# Longman Dictionary of the English Language

# Longman Dictionary of the English Language

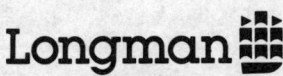
Longman

**Longman Group Limited,**
*Longman House, Burnt Mill, Harlow,*
*Essex CM20 2JE, England*
*and Associated Companies throughout the world.*

© Merriam-Webster Inc. 1984

First published 1984
Reprinted 1985 (twice)
ISBN 0 582 55511 6 (standard edition)
ISBN 0 582 55578 7 (thumb-index edition)
ISBN 0 582 89250 3 (Japanese standard edition)
ISBN 0 582 89267 8 (Japanese thumb-index edition)

*British Library Cataloguing in Publication Data*

Longman dictionary of the English language.
1. English language—Dictionaries
423    PE1625
ISBN 0-582-55511-6
ISBN 0-582-55578-7 (thumb-index)

Set in Monophoto Times NR. 7/7½ pt.

Printed in Great Britain
by Wm. Clowes Limited, Beccles & London

# Contents

# Acknowledgments

*Editorial*

Heather Gay
Brian O'Kill
Katherine Seed
Janet Whitcut

*Design and Production*

Giles Davies
Clive McKeough
Paul Price-Smith
Geoff Sida

We would also like to thank the many other individuals who have helped in the compilation of this dictionary, particularly:

Peter Adams, BBC Pronunciation Unit, Jacky Billington, Philip Brew, Barbara Burge, Carey Chapman, James Coakley, Jill Davies, Valerie Dudley, Doris Dunning, Jane Freebury, Vera Grant, James Harpur, Bonnie Hearn, Pat Hill, Susan M. Lloyd, Anna Lumley, Sylvia Mansfield, Margaret Penney, Gillian Rathbone, Michael Scherk, Stella Stiegeler, Gordon Walsh, Cliff Waterman, Elizabeth Webster.

*Publishing*

Sheila Dallas
Anna Hodson
Kathy Rooney

*Administration*

Melanie Ashurst
Carol Hawthorne
Linda O'Donnell
Ursula Springham

We would like to acknowledge the services of the panel of eminent linguists who have provided invaluable guidance in the compilation of Longman dictionaries:

Professor Randolph Quirk    *Chairman*

*Computer Systems*

Christine Barnes
Kent Barnett
Ken Moore
Steven Parish

Louis Alexander
Professor Dwight Bolinger
Professor Christopher Candlin
Reg Close
Professor David Crystal
Professor A C Gimson
Denis Girard
Dr Philip Johnson-Laird
Professor Geoffrey Leech

Professor John Lyons
Philip J Scholefield
Professor Barbara Strang
Professor Jan Svartvik
Dr Walter Voigt
Owen Watson
David Wilkins
Professor Yorick Wilks

The publishers are indebted to past members of the Longman Lexicographic Unit and Dictionary and Reference Book Department for their contribution to the dictionary, particularly:

Paul Procter
John Ayto
Beverley Britton
Ann Brown
Timothy Burton
Faye Carney
James Clarke
Roger Cohen
Bob Cole
David Fairlamb
Catherine Freer
Norman Gill
Anne Gilpin
Christine Hatt
Jan Hulston
Robert F. Ilson
Malcolm Jones

Hazel Leigh
Charles McCormack
Robin Mann
Barbara Mansergh
Robert Mansergh
Nick Murr
Joyce Nairn
Sean O'Boyle
Yvonne O'Leary
Sarah Overton
Ellayne Parker
Elaine Roberts
Penelope Stock
Paul Surzyn
Ruth Swan
Ann Tierney

Our gratitude is due also to the members of the Longman Advisory Board, who have given generously of their advice, encouragement, and constructive criticism in the compilation and presentation of Longman dictionaries:

Lord Briggs    *Chairman*
Melvyn Bragg
Alan Brien
Ernestine Carter
Sir Frederick Dainton
Bernard Dixon
Derek Dougan
Clement Freud
Professor L C B Gower
Germaine Greer
John Gross
Professor S M Hall
Antony Hopkins
Clive Jenkins
Elizabeth Jennings

Professor Frank Kermode
Dr R D Laing
Professor Peter Lasko
Sir Jack Longland
George Melly
Mike Molloy
Dipak Nandy
Anne Nightingale
Michael O'Donnell
Professor Randolph Quirk
Dr John Robinson
Audrey Slaughter
Janet Street-Porter
John Treasure
Jeff Wayne

# Consultants

The compilers have made extensive use of consultants to ensure the accuracy of the dictionary's definitions and tables, and would like to express their thanks to the following:

*Aeronautics*
Dr R Hillier,
Imperial College of Science and Technology, London

*Agriculture*
Dr E J Evans,
Department of Agriculture, University of Newcastle upon Tyne
Frank H Garner,
Formerly Lecturer in Agriculture, Cambridge, and Principal of the Royal Agricultural College, Cirencester
Dr Peter Rowlinson,
Department of Agriculture, University of Newcastle upon Tyne

*Anthropology*
R Angus Downie

*Archaeology*
Malcolm Jones,
Formerly Curator, Wiltshire Folk Life Museum

*Architecture*
R H Franks, ARIBA,
Senior Lecturer, Polytechnic of North London

*Arts and Crafts*
Frank Hilton

*Astronomy*
Harry Whitcut

*Australian English*
Dr J R L Bernard,
Macquarie University

*Botany*
Dr C J Humphries,
British Museum (Natural History)

*Building Science*
C R Bassett, FCIOB,
Formerly Principal Lecturer, Guildford County College of Technology

*Canadian English*
The late Walter S Avis, BA MA PhD,
Professor of English and·Dean, Canadian Forces Military College, Royal Military College of Canada, Kingston, Ontario

*Cartography*
J S Keates,
Reader in Geography, University of Glasgow

*Chinese Etymology*
Richard Szu-cheng Wang,
Formerly Assistant Director of Research in Chinese, University of Cambridge

*Civil Engineering*
Professor W Fisher Cassie,
University of Newcastle upon Tyne

*Clothing*
Ernestine Carter, OBE
Ann Thomas

*Commerce*
Alison Farrow
Gordon Heald

*Dancing*
John Allen

*Dentistry*
Professor Malcolm Harris,
Institute of Dental Surgery, University of London

*Domestic Science*
Annette Thomas

*Drugs*
Richard O'Neill,
Department of Pharmaceutics, The School of Pharmacy, University of London

*Economics*
D Deadman,
Lecturer, University of Leicester

*Education*
Professor Roy Niblett,
Formerly Dean, University of London, Institute of Education

*Electrical Engineering*
Dr A R Bean,
Formerly Head of Department, Electrical Engineering and Applied Physics, Chelmer Institute of Higher Education

*Entomology*
Dr J D Bradley,
Commonwealth Institute of Entomology, London

*Firearms*
Colin Hayes

*Food and Drink*
Elma McLean,
Essex Education Authority

*Forestry*
Professor F T Last,
Institute of Terrestrial Ecology, Penicuik, Midlothian

*Games*
Elizabeth Webster

*Glass and Ceramics*
Geoffrey Payton

*History*
L E Snellgrove

*Horse-riding*
Bridget Hamilton
Kate Reddick

*Hunting and Fishing*
Dr William B Currie,
Edinburgh Language Foundation

*Industrial Relations*
Dr S R Hill,
London School of Economics

*Insurance*
A G Andrusier,
Director, Sheldon Monk & Co Ltd, Insurance Brokers

*Journalism*
Bob James,
Westminster Press, London

*Law*
Angus Murray,
Publisher, Butterworth & Co (Publishers) Ltd

*Linguistics*
R Angus Downie

*Manufacturing*
Rodney Dale

*Mechanical Engineering*
Rayner Joel,
BSc(Eng) CEng FIMechE FIMarE

*Metallurgy*
Professor J G Ball,
Imperial College of Science and Technology, London

*Meteorology*
R P W Lewis,
Meteorological Office

*Military Ranks*
David Bradley,
National Military Museum
Nigel Der Lee,
Royal Military Academy, Sandhurst

*Mineralogy*
M P Jones, Mineral Resources Engineering Department,
Imperial College of Science and Technology, London

*Mining*
Dr John Stocks,
Royal School of Mines, London

*Motoring*
Rayner Joel

*Music*
Peter Holman
Rosalyn Asher

*Nautical Terms*
Gordon Fairley,
Royal Yachting Association

*New Zealand English*
C C Bowley,
University of Auckland

*Numbers*
David Walker,
Simon Balle School, Hertford

*Pharmacy*
V Osbourne, MPS,
The Boots Company Ltd, Nottingham
Dr M A Simmonds,
The School of Pharmacy, University of London

*Philosophy*
Michael Luntley,
Linacre College, Oxford

*Photography*
Trevor Clifford

*Physics*
David Pritchard,
The Blackett Laboratory, Imperial College of Science and
Technology, London

*Political Science*
D M Shapiro,
Reader in Government, Brunel University

*Printing*
Walter Partridge

*Psychology*
Dr H G Procter,
Senior Clinical Psychologist, Southwood House, Bridgwater,
Somerset
Helen Weinreich-Haste,
Lecturer, University of Bath

*Railways*
D W Peacock, BSc CEng,
British Railways Research Dept (Retd)

*Scottish English*
Professor Tom McArthur,
Université du Québec

*Scouting*
Anthony Eyre

*South African English*
Pieter D Williams,
Department of English, University of the Orange Free State

*Sports*
Norman Barrett, MA
John Goodbody
Andrew F Wilson

*Stamp and Coin Collecting*
James A Mackay,
Numismatic and Philatelic Columnist of the *Financial Times*

*Statistics*
Dr David Jones

*Textiles*
Dr E Dyson,
Chairman and Reader in Textile Engineering, Postgraduate
School of Studies in Textile Technology, University of Bradford

*Theatre*
Professor John Allen OBE,
Visiting Professor of Drama, Westfield College, University of
London

*Tobacco*
J W Drummond,
British-American Tobacco Company Ltd, 7 Millbank, London

*Transport*
Peter Levy

*Video*
Editor, *Professional Video*

*Weights and Measures*
David Walker,
Simon Balle School, Hertford

*Zoology*
Dr Ian Bishop
Dr Heather M Gay

# Foreword

Good dictionaries proceed from a controlled interaction of tradition and innovation. Too much of the one results in being locked into out-dated practice and presentation. Too much of the other results in a book where the reader misses familiar forms of guidance. The present volume has achieved a superb balance – as well it might, in view of its lineage.

For this book is a very special member of a very special family. Part of what is special about the family is that there is a distinguished genealogy, since it was of course the house of Longman that published Samuel Johnson's monumental dictionary in 1755; and the Longman list includes another historic contribution to lexicology, the *Roget's Thesaurus*.

But to come down to the present day, there have been outstanding new additions to the 'family' since the 1970s: the *Longman Dictionary of Contemporary English* – a strikingly innovative work designed primarily for the mature learner; the *New Generation Dictionary* – an attractive small book for younger learners; the *New Universal Dictionary* – a major and very enjoyable work for everyone in the home.

And now the *Longman Dictionary of the English Language* (the *Longman Webster English College Dictionary*). What is so 'very special' about this latest member of this very special family? It is special because it is the most representative of the rich storehouse of lexical information (the Longman database) from which others have proceeded. Reversing the biological process of germination, we now have the birth of the parent book of which the earlier dictionaries are the offspring.

But the *Longman Dictionary of the English Language* is not merely larger: though this it certainly is, with nearly a quarter of a million lexical definitions, and an extraordinarily wide coverage of the English used in the major English-speaking countries and in the major fields of activity from sport to science. At least as significant as the size and coverage, however, is the firm grasp on a first-class lexicographical method that reflects the most recent scholarly work in this field: meticulous care with sense differentiation, precision of definition, detailed etymology, abundant cross-reference – the whole being computer-checked for accuracy. The discerning user who is concerned to write with discrimination is well served with comprehensive usage notes (especially on points of English where usage is disputed) and with essays explaining the nuances involved in words of similar or contrastive meaning.

Randolph Quirk
*Vice-Chancellor, University of London,*
Senate House, London WC1, 4 May 1984

# Preface

The earliest English dictionary (excluding glossaries and bilinguals) was a small volume compiled by Robert Cawdrey, an obscure schoolmaster, with the assistance of his son Thomas, which was published in 1604 as *A Table Alphabeticall, Contayning and Teaching the True Writing and Understanding of Hard Usuall English Wordes*. In the centuries since that modest pioneering work, dictionaries have developed greatly. The goal of a modern monolingual dictionary, in very general terms, remains similar to that of Cawdrey: to collect and describe the vocabulary of a language in order to serve the users of that language in their daily need to comprehend and interpret the civilization in and through which they live. Its scale is far more comprehensive, however, for Cawdrey's work did not aim to provide a full description of the language and contained barely three thousand entries. Moreover, the evolution of scholarly and scientific method, and civilization in general, have contributed to the growth of the dictionary. Whereas many principles of lexicography have long been established, there has also been a continuing process of refining old techniques and evolving new ones. A new dictionary is thus aided by accumulated experience and the substantial advances in linguistic analysis made during the last hundred years, quite apart from the improved methods of collecting, storing, and retrieving information which are made possible by new technology.

The needs and skills of dictionary-users have also changed. Cawdrey's dictionary, written long before the time of universal education and increasing social equality, was professedly intended 'for the benefit & helpe of Ladies, Gentlewomen, or any other unskilfull persons'. A comprehensive modern dictionary contains many special features evolved in response to the manifold and increasingly sophisticated requirements of users, ranging from the student to the solver of crossword puzzles. It has to answer innumerable purposes and to function in homes, libraries, educational establishments, and places of work as a source of knowledge of many kinds. While remaining preeminently a listing of words and their meanings, it must also contain elements of more specialized reference works in order to provide a full, accurate, and up-to-date record of our language and our world.

## The range of English vocabulary

Cawdrey's *A Table Alphabeticall* set a very limiting precedent for other seventeenth-century dictionaries, such as John Bullokar's *An English Expositor* (1616) and Henry Cockeram's *The English Dictionarie* (1623). Dealing exclusively with 'hard' words (mostly neologisms or nonce-terms of Latin and Greek derivation), they included such polysyllabic monsters as *obsalutrate* and *embriolate*, but not *take* or *want*. Not until the eighteenth century –

sketchily in John Kersey's *A New English Dictionary* (1702), more thoroughly in Nathan Bailey's *Universal Etymological English Dictionary* (1721) – did any lexicographer attempt to cover the full range of English vocabulary. Even then, the legacy of the 'hard words' tradition remained for many years more, as successive dictionaries inherited from their predecessors words which had no currency in actual usage.

In the later part of the twentieth century, however, we face the problem that the corpus of English is so vast, ever-expanding, and impossible to demarcate precisely, that it is a hopeless ambition to include it all in one dictionary. Realistically, a practical dictionary can aim to include all the language which its users might expect to encounter in speech or writing, outside highly technical contexts or untypical circumstances. It must certainly describe the common core of familiar English as well as a large number of more specialized words. Yet in one respect there may be a significant parallel between our own age and the era of the 'hard words' dictionaries. Both are, in many people's opinion, periods of rapid and bewildering changes in the English language; times of notable social, cultural, and linguistic developments, with inventions, novel ideas, and an increased accessibility of foreign lands bringing a multitude of new words and usages into English.

Reflecting and responding to this situation, the *Longman Dictionary of the English Language* pays special attention to three areas of vocabulary inadequately covered in many older dictionaries. First, there is extensive treatment of scientific and technical words: the burgeoning terminology, much of it no longer exclusive to specialists but entering our daily speech, of a radical change in our daily lives – our domestic life, our health, work, leisure – and in our conceptions of the universe. Secondly, particular consideration has been given to English as it is used throughout the world. The English written and spoken in Britain must now be classified as only one variety of a language spoken by more than 300 million people throughout the world, of which there are other major varieties in the USA, Canada, Australia, New Zealand, the Caribbean, and South Africa, beside minor varieties elsewhere and an infinite number of the local subvarieties commonly known as dialects. In the age of the 'global village', and with English continuing to grow in importance as a medium of international communication, a dictionary cannot afford to be insular; hence this work provides an exceptionally full treatment of significant features of vocabulary, grammar, and spelling occurring in non-British English. Thirdly, many items have been included from colloquial and idiomatic English: the common currency of our speech, yet an elusive or ambiguous area of language which can produce many misunderstandings and can be most difficult for the lexicographer to identify and describe.

## Clarity in definitions

The modern dictionary is, then, far more inclusive than its ancestors; it is also a much more reliable and efficient tool of explication. Using the sophisticated defining techniques of contemporary lexicography, the compilers of the *Longman Dictionary of the English Language* have striven to ensure accuracy, clarity, and consistency of presentation. Accuracy derives from the assembling and rigorous anatomy of a mass of data, and from the advice of expert consultants; clarity from the persistent effort to make the language of definitions readily comprehensible without distorting or omitting information; and consistency from a firm framework of working principles and a thorough system of cross-checking.

More specifically, the pursuit of clarity in this dictionary has produced an innovative treatment of certain definitions. Although it has long been an axiom of lexicography that a definition should employ, in Samuel Johnson's words, 'terms less abstruse than that which is to be explained', this goal sometimes proves very difficult to accomplish. Many basic words (such as *sky, house, anger*) can scarcely be explained except by means of more elaborate words; Johnson's own treatment of *network* ('any thing reticulated or decussated, at equal distances, with interstices between the intersections') is a notorious example of this tendency. Moreover, there is the problem posed by relatively abstruse words, or words pertaining to specialized subjects, the explanation of which, in conventional dictionaries, involves the use of other words which are probably known only to someone already well-acquainted with the subject or possessing an uncommonly extensive vocabulary.

The special system employed in this dictionary has previously been restricted to a few dictionaries intended primarily for learners of English. But learning words is, even for the native speaker and regardless of educational qualifications, an inexhaustible process that continues throughout our lives; it is therefore reasonable to assume that anyone consulting a dictionary may be, for the nonce, a learner who needs guidance. Many dictionaries are not genuinely accessible. Most users are familiar with the problems of complete disorientation when faced with a definition in purely technical terms, and of frustration when having to hunt through a dictionary in order to find explanations of purported explanations. In this dictionary, however, the technique of combining a technical, specialized, or abstruse defining term with a brief non-technical gloss should enable all readers to grasp without difficulty or distraction the essence of the definition. At the same time, individual readers can approach such definitions on different levels, depending on their existing knowledge of the field of terminology being explained. A biochemist looking up a biochemical term will find an accurate scientific definition; an architect knowing little or nothing about biochemistry will find that same term explained simply and comprehensibly and can obtain more detailed information by consulting entries for those specialized terms distinguished by being printed in a different typeface.

## Words in context: grammar and usage

Although the main principle of a dictionary assumes that the basic unit of discourse is the word, it is not sufficient to offer merely explanations of individual words (the *lexis* of a language) in isolation. In actual use, words normally exist in context, in syntactical relationship with other words within a phrase or sentence. A full treatment of these relationships is strictly the domain of a *grammar*, but a dictionary should aim to offer as much detail as possible: indicating not only irregular inflections (plurals of nouns, tenses of verbs, comparison of adjectives and adverbs), but also concordance, restricted collocations, and other peculiarities of construction. On such subjects the *Longman Dictionary of the English Language* provides unusually full information, not only through a precise system of description but also through its use of thousands of illustrative quotations showing words within context.

Further, a dictionary may serve as a *usage book*, by providing reliable guidance on such topics as frequently raise dispute about 'good English'. As a continuing flow of letters to newspapers and the BBC testifies, the question of correctness in language remains very much a live issue, and a complex one often involving social and cultural attitudes. At the extreme ends of the popular debate are 'purists' maintaining that there exists an immutable standard of the language from which any change marks a decline towards barbarism, and 'permissives' holding that many traditional 'rules' are artificial barriers against the natural flow of the language and free self-expression. On a more academic level, linguists still debate the opposing principles of prescriptivism (believing that a dictionary, grammar, or similar work ought to propound authoritative rules of correctness) and descriptivism (contending that such a work should objectively describe existing usage, without seeking to fix or judge standards). The compilers of the present work believe that a contemporary dictionary can best serve its readers by being, as it were, descriptive about prescriptivism. Since attitudes towards language are part of the facts of usage, a responsible dictionary should at least discuss the controversies surrounding the use of some words and constructions. The wholly original usage notes offered in this dictionary are based not on individual prejudices but on a vast body of information about usage and attitudes. Thus they are authoritative but not authoritarian; typically they analyse the grounds of controversy, adduce valuable evidence of usage from historical and modern sources, and provide helpful advice to the speaker and writer.

'Correctness' may often be largely a matter of appropriateness to context or circumstance. Semantically, *quid* and *sidewalk* are equivalent to *pound* and *pavement*, but they would not be acceptable substitutes in certain types of discourse. Many other words are similarly restricted in use to a particular time, place, or circumstance. They may be archaic or obsolete, peculiar to a regional variety of English, used wholly or largely in specific types of communication (e g poetic, journalistic), or indicative of a certain attitude (e g derogatory, euphemistic) or 'level' of language (formal, informal, slang). Since plain definitions may fail to reveal these limitations, a dictionary must seek to identify and label all such restricted items. Indeed, such labelling appeared, albeit unsystematically, in the earliest English dictionaries, and it has generally been accepted as an essential technique of lexicography. Objections are sometimes raised that it is inevitably both arbitrary and ephemeral. While it is true that no word belongs intrinsically to a particular register of language, a consensus about its status at a given time can justifiably be noted in a dictionary which is based on plentiful evidence of prevailing usage and attitude. It is also true that, as a glance at any older dictionary will show, the status of a word can alter amid the general process of linguistic change. Words labelled 'barbarous' or 'low and ludicrous' by Johnson are now an accepted part of our language; words which only a few years ago were used exclusively in North America have become naturalized in British English; yesterday's slang may become today's standard English. Yet this very transience – together with, more obviously, the introduction to the language of new words and meanings – provides a prime justification for the production of a brand-new dictionary, based on the latest available information. For practical purposes an outdated dictionary is a blunt and rusty tool – worse, even, for its deficiencies may not be immediately apparent.

## Explicit and implied meanings

Many words in our language have not only a denotation (an explicit, direct, or exact meaning) but also a connotation (an implied, suggested, or associative meaning); consider, for example, the different implications of *my house* and *my home*. Restrictive labels indicate some of these subtler nuances, but there are two further ways in which this dictionary reveals them. In the first place, it functions as a *thesaurus* and *synonymy*. Frequently it provides lists of groups of words of similar and opposite meaning (synonyms and antonyms); in addition, it often draws attention to commonly confused words of similar appearance but different meaning. More particularly, it features an extended treatment of several hundred groups of synonyms (such as *secret, covert, clandestine, furtive, surreptitious, stealthy,* and *underhand*), whose meanings are precisely distinguished by analysis and illustration. This aspect of the dictionary, partly based on work for Longman's recent new edition of the famous *Roget's Thesaurus*, should prove a special attraction to all those who value the rich subtleties of English or need to use it with clarity and precision.

The second important treatment of connotations lies in the use of examples illustrating a word within the context of a phrase or sentence. By using illustrative quotations which give typical instances of a particular use of a word, the dictionary can readily distinguish nuances of meaning, show the kind of context in which a word characteristically occurs, and illustrate grammatical relationships and structures. This invaluable lexicographic technique was first used in English in Samuel Johnson's *A Dictionary of the English Language* (1755); earlier English dictionaries had merely sometimes cited sources as authorities for the existence of a word or sense. The method has rarely been employed so thoroughly and discriminatingly, save in large historical dictionaries, as in the *Longman Dictionary of the English Language*. Of the many thousand illustrative examples given here, most are actual quotations from a wide variety of named sources or have been adapted from genuine quotations to clarify a point.

## Dictionaries and encyclopedias

Inevitably, a dictionary partly overlaps an *encyclopedia*. In contrast to most dictionaries produced in America, France, and other countries, British dictionaries of the nineteenth and twentieth centuries have generally eschewed what their compilers regarded as encyclopedic content. Theoretical distinctions suggest that the true province of a dictionary is words, not things; or purely lexical, not technical or factual, information; or generic, not specific, entities. In practice, however, no clear dividing line can be drawn between the two types of book. The dictionary definition of any entity must involve an account of its typical composition, attributes, and functions sufficiently detailed to distinguish it from other entities; the modern reader can scarcely be content with such vague identifications as '*mackerel* a sea-fish' (Johnson) or '*laurel* the tree so called' (Dyche, 1768). The compilers of the *Longman Dictionary of the English Language* have aimed, especially in dealing with terms from scientific and technical subjects, to provide that fullness of factual information which many readers expect to find in a comprehensive dictionary. As for proper names, although they may more justifiably be withheld from the main text of a dictionary, they are nonetheless an important component of our vocabulary and have not been neglected here; two separate sections – a concise *biographical dictionary* and a *gazetteer* – present key facts about thousands of eminent people from all ages and many spheres of human activity, and about the nations, chief cities, rivers, mountains, and other physical features of our planet.

## Historical information

Two contrasting methods of describing a language are recognized by linguists: synchronic (or contemporary) and diachronic (or historical). The former involves isolating for examination the language at one point in time, ignoring its historical roots; the second is principally concerned to chronicle the development of the language, including all those parts of it (forms, meanings, and words) which have become obsolete. Although a dictionary such as the present work is fundamentally synchronic, emphasizing words in current use, it yet incorporates some features of a more specialized *historical dictionary* which are relevant to the user's practical needs. It does not ignore that important substratum, lying beneath the active vocabulary of the present day, of archaic or obsolete words and senses maintaining a ghostly existence in special contexts and old literature; it includes those elements of the language of Shakespeare, the Authorized Version of the Bible, and other sources which are still encountered in our times. Nor does this dictionary sever the living language from its deepest sources; in concise yet detailed etymologies, it uncovers the varied origins of the English vocabulary – presenting to the scholar a valuable mine of information, and to the general reader a store of interesting and often unexpected material that reveals a great deal about the social and cultural history of the English-speaking peoples.

## Pronunciations

A general dictionary also subsumes a *pronouncing dictionary*, recording the exact pronunciation(s) of words. This is a surprisingly late development in English lexicography. Even the major eighteenth-century dictionaries of Nathan Bailey (1727) and Samuel Johnson (1755) had usually merely marked the main stresses of words. No significant systematic attempt to indicate the actual sounds of words was made before Thomas Sheridan's *General*

*Dictionary of the English Language*, published in 1780. Since then, many systems of transcribing pronunciations have been tried, yet few have achieved ready comprehensibility while avoiding ambiguity or inaccuracy. The International Phonetic Alphabet has been commonly used by professional phoneticians in recent years, but its special symbols undoubtedly constitute a stumbling block and source of confusion to many readers. To overcome these problems, a new method of transcription has been devised for Longman dictionaries. Dispensing with nearly all unfamiliar characters, it provides a precise, consistent, and accessible record (with wide coverage of variations and special treatment of pronunciations sometimes considered incorrect) of English as it is spoken.

## Creating the dictionary

The creation of a general-purpose modern English dictionary is a massive task, and one that could never be accomplished by a person, or group of people, sitting isolated in a room, starting with the letter *a* and writing down all the words that come to mind. Since it is primarily a record or inventory of the English language as it is really used in writing and speech, the dictionary must arise from a solid foundation of reliable evidence about the language. The compilers of the *Longman Dictionary of the English Language* have indeed been fortunate to have access to the immense fund of linguistic data assembled by Merriam-Webster Inc., the publishers since the 1840s of successive editions of the internationally famous Webster's Dictionary. Their file of over thirteen million citations from all kinds of material, and from all parts of the globe where English is used, has been of indispensable service to this work; so, too, have been the justly renowned scholarship and lexicographic expertise of their staff. Another invaluable source has been the massive corpus of spoken and written material collected by the Survey of English Usage at University College London. Much additional evidence of language use has been collected by Longman's dictionary department; and it is on the resulting vast and constantly updated collection of specimens of English that this dictionary is securely based.

The *Longman Dictionary of the English Language* is a fruit of a carefully planned project which has extended over almost ten years and, in a sense, has roots much deeper in the history of dictionaries. In the eighteenth century, Thomas Longman was one of the five collaborating publishers of Samuel Johnson's great *Dictionary* (according to Boswell, Johnson described them as 'generous liberal-minded men'); his heirs published such celebrated reference works as Peter Mark Roget's *Thesaurus* and Ephraim Chambers' *Cyclopedia*. Within the last decade, Longman's Dictionary and Reference Book Department has produced the much-acclaimed *Longman Dictionary of Contemporary English* (principally intended for foreign learners of English), the *New Generation Dictionary* (meeting the special needs of the 11-16 age group), the concise *Longman New Universal Dictionary*, and a number of more specialized reference books. The present work has brought together a variety of resources: the experience and dedication of a team of full-time staff; the expert knowledge of more than eighty consultants on special subjects; the counsel of a panel of eminent academic linguists and of an advisory body of public figures having a lively practical concern with language; and the facilities offered by an advanced data-processing system. All these have combined to collect, sift, analyse, and interpret a vast mass of information about our incomparably rich language.

# Explanatory chart   Numbers in brackets refer to paragraphs in the guide to the dictionary (p xvii).

**angle brackets** enclosing an example of an entry used in context (**7**)

**aah, ah** /ah *often prolonged*/ *vi* to exclaim in amazement, joy, or surprise   < *oohing and* ~*ing . . .* >

**abase** /ə'bays/ *vt* . . .
*antonym* extol ——————————————— **antonym** (**8.6**)

**capitalization** (**5**)

**academy** /ə'kadəmi/ *n* **1** *cap* **a** *the* school for advanced education founded by Plato **b** the philosophical doctrines associated with Plato's Academy

usage note indicating the phrase (**collocation**) in which a verb frequently appears (**8.7**)

**acquiesce** /,akwee'es/ *vi* to submit or comply tacitly or passively – often + *in*

**Acts** /akts/, **Acts of the Apostles** *n taking sing vb* the fifth book of the New Testament narrating the beginnings of the Christian Church

**grammatical information** about an entry (**4.1**)

**adrift** /ə'drift/ *adv or adj* **1** afloat without motive power or mooring and at the mercy of winds and currents **2** in or into a state of being unstuck or unfastened; loose – *esp in come adrift*

usage note indicating the phrase (**collocation**) in which an entry is frequently found (**8.7**)

arrow indicating the part of speech formed when a **combining form** is added to a word or word part (**10**)

**-agogue** /-əgog/ *comb form* (→*n*) **1** leader; guide <*peda*gogue> – sometimes derog <*dema*gogue> **2** substance that promotes the secretion or expulsion of <*emmen*agogue>

**agranulocyte** /ay'granyoolə,siet/ *n* any of various WHITE BLOOD CELLS that have no conspicuous granules in the CYTOPLASM (jellylike material surrounding the nucleus) – compare GRANULOCYTE

**cross-reference** recommending the user to look up a related entry (**9**)

**cross-reference** recommending the user to look up the main form of an affix or combining form (**9**)

**al-** – see AD-

**alternative society** *n* *the* group of people who reject conventional social institutions, practices, and values in favour of a life-style based esp on communal ownership and self-sufficiency – compare COUNTERCULTURE

italicized **definite article** indicating that an entry is always preceded by *the* (**8.7**)

**²amount** . . .
*usage* **Amount** and **quantity** are correctly used of mass nouns with no plural, and of abstractions that cannot be counted, in the way that **number** is used of plurals. Compare <*a large* **quantity** *of butter*> <*a certain* **amount** *of influence*> <*a large* **number** (*not* **amount**) *of people*> <*a certain* **number** (*not* **amount**) *of mistakes*>.

**essay** discussing a problem of correctness (**8.6**)

**amorous** /'amərəs/ *adj* . . .
*synonyms* **Amatory** describes behaviour or art expressing or inspired by sexual love, while **amorous** relates specifically to sexual desire <**amatory** *poetry*> <**amorous** *advances*>.

**essay** comparing two or more words of similar meaning (**8.6**)

**anabatic** /,anə'batik/ *adj* moving upwards, esp up a slope; rising <*an* ~ *wind*> [Gk *anabatos*, verbal of *anabainein*]

**etymology** showing history of an entry (**12**)

**antebellum** /,anti'beləm/ *adj* existing before the war; *esp* existing before the US Civil War <*an* ~ *brick mansion*>

**example** showing an entry used in a typical context (**7**)

**example** consisting of an illustrative quotation showing the use of an entry in an actual context (**7**)

**assignation** /,asig'naysh(ə)n/ *n* **1** the act of assigning; *also* the assignment made **2** a meeting, esp a secret one with a lover <*returned from an* ~ *with his mistress* – W B Yeats>

**author** /'awthə/, [ fem **authoress** ] /'awthəris, awthə'res, '---/ n
**1a** the writer of a literary work ...
— **feminine form** of an entry (**2**)

**homograph number (1.1)** —— [ 1 ] **ban** /ban/ vt **-nn-** to prohibit, esp by legal means or social pressure

**bandwagon** /'band‚wagən/ n **1** a party, movement, cause, or enterprise that ... [ – **climb/jump on the bandwagon** ] to attach oneself to a successful or popular cause, enterprise, etc, esp in the hope of personal gain
— **idiom** (**1.3**)

**¹bare** /beə/ adj ... [ – see also **with one's bare** HANDS, **under bare** POLES ]
— **cross-reference to an idiom,** specifying the entry at which it appears (**1.3**)

**inflection (4)** —— **²barrel** vb [ **-ll-** (NAm **-l-, -ll-**) ] to put or pack in a barrel

**blew** /blooh/ [ past of BLOW ]
— **inflectional cross-reference** giving an inflected form of an entry (**9**)

**irregular plural (4.1)** —— **boletus** /bə'leetəs, boh -/ n, pl **boletuses,** [ **boleti** /-ti/ ] any of a genus (Boletus) of fleshy fungi (class Basidiomycetes), some of which are edible

**¹bolshie, bolshy** /'bolshi/ n, [ informal ] a Bolshevik
— usage note indicating the style, attitude, or level of formality of an entry (**8.4**)

**main entry (1.1)** —— [ **¹bolt-‚hole** ] n **1** a hole into which an animal runs for safety **2** a place of refuge

**object** of a verb (**6.3**) —— **³bond** vt **1** to overlap [ (e g bricks) ] for solidity of construction **2** to put [ (goods) ] in bond until duties and taxes are paid

**part of speech (3)** —— **bonfire** /'bonfie-ə/ [ n ] a large fire built in the open air

**two parts of speech** shown in combination (**3**) —— **¹bop** /bop/ [ vt or n ] **-pp-** informal (to strike with) a blow (e g of the fist)

**bottom drawer** n, [ Br ] (a place for storing) a woman's collection of clothes and esp household articles and furnishings (e g linen and tableware) kept in anticipation of her marriage
— **regional label,** in this case indicating that the entry is used only in British English (**8.3**)

**²buoy** vt **1** to mark (as if) with a buoy **2a** to keep afloat **b** to support, sustain <an economy ~ed up by the dramatic postwar growth of industry> **3** to raise the spirits of <hope ~s him up> [ □ (2&3) usu + up ]
— **usage note** applying to more than one sense (**8.1**)

**cacophony** /kə'kofəni/ n harsh or discordant sound; dissonance ... [ – **cacophonous** adj ]
— **undefined run-on** entry (**1.2**)

**sense number (6.1)** —— **cadet** /ka'det/ n [ 1 ] **a** a younger brother or son [ b ] (a member of) a younger branch of a family
— **sense letter (6.1)**

— **sense divider (6.1)**

**caff** /kaf/ n, Br informal a café; [ esp ] a cheap plain one

**usual/only subject** of a verb —— **¹call** /kawl/ vi **1** ... **c** [ of an animal ] to utter a characteristic note or cry ...

**phrasal** verbs listed separately after the entry for their main verb (**1.4**) —— **¹cry** /krie/ vi **1** to call loudly ...
[ **cry down** ] vt to disparage ...

**¹daring** /'deəring/ adj adventurously bold in action or thought [ <~ acrobats> <~ crimes> ]
— **swung dash** replacing entry in an example (**7**)

**synonymous cross-reference** to a compound entry (**9**) —— **dateline** /'dayt‚lien/ n **1** a line in a written document or publication giving the date and place of composition or issue **2** [ INTERNATIONAL DATE LINE ] – **dateline** vt

**daystar** /'day‚stah/ n **1** MORNING STAR **2** [ SUN 1a ]
— **synonymous cross-reference** to a particular sense (**9**)

**temporal label** showing that the use of a word or meaning is limited to special contexts (**8.2**) —— **deer** /diə/ n, pl **deer** also **deers 1** any of several RUMINANTS ... **2** [ archaic ] an animal; esp a small mammal
— **verb entry ending in -ize** separated by a comma from **-ise,** indicating that the two forms are **equal variants** (**2**)

[ **depersonal·ize, -ise** ] /‚dee'puhsənl·iez/ vt **1** to deprive of the sense of personal identity ...

two entries separated by a comma indicating that they are **equal variants (2)**

**dermat-** /duhmət-/, **dermato-** *comb form* skin <dermat*itis*> <dermato*logy*>

**regional variant**, in this case indicating that the second form is used chiefly in the USA and Canada (2)

**diaeresis**, *chiefly NAm* **dieresis** /die'erəsis, -'irəsis/ *n, pl* **diaereses** /-əseez/ **1** a mark‾ placed over a vowel to indicate that it is pronounced as a separate syllable

two entries separated by *also* indicating that the latter is a **secondary variant (2)**

**¹diagnostic** /ˌdie·əg'nostik/ *also* **diagnostical** /-kl/ *adj* of or involving diagnosis

**²diffuse** ...
⚠ defuse

**warning** sign, in this case indicating that the entry should not be confused with an apparently similar word **(8.6)**

**specialized word**, often followed by a sense number, in small capital letters in round brackets **(6.3)**

**DNA** *n* a chemical compound ... that ... consists of long strands of phosphate groups alternating with sugar (DEOXYRIBOSE) groups ... The DNA chains typically occur as pairs in a DOUBLE HELIX (spiral of two parallel strands round the same central axis).

**explanation** in round brackets of specialized word in small capital letters **(6.3)**

**-fy** /-fie/, **-ify** *suffix* (→*vb*) ...

**arrow** indicating the part of speech formed when a **suffix** is added to a word or word part **(10)**

# Explanatory chart – pronunciations

**controversy** /'kontrəˌvuhsi, kən'trovəsi USE *the last pron is disliked by some speakers*/ *n* ...

two pronunciations followed by note indicating usage **(11.5)**

**controvert** /'kontrəˌvuht, ˌ--'-/

another **stress pattern** that can be used without otherwise changing the pronunciation **(11.3)**

**oblique lines** enclosing a pronunciation **(11.2)**

**hiss** /his/ *vi* ...

**¹hire** /hie·ə/ *n* ...

pronunciation containing a **centred dot (11.4)**

**Deutsche Mark** /'doychˌmahk (*Ger* dɔɪtʃə mark)/ *n* ...

**entente** /on'tont (*Fr* ɑ̃tɑ̃ːt)/ *n* ...

**foreign pronunciations (11.9)**

**honorary** /'on(ə)rəri/ *adj* ...

pronunciation containing (ə) **(11.4)**

**specialist pronunciation**, in this case indicating that the word is pronounced differently by sailors **(11.5)**

**¹leeward** /'leewood; *naut* 'looh·əd/ *adj or adv* ...

**stress mark** showing primary stress **(11.3)**

**hoodwink** /'hoodˌwingk/ *vt* ...

**hoofˌbeat** /-ˌbeet/ ...

**stress mark** showing secondary stress **(11.3)**

**stress pattern** shown in compound words and phrases **(11.3)**

**swung dash** indicating that the plural is pronounced in the same way as the singular **(11.4)**

**hors d'oeuvre** /ˌaw'duhv (*Fr* ɔːr dœvr)/ *n, pl* **hors d'oeuvres** *also* **hors d'oeuvre** /aw'duhv(z) (*Fr* ~)/ ...

two pronunciations separated by *often*, indicating that they are **variants** but that the second is considered incorrect by many speakers **(11.5)**

**gypsophila** /jip'sofilə; *often* ˌjipsə'fili·ə/ *n* ...

**lieutenant** /lef'tenənt; *Royal Navy* lə'tenənt; *NAm* looh'tenənt/

pronunciation showing specialist and **regional variant (11.5)**

two pronunciations separated by *also*; indicating that they are **variants** but that the second is less common, or is considered less correct by some speakers **(11.5)**

**longitude** /'lonjityoohd; *also* 'long-giˌtyoohd/ *n* ...

*usage* The pronunciation /'lonjityoohd/ is recommended for BBC broadcasters.

advice as to the 'safer' choice where there is some **dispute** over a pronunciation **(11.5)**

# How to use this dictionary

## 1 How to find the word you want

Most of the words defined in this dictionary, both single words and compounds, are entered as main entries in alphabetical order. Words that are not defined, because their meaning can easily be guessed from their base form plus an added word-part, are entered either under their base form for words with suffixes or in a separate alphabetical list for words with pre-fixes (see 1.2). Idiomatic phrases are entered under the main word in the phrase (see 1.3). Phrasal verbs are entered under their base verb (see 1.4).

### 1.1 Main entries

1  Alphabetical order of entry, letter by letter, applies to all main entries, whether they are single words, hyphenated words, or compounds consisting of two or more individual words. This means that, for example, **giveaway** comes between **give-and-take** and **given**:

²**give** *n*
**giveaway** ... *n*
**given** ... *adj*
**given name** *n*

2  A main entry with a number in it comes before a main entry with a letter in the same position:

**mi-**
**MI5**
**MI6**
**Miami**

But main entries that *begin* with a number are listed as if the number were spelt out as a word:

,**two-'fisted**
**2,4,5-T**
,**two-'handed**

3  Main entries beginning with Mc- are listed as if they were spelt **Mac-**.

4  Main entries beginning with St are shown with the abbreviation spelt out in full:

**Saint Vitus's dance**

5  Many words that share the same spelling have a different pronunciation or a different history, or are different in grammar. Such words are shown separately in this dictionary, with superior figures in front to distinguish them:

¹**head** *n*
²**head** *adj*
³**head** *vt*

These words are generally listed in historical order, according to when they first appeared in English.

### 1.2 Undefined words

Words whose meaning can easily be guessed, because they consist of a base form plus an added ending, are not given definitions. These words are shown at the end of the definition of their base form, and after the etymology, if there is one:

**charitable** ... *adj* ... – **charitableness** *n*, **charitably** *adv*

This means that the meaning of **charitableness** can be guessed from the meaning of **charitable** plus the meaning of the ending **-ness**, which can also be found at its own place in the dictionary. Sometimes the undefined entry has the same form as its base, but a different part of speech:

**miaow** *n* **1** the characteristic cry of a cat ... – **miaow** *vi*

This means that the verb **miaow** is obviously related to the noun **miaow** – 'to make the characteristic cry of a cat'.

Words whose meaning can be guessed because they consist of a base form plus **anti-, non-, over-, re-, self-,** or **un-** are entered alphabetically, without definitions, in separate lists.

### 1.3 Idiomatic phrases

An idiom is a fixed phrase whose meaning cannot be guessed from the meanings of the individual words from which it is made up. Idioms are shown at the end of an entry, after the etymology and any derived undefined words:

¹**spade** *n* ... – **call a spade a spade 1** to call a thing by its right name however coarse ...

They are entered at the first noun they contain; hence **on the ball** appears at **ball, in spite of** is shown at **spite,** and **apple of somebody's eye** is entered at **apple.** If they contain no noun, they are entered at their first adjective; hence **contrary to** is shown at ²**contrary.** If they contain no adjective, they are entered under their first adverb; if they contain no adverb, they are entered under their first verb; and if they contain no verb, they are entered under their first word.

When an idiom has more than one accepted form, it is entered at the first invariable meaningful word it contains, regardless of the above hierarchy. The alternative form is shown after an oblique ( / ):

**breathe** ... *vi* ... – **breathe easily/freely** ...

### 1.4 Phrasal verbs

Compound verbs consisting of a base verb followed by an adverb, a preposition, or both, are entered in a separate alphabetical list at the end of the entry for their main verb. Hence **pick at, pick off, pick on, pick out, pick over,** and **pick up** can all be found at the end of the entry for the verb **pick.**

### 1.5 Abbreviations

Abbreviations that are commonly used in English are listed separately (pp 1761–74). However, some abbreviations that are used like ordinary words, such as the noun **IOU** and the verb **KO,** are entered at their alphabetical places in the main body of the text. You should check in both places when in doubt.

## 2 Alternative versions of words

Many words come in pairs, or even trios, that are nearly identical. They may differ only in spelling (e g **judgment**, **judgement**), or in their ending (e g **polyphonic, polyphonous**), or even in the presence or absence of a complete word in a compound (e g **silk screen, silk-screen printing**). In this dictionary, common variant forms of a word are shown immediately after the main entry.

1 When the variant is preceded by a comma, it is about as common as the main entry in current standard usage:

**judgment, judgement** *n*

When the variant is preceded by *also*, it is rather less common:

**poky** *also* **pokey** *adj*

These alternative forms are shown separately as main entries only if they fall more than ten places away from their main form in the alphabetical list.

2 Variant spellings of the **-ize/-ise** type are shown in abbreviated form. The variant **-ize** is taken as the main entry:

**computer·ize, -ise** . . . *vt*
**liquid·izer, -iser** . . . *n*

This means that **computerize** can also be spelt **computerise.**

3 Feminine forms of words are shown in the same way as other variants:

**author** . . . *fem* **authoress** . . . *n*

4 Individual meanings, as well as whole main entries, can have variant forms:

**¹top** *n* . . . **8 top, top gear** *Br* the transmission gear of a motor vehicle giving the highest ratio of propeller-shaft to engine-shaft speed . . .

5 Variant forms that are entirely or partially restricted to British or American English are labelled *Br* or *NAm*:

**jail,** *Br also* **gaol** . . . *n* . . .
**gaol** . . . *vb or n, chiefly Br* (to) jail

This means that the spelling **jail** is used everywhere in the English-speaking world, but British English also uses **gaol** (see 8.3).

6 If the variable part of a pair of words is shown as a main entry in its own right, then this variation is *not* shown in the entry for the word formed from it. Hence **hemorrhage**, the American variant spelling of **haemorrhage**, is not shown because **hemo-** is already entered as the American variant of **haemo-.**

7 There are also, of course, many instances of pairs of words that mean the same but are not otherwise closely related to each other. In such cases, we give the definition at the entry for the commoner alternative, and refer to the less common one with the note '– called also . . .':

**gudgeon pin** *n* a metal pin linking the piston and CONNECTING ROD . . . – called also PISTON PIN

## 3 Parts of speech

Sometimes two or more parts of speech are combined:

**zilch** . . . *adj or n, chiefly NAm slang* zero

These are the various word classes to which the entries in this dictionary belong:

| | | |
|---|---|---|
| *adj* | adjective: | **energetic, durable** |
| *adv* | adverb: | **very, happily** |
| *comb form* | combining form: | **Anglo-, psych-** |
| *conj* | conjunction: | **but, insofar as** |
| *interj* | interjection: | **hey, bravo** |
| *n* | noun: | **dynamite, bird of paradise** |
| *prefix* | | **pre-, trans-** |
| *prep* | preposition: | **for, to** |
| *pron* | pronoun: | **herself, ours** |
| *suffix* | | **-ful, -ness** |
| *trademark* | | **Hoover, Valium** |
| *vb* | verb (both transitive and intransitive): | **agglomerate, americanize** |
| *vb impersonal* | impersonal verb: | **methinks** |
| *verbal auxiliary* | | **can, must** |
| *vi* | intransitive verb: | **arise, arrive** |
| *vt* | transitive verb: | **indicate, thank** |

## 4 Inflections

The dictionary shows only those inflections which are irregular and may cause difficulty. They are written out in full, unless they involve merely the doubling of a consonant or the change of **-c-** to **-ck-**:

**¹mouse** . . . *n, pl* **mice**
**¹swat** . . . *vt* **-tt-**
**²picnic** . . . *vi* **-ck-**

This means that the present participle and past of **swat** are **swatting** and **swatted**, and those of **picnic** are **picnicking** and **picnicked**.

### 4.1 Nouns

Regular plurals of nouns (e g **cats, matches, spies**) are not shown. All other plurals (e g **louse, lice; sheep, sheep; graffito, graffiti**) are given.

1 Sometimes alternative plurals are possible:

**salmon** . . . *n, pl* **salmon,** *esp for different types* **salmons**

2 A plural may have an alternative pronunciation:

**¹bath** /bahth/ *n, pl* **baths** /bahths; *sense 3 also* bahdhz/

3 Some plurals are regular but might have been expected to be irregular:

**coleus** . . . *n, pl* **coleuses** . . .

4 Nouns that are always plural are shown as follows:

**environs** . . . *n pl* . . .

5 Sometimes an individual sense of a noun is exclusively plural:

**¹victual** . . . *n* . . . **2** *pl* supplies of food . . .

6 Some plural nouns do not always take a plural verb. This is shown as follows:

**genetics** *n taking sing vb* . . .
**forty winks** *n taking sing or pl vb* . . .

This means that one says 'Genetics is . . .' but one says either 'Forty winks is . . .' or 'Forty winks are . . .'.

7 Some nouns have no recognizable plural form, but nevertheless can take a plural verb:

**¹police** *n* . . . **2a** . . . **b** *taking pl vb* policemen
**silent majority** *n taking sing or pl vb* . . .

This means that one says 'Several police are . . .' but one says either 'The silent majority is . . .' or '. . . are . . .'.

## 4.2 Verbs

Regular verb forms (e g **halted, cadged, carrying**) are not shown. All other verb inflections (e g **rang, rung**) are shown.

1 A verb is counted as irregular if it ends in a vowel other than *-e*:

**²visa** *vt* **visas; visaing; visaed**

or if it keeps its final *-e* before the inflection:

**singe** . . . *vt* **singeing; singed**

2 There may be alternative inflections:

**²spell** *vb* **spelt** . . . *NAm chiefly* **spelled**

Inflections are shown in the following order:

present: 1st, 2nd, and 3rd person singular; plural; present subjunctive; present participle; past: 1st, 2nd, and 3rd person singular; plural; past subjunctive; past participle.

3 For any given verb, only the irregular inflections are shown. Certain forms (e g the entire past tense, or the past tense and the past participle) are combined if they are identical. Thus in

**¹run** . . . *vb* **-nn-; ran; run**

the present participle is **running**, the entire past tense is **ran**, and the past participle is **run**.

4 Irregular American and archaic inflections are listed as separate entries in the dictionary, but are not shown at the main form of the verb:

**²dove** /dohv/ *NAm past of* DIVE
**hath** . . . *archaic pres 3 sing of* HAVE

## 4.3 Adjectives and adverbs

Adjectives and adverbs whose comparative and superlative are formed with **more** and **most**, or by adding **-(e)r** and **-(e)st** (e g **nicer, fastest, happier**) are not shown. All other inflections are shown:

**¹good** . . . *adj* **better** . . . **best** . . .

Inflections that involve a change of pronunciation are shown:

**¹young** /yung/ *adj* **younger** /'yung·gə/; **youngest** /'yung·gist/

so are alternative inflections:

**¹shy** . . . *adj* **shier, shyer; shiest, shyest** . . .

## 4.4 Pronouns

Inflections of pronouns are entered at their alphabetical place in the dictionary and cross-referred to their main form:

**²her** *pron, objective case of* SHE

# 5 Capitalization

Some words, or meanings of words, can be used with or without a capital letter, and we show this with the notes *often cap* and *often not cap*. In the case of compound words, the note specifies which parts are capitalized:

**pop art** *n, often cap P&A* . . .

# 6 How the meanings of words are shown

Sometimes, instead of giving a definition, the dictionary describes how a word is used:

**²after** *prep* . . . **3** – used to indicate the goal or purpose of an action <*go ~ gold*>

Trademarks are treated in the same way:

**Hoover** . . . *trademark* – used for a vacuum cleaner

Most words, however, are given ordinary dictionary definitions, with one or more meanings.

## 6.1 The numbering of meanings

1 The main meanings of a word are numbered:

**tress** . . . *n* **1** a plait of hair . . . **2** *usu pl* a long lock of hair . . .

2 When a numbered main meaning of a word is divided into subsenses, they are introduced by letters:

**¹title** . . . *n* **1** . . . **2a** something that justifies or substantiates a claim **b** an alleged or recognized right . . .

3 Divisions of a subsense are indicated by bracketed numbers:

**¹take** . . . *vb* . . . **1a** . . . **c(1)** to move against (e g an opponent's piece in chess) and remove from play . . . **(2)** to win in a card game . . .

4 When a definition is followed by a colon and two or more subsenses, this indicates that the meaning of the subsenses is covered by the introductory definition. The colon may be followed by e g when the subsenses are a representative sample rather than a complete list of meanings:

**activate** *vt* **1** to make (more) active or reactive, esp in chemical or physical properties: e g **a** to make (a substance) radioactive **b** to treat (e g carbon) . . .

5 When two meanings of a word are very closely related, they are not separated off with numbers or letters, but run together, with the word *esp, specif, also,* or *broadly* between them to show the way in which they are related:

**aggression** . . . *n* . . . **2** attack, encroachment; *esp* unprovoked violation by one country of the territorial integrity of another . . .

## 6.2 The order in which senses are shown

Those meanings that would be understood anywhere in the English-speaking world are shown first, in their historical order: the older senses before the newer. After these come the meanings whose usage is restricted in some way (e g because they are used in only one area, or have gone out of current use).

## 6.3 Brackets

Round brackets are used in seven main ways in definitions in this dictionary. They:

a) enclose the object of a verb:

**²contract** . . . *vt* . . . **2a** to catch (a disease) . . .

b) give extra information:

**³nap** *n* a hairy or downy surface (e g on a woven fabric)

c) separate the parts of a combined definition that relate to different parts of speech:

**cheep** . . . *vi or n* (to utter) a faint shrill sound characteristic of a young bird

d) enclose optional wording:

**afloat** . . . *adj or adv* **1a** borne (as if) on the water or air . . .

This indicates that **afloat** means both 'borne on the water or air' and 'borne as if on the water or air'.

e) enclose scientific Latin names for plants and animals:

**timothy** . . . *n* a European grass (*Phleum pratense*) that has long cylindrical spikes . . .

f) give brief explanations of words in small capital letters:

**²dominant** *n* . . . **2** the fifth note of a DIATONIC scale (ordinary 8-note musical scale) represented in sol-fa by *soh* . . .

The small capital letters mark specialized words which the reader can look up for more detailed information.

g) enclose specialized words in small capital letters, either to mark them out as useful items for further reference, or, when they are followed by a sense number, to lead the reader to a particular sense of that word:

**beating reed** *n* a thin flat piece of metal, cane, etc (REED 6a) in a musical instrument, that vibrates against the edges of an air opening . . . to which it is attached

# 7 Examples

Definitions in this dictionary, particularly of those words with several different senses, may be followed by an example phrase or sentence illustrating a typical use of the word in context. Many of these are actual quotations from a written, or spoken, source; in such cases the author or source is given.

1 Examples are printed in italics between angle brackets (< >). The word being illustrated is represented by a swung dash (~):

**highroad** . . . *n* **1** *the* easiest course *to* <*the ~ to success*>
**³tip** . . . *vt* . . . **3** . . . **b** to transfer by tilting <*~ in some of the cooking juices* – Jane Grigson>

2 When an inflected form of the main entry is being illustrated, it is shown by a swung dash followed by the inflection:

**¹dare** . . . *vt* **1a** . . . **b** to confront boldly; defy <*~* d *the anger of her family*>

The complete example is therefore 'dared the anger of her family'.

3 When the inflection changes the spelling of the base form of the word it is written out in full:

**come** . . . **1a** . . . <came *running to her mother*>

# 8 Usage

There is more to a complete description of a word than a definition of its meaning; many words have peculiarities of usage that a dictionary must take account of. They may be restricted to a particular geographical area; they may have fallen out of use; and there may be limitations on the sort of context in which they are used.

## 8.1 The ways in which usage is shown

1 Words, or meanings, that are limited to a particular period, area, or level of usage are identified by an italic label:

**²fain** *adv, archaic* **1** with pleasure . . .
**howff** . . . *n, Scot* a haunt, resort; *esp* a pub
**thrasonical** . . . *adj, formal* bragging, boastful

2 Italic labels are also used to identify the subject area to which a word or meaning belongs:

**³quadruple** *adj* . . . **3** *music* marked by four beats per bar . . .

3 When an italic label comes between the main entry and the first definition it refers to all meanings of the word; otherwise, it applies to all subsenses of the number or letter it follows.

4 All other information of relatively limited scope on usage is given in a note at the end of a definition:

**¹dolly** . . . *n* **1** a child's doll – used chiefly by or to children

5 When a usage note applies to all or several meanings of a word, it follows the last definition, and is introduced by the symbol □:

**³rag** *vb* **-gg-** *chiefly Br informal vt* **1** to scold **2** to torment, tease *~ vi* to indulge in horseplay; behave noisily <*Evans and Jones were ~ging in the corridor*> □ no longer in vogue [origin unknown]

6 Longer statements about a word's usage are given in short essays at the end of an entry, headed *usage* or *synonyms* (see 8.6).

## 8.2 Words that are no longer in current use

1 The label *obs* for 'obsolete' means there is no evidence of use for a word or meaning since 1755 (the date of publication of Samuel Johnson's Dictionary):

**choler** . . . *n* . . . **3** *obs* biliousness

The label *obs* is a comment on the word being defined, not on the thing it designates.

2 When a thing, as opposed to the word for it, is obsolete, this is indicated in the definition:

**peruke** . . . *n* a long curly wig worn by men in the 17th, 18th, and early 19th centuries

3 The label *archaic* means that a word or meaning once in common use is found today only in special contexts, such as poetry or historical fiction, where it is used to introduce a flavour of the past:

**egad** . . . *interj, archaic* – used as a mild oath
**¹travail** . . . *n* . . . **2** *archaic* the pains of childbirth; labour

4 Some of the more common archaisms that tend to linger on in poetic diction are labelled *poetic*:

**e'en** . . . *adv, poetic* even

5 Comparatively modern terms which have become old-fashioned because they belong to rapidly changing areas of vocabulary such as science and technology, or casual everyday speech, are treated more explicitly by means of a note:

**matron** . . . *n* . . . **2** *Br* a woman in charge of the nursing in a hospital – not now used technically
**cripes** . . . *interj, chiefly Br slang* – used for expressing surprise or amazement; no longer in vogue

## 8.3 Words that are not used throughout the English-speaking world

1 A word or sense limited in use to one or more of the countries of the English-speaking world is labelled accordingly:

**³crook** *adj, Austr & NZ informal* **1a** bad, unpleasant

The label *Br* indicates that a word or meaning is used in Britain and also usually the Commonwealth countries of Australasia. The label *NAm* indicates the use of a word or meaning in both the USA and Canada.

2 A word or meaning whose use is limited to a particular part of Britain, or occasionally of the USA, is labelled accordingly:

**²hinny** . . . *n, Scot & N Eng* **³DEAR 1b**
**you-all** *pron, chiefly S US* you

3 The label *dial* for 'dialect' indicates that a word or meaning belongs to the common local speech of several different places:

**critter** . . . *n, dial* a creature

4 All the abbreviations used in such labels as these are explained on pp xxvii–xxviii.

## 8.4 Words that suggest a particular style, attitude, or level of formality

It is not the role of a responsible modern dictionary to dictate usage; it can only make statements, based on reference to a large stock of spoken and written data, as to how a word is being used by the community at large. However, most English words can be generally used in both speech and writing, but some would be traditionally described as 'informal' or 'slang', and others, perhaps, as 'formal'.

It is always hard to apply such descriptions consistently, since the status of these words is constantly shifting with the passage of time, and others are also frequently used in an incongruous setting for stylistic effect.

1 The label *informal* is used for words or senses that are characteristic of conversational speech and casual writing (e g between friends and contemporaries) rather than of official or 'serious' speech or writing:

**snifter** ... *n, informal* **1** a small drink of spirits ...
**²creepy-crawly** *n, Br informal* a small creature (e g an insect or worm); *esp* one that does not fly

2 The label *slang* is used for words or meanings found in contexts of extreme informality. Such words may be, or may have been until recently, used by a particular social group such as criminals, drug users, or the armed forces. They often refer to topics that are thought of as risqué or 'low':

**porridge** ... *n* ... **2** *Br slang* time spent in prison
**pissed** ... *Br slang* drunk

3 At the opposite end of the scale, the label *formal* is used for words or meanings characteristic of written rather than spoken English, and particularly of official or academic writings:

**importunate** ... *adj, chiefly formal* ... extremely persistent in request or demand

4 Some labels describe the attitude or tone of the user of a word:

**egghead** ... *n, derog or humorous* an intellectual, highbrow
**working girl** *n, euph* a prostitute

**8.5 Warnings about words**
Many people would disapprove of the use of some of the words we have described as *slang* or *informal*, and there are contexts in which their use would be quite inappropriate; but there is a further distinct class of words that are generally felt to be 'incorrect'. Such words are likely to arouse controversy or disapproval.

1 The label *nonstandard* is used for words or meanings that are quite commonly used in standard English but are considered incorrect by many speakers:

**¹lay** ... ~*vi* ... **5** *nonstandard* ¹LIE

2 The label *substandard* is used for words or meanings that are widely used but are not part of standard English:

**learn** ... *vb* ... **2** *substandard* to teach <*that teacher never* ~t *me nothing*>

3 Certain highly controversial words or meanings have a warning note '– disapproved of by some speakers':

**disinterested** ... *adj* **1** uninterested – disapproved of by some speakers

4 A word that might easily be confused with another, perhaps better-known, word is marked with the warning symbol △ before the one with which it might be confused:

**formication** ... *n* ... △ fornication

**8.6 Advice on usage**
More complex problems about the use of words are dealt with in short essays headed *usage*. These discuss areas where the user may be in real doubt, as with the question of whether to use a singular or plural verb after **each**, or the difference between **its** and **it's**, and difficulties caused by change in the language, as with **hopefully**.

1 The symbol △ is used in examples of 'what *not* to do':

**comprise** ... *vt* ... < △ *a chess set is* **comprised** *of 32 chessmen*>

2 Groups of words whose meanings must be delicately distinguished are treated together in short essays headed *synonyms*, at the entry for one of the words in the group, as with the discussion of **abandon, desert**, and **forsake** at **¹abandon**. The synonym is printed in small capitals:

**¹abandon** *vt* ... *synonyms* see FORSAKE

3 A word of opposite meaning to another is marked *antonym*:

**practicable** ... *adj* ... *antonym* impracticable

**8.7 The context in which a word can appear**
Many words or meanings can be used only in certain contexts within a sentence: some verbs are used only in the passive: some words can appear only in the negative, along with *not, never,* etc; others are always used with particular prepositions or adverbs, or in certain fixed phrases. Such restrictions are shown in a note following a definition:

**abide** ... *vt* **1a** to bear patiently; tolerate – used negatively
**agree** ... *vi* ... **2a** to be of one mind ... – often + *with* <*I* ~ *with you*>
**dumps** ... *n pl, informal* a gloomy state of mind; despondency – esp in *in the dumps*

Sometimes a word that is commonly used with the main entry word in a sentence is printed in italic within the definition:

**allude** ... *vi* to make indirect, casual, or implicit reference *to*
**²altogether** *n the* nude <*posed in the* ~> – *infml*

This means that **allude** is almost always used in the phrase *allude to*, and that the noun **altogether** is almost always used with *the*.

# 9 Cross-references

Cross-references draw your attention to a related word in another part of the dictionary. They are printed in SMALL CAPITAL letters.

A cross-reference may constitute an entire definition. This happens either when the word used in the definition has more than one meaning, and it is necessary to specify which meaning is referred to:

**²flash** *n* ... **5a** ... **c** FLASHLIGHT 2

or when the word used in the definition is a compound that is a main entry in the dictionary:

**rubella** ... *n* GERMAN MEASLES

A cross-reference that refers you to another entry that is related to the one you have looked up, or that may give you additional useful information, is introduced by 'compare':

**,white-'collar** *adj* ... – compare BLUE-COLLAR

Variant forms of prefixes and combining forms – that is to say, alternative spellings used when combining with different base forms (e g the **im-** form of **in-** in words like **impossible**) – are shown as follows in the alphabetical list:

**con-** – see COM-

Small capitals are also used for synonyms (see 8.6).

# 10 Prefixes, suffixes, and combining forms

Word elements that can be used to form new words in English are entered at their alphabetical place in the dictionary. These elements are prefixes (e g **pre-**, **un-**), suffixes (e g **-ous**, **-ly**), and combining forms (e g **Anglo-**, **-logy**).

Suffixes and combining forms added to the end of a word may alter the grammatical function as well as the meaning of the word. Where appropriate, this change of part of speech is indicated as follows:

¹-ful ... *suffix* 1 (*n → adj*) full of <*eventful*> <*colourful*>

This means that the suffix **-ful** is added to nouns to make adjectives.

# 11 Pronunciation

## 11.1 Type of pronunciation represented
The dictionary attempts to give all the most common variant pronunciations of each word. It is not, however, possible to include all the many regional and social variants, and so the pronunciation represented here is what may be called a 'standard' or 'neutral British-English' accent: the type of speech characteristic of those people often described as having 'no accent'. A better definition would be that it is an accent that betrays nothing of the region to which the speaker belongs.

Different age groups may also pronounce words differently. Some pronunciations that have become so old-fashioned as to be used only by the elderly have been excluded, as have certain others which have recently come into vogue amongst the young but which are not yet sufficiently established to be worthy of inclusion.

## 11.2 Choice of symbols
English spelling is often a poor guide to the pronunciation of a word. In **bough, cough, rough, thorough, though, thought,** and **through,** the sequence **ough** represents seven different sounds. There are in fact 23 vowel sounds in English (see the chart below) and only five letters (a, e, i, o, u) in the spelling to represent these sounds. Nevertheless, by choosing those combinations of letters which are regularly used in English spelling to represent a particular sound, it is possible to produce a pronunciation system that is quick and easy to learn.

| *Vowels* | | | *Consonants* | | |
|---|---|---|---|---|---|
| a | as in | bad, fat | b | as in | bad |
| ah | ,, | father, oompah | ch | ,, | cheer |
| aw | ,, | saw, awful | d | ,, | day |
| ay | ,, | make, hay | dh | ,, | they |
| e | ,, | bed, head | f | ,, | few |
| ee | ,, | sheep, key | g | ,, | gay |
| eə | ,, | there, hair | h | ,, | hot |
| i | ,, | ship, lick | j | ,, | jump |
| ie | ,, | bite, lied | k | ,, | king |
| ie·ə | ,, | fire, liar | kh | ,, | loch |
| iə | ,, | here, fear | l | ,, | led |
| o | ,, | pot, crop | m | ,, | man |
| oh | ,, | note, Joan | n | ,, | sun |
| oo | ,, | put, cook | ng | ,, | sung |
| ooh | ,, | boot, lute | nh | ,, | restaurant |
| ooə | ,, | jury, cure | p | ,, | pot |
| ow | ,, | now, bough | r | ,, | red |
| owə | ,, | our, power | s | ,, | soon |
| oy | ,, | boy, loiter | sh | ,, | fish |
| oyə | ,, | lawyer, sawyer | t | ,, | tea |
| u | ,, | cut, luck | th | ,, | thing |
| uh | ,, | bird, absurd | v | ,, | view |
| ə | ,, | mother, about | w | ,, | wet |
| | | | y | ,, | yet |
| | | | z | ,, | zero |
| | | | zh | ,, | pleasure |

All pronunciations are shown within slant lines (/    /): so for instance /ie/ is pronounced as it is spelt in **lied, spied, cried,** although this same sound may also be spelt in other ways (e g **cry, giant, right**), and /ee/ is pronounced as it is spelt in **meet, street, feet,** etc, although this same sound may also be spelt as in **stream, key, quay,** and **people.** Below are a few examples:

| | | | |
|---|---|---|---|
| cheat | /cheet/ | fountain | /'fowntin/ |
| luck | /luk/ | measure | /'mezhə/ |
| lute | /looht/ | thought | /thawt/ |
| rhyme | /riem/ | rough | /ruf/ |
| hair | /heə/ | knight | /niet/ |

## 11.3 Stress

1 *Primary stress*
In all English words of two or more syllables one syllable is more prominent than the others, and we say it has greater stress or *primary stress*. For instance, in the word **paper** the first syllable **pa-** has greater stress than the second syllable **-per**, and in **complete** the second syllable has greater stress than the first.
In the pronunciation entries the symbol /'/ is placed *before* the syllable with primary stress:

**paper** /'paypə/
**complete** /kəm'pleet/

2 *Secondary stress*
Some longer words also have *secondary stress* on another syllable; that is, the syllable has some prominence but not so much as that syllable with primary stress. The symbol /,/ is used before such syllables. For instance, in **university** the syllable **-ver-** has primary stress, but the first syllable also has some stress. This is secondary stress, and we show the pronunciation in **university** as /,yoohni'vuhsəti/.

3 *Stress on compounds*
Some main entries in the dictionary consist of two or more words separated by a hyphen. If each of these words is listed and given a pronunciation at its own alphabetical place in the dictionary, the hyphenated word is not given a full pronunciation, but only a 'stress pattern':

**'cover-,up**

A main entry which consists of two or more words separated by spaces will not be given a stress pattern.

Main entries consisting of two or more individual words are not normally given a full pronunciation. Since the pronunciation in **lighthouse** may be partially guessed from that of **light**, only the pronunciation of the latter part of the compound is shown, together with a stress pattern:
**light** /liet/
**lighthouse** /-,hows/

4 *Alternative stress patterns*
It is sometimes convenient to show alternative stress patterns by using a hyphen to represent each syllable:

**impracticality** /im,prakti'kaləti, ,---'---/

showing that the secondary stress may be either on the second syllable /prak/ or the first syllable /im/.

5 *Stress shift*
There are certain words for which the stress pattern changes according to the position of the word within a phrase or sentence. For example, **brigadier** has primary stress on the last syllable **-dier**, but when this word is used in the phrase **brigadier general**, the primary stress shifts to the first syllable of **general**, and there is now secondary stress on the first syllable of **brigadier**. The stress pattern shown in this dictionary is always that which would be used if the word were read out by itself.

## 11.4 Special symbols

1 *The symbol /ə/*
This is the only special phonetic character used in this dictionary. It represents the unstressed vowel sound in **mother**, **about**, **purpose**, and may correspond to many different vowels in ordinary spelling.

2 *Bracketed* (ə)
This symbol is used when the sound /ə/ may be either pronounced or missed out, or where its presence or absence is
uncertain. Most syllables of English contain a vowel:
**telephone** /'telifohn/ has three syllables and three vowels, /e/,
/i/, and /oh/. But certain consonants can form a syllable by
themselves: **cattle** /'katl/ has two syllables, /'kat/ and /l/. In a
word such as **memory** /'mem(ə)ri/, a bracketed /(ə)/ is used, to
show that the /r/ may or may not form a syllable: one can say
/'memri/, /'meməri/, or /'memr·i/. Similarly, **sudden** /'sud(ə)n/
may be pronounced /'sudn/ or /'sudən/.

The bracketed symbol (ə) may also be used after the vowel
/ie/:

**giro** /'jie(ə)roh/

This means that some people pronounce the vowel as /ie·ə/
and others simply as /ie/.

3 *Hyphens*
A hyphen in the spelling of a word is not shown in its pronunciation. However, a hyphen is used in pronunciation entries in
the following cases:

a) to show that the pronunciation is not a full word and cannot
stand alone (e g for prefixes or suffixes):

**pre-** /,pree-, pri-/
**-tion** /-sh(ə)n/

b) to show that part of the pronunciation has not been
repeated:

**²digest** /di'jest, die-/

Since the syllable /-'jest/ is the same for both variants it is not
written twice.

4 *Centred dot*
A centred dot (·) separates pairs of letters that might otherwise be wrongly read as one sound. It separates /n/ from /g/
where the sound /ng/ as in **sing** is not intended, or /t/ from /h/
where /th/ as in **through** is not intended:

**knighthood** /'niet·hood/

The centred dot may also occur within a single syllable:

**fire** /fie·ə/

This shows that the sequence /ieə/ should not be read /i·eə/ as
in **Riviera**.

5 *Swung dash*
A swung dash means that one or more whole words have not
been repeated in the pronunciation line. It is used in the
following cases:

a) where the plural form of a word although spelt differently
has the same pronunciation as the singular:

**hors d'oeuvre** /aw 'duhv (*Fr* ɔːr dœvr)/ *n, pl* **hors d'oeuvres**
*also* **hors d'oeuvre** /aw 'duhv(z) (*Fr* ~)/

Here the French pronounce the singular and plural in the same
way although when anglicized the plural form may be different
from the singular.

b) where the pronunciation of a word has been shown previously and is not repeated when that word occurs within a
phrase:

**mousseline** /'moohsleen (*Fr* muslin)/
**mousseline de soie** /~ də 'swah (*Fr*~ də swa)/
**cheval-de-frise** /shə,val də 'freez (*Fr* ʃəval də friz)/ **chevaux-
de-frise** /shə,voh ~ (*Fr* ʃəvo~)/

**11.5 Variant pronunciations**

1 *Alternative pronunciations*
In general, the first variant shown is considered to be the most
usual, although even if two or more pronunciations are
genuinely equal in acceptability, it is inevitable because of the
nature of print that one must be placed first on the page. All

pronunciations shown may be safely used, with the following
exceptions:

a) a pronunciation preceded by *also* is not so usual as th
other pronunciation(s) given.

b) when a pronunciation in general usage is disliked or considered to be incorrect by some speakers a note to this effect
follows the pronunciation:

**controversy** /'kontrə,vuhsi, kən'trovəsi USE *the last pron is
disliked by some speakers*/

Sometimes, further advice on a disputed pronunciation is
given in a note headed *usage* (see 8.6). Many of these notes
refer to the pronunciation recommended for use by BBC
broadcasters, which may be taken as a widely acceptable form.

2 *linking r*
In the neutral British-English accent we show in this dictionary, the final **r** is pronounced only if a vowel follows:

**far** /fah/
**faraway** /,fahrə'way/

Word-final **r** is not therefore shown on single words in this
dictionary.

Some people also pronounce r between two vowels in phrases
like **Shah of Iran** and **china and porcelain**.

This 'intrusive r' is usually considered incorrect and is not
shown in this dictionary.

3 *Feminine variants*
A separate pronunciation is not given for feminine variants
where it may be readily inferred:

**postmaster** /'–,mahstə/, *fem* **postmistress** [no pron] . . .

4 *wh forms*
Some people pronounce a sound like /hw/ at the beginning of
words such as **which, what, who**. Since this is a rare pronunciation nowadays it is not shown:

**which** /wich/

5 *Common variants that are not shown*
There are many words which some speakers pronounce
slightly differently from other speakers. Where such
differences are very slight, as in the cases below, it has been
decided not to show both variants, although each may be quite
usual. The fact that the other variant does not appear does not
mean that it is in any way undesirable.

*i/ə*
The two sounds /i/ and /ə/ are often variants within a word.
Some people pronounce the final syllable of **bargain, painless,
meanness** with an /i/ and others with /ə/. Because such words
are so very numerous, normally either /i/ or /ə/ is shown but not
both.

*i/y*
Words like **apiary, anaemia** may be pronounced with either /i/
or /y/:

**apiary** /'aypi·əri/

For such words only one variant is usually given:

*n/ng*
When a prefix such as **un-** is followed by a /k/ or a /g/ sound, the
*n* may be pronounced either as /n/ or as /ng/:

**ungainly** /un'gaynli/ or /ung'gaynli/.

Only one variant is normally shown.

6 *Foreign and specialized pronunciations*
French, German, and Spanish pronunciations (*Fr, Ger, Sp*)
are given where appropriate in the International Phonetic
Alphabet (IPA) (see 11.10). Pronunciations marked *naut* and

*tech* are those used by experts within the field to which the word belongs:

**leeward** /'leewood; *naut* 'looh·əd/

Here, lay people may say /'leewood/ but sailors would say /'looh·əd/

### 11.6 Main entries which are abbreviations

If the main entry consists merely of a sequence of capital letters, such as **BA** or **ESP**, the pronunciation is obvious, and so need not be given. However, abbreviations which may be pronounced as a word do receive a pronunciation:

**UFO** /'yooh,foh, ,yooh ef 'oh/

### 11.7 Inflections

Regular inflections are not given a pronunciation unless they are a main entry. Irregular inflections are given pronunciations throughout.

### 11.8 Strong and weak forms

Some common words have both a *strong form* and a *weak form*. The strong form is used only when the word is stressed or carries emphasis. Otherwise the weak form is used.

For instance, if I say 'I am going out', **am** is pronounced in its unstressed or weak form /əm/. But if someone denies that I am going out, I may repeat the same sentence with a different emphasis and say 'I *am* going out.' Here I have stressed the verb **am**, and the *strong form* /am/ is used.

Since the weak form is the most usual form of the word, this is given first in pronunciation entries and the strong form follows the word *strong*:

**am** /əm, m; *strong* am/
**¹her** /hə, ə; *strong* huh/

### 11.9 Foreign words and phrases

1 *American pronunciations*
American pronunciation often differs from that of British-English speakers, but a specifically American pronunciation is only shown when a word is pronounced in such a way that it might not be recognized by British speakers:

**clerk** /klahk; *NAm* kluhk/
**lieutenant** /lef'tenənt; *Royal Navy* lə'tenənt; *NAm* looh'tenənt/

Some American-influenced pronunciations are gaining popularity in Britain in such words as **temporary** /'tempəreri/, **temporarily** /,tempə'rerəli/, or **mandatory** /man'dayt(ə)ri/ instead of the more conventionally British-English /'temprəri/, /temprərəli/, and /'mandət(ə)ri/. Such pronunciations are shown only when they are considered to be sufficiently usual to have gained general acceptance.

2 *Latin words and phrases*
There are at least two distinct systems of pronouncing Latin words in English. Until the late nineteenth century the pronunciation system taught in most schools and universities was one which had developed together with the English language and which differed considerably from the original Roman Latin. This system has now been largely displaced by a reformed pronunciation which is believed to be closer to that of the original. The reformed Latin pronunciation system has been applied in this dictionary to words or phrases for which no conventional pronunciation has become established.

### 11.10 Borrowed words and phrases

Where English has 'borrowed' a word or phrase from a foreign language it eventually acquires an anglicized pronunciation. All such words in this dictionary are given a pronunciation which may be easily used by native English speakers who know nothing of the language from which the word is borrowed. However, many of these words are normally pronounced in a manner that is closer to the original

pronunciation, and in these cases the foreign pronunciation is also given within round brackets, using the International Phonetic Alphabet (IPA). This is because many foreign sounds cannot be adequately represented using the English alphabet. The IPA symbols used are as follows:

| Symbol | as in: | | Nearest English Equivalent |
|---|---|---|---|
| | FRENCH | GERMAN | |
| i | *nid* | *Inhalt* | heat |
| i: | — | *riechen* | feed |
| ɪə | — | *Bier* | beer |
| e | *été* | *Medikament* | day |
| e: | — | *mehr* | fair |
| ɛ | *sept* | *Kette* | pet |
| ɛ: | — | *Rätsel* | fair |
| eə | — | *Wiedersehen* | fair |
| a | *patte* | *Album* | cart |
| aɪ | — | *Fräulein* | tie |
| aʊ | — | *auf* | cow |
| ɑ | *bas* | *Ahnung* | card |
| ɔ | *tonne* | *Post* | hot |
| ɔɪ | — | *Fräulein* | toy |
| o | *chaud* | *Tomate* | coat |
| o: | *rose* | *Kohle* | code |
| ʊ | — | *unter* | put |
| u | *coup* | — | cool |
| u: | *rouge* | *Uhr* | cool |
| y | *cru* | *Führer* | crude |
| y: | *buche* | *physisch* | crude |
| ø | *bleu* | *öffnen* | early |
| ø: | *jeune* | *böse* | early |
| œ | *seul* | — | early |
| ə | *le* | *genug* | ado |
| ɛ̃ | *vin* | — | — |
| ɑ̃ | *blanc* | — | restaura*nt* |
| ɔ̃ | *non* | — | — |
| œ̃ | *brun* | — | — |
| ɥ | *nuit* | — | *whea*t |
| ç | — | *ich* | loch |
| x | — | *nach* | loch |
| ɲ | *pagne* | — | new |
| ŋ | — | *ringen* | pa*ng* |
| ʒ | *journal* | *Genie* | pleasure |
| ʃ | *chat* | *Strasse* | show |
| tʃ | *(tcheque)* | — | cheat |
| j | *mieux* | *Jahr* | you |

# 12 Etymologies

An etymology, or history of a word, is shown in square brackets [ ] after the definition, but before any derived undefined words or idioms (unless an idiom itself has been given an etymology).

### 12.1 Usual features

The etymology usually aims to trace a word's origin, together with any changes that have taken place in its form and meaning, as far as possible within the recorded history of language, working backwards step by step from its immediate source to the final point where its history becomes obscure. The chief features commonly described are:

1 *Earlier forms in English*
Whenever an etymologized word is descended from a word recorded in either or both of the earlier periods of English (i e Old English and Middle English), its occurrence in the earlier period(s) is shown, and its earlier form and meaning are presented if they differ from the form of the main entry and from the earliest sense defined:

**¹above** ... [ME, fr OE *abufan* ...]
**¹addle** ... [ME *adel* filth, fr OE *adela* ...]

## 2 Loanwords

When a word has been borrowed into English at any period from another language, the source-language is identified, and the form and meaning of the source-word are stated if they differ from those shown for the English word:

¹**join** . . . [ME *joinen,* fr OF *joindre* . . .]
**polo** . . . [Balti, ball]

## 3 Earlier history of loanwords

In the case of most words which belong to the general vocabulary of English, the earlier history of a foreign source-word is traced as far back as possible:

**dine** . . . [ME *dinen,* fr OF *diner,* fr (assumed) VL *disjejunare* to break one's fast, fr L *dis-* + LL *jejunare* to fast, fr L *jejunus* fasting]

Specialized or 'exotic' words which have entered English, such as **hummus** and **sargasso**, are often treated less fully, and with few exceptions a word from a language outside the Indo-European family is not traced any further back.

## 4 Prehistory and use of 'akin to'

Sometimes when a word has been traced back to its earliest recorded ancestor, an indication of its ultimate origin is given in the form of one or more significant words which are related to it by common descent (e g from Proto-Indo-European or Proto-Germanic); these related words (cognates) are introduced by the phrase 'akin to'.

The formula 'of [Celtic, Scandinavian, etc] origin; akin to . . .' is used when a word is known to have been borrowed from some word in a certain group of languages (e g Celtic or Scandinavian), but its origin cannot assuredly be traced to any particular known word in any particular language of that group. In this case, 'akin to' introduces words which belong to the named group and are related to the word in question. For example:

**skulk** . . . [ME *skulken,* of Scand origin; akin to Dan *skulke to* shirk, play truant]

The word **skulk** came into English in the 13th century, but there is no record of a related Scandinavian word as early as that; however, modern Danish *skulke* points to the existence of an earlier Scandinavian form from which the English word was borrowed.

## 12.2 Implied information

1 In etymologies, word or word-elements in *italics* are the source from which the main entry is derived. An English word or phrase in ordinary type after such a source-word explains its meaning or function.

**eulogy** . . . [. . . Gk *eulogia* praise . . .]
**parturition** . . . [. . . L *parturitus,* pp of *parturire* . . .]

When only certain letters or parts of a source-word are directly relevant to the etymology, those sections are shown in italic but the rest of the word appears in ordinary type.

2 If a source-word had the same form as the English word that comes from it, but a different meaning, that meaning is given:

**nimbus** . . . [L, rainstorm, cloud . . .]

3 If a source-word had the same meaning as the English word but a different form, that form is given.

**gracile** . . . [L *gracilis*]

4 If the source-word had the same form and meaning as the English word, it appears like this:

**scabies** . . . [L]

5 If there is no language-label before the first word in italics, it is English.

6 The same principles are applied throughout an etymology: when no meaning, form, or language-label is attached to an italicized word, then the meaning, form, and language of the word are to be taken as identical with that of the word preceding it. Take, for example, the etymology for **famous**:

[ME, fr MF *fameux,* fr L *famosus,* fr *fama* fame]

If this had to be written out in full, it would appear as:

[ME *famous* well-known, fr MF *fameux* well-known, fr L *famosus* well-known, fr L *fama* fame]

## 12.3 Cross-references

An explicit cross-reference such as 'more at SHILLING' directs you to another main entry where further information about etymology is to be found.

A cross-reference is implied when the same italicized form occurs in two or more etymologies which are not further than ten entries apart; to save repetition, full information about it is given only in one place, so that it is sometimes necessary to look at nearby entries for further details.

Cross-references introduced by 'cf' (compare) are sometimes used to link two or more words which have the same origin or a similar history.

## 12.4 Sub-etymologies

When one (or more than one) of the numbered meanings of a word has an origin which is not strictly identical with that of the other meaning(s), although not sufficiently different to justify listing it as a separate main entry, extra information about it is given:

**attrition** . . . [L *attrition-, attritio,* fr *attritus,* pp of *atterere* to rub against, fr *ad-* + *terere* to rub – more at THROW; (1) ME *attricioun,* fr (assumed) ML *attrition-, attritio,* fr L]

**walking** . . . [(1, 3, 4) fr prp of ¹*walk*; (2) fr gerund of ¹*walk*]

## 12.5 Explanatory etymologies

Sometimes, in place of or in addition to the history of a word, an etymology offers an explanation of *why* that word is used with a particular meaning. Such explanations are always introduced by 'fr':

**candidate** . . . [L *candidatus,* fr *candidatus* clothed in white, fr *candidus* white; fr the white toga worn by a candidate for office in ancient Rome]

**kiss of death** . . . [fr the kiss with which Judas betrayed Jesus (Mk 14:44–46)]

## 12.6 Special terminology

a) fr = from. This indicates various kinds of relationship between one word and another: e g borrowing, compounding, or grammatical change.

b) deriv = derivative. This means that at least one intermediate step has been left out in tracing the history of a word:

**apricot** . . . [alter. of earlier *abrecock,* deriv of Ar *al-birqūq* the apricot]

Here, the Arabic word may have reached us through Catalan, Italian, French, Spanish, or Portuguese.

c) alter. = alteration. This means that there has been a change of form, within a single language, following no regular pattern of linguistic change, as with **apricot**.

d) modif = modification. This means that there has been the same kind of change in a word borrowed from another language:

**boulevard** . . . [Fr, modif of MD *bolwerc* bulwark]

e) blend. This describes a word formed from two or more constituents which has at least one letter or sound in common with those constituents, or in which part of one constituent is inserted into the other:

**smog** . . . [blend of *smoke* and *fog*]

Compounds which do not meet these special conditions are treated differently:

**brunch** ... [*breakfast* + *lunch*]

## 12.7  Other languages

Abbreviations used in etymologies for the names of languages are listed on pp xxvii–xxviii. In addition, the following points may be noted:

1  Many technical terms used in the sciences and other specialized studies consist of words or word-elements which are current in at least two languages, with whatever minor changes of form are needed to adapt them to the structure of each individual language. Frequently it is not known which particular language they were originally formed in. The label ISV (International Scientific Vocabulary) is therefore attached to any such term which is not positively known to have originated in English.

2  The labelling and representation in writing of words from the Indian subcontinent presents a problem. When they were borrowed into English, the language of most of them was generally called Hindustani; but since partition in 1947, more commonly the names Hindi and Urdu have been used to denote the two similar but divergent main forms. Hindi, written in the Sanskritic (Devanagari) alphabet, is the form adopted in India; Urdu, written in Perso-Arabic characters, is the form adopted in Pakistan. In this dictionary, the label Hindi has generally been used in the wider sense formerly conveyed by Hindustani: 'a group of Indic dialects of northern India of which literary Hindi and Urdu are considered diverse written forms'. Words thus labelled are either common to Hindi and Urdu (e g **lac, sari**) or specifically Urdu (e g **lascar, sahib**); specifically Hindi words have usually been labelled Sanskrit, whether they came into English directly from Sanskrit (e g **Upanishad**) or via Hindustani (e g **maharishi**).

3  With a few special exceptions, a word borrowed from Latin or Greek is ascribed to the earliest period in which it is recorded in either of those languages with the same meaning that it has in the borrowing language, regardless of the date of the borrowing. Borrowings from other languages divided into historical periods, such as 'Old' and 'Middle', are attributed to the period corresponding to the date of the word's first recorded borrowing. In the cases of 'Old Italian', 'Old Portuguese', and 'Old Spanish', however, the term 'Old' does not denote a definable period, but indicates a form in Italian, Portuguese, or Spanish which was borrowed into the Old or Middle period of another language.

4  In many Latin and Greek nouns, the final consonant of the nominative singular case differs from the final stem consonant of other cases: e g Latin *nox* (meaning 'night') has the genitive form *noctis*. Such nouns are shown with the stem of the oblique cases preceding the nominative singular form (e g L *noct-, nox*)

5  The label 'native name', followed by the name of a country or region, is used in a few instances when it has been impossible to determine which particular language of that place the word comes from:

**koala** ... [native name in Australia]

## 12.8  Other alphabets

All forms from non-Roman alphabets (Hebrew, Arabic, Greek, Sanskrit, Chinese, Cyrillic, etc) are presented in conventional transliteration. Chinese words are shown in the Pinyin system, followed in parentheses by their equivalents in the older Wade-Giles system. In the Wade-Giles transliterations, as in representations of words from other tone languages where variations in the pitch of a sound serve to distinguish words of different meaning, small superscript numbers are used to indicate the tone of the word or syllable which they follow.

## 12.9  Main entries without an etymology

When lack of evidence makes it impossible to supply any satisfactory etymology, the phrase '[origin unknown]' is used. When a word is given no etymology, this is usually not because of lack of evidence but because it is considered that an etymology is unnecessary. This applies to any word which is:

a)  a trademark (e g **Vaseline**)

b)  the name of a tribe or people in its own language (e g **Zulu**)

c)  an interjection which is a natural non-linguistic sound (e g **bah, ugh, whee**)

d)  derived from the name of a person or place fully identified in the definition (e g **Tokay**)

e)  a shortened or contracted form (e g **exam, o'er**)

f)  a spelling variant of another word to which it is cross-referred (e g **kadi, kaftan**)

g)  an inflected form of a verb, noun, or adjective to which it is cross-referred (but special forms, such as **better** and **went**, and forms of the verb **be**, do have etymologies)

h)  a compound, derivative, or phrase created in English by the combination of forms listed in this dictionary, provided that the identity of each component is clear. Thus no etymology is given for **toothpaste** (from *tooth* + *paste*), for **dehumanize** (from *de-* + *humanize*), or for **polygamy** (from *poly-* + *-gamy*).

i)  formed by the addition of an easily-recognizable suffix to an English word, although it may have been formed in a language other than English. Thus **depression** has no etymology because it is an obvious derivative of **depress**, although in strict point of fact it was borrowed into English from French or Late Latin. In the same way, undefined related words (runons) have no etymology, even though in some cases such words may have been borrowed from another language rather than formed in English.

j)  created in English by change of grammatical function (as the verb **talk** led to the noun **talk**) from another main entry.

# Abbreviations used in this dictionary

Abbreviations and symbols used in the dictionary itself are listed below:

## A

**ab** about
**abbr** abbreviation
**abl** ablative
**acc** accusative
**AD** Anno Domini
**adj** adjective
**adv** adverb
**AF** Anglo-French
**Afrik** Afrikaans
**alter.** alteration
**am** ante meridiem
**AmerF** American French
**AmerInd** American Indian
**AmerSp** American Spanish
**amt** amount
**apprec** appreciative
**approx** approximate, approximately
**Ar** Arabic
**Arab** Arabian
**Aram** Aramaic
**arch.** archaic
**Arm** Armenian
**attrib** attributive
**aug** augmentative
**Austr** Australian
**AV** Authorized Version

## B

**b** born
**BC** before Christ
**Br** British
**Bret** Breton
**Btu** British thermal unit

## C

**c** centi-
**c** century
**C** Celsius, centigrade
**Can** Canadian
**CanF** Canadian French
**Cant** Cantonese
**cap** capital, capitalized
**Catal** Catalan
**Celt** Celtic
**cf** compare
**cgs** centimetre-gram-second
**Chin** Chinese
**comb** combining
**compar** comparative

**conj** conjunction
**constr** construction
**contr** contraction

## D

**D** Dutch
**Dan** Daniel
**Dan** Danish
**dat** dative
**deriv** derivative
**derog** derogatory
**dial.** dialect
**dim.** diminutive

## E

**E** East, Eastern
**E** English
**e g** for example
**Egypt** Egyptian
**Eng** English, England
**esp** especially
**etc** etcetera
**euph** euphemistic

## F

**f** femto-
**F** Fahrenheit
**fem** feminine
**fl** floruit (flourished)
**Flem** Flemish
**fr** from
**Fr** French
**freq** frequentative
**Fris** Frisian

## G

**Gael** Gaelic
**gen** genitive
**Gen** Genesis
**Ger** German
**Gk** Greek [to AD 200]
**Gmc** Germanic
**Goth** Gothic

## H

**hp** horsepower
**Heb** Hebrew
**Hitt** Hittite
**Hung** Hungarian

## I

**Icel** Icelandic
**i e** that is
**IE** Indo-European
**imit** imitative
**imper** imperative
**incho** inchoative
**Ind** Indian
**indef** indefinite
**indic** indicative
**infin** infinitive
**interj** interjection
**interrog** interrogative
**IrGael** Irish Gaelic
**irreg** irregular, irregularly
**Isa** Isaiah
**ISV** International Scientific Vocabulary
**It** Italian

## J

**J** joule
**Jap** Japanese
**Jav** Javanese

## K

**k** kilo-

## L

**L** Latin [to AD 200]
**LaF** Louisiana French
**lat** latitude
**Lat** Latin
**LG** Low German
**LGk** Late Greek [201–600]
**LHeb** Late Hebrew
**lit.** literally
**Lith** Lithuanian
**Lk** Luke
**LL** Late Latin [201–600]
**long** longitude

## M

**m** milli-
**M** mega-
**masc** masculine
**MBret** Middle Breton
**MD** Middle Dutch [1100–1500]
**ME** Middle English [1151–1500]
**MexSp** Mexican Spanish
**MF** Middle French [1301–1600]
**MFlem** Middle Flemish [1301–1600]
**MGk** Middle Greek [601–1500]
**MHeb** Middle Hebrew
**MHG** Middle High German [1101–1500]
**Mid Eng** Midlands
**Mid US** Mid United States
**MIr** Middle Irish [1001–1500]
**ML** Medieval Latin [601–1500]
**MLG** Middle Low German [1100–1500]
**modif** modification
**MPer** Middle Persian
**Mt** Matthew
**Mt** Mount
**MW** Middle Welsh [1151–1500]

## N

**n** nano-
**n** noun
**N** North, Northern
**NAm** North American
**naut** nautical
**NE Eng** North East England
**neg** negative
**N Eng** North England
**neut** neuter
**New Eng US** New England, United States
**NGk** New Greek [1501–]
**NHeb** New Hebrew [19th–20th century]
**NL** New Latin [1501–]
**nom** nominative
**Norw** Norwegian
**NW Eng** North West England
**NW US** North West United States
**NZ** New Zealand

# O

**obs** obsolete
**occas** occasionally
**OCatal** Old Catalan
**OE** Old English [–1150]
**OF** Old French [–1300]
**OFris** Old Frisian [–1500]
**OHG** Old High German [–1100]
**OIr** Old Irish [601–1100]
**OIt** Old Italian
**OL** Old Latin
**ON** Old Norse [–*ab* 1350]
**ONF** Old North French
**OPer** Old Persian
**OPg** Old Portuguese
**OProv** Old Provençal
**OPruss** Old Prussian
**orig** original, originally
**ORuss** Old Russian [1101–1500]
**OS** Old Saxon [–12th century]
**OSlav** Old Slavonic
**OSp** Old Spanish
**OSw** Old Swedish
**OW** Old Welsh [–*ab* 1150]

# P

**p** pence
**p** pico-
**PaG** Pennsylvania German
**part** participle
**pass** passive
**Pek** Pekingese
**Per** Persian

**perf** perfect
**perh** perhaps
**pers** person
**Pg** Portuguese
**phr(s)** phrase(s)
**pl** plural
**pm** post meridiem
**pp** past participle
**prep** preposition
**pres** present
**prob** probably
**pron** pronoun *or* pronunciation
**Prov** Provençal
**prp** present participle

# R

**RC** Roman Catholic
**redupl** reduplication
**refl** reflexive
**rel** relative
**Rom** Roman
**RSV** Revised Standard Version
**Russ** Russian
**RV** Revised Version

# S

**S** South, Southern
**SAfr** South Africa, South African
**Sc** Scots
**Scand** Scandinavian

**ScGael** Scottish Gaelic
**Scot** Scotland, Scottish
**Sem** Semitic
**Serb** Serbian
**SEU S** Survey of English Usage (spoken)
**SEU W** Survey of English Usage (written)
**Shak** Shakespeare
**SI** Système International d'Unités
**sing.** singular
**Skt** Sanskrit
**Slav** Slavonic
**Sp** Spanish
**specif** specifically
**St** Saint
**Ste** Sainte
**subj** subjunctive
**superl** superlative
**S US** Southern US
**Sw** Swedish
**SW Eng** South West England
**SW US** South Western United States

# T

**tech** technical
**TES** Times Educational Supplement
**THES** Times Higher Educational Supplement

**TLS** Times Literary Supplement
**trans** translation
**Turk** Turkish

# U

**UK** United Kingdom
**US** United States
**USA** United States of America
**usu** usually

# V

**va** verbal auxiliary
**var** variant
**vb** verb
**vi** verb intransitive
**VL** Vulgar Latin (used only for assumed forms)
**voc** vocative
**vt** verb transitive
**vulg** vulgar

# W

**W** Welsh
**W** West, Western
**WI** West Indian
**WUS** Western United States

# A

**¹a, A** /ay/ *n, pl* **a's** *also* **as, A's, As 1a** the 1st letter of the English alphabet **b** a graphic representation of or device for reproducing the letter *a* **c** a speech counterpart of printed or written *a* **2** the 6th note of a C-major musical scale **3** one designated *a*, *esp* as the first in an order or class ⟨A, *B and C left at intervals of one hour*⟩ **4a** a first-class mark or a grade rating a student's work as superior in quality **b** one who or that which is graded or rated with an A, *esp* as a mark of superior status ⟨*is this road an A?*⟩ **5** something shaped like the letter A – **from A to B** *informal* from one place to some other place ⟨*I just use it for getting from A to B*⟩ – **from A to Z 1** *informal* from beginning to end **2** including everything

**²a** /ə; *strong* ay/ *indefinite article* **1** ONE – used before singular nouns when the referent is unspecified ⟨~ *man overboard*⟩ ⟨~ *friend of John's*⟩ and before number collectives and some numbers ⟨~ *great many*⟩ ⟨~ *dozen*⟩ **2** the same ⟨*birds of ~ feather*⟩ ⟨*swords all of ~ length*⟩ **3a(1)** ANY ⟨~ *bicycle has two wheels*⟩ **a(2)** one single ⟨*can't see ~ thing*⟩ **b** – used before a mass noun to denote a particular type, instance, or unit ⟨~ *dessert wine*⟩ ⟨*glucose is ~ simple sugar*⟩ ⟨*two teas and ~ coffee*⟩ **c** – used before a noun formed from a verb to denote a period or occurrence of the activity concerned ⟨*had ~ little weep*⟩ ⟨*heard ~ crashing of gears*⟩ **4** – used before a proper name to denote (1) membership of a class ⟨*I was ~ Burton before my marriage – SEU S*⟩ (2) resemblance ⟨~ *Daniel come to judgment*⟩ (3) something made ⟨~ *Rembrandt*⟩ ⟨~ *Stradivarius*⟩ (4) one named but not otherwise known ⟨~ *Mrs Jones*⟩ **5** – used before a pair of items to be considered as a unit ⟨~ *cap and gown*⟩ □ used before words or letters with an initial consonant sound ⟨~ *BBC spokesman*⟩; compare ¹AN [ME, fr OE *ān* one – more at ONE]

*usage* **1** The strong pronunciation /ay/ has always been common in conversational speech when the speaker pauses to select the following noun, but its introduction into more formal speaking (eg by broadcasters) as if in imitation of conversational style is widely disliked. In any case, a is often pronounced /ay/ to express contrast ⟨*it's not a very good job, but it's a job*⟩. **2** A should be capitalized if it is the first word of a title ⟨*A E Housman wrote A Shropshire Lad*⟩.

**³a** /ə/ *prep* **1** PER 1 ⟨*twice ~ week*⟩ ⟨18p ~ *dozen*⟩ **2** *chiefly dial* on, in, at □ used before words or letters with an intial consonant sound; compare ³AN [ME, fr OE *a-, an, on*]

**A** /ay/ *n or adj* (a film) certified in Britain as suitable for all ages but requiring parental guidance for children under 14 – not used technically since December 12 1982; compare PG [adult]

**¹A1** *adj* **1** *of a ship* in first-class condition as defined in Lloyd's Register of Shipping **2** *informal* in very good health; in peak physical condition **3** *informal* excellent, first-class

**²A1** *n* a standard size of paper 594 × 840 millimetres (about 23¹/₂ × 33 inches)

**A2** *n* a standard size of paper 594 × 420 millimetres (about 23¹/₂ × 16¹/₂ inches)

**A3** *n* a standard size of paper 297 × 420 millimetres (about 11³/₄ × 16¹/₂ inches)

**A4** *n* a standard size of paper 297 × 210 millimetres (about 11³/₄ × 8¹/₄ inches)

**A5** *n* a standard size of paper 148 × 210 millimetres (about 5⁷/₈ × 8¹/₄ inches)

**¹a-** /ə-/ *prefix* **1** on; in; at; to ⟨*abed*⟩ ⟨*ajar*⟩ **2** in (such) a state or condition ⟨*ablaze*⟩ **3** in (such) a manner ⟨*aloud*⟩ **4** in the act or process of ⟨*gone a-hunting*⟩ ⟨*atingle*⟩ □ in predicative adjectives and adverbs [ME, fr OE]

**²a-** /ay-, a-/, **an-** /an-/ *prefix* not; without ⟨*asexual*⟩ ⟨*amoral*⟩ – a- used before consonants other than *h*, *an-* before vowels and usu before *h* ⟨*achromatic*⟩ ⟨*ahistorical*⟩ ⟨*anaesthetic*⟩ ⟨*anhedral*⟩ [L & Gk; L, fr Gk – more at UN-]

**-a-** *comb form* replacing carbon, esp in a ring ⟨*aza-*⟩ [ISV]

**-a** /-ə/ *suffix* (→ *n*) oxide ⟨*thoria*⟩ ⟨*alumina*⟩ [NL, fr *-a* (as in *magnesia*)]

**AA** *n or adj* (a film) certified in Britain as suitable for people over 14 – not used technically since December 12 1982; compare 15

**aah, ah** /ah *often prolonged*/ *vi* to exclaim in amazement, joy, or surprise ⟨*oohing and ~ing over the exciting new dresses*⟩ – **aah** *n*

**aardvark** /'ahd,vahk/ *n* a large burrowing nocturnal African mammal (*Orycteropus afer* of the order Tubulidentata) that has an extendable tongue, powerful claws, large ears, and heavy tail and feeds on ants and termites [obs Afrik, fr Afrik *aard* earth + *vark* pig]

**aardwolf** /'ahd,woolf/ *n* a striped mammal (*Proteles cristata*) of southern and eastern Africa that resembles the hyenas and feeds chiefly on carrion and insects [Afrik, fr *aard* + *wolf*]

**Aaronic** /eə'ronik/ *adj* of or stemming from Aaron, the brother of Moses; *specif* relating to various clerical orders so called in recognition of his archetypal priesthood

**Aaron's beard** /'eərənz/ *n* any of various plants having flower parts or other structures resembling hair; *esp* a Saint-John's-wort (*Hypericum calycinum*) that is a creeping shrub with bright yellow flowers [fr the reference to the beard of Aaron, brother of Moses, in Ps 133:2]

**Aaron's rod** *n* any of various plants that have long tall stems; *esp* a plant (*Verbascum thapsus*) of the foxglove family that has spikes of yellow flowers [fr the rod belonging to Aaron which miraculously blossomed (Num 17:1–8)]

**Ab** /ab/ *n* – see MONTH table [Heb *Ābh*]

**ab-** /ab-, əb-/ *prefix* from; away; off ⟨*abaxial*⟩ ⟨*abduct*⟩ [ME, fr OF & L; OF, fr L *ab-, abs-, a-*, fr *ab, a* – more at OF]

**aba, abba** /ə'bah, ah'bah/ *n* **1** a fabric woven from the hair of camels or goats **2** a loose sleeveless outer garment worn by Arabs [Ar *'abā'*]

**abaca** /,abə'kah/ *n* a fibre obtained from the leafstalk of a banana (*Musa textilis*) native to the Philippines; *also* the plant that yields abaca [Sp *abacá*, fr Tagalog *abaká*]

**aback** /ə'bak/ *adv* **1** in a position to catch the wind on what is normally the leeward side **2** by surprise; unawares – + *take* ⟨*was taken ~ by her sharp retort*⟩ **3** *archaic* backwards, back

**abacterial** /,aybak'tiəriəl/ *adj* not caused by or characterized by the presence of bacteria ⟨*an ~ inflammation*⟩

**abacus** /'abəkəs/ *n, pl* **abaci** /'abəkie, -sie/, **abacuses 1** a slab that forms the uppermost component of the capital of a column or pier **2** an instrument for performing calculations by sliding bead counters along rods or in grooves [L, fr Gk *abak-, abax*, lit., slab]

**¹abaft** /ə'bahft/ *adv* towards or at the stern; aft [¹*a-* + *baft* (aft)]

**²abaft** *prep* to the rear of; *specif* towards the stern from ⟨*stands just ~ the mainmast*⟩

**abalone** /,abə'lohni/ *n* any of a genus (*Haliotis* of the class Gastropoda) of edible rock-clinging INVERTEBRATE animals related to the snails and limpets, that have a flattened shell slightly spiral in form, lined with a type of mother-of-pearl, and used for decoration and ornament (eg in jewellery) [AmerSp *abulón*]

**¹abandon** /ə'band(ə)n/ *vt* **1** to give up with the intention of never resuming, reclaiming, or rescuing ⟨~*ed his studies*⟩ ⟨~*ed to horrible deaths*⟩ **2** to withdraw from, often in the face of danger or encroachment ⟨~ *ship*⟩ ⟨~ *their position*⟩ **3** to forsake or desert, esp in spite of an allegiance, duty, or responsibility ⟨*endure the ignominy of his ~ing her –* D H Lawrence⟩ **4** to surrender (oneself) unrestrainedly to a feeling, emotion, or activity – + *to* **5a** to cease from maintaining, practising, or using ⟨*immigrants slow to* ~ *their native language*⟩ ⟨ ~ *Islam for Christianity*⟩ **b** to cease intending or attempting to perform ⟨~ed *their attempts to escape*⟩ **6** to surrender (insured property) to the underwriter where there has been a partial loss so that the insured may claim a total loss – + *to synonyms* see FORSAKE [ME *abandounen*, fr MF *abandoner*, fr *abandon*, n, surrender, fr *a bandon* in one's power] – **abandoner** *n*, **abandonment** *n*

²**abandon** *n* a thorough yielding to natural impulses ⟨*danced with gay* ~⟩

**abandoned** /ə'bandənd/ *adj* **1** given up; forsaken ⟨*left* ~ *with nothing but the clothes he was wearing*⟩ **2** wholly free from restraint ⟨*an* ~ *party*⟩

**abandonee** /ə,bandə'nee/ *n* one who holds or claims abandoned property; *specif* the person (eg the insurer in marine insurance) to whom property or rights are relinquished

**à bas** /ah 'bah (*Fr* ə bə)/ *interj* down with ⟨à bas *the profiteers*⟩ [Fr]

**abase** /ə'bays/ *vt* **1** to bring lower in rank, office, prestige, or esteem **2** *archaic* to bring lower physically *synonyms* see ²HUMBLE *antonym* extol [ME *abassen*, fr MF *abaisser*, fr *a-* (fr L *ad-*) + (assumed) VL *bassiare* to lower] – **abasement** *n*

**abash** /ə'bash/ *vt* to destroy the self-possession or self-confidence of; disconcert [ME *abaishen*, fr (assumed) MF *abaiss-*, *abair* to astonish, alter. of MF *esbair*, fr *ex-* + *baer* to yawn – more at ABEYANCE] – **abashment** *n*

**abate** /ə'bayt/ *vt* **1** to put an end to; abolish ⟨ ~ *a nuisance*⟩ **2a** to reduce in degree or intensity; moderate ⟨*further research ... has by no means* ~d *his enthusiasm – TLS*⟩ **b** to reduce in value or amount; make less, esp so as to bring relief ⟨ ~ *a tax*⟩ **3** to deduct, omit ⟨ ~ *part of the price*⟩ **4** to beat down or cut away so as to leave a figure in relief (eg in metalwork) ~ *vi* **1** to decrease in force or intensity ⟨*the wind has* ~d⟩ **2** to become defeated or become null or void [ME *abaten*, fr OF *abattre* to beat down, slaughter – more at REBATE]

**abatement** /ə'baytmənt/ *n* **1** the act or process of abating; the state of being abated ⟨*noise* ~⟩ **2** an amount abated; *esp* a deduction from the full amount of a tax

**abatis, abattis** /'abətee, -tis; *mil* ,abə'tee/ *n*, *pl* **abatis, abatises, abattises** a defensive obstacle made of felled trees with sharpened branches facing the enemy [Fr, fr *abattre*]

**abattoir** /'abə,twah/ *n* a slaughterhouse [Fr, fr *abattre*]

**abaxial** /ab'aksi·əl/ *adj* situated outside or directed away from the AXIS of an organ, plant part, or organism – compare ADAXIAL

**abaya** /ə'bah·yah, ah-/ *n* ABA (Arab garment or cloth) [Ar *'abā'ah*]

**abba** /ə'bah, ah'bah/ *n* ABA (Arab garment or cloth)

**abbacy** /'abəsee/ *n* the office, dignity, jurisdiction, or tenure of an abbot or abbess [ME *abbatie*, fr LL *abbatia*]

**Abbasid** /'abəsid, ə'basid/ *n* a member of a dynasty of caliphs ruling the Muslim Empire (750–1258) and claiming descent from Abbas the uncle of Muhammad – **Abbasid** *adj*

**abbatial** /ə'baysh(ə)l/ *adj* of an abbey, abbess, or abbot

**abbé** /'abay/ *n* a member of the French secular clergy in major or minor orders – used as a title [Fr, fr LL *abbat-*, *abbas*]

**abbess** /'abes/ *n* a woman who is the superior of a convent of nuns [ME *abbesse*, fr OF, fr LL *abbatissa*, fem of *abbat-*, *abbas*]

**Abbevillian** /,ab(ə)'vilyən/ *adj* of the earliest Palaeolithic culture in Europe, characterized esp by crudely chipped stone hand axes [*Abbeville*, town in N France]

**abbey** /'abi/ *n* **1a** a monastery ruled by an abbot **b** a convent ruled by an abbess **2** the buildings, esp the church, of a former abbey ⟨*Westminster* Abbey⟩ [ME, fr OF *abaïe*, fr LL *abbatia* abbey, fr *abbat-*, *abbas*]

**abbo** /'aboh/ *n* ABO (Australian aborigine)

**abbot** /'abət/ *n* the superior of a monastery for men [ME *abbod*, fr OE, fr LL *abbat-*, *abbas*, fr LGk *abbas*, fr Aram *abbā* father]

**abbreviate** /ə'breeviayt/ *vt* to make briefer; *esp* to reduce to a shorter form intended to stand for the whole [ME *abbreviaten*, fr LL *abbreviatus*, pp of *abbreviare* – more at ABRIDGE] – **abbreviator** *n*

**abbreviated** /ə'breevi,aytid/ *adj* **1** made briefer or shortened **2** shorter and skimpier than normal ⟨*an* ~ *swimming costume*⟩

**abbreviation** /ə,breevi'aysh(ə)n/ *n* **1** the act or result of abbreviating; an abridgment **2** a shortened form of a written word or phrase used in place of the whole ⟨*amt is an* ~ *for* amount⟩

**ABC** *n* **1** ABC, *NAm chiefly* **ABC's**, **ABCs** *pl* an alphabet **2a** ABC, *NAm chiefly* **ABC's**, **ABCs** *pl* the rudiments of a subject, esp of reading, writing, and spelling **b** *Br* a handbook of time-tables or maps that usu has an index

**Abdias** /ab'die·əs/ *n* – see BIBLE table [LL, Obadiah]

**abdicate** /'abdikayt/ *vt* to relinquish (eg sovereign power or responsibility) formally ~ *vi* to renounce a throne, high office, dignity, or function [L *abdicatus*, pp of *abdicare*, fr *ab-* + *dicare* to proclaim – more at DICTION] – **abdicable** *adj*, **abdication** *n*, **abdicator** *n*

**abdomen** /'abdəmən, əb'dohmən/ *n* **1** the part of the body between the THORAX (usu middle body part behind the head) and the pelvis; the belly; *also* the cavity of this part of the trunk containing the liver, gut, etc **2** the rear part of the body behind the THORAX in a lobster, spider, insect, or other ARTHROPOD [MF & L; MF, fr L] – **abdominal** *adj*, **abdominally** *adv*

**abducens** /əb'dyoohsəns, -kenz/ *n*, *pl* **abducentes** /,abdyooh'-senteez/ ABDUCENS NERVE

**abducens nerve** *n* either of the 6th pair of CRANIAL NERVES that supply one of the muscles of the eye [NL *abducent-*, *abducens*, fr L, prp]

**abducent** /əb'dyoohsənt/ *adj*, *of a muscle* serving to abduct [L *abducent-*, *abducens*, prp of *abducere*]

**abduct** /əb'dukt/ *vt* **1** to carry off (esp a women or child) secretly or by force – compare KIDNAP **2** to draw away (eg a limb) from a position near or parallel to the central axis of the body; *also* to move (similar parts) apart [L *abductus*, pp of *abducere*, lit., to lead away, fr *ab-* + *ducere* to lead – more at TOW] – **abductor** *n*

**abduction** /əb'duksh(ə)n/ *n* **1** *anatomy* the action of abducting; the state of being abducted **2** the unlawful carrying away of a woman for marriage or intercourse

**abeam** /ə'beem/ *adv or adj* on a line at right angles to a ship's or aircraft's length ⟨*the island lay* ~ *of us*⟩

¹**abecedarian** /aybeesee'deəriən/ *n* one learning the rudiments of the alphabet; *broadly* one learning the rudiments of anything [ME *abecedary*, fr ML *abecedarium* alphabet, fr LL, neut of *abecedarius* of the alphabet, fr the letters *a + b + c + d*]

²**abecedarian** *adj* **1a** of the alphabet **b** alphabetically arranged ⟨*medieval* ~ *poems in which the first line begins with A, the second with B, and so on*⟩ **2** rudimentary

**abed** /ə'bed/ *adv or adj* in bed

**Abel** /'aybl/ *n* a son of Adam and Eve, killed by his brother Cain [LL, fr Gk, fr Heb *Hebhel*]

**abele** /ə'beel/ *n* the white poplar (*Populus alba*), a Eurasian tree having leaves covered in silvery-white hairs [D *abeel*, fr MD, fr ONF *abiel*, irreg fr L *albus* white]

**Abelian** /ə'beelyən/ *adj*, *maths* COMMUTATIVE 2 ⟨ ~ *group*⟩ ⟨ ~ *ring*⟩ [Niels *Abel* †1829 Norw mathematician]

**abelmosk** /'aybl,mosk/ *n* a bushy plant (*Hibiscus moschatus*) of the hollyhock family native to tropical Asia and the East Indies, whose musky seeds are used in perfumery and in flavouring coffee [deriv of Ar *abū-l-misk* father of the musk]

**Aberdeen Angus** /,abədeen 'ang·gəs/ *n* (any of) a breed of black hornless beef cattle originating in Scotland [*Aberdeen & Angus*, former counties in Scotland]

¹**aberrant** /ə'berənt/ *adj* **1** deviating from the right or normal way ⟨ ~ *behaviour*⟩ **2** diverging from the usual or natural type; not typical [L *aberrant-*, *aberrans*, prp of *aberrare* to go astray, fr *ab-* + *errare* to wander, err] – **aberrance** *n*, **aberrancy** *n*, – **aberrantly** *adv*

²**aberrant** *n* **1** an aberrant natural group, individual, or structure **2** a person whose behaviour departs substantially from the acceptable standard

**aberrated** /'abəraytid/ *adj*, *biology* aberrant [L *aberratus*]

**aberration** /,abə'raysh(ə)n/ *n* **1** the act or state of being aberrant, esp from a moral standard or normal state ⟨*it was just some momentary* ~⟩ **2** the failure of a mirror, refracting surface, or lens to produce exact correspondence between an object and its image **3** (an instance of) unsoundness or disorder of the mind **4** a small periodic change of apparent position in celestial bodies due to the combined effect of the velocity of light and the motion of the observer **5** an aberrant organ or individual; SPORT 5 [L *aberratus*, pp of *aberrare*] – **aberrational** *adj*

**abet** /ə'bet/ *vt* **-tt-** to give active encouragement or approval to ⟨*aided and* ~ted *in the crime by his wife*⟩ *antonyms* deter, hinder [ME *abetten*, fr MF *abeter*, fr OF, fr *a-* (fr L *ad-*) + *beter* to bait, of Gmc origin; akin to OE *bǣtan* to bait] – **abetment** *n*, **abetter**, **abettor** *n*

**ab extra** /ab 'ekstrə/ *adv* from outside [LL]

**abeyance** /ə'bayəns/ *n* **1** a lapse in succession during which there is nobody in whom a title is vested ⟨*a peerage in* ∼⟩ **2** temporary inactivity; suspension ⟨*a rule in* ∼ *since 1935*⟩ [MF *abeance* expectation, fr *abaer* to desire, fr *a-* + *baer* to yawn, fr ML *batare*] – **abeyant** *adj*

**abhor** /əb'(h)aw/ *vt* **-rr-** to regard with extreme repugnance; loathe; *also* reject *synonyms* see ²HATE *antonyms* admire, delight in [ME *abhorren*, fr L *abhorrēre*, fr *ab-* + *horrēre* to shudder – more at HORROR] – **abhorrer** *n*

**abhorrence** /əb'(h)orəns, əb'(h)aw-/ *n* **1** the feeling or state of abhorring **2** one who or that which is abhorred ⟨*my pet* ∼⟩

**abhorrent** /əb'(h)orənt, əb'(h)awrənt/ *adj* **1** opposed, contrary – + *to* ⟨*a notion* ∼ *to their philosophy*⟩ **2** causing horror; repugnant ⟨*acts* ∼ *to every right-minded person*⟩ **3** *archaic* feeling or showing abhorrence – + *of antonym* congenial [L *abhorrent-, abhorrens*, prp of *abhorrēre*] – **abhorrently** *adv*

**abidance** /ə'bied(ə)ns/ *n* **1** an act or state of abiding; continuance **2** compliance ⟨∼ *by the rules*⟩

**abide** /ə'bied/ *vb* **abode** /ə'bohd/, **abided** *vt* **1a** to bear patiently; tolerate – used negatively ⟨*can't* ∼ *such bigots*⟩ **b** *archaic* to sustain without yielding; withstand **2** *archaic* to wait for; await ∼ *vi* **1** to remain stable or fixed in a state ⟨*if any man's work* ∼ – I Cor 3:14 AV⟩ **2** *archaic* to continue to be present; sojourn ⟨*We* abode *in tents three days* – Ezra 8:15 AV⟩ *synonyms* see ³STAY, ²BEAR, CONTINUE [ME *abiden*, fr OE *ābīdan*, fr *ā-*, perfective prefix + *bīdan* to bide] – **abider** *n*

**abide by** *vt* **1** to acquiesce in; comply with ⟨*you must* abide by *the rules*⟩ **2** to be faithful to ⟨*you must* abide by *your oath*⟩

**abiding** /ə'bieding/ *adj* enduring, continuing ⟨*an* ∼ *interest in nature*⟩ – **abidingly** *adv*

**abigail** /'abigayl/ *n* a lady's personal maid – esp in historical contexts [*Abigail*, servant in *The Scornful Lady*, a play by Francis Beaumont †1616 & John Fletcher †1625 E dramatists]

**ability** /ə'biləti/ *n* **1a** the quality or state of being able; *esp* physical, mental, or legal power to perform ⟨*doubted her* ∼ *to walk so far*⟩ **b** natural or acquired competence in doing; skill ⟨*a man of great* ∼⟩ **2 abilities, ability** natural talent; aptitude ⟨*children whose* abilities *warrant higher education*⟩ [ME *abilite*, fr MF *habilité*, fr L *habilitat-, habilitas*, fr *habilis* apt, skilful – more at ABLE]

usage The normal construction is **ability** *to* do something, not **ability** *of* doing something ⟨△ the **ability** *which was so prevalent among the rural community of practising their traditional crafts*⟩ *synonyms* see CAPABILITY *antonym* inability

**-ability** *also* **-ibility** /-ə'biləti/ *suffix* (→ *n*) capacity, suitability, or tendency to (so act or be acted on) ⟨*readability*⟩ ⟨*excitability*⟩ [ME *-abilite, -ibilite*, fr MF *-abilité, -ibilité*, fr L *-abilitas, -ibilitas*, fr *-abilis, -ibilis*, *-able* + *-tas* -ty]

**ab initio** /ˌab i'nishioh/ *adv* from the beginning [L]

**ab intra** /ˌab 'intrə/ *adv* from within [NL]

**abiogenesis** /ˌay,bie·oh'jenəsis/ *n* the supposed spontaneous origination of living organisms directly from lifeless matter [NL, fr ²*a-* + *bio-* + L *genesis*] – **abiogenetic** *adj*, **abiogenetically** *adv*, **abiogenist** *n*

**abiotic** /ˌaybie'otik/ *adj* not involving or produced by living organisms ⟨∼ *material*⟩ – **abiotically** *adv*

**abject** /'abjekt/ *adj* **1a** *of a condition* showing utter hopelessness and degradation; deserving great pity ⟨∼ *poverty*⟩ **b** *of people or behaviour* showing lack of self-respect; servile, spiritless ⟨*your* ∼ *slave*⟩ ⟨∼ *surrender*⟩ **2** expressed or offered in a humble and often ingratiating spirit ⟨∼ *flattery*⟩ ⟨*an* ∼ *apology*⟩ *synonyms* see ¹MEAN [ME, fr L *abjectus*, fr pp of *abicere* to cast off, fr *ab-* + *jacere* to throw – more at ²JET] – **abjectly** *adv*, **abjectness** *n*

**abjection** /əb'jeksh(ə)n/ *n* **1** a low or downcast state; degradation **2** *formal* the act of making abject; humbling, subjection ⟨*I protest . . . this vile* ∼ *of youth to age* – G B Shaw⟩

**abjuration** /ˌabjə'raysh(ə)n/ *n* **1** the act or process of abjuring **2** an oath of abjuring

**abjure** /əb'jooə/ *vt* **1a** to renounce on oath or reject formally (e g a claim, opinion, or allegiance) ⟨*this rough magic I here* ∼ – Shak⟩ **b** to swear to leave (a country) **2** to abstain from; avoid ⟨∼ *extravagance*⟩ △ adjure [ME *abjuren*, fr MF or L; MF *abjurer*, fr L *abjurare*, fr *ab-* + *jurare* to swear – more at JURY] – **abjurer** *n*

**ablate** /ə'blayt/ *vt* to remove by cutting, erosion, melting, evaporation, or vaporization ∼ *vi* to become ablated [L *ablatus* (suppletive pp of *auferre* to remove, fr *au-* away + *ferre* to carry), fr *ab-* + *latus*, suppletive pp of *ferre* – more at UKASE, BEAR, TOLERATE]

**ablation** /ə'blaysh(ə)n/ *n* the process of ablating: e g **a** a surgical removal **b** removal of a part (e g the outside of a NOSE CONE of a rocket) by melting or vaporization **c** the loss of snow, ice, or water from a glacier

¹**ablative** /ə'blətiv/ *n* (a form in) a grammatical case expressing typically the relations of separation and source and also frequently such relations as cause or instrument – **ablative** *adj*

²**ablative** /ə'blaytiv/ *adj* **1** relating to ablation **2** tending to ablate ⟨∼ *material on a nose cone*⟩ – **ablatively** *adv*

**ablative absolute** /'ablətiv/ *n* a construction in Latin in which a noun or pronoun and its adjunct, both in the ablative case, form together an adverbial phrase expressing generally the time, cause, or an attendant circumstance of an action

**ablator** /ə'blaytə/ *n* a material that provides protection (e g to the outside of a spacecraft on re-entry) by ablating

**ablaut** /'aplowt, 'ab-/ *n* a systematic gradation of vowels in the same root, esp in the Indo-European languages, that is usu accompanied by differences in use or meaning (e g in *sing, sang, sung, song*) – compare UMLAUT [Ger, fr *ab* away from + *laut* sound]

**ablaze** /ə'blayz/ *adj or adv* **1** (being) on fire **2** radiant with light or bright colour; glowing ⟨*his face all* ∼ *with excitement* – Bram Stoker⟩

**able** /'aybl/ *adj* **1a** having sufficient power, skill, resources, or qualifications – used + *to* and an infinitive, esp to replace missing tenses of *can* ⟨*as I had more money I was better* ∼ *to help her*⟩ ⟨*am* ∼ *to baptize people*⟩ **b** susceptible to action or treatment ⟨∼ *to be fried*⟩ **2** marked by intelligence, knowledge, skill, or competence ⟨*the* ∼st *lawyer in London*⟩ [ME, fr MF, fr L *habilis* apt, fr *habēre* to have – more at GIVE]

usage The use of **able** as in sense **1b** with a passive infinitive, and particularly with a nonhuman subject, sounds awkward; perhaps because **able** suggests a skill or expertness more appropriate to a person who performs an action than to a person or thing that undergoes it. The construction can be avoided either by using *can* or *could* ⟨*it can be fried*⟩ or, where this is impossible, by recasting the sentence ⟨*we'll be* **able** *to fry it*⟩.

**-able** *also* **-ible** /-əbl/ *adj suffix* (→ *adj*) **1** fit for, able to, liable to, or worthy to (so act or be acted upon) ⟨*breakable*⟩ ⟨*reliable*⟩ ⟨*get-at-able*⟩ **2** marked by, providing, or possessing (a specified quality or attribute) ⟨*knowledgeable*⟩ ⟨*comfortable*⟩ [ME, fr OF, fr L *-abilis*, fr *-a-, -i-*, verb stem vowels + *-bilis* capable or worthy of] – **-ably** *also* **-ibly** *adv*

usage **-able** is the commoner form of this suffix, and is always used for words such as *packable* and *drinkable* that are built up from other English words. The rarer form **-ible** is used for certain borrowed words of Latin origin, such as *credible*.

,**able-'bodied** *adj* physically strong and healthy; fit

**able seaman, able-bodied seaman** *n* – SEE MILITARY RANKS table

**abloom** /ə'bloohm/ *adj* abounding with blooms; blooming ⟨*parks* ∼ *with roses*⟩

**ablution** /ə'bloohsh(ə)n/ *n* **1 ablutions** *pl*, **ablution** the washing of one's body or part of it, esp in a ritual purification; *also* a wash ⟨*performed his* ∼s⟩ **2** *pl* a building housing washing and toilet facilities (e g in a camp) [ME, fr MF or L; MF, fr L *ablution-, ablutio*, fr *ablutus*, pp of *abluere* to wash away, fr *ab-* + *lavere* to wash – more at LYE] – **ablutionary** *adj*

**ably** /'aybli/ *adv* in an able manner; capably and competently

**ABM** *n* ANTIBALLISTIC MISSILE

**Abnaki** /ab'nahki/ *n, pl* **Abnakis**, *esp collectively* **Abnaki** a member, or the Algonquian language, of an American Indian people of Maine and S Quebec

**abnegate** /'abnigayt/ *vt* **1** to surrender, relinquish ⟨∼d *his powers*⟩ **2** to renounce (a belief or idea) ⟨∼d *his God*⟩ [backformation fr *abnegation*, fr LL *abnegation-, abnegatio*, fr L *abnegatus*, pp of *abnegare* to refute, fr *ab-* + *negare* to deny – more at NEGATE] – **abnegation** *n*, **abnegator** *n*

**abnormal** /ˌab'nawməl, əb-/ *adj* deviating from the normal or average; *esp* markedly and disturbingly irregular ⟨∼ *behaviour*⟩ [alter. of earlier *anormal*, fr Fr, fr ML *anormalis*, fr L *a-* + LL *normalis* normal] – **abnormally** *adv*

synonyms What differs from the normal in standards, behaviour, and so on is **abnormal**; what fails to reach the normal is **subnormal** ⟨*subnormal intelligence*⟩ ⟨*subnormal temperatures*⟩, while what goes beyond the normal is **supernormal**.

**abnormality** /,abnaw'malǝti/ n 1 the quality or state of being abnormal 2 something abnormal

**abnormal psychology** n the psychology of mental and behavioural disorder; psychopathology

**abnormity** /ǝb'nawmǝti/ n abnormality; also a monstrosity [LL abnormitas, fr L abnormis irregular, abnormal, fr ab- + norma rule, pattern]

**abo, abbo** /'aboh/ n, pl abos, abbos often cap, Austr chiefly derog an aborigine – **abo, abbo** adj

¹**aboard** /ǝ'bawd/ adv 1 on, onto, or within a ship, aircraft, train, or road vehicle ⟨climb ∼⟩ ⟨all ∼!⟩ 2 archaic alongside

²**aboard** prep on, onto, within ⟨go ∼ ship⟩ ⟨∼ a plane⟩

**ABO blood group** n ABO SYSTEM

¹**abode** /ǝ'bohd/ n 1 a continued stay; a sojourn 2 formal a home, residence ⟨of no fixed ∼⟩ [ME abod, fr abiden to abide]

²**abode** past of ABIDE

**abolish** /ǝ'bolish/ vt to do away with (eg a law or custom) wholly; annul [ME abolisshen, fr MF aboliss-, stem of abolir, fr L abolēre, prob back-formation fr abolescere to disappear, fr ab- + -olescere (as in adolescere to grow up) – more at ADULT] – **abolishable** adj, **abolisher** n, **abolishment** n

**synonyms** Abolish, annihilate, and extinguish mean "make nonexistent, do away with". Abolish deals with institutions, customs and the human condition rather than with things or people ⟨a campaign to abolish low pay⟩. Annihilate may apply to abstract concepts, things, or people, and suggests a destruction so complete as to preclude reconstruction or revival ⟨one bomb can now annihilate an entire city⟩. Extinguish stresses the process of abolition, suggesting suppressing and overwhelming, as one puts out a fire ⟨the authorities tried to extinguish the cult, without success⟩. See EXTERMINATE **antonym** establish

**abolition** /,abǝ'lish(ǝ)n/ n 1 the act of abolishing; the state of being abolished 2 chiefly NAm the abolishing of slavery in the USA [MF, fr L abolition-, abolitio, fr abolitus, pp of abolēre] – **abolitionary** adj

**abolitionism** /,abǝ'lishǝniz(ǝ)m/ n principles or measures fostering abolition (eg of slavery in the USA) – **abolitionist** n or adj

**abomasum** /,abǝ'mays(ǝ)m/ n, pl abomasa /-sǝ/ the fourth or true digestive stomach of a RUMINANT (cud-chewing animal) [NL, fr L ab- + omasum tripe of a bullock] – **abomasal** adj

**A-bomb** /ay/ n ATOM BOMB – **A-bomb** vb

**abominable** /ǝ'bominǝbl/ adj 1 worthy of or causing disgust or hatred; detestable ⟨the ∼ treatment of the poor⟩ 2 very disagreeable or unpleasant – esp in colloquial exaggeration ⟨∼ weather⟩ [ME, fr MF, fr L abominabilis, fr abominari, lit., to deprecate as an ill omen, fr ab- + omin-, omen omen] – **abominably** adv

**abominable snowman** n, often cap A&S a large animal reported as existing in the high Himalayas and usu thought to be bear-or ape-like – called also YETI

**abominate** /ǝ'bominayt/ vt to hate or loathe intensely and unremittingly; abhor **synonyms** see ²HATE [L abominatus, pp of abominari ] – **abominator** n

**abomination** /ǝ,bomi'naysh(ǝ)n/ n 1 something abominable; esp a detestable or shameful action 2 extreme disgust and hatred; loathing

**aboral** /ab'awrǝl/ adj situated opposite to or away from the mouth [ab- + oral] – **aborally** adv

¹**aboriginal** /,abǝ'rijin(ǝ)l/ adj 1 being the first known inhabitants of a region and usu more primitive than later types 2 of aborigines **synonyms** see ¹NATIVE – **aboriginally** adv

²**aboriginal** n an (Australian) aborigine

**aborigine** /,abǝ'rijinee/ n 1 an aboriginal inhabitant, esp as contrasted with an invading or colonizing people; specif, often cap an Australian aborigine 2 pl the original animals and plants of a geographical area [L aborigines, pl, prob fr ab origine from the beginning]

**aborning** /ǝ'bawning/ adv, NAm while being born or produced ⟨a resolution that died ∼⟩ [¹a- + E dial. borning birth]

¹**abort** /ǝ'bawt/ vi 1 to bring forth premature nonviable offspring 2 to fail to develop completely; shrink away ∼ vt 1a to give birth to prematurely; also to induce the abortion of (a foetus) b to terminate the pregnancy of before term 2a to end prematurely; cancel ⟨∼ a project⟩ ⟨∼ a spaceflight⟩ b to stop in the early stages ⟨∼ a disease⟩ [L abortare, fr abortus, pp of aboriri to miscarry, fr ab- + oriri to rise, be born – more at RISE]

²**abort** n the premature termination of the flight of an aircraft on a combat or bombing mission; also such termination of a rocket or spacecraft mission ⟨a launch ∼⟩

**abortifacient** /ǝ,bawti'fayshǝnt/ n or adj (a drug or other agent) inducing abortion

**abortion** /ǝ'bawsh(ǝ)n/ n 1 the expulsion of a nonviable foetus: eg 1a spontaneous expulsion of a human foetus during the first 12 weeks of gestation – compare MISCARRIAGE 2 b the induced expulsion of a foetus for the purposes of terminating a pregnancy 2 a monstrosity ⟨monstrously carved ∼s – Country Life⟩ 3 arrest of development (eg of an organ or process) resulting in imperfection; also a result of such an arrest

**abortionist** /ǝ'bawsh(ǝ)nist/ n one who induces abortions, esp illegally; also one in favour of a woman's right to procure an abortion on demand

**abortive** /ǝ'bawtiv/ adj 1 fruitless, unsuccessful ⟨an ∼ attempt⟩ 2 imperfectly formed or developed 3 inducing abortion – **abortively** adv, **abortiveness** n

**ABO system** n the basic system of ANTIGENS (substances that induce the production of antibodies) of human blood which determine any of the four blood groups A, B, AB, or O

**aboulia, abulia** /ay'byoohli-ǝ/ n pathological loss of willpower [NL, fr ²a- + Gk boulē will]

**abound** /ǝ'bownd/ vi 1 to be present in large numbers or in great quantity; be abundant ⟨has ∼ing energy⟩ 2 to be amply supplied – + in ⟨the city ∼s in historic remains⟩ 3 to be crowded or infested with ⟨the attics ∼ with rats⟩ [ME abounden, fr MF abonder, fr L abundare, fr ab- + unda wave (cf SURROUND, REDOUND)]

¹**about** /ǝ'bowt/ adv 1 on or to all sides; ROUND 2 2 round the outside 3a in the neighbourhood of; approximately ⟨cost ∼ £5⟩ b almost ⟨∼ starved⟩ – often used ironically ⟨∼ as interesting as a wet Sunday⟩ 4a HERE AND THERE 1 ⟨went ∼ together⟩ b in the vicinity; near ⟨there was nobody ∼⟩ 5 in succession or rotation; alternately ⟨turn ∼ is fair play⟩ 6 ROUND 3c ⟨∼ turn⟩ [ME, fr OE abūtan, fr ¹a- + būtan outside – more at BUT]

²**about** prep 1a on every side of; round, surrounding ⟨the wall ∼ the prison⟩ b in the vicinity of; near c in spatial relation to ⟨symmetry ∼ a plane⟩ 2a on or near the person of ⟨have you a match ∼ you?⟩ b in the makeup of ⟨a mature wisdom ∼ him⟩ c at the command of ⟨has his wits ∼ him⟩ 3a engaged in ⟨knows what she's ∼⟩ b on the verge of – + to ⟨∼ to join the army⟩ 4a with regard to; concerning ⟨a story ∼ rabbits⟩ b intimately concerned with ⟨politics is ∼ capturing votes⟩ 5 over or in different parts of ⟨walked ∼ the streets⟩ 6 chiefly NAm – used with the negative to express intention or determination ⟨is not ∼ to quit⟩ **usage** see ²AROUND

³**about** adj 1 moving from place to place; specif out of bed ⟨good to see you up and ∼ again⟩ 2 in existence, evidence, or circulation ⟨skateboards weren't ∼ long⟩

**a,bout-'face** vi or n, chiefly NAm (to) about-turn [fr the military command about face, fr ¹about + ²face]

**a,bout-'turn** n 1 a 180° turn to the right from the position of attention, esp as a drill movement 2 chiefly Br a reversal of direction, policy, or opinion ⟨a massive ∼ on the Stock Exchange – Daily Mirror⟩ [fr the military command about turn] – **about-turn** vi

¹**above** /ǝ'buv/ adv 1a in the sky; overhead b in or to heaven 2a in or to a higher place b higher on the same or an earlier page c upstairs ⟨the flat ∼⟩ 3 in or to a higher rank or number ⟨30 and ∼⟩ 4 upstage 5 archaic in addition, besides [ME, fr OE abufan, fr a- + bufan above, fr be- + ufan above; akin to OE ofer over]

²**above** prep 1a higher than the level of ⟨∼ water⟩ ⟨rose ∼ the clouds⟩ ⟨∼ the noise⟩ ⟨∼ the Mason-Dixon line⟩ b upstream from 2a superior to (eg in rank) b OVER 3 ⟨∼ 1,000 people⟩ c beyond, transcending ⟨∼ criticism⟩ d in preference to ⟨values safety ∼ excitement⟩ e too proud or honourable to stoop to ⟨I hope I'm ∼ that kind of pettiness⟩ 3 more than ⟨nothing ∼ 5⟩ – see also OVER **and above** – **above all** before every other consideration; especially – **above oneself** excessively self-satisfied

³**above** n, pl above 1a a thing or place that is above ⟨a cry from ∼⟩ ⟨the ∼ are the main facts⟩ b a person whose name is written above ⟨the ∼ are to report to me forthwith⟩ 2a a higher authority b heaven

⁴**above** adj written or discussed higher on the same or an earlier page ⟨the ∼ sentence⟩

**aboveboard** /ǝ,buv'bawd/ adj free from all traces of deceit or duplicity; open ⟨it's all open and ∼⟩ [fr the difficulty of cheating at cards when the hands are above the table] – **above board** adv

**aboveground** /ə͵buv'grownd/ adj 1 located on or above the surface of the ground 2 not yet buried; alive – **above ground** adv

**abovementioned** /ə'buv͵menshənd/ adj aforementioned

**ab ovo** /ab 'ohvoh/ adv from the beginning [L, lit., from the egg]

**abracadabra** /͵abrəkə'dabrə/ n 1 a magical charm or incantation – used interjectionally as an accompaniment to conjuring tricks 2 unintelligible language; gibberish, gobbledygook [LL]

**abradant** /ə'braydənt/ n an abrasive

**abrade** /ə'brayd/ vt 1a to rub or wear away, esp by friction; erode b to irritate or roughen by rubbing 2 to wear down in spirit; weary ~ vi to undergo abrasion [L abradere to scrape off, fr ab- + radere to scrape – more at RAT] – **abradable** adj, **abrader** n

**Abraham** /'aybrəham, -həm/ n an Old Testament patriarch and founder of the Hebrew people [LL, fr Gk Abraam, fr Heb 'Abhrāhām]

**abrasion** /ə'brayzh(ə)n/ n 1 a wearing, grinding, or rubbing away by friction 2 an abraded area of the skin or the lining of body cavities [ML abrasion-, abrasio, fr L abrasus, pp of abradere]

**¹abrasive** /ə'braysiv, -ziv/ adj tending to abrade; causing irritation ⟨an ~ personality⟩ – **abrasively** adv, **abrasiveness** n

**²abrasive** n a substance (e g emery or pumice) that abrades and may be used for grinding away, smoothing, or polishing

**abreaction** /͵abri'aksh(ə)n/ n the release, esp during psychoanalysis, of mental tension due to a repressed emotion by means of reliving in words or action the situation in which the tension originally occurred [part trans of Ger abreagierung, fr ab away from + reagierung reaction] – **abreact** vt

**abreast** /ə'brest/ adv or adj 1 side by side and facing in the same direction ⟨columns of men five ~⟩ 2 up-to-date in attainment or information ⟨keeps ~ of the latest trends⟩

**abridge** /ə'brij/ vt 1 to reduce in scope; curtail ⟨attempts to ~ the right of free speech⟩ 2 to shorten by omission of words without sacrifice of sense; condense 3 archaic to deprive [ME abregen, fr MF abregier, fr LL abbreviare, fr L ad- + brevis short – more at BRIEF] – **abridger** n

**abridgment, abridgement** /ə'brijmənt/ n 1 the action of abridging; the state of being abridged 2 a shortened form of a work retaining the sense and unity of the original – compare ²ABSTRACT, SYNOPSIS, CONSPECTUS, EPITOME, ¹PRÉCIS, ²CONTRACT antonym expansion

**abroach** /ə'brohch/ adv or adj 1 in a condition for letting out liquid (e g wine) ⟨a cask set ~⟩ 2 archaic in action or agitation; astir ⟨mischiefs that I set ~ – Shak⟩

**¹abroad** /ə'brawd/ adv or adj 1 over a wide area; widely 2 away from one's home; out of doors ⟨few people ~ at this hour⟩ 3 beyond the boundaries of one's country 4 in wide circulation; about ⟨the idea has got ~⟩ 5 archaic wide of the mark; astray [ME abrood, fr ¹a- + brood broad]

**²abroad** n, Br informal places outside one's country ⟨God, how I hate ~, I'll never go there again – M Drabble⟩

**abrogate** /'abrəgayt/ vt to abolish by authoritative action; annul, repeal [L abrogatus, pp of abrogare, fr ab- + rogare to ask, propose a law – more at RIGHT] – **abrogation** n

synonyms Abrogate, nullify, negate, cancel, annul, and invalidate all mean "deprive of effectiveness or validity". Nullify and negate both completely counteract the force, value, or operability of something; negate also suggests two mutually exclusive forces cancelling each other out. Annul is mostly used in a legal or official sense. To invalidate something is to render it ineffective for a specific reason ⟨the lack of a signature invalidated the form⟩ ⟨the girl's obvious good health invalidated her excuse for absence⟩. Abrogate expresses formal or legal action to nullify treaties, official privileges, etc. Cancel (sense 2) has a similar meaning in a less formal context ⟨cancel a contract⟩ ⟨cancel an order⟩. Compare REPEAL
△ arrogate

**abrupt** /ə'brupt/ adj 1 ending as if sharply cut or broken off; truncated ⟨~ plant filaments⟩ 2a occurring without warning; unexpected ⟨~ weather changes⟩ b unceremoniously curt ⟨an ~ manner⟩ c marked by sudden changes in subject matter; disconnected ⟨an ~ style of writing⟩ 3 rising or dropping sharply; steep ⟨a high ~ bank bounded the stream⟩ synonyms see BRUSQUE antonyms unctuous, bland [L abruptus, fr pp of abrumpere to break off, fr ab- + rumpere to break – more at BEREAVE] – **abruptly** adv, **abruptness** n

**abruption** /ə'brupsh(ə)n/ n a sudden breaking of a portion from a mass

**abscess** /'abses, -sis/ n a pocket of pus surrounded by inflamed tissue [L abscessus, lit., act of going away, fr abscessus, pp of abscedere to go away, fr abs-, ab- + cedere to go – more at CEDE] – **abscessed** adj

**abscise** /əb'siez/ vb to cut off or become separated by abscission [L abscisus, pp of abscidere, fr abs- + caedere to cut – more at CONCISE]

**abscisic acid** /ab'sisik, -'siz-/ n a plant hormone, $C_{15}H_{20}O_4$, that is widespread in nature and is also made synthetically, and that typically causes leaves to fall off and inhibits growth of the plant, development of new buds, etc – called also DORMIN [abscision (var of abscission) + -ic]

**abscisin** also **abscissin** /ab'sisin, əb'sisin/ n ABSCISIC ACID or a similar plant hormone that tends to cause leaves to fall off and inhibits various growth processes [abscision, abscission + -in]

**abscissa** /əb'sisə, ab-/ n, pl **abscissas** also **abscissae** /əb'sisi, ab-/ maths the coordinate of a point in a CARTESIAN COORDINATE system (having only an x-axis and a y-axis) obtained by measuring parallel to the x-axis – compare ORDINATE [NL, fr L, fem of abscissus, pp of abscindere to cut off, fr ab- + scindere to cut – more at SHED]

**abscission** /ab'sish(ə)n, əb-/ n 1 the natural separation of flowers, fruit, or leaves from plants at a special separation layer 2 formal the act or process of cutting off; removal [L abscission, abscissio, fr abscissus]

**abscond** /əb'skond/ vi to depart secretly and hide oneself, esp so as to evade retribution ⟨~ed with the funds⟩ [L abscondere to hide away, fr abs- + condere to store up, conceal – more at CONDIMENT] – **absconder** n

**abseil** /'apsiel/ vi to descend a vertical surface, esp a cliff face, by sliding down a rope passed under one thigh, across the body, and over the opposite shoulder; broadly to descend a vertical surface using a rope [Ger abseilen to descend by a rope, fr ab- down + seil rope] – **abseil** n

**absence** /'absəns/ n 1 the state of being absent 2 the period of time that one is absent 3 a want, lack ⟨an ~ of detail⟩ synonyms see ¹LACK antonym presence

**absence of mind** n inattention to present surroundings or occurrences

**¹absent** /'absənt/ adj 1 not present or attending; missing ⟨~ from school last Wednesday⟩ ⟨~ without leave⟩ 2 not existing; lacking ⟨a species totally ~ in the Great Lakes⟩ 3 inattentive, preoccupied [ME, fr MF, fr L absent-, absens, prp of abesse to be absent, fr ab- + esse to be – more at IS] – **absently** adv

**²absent** /əb'sent/ vt to take or keep (oneself) away – + from ⟨~ed himself from morning prayers⟩

**absentee** /͵abz(ə)n'tee/ n one who is absent or who absents him-/herself – **absentee** adj

**absentee ballot** n a ballot submitted (e g by post) in advance of an election by a voter who is unable to be present at the polls

**absenteeism** /͵abzən'tee͵iz(ə)m/ n 1 prolonged esp irresponsible absence from one's property or source of income 2 persistent and deliberate absence from work or duty

**absentminded** /͵absənt'miendid/ adj lost in thought and unaware of one's surroundings or actions; preoccupied; also given to absence of mind ⟨~ professor⟩ synonyms see ABSTRACTED – **absentmindedly** adv, **absentmindedness** n

**absinthe, absinth** /'absinth/ (Fr absɛt)/ n 1 WORMWOOD 1 (plant yielding a bitter oil) 2 a green liqueur flavoured with wormwood or a substitute, anise, and other aromatics [Fr absinthe, fr L absinthium, fr Gk apsinthion]

**¹absolute** /'absəlooht, -lyooht, ͵--'-/ adj 1a free from imperfection; perfect, unalloyed ⟨~ bliss⟩ b (relatively) free from mixture; pure ⟨~ alcohol⟩ c outright, unmitigated ⟨an ~ lie⟩ 2 being, governed by, or characteristic of a ruler or authority completely free from restraint (e g by a constitution); despotic 3a standing apart from a usual syntactical relation with other words or sentence elements ⟨this being the case, in the sentence "this being the case, let us go", is an example of the ~ construction⟩ b of an adjective or possessive pronoun standing alone without a modified substantive ⟨blind in "help the blind" and ours in "your work and ours" are ~⟩ c of a verb having no object in the particular construction under consideration, though normally transitive ⟨kill in "if looks could kill" is an ~ verb⟩ 4 having no restriction, exception, or qualification ⟨an ~ requirement⟩ ⟨~ ownership⟩ 5 positive, unquestionable ⟨~ proof⟩ 6a independent of arbitrary standards of measurement

**b** relating to or derived in the simplest manner from the fundamental units of length, mass, and time ⟨~ *electric units*⟩ **c** relating to a temperature scale that has ABSOLUTE ZERO as its lower reference point ⟨*10°* ~⟩ **9** self-sufficient and free of external references or relationships ⟨*an* ~ *term in logic*⟩ ⟨*improve their position – both* ~ *and relative – on the domestic and foreign markets – Handbook for Managers*⟩ **10** measuring or representing the distance from an aircraft to the ground or water beneath ⟨~ *altimeter*⟩ [ME *absolut*, fr L *absolutus*, fr pp of *absolvere* to set free, absolve] – **absoluteness** *n*

²**absolute** *n* **1** something that is absolute, esp as being independent of human perception or valuation **2** *usu cap* the transcendent or underlying unity of spirit and matter

**absolute ceiling, ceiling** *n* the maximum height above sea level at which a particular aircraft can maintain horizontal flight under standard air conditions

**absolute discharge** *n* a nominal penalty that consists in being set free and is imposed by a court for a minor or technical offence where punishment is inappropriate – compare CONDITIONAL DISCHARGE

**absolute humidity** *n* VAPOUR CONCENTRATION (water vapour present in a given volume of air)

**absolutely** /ˌabsəˈloohtli, ˈ----, -lyooh-/ *adv* totally, completely – often used alone to express emphatic agreement

**absolute magnitude** *n* the intrinsic brightness of a star or other celestial body if viewed from a distance of 10 parsecs (32.6 light years)

**absolute majority** *n* a number of votes greater than half of the total cast in an election; *also* the number by which this exceeds the total votes of other candidates

**absolute pitch** *n* **1** the pitch of a note determined by its rate of vibration **2** the ability to sing or name a note asked for or heard

**absolute scale** *n* a temperature scale based on ABSOLUTE ZERO

**absolute space** *n* SPACE 4b

**absolute temperature** *n* temperature measured on the ABSOLUTE SCALE

**absolute value** *n, maths* the magnitude of a number, usu indicated by a vertical line on each side of the number: **a** the numerical magnitude of a REAL NUMBER irrespective of sign ⟨$|6|=|-6|=6$⟩ **b** the positive square root of the sum of the squares of the REAL PARTS and IMAGINARY PARTS of a COMPLEX NUMBER ⟨$|a + ib| = +\sqrt{a^2 + b^2}$⟩

**absolute zero** *n* the lowest temperature theoretically possible, at which the particles whose motion constitutes heat are at rest and which is defined to be 0° kelvin (about −273.15°C celsius or −459.69° fahrenheit)

**absolution** /ˌabsəˈloohsh(ə)n, -bz-, -ps-, -ˈlyooh-/ *n* the act of absolving; *specif* a declaration of forgiveness of sins pronounced by a priest

**absolutism** /ˌabsəˈloohtiz(ə)m, -bz-, -ps-, ˈ---,--/ *n* **1a** the political theory that absolute power should be vested in one or more rulers **b** government by an absolute ruler or authority; despotism **2** an absolute standard or principle – **absolutist** *n or adj*

**absolut·ize, -ise** /ˌabsəˈloohtiez, -ˈlyooh- ˈ---,-/ *vt* to make absolute; convert into an absolute

**absolve** /əbˈzolv/ *vt* **1** to set free *from* an obligation or the consequences of guilt **2** to remit (a sin) by absolution [ME *absolven*, fr L *absolvere*, fr ab- + *solvere* to loosen – more at SOLVE] – **absolver** *n*

**absorb** /əbˈzawb; *also* -bs-/ *vt* **1** to take in and make part of an existent whole ⟨~ *new entrants easily into school life* – H C Dent⟩ **2a** to suck up or take up ⟨*charcoal* ~s *gas*⟩ ⟨*plant roots* ~ *water*⟩ **b** to assimilate; TAKE IN 6 ⟨*beliefs* ~ed *in early youth*⟩ **3** to consume or occupy wholly ⟨*his work* ~s *him utterly*⟩ **4a** to receive without reflecting or transmitting ⟨*a sound-absorbing surface*⟩ **b** to transform (light or other form of RADIANT ENERGY) into a different form, usu with a resulting rise in temperature ⟨*the earth* ~s *the sun's rays*⟩ **5** to take over (a cost) [MF *absorber*, fr L *absorbēre*, fr ab- + *sorbēre* to suck up; akin to Gk *rhophein* to suck up] – **absorbability** *n*, **absorbable** *adj*, **absorber** *n*

**absorbed** /əbˈzawbd; *also* -bs-/ *adj* intensely engrossed or preoccupied *synonyms* see ABSTRACTED – **absorbedly** *adv*

**absorbency** /əbˈzawb(ə)nsi; *also* -bs-/ *n* **1** the quality or state of being absorbent **2** **absorbency, absorbancy** *also* **absorbance** the ability of a layer of a substance to absorb radiation expressed mathematically as the logarithm to base 10 of the TRANSMITTANCE

**absorbent** *also* **absorbant** /əbˈzawb(ə)nt; *also* -bs-/ *adj* able to absorb ⟨*as* ~ *as a sponge*⟩ [L *absorbent-, absorbens*, prp of *absorbēre*] – **absorbent** *also* **absorbant** *n*

**absorbing** /əbˈzawbing; *also* -bs-/ *adj* engaging one's full attention; engrossing ⟨*an* ~ *novel*⟩ – **absorbingly** *adv*

**absorptance** /əbˈzawpt(ə)ns; *also* -bs-/ *n* the ratio of the RADIANT ENERGY (e g light) absorbed by a body to that falling upon it [*absorption* + *-ance*]

**absorption** /əbˈzawpsh(ə)n; *also* əbˈsawpsh(ə)n/ *n* **1a** the process of absorbing or of being absorbed – compare ADSORPTION **b** interception of RADIANT ENERGY (e g light) or sound waves **2** total involvement of the mind ⟨~ *in his work*⟩ [Fr & L; Fr, fr L *absorption-, absorptio*, fr *absorptus*, pp of *absorbēre*] – **absorptional** *adj*, **absorptive** *adj*

**absquatulate** /əbˈskwochəlayt/ *vi, humorous* to decamp, abscond [prob based on *abscond* + *squat* + *-ulate* (as in *perambulate*)]

**abstain** /əbˈstayn/ *vi* **1** to refrain deliberately and often with an effort of self-denial *from* ⟨*I* ~ *from all alcohol*⟩ **2** to refrain from using one's vote [ME *absteinen*, fr MF *abstenir*, fr L *abstinēre*, fr *abs-, ab-* + *tenēre* to hold – more at THIN]

**abstainer** /əbˈstaynə/ *n* one who abstains, specif from intoxicating beverages ⟨*a total* ~⟩

**abstemious** /əbˈsteemi·əs/ *adj* **1** sparing, esp in eating or drinking; marked by abstinence ⟨~ *habits*⟩ **2** sparingly used or indulged in ⟨~ *diet*⟩ [L *abstemius*, fr abs- + *temetum* mead, strong drink] – **abstemiously** *adv*

**abstention** /əbˈstensh(ə)n/ *n* **1** the act or practice of abstaining – often + *from* **2** an instance of withholding a vote [LL *abstention-, abstentio*, fr L *abstentus*, pp of *abstinēre*] – **abstentionist** *n*, **abstentious** *adj*

**abstinence** /ˈabstinəns/ *also* **abstinency** /-si/ *n* **1** voluntary forbearance, esp from indulgence of appetite or from eating some foods; abstention – often + *from* **2** habitual abstaining from intoxicating beverages – chiefly in *total abstinence* [ME, fr OF, fr L *abstinentia*, fr *abstinent-, abstinens*, prp of *abstinēre*] – **abstinent** *adj*, **abstinently** *adv*

*synonyms* Abstinence, sobriety, temperance, continence, and self-denial all refer to the voluntary restraint of one's natural appetites. To practise **abstinence** is to refrain completely from indulgence, on a given occasion or habitually. **Sobriety** and **temperance** imply indulgence tempered by judgment, especially with regard to alcohol, while **continence** is often associated with sexual indulgence. **Self-denial** emphasizes the deliberate giving up of a specific pleasure for moral or religious reasons ⟨*Christians practise self-denial during Lent*⟩. *antonym* self-indulgence

¹**abstract** /ˈabstrakt/ *adj* **1a** detached from any specific instance or object ⟨~ *entity*⟩ **b** difficult to understand; abstruse ⟨~ *problems*⟩ **c** ideal ⟨~ *justice*⟩ **2** of a *noun* naming a quality, state, or action rather than a thing; not concrete ⟨*the word* poem *is concrete*, poetry *is* ~⟩ **3a** dealing with a subject in its abstract aspects; theoretical rather than practical or applied ⟨~ *science*⟩ **b** impersonal, detached ⟨*the* ~ *compassion of a surgeon – Time*⟩ **4** having only intrinsic form with little or no element of pictorial representation ⟨~ *painting*⟩ [ML *abstractus*, fr L, pp of *abstrahere* to draw away, fr abs-, ab- + *trahere* to draw] – **abstractly** *adv*, **abstractness** *n*

²**abstract** *n* **1** a summary of points (e g of a piece of writing) **2** an abstract concept or state **3** an abstract composition or creation in art [ME, fr L *abstractus*]

³**abstract** /əbˈstrakt/ *vt* **1** to remove, separate **2** to consider apart from application to a particular instance **3** to make an abstract of; summarize **4** to draw away the attention of; *also* to draw away (the attention) **5** *euph* to steal, purloin ~ *vi* to make an abstraction ⟨*a tendency to conceptualize and* ~ *– The Listener*⟩ – **abstractable** *adj*, **abstractor, abstracter** *n*

**abstracted** /əbˈstraktid/ *adj* preoccupied, absentminded ⟨*the* ~ *look of a professor*⟩ – **abstractedly** *adv*, **abstractedness** *n*

*synonyms* Someone who is **abstracted, preoccupied, absorbed, oblivious, inattentive,** or **absentminded** is unaware of his/her surroundings. The first three words suggest the reasons for this: **abstracted** means ''lost in thought'', often serious thought; **preoccupied** describes a mind busy with its own problems and ideas, while **absorbed** involves giving all one's attention to something found fascinating ⟨*so absorbed in watching the goldfish, I did not hear you come in*⟩. A person may be described as **oblivious** if absorption makes him/her unaware of what is happening, or **inattentive** if preoccupation prevents him/her from paying proper attention. **Absentminded** behaviour accompanies **abstraction,** either on one occasion or habitually.

**abstract expressionism** *n* art in which the artist attempts to express his/her attitudes and emotions through nonrepresentational means – **abstract expressionist** *n*

**abstraction** /əb'straksh(ə)n/ *n* **1a** the act or process of abstracting; the state of being abstracted **b** an abstract idea or term rigorously stripped of any concrete application or reference **2** absentmindedness **3** the quality of being abstract **4** an abstract work of art – **abstractional** *adj*, **abstractive** *adj*

**abstractionism** /əb'strakshəniz(ə)m/ *n* the principles or practice of creating abstract art – **abstractionist** *adj or n*

**abstract of title** *n* a chronological summary statement of the events and facts (e g successive conveyances) on which a person's legal title to a piece of land rests

**abstriction** /əb'striksh(ə)n/ *n* the formation of spores in certain fungi by the cutting off of portions of the SPOROPHORE (spore-bearing structure) through the growth of SEPTA (dividing membranes) [*ab-* + LL *striction-, strictio* act of pressing together, fr L *strictus*, pp of *stringere* to draw tight]

**abstruse** /əb'stroohs/ *adj* difficult to understand; recondite ⟨*the ~ calculations of mathematicians*⟩ **synonyms** see ¹OBSCURE [L *abstrusus*, fr pp of *abstrudere* to conceal, fr *abs-, ab-* + *trudere* to push – more at THREAT] – **abstrusely** *adv*, **abstruseness** *n*

¹**absurd** /əb'suhd, -bz-/ *adj* **1** ridiculously unreasonable, unsound, or incongruous; silly **2** lacking order or value; meaningless **synonyms** see LAUGHABLE [MF *absurde*, fr L *absurdus*, fr *ab-* + *surdus* deaf, stupid – more at SURD] – **absurdly** *adv*, **absurdness** *n*

²**absurd** *n* the condition of human beings in a universe considered as irrational and meaningless, and where life has no significance beyond itself

**absurdity** /əb'suhdəti, -bz-/ *n* **1** the quality or state of being absurd; absurdness **2** something absurd

**absurd theatre** *n* THEATRE OF THE ABSURD

**abulia** /ay'byoohli-ə/ *n* ABOULIA (loss of willpower)

**abundance** /ə'bund(ə)ns/ *n* **1** a great quantity; a profusion ⟨*the presence of an ~ of woodmice – Scottish Field*⟩ **2** affluence, wealth **3** relative plentifulness ⟨*the low ~ of uranium in the area*⟩ **4** a bid in SOLO WHIST to win at least nine tricks

**abundant** /ə'bund(ə)nt/ *adj* **1a** marked by great plenty (e g of resources) ⟨*a fair and ~ land*⟩ **b** plentifully supplied *with*; abounding *in* ⟨*~ in natural food for trout*⟩ **2** occurring in abundance ⟨*~ rainfall*⟩ **synonyms** see PLENTIFUL **antonyms** scanty, scarce [ME, fr MF, fr L *abundant-, abundans*, prp of *abundare* to abound] – **abundantly** *adv*

¹**abuse** /ə'byoohz/ *vt* **1** to attack in words; insult **2** to put to a wrong or improper use; misuse ⟨*~ a privilege*⟩ **3** to use so as to injure or damage; maltreat ⟨*~ a dog*⟩ **4** *obs* to deceive **synonyms** see ¹MISUSE, ²SCOLD □ compare ²MALIGN [ME *abusen*, fr MF *abuser*, fr L *abusus*, pp of *abuti*, fr *ab-* + *uti* use] – **abusable** *adj*, **abuser** *n*

²**abuse** /ə'byoohs/ *n* **1** a corrupt practice or custom **2** improper use or treatment; misuse ⟨*drug ~*⟩ **3** vehemently expressed condemnation or disapproval ⟨*greeted them with a torrent of ~*⟩ **4** physical maltreatment **5** *obs* a deceitful act; deception
*synonyms* Invective, vituperation, and scurrility are all forms of abuse (sense 3), which is the general term, applied to private exchanges. Invective is public or literary abuse, and may be oratorical and even dignified in tone, while abuse implies coarseness and crudity. Vituperation is a sustained flow of abuse. Obloquy is defamatory abuse directed against one by many. It is now usually used to express rather the disgrace resulting from this. *antonym* adulation

**abusive** /ə'byoohsiv, -ziv/ *adj* **1** characterized by wrong or improper use or action; corrupt ⟨*~ financial practices*⟩ **2a** using or consisting of verbal abuse **b** physically injurious ⟨*received ~ treatment*⟩ – **abusively** *adv*, **abusiveness** *n*

**abut** /ə'but/ *vb* **-tt-** *vi* **1** *of an area* to touch along a border or with a projecting part – + *on* or *upon* ⟨*land ~s on the road*⟩ **2a** *of a structure* to terminate at a point of contact; be adjacent – + *on* or *against* ⟨*the town hall ~s on the church*⟩ **b** to lean for support – + *on* or *upon* ⟨*the neighbours' shed ~s on our wall*⟩ ~ *vt* **1** to border on; touch **2** to cause to abut [ME *abutten*; partly fr OF *aboter* to border on, fr *a-* (fr L *ad-*) + *bout* blow, end, fr *boter* to strike; partly fr OF *abuter* to come to an end, fr *a-* + *but* end, aim – more at ¹BUTT, ³BUTT] – **abuttal** *n*, **abutter** *n*

**abutilon** /ə'byoohtilən/ *n* any of a genus (*Abutilon*) of quick-growing shrubs of the hollyhock family; *esp* the flowering maple (*Abutilon hybridum*) [NL, genus name, fr Ar *awbūtīlūn*]

**abutment** /ə'butmənt/ *n* **1** the place at which abutting occurs **2a** a part of a structure that directly receives thrust or pressure (e g from an arch) **b** an anchorage for the cables of a suspension bridge or aerial railway

**abutting** /ə'buting/ *adj* that abuts or serves as an abutment; adjoining, bordering

**abuzz** /ə'buz/ *adj* filled or resounding (as if) with a buzzing sound ⟨*a lake ~ with speedboats*⟩ ⟨*studio was ~ with the news*⟩

**aby, abye** /ə'bie/ *vt*, *archaic* to suffer a penalty for (an offence) [ME *abien*, fr OE *ābycgan*, fr *ā-*, perfective prefix + *bycgan* to buy]

**abysm** /ə'bizəm/ *n* an abyss ⟨*the dark backward and ~ of time* – Shak⟩ [ME *abime*, fr OF *abisme*, modif of LL *abyssus*]

**abysmal** /ə'bizməl/ *adj* **1** having immense or unfathomable extension, esp downwards ⟨*an ~ cliff*⟩ **2a** deplorably great; profound ⟨*~ ignorance*⟩ **b** immeasurably bad ⟨*standard of writing was ~ – Punch*⟩ – **abysmally** *adv*

**abyss** /ə'bis/ *n* **1** the infernal regions or chaos of old theories of the universe, thought of as a bottomless pit **2a** an immeasurably deep gulf or great space **b** moral or emotional depths ⟨*an ~ of hopelessness*⟩ [ME *abissus*, fr LL *abyssus*, fr Gk *abyssos*, fr *abyssos* bottomless, fr *a-* + *byssos* depth; akin to Gk *bathys* deep – more at BATHY-]

**abyssal** /ə'bis(ə)l/ *adj* **1** unfathomable, incomprehensible **2** of the bottom waters of the ocean depths **3** *of a rock* PLUTONIC (formed deep within the earth)

**Abyssinian cat** /ˌabi'siniən/ *n* (any of) a breed of small slender cats of African origin with short brownish hair flecked with darker colour [*Abyssinia* (Ethiopia), country in E Africa]

¹**-ac** /-ak, -ək/ *suffix* (→ *n*) one affected with ⟨*maniac*⟩ ⟨*hypochondriac*⟩ [NL *-acus* of or relating to, fr Gk *-akos*]

²**-ac, -acal** *suffix* (→ *adj*) relating to ⟨*cardiac*⟩ ⟨*iliac*⟩

**acacia** /ə'kaysh(y)ə/ *n* **1** any of a genus (*Acacia*) of woody plants of the pea family, of warm regions, with white or yellow flowers **2** GUM ARABIC (gum obtained from the acacia, esp *Acacia senegal*) [NL, genus name, fr L, acacia tree, fr Gk *akakia* shittah]

**academe** /'akədeem/ *n, chiefly NAm* a college; *also* the university community ⟨*the groves of ~*⟩ [irreg fr NL *academia*]

**academese** /əˌkadə'meez/ *n* a style of writing held to be characteristic of those in academic life ⟨*the usual scholarly biography, written in barbarous ~* – Dwight Macdonald⟩

**academia** /ˌakə'deemiə/ *n, chiefly NAm* the university community [NL, fr L, academy]

¹**academic** /ˌakə'demik/ *also* **academical** /-kl/ *adj* **1a** of or associated with an institution of higher learning ⟨*~ jobs are no longer safe*⟩ **b** formed by education; scholarly **c** very learned but inexperienced in practical matters ⟨*~ thinkers*⟩ **d** relating to formal study ⟨*high ~ standards*⟩ **2** of liberal education rather than technical or vocational studies **3** conforming to the traditions or rules of a school (e g of literature or art) or official academy; conventional ⟨*an ~ painting*⟩ **4** theoretical with no practical or useful bearing; *broadly* irrelevant ⟨*an ~ question*⟩ ⟨*whether he comes or not is ~*⟩ – **academically** *adv*, **academicize** *vt*

²**academic** *n* a member (of the teaching staff) of an institution of higher learning; *also* one who is academic in outlook

**academicals** /ˌakə'demiklz/ *n pl* the cap, gown, hood, etc worn as formal academic dress

**academic freedom** *n* freedom to teach or to learn without interference (e g by government control)

**academician** /əˌkadə'mish(ə)n/ *n* **1** one who is admitted to membership of an academy for the advancement of science, art, or literature **2** a follower of an artistic or philosophical tradition or a promoter of its ideas

**academicism** /əˌkadə'demisiz(ə)m/ *also* **academism** /ə'kadəmiz(ə)m/ *n* **1** conformity to official or conventional tradition in art or literature **2** purely speculative thought and attitudes

**academic year** *n* the annual period of sessions of an educational institution, usu beginning in the autumn and ending in the summer

**academy** /ə'kadəmi/ *n* **1a** *cap the* school for advanced education founded by Plato **b** *the* philosophical doctrines associated with Plato's Academy; *esp* PLATONISM **2a** a school usu above the elementary level; *esp* a private high school – now used only in names **b** a college in which special subjects or skills are taught ⟨*an ~ of music*⟩ – compare MILITARY ACADEMY **3** a society of learned people organized to promote the arts or sciences [L *academia,* fr Gk *Akadēmeia,* fr *Akadēmeia,* gymnasium where Plato taught, fr *Akadēmos* Attic mythological hero; (2–3) largely fr Fr *académie* university, fr NL *academia*]

**Acadian** /ə'kaydi·ən/ *n* 1 a native or inhabitant of Acadia 2 an inhabitant of Louisiana descended from French-speaking immigrants from Acadia [*Acadia,* former Fr colony in N America, fr Fr *Acadie*] – **Acadian** *adj*

**acajou** /'akəzhooh/ *n* a cashew [Fr, fr Pg *acajú* – more at CASHEW]

**-acal** /-əkl/ – see ²-AC

**acanth-** /əkanth-/, **acantho-** *comb form* thorn; spine ⟨acanthous⟩ [NL, fr Gk *akanth-, akantho-,* fr *akantha;* akin to ON *ögn* awn – more at AWN]

**acanthocephalan** /ə,kanthoh'sefələn/ *n* SPINY-HEADED WORM [deriv of *acanth-* + Gk *kephalē* head – more at CEPHALIC] – **acanthocephalan** *adj*

**acanthopterygian** /,akən,thoptə'rijiən/ *n* any of a major division (Acanthopterygii) of BONY FISHES having spiny fins that includes most of the salt-water fishes (e g basses, perches, and mackerels) [deriv of *acanth-* + Gk *pteryg-, pteryx* wing, fin – more at PTERYGOID] – **acanthopterygian** *adj*

**acanthus** /ə'kanthəs/ *n, pl* **acanthuses** *also* **acanthi** /ə'kanthie/ 1 any of a genus (*Acanthus* of the family Acanthaceae, the acanthus family) of usu large prickly plants esp of the Mediterranean region, having spiny leaves and white or purple flower spikes 2 an architectural ornament (e g on a Corinthian capital) representing or suggesting the leaves of the acanthus [NL, genus name, fr Gk *akanthos,* a hellebore, fr *akantha*]

**a cappella** *also* **a capella** /,ah kə'pelə/ *adv or adj* without instrumental accompaniment [It *a cappella* in chapel style]

**acariasis** /,akə'rie·əsis/ *n* infestation with or disease caused by mites [NL]

**acarid** /'akərid/ *n* any of an order (Acarina of the phylum Arachnida) of INVERTEBRATE animals related to the spiders and scorpions including the mites and ticks; *esp* a typical mite (family Acaridae) – **acarid** *adj,* **acarine** *adj*

**acarus** /'akərəs/ *n, pl* **acari** /-rie/ a mite; *esp* any of a formerly extensive genus (*Acarus*) [NL, genus name, fr Gk *akari,* a mite]

**acatalectic** /ə,katə'lektik/ *adj* having the full number of syllables; not catalectic ⟨~ *verse*⟩ [LL *acatalecticus,* fr *acatalectus,* fr Gk *akatalēktos,* fr *a-* + *katalēgein* to leave off – more at CATALECTIC] – **acatalectic** *n*

**acaulescent** /,akaw'les(ə)nt/ *adj* having or appearing to have no stem [*a-* + L *caulis* stem – more at HOLE] – **acaulescence** *n*

**accede** /ək'seed/ *vi* 1a to become a party (e g to a treaty) b to express approval or give consent often in response to urging; concede 2 to enter upon an office or position; *esp* to become monarch ⟨~ *to the throne*⟩ **synonyms** see ¹ASSENT **antonym** demur △ exceed [ME *acceden* to approach, fr L *accedere* to go to, be added, fr *ad-* + *cedere* to go – more at CEDE]

**accelerando** /ək,selə'randoh/ *n, adv, or adj, pl* **accelerandos, accelerandi** (a musical passage that gets) gradually faster [It, lit., accelerating, fr L *accelerandum,* gerund of *accelerare*]

**accelerant** /ək'selərənt/ *n* ACCELERATOR C

**accelerate** /ək'selərayt/ *vt* 1 to bring about at an earlier time 2 to cause to move faster; *also* to cause to undergo acceleration 3 to hasten the progress, development, or growth of ~ *vi* 1 to move faster; gain speed 2 to increase more rapidly ⟨*believed inflation was* accelerating⟩ [L *acceleratus,* pp of *accelerare,* fr *ad-* + *celer* swift – more at HOLD] – **acceleratingly** *adv*

**acceleration** /ək,selə'raysh(ə)n/ *n* 1 the act or process of accelerating; the state of being accelerated 2 increase in speed or velocity; *specif* the rate of change of velocity with respect to time ⟨*this car has good* ~⟩

**acceleration principle** *n* a theory in economics: the level of net investment varies directly with the rate of change of income or output

**accelerative** /ək'selərətiv/ *adj* relating to or tending to cause acceleration; accelerating

**accelerator** /ək'seləraytə/ *n* something that accelerates: e g a a muscle or nerve that speeds up the performance of an action b a pedal in a motor vehicle that varies the supply of fuel-air mixture to the combustion chamber in order to control the speed of the motor c a substance that speeds up a chemical reaction d an apparatus for imparting high velocities and hence high energies to electrically charged particles (e g electrons)

**accelerometer** /ək,selə'romitə/ *n* an instrument for measuring

acceleration or for detecting and measuring vibrations [ISV *acceler*ation + *-o-* + *-meter*]

**¹accent** /'aksənt/ *n* 1 a distinctive manner of expression: e g **1a** accents *pl,* **accent** an individual inflection, tone, or choice of words ⟨*in plaintive* ~ s⟩ b sounds characteristic of regional or national speech ⟨*an Irish* ~⟩ 2 an emphasis made in the course of speech to give prominence in stress or pitch to one syllable over others; *also* the prominence thus given to a syllable 3 the stress given to the syllables of a verse usu at regular intervals, pointing up the rhythm **4a** a mark added to a letter (e g as in *à, ń, ĉ*) to indicate a specific sound value, stress, or pitch, to distinguish words otherwise identically spelt, or to indicate that an ordinarily silent vowel should be pronounced – compare DIACRITIC b an accented letter **5a** greater stress given to one musical note than to its neighbours b the principle of regularly recurring stresses which serve to distribute a succession of pulses into measures c ACCENT MARK 2 **6a** a sharply contrasting detail b a substance or object used for emphasis 7 a mark placed to the right of a letter or number and usu slightly above it; *esp* any of those used singly with numbers to denote minutes or feet and doubly to denote seconds or inches ⟨*the* ~s *on 12′ 6″* can be read as 12 feet 6 inches or 12 minutes 6 seconds of either time or angle⟩ 8 special concern or attention; an emphasis ⟨*an* ~ *on youth*⟩ [MF, fr L *accentus,* fr *ad-* + *cantus* song, fr *cantus,* pp of *canere* to sing – more at CHANT] – **accentless** *adj*

**²accent** /ək'sent, 'aksent/ *vt* **1a** to pronounce (a vowel, syllable, or word) with accent; stress b to mark with a written or printed accent 2 to give prominence to; make more prominent

**accent mark** /'aksənt/ *n* 1 ACCENT 4a, 7 2 a symbol used to indicate musical stress

**accentor** /ək'sentaw, -tə/ *n* any of a genus (*Prunella* of the family Prunellidae) of rather drab birds (e g the dunnock) resembling sparrows [NL, fr ML, one who sings with another, fr L *ad-* + *cantor* singer]

**accentual** /ək'sentyoo·əl, -choo·əl/ *adj* relating to rhythmical accent; *specif,* of verse metre based on the recurrence of stress rather than on that of syllables – compare QUANTITATIVE [L *accentus*] – **accentually** *adv*

**accentuate** /ək'sentyoo·ayt, -choo·ayt/ *vt* to accent, emphasize [ML *accentuatus,* pp of *accentuare,* fr L *accentus*] – **accentuation** *n*

**accept** /ək'sept/ *vt* **1a** to agree to receive ⟨~ *a gift*⟩ ⟨~ *a suitor*⟩; *also* to agree to ⟨~ *an invitation*⟩ b to be able or designed to take or hold (something applied or inserted) ⟨*a surface that will not* ~ *ink*⟩ ⟨*the machine* ~s *only pennies*⟩ 2 to give admittance or approval to ⟨~ *her as one of the group*⟩ **3a** to endure without protest; accommodate oneself to ⟨~ *poor living conditions*⟩ b to regard as proper, normal, or inevitable ⟨*the idea of universal education is widely* ~ed⟩ c to consider as true or adequate ⟨*refused to* ~ *my explanation*⟩ ⟨*what will you* ~ *as evidence?*⟩ d to recognize as a fact ⟨*users of a language* ~ *words to mean certain things*⟩ ⟨*I cannot* ~ *that you have met the conditions*⟩ 4 to undertake the responsibility of ⟨~ *a job*⟩ 5 to assume formal obligation to pay 6 *of a deliberative body* to receive (e g a report) officially as being adequate ~ *vi* to receive favourably when it is offered △ except [ME *accepten,* fr MF *accepter,* fr L *acceptare,* fr *acceptus,* pp of *accipere* to receive, fr *ad-* + *capere* to take – more at HEAVE]

**acceptable** /ək'septəbl/ *adj* 1 capable or worthy of being accepted ⟨*no compromise would be* ~⟩ 2 welcome or pleasing to the receiver ⟨*compliments are always* ~⟩ 3 barely adequate ⟨*performances varied from excellent to* ~⟩ – **acceptability** *n,* **acceptableness** *n,* **acceptably** *adv*

**acceptance** /ək'sept(ə)ns/ *n* 1 the act of accepting; approval 2 the fact or state of being accepted or acceptable; acceptability 3 agreement, either outright or by conduct, to the act or offer of another, so that a contract is concluded and the parties become legally bound **4a** the act of accepting a time draft or bill of exchange for payment when due according to the specified terms b an accepted draft or bill of exchange

**acceptance house** *n* ACCEPTING HOUSE

**acceptant** /ək'sept(ə)nt/ *adj* willing to accept; receptive – often + *of*

**acceptation** /,aksep'taysh(ə)n/ *n* 1 acceptance; *esp* favourable reception or approval 2 a generally accepted meaning of a word or concept

**accepted** /ək'septid/ *adj* generally approved or used; customary – **acceptedly** *adv*

**accepter** /ək'septə/ *n* 1 one who or that which accepts 2 ACCEPTOR 2

**accepting house** /ək'septing/ n a bank that specializes in handling bills of exchange

**acceptor** /ək'septaw, -tə/ n 1 ACCEPTER 1 2 one who accepts an order or a bill of exchange **3a** a chemical compound, element, etc with an affinity for another entity (eg an electron, atom, or chemical group) **b acceptor, acceptor impurity** *electronics* an impurity (eg aluminium in germanium) added to a SEMICONDUCTOR to change its conduction properties to those of a P-TYPE semiconductor – compare DONOR 3b **4** a horse that has been entered for a race

¹**access** /'akses, -səs/ n **1a** a sudden attack esp of a disease, fever, etc **b** a fit *of* intense feeling; an outburst ⟨*an ~ of supernatural power was helping their curses to take effect* – Keith Thomas⟩ **2a** freedom to approach, reach, or communicate with somebody or something **b** freedom to obtain or make use of something ⟨*~ to classified information*⟩ **c** a means (eg a doorway or channel) of access **d** the state of being readily reached or obtained ⟨*the building is not easy of ~*⟩ **3** an increase by addition; ACCESSION 1 △ excess [ME, fr MF & L; MF *acces* arrival, fr L *accessus* approach, fr *accessus*, pp of *accedere* to approach – more at ACCEDE]

²**access** *vt* to take information from or write information into (a computer storage area or memory) ⟨*accumulator and index registers can be ~ed by the programmer* – Datamation⟩

³**access** *adj* made by members of the general public as opposed to professional broadcasters; *also* featuring programmes made in this way ⟨*we have a new ~ channel*⟩ ⟨*~ television*⟩

**accessary** /ək'ses(ə)ri/ n or adj (an) accessory

**accessible** /ək'sesəbl/ adj **1a** capable of being reached ⟨*~ by rail*⟩ **b** of a form that can be readily grasped intellectually ⟨*prose is too lucid, too ~, to be exciting to him* – TLS⟩ **2** able to be influenced; open ⟨*~ to persuasion*⟩ **3** available to be visited or consulted; approachable ⟨*should be readily ~ to his students at all times*⟩ – **accessibility** n, **accessibleness** n, **accessibly** adv

¹**accession** /ək'sesh(ə)n/ n **1** something added, esp to a collection; an acquisition; *specif* a book added to a library **2** the act by which one nation becomes party to an agreement already in force between other powers **3** increase by something added; *specif* acquisition of additional property by growth, increase, etc **4** the act of entering upon a high office or position of honour ⟨*his ~ to the Papacy*⟩ **5** a sudden fit or outburst; ACCESS 1b **6** *formal* the act of assenting or agreeing ⟨*his ~ to our demands*⟩ – **accessional** adj

²**accession** *vt* to record (eg a book) as having been acquired, esp by a library or museum

**accessorial** /ˌakse'sawriəl/ adj **1** relating to an accessory ⟨*~ liability*⟩ **2** relating to or constituting an accession; supplementary ⟨*~ services*⟩

**accessor·ize, -ise** /ək'sesəriez/ vt to furnish with accessories

¹**accessory** /ək'sesəri/ n **1a** a thing of lesser importance; an adjunct **b** an object or device not essential in itself but adding to the beauty, convenience, or effectiveness of something else; *specif* a minor part of esp female dress (eg gloves, handbag, hat, etc) ⟨*car accessories*⟩ ⟨*a lilac dress with matching accessories*⟩ **2 accessory, accessary** *law* **2a** ACCESSORY AFTER THE FACT **b** ACCESSORY BEFORE THE FACT

²**accessory** adj **1** aiding or contributing in a secondary way; supplementary **2 accessory, accessary** *law* assisting as a subordinate; *esp* contributing to a crime but not as the chief party **3** present in a minor amount and not an essential constituent ⟨*an ~ mineral in a rock*⟩

**accessory after the fact** n, *law* a person who knowing that a crime has been committed aids or shelters the offender with the intention of securing his/her escape – no longer used technically

**accessory before the fact** n, *law* a person who instigates or provides the means to commit a crime but is not actually present when it is committed – no longer used technically

**accessory fruit** n a fruit (eg the apple) of which the major part consists of tissue other than that of the ripened OVARY (seed producing structure) – called also PSEUDOCARP

**accessory nerve** n either of the 11th pair of CRANIAL NERVES that supply chiefly the PHARYNX (muscular tube joining the mouth to the upper part of the digestive tract) and muscles of the upper chest, back, and shoulders

**accessory shoe** n SHOE 4 (device on a camera)

**access road** n a road that provides access to a particular area

**access time** n the time lag between the request and delivery of stored information (eg in a computer)

**acciaccatura** /əˌchakə'tooərə/ n, pl **acciaccaturas, acciaccature** a discordant note sounded with or before a principal note or chord and immediately released [It, lit., crushing, fr *acciaccare* to crush]

**accidence** /'aksid(ə)ns/ n that part of grammar which deals with INFLECTIONS (the variable parts of words) [L *accidentia* inflections of words, nonessential qualities, pl of *accident-, accidens*, n]

**accident** /'aksid(ə)nt/ n **1a** an event occurring by chance or arising from unknown causes **b** lack of intention or necessity; chance ⟨*met by ~ rather than by design*⟩ **2** *insurance* an unfortunate mishap causing loss or injury; *specif* one which is not due to any fault or misconduct on the part of the person injured, but from the consequences of which he/she may be entitled to some legal relief **3** a nonessential property, quality, or condition of something ⟨*the ~ of appearance*⟩ **4** an irregularity of a surface (eg of the moon) [ME, fr MF, fr L *accident-accidens* nonessential quality, chance, fr prp of *accidere* to happen, fr *ad- + cadere* to fall – more at CHANCE]

¹**accidental** /ˌaksi'dentl/ adj **1** arising from incidental causes; nonessential **2a** occurring unexpectedly or by chance **b** happening without intent or through carelessness and often with unfortunate results **synonyms** see FORTUITOUS, ¹INCIDENTAL **antonyms** planned, intentional – **accidentally** adv, **accidentalness** n

²**accidental** n **1** a nonessential quality; ACCIDENT 3 **2a** a musical note that is prefaced by a sharp, flat, or natural sign and is adjusted accordingly in playing or singing **b** a sign written in front of such a note to indicate that it is an accidental

'**accident-,prone** adj **1** having a greater than average number of accidents **2** having the sort of personality traits that make a person more liable to accidents

**accidie** /'aksidi/ n a condition of hopeless listlessness; spiritual apathy [ME, fr OF, fr ML *accidia*, alter. of LL *acedia* – more at ACEDIA]

**accipiter** /ək'sipitə/ n any of a genus (*Accipiter*) of medium-sized short-winged long-legged hawks (eg the sparrow hawk) having a low darting type of flight; *broadly* a hawk of similar appearance or habit of flight [NL, genus name, fr L, hawk]

**accipitrine** /ək'sipitrien, -trin/ *also* **accipitral** /-trəl/ adj relating to or resembling the hawks – **accipitrine** n

¹**acclaim** /ə'klaym/ vt **1** to applaud, praise **2** to hail or proclaim by acclamation ⟨*~ed her Queen*⟩ [L *acclamare*, lit., to shout at, fr *ad- + clamare* to shout – more at CLAIM] – **acclaimer** n

²**acclaim** n **1** the act of acclaiming; the state of being acclaimed **2** ACCLAMATION

**acclamation** /ˌaklə'maysh(ə)n/ n **1** *often pl* a loud expression of praise, goodwill, or assent **2** an overwhelming affirmative vote by cheers, shouts, or applause rather than by ballot ⟨*motion was carried by ~*⟩ [L *acclamation-, acclamatio*, fr *acclamatus*, pp of *acclamare*]

**acclimate** /'aklimayt, ə'kliemət/ vb, NAm to acclimatize [Fr *acclimater*, fr a- (fr L ad-) + *climat* climate] – **acclimation** n

**acclimation** /akli'maysh(ə)n/ n acclimatization esp under controlled (eg laboratory conditions)

**acclimat·ize, -ise** /ə'kliemətiez/ vt to adapt to a new climate or situation ⟨*he ~d himself to a life of comparative leisure during his retirement*⟩ ~ vi to become acclimatized – **acclimatization, acclimatizer** n

**acclivity** /ə'klivəti/ n, *formal* an ascending slope (eg of a hill) – compare DECLIVITY [L *acclivitas*, fr *acclivis* ascending, fr *ad-* + *clivus* slope – more at DECLIVITY]

**accolade** /'akəlayd/ n **1** a ceremony or salute that marks the conferring of knighthood and consists of a light blow to each of the candidate's shoulders with a ceremonial sword **2** a mark of acknowledgment or honour; an award **3** (an expression of) enthusiastic praise [Fr, fr *accoler* to embrace, fr (assumed) VL *accollare*, fr L *ad- + collum* neck – more at COLLAR]

**accommodate** /ə'komədayt/ vt **1** to make fit, suitable, or appropriate *to* ⟨*~d himself to circumstances*⟩ **2** to bring into agreement or concord; reconcile **3** to furnish with something desired, needed, or necessary: **3a** to grant a loan to, esp without security **b** to provide with lodgings; house **4a** to make room for **b** to hold without crowding or inconvenience **5** to give consideration to; allow for ⟨*~ the special interests of various groups*⟩ ~ vi to adapt oneself; *also, of the eye* to undergo visual accommodation [L *accommodatus*, pp of *accommodare*, fr *ad- + commodare* to make fit, fr *commodus* suitable – more at COMMODE] – **accommodative** adj

**accommodating** /ə'komədayting/ *adj* helpful, obliging – **accommodatingly** *adv*

**accommodation** /ə,komə'daysh(ə)n/ *n* **1 accommodation,** *NAm chiefly* **accommodations** *pl* something supplied for convenience or to satisfy a need: e g **1a(1)** lodging, housing; *also* space, premises ⟨*office* ~⟩ ⟨*2,552 were in* ~ *provided by the University – The Univ of Birmingham*⟩ **a(2)** *chiefly NAm* a space (e g a seat or berth) occupied during travel ⟨*tourist* ~s *on the boat*⟩ **b** a loan of money; *esp* one made as a favour by a bank **2** the act of accommodating; the state of being accommodated: e g **2a** the provision of housing or seating **b** adaptation, adjustment **c** an adjustment of differences; a settlement **d** the automatic adjustment made by the eye in order to see at different distances, which is effected in humans chiefly by changes in the degree of curvature of the crystalline lens; *also* the range over which such adjustment is possible – **accommodational** *adj*

**accommodation address** *n* an address to which letters may be sent to be collected by or forwarded to someone who does not give his/her real address

**accommodation agency** *n* an office that finds tenants for rented accommodation

**accommodation bill** *n* a bill, draft, or note made, drawn, accepted, or endorsed by one person for another without VALUABLE CONSIDERATION to enable that other to raise money or obtain credit

**accommodation ladder** *n* a light ladder or stairway hung over the side of a ship for ascending from or descending to small boats

**accommodation road** *n* a road provided for access to a place not on the public highway

**accompaniment** /ə'kump(ə)nimənt/ *n* **1** an instrumental or vocal part supporting or complementing a principal voice or instrument **2a** an addition intended to give completeness; a complement **b** an accompanying situation or occurrence; a concomitant

**accompanist** /ə'kumpənist/ *n* a player of an accompaniment (e g on a piano)

**accompany** /ə'kump(ə)ni/ *vt* **1** to go with as an escort or companion **2** to perform a musical accompaniment to or for **3a** to supplement *with* ⟨accompanied *his advice with a warning*⟩ **b** *of a thing* to be in association with ⟨*the pictures that* ~ *the text*⟩ ~ *vi* to perform a musical accompaniment [ME *accompanien*, fr MF *acompaignier*, fr *a-* (fr L *ad-*) + *compaing* companion, fr LL *companio*]

*synonyms* **Accompany** is a general term. It assumes an equal relationship, whereas **attend** suggests a subordinate one ⟨*the princess was* **attended** *everywhere by her lady-in-waiting*⟩. **Escort** and **convoy** mean "accompany in order to protect", but **convoy** is usually limited to military contexts. **Conduct** includes the idea of guidance, and may suggest some compulsion ⟨*the host* **conducted** *this gatecrasher to the door*⟩. In ⟨*he* **escorted** *his visitor to the door*⟩, the action is one of courtesy and respect. To **chaperon** young people is to **accompany** them as a protector and moral guardian. *usage* A person is **accompanied** *by* a companion ⟨*the Mayor was* **accompanied** *by her husband*⟩ or by an **accompanist**; a thing or a state of affairs is **accompanied** *with* another ⟨*veal* **accompanied** *with spaghetti*⟩.

**accomplice** /ə'kumplis, -'kom-/ *n* one who collaborates with another, esp in wrongdoing [alter. (prob by incorrect division of *a complice*) of *complice*]

**accomplish** /ə'kumplish, -'kom-/ *vt* **1** to bring to a successful conclusion; carry to completion ⟨*when they had* ~ed *their mission*⟩ ⟨*I hope to* ~ *much more today*⟩ **2** to attain (a measure of time or distance); cover ⟨*at that rate will* ~ *only half the distance*⟩ *synonyms* see PERFORM, ¹REACH [ME *accomplisshen*, fr MF *acompliss-*, stem of *acomplir*, fr (assumed) VL *accomplēre*, fr L *ad-* + *complēre* to fill up – more at COMPLETE] – **accomplishable** *adj*, **accomplisher** *n*

**accomplished** /ə'kumplisht, 'kom-/ *adj* **1** fully ⟨effected; completed ⟨*an* ~ *fact*⟩ **2a** complete in skills of a specified kind as the result of practice or training ⟨*an* ~ *dancer*⟩ **b** having many social accomplishments

**accomplishment** /ə'kumplishmənt, -'kom-/ *n* **1** the act of accomplishing; completion **2** something accomplished; an achievement **3a** an acquired quality or ability equipping one for society **b** the fact or degree of being socially accomplished

¹**accord** /ə'kawd/ *vt* **1a** to grant as suitable or proper; concede ⟨~ed *them permission*⟩ **b** to confer, give ⟨~ed *her a warm welcome*⟩ **2** *archaic* to bring into agreement; reconcile ~ *vi* **1**

to be consistent; fit harmoniously *with* ⟨*I'm afraid that could never* ~ *with my principles*⟩ **2** *archaic* to arrive at an agreement *synonyms* see AGREE [ME *accorden* to reconcile, agree, fr OF *acorder*, fr (assumed) VL *accordare*, fr L *ad-* + *cord-, cor* heart – more at HEART] – **according as 1** proportionately as; depending on how **2** depending on whether ⟨*they move up according* as *they pass or fail the examination*⟩ – **according to 1** in conformity with **2** as stated or attested by ⟨according to *George, it's impossible*⟩ **3** depending on

²**accord** *n* **1a** agreement, conformity ⟨*acted in* ~ *with the company's policy*⟩ **b** a formal act of agreement; a treaty **2** balanced interrelationship (e g of colours or sounds); harmony **3** *obs* assent *usage* see ¹ACCOUNT [ME, fr OF *acort*, fr *acorder*] – **of one's own accord** voluntarily, unbidden ⟨*gave generously of their own accord*⟩ – **with one accord** with the consent or agreement of all

**accordance** /ə'kawd(ə)ns/ *n* **1** agreement, conformity ⟨*in* ~ *with a rule*⟩ **2** the act of granting

**accordant** /ə'kawd(ə)nt/ *adj* **1** consonant, agreeing *with* ⟨~ *with your orders*⟩ **2** harmonious, correspondent – **accordantly** *adv*

**accordingly** /ə'kawdingli/ *adv* **1** as suggested; appropriately ⟨*told him to lock it and he acted* ~⟩ **2** consequently, so

¹**accordion** /ə'kawdiən/ *n* a portable keyboard wind instrument in which the wind is forced past free reeds by means of a hand-operated bellows of pleated structure – compare CONCERTINA [Ger *akkordion*, fr *akkord* chord, fr Fr *accord*, fr OF *acort*] – **accordionist** *n*

²**accordion** *adj* folding, creased, or hinged to fold like an accordion ⟨~ *pleats*⟩ ⟨~ *wall*⟩

**accost** /ə'kost/ *vt* **1** to approach and speak to, esp boldly or challengingly **2** *of a prostitute* to solicit [MF *accoster*, deriv of L *ad-* + *costa* rib, side – more at COAST]

**accouchement** /ə'koohshmənt, a'koohshmonh (*Fr* akuʃma)/ *n* lying-in; *esp* PARTURITION (act or process of birth) [Fr, fr *accoucher* to deliver a child, fr OF *acouchier* to lie down]

**accoucheur** /ə,kooh'shuh (*Fr* akuʃœːr)/ *fem* **accoucheuse** /ə,kooh'shuhz (*Fr* akuʃœːz)/ *n* one who assists at a birth [Fr, fr *accoucher*]

¹**account** /ə'kownt/ *n* **1a** a chronological record of debit and credit entries to cover transactions involving a particular item or a particular person or concern **b** a statement of transactions during a financial period **2 accounts** *pl*, **account** a list of items of expenditure to be balanced against income ⟨*doing her monthly* ~s⟩ **3** a statement explaining one's conduct or one's discharge of a responsibility ⟨*you will be required to give an* ~ *of your behaviour*⟩ ⟨*he will soon be called to* ~⟩ **4a** a facility offered by some businesses to customers considered creditworthy, by means of which they may have goods on credit subject to payment of bills detailing their purchases presented periodically by the businesses ⟨*it's on* ~⟩ ⟨*have you an* ~ *with us?*⟩ **b** business, patronage ⟨*glad to get that customer's* ~⟩ **5** value, importance ⟨*a man of no* ~⟩ **6** profit, advantage ⟨*turned his wit to good* ~⟩ **7a** an explanation of reasons, causes, grounds, or motives ⟨*no satisfactory* ~ *of these phenomena*⟩ **b** a reason for an action ⟨*on that* ~ *alone, you must do it*⟩ **c** careful thought; consideration ⟨*left nothing out of* ~⟩ ⟨*take* ~ *of his extreme youth*⟩ **8** a report of facts or events; a relation ⟨*a newspaper* ~⟩ **9 accounts** *pl*, **account** hearsay, report ⟨*by all* ~s *a rich man*⟩ **10** a sum of money or its equivalent deposited in the common cash of a bank and able to be withdrawn usu on demand by the depositor **11** a version, rendering ⟨*the pianist's sensitive* ~ *of it*⟩ **12** *archaic* a reckoning, computation – **bring/call somebody to account** to ask or demand that somebody should give an explanation for his/her words or actions; *broadly* to reprimand somebody – **go to one's (last) account** *euph* to die – **give a good account of oneself** to acquit oneself well – **hold to account** to hold responsible – **on account of** for the sake of; because of – **on no account/not on any account** under no circumstances – **on one's own account 1** on one's own behalf **2** at one's own risk – **on somebody's account** for the sake of somebody – **take account of** TAKE INTO ACCOUNT – **take into account** to make allowances for ⟨*took the boy's age into account*⟩
*usage* **Of one's own accord** is sometimes confused with **on one's own account** (e g by using *on* for *of*).

²**account** *vt* to consider; COUNT **2** ⟨~s *himself lucky*⟩ ~ *vi* **1** to explain one's conduct or the discharge of one's duties **2** to explain a cause **3a** to be the sole or primary explanation **b** to bring about the capture, death, or destruction of something

⟨~ed *for two rabbits*⟩ □ *(vi)* + *for* [ME *accounten*, fr MF *acompter*, fr *a*- (fr L *ad*-) + *compter* to count]

**accountability** /ə,kowntə'biləti/ *n* 1 the quality or state of being accountable 2 an area for which one is responsible; a responsibility ⟨*distinguished their individual* account-abilities *from their joint* accountabilities – *Handbook for Managers*⟩

**accountable** /ə'kowntəbl/ *adj* 1 liable to be required to give an account; answerable ⟨~ *to your mother for your safety*⟩ 2 capable of being accounted for; explainable – **accountableness** *n*, **accountably** *adv*

**accountancy** /ə'kownt(ə)nsi/ *n* the profession or duties of an accountant

**accountant** /ə'kownt(ə)nt/ *n* one who is skilled in the practice of accounting or who is in charge of accounts – **accountant-ship** *n*

**account book** *n* a book in which accounts are kept; a ledger

**account executive** *n* a business executive (eg in an advertising agency) responsible for the management of a client's account

**accounting** /ə'kownting/ *n* 1 the system of recording and summarizing business and financial transactions in special ledgers and analysing, verifying, and reporting the results; *also* the principles and procedures of accounting 2 the practical application of accounting; *also* an instance of this

**account payable** *n, pl* **accounts payable** the balance due to a creditor on a current account

**account receivable** *n, pl* **accounts receivable** a balance due from a debtor on a current account

**accoutre**, *NAm also* **accouter** /ə'koohtə/ *vt* to provide with equipment, esp in the form of military costume and trappings; outfit [Fr *accoutrer*, fr MF *acoustrer*, fr *a*- + *cousture* sewing, seam – more at COUTURE]

**accoutrement** /ə'koohtrəmənt/, *NAm also* **accouterment** /ə'koohtəmənt/ *n* 1 the act of accoutring; the state of being accoutred 2a an article of equipment or dress, esp when used as an accessory **b accoutrements** *pl*, **accoutrement** equipment, trappings; *specif* a soldier's outfit usu not including clothes and weapons

**accredit** /ə'kredit/ *vt* 1 to give official authorization to or approval of: **1a** to provide with credentials; *esp* to send (an envoy) with letters of authorization **b** to recognize or vouch for as conforming to a standard ⟨*an* ~ed *dairy herd*⟩ 2 to credit *with*, attribute *to* ⟨~ed *him with the discovery of Tasmania*⟩ ⟨~ed *the discovery to him*⟩ [Fr *accréditer*, fr *ad*- + *crédit* credit] – **accreditable** *adj*, **accreditation** *n*

**accrete** /ə'kreet/ *vi* to grow or become attached by accretion ~ *vt* to cause to stick or become attached; accumulate ⟨*a Parliamentary programme is* ~d *piecemeal* – *Punch*⟩ [back-formation fr *accretion*]

**accretion** /ə'kreesh(ə)n/ *n* 1 the process of growth or enlargement: eg **1a** increase by external addition or by accumulation of external parts or particles **b** the increase of land by the gradual or imperceptible action of natural forces 2 a product of accretion; *broadly* an overlying layer ⟨~s *of grime*⟩ 3 (a mass formed by) the sticking together of separate particles; a concretion 4 *law* a rise in the value of property increased by accretion; *also* an increased share of a property, estate, etc devolving upon an heir by default (eg when another heir does not take up his/her share) [L *accretion-, accretio*, fr *accretus*, pp of *accrescere*] – **accretionary** *adj*, **accretive** *adj*

**accrue** /ə'krooh/ *vi* 1 to come into existence as a legally enforceable right or claim 2 to come by way of increase or addition; to arise as a growth or a result ⟨*advantages that have* ~d *to society from the freedom of the press*⟩ 3 to be periodically accumulated whether as an increase or a decrease ⟨*taxes have* ~d⟩ ~ *vt* to collect, accumulate [ME *acreuen*, prob fr MF *acreue* increase, fr *acreistre* to increase, fr L *accrescere*, fr *ad*- + *crescere* to grow – more at CRESCENT] – **accruable** *adj*, **accrual** *also* **accruement** *n*

**acculturation** /ə,kulchə'raysh(ə)n/ *n* a process of interaction and diffusion of cultural values and traditions between individuals or societies, resulting in the acquisition of new cultural characteristics – compare SOCIALIZATION – **acculturational** *adj*, **acculturate** *vt*, **acculturative** *adj*

**accumulate** /ə'kyoohmyoo,layt/ *vt* to heap or pile up; amass, collect ⟨~ *a fortune*⟩ ~ *vi* to increase in quantity or number, esp so as to form a mass [L *accumulatus*, pp of *accumulare*, fr *ad*- + *cumulare* to heap up – more at CUMULATE]

**accumulation** /ə,kyoohmyoo'laysh(ə)n/ *n* 1 the action or

process of accumulating; the state of being or having accumulated 2 increase or growth by addition, esp when continuous or repeated ⟨~ *of interest*⟩ 3 something that has accumulated or has been accumulated ⟨*age may bring* ~s *of respect* – *Observer Review*⟩

**accumulative** /ə'kyoohmyoolətiv/ *adj* 1 cumulative ⟨*an age of rapid and* ~ *change*⟩ 2 tending or given to accumulation; acquisitive; *also* intended to accumulate – **accumulatively** *adv*, **accumulativeness** *n*

**accumulator** /ə'kyoohmyoo,laytə/ *n* one who or that which accumulates: eg **a** *Br* STORAGE CELL (battery or other device storing electric charge); *also* a connected set of these **b** a section of a computer's main memory where numbers are totalled or stored **c** a bet (eg on horse races) in which the winnings from the first of a series of events are staked on the next event; *esp* such a bet covering four or more selections

**accuracy** /'akyoorəsi/ *n* 1 freedom from error; correctness 2 conformity to a standard; exactness; *also* the degree of such conformity ⟨*measurements within 2 percent* ~⟩ **synonyms** see TRUTH

**accurate** /'akyoorət/ *adj* 1 free from error, esp as the result of care ⟨*an* ~ *estimate*⟩ 2 conforming precisely to a measurable standard; exact ⟨~ *instruments*⟩ [L *accuratus*, fr pp of *accurare* to take care of, fr *ad*- + *cura* care] – **accurately** *adv*, **accurateness** *n*

**accursed** /ə'kuhst, ə'kuhsid/ *adj* 1 under a curse; ill-fated 2 damnable, detestable [ME *acursed*, fr pp of *acursen* to consign to destruction with a curse, fr *a*- (fr OE *ā*, perfective prefix) + *cursen* to curse] – **accursedly** *adv*, **accursedness** *n*

**accurst** /ə'kuhst/ *adj, archaic* accursed

**accusal** /ə'kyoohz(ə)l/ *n* (an) accusation

**accusation** /,akyoo'zaysh(ə)n/ *n* 1 the act of accusing; the state or fact of being accused **2a** a charge of wrongdoing; an allegation **b** the specific offence charged ⟨*the* ~ *was piracy*⟩

¹**accusative** /ə'kyoohzətiv/ *adj* 1 relating to or being the grammatical accusative 2 accusatory [ME, fr MF or L; MF *accusatif*, fr L *accusativus*, fr *accusatus*, pp of *accusare*]

²**accusative** *n* a grammatical case expressing the direct object of a verb or of any of several prepositions; *also* a form (eg *me*) in this case

**accusatorial** /ə,kyoohzə'tawri·əl/ *adj* relating to the system of examination before a judge who is not himself the prosecutor – compare INQUISITORIAL

**accusatory** /ə'kyoohzət(ə)ri/ *adj* containing or expressing accusation; accusing

**accuse** /ə'kyoohz/ *vt* 1 to charge with a fault or offence; blame 2 to charge with an offence formally, esp in a court of law – often + *of* ~ *vi* to bring an accusation [ME *accusen*, fr OF *acuser*, fr L *accusare* to call to account, fr *ad*- + *causa* lawsuit, cause] – **accuser** *n*, **accusingly** *adv*

**synonyms** Accuse, charge, arraign, indict, and impeach mean "declare publicly that someone is guilty of a fault or an offence". Accuse, the most general, suggests direct, personal action, while charge is more formal and used for serious offences. An accusation (eg of stealing) in private becomes a charge in a court of law. Arraign, indict, and impeach are all legal terms in this sense. To arraign someone is to bring him/her before a court to be indicted, that is, to be formally charged ⟨*I hereby* indict *you for treason*⟩. Impeach implies a charge of corruption or poor judgment, which requires an answer.

**accused** /ə'kyoohzd/ *n, pl* **accused** the person charged with an offence; *esp* the defendant in a criminal case ⟨*the* ~ *will stand*⟩

**accustom** /ə'kust(ə)m/ *vt* to make familiar through use or experience; habituate – usu + *to* [ME *accustomen*, fr MF *acostumer*, fr *a*- (fr L *ad*-) + *costume* custom]

**accustomed** /ə'kustəmd/ *adj* 1 familiar through use or experience; habitual, usual ⟨*her* ~ *cheerfulness*⟩ 2 in the habit or custom; used ⟨~ *to making decisions*⟩ **synonyms** see USUAL **antonym** unaccustomed – **accustomedness** *n*

**AC/DC** /,-- '--/ *adj, informal* BISEXUAL 1b [alternating *c*urrent, *d*irect *c*urrent]

¹**ace** /ays/ *n* **1a** the face of a die marked with one spot **b** a playing card marked in its centre with one large pip ⟨*the* ~ *of hearts*⟩ **c** a domino end marked with one spot **2a** a score made by a single stroke; *specif* a point scored on a shot (eg a service in tennis or squash) that an opponent fails to touch **b** *chiefly NAm* HOLE IN ONE 3 a combat pilot who has brought down at least five enemy aircraft 4 one who excels; a leading performer in a specified field ⟨*an* ~ *at tennis*⟩ – used as a generalized

term of approval [ME *as*, fr OF, fr L, unit, a copper coin] –
**ace in the hole 1** *NAm* an ace dealt face down to a player (e g
in STUD POKER) and not exposed until the showdown **2** ACE UP
ONE'S SLEEVE – **ace up one's sleeve** *Br* an effective and decisive
argument or resource held in reserve – **within an ace of** extremely close to but just missing ⟨*came* within an ace of *winning*⟩

²**ace** *vt* to score an ace against (an opponent); *broadly* to deliver
a decisive retort to

³**ace** *adj, informal* of first or high rank or quality; excellent
⟨*he's* ~ *at ice hockey*⟩

**-aceae** /-'aysh(y)ə/ *suffix* (→ *n pl*) members of the family of
⟨*Rosaceae*⟩ – in most names of plant families; formerly in
names of orders of plants [NL, fr L, fem pl of *-aceus* -aceous]

**acedia** /ə'seedyə/ *n* ACCIDIE (listlessness, apathy) [LL, fr Gk
*akēdeia*, fr *a-* + *kēdos* care, grief – more at HATE]

**acellular** /,ay'selyoolə/ *adj* containing no cells; not divided into
cells

**acentric** /,ay'sentrik/ *adj* of or being a CHROMOSOME (strand of
gene-carrying material in a cell) that lacks a CENTROMERE

**-aceous** /-'aysi-əs, -'aysh(y)əs/ *suffix* (→ *adj*) **1a** having the
characteristics of ⟨*herb*aceous⟩ ⟨*tuff*aceous⟩ **b** consisting of
⟨*carbon*aceous⟩ ⟨*set*aceous⟩; containing ⟨*farin*aceous⟩ ⟨*argilla*ceous⟩ **2a** relating to a group of animals typified by (a specified
form) ⟨*cet*aceous⟩ or characterized by (a specified feature)
⟨*crust*aceous⟩ **b** relating to a plant family typified by (a specified genus) ⟨*ros*aceous⟩ [L *-aceus*]

**acephalous** /ə'sefələs, ,ay-/ *adj* **1** lacking a head or having the
head reduced **2** lacking a governing head or chief [Gk *akephalos*, fr *a-* + *kephalē* head – more at CEPHALIC]

**acerbate** /'asəbayt/ *vt* **1** to make sour **2** to irritate, exasperate
– compare EXACERBATE

**acerbic** /ə'suhbik/ *also* **acerb** *adj* **1** acid or sour to the taste **2**
acid in temper, mood, or tone *synonyms see* ACRIMONY *antonym* mellow [Fr or L; Fr *acerbe*, fr L *acerbus*, fr *acer*] – **acerbically** *adv*, **acerbity** *n*

**acerose** /'asərohs/ *also* **acerous** /-rəs/ *adj* shaped like a needle
⟨~ *leaves*⟩ [L *acer* sharp – more at EDGE]

**acervate** /ə'suhvayt, -vət/ *adj* growing in heaps or closely
compacted clusters ⟨~ *fungal sporophores*⟩ [L *acervatus*, pp of
*acervare* to heap up, fr *acervus* heap] – **acervately** *adv*, **acervation** *n*

**acescent** /ə'kes(ə)nt, -'ses-/ *adj* turning sour; somewhat acid
[Fr, fr L *acescent-*, *acescens*, prp of *acescere* to turn sour, incho
of *acēre* to be sour, fr *acer* sharp] – **acescence** *also*
**acescency** *n*

**acet-** /əseet-/, **aceto-** *comb form* acetic acid; acetic ⟨acet*yl*⟩ [Fr
& L; Fr *acét-*, fr L *acet-*, fr *acetum* vinegar, fr *acēre*]

**acetabularia** /,asitəbyoo'leəri-ə, ,asi,tabyoo'leəri-ə/ *n* a large
single-celled green alga (genus *Acetabularia*) of warm seas that
resembles a small mushroom in form [NL, genus name, fr L
*acetabulum* vinegar cup]

**acetabulum** /,asi'tabyooləm/ *n, pl* **acetabulums, acetabula**
/-lə/ **1a** the cup-shaped socket in the hipbone into which the
head of the thighbone fits **b** the cavity in the body of an insect
into which a leg fits **2** a round saucer of a leech, flatworm, or
other INVERTEBRATE animal [L, lit., vinegar cup, fr *acetum*
vinegar] – **acetabular** *adj*

**acetal** /'asitl/ *n* any of various chemical compounds containing
the chemical group $C(OR)_2$ [Ger *azetal*, fr *azet-* acet- + *alko-*
hol alcohol]

**acetaldehyde** /,asi'taldihied/ *n* a colourless readily vaporizing
liquid chemical compound $CH_3CHO$, that is an ALDEHYDE used
chiefly in the synthesis of other organic chemical compounds
[ISV]

**acetamide** /ə'setəmied, ,asi'tamid, -mied/ *n* a white solid
chemical compound, $CH_3CONH_2$, that is an AMIDE of acetic
acid and is used esp in the synthesis of other organic chemical
compounds [Ger *azetamid*, fr *azet-* + *amid* amide]

**acetaminophen** /,asitə'minəfən/ *n, chiefly NAm* PARACETAMOL
(type of pain-killing drug) [*acet-* + *amino-* + *phenol*]

**acetanilide** /,asi'tanilied/, **acetanilid** /-lid/ *n* a chemical compound, $C_6H_5NHCOCH_3$, derived from ANILINE that is used in
the synthesis of other organic chemical compounds and was
formerly used as a painkiller [ISV]

**acetate** /'asitayt/ *n* **1** any of various chemical compounds
(SALTS or ESTERS) formed by combination between ACETIC ACID
and a metal atom, an alcohol, or another chemical group **2** the
chemical compound CELLULOSE ACETATE; *also* a product (e g a
textile fibre) made from this *synonyms see* NYLON

**acetic** /ə'seetik, -'set-/ *adj* of or producing ACETIC ACID or vinegar [Fr *acétique*, fr L *acetum* vinegar]

**acetic acid** *n* a colourless pungent liquid acid, $CH_3CO_2H$,
that is the major acid in vinegar and is used esp in synthesis
(e g of plastics)

**acetify** /ə'seetifie, -'set-/ *vb* to turn or be turned into ACETIC
ACID or vinegar – **acetification** *n*, **acetifier** *n*

**acetoacetic acid** /,asitoh-ə'seetik, -'setik, ə,seetoh-/ *n* an unstable acid, $CH_3COCH_2CO_2H$, that is formed as an intermediate compound in the synthesis and breakdown of many
substances in the body and is one of the chemical compounds
(KETONE BODIES) whose presence in the urine is a sign of
diabetes [part trans of Ger *azetessigsäure*, fr *azet-* acet-+
*essigsäure* acetic acid]

**acetone** /'asitohn/ *n* a colourless readily vaporizing fragrant
inflammable liquid, $(CH_3)_2CO$, that is used as a solvent (e g in
varnishes) and is one of the chemical compounds (KETONE
BODIES) whose presence in the urine is a sign of diabetes
[Ger *azeton*, fr L *acetum*] – **acetonic** *adj*

**acetophenetidin** /,asitohfə'netədin, ə,seetoh-/ *n* PHENACETIN
(compound formerly used as a painkiller) [ISV]

**acetous** /'asitəs, ə'setose/ *also* **acetose** /-tohs/ *adj* relating to or producing
vinegar; *also* sour, vinegary [Fr *acéteux*, fr LL *acetosus*, fr L
*acetum*]

**acetyl** /'asitil, ə'si-, ə'see-, -tiel/ *n* the chemical group, $CH_3CO$,
that is characteristic of ACETIC ACID

**acetylate** /ə'seetl,layt, -'set-/ *vt* to introduce one or more acetyl
groups into (a chemical compound) – **acetylation** *n*, **acetylative** *adj*

**acetylcholine** /,asitil'kohleen, -lin/ *n* a chemical compound,
$(CH_3)_3NCH_2CH_2OOCCH_3$, that is released at the ends of
some nerves in the AUTONOMIC NERVOUS SYSTEM and all nerves
that control VOLUNTARY MUSCLES, and that transmits nerve
impulses from one nerve to another or from a nerve to a muscle
[ISV] – **acetylcholinic** *adj*

**acetylcholinesterase** /,asitil,kohli'nestərayz, ə,see-, ə,se-/ *n*
an ENZYME (e g occurring in some nerve endings and in the
blood) that promotes the breakdown of acetylcholine [*acetylcholine* + *esterase*]

**acetyl-coA** /-koh'ay/ *n* ACETYL COENZYME A

**acetyl coenzyme A** *n* a chemical compound,
$C_{25}H_{38}N_7O_{17}P_3S$, formed in all living cells as an essential
intermediate in the processes (e g the breakdown of sugars and
fats) by which cells produce energy

**acetylene** /ə'setileen, -lin/ *n* a colourless inflammable gas,
$HC{\equiv}CH$, used chiefly as a fuel (e g in oxyacetylene torches)
and in the synthesis of other organic chemical compounds –
**acetylenic** *adj*

**acetylsalicylate** /,asitil,sali'silayt, -sə'lisilayt, ə,see-/ *n* any of
various chemical compounds (SALTS or ESTERS) formed by
combination between ACETYLSALICYLIC ACID and a metal atom,
an alcohol, or another chemical group

**acetylsalicylic acid** /,asitil,sali'silik/ *n* aspirin [ISV]

**Achates** /ə'kayteez/ *n* a faithful friend [*Achates*, the companion
of Aeneas in the epic poem *The Aeneid* by Vergil †19 BC
Roman poet]

¹**ache** /ayk/ *vi* **1a** to suffer a usu dull persistent pain **b** to feel
distressed compassion ⟨*heart* ~ d *for her*⟩ **2** to yearn painfully
⟨*aching with desire to see you*⟩ [ME *aken*, fr OE *acan*; akin to
LG *äken* to hurt] – **achingly** *adv*

²**ache** *n* **1** a usu dull persistent pain **2** a painful distress or
yearning

**achene** *also* **akene** /ə'keen/ *n* a small dry 1-seeded fruit (e g
that of the dandelion) that does not split open at maturity (is
INDEHISCENT) [NL *achaenium*, fr *a-* + Gk *chainein* to yawn
– more at YAWN] – **achenial** *adj*

**Acheron** /'akərən/ *n* a river in Hades [L, fr Gk *Acherōn*]

**Acheulian, Acheulean** /ə'shoohli-ən/ *adj or n* (of) a Lower
Palaeolithic culture characterized by two-faced tools with
round cutting edges and, in Europe, falling between the Abbevillian and Mousterian periods [Fr *Acheuléen*, fr St *Acheul*,
site near Amiens in France]

**à cheval** /,ah shə'val/ *adv* **1** with a leg on each side; astride **2**
in such a way as to straddle a line on the layout of a game of
chance (e g roulette) or be split evenly between two numbers,
cards, or events [Fr, lit., on horseback]

**achieve** /ə'cheev/ *vt* **1** to carry out successfully; accomplish
⟨~ *a low unemployment rate*⟩ **2** to obtain by exertion; win ⟨~
*greatness*⟩ ~ *vi* to attain a desired end or level of performance
*synonyms see* PERFORM, ¹REACH [ME *acheven*, fr MF *achever*

to finish, fr *a-* (fr L *ad-*) + *chief* end, head – more at CHIEF] – **achievable** *adj*, **achiever** *n*

**achievement** /ə'cheevmənt/ *n* **1** the act of achieving; successful completion; accomplishment **2** a result brought about by such qualities as determination, persistence, or bravery; a feat ⟨*that was quite an* ∼⟩ **3** performance in a test or academic course **4** a coat of arms displayed with its adjuncts (e g helm, crest, and supporters)

**Achilles** /ə'kileez, -liz/ *n* the greatest warrior among the Greeks at Troy and slayer of Hector in Greek legend [L, fr Gk *Achilleus*]

**Achilles' heel** *n* the only vulnerable point ⟨*fast cars were his* ∼⟩ [fr the story that Achilles was vulnerable only in the heel]

**Achilles tendon** *n* the strong tendon joining the muscles in the calf of the leg to the bone of the heel

**achlamydeous** /ˌaklə'midiəs/ *adj, of a plant* lacking both petals and SEPALS (leaflike structures protecting developing flower bud) [²*a-* + Gk *chlamyd-, chlamys* mantle]

**achlorhydria** /ˌayklaw'hiedriə/ *n* abnormal absence of HYDROCHLORIC ACID from the digestive liquid in the stomach [NL, fr ²*a-* + *chlorine* + *hydrogen*] – **achlorhydric** *adj*

**achondrite** /ˌay'kondriet/ *n* a rare type of stony meteorite without rounded grains (CHONDRULES) – **achondritic** *adj*

**achondroplasia** /ˌay,kondrə'playzh(y)ə/ *n* the failure of normal development of cartilage in humans, resulting in dwarfism [NL] – **achondroplastic** *adj*

**achromat** /'akroh,mat/ *n* ACHROMATIC LENS

**achromat-, achromato-** *comb form* achromatic ⟨achromatism⟩ [Gk *achrōmatos* colourless, fr *a-* + *chrōmat-, chrōma* colour – more at CHROMATIC]

**achromatic** /ˌakroh'matik, -krə-/ *adj* **1** transmitting light without dispersing it into its constituent colours; free from or corrected for CHROMATIC ABERRATION **2** not readily coloured by the usual biological staining agents **3** possessing no colour; black, grey, or white; neutral – **achromatically** *adv*, **achromaticity** *n*, **achromatism** *n*, **achromatize** *vt*

**achromatic lens** *n* a lens made by combining lenses of different glasses having different focal powers, so that the light emerging from the lens forms an image practically free from unwanted colours

**achy** /'ayki/ *adj* afflicted with aches – **achiness** *n*

**acicula** /ə'sikyoolə/ *n, pl* **aciculae** /-lee, -lie/, **aciculas** a needlelike spine, bristle, or crystal [NL, fr LL, ornamental pin – more at AGLET] – **acicular** *adj*, **aciculate** *adj*

¹**acid** /'asid/ *adj* **1a** sour or sharp to the taste **b** sharp, cutting, or sour in speech, manner, or disposition; caustic ⟨*an* ∼ *wit*⟩ **c** piercingly intense ⟨∼ *yellow*⟩ **2a** of, being, like, or containing a chemical acid ⟨∼ *soil*⟩ ⟨*an* ∼ *solution*⟩ **b** being a chemical compound (SALT or ESTER) formed by the replacement of some but not all of the hydrogen atoms in a molecule of an acid by one or more metal atoms or other chemical groups ⟨∼ *sodium carbonate NaHCO₃*⟩ **3** of, being, or made by a steelmaking process in which the furnace is lined with acidic material **4** *of rock* rich in silica [Fr or L; Fr *acide*, fr L *acidus*, fr *acēre* to be sour – more at ACESCENT] – **acidly** *adv*, **acidness** *n*

²**acid** *n* **1a** a sour substance **b** any of various sour typically water-soluble chemical compounds that are capable of reacting with an alkali or other chemical base (BASE 7) to form a salt; *specif* a compound capable of giving a hydrogen ion to a base or taking up a pair of electrons from a base **2** something incisive, biting, or sarcastic ⟨*a social satire dripping with* ∼⟩ **3** *slang* LSD

**acid drop** *n* a hard tart sweet made with sugar and tartaric acid

**acidhead** /'asid,hed/ *n, slang* a person who takes LSD – no longer in vogue

**acidic** /ə'sidik/ *adj* **1** acid-forming **2** acid

**acidify** /ə'sidifie/ *vt* to make or convert into (an) acid ∼ *vi* to become acid – **acidifer** *n*, **acidification** *n*

**acidimeter** /ˌasi'dimitə/ *n* an apparatus for measuring the strength or the amount of acid in a mixture or solution – **acidimetry** *n*, **acidimetric** *adj*

**acidity** /ə'sidəti/ *n* **1** the quality, state, or degree of being acid; tartness **2** the quality or state of being excessively or abnormally acid

**acidophil** /ə'sidəfil, -doh-/, **acidophile** /-fiel/ *n* something (e g a tissue or organism) acidophilic; *esp* a WHITE BLOOD CELL that stains readily with the acid biological dye EOSIN

**acidophilic** /ˌasidoh'filik/ *adj* **1** staining readily with acid biological dyes **2** preferring or thriving in an acid environment – **acidophilia** *n*

**acidophilus milk** /ˌasi'dofiləs/ *n* milk fermented by any of several species of bacteria (esp *Lactobacillus acidophilus*) and used in the treatment of some disorders of the digestive system to alter the type of bacteria growing in the intestines [NL *Lactobacillus acidophilus*, lit., acidophilic Lactobacillus]

**acidosis** /ˌasi'dohsis/ *n* a disorder in which the blood, tissues, etc are unusually acid [NL] – **acidotic** *adj*

**acid rock** *n* rock music marked by long passages of electronic musical effects intended to convey the atmosphere of drug-induced hallucinations

**acid test** *n* a severe or crucial test (e g of value or suitability) [fr the use of nitric acid to test for gold]

**acidulate** /ə'sidyoolayt/ *vt* to make (slightly) acid ⟨∼d *water*⟩ [L *acidulus*] – **acidulation** *n*

**acidulous** /ə'sidyooləs/, **acidulent** /-lənt/ *adj* somewhat acid in taste or manner; harsh, caustic [*acidulous* fr L *acidulus* sourish, fr *acidus; acidulent* fr Fr *acidulant*, fr prp of *aciduler* to acidulate, fr L *acidulus*] – **acidulosity** *n*

**acinar** /'asinə, -nah/ *adj* relating to or comprising an acinus ⟨*pancreatic* ∼ *cells*⟩

**acinus** /'asinəs/ *n, pl* **acini** /-ni/ any of the small sacs lined with secreting cells found in a RACEMOSE GLAND (compound gland made up of grapelike clusters) [NL, fr L, berry, berry seed] – **acinous** *adj*

¹**ack-ack** /ˌak 'ak/ *n* an antiaircraft gun; *also* antiaircraft fire [signallers' terms for *AA*, abbr of *antiaircraft*]

²**ack-ack** *adj* antiaircraft

**ackee, akee** /'akee, a'kee/ *n* (the red fruit, edible when cooked, of) a tropical tree (*Blighia sapida* of the family Sapindaceae) [Kru *ā-kee*]

**ack emma** /ˌak 'emə/ *adj, informal* in the morning; ANTE MERIDIEM – no longer in vogue [signallers' terms for *AM*]

**acknowledge** /ək'nolij/ *vt* **1** to own or admit knowledge of; concede to be true or valid **2** to recognize the status or claims of **3a** to express gratitude or obligation for **b** to show recognition of (e g by smiling or nodding) **c** to confirm receipt of **4** to recognize as genuine or valid ⟨∼ *a debt*⟩ ◻ compare ASSERT [*ac-* (as in *accord*) + *knowledge*] – **acknowledgeable** *adj*
*synonyms* Acknowledge, admit, own, concede, and confess all mean "agree unwillingly that something is so". Acknowledge suggests accepting responsibility without necessarily implying a fault ⟨*she* **acknowledged** *her fondness for the child, but denied that she spoilt him*⟩. Own suggests a more private and reluctant acknowledgment ⟨*she* **owned** *to her friend in some embarrassment that she had bought him a bicycle*⟩. Admit and concede suggest an acknowledgment drawn out under pressure; admit is used of facts and actions, and concede for demands, claims, and in argument. ⟨*Although she* **admitted** *buying the boy a bicycle, she would not* **concede** *that this was spoiling him*⟩. One **confesses** to something of which one is ashamed ⟨*she* **confessed** *it was a bicycle which she could not really afford*⟩. **antonym** deny

**acknowledged** /ək'nolijd/ *adj* generally recognized, accepted, or admitted – **acknowledgedly** *adv*

**acknowledgment** *also* **acknowledgement** /-mənt/ *n* **1a** the act of acknowledging **b** recognition or favourable reception of an act or achievement **2** a thing done or given in recognition of something received **3** a declaration or avowal of one's act or of a fact to give it legal validity **4** *pl* an author's list of others to whom he/she is indebted

**aclinic line** /ə'klinik/ *n* an imaginary line roughly parallel to the geographical equator and connecting all points at which the magnetic DIP (angle formed with the horizon by a magnetic needle freely rotating in a vertical plane) is zero – called also DIP EQUATOR, MAGNETIC EQUATOR [²*a-* + *-clinic*]

**acme** /'akmi/ *n* the highest point or stage; *esp* a perfect representative of a specified class or thing ⟨*he was the* ∼ *of courtesy*⟩ *synonyms* see SUMMIT [Gk *akmē* point, highest point – more at EDGE]

**acmite** /'akmiet/ *n* AEGIRINE (type of mineral) [Ger *achmit*, fr Gk *akmē* point; fr its pointed crystals]

**acne** /'akni/ *n* a skin disorder found esp among adolescents, characterized by inflammation of the skin glands and hair follicles and causing red pimples, esp on the face and neck [Gk *aknē* eruption of the face, MS var of *akmē*, lit., point] – **acned** *adj*

**acock** /ə'kok/ *adj or adv* in a cocked position ⟨*a dog listening with ears* ∼⟩

**acoelomate** /ˌay'seeləmayt, -mət/ *n or adj* (a jelly fish, flatworm, or other primitive animal) having no COELOM (separate cavity between the digestive tract and the body wall)

**acold** /ə'kohld/ *adj, archaic* cold, chilled [ME]

**acolyte** /'akəliet/ *n* 1 an assistant who helps a member of the clergy in a service of worship by performing minor duties 2 one who attends or assists; a follower [ME *acolite*, fr OF & ML; OF, fr ML *acoluthus*, fr MGk *akolouthos*, fr Gk, adj, following, fr *a-*, *ha-* (akin to Gk *homos* same) + *keleuthos* path]

**aconite** /'akəniet/ *n* 1 MONKSHOOD (plant of the buttercup family) 2 the dried tuberous root of a MONKSHOOD (*Aconitum napellus*) that yields a drug formerly used to reduce fever [MF, fr L *aconitum*]

**aconitum** /,akə'nietəm/ *n* 1 any of a genus (*Aconitum*) of usu bluish flowered poisonous plants (e g MONKSHOOD) of the buttercup family 2 ACONITE 2 [NL, genus name, fr L *aconitum*, fr Gk *akoniton*]

**acorn** /'ay,kawn/ *n* the nut of the oak, usu seated in or surrounded by a hard woody cup [ME *akern*, fr OE *æcern*; akin to MHG *ackeran* acorns collectively, Russ *yagoda* berry]

**acorn barnacle** *n* any of numerous barnacles (family Balanidae) that commonly form an incrustation on rocks on the seashore

**acorn worm** *n* any of a group (Enteropneusta) of burrowing wormlike marine animals having an acorn-shaped PROBOSCIS (tubular structure projecting from the head)

¹**acoustic** /ə'koohstik/ *also* **acoustical** /-kl/ *adj* 1 of the sense of hearing, sound, or the science of sounds ⟨∼ *apparatus of the ear*⟩ ⟨∼ *energy*⟩: e g **1a** deadening or absorbing sound ⟨∼ *panelling*⟩ **b** operated by or utilizing sound waves ⟨*the ship was blown up by an* ∼ *mine*⟩ 2 of or being a musical instrument whose sound is not electronically modified ⟨*an* ∼ *guitar*⟩ [Gk *akoustikos* of hearing, fr *akouein* to hear – more at HEAR] – **acoustically** *adv*

²**acoustic** *n* 1 *pl but taking sing vb* a science that deals with the nature and properties of sound and the effects that it undergoes and produces 2 **acoustics** *pl*, **acoustic** the properties of an enclosed space (e g a room or hall) that govern the quality of sound heard – **acoustician** *n*

**acquaint** /ə'kwaynt/ *vt* to cause to know firsthand ⟨∼ *oneself with the law*⟩ [ME *aquainten*, fr OF *acointier*, fr ML *accognitare*, fr LL *accognitus*, pp of *accognoscere* to know perfectly, fr L *ad-* + *cognoscere* to know – more at COGNITION]

**acquaintance** /ə'kwaynt(ə)ns/ *n* 1 personal knowledge; familiarity ⟨*my* ∼ *with the subject is slight*⟩ **2a** the people with whom one is acquainted ⟨*among my numerous* ∼⟩ **b** a person whom one knows but who is not a particularly close friend – **acquaintanceship** *n* – **make somebody's acquaintance/the acquaintance of somebody** to meet or get to know somebody, esp as a result of being formally introduced

**acquainted** /ə'kwayntid/ *adj* having met (each other) socially; familiar *with* (each other) ⟨*we are not* ∼⟩ ⟨*is* ∼ *with the mayor*⟩

**acquiesce** /,akwee'es/ *vi* to submit or comply tacitly or passively – often + *in synonyms* see ¹ASSENT *antonym* object [Fr *acquiescer*, fr L *acquiescere*, fr *ad-* + *quiescere* to be quiet, fr *quies* rest, quiet] – **acquiescence** *n*, **acquiescent** *adj*, **acquiescently** *adv*

**acquire** /ə'kwie·ə/ *vt* **1a** to gain or come into possession of, often by unspecified means; *also, euph* to steal **b** to come to have as a new or additional characteristic or ability (e g by conscious effort or through environmental influences) ⟨∼ *fluency in French*⟩ ⟨*bacteria that* ∼ *tolerance to antibiotics*⟩ **2** to locate and hold (a desired object) in a detector ⟨∼ *a target by radar*⟩ *synonyms* see ¹WIN *antonym* forfeit [ME *aqueren*, fr MF *aquerre*, fr L *acquirere*, fr *ad-* + *quaerere* to seek, obtain] – **acquirable** *adj*, **acquirement** *n*

**acquired taste** *n* something that one must learn to like ⟨*oysters are an* ∼⟩ ⟨*many people find opera an* ∼⟩

**acquisition** /,akwi'zish(ə)n/ *n* 1 the act of acquiring or gaining 2 somebody or something that is acquired or gained, esp to advantage ⟨*Martin is a great* ∼ *for the department*⟩ [ME *acquisicioun*, fr MF or L; MF *acquisition*, fr L *acquisition-, acquisitio*, fr *acquisitus*, pp of *acquirere*] – **acquisitional** *adj*, **acquisitor** *n*

**acquisitive** /ə'kwizətiv/ *adj* keen or tending to acquire and possess – **acquisitively** *adv*, **acquisitiveness** *n*

**acquit** /ə'kwit/ *vt* **-tt-** 1 to free from responsibility or obligation; *specif* to declare not guilty ⟨*the court* ∼ted *him of the charge*⟩ 2 to conduct (oneself) in a specified, usu praiseworthy,

manner ⟨*the recruits* ∼ted *themselves like veterans*⟩ **3a** *archaic* to pay off (e g a claim or debt) **b** *obs* to repay (a person) [ME *aquiten*, fr OF *aquiter*, fr *a-* (fr L *ad-*) + *quite* free of – more at QUIT] – **acquitter** *n*

**acquittal** /ə'kwitl/ *n* a judicial release from a criminal charge, esp by a verdict of not guilty

**acquittance** /ə'kwit(ə)ns/ *n* (a document giving proof of) a discharge from an obligation, esp debt

**acr-** /akr-/, **acro-** *comb form* 1 beginning; end ⟨acro*nym*⟩ ⟨acro*stic*⟩ **2a** top; peak; summit; apex ⟨acro*dont*⟩ ⟨acro*polis*⟩ ⟨acro*petal*⟩ **b** height ⟨acro*phobia*⟩ ⟨acro*bat*⟩ **c** extremity ⟨acro*megaly*⟩ ⟨acro*gen*⟩ [MF or Gk; MF *acro-*, fr Gk *akr-*, *akro-*, fr *akros* topmost, extreme; akin to Gk *akmē* point – more at EDGE]

**acrasin** /'akrəsin/ *n* a chemical substance (e g CYCLIC AMP) that is secreted by the individual amoebalike cells of a SLIME MOULD (funguslike organism) and causes them to aggregate in a many-celled mass [NL *Acrasia*, genus of fungi related to the slime moulds + *-in*]

**acre** /'aykə/ *n* **1** *pl* lands, fields ⟨*England's green* ∼s *glided by beneath them*⟩ **2** any of various units of area; *esp* a unit equal to 4840 square yards (4046.86 square metres) ⟨*a lake of 9* ∼s⟩ **3** *pl, informal* great quantities ⟨∼s *of time devoted to trivia*⟩ **4** *archaic* a field, esp of arable or pasture land [ME, fr OE *æcer*; akin to OHG *ackar* field, L *ager*, Gk *agros*, L *agere* to drive – more at AGENT]

**acreage** /'ayk(ə)rij/ *n* area in acres

**acre-'foot** *n* the volume (e g of irrigation water) that would cover one acre to a depth of one foot

**acrid** /'akrid/ *adj* 1 unpleasantly pungent in taste or smell; irritating, corrosive 2 violently bitter in manner or language; acrimonious ⟨*an* ∼ *denunciation*⟩ [modif (influenced by *acid*) of L *acr-*, *acer* sharp – more at EDGE] – **acridly** *adv*, **acridness** *n*, **acridity** *n*

**acridine** /'akrideen, -dien, -din/ *n* a colourless solid chemical compound, $C_{13}H_9N$, that occurs in COAL TAR and is used in the manufacture of dyes and antiseptics

**acriflavine** /,akri'flayveen, -vin/ *n* a red or orange dye, $C_{14}H_{14}NO_3Cl$, that is used as a skin disinfectant and antiseptic [*acridine* + *flavine*]

**Acrilan** /'akrilan/ *trademark* – used for an acrylic fibre *synonyms* see NYLON

**acrimony** /'akriməni/ *n* caustic sharpness of manner or language resulting from anger or ill nature [MF or L; MF *acrimonie*, fr L *acrimonia*, fr *acr-*, *acer*] – **acrimonious** *adj*, **acrimoniously** *adv*, **acrimoniousness** *n*

**synonyms** Acrimony, **acerbity**, and **asperity** all mean the expression of anger or irritation in temper or language. Acrimony and acrimonious suggest deep resentment and bitterness, resulting in sharpness of manner and caustic language ⟨*an* acrimonious quarrel⟩. Acerbity includes sourness as well as bitterness; an acerbic remark may be due to a sour nature or be an acid response to something irritating. Asperity means harshness of manner rather than bitterness of nature, though it also conveys irritation ⟨*she replied with some* asperity *that her produce was always fresh*⟩. **antonym** suavity

**acro-** – see ACR-

**acrobat** /'akrəbat/ *n* 1 one who performs gymnastic feats requiring skilful control of the body 2 one who nimbly and often too readily changes his/her position or viewpoint ⟨*a political* ∼⟩ [Fr & Gk; Fr *acrobate*, fr Gk *akrobatēs*, fr *akrobatos* walking on tiptoe, fr *akros* + *bainein* to go – more at COME]

**acrobatic** /,akrə'batik/ *adj* 1 of or like an acrobat 2 very mobile ⟨∼ *eyebrows* – *Punch*⟩ – **acrobatically** *adv*

**acrobatics** /,akrə'batiks/ *n pl* 1 *taking sing or pl vb* the art, performance, or activity of an acrobat 2 a spectacular performance involving great agility ⟨*contralto's vocal* ∼⟩

**acrocarpous** /,akrə'kahpəs/ *adj, of a moss* having the female sex organs, and hence the spore-containing capsules, at the end of the stem [NL *acrocarpus*, fr Gk *akrokarpos* bearing fruit at the top, fr *akr-* acr- + *-karpos* -carpous]

**acrocentric** /,akrə'sentrik, ,akroh-/ *adj* of or being a CHROMOSOME (strand of gene-carrying material in a cell) that has the CENTROMERE situated so that one arm of the chromosome is much shorter than the other [*acr-* + *-centric*] – **acrocentric** *n*

**acrodont** /'akrə,dont/ *adj, of a tooth of certain reptiles, fishes, etc* fused with the bony ridge of the jaw rather than growing from a socket – compare PLEURODONT [*acr* + *-odont*]

**acrolein** /ə'krohli·in/ *n* a colourless irritant pungent liquid chemical compound, $CH_2$:CHCHO, used in manufacturing plastics and perfumes and in the synthesis of other organic chemical compounds [ISV *acr-* (fr L *acr-*, *acer*) + L *olēre* to smell – more at ODOUR]

**acromegaly** /ˌakroh'megəli, ˌakrə-/ *n* a long-lasting progressive disorder marked by abnormal enlargement of the hands, feet, and face, caused by excessive production of GROWTH HORMONE by the PITUITARY GLAND [Fr *acromégalie*, fr *acr-* + Gk *megal-*, *megas* large – more at MUCH] – **acromegalic** *adj* or *n*

**acronychal** /ˌakroh'niekl, ˌakrə-/ *adj*, *of the rising or setting of a star* occurring at sunset [Gk *akronychos*, fr *akr-* acr- + *nyx* night]

**acronym** /'akrənim/ *n* a word (e g *radar* or *snafu*) formed from the initial letters of other words [*acr-* + *-onym* (as in *homonym*)] – **acronymic** *adj*, **acronymically** *adv*

**acropetal** /ə'kropitl/ *adj* proceeding or developing from the base towards the tip of a plant ⟨*an* ~ *inflorescence*⟩ – compare BASIPETAL [*acr-* + *-petal* (as in *centripetal*)] – **acropetally** *adv*

**acrophobia** /ˌakrə'fohbi-ə/ *n* abnormal dread of being at a great height [NL]

**acropolis** /ə'kropəlis/ *n* the citadel of an ancient Greek city (e g Athens) [Gk *akropolis*, fr *akr-* acr- + *polis* city – more at POLICE]

**¹across** /ə'kros/ *adv* **1a** in a position reaching from one side to the other; crosswise **b** in distance from one side to the other ⟨*the stream is six feet* ~⟩ **2** to or on the opposite side **3** so as to be understandable, acceptable, or successful – compare GET ACROSS [ME *acros*, fr AF *an crois*, fr *an* in (fr L *in*) + *crois* cross, fr L *crux* – more at IN, RIDGE]

**²across** *prep* **1a** from one side to the opposite side of; over, through ⟨*swam* ~ *the river*⟩ **b** on the opposite side of ⟨*lives* ~ *the street from us*⟩ **2** so as to intersect or pass through at an angle ⟨*sawed* ~ *the grain of the wood*⟩ **3** into transitory contact with ⟨*ran* ~ *an old friend*⟩

**a,cross-the-'board** *adj* **1** embracing all classes or categories; blanket ⟨*an* ~ *pay rise*⟩ **2** *NAm* placed in combination to win or to come in the first three or four ⟨*an* ~ *racing bet*⟩ – **across the board** *adv*

**acrostic** /ə'krostik/ *n* **1** a composition, usu in verse, in which sets of letters (e g the initial or final letters of the lines) taken in order form a word or phrase or a regular sequence of letters of the alphabet **2** a puzzle consisting of lines of rhyming verse that are clues leading to words, of which the initial and sometimes other (e g final) letters, when read vertically downwards, spell out the answer to the puzzle – compare WORD SQUARE [MF & Gk; MF *acrostiche*, fr Gk *akrostichis*, fr *akr-* acr- + *stichos* line; akin to *steichein* to go – more at STAIR] – **acrostic** *also* **acrostical** *adj*, **acrostically** *adv*

**acroter** /ə'krohtə, 'akrətə/ *n* a PEDESTAL (base) resting on the centre or side of a PEDIMENT (triangular gable) to support an ornament (e g a statue); *broadly* this and the object placed on it [Fr *acrotère*, fr L *acroterium*, fr Gk *akrōtērion*, fr *akros* topmost, extreme]

**acroterion** /ˌakrə'tiərion, -riən/ *n* an acroter [Gk *akrōtērion*]

**acrylate** /'akrilayt/ *n* **1** any of various chemical compounds (SALTS or ESTERS) formed by combination between ACRYLIC ACID and a metal atom, an alcohol, or another chemical group **2** ACRYLIC RESIN

**¹acrylic** /ə'krilik/ *adj* of ACRYLIC ACID or its derivatives ⟨~ *polymers*⟩ [ISV *acrolein* + *-yl* + *-ic*]

**²acrylic** *n* **1a** ACRYLIC RESIN **b** (a painting done in) a paint containing an ACRYLIC RESIN **2** ACRYLIC FIBRE

**acrylic acid** *n* a colourless liquid acid, $CH_2$:CHCOOH, used in the manufacture of ACRYLIC RESINS and other plastics

**acrylic fibre** *n* a synthetic textile fibre made from acrylonitrile and usu other POLYMERS (complex chemical compounds composed of repeating linked subunits) *synonyms* see NYLON

**acrylic resin** *n* a glasslike plastic made by causing (a derivative of) ACRYLIC ACID or METHACRYLIC ACID to react to form a POLYMER (complex chemical compound composed of repeating linked subunits) and used for cast and moulded parts or as coatings and adhesives

**acrylonitrile** /ˌakriloh'nietril/ *n* a colourless readily vaporizing inflammable liquid chemical compound, $H_2C$:CHCN, that is a NITRILE used chiefly in the manufacture of plastics and adhesives

**¹act** /akt/ *n* **1a** a thing done; a deed **b** the outward sign (e g a prayer) of an inward condition ⟨*make an* ~ *of contrition*⟩ **2** the formal product of a legislative body; a statute ⟨*Parliament*

*passed an* ~⟩; *also* a decree, edict **3** the process of doing ⟨*caught in the very* ~⟩ **4** *often cap* a formal record of something done or transacted – usu in *one's act and deed* **5a** any of the principal divisions of a play or opera – compare SCENE **b** any of the successive parts or performances in an entertainment (e g a variety show or circus) **6** a display of affected behaviour; a pretence **7** *Austr* a fit of temper [ME; partly fr L *actus* doing, act, fr *actus*, pp of *agere* to drive, do; partly fr L *actum* thing done, record, fr neut of *actus*, pp – more at AGENT] – **be/get in on the act** to be or deliberately become involved in a situation or undertaking, esp for one's own advantage

synonyms **Act, action, deed, feat**, and **exploit** all describe something done. **Act** is a neutral word, sometimes used to stress a single occurrence ⟨*he suffered for this* **act** *of youthful irresponsibility for the rest of his life*⟩. **Action** tends to be used for the accomplishing of something, stressing the process. In the plural, like **deeds**, it may mean "conduct". **Deed, exploit**, and **feat** are all used for praiseworthy achievements. **Deed** is becoming less usual ⟨*the noble* **deeds** *of knights of old*⟩, except in the phrase "good **deed**". **Exploit** usually refers to physical achievement, and implies heroism or courage. **Feat** may refer to mental prowess as well ⟨*to remember the names of all her pupils was no mean* **feat**⟩.

**²act** *vt* **1** to represent or perform by action, esp on the stage **2** to stimulate, affect ⟨~ed *an emotion he did not feel*⟩ **3** to play the part of; behave as ⟨~ *the fool*⟩ **4** to behave in a manner suitable to ⟨~ *your age*⟩ **5** *obs* to actuate, animate ~ *vi* **1a** to perform on the stage; engage in acting **b** to behave insincerely **2** to take action; move ⟨*think before* ~ing⟩ **3** to function in a specified manner; behave ⟨~ed *generously*⟩ **4** to perform a specified function; serve *as* ⟨*trees* ~ing *as a windbreak*⟩ ⟨~ *as chairman*⟩ **5** to be a substitute or representative *for* **6** to produce an effect; work ⟨*wait for a medicine to* ~⟩ – **actable** *adj*, **actability** *n*

**act out** *vt* **1a** to represent in action ⟨*children act out what they read*⟩ **b** to translate into action ⟨*unwilling to* act out *their beliefs*⟩ **2** to express (repressed or unconscious impulses) in overt behaviour without awareness or insight, esp during psychoanalytic investigation

**act up** *vi* **1** *informal* to behave in an unruly manner; PLAY UP **2** to give pain or trouble ⟨*this typewriter is* acting up *again*⟩

**-acter** /-aktə/ *comb form* (→ *n*) something, esp a play, containing a specified number of acts ⟨*a one* -acter⟩

**ACTH** *n* ADRENOCORTICOTROPHIC HORMONE [*adrenocorticotrophic hormone*]

**actin** /'aktin/ *n* a protein that is found in most cells, esp muscle, and that combines with MYOSIN in producing muscular contraction – compare ACTOMYOSIN [ISV, fr L *actus*]

**actin-** /aktin-/, **actini-, actino-** *comb form* **1** having a radiate form ⟨Actino*myces*⟩ **2** actinian ⟨actin*iform*⟩ [NL, ray, fr Gk *aktin-*, *aktino-*, fr *aktin-*, *aktis*; akin to OE *ūhte* morning twilight, L *noct-*, *nox* night – more at NIGHT]

**¹acting** /'akting/ *adj* holding a specified rank or position temporarily ⟨~ *president*⟩

**²acting** *n* the art or practice of representing a character in a dramatic production

**actinia** /ak'tiniə/ *n*, *pl* **actiniae** /-ni,ie/, **actinias** any of a genus (*Actinia*) of SEA ANEMONES [NL, genus name, fr *actin-* + *-ia*] – **actinian** *adj*

**actinide** /'aktinied/ *n* any of a series of 15 radioactive chemical elements beginning with actinium of ATOMIC NUMBER 89 and ending with lawrencium of ATOMIC NUMBER 103 [ISV]

**actinism** /'aktiniz(ə)m/ *n* the property of RADIANT ENERGY, esp in the visible and ultraviolet spectral regions, by which chemical changes are produced – **actinic** *adj*, **actinically** *adv*

**actinium** /ak'tini-əm/ *n* a radioactive metallic chemical element that has a VALENCY of three, that resembles lanthanum in chemical properties, and that is found esp in pitchblende [NL]

**actino** – see ACTIN-

**actinolite** /ak'tinəliet/ *n* a bright or greyish green AMPHIBOLE (type of mineral) occurring in elongated or needlelike forms

**actinometer** /ˌakti'nomitə/ *n* an instrument used, esp formerly, for measuring the intensity of esp solar radiation – **actinometry** *n*, **actinometric** *adj*

**actinomorphic** /ˌaktinoh'mawfik/ *also* **actinomorphous** /-fəs/ *adj*, *of an organism or part* capable of being divided symmetrically by more than one plane passing lengthways through the central axis; radially symmetrical ⟨*an* ~ *flower*⟩ [ISV] – **actinomorphy** *n*

**actinomyces** /ˌaktinoh'mieseez/ *n*, *pl* **actinomyces** any of a genus (*Actinomyces*) of threadlike bacteria including both soil-inhabiting SAPROPHYTES (organisms that feed on dead or decaying animal and plant matter) and disease-producing parasites [NL, genus name, fr *actin-* + Gk *mykēt-, mykēs* fungus; akin to Gk *myxa* mucus – more at MUCUS] – **actinomycetal** *adj*

**actinomycete** /ˌaktinoh'mieseet, ˌ----'-/ *n* any of an order (Actinomycetales) of threadlike or rod shaped bacteria including the actinomyces and STREPTOMYCES [deriv of Gk *aktin-, aktis* + *mykēt-, mykēs*] – **actinomycetous** *adj*

**actinomycin** /ˌaktinoh'miesin/ *n* any of various red or yellow-red antibiotics that are obtained from soil bacteria (esp *Streptomyces antibioticus*)

**actinomycosis** /ˌaktinohmie'kohsis/ *n* infection with or disease caused by actinomycetes; *esp* a long-lasting disease of cattle, pigs, and human beings characterized by hard swollen masses of tissue, usu in the mouth and jaw [NL] – **actinomycotic** *adj*

**actinon** /'aktinon/ *n* a gaseous radioactive ISOTOPE (form in which an atom can occur) of the chemical element RADON that has a HALF-LIFE (time required for half the atoms of a quantity of a radioactive substance to disintegrate) of about 4 seconds [NL, fr *actinium*]

**actinouranium** /ˌaktinoh·yoo'raynyəm/ *n* the ISOTOPE (form in which an atom can occur) of the chemical element uranium, having a MASS NUMBER of 235 [NL, fr *actinium* + *uranium*]

**actinozoan** /-'zoh·ən/ *n* ANTHOZOAN (coral, SEA ANEMONE or related animal) [*actin-* + Gk *zōion* animal; akin to Gk *zōē* life – more at QUICK] – **actinozoan** *adj*

¹**action** /'aksh(ə)n/ *n* **1** a civil proceeding in a court of law by which one demands or enforces one's legal rights **2a** the state or process of acting or being active ⟨~ *photography*⟩ **b** the process of acting or working, esp to produce alteration by force or through a natural agency ⟨~ *of acid on metal*⟩ **3a** the manner of movement of the body ⟨*a horse's* ~⟩ **b** a function of (a part of) the body **4** a voluntary act; a deed ⟨*a kind* ~⟩ ⟨*know him by his* ~s⟩ **5a** the state of functioning actively ⟨*machine is out of* ~⟩ **b** practical, often militant activity usu directed towards a particular aim ⟨*an* ~ *group*⟩ ⟨*take decided* ~⟩ **c** initiative, enterprise ⟨*a man of* ~⟩ **6a(1)** an engagement between troops or ships **a(2)** combat in war ⟨*gallantry in* ~⟩ – compare ¹BATTLE **b** (the unfolding of) the events in a play or work of fiction; plot ⟨*the* ~ *takes place in Europe*⟩ **7** an operating mechanism (eg of a gun or piano); *also* the manner in which it operates **8** *informal* lively activity; *esp* the most exciting activity in an area ⟨*go where the* ~ *is*⟩ ⟨*a piece of the* ~⟩ *synonyms* see ¹ACT [ME *accioun*, fr MF *action*, fr L *action-, actio*, fr *actus*, pp of *agere* to drive, do] – **take action 1** to begin to act **2** to begin legal proceedings

²**action** *vt* to take action on; implement

**actionable** /-əbl/ *adj* giving grounds for an action at law ⟨*his conduct was* ~⟩ – **actionably** *adv*

**action painting** *n* ABSTRACT EXPRESSIONISM in art marked esp by the use of spontaneous techniques (eg dribbling, splattering, or smearing paint on a canvas)

**action potential** *n* a momentary change in electrical POTENTIAL (amount of electrical intensity) across the membrane of a (nerve) cell resulting from activation by a stimulus

**action replay** *n* a videotape recording of a televised incident (eg in a sports event) played back on television usu immediately after the event and often in slow motion

**activate** /'aktivayt/ *vt* **1** to make (more) active or reactive, esp in chemical or physical properties: eg **1a** to make (a substance) radioactive **b** to treat (eg carbon) so as to improve its properties of ADSORPTION (adhesion of molecules of one substance to another) **c** to aerate (sewage) so as to favour the growth of organisms that decompose organic matter **d** to convert (eg a provitamin) into a biologically active derivative **2** *NAm* to put (troops) on active duty; mobilize – **activator** *n*, **activation** *n*

**activated carbon** *n* a powdered or granular carbon made usu by CARBONIZATION (breakdown of coal by heat) and chemical activation and used chiefly for removing impurities (eg from alcohol) by ADSORPTION (adhesion of molecules of one substance to another)

**activated charcoal** *n* ACTIVATED CARBON

**activation analysis** /ˌakti'vaysh(ə)n/ *n* analysis to determine the chemical composition of a material by bombarding it with neutrons to produce radioactive atoms whose radiations are characteristic of the chemical elements present

¹**active** /'aktiv/ *adj* **1** characterized by practical action rather than by contemplation or speculation ⟨*took an* ~ *interest in the project*⟩ ⟨~ *hostility*⟩ **2** quick in physical movement; lively, agile **3** marked by vigorous activity; busy, brisk ⟨*the stock market was* ~⟩ **4** requiring vigorous action or exertion ⟨~ *sports*⟩ **5** marked by current and practical action, use, or effect ⟨~ *club members*⟩ ⟨~ *accounts*⟩ **6** having practical operation or results; effective ⟨*an* ~ *law*⟩ **7** liable to erupt; not extinct ⟨*an* ~ *volcano*⟩ **8a** *of a verb form or voice* having as the subject the person or thing doing the action (eg *hit* in "she hit the ball") **b** *of a sentence* containing an active verb form **9** of, in, or being full-time service, esp in the armed forces ⟨~ *duty*⟩ **10a** capable of acting or reacting; activated ⟨~ *nitrogen*⟩ **b** tending to progress or to cause degeneration; not cured ⟨~ *tuberculosis*⟩ **c** *of a chemical substance* exhibiting OPTICAL ACTIVITY **11a** operating by emitting signals and acting on their interpretation on reflection from a target ⟨*an* ~ *homing missile*⟩ – compare PASSIVE 2f **b** *of an electronic device* using electrical power for amplifying or controlling an electrical signal ⟨*transistors and valves are* ~ *devices*⟩ – compare PASSIVE 2d *synonyms* see LIVELY *antonyms* inactive, lethargic [ME, fr MF or L; MF *actif*, fr L *activus*, fr *actus*, pp of *agere* to drive, do – more at AGENT] – **actively** *adv*, **activeness** *n*

²**active** *n* **1** an active verb form **2** the active VOICE of a language

**active immunity** *n* immunity that is usu long-lasting and is acquired through production of antibodies within a living organism in response to the presence of ANTIGENS (substances causing the production of specific antibodies) – compare PASSIVE IMMUNITY

**active site** *n* a part of the surface of an ENZYME molecule that is shaped so as to fit closely with a molecule of the chemical compound that the enzyme acts on

**active transport** *n* movement of a chemical substance across a (cell) membrane in living tissue by the expenditure of energy esp against a gradient of concentration or electrical potential and usu opposite to the direction of normal diffusion

**activism** /'aktiviz(ə)m/ *n* a doctrine or practice that emphasizes direct vigorous action (eg the use of mass demonstrations) in support of or opposition to one side of a controversial issue – **activist** *n or adj*, **activistic** *adj*

**activity** /ak'tivəti/ *n* **1** the quality or state of being active **2** vigorous or energetic action; liveliness, assiduity **3** natural or normal function: eg **3a** a process (eg digestion) that an organism carries on or participates in by virtue of being alive **b** a process actually or potentially involving mental function; *specif* an educational procedure designed to stimulate learning by firsthand experience **4** *usu pl* a pursuit in which a person is active ⟨*social* activities⟩

**act of faith** *n* an action demonstrating the strength of one's esp religious convictions

**act of God** *n* a sudden event, esp a catastrophe, brought about by uncontrollable natural forces

**actomyosin** /ˌaktoh'mie·əsin/ *n* a protein complex in muscle formed by the linkage of ACTIN and MYOSIN that is involved together with the energy-storing chemical compound ATP in muscular contraction [ISV *actin* + *-o-* + *myosin*]

**actor** /'aktə/, *fem* **actress** /'aktris/ *n* one who represents a character in a dramatic production; *esp* one whose profession is acting – **actorish** *adj*

**Acts** /akts/, **Acts of the Apostles** *n taking sing vb* the fifth book of the New Testament narrating the beginnings of the Christian Church

**actual** /'aktyoo(ə)l, -choo(ə)l/ *adj* **1** existing in fact or reality rather than as something potential, apparent, or imagined; genuine ⟨~ *poverty*⟩ ⟨~ *and imagined conditions*⟩ **2** existing or occurring at the time; current ⟨*caught in the* ~ *commission of a crime*⟩ **3** *obs* active *antonyms* ideal, imaginary [ME *actuel*, fr MF, fr LL *actualis*, fr L *actus* act] – **actualize** *vt*, **actualization** *n*

**actual cash value** *n* the amount necessary to replace or restore lost, stolen, or damaged property (eg a car); replacement value

**actuality** /ˌaktyoo'aləti, ˌakchoo-/ *n* **1** the quality or state of being actual; reality **2** *often pl* an existing circumstance; a real fact ⟨*possible risks which have been seized upon as* actualities – T S Eliot⟩

**actually** /-li/ *adv* **1** in act or in fact; really ⟨*nominally but not* ~ *independent*⟩ ⟨*I'm not hungry,* ~*!*⟩ **2** at the present moment ⟨*the party* ~ *in power*⟩ **3** strange as it may seem; even ⟨*she* ~ *spoke Latin*⟩

**actuary** /'aktyoo(ə)ri, 'akchoo-/ *n* **1** a statistician who calculates insurance risks, premiums, annuities, etc **2** *obs* a clerk, registrar [L *actuarius* shorthand writer, fr *actum* record – more at ACT] – **actuarial** *adj*, **actuarially** *adv*

**actuate** /'aktyooayt, -choo-/ *vt* **1** to put into (mechanical) action or motion **2** to incite to action ⟨~d *by greed*⟩ [ML *actuatus*, pp of *actuare*, fr L *actus* act] – **actuator** *n*, **actuation** *n*

**acuity** /ə'kyooh•əti/ *n, formal* keenness of perception; sharpness [MF *acuité*, fr OF *agüeté*, fr *agu* sharp, fr L *acutus*]

**aculeate** /ə'kyoohli•ət/ *adj* having a sting ⟨~ *insects*⟩ [L *aculeatus* having stings, fr *aculeus*, dim. of *acus*]

**acumen** /'akyoomən/ *n* keenness and depth of perception, discernment, or discrimination, esp in practical matters; shrewdness *synonyms* see DISCERNMENT [L *acumin-, acumen*, lit., point, fr *acuere*]

**acuminate** /ə'kyoohminayt/ *adj* tapering to a slender point ⟨*an* ~ *leaf*⟩

**acupuncture** /'ak(y)oo,pungkchə/ *n* an originally Chinese practice of puncturing the body at particular points with needles, esp to cure disease, relieve pain, or produce anaesthesia [L *acus* + E *puncture*] – **acupuncturist** *n*

**acushla** /ə'koohshlə/ *n, Irish* darling – usu used as a term of address [IrGrael *a cuisle* o darling, fr *a* o + *cuisle* darling, lit., pulse]

¹**acute** /ə'kyooht/ *adj* **1a** *of an angle* measuring less than 90° **b** composed of acute angles ⟨*an* ~ *triangle*⟩ **2a** marked by keen discernment or intellectual perception, esp of subtle distinctions; penetrating ⟨*an* ~ *thinker*⟩ **b** responsive to slight impressions or stimuli ⟨~ *eyesight*⟩ **3** intensely felt or perceived ⟨~ *pain*⟩ **4a** *esp of an illness, disease, etc* having a sudden onset, sharp rise, and short course; *also* suffering from or affected by acute illness ⟨*an* ~ *patient*⟩ ⟨*an* ~ *abdomen*⟩ – compare CHRONIC 1a **b** lasting a short time ⟨~ *experiments*⟩ **5** demanding urgent attention; severe ⟨*an* ~ *housing shortage*⟩ **6** being or marked with an acute accent *synonyms* see ¹SHARP *antonyms* obtuse (for 1) chronic (for 4a) [L *acutus*, pp of *acuere* to sharpen, fr *acus* needle; akin to L *acer* sharp – more at EDGE] – **acutely** *adv*, **acuteness** *n*

²**acute, acute accent** *n* an accent mark placed over certain vowels in some languages (e g French) to denote a particular sound quality or stress

**acyclic** /,ay'sieklik, ,ay'siklik/ *adj* **1** not cyclic; *esp, of a flower part* not arranged in cycles or whorls **2** (of or being a chemical compound) that does not contain a ring of atoms in the molecular structure; *esp* ALIPHATIC

**acyl** /'as(i)l, 'asiel/ *n* a chemical group derived from an organic chemical acid (e g ACETIC ACID) by removal of the HYDROXYL group (group containing an atom of hydrogen and an atom of oxygen) [ISV, fr *acid*]

¹**ad** /ad/ *n, informal* an advertisement

²**ad** *n, chiefly NAm* ADVANTAGE 4

**ad-, ac-, af-, ag-, al-, ap-, as-, at-** *prefix* **1** to; towards – usu *ac-* before *c, k,* or *q* ⟨*acculturation*⟩, *af-* before *f* ⟨*affiliate*⟩, *ag-* before *g* ⟨*aggrade*⟩, *al-* before *l* ⟨*alliteration*⟩, *ap-* before *p* ⟨*approximate*⟩, *as-* before *s* ⟨*assuage*⟩, *at-* before *t* ⟨*at*tune⟩, and *ad-* before other sounds but sometimes *ad-* even before one of the listed consonants ⟨*ad*sorb⟩ **2** near; adjacent to – in this sense always in the form *ad-* ⟨*ad*renal⟩ [ME, fr MF, OF & L; MF, fr OF, fr L, fr *ad* – more at AT]

**-ad** /-əd, -ad/ *suffix* (→ *adv*) in the direction of; towards ⟨*cephal*ad⟩ [L *ad*]

**ADA, Ada** /'aydə/ *n* a HIGH-LEVEL computer programming language similar to PASCAL that is designed for REAL-TIME applications (applications requiring very rapid responses by a computer to changing conditions) and to control the simultaneous performance of several operations, and that has been developed to be used primarily for military purposes (e g in missile guidance systems) [*Ada* Lovelace (née Byron) †1852 E mathematician & assistant to the inventor of a computer, Charles Babbage]

**adage** /'adij/ *n* a maxim or proverb that embodies a commonly accepted observation [MF, fr L *adagium*, fr *ad-* + *-agium* (akin to *aio* I say); akin to Gk *ē* he spoke]

¹**adagio** /ə'dahjioh/ *adv or adj* in an easy slow graceful manner – used chiefly as a TEMPO (speed) direction in music [It, fr *ad* at, to + *agio* ease]

²**adagio** *n, pl* **adagios** **1** a musical composition or movement in adagio tempo **2** ballet dancing, esp a PAS DE DEUX, involving difficult feats of balance, lifting, or spinning

¹**Adam** /'adəm/ *n* **1** the first man and father by Eve of Cain and Abel according to the Bible **2** the sinful nature inherent in human beings – esp in *the old Adam* [Adam, the first man (Gen 2–5), fr ME, fr LL, fr Gk, fr Heb *Adhām*] – **Adamic, Adamical** *adj* – **not know somebody from Adam** to have no idea who somebody is

²**Adam** *adj* of a decorative style of furniture and architecture that originated in the 18th century and is characterized by straight lines, surface decoration, and conventional designs (e g garlands and medallions) [Robert *Adam* †1792 & James *Adam* †1794 Sc architects & designers]

¹**adamant** /'adəmənt/ *n* a stone formerly believed to be of impenetrable hardness and sometimes identified with the diamond; *broadly* any very hard unbreakable substance [ME, fr OF, fr L *adamant-, adamas* hardest metal, diamond, fr Gk (cf DIAMOND)]

²**adamant** *adj* unshakable in determination; unyielding – **adamancy** *n*, **adamantly** *adv*

**adamantine** /,adə'mantien/ *adj* **1** made of or like adamant **2** rigidly firm; unyielding **3** resembling the diamond in hardness or lustre [ME, fr L *adamantinus*, fr Gk *adamantinos*, fr *adamant-, adamas*]

**Adamic** /ə'damik/ *adj* of or resembling the epoch of Adam; primeval

**Adamite** /'adəmiet/ *n* **1** a human being **2** a member of a nudist sect [(2) fr Adam's nakedness before his fall from grace (Gen 2 & 3)]

**Adam's ale** *n* water as a drink [fr the assumption that it was the only drink available to the biblical Adam]

**Adam's apple** *n* the projection in the front of the neck formed by the largest cartilage of the LARYNX (organ of vocalization) [prob fr the legend that it was caused by a piece of the forbidden fruit sticking in Adam's throat]

**adapt** /ə'dapt/ *vb* to make or become fit or suitable, (e g for a specific or new use or situation) often by modification *synonyms* see ¹PLASTIC △ adopt [Fr or L; Fr *adapter*, fr L *adaptare*, fr *ad- + aptare* to fit, fr *aptus* apt, fit] – **adaptable** *adj*, **adaptedness** *n*, **adaptability** *n*

**adaptation** /,adap'taysh(ə)n/ *n* **1** adapting or being adapted **2a** adjustment of a SENSE ORGAN to the intensity or quality of stimulation **b** modification of an organism or its parts fitting it better for existence and successful breeding under the conditions of its environment **3** something that is adapted; *specif* a composition rewritten into a new form or for a different medium – **adaptational** *adj*, **adaptationally** *adv*

**adapter** *also* **adaptor** /ə'daptə/ *n* **1** one (e g a writer) who adapts something **2** a device **2a** for connecting two pieces of apparatus not originally intended to be joined **b** for converting a tool or piece of apparatus to some new use **c** for connecting several pieces of electrical apparatus to a single power point, or connecting a plug of one type to a socket of a different type

**adaption** /ə'dapsh(ə)n/ *n* (an) adaptation

**adaptive** /ə'daptiv/ *adj, of an organism* showing or having a capacity for or tendency towards adaptation – **adaptively** *adv*, **adaptiveness** *n*, **adaptivity** *n*

**adaptive radiation** *n* RADIATION 4 (evolution from a common ancestor of organisms adapted to different environments)

**Adar** ah'dah, 'ah-/ *n* – see MONTH table [ME, fr Heb *Adhār*]

**adaxial** /,ad'aksi•əl/ *adj* situated on the same side as or facing the AXIS of an organ, plant or part, or organism ⟨*upper side of a leaf stalk is known as the* ~ *surface* – R E Torrey⟩ – compare ABAXIAL

**add** /ad/ *vt* **1** to join or unite so as to bring about an increase or improvement ⟨~s *60 acres to his land*⟩ ⟨*wine* ~s *a creative touch to cooking*⟩ **2** to say or write further **3** to combine (numbers) into an equivalent single number; find the sum of – often + *up* ~ *vi* **1a** to perform addition **b** to come together or unite by addition **2** to make or serve as an addition *to* [ME *adden*, fr L *addere*, fr *ad- + -dere* to put – more at DO ] – **addable, addible** *adj*

**add in** *vt* to include as a member or item ⟨add in *the cost of the beer*⟩

**add up** *vi* **1** to amount *to* in total or substance ⟨*the play* adds up *to a lot of laughs*⟩ **2** to come to the expected total ⟨*the bill doesn't add up*⟩ **3** to be internally consistent; make sense

**addend** /'adend, ə'dend/ *n* a number to be added to another [short for *addendum*]

**addendum** /ə'dendəm/ *n, pl* **addenda** /-də/ **1** a thing added; an addition **2** *often pl but taking sing vb* a supplement to a book [L, neut of *addendus*, gerundive of *addere*]

# add

¹**adder** /'adə/ *n* the common venomous viper (*Vipera berus*) of Europe; *broadly* a ground-living viper (family Viperidae) [ME, alter. (by incorrect division of *a naddre*) of *naddre*, fr OE *nǣdre;* akin to OHG *nātara* adder, L *natrix* water snake]

²**adder** *n* one who or that which adds; *esp* a device (eg in a computer) that performs addition

**'adder's-,tongue** *n* a fern (genus *Ophioglossum*) whose fruiting spike resembles a snake's tongue

¹**addict** /ə'dikt/ *vt* 1 to devote or surrender (oneself) to something (eg a taste, practice, or pursuit) habitually or obsessively ⟨~ed *to gambling*⟩ 2 to cause (a person or animal) to become physiologically dependent upon a drug [L *addictus,* pp of *addicere* to favour, fr *ad-* + *dicere* to say – more at DICTION] – **addictive** *adj,* **addictiveness** *n,* **addiction** *n*
usage One is **addicted** *to* something, or *to* doing it, but not *to* do it ⟨⚠ *he's* **addicted** *to lie*⟩

²**addict** /'adikt/ *n* 1 one who is addicted to a drug 2 DEVOTEE 2 ⟨*a detective-novel* ~⟩ – compare DEVOTEE, BUFF, FAN, ENTHUSIAST

**adding machine** /'ading/ *n* a keyboard machine which is usu operated manually and performs various simple mathematical calculations

**Addison's disease** /'adis(ə)nz/ *n* a disease marked by deficient secretion of the hormones (eg ALDOSTERONE and HYDROCORTISONE) of the CORTEX (outer region) of the ADRENAL GLAND and characterized by extreme weakness, loss of weight, low blood pressure, disturbances of the stomach and intestines, and brownish pigmentation of the skin [Thomas *Addison* †1860 E physician]

**addition** /ə'dish(ə)n/ *n* 1 somebody or something added, esp as an improvement 2 an act, process, or instance of adding; *esp* the operation of combining numbers so as to obtain a single equivalent number 3 direct chemical combination of substances into a single product 4 *NAm* a room added to a house or other building [ME, fr MF, fr L *addition-, additio,* fr *additus,* pp of *addere*] – **in addition** besides, also ⟨*bought a new carpet and a rug* in addition⟩ – **in addition to** as well as ⟨*a telephone in the kitchen* in addition to *the one in the hall*⟩

**additional** /ə'dish(ə)nl/ *adj* existing by way of addition; supplementary – **additionally** *adv*

¹**additive** /'adətiv/ *adj* 1 of or characterized by addition 2 produced by addition – **additively** *adv,* **additivity** *n*

²**additive** *n* a substance added to another in relatively small amounts to give desirable properties or suppress undesirable ones ⟨*food* ~s⟩

¹**addle** /'adl/ *adj* 1 of an egg rotten 2 confused, muddled – usu in combination ⟨*an* addle-*headed scheme*⟩ [ME *adel* filth, fr OE *adela;* akin to MLG *adele* liquid manure]

²**addle** *vt* to throw into confusion – *vi* 1 of an egg to become rotten 2 to become confused or muddled

³**addle** *vt, N Eng* to earn by labour, gain [ME *addlen,* fr ON *öthlask* to acquire as property, fr *ōthal* property]

**addlepated** /'adl,paytid, ,--'--/ *adj* confused or muddled in mind

¹**address** /ə'dres/ *vt* 1a to direct the efforts or attention of (oneself) ⟨*will* ~ *himself to the problem*⟩ b to deal with; treat 2a to communicate directly ⟨~ed *his thanks to his host*⟩ b to speak or write directly to; *esp* to deliver a formal speech to ⟨~ed *the audience*⟩ 3 to mark directions for delivery on ⟨~ *a letter*⟩ 4 to greet by a prescribed form ⟨~ed *him as "My Lord"*⟩ 5 to take one's stance and adjust the club before hitting (a golf ball) 6 *archaic* to make ready ⟨~ed *himself to leave*⟩ 7 *archaic* to approach as a suitor; woo [ME *adressen,* fr MF *adresser,* fr *a-* (fr L *ad-*) + *dresser* to arrange – more at DRESS] – **addresser** *n*

²**address** /ə'dres/ *n* 1 *pl* dutiful and courteous attention, esp in courtship ⟨*paid his* ~es *to her*⟩ 2 readiness and capability for coping (eg with a person or problem) skilfully and smoothly; adroitness 3 a formal communication; *esp* a prepared speech delivered to an audience 4a a place of residence; *esp* one where a person or organization may be communicated with b directions for delivery on the outside of an object (eg a letter or package) – compare TELEGRAPHIC ADDRESS c the designation of place of origin or delivery at the head of a letter 5 a preparatory position of the player and club in golf 6 any of many locations in a computer memory where data can be stored; *also* the number identifying such a location 7 *archaic* manner of expressing or bearing oneself ⟨*a man of rude* ~⟩ 8 *obs* a making ready; *also* a state of preparedness

**addressable** /ə'dresəbl/ *adj* accessible by an address ⟨~ *registers in a computer*⟩

**addressee** /,adre'see/ *n* one to whom something is addressed for posting

**Addressograph** /ə'dresə,grahf, -,graf, -soh-/ *trademark* – used for a device that prints addresses on envelopes

**adduce** /ə'dyoohs/ *vt, formal* to offer as example, reason, or proof in discussion or analysis [L *adducere,* lit., to lead to, fr *ad-* + *ducere* to lead – more at TOW] – **adducer** *n,* **adduction** *n*

**adducent** /ə'dyoohs(ə)nt/ *adj* serving to adduct ⟨*an* ~ *muscle*⟩ [L *adducent-, adducens,* prp of *adducere*]

**adduct** /ə'dukt/ *vt* to draw (eg a limb) towards or past the central axis of the body; *also* to bring together (similar parts) ⟨~ *the fingers*⟩ [L *adductus,* pp of *adducere*] – **adductive** *adj,* **adduction** *n*

**adductor** /ə'duktə/ *n* 1 a muscle that draws a part towards the central line of the body or towards the axis of a limb or other extremity 2 a muscle that closes the shell of a mussel, clam, oyster, or related animal [NL, fr L, something that draws towards, fr *adductus*]

**-ade** /-ayd/ *suffix* (→ *n*) 1a act or action of ⟨*block*ade⟩ ⟨*escap*ade⟩ b individual or group of people involved in (a specified action) ⟨*cavalc*ade⟩ ⟨*reneg*ade⟩ 2 product; *esp* sweet drink made from (a specified fruit) ⟨*lim*eade⟩ [ME, fr MF, fr OProv *-ada,* fr LL *-ata,* fr L, fem of *-atus* -ate]

**Adélie penguin** /ə'dayli/ *n* a small antarctic penguin (*Pygoscelis adeliae*) [*Adélie* Coast, Antarctica]

**-adelphous** /-ə'delfəs/ *comb form* (→ *adj*) having (such or so many) bundles of stamens ⟨*mona*delphous⟩ [deriv of Gk *adelphos* brother, fr *ha-, a-* (akin to *homos* same) + *delphys* womb – more at SAME, DOLPHIN]

**ademption** /ə'dempsh(ə)n/ *n, law* the withdrawal of all or part of a legacy by the writer of a will while he/she is still alive (other than by revoking the will), esp by selling the property [L *ademption-, ademptio* taking away, fr *ademptus,* pp of *adimere* to take away, fr *ad-* + *emere* to take, buy]

**aden-** /adən-/, **adeno-** *comb form* gland ⟨*aden*itis⟩ [NL, fr Gk, fr *aden-, adēn;* akin to L *inguen* groin, Gk *nephros* kidney]

**adenine** /'adəneen, -nin/ *n* a chemical compound, $C_5H_3N_4.NH_2$, that is a PURINE and is one of the four BASES whose order in the molecular chain of DNA or RNA codes genetic information – compare CYTOSINE, GUANINE, THYMINE, URACIL [ISV; fr its presence in glandular tissue]

**adenitis** /,adə'nietəs/ *n* inflammation of a gland; *specif* LYMPHADENITIS (inflammation of a LYMPH NODE) [NL]

**adenocarcinoma** /,adənoh,kahsi'nohmə/ *n* a cancerous tumour originating in the tissue lining a gland [NL] – **adenocarcinomatous** *adj*

**adenohypophysis** /,adənoh-hie'pofəsis/ *n, pl* **adenohypophyses** /-seez/ the front lobe of the PITUITARY GLAND that secretes several protein hormones including GROWTH HORMONE and THYROID-STIMULATING HORMONE – compare NEUROHYPOPHYSIS [NL] – **adenohypophyseal, adenohypophysial** *adj*

**adenoidal** /,adə'noydl/ *adj* 1 of the adenoids 2 typical or suggestive of somebody affected with abnormally enlarged adenoids ⟨*an* ~ *tenor*⟩ ⟨~ *breathing*⟩ – **adenoidally** *adv*

**adenoidectomy** /,adənoy'dektəmi/ *n* surgical removal of the adenoids

**adenoids** /'adənoydz/ *n pl,* **adenoid** *n* an enlarged mass of glandular tissue at the back of the PHARYNX (muscular tube joining the mouth to the upper portion of the digestive tract) that characteristically obstructs breathing [Gk *adenoeidēs* glandular, fr *adēn*] – **adenoid** *adj*

**adenoma** /,adə'nohmə/ *n, pl* **adenomas, adenomata** /-mətə/ a mild nonlethal tumour of a glandular structure or of glandular origin [NL *adenomat-, adenoma*] – **adenomatous** *adj*

**adenosine** /ə'denəseen, -sin/ *n* a chemical compound (NUCLEOSIDE), $C_{10}H_{13}N_5O_4$, that forms part of RNA and contains adenine attached to the sugar RIBOSE [ISV, blend of *adenine* and *ribose*]

**adenosine diphosphate** *n* ADP

**adenosine monophosphate** /,monoh'fosfayt/ *n* 1 AMP 2 CYCLIC AMP

**adenosine triphosphate** *n* ATP

**adenovirus** /,adənoh'vie-ərəs/ *n* any of a group of DNA-containing viruses originally identified in human adenoid tissue, causing respiratory diseases (eg colds), and including some capable of inducing cancerous tumours in experimental animals [*adenoid* + *-o-* + *virus*] – **adenoviral** *adj*

**adenyl** /'adənil/ *n* a chemical group, $C_5H_4N_5$, that is derived from ADENINE and has a VALENCY of one

**adenylate cyclase** /ə,denilayt 'sieklayz/ *n* ADENYL CYCLASE

**adenyl cyclase** /,adənil 'sieklayz/ *n* an ENZYME that promotes the formation of CYCLIC AMP from ATP

**adenylic acid** /,adə'nilik/ *n* AMP

¹**adept** /'adept, ə'dept/ *n* a highly skilled or well-trained performer; an expert ⟨*an ~ at chess*⟩ [NL *adeptus,* alchemist who has discovered how to change base metals into gold, fr L, pp of *adipisci* to attain, fr *ad-* + *apisci* to reach – more at APT]

²**adept** *adj* thoroughly proficient; expert *at synonyms* see PROFICIENT – **adeptly** *adv*, **adeptness** *n*

**adequacy** /'adikwəsi/ *n* the quality or state of being adequate

**adequate** /'adikwət/ *adj* sufficient for a specific requirement ⟨*a solution ~ to the problem*⟩; *esp* barely sufficient or satisfactory ⟨*her first performance was merely ~*⟩ *synonyms* see SUFFICIENT *antonym* inadequate [L *adaequatus,* pp of *adaequare* to make equal, fr *ad-* + *aequare* to equal, fr *aequus* level, equal] – **adequately** *adv*, **adequateness** *n*

**ad eundem** /,ad ay'oondəm/, **ad eundem gradum** /'grahdəm/ *adv or adj* to, in, or of the same rank – used esp of the granting without examination of a university degree to the holder of the same degree at another university [NL *ad eundem gradum*]

**à deux** /ah 'duh *(Fr* a dœ)/ *adj or adv* with only two people present ⟨*a cosy evening ~*⟩ [Fr]

**adhere** /əd'(h)iə/ *vi* **1** to give continued support; maintain loyalty *to* ⟨*~ to our original plan*⟩ **2** to hold fast or stick (as if) by gluing, suction, grasping, or fusing **3** to bind oneself to joining or observing something ⟨*~d to the treaty*⟩ **4** *obs* to be consistent; accord ~ *vt* to cause to stick fast [MF or L; MF *adhérer,* fr L *adhaerēre,* fr *ad-* + *haerēre* to stick – more at HESITATE] – **adherence** *n*

¹**adherent** /ə'diərənt, əd'hiə-/ *adj* **1** tending to adhere **2** contractually bound or associated **3** ADNATE (growing close to another flower part) [ME, fr MF or L; MF *adhérent,* fr L *adhaerent-, adhaerens,* prp of *adhaerēre*] – **adherently** *adv*

²**adherent** *n* one who adheres (e g to a cause)

**adhesion** /ə'deezh(ə)n, əd'hee-, ad-/ *n* **1** steady attachment; adherence **2** the action or state of adhering; *specif* a union of bodily parts by growth **3** *pl* an abnormal union of usu separated tissues by the formation of fibrous tissue; *also* the tissues so united **4** agreement to join **5** the molecular attraction exerted between the surfaces of bodies in contact [Fr or L; Fr *adhésion,* fr L *adhaesion-, adhaesio,* fr *adhaesus,* pp of *adhaerēre*] – **adhesional** *adj*

¹**adhesive** /əd'(h)eeziv, -siv/ *adj* **1** tending to adhere or cause adherence **2** prepared for adhering; sticky – **adhesively** *adv*, **adhesiveness** *n*

²**adhesive** *n* an adhesive substance (e g glue or cement)

**adhibit** /əd'hibit/ *vt* **1** to attack **2** to administer (e g a medicine) [L *adhibitus,* pp of *adhibēre* to bring to, apply, fr *ad-* + *habēre* to hold – more at GIVE]

**ad hoc** /,ad 'hok/ *adj or adv* for the particular end or purpose in hand and without consideration of wider applications ⟨*set up the committee ~*⟩ ⟨*an ~ investigating committee*⟩ [L, for this]

**ad hoccery, ad hocery** /ad 'hokəri/ *n, informal* practical and immediate action based on a decision made ad hoc; pragmatism [*ad hoc* + *-ery*]

**ad hominem** /,ad 'hominem/ *adj* **1** appealing to a person's feelings or prejudices rather than his/her intellect **2** marked by an attack on an opponent's character rather than on an answer to his/her arguments ⟨*an ~ remark*⟩ [NL, lit., to the man] – **ad hominem** *adv*

**adiabatic** /,adi-ə'batik/ *adj* occurring without loss or gain of heat ⟨*~ expansion of a body of air*⟩ [Gk *adiabatos* impassable, fr *a-* + *diabatos* passable, fr *diabainein* to go across, fr *dia-* + *bainein* to go – more at COME] – **adiabatically** *adv*

**adieu** /ə'dyooh, ə'dyuh *(Fr* adjœ)/ *n, pl* **adieus, adieux** /ə'dyooh(z), ə'dyuh(z) *(Fr ~*)/ *chiefly poetic* a farewell – often used interjectionally [ME, fr MF, fr *a* (fr L *ad*) + *Dieu* God, fr L *Deus* – more at AT, DEITY]

**ad infinitum** /,ad infi'nietəm/ *adv or adj* without end or limit [L, to an infinite extent]

**ad interim** /ad 'intərim/ *adj or adv* for the meantime; pending permanent arrangements [L]

**adios** /adi'ohs, -'os/ *interj* – used to express farewell [Sp *adiós,* fr *a* (fr L *ad*) + *Dios* God, fr L *Deus*]

**adipic acid** /ə'dipik/ *n* an organic chemical acid, $HOOC(CH_2)_4COOH$, used esp in manufacturing resins and plastics (e g nylon) [deriv of L *adip-, adeps*]

**adipose** /'adipohs, -pohz/ *adj* of or resembling animal fat; fatty [NL *adiposus,* fr L *adip-, adeps* fat, fr Gk *aleipha;* akin to Gk *lipos* fat – more at LEAVE] – **adiposity** *n*

**adipose tissue** *n* an animal tissue in which fat is stored, consisting of CONNECTIVE TISSUE cells each containing a large globule of fat

**adit** /'adit/ *n* a nearly horizontal passage from the surface into a mine [L *aditus* approach, fr *aditus,* pp of *adire* to go to, fr *ad-* + *ire* to go – more at ISSUE]

¹**adjacent** /ə'jays(ə)nt/ *adj* **1a** not distant; nearby ⟨*the city and ~ suburbs*⟩ **b** having a common boundary or border ⟨*gardens ~ to ours*⟩ **2** *of two angles* having the point from which the lines diverge and one side in common *synonyms* see ²NEXT [ME, fr MF or L; MF, fr L *adjacent-, adjacens,* prp of *adjacēre* to lie near, fr *ad-* + *jacēre* to lie; akin to L *jacere* to throw – more at ²JET] – **adjacency** *n*, **adjacently** *adv*

²**adjacent** *n* the side of a right-angled triangle that with the hypotenuse makes a specified angle

**adjectival** /,ajik'tievl/ *adj* **1** adjective **2** of or characterized by the use of adjectives – **adjectivally** *adv*

¹**adjective** /'ajiktiv/ *adj* **1** of or functioning as an adjective ⟨*an ~ clause*⟩ **2** requiring or employing a MORDANT (substance which fixes colours) ⟨*~ dyes*⟩ **3** concerned with court procedure rather than legal principles ⟨*~ law*⟩ [ME, fr MF or LL; MF *adjectif,* fr LL *adjectivus,* fr L *adjectus,* pp of *adjicere* to throw to, fr *ad-* + *jacere* to throw – more at ²JET] – **adjectively** *adv*

²**adjective** *n* a word typically serving as a modifier of a noun to denote a quality of what is named, to indicate its quantity or extent, or to specify it as distinct from something else

**adjoin** /ə'joyn/ *vt* **1** to be next to or in contact with **2** *formal* to affix ~ *vi* to be next to or in contact with one another *synonyms* see ²NEXT [ME *adjoinen,* fr MF *adjoindre,* fr L *adjungere,* fr *ad-* + *jungere* to join – more at YOKE]

**adjoining** /ə'joyning/ *adj* touching or having a common boundary at a point or line ⟨*the ~ room*⟩

**adjoint** /'ajoynt/ *n* the TRANSPOSE (mathematical matrix formed by interchanging the rows and columns) of a matrix in which each element has been replaced by its COFACTOR [Fr, fr pp of *adjoindre* to adjoin]

**adjourn** /ə'juhn/ *vt* **1** to suspend (e g a session of a court) indefinitely or until a later stated time **2** to defer discussion of (a question) until a future time ~ *vi* **1** of a group, esp a court, in session to postpone or suspend proceedings and disband ⟨*the finance committee ~ed until the following day*⟩ **2** *informal* to move to another place ⟨*we ~ed to the library*⟩ [ME *ajournen,* fr MF *ajourner,* fr *a-* (fr L *ad-*) + *jour* day – more at JOURNEY] – **adjournment** *n*

**adjudge** /ə'juj/ *vt* **1a** to decide or rule upon as a judge; adjudicate **b** to pronounce formally and esp judicially; rule ⟨*~ him guilty of manslaughter*⟩ **2** to hold or pronounce to be; deem ⟨*~ the book a success*⟩ **3** to award or grant (e g costs) judicially **4** *archaic* to sentence, condemn *synonyms* see ¹JUDGE [ME *ajugen,* fr MF *ajugier,* fr L *adjudicare,* fr *ad-* + *judicare* to judge – more at JUDGE]

**adjudicate** /ə'joohdikayt/ *vt* to make a judicial decision on ~ *vi* to act as judge or arbitrator [L *adjudicatus,* pp of *adjudicare*] – **adjudicator** *n*, **adjudicative** *adj*

**adjudication** /ə,joohdi'kaysh(ə)n/ *n* **1** the act or process of adjudicating **2a** a judicial decision or sentence **b** a formal judgment or decision; *esp* a decree declaring someone bankrupt – **adjudicatory** *adj*

¹**adjunct** /'ajungkt/ *n* **1** something joined to another thing as an incidental accompaniment rather than as an essential part of it **2** a person, usu in a subordinate or temporary capacity, assisting another to perform some duty or service **3** a word (e g an adverb) or word group (e g a prepositional phrase) that qualifies or completes the meaning of another word or other words and is not itself one of the principal structural elements in its sentence **4** an adverbial linguistic form (e g *now* in "he can *now* swim") that is integrated within a clause – compare CONJUNCT, DISJUNCT [L *adjunctum,* fr neut of *adjunctus,* pp of *adjungere*] – **adjunctive** *adj*, **adjunctively** *adv*

²**adjunct** *adj* attached in a subordinate or temporary capacity to a staff; auxiliary ⟨*an ~ psychiatrist*⟩

**adjure** /ə'jooə/ *vt, formal* **1** to charge or command solemnly (as if) under oath or penalty of a curse **2** to entreat or advise earnestly △ abjure [ME *adjuren,* fr MF & L; MF *ajurer,* fr L *adjurare,* fr *ad-* + *jurare* to swear – more at JURY] – **adjuratory** *adj*, **adjuration** *n*

**adjust** /ə'just/ *vt* **1a** to bring to a more satisfactory or correct state by minor change or adaption ⟨~ing *over immigration policy*⟩ **b** to settle, resolve ⟨~ *a conflict*⟩ **c** to regulate the position or the relationship between the parts of ⟨~ *a carburettor*⟩ ⟨~ *a radio dial*⟩ ⟨~ed *his hat*⟩ **2** to determine the amount to be paid under an insurance policy in settlement of (a loss) ~ *vi* **1** to adapt or conform oneself (eg to climate, food, or new working hours) **2** to achieve mental and behavioural balance between one's own needs and the demands of others [Fr *ajuster*, fr *a-* + *juste* exact, just] – **adjustable** *adj*, **adjustive** *adj*, **adjustability** *n*

**adjusted** /ə'justid/ *adj* having achieved a harmonious relationship with the environment or with other individuals – often in combination ⟨*a well-adjusted child*⟩

**adjuster** *also* **adjustor** /ə'justə/ *n* one who or that which adjusts; *esp* an insurance agent who investigates personal or property damage and makes estimates for reaching settlements

**adjustment** /-mənt/ *n* **1** adjusting or being adjusted **2** a settlement of a disputed claim or debt; *esp* one fixing the proportion each underwriter must pay on a policy of marine insurance **3** a means (eg a mechanism) by which things are adjusted – **adjustmental** *adj*

**adjutant** /'ajoot(ə)nt/ *n* **1** a staff officer who assists the commanding officer and is responsible esp for correspondence **2** one who helps; an assistant [L *adjutant-, adjutans*, prp of *adjutare* to help – more at AID] – **adjutancy** *n*

**adjutant general** *n, pl* **adjutants general 1** the chief administrative officer of an army who is responsible esp for the administration and preservation of personnel records **2** the chief administrative officer of a major military unit (eg a division or corps)

¹**adjuvant** /'ajoovənt/ *adj, formal* serving to aid or contribute; auxiliary [Fr or L; Fr, fr L *adjuvant-, adjuvans*, prp of *adjuvare* to aid – more at AID]

²**adjuvant** *n, formal* one who or that which helps or facilitates; *esp* something that enhances the effectiveness of medical treatment

**Adlerian** /ad'liəriən/ *adj* of or being a theory and technique of psychotherapy emphasizing the importance of feelings of inferiority and ascribing neurotic disorders to overcompensation for such feelings [Alfred *Adler* †1937 Austrian psychiatrist] – **Adlerian** *n*

¹**ad-lib** /,ad 'lib/ *adj* spoken, composed, or performed without preparation; impromptu [*ad lib*]

²**ad-lib** *vb* **-bb-** *vt* to deliver spontaneously ~ *vi* to improvise lines or a speech – **ad lib** *n*

**ad lib** *adv* **1** in accordance with one's wishes; as desired **2** without restraint or limit [NL *ad libitum* in accordance with desire]

¹**ad libitum** /,ad 'libitəm/ *adv* AD LIB

²**ad libitum** *adj* to be played or sung if desired – used as a direction in music; compare OBBLIGATO

**adman** /'ad,man/ *n, informal* a member of the advertising profession

**admass** /'ad,mas/ *n, chiefly Br* the section of society readily influenced by mass-media advertising – compare CONSUMER SOCIETY [*advertising* + *mass*]

**admeasure** /ad'mezhə, əd-/ *vt, formal* to assign in shares; portion out [ME *amesuren*, fr MF *amesurer*, fr *a-* (fr L *ad-*) + *mesurer* to measure] – **admeasurement** *n*

**admin** /'admin/ *n, chiefly Br informal* administration; *esp* administrative work

**administer** /əd'ministə/ *vt* **1** to manage or supervise the execution, use, or conduct of ⟨~ *a trust fund*⟩ **2a** to mete out; dispense ⟨~ *punishment*⟩ **b** to give or perform ritually ⟨~ *the last rites*⟩ **c** to give remedially ⟨~ *a dose of medicine*⟩ ~ *vi* **1** to perform the office of administrator; manage affairs **2** to furnish a benefit; minister ⟨~ *to his ailing friend*⟩ [ME *administren*, fr MF *administrer*, fr L *administrare*, fr *ad-* + *ministrare* to serve, fr *minister* servant – more at MINISTER] – **administrable** *adj*, **administrant** *n*

**usage** Some writers on usage advise that **minister** rather than **administer** should be used for the sense "furnish a benefit *to*".

**administrate** /əd'ministrayt/ *vt* to administer [L *administratus*, pp of *administrare*]

**administration** /əd,mini'straysh(ə)n/ *n* **1** the act or process of administering **2** performance of executive duties, esp in a business organization; management **3** the execution of public affairs as distinguished from the making of policy **4** the term of office of an official or body ⟨*during the Carter* ~⟩ **5** *law* the management of the estate of a deceased person **6** *taking sing or pl vb* **6a** a body of people who administer **b** *cap, chiefly NAm* a group constituting the political executive in a government **c** *NAm* a governmental agency or board – **administrational** *adj*, **administrationist** *n*

**administrative** /əd'ministrativ/ *adj* **1** relating to (an) administration; executive **2** relating to the formulation of policy rather than to its detailed application – compare EXECUTIVE – **administratively** *adv*

**administrative law** *n* law dealing with the establishment, duties, and powers of and available remedies against governmental administrative agencies

**administrator** /əd'mini,straytə/ *n* **1** *law* a person legally authorized to administer an estate, esp of a deceased person **2** one who administers esp business, school, or governmental affairs

**administratrix** /əd'ministrətriks/ *n, pl* **administratrices** /əd,mini'straytrəseez/ a female administrator, esp of an estate [NL]

**admirable** /'admərəbl/ *adj* **1** deserving the highest esteem; excellent **2** *obs* exciting wonder; surprising – **admirableness** *n*, **admirably** *adv*, **admirability** *n*

**admiral** /'admərəl/ *n* **1a** – see MILITARY RANKS table **b** a senior naval officer of the rank of REAR ADMIRAL or above **2** *archaic* the commander in chief of a navy – compare LORD HIGH ADMIRAL **3** any of several brightly coloured butterflies (family Nymphalidae) ⟨*a Red* ~⟩ **4** *archaic* a flagship [ME, fr MF *amiral* admiral & ML *admiralis* emir, *admirallus* admiral, fr Ar *amīr-al-* commander of the (as in *amīr-al-baḥr* commander of the sea)]

**admiral of the fleet** *n* – see MILITARY RANKS table

**admiralty** /'admərəlti/ *n* **1** *taking sing or pl vb, cap* the executive department or officers formerly having general authority over British naval affairs; *also* ADMIRALTY BOARD **2** the courts of law having jurisdiction over maritime affairs; *also* the system of law administered by the admiralty courts

**Admiralty Board** *n taking sing or pl vb* the department of the Ministry of Defence that administers the British navy

**Admiralty mile** *n* NAUTICAL MILE (a unit of distance used for sea and air navigation)

**admiration** /,admə'raysh(ə)n/ *n* **1** one who or that which is admired ⟨*was the* ~ *of the whole school*⟩ **2a** a feeling of delighted or astonished approval **b** the act or process of regarding with delighted or astonished approval **3** *archaic* wonder

**admire** /əd'mie•ə/ *vt* **1a** to regard with admiration **b** to think highly of, often in a somewhat impersonal manner ⟨~ *a man's capacity for work*⟩ **2** *chiefly Br* to express admiration for ⟨*loudly* ~d *the new curtains*⟩ **3** *archaic* to marvel at **synonyms** see ²REGARD [MF *admirer*, fr L *admirari*, fr *ad-* + *mirari* to wonder – more at SMILE] – **admiringly** *adv*

**admirer** /əd'mie•ərə/ *n* one who admires; *esp* a woman's lover or suitor

**admissible** /əd'misəbl/ *adj* **1a** capable of being allowed or conceded; permissible ⟨*behaviour that was hardly* ~⟩ **b** acceptable as legal evidence **2** entitled or worthy to be allowed to enter ⟨*foreign products* ~ *to a domestic market*⟩ [Fr, fr ML *admissibilis*, fr L *admissus*, pp of *admittere*] – **admissibility** *n*

**admission** /əd'mish(ə)n/ *n* **1a** the granting of an argument or position not fully proved **b** acknowledgment that a fact or allegation is true ⟨~ *of guilt*⟩ **2a** the act of accepting into something (eg an office or organization) **b** permission or right to enter or to be received as a member **c** a fee paid on or for entrance – **admissive** *adj*

**admit** /əd'mit/ *vb* **-tt-** *vt* **1a** to allow scope for; permit **b** to concede as true or valid ⟨*compelled to* ~ *his failure*⟩ **2** to allow entry (eg to a place, fellowship, or privilege) ⟨*each ticket* ~s *two persons*⟩ ⟨~ted *to the university*⟩ ~ *vi* **1** to give entrance or access **2a** to allow, permit ⟨*this passage* ~s *of two interpretations*⟩ **b** to make acknowledgment – + *to* ⟨~ted *to the crime*⟩ [ME *admitten*, fr L *admittere*, fr *ad-* + *mittere* to send]

**usage** When **admit** means "acknowledge" or "confess", some writers prefer to use it as a transitive verb, without *to* ⟨*he admitted having* (not *to having*) *opened the letter*⟩. **synonyms** see ACKNOWLEDGE **antonym** deny

**admittance** /əd'mit(ə)ns/ *n* **1a** permission to enter a place **b** access, entrance **2** the ease with which an ALTERNATING CURRENT can pass through an electrical circuit; the reciprocal of the IMPEDANCE

**admittedly** /əd'mitidli/ *adv* as must reluctantly be admitted

**admix** /əd'miks/ *vt* to mingle, blend [back-formation fr obs *admixt* mingled (with), fr ME, fr L *admixtus*]

**admixture** /əd'mikschə, 'admikschə/ *n* **1a** the act of mixing **b** the fact of being mixed **2a** a component added by mixing **b** a substance produced by mixing; mixture [L *admixtus*, pp of *admiscēre* to mix with, fr *ad-* + *miscēre* to mix – more at MIX]

**admonish** /əd'monish/ *vt* **1** to advise or urge to 〈~ed *me to work harder*〉 **2** to warn about remissness or error, esp gently; reprove **synonyms** see WARN [ME *admonesten*, fr MF *admonester*, fr (assumed) VL *admonestare*, alter. of L *admonēre* to warn, fr *ad-* + *monēre* to warn – more at MIND] – **admonisher** *n*, **admonishingly** *adv*, **admonishment** *n*

**admonition** /ˌadmə'nish(ə)n/ *n* (a) gentle friendly reproof, counsel, or warning [ME *amonicioun*, fr MF *amonition*, fr L *admonition-*, *admonitio*, fr *admonitus*, pp of *admonēre*] – **admonitory** *adj*, **admonitorily** *adv*

**adnate** /'adnayt/ *adj*, *of a plant or animal part* attached to or growing into a usu unlike part, esp along a margin 〈*a calyx* ~ *to the ovary*〉 [L *adgnatus*, pp of *adgnasci* to grow on, fr *ad-* + *nasci* to be born (cf AGNATE)] – **adnation** *n*

**ad nauseam** /ˌad 'nawzi·əm, -si·əm/ *adv* to a disgusting degree; sickeningly often [L, to sickness]

**adnexa** /ad'neksə/ *n pl* linked, associated, or closely related anatomical parts; appendages; *specif* the embryonic membranes and other temporary structures of the embryo [NL, fr L *annexa*, neut pl of *annexus*, pp of *annectere* to bind to – more at ANNEX] – **adnexal** *adj*

**adnominal** /əd'nominl/ *adj*, *of a noun* functioning as an adjective; adjectival

**adnoun** /'adnown/ *n* an adjective functioning as a noun; an absolute adjective [*ad-* + *noun*]

**ado** /ə'dooh/ *n* time-wasting activity; fuss 〈*much* ~ *about nothing*〉 〈*wrote the paper without further* ~〉 **synonyms** see ¹FUSS [ME, fr *at do*, fr *at* + *don, do* to do]

**adobe** /ə'dohbi/ *n* **1** a brick or building material made from sun-dried earth and straw **2** a heavy clay used in making adobe bricks **3** a structure made of adobe bricks [Sp, fr Ar *aṭ-ṭūb* the brick, fr Copt *tōbe* brick]

**adolescence** /ˌadə'les(ə)ns/ *n* the period of human life from puberty to maturity ending legally at the age of majority

¹**adolescent** /ˌadə'les(ə)nt/ *n* a person who is in the period of life from puberty to maturity [Fr, fr L *adolescent-*, *adolescens*, prp of *adolescere* to grow up – more at ADULT]

²**adolescent** *adj* **1** of or in adolescence **2** immature, puerile 〈*his* ~ *behaviour at the party*〉 **synonyms** see ¹YOUNG – **adolescently** *adv*

**Adonai** /ˌadə'nie, ˌadə'nay·ie/ *n* – used as the sacred title of the God of the Jews, only pronounced in solemn prayer and with the head covered [Heb *ǎdhōnāy*]

**Adonis** /ə'dohnis/ *n* **1** a handsome youth loved by Aphrodite who was killed by a wild boar and restored to Aphrodite from Hades **2** an exceptionally handsome young man [*Adonis* (Gk *Adōnis*), a beautiful youth in Greco-Roman mythology] – **adonic** *adj*

**adopt** /ə'dopt/ *vt* **1** to take by choice into a new relationship; *specif* to take voluntarily (a child of other parents) as one's own child **2** to take up and practise or use as one's own; assume 〈~ *another's mannerisms*〉 **3** to vote or choose to accept 〈~ *a constitutional amendment*〉 **4** to assume responsibility for the maintenance of (a road) 〈*the town council won't* ~ *Meadow Lane*〉 **5** *of a constituency* to nominate as a Parliamentary candidate **usage** see ADOPTIVE △ adapt [MF or L; MF *adopter*, fr L *adoptare*, fr *ad-* + *optare* to choose – more at OPTION] – **adoptable** *adj*, **adopter** *n*, **adoption** *n*, **adoptability** *n*, **adoptee** *n*

**adoptionism, adoptianism** /ə'dopshəniz(ə)m/ *n*, *often cap* the doctrine that Jesus was appointed to be the Son of God after his birth – **adoptionist** *n*, *often cap*

**adoptive** /ə'doptiv/ *adj* **1** of adoption **2** made or acquired by adoption 〈*the* ~ *father*〉 **3** tending to adopt – **adoptively** *adv*
*usage* Parents are **adoptive**; children are **adopted**.

**adorable** /ə'dawrəbl/ *adj* **1** worthy of being adored **2** extremely charming 〈*an* ~ *child*〉 – **adorableness** *n*, **adorably** *adv*, **adorability** *n*

**adore** /ə'daw/ *vt* **1** to worship or honour as a deity or as divine **2** to regard with reverent admiration and devotion 〈*at 40 he still* ~d *his father*〉 **3** *informal* to be extremely fond of 〈*I really* ~ *banana sandwiches*〉 **synonyms** see ¹REVERE [MF *adorer*, fr L *adorare*, fr *ad-* + *orare* to speak, pray – more at ORATION] – **adorer** *n*, **adoration** *n*

**adorn** /ə'dawn/ *vt* **1** to decorate, esp with ornaments **2** to add to the pleasantness or attractiveness of 〈*the admiral's daughter* ~ed *the gathering*〉 **synonyms** see DECORATE **antonym** disfigure [ME *adornen*, fr MF *adorner*, fr L *adornare*, fr *ad-* + *ornare* to furnish – more at ORNATE] – **adornment** *n*

**ADP** *n* a chemical compound, $C_{10}H_{12}N_5O_3H_3P_2O_7$, that is a NUCLEOTIDE of ADENINE containing two PHOSPHATE groups and that is converted to ATP by the addition of another phosphate group in a reaction that stores some of the energy produced inside a cell (e g from the breakdown of glucose or fats) in the form of ATP [adenosine *di*phosphate]

**adpressed** /ad'prest/ *adj*, *botany* APPRESSED (pressed together without being united)

**ad rem** /ˌad 'rem/ *adv or adj* to the point or purpose [L, to the matter]

**adren-, adreno-** *comb form* **1** adrenal 〈adreno*cortical*〉 **2** adrenalin 〈adren*ergic*〉 [*adrenal*]

**adrenal** /ə'dreenl/ *adj* **1** adjacent to the kidneys **2** of or derived from ADRENAL GLANDS [*ad-* + *renal*] – **adrenally** *adv*

**adrenalectomy** /ə,dreenə'lektəmi/ *n* surgical removal of one or both ADRENAL GLANDS – **adrenalectomized** *adj*

**adrenal gland, adrenal** *n* either of a pair of complex ENDOCRINE GLANDS near the upper central border of the kidney consisting of a CORTEX (outer region) that secretes STEROID hormones and a MEDULLA (inner region) that secretes adrenalin

**adrenalin, adrenaline** /ə'drenəlin/ *n* a hormone, $(OH)_2C_6H_3CH(OH)CH_2 NHCH_3$, that is produced by the MEDULLA (inner region) of the ADRENAL GLAND, and is released into the blood when the SYMPATHETIC NERVOUS SYSTEM is stimulated, occurs as a NEUROTRANSMITTER (substance transmitting impulses between nerve endings) in the sympathetic nervous system, and gives the effects of some stimulation of the sympathetic nervous system (e g constriction of blood vessels, stimulation of the heart, and relaxation of SMOOTH MUSCLE) when administered medically

**adrenergic** /ˌadri'nuhjik/ *adj* **1** liberating or activated by (a substance like) adrenalin (e g NORADRENALIN) 〈*an* ~ *nerve*〉 **2** *of a drug* resembling adrenalin [*adren-* + Gk *ergon* work – more at WORK]

**adrenocortical** /ə,dreenoh'kawtikl/ *adj* of or derived from the outer region (CORTEX) of the adrenal glands

**adrenocorticosteroid** /ə,dreenoh,kawtikoh'stiəroyd/ *n* a STEROID drug or hormone (e g hydrocortisone) obtained from, resembling, or having effects on the body like those produced by the outer region (CORTEX) of the ADRENAL GLANDS

**adrenocorticotrophic** /ə,dreenoh,kawtikoh'trohfik/, **adrenocorticotropic** /-'trohpik, -'tropik/ *adj* acting on or stimulating the outer region (CORTEX) of the ADRENAL GLAND

**adrenocorticotrophic hormone** *n* a hormone produced by the front lobe of the PITUITARY GLAND that stimulates the outer region (CORTEX) of the ADRENAL GLAND – called also ACTH

**adrenocorticotrophin** /-'trohfin/ *n* ADRENOCORTICOTROPHIC HORMONE

**adriamycin** /ˌaydriə'miesin/ *trademark* – used for the anticancer drug DOXORUBICIN

**adrift** /ə'drift/ *adv or adj* **1** afloat without motive power or mooring and at the mercy of winds and currents **2** in or into a state of being unstuck or unfastened; loose – esp in *come adrift* **3** *informal* astray 〈*his reasoning's gone completely* ~〉

**adroit** /ə'droyt/ *adj* **1** dexterous; nimble **2** marked by shrewdness, readiness, and/or resourcefulness in coping with difficulty or danger **synonyms** see CLEVER **antonyms** clumsy, awkward [Fr, fr *à droit* properly, fr *à* to, at + *droit* right ] – **adroitly** *adv*, **adroitness** *n*

**adscititious** /ˌadsi'tishəs/ *adj*, *formal* derived or acquired from outside; additional [L *adscitus*, fr pp of *adsciscere* to receive, fr *ad-* + *sciscere* to accept, incho of *scire* to know – more at SCIENCE]

**adsorb** /əd'zawb/ *vt* to take up and hold by adsorption ~ *vi* to become adsorbed △ absorb [*ad-* + *-sorb* (as in *absorb*)] – **adsorbable** *adj*, **adsorbent** *adj or n*

**adsorbate** /əd'zawbət, -bayt/ *n* an adsorbed substance

**adsorption** /əd'zawpsh(ə)n/ *n* the adhesion of molecules (e g of gases or liquids) in an extremely thin layer to the surfaces of solid bodies or liquids with which they are in contact – compare ABSORPTION [fr *adsorb*, by analogy to *absorb* : *absorption*] – **adsorptive** *adj*

**adularia** /ˌadyoo'leəriə/ *n* a transparent or translucent

ORTHOCLASE (type of mineral) [It, fr Fr *adulaire*, fr *Adula*, Swiss mountain group]

**adulate** /'adyoolayt/ *vt* to flatter or admire excessively or slavishly [back-formation fr *adulation*, fr ME, fr MF, fr L *adulation-, adulatio*, fr *adulatus*, pp of *adulari* to flatter] – **adulator** *n*, **adulatory** *adj*, **adulation** *n*

¹**adult** /'adult, ə'dult/ *adj* 1 fully developed and mature; grown-up **2a** of or befitting adults ⟨*an ~ approach to a problem*⟩ **b** suitable only for adults; *broadly* salacious, pornographic ⟨*~ films*⟩ [L *adultus*, pp of *adolescere* to grow up, fr *ad- + olescere* (fr *alescere* to grow) – more at OLD] – **adulthood** *n*, **adultlike** *adj*, **adultness** *n*

usage The pronunciation /'adult/ is recommended for BBC *broadcasters*.

²**adult** *n* a person or creature that is adult; *esp* a person who has reached or passed an age specified by law (eg in Britain, 18)

**adult education** *n* mainly non-vocational courses for adults with classes often held in the evenings

¹**adulterate** /ə'dultərəyt/ *vt* to corrupt, debase, or make impure by the addition of a foreign or inferior substance [L *adulteratus*, pp of *adulterare*, fr *ad- + alter* other – more at ELSE] – **adulterant** *n or adj*, **adulterator** *n*, **adulteration** *n*

²**adulterate** /ə'dultərət/ *adj* 1 adulterous 2 adulterated, debased, or impure

**adulterer** /ə'dultərə/, *fem* **adulteress** /ə'dult(ə)ris/ *n* someone who commits adultery

**adulterine** /ə'dultərin, -rien/ *adj* 1 marked by adulteration; fake 2 born of adultery ⟨*an ~ son*⟩

**adulterous** /ə'dultərəs/ *adj* of, characterized by, or given to adultery – **adulterously** *adv*

**adultery** /ə'dultəri/ *n* voluntary sexual intercourse between a married person and someone other than his/her spouse [ME, alter. of *avoutrie*, fr MF, fr L *adulterium*, fr *adulter* adulterer, back-formation fr *adulterare*]

**adumbrate** /'adəmbrayt/ *vt, formal* 1 to foreshadow (a future event) vaguely 2 to outline broadly without details 3 to cast a shadow over; obscure [L *adumbratus*, pp of *adumbrare*, fr *ad- + umbra* shadow – more at UMBRAGE] – **adumbration** *n*, **adumbrative** *adj*, **adumbratively** *adv*

**adust** /ə'dust/ *adj, archaic* 1 scorched, burned 2 of a sunburned appearance 3 of a gloomy appearance or disposition [ME, fr L *adustus*, pp of *adurere* to set fire to, fr *ad- + urere* to burn (cf COMBUST)]

**ad valorem** /,ad va'lawrəm/ *adj or adv, of a tax* imposed at a rate proportional to the stated or estimated value ⟨*an ~ tax on goods*⟩ [L, according to the value]

¹**advance** /əd'vahns/ *vt* 1 to bring or move forwards in position or time ⟨*~ the date of the meeting*⟩ 2 to accelerate the growth or progress of; further 3 to raise in rank; promote 4 to supply (money or goods) ahead of time or as a loan 5 to bring (an opinion or argument) forward for notice; propose 6 to raise in rate; increase ⟨*~ the price*⟩ 7 *archaic* to lift up; promote ~ *vi* 1 to go forwards; proceed 2 to make progress; increase, grow ⟨*~ in age*⟩ 3 to rise in rank, position, or importance 4 to rise in rate or price [ME *advauncen*, fr OF *avancier*, fr (assumed) VL *abantiare*, fr L *abante* before, fr *ab- + ante* before – more at ANTE-] – **advancer** *n*

²**advance** *n* 1a a forward movement b a signal for troops to advance **2a** progress in development; improvement ⟨*an ~ in medical technique*⟩ **b** a progressive step; an advancement ⟨*an ~ in rank*⟩ 3 a rise in price, value, or amount 4 *usu pl* a friendly or amorous approach or overture ⟨*her attitude discouraged all ~s*⟩ 5 (a provision of) money or goods supplied before a payment is received *synonyms* see ADVANCEMENT – **in advance** beforehand – **in advance of** ahead of, before

³**advance** *adj* 1 made, sent, or provided ahead of time ⟨*an ~ payment*⟩ 2 going or situated ahead of others ⟨*an ~ party of soldiers*⟩

**advanced** /əd'vahnst/ *adj* 1 far on in time or course ⟨*a man ~ in years*⟩ **2a** beyond the elementary or introductory ⟨*~ chemistry*⟩ **b** beyond others in progress or development ⟨*an ~ country*⟩ 3 ahead of the times; modern ⟨*~ ideas*⟩

**Advanced level** *n, often cap L* an examination in any of many subjects that is the second of the three levels of the British General Certificate of Education, is usu taken at about the age of 18, and is a partial qualification for university entrance; *also* a subject taken in this examination – compare ORDINARY LEVEL, SCHOLARSHIP LEVEL

**advancement** /-mənt/ *n* 1 advancing or being advanced: **1a**

(a) promotion or elevation to a higher rank or position **b** furtherance towards perfection or completeness ⟨*the ~ of knowledge*⟩ 2 an advance of money or value

synonyms Advancement is action taken to **advance** something ⟨*work towards the* **advancement** *of my favourite cause*⟩ whereas an **advance** is the way something is **advancing**.

¹**advantage** /əd'vahntij/ *n* 1 superiority of position or condition ⟨*higher ground gave the enemy the ~*⟩ – often + *of* or *over* ⟨*has the ~ over heavier jockeys*⟩ 2 benefit, gain; *esp* benefit resulting from some course of action ⟨*a mistake which turned out to his ~*⟩ ⟨*could be shortened with ~*⟩ 3 a factor or circumstance of benefit to its possessor ⟨*lacked the ~s of an education*⟩ 4 the first point won in tennis after DEUCE (score of 40 all); *also* the resulting score ⟨*~ Smith*⟩ [ME *avantage*, fr MF, fr *avant* before, fr L *abante*] – **have the advantage of somebody** to have superiority over somebody; *specif* to have personal unreciprocated knowledge of somebody ⟨*I'm afraid you* have the advantage of me⟩ – **take advantage of 1** to make use of the opportunity provided by ⟨*took advantage of the good weather to mow the lawn*⟩ 2 to impose on; exploit 3 *euph* to seduce – **to advantage** so as to produce a favourable impression or improvement ⟨*could lose a few pounds to advantage*⟩

²**advantage** *vt, formal* to be of service or profit to; benefit

**advantageous** /,adv(ə)n'tayjəs/ *adj* providing an opportunity or benefit; favourable *synonyms* see BENEFICIAL *antonyms* disadvantageous, detrimental – **advantageously** *adv*, **advantageousness** *n*

**advection** /əd'veksh(ə)n/ *n* the horizontal movement of a mass of air that causes changes in the physical properties (eg temperature) of the air [L *advection-, advectio* act of bringing, fr *advectus*, pp of *advehere* to carry to, fr *ad- + vehere* to carry –more at WAY] – **advective** *adj*

**Advent** /'advent, -vənt/ *n* 1 the period between the fourth Sunday before Christmas and Christmas itself **2a** the coming of Christ in the flesh **b** SECOND COMING (return of Christ to earth at the Last Judgment) 3 *not cap* a coming into being; an arrival ⟨*the ~ of spring*⟩ [ME, fr ML *adventus*, fr L, arrival, fr *adventus*, pp]

**Adventism** /'adventiz(ə)m, -vən-/ *n* the doctrine that the SECOND COMING (return of Christ to earth at the Last Judgment) and the end of the world are at hand – **Adventist** *adj or n*

**adventitious** /,advən'tishəs, -ven-/ *adj* 1 coming accidentally or unexpectedly from another source; not inherent or innate 2 arising or occurring sporadically or in other than the usual location ⟨*~ buds on a plant*⟩ *synonyms* see ¹INCIDENTAL *antonym* inherent [L *adventicius*, fr *adventus*, pp] – **adventitiously** *adv*, **adventitiousness** *n*

**adventive** /əd'ventiv/ *adj* 1 *of an organism* introduced but not fully naturalized 2 ADVENTITIOUS 2 – **adventive** *n*, **adventively** *adv*

**Advent Sunday** *n* the first Sunday in Advent

¹**adventure** /əd'venchə/ *n* **1a** an undertaking involving danger, risks, and uncertainty of outcome **b** the encountering of exciting risks ⟨*the spirit of ~*⟩ 2 an exciting or remarkable experience ⟨*an ~ in exotic dining*⟩ 3 an enterprise involving financial risk [ME *aventure*, fr OF, fr (assumed) VL *adventura*, fr L *adventus*, pp of *advenire* to arrive, fr *ad- + venire* to come – more at COME] – **adventuresome** *adj*, **adventuresomeness** *n*, **adventurous** *adj*, **adventurously** *adv*, **adventurousness** *n*

synonyms Adventurous and venturesome describe people who seek, or activities which offer, adventure; venturesome suggests a greater danger. Bold, daring, and audacious describe a readiness to face danger or take risks either generally, as a characteristic, or in a given situation. They are usually terms of approval, though audacious, which is the strongest, may sometimes suggest too great a readiness to take risks. It sometimes implies breathtaking ingenuity ⟨*an* audacious *plan to enter the castle inside casks of beer*⟩. Reckless, rash, and foolhardy are usually disapproving: rash suggests imprudent haste or boldness and reckless utter disregard of the consequences. Foolhardy is less strong than reckless, and emphasizes rather the foolishness of the action than the attitude of the person taking it ⟨*it was rather* foolhardy *to climb the mountain in plimsolls*⟩. Daredevil expresses ostentatious daring, in feats or their performers ⟨*a daredevil trapeze act*⟩. Compare BRAVE *antonyms* timid, fainthearted, unadventurous, cautious

²**adventure** *vt* 1 to expose to danger or loss; venture, risk 2 to venture upon; dare to try ~ *vi* 1 to hazard oneself; dare to go or enter – usu + *into, on*, or *upon* 2 to take a risk

**adventure playground** *n, chiefly Br* a playground equipped with often old or disused objects (e g tyres, pipes, or vehicles) with which children can create their own amusement

**adventurer** /əd'venchərə/, *fem* **adventuress** /-ris/ *n* **1** one who or that which adventures: e g **1a** SOLDIER OF FORTUNE (one who pursues a military career for profit or pleasure) **b** one who engages in risky commercial enterprises for profit **2** one who seeks wealth or position, esp by unscrupulous means

**adventurism** /əd'venchə,riz(ə)m/ *n* ill-considered or rash improvisation or experimentation, esp in politics – **adventurist** *n*, **adventuristic** *adj*

**adverb** /'advuhb/ *n* a word that modifies a verb an adjective, another adverb, a preposition, a phrase, a clause, or a sentence, and that typically answers such questions as how? when? or where? or expresses affirmation or denial [MF *adverbe*, fr L *adverbium*, fr *ad-* + *verbum* word – more at WORD]

**adverbial** /əd'vuhbi·əl/, **adverb** *adj* of or functioning as an adverb ⟨*an* ∼ *clause*⟩ – **adverbial** *n*, **adverbially** *adv*

**ad verbum** /ad 'vuhbəm/ *adv* in the exact words; verbatim [L, to a word]

¹**adversary** /'advəs(ə)ri; *also* əd'vuhs(ə)ri USE *the last pron is disliked by some speakers*/ *n* an enemy, opponent, or opposing faction – **adversariness** *n*

²**adversary** *adj* **1** of or involving an adversary **2** having or involving antagonistic parties or interests ⟨ ∼ *politics*⟩

**adversative** /əd'vuhsətiv/ *adj* expressing contrast, opposition, or adverse circumstance ⟨*the* ∼ *conjunction* but⟩ – **adversative** *n*, **adversatively** *adv*

**adverse** /'advuhs, əd'vuhs/ *adj* **1** acting against or in a contrary direction ⟨*hindered by* ∼ *winds*⟩ **2** unfavourable ⟨ ∼ *criticism*⟩ **3** *archaic* opposite in position △ averse [ME, fr MF *advers*, fr L *adversus*, pp of *advertere*] – **adversely** *adv*, **adverseness** *n*

**adversity** /əd'vuhsəti/ *n* **1** suffering, destitution, or affliction **2** a calamitous or disastrous experience *antonym* prosperity

¹**advert** /əd'vuht/ *vi, formal* **1** to pay heed or attention **2** to make a glancing reference in speech or writing □ + *to* [ME *adverten*, fr MF & L; MF *advertir*, fr L *advertere*, fr *ad-* + *vertere* to turn (cf AVERT)]

²**advert** /'advuht/ *n, chiefly Br informal* an advertisement

**advertence** /əd'vuht(ə)ns/, **advertency** /-si/ *n* attention, heedfulness

**advertent** /əd'vuht(ə)nt/ *adj* giving attention; heedful [L *advertent-, advertens*, prp of *advertere*] – **advertently** *adv*

**advertise** /'advətiez/ *vt* **1** to make publicly and generally known ⟨∼d *her presence by sneezing*⟩ **2** to announce (e g an article for sale or a vacancy) publicly, esp in the press or by a printed notice ⟨ ∼ *the post of editor*⟩ **3** to describe and praise (a product, service, etc) publicly in the mass media in order to encourage sales or patronage ⟨ ∼ *a new washing powder on television*⟩ ∼ *vi* **1** to describe and praise a product, service, etc in the mass media in order to encourage sales or patronage **2** to seek by means of advertising – + *for* ⟨ ∼ *for a secretary*⟩ [ME *advertisen*, fr MF *advertiss-*, stem of *advertir*] – **advertiser** *n*

**advertisement** /əd'vuhtismənt, -tiz-, 'advə,tiezmənt/ *n* **1** the act or process of advertising **2** a public notice; *esp* one published, broadcast, or displayed publicly to advertise a product, service, etc

**advertising** /'advə,tiezing/ *n* **1** the action of calling something to the attention of the public esp by means of broadcast or published announcements **2** ADVERTISEMENTS 2 ⟨*the magazine contains a lot of* ∼⟩ **3** the profession of preparing advertisements for publication or broadcast

**advice** /əd'vies/ *n* **1** recommendation regarding a decision or course of conduct; counsel ⟨*my* ∼ *to you is – don't do it*⟩ ⟨*take medical* ∼⟩ **2** *usu pl* communication, esp from a distance **3** an official notice concerning a business transaction ⟨*a remittance* ∼⟩ [ME, fr OF *avis* opinion, prob fr the phrase *ce m'est a vis* that appears to me, part trans of L *mihi visum est* it seemed so to me, I decided]

**advisable** /əd'viezəbl/ *adj* worthy to be advised or done; prudent – **advisableness** *n*, **advisably** *adv*, **advisability** *n*

**advise** /əd'viez/ *vt* **1a** to give advice to; counsel ⟨ ∼ *her to try a drier climate*⟩ **b** to caution, warn ⟨ ∼ *him against going*⟩ **c** to recommend ⟨ ∼ *prudence*⟩ ⟨*I* ∼ *you to give up smoking*⟩ **2** *formal or commercialese* to give information or notice to; inform ⟨ ∼ *his friends of his intentions*⟩ ∼ *vi* **1** to give advice ⟨ ∼ *on legal matters*⟩ **2** *chiefly NAm* to take counsel; consult ⟨ ∼ *with one's parents*⟩ [MF *advisen*, fr OF *aviser*, fr *avis*]

**advised** /əd'viezd/ *adj* **1a** judicious – chiefly in *ill-advised, well-advised* ⟨*you'd be well-*advised *not to travel today*⟩ **b** thought out; considered – usu in combination ⟨*ill-*advised *plans*⟩ **2** informed – esp in *keep someone advised* – **advisedly** *adv*

**advisement** /əd'viezmənt/ *n, NAm* careful consideration; deliberation

**adviser, advisor** /əd'viezə/ *n* one who gives advice, esp professionally in a specialized field ⟨*medical* ∼ *to the Queen*⟩

**advisory** /əd'viez(ə)ri/ *adj* **1** having or exercising power to advise **2** containing or consisting of advice

**advocaat** /'advəkah/ *n* a sweet thick yellow liqueur consisting chiefly of brandy and eggs [D, short for *advocatenborrel*, fr *advocaat* lawyer + *borrel* drink, bubble, fr *borrelen* to bubble]]

**advocacy** /'advəkəsi/ *n* **1** the act or process of advocating; active support or pleading ⟨*his* ∼ *of reform*⟩ **2** the work or function of an advocate

¹**advocate** /'advəkət/ *n* **1** a person who pleads the cause of another before a tribunal or judicial court ⟨*the* ∼ *for the defence*⟩; *specif, Scot* a barrister **2** one who defends or maintains a cause or proposal ⟨*an* ∼ *of monetarism*⟩ [ME *advocat*, fr MF, fr L *advocatus*, fr pp of *advocare* to summon, fr *ad-* + *vocare* to call – more at VOICE]

²**advocate** /'advəkayt/ *vt* to plead in favour of *synonyms* see ¹SUPPORT – **advocator** *n*, **advocation** *n*, **advocative** *adj*, **advocatory** *adj*

**advowson** /əd'vowz(ə)n/ *n* the right of presenting a clergyman for a vacant position (BENEFICE) in the CHURCH OF ENGLAND [ME, fr OF *avoueson*, fr ML *advocation-, advocatio*, fr L, act of calling, fr *advocatus*, pp]

**adytum** /'aditəm/ *n, pl* **adyta** /-tə/ the innermost sanctuary in an ancient temple; the sanctum [L, fr Gk *adyton*, neut of *adytos* not to be entered, fr *a-* + *dyein* to enter; akin to Skt *upā-du* to put on]

**adze, NAm chiefly adz** /adz/ *n* a tool that has a blade at right angles to the handle and is used chiefly for cutting and shaping wood [ME *adse*, fr OE *adesa* ]

**ae** /ay/ *adj, chiefly Scot* one [ME (northern) *a*, alter. of *an*]

**-ae** /-i, -ee, -ie/ *suffix* (→ *n pl*) members of the family or subfamily of ⟨*Compositae*⟩ – in names of animal and some plant families and plant subfamilies [NL, fr L, pl of *-a*, ending of fem nouns & adjectives]

**aeciospore** /'eesiə,spaw/ *n* any of the spores arranged within an aecium in a series like a chain

**aecium** /'eeshiəm, 'eesiəm/ *n, pl* **aecia** /-iə/ the FRUITING BODY of a rust fungus in which the first spores are usu produced [NL, fr Gk *aikia* assault, fr *aeikēs* unseemly, fr *a-* + *eikōs* seemly, fr participle of *eikenai* to seem] — **aecial** *adj*

**aedeagus** /ee'dee·əgəs, ,eedi'aygəs/ *n* the part of the male genitalia of an insect that is inserted into the female during copulation [NL, fr Gk *aidoia* genitals + *agos* leader, fr *agein* to lead]

**aëdes** /ay'eedeez/ *n, pl* **aëdes** any of a genus (*Aëdes*) of mosquitoes including the carriers of various diseases (e g YELLOW FEVER and DENGUE) [NL, genus name, fr Gk *aēdēs* unpleasant, fr *a-* + *ēdos* pleasure; akin to Gk *hēdys* sweet – more at SWEET] – **aedine** *adj*

**aedile** /'aydiel/ *n* an official in ancient Rome in charge of public works and games, the police, and the grain supply [L *aedilis*, fr *aedes* temple – more at EDIFY]

**Aegean** /i'jee·ən/ *adj* **1** of the Aegean sea **2** of the chiefly BRONZE AGE civilization of the islands of the Aegean sea and the countries adjacent to it [L *Aegaeus*, fr Gk *Aigaios*]

**aegirine** /'aygərien, 'eejə-, -rin/ *n* a green to black mineral, NaFeSi₂O₆, that contains iron, sodium, silicon, and oxygen, belongs to the PYROXENE group of minerals, and occurs in various IGNEOUS rocks [Ger *aegirin*, fr *Aegir*, ancient Scand sea-god]

**aegis** /'eejis/ *n* auspices, sponsorship ⟨*under the* ∼ *of the education department*⟩ [L, shield of Jupiter or Minerva, protection, fr Gk *aigis* goatskin, shield of Zeus, perh fr *aig-, aix* goat; akin to Arm *aic* goat]

**Aegisthus** /ee'jisthəs/ *n* a lover of Clytemnestra, the wife of Agamemnon, who was slain with her by her son Orestes [L, fr Gk *Aigisthos*]

**aegrotat** /'egrətat/ *n* an unclassified degree awarded in British universities to a student prevented by illness from taking some or all of his/her examinations [L, he is ill, fr *aegrotare* to be ill, fr *aegr-, aeger* ill]

**-aemia, chiefly NAm -emia** /-'eemyə, -'eemi·ə/ *comb form*

(→ *n*) **1** condition of having (such) blood ⟨*leuk*aemia⟩ **2** condition of having (something specified) in the blood ⟨*ur*aemia⟩ [NL, fr Gk *-aimia*, fr *haima* blood]

**Aeneolithic, Eneolithic** /ay,eeniə'lithik/ *adj* of a transitional period between the NEOLITHIC age and the BRONZE AGE, esp in Europe and Asia, in which the use of copper became more widespread [L *aeneus* of copper or bronze, fr *aes* copper, bronze – more at ORE]

**aeolian** /ee'ohli·ən/ *adj* **1** *often cap* of Aeolus or the winds generally **2** giving forth or marked by a sighing sound or musical tone produced (as if) by the wind **3** borne, deposited, produced, or eroded by the wind [*Aeolus* (Gk *Aiolos*), Gk god of the winds]

¹**Aeolian** /ee'ohliən/, **Aeolic** /ee'ohlik/ *adj* of Aeolis or its inhabitants [*Aeolis, Aeolia*, ancient district of Asia Minor, fr L, fr Gk *Aiolis*]

²**Aeolian** *n* **1** a member of a group of Greek peoples of Thessaly and Boeotia that colonized Lesbos and the adjacent coast of Asia Minor **2 Aeolic, Aeolian** a group of ancient Greek dialects used by the Aeolians

**aeolian harp** *n* a box-shaped musical instrument with strings stretched over it which produce sounds when wind or air blows over them [*aeolian*]

**aeolian mode** *n*, *often cap A* a MODE (fixed arrangement of eight notes) which may be represented on the white keys of the piano on a scale from A to A [*Aeolian*]

**aeolotropic** /,ee·əloh'tropik/ *adj*, *of crystalline material* ANISOTROPIC (having physical properties dependent on the direction of the crystal axes) [Gk *aiolos* variegated] – **aeolotropy** *n*

**aeon** /'ee·ən, 'ee,on/ *n* **1** an immeasurably or indefinitely long period of time; an age **2** a unit of geological time equal to a thousand million years [L, fr Gk *aiōn* – more at AYE]

**aeonian** /ee'ohnyən/, **aeonic** /-nik/ *adj*, *poetic* lasting for an immeasurably long time

**aer-** /eər-/, **aero-** *comb form* **1a** air; atmosphere ⟨*aer*ate⟩ ⟨*aero*biology⟩ **b** aerial and ⟨*aero*marine⟩ **2** gas ⟨*aero*sol⟩ **3** aircraft ⟨*aero*drome⟩ [ME *aero-*, fr MF, fr L, fr Gk *aer-, aero-*, fr *aēr*]

**aerate** /'eərayt, -'-/ *vt* **1** to supply (the blood) with oxygen by respiration **2** to supply or impregnate (e g the soil or a liquid) with air **3a** to combine or charge with a gas (e g CARBON DIOXIDE) **b** to make effervescent – **aeration** *n*, **aerator** *n*

**aerenchyma** /eə'rengkimə/ *n* a spongy plant tissue, in which there are large gas-filled cavities between cells, that occurs in many water plants and helps to keep floating parts buoyant and to increase the rate at which the gases CARBON DIOXIDE and oxygen are taken in or given out [NL]

¹**aerial** /'eəri·əl/ *adj* **1a** of or occurring in the air or atmosphere **b** consisting of air ⟨~ *particles*⟩ **c** existing or growing in the air rather than in the ground or in water ⟨~ *roots on a tropical orchid*⟩ **d** operating overhead on elevated cables or rails ⟨*an* ~ *railway*⟩ **2** lacking substance; thin, unreal **3a** of aircraft ⟨~ *navigation*⟩ **b** designed for use in, taken from, or operating from or against aircraft ⟨~ *photograph*⟩ **c** effected by means of aircraft ⟨~ *transportation*⟩ **4** *poetic* lofty ⟨~ *spires*⟩ **5** *poetic* ethereal ⟨*visions of* ~ *joy* – P B Shelley⟩ [L *aerius*, fr Gk *aerios*, fr *aēr*] – **aerially** *adv*

²**aerial** *n* a conductor (e g a wire) or arrangement of conductors designed to radiate or receive radio waves

**aerial perspective** *n* the manner of showing distance in painting and drawing by gradation of colour and tone

**aerie** /'eəri, 'iəri/ *n* an eyrie

**aeriform** /'eəri,fawm/ *adj* **1** consisting or having the form of air **2** lacking substance; thin, unreal

**aero** /'eəroh/ *adj* **1** of aircraft or aeronautics ⟨*an* ~ *engine*⟩ **2** designed for aerial use ⟨*an* ~ *lens*⟩ [*aero-*]

**aero-** – see AER-

**aeroballistics** /,eərohbə'listiks/ *n taking sing or pl vb* the BALLISTICS (study of the flight of projectiles, esp from weapons) of missiles and projectiles in the atmosphere – **aeroballistic** *adj*

**aerobatics** /,eərə'batiks/ *n taking sing or pl vb* the performance of stunts in an aircraft [blend of *aer-* and *acrobatics*] – **aerobatic** *adj*

**aerobe** /'eərohb/ *n* an aerobic organism (e g a bacterium) [Fr *aérobie*, fr *aér-* aer- + *-bie* (fr Gk *bios* life) – more at QUICK]

**aerobic** /eə'rohbik/ *adj* **1** living, active, or occurring only in the presence of oxygen ⟨~ *respiration*⟩ **2** of or induced by aerobes ⟨~ *fermentation*⟩ – **aerobically** *adv*

**aerobiosis** /,eərohbie'ohsis/ *n*, *pl* **aerobioses** /-seez/ life in the presence of air or oxygen [NL] – **aerobiotic** *adj*, **aerobiotically** *adv*

**aerodrome** /'eərə,drohm/ *n*, *chiefly Br* a usu small airfield

**aerodynamics** /,eərohdie'namiks, -di-/ *n taking sing or pl vb* a branch of DYNAMICS that deals with the motion of gases, esp air, and with the forces acting on solid bodies moving through such gases – **aerodynamic, aerodynamical** *adj*, **aerodynamically** *adv*, **aerodynamicist** *n*

**aerodyne** /'eəroh,dien/ *n* a heavier-than-air aircraft that derives its lift in flight from forces resulting from its motion through the air – compare AEROSTAT [*aerodynamic*]

**aeroembolism** /,eəroh'embəliz(ə)m/ *n* an abnormal condition characterized by the presence of nitrogen gas bubbles in the blood and body tissues and caused by moving too rapidly from an atmosphere where air pressure is high to one where it is low – compare CAISSON DISEASE

**aerofoil** /'eərə,foyl, -roh-/ *n*, *chiefly Br* a body (e g an aircraft wing or propeller blade) designed to act on the air through which it moves in such a way as to move forward, lift, steer, etc the vehicle to which it is attached [*aer-* + ³*foil*]

**aerogram, aerogramme** /'eərə,gram/ *n* **1** AIR LETTER 2 **2** RADIOGRAM 2

**aerographer** /eə'rogrəfə/ *n*, *NAm* a naval officer who observes and forecasts weather and surf conditions

**aerography** /eə'rogrəfi/ *n* meteorology

**aerolite** /'eərə,liet/ *n* a stony meteorite – **aerolitic** *adj*

**aerolith** /'eərə,lith/ *n* an aerolite

**aerology** /eə'roləji/ *n* meteorology; *specif* a branch of this dealing esp with the upper atmosphere – **aerologist** *n*, **aerological** *adj*

**aeromagnetic** /,eərohmag'netik/ *adj* of or derived from a study of the earth's MAGNETIC FIELD, esp from the air ⟨*an* ~ *survey*⟩

**aeromechanics** /,eərohmə'kaniks/ *n taking sing or pl vb* mechanics that deals with the equilibrium and motion of gases and of solid bodies immersed in them

**aerometer** /eə'romitə/ *n* an instrument for determining the weight or density of a gas, esp air

**aeromodelling** /'eəroh,modl·ing/ *n* the hobby of making miniature aircraft

**aeronaut** /'eərə,nawt/ *n* one who operates or travels in an airship or balloon [Fr *aéronaute*, fr *aér-* aer- + Gk *nautēs* sailor – more at NAUTICAL]

**aeronautics** /,eərə'nawtiks/ *n taking sing vb* the art or science of flight – **aeronautic, aeronautical** *adj*, **aeronautically** *adv*

**aeropause** /'eərə,pawz/ *n* the level above the earth's surface beyond which normal aircraft are not able to fly

**aeroplane** /'eərəplayn/ *n*, *chiefly Br* an aircraft that is heavier than air, has nonrotating wings from which it derives its lift, and is mechanically propelled (e g by a propeller or jet engine) [Fr *aéroplane*, fr *aér-* + *plan*, *adj*, plane]

¹**aerosol** /'eərəsol/ *n* **1** a suspension of fine solid or liquid particles in gas ⟨*smoke, fog, and mist are* ~s⟩ **2** a substance (e g an insecticide or deodorant) dispensed from a pressurized container as an aerosol **3 aerosol, aerosol container** a metal container for substances in aerosol form [*aer-* + ⁴*sol*]

²**aerosol** *vt* **-ll-** to write or paint with an aerosol ⟨*a slogan* ~*led on a wall*⟩

¹**aerospace** /'eəroh,spays/ *n* **1** the earth's atmosphere and the space beyond **2** a branch of PHYSICAL SCIENCE (science concerned with nonliving materials) that deals with aerospace **3** the branch of industry involved in the manufacture of vehicles, weapons, etc used in aerospace

²**aerospace** *adj* relating to aerospace, to vehicles used in aerospace or the manufacture of such vehicles, or to travel in aerospace ⟨~ *research*⟩ ⟨~ *medicine*⟩

**aerostat** /'eərə,stat/ *n* an aircraft (e g a balloon) that is lighter than the surrounding air – compare AERODYNE [Fr *aérostat*, fr *aér-* + *-stat*]

**aerostatics** /,eərə'statiks/ *n taking sing or pl vb* a branch of STATICS that deals with the equilibrium of gases and of solid bodies immersed in them [modif of NL *aerostatica*, fr *aer-* + *statica* statics]

**Aertex** /'eə,teks/ *trademark* – used for a cellular cotton fabric

¹**aery** /'eəri, 'iəri/ *adj*, *poetic* lofty, ethereal ⟨~ *visions*⟩ [L *aerius* – more at AERIAL] – **aerily** *adv*

²**aery** *n* an eyrie

**Aesculapian** /,eskyoo'laypi·ən/ *adj* of Aesculapius or the healing art; medical [*Aesculapius*, Greco-Roman god of medicine, fr L, fr Gk *Asklēpios*]

**Aesir** /'aysiə, 'eesiə/ *n pl* the principal race of Norse gods [ON *Æsir*, pl of *āss* god]

**Aesopian** /ee'sohpyən/ *also* **Aesopic** /-pik/ *adj* (characteristic) of Aesop or his fables [*Aesop* † *ab* 560 BC Gk writer of fables]

**aesthesia**, *NAm* **esthesia** /ees'theezyə, -zh(y)ə/ *n* the capacity for sensation and feeling; sensibility [NL, back-formation fr *anaesthesia*]

**aesthesio-**, *NAm chiefly* **esthesio-** *comb form* sensation 〈*aesthesiology*〉 [NL, fr Gk *aisthēsis* sensation, perception, fr *aisthanesthai*]

**aesthesis** /ees'theesis/ *n* AESTHESIA [NL, fr Gk *aisthēsis*]

**aesthete**, *NAm also* **esthete** /'ees,theet/ *n* 1 one who has or professes a developed sensitivity to the beautiful in art or nature 2 one who affects concern for the arts and indifference to practical affairs [back-formation fr *aesthetic*]

¹**aesthetic** /ees'thetik, -es, əs-/ *also* **aesthetical** /-kl/, *NAm also* **esthetic** *also* **esthetical** *adj* **1a** of or dealing with aesthetics or the appreciation of the beautiful 〈~ *theories*〉 **b** artistic 〈*a work of ~ value*〉 **2** having a developed sense of beauty *synonyms* see ARTISTIC [Ger *ästhetisch*, fr NL *aestheticus*, fr Gk *aisthētikos* of sense perception, fr *aisthanesthai* to perceive – more at AUDIBLE] – **aesthetically** *adv*

²**aesthetic**, *NAm also* **esthetic** /ees'thetik, es-, əs-/ *n* 1 *pl but taking sing or pl vb* a branch of philosophy dealing with the nature of the beautiful and with judgments concerning beauty 2 the description and explanation of artistic phenomena and aesthetic experience by means of other sciences (e g psychology, sociology, or history) 3 a particular philosophical theory or conception of art or beauty 〈*the grim Calvinist* ~〉 – **aesthetician** *n*

**aestheticism** /ees'thetisiz(ə)m/, *NAm also* **estheticism** /ees-, es-/ *n* 1 the doctrine that the principles of beauty form a fundamental standard prior to other, esp moral, principles 2 devotion to or emphasis on beauty or the cultivation of the arts

**aestival** /ee'stievl/ *adj, formal* relating to the summer [ME *estival*, fr MF or L; MF, fr L *aestivalis*, fr *aestivus* of summer, fr *aestas* summer – more at EDIFY]

**aestivate** /'eestivayt/ *vi* 1 *of an animal, esp an insect* to pass the summer in a state of torpor – compare HIBERNATE 2 *formal* to spend the summer, esp at one place [L *aestivatus*, pp of *aestivare*, fr *aestivus*]

**aestivation** /,eesti'vaysh(ə)n/ *n* 1 the act or state of aestivating 2 the arrangement of floral parts in a bud – compare VERNATION

**aether** /'eethə/ *n* ETHER 1, 2

**aetiology**, *chiefly NAm* **etiology** /,eeti'oləji/ *n* 1 a cause, origin; *specif* all the causes of a disease or abnormal condition 2 the study of the causes of anything, esp diseases [ML *aetiologia* statement of causes, fr Gk *aitiologia*, fr *aitia* cause] – **aetiologic, aetiological** *adj*, **aetiologically** *adv*

**af-** – see AD-

¹**afar** /ə'fah/ *adv* from, to, or at a great distance – often + *off* 〈*roamed* ~〉 〈*saw him* ~ *off*〉 [ME *afer*, fr *on fer* at a distance & *of fer* from a distance]

²**afar** *n* a great distance 〈*saw him from* ~〉

**afeard, afeared** /ə'fiəd/ *adj, dial* afraid [ME *afered*, fr OE *āfǣred*, pp of *āfǣran* to frighten, fr *ā-*, perfective prefix + *fǣran* to frighten – more at FEAR]

**affable** /'afəbl/ *adj* 1 pleasant and relaxed in talking to others 2 characterized by ease and friendliness; benign *antonyms* reserved, unsociable [MF, fr L *affabilis*, fr *affari* to speak to, fr *ad-* + *fari* to speak – more at BAN] – **affably** *adv*, **affability** *n*

**affair** /ə'feə/ *n* **1a** *pl* commercial, professional, or public business or matters 〈*world* ~s〉 **b** a particular or personal concern 〈*that's my* ~, *not yours*〉 **2a** a procedure, action, or occasion only vaguely specified 〈*the whole* ~ *only lasted an hour*〉 **b** a social event; a party 〈*a sit-down* ~〉 **3** *also* **affaire** a romantic or passionate attachment between two people who are not married to each other, often of considerable but limited duration; a liaison **4** a matter occasioning public anxiety, controversy, or scandal; a case 〈*the Dreyfus* ~〉 **5** *informal* an object or collection of objects only vaguely specified – used with a descriptive or qualifying term 〈*the house was a 2-storey* ~〉 [ME & MF; ME *affaire*, fr MF, fr *a faire* to do; (3) Fr *affaire*, fr MF]

**affair of honour** *n* a duel [trans of Fr *affaire d'honneur*]

¹**affect** /'afekt/ *n* 1 *psychology* the conscious subjective aspect of emotion or feeling considered apart from bodily changes 2 *obs* feeling, affection [(1) Ger *affekt*, fr L *affectus* (2) L *affectus*, fr *affectus*, pp] – **affectless** *adj*, **affectlessness** *n*

²**affect** /ə'fekt/ *vt* 1 to be given to; prefer 〈~ *flashy clothes*〉 2 to make a usu pretentious display of liking, using, or having; cultivate 〈~ *a worldly manner*〉 **3a** to put on a pretence of; feign 〈~ *indifference*〉 **b** to assume the character, attitude, etc of 〈~ *the experienced traveller*〉 **4** to tend towards 〈*drops of water* ~ *roundness*〉 **5** to be habitually found in; frequent **6** *archaic* to aim at **7** *archaic* to have affection for ~ *vi, obs* INCLINE 2 *synonyms* see ¹PRETEND [MF & L; MF *affecter*, fr L *affectare*, fr *affectus*, pp of *afficere* to influence, fr *ad-* + *facere* to do – more at DO]

³**affect** *vt* 1 to produce a material effect upon or alteration in 〈*paralysis* ~ed *his limbs*〉 2 to act on (e g a person or his/her mind or feelings) so as to bring about a response 〈*was deeply* ~ed *by the news*〉 [L *affectus* pp] – **affectability** *n*, **affectable** *adj*

*usage* To **affect** somebody or something is to "influence" him/her/it; to **effect** something (e g a result or purpose) is to "bring it about" or "carry it out". *synonyms* see ¹MOVE **antonym** leave cold

**affectation** /,afek'taysh(ə)n/ *n* 1 an insincere display (e g of a quality not really possessed) 〈*the* ~ *of righteous indignation*〉 2 a deliberately assumed peculiarity of speech or conduct; artificiality 〈*his silly* ~s〉 3 *obs* a striving after

**affected** /ə'fektid/ *adj* **1a** given to affectation **b** assumed artificially or falsely; pretended 〈*an* ~ *interest in art*〉 2 *archaic* inclined, disposed *towards* – **affectedly** *adv*, **affectedness** *n*

**affecting** /ə'fekting/ *adj* evoking a strong emotional response; moving – **affectingly** *adv*

¹**affection** /ə'feksh(ə)n/ *n* 1 affection, affections *pl* emotion as compared with reason 2 tender and lasting attachment; fondness 〈*she had a deep* ~ *for her parents*〉 3 *psychology* the subjective aspect (e g in pleasure or displeasure) of emotion 4 *archaic* a propensity, disposition **b** AFFECTATION 2 [ME, fr MF *affection*, fr L *affection-*, *affectio*, fr *affectus*, pp] – **affectional** *adj*, **affectionally** *adv*, **affectionless** *adj*

²**affection** *n* 1 affecting or being affected 2 a disease, malady, or other bodily condition

**affectionate** /ə'feksh(ə)nət/ *adj* 1 showing affection or warm regard; loving 2 proceeding from affection; tender 〈~ *care*〉 3 *obs* mentally or emotionally disposed or inclined *synonyms* see LOVING **antonyms** chilly, frigid – **affectionately** *adv*

**affective** /ə'fektiv/ *adj* 1 *psychology* of, arising from, or influencing affect; emotional 〈~ *disorders*〉 2 expressing emotion 〈~ *language*〉 – **affectively** *adv*, **affectivity** *n*

**affenpinscher** /'afən,pinshə/ *n* (any of) a breed of small dogs with a stiff red, grey, or black coat, pointed ears, and bushy eyebrows, chin tuft, and moustache [Ger, fr *affe* monkey + *pinscher*, a breed of hunting dog]

**afferent** /'afərənt/ *adj* bearing or conducting inwards; *specif* conveying nervous impulses towards a NERVE CENTRE (e g the brain) – compare EFFERENT [L *afferent-*, *afferens*, prp of *afferre* to bring to, fr *ad-* + *ferre* to bear – more at ²BEAR] – **afferently** *adv*

¹**affiance** /ə'fie·əns/ *n, archaic* 1 trust, confidence 2 a pledge; *specif* a marriage contract [ME, fr MF, fr *affier* to pledge, trust, fr ML *affidare* to pledge, fr L *ad-* + (assumed) VL *fidare* to trust – more at FIANCÉ]

²**affiance** *vt* to promise (oneself or another) solemnly in marriage; betroth

**affiant** /ə'fie·ənt/ *n, NAm* one who swears to an affidavit; *broadly* DEPONENT (person who gives evidence) [MF, fr prp of *affier*]

**afficionado** /ə,fish(y)ə'nahdoh/ *n, pl* **afficionados** AFICIONADO (devotee)

**affidavit** /,afi'dayvit/ *n* a sworn statement in writing for use as proof in law [ML, he has made an oath, fr *affidare*]

¹**affiliate** /ə'filiayt/ *vt* 1 to attach or adopt as a member or branch – + *to* or *with* 〈*the union is* ~d *to the TUC*〉 2 to judicially establish the paternity of (an illegitimate child) – + *on* or *to* ~ *vi* to connect or associate oneself *with* another, often in a dependent or subordinate position; combine 〈*the two branches* ~d〉 [ML *affiliatus*, pp of *affiliare* to adopt as a son, fr L *ad-* + *filius* son – more at FEMININE] – **affiliation** *n*

²**affiliate** /ə'filiayt, -ət/ *n* an affiliated person or organization 〈*an* ~ *member*〉

**affiliation order** /ə,fili'aysh(ə)n/ *n* a legal order requiring that the father of an illegitimate child make specified regular payments towards its maintenance

**affine** /ə'fien, a-/ *adj* of or being a TRANSFORMATION (change in the size, shape, etc of something made according to given mathematical rules) that preserves straightness and parallelism of lines but may alter distances between points and angles between lines ⟨~ *geometry*⟩ [L *affinis* related] – **affinely** *adv*

**affined** /ə'fiend/ *adj* joined in a close relationship; connected

**affinity** /ə'finəti/ *n* **1** relationship by marriage **2a** sympathy of interest; kinship ⟨*this mysterious ~ between us*⟩ **b** attraction; *esp* an attractive force between substances or particles that causes them to enter into and remain in chemical combination **3a** likeness based on relationship or causal connection **b** a relation between biological groups involving resemblance in structural plan and indicating descent from a common ancestor [ME *affinite*, fr MF or L; MF *afinité*, fr L *affinitas*, fr *affinis* bordering on, related by marriage, fr *ad-* + *finis* end, border] **usage** An **affinity** exists *between* two things or people, or *with* another thing or person. Some writers on usage have objected to the use of *to* or *for*; but this has long been established ⟨*whatever bears* **affinity** *to cunning is despicable* – Jane Austen⟩ and is becoming increasingly usual in scientific writing.

**affirm** /ə'fuhm/ *vt* **1a** to validate, confirm **b** to state positively **2** to assert (e g a contract or a judgment of a lower court) as valid or confirmed; ratify **3** to express commitment to ⟨~ *life by refusing to kill*⟩ ~ *vi* **1** to testify or declare by affirmation – compare SWEAR **2** to uphold a judgment or decree of a lower court *synonyms* see ASSERT *antonym* deny [ME *affermen*, fr MF *afermer*, fr L *affirmare*, fr *ad-* + *firmare* to make firm, fr *firmus* firm – more at FIRM] – **affirmable** *adj*, **affirmatory** *adj*

**affirmation** /,afə'maysh(ə)n/ *n* **1a** affirming **b** something affirmed; a positive assertion **2** *law* a solemn declaration made by a person who conscientiously declines taking an oath

¹**affirmative** /ə'fuhmətiv/ *adj* **1** *philosophy* asserting a PREDICATE of a subject **2** asserting or answering that the fact is so ⟨*gave an ~ nod*⟩ **3** favouring or supporting a proposition or motion ⟨*an ~ vote*⟩ **4** *chiefly NAm* positive ⟨*an ~ responsibility*⟩ – **affirmatively** *adv*

²**affirmative** *n* **1** an expression (e g the word *yes*) of affirmation or assent **2** an affirmative proposition

¹**affix** /ə'fiks/ *vt* **1** to attach physically ⟨~ *a stamp to a letter*⟩ **2** to attach in any way; *esp* to add in writing ⟨~ *a signature to a document*⟩ **3** IMPRESS 1a ⟨~ed *his seal*⟩ [ML *affixare*, fr L *affixus*, pp of *affigere* to fasten to, fr *ad-* + *figere* to fasten – more at DYKE] – **affixable** *adj*, **affixment** *n*, **affixture** *n*, **affixation** *n*

²**affix** /'afiks/ *n* **1** an addition to the beginning or end of, or an insertion in, a word, a root, or a whole phrase, serving to produce a derivative word or an inflectional form: **1a** an infix **b** a prefix **c** a suffix **2** an appendage – **affixal, affixial** *adj*

**afflatus** /ə'flaytəs/ *n* a divine bestowing of knowledge or mental power; inspiration [L, act of blowing or breathing on, fr *afflatus*, pp of *afflare* to blow on, fr *ad-* + *flare* to blow – more at BLOW]

**afflict** /ə'flikt/ *vt* **1** to distress so severely as to cause persistent suffering **2** to trouble ⟨~ed *with shyness*⟩ *usage* see INFLICT [ME *afflicten* to overthrow, fr L *afflictus*, pp of *affligere* to cast down, fr *ad-* + *fligere* to strike (cf CONFLICT, INFLICT)]

**affliction** /ə'fliksh(ə)n/ *n* **1** the state of being afflicted; great suffering **2** a cause of persistent pain or distress – **afflictive** *adj*, **afflictively** *adv*

**affluence** /'aflooəns/, **affluency** /'aflooənsi/ *n* **1** profusion; *esp* an abundance of wealth **2** a flow to or towards a point; an influx

¹**affluent** /'aflooənt/ *adj* **1** flowing in abundance; copious **2** having a generously sufficient and typically increasing supply of material possessions ⟨*our ~ society*⟩ *antonyms* impecunious, hard up [ME, fr MF, fr L *affluent-, affluens*, prp of *affluere* to flow to, flow abundantly, fr *ad-* + *fluere* to flow – more at FLUID] – **affluently** *adv*

²**affluent** *n* a tributary stream

**afflux** /'afluks/ *n* AFFLUENCE 2 [Fr or L; Fr, fr L *affluxus*, pp of *affluere*]

**afforce** /ə'faws/ *vt* to reinforce (a jury or other group) by the addition of experts, esp in former times [ML *afforciare*, fr OF *aforcier* to strengthen, increase, fr *a-* (fr L *ad-*) + *forcier, forcer* to force]

**afford** /ə'fawd/ *vt* **1a** to manage to bear without serious detriment – usu + *can, could,* or *able to* ⟨*you can't ~ to neglect your health*⟩ **b** to be able to bear the cost of ⟨*he can't ~ to go to Paris*⟩ ⟨~ *a new coat*⟩ **2** *formal* to make available; furnish ⟨*the roof ~*ed *a fine view*⟩ ⟨*history ~*s *us many examples*⟩

[ME *aforthen*, fr OE *geforthian* to carry out, fr *ge-*, perfective prefix + *forthian* to carry out, fr *forth* – more at CO-, FORTH] – **affordable** *adj*

**afforest** /a'forist, ə-/ *vt* to establish a forest on; *specif, chiefly Br* to convert into forest by seeding or planting [ML *afforestare*, fr L *ad-* + ML *forestis, foresta* forest – more at FOREST] – **afforestation** *n*

**affranchise** /ə'franchiez/ *vt* to set free from servitude or obligation; ENFRANCHISE 1 [modif of MF *afranchiss-*, stem of *afranchir*, fr *a-* (fr L *ad-*) + *franchir* to free – more at FRANCHISE]

¹**affray** /ə'fray/ *n, law* a brawl in a public place [ME, fr MF, fr *affreer* to startle]

²**affray** *vt, archaic* to startle, frighten [ME *affraien*, fr MF *affreer*, fr (assumed) VL *exfridare*, fr L *ex-* + a word of Gmc origin akin to OHG *fridu* peace (cf AFRAID)]

**affreightment** /ə'fraytmənt/ *n* the hiring of a vessel for the carriage of goods by sea [modif of Fr *affrètement*, fr *affréter* to hire a ship to carry goods, fr *a-* (fr L *ad-*) + *fréter* to freight, fr *fret* freight, fr OF, fr MD *vracht, vrecht*]

**affricate** /'afrikət/ *n* a composite speech sound consisting of a plosive consonant (STOP 7) and its immediately following FRICATIVE (e g the /t/ and /sh/ that are the constituents of the /tsh/in *why choose*) [deriv of L *affricatus*, pp of *affricare* to rub against, fr *ad-* + *fricare* to rub – more at FRICTION] – **affricative** *n or adj*

**affrication** /,afri'kaysh(ə)n/ *n* conversion (e g of a simple stop sound) into an affricate

¹**affright** /ə'friet/ *vt, archaic* to frighten, alarm [ME *afyrht, afright* frightened, fr OE *āfyrht*, pp of *āfyrhtan* to frighten, fr *ā-*, perfective prefix + *fyrhtan* to fear; akin to OE *fyrhto* fright – more at FRIGHT]

²**affright** *n, archaic* sudden terror

¹**affront** /ə'frunt/ *vt* **1a** to insult by openly insolent or disrespectful behaviour or language; give offence to **b** to appear directly before as a visible offence ⟨*sky-line is ~*ed *by tower blocks* – *Observer Magazine*⟩ **2** *archaic* to face in defiance; confront ⟨~ *death*⟩ [ME *afronten*, fr MF *afronter* to defy, fr (assumed) VL *affrontare*, fr L *ad-* + *front-, frons* forehead – more at BRINK]

²**affront** *n* a deliberate insult ⟨*an ~ to his dignity*⟩

**affusion** /ə'fyoohzh(ə)n/ *n* an act of pouring a liquid on (e g in baptism) [LL *affusion-, affusio*, fr L *affusus*, pp of *affundere* to pour on, fr *ad-* + *fundere* to pour – more at FOUND]

**Afghan** /'afgan/ *n* **1** a native or inhabitant of Afghanistan **2** PASHTO (language of Afghanistan and Pakistan) **3** *not cap* **3a** a blanket or shawl of coloured wool knitted or crocheted in strips or squares **b** an embroidered sheepskin coat with a long shaggy pile on the inside **4** *not cap* a large carpet of long pile woven in geometric designs, made in the eastern USSR **5 Afghan, Afghan hound** a tall slim swift hunting dog with silky thick hair [Pashto *afghānī*] – **Afghan** *adj*

**afghani** /af'gahni, -'gani/ *n* – see MONEY table [Pashto *afghāni*, lit., Afghan]

**aficionado** /ə,fishyə'nahdoh/, *fem* **aficionada** /ə,fishyə'nada/ *n, pl* **aficionados**, *fem* **aficionadas** a devotee, fan ⟨~s *of the bullfight*⟩ ⟨*cinema ~*s⟩ [Sp, fr pp of *aficionar* to inspire affection, fr *afición* affection, fr L *affection-, affectio* – more at AFFECTION]

**afield** /ə'feeld/ *adv or adj* **1** to, in, or on the field (e g of battle or sport) **2** away from home; abroad **3** out of the way; astray ⟨*irrelevant remarks that carried us far ~*⟩

**afire** /ə'fie-ə/ *adj or adv* on fire; inflamed ⟨~ *with enthusiasm*⟩

**aflame** /ə'flaym/ *adj or adv* afire

**aflatoxin** /,aflə'toksin/ *n* any of several very poisonous substances (MYCOTOXINS) that are produced (e g in badly stored peanuts) by moulds (e g *Aspergillus flavus*) and cause liver cancers [NL *Aspergillus flavus*, species of mould + E *toxin*]

**afloat** /ə'floht/ *adj or adv* **1a** borne (as if) on the water or air **b** at sea or on shipboard **2** free of debt **3** circulating about; rumoured ⟨*nasty stories were ~*⟩ **4** flooded with or submerged under water; awash [ME *aflot*, fr OE *on flot*, fr *on* + *flot* deep water, sea; akin to OE *flēotan* to float – more at FLEET]

**aflutter** /ə'flutə/ *adj* **1** fluttering; *also* with things fluttering ⟨*roofs ~ with flags*⟩ **2** nervously excited

**afoot** /ə'foot/ *adv or adj* **1** on foot **2** happening, astir ⟨*there's trouble ~*⟩

**afore** /ə'faw/ *adv, conj, or prep, chiefly dial* before [ME, fr OE *onforan*, fr *on* + *foran* before – more at BEFORE]

**aforementioned** /ə'faw,mensh(ə)nd/ *adj* mentioned previously

**aforesaid** /ə'faw,sed/ *adj* aforementioned

**aforethought** /ə'faw,thawt/ *adj, formal* premeditated, deliberate – chiefly in *with malice aforethought*

**a fortiori** /,ay fawti'awri/ *adv* with still greater reason; all the more – used in drawing a conclusion that is inferred to be even more certain than another ⟨*if he can afford a house, ~, he can afford a tent*⟩ [NL, lit., from the stronger (argument)]

**afoul** /ə'fowl/ *adv* in or into collision or conflict – + *of*

**Afr-, Afro-** *comb form* African ⟨*Afro-American*⟩; African and ⟨*Afro-Asiatic*⟩ [L, *Afr-, Afer*]

**afraid** /ə'frayd/ *adj* 1 filled with fear or apprehension ⟨*~ of machines*⟩ ⟨*was ~ it would bite*⟩ 2 regretfully of the opinion – used in apology for an utterance ⟨*I'm ~ I won't be able to go*⟩ *antonyms* unafraid, intrepid [ME *affraied*, fr pp of *affraien* to frighten – more at AFFRAY]

**afreet** /'afreet, ə'freet/, **afrit** /ə'frit/ *n* a powerful evil spirit or monster in Arabic mythology [Ar '*ifrīt*]

**afresh** /ə'fresh/ *adv* anew, again

**African** /'afrikən/ *n* 1 a native or inhabitant of Africa 2 an individual of African ancestry; *esp* a Negro [ME, fr OE, fr L *Africanus*, fr *Africa*] – **African** *adj*, **Africanness** *n*

**Africana** /,afri'kahnə/ *n pl* (a collection of) materials concerning or characteristic of Africa

**Africander, Afrikander** /,afri'kandə/ *n* (any of) a breed of tall red large-horned humped southern African cattle [Afrik *Afrikaner, Afrikaander*, lit., Afrikaner]

**Africanism** /'afrikə,niz(ə)m/ *n* 1 a characteristic feature (eg a custom or belief) of Africans or African culture 2 a characteristic feature of an African language occurring in a non-African language 3 allegiance to the traditions, interests, or ideals of Africa

**Africanist** /'afrikənist/ *n* a specialist in African cultures or languages

**African·ize, -ise** /'afrikə,niez/ *vt* to make African; *esp* to bring under Black African control – **Africanization** *n*

**African lily** *n* an agapanthus

**African marigold** *n* a yellow to orange marigold (*Tagetes erecta*) commonly grown in gardens [formerly believed to come from Africa, but in fact native to Mexico]

**African violet** *n* any of several tropical African plants (esp *Saintpaulia ionantha*) of the gloxinia family widely grown as a houseplant for their purple, pink, or white flowers

**Afrikaans** /,afri'kahnz/ *n* a language of S Africa developed from 17th-century Dutch [Afrik, fr *afrikaans*, adj, African, fr obs Afrik *afrikanisch*, fr L *africanus*] – **Afrikaans** *adj*

**Afrikander** /,afri'kandə/ *n* an Africander

**Afrikaner** /,afri'kahnə/ *n* an Afrikaans-speaking S African of European, esp Dutch, descent [Afrik, lit., African, fr L *africanus*]

**Afrikanerdom** /,afri'kahnədəm/ *n* the political and social supremacy of Afrikaners in S Africa ⟨*not allowing the ideals of ~ to be submerged* – N E Davis⟩

**afrit** /ə'frit/ *n* AFREET (evil spirit)

**Afro** /'afroh/ *n or adj, pl* **Afros** (a man's or woman's hairstyle) shaped into a round curly bushy mass [prob fr *Afro-American*]

**Afro-** /afroh-/ – see AFR-

**,Afro-A'merican** *n* an American of African, esp Negroid, descent – **Afro-American** *adj*

**,Afro-Asi'atic** *adj* of or constituting a family of languages of SW Asia and N Africa comprising Semitic, Egyptian, Berber, Cushitic, and Chad

**afrormosia** /,afraw'mohzyə, -zh(y)ə/ *n* any of a genus (*Afrormosia*) of N and W African trees of the pea family; *also* the dark hard teaklike wood of this tree used for furniture [NL, genus name, fr *Afr-* + *Ormosia*, a genus of trees, fr Gk *hormos* chain, necklace]

**¹aft** /ahft/ *adv or adj* near, towards, or in the stern of a ship or the tail of an aircraft ⟨*called all hands ~*⟩ [ME *afte* back, fr OE *æftan* from behind, behind; akin to OE *æfter*]

**²aft** *adv, Scot* often [var of *oft*]

**¹after** /'ahftə/ *adv* 1 in the rear; behind ⟨*mourners follow ~ – SEU S*⟩ 2 afterwards ⟨*arrived shortly ~*⟩ [ME, fr OE *æfter*; akin to OHG *aftar* after]

  *usage* The use of **after** for "afterwards" ⟨*had dinner and went home after*⟩ should be avoided in formal writing unless there is an accompanying adverb such as *soon* or *shortly* ⟨*went home shortly after*⟩.

**²after** *prep* 1 behind in place or order ⟨*name comes ~ mine*⟩ ⟨*shut the door ~ you*⟩ – used in yielding precedence ⟨*~ you!*⟩

or in asking for the next turn ⟨*~ you with the pencil*⟩ 2a following in time; later than ⟨*~ breakfast*⟩ b continuously succeeding ⟨*saw play ~ play*⟩ c in view or in spite of (something preceding) ⟨*~ all our advice*⟩ 3 used to indicate the goal or purpose of an action ⟨*go ~ gold*⟩ 4 next in importance to ⟨*put quantity ~ quality*⟩ 5 so as to resemble: e g 5a in accordance with b approximating to ⟨*something ~ the order of 10*⟩ c in allusion to the name of d in the characteristic manner of e in imitation of 6 about, concerning ⟨*ask ~ his health*⟩ – **after all** 1 in spite of all expectations or exertions ⟨*she was right after all*⟩ 2 – used for introducing or acknowledging matter to be taken into consideration ⟨*after all, he's a busy man*⟩

**³after** *conj* later than the time when

**⁴after** *adj* 1 later, subsequent ⟨*in ~ years*⟩ – often in combination ⟨*an after-event*⟩ 2 located towards the rear or stern of a ship or tail of an aircraft ⟨*the ~ cabin*⟩

**afterbirth** /'ahftə,buhth/ *n* the placenta and foetal membranes expelled after delivery of offspring

**afterburner** /'ahftə,buhnə/ *n* 1 a device in a jet engine for burning unburnt fuel to provide extra power 2 a device for burning or otherwise destroying unburnt or partially burnt carbon compounds in exhaust fumes (eg from a motor car engine) in order to minimize pollution – **afterburning** *n*

**aftercare** /'ahftə,keə/ *n* the care, treatment, help, or supervision given to people discharged from a hospital or other institution; *esp* the assistance given to criminals on their release from prison

**afterdamp** /'ahftə,damp/ *n* a poisonous gas mixture remaining after an explosion of firedamp in a mine

**aftereffect** /'ahftəri,fekt/ *n* an effect that follows its cause after an interval or later than the primary effect

**afterglow** /'ahftə,gloh/ *n* 1 a glow remaining (eg in the sky after sunset) where a light source has disappeared 2 a vestige of past splendour, success, or happy emotion

**,after-'hours** *adj* done or operating after closing time ⟨*~ drinking*⟩ – **after-hours** *adv*

**afterimage** /'ahftə,rimij/ *n* a usu visual sensation occurring after stimulation (eg of the retina) has ceased

**afterlife** /'ahftə,lief/ *n* 1 an existence after death 2 a later period in one's life

**aftermath** /'ahftə,mahth, -math/ *n* 1 a second crop of grass, clover, or other grazing crop that grows on the same soil as an earlier crop 2 a consequence, result ⟨*stricken with guilt as an ~ of the accident*⟩ 3 the period immediately following a usu ruinous event ⟨*in the ~ of the war*⟩ [⁴*after* + *math* (mowing, crop), fr OE *mæth*]

**aftermost** /'ahftə,mohst/ *adj* farthest aft ⟨*the ~ cabin*⟩

**afternoon** /,ahftə'noohn/ *n* 1 the time between noon and sunset 2 a relatively late period (eg of time or life) ⟨*in the ~ of the 19th century*⟩ – **afternoon** *adj*

**afternoons** /,ahftə'noohnz/ *adv, chiefly NAm* in the afternoon repeatedly; on any afternoon ⟨*~ he usually slept*⟩

**afterpiece** /'ahftə,pees/ *n* a short usu comic entertainment performed after a play

**afters** /'ahftəz/ *n pl, Br informal* dessert ⟨*mum's cooked apple pie for ~*⟩

**'after-,shave** *n* a usu scented lotion for use on the face after shaving

**aftertaste** /'ahftə,tayst/ *n* persistence of a flavour or impression after the stimulating agent or experience has gone ⟨*the bitter ~ of a quarrel*⟩

**'after-,tax** *adj* remaining after payment of taxes, esp income tax ⟨*an ~ profit*⟩

**afterthought** /'ahftə,thawt/ *n* 1 an idea occurring later 2 a part, feature, or device not thought of originally

**afterwards** /'ahftəwədz/, *NAm also* **afterward** /,ahftəwəd/ *adv* after that; subsequently, thereafter ⟨*for years ~*⟩

**afterword** /'ahftə,wuhd/ *n* EPILOGUE 1

**afterworld** /'ahftə,wuhld/ *n* a future world; a world after death

**ag** /ahkh (*Afrikaans* ax)/ *interj, SAfr* OH 1 [Afrik, fr D *ach*]

**again** /ə'gayn, ə'gen/ *adv* 1a so as to be as before ⟨*put it back ~*⟩ b in response ⟨*hills echoed ~*⟩ 2 another time; once more 3 on the other hand ⟨*he might go, and ~ he might not*⟩ 4 further; IN ADDITION ⟨*could eat as much ~*⟩ [ME, opposite, again, fr OE *ongēan* opposite, back, fr *on* + *gēn, gēan* still, again; akin to OE *gēan-* against, OHG *gegin* against, towards]

**again and again** *adv* often, repeatedly

**¹against** /ə'gaynst, ə'genst/ *prep* 1 directly opposite; facing 2a in opposition or hostility to ⟨*a war ~ Carthage*⟩ ⟨*the rule ~*

*smoking*⟩ ⟨*he's ~ devolution*⟩ **b** unfavourable to ⟨*told jokes ~ herself*⟩ ⟨*his appearance is ~ him*⟩ **c** as a defence or protection from ⟨*warned them ~ opening the box*⟩ ⟨*shots ~ typhoid*⟩ **3** compared or contrasted with ⟨*cost only £2, as ~ £3 at home*⟩ **4a** in preparation or provision for ⟨*saving ~ his retirement*⟩ **b** with respect to; towards ⟨*customs which had the force of law ~ both landlord and tenant*⟩ **5a** in the direction of and into contact with ⟨*rain beat ~ the windows*⟩ **b** in contact with ⟨*leaning ~ the wall*⟩ **6** in a direction opposite to the motion or course of; counter to ⟨*swam ~ the tide*⟩ **7a** in exchange for **b** as a charge on **8** before the background of **9** *obs* exposed to [ME, alter. of *againes*, fr *again* + *-es, -s*, adv suffix (cf AMIDST, AMONGST, WHILST)]

²**against** *conj, archaic* in preparation for the time when ⟨*throw on another log of wood ~ father comes home* – Charles Dickens⟩

³**against** *adj* **1** opposed to a motion or measure **2** unfavourable to a specified degree; *esp* unfavourable to a win ⟨*the odds are 2 to 1 ~* ⟩

**Aga Khan** /ˌahgə 'kahn/ *n* the leader of a Shiite sect of Muslims [Turk *ağa* lord, master]

**agamic** /ay'gamik, ə-/, **agamous** /ay'gaməs, ə-/ *adj* reproducing without fertilization; PARTHENOGENETIC [Gk *agamos* unmarried, fr *a-* + *gamos* marriage – more at BIGAMY] – **agamically** *adv*

**agamid** /ay'gamid, ə-/ *n* any of various lizards (family Agamidae) found in Australia and tropical Africa and Asia [NL *Agama*, type genus of the family, fr Carib]

**agammaglobulinaemia** /ˌay,gamə,globyooli'neemiə/ *n* a condition in which the body forms few or no GAMMA GLOBULINS (specialized complex proteins found in the blood) or antibodies [NL, fr²*a-* + ISV *gamma globulin* + NL *-aemia*]

**agamogenesis** /ˌay,gamə'jenəsis/ *n* reproduction without fertilization [NL, fr Gk *agamos* + L *genesis*]

**agamospermy** /ay'gamə,spuhmi/ *n, botany* APOGAMY (reproduction without fertilization by a male reproductive cell); *specif* the production (e g in some higher plants) of seeds without fertilization [Gk *agamos* + E *-spermy*]

**agapanthus** /ˌagə'panthəs/ *n* any of several African plants (genus *Agapanthus*) of the lily family cultivated for their clusters of showy blue or purple flowers [NL, genus name, fr Gk *agapē* + *anthos* flower – more at ANTHOLOGY]

¹**agape** /ə'gayp/ *adj* **1** wide open; gaping ⟨*young birds with mouths ~ in expectation of food*⟩ **2** in a state of wonder ⟨*~ with expectation*⟩

²**agape** /ə'gahpah, 'ahgə,pah/ *n* **1** LOVE **4a 2** LOVE FEAST [LL, fr Gk *agapē*, lit., love, fr *agapan* to welcome, love] – **agapeic** *adj*

**agar-agar** /ˌaygahr 'aygay/, **agar**, **agar jelly** *n* a jelly extracted from any of various RED ALGAE (e g of the genera *Gelidium*, *Gracilaria*, and *Eucheuma*) used esp in culture media (e g for growing bacteria) or as a gelling and thickening agent in food (e g soup) [Malay *agar-agar*]

**agaric** /'agərik, ə'garik/ *n* **1a** any of several fungi (genus *Fomes*) with spore tubes rather than gills **b** the dried FRUITING BODY of a fungus (*Fomes officinalis*) formerly used in medicine **2** any of a family (Agaricaceae) of fungi, including the common edible mushroom, with the cap usu resembling an umbrella and with numerous LAMELLAE (radiating gills) on the underside of the cap [L *agaricum*, a fungus, fr Gk *agarikon*]

**agate** /'agayt, 'agət/ *n* **1** a mineral that is a fine-grained variegated mixture of quartz and chalcedony with its colours arranged in stripes, bands, or mosslike forms **2** something made of or fitted with agate; *esp* a device (DRAWPLATE) with holes used for making gold wire [MF, fr L *achates*, fr Gk *achatēs*]

**agateware** /'agayt,weə, 'agət/ *n* pottery veined and marbled to resemble agate

**agave** /ə'gayvi/ *n* any of a N or S American genus (*Agave*) of plants of the daffodil family with spiny leaves and flowers in tall spreading flat clusters, including some cultivated for their fibre or for ornament [NL *Agave*, genus name, fr L, a daughter of Cadmus in mythology, fr Gk *Agauē*]

**agaze** /ə'gayz/ *adj* gazing

¹**age** /ayj/ *n* **1a(1)** the length of an existence measured from the beginning to any given time ⟨*a boy 10 years of ~*⟩ **a(2)** the length of time that an individual or species lives; a lifetime **b** the time of life at which some particular qualification, power, or capacity arises ⟨*the voting ~ is 18*⟩ **c** a stage of life ⟨*the seven ~s of man*⟩ **d** feebleness or infirmity resulting from advanced age ⟨*eyes dim with ~*⟩ **2a** the period contemporary

with a person's lifetime ⟨*leading poet of his ~*⟩ **b** a generation ⟨*the ~s to come*⟩ **3** a period of time dominated by a central figure or prominent feature ⟨*the ~ of Pericles*⟩: e g **3a** a period in history or human progress ⟨*the steam ~*⟩ ⟨*the ~ of exploration*⟩ **b** a cultural period marked by the prominence of a particular item ⟨*entering the atomic ~*⟩ **c** a division of geological time that is usu shorter than an epoch **4** an individual's development, esp in a specified area, that is measured in terms of the years required for like development of an average individual ⟨*an emotional ~ of eight*⟩ **5** *informal* a long time – usu pl ⟨*haven't seen him for ~*s⟩ [ME, fr OF *aage*, fr (assumed) VL *aetaticum*, fr L *aetat-, aetas*, fr *aevum* lifetime – more at AYE] – **of age** having legal adult status

²**age** *vb* **aging, ageing** *vi* **1** to become old; show the effects or the characteristics of increasing age ⟨*he's ~d terribly since you last saw him*⟩ **2** to become mellow or mature; *esp* to ripen ⟨*this cheese has ~d for nearly two years*⟩ ~ *vt* **1** to cause to seem old, esp prematurely ⟨*illness has ~d him*⟩ **2** to bring to a state fit for use or to maturity

**-age** /-ij/ *suffix* (→ *n*) **1** aggregate or collection of ⟨*baggage*⟩ ⟨*acreage*⟩ **2a** action or process of ⟨*haulage*⟩ **b** cumulative result of ⟨*breakage*⟩ ⟨*spillage*⟩ **c** rate or amount of ⟨*dosage*⟩ **3** house or place of ⟨*orphanage*⟩ **4** condition or rank of ⟨*bondage*⟩ ⟨*peerage*⟩ **5** fee or charge for ⟨*postage*⟩ ⟨*wharfage*⟩ [ME, fr OF, fr L *-aticum*]

**aged** /'ayjid; *sense 1b&c* ayjd/ *adj* **1** grown old: e g **1a** of an advanced age **b** having attained a specified age ⟨*a man ~ 40 years*⟩ **c** of a geographic feature, *esp a river bed* well advanced towards reduction to BASELEVEL (lowest land level produced by erosion) **2** typical of old age ⟨*his ~ steps*⟩ **synonyms** see ¹OLD **antonym** youthful – **agedness** *n*

'**age-,group** *n* a segment of a population that is of approximately the same age or is within a specified range of ages

**ageism** /'ay,jiz(ə)m/ *n* discrimination on grounds of age, esp of advanced age – **ageist** *adj or n*

**ageless** /'ayjlis/ *adj* **1** never growing old or showing the effects of age **2** timeless, eternal ⟨*~ truths*⟩ – **agelessly** *adv*, **agelessness** *n*

**agen** /ə'gen/ *adv, dial* again

**agency** /'ayjənsi/ *n* **1** a power or force through which a result is achieved; instrumentality ⟨*communicated through the ~ of his ambassador*⟩ **2** the function of an agent or representative **3a** an establishment that does business for another ⟨*an advertising ~*⟩ ⟨*an estate ~*⟩ **b** the headquarters or place of business of an agent or representative **4** an administrative division (e g of the United Nations)

**agenda** /ə'jendə/ *n* **1** a list of items to be discussed or business to be transacted (e g at a meeting) **2** a plan of procedure; a programme [L, pl of *agendum*, neut of *agendus*, gerundive of *agere*] – **agendaless** *adj*

    **usage** Although **agenda** is a Latin plural, it is now always treated as a singular noun ⟨*this long* **agenda**⟩. One can speak of any of its parts as ⟨*an item on the* **agenda**⟩, rather than using the Latin singular *agendum*.

**agene** /'ay,jeen/ *n* a chemical compound consisting of nitrogen with three chlorine atoms [fr *Agene*, a trademark]

**agenesis** /ay'jenəsis/ *n* lack or failure of development (e g of a body part) [NL, fr ²*a-* + *genesis*]

**agent** /'ayjənt/ *n* **1a** the producer of an effect; the active or efficient cause **b** a chemically, physically, or biologically active substance **2a** one who or that which acts or exerts power as contrasted with one who or that which is acted on – compare PATIENT **b** *linguistics* a person or thing (e g *tiger* in "He was eaten by a tiger") that performs an action, esp without being a grammatical subject **3** a person who acts for or in the place of another by authority from him/her: e g **3a** a representative or emissary of a government ⟨*a secret ~*⟩ **b** a paid worker for a British political party ⟨*an election ~*⟩ **c(1)** a business representative **c(2)** one who carries out business transactions on behalf of a client – compare TRAVEL AGENT **d** one employed by or controlling an agency ⟨*my literary ~*⟩ [ME, fr ML *agent-, agens*, fr L, prp of *agere* to drive, lead, act, do; akin to ON *aka* to travel in a vehicle, Gk *agein* to drive, lead]

**agentive** /'ayjəntiv/, **agential** /ay'jensh(ə)l/ *adj* of or being a linguistic form indicating the doer of an action ⟨*the suffix -er in singer is ~*⟩ – **agentive** *n*

**agent provocateur** /ˌahzhonh provokə'tuh, ˌayjənt (*Fr* aʒɑ provɔkatœːr)/ *n, pl* **agents provocateurs** /~/ a person employed to associate with suspected people and, by pretended sympathy with their aims, to incite them to some open action that will make them liable to punishment [Fr, lit., provoking agent]

**age of consent** *n* the age at which one is legally allowed to give consent; *specif* that at which a girl may legally consent to sexual intercourse

**age of reason** *n* **1** a period characterized by belief in the use of reason and a willingness to reject those social, religious, and philosophical beliefs not justifiable by reason; *esp, often cap A&R* the 18th century in Europe – compare ENLIGHTENMENT 2 **2** the time of life when one begins to be able to distinguish right from wrong

**,age-'old** *adj* having existed for ages; ancient

**ageratum** /,ajə'rahtəm, -'raytəm/ *n, pl* **ageratums** (any of) a large genus (*Ageratum*) of tropical American plants of the daisy family often cultivated for their small showy heads of blue or white flowers [NL, genus name, fr Gk *agēratos* ageless, fr *a-* + *gēras* old age – more at CORN]

**Aggada** /ə'gahdə/ *n* HAGGADAH (Jewish lore or ritual)

**aggiornamento** /ə,jawnə'mentoh/ *n, pl* **aggiornamentos** a bringing up to date; *specif* the modernization of the Roman Catholic church [It, fr *aggiornare* to bring up to date, fr *a* to (fr L *ad-*) + *giorno* day, fr LL *diurnum* day – more at JOURNEY]

**¹agglomerate** /ə'glomərayt/ *vb* to gather into a mass or disorderly cluster [L *agglomeratus*, pp of *agglomerare* to heap up, join, fr *ad-* + *glomer-, glomus* ball]

**²agglomerate** /ə'glomərət/ *adj* gathered into a ball, mass, or cluster *specif* clustered or growing together but not joined ⟨*an ~ flower head*⟩

**³agglomerate** /ə'glomərət/ *n* **1** a jumbled mass or collection **2** a rock composed of irregular volcanic fragments

**agglomeration** /ə,glomə'raysh(ə)n/ *n* **1** the action or process of collecting in a mass **2** a mass or cluster of disparate elements ⟨*urban ~s knit together by the new railways – TLS*⟩ – **agglomerative** *adj*

**agglutinate** /ə'gloohti,nayt/ *vt* **1** to cause to stick; fasten together (as if) with glue **2** *linguistics* to combine into a compound; attach to a base as an affix **3** *physiology* to cause (eg blood cells or bacteria) to undergo agglutination ~ *vi* **1** to unite or combine together **2** to form words by agglutination [L *agglutinatus*, pp of *agglutinare* to glue to, fr *ad-* + *glutinare* to glue, fr *glutin-, gluten* glue – more at GLUTEN] – **agglutinability** *n*

**agglutination** /ə,gloohti'naysh(ə)n/ *n* **1a** the action or process of agglutinating; sticking together **b** the state of being thus united **2** a mass or group formed by the adherence of separate elements **3** the formation of words by putting together constituents of which each expresses a single definite meaning and is relatively fixed in form – compare POLYSYNTHETIC **4** a reaction in which particles (eg RED BLOOD CELLS or bacteria) suspended in a liquid collect into clumps and which occurs esp as a response to a specific antibody

**agglutinative** /ə'gloohtinətiv/ *adj* **1** adhesive **2** **agglutinative, agglutinate** characterized by agglutination

**agglutinin** /ə'gloohtinin/ *n* a substance (eg an antibody) producing agglutination [ISV *agglutin*ation + *-in*]

**agglutinogen** /ə,glooh'tinəjən/ *n* an ANTIGEN (substance that generates antibodies) whose presence results in the formation of an agglutinin [*agglutin*in + *-o-* + *-gen*] – **agglutinogenic** *adj*

**aggrade** /ə'grayd/ *vt* to fill with loose eroded material ⟨*silt has ~d the river bed*⟩ [*ad-* + *grade*] – **aggradation** *n*

**aggrand·ize, -ise** /ə'grandiez, 'agrəndiez/ *vt* **1** to increase the size of **2** to give a false air of greatness to; praise highly ⟨*~d the one and disparaged the other*⟩ **3** to enhance the power, wealth, position, or reputation of ⟨*exploited the situation to ~ himself*⟩ [Fr *agrandiss-*, stem of *agrandir*, fr *a-* (fr L *ad-*) + *grandir* to increase, fr L *grandire*, fr *grandis* great] – **aggrandizement** *n*

**aggravate** /'agrəvayt/ *vt* **1** to make worse or more severe; intensify unpleasantly ⟨*problems have been ~d by neglect*⟩ **2a** to annoy, irritate – disapproved of by some speakers **b** to produce inflammation in [L *aggravatus*, pp of *aggravare* to make heavier, fr *ad-* + *gravare* to burden, fr *gravis* heavy – more at GRIEVE] – **aggravation** *n*

*usage* Though disapproved of by some people, sense 2a has been firmly established in English since the early 17th century ⟨*to aggravate her parents* – Samuel Richardson⟩. *synonyms* see INTENSIFY, IRRITATE *antonyms* mitigate, alleviate

**¹aggregate** /'agrigət/ *adj* formed by the collection of units or particles into a body, mass, or amount: eg **a** *of a flower* clustered in a dense mass or head **b** *of a fruit* (eg a raspberry) formed from the several OVARIES (female reproductive structures) of a single flower **c** composed of closely packed mineral crystals of one or more kinds or of mineral rock fragments **d** taking all units as a whole; total ⟨*~ earnings*⟩ ⟨*~ sales*⟩ [ME *aggregat*, fr L *aggregatus*, pp of *aggregare* to add to, fr *ad-* + *greg-, grex* flock – more at GREGARIOUS]

**²aggregate** /'agri,gayt/ *vt* **1** to bring together into a mass or whole **2** to amount to (a specified total) – **aggregative** *adj*, **aggregation** *n*, **aggregational** *adj*

**³aggregate** /'agrigət/ *n* **1** a mass of loosely associated parts; an assemblage **2** the whole amount; SUM TOTAL **3a** an aggregate rock **b** any of several hard materials (eg sand, gravel, or slag) used for mixing with cement to make concrete, mortar, or plaster **c** a clustered mass of individual particles of various shapes and sizes that is considered to be the basic structural unit of soil **4** *maths* SET 19 – **in the aggregate** considered as a whole; collectively

**aggress** /ə'gres/ *vi* to commit aggression; act aggressively

**aggression** /ə'gresh(ə)n/ *n* **1** a hostile attack or encroachment, esp when intended to dominate unjustly **2** attack, encroachment; *esp* unprovoked violation by one country of the territorial integrity of another **3** *psychology* hostile, injurious, or destructive behaviour or outlook [L *aggression-, aggressio*, fr *aggressus*, pp of *aggredi* to attack, fr *ad-* + *gradi* to step, go – more at GRADE] – **aggressor** *n*

**aggressive** /ə'gresiv/ *adj* **1a** tending towards or practising aggression ⟨*an ~ foreign policy*⟩ **b** ready to attack ⟨*an ~ fighter*⟩ **2a** marked by driving forceful energy and enterprise ⟨*an ~ salesman*⟩ **b** marked by obtrusive energy and swagger – **aggressively** *adv*, **aggressiveness** *n*

**aggrieve** /ə'greev/ *vt* **1** to give pain or trouble to; distress **2** to inflict injury on □ usu in passive [ME *agreven*, fr MF *agrever*, fr L *aggravare* to make heavier]

**aggrieved** /ə'greevd/ *adj* **1** showing or expressing resentment; hurt ⟨*an ~ yell*⟩ **2** suffering from an infringement or denial of legal rights ⟨*~ minority groups*⟩ – **aggrievedly** *adv*

**aggro** /'agroh/ *n, chiefly Br informal* **1** provocation, hostility **2** deliberate aggression or violence ⟨*he's always full of ~ on Monday mornings*⟩ [by shortening & alter. fr *aggravation* or *aggression*]

**Aghan** /ə'gahn/ *n* – see MONTH table [Hindi, fr Skt *Agrahāyaṇa*]

**aghast** /ə'gahst/ *adj* suddenly struck with terror, amazement, or horror; shocked ⟨*stood by ~ as the building collapsed*⟩ [ME *agast*, fr pp of *agasten* to frighten, fr *a-* (perfective prefix) + *gasten* to frighten, fr *gast, gost* ghost]

**agile** /'ajiel/ *adj* **1** quick, easy, and graceful in movement **2** mentally quick and resourceful *synonyms* see NIMBLE *antonyms* awkward, clumsy [MF, fr L *agilis*, fr *agere* to drive, act – more at AGENT] – **agilely** *adv*, **agility** *n*

**agin** /ə'gin/ *prep, dial Br* against; *esp* stubbornly or unreasonably opposed to ⟨*~ everything they don't understand*⟩

**aging** /'ayjing/ *pres part of* AGE

**aginner** /ə'ginə/ *n, Br informal* one who opposes change [*agin* + *-er*]

**agio** /,ajoh, 'ajioh, 'ahjoh/ *n, pl* **agios** a premium or percentage paid for the exchange of one currency for another; *also* the premium or discount on foreign bills of exchange [It, perh alter. of It dial. *lajjë*, fr MGk *allagion* exchange, fr Gk *allagē* exchange, fr *allos* other – more at ELSE]

**agiotage** /'ajətij/ *n* **1** the business of money exchange **2** STOCKJOBBING (dealing as a middleman between stockbrokers) **3** speculative buying or selling of shares [Fr, fr *agioter* to practise stockjobbing, fr *agio* stockjobbing, fr It]

**agistment** /ə'jistmənt/ *n* pastureland available for rent; *also* the practice of sending or receiving livestock to be pastured on land rented for the purpose [MF *agistement*, fr *agister* to take in livestock for payment, fr *a-* (fr L *ad-*) + *gister* to give lodging, deriv of L *jacēre* to lie – more at ADJACENT]

**agitate** /'ajitayt/ *vt* **1a** to give rhythmic motion to ⟨*washing machine ~s the clothes*⟩ **b** to move with irregular, rapid, or violent action ⟨*tremors ~d his frame*⟩ **2** to excite and often trouble the mind or feelings of; disturb **3** to discuss (a question or project) excitedly and earnestly ~ *vi* to work to arouse public feeling for or against a cause ⟨*~d for better schools*⟩ *synonyms* see ¹SHAKE [L *agitatus*, pp of *agitare*, freq of *agere* to drive – more at AGENT] – **agitatedly** *adv*, **agitation** *n*, **agitational** *adj*

**agitato** /ˌaji'tahtoh, ˌahji-/ *adv or adj* in a restless and agitated manner – used as a TEMPO (speed) direction in music [It, lit., agitated, fr L *agitatus*]

**agitator** /'ajitaytə/ *n* one who or that which agitates: e g a one who stirs up public feeling on controversial issues ⟨*political* ~s⟩ **b** a device or apparatus for stirring or shaking

**agitprop** /'ajit,prop, ˌ--'-/ *n* political propaganda, esp procommunist, through literature, drama, music, art, etc ⟨~ *drama*⟩ [Russ, office of agitation and propaganda, fr *agitatsiya* agitation + *prop*aganda] – **agitprop** *adj*

**aglare** /ə'gleə/ *adj* glaring ⟨*his eyes* ~ *with fury*⟩

**agleam** /ə'gleem/ *adj* gleaming

**aglet** /'aglət/ *n* **1** an often metal tag attached to the end of a lace, cord, or ribbon **2** any of various ornamental studs, cords, or pins worn on clothing [ME, fr MF *aguillette, aiguillette*, dim. of *aguille, aiguille* needle, fr LL *acicula, acucula* ornamental pin, dim. of L *acus* needle, pin – more at ACUTE]

**agley** /ə'glay, ə'glee/ *adv, chiefly Scot* awry, wrong ⟨*the best-laid schemes o' mice an' men gang aft* ~ – Robert Burns⟩ [Sc, lit., squintingly, fr ¹*a*- + *gley* to squint, fr ME (northern) *gleyen*]

**aglimmer** /ə'glimə/ *adj* glimmering

**aglitter** /ə'glitə/ *adj* glittering

**aglow** /ə'gloh/ *adj* glowing

**aglucone** /ə'gloohkohn/, **aglucon** /ə'gloohkon/ *n* an aglycone; *esp* one combined with glucose in a GLUCOSIDE (sugar derivative containing glucose)

**aglycone** /ə'gliekohn/, **aglycon** /ə'gliekon/ *n* a PHENOL, alcohol, or similar chemical compound that is combined with a sugar to form a GLYCOSIDE (sugar derivative) [ISV *a*- (fr Gk *ha-, a-* together) + *glyc*- + *-one, -on*]

**AGM** *n* an annual general meeting (e g of a society or company)

**agnail** /'agnayl/ *n* a sore or inflammation about a fingernail or toenail; *also* a hangnail [ME, corn on the foot or toe, fr OE *angnægl*, fr *ang*- (akin to *enge* tight, painful) + *nægl* metal nail – more at ANGER, NAIL]

¹**agnate** /'agnayt/ *n* a relative whose kinship is traceable exclusively through males; *broadly* any paternal kinsman – compare COGNATE [L *agnatus*, fr pp of *agnasci* to be born in addition to, fr *ad*- + *nasci* to be born – more at NATION]

²**agnate** *adj* **1** related through male descent or on the father's side **2** allied, akin – **agnatic** *adj*, **agnatically** *adv*, **agnation** *n*

**agnosia** /ag'nohzh(y)ə/ *n* disturbance of perception caused esp by faulty functioning of nerves [NL, fr Gk *agnōsia* ignorance, fr *a*- ²*a*- + *gnōsis* knowledge]

¹**agnostic** /ag'nostik, əg-/ *n* one who holds the view that any ultimate reality is unknown and probably unknowable; *broadly* one who doubts the existence of God – compare ATHEIST [modif of Gk *agnōstos* unknown, unknowable, fr *a*- + *gnōstos* known, fr *gignōskein* to know – more at KNOW] – **agnosticism** *n*

²**agnostic** *adj* **1** of or being an agnostic or the beliefs of agnostics **2** noncommittal, undogmatic

**Agnus Dei** /ˌagnəs 'day·ee/ *n* a liturgical prayer addressed to Christ as Saviour, often set to music ⟨*the* ~ *from Bach's B Minor Mass*⟩ [ME, fr LL, lamb of God; fr its opening words]

**ago** /ə'goh/ *adj or adv* earlier than now – not used with tenses formed with *to have* ⟨*how long* ~ *did he leave?*⟩ [ME *agon, ago*, fr pp of *agon* to pass away, fr OE *āgān*, fr *ā*- (perfective prefix) + *gān* to go]

*usage* Some authorities recommend the use of *that* rather than *since* after ago ⟨*it is nearly 40 years ago that World War II ended*⟩.

**agog** /ə'gog/ *adj* full of intense anticipation or excitement; eager ⟨*the . . .court was* ~ *with gossip, scandal and intrigue* – TLS⟩ [MF *en gogues* in mirth]

**a-go-go** /ə 'goh goh/ *adj* of or being a discotheque or the music or dances performed there

**-agogue** /-əgog/ *comb form* (→ *n*) **1** leader; guide ⟨*ped*agogue⟩ – sometimes derog ⟨*dema*gogue⟩ **2** substance that promotes the secretion or expulsion of ⟨*emmena*gogue⟩ [deriv of Gk *agōgos*, fr *agein* to lead – more at AGENT]

**agon** /'ahgon, -'-, 'aygon/ *n* a contest, conflict; *specif* the dramatic conflict between the chief characters in a literary work [Gk *agōn*]

**agone** /ə'gon/ *adj or adv, archaic* ago

**agonic** /ə'gonik/, **agonic line** *n* an imaginary line connecting points where a compass needle always points to true as well as to MAGNETIC NORTH [Gk *agōnos* without angle, fr *a*- + *gōnia* angle – more at -GON]

**agonist** /'agənist/ *n* **1a** one who is engaged in an action (e g a

struggle) **b** a character in a literary work **2a** a muscle that is controlled by the action of another muscle (ANTAGONIST) with which it is paired **b** a chemical substance capable of combining with a RECEPTOR on the surface of a cell, esp a nerve cell, and initiating a reaction – compare ANTAGONIST [LL *agonista* competitor, fr Gk *agōnistēs*, fr *agōnizesthai* to contend, fr *agōn*; (2) back-formation fr *antagonist*]

**agonistic** /ˌagə'nistik/, **agonistical** /-kl/ *adj* **1** argumentative **2** of or being aggressive or defensive social interaction (e g fighting, fleeing, or submitting) between individuals usu of the same species – **agonistically** *adv*

**agon·ize, -ise** /'agəniez/ *vt* to cause to suffer agony; torture ~ *vi* **1** to suffer agony, torture, or anguish ⟨~s *over every decision*⟩ **2** to make a great effort

**agon·ized, -ised** /'agəniezd/ *adj* characterized by, suffering, or expressing agony

**agon·izing, -ising** /'agəniezing/ *adj* causing agony; painful ⟨*an* ~ *reappraisal of his policies*⟩ – **agonizingly** *adv*

**agony** /'agəni/ *n* **1a** intense and often prolonged pain of mind or body; anguish, torture **b** *often cap* the sufferings of Jesus in the garden of Gethsemane **c** the struggle that precedes death ⟨*his last* ~⟩ **2** a violent struggle or contest **3** a strong sudden onset (e g of mental excitement, joy, or delight) [ME *agonie*, fr LL *agonia*, fr Gk *agōnia* struggle, anguish, fr *agōn* gathering, contest for a prize, fr *agein* to lead, celebrate – more at AGENT] – **agonal** *adj*

¹**agora** /'agərə/ *n, pl* **agoras, agorae** /'agəri/ a gathering place for popular political assembly in ancient Greece; *esp* a marketplace [Gk – more at GREGARIOUS]

²**agora** /ˌagə'rah/ *n, pl* **agorot** /ˌagə'roht/ – see *shekel* at MONEY table [NHeb *ăgōrāh*, fr Heb, a small coin]

**agoraphobia** /ˌag(ə)rə'fohbi·ə/ *n* abnormal dread of being in open spaces [NL, fr Gk *agora* + NL *phobia*] – **agoraphobe** *n*, **agoraphobic** *n or adj*

**agouti** /ə'goohti/ *n, pl* **agoutis**, *esp collectively* **agouti 1** a tropical American rodent (genus *Dasyprocta* or *Myoprocta*) about the size of a rabbit **2** a colour of fur resulting from the barring of each hair in several alternate dark and light bands [Fr, fr Sp *aguti*, fr Guarani]

**agranulocyte** /ay'granyoolə,siet/ *n* any of various WHITE BLOOD CELLS that have no conspicuous granules in the CYTOPLASM (jellylike material surrounding the nucleus) – compare GRANULOCYTE, LYMPHOCYTE, MONOCYTE – **agranulocytic** *adj*

**agranulocytosis** /ay,granyoolohsie'tohsis/ *n* a serious and often fatal condition marked by severe decrease in the granule-containing cells (GRANULOCYTES) in the blood and often associated with the administration of certain drugs [NL]

**agrapha** /'agrafə/ *n pl* sayings of Jesus not in the canonical gospels but found in other early Christian writings [Gk, neut pl of *agraphos* unwritten, fr *a*- + *graphein* to write – more at CARVE]

**agraphia** /ay'grafiə/ *n* total or partial loss of the ability to write due to an injury to the brain – compare APHASIA [NL, fr ²*a*- + Gk *graphein* to write]

¹**agrarian** /ə'greəri·ən/ *adj* **1** of fields or lands or their tenure **2a** of or characteristic of farmers or agricultural life **b** organized to promote agricultural interests ⟨*an* ~ *political party* ⟩ ⟨~ *reforms*⟩ [L *agrarius*, fr *agr-, ager* field – more at ACRE]

²**agrarian** *n* a member of an agrarian party or movement

**agrarianism** /ə'greəri·ə,niz(ə)m/ *n* a social or political movement designed to bring about land reforms or to improve the economic status of farmers (e g by the redistribution of land)

**agree** /ə'gree/ *vt* **1a** to admit, concede – usu + a clause ⟨*I* ~ *that you're right*⟩ **b** to consent ⟨~d *to go away*⟩ **2** to bring into harmony ⟨~ *the totals with the estimate*⟩ **3** *chiefly Br* to come to terms on, typically after discussion; plan by agreement ⟨*the following articles were* ~d – Sir Winston Churchill⟩ ~ *vi* **1** to give assent; accede – often + *to* ⟨~ *to your proposal*⟩ **2a** to be of one mind; share the same opinion ⟨*can't* ~ *in our choice*⟩ – often + *with* ⟨*I* ~ *with you*⟩ **b** to get along together **c** to come to terms; decide together ⟨~ *on blue for the kitchen*⟩ **3a** to be similar; correspond ⟨*both copies* ~⟩ **b** to be consistent ⟨*the story* ~s *with the facts*⟩ **4** to be compatible or healthful; suit the constitution – + *with* ⟨*onions don't* ~ *with me*⟩ **5** to correspond in grammatical gender, number, case, or person – often + *with*; see "Ten Vexed Points" [ME *agreen*, fr MF *agreer*, fr *a-* (fr L *ad-*) + *gre* will, pleasure, fr L *gratum*, neut of *gratus* pleasing, agreeable – more at GRACE]

*synonyms* Agree, conform, correspond, coincide, accord, harmonize: agree may express slight or great similarity. It has the widest range of meanings and may stand in for the other terms. **Conform** suggests close resemblance to something else in form, ideas, or basic characteristics ⟨*this poem* conforms *to the Romantic tradition*⟩. **Correspond** is used when two otherwise disparate things match in some particular, either because they are analogous or proportionate, or because they belong to the same class ⟨*a bird's wing* corresponds *to the human arm*⟩ ⟨*the length of an essay does not always* correspond *to the time it takes to write*⟩. Things which **coincide** match exactly ⟨*her arrival* coincided *with my departure*⟩⟨*his wishes* coincided *with those of his parents*⟩. **Accord** suggests harmony and lack of friction in a relationship or association ⟨*their sentiments* accorded *perfectly with those of the ruling party*⟩. When things **harmonize**, they relate so well to each other in spite of their differences that they produce a pleasant or satisfying result ⟨*the greyness of the landscape* harmonized *with her inmost thoughts*⟩.

*usage* The chiefly British use of **agree** as a transitive verb, as in *vt* 3, though still disapproved of by some writers on usage, is now well established in English. See also ¹ASSENT. *antonyms* protest, differ (from)

**agreeable** /ə'gree-əbl/ *adj* 1 pleasing to the mind or senses; to one's liking ⟨*an* ~ *companion*⟩ ⟨*an* ~ *smell*⟩ 2 willing to agree or consent 3 in harmony; consonant *antonyms* disagreeable, unpleasant – **agreeableness** *n*, **agreeably** *adv*

**agreed** /ə'greed/ *adj* 1 arranged by consent ⟨*the* ~ *time*⟩ 2 of the joint opinion ⟨*in this we are* ~⟩

**agreed syllabus** *n* a nondenominational form of religious education

**agreement** /ə'greemənt/ *n* 1a the act or fact of agreeing b harmony of opinion or feeling c correspondence ⟨~ *between the data and the hypothesis*⟩ 2a an arrangement as to a course of action b a compact, treaty 3a a legally binding common intention expressed in spoken words or a written document b COLLECTIVE AGREEMENT]

**agrement, agrément** /ə'graymonh/ *n* 1 an agreeable quality or circumstance 2 a musical ornament; GRACE NOTE 3 acceptance by a state of the diplomatic representative of another [Fr *agrément* pleasure, ornament, approval, fr MF *agrement*, fr *agreer*

**agrestic** /ə'grestik/ *adj* 1 rustic 2 uncouth [L *agrestis*, lit., of a field, fr *agr-, ager* field]

**agribusiness** /'agri,biznis/ *n* all the industries involved in farming [*agriculture* + *business*]

**agriculture** /'agri,kulchə/ *n* the theory and practice of cultivating the soil, producing crops, and raising livestock, and in varying degrees the preparation of these products for sale [Fr, fr L *agricultura*, fr *agr-, ager* field + *cultura* cultivation – more at ACRE, CULTURE] – **agricultural** *adj*, **agriculturally** *adv*, **agriculturist, agriculturalist** *n*

**agrimony** /'agrimoni/ *n* a common yellow-flowered plant (genus *Agrimonia*) of the rose family, with flowers in spikes and fruits like burs; *also* a similar or related plant [ME, fr MF & L; MF *aigremoine*, fr L *agrimonia*, MS var of *argemonia*, fr Gk *argemōnē*]

**agro-** *comb form* 1 fields; soil; agriculture ⟨*agrology*⟩ 2 agricultural and ⟨*agro-industrial*⟩ [Fr, fr Gk, fr *agros* field – more at ACRE]

**agrobiology** /,agrohbie'olǝji/ *n* a branch of biology dealing with plant nutrition and growth and crop production in relation to soil management – **agrobiologic, agrobiological** *adj*, **agrobiologically** *adv*

**agronomy** /ə'gronəmi/ *n* a branch of agriculture dealing with field-crop production and soil management [prob fr Fr *agronomie*, fr *agro-* + *-nomie* -nomy] – **agronomist** *n*, **agronomic, agronomical** *adj*, **agronomically** *adv*

**aground** /ə'grownd/ *adv or adj* 1 on or onto the shore or the bottom of a body of water ⟨*the ship ran* ~⟩ 2 on the ground ⟨*planes aloft and* ~⟩

**ague** /'aygyooh/ *n* 1 a fever (e g malaria) marked by regularly recurring attacks of chills, fever, and sweating 2 a fit of shivering [ME, fr MF *aguë*, fr ML (*febris*) *acuta*, lit., sharp fever, fr L, fem of *acutus* sharp – more at ACUTE] – **aguish** *adj*

**ah** /ah *often prolonged*/ *interj* 1 – used to express delight, relief, regret, or contempt 2 *dial Br* – used to express agreement – **ah** *vi*

**aha** /ah'hah/ *interj* – used to express surprise, triumph, derision, or amused discovery

**ahead** /ə'hed/ *adv or adj* 1a in a forward direction; forwards b in front ⟨*the road* ~⟩ 2 in, into, or for the future ⟨*plan* ~⟩ ⟨*the years* ~⟩ 3 in or towards a better position ⟨*get* ~ *of the rest*⟩ – **ahead of** 1 in front or advance of ⟨*ahead of his time*⟩ 2 better than

**ahem** /ə'həm/ *interj* – used esp to attract attention or express mild disapproval

**ahimsa** /ə'himsah/ *n* the Hindu and Buddhist doctrine of refraining from harming any living being [Skt *ahiṃsā* noninjury]

**ahistorical** /,ayhi'storikl/, **ahistoric** /-storik/ *adj* without regard to history or tradition; concerned only with the present ⟨*the* ~ *attitudes of the radicals*⟩

**'A-ho,rizon** /ay/ *n* the surface usu dark-coloured layer of soil consisting of mineral material mixed with humus

**ahoy** /ə'hoy/ *interj* – used chiefly by seamen as a greeting or warning ⟨*ship* ~⟩ [*a-* (as in *aha*) + *hoy*, interj, a cry for attention]

**Ahriman** /'ahrimən/ *n* Ahura Mazda's antagonist who is a spirit of darkness and evil in Zoroastrianism [Per, modif of Avestan *aŋrō mainyuš* hostile spirit]

**Ahura Mazda** /ə,hooərə 'mazdə, ,ah·hooərə/ *n* the Supreme Being represented as a deity of goodness and light in Zoroastrianism [Avestan *Ahuramazda*, lit., wise god]

**ai** /ie, ah'ee/ *n* THREE-TOED SLOTH [Pg *ai* or Sp *ai*, fr Tupi *ai*]

**aiblins** /'ayblinz/ *adv, chiefly Scot* perhaps [*able* + *-lings, -lins -lings*]

**¹aid** /ayd/ *vt* 1 to afford assistance to 2 to bring about the accomplishment of; facilitate ⟨~ *his recovery*⟩ ~ *vi* to be of assistance *synonyms* see HELP¹ *antonym* hinder [ME *eyden*, fr MF *aider*, fr L *adjutare*, fr *adjutus*, pp of *adjuvare*, fr *ad-* + *juvare* to help] – **aider** *n*

**²aid** *n* 1 a subsidy granted to the king by the English parliament until the 18th century for a specific purpose 2a the act of helping b help given; assistance; *specif* tangible means of assistance (e g money or supplies) 3a a helper – compare AIDE b something that helps; an assisting device ⟨*an* ~ *to understanding*⟩ ⟨*a visual* ~⟩; *specif* HEARING AID 4 a tribute paid by a vassal to his/her lord 5 a signal or means (e g voice, whip, or leg pressure) that a rider uses to convey his/her instructions to the horse and that the horse is taught to obey – **in aid of** 1 in order to aid; for the use of ⟨*sold her jewels in aid of charity*⟩ 2 *Br informal* for the purpose of ⟨*what's this in aid of?*⟩

**aide** /ayd, ed/ *n* an assistant; *esp, chiefly NAm* an aide-de-camp [short for *aide-de-camp*]

**,aide-de-'camp** /də 'kamp/ *n, pl* **aides-de-camp** /~/ an officer in the armed forces acting as a confidential personal assistant to a senior officer [Fr *aide de camp*, lit., camp assistant]

**aided school** /'aydid/ *n* a VOLUNTARY SCHOOL whose managers retain control over religious instruction and over appointments of teachers and are responsible for part of the cost both of structural maintenance and of obligatory structural improvements

**aide-mémoire** /,ayd mem'wah, ed/ *n, pl* **aides-mémoire** /~/ 1 an aid to the memory (e g a note or sketch) 2 a written summary of a proposed agreement or communication; a memorandum [Fr, fr *aider* to aid + *mémoire* memory]

**aigrette** /ay'gret/ *n* 1 a spray of feathers (e g of the egret) that ornaments the head 2 a spray of gems worn on a hat or in the hair 3 a deep-fried puff of choux pastry [Fr – more at EGRET]

**aiguille** /ay'gweel, '--/ *n* a sharp-pointed pinnacle of rock [Fr, lit., needle – more at AGLET]

**aiguillette** /,aygwi'let/ *n* a tag, cord, or pendant; *specif* a shoulder cord worn on certain military uniforms – compare FOURRAGÈRE [Fr – more at AGLET]

**aikido** /ay'keedoh, ie-/ *n* a classical Japanese MARTIAL ART employing locks and holds and using nonresistance to cause an opponent's own momentum to work against him/her [Jap *aikidō*, fr *ai-* together, mutual + *ki* spirit + *dō* art]

**ail** /ayl/ *vt* to give physical or emotional pain, discomfort, or trouble to ~ *vi* to have something the matter; *esp* to be unwell [ME *eilen*, fr OE *eglan*; akin to MLG *egelen* to annoy]

**ailanthus** /ay'lanthəs, ie-/ *n* any of a small Asiatic genus (*Ailanthus*, family Simaroubaceae) of chiefly tropical trees with unpleasant-smelling greenish flowers – compare TREE OF HEAVEN [NL, genus name, fr Amboinese *ai lanto*, lit., tree (of) heaven]

**aileron** /,ayləron, -rən/ *n* a movable control surface of an aircraft wing or a movable aerofoil external to the wing at the trailing edge for giving a rolling motion and thus providing lateral control [Fr, fr dim. of *aile* wing – more at AISLE] – **aileroned** *adj*

**ailment** /'aylmənt/ *n* a bodily disorder or long-lasting disease

**ailurophile** /ay'looərə,fiel, ie-, -'lyooə-/ *n* a cat fancier; a lover of cats [Gk *ailouros* cat]

**ailurophobe** /ay'looərə,fohb, ie-, -'lyooə-/ *n* one who hates or fears cats – **ailurophobia** *n*

¹**aim** /aym/ *vi* **1** to direct a course; *specif* to point a weapon at an object **2** to channel one's efforts; aspire ⟨~ *at promotion*⟩ ⟨~ *high*⟩ **3** to have the intention; mean ⟨~s *to marry a duke*⟩ ~ *vt* **1** to direct or point (eg a weapon or missile) at a target **2** to direct at or towards a specified goal; intend ⟨*shows* ~ed *at children*⟩ [ME *aimen*, fr MF *aesmer* & *esmer;* MF *aesmer*, fr OF, fr *a-* (fr L *ad-*) + *esmer* to estimate, fr L *aestimare*] – **aimer** *n*

²**aim** *n* **1a** the pointing of a weapon at a mark, object, or target **b** the ability to hit a target ⟨*his* ~ *was deadly*⟩ **c** a weapon's accuracy or effectiveness **2** a clearly directed intention or purpose – **aimless** *adj*, **aimlessly** *adv*, **aimlessness** *n*

**ain** /ayn/ *adj, Scot* own [prob fr ON *eiginn*]

**ain't** /aynt/ **1** *nonstandard* **1a** are not **b** is not **c** am not **2** *substandard* **2a** have not **b** has not

usage The humorous use of **ain't**, as in ⟨things **ain't** what they used to be⟩, is the only one now recognized as acceptable in educated British usage. **Ain't** *I* meaning "Am I not" is used by educated speakers of certain American dialects who wish to avoid the alternative **Aren't** *I*; but all senses of **ain't** should always be avoided in formal writing

**Ainu** /'ienooh/ *n, pl* **Ainus,** *esp collectively* **Ainu 1** (a member of) a hairy aboriginal people of N Japan who have retained many customs and beliefs to the present day **2** the language of the Ainu [Ainu, lit., man]

**aïoli** /ie'ohli/ *n* a golden-coloured garlic mayonnaise (eg for seafood) [Fr, fr Prov, fr *ai* garlic + *oli* oil]

¹**air** /eə/ *n* **1a** the mixture of invisible odourless tasteless gases, containing esp nitrogen and oxygen, that surrounds the earth **b** a light breeze **2a** empty unconfined space ⟨*jumped into the* ~⟩ – compare OPEN AIR **b** nothingness ⟨*vanished into thin* ~⟩ **3** COMPRESSED AIR **4a(1)** aircraft ⟨*go by* ~⟩ **a(2)** aviation ⟨~ *safety*⟩ ⟨~ *rights*⟩ **b** the hypothetical medium of transmission of radio waves; *also* radio, television ⟨*went on the* ~⟩ **5a** the look, appearance, or bearing of a person; demeanour ⟨*an* ~ *of dignity*⟩ **b** *pl* an artificial or affected manner; haughtiness ⟨*to put on* ~s⟩ **c** any of various complicated movements of advanced dressage **d** outward appearance of a thing ⟨*an* ~ *of luxury*⟩ **e** a surrounding or pervading influence; an atmosphere ⟨*an* ~ *of mystery*⟩ **6a** an Elizabethan or Jacobean accompanied song or melody, usu repeating the same music for successive stanzas **b** a tune, melody [ME, fr OF, fr L *aer*, fr Gk *aēr;* (5) Fr, fr OF; (6) prob trans of It *aria*, modif of L *aer*] – **in the air 1** not yet settled; uncertain **2** being generally spread round or hinted at ⟨*rumours* in the air *that he will be promoted*⟩; see also CLEAR the air

²**air** *vt* **1** to expose to the air for drying, freshening, etc; ventilate **2** to expose to public view or bring to public notice **3** to transmit by radio or television ⟨~ *a programme*⟩ **4** *chiefly Br* to expose to heat so as to warm or finish drying ⟨~ *the sheets round the fire*⟩ ~ *vi* to become exposed to the open air

**air base** *n* a base of operations for military aircraft

**air bed** *n, chiefly Br* an inflatable mattress used esp for floating on water or for sleeping on

**air bladder** *n* a pouch containing gas, esp air; *esp* an organ present in most BONY FISHES that functions esp in the control of buoyancy

**airborne** /'eə,bawn/ *adj* supported or transported by air

**air brake** *n* **1** a brake operated by a piston pressurized by compressed air **2** a movable surface that may be projected into the airstream for slowing an aircraft

**air brick** *n* a building brick or brick-sized metal box perforated to allow ventilation

**airbrush** /'eə,brush/ *n* an atomizer for spraying paint – **airbrush** *vt*

**airburst** /'eə,buhst/ *n* the explosion of a shell, bomb, or missile in the air

**airbus** /'eə,bus/ *n* a subsonic jet passenger aeroplane designed for short intercity flights

**air chief marshal** *n* – see MILITARY RANKS table

**air commodore** *n* – see MILITARY RANKS table

**air-con·dition** *vt* to equip (eg a building) with an apparatus for cleaning air and controlling its humidity and temperature; *also* to subject (air) to these processes [back-formation fr *air conditioning*] – **air conditioner** *n*

'**air-cool** *vt* to cool the cylinders of (an INTERNAL-COMBUSTION ENGINE) directly by air without the use of an intermediate medium (eg water) [back-formation fr *air-cooled* & *air cooling*]

**aircraft** /'eə,krahft/ *n, pl* **aircraft** a weight-carrying structure that can travel through the air and is supported either by its own buoyancy or by the dynamic action of the air against its surfaces

**aircraft carrier** *n* a warship designed so that aircraft can be operated from it

**aircraftman** /'eə,krahftmən/, *fem* **aircraftwoman** /-,woomən/ *n* – see MILITARY RANKS table

**aircrew** /'eə,krooh/ *n* the crew manning an aeroplane

**air-cushion vehicle** *n, chiefly NAm* a hovercraft

**airdrop** /'eə,drop/ *n* delivery of cargo or personnel by parachute from an aircraft in flight – **air-drop** *vt*, **air-droppable** *adj*

'**air-,dry** *adj* so dry that no further moisture is given up on exposure to air

**Airedale** /'eə,dayl/, **Airedale terrier** *n* (any of) a breed of large terriers with a hard wiry coat that is dark on the back and sides and tan elsewhere [*Airedale*, district in Yorkshire, England]

**airer** /'eərə/ *n* one who or that which airs; *specif, Br* a freestanding usu collapsible framework for airing or drying clothes and linen; a clotheshorse

**airfare** /'eə,feə/ *n* a fare paid to enable one to travel on an aircraft

**airfield** /'eə,feeld/ *n* an area of land that is maintained for the landing and takeoff of aircraft and that usu has facilities for their sheltering and maintenance

**airflow** /'eə,floh/ *n* the motion of air round a moving object (eg an aeroplane in flight) or a stationary one (eg in wind)

**airfoil** /'eə,foyl/ *n, chiefly NAm* an aerofoil

**air force** *n* the branch of a country's armed forces for air warfare

**airframe** /'eə,fraym/ *n* the structure of an aircraft or missile, without the power plant [*aircraft* + *frame*]

**airfreight** /'eə,frayt/ *n* (the charge for) freight transport by air – **airfreight** *vb*

**airglow** /'eə,gloh/ *n* light that is observed, esp during the night, that originates in the high atmosphere, and that is associated with reactions of gases caused by the sun's radiation

**air gun** *n* **1** a gun from which a projectile is propelled by compressed air **2** any of various hand tools that work by compressed air; *esp* an airbrush

**air hole** *n* **1** a hole to admit or discharge air **2** AIR POCKET

**air hostess** *n* a stewardess on an airliner

**airily** /'eərəli/ *adv* in an airy manner; jauntily; lightly

**airing** /'eəring/ *n* exposure to air; *esp* a walk, ride, or drive in the open air

**airing cupboard** *n* a heated cupboard in which esp household linen is aired and kept dry

**air lane** *n* a path customarily followed by aircraft

**airless** /'eəlis/ *adj* **1** still, windless **2** lacking fresh air; stuffy

**air letter** *n* **1** an airmail letter **2** a sheet of airmail stationery that can be folded and sealed with the message inside and the address outside

**airlift** /'eə,lift/ *n* the transport of cargo or passengers by aircraft, usu to an otherwise inaccessible area – **airlift** *vt*

**airline** /'eə,lien/ *n* an organization that provides usu regular public air transport

**air line** *n, chiefly NAm* a beeline

**airliner** /'eə,lienə/ *n* a passenger aircraft operated by an airline

**air lock** *n* **1** an airtight intermediate chamber (eg in a spacecraft) which provides entrance to a pressurized chamber without loss of internal pressure **2** a stoppage of flow caused by air being in a part where liquid ought to circulate

**airmail** /'eə,mayl/ *n* (the postal system using) mail transported by aircraft – **airmail** *vt*

**airman** /'eəmən/ *fem* **airwoman** /-,woomən/ *n* **1** – see MILITARY RANKS table **2** a civilian or military pilot, aviator, or aviation technician

**airman basic** *n* – see MILITARY RANKS table

**airman first class** *n* – see MILITARY RANKS table

**airman second class** *n* – see MILITARY RANKS table

**airmanship** /'eəmənship/ *n* skill in piloting or navigating aircraft

**airman third class** *n* – see MILITARY RANKS table

**air marshal** *n* – see MILITARY RANKS table

**air mass** *n* a very large body of air maintaining as it travels nearly uniform conditions of temperature and humidity at any given level

**air mattress** *n, chiefly NAm* AIR BED

**airmobile** /'eəmə,beel, -moh-/ *adj* of or being a military unit whose members are transported to combat areas usu by helicopter [*air* + ¹*mobile*]

**air pistol** *n* a pistol from which a projectile is propelled by compressed air

**airplane** /'eə,playn/ *n, chiefly NAm* an aeroplane [by alter.]

**air plant** *n* EPIPHYTE (plant growing nonparasitically on the surface of another)

**airplay** /'eə,play/ *n* a broadcast (e g of a gramophone record), esp by a radio station

**air pocket** *n* a region of down-flowing or rarefied air that causes an aircraft to drop suddenly

**airport** /'eə,pawt/ *n* a fully-equipped airfield, esp with a customs house, that is used as a base for the transport of passengers and cargo by air

**airportable** /'eə,pawtəbl/ *adj* suitable for transport by aircraft

**airpost** /'eə,pohst/ *n* airmail

**air power** *n* the military strength of an air force

**air pump** *n* a pump for removing air from a closed space or for compressing air or forcing it through other apparatus

**air raid** *n* an attack by armed aircraft on a surface target

**air rifle** *n* an AIR GUN with a rifled bore

**air right** *n* a property right to the airspace owned by a person over his/her land and building(s) subject to the public right of air navigation over the property at a legally prescribed altitude

**air sac** *n* **1** any of the air-filled spaces in the body of a bird connected with the air passages of the lungs **2** ALVEOLUS b (cavity in the lungs) **3** a thin-walled expanded portion of a TRACHEA (breathing tube) that occurs in many insects

**airscrew** /'eə,skrooh/ *n* an aircraft propeller

**airship** /'eə,ship/ *n* a gas-filled lighter-than-air self-propelled aircraft that has a steering system

**air shot** *n, Br* a golf or tennis stroke that misses the ball

**airsick** /'eə,sik/ *adj* suffering from the MOTION SICKNESS associated with flying – **airsickness** *n*

**airspace** /'eə,spays/ *n* the space lying above the earth or above a certain area of land or water; *esp* the space lying above a nation and coming under its jurisdiction

**air space** *n* an enclosed space for or containing air: e g **a** the space (e g in a room) available for respiration **b** a space (e g between two walls or panes of glass) that provides insulation or protects against dampness

**airspeed** /'eə,speed/ *n* the speed (e g of an aircraft) relative to the air – compare GROUND SPEED

**airstream** /'eə,streem/ *n* a current of air; *specif* an airflow

**airstrip** /'eə,strip/ *n* a runway without normal airfield or airport facilities

¹**airt** /eət/ *n, chiefly Scot* a compass point; a direction [ME *art*, fr ScGael *āird*]

²**airt** *vt, chiefly Scot* to direct, guide

**air terminal** *n* the building, usu in a city centre, where passengers assemble to be taken to an airport by bus or train

**airtight** /'eə,tiet/ *adj* **1** (nearly) impermeable to air **2** unassailable – **airtightness** *n*

**airtime** /'eə,tiem/ *n* the broadcasting of something (e g a gramophone record) on the radio; *also* access to or the duration of this

,**air-to-'air** *adj* launched from one aircraft in flight at another; involving aircraft in flight ⟨~ *rockets*⟩ ⟨~ *combat*⟩

**air trap** *n* a device that prevents the escape of foul air from a drain or sewer

**air vice-marshal** *n* – see MILITARY RANKS table

**airwaves** /'eə,wayvs/ *n pl* the hypothetical medium of radio and television transmission

**airway** /'eə,way/ *n* **1** a passage for a current of air (e g in a mine or to the lungs) **2** a designated route along which aircraft fly from airport to airport; *esp* such a route equipped with navigational aids

**airworthy** /'eə,wuhdhi/ *adj* fit for operation in the air ⟨*an* ~ *aircraft*⟩ – **airworthiness** *n*

**airy** /'eəri/ *adj* **1a** not having solid foundation; illusory ⟨~ *promises*⟩ **b** showing lack of concern; flippant **2** light and graceful in movement or manner; sprightly, vivacious **3** delicately thin in texture **4** open to the free circulation of air; breezy **5** *poetic* high in the air; lofty ⟨~ *perches*⟩ – **airiness** *n*

,**airy-'fairy** *adj, chiefly Br* whimsically unrealistic ⟨*too much* ~ *idealism*⟩

**aisle** /iel/ *n* **1** the side division of a church or basilica separated from the nave by columns or piers **2** *chiefly NAm* a gangway [alter. (influenced by E *isle* & Fr *aile* wing) of ME *ele, ile,* fr MF *ele, aile* wing, fr L *ala;* akin to OE *eaxl* shoulder, L *axilla* armpit – more at AXIS] – **aisleless** *adj*

**ait** /ayt/ *n, Br* a little island, esp in a river [ME *eyt, eit,* alter. of OE *īgeoth,* fr *īg* island – more at ISLAND]

**aitch** /aych/ *n* the letter *h* [Fr *hache,* fr (assumed) VL *hacca*]

**aitchbone** /'aych,bohn/ *n* **1** the hipbone, esp of cattle **2** the cut of beef containing the aitchbone [ME *hachbon,* alter. (by incorrect division of *a nachebon*) of (assumed) ME *nachebon,* fr ME *nache* buttock (fr MF, fr LL *natica,* fr L *natis*) + *bon* bone – more at NATES]

**ajar** /ə'jah/ *adj or adv, esp of a door* slightly open [earlier *on char,* fr *on* + *char* turn, piece of work, fr OE *cierr*]

**Akan** /'ahkahn/ *n, pl* **Akans,** *esp collectively* **Akan 1** (a member of) a group of peoples of the Guinea coast, esp of Ghana **2** the Kwa language of these peoples

**Akela** /ə'kaylə/ *n* the adult leader of a cub-scout pack [*Akela,* leader of a wolf-pack in the stories *The Jungle Book* by Rudyard Kipling †1936 E writer]

**akimbo** /ə'kimboh/ *adj or adv* having the hands on the hips and the elbows turned outwards [ME *in kenebowe,* prob fr (assumed) ON *i keng boginn* bent in a curve]

**akin** /ə'kin/ *adj* **1** related by blood; descended from a common ancestor or prototype **2** essentially similar, related, or compatible □ often + *to*

**Akkadian** /ə'kaydi-ən/ *n* **1** a member of a Semitic people inhabiting central Mesopotamia before 2000 BC **2** an ancient Semitic language of Mesopotamia [*Akkad,* northern region of ancient Babylonia] – **Akkadian** *adj*

**al-** – see AD-

¹**-al** /-(ə)l/, **-ial** *suffix* (*n* → *adj*) of or having the character of ⟨*directional*⟩ ⟨*fictional*⟩ [ME, fr OF & L; OF, fr L *-alis*]

²**-al** *suffix* (*vb* → *n*) action or process of ⟨*rehearsal*⟩ ⟨*withdrawal*⟩ [ME *-aille,* fr OF, fr L *-alia,* neut pl of *-alis*]

³**-al** /-al, -(ə)l/ *suffix* (→ *n*) **1** aldehyde ⟨*butanal*⟩ **2** acetal ⟨*butyral*⟩ [Fr, fr *alcool* alcohol, fr ML *alcohol*]

**ala** /'aylə/ *n, pl* **alae** /'ayli/ a wing or a winglike anatomical projection or part [L – more at AISLE] – **alary** *adj,* **alate** *also* **alated** *adj,* **alation** *n*

**a la, à la** /'ah lah/ *prep* **1** in the manner of ⟨*public spending* ~ *Roosevelt*⟩ **2** prepared, flavoured, or served with ⟨*spinach* ~ *creme*⟩ [Fr *à la*]

*usage* Although *la* is feminine in French, *à la* is correctly used in English irrespective of the sex of the person whose name it introduces.

**alabaster** /'alə,bastə, -,bahstə/ *n* **1** a compact fine-textured usu white and translucent chalky stone (GYPSUM) often carved into vases and ornaments **2** a translucent mineral (CALCITE or ARAGONITE) that occurs in STALAGMITES and is sometimes banded [ME *alabastre,* fr MF, fr L *alabaster* vase of alabaster, fr Gk *alabastros*] – **alabaster, alabastrine** *adj*

**à la bonne heure** /,ah lah ,bon 'uh (*Fr* a la bɔn œr)/ *adv* at a good time; well and good; all right [Fr, lit., at the good hour]

**à la carte** /,ah lah 'kaht/ *adv or adj* according to a menu that prices each item separately – compare TABLE D'HÔTE [Fr, by the bill of fare]

**alack** /ə'lak/ *interj, archaic* – used to express sorrow or regret [ME, prob fr *a* ah + *lack* fault, loss]

**alacrity** /ə'lakrəti/ *n, formal* promptness in response; cheerful readiness ⟨*accepted the invitation with* ~⟩ [L *alacritas,* fr *alacr-, alacer* lively, eager; akin to OE & OHG *ellen* zeal] – **alacritous** *adj*

**Aladdin's cave** /ə'ladinz/ *n* a hoard of precious things [*Aladdin,* hero of a tale in *The Arabian Nights,* who gains access to a cave filled with treasure]

**alalia** /,ay'laylyə, ə-/ *n* loss of the ability to speak [NL, fr ²*a-* + *-lalia*]

**alameda** /,alə'meedə, 'maydə/ *n* a public promenade bordered with trees [Sp, fr *álamo* poplar]

**à la mode** /,ah lah 'mod, 'mohd/ *adj* **1** fashionable, stylish **2** *of beef* braised with vegetables and served with a rich brown sauce **3** *chiefly NAm* served with ice cream [Fr, according to the fashion]

**alanine** /'aləneen, -nien/ *n* an AMINO ACID, $CH_3CH(NH_2)COOH$, found in most proteins [Ger *alanin,* irreg fr *aldehyd* aldehyde]

**alanyl** /'alənil/ *n* a chemical group derived from a molecule of alanine [ISV *alanine* + *-yl*]

**alar** /'aylə/ *adj* of or resembling a wing or wings [L *alaris,* fr *ala* wing – more at AISLE]

¹**alarm** /ə'lahm/ *n* **1** a signal (e g a loud noise or flashing light)

that warns or alerts; *also* an automatic device, esp a clock, that warns, rouses, or signals ⟨*set the* ∼ *to wake me at seven*⟩ 2 sudden sharp fear resulting from the perception of imminent danger 3 *obs* ALARUM 2 *synonyms* see ¹FEAR *antonyms* reassurance, composure [ME *alarme, alarom* call to arms, fr MF *alarme*, fr OIt *all'arme*, lit., to the weapon]

²**alarm** *vt* 1 to give warning to 2 to strike with fear

**alarm clock** *n* a clock that can be set to sound an alarm at a desired time

**alarmingly** /ə'lahmingli/ *adv* 1 in a manner or to a degree that disturbs or alarms 2 as seems alarming ⟨∼, *the treaty has been rejected*⟩

**alarmism** /ə'lah,miz(ə)m/ *n* the often unwarranted arousing of fears or prophesying of calamity – **alarmist** *n or adj*

**alarm reaction** *n* the complex of reactions (e g increased hormonal activity) of an organism to stress

**alarum** /ə'larəm/ *n* 1 ALARM 1 – now used chiefly with reference to clocks 2 *obs* a call to arms

**alarums and excursions** *n pl* 1 martial sounds and the movement of soldiers across the stage – used as a stage direction in Elizabethan drama 2 clamour, excitement, and feverish or disordered activity

**alas** /ə'las, ə'lahs/ *interj* – used to express unhappiness, pity, or disappointment [ME, fr OF, fr *a* ah + *las* weary, fr L *lassus* – more at LET]

**Alaskan malamute** /ə'laskən/ *n* (any of) a breed of powerful heavy-coated deep-chested dogs of Alaskan origin with erect ears, heavily cushioned feet, and plumy tail [*Alaska*, state of USA]

**alb** /alb/ *n* a full-length white linen vestment with long tight sleeves that is held at the waist with a girdle (CINCTURE) and worn by a priest at Mass [ME *albe*, fr OE, fr ML *alba*, fr L, fem of *albus* white]

**albacore** /'albə,kaw/ *n, pl* **albacores**, *esp collectively* **albacore** a large tuna fish (*Thunnus alalunga*) with long PECTORAL FINS that is a source of canned tuna; *broadly* any of various tunas (e g a bonito) [Pg *albacor*, fr Ar *al-bakūrah* the albacore]

**Albanian** /,al'baynyən, -ni·ən/ *n* 1 a native or inhabitant of Albania 2 the Indo-European language of the Albanians [*Albania*, country in SE Europe] – **Albanian** *adj*

**albatross** /'albətros/ *n, pl* **albatrosses**, *esp collectively* **albatross** 1 any of various large web-footed seabirds (family Diomedeidae) that are related to the petrels and include the largest seabirds 2 an encumbrance, handicap 3 *Br* a golf score of three strokes less than par on a hole [prob alter. of *alcatras* (water bird), fr Pg or Sp *alcatraz* pelican; (2) fr the dead albatross hung round the neck of a sailor in the poem *The Ancient Mariner* by S T Coleridge †1834 E poet; (3) suggested by *birdie* & *eagle*]

**albedo** /al'beedoh/ *n, pl* **albedos** reflective power; *specif* the fraction of light or other ELECTROMAGNETIC RADIATION that is reflected by a surface or body (e g the moon or a cloud) on which it falls [LL, whiteness, fr L *albus*]

**albeit** /awl'bee·it/ *conj, formal* even though [ME, lit., all though it be]

**albert** /'albət/ *n* a watch chain worn across the front of a waistcoat [Prince *Albert* †1861 consort of Queen Victoria]

**albescent** /al'bes(ə)nt/ *adj* becoming or tending to white [L *albescent-, albescens*, prp of *albescere* to become white, incho of *albēre* to be white, fr *albus*]

**Albigenses** /,albi'jenseez/ *n pl* members of a CATHARISTIC sect of S France between the 11th and 13th centuries [ML, pl of *Albigensis*, lit., inhabitant of Albi, fr *Albiga* (Albi), commune in S France] – **Albigensian** *adj or n*, **Albigensianism** *n*

**albino** /al'beenoh/ *n, pl* **albinos** an organism with deficient pigmentation; *esp* a human being or other animal that has deficient pigmentation from birth and usu has a milky or translucent skin, white or colourless hair, and eyes with a pink pupil [Pg, fr Sp, fr *albo* white, fr L *albus*] – **albinic** *adj*, **albinism** *n*, **albinotic** *adj*

**Albion** /'albi·ən/ *n, poetic* 1 Great Britain 2 England [ME, fr OE, fr L, fr Gk *Aloviōn*, of Celt origin; akin to IrGael *Alba* Scotland]

**albite** /'albiet/ *n* a usu white to grey FELDSPAR (type of mineral) that consists of the chemical compound sodium aluminium silicate, $NaAlSi_3O_8$, and that is a common constituent of various rocks (e g granite) [Sw *albit*, fr L *albus*] – **albitic** *adj*

**album** /'albəm/ *n* 1a a book with blank pages used for making a collection (e g of autographs, stamps, or photographs) b a recording or collection of recordings issued on one or more long-playing gramophone records or cassettes 2 a book of literary selections, musical compositions, or pictures; an anthology [L, a white tablet, fr neut of *albus*]

**albumen** /'albyoomin, al'byoohmin/ *n* 1 the white of an egg 2 albumin [L, fr *albus*]

**albumin** /'albyoomin, al'byoohmin/ *n* any of numerous simple proteins that occur in large quantities in animal substances (e g blood plasma, muscle, or milk) and in many plant tissues and fluids, and are coagulated by heat and soluble in water [ISV *albumen* + *-in*]

¹**albuminoid** /al'byoohminoyd/ *adj* resembling albumin; protein

²**albuminoid** *n* protein; esp SCLEROPROTEIN (protein occurring in bones and CONNECTIVE TISSUE)

**albuminous** /al'byoohminəs/ *adj* relating to, containing, or having the properties of albumen or albumin

**albuminuria** /al,byoohmi'nyooəri·ə/ *n* the presence of albumin in the urine, usu symptomatic of kidney disease [NL] – **albuminuric** *adj*

**alburnum** /al'buhnəm/ *n* SAPWOOD (young soft wood lying next to the bark of a tree) [L, fr *albus* white]

**alcaic** /al'kayik/ *adj, often cap* relating to or written in a four-line stanza of which each line contains four IAMBIC feet (e g "The night/was dark,/the way/was cold" – Sir Walter Scott) [LL *Alcaicus* of Alcaeus, fr Gk *Alkaïkos*, fr *Alkaios* Alcaeus, *fl ab* 600 BC Gk poet] – **alcaic** *n*

**alcaide, alcayde** /ahl'kaydi/ *n* a commander of a Spanish, Portuguese, or Moorish castle, fortress, or prison [Sp *alcaide*, fr Ar *al-qā'id* the captain]

**alcalde** /ahl'kahldi, al-/ *n* the chief administrative and judicial officer of a Spanish town [Sp, fr Ar *al-qādī* the judge]

**alcazar** /al'kazə, ahl'kahzə, al'kahzə, 'alkə,zah/ *n* a Spanish fortress or palace [Sp *alcázar*, fr Ar *al-qaṣr* the castle]

**alchem·ize, -ise** /'alkəmiez/ *vt* to change by alchemy; transmute

**alchemy** /'alkəmi/ *n* 1 a medieval chemical science and philosophical doctrine aiming to achieve the transmutation of the base metals into gold and the discovery of a universal cure for disease and a means of achieving immortality 2 the transformation of something common into something precious [ME *alkamie, alquemie*, fr MF or ML; MF *alquemie*, fr ML *alchymia*, fr Ar *al-kīmiyā'*, fr *al* the + *kīmiyā'* alchemy, fr LGk *chēmeia*] – **alchemist** *n*, **alchemic, alchemical** *adj*, **alchemically** *adv*

**alcohol** /'alkəhol/ *n* 1 *also* **ethyl alcohol** ETHANOL 2 any of various chemical compounds (e g methanol) that are analogous to ETHYL ALCOHOL in constitution and are HYDROXYL derivatives of HYDROCARBONS (chemical compounds composed only of hydrogen and carbon) 3 intoxicating drink containing alcohol; *esp* spirits [NL, fr ML, powdered antimony, fr OSp, fr Ar *al-kuḥul* the powdered antimony]

¹**alcoholic** /,alkə'holik/ *adj* 1a of or caused by alcohol b containing alcohol 2 affected with alcoholism – **alcoholically** *adv*

²**alcoholic** *n* someone who is affected with alcoholism

**alcoholism** /'alkəhə,liz(ə)m/ *n* 1 continued excessive or compulsive use of alcoholic drinks 2 poisoning by alcohol; *esp* a complex long-lasting psychological and nutritional disorder associated with excessive and usu compulsive drinking

**alcohol·ize, -ise** /'alkəhə,liez/ *vt* to treat or saturate with alcohol

**alcoholometer** /,alkəho'lomitə/ *n* a device for determining the alcoholic strength of liquids [Fr *alcoolomètre*, fr *alcool* alcohol + *-o-* + *-mètre* -meter] – **alcoholometry** *n*

**Alcoran** /'alkə,ran/ *n, archaic* the Koran [ME, fr MF or ML; MF & ML, fr Ar *al-qur'ān*, lit., the reading]

**alcove** /'alkohv/ *n* 1a a nook or recess off a larger room b a niche or arched opening (e g in a wall or hedge) 2 *archaic* a summerhouse [Fr *alcôve*, fr Sp *alcoba*, fr Ar *al-qubbah* the arch] – **alcoved** *adj*

**alcyonarian** /,alsiə'neəriən/ *n* any of a subclass (Alcyonaria of the class Anthozoa) of marine INVERTEBRATE animals related to the SEA ANEMONES and stony corals that form colonies and include the soft horny corals, the SEA PENS and SEA FEATHERS [NL *Alcyonium*, genus of soft corals, fr Gk *alkyoneios*, a type of coral, deriv of *alkyōn* kingfisher; fr its resemblance to a kingfisher's nest]

**aldehyde** /'aldi,hied/ *n* any of various highly reactive chemical compounds (e g acetaldehyde) characterized by the group CHO [Ger *aldehyd*, fr NL *al dehyd*, abbr of *alcohol dehydrogenatum* dehydrogenated alcohol] – **aldehydic** *adj*

**al dente** /al 'denti/ *adj, esp of pasta and vegetables* cooked but firm when bitten [It, lit., to the tooth]

**alder** /'awldə/ *n* any of a genus (*Alnus*) of toothed-leaved trees or shrubs of the birch family that grow in moist ground and have wood suitable for turning and bark used in dyeing and tanning [ME, fr OE *alor;* akin to OHG *elira* alder, L *alnus*]

**alder fly** *n* any of several net-winged insects (order Megaloptera)

**alderman** /'awldəmən/ *n, pl* **aldermen 1** a person governing a kingdom, district, or shire as viceroy for an Anglo-Saxon king **2** a senior member of a county or borough council elected by the other councillors – not used officially in Britain after 1974 [ME, fr OE *ealdorman,* fr *ealdor* parent (fr *eald* old) + *man* – more at OLD] – **aldermanic** *adj*

**Alderney** /'awldəni/ *n* any of several breeds of Channel Island dairy cattle (e g Jersey or Guernsey) [*Alderney,* one of the Channel Islands]

**Aldis lamp** /'awldis/ *n* a hand-held lamp for signalling (e g in Morse code) [fr *Aldis,* a trademark]

**aldol** /'aldol, 'aldohl/ *n* **1** a colourless oily liquid that is an aldehyde, $CH_3CH(OH)CH_2CHO$, and is used as a solvent **2** any of various organic chemical compounds containing a HYDROXYL group and an aldehyde group bound to adjacent carbon atoms in the molecular structure [ISV *ald*ehyde + *-ol*] – **aldolization** *n*

**aldose** /'al,dohs/ *n* a sugar containing one aldehyde group per molecule [ISV *ald*ehyde + *-ose*]

**aldosterone** /al'dostə,rohn, 'aldohstiə,rohn/ *n* a STEROID hormone, $C_{21}H_{28}O_5$, produced by the CORTEX (outer region) of the ADRENAL GLANDS that functions in the regulation of the salt and water balance of the body [*ald*ehyde + *-o-* + *ster*ol + *-one*]

**aldosteronism** /al'dostəroh,niz(ə)m/ *n* a condition that is characterized by excessive production and excretion of aldosterone and typically by loss of body potassium, muscular weakness, and high blood pressure

**aldrin** /'awldrin/ *n* a brown or white chlorine-containing insecticide, $C_{12}H_8Cl_6$, that is very poisonous to human beings [Kurt *Alder* †1958 Ger chemist + E *-in*]

**ale** /ayl/ *n* **1** beer **2** a malted alcoholic drink flavoured with hops that is usually more bitter, stronger, and heavier than beer [ME, fr OE *ealu;* akin to ON *öl* ale]

**aleatoric** /,ali·ə'torik/ *adj* improvisatory, random; *specif, of esp electronic music* containing random improvisatory elements within controlled limits that produce chance effects [L *aleatorius* of a gambler]

**aleatory** /'ayli-ət(ə)ri, 'ali-/ *adj* **1** depending on chance ⟨*an ~ contract*⟩ **2** relating to luck, esp bad luck **3** aleatoric [L *aleatorius* of a gambler, fr *aleator* gambler, fr *alea,* a dice game]

**alebench** /'ayl,bench/ *n* a bench in or outside an alehouse

**alee** /ə'lee/ *adv* on or towards the leeward side – compare AWEATHER

**alegar** /'aligə/ *n* vinegar made from ale; sour ale [*ale* + *vinegar*]

**alehouse** /'ayl,hows/ *n* a pub, esp in former times

**Alemannic** /,alə'manik/ *n* the group of German dialects spoken in Alsace, Switzerland, and SW Germany [LL *alemanni,* pl, a Germanic people (of Gmc origin; akin to Goth *alamans* totality of people)]

**alembic** /ə'lembik/ *n* **1** an apparatus formerly used in distillation **2** a means of refining or transmuting [ME, fr MF & ML; MF *alambic* & ML *alambicum,* fr Ar *al-anbīq,* fr al the + *anbīq* still, fr LGk *ambik-, ambix* alembic, fr Gk, cap of a still]

**aleph** /'ahlef, 'aylef/ *n* the 1st letter of the Hebrew alphabet [Heb *āleph,* prob fr *eleph* ox]

**,aleph-'null, aleph nought** *n* the CARDINAL NUMBER of the set of NATURAL NUMBERS (1, 2, 3, 4, etc), usu indicated by the symbol $\aleph_0$

¹**alert** /ə'luht/ *adj* **1** watchful and prompt to act **2** active, brisk [Fr *alerte,* fr It *all' erta,* lit., on the ascent] – **alertly** *adv,* **alertness** *n*

²**alert** *n* **1** a signal that warns of danger (e g from hostile aircraft) **2** the danger period during which an alert is in effect – **on the alert** on the lookout, esp for danger or opportunity

³**alert** *vt* **1** to call to a state of readiness; warn **2** to make aware (e g of a need or responsibility)

**-ales** /-'ayleez, -ahleez/ *suffix* (→ *n pl*) plants consisting of or related to – in the names of taxonomic orders [NL, fr L, pl of *-alis* -al]

**aleurone** /'alyoorohn/ *n* minute storage granules of protein occurring in seeds in the nutritive tissue (ENDOSPERM) or in a special outer layer [Ger *aleuron,* fr Gk, flour; akin to Arm *alam* I grind] – **aleuronic** *adj*

**Aleut** /ə'l(y)ooht, 'al(y)ooht, ə'looht/ *n* **1** a member of a people of the Aleutian and Shumagin islands and W Alaska **2** the language of the Aleuts [Russ]

**A level** /ay/ *n* ADVANCED LEVEL

**alevin** /'alivin/ *n* a young fish; *esp* the newly hatched salmon when still attached to the YOLK SAC [Fr, fr OF, fr *alever* to lift up, rear (offspring), fr L *allevare,* fr *ad-* + *levare* to raise – more at LEVER]

**alexanders** /,alig'zahndəz/ *n, pl* **alexanders** a European plant (*Smyorium olusatrum*) of the carrot family with flat clusters of yellowish-green flowers and black seeds [ME *alexaundre,* fr OF & ML; OF *alexandre,* fr ML *alexandrum,* prob by folk etymology fr L *holys atrum* black vegetable]

**Alexandrian** /,alig'zahndri-ən/ *adj* **1** of Alexander the Great **2** HELLENISTIC (of ancient Greek culture) [(1)*Alexander* the Great †323 BC king of Macedonia; (2) *Alexandria,* city in Egypt founded by Alexander the Great which was the centre of Hellenistic culture]

**alexandrine** /,alig'zahndrin/ *n, often cap* a line of verse of 12 syllables consisting of six IAMBICS (pairs of syllables with the first shorter or less stressed than the second) with a pause after the third iambic (e g "That, like/a wound/ed snake,/drags its/slow length/along" – Alexander Pope) [MF *alexandrin,* adj, fr *Alexandre* Alexander the Great; fr its use in a 12th- or 13th-c poem on Alexander] – **alexandrine** *adj*

**alexandrite** /,alig'zahndriet/ *n* a green variety of the mineral CHRYSOBERYL that is used as a gem and shows a red colour by transmitted light [Ger *alexandrit,* fr *Alexander I* †1825 tsar of Russia]

**alexia** /ə'leksi-ə/ *n* total or partial loss of the ability to read owing to brain damage – compare APHASIA, DYSLEXIA [NL, fr *a-* + Gk *lexis* speech, fr *legein* to speak – more at LEGEND]

**Alfa** /'alfə/ Alpha

**alfalfa** /al'falfə/ *n, NAm* LUCERNE (plant of pea family used as fodder) [Sp, modif of Ar dial. *al-fasfaṣah* the alfalfa]

**alfresco** *also* **al fresco** /al'freskoh/ *adj or adv* taking place in the open air ⟨*an ~ lunch*⟩ [It]

**alg-** /alg-, alj-/, **algo-** *comb form* pain ⟨*algophobia*⟩ [NL, fr Gk *alg-,* fr *algos*]

**alga** /'algə/ *n, pl* **algae** /'alji, -gi/ *also* **algas** any of a group (Algae) of chiefly aquatic simple plants (e g seaweeds and pond scums) that lack differentiated stems, roots, and leaves and that often contain a brown or red pigment in addition to chlorophyll; *also* BLUE-GREEN ALGA [L, seaweed] – **algal** *adj,* **algoid** *adj*

**algebra** /'aljibrə/ *n* **1** a branch of mathematics in which letters, symbols, etc representing numbers, sets of numbers, or similar entities are manipulated according to special rules of operation **2** a system of representing logical arguments in symbols [ML, fr Ar *al-jabr,* lit., the reduction] – **algebraist** *n*

**algebraic** /,alji'brayik/ *adj* **1** relating to, involving, or according to the laws of algebra **2** involving only a finite rather than an infinite number of repetitions of addition, subtraction, multiplication, division, extraction of roots, and raising to powers ⟨*an ~ equation*⟩ – compare TRANSCENDENTAL – **algebraically** *adv*

**algebraic number** *n* a number that can be the answer to an algebraic equation containing only numbers that can be expressed as ratios, roots, or powers of integers; a number that is not a TRANSCENDENTAL NUMBER

**Algerish** /'aljərish/ *adj, NAm* (characteristic) of the works of the American writer Horatio Alger in which success is achieved through self-reliance and hard work [Horatio *Alger* †1899 US writer of fiction for children]

**-algia** /-'aljə/ *comb form* (→ *n*) pain ⟨*neuralgia*⟩ [Gk, fr *algos*]

**algicide** /'aljisied/ *n* something, esp a chemical, that kills algae [*alga* + *-i-* + *-cide*] – **algicidal** *adj*

**algid** /'aljid/ *adj* chill, cold [L *algidus,* fr *algēre* to feel cold; akin to Icel *elgur* slush] – **algidity** *n*

**algin** /'aljin/ *n* ALGINIC ACID, an alginate, or a similar substance obtained from seaweed or other marine BROWN ALGAE

**alginate** /'aljinayt/ *n* a chemical compound [(SALT)] formed by combination between ALGINIC ACID and a metal atom and used as a stabilizing, gelling, or thickening agent in the manufacture of ice cream, dyes, plastics, etc

**alginic acid** /al'jinik/ *n* an insoluble acid, $(C_6H_8O_6)_n$, that forms a thick jelly-like paste when mixed with water, and that, in the form of alginates, is a constituent of the CELL WALLS of seaweed and other BROWN ALGAE [ISV *algin* + *-ic*]

**algo-** – see ALG-

**¹Algol** /'algol/ *n* a BINARY STAR in the constellation Perseus consisting of a larger dimmer star which revolves round a smaller brighter star, causing periodic variations in brightness [Ar *al-ghūl*, lit., the ghoul]

**²Algol, ALGOL** /'algol/ *n* a HIGH-LEVEL language (language more like English than the code recognized by a computer) for programming a computer, used primarily for solving mathematical and scientific problems [*algorithmic language*]

**algolagnia** /ˌalgoh'lagniə/ *n* the finding of sexual pleasure in inflicting or suffering pain – compare MASOCHISM, SADISM, SADOMASOCHISM [NL, fr *alg-* + Gk *lagneia* lust] – **algolagnic** *adj*, **algolagnist** *n*

**algology** /al'goləji/ *n* a branch of biology dealing with algae – **algologist** *n*, **algological** *adj*, **algologically** *adv*

**algometer** /al'gomitə/ *n* an instrument for measuring the smallest pressure that causes pain – **algometry** *n*, **algometric**, **algometrical** *adj*

**¹Algonkian** /al'gongkiən/ *n* (an) Algonquian

**²Algonkian** *n* PROTEROZOIC (geological era) – not now used technically [fr the occurrence of proterozoic rocks in a territory of the Algonquian Indians]

**Algonkin** /al'gongkin/ *n* (an) Algonquian

**Algonquian** /al'gongkwi·ən/ *n* 1 ALGONQUIN 1 2 a group of American Indian languages spoken esp in the eastern parts of Canada and USA 3 a member of any of the American Indian peoples who speak Algonquian languages [CanF *Algonquin*]

**Algonquin** /al'gongkwin/ *n* 1 a dialect of Ojibwa 2 ALGONQUIAN 2,3

**algophobia** /ˌalgə'fohbyə/ *n* abnormal dread of pain [NL]

**algorithm** /'algəˌridhəm/ *n* a systematic procedure for solving a mathematical problem in a limited number of steps, usu involving the repetition of a single operation several times; *broadly* a step-by-step procedure for solving a problem or accomplishing some end [alter. (influenced by Gk *arithmos* number) of ME *algorisme*, fr OF & ML; OF, fr ML *algorismus*, fr Ar *al-khuwārizmi*, fr *al-Khuwārizmi fl*825 Arab mathematician] – **algorithmic** *adj*

**Alhambra** /al'hambrə/ *n* the palace of the Moorish kings at Granada in Spain, noted for its intricate ornamentation [Sp, fr Ar *al-ḥamrā'* the red house] – **Alhambraic, Alhambresque** *adj*

**ali-** /ayli-/ *comb form* wing ⟨*aliform*⟩ [L, fr *ala* – more at AISLE]

**¹alias** /'ayli·əs/ *adv* otherwise called or known as ⟨*Hancock ~ Jones*⟩ [L, otherwise, fr *alius* other – more at ELSE]

**²alias** *n* a name taken by somebody who wishes his/her real identity to remain unknown

**¹alibi** /'aləbie/ *n* 1 (the evidence supporting) the legal plea of being unassociated with a crime by reason of being elsewhere when the crime was committed; *also* such a claim made in a nonlegal context 2 a plausible excuse usu intended to avert blame or punishment (e g for failure or negligence) *synonyms* see ²EXCUSE [L, elsewhere, fr *alius*]

**²alibi** *vt* **alibies; alibiing; alibied** to show to be innocent by an alibi

*usage* The use of **alibi** as a noun meaning "an excuse" or as an intransitive verb meaning "to offer an excuse" is widely disliked.

**alicyclic** /ˌali'sieklik, -'siklik/ *adj* of or being an organic chemical compound that contains a ring of atoms in its molecular structure that is not a BENZENE RING or a benzene-like ring; of or being an ALIPHATIC compound containing carbon atoms arranged in a ring – compare AROMATIC [ISV *ali*phatic + *cyclic*]

**alidade** /'alidayd/ *n* an instrument with measurements marked off on it and sights, used to determine direction in astronomy, surveying, navigation, etc (e g as part of an ASTROLABE) [ME *allidatha*, fr ML *alhidada*, fr Ar *al-'iḍādah* the revolving radius of a circle]

**¹alien** /'ayli·ən/ *adj* **1a** of or belonging to another person, place, or thing; strange **b** relating, belonging, or owing allegiance to another country or its citizens; foreign **2** differing in nature or character, esp so as to be repugnant – + *to* ⟨*ideas quite ~ to ours*⟩ [ME, fr OF, fr L *alienus*, fr *alius*] – **alienly** *adv*, **alienness** *n*

*usage* The construction **alien** *from* is common in the work of earlier writers but has been superseded.

**²alien** *n* 1 a person from another family, race, or nation; *also*

a being from another world 2 a resident of a country who is a subject or citizen of a foreign country; *broadly* a foreign-born citizen

**alienable** /'ayli·ənəbl, 'aylyənəbl/ *adj* legally capable of being sold or transferred to the ownership of another – **alienability** *n*

**alienate** /'ayli·əˌnayt, 'aylyə-/ *vt* 1 to convey or transfer (e g property or a right) to another, usu by a specific act (e g a deed or will) or the due course of law (e g a judgment order) 2 to make unfriendly, hostile, or indifferent where attachment or support formerly existed ⟨~d *from their mothers*⟩ 3 to cause to be withdrawn or diverted ⟨~ *her affections*⟩ [L *alienatus*, pp of *alienare* to estrange, fr *alienus*] – **alienative** *adv*, **alienator** *n*

**alienation** /ˌayli·ə'naysh(ə)n, ˌaylyə-/ *n* 1 a transfer of property to another 2a a withdrawal or separation of a person or his/her affections from an object or position of former attachment; isolation ⟨~ *from the process of work and the values of one's society*⟩ **b** a feeling of estrangement from, apathy or disaffection towards, and powerlessness to influence one's social existence – compare ANOMIE

**alienee** /ˌayliə'nee, ˌaylyə-/ *n* somebody to whom property is legally transferred

**alienist** /'ayli·ənist, 'aylyə-/ *n* 1 one who treats diseases of the mind; a psychiatrist – not now used technically 2 *NAm* a specialist in legal aspects of psychiatry [Fr *aliéniste*, fr *aliéné* insane, fr L *alienatus*, pp]

**alienor** /'ayliənaw, 'aylyə-, ˌ---'-/ *n* somebody who transfers property legally to another

**aliform** /'ayliˌfawm/ *adj* wing-shaped or having wing-shaped parts

**¹alight** /ə'liet/ *vi* **alighted** *also* **alit** /ə'lit/ 1 to come down from something: e g **1a** to dismount **b** to disembark 2 to descend from the air and settle; land 3 *archaic* to come by chance *upon;* ⁶LIGHT 3 [ME *alighten*, fr OE *ālīhtan*, fr *ā-* (perfective prefix) + *līhtan* to alight – more at LIGHT] – **alightment** *n*

**²alight** *adj* 1 animated, alive ⟨*see the place ~ with merriment – Punch*⟩ 2 lit up; illuminated 3 *chiefly Br* on fire; ignited ⟨*the paper caught ~*⟩ [prob fr ¹*a-* + ¹*light*]

**align** *also* **aline** /ə'lien/ *vt* 1 to bring into alignment; *specif* to place (three or more points) in a straight line 2 to array or position (e g a country or organization) on the side of or against a cause or another party ⟨*nations ~ed against fascism*⟩ ~ *vi* 1 to join with others in a common cause 2 to be in or come into alignment [Fr *aligner*, fr OF, fr *a-* (fr L *ad-*) + *ligne* line, fr L *linea*] – **aligner** *n*

**alignment** *also* **alinement** /ə'lienmənt/ *n* 1 aligning or being aligned; *esp* the proper state of adjustment (e g of an electronic device) or positioning of parts (e g of a mechanical device) or points in relation to each other 2 the line formed by aligning things, points etc 3 the ground plan (e g of a railway or road network) as distinguished from the profile **4a** the action of associating oneself with a usu political party or cause **b** an arrangement of groups or forces in relation to one another ⟨*sectional ~s within a political party*⟩

**¹alike** /ə'liek/ *adj* similar without being identical ⟨*were ~ in their beliefs*⟩ [ME *ilik* (alter. of *ilich*) & *alik*, alter. of OE *onlīc*, fr *on* + *līc* body – more at LIKE] – **alikeness** *n*

**²alike** *adv* in the same manner, form, or degree; equally ⟨*peasants and nobility ~ – SEU W*⟩

**aliment** /'alimənt/ *n, formal* food or nutriment; *also* sustenance [ME, fr L *alimentum*, fr *alere* to nourish – more at OLD] – **aliment** *vt*

**alimentary** /ˌali'ment(ə)ri/ *adj* 1 of nourishment or nutrition 2 connected with or providing sustenance or maintenance

**alimentary canal** *n* the tubular passage that extends from mouth to anus, including the gullet, stomach, and intestines, and that functions in the digestion and absorption of food and the elimination of residual waste

**alimentation** /ˌalimən'taysh(ə)n/ *n, formal* the act or process of giving nourishment; *also* being nourished – **alimentative** *adj*

**alimony** /'aliməni/ *n* 1 payments for the support of one spouse by another, esp of a woman by a man, pending or following legal separation or divorce 2 the means of living; maintenance [L *alimonia* sustenance, fr *alere*]

**aline** /ə'lien/ *vb* to align

**'A-ˌline** *adj, of a garment* shaped like the lower part of an A with the bottom being wider than the top ⟨*an ~ skirt*⟩

**alinement** /ə'lienmənt/ *n* alignment

**aliphatic** /ˌaliˈfatik/ *adj* 1 of or derived from fat 2 of or being an organic chemical compound that does not contain a BENZENE RING or a benzene-like ring in its molecular structure; not AROMATIC; *esp* of or being a compound (eg an alkane, alkene, or alkyne) containing only straight or branched chains of carbon atoms in its structure – compare AROMATIC, ALICYCLIC [ISV, fr Gk *aleiphat-, aleiphar* oil, fr *aleiphein* to smear; akin to Gk *lipos* fat – more at LEAVE]

¹**aliquot** /ˈalikwot/ *adj* 1 of a divisor or part contained an exact number of times in a larger whole ⟨*5 is an ~ part of 15*⟩ 2 constituting a fraction of a whole ⟨*an ~ part of invested capital*⟩ [ML *aliquotus*, fr L *aliquot* some, several, fr *alius* other + *quot* how many – more at ELSE, QUOTE]

²**aliquot** *n* 1 a small part that is contained (an exact number of times) in a whole 2 a small sample, esp one of a series of samples, that is taken out from a mass of material (eg a mixture undergoing a chemical reaction) for testing to determine what changes have occurred, the stage reached in an experiment, etc

**alive** /əˈliev/ *adj* 1 having life; not dead or inanimate 2a still in existence, force, or operation; active ⟨*kept hope ~*⟩ b connected to a source of electric power; LIVE 3b 3 aware of a possibility, opportunity, etc; sensitive ⟨*~ to the danger*⟩ 4 not dull or inactive; alert 5 showing much life, animation, or activity; swarming ⟨*sea was ~ with large whales* – Herman Melville⟩ 6 of all those living – used as an intensive following the noun ⟨*the proudest boy ~*⟩ [ME, fr OE *on life*, fr *on + līf* life] – **aliveness** *n* – **come alive 1** to become animated or responsive 2 COME TO LIFE 2

**aliyah** /ˈahleeyah, --ˈ-, əˈleeyə/ *n* the ceremonial calling up of a member of the congregation in a synagogue to the reading desk to read from the Scriptures; *also* the action of such a member in going up to the reading desk [NHeb *'alīyāh*, fr Heb, ascent]

**alizarin** /əˈlizərin/ *n* an orange or red chemical compound, $C_{14}H_8O_4$, formerly prepared from the madder plant but now made synthetically, and used as a dye and in the manufacture of other dyes, esp stains for wood [Fr *alizarine*, fr *alizari* madder, fr Sp, prob fr Ar *al-'aṣārah* the juice]

**alkahest** /ˈalkəhest/ *n* the universal solvent that the alchemists believed to exist [NL *alchahest*, prob coined by Theophrastus Paracelsus †1541 Swiss alchemist & physician] – **alkahestic** *adj*

**alkalescence** /ˌalkəˈles(ə)ns/ *n* the property or degree of being alkaline – **alkalescent** *adj*

**alkali** /ˈalkəlie/ *n, pl* **alkalies, alkalis** 1 any of various chemical compounds (eg the HYDROXIDE or CARBONATE of lithium, sodium, potassium, etc) that combine with acids to form salts and are soluble in water – compare ACID 1b, BASE 7a 2 a soluble chemical SALT or a mixture of soluble salts (eg CALCIUM CARBONATE or SODIUM CHLORIDE) that is present in some soils of dry regions and prevents the growth of agricultural crop plants [ME, fr ML, fr Ar *al-qili* the ashes of the plant saltwort]

**alkalify** /alˈkalifie, ˈalkəlifie/ *vt* to convert or change into an alkali; make alkaline ~ *vi* to become alkaline

**alkali metal** *n* any of a group of chemical elements, comprising lithium, sodium, potassium, rubidium, caesium, and francium, that are metals, have a VALENCY of one, and whose HYDROXIDES dissolve in water to form strong and often caustic alkaline solutions

**alkalimeter** /ˌalkəˈlimitə/ *n* an apparatus for measuring the strength or amount of alkali in a mixture or solution [Fr *alcalimètre*, fr *alcali* alkali + *-mètre* -meter] – **alkalimetry** *n*

**alkaline** /ˈalkəlien/ *adj* of or having the properties of an alkali; *also, of a solution* containing an alkali – **alkalinity** *n*

**alkaline earth** *n* 1 a chemical compound that is an oxide of any of the alkaline earth metals 2 **alkaline earth, alkaline-earth metal** any of a group of chemical elements, comprising beryllium, magnesium, calcium, strontium, barium, and radium, that are metals, have a VALENCY of two, and whose HYDROXIDES dissolve to a small extent in water to form alkaline solutions

**alkaloid** /ˈalkəloyd/ *n* any of numerous nitrogen-containing naturally occurring organic chemical compounds (eg morphine or quinine), that are usually chemical BASES, are obtained from plants, and are extensively used as drugs – **alkaloidal** *adj*

**alkalosis** /ˌalkəˈlohsis/ *n* a medical disorder in which the blood and liquid bathing the body tissues are abnormally alkaline [NL]

**alkane** /ˈalkayn/ *n* any of a series of chemical compounds (eg methane, ethane, propane, butane, or octane) that contain only carbon and hydrogen, have only straight or branched chains of carbon atoms in the molecular structure, and have only single chemical bonds joining adjacent carbon atoms – compare ALKENE, ALKYNE [*alkyl + -ane*]

**alkanet** /ˈalkənet/ *n* 1 any of several European plants (genera *Alkanna, Pentaglottis*, or *Anchusa*) of the forget-me-not family; *esp* a S European plant (*Alkanna tinctoria*) whose roots yield a strong red dye used to stain wood, colour the liquid in thermometers, etc; *also* the dye obtained from alkanet 2 BUGLOSS (plant of the forget-me-not family) [ME, fr OSp *alcaneta*, dim. of *alcana* henna shrub, fr ML *alchanna*, fr Ar *al-ḥinnā'* the henna]

**alkene** /ˈalkeen/ *n* any of a series of chemical compounds (eg ethylene or propylene) that contain only carbon and hydrogen, have only straight or branched chains of carbon atoms in the molecular structure, and that have one DOUBLE BOND joining one pair of adjacent carbon atoms – compare ALKANE, ALKYNE; called also OLEFIN [*alkyl + -ene*]

**alkie, alky** /ˈalki/ *n, informal* an alcoholic [by shortening & alter.]

**alkyd** /ˈalkid/, **alkyd resin** *n* any of numerous plastics that are made by heating chemical ALCOHOLS containing more than one HYDROXYL (alcohol) group with acids containing more than one CARBOXYL (acid) group, and that are used to make paints and tough protective coatings [blend of *alkyl* and *acid*]

**alkyl** /ˈalkil/ *n* 1 a chemical group with a general formula of $C_nH_{2n+1}$ (eg methyl or ethyl) and a VALENCY of one, derived from an alkane (eg methane or ethane) by the removal of a single hydrogen atom 2 a compound of several alkyl chemical groups with a metal atom ⟨*aluminium ~s*⟩ [prob fr Ger, fr *alkohol* alcohol, fr ML *alcohol*] – **alkylic** *adj*

**alkylate** /ˈalkilayt/ *vt* to subject (a chemical compound) to a reaction that introduces one or more alkyl groups into the molecular structure

**alkylation** /ˌalkiˈlaysh(ə)n/ *n* the act or process of alkylating; *specif* a process carried out at oil refineries in which an alkane and an alkene are made to react chemically to produce a high-octane motor fuel

**alkyne** /ˈalkien/ *n* any of a series of chemical compounds (eg acetylene) that contain only carbon and hydrogen, have only straight or branched chains of carbon atoms in the molecular structure, and that have one TRIPLE BOND joining one pair of adjacent carbon atoms – compare ALKANE, ALKENE [*alkyl + -yne*, var of ²*-ine*]

¹**all** /awl/ *adj* **1a** the whole amount or quantity of ⟨*sat up ~ night*⟩ ⟨*ate it ~*⟩ ⟨*can't eat ~ that*⟩ ⟨*~ the year round*⟩ b as much as possible ⟨*spoke in ~ seriousness*⟩ ⟨*came with ~ speed*⟩ 2 every one of (more than two) ⟨*~ men will go*⟩ ⟨*~ the five children were present*⟩ ⟨*not ~ berries are edible*⟩ ⟨*we're ~ hungry*⟩ 3 the whole number or sum of ⟨*~ kinds of things*⟩ ⟨*~ the angles of a triangle are equal to 180°*⟩ 4 every ⟨*~ manner of hardship*⟩ 5 any whatever ⟨*beyond ~ doubt*⟩ **6a** given to or displaying only ⟨*became ~ attention*⟩ ⟨*was ~ sympathy*⟩ b having or seeming to have or use (some physical feature) conspicuously or excessively ⟨*~ thumbs*⟩ ⟨*~ ears*⟩ 7 *chiefly NAm* being more than one person or thing ⟨*who ~ was there?*⟩ [ME, *al, al,* fr OE *eall;* akin to OHG *al* all] – **all along** all the time ⟨*knew the truth* all along⟩ – **all out** with maximum determination, enthusiasm, or effort; FLAT OUT – chiefly in *go all out* – **all over 1** over the whole extent ⟨*decorated* all over *with a flower pattern*⟩ 2 everywhere ⟨*looked* all over *for the missing book*⟩ 3 in every respect – used when a person, organization, etc behaves typically ⟨*that's Paul* all over⟩ 4 *informal* everywhere on the outside, esp of one's body ⟨*I'm* all over *bruises*⟩

²**all** *adv* **1a** wholly, altogether ⟨*sat ~ alone*⟩ ⟨*~ too soon*⟩ – often used as an intensive ⟨*I'm ~ for freedom of conscience*⟩ b to a supreme degree – usu in combination ⟨*all-knowing*⟩ 2 for each side; apiece ⟨*the score is two ~*⟩ – **all but** very nearly; almost ⟨*he* all but *disappeared from public notice*⟩ – **all right 1** well enough ⟨*does* all right *at school*⟩ **2a** very well; yes ⟨*all right, let's go*⟩ b – used in indignant or menacing response ⟨*all right! Just you wait*⟩ 3 beyond doubt; certainly ⟨*he has pneumonia* all right⟩ **4a** satisfactory, acceptable ⟨*the film is* all right *for children*⟩ b safe, well ⟨*he was ill but he's* all right *now*⟩ 5 agreeable, pleasing – used as a generalized term of approval – **all round 1** in every respect 2 to or for everyone present ⟨*ordered drinks* all round⟩ – **all that** to a specified or implied extent or degree; very – chiefly in negatives and questions ⟨*I didn't take his threat* all that *seriously*⟩ – **all the** as much of

something specified as ⟨all the *home I ever had*⟩ – **(not) all there** *informal* (not) having normal mental abilities – **all very well** – used in rejection of advice or sympathy ⟨*it's* all very well *for you to talk*⟩

³**all** *pron, pl* **all 1** the whole number, quantity, or amount; totality ⟨~ *of us*⟩ ⟨~ *that I have*⟩ ⟨*it was* ~ *I could do not to cry*⟩ **2** everybody, everything ⟨*sacrificed* ~ *for love*⟩ – **all in all 1** generally; ON THE WHOLE | **2** supremely important ⟨*she was* all in all *to him*⟩ – **all of** fully; AT LEAST ⟨*lost* all of *£50*⟩ – **all the same** JUST THE SAME

*usage* **1** In British English the forms ⟨**all** *the people*⟩ ⟨**all** *the year* [*round*]⟩ are generally preferred; in American English ⟨**all of** *the people*⟩ ⟨**all** *year*⟩ are common, but disliked for formal writing. **2** Writers on usage recommend ⟨**all** *the houses have garages*⟩ rather than ⟨**all** *the houses have a garage*⟩. **3** Compare ⟨*they're* **all ready** (= all of them)⟩ ⟨*they've* **already** *gone*⟩; ⟨*they sang* **all together**⟩ ⟨*it's* **altogether** (= completely) *different*⟩; ⟨*it's* **all most** (= all of it is very) *persuasive*⟩ ⟨*it's* **almost** (= nearly) *persuasive*⟩; see ALRIGHT

⁴**all** *n* the whole of one's possessions or of what one prizes ⟨*gave his* ~ *for the cause*⟩

**all-** /əl-, al-/, **allo-** *comb form* **1** other; different; atypical ⟨*allo*gamous⟩ ⟨*allo*pathy⟩ **2** being one of a (specified) group whose members together constitute a structural unit, esp of a language ⟨*allo*phone⟩ [Gk, fr *allos* other – more at ELSE]

¹**alla breve** /ˌalə 'brevi/ *adv or adj, of music* in a time having two or four beats in a bar with a single beat represented by a minim [It, lit., according to the breve]

²**alla breve** *n* (the sign marking) a musical piece or passage to be played ALLA BREVE

**Allah** /'alah, 'alə/ *n* GOD **1** – used by Muslims or in reference to the Islamic religion [Ar *allāh*]

**all-A'merican** *adj* representative of the ideals of the USA ⟨*an* ~ *boy*⟩

**allanto-chorion** /əˌlantoh 'kawriən/ *n* a membrane that forms during the development of the foetus, consists of the CHORION (outer membrane of foetus) fused with part of the allantois, and constitutes part of the placenta

**allantois** /ə'lantoh·is/ *n, pl* **allantoides** /əˌlan'toh·ideez/ a membrane that surrounds the foetus in reptiles, birds, and mammals and that in some mammals (e g humans) combines with the CHORION to form the placenta [NL, deriv of Gk *allan-toeidēs* sausage-shaped, fr *allant-, allas* sausage] – **allantoic** *adj*

**allargando** /ˌahlah'gandoh/ *adj or adv, music* becoming gradually slower and fuller with the same or greater loudness [It, widening, verbal of *allargare* to widen, fr *al-* (fr L *ad-*) + *largare* to widen]

**all-a'round** *adj, chiefly NAm* all-round

**allay** /ə'lay/ *vt* **1** to reduce the severity of; alleviate ⟨*the drink* ~ed *her thirst*⟩ **2** to make quiet; pacify ~ *vi obs* to diminish in strength; subside *synonyms* see RELIEVE *antonym* intensify [ME *alayen*, fr OE *ālecgan*, fr *ā-* (perfective prefix) + *lecgan* to lay – more at LAY]

**All Black** *n* a member of the New Zealand Rugby Union team [fr the colour of the team's shirts, shorts, and socks]

**all clear** *n* a signal that a danger has passed or that it is safe to proceed

**allegation** /ˌali'gaysh(ə)n/ *n* **1** the act of alleging **2** something alleged or asserted without proof; *specif* a statement made by the prosecution in a legal action of what it undertakes to prove

**allege** /ə'lej/ *vt* **1** to assert without proof or before proving ⟨*the newspaper* ~s *the mayor's guilt*⟩ **2** to put forward (e g a plea) as a reason or excuse **3** *archaic* to adduce as a source or authority [ME *alleggen*, fr OF *alleguer*, fr L *allegare* to dispatch, cite, fr *ad-* + *legare* to depute – more at LEGATE]

**alleged** /ə'lejd, ə'lejid/ *adj* claimed or asserted without proof to exist, to be true, or to be something specified ⟨*an* ~ *antique vase*⟩

**allegedly** /ə'lejidli/ *adv* according to allegation – used in reporting statements of whose truth one is uncertain

**allegiance** /ə'leejəns/ *n* **1a** the loyalty owed by a subject (VASSAL) in a feudal society to his lord **b** the loyalty owed by a subject or citizen to his/her sovereign or country **2** dedication to or dutiful support of a person, group, cause, etc [ME *allegeaunce*, modif of MF *ligeance*, fr OF, fr *lige* liege] – **allegiant** *adj*

**allegorical** /ˌali'gorikl/, **allegoric** /-gorik/ *adj* **1** of, occurring in, or constituting allegory **2** having hidden spiritual meaning

that transcends the literal sense of a sacred text – **allegorically** *adv*, **allegoricalness** *n*

**allegorist** /'aligərist/ *n* one who uses or writes allegory

**allegor-ize, -ise** /'aligəriez/ *vt* **1** to make into or treat or interpret as allegory ~ *vi* **2** to compose, use, or give explanations in allegory – **allegorizer** *n*, **allegorization**

**allegory** /'alig(ə)ri/ *n* **1** the expression by means of symbolic figures and actions of truths or generalizations about human existence; *also* an instance (e g a painting, or a story like Bunyan's *Pilgrim's Progress*) of such expression **2** symbolic representation; an emblem [ME *allegorie*, fr L *allegoria*, fr. Gk *allēgoria*, fr *allēgorein* to speak figuratively, fr *allos* other + *-agorein* to speak publicly, fr *agora* assembly – more at ELSE, GREGARIOUS]

**allegretto** /ˌali'gretoh/ *n, adv or adj, pl* **allegrettos** (a musical composition or movement to be played) at a speed faster than ANDANTE (moderately slow) but not as fast as allegro – used as a TEMPO (speed) direction in music [It, fr *allegro*]

**allegro** /ə'legroh/ *n, adv or adj, pl* **allegros** (a musical composition or movement to be played) in a brisk lively manner – used as a TEMPO (speed) direction in music [It, merry, fr (assumed) VL *alecrus* lively, alter. of L *alacr-, alacer* – more at ALACRITY]

**allele** /ə'leel/ *n* **1** any of two or more genes that can occur as alternatives at a particular place on a CHROMOSOME (strand of gene-carrying material) and that are responsible for coding for alternative versions of the same inheritable characteristic (e g eye colour) **2** any of two or more versions of an inheritable characteristic (e g blue eyes or brown eyes), that can occur as alternatives and are usu controlled by genes that are alleles [Ger *allel*, short for *allelomorph*] – **allelic** *adj*, **allelism** *n*

**allelomorph** /ə'le(e)lə,mawf/ *n* an allele [Gk *allēlōn* of each other (fr *allos ... allos* one ... the other, fr *allos* other) + *morphē* form] – **allomorphism** *n*, **allelomorphic** *adj*,

**alleluia** /ˌali'looh·yə/ *interj* hallelujah [ME, fr LL, fr Gk *allēlouia*, fr Heb *halălūyāh*]

**allemande** /'aləmand/ *n, often cap* **1** a 17th- and 18th-century COURT DANCE developed in France from a German folk dance **2** a musical composition or movement found in the 17th- and 18th-century baroque suite in moderate TEMPO (speed) with four beats in the bar [Fr, fr fem of *allemand* German]

**all-em'bracing** *adj* complete, sweeping

**allergen** /'aləjən, -jen/ *n* a substance that induces allergy – **allergenic** *adj*, **allergenicity** *n*

**allergic** /ə'luhjik/ *adj* **1** of or inducing allergy **2** *informal* averse or antipathetic *to* ⟨~ *to marriage*⟩

**allergist** /'aləjist/ *n* a specialist in allergy

**allergy** /'aləji/ *n* **1** altered reactivity (e g increased sensitivity) of the body to a particular substance (ANTIGEN) in response to a first exposure to the substance ⟨*his bee-venom* ~ *may make a second sting fatal*⟩ **2** exaggerated reaction (e g by sneezing, asthma, itching, or skin rashes) to substances that have no such effect on the average individual **3** *informal* an aversion, repugnance [Ger *allergie*, fr *all-* + Gk *ergon* work – more at WORK]

**allethrin** /'aləthrin/ *n* a light-yellow oily liquid, $C_{19}H_{26}O_3$, used esp as an insecticide in household aerosol sprays [*allyl* + *pyrethrin*]

**alleviate** /ə'leevi,ayt/ *vt* to make (a troublesome situation or state of mind) more bearable; partially relieve, remove, or correct *synonyms* see RELIEVE *antonyms* aggravate, arouse, intensify [LL *alleviatus*, pp of *alleviare*, fr L *ad-* + *levis* light – more at LIGHT] – **alleviator** *n*, **alleviative, alleviatory** *adj*, **alleviation** *n*

¹**alley** /'ali/ *n* **1** a garden walk bordered by trees or a hedge **2** BOWLING ALLEY **3** alley, alleyway a narrow back street or passageway between buildings [ME, fr MF *alee*, fr OF, fr *aler* to go, modif of L *ambulare* to walk] – **up/down somebody's alley** UP SOMEBODY'S STREET

²**alley** *n* a marble for playing the game of marbles; *esp* one of superior quality [by shortening & alter. fr *alabaster*]

**all-firedly** /ˌawl 'fieədli/ *adv, chiefly NAm informal* extremely, insufferably [*all-fired*, euphemism for *hell-fired*] – **all-fired** *adj*

**All Fools' Day** *n* APRIL FOOLS' DAY

**all fours** *n pl* **1** all four legs of an animal **2** both legs and both arms of a person when used to support the body ⟨*crawling on* ~⟩

**all hail** *interj* – used as a formal greeting or acclamation

**Allhallows** /awl'halohz/ *n, pl* **Allhallows** ALL SAINTS' DAY (November 1) [short for *All Hallows' Day*]

**allheal** /'awl,heel/ *n* any of several plants (e g valerian or self-heal) used in folk medicine for their supposed healing properties

**alliaceous** /ˌaliˈayshəs/ adj resembling garlic or onion, esp in smell or taste [L *allium* garlic]

**alliance** /əˈlie·əns/ n **1a** allying or being allied **b** a bond or connection between states, groups, parties, or individuals; *esp* a union of families by marriage **2** an association to further the common interests of the members; *specif* (a treaty signed by the members of) a confederation of nations, esp for purposes of defence ⟨*the Western* ∼⟩ **3** an affinity or union between related properties or qualities ⟨*the* ∼ *between aesthetic and religious feeling*⟩

**allied** /ˈalied, əˈlied/ adj **1** in close association; united ⟨*a strong personal pride* ∼ *with the utmost probity*⟩ ⟨*two families* ∼ *by marriage*⟩ **2a** joined in alliance by agreement or treaty **b** *cap* of the Allies in World War I or World War II **3a** related by resemblance or common properties; associated ⟨*heraldry and* ∼ *subjects*⟩ **b** related genetically

**Allies** /ˈaliez/ n pl **1** the countries, including Britain, Russia, France, and the USA united against the Central European powers in World War I **2** the countries, including Britain, the Commonwealth countries, the USA, and the Soviet Union united against the Axis powers (Germany, Italy, and Japan) in World War II

**alligator** /ˈaliˌgaytə/ n **1** either of two large American or Chinese flesh-eating aquatic reptiles (genus *Alligator*) that differ from the related crocodiles in having broad heads that do not taper to the snout and by having a special pocket in the upper jaw for reception of the enlarged lower fourth tooth **2** leather made from alligator hide [Sp *el lagarto* the lizard, fr *el* the (fr L *ille* that) + *lagarto* lizard, fr (assumed) VL *lacartus*, fr L *lacertus, lacerta* – more at LIZARD]

**alligator pear** n an avocado [by folk etymology fr *avocado pear*]

**ˌall-imˈportant** adj of very great or the greatest importance ⟨*an* ∼ *question*⟩

**ˌall-ˈin** adj **1** *chiefly Br* all-inclusive; *esp* including all costs ⟨*an* ∼ *holiday in Greece*⟩ **2** *of wrestling* having almost no holds barred

**all in** adj, *informal* exhausted ⟨*was* ∼ *after a day on the building site*⟩

**ˌall-inˈclusive** adj including everything ⟨*a broader and more* ∼ *view*⟩ – **all-inclusiveness** n

**alliterate** /əˈlitərayt/ vi **1** to constitute an alliteration ⟨*"cat"* ∼s *with "king"*⟩ **2** to write or speak alliteratively ∼ vt to arrange or place so as to make alliteration ⟨∼ *syllables in a sentence*⟩ [back-formation fr *alliteration*]

**alliteration** /əˌlitəˈraysh(ə)n/ n the repetition of usu initial consonant sounds in two or more neighbouring words or syllables (e g *w*ild and *w*oolly, *thr*eatening *thr*ongs of *thr*eshers) [*ad-* + L *litera, littera* letter] – **alliterative** adj, **alliteratively** adv

**allium** /ˈali·əm/ n any of a large genus (*Allium*) of plants of the lily family including the onion, garlic, chives, leek, and shallot [NL, genus name, fr L, garlic]

**ˌall-ˈnight** adj **1** lasting throughout the night ⟨*an* ∼ *poker game*⟩ **2** open throughout the night ⟨*an* ∼ *café*⟩

**allo-** – see ALL-

**alloantigen** /ˌalohˈantijən/ n, *biology* ISOANTIGEN

**allocable** /ˈaləkəbl/ adj **1** capable of being allocated **2** assignable in accounting to a particular account or to a particular period of time

**allocate** /ˈaləkayt/ vt **1** to share out (e g money or responsibility) **2** to assign (something limited in supply) as a share ⟨*we've been* ∼d *the top flat*⟩ **3** to set apart or earmark (e g space); designate ⟨∼ *a section of the building for research purposes*⟩ **synonyms** see ALLOT [ML *allocatus*, pp of *allocare*, fr L *ad-* + *locare* to place, fr *locus* place – more at STALL] – **allocator** n, **allocatable** adj, **allocative** adj, **allocation** n

**allochthonous, allocthonous** /əˈlokthənəs/ adj of foreign origin or originating elsewhere; *specif*, *of a plant, animal, etc* entering a particular ecological region from an outside source – compare AUTOCHTHONOUS [*all-* + *-chthonous* (as in *autochthonous*)]

**allocution** /ˌaləˈkyoohsh(ə)n/ n a formal speech; *esp* an authoritative or stirring address [L *allocution-, allocutio*, fr *allocutus*, pp of *alloqui* to speak to, fr *ad-* + *loqui* to speak]

**allodium, alodium** /əˈlohdiəm/ n land held in absolute ownership free from obligations to an overlord [ML, fr OHG *alōd*, fr *al* all + *-ōd* property] – **allodial** adj

**allogamous** /əˈlogəməs/ adj reproducing by CROSS-FERTILIZATION – compare AUTOGAMY – **allogamy** n

**allogeneic** /ˌalohjəˈneeik, -ˈnayik/ adj, *of a type of living cell, tissue, etc* sufficiently different from another living cell, tissue, etc to have different ANTIGENS (substances stimulating antibody production) [*all-* + *-geneic* (as in *syngeneic*)]

**allograft** /ˈaləˌgrahft, -ˌgraft/ n a graft of tissue between two genetically unlike members of the same species

**allograph** /ˈaləˌgrahf, -ˌgraf/ n a letter or combination of letters that is one of several ways of representing one sound (e g *pp* in *hopping* representing the sound /p/) – **allographic** adj

**allomerism** /əˈloməriz(ə)m/ n the tendency of a chemical substance to retain the same crystalline form while varying in chemical constitution – **allomeric, allomerous** adj

**allometry** /əˈlomətri/ n (the measurement and study of) the relative growth of a part in relation to a whole living organism – **allometric** adj

**¹allomorph** /ˈaləˌmawf/ n any of two or more distinct crystalline forms that the same chemical substance can take [ISV] – **allomorphism** n, **allomorphic** adj

**²allomorph** n any of two or more alternative forms of a unit of meaning (e g the MORPHEME *-es* in *dishes*, and the *-s* in *dreams*) that varies with its environment [*allo-* + *morph*eme] – **allomorphism** n, **allomorphic** adj

**allonge** /əˈlonj/ n RIDER 2a (addition to a legal document) [Fr, lit., lengthening]

**allopath** /ˈaləˌpath/ n one who practises allopathy

**allopathy** /əˈlopəthi/ n **1** a system of medical practice that combats disease by treatments that produce effects different from those produced by the disease – compare HOMOEOPATHY **2** a system of medical practice making use of all measures proved of value in treatment of disease; conventional medicine exclusive of HOMOEOPATHY [Ger *allopathie*, fr *all-* + *-pathie* - pathy] – **allopathic** adj, **allopathically** adv

**allopatric** /ˌaləˈpatrik, -ˈpay-/ adj occurring in different areas or in only one area; *esp*, *of different groups of the same species* not interbreeding as a result of living or growing in different places – compare SYMPATRIC [*all-* + Gk *patra* fatherland, fr *patēr* father – more at FATHER] – **allopatrically** adv **allopatry** n

**allophane** /ˈaləˌfayn/ n a usu blue or white very soft noncrystalline mineral that consists essentially of aluminium silicate chemically combined with water and that occurs esp in clays [Gk *allophanēs* appearing otherwise, fr *all-* + *phainesthai* to appear, passive of *phainein* to show – more at FANCY]

**allophone** /ˈaləfohn/ n any of two or more alternative forms of a PHONEME (e g the aspirated /p/ of *pin* and the nonaspirated /p/ of *spin*) that varies with its environment [*allo-* + *phone*] – **allophonic** adj

**allopolyploid** /ˌaləˈpoliployd/ n a living organism whose cells contain more than one set of CHROMOSOMES (strands of gene-carrying material) that are not all derived from the same parent species of organism – compare AUTOPOLYPLOID – **allopolyploid** adj, **allopolyploidy** n

**allopurinol** /ˌaləˈpyooərinol/ n a drug, $C_5H_4N_4O$, used (e g in the treatment of gout) to reduce the formation of URIC ACID in the body [*all-* + *purine* + *-ol*]

**ˌall-orˈnone** adj giving or marked by an effect or response that can only be either nonexistent or present at a single maximum level ⟨*stimulation of a nerve cell gives an* ∼ *response; the cell either fires or it remains unaffected*⟩

**ˌall-orˈnothing** adj **1** all-or-none **2a** accepting no compromises ⟨*he's an* ∼ *perfectionist*⟩ **b** risking or staking everything ⟨*playing an* ∼ *game*⟩

**allosteric** /ˌaləˈsterik, -ˈloh-, -ˈstiərik/ adj of or being an ENZYME whose activity in increasing the rate of a biochemical reaction is inhibited or stimulated by the combining of a molecule with the enzyme molecule at a point on its surface other than its ACTIVE SITE (site that combines with the substance that the enzyme acts on); *also* of or being the inhibition or stimulation of an enzyme in this way [*all-* + *steric*] – **allosterically** adv, **allostery** n

**allot** /əˈlot/ vt **-tt-** to set apart or earmark; allocate ⟨∼ *ten minutes for the speech*⟩ [ME *alotten*, fr MF *aloter*, fr *a-* (fr L *ad-*) + *lot*, of Gmc origin; akin to OE *hlot* lot] – **allotter** n

**synonyms** Allot, allocate, apportion, and assign all deal with the giving out or distribution of roles or portions. **Allot** is the least specific and suggests an arbitrary sharing out which may be unfair. **Assign** adds a suggestion of authority to **allot**, while **apportion** suggests a fairer, often proportionate division. One **allocates** a particular sum, power, or thing for a specific purpose or to a particular person or group.

**allotment** /ə'lotmənt/ n 1 allotting or being allotted 2 something that is allotted; specif, Br any of many similar small plots of land into which a larger piece of land, usu in a built-up area is divided, that are let out to individuals (eg by a town council) for cultivation

**allotrope** /'alə,trohp/ n a form of a substance that shows allotropy ⟨graphite and diamond are ~s of carbon⟩ [ISV, back-formation fr allotropy] – **allotropic** adj, **allotropically** adv

**allotropy** /ə'lotrəpi/ n the property of a substance, esp a chemical element, of existing in two or more different forms that have different physical properties (eg different crystal structures) [all- + -tropy]

**allottee** /ə,lo'tee/ n one to whom an allotment is made

**,all-'out** adj using maximum effort and resources ⟨an ~ effort to win the contest⟩

**all out** adv with maximum determination, enthusiasm, or effort; FLAT OUT – chiefly in go all out

**allover** /,awl'ohvə/ adj covering the whole extent or surface ⟨a sweater with an ~ pattern⟩

**allow** /ə'low/ vt 1a(1) to assign as a share or suitable amount (eg of time or money) ⟨~ an hour for lunch⟩ a(2) to grant as an allowance ⟨~ ed him 500 a year⟩ b to reckon as a deduction or an addition ⟨~ a gallon for leakage⟩ 2a to admit as true or valid; acknowledge ⟨we cannot ~ your claim⟩ b to admit the possibility of ⟨the facts ~ only one explanation⟩ 3 to permit: eg 3a to make it possible for; to enable ⟨the gift will ~ me to buy a car⟩ b to fail to prevent ⟨he ~ed himself to get fat⟩ c to give freedom to go ⟨not ~ed out⟩ 4 dial NAm to be of the opinion that; think ~ vi 1 to admit the possibility of ⟨evidence that ~s of only one conclusion⟩ 2 to make allowance for ⟨~ for expansion⟩ [ME allowen, fr MF alouer to place (fr ML allocare) & allouer to approve, fr L adlaudare to extol, fr ad- + laudare to praise – more at ALLOCATE, LAUD]

**allowable** /ə'lowəbl/ adj 1 permissible 2 assigned as an allowance ⟨expenses ~ against tax⟩ – **allowableness** n, **allowably** adv

**¹allowance** /ə'lowəns/ n 1a a share or portion allotted or granted ⟨an ~ for depreciation⟩ b a sum paid as a reimbursement or for expenses ⟨the salary includes a cost-of-living ~⟩; esp a sum regularly provided for personal or household expenses – compare WEIGHTING c a fixed or limited amount; a ration ⟨we provide an ~ of time for recreation⟩ d a reduction from a list price or stated price ⟨a trade-in ~⟩ 2 an imposed handicap (eg in a horse race) 3 an act of allowing; eg 3a permission, sanction b acknowledgment ⟨the ~ of your claim will not be possible⟩ 4 allowances pl, **allowance** the taking into account of mitigating circumstances ⟨make ~s for his youth⟩

**²allowance** vt to provide or supply in a fixed or limited quantity

**allowedly** /ə'lowidli/ adv as is allowed; admittedly

**alloxan** /ə'loksən/ n a drug, $C_4H_2N_2O_4$, used to induce diabetes in experimental animals; also a chemical compound made from alloxan that acts similarly [Ger, fr allantoin, a chemical found in the allantoic membrane of cows + oxalsäure oxalic acid + -an]

**¹alloy** /'aloy/ n 1 the proportion of gold or silver in a mixture with a less precious metal 2 a metallic substance (eg steel or brass) composed of an intimate mixture of two or more metals or of a metal and a nonmetal; also the state of union of the components of an alloy 3 a metal mixed with a more valuable metal 4 an addition that impairs or debases ⟨happiness without ~⟩ [MF aloi, fr aloier to combine, fr L alligare to bind – more at ALLY]

**²alloy** /ə'loy/ vt 1 to reduce the purity or value of by adding something; debase, impair 2 to mix (eg metals) so as to form an alloy 3 to diminish, moderate

**,all-'powerful** adj having total or sole power; omnipotent

**,all-'purpose** adj suited for many purposes or uses; not specialized

**,all-'round** adj 1 competent or useful in many fields ⟨an ~ athlete⟩ 2 considered in or encompassing many aspects; comprehensive, inclusive ⟨~ ability⟩

**,all-'rounder** n one who is competent in many fields; specif a cricketer who bats and bowls to a relatively high standard

**All Saints' Day** n November 1 observed by Western churches as a Christian festival in honour of all the saints

**allseed** /'awl,seed/ n any of several plants (eg knotgrass) that produce many seeds

**All Souls' Day** n November 2 observed by Christian churches as a day of prayer for the souls of believers who have died

**allspice** /'awl,spies/ n 1 the berry of a W Indian tree (Pimenta dioica) of the eucalyptus family 2 a mildly pungent and aromatic spice prepared from allspice berries [all + spice; fr its supposed combination of the flavours of cinnamon, cloves, and nutmeg]

**,all-'star** adj composed of or taken part in wholly or chiefly by stars of the theatre, cinema, etc

**all the best** interj – used as an expression of goodwill and usu farewell

**'all-,time** adj exceeding all others yet known ⟨an ~ best seller⟩

**allude** /ə'l(y)oohd/ vi to make indirect, casual, or implicit reference to [L alludere, lit., to play with, fr ad- + ludere to play – more at LUDICROUS]

**'all-,up** adj being the total inclusive of everything necessary for operation ⟨the ~ weight of the aircraft⟩

**¹allure** /ə'l(y)ooə/ vt to entice by charm or attraction **antonym** repel [ME aluren, fr MF alurer, fr OF, fr a- (fr L ad-) + loire lure – more at LURE] – **allurement** n

**²allure** n power of attraction or fascination; charm

**allus** /'aləs, 'awləs/ adv, dial always

**allusion** /ə'lyooh-zh(ə)n, -'looh-/ n 1 the act of alluding or hinting at 2 an implied or indirect reference, esp when used in literature; also the use of such references ⚠ illusion [LL allusion-, allusio, fr L allusus, pp of alludere] – **allusive** adj, **allusively** adv, **allusiveness** n

**¹alluvial** /ə'l(y)oohviəl/ adj of, forming, or found in alluvium ⟨~ soil⟩ ⟨~ diamonds⟩

**²alluvial** n a deposit of alluvium

**alluvial fan** n the large fan-shaped deposit of alluvium made by a stream where it flows from a steep gorge onto a plain or where it joins a much larger stream

**alluvion** /ə'l(y)oohvi·ən/ n 1 the wash or flow of water against a shore 2 a flood or inundation; esp the flooding of a river 3 alluvium 4 new land formed by the gradual addition of matter (eg by deposit of alluvium) to existing land and belonging to the owner of the land to which it is added; also the formation of such land [L alluvion-, alluvio, fr alluere to wash against, fr ad- + lavere to wash – more at LYE]

**alluvium** /ə'lyoohvi·əm, -'looh-/ n, pl **alluviums, alluvia** /-vi·ə/ clay, silt, sand, gravel, or similar material formed by the disintegration of rock, that has been deposited by running water [LL, neut of alluvius alluvial, fr L alluere]

**,all-'weather** adj of, for, during, or usable in all kinds of weather

**¹ally** /ə'lie; also ə'lie/ vt 1 to join or unite (eg by marriage or treaty) – + with or to ⟨allied himself with a wealthy family by marriage⟩ 2 to relate to by resemblance or common properties ⟨its beak allies it to the finches⟩ ~ vi to form or enter into an alliance [ME allien, fr OF alier, fr L alligare to bind to, fr ad- + ligare to bind – more at LIGATURE]

**²ally** /'alie/ n 1 a monarch, state, country, etc allied with another (eg by treaty) 2 a person, organization, etc associated with another as an auxiliary helper

*usage* The pronunciations /'alie/ for the noun and /ə'lie/ for the *verb are recommended for BBC broadcasters.*

**-ally** /-(ə)li/ suffix (→ adv) ²-LY ⟨terrifically⟩ – used to form adverbs from adjectives that end in -ic and have no alternative form ending in -ical [¹-al + -ly]

**allyl** /'alil/ n an organic chemical group, $CH_2CHCH_2$, that has a VALENCY of one and occurs in the compounds that give the characteristic pungency to garlic and mustard ⟨~ alcohol⟩ [ISV, fr L allium garlic] – **allylic** adj

**almagest** /'alməjest/ n any of several treatises written in early medieval times on a branch of knowledge (eg alchemy or astronomy) [ME almageste, fr MF & ML, fr Ar al-majusti the almagest, fr al the + Gk megistē, fem of megistos, superl of megas great – more at MUCH]

**alma mater** /,almə 'mahtə, 'maytə/ n a school, college, or university which one has attended [L, fostering mother]

**almanac**, Br also **almanack** /'awlmənak/ n any of various publications giving information, esp in the form of tables, for a particular year; esp a publication giving meteorological and astronomical information (eg the times of high tide and the phases of the moon) for each day in a particular year [ME almenak, fr ML almanach, prob fr Ar al-manākh the calendar]

**almandine** /'alməndeen, -dien/ *n* **1** a deep violet to red iron- and aluminium-containing garnet, $Fe_3Al_2$ $(SiO_4)_3$, used as a gem; the major gem form of garnet **2** a violet variety of the mineral SPINEL, used as a gem [ME *alabandine*, fr ML *ala-bandina*, fr *Alabanda*, ancient city in Asia Minor]

**almandite** /'alməndiet/ *n* almandine [by alter.]

¹**almighty** /awl'mieti/ *adj* **1** *often cap* having absolute power over all ⟨Almighty *God*⟩ **2** relatively unlimited in power ⟨*the ~ dollar*⟩ **3** *informal* great in extent, seriousness, force, etc ⟨*an ~ crash*⟩ [ME, fr OE *ealmihtig*, fr *eall* all + *mihtig* mighty] – **almightiness** *n*, *often cap*, **almightiest** *adj*

²**almighty** *adv*, *informal* to a great degree; mighty ⟨*although he did not exactly starve, he was ~ hungry*⟩

**Almighty** *n* GOD 1 – + *the*

¹**almond** /'ahmənd; *also* 'awl-/ *n* a small tree (*Prunus amygdalus*) of the rose family whose fruit is an edible nut; *also* the flattened oval nut of the almond [ME *almande*, fr OF, fr LL *amandula*, alter. of L *amygdala*, fr Gk *amygdalē*]

²**almond** *adj* containing, made with, or having the character- istic smell or flavour of almonds ⟨*~ icing*⟩

**almond-'eyed** *adj* having narrow slanting almond-shaped eyes

**almoner** /'ahmənə, 'al-/ *n* **1** one who distributes alms **2** a social worker attached to a British hospital who attends to the needs of the sick – not now used technically [ME *almoiner*, fr OF *almosnier*, fr *almosne* alms, fr LL *eleemosyna*]

**almost** /'awlmohst/ *adv* very nearly but not exactly or entirely – not used after *not*, *pretty*, or *very* ⟨*~ any bus will do*⟩ *usage* see ³ALL [ME, fr OE *ealmǣst*, fr *eall* + *mǣst* most]

**alms** /'ahmz/ *n taking sing or pl verb* money, food, etc given to help the poor [ME *almesse*, *almes*, fr OE *ælmesse*, *ælms*; akin to OHG *alamuosan* alms; both fr a prehistoric WGmc word borrowed fr LL *eleemosyna* alms, fr Gk *eleēmosynē* pity, alms, fr *eleēmōn* merciful, fr *eleos* pity] – **almsgiver** *n*, **almsgiving** *n*

**almshouse** /'ahmz,hows/ *n* **1** *Br* a house founded and financed by charity in which a poor or old person can live cheaply or free **2** *archaic* a poorhouse

**almsman** /'ahmzmən/, *fem* **almswoman** /-,woomən/ *n* a person supported by alms

**Alnico** /'alnikoh/ *trademark* – used for an alloy containing iron, nickel, aluminium, and often also cobalt, copper, and titanium, from which permanent magnets are made

**alodium** /ə'lohdiəm/ *n* ALLODIUM

**aloe** /'aloh/ *n* **1** *pl but taking sing vb* the fragrant wood of an E Indian tree (*Aquilaria agallocha* of the family Thymelaeaceae) **2a** any of a large genus (*Aloe*) of succulent chiefly S African plants of the lily family with tall spikes of flowers **b** *pl but taking sing vb* the dried juice of the leaves of various aloes, used esp as a laxative [ME, fr LL, fr L, dried juice of aloe leaves, fr Gk *aloē*]

**aloft** /ə'loft/ *adv* **1** at or to a great height **2** in the air; *esp* in flight (e g in an aeroplane) ⟨*meals served ~*⟩ **3** at, on, or to the upper rigging or the top of the mast of a ship – compare ALOW [ME, fr ON *ā lopt*, fr *ā* on, in + *lopt* air – more at ON, LOFT]

**aloha** /ə'loh·hə, ə'loh·ə/ *interj* – used to express greeting or farewell [Hawaiian, fr *aloha* love]

**aloin** /'alohin/ *n* a bitter chemical compound obtained from various aloes and used as a laxative [*aloe* + *-in*]

**alone** /ə'lohn/ *adj or adv* **1** separated from others; isolated ⟨*the house stands ~*⟩ **2** exclusive of other factors ⟨*time ~ will show*⟩ **3a** considered without reference to any other; *esp* un- assisted ⟨*the children ~ would eat that much*⟩ **b** free from interference ⟨*leave my bag ~*⟩ **c** incomparable, unique ⟨*she stood ~ in her ability to solve fiscal problems*⟩ [ME, fr *al* all + *one* one]

*usage* The position of **alone** in a sentence affects its meaning. Com- pare ⟨he **alone** (= only he) *can lift it*⟩⟨*he can lift it* **alone** (= unassisted)⟩.

¹**along** /ə'long/ *prep* **1** in a line parallel with the length or direction of **2** in the course of (a route or journey) **3** in accord- ance with ⟨*something ~ these lines*⟩ [ME, fr OE *andlang*, fr *and-* against + *lang* long – more at ANTE-]

²**along** *adv* **1** forward, on ⟨*bicycled ~*⟩ ⟨*move ~*⟩ **2** from one to another ⟨*word was passed ~*⟩ **3** as a companion or a neces- sary or pleasant addition; with one ⟨*brought his wife ~*⟩ ⟨*take your flute ~*⟩ **4a** in company and simultaneously – + *with* ⟨*pay a penny a week ~ with all the other village boys* – SEU S⟩ **b** also; IN ADDITION – often + *with* ⟨*a bill came ~ with the parcel*⟩ **5** at or to a specified or advanced point ⟨*our plans are far ~*⟩ **6** on hand; there ⟨*I'll be ~ in five minutes*⟩

*usage* The combination **along** with is widely disliked.

**along of** *prep* **1** *dial Br* in company with **2** *dial* BECAUSE OF [ME *ilong on*, fr OE *gelang on*, fr *ge-*, associative prefix + *lang* – more at CO-]

**alongshore** /ə,long'shaw/ *adv or adj* along the shore or coast ⟨*walked ~*⟩ ⟨*~ currents*⟩

¹**alongside** /ə-'sied/ *adv* **1** along the side in a parallel position **2** at the side; close by ⟨*a guard with a prisoner ~*⟩

²**alongside, alongside of** *prep* **1** side by side with; *specif* parallel to **2** concurrently with

*usage* The combination **alongside** of is widely disliked.

¹**aloof** /ə'loohf/ *adv* at a distance; out of involvement ⟨*we kept ~*⟩ [obs *aloof* to windward, fr ¹*a-* + *loof*, var of *luff*]

²**aloof** *adj* distant in interest or feeling; reserved, unsympathetic *antonyms* sociable, friendly – **aloofly** *adv*, **aloofness** *n*

**alopecia** /,alə'peeshə/ *n* usu abnormal baldness in humans or loss of hair, wool, feathers, etc in animals [ME *allopicia*, fr L *alopecia*, fr Gk *alōpekia*, fr *alōpek-*, *alōpēx* fox – more at VULPINE] – **alopecic** *adj*

**aloud** /ə'lowd/ *adv* **1** with a normal speaking voice; not in a whisper **2** *archaic* loudly [ME, fr ¹*a-* + *loud*]

**à l'outrance** /,ah looh'trons/ (*Fr* a lutra:s) *adv* À OUTRANCE (to the bitter end)

**alow** /ə'loh/ *adv* below, esp in a ship; ⟨*~ in the ship's hold*⟩; *also* on or near the deck – compare ALOFT [ME, fr ¹*a-* + *low*]

**alp** /alp/ *n* a high mountain [back-formation fr *Alps*, mountain system in Europe]

**alpaca** /al'pakə/ *n* **1** (the fine long woolly hair of) a mammal related to the llama that is bred esp in Peru **2** (cloth resembling) a fine thin cloth made of or containing the wool of the alpaca [Sp, fr Aymara *allpaca*]

**alpenglow** /'alpən,gloh/ *n* a reddish glow seen near sunset or sunrise on the summits of mountains [prob part trans of Ger *Alpenglühen*, fr *Alpen* Alps + *glühen* glow]

**alpenhorn** /-,hawn/ *n* a long straight wooden horn used, esp formerly, by Swiss herdsmen for communicating with each other and to call cattle [Ger, fr *Alpen* + *horn* horn]

**alpenstock** /-,stok/ *n* a long iron-pointed staff, formerly used in mountain climbing but now superseded by the ice axe [Ger, fr *Alpen* + *stock* staff

**alpestrine** /al'pestrin/ *adj* growing high on mountains but not above the TREE LINE (highest point at which trees grow) [ML *alpestris* mountainous, fr L *Alpes* Alps]

¹**alpha** /'alfə/ *n* **1** the 1st letter of the Greek alphabet **2** one who or which is first (e g in a series or order); a beginning – compare OMEGA **2 3** – used to designate the chief or brightest star of a constellation **4** ¹A 4a [ME, fr L, fr Gk, of Sem origin; akin to Heb *āleph* aleph]

²**alpha**, α *adj* **1** of or being an atom or chemical group closest to a particular major or conspicuous atom or group in the molecular structure of an organic chemical compound **2** of or being a chemical compound closely related in structure and having the same number of each type of atom as a specified chemical compound ⟨*α-naphthol*⟩

³**alpha** *adj* alphabetical ⟨*put them in ~ order*⟩

**Alpha, Alfa** – used as a communications code word for the letter *a*

**alpha-adre'nergic** /adrə'nuhjik/ *adj* of, stimulating, or being an ALPHA-RECEPTOR ⟨*~ blocking action*⟩

**alpha-adrenergic receptor** *n* ALPHA-RECEPTOR

**alpha and omega** *n* **1** the beginning and ending **2** the principal or essential part of something [fr the first and last letters of the Greek alphabet]

**alphabet** /'alfəbet/ *n* **1a** (an arrangement in a conventional order of) a set of characters, esp letters, used to write or print one or more languages **b** a system of signs or signals that can be used in place of letters ⟨*the deaf and dumb ~*⟩ **2** ABC 2a [ME *alphabete*, fr LL *alphabetum*, fr Gk *alphabētos*, fr *alpha* + *bēta* beta]

**alphabetical** /,alfə'betikl/, **alphabetic** /-betik/ **1** of or employing an alphabet **2** in or being the order that the letters of the alphabet are conventionally arranged – **alphabetically** *adv*

**alphabet·ize, -ise** /'alfəbe,tiez/ *vt* to arrange in alphabet order – **alphabetizer** *n*, **alphabetization** *n*

**alpha-'helix** *n* a coiled structural arrangement of parts of the molecules of many proteins, consisting of a single chain of AMINO ACIDS arranged in a spiral

**alphameric** /,alfə'merik/, **alphamerical** /-kl/ *adj* ALPHA- NUMERIC [*alpha*bet + *numeric*, *numerical*]

**alphanumeric** /ˌalfənyooh'merik/ also **alphanumerical** /-kl/ adj 1 consisting of both letters and numbers and often other symbols (e g punctuation marks and mathematical symbols) ⟨RT756 is the ~ code⟩; also being a character in an alphanumeric system 2 able to display, use, or interpret alphanumeric characters ⟨an ~ printer for a computer⟩ [alphabet + numeric, numerical] – **alphanumerically** adv

**alpha particle** n a tiny particle identical with the nucleus of a helium atom that carries a positive electric charge, consists of two protons and two neutrons, and is ejected at high speed from some radioactive substances

**alpha ray** n a continuous stream of ALPHA PARTICLES esp emitted by some radioactive substances

**'alpha-reˌceptor** n a site (RECEPTOR) on the surface of a cell to which adrenalin and similar chemical substances (e g NOR-ADRENALIN) bind, causing the stimulation of those body actions (e g the constriction of small blood vessels, the contraction of uterine and bronchial muscle, an increase in blood pressure, and the relaxation of intestinal muscle) that are activated by the SYMPATHETIC NERVOUS SYSTEM – compare BETA-RECEPTOR; called also ALPHA-ADRENERGIC RECEPTOR

**alpha wave** n a variation in an ELECTROENCEPHALOGRAM (record of the electrical activity of the brain) of a frequency of about 10 hertz, that is often associated with states of waking relaxation

**alphorn** /'alp,hawn/ n an alpenhorn

**alpine** /'alpien/ n 1 a plant that grows naturally in alpine or northern parts of the N hemisphere; esp such a plant grown for ornament 2 cap a person possessing Alpine physical characteristics

**Alpine** adj 1 often not cap of, growing in, or like the Alps; broadly of or like any mountains 2 often not cap of or growing in high mountain areas above the TREE LINE (highest point at which trees grow) 3 of or being a type of stocky broad-headed white person of medium height with brown hair or eyes 4 of or being competitive ski events consisting of SLALOM (skiing between obstacles) and downhill racing – compare NORDIC

**alpinism** /'alpiniz(ə)m/ n, often cap the climbing of high mountains, esp in the Alps – **alpinist** n

**already** /awl'redi/ adv 1 no later than now or then; even by this or that time ⟨John can't crawl yet, but Ann can ~ walk⟩ ⟨was he still there? No, he'd ~ left⟩ 2 before, previously ⟨I have seen the film ~ so I won't go again⟩ usage see ³ALL [ME al redy, fr al redy, adj, wholly ready, fr al all + redy ready]

**alright** /awl'riet/ adv or adj ALL RIGHT ⟨the first two years of the medical school were ~ Gertrude Stein⟩
usage This frequent spelling of all right is disapproved of by many people; though some would defend it, by analogy with altogether and already, as a means of distinguishing between ⟨the answers are all (= all of them are) right⟩ and ⟨the answers are alright (= OK)⟩.

**Alsace** /al'zas/ n a white wine made in Alsace

**Alsatian** /al'saysh(ə)n/ n (any of) a breed of large working dogs that are intelligent and responsive and are often used as police or guard dogs [ML Alsatia Alsace, region in France (formerly in Germany)]

**alsike clover** /'alsiek, 'awl-, -sik/ n a European clover (Trifolium hybridum) often grown for animal feed [Alsike, town in Sweden]

**also** /'awlsoh/ adv as an additional circumstance; too [ME, fr OE eallswā, fr eall all + swā so – more at SO]
usage Also should not correctly be used instead of and, although the combination and also is permissible ⟨⚠ likes bubble and squeak, also onions⟩.

**'also-ˌran** n 1 a horse, dog, etc that finishes out of the first three places in a race 2 a contestant that does not win 3 a competitor of little importance ⟨he was just an ~ in the fight for privileges⟩

**Altaic** /al'tayik/ adj of or constituting a language family comprising Turkic, Tungusic, and Mongolian [Altai mountains, range in central Asia]

**altar** /'awltə/ n 1 a usu raised structure or place on which sacrifices are offered or incense is burnt in worship 2 Christianity a table on which the bread and wine used in communion are consecrated or which serves as a centre of worship or ritual [ME alter, fr OE altar, fr L altare; akin to L adolēre to burn up]

**altar boy** n a boy who assists a priest in celebrating a Christian service

**altarpiece** /-ˌpees/ n a work of art that decorates the space above and behind an altar

**altar stone** n a stone slab with a compartment containing the relics of martyrs that forms part of the altar in some Roman Catholic churches

**altazimuth** /al'taziməth/ n a telescope or similar instrument mounted so that it can swing horizontally and vertically [ISV altitude + azimuth]

**alter** /'awltə/ vt 1 to make different without changing into something else 2 chiefly NAm euph to castrate, spay ~ vi to become different synonyms see CHANGE¹ [ME alteren, fr MF alterer, fr ML alterare, fr L alter other (of two); akin to L alius other – more at ELSE] – **alterable** adj, **alterably** adv, **alterer** n, **alterability** n

**alteration** /ˌawltə'raysh(ə)n/ n (the act or result of) altering or being altered; (a) modification

**altercation** /ˌawltəkaysh(ə)n/ n a noisy heated quarrel; also quarrelling [ME altercacioun, fr MF altercation, fr L altercation-, altercatio, fr altercatus, pp of altercari to quarrel, dispute, fr (assumed) altercus contending, fr alter other] – **altercate** vi

**alter ego** /'altə/ n 1 a second self (e g the part played by an actor when considered in relation to the actor him- or herself) 2 a trusted friend [L, lit., second I]

**¹alternate** /awl'tuhnət/ adj 1 occurring or succeeding each other by turns ⟨a day of ~ sunshine and rain⟩ 2a of plant parts arranged singly first on one side and then on the other at a different height or point along a stem, flower stalk, etc ⟨~ leaves⟩ – compare OPPOSITE b arranged one above or alongside the other; forming or constituting an alternating series ⟨~ layers of brick and stone⟩ 3 every other; every second ⟨he works on ~ days⟩ 4 being either of a particular pair of angles lying on opposite sides (e g of intersecting or parallel lines): 4a being either of a pair of angles lying between the two lines that are crossed b being either of a pair of angles lying outside the two lines that are crossed 5 alternative ⟨took the ~ route home⟩ [L alternatus, pp of alternare to alternate, fr alternus alternate, fr alter] – **alternately** adv
usage The use of alternate and alternately to mean "offering a choice" ⟨took the alternate route home⟩ is widely disliked.

**²alternate** /'awltəˌnayt/ vt 1 to interchange with something else in turn ⟨~ work with sleep⟩ 2 to cause to alternate ~ vi 1 to occur or succeed each other by turns ⟨work and sleep ~⟩; also to take turns ⟨singers who ~ in the leading role⟩ 2 to happen or appear in turn with something else ⟨storms ~ with sunshine⟩ 3 to undergo or consist of repeated change from one thing to another ⟨he ~ s between work and sleep⟩

**³alternate** /awl'tuhnət/ n, chiefly NAm one who substitutes for or alternates with another; a deputy

**alternating current** /'awltənayting/ n an electric current that reverses its direction at regularly recurring intervals; the electric current provided by most mains electricity supplies

**alternation** /ˌawltə'naysh(ə)n/ n 1 alternating or being alternated 2 INCLUSIVE DISJUNCTION

**alternation of generations** n the occurrence of two or more forms in the LIFE CYCLE of a plant or animal (e g a jellyfish or fern) usu involving the regular alternation of a generation produced by SEXUAL REPRODUCTION and a generation produced by asexual means

**¹alternative** /awl'tuhnətiv/ adj 1 giving a choice, esp between mutually exclusive options ⟨several ~ plans⟩ 2 constituting an alternative ⟨we will adopt your ~ suggestion⟩ 3 of or catering for the alternative society ⟨the ~ press⟩ 4 not based on traditional techniques; specif using methods other than the burning of fossil fuels (e g oil and coal) to provide power ⟨~ energy⟩ ⟨~ technology⟩ – **alternatively** adv **alternativeness** n
usage The use of alternative(ly) for alternate(ly) ⟨⚠ they laughed and cried alternatively⟩ is a common confusion.

**²alternative** n 1 an opportunity or need for deciding between two or more possible courses of action, things, etc 2 any of several things, propositions, or possibilities of which one is to be chosen
usage Some writers on usage still maintain that there should be no more than two alternatives, because the word is ultimately derived from the Latin alter = "other" (of two); but times have changed. Today it is legitimate to speak of several alternatives ⟨our three alternatives – T E Lawrence⟩ synonyms see ¹CHOICE

**alternatively** /awl'tuhnətivli/ adv as an alternative; otherwise

**alternative society** *n the* group of people who reject conventional social institutions, practices, and values in favour of a life-style based esp on communal ownership and self-sufficiency – compare COUNTERCULTURE

**alternator** /'awltə,naytə/ *n* an electric generator for producing ALTERNATING CURRENT; *also* such a device together with a set of RECTIFIERS that converts the alternating current into a DIRECT CURRENT, used esp in motorcar engines

**althaea,** *chiefly NAm* **althea** /al'theeə/ *n* a hollyhock, marshmallow, or related plant (genus *Althaea*) [L *althaea* marshmallow, fr Gk *althaia*]

**although** *also* **altho** /awl'dhoh/ *conj* in spite of the fact or possibility that; though *synonyms* see ¹THOUGH [ME *although*, fr *al* all + *though*]

**altimeter** /'alti,meetə/ *n* an instrument (e g fitted to an aircraft) for measuring altitude; *specif* a barometer that registers altitude by responding to the changes in atmospheric pressure that accompany changes in height [L *altus* + E *-meter*] – **altimetry** *n*

**altitude** /'altityoohd/ *n* **1a** the vertical angle between a planet, star, or other celestial body and a horizontal plane containing the horizon, used with the AZIMUTH to fix the exact position of a celestial body; *also* the vertical angle between a high object and a horizontal plane containing an observer, used to fix the position of objects in surveying **b(1)** the height of an object (e g an aircraft) or a place (e g on a mountain), esp above sea level **b(2)** height ⟨*the ∼ of the mercury in the tube*⟩ **c** the perpendicular distance from the base of a geometric figure (e g a triangle or cone) to its apex or to a side parallel to the base; *also* a line drawn on a geometric figure corresponding to such an altitude **2 altitudes** *pl.* altitude a high place or region [ME, fr L *altitudo* height, depth, fr *altus* high, deep – more at OLD] – **altitudinal, altitudinous** *adj*

**altitude sickness** *n* dizziness, nosebleed, nausea, etc caused by the lack of oxygen in the thin air of high altitudes, that often affects climbers and pilots above heights of about 4000 metres (12 500 feet)

¹**alto** /'altoh/ *n, pl* **altos 1a** COUNTERTENOR (high male singing voice) **b** CONTRALTO (low female singing voice) **2** the second highest part in conventional 4-part harmony **3** a member of a family of instruments (e g clarinets or saxophones) having a range lower than that of the treble or soprano and higher than that of the tenor [It, lit., high, fr L *altus*]

²**alto** *adj* of, being, or having the range or part of an alto

**alto clef** *n* a C CLEF designating a note written on the middle line of the stave as MIDDLE C

**altocumulus** /,altoh'kyoohmyooləs/ *n, pl* **altocumuli** /-lie/ a fleecy cloud formation consisting of large whitish globular clouds at a higher level than CUMULUS cloud, between about 2000 metres and 7000 metres (about 6500 feet and 23 000 feet) [NL, fr L *altus* + NL *-o-* + *cumulus*]

¹**altogether** /,awltə'gedhə/ *adv* **1** wholly, thoroughly ⟨*an ∼ different problem*⟩ **2a** ALL TOLD **b** in every way ⟨*more complicated ∼*⟩ **3** in the main; ON THE WHOLE *usage* see ³ALL [ME *altogedere*, fr *al* all + *togedere* together]

²**altogether** *n* – **in the altogether** nude, naked ⟨*he posed in the altogether*⟩

**alto-rilievo** /,altoh-ri'leevoh/ *n, pl* **alto-rilievi** /-ri'leevi/ HIGH RELIEF (sculpture with projecting design) [It *alto rilievo*]

**altostratus** /,altoh'strahtəs/ *n, pl* **altostrati** /-tie/ a cloud formation that consists of a continuous dark layer between about 2000 metres and 7000 metres (about 6500 feet and 23 000 feet) [NL, fr L *altus* + NL *-o-* + *stratus*]

**altricial** /al'trish(ə)l/ *adj, of a bird* (having the young) hatched in a very immature and helpless condition so as to require care for some time – compare PRECOCIAL [L *altric-, altrix*, fem of *altor* one who nourishes, fr *altus*, pp of *alere* to nourish – more at OLD]

**altruism** /'altrooh,iz(ə)m/ *n* unselfish regard for or devotion to the welfare of others [Fr *altruisme*, fr *autrui* other people, fr OF, oblique case form of *autre* other, fr L *alter*] – **altruist** *n*, **altruistic** *adj*, **altruistically** *adv*

**alula** /'alyoolə/ *n, pl* **alulae** /-li/ BASTARD WING (part of a bird's wing corresponding to the thumb) [NL, fr L, dim. of *ala* wing – more at AISLE] – **alular** *adj*

**alum** /'aləm/, **potash alum** *n* (any of various chemical compounds with a similar chemical formula and crystal structure to) a sulphate of aluminium with potassium or ammonium, $AlK(SO_4)_2.12H_2O$ or $NH_4Al(SO_4)_2.12H_2O$, used esp in the manufacture of leather and paper and in medicine as a STYPTIC

(substance that stops minor bleeding when applied to the skin) [ME, fr MF *alum, alun,* fr L *alumen*]

**alumina** /ə'l(y)oohminə/ *n* aluminium oxide, $Al_2O_3$, that occurs naturally esp as CORUNDUM (mineral of which sapphire and ruby are forms) and BAUXITE (major ore of aluminium) [NL, fr L *alumin-, alumen* alum]

**aluminate** /ə'l(y)oohminayt/ *n* a chemical compound formed between aluminium oxide and another metal ⟨*sodium ∼ is Na* $AlO_2$⟩

**aluminiferous** /ə,l(y)oohmi'nifərəs/ *adj* containing alum or aluminium

**aluminium** /,alyooh'mini-əm, -yoo-/ *n* a silvery-white very light and easily shaped metallic chemical element that has a VALENCY of three, conducts heat and electricity well, is very resistant to rusting, and is used esp in kitchen utensils and lightweight alloys (e g for aircraft parts) [NL, fr *alumina*]

**aluminium sulphate** *n* a chemical compound, $Al_2(SO_4)_3$, used in water purification and in the manufacture of paper and leather

**alumin·ize, -ise** /ə'l(y)oohmi,niez/ *vt* to treat or coat with aluminium

**aluminous** /ə'l(y)oohminəs/ *adj* of or containing alum or aluminium

**aluminum** /ə'loohminəm/ *n, NAm* aluminium

**alumnus** /ə'lumnəs/, *fem* **alumna** /ə'lumnə/ *n, pl* **alumni** /-nie/ *fem* **alumnae** /-ni/ *chiefly NAm* a former student of a particular school, college, or university; *broadly* a former member of any organization [L, foster son, pupil, fr *alere* to nourish – more at OLD]

*usage* A mixed group of male and female former students are alumni.

**alunite** /'alyooniet/ *n* a mineral consisting of a potassium aluminium sulphate chemically combined with water, $K(AlO)_3$ $(SO_4)_2.3H_2O$, that is used esp to make alum and other aluminium compounds [Fr, fr *alun* alum]

**alveolar** /,alvi'ohlə, al'vee-ələ/ *adj* **1** of, resembling, made up of, or having alveoli or an alveolus **2** *of a consonant* articulated with the tip or blade of the tongue touching or near the ALVEOLAR RIDGE – **alveolarly** *adv*

**alveolar ridge** *n* a flesh-covered ridge of bone behind the upper front teeth

**alveolate** /al'vee-alət, -layt/ *adj* having regularly arranged deep pits like a honeycomb – **alveolation** *n*

**alveolus** /,alvi'ohləs, al'vee-ələs/ *n, pl* **alveoli** /-lie/ a small cavity or pit, esp in a body part: e g **a** a socket for a tooth **b** any of the many tiny air cells in the lungs where oxygen is absorbed into the blood **c** a cell or compartment of a honeycomb **d** a socket from which a bristle, hair, etc arises [NL, fr L, dim. of *alveus* cavity, hollow, fr *alvus* belly; akin to ON hvannjōli stalk of angelica, Gk *aulos*, a reed instrument]

**alway** /'awlway/ *adv, archaic* always

**always** /'awlwayz, -wiz/ *adv* **1a** at all times ⟨*I have ∼ lived here*⟩ **b** in all cases ⟨*they ∼ have long tails*⟩ **2** on every occasion; repeatedly ⟨*we ∼ go to Blackpool*⟩ – often used with continuous tenses to express exasperation ⟨*he's ∼ complaining*⟩ **3** forever, perpetually ⟨*she will ∼ love you*⟩ **4** as a last resort; AT ANY RATE ⟨*they could ∼ eat cake*⟩ [ME *alway, alwayes,* fr OE *ealne weg,* lit., all the way, fr *ealne* (acc of *eall* all) + *weg* (acc) way – more at WAY]

**alyssum** /'alisəm/ *n* **1** any of a genus (*Alyssum*) of Eurasian and African plants of the cabbage family that are grown in gardens for their clusters of small white or yellow flowers – called also MADWORT **2** SWEET ALYSSUM (European flower) [NL, fr Gk *alysson*, plant believed to cure rabies, fr neut of *alyssos* curing rabies, fr *a-* + *lyssa* rabies]

**am** /əm, m; *strong* am/ *pres 1 sing of* BE [ME, fr OE *eom;* akin to ON *em* am, L *sum,* Gk *eimi,* OE *is* is]

**AM** /,ay 'em/ *adj* of or being a radio broadcasting or receiving system using AMPLITUDE MODULATION (transmission of a signal by variation of the amplitude rather than the frequency of a carrier wave)

**ama** /'ahmə, 'ahmah/ *n, pl* **amas, ama** a Japanese diver, esp for pearls [Jap]

**amah** /'amə, 'ahmə/ *n* a female servant in the far East, esp formerly; *esp* a Chinese nursemaid [Pg *ama* wet nurse, fr ML *amma*]

**amain** /ə'mayn/ *adv, archaic or poetic* **1** with all one's strength **2** in great haste; precipitately **3** to a high degree; exceedingly [¹*a-* + ¹*main*]

**amalgam** /ə'malgəm/ *n* **1** an alloy of mercury with another metal (e g silver) that is solid or liquid at room temperature according to the proportion of mercury present and is used esp in making fillings for teeth **2** a mixture or blend ⟨*an* ~ *of wisdom and nonsense*⟩ [ME *amalgame*, fr MF, fr ML *amalgama*, prob deriv of Gk *malagma* emollient, fr *malassein* to soften]

**amalgamate** /ə'malgəmayt/ *vb* to unite in or as if in a mixture or blend; *esp* to combine (different things) into a single body – **amalgamator** *n*

**amalgamation** /ə,malgə'maysh(ə)n/ *n* **1** amalgamating or being amalgamated; uniting **2** the result of amalgamating; an amalgam **3** a consolidation, merger ⟨*on* ~ *of two companies*⟩ – **amalgamative** *adj*

**amanita** /,amə'nietə/ *n* any of a genus (*Amanita*) of large mostly poisonous fungi related to the common mushroom that includes the DEATH CAP (extremely poisonous toadstool) [NL, genus name, fr Gk *amanitai*, pl, a kind of fungus]

**amantadine** /ə'mantədeen/ *n* a synthetic drug, $C_{10}H_{17}N$, used esp to prevent viral infections (e g influenza) by interfering with the penetration of the virus into the cells of the body [ISV *adamant*ane ($C_{10}H_{16}$) + am*ine*]

**amanuensis** /ə,manyooh'ensis/ *n, pl* **amanuenses** /-seez/ one employed to write from dictation or to copy a manuscript [L, fr (*servus*) *a manu* slave with secretarial duties]

**amaranth** /'aməranth/ *n* **1** any of a genus (*Amaranthus* of the family Amaranthaceae, the amaranth family) of large plants some of which are grown in gardens for their purple flowers **2** a dark reddish-purple colour **3** *chiefly poetic* an imaginary flower that never fades [L *amarantus*, a flower, fr Gk *amaranton*, fr neut of *amarantos* unfading, fr *a-* + *marainein* to waste away – more at SMART] – **amaranthine** *adj*

**amaryllis** /,amə'rilis/ *n* any of a genus (*Amaryllis*) of African plants of the daffodil family that grow from bulbs and have bright reddish or white lily-like flowers; *also* a plant of any of several related genera (e g *Hippeastrum*) [NL, genus name, prob fr L, name of a shepherdess in Vergil's *Eclogues*]

**amass** /ə'mas/ *vt* **1** to collect for oneself; accumulate ⟨~ *a great fortune*⟩ **2** to bring together into a mass; gather ⟨~ *the wool into a large ball*⟩ to come together; assemble [MF *amasser*, fr OF, fr a- (fr L *ad-*) + *masser* to gather into a mass, fr *masse* mass] – **amasser** *n*, **amassment** *n*

**amateur** /'amətə, -chə/ *n* **1** a devotee, admirer **2** one who engages in a pursuit (e g a study, science, or sport) as a pastime rather than as a profession; *esp* a sportsman or sportswoman who has never competed for money **3** one who practises an art or science unskilfully; a dabbler *antonyms* professional, expert [Fr, fr L *amator* lover, fr *amatus*, pp of *amare* to love] – **amateur** *adj*, **amateurish** *adj*, **amateurishly** *adv* **amateurishness** *n*, **amateurism** *n*

**amative** /'amətiv/ *adj, formal* disposed to love; amorous [ML *amativus*, fr L *amatus*] – **amatively** *adv*, **amativeness** *n*

**amatol** /'amətol/ *n* an explosive consisting of a mixture of AMMONIUM NITRATE and TNT used esp in bombs and shells [ISV *ammoni*um + *a-* + trinitro*tol*uene]

**amatory** /'amət(ə)ri/ *adj* of or expressing sexual love or desire *synonyms* see AMOROUS

**amaurosis** /,amaw'rohsis/ *n, pl* **amauroses** /-seez/ decay of sight, esp owing to disease of certain nerves or the RETINA (light-sensitive part at the back of the eye), without obvious change or damage to the eye [NL, fr Gk *amaurōsis*, lit., dimming, fr *amauroun* to dim, fr *amauros* dim] – **amaurotic** *adj*

¹**amaze** /ə'mayz/ *vt* **1** to fill with wonder; astonish, astound **2** *obs* to bewilder, perplex ~ *vi* to cause astonishment ⟨*her calmness continues to* ~⟩ *synonyms* see ²SURPRISE [ME *amasen*, fr OE *āmasian*, fr *ā-* (perfective prefix) + (assumed) *masian* to confuse]

²**amaze** *n, archaic* amazement

**amazement** /-mənt/ *n* **1** great astonishment, wonder, or surprise **2** *obs* consternation, bewilderment

**amazing** /ə'mayzing/ *adj* – used as a generalized term of approval ⟨*she has the most* ~ *vintage car*⟩

**amazingly** /ə'mayzingli/ *adv* **1** to an amazing degree **2** as is amazing ⟨~, *she believed his story*⟩

**amazon** /'aməz(ə)n/ *n* **1** *cap* a member of a race of female warriors who repeatedly warred with the Greeks of classical mythology **2** *often cap* a tall strong athletic usu assertive or aggressive woman [ME, fr L, fr Gk *Amazōn*]

**Amazonian** /,amə'zohnyən, -niən/ *adj* **1a** of, resembling, or befitting an Amazon warrior **b** *not cap, esp of a woman* strong, assertive, or aggressive **2** of the Amazon river or its valley [(2) *Amazon* river in S America]

**amazonite** /'aməz(ə)n,iet/ *n* an apple-green or bluish-green MICROCLINE (mineral of the feldspar group) sometimes used as a gem [*Amazon* river in S America]

**amazonstone** /'aməz(ə)n,stohn/ *n* amazonite

**ambage** /'ambij/ *n, pl* **ambages** /am'bayjeez, 'ambijiz/ *archaic* **1 ambages** *pl*, **ambage** ambiguity; circumlocution **2** *pl* indirect ways or proceedings [back-formation fr ME *ambages*, fr MF or L; MF, fr L, fr *ambi-* + *agere* to drive – more at AGENT] – **ambagious** *adj*

**ambassador** /am'basədə/ *n* **1** an official envoy: e g **1a** a top-ranking diplomat accredited to a foreign government or sovereign as a resident representative **b** one similarly appointed for a special and often temporary diplomatic assignment **2** a representative, messenger [ME *ambassadour*, fr MF *ambassadeur*, of Gmc origin; akin to OHG *ambaht* service] – **ambassadorship** *n*, **ambassadorial** *adj*

**am,bassador-at-'large** *n, pl* **ambassadors-at-large** a diplomat or minister of the highest rank who represents the government of the USA in negotiations with foreign governments but is not accredited to any particular foreign government

**ambassadress** /am'basədris/ *n* **1** a female representative, authorized messenger, or ambassador **2** the wife of an ambassador

**amber** /'ambə/ *n* **1** a hard yellowish to brownish translucent substance that is the fossilized resin of some extinct trees, takes a fine polish, and is used chiefly for ornaments and jewellery **2** the colour of amber **3** a yellow traffic light meaning "caution" that comes on for a short time between red and green [ME *ambre*, fr MF, fr ML *ambra*, fr Ar *'anbar* ambergris] – **amber** *adj*

**ambergris** /-,grees, -,gris/ *n* a waxy substance found floating in tropical waters, that originates in the intestines of the SPERM WHALE and is used in perfumery as a FIXATIVE [ME *ambregris*, fr MF *ambre gris*, fr *ambre* + *gris* grey – more at GRIZZLE]

**ambi-** /ambi-/ *prefix* both; two ⟨ambi*valent*⟩ ⟨ambi*guous*⟩ [L *ambi-*, *amb-* both, round; akin to L *ambo* both, Gk *amphō* both, *amphi* round – more at BY]

**ambidexterity** /,ambidek'sterəti/ *n* the quality or state of being ambidextrous

**ambidextrous** /,ambi'dekstrəs/ *adj* **1** capable of using either hand with equal ease for tasks normally done with a particular hand **2** unusually skilful; versatile **3** characterized by deceitfulness and double-dealing [LL *ambidexter*, fr L *ambi-* + *dexter* on the right, skilful] – **ambidextrously** *adv*

**ambience, ambiance** /'ambi-əns (*Fr* abias)/ *n* a surrounding or pervading atmosphere characteristic of a particular place; environment, milieu [F *ambiance*, fr *ambiant* ambient, fr L *ambient-*, *ambiens*]

¹**ambient** /'ambi-ənt/ *adj* **1** surrounding on all sides; encompassing ⟨*to exist in the* ~ *matter of space* – Joseph Conrad⟩ **2** of the immediate surroundings ⟨*the* ~ *temperature*⟩ [L *ambient-*, *ambiens*, prp of *ambire* to go round, fr *ambi-* + *ire* to go – more at ISSUE]

²**ambient** *n, formal* ambience

**ambiguity** /,ambi'gyooh-əti/ *n* **1** (a word or expression with) the quality of being ambiguous or imprecise in meaning ⟨~ *is often an intentional feature of poetry*⟩ **2** uncertainty of meaning or of relative position ⟨*the basic* ~ *of her political stance*⟩

**ambiguous** /am'bigyoo-əs/ *adj* **1** vague, indistinct, obscure, or difficult to classify ⟨*eyes of an* ~ *colour*⟩ **2** capable of two or more interpretations *synonyms* see ¹OBSCURE *antonyms* unambiguous, explicit △ ambivalent [L *ambiguus*, fr *ambigere* to wander about, fr *ambi-* + *agere* to drive – more at AGENT] – **ambiguously** *adv*, **ambiguousness** *n*

**ambit** /'ambit/ *n* **1** a limiting circumference ⟨*everywhere within an* ~ *of four yards*⟩ **2** the bounds or limits of a place; the precincts **3** a sphere of influence; a scope [ME, fr L *ambitus*, fr *ambitus*, pp of *ambire*]

**ambition** /am'bish(ə)n/ *n* **1a** a strong desire for status, fame, wealth, power, or success **b** a desire to achieve a particular end ⟨*her* ~ *to climb the Matterhorn*⟩ **2** an end, goal, etc that is an object of ambition [ME, fr MF or L; MF, fr L *ambition-*, *ambitio*, lit., going around, fr *ambitus*, pp] – **ambitionless** *adj*

**ambitious** /am'bishəs/ *adj* **1a** having or motivated by ambition for wealth, success, fame, etc **b** having a desire; aspiring – usu + of ⟨~ *of honours*⟩ **2** resulting from or showing ambition ⟨*an* ~ *attempt*⟩ **3** elaborate ⟨*cooked nothing more* ~ *than boiled eggs*⟩ – **ambitiously** *adv*, **ambitiousness** *n*

**ambivalence** /am'bivələns/ *n* **1** simultaneous attraction towards and repulsion from an object, person, or action **2** uncertainty or indecisiveness in choosing between alternatives **3** ambiguity [ISV] – **ambivalent** adj, **ambivalently** adv

**ambivert** /'ambi,vuht/ n a person having the characteristics of both an extrovert and an introvert [ambi- + -vert (as in introvert)] – **ambiversion** n, **ambiversive** adj

¹**amble** /'ambl/ vi to go (as if) at an amble; saunter [ME amblen, fr MF ambler, fr L ambulare to walk] – **ambler** n

²**amble** n **1** an easy gait of a horse in which the legs on the same side of the body move together **2** a leisurely manner of walking **3** a leisurely stroll

**amblyopia** /,ambli'ohpi·ə/ n poor sight without obvious change or damage to the eye, associated esp with poisoning or a deficiency of essential substances (eg VITAMIN A) in the diet [NL, fr Gk amblyōpia, fr amblys blunt, dull + -ōpia -opia] – **amblyopic** adj

**ambo** /'amboh/ n, pl **ambos**, **ambones** /am'bohneez/ a raised platform in an early Christian church, usu with various levels from which different parts of the service were conducted [ML ambon-, ambo, fr LGk ambōn, fr Gk, rim]

**Amboinese** /,amboh·i'neez, ,amboy'neez/ n, pl **Amboinese 1** a native or inhabitant of the Indonesian island of Ambon **2** the language of the people of Ambon [Amboina (Ambon) + ese]

**Ambonese** /,ambə'neez/ n, pl **Ambonese** Amboinese

**ambrosia** /am'brohzi·ə, -zh(y)ə/ n **1** the food of the Greek and Roman gods **2** something extremely pleasing to eat or smell [L, fr Gk, lit., immortality, fr ambrotos immortal, fr a- + -mbrotos (akin to brotos mortal) – more at MURDER] – **ambrosial** adj, **ambrosially** adv

**ambrosia beetle** n any of several BARK BEETLES (family Scolytidae) that bore holes in the wood of trees, into which they introduce a fungus on which they feed [ambrosia (fungus), a fungus]

**ambry** /'ambri/ n **1** a recess in a church wall for holding the cup, plate, etc used in communion **2** archaic chiefly Br a pantry or cupboard [ME armarie, fr OF, fr L armarium, cabinet, cupboard, fr arma weapons, tools – more at ARM]

**ambsace** /'aymzayz, 'amzays/ n, archaic the lowest throw at dice; also something worthless or unlucky [ME ambes as, fr OF, fr ambes both + as aces]

**ambulacral** /,ambyoo'laykrəl/ adj of or being any of the radiating areas of starfishes, sea urchins, and other ECHINODERMS along which run the main nerves, blood vessels, etc [ambulacrum fr NL, fr L, alley, fr ambulare to walk] – **ambulacrum** n

**ambulance** /'ambyoolǝns/ n a vehicle equipped for transporting injured or sick people, animals, etc [Fr, field hospital, fr ambulant itinerant, fr L ambulant-, ambulans, prp of ambulare]

**ambulanceman** /'ambyoolǝnsmǝn/, fem **ambulancewoman** /-,woomǝn/ n a member of the crew of an ambulance

**ambulant** /'ambyoolǝnt/ adj **1** of a patient not confined to bed; able to walk **2** moving about [L ambulant-, ambulans]

**ambulate** /'ambyoolayt/ vi, formal to move from place to place; walk, stroll [L ambulatus, pp of ambulare] – **ambulation** n

¹**ambulatory** /'ambyoolǝt(ǝ)ri/ adj **1** of or adapted to walking; also occurring while walking **2** moving or movable from place to place; not fixed or stationary **3** archaic, law capable of being altered (a will is ~ until the testator's death) **4a** AMBULANT 1 **b** of or for one who is able to walk about (~ medical care) – **ambulatorily** adv

²**ambulatory** n a covered area (eg in a cloister or aisle) for walking; specif a passage surrounding the east end of a church

**ambuscade** /,amboo'skayd/ n an ambush [MF embuscade, modif of OIt imboscata, fr imboscare to place in ambush, fr in (fr L) + bosco forest, perh of Gmc origin; akin to OHG busc forest – more at IN, BUSH] – **ambuscade** vb, **ambuscader** n

¹**ambush** /'amboosh/ vt to attack from an ambush; waylay to lie in wait; lurk [ME embushen, fr OF embuschier, fr en in (fr L in) + busche wood] – **ambusher** n, **ambushment** n

²**ambush** n **1** the concealment of soldiers, police, etc in order to carry out a surprise attack from a hidden position; also an attack from such a position **2** taking sing or pl vb (the concealed position of) people stationed in ambush

**ameba** /ə'meebə/ n, pl **amebae** /ə'meebi/, **amebas** NAm an amoeba – **ameban**, **amebic** adj, **ameboid** adj

**ameer** /ə'miə/ n an emir

**ameliorate** /ə'meelyǝrayt/ vb to make or become better or more tolerable antonym worsen, deteriorate [alter. of meliorate]

– **ameliorator** n, **amelioratory, ameliorative** adj, **amelioration** n

**amen** /,ah'men, ,ay-, '-,-/ interj – used to express solemn reinforcement or agreement (eg with an expression of faith) or hearty approval (eg of an assertion) [ME, fr OE, fr LL, fr Gk amēn, fr Heb āmēn]

**amenable** /ə'meenǝbl/ adj **1** liable to be made to account for one's behaviour; answerable (citizens ~ to the law) **2a** capable of submission (eg to judgment or test) (the data is ~ to analysis) **b** readily persuaded to yield, submit, or agree; tractable [deriv of MF amener to lead up, fr OF, fr a- (fr L ad-) + mener to lead, fr L minare to drive, fr minari to threaten – more at MOUNT] – **amenably** adv, **amenability** n

usage One is amenable to something (amenable to persuasion).

synonyms see OBEDIENT antonyms recalcitrant, refractory

**amend** /ə'mend/ vt **1** to put right; specif to make corrections to (eg a text) **2a** to change or modify for the better; improve **b** to alter esp the wording of; specif to alter (legislation) formally by modification, deletion, or addition (~ the constitution) ~ vi to reform oneself antonym impair [ME amenden, fr OF amender, modif of L emendare, fr e, ex out + menda fault; akin to L mendax lying, mendicus beggar, Skt mindā physical defect] – **amendable** adj, **amender** n

**amendatory** /ə'mendǝt(ǝ)ri/ adj, chiefly NAm corrective [amend + -atory (as in emendatory)]

**amendment** /-mǝnt/ n **1** the act of amending, esp for the better; correction **2a** the process of amending a bill, law, motion, etc by parliamentary or constitutional procedure **b** an alteration made or proposed by this process (several ~s to the Bill)

**amends** /ə'mendz/ n taking sing or pl vb compensation for a loss or injury; recompense (make ~) [ME amendes, fr OF, pl of amende reparation, fr amender]

¹**amenity** /ə'menǝti, ǝ'mee-/ n **1** usu pl something (eg a public facility) that provides or improves material comfort (urban amenities – roads, water, sewerage, and power – National Times (Sydney)) **2** usu pl something (eg a courteous social gesture) conducive to pleasantness and ease of conversation on a social occasion **3** formal the quality or degree of being pleasant or agreeable; esp pleasantness of surroundings [ME amenite pleasantness, fr L amoenitat-, amoenitas, fr amoenus pleasant]

²**amenity** adj of or providing amenity (an ~ area)

**amenorrhoea**, NAm **amenorrhea** /ə,menǝ'riə, ay-/ n, medicine abnormal absence of menstruation [NL, fr ²a- + Gk mēn month + NL -o- + -rrhoea] – **amenorrhoeic** adj

¹**ament** /'amǝnt, 'aymǝnt/ n a catkin [NL amentum, fr L, thong, strap] – **amentaceous** adj, **amentiferous** adj

²**ament** /ə'ment, 'aymǝnt/ n a person who suffers from amentia [L ament-, amens mad]

**amentia** /ə'menshǝ/ n severe mental deficiency, esp when present from birth [NL, fr L, madness, fr ament-, amens mad, fr a- (fr ab-) + ment-, mens mind – more at MIND]

**amerce** /ə'muhs/ vt, archaic to punish by a fine whose amount is fixed at the court's discretion; broadly punish [ME amercien, fr AF amercier, fr OF a merci at (one's) mercy] – **amercement** n, **amerciable** adj

¹**American** /ə'merikǝn/ n **1** a N or S American Indian **2** a native or inhabitant of N or S America; specif a citizen of the USA **3** American, American English English as spoken and written in the USA and in areas influenced by American culture – often taken to include Canadian English insofar as it does not differ from that of the USA [America, western continent, fr NL, fr Americus Vespucius (Amerigo Vespucci) †1512 It explorer once believed to have discovered its mainland]

²**American** adj **1** of or characteristic of N or S America **2** of or characteristic of the USA **3** of the N or S American Indians

**Americana** /ə,meri'kahnə/ n pl (a collection of) materials concerning or characteristic of America, its civilization, or its culture

**American cloth** n, Br a strong cotton cloth with a glossy waterproof surface

**American Dream** n the ideals of democracy, equality, freedom, material prosperity, etc on which the USA was founded – usu + the (people are aware of the erosion of the ~)

**American football** n a football game resembling rugby that is played with an oval football between teams of 11 players each wearing heavy padding and helmets and that features the running, forward passing, and kicking of the ball

**American Indian** n a member of any of the indigenous peoples of N, S, or Central America, usu with the exception of the Eskimos, constituting one of the divisions of the Mongoloid peoples

**Americanism** /ə'merikəniz(ə)m/ n **1** a custom, belief, word, pronunciation, etc characteristic of the USA or of its citizens, culture, or language **2a** adherence or attachment to America or to its culture, customs, tastes, or ideas **b** the promotion of American political policies

**Americanist** /ə'merikənist/ n one who studies the languages or cultures of American Indians

**Americanization** /ə,merikəniˈzaysh(ə)n/ n the act or process of Americanizing; *specif* instruction received by immigrants to the USA in English and US culture

**american·ize, -ise** /əˈmerikəniez/ vb, *often cap* to (cause to) have, acquire, or conform to American customs, tastes, characteristics, etc – **americanizer** n, *often cap*

**American organ** n a melodeon

**American plan** n a method of charging for a hotel room whereby meals are included in the standard daily rate – compare EUROPEAN PLAN, PENSION

**American saddle horse** n (any of) a breed of riding horse developed chiefly in Kentucky in the USA from Thoroughbreds

**americium** /,aməˈrisi·əm/ n a radioactive metal that is a chemical element produced by bombarding a piece of uranium with very fast ALPHA PARTICLES [NL, fr *America* + NL *-ium*]

**Amerindian** /,aməˈrindi·ən/ n, *chiefly NAm* AMERICAN INDIAN [*American* + *Indian*] – **Amerindian, Amerindic** adj **Amerind** n

**Ames test** /aymz/ n a test in which the number of genetic changes caused by a chemical when it is exposed to a group of bacteria is determined and which probably indicates how likely the chemical is to cause cancer [Bruce *Ames* b 1928 US biochemist]

**amethopterin** /,amiˈthoptərin/ n METHOTREXATE (anticancer drug) [*amin-* + *meth-* + *pteroic* acid + *-in*]

**amethyst** /aˈməthist/ n **1** a clear purple or bluish-violet variety of quartz that is much used as a gemstone **2** the colour of amethyst [ME *amatiste*, fr OF & L; OF, fr L *amethystus*, fr Gk *amethystos*, lit., remedy against drunkenness, fr *a-* + *methyein* to be drunk, fr *methy* wine – more at MEAD] – **amethystine** adj

**ametropia** /,amiˈtrohpiə/ n an abnormal condition of the eye in which images, are not focused properly on the RETINA (lightsensitive membrane at the back of the eye), resulting esp in shortsightedness or farsightedness [NL, fr Gk *ametros* without measure (fr *a-* + *metron* measure) + NL *-opia* – more at MEASURE] – **ametropic** adj

**Amharic** /amˈharik/ n an Ethiopian Semitic language [*Amhara*, province of Ethiopa] – **Amharic** adj

**amiability** /,aymiəˈbiləti/ n **1** the quality or state of being amiable **2** a small gesture of social politeness

**amiable** /ˈaymi·əbl/ adj **1** being or seeming agreeable and wellintentioned; devoid of anything contentious or offensive ⟨an ~ *musical comedy*⟩ **2** friendly, congenial [ME, fr MF, fr LL *amicabilis* friendly, fr L *amicus* friend; akin to L *amare* to love] – **amiableness** n, **amiably** adv

**amianthus** /,amiˈanthəs/, **amiantus** /-təs/ n fine silky asbestos [L *amiantus*, fr Gk *amiantos*, fr *amiantos* unpolluted, fr *a-* + *miainein* to pollute]

**amicable** /ˈamikəbl; *also* əˈmikəbl USE *the last pron is disliked by some speakers*/ adj characterized by friendly goodwill; peaceable *antonym* antagonistic [ME, fr LL *amicabilis*] – **amicableness** n, **amicably** adv, **amicability** n

**amice** /ˈamis/ n a vestment made of an oblong piece of cloth, usu white linen, worn by a priest round the neck and shoulders and partly under the full-length white vestment (ALB) [ME *amis*, prob fr MF, pl of *amit*, fr ML *amictus*, fr L, cloak, fr *amictus*, pp of *amicire* to wrap round, fr *am-*, *amb-* around + *jacere* to throw – more at AMBI-, JET]

**amid** /əˈmid/ prep, *formal* **1** in or to the middle of; among ⟨~ *the bosky shade* – *The Observer*⟩ **2** during [ME *amidde*, fr OE *onmiddan*, fr *on* + *middan*, dat of *midde* mid]

**amid-, amido-** comb form **1** containing an amide group ⟨*amidosulphuric*⟩ **2** amin- ⟨*amidopyrene*⟩ [ISV, fr *amide* ]

**Amida Buddha** n the principal object of faith of Japanese Mahayana Buddhists promising life in paradise for all who invoke his name

**amidase** /ˈamidayz, -ays/ n an ENZYME that promotes the breakdown of acid amides in a chemical reaction in which ammonia gas is usu produced [ISV *amide* + *-ase*]

**amide** /ˈamied, ˈamid/ n any of various usu organic chemical

compounds resulting from replacement of an atom of hydrogen in ammonia by a chemical element or chemical group, or of one or more atoms of hydrogen in ammonia by acid groups having a VALENCY of one – compare IMIDE [ISV, fr NL *ammonia*] – **amidic** adj

**amido** /ˈamidoh, əˈmeedoh/ adj of or containing the chemical group $NH_2$ or a substituted group NHR or $NR_2$ united to an acid group – compare AMINO [*amid-*]

**Amidol** /ˈamidol, -ohl/ *trademark* – used for a colourless chemical compound, $C_6H_3(NH_2)_2OH.2HCL$, that is used chiefly as a photographic developer

**amidships** /əˈmid,ships/ adv **1** in or towards the part of a ship midway between the bow and the stern **2** in or towards the middle

**amidst** /əˈmidst/ prep amid [alter. of ME *amiddes*, fr *amidde* + *-es, -s*, adv suffix (cf AGAINST, AMONGST, WHILST)]

**amigo** /əˈmeegoh/ n, pl **amigos** a friend [Sp, fr L *amicus* – more at AMIABLE]

**amin-, amino-** comb form containing an amino group ⟨*aminomethane*⟩ [ISV, fr *amine*]

**amine** /ˈameen, əˈmeen/ n any of various chemical compounds that are chemical BASES derived from ammonia by replacement of hydrogen by one or more carbon- and hydrogen-containing groups with a VALENCY of one [ISV, fr NL *ammonia*] – **aminic** adj

**amino** /əˈmeenoh/ adj of or containing the chemical group $NH_2$ or a substituted group NHR or $NR_2$ united to a group other than an acid group – compare AMIDO [*amin-*]

**amino acid** n an organic acid containing the amino group $NH_2$; *esp* any of the amino acids that are the chief components of proteins and are synthesized by living cells or are obtained as essential components of the diet

**aminobenzoic acid** /ə,meenohbenˈzoh·ik, ,aminoh-/ n any of three derivatives, $NH_2C_6H_4COOH$, of BENZOIC ACID of which one (PARA-AMINOBENZOIC ACID) is a factor of the VITAMIN B COMPLEX [ISV]

**aminophylline** /ə,meenohˈfileen, ,aminoh-, ,amiˈnofileen/ n a derivative, $(C_7H_8N_4O_2)_2C_2H_4(NH_2)_2$, of the chemical compound THEOPHYLLINE used esp to treat heart failure and respiratory disorders [*amin-* + *theophylline*]

**aminopyrine** /ə,meenohˈpiereen, ,aminoh-/ n a synthetic drug, $C_{13}H_{17}N_3O$, that is used to relieve fever and pain and that can cause a dangerous blood disorder in some users [ISV, fr *amin-* + anti*pyrine*]

**aminosalicylic acid** /ə,meenoh,saliˈsilik, ,aminoh-/ n any of the four amino derivatives of SALICYLIC ACID; *esp* the drug PARA-AMINOSALICYLIC ACID used to treat tuberculosis

**amir** /əˈmiə/ n an emir

**Amish** /ˈahmish, ˈamish/ adj of a strict sect of Mennonite followers of Amman in America [prob fr Ger *amisch*, fr Jacob *Amman* or *Amen* fl 1693 Swiss Mennonite bishop] – **Amish** n

**¹amiss** /əˈmis/ adv **1** in a mistaken way; wrongly ⟨*if you think he is guilty, you judge* ~⟩ **2** in a faulty way; imperfectly **3** out of place in given circumstances – usu + a neg ⟨*a few pertinent remarks may not come* ~ *here*⟩ [ME *amis*, fr *¹a-* + *mis* mistake, wrong, fr *missen* to miss] – **take amiss** to impute a wrong motive or a bad meaning or intention to; take offence at

**²amiss** adj out of order; at fault

**amitosis** /,amiˈtohsis/ n CELL DIVISION by simple splitting of the nucleus and division of the CYTOPLASM (jellylike substance filling a cell) without the appearance of CHROMOSOMES (strands of gene-carrying material) [NL, fr *²a-* + *mitosis*] – **amitotic** adj, **amitotically** adv

**amitriptyline** /,amiˈtriptəleen/ n an antidepressant drug, $C_{20}H_{23}N$ [*amin-* + *trypt*amine + methyl + *-ine*]

**amity** /ˈamiti/ n friendship; *esp* friendly relations between nations [ME *amite*, fr MF *amité*, fr ML *amicitas*, fr L *amicus* friend – more at AMIABLE]

**ammeter** /ˈameetə/ n an instrument for measuring electric current in amperes [*ampere* + *-meter*]

**ammine** /ˈameen, əˈmeen/ n **1** a molecule of ammonia as it exists in a COORDINATION COMPLEX (molecular structure usu involving a central metallic atom) ⟨*hex-ammine-cobalt chloride* $CON_6H_{18}Cl_3$⟩ **2** an ammino chemical compound [ISV *ammonia* + *-ine*]

**ammino** /ˈaminoh, əˈmeenoh/ adj of or being an ammine [ISV *ammino-*, fr *ammonia*]

**ammo** /ˈamoh/ n, *informal* ammunition [by shortening & alter.]

**ammocoete** /ˈaməseet/ n the larva of any of various LAMPREYS (eel-like animals with sucking mouthparts) [deriv of Gk *ammos* sand + *koitē* bed, fr *keisthai* to lie]

**ammonia** /ə'mohnyə, -ni•ə/ *n* **1** a pungent colourless gas that is a chemical compound of nitrogen and hydrogen, NH$_3$, is very soluble in water, forming an alkaline solution, and is used in the manufacture esp of fertilizers, synthetic fibres, and explosives **2 ammonia water, ammonia** a water solution of ammonia [NL, fr L *sal ammoniacus* sal ammoniac, lit., salt of Ammon, fr Gk *ammōniakos* of Ammon, fr *Ammōn* Ammon, Amen, an Egyptian god near one of whose temples it was prepared]

**ammoniac** /ə'mohni•ak/ *n* an aromatic GUM RESIN obtained from an Asian plant (*Dorema ammoniacum*) of the carrot family and used formerly in medicine as a stimulant and expectorant – called also GUM AMMONIAC [ME & L; ME, fr L *ammoniacum,* fr Gk *ammōniakon,* fr neut of *ammōniakos* of Ammon]

**ammoniacal** /,amə'nie•əkl/, **ammoniac** /ə'mohni,ak/ *adj* of, containing, or having the properties of ammonia

**ammoniate** /ə'mohni,ayt/ *vt* **1** to combine or impregnate with ammonia or an ammonium chemical compound **2** to subject to decomposition by ammonification – **ammoniation** *n*

**ammonification** /ə,mohnifi'kaysh(ə)n/ *n* **1** the act or process of ammoniating **2** decomposition with production of ammonia or ammonium chemical compounds, esp by the action of bacteria on nitrogen-containing organic matter – **ammonifier** *n*, **ammonify** *vb*

**ammonite** /'aməniet/ *n* any of numerous flat spiral fossil shells of a group (order Ammonoidea of the class Cephalopoda) of INVERTEBRATE animals related to the squids and octopuses, that were abundant esp in the MESOZOIC geological age [NL *ammonites,* fr L *cornu Ammonis,* lit., horn of Ammon (ie the ram's horns conventionally shown in pictures of Ammon)] – **ammonitic** *adj*

**ammonium** /ə'mohnyəm, -ni•əm/ *n* an ion, NH$_4$$^+$, or chemical group, NH$_4$, derived from ammonia by combination with a hydrogen ion or atom and known in chemical compounds (eg salts) that resemble in properties the compounds of the ALKALI METALS and in organic chemical compounds (eg quaternary ammonium compounds) [NL, fr *ammonia*]

**ammonium carbonate** *n* a chemical compound, (NH$_4$)$_2$CO$_3$, that is a CARBONATE of ammonium; *specif* the commercial mixture of the BICARBONATE and CARBAMATE used esp in smelling salts

**ammonium chloride** *n* a white readily vaporizing chemical compound, NH$_4$Cl, that is used in dry-cell batteries and as a medicine that helps to clear phlegm from the chest or lungs

**ammonium hydroxide** *n* a chemical compound, NH$_4$OH, that is formed when ammonia dissolves in water and that exists only in solution

**ammonium nitrate** *n* a colourless chemical compound, NH$_4$NO$_3$, used in explosives and fertilizers

**ammonium phosphate** *n* a chemical compound that is a PHOSPHATE of ammonium; *esp* a white compound, (NH$_4$)$_2$HPO$_4$, used esp as a fertilizer and as a fire retardant

**ammonium sulphate** *n* a white chemical compound, (NH$_4$)$_2$SO$_4$, used esp as a nitrogen-containing fertilizer

**ammonoid** /'amənoyd/ *n* AMMONITE (type of fossil shell)

**ammunition** /,amyoo'nish(ə)n/ *n* **1a** the projectiles, together with their fuses, primers, and propelling charges, used in the firing of guns **b** items (eg bullets, shells, grenades, or bombs) propelled by or containing explosives **2** material used to defend or attack a point of view ⟨his indiscretions provided ∼ for the press⟩ [obs Fr *amunition,* fr MF, alter. of *munition*]

**amnesia** /am'neezyə, -zh(y)ə/ *n* a loss of memory (eg due to brain injury) ⟨*suffered from* ∼ *after the car crash*⟩; *broadly* a gap in one's memory [NL, fr Gk *amnēsia* forgetfulness, prob alter. of *amnēstia*] – **amnesiac, amnesic** *adj or n,* **amnestic** *adj*

**amnesty** /'amnəsti/ *n* a pardon granted to a large group of individuals, esp for political offences [Gk *amnēstia* forgetfulness, fr *amnēstos* forgotten, fr *a-* + *mnasthai* to remember – more at MIND] – **amnesty** *vt*

**amniocentesis** /,amniohsen'teesis/ *n* the surgical insertion of a hollow needle through the abdominal wall and uterus of a pregnant female, esp to obtain amniotic fluid from which the sex of the foetus can be determined and any abnormality in its CHROMOSOMES (strands of gene-carrying material in the cells) can be detected [NL, fr *amnion* + *centesis* puncture, fr Gk *kentesis,* fr *kentein* to prick – more at CENTRE]

**amnion** /'amni•ən/ *n, pl* **amnions, amnia** /'amni•ə/ **1** a thin membrane forming a closed sac round the embryos of reptiles, birds, and mammals and containing a watery fluid in which the embryo is immersed **2** a membrane analogous to the mammalian amnion and occurring in various INVERTEBRATE animals [NL, fr Gk, caul, prob fr dim. of *amnos* lamb] – **amniote** *adj or n,* **amniotic** *adj*

**amoeba, chiefly NAm ameba** /ə'meebə/ *n, pl* **amoebas, amoebae** /ə'meebee/ any of a large genus (*Amoeba* of the class Rhizopodea) of PROTOZOANS (single-celled organisms) that have temporary lobed projections (PSEUDOPODIA), with which they feed and move, and that are widely distributed in fresh and salt water and moist terrestrial habitats; *broadly* an amoeboid protozoan [NL, genus name, fr Gk *amoibē* change, fr *ameibein* to change – more at MIGRATE] – **amoebic** *also* **amoeban** *adj*

**amoebiasis** /,amee'bie•əsis/ *n* infection, or disease, esp of the intestines, caused by amoebas [NL]

**amoebic dysentery** /ə'meebik/ *n* a short-lived serious intestinal disease of human beings caused by an amoeba (*Entamoeba histolytica*) and marked by dysentery, griping pain, and erosion of the intestinal wall

**amoebocyte** /ə'meebə,siet/ *n* a cell (eg a PHAGOCYTE) having amoeboid form or movements

**amoeboid** /ə'mee,boyd/ *adj* resembling an amoeba, specif in moving or changing in shape by means of the flow of PROTOPLASM (internal cellular material)

**amok** /ə'muk/ *adv* **1** in a murderous frenzy; raging violently **2** OUT OF HAND □ chiefly in *run amok* [Malay]

**among** /ə'mung/ *prep* **1** in or through the midst of; surrounded by **2** in company or association with ⟨*living* ∼ *artists*⟩ **3** by or through the whole group of ⟨*discontent* ∼ *the poor*⟩ **4** in the number or class of ⟨*wittiest* ∼ *poets*⟩ ⟨∼ *other things she was captain of the hockey team*⟩ **5** in shares to each of; between – used for more than two ⟨*divided* ∼ *the heirs*⟩ **6** through the common or reciprocal action of; between – used for more than two ⟨*made a fortune* ∼ *themselves*⟩ [ME, fr OE *on gemonge,* fr *on* + *gemonge,* dat of *gemong* crowd, fr *ge-* (associative prefix) + *-mong* (akin to OE *mengan* to mix) – more at MINGLE]

*usage* Where only two participants are involved, **between** is used instead of **among** ⟨*divided it* **between** *John and Anne*⟩. The use of **between**, rather than **among**, for more than two has been established in English since the 10th century ⟨*two or more possible arrangements* **between** *which a choice must be consciously made* – H W Fowler⟩ and is objected to only by very conservative writers on usage. When we speak of exact position or of precise individual relationships, **between** is the only choice ⟨*Ecuador lies* **between** *Colombia, Peru, and the Pacific Ocean*⟩ ⟨*a treaty* **between** *four European Powers*⟩.

**amongst** /ə'mungst/ *prep* among [alter. of ME *amonges,* fr *among* + *-es, -s,* adv suffix (cf AGAINST, AMIDST, WHILST)]

**amontillado** /ə,monti'lahdoh/ *n, pl* **amontillados** a pale fairly dry sherry [Sp, fr *a* to + *montilla* Montilla]

**amoral** /a(y)'morəl, ə-/ *adj* **1** neither moral nor immoral; *specif* lying outside the sphere of ethical judgments **2** having no understanding of, or unconcerned with, morals □ compare IMMORAL – **amoralism, amorally** *adv,* **amorality** *n*

**amorist** /'amərist/ *n* **1** a devotee of sexual love; a gallant **2** one who writes about romantic love – **amoristic** *adj*

**amorous** /'amərəs/ *adj* **1** relating to love **2** moved by, inclined to, or indicative of love or desire [ME, fr MF, fr ML *amorosus,* fr L *amor* love, fr *amare* to love] – **amorously** *adv,* **amorousness** *n*

*synonyms* **Amatory** describes behaviour or art expressing or inspired by sexual love, while **amorous** relates specifically to sexual desire ⟨*amatory poetry*⟩ ⟨*amorous advances*⟩.

**amorphous** /ə'mawfəs/ *adj* **1a** having no definite form; shapeless ⟨*an* ∼ *cloud mass*⟩ **b** without definite character or nature; unclassifiable **c** lacking organization or unity **2** having no real or apparent crystalline form; uncrystallized ⟨*an* ∼ *mineral*⟩ [Gk *amorphos,* fr *a-* + *morphē* form] – **amorphism** *n,* **amorphously** *adv,* **amorphousness** *n*

**amort·ize, -ise** /ə'mawtiez/ *vt* to provide for the gradual paying off of (eg a mortgage), usu by periodic contributions to a fund of money (SINKING FUND) set aside for the purpose [ME *amortisen* to deaden, alienate in mortmain, modif of MF *amortiss-,* stem of *amortir,* fr (assumed) VL *admortire* to deaden, fr L *ad-* + *mort-, mors* death – more at MURDER] – **amortizable** *adj,* **amortization** *n*

**Amos** /'aymos/ *n* – see BIBLE table [(a prophetic book of the

Old Testament attributed to) a Hebrew prophet of the 8th century BC]

**¹amount** /ə'mownt/ *vi* **1** to be equal in number or quantity *to* ⟨*the bill* ~*s to £10*⟩ **2** to be equivalent in significance *to* ⟨*acts that* ~ *to treason*⟩ [ME *amounten*, fr OF *amonter*, fr *amont* upwards, fr *a-* (fr L *ad-*) + *mont* mountain – more at MOUNT]

**²amount** *n* **1** the total quantity; the aggregate **2** the quantity at hand or under consideration ⟨*has an enormous* ~ *of energy*⟩ **3** a sum of money on which interest is earned, together with the interest on it

*usage* Amount and quantity are correctly used of mass nouns with no plural, and of abstractions that cannot be counted, in the way that **number** is used of plurals. Compare ⟨*a large* **quantity** *of butter*⟩⟨*a certain* **amount** *of influence*⟩⟨*a large* **number** (not **amount**) *of people*⟩⟨*a certain* **number** (not **amount**) *of mistakes*⟩.

**amour** /ə'maw, ə'mooə (*Fr* amur)/ *n* a love affair, esp when illicit [ME, love, affection, fr OF, fr OProv *amor*, fr L, fr *amare* to love]

**amour propre** /'proprə (*Fr* prɔpr)/ *n* self-esteem [Fr *amour-propre*, lit., love of oneself]

**amp** /amp/ *n* **1** an ampere **2** *informal* an amplifier

**AMP** *n* a chemical compound that is a MONONUCLEOTIDE of ADENINE, $C_{10}H_{12}N_5O_3H_2PO_4$, and that is reversibly convertible in cells to the energy-storing compounds ADP and ATP – compare CYCLIC AMP [*adenosine monophosphate*]

**amperage** /'amp(ə)rij/ *n* the strength of a current of electricity expressed in amperes

**ampere** /'ampeə/ *n* the SI unit of electric current equal to a constant current that when maintained in two straight parallel conductors of infinite length and negligible circular cross-section one metre apart in a vacuum produces between the conductors a force equal to 2 x $10^{-7}$ newton per metre of length [André *Ampère* †1836 Fr physicist]

**‚ampere-'hour** *n* a unit quantity of electricity equal to the quantity carried past any point of a circuit by a steady current of one ampere flowing for one hour

**‚ampere-'turn** *n* a unit of MAGNETOMOTIVE FORCE equal to the magnetomotive force produced by a current of one ampere flowing through one turn of a coil in an electromagnet

**ampersand** /'ampə‚sand/ *n* a sign, typically &, standing for the word *and* [alter. of *and* (&) *per se and*, lit., (the character) & by itself (is the word) *and*]

**amphetamine** /am'fetəmeen, -min/ *n* a synthetic drug, $C_6H_5CH_2CH(NH_2)CH_3$, that is a powerful stimulant of the CENTRAL NERVOUS SYSTEM and that can be strongly addictive if abused; *also* any of several derivatives of amphetamine (e g DEXTROAMPHETAMINE SULPHATE) that have similar properties and uses and have also been used in the treatment of obesity [ISV *alpha* + *methyl* + *phen-* + *ethyl* + *amine*]

**amphi-** /amfi-/, **amph-** *prefix* **1** on both sides; round ⟨*amphitheatre*⟩ **2** of both kinds; both ⟨*amphi*bian⟩ [L *amphi-* round, on both sides, fr Gk *amphi-*, *amph-*, fr *amphi* – more at AMBI-]

**amphibian** /am'fibi·ən/ *n, pl* **amphibians, amphibia** /-biə/ **1** an amphibious organism; *esp* any of a class (Amphibia) of cold-blooded VERTEBRATE animals (e g frogs, toads, or newts) intermediate in many characteristics between fishes and reptiles and having gilled aquatic larvae and air-breathing adults **2** a vehicle (e g an aeroplane or tank) designed to operate on or from both land and water [deriv of Gk *amphibion* amphibious being, fr neut of *amphibios*] – **amphibian** *adj*

**amphibious** /am'fibi·əs/ *adj* **1** able to live both on land and in water ⟨~ *plants*⟩ **2a** relating to or designed for both land and water ⟨~ *vehicles*⟩ **b** involving or trained for coordinated action of land, sea, and air forces organized for invasion ⟨~ *forces*⟩ **3** combining two positions or qualities [Gk *amphibios*, lit., living a double life, fr *amphi-* + *bios* mode of life – more at QUICK] – **amphibiously** *adv*, **amphibiousness** *n*

**amphibole** /'amfi‚bohl/ *n* any of a group of complex rock-forming minerals that are SILICATES with similar crystal structures usu containing three groups of metal ions; *esp* HORN-BLENDE [Fr, fr LL *amphibolus*, fr Gk *amphibolos* ambiguous, fr *amphiballein* to throw round, doubt, fr *amphi-* + *ballein* to throw – more at DEVIL] – **amphibolitic** *adj*

**amphibolite** /am'fibəliet/ *n* a coarse-grained usu METAMORPHIC rock consisting essentially of amphibole – **amphibolitic** *adj*

**amphibology** /‚amfi'boləji/ *n* ambiguity of sentence construction (e g in "are the children at home safe?") [ME *amphibologie*, fr LL *amphibologia*, alter. of *amphibolia*, fr Gk, fr *amphibolos*]

**amphibrach** /'amfi‚brak/ *n* a unit of poetic metre (FOOT) consisting of a long syllable between two short syllables [L *amphi-*

*brachys*, fr Gk, lit., short at both ends, fr *amphi-* + *brachys* short – more at BRIEF] – **amphibrachic** *adj*

**amphidiploid** /‚amfi'diployd/ *n or adj* (an interspecific hybrid plant or animal) having a complete double (DIPLOID) set of CHROMOSOMES (strands of gene-carrying material in cells) from each parent strain – **amphidiploidy** *n*

**amphimacer** /am'fimasə, 'amfi‚maysə/ *n* a unit of poetic metre (FOOT) consisting of a short syllable between two long syllables [L *amphimacrus*, fr Gk *amphimakros*, lit., long at both ends, fr *amphi-* + *makros* long – more at MEAGRE]

**amphimictic** /‚amfi'miktik/ *adj* capable of interbreeding freely and of producing fertile offspring [ISV *amphi-* + Gk *miktos* blended, fr *mignynai*] – **amphimictically** *adv*

**amphimixis** /‚amfi'miksis/ *n, pl* **amphimixes** /-'mickseez/ (the union of reproductive cells in) SEXUAL REPRODUCTION – compare APOMIXIS [NL, fr *amphi-* + Gk *mixis* mingling, fr *mignynai* to mix – more at MIX]

**amphioxus** /‚amfi'oksəs/ *n, pl* **amphioxi** /-'oksie/, **amphioxuses** any of a genus (*Branchiostoma*) of LANCELETS (small fishlike marine animals); *broadly* a lancelet [NL, fr *amphi-* + Gk *oxys* sharp]

**amphiploid** /'amfi‚ployd/ *adj, of a hybrid* having at least one complete double (DIPLOID) set of CHROMOSOMES (strands of gene-carrying material in cells) derived from each ancestral species – **amphiploid** *n*, **amphiploidy** *n*

**amphipod** /'amfi‚pod/ *n* any of a large group (Amphipoda of the class Crustacea) of small shrimplike INVERTEBRATE animals (e g the sandhopper) with a body flattened sideways [deriv of Gk *amphi-* + *pod-, pous* foot – more at FOOT] – **amphipod** *adj*

**amphiprostyle** /‚amfi'proh‚stiel/ *adj* having columns at each end but not at the sides ⟨*a* ~ *temple*⟩ [L *amphiprostylos*, fr Gk, fr *amphi-* + *prostylos* having pillars in front, fr *pro-* + *stylos* pillar – more at STEER] – **amphiprostyle** *n*

**amphisbaena** /‚amfis'beenə/ *n* a serpent in classical mythology having a head at each end and capable of moving in either direction [L, fr Gk *amphisbaina*, fr *amphis* on both sides (fr *amphi* round) + *bainein* to walk, go – more at BY, COME] – **amphisbaenic** *adj*

**amphisbaenian** /‚amfis'beenyən/ *n* any of various modified wormlike burrowing reptiles (genus *Amphisbaena*) that live in warm or tropical countries [NL *Amphisbaena*, genus name, fr L, amphisbaena] – **amphisbaenian** *adj*

**amphitheatre** /'amfi‚thiətə/ *n* **1a** an oval or circular building with rising tiers of seats ranged about an arena and used in ancient Rome esp for contests and public spectacles **b** an arena where public games, contests, etc are held **2** a semicircular gallery in a theatre **3** a flat or gently sloping area surrounded by abrupt slopes **4** a room with a gallery from which doctors and students may observe surgical operations [L *amphitheatrum*, fr Gk *amphitheatrou*, fr *amphi-* + *theatron* theatre] – **amphitheatric, amphitheatrical** *adj*, **amphitheatrically** *adv*

**amphora** /'amfərə/ *n, pl* **amphorae** /'amfəri, -rie/, **amphoras** a 2-handled oval jar or vase with a narrow neck and base, originally used by the ancient Greeks and Romans for holding oil or wine [L, modif of Gk *amphoreus, amphiphoreus*, fr *amphi-* + *phoreus* bearer, fr *pherein* to bear – more at BEAR]

**amphoteric** /‚amfə'terik/ *adj* partly one and partly the other; *specif* capable of reacting chemically either as an acid or as a BASE [ISV, fr Gk *amphoteros* each of two, fr *amphō* both – more at AMBI-]

**amphotericin** /‚amfə'terəsin/ *n* either of two antibiotic drugs obtained from a soil bacterium (*Streptomyces nodosus*); *esp* one used against deep-seated and nonlocalized fungal infections [*amphoteric* + *-in*]

**ampicillin** /‚ampi'silin/ *n* a penicillin that is effective against a wide variety of bacteria and is used esp to treat respiratory infections (e g bronchitis) [*amin-* + *penicillin*]

**ample** /'ampl/ *adj* **1** generous or more than adequate in size, scope, or capacity **2** generously sufficient to satisfy a requirement or need; abundant ⟨*they had* ~ *money for the trip*⟩ **3** *euph* buxom, portly ⟨*an* ~ *figure*⟩ **synonyms** see PLENTIFUL, SUFFICIENT *antonyms* insufficient, meagre, scant, scanty [MF, fr L *amplus*] – **ampleness** *n*, **amply** *adv*

**amplexicaul** /am'pleksi‚kawl/ *adj, of a leaf* having no stalk and surrounding the plant stem with its base [NL *amplexicaulis*, fr L *amplexus* (pp of *amplecti* to entwine, fr *ambi-* + *plectere* to braid) + *-i-* + *caulis* stem – more at HOLE]

**amplexus** /am'pleksəs/ *n* the mating embrace of frogs or toads during which eggs are shed into the water and there fertilized [NL, fr L, embrace, fr *amplexus*, pp]

**amplification** /ˌamplifiˈkaysh(ə)n/ *n* **1** an act, example, or product of amplifying **2a** the particulars used to expand a statement **b** an expanded statement

**amplifier** /ˈampliˌfie·ə/ *n* **1** one who or that which amplifies **2** a device usu employing transistors or valves to obtain amplification of voltage, current, or power; *specif* such a device whose output is used to produce amplified sound

**amplify** /ˈampliˌfie/ *vt* **1** to expand (e g a statement) by the use of detail or illustration or by closer analysis **2** to make larger or greater (e g in amount, importance, or intensity); increase **3** to increase the magnitude of (an electrical signal or other input of power) ~ *vi* to expand on one's remarks or ideas *synonyms* see EXPAND *antonyms* abridge, condense [ME *amplifien*, fr MF *amplifier*, fr L *amplificare*, fr *amplus*]

**amplitude** /ˈamplityoohd, -choohd/ *n* **1** largeness of dimensions or scope; abundance **2a** the extent of a vibration or oscillation measured from the average position to a maximum **b** the maximum departure of the value of an ALTERNATING CURRENT or wave (e g a radio wave) from the average value **3** the position of the horizon between the true east or west point and the foot of a vertical circle passing through any star or object

**amplitude modulation** *n* a MODULATION (controlled alteration in size or state) of the strength (AMPLITUDE) of a wave, esp a radio carrier wave, by the characteristics of the signal carried; *also* a method of transmitting using this – compare FREQUENCY MODULATION

**ampoule**, *chiefly NAm* **ampul**, **ampule** /ˈampoohl/ *n* a sealed airtight small bulbous glass vessel that is used esp to hold a sterile solution for hypodermic injection [ME *ampulle* flask, fr OE *ampulle* & OF *ampoule*, fr L *ampulla*]

**ampulla** /amˈpoolə/ *n, pl* **ampullae** /-li/ **1** a 2-handled globular flask of glass or earthenware used esp by the ancient Romans to hold ointment, perfume, or wine **2** a saclike anatomical swelling or pouch [ME, fr OE, fr L, dim. of *amphora*] – **ampullar** *adj*

**amputate** /ˈampyootayt/ *vt* to cut or lop off; *esp* to cut (e g a damaged or diseased limb) from the body [L *amputatus*, pp of *amputare*, fr *am-, amb-* round + *putare* to cut, prune – more at AMBI-, PAVE] – **amputator** *n*, **amputation** *n*

**amputee** /ˌampyooˈtee/ *n* somebody who has had a limb amputated

**amuck** /əˈmuk/ *adv* amok

**amulet** /ˈamyoolit/ *n* a charm often inscribed with a magic incantation or symbol to aid the wearer or protect him/her against evil [L *amuletum*]

**amuse** /əˈmyoohz/ *vt* **1a** to entertain or occupy in a light, playful, or pleasant manner ⟨~ *the child with a story*⟩ **b** to appeal to the sense of humour of ⟨*the joke doesn't* ~ *me*⟩ **2a** *archaic* to divert the attention of so as to deceive; bemuse **b** *obs* to occupy the attention of; absorb **c** *obs* to distract, bewilder *antonym* bore [MF *amuser*, fr OF, fr *a-* (fr L *ad-*) + *muser* to muse] – **amuser** *n*, **amusing** *adj*, **amusingly** *adv*, **amusingness** *n*, **amusedly** *adv*

**amusement** /əˈmyoohzmənt/ *n* **1** a means of entertaining or occupying; a pleasurable diversion ⟨*plays the piano for his own* ~⟩ **2** the condition of being amused; enjoyment ⟨*his* ~ *knew no bounds*⟩ **3** a mechanical device (e g a roundabout or big wheel) for entertainment at a fair ⟨*go on all the* ~s⟩

**amusement arcade** *n, chiefly Br* a covered area containing coin-operated games machines for recreation

**amusement park** *n* a commercially operated enclosed park where various amusements (e g roundabouts or sideshows) are permanently set up

**amygdala** /əˈmigdələ/ *n, pl* **amygdalae** /-li, -lie/ an almond-shaped mass of nerve tissue (GREY MATTER) in the roof of a cavity (VENTRICLE) in the side of the brain [NL, fr L, almond, fr Gk *amygdalē*]

**amygdalin** /əˈmigdəlin/ *n* a GLUCOSIDE (derivative of sugar), $C_{20}H_{27}NO_{11}$, that produces cyanide, is found esp in the bitter almond (*Amygdalus communis amara*), and is held to be of use in treating cancer [NL *Amygdalus*, genus name, fr LL, almond tree, fr Gk *amygdalos*; akin to Gk *amygdalē*]

**¹amygdaloid** /əˈmigdəloyd/ *n* a usu volcanic rock originally containing small cavities filled with deposits of different minerals (e g chalcedony or calcite) [Gk *amygdaloeidēs*, adj] – **amygdaloidal** *adj*

**²amygdaloid** *adj* **1** almond-shaped **2** of an amygdala [Gk *amygdaloeidēs*, fr *amygdalē* almond]

**amyl** /ˈamil, ˈamiel/ *n* PENTYL (type of chemical compound) [blend of *amyl-* and *-yl*]

**amyl-, amylo-** *comb form* starch ⟨*amylase*⟩ [LL *amyl-*, fr L *amylum*, fr Gk *amylon*, fr neut of *amylos* not ground at the mill, fr *a-* + *mylē* mill – more at MEAL]

**amylaceous** /ˌamiˈlayshəs/ *adj* of or having the characteristics of starch; starchy

**amyl acetate** *n* a colourless liquid ACETATE, $CH_3COOC_5H_{11}$, of AMYL ALCOHOL that has a pleasant fruity smell and is used as a solvent and in manufacturing (e g of artificial fruit essences and artificial silk and leather) – called also BANANA OIL

**amyl alcohol** *n* any of eight related alcohols, $C_5H_{11}OH$, used esp as solvents and in making other chemical compounds (ESTERS)

**amylase** /ˈamilayz, -lays/ *n* any of the ENZYMES (e g amylopsin) that accelerate the breakdown of starch and glycogen, or their products, into simple sugars

**¹amyloid** /ˈamiloyd/, **amyloidal** /ˌamiˈloydl/ *adj* resembling or containing amylum

**²amyloid** *n* a hard waxy translucent substance consisting of protein in combination with POLYSACCHARIDES (complex carbohydrates) that is deposited in some animal organs under abnormal conditions (e g when affected by disease)

**amyloidosis** /ˌamiloyˈdohsis/ *n* a condition characterized by the deposition of amyloid in organs or tissues [NL]

**amylolysis** /ˌamiˈloləsis/ *n* the conversion of starch into soluble products (e g sugars), esp by ENZYMES [NL] – **amylolytic** *adj*

**amylopectin** /ˌamilohˈpektin/ *n* a component of starch characterized by its branched chains of glucose units, its high MOLECULAR WEIGHT, and the lack of tendency of its aqueous solutions to gel

**amylopsin** /ˌamiˈlopsin/ *n* the amylase of the PANCREATIC JUICE [*amyl-* + *-psin* (as in *trypsin*)]

**amylose** /ˈamilohz, -lohs/ *n* **1** any of various POLYSACCHARIDES (complex carbohydrates) (e g starch or cellulose) **2** a component of starch characterized by its straight chains of glucose units and by the tendency of its aqueous solutions to set to a stiff gel **3** any of various chemical compounds, $(C_6H_{10}O_5)_n$, obtained by the breakdown of starch

**amylum** /ˈamiləm/ *n* STARCH **1** [L – more at AMYL-]

**amyotonia** /ˌaˌmie·əˈtohnyə/ *n* deficiency of muscle tone [NL, fr ²*a-* + *myotonia*]

**¹an** /(ə)n; *strong* an/ *indefinite article* ²A – used (1) before words or letter sequences with an initial vowel sound ⟨~ *oak*⟩ ⟨~ *honour*⟩ ⟨~ *RAF officer*⟩ (2) frequently, esp formerly or in the USA, before words whose initial /h/ sound is often lost before the *an* ⟨~ *hotel*⟩ (3) sometimes, esp formerly in British writing, before words like *union* or *European* whose initial sound is /y/ [ME, fr OE *ān* one – more at ONE]

**²an, an'** *conj* **1** and **2** *archaic* if

**³an** *prep* ³A – used under the same conditions as ¹AN

**an-** /an-/ – see ²A-

**¹-an** /-ən/, **-ian** *also* **-ean** *suffix* (→ *n*) **1** one who is of or belonging to ⟨*Mancun*ian⟩ ⟨*republic*an⟩ **2** one skilled in or specializing in ⟨*phonetic*ian⟩ [*-an* & *-ian* fr ME *-an, -ian,* fr OF & L; OF *-ien,* fr L *-ianus,* fr *-i-* + *-anus,* fr *-anus,* adj suffix; *-ean* fr such words as *Mediterranean, European*]

**²-an, -ian** *also* **-ean** *suffix* (→ *adj*) **1** of or belonging to ⟨*Americ*an⟩ ⟨*Christi*an⟩ **2** characteristic of; resembling ⟨*Mozart*ean⟩ ⟨*Shavi*an⟩

**³-an** *suffix* (→ *n*) **1** unsaturated carbon chemical compound ⟨*tol*an⟩ ⟨*fur*an⟩ **2** polymeric anhydride of (a specified carbohydrate) ⟨*dextr*an⟩ [ISV *-an, -ane,* alter. of *-ene, -ine,* & *-one*]

**¹ana** /ˈanə/ *adv* of each an equal quantity – used formerly in prescriptions and usu abbreviated to āā or ĀĀ [ME, fr ML, fr Gk, at the rate of, lit., up]

**²ana** /ˈahnə/ *n, pl* **ana, anas** (an item in) a collection of anecdotes or interesting or curious information about a person or a place [*-ana*]

**ana-** /anə-/, **an-** *prefix* **1** up; upwards ⟨*anabasis*⟩ **2** back; backwards ⟨*anatropous*⟩ **3** again ⟨*anabaptism*⟩ [L, fr Gk, up, back, again, fr *ana* up – more at ON]

**-ana** /-ˈahnə/, **-iana** /-iˈahnə/ *suffix* (→ *n pl*) collected objects or information relating to or characteristic of (a specified topic or individual) ⟨*Victori*ana⟩ ⟨*Johnsoni*ana⟩ [NL, fr L, neut pl of *-anus* -an & *-ianus* -ian]

**anabaptism** /ˌanəˈbaptiz(ə)m/ *n* **1** *cap* the (doctrine or practices of the) Anabaptist movement **2** the baptism of one previously baptized, esp as practised by Anabaptists [NL *anabaptismus,* fr LGk *anabaptismos* rebaptism, fr *anabaptizein* to rebaptize, fr *ana-* again + *baptizein* to baptize]

**Anabaptist** /ˌanəˈbaptist/ n or adj (a member) of a radical protestant movement which arose in Zurich in 1524 and advocates the baptism of adult believers only, nonresistance, and the separation of church and state

**anabas** /ˈanəbəs, -bas/ n any of a genus (*Anabas*) of fishes; *esp* CLIMBING PERCH [NL, genus name, fr Gk *anabainein* to go up]

**anabasis** /əˈnabəsis/ n, pl **anabases** /-seez/ 1 an esp military advance 2 a difficult and dangerous military retreat [Gk, inland march, fr *anabainein* to go up or inland, fr *ana-* + *bainein* to go – more at COME; (2) fr the retreat of Gk mercenaries in Asia Minor described in the *Anabasis* by Xenophon † ab 355 BC Gk historian]

**anabatic** /ˌanəˈbatik/ adj moving upwards, esp up a slope; rising 〈*an ∼ wind*〉 [Gk *anabatos*, verbal of *anabainein*]

**anabiosis** /ˌanəbieˈohsis/ n, pl **anabioses** /-seez/ a state of suspended animation or apparent death induced in some organisms (eg by desiccation) and from which they can be revived [NL, fr Gk *anabiōsis* return to life, fr *anabioun* to return to life, fr *ana-* + *bios* life – more at QUICK] – **anabiotic** adj

**anabolic steroid** /ˌanəˈbolik/ n any of several synthetic STEROID hormones that cause a rapid increase in the size and weight of skeletal muscle and are used esp to increase strength (eg by athletes)

**anabolism** /əˈnabəˌliz(ə)m/ n constructive METABOLISM (life-supporting chemical reactions) involving the utilization of energy and resulting in the synthesis of complex materials (eg proteins) within the organism [ISV *ana-* + *-bolism* (as in *metabolism*)] – **anabolic** adj

**anabranch** /ˈanəˌbrahnch/ n a diverging branch of a river which reenters the river or which sinks into the ground downstream

**anachronism** /əˈnakrəˌniz(ə)m/ n 1 an error in CHRONOLOGY (arrangement of events, dates, etc in order of occurrence); *esp* a chronological misplacing of people, events, objects, or customs 2 somebody or something that seems misplaced in time [prob fr MGk *anachronismos*, fr *anachronizesthai* to be an anachronism, fr LGk *anachronizein* to be late, fr Gk *ana-* + *chronos* time] – **anachronistic** *also* **anachronic, anachronous** adj, **anachronistically** *also* **anachronously** adv

**anaclitic** /ˌanəˈklitik/ adj of or being a relationship in which an object of attraction resembles the protective figures of early infancy [Gk *anaklitos* for reclining, fr *anaklisis* act of reclining, fr *anaklinein* to lean upon] – **anaclisis** n

**anacoluthon** /ˌanəkəˈloohˌthon/ n, pl **anacolutha** /-thə/, **anacoluthons** inconsistency in the way in which words are put together to form phrases, sentences, etc; *esp* the shift from one construction to another (eg in "you really ought – well, do it your own way") [LL, fr LGk *anakolouthon* inconsistency in logic, fr Gk, neut of *anakolouthos* inconsistent, fr *an-* + *akolouthos* following, fr *ha-, a-* together + *keleuthos* path; akin to Gk *hama* together – more at SAME] – **anacoluthic** adj, **anacoluthically** adv

**anaconda** /ˌanəˈkondə/ n a large semiaquatic snake (*Eunectes murinus*) of the boa family of tropical S America that crushes its prey in its coils; *broadly* a large constricting snake [prob modif of Sinhalese *henakandayā* a slender green snake]

**anacreontic** /əˌnakriˈontik/ n or adj, often cap (a poem or song) in the manner of Anacreon, esp in dealing with love or drink [L *anacreonticus*, fr *Anacreont-, Anacreon* Anacreon † ab 488 BC Gk poet, fr Gk *Anakreont-, Anakreōn*]

**anacrusis** /ˌanəˈkroohsis/ n, pl **anacruses** 1 one or more unstressed syllables at the beginning of a line of poetry not included in the metrical scheme 2 UPBEAT (musical beat before an accented note); *specif* one or more notes preceding the first downbeat of a musical phrase [NL, fr Gk *anakrousis* beginning of a song, fr *anakrouein* to begin a song, fr *ana-* + *krouein* to strike, beat; akin to Lith *krušti* to stamp]

**anadem** /ˈanədem, -dəm/ n, archaic a garland [L *anadema*, fr Gk *anadēma*, fr *anadein* to wreathe, fr *ana-* + *dein* to bind – more at DIADEM]

**anadiplosis** /ˌanədiˈplohsis/ n, pl **anadiploses** /-seez/ repetition of a prominent and usu final word in one phrase or clause at the beginning of the next (eg in "rely on his honour – honour such as his?") [LL, fr Gk *anadiplōsis*, lit., repetition, fr *anadiploun* to double, fr *ana-* + *diploun* to double – more at DIPLOMA]

**anadromous** /əˈnadrəməs/ adj, of a fish ascending rivers from the sea for breeding 〈*salmon are ∼*〉 [Gk *anadromos* running upward, fr *anadramein* to run upward, fr *ana-* + *dramein* to run – more at DROMEDARY]

**anaemia,** *chiefly NAm* **anemia** /əˈneemyə, -miˈə/ n **1a** a condition in which the blood is deficient in RED BLOOD CELLS, haemoglobin, or total volume **b** inadequate blood supply to a particular organ **2** lack of vitality [NL, fr Gk *anaimia* bloodlessness, fr *an-* + *haima* blood] – **anaemic** adj, **anaemically** adv

**anaerobe** /əˈneərohb, 'anəˌrohb/ n an organism (eg a bacterium) that lives only in the absence of oxygen [ISV]

**anaerobic** /ˌanəˈrohbik, ˌaneə-/ adj **1** living, active, or occurring in the absence of oxygen 〈*∼ bacteria*〉 〈*∼ respiration*〉 **2** of or induced by anaerobes 〈*∼ breakdown of organic matter*〉 – **anaerobically** adv

**anaerobiosis** /ˌanərohbieˈohsis/ n pl **anaerobioses** /-seez/ life in the absence of air or oxygen [NL]

**anaesthesia,** *chiefly NAm* **anesthesia** /ˌanəsˈtheezh(y)ə, -zyə/ n loss of sensation, esp loss of sensation of pain, resulting either from injury or a disorder of the nerves or from the action of drugs – compare ANALGESIA [NL, fr Gk *anaisthēsia*, fr *an-* + *aisthēsis* sensation, fr *aisthanesthai* to perceive – more at AUDIBLE]

**anaesthesiology** /ˌanəsˌtheeziˈoləji/ n, *NAm* ANAESTHETICS 2

**¹anaesthetic,** *chiefly NAm* **anesthetic** /ˌanəsˈthetik/ adj of or capable of producing anaesthesia – **anaesthetically** adv

**²anaesthetic** n **1** a substance (eg HALOTHANE or LIGNOCAINE) that produces anaesthesia, esp so that surgery can be carried out painlessly **2** pl but taking sing vb a branch of medical science dealing with anaesthesia and anaesthetics

**anaesthet·ize, -ise** /əˈneesthəˌtiez/ vt to subject to anaesthesia, esp for purposes of surgery – **anaesthetist** n

**anaglyph** /ˈanəˌglif/ n **1** a sculptured or embossed ornament in low relief **2** a moving or still picture in which two images in contrasting colours are superimposed to produce a three-dimensional effect when viewed through filters of these same colours in the form of spectacles [LL *anaglyphus* embossed, fr Gk *anaglyphos*, fr *anaglyphein* to emboss, fr *ana-* + *glyphein* to carve – more at CLEAVE] – **anaglyphic** adj

**anagoge, anagogy** /ˈanəˌgohji/ n, pl **anagoges, anagogies** interpretation of a word or text (eg of Scripture or poetry) that finds beyond the literal, allegorical, and moral senses a fourth and ultimate spiritual or mystical sense [LL *anagoge*, fr LGk *anagōgē*, fr Gk, reference, fr *anagein* to refer, fr *ana-* + *agein* to lead – more at AGENT] – **anagogic, anagogical** adj, **anagogically** adv

**anagram** /ˈanəˌgram/ n a word or phrase made by rearranging the letters of another [MF *anagramme*, fr NL *anagrammat-, anagramma*, modif of Gk *anagrammatismos*, fr *anagrammatizein* to transpose letters, fr *ana-* + *grammat-, gramma* letter – more at GRAM] – **anagrammatic, anagrammatical** adj, **anagrammatically** adv

**anagrammat·ize, -ise** /ˌanəˈgramətiez/ vt to rearrange (eg letters in a word) so as to form an anagram – **anagrammatization** n

**anal** /ˈaynl/ adj **1** of or situated near the anus **2** of or characterized by (parsimony, meticulousness, or other personality traits typical of) the stage of psychosexual development during which the child is concerned esp with the anal region and its function, and with faeces – compare ORAL, GENITAL – **anally** adv, **anality** n

**analcime** /əˈnalseem, -siem/ n a white or slightly coloured ZEOLITE mineral, $NaAlSi_2O_6.H_2O$, occurring in various IGNEOUS rocks [Fr, fr Gk *analkimos* weak, fr *an-* + *alkimos* strong, fr *alkē* strength] – **analcimic** adj

**analcite** /əˈnalsiet, 'anəlsiet/ n analcime

**analects** /ˈanəˌlekts/ *also* **analecta** /ˌanəˈlektə/ n pl selected miscellaneous writings [NL *analecta*, fr Gk *analekta*, neut pl of *analektos*, verbal of *analegein* to collect, fr *ana-* + *legein* to gather – more at LEGEND]

**analemma** /ˌanəˈlemə/ n a graduated scale having the shape of a figure 8 and showing the sun's angular distance from the CELESTIAL EQUATOR and the difference between the actual time and the time shown by the sun for each day of the year [L, sundial on a pedestal, fr Gk *analēmma*, lofty structure, sundial, fr *analambanein* to take up, fr *ana-* + *lambanein* to take – more at LATCH] – **analemmatic** adj

**analeptic** /ˌanəˈleptik/ adj, esp of a medicine stimulating the CENTRAL NERVOUS SYSTEM; restorative [Gk *analēptikos*, fr *analambanein* to take up, restore] – **analeptic** n

**anal fin** n a central unpaired fin of a fish situated behind the vent on the lower side of the body

**analgesia** /ˌanlˈjeezh(y)ə, -zyə/ n insensibility to pain without loss of consciousness – compare ANAESTHESIA [NL, fr Gk *analgēsia*, fr *an-* + *algēsis* sense of pain, fr *algein* to suffer pain, fr *algos* pain] – **analgesic** *adj or n*, **analgetic** *adj or n*

**analogical** /ˌanə'lojikl/ *also* **analogic** *adj* 1 of or based on analogy 2 expressing or implying an analogy – **analogically** *adv*

**analogist** /ə'naləjist/ *n* one who searches for or reasons from analogies

**analog·ize, -ise** /ə'naləjiez/ *vb* to compare by or use analogy

**analogous** /ə'naləgəs *also* -jes/ *adj* 1 corresponding by analogy 2 being or related to as an analogue ⟨*the wings of a bird and those of an aeroplane are* ~⟩ [L *analogus*, fr Gk *analogos*, lit., proportionate, fr *ana-* + *logos* reason, ratio, fr *legein* to gather, speak – more at LEGEND] – **analogously** *adv*, **analogousness** *n usage* Things are **analogous** *in* stated respects *to* or *with* each other.

¹**analogue**, *NAm also* **analog** /'analog/ *n* 1 something that is analogous or parallel to something else 2 an organ similar in function to an organ of another animal or plant but different in structure and origin 3 a chemical compound structurally similar to another but differing often by a single chemical element of the same VALENCY and group of the PERIODIC TABLE as the element it replaces [Fr *analogue*, fr *analogue* analogous, fr Gk *analogos*]

²**analogue**, *NAm also* **analog** *adj* of an ANALOGUE COMPUTER

**analogue computer** *n* a computer that operates with numbers represented by directly measurable quantities (e g voltages or mechanical rotations) – compare DIGITAL COMPUTER

**analogy** /ə'naləji/ *n* 1 inference from a parallel case 2 resemblance in some particulars; similarity 3 the tendency for new words or linguistic forms to be created in imitation of existing patterns 4 correspondence in function between anatomical parts of different structure and origin – compare HOMOLOGY [prob fr Gk *analogia* mathematical proportion, correspondence, fr *analogos*] – **analogic, analogical** *adj*, **analogically** *adv usage* There may be an **analogy** *in* stated respects *between* things, or *of* one *to* or *into* another.

**analphabet** /ˌan'alfəbet/ *n* one who cannot read; an illiterate [Gk *analphabētos* not knowing the alphabet, fr *an-* + *alphabētos* alphabet] – **analphabetism** *n*, **analphabetic** *adj or n*

**analysand** /ə'nali,sand/ *n* somebody undergoing psychoanalysis [*analyse* + *-and* (as in *multiplicand*)]

**analyse**, *NAm chiefly* **analyze** /'analiez/ *vt* 1 to subject to analysis 2 to determine by analysis the constitution or structure of ⟨~ *a traffic pattern*⟩ 3 to psychoanalyse [prob irreg fr *analysis*] – **analysable** *adj*, **analysability** *n*

**analysis** /ə'naləsis/ *n, pl* **analyses** /-seez/ **1a** examination and identification of the constituents of a complex whole and their relationship to one another – compare SYNTHESIS **b** a statement of such an analysis 2 the use of FUNCTION WORDS instead of changing word endings (INFLECTIONS) as a characteristic device of a language 3 a branch of mathematics concerned with the RIGOROUS treatment of the ideas of LIMITS, FUNCTIONS, CALCULUS, etc 4 a method in philosophy of resolving complex expressions into simpler or more basic ones 5 psychoanalysis [NL, fr Gk, fr *analyein* to break up, fr *ana-* + *lyein* to loosen – more at LOSE] – **in the final/last analysis** everything having been duly considered; ultimately

**analysis of variance** *n* analysis of variation in an experimental outcome, esp a statistical variation (VARIANCE 5), in order to determine the contributions of given factors or variables to it

**analyst** /'analist/ *n* 1 a person who analyses or who is skilled in analysis 2 a psychoanalyst 3 SYSTEMS ANALYST [irreg fr *analyse* or *analysis*]

**analytic** /ˌanə'litik/, **analytical** /-kl/ *adj* 1 of analysis or analytics; *esp* separating something into constituents 2 skilled in or using analysis, esp in reasoning ⟨*a keenly* ~ *man*⟩ 3 asserting something of a subject which is part of the meaning of that subject; tautologous ⟨*"all women are female" is an* ~ *truth*⟩ – compare SYNTHETIC 2a 4 *linguistics* characterized by the use of separate words (e g the preposition *of*) rather than by the addition of inflections (e g the English possessive *-'s*) to show a word's function in a sentence ⟨~ *languages such as English*⟩ 5 psychoanalytic 6 treated or solvable by or using the methods of mathematical ANALYSIS ⟨*the* ~ *solution*⟩ 7 *maths, of a function of a complex variable* being defined and having a DERIVATIVE at a specified point or at all points of some region [LL *analyticus*, fr Gk *analytikos*, fr *analyein*] – **analytical** *adj*, **analytically** *adv*, **analyticity** *n*

**analytical geometry** /ˌanə'litikl/ *n* the study of geometric properties by means of algebraic operations on COORDINATES (numbers specifying the position of points) in a coordinate system – called also COORDINATE GEOMETRY

**analytics** /ˌanə'litiks/ *n taking sing or pl vb* logical analysis

**anamnesis** /ˌanəm'neesis/ *n, pl* **anamneses** /-seez/ 1 a recalling to mind; recollection; *specif* recall of innate knowledge in Platonic philosophy 2 a preliminary case history of a medical or psychiatric patient [NL, fr Gk *anamnēsis*, fr *anamimnēskesthai* to remember, fr *ana-* + *mimnēskesthai* to remember – more at MIND]

**anamnestic** /ˌanəm'nestik/ *adj* 1 of an anamnesis 2 of or being a secondary response to an immunity-producing substance (e g a vaccine) after serum antibodies can no longer be detected in the blood [Gk *anamnēstikos* easily recalled, fr *anamimnēskesthai*] – **anamnestically** *adv*

**anamorphic** /ˌanə'mawfik/ *adj, of (the image produced by) an optical instrument* producing or having different magnification of the image in each of two perpendicular directions [NL *anamorphosis* distorted optical image, deriv of Gk *ana-* + *morphē* form]

**ananas** /'anənəs, -nas/ *n* PINEAPPLE 1 [Fr or Sp; Fr, fr Sp *ananás*, fr Pg, modif of Guarani *naná*]

**Ananias** /ˌano'nie·əs/ *n* a liar [*Ananias*, an early Christian struck dead for lying (Acts 5:1–11)]

**anapaest**, *NAm chiefly* **anapest** /'anə,pest, -,peest/ *n* a unit of poetic metre (FOOT) consisting of two short syllables followed by one long syllable [L *anapaestus*, fr Gk *anapaistos*, lit., struck back (i e a dactyl reversed), fr (assumed) Gk *anapaiein* to strike back, fr Gk *ana-* + *paiein* to strike] – **anapaestic** *adj*

**anaphase** /'anə,fayz/ *n* the stage of MITOSIS and MEIOSIS (types of CELL DIVISION) in which the CHROMOSOMES (strands of gene-carrying material) move towards the ends of the SPINDLE (arrangement of fibres formed in a dividing cell) [ISV] – **anaphasic** *adj*

**anaphora** /ə'nafərə/ *n* 1 repetition of a word or phrase at the beginning of successive clauses or verses, esp for rhetorical or poetic effect (e g in *for you we worked, for you we fought, for you we went hungry*) – compare EPISTROPHE 2 the use of a grammatical form (e g a pronoun) to refer to a preceding word or group of words [LL, fr LGk, fr Gk, act of carrying back, reference, fr *anapherein* to carry back, refer, fr *ana-* + *pherein* to carry – more at BEAR]

**anaphoric** /ˌanə'forik/ *adj* referring to a preceding word or group of words ⟨*the* ~ *so in "so do I"*⟩ – **anaphorically** *adv*

**anaphrodisia** /ˌanafrə'diziə/ *n* absence or impairment of sexual desire [NL, fr *a-* + Gk *aphrodisios* sexual – more at APHRODISIAC]

**anaphrodisiac** /ˌanafrə'diziak/ *n* 1 a painkilling drug 2 something, esp a drug, producing anaphrodisia – **anaphrodisiac** *adj*

**anaphylactic** /ˌanəfə'laktik/ *adj* of, affected by, or causing anaphylaxis ⟨~ *shock*⟩ – **anaphylactically** *adv*

**anaphylactoid** /ˌanəfə'laktoyd/ *adj* resembling anaphylaxis

**anaphylaxis** /ˌanəfə'laksis/ *n, pl* **anaphylaxes** /-'lakseez/ sometimes fatal hypersensitivity to foreign substances (e g drugs or insect venom) due to sensitization resulting from earlier contact with the causative agent [NL, fr *ana-* + *-phylaxis* (as in *prophylaxis*)]

**anaplasia** /ˌanə'playzyə, -zh(y)ə/ *n* reversion of cells in an organism to a more primitive or undifferentiated form (e g in some tumour cells) [NL] – **anaplastic** *adj*

**anaptotic** /ˌanap'totik/ *adj, of a language* tending to become less inflected [Gk *ana* up, back + *ptōtikos* of grammatical case]

**anaptyxis** /ˌanap'tiksis/ *n* the development of a vowel between two consonants (e g *a* in "thataway") [NL, fr Gk, act of unfolding, fr *anaptyssein* to unfold, fr *ana-* + *ptyssein* to fold]

**anarch** /'anahk/ *n, archaic* a leader or advocate of revolt or anarchy [back-formation fr *anarchy*]

**anarchic** /a'nahkik/ *adj* **1a** of or advocating anarchy **b** likely to bring about anarchy ⟨~ *violence*⟩ 2 lacking order, regularity, or definiteness ⟨~ *art forms*⟩

**anarchism** /'anə,kiz(ə)m/ *n* 1 a political theory holding that all forms of governmental authority are unnecessary and undesirable and advocating a society based on voluntary cooperation and free association of individuals and groups 2 the attacking of the established social order or laws; rebellion

**anarchist** /'anəkist/ *n* 1 one who attacks the established social order or laws; a rebel 2 one who believes in, advocates, or promotes anarchism or anarchy; *esp* one who uses violent means to overthrow the established order – **anarchist, anarchistic** *adj*

**anarchy** /'anəki/ *n* **1a** absence of government **b** a state of lawlessness or political disorder due to the absence of governmental authority; *broadly* general confusion or disorder **c** an imaginary ideal society in which there is complete freedom and no government **2** anarchism [ML *anarchia*, fr Gk, fr *anarchos* having no ruler, fr *an-* + *archos* ruler – more at ARCH-]

**anarthria** /a'nahthriə/ *n* inability to speak words as a result of brain injury – compare APHASIA [NL, fr Gk *anarthros* inarticulate, fr *an-* + *arthron* joint – more at ARTHR-]

**anarthrous** /a'nahthrəs/ *adj* having no distinct joints

**anasarca** /,anə'sahkə/ *n* generalized OEDEMA (swelling) with accumulation of serum in the CONNECTIVE TISSUE [NL, fr *ana-* + Gk *sark-, sarx* flesh – more at SARCASM] – **anasarcous** *adj*

**anastigmat** /ə'nastigmat, anə'stigmat/ *n* an anastigmatic lens [Ger, back-formation fr *anastigmatisch* anastigmatic]

**anastigmatic** /,anəstig'matik, ə,nastig'matik/ *adj, esp of a lens* not ASTIGMATIC (defective and hence producing distorted images) [ISV]

**anastomose** /ə'nastə,mohz/ *vb* to interconnect or join by anastomosis [prob back-formation fr *anastomosis*]

**anastomosis** /ə,nastə'mohsis/ *n, pl* **anastomoses** /-seez/ **1** the union of parts or branches (eg of streams, blood vessels, or leaf veins) so as to intercommunicate **2** a product of anastomosis; a network **3** the surgical joining of two hollow organs (eg the rejoining of the gut after part has been removed) [LL, fr Gk *anastomōsis*, fr *anastomoun* to provide with an outlet, fr *ana-* + *stoma* mouth, opening – more at STOMACH] – **anastomotic** *adj*

**anastrophe** /ə'nastrəfi/ *n* reversal of the usual order of words [ML, fr Gk *anastrophē*, lit., turning back, fr *anastrephein* to turn back, fr *ana-* + *strephein* to turn – more at STROPHE]

**anatase** /'anətays/ *n* a blue or black mineral consisting essentially of the chemical compound TITANIUM DIOXIDE, $TiO_2$, and used esp as a white pigment [Fr, fr Gk *anatasis* extension, fr *anateinein* to extend, fr *ana-* + *teinein* to stretch – more at THIN]

**anathema** /ə'nathəmə/ *n* **1a** a ban or curse solemnly pronounced by ecclesiastical authority and accompanied by excommunication **b** a vigorous denunciation; a curse **2a** the object of a curse by ecclesiastical authority **b** someone or something intensely disliked or loathed ⟨*his opinions are* ~ *to me*⟩ [LL *anathemat-, anathema*, fr Gk, thing devoted to evil, curse, fr *anatithenai* to set up, dedicate, fr *ana-* + *tithenai* to place, set – more at DO]

**anathemat-ize, -ise** /ə'nathəmə,tiez/ *vt* to pronounce an anathema on

**Anatolian** /,anə'tohlyən/ *n* **1** a native or inhabitant of Anatolia, specif of the western plateau lands of Turkey in Asia **2** a branch of the Indo-European language family including a group of extinct languages of ancient Anatolia [*Anatolia* Asia Minor] – **Anatolian** *adj*

**anatomico-, anatomo-** *comb form* anatomical; anatomical and ⟨anatomico*pathological*⟩ ⟨anatomo*clinical*⟩

**anatomist** /ə'natəmist/ *n* **1** a student of anatomy; *esp* one skilled in dissection **2** one who analyses minutely and critically ⟨*an* ~ *of urban society*⟩

**anatom-ize, -ise** /ə'natəmiez/ *vt* **1** to cut in pieces in order to display or examine the structure and use of the parts; dissect **2** to analyse, esp critically

**anatomy** /ə'natəmi/ *n* **1** a branch of biology that deals with the structure of organisms **2** a treatise on anatomic science or art **3** the art of separating the parts of an animal or plant in order to ascertain their position, relations, structure, and function; dissection **4** structural makeup, esp of an organism or any of its parts **5** an analysis ⟨*the* ~ *of English society*⟩ **6** the human body – not used technically [LL *anatomia* dissection, fr Gk *anatomē*, fr *anatemnein* to dissect, fr *ana-* + *temnein* to cut – more at TOME] – **anatomic, anatomical** *adj*, **anatomically** *adv*

**anatropous** /ə'natrəpəs/ *adj* of or being an OVULE (developing plant seed) that is bent over against the stalk

**-ance** /-əns/ *suffix* (→ *n*) **1** action or process of ⟨*further*ance⟩; *also* instance of (a specified action or process) ⟨*perform*ance⟩ **2** quality or state of ⟨*brilli*ance⟩; *also* instance of (a specified quality or state) ⟨*protuber*ance⟩ **3** amount or degree of ⟨*conduct*ance⟩ [ME, fr OF, fr L *-antia*, fr *-ant-, -ans* -ant + *-ia* -y]

**ancestor** /'ansestə, -səs-/, *fem* **ancestress** /-tris/ *n* **1a** one from

whom a person is descended, usu more distant than a grandparent **b** FOREFATHER 2 **2** a forerunner, prototype **3** a progenitor of a more recent or existing species or organism [ME *ancestre*, fr OF, fr L *antecessor* one who goes before, fr *antecessus*, pp of *antecedere* to go before, fr *ante-* + *cedere* to go – more at CEDE]

**ancestral** /an'sestrəl, '---/ *adj* of or inherited from an ancestor ⟨~ *estates*⟩ – **ancestrally** *adv*

**ancestry** /'ansestri, -səs-/ *n* **1** line of esp honourable or noble descent; lineage **2** *taking pl vb* people comprising a line of descent; ancestors

**anchoïade** /,onshwah'yahd (*Fr* ɑ̃ʃwajad)/ *n* a type of fish pâté made from anchovies, olive oil, garlic, and herbs [Fr, fr *anchois* anchovy]

**¹anchor** /'angkə/ *n* **1** a device usu of metal attached to a ship or boat by a chain or cable and dropped overboard to hold it in a particular place **2** a reliable support; a mainstay **3** something that serves to hold an object firmly **4** an object shaped like a ship's anchor **5** *pl, slang* the brakes of a motor vehicle [ME *ancre*, fr OE *ancor*, fr L *anchora*, fr Gk *ankyra*; akin to L *uncus* hook – more at ANGLE] – **anchorless** *adj* – **cast anchor** to lower the anchor

**²anchor** *vt* **1** to hold in place in the water by an anchor **2** to secure firmly; fix **3** *chiefly NAm* to serve as an anchorman on ⟨~ *ing a television spectacular*⟩ ~ *vi* **1** to drop anchor **2** to become fixed; settle

**anchorage** /'angkərij/ *n* **1a** the act of anchoring; the condition of lying at anchor **b** a place where vessels anchor; a place suitable for anchoring **c** a charge made for anchoring **2** a source of trust or reassurance **3** something that provides a secure hold or attachment [ME *ankeresse*, fr *anker* hermit, fr OE *ancor*, fr OIr *anchara*, fr LL *anachoreta*]

**anchoret** /'angkərət/ *n* an anchorite

**anchorite** /'angkə,riet/, *fem* **anchoress** /'angk(ə)ris/ **ancress** /'angkris/ *n* one who lives in seclusion, usu for religious reasons [ME *ancorite*, fr ML *anchorita*, alter. of LL *anachoreta*, fr LGk *anachōrētēs*, fr Gk *anachōrein* to withdraw, fr *ana-* + *chōrein* to make room, fr *chōros* place] – **anchoritic** *adj*, **anchoritically** *adv*

**anchorman** /'angkəmən, -,man/ *n* **1a** the member of a team who competes last ⟨*the* ~ *on a relay team*⟩ **b** the member of a tug-of-war team furthest from the centre of the rope **2** a television or radio linkman

**anchovy** /'anchəvi/ *n, pl* **anchovies, anchovy** any of numerous small fishes (family Engraulidae) resembling herrings; *esp* a common Mediterranean fish (*Engraulis encrasicholus*) used esp in appetizers, as a garnish and for making a salty paste [Sp *anchova*, prob fr It dial. *ancioa*, fr (assumed) VL *apjua*, fr Gk *aphyē* small fry]

**ancien régime** /,ahnsyen ray'zheem (*Fr* ɑ̃sjɛ reʒim)/ *n* **1** the political and social system of France before the Revolution of 1789 **2** a system or arrangement which has been superseded [Fr, lit., old regime]

**¹ancient** /'aynsh(ə)nt, -chənt/ *adj* **1** having existed for many years **2** of a remote period or those living in such a period; *specif* of the historical period beginning with the earliest known civilizations and extending to the fall of the western Roman Empire in AD 476 **3** old-fashioned, antique *synonyms* see ¹OLD *antonym* modern [ME *ancien*, fr MF, fr (assumed) VL *anteanus*, fr L *ante* before – more at ANTE-] – **ancientness** *n*

**²ancient** *n* **1a** somebody who lived in ancient times **b** *pl the* members of a civilized, esp a classical, nation of antiquity **2** *archaic* an aged person ⟨*a penniless* ~⟩

**³ancient** *n* **1** *archaic* an ensign, standard **2** *obs* the bearer of an ensign [alter. of *ensign*]

**ancient history** *n* **1** the history of the classical civilizations of Greece and Rome **2** *informal* something which has been common knowledge for a long time

**ancient lights** *n taking sing vb* the legally enforceable right to receive unobstructed daylight into a building from a window which has remained unobstructed for at least twenty years

**anciently** /'aynsh(ə)ntli, -chən-/ *adv* in ancient times; long ago

**ancientry** /'aynsh(ə)ntri, -chən-/ *n* antiquity, ancientness

**ancilla** /an'silə/ *n, pl* **ancillae** /an'silee/ something that assists [L, female servant, fem dim. of *anculus* servant]

**¹ancillary** /an'siləri; *NAm usu* 'ansə,leri/ *adj* **1** subordinate, subsidiary **2** auxiliary, supplementary

**²ancillary** *n, Br* one who assists; a helper

**ancon** /'angkon/ *n, pl* **ancones** /ang'kohneez/ either of the carved brackets used to support a classical door CORNICE (moulded projection at the top) [L, fr Gk *ankōn* elbow; akin to L *uncus* hook]

**ancress** /'angkris/ *n* a female ANCHORITE (hermit) [ME *ankeresse*, fem, fr *anker* hermit, fr OE *ancor*, fr OIr *anchara*, fr LL *anachoreta* – more at ANCHORITE]

**-ancy** /-ənsi/ *suffix* (→ *n*) quality or state of ⟨*piquancy*⟩ ⟨*expectancy*⟩ [L *-antia* – more at -ANCE]

**ancylostomiasis** /,angkilohstoh'mie-əsis, -siloh-, ,angki,lostə-/ *n, pl* **ancylostomiases** /-seez/ infestation with or disease caused by hookworms; *esp* a lethargic anaemic state in human beings due to blood loss caused by the feeding of hookworms in the SMALL INTESTINE – called also UNCINARIASIS [NL, fr *Ancylostoma*, genus of hookworms, fr Gk *ankylos* hooked (akin to L *uncus* hook) + *stoma* mouth – more at ANGLE, STOMACH]

**and** /(ə)n, (ə)nd; *strong* and/ *conj* **1a** – used to join coordinate sentence elements of the same class or function expressing addition or combination ⟨*cold ~ hungry*⟩ ⟨*sang ~ shouted*⟩ ⟨*John ~ I*⟩ **b(1)** – used, esp in British speech, before the numbers 1 to 99 and after the number 100 ⟨*three hundred ~ seventeen*⟩; used also originally between tens and units ⟨*five ~ twenty blackbirds*⟩ **b(2)** plus ⟨*three ~ three make six*⟩ **2a** – used to introduce a second clause expressing sequence in time ⟨*came to tea ~ stayed to dinner*⟩, consequence ⟨*water the seeds ~ they will grow*⟩, contrast ⟨*he's old ~ I'm young*⟩, or supplementary explanation ⟨*she's ill ~ can't travel*⟩ **b** – used to join words expressing continuation or progression ⟨*ran ~ ran*⟩ ⟨*waited hours ~ hours*⟩ ⟨*came nearer ~ nearer*⟩ **c** – used to join repeated words expressing contrast of type or quality ⟨*there are aunts ~ aunts*⟩ ⟨*gynaecology of one sort ~ another* – Jan Morris⟩ **d** – used instead of *to* to introduce an infinitive after *come, go, run, stop, try* ⟨*come ~ look*⟩ **3** *archaic* if – **and all (that)** AND SO FORTH – **and how** – used to emphasize the preceding idea – **and so forth/on 1** and others or more of the same kind **2** and further in the same manner **3** and the rest **4** and other things – **and that** *chiefly Br nonstandard* AND SO FORTH [ME, fr OE; akin to OHG *unti* and]

*usage* There are many occasions on which it is perfectly legitimate and very effective to begin a sentence with **and**.

**Andalusian** /,andə'loohzh(ə)n, -zyən/ *adj* of or being a (breed of) riding horse of Oriental origin developed in Spain [*Andalusia*, region in S Spain]

**andalusite** /,andə'loohsiet/ *n* a mineral, $Al_2SiO_5$, consisting of a SILICATE of aluminium and occurring in thick nearly square prisms of various colours [Fr *andalousite*, fr *Andalousie* Andalusia]

**andante** /an'danti/ *n, adv, or adj* (a musical composition or movement to be played) moderately slow – used as a TEMPO (speed) direction in music [It, lit., going, prp of *andare* to go]

**andantino** /,andan'teenoh/ *n, adv or adj pl* **andantinos** (a musical composition or movement to be played) slightly faster than andante – used as a TEMPO (speed) direction in music [It, dim of *andante*]

**andesine** /'andəzeen/ *n* a FELDSPAR (type of mineral) that is one of the PLAGIOCLASE series and composed of a mixture of sodium, calcium, and aluminium SILICATES [Ger *andesin*, fr *Andes*, mountain range in S America]

**andesite** /'andəziet/ *n* a fine-grained volcanic usu dark greyish rock consisting essentially of the mineral OLIGOCLASE [Ger *andesit*, fr *Andes*] – **andesitic** *adj*

**andiron** /'andie-ən/ *n* either of a pair of metal stands used on a hearth to support burning wood [ME *aundiren*, modif (influenced by ME *iren* iron) of OF *andier*, fr (assumed) Gaulish *anderos* young bull; akin to W *anner* heifer]

**and/or** *conj* – used to indicate that two words or expressions are to be taken either together or individually

*usage* **And/or** is useful in legal and commercial contexts, since ⟨*soldiers and/or sailors*⟩ is shorter than ⟨*soldiers or sailors or both*⟩, but its use in general writing is widely disliked.

**andr-, andro-** *comb form* **1** man ⟨*androgynous*⟩ **2** male ⟨*androecium*⟩ [MF, fr L, fr Gk, fr *andr-*, *anēr* man (male); akin to Oscan *ner* man, Skt *nr*, OIr *nert* strength]

**andradite** /'andrədiet/ *n* a garnet, $Ca_3Fe_2(SiO_4)_3$, of any of various colours ranging from yellow and green to brown and black [José de *Andrada* e Silva †1838 Brazilian geologist]

**Androcles** /'andrəkleez/ *n* a slave in a Roman fable spared in the arena by a lion from whose foot he had years before extracted a thorn [L, fr Gk *Androklēs*]

**androecium** /,an'dreesyəm, -sh(y)əm/ *n, pl* **androecia** /-syə, -sh(y)ə/ all the STAMENS (male reproductive organs) collectively

in the flower of a SEED PLANT [NL, fr *andr-* + Gk *oikion*, dim. of *oikos* house – more at VICINITY]

**androgen** /'andrəjən/ *n* a male SEX HORMONE (e g testosterone) [ISV] – **androgenic** *adj*

**androgyne** /'andrə,jien/ *n or adj* (a) hermaphrodite [MF, fr L *androgynus*]

**androgynous** /an'drojənəs/ *adj* **1** having the characteristics or nature of both the male and female forms **2** bearing both male and female flowers in the same cluster [L *androgynus* hermaphrodite, fr Gk *androgynos*, fr *andr-* + *gynē* woman – more at QUEEN] – **androgyny** *n*

**android** /'androyd/ *n* an automaton externally indistinguishable from a human [LGk *androeidēs* manlike, fr Gk *andr-* + *-oeides* -oid]

**androsterone** /an'drostərohn/ *n* an androgenic STEROID hormone, $C_{19}H_{30}O_2$, that is found in the testes and in esp male urine [ISV *andr-* + *sterol* + *-one*]

**-androus** /-andrəs/ *comb form* (→ *adj*) having (such or so many) stamens ⟨*monandrous*⟩ [NL *-andrus*, fr Gk *-andros* having (such or so many) men, fr *andr-*, *anēr*]

**ane** /ayn/ *adj, n, or pron, chiefly Scot* one [ME (northern) *an*, fr OE *ān* – more at ONE]

**-ane** /-ayn/ *suffix* (→ *n*) saturated carbon chemical compound; *esp* a hydrocarbon of the ALKANE series ⟨*methane*⟩ ⟨*hexane*⟩ [ISV *-an*, *-ane*, alter. of *-ene*, *-ine*, & *-one*]

**anecdotage** /,anik'dohtij/ *n* **1** (the telling of) anecdotes **2** *humorous* advanced age accompanied by a tendency to tell too many anecdotes ⟨*in his ~*⟩ [(1) anecdote + -age; (2) blend of *anecdote* and *dotage*]

**anecdotal** /,anik'dohtl/ *adj* **1** of or containing anecdotes **2** consisting of or depicting an anecdote ⟨*~ art*⟩ – **anecdotally** *adv*

**anecdote** /'anik,doht/ *n* a usu short narrative about an interesting or amusing person or incident △ antidote [Fr, fr Gk *anekdota* unpublished items, fr neut pl of *anekdotos* unpublished, fr *a-* + *ekdidonai* to publish, fr *ex* out + *didonai* to give – more at EX-, DATE]

**anecdotic** /,anik'dotik/, **anecdotical** /-kl/ *adj* **1** anecdotal **2** given to or skilled in telling anecdotes – **anecdotically** *adv*

**anecdotist** /'anik,dohtist/, **anecdotalist** *n* one given to or skilled in telling anecdotes

**anechoic** /,ani'koh-ik, ane-/ *adj* free from echoes and reverberations ⟨*an ~ chamber*⟩

**anem-** /anim-/, **anemo-** *comb form* wind ⟨*anemometer*⟩ [Gk *anem-*, *anemo-*, fr *anemos* – more at ANIMATE]

**anemia** /ə'neemyə, -mi-ə/ *n, chiefly NAm* anaemia – **anemic** *adj*, **anemically** *adv*

**anemogram** /ə'nemagram/ *n* an anemographic tracing

**anemograph** /ə'nemə,grahf, -,graf/ *n* a recording anemometer – **anemographic** *adj*

**anemometer** /,ani'momitə/ *n* an instrument for measuring and indicating the force or speed of the wind – **anemometric** *also* **anemometrical** *adj*

**anemometry** /,ani'momətri/ *n* the act or process of ascertaining the force, speed, and direction of wind

**anemone** /ə'nemoni/ *n* **1** any of a large genus (*Anemone*) of plants of the buttercup family with lobed or divided leaves and showy flowers **2** SEA ANEMONE [L, fr Gk *anemōnē*, perh by folk etymology fr a word of Sem origin; akin to Heb *Na'āmān*, epithet of Adonis]

**anemophilous** /,ani'mofələs/ *adj* pollinated by the wind – **anemophily** *n*

**anencephaly** /,anin'sefəli, -'kef-/ *n* a birth defect in which part or all of the brain is absent – **anencephalic** *adj*

**anent** /ə'nent/ *prep, chiefly archaic or humorous* about, concerning [ME *onevent*, *anent*, fr OE *on efen* alongside, fr *on* + *efen* even]

**aneroid** /'anəroyd/ *adj* containing no liquid or operated without the use of liquid ⟨*an ~ manometer*⟩ [Fr *anéroïde*, fr Gk *a-* + LGk *nēron* water, fr Gk, neut of *nearos*, *nēros* fresh; akin to Gk *neos* new – more at NEW]

**aneroid barometer** *n* a barometer in which the action of atmospheric pressure in compressing an evacuated metal capsule is made to move a pointer

**anesthesia** /,anəs'theezyə, -zh(y)ə/ *n, chiefly NAm* anaesthesia – **anesthetic** *n or adj*, **anesthetist** *n*, **anesthetize** *vt*

**anesthesiology** /,anəs,theezi'oləji/ *n, NAm* anaesthesiology – **anesthesiologist** *n*

¹**aneuploid** /'anyooployd, ə'nyooh-/ *adj* having a CHROMOSOME NUMBER (normal amount of genetic material in a cell) that is

not an exact multiple of the HAPLOID number (amount of genetic material in a reproductive cell) – compare EUPLOID [*an-* + *euploid*]

**²aneuploid** *n* a single cell, individual, or generation that is aneuploid – **aneuploidy** *n*

**aneurine, aneurin** /'anyooreen/ *n* THIAMINE (type of vitamin B) [ISV ²*a-* + *neur-* + *-ine*]

**aneurysm** *also* **aneurism** /'anyoo,riz(ə)m/ *n* a permanent abnormal blood-filled swelling of a blood vessel (eg the aorta) resulting from disease of the vessel wall [Gk *aneurysma*, fr *aneurynein* to dilate, fr *ana-* + *eurynein* to stretch, fr *eurys* wide – more at EURY-] – **aneurysmal** *adj*

**anew** /ə'nyooh/ *adv* 1 for an additional time; afresh 2 in a new form or way [ME *of newe*, fr OE *of nīwe*, fr *of* + *nīwe* new]

**anfractuosity** /,an,fraktyoo'osəti/ *n* 1 the quality or state of being anfractuous 2 something (eg a path) that winds

**anfractuous** /an'fraktyooəs/ *adj* full of windings and intricate turnings; tortuous [Fr *anfractueux*, fr LL *anfractuosus*, fr L *anfractus* coil, bend, fr *anfractus* crooked, fr *an-* (fr *ambi-* round) + *fractus*, pp of *frangere* to break – more at AMBI-, BREAK]

**angary** /'ang·gəri/ *n* the right in international law of a nation at war to seize, use, or destroy property of neutrals if necessary for military purposes, subject to the payment of compensation [LL *angaria* service to a lord, fr Gk *angareia* compulsory public service, fr *angaros* Persian courier, of Iranian origin]

**angel** /'aynj(ə)l/ *n* 1a a spiritual being, usu depicted as being winged, serving as God's intermediary or acting as a heavenly worshipper b *pl* the lowest of the nine orders of angelic beings in the CELESTIAL HIERARCHY 2 an attendant spirit or guardian 3 a messenger, harbinger ⟨~ *of death*⟩ 4 a very kind, innocent, or loving person, esp a woman or girl 5 a former English gold coin portraying St Michael killing a dragon 6 *informal* a financial backer of a theatrical venture or other enterprise [ME, fr OF *angele*, fr LL *angelus*, fr Gk *angelos*, lit., messenger] – **angelic, angelical** *adj*, **angelically** *adv*

**angelfish** /-,fish/ *n* 1 any of several flattened brightly coloured BONY FISHES (family Chaetodontidae) that live in warm seas 2 SCALARE (type of black and silver fish)

**angelica** /an'jelikə/ *n* 1 any of a genus (*Angelica*) of plants of the carrot family; *esp* one (*Angelica archangelica*) whose roots and fruit are used to produce a flavouring oil 2 candied stalks of angelica often used as a decoration on cakes and desserts [NL, genus name, fr ML, short for *herba angelica*, lit., angelic plant; fr its supposed medicinal properties]

**angelology** /,aynjə'loləji/ *n* the doctrine or theory of angels and their hierarchy [NL *angelologia*, fr LL *angelus* angel + NL *-o-* + *-logia* -logy]

**angels on horseback** *n taking sing vb* oysters rolled in bacon, grilled, and served (eg on cocktail sticks or toast) as an appetizer or a savoury – compare DEVILS ON HORSEBACK

**angel top** *n* a usu woollen top worn by babies and toddlers

**Angelus** /'anjələs/ *n* 1 a devotion of the Roman Catholic church that commemorates the Incarnation and is said at morning, noon, and evening 2 a bell announcing the time for the Angelus [ML, fr LL, angel; fr the first word of the opening versicle]

**¹anger** /'ang·gə/ *n* a strong feeling of displeasure aroused by real or imaginary injury and usu accompanied by the desire to retaliate [ME, affliction, anger, fr ON *angr* grief; akin to OE *enge* narrow, L *angere* to strangle, Gk *anchein*] – **angerless** *adj*

**synonyms** Anger, rage, fury, wrath, ire, indignation: anger is the most general term, and may be strong or mild. Indignation implies justly provoked anger, while rage and fury can suggest barely restrained passion, as well as its violent expression. Ire is a literary term for anger; wrath, also somewhat literary, suggests rage or indignation with a strong sense of grievance, which seeks to avenge or punish ⟨fear the wrath of God⟩. Compare IRRITATION. Angry, indignant, wrathful, and furious have very similar connotations to their related nouns. Irate stresses explicit anger in people and their expressions, and may suggest a comic disparity between the cause of this anger and the strong reaction it provokes ⟨an irate Dr Brown demanded to know what they had done with his hat⟩. The informal mad and livid both express extreme anger, but livid, suggesting apoplectic rage, is the stronger of the two.

**²anger** *vb* to make or become angry

**Angevin** /'anjivin/ *adj* (characteristic) of Anjou or the Plantagenets [Fr, fr OF, fr ML *andegavinus*, fr *Andegavia* Anjou, former province of France] – **Angevin** *n*

**angi-** /anji-/, **angio-** *comb form* 1 blood or lymph vessel

⟨*angioma*⟩; blood vessels and ⟨*angiocardiography*⟩ 2 seed vessel ⟨*angiocarpous*⟩ [NL, fr Gk *angei-*, *angeio-*, fr *angeion* vessel, blood vessel, dim. of *angos* vessel]

**angina** /an'jienə/ *n* a disease marked by spasmodic attacks of intense pain and the feeling of suffocation: eg a a severe inflammatory or ulcerated condition of the mouth or throat b ANGINA PECTORIS [L, quinsy, fr *angere*] – **anginal** *adj*, **anginose** *adj*

**angina pectoris** /'pektəris, pek'tawris/ *n* a disease marked by brief paroxysmal attacks of chest pain, esp on exertion, brought on by deficient oxygenation of the heart muscles [NL, lit., angina of the chest]

**angiocarpous** /,anjioh'kahpəs/, **angiocarpic** /-'kahpik/ *adj* having or being fruit enclosed within an external covering – **angiocarpy** *n*

**angiography** /,anji'ogrəfi/ *n* the examination of the blood vessels by X-ray photography after injection of a substance through which X rays do not pass – **angiographic** *adj*

**angiology** /,anji'oləji/ *n* the study of blood and lymph vessels

**angioma** /,anji'ohmə/ *n* a tumour composed chiefly of blood or lymph vessels [NL] – **angiomatous** *adj*

**angiosarcoma** /,anjiohsah'kohmə/ *n* a rare form of cancerous tumour affecting the liver

**angiosperm** /'anji·ə,spuhm/ *n* any of a class (Angiospermae) of SEED PLANTS (eg buttercups, orchids, roses, oaks, or grasses) having the seeds in a closed ovary – called also FLOWERING PLANT; compare GYMNOSPERM [deriv of NL *angi-* + Gk *sperma* seed – more at SPERM] – **angiospermous** *adj*

**angiotensin** /,anji·ə'tensin/ *n* either of two related hormones that influence the fluid balance of the body and cause constriction of the small blood vessels; *also* a synthetic chemical compound (AMIDE) used to treat some forms of low blood pressure – compare RENIN [*angi-* + hyper*tension* + *-in*]

**angiotensinase** /,anjiə'tensinayz, -ays/ *n* any of several ENZYMES in the blood that promote the breakdown of angiotensin

**¹angle** /'ang·gl/ *n* 1 a corner whether constituting a projecting part or a partially enclosed space ⟨they sheltered in an ~ of the building⟩ 2a the geometrical figure formed by 2a(1) two esp straight lines diverging from a point a(2) two intersecting planes b a measure of the amount of turning necessary to bring one line or plane into coincidence with or parallel to another 3a a precise viewpoint from which something is observed or considered; *also* the aspect seen from such an angle b a special approach, point of attack, or technique for accomplishing an objective 4 a divergent course or position; a slant – esp in at an angle 5 NAm informal an often improper or illicit method of obtaining advantage ⟨he always had an ~ to beat the other fellow⟩ [ME, fr MF, fr L *angulus*; akin to OE *anclēow* ankle] – **angled** *adj*

**²angle** *vb* 1 to place, move, or direct obliquely 2 to present (eg a news story) from a particular or prejudiced point of view; slant ~ *vi* to turn or proceed at an angle

**³angle** *vi* 1 to fish with a hook and line 2 to use artful means to attain an objective ⟨~d for an invitation⟩ [ME *angelen*, fr *angel* fishhook, fr OE, fr *anga* hook; akin to OHG *ango* hook, L *uncus*, Gk *onkos* barbed hook, *ankos* glen] – **angler** *n*

**Angle** *n* a member of a Germanic people that invaded England together with the Saxons and Jutes in the 5th century AD and merged with them to form the Anglo-Saxon people [L *Angli*, pl, of Gmc origin; akin to OE *Engle* Angles]

**angle bracket** *n* 1 either of a pair of punctuation marks ⟨ ⟩ used to enclose matter 2 a usu metal bracket used to support shelving

**angle iron** *n* 1 an iron piece for joining parts of a structure at an angle 2 a rolled-steel structural bar having an L-shaped cross-section

**angle of attack** *n* the acute angle between the direction of the relative airflow and an imaginary straight line (CHORD) joining the leading and trailing edges of an aerofoil

**angle of depression** *n* the angle formed by the line of sight and the horizontal plane for an object below the horizontal

**angle of elevation** *n* the angle formed by the line of sight and the horizontal plane for an object above the horizontal

**angle of incidence** *n* the angle between the direction of a moving body or ray of light where it meets a surface, and a perpendicular at that point

**angle of reflection** *n* the angle between the direction of a moving body or ray of light after reflection from a point on a surface, and a perpendicular at that point

**angle of refraction** *n* the angle between a refracted ray and a perpendicular at the point where the ray meets the interface at which refraction occurs

**Anglepoise** /'ang-gl,poyz/ *trademark* – used for a lamp with a jointed support that can be moved into various positions

**angler fish** /'ang·glə/ *n* any of several highly specialized marine fishes (order Pediculati); *esp* one (*Lophius piscatorius*) having a large flattened head and wide mouth with a lure on the head and fleshy projections round the mouth used to attract smaller fishes as prey

**angle shades moth** *n* a large moth (*Phlogophora meticulosa*) the caterpillar of which causes serious damage to garden flowers

**angle shot** *n* a shot in squash which hits a side wall before hitting the front wall

**anglesite** /'ang·gl,siet/ *n* a mineral consisting of the chemical compound lead sulphate, $PbSO_4$, that is formed from GALENA (important ore of lead) [Fr *anglêsite*, fr *Anglesey* island, Wales]

**Anglian** /'ang·gliən/ *n* 1 an Angle 2 the Old English dialects of Mercia and Northumbria – **Anglian** *adj*

**Anglican** /'ang·glikən/ *adj* of the body of churches including the established episcopal Church of England and churches of similar faith and forms of worship in communion with it [ML *anglicanus*, fr *anglicus* English, fr LL *Angli* English people, fr L, Angles] – **Anglican** *n*, **Anglicanism** *n*

**Anglican chant** *n* a harmonized chant consisting of one 3-bar and one 4-bar strain in each of which the first bar contains a single reciting note and the remaining bars a cadence sung in strict rhythm

**anglice** /'ang·glisi/ *adv*, *often cap* in English; *esp* in readily understood English 〈*the city of Napoli*, ~ *Naples*〉 [ML, adv of *anglicus*]

**anglicism** /'angli,siz(ə)m/ *n*, *often cap* 1 a characteristic feature (e g a word or phrase) of English occurring in another language 2 a characteristic feature (e g a custom or belief) of the English people or English culture 3 adherence or attachment to England or to English customs, tastes, or ideas [ML *anglicus* English]

**Anglicist** /'ang·glisist/ *n* a specialist in English language, literature, or culture – not usu used for native speakers of English

**anglic·ize, -ise** /'ang·gli,siez/ *vb*, *often cap* *vt* 1 to make English in tastes or characteristics 2 to adapt (a foreign word or phrase) to English usage ~ *vi* to take on English tastes or characteristics – **anglicization** *n*, *often cap*

**angling** /'ang·gling/ *n* the act of one who angles; *esp* the act or sport of fishing with hook and line

**Anglist** /'ang·glist/ *n* an anglicist

**Anglo** /'ang·gloh/ *n*, *pl* **Anglos** *chiefly Can* a Canadian whose first language is English [short for *Anglo-Canadian*]

**Anglo-** /,ang·gloh-/ *comb form* 1 English nation, people, or culture 〈Anglo*phobia*〉 2 English and 〈Anglo-*Japanese*〉 [NL, fr LL *Angli*]

**Anglo-American** /,ang·gloh-/ *n* an inhabitant of the USA of English origin or descent – **Anglo-American** *adj*

**Anglo-'Catholic** *adj* of a High Church movement in Anglicanism fostering Catholic traditions of belief and forms of worship – **Anglo-Catholic** *n*, **Anglo-Catholicism** *n*

**Anglo-'French** *n* the French language used in medieval England

**Anglo-'Indian** *n* 1 a British person who lived for a long time in India 2 a Eurasian of mixed British and Indian birth or descent – **Anglo-Indian** *adj*

**Anglo-'Irish** *n taking pl vb* the once dominant group of English Protestant settlers in Ireland – **Anglo-Irish** *adj*

**Anglomania** /,ang·glə'maynyə/ *n* excessive fondness for what is English (e g English customs and institutions)

**Anglo-'Norman** *n* 1 a Norman living in England after the Conquest 2 the form of Anglo-French used by Anglo-Normans

**anglophile** /'ang·gləfiel, -fil/ *also* **anglophil** /-fil/ *n, often cap* a foreigner who greatly admires or favours England and things English [Fr, fr *anglo-* + *-phile*] – **anglophilia** *n, often cap*, **anglophilic** *adj, often cap*, **anglophilism** *n, often cap*, **anglophily** *n*

**anglophobe** /'ang·glə,fohb/ *n, often cap* a foreigner who is averse to England and things English [prob fr Fr, fr *anglo-* + *-phobe*] – **anglophobia** *n, often cap*, **anglophobic** *adj, often cap*

**anglophone** /-,fohn/ *adj, often cap* consisting of or belonging to an English-speaking population – **Anglophone** *n*

**Anglo-'Saxon** *n* 1 a member of the Germanic peoples that conquered England in the 5th century AD and formed the ruling group until the Norman conquest – compare ANGLE, JUTE, SAXON 2 an Englishman; *specif* a person descended from the Anglo-Saxons 3 OLD ENGLISH 1a 4 *informal* direct blunt English [NL *Anglo-Saxones*, pl, alter. of ML *Angli Saxones*, fr L *Angli* Angles + LL *Saxones* Saxons] – **Anglo-Saxon** *adj*

**angora** /ang'gawrə/ *n* 1 the hair of the Angora rabbit or Angora goat 2 a fabric or yarn made wholly or in part of Angora rabbit hair used esp for knitting – compare MOHAIR 3 *cap* 3a ANGORA CAT b ANGORA GOAT c ANGORA RABBIT [*Angora* (Ankara), capital city of Turkey]

**Angora cat** *n* a long-haired domestic cat

**Angora goat** *n* (any of) a breed of the domestic goat raised for its long silky hair which is the true mohair

**Angora rabbit** *n* a long-haired usu white rabbit with red eyes that is raised for its fine wool

**angostura bark** /,ang·gə'stooərə/ *n* the aromatic bitter bark of either of two S American trees (*Galipea officinalis* and *Cusparia trifoliata*) of the orange family that is used to make ANGOSTURA BITTERS and to treat fever [*Angostura* (now Ciudad Bolivar), town in Venezuela]

**Angostura bitters** *trademark* – used for a bitter aromatic tonic added to alcoholic drinks as a flavouring

**angoumois grain moth** /ong'goohmwah, ahn-/ *n* a moth (*Sitotroga cerealella*) the caterpillar of which causes severe damage to grain (e g wheat and maize) both in the field and in store [*Angoumois*, former province of France]

**angry** /'ang·gri/ *adj* 1 feeling or showing anger; wrathful 〈 ~ *with his brother*〉 〈 ~ *at his rude remark*〉 2a proceeding from anger 〈 ~ *words*〉 b seeming to show or typify anger 〈*an* ~ *sky*〉 3 painfully inflamed 〈*an* ~ *rash*〉 – **angrily** *adv*, **angriness** *n*

**usage** Traditionally, one is **angry** *at* or *about* things or events and **angry** *with* people 〈*she was* **angry** *at the delay and* **angry** *with me for causing it*〉; but if one is **angry** *with* people they have displeased one, while if one is **angry** *about* them one is displeased at what has befallen them. **synonyms** see [1]ANGER

**angry young man** *n* 1 *often cap A, Y, &M* any of a group of mid-20th century British authors whose works express the bitterness of the lower classes towards the established social system and towards the mediocrity and hypocrisy of the middle and upper classes 2 a rebellious young man

**angst** /angst/ *n* a feeling of generalized anxiety and anguish, caused esp by considering the state of the world and the human condition [Dan & Ger; Dan, fr Ger; akin to L *angustus*]

**angstrom** /'angstrəm, -,strom/ *n* a unit of length equal to $10^{-10}$ of a metre – not now in technical use [Anders J *Ångström* †1874 Sw physicist]

**anguine** /'ang·gwin/ *adj* of or resembling a snake [L *anguinus*, fr *anguis* snake]

**anguish** /'ang·gwish/ *n* extreme physical pain or mental distress **synonyms** see GRIEF *antonym* relief [ME *angwisshe*, fr OF *angoisse*, fr L *angustiae*, pl, straits, distress, fr *angustus* narrow; akin to OE *enge* narrow – more at ANGER]

**anguished** /'ang·gwisht/ *adj* 1 suffering anguish; tormented 〈*the* ~ *martyrs*〉 2 expressing anguish; agonized 〈 ~ *cries*〉

**angular** /'ang·gyoolə/ *adj* 1a having one or more angles b forming an angle; sharp-cornered 2 measured by an angle 〈 ~ *distance*〉 〈 ~ *separation*〉 3a stiff in character or manner; awkward b lean, bony [MF or L; MF *angulaire*, fr L *angularis*, fr *angulus* angle] – **angularly** *adv*

**angularity** /,ang·gyoo'larəti/ *n* 1 the quality of being angular 2 *pl* angular outlines or characteristics

**angular leaf spot** *n* a plant disease characterized by dark angular spots on leaves and caused by any of several bacteria (e g *Pseudomonas lachrymans* in cucumber and *Pseudomonas angulata* in tobacco)

**angular momentum** *n* a VECTOR (quantity having both magnitude and direction) that is equal to the ANGULAR VELOCITY of a rotating body or system multiplied by its MOMENT OF INERTIA with respect to the rotation axis or to the VECTOR PRODUCT of a body's momentum and position relative to a specified point

**angular velocity** *n* a VECTOR (quantity having both magnitude and direction) that is equal to the rate of change of angular position with time and that has direction and sense such that the motion appears clockwise to someone looking in the direction of the vector

**angulation** /ˌang·gyoo'laysh(ə)n/ *n* **1** the action of making angular **2** an angular position, formation, or shape

**Angus** /'ang·gəs/ *n* ABERDEEN ANGUS [*Angus*, former county of Scotland]

**angwantibo** /ang'gwantiboh/ *n* a small lemur (*Arctocebus calabarensis*) of W Africa [native name in Nigeria]

**anhedral** /an'heedrəl/ *n* the angle between a downwardly inclined aircraft wing and a horizontal line – compare DIHEDRAL [*an-* + *-hedral*]

**anhydride** /an'hiedried/ *n* a chemical compound derived from another, esp an acid, by removal of the elements of water

**anhydrite** /an'hiedriet/ *n* a white or slightly coloured mineral, CaSO₄, consisting of an anhydrous chemical compound of calcium sulphate [Ger *anhydrit*, fr Gk *anydros*]

**anhydrous** /an'hiedrəs/ *adj* free from water, esp WATER OF CRYSTALLIZATION [Gk *anydros*, fr *a-* + *hydōr* water – more at WATER]

**aniconic** /ˌanie'konik/ *adj* symbolic (e g of an object of worship) rather than literally representational [*an-* + *iconic*]

**anicut** /'anikut/ *n* a dam made in a stream for regulating irrigation and found esp in S India [Tamil *aṇaikkaṭṭu*, fr *aṇai* dam + *kaṭṭu* building]

**anil** /'anil/ *n* a shrub (*Indigofera suffruticosa*) of the pea family found in the W Indies which is a source of indigo dye [Fr F, fr Pg, fr Ar *an-nīl* the indigo plant, fr Skt *nīlī* indigo, fr fem of *nīla* dark blue]

**anile** /'aniel, 'ay/ *adj* of or resembling a silly old woman [L *anilis*, fr *anus* old woman; akin to OHG *ano* grandfather] – **anility** *n*

**aniline** /'anilin, -leen/ *n* an oily liquid poisonous chemical compound, C₆H₅NH₂, that is an AMINE obtained from NITROBENZENE and is used chiefly in organic synthesis (e g of dyes) [Ger *anilin*, fr *anil*]

**aniline dye** *n* a synthetic organic dye; *specif* one made from or chemically related to aniline

**anilingus** /ˌayni'ling·gəs/, **anilinctus** /-'lingktəs/ *n* erotic stimulation of the anus with the mouth [NL, fr *anus* + *-i-* + *-lingus*, *-linctus* (as in *cunnilingus*, *cunnilinctus*)]

**anima** /'animə/ *n* an individual's true inner self that, according to the analytic psychology of C G Jung, reflects archetypal ideals of conduct; *also* an inner feminine part of the male personality – compare ANIMUS 3, PERSONA 2 [NL, fr L, soul]

**animadversion** /ˌanimad'vuhsh(ə)n/ *n, formal* **1** a critical and usu censorious remark **2** hostile criticism [L *animadversion-*, *animadversio*, fr *animadversus*, pp of *animadvertere*]

**animadvert** /ˌanimad'vuht/ *vi, formal* to comment critically or adversely – usu + *on* or *upon* [L *animadvertere* to pay attention to, censure, fr *animum advertere*, lit., to turn the mind to]

**¹animal** /'animəl/ *n* **1** any of a kingdom (Animalia) of living things typically differing from plants in capacity for spontaneous movement and rapid response to stimulation **2a** one of the lower animals as distinguished from human beings **b** a mammal – not used technically **3** a person considered as a purely physical being; a creature [L, fr *animale*, neut of *animalis* animate, fr *anima* soul] – **animal-like** *adj*, **animalness** *n*

**²animal** *adj* **1** of or derived from animals **2** relating to the ANIMAL POLE of an egg or to the part from which ECTODERM (outer layer of tissue of an embryo) normally develops **3** *chiefly derog* of the body as opposed to the mind or spirit – **animally** *adv*

**animalcule** /ˌani'malkyoohl/ *n* a minute usu microscopic organism [NL *animalculum*, dim. of L *animal*] – **animalcular** *adj*

**animalculum** /ˌani'malkyooləm/ *n, pl* **animalcula** /-lə/ an animalcule

**animal husbandry** *n* a branch of agriculture concerned with the breeding and care of domestic animals

**animalism** /'animəˌliz(ə)m/ *n* **1a** (the state of having) qualities typical of animals **b** preoccupation with the satisfaction of physical drives (e g towards food, sex, or slaughter); sensuality **2** a theory that human beings are nothing more than animals – **animalist** *n*, **animalistic** *adj*

**animality** /ˌani'maləti/ *n* **1** ANIMALISM 1a **2a** the state of being an animal **b** animal nature as contrasted with rationality **3** ANIMAL KINGDOM

**animal·ize, -ise** /'animəˌliez/ *vt* **1** to brutalize ⟨*men ~d by the war*⟩ **2** to sensualize ⟨*~d by passion*⟩ – **animalization** *n*

**animal kingdom** *n* that one of the three fundamental groups of natural objects that includes all living and extinct animals – compare MINERAL KINGDOM, PLANT KINGDOM

**animal magnetism** *n* **1** a force held to be present in some

individuals by which a strong hypnotic influence can be exerted **2** physical charm

**animal pole** *n* the point on the surface of an egg that is directly opposite the VEGETAL POLE and is usu the place of the most active CELL DIVISION and tissue growth

**animal starch** *n* GLYCOGEN (type of carbohydrate)

**¹animate** /'animət/ *adj* **1** possessing life; alive **2** of animal life as opposed to plant life **3** full of life; animated [ME, fr L *animatus*, pp of *animare* to give life to, fr *anima* breath, soul; akin to OE *ōthian* to breathe, L *animus* spirit, mind, courage, Gk *anemos* wind] – **animately** *adv*, **animateness** *n*

**²animate** /'animayt/ *vt* **1** to give spirit and support to; encourage **2a** to give life to **b** to give vigour and zest to **3** to move to action; incite **4a** to make or design in such a way that lifelike movement is effected **b** to produce in the form of an animated cartoon

**animated** /'animaytid/ *adj* **1a** endowed with life or the qualities of life; alive ⟨*viruses that can behave as ~ bodies or inert crystals*⟩ **b** full of bustle and activity **c** full of vigour and spirit; vivacious ⟨*an ~ discussion*⟩ **2** appearing to be alive; moving or seeming to move – **animatedly** *adv*

**animated cartoon** /'aniˌmaytid/ *n* a film that creates the illusion of movement by photographing successive positional changes (e g of drawings or inanimate objects)

**animation** /ˌani'maysh(ə)n/ *n* **1** the act of animating **2** vigorous liveliness; ardour **3** (the preparation of) an animated cartoon

**animato** /ˌani'mahtoh/ *adv or adj* with liveliness and vigour – used as a direction in music [It, fr L *animatus*]

**animator** /'animaytə/ *n* an artist responsible for the production of the illusion of movement in animated cartoons

**animism** /'animiz(ə)m/ *n* **1** a doctrine that the soul is the vital principle of organic development **2** attribution of conscious life or spirits to nature or natural objects or phenomena (e g earthquakes) **3** belief in the existence of spirits separable from bodies [Ger *animismus*, fr L *anima* soul] – **animist** *n*, **animistic** *adj*

**animosity** /ˌani'mosəti/ *n* ill will or resentment tending towards active hostility **synonyms** see ENMITY [ME *animosite*, fr MF or LL; MF *animosité*, fr LL *animositat-*, *animositas*, fr L *animosus* spirited, fr *animus*]

**animus** /'animəs/ *n* **1** a pervading attitude or tendency **2** animosity **3** an inner masculine part of the female personality according to the analytic psychology of C G Jung – compare ANIMA **synonyms** see ENMITY [L, spirit, mind, courage, anger]

**anion** /'anˌie·ən/ *n* the ion in an ELECTROLYSED (chemically decomposed by an electric current) solution that travels towards the positive electrode (ANODE); *broadly* an ion with a negative electric charge [Gk, neut of *aniōn*, prp of *anienai* to go up, fr *ana-* + *ienai* to go – more at ISSUE]

**anionic** /ˌanie'onik/ *adj* **1** of anions **2** characterized by an active anion; esp a surface-active anion – **anionically** *adv*

**anis** /'anees, 'ani/ (*Fr* ani) *n* anisette [Fr, anise]

**anis-** /anˌies-/, **aniso-** *comb form* unequal; unlike ⟨*anisodactylous*⟩ ⟨*anisometropia*⟩ [NL, fr Gk, fr *anisos*, fr *a-* + *isos* equal]

**anise** /'anis/ *n* a plant (*Pimpinella anisum*) of the carrot family having aromatic seeds with a liquorice-like flavour; *also* aniseed [ME *anis*, fr OF, fr L *anisum*, fr Gk *annēson*, *anison*]

**aniseed** /'anəseed/ *n* the seed of anise used esp as a flavouring in drinks (e g in liqueurs) and in cooking [ME *anis seed*, fr *anis* + *seed*]

**aniseikonia** /ˌaniesie'kohnyə/ *n* a defect of binocular vision in which the image of an object seen by one eye differs in size from that seen by the other [NL, fr *anis-* + Gk *eikōn* image – more at ICON] – **aniseikonic** *adj*

**anisette** /ˌani'set/ (*Fr* aniset) *n* a usu colourless liqueur flavoured with aniseed [Fr, fr *anis*]

**anisogamous** /ˌanie'sogəməs/, *also* **anisogamic** /ˌanˌiesə'gamik/ *adj* characterized by fusion of unlike reproductive cells (GAMETES) or of individuals that usu differ chiefly in size ⟨*~ reproduction*⟩ – **anisogamy** *n*

**anisometric** /ˌanˌiesə'metrik/ *adj, of a crystal* having three unequal axes

**anisometropia** /ˌanˌiesəmə'trohpiə/ *n* an abnormal condition in which there is unequal power to deflect rays of light in the two eyes [NL, fr Gk *anisometros* of unequal measure (fr *anis-* + *metron* measure) + NL *-opia* – more at MEASURE] – **anisometropic** *adj*

**anisopteran** /ˌanie'soptərən/ *n* a dragonfly [deriv of Gk *anisos* + *pteron* wing]

**anisotropic** /ˌaniesoh'trohpik, -'tropik/ *adj, of a crystal or crystalline material* exhibiting properties with different values when measured in different directions – **anisotropically** *adv,* **anisotropy, anisotropism** *n*

**ankerite** /'angkəriet/ *n* a brown iron-containing DOLOMITE (type of mineral), Ca(Fe,Mg,Mn)(CO₃)₂ [Ger *ankerit,* fr M J *Anker* †1843 Austrian mineralogist]

**ankh** /angk/ *n* a cross having a loop for its upper vertical arm and serving, esp in ancient Egypt, as an emblem of life [Egypt *'nh*]

**ankle** /'angkl/ *n* **1** the joint between the foot and the leg; *also* the region of this joint; TARSUS **2** the joint between the CANNON BONE and PASTERN (eg in the horse) [ME *ankel,* fr OE *anclēow;* akin to OHG *anchlāo* ankle, L *angulus* angle]

**anklebone** /'angkl,bohn/ *n* ²TALUS 1

**anklet** /'angklit/ *n* an ornamental band or chain worn round the ankle

**ankylose** /'angkilohz, -lohs/ *vt* to unite or stiffen by ankylosis ~ *vi* to undergo ankylosis [back-formation fr *ankylosis*]

**ankylosis** /ˌangki'lohsis/ *n, pl* **ankyloses** /-seez/ **1** abnormal or surgical union of the bones in a joint resulting in a stiffness or fixation **2** union of separate bones or hard parts to form a single bone or part [NL, fr Gk *ankylōsis,* fr *ankyloun* to make crooked, fr *ankylos* crooked; akin to L *uncus* hooked – more at ANGLE] – **ankylotic** *adj*

**ankylostomiasis** /ˌangkilohstoh'mie-əsis, -siloh-, ˌangki,lostə-/ *n* ANCYLOSTOMIASIS (infestation with or disease caused by hookworms)

**anlace** /'anlis, 'anlays/ *n* a short and tapering medieval dagger [ME *anlas,* perh fr OF *alenaz,* aug of *alesne* awl, of Gmc origin]

**anlage** /'an,lahgə/ *n, pl* **anlagen** /-gən/ *also* **anlages** the foundation of a subsequent development; *specif, biology* the first structure indicating growth of a part or organ; PRIMORDIUM [Ger ]

**anna** /'anə/ *n* **1** a former monetary unit of Burma, India, and Pakistan worth ¹/₁₆ rupee **2** a coin representing one anna [Hindi *ānā*]

**annabergite** /'anə,buhgiet/ *n* an apple-green mineral, Ni₃As₂O₈.8H₂O, consisting of a chemical compound of nickel arsenate [*Annaberg,* town in Germany]

**annalist** /'anl-ist/ *n* a writer of annals; a historian – **annalistic** *adj*

**annals** /'anlz/ *n pl* **1** a record of events arranged in yearly sequence **2** historical records; chronicles **3** records of the activities of an organization (eg a learned society) [L *annales,* fr pl of *annalis* yearly – more at ANNUAL]

**Annamese** /ˌanə'meez/ *n, pl* **Annamese 1** a member of a Mongolian people inhabiting Vietnam **2** the language of the Annamese; Vietnamese [*Annam,* region of Vietnam] – **Annamese** *adj,* **Annamite** *adj*

**annatto** /ə'natoh/ *n* a yellowish red dyestuff made from the pulp round the seeds of a tropical tree (*Bixa orellana,* family Bixaceae) [of Cariban origin; akin to Galibi *annoto* tree producing annatto]

**anneal** /ə'neel/ *vt* **1** to heat (eg glass) in order to fix colours **2** to heat and then cool (eg steel or glass), usu for toughening by softening and making less brittle **3** to temper, toughen [ME *anelen,* fr OE *onǣlan,* fr *on* + *ǣlan* to set on fire, burn, fr *āl* fire; akin to OE *ād* funeral pyre – more at EDIFY]

**annelid** /'anəlid/ *n* any of a phylum (Annelida) of usu elongated segmented INVERTEBRATE animals that includes the earthworms, various marine worms, and leeches [deriv of L *anellus* little ring – more at ANNULET] – **annelid** *adj,* **annelidan** *adj or n*

¹**annex** /ə'neks/ *vt* **1** to attach as a consequence or condition **2** to subjoin, append **3** to incorporate (sovereign territory) within the domain of a state **4** to gain exclusive possession or control of; appropriate [ME *annexen,* fr MF *annexer,* fr OF, fr *annexe* joined, fr L *annexus,* pp of *annectere* to bind to, fr *ad-* + *nectere* to bind] – **annexation** *n,* **annexational** *adj,* **annexationist** *n*

²**annex,** *chiefly Br* **annexe** /'aneks/ *n* **1** something (eg an addition to a document) annexed or appended **2** a separate or attached extra structure; *esp* a building providing extra accommodation

**annihilate** /ə'nie-ə,layt/ *vt* **1** to destroy entirely; put completely out of existence **2** to destroy a considerable part of ⟨*the army was* ~*d*⟩ **3** to defeat conclusively; rout ⟨*his team was* ~*d in the quarterfinals*⟩ **4** *archaic* to cause or consider to be of no

effect; nullify ⟨~ *a law*⟩ *synonyms* see ABOLISH [LL *annihilatus,* pp of *annihilare* to reduce to nothing, fr L *ad-* + *nihil* nothing – more at NIL] – **annihilator** *n,* **annihilative** *adj,* **annihilatory** *adj,* **annihilation** *n*

**anni mirabiles** /ˌani mi'rahbilayz, -leez/ *pl of* ANNUS MIRABILIS

**anniversary** /ˌani'vuhs(ə)ri/ *n* **1** a day marking the annual recurrence of the date of a notable event **2** the celebration of an anniversary ⟨*an* ~ *party*⟩ [ME *anniversarie,* fr ML *anniversarium,* fr L, neut of *anniversarius* returning annually, fr *annus* year + *versus,* pp of *vertere* to turn – more at ANNUAL, WORTH]

**anno Domini** /ˌanoh 'dominie/ *adv, often cap A* – used to indicate that a time division falls within the Christian era [ML, in the year of the Lord]

**anno hegirae** /hi'jie-əri/ *adv, often cap A&H* – used to indicate that a time division falls within the Muhammadan era [NL, in the year of the Hegira]

**annotate** /'anətayt, 'anoh-/ *vt* to make or provide critical or explanatory notes for or comment on (eg a literary work) [L *annotatus,* pp of *annotare,* fr *ad-* + *notare* to mark – more at NOTE] – **annotative** *adj,* **annotator** *n*

**annotation** /ˌanə'taysh(ə)n/ *n* a note added as a comment or explanation

**announce** /ə'nowns/ *vt* **1** to make known publicly ⟨~*d their engagement*⟩ **2a** to give notice of the arrival, presence, or readiness of ⟨~ *dinner*⟩ **b** to give evidence of; indicate by action or appearance **3** *chiefly NAm* to serve as a television or radio announcer of ~ *vi* **1** *NAm* to act as an announcer **2** to declare one's candidacy; give one's political support – usu + *for* [ME *announcen,* fr MF *annoncer,* fr L *annuntiare,* fr *ad-* + *nuntiare* to report, fr *nuntius* messenger]

**announcement** /ə'nownsmənt/ *n* **1** announcing or being announced **2** a public notification or declaration

**announcer** /ə'nownsə/ *n* one who announces; *esp* somebody who introduces programmes, makes commercial announcements, reads news summaries, etc on television or radio

**annoy** /ə'noy/ *vt* to vex, irritate, or harass, esp by repeated acts or attacks ⟨~*ed with her brother*⟩ ~ *vi* to be a source of annoyance [ME *anoien,* fr OF *enuier,* fr LL *inodiare* to make loathsome, fr L *in* + *odium* hatred – more at ODIUM] – **annoying** *adj,* **annoyingly** *adv*

*synonyms* Annoy, bother, vex, irk: bother is the mildest term, suggesting a fairly mild interference with one's peace of mind ⟨bothered *while shopping over whether he had left the door unlocked*⟩. Annoy stresses displeasure and/or dislike for whatever has made one lose one's patience or one's equanimity ⟨*his habitual nonchalance* annoyed *her*⟩. Vex is the strongest term, suggesting both greater provocation and a deeper disturbance as a result ⟨*Her silence on the subject* vexed *him. What could be the cause of it?*⟩ Irk usually emphasizes the continued nature of the irritation ⟨*The whine of the engines soon began to* irk *her*⟩. Compare WORRY, IRRITATE *antonym* soothe

**annoyance** /ə'noyəns/ *n* **1** the act of annoying **2** the state or feeling of being annoyed **3** a source of irritation; a nuisance

¹**annual** /'anyoo(ə)l/ *adj* **1a** reckoned by the year ⟨~ *rainfall*⟩ **b** based on a year ⟨*the sun's* ~ *course*⟩ **2** occurring or performed once a year ⟨*an* ~ *reunion*⟩ **3** *of a plant* completing the LIFE CYCLE in one growing season – compare PERENNIAL [ME, fr MF & LL; MF *annuel,* fr LL *annualis,* blend of L *annuus* yearly and *annalis* yearly (both fr *annus* year); akin to Goth *athnam* (dat pl) years, Skt *atati* he walks, goes] – **annually** *adv*

²**annual** *n* **1** a publication (eg a book) appearing yearly ⟨*buying the kids' Christmas* ~*s*⟩ **2** an event that occurs yearly **3** something that lasts one year or season; *specif* an annual plant

**annual ring** *n* the layer of wood produced by a single year's growth that can be seen in a cross-section of the stem or trunk of a woody plant

**annuitant** /ə'nyooh-it(ə)nt/ *n* a beneficiary of an annuity

**annuity** /ə'nyooh-əti/ *n* **1** an amount payable at regular intervals, esp yearly **2** the right to receive or the obligation to pay an annuity **3** a contract or agreement providing for the payment of an annuity [ME *annuite,* fr MF *annuité,* fr ML *annuitat-, annuitas,* fr L *annuus* yearly]

**annul** /ə'nul/ *vt* **-ll- 1** to reduce to nothing; cancel **2** to declare or make legally invalid or void ⟨*wants his marriage* ~*led*⟩ *synonyms* see ABROGATE [ME *annullen,* fr MF *annuller,* fr LL *annullare,* fr L *ad-* + *nullus* not any – more at NULL]

**annular** /'anyoolə/ *adj* of or forming a ring [MF or L; MF *annulaire*, fr L *annularis*, fr *annulus*] – **annularity** *n*, **annularly** *adv*

**annular eclipse** *n* an eclipse in which a thin outer ring of the sun's disc remains visible round the smaller dark disc of the moon

**annulate** /'anyoolət/, **annulated** /-,laytid/ *adj* having or composed of rings – **annulately** *adv*

**annulation** /,anyoo'laysh(ə)n/ *n* the formation of rings; *also* a ringlike structure

**annulet** /'anyoolət/ *n* a small ring or circle [modif of MF *annelet*, dim. of *anel*, fr L *anellus*, dim. of *annulus*]

**annulment** /ə'nulmənt/ *n* **1** annulling or being annulled **2** a legal pronouncement declaring a legal matter (e g a marriage or a bankruptcy order) invalid

**annulus** /'anyooləs/ *n, pl* **annuli** /'anyoolie/ *also* **annuluses 1** a ring **2** a part, structure, or marking resembling a ring: e g **2a** a line of cells round a fern SPORANGIUM (walled structure containing spores) that ruptures the sporangium by contracting **b** a GROWTH RING (e g on the scale of a fish) that can be used in estimating age; ANNUAL RING [L, dim. of *anus* ring, anus – more at ANUS]

**annunciate** /ə'nunsi·ayt/ *vt, formal* to announce [L *annuntiatus*, pp]

**annunciation** /ə,nunsi'aysh(ə)n/ *n* **1** *cap* the announcement of the Incarnation to the Virgin Mary related in Luke 1:26–28; *also* March 25 observed as a church festival in commemoration of this **2** an announcement [ME *annunciacioun*, fr MF *anunciation*, fr LL *annuntiation-*, *annuntiatio*, announcement, fr L *annuntiatus*, pp of *annuntiare* – more at ANNOUNCE]

**annus mirabilis** /,anəs mi'rahbilis/ *n, pl* **anni mirabiles** /,anie mi'rahbilayz, -eez/ a remarkable or wonderful year [NL]

**anoa** /ə'noh·ə/ *n* a small wild ox (*Anoa depressicornis*) of Celebes, an island in Indonesia [native name in Celebes]

**anode** /'anohd/ *n* **1** the ELECTRODE (wire, plate, etc that conducts an electric current) by which electrons leave a device and enter an external circuit: e g **1a** the electrode having a positive electrical charge of a chemical cell undergoing ELECTROLYSIS (chemical decomposition of a substance by an electric current) **b** the negative terminal of a PRIMARY CELL or of a storage battery that is delivering current **2** the electrode in a THERMIONIC VALVE or similar electronic device which collects the electrons **3** a positive electrode used to accelerate a beam of electrons in an ELECTRON GUN □ compare CATHODE [Gk *anodos* way up, fr *ana-* + *hodos* way – more at CEDE] – **anodic, anodal** *adj*, **anodically, anodally** *adv*

**anod-ize, -ise** /'anohdiez, 'anədiez/ *vt* to coat (a piece of metal) with a protective or decorative film by ELECTROLYSIS (chemical decomposition of a substance by an electric current) by making it the anode – compare ELECTROPLATING – **anodization** *n*

**anodontia** /,anə'donsh(y)ə, ,anoh-/ *n* an abnormal condition in which the teeth fail to develop [NL]

**¹anodyne** /'anədien/ *adj* mentally or emotionally soothing [L *anodynos*, fr Gk *anōdynos*, fr *a-* + *odynē* pain; akin to OE *etan* to eat]

**²anodyne** *n* **1** a pain-relieving drug **2** something that soothes, calms, or comforts – **anodynic** *adj*

**anoestrous** /a'neestrəs/ *adj* **1** not exhibiting OESTRUS (period of sexual activity) **2** of anoestrus

**anoestrus** /a'neestrəs/ *n* the period of sexual quiescence between two periods of sexual activity in mammals that have breeding cycles – compare OESTRUS [NL, fr ²*a-* + *oestrus*]

**anoint** /ə'noynt/ *vt* **1** to smear or rub with oil or an oily substance **2** to apply oil to as a sacred rite, esp for consecration [ME *anointen*, fr MF *enoint*, pp of *enoindre*, fr L *inunguere*, fr *in-* + *unguere* to smear – more at OINTMENT] – **anointer** *n*, **anointment** *n*

**anointing of the sick** *n* the chiefly Roman Catholic and Eastern Orthodox sacrament of anointing and praying over a sick or elderly person, esp one who is in danger of death – called also EXTREME UNCTION

**anomalistic** /ə,nomə'listik/, **anomalistical** /-kl/ *adj* relating to the astronomical anomaly

**anomalistic month** *n* the average time taken by the moon to travel from the point (PERIGEE) in its orbit nearest the earth round to that point again; about $27^1/_2$ days

**anomalistic year** *n* the average time taken by the earth to travel from the point (PERIHELION) in its orbit nearest the sun round to that point again; about 365 days, 6 hours, 13 minutes, and 53 seconds

**anomalous** /ə'nomələs/ *adj* **1** deviating from a general rule or

standard; abnormal **2** inconsistent with accepted ideas of fitness or order; incongruous [LL *anomalus*, fr Gk *anōmalos*, lit., uneven, fr *a-* + *homalos* even, fr *homos* same – more at SAME] – **anomalously** *adv*

**anomaly** /ə'noməli/ *n* **1a** the angle between an imaginary line joining a planet to the sun at the nearest point (PERIHELION) in its orbit and another line joining the planet to the sun at any other point in its orbit **b** the angle between an imaginary line joining a satellite to the earth at the nearest point (PERIGEE) in its orbit and another line joining the satellite to the earth at any other point in its orbit **2** deviation from the normal or usual rule; an irregularity, incongruity **3** something or somebody anomalous; *esp* something (e g an organism) that deviates in excess of normal variation

**anomie, anomy** /'anomi/ *n* the lack, in a society or individual, of moral or social standards of conduct and belief [Fr *anomie*, fr Gk *anomia* lawlessness, fr *anomos* lawless, fr *a-* + *nomos* law, fr *nemein* to distribute – more at NIMBLE] – **anomic** *adj*

**anon** /ə'non/ *adv* **1** at another time **2** *archaic* soon, presently **3** *obs* at once; immediately [ME, at once fr OE *on ān*, fr *on* in + *ān* one – more at ON, ONE]

**anonym** /'anənim/ *n* **1** an anonymous person or book **2** a pseudonym

**anonymous** /ə'nonəməs/ *adj* **1** having or giving no name ⟨*an ~ author*⟩ **2** of unknown or unnamed origin or authorship ⟨*~ gifts*⟩ **3** lacking individuality or personality ⟨*~ sandwiches – Punch*⟩ [LL *anonymus*, fr Gk *anōnymos*, fr *a-* + *onyma* name – more at NAME] – **anonymously** *adv*, **anonymousness** *n*, **anonymity** *n*

**anopheles** /ə'nofileez/ *n* any of a genus (*Anopheles*) of mosquitoes that includes all those which transmit malaria to human beings [NL, genus name, fr Gk *anōphelēs* useless, fr *a-* + *ophelos* advantage, help; akin to OE *ō-* behind, Skt *ā-* towards and to Skt *phalam* fruit, profit] – **anopheline** *adj or n*

**anorak** /'anərak/ *n, chiefly Br* a short weatherproof coat with a hood and often a pouch pocket [Greenland Esk *ánorâq*]

**anorectic** /,anə'rektik/ *adj* lacking appetite: **a** suffering from ANOREXIA NERVOSA **b** causing loss of appetite [Gk *anorektos*, fr *a-* + *orektos* desired, fr *oregein*] – **anorectic** *n*

**anorexia** /,anə'reksi·ə/ *n* **1** loss of appetite, esp when prolonged **2 anorexia nervosa, anorexia** abnormal and potentially fatal aversion to food induced by emotional or psychological disturbance [NL, fr Gk, fr *a-* + *orexis* appetite, fr *oregein* to stretch out, reach after – more at RIGHT; *anorexia nervosa* fr NL, lit., nervous anorexia] – **anorexigenic** *adj*

**anorexic** /,anə'reksik/ *n or adj* (a person) suffering from ANOREXIA NERVOSA; (an) anorectic

**anorthite** /ə'nawthiet/ *n* a white, greyish, or reddish FELDSPAR (type of mineral), $CaAl_2Si_2O_8$, of the PLAGIOCLASE series that is a chemical compound of calcium aluminium silicate occurring in many IGNEOUS rocks [Fr, fr *a-* + Gk *orthos* straight – more at ARDUOUS; fr its oblique crystals] – **anorthitic** *adj*

**anorthoclase** /ə'nawthəklayz, -klays/ *n* a bluish iridescent FELDSPAR (type of mineral) consisting mainly of the chemical compound sodium potassium aluminium silicate and used esp for facing buildings [ISV]

**anorthosite** /ə'nawthəsiet/ *n* a coarse-grained IGNEOUS rock composed almost exclusively of a soda-lime FELDSPAR (type of mineral) (e g labradorite) [Fr *anorthose* anorthoclase, fr *a-* + Gk *orthos*]

**anosmia** /a'nozmi·ə/ *n* (partial) loss of the sense of smell [NL, fr *a-* + Gk *osmē* smell – more at ODOUR] – **anosmic** *adj*

**¹another** /ə'nudhə/ *adj* **1** being a different or distinct one ⟨*the same scene viewed from ~ angle*⟩ **2** some other; later ⟨*do it ~ time*⟩ **3** being one additional; further ⟨*have ~ piece of pie*⟩ **4** patterned after; a second ⟨*~ Napoleon*⟩

*usage* The combinations **another** *from* and **another** *to* are widely disliked. Writers on usage recommend **another** *than* ⟨**another** *century than ours*⟩.

**²another** *pron, pl* **others 1** an additional one; one more **2** a different one ⟨*she loved ~*⟩ ⟨*for one reason or ~*⟩ – compare OTHER, ONE ANOTHER

**anovulant** /ə'novyoolənt/ *n* a drug that suppresses ovulation [²*a-* + *ovulate* + *-ant*] – **anovulant** *adj*

**anovulatory** /ə'novyoolət(ə)ri/ *adj* **1** not involving or associated with ovulation ⟨*~ vaginal bleeding*⟩ **2** suppressing ovulation [²*a-* + *ovulate* + *-ory*]

**anoxaemia** /,anok'seemyə/ *n* a condition in which the blood in the arteries does not carry enough oxygen [NL, fr ²*a-* + *ox-* + *-aemia*]

**anoxia** /ə'noksi-ə/ n oxygen deficiency (HYPOXIA), esp of such severity as to result in permanent physiological damage [NL] – **anoxic** adj

**anschluss** /'anshloos (Gr anʃlʊs)/ n political union; specif, often cap that between Germany and Austria in 1938 [Ger, union, fr anschliessen to join]

**anserine** /'ansərien, -rin/ adj of or resembling a goose [L anserinus, fr anser goose – more at GOOSE]

¹**answer** /'ahnsə/ n 1 a spoken or written reply to a question, remark, examination question, etc **2a** a reply to a charge; a legal defence **b** a formal reply made by the defendant in a legal case in reply to the facts alleged by the plaintiff 3 something done in response 〈her only ∼ was to walk out〉 4 a solution to a problem 〈the ∼ to a chess problem〉; specif a correct solution 5 someone or something thought of as or intended to be a close equivalent or rival of another 〈Scotland's ∼ to Andy Williams〉 6 an appropriate procedure for dealing with something 〈force isn't the ∼〉 [ME, fr OE andswaru; akin to ON andsvar answer; both fr a prehistoric WGmc-NGmc compound whose first constituent is represented by OE and- against, and whose second is akin to OE swerian to swear]

²**answer** vi 1 to speak or write in reply **2a** to be or make oneself responsible or accountable for 〈can't ∼ for the consequences〉 **b** to make amends; atone for 3 to conform or correspond to 〈∼ed to the description〉 4 to act in response 〈dog ∼s to his name〉 〈telephoned but nobody ∼ed〉 5 to be adequate or usable; serve the purpose 〈this paper clip will ∼ for the time being〉 ∼ vt **1a** to speak or write in reply to **b** to say or write by way of reply **c** to write an answer to (a question designed to test knowledge) 2 to reply to in rebuttal, justification, or explanation 〈∼ a charge〉 **3a** to correspond to **b** to be adequate or usable for 4 to act in response to 〈∼ the door〉 5 to offer a solution for; esp to solve 〈∼ a riddle〉 – **answerer** n

**synonyms** Answer, reply, respond, rejoin, retort, riposte: answer is the most general of this group, and may be used, suitably qualified, in place of any of the others. To **respond** is to react positively to a stimulus of some kind, in words or behaviour 〈respond to an appeal〉〈the horse responded to the jockey's whip〉. Reply is used for giving an answer to a specific question, or for responding to words or behaviour in a similar tone or way 〈babies soon learn to reply to a smile〉. To **rejoin**, or make a **rejoinder**, is to reply to another's reply, or to reply in a way that implies disagreement or criticism 〈I composed a suitable rejoinder to their reply〉〈"You cannot sit there either", snapped the attendant. "It seems I cannot sit anywhere", rejoined the visitor〉. Retort is stronger than rejoin and suggests a counterattack 〈"You should not be here". "Neither should you", she retorted〉. Riposte comes from fencing and is used for retorting in a sharp or witty manner.

**answer back** vb, esp of a child to reply rudely (to)

**answerability** /,ahns(ə)rə'biləti/ n accountability, responsibility 〈ministerial ∼〉

**answerable** /'ahns(ə)rəbl/ adj **1a** responsible 〈∼ for her son's debts〉 **b** having to account for one's actions 〈∼ only to the Prime Minister〉 2 capable of being answered or refuted 3 archaic suitable, fitting 4 archaic corresponding, esp in quantity or degree

**ant** /ant/ n any of a family (Formicidae) of HYMENOPTEROUS insects related to the bees and wasps that live in large colonies with a complex social organization and a hierarchy in which different castes perform special duties [ME ante, emete, fr OE æmette; akin to OHG āmeiza ant]

**ant-** /ant-/ – see ANTI-

¹**-ant** /-(ə)nt/ suffix (→ n) **1a** one who or that which performs (a specified action) 〈claimant〉 〈deodorant〉 **b** thing that causes (a specified action or process) 〈expectorant〉 2 one connected with 〈annuitant〉 3 thing that is used or acted on (in a specified manner) 〈inhalant〉 [ME, fr OF, fr -ant, prp suffix, fr L -ant, -ans, prp suffix of first conjugation, fr -a- (stem vowel of first conjugation) + -nt-, -ns, prp suffix; akin to OE -nde, prp suffix, Gk -nt-, -n, participle suffix]

²**-ant** suffix (→ adj) 1 performing (a specified action) or being (in a specified condition) 〈repentant〉 〈somnambulant〉 2 causing (a specified action or process) 〈expectorant〉

**anta** /'antə/ n, pl antas, antae /'anti/ a column formed at the edge of a projecting wall (eg of a portico) [L; akin to ON önd anteroom]

**antacid** /ant'asid/ adj correcting excessive activity (eg in the stomach) – **antacid** n

**antagonism** /an'tagəni(ə)m/ n **1a** hostility or antipathy, esp when actively expressed **b** opposition of a conflicting force, tendency, or principle 2 opposition in physiological action; esp interaction of two or more substances such that the action of any one of them on living cells or tissues is lessened **synonyms** see ENMITY **antonyms** amicability, accord

**antagonist** /an'tagənist/ n 1 an opponent, adversary 2 an agent of physiological antagonism: eg **2a** a muscle that contracts with and limits the action of another (AGONIST) with which it is paired **b** a drug that opposes the action of another drug or of a substance (eg one transmitting nerve impulses) that occurs naturally in the body □ (2) compare AGONIST

**antagonistic** /an,tagə'nistik, ,---'--/ adj characterized by or resulting from antagonism; opposing – **antagonistically** adv

**antagonistic muscle** n ANTAGONIST 2a

**antagon·ize, -ise** /an'tagəniez/ vt 1 to oppose, counteract 2 to provoke the hostility of [Gk antagōnizesthai, fr anti- + agōnizesthai to struggle, fr agōn contest – more at AGONY]

**antarctic** /an'tahktik; also an'tahtik/ adj, often cap of the South Pole or the surrounding region [ME antartik, fr L antarcticus, fr Gk antarktikos, fr anti- + arktikos arctic]

**usage** The pronunciation /an'tahktik/ is recommended for BBC broadcasters.

**Antarctic** n the most southern part of the world, south of the Antarctic circle

**antarctic circle** n, often cap A&C the parallel of latitude that is about $66^1/_2$ degrees south of the earth's equator and that is the limit of the south polar region

**ant bear** n an aardvark

**ant cow** n an aphid from which ants obtain honeydew

¹**ante** /'anti/ n 1 a poker stake usu put up before the deal to build the pot 〈the dealer called for a dollar ∼〉 2 chiefly NAm informal an amount paid; a price 〈these improvements would raise the ∼〉 [ante-]

²**ante** vt anteing; anted to pay or produce (an ante)

**ante up** vb, chiefly NAm PAY UP

**ante-** /'anti-/ prefix **1a** prior; before 〈antecedent〉 〈antedate〉 **b** anterior; situated before 〈anteroom〉 2 prior to; earlier than 〈antediluvian〉 □ compare ANTI- [ME, fr L, fr ante before, in front of; akin to OE and- against, Gk anti before, against – more at END]

**anteater** /'ant,eetə/ n any of several mammals that feed largely or entirely on ants and termites: eg **a** any of various EDENTATE mammals with a long narrow snout, a long tongue, and enormous salivary glands (eg the pangolin); specif GIANT ANTEATER **b** ECHIDNA **c** an aardvark

**antebellum** /,anti'beləm/ adj existing before the war; esp existing before the US Civil War 〈an ∼ brick mansion〉 [L ante bellum before the war]

**antecede** /,anti'seed/ vt to precede [L antecedere, fr ante- + cedere to go – more at CEDE]

**antecedence** /,anti'seed(ə)ns/ n priority, precedence

¹**antecedent** /,anti'seed(ə)nt/ n 1 a word, phrase, or clause functioning as a noun and referred to by a pronoun (eg John in "I saw John and spoke to him"); broadly a word or group of words replaced and referred to by a substitute 2 the premise of a conditional proposition (eg if A in "if A, then B") – compare CONSEQUENT 3 the first term of a mathematical ratio (eg a in "a : b") – not used technically **4a** a preceding event, condition, or cause **b** pl the significant events and conditions of one's earlier life **5a** something that came earlier in a series; esp a model or stimulus for later developments 〈a stringed instrument that was an ∼ to the banjo〉 **b** pl family origins; parentage **synonyms** see ¹CAUSE [ME, fr ML & L; ML antecedent-, antecedens, fr L, logical antecedent, lit., that which goes before, fr neut of antecedent-, antecedens, prp of antecedere]

²**antecedent** adj 1 prior in time or order 2 causally or logically prior – **antecedently** adv

**antecessor** /'anti,sesə, ,--'--/ n, formal a predecessor [ME antecessour, fr L antecessor – more at ANCESTOR]

**antechamber** /'anti,chaymbə/ n a usu small room leading to another room; ANTEROOM [Fr antichambre, fr MF, fr It anti- (fr L ante-) + MF chambre room – more at CHAMBER]

**antechapel** /'anti,chapl/ n a porch or lobby at the west end of a chapel

**antechoir** /'anti,kwie·ə/ n a space enclosed or reserved for the clergy and choristers at the entrance to a choir

**ante-com'munion** n the part of an Anglican service of Communion that comes before the consecration of the bread and wine

**antedate** /'anti,dayt/ vt 1 to attach or assign a date earlier than the true one to (eg a document), esp with intent to deceive

⟨~ *an insurance eertificate*⟩ **2** to precede in time ⟨*her death* ~d *her brother's*⟩ **3** *archaic* to anticipate – **antedate** *n*

**antediluvian** /ˌantidiˈloohvi-ən/ *adj* **1** of the period before the flood described in the Bible **2** utterly out-of-date; antiquated ⟨*an ~ car*⟩ **synonyms** see ¹OLD [*ante-* + L *diluvium* flood – more at DELUGE] – **antediluvian** *n*

**antefix** /ˈantiˌfiks/ *n* an ornamental block at the eaves of a classical building that conceals the ends of the roofing tiles [L *antefixum*, fr neut of *antefixus*, pp of *antefigere* to fasten before, fr *ante-* + *figere* to fasten – more at DYKE] – **antefixal** *adj*

**antelope** /ˈantilohp/ *n, pl* **antelopes**, *esp collectively* **antelope 1** any of various African and Eurasian RUMINANT (cud-chewing) mammals (family Bovidae) that are related to the oxen but differ esp in having a lighter racier build and horns directed upwards and backwards **2** leather made from antelope hide [ME, fabulous heraldic beast, prob fr MF *antelop* savage animal with sawlike horns, fr ML *anthalopus*, fr LGk *antholop-, antholops*]

**ante meridiem** /ˌanti məˈridi-əm/ *adj* being before noon – abbr *am*; compare POST MERIDIEM [L]

**antemortem** /-ˈmawtəm/ *adj* preceding death [L *ante mortem*]

**antenatal** /-ˈnaytl/ *adj* of or concerned with an unborn child, pregnancy, or a pregnant woman ⟨*an ~ clinic*⟩

**antenna** /anˈtenə/ *n, pl* **antennae** /anˈteni/, **antennas 1** a movable segmented SENSE ORGAN on the head of insects, MYRIAPODS (e g centipedes and millipedes), and CRUSTACEANS (e g shrimps, crabs and wood-lice) **2** an aerial – chiefly used in Br with reference to complex aerials **3** means of perception or of intuition ⟨*the sensitive ~ of a poet*⟩ [ML, fr L, sail yard] – **antennal** *adj*

**antennule** /anˈtenyool/ *n* a small antenna or similar body part

**antepenult** /ˌantipiˈnult/ *also* **antepenultima** /-ˈultimə/ *n* the 3rd from the last syllable in a word (e g *cu* in *accumulate*) [LL *antepaenultima*, fem of *antepaenultimus* preceding the next to last, fr L *ante-* + *paenultimus* penultimate] – **antepenultimate** *adj or n*

**ante-post** /ˈanti ˌpohst/ *adj, Br* **1** *of a horse-racing bet* placed before the runners' numbers are put up on the board **2** of or occurring in the period before the day of a horse race ⟨*the ~ favourite*⟩

**anterior** /anˈtiəri-ə/ *adj* **1a** situated before or towards the front **b** *of a plant part* (on the side) facing away from the stem or axis; *also* ABAXIAL, INFERIOR 4c **c** *of an animal part* relating to or situated near the head; CEPHALIC **d** *of the human body or its parts* relating to or situated in the front part of the body; VENTRAL **2a** preceding in time; antecedent **b** logically prior □ compare POSTERIOR [L, compar of *ante* before – more at ANTE-] – **anteriorly** *adv*

**antero-** *comb form* **1** anterior ⟨antero*parietal*⟩; anterior and ⟨antero*lateral*⟩ **2** from front to ⟨antero*posterior*⟩ [NL, fr L *anterior*]

**anteroom** /ˈantiˌroohm, -room/ *n* **1** an outer room that leads to another usu more important room, often used as a waiting room **2** *Br* the sitting room in an officers' mess

**anth-** – see ANTI-

**anthelion** /antˈheelyən, anˈthee-/ *n, pl* **anthelia** /antˈheelyə, anˈtheelyə/, **anthelions** a luminous spot appearing on the PARHELIC CIRCLE opposite the sun – compare PARHELION [Gk *anthēlion*, fr neut of *anthēlios* opposite the sun, fr *anti-* + *hēlios* sun – more at SOLAR]

**anthelmintic** /ˌantˈhelˈmintik, ˌanthel-/ *adj, esp of a drug* expelling or destroying parasitic worms (e g tapeworms), esp of the intestine [*anti-* + Gk *helminth-, helmis* worm – more at HELMINTH] – **anthelmintic** *n*

**anthem** /ˈanthəm/ *n* **1a** ANTIPHON **b** a piece of church music for voices that has words usu taken from the Bible **2** a song or hymn of praise or gladness; *specif* one included in the Anglican church service for choir and sometimes solos accompanied by the organ [ME *antem*, fr OE *antefn*, fr LL *antiphona*, fr LGk *antiphōna*, pl of *antiphōnon*, fr Gk, neut of *antiphōnos* responsive, fr *anti-* + *phōnē* sound – more at BAN]

**anthemion** /anˈtheemyən/ *n, pl* **anthemia** /anˈtheemyə/ an ornamental design (e g on an architectural moulding, or a painting) that consists of formal flower and leaf patterns [Gk, fr dim. of *anthemon* flower, fr *anthos* – more at ANTHOLOGY]

**anther** /ˈanthə/ *n* the part of a STAMEN (male reproductive organ of a plant) that develops and contains pollen and is usu borne on a stalk [NL *anthera*, fr L, medicine made of flowers, fr Gk *anthēra*, fr fem of *anthēros* flowery, fr *anthos*] – **antheral** *adj*

**antheridium** /ˌanthəˈridi-əm/ *n, pl* **antheridia** /ˌanthəˈridiə/ the male reproductive organ of a plant (e g a fern or a moss) that reproduces by spores and not seeds [NL, fr *anthera* + *-idium*] – **antheridial** *adj*

**anthesis** /anˈtheesis/ *n* the action or period of opening of a flower [NL, fr Gk *anthēsis* bloom, fr *anthein* to flower, fr *anthos*]

**anthill** /ˈantˌhil/, **antheap** /ˈantˌheep/ *n* **1** a mound thrown up by ants or termites in digging their nest **2** a place (e g a city) that is overcrowded and incessantly busy ⟨*the human ~* H G Wells⟩

**anthocyan** /ˌanthohˈsie-an/ *n* anthocyanin

**anthocyanin** /ˌanthohˈsie-ənin/ *n* any of various soluble pigments that produce the blue and red colouring in flowers and plants [Gk *anthos* + *kyanos* dark blue]

**anthologist** /anˈtholəjist/ *n* a compiler of an anthology

**antholog·ize, -ise** /anˈtholəˌjiez/ *vt* to compile or publish in an anthology – **anthologizer** *n*

**anthology** /anˈtholəji/ *n* **1** a collection of selected literary pieces or passages **2** a collection or presentation of selected non-literary works ⟨*a fine ~ of Byzantine icons*⟩ [NL *anthologia* collection of epigrams, fr MGk, fr Gk, flower gathering, fr *anthos* flower (akin to Skt *andha* herb) + *logia* collecting, fr *legein* to gather – more at LEGEND]

**anthophagous** /anˈthofəgəs/ *adj* feeding on flowers [Gk *anthos* + E *-phagous*] – **anthophagy** *n*

**anthophyllite** /ˌanthohˈfiliet, anˈthofiliet/ *n* a grey-brown mineral of the AMPHIBOLE group [Ger *anthophyllit*, fr NL *anthophyllum*, fr Gk *anthos* + *phyllon* leaf]

**anthozoan** /ˌanthəˈzoh-ən/ *n* any of a class (Anthozoa of the phylum Coelenterata) of marine INVERTEBRATE animals including the corals and SEA ANEMONES that have cylindrical bodies (POLYPS) bearing tentacles and that live attached to rocks or other stationary objects [deriv of Gk *anthos* + *zōion* animal; akin to Gk *zōē* life – more at QUICK] – **anthozoan** *adj*

**anthracene** /ˈanthrəˌseen/ *n* a carbon- and hydrogen-containing chemical compound, $C_{14}H_{10}$, with a molecular structure consisting of three joined rings of atoms that is obtained from the distillation of coal-tar and is an important source of dye-stuffs

**anthracite** /ˈanthrəˌsiet/ *n* a hard slow-burning natural coal that differs from BITUMINOUS COAL in burning with a nearly smokeless flame and in producing very little ash [Gk *anthrakitis*, fr *anthrak-, anthrax* coal] – **anthracitic** *adj*

**anthracnose** /anˈthraknohs/ *n* any of numerous destructive plant diseases caused by certain fungi (IMPERFECT FUNGI) and characterized by the appearance of dark sunken spots or blisters on the plant [Fr, fr Gk *anthrak-, anthrax* + *nosos* disease]

**anthraquinone** /ˌanthrəˈkweenohn, -ˈkwi-/ *n* a chemical compound, $C_{14}H_8O_2$, that is a KETONE with a molecular structure consisting of three rings of atoms joined together that is derived from anthracene and used esp in the manufacture of dyes [prob fr Fr, fr *anthracene* + *quinone*]

**anthrax** /ˈanthraks/ *n* a severe and often fatal infectious disease of warm-blooded animals (e g cattle and sheep) caused by a spore-forming bacterium (*Bacillus anthracis*), transmissible to humans, esp by the handling of infected products (e g hair) and characterized by large ulcers on the body or by damage to the lungs [ME *antrax* carbuncle, fr L *anthrax*, fr Gk, coal, carbuncle]

**anthrop-, anthropo-** *comb form* human being; man ⟨*anthropology*⟩ [L *anthropo-*, fr Gk *anthrōp-, anthrōpo-*, fr *anthrōpos*]

**anthropic** /anˈthropik/, **anthropical** /-kl/ *adj* of the human race or the period of its existence on earth [Gk *anthrōpikos*, fr *anthrōpos*]

**anthropocentric** /ˌanthrəpəˈsentrik, -poh-/ *adj* **1** considering human beings to be the most significant entities in the universe **2** interpreting or regarding the world in terms of human values and experiences – **anthropocentrically** *adv*, **anthropocentricity** *n*

**anthropogenesis** /ˌanthrəpohˈjenəsis/ *n* the study of the origin and development of the human race [NL, fr *anthrop-* + L *genesis*] – **anthropogenetic** *adj*

**anthropogenic** /ˌanthrəpəˈjenik, -poh-/ *adj* of or influenced by the impact of humans on nature ⟨*~ ecosystems*⟩

**anthropogeny** /ˌanthrəˈpojəni/ *n* anthropogenesis

**anthropogeography** /ˌanthrəpohji'ogrəfi/ *n* anthropography

**anthropography** /ˌanthrəˈpogrəfi/ *n* a branch of anthropology dealing with the distribution of humans as distinguished by physical character, language, institutions, and customs

**¹anthropoid** /'anthrǝ,poyd/ *adj* **1** resembling humans or the ANTHROPOID APES (eg in form or behaviour); apelike **2** *of a human* resembling an ape ⟨~ *gangsters*⟩ [Gk *anthrōpoeidēs*, fr *anthrōpos*]

**²anthropoid** *n* APE 1b

**anthropoid ape** *n* APE 1b

**anthropology** /,anthrǝ'polǝji/ *n* **1** the science of the human race; *esp* the study of the human race in relation to distribution, origin, classification, and relationship of races, physical characteristics, environmental and social relations and culture [NL *anthropologia*, fr *anthrop-* + *-logia* -logy] – **anthropologist** *n*, **anthropological** *adj*, **anthropologically** *adv*

**anthropometry** /,anthrǝ'pomǝtri/ *n* the study of the measurements of the human body, esp on a comparative basis [Fr *anthropométrie*, fr *anthrop-* + *-métrie* -metry] – **anthropometric, anthropometrical** *adj*, **anthropometrically** *adv*

**anthropomorphic** /,anthrǝpǝ'mawfik/, **anthropomorphous** /-ǝs/ *adj* **1** having a human form or human attributes ⟨~ *deities*⟩ **2** ascribing human characteristics to nonhuman things ⟨~ *supernaturalism*⟩ [LL *anthropomorphus* of human form, fr Gk *anthrōpomorphos*, fr *anthrōp-* + *-morphos* -morphous] – **anthropomorphically** *adv*

**anthropomorphism** /,anthrǝpǝ'mawfiz(ǝ)m/ *n* the ascribing of human behaviour, form, etc to what is not human (eg a god or animal) – **anthropomorphist** *n*

**anthropomorph·ize, -ise** /,anthrǝpǝ'mawfiez/ *vt* to attribute human form or personality to

**anthropopathism** /,anthrǝ'popǝthiz(ǝ)m/, **anthropopathy** /-'popǝthi/ *n* the ascribing of human feelings to what is not human (eg to God) [LGk *anthrōpopatheia* humanity, fr Gk *anthrōpopathēs* having human feelings, fr *anthrōp-* + *pathos* experience – more at PATHOS]

**anthropophagous** /,anthrǝ'pofǝgǝs/ *adj* feeding on human flesh; cannibal – **anthropophagy** *n*

**anthropophagus** /,anthrǝ'pofǝgǝs/ *n, pl* **anthropophagi** /-ǝgie/ a cannibal, man-eater [L, fr Gk *anthrōpophagos*, fr *anthrōp-* + *-phagos* -phagous]

**¹anti** /'anti/ *n, pl* **antis** one who is opposed to a practice or policy [*anti-*]

**²anti** *prep* opposed or antagonistic to

**anti-** /anti-/, **ant-, anth-** *prefix* **1a** of the same kind but situated opposite; in the opposite direction to ⟨*antipodes*⟩ ⟨*anticlockwise*⟩ **b** opposite in kind to ⟨*anticlimax*⟩ ⟨*anti-hero*⟩ **2a** opposing or hostile to in opinion, sympathy, or practice ⟨*antiSemite*⟩ ⟨*antislavery*⟩ **b** opposing in effect or activity; preventing ⟨*antiseptic*⟩ ⟨*anti-thief device*⟩ **c** being an antibody or serum immunologically active against antigen from the tissues or protein of (a specified animal) ⟨*anti-rat gamma globulin*⟩ **d** being the antimatter counterpart of ⟨*antineutrino*⟩ ⟨*antigalaxy*⟩ **3** combatting or defending against ⟨*antiaircraft*⟩ ⟨*antitank*⟩ □ compare ANTE- [*anti-* fr ME, fr OF & L; OF, fr L, against, fr Gk, fr *anti-*; *ant-* fr ME, fr L, against, fr Gk, fr *anti*; *anth-* fr L, against, fr Gk, fr *anti* – more at ANTE-]

*usage* The pronunciation /'anti/ rather than /'antie/ is recommended for BBC broadcasters.

**antiaircraft** /,anti'eǝkrahft/ *adj* designed for or concerned with defence against aircraft ⟨*an ~ missile*⟩

**antiarrhythmic** /,anti-ǝ'ridhmik/ *adj* counteracting or preventing ARRHYTHMIA (irregular heartbeat)

**antiauxin** /,anti'awksin/ *n* a plant substance that opposes or suppresses the natural effect of an AUXIN (plant growth hormone)

**antibacterial** /,antibak'tiǝriǝl/ *adj* directed or effective against bacteria

**antiballistic missile** /,antibǝ'listik/ *n* a missile for intercepting and destroying ballistic missiles

**antibiosis** /-bie'ohsis/ *n* antagonistic association between organisms to the detriment of one of them or between one organism and a metabolic product of another [NL, fr *anti-* + *-biosis*]

**antibiotic** /-bie'otik/ *n* a substance that is produced by a microorganism and is able to inhibit the growth of or kill another microorganism – **antibiotic** *adj*, **antibiotically** *adv*

**antibody** /-,bodi/ *n* any of the specialized proteins (IMMUNOGLOBULINS) in the body that are produced in response to specific ANTIGENS (eg toxins, viruses, bacteria, or other harmful substances) and that combine with them chemically to counteract their effect

**¹antic** /'antik/ *n* **1** *usu pl* a strange, silly, or absurd act or action, esp with odd or amusing body movements; a caper ⟨*childish ~* s⟩ **2** *archaic* a performer of a grotesque or ludicrous part; a buffoon

**²antic** *adj, archaic* grotesque, bizarre [It *antico* ancient, fr L *antiquus* – more at ANTIQUE] – **antically** *adv*

**anticancer** /,anti'kansǝ/ *also* **anticancerous** /-'kans(ǝ)rǝs/ *adj* used or effective in the treatment of cancer ⟨~ *drugs*⟩

**anticatalyst** /,anti'katl-ist/ *n* **1** a substance that slows down a chemical reaction **2** a substance that prevents the action of a catalyst

**anticholinergic** /,antikoli'nuhjik, -koh-/ *adj* counteracting or blocking the physiological action of ACETYLCHOLINE (substance that transmits impulses between nerve endings) – **anticholinergic** *n*

**anticholinesterase** /,antikoli'nestǝrayz, -koh-, -ays/ *n* any of various substances (eg NEOSTIGMINE) that inhibit a CHOLINESTERASE (enzyme that promotes the breakdown of substances that transmit nerve impulses) some of which can be used to reverse the effects of muscle relaxant drugs

**Antichrist** /-,kriest/ *n* an enemy of Christ; *specif* a great personal opponent of Christ expected to appear shortly before the end of the world – usu + *the* [ME *anticrist*, fr OF & LL; OF, fr LL *Antichristus*, fr Gk *Antichristos*, fr *anti-* + *Christos* Christ]

**anticipant** /an'tisipǝnt/ *adj* expectant, anticipating – usu + *of* – **anticipant** *n*

**anticipate** /an'tisipayt/ *vt* **1** to give advance thought, discussion, or treatment to **2** to meet (an obligation) before a due date **3** to foresee and deal with in advance; forestall **4** to use, expend, act on, tell, or write before the proper or natural time **5** to act before (another) often so as to thwart ⟨*we ~d them and seized the bridge*⟩ **6** to look forward to as certain; expect ~ *vi* to speak or write in knowledge or expectation of something coming later or due to happen [L *anticipatus*, pp of *anticipare*, fr *ante-* + *-cipare* (fr *capere* to take) – more at HEAVE] – **anticipatable** *adj*, **anticipator** *n*, **anticipative** *adj*, **anticipatively** *adv*, **anticipatory** *adj*

*usage* The very common sense 6 "expect" has been established in English since the 18th century, and does not appear to lead to confusion with the other senses. Since it is, however, widely disliked, one may prefer to express this idea by using expect or foresee.

**anticipation** /an,tisi'paysh(ǝ)n, ,---'--/ *n* **1** the use of money before it is available; *esp* the taking of the income of a trust estate before it is due **2** an act of looking forward ⟨*police assembled in ~ of a riot*⟩; *specif* pleasurable expectation ⟨*beaming in ~*⟩ **3** the sounding of one or more notes of a chord before the rest of the chord – compare SUSPENSION

| | | | |
|---|---|---|---|
| antiacademic *adj or n* | antiauthority *adj* | anticapitalistic *adj* | anticommunism *n* |
| antiadministration *adj* | antibiblical *adj* | anticarcinogenic *adj* | anticommunist *adj or n* |
| antiaggression *adj* | anti-Bolshevik *adj or n* | anti-Catholic *adj or n* | anticonscription *adj* |
| antiaging *adj* | anti-Bolshevism *n* | anti-Catholicism *n* | anticonservation *adj* |
| antialien *adj* | anti-Bolshevist *adj or n* | anticensorship *n* | anticonservationist *n* |
| antiallergenic *adj* | antibourgeois *adj* | anti-Christian *adj or n* | anticonstitutional *adj* |
| antianxiety *adj* | anti-British *adj or n* | antichurch *adj* | anticonsumerism *n* |
| antiapartheid *adj* | antibugging *adj or n* | anticigarette *adj* | anticonventional *adj* |
| antiaristocracy *adj or n* | antibureaucratic *adj* | anticlassical *adj* | anticorporate *adj* |
| antiaristocratic *adj* | antiburglar *adj* | anticlotting *adj* | anticorrosion *adj* |
| antiarthritic *adj or n* | antiburglary *adj* | anticolonial *adj or n* | anticorrosive *adj* |
| antiassimilation *adj* | anticaking *adj* | anticolonialism *n* | anticorruption *adj* |
| antiauthoritarian *adj or n* | anticapitalism *n* | anticolonialist *adj or n* | anticreative *adj* |
| antiauthoritarianism *n* | anticapitalist *adj or n* | anticommercialism *n* | anticrime *adj* |

**anticlerical** /-'klerikl/ *adj* opposed to the influence of the clergy or church in secular affairs – **anticlerical** *n*, **anticlericalism** *n*, **anticlericalist** *n*

**anticlimax** /-'kliemaks/ *n* **1** (an instance of) the usu sudden or ludicrous descent in writing or speaking from a significant to a trivial idea **2** an event (eg at the end of a series) that is strikingly less dignified, important, or exciting than might have been expected – **anticlimactic** *also* **anticlimactical** *adj*, **anticlimactically** *adv*

**anticlinal** /,anti'klienl/ *adj* inclining in opposite directions; *specif* of a geological anticline [*anti*- + Gk *klinein* to lean – more at LEAN]

**anticline** /-,klien/ *n* an arch of stratified rock in which the layers bend downwards in opposite directions from the crest – compare SYNCLINE [back-formation fr *anticlinal*]

**anticlockwise** /-'klokwiez/ *adj or adv* in a direction opposite to that in which the hands of a clock rotate as viewed from in front

**anticoagulant** /-koh'agyoolənt/ *n* a substance that inhibits the clotting of blood – **anticoagulant** *adj*

**anticoagulate** /,antikoh'agyoolayt/ *vt* to inhibit the clotting of the blood of esp by treatment with an anticoagulant [back-formation fr *anticoagulant*] – **anticoagulation** *n*

**anticodon** /-'kohdon/ *n* a group of three BASES in TRANSFER RNA that identifies the AMINO ACID carried by the transfer RNA molecule and binds to a complementary group (CODON) in MESSENGER RNA during protein synthesis at a RIBOSOME (specialized cell part) [*anti*- + *codon*]

**anticollision** /,antikə'lizh(ə)n/ *adj* tending to minimize the risk of collision ⟨*radar is an ∼ device*⟩

**anticonvulsant** /-kən'vuls(ə)nt/, **anticonvulsive** /-siv, -ziv/ *adj* used in treating, controlling, or preventing convulsions (eg in epilepsy) – **anticonvulsant** *n*

**anticyclone** /-'sieklohn/ *n* **1** a system of winds that rotates about a centre of high atmospheric pressure, clockwise in the northern hemisphere and anticlockwise in the southern **2** HIGH **2** – **anticyclonic** *adj*

**antidepressant** /-di'pres(ə)nt/, **antidepressive** /-siv/ *adj, esp of a drug* used to relieve or prevent mental depression – **antidepressant** *n*

**antiderivative** /,antidi'rivativ/ *n, maths* INDEFINITE INTEGRAL

**antidiuretic** /,antidieyoo'retik/ *n* a substance that tends to reduce the formation of urine – **antidiuretic** *adj*

**antidiuretic hormone** *n* VASOPRESSIN

**antidote** /'anti,doht/ *n* **1** a remedy that counteracts the effects of poison **2** something that relieves, prevents, or counteracts esp an unwanted or unpleasant state or condition ⟨*an ∼ to the mechanization of our society*⟩ [ME *antidot*, fr L *antidotum*, fr Gk *antidotos*, fr fem of *antidotos* given as an antidote, fr *antididonai* to give as an antidote, fr *anti*- + *didonai* to give – more at DATE] – **antidotal** *adj*, **antidotally** *adv*

  *usage* One thing may be an **antidote** *to, for,* or *against* another. ⚠ anecdote

**antidromic** /-'dromik/ *adj, esp of a nerve impulse or fibre* proceeding or conducting in a direction opposite to the usual one [*anti*- + *drom*- (fr Gk *dromos* course, racecourse, running) + *-ic* – more at DROMEDARY] – **antidromically** *adv*

**antienzyme** /'anti,enziem/ *n* an inhibitor of ENZYME action; *esp* one produced by living cells

**antiestablishment** /,anti·i'stablishmənt/ *adj* opposed or hostile to the social, political, economic, or moral principles of a ruling class (eg of a nation)

**anti-'federalist** *n, often cap A&F* a member of the group that opposed the adoption of the US Constitution

**antifertility** /,antifuh'tiləti/ *adj* intended to control fertility, esp in mammals; contraceptive

**antiflash** /,anti'flash, '--,-/ *adj* designed to reduce the effect of flash from an explosion

**antifouling** /,anti'fowling/ *n or adj* (any specially prepared composition) intended to prevent the growth of barnacles, seaweed, etc on underwater structures (eg the bottoms of ships) ⟨∼ *paint*⟩

**antifreeze** /-,freez/ *n* a substance added to a liquid (eg the water in a car radiator) to lower its freezing point

**antifungal** /,anti'fung·g(ə)l/ *adj* directed or effective against fungi; fungicidal ⟨∼ *drugs*⟩

**antigen** /'antijən/ *n* a usu protein or carbohydrate substance (eg a toxin or an enzyme) that when introduced into the body stimulates the production of an antibody [ISV] – **antigenic** *adj*, **antigenically** *adv*, **antigenicity** *n*

**antiglobulin** /,anti'globyoolin/ *n* an antibody that combines with and forms a solid insoluble chemical compound with GLOBULIN (type of protein)

¹**antigravity** /,anti'gravəti/ *adj* reducing or cancelling the effect of gravity or protecting against it

²**antigravity** /'anti,gravəti/ *n* a hypothetical property that reduces or cancels the effect of gravity

**antihaemophilic** /,anti,heemə'filik/ *adj* counteracting the bleeding tendency in haemophilia ⟨*an ∼ drug*⟩

**'anti-,hero**, *fem* **'anti-,heroine** *n* a principal character (eg in a novel or play) who lacks the noble qualities (eg courage or unselfishness) traditionally attributed to the hero or heroine – **anti-heroic** *adj*

**antihistamine** /-'histəmin/ *n* any of various chemical compounds that oppose the actions of HISTAMINE and are used esp for treating allergies (eg in hay fever) and motion sickness – **antihistaminic** *adj or n*

**antihypertensive** /,anti,hiepə'tensiv/ *n* a substance that reduces high blood pressure – **antihypertensive** *adj*

**anti-in'flammatory** *adj* counteracting inflammation

**antiknock** /-'nok/ *n* a substance used as a fuel or fuel additive to prevent knocking in an INTERNAL-COMBUSTION ENGINE

**antileukaemic** /,antilooh'keemik, -lyooh-/ *adj* counteracting the effects of leukaemia

**antilog** /-,log/ *n* an antilogarithm

**antilogarithm** /-'logə,ridhəm/ *n* the number whose logarithm is a given number

**antilogy** /an'tiləji/ *n* a contradiction in terms [Gk *antilogia*, fr *anti*- + *-logia* -logy]

**antilymphocyte serum** /,anti'limfəsiet/, **antilymphocytic serum** /,anti,limfə'sitik/ *n* a serum containing antibodies against LYMPHOCYTES (types of white blood cell) that is used for suppressing the natural tendency of the body to reject tissue or organ transplants

**antimacassar** /-mə'kasə/ *n* a cover put over the backs or arms of upholstered seats for decoration or esp protection [*anti*- + *Macassar* (*oil*)]

**antimagnetic** /,antimag'netick/ *adj, of a watch* having a balance unit composed of alloys that will not remain magnetized

**antimalarial** /,antimə'leəriəl/ *adj* serving to prevent, check, or cure malaria – **antimalarial** *n*

**antimasque, antimask** /'anti,mahsk/ *n* an additional masque usu preceding the main masque (in 16th- and 17th-century drama) and often introduced for comic or grotesque effect

| | | | |
|---|---|---|---|
| **anticruelty** *adj* | **antielitist** *adj or n* | **antifogging** *adj* | **antihumanist** *adj or n* |
| **anti-Darwinian** *adj or n* | **antierosion** *adj* | **antiforeigner** *adj or n* | **antihumanistic** *adj* |
| **anti-Darwinism** *n* | **antierosive** *adj* | **antifraud** *adj* | **antihumanitarian** *adj or n* |
| **antidemocratic** *adj* | **antievolution** *adj* | **antifriction** *adj* | **antihumanity** *adj* |
| **antidepression** *adj or n* | **antievolutionary** *adj* | **antifundamentalist** *adj or n* | **antihunting** *adj* |
| **antidesegregation** *adj* | **antievolutionism** *n* | **antigambling** *adj* | **anti-icing** *adj* |
| **antidiabetic** *adj* | **antievolutionist** *adj or n* | **antigay** *adj or n* | **anti-imperialism** *n* |
| **antidiarrhoeal** *adj* | **antifaction** *adj* | **antiglare** *adj* | **anti-imperialist** *adj or n* |
| **antidiscrimination** *adj* | **antifamily** *adj* | **antigovernment** *adj* | **anti-infective** *adj* |
| **antidissident** *adj or n* | **antifascism** *n* | **antigrowth** *adj* | **anti-inflation** *adj* |
| **antidraft** *adj* | **antifascist** *adj or n* | **antiguerrilla** *adj* | **anti-inflationary** *adj* |
| **antiecclesiastical** *adj* | **antifebrile** *adj or n* | **antigun** *adj* | **anti-institutional** *adj* |
| **antieducational** *adj* | **antifemale** *adj* | **antihierarchical** *adj* | **anti-integration** *adj* |
| **antiegalitarian** *adj* | **antifeminism** *n* | **antihomosexual** *adj or n* | **anti-Jewish** *adj* |
| **antielite** *adj or n* | **antifeminist** *adj or n* | **antihuman** *adj* | **antilabour** *adj* |
| **antielitism** *n* | **antifoaming** *adj* | **antihumanism** *n* | **antileft** *adj* |

(*anti-* (ante-), fr MF, fr ML, fr L *ante-*]

**antimatter** /-ˌmatə/ *n* matter composed of the counterparts of ordinary matter, antiprotons instead of protons, positrons instead of electrons, and antineutrons instead of neutrons

**antimetabolite** /-mə'tabəˌliet/ *n* a substance (eg a sulpha drug) that disrupts the METABOLISM (life-supporting chemical processes) of an organism by specifically inhibiting a particular reaction and that is used esp to inhibit the growth of a microorganism (eg a bacterium)

**antimicrobial** /ˌantimie'krohbiəl/ *adj* destroying or inhibiting the growth of microorganisms – **antimicrobial** *n*

**antimissile** /ˌanti'misiel/ *adj* directed against or used for intercepting a missile attack ⟨an ∼ system⟩ – **antimissile** *n*

**antimitotic** /ˌantimie'totik/ *adj* inhibiting or disrupting MITOSIS (type of CELL DIVISION producing two new cells) ⟨∼ agents⟩ ⟨∼ activity⟩ – **antimitotic** *n*

**antimonial** /ˌanti'mohnyəl/ *adj* of or containing antimony – **antimonial** *n*

**antimonic** /ˌanti'monik, -'moh-/ *adj* of or derived from antimony when having a VALENCY of five

**antimonious** /ˌanti'mohnyəs/ *adj* of or derived from antimony when having a VALENCY of three

**antimonite** /'antiməˌniet/ *n* STIBNITE (type of mineral) [Ger *antimonit*, fr *antimon* antimony]

**antimony** /'antiməni/ *NAm* 'antiˌmohni/ *n* 1 a blue-white naturally occurring metal that is present as crystals or shapeless masses 2 a silvery white, crystalline, and brittle metallic chemical element that has a VALENCY of three or five and is used esp as a constituent of alloys and in medicine [ME *antimonie*, fr ML *antimonium*, perh modif of Ar *ithmid*, of Hamitic origin]

**antimony glance** *n* STIBNITE (type of mineral)

**antimycin** /ˌanti'miesin/ *n* any of several antibiotics used experimentally to kill fungi, insects, and mites

**antineoplastic** /ˌantiˌnee-ə'plastik/ *adj* inhibiting the growth and spread of tumours (NEOPLASMS) or cancerous cells

**antineutron** /ˌanti'nyoohtron/ *n* an uncharged particle of mass equal to that of the neutron but having a MAGNETIC MOMENT in the opposite direction

**anting** /'anting/ *n* the deliberate placing by some songbirds of living ants among their feathers

**antinode** /-ˌnohd/ *n* a region, point, etc on or in a vibrating body (eg a string of a musical instrument) at which the vibration is at a maximum – compare NODE [ISV] – **antinodal** *adj*

**antinomian** /-'nohmi-ən/ *n* one who denies the universality of moral laws; *specif* an adherent of the (heretical) view that those whose salvation is preordained are freed from all moral restraints [ML *antinomus*, fr L *anti-* + Gk *nomos* law] – **antinomian** *adj*, **antinomianism** *n*

**antinomy** /an'tinəmi/ *n* 1 a contradiction between (the inferences correctly drawn from) two apparently valid principles 2 conflict (eg of principles, ideas, or aspirations) insoluble in the light of available knowledge [Ger *antinomie*, fr L *antinomia* conflict of laws, fr Gk, fr *anti-* + *nomos* law – more at NIMBLE]

'**anti-ˌnovel** *n* a work of fiction that lacks most or all of the traditional features of the novel (eg coherent structure or character development)

**antioxidant** /-'oksid(ə)nt/ *n* a substance that opposes the chemical combination (OXIDATION) of a substance with oxygen and is used to prevent deterioration in food, petrol, rubber, etc – **antioxidant** *adj*

**antiparasitic** /ˌantiˌparə'sitik/ *adj* acting against parasites

**antiparticle** /-'pahtikl/ *n* an ELEMENTARY PARTICLE (minute particle of matter) that is identical to another elementary particle in mass and SPIN but opposite to it in electric and magnetic properties and that when brought together with its counterpart can produce mutual annihilation

**antipasto** /'antiˌpastoh/ *n, pl* **antipastos** HORS D'OEUVRE – used esp with reference to Italian food [It, fr *anti-* (fr L *ante-*) + *pasto* food, fr L *pastus*, fr *pastus*, pp of *pascere* to feed – more at FOOD]

**antipathetic** /-pə'thetik/ *adj* having, showing, or arousing a natural aversion or opposition ⟨a person ∼ to violence⟩ [*antipathy* + *-etic* (as in *pathetic*)] – **antipathetically** *adv*

**antipathy** /an'tipəthi/ *n* 1 a settled aversion or dislike; distaste 2 an object of aversion 3 *obs* natural incompatibility *synonyms* see ENMITY *antonyms* taste (for), affection (for) [L *antipathia*, fr Gk *antipatheia*, fr *antipathēs* of opposite feelings, fr *anti-* + *pathos* experience – more at PATHOS]

**antipersonnel** /-puhsə'nel/ *adj, of a weapon* (designed) for use against people ⟨an ∼ mine⟩

**antiperspirant** /-'puhspirənt/ *n* a substance used to stop excessive perspiration

**antiphlogistic** /ˌantifloh'jistik/ *adj* counteracting inflammation – **antiphlogistic** *n*

**antiphon** /'antifən, -fon/ *n* 1 a psalm, anthem, or verse sung as a set of responses 2 a verse, usu from Scripture, said or sung before and after a canticle, psalm, or psalm verse as part of the liturgy [LL *antiphona* – more at ANTHEM]

**antiphonal** /an'tifənl/ *adj* consisting of or relating to music that uses the effect of two separated groups of performers or singers

**antiphonary** /an'tifən(ə)ri/, **antiphonal** /an'tifənl/ *n* a book containing the choral parts of the DIVINE OFFICE

**antiphony** /an'tifəni/ *n* musical alternation between two groups of performers or singers or between a single voice and a group

**antiphrasis** /an'tifrəsis/ *n, pl* **antiphrases** /-eez/ the use of words in senses opposite to the generally accepted meanings, usu for ironic or humorous effect (eg in "the child is a giant of 3 feet 4 inches") [LL, fr Gk, fr *anti-* + *phrasis* diction – more at PHRASE]

¹**antipodal** /an'tipədl/ *adj* 1a of the antipodes b situated at the opposite side of the earth or moon ⟨an ∼ meridian⟩ ⟨an ∼ continent⟩ 2 diametrically opposite ⟨an ∼ point on a sphere⟩ 3 widely different

²**antipodal** *n* any of three cells that are grouped at the end of the EMBRYO SAC farthest from the MICROPYLE (opening that allows pollen to enter) in the female reproductive cell of most FLOWERING PLANTS

**antipode** /'antiˌpohd/ *n, pl* **antipodes** /an'tipədeez/ *chiefly NAm* the exact opposite or contrary [back-formation fr *antipodes*]

**antipodean** /anˌtipə'dee-ən/ *n* an Australian or New Zealander – **antipodean** *adj*

**antipodes** /an'tipəˌdeez/ *n pl* the region of the earth diametrically opposite; *specif, often cap* Australasia [ME *antipodes*, pl, people dwelling at opposite points on the globe, fr L, fr Gk, fr pl of *antipod-*, *antipous* with feet opposite, fr *anti-* + *pod-*, *pous* foot – more at FOOT] – **antipodean** *adj*

**antipope** /'antiˌpohp/ *n* somebody elected or claiming to be pope in opposition to the legitimately elected pope [MF *antipape*, fr ML *antipapa*, fr *anti-* + *papa* pope]

---

| | | | |
|---|---|---|---|
| antileprosy *adj* | antimilitaristic *adj* | antipacifist *adj or n* | antiprostitution *adj* |
| antiliberal *adj* | antimodernist *adj or n* | antipapal *adj* | anti-Protestant *adj or n* |
| antiliberalism *n* | antimonarchic *adj* | antiparty *adj* | antirabies *adj* |
| antiliteracy *adj* | antimonarchical *adj* | antipathogen *n* | antiracism *n* |
| antiliterate *adj* | antimonarchist *adj or n* | antipathogenic *adj* | antiracist *adj or n* |
| antilitter *adj* | antimonopolist *adj or n* | antipesticide *adj or n* | antiradar *adj* |
| antilittering *adj* | antimonopoly *adj* | antiprohibition *adj* | antiradical *adj or n* |
| antiliturgical *adj* | antimosquito *adj* | antiprohibitionist *adj or n* | antiradicalism *n* |
| antimale *adj* | antinarcotic *adj* | antipiracy *adj* | antirape *adj* |
| antimanagement *adj* | antinational *adj* | antipolitical *adj* | antirational *adj* |
| antimaterialism *n* | antinationalist *adj or n* | antipolitics *adj* | antirationalism *n* |
| antimaterialist *adj or n* | antinationalistic *adj* | antipollution *adj or n* | antirationalist *adj or n* |
| antimaterialistic *adj* | anti-Nazi *adj or n* | antipornography *adj* | antirationality *adj or n* |
| antimerger *adj* | antinoise *adj* | antipoverty *adj* | antirealism *n* |
| antimilitarism *n* | antiobscenity *adj* | antiprofiteering *adj* | antirealistic *adj* |
| antimilitarist *adj or n* | antiorganization *adj* | antiprogressive *adj or n* | antirecession *adj* |

**antpsychiatry** /ˌantisie'kie•ətri/ *n* an approach to psychiatry that rejects the traditional model of physical medicine and does not rely on treatment by physical means (e g drugs)

**antipyretic** /ˌantipie(ə)'retik/ *n* something, esp a drug, that reduces fever – **antipyretic** *adj*

**antipyrine** /ˌanti'piereen/, **antipyrin** /-'pierin/ *n* a chemical compound, $C_{11}H_{12}N_2O$, used to relieve fever and pain [fr *Antipyrine*, a trademark]

**¹antiquarian** /ˌanti'kweəri•ən/, **antiquary** /'antikwəri/ *n* somebody who collects or studies antiquities

**²antiquarian** *adj* **1** of antiquarians or antiquities **2** *of books or prints* old; *esp* old and rare **3** dealing in antiquarian books or prints – **antiquarianism** *n*

**antiquate** /'antikwayt/ *vt* to make (seem) old or obsolete [LL *antiquatus*, pp of *antiquare*, fr L *antiquus*] – **antiquation** *n*

**antiquated** /'antiˌkwaytid/ *adj* **1** outmoded or discredited by reason of age; out-of-date ⟨~ *methods of farming*⟩ **2** advanced in age *synonyms* see ¹OLD

**¹antique** /an'teek/ *adj* **1** belonging to or surviving from earlier, esp classical, times; ancient ⟨*ruins of an* ~ *city*⟩ **2** old-fashioned ⟨~ *manners and graces*⟩ **3** made in an earlier period and therefore valuable ⟨~ *mirrors*⟩; *also* suggesting the crafts of an earlier period [MF, fr L *antiquus*, fr *ante* before – more at ANTE-] *synonyms* see ¹OLD *antonyms* new, modern, contemporary, up-to-date

**²antique** *n* **1** a relic or object of ancient, esp classical, times **2** a work of art, piece of furniture, or decorative object surviving from an earlier period that is sought by collectors **3** *the* ancient Greek or Roman style in art **4** a rough-surfaced relatively bulky paper used esp for books

**³antique** *vt* to finish or refinish (e g furniture) in antique style; give an appearance of age to

**antiquity** /an'tikwəti/ *n* **1** ancient times; *esp* the period before the Middle Ages **2** the quality of being ancient **3** *pl* relics or monuments (e g coins, statues, or buildings) of ancient times **4** the people of ancient times

**antirachitic** /ˌantira'kitik/ *adj* counteracting or preventing the development of rickets ⟨*an* ~ *vitamin*⟩ – **antirachitic** *n*

**anti-roll bar** *n* a rod connecting the suspension system on one side of a motor vehicle to that on the other, intended to reduce rolling while cornering

**antirrhinum** /ˌanti'rienəm/ *n* any of a large genus (*Antirrhinum*) of plants (e g the snapdragon) of the foxglove family with bright-coloured two-lipped flowers [NL, genus name, fr L, snapdragon, fr Gk *antirrhinon*, fr *anti-* like (fr *anti* against, equivalent to) + *rhin-*, *rhis* nose – more at ANTI-]

**antiscorbutic** /ˌantiskaw'byoohtik/ *adj* counteracting or preventing the development of scurvy ⟨*vitamin C is the* ~ *vitamin*⟩ – **antiscorbutic** *n*

**anti-'Semitism** *n* hostility towards or discrimination against Jews – **anti-Semitic** *adj*, **anti-Semite** *n*

**antisepsis** /ˌanti'sepsis/ *n* the inhibiting of the growth and multiplication of microorganisms by the use of antiseptic chemicals or methods [NL]

**¹antiseptic** /-'septik/ *adj* **1a** opposing SEPSIS, putrefaction, or decay; *esp* preventing or arresting the growth of microorganisms (e g on living tissue) **b** acting or protecting like an antiseptic **2** relating to or characterized by the use of antiseptics **3a** scrupulously clean; aseptic **b** extremely neat or orderly; *esp* neat to the point of being bare or uninteresting **c** free from moral contamination **4** (coldly) impersonal or detached ⟨*"acceptable losses on the battlefield" is another* ~ *phrase*⟩ [*anti-* + Gk *sēptikos* putrefying, septic] – **antiseptically** *adv*

**²antiseptic** *n* a substance that checks the growth or action of microorganisms, esp in or on living tissue; *also* a germicide

**antiserum** /'antiˌsiərəm, ˌ--'--/ *n* a serum containing antibodies [ISV]

**antisocial** /-'sohsh(ə)l/ *adj* **1** hostile or harmful to organized society; *esp* being or marked by behaviour which is outside the social norm **2a** averse to the society of others; unsociable **b** *Br* impeding the enjoyment of social life or pleasant social relations; *specif* UNSOCIAL 2 ⟨*working* ~ *hours away from their families*⟩ *synonyms* see UNSOCIAL

**antispasmodic** /ˌantispaz'modik/ *adj* preventing or relieving spasms or convulsions – **antispasmodic** *n*

**antistatic** /ˌanti'statik/ *adj* reducing the accumulation or effects of static electricity

**antistrophe** /an'tistrəfi/ *n* a movement in Greek choral dance exactly answering to a previous STROPHE; *also* the part of a choral song delivered during this movement [LL, fr Gk *antistrophē*, fr *anti-* + *strophē* strophe] – **antistrophic** *adj*, **antistrophically** *adv*

**antisubmarine** /ˌanti,submə'reen/ *adj* designed or waged to destroy submarines ⟨~ *warfare*⟩

**antisymmetric** /-si'metrik/ *adj* **1** of or being a (mathematical) relation (e g "is a subset of") such that if $x * y$ and $y * x$ then $x = y$, where * denotes the relation **2** having a form which would be symmetric if the signs of the numbers describing one half were reversed ⟨*an* ~ *equation*⟩ – **antisymmetry** *n*

**antitank** /ˌanti'tangk/ *adj* designed for use against armoured vehicles, esp tanks

**antithesis** /an'tithəsis/ *n, pl* **antitheses** /-eez/ **1a** a contrast of ideas expressed by a parallel arrangement of words, clauses, or sentences (e g in "action, not words" or "they promised freedom and provided slavery") **b** opposition, contrast ⟨*the* ~ *of prose and verse*⟩ **c** the direct opposite ⟨*her ideas are the* ~ *of mine*⟩ **2** the second stage of a reasoned argument, in contrast to the thesis – compare SYNTHESIS [LL, fr Gk, lit., opposition, fr *antitithenai* to oppose, fr *anti-* + *tithenai* to set – more at DO]

**antithetical** /ˌanti'thetikl/, **antithetic** *adj* **1** constituting or marked by antithesis **2** directly opposed – **antithetically** *adv*

**antithyroid** /ˌanti'thieroyd/ *adj* counteracting excessive activity (e g hormone production) of the thyroid gland

**antitoxic** /ˌanti'toksik/ *adj* **1** counteracting poison **2** of or being an antitoxin

**antitoxin** /-'toksin/ *n* an antibody that is capable of neutralizing the specific toxin that stimulated its production in the body and may be used therapeutically for this; *also* a serum produced commercially containing antitoxins [ISV]

**antitrades** /-'traydz/ *n pl* westerly winds that move counter to and above the trade winds and which descend beyond the trade winds to become the prevailing westerly winds of middle latitudes

**antitrust** /-'trust/ *adj* of or being legislation in the USA protecting trade and commerce from monopolies or unfair business practices

**antituberculous** /ˌantityoo'buhkyoolǝs/ *also* **antitubercular** *adj* used or effective in the treatment of tuberculosis

**antitumour** /ˌanti'tyoohmǝ/, **antitumoural** *adj* anticancer

**antitussive** /-'tusiv/ *n or adj* (something) that controls or prevents coughing

**antitype** /-ˌtiep/ *n* **1** TYPE 1a,b **2** an opposite type ⟨*she was hardly a caring nurse … the … to Florence Nightingale*⟩ [deriv of Gk *antitypos* repelled by a hard body, corresponding to a die, fr *antitypoun* to strike against, fr *anti-* + *typoun* to stamp, fr *typos* – more at TYPE]

**antivenin** /-'venin/ *n* an antitoxin to a venom (e g a snake

| | | | |
|---|---|---|---|
| **antirecessionary** *adj* | **antirust** *adj* | **antistatism** *n* | **antitraditional** *adj* |
| **antireform** *adj* | **antiscience** *adj* | **antistick** *adj* | **antityphoid** *adj* |
| **antireligion** *adj or n* | **antiscientific** *adj* | **antistress** *adj* | **antiunemployment** *adj* |
| **antireligious** *adj* | **antisegregation** *adj* | **antistrike** *adj* | **antiunion** *adj* |
| **antirepublican** *adj or n* | **antiseparatist** *adj or n* | **antitarnish** *adj* | **antiviolence** *adj or n* |
| **antiresonance** *adj* | **antiship** *adj* | **antitarnishing** *adj* | **antivivisection** *n* |
| **antirevolutionary** *adj or n* | **antishock** *adj* | **antitax** *adj* | **antivivisectionist** *adj or n* |
| **antirheumatic** *adj or n* | **antislavery** *adj or n* | **antitechnological** *adj* | **antiwar** *adj* |
| **antirights** *adj* | **antislip** *adj* | **antitechnology** *adj* | **anti-West** *adj* |
| **antiriot** *adj* | **antismog** *adj* | **antiterrorism** *n* | **anti-Western** *adj* |
| **antiritualism** *n* | **antismoke** *adj* | **antiterrorist** *adj* | **antiwhite** *adj* |
| **antiromantic** *adj or n* | **antismoking** *adj or n* | **antitetanus** *adj* | **antiwrinkle** *adj* |
| **antiromanticism** *n* | **anti-Soviet** *adj or n* | **antitheft** *adj* | **anti-Zionist** *adj or n* |
| **antiroyalist** *adj or n* | **antispiritual** *adj* | **antitobacco** *adj* | |
| **anti-Russian** *adj or n* | **antistate** *adj* | **antitotalitarian** *adj* | |

venom); *also* an antiserum containing such antitoxin [ISV]

**antiviral** /ˌanti'vie-ərəl/ *adj* directed or effective against viruses – **antiviral** *n*

**antivitamin** /ˌanti'vitəmin, -'vie-/ *n* a substance that makes a vitamin nutritionally ineffective

**antler** /'antlə/ *n* the solid (much branched) horn of an animal of the deer family that is periodically shed; *also* a branch of this horn [ME *aunteler*, fr MF *antoillier*, prob fr (assumed) VL *anteoculare*, fr neut of *anteocularis* located before the eye, fr L *ante-* + *oculus* eye – more at EYE] – **antlered** *adj*

**antler moth** *n* a brownish moth (*Cerapteryx graminis*) with white markings whose caterpillar devastates grasslands

**ant lion** *n* any of various net-winged insects (order Neuroptera and esp genus *Myrmeleon*) having a long-jawed larva that digs a conical pit in which it lies in wait to catch insects (e g ants) on which it feeds

**Antonian** /an'tohnyən/ *n* a member of any of several monastic communities (e g the Armenian Antonians) that follow a rule derived from St Anthony [L *Antonius* Anthony]

**antonomasia** /ˌantonə'mayzh(y)ə, -zyə/ *n* **1** the use of an epithet or title to identify a person, rather than a proper name (e g "Her Majesty" for the Queen) **2** the use of a personal name to identify a class (e g "a Solomon" for a wise ruler) [L, fr Gk, *antonomazein* to name instead, fr *anti-* instead, against + *onomazein* to name, fr *onoma* name]

**antonym** /'antənim/ *n* a word of opposite meaning (e g "good" is the usual antonym of "bad", "hot" of "cold") – **antonymous** *adj*, **antonymy** *n*

**antre** /'antə/ *n, archaic* CAVE 1 [Fr, fr L *antrum*]

**antrorse** /an'traws/ *adj, biology* directed forwards or upwards – compare RETRORSE [NL *antrorsus*, irreg fr L *anterior* + *-orsus* (as in *dextrorsus* towards the right) – more at DEXTRORSE] – **antrorsely** *adv*

**antrum** /'antrəm/ *n, pl* **antra** /'antrə/ the cavity of a hollow organ or a sinus [LL, fr L, cave, fr Gk *antron*] – **antral** *adj*

**Anubis** /'anyoobis, ə'nyoohbis/ *n* an ancient Egyptian god of the dead with the body of a man and the head of a jackal [L, fr Gk *Anoubis*, fr Egypt *Aṅpu, Aṅp*]

**anuran** /ə'nyooərən/ *n* SALIENTIAN (frog, toad, etc) [deriv of *a-* + Gk *oura* tail – more at SQUIRREL] – **anuran** *adj*

**anuria** /ə'nyooəriə/ *n* pathological failure or deficiency in the excretion of urine [NL] – **anuric** *adj*

**anurous** /ə'nyooərəs/ *adj* having no tail

**anus** /'aynəs/ *n* the rear opening of the digestive tract through which faeces are extruded [L; akin to OIr *áinne* anus]

**anvil** /'anvil/ *n* **1** a heavy, usu steel-faced, iron block on which metal is shaped during forging **2** INCUS (bone in the ear) **3** a towering anvil-shaped cloud, usu associated with a thunder storm [ME *anfilt*, fr OE; akin to OHG *anafalz* anvil; both fr a prehistoric WGmc compound whose first constituent is represented by OE *an* on, and whose second is akin to Sw dial. *filta* to beat; akin to L *pellere* to beat – more at ON, FELT]

**anxiety** /ang'zie-əti/ *n* **1a** apprehensive uneasiness of mind, usu over an impending or anticipated ill **b** an ardent or earnest wish ⟨~ *to please*⟩ **c** a cause of anxiety **2** *psychology* an abnormal and overwhelming sense of apprehension and fear often associated with tension, fatigue, and physical symptoms such as palpitations and breathlessness ⟨~ *state*⟩ *synonyms* see [1]CARE *antonym* security [L *anxietas*, fr *anxius*]

**anxious** /'ang(k)shəs/ *adj* characterized by or resulting from uneasiness of mind or brooding fear; worried **2** causing anxiety; worrying ⟨*several* ~ *days passed while they awaited the results*⟩ **3** ardently or earnestly wishing *to* [L *anxius*; akin to L *angere* to strangle, distress – more at ANGER] – **anxiously** *adv*, **anxiousness** *n*

*usage* One is anxious *about* something, anxious *for* something to happen, anxious *that* something should happen, or anxious (= eager) *to* do something. This last construction, though disliked by some writers on usage, has been established in English since the 18th century ⟨*a kindhearted landlord ever* anxious *to ameliorate the condition of the poor* – Anthony Trollope⟩ *antonyms* carefree, untroubled, secure, composed

**[1]any** /'eni/ *adj* **1a** one or some indiscriminately; whichever is chosen ⟨*ask* ~ *woman*⟩ ⟨~ *plan is better than none*⟩ **b** one, some, or all; whatever: e g **b(1)** no matter how great ⟨*at* ~ *cost*⟩ ⟨~ *quantity you desire*⟩ **b(2)** no matter how commonplace or deficient ⟨*wear just* ~ *old thing*⟩ – compare IN ANY CASE, AT ANY RATE **2a** of whatever number or quantity; being even the smallest number or quantity of – chiefly in negatives and questions ⟨*have you* ~ *money?*⟩ ⟨*isn't* ~ *use*⟩ ⟨*never get* ~ *letters*⟩ **b** being an appreciable number, part, or amount of – not used in positive statements ⟨*could not endure it* ~ *length of time*⟩ [ME, fr OE *ǣnig*; akin to OHG *einag* any, OE *ān* one – more at ONE]

**[2]any** *pron, pl* **any 1** any person; anybody ⟨~ *of us*⟩ **2a** any thing **b** any part, quantity, or number ⟨*hardly* ~ *of it*⟩

*usage* **1** Even when any is used as an adjective with a singular noun, it is sometimes followed by a plural pronoun ⟨*he would at no time be a willing party to* any *artist breaking their contract – The Times*⟩. This avoids using either *he* for both sexes or the awkward *he or she*. When any is a pronoun, it can be plural in a plural context ⟨*are* any *of them ready?*⟩ **2** The use of any in comparing things of the same class ⟨*a better dentist than* any *I know*⟩ ⟨*the most beautiful of* any *English cathedral*⟩ is disapproved of by some people, who prefer to replace it by any other, or by all ⟨*a better dentist than* any other *I know*⟩ ⟨*the most beautiful of all English cathedrals*⟩. See ANYMORE, ANYONE

**[3]any** *adv* to any extent or degree; AT ALL ⟨*not feeling* ~ *better*⟩ ⟨*were you* ~ *the wiser?*⟩

*usage* The informal use of any as an adverb standing alone, with no following adjective ⟨*you certainly aren't helping me* any⟩ is disliked by some British people as an Americanism.

**anybody** /'eniˌbodi, -bədi/ *pron* any person ⟨*ask* ~⟩ ⟨*has* ~ *lost their glasses?*⟩

*usage* Since anybody and anyone are used with a singular verb, it seems logical that they should be followed by a singular pronoun ⟨*has* anybody *lost his glasses?*⟩ and this singular construction should be preferred for formal writing. The plural pronoun ⟨*has* anybody *lost their glasses?*⟩ is often used today, however, to avoid using either *he* for both sexes or the awkward *he or she*. See ELSE

**anyhow** /-ˌhow/ *adv* **1** in a haphazard manner ⟨*thrown down all* ~⟩ **2** anyway

**anymore** /ˌeni'maw/ *adv, chiefly NAm* by the present time; any longer – usu neg

*usage* Compare ⟨*they don't live here* anymore (= any longer)⟩ ⟨*I can't eat any* more (= even the smallest quantity)⟩

**anyone** /-wun, -wən/ *pron* anybody

*usage* Compare ⟨*marry* anyone (= anybody) *you like*⟩ ⟨*open any one of the three boxes*⟩. See ANYBODY

**anyplace** /-ˌplays/ *adv, NAm* anywhere

**anyroad** /-ˌrohd/ *adv, Br nonstandard* anyway

**[1]anything** /-ˌthing/ *pron* any thing whatever ⟨*do* ~ *for a quiet life*⟩ ⟨*don't believe* ~ *he says*⟩ – compare IF ANYTHING – **anything but** not at all; far from

**[2]anything** *adv* in any degree; AT ALL – **anything like** to any extent; anything ⟨*isn't* anything like *so cold*⟩

**anyway** /-ˌway/ *adv* **1** inevitably; IN ANY CASE ⟨*going to be hanged* ~⟩ **2** – used when resuming a narrative ⟨*well,* ~, *I rang the bell . . .*⟩

*usage* Compare ⟨*I'm not going* anyway (= in any case)⟩ ⟨*any way* (= any direction) *we go will involve climbing*⟩.

**anyways** /'eniˌwayz/ *adv, chiefly dial NAm* anyway

**[1]anywhere** /-ˌweə/ *adv* **1** in, at, or to any place ⟨*sit* ~ *you like*⟩ ⟨*too late to go* ~⟩ **2** to any extent; AT ALL ⟨*isn't* ~ *near ready*⟩ **3** – used to indicate limits of variation ⟨~ *from 40 to 60 students*⟩

**[2]anywhere** *n* any place

**anywise** /'eniwiez/ *adv, chiefly NAm* in any way whatever; AT ALL

**Anzac** /'anzak/ *n* a soldier from Australia or New Zealand, esp in World War I [*A*ustralian and *N*ew *Z*ealand *A*rmy *C*orps]

**ao dai** /ˌah-oh 'die/ *n, pl* **ao dais** a garment, similar in style to a cheongsam, worn by women in SE Asia [Vietnamese *áo dái*, fr *áo* blouse, jacket + *dái* long]

**A-OK** /ˌay oh 'kay/ *adv or adj, chiefly NAm informal* in fully satisfactory condition or ready to work; absolutely OK

**aorist** /'ayərist, 'eərist/ *n* a verb inflection (e g in Greek) expressing simple occurrence of a past action without reference to its completeness, duration, or repetition [LL & Gk; LL *aoristos*, fr Gk, fr *aoristos* undefined, fr *a* + *horistos* definable, fr *horizein* to define – more at HORIZON] – **aorist, aoristic** *adj* **aoristically** *adv*

**aort-, aorto-** *comb form* **1** aorta **2** aortic and ⟨*aortooesophageal*⟩

**aorta** /ay'awtə/ *n, pl* **aortas, aortae** /ay'awti/ the large main artery that carries blood from the heart to be distributed by smaller arteries through the body [NL, fr Gk *aortē*, fr *aeirein* to lift] – **aortal** *adj*, **aortic** *adj*

**aortic arch** /ay'awtik/ *n* any of the arterial branches in the embryos of VERTEBRATE animals that exist in a series of pairs with one on each side of the embryo in front of the heart. They connect the front and back arterial systems and persist in a complete form only in adult fishes.

**aortic valve** *n* the valve between the left VENTRICLE (chamber of the heart) and the aorta that stops blood flowing back into the left ventricle

**à outrance** /,ah 'oohtronhs (*Fr* a utrãs)/ *adv* to the bitter end; unsparingly [Fr, lit., to excess]

**¹ap-** – see AD-

**²ap-** – see APO-

**apace** /ə'pays/ *adv* at a quick pace; swiftly [ME, prob fr MF *à pas* on step]

**Apache** /ə'pachi; *sense 3* ə'pash/ *n, pl* **Apaches,** *esp collectively* **Apache 1** a member of a group of American Indian peoples of the southwestern USA **2** any of the Athapaskan languages of the Apache people **3** *not cap* a member of a gang of (Parisian) criminals [Sp, prob fr Zuni *Apachu*, lit., enemy; (3) Fr, fr *Apache* Apache Indian]

**apagoge** /,apə'gohji/ *n* proof by showing the absurdity of the alternative [Gk *apagōgē*, lit., act of leading away, fr *apo-* + *agōgē* leading, fr *agein* to lead ] – **apagogic, apagogical** *adj*, **apagogically** *adv*]

**apanage** /'apənij/ *n* APPANAGE

**aparejo** /,apə'rayoh, -hoh/ *n, pl* **aparejos** a packsaddle of stuffed leather or canvas [AmerSp, fr Sp, equipment, fr *aparejar* to prepare]

**apart** /ə'paht/ *adv or adj* **1a** at a little distance ⟨*tried to keep ~ from the family squabbles*⟩ **b** away from one another in space or time ⟨*towns 20 miles ~*⟩ **c** at a distance in character or opinions ⟨*their ideas are worlds ~*⟩ **2a** in reserve ⟨*a room set ~ for study*⟩ **b** so as to separate one from another ⟨*can't tell the twins ~*⟩ **3** excluded from consideration ⟨*joking ~, what shall we do?*⟩ **4** in or into two or more parts ⟨*had to take the engine ~*⟩ [ME, fr MF *a part*, lit., to the side] – **apart from 1** in addition to; besides ⟨*haven't time to go, quite apart from the cost*⟩ **2** EXCEPT FOR ⟨*excellent apart from a few blemishes*⟩

**apartheid** /ə'pahtayt, ə'paht·hayt, -iet, -ied/ *n* a policy of keeping different racial groups separate from each other; *specif* a policy of segregation and political, economic, and social discrimination against non-European groups in the Republic of S Africa [Afrik, lit., separateness]

*usage* The pronunciation /ə'paht·hayt/ is recommended for BBC broadcasters.

**apartment** /ə'pahtmənt/ *n* **1** a single room in a building **2** *pl* a suite of rooms used for living quarters ⟨*the Royal ~s*⟩ **3** *chiefly NAm* a flat [Fr *appartement*, fr It *appartamento*, fr *appartare* to put aside, separate] – **apartmental** *adj*

**apartment building, apartment house** *n, NAm* a block of flats

**apathetic** /,apə'thetik/ *adj* **1** having or showing little or no motivation and energy **2** lacking interest or concern; indifferent ⟨*denounced them as too ~ to vote*⟩ **synonyms** see INDIFFERENT **antonyms** interested, eager [*apathy* + *-etic* (as in *pathetic*)] – **apathetically** *adv*

**apathy** /'apəthi/ *n* absence of motivation, energy, enthusiasm, interest, concern, etc [Gk *apatheia*, fr *apathēs* without feeling, fr *a-* + *pathos* emotion – more at PATHOS]

**apatite** /'apətiet/ *n* any of a group of minerals containing the chemical compound CALCIUM PHOSPHATE, of the approximate general formula $Ca_5(PO_4)_3(F,Cl,OH)$, occurring variously as crystals, as granular masses, or in fine-grained masses as the chief constituent of phosphate rock and of bones and teeth; *specif* the mineral calcium fluoro-phosphate, $Ca_5F(PO_4)_3$ [Ger *apatit*, fr Gk *apatē* deceit; fr its being easily mistaken for other minerals]

**¹ape** /ayp/ *n* **1a** a monkey; *esp* one of the larger tailless or short-tailed forms from Africa and Eurasia **b** any of a family (Pongidae) of large semierect primates (e g the chimpanzee or gorilla) – called also ANTHROPOID APE **2a** a mimic **b** a large uncouth person [ME, fr OE *apa*; akin to OHG *affo* ape] – **apelike** *adj* – **go ape 1** to run amok; lose control ⟨*fuses can blow and computers can go ape*⟩ **2** to become highly excited or enthusiastic

**²ape** *vt* to imitate closely but often clumsily and ineptly – **aper** *n*

**apeak** /ə'peek/ *adj or adv* in a vertical position ⟨*with oars ~*⟩ [alter. of earlier *apike*, prob fr *a-* + *pike* mountain]

**'ape-,man** *n* a prehistoric man (e g JAVA MAN) intermediate in character between modern man and the higher apes

**aperçu** /apuh'sooh (*Fr* apɛrsy)/ *n, pl* **aperçus** /~/ **1** an immediate impression; *esp* an insight **2** a brief survey or conspectus; an outline [Fr, fr pp of *apercevoir* to perceive]

**aperient** /ə'piəri·ənt/ *n or adj* (a) laxative [adj L *aperient-, aperiens,* prp of *aperire;* n fr adj]

**aperiodic** /,aypiəri'odik/ *adj* **1** occurring irregularly ⟨*~ floods*⟩ **2** not having periodic vibrations; not oscillatory – **aperiodically** *adv,* **aperiodicity** *n*

**aperitif** /ə,perə'teef, -'---/ *n* an alcoholic drink taken before a meal to stimulate the appetite [Fr *apéritif* aperient, aperitif, fr MF *aperitif*, adj, aperient, fr ML *aperitivus*, irreg fr L *aperire*]

**aperture** /'apəchə/ *n* **1** an open space; a hole, gap **2a** (the width of) the opening in a photographic lens that admits the light **b** the diameter of the OBJECTIVE lens or mirror of a telescope [ME, fr L *apertura*, fr *apertus*, pp of *aperire* to open – more at WEIR]

**apery** /'aypəri/ *n* **1** mimicry **2** a monkey house in a zoo

**apetalous** /ə'petələs/ *adj* having no petals – **apetaly** *n*

**apex** /'aypeks/ *n, pl* **apexes, apices** /'aypəseez/ **1a** the uppermost peak; the vertex ⟨*the ~ of a mountain*⟩ **b** the narrowed or pointed end; the tip ⟨*the ~ of the tongue*⟩ **2** the highest or culminating point ⟨*the ~ of her career*⟩ **synonyms** see SUMMIT [L, summit, small rod at top of priest's cap; prob akin to L *aptus* fastened – more at APT]

**aphaeresis** /ə'ferəsis, ə'fiə-/ *n, pl* **aphaereses** /ə'ferəseez, ə'fiə-/ the loss of one or more sounds or letters at the beginning of a word (e g in *bus* for *omnibus*) [LL, fr Gk *aphairesis*, lit., taking off, fr *aphairein* to take away, fr *apo-* + *hairein* to take] – **aphaeretic** *adj*

**aphanite** /'afəniet/ *n* a dark IGNEOUS rock of such fine-grained texture that its separate grains are invisible to the naked eye [Fr, fr Gk *aphanēs* invisible, fr *a-* + *phainesthai* to appear – more at PHENOMENON] – **aphanitic** *adj*

**aphasia** /ə'fayzh(y)ə, -zyə/ *n* total or partial loss of the power to use or understand words, usu resulting from brain damage – compare ALEXIA, DYSPHASIA [NL, fr Gk, fr *a-* + *-phasia*] – **aphasic** *n or adj*

**aphelion** /ap'heelyən, a'fee-/ *n, pl* **aphelia** /-lyə/ the point in the path of a planet, comet, etc that is farthest from the sun – compare PERIHELION [NL, fr *apo-* + Gk *hēlios* sun – more at SOLAR]

**aphesis** /'afəsis/ *n, pl* **apheses** /'afəseez/ aphaeresis consisting of the gradual loss of a short unstressed vowel (e g in *lone* for *alone*) [NL, fr Gk, release, fr *aphienai* to let go, fr *apo-* + *hienai* to send – more at JET] – **aphetic** *adj,* **aphetically** *adv*

**aphid** /'ayfid/ *n* any of a superfamily (Aphidoidea) of small insects (e g the greenfly) that suck the juices of plants

**aphis** /'ayfis/ *n, pl* **aphides** /'ayfideez/ an aphid of a common genus (*Aphis*); *broadly* an aphid [NL *Aphid-, Aphis,* genus name, fr NGk *aphis,* perh alter. of Gk *koris* bug]

**aphonia** /ə'fohnyə/ *n* loss of voice due to disease or defects in the vocal organs rather than to brain damage [NL, fr Gk *aphōnia,* fr *aphōnos* voiceless, fr *a-* + *phōnē* sound – more at BAN] – **aphonic** *adj*

**aphorism** /'afəriz(ə)m/ *n* a concise pithy saying that expresses a truth; an adage [MF *aphorisme,* fr LL *aphorismus,* fr Gk *aphorismos* definition, aphorism, fr *aphorizein* to define, fr *apo-* + *horizein* to bound – more at HORIZON] – **aphorist** *n,* **aphoristic** *adj,* **aphoristically** *adv*

**aphor·ize, -ise** /'afəriez/ *vi* to write or speak (as if) in aphorisms

**aphotic** /,ay'fohtik/ *adj* lacking light ⟨*the ~ regions of the ocean*⟩

**aphrodisiac** /,afrə'diziak/ *n or adj* (a substance) that stimulates sexual desire [Gk *aphrodisiakos* sexual, fr *aphrodisia* sexual pleasures, fr neut pl of *aphrodisios* of Aphrodite, fr *Aphroditē,* Gk goddess of love and beauty] – **aphrodisiacal** *adj*

**aphyllous** /ə'filəs/ *adj* having no foliage leaves [Gk *aphyllos,* fr *a-* + *phyllon* leaf – more at BLADE] – **aphylly** *n*

**apian** /'aypi·ən/ *adj* of, concerning, or resembling bees [L *apianus,* fr *apis*]

**apiarian** /,aypi'eari·ən/ *adj* of beekeeping or bees

**apiarist** /'aypi·ərist/ *n* a beekeeper

**apiary** /'aypi·əri/ *n, pl* **apiaries** a place where bees are kept; *esp* a collection of hives or colonies of bees kept for their honey [L *apiarium,* fr *apis* bee]

**apical** /'aypikl, a-/ *adj* **1** of, situated at, or forming an apex **2** *of a consonant* of or formed with the tip of the tongue ⟨n, l, and r are ~ consonants⟩ [deriv of L *apic-, apex*] – **apically** *adv*

**apical dominance** *n* inhibition of the growth of side buds on the stem of a plant by the presence of a bud at the end of the stem

**apiculate** /ə'pikyoolət, -layt/ *adj, of a leaf* ending abruptly in a small distinct point [NL *apiculus*, dim. of L *apic-, apex*]

**apiculture** /'aypi,kulchə/ *n* the keeping of bees, esp on a large scale [prob fr Fr, fr L *apis* bee + Fr *culture*] – **apicultural** *adj*, **apiculturist** *n*

**apiece** /ə'pees/ *adv* for each one; individually

**à pied** /ah 'pyay (*Fr* a pje)/ *adv* on foot [Fr]

**apish** /'aypish/ *adj* resembling an ape: eg **a** a slavishly imitative **b** extremely silly or affected – **apishly** *adv*, **apishness** *n*

**aplacental** /,ayplə'sentl, ,aplə-/ *adj* having or developing no placenta ⟨*the lowest mammals are* ∼⟩

**aplanatic** /,ayplə'natik/ *adj, esp of a lens (system)* free from or corrected for SPHERICAL ABERRATION and hence producing undistorted images [*a-* + Gk *planasthai* to wander – more at PLANET]

**aplasia** /ay'playzh(y)ə, -zyə/ *n* incomplete or faulty development of a body organ or part (eg bone marrow) [NL, fr ²*a-* + *-plasia*] – **aplastic** *adj*

**aplenty** /ə'plenti/ *adj or adv* 1 enough and to spare; in abundance ⟨*had money* ∼⟩ 2 *chiefly NAm* in plenty ⟨*was scared* ∼⟩

**aplite** /'apliet/ *n* a fine-grained light-coloured granite consisting almost entirely of the minerals quartz and feldspar [prob fr Ger *aplit*, fr Gk *haploos* simple – more at HAPL-] – **aplitic** *adj*

**aplomb** /ə'plum, ə'plom/ *n* complete composure or self-assurance; poise ⟨*he parried her difficult questions with* ∼⟩ [Fr, lit., perpendicularity, fr MF, fr *a plomb*, lit., according to the plummet]

**apnoea**, *chiefly NAm* **apnea** /'apni-ə/ *n* 1 brief and temporary cessation of breathing 2 asphyxia – **apnoeic** *adj*

**apo-, ap-** *prefix* 1 away from; off ⟨*aphelion*⟩ ⟨*apogee*⟩ 2 detached; separate ⟨*apocarpous*⟩ 3 obtained from; related to ⟨*apomorphine*⟩ [ME, fr MF & L; MF, fr L, fr Gk, fr *apo* – more at OF]

**apocalypse** /ə'pokəlips/ *n* **1a** any of a number of early Jewish and Christian writings, characterized by symbolic imagery and written esp under an assumed name, that describe the establishment of God's kingdom **b** *cap* REVELATION – usu + *the*; see BIBLE table 2 something viewed as a prophetic revelation [ME, revelation, Revelation, fr LL *apocalypsis*, fr Gk *apokalypsis*, fr *apokalyptein* to uncover, fr *apo-* + *kalyptein* to cover – more at HELL]

**apocalyptic** /ə,pokə'liptik/ *also* **apocalyptical** /-kl/ *adj* 1 of or resembling an apocalypse 2 forecasting the ultimate destiny of the world; prophetic 3 foreboding imminent disaster; terrible 4 ultimately decisive; climactic [LGk *apokalyptikos*, fr Gk *apokalyptein*] – **apocalyptically** *adv*

**apocalypticism** /ə,pokə'liptəsiz(ə)m/, **apocalyptism** /ə,pokə'liptiz(ə)m/ *n* apocalyptic expectation; *esp* a doctrine concerning an imminent end to the world and an ensuing general resurrection and final judgment

**apocalyptist** /ə,pokə'liptist/ *n* the writer of an apocalypse

**apocarpous** /,apə'kahpəs/ *adj, of a flower* having the CARPELS (female reproductive parts) separate or partially joined – **apocarpy** *n*

**apochromatic** /,apəkrə'matik/ *adj, esp of a lens (system)* free from CHROMATIC ABERRATION and SPHERICAL ABERRATION and hence producing undistorted and clear images [ISV]

**apocope** /ə'pokəpi/ *n* the loss of the end of a word (eg in *sing* from Old English *singan*) [LL, fr Gk *apokopē*, lit., cutting off, fr *apokoptein* to cut off, fr *apo-* + *koptein* to cut – more at CAPON]

**apocrine** /'apəkrin, -kreen/ *adj, of a gland* producing a fluid secretion by separation of part of the CYTOPLASM (jellylike material filling a cell) from the secreting cells; *also* produced by an apocrine gland – compare HOLOCRINE, MEROCRINE [ISV *apo-* + Gk *krinein* to separate – more at CERTAIN]

**apocrypha** /ə'pokrifə/ *n* 1 (a collection of) writings or statements of dubious authenticity 2 *taking sing or pl vb, cap* books included in the Septuagint and Vulgate but excluded from the Jewish and Protestant canons of the Old Testament – usu + *the*; see BIBLE table [ML, fr LL, neut pl of *apocryphus* secret, not canonical, fr Gk *apokryphos* obscure, fr *apokryptein* to hide away, fr *apo-* + *kryptein* to hide – more at CRYPT]

**apocryphal** /ə'pokrif(ə)l/ *adj* 1 *often cap* of or resembling the Apocrypha 2 of doubtful authenticity – **apocryphally** *adv*, **apocryphalness** *n*

**apocynthion** /,apə'sinthiən/ *n* APOLUNE (point in an orbit of the moon that is furthest from the centre of the moon) [NL, fr *apo-* + *Cynthia*]

**apodal** /'apədl/ *adj* having no feet or analogous structures ⟨*eels are* ∼⟩ [Gk *apod-, apous*, fr *a-* + *pod-, pous* foot – more at FOOT]

**apodeictic** /,apə'diektik/ *adj* APODICTIC

**apodictic** /,apə'diktik/ *adj* expressing or possessing necessary truth or absolute certainty – used esp of propositions in logic [L *apodicticus*, fr Gk *apodeiktikos*, fr *apodeiknynai* to demonstrate, fr *apo-* + *deiknynai* to show – more at DICTION] – **apodictically** *adv*

**apodosis** /ə'podəsis/ *n, pl* **apodoses** /ə'podəseez/ the main clause of a conditional sentence (eg "I'd go" in "If I were you, I'd go") – compare PROTASIS [NL, fr Gk, fr *apodidonai* to give back, deliver, fr *apo-* + *didonai* to give – more at DATE]

**apodous** /'apədəs/ *apodal; specif, of an insect larva* having no feet – compare ERUCIFORM, SCARABAEIFORM, CAMPODEIFORM

**apoenzyme** /,apoh'enziem/ *n* a protein that forms an active ENZYME by combination with a nonprotein portion (COENZYME) and determines the specificity of this enzyme for a particular substance (SUBSTRATE) on which it will act [ISV]

**apogamy** /ə'pogəmi/ *n* development of a plant embryo from a female reproductive cell (GAMETOPHYTE) without fertilization (eg in some ferns) [ISV] – **apogamous, apogamic** *adj*

**apogee** /'apəjee/ *n* 1 the point in an orbit round the earth (eg of a satellite) that is at the greatest distance from the centre of the earth; *also* the farthest point from a planet, satellite, or other celestial body reached by any object orbiting it – compare PERIGEE 2 the farthest or highest point; the culmination ⟨*Aegean civilization reached its* ∼ *in Crete*⟩ [Fr *apogée*, fr NL *apogaeum*, fr Gk *apogaion*, fr neut of *apogeios, apogaios* far from the earth, fr *apo-* + *gē* earth] – **apogean** *adj*

**apolitical** /,aypə'litikl/ *adj* 1 having an aversion to or no interest or involvement in political affairs 2 having no political significance – **apolitically** *adv*

**Apollonian** /,apə'lohnyən/ *adj* harmonious, measured, ordered, or balanced in character [*Apollo*, Greco-Roman god of the sun, healing, prophecy, music, & poetry, fr L, fr Gk *Apollōn*]

**apologetic** /ə,polə'jetik/ *adj* **1a** offered in defence or vindication ⟨*the* ∼ *writings of the early Christians*⟩ **b** offered by way of excuse or apology ⟨*an* ∼ *smile*⟩ 2 regretfully acknowledging fault or failure; contrite ⟨*was most* ∼ *about his mistake*⟩ [LL *apologeticus*, fr Gk *apologētikos*, fr *apologeisthai* to defend, fr *apo-* + *logos* speech] – **apologetically** *adv*

**apologetics** /ə,polə'jetiks/ *n taking sing or pl vb* 1 systematic reasoned argument in defence (eg of a doctrine) 2 a branch of theology devoted to the rational defence of Christianity

**apologia** /,apə'lohjyə/ *n* a reasoned defence or vindication in speech or writing, esp of a faith, cause, belief, or institution ⟨*the finest* ∼ *of the party's revolutionary policies*⟩ [LL]

**apologist** /ə'poləjist/ *n* somebody who speaks or writes in defence of a faith, cause, belief, or institution

**apolog-ize, -ise** /ə'poləjiez/ *vi* to make an apology – **apologizer** *n*

**apologue** /'apəlog/ *n* an allegorical narrative usu intended to convey a moral *synonyms* see ALLEGORY [Fr, fr L *apologus*, fr Gk *apologos*, fr *apo-* + *logos* speech, narrative]

**apology** /ə'poləji/ *n* **1a** an apologia **b** EXCUSE 2a 2 an admission of error or discourtesy accompanied by an expression of regret 3 a poor substitute *for synonyms* see ²EXCUSE [MF or LL; MF *apologie*, fr LL *apologia*, fr Gk, fr *apo-* + *logos* speech – more at LEGEND]

**apolune** /'apəloohn/ *n* the point in the path of a body orbiting the moon that is farthest from the centre of the moon – compare PERILUNE [*apo-* + L *luna* moon – more at LUNAR]

**apomict** /'apəmikt/ *n* an organism produced or reproducing by apomixis [prob back-formation fr ISV *apomictic*, fr *apo-* + Gk *mignynai* to mix – more at MIX] – **apomictic** *adj*, **apomictically** *adv*

**apomixis** /,apə'miksis/ *n, pl* **apomixes** /,apə'mikseez/ reproduction (eg APOGAMY or PARTHENOGENESIS) involving the production of seed without fertilization [NL, fr *apo-* + Gk *mixis* act of mixing, fr *mignynai*]

**apomorphine** /,apə'mawfeen/ *n* a chemical compound (ALKALOID), $C_{17}H_{17}NO_2$, made synthetically from morphine that is injected under the skin to induce vomiting in many cases of poisoning [ISV]

**apophthegm** /'apə,them/ *n* a short, pithy, and instructive saying [Gk *apophthegma*, fr *apophthengesthai* to speak out, fr *apo-* + *phthengesthai* to utter]

**apophyllite** /ə'pofiliet, ,apə'filiet/ *n* a mineral, $KCa_4Si_8O_{20}(F,OH).8H_2O$, composed of a chemical compound of potassium calcium silicate related to the ZEOLITES and usu found in transparent square prisms or white or greyish masses [Fr, fr *apo-* + Gk *phyllon* leaf]

**apophysis** /ə'pofəsis/ *n, pl* **apophyses** /-eez/ an expanded or projecting part; *esp* a projection from a bone on which muscles attach [NL, fr Gk, fr *apo-* + *phyein* to bring forth – more at BE] – **apophyseal** *adj*

**apoplectic** /,apə'plektik/ *adj* **1** of or causing apoplexy **2** affected with, inclined to, or showing symptoms of apoplexy **3** violently excited (eg from rage) [Fr or LL; Fr *apoplectique*, fr LL *apoplecticus*, fr Gk *apoplēktikos*, fr *apoplēssein*] – **apoplectically** *adv*

**apoplexy** /'apə,pleksi/ *n, medicine* [2]STROKE 5 [ME *apoplexie*, fr MF & LL; MF, fr LL *apoplexia*, fr Gk *apoplēxia*, fr *apoplēssein* to cripple by a stroke, fr *apo-* + *plēssein* to strike – more at PLAINT]

**aport** /ə'pawt/ *adv* on or towards the left-hand side of a ship ⟨*put the helm hard* ~⟩

**aposelene** /,apohsə'leeni/ *n* APOLUNE (point in an orbit of the moon that is farthest from the centre of the moon) [ISV *apo-* + Gk *selēnē* moon – more at SELENIUM]

**aposematic** /,apəsi'matik/ *adj, esp of the coloration of insects* conspicuous and serving to warn [*apo-* + Gk *sēmat-, sēma* sign] – **aposematically** *adv*

**aposiopesis** /,apəzie-ə'peesis/ *n, pl* **aposiopeses** /-eez/ the leaving incomplete of a thought, usu by a sudden breaking off of a sentence (eg in *her behaviour was – but I blush to mention that*) [LL, fr Gk *aposiōpēsis*, fr *aposiōpan* to be quite silent, fr *apo-* + *siōpan* to be silent, fr *siōpē* silence] – **aposiopetic** *adj*

**apostasy** /ə'postəsi/ *n* **1** renunciation of a religious faith **2** abandonment of a previous loyalty; defection [ME *apostasie*, fr LL *apostasia*, fr Gk, lit., revolt, fr *aphistasthai* to revolt, fr *apo-* + *histasthai* to stand – more at STAND]

**apostate** /ə'postayt/ *n* somebody who commits apostasy – **apostate** *adj*

**apostat·ize, -ise** /ə'postətiez/ *vi* to commit apostasy

**a posteriori** /,ay po,stiəri'awri/ *adj* **1** INDUCTIVE **2** relating to or derived by reasoning from observed facts – compare A PRIORI [L, lit., from the latter] – **a posteriori** *adv*

**apostle** /ə'pos(ə)l/ *n* **1a** one sent on a mission; *esp* any of a group of men, recorded in the New Testament of the Bible, who were sent out to preach the gospel. They comprised Jesus's original 12 disciples and Paul. **b** the first prominent Christian missionary to a region or group **2a** somebody who initiates a great moral reform or who first advocates an important belief or system **b** an ardent supporter; an adherent ⟨*an* ~ *of liberal tolerance*⟩ **3** a member of a Mormon administrative council of 12 men [ME, fr OF *apostle* & OE *apostol*, fr LL *apostolus*, fr Gk *apostolos*, lit., messenger, fr *apostellein* to send away, fr *apo-* + *stellein* to send – more at STALL] – **apostleship** *n*

**Apostles' Creed** *n* a Christian statement of belief used in the Western church, esp in public worship

**apostolate** /ə'postələt, -ayt/ *n* **1** the office or mission of an apostle **2** an association of people dedicated to the propagation of a religion or doctrine [LL *apostolatus*, fr *apostolus*]

**apostolic** /,apə'stolik/ *adj* **1** of or conforming to an apostle, the New Testament apostles, or their teachings **2a** of the authority originally vested in the apostles and held (eg by Roman Catholics, Anglicans, and Eastern Orthodox Christians) to be handed down through the successive ordinations of bishops **b** of the Pope as the successor to the apostolic authority vested in St Peter – **apostolicity** *n*

**apostolic delegate** *n* an ecclesiastical representative of the HOLY SEE in a country with which it has no formal diplomatic relations

[1]**apostrophe** /ə'postrəfi/ *n* the addressing, rhetorically, of a usu absent person or a usu personified thing (eg in Carlyle's "O Liberty, what things are done in thy name!") [L, fr Gk *apostrophē*, lit., act of turning away, fr *apostrephein* to turn away, fr *apo-* + *strephein* to turn – more at STROPHE] – **apostrophic** *adj*

[2]**apostrophe** *n* a punctuation mark ' used to indicate the omission of letters or figures, the possessive case, or the plural of letters or figures [MF & LL; MF, fr LL *apostrophus*, fr Gk *apostrophos*, fr *apostrophos* turned away, fr *apostrephein*] – **apostrophic** *adj*

**apostroph·ize, ise** /ə'postrəfiez/ *vt* to address by or in apostrophe ~ *vi* to make use of apostrophe

**apothecaries' measure** /ə'pothək(ə)riz/ *n* a measure of capacity used formerly by pharmacists and based on the fluid ounce of 8 drachms and the drachm of 60 minims

**apothecaries' weight** /ə'pothək(ə)riz/ *n* the series of units of weight used formerly by pharmacists and based on the ounce of 8 drachms and the drachm of 3 scruples or 60 grains

**apothecary** /ə'pothək(ə)ri/ *n, archaic or NAm* **1** a pharmacist **2** PHARMACY 2 [ME *apothecarie*, fr ML *apothecarius*, fr LL, shopkeeper, fr L *apotheca* storehouse, fr Gk *apothēkē*, fr *apotithenai* to put away, fr *apo-* + *tithenai* to put – more at DO]

**apothecium** /,apə'theesiəm/ *n, pl* **apothecia** /-siə/ a spore-bearing structure in many lichens and fungi consisting of a disc-shaped or cupped body bearing spore sacs on the exposed flat or concave surface [NL, fr L *apotheca*] – **apothecial** *adj*

**apothegm** /'apəthem/ *n, NAm* APOPHTHEGM – **apothegmatic, apothegmatical** *adj*, **apothegmatically** *adv*

**apothem** /'apəthem/ *n* the perpendicular from the centre of a regular polygon to one of the sides [ISV *apo-* + *-them* (fr Gk *thema* something laid down, theme)]

**apotheosis** /ə,pothi'ohsis/ *n, pl* **apotheoses** /-eez/ **1** deification **2** the perfect example; the quintessence ⟨*she is the* ~ *of wit*⟩ [LL, fr Gk *apotheōsis*, fr *apotheoun* to deify, fr *apo-* + *theos* god] – **apotheosize** *vt*

**apotropaic** /,apətrə'payik/ *adj* designed to avert evil ⟨*an* ~ *ritual*⟩ [Gk *apotropaios*, fr *apotrepein* to avert, fr *apo-* + *trepein* to turn – more at TROPE] – **apotropaically** *adv*

**appal, appall** *NAm chiefly* **appall** /ə'pawl/ *vt* **-ll-** to overcome with consternation, horror, or dismay [ME *appallen* to make pale, fr MF *apalir*, fr OF, fr *a-* (fr L *ad-*) + *palir* to grow pale, fr L *pallescere*, incho of *pallēre* to be pale – more at FALLOW]

**Appalachian dulcimer** /,apə'laychən, -'lachən/ *n* an American folk instrument with three or four strings stretched over a long FRETTED (ridged) sound box held on the lap and played by plucking or strumming [*Appalachia*, region in E USA]

**appalling** /ə'pawling/ *adj* inspiring horror, dismay, or disgust ⟨*living under* ~ *conditions*⟩ – **appallingly** *adv*

**Appaloosa** /,apə'loohsə, -zə/ *n* (any of) a N American breed of rugged saddle horses with a mottled skin and vertically striped hooves [prob fr *Palouse*, an Indian people of Washington and Idaho, USA]

**appanage, apanage** /'apənij/ *n* **1** a grant (eg of land or revenue) made by a sovereign or legislative body to a dependent member of the royal family or a principal vassal **2** a usual adjunct or accompaniment [Fr *apanage*, fr OF, fr *apaner* to provide for a younger offspring, fr OProv *apanar* to support, fr *a-* (fr L *ad-*) + *pan* bread, fr L *panis* – more at FOOD]

**apparat** /'apərat, ,--'-/ *n* APPARATUS 2 [Russ]

**apparatchik** /,apə'rachik/ *n, pl* **apparatchiks, apparatchiki** /'rachiki/ a member of a Communist APPARAT; *broadly* a bureaucrat [Russ, fr *apparat*]

**apparatus** /'apəraytəs, --'--; *NAm also* -'ratəs/ *n, pl* **apparatuses, apparatus 1a** a set of materials or equipment designed for a particular use **b** an instrument or appliance designed for a specific operation **c** a group of anatomical parts or organs having a common function **2** the administrative bureaucracy of an organization, esp a political party [L, fr *apparatus*, pp of *apparare* to prepare, fr *ad-* + *parare* to prepare – more at PARE]

[1]**apparel** /ə'parəl/ *vt* **-ll-** (*NAm* **-l-, -ll-**) **1** *chiefly formal* to put clothes on; dress **2** *chiefly poetic* to adorn, embellish [ME *appareillen*, fr OF *apareillier* to prepare, fr (assumed) VL *appariculare*, irreg fr L *apparare*]

[2]**apparel** *n* **1** *chiefly formal* personal attire; clothing **2** *chiefly poetic* something that clothes or adorns ⟨*the bright* ~ *of spring*⟩ **3** *archaic* the sails and rigging of a ship

**apparent** /ə'parənt/ *adj* **1** easily seen or understood; plain, evident **2** seemingly real but not necessarily so ⟨*his* ~ *absorption was belied by his rigid pose*⟩ **3** having a clear right to succeed to a title or estate ⟨*the heir* ~⟩ [ME, fr OF *aparent*, fr L *apparent-, apparens*, prp of *apparēre* to appear] – **apparently** *adv*, **apparentness** *n*

*synonyms* **Apparent, illusory, seeming**, and **ostensible** all suggest that things are not really what they appear to be. **Apparent** contrasts what is perceived by the senses with what is true or known to be true ⟨*the* **apparent** *motion of the sun around the earth*⟩. **Illusory** stresses the deceptive nature of what is perceived or thought to be true ⟨**illusory** *pools shimmering in the desert heat*⟩. **Seeming** puts the emphasis on what is seen, rather than on how it is perceived, and suggests an appearance so close to reality as to be mistaken for it ⟨*the* **seeming** *blueness of distant hills*⟩ ⟨*his* **seeming** *prosperity was a front, put on to impress his bank manager*⟩. **Ostensible** suggests that something outwardly what it purports to be has a hidden aim or motive ⟨*though the* **ostensible** *purpose of the procession was to celebrate the anniversary of independence, it was really a public demonstration against the regime*⟩. See EVIDENT **antonyms** unintelligible (for 1), real, actual (for 2)

**apparent horizon** *n* HORIZON 1a (meeting of earth and sky)

**apparent time** *n* the time of day indicated by a sundial

**apparition** /apə'rish(ə)n/ *n* **1a** an unusual or unexpected sight; a phenomenon **b** a ghostly figure **2** the act of becoming visible; appearance [ME *apparicioun*, fr LL *apparition-, apparitio* appearance, fr L *apparitus*, pp of *apparēre*] – **apparitional** *adj*

**[1]appeal** /ə'peel/ *n* **1** a legal proceeding by which a case is brought from a lower to a higher court for review **2a(1)** an application (eg to a recognized authority) for corroboration, vindication, or decision **a(2)** a call by members of the fielding side in cricket, esp the bowler, for the umpire to decide if the batsman is out **b** an earnest plea or call for aid or mercy; an entreaty **3** the power of arousing a sympathetic response; attraction ⟨*the theatre has lost its ~ for him*⟩

**[2]appeal** *vt* to take proceedings to have (a case) reheard in a higher court ~ *vi* **1** to take a case to a higher court for review **2a** to call on someone for corroboration, vindication, or decision ⟨*~ed to the king*⟩ **b** to make an appeal in cricket **3** to make an earnest plea or request **4** to arouse a sympathetic response ⟨*a child's plea that ~s to one's humanity*⟩ [ME *appelen* to accuse, appeal, fr MF *apeler*, fr L *appellare*, fr *appellere* to drive to, fr *ad-* + *pellere* to drive – more at FELT] – **appealer** *n*, **appealable** *adj*, **appealability** *n*

**appealing** /ə'peeling/ *adj* **1** having appeal; pleasing **2** marked by earnest entreaty; imploring – **appealingly** *adv*

**appear** /ə'piə/ *vi* **1a** to be or become visible or evident ⟨*the sun ~s on the horizon*⟩ **b** to arrive ⟨*~s promptly at eight each day*⟩ **2** to come formally before an authoritative body ⟨*must ~ in court today*⟩ **3** to give the impression of being; seem, look ⟨*~s happy enough*⟩ **4** to come into public view ⟨*first ~ed on a television variety show*⟩ **5** to come into existence ⟨*man ~s late in the evolutionary chain*⟩ [ME *apperen*, fr OF *aparoir*, fr L *apparēre*, fr *ad-* + *parēre* to show oneself; akin to Gk *peparein* to display]

**appearance** /ə'piərəns/ *n* **1a** an instance or the act, action, or process of appearing **b** the coming into court of a party in an action or his/her legal representative; *also* notice of intent to defend an action ⟨*enter an ~*⟩ **2** a visit or attendance that is seen or noticed by others ⟨*put in an ~ at the party*⟩ **3a** an outward aspect; a look ⟨*had a fierce ~*⟩ **b** an external show; a semblance ⟨*although hostile, he tried to preserve an ~ of neutrality*⟩ **c** *pl* outward or superficial indication that hides the real situation ⟨*would do anything to keep up ~s*⟩

**appease** /ə'peez/ *vt* **1** to bring to a state of peace or quiet; pacify, calm **2** to cause to subside; allay, satisfy ⟨*~ his hunger*⟩ **3** to accede to the demands of (an aggressor) by concessions, usu including the sacrifice of principles [ME *appesen*, fr OF *apaisier*, fr *a-* (fr L *ad-*) + *pais* peace – more at PEACE] – **appeasable** *adj*, **appeasement** *n*, **appeaser** *n*

**[1]appellant** /ə'pelənt/ *adj* of an appeal; appellate

**[2]appellant** *n* one who or that which appeals; *specif* one who appeals against a judicial decision

**appellate** /ə'pelət/ *adj* of or recognizing appeals; *specif* having the power to review the judgment of another tribunal ⟨*an ~ court*⟩ [L *appellatus*, pp of *appellare*]

**appellation** /,apə'laysh(ə)n/ *n* **1** an identifying name or title; a designation **2** *archaic* the act of naming

**appellation contrôlée** /,apə,laysh(ə)n ,kontroh'lay/ (*Fr* apəlasjɔ̃ kõtrole)/ *n* a government certification of a French wine guaranteeing that it originates from a specified geographical area and meets that locality's standards of production [Fr, lit., controlled appellation]

**appellative** /ə'pelətiv/ *adj* of or being a common noun – **appellative** *n*, **appellatively** *adv*

**append** /ə'pend/ *vt, formal* to attach, affix, or add, esp as a supplement or appendix [Fr *appendre*, fr LL *appendere* fr L, to weigh, fr *ad-* + *pendere* to weigh – more at PENDANT]

**appendage** /ə'pendij/ *n* **1** something appended to something larger or more important **2** a part or organ (eg a leg, wing, or antenna) that projects from the trunk or central part of the body of an animal **3** a subsidiary or supplementary part of a plant (eg a branch or leaf)

**appendant** /ə'pend(ə)nt/ *adj* **1** associated as an accompani-

ment or attendant circumstance **2** attached as an appendage ⟨*a seal ~ to a document*⟩ – **appendant** *n*

**appendectomy** /,apən'dektəmi, ,apen-/ *n, chiefly NAm* an appendicectomy

**appendicectomy** /ə,pendi'sektəmi/ *n* surgical removal of the appendix [L *appendic-, appendix* + E *-ectomy*]

**appendicitis** /ə,pendi'sietəs/ *n* inflammation of the appendix [NL]

**appendicular** /,apən'dikyoolə, ,apen-/ *adj* of an appendage, esp a limb ⟨*the ~ skeleton*⟩

**appendix** /ə'pendiks/ *n, pl* **appendixes, appendices** /ə'pendi,seez/ **1** a supplement, esp of biographical, statistical, or explanatory material, usu attached at the end of a piece of writing **2** an outgrowth or projection from the body or a body part; *specif* VERMIFORM APPENDIX [L *appendic-, appendix* appendage, fr *appendere*]

**apperception** /,apuh'sepsh(ə)n/ *n* **1** introspective self-consciousness **2** mental perception; *esp* the process of understanding something perceived in terms of previous experience [Fr *aperception*, fr *apercevoir* to perceive, fr OF *aperceivre*, fr *a-* (fr L *ad-*) + *perceivre* to perceive] – **apperceive** *vt*, **apperceptive** *adj*

**appertain** /,apə'tayn/ *vi* to belong or be connected as a rightful or customary part, possession, or attribute; pertain – usu + *to* [ME *apperteinen*, fr MF *apartenir*, fr LL *appertinēre*, fr L *ad-* + *pertinēre* to belong – more at PERTAIN]

**appetence** /'apitəns/, **appetency** /'apitənsi/ *n* **1** a fixed and strong desire; an appetite, craving **2** a natural attraction or affinity (eg between chemicals) [L *appetentia*, fr *appetent-, appetens*, prp of *appetere*] – **appetent** *adj*

**appetite** /'apətiet/ /'apətiet/ *n* **1** a desire to satisfy an internal bodily need ⟨*strong sexual ~s*⟩; *esp* a desire for food or for food and drink, usu accompanied by eager anticipation **2a** a strong desire demanding satisfaction ⟨*an insatiable ~ for work*⟩ **b** a taste, preference ⟨*the prevailing cultural ~s*⟩ [ME *apetit*, fr MF, fr L *appetitus*, fr *appetitus*, pp of *appetere* to strive after, fr *ad-* + *petere* to go to – more at FEATHER] – **appetitive** *adj*

**appet·izer, -iser** /'apətiezə/ *n* a food or drink that stimulates the appetite and is usu served before a meal; *broadly* something to increase pleasurable anticipation

**appet·izing, -ising** /'apətiezing/ *adj* appealing to the appetite, esp in appearance or aroma – **appetizingly** *adv*

**applaud** /ə'plawd/ *vi* to express approval, esp by clapping the hands ~ *vt* **1** to express approval of ⟨*a foreign policy we can ~*⟩ **2** to show approval of, esp by clapping the hands ⟨*the procession was ~ed through the streets*⟩ [MF or L; MF *applaudir*, fr L *applaudere*, fr *ad-* + *plaudere* to applaud (cf EXPLODE)] – **applaudable** *adj*, **applaudably** *adv*, **applauder** *n*

**applause** /ə'plawz/ *n* **1** approval publicly expressed (eg by clapping the hands) **2** praise, acclaim ⟨*all creative writers want ~*⟩ [ML *applausus*, fr L, clashing noise, fr *applausus*, pp of *applaudere*]

**apple** /'apl/ *n* **1a** any of a genus (*Malus*) of trees of the rose family widely cultivated for their edible fruit **b** the fleshy edible usu rounded red, yellow, or green fruit of an apple tree **2** a fruit or other plant structure resembling an apple ⟨*oak ~*⟩ [ME *appel*, fr OE *æppel*; akin to OHG *apful* apple, OSlav *ablŭko*] – **apple of somebody's eye** somebody or something greatly cherished ⟨*his daughter is the* apple of his eye⟩ [orig applied to the pupil of the eye] – **she's apples** *Austr informal* everything's fine [rhyming slang *apples (and rice)* nice]

**apple green** *adj or n* (of) a light yellowish-green colour

**applejack** /'apl,jak/ *n, chiefly NAm* brandy distilled from cider

**,apple-'pie** *adj* excellent, perfect ⟨*~ order*⟩

**apple-pie bed** *n, Br* a bed made as a practical joke with the sheet so folded that one cannot lie out straight

**'apple-,polish** *vb, NAm vi* to attempt to ingratiate oneself ~ *vt* to curry favour with (eg by flattery) [fr the tradition of schoolchildren giving a shiny apple to their teacher] – **apple-polisher** *n*

**apples and pears** *n pl, Br slang* stairs [rhyming slang]

**Appleton layer** /'aplt(ə)n/ *n* F LAYER (layer of the atmosphere) [Sir Edward *Appleton* †1965 E physicist]

**appliance** /ə'pliəns/ *n* **1** an act of applying **2** an instrument or device designed for a particular use: eg **2a** a domestic machine or device powered by gas or electricity (eg a food mixer, vacuum cleaner, or cooker) **b** an artificial limb, dental brace, or other device worn to replace a missing body part, correct a deformity, etc **3** FIRE ENGINE *synonyms* see ¹TOOL

**applicable** /ˈaplikəbl, əˈplikəbl/ *also* **applicative** /əˈplikətiv/ *adj* capable of or suitable for being applied; appropriate ⟨*there are several statutes ~ to the case*⟩ – **applicableness** *n*, **applicably** *adv*, **applicability** *n*
  **usage** The pronunciation /ˈaplikəbl/ is recommended for BBC broadcasters. *synonym* see RELEVANT *antonym* inapplicable

**applicant** /ˈaplikənt/ *n* one who applies for a job, posting, grant, etc

**application** /ˌapliˈkaysh(ə)n/ *n* **1a** an act of applying ⟨*~ of new techniques*⟩ ⟨*~ of paint to a house*⟩ **b** a use to which something is put ⟨*new ~s for plastics*⟩ **c** close attention; diligence ⟨*succeeds by ~ to his studies*⟩ **2a** a request, petition ⟨*an ~ for financial aid*⟩ **b** a form used in making a request ⟨*tore up his ~*⟩ **3** a medicated or protective layer or material ⟨*an oily ~ for dry skin*⟩ **4** capacity for practical use; relevance ⟨*words of varied ~*⟩ [ME *applicacioun*, fr L *application-, applicatio* inclination, fr *applicatus*, pp of *applicare*]

**applicator** /ˈaplikaytə/ *n* one who or that which applies; *specif* a device for applying a substance (eg medicine or polish)

**applicatory** /əˈplikət(ə)ri/ *adj* applicable

**applied** /əˈplied/ *adj* put to practical use; *esp* applying general principles to solve definite problems ⟨*~ sciences*⟩

¹**appliqué** /əˈpleekay, apleeˈkay/ *n* **1** a decoration that is cut from one material and fastened by sewing, glueing, etc to a larger piece of material; *also* the decorative work formed in this manner **2** the method or technique of decorating or ornamenting using appliqué [Fr, pp of *appliquer* to put on, fr L *applicare*] – **appliqué** *adj*

²**appliqué** *vt* **appliquéing** /-kaying/ to apply (eg a decoration or ornament) to a larger surface

**apply** /əˈplie/ *vt* **1a** to put to use, esp for some practical purpose ⟨*~ pressure to get what they want*⟩ **b** to put into operation or bring into effect ⟨*~ the brakes*⟩ **c** to lay or spread on ⟨*~ varnish to a table*⟩ **2** to devote (eg oneself) with earnestness, close attention, or diligence – usu + *to* ⟨*should ~ himself to his work*⟩ ~ *vi* **1** to have relevance or a valid connection – usu + *to* ⟨*this rule applies to new members only*⟩ **2** to make an appeal or request, esp in writing ⟨*~ for a job*⟩ [ME *applien*, fr MF *aplier*, fr L *applicare*, fr *ad-* + *plicare* to fold – more at PLY] – **applier** *n*

**appoggiatura** /əˌpojəˈtooərə/ *n* an embellishing note or tone preceding an essential melodic note, used chiefly in the 18th century [It, lit., support, fr *appoggiare* to cause to lean, fr (assumed) VL *appodiare*, fr L *ad-* + *podium* support]

**appoint** /əˈpoynt/ *vt* **1a** to fix or name officially ⟨*~ a trial date*⟩ **b** to select for an office or position ⟨*will ~ her director*⟩ **2** *law* to nominate a person in a deed or will to decide the destination of (an estate) **3** *archaic* to arrange [ME *appointen*, fr MF *apointier* to arrange, fr *a-* (fr L *ad-*) + *point*]

**appointed** /əˈpoyntid/ *adj* (appropriately or elegantly) furnished or equipped

**appointee** /əˌpoynˈtee, əˌpoynˈtee/ *n* **1** one who is appointed **2** *law* a person to whom an estate is appointed

**appointive** /əˈpoyntiv/ *adj* of or filled by appointment ⟨*an ~ office*⟩

**appointment** /əˈpoyntmənt/ *n* **1a** an act of appointing; a designation ⟨*fill a vacancy by ~*⟩ **b** *law* the designation of a person to have part or all of an estate by one having a power of appointing under a settlement or trust **2** an office or position held by somebody who has been appointed to it rather than elected **3** an arrangement for a meeting ⟨*~ at the doctor's for six o'clock*⟩ **4** *pl* equipment, furnishings

**apportion** /əˈpawsh(ə)n/ *vt* to divide and share out in just proportion or according to a plan; allot *synonyms* see ALLOT [MF *apportionner*, fr *a-* (fr L *ad-*) + *portionner* to portion]

**apportionment** /əˈpawsh(ə)nmənt/ *n* an act or result of apportioning; *esp*, *NAm* the apportioning of representatives or taxes among the states according to population

**appose** /əˈpohz/ *vt* **1** to place (something) next to another; *also* to place side by side **2** *archaic* to apply (one thing) to another ⟨*~ a seal to a document*⟩ [MF *aposer*, fr OF, fr *a-* + *poser* to put – more at POSE]

**apposite** /ˈapəzit/ *adj* highly pertinent or appropriate; apt *synonyms* see RELEVANT *antonyms* inapposite, inapt △ opposite [L *appositus*, fr pp of *apponere* to place near, fr *ad-* + *ponere* to put – more at POSITION] – **appositely** *adv*, **appositeness** *n*

**apposition** /ˌapəˈzish(ə)n/ *n* **1a** a grammatical construction in which two usu adjacent nouns or noun phrases refer to the same person or thing and are used grammatically in the same way (eg *the poet* and *Burns* in "a biography of the poet Burns") **b** the relation of one of such a pair of nouns or noun phrases to the other **2a** an act or instance of apposing; *specif* the deposition of successive layers upon those already present (eg in plant cell walls) **b** the state of being apposed – **appositional** *adj*, **appositionally** *adv*

**appositive** /əˈpozətiv, a-/ *adj* of or standing in grammatical apposition – **appositive** *n*, **appositively** *adv*

**appraisal** /əˈprayz(ə)l/ *n* an act or instance of appraising; *esp* a valuation of property by an authorized person

**appraise** /əˈprayz/ *vt* **1** to set a value on ⟨*~ the damage caused by the fire*⟩ **2** to evaluate the worth, significance, or status of; *esp* to give an expert judgment of the value or merit of ⟨*~ the political effects of the royal tour*⟩ △ apprise, apprize [ME *appreisen*, fr MF *aprisier* – more at APPRIZE] – **appraisement** *n*, **appraiser** *n*, **appraising** *adj*, **appraisingly** *adv*

**appreciable** /əˈpreesh(y)əbl/ *adj* **1** capable of being perceived or measured **2** fairly large ⟨*an ~ distance*⟩ *synonyms* see PERCEPTIBLE *antonym* inappreciable – **appreciably** *adv*

**appreciate** /əˈpreeshiayt; *also* -siayt USE *the last pron is disliked by some speakers*/ *vt* **1a** to understand the nature, worth, quality, or significance of ⟨*can't ~ the difference between right and wrong*⟩ **b** to value or admire highly ⟨*must appreciate it to ~ it*⟩ **c** to recognize with gratitude ⟨*certainly ~s your kindness*⟩ **2** to increase the value of to increase in value [LL *appretiatus*, pp of *appretiare*, fr L *ad-* + *pretium* price – more at PRICE] – **appreciator** *n*, **appreciatory** *adj*

**appreciation** /əˌpreeshiˈaysh(ə)n, -si-/ *n* **1a** sensitive awareness; *esp* recognition of aesthetic values **b** a judgment, evaluation; *esp* a favourable critical estimate **c** an expression of admiration, approval, or gratitude **2** increase in value – **appreciative** *adj*, **appreciatively** *adv*, **appreciativeness** *n*

**apprehend** /ˌapriˈhend/ *vt* **1** to arrest, seize ⟨*~ a thief*⟩ **2a** to become aware of; grasp the meaning of **b** to anticipate, esp with anxiety, unease, or fear ~ *vi* to understand [ME *apprehenden*, fr L *apprehendere*, lit., to seize, fr *ad-* + *prehendere* to seize – more at PREHENSILE]

**apprehensible** /ˌapriˈhensəbl/ *adj* capable of being apprehended – **apprehensibly** *adv*

**apprehension** /ˌapriˈhensh(ə)n/ *n* **1** anxiety or fear, esp of future evil; foreboding **2** arrest, seizure – used technically in Scottish law **3** *chiefly formal* **3a** the act or power of perceiving or comprehending ⟨*a man of dull ~*⟩ **b** understanding, conception ⟨*according to popular ~*⟩ [ME LL *apprehension-, apprehensio*, fr L *apprehensus*, pp of *apprehendere*]

**apprehensive** /ˌapriˈhensiv, -ziv/ *adj* **1** *chiefly formal* **1a** capable of apprehending, esp quickly **b** having understanding; conscious – usu + *of* **2** viewing the future with anxiety, unease, or fear – often + *for* or *of synonyms* see TIMID *antonym* confident – **apprehensively** *adv*, **apprehensiveness** *n*

¹**apprentice** /əˈprentis/ *n* **1** one who is learning an art or trade **1a** from an employer to whom he/she is bound by a formal contract **b** by practical experience under skilled workers **2** an inexperienced person; a novice ⟨*an ~ in cooking*⟩ [ME *aprentis*, fr MF, fr OF, fr *aprendre* to learn, fr L *apprendere*, *apprehendere*] – **apprenticeship** *n*

²**apprentice** *vt* to set at work as an apprentice; *esp* to bind to an apprenticeship by a contract

**appressed** /əˈprest/ *adj* pressed close to or lying flat against something ⟨*leaves ~ to the stem*⟩ [L *appressus*, pp of *apprimere* to press to, fr *ad-* + *premere* to press – more at PRESS]

**apprise** /əˈpriez/ *vt*, *formal* to give notice to; tell – often + *of* △ appraise [Fr *appris*, pp of *apprendre* to learn, teach, fr OF *aprendre*]

**apprize** /əˈpriez/ *vt* to value, appreciate △ appraise [ME *apprisen*, fr MF *aprisier*, fr OF, fr *a-* (fr L *ad-*) + *prisier* to value – more at PRIZE]

**appro** /ˈaproh/ *n*, *Br* – **on appro** *informal* ON APPROVAL

¹**approach** /əˈprohch/ *vt* **1a** to draw closer to ⟨*~ the podium*⟩ **b** to come very near to; be almost the same as in quality, character, etc **2a** to make advances to, esp in order to create a desired result ⟨*was ~ed by several film producers*⟩ **b** to take preliminary steps towards consideration, accomplishment, or experience of ⟨*~ the subject with an open mind*⟩ ~ *vi* to draw nearer ⟨*dawn ~es*⟩ [ME *approchen*, fr OF *aprochier*, fr LL *appropiare*, fr L *ad-* + *prope* near; akin to L *pro* before – more at FOR]

²**approach** *n* **1a** an act or instance of approaching ⟨*the ~ of*

summer⟩ ⟨*long-jumpers ... have seldom exceeded 150 feet in their* ~ – G Dyson⟩ **b** an approximation ⟨*in this book he makes his closest* ~ *to greatness*⟩ **2** a manner or method of doing something, esp for the first time ⟨*experimenting with new lines of* ~⟩ ⟨*a highly individual* ~ *to marketing*⟩ **3** a means of access ⟨*the* ~*es to the city*⟩ **4a** a golf shot from the fairway towards the green **b** (the steps taken on) the part of the bowling alley from which the bowler must deliver the ball **5** the final part of an aircraft flight before landing **6** *usu pl* an advance made to establish personal or business relations

**approachable** /ə'prohchəbl/ *adj* capable of being approached; *specif* easy to meet or deal with **approachability** *n*

**approbate** /'aprəbayt/ *vt, chiefly NAm* to approve, sanction [ME *approbaten*, fr L *approbatus*, pp of *approbare*] – **approbatory** *adj*

**approbation** /,aprə'baysh(ə)n/ *n* **1** formal or official approval; sanction, commendation **2** *obs* proof

¹**appropriate** /ə'prohpri,ayt/ *vt* **1** to take exclusive possession of ⟨*no one should* ~ *a common benefit*⟩ **2** to set apart for or assign to a particular purpose or use ⟨~ *money for the research programme*⟩ **3** to take or make use of without authority or right; steal [ME *appropriaten*, fr LL *appropriatus*, pp of *appropriare*, fr L *ad-* + *proprius* own] – **appropriable** *adj*, **appropriator** *n*

²**appropriate** /ə'prohpriət/ *adj* especially suitable or compatible; fitting, proper *synonyms* see ³FIT *antonym* inappropriate – **appropriately** *adv*, **appropriateness** *n*

**appropriate technology** *n* technology that requires little sophisticated knowledge to use or maintain, is cheap, and is suitable as aid for developing countries

**appropriation** /ə,prohpri'aysh(ə)n/ *n* **1** an act or instance of appropriating **2** something appropriated; *specif* money set aside by formal action for a specific use – **appropriative** *adj*

**approval** /ə'proohvl/ *n* **1** an act or instance of approving **2** favourable opinion or judgment **3** formal or official permission – **on approval** to be returned without payment if found unsatisfactory – used of goods supplied commercially

**approve** /ə'proohv/ *vt* **1** to have or express a favourable opinion of ⟨*couldn't* ~ *their conduct*⟩ **2a** to accept as satisfactory **b** to give formal or official sanction to; ratify ⟨*Parliament* ~d *the proposed policy*⟩ **3** *obs* to prove, attest ~ *vi* to take a favourable view – often + *of* ⟨*doesn't* ~ *of fighting*⟩ [ME *approven*, fr OF *aprover*, fr L *approbare*, fr *ad-* + *probare* to prove – more at PROVE] – **approvingly** *adv*

**approved school** /ə'proohvd/ *n, Br* a boarding school for juvenile delinquents – no longer used technically; compare COMMUNITY HOME

¹**approximate** /ə'proksimət/ *adj* **1** nearly correct or exact **2** located close together ⟨~ *leaves*⟩ [LL *approximatus*, pp of *approximare* to come near, fr L *ad-* + *proximare* to come near – more at PROXIMATE] – **approximately** *adv*

²**approximate** /ə'proksimayt/ *vt* **1a** to bring near or close; cause to approach – often + *to* **b** to bring (cut edges of body tissue) together – used technically **2** to come near to; approach, esp in quality, number, performance, etc ~ *vi* to come close – usu + *to*

**approximation** /ə,proksi'maysh(ə)n/ *n* **1** the act or process of drawing together **2** the quality or state of being close or near ⟨*an* ~ *to the truth*⟩ **3** something that is approximate; *esp* a mathematical quantity that is close in value but not equal to a desired quantity – **approximative** *adj*, **approximatively** *adv*

**appui** /ə'pwee, a'pwee/ *n* the reciprocal pressure between a horse's mouth and the rider's hand [Fr, support, fr *appuyer* to support, fr OF *apuyer*, fr (assumed) VL *appodiare* – more at APPOGGIATURA]

**appurtenance** /ə'puhtinəns/ *n* **1** a subordinate part or adjunct ⟨*the* ~ *of welcome is fashion and ceremony* – Shak⟩ **2** an accessory

**appurtenant** /ə'puhtinənt/ *adj* auxiliary, accessory [ME *apertenant*, fr MF, fr OF, prp of *apartenir* to belong – more at APPERTAIN] – **appurtenant** *n*

**apraxia** /,ay'praksiə/ *n* loss or impairment of the ability to execute complex coordinated movements [NL, fr Gk, inaction, fr *a-* + *praxis* action, fr *prassein* to do – more at PRACTICAL] – **apractic, apraxic** *adj*

**après-ski** /,apray 'skee (*Fr* apre ski)/ *adj or n* (of or for) social activity after a day's skiing [Fr *après* after + *ski* ski, skiing]

**apricot** /'ayprikot, -kət/ *n* **1a** a tree (*Prunus armeniaca*) of the rose family, that is closely related to the peach and plum and is widely cultivated in temperate regions for its edible fruit **b** the rounded juicy yellow to orange-coloured single-stoned fruit

of the apricot tree **2** an orange pink colour [alter. of earlier *abrecock*, deriv of Ar *al-birqūq* the apricot]

**April** /'ayprəl/ *n* the 4th month of the year according to the GREGORIAN CALENDAR (standard Western calendar) – see MONTH table [ME, fr OF & L; OF *avrill*, fr L *Aprilis*, perh deriv of Gk *Aphrō*, short for *Aphroditē* Aphrodite, Gk goddess of love and beauty]

**April fool** *n* the victim of a joke or trick played on April Fools' Day; *also, NAm* such a joke or trick

**April Fools' Day** *n* April 1, characteristically marked by the playing of practical jokes

**a priori** /,ay pree'awri, ,ah, -rie/ *adj* **1a** deductive ⟨*an* ~ *argument*⟩ **b** of or derived by reasoning from self-evident propositions – compare A POSTERIORI **c** of or referring to something that can be known by reason alone ⟨~ *geometrical propositions*⟩ **d** true or false by definition or convention alone ⟨~ *statements*⟩ **2** without examination or analysis; presumptive ⟨~ *acceptance of the greatness of the book*⟩ [L, from the former] – **a priori** *adv*, **apriority** *n*

**apron** /'ayprən/ *n* **1** a garment usu tied round the waist and used to protect clothing **2** something that suggests or resembles an apron in shape, position, or use: eg **2a** the lower piece under the sill of the interior casing of a window **b** an upward or downward vertical extension of a sink or lavatory **c** a covering (eg of sheet metal) for protecting parts of machinery **d** an extensive fan-shaped deposit of sand, gravel, etc; ALLUVIAL FAN **e** the part of the stage in front of the proscenium arch **f** a shield (eg of concrete, planking, or brushwood) along the bank of a river, along a seawall, or below a dam **g** the extensive surfaced part of an airport immediately adjacent to the terminal area or hangars [ME, alter. by incorrect division of *a napron*) of *napron*, fr MF *naperon*, dim. of *nape* cloth, modif of L *mappa* napkin, towel]

**apron strings** *n pl* dominance or control, esp of a man by his mother or wife

¹**apropos** /,aprə'poh/ *adv* **1** at an opportune time **2** BY THE WAY [Fr *a propos*, lit., to the purpose]

²**apropos** *adj* both relevant and opportune *synonyms* see RELEVANT

³**apropos, apropos of** *prep* concerning; WITH REGARD TO

**apse** /aps/ *n* **1** a usu vaulted semicircular or polygonal projecting part of a building, esp a church **2** APSIS 1 [ML & L; ML *apsis*, fr L]

**apsidal** /'apsidl/ *adj* of an apse

**apsis** /'apsis/ *n, pl* **apsides** /'apsideez/ **1** the point in an astronomical orbit at which the distance of the body from the centre of attraction is either greatest or least **2** APSE 1 [NL *apsid-, apsis*, fr L, arch, orbit, fr Gk *hapsid-, hapsis*, fr *haptein* to fasten]

**apt** /apt/ *adj* **1** ordinarily disposed; inclined, likely – usu + *to* ⟨~ *to accept what is plausible as true*⟩ **2** suited to a purpose; *esp* relevant ⟨*an* ~ *quotation*⟩ **3** keenly intelligent and responsive ⟨*an* ~ *pupil*⟩ *synonyms* see ³FIT, RELEVANT [ME, fr L *aptus*, lit., fastened, fr pp of *apere* to fasten; akin to L *apisci* to reach, *apud* near, Skt *āpta* fit] – **aptly** *adv*, **aptness** *n*

**apterous** /'aptərəs/ *adj* **1** lacking wings; wingless ⟨~ *insects*⟩ **2** *botany* having no winglike expansions ⟨*an* ~ *seed*⟩ [Gk *apteros*, fr *a-* + *pteron* wing – more at FEATHER]

**apterygial** /,aptə'rijiəl/ *adj* without paired limbs (eg wings or fins)

**apterygote** /ap'terəgoht, ay'te-/ *n* any of a subclass (Apterygota) of insects that includes the primitive wingless forms (eg a bristletail or springtail) – compare PTERYGOTE [deriv of Gk *a-* + *pterygōtos* winged, fr *pteryg-, pteryx* wing] – **apterygote** *adj*

**apteryx** /'aptəriks/ *n* KIWI (New Zealand bird) [NL, fr *a-* + Gk *pteryx* wing; akin to Gk *pteron*]

**aptitude** /'aptityoohd, -choohd/ *n* **1** a natural ability; talent, esp for learning **2** an inclination, tendency **3** general fitness or suitability □ usu + *for* – **aptitudinal** *adj*, **aptitudinally** *adv*

**aqua** /'akwə/ *n, pl* **aquae** /'akwee, 'akwie/, **aquas** water – used, esp formerly, in names for solutions of a substance in water ⟨~ *ammonia*⟩ [L – more at ISLAND]

**aquaculture** /'akwə,kulchə/ *n* AQUICULTURE

**Aquadag** /'akwə,dag/ *trademark* – used for a suspension of fine particles of graphite in water for use as a lubricant

**aqua fortis** /,akwə 'fawtis/ *n, archaic* NITRIC ACID [NL, lit., strong water]

**aqualung** /'akwə,lung/ *n* an apparatus that usu consists of cylinders of compressed air or an oxygen mixture carried on the back and connected to a face mask for breathing underwater [L *aqua* + E *lung*]

**aquamarine** /ˌakwəməˈreen/ *n* 1 a transparent blue, blue-green, or green variety of the mineral beryl used as a gemstone 2 a pale blue to light greenish-blue colour [NL *aqua marina*, fr L, sea water]

**aquanaut** /ˈakwəˌnawt/ *n* a diver who lives and works both inside and outside an underwater shelter for an extended period [L *aqua* + E *-naut* (as in *aeronaut*)]

¹**aquaplane** /ˈakwəˌplayn/ *n* a board on which someone stands to be towed behind a fast motorboat

²**aquaplane** *vi* 1 to ride on an aquaplane 2 *of a car* to go out of control by sliding on a thin layer of water lying on the surface of a wet road

**aqua regia** /ˌakwə ˈrejiə, ˈreejiə/ *n* a corrosive liquid mixture of NITRIC ACID and HYDROCHLORIC ACID that dissolves gold and platinum [NL, lit., royal water]

**aquarelle** /ˌakwəˈrel/ *n* a painting in thin, usu transparent, watercolours [Fr, fr obs It *acquarella* (now *acquerello*), fr *acqua* water, fr L *aqua*] – **aquarellist** *n*

**aquarist** /ˈakwərist/ *n* one who keeps an aquarium

**aquarium** /əˈkweəriəm/ *n*, *pl* **aquariums, aquaria** /əˈkweəriə/ 1 a glass tank, artificial pond, etc in which living aquatic animals or plants are kept 2 an establishment where collections of living aquatic organisms are kept and exhibited [fr neut of L *aquarius* of water, fr *aqua*]

**Aquarius** /əˈkweəriəs/ *n* 1 a constellation of the ZODIAC (imaginary belt in the heavens) lying between Capricornus and Pisces and represented as a man pouring water 2a the 11th sign of the zodiac in astrology, held to govern the period January 21-February 19 approx **b** somebody born under this sign [L, lit., water carrier] – **Aquarian** *adj or n*

¹**aquatic** /əˈkwotik, əˈkwatik/ *adj* 1 growing, living in, or frequenting water 2 taking place in or on water ⟨*∼ sports*⟩ [MF *aquatique*, fr L *aquaticus*, fr *aqua*] – **aquatically** *adv*

²**aquatic** *n* 1 an aquatic animal or plant 2 *pl taking sing or pl vb* water sports

**aquatint** /ˈakwətint/ *n* (a print made by) a method of etching a printing plate so that tones similar to watercolour washes can be reproduced [It *acqua tinta* dyed water] – **aquatint** *vt*, **aquatinter** *n*, **aquatintist** *n*

**aquavit** /ˈakwəvit/ *n* a colourless Scandinavian spirit flavoured with caraway seeds [Sw, Dan & Norw *akvavit*, fr ML *aqua vitae*]

**aqua vitae** /ˌakwə ˈveetie, ˈvietie/ *n* 1 ETHANOL 2 a strong spirit (e g brandy or whisky) [ME, fr ML, lit., water of life]

**aqueduct** /ˈakwiˌdukt/ *n* 1a a conduit for water; *esp* one for carrying a large quantity of water flowing by gravity **b** a usu arched structure for conveying such a conduit or canal over a valley, river, etc 2 a canal or passage in a body part or organ [L *aquaeductus*, fr *aquae* (gen of *aqua*) + *ductus* act of leading – more at DUCT]

**aqueous** /ˈakwiəs, ˈaykwiəs/ *adj* 1 of, containing, or resembling water 2 made from, with, or by water ⟨*an ∼ solution*⟩ [ML *aqueus*, fr L *aqua*] – **aqueously** *adv*

**aqueous humour** *n* the transparent watery liquid that fills the front part of the eyeball between the cornea and the lens

**aquiculture** /ˈakwiˌkulchə/, **aquaculture** /ˈakwəˌkulchə/ *n* 1 the cultivation of aquatic plants or animals for use by humans 2 HYDROPONICS (cultivation of plants in water containing nutrients) [L *aqua* + E *-culture* (as in *agriculture*)] – **aquicultural** *adj*

**aquifer** /ˈakwifə/ *n* a water-bearing layer of permeable rock, sand, or gravel [NL, fr L *aqua* + *-fer*] – **aquiferous** *adj*

**aquilegia** /ˌakwiˈleej(y)ə/ *n* COLUMBINE (plant of the buttercup family) [NL]

**aquiline** /ˈakwilien/ *adj* 1 of or resembling an eagle 2 *of the human nose* curving like an eagle's beak; hooked [L *aquilinus*, fr *aquila* eagle] – **aquilinity** *n*

**aquiver** /əˈkwivə/ *adj* marked by trembling or quivering

¹**-ar** /-ə/ *suffix* (*n → adj*) of or being ⟨*molecul*ar⟩ ⟨*spectacul*ar⟩; resembling ⟨*oracul*ar⟩ [ME, fr L *-aris*, alter. of *-alis* -al]

²**-ar** *suffix* (*→ n*) ²-ER ⟨*beggar*⟩ ⟨*scholar*⟩

**Arab** /ˈarəb/ *n* 1a a member of a Semitic people originally of the Arabian peninsula but now widespread throughout the Middle East and N Africa **b** a member of an Arabic-speaking people 2 *not cap* 2a a homeless vagabond; *esp* an outcast boy or girl **b** a mischievous or annoying child 3 a typically graceful, swift, intelligent, and spirited horse of an Arabian stock [ME, fr L *Arabus, Arabs,* fr Gk *Arab-, Araps,* fr Ar *'Arab*] – **Arab** *adj*

¹**arabesque** /ˌarəˈbesk/ *adj* of or being in the style of arabesque [Fr, fr It *arabesco* in Arabian style, fr *Arabo* Arab, fr L *Arabus*]

²**arabesque** *n* 1a a decorative design or style that combines natural objects (e g flowers or foliage) to form an intricate pattern **b** an intricate pattern (e g of words or music) ⟨*∼s of assonance*⟩ 2 a posture in ballet in which the dancer stands on one leg with one arm extended forwards and the other arm and leg backwards

**Arabian** /əˈraybiən/ *n* 1 a native or inhabitant of Arabia 2 an Arab horse [*Arabia,* peninsula in SW Asia] – **Arabian** *adj*

¹**Arabic** /ˈarəbik/ *adj* 1 (characteristic) of Arabia, Arabians, or the Arabs 2 of or being the Arabic language 3 *often not cap* of ARABIC NUMERALS

²**Arabic** *n* a Semitic language, now the prevailing speech of Arabia, Jordan, Lebanon, Syria, Iraq, Egypt, and parts of N Africa

**arabic·ize, -ise** /əˈrabisiez/ *vt, often cap* 1 to adapt (a language or elements of a language) to Arabic usage 2 ARABIZE 1

**Arabic numeral** *n, often not cap A* any of the number symbols 0, 1, 2, 3, 4, 5, 6, 7, 8, 9

**arabinose** /əˈrabinohs, ˈarəbinohs/ *n* a PENTOSE sugar (sugar containing five carbon atoms), $C_5H_{10}O_5$, occurring in PECTIN (constituent of plant cell walls), gums, and similar compounds produced by plants [ISV *arabin* (the solid principle in gum arabic, fr *gum arabic* + *-in*) + *-ose*]

**Arabist** /ˈarəbist/ *n* a specialist in Arabic language, literature, or culture

**arab·ize, -ise** /ˈarəbiez/ *vt, often cap* 1a to cause to acquire Arabic customs, manners, speech, or outlook **b** to modify (a people) by an admixture of Arab blood 2 ARABICIZE 1 – **arabization** *n, often cap*

**arable** /ˈarəbl/ *n or adj* (land) farmed for or fit for crops [adj MF or L; MF, fr L *arabilis*, fr *arare* to plough; akin to OE *erian* to plough, Gk *aroun*; n fr adj] – **arability** *n*

**arachis oil** /ˈarəkis/ *n* PEANUT OIL [NL *Arachis*, genus of plants including the peanut]

**arachnid** /əˈraknid/ *n* any of a class (Arachnida of the phylum Arthropoda) of INVERTEBRATE animals including the spiders, scorpions, mites, and ticks, that have a segmented body divided into two regions of which the front bears four pairs of legs but no antennae [deriv of Gk *arachnē* spider] – **arachnid** *adj*

¹**arachnoid** /əˈraknoyd/ *n* a thin membrane that is the middle one of the three membranes (the MENINGES) that surround the brain and SPINAL CORD – compare DURA MATER, PIA MATER [NL *arachnoides;* fr Gk *arachnoeidēs* like a cobweb, fr *arachnē* spider, spider's web]

²**arachnoid** *adj* 1 of the arachnoid membrane 2 *esp of a plant part* covered with or composed of soft loose hairs or fibres

³**arachnoid** *adj* resembling or related to the arachnids [deriv of Gk *arachnē*]

**aragonite** /ˈarəgəˌniet, əˈragəniet/ *n* a colourless or whitish mineral consisting of CALCIUM CARBONATE, $CaCO_3$, that occurs as a deposit near hot springs and is the form of calcium carbonate normally found in pearls [Ger *aragonit*, fr *Aragon*, region in NE Spain] – **aragonitic** *adj*

**arak** /ˈarak, ˈarək/ *n* ARRACK (Asian alcoholic spirit)

**Araldite** /ˈarəldiet/ *trademark* – used for any of various, esp adhesive, EPOXY RESINS

**Aramaean** /ˌarəˈmeeən/ *n* 1 a member of a pre-Christian Semitic people of Syria and Upper Mesopotamia 2 Aramaic [L *Aramaeus*, fr Gk *Aramaios*, fr Heb *'Arām* Aram, ancient name for Syria] – **Aramaean** *adj*

**Aramaic** /ˌarəˈmayik/ *n* a Semitic language of the Aramaeans that was used extensively in SW Asia by various non-Aramaean peoples, including the Jews after the Babylonian exile

**Aran** /ˈarən/ *n* a style of knitting that produces a fabric consisting of vertical patterned bands and that is usu in a thick cream-coloured wool [*Aran* Islands, Ireland]

**Arapaho, Arapahoe** /əˈrapəhoh/ *n, pl* **Arapahos, Arapahoes,** *esp collectively* **Arapaho, Arapahoe** a member of an American Indian people of the plains region of N America

**Araucanian** /ˌarawˈkaynyən, ˌaraw-/ *also* **Araucan** /əˈrawkən/ *n* a member, or the language, of a group of American Indian peoples of S central Chile and adjacent regions of Argentina [Sp *araucano*, fr *Arauco*, province in Chile] – **Araucanian** *adj*

**araucaria** /ˌarawˈkeəriə/ *n* any of a genus (*Araucaria* of the family Araucariaceae) of S American or Australian coniferous

trees; *esp* the monkey-puzzle [NL, genus name, fr *Arauco*] –
**araucarian** *adj*

**Arawak** /'arǝwak, -wahk/ *n, pl* **Arawaks,** *esp collectively*
**Arawak** a member, or the language, of an American Indian
people living chiefly along the coast of Guyana

**Arawakan** /,arǝ'wakǝn, -'wahkǝn/ *n, pl* **Arawakans,** *esp collectively* **Arawakan** a member, or the language family, of a
group of American Indian peoples of S America and the W
Indies

**arbalest, arbalist** /'ahbǝlist/ *n* a large medieval military crossbow with a steel bow [ME *arblast,* fr OE, fr OF *arbaleste,* fr
LL *arcuballista,* fr L *arcus* bow + *ballista* – more at ARROW] –
**arbalester** *n*

**arbiter** /'ahbitǝ/ *n* 1 a person with power to decide a dispute 2
a person or agency with absolute power of judging and determining [ME *arbitre,* fr MF, fr L *arbitr-, arbiter*]

**arbitrage** /'ahbitrij, 'ahbitrahzh/ *vi or n* (to engage in) the
simultaneous purchase and sale of the same or equivalent
security in different markets in order to profit from price discrepancies [Fr, fr MF, arbitration, fr OF, fr *arbitrer* to give
judgment, fr L *arbitrari,* fr *arbitr-, arbiter*] – **arbitrager** *n*

**arbitral** /'ahbitrǝl/ *adj* of arbiters or arbitration

**arbitrament** /'ahbitrǝmǝnt/ *n* the award made by an arbitrator
[ME, fr MF *arbitrement,* fr *arbitrer*]

**arbitrary** /'ahbitrǝri, 'ahbitri/ *adj* 1 depending on choice or
discretion; *specif* determinable by decision of a judge or tribunal rather than by statute 2a arising from unrestrained
exercise of the will; capricious **b** based on random or convenient selection or choice rather than reason 3 despotic, tyrannical
⟨~ *rule*⟩ – **arbitrarily** *adv,* **arbitrariness** *n*

**arbitrate** /'ahbitrayt/ *vi* to act as arbitrator ⟨*a committee appointed to* ~ *between the company and the union*⟩ ~ *vt* 1 to
act as arbiter upon 2 to submit or refer for decision to an
arbiter ⟨*they agreed to* ~ *their differences*⟩ – **arbitrable** *adj,*
**arbitrative** *adj*

**arbitration** /,ahbi'traysh(ǝ)n/ *n* the act of arbitrating; *esp* the
hearing and determination of a disputed issue by a person
chosen by the parties or appointed under statutory authority –
**arbitrational** *adj*

**arbitrator** /'ahbi,traytǝ/ *n* 1 a person chosen to settle differences between two parties in dispute 2 an arbiter

¹**arbor** /'ahbǝ/ *n, chiefly NAm* an arbour

²**arbor** *n* 1a a main shaft or beam **b** a spindle or axle of a
wheel 2 *chiefly NAm* a shaft on which a workpiece (eg on a
lathe) is mounted [L, tree, shaft]

**arboreal** /,ah'bawriǝl/ *adj* 1 of or resembling a tree 2 *esp of a
mammal* (adapted for) living in or among trees [L *arboreus* of
a tree, fr *arbor*] – **arboreally** *adv*

**arboreous** /,ah'bawriǝs/ *adj* 1 wooded 2 arboreal

**arborescent** /,ahbǝ'res(ǝ)nt/ *adj* resembling a tree in properties, growth, structure, or appearance – **arborescence** *n,*
**arborescently** *adv*

**arboretum** /,ahbǝ'reetǝm, ah'boritǝm/ *n, pl* **arboretums,**
**arboreta** /-tǝ/ a place where trees and shrubs are cultivated for
study and display [NL, fr L, place grown with trees, fr *arbor*]

**arboriculture** /'ahbǝri,kulchǝ/ *n* the cultivation of trees and
shrubs [²*arbor + -i- + culture*] – **arboriculturist** *n*

**arborist** /'ahbǝrist/ *n* a specialist in the care and cultivation of
trees

**arbor·ization, -isation** /,ahbǝrie'zaysh(ǝ)n/ *n* a branching or
treelike figure or arrangement (eg in a mineral or fossil); *also*
formation of or into such a figure

**arbor·ize, -ise** /'ahbǝriez/ *vi* to assume a treelike appearance
⟨*the nerve fibres* ~d⟩

**arborvitae** /,ahbaw'vietee, -'veetee/ *n* any of various N
American and E Asian evergreen conifer trees (esp genus
*Thuja*) of the cypress family that have tiny scalelike leaves and
oblong or egg-shaped cones, and that are often grown for
ornament or for their soft durable yellowish to reddish-brown
wood [NL *arbor vitae,* lit., tree of life]

**arbour, NAm chiefly arbor** /'ahbǝ/ *n* a shady retreat (eg in a
garden) protected by trees or climbing plants grown over
trelliswork [ME *erber* plot of grass, arbour, fr OF *herbier* plot
of grass, fr *herbe* herb, grass, fr L *herba*]

**arbovirus** /'ahboh,vieǝrǝs/ *n* any of various viruses, including
the causative agents of YELLOW FEVER and ENCEPHALITIS (inflammation of the brain), that multiply in and are subsequently
transmitted to VERTEBRATE animals by mosquitoes, ticks, and
other ARTHROPODS [arthropod-*borne virus*]

**arbutus** /ah'byoohtǝs/ *n* any of a genus (*Arbutus*) of shrubs

and trees of the heather family with white or pink flowers and
scarlet berries [NL, genus name, fr L, strawberry tree]

¹**arc** /ahk/ *n* 1 the apparent path, both above and below the
horizon, of a star, planet, or other celestial body 2 something
arched or curved 3 a sustained discharge of electricity, visible
as light, that is produced by the passage of an electric current
across a gap between two parts of a circuit or between
ELECTRODES (wires, plates, etc that conduct electricity); *also*
ARC LAMP 4 a portion of a curve (eg part of a circumference)
[ME *ark,* fr MF *arc* bow, fr L *arcus* bow, arch, arc – more at
ARROW]

²**arc** *vi* to form an electric arc

³**arc** *adj* mathematically inverse – used of TRIGONOMETRIC
FUNCTIONS and HYPERBOLIC FUNCTIONS ⟨~ *sine*⟩ ⟨*if* y *is
the cosine of* θ *then* θ *is the* ~ *cosine of* y⟩ [*arc sine* arc or
angle (corresponding to the) sine (of so many degrees)]

**arcade** /ah'kayd/ *n* 1 a long building or gallery with a roof
supported by arches 2 a covered passageway or avenue (eg
between shops) 3 a series of arches with their columns or piers
[Fr, fr It *arcata,* fr *arco* arch, fr L *arcus*]

**arcaded** /ah'kaydid/ *adj* formed in or furnished or decorated
with arches or arcades

**Arcadia** /ah'kaydiǝ/ *n* a usu idealized rural region or scene of
simple pleasure and peace [*Arcadia,* pastoral region of ancient
Greece, fr L, fr Gk *Arkadia*]

¹**Arcadian** /ah'kaydiǝn/ *n* 1 *often not cap* a person who lives a
simple, quiet, esp rustic, life 2 a native or inhabitant of Arcadia
3 the dialect of ancient Greek used in Arcadia

²**Arcadian** *adj, sometimes not cap* of Arcadia, Arcadians, or
Arcadian

**arcading** /ah'kayding/ *n* a series of arches or arcades used in
the construction or decoration of a building

**Arcady** /'ahkǝdi/ *n* Arcadia

**arcane** /ah'kayn/ *adj* known or knowable only to an initiate
⟨~ *rites*⟩ [L *arcanus*]

**arcanum** /ah'kaynǝm/ *n, pl* **arcana** /-nǝ/ 1 a secret or mystery
known only to those who have been initiated 2 an extract of
the vital nature of something; an elixir [L, fr neut of *arcanus*
secret, fr *arca* chest – more at ARK]

¹**arch** /ahch/ *n* 1 a typically curved structure spanning an
opening and serving usu as a support (eg for the wall or other
weight above the opening) 2a something resembling an arch in
form or function **b** a curved or arched anatomical structure or
part; *esp* the arched bony structure of the foot 3 an archway
[ME *arche,* fr OF, fr (assumed) VL *arca,* fr L *arcus* – more at
ARROW]

²**arch** *vt* 1 to cover, span, or provide with an arch 2 to form or
bend into an arch ~ *vi* to form an arch

³**arch** *adj* 1 principal, chief ⟨*an arch-villain*⟩ ⟨*an* ~ *rebel*⟩ 2a
cleverly sly and alert **b** playfully saucy [*arch-*; (2) prob suggested by *archrogue*] – **archly** *adv,* **archness** *n*

¹**arch-** /ahch-/ *prefix* 1 chief; principal ⟨arch*bishop*⟩ 2 extreme;
most fully embodying the qualities of a (specified, usu undesirable, human type) ⟨arch*enemy*⟩ ⟨arch*rogue*⟩ [ME *arche-, arch-,*
fr OE *arce-* & OF *arch-,* fr LL *arch-* & L *archi-,* fr Gk *arch-,
archi-,* fr *archein* to begin, rule; akin to Gk *archē* beginning,
rule, *archos* ruler]

²**arch-** /ahk-/ – see ARCHI-

**-arch** /-ahk/ *comb form* (→ *n*) ruler; leader ⟨matri*arch*⟩
⟨olig*arch*⟩ [ME *-arche,* fr OF & LL & L; OF *-arche,* fr LL
*-archa,* fr L *-arches, -archus,* fr Gk *-archēs, -archos,* fr *archein*]

**archae-** /ahki-/, **archaeo-,** *chiefly NAm* **arche-, archeo-** *comb
form* ancient; primitive ⟨*Archaeopteryx*⟩ ⟨*archaeology*⟩ [Gk
*archaio-,* fr *archaios* ancient, fr *archē* beginning]

**Archaean** /ah'keeǝn/ *adj* of or being the oldest known group
of rocks formed in (the earlier part of) the PRECAMBRIAN geological era

**archaeology** /,ahki'olǝji/ *n* 1 the scientific study of material
remains (eg fossil relics, artefacts, and dwellings) of past
human life and activities 2 the remains of the culture of a
people [Fr *archéologie,* fr LL *archaeologia* antiquarian lore, fr
Gk *archaiologia,* fr *archaio- + -logia* -logy] – **archaeological**
*adj,* **archaeologically** *adv,* **archaeologist** *n*

**archaeopteryx** /,ahki'optǝriks/ *n* any of an extinct genus
(*Archaeopteryx*) of small primitive birds with many characteristics of reptiles, that occurred in the later part of the JURASSIC
geological period [NL, genus name, fr *archae- +* Gk *pteryx*
wing; akin to Gk *pteron* wing – more at FEATHER]

**Archaeozoic** /,ahkiǝ'zoh·ik/ *adj or n* (of or being) the earliest
era of geological history, equivalent to the earlier division of

the PRECAMBRIAN, or the system of rocks formed in this era; *also* PRECAMBRIAN

**archaic** /ah'kayik/ *adj* **1** (characteristic) of an earlier or more primitive time; antiquated 〈~ *legal traditions*〉 **2** having the characteristics of the language of the past and surviving chiefly in specialized uses; no longer used in ordinary speech or writing **3** surviving essentially unchanged from an earlier period *synonyms* see ¹OLD *antonyms* current, up-to-date [Fr or Gk; Fr *archaïque*, fr Gk *archaïkos*, fr *archaios*] – **archaically** *adv*

**archaism** /ah'kayiz(ə)m/ *n* **1** the use of archaic speech or writing **2** an instance of archaic usage; *esp* an archaic word or expression **3** something that is outmoded or old-fashioned 〈*judicial* ~〉 [NL *archaïsmus*, fr Gk *archaïsmos*, fr *archaios*] – **archaist** *n*, **archaize** *vb*, **archaistic** *adj*

**archangel** /,ahk'aynj(ə)l/ *n* **1** a chief angel **2** *pl* the eighth of the nine orders of angelic beings in the CELESTIAL HIERARCHY ranking immediately below PRINCIPALITIES and above ANGELS [ME, fr OF or LL; OF *archangele*, fr LL *archangelus*, fr Gk *archangelos*, fr *arch-* + *angelos* angel] – **archangelic** *adj*

**archbishop** /,ahch'bishəp/ *n* a bishop of the highest rank [ME, fr OE *arcebiscop*, fr LL *archiepiscopus*, fr LGk *archiepiskopos*, fr *archi-* + *episkopos* bishop – more at BISHOP]

**archbishopric** /ahch'bishəprik/ *n* the office of or the area under the care of an archbishop

**archdeacon** /ahch'deekən/ *n* a clergyman ranking just below a bishop and helping esp in administrative work [ME *archedeken*, fr OE *arcediacon*, fr LL *archidiaconus*, fr LGk *archidiakonos*, fr Gk *archi-* + *diakonos* deacon] – **archdeaconate** *n*

**archdeaconry** /ahch'deekənri/ *n* the office or district of an archdeacon

**archdiocese** /ahch'dieəsis/ *n* the area under the care of an archbishop – **archdiocesan** *adj*

**archducal** /ahch'dyoohkəl/ *adj* of an archduke or archduchy [Fr *archiducal*, fr *archiduc*]

**archduchess** /ahch'duchis/ *n* **1** the wife or widow of an archduke **2** a woman having in her own right the rank of an archduke [Fr *archiduchesse*, fem of *archiduc* archduke, fr MF *archeduc*]

**archduchy** /ahch'duchi/ *n* the territory of an archduke or archduchess [Fr *archiduché*, fr MF *archeduché*, fr *arche-* arch- + *duché* duchy]

**archduke** /ahch'dyoohk/ *n* a duke over other dukes; *specif* (the title of) a prince of the imperial family of Austria [MF *archeduc*, fr *arche-* arch- + *duc* duke] – **archdukedom** *n*

**arche-** /ahki-/, **archeo-** *comb form, chiefly NAm* archae-, archaeo-

**archegonium** /,ahki'gohnyəm/ *n, pl* **archegonia** /-nyə/ the flask-shaped female sex organ of mosses, ferns, and some conifers and related plants, that consists of a neck and a swollen base (VENTER) that contains a single egg cell [NL, fr Gk *archegonos* originator, fr *archein* to begin + *gonos* procreation; akin to Gk *gignesthai* to be born – more at ARCH-, KIN] – **archegonial** *adj*, **archegoniate** *n or adj*

**archenemy** /ahch'enəmi/ *n* **1** a principal enemy **2** *often cap the* Devil

**archenteron** /,ahk'enteron/ *n* the central cavity of the GASTRULA (animal embryo at an early stage of development) [NL]

**archer** /'ahchə/ *n* **1** one who uses or is skilled in using a bow and arrow **2** *cap* the constellation or sign of the zodiac Sagittarius [ME, fr OF, fr LL *arcarius*, alter. of *arcuarius*, fr *arcuarius* of a bow, fr L *arcus* bow – more at ARROW]

**archerfish** /'ahchə,fish/ *n, pl* **archerfish** a small fish (*Toxotes jaculator*) of the E Indies that catches insects by stunning them with drops of water ejected from its mouth; *also* any of various related fishes of similar habits

**archery** /'ahchəri/ *n* **1** the art, practice, skill, or sport of shooting arrows from a bow **2** an archer's weapons **3** *taking sing or pl vb* a body of archers

**archespore** /'ahkə,spaw/, **archesporium** /-'spawriəm/ *n, pl* **archespores**, **archesporia** /-'spawriə/ the cell or group of cells (e g in fungi) from which cells that divide to form spores develop [NL *archesporium*, fr *arche-* (as in *archegonium*) + *-sporium* (fr *spora* spore)] – **archesporial** *adj*

**archetype** /'ahki,tiep/ *n* **1a** the original pattern or model of which all things of the same type are representations or copies; a prototype **b** a typical or perfect model or specimen **2** IDEA 1 – used in Platonic philosophy **3** *psychology* an inherited idea or way of thinking that, according to Jungian psychology, is derived from the COLLECTIVE UNCONSCIOUS (part of the unconscious mind that all people have in common) [L *archetypum*, fr Gk *archetypon*, fr neut of *archetypos* archetypal, fr *archein* + *typos* type] – **archetypal**, **archetypical** *adj*, **archetypally**, **archetypically** *adv*

**archfiend** /,ahch'feend/ *n* a chief fiend

**archi-** /ahki-/, **arch-** *prefix* **1** chief; principal 〈*archi*trave〉 **2** primitive; original; primary 〈*archicarp*〉 [Fr or L; Fr, fr L, fr Gk – more at ARCH-]

**archicarp** /'ahki,kahp/ *n* the female sex organ of an ASCOMYCETE fungus that develops usu as a spirally coiled side branch from a filament (HYPHA) making up the body of the fungus and bears an ASCOGONIUM (cell in which fertilization occurs)

**archidiaconal** /,ahkdie'akənl/ *adj* of an archdeacon [LL *archidiaconus* archdeacon]

**archiepiscopal** /,ahki-i'piskəpl/ *adj* of an archbishop [ML *archiepiscopalis*, fr LL *archiepiscopus* archbishop – more at ARCHBISHOP ] – **archiepiscopally** *adv*, **archiepiscopate** *n*

**archil** /'ahkəl/ *n* ORCHIL (dye or a lichen that yields it)

**archimandrite** /,ahki'mandriet/ *n* the superior of a large monastery or group of monasteries in the Eastern Orthodox branch of the Christian faith [LL *archimandrites*, fr LGk *archimandritēs*, fr Gk *archi-* + LGk *mandra* monastery, fr Gk, fold, pen]

**Archimedes' screw** /,ahki'meediz/ *n* a primitive device for raising water, consisting typically of a broad-threaded screw encased by a cylinder [*Archimedes* †212 BC Gk mathematician & inventor]

**archipelago** /,ahki'peləgoh, ,ahchi-/ *n, pl* **archipelagoes**, **archipelagos** **1** an expanse of water with many scattered islands **2** a group of islands [*Archipelago* Aegean sea, fr It *Arcipelago*, lit., chief sea, fr *arci-* (fr L *archi-*) + Gk *pelagos* sea – more at FLAKE] – **archipelagic** *adj*

**architect** /'ahkitekt/ *n* **1a** a person who designs buildings and supervises their construction **b** a person who designs ships 〈*a naval* ~〉 **2** a person who devises, plans, and achieves a difficult objective 〈*the* ~ *of a military victory*〉 [MF *architecte*, fr L *architectus*, fr Gk *architektōn* master builder, fr *archi-* + *tektōn* builder, carpenter – more at TECHNICAL]

**architectonic** /,ahkitek'konik/ *adj* **1** of or according with the principles of architecture **2a** resembling architecture in structure or organization **b** of architectonics [L *architectonicus*, fr Gk *architektonikos*, fr *architektōn*] – **architectonically** *adv*

**architectonics** /,ahkitek'toniks/ *n taking sing or pl vb also* **architectonic** *n* **1** the art or science of architecture **2** *philosophy* the systematic arrangement of knowledge **3a** the structural design of a construction or work **b** the system of structure; plan of order

**architectural** /,ahki'tekchərəl/ *adj* of or conforming to the rules of architecture – **architecturally** *adv*

**architecture** /'ahki,tekchə/ *n* **1** the art, science, practice, or profession of designing and erecting buildings **2** the design, formation, or construction of something 〈*the careful* ~ *of the story*〉 **3** a product or work of architecture **4** a method or style of building

**architrave** /'ahki,trayv/ *n* **1** the lowest part of a classical Greek architectural ENTABLATURE, resting directly on the top of the column **2** a decorative moulded frame around a door, window, or other rectangular recess or opening [MF, fr OIt, fr *archi-* + *trave* beam, fr L *trabs*]

**archival** /ah'kievl/ *adj* of, contained in, or being archives

¹**archive** /'ahkiev/ *n*, **archives** *n pl* a place in which records or documents of interest to a government, institution, family, etc are preserved; *also* the material (e g books, papers, or magnetic tape) so preserved [Fr & L; Fr, fr L *archivum*, fr Gk *archeion* government house (in pl, official documents), fr *archē* rule, government – more at ARCH-]

²**archive** *vt* to file or collect (e g records or documents) in an archive or other collection

**archivist** /'ahkivist/ *n* a person in charge of archives

**archivolt** /'ahkivolt, -vohlt/ *n* **1** an ornamental moulding round an arch **2** the underside of an arch [It *archivolto*, prob fr *arco* arch + *volta* vault]

**archon** /'ahkon/ *n* a chief magistrate in ancient Athens [L, fr Gk *archōn*, fr prp of *archein*]

**archpriest** /,ahch'preest/ *n* a priest who occupies a preeminent position

**archway** /'ahch,way/ *n* a way or passage that runs beneath arches; *also* an arch over a passage

**-archy** /-ahki/ *comb form* (→ *n*) rule; government ⟨*monarchy*⟩ [ME *-archie*, fr MF, fr L *-archia*, fr Gk, fr *archein* to rule – more at ARCH-]

**arc lamp** /ahk/ *also* **arc** *n* an electric lamp that uses the ARC produced when a current passes between two incandescent carbon rods or other electrically conducting ELECTRODES as the source of an intensely bright white light

**arc light** *n* ARC LAMP

¹**arctic** /'ahktik; *also* 'ahtik/ *adj* **1** *often cap* of the North Pole or the surrounding region **2a** extremely cold; frigid **b** cold in temper or mood [ME *artik*, fr L *arcticus*, fr Gk *arktikos*, fr *arktos* bear, Ursa Major, north; akin to L *ursus* bear] – **arctically** *adv*

   *usage* The pronunciation /'ahktik/ is recommended for BBC broadcasters.

²**arctic** *n, NAm* a rubber overshoe reaching to the ankle or above

**Arctic** *n – the* most northern part of the world, north of the Arctic Circle

**arctic circle** *n, often cap A&C* the parallel of latitude that is about $66\frac{1}{2}$ degrees north of the earth's equator and that goes round the northern polar region

**arctic fox** *n, often cap A* a small fox (*Alopex lagopus*) of arctic regions that is either brownish in summer and white in winter or grey in summer and a light grey-blue in winter

**arctic skua** *n, often cap A* a SKUA (large dark-coloured seabird) (*Stercorarius parasiticus*) having prominent pointed middle tail feathers

**arctic tern** *n, often cap A* a tern (*Sterna paradisaea*) resembling the common tern but breeding in the Arctic and migrating to southern Africa and S America

**arctophile** /'ahktə,fiel/ *n* a person who likes or collects teddy bears [Gk *arktos* bear + E *-phile*] – **arctophilia** *n*

**arcuate** /'ahkyooət, -ayt/ *adj* curved like a bow ⟨*an ~ cloud*⟩ ⟨*~ veins in a leaf*⟩ [L *arcuatus*, pp of *arcuare* to bend like a bow, fr *arcus* bow] – **arcuately** *adv*

**arc weld** *n* a weld made by ARC WELDING

**arc welding** *n* the welding of metal parts using the heat produced by an electric ARC formed by the passage of an electric current between two metal rods or between one rod and the metal being worked on – **arc-weld** *vt*

**-ard** /-əd/ *also* **-art** /-ət/ *suffix* (→ *n*) one characterized by or associated with a (usu undesirable specified action, state, or quality) ⟨*braggart*⟩ ⟨*dullard*⟩ ⟨*pollard*⟩ ⟨*wizard*⟩ [ME, fr OF, of Gmc origin; akin to OHG *-hart* (in personal names such as *Gērhart* Gerard), OE *heard* hard]

**ardeb** /'ahdeb/ *n* any of numerous Egyptian units of capacity; *esp* the customs unit equal to 197.9 litres (5.44 bushels) [Ar *ardabb, irdabb*]

**ardent** /'ahd(ə)nt/ *adj* **1** characterized by warmth of feeling, typically expressed by eager fervent support or activity; passionate **2** shining, glowing ⟨*~ eyes*⟩ *antonym* cool [ME, fr MF, fr L *ardent-, ardens,* prp of *ardēre*] – **ardency** *n*, **ardently** *adv*

**ardent spirits** *n pl* strong distilled alcoholic drinks

**ardour**, *NAm chiefly* **ardor** /'ahdə/ *n* **1** an often restless or transitory warmth of feeling ⟨*the sudden ~s of youth*⟩ **2** extreme vigour or intensity; zeal **3** strong or burning heat *synonyms* see PASSION [ME *ardour*, fr MF & L; MF, fr L *ardor,* fr *ardēre* to burn; akin to OHG *essa* forge, L *aridus* dry]

**arduous** /'ahdyooəs/ *adj* **1a** hard to accomplish or achieve **b** marked by great labour or effort; strenuous **2** hard to climb; steep ⟨*an ~ mountain path*⟩ *synonyms* see ¹HARD *antonym* light [L *arduus* high, steep, difficult; akin to ON *örthigr* high, steep, Gk *orthos* straight] – **arduously** *adv*, **arduousness** *n*

¹**are** /ə; *strong* ah/ *pres 2 sing or pres pl of* BE [ME, fr OE *earun;* akin to ON *eru, erum* are, OE *is* is]

²**are** /ah/ *n* a metric unit of square measure equal to 100 square metres [Fr, fr L *area*]

**area** /'eəriə/ *n* **1** a level piece of ground (set aside for a specific purpose) ⟨*a car parking ~*⟩ **2a** the surface included within a boundary, geometrical drawing, set of lines, etc **b** the extent of a surface as measured in an equivalent number of squares of standard size ⟨*the ~ of the tabletop is 1.5 square metres*⟩ **3** *NAm chiefly* **areaway** a sunken space providing access, ventilation, and light to a cellar or basement **4** a particular extent of space or surface or one serving a special function ⟨*a large kitchen ~*⟩ ⟨*wash that ~ of your body*⟩ ⟨*the ~ round London*⟩ **5** the extent, range, or scope of a concept, operation, or activity ⟨*the whole ~ of foreign policy*⟩ [L, piece of level ground,

threshing floor, fr *arēre* to be dry; akin to L *ardor*] – **areal** *adj*, **areally** *adv*

**areca** /ə'reekə, 'arikə/ *n* any of several tropical Asian palms (*Areca* or related genera); *esp* BETEL PALM [NL, genus name, fr Pg, fr Malayalam *atekka*]

**arena** /ə'reenə/ *n* **1** the area in the central part of a Roman amphitheatre for gladiatorial combats and other spectacles **2a** an enclosed area used for public entertainment **b** a building containing such an enclosed area and used esp for sporting events **3** a sphere of usu intense interest, activity, or controversy ⟨*the political ~*⟩ [L *harena, arena* sand, sandy place]

**arenaceous** /,ari'nayshəs/ *adj* **1** resembling, made of, or containing sand or sandy particles ⟨*~ rocks*⟩ **2** growing or living in sandy places ⟨*~ plants*⟩ [L *arenaceus,* fr *arena*]

**arenicolous** /,ari'nikələs/ *adj* living, burrowing, or growing in sand [L *arena* + E *-i-* + *-colous*]

**arenite** /'arəniet, ə'ree-/ *n* a rock composed largely of cemented sand or sand particles; a sandstone

**aren't** /ahnt/ **1** are not **2** am not – used in questions

**areocentric** /,ariə'sentrik/ *adj* having or relating to the planet Mars as a centre [Gk *Areios* of Ares, fr *Arēs,* Ares, Gk god of war (equivalent to the Roman god Mars)]

**areola** /ə'reeələ/ *n, pl* **areolae** /-li/, **areolas** *biology* **1** a small defined area or space (eg between the veins of a leaf or the fibres of some tissues) **2** a coloured ring (eg round the human nipple or a pimple) [NL, fr L, small open space, dim. of *area*] – **areolar** *adj*, **areolate** *adj*, **areolation** *n*

**areole** /'eəriohl/ *n* **1** an areola **2** a small pit or cavity, esp in a plant

**Areopagus** /,ari'opəgəs/ *n* the supreme tribunal of ancient Athens [L, fr Gk *Areios pagos,* fr *Areios pagos* (lit., hill of Ares), a hill in Athens where the tribunal met]

**arête** /ə'ret, ə'rayt/ *n* a sharp-crested mountain ridge, esp between two steep-sided round valleys (CIRQUES) [Fr, lit., fish bone, fr LL *arista,* fr L, beard of grain]

**argali** /,ahgəli/ *n, pl* **argalis**, *esp collectively* **argali** a large wild sheep (*Ovis ammon*) of mountainous central and eastern Asia, noted for its immense horns; *also* any of several other large wild sheep (eg the bighorn) [Mongolian]

**Argand diagram** /'ahgənd, 'ahgand/ *n* a graph consisting of two axes, on which a COMPLEX NUMBER $x + iy$ (where $i = \sqrt{-1}$) can be represented, the x-axis being taken to be the REAL axis, and the y-axis being taken to be the IMAGINARY axis [Jean Robert *Argand* †1822 Swiss mathematician]

**argent** /'ahjənt/ *n* **1** a silver colour; *also,* HERALDRY white **2** *archaic* the metal silver [ME, fr MF & L; MF, fr L *argentum;* akin to L *arguere* to make clear, Gk *argyros* silver, *argos* white] – **argent** *adj*

**argentic** /ah'jentik/ *adj* of or containing silver, esp with a VALENCY of two

**argentiferous** /,ahjən'tifərəs/ *adj* producing or containing silver ⟨*~ rock*⟩

**argentine** /'ahjəntien/ *adj* silver, silvery

**argentite** /'ahjəntiet/ *n* a dark lead-grey mineral that consists of silver sulphide, $Ag_2S$, and is a valuable ore of silver

**argentous** /,ah'jentəs/ *adj* of or containing silver, esp with a VALENCY of one

**argie-bargie** /,ahji 'bahji/ *n* an argy-bargy

**argil** /'ahjil/ *n* clay; *esp* potter's clay [ME, fr L *argilla,* fr Gk *argillos;* akin to Gk *argos* white]

**argillaceous** /,ahji'layshəs/ *adj* of or containing clay or clay minerals ⟨*~ rocks*⟩ [L *argillaceus,* fr *argilla*]

**argillite** /'ahjiliet/ *n* a compact rock composed largely of clay or clay minerals

**arginase** /'ahjinayz/ *n* an enzyme that converts arginine into urea and the AMINO ACID ornithine in the process by which the nitrogen-containing waste products of protein breakdown are removed from the cell [ISV]

**arginine** /'ahjinien/ *n* an AMINO ACID, $HOOCCH(NH_2)(CH_2)_3NHC(NH_2)NH$, that is a chemical BASE (compound that can react with an acid to form a salt) occurring in most proteins [Ger *arginin,* perh fr Gk *arginoeis* bright, white]

**Argive** /'ahgiev, 'ahjiev/ *adj* of the Greeks or Greece, esp the Achaean city of Argos or the surrounding territory of Argolis [L *Argivus,* fr Gk *Argeios,* lit., of Argos, fr *Argos,* city-state of ancient Greece] – **Argive** *n*

**argol** /'ahgol/ *n* crude TARTAR (substance in grape juice) deposited as a brownish-red crust on wine casks during the aging of wine [ME *argoile,* prob fr AF *argoil*]

**argon** /'ahgon/ *n* a colourless odourless gaseous chemical element that is one of the NOBLE GASES (group of chemically unreactive gases), is found in the air and in volcanic gases, and is used esp in electric light bulbs, valves, television tubes, etc [Gk, neut of *argos* idle, lazy, fr *a-* + *ergon* work – more at WORK; fr its relative inertness]

**argonaut** /'ahgə,nawt/ *n* PAPER NAUTILUS (animal related to the octopus) [*Argonaut* (one of a band of legendary heroes who sailed in quest of the Golden Fleece), fr L *Argonautes*, fr Gk *Argonautēs*, fr *Argō*, ship in which the Argonauts sailed + *nautēs* sailor – more at NAUTICAL]

**argosy** /'ahgəsi/ *n* a large merchant ship, esp carrying a valuable cargo; *also, taking sing or pl vb* a fleet of such ships [modif of It *ragusea* Ragusan vessel, fr *Ragusa*, city & seaport in Dalmatia (now Dubrovnik, Yugoslavia)]

**argot** /'ahgoh/ *n* an often more or less secret vocabulary and idiom peculiar to a particular group ⟨*the ∼ of the prison*⟩ *synonyms* see DIALECT [Fr]

**arguable** /'ahgyoo͞əbl/ *adj* 1 open to argument, dispute, or question 2 as can be supported by argument ⟨*it is ∼ that they are the best band at present*⟩ – **arguably** *adv*

   *usage* The use of **arguable** and **arguably** to mean "as can be argued" ⟨*arguably a real danger to the economy*⟩ is disliked by some people.

**argue** /'ahgyooh/ *vi* 1 to give reasons for or against something; reason 2 to contend or disagree in words ∼ *vt* 1 to give evidence of; indicate 2 to consider the reasons for and against; discuss 3 to prove or try to prove by giving reasons; maintain 4 to persuade by giving reasons ⟨*∼d them out of going*⟩ [ME *arguen*, fr MF *arguer* to accuse, reason & L *arguere* to make clear; MF *arguer*, fr L *argutare* to prate, fr *argutus* clear, noisy, fr pp of *arguere*] – **arguer** *n*

**argufy** /'ahgyoofie/ *vb, informal* to dispute, esp excessively; debate – **argufier** *n*

**argument** /'ahgyoomənt/ *n* 1 a reason given in proof or rebuttal 2a the act or process of arguing; argumentation, debate **b** a coherent series of reasons offered 3 a quarrel, disagreement 4 an abstract or summary, esp of a literary work ⟨*a later editor added an ∼ to the poem*⟩ 5 *maths* 5a INDEPENDENT VARIABLE **b** the angle between the line joining the representation of a COMPLEX NUMBER on an ARGAND DIAGRAM with the point where the axes cross and the horizontal axis taken in the positive direction [ME, fr MF, fr L *argumentum*, fr *arguere*]

**argumentation** /,ahgyoomən'taysh(ə)n, -men-/ *n* 1 the act or process of forming reasons and of drawing conclusions and applying them to a case in discussion 2 debate, discussion

**argumentative** /,ahgyoo'mentətiv/ *adj* 1 characterized by argument 2 given to or liking argument – **argumentatively** *adv*, **argumentativeness** *n*

**argumentum** /,ahgyoo'mentəm/ *n, pl* **argumenta** /-tə/ ARGUMENT 2b [L]

**Argus** /'ahgəs/ *n* 1 a 100-eyed monster of Greek legend 2 a watchful guardian [L, fr Gk *Argos*]

**Argus-'eyed** *adj* vigilant

**argy-bargy** /,ahji 'bahji/ *n, chiefly Br informal* a lively discussion; an argument, dispute [redupl of Sc & E dial. *argy*, alter. of *argue*]

**arhat** /'ah,haht/ *n* a Buddhist who has reached a state of absolute blessedness and release from the cycle of reincarnation (NIRVANA) [Skt, fr prp of *arhati* he deserves; akin to Gk *alphein* to gain] – **arhatship** *n*

**aria** /'ahriə/ *n* a melody, tune; *specif* an accompanied elaborate melody sung (eg in an opera) by a single voice [It, lit., atmospheric air, modif of L *aer*]

**Arian** /'eəriən/ *adj* of Arius or Arianism [*Arius* †336 Gk theologian]

**-arian** /-'eəriən/ *suffix* (→ *n*) 1 believer in ⟨*Unitarian*⟩; advocate of ⟨*vegetarian*⟩ 2 one who pursues (a specified interest or activity) ⟨*antiquarian*⟩ ⟨*librarian*⟩ 3 one who is (so many decades) old ⟨*octogen*arian⟩ [L *-arius* -ary]

**Arianism** /'eəriə,niz(ə)m/ *n* the doctrine, declared heretical by the established Christian Church in the 4th century AD, that Jesus Christ is not as divine as God

**arid** /'arid/ *adj* 1 excessively dry; *specif* having insufficient rainfall to support agriculture 2 lacking in interest and life [Fr or L; Fr *aride*, fr L *aridus* – more at ARDOUR] – **aridness** *n*, **aridity** *n*

**ariel** /'eəriəl/ *n* an Asian and African gazelle (*Gazella arabica*) [Ar *aryal*, var of *ayyil* stag]

**Aries** /'eəriz, 'eəreez/ *n* 1 a small constellation of the ZODIAC

(imaginary belt in the heavens) lying between Taurus and Pisces and represented as a ram 2a the 1st sign of the zodiac in astrology, held to govern the period March 21-April 20 approx **b** somebody born under this sign [L, lit., ram; akin to Gk *eriphos* kid, OIr *heirp* doe] – **Arian** *adj or n*

**arietta** /,ari'etə, ,ahri-/ *n* a short relatively simple aria [It, dim. of *aria*]

**aright** /ə'riet/ *adv* rightly, correctly ⟨*if I remember ∼*⟩ [ME, fr OE *ariht*, fr ¹*a-* + *riht* right]

**aril** /'aril/ *n* an additional exterior covering or outgrowth developed by some seeds (eg those of the yew tree) after fertilization [prob fr NL *arillus*, fr ML, raisin, grape seed] – **ariled** *adj*, **arillate** *adj*

**arioso** /,ahri'ohsoh, ,ari-, -zoh/ *n, pl* **ariosos** *also* **ariosi** /-si/ a musical passage or composition having a mixture of free spoken narrative and rhythmic song in verse [It, fr *aria*]

**arise** /ə'riez/ *vi* **arose** /ə'rohz/; **arisen** /ə'riz(ə)n/ **1a** to originate from a source – often + *from* **b** to come into being or to attention 2 to ascend 3 *formal* to get up, rise [ME *arisen*, fr OE *ārīsan*, fr *ā-*, perfective prefix + *rīsan* to rise]

**arista** /ə'ristə/ *n, pl* **aristae** /-ti/, **aristas** a bristlelike structure: eg **a** a narrow spiked projection from the tip of a leaf **b** a bristle near or at the tip of the antenna of some flies [NL, fr L, beard of grain] – **aristate** *adj*

**aristo** /ə'ristoh/ *n, chiefly Br informal* ARISTOCRAT 1

**aristocracy** /,ari'stokrəsi/ *n* 1 government by the best individuals or by a small privileged usu hereditary noble class 2a a government in which power is vested in a small privileged usu hereditary noble class **b** a state with such a government 3 *taking sing or pl vb* 3a a governing body or upper class, usu made up of a hereditary nobility **b** all those people believed to be superior for reasons of wealth, birth, intellect, etc [MF & LL; MF *aristocratie*, fr LL *aristocratia*, fr Gk *aristokratia*, fr *aristos* best + *-kratia* -cracy]

**aristocrat** /'aristəkrat; *also* ə'ri- USE *the last pron is disliked by some speakers*/ *n* 1 a member of an aristocracy; *esp* a noble 2a a person who has the bearing and viewpoint typical of the aristocracy **b** a person who favours an aristocratic form of government

**aristocratic** /,aristə'kratik; *also* ə,ri-/ *adj* 1 belonging to, having the qualities of, or favouring aristocracy ⟨*an ∼ government*⟩ 2a socially exclusive ⟨*an ∼ neighbourhood*⟩ **b** snobbish [MF *aristocratique*, fr ML *aristocraticus*, fr Gk *aristokratikos*, fr *aristos* + *-kratikos* -cratic] – **aristocratically** *adv*

**Aristotelian, Aristotelean** /,aristə'teelyən, -stoh-/ *adj* of Aristotle, his doctrines, or his principles of logic [*Aristotle* † 322 BC Gk philosopher] – **Aristotelian** *n*, **Aristotelianism** *n*

**arithmetic** /ə'rithmətik/ *n* **1a** a branch of mathematics that deals with the operations of addition, multiplication, subtraction, and division **b** skill in using numbers 2 calculation using numbers [ME *arsmetrik*, fr OF *arismetique*, fr L *arithmetica*, fr Gk *arithmētikē*, fr fem of *arithmētikos* arithmetical, fr *arithmein* to count, fr *arithmos* number; akin to Gk *arariskein* to fit] – **arithmetic, arithmetical** *adj*, **arithmetically** *adv*, **arithmetician** *n*

**arithmetic mean** /,arith'metik/ *n* the value found by dividing the sum of a set of terms by the number of terms ⟨*the ∼ of 4, 5, and 9 is 6*⟩

**arithmetic progression** *n* a sequence (eg 3, 5, 7, 9) in which each number differs from the one in front of it by a constant amount

**-arium** /-'eəriəm/ *suffix* (→ *n*), *pl* **-ariums, -aria** /-'eəriə/ thing or place relating to or connected with ⟨*planet*arium⟩ ⟨*aquarium*⟩ [L, fr neut of *-arius* -ary]

**ark** /ahk/ *n* 1 a boat or ship; *esp* (one like) the one built by Noah to preserve himself, his family, and representative animals, birds, etc from the biblical Flood 2a **Ark, Ark of the Covenant** the sacred chest representing to the Hebrews the presence of God among them and containing the laws of their religion **b** a repository (eg a chest or cupboard in a synagogue) for the scrolls containing the body of Jewish tradition and sacred writings (the TORAH) [fr OE *arc*; akin to OHG *arahha* ark; both fr a prehistoric Gmc word borrowed fr L *arca* chest; akin to L *arcēre* to hold off, defend, Gk *arkein*]

**arkose** /'ahkohs, -ohz/ *n* a coarse-grained sandstone containing a high proportion of FELDSPAR fragments in addition to quartz and derived from the rapid disintegration of granite or GNEISS [Fr] – **arkosic** *adj*

**¹arm** /ahm/ *n* 1 a human upper limb; *esp* the part between the shoulder and the wrist **2** something like or corresponding to an arm: e g **2a** the forelimb of a VERTEBRATE animal (e g a monkey or bear) **b** a limblike part of an INVERTEBRATE animal (e g a starfish or octopus) **c** a slender part of a structure, machine, or instrument projecting from a main part, axis, or fulcrum ⟨*either ~ of a beam balance*⟩ ⟨*the ~ of a rotary clothes line*⟩ **d** a yardarm on the mast of a sailing ship **3** an inlet of water (e g from the sea) **4** might, authority ⟨*the long ~ of the law*⟩ **5** a support (e g on a chair) for the elbow and forearm **6** a sleeve **7** a functional division of a group or activity ⟨*the transport ~ of the air force*⟩ [ME, fr OE *earm;* akin to L *armus* shoulder, Gk *harmos* joint, L *arma* weapons, *ars* skill, Gk *arariskein* to fit] – **armed** *adj,* **armless** *adj,* **armlike** *adj* – **chance one's arm** to attempt something dangerous or difficult; take a risk – **keep somebody at arm's length** to avoid intimacy with somebody – **twist somebody's arm** to bring strong pressure to bear on somebody – see also SHOT **in the arm**

²**arm** *vt* **1** to supply or equip with weapons **2** to provide with something that strengthens or protects **3** to fortify morally **4** to equip or ready for action or operation ⟨*~ a bomb*⟩ ~ *vi* to prepare oneself for struggle or resistance [ME *armen,* fr OF *armer,* fr L *armare,* fr *arma* weapons, tools]

³**arm** *n* **1a** *usu pl* a weapon; *esp* a firearm **b** *taking sing or pl vb* a particular, usu combat, branch (e g the infantry or cavalry) of the armed forces **2** *pl* the heraldic insignia of a group or body (e g a family or government) **3** *pl* **3a** active hostilities; warfare **b** military service; the military profession [ME *armes* (pl) weapons, fr OF, fr L *arma*] – **slope arms** to rest a rifle at an angle on the shoulder in military drill – **up in arms** angrily rebellious and protesting strongly ⟨*the entire community is* up in arms *about the proposed airport*⟩

**armada** /ah'mahdə/ *n* **1** a fleet of warships; *specif, cap* the fleet sent against England by Spain in 1588 **2** a large force of moving things ⟨*an ~ of fishing boats*⟩ [Sp, fr ML *armata* army, fleet, fr L, fem of *armatus,* pp of *armare*]

**armadillo** /ˌahmə'diloh/ *n, pl* **armadillos** any of several burrowing chiefly nocturnal S American EDENTATE mammals (family Dasypodidae) related to the anteaters and sloths, that have the body and head encased in an armour of small bony or horny plates [Sp, fr dim. of *armado* armed one, fr L *armatus*]

**Armageddon** /ˌahmə'ged(ə)n/ *n* **1a** a final and conclusive battle between the forces of good and evil **b** the site or time of this **2** a vast decisive conflict [Gk *Armageddōn, Harmagedōn,* scene of the battle foretold in Rev 16:14–16]

**Armagnac** /'ahmənyak/ *n* a dry brandy produced in the Gers district of France [Fr, fr *Armagnac,* region in SW France]

**armament** /'ahməmənt/ *n* **1** a military or naval force **2a** the whole military strength of a nation **b** the total amount of arms and equipment (e g of a ship, fort, or combat unit) **3** the process of preparing for war [Fr *armement,* fr L *armamenta* (pl) utensils, military or naval equipment, fr *armare* to arm, equip]

**armamentarium** /ˌahməmən'teəriəm/ *n, pl* **armamentaria** /-riə/ the equipment and methods available, esp for medical treatment [L, armoury, fr *armamenta*]

**armature** /'ahməchə/ *n* **1** a plant or animal structure (e g a tooth or thorn) used for attack or esp for protection or defence **2a** a piece of soft iron or steel placed across the poles of a permanent magnet in order to close the magnetic circuit and prevent demagnetization of the magnet – called also KEEPER **b** the part of an electric motor or of a generator that consists of a metal core wound with coils of insulated wire through which, in a motor, a current flows to produce turning and in which, in a generator, a current is induced by the mechanical rotation of the core – called also ROTOR **c** the part of an electromagnetic device that moves or vibrates under the influence of a MAGNETIC FIELD (e g in an electric bell or loudspeaker), or whose movement in a magnetic field causes an electric current to flow (e g in a microphone) **d** a framework on which clay or other plastic material is supported during sculpture, modelling, etc [L *armatura* armour, equipment, fr *armatus*]

**armband** /'ahmˌband/ *n* a band of material, esp cloth, attached over the upper sleeve, usu denoting status (e g authority) or condition (e g mourning)

¹**armchair** /'ahmˌcheə/ *n* a usu comfortable and upholstered chair with armrests

²**armchair** *adj* **1** remote from direct dealing with practical problems ⟨*~ strategists*⟩ **2** sharing in another's experiences as if they were one's own ⟨*an ~ traveller*⟩ **3** seen or experienced at home ⟨*the ~ theatre*⟩

**armed forces** /ahmd/ *n pl* the military, naval, and air forces of a nation

**Armenian** /ah'meenyən/ *n* **1** a member of a people dwelling chiefly in Armenia **2** the Indo-European language of the Armenians [*Armenia* (fr L, fr Gk), former kingdom in W Asia, now divided between USSR, Turkey, & Iran] – **Armenian** *adj*

**armful** /'ahmf(ə)l/ *n, pl* **armfuls, armsful** as much as the arm can hold

**armhole** /'ahmˌhohl/ *n* an opening for the arm in a garment

**armiger** /'ahmijə/ *n* **1** a squire for a medieval knight **2** a person entitled to bear heraldic arms [ML, fr L, armour-bearer, fr *armiger* bearing arms, fr *arma* arms + *-ger* -gerous] – **armigeral** *adj*

**armigerous** /ah'mijərəs/ *adj* bearing heraldic arms

**armillary sphere** /'ahmiləri, -'---/ *n* an old astronomical instrument composed of rings that form a hollow globe and represent the positions of the celestial equator, ecliptic, meridian, etc [Fr *sphère armillaire,* fr ML *armilla,* fr L, bracelet, iron ring, fr *armus* arm, shoulder; akin to OE *earm*]

**armistice** /'ahmistis/ *n* a temporary suspension of hostilities by agreement between the opponents, esp to discuss peace [Fr or NL; Fr, fr NL *armistitium,* fr L *arma* + *-stitium* (as in *solstitium* solstice)]

**Armistice Day** *n* **1** *Br* November 11 celebrated in commemoration of the armistice terminating World War I – used before the official adoption of REMEMBRANCE SUNDAY after World War II **2** *NAm* VETERANS DAY – used before the official adoption of *Veterans Day* in 1954 [fr the armistice terminating World War I on November 11, 1918]

**armlet** /'ahmlit/ *n* **1** a band (e g of cloth or metal) worn round the upper arm **2** a small arm (e g of the sea)

**armoire** /ah'mwah, -'-/ *n* a usu large cupboard or wardrobe [MF, fr OF *armaire,* fr L *armarium,* fr *arma*]

**armorial** /ah'mawriəl/ *adj* of or bearing heraldic arms [*armory* (heraldry), fr MF *armoierie,* fr OF, fr *armoier* to blazon, fr *armes* arms] – **armorially** *adv*

**Armorican** /ah'morikən, -'maw-/, **Armoric** /ah'morik, -'maw-/ *n* a native or inhabitant of Armorica; *esp* a Breton [L *Armoricae* (pl) Armorica, coastal region of Gaul, of Gaulish origin] – **Armorican, Armoric** *adj*

¹**armour,** *NAm chiefly* **armor** /'ahmə/ *n* **1a** defensive covering for the body; *esp* a covering (e g of metal) worn in combat **b** a usu metallic protective covering (e g for a ship, tank, or aircraft) **2** a protective covering (e g a diver's suit, the covering of a plant or animal, or a sheathing for wire or cable) **3** *taking sing or pl vb* armoured forces and vehicles (e g tanks) [ME *armure,* fr OF, fr L *armatura* – more at ARMATURE] – **armourless** *adj*

²**armour** *vt* to provide or equip with armour

**armour-'clad** *adj* sheathed in or protected by armour

**armoured** /'ahməd/ *adj* **1** protected by armour plate or armour **2** consisting of or equipped with armoured vehicles ⟨*an ~ division*⟩

**armourer** /'ahmərə/ *n* **1** somebody who makes or looks after armour or arms **2** somebody who repairs, assembles, and tests firearms

**armour plate** *n* a defensive covering of hard metal plates for combat vehicles and vessels

**armoury** /'ahməri/ *n* **1a** a collection or array of arms **b** a place where arms and military equipment are manufactured or stored **2** a collection of available resources

**armpit** /'ahmˌpit/ *n* the hollow beneath the junction of the arm and shoulder – see also UP **to one's armpits**

**armrest** /'ahmˌrest/ *n* a support for the arm

'**arm-ˌtwisting** *n* the use of direct personal pressure in order to achieve a desired end

**arm wrestling** *n* a contest in which two opponents sit face to face gripping each other's usu right hands and setting corresponding elbows on a surface (e g a tabletop) in an attempt to force each other's arm down

**army** /'ahmi/ *n taking sing or pl vb* **1a** a large organized force for war on land **b** a military unit capable of independent action and consisting usu of two corps **c** *often cap* the complete military organization of a nation for land warfare **2** a great multitude ⟨*an ~ of bicycles*⟩ **3** a body of people organized to advance a cause ⟨*the Salvation* Army⟩ [ME *armee,* fr MF, fr ML *armata* – more at ARMADA]

**army ant** *n* any of a subfamily (Dorylinae) of ants that travel in huge groups destroying plants and animals in their path

**armyworm** /'ahmiˌwuhm/ *n* the larva of any of several moths (family Noctuidae) esp of the USA and E Africa, that travels in large numbers from field to field destroying crops (e g corn, sugarcane, and cotton)

**arnica** /'ahnikə/ *n* **1** any of several related plants (genus *Arnica*) of the daisy family that typically have bright yellow to orange flower heads **2** the dried flower heads of an arnica (esp *Arnica montana*), that contain an oil used esp in the form of a TINCTURE (solution in alcohol) for treating sprains, bruises, etc; *also* this tincture [NL, genus name]

**'A-,road** *n* a main road of high standard

**aroint** /ə'roynt/ *vb imper, archaic* to begone ⟨∼ *thee, witch* – Shak⟩ [origin unknown]

**aroma** /ə'rohmə/ *n* **1a** a distinctive pervasive usu pleasant or savoury smell **b** the fragrance (BOUQUET) of a wine **2** a distinctive quality or atmosphere ⟨*an* ∼ *of mystery hung over the place*⟩ **synonyms** see ²SMELL [ME *aromat* spice, fr OF, fr L *aromat-, aroma*, fr Gk *arōmat-, arōma*]

**aromatherapy** /ə'rohmə,therəpi/ *n* treatment that combines the use of natural oils with massage to reduce tension

**¹aromatic** /,arə'matik/ *adj* **1** of or having an aroma: **1a** fragrant **b** having a strong esp pungent or spicy smell **2** of or being an organic chemical compound containing a BENZENE RING in its molecular structure, or a ring of atoms that has properties similar to those of a benzene ring – compare ALICYCLIC, ALIPHATIC – **aromatically** *adv*, **aromaticness** *n*, **aromaticity** *n*

**²aromatic** *n* **1** an aromatic plant, drug, medicine, etc **2** an aromatic chemical compound containing mainly carbon and hydrogen atoms

**aromat·ize, -ise** /ə'rohmətiez/ *vt* **1** to make aromatic; flavour ⟨∼ *the casserole with spices*⟩ **2** to convert into one or more aromatic chemical compounds – **aromatization** *n*

**arose** /ə'rohz/ *past of* ARISE

**¹around** /ə'rownd/ *adv, chiefly NAm* **1** round **2** ABOUT (except 3b) [ME, fr ¹*a-* + *round*, n]

**²around** *prep, chiefly NAm* **1** round **2** ABOUT **5** ⟨*the parentheses* ∼ *the asterisks* – Journal of Linguistics⟩

*usage* In British English the use of **around** for "approximately" ⟨**around** *50 cars*⟩ is still felt by some people to be an Americanism, and such people may prefer to use **about** for this sense. British speakers often prefer to use **round** for the idea of "revolving" ⟨*wheels go* **round**⟩ or of "a circuitous route" ⟨**round** *the corner*⟩, but are willing to use **around** as the Americans do for "surrounding" ⟨*seated* **around** *the table*⟩ ⟨*Country Walks* **Around** *London* – London Transport⟩ or for "here and there" ⟨*travelling* **around**⟩.

**³around** *adj, chiefly NAm* **1** ABOUT 1 ⟨*has been up and* ∼ *for two days*⟩ **2** in existence, evidence, or circulation ⟨*the most intelligent of the artists* ∼ *today* – R M Coates⟩

**arouse** /ə'rowz/ *vt* **1** to awaken from sleep **2** to rouse to action; excite, esp sexually [*a-* (as in *arise*) + *rouse*] – **arousal** *n*

**arpeggio** /ah'pejioh/ *n, pl* **arpeggios 1** production of the notes of a chord in succession and not simultaneously **2** a chord played in arpeggio [It, fr *arpeggiare* to play on the harp, fr *arpa* harp, of Gmc origin; akin to OHG *harpha* harp]

**arpent** /'ahpənt/ *n* any of various old French units of land area; *esp* one used in French sections of Canada and the USA equal to about 3440 square metres (about 0.85 acre) [MF]

**arquebus** /'ahkwibəs/ *n* a heavy but portable 15th-century matchlock gun, usu fired from a support [MF *harquebuse, arquebuse*, deriv of MLG *hakebusse*, fr *haken* hook + *busse* gun] – **arquebusier** *n*

**arrack, arak** /'arak, 'arək/ *n* an Asian alcoholic spirit that is a distillation of the fermented mash of rice and molasses and to which has been added the fermented sap of the coconut palm [Ar '*araq* sweat, juice, liquor]

**arraign** /ə'rayn/ *vt* **1** to call before a court to answer a charge or accusation **2** to accuse of wrong, inadequacy, or imperfection **synonyms** see ACCUSE [ME *arreinen*, fr MF *araisner*, fr OF, fr *a-* (fr L *ad-*) + *raisnier* to speak, fr (assumed) VL *rationare*, fr L *ration-, ratio* reason – more at REASON] – **arraignment** *n*

**arrange** /ə'raynj/ *vt* **1** to put into a proper order or into a correct or suitable sequence, relationship, or adjustment ⟨∼ *flowers in a vase*⟩ ⟨∼ *cards alphabetically*⟩ **2** to make preparations for; plan ⟨∼d *a reception for the visitor*⟩ **3** to bring about an agreement or understanding concerning ⟨∼ *an exchange of war prisoners*⟩ **4a** to adapt (a musical composition) for voices or instruments other than those originally intended **b** to orchestrate ∼ *vi* **1** to bring about an agreement or understanding ⟨∼d *to have a table at the restaurant*⟩ **2** to make

preparations ⟨∼d *for a vacation with his family*⟩ [ME *arangen*, fr MF *arangier*, fr OF, fr *a-* + *rengier* to set in a row, fr *reng* row – more at RANK] – **arranger** *n*

**arrangement** /ə'raynjmənt/ *n* **1a** the act of arranging ⟨*the* ∼ *of the details was quickly accomplished*⟩ **b** the state of being arranged; order ⟨*everything in neat* ∼⟩ **2** something arranged: e g **2a** a preliminary measure; a preparation ⟨*travel* ∼s⟩ **b** an adaptation of a musical composition for voices or instruments other than those for which it was written **c** an informal agreement or settlement, esp on personal, social, or political matters ⟨∼s *under the new regime*⟩ **d** an agreement with a bank that allows one to draw money without notice from a branch other than that at which one has one's account ⟨*have you got an* ∼?⟩ **3** something made by arranging things together ⟨*a floral* ∼⟩

**arrant** /'arənt/ *adj* notoriously without moderation; extreme ⟨*we are* ∼ *knaves, all; believe none of us* – Shak⟩ ⟨∼ *nonsense*⟩ [alter. of *errant*] – **arrantly** *adv*

**arras** /'arəs/ *n, pl* **arras** a wall hanging or screen made of tapestry [ME, fr *Arras*, city in N France]

**¹array** /ə'ray/ *vt* **1** to set or place in order; marshal **2** to dress or decorate, esp in splendid or impressive attire [ME *arrayen*, fr OF *arayer*, fr (assumed) VL *arredare*, fr L *ad-* + a base of Gmc origin; akin to Goth *garaiths* arranged – more at READY] – **arrayer** *n*

**²array** *n* **1a** a regular and often imposing grouping or arrangement; order **b** military order ⟨*forces in* ∼⟩ **c** an orderly listing of people summoned for jury service **2a** clothing, attire **b** rich or beautiful apparel; finery **3** an imposing group; a large number ⟨*faced a whole* ∼ *of problems*⟩ **4** an arrangement of mathematical or statistical data in a specific order; *specif* an arrangement of numbers, symbols or other mathematical elements in rows and columns **5** a set of similar pieces of data in a computer memory, that comprises a single unit of which each member can be acted on by a single instruction in a programming language

**arrearage** /ə'riərij/ *n* **1** the condition of being in arrears **2** something that is in arrears; *esp* something unpaid and overdue

**arrears** /ə'riəz/ *n taking sing or pl vb* **1** the state of being behind in the discharge of obligations ⟨*in* ∼ *with his payments*⟩ **2a** an unfinished duty ⟨∼ *of work that have piled up*⟩ **b** an unpaid and overdue debt ⟨*paying off the* ∼ *of the past several months*⟩ [ME *arrere* behind, backwards, fr MF, fr (assumed) VL *ad retro* backwards, fr L *ad* to + *retro* backwards, behind – more at AT, RETRO-]

**¹arrest** /ə'rest/ *vt* **1a** to bring to a stop ⟨*sickness* ∼ed *his activities*⟩ **b** to check, slow **c** to make inactive or less active; slow or stop the course of growth of (a disease or disease condition) ⟨*an* ∼ed *tumour*⟩ **2** to seize, capture; *specif* to take or keep in custody by authority of law **3** to catch and fix or hold ⟨*to* ∼ *the attention*⟩ [ME *aresten*, fr MF *arester* to rest, arrest, fr (assumed) VL *arrestare*, fr L *ad-* + *restare* to remain, rest] – **arrester, arrestor** *n*, **arrestment** *n*

**²arrest** *n* **1** stopping or being stopped **2** the taking or detaining of somebody in custody by authority of law **3** a device for arresting motion – **under arrest** in legal custody

**arrestable offence** /ə'restəbl/ *n* a serious offence for which anyone can make an arrest without a warrant

**arresting** /ə'resting/ *adj* catching the attention; striking, impressive – **arrestingly** *adv*

**arrhythmia** /ə'ridhmiə/ *n* a usu abnormal alteration in the rhythm of the heartbeat [NL, fr Gk, lack of rhythm, fr *arrhythmos* unrhythmical, fr *a-* + *rhythmos* rhythm]

**arrhythmic** /ə'ridhmik/, **arrhythmical** /-kl/ *adj* **1** lacking rhythm or regularity **2** characterized by arrhythmia ⟨*an* ∼ *heartbeat*⟩ [Gk *arrhythmos*] – **arrhythmically** *adv*

**arrière-ban** /,ariეə 'bonh/ (*Fr* arjɛːr bã) *n* a proclamation of a king, esp of France, calling his vassals to arms; *also, taking sing or pl vb* all the vassals so summoned [Fr, fr OF *arriereban*, alter. (influenced by *arriere* behind) of *herban*, of Gmc origin; akin to OHG *heri* army & *ban* proclamation – more at HARRY, BAN]

**arrière-pensée** /,ariეə 'ponsay, ,--- -'- (*Fr* arjɛːr p�õse) *n* a mental reservation [Fr, fr *arrière* behind + *pensée* thought]

**arris** /'aris/ *n, pl* **arris, arrises** the sharp ridge or prominent angle formed by the meeting of two surfaces, esp in mouldings [prob modif of MF *areste*, lit., fishbone, fr LL *arista* – more at ARÊTE]

**arrival** /ə'rievl/ *n* **1** the act of arriving **2** the attainment of an end or state ⟨~ *at a decision*⟩ **3** a person or thing that has arrived ⟨*welcome the new* ~s⟩

**arrive** /ə'riev/ *vi* **1a** to reach a destination **b** to make an appearance ⟨*all the guests have* ~d⟩; *also, informal* to be born **2** to be near in time; come ⟨*the moment has* ~d⟩ **3** to achieve success [ME *ariven*, fr OF *ariver*, fr (assumed) VL *arripare* to come to shore, fr L *ad-* + *ripa* shore – more at RIVE] – **arriver** *n* **arrive at** to reach by effort or thought ⟨*have* arrived at *a decision*⟩

**arrivederci** /ˌarivə'deəchi/ *interj* – used to express farewell [It, lit., till seeing again]

**arriviste** /ˌaree'veest/ *n* a person who is a new, ambitious, and often unscrupulous arrival [Fr, fr *arriver* to arrive, fr OF *ariver*]

**arroba** /ə'rohbə/ *n* **1** an old Spanish unit of weight equal to about 11.34 kilograms (25 pounds) used in some Spanish-American countries **2** an old Portuguese unit of weight equal to about 14.5 kilograms (32 pounds) used in Brazil [Sp & Pg, fr Ar *ar-rub'*, lit., the quarter]

**arrogance** /'arəgəns/ *n* a feeling of superiority manifested in a haughty overbearing manner or in presumptuous claims *antonyms* meekness, humility

**arrogant** /'arəgənt/ *adj* **1** exaggerating or disposed to exaggerate one's own worth or importance in an overbearing conceited manner ⟨*an* ~ *official*⟩ **2** proceeding from or characterized by arrogance ⟨~ *manners*⟩ *synonyms* see PROUD [ME, fr L *arrogant-, arrogans*, prp of *arrogare*] – **arrogantly** *adv*

**arrogate** /'arəgayt/ *vt* **1a** to claim or seize without justification **b** to make undue claims to having ⟨*the unwarranted importance* ~d *to themselves by public men*⟩ **2** to claim on behalf of another without just reason △ abrogate [L *arrogatus*, pp of *arrogare*, fr *ad-* + *rogare* to ask – more at RIGHT] – **arrogation** *n*

**arrondissement** /ˌarən'deesmənt (*Fr* arɔ̃dismɑ̃)/ *n* **1** a parliamentary division of a French DEPARTMENT (territorial and administrative region) **2** an administrative district of some large French cities, esp Paris [Fr, lit., rounding, fr *arrondiss-*, stem of *arrondir* to make round]

¹**arrow** /'aroh/ *n* **1** a projectile shot from a bow and usu having a slender shaft, a pointed head, and stabilizing feathers at the tail end **2** something shaped like an arrow; *esp* a mark (eg on a map or signboard) to indicate direction [ME *arwe*, fr OE; akin to Goth *arhwazna* arrow, L *arcus* bow, arch, arc]

²**arrow** *vt* to indicate with an arrow ⟨*the location is* ~ed *on the map*⟩

**arrowhead** /'aroh,hed/ *n* **1** the usu pointed or wedge-shaped striking end of an arrow **2** something shaped like an arrowhead **3** any of several freshwater plants (genus *Sagittaria*, esp *Sagittaria sagittifolia*) with leaves shaped like arrowheads

**arrowroot** /'aroh,rooht/ *n* **1a** any of a genus (*Maranta* of the family Marantaceae, the arrowroot family) of tropical American plants with fleshy roots adapted for food storage; *esp* one (*Maranta arundinacea*) whose roots yield a nutritious starch **b** any of several tropical plants that yield starch **2** the starch yielded by an arrowroot and used esp as a thickening agent in cooking [fr its use by American Indians to heal wounds made by poisoned arrows]

**arrowworm** /'aroh,wuhm/ *n* CHAETOGNATH (small wormlike marine animal)

**arroyo** /ə'roh·yoh, ə'royoh/ *n, pl* **arroyos** *NAm* a gully or channel carved by running water; *also* a brook or stream in a very dry region [Sp]

**arse** /ahs/ *n, vulg* **1a** the buttocks **b arse, arsehole** the anus **2 arse, arsehole** a foolish or stupid person [ME *ars, ers*, fr OE *ærs, ears*; akin to OHG & ON *ars* buttocks, Gk *orrhos*, OIr *err* tail]

'**arse-,licker** *n, vulg* a toady, creep – **arse-licking** *n or adj*

**arsenal** /'ahsənl, 'ahsənəl/ *n* **1a** an establishment for the manufacture or storage of arms and military equipment **b** a collection of weapons **2** a store, repertory ⟨*the team's* ~ *of experienced players*⟩ [It *arsenale*, modif of Ar *dār ṣinā'ah* house of manufacture]

**arsenate** /'ahsənayt, -ət/ *n* any of various chemical compounds (SALTS or ESTERS) formed by combination between an arsenic acid and a metal atom, an alcohol, or another chemical group

¹**arsenic** /'ahsnik/ *n* **1** a solid poisonous chemical element that occurs in various forms of which the commonest form is metallic steel-grey, crystalline, and brittle **2** ARSENIC TRIOXIDE – not used technically in chemistry [ME, fr MF & L; MF, fr L *arsenicum*, fr Gk *arsenikon, arrhenikon* yellow orpiment, fr Syr

*zarnīg*, of Iranian origin; akin to Avestan *zaranya* gold, Skt *hari* yellowish – more at YELLOW]

²**arsenic** /ah'senik; *for names of compounds beginning with* arsenic *the usu pron is* /'ahsnik/ *except for* arsenic acid *which is usu pronounced* /ah'senik// *adj* of or containing arsenic, esp with a VALENCY of five

**arsenical** /ah'senikl/ *adj* of or containing arsenic ⟨*an* ~ *drug*⟩ – **arsenical** *n*

**arsenical nickel** *n* NICCOLITE (copper-coloured nickel mineral)

**arsenic trioxide** *n* an extremely poisonous chemical compound, $As_2O_3$, that is a TRIOXIDE of arsenic used, esp formerly, in insecticides and weed killers

**arsenic trisulphide** *n* a yellow chemical compound, $As_2S_3$, that occurs naturally as the mineral ORPIMENT or can be prepared artificially and used in manufacturing (e g of glass and lino) and as a pigment

**arsenide** /'ahsənied/ *n* a chemical compound of arsenic with one other chemical element ⟨*silver* ~⟩

**arsenious** /ah'seenyəs/ *adj* of or containing arsenic, esp with a VALENCY of three

**arsenite** /'ahsəniet/ *n* any of various chemical compounds (SALTS or ESTERS) formed by combination between an arsenious acid and a metal atom, an alcohol, or another chemical group

**arsenopyrite** /ˌahsənoh'pie·əriet, ah,senoh-/ *n* a metallic mineral, FeAsS, that consists of a sulphide of iron and arsenic and is a principal ore of arsenic

**arshin** /ah'sheen/ *n* a Russian unit of length equal to 28 inches (about 0.71 metre) [Russ, of Turkic origin]

**arsine** /'ahseen/ *n* an unstable colourless inflammable extremely poisonous gas, $AsH_3$, with a smell like garlic [ISV, fr *arsenic*]

**arsis** /'ahsis/ *n, pl* **arses** /'ahsees/ **1** a stressed syllable in a metrical foot of poetic verse **2** the unaccented part of a musical bar – compare THESIS [LL & Gk; LL, raising of the voice, accented part of foot, fr Gk, upbeat, unaccented part of foot, lit., act of lifting, fr *aeirein, airein* to lift]

**arson** /'ahsən/ *n* the criminal act of setting fire to property in order to cause destruction [obs Fr, fr OF, fr *ars*, pp of *ardre* to burn, fr L *ardēre* – more at ARDOUR] – **arsonist** *n*

**arsphenamine** /ˌahs'fenəmeen, ,---'-, -fen'amin/ *n* a poisonous light yellow arsenic-containing chemical compound, $C_{12}Cl_2H_{14}As_2N_2O_2$, formerly used as a drug in the treatment of syphilis and related diseases caused by SPIROCHAETE bacteria [ISV *arsenic* + *phen-* + *amine*]

**arsy-versy** /ˌahsi 'vuhsi/ *adv or adj, chiefly informal* topsy-turvy [*arse* + L *versus*, pp of *vertere* to turn]

¹**art** /aht/ *archaic pres 2 sing of* BE [ME, fr OE *eart*; akin to ON *est, ert* (thou) art, OE *is* is]

²**art** *n* **1** skill acquired by experience, study, or observation ⟨*the* ~ *of making friends*⟩ ⟨*the* ~ *of organ building*⟩ **2** *pl* **2a** any of the academic subjects that are not considered to be a science (e g literature, languages, or philosophy) **b** LIBERAL ARTS **3a** the conscious use of skill and creative imagination, esp in the production of aesthetic objects; *also* works so produced **b(1)** FINE ARTS **b(2)** any of the fine arts **b(3)** any of the graphic arts **4** the quality or state of being artful **5** artwork in printed matter **6** *archaic* learning, scholarship **7** *archaic* a skilful plan [ME, fr OF, fr L *art-, ars* – more at ARM]

³**art** *adj* **1** composed, designed, or created with conscious artistry ⟨*an* ~ *song*⟩ **2** designed for decorative purposes ⟨~ *pottery*⟩

**-art** – see -ARD

**art deco** /ˌah(t) 'dekoh/ *n, often cap A&D* a decorative style of the 1920s and 1930s characterized esp by bold outlines, streamlined and rectilinear forms, and the use of new materials (e g plastic) [Fr *Art Déco*, fr *Exposition Internationale des Arts Décoratifs*, an exhibition of decorative arts held in Paris in 1925]

**artefact, artifact** /'ahtifakt/ *n* **1a** a usu simple object (e g a tool, weapon, or ornament) produced by human workmanship **b** a product of civilization ⟨*an* ~ *of the jet age*⟩ **2** a structure, substance, etc that appears in a biological specimen (e g a tissue or cell) as a result of its preparation (e g staining) but that is not naturally present in the living specimen; *broadly* something artificial that is produced or occurs (e g in an experiment) as a result of extraneous influences [L *arte* by skill (abl of *art-, ars* skill) + *factum*, neut of *factus*, pp of *facere* to make, do] – **artefactual** *adj*

**artel** /ah'tel/ *n* a workers' or peasants' cooperative in the USSR [Russ *artel'*, fr It *artieri*, pl of *artiere* artisan, fr *arte* art]

**artemisia** /ˌahtə'miziˑə, -'misiˑə, -'mizh(y)ə/ *n* any of a genus (*Artemisia*) of plants (e g wormwood) of the daisy family with strong-smelling foliage [NL, genus name, fr L, artemisia, fr Gk]

**arteri-** /ahtiəri-/, **arterio-** *comb form* 1 artery ⟨arterio*logy*⟩ ⟨arteri*tis*⟩ 2 arterial and ⟨arterio*venous*⟩ [MF, fr LL, fr Gk *artēri-*, *artērio-*, fr *artēria* artery]

**arterial** /ah'tiəriˑəl/ *adj* **1a** of or affecting an artery **b** of or being the bright red oxygen-rich blood that circulates in the arteries after passing through the lungs or gills **2** of or being a main road – **arterially** *adv*

**arterial·ize**, **-ise** /ah'tiəriˑəliez/ *vt* to transform (oxygen-depleted venous blood) into arterial blood by oxygenation – **arterialization** *n*

**arteriography** /ahˌtiəri'ogrəfi/ *n* X-ray photography of an artery after the injection of a substance that prevents the passage of X rays [ISV] – **arteriographic** *adj*

**arteriole** /ah'tiəriohl/ *n* any of the very small arteries that connect larger arteries with the network of CAPILLARIES (tiny blood vessels connecting arteries and veins) [Fr *artériole* (dim. of *artère* artery, fr L *arteria*) or NL *arteriola*, dim. of L *arteria*] – **arteriolar** *adj*

**arteriosclerosis** /ahˌtiəriohsklə'rohsis/ *n* a condition characterized by abnormal thickening and hardening of the walls of the arteries [NL] – **arteriosclerotic** *adj or n*

**arteritis** /ˌahtə'rietəs/ *n* inflammation of an artery [NL]

**artery** /'ahtəri/ *n* **1** any of the tubular branching vessels that have elastic muscular walls and that, with the exception of the PULMONARY ARTERY, carry blood containing a high proportion of oxygen from the heart to all parts of the body – compare VEIN **2** an esp main channel (e g a river or highway) of transport or communication [ME *arterie*, fr L *arteria*, fr Gk *artēria*; akin to Gk *aortē* aorta]

**artesian well** /ah'teezh(ə)n, -ziˑən/ *n* a well made by boring a hole in the ground at a strategic point where water will be forced to the surface and will require little or no pumping [Fr *artésien*, lit., of Artois, fr OF, fr *Arteis* Artois, region in N France]

**art film** *n* a film produced for predominantly aesthetic rather than commercial purposes

**art form** *n* a recognized form (e g a symphony) or medium (e g sculpture) of artistic expression

**artful** /'ahtf(ə)l/ *adj* **1** adroit in attaining an end, often by deceitful or indirect means; wily, crafty **2** *archaic* performed with or showing art or skill ⟨an ~ *performance on the violin*⟩ synonyms see SLY *antonym* artless – **artfully** *adv*, **artfulness** *n*

**art history** *n* the study of the history of art – **art historian** *n*, **art-historical** *adj*

**art house** *n* a cinema that shows art films

**arthr-** /ahthr-/, **arthro-** *comb form* joint ⟨arth*ritis*⟩ ⟨arthro*pod*⟩ [L, fr Gk, fr *arthron;* akin to Gk *arariskein* to fit – more at ARM]

**arthralgia** /ah'thraljə/ *n* pain in a joint that originates in the nerves supplying the joint [NL] – **arthralgic** *adj*

**arthritic** /ah'thritik/ *adj* of or affected with arthritis – **arthritic** *n*, **arthritically** *adv*

**arthritis** /ah'thrietəs/ *n, pl* **arthritides** /ah'thrietiˌdeez/ usu painful inflammation of one or more joints causing stiffness in the affected areas [L, fr Gk, fr *arthron*]

**arthrodesis** /ah'throdisis/ *n, pl* **arthrodeses** /-seez/ the surgical immobilization of a joint so that the bones grow solidly together [NL, fr *arthr-* + Gk *desis* binding, fr *dein* to bind]

**arthromere** /'ahthrəmiə/ *n* any of the segments making up the body of an arthropod

**arthropathy** /ah'thropəthi/ *n* a disease or abnormal condition of a joint

**arthropod** /'ahthrəˌpod/ *n* any of a phylum (Arthropoda) of INVERTEBRATE animals including the insects, ARACHNIDS (spiders, scorpions, etc), CRUSTACEANS (crabs, lobsters, shrimps, etc), and MYRIAPODS (centipedes, millipedes, etc), that have a body divided into segments, jointed limbs, and a hard horny outer covering (EXOSKELETON) that is usu made of CHITIN and is periodically shed to allow for growth [NL *Arthropoda*, group name, fr *arthr-* + Gk *pod-*, *pous* foot – more at FOOT]

**arthrosis** /ah'throhsis/ *n, pl* **arthroses** /-seez/ a joint between bones or a line of juncture between two fused bones;

ARTICULATION 2a(1) [NL, fr Gk *arthrōsis* jointing, articulation, fr *arthroun* to articulate, fr *arthron*]

**arthrospore** /'ahthrəˌspaw/ *n* **1** a thick-walled RESTING (not dividing to produce new cells) spore formed by some BLUE-GREEN ALGAE (e g of the genus *Nostoc*) **2** OIDIUM 1b (type of spore formed by various fungi) – **arthrosporic, arthrosporous** *adj*

**Arthur** /'ahthə/ *n* a legendary king of Britain whose story is based on traditions of a military leader who led a Celtic resistance against the invading Saxons in the sixth century AD

**Arthurian** /ah'th(y)ooəriən/ *adj* of the legend of King Arthur and his royal court

**artic** /ah'tik/ *n*, *Br informal* an articulated lorry

**artichoke** /'ahtiˌchohk/ *n* **1a** a tall plant (*Cynara scolymus*) of the daisy family that resembles a thistle **b** the partly edible flower head of the artichoke used as a vegetable; GLOBE ARTICHOKE **2** JERUSALEM ARTICHOKE [It dial. *articiocco*, fr Ar *al-khurshūf* the artichoke]

**¹article** /'ahtikl/ *n* **1a(1)** a separate clause, item, provision, or point in a document **a(2)** a stipulation in a document (e g a contract or a creed) ⟨~s *of faith*⟩ **a(3)** *pl* a written agreement specifying conditions of apprenticeship **b** a nonfictional prose composition usu forming an independent part of a publication (e g a magazine) **2** an item of business; a matter **3** any of a small set of words or affixes (e g *a*, *an*, and *the*) used with nouns to specify definiteness or indefiniteness **4** a member of a class of things; *esp* an item of merchandise ⟨~s *of value*⟩ **5** a thing of a particular and distinctive kind ⟨*the genuine* ~⟩ **6** *informal* an object, entity, or person not clearly designated ⟨*that son of mine's a useless* ~⟩ [ME, fr OF, fr L *articulus* joint, division, dim. of *artus* joint; akin to Gk *arariskein* to fit – more at ARM]

**²article** *vt* to bind by articles (e g of apprenticeship)

**articles of association** *n pl* the regulations governing the internal management of a company that are registered when the company is formed and are binding on each company member

**articulable** /ah'tikyoolәbl/ *adj* capable of being articulated

**articular** /ah'tikyoolə/ *adj* of, affecting, or associated with a joint (~ *cartilage*) [ME *articuler*, fr L *articularis*, fr *articulus*]

**¹articulate** /ah'tikyoolət/ *adj* **1a** divided into syllables or words which are meaningfully arranged; intelligible **b** having the power of speech **c** expressing oneself readily, clearly, or effectively; *also* expressed in this manner ⟨*the primitive poet . . . was used by the community to make its spiritual needs* ~ – C Day Lewis⟩ **2** having joints or segments united by joints; jointed ⟨*insects are* ~ *animals*⟩ [NL *articulatus*, fr L *articulus*] – **articulately** *adv*, **articulateness** *n*, **articulacy** *n*

**²articulate** /ah'tikyoolayt/ *vt* **1a** to utter distinctly ⟨articulating *each note in the musical phrase*⟩ **b** to give clear and effective utterance to ⟨~ *one's grievances*⟩ **2** to unite by means of a joint ~ *vi* **1** to utter articulate sounds **2** to be united or connected (as if) by a joint ⟨*the thigh* ~s *with the pelvic girdle*⟩ [L *articulatus*, pp of *articulare*, fr *articulus*] – **articulator** *n*, **articulative** *adj*, **articulatory** *adj*

**articulated** /ah'tikyoolaytid/ *adj*, *chiefly Br* having two parts flexibly connected and intended to operate as a unit ⟨*an* ~ *lorry*⟩

**articulation** /ahˌtikyoo'laysh(ə)n, ---'--/ *n* **1a** the action or manner of jointing or interrelating ⟨*a sketch showing the* ~ *of the limbs*⟩ **b** the state of being jointed or interrelated **2a(1)** a joint or juncture between bones or cartilages in the skeleton of a VERTEBRATE animal **a(2)** a movable joint between rigid parts of an INVERTEBRATE animal **b(1)** a joint (e g the base of a leafstalk) between two separable plant parts **b(2)** a joint on a plant stem, or the stem between two such joints **3a** the act of giving utterance or expression ⟨*a minority's* ~ *of cultural identity*⟩ **b** the act or manner of articulating sounds **c** an articulated utterance or sound; *specif* a consonant **4** OCCLUSION 1b (the meeting of the opposing surfaces of the upper and lower front teeth)

**artifact** /'ahtifakt/ *n* an artefact

**artifice** /'ahtifis/ *n* **1a** an artful device, expedient, or stratagem; a trick **b** false or insincere behaviour ⟨*social* ~⟩ **2** clever or artful skill; ingenuity ⟨*not a show of* ~ *. . . but a genuine creative effort* – H Hervey⟩ [MF, fr L *artificium*, fr *artific-*, *artifex* artificer, fr L *art-*, *ars* + *facere* to make, do – more at ARM, DO]

**artificer** /ah'tifisə, 'ahtifisə/ *n* **1** a skilled or artistic worker or craftsman **2** one who makes or contrives; a deviser ⟨*had been the* ~ *of his own fortunes* – TLS⟩ **3** a military or naval mechanic

**artificial** /ˌahti'fish(ə)l/ *adj* 1 made by human skill and labour, often to a natural model; man-made ⟨*an* ~ *limb*⟩ ⟨~ *diamonds*⟩ 2a feigned, assumed ⟨*in an* ~ *manner*⟩ b lacking in natural quality; AFFECTED ⟨*the* ~ *smile of one who is not really enjoying himself*⟩ c imitation, sham ⟨~ *colouring*⟩ 3 *biology* based on features not necessarily indicative of natural relationships – used esp in the classification of living things; compare NATURAL 2b 4 *obs* artful, cunning – **artificially** *adv*, **artificialness** *n*, **artificiality** *n*

   *synonyms* With man-made substances and things, **artificial** tends to be used of something which is of quite different origin from what it imitates ⟨*artificial flowers cut from paper*⟩. **Synthetic,** on the other hand, usually signifies "highly-processed", but tends to modify nouns which are really what they claim to be ⟨*synthetic fibres*⟩. *antonym* natural

**artificial horizon** *n* 1 *astronomy* HORIZON 1c (level mirror used for observing altitudes of stars, planets, etc) 2 an aeronautical instrument based on a gyroscope and designed to indicate an aircraft's position in relation to the horizontal plane

**artificial insemination** *n* the introduction of semen into the female reproductive tract by other than natural means

**artificiality** /ˌahtiˌfishi'aləti/ *n* 1 the quality or state of being artificial 2 something artificial

**artificial respiration** *n* the rhythmic forcing of air into and out of the lungs of a person whose breathing has stopped

**artificial silk** *n* a man-made fibre originally designed to imitate silk; *esp* rayon – not used technically

**artillerist** /ah'tilərist/ *n* a gunner, artilleryman

**artillery** /ah'tiləri/ *n* 1 weapons (e g bows, slings, and catapults) for discharging missiles 2 large-calibre mounted firearms (e g guns, howitzers, and missiles) 3 *taking sing or pl vb* a branch of an army armed with artillery [ME *artillerie*, fr MF, fr OF, fr *artillier* to equip, arm, prob alter. of *atillier, atirier* to equip – more at ATTIRE]

**artilleryman** /ah'tilərimən/ *n* a soldier who is assigned to the artillery

**artiodactyl** /ˌahtioh'daktil/ *n* any of an order (Artiodactyla) of hoofed mammals (e g the pig, camel, and ox) with an even number of functional toes on each foot [deriv of Gk *artios* fitting, even-numbered + *daktylos* finger, toe] – **artiodactyl, artiodactylous** *adj*

**artisan** /'ahti,zan, ,--'-, 'ahtiz(ə)n/ *n* 1 a manual worker (e g a carpenter, plumber, or tailor) skilled in a particular trade or craft 2 a member of the lower class in society; *specif* an industrial worker [MF, fr OIt *artigiano*, fr *arte* art, fr L *art, ars*]

**artist** /'ahtist/ *n* 1a one who professes and practises an imaginative art b a person skilled in one of the fine arts 2 a skilled performer; *specif* an artiste 3 *informal* one who is proficient in a specified and usu dubious activity; an expert ⟨*rip-off* ~⟩ 4 *Austr & NAm informal* a fellow or character, esp of a specified sort 5a *archaic* an artisan b *obs* one skilled or versed in learned arts; *esp* a physician

**artiste** /ah'teest/ *n* a skilled public performer; *specif* a musical or theatrical entertainer [Fr, artist]

**artistic** /ah'tistik/ *adj* 1 (characteristic) of art or artists ⟨~ *subjects*⟩ 2 showing imaginative skill in arrangement or execution ⟨~ *photography*⟩ – **artistically** *adv*

   *synonyms* **Artistic, aesthetic, arty, arty-crafty: aesthetic** concerns the appreciation of beauty, whether natural or man-made, and regardless of whether it is useful or morally desirable. **Artistic** refers to the (gift of) making something beautiful, particularly in a minor way, or describes what has been made attractive ⟨*an artistic flower arrangement• window display*⟩. **Aesthetic** suggests beauty of a higher order; it speaks to the mind and soul, as well as to the senses. Something **arty** is rather too obviously **artistic,** while **arty-crafty** suggests the self-conscious rusticity of some practitioners of arts and crafts such as pottery and weaving. *antonyms* inartistic, unattractive

**artistry** /'ahtistri/ *n* 1 artistic quality of workmanship ⟨*the* ~ *of his novel*⟩ 2 artistic ability ⟨*the* ~ *of the violinist*⟩

**artless** /'ahtlis/ *adj* 1 lacking art, knowledge, or skill; uncultured 2a made without skill; crude b free from artificiality; natural ⟨~ *grace*⟩ 3 free from deceit, guile, or craftiness; sincerely simple *synonyms* see ¹NATURAL *antonym* artful – **artlessly** *adv*, **artlessness** *n*

**art nouveau** /ˌah(t) nooh'voh/ *n, often cap A&N* a decorative style of late 19th-century origin, characterized esp by curved lines and plant motifs [Fr, lit., new art]

**art paper** *n, Br* paper coated with china clay to create a smooth finish

**arts and crafts** *adj, often cap A&C* of or being a late 19th-century design movement that stressed craftsmanship and the use of everyday themes for decorative work (e g in bookbinding, weaving, and needlework)

**artsy-craftsy** /ˌahtsi 'krahftsi/ *adj, chiefly NAm informal* arty-crafty

**artwork** /'aht,wuhk/ *n* 1a an artistic creation ⟨*an 8-foot metal* ~⟩ b paintings, drawings, etc collectively ⟨~ *being sold at a street market*⟩ 2 illustrations, graphs, etc in printed material

**arty** /'ahti/ *adj* showily or pretentiously artistic ⟨~ *lighting and photography*⟩ *synonyms* see ARTISTIC *antonym* simple – **artily** *adv*, **artiness** *n*

**arty-crafty** /ˌahti 'krahfti/ *adj, informal* arty; *esp* affectedly simple or rustic in style ⟨~ *furniture*⟩ [fr the phrase *arts and crafts*] *synonyms* see ARTISTIC

**arum** /'eərəm, 'arəm/ *n* 1 any of a genus (*Arum* of the family Araceae, the arum family) of European and Asian plants (e g cuckoopint) with a spike (SPADIX) of tiny densely packed flowers enclosed by a large fleshy leaflike part (SPATHE) 2 **arum lily** *also* **arum** CALLA a [NL, genus name, fr L, arum, fr Gk *aron*]

**arvo** /'ahvoh/ *n, Austr & NZ informal* the afternoon ⟨*see him at the Saturday* ~ *game with the boys* – Mark Butler⟩ [by shortening & alter.]

**¹-ary** /-(ə)ri, -eri/ *suffix* (→ *n*) 1 thing belonging to or connected with ⟨*ovary*⟩; *esp* place of keeping for ⟨*library*⟩ ⟨*aviary*⟩ 2 one belonging to, connected with, or engaged in ⟨*functionary*⟩ ⟨*missionary*⟩ [ME *-arie*, fr OF & L; OF *-aire, -arie*, fr L *-arius, -aria, -arium*, fr *-arius*, adj suffix]

**²-ary** *suffix* (→ *adj*) of or connected with ⟨*budgetary*⟩ ⟨*military*⟩ [ME *-arie*, fr MF & L; MF *-aire*, fr L *-arius*]

**¹Aryan** /'eəri-ən, 'ahri-ən/ *adj* 1 *of language* Indo-European 2 of speakers of Indo-European languages 3a of a supposed ethnic type represented by early speakers of Indo-European languages b Nordic [Skt *ārya* noble, belonging to the people speaking an Indo-European dialect who migrated into N India]

**²Aryan** *n* 1 a member of the Indo-European-speaking people that occupied the Iranian plateau or entered India and conquered and merged with the earlier non-Indo-European inhabitants in prehistoric times 2 a member of a people speaking an Indo-European language 3 a member of a non-Jewish race that were of the Nordic type and in Nazi ideology were held to be a superior people

**aryl** /'aril/ *adj or n* (of, being, or containing) a chemical group (e g phenyl) derived from an AROMATIC compound (e g benzene) containing only carbon and hydrogen by the removal of one hydrogen atom [ISV *aromatic* + *-yl*]

**arytenoid** /ˌari'teenoyd, ə'ritənoyd/ *adj* 1 of or being either of a pair of small cartilages in the larynx to which the vocal cords are attached 2 of or being either of a pair of small muscles or an unpaired muscle of the larynx [NL *arytaenoides*, fr Gk *arytainoeidēs*, lit., ladle-shaped, fr *arytaina* ladle, cup, funnel, fr *aryein* to draw (water)] – **arytenoid** *n*

**¹as** /əz; *strong* az/ *adv* 1 to the same degree or amount; equally ⟨~ *deaf as a post*⟩ ⟨*I thought* ~ *much*⟩ 2 FOR EXAMPLE ⟨*wore gloves for dirty work,* ~ *when gardening*⟩ 3 when considered in a specified form or relation – usu used before a preposition or a participle ⟨*my opinion* ~ *distinguished from his*⟩ [ME, fr OE *eallswā* likewise, just as – more at ALSO] – **as against** in esp striking contrast to – **as for** concerning; IN REGARD TO – used esp in making a contrast ⟨as for *the others, they'll arrive later*⟩ – **as from** not earlier or later than ⟨*takes effect* as from *July 1*⟩ – **as of** *chiefly NAm* AS FROM ⟨*takes effect* as of *July 1*⟩ – **as to** 1a with regard or reference to; about – used esp with questions and speculations ⟨*at a loss* as to *how to explain the mistake*⟩ b AS FOR 2 ACCORDING TO; by ⟨*graded* as to *size and colour*⟩

**²as** *conj* 1a to the same degree that ⟨*deaf* ~ *a post*⟩ – usu used together with *as* or *so* to introduce a comparison ⟨*as long ago* ~ *1930*⟩ or a result ⟨*so clearly guilty* ~ *to leave no doubt*⟩ b – used after *same* or *such* to introduce an example or comparison ⟨*tears such* ~ *angels weep* – John Milton⟩ ⟨*in the same building* ~ *my brother*⟩ c – used after *so* to introduce the idea of purpose ⟨*he hid so* ~ *not to get caught*⟩ 2 in the way that ⟨*don't do* ~ *I do, do* ~ *I say!*⟩ ⟨*2 is to 4* ~ *8 is to 16*⟩ – used before *so* to introduce a parallel ⟨~ *the French like their wine, so the British like their beer*⟩ 3 in accordance with how or what ⟨*quite good* ~ *boys go*⟩ ⟨*late,* ~ *usual*⟩ ⟨~ *he lived, so he died*⟩ ⟨~ *you know, he writes plays*⟩ 4 while, when ⟨*spilt the milk* ~ *she* *got up*⟩ **5** regardless of the fact that; though ⟨*naked ~ I was, I rushed out*⟩ **6** for the reason that; seeing ⟨*~ it's raining, let's stay indoors*⟩ **7** *archaic* AS IF ⟨*looks ~ he had seen a ghost* – S T Coleridge⟩ – **as far as** INSOFAR AS – **as if 1** as it would be if ⟨*it was as if he had lost his best friend*⟩ **2** as one would do if ⟨*shook his head* as if *to say no*⟩ **3** that ⟨*it looks* as if *we'll have to walk*⟩ ⟨*it's not* as if *she's poor*⟩ **4** – used in emphatic rejection of a notion ⟨*as if I cared!*⟩ – **as** is *chiefly informal* in the present condition without modification ⟨*bought the clock at an auction* as is⟩ – **as it is** in truth; actually – **as it were** SO TO SPEAK – **as much as even;** SO MUCH AS – **as often as not** at least half the time – **as though** AS IF – **as yet** up to this or that time

³**as** *pron* **1a** a fact that; and this ⟨*is a foreigner, ~ is evident from his accent*⟩ ⟨*unaccustomed ~ I am to public speaking . . .*⟩ **b** which also; and so ⟨*plays football, ~ do his brothers*⟩ **2** *chiefly dial* that, who ⟨*that kind of fruit ~ maids call medlars* – Shak⟩

⁴**as** *prep* **1a** LIKE 2 ⟨*all rose ~ one man*⟩ **b** LIKE 1a ⟨*his face was ~ a mask* – Max Beerbohm⟩ **2** in the capacity, character, role, or state of ⟨*works ~ an editor*⟩ ⟨*they regard her ~ clever*⟩ ⟨*costs £1000 ~ a minimum*⟩ ⟨*~ a father, I must protest*⟩
***usage 1*** Since **as** is a conjunction as well as a preposition, **as** *I/he/she/we/they* are preferable, in formal writing, to **as** *me/him/her/us/them* ⟨*she was as distinguished* **as** *he*⟩. **2** The construction ⟨*he's* **as** *fat or fatter than Jane*⟩ is disapproved of by some people, who prefer ⟨*he's* **as** *fat* **as** *or fatter than Jane*⟩ or ⟨*he's* **as** *fat* **as** *Jane, or fatter*⟩. **3** Some writers on usage have preferred **so . . . as** for negative comparisons ⟨*she's not so pretty* **as** *her sister*⟩, but today **as . . . as** is perfectly legitimate ⟨*she's not* **as** *pretty* **as** *her sister*⟩. **4** One should be careful to avoid ambiguity where **as** can mean "while" or "because". A sentence such as ⟨**as** *Anne was working I bathed the baby*⟩ has two meanings. **5** The use of **as** for *that* is nonstandard ⟨ △ *not* **as** *I know of*⟩. See ⁷LIKE

⁵**as** /as/ *n, pl* **asses 1** LIBRA 2a (Roman unit of weight) **2** a bronze coin of ancient Rome; *also* an equivalent unit of value [L (cf ACE)]

**as-** – see AD-

**asafoetida, assafoetida,** *NAm chiefly* **asafetida** / ˌasə'fetidə/ *n* a GUM RESIN obtained from any of various oriental plants (genus *Ferula*) of the carrot family, that has a strong unpleasant onion-like smell, is used in esp Indian and middle Eastern cookery to flavour curries, pickles, etc, and was formerly used in medicine [ME *asafetida*, fr ML *asafoetida*, fr Per *azā* mastic + L *foetida*, fem of *foetidus* fetid]

**Asarh** /'ahsah, -'-/ *n* – see MONTH table [Hindi *Asāṛh*, fr Skt *Aṣāḍha*]

**asbestos** /ə'spestos, -zb-, -sb-/, *NAm also* **asbestus** /-əs/ *n* any of various minerals (e g an amphibole or serpentine) that readily separate into long thin flexible fibres suitable for use as noncombustible, nonconducting, or chemically resistant materials [ME *albestron* mineral supposed to be inextinguishable when set on fire, fr MF, fr ML *asbeston*, alter. of L *asbestos*, fr Gk, unslaked lime, fr *asbestos* inextinguishable, fr *a-* + *sbennynai* to quench; akin to Lith *gesti* to be extinguished]

**asbestosis** /ˌaspe'stohsis, -zb-, -sb-/ *n, pl* **asbestoses** /-seez/ a diseased condition of the lungs due to the breathing in of asbestos particles [NL]

**asc-, asco-** *comb form* ascomycete ⟨*ascocarp*⟩ ⟨*ascus*⟩ [NL, fr *ascus*]

**ascariasis** /ˌaskə'rie·əsis/ *n, pl* **ascariases** /-seez/ infestation with or disease caused by ascarids [NL]

**ascarid** /'askərid/ *n* any of a family (Ascaridae) of NEMATODE worms (unsegmented round-bodied worms) including the common roundworm (*Ascaris lumbricoides*) that is parasitic in the human intestine [deriv of LL *ascarid-*, *ascaris* intestinal worm, fr Gk *askarid-*, *askaris;* akin to Gk *skairein* to gambol – more at CARDINAL]

**ascaris** /'askəris/ *n, pl* **ascarides** /a'skarideez/ an ascarid [LL]

**ascend** /ə'send/ *vi* **1** to move or slope gradually upwards; rise **2a** to rise from a lower level or degree ⟨*~ to power*⟩ **b** to go back in time or in order of genealogical succession *~ vt* **1** to go or move up **2** to succeed to; begin to occupy – esp in *ascend the throne* **antonym** descend [ME *ascenden*, fr L *ascendere*, fr *ad-* + *scandere* to climb – more at SCAN] – **ascendable, ascendible** *adj*

**ascendance** *also* **ascendence** /ə'send(ə)ns/ *n* ascendancy

**ascendancy** *also* **ascendency** /ə'send(ə)nsi/ *n* a governing or controlling influence; domination

¹**ascendant** *also* **ascendent** /ə'send(ə)nt/ *n* **1** the part of the zodiac that rises above the eastern horizon at any particular moment (e g at one's birth) **2** a state or position of dominant power or importance – esp in *in the ascendant* ⟨*his ideas are now in the ~*⟩ **3** an ancestor [ME *ascendent*, fr ML *ascendent-, ascendens*, fr L, prp of *ascendere*]

²**ascendant** *also* **ascendent** *adj* **1a** moving upwards; rising **b** ASCENDING 2 **2** superior, dominant – **ascendantly** *adv*

**ascender** /ə'sendə/ *n* the part of a noncapital letter (e g b) that rises above the main body of the letter; *also* a letter that has such a part

**ascending** /ə'sending/ *adj* **1a** rising or sloping upwards **b** seen as being in an upward direction **2** *botany* rising upwards, usu from a more or less horizontal base or point of attachment ⟨*an ~ stem*⟩

**ascension** /ə'sensh(ə)n/ *n* **1** the act or process of ascending **2** *often cap* Christ's ascent to Heaven after He had risen from the dead [ME, fr L *ascension-, ascensio,* fr *ascensus,* pp of *ascendere*]

**Ascension Day** *n* the Thursday 40 days after Easter commemorating Christ's ascension

**ascent** /ə'sent/ *n* **1a** the act of rising or travelling upwards **b** a way up; an upward slope or rising gradient **c** the degree of elevation; an inclination, gradient **2** an advance in social status or reputation; progress **3** a going back in time, esp in an order of genealogical succession back to an ancestor [fr *ascend,* by analogy to *descend: descent*]

**ascertain** /ˌasə'tayn/ *vt* **1** to find out or learn with certainty **2** *archaic* to make certain, exact, or precise [ME *acertainen,* fr MF *acertainer,* fr *a-* (fr L *ad-*) + *certain*] – **ascertainable** *adj*, **ascertainment** *n*

**ascetic** /ə'setik/ *also* **ascetical** /-kl/ *adj* **1** practising strict self-denial as a measure of personal, esp spiritual, discipline **2** austere in appearance, manner, or attitude **antonym** sybaritic [Gk *askētikos,* lit., laborious, fr *askētēs* one who exercises, hermit, fr *askein* to work, exercise] – **ascetic** *n,* **ascetically** *adv,* **asceticism** *n*

**asci** /'askie, -si/ *pl of* ASCUS (spore-bearing structure in ascomycete fungi)

**ascidian** /ə'sidi·ən/ *n* any of an order (Ascidiacea of the subphylum Urochordata) of marine INVERTEBRATE animals with a tough outer membrane (e g the sea squirt) the adults of which remain attached to rocks; *broadly* TUNICATE [NL *Ascidia,* genus name, fr Gk *askidion*]

**ascidium** /ə'sidiəm/ *n, pl* **ascidia** /-diə/ a pitcher-shaped or flask-shaped organ or appendage of a plant, which in some plants is used for trapping insects [NL, fr Gk *askidion,* dim. of *askos* wineskin, bladder]

**ASCII** /'aski/ *n, computers* a standard system for representing characters (e g A,B,C,1,2,3...) as binary numbers storable in a computer memory [*American Standard Code for Information Interchange*]

**ascites** /ə'sieteez/ *n, pl* **ascites** accumulation of usu SEROUS fluid (watery substance derived from the blood) in the abdominal cavity [ME *aschytes,* fr LL *ascites,* fr Gk *askitēs,* fr *askos*] – **ascitic** *adj*

**asclepiad** /ə'skleepiad, -əd/ *n* a Greek lyric verse consisting of a SPONDEE, (foot of two long syllables), two or three CHORIAMBS (feet of four syllables having long, short, short, long stresses), and an IAMB (foot of one short syllable followed by one long syllable) [Gk *asklēpiadeios,* fr *asklēpiadeios* of Asclepiades, fr *Asklēpiadēs* Asclepiades, 3rd-c BC Gk poet]

**asco-** – see ASC-

**ascocarp** /'askoˌkahp/ *n* the usu spherical, flask-shaped, or saucer-shaped FRUITING BODY of an ascomycete fungus, that consists of HYPHAE (fungal threads) and is developed as a protective covering for the asci and their enclosed spores – **ascocarpous** *adj*

**ascogenous** /a'skojinəs, ə-/ *adj* producing or giving rise to asci

**ascogonium** /ˌaskə'gohniəm/ *n, pl* **ascogonia** /-niə/ the usu single-celled reproductive part of the ARCHICARP (female sex organ) of an ascomycete fungus, in which fertilization occurs and from which the asci develop [NL, fr *asc-* + Gk *gonos* procreation – more at GON-]

**ascomycete** /ˌaskəmie'seet/ *n* any of the largest class (Ascomycetes) of fungi (e g yeast and truffles) in which the spores are formed inside asci [deriv of Gk *askos* + *mykēt-, mykēs* fungus; akin to L *mucus*] – **ascomycetous** *adj*

**ascorbate** /ə'skawbayt/ *n* a chemical compound (SALT) formed by combination between ASCORBIC ACID and a metal atom or other chemical group

**ascorbic acid** /ə'skawbik/ *n* VITAMIN C [a- + NL *scorbutus* scurvy – more at SCORBUTIC]

**ascospore** /'askə,spaw/ *n* any of the spores produced and contained in an ascus of an ascomycete fungus – **ascosporic, ascosporous** *adj*

**ascot** /'askot, -ət/ *n* a broad cravat that is tied under the chin [*Ascot* Heath, racecourse near Ascot in S England]

**ascribe** /ə'skrieb/ *vt* to refer or attribute (something) *to* a supposed cause, source, or author ⟨~d *her success to hard work*⟩ [ME *ascriven*, fr MF *ascrivre*, fr L *ascribere*, fr *ad-* + *scribere* to write – more at SCRIBE] – **ascribable** *adj*

  **synonyms** Ascribe, attribute, impute, assign, refer, credit, charge all mean "lay something to the account of a person or thing". The first three are often interchangeable, but while **ascribe** is neutral, **attribute** is increasingly used with good implications, and **impute** with bad ones ⟨**attributed** *his longevity to drinking real ale*⟩ but ⟨**imputed** *her dishonesty to bad upbringing*⟩. **Credit** and **charge** deal more emphatically with good and bad qualities respectively. **Assign** and **refer** are used for placing things, rather than people, in categories.

**ascription** /ə'skripsh(ə)n/ *n* the act of ascribing; an attribution [LL *ascription-, ascriptio*, fr L, written addition, fr *ascriptus*, pp of *ascribere*]

**ascus** /'askəs/ *n, pl* **asci** /'askie/ a membranous oval or tubular single-celled structure that develops in an ascomycete fungus from a fertilized ascogonium and in which usu eight spores are produced [NL, fr Gk *askos* wineskin, bladder]

**asdic** /'azdik/ *n* SONAR (echo-sounding device for detecting submerged objects) [*A*nti-*S*ubmarine *D*etection *I*nvestigation *C*ommittee]

**-ase** /-ayz, -ays, -əz/ *suffix* (→ *n*) enzyme ⟨prot*ease*⟩ ⟨amyl*ase*⟩ [Fr, fr di*astase*]

**aseity** /ə'see-əti/ *n, philosophy* the quality or state of being self-derived; *specif* the absolute self-sufficiency of God [ML *aseitas*, fr L *a se* from oneself]

**asepsis** /ay'sepsis, ə-, a-/ *n* **1** the condition of being aseptic **2** the methods of making or keeping something aseptic [NL]

**aseptic** /ay'septik, ə-, a-/ *adj* **1a** preventing infection ⟨~ *techniques*⟩ **b** free or freed from disease-causing microorganisms ⟨*an ~ operating theatre*⟩ **2a** lacking vitality, emotion, or warmth ⟨~ *essays*⟩ **b** detached, objective ⟨*an ~ view of civilization*⟩ [ISV] – **aseptically** *adv*

**asexual** /ay'seksyooəl, -'seksh(ə)l, ə-/ *adj* **1** lacking sex or functional sexual organs **2** produced without sexual action or differentiation **3** without sexuality; *specif* without expression of or reference to sexual interest – **asexually** *adv*

**asexual reproduction** *n* reproduction (eg CELL DIVISION, spore formation, or budding) without the union of individuals or the joining of a female GAMETE (eg an egg cell) with a male gamete (eg a sperm cell)

¹**ash** /ash/ *n* **1** any of a genus (*Fraxinus* of the family Oleaceae, the ash family) of tall trees with PINNATE leaves, grey-green thin furrowed bark, and winged seeds that hang in clusters **2** the tough elastic wood of an ash **3** the letter *æ* used in Old English to represent a low front vowel sound, similar to /a/ as in *fat* [ME *asshe*, fr OE *æsc*; akin to OHG *ask* ash, L *ornus* wild mountain ash; (2) OE *æsc*, name of the corresponding runic letter]

²**ash** *n* **1a** the solid residue left when material is thoroughly burned or is oxidized by chemical means **b** fine particles of mineral matter from a volcano **2** *pl* the remains of something that has been destroyed, esp by fire; the ruins ⟨*a new city built on the ~es of the old*⟩ **3** *pl* the remains of a dead body after cremation or disintegration [ME *asshe*, fr OE *asce*; akin to OHG *asca* ash, L *aridus* dry – more at ARDOUR] – **ashless** *adj*

³**ash** *vt* to convert into ash

**ashamed** /ə'shaymd/ *adj* **1** feeling shame, guilt, or disgrace **2** restrained by anticipation or fear of shame ⟨*was ~ to beg*⟩ [ME, fr OE *āscamod*, pp of *ascamian* to shame, fr *ā-* (perfective prefix) + *scamian* to shame, fr *scamu* shame – more at SHAME] – **ashamedly** *adv*

**Ashanti** /ə'shanti/ *n, pl* **Ashantis**, *esp collectively* **Ashanti 1** a member of a W African people of Ghana **2** the dialect of Akan spoken by the Ashanti people [Ashanti *A¹san³te¹*]

**ash can** *n, NAm* a dustbin

**ashcan school** *n, often cap A&S* a group of early 20th-century American painters characterized by their realistic depiction of city life

¹**ashen** /'ash(ə)n/ *adj* of or made from the wood of the ash tree

²**ashen** *adj* **1** consisting of or resembling ashes **2** deadly pale; blanched ⟨*his face was ~ with fear*⟩

**Ashes** /'ashiz/ *n pl* a trophy played for in a series of cricket test matches between England and Australia – + *the* [fr a jesting reference to the ashes of the dead body of English cricket after an Australian victory in 1882]

**ashet** /'ashit/ *n, chiefly Scot & NZ* a large plate; a platter [Fr *assiette*]

**ashiver** ə'shivə/ *adj, poetic* quivering ⟨*sails ~*⟩

**Ashkenazi** /ˌashkə'nahzi/ *n, pl* **Ashkenazim** /-zim/ a member of one of the two great divisions of Jewish people comprising the northern European Yiddish-speaking Jews – compare SEPHARDI [Heb *Ashkĕnāzī*] – **Ashkenazic** *adj*

**ashlar** /'ashlə/ *n* **1** hewn or squared stone; *also* masonry of such stone **2** a thin squared and smoothed stone for facing a wall of rubble or brick [ME *asheler*, fr MF *aisselier* a transverse beam, fr OF, fr *ais* board, fr L *axis*, alter. of *assis*]

**ashore** /ə'shaw/ *adv* on or to the shore

**ashpan** /'ash,pan/ *n* a tray that is fitted under the grate in a fire and into which ashes fall

**ashram** /'ashrəm, -ram/ *n* the hermitage of a Hindu wise man; *broadly* any Hindu religious retreat [Skt *āśrama*, fr *ā* towards + *śrama* religious exercise]

**ashtray** /'ash,tray/ *n* a small receptacle for tobacco ash and for cigar and cigarette ends

**Ash Wednesday** *n* the first day of Lent [fr the ashes sprinkled on the heads of penitents]

**ashy** /'ashi/ *adj* **1** of ashes **2** deadly pale

**Asian** /'aysh(ə)n, 'ayzh(ə)n/ *adj* (characteristic) of the continent of Asia or its people [L *Asianus*, fr Gk *Asianos*, fr *Asia*] – **Asian** *n*

**Asiatic** /ˌayzhi'atik; *also* ˌayzi- USE *the last pron is disliked by some speakers*/ *adj* Asian – **Asiatic** *n*

  **usage** Asian is the preferred word for the peoples and cultures of Asia.

**Asiatic cholera** *n* CHOLERA 1 (epidemic often fatal disease)

¹**aside** /ə'sied/ *adv or adj* **1** to or towards the side ⟨*stepped ~*⟩ **2** out of the way ⟨*put his work ~*⟩ ⟨*took me ~ for a private chat*⟩ **3** IN RESERVE, APART 2a **4** APART 3 – **aside from** *chiefly NAm* APART FROM – **put aside** to reserve for a purpose; SET ASIDE 2 – **set aside 1** to put to one side; discard **2** to reserve for a particular purpose; save **3** to reject from consideration **4** to annul (a legal sentence, order, or verdict)

²**aside** *prep, obs* beyond, past

³**aside** *n* **1** an utterance meant to be inaudible to someone; *esp* an actor's speech heard by the audience but supposedly not by other characters on stage **2** a straying from the theme; digression ⟨*a somewhat discursive essay with a good many ~s*⟩

**asiento** /asi'entoh/ *n, pl* **asientos** a commercial treaty; *specif, often cap* a treaty concluded in 1713 between England and Spain for the provision of slaves to the Spanish colonies in America [Sp, seat, treaty, contract, fr *asentar* to seat, make an agreement, fr *a-* (fr L *ad-*) + *sentar* to seat]

**Asin** /'ah,sin/ *n* – see MONTH table [Hindi *Asin*, fr Skt *Āśvina*]

**asinine** /'asinien/ *adj* stupid, unintelligent ⟨*an ~ excuse*⟩ ⟨*so ~ that he looks for gratitude in this world* – H L Mencken⟩ [L *asininus* of or like an ass, fr *asinus* ass] **asininely** *adv*, **asininity** *n*

**ask** /ahsk/ *vt* **1a** to call on for an answer ⟨*I ~ed him about his trip*⟩ **b** to put a question about ⟨*I ~ed his whereabouts*⟩ **c** to put or frame (a question) ⟨*~ a question of him*⟩ **2a** to make a request of ⟨*he ~ed her to accompany him*⟩ **b** to make a request for ⟨*she ~ed to be included*⟩ **3** to behave in such a way as to provoke (an unpleasant response) ⟨*just ~ing to be given a good hiding*⟩ **4** to set as a price ⟨*~ed £1500 for the car*⟩ **5** to invite ⟨*~ him to dinner*⟩ ~ *vi* **1** to seek information ⟨*she ~ed after the old man's health*⟩ **2** to make a request – usu + *for* ⟨*he ~ed for forgiveness*⟩ [ME *asken*, fr OE *āscian*; akin to OHG *eiscōn* to ask, L *aeruscare* to beg] – **asker** *n*

  **synonyms** Ask, request. **Ask** conveys a simple making known of one's wants. **Request** is more formal and polite, and courteously leaves room for a refusal. Compare DEMAND **usage** The pronunciation /ahst/ for the past tense should be avoided in careful speech.

**askance** /ə'skahns/ *adv* **1** with a side glance; obliquely **2** with disapproval or distrust; scornfully – esp in **look askance** [perh fr It *a scancio* obliquely]

**askari** /ə'skahri, 'askəri/ *n* an E African native soldier or policeman, esp when employed by a European power [Ar *'askarī*]

**askew** /ə'skyooh/ *adv or adj* out of line; awry ⟨*the picture hung* ~⟩ [prob fr *a-* + *skew*] – **askewness** *n*

**asking price** /'ahsking/ *n* the price at which something is offered for sale

¹**aslant** /ə'slahnt/ *adv or adj* in a slanting direction; obliquely

²**aslant** *prep* over or across in a slanting direction

¹**asleep** /ə'sleep/ *adj* 1 in a state of sleep 2 lacking sensation; numb 3 not alert; inactive, sluggish ⟨*a weak timid lethargic government usually* ~ – Sir Winston Churchill⟩ 4 *euph* dead

²**asleep** *adv* 1 into a state of sleep 2 into a state of inactivity, sluggishness, or indifference 3 *euph* into the state of death

**aslope** /ə'slohp/ *adj or adv* in a sloping or slanting position or direction

**asocial** /ay'sohsh(ə)l/ *adj* not social: eg a rejecting or lacking the capacity for social interaction; recluse b antisocial *synonyms* see UNSOCIAL

¹**asp** /asp/ *n, archaic* an aspen tree [ME]

²**asp** *n* a small venomous snake of Egypt, variously identified as the CERASTES (type of viper) or a small African cobra (*Naja haje*) [ME *aspis*, fr L, fr Gk]

**asparagine** /ə'sparəjeen, -jin/ *n* an AMINO ACID, $NH_2COCH_2CH(NH_2)COOH$, that is derived from ASPARTIC ACID and is found in many plants [Fr, fr L *asparagus*]

**asparagus** /ə'sparəgəs/ *n* any of a genus (*Asparagus*) of European and Asian plants of the lily family; *esp* a tall plant (*Asparagus officinalis*) widely cultivated for its young shoots that are edible when cooked [NL, genus name, fr L, asparagus plant, fr Gk *asparagos;* akin to Gk *spargan* to swell – more at SPARK]

**aspartate** /ə'spahtayt/ *n* any of various chemical compounds (SALTS or ESTERS) formed by combination between ASPARTIC ACID and a metal atom, an alcohol, or another chemical group

**aspartic acid** /ə'spahtik/ *n* an AMINO ACID, $COOHCH_2CH(NH_2)COOH$, found esp in plants that forms part of many proteins [ISV, irreg fr L *asparagus*]

**aspect** /'aspekt/ *n* **1a** the position of planets or stars with respect to one another, held by astrologers to influence human affairs; *also* the apparent position (eg conjunction) of a body in the solar system with respect to the sun **b** a position facing a particular direction ⟨*the house has a southern* ~⟩ **c** the manner of presentation of an aerofoil, hydrofoil, etc to (the current of) a gas or liquid through which it is moving **2a(1)** appearance to the eye or mind **a(2)** a particular appearance of countenance; a facial expression ⟨*a man surly in* ~⟩ **b** a particular feature of a situation, state of affairs, plan, or point of view as it can be brought to the attention or regarded ⟨*studied every* ~ *of the problem*⟩ **3** the nature of the action of a verb as to its beginning, duration, completion, or repetition and without reference to its position in time ⟨*"I swim" differs from "I am swimming" in* ~⟩ **4** *archaic* a glance, look *synonyms* see ¹VIEW [ME, fr L *aspectus*, fr *aspectus*, pp of *aspicere* to look at, fr *ad-* + *specere* to look – more at SPY] – **aspectual** *adj*

**aspect ratio** *n* a ratio of one dimension to another: eg **a** the ratio of the length to the average width of an aircraft's wing or other aerofoil **b** the ratio of the width to the height of a television or film screen or of the image on it

**aspen** /'aspən/ *n* any of several poplar trees (genus *Populus*) with leaves that flutter in the lightest wind because of their flattened stalks [alter. of ME *asp*, fr OE *æspe;* akin to OHG *aspa* aspen, Latvian *apsa*] – **aspen** *adj*

**asperges** /ə'spuhjeez/ *n* a worship service prescribed by a church in which the altar, clergy, and people are sprinkled with holy water [L, thou wilt sprinkle, fr *aspergere*]

**aspergillosis** /ə,spuhji'lohsis/ *n, pl* **aspergilloses** /-seez/ infection (eg of the lungs) with or disease caused by aspergillus moulds (eg in poultry) [NL]

**aspergillum** /,aspə'jiləm/ *n, pl* **aspergilla** /-lə/, **aspergillums** a brush or small perforated container with a handle that is used for sprinkling holy water [NL, fr L *aspergere* to sprinkle]

**aspergillus** /,aspə'jiləs/ *n, pl* **aspergilli** /-lie/ any of a genus (*Aspergillus*) of ASCOMYCETE fungi including many common moulds, whose asexual spores are borne in chains on stalks (STERIGMATA) that radiate out from the tip of a CONIDIOPHORE (specialized fungal filament) [NL, genus name, fr *aspergillum*]

**asperity** /ə'sperəti/ *n* 1 rigour, hardship 2a roughness of surface; unevenness b roughness of sound 3 roughness of manner or of temper; harshness, acrimony *synonyms* see ACRIMONY *antonym* gentleness [ME *asprete*, fr OF *aspreté*, fr *aspre* rough, fr L *asper*]

**asperse** /ə'spuhs/ *vt* 1 to sprinkle, esp with holy water 2 to attack with evil reports or false or injurious charges [L *aspersus*, pp of *aspergere*, fr *ad-* + *spargere* to scatter – more at SPARK]

**aspersion** /ə'spuhsh(ə)n/ *n* 1 a sprinkling with water, esp in religious ceremonies 2a the act of slander; defamation b a slanderous or unwarranted doubt ⟨*he cast* ~ s *on her integrity*⟩ *synonyms* see ²MALIGN

**asphalt** /'asfalt, -felt, ash-; *NAm* 'asfawlt/ *n* 1 a brown to black bitumen-containing substance that is found naturally and is also obtained as a residue in petroleum or coal-tar refining 2 a mixture of asphalt and sand or gravel used for surfacing roads and as a waterproof cement [ME *aspalt*, fr LL *aspaltus*, fr Gk *asphaltos*] – **asphaltic** *adj*

**asphalt jungle** *n* a big city or a specified part of a big city

**asphaltum** /'asfaltəm, -ash, -felt-; *NAm* 'asfawltəm/ *n* asphalt [alter. of ME *aspaltoun*, *aspalt*]

**aspherical** /,ay'sferikl, ay'sfiarikl/ *also* **aspheric** *adj* 1 departing slightly from the spherical form ⟨*the* ~ *surface of a lens*⟩ 2 free from the ABERRATION (faulty image formation) caused by a spherical surface ⟨*an* ~ *lens*⟩

**asphodel** /'asfə,del/ *n* any of various S European plants (esp genera *Asphodelus* and *Asphodeline*) of the lily family with long erect unbranched stems bearing flowers on short stalks [L *asphodelus*, fr Gk *asphodelos* (cf DAFFODIL)]

**asphyxia** /ə'sfiksi-ə/ *n* a lack of oxygen or excess of carbon dioxide in the body, usu caused by interruption of breathing, and resulting in unconsciousness or death [NL, fr Gk, stopping of the pulse, fr *a-* + *sphyzein* to throb]

**asphyxiate** /ə'sfiksiayt/ *vt* to cause asphyxia in; *also* to kill or make unconscious through an obstruction to normal breathing (eg by depriving of adequate oxygen through smothering) ~ *vi* to become asphyxiated – **asphyxiator** *n*, **asphyxiant** *n*, **asphyxiation** *n*

¹**aspic** /'aspik/ *n, obs* ²ASP (small venomous snake) [MF, alter. of *aspe*, fr L *aspis*]

²**aspic** *n* a clear savoury jelly (eg of fish or meat stock) used as a garnish or to make a meat, fish, or vegetable mould [Fr, lit., asp]

**aspidistra** /,aspi'distrə/ *n* any of various Asian plants (genus *Aspidistra*) of the lily family that have large leaves that grow from the base of the stem and that are often grown as house plants [NL, irreg fr Gk *aspid-, aspis* shield; fr the shape of the leaves]

¹**aspirant** /'aspirənt, ə'spie·ərənt/ *n* one who aspires ⟨*presidential* ~s⟩

²**aspirant** *adj* seeking to attain a desired position or status

¹**aspirate** /'aspirət/, **aspirated** /'aspiraytid/ *adj* pronounced by adding a *h*-sound [L *aspiratus*, pp of *aspirare*]

²**aspirate** /'aspirayt/ *vt* 1 to pronounce (a vowel, consonant, or word) with an accompanying forceful *h*-sound 2a to draw in or up by suction; *esp* to breathe (foreign matter) into the lungs b to remove (eg liquid on the lungs) by suction

³**aspirate** /'aspirət/ *n* 1 an independent sound /h/ or a character (eg the letter h) representing it 2 an aspirated consonant (eg the *p* of *pit*) 3 (unwanted or foreign) matter removed from a body cavity (eg the lungs) by aspiration

**aspiration** /,aspi'raysh(ə)n/ *n* 1 the pronunciation or addition of an aspirate; *also* the aspirate or its symbol 2 a drawing of something in, out, up, or through (as if) by suction: eg 2a the act of breathing in b the withdrawal of pus, blood, air, etc from a body cavity (eg the lungs) c the breathing or sucking in of foreign matter (eg vomit or dust) into the lungs 3a a strong desire to achieve something high or great b an object of such desire

**aspirator** /'aspiraytə/ *n* 1 one who or that which aspirates 2 an apparatus for producing suction or moving or collecting materials by suction; *esp* a hollow tubular instrument used to remove liquid, foreign bodies, etc from a body cavity by suction

**aspire** /ə'spie·ə/ *vi* 1 to seek to attain or accomplish a particular goal – usu + *to* ⟨~d *to a career in medicine*⟩ 2 *poetic* ascend, soar [ME *aspiren*, fr MF or L; MF *aspirer*, fr L *aspirare*, lit., to breathe upon, fr *ad-* + *spirare* to breathe – more at SPIRIT] – **aspirer** *n*, **aspirant** *n or adj*

**aspirin** /'asprin/ *n, pl* **aspirin, aspirins** 1 a chemical compound, $HOOCC_6H_4OCOCH_3$, derived from SALICYLIC ACID that is used as a drug for relief of pain and fever – called also ACETYLSALICYLIC ACID 2 a tablet of aspirin [ISV, fr *a*cetyl + *spir*aeic acid (former name of salicylic acid), fr NL *Spiraea*, genus of shrubs – more at SPIRAEA]

**¹ass** /as/ n **1** any of several long-eared hardy mammals (genus *Equus*) (e g the donkey) that are related to and smaller than the horse **2** a stupid, obstinate, or perverse person or thing ⟨*saying that the law is an* ~⟩ [ME, fr OE *assa*, deriv of L *asinus*]

**²ass** n, chiefly NAm the arse [by alter.]

**assafoetida** /,asə'fetidə/ n ASAFOETIDA (strong-smelling plant product)

**assagai** /'asigie/ n ASSEGAI (light hardwood spear)

**assai** /a'sie/ adv very – used with a tempo direction in music ⟨*allegro* ~⟩ [It, fr (assumed) VL *ad satis* enough – more at ASSET]

**assail** /ə'sayl/ vt **1** to attack violently with blows or words **2** to prey on ⟨~ed *by doubts*⟩ *synonyms* see ¹ATTACK [ME *assailen*, fr OF *asaillir*, fr (assumed) VL *assalire*, alter. of L *assilire* to leap upon, fr *ad-* + *salire* to leap – more at SALLY] – **assailable** adj, **assailant** n

**Assamese** /,asa'meez/ n, pl **Assamese 1** a native or inhabitant of Assam in India **2** the Indic language of Assam

**assassin** /ə'sasin/ n **1** cap any of a secret order of Muslims who at the time of the Crusades terrorized Christians and other enemies by secret murders committed under the influence of the drug hashish **2** a murderer; *esp* one who murders a politically important or famous person for money or from fanatical motives [ML *assassinus*, fr Arḥashshāshīn, pl of ḥashshāsh one who smokes or chews hashish, fr ḥashīsh hashish]

**assassinate** /ə'sasinayt/ vt **1** to murder by sudden or secret premeditated attack, usu for political or religious reasons **2** to injure or destroy (a person's reputation, character, etc) unexpectedly and treacherously *synonyms* see ¹KILL – **assassinator** n, **assassination** n

**assassin bug** n any of a family (Reduviidae) of long-legged insects that usu prey on other insects and often suck the blood of mammals

**¹assault** /ə'sawlt/ n **1** a violent physical or verbal attack **2a** an attempt to do or immediate threat of doing unlawful personal violence to another ⟨*it would be an* ~ *in law to threaten someone with a knife*⟩ – compare BATTERY 1 **b** INDECENT ASSAULT **c** rape **3** a sudden military attack, usu on a fortification [ME *assaut*, fr OF, fr (assumed) VL *assaltus*, fr *assaltus*, pp of *assalire*]

**²assault** vt **1** to make an assault on; *specif* to make an indecent assault on **2** to rape *synonyms* see ¹ATTACK – **assaulter** n, **assaultive** adj

**assault gun** n a self-propelled gun used esp by infantry troops as a support weapon

**¹assay** /ə'say/ n **1** examination and determination as to characteristics (e g weight, measure, or quality) **2** an analysis (e g of a metal ore or drug) to determine the presence, absence, or quantity of one or more components **3** a substance to be assayed; *also* the written results of an analysis **4** archaic a trial, attempt △ essay [ME, fr OF *essai*, *assai* test, effort – more at ESSAY]

**²assay** vt **1a**(1) to analyse (e g an ore) for one or more components **a**(2) to determine the purity of (gold, silver, or another precious metal) **b** to judge the worth or quality of; estimate, evaluate **2** formal to try, attempt – **assayer** n

**assegai, assagai** /'asigie/ n a slender hardwood spear or light javelin usu tipped with iron and used by southern African tribes [deriv of Ar *az-zaghāya* the assegai, fr *al-* the + *zaghāya* assegai]

**assemblage** /ə'semblij/ n **1** a collection of people or things; a gathering **2** the act of assembling or the state of being assembled **3** a three-dimensional collage made from scraps, junk, and odds and ends (e g of paper, cloth, wood, stone, or metal)

**assemble** /ə'sembl/ vt **1** to bring together (e g in a particular place or for a particular purpose) **2** to fit together the parts of ~ vi to gather together; convene *synonyms* see ¹GATHER *antonym* dismiss [ME *assemblen*, fr OF *assembler*, fr (assumed) VL *assimulare*, fr L *ad-* + *simul* together – more at SAME]

**assemblé** /,asom'blay (Fr asåble)/ n a leaping movement in ballet in which one leg is extended and the feet are brought together crossed with the toes turned outwards [Fr, fr pp of *assembler* to assemble]

**assembler** /ə'semblə/ n **1** one who or that which assembles **2** a computer program that automatically converts instructions written in ASSEMBLY LANGUAGE into the equivalent MACHINE CODE (information in a form directly usable by a computer) **3** ASSEMBLY LANGUAGE

**assembly** /ə'sembli/ n **1** a company of people gathered for deliberation and legislation, worship, or entertainment; *specif* a morning gathering of a school for prayers and/or giving out of notices **2** cap a legislative body **3** ASSEMBLAGE 1,2 **4** a signal (e g given by drum or bugle) for troops to assemble or fall in **5** the fitting together of manufactured parts into a complete machine, structure, or unit of a machine; *also* the collection of parts so assembled **6** the translation of ASSEMBLY LANGUAGE into MACHINE CODE (information in a form directly usable by a computer) by an assembler [ME *assemblee*, fr MF, fr OF, fr *assembler*]

**assembly language** n a LOW-LEVEL computer language that is a close approximation of MACHINE CODE (information in a form directly usable by a computer) and in which each instruction typically corresponds to a single instruction in machine code

**assembly line** n **1** an arrangement of machines, equipment, and usu workers in which work passes in a direct line through successive operations until the product is assembled **2** a process for turning out a finished product in a mechanically efficient but often hasty manner ⟨*academic* assembly lines⟩

**assemblyman** /ə'sembliman/, fem **assemblywoman** /,woomən/ n a member of an assembly

**Assembly of God** n a congregation belonging to a Pentecostal church founded in the USA in 1914

**¹assent** /ə'sent/ vi to agree to something, esp after thoughtful consideration [ME *assenten*, fr OF *assenter*, fr L *assentari*, fr *assentire*, fr *ad-* + *sentire* to feel – more at SENSE] – **assentor**, **assenter** n

*synonyms* **Assent, consent, acquiesce, concur, accede**, and **agree** all mean "go along with what has been proposed". **Assent** and **consent** imply a free choice but not necessarily approval. **Assent** is more formal and impersonal, and usually used for statements or facts, while **consent** involves the will and the feelings ⟨*she* **assented** *that it was a fine day, but would not* **consent** *to go for a walk*⟩. **Acquiesce** suggests less freedom of choice, and compliance with what has been suggested in spite of reservations, or because of a willingness to object ⟨*successive governments have* **acquiesced** *in this appalling trade*⟩. **Agree** has a wider sense than the other terms, but often suggests a position arrived at after disagreement. **Concur** stresses agreement *with* someone or *in* their views. **Accede** implies a yielding of one's own wishes in giving consent. *antonyms* dissent, demur

**²assent** n an act of assenting; acquiescence, agreement

**assentation** /,asen'taysh(ə)n/ n ready assent, esp when insincere or servile

**assert** /ə'suht/ vt **1** to state or declare positively and often forcefully or aggressively ⟨*in spite of my arguments he continued to* ~ *that it wouldn't work*⟩ **2a** to demonstrate the existence of ⟨~ *his manhood* – James Joyce⟩ **b** to postulate [L *assertus*, pp of *asserere*, fr *ad-* + *serere* to join – more at SERIES]

*synonyms* **Assert, declare, profess, affirm, aver, avow**, and **protest** all mean "state positively and forcefully, often in the face of doubts or objections". **Assert** suggests something which one cannot prove but which one claims is true ⟨*he* **asserted** *that the factory was a happier place since the introduction of piped music*⟩. **Declare** and **profess** describe public assertions. **Declare** is the more formal; **profess** sometimes carries implications of hypocrisy ⟨*the politician* **declared** *his support for the campaign*⟩ ⟨*all politicians* **profess** *an interest in little children*⟩. **Affirm** and the formal **aver** are less forceful than the preceding terms: both imply that the speaker is convinced of the truth of his/her statement, but **aver** also suggests that this truth may be questioned ⟨*she* **averred** *that his brief stay in prison had done him a world of good*⟩. **Protest** expresses an emphatic affirmation in the face of actual or expected doubt or objections ⟨*she* **protested** *her innocence/that she was innocent*⟩. **Avow** is an open, emphatic declaration expressing full personal responsibility for the position taken. It often carries a sense of confession or admission ⟨**avowed** *his love for the foreign spy*⟩. *antonym* deny

**assertion** /ə'suhsh(ə)n/ n the act of asserting; *also* a declaration, affirmation

**assertive** /ə'suhtiv/ adj disposed to or characterized by bold or confident assertion; dogmatic *antonyms* retiring, acquiescent – **assertively** adv, **assertiveness** n

**assertoric** /,asuh'torik/ adj, philosophy asserted as true – used of propositions in logic [L *assertor* declarer, fr *assertus*]

**asses** /'asiz/ /'aseez, 'asiz/ pl of AS or of ASS

**assess** /ə'ses/ vt **1a** to determine the rate or amount of (e g a tax) ⟨~ *damages after an accident*⟩ **b** to impose (e g a tax) according to an established rate **2** to make an official valuation of (property) for the purposes of taxation **3** to determine the importance, size, or value of [ME *assessen,* fr ML *assessus,* pp of *assidēre,* fr L, to sit beside, assist in the office of a judge – more at ASSIZE] – **assessable** *adj*

**assessment** /ə'sesmənt/ *n* **1** the act or an instance of assessing; (an) appraisal **2** the amount assessed

**assessment centre** *n, Br* a centre where juvenile offenders and young people in need of care or protection are sent temporarily while their situation or condition is assessed and until suitable longer-term accommodation is available

**assessor** /ə'sesə/ *n* **1** a specialist who advises a court of law on scientific or technical matters **2** an official who assesses property for taxation **3** *chiefly Br* a person who investigates and values insurance claims

**asset** /'aset/ *n* **1a(1)** *pl* the total property of a person, company, or institution; *esp* that part which can be used to pay debts **a(2)** a single item of property **b** *pl* the property of a deceased person subject, by law, to the payment of his/her debts and legacies **2** an advantage, resource ⟨*his wit is his chief* ~⟩ **3** *pl* the items on a balance sheet showing the value of property owned by a firm or organization and money owing to it [back-formation fr *assets,* sing., sufficient property to pay debts and legacies, fr AF *asetz,* fr OF *assez* enough, fr (assumed) VL *ad satis,* fr L *ad* to + *satis* enough – more at AT, SAD]

**asset-stripping** *n* the practice of selling the assets of a profitable enterprise in order to maximize short-term profits; *specif* the buying of a company whose assets are greater than its current stock-market value in order to make a profit from the sale of those assets

**asseverate** /ə'sevərayt/ *vt, formal* to affirm solemnly or earnestly [L *asseveratus,* pp of *asseverare,* fr *ad-* + *severus* severe] – **asseverative** *adj,* **asseveration** *n*

**assibilate** /ə'sibilayt/ *vt* to pronounce with or change into a SIBILANT (/s/- or /sh/ -like speech sound) ~ *vi* to become SIBILANT [*ad-* + *sibilate*]

**assiduity** /,asi'dyooh·əti/ *n* **1** the quality or state of being assiduous; diligence **2** solicitous or obsequious attention to a person

**assiduous** /ə'sidyoo·əs/ *adj* marked by careful unremitting attention or persistent application; constant ⟨~ *patrons of the opera*⟩ **synonyms** see [1]BUSY **antonym** desultory [L *assiduus,* fr *assidēre*] – **assiduously** *adv,* **assiduousness** *n*

[1]**assign** /ə'sien/ *vt* **1** to transfer (property) to another, esp in trust or for the benefit of creditors **2a** to appoint to a post or duty **b** to prescribe ⟨*rifles are* ~ed *for guard duty*⟩ **3** to fix authoritatively; specify, designate ⟨~ *a limit*⟩ **4** to ascribe with assurance esp as the motive or reason □ + *to* **synonyms** see ASCRIBE, ALLOT [ME *assignen,* fr OF *assigner,* fr L *assignare,* fr *ad-* + *signare* to mark, fr *signum* mark, sign] – **assignable** *adj,* **assignability** *n,* **assigner, assignor** *n*

[2]**assign** *n* **1** ASSIGNEE 1, 2 **2** a person to whom property is legally transferred – chiefly in *heirs and assigns*

**assignat** /'asignat, ,ahsee'nyah (Fr asiɲa)/ *n* a paper note issued as currency by the French Revolutionary government (1789–96) on the security of land and property confiscated from the Church and the aristocracy [Fr, fr L *assignatus,* pp of *assignare*]

**assignation** /,asig'naysh(ə)n/ *n* **1** the act of assigning; *also* the assignment made **2** a meeting, esp a secret one with a lover ⟨*returned from an* ~ *with his mistress* – W B Yeats⟩ – **assignational** *adj*

**assignee** /,asie'nee/ *n* **1** a person to whom an assignment is made **2** a person appointed to act for another **3** ASSIGN 2

**assignment** /ə'sienmənt/ *n* **1** the act of assigning **2a** a position, post, or job to which one is assigned **b** a specified task or amount of work assigned by authority **3** the legal transfer of property; *also* a document by which such a transfer is made **synonyms** see [1]TASK

**assimilable** /ə'similəbl/ *adj* capable of being assimilated – **assimilability** *n*

**assimilate** /ə'siməlayt/ *vt* **1a** to absorb and utilize (food substances); take in and incorporate into the body tissues **b** to absorb and thoroughly comprehend (information) **2a** to make similar – usu + *to* or *with* ⟨~ *our law in this respect to the law of Scotland* – J Bright⟩ **b** to alter by assimilation ⟨*the prefix* im- *is an* ~d *form of* in-⟩ **c** to absorb into the cultural tradition of a population or group ⟨*the community* ~d *many immigrants*⟩ **3** to compare, liken – usu + *to* or *with* ~ *vi* to become

assimilated [ML *assimilatus,* pp of *assimilare,* fr L *assimulare* to make similar, fr *ad-* + *simulare* to make similar, simulate] – **assimilator** *n*

**assimilation** /ə,simə'laysh(ə)n/ *n* **1a** an act, process, or instance of assimilating **b** the state of being assimilated **2** the incorporation or conversion of nutrients into living matter. In animals this process follows digestion and absorption and in plants involves usu both photosynthesis and absorption of water and minerals from the soil by the roots **3** adaptation of a sound to an adjacent sound ⟨*in* cupboard *the* /p/ *sound of* cup *has undergone complete* ~⟩

**assimilatory** /ə'similətri/, **assimilative** /ə'similətiv/ *adj* of or causing assimilation

[1]**assist** /ə'sist/ *vi* **1** to give support or aid **2** to be present as a spectator ~ *vt* to give support or aid to ⟨~ *a disabled person up the stairs*⟩ **synonyms** see [1]HELP **antonyms** hamper, impede [MF or L; MF *assister* to help, stand by, fr L *assistere,* fr *ad-* + *sistere* to cause to stand; akin to L *stare* to stand – more at STAND]

[2]**assist** *n* the officially recorded action of a player who by throwing a ball in baseball enables a teammate to put an opponent out or by passing a ball or puck in basketball, lacrosse, or ice hockey enables a teammate to score a goal

**assistance** /ə'sist(ə)ns/ *n* the act of assisting or the help supplied; aid ⟨*financial and technical* ~⟩

**assistant** /ə'sist(ə)nt/ *n* one who assists; a helper; *also* an auxiliary device or substance – **assistant** *adj*

**assistant professor** *n* a member of an American college or university staff who ranks below an associate professor – **assistant professorship** *n*

**assistantship** /ə'sist(ə)nt,ship/ *n* an appointment awarded on an annual basis to a graduate student that requires part-time teaching, research, or duties in a hall of residence and carries a salary

**assistant teacher** *n* a schoolteacher who is not the head of a school

**assize** /ə'siez/ *n* **1** assizes *pl,* **assize** *often cap* **1a** the periodical sessions of the superior courts formerly held in every English county for the trial of civil and criminal cases by a judge of the High Court on circuit ⟨*Shrewsbury* Assizes⟩ ⟨*an* ~ *court*⟩ – compare CROWN COURT **b** the time or place of holding such a court, the court itself, or a session of it **2** a fixed or customary standard (e g of quantity, quality, or price) [ME *assise,* fr OF, session, settlement, fr *asseoir* to seat, fr (assumed) VL *assedēre,* fr L *assidēre* to sit beside, assist in the office of a judge, fr *ad-* + *sedēre* to sit – more at SIT]

**associable** /ə'soh·sh(y)əbl, -si·əbl/ *adj* capable of being associated, joined, or connected in thought

[1]**associate** /ə'sohs(h)iayt/ *vt* **1** to join as a friend, companion, or partner in business ⟨~ *ourselves with a larger firm*⟩ **2** to connect in any of various ways (e g in memory, thought, or imagination) ⟨*buttercups are* ~d *with acid soils*⟩ ⟨*sunny days are* ~d *with happy times*⟩ **3** to join or connect together; combine; *specif* to subject to chemical association **4** *obs* to keep company with; attend ~ *vi* **1** to come together as partners, friends, or companions **2** to combine or join with other parties; unite □ (*except 4*) usu + *with* **synonyms** see [1]JOIN [ME *associat* associated, fr L *associatus,* pp of *associare* to unite, fr *ad-* + *sociare* to join, fr *socius* companion – more at SOCIAL] – **associatory** *adj*

[2]**associate** /ə'sohs(h)i·ət/ *adj* **1** closely connected (e g in function or office) with another **2** closely related, esp in the mind **3** having secondary or subordinate status ⟨~ *membership in a society*⟩

[3]**associate** /ə'sohs(h)i·ət, -ayt/ *n* **1** a fellow worker; a partner, colleague **2** a companion, comrade **3** something closely connected with or usu accompanying another **4** one admitted to a subordinate degree of membership ⟨*an* ~ *of the Royal Academy*⟩ **5** *NAm, often cap* a degree conferred esp by a junior college ⟨~ *in arts*⟩ – **associateship** *n*

**associate professor** *n* a member of an American college or university staff who ranks above an assistant professor and below a professor – **associate professorship** *n*

**association** /ə,sohsi'aysh(ə)n, -shi-/ *n* **1a** the act of associating **b** the state of being associated; partnership, combination **2** an organization of people having a common interest; a society, league, union **3** something linked in memory, thought, or imagination with a thing or person; a connotation **4** *psychology* the process of forming mental connections or bonds between sensations, ideas, memories, etc **5** *chemistry* the formation of aggregates of molecules, ions, etc in solution, in which the constituents are held loosely together by weak chemical bonds (e g HYDROGEN BONDS) **6** *ecology* a plant community (e g heath) that forms a division of a larger ecological unit and is characterized usu by two or more dominant species that remain unchanged and stable in numbers – **associational** *adj*

**association football** *n* soccer

**associationism** /ə₋sohs(h)ī·əyshəniz(ə)m, -shi-/ *n*, *philosophy* a theory that seeks to explain mental life in terms of the association of simple discrete ideas

**associative** /ə'sohs(h)ī·ətiv/ *adj* **1** of or inducing association, esp of ideas or images **2a** dependent on or characterized by association ⟨an ~ reaction⟩ **b** acquired by a process of learning ⟨an ~ reflex⟩ **3** of or being a mathematical operation (e g addition or multiplication) such that $(x^*y)^*z = x^*(y^*z)$, where * denotes the operation – **associatively** *adv*, **associativity** *n*

**assoil** /ə'soyl/ *vt, archaic* **1** to absolve, pardon **2** to atone for (e g wrongdoing) [ME *assoilen*, fr OF *assoldre*, fr L *absolvere* to absolve] – **assoilment** *n*

**assonance** /'asənəns/ *n* a similarity of sound between words or syllables, esp as used as an alternative to rhyme in poetry by means of a repetition of vowels without repetition of consonants (e g in *stony* and *holy*) **b** repetition of consonants without repetition of vowels (e g in *held* and *healed* and in *spanner* and *spinner*) [Fr, fr L *assonare* to answer with the same sound, fr *ad-* + *sonare* to sound – more at SOUND] – **assonant** *adj or n*

**assonate** /'asənayt/ *vi* to correspond in sound by assonance [L *assonatus*, pp of *assonare*]

**assort** /ə'sawt/ *vt* **1** to distribute into groups of a like kind; classify **2** to supply with an assortment or variety (e g of goods) ~ *vi, formal* **1** to agree in kind; harmonize, match **2** to keep company; associate [MF *assortir*, fr *a-* (fr L *ad-*) + *sorte* sort] – **assortative** *adj*, **assorter** *n*

**assorted** /ə'sawtid/ *adj* **1** consisting of various kinds **2** suited by nature, character, or design; matched ⟨an ill-assorted pair⟩

**assortment** /ə'sawtmənt/ *n* **1a** the act of assorting **b** the state of being assorted **2** a collection of assorted things or people

**assuage** /ə'swayj/ *vt* **1** to lessen the intensity of (pain, suffering, desire, etc); ease **2** to pacify, quiet **3** to put an end to by satisfying; appease, quench ⟨he ~d his hunger with a sandwich⟩ *synonyms* see RELIEVE *antonyms* exacerbate, intensify [ME *aswagen*, fr OF *assouagier*, fr (assumed) VL *assuaviare*, fr L *ad-* + *suavis* sweet – more at SWEET] – **assuagement** *n*

**assuasive** /ə'swaysiv, -ziv/ *adj* having a pleasantly soothing quality or effect; calming [*ad-* + *suasive*]

**assume** /ə'syoohm/ *vt* **1** to take up or in; receive ⟨on marrying she ~d a new surname⟩ **2a** to take to or upon oneself; undertake ⟨he ~d the role of leader⟩ **b** to put on (e g clothing or facial expression); don ⟨she ~d a different guise for each character that she played⟩ **3** to seize, usurp **4** to pretend to have or be; feign ⟨~d an air of confidence in spite of his dismay⟩ **5** to take as granted or true; suppose – often + that ⟨we simply ~d that we were going to be married⟩ **6** to take over (the debts of another) as one's own *synonyms* see ¹PRETEND, PRESUME [ME *assumen*, fr L *assumere*, fr *ad-* + *sumere* to take – more at CONSUME] – **assumable** *adj*

**assuming** /ə'syoohming/ *adj* presumptuous, arrogant

**assumption** /ə'sumsh(ə)n, ə'sump-/ *n* **1a** the taking up of a person into heaven **b** *cap* August 15 observed in commemoration of the Assumption of the Virgin Mary **2** a taking upon oneself ⟨a delay in the ~ of his new position⟩ **3** the act of laying claim to or taking possession of something ⟨the ~ of power⟩ **4** arrogance, presumption **5a** the supposition that something is true **b** a fact or statement (e g a proposition, postulate, or established principle) taken to be true without proof **6** the taking over of another's debts [ME, fr LL *assumption-, assumptio*, fr L, taking up, fr *assumptus*, pp of *assumere*]

**assumptive** /ə'sum(p)tiv/ *adj* **1** taken for granted or inclined to take for granted ⟨~ beliefs⟩ **2** assuming

**assurance** /ə'shawrəns, -'shooə-/ *n* **1a** the act or action of assuring **b** a pledge, guarantee **2** the state of being assured: e g **2a** the quality or state of being sure or certain; freedom from doubt ⟨the puritan's ~ of salvation⟩ **b** confidence of mind or manner; *also* excessive self-confidence; brashness **3** something that inspires or tends to inspire confidence ⟨gave repeated ~s of his goodwill⟩ **4** *chiefly Br* insurance where it is certain that the insurer will have to pay out money at some time – used

esp with reference to life insurance *synonyms* see CERTAINTY *antonyms* mistrust, diffidence

**assure** /ə'shaw, -'shooə/ *vt* **1** to secure in the face of risk; ensure ⟨capable of assuring the safety of the Queen⟩ **2** to give confidence to; reassure **3** to make sure or certain; convince **4** to inform positively ⟨~d her of his fidelity⟩ **5** to make certain the coming or attainment of; guarantee ⟨worked hard to ~ accuracy⟩ □ (3&4) often + of or that [ME *assuren*, fr MF *assurer*, fr ML *assecurare*, fr L *ad-* + *securus* secure]

¹**assured** /ə'shawd, ə'shooəd/ *adj* **1** characterized by certainty or security; guaranteed ⟨an ~ market⟩ **2** characterized by self-confidence ⟨an ~ dancer⟩ **3** satisfied as to the certainty or truth of a matter; convinced *synonyms* see ¹SURE – **assuredly** *adv*, **assuredness** *n*

²**assured** *n, pl* **assured, assureds** a beneficiary of an assurance policy

**assurer, assuror** /ə'shawrə, ə'shooərə/ *n* a person or firm that assures; an insurer

**assurgent** /ə'suhj(ə)nt/ *adj* moving upwards; rising; *esp* ASCENDANT 1b [L *assurgent-, assurgens*, prp of *assurgere* to rise, fr *ad-* + *surgere* to rise – more at SURGE]

**Assyrian** /ə'siri·ən/ *n* **1** a member of an ancient Semitic race forming the Assyrian nation **2** the Semitic language of the Assyrians [*Assyria*, ancient empire in W Asia] – **Assyrian** *adj*

**Assyriology** /ə₋siri'oləji/ *n* the science or study of the history, language, and relics of ancient Assyria and Babylonia – **Assyriologist** *n*, **Assyriological** *adj*

**-ast** /-ast/ *suffix* (→n) one practising or given to ⟨iconoclast⟩ ⟨enthusiast⟩ [ME, fr L *-astes*, fr Gk *-astēs*, fr verbs in *-azein*]

**astable** /₋ay'staybl/ *adj, of an electrical circuit* having no permanently stable state

**astarboard** /ə'stahbəd, -₋bawd/ *adv* on or towards the right-hand side of a ship ⟨put the helm ~⟩

**astatic** /ə'statik, ay-/ *adj* **1** not static; not stable or steady **2** *physics* having little or no tendency to take a fixed or definite position or direction – **astatically** *adv*, **astaticism** *n*

**astatic galvanometer** *n* a GALVANOMETER (instrument that detects small electric currents) whose functioning is not affected by an external MAGNETIC FIELD (e g that of the earth)

**astatine** /'astəteen, -tin/ *n* a radioactive chemical element of the HALOGEN group (group of elements including fluorine, chlorine, and iodine) that occurs naturally in minute amounts as a product of the radioactive decay of uranium and thorium and is usu produced synthetically by bombarding the chemical element bismuth with ALPHA PARTICLES [Gk *astatos* unsteady, fr *a-* + *statos* standing, fr *histanai* to cause to stand – more at STAND]

**aster** /'astə/ *n* **1** any of various leafy-stemmed chiefly autumn-blooming plants (*Aster* and related genera) of the daisy family with often showy daisylike heads of flowers **2** *genetics* a star-shaped group of minute threadlike tubes (MICROTUBULES) that radiate from the CENTROSOME at each end of the SPINDLE (spindle-shaped bunch of fibres) formed in a cell undergoing MITOSIS (division of a cell and its contents into two new cells) [(1) NL, genus name, fr L, aster, fr Gk *aster-, astēr* star, aster; (2) NL, fr Gk *aster-, astēr* – more at STAR]

**-aster** /-a(h)stə, -əstə/ *suffix* (n → n) one who is an inferior, worthless, or false kind of ⟨criticaster⟩ ⟨poetaster⟩ [ME, fr L, suffix denoting partial resemblance]

**asteria** /ə'stiəri·ə/ *n* a gemstone cut to show asterism [L, a precious stone, fr Gk, fem of *asterios* starry, fr *aster-, astēr*]

**asteriated** /ə'stiəriaytid/ *adj* exhibiting asterism ⟨~ sapphire⟩ [Gk *asterios*]

¹**asterisk** /'astərisk/ *n* the character * used as a reference mark, esp to denote the omission of letters or words, or to show that something is doubtful or absent [LL *asteriscus*, fr Gk *asteriskos*, lit., little star, dim. of *aster-, astēr*]

²**asterisk** *vt* to mark with an asterisk; star

**asterism** /'astəriz(ə)m/ *n* **1a** a constellation **b** a small group of stars **2** a star-shaped figure visible in some crystals under reflected light (e g in a STAR SAPPHIRE) or transmitted light (e g in some varieties of the mineral mica) **3** three asterisks arranged in the form of a pyramid (e g *⁎* or *⁎*), used esp to direct attention to a following passage [Gk *asterismos*, fr *asterizein* to arrange in constellations, fr *aster-, astēr*]

**astern** /ə'stuhn/ *adv or adj* **1** behind the stern of a ship; to the rear ⟨sailed due east, with the setting sun directly ~⟩ **2** at or towards the stern of a ship ⟨went ~ and gazed at the wake⟩ **3** backwards ⟨full speed ~⟩

<sup>1</sup>**asteroid** /'astəroyd/ n **1** any of thousands of small planets between Mars and Jupiter **2** a starfish [Gk *asteroeidēs* starlike, fr *aster-, astēr*] – **asteroidal** adj

<sup>2</sup>**asteroid** adj **1** starlike **2** of or like a starfish

**asthenia** /əs'theenyə, -ni·ə/ n lack or loss of strength; debility [NL, fr Gk *astheneia*, fr *asthenēs* weak, fr *a-* + *sthenos* strength]

**asthenic** /əs'thenik/ adj **1** of or exhibiting asthenia; weak **2** characterized by slender build, long limbs, and slight muscular development; ECTOMORPHIC

**asthenosphere** /əs'theenə,sfiə/ n a hypothetical zone of the earth beneath the LITHOSPHERE (outer rocky zone of the earth's crust) within which the material is believed to yield readily under stress [Gk *asthenēs* weak + E -o- + *sphere*]

**asthma** /'as(th)mə/ n a condition, often of allergic origin, that is marked by attacks of laboured breathing accompanied by wheezing and usu coughing, gasping, and a sense of constriction in the chest [ME *asma*, fr ML, modif of Gk *asthma*] – **asthmatic** adj or n, **asthmatically** adv

**astigmatic** /,astig'matik/ adj **1** affected with or correcting astigmatism **2** showing incapacity for observation or discrimination ⟨an ~ approach to his work⟩ [a- + Gk *stigmat, stigma* mark – more at STIGMA] – **astigmatically** adv

**astigmatism** /a'stigmatiz(ə)m, ə-/ n **1** a defect of an optical system (e g a lens) as a result of which light rays from a single point fail to converge at a single FOCAL POINT, resulting in a blurred and imperfect image **2** a defect of vision due to astigmatism of the lens of the eye **3** distorted understanding suggestive of the blurred vision of an astigmatic person

**astilbe** /ə'stilbi/ n any of several plants (genus *Astilbe*) of the saxifrage family grown in gardens for their showy white or purple flowers [NL, genus name, fr <sup>2</sup>a- + Gk *stilbē*, fem of *stilbos* glistening]

**astir** /ə'stuh/ adj **1** in a state of bustle or excitement **2** out of bed; up

**Asti spumante** /,asti spoo'manti, spyooh-/ n an Italian sparkling white wine [It, lit., sparkling Asti, fr *Asti*, town in Italy]

**astonied** /ə'stoneed/ adj, archaic **1** temporarily unable to move; dazed, stunned **2** filled with consternation or dismay [ME, fr pp of *astonien*]

**astonish** /ə'stonish/ vt **1** to strike with sudden wonder or surprise **2** obs to strike with sudden fear synonyms see <sup>2</sup>SURPRISE [prob fr earlier *astony* (fr ME *astonen, astonien*, fr OF *estoner*, fr – assumed – VL *extonare*, fr L *ex-* + *tonare* to thunder) + -ish (as in *abolish*) – more at THUNDER]

**astonishing** /ə'stonishing/ adj causing astonishment; surprising – **astonishingly** adv

**astonishment** /ə'stonishmənt/ n **1a** the state of being astonished **b** great surprise or wonder; amazement **2** a cause of amazement or wonder

**astound** /ə'stownd/ vt to fill with bewilderment and wonder synonyms see <sup>2</sup>SURPRISE [prob fr arch. *astound*, adj, fr ME *astoned*, fr pp of *astonen*]

**astounding** /ə'stownding/ adj causing astonishment or amazement – **astoundingly** adv

**astr-** /astr-/, **astro-** comb form **1** star; heavens; outer space ⟨astrophysics⟩ **2** ASTER of a cell ⟨astrosphere⟩ [ME *astro-*, fr OF, fr L *astr-, astro-*, fr Gk, fr *astron* – more at STAR]

<sup>1</sup>**astraddle** /ə'stradl/ adv with one leg on each side; astride

<sup>2</sup>**astraddle** prep with one leg on each side of; astride

**astragal** /'astrəgl/ n **1** a narrow convex often carved moulding used esp in architecture of the Greek and Roman style **2** a projecting strip on the edge of a folding door [L *astragalus*, fr Gk *astragalos* anklebone, moulding]

**astragalus** /a'stragələs, ə-/ n, pl **astragali** /-lie/ **1** a bone of the TARSUS of the foot of a bird, mammal, etc that corresponds to the ankle bone (<sup>2</sup>TALUS 1) in humans – compare <sup>2</sup>TALUS 2 an astragal [NL, fr Gk *astragalos*]

**astrakhan, astrachan** /,astrə'kahn, -'kan, -kən/ n, often cap **1** KARAKUL (fur from the fleece of karakul lambs) of Russian origin **2** a woollen cloth with curled and looped pile resembling the fleece of the karakul lambs [*Astrakhan*, city in USSR]

**astral** /'astrəl/ adj **1a** of the stars **b** consisting of stars **2** of an ASTER (star-shaped structure seen in a dividing cell) **3** philosophy (consisting of a spiritual substance held in THEOSOPHY (belief in knowing God by intuitive insight and meditation) to be the material of which somebody's supposed second body is made up, that can be seen by specially gifted people ⟨~ body⟩ [LL *astralis*, fr L *astrum* star, fr Gk *astron* – more at STAR] – **astrally** adv

**astray** /ə'stray/ adv or adj **1** off the right path or route; straying **2** in error; away from a proper or desirable course or development [ME, fr MF *estraié* wandering, fr *estraier* to stray – more at STRAY]

<sup>1</sup>**astride** /ə'stried/ adv **1** with one leg on each side ⟨rode her horse ~⟩ **2** with the legs wide apart ⟨standing ~ with arms folded⟩

<sup>2</sup>**astride** prep **1** on or above and with one leg on each side of **2** placed or lying on both sides of **3** extending over or across; spanning, bridging

**astringe** /ə'strinj/ vt to bind together; constrict, compress [L *astringere*]

<sup>1</sup>**astringent** /ə'strinj(ə)nt/ adj **1a** capable of making firm the soft tissues of the body; contracting, constricting ⟨~ lotions⟩ **b** checking secretion and discharge (e g of SERUM or mucus); styptic **2** rigidly severe; austere ⟨dry ~ comments⟩ **3** sharply refreshing [MF, fr L *astringent-, astringens*, prp of *astringere* to bind fast, fr *ad-* + *stringere* to bind tight – more at STRAIN] – **astringency** n, **astringently** adv

<sup>2</sup>**astringent** n an astringent agent or substance

**astro-** – see ASTR-

**astrocompass** /'astroh,kumpəs/ n an instrument for determining the direction of travel of something (e g a spacecraft) by assessing its position in relation to an imaginary line drawn from the centre of the earth to a particular star

**astrocyte** /'astrə,siet/ n a star-shaped cell (e g of the supporting tissue in the nervous system) [ISV] – **astrocytic** adj

**astrocytoma** /,astrohsie'tomə/ n, pl **astrocytomas, astrocytomata** /-mətə/ a tumour of nervous tissue composed of astrocytes [NL]

**astrodome** /'astrə,dohm/ n a transparent dome in the upper surface of an aeroplane for making observations, esp of the stars [ISV]

**astrolabe** /'astrə,layb/ n an instrument used to observe the position of stars and planets before the invention of the SEXTANT [ME, fr MF & ML; MF, fr ML *astrolabium*, fr LGk *astrolabion*, dim. of Gk *astrolabos*, fr *astr-* + *lambanein* to take – more at LATCH]

**astrology** /ə'strolaji/ n **1** the art or practice of determining the supposed influences of the planets on human affairs by virtue of their positions and aspects **2** obs astronomy [ME *astrologie*, fr MF, fr L *astrologia*, fr Gk, fr *astr-* + *-logia* -logy] – **astrologer, astrologist** n, **astrological** adj, **astrologically** adv

**astronaut** /'astrə,nawt/ n a person who travels in space; also a trainee for spaceflight [*astr-* + *-naut* (as in *aeronaut*)]

**astronautics** /,astrə'nawtiks/ n taking sing vb **1** the science of the construction and operation of vehicles for travel in space **2** navigation in space – **astronautic, astronautical** adj, **astronautically** adv

**astronavigation** /,astrə,navi'gaysh(ə)n/ n navigation using the position of the stars – called also CELESTIAL NAVIGATION

**astronomer** /ə'stronəmə/ n one who is skilled in astronomy or who makes observations of stars, planets, comets, etc

**astronomical** /,astrə'nomikl/, **astronomic** /-'nomik/ adj **1** of astronomy **2** informal enormously or inconceivably large ⟨some ~ figure like 2 billion⟩ – **astronomically** adv

**astronomical unit** n a unit of length used in astronomy equal to the average distance of the earth from the sun or about 149 600 000 kilometres (about 93 million miles)

**astronomy** /ə'stronəmi/ n a branch of science dealing with the universe and its stars, planets, comets, etc [ME *astronomie*, fr OF, fr L *astronomia*, fr Gk, fr *astr-* + *-nomia* -nomy]

**astrophotography** /,astrohfə'togrəfi/ n photography as used in astronomical investigations [ISV]

**astrophysics** /,astroh'fiziks/ n taking sing vb a branch of astronomy dealing with the physical and chemical properties of the planets, stars, etc [ISV] – **astrophysical** adj, **astrophysicist** n

**astrosphere** /'astrə,sfiə/ n, genetics an ASTER (star-shaped structure seen in a dividing cell) exclusive of the CENTROSOME from which it radiates [ISV]

**Astroturf** /'astrə,tuhf/ trademark – used for an artificial grasslike surface that is used for lawns and sports fields

**astute** /ə'styooht, ə'schooht/ adj exhibiting combined shrewdness and acute perception, often to the point of being artful or crafty ⟨an ~ observer⟩ ⟨an ~ appeal to the weakness of his victim⟩ synonyms see SHREWD antonym gullible [L *astutus*, fr *astus* craft] – **astutely** adv, **astuteness** n

**asunder** /ə'sundə/ adv or adj **1** into parts ⟨torn ~⟩ **2** apart from each other in position ⟨wide ~⟩

**aswarm** /ə'swawm/ *adj* swarming ⟨*streets ~ with people*⟩

**aswoon** /ə'swoohn/ *adj* in a swoon; dazed

**asyllabic** /,aysi'labik/ *adj* not syllabic

**asylum** /ə'sieləm/ *n* **1** an inviolable place of refuge and protection formerly giving shelter to criminals and fugitives; SANCTUARY 2a(1) **2** a place of retreat and security; a shelter **3a** the protection or inviolability afforded by an asylum; refuge **b** protection from arrest and extradition given, esp to political refugees, by a nation or by an agency (eg an embassy) enjoying diplomatic immunity **4** an institution for the relief or care of those who are destitute or ill, esp the insane [ME, fr L, fr Gk *asylon*, neut of *asylos* inviolable, fr *a-* + *sylon* right of seizure]

**asymmetric** /aysi'metrik/, **asymmetrical** /-kl/ *adj* **1** not symmetrical **2a** *of a carbon atom* attached to four different atoms or chemical groups **b** *of a molecule or chemical group* containing an asymmetric carbon atom [Gk *asymmetria* lack of proportion, fr *asymmetros* ill-proportioned, fr *a-* + *symmetros* symmetrical – more at SYMMETRY] – **asymmetrically** *adv*, **asymmetry** *n*

**asymmetric bars** *n pl* **1** a pair of wooden bars supported horizontally, one 1.5 metres (about 5 feet) and the other 2.3 metres (about 7 feet 6 inches) above the floor, usu by a common base and used by women in gymnastics **2** *taking sing vb* a gymnastics event in which the asymmetric bars are used

**asymptomatic** /,aysimptə'matik/ *adj* presenting no symptoms of disease – **asymptomatically** *adv*

**asymptote** /'asimtoht/ *n, maths* a straight line which is approached more and more closely by a curve such that the tangent to the curve comes nearer and nearer to coinciding with the line, but meets the line only at infinity [deriv of Gk *asymptōtos*, fr *asymptōtos* not meeting, fr *a-* + *sympiptein* to meet – more at SYMPTOM] – **asymptotic** *adj*, **asymptotically** *adv*

**asynapsis** /,aysi'napsis/ *n, pl* **asynapses** /-seez/ *genetics* the failure of identical (HOMOLOGOUS) chromosomes to pair during MEIOSIS (division of a cell and its contents to form four new cells) in which one chromosome from the male parent and one from the female parent associate in pairs [NL ²*a-* + *synapsis*]

**asynchronous** /,ay'singkrənəs/ *adj* not synchronous – **asynchronously** *adv*

**asynchrony** /ay'singkrəni/, **asynchronism** /-,niz(ə)m/ *n* the quality or state of being asynchronous; an absence or lack of concurrence in time

**asyndeton** /ə'sindətən, ay-/ *n, pl* **asyndetons**, **asyndeta** /-tə/ the omission of *and, or,* or other conjunctions (eg in "I came, I saw, I conquered") [LL, fr Gk, fr neut of *asyndetos* unconnected, fr *a-* + *syndetos* bound together, fr *syndein* to bind together, fr *syn-* + *dein* to bind – more at DIADEM] – **asyndetic** *adj*

¹**at** /ət; *strong* at/ *prep* **1** – used to indicate presence or occurrence in, on, or near a place imagined as a point ⟨*~ a hotel*⟩ ⟨*~ Blackpool*⟩ ⟨*~ a party*⟩ ⟨*~ the bottom*⟩ ⟨*sick ~ heart*⟩; compare IN 1a(3) **2** – used to indicate the goal or direction of an action ⟨*aim ~ the target*⟩ ⟨*laugh ~ him*⟩ ⟨*creditors are ~ him again*⟩; compare TO 1 **3a** – used to indicate occupation or employment ⟨*~ work*⟩ ⟨*~ the controls*⟩ ⟨*~ school*⟩ ⟨*~ tea*⟩ **b** when it comes to (an occupation or employment); AS REGARDS ⟨*an expert ~ chess*⟩ ⟨*good ~ arranging flowers*⟩ **4** – used to indicate situation or condition ⟨*~ liberty*⟩ ⟨*~ risk*⟩ ⟨*~ sea*⟩ ⟨*~ grass*⟩ ⟨*~ war*⟩ ⟨*~ rest*⟩ **5** in response to ⟨*laugh ~ his jokes*⟩ ⟨*impatient ~ the delay*⟩ ⟨*act ~ your own discretion*⟩ ⟨*shoot ~ sight*⟩ **6** – used to indicate position on a scale (eg of cost, speed, or age) ⟨*sold ~ 25p a dozen*⟩ ⟨*~ 90 miles/hour*⟩ ⟨*the temperature ~ 90*⟩ ⟨*retire ~ 65*⟩ **7** – used to indicate position in time imagined as a point ⟨*~ three o'clock*⟩ ⟨*~ weekends*⟩ **8** from a distance of ⟨*shot him ~ 30 paces*⟩ [ME, fr OE *æt*; akin to OHG *az* at, L *ad*] – **at a** as a result of only one; by or during only one ⟨*drank it a a gulp*⟩ ⟨*reduce prices* at *a stroke*⟩ ⟨*two at a time*⟩ – **at all** in any way or respect; to the least extent or degree; under any circumstances ⟨*not at all fat*⟩ ⟨*very seldom if at all*⟩ ⟨*have you a religion at all?*⟩ – compare NOT AT ALL – **at it** doing it; *esp* busy ⟨*been hard* at it *all day*⟩ – **at that 1** at that point and no further ⟨*let it go* at that⟩ **2** which makes it more surprising; IN ADDITION ⟨*she says sack him, and maybe I will* at that⟩

²**at** /aht/ *n, pl* **at** – see *kip* at MONEY table [Thai]

**at-** – see AD-

**atacamite** /ə'takəmiet, ,atə'kamiet/ *n* a mineral, $Cu_2Cl(OH)_3$, consisting of a chloride of copper [Fr, fr the *Atacama* desert in N Chile]

**ataman** /'atəmən/ *n* HETMAN (a leader of the Cossacks) [Russ]

**ataractic** /,atə'raktik/ *n* TRANQUILLIZER 2 [Gk *ataraktos* calm, fr *a-* + *tarassein* to disturb] – **ataractic** *adj*

**ataraxic** /,atə'raksik/ *n* TRANQUILLIZER 2 [Gk *ataraxia* calmness, fr *a-* + *tarassein*] – **ataraxic** *adj*

**atavism** /'atəviz(ə)m/ *n* **1** the recurrence in an organism of a form typical of ancestors more remote than the parents; *broadly* the recurrence of primitive characteristics from the remote past **2** an individual or character manifesting atavism; a throwback [Fr *atavisme*, fr L *atavus* ancestor] – **atavist** *n*, **atavistic** *adj*, **atavistically** *adv*

**ataxia** /ə'taksi·ə/ *n* **1** a lack of order; confusion **2** an inability to coordinate voluntary muscular movements that is a symptom of some nervous disorders [Gk, fr *a-* + *tassein* to put in order – more at TACTICS] – **ataxic** *adj*

¹**ate** /et/; *also* ayt/ *past of* EAT *usage* see EAT

²**ate** /'ahtay, -ti/ *n* blind impulse, reckless ambition, or excessive folly that drives people to ruin [Gk *atē*]

¹**-ate** /-ət, -ayt/ *suffix* (→ *n*) **1** product of (a specified process) ⟨*distill*ate⟩ ⟨*condens*ate⟩ **2** chemical compound or complex ANION (negatively charged atom or group of atoms) derived from (a specified compound or element) ⟨*phenol*ate⟩ ⟨*ferr*ate⟩; *esp* SALT or ESTER of (a specified acid with a name ending in *-ic* and not beginning with *hydro-*) ⟨*sulph*ate⟩ [ME *-at*, fr OF, fr L *-atus, -atum*, masc & neut of *-atus*, pp ending; (2) NL *-atum*, fr L]

²**-ate** *suffix* (→ *n*) **1** office, function, or rank of ⟨*consul*ate⟩ ⟨*doctor*ate⟩ **2** individual or group of people holding (a specified office or rank) or having (a specified function) ⟨*elector*ate⟩ ⟨*candid*ate⟩ [ME *-at*, fr OF, fr L *-atus*, fr *-atus*, pp ending]

³**-ate, -ated** *suffix* (→ *adj*) **1** being in or brought to (a specified state) ⟨*passion*ate⟩ ⟨*inanim*ate⟩ **2** marked by having ⟨*crani*ate⟩ ⟨*locul*ated⟩ **3** resembling; having the shape of ⟨*pinn*ate⟩ ⟨*foli*ate⟩ [ME *-at*, fr L *-atus*, fr pp ending of 1st conjugation verbs, fr *-a-*, stem vowel of 1st conjugation + *-tus*, pp suffix – more at -ED]

⁴**-ate** *suffix* (→ *vb*) **1** act (in a specified way) ⟨*pontific*ate⟩ ⟨*remonstr*ate⟩ **2** act (in a specified way) upon ⟨*insul*ate⟩ ⟨*assassin*ate⟩ **3** cause to become; cause to be modified or affected by ⟨*activ*ate⟩ ⟨*pollin*ate⟩ **4** provide with ⟨*substanti*ate⟩ ⟨*aer*ate⟩ [ME *-aten*, fr L *-atus*, pp ending]

**atelectasis** /,ati'lektəsis/ *n, pl* **atelectases** /-seez/ the collapse of an expanded lung; *also* defective expansion of the lungs at birth [NL, fr Gk *atelēs* incomplete, defective (fr *a-* ²*a-* + *telos* end) + *ektasis* extension, fr *ekteinein* to stretch out, fr *ex-* + *teinein* to stretch – more at WHEEL, THIN]

**atelier** /ə'teliay, 'atəlyay/ *n* an artist's or designer's studio or workroom [Fr]

**a tempo** /,ah 'tempoh/ *adv or adj* in the original tempo – used as a direction in music to return to the original tempo [It]

**Aterian** /ə'tiəriən/ *adj* of a PALAEOLITHIC culture of N Africa characterized by tanged arrow points and leaf-shaped spearheads [Fr *atérien*, fr Bir el-*Ater* (Constantine), city in Algeria]

**Athabascan, Athabaskan** /,athə'baskən/ *n* (an) Athapaskan

**Athanasian Creed** /,athə'nayzh(ə)n, -sh(ə)n/ *n* a Christian statement of belief originating in Europe about AD 400 that defines esp the threefold nature of God in the Trinity and the Incarnation of God as Jesus Christ [St *Athanasius* †373 Gk patriarch & theologian, formerly believed to have written it]

**Athapaskan, Athapascan** /,athə'paskən/ *n* **1** one of three languages families of the Na-dene grouping of N American Indian languages **2** a member of a people speaking an Athapaskan language [Cree *Athap-askaw*, an Athapaskan people, lit., grass or reeds here and there]

**atheism** /'aythi·iz(ə)m/ *n* **1a** disbelief in the existence of God and any other gods **b** the doctrine that there is no God **2** *archaic* ungodliness, wickedness [MF *athéisme*, fr *athée* atheist, fr Gk *atheos* godless, fr *a-* + *theos* god]

**atheist** /'aythi·ist/ *n* one who denies the existence of God – compare AGNOSTIC *antonym* theist – **atheistic, atheistical** *adj*, **atheistically** *adv*

**atheling** /'athəling/ *n* an Anglo-Saxon prince or nobleman; *esp* the heir apparent or a prince of the royal family – often placed after the Christian name as a title ⟨*Edward* Atheling⟩ [ME, fr OE *ætheling*, fr *æthelu* nobility; akin to OHG *adal* nobility]

**athematic** /,aythee'matik/ *adj, of a verb form* containing no connecting vowel between the stem and its inflection (eg in Latin *est* "he is", where *es-* is the stem and *-t* the inflection)

**athenaeum, atheneum** /,athə'nee·əm, ə'theeni·əm/ *n* **1** a literary or scientific association **2** a building or room in which books, periodicals, and newspapers are kept for use [L *Athenaeum*, a school in ancient Rome for the study of arts, fr Gk *Athēnaion*, a temple of Athena, fr *Athēnē* Athena, Gk goddess of wisdom and war]

**Athenian** /ə'theenyən, -ni-ən/ *n or adj* (a native or inhabitant) of Athens [*Athens*, city in Greece, fr L *Athenae*, fr Gk *Athēnai*]

**atherogenesis** /,athəroh'jenəsis/ *n* the production of atheroma

**atherogenic** /,athəroh'jenik/ *adj* of or producing degenerative changes in the walls of the arteries ⟨*an* ~ *diet*⟩ [*athero*ma + *-genic*]

**atheroma** /,athə'rohmə/ *n* the deposition of fatty substances on the inner lining of the arteries [NL *atheromat-, atheroma*, fr L, a tumour containing matter like gruel, fr Gk *athērōma*, fr *athēra* gruel] – **atheromatosis** *n*, **atheromatous** *adj*

**atherosclerosis** /,athərohsklə'rohsis/ *n* ARTERIOSCLEROSIS (thickening and hardening of the artery walls) characterized by the deposition of fatty substances in the arteries [NL, fr *athero*ma + *sclerosis*] – **atherosclerotic** *adj*, **atherosclerotically** *adv*

**athirst** /ə'thuhst/ *adj* **1** having a strong eager desire ⟨*I that for ever feel* ~ *for glory* – John Keats⟩ **2** *archaic* thirsty [ME, fr OE *ofthyrst*, pp of *ofthyrstan* to suffer from thirst, fr *of* off, from + *thyrstan* to thirst – more at OF]

**athlete** /'athleet/ *n* one who is trained or skilled in or takes part in exercises, sports, or games that require physical strength, agility, or stamina [ME, fr L *athleta*, fr Gk *athlētēs*, fr *athlein* to contend for a prize, fr *athlon* prize, contest]

**athlete's foot** *n* RINGWORM (fungal infection) of the feet

**athletic** /ath'letik/ *adj* **1** of athletes or athletics **2** characteristic of an athlete; *esp* vigorous, active **3** characterized by heavy frame, large chest, and powerful muscular development; MESOMORPHIC – **athletically** *adv*, **athleticism** *n*

**athletics** /ath'letiks/ *n taking sing vb* exercises, sports, or games engaged in by athletes; *specif, Br* competitive walking, running, throwing, and jumping sports collectively

**athletic support** *n* a jockstrap

**athodyd** /'athə,did/ *n* RAMJET (type of jet engine) [*aero-thermodynamic duct*]

**at home** *n* a reception given at one's home

**-athon** /-əthən, -athon/ *comb form* (→ *n*) contest of endurance ⟨*talk*athon⟩ [*marathon*]

**athrocyte** /'athrə,siet/ *n* a cell capable of picking up foreign material and storing it in granular form in the CYTOPLASM (jellylike material outside the cell nucleus) [Gk *athroos* together, collected + ISV *-cyte*] – **athrocytosis** *n*

**¹athwart** /ə'thwawt/ *adv* **1** across, esp in an oblique direction **2** across a ship at right-angles to the fore-and-aft line **3** in opposition to the right or expected course ⟨*and quite* ~ *goes all decorum* – Shak⟩

**²athwart** *prep* **1** across **2** in opposition to

**athwartships** /ə'thwawt,ships/ *adv* across the ship from side to side

**atilt** /ə'tilt/ *adv or adj* **1** in a tilted position **2** in a jousting encounter; with lance in hand ⟨*run* ~ *at death* – Shak⟩

**atingle** /ə'ting·gl/ *adj* tingling, esp with excitement or exhilaration

**-ation** /-'aysh(ə)n/ *suffix* (*vb* → *n*) **1** action or process of ⟨*flirta*tion⟩ ⟨*computa*tion⟩ **2** result or product of (a specified action or process) ⟨*altera*tion⟩ ⟨*planta*tion⟩ **3** state or condition of ⟨*vexa*tion⟩ ⟨*starva*tion⟩ [ME *-acioun*, fr OF *-ation*, fr L *-ation-, -atio*, fr *-atus* -ate + *-ion-, -io* -ion]

**-ative** /-ətiv, -aytiv/ *suffix* (*vb, n* → *adj*) **1** of or connected with ⟨*authorit*ative⟩ **2** tending to; disposed to ⟨*talk*ative⟩ ⟨*lax*ative⟩ [ME, fr MF *-atif*, fr L *-ativus*, fr *-atus* + *-ivus* -ive]

**¹Atlantean** /ət'lantiən/ *adj* of or resembling Atlas; strong

**²Atlantean** *adj* of the legendary island of Atlantis

**Atlantic** /ət'lantik/ *adj* **1** of or found in, on, or near the Atlantic ocean **2** of the nations that border the Atlantic ocean ⟨*the* ~ *community*⟩ [L *Atlanticus*, fr Gk *Atlantikos*, fr *Atlantis* Atlantic ocean, fr *Atlant-, Atlas* Atlas (or the Atlas Mountains in NW Africa)]

**Atlanticism** /ət'lanti,siz(ə)m/ *n* a policy of military cooperation between European and N American powers [*Atlantic* (*ocean*)] – **Atlanticist** *n*

**Atlantis** /ət'lantis/ *n* a legendary island that was traditionally situated west of the Straits of Gibraltar and was swallowed up by the sea [L, fr Gk, prob fr *Atlantis* Atlantic ocean]

**atlas** /'atləs/ *n* **1** *cap* one who bears a heavy burden **2a** a bound collection of maps **b** a bound collection of tables and charts **3** the first vertebra of the neck that supports the skull **4** *pl* **atlantes** *building* a figure or half figure of a man used as a column to support an ENTABLATURE (upper part of a wall displaying decorative work) – compare CARYATID [*Atlas*, a Titan in Gk mythology who was forced to bear the heavens on his shoulders, fr L *Atlant-, Atlas*, fr Gk; (2) fr the title of a book of maps by Gerhardus Mercator †1594 Flemish cartographer]

**Atlas moth** *n* the largest Asian moth (*Attacus atlas*) that is cultivated for silk in some places

**atlatl** /'at,latl/ *n* a device used by Central American Indians for throwing a spear or dart that consists of a rod or board with a projection (e g a hook or thong) at the rear end to hold the weapon in place until released [of Uto-Aztecan origin; akin to Nahuatl *atlatl* atlatl]

**atman** /'ahtmən/ *n, often cap, Hinduism* **1** the innermost essence of each individual **2** the supreme universal self; BRAHMAN 1b [Skt *ātman*, lit., breath, soul; akin to OHG *ātum* breath]

**atmosphere** /'atməsfiə/ *n* **1a** a mass of gas enveloping a planet, moon, etc **b** the total mass of air surrounding the earth **2** the air of a locality **3** a surrounding influence or environment ⟨*an* ~ *of mutual trust*⟩ **4** a unit of pressure that corresponds to the average pressure of the air at sea level and is equal to 101 325 newtons per square metre (about 14.7 pounds per square inch) **5a** the overall aesthetic effect of a work of art **b** a dominant aesthetic or emotional effect or appeal – see also CLEAR the atmosphere [NL *atmosphaera*, fr Gk *atmos* vapour (akin to Gk *aēnai* to blow) + L *sphaera* sphere – more at WIND] – **atmosphered** *adj*

**atmospheric** /,atmə'sferik/ *adj* **1** of, occurring in, or like the atmosphere **2** having, marked by, or contributing aesthetic or emotional atmosphere ⟨~ *music*⟩ – **atmospherically** *adv*

**atmospherics** /,atmə'sferiks/ *n pl* the audible disturbances produced in a radio receiver by electrical atmospheric phenomena (e g lightning); *also* the electrical phenomena causing these disturbances

**atmospheric tide** *n* TIDE 1a(4) (waves of movement in the atmosphere)

**atoll** /'atol, ə'tol/ *n* a coral reef surrounding a lagoon [*atolu*, native name in the Maldive islands]

**atom** /'atəm/ *n* **1** any of the minute indivisible particles which, in the theories of early Greek and Roman MATERIALISTS (philosophers holding that the universe contains nothing but physical objects or phenomena caused by them), are the basic components of the universe **2a** a tiny particle; a mote **b** a bit, scrap ⟨*not an* ~ *of truth in it*⟩ **3a** the smallest subdivision of a chemical element that can exist alone or in combination, consisting of various numbers of electrons, protons, and neutrons **b** a group of such particles constituting the smallest quantity of a chemical group **4** the atom considered as a source of energy; nuclear power [ME, fr L *atomus*, fr Gk *atomos*, fr *atomos* indivisible, fr *a-* + *temnein* to cut – more at TOME]

**atom bomb, atomic bomb** *n* a bomb whose violent explosive power is due to the sudden release of ATOMIC ENERGY resulting from the splitting of nuclei of a heavy chemical element (e g plutonium or uranium) by neutrons in a very rapid CHAIN REACTION; *broadly* any bomb the explosive power of which is derived from atomic energy – **atom-bomb** *vt*

**atomic** /ə'tomik/ *adj* **1** of, concerned with, or making use of atoms, ATOMIC ENERGY, or ATOM BOMBS **2** *of a chemical element* existing in a state in which the atoms are separate rather than combined with one another or with the atoms of another element – **atomically** *adv*

**atomic clock** *n* a very accurate form of clock which is regulated by the natural frequency of vibration of some atomic system (e g a beam of caesium atoms)

**atomic energy** *n* energy that can be liberated by changes in the nucleus of an atom, esp by splitting (FISSION) of a heavy nucleus or fusion of light nuclei into heavier ones with accompanying loss of mass

**atomicity** /,atə'misəti/ *n* **1a** the number of atoms in the molecule of a (gaseous) chemical element **b** the number of replaceable atoms or groups in the molecule of a chemical compound **2** the state of consisting of atoms

**atomic mass** *n* the mass of an atom, usu expressed in ATOMIC MASS UNITS

**atomic mass unit** *n* a unit of mass for expressing masses of atoms, molecules, or nuclear particles equal to $^1/_{12}$ of the ATOMIC MASS of the most abundant ISOTOPE (form in which an atom can occur) of carbon, $_6C^{12}$

**atomic number** *n* an experimentally determined number

characteristic of a chemical element that represents the number of protons in the nucleus (which in a neutral atom equals the number of electrons outside the nucleus), and that determines the place of the element in the PERIODIC TABLE

**atomic pile** *n* REACTOR 3b

**atomics** /ə'tomiks/ *n taking sing vb, chiefly NAm* a branch of physics dealing with the properties of atoms, esp those that have applications in the development of ATOMIC ENERGY

**atomic theory** *n* **1** a theory of the nature of matter: all material substances are composed of minute particles or atoms of a comparatively small number of kinds and all the atoms of the same kind are uniform in size, weight, and other properties **2** any of several theories of the structure of the atom; *esp* one based on experimentation and theoretical considerations holding that the atom is composed essentially of a small positively charged comparatively heavy nucleus surrounded by a comparatively large arrangement of electrons

**atomic weight** *n* the ratio of the average mass of one atom of a chemical element to the mass of the $_6C^{12}$ carbon atom that is taken as 12

**atomism** /'atəmiz(ə)m/ *n* a doctrine that the universe is composed of simple indivisible minute particles – **atomist** *n*

**atomistic** /atə'mistik/ *adj* **1** of atoms or atomism **2** composed of many simple elements; *also* divided into unconnected or antagonistic fragments ⟨*an ~ society*⟩ – **atomistically** *adv*

**atom-ize, -ise** /'atəmiez/ *vt* **1** to reduce to minute particles or to a fine spray **2** to treat as made up of many discrete units – **atomization** *n*

**atom-izer, -iser** /'atəmiezə/ *n* an instrument used to reduce a liquid to a fine spray: eg **a** a (pressurized) container with a narrow outlet used to spray a perfume, disinfectant, pesticide, etc **b** a nozzle or valve through which oil is forced into a furnace to form fine particles so that it will burn more efficiently

**atom smasher** *n, informal* ACCELERATOR (device for speeding up electrically charged particles)

**atonal** /a'tohnl, ay-/ *adj* marked by avoidance or rejection of musical tonality; *esp* organized without reference to musical key and using all the 12 notes of the CHROMATIC SCALE (musical scale consisting of semitones) – **atonalism** *n*, **atonalist** *n*, **atonally** *adv*, **atonalistic** *adj*, **atonality** *n*

**atone** /ə'tohn/ *vt* **1** to supply satisfaction for; expiate **2** *obs* to reconcile ~ *vi* to make amends *for* ⟨*the crime must be* ~d *for*⟩ [ME *atonen* to become reconciled, fr *at on* in harmony, fr *at + on* one]

**atonement** /ə'tohnmənt/ *n* **1** *sometimes cap, Christianity* the reconciliation of God and mankind through the life and death of Christ; *also* the removal of mankind's burden of original sin through the death of Christ **2** reparation for an offence or injury; satisfaction ⟨*made ~ for his cruelty*⟩ **3** *obs* reconciliation

**atonic** /ə'tonik, a-/ *adj* **1** characterized by atony **2** *linguistics* not accented – **atonicity** *n*

**atony** /'atəni/ *n* lack of physiological TONE (healthy condition of tension and elasticity), esp in a muscle or muscular organ capable of contraction ⟨*post-partum haemorrhage due to uterine ~*⟩ [LL *atonia*, fr Gk, fr *atonos* without tone, fr *a-* + *tonos* tone]

**atop** /ə'top/ *prep* at the top of; on top of

**atopy** /'atəpi/ *n* a probably hereditary tendency to allergy in which usu several substances produce allergic symptoms (eg asthma or hay fever) [Gk *atopia* uncommonness, fr *atopos* out of the way, uncommon, fr *a-* + *topos* place – more at TOPIC] – **atopic** *adj*

**-ator** /-aytə/ *suffix* (→ *n*) ¹-OR ⟨*totalizator*⟩ [ME *-atour*, fr OF & L; OF, fr L *-ator*, fr *-atus* -ate + *-or*]

**ATP** *n* a chemical compound, $C_{10}H_{12}N_5O_3H_4P_3O_{10}$, that is a NUCLEOTIDE of ADENINE containing three PHOSPHATE groups and that is reversibly converted esp to ADP with the release of energy required for many life-supporting chemical reactions (eg protein synthesis) occurring in cells [*adenosine triphosphate*]

**ATPase** /,ay tee 'pee,ayz/ *n* an ENZYME that promotes the breakdown of ATP; esp one that breaks down ATP to ADP and a PHOSPHATE group

**atrabilious** /,atrə'biliəs/ *adj, formal* melancholic, ill-humoured – **atrabiliousness** *n* [L *atra bilis* black bile (cf MELANCHOLY)]

**atremble** /ə'trembl/ *adj* trembling

**atresia** /ə'treezyə, -zh(y)ə/ *n* **1** absence or closure of a natural passage (eg the anus) of the body **2** atrophy or disappearance of a part, esp a GRAAFIAN FOLLICLE (spherical body in the ovary containing a developing egg), by degeneration [NL, fr ²*a-* + Gk *trēsis* perforation, fr *tetrainein* to pierce – more at THROW]

**atrioventricular** /,aytriohven'trikyoolə, ,atri-/ *adj* of or located between an atrium and a lower chamber (VENTRICLE) of the heart [NL *atrium* + E *ventricular*]

**atrium** /'atri-əm, 'ay-/ *n, pl* **atria** /'atri-ə, 'ay-/ *also* **atriums** **1** an inner courtyard open to the sky (eg in a Roman house) **2** an anatomical cavity or passage; *esp* a chamber of the heart that receives blood directly from the veins and forces it backwards or downwards into a VENTRICLE (chamber from which blood is pumped to the veins) [(1) L; (2) NL, fr L] – **atrial** *adj*

**atrocious** /ə'trohshəs/ *adj* **1** extremely wicked, brutal, or cruel; barbaric **2** appalling, horrifying ⟨*the ~ weapons of modern war*⟩ ⟨*~ working conditions*⟩ **3** of very poor quality ⟨*~ handwriting*⟩ [L *atroc-, atrox* gloomy, cruel, fr *atr-, ater* black + *-oc-, -ox* looking, appearing (akin to Gk *ōps* eye) – more at EYE] – **atrociously** *adv*, – **atrociousness** *n*

**atrocity** /ə'trosəti/ *n* **1** the quality or state of being atrocious **2** an atrocious act, object, or situation; *esp* an act contrary to the rules of war (eg the killing of noncombatants)

¹**atrophy** /'atrəfi/ *n* **1** decrease in size or wasting away of a body part or tissue; *also* arrested development or loss of a part or organ incidental to the normal development or life of an animal or plant **2** a wasting away or progressive decline, esp from lack of use; degeneration ⟨*the ~ of freedom*⟩ [LL *atrophia*, fr Gk, fr *atrophos* ill-fed, fr *a-* + *trephein* to nourish; akin to Gk *thrombos* clot, curd] – **atrophic** *adj*

²**atrophy** *vb* to (cause to) undergo atrophy

**atropine** /'atrəpeen, -pin/ *n* a poisonous chemical compound (ALKALOID), $C_{17}H_{23}NO_3$, obtained from any of several related plants (family Solanaceae) including DEADLY NIGHTSHADE and used in medicine, esp to inhibit the actions of ACETYLCHOLINE (substance that transmits impulses between nerve endings) in the PARASYMPATHETIC NERVOUS SYSTEM (eg to dilate the pupil of the eye and to reduce salivation in premedication for a general anaesthetic) [Ger *atropin*, fr NL *Atropa*, genus name of deadly nightshade, fr Gk *Atropos*, one of the three mythical Fates]

**attaboy** /'atə,boy/ *interj, chiefly NAm* – used to encourage or express admiration [alter. of *that's the boy*]

**attach** /ə'tach/ *vt* **1** to seize (a person or property) by legal authority, esp under a writ **2** to bring (oneself) into an association **3** to order or appoint to serve with a unit or organization for special duties or for a temporary period ⟨*she was ~ed to NATO for the duration of the exercise*⟩ **4** to bind by personal ties (eg of affection or sympathy) ⟨*was strongly ~ed to his family*⟩ **5** to make fast (eg by tying or gluing) ⟨*~ a label to a package*⟩ **6** to ascribe, attribute ⟨*~ed great importance to public opinion polls*⟩ ~ *vi* **1** to become attached; adhere **2** *of an insurance policy* to come into legal effect (eg when certain specified conditions are met) ⟨*if a false declaration of the value of the property is made, the policy will not ~*⟩ often + *to* [ME *attachen*, fr MF *attacher*, fr OF *estachier*, fr *estache* stake, of Gmc origin; akin to OE *staca* stake] – **attachable** *adj*

**attaché** /ə'tashay/ *n* a technical expert on the staff of an embassy or legation ⟨*a military ~*⟩ [Fr, pp of *attacher*]

**attaché case** *n* a small thin case used esp for carrying papers and documents

**attached** /ə'tacht/ *adj* **1** feeling affection or liking **2** fixed or joined to something ⟨*please fill in the ~ form and return it within 7 days*⟩

**attachment** /ə'tachmənt/ *n* **1** a seizure of a person or property by legal process **2a** being personally attached; fidelity ⟨*~ to a cause*⟩ **b** an affectionate regard ⟨*a deep ~ to the Lake district*⟩ **3** a device attached to a machine or implement; *esp* one which enables some new function to be performed ⟨*a sanding ~ for an electric drill*⟩ **4** the physical connection by which one thing is attached to another **5** a temporary posting or tour of duty in an organization, branch of an organization, or military unit other than that in which one is normally employed ⟨*working in the BBC on ~ from Radio Zimbabwe*⟩ □ (2) often + *to*

¹**attack** /ə'tak/ *vt* **1a** to make a physical assault upon ⟨*Israeli troops ~ed PLO bases in Lebanon*⟩ **b** to open hostilities against; direct armed forces against ⟨*on the morning of June 22 1941 Germany ~ed Russia on a wide front*⟩ **2** to take the initiative against in a game or contest **3** to assail with unfriendly or bitter words **4** to begin to affect or to act on injuriously **5** to set to work on, esp vigorously ~ *vi* to make an attack [MF *attaquer*, fr OIt *attaccare* to attach, fr

(assumed) OIt *stacca* stake, of Gmc origin; akin to OE *staca*] –
**attacker** *n*
  **synonyms Attack, assail, assault, bombard,** and **storm** are all
  comparable literally and figuratively when they mean "make a violent
  attack on". **Attack** implies violent and vigorous aggression, especially taking the initiative in such aggression. **Assail** suggests a series
  of attacking blows ⟨**assailed** *by doubts/wave after wave of infantry*⟩. **Assail** stresses violence and refers to an attack at close
  quarters ⟨*ears suddenly* **assaulted** *by a blast of rock music*⟩ and
  particularly to rape. **Bombard** means to assail repeatedly with shells
  or bombs, and so by extension to importune unremittingly with a
  series of similar requests or items ⟨*planes* **bombarded** *the city for
  three days and nights*⟩ ⟨*the producer was* **bombarded** *with requests
  for tickets*⟩. **Storm** stresses the violence, rush, and effectiveness of
  an **attack**, suggesting that opposition is swept aside ⟨**stormed** *the
  citadel and occupied the town*⟩.
²**attack** *n* 1 the act of attacking; an assault 2a a belligerent
  or antagonistic action b a verbal assault; an argument against
  or criticism of something or someone ⟨*the Opposition* ~ *on
  the Chancellor's Budget policy*⟩ 3 the beginning of destructive
  action (e g by a chemical agent) 4 the setting to work on some
  undertaking ⟨*made a new* ~ *on the problem*⟩ 5 the act or
  manner of beginning a musical note or phrase; *specif* cleanness
  and decisiveness in beginning a note or passage 6 a fit of sickness; *esp* an active period of a long-lasting or recurrent disease
  ⟨*a heart* ~⟩ ⟨*an* ~ *of gout*⟩ 7a an attempt to score or gain
  ground or an advantage in a game b *taking sing or pl vb* the
  attacking players in a team or the positions they occupy; *also*
  the bowlers in a cricket team ⟨*the England* ~ *could make little
  headway against the West Indian batting*⟩ □ *(2 & 4)* often +
  *on*
**attack trainer** *n* a military aircraft suitable for both training
  and ground-attack roles
**attain** /ə'tayn/ *vt* to reach as an end; achieve ⟨~ *his heart's
  desire*⟩ ~ *vi* to come or arrive by motion, growth, or effort –
  + *to synonyms* see ¹REACH [ME *atteynen*, fr OF *ataindre*, fr
  (assumed) VL *attangere*, fr L *attingere*, fr *ad-* + *tangere* to
  touch – more at TANGENT] – **attainable** *adj*, **attainableness** *n*,
  **attainability** *n*
**attainder** /ə'tayndə/ *n* 1 a penalty enforced until 1870 against
  a person sentenced to death or outlawry, usu after a conviction
  of treason, by which he/she forfeited his/her property and civil
  rights 2 *obs* dishonour [ME *attaynder*, fr MF *ataindre* to
  accuse, attain]
**attainment** /ə'taynmənt/ *n* 1 something attained; an accomplishment 2 the quality and quantity of a pupil's work and
  knowledge ⟨*an* ~ *test*⟩
**attaint** /ə'taynt/ *vt* 1 to subject to the penalty of attainder 2
  *archaic* to infect, corrupt, or taint [ME *attaynten*, fr MF *ataint*,
  pp of *ataindre*]
**attainture** /ə'taynchə/ *n*, *obs* attainder
**attar** /'atə/ *n* a fragrant ESSENTIAL OIL (e g from rose petals);
  *also* a fragrance [Per '*atir* perfumed, fr Ar, fr '*iṭr* perfume]
¹**attempt** /ə'tempt/ *vt* 1 to make an effort to do, accomplish,
  solve, or effect, esp without success ⟨~ed *to swim the swollen
  river*⟩ 2 to try 2a to climb ⟨*three teams will* ~ *the North Face
  of the Eiger*⟩ b to better or break (a record) ⟨*at least three
  athletes have a chance of* ~ing *the 1500m record this summer*⟩
  [L *attemptare*, fr *ad-* + *temptare* to touch, try – more at TEMPT]
  – **attemptable** *adj*
²**attempt** *n* 1 the act or an instance of attempting; *esp* an unsuccessful effort ⟨*embarrassed about his* ~s *at gardening*⟩ 2 an
  attack, assault – often + *on* ⟨*the recent* ~ *on the Pope*⟩
**attend** /ə'tend/ *vt* 1 to take charge of; LOOK AFTER 2 to be in
  store for 3a to go or stay with as a companion, nurse, or servant b *of a doctor* to visit professionally 4 to be present with;
  accompany, escort 5 to be present at ⟨~ *school*⟩ 6 *archaic* to
  give heed to ~ *vi* 1 to apply oneself – often + *to* ⟨~ *to your
  work*⟩ 2 to apply the mind or pay attention; heed – often +
  *to* 3 to be ready for service – often + *on usage* see ¹TEND
  *synonyms* see ACCOMPANY [ME *attenden*, fr OF *atendre*, fr L
  *attendere*, lit., to stretch to, fr *ad-* + *tendere* to stretch – more
  at THIN] – **attender** *n*
  **attend to** *vt* to deal with; handle ⟨*we can* attend to *that
  problem tomorrow*⟩
**attendance** /ə'tend(ə)ns/ *n* 1 the number of people attending
  ⟨*daily* ~ *at the exhibition dwindled*⟩ 2 the number of times a
  person attends, usu out of a possible maximum ⟨*poor* ~ *because of his illness*⟩
**attendance centre** *n* a centre at which a young offender is

obliged to attend regularly as an alternative to being sent to
prison or borstal
¹**attendant** /ə'tend(ə)nt/ *adj* accompanying or following as a
  consequence
²**attendant** *n* one who attends another to perform a service;
  *esp* an employee who waits on customers ⟨*a car park* ~⟩
**attending** /ə'tendiŋ/ *adj*, *NAm* serving as a physician on the
  staff of a teaching hospital ⟨*an* ~ *surgeon*⟩
**attention** /ə'tensh(ə)n/ *n* 1 attending, esp by concentrating on
  an object of sense or thought 2 consideration with a view to
  action ⟨*a problem requiring your prompt* ~⟩ 3a *usu pl* civility
  or courtesy, esp in courtship ⟨*his constant* ~s *were unmistakable*⟩ b sympathetic consideration of the needs and wants of
  others 4 a formal drill position of readiness assumed by a
  soldier – often as a command [ME *attencioun*, fr L *attention-,
  attentio*, fr *attentus*, pp of *attendere*] – **attentional** *adj*
**attention span** *n* the length of time that an individual can
  concentrate with full efficiency on a particular task
**attentive** /ə'tentiv/ *adj* 1a observant, concentrating ⟨*goes
  about his work in an* ~ *manner*⟩ b paying attention; listening
  ⟨*an* ~ *audience*⟩ 2 solicitous 3 paying attentions (as if) in the
  role of a suitor *antonyms* inattentive, careless, abstracted,
  negligent – **attentively** *adv*, **attentiveness** *n*
¹**attenuate** /ə'tenyooayt/ *vt* 1 to make thin or slender 2 to
  lessen the amount, force, or value of; weaken 3 to reduce the
  severity, virulence, or vitality of 4 to make thin in consistency;
  rarefy ~ *vi* to become thin, fine, or less [L *attenuatus*, pp of
  *attenuare* to make thin, fr *ad-* + *tenuis* thin – more at THIN] –
  **attenuation** *n*
²**attenuate** /ə'tenyooət, -ayt/ *adj* 1 attenuated, esp in thickness,
  density, or force 2 tapering gradually, usu to a long slender
  point ⟨~ *leaves*⟩
**attenuator** /ə'tenyoo,aytə/ *n* a device for attenuating; *esp* one
  for reducing the AMPLITUDE (strength or height of a wave) of
  an electrical signal without appreciable distortion
**attest** /ə'test/ *vt* 1a to affirm to be true or genuine; *specif* to
  authenticate (e g a will) by signing as a witness b to authenticate, esp officially 2 to establish as existing or being valid ⟨*a
  usage* ~ed *by several eminent authors*⟩ 3 to be proof of; bear
  witness to ⟨*the ruins of the city* ~ *its ancient magnificence*⟩
  ~ *vi* to bear witness; testify ⟨~ *to the truth of the statement*⟩
  [MF *attester*, fr L *attestari*, fr *ad-* + *testis* witness – more at
  TESTAMENT] – **attester, attestor** *n*, **attestation** *n*
**attic** /'atik/ *n* 1 a low storey above the CORNICE (line of projecting moulding or brickwork running between the eaves) at
  the front of a classical building 2 a room or space immediately
  under the roof of a building [Fr *attique*, fr *attique* of Attica, fr
  L *Atticus*; fr its usu conforming to the Attic order of archi-
  tecture]
¹**Attic** *adj* 1 (characteristic) of Attica or Athens 2 showing
  simplicity, purity, and refinement ⟨*an* ~ *prose style*⟩ [L *Atticus*, fr Gk *Attikos*, fr *Attikē* Attica, state of ancient Greece]
²**Attic** *n* a Greek dialect of ancient Attica which became the
  literary language of the Greek-speaking world
**atticism** /'ati,siz(ə)m/ *n*, *often cap* 1 a characteristic feature of
  Attic Greek occurring in another language or dialect 2 a witty
  or well-turned phrase
¹**attire** /ə'tie•ə/ *vt, formal* to put garments on; dress, array; *esp*
  to clothe in fancy or rich garments [ME *attiren*, fr OF *atirier*,
  fr *a-* (fr L *ad-*) + *tire* order, rank, of Gmc origin; akin to OE
  *tīr* glory; akin to L *deus* god – more at DEITY]
²**attire** *n* 1 the antlers (and scalp) of a stag or buck 2 *formal*
  dress, clothes; *esp* splendid or decorative clothing
**attitude** /'atityoohd/ *n* 1 the arrangement of the parts of a
  body or figure; a posture 2 a feeling, emotion, or mental position with regard to a fact or state 3 a manner assumed for a
  specific purpose ⟨*adopted a threatening* ~⟩ 4 a ballet position
  in which the dancer balances on one leg with the other raised
  behind and bent at the knee 5 the position of an aircraft or
  spacecraft relative to a particular point of reference (e g the
  horizon) 6 a state of readiness of a living organism to respond
  in a characteristic way to a stimulus (e g an object, concept, or
  situation) [Fr, fr It *attitudine*, fr *attitudine* aptitude, fr LL *apti-
  tudin-, aptitudo* fitness, fr L *aptus* fit – more at APT]
**attitudinal** /,ati'tyoohdinl/ *adj* relating to, based on, or expressive of personal attitudes or feelings ⟨*an* ~ *survey*⟩ [*attitude* + *-inal* (as in *aptitudinal*, fr L *aptitudin-, aptitudo*)]
**attitudin-ize, -ise** /,ati'tyoohdiniez/ *vi* to assume an affected
  mental attitude; pose
**atto-** *comb form* one million million millionth $(10^{-18})$ part of

(a specified unit) ⟨atto*gram*⟩ [ISV, fr Dan or Norw *atten* eighteen, fr ON *āttjān*; akin to OE *eahtatīene* eighteen]

**attorn** /ə'tuhn/ *vi* to formally agree to continue a tenancy under a new owner or landlord [ME *attournen*, fr MF *atorner*, fr OF, fr *a-* (fr L *ad-*) + *torner* to turn] – **attornment** *n*

**attorney** /ə'tuhni/ *n* **1** a person legally appointed by another to act on his/her behalf **2** *NAm* a lawyer combining the functions of the English barrister and solicitor [ME *attourney*, fr MF *atorné*, pp of *atorner*] – **attorneyship** *n*

**attorney general** *n*, *pl* **attorneys general, attorney generals** *often cap A&G* the chief legal officer of a nation or state who represents the government in its legal actions and serves as its principal legal advisor

**attract** /ə'trakt/ *vt* **1** to cause to approach or adhere: eg **1a** to pull to or towards oneself or itself ⟨*a magnet ~ s iron*⟩ **b** to draw by appeal to natural or excited interest, emotion, or aesthetic sense; charm ⟨*~ attention*⟩ **2** to be liable for – used in law and insurance ⟨*estates passing between spouses because of death do not ~ capital transfer tax*⟩ *~ vi* to possess or exercise the power of attraction ⟨*opposites ~*⟩ *antonym* repel [ME *attracten*, fr L *attractus*, pp of *attrahere*, fr *ad-* + *trahere* to draw – more at DRAW] – **attractable** *adj*, **attractor** *n*

**attractant** /ə'trakt(ə)nt/ *n* something that attracts; *esp* a substance (eg a pheromone) that attracts insects or other animals

**attraction** /ə'traksh(ə)n/ *n* **1a** *usu pl* a characteristic that causes interest or admiration **b** personal charm **2** the action or power of drawing forth a response (eg interest or affection); an attractive quality **3** a force (eg between unlike electric charges, unlike magnetic poles, or particles of matter) tending to resist separation **4** something that attracts or is intended to attract people by appealing to their desires and tastes ⟨*the presidential candidate will be the main ~*⟩

**attractive** /ə'traktiv/ *adj* **1** having or relating to the power to attract ⟨*~ forces between molecules*⟩ ⟨*an ~ offer*⟩ **2** arousing interest or pleasure; charming ⟨*an ~ smile*⟩ – **attractively** *adv*, **attractiveness** *n*, **attractivity** *n*

**¹attribute** /'atribyooht/ *n* **1** a characteristic feature, property, or quality ⟨*wisdom is one of his ~ s*⟩; *also, philosophy* a property possessed by a concept or object but which is not one of the characteristics by means of which the concept or object is defined ⟨*if man is defined as the language-using animal, then his bipedality can be seen only as an ~*⟩ **2** an object closely associated with or belonging to a specific person, thing, or office ⟨*a sceptre is the ~ of power*⟩; *esp* such an object used to show the identity of a figure in painting or sculpture (eg an owl for Athene) **3** *linguistics* a subordinate word or phrase that limits the meaning of another; *esp* an adjective *synonyms* see ¹QUALITY [ME, fr L *attributus*, pp of *attribuere* to attribute, fr *ad-* + *tribuere* to bestow – more at TRIBUTE]

**²attribute** /ə'tribyooht/ *vt* to reckon as made or originating in an indicated fashion – *usu* + *to* ⟨*~ d the invention to a Russian*⟩ ⟨*a manuscript ~ d to the 10th century*⟩ *synonyms* see ASCRIBE – **attributable** *adj*, **attributer** *n*

**attribute to** *vt* **1** to explain by indicating as a cause ⟨*attributed his success to his coach*⟩ **2** to regard as a characteristic of (a person or thing) ⟨*attributed feelings of jealousy to her cousin*⟩

**attribute with** *vt* to regard as having (a characteristic) ⟨*attributed her cousin with feelings of jealousy*⟩

**attribution** /,atri'byooohsh(ə)n/ *n* the act of attributing; *esp* the ascribing of a work (eg of literature or art) to a particular author, artist, or period – **attributional** *adj*

**attributive** /ə'tribyootiv/ *adj* **1** relating to or of the nature of an attribute **2** directly preceding a noun, without a linking verb such as *be* or *become* ⟨*city* in "city *streets*" is an *~ noun*⟩ ⟨*red* in "red *dress*" is in the *~ position*⟩ – compare PREDICATIVE – **attributive** *n*, **attributively** *adv*

**attrited** /ə'trietid/ *adj* worn by attrition

**attrition** /ə'trish(ə)n/ *n* **1** *Christianity* sorrow for one's sins that arises from a motive other than that of the love of God (eg fear of punishment) – compare CONTRITION **2** the act of rubbing together; friction; *also* the act of wearing or grinding down by friction **3** the act of weakening or exhausting by constant harassment or abuse ⟨*war of ~*⟩ [L *attrition-, attritio*, fr *attritus*, pp of *atterere* to rub against, fr *ad-* + *terere* to rub – more at THROW; (1) ME *attricioun*, fr (assumed) ML *attrition-, attritio*, fr L] – **attritional** *adj*

**attune** /ə'tyoohn/ *vt* **1** to cause or allow to become used, accustomed, or acclimatized – *usu* + *to* ⟨*the expedition rested to ~ the climbers to the altitude*⟩ **2** to bring into harmony; tune – **attunement** *n*

**atwitter** /ə'twitə/ *adj* nervously excited ⟨*the whole village was all ~ at the news*⟩

**atypical** /,ay'tipikl/ *adj* not typical; deviating from a standard or usual type – **atypically** *adv*, **atypicality** *n*

**aubade** /'oh,bahd/ *n* a (love) story or poem associated with morning or the dawn [Fr, fr (assumed) OProv *aubada*, fr OProv *alba, auba* dawn, fr (assumed) VL *alba*, fr L, fem of *albus* white]

**aubergine** /'ohbəzheen, -jeen/ *n* **1** (the edible usu smooth dark purple egg-shaped fruit of) the eggplant **2** a deep reddish-purple colour [Fr, fr Catal *albergínia*, fr Ar *al-bādhinjān* the eggplant, fr *al* the + *bādhinjān* eggplant, fr Per *bādingān*]

**aubrietia** *also* **aubretia** /aw'breeshə/ *n* any of various colourful trailing spring-flowering rock plants (genus *Aubrietia*) of the cabbage family [NL *Aubrietia*, genus name, fr Claude *Aubriet* †1742 Fr painter of flowers & animals]

**auburn** /'awbən/ *adj or n* (of) a reddish-brown colour [adj ME *aborne* blond, fr MF *auborne*, fr ML *alburnus* whitish, fr L *albus* white; n fr adj]

**au courant** /,oh kooh'ronh (*Fr o kurã*)/ *adj* **1** fully informed; up-to-date **2** fully familiar; conversant [Fr, lit., in the current]

**¹auction** /'awksh(ə)n/ *n* **1** a public sale of property in which prospective buyers bid against one another and the sale is made to the buyer offering the highest bid **2** the act or process of bidding in some card games [L *auction-, auctio*, lit., increase, fr *auctus*, pp of *augēre* to increase – more at EKE OUT]

**²auction** *vt* to sell at auction – often + *off* ⟨*~ ed off the family silver*⟩

**auction bridge** *n* a form of bridge differing from CONTRACT BRIDGE in that tricks made in excess of the number one has undertaken to try to win are also scored towards game

**auctioneer** /,awksh(ə)n'iə/ *n* an agent who sells goods at auction – **auctioneer** *vt*

**auctorial** /awk'tawriəl/ *adj* of an author [L *auctor* author – more at AUTHOR]

**audacious** /aw'dayshəs/ *adj* **1a** intrepidly daring; adventurous ⟨*an ~ mountain climber*⟩ **b** recklessly bold; rash **2** contemptuous of law, religion, or decorum; insolent *synonyms* see ¹ADVENTURE *antonym* timorous [MF *audacieux*, fr *audace* boldness, fr L *audacia*, fr *audac-, audax* bold, fr *audēre* to dare, fr *avidus* eager – more at AVID] – **audaciously** *adv*, **audaciousness** *n*, **audacity** *n*

**audible** /'awdəbl/ *adj* (capable of being) heard [LL *audibilis*, fr L *audire* to hear; akin to Gk *aisthanesthai* to perceive, Skt *āvis* evidently] – **audibly** *adv*, **audibility** *n*

**audience** /'awdi-əns/ *n* **1a** a formal hearing or interview ⟨*an ~ with the pope*⟩ **b** an opportunity of being heard ⟨*the court refused him ~*⟩ **2** *taking sing or pl vb* a group of listeners or spectators ⟨*the pianist played to an appreciative ~*⟩ [ME, fr MF, fr L *audientia*, fr *audient-, audiens*, prp of *audire*]

**¹audio** /'awdioh/ *adj* **1** of or being acoustic, mechanical, or electrical frequencies corresponding to normally audible sound waves which are of frequencies approximately from 20 to 20,000 hertz **2a** of sound or its reproduction, esp high-fidelity reproduction **b** relating to or used in the transmission or reception of sound – compare VIDEO [*audio-*]

**²audio** *n* the transmission, reception, or reproduction of sound

**audio-** *comb form* **1** hearing ⟨*audiometer*⟩ **2** sound ⟨*audiophile*⟩ **3** auditory and ⟨*audiovisual*⟩ [L *audire* to hear]

**audiogenic** /,awdiə'jenik, ,awdioh-/ *adj, esp of an epileptic fit* produced by frequencies corresponding to sound waves

**audio-'lingual** *adj* involving a drill routine of listening and speaking in language learning

**audiology** /,awdi'oləji/ *n* a branch of biology dealing with hearing; *specif* diagnosis and therapy of hearing defects – **audiologist** *n*, **audiological** *adj*

**audiometer** /,awdi'omitə/ *n* an instrument used in measuring a person's sensitivity to the frequency and intensity of sound – **audiometry** *n*, **audiometric** *adj*

**audiophile** /'awdiə,fiel, 'awdioh-/ *n* someone with a keen interest in the reproduction of sound, esp of music from high-fidelity broadcasts or recordings

**audiovisual** /,awdioh'viz(h)yoosl/ *adj* of or involving both hearing and sight – used esp of teaching methods that employ a combination of film strips or slides and recordings

**¹audit** /'awdit/ *n* **1a** a formal or official examination and certification of the correctness of an account book **b** a methodical examination and review of a situation (eg within a business enterprise) **2** the final report of an examination of account

# aud

94

books by properly qualified accountants [ME, fr L *auditus* act of hearing, fr *auditus*, pp] – **auditable** *adj*

²**audit** *vt* to perform an audit on ⟨~ *the account books*⟩

¹**audition** /aw'dish(ə)n/ *n* **1** the power or sense of hearing **2** a trial performance to appraise an entertainer's abilities or judge his/her suitability for a particular role [MF or L; MF, fr L *audition-*, *auditio*, fr *auditus*, pp of *audire*]

²**audition** *vt* to test (eg for a role) in an audition ~ *vi* to give a trial performance – usu + *for* ⟨*I* ~ed *for the part but didn't get it*⟩

**auditive** /'awditiv/ *adj* auditory

**auditor** /'awditə/ *n* **1** one who hears or listens; *esp* a member of an audience **2** one authorized to audit accounts **3** *NAm* one who attends a course of study without wishing or expecting to receive formal qualifications

**auditorium** /,awdi'tawri-əm/ *n*, *pl* **auditoriums**, **auditoria** /-riə/ **1** the part of a building from which an audience views a play, film, concert, etc ⟨*the actors entered from the back of the* ~ *and mingled with the audience*⟩ **2** (a large room in) a building for meetings, public lectures, etc ⟨*the college's main* ~⟩ [L, fr *auditus*, pp]

¹**auditory** /'awdit(ə)ri/ *n*, *archaic* **1** AUDIENCE 2 **2** an auditorium [ME *auditorie*, fr L *auditorium*]

²**auditory** *adj* of or experienced through hearing [LL *auditorius*, fr L *auditus*]

**auditory nerve** *n* either of the 8th pair of CRANIAL NERVES that transmit impulses concerned with hearing and balance from the INNER EAR to the brain

**au fait** /,oh 'fay/ *adj* **1** fully competent; capable **2** fully informed; familiar – + *with* [Fr, lit., to the point]

**Aufklärung** /'owf,kleərəng (*Ger* aʊfkleːrʊŋ)/ *n* ENLIGHTENMENT 2 [Ger, fr *aufklären* to enlighten, clear up]

**au fond** /oh 'fonh (*Fr* o fɔ̃)/ *adv* at bottom; fundamentally [Fr]

**auf Wiedersehen** /,owf 'veedzayn (*Ger* aʊf viːdərzeːən) /*interj* – used to express farewell [Ger, lit., till seeing again]

**Augean stable** /aw'jee-ən/ *n*, **Augean stables** *n pl* a condition or place marked by great accumulation of filth or corruption ⟨*every government should attend to cleaning its own Augean stables*⟩ [fr the Gk myth of *Augeas*, king of Elis in Greece, whose stable was uncleaned for 30 years until Hercules cleaned it]

**auger** /'awgə/ *n* **1** a tool for boring large holes in wood consisting of a shank with a crosswise handle, a central tapered screw which drives the tool into the wood, a pair of cutting lips with projecting spurs that cut the edge of the hole, and a wide spiral channel to carry away the wood removed – compare GIMLET **2** any of various instruments or devices shaped like an auger: eg **2a** any of various tools having wide spiral channels used for digging or drilling holes in the ground **b** a wide-spiralled component of various machines used to convey or mix materials, or to force them through an opening ⟨*the* ~ *used to force meat through the blades of a mincer*⟩ △ augur [ME, alter. (by incorrect division of *a nauger*) of *nauger*, fr OE *nafogār*, fr *nafu* nave + *gār* spear; fr its being orig used to bore the naves of wheels]

¹**aught** /awt/ *pron* **1** all ⟨*for* ~ *I care*⟩ **2** *archaic* anything [ME, fr OE *āwiht*, fr *ā* ever + *wiht* creature, thing – more at WIGHT]

²**aught** *n* zero, nought [alter. (by incorrect division of *a naught*) of *naught*]

**augite** /'awjiet/ *n* **1** a mineral consisting of an aluminium-containing usu black or dark green PYROXENE that is found in IGNEOUS rocks **2** PYROXENE [L *augites*, a precious stone, fr Gk *augitēs*, fr *augē* brightness] – **augitic** *adj*

¹**augment** /awg'ment/ *vt* **1** to make (something well or adequately developed) greater, more numerous, larger, or more intense **2** to add an augment to; *also* to make (a musical note) augmented ~ *vi* to become augmented **synonyms** see ¹INCREASE [ME *augmenten*, fr MF *augmenter*, fr LL *augmentare*, fr *augmentum* increase, fr *augēre* to increase – more at EKE OUT] – **augmentable** *adj*, **augmenter**, **augmentor** *n*, **augmentation** *n*

²**augment** /'awgment/ *n* a prefixed or lengthened initial vowel marking past tense, esp in Greek and Sanskrit verbs

¹**augmentative** /awg'mentətiv/ *adj* **1** able to augment **2** having or being an augmentative

²**augmentative** *n* (a word containing) an affix or particle indicating greatness or largeness and sometimes awkwardness or unattractiveness

**augmented** /awg'mentid/ *adj*, *of a musical interval* made one semitone greater than MAJOR or PERFECT ⟨*an* ~ *fifth*⟩ – compare DIMINISHED, MAJOR 5c, MINOR 3c, PERFECT 5a

**au gratin** /,oh 'gratin (*Fr* o gratɛ̃)/ *adj* covered with breadcrumbs or grated cheese and browned (eg under a grill) [Fr, lit., with the burnt scrapings from the pan]

¹**augur** /'awgə/ *n* someone who foretells events by omens; a soothsayer; *specif* an official of ancient Rome responsible for establishing the auspiciousness of public events by reference to accepted omens and portents △ auger [L; prob akin to L *augēre*]

²**augur** *vt* **1** to foretell, esp from omens **2** to give promise of; presage ⟨*higher pay* ~s *a better future*⟩ ~ *vi* to predict the future, esp from omens **synonyms** see FORETELL

**augury** /'awgyoori/ *n* **1** divination from omens, portents, or chance events (eg the fall of lots) **2** an omen, portent

**august** /aw'gust/ *adj* majestically dignified or grand [L *augustus*; akin to L *augēre* to increase] – **augustly** *adv*, **augustness** *n*

**August** /'awgəst/ *n* the 8th month of the year according to the GREGORIAN CALENDAR (standard Western calendar) – see MONTH table [ME, fr OE, fr L *Augustus*, fr *Augustus* Caesar]

**Augustan** /aw'gust(ə)n/ *adj* **1** (characteristic) of Augustus Caesar or his period; *also* (characteristic) of the literature of his reign (eg the works of Virgil and Ovid) **2** (characteristic) of a period in a country's art and literature which takes the Roman Augustans as its model and is marked by a rather heavy or stately refinement and elegance (eg the period of Corneille and Racine in France and of Dryden, Pope, and Johnson in England) [*Augustus* Caesar †14 AD first Roman emperor (reigned 27 BC–14 AD)] – **Augustan** *n*

**August Bank Holiday** *n* a public holiday in England, Wales, and N Ireland which formerly took place on the first Monday in August, but which is now observed on the last Monday

¹**Augustinian** /,awgə'stini-ən/ *adj* **1** of St Augustine of Hippo or his doctrines **2** of any of several religious orders following a monastic way of life traditionally held to have been laid down by St Augustine [St *Augustine* †430 Numidian church father & Bishop of Hippo in N Africa] – **Augustinianism** *n*

²**Augustinian** *n* **1** a follower of St Augustine **2** a member of an Augustinian order; *specif* a friar of the Hermits of St Augustine founded in 1256 and devoted to educational, missionary, and parish work

**au jus** /oh 'zhooh (*Fr* o ʒy)/ *adj*, *of meat* served in the juice or sauce obtained from roasting [Fr, lit., with juice]

**auk** /awk/ *n* any of several black and white short-necked diving seabirds (family Alcidae of the order Charadriiformes) that breed in colder parts of the northern hemisphere [Norw or Icel *alk*, *alka*, fr ON *ālka*; akin to L *olor* swan]

**au lait** /oh 'lay (*Fr* o lɛ)/ *adj* (made or served) with milk [Fr]

**auld** /awld/ *adj*, *chiefly Scot* old [ME (northern), var of ME *ald*, fr OE *eald* – more at OLD]

**auld lang syne** /awld lang 'sien; USE *the pronunciation* zien *is often used but is disapproved of by purists*/ *n* the past, esp viewed nostalgically; the good old days [Sc, lit., old long ago]

**aumbry** /'awmbri/ *n*, *archaic* AMBRY (recess in a church wall for holding vessels used in Holy Communion)

**au naturel** /,oh natyoo'rel/ *adj* **1** in natural style or condition **2** uncooked or cooked plainly **3** *euph* naked [Fr]

**aunt** /ahnt/ *n* **1a** the sister of one's father or mother **b** the wife of one's uncle **2** – used as a term of courtesy or affection for a woman who is a close friend of a young child or its parents [ME, fr OF *ante*, fr L *amita*; akin to OHG *amma* mother, nurse, Gk *amma* nurse] – **aunthood** *n*, **auntlike** *adj*, **auntly** *adj*

**auntie, aunty** /'ahnti/ *n*, *informal* an aunt

**Aunt Sally** /'sali/ *n* **1** an effigy of a woman usu smoking a pipe, at which objects are thrown at a fair **2** *Br* an easy target of criticism or attack; *esp* an argument or adversary set up or devised only to be easily demolished

**au pair** /oh 'peə (*Fr* o pɛr)/, **au pair girl** *n* a foreign girl who does domestic work for a family in return for room and board and the opportunity to learn her hosts' language [Fr *au pair* on equal terms] – **au pair** *vi*

**aur-** /awr-/, **auri-** *comb form* **1** ear ⟨*aural*⟩ ⟨*auriscope*⟩ **2** aural and ⟨*aurinasal*⟩ [L, fr *auris* – more at EAR]

**aura** /'awrə/ *n* **1a** a faint odour ⟨*an* ~ *of roses*⟩ **b** a distinctive atmosphere or quality associated with a person or thing ⟨*the place had an* ~ *of mystery*⟩ **2a** a luminous radiation surrounding a person or thing; NIMBUS **b** a usu coloured radiance held (eg by spiritualists) to be produced by and surround a person or thing and to be visible only to those with highly developed psychic powers **3** a sensation preceding and giving warning of an attack of epilepsy or similar convulsive disorder which may affect sight, hearing, taste, etc (eg such that the sufferer sees flashing lights or has a ringing sensation in the ears) [ME, fr L, air, breeze, fr Gk; akin to Gk *aēr* air]

**aural** /'awrəl/; USE aural *is sometimes pronounced* 'owrəl *in order to distinguish it from* oral/ *adj* of the ear or the sense of hearing – **aurally** *adv*

**aurar** /'owrah, 'awrah/ *n pl, sing* **eyrir** /'ayriə/ – see *krona* at MONEY table [Icel]

**aureate** /'awriət, -ayt/ *adj* 1 of a golden colour or brilliance 2 *of literary style* over elaborate or pompously florid [ME *aureat*, fr ML *aureatus* decorated with gold, fr L *aureus* golden – more at ORIOLE]

**aureola** /aw'ree·ələ/ *n, pl* **aureolas, aureolae** /-lie/ an aureole

**aureole** /'awriohl/ *n* 1 a radiant light surrounding the head or body of a representation of a holy figure – compare NIMBUS 2 a radiance, aura ⟨*had about him an* ~ *of youth and health*⟩ 3 the halo surrounding the sun, moon, or other bright light when seen through thin cloud or mist; CORONA **4 aureole, metamorphic aureole** a ring-shaped zone of rock that surrounds a mass (INTRUSION) of a different type of rock [ME, heavenly crown worn by saints, fr ML *aureola*, fr L, fem of *aureolus* golden – more at ORIOLE] – **aureole** *vt*

**Aureomycin** /ˌawrioh'miesin/ *trademark* – used for the antibiotic drug CHLORTETRACYCLINE

**au revoir** /ˌoh rə'vwah (*Fr* o rəvwa:r)/ *interj* – used to express farewell [Fr, lit., till seeing again]

**auric** /'awrik/ *adj* of or derived from gold, esp when having a VALENCY of three [L *aurum* gold – more at ORIOLE]

**auricle** /'awrikl/ *n* 1a PINNA (external part of the ear) b an ATRIUM (upper chamber) of the heart – not now used technically 2 an angular or ear-shaped anatomical lobe or process (eg one at the top of the atrium of the heart) [L *auricula*, fr dim. of *auris* ear] – **auriculate** *adj*

**auricula** /ə'rikyoolə/ *n* a yellow-flowered Alpine primrose (*Primula auricula*) [NL, fr L, external ear; fr the shape of its leaves]

**auricular** /aw'rikyoolə/ *adj* 1 of or using the ear or the sense of hearing 2 told privately ⟨*an* ~ *confession*⟩ 3 understood or recognized by the sense of hearing **4a** of or shaped like an ear **b** ATRIAL

**auriferous** /aw'rifərəs/ *adj, of rock* gold-bearing [L *aurifer*, fr *aurum* + *-fer* -ferous]

**Aurignacian** /ˌawrig'naysh(ə)n/ *adj* of a culture of the late PALAEOLITHIC period in the development of the human race, characterized by finely made artefacts of stone and bone, cave paintings, and engravings [Fr *aurignacien*, fr *Aurignac*, village in SW France]

**aurist** /'awrist/ *n* an ear specialist

**aurochs** /'awroks/ *n, pl* **aurochs** an extinct large long-horned wild ox (*Bos taurus primigenius*) of the German forests held to be a wild ancestor of domestic cattle [Ger, fr OHG *ūrohso*, fr *ūro* aurochs + *ohso* ox; akin to OE *ūr* aurochs – more at OX]

**aurora** /aw'rawrə/ *n, pl* **auroras, aurorae** /-rie/ 1 *dawn; also, cap* dawn personified **2a aurora borealis** /ˌbawri'ahlis/, **aurora** a luminous phenomenon held to be of electrical origin that consists of streamers or arches of light in the sky and is ordinarily best viewed at night in high northern latitudes **b aurora australis** /aw'strahlis/, **aurora** a luminous phenomenon in the southern hemisphere corresponding to the aurora borealis in the northern hemisphere [L – more at EAST; (2a) NL, lit., northern dawn; (2b) NL, lit., southern dawn] – **auroral, aurorean** *adj adj*

**aurous** /'awrəs/ *adj* of or containing gold, esp when having a VALENCY of one [ISV, fr L *aurum* gold – more at ORIOLE]

**auscultate** /'awskəltayt/ *vt* to examine by auscultation [backformation fr *auscultation*] – **auscultatory** *adj*

**auscultation** /ˌawskəl'taysh(ə)n/ *n* the medical act or practice of listening to and interpreting sounds produced within the body (eg those produced by the lungs in breathing or the heartbeats of an unborn baby) using the ear alone, a stethoscope, or a microphone and some form of amplification system as an aid to diagnosis and treatment [L *auscultation-, auscultatio* act of listening, fr *auscultatus*, pp of *auscultare* to listen; akin to L *auris* ear – more at EAR]

**auslese** /'ows,layzə (*Ger* ᴀᴜsle:zə)/ *n, often cap* a usu sweetish German or Austrian white table wine made only from selected late-gathered ripe grapes [Ger, selection, choice, choice wine]

**auspice** /'awspis/ *n* 1 *pl* the observation of some recognized prophetic phenomenon (eg the flight or feeding of birds) often as part of some more general ritual by an augur or other official soothsayer, usu to determine whether some course of action will have a favourable outcome – often in *take/consult the auspices* 2 a usu favourable omen or sign 3 *pl* kindly patronage and guidance ⟨*under the* ~s *of the BBC*⟩ [L *auspicium*, fr *auspic-, auspex* diviner by birds, fr *avis* bird + *specere* to look, look at – more at AVIARY, SPY]

**auspicious** /aw'spish(ə)s/ *adj* 1 affording a favourable auspice; propitious ⟨*made an* ~ *beginning by getting an A*⟩ 2 attended by good auspices; prosperous ⟨*an* ~ *year*⟩ – **auspiciously** *adv*, **auspiciousness** *n*

**Aussie** /'ozi/ *n, informal* 1 a native or inhabitant of Australia 2 *Austr* Australia [*Australian* + *-ie*]

**austenite** /'awstə,niet/ *n* a solid solution in iron of carbon and sometimes other dissolved substances that occurs as a constituent of steel under certain conditions [Fr, fr Sir W C Roberts-*Austen* †1902 E metallurgist] – **austenitic** *adj*

**austere** /aw'stiə, o'stiə/ *adj* **1a** stern and forbidding in appearance and manner ⟨~ *Puritan colonists*⟩ **b** sombre, grave ⟨*dressed all in* ~ *black for the funeral*⟩ 2 joylessly abstemious; ascetic ⟨*an* ~ *old hermit living on berries and roots*⟩ 3 unadorned, simple ⟨*an* ~ *chair with a straight back*⟩ [ME, fr MF, fr L *austerus*, fr Gk *austēros* harsh, severe; akin to Gk *hauos* dry – more at SERE] – **austerely** *adv*, **austereness** *n*

**austerity** /aw'sterəti, os-/ *n* **1a** an austere act, manner, or attitude **b** an ascetic practice 2 enforced or extreme economy

**Austin** /'ostin/ *n or adj* (an) Augustinian [ME *Austyn*, modif of LL *Augustinus* Augustine]

[1]**Austr-, Austro-** *comb form* 1 south; southern ⟨Austro*asiatic*⟩ 2 Australian and ⟨Austro-*Malayan*⟩ [ME *austr-*, fr L, fr *Austr-, Auster* south wind; akin to L *aurora* dawn – more at EAST]

[2]**Austr-, Austro-** *comb form* Austrian and ⟨Austro-*Hungarian*⟩ [NL, fr *Austria*]

**austral** /'awstrəl/ *adj* southern [ME, fr L *australis*, fr *austr-, auster*]

**Australasian** /ˌostrə'layzh(y)ən; *also* ˌaw-/ *n or adj* (a native or inhabitant) of Australasia, the area comprising Australia, Tasmania, New Zealand, and islands in the central and S Pacific

**Australia Day** /o'straylyə; *also* aw-/ *n* the first Monday after January 25 observed as a national holiday in Australia in commemoration of the landing of the British at Sydney Cove on January 26, 1788

[1]**Australian** /o'straylyən; *also* aw-/ *n* 1 a native or inhabitant of Australia **2a** the speech of the aboriginal inhabitants of Australia **b** English as spoken and written in Australia [*Australia*, continent of the southern hemisphere]

[2]**Australian** *adj* 1 (characteristic) of Australia, its inhabitants, or the languages spoken there 2 of or being a biological and geographic region that comprises Australia, the islands north of it from the Celebes eastwards, Tasmania, New Zealand, and Polynesia

**Australianism** /o'straylyəniz(ə)m; *also* aw-/ *n* a characteristic feature of Australian English

**Australian Rules football** *n* a game played between two teams of 18 players on an oval field from 180 to 190 yards (about 165 to 175 metres) long with four goalposts at each end using a ball similar to a rugby ball which may be passed from player to player by kicking or by striking it with the clenched fist

**Australian terrier** *n* a small rather short-legged usu greyish wirehaired terrier of Australian origin

**Australoid** /'ostrəloyd/ *adj* of an ethnic group including the Australian aborigines and other peoples of southern Asia and Pacific islands sometimes including the AINU (aboriginal inhabitants of Japan) [*Australia* + E *-oid*] – **Australoid** *n*

**australopithecine** /ˌostrəloh'pithəseen/ *adj* of extinct S African HOMINIDS (esp genus *Australopithecus*) with nearhuman dentition and a relatively small brain [deriv of L *australis* southern (fr *Austr-, Auster*) + Gk *pithēkos* ape – more at PITHECANTHROPUS] – **australopithecine** *n*

**Australorp** /'ostrə,lawp/ *n* a usu black domestic fowl developed in Australia and valued for egg production [*Australia* + *Orp*ington]

**Austro-** – see AUSTR-

**Austroasiatic** *also* **Austro-Asiatic** /ˌostroh,ayzi'atik, -,ayzhi-/ *adj* of or constituting a family of languages once widespread over NE India and SE Asia

**Austronesian** /ˌostrə'neezh(ə)n/ *adj* of or constituting a family of Pacific languages including Indonesian, Melanesian, Micronesian, and Polynesian but not the Australian, Papuan, or Negrito languages [*Austronesia*, islands of the S Pacific]

**aut-** /-/awt-/, **auto-** *comb form* **1** self; same one; of or by oneself ⟨auto*biography*⟩ ⟨auto*didact*⟩ **2** automatic; self-acting; self-regulating ⟨auto*dyne*⟩ ⟨auto*stop*⟩ [Gk, fr *autos* same, -self, self]

**autacoid** /'awtə,koyd/ *n* a specific organic chemical substance (e g a hormone) forming in one part of the body, moving in the body fluid or the sap, and modifying the activity of the cells of another part [*aut-* + Gk *akos* remedy; akin to OIr *hícc* healing] – **autacoidal** *adj*

**autarchic** /,aw'tahkik/, **autarchical** *adj* of or marked by autarchy

**autarchy** /'awtahki/ *n* **1** absolute sovereignty **2** absolute or autocratic rule [Gk *autarchia*, fr *aut-* + *-archia* -archy]

**autarkic** /aw'tahkik/, **autarkical** *adj* of or marked by autarky

**autarky** /'awtahki/ *n* **1** self-sufficiency, independence; *specif* national economic self-sufficiency and independence ⟨*under a system of* ∼, *trade between nations would come to a halt*⟩ **2** a policy of establishing national economic independence (e g by reducing or stopping imports) **3** a state which is economically self-sufficient [Ger *autarkie*, fr Gk *autarkeia*, fr *autarkēs* self-sufficient, fr *aut-* + *arkein* to defend, suffice – more at ARK]

**autecology** /,awti'koləji/ *n* ecology dealing with a single organism or a single species of organism [ISV] – **autecological** *adj*

**auteur theory** /aw'tuh/ *n* a theory in film criticism that views a particular film in the light of its contribution to the development of a set of themes or preoccupations characteristic of its director [part trans of Fr *politique des auteurs*, fr *auteur* author; fr the view that directors are the true authors of a film]

**authentic** /aw'thentik/ *adj* **1** representing facts accurately or reliably; trustworthy ⟨∼ *testimony*⟩ **2** not imaginary, false, or imitation; genuine ⟨*one of the few remaining* ∼ *colonial buildings*⟩ **3** *of a* CHURCH MODE (*musical scale*) ranging upward from the KEYNOTE (note on which the mode is based) – compare PLAGAL 1 **synonyms** see GENUINE **antonyms** fraudulent, spurious [ME *autentik*, fr MF *autentique*, fr LL *authenticus*, fr Gk *authentikos*, fr *authentēs* perpetrator, master, fr *aut-* + *-hentēs* (akin to Gk *anyein* to accomplish, Skt *sanoti* he gains)] – **authentically** *adv*, **authenticity** *n*

**authenticate** /aw'thentikayt/ *vt* to (serve to) prove the authenticity of **synonyms** see CONFIRM **antonyms** dispute, impugn – **authenticator** *n*, **authentication** *n*

**author** /'awthə/, *fem* **authoress** /'awthəris, awthə'res, '---/ *n* **1a** the writer of a literary work **b** a person whose profession is writing **c** a writer's books ⟨*found the right words in their favourite* ∼⟩ **2** one who or that which originates or gives existence; a source ⟨*trying to track down the* ∼ *of the rumour*⟩ ⟨*the* ∼ *of a theory*⟩ *usage* see -ESS [ME *auctour*, fr ONF, fr L *auctor* promoter, originator, writer, fr *auctus*, pp of *augēre* to increase – more at EKE OUT]

**authoritarian** /aw,thori'teəri-ən/ *adj* **1** of or favouring blind submission to authority ⟨*had* ∼ *parents*⟩ **2** of or favouring a concentration of power in a leader or an elite not constitutionally responsible to the people **3** of a personality syndrome characterized by deference to superiors and dictatorial behaviour towards inferiors – **authoritarian** *n*, **authoritarianism** *n*

**authoritative** /aw'thoritətiv/ *adj* **1a** having or proceeding from authority; official ⟨∼ *church doctrine*⟩ **b** entitled to credit or acceptance; conclusive ⟨*the* ∼ *interpretation of the Russian revolution*⟩ **2** dictatorial, peremptory, commanding – **authoritatively** *adv*, **authoritativeness** *n*

**authority** /aw'thorəti/ *n* **1a(1)** a citation (e g from a book or file) used in defence or support of one's actions, opinions, or beliefs **a(2)** the source from which the citation is drawn **b(1)** a conclusive statement or set of statements (e g an official decision of a court) **b(2)** a recognized source (e g a statute, previous judicial decision, rule of court, or the opinion of a noted jurist) used to establish a principle of law **c** an individual cited or appealed to as an expert **2a** power to require and receive submission; the right to expect obedience **b** delegated power over others; authorization **c** right granted by someone to another to act on his/her behalf **3a** *pl* people in command; *specif* a governmental or law-enforcing agency ⟨*reported him to the authorities*⟩ **b** *often cap* a governmental body that administers a public service or enterprise ⟨*the Inner London Education Authority*⟩ ⟨*the Thames Water* Authority⟩ **4a** grounds, warrant ⟨*had excellent* ∼ *for his strange actions*⟩ **b** power to influence or command thought, opinion, or behaviour ⟨*Vol-*

*taire had his enemies but his* ∼ *could not be denied*⟩ **c** convincing force; weight ⟨*his strong tenor lent* ∼ *to the performance*⟩ [ME *auctorite*, fr OF *auctorité*, fr L *auctoritat-*, *auctoritas* opinion, decision, power, fr *auctor*]

**author·ization, -isation** /,awthəriz'zaysh(ə)n, -ri-/ *n* **1** the act of authorizing **2** a legal instrument or document that authorizes; sanction

**author·ize, -ise** /'awthəriz/ *vt* **1** to give authority or legal power to; empower – often + infin ⟨∼d *to act for her father*⟩ **2** to establish (as if by) authority; sanction ⟨*a custom* ∼d *by time*⟩ ⟨*Queen Isabella* ∼d *the first voyage*⟩ – **authorizer** *n*

**Authorized Version** *n* an English version of the Bible prepared under James I, published in 1611, and widely used by Protestants

**authorship** /'awthəship/ *n* **1** the profession or activity of writing **2a** the identity of the author of a literary work ⟨*the* ∼ *of* Hamlet *is not seriously disputed*⟩ **b** the state or act of creating or causing ⟨*the* ∼ *of the crime*⟩

**autism** /'awtiz(ə)m/ *n* **1** absorption in self-centred mental activity (e g daydreams, fantasies, delusions, and hallucinations), esp when accompanied by marked withdrawal from reality **2** a disorder of childhood development marked by inability to form relationships with other people and severe educational backwardness not related to low intelligence [NL *autismus*, fr *aut-* + *-ismus* -ism] – **autistic** *adj*

**autistic** /aw'tistik/ *n* a sufferer from childhood autism

**auto** /'awtoh/ *n*, *pl* **autos** *chiefly NAm* a car [short for ²*automobile*]

**¹auto-** – see AUT-

**²auto-** *comb form* motor; self-propelling; automotive ⟨auto*rickshaw*⟩ [¹*automobile*]

**autoantibody** /,awtoh'antibodi/ *n* an antibody against one of the constituents of the tissues of the individual that produces it

**autobahn** /'awtoh,bahn/ *n* a German motorway [Ger, fr *auto* + *bahn* track, way]

**autobiographical** /,awtə,bie-ə'grafikl/, **autobiographic** *adj* of (the nature of) an autobiography – **autobiographically** *adv*

**autobiography** /,awtəbie'ografi/ *n* **1** the biography of a person written by him-/herself **2** autobiographical writing as a literary genre – **autobiographer** *n*

**autocatalysis** /,awtohkə'taləsis/ *n*, *pl* **autocatalyses** /-seez/ the speeding up of a chemical reaction by one of the products of the reaction acting as a catalyst [NL] – **autocatalytic** *adj*

**autocephalous** /,awtoh'sefələs/ *adj*, *esp of Eastern national churches* governed by a national synod with the power to appoint its own bishops; independent of any larger church body [LGk *autokephalos*, fr Gk *aut-* + *kephalē* head – more at CEPHALIC]

**autochthon** /aw'tokthən/ *n*, *pl* **autochthons**, **autochthones** /aw'toktha,neez/ **1** an aborigine, native; *esp* any of the earliest recorded inhabitants of a particular region **2** something (e g a plant or animal) that is autochthonous [Gk *autochthōn*, fr *aut-* + *chthōn* earth – more at HUMBLE] – **autochthonism** *n*

**autochthonous** /aw'tokthənəs/ *adj*, *of a plant, animal, or substance* naturally occurring in a particular ecological region (e g a river or geological stratum); native, indigenous – compare ALLOCHTHONOUS **synonyms** see ¹NATIVE – **autochthonously** *adv*, **autochthony** *n*

**autoclave** /'awtəklayv/ *n* **1** an apparatus using superheated steam under pressure (e g for sterilizing surgical instruments) **2** a strong sealable vessel used for chemical reactions requiring high temperatures and pressures [Fr, fr *aut-* + L *clavis* key – more at CLAVICLE] – **autoclave** *vt*

**autocracy** /aw'tokrəsi/ *n* **1** government in which one person possesses unlimited power **2** the authority or rule of an autocrat **3** a community or state governed by autocracy

**autocrat** /'awtəkrat/ *n* **1** a person (e g a monarch) ruling with unlimited power **2** a dictatorial person ⟨*he was the* ∼ *of his household*⟩ [Fr *autocrate*, fr Gk *autokratēs* ruling by oneself, absolute, fr *aut-* + *kratos* strength, power – more at HARD] – **autocratic, autocractical** *adj*, **autocratically** *adv*

**autocross** /'awtoh,kros/ *n* the sport of racing cars across country (e g on grass tracks) against the clock – compare RALLYCROSS [*auto* + *cross* country]

**autocue** /'awtoh,kyooh/ *n* an electronic device that enables a person (e g a newsreader) being televised to read a script without looking away from the camera, by automatically magnifying and displaying the script a line at a time

**autocycle** /'awtoh,siekl/ *n* a bicycle fitted with a small auxiliary engine that was in common use between about 1920 and 1960

**auto-da-fé** /ˌawtoh dah 'fay/ *n, pl* **autos-da-fé** the ceremony accompanying the pronouncement of judgment on a heretic by the Spanish Inquisition and followed by the execution of sentence by the civil authorities; *broadly* the burning of a heretic [Pg *auto da fě*, lit., act of the faith]

**autodidact** /-'diedakt/ *n* a self-taught person [Gk *autodidaktos* self-taught, fr *aut-* + *didaktos* taught, fr *didaskein* to teach – more at DOCILE] – **autodidactic** *adj*

**autodyne** /'awtəˌdien/ *n* a HETERODYNE radio receiver in which the same components function as oscillator and detector [ISV *aut-* + hetero*dyne*]

**autoecious** /ˌawt'eeshəs/ *adj, of a parasitic organism, esp a fungus* passing through all life stages on the same host ⟨~ *rusts*⟩ – compare HETEROECIOUS [*aut-* + Gk *oikia* house – more at VICINITY] – **autoeciously** *adv*, **autoecism** *n*

**autoeroticism** /-i'rotisiz(ə)m/, **autoerotism** /-'eərətiz(ə)m/ *n* sexual arousal and/or gratification obtained without the participation of another person; *broadly* MASTURBATION – **autoerotic** *adj*, **autoerotically** *adv*

**autogamy** /aw'togəmi/ *n* self-fertilization: eg **a** pollination of a flower by its own pollen **b** CONJUGATION (process of sexual reproduction) of two single-celled organisms (PROTOZOANS) or their nuclei originating from the division of the same individual – compare ALLOGAMY [ISV] – **autogamous** *adj*

**autogenesis** /ˌawtoh'jenəsis/ *n* ABIOGENESIS (spontaneous arising of life from inorganic matter) [NL] – **autogenetic** *adj*, **autogenetically** *adv*

**autogenous** /aw'tojənəs/, **autogenic** /ˌawtə'jenik/ *adj* **1** produced independently of external influence or aid; endogenous **2** *medicine* originating or derived from sources within the same individual ⟨*an* ~ *graft*⟩ **3** *of a female insect* not requiring a meal (of blood) to produce viable eggs ⟨~ *mosquitoes*⟩ [Gk *autogenēs*, fr *aut-* + *-genēs* born, produced – more at -GEN] – **autogenously** *adv*

**autogiro** *also* **autogyro** /ˌawtə'jie-əroh/ *n* an aircraft that resembles a helicopter and has a propeller for forward motion and a freely rotating horizontal rotor for lift [fr *Autogiro*, a trademark]

**autograft** /'awtəˌgrahft, -ˌgraft/ *n* a tissue or organ that is transplanted from one place to another within the same body – **autograft** *vt*

**¹autograph** /'awtəˌgrahf, -ˌgraf/ *n* something written or made with one's own hand: eg **a** an original manuscript or work of art **b** a person's handwritten signature; *esp* that of a celebrity ⟨*a collector of* ~*s*⟩ [LL *autographum*, fr L, neut of *autographus* written with one's own hand, fr Gk *autographos*, fr *aut-* + *-graphos* written – more at -GRAPH] **autographic** *adj*, **autographically** *adv*, **autography** *n*

**²autograph** *vt* **1** to write in one's own hand **2** to write one's signature in or on

**Autoharp** /'awtoh,hahp/ *trademark* – used for a zither with button-controlled dampers which stop selected strings sounding so that chords can be played

**autohypnosis** /ˌawtoh-hip'nohsis/ *also* **autohypnotism** /'hipnətiz(ə)m/ *n* self-induced hypnosis [NL] – **autohypnotic** *adj*

**autoimmune** /ˌawtohi'myoohn/ *adj* of or caused by AUTOANTIBODIES ⟨~ *diseases*⟩ – **autoimmunity** *n*, **autoimmunization** *n*

**autoinfection** /ˌawtoh-in'feksh(ə)n/ *n* reinfection with larvae produced by parasitic worms already in the body [ISV]

**autoinoculation** /ˌawtoh-iˌnokyoo'laysh(ə)n/ *n* **1** inoculation with vaccine prepared from material from the same body as that which it is used to treat **2** spread of infection from one part to other parts of the same body [ISV

**autointoxication** /ˌawtoh-inˌtoksi'kaysh(ə)n/ *n* a state of being poisoned by toxic substances produced by the body's own action [ISV]

**autologous** /aw'toləgəs/ *adj* derived from the same individual ⟨*an* ~ *skin graft*⟩ [*aut-* + *-ologous* (as in *homologous*)]

**autolysate** /aw'tolisayt/ *n* a product of autolysis

**autolysin** /aw'tolisin/ *n* a substance that produces autolysis

**autolysis** /aw'toləsis/ *n* breakdown of all or part of a cell or tissue by self-produced ENZYMES (eg after death) [NL] – **autolyse**, *NAm chiefly* **autolyze** *vb*, **autolytic** *adj*

**Automat** /'awtəˌmat/ *trademark* – used in the USA for a cafeteria in which food is obtained from coin-operated compartments

**automate** /'awtəmayt/ *vt* **1** to operate by automation **2** to convert to largely automatic operation ~ *vi* to undergo automation [back-formation fr *automation*] – **automatable** *adj*

**¹automatic** /ˌawtə'matik/ *adj* **1a** largely or wholly involuntary; *esp* REFLEX 5 ⟨~ *blinking of the eyelids*⟩ **b** acting or performed spontaneously or unconsciously **c** resembling an automaton; mechanical ⟨*knew the lesson so well that her answers were* ~⟩ **2** having a self-acting or self-regulating mechanism ⟨*an* ~ *car with* ~ *transmission*⟩ **3** *of a firearm* using either gas pressure or the force of recoil together with mechanical spring action for repeatedly ejecting the empty cartridge shell, introducing a new cartridge, and firing it **synonyms** see SPONTANEOUS [Gk *automatos* self-acting, fr *aut-* + *-matos* (akin to L *ment-*, *mens* mind) – more at MIND ] – **automatically** *adv*, **automaticity** *n*

**²automatic** *n* a machine or apparatus that operates automatically: eg **a** an automatic firearm **b** (a motor vehicle employing) an automatic gear-changing mechanism

**automatic pilot** *n* a device for automatically steering ships, aircraft, and spacecraft

**automation** /awtə'maysh(ə)n/ *n* **1** the technique of making an apparatus, process, or system operate automatically **2** the state of being operated automatically **3** automatically controlled operation of an apparatus, process, or system by mechanical or electronic devices that take the place of human monitoring, decision-making, and labour [¹*automatic*]

**automatism** /aw'tomətiz(ə)m/ *n* **1a** the quality or state of being automatic **b** an automatic action **2** a theory of behaviour which ascribes all activity to physical or physiological processes within the body which can be neither initiated, controlled, nor influenced by mental processes **3** *psychology* a state in which an individual is driven to the performance of certain actions without intending or wanting to do so ⟨*ambulatory* ~, *in which the patient is found wandering about with no clear idea of where he is going or why*⟩ **4** (a technique involving) the suspension of the control of the conscious mind over the free flow of thoughts, associations, and images used by certain groups of writers and artists, esp the Surrealists [Fr *automatisme*, fr *automate* automaton, fr L *automaton*] – **automatist** *n*

**automaton** /aw'tomət(ə)n; *also* ˌawtə'mayt(ə)n/ *n, pl* **automatons**, **automata** /-tə/ **1** a mechanism having its own power source; *also* a robot **2** a machine or control mechanism designed to carry out a predetermined sequence of operations or respond to a set of encoded instructions automatically **3** a person who acts in a mechanical fashion [L, fr Gk, neut of *automatos*]

**¹automobile** /'awtəməˌbeel/ *adj* automotive [Fr, fr *aut-* + *mobile*]

**²automobile** *n* a car – **automobile** *vi*

**automorphism** *n, maths* an ISOMORPHISM that maps a set onto itself

**automotive** /-'mohtiv/ *adj* **1** self-propelled **2** of or concerned with automotive vehicles or machines

**autonomic** /-'nomik/ *adj* **1a** acting or occurring involuntarily ⟨~ *reflexes*⟩ **b** relating to, affecting, or controlled by the AUTONOMIC NERVOUS SYSTEM **2** due to internal causes or influences; spontaneous – **autonomically** *adv*

**autonomic nervous system** *n* a part of the nervous system of VERTEBRATE animals that supplies SMOOTH MUSCLE, heart muscle, and glandular tissues with nerves, regulates involuntary actions, and consists of the SYMPATHETIC NERVOUS SYSTEM and the PARASYMPATHETIC NERVOUS SYSTEM

**autonomous** /aw'tonəməs/ *adj* **1** of or marked by autonomy **2** having the right or power of self-government; possessing a certain degree of (political) independence ⟨*an* ~ *school system*⟩ **3a** (capable of) existing independently ⟨*an* ~ *zooid*⟩ **b** responding, reacting, or developing independently of the whole ⟨*an* ~ *growth*⟩ **4** controlled by the AUTONOMIC NERVOUS SYSTEM [Gk *autonomos* independent, fr *aut-* + *nomos* law – more at NIMBLE] – **autonomously** *adv*

**autonomy** /aw'tonəmi/ *n* **1** self-government; *specif* the degree of self-determination or political independence possessed by a minority group, territorial division, or political unit in its relations with the state or political community of which it forms a part ⟨*a solution giving the Palestinians some degree of* ~⟩ **2** personal freedom to make moral choices; *broadly* moral maturity ⟨*in his relationship with his family he showed all the* ~ *of a 4 year-old child*⟩

**autophyte** /'awtoh,fiet/ *n* a plant that is an AUTOTROPH (organism that can synthesize its own nutrients) – compare

HETEROPHYTE, SAPROPHYTE – **autophytic** *adj*, **autophytically** *adv*

**autopilot** /'awtoh,pielət/ *n* AUTOMATIC PILOT

**autoplastic** /'awtoh,plastik; *also* -,plahstik/ *adj* of or involving surgical repair (eg skin grafting) using tissue taken from the body of the patient rather than from a donor – **autoplastically** *adv*, **autoplasty** *n*

**autopolyploid** /,awtoh'poliployd/ *n* a living organism whose cells contain more than one set of CHROMOSOMES (strands of gene-carrying material) that are derived from a single parent species – compare ALLOPOLYPLOID – **autopolyploid** *adj*, **autopolyploidy** *n*

**autopsy** /'awtopsi/ *n* POSTMORTEM 1 [Gk *autopsia* act of seeing with one's own eyes, fr *aut-* + *opsis* sight, fr *opsesthai* to be going to see – more at OPTIC] – **autopsy** *vt*

**autoradiograph** /,awtoh'raydi-ə,grahf, -,graf/, **autoradiogram** /-,gram/ *n* an image produced on a photographic film or plate by the radiations from a radioactive substance in an object which is in close contact with the emulsion [ISV] – **autoradiographic** *adj*, **autoradiography** *n*

**autorotation** /,awtoh·roh'taysh(ə)n/ *n* the turning of the rotor of an autogiro or helicopter with the resulting lift caused solely by the aerodynamic forces induced by motion of the rotor along its flight path – **autorotational** *adj*, **autorotate** *vi*

**autoroute** /-,rooht/ *n* a French motorway [Fr, fr *auto*mobile + *route* road – more at ROUTE]

**autos-da-fé** /,awtoh dah 'fay/ *pl of* AUTO-DA-FÉ

**autosome** /'awtə,sohm/ *n* a CHROMOSOME (strand of gene-carrying material in a cell) that is not a SEX CHROMOSOME – **autosomal** *adj*, **autosomally** *adv*

**autosport** /'awtoh,spawt/ *n* motorcycle and motor-vehicle racing and rallying

**autostrada** /-,strahdə/ *n*, *pl* **autostradas**, **autostrade** /-,strahday/ an Italian motorway [It, fr *auto*mobile + *strada* street, fr LL *strata* paved road – more at STREET]

**autosuggestion** /-sə'jeschən/ *n* an influencing of one's attitudes, behaviour, or physical condition by suggestion arising from one's own mind [ISV] – **autosuggest** *vb*, **autosuggestive** *adj*

**autotelic** /,awtoh'telik/ *adj* having a purpose in itself [Gk *autotelēs*, fr *aut-* + *telos* end – more at WHEEL]

**autotetraploidy** /,awtoh'tetrəploydy/ *n* the state of having four instead of two HAPLOID sets of CHROMOSOMES (strands of gene-carrying material) in each cell due to doubling of the ancestral chromosome complement – **autotetraploid** *adj or n*

**autotomy** /aw'totəmi/ *n* reflex separation of a part (eg a lizard's tail) from the body; spontaneous division of the body into two or more pieces [ISV] – **autotomous, autotomic** *adj*

**'auto-trans,former** *n* a TRANSFORMER (device for changing the voltage of a current) in which the primary and secondary coils have part or all of their turns in common

**autotransplant** /,awtoh'trahnsplahnt, -trans-, -plant/ *n* AUTOGRAFT – **autotransplant** *vt*, **autotransplantation** *n*

**autotroph** /'awtə,trohf/ *n* an autotrophic organism [Ger, fr *autotroph* autotrophic, fr Gk *autotrophos*] – **autotrophy** *n*

**autotrophic** /,awtə'trofik/ *adj* 1 *of a living organism* able to manufacture organic materials and nutrients from water, CARBON DIOXIDE, an inorganic source of nitrogen (eg a nitrate), and inorganic salts usu with sunlight as a source of energy ⟨*most green plants are* ∼⟩ – compare HETEROTROPHIC 2 not requiring a specified external factor for normal METABOLISM (life-supporting processes) [deriv of Gk *autotrophos* supplying one's own food, fr *aut-* + *trephein* to nourish – more at ATROPHY] – **autotrophically** *adv*

**autrefois acquit** /,ohtrəfwah a'kee (*Fr* otrəfwa aki)/ *n* a special plea in a criminal prosecution that the accused has already been tried and acquitted of the same offence [AF, formerly acquitted]

**autrefois convict** /kən'vikt (*Fr* kõvikt)/ *n* a special plea in a criminal prosecution that the accused has already been tried and convicted of the same offence [AF, formerly convicted]

**autumn** /'awtəm/ *n* 1 the season between summer and winter which in the N hemisphere is usu taken to comprise the months of September, October, and November; *also* the period from the September EQUINOX (time when day and night are of equal length) to the December SOLSTICE (shortest day of the year) 2 a period of maturity passing into decline ⟨*the long* ∼ *of Liberal England*⟩ [ME *autumpne*, fr. L *autumnus*] – **autumnal** *adj*, **autumnally** *adv*

**autumn crocus** *n* MEADOW SAFFRON

**autunite** /'awtəniet/ *n* a fluorescent radioactive lemon-yellow mineral, $Ca(UO_2)(PO_4)_2.10–12H_2O$, found in many uranium ores [*Autun*, town in E France]

**auxanometer** /,awksə'nomitə/ *n* an instrument for measuring the rate of growth of plants [ISV *auxano-* (fr Gk *auxanein* to increase) + *-meter*]

**auxesis** /awk'seesis, -gz-/ *n* 1 growth; *specif* increase of cell size without CELL DIVISION 2 intensification of meaning; hyperbole [NL, fr Gk *auxēsis* increase, growth, fr *auxein* to increase – more at EKE OUT] – **auxetic** *adj*, **auxetically** *adv*

**¹auxiliary** /awg'zilyəri/ *adj* 1 functioning in a subsidiary capacity ⟨*an* ∼ *branch of the university*⟩ 2 *of a verb* accompanying or sometimes replacing another verb and typically expressing person, number, mood, voice, or tense ⟨be, do, *and* may *are* ∼ *verbs*⟩ 3a supplementary ⟨*with* ∼ *instruments the new telescope has more power*⟩ **b** reserve ⟨*an* ∼ *power plant*⟩ ⟨*an* ∼ *petrol tank*⟩ 4 *of a sailing vessel* having a usu inboard engine for occasional use 5 *archaic* offering or providing help – usu + *to* [L *auxiliaris*, fr *auxilium* help; akin to Gk *auxein* to increase]

**²auxiliary** *n* 1 an auxiliary person, group, or device 2 an auxiliary verb 3 a member of a foreign force serving under another nation

**auxin** /'awksin/ *n* a naturally occurring plant hormone (eg INDOLEACETIC ACID) or man-made product (eg 2,4 D) that in low concentrations affects the growth of plants, esp by causing plant shoots to become elongated [ISV, fr Gk *auxein*] – **auxinic** *adj*, **auxinically** *adv*

**auxotroph** /'awksə,trohf/ *n* an auxotrophic strain or individual – **auxotrophy** *n*

**auxotrophic** /,awksə'trohfik/ *adj* requiring a specific growth substance beyond the minimum required for normal METABOLISM (life-supporting processes) and reproduction ⟨∼ *mutants of bacteria*⟩ [Gk *auxein* to increase + *-o-* + E *-trophic*]

**¹avail** /ə'vayl/ *vb* to be of use or advantage (to) [ME *availen*, alter. (prob influenced by *a-* in such words as *abate, amount*) of *vailen*, fr OF *vail-*, stem of *valoir* to be of worth, fr L *valēre* to be strong, be of worth] – **avail oneself of** to make use of; take advantage of

**²avail** *n* 1 advantage in attaining an object or goal; use – chiefly after *of* or *to* and in negative contexts ⟨*his effort was of little* ∼⟩ 2 *pl*, *archaic* profits or proceeds, esp from a business or from the sale of property

**available** /ə'vayləbl/ *adj* 1 present or ready for immediate use or consultation ⟨*meal vouchers will be* ∼ *for those who do not wish to eat in the hotel*⟩ ⟨*the doctor is* ∼ *after 3.15*⟩ 2 accessible, obtainable ⟨*whisky was* ∼, *but only on the black market*⟩ 3 present in a chemical or physical form which allows its immediate use (eg by a living organism) ⟨∼ *nitrogen*⟩ ⟨∼ *water*⟩ 4 *NAm* qualified or willing to do something (eg stand for political office) or to assume a responsibility ⟨∼ *candidates*⟩ 5 *archaic* having a beneficial effect; being of avail – **availableness** *n*, **availably** *adv*, **availability** *n*

**avalanche** /'avəlahnch/ *n* 1 a large mass of snow, ice, rock, etc falling rapidly down a mountain ⟨*a sand* ∼⟩; *specif* a mass of snow which has become detached from high up a mountain falling into a valley accumulating more snow as it falls, bringing rock and earth with it, and causing great destruction in its path – compare LANDSLIDE 2 a sudden great or overwhelming rush or accumulation of something ⟨*tied down with an* ∼ *of paper work*⟩ 3 a cumulative process in which a high-energy particle (eg an electron) is accelerated by an electric field to produce additional particles through collisions (eg with gas molecules) [Fr, fr Fr dial. *lavantse, avalantse*] – **avalanche** *vi*

**¹avant-garde** /,avong 'gahd/ *n* the group of people that create or apply new and esp experimental ideas and techniques in any field, particularly in the arts; *also* such a group that is extremist and bizarre, or arty and affected – usu + *the* [Fr, vanguard] – **avant-gardism** *n*, **avant-gardist** *n*

**²avant-garde** *adj* of the avant-garde or artistic work that is new and experimental ⟨*found the decoration of their bedroom very* ∼⟩

**avarice** /'avəris/ *n* excessive or insatiable desire to accumulate wealth; greediness, cupidity [ME, fr OF, fr L *avaritia*, fr *avarus* avaricious, fr *avēre* to covet – more at AVID]

**avaricious** /,avə'rishəs/ *adj* excessively acquisitive, esp in seeking to hoard riches; tightfisted – **avariciously** *adv*, **avariciousness** *n*

**avascular** /,ay'vaskyoolə/ *adj*, *of body tissue* lacking a supply of blood or lymph vessels

**avast** /ə'vahst/ *vb imper* – a nautical command to stop or cease, used esp to countermand a previous order or to order the discontinuation of some action or process [perh fr D *houd vast* hold fast]

**avatar** /'avətah/ *n* **1** an incarnation of a Hindu deity, esp Vishnu, usu in human form **2** an embodiment (eg of a concept or philosophy), usu in a person 〈∼s *of new hard-line economic theories*〉 [Skt *avatāra* descent, fr *avatarati* he descends, fr *ava-* away + *tarati* he crosses over]

**avaunt** /ə'vawnt/ *interj, archaic* begone! [ME, fr MF *avant*, fr L *abante* forward, before, fr *ab* from + *ante* before]

**ave** /'ahvay, -vi/, **Ave Maria** /mə'ree-ə/ *n, often cap* HAIL MARY (Roman Catholic prayer) [ME, fr L *ave* hail! & ML *ave Maria* hail, Mary!]

**avenge** /ə'venj/ *vt* **1** to take vengeance on behalf of 〈∼d *his brother*〉 **2** to exact satisfaction for (a wrong) by punishing the wrongdoer 〈∼d *his brother's murder*〉 [ME *avengen*, prob fr *a-* (as in *abaten* to abate) + *vengen* to avenge, fr OF *vengier* – more at VENGEANCE] – **avenger** *n*

**avens** /'avinz/ *n, pl* **avens** /∼/ any of a genus (*Geum*) of plants of the rose family with white, purple, or yellow flowers [ME *avence*, fr OF]

**aventurine** /ə'ventyoorin, -reen/ *n* **1** glass containing opaque sparkling particles of foreign material, usu copper or chromic oxide **2** a translucent quartz spangled throughout with scales of mica or other mineral [Fr, fr *aventure* chance – more at ADVENTURE; fr its accidental discovery]

**avenue** /'avənyooh/ *n* **1** a way of access; a route 〈*the* ∼ *to India*〉 **2** a channel for pursuing a desired object 〈∼s *of communication*〉 **3** a broad passageway bordered by trees **4** a usu broad street or road **5** *chiefly Br* a tree-lined walk or driveway to a large country house situated off a main road [MF, fr fem of *avenu*, pp of *avenir* to approach, fr L *advenire* – more at ADVENTURE]

**aver** /ə'vuh/ *vt -rr-* **1** to allege or assert as a fact in pleading in a court of law **2** *formal* to declare positively *synonyms* see ASSERT [ME *averren*, fr MF *averer*, fr ML *adverare* to confirm as authentic, fr L *ad-* + *verus* true – more at VERY]

**¹average** /'avərij, 'avrij/ *n* **1a** a partial loss or damage sustained by a ship or cargo **b** the fair distribution of the costs resulting from the loss or damage of a ship's cargo at sea between all those bearing some responsibility for it **2** a single value that summarizes or represents the general significance of a set of unequal values; *esp* ARITHMETIC MEAN **3** a level (eg of intelligence, height, or income) typical of a group, class, or series 〈*above the* ∼〉 **4** a ratio expressing the average performance esp of an athletic team or an athlete computed according to the number of opportunities for successful performance 〈*an* ∼ *of over 50 in Test Matches*〉 [modif of MF *avarie* damage to ship or cargo, fr OIt *avaria*, fr Ar *'awārīyah* damaged merchandise] – **on average, on the average** taking the mean of unequal numbers or quantities; taking the typical example of the group under consideration 〈*these are* on the average, *a better class of article*〉

**²average** *adj* **1** equalling an ARITHMETIC MEAN **2a** about midway between extremes 〈*a man of* ∼ *height*〉 **b** not out of the ordinary; common, typical 〈*the* ∼ *person*〉 – **averagely** *adv*, **averageness** *n*

**³average** *vi* **1** to be or come to an average – usu + *out at* or *out to* 〈*the gain* ∼d *out to 20 per cent*〉 **2** to buy additional shares or commodities on a falling market, or sell them on a rising market, so as to obtain a more favourable average price – usu + *down* or *up* ∼ *vt* **1a** to do, get, or have on average or as an average sum or quantity 〈∼s *12 hours of work a day*〉 〈∼s *over 50 in Test Matches*〉 **b** to have a mid value of 〈*a colour* averaging *a pale purple*〉 〈*an earthquake* averaging *6.4 on the Richter Scale*〉 **2** to find the ARITHMETIC MEAN of (a series of unequal quantities) **3** to bring towards the average

**averment** /ə'vuhmənt/ *n, formal* **1** the act of averring **2** something that is averred; an affirmation

**averse** /ə'vuhs/ *adj* having an active feeling of repugnance or distaste – usu + *to* 〈*not* ∼ *to strenuous exercise*〉 [L *aversus*, pp of *avertere*] – **aversely** *adv*, **averseness** *n*

 *usage* Some older writers on usage advised *from* as the right preposition after **averse** or **aversion**, because the Latin preposition *a* means "away"; but **averse** *to*, **an aversion** *to* are now the usually accepted forms.△ **adverse**

**aversion** /ə'vuhsh(ə)n, -zh(ə)n/ *n* **1** a feeling of repugnance towards or settled dislike for something; antipathy 〈*regards drunkenness with* ∼〉 〈*expressed an* ∼ *to parties*〉 **2** *chiefly Br*

someone or something that is the object of aversion; a cause of repugnance 〈*what are your pet* ∼s?〉 **3** *obs* the act of turning away

**aversion therapy** *n* therapy intended to change a distressing habit or antisocial behaviour (eg alcoholism) by associating it with unpleasant sensations

**aversive** /ə'vuhsiv, -ziv/ *adj* causing or tending to cause avoidance; *esp* of, being, or using an unpleasant or punishing stimulus that tends to cause avoidance 〈*behaviour modification by* ∼ *stimulation*〉

**avert** /ə'vuht/ *vt* **1** to turn (eg the eyes) away or aside in avoidance **2** to see coming and ward off; avoid, prevent 〈∼ *evil*〉 [ME *averten*, fr MF *avertir*, fr L *avertere*, fr *ab-* + *vertere* to turn – more at WORTH]

**Avesta** /ə'vestə/ *n* the book of the sacred writings of Zoroastrianism [MPer *Avastāk*, lit., original text]

**Avestan** /ə'vest(ə)n/ *n* that one of the two ancient languages of Old Iranian in which the sacred books of Zoroastrianism were written – **Avestan** *adj*

**avian** /'ayvi-ən/ *adj* of or derived from birds [L *avis*]

**aviary** /'ayvyəri/ *n* a place for keeping birds confined [L *aviarium*, fr *avis* bird; akin to Gk *aetos* eagle]

**aviation** /,ayvi'aysh(ə)n/ *n* **1** the operation of heavier-than-air aircraft **2** aircraft manufacture, development, and design [Fr, fr L *avis* bird]

**aviator** /'ayviaytə/, *fem* **aviatrix** /'ayviətriks/ *n, pl* **aviators**, *fem* **aviatrixes, aviatrices** /-treesiz/ the pilot of an aircraft

**aviculture** /'ayvi,kulchə/ *n* the raising and care of birds, esp of wild birds in captivity [L *avis* + E *culture*] – **aviculturist** *n*

**avid** /'avid/ *adj* **1** urgently or greedily eager; greedy 〈∼ *fondness for publicity*〉 〈∼ *for the next instalment of the serial*〉 **2** strongly interested; enthusiastic 〈∼ *readers of detective fiction*〉 *antonyms* indifferent, averse [Fr or L; Fr *avide*, fr L *avidus*, fr *avēre* to covet; akin to Goth *awiliuth* thanks, Gk *enēēs* gentle] – **avidly** *adv*, **avidness** *n*

**avidin** /'avidin, ə'vidin/ *n* a protein found in white of egg that combines with BIOTIN (B vitamin found in egg yolks) and makes it inactive [fr its avidity for biotin]

**avidity** /ə'vidəti/ *n* **1** the quality or state of being avid: **1a** keen eagerness **b** consuming greed **2a** the strength of an acid or chemical base dependent on its degree of dissociation **b** AFFINITY (attraction between substances causing them to combine chemically)

**avifauna** /,ayvi'fawnə/ *n* the (kinds of) birds of a region, period, or environment [NL, fr L *avis* + NL *fauna*] – **avifaunal** *adj*, **avifaunally** *adv*, **avifaunistic** *adj*

**avionics** /,ayvi'oniks/ *n taking sing or pl vb* the development and production of electrical and electronic devices for use in aeronautics and astronautics; *also, taking pl vb* the devices and systems so developed [*aviation electronics*] – **avionic** *adj*

**avirulent** /,ay'viryoolənt, ,a-/ *adj* not virulent – compare NONPATHOGENIC [ISV]

**avitaminosis** /,ay,vitəmi'nohsis, ,a-/ *n, pl* **avitaminoses** /-seez/ disease (eg rickets) resulting from a deficiency of one or more vitamins in the diet [NL] – **avitaminotic** *adj*

**avo** /'avooh/ *n, pl* **avos** – see *pataca* at MONEY table [Pg, fr *avo* fractional part, fr *-avo* ordinal suffix (as in *oitavo* eighth, fr L *octavus*) – more at OCTAVE]

**avocado** /,avə'kahdoh/, **avocado pear** *n, pl* **avocados** *also* **avocadoes** the pulpy green or purple edible pear-shaped fruit of various tropical American trees (genus *Persea*) of the laurel family; *also* a tree bearing avocados [Sp, alter. (influenced by *avocado* advocate) of *aguacate*, fr Nahuatl *ahuacatl*, lit., testicle]

**avocation** /,avə'kaysh(ə)n/ *n* **1** a subordinate interest pursued in addition to one's vocation, esp for enjoyment; a hobby **2** customary employment; vocation **3** *archaic* a diversion, distraction [L *avocation-, avocatio*, fr *avocatus*, pp of *avocare* to call away, fr *ab-* + *vocare* to call, fr *voc-, vox* voice – more at VOICE] – **avocational** *adj*, **avocationally** *adv*

**avocet** /'avəset/ *n* a large long-legged black and white wading bird (*Recurvirostra avosetta*) with webbed feet and a slender upward-curving bill [Fr & It; Fr *avocette*, fr It *avocetta*]

**Avogadro's constant** /,avə'gadrohz/ *n* the number of molecules that occurs in one MOLE (unit of amount) of substance; $6.023 \times 10^{23}$ [Count Amedeo *Avogadro* †1856 It chemist & physicist]

**Avogadro's number** *n* AVOGADRO'S CONSTANT

**avoid** /ə'voyd/ *vt* **1** to make legally void; annul 〈∼ *a plea*〉 **2a** to keep away from; shun **b** to prevent the occurrence or effectiveness of ⟨*couldn't ~ hitting it*⟩ **c** to refrain from ⟨ *~ putting hot dishes directly on the table*⟩ **3** *archaic* to depart or withdraw from; leave **synonyms** see ¹ESCAPE [ME *avoiden,* fr OF *esvuidier,* fr *es-* (fr L *ex-*) + *vuidier* to empty – more at VOID] – **avoidable** *adj,* **avoidably** *adv,* **avoider** *n*

**avoidance** /ə'voyd(ə)ns/ *n* **1** annulment **2** an act or practice of avoiding

**avoirdupois** /ˌavwahdooh'pwah, ˌavədə'poyz/ *n* **1** AVOIRDU-POIS WEIGHT **2** *chiefly NAm* weight, heaviness; *esp* personal weight [ME *avoir de pois* goods sold by weight, fr OF, lit., goods of weight]

**avoirdupois weight** *n* the series of units of weight based on the pound of 16 ounces and the ounce of 16 drams

**avouch** /ə'vowch/ *vt, archaic or formal* **1** to declare as a matter of fact; affirm **2** to vouch for; corroborate **3a** to acknowledge (e g an act) as one's own **b** to confess, avow [ME *avouchen* to cite as authority, fr MF *avochier* to summon, fr L *advocare* – more at ADVOCATE] – **avouchment** *n*

**avow** /ə'vow/ *vt* **1** to declare assuredly ⟨*loudly ~*ing *their support*⟩ **2** to acknowledge openly, bluntly, and without shame ⟨*ever ready to ~ his reactionary outlook*⟩ **synonyms** see ASSERT **antonym** disavow [ME *avowen,* fr OF *avouer,* fr L *advocare*] – **avower** *n,* **avowedly** *adv*

**avowal** /ə'vowəl/ *n* an open declaration or acknowledgment

**avulse** /ə'vuls/ *vt* to separate by avulsion [L *avulsus,* pp of *avellere* to tear off, fr *ab-* + *vellere* to pluck – more at VUL-NERABLE]

**avulsion** /ə'vulsh(ə)n/ *n* a forcible separation or detachment: e g a a tearing away of a body part accidentally or surgically **b** a sudden cutting off of land by flood, currents, or change in course of a body of water; *esp* one separating land from one person's property and joining it to another's

**avuncular** /ə'vungkyoolə/ *adj* **1** of an uncle **2** kindly, genial ⟨ *~ indulgence*⟩ [L *avunculus* maternal uncle – more at UNCLE]

**aw** /aw/ *interj, chiefly NAm* – used to express mild sympathy, remonstrance, incredulity, or disgust

**awa** /ə'wah, ə'waw/ *adv, Scot* away

**await** /ə'wayt/ *vt* **1** to wait for ⟨*a treaty ~*ing *ratification*⟩ **2** to be in store for ⟨*wondered what ~*ed *him at the end of his journey*⟩ **3** *obs* to lie in wait for *~ vi* **1** to stay or be in waiting; wait **2** to be in store **usage** see ¹WAIT [ME *awaiten,* fr ONF *awaitier,* fr L *ad-*) + *waitier* to watch – more at WAIT]

¹**awake** /ə'wayk/ *vb* awoke /ə'wohk/ *also* awaked; awaken /ə'wohkən/ *vi* **1** to emerge from sleep or a sleeplike state **2** to become conscious or aware of something *– + to* ⟨*awoke to their danger*⟩ *~ vt* **1** to arouse from sleep or a sleeplike state **2** to make active; stir up ⟨*awoke old memories*⟩ [ME *awaken* (fr OE *awacan,* fr ¹*a-* + *wacan* to awake, rise, be born) & *awakien,* fr OE *awacian,* fr ¹*a-* + *wacian* to be awake, watch – more at WAKE]

²**awake** *adj* **1** roused (as if) from sleep **2** fully conscious; awake *– + to* ⟨*they went forward quite ~ to the dangers of their undertaking*⟩

**awaken** /ə'waykən/ *vb* to awake [ME *awakenen,* fr OE *awæcnian,* fr a- + *wæcnian* to waken] – **awakener** *n*

¹**award** /ə'wawd/ *vt* **1** to give by judicial decree ⟨*the court ~*ed *him substantial damages*⟩ **2** to confer or bestow as being deserved, merited, or needed ⟨ *~ a scholarship*⟩ [ME *awarden* to decide, fr ONF *eswarder,* fr *es-* (fr L *ex-*) + *warder* to guard, of Gmc origin; akin to OHG *wartēn* to watch – more at WARD] – **awardable** *adj,* **awarder** *n*

²**award** *n* **1** a judgment or final decision; *esp* a grant of damages in a civil court case **2** something that is conferred or bestowed, esp on the basis of merit or need

**awardee** /ə,waw'dee/ *n* a person who receives an award

**aware** /ə'weə/ *adj* **1** having or showing realization, perception, or knowledge; conscious, cognizant *– often + of* **2** *archaic* watchful, wary [ME *iwar,* fr OE *gewær,* fr *ge-* (associative prefix) + *wær* wary] – **awareness** *n*

**awash** /ə'wosh/ *adj* **1a** floating in and washed over by waves **b** covered with water; flooded ⟨*the streets were ~ after the sudden storm*⟩ **2** marked by an abundance ⟨*a post office ~ with holiday mail*⟩

¹**away** /ə'way/ *adv* **1** on the way; along ⟨*get ~ early*⟩ **2a** from here or there; hence, thence ⟨*he's ~ for the weekend*⟩ ⟨*go ~ and leave me in peace!*⟩ **b** on an opponent's ground ⟨*Liverpool won ~ and have goals in hand for the home leg*⟩ **3** so as to be separated; off ⟨*cut the dead branch ~*⟩ **4a** in a secure place or manner ⟨*locked ~*⟩ ⟨*tucked ~*⟩ **b** in another direction; aside ⟨*looked ~*⟩ **5** out of existence; to an end ⟨*water's boiled ~*⟩

⟨*laze ~ the afternoon*⟩ **6** from one's possession ⟨*gave ~ a fortune*⟩ **7a** on, uninterruptedly ⟨*clocks ticking ~*⟩ **b** without hesitation or delay ⟨*do it right ~*⟩ **8** by a long distance or interval; far ⟨ *~ back in 1910*⟩ [ME, fr OE *aweg, onweg,* fr *a-, on* + *weg* way]

²**away** *adj* **1** absent from a place; gone ⟨ *~ for the weekend*⟩ **2** distant ⟨*a lake 10 miles ~*⟩ **3** played or scored on an opponent's grounds ⟨*not lost in their last 23 ~ matches*⟩ ⟨*won on the ~ goals rule*⟩ – **awayness** *n*

¹**awe** /aw/ *n* **1** an emotion compounded of dread, veneration, and wonder inspired by authority, or by something sacred or sublime ⟨*stood in ~ of the director*⟩ ⟨*filled with ~ by the B Minor Mass*⟩ **2** *archaic* (the power to inspire) dread or terror [ME, fr ON *agi;* akin to OE *ege* awe, Gk *achos* pain]

²**awe** *vt* to inspire with awe

**aweather** /ə'wedhə/ *adv, nautical* on or towards the side from which the wind is blowing – compare ALEE

**awed** /awd/ *adj* showing awe ⟨ *~ respect*⟩

**aweigh** /ə'way/ *adj, of an anchor* raised just clear of the bed of a body of water △ away

**aweless, awless** /'awlis/ *adj* **1** feeling no awe **2** *obs* inspiring no awe

**awesome** /'aws(ə)m/ *adj* **1** expressing awe ⟨ *~ tribute*⟩ **2** inspiring awe ⟨*an ~ sight*⟩ – **awesomely** *adv,* **awesomeness** *n*

**awestruck** /-ˌstruk/ *also* **awestricken** /-ˌstrikən/ *adj* filled with awe

¹**awful** /'awf(ə)l/ *adj* **1** extremely disagreeable or objectionable **2** filled with awe: e g **2a** deeply respectful or reverential **3** *obs* afraid, terrified **3** *informal* exceedingly great – used as an intensive ⟨*they took an ~ chance*⟩ **4** *archaic* inspiring awe – **awfully** *adv,* **awfulness** *n*

    **usage** The modern senses of **awful** and **awfully** are disapproved of by some people, who would prefer to confine these words to their original meanings associated with **awe**; but as today one could scarcely use the **awe** senses without danger of misunderstanding it may be safer to avoid the words altogether in formal writing.

²**awful** *adv, nonstandard* very, extremely ⟨ *~ tired*⟩

**awhile** /ə'wiel/ *adv* for a while

    **usage** Since **awhile** is an adverb it should not be confused with the noun *a* while. One can ⟨*rest awhile*⟩ or ⟨*rest for a while*⟩, but not ⟨△ *rest for* awhile⟩.

**awkward** /'awkwəd/ *adj* **1a** lacking dexterity or skill, esp in the use of hands; clumsy ⟨ *~ with a needle and thread*⟩ **b** showing lack of expertness ⟨*his landing was ~, but it was only the second time he'd flown solo*⟩ **2a** lacking ease or grace (e g of movement or expression) ⟨*played an ~ stroke*⟩ **b** lacking the right proportions, size, or harmony of parts; ungainly ⟨*the new double garage made an ~ addition to the house*⟩ **3a** lacking social grace and assurance **b** causing embarrassment ⟨*an ~ moment*⟩ **4** poorly adapted for use or handling **5** requiring caution ⟨*an ~ diplomatic situation*⟩ **6** deliberately obstructive ⟨*the shareholders decided to be ~ and declined to attend the meeting – The Times*⟩ **7** *archaic* unfavourable, adverse **8** *obs* perverse **synonyms** see CLUMSY **antonyms** deft, graceful, skilful [ME *awkeward* in the wrong direction, fr *awke* turned the wrong way, fr ON *ǫfugr;* akin to OHG *abuh* turned the wrong way, L *opacus* obscure] – **awkwardly** *adv,* **awkwardness** *n*

**awl** /awl/ *n* a pointed instrument for marking surfaces or piercing small holes (e g in leather or wood) [ME *al,* fr ON *alr;* akin to OHG *āla* awl, Skt *ārā*]

**awn** /awn/ *n* any of the slender bristles at the end of the flower spikelet in some cereals and grasses (e g barley); *broadly* a small pointed projecting part [ME, fr OE *agen,* fr ON *ǫgn;* akin to OHG *agana* awn, OE *ecg* edge – more at EDGE] – **awned** *adj,* **awnless** *adj*

**awning** /'awning/ *n* **1** a rooflike cover, often made of canvas, put up (e g over the deck of a ship or in front of a window) as a protection from sun or rain **2** a shelter resembling an awning [origin unknown]

**awoke** /ə'wohk/ *past of* AWAKE

**awoken** /ə'wohkən/ *past part of* AWAKE

**AWOL** /'aywol/ *n or adj, often not cap* (someone who is) absent without leave [*absent without leave*]

**awry** /ə'rie/ *adv or adj* **1** in a turned or twisted position or direction; askew **2** out of the right or hoped-for course; amiss [ME *on wry,* fr *on* + *wry*]

¹**axe,** *NAm chiefly* **ax** /aks/ *n* **1a** a tool that has an edged head fixed to a handle with the cutting edge parallel to the handle and that is used esp for felling trees and chopping and splitting

wood **b** ICE AXE **2** drastic or abrupt removal (e g from employment or from a budget) [ME, fr OE *æx;* akin to OHG *ackus* axe, L *ascia,* Gk *axinē* ] – **axe to grind** an ulterior motive, often based on some real or imagined grievance

²**axe,** *NAm chiefly* **ax** *vt* **1a** to shape, dress, or trim with an axe **b** to chop, split, or sever with an axe **2** to remove abruptly (e g from employment or from a budget) ⟨*the daily afternoon show is being* ~ d⟩

**axel** /'aksl/ *n* a jump in ice-skating from the outside forward edge of one skate with $1^1/_2$ turns in the air and a return to the outside backward edge of the other skate [*Axel* Paulsen *fl* 1890 Norw figure skater]

**axeman** /-ˌman/ *n* one who wields an axe; *specif* a usu psychopathic criminal whose habitual weapon is an axe ⟨*the mad* ~ *of Barnsley*⟩

**axenic** /ˌay'zenik, -'zeenik, ˌaks-/ *adj* free from other living organisms ⟨*an* ~ *culture*⟩ [*a-* + Gk *xenos* strange] – **axenically** *adv*

**axial** /'aksi·əl/, **axal** /'aksl/ *adj* **1** of or functioning as an axis **2** situated round, in the direction of, on, or along an axis – **axially** *adv,* **axiality** *n*

**axial skeleton** *n* the skeleton of the trunk and head

**axil** /'aksl/ *n* the angle between a branch or leaf and the main stem from which it arises [NL *axilla,* fr L]

**axilla** /ak'silə/ *n, pl* **axillas, axillae** /-lie/ the armpit [L]

**axillar** /ak'silə/ *n* an axillary part (e g a vein, nerve, or feather)

¹**axillary** /ak'siləri/ *adj* **1** of or located near the armpit **2** situated in or growing from an axil

²**axillary** *n* an axillar; *esp* any of the feathers arising from the area where the wing joins the body and closing the space between the flight feathers and body of a flying bird

**axillary bud** *n* LATERAL BUD

**axiology** /ˌaksi'oləji/ *n* inquiry into the nature, types, and criteria of values, esp in ethics [Gk *axios* + ISV *-logy*] – **axiological** *adj*

**axiom** /'aksi·əm/ *n* **1** a principle, rule, or maxim widely accepted on its intrinsic merit; a generally recognized truth **2a** a proposition regarded as a self-evident truth **b** *maths & philosophy* a postulate [L *axioma,* fr Gk *axiōma,* lit., honour, fr *axioun* to think worthy, fr *axios* worth, worthy; akin to Gk *agein* to drive – more at AGENT]

**axiomatic** /ˌaksi·ə'matik/ *adj* (having the nature) of an axiom; *esp* self-evident [MGk *axiōmatikos,* fr Gk, honourable, fr *axiōmat-, axiōma*] – **axiomatically** *adv*

**axis** /'aksis/ *n, pl* **axes** /'akseez/ **1a** a straight line about which a body or a geometric figure rotates or may be supposed to rotate **b** a straight line with respect to which a body or figure is symmetrical **c** a straight line about which a line, curve, or plane figure revolves in generating a SOLID OF REVOLUTION **d** any of the reference lines of a system (e g a graph) for denoting position on a plane or in space **2a** the second vertebra of the neck on which the head and first vertebra turn as on a pivot **b** any of various parts that are central or fundamental or that lie on or constitute an axis **3** a plant stem **4** any of several imaginary reference lines used in describing the positions of the planes by which a crystal is bounded and the positions of atoms in the structure of the crystal **5** a main line of direction, motion, growth, or extension ⟨*the* ~ *of the city*⟩ **6** *often cap the* alliance between Germany, Italy, and Japan before and during World War II; *also, not cap* a similar political partnership [L, axis, axle; akin to OE *eax* axis, axle, Gk *axōn,* L *axilla* armpit, *agere* to drive – more at AGENT]

**axis deer** *n* any of several species (e g *Axis axis*) of whitespotted deer of India and other parts of S Asia [NL *axis,* fr L, a wild animal of India]

**axisymmetric** /ˌaksisi'metrik/ *also* **axisymmetrical** /-kl/ *adj* symmetric about an axis [*axis* + *symmetric*] – **axisymmetrically** *adv,* **axisymmetry** *n*

**axle** /'aksl/ *n* **1** a shaft on or with which a wheel revolves **2** a rod connecting a pair of wheels of a vehicle; *also* an axletree [ME *axel-* (as in *axeltre*)]

**axletree** /-ˌtree/ *n* a fixed bar or beam with bearings at each end on which wheels (e g of a cart) revolve [ME *axeltre,* fr ON *öxultrē,* fr *öxull* axle + *trē* tree]

**Axminster** /'aksˌminstə/ *n* **1** a carpet weave in which pile tufts are inserted into a backing during its weaving according to a predetermined arrangement of colours and patterns – compare WILTON **2** a carpet woven by the Axminster method [*Axminster,* town in Devon, England]

**axolotl** /'aksəlotl, ˌaksə'lotl/ *n* any of several salamanders

(genus *Ambystoma*) of mountain lakes of Mexico that mature sexually in the larval stage [Nahuatl, lit., water doll]

**axon** /'akson/ *n* a usu long projecting part of a nerve cell that usu conducts nerve impulses away from the cell body [NL, fr Gk *axōn* axis] – **axonal, axonic** *adj*

**axonometric projection** /ˌaksənoh'metrik/ *n* a method of drawing a three-dimensional object in such a way that a rectangular solid appears as inclined and shows three faces [Gk *axōn* axis + E *-metric*]

**axoplasm** /'aksəplaz(ə)m/ *n* the PROTOPLASM (nucleus and jellylike contents of cells) of an axon [*axon* + *-plasm* ] – **axoplasmic** *adj*

**ayah** /'ie·ə/ *n* a native nurse or maid in India [Hindi *āyā,* fr Pg *aia,* fr L *avia* grandmother]

**ayatollah** /ˌie·ə'tolə/ *n* a SHIITE religious leader in Iran, often exercising considerable political power and influence [Per *āyatollāh,* fr Ar *āyatullāh* manifestation of God]

¹**aye** *also* **ay** /ay/ *adv* ever, always, continually ⟨*love that will* ~ *endure* – W S Gilbert⟩ [ME, fr ON *ei;* akin to OE *ā* always, L *aevum* age, lifetime, Gk *aiōn* age]

²**aye** *also* **ay** /ie/ *adv* yes – used as the correct formal response to a naval order ⟨~, ~, *sir!*⟩ [perh fr ME *ye, yie* – more at YEA]

³**aye** *also* **ay** /ie/ *n* an affirmative vote or voter ⟨*the* ~s *have it*⟩

¹**aye-aye** /'ie ˌie/ *n* a nocturnal LEMUR (small monkeylike mammal) (*Daubentonia madagascariensis*) of Madagascar [Fr, fr Malagasy *aiay,* of imit origin]

²ˌ**aye-'aye** *interj* – used for expressing amused surprise [*ay,* interj expressing surprise or sorrow, fr ME *ey*]

**ayin** /'ie·in/ *n* the 16th letter of the Hebrew alphabet [Heb *'ayin,* lit., eye]

**Aylesbury** /'aylzb(ə)ri/ *n* (any of) a breed of large white domestic ducks [*Aylesbury,* town in Buckinghamshire, England]

**Aymara** /'ieməˌrah/ *n, pl* **Aymaras,** *esp collectively* **Aymara 1** a member of an American Indian people of Bolivia and Peru **2** the language of the Aymara people, belonging to the Quechumaran stock [Sp *aymará*]

**ayont** /ə'yont/ *adv or prep, Scot* beyond [¹*a-* + *yont,* var of *yond*]

**ayre** /eə/ *n, archaic* AIR 6a

**Ayrshire** /'eəˌshiə/ *n* (any of) a breed of hardy dairy cattle that are reddish-brown and white in colour [*Ayrshire,* former county of Scotland]

**A-Z** /ˌay tə 'zed/ *n, Br* an indexed street atlas of a town

**az-** /əz-, az-/, **azo-** *comb form* containing nitrogen, esp as the group N=N that has a VALENCY of two ⟨*azobenzene*⟩ [ISV, fr *azote*]

**aza-, az-** *comb form* having a nitrogen atom instead of a carbon atom in the molecular structure; *specif* containing the chemical group NH in place of the chemical group $CH_2$ or a single nitrogen atom in place of the chemical group CH ⟨*azaguanine*⟩ [ISV *az-* + *-a-*]

**azalea** /ə'zaylyə/ *n* any of a genus or subgenus (*Azalea*) of rhododendrons with showy trumpet-shaped flowers and usu deciduous leaves [NL, genus name, fr Gk, fem of *azaleos* dry; akin to L *aridus* dry – more at ARDOUR]

**azathioprine** /ˌazə'thie·əpreen, -prin/ *n* a drug, $C_9H_7N_7O_2S$, that is used esp to suppress antibody production (e g to prevent a transplanted organ from being rejected) [*aza-* + *thio-* + *purine*]

**azeotrope** /ə'zee·ətrohp/ *n* a mixture of liquids whose boiling point does not change during distillation [ISV ²*a-* + *zeo-* (fr Gk *zein* to boil) + *-trope,* fr Gk *tropos* turn, way – more at YEAST, TROPE] – **azeotropic** *adj*

**azide** /'ayˌzied, 'a-/ *n* a chemical compound containing the group $N_3$ combined with another chemical element or group – **azido** *adj*

**azimuth** /'azimɘth/ *n* **1** the horizontal angle between a plane passing through an observer and the poles of the earth and a plane passing through an observer and a given object (e g a planet) and cutting the horizon at 90°. This angle is usu measured clockwise between true North or South and is used with the ALTITUDE to fix the exact position of a celestial body. **2** horizontal direction expressed as the angular distance between the direction of a fixed point (e g the observer's heading) and the direction of the object; the angular distance between the vertical circle of an object (e g a celestial body) and a fixed vertical circle [ME, fr (assumed) ML, fr Ar *as-sumūt* the azimuth, pl of *as-samt* the way] – **azimuthal** *adj,* **azimuthally** *adv*

**azimuthal equidistant projection** /ˌaziˈmoohthl/ *n* a map projection of the surface of the earth so centred at any given point that a straight line radiating from the centre to any other point represents the shortest distance and can be measured to scale – called also ZENITHAL EQUIDISTANT PROJECTION

**azimuthal projection** *n* a map projection onto a tangent plane of a part of a globe, in which all points have their true compass directions from the central point of the projection – called also ZENITHAL PROJECTION

**azine** /ˈazeen, -in/ *n* any of numerous organic chemical compounds whose molecular structure includes a ring containing six atoms at least one of which is a nitrogen atom

**azo** /ˈayzoh, ˈa-/ *adj* of or containing in the molecular structure the chemical group $N = N$ linked at both ends to carbon atoms [*az-*]

**azo-** – see AZ-

**azo dye** *n* any of numerous synthetic dyes containing nitrogen in the form of an azo group that have widespread commercial use

**azoic** /ayˈzohˈik, a-/ *adj* having no (form of) life; *specif* of the part of geological time that antedates life – compare ARCHAEAN [*a-* + Gk *zōē* life – more at QUICK]

**azole** /ˈazohl, əˈzohl/ *n* any of numerous organic chemical compounds whose molecular structure includes a ring containing five atoms at least one of which is a nitrogen atom

**azonal** /ayˈzohnl/ *adj* of or being a soil or a class of soils that lack well-developed layers (e g because they have only recently been deposited) – compare INTRAZONAL, ZONAL

**azotaemia** /ˌazəˈteemyə/ *n* URAEMIA (excess of waste products in the blood) [ISV *azote* + NL *-aemia*]

**azote** /ˈazoht,əˈzoht/ *n* nitrogen – not now used technically [Fr, irreg fr *a-* + Gk *zōē* life]

**azoth** /ˈazoth/ *n* **1** mercury when regarded by alchemists as the fundamental constituent of all metals **2** the universal remedy postulated by the alchemist Paracelsus [Ar *az-zāˈūq* the mercury]

**azotobacter** /əˈzohtə,baktə, ay-/ *n* any of a genus (*Azotobacter*) of large rod-shaped or spherical bacteria that occur in soil and sewage and carry out NITROGEN FIXATION [NL, genus name, fr ISV *azote* + NL *bacterium*]

**azoturia** /ˌazəˈtyooəriə/ *n* an excess of urea or other nitrogen-containing substances in the urine [ISV *azote* + NL *-uria*]

**Aztec** /ˈaztek/ *n* **1a** a member of the Nahuatlan people that founded the Mexican empire conquered by Cortes in 1519 **b** a member of any people under Aztec influence **2a** the language of the Aztecs **b** NAHUATL [Sp *azteca,* fr Nahuatl, pl of *aztecatl*] – **Aztecan** *adj*

**Aztec-Tanoan** /ˌaztek ˈtahnoh-ən/ *n* an American Indian group of related language families including the Tanoan and Zuni families – **Aztec-Tanoan** *adj*

**azure** /ˈazyooə, ˈay-, -zhə/ *n* **1a** SKY BLUE **b** the heraldic colour blue **2** *poetic* the unclouded sky **3** *archaic* LAPIS LAZULI (blue stone) [ME *asur,* fr OF *azur,* prob fr OSp, modif of Ar *lāzaward,* fr Per *lāzhuward*] – **azure** *adj*

**azurite** /ˈazyooriet, ˈay-, -zhə-/ *n* a blue mineral, $Cu_3(OH)_2(CO_3)_2$, consisting of the chemical compound copper carbonate used as a source of copper and, formerly, as a pigment in painting; *also* a semiprecious stone made from this mineral [Fr, fr *azur* azure]

**azygous, azygos** /ayˈziegəs/ *adj, biology* not one of a pair; single ⟨*an* ~ *vein*⟩ [NL *azygos,* fr Gk, unyoked, fr a- + *zygon* yoke – more at YOKE]

# B

**¹b, B** /bee/ *n, pl* **b's, bs, B's, Bs 1a** the 2nd letter of the English alphabet **b** a graphic representation of or device for reproducing the letter *b* **c** a speech counterpart of printed or written *b* **2** the 7th note of a C-major musical scale **3** one designated *b*, esp as the 2nd in order or class **4a** a second-class mark or grade rating a pupil's or student's work as good but short of excellent **b** one who or that which is graded or rated with a B **5** something that is the supporting item of two things ⟨*the B side of a record*⟩ **6** – used euphemistically for any offensive word beginning with the letter *b* **7** something shaped like the letter B

**²b** *adj, of a film* second-rate

**baa, ba** /bah/ *vi or n* (to make) the characteristic bleating sound of a sheep [imit]

**Baal** /bahl, 'bay·əl/ *n, pl* **Baals, Baalim** /-im/ **1** the universal god of fertility and most important god of the Canaanites and Phoenicians **2** *often not cap* a false god [Heb *ba'al* lord] – **baalism** *n, often cap*

**baas** /bahs/ *n, SAfr* a master, boss – used esp by nonwhites when speaking to or about Europeans in positions of authority [Afrik, fr D – more at BOSS]

**baasskap** /'bah,skap/ *n, SAfr* WHITE SUPREMACY ⟨ . . . *the old ~ mentality of the earlier governments* – N E Davis⟩ [Afrik, lit., mastership, fr *baas*]

**baba** /'bahbə/ *n* a rich yeast-leavened cake usu soaked in a rum and sugar syrup [Fr, fr Polish, lit., old woman]

**babassu** /,babə'sooh, '--,-/ *n, pl* **babassus** a tall palm (*Orbignya speciosa* or *Orbignya martiana*) of NE Brazil with hard-shelled nuts that yield a valuable oil [Pg *babaçu*]

**¹babbitt** /'babit/ *n* a babbitt-metal lining for a mechanical bearing

**²babbitt** *vt* to line with BABBITT METAL

**Babbitt** *n, chiefly NAm derog* a business or professional person who conforms unthinkingly to bourgeois standards and ideals, esp of materialism [George F *Babbitt*, character in the novel *Babbitt* by Sinclair Lewis †1951 US novelist] – **Babbittry** *n*

**babbitt metal** *n* an alloy, esp of tin, copper, antimony, and lead, used for lining mechanical bearings [Isaac *Babbitt* †1862 US inventor]

**babble** /'babl/ *vi* **1a** to utter meaningless or unintelligible sounds **b** to talk foolishly; chatter **2** to make a continuous murmuring sound ⟨*a babbling brook*⟩ ~ *vt* **1** to utter in an incoherent manner **2** to disclose (e g secrets) by talk that is too free [ME *babelen*, prob of imit origin] – **babble** *n*, **babblement** *n*

**babbler** /'bablə/ *n* **1** any of various songbirds (family Timaliidae) found in tropical areas of Europe, Asia, and Africa that have a loud persistent cry **2** *Austr slang* a cook on a sheep station or in a camp [(2) fr rhyming slang *babbling brook* cook]

**Babcock test** /'babkok/ *n* a test for determining the fat content of milk and milk products [Stephen M *Babcock* †1931 US agricultural chemist]

**babe** /bayb/ *n* **1** a naive inexperienced person **2a** *chiefly poetic* an infant, baby **b** *chiefly NAm slang* a girl, woman – usu as a noun of address [ME, baby, prob of imit origin]

**Babel** /'baybl/ *n* **1** a city, probably Babylon, where according to Genesis the building of a tower intended to reach Heaven incurred the wrath of God, who punished the builders by making their speech mutually unintelligible **2** *often not cap* **2a** a confusion of sounds or voices **b** a scene of noise or confusion [Heb *Bābhel*, fr Assyrian-Babylonian *bāb-ilu* gate of god]

**babesia** /bə'beezh(y)ə/ *n* any of a family (Babesiidae, esp genus *Babesia*) of single-celled organisms (PROTOZOANS) that are parasites found in the RED BLOOD CELLS of mammals, are transmitted by the bite of a tick, and cause serious diseases in cattle (e g RED-WATER FEVER) [NL, genus name, fr Victor *Babeş* †1926 Romanian bacteriologist]

**babirusa, babirussa, babiroussa** /,babə'roohsə/ *n* a large wild pig (*Babirousa babyrussa*) of the E Indies, the male of which has large backward-curving tusks [Malay *bābīrūsa*, fr *bābī* hog + *rūsa* deer]

**baboon** /bə'boohn/ *n* any of several large African and Asiatic primates (*Papio* and related genera of the family Cercopithecidae) with doglike muzzles and usu short tails [ME *babewin*, fr MF *babouin*, fr *baboue* grimace] – **baboonish** *adj*

**babouche** /bə'boohsh/ *n* an oriental slipper without a heel [Fr, fr Ar *bābūj, bābūsh*, fr Per *pāpūsh*]

**babu** /'bah,booh/ *n, pl* **babus 1a** a Hindu gentleman b – used as a form of address in India corresponding to *Mr* **2a** an Indian clerk who writes English **b** *chiefly derog* an Indian with some knowledge of English [Hindi *bābū*, lit., father]

**babul** /bah'boohl, '- -/ *n* an acacia tree (*Acacia arabica*) widespread in N Africa and across Asia that yields GUM ARABIC and tannins as well as fodder and timber [Per *babūl*]

**¹baby** /'baybi/ *n* **1a(1)** a very young child; *esp* an infant **a(2)** an unborn child ⟨*my ~ started kicking before I was four months pregnant*⟩ **a(3)** a very young animal **b** the youngest of a group **2** an infantile person **3** *informal* a person or thing for which one feels special responsibility or pride ⟨*the plan for the community centre was the mayor's ~*⟩ **4** *slang* a person; *esp* a girl, woman – usu as a noun of address [ME, fr *babe*] – **babyhood** *n*, **babyish** *adj* – **be left holding the baby** to be left to bear alone a responsibility that should have been shared by others

**²baby** *adj* very small ⟨*use ~ mushrooms*⟩

**³baby** *vt* to tend or indulge with often excessive or inappropriate care and solicitude ⟨*the urge to ~ an only child*⟩

**baby buggy** *n* **1** a lightweight foldable pushchair **2** *NAm* a pram

**baby carriage** *n, chiefly NAm* a pram

**Babycham** /'baybi,sham/ *trademark* – used for a type of sweet sparkling alcoholic perry

**baby grand** *n* a small grand piano about 2 metres (5 to 6 feet) long

**Babylon** /'babilən, -lon/ *n* a city given to materialism and the pursuit of sensual pleasure [*Babylon*, ancient city of Babylonia, ancient country of SW Asia]

**¹Babylonian** /,babi'lohnyən, -niən/ *n* **1** a native or inhabitant of ancient Babylonia or Babylon **2** the Akkadian language of ancient Babylonia

**²Babylonian** *adj* **1** of or characteristic of ancient Babylon, Babylonia, or its language or people **2** luxurious, sumptuous

**'baby-,minder** *n, chiefly Br* a person who looks after babies or preschool children – **baby-minding** *n*

**'baby-,sit** *vi* **-tt-; baby-sat** to care for a child usu for a short period while the parents are out [back-formation fr *baby-sitter*] – **baby-sitter** *n*

**baby sling** *n* a harness for carrying a baby that can be worn usu on the front or the back leaving the arms free

**'baby-,snatcher** *n* someone who steals a baby from its pram

**baby talk** *n* the imperfect speech of very young children learning to talk; *also* imitation of this, esp as used by adults in speaking to young children

**baby tooth** *n* MILK TOOTH

**bacalao** /,bakə'low, '--,-/ *n* dried salted cod, often formed into flat slabs [Sp]

**bacca** /'bakə/ *n, pl* **baccae** /'bakie/ BERRY 1c (coffee bean or similar dry seed) [NL, fr L *baca, bacca* berry] – **bacciferous** *adj*

**baccalaureate** /,bakə'lawri·ət/ *n* the academic degree of bachelor conferred by universities and colleges [ML *baccalaureatus*, fr *baccalaureus* bachelor, alter. (influenced by L *bacca* berry & *laureus* laurel) of *baccalarius*]

**baccarat** /'bakərah, --'-/ *n* a card game in which three hands are dealt and players may bet on either or both hands against the banker's hand [Fr *baccara*]

**baccate** /'bakayt/ *adj* 1 pulpy throughout like a berry 2 bearing berries [L *bacca* berry]

**Bacchae** /'bakee, 'bakie/ *n pl* the female attendants or priestesses of Bacchus, the Graeco-Roman god of wine [L, fr Gk *Bakchai*, fr *Bakchos* Bacchus]

**bacchanal** /'bakənl/ *n* 1a a follower of Bacchus; *esp* one who celebrates the Bacchanalia **b** a reveller 2 drunken revelry; bacchanalia [L *bacchanalis* of Bacchus] – **bacchanal** *adj*

**bacchanalia** /ˌbakə'naylyə/ *n, pl* **bacchanalia** 1 *pl, cap* a Roman festival of Bacchus celebrated with dancing, singing, and revelry 2 a drunken feast; an orgy [L, pl, fr neut pl of *bacchanalis*] – **bacchanalian** *adj or n*

**bacchant** /'bakənt/ *n, pl* **bacchants, bacchantes** a bacchanal [L *bacchant-, bacchans*, fr prp of *bacchari* to celebrate the festival of Bacchus] – **bacchant, bacchantic** *adj*

**bacchante** /bə'kanti/ *n* a priestess or female follower of Bacchus [Fr, fr L *bacchant-, bacchans*]

**bacchic** /'bakik/ *adj, often cap* of or characteristic of Bacchus or the Bacchanalia

**baccy** /'baki/ *n, chiefly Br informal* tobacco [by shortening & alter.]

¹**bach** /bach/ *vi, Austr & NZ* to keep house alone [short for *bachelor*]

²**bach** /bakh/ *n, NZ* a simple dwelling; *specif* a holiday house [prob fr ¹*bach*]

³**bach** /bahkh/ *n, Welsh* – used as a term of endearment, usu after a person's name ⟨*how are you Dai ~?*⟩ [W, lit., little (one)]

**bachelor** /'bachələ, 'bachlə/ *n* 1a **bachelor-at-arms, bachelor** a young knight who followed the banner of another in medieval times **b** KNIGHT BACHELOR 2 a person awarded what is usu the lowest degree conferred by a college or university ⟨*Bachelor of Arts*⟩ 3a a man who has never been married **b** a man past the usual age for marrying or one who seems unlikely to marry ⟨*a confirmed ~*⟩ 4 a male animal (eg a FUR SEAL) without a mate during breeding time [ME *bacheler*, fr OF, prob fr ML *baccalarius* tenant farmer, squire, advanced student, of Celtic origin; akin to IrGael *bachlach* shepherd, peasant, fr OIr *bachall* staff, fr L *baculum*] – **bachelorhood** *n*, **bachelordom** *n*

**bachelor girl** *n* an unmarried girl or woman who lives independently

**bacillary** /bə'siləri/, **bacillar** /bə'silə, 'basilə/ *adj* 1 of or caused by bacilli 2 *also* **bacilliform** /bə'sili,fawm/ *biology* shaped like a rod; *also* consisting of small rods [ML & NL *bacillus*]

**bacillus** /bə'siləs/ *n, pl* **bacilli** /-li/ a usu rod-shaped bacterium; *esp* one that causes disease [NL, fr ML, small staff, rod, dim. of L *baculus* staff, alter. of *baculum* – more at BACTERIUM]

**bacitracin** /ˌbasi'traysin/ *n* an antibiotic obtained from certain strains of two bacteria (*Bacillus subtilis* and *Bacillus licheniformis*) and used esp in treating bacterial skin and throat infections [NL *Bacillus subtilis* (species of bacillus producing the toxin) + Margaret *Tracy* b *ab*1936 US child in whose tissues it was found]

¹**back** /bak/ *n* 1a the rear part of the human body, esp from the neck to the base of the spine **b** the corresponding part of another animal; the dorsal surface of an animal **c** SPINAL COLUMN **d** the edge of a book along which the sections are secured in binding 2a(1) the side or surface behind the front or face; the rear part; *also* the farther or reverse side **a(2)** the upper, outer, or convex side of something ⟨*the ~ of the hand*⟩ **b** something at or on the back for support ⟨*the ~ of a chair*⟩ 3 (the position of) a primarily defensive player behind a forward in ball games such as soccer, hockey, etc [ME, fr OE *bæc*; akin to OHG *bah* back] – **backless** *adj* – **break one's back** to exhaust oneself; overwork – **break the back of** to complete or carry out the largest or most difficult part of (a job, task, etc) ⟨*we've broken the back of the decorating now*⟩ – **have one's back to the wall** to be in a difficult or desperate situation which allows one little or no choice of action – **put one's back into** to work with zest and energy at – **turn one's back on** 1 to abandon, reject ⟨*turned his back on his former friends*⟩ 2 to turn away from in disgust or fury – see also SLAP on the back, STAB in the back

²**back** *adv* 1a(1) to, towards, or at the rear ⟨*tie one's hair ~*⟩ **a(2)** away (eg from the speaker) ⟨*stand ~ and give him air*⟩ **b(1)** in or into the past; ago **b(2)** nearer the beginning (eg of a book) ⟨*six pages ~*⟩ **c** in or into a reclining position ⟨*lie ~*⟩ **d(1)** under restraint ⟨*hold ~ his tears*⟩ **d(2)** in or into a delayed or retarded condition ⟨*set them ~ on the schedule*⟩ **2a** to, towards, or in the original place from which somebody or something came ⟨*put it ~ on the shelf*⟩ **b** to or towards a former state ⟨*thought ~ to her childhood*⟩ **c** in return or reply ⟨*ring me ~*⟩ – **back and forth** backwards and forwards repeatedly

³**back** *adj* 1a being at or in the back ⟨*~ door*⟩ **b** distant from a central or main area; remote ⟨*a ~ road*⟩ **c** *of a speech sound* articulated at or towards the back of the oral passage 2 being in arrears; overdue ⟨*~ pay*⟩ 3 moving or operating backwards 4 not current; relating to the past ⟨*~ number of a magazine*⟩ ⟨*back-data*⟩ 5 being the last 9 holes of an 18-hole golf course

⁴**back** *vt* 1a to support by giving material or moral assistance – often + *up* **b** to substantiate – often + *up* ⟨*~ed up her argument with written evidence*⟩ **c(1)** to countersign, endorse **c(2)** to assume financial responsibility for ⟨*~ a new company*⟩ 2 to cause to go back or in reverse 3a to provide with a back **b** to be at the back of **c** to provide a musical backing for 4 to get upon the back of, esp for the first time; mount 5 to place a bet on (eg a horse) ⟨*~ed five winners*⟩ 6 to cause (a sail) to have the wind blowing onto the front of it in order to slow progress **~ vi** 1 to move backwards 2 *of the wind* to shift anticlockwise – compare VEER 3 to have the back in the direction of something ⟨*my house ~s onto the golf course*⟩ **synonyms** see ¹SUPPORT – **back and fill** 1 to manage the sails of a ship so that the wind alternately fills and empties them in order to achieve maximum manoeuvrability 2 to constantly change one's opinion

**back away** *vi* to recoil, withdraw

**back down** *vi* to retract an earlier claim; give up a previous opinion

**back off** *vi* to retreat; shy away

**back out** *vi* to withdraw, esp from an obligation, agreement, or contest

**back up** *vt* 1 to hold back ⟨*a dam backing up a huge lake*⟩ 2 to support (somebody), esp in argument or in playing a team game – *vi* 1 to back up a teammate 2 to accumulate in a congested manner ⟨*traffic backed up for miles*⟩

**backache** /'bak,ayk/ *n* a (dull persistent) pain in the back

**back bacon** *n* bacon from the loin of a pig

**back bench** *n usu pl* any of the benches in Parliament on which members who do not hold office in the government or opposition sit ⟨*speaking from the Labour back benches*⟩ – compare FRONT BENCH – **backbencher** *n*

**backbite** /'bak,biet/ *vb* **backbit** /-,bit/; **backbitten** /-,bit(ə)n/ to say mean or spiteful things about (somebody) – **backbiter** *n*

**backblocks** /'bak,bloks/ *n pl, Austr & NZ* remote or culturally backward areas ⟨*a bush nurse in Queensland's ~ – Australian Women's Weekly*⟩ [fr *block* in the sense "tract of land"] – **backblock** *adj*

**backboard** /'bak,bawd/ *n* a board placed at or serving as the back of something; *specif* a rounded or rectangular board positioned behind the basket on a basketball court

**back boiler** *n, chiefly Br* a boiler fitted at the back of a usu coal or gas fire for heating a domestic water supply

**backbone** /'bak,bohn/ *n* 1 the spine; SPINAL COLUMN 2a the chief or central mountain ridge or range of a country, region, etc **b** the most substantial or sturdiest part of something; the foundation 3 courage and determination; strength of character

**backbreaking** /-,brayking/ *adj* physically taxing or exhausting

**backchat** /-,chat/ *n, chiefly Br informal* impudent answering back, esp by a subordinate

**backcloth** /-,kloth/ *n, Br* a large painted cloth hung across the rear of a stage

**backcomb** /-,kohm/ *vt* to comb (the hair) against the direction of growth, starting near the roots, in order to produce a bouffant effect

**back country** *n, chiefly Austr* a sparsely populated rural area

**backcourt** /'bak,kawt/ *n* the area near or nearest the back boundary lines or back wall in a net or court game

**backcross** /'bak,kros/ *vt* to cross (a first-generation hybrid) with one parent [²*back*] – **backcross** *n*

**backdate** /-,dayt/ *vt* to apply (eg a pay rise) retrospectively – compare POSTDATE

**back dive** *n* a dive from a standing position facing away from the water with backward rotation of the body – compare FORWARD DIVE, INWARD DIVE, REVERSE DIVE

**back door** *n* an indirect, unfair, or underhand means of access – **backdoor** *adj*

**backdrop** /-ˌdrop/ *n* **1** a backcloth **2** BACKGROUND 1a, 3a, b

**back end** *n, dial Br* the end of a period of time; *esp* late autumn

**backer** /'bakə/ *n* **1** a person who provides esp financial support **2** *Br* a person who places a bet

**backfill** /'bak,fil/ *vb* to replace (soil) in a hole or trench, esp after an archaeological investigation

**¹backfire** /-ˌfie·ə/ *n* **1** a controlled fire that checks an advancing forest or prairie fire by clearing an area **2** a premature explosion in the cylinder or an explosion in the exhaust system of an internal-combustion engine

**²backfire** /ˌbak'fie·ə/ *vi* **1** *of an internal-combustion engine* to make a sudden loud noise as a result of a backfire **2** to have the reverse of the desired or expected effect ⟨*her scheme* ∼d *on her*⟩

**'back-for,mation** *n* the formation of a word by removing a real or supposed affix from an already existing longer word; *also* a word so formed (e g *burgle* from *burglar*)

**backgammon** /-ˌgamən/ *n* a board game played with dice and counters in which each player tries to move his/her counters along the board and at the same time to block or capture his/her opponent's counters [perh fr ³*back* + ME *gamen, game* game]

**background** /-ˌgrownd/ *n* **1a** the scenery or ground behind something **b** the part of a painting or photograph representing what lies behind objects in the foreground **2** an inconspicuous position ⟨*remain in the* ∼⟩ **3a** the conditions that form the setting within which something is experienced **b** the circumstances or events immediately related or leading up to a phenomenon or development ⟨*investigate the* ∼ *to a murder*⟩ **c** information essential to the understanding of a problem or situation **d(1)** the social factors (e g class, education, and family) that go to form a person, esp in early life ⟨*comes from a working-class* ∼⟩ **d(2)** a person's previous experience and training ⟨*she has a* ∼ *in computers*⟩ **4** BACKGROUND NOISE

**background music** *n* music to accompany the dialogue or action of a film or radio or television drama; *broadly* any music played in order to create a certain atmosphere (e g in a restaurant or airport)

**background noise** *n* intrusive sound that interferes with received or recorded electronic signals; NOISE 2b, 2c

**¹backhand** /-ˌhand/ *n* **1** a stroke in tennis, squash, etc made with the back of the hand turned in the direction of movement; *also* the side on which such strokes are made **2** handwriting whose strokes slant downwards from left to right

**²backhand, backhanded** /ˌ-'--/ *adv* with a backhand

**³backhand** *vt* to do, hit, or catch backhand

**backhanded** /-'handid/ *adj* **1** using or made with a backhand **2** *of writing* slanting downwards from left to right **3** indirect, devious; *esp* sarcastic ⟨*a* ∼ *compliment*⟩ – **backhandedly** *adv*

**backhander** /-ˌhandə/ *n* **1** a backhanded blow or stroke **2** *Br informal* a bribe

**backhouse** /'bak,hows/ *n, chiefly NAm* an outdoor toilet

**backing** /'baking/ *n* **1** something forming a back (e g to strengthen or protect) **2a** support, aid ⟨*the project had government* ∼⟩ **b** endorsement; *esp* endorsement of a warrant, by a magistrate **3** a musical accompaniment, esp for a vocalist

**backlash** /-ˌlash/ *n* **1** a sudden violent backward movement or reaction **2a** the clearance, slack, or play between adjacent movable parts of a mechanical system or machine **b** a jarring reaction in a mechanism caused by worn or badly fitting parts or by uneven operating **3** a strong adverse reaction (e g to a recent political or social development)

**backlift** /-ˌlift/ *n* a backswing

**backlist** /'bak,list/ *n* a list of publications that are still in print (e g because of continuing public demand)

**backlog** /-ˌlog/ *n* **1** a reserve (e g of resources or orders) that promises continuing work and profit **2** an accumulation of work, orders, cases, etc still to be completed or processed **3** *chiefly Nam* a large log at the back of a hearth fire

**backmost** /-ˌmohst/ *adj* farthest back

**back mutation** *n* mutation of a previously mutated gene back to its previous form

**back number** *n* an out-of-date issue of a periodical, newspaper, or magazine

**back of beyond** *n* a remote inaccessible place ⟨*lives in the* ∼⟩

**¹backpack** /-ˌpak/ *n* **1a** a load carried on the back **b** a piece of equipment designed to be carried on the back while in use ⟨*an oxygen* ∼ *for lunar exploration*⟩ **2** *chiefly NAm* a rucksack **synonyms** see RUCKSACK

**²backpack** *vb, chiefly NAm* **vi** to hike carrying food, equipment, etc in a backpack ∼ *vt* to carry on the back – **backpacker** *n*

**back passage** *n, chiefly Br euph* the rectum

**backpedal** /-ˌpedl/ *vi* **-ll-** (*NAm* **-l-** *also* **-ll-**) **1** to press backwards on the pedals of a bicycle (e g in order to brake) **2** to retreat or move backwards (e g in boxing) **3a** to hold back from going through with an action or enterprise **b** to back down from or reverse a previous opinion or stand

**backplate** /-ˌplayt/ *n* a metal plate worn as defensive armour for the back

**back projection** *n* a method of providing a background for a film or play by projecting a film or slides on to a screen placed behind the actors (e g in order to provide the illusion of movement)

**backrest** /'bak,rest/ *n* a support for the back

**backroom** /-'roohm, -'room/ *adj* **1** of or being a directing group that exercises its authority in an inconspicuous and indirect way **2** *chiefly Br* of or being an expert who works behind the scenes, esp a scientist engaged in scientific research ⟨∼ *boys*⟩

**backscattering** /-ˌskatəring/, **backscatter** /-ˌskatə/ *n* the scattering of radiation (e g X rays) backwards due to reflection from particles of the medium through which it is passing; *also* the radiation so scattered

**back seat** *n* **1** a seat in the back (e g of a car) **2** an inferior or unobtrusive position ⟨*won't take a* ∼ *to anyone*⟩

**back-seat driver** *n* a passenger in a motor car who offers unwanted advice to the driver; *broadly* a person who interferes in matters outside his/her responsibility or competence

**backset** /'bak,set/ *n, NAm* a setback

**backside** /-'sied/ *n, informal* the buttocks

**backsight** /-ˌsiet/ *n* the sight nearest the eye when aiming a firearm

**back slang** *n* British slang created by spelling a word backwards and pronouncing it accordingly (e g *yob* for "boy")

**backslap** /-ˌslap/ *vi* **-pp-** to display excessive heartiness – **backslapper** *n*

**backslide** /-ˌslied/ *vi* **backslid** /-slid/; **backslid, backslidden** /-ˌslid(ə)n/ to lapse morally or in the practice of religion – **backslider** *n*

**backspace** /-ˌspays/ *vi* to press a key on a typewriter which causes the carriage to move back one space

**backspin** /-ˌspin/ *n* spin of a moving ball (e g in tennis) in a direction opposite to that of its forward motion – compare TOP SPIN

**¹backstage** /-'stayj/ *adv* **1** in or to a backstage area **2** in private, secretly

**²backstage** /'bak,stayj/ *adj* **1** of or occurring in the parts of a theatre (e g the wings or dressing rooms) that cannot be seen by the audience **2a** of or being the inner workings of an organization (e g the government) **b** out of the public eye

**backstairs** /-ˌsteəz/ *adj* **1** secret, furtive ⟨∼ *political deals*⟩ **2** sordid, scandalous ⟨∼ *gossip*⟩

**backstay** /-ˌstay/ *n* **1** a stay extending aft from a masthead to the stern or side of a ship to support the mast **2** a strengthening or supporting device at the back (e g of a machine or shoe)

**backstitch** /-ˌstich/ *n* a strong hand sewing stitch made by inserting the needle at the beginning or middle of the previous stitch and bringing it out a stitch length in front – **backstitch** *vb*

**backstop** /-ˌstop/ *n* **1a** a screen or fence for keeping a ball from leaving the field of play (e g in baseball) **b** a stop that prevents backward movement (e g on the sliding seat of a rowing boat) **2** a player, esp the catcher in baseball, whose position is behind the batter

**back straight** *n* the straight part of a racecourse or racetrack on the opposite side of the field from the finishing post

**¹backstreet** /'bak,street/ *n* a usu narrow street, esp between the backs of houses

**²backstreet** *adj* made, carried out, or acting illegally or surreptitiously ⟨∼ *abortion*⟩

**backstroke** /-ˌstrohk/ *n* a swimming stroke executed on the back using reverse overarm strokes and kicking movements of the feet – **backstroker** *n*

**backswept** /'bak,swept/ *adj* swept or slanting backwards

**back swimmer** *n* a TRUE BUG (family Notonectidae) that lives in water and swims on its back by means of long oarlike legs

**backswing** /-,swing/ *n* the movement of a club, racket, bat, etc backwards to a position from which the forward or downward swing is made

**backsword** /-,sawd/ *n* 1 a single-edged broad-bladed sword 2 a stick (SINGLESTICK) used instead of a sword in fencing

**back talk** *n*, *NAm* backchat

**back-to-'back** *n*, *Br* a two-storey terraced house built with its back against the back of a parallel terrace

**back to front** *adv* 1 in such a way that the back and the front are reversed in position 2 being a mirror image ⟨*this photograph is* ~⟩ 3 thoroughly; INSIDE OUT ⟨*learnt the Highway Code* ~⟩

**backtrack** /-,trak/ *vi* 1 to retrace a path or course 2 to reverse an opinion or stance

**backup** /-,up/ *n* 1 somebody or something that serves as a substitute, auxiliary, or alternative ⟨*a* ~ *for a rocket*⟩ 2 somebody or something that gives support

**backveld, backveldt** /-velt, -felt/ *n*, *SAfr* a remote or culturally backward area – compare BUNDU [³*back* + Afrik *veld* country] – **backvelder** *n*

**backward** /-wood/ *adj* 1a directed or turned backwards **b** done or executed backwards ⟨*a* ~ *somersault*⟩ 2 retarded in development (eg physical, mental, or economic) 3 of or occupying a fielding position in cricket behind the batsman's wicket ⟨~ *short leg*⟩ 4 chiefly *NAm* diffident, shy – **backwardly** *adv*, **backwardness** *n*

**backwardation** /,bakwoo'daysh(ə)n/ *n*, *Br* 1 a premium paid by a seller to a buyer of shares to postpone delivery until a future day of settlement – compare CONTANGO 2 the amount by which the SPOT PRICE of a commodity exceeds its FORWARD PRICE [*backward* + -*ation*]

**backwards** /'bakwədz/, chiefly *NAm* **backward** *adv* 1 towards the back 2 with the back foremost 3 in a reverse direction; towards the beginning ⟨*say the alphabet* ~⟩ 4 perfectly; BY HEART ⟨*knows it all* ~⟩ 5 towards the past 6 towards a worse state – **bend/fall/lean over backwards** to make extreme efforts, esp in order to please or conciliate

**¹backwash** /'bak,wosh/ *n* 1a backward movement of water, air, etc produced by a propelling force (eg the motion of oars) **b** the backward movement of a receding wave 2 a usu unwelcome consequence or by-product of an event; an aftermath

**²backwash** *vt* to wash (combed wool) before or after preliminary processing in order to remove oil

**backwater** /-,wawtə/ *n* 1 a stagnant pool or inlet kept filled by the opposing current of a river; *broadly* a body of water turned back in its course by a dam, tide, etc 2 a place or condition that is isolated or backward, esp intellectually

**backwoods** /-woodz/ *n taking sing or pl vb* 1 a remote or culturally backward area – usu + *the* 2 chiefly *NAm* wooded or partly cleared land on the outskirts of settled or developed areas – **backwoodsman** *n*

**backyard** /bak'yahd/ *n* a yard at the rear of a house

**bacon** /'baykən/ *n* (the meat cut from) the cured and often smoked side of a pig [ME, fr MF, of Gmc origin; akin to OHG *bahho* side of bacon, *bah* back]

**bacon pig** *n* a pig reared to produce a certain proportion of lean meat to fat suitable for being made into bacon, gammon, and ham

**bacteraemia** /,baktə'reemi·ə/ *n* the abnormal and usu temporary presence of microorganisms, esp bacteria, in the blood [NL, alter. of *bacteriaemia*, fr *bacteri-* + -*aemia*]

**bacteri-** /baktiəri-/, **bacterio-** *comb form* bacteria ⟨bacteria*l*⟩ ⟨bacterio*lysis*⟩ [NL *bacterium*]

**bacterial** /bak'tiəriəl/ *adj* of or caused by bacteria ⟨*a* ~ *chromosome*⟩ ⟨~ *infection*⟩ – **bacterially** *adv*

**bactericide** /bak'tiəri,sied/ *n* something that kills bacteria – **bactericidal** *adj*, **bactericidally** *adv*

**bacterin** /'baktərin/ *n* a vaccine prepared from bacteria that are dead or can no longer cause infection

**bacteriochlorophyll** /bak,tiərioh'klorəfil/ *n* a chemical compound formed from PYRROLE that is found in photosynthetic bacteria and is similar to the chlorophyll of higher plants

**bacteriocin** /bak'tiəriəsin/ *n* an antibiotic (eg COLICIN) produced by bacteria [ISV *bacteri-* + -*cin* (as in *colicin*)]

**bacteriology** /bak,tiəri'oləji/ *n* 1 the study of bacteria 2 bacterial life and phenomena ⟨*the* ~ *of a water supply*⟩ [ISV] – **bacteriologist** *n*, **bacteriological** *adj*, **bacteriologically** *adv*

**bacteriolysis** /bak,tiəri'oləsis/ *n* destruction of bacterial cells esp by antibodies [NL] – **bacteriolytic** *adj*

**bacteriophage** /bak'tiəriə,fayj/ *n* any of various viruses that are parasitic in and eventually destructive to bacteria [ISV] – **bacteriophagic** *adj*, **bacteriophagous** *adj*, **bacteriophagy** *n*

**bacteriostasis** /bak,tiərioh'staysis/ *n* inhibition of the growth and multiplication of bacteria without their destruction [NL]

**bacteriostat** /bak'tiəriə,stat/ *n* something, esp a chemical, that causes bacteriostasis – **bacteriostatic** *adj*, **bacteriostatically** *adv*

**bacterium** /bak'tiəri·əm/ *n, pl* **bacteria** /-riə/ any of a class (Schizomycetes) of microscopic organisms that have round, rodlike, spiral, or filamentous single-celled bodies and often move by means of FLAGELLA (whiplike structures). They live in soil, water, organic matter, or the bodies of plants and animals and are important to human beings because of their chemical effects and because many of them cause diseases. [NL, fr Gk *baktērion* staff; akin to L *baculum* staff]

**bacteriuria** /bak,tiəri'yooəriə, -yoo'ree·ə/ *n* the presence of bacteria in the urine [NL]

**bacteroid** /'baktəroyd/ *n* an irregularly shaped bacterium (eg a RHIZOBIUM) found esp in root nodules of certain plants (eg beans or clover)

**Bactrian camel** /'baktri·ən/ *n* CAMEL 1b (camel with two humps) [*Bactria*, ancient country in SW Asia]

**¹bad** /bad/ *adj* **worse** /wuhs/, **worst** /wuhst/ 1a failing to reach an acceptable standard; poor, inadequate ⟨*a* ~ *repair job*⟩ ⟨~ *lighting*⟩ **b** unfavourable ⟨*a* ~ *omen*⟩ **c** rotten, decayed; in disrepair ⟨~ *fish*⟩ ⟨*the house was in a* ~ *condition*⟩ 2a morally objectionable; evil ⟨*good deeds and* ~ *deeds*⟩ **b** mischievous, disobedient 3 unskilful, incompetent – often + *at* ⟨~ *at arithmetic*⟩ 4 distressing, unpleasant ⟨~ *news*⟩ 5a injurious, harmful ⟨*excessive alcohol is* ~ *for you*⟩ **b** severe ⟨*Humpty Dumpty had a* ~ *fall*⟩ 6 incorrect, faulty ⟨~ *grammar*⟩ 7a suffering pain or distress; unwell ⟨*he felt* ~ *because of his cold*⟩ **b** unhealthy, diseased ⟨~ *teeth*⟩ 8 sorry, remorseful ⟨*felt* ~ *about losing her temper*⟩ 9 invalid, worthless ⟨*a* ~ *cheque*⟩ ⟨*a* ~ *coin*⟩ 10 of a debt not collectible – see also in somebody's bad BOOKS, **give a** DOG **a bad name, take something in bad** PART, **turn up like a bad** PENNY, **bad** SHOW [ME, perh fr OE *bæddel* hermaphrodite] – **bad** *adv*, **badly** *adv*, **badness** *n*

> **synonyms** Bad, evil, wicked, sinful, and naughty all describe ethically or morally unacceptable behaviour, or the people who perpetrate such behaviour. **Bad** is the most general and usually the mildest term ⟨bad *behaviour will not be tolerated at this school*⟩. **Evil** has a sinister ring, and suggests an inherent predisposition or capacity for wrongdoing or harmfulness. A **wicked** person or **wicked** deed consciously and deliberately contravene ethical codes or moral laws. **Sinful**, often interchangeable with **wicked**, stresses the breaking of religious or moral taboos. In a religious context **sinful** contrasts the proneness to evil of human beings with the purity of God. **Naughty** suggests by comparison trivial disobedience, and is usually reserved for children or animals. **Bad, wicked,** and **naughty** are sometimes used playfully ⟨bad *girl, be quiet, stay out late!*⟩. **Naughty** can also mean "risqué". *usage* The adjective **bad** is correctly used after linking (copula) verbs ⟨taste bad⟩ ⟨look bad⟩, though ⟨feel badly⟩ is common in speech. The adverb **badly,** not **bad,** is appropriate after ordinary verbs ⟨it hurts badly⟩ and where it means "desperately" ⟨want it badly⟩. *antonym* good

**²bad** *n* 1 a state of moral deterioration 2 an unpleasant or unfortunate state of affairs ⟨take the ~ with the good⟩ – **go to the bad** to embark upon an evil life

**bad blood** *n* ill feeling; bitterness

**bad debt** *n* a debt which is unlikely to be repaid

**baddie, baddy** /'badi/ *n, informal* somebody or something that is bad; *esp* an opponent of the hero (eg in fiction or the cinema)

**bade** /bed, bad/ *past of* BID

**badge** /baj/ *n* 1 a device, mark, or token, esp of authority, allegiance, or membership of a society or group 2 a characteristic mark 3 an emblem awarded for a particular accomplishment [ME *bage, bagge*] – **badge** *vt*

**¹badger** /'bajə/ *n* 1 any of several sturdy burrowing nocturnal mammals (esp the genera *Meles* and *Taxidea* of the family Mustelidae) that are widely distributed in the northern hemisphere, and are usu grey in colour with white striped facial markings 2 the pelt or fur of a badger [prob fr *badge;* fr the white mark on its forehead]

**²badger** *vt* to harass or annoy persistently [fr the sport of baiting badgers]

**bad hat** *n, chiefly Br* BAD LOT

**badinage** /'badi,nahzh, -nij/ *n* playful repartee; banter [Fr, fr *badiner* to joke]

**badlands** /'bad,landz/ *n pl, NAm* a barren region characterized by extensive rock erosion and spectacular hill formations

**bad language** *n* (the use of) swearwords

**bad lot** *n* a disreputable or dishonest person

**badly off** /'badli/ *adj* in an unsatisfactory condition; *esp* not having enough money

**badminton** /'badmint(ə)n/ *n* a court game played with light long-handled rackets and a shuttle volleyed over a high net [*Badminton,* estate in Gloucestershire, where it was first played]

'**bad-,mouth** *vt, chiefly NAm informal* to criticize or speak badly of ⟨*so why do we keep* ~ing *ourselves all the time? – Punch*⟩

**Baedeker** /'baydikə/ *n* any of a series of guidebooks mainly on European countries and cities [Karl *Baedeker* †1859 Ger publisher of guidebooks]

¹**baffle** /bafl/ *vt* **1a** to defeat or frustrate (eg a person or his/her plans) **b** to perplex or confuse ⟨*her clever arguments* ~ *him*⟩ **2a** to check or break the force or flow of (as if) by a baffle **b** to prevent (sound waves) from interfering with each other (eg by a baffle) *synonyms* see ¹PUZZLE [prob alter. of ME (Sc) *bawchillen* to denounce, discredit publicly] – **baffling** *adj*, **bafflingly** *adv*, **bafflement** *n*

²**baffle** *n* **1** a device (eg a plate, wall, or screen) to deflect, check, or regulate flow (eg of a fluid or light) **2** a part of a loudspeaker that prevents unwanted reflection of sound waves

**baffling wind** /'bafling/ *n* a light wind that frequently shifts from one point to another

¹**bag** /bag/ *n* **1** a usu flexible container for holding, storing, or carrying something: eg **1a** a handbag or shoulder bag **b** a suitcase **2a** a pouched or hanging body part or organ; *esp* an udder **b** a puffed-out sag or bulge, esp in cloth **3** a bagful **4a** a quantity of game taken or permitted to be taken **b** spoils, loot **5** *pl, informal* lots, masses ⟨*~s of time to do my homework*⟩ **6** *slang* an unpleasant or unattractive woman ⟨*silly old* ~⟩ **7** *slang* something one particularly likes or does very well ⟨*crosswords were her* ~⟩ [ME *bagge,* fr ON *baggi*] – **in the bag** *informal* as good as achieved; already assured of success

²**bag** *vb* **-gg-** *vi* **1** to swell out; bulge **2** to hang loosely ~ *vt* **1** to cause to swell **2** to put into a bag **3a** to take (animals) as game **b** to get possession of, seize; *also* to steal **c** to shoot down; destroy **4** *informal* to reserve the right to do or have ⟨*she* ~ged *the first turn*⟩ **5** *Austr slang* to criticize

**bag and baggage** *adv* **1** with all one's belongings **2** entirely, wholesale

**bagasse** /bə'gas/ *n* the residue of sugarcane, grapes, etc left after a product (eg juice) has been extracted [Fr, deriv of L *baca, bacca* berry]

**bagatelle** /,bagə'tel/ *n* **1** something of no consequence; a trifle ⟨*a mere* ~⟩ **2** a game in which balls must be put, by means of a cue, into cups or through arches at one end of an oblong table [Fr, fr It *bagattella,* prob fr L *baca, bacca*]

**bagel** /'baygl/ *n* a hard glazed ring-shaped bread roll [Yiddish *beygel,* deriv of OHG *boug* ring; akin to OE *bēag* ring – more at BEE]

**bagful** /'bagf(ə)l/ *n, pl* **bagfuls** *also* **bagsful** the amount contained in a bag

**baggage** /'bagij/ *n* **1** portable equipment, esp of a military force **2** superfluous or useless ideas or practices **3** *NAm* luggage, esp for travel by sea or air **4** *informal* **4a** a worthless or immoral woman **b** a pert or impudent young woman or girl – no longer in vogue [ME *bagage,* fr MF, fr *bague* bundle; (4) prob modif of MF *bagasse,* fr OProv *bagassa*]

**bagging** /'baging/ *n* material for making bags; *specif* coarse woven cloth

**baggy** /'bagi/ *adj* loose, puffed out, or hanging like a bag ⟨~ *trousers*⟩ – **baggily** *adv*, **bagginess** *n*

**bagman** /'bagmən/ *n* **1** *NAm* a person who collects or distributes dishonestly or illegally gained money on behalf of another **2** *Austr* a swagman or tramp **3** *archaic chiefly Br* TRAVELLING SALESMAN

**bagnio** /'bahnyoh/ *n, pl* **bagnios** **1** a brothel **2** *obs* an oriental prison, esp for slaves [It *bagno,* lit., public baths, fr L *balneum,* fr Gk *balaneion;* akin to OHG *quellan* to gush – more at DEVIL; (2) fr the use of Roman baths at Constantinople for imprisonment of Christian prisoners by the Turks]

**bag of waters** *n* the double-walled liquid-filled sac that encloses and protects the foetus in the womb and that breaks, releasing its liquid, during the birth process – not used technically

**bagpipes** /'bag,pieps/ *n taking sing or pl vb,* **bagpipe** *n, pl* **bagpipes** a wind instrument consisting of a reed melody pipe and three or four drone pipes that are provided with wind from a leather bag inflated either by a valve-stopped mouth tube or by a small bellows held under the arm – **bagpiper** *n*

**bags** /bagz/ *n pl* OXFORD BAGS

**bags** I *interj, chiefly Br informal* – used esp by children to claim the right to have or do something ⟨~ *have the last sweet*⟩

**baguette** /ba'get/ *n* **1** a small architectural moulding like, but smaller than, the astragal **2** (a gem having) the shape of a long narrow rectangle **3** a long thin crusty French loaf [Fr, lit., rod]

**bagwig** /'bag,wig/ *n* an 18th-century wig with the back hair enclosed in a small silk bag

**bagworm** /'bag,wuhm/ *n* any of a family (Psychidae) of moths with wingless wormlike females and plant-feeding larvae that live in a silk case covered with plant debris

**bah** /bah/ *interj* – used to express disdain or contempt

**bahadur** /bə'hahdə/ *n, often cap* a distinguished person – used as a title of respect in India; often after a person's name [Hindi *bahādur* hero, champion, fr Per]

**Baha'i** /bə'hah·i/ *n, pl* **Baha'is** a member of a religious movement founded by Bahā' Allah, a Persian prophet, in the mid-19th century that proclaims the necessity and the inevitability of the spiritual unification of humankind [Per *bahā'ī,* lit., of glory, fr *bahā* glory] – **Baha'i** *adj,* **Bahaism** *n,* **Bahaist** *n*

**Bahasa Indonesia** /bah'hahsə/ *n* the official language of the Republic of Indonesia, based on Malay – called also INDONESIAN [Indonesian *bahasa indonésia,* lit., Indonesian language]

**baht** /baht/ *n, pl* **bahts, baht** – see MONEY table [Thai *bāt*]

¹**bail** /bayl/ *n* **1** security deposited as a guarantee that a person temporarily freed from custody will return to stand trial when required ⟨*released on* ~ *of £2,000*⟩ **2** the temporary release of a prisoner on bail ⟨*he hasn't a hope of* ~⟩ **3** someone who provides bail △ **bale** [ME, custody, security for appearance, fr MF, custody, fr *baillier* to have in charge, deliver, fr ML *bajulare* to control, fr L, to carry a load, fr *bajulus* porter]

²**bail** *vt* **1** to deliver (property) in trust to another for a special purpose and for a limited period **2** to release on bail **3** to procure the release of (a person in custody) by giving bail – often + *out* [(1) AF *baillier,* fr Fr, to deliver; (2, 3) ¹*bail*]

³**bail** *n* **1** either of the two crosspieces that lie on the stumps to form the wicket in cricket **2** a movable open shed, often on wheels, that is used for milking cows **3** *chiefly Br* a partition or bar for separating animals in a stable **4** *Austr & NZ* a frame for holding a cow's head during milking [ME *baille* bailey, fr OF]

⁴**bail,** *Br also* **bale** *n* a container used to remove water from a boat [ME *baille,* fr MF, bucket, fr ML *bajula* water vessel, fr fem of L *bajulus*]

⁵**bail,** *Br also* **bale** *vt* to clear (water) from a boat by collecting in a bail, bucket, etc and throwing over the side ~ *vi* to parachute from an aircraft □ usu + *out* – **bailer** *n*

**bail out** *vt* to help from a predicament; release from difficulty

**bail up** *vb, Austr & NZ vt 1* to secure (a cow's head) in a bail **2** to make captive (eg by force or by engaging in conversation) ⟨*had bailed up a bloke and his wife – The Sun (Melbourne)*⟩ ~ *vi, informal* to surrender ⟨*bail up, you! Come on, put your hands up – Ned Kelly*⟩

⁶**bail** *n* **1** a supporting half hoop, esp for a wagon cover **2** a movable hinged bar for holding the paper in position on a typewriter **3** the usu semicircular arched handle of a kettle, bucket, etc [ME *beil, baile,* prob fr Scand origin; akin to Sw *bygel* bow, hoop; akin to OE *būgan* to bend – more at BOW]

**bailable** /'baylabl/ *adj* eligible for bail ⟨*a* ~ *offence*⟩

**bailee** /bay'lee/ *n* the person to whom property is bailed

**bailey** /'bayli/ *n* **1** the outer wall of a castle or any of several walls surrounding the keep **2** the space immediately within the external wall or between two outer walls of a castle – compare WARD 3a [ME *bailli,* fr OF *baille, balie* palisade, bailey]

**Bailey bridge** *n* a prefabricated bridge built from interchangeable latticed steel panels that are coupled together with steel pins [Sir Donald *Bailey* b 1901 E engineer]

**bailie** /'bayli/ *n* a Scottish municipal magistrate [ME]

**bailiff** /'baylif/ *n* **1** an official employed by a sheriff to serve writs, make arrests, etc **2** *chiefly Br* one who manages an estate or farm [ME *baillif, bailie,* fr OF *baillif,* fr *bail* custody, jurisdiction – more at BAIL] – **bailiffship** *n*

**bailiwick** /'bayliwik/ *n* **1** the area of jurisdiction of a bailie or bailiff **2** a person's special skill or area of knowledge [ME *baillifwik,* fr *baillif* + *wik* dwelling place, village, fr OE *wīc;* akin to OHG *wīch* dwelling place, town; both fr a prehistoric WGmc word borrowed fr L *vicus* village – more at VICINITY]

**bailment** /'baylmənt/ *n* the delivery by a bailor to a bailee of personal property in trust for a specific period or purpose

**bailor,** *NAm also* **bailer** /'baylə/ *n* a person who delivers property to another in trust

**bailsman** /'baylzmən/ *n* one who gives bail for another

**bain-marie** /banh mə'ree (*Fr* bɛ̃ mari)/ *n* a vessel (eg a saucepan) of hot or boiling water into which a bowl or other vessel containing food is placed in order to cook or heat the food gently (eg to prevent curdling) – compare DOUBLE BOILER [Fr, fr MF, lit., bath (of) Mary]

**bairn** /beən/ *n, chiefly Scot & N Eng* a child [ME *bern, barn,* fr OE *bearn* & ON *barn;* akin to OHG *barn* child]

**Baisakh** /'biesahk/ *n* – see MONTH table [Hindi, fr Skt *Vaiśākha*]

**¹bait** /bayt/ *vt* **1** to provoke, tease, or exasperate with unjust, nagging, or persistent remarks **2** to harass (eg a chained animal) with dogs, usu for sport **3a** to put bait on or in ⟨~ *a hook*⟩ **b** to entice, lure **4** to give food and drink to (an animal), esp during a break in a journey ~ *vi, archaic* to stop for food and rest when travelling △ bate [ME *baiten,* fr ON *beita;* akin to OE *bǣtan* to bait, *bītan* to bite] – **baiter** *n*

**²bait** *n* **1a** something used to lure an animal, fish, etc, esp to a hook or trap **b** a poisonous material placed where it will be eaten by pests **2** a lure, temptation [ON *beit* pasturage & *beita* food; akin to OE *bītan* to bite]

**baiza** /'biezə/ *n* – see *rial* at MONEY table [colloq Ar, fr Hindi *paisā*]

**baize** /bayz/ *n* a lightweight woollen or cotton cloth resembling felt, used chiefly for covering or lining something (eg table tops or the inside of drawers) [MF *baies,* pl of *baie* baize, fr fem of *bai* bay-coloured]

**¹bake** /bayk/ *vt* **1** to cook (eg food) by dry heat, esp in an oven **2** to dry or harden by subjecting to heat ~ *vi* **1** to cook food (eg bread and cakes) by baking **2** to become baked **3** *informal* to become extremely hot ⟨*I'll have to stop sunbathing, I'm* baking⟩ [ME *baken,* fr OE *bacan;* akin to OHG *bahhan* to bake, Gk *phōgein* to roast] – **baker** *n*

**²bake** *n* **1** a batch of goods baked at one time **2** *NAm* a social gathering at which (baked) food is served

**bakehouse** /-,hows/ *n* a place for baking food, esp bread [ME *bakhous,* fr *baken* to bake + *hous* house]

**Bakelite** /'baykəliet/ *trademark* – used for any of various synthetic resins and plastics used esp for electrical insulation

**baker's dozen** /'baykəz/ *n* thirteen [prob fr a former practice of selling 13 loaves for the price of 12 to prevent accusations of giving short weight]

**bakery** /'bayk(ə)ri/ *n* a place for baking or selling baked goods, esp bread and cakes

**baking powder** /'bayking/ *n* a powder used in place of yeast as a raising agent in making scones, cakes, etc that consists of a BICARBONATE and an acid substance

**baking soda** *n* SODIUM BICARBONATE used as an ingredient of BAKING POWDER

**bakkie** /bə'kee/ *n, SAfr* a light lorry with an open back and low sides; a pickup truck [Afrik *bak* container]

**baklava** /bə'klahvə/ *n* a sweet rich dessert of Turkish origin, made of thin layers of pastry containing nuts and honey [Turk]

**baksheesh** /'bak,sheesh, - '-/ *n, pl* **baksheesh** money given as a tip or donation in some Eastern countries [Per *bakhshīsh,* fr *bakhshīdan* to give; akin to Gk *phagein* to eat, Skt *bhajati* he allots]

**BAL** *n* a chemical compound, HSCH(CH₂SH)CH₂OH, developed originally as an antidote to LEWISITE (gas used in warfare), and used to treat poisoning by certain metals (eg arsenic) [British Anti-Lewisite]

**balaclava** /,balə'klahvə/ *also* **balaclava helmet** *n, often cap B* a knitted pull-on hood that covers the ears, neck and throat [*Balaclava* (*Balaklava*), village in the Crimea, USSR, site of a battle in the Crimean War]

**balalaika** /,balə'liekə/ *n* a musical instrument of Russian origin, usu having three strings and a triangular body and played by plucking [Russ]

**¹balance** /'baləns/ *n* **1** an instrument for weighing: eg **1a** a beam that is supported freely in the centre and has two scale-pans of equal weight suspended from its ends **b** a device that measures weight or force (eg by using the elasticity of a spiral spring) **2** *cap* Libra **3** a counterbalancing weight, force, or influence **4 balance wheel, balance** an oscillating wheel acting against the tension of a hairspring to regulate the movement of a timepiece **5a** stability produced by even distribution of weight on each side of a vertical axis **b** equilibrium between contrasting, opposing, or interacting elements ⟨*necessary to create a* ~ *between the practical and the ideal*⟩ **c** equality between the totals of the two sides of an account **6** an aesthetically pleasing integration of elements **7** the ability to retain one's physical equilibrium **8** the power to make authoritative judgments ⟨*hold the* ~⟩ **9** the weight or force of one side in excess of another ⟨*the* ~ *of the evidence lay on the side of the defendant*⟩ **10a** (a statement of) the difference between credits and debits in an account **b** something left over; a remainder **c** an amount in excess, esp on the credit side of an account **11** mental and emotional steadiness **12** the point on the trigger side of a rifle at which the weight of the ends balance each other [ME, fr OF, fr (assumed) VL *bilancia,* fr LL *bilanc-, bilanx* having two scalepans, fr L *bi-* + *lanc-, lanx* plate; akin to OE *eln* ell] – **balanced** *adj* – **in the balance** with the fate or outcome about to be determined ⟨*her future hung in the balance*⟩ – **off balance** unevenly weighted; unstable – **on balance** all things considered

*usage* The use of **balance,** as in **10b,** to mean "remainder" is disliked by some people, who feel that the word should be used only when a clear comparison is made between two amounts, especially of money. Compare ⟨*bought some shoes and spent the* **balance** *of what you gave me on beer*⟩ ⟨△ *read the* **balance** *of the chapter tomorrow*⟩.

**²balance** *vt* **1a(1)** to compute the difference between the debits and credits of (an account) **a(2)** to pay the amount due on; settle **b(1)** to arrange so that one set of mathematical elements exactly equals another ⟨~ *an equation*⟩ **b(2)** to complete (a chemical equation) so that the same number of atoms of each kind appears on each side **2a** to counterbalance, offset **b** to equal or equalize in weight, number, or proportion **3a** to weigh in a balance **b** to compare the relative importance, value, force, or weight of; ponder ⟨~ *the various probabilities*⟩ **4a** to bring to a state or position of equilibrium **b** to bring into harmony or proportion ~ *vi* **1** to become balanced or established in balance ⟨*sat* balancing *on the fence*⟩ **2** to be an equal counterbalance – often + *with* – **balancer** *n*

**balance beam** *n* a narrow horizontal wooden beam supported 1.2 metres (about 4 feet) above the floor and used for balancing feats in gymnastics; *also* a gymnastics event using this

**balanced budget multiplier** *n* the ratio of the change in national income to an increase in government expenditure where this expenditure is matched by an equal rise in tax revenues – compare MULTIPLIER

**balance of payments** *n* **1** the balance of supply and demand for a country's currency in foreign exchange markets **2** a record of all financial dealings in goods, services, and capital assets between one country's residents and those of other countries over an accounting period, normally one year

**balance of power** *n* an equilibrium of power sufficient to discourage or prevent one nation or political party from imposing its will upon or interfering with the interests of another

**balance of terror** *n* an equilibrium of military power (eg nuclear capability) between potentially opposing nations sufficient to deter one nation from waging war on another

**balance of trade** *n* the difference in value between a country's imports and exports

**balancer** /'balənsə/ *n* one who or that which balances or assists in balancing; *specif* HALTERE (modified hind wing of an insect used to balance)

**balance sheet** *n* a statement of the financial condition of an enterprise at a given date

**Balante** /bə'lahnt/ *n, pl* **Balantes,** *esp collectively* **Balante** a member, or the language, of a Negro people of Senegal and Angola [Fr, fr Balante *Bulanda*]

**balas** /'baləs/ *n* a gemstone that is a variety of the mineral SPINEL and has a pale rose-red or orange colour [ME, fr MF *balais,* fr Ar *balakhsh,* fr *Balakhshān,* ancient region of Afghanistan]

**balata** /bə'lahtə/ *n* the dried juice of tropical American trees (esp *Manilkara bidentata*) of the sapodilla family that is used in its rubberlike gum form as an alternative to GUTTA-PERCHA, esp in making belting and golf balls; *also* a tree yielding balata [Sp, of Cariban origin; akin to Galibi *balata*]

**balboa** /bal'boh-ə/ *n* – see MONEY table [Sp, fr Vasco Núñez de *Balboa* †1517 Sp explorer]

**balbriggan** /bal'brigən/ *n* a knitted cotton fabric used esp for underwear or hosiery [*Balbriggan*, town in Ireland]

**balcony** /'balkəni/ *n* **1** a raised platform built out from the wall of a building and enclosed by a railing or low wall **2** a raised platform built out from the wall inside a public building (e g a theatre) [It *balcone*, fr OIt, scaffold, of Gmc origin; akin to OHG *balko* beam – more at BALK] – **balconied** *adj*

**bald** /bawld/ *adj* **1a** lacking a natural or usual covering (e g of hair, vegetation, or nap) **b** having little or no tread ⟨~ *tyres*⟩ **2a** unadorned ⟨*the* ~ *facts*⟩ **b** undisguised, blatant ⟨*a* ~ *lie*⟩ **3** *of an animal or bird* marked with white, esp on the head or face *synonyms* see ¹BARE [ME *balled;* akin to OE *bæl* fire, pyre, Dan *bældet* bald, L *fulica* coot, Gk *phalios* having a white spot] – **baldish** *adj*, **baldly** *adv*, **baldness** *n*

**baldachin, baldaquin** /'baldəkin/, **baldachino** /ˌbawld-ə'keenoh/ *n, pl* **baldachins, baldaquins, baldachinos** **1** a richly embroidered fabric of silk and gold **2** a cloth canopy fixed or carried over an important person or a sacred object **3** an ornamental structure resembling a canopy, esp over an altar or shrine in a Christian church [It *baldacchino*, fr *Baldacco* Baghdad, city in Iraq]

**bald eagle** *n* an eagle (*Haliaeetus leucocephalus*) of N America that feeds on fish and carrion and is brown when young but has a white head and tail when mature

**balderdash** /'bawldədash/ *n* nonsense – often used interjectionally to express strong disagreement [origin unknown]

**'bald-, faced** *adj, NAm* barefaced

**baldie** /'bawldi/ *n, informal* a bald person – usu as a noun of address

**balding** /'bawlding/ *adj* becoming bald

**baldpate** /'bawld,payt/ *n* a bald person

**baldric** /'bawldrik/ *n* a wide often ornamented sash or belt worn over one shoulder and across the body to support a sword, bugle, etc [ME *baudry, baudrik*]

**¹bale** /bayl/ *n* **1** great evil **2** *archaic* woe, sorrow [ME, fr OE *bealu;* akin to OHG *balo* evil, OSlav *bolŭ* sick man]

**²bale** *n* a large bundle of goods; *specif* a large closely pressed package of merchandise usu wrapped or bound by rope, wire, etc for storage or transport ⟨*a* ~ *of paper*⟩ ⟨*a* ~ *of hay*⟩ [ME, fr OF, of Gmc origin; akin to OHG *balla* ball]

**³bale** *vt* to make up into a bale – **baler** *n*

**⁴bale** *vt or n, Br* ⁴,⁵BAIL

**baleen** /bə'leen/ *n* whalebone [ME *baleine* whale, baleen, fr L *balaena* whale, fr Gk *phallaina;* akin to Gk *phallos* penis – more at BLOW]

**baleen whale** *n* WHALEBONE WHALE

**balefire** /'bayl,fie-ə/ *n* an outdoor fire often used as a signal fire; *also* a funeral pyre [ME, fr OE *bælfyr* funeral fire, fr *bæl* pyre + *fyr* fire – more at BALD]

**baleful** /'baylf(ə)l/ *adj* **1** deadly or wicked in influence; threatening great evil **2** very gloomy, esp as if expecting the worst *synonyms* see SINISTER ⚠ baneful – **balefully** *adv*, **balefulness** *n*

**¹balk, ** *chiefly Br* **baulk** /bawlk, bawk/ *n* **1** a ridge of land left unploughed, esp to mark off an area of land or prevent erosion **2** a large roughly squared beam of timber **3** a hindrance, obstacle **4** an illegal motion of the pitcher in baseball **5** *NAm* ²BAULK [ME *balke*, fr OE *balca;* akin to OHG *balko* beam, L *fulcire* to prop, Gk *phalanx* log, phalanx]

**²balk, ** *chiefly Br* **baulk** *vt* **1** to ignore, evade ⟨~ *his duty*⟩ **2** to check or stop (as if) by an obstacle; hinder, thwart ~ *vi* **1** to stop short and refuse to proceed **2** to draw back; recoil – often + *at* ⟨~ed *at the suggestion*⟩ **3** to commit a balk in baseball *synonyms* see ¹HINDER – **balker** *n*, **balky** *adj*

**balkan·ize, -ise** /'bawlkəniez/ *vt, often cap* to divide (e g a region) into smaller and often mutually hostile units [*Balkan* peninsula, SE Europe; fr the division of this territory into many small states] – **balkanization** *n, often cap*

**¹ball** /bawl/ *n* **1** a round or roundish body or mass ⟨~ *of wool*⟩ ⟨~ *of soil*⟩: e g **1a** a solid or hollow spherical or egg-shaped body used in a game or sport **b** a spherical or conical projectile; *also* projectiles used in firearms ⟨*powder and* ~⟩ **c** the rounded slightly raised fleshy area at the base of the thumb or big toe **2** a delivery or play of the ball in cricket, baseball, etc ⟨*the batsman was bowled by a good* ~⟩ **3** a game in which a ball is thrown, kicked, or struck; *specif, NAm* baseball **4** *pl,*

*slang* nonsense, rubbish – often used interjectionally **5** *pl, slang* audacity, gall ⟨*she even had the* ~s *to tell her boss he was lazy*⟩ **6** *usu pl, vulg* a testicle [ME *bal*, fr ON *böllr;* akin to OE *bealluc* testis, OHG *balla* ball, OE *bula* bull] – **keep the ball rolling** to keep something going; maintain the rate of something – **on the ball** *informal* alert and competent – **play ball** *chiefly NAm informal* to cooperate – **start/set/get the ball rolling** to set something in motion; get an activity underway

**²ball** *vb* **1** to form or gather into a ball ⟨~ed *the paper into a wad*⟩ **2** *chiefly NAm vulg* to have sexual intercourse (with)

**³ball** *n* **1** a large formal gathering for social dancing **2** *informal* a very pleasant experience; a marvellous time ⟨*have a* ~⟩ [Fr *bal*, fr OF, fr *baller* to dance, fr LL *ballare*, fr Gk *ballizein;* akin to Skt *balbalīti* he whirls]

**ballad** /'baləd/ *n* **1a** a narrative composition in rhythmic verse suitable for singing **b** a simple narrative song; *esp* a traditional ballad set to music **2** a slow, romantic, or sentimental popular song, esp one with a narrative [ME *balade* song sung while dancing, song, fr MF, fr OProv *balada* dance, song sung while dancing, fr *balar* to dance, fr LL *ballare*] – **balladry** *n*, **balladic** *adj*

**ballade** /bə'lahd, ba-/ *n* **1** a fixed verse form consisting usu of three stanzas with recurrent rhymes, a short concluding verse, and an identical refrain for each part **2** a musical composition, usu for piano, suggesting the epic ballad [ME *balade*, fr MF, ballad, ballade]

**balladeer** /ˌbalə'diə/ *n* a singer of ballads

**ball-and-socket joint** *n* **1** a mechanical joint in which a ball moves within a socket so as to allow rotary motion in every direction within certain limits **2** a joint (e g in the hip) in which the rounded head of one bone fits into a cuplike cavity of the other and that allows movement in many directions; *also* an artificial joint that allows the same degree of movement

**¹ballast** /'baləst/ *n* **1a** heavy material (e g gravel or water) carried in a ship to improve stability **b** heavy material carried on a balloon or airship to steady it that can be jettisoned to control the rate of descent **2** (something that gives) stability, esp in character or conduct ⟨*felt that his marriage had given him* ~⟩ **3** gravel or broken stone used as a bed for railway lines or as the bottom layer of roads **4** a device (e g a RESISTOR, CAPACITOR, or INDUCTOR) used to stabilize the current in an electrical circuit [prob fr LG, of Scand origin; akin to Dan & Sw *barlast* ballast; akin to OE *bær* bare & to OE *blæst* load – more at LAST] – **in ballast** *of a ship* having only ballast for a load

**²ballast** *vt* **1** to steady or equip (as if) with ballast **2** to fill in or make (e g a railway bed) with ballast

**ball bearing** *n* a circular bearing inside which friction is reduced by metal balls running easily in a groove around the shaft or rod being supported; *also* any of the balls in such a bearing

**ball boy**, *fem* **ball girl** *n* a person who retrieves balls for the players on a tennis court

**ballbreaker** /'bawl,braykə/ *n, slang* a very difficult or demanding task

**ball cock** *n* an automatic valve worked by a lever with a hollow floating ball attached to it that controls a flow of water (e g into a cistern) by opening and closing as the ball rises and falls with the level of the water

**ballerina** /ˌbalə'reenə/ *n* a female ballet dancer [It, fr *ballare* to dance, fr LL]

**ballet** /'balay; *NAm also* ba'lay/ *n* **1a** artistic dancing in which set conventional poses and steps are combined with light flowing movements and gestures (e g leaps and turns) **b** a theatrical art form using ballet dancing, music, and scenery to convey a story, theme, or atmosphere **2** music for a ballet **3** a group that performs ballets [Fr, fr It *balletto*, dim. of *ballo* dance, fr *ballare*] – **balletic** *adj*

**balletomania** /ˌbalitə'maynyə/ *n* (excessive) enthusiasm for ballet – **balletomane** *n*

**ball game** *n, chiefly NAm informal* a state of affairs; a way of thinking ⟨*compared to simply living with somebody marriage is a whole new* ~⟩

**ballista** /bə'listə/ *n, pl* **ballistae** /-tie/ a piece of ancient military equipment, often in the form of a crossbow, for hurling large missiles (e g boulders) [L, fr (assumed) Gk *ballistēs*, fr *ballein* to throw – more at DEVIL]

**ballistic** /bə'listik/ *adj* **1** of ballistics or a body in motion according to the laws of ballistics **2** *of a measurement or measuring instrument* sensitive to a sudden impulse (e g one caused by the passage of an electric current) [L *ballista*] – **ballistically** *adv*

**ballistic galvanometer** *n* a GALVANOMETER (instrument for measuring electric currents) that indicates a momentary current by a delayed and oscillatory deflection of the indicator

**ballistic missile** *n* a self-propelled missile guided in the ascent of a high-arch trajectory and falling freely in the descent

**ballistics** /bə'listiks/ *n taking sing or pl vb* **1a** the science of the physical laws according to which projectiles move in flight **b** the flight characteristics (e g the degree to which it is streamlined) of a particular projectile **2a** the study of the processes that occur within a firearm when it is fired **b** the firing characteristics of a particular firearm or cartridge

**ballistocardiogram** /bə,listoh'kahdiəgram/ *n* the results recorded by a ballistocardiograph

**ballistocardiograph** /bə,listoh'kahdiəgrahf, -graf/ *n* a device for measuring the amount of blood passing through the heart over a certain period of time [*ballistic* + *-o-* + *cardiograph*] – **ballistocardiographic** *adj*, **ballistocardiography** *n*

**ball joint** *n* BALL-AND-SOCKET JOINT

**ball lightning** *n* a rare form of lightning consisting of luminous balls that move horizontally and explode after a few seconds

**ballock** /'bolək, 'bawlək/ *n usu pl, Br slang* a bollock – often used interjectionally to express strong disagreement or annoyance

**ballonet** /,balə'net/ *n* a gas or air compartment of variable volume within the interior of a balloon or airship used to control ascent and descent [Fr *ballonnet*, dim. of *ballon*]

¹**balloon** /bə'loohn/ *n* **1** a large airtight bag filled with hot air or a gas that is lighter than air, so that it rises and floats in the atmosphere; *esp* one with a large basket attached for carrying passengers **2** an inflatable bag of various shapes and sizes made of thin usu brightly coloured rubber and used as a toy or for decoration **3** a line usu enclosing words spoken or thought by a character, esp in a cartoon [Fr *ballon* large football, balloon, fr It dial. *ballone* large football, aug of *balla* ball, of Gmc origin]

²**balloon** *vt* to inflate, distend ∼ *vi* **1** to ascend or travel in a balloon **2** to swell or puff out; expand – often + *out* **3** to increase rapidly **4** to travel in a high curving arc

³**balloon** *adj* relating to, resembling, or suggesting a balloon ⟨a ∼ *sleeve*⟩

**balloon glass** *n, chiefly Br* a short-stemmed drinking glass used esp for brandy that has a large pear-shaped bowl that narrows towards the top so as to retain the aroma of the contents

**ballooning** /bə'loohning/ *n* the act or sport of riding in a balloon – **balloonist** *n*

**balloon tyre** *n* a large flexible tyre inflated with air at a low pressure in order to provide cushioning over rough surfaces

¹**ballot** /'balət/ *n* **1a** a small ball formerly used for casting a vote in secret **b** a slip of paper, ticket, etc used for casting a vote in secret **2a** the system of voting in secret **b** the act or an instance of voting in secret **3** the right to vote **4** the number of votes cast [It *ballotta*, fr It dial., dim. of *balla* ball]

²**ballot** *vi* to vote or decide by ballot ∼ *vt* to obtain a vote in secret from ⟨*the union* ∼ed *the members*⟩ – **balloter** *n*

**ballottement** /bə'lotmənt/ *n* a method for detecting pregnancy by pushing sharply with a finger on the wall of the uterus and feeling the return impact of the displaced foetus; *also* a similar procedure for detecting a kidney that is out of its normal position [Fr, lit., act of tossing, shaking, fr *ballotter* to toss, fr MF *baloter*, fr *balotte* little ball, fr It dial. *ballotta*]

**ball park** *n, NAm* **1** a park in which ball games, esp baseball, are played **2** *informal* the approximately correct area ⟨*a figure of 60,000 is in the right* ∼ – *Saturday Review*⟩

'**ball-,point, ball-point pen** *n* a pen that has a small rotating metal ball as the writing point that inks itself by contact with a thin plastic inner tube containing ink

**ballroom** /'bawlroohm, -room/ *n* a large room for dances

**ballroom dancing** *n* a usu formal type of dancing that is done by couples or groups to music with conventional rhythms (e g the waltz or foxtrot) for recreation, exhibition, or competition

'**balls-,up, NAm ball-up** *n, slang* a state of muddled confusion usu caused by a mistake

**balls up, NAm ball up** *vb, slang* to make a mess (of); botch (something) ⟨*incompetents who ballsed up the whole programme*⟩

**ball valve** *n* a one-way valve consisting of a ball that rests inside a cylindrical seating over a hole and rises and falls by means of a spring, its own weight, or pressure of gases or liquids

**bally** /'bali/ *adj or adv, Br euph* ¹BLOODY 6, ³BLOODY [euphemism]

**ballyhoo** /,bali'hooh/ *n, pl* **ballyhoos** **1** a noisy, esp meaningless, demonstration or talk **2** flamboyant, exaggerated, or sensational advertising or propaganda [origin unknown] – **ballyhoo** *vt*

**ballyrag** /'bali,rag/ *vb* **-gg-** to bullyrag

**balm** /bahm/ *n* **1** a sweet-smelling oily resin obtained from various tropical trees (genus *Commiphora* of the family Burseraceae) and used for medicinal purposes (e g in soothing lotions); *also* a tree (e g BALM OF GILEAD) that yields this resin **2** an aromatic preparation used for soothing or healing **3** any of various aromatic plants (e g of the genera *Melissa* or *Monarda* of the mint family); *esp* LEMON BALM **4** a spicy aromatic odour **5** something that is physically, emotionally, or spiritually soothing or healing ⟨*praise is a* ∼ *to the wounded ego*⟩ [ME *basme, baume*, fr OF, fr L *balsamum* balsam, fr Gk *balsamon*]

**balm of Gilead** /'giliad/ *n* **1** a small evergreen African and Asian tree (*Commiphora opobalsamum* of the family Burseraceae) with sweet-smelling leaves; *also* a fragrant oily resin obtained from this tree and used esp in making perfumes **2** either of two poplars: **2a** a hybrid N American female tree (*Populus gileadensis*) with broad heart-shaped leaves **b** BALSAM POPLAR [*Gilead*, region of ancient Palestine known for its balm (Jer 8:22)]

**balmoral** /bal'morəl/ *n, often cap* a round flat brimless Scottish cap made of wool and with a plume on one side [*Balmoral* Castle in Scotland]

**balmy** /'bahmi/ *adj* **1a** having the qualities of balm; *esp* soothing **b** mild ⟨a ∼ *breeze*⟩ **2** barmy [(2) by alter.] – **balmily** *adv*, **balminess** *n*

**balneology** /,balni'oləji/ *n* the branch of medicine concerned with the therapeutic use of baths and mineral springs [ISV, fr L *balneum* bath – more at BAGNIO] – **balneal** *adj*, **balneological** *adj*

**baloney** /bə'lohni/ *n* nonsense – often used to express disagreement [perh alter. of *bologna* (*sausage*)]

**balsa** /'bawlsə, 'bolsə/ *n* **1a** a tropical American tree (*Ochroma pyramidale*) of the baobab family **b** balsawood, balsa the extremely light strong wood of this tree used esp for making rafts, fitting out aeroplanes, etc **2** a canoe or raft constructed of logs of balsawood [Sp]

**balsam** /'bawls(ə)m/ *n* **1a** an aromatic usu oily resinous substance secreted by various plants (e g BALSAM OF PERU and BALSAM OF TOLU); *esp* any of several resinous substances containing BENZOIC ACID or CINNAMIC ACID and used esp in making perfumes and certain medical preparations **b** any of various medical preparations containing resinous substances and smelling like balsam **2a** any of several trees yielding balsam **b** any of a widely distributed genus (*Impatiens* of the family Balsaminaceae, the balsam family) of often cultivated plants (e g busy lizzie) with watery translucent stems **3** BALM **5** [L *balsamum*] – **balsamic** *adj*

**balsam fir** *n* a N American fir tree (*Abies balsamea*) from which CANADA BALSAM is obtained

**balsam of Peru** *n* a balsam obtained from a tropical American tree (*Myroxylon pereirae*) of the pea family and used in making perfumes and in medicine, esp as an antiseptic [*Peru*, country in S America]

**balsam of Tolu** /tə'looh/ *n* a balsam obtained from a tropical American tree (*Myroxylon balsamum*) of the pea family and used esp in making cough syrups and perfumes [Santiago de *Tolú*, town in Colombia]

**balsam poplar** *n* a N American poplar (*Populus balsamifera*) that is often cultivated as a SHADE TREE and that has buds thickly coated with a sweet-smelling resin

**Balti** /'bahlti, 'bawlti/ *n* a Tibeto-Burman language of N Kashmir

**Baltic** /'bawltik, 'bol-/ *adj* **1** of the Baltic sea or Lithuania, Latvia, and Estonia ⟨*the* ∼ *states of the Soviet Union*⟩ **2** of a branch of the Indo-European languages that includes Latvian, Lithuanian, and Old Prussian [ML (*mare*) *balticum* Baltic sea]

**Balto-Slavonic** /,bawltoh, ,bol-/ *n* a hypothetical subfamily of Indo-European languages consisting of the Baltic and the Slavonic branches

**Baluchi** /bə'loohchi/ *n, pl* **Baluchis,** *esp collectively* **Baluchi** **1**

a member of an Indo-Iranian people of Baluchistan, a mountainous region in SW Asia **2** the Iranian language of the Baluchi people [Per *Balūchī*]

**baluster** /'balostə/ *n* **1** an upright rounded, square, or vase-shaped pillar supporting a railing (e g of a staircase or balcony) **2** a vase-shaped vertical support (e g the leg of a table or the stem of a glass) [Fr *balustre*, fr It *balaustro*, fr *balaustra* wild pomegranate flower, fr L *balaustium*, fr Gk *balaustion;* fr its shape]

**balustrade** /ˌbalə'strayd, 'balə,strayd/ *n* a row of balusters topped by a rail; *also* a usu low parapet or barrier [Fr, fr It *balaustrata*, fr *balaustro*]

**Bambara** /bam'bahrə/ *n, pl* **Bambaras**, *esp collectively* **Bambara** a member, or the MANDE language, of a Negroid people of the upper Niger

**bambino** /bam'beenoh/ *n, pl* **bambinos, bambini** /-ni/ **1** a representation of the infant Christ in religious art **2** *informal* a young child, esp in Italy [It, dim. of *bambo* child]

**bamboo** /bam'booh/ *n, pl* **bamboos** any of various chiefly tropical giant treelike grasses (e g of the genera *Bambusa, Arundinaria,* and *Dendrocalamus*), the hollow stems of which are used for building, furniture, or utensils and the young shoots for food [Malay *bambu*] – **bamboo** *adj*

**bamboo curtain** *n, often cap B&C* a political, military, and ideological barrier to communications between China and territories not under her influence

**bamboozle** /bam'boohzl/ *vt, informal* **1** to trick or mislead **2** to confuse, muddle [origin unknown] – **bamboozlement** *n*

**¹ban** /ban/ *vt* **-nn-** to prohibit, esp by legal means or social pressure [ME *bannen* to summon, curse, fr OE *bannan* to summon; akin to OHG *bannan* to command, L *fari* to speak, Gk *phanai* to say, *phōnē* sound, voice]

**²ban** *n* **1** the summoning of the king's vassals for military service in feudal times **2** a prohibition; *esp* an official prohibition that can be legally enforced ⟨*a 30-day* ~ *was introduced on all public marches*⟩ **3** *archaic* an ecclesiastical denunciation; excommunication [ME, partly fr *bannen* & partly fr OF *ban*, of Gmc origin; akin to OHG *bannan* to command]

**³ban** *n, pl* **bani** – see *leu* at MONEY table [Romanian]

**banal** /bə'nahl/ *adj* **1** lacking originality, freshness, or novelty; trite, hackneyed **2** common, ordinary ⟨~ *symptoms*⟩ – used in medicine [Fr, fr MF, of compulsory feudal service, possessed in common, commonplace, fr *ban*] – **banally** *adv*, **banality** *n*

**banana** /bə'nahnə/ *n* an elongated usu slightly curved tropical fruit with edible pulpy flesh enclosed in a soft rind that is yellow when ripe; *also* the widely cultivated plant (genus *Musa* of the family Musaceae, the banana family) that bears bananas in compact hanging bunches [Sp or Pg; Sp, fr Pg, of African origin; akin to Wolof *banäna* banana]

**banana oil** *n* AMYL ACETATE (chemical compound used in solvents and in food manufacturing)

**banana republic** *n, chiefly derog* a small country (e g in Central America) that is politically unstable and usu economically dependent on foreign aid [fr the dependence of some small tropical countries on their fruit-exporting trade]

**bananas** /bə'nahnəz/ *adj, informal* mad, crazy ⟨*call him that and he goes* ~⟩ [prob fr *banana oil* (nonsense, insincere or mad talk)]

**banausic** /bə'nawsik, -zik/ *adj* **1** dull, mechanical ⟨*a* ~ *performance*⟩ **2** materialistic ⟨*a* ~ *civilization*⟩ [Gk *banausikos* of an artisan, nonintellectual, vulgar, fr *banausos* artisan]

**Banbury cake** /'banb(ə)ri/ *n, Br* a cake consisting of a pastry casing filled with currants, raisins, etc [*Banbury*, town in Oxfordshire, England]

**¹band** /band/ *n* **1** a strip, ribbon, etc used to join or hold two or more parts together: e g **1a** BELT **2** (moving belt in a machine) **b** a cord across the back of a book to which the page sections are sewn **2** a thin flat encircling strip used esp to hold loose objects together or in place: e g **2a** RUBBER BAND **b** a bandeau **3** a strip, layer, or usu broad stripe differing in colour, texture, composition, etc from the areas on either side **4** a section or category within a larger set of people, things, values, etc ⟨*the under-16 age* ~⟩: e g **4a** a narrow range of wavelengths or frequencies of light waves, radio waves, sound waves, etc ⟨*the medium-wave* ~⟩ **b** *Br* a group of pupils of broadly similar ability – compare STREAM **5** **5a** a narrow strip or circle of cloth, paper, etc put on or round something (e g a hat or cigar), esp for decoration **b** a strip of material attached to a garment for decoration, strengthening, or to hold gathered material together (e g at the cuffs or neck) **c** *pl* a pair of cloth

strips or ribbons worn hanging down from the front of the neck as part of legal, academic, or, esp formerly, clerical dress **6** *archaic* something that restrains, constricts, or binds either physically or morally, legally, etc; a tie, bond [ME *bande* strip, fr MF, fr (assumed) VL *binda*, of Gmc origin; akin to OHG *binta* fillet; akin to OE *bend* fetter, *bindan* to bind; (6) ME *band, bond,* fr ON *band;* akin to OE *bindan*]

**²band** *vt* **1** to fix a band to or hold together with a band **2** to gather together for a purpose ⟨*he* ~ed *his resources*⟩ **3** *Br* to divide into bands or categories ~ *vi* **1** to unite, esp for a common purpose ⟨*they all* ~ed *together to fight the enemy*⟩ **2** *Br* to divide esp pupils into bands or categories □ *(vt 2; vi 1)* often + *together*

**³band** *n taking sing or pl vb* **1** a group of animals, things, or esp people having a common purpose or acting together **2** any of various groups of musicians, usu smaller than an orchestra, who typically play marches, dances, jazz, rock, or other nonclassical music: e g **2a** BRASS BAND **b** STEEL BAND **c** a pop or rock group **3** *Can* a group of Canadian Indians; *esp* such a group living on a reservation and recognized as a unit for administrative purposes [MF *bande* troop]

**¹bandage** /'bandij/ *n* **1** a strip of soft fabric used to dress wounds, hold a broken limb in position, etc **2** a flexible strip used to cover, strengthen, or compress something [MF, fr *bande* strip]

**²bandage** *vt* to bind, dress, or cover with a bandage – **bandager** *n*

**'Band-,Aid** *trademark* – used for a small adhesive plaster with a gauze pad

**bandanna, bandana** /ban'danə/ *n* a large colourful patterned handkerchief [Hindi *bādhnū* tie-dyeing, tie-dyed cloth, fr *bādhnā* to tie, fr Skt *badhnāti* he ties; akin to OE *bindan*]

**bandbox** /-,boks/ *n* a usu cylindrical box of cardboard or thin wood for holding light articles of clothing, esp hats

**bandeau** /'bandoh; *NAm* -'-/ *n, pl* **bandeaux** /'bandoh(z); *NAm* ban'doh(z)/ a band or ribbon of material worn round the head to keep the hair in place [Fr, dim. of *bande* strip]

**banded** /'bandid/ *adj* having or marked with bands

**banded anteater** *n* NUMBAT (small Australian marsupial mammal)

**banderilla** /ˌbandə'ree(l)yə/ *n* a decorated barbed dart that is thrust into the neck or shoulders of the bull in a bullfight [Sp, dim. of *bandera* banner]

**banderillero** /ˌbandəree(l)'yeəroh/ *n, pl* **banderilleros** a bullfighter's assistant who thrusts banderillas into the bull [Sp, fr *banderilla*]

**banderole, banderol** /ˌbandə'rohl/ *n* a long narrow usu forked flag or streamer; *esp* one attached to a knight's lance or flown from the top of a mast – called also BANNEROL [Fr *banderole,* fr It *banderuola,* dim. of *bandiera* banner, of Gmc origin; akin to Goth *bandwo* sign – more at BANNER]

**bandicoot** /'bandikooht/ *n* **1** bandicoot, bandicoot rat any of several very large burrowing rats (*Nesokia* and related genera) of India and Ceylon that cause damage to rice fields and gardens **2** any of various small insect- and plant-eating marsupial mammals (family Peramelidae) of Australia, Tasmania, and New Guinea, that have a long tail and a pointed snout, and that dig pits in search of food [Telugu *pandikokku*]

**bandit** /'bandit/ *n, pl* **bandits** *also* **banditti** /ban'deeti/ **1** an outlaw; *esp* a member of a band of armed robbers or marauders **2** a political terrorist; a guerrilla [It *bandito* (pl *banditi*), fr pp of *bandire* to banish, of Gmc origin; akin to OHG *bannan* to command – more at BAN] – **banditry** *n*

**bandleader** /'band,leedə/ *n* a conductor of a small orchestra, dance band, etc that plays light popular music

**bandmaster** /'band,mahstə/ *n* a conductor of a brass band, military band, etc

**bandolier, bandoleer** /ˌbandə'liə/ *n* a belt worn over the shoulder and across the chest with pockets or loops, esp for holding cartridges [MF *bandouliere*, deriv of OSp *bando* band, of Gmc origin; akin to Goth *bandwo*]

**bandora** /ban'dawrə/ *n* a bandore

**bandore** /ban'daw, '--/ *n* a Renaissance stringed instrument resembling a lute or guitar with scalloped sides [Sp *bandurria* or Pg *bandurra,* fr LL *pandura* three-stringed lute, fr Gk *pandoura*]

**band saw** *n* a motor-driven saw whose blade consists of a steel loop running over pulleys

**bandsman** /'bandzmən/ *n* a member of a brass band, military band, etc

**band spectrum** *n* a SPECTRUM that is produced by molecules and consists of a series of bands each composed of a group of regularly spaced lines – compare CONTINUOUS SPECTRUM, LINE SPECTRUM

**bandstand** /'band,stand/ *n* a usu roofed stand or raised platform on which a band or orchestra performs

**bandwagon** /'band,wagən/ *n* 1 a party, movement, cause, or enterprise that attracts supporters or followers by its rapid success or gain in popularity 2 *NAm* a usu ornate high wagon on which a band of musicians play, esp in a parade – **climb/jump on the bandwagon** to attach oneself to a successful or popular cause, enterprise, etc, esp in the hope of personal gain

**bandwidth** /'band,width/ *n* 1 the range of frequencies within which an electronic device (eg an amplifier) operates at or near its maximum efficiency 2 the range of wavelengths or frequencies that make up the signal of a particular radio station, television channel, etc

¹**bandy** /'bandi/ *vt* 1 to bat, toss, or pass to and fro, from side to side, or from one to another, esp in a casual or careless manner 2 to exchange (blows, insults, etc); *esp* to exchange (words) argumentatively 3 to use or discuss in a glib or offhand manner – often + *about* ⟨*easy to ~ statistics about but it's harder to interpret them*⟩ [prob fr MF *bander* to be tight, to bandy, fr *bande* strip – more at BAND]

²**bandy** *n* a game similar to ice hockey, played esp in the Baltic countries [perh fr MF *bandé*, pp of *bander*]

³**bandy** *adj* 1 *of legs* curved outwards at the knees 2 **bandy-legged**, **bandy** *of a person* having bandy legs; bowlegged [prob fr *bandy* (hockey stick)]

**bane** /bayn/ *n* 1 (a) poison – usu in combination ⟨*ratsbane*⟩ 2 something that kills or destroys; *also, archaic or poetic* destruction, death ⟨*money, thou ~ of bliss, and source of woe* – George Herbert⟩ 3 a cause of harm, ruin, or trouble ⟨*you're the ~ of my life*⟩ [ME, fr OE *bana;* akin to OHG *bano* death, Avestan *banta* ill]

**baneberry** /'baynb(ə)ri/ *n* 1 an unpleasant-smelling plant (*Actaea spicata*) of the buttercup family, that has small white flowers and black shiny poisonous berries – called also HERB CHRISTOPHER 2 the berry of the baneberry plant

**baneful** /'baynf(ə)l/ *adj* 1 seriously harmful; destructive ⟨*a ~ influence*⟩ 2 *archaic* poisonous △ baleful – **banefully** *adv*

¹**bang** /bang/ *vt* 1 to strike sharply; bump ⟨*fell and ~ed his knee*⟩ 2a to knock, beat, or hit sharply, esp with a loud noise ⟨*~ the drum*⟩ b to thrust, push, or put with force or a loud noise into a usu specified place ⟨*~ed the book down on the table*⟩; *also* to close (eg a door) with a bang ~ *vi* 1 to strike with a sharp noise or thump ⟨*the falling chair ~ed against the wall*⟩ 2a to produce a sharp often explosive noise or a series of such noises b to close with a bang 3 *informal* to produce very quickly ⟨*~ out an essay*⟩ 4 *vulg* to have sexual intercourse with [prob of Scand origin; akin to Icel *banga* to hammer]

**bang away** *vi* to work with persistent determined effort

**bang up** *vt* 1 to cause extensive damage to 2 *chiefly Br* to raise, increase ⟨*bang an executive's salary* up⟩

²**bang** *n* 1 a resounding blow or knock; a thump 2 a sudden loud noise – often used interjectionally or in imitation 3a a striking effect or impact b a quick burst of energy or activity ⟨*start off with a ~*⟩ c *NAm informal* a thrill ⟨*do they really get a ~ out of this?*⟩ 4 *vulg* an act of sexual intercourse

³**bang** *adv* 1 directly, abruptly ⟨*ran ~ up against more trouble*⟩ 2 exactly, precisely ⟨*arrived ~ on six o'clock*⟩ ⟨*~ on target*⟩

⁴**bang** *adj, Austr & NZ* – used as an intensive ⟨*the whole ~ lot of them* – Frank Sargeson⟩

⁵**bang** *n*, **bangs** *n pl* a short fringe cut squarely across the forehead [prob short for *bangtail*]

⁶**bang** *vt* to cut (hair) in a bang

⁷**bang** *n* BHANG (form of cannabis)

**banger** /'bang-ə/ *n, Br* 1 a firework that explodes with a loud bang 2 *informal* a sausage 3 *informal* an old dilapidated car

**Bangladeshi** /,bang-glə'deshi/ *adj* (characteristic) of Bangladesh [*Bangladesh* (formerly E Pakistan), country in S Asia]

**bangle** /'bang-gl/ *n* a rigid usu ornamental bracelet or anklet slipped or clasped on [Hindi *ba·nglī*]

,**bang-'on** *adj, Br informal* just what is needed; first-rate, excellent [³BANG]

**Bang's disease** /bangz/ *n* BRUCELLOSIS (infectious disease) causing abortion in cattle [Bernhard L F *Bang* †1932 Dan veterinarian]

**bangtail** /'bang,tayl/ *n* 1 a horse's tail cut across in a straight line below the bone 2 a horse with a bangtail [prob fr ¹*bang*]

,**bang-'up** *adj, NAm informal* bang-on

**bani** /'bahni/ *pl of* BAN

**banian** /'banyən/ *n* BANYAN (E Indian tree)

**banish** /'banish/ *vt* 1 to require by authority to leave a place, esp a country – compare ²EXILE, DEPORT, ¹TRANSPORT, ¹EXPATRIATE, EXTRADITE 2 to compel to depart; drive away ⟨*~ed such thoughts from his head*⟩ [ME *banishen*, fr MF *baniss-*, stem of *banir*, of Gmc origin; akin to OHG *bannan* to command – more at BAN] – **banisher** *n*, **banishment** *n*

**banister** *also* **bannister** /'banistə/ *n* 1 any of the upright supporting posts of a handrail alongside a staircase 2 **banister**, **banisters** *pl* a handrail alongside a staircase; *esp* such a rail together with its upright supports [alter. of *baluster*]

**banjax** /'banjaks/ *vt, chiefly Irish informal* to damage, harm [origin unknown]

**banjo** /'banjoh, -'-/ *n, pl* **banjos** *also* **banjoes** a musical instrument with a circular drumlike body, a long neck like that of a guitar, and four or more strings that are strummed or plucked, usu with the fingers [prob of African origin; akin to Kimbundu *mbanza*, a similar instrument] – **banjoist** *n*

¹**bank** /bangk/ *n* 1a a mound, pile, or ridge (eg of earth or snow) b a thick mass of cloud or fog c an underwater mound of sand, mud, etc which rises esp from the seabed and over which the water is fairly shallow 2a the rising ground bordering a lake or river or forming the edge of a hollow b the ground round the top of a mine shaft 3a a steep slope (eg of a hill) b(1) a slope given to a curve of a road, track, etc so that the outside edge is higher than the centre or inner edge and the likelihood of skidding or going off course is reduced b(2) the sideways tilt of a vehicle (eg an aeroplane) when turning or following a curved path 4 *NAm* a protective or cushioning rim or piece; *esp* the cushion round the edge of a billiard table [ME, prob of Scand origin; akin to ON *bakki* bank; akin to OE *benc* bench – more at BENCH]

²**bank** *vt* 1a to surround or border with a bank b to cover (a fire) with enough fresh fuel to ensure slow burning c to build (a curved part of a road, track, etc) with the outside edge higher than the inner d to cause (eg an aeroplane) to tilt sideways when moving round a curve 2 to heap or pile in a bank or mound 3 to form or group in a row, series, or tier 4 *NAm* to drive (a ball in billiards) into the cushion round the edge of the table ~ *vi* 1 to rise in or form a bank 2a(1) to tilt an aeroplane, motorbike, etc sideways when moving round a curve a(2) to tilt sideways when moving round a curve b to follow a sloping curve or bank, esp at high speed ⟨*skiers ~ing round the turn*⟩ □ (*vt 1b & 2; vi 1*) often + *up*

³**bank** *n* 1 a bench for the rowers of a galley 2 a group or series of objects arranged near together in a row or tier ⟨*the ~ of keys on a typewriter*⟩ [ME, fr OF *banc* bench, of Gmc origin; akin to OE *benc*]

⁴**bank** *n* 1 a place for or an organization dealing with the custody, loan, exchange, issue, or transfer of money, and the giving of credit 2 a supply of something held in reserve: eg 2a the funds (eg in the form of money, chips, or pieces) held by the banker, dealer, or gaming house for use in a gambling game b a fund of pieces, tokens, etc belonging to a game (eg dominoes) from which the players draw 3 a person who runs a game or gaming house; *specif* ¹BANKER 2 4 a place where something (eg data) is held available; *esp* a depot where blood, corneas of eyes, sperm, etc are collected and stored for medical use [ME, fr MF or OIt; MF *banque*, fr OIt *banca*, lit., bench, of Gmc origin; akin to OE *benc*] – **break the bank** to cause financial ruin

⁵**bank** *vi* 1 to keep or engage in the business of a bank 2 to deposit money or have an account in a bank ⟨*where do you ~?*⟩ 3 to manage the bank in a game ~ *vt* to deposit in a bank
*synonyms* see RELY ON

**bank on** *vt* to depend or rely on; COUNT ON

**bankable** /'bangkəbl/ *adj* acceptable to or at a bank

**bank bill** *n* a BILL OF EXCHANGE (written order to pay money at a certain date) which is issued by one bank to another or for which payment of the money is guaranteed by a bank

**bankbook** /'bangk,book/ *n* a book given to a customer with a DEPOSIT ACCOUNT, in which a bank enters a record of deposits, withdrawals, and interest paid

¹**banker** /'bangkə/ *n* 1 one who or that which engages in the business of banking 2 the player who keeps the bank in various games 3 a match-result forecast or an answer to a competition-puzzle clue which a competitor chooses from a number of alternatives and keeps constant through a series of entries (eg in a football pool or crossword contest) [⁵*bank* + ²*-er*]

**²banker** *n* **1** a man or boat employed in the cod fishery on the Newfoundland banks **2** *Austr* a river that has overflown its banks [¹*bank* + ²*-er*]

**³banker** *n* a sculptor's or stonemason's workbench [³*bank* + ²*-er*]

**banker's card** *n* CHEQUE CARD

**banker's order** *n* a STANDING ORDER from a customer to a bank to make a regular payment on his/her behalf

**bank holiday** *n* **1** *often cap B&H* a public holiday in the British Isles on which banks and most businesses are closed by law **2** *NAm* a period when banks are closed, often by order of the government

**banking** /'bangking/ *n* the business of a bank or a banker

**bank note** *n* a piece of paper issued by a bank (eg the Bank of England) that states that the bank owes the holder the amount shown, and that is used as money; a piece of paper money

**bank rate** *n* MINIMUM LENDING RATE (the minimum rate of interest charged by the Bank of England or another country's central bank) – not now in technical use

**¹bankroll** /'bangk,rohl/ *n, NAm* a supply of money; funds

**²bankroll** *vt, NAm informal* to supply the capital for or pay the cost of (a business or project) – **bankroller** *n*

**¹bankrupt** /'bangkrupt/ *n* **1** a person who becomes financially ruined; *specif* one who has been declared by a court of law to have insufficient funds or assets to pay his/her debts and whose property is administered or divided for the benefit of his/her creditors **2** one who totally lacks a usu specified quality or thing ⟨*a moral* ~⟩ [modif of MF & OIt; MF *banqueroute* bankruptcy, fr OIt *bancarotta*, fr *banca* bank + *rotta* broken, fr L *rupta*, fem of *ruptus*, pp of *rumpere* to break – more at BANK, BEREAVE]

**²bankrupt** *vt* to reduce to bankruptcy

**³bankrupt** *adj* **1** reduced to a state of financial ruin; *specif* legally declared to be in this state ⟨*the company went* ~⟩ **2a** lacking or having lost a necessary or desirable quality; failed, ruined **b** destitute *of*; totally lacking *in* ⟨~ *of all merciful feelings*⟩

**bankruptcy** /'bangk,rupsi/ *n* **1** the quality or state of being financially bankrupt **2** utter failure or destitution

**banksia** /'bangksiə/ *n* any of a genus (*Banksia* of the family Proteaceae) of Australian evergreen trees and shrubs with tough leathery leaves and yellowish flowers [NL, genus name, fr Sir Joseph *Banks* †1820 E naturalist]

**¹banner** /'banə/ *n* **1a** a usu square flag carried on a pole, bearing the heraldic arms of a monarch, feudal lord, or commander, and originally used as a rallying point in battle **b** a flag (eg of a country) **c** a flag displaying a distinctive symbol, motto, etc; *esp* one attached to a pole or suspended between two poles for carrying in a procession (eg by a church or guild) **2 banner headline, banner** a headline in large type running across the full width of a newspaper page **3** a strip of cloth on which a sign, slogan, etc is displayed ⟨*welcome* ~s *stretched across the street*⟩ **4** a name, slogan, or goal associated with a particular group or cause ⟨*minorities uniting under the* ~ *of freedom*⟩ [ME *banere*, fr OF, of Gmc origin; akin to Goth *bandwo* sign; akin to ON *benda* to give a sign]

**²banner** *adj, NAm* distinguished from all others, esp in excellence ⟨*a* ~ *year for business*⟩

**¹banneret** /,banə'ret/ *n, often cap* a knight entitled to lead his men into battle under his own banner and therefore ranking above a KNIGHT BACHELOR [ME *baneret*, fr OF, fr *banere*]

**²banneret** *also* **bannerette** *n* a small banner [ME *banerett*, fr MF *banerete*, dim. of *banere*]

**bannerol** /,banə'rohl/ *n* BANDEROLE (narrow flag) [MF, var of *banderole*]

**bannister** /'banistə/ *n* a banister

**bannock** /'banək/ *n* a flat cake or biscuit of oatmeal or barley meal [ME *bannok*, prob fr ScGael *bannach*]

**banns** /banz/ *n pl* the public announcement of a proposed marriage, usu made in church on three consecutive Sundays [pl of *bann*, fr ME *bane*, *ban* proclamation, ban]

**¹banquet** /'bangkwit/ *n* an elaborate ceremonial meal for many people, often in honour of a person; *broadly* a lavish feast [MF, fr OIt *banchetto*, fr dim. of *banca* bench, bank]

**²banquet** *vt* to provide or honour with a banquet ~ *vi* to take part in a banquet; feast – **banqueter** *n*

**banquette** /bang'ket/ (*Fr* bãkεt) *n* **1** a raised step along the inside of a parapet or trench for soldiers or guns **2** a long upholstered seat, esp along a wall [Fr, fr Prov *banqueta*, dim. of *banc* bench, of Gmc origin; akin to OE *benc* bench]

**banshee** /'banshee *also* -'-/ *n* a female spirit in Gaelic folklore whose appearance or wailing warns of approaching death in a household [ScGael *bean-sìth*, fr or akin to OIr *ben sìde* woman of fairyland]

**bantam** /'bant(ə)m/ *n* **1** any of numerous small or miniature breeds of DOMESTIC FOWL **2** a small, usu argumentative, person [*Bantam*, former residency in Java]

**bantamweight** /'bant(ə)m,wayt/ *n* a boxer who weighs not more than 8 stone 6 pounds (about 53-5 kilograms) if professional, or between 51 and 54 kilograms (between about 8 stone and 8 stone 7 pounds) if amateur

**banteng** /'banteng/ *n* a wild ox (*Bos banteng*) of SE Asia that has slender curved horns, a ridge along its back, and a small hump behind the neck [Malay *banteng, banting*]

**¹banter** /'bantə/ *vb* to speak (to) in a playful, witty, or teasing manner [origin unknown] – **banterer** *n*, **banteringly** *adv*

**²banter** *n* good-natured usu witty and animated talk or joking

**banting** /'banting/ *n, archaic* a method of slimming based on a low carbohydrate and fat diet [William *Banting* †1878 E undertaker & writer on dieting]

**bantling** /'bantling/ *n* a very young child [perh modif of Ger *bänkling* bastard, fr *bank* bench, fr OHG – more at BENCH]

**Bantu** /'bantooh; *also* -'-/ *n, pl (1)* **Bantus**, *esp collectively* **Bantu 1** a member of a family of Negroid peoples occupying central, eastern, and southern Africa **2** a group of African languages spoken generally at and south of the Equator

**bantustan** /,bantooh'stan, -'stahn/ *n, often cap* a partly self-governing area in the Republic of S Africa, reserved for occupation by black citizens [*Bantu* + *-stan* land (as in *Hindustan*)]

**banyan, banian** /'banyan/ *n* an E Indian tree (*Ficus bengalensis*) of the fig family with branches that send out shoots which grow down to the soil and root to form secondary trunks [earlier *banyan* Hindu merchant, fr Hindi *baniyā*; fr a pagoda erected by merchants under a tree of the species in Iran]

**banzai** /ban'zie/ *interj* – used as a Japanese cheer or battle cry [Jap, lit., 10,000 years]

**baobab** /'bayoh,bab, 'bayə-, 'bow,bab/ *n* a broad-trunked tropical tree (*Adansonia digitata* of the family Bombacaceae, the baobab family) of Africa, India, and Australia, that has a hard-rinded fruit with an edible acid pulp and bark used in making paper, cloth, and rope [prob native name in Africa]

**bap** /bap/ *n* a soft thin-crusted bread roll that is usu dusted with flour and is made in various shapes and sizes according to regional custom [origin unknown]

**baptism** /'baptiz(ə)m/ *n* **1a** a religious rite using water as a symbol of purification; *specif* the Christian ceremony (SACRAMENT 1), generally including the giving of a name, in which a person, often a baby, is sprinkled with or immersed in water to symbolize the washing away of sin and to proclaim his/her admission to the Christian church **b** an act of baptizing somebody or of being baptized **2** an act, experience, or ordeal by which one is purified, initiated, or named – **baptismal** *adj*, **baptismally** *adv*

**baptismal name** /bap'tizmal/ *n* CHRISTIAN NAME 1

**baptism of fire** *n* an initial experience that is a severe ordeal; *esp* a soldier's first battle [orig meaning (fr trans of LGk *baptisma pyros*), a spiritual baptism by gift of the Holy Spirit; now usu taken to refer to artillery fire]

**baptist** /'baptist/ *n* **1** one who baptizes **2** *cap* a member of a Protestant denomination practising the baptism, by total immersion in water, only of people old enough to hold firm beliefs – **Baptist** *adj*

**baptistery, baptistry** /'baptistri/ *n* **1** a part of a church, or formerly a separate building, used for baptisms **2** a large tank in a Baptist church, used for baptisms

**bapt-ize, -ise** /bap'tiez, '--/ *vt* **1** to administer baptism to **2a** to purify or cleanse spiritually, esp by a purging experience or ordeal **b** to initiate, launch **3** to give a name to (eg at baptism); christen ~ *vi* to administer baptism [ME *baptizen*, fr OF *baptiser*, fr LL *baptizare*, fr Gk *baptizein* to dip, baptize, fr *baptos* dipped, fr *baptein* to dip; akin to ON *kafa* to dive] – **baptizer** *n*

**¹bar** /bah/ *n* **1a** a straight piece of wood, metal, etc that is longer than it is wide and has any of various uses (eg as a lever, support, barrier, or fastening) **b** a solid piece or block of material that is usu rectangular and longer than it is wide ⟨*a* ~ *of chocolate*⟩ **c** a long narrow rigid piece of wood, metal, etc used as a handle or support; *esp* BARRE (handrail used by ballet dancers) **d** the crossbar joining the upright posts of a goal in soccer, rugby, etc **e** a usu rod-shaped heating element in an electric fire **2** the part of the wall of a horse's hoof that bends inwards towards the centre of the sole **3** something that obstructs or prevents passage, progress, or action: eg **3a** the loss (eg by the expiry of a time limit) of a right to bring legal action or make a legal claim; *also* a plea or objection demonstrating such a loss **b** a nonphysical restriction, obstacle, or impediment **c** a submerged or partly submerged bank of sand, shingle, etc along a shore, in a river, or across the entrance of a bay, harbour, etc **4a(1)** the place in a law court where a prisoner stands; [6]DOCK **a(2)** a particular court or system of courts **a(3)** an authority that judges or evaluates ⟨*the ~ of public opinion*⟩ **b** the area or partition in a court of law that separates the judges and QUEEN'S COUNSEL (senior barristers) from the solicitors, general public, etc **c** *often cap* **c(1)** *taking sing or pl vb* the whole body of barristers or lawyers ⟨*the Spanish ~*⟩ **c(2)** the profession of barrister **d** a rail or line marking off the boundary in either of the Houses of Parliament beyond which nonmembers may not pass **5** a straight stripe, band, or line longer than it is wide: eg **5a** any of two or more horizontal stripes on a heraldic shield **b** *NAm* a metal or embroidered strip worn on a military uniform, esp to indicate rank or service; [2]STRIPE 2 **c** a device (eg a strip of silver) attached to a military medal to indicate an additional award of the medal ⟨*MC and ~*⟩ **6a** a solid unjointed mouthpiece of a bridle **b** the space between a horse's teeth in which the mouthpiece of a bridle fits **7a** a place or counter where a particular kind of food or drink is sold ⟨*a sandwich ~*⟩; *specif* a counter at which alcoholic drinks are served **b** a room or building with a counter for the sale of alcoholic drinks to be drunk on the premises **c** a counter (eg in a department store) where goods of a particular type are sold or a service is provided ⟨*a shoe ~*⟩ **8a** BAR LINE (vertical line separating musical bars) **b** a group of musical notes and rests that add up to a prescribed time value and when written on the stave are bounded by BAR LINES **9** a small loop or crosspiece of oversewn threads used, esp on clothes, as a fastening (eg for a hook) or for strengthening something (eg the end of a buttonhole, zip, or slit) – compare [2]BRIDE [ME *barre*, fr OF] – **called to the bar** formally made a barrister

[2]**bar** *vt* -**rr**- **1a** to fasten with a bar ⟨*~ the gate*⟩ **b** to prevent movement into, out of, through or along (as if) by placing bars across; block, obstruct **2** to mark with bars; stripe **3a** to confine or shut in or out (as if) by bars **b** to keep out; exclude (*~red from the club*) **4a** to make or act as a legal objection to (a claim); *also* to make or act as a legal objection to the claim of (a person) **b** to prevent, forbid ⟨*no holds ~*red⟩ **synonyms** see [1]HINDER

[3]**bar** *prep* except for ⟨*a lovely day ~ the rain*⟩

[4]**bar** *adv* except for those competitors named – used when stating odds in betting ⟨*20 to 1 ~*⟩

[5]**bar** *n* a unit of pressure equal to 100,000 newtons per square metre (about 14.5 pounds per square inch) [Ger, fr Gk *baros*]

**bar-, baro-** *comb form* weight; pressure ⟨*baro*meter⟩ [Gk *baros*; akin to Gk *barys* heavy – more at GRIEVE]

**barathea** /ˌbarəˈthiə, -ˈthee-ə/ *n* a fabric with a rough pebbly texture that is made of silk, wool, a synthetic fibre, or a combination of these, and is used esp for coats and jackets [fr *Barathea*, a trademark]

[1]**barb** /bahb/ *n* **1** a sharp point or spike that extends backwards from the point of an arrow, fishhook, etc and prevents easy extraction; *broadly* a sharp projecting point **2** a biting or pointedly critical remark or comment **3** any of the side branches of the shaft of a feather **4** a plant or animal hair or bristle ending in a hook [ME *barbe* barb, beard, fr MF, fr L *barba* – more at BEARD]

[2]**barb** *vt* to provide (eg an arrow or hook) with a barb

[3]**barb** *n* any of a N African breed of horses noted for speed and endurance that are related to the Arab horse [Fr *barbe*, fr It *barbero*, fr *barbero* of Barbary, fr *Barberia* Barbary, coastal region in N Africa]

[4]**barb** *n, informal* a barbiturate

**barbarian** /bah'beəri-ən/ *adj* **1** (characteristic) of or being a land, culture, or people alien to one's own and believed to be inferior, less civilized, and more savage **2** lacking refinement, sensitivity, learning, or artistic or literary culture; uncivilized [L *barbarus*] – **barbarian** *n*, **barbarianism** *n*

*synonyms* **Barbarian, barbaric,** and **barbarous** all mean "uncultured" or "savage", but **barbarian** is the most neutral. **Barbaric**

may be either condemnatory ⟨**barbaric** *cruelty*⟩ or admiring ⟨**barbaric** *splendour*⟩. **Barbarous** is strongly derogatory ⟨**barbarous** *treatment/ignorance*⟩. **antonyms** civilized, cultured

**barbaric** /bah'barik/ *adj* **1** (characteristic) of barbarians; *esp* uncivilized ⟨*~ habits*⟩ **2a** vicious and cruel; barbarous ⟨*~ punishment*⟩ **b** having a bizarre, primitive, or unsophisticated quality – **barbarically** *adv* **synonyms** see BARBARIAN

**barbarism** /'bahbə,riz(ə)m/ *n* **1** an idea, act, attitude, or expression that offends against contemporary standards of good taste or acceptability; *also* the use or display of these **2** an uncivilized, primitive, or backward condition

**barbarity** /bah'barəti/ *n* **1** (a) barbarism **2** (an act or instance of) barbarous cruelty or inhumanity

**barbar-ize, -ise** /'bahbəriez/ *vb* to make or become barbarous – **barbarization** *n*

**barbarous** /'bahb(ə)rəs/ *adj* **1a** uncivilized, primitive **b** lacking culture or refinement; philistine **2** mercilessly harsh or cruel; brutal **synonyms** see BARBARIAN **antonyms** civilized, clement (for 2) [L *barbarus*, fr Gk *barbaros* foreign, ignorant] – **barbarously** *adv*, **barbarousness** *n*

**Barbary ape** /'bahbəri/ *n* a tailless monkey (*Macaca sylvana*) of N Africa and Gibraltar [*Barbary*, region in N Africa

**barbate** /'bahbayt/ *adj, esp of a plant* having a tuft or tufts of long stiff hairs [L *barbatus* bearded, fr *barba*]

[1]**barbecue** /'bahbi,kyooh/ *n* **1** an often portable fireplace or grill over which meat, poultry, etc is roasted **2** food, esp meat, roasted over an open fire **3** a meal or party, esp outdoors, at which barbecued food is served [AmerSp *barbacoa*, prob fr Taino]

[2]**barbecue** *vt* **1** to roast or grill on a rack over hot coals or on a revolving spit in front of or over a source of heat, esp an open fire **2** to cook in a highly seasoned spicy sauce – **barbecuer** *n*

**barbed** /bahbd/ *adj* **1** having a barb or barbs **2** characterized by pointed and biting criticism ⟨*a ~ comment*⟩ – **barbedness** *n*

**barbed wire** *n* wire consisting of two or more twisted strands armed at intervals with sharp points

[1]**barbel** /'bahbl/ *n* (any of various fishes of the same genus as) a European freshwater fish (*Barbus barbus*) that has four barbels on its upper jaw and is related to the carp and tench [ME, fr MF, fr (assumed) VL *barbellus*, dim. of L *barbus* barbel, fr *barba* beard – more at BEARD]

[2]**barbel** *n* a slender sensitive projection on the lips of certain fishes (eg catfish) used to feel for food on the bottom of the river, lake, etc [obs Fr, fr MF, dim. of *barbe* barb, beard]

**barbell** /'bah,bel/ *n* a bar with adjustable disc-shaped weights attached to each end that is used for exercise and in weightlifting

**barbellate** /'bahbilayt, bah'belayt, -it/ *adj, of (a part of) a plant or animal* having short stiff hooked bristles or hairs [NL *barbella* short stiff hair, dim. of L *barbula*, dim. of *barba*]

[1]**barber** /'bahbə/ *n* a person, esp a man, whose occupation is cutting and styling men's hair, shaving or trimming beards, etc [ME, fr MF *barbeor*, fr *barbe* beard – more at BARB]

[2]**barber** *vt* to cut or trim the hair or beard of

**barberry** /'bahb(ə)ri, -,beri/ *n* any of a genus (*Berberis* of the family Berberidaceae, the barberry family) of shrubs having thorny stems, yellow flowers, and oblong red berries [by folk etymology (influenced by *berry*) fr ME *barbere*, fr MF *barbarin*, fr Ar *barbārīs*]

**barbershop** /'bahbə,shop/ *adj* of, characterized by, or being a style of unaccompanied singing of popular romantic songs, that is performed esp by a male quartet and is marked by harmony in which the notes are close together [fr the old custom of men in barbershops forming quartets for impromptu singing] – **barbershop** *n*

**barber's itch** *n* RINGWORM (fungus infection) of the face and neck

**barber's pole** *n* a pole with red and white spiral stripes, fixed to the front of a barber's shop

**barbette** /bah'bet/ *n* **1** a mound of earth or a protected platform from which guns fire over a parapet **2** the armour protection of a turret on a warship [Fr, dim. of *barbe* headdress]

**barbican** /'bahbikən/ *n* a structure outside a city or castle used for defence; *esp* a tower at a gate or bridge [ME, fr OF *barbacane*, fr ML *barbacana*]

**barbicel** /'bahbisel/ *n* any of the small hooks on a barbule of a feather that interlock with those on adjacent barbules to give a flat surface to the feather [NL *barbicella*, dim. of L *barba*]

**bar billiards** *n*, *Br* a form of billiards in which balls are driven into holes in the table, some of which are guarded by obstacles, and in which an automatic device prevents the use of the balls after a certain time [¹*bar* 1a & ¹*bar* 7b]

**barbital** /'bahbi,tal/ *n*, *NAm* barbitone [*barbit*uric + *-al* (as in *Veronal*)]

**barbitone** /'bahbi,tohn/ *n*, *Br* a barbiturate, $C_8H_{12}N_2O_3$, formerly much used in sleeping pills [*barbit*uric + *-one*]

**barbiturate** /bah'bityoorət/ *n* 1 any of various chemical compounds (SALTS or ESTERS) formed by combination between BARBITURIC ACID and a metal atom, an alcohol, or another chemical group 2 any of several drugs (eg phenobarbitone) derived from BARBITURIC ACID, that have a calming effect and are used esp in sleeping tablets and as sedatives (eg in the treatment of insomnia and epilepsy)

**barbituric acid** /,bahbi'tyooərik/ *n* an acid, $C_4H_4N_2O_3$, used in the manufacture of barbiturate drugs and some plastics [part trans of Ger *barbitursäure*, irreg fr the name *Barbara* + ISV *uric* + Ger *säure* acid]

**barbola** /bah'bohlə/, **barbola work** *n* the decoration of small articles (eg of wood or glass) by the attachment of coloured moulded representations of flowers, fruit, etc [fr *Barbola*, a trademark]

**barbule** /'bah,byoohl/ *n* a minute spike or hooked bristle; *esp* any of the small outgrowths that fringe the side branches (¹BARBS 3) of a feather [L *barbula* little beard]

**barbwire** /,bahb'wie-ə/ *n*, *NAm* BARBED WIRE

**bar car** *n*, *NAm* BUFFET CAR

**barcarole, barcarolle** /,bahkə'rohl/ *n* 1 a Venetian boat song usu with two or four dotted beats to the bar, characterized by the alternation of a strong and weak beat that suggests a rowing rhythm 2 a musical composition imitating a barcarole [Fr *barcarolle*, fr It *barcarola*, fr *barcarolo* gondolier, fr *barca* bark, fr LL]

**bar code** *n* a code printed on the label of a product for sale, esp a food, consisting of parallel lines of varying thickness that indicate price, make, etc and can be read by a computer to automatically register a price on a cash register or for automatic stock control

**¹bard** /bahd/ *n* **1a** a Celtic poet-singer of former times, gifted in composing and reciting verses about heroes and their deeds **b** a composer, singer, or reciter of epic or heroic verse 2 a poet; *specif* one recognized or honoured at an eisteddfod 3 *cap* Shakespeare – + *the* [ME, fr ScGael & MIr; akin to W *bardd* poet] – **bardic** *adj*

**²bard, barde** *n* a strip of pork fat, bacon, etc for covering lean meat before roasting to prevent it drying out – compare LARDOON [MF *barde* armour or ornamental covering for a horse, fr OSp *barda*, fr Ar *barda'ah*]

**³bard, barde** *vt* to cover (meat) with bards

**bardolatry** /bah'dolətri/ *n* idolatry of Shakespeare [*Bard (of Avon)*, epithet of Shakespeare + id*olatry*] – **bardolater** *n*

**¹bare** /beə/ *adj* **1** lacking a natural, usual, or appropriate covering (*a ~ tree*) (*~ walls*) **b** lacking clothing; uncovered (*~ legs*) 2 open to view; unconcealed – usu in *lay bare* **3a** lacking the usual or appropriate furnishings or supplies; empty (*the cupboard was ~*) **b** lacking; destitute *of* (*~ of all social graces*) **4a** having nothing left over or added; scant, meagre (*the ~ necessities*) **b** without anything added; unadorned, simple (*the ~ facts*) **c** very slight (*the ~st chance of success*) – see also **with one's bare** HANDS, **under bare** POLES [ME, fr OE *bær*; akin to OHG *bar* naked, Lith *basas* barefoot] – **bareness** *n*

**synonyms** Bare, naked, nude, bald, and barren all denote the absence of an expected covering. Bare, naked, and nude are comparable as they refer to the human body: bare refers to parts of the body (*bare feet*), while naked refers to the whole body, and has connotations which are not present in bare, of primitive naturalness, poverty, unprotectedness, shamelessness, or desirability. It may also be simply factual (*a naked body found by police*). Figuratively, bare stresses omission of ornament and nonessentials, while naked implies that nothing is being concealed. Nude may be a euphemism for naked, but is generally restricted to artistic contexts, and more common as a noun. Bald and barren, like bare, stress the lack of natural covering. In people and animals, bald refers to the absence of hair on the head, or of fur or feathers. It can be applied by extension to textiles or vegetation (*a bald patch on the elbow of his jacket*). Used metaphorically, it contrasts with naked to suggest an uncompromising truthfulness which repels rather than pleases. Barren suggests infertility and sterility (*a barren landscape, devoid of trees and interest*). **antonym** covered

**²bare** *vt* to make or lay bare; uncover, reveal

**³bare** *archaic past of* BEAR

**bareback** /'beə,bak/, **barebacked** *adv or adj* on the bare back of a horse; without a saddle

**bare bones** *n pl* the barest essentials or facts (*got down to the ~ of the subject*)

**barefaced** /,beə'fayst/ *adj* blatant, shameless (*a ~ lie*) – **barefacedly** *adv*, **barefacedness** *n*

**barefoot** /'beə,foot/, **barefooted** /,beə'footid/ *adv or adj* with the feet bare; without shoes or other covering for the feet

**barefoot doctor** *n* a villager, esp in Asia, who has been given some medical training and who is the first person consulted by sick people in his/her community

**barège** /ba'rezh/ (*Fr* barɛʒ)/ *n* a lightweight silky loosely woven fabric usu made of wool with silk or cotton and used for dresses, blouses, etc [Fr, fr *Barèges*, town in SW France]

**bare-'handed** *adv or adj* 1 without gloves 2 without tools or weapons (*fight an animal ~*)

**bareheaded** /,beə'hedid/ *adv or adj* without a hat or other covering for the head

**bare knuckle** *adj or adv* without wearing boxing gloves (*a ~ fight*)

**barely** /'beəli/ *adv* 1 scarcely, hardly (*~ enough money to cover expenses*) 2 in a meagre manner; scantily (*a ~ furnished room*) *usage* see HARDLY

**barfly** /'bah,flie/ *n*, *informal* one who frequents bars

**¹bargain** /'bahgin, -gən/ *n* 1 an agreement between parties setting out what each gives or receives in a transaction between them or what course of action or policy each pursues in respect to the other **2a** something acquired (as if) by bargaining **b** something bought or offered for sale that is good value for money; an advantageous purchase 3 a transaction, situation, or event regarded in the light of its good or bad results (*make the best of a bad ~*) – **into the bargain** also; IN ADDITION

**²bargain** *vi* 1 to negotiate the terms of a purchase, agreement, or contract; haggle 2 to come to terms; agree ~ *vt* to sell, exchange, or agree (as if) by bargaining; barter [ME *bargainen*, fr MF *bargaignier*, of Gmc origin; akin to OE *borgian* to borrow] – **bargainer** *n*

**bargain for** *vt* to be prepared for; expect, anticipate (*more trouble than we had* bargained *for*)

**bargain basement** *n* a section of a department store (eg the basement) where goods are sold at reduced prices

**¹barge** /bahj/ *n* any of various boats: eg **a** a large flat-bottomed boat used chiefly for the transport of goods on canals and rivers or sometimes between ships and the shore that is usu powered by an engine but was formerly towed by a horse **b** a flat-bottomed freight-carrying sailing vessel that travels along or near the coast **c** a large naval motorboat, usu carried on board a battleship, for use by an admiral **d** an ornate carved boat propelled by oars and used on ceremonial occasions (*the ~ she sat in, like a burnished throne, burned on the water* – Shak) [ME, fr OF, fr LL *barca* (cf ⁵BARK)]

**²barge** *vi* 1 to move in a headlong or clumsy fashion 2 to interrupt rudely or unceremoniously – + *in* or *into* (*~d in on them while they were in conference*) ~ *vt* to make (one's way) by pushing and shoving (*~s his way through the crowd*) [fr the slow heavy motion of a barge]

**bargeboard** /'bahj,bawd/ *n* an often ornamented board attached to the sloping edge of a gabled roof to protect and conceal projecting rafters [origin unknown]

**bargee** /bah'jee/ *n*, *Br* one who works on or is in charge of a barge

**baric** /'barik/ *adj* of or containing barium

**barilla** /bə'rilə/ *n* 1 either of two European saltworts (*Salsola kali* and *Salsola soda*) or a related Algerian plant (*Halogeton soda*) formerly burned to obtain an ash rich in SODIUM CARBONATE 2 an impure form of SODIUM CARBONATE made from barilla ashes and formerly used in making soap and glass [Sp *barrilla*]

**barite** /'beəriet/ *n* BARYTES (commonest barium mineral) [Gk *barytēs* weight, fr *barys*]

**¹baritone** /'baritohn/ *n* 1 (a person with) a singing voice of medium range between bass and tenor, that is the second lowest adult male singing voice 2 a member of a family of instruments (eg saxophones) having a range next below that of the TENOR; *esp* a SAXHORN (brass instrument) similar in range and tone to the euphonium [Fr *baryton* or It *baritono*, fr Gk *barytonos* deep sounding, fr *barys* heavy + *tonos* tone – more at GRIEVE] – **baritonal** *adj*

²**baritone** *adj* relating to or having the range or part of a baritone

**barium** /'beəri·əm/ *n* a silver-white soft poisonous metal that is a chemical element having a VALENCY of two and belonging to the group containing calcium, strontium, and radium (ALKALINE-EARTH group) [NL, fr *bar-*]

**barium meal** *n* a solution of BARIUM SULPHATE that is swallowed by a patient before X-ray photographs are taken, to make the stomach and intestines visible

**barium sulphate** *n* a white compound, $BaSO_4$, that occurs naturally as the mineral barytes and is used in X-ray photography to make the internal organs visible and as a pigment in paint

¹**bark** /bahk/ *vi* 1 to make (a sound similar to) the short loud cry characteristic of a dog or some other animals (e g a seal) 2 to speak in a curt, loud, and usu angry tone 3 *informal* to cough ~ *vt* 1 to utter in a curt, loud, and usu angry tone 2 to advertise by calling out loudly and persistently ⟨*newsboys* ~ed *their wares*⟩ – see also **bark up the wrong** TREE [ME *berken,* fr OE *beorcan;* akin to ON *berkja* to bark, Lith *burgéti* to growl]

²**bark** *n* 1 (a sound similar to) the sound made by a barking dog 2 a short sharp peremptory utterance 3 *informal* a cough – **barkless** *adj*

³**bark** *n* 1 the tough outer corky covering of a tree trunk, branches, or a woody root 2 the bark of any of several trees used in dyeing or tanning [ME, fr ON *bark-, börkr;* akin to MD & MLG *borke* bark] – **barkless** *adj,* **barky** *adj*

⁴**bark** *vt* 1 to tan or treat with extracts obtained from some barks 2 to strip the bark from 3 to rub off or abrade the skin of ⟨~ed *his shins*⟩

⁵**bark** *n* 1 *chiefly NAm* BARQUE (a sailing ship) 2 *poetic* a boat [ME, fr MF *barque,* fr OProv *barca,* fr LL (cf BARGE)]

**bark beetle** *n* any of several beetles (family Scolytidae) that bore passages under the bark of trees, often causing extensive damage

**barkeeper** /'bah,keepə/, **barkeep** /'bah,keep/ *n, NAm* a bartender

**barker** /'bahkə/ *n* a person or animal that barks; *esp* a person who stands outside a circus, fair, etc and shouts to encourage people to go in

**barley** /'bahli/ *n* 1 a widely cultivated cereal grass (genus *Hordeum,* esp *Hordeum vulgare* or *Hordeum distichon*) having dense spikes of flowers interspersed with long stiff bristles (AWNS) 2 the seed of barley used in foods (e g breakfast cereals and soups), stock feeds, and to make malt [ME *barly,* fr OE *bærlic* of barley; akin to OE *bere* barley, L *far* spelt]

**barleycorn** /'bahli,kawn/ *n* 1 a grain of barley 2 an old unit of length equal to $1/3$ inch (about 0.85 centimetres)

**barley sugar** *n* a brittle semitransparent amber-coloured sweet made of boiled sugar [fr its having been made formerly by boiling sugar in a decoction of barley]

**barley water** *n* a drink made by boiling barley in water

**barley wine** *n* a type of strong ale

**bar line, bar** *n* a vertical line across a musical stave separating one bar of music from the next

**barm** /bahm/ *n* yeast; *esp* the froth of yeast formed on top of fermenting alcoholic drinks made from malt [ME *berme,* fr OE *beorma;* akin to L *fermentum* yeast, *fervēre* to boil – more at BURN]

**barmaid** /'bahmayd/, *masc* **barman** /'bahmən/ *n* a woman or girl who serves drinks in a bar – **barmaid** *vi*

**Barmecidal** /,bahmi'siedl/ *adj* providing only the illusion of plenty or abundance ⟨a ~ *feast*⟩ [*Barmecide,* a wealthy Persian, who, in a tale of *The Arabian Nights,* invited a beggar to a feast of imaginary food]

**Barmecide** /'bahmisied/ *adj* Barmecidal

**bar mitzvah** /,bah 'mitsvə/ *n, fem* **bas mitzvah** /bahs/ *also* **bat mitzvah** /baht/ *often cap B&M* 1 a Jewish boy who reaches his 13th birthday and thus, in Jewish law, assumes adult religious obligations and responsibilities 2 the initiatory ceremony recognizing a boy as a bar mitzvah [Heb *bar miṣwāh,* lit., son of the (divine) law]

**barmy** /'bahmi/ *adj* 1 frothy with yeast 2 *informal* slightly mad; foolish – **barminess** *n*

**barn** /bahn/ *n* 1a a usu large farm building used chiefly for storing feed and farm products (e g cereal crops) and sometimes for housing animals b an unusually large, usu bare, building ⟨*a great* ~ *of a house*⟩ 2 a unit of area that equals $10^{-28}$ square metres, used esp in nuclear physics for measuring the cross

sections of the nuclei of atoms 3 *NAm* a large building in which vehicles (e g lorries or railway carriages) are housed [ME *bern,* fr OE *bereærn,* fr *bere* barley + *ærn* place; (2) fr its having been considered "as big as a barn" for the purposes of nuclear bombardment]

**barnacle** /'bahnəkl/ *n* any of numerous marine INVERTEBRATE animals (subclass Cirripedia of the class Crustacea) that as adults have a thick hard shell and live fixed to rocks or solid floating objects [fr the former belief that the barnacle (goose) was generated from this animal] – **barnacled** *adj*

**barnacle goose** *n* a European goose (*Branta leucopsis*) with grey wings, a black neck, and a white face, that breeds in the Arctic and is smaller than the related CANADA GOOSE [ME *barnakille,* alter. of *bernake,* fr ML *bernaca*]

**barn dance** *n* 1 a country-dance in which the dancers form and move round the floor in a large circle, often changing partners at regular intervals 2 a social gathering, originally held in a barn, at which country-dances (e g SQUARE DANCES and ROUND DANCES) are performed to the accompaniment of traditional music and called instructions to the dancers

**barn door** *n* a movable flap set in front of a stage light to control the shape of the beam

**barney** /'bahni/ *vi or n, Br informal* (to) quarrel, row [perh fr the name *Barney*]

**barn owl** *n* an owl (*Tyto alba*) found in most parts of the world, that has mottled buff, brown, and grey upper plumage and a chiefly white underside, nests in barns and other buildings, and eats mice, shrews, and similar small animals

**barnstorm** /'bahn,stawm/ *vb, chiefly NAm* *vi* 1 to tour rural districts staging usu one-night theatrical performances 2 to travel from place to place making brief stops (e g in the course of a political campaign) 3 to take people for brief trips in an aeroplane or stage informal or unscheduled exhibitions of flying stunts, esp at local country shows ~ *vt* to travel across while barnstorming [*barn* + ²*storm;* fr touring actors performing in barns] – **barnstormer** *n*

**barnyard** /'bahn,yahd/ *n* a farmyard

**baro-** – see BAR-

**barogram** /'barəgram/ *n* the record made by a barograph [ISV]

**barograph** /'barə,grahf, -,graf/ *n* a barometer that gives a permanent record of its reading (e g by tracing a line on paper) [ISV] – **barographic** *adj*

**barometer** /bə'romitə/ *n* 1 an instrument that measures the pressure of the atmosphere and is used for predicting changes in the weather or for measuring height above sea level 2 something that registers fluctuations (e g in public opinion) – **barometry** *n,* **barometric, barometrical** *adj,* **barometrically** *adv*

**barometric pressure** /,barə'metrik/ *n* the pressure of the atmosphere as shown by a barometer

**baron** /'barən/ *n* 1 a member of a class of tenants who, in former times, held his land and title directly from a superior (e g the king) by virtue of military or other honourable service 2 a nobleman of any of various ranks; *esp* a member of the lowest grade of the peerage in Britain 3 a man of great power, influence, or wealth in a specified field of activity or business; a magnate ⟨*a cattle* ~⟩ 4 **baron of beef, baron** a joint of beef consisting of two sirloins joined by the backbone [ME, fr OF, of Gmc origin; akin to OHG *baro* freeman; (4) prob suggested by *sirloin,* commonly taken to be "Sir Loin"]

**baronage** /'barənij/ *n* the whole body of barons or peers; the nobility

**baroness** /,barə'nes, 'barənis/ *n* 1 the wife or widow of a baron 2 a woman having in her own right the rank of a baron

**baronet** /,barə'net, 'barənit/ *n* the holder of a hereditary title ranking below a baron and above a knight

**baronetage** /'barənətij/ *n* 1 baronetcy 2 the whole body of baronets

**baronetcy** /'barənətsi/ *n* the rank of a baronet

**barong** /ba'rong/ *n* a thick-backed thin-edged knife or sword used by the Moro peoples of the Philippines [native name in the Philippines]

**baronial** /bə'rohni·əl/ *adj* 1 of or befitting a baron or barons 2 stately, spacious ⟨*a* ~ *hall*⟩

**barony** /'barəni/ *n* 1 the rank of a baron 2 the land held by a baron or over which his rights extend

**baroque** /bə'rok/ *adj* (characteristic) of a style of artistic expression prevalent esp in the 17th century that is marked by extravagant forms and elaborate and sometimes grotesque ornamentation – compare ROCOCO [Fr, lit., irregular, fr Pg *barroco* or Sp *barrueco* irregular pearl] – **baroquely** *adv*

**baroreceptor** /'barohri,septə/ *n* a SENSE ORGAN (specialized part of the body that receives stimuli), esp in the wall of a large artery, that is sensitive to changes in pressure (e g of the blood) [*bar-* + *receptor*]

**barouche** /bə'roohsh/ *n* a 4-wheeled horse-drawn carriage with a high driver's seat at the front and a folding top over the rear seats [Ger *barutsche*, fr It *biroccio*, deriv of LL *birotus* two-wheeled, fr L *bi-* + *rota* wheel – more at ROLL]

**barque**, *chiefly NAm* **bark** /bahk/ *n* a sailing ship with usu three or sometimes more masts, of which all but the rearmost have sails set across the mast and with the rearmost having sails set behind the mast pointing in the direction of the stern [ME *bark* – more at ⁵BARK]

**barquentine** /'bahkən,teen/ *n* a sailing ship with three or more masts, the front mast having sails set across the mast and the other masts having sails set behind the mast pointing in the direction of the stern [*barque* + *-entine*, alter. of *-antine* (as in *brigantine*)]

¹**barrack** /'barək/ *vt* to lodge in barracks

²**barrack** *vb* 1 *chiefly Br* to jeer or scoff (at) 2 *chiefly Austr & NZ* to support (e g a sports team) by cheering or shouting encouragement [prob fr *borak* nonsense, banter (in a native language of Australia)] – **barracker** *n*

**barrack-room lawyer** *n* an opinionated person who persistently and pettily argues over details without having the knowledge or authority to do so

**barracks** /'barəks/ *n taking sing or pl vb*, **barrack** *n, pl* **barracks** 1 (the area or set of buildings that includes) the living accommodation for soldiers at their home base 2 a large extremely plain or bleak building (e g a house) [Fr *baraque* hut, fr Catal *barraca*]

**barrack square** *n* an area for drill practice within an army barracks

**barracoon** /,barə'koohn/ *n* an enclosure or barracks formerly used for the temporary confinement of slaves or convicts [Sp *barracón*, aug of *barraca* hut, fr Catal]

**barracouta** /,barə'koohtə/ *n* a large food fish (*Thyrsites atun*) of Pacific seas [modif of AmerSp *barracuda*]

**barracuda** /,barə'kyoohdə/ *n, pl* **barracuda**, *esp for different types* **barracudas** any of several fishes (genus *Sphyraena* of the family Sphyraenidae) of warm seas that prey on other fishes (e g mullet and anchovies) and include some excellent food fishes as well as forms regarded as poisonous [AmerSp]

¹**barrage** /'barahzh/ *n* an artificial dam placed across a watercourse (e g a river) or estuary to increase the depth of water or to divert it into a channel to aid navigation or for irrigation [Fr, fr *barrer* to bar, fr *barre* bar]

²**barrage** *n* 1 an intensive prolonged bombardment of an area with shells, bullets, etc to hinder enemy action 2 a rushed outpouring or rapid series or delivery (e g of phone calls or questions) [Fr (*tir de*) *barrage* barrier fire]

³**barrage** *vt* to deliver a barrage against; attack or overwhelm with a barrage

**barrage balloon** *n* a large balloon that is attached to the ground by ropes and is used to support wires or nets to prevent the approach of low-flying enemy aircraft

**barramunda** /,barə'moondə/ *n, pl* **barramunda**, *esp for different types* **barramundas** any of several Australian freshwater fishes used for food; *esp* a large red-fleshed lungfish (*Neoceratodus forsteri*) [native name in Australia]

**barramundi** /,barə'moondi/ *n, pl* **barramundi**, *esp for different types* **barramundis**, **barramundies** a barramunda

**barrator** /'barətə/ *also* **barrater** *n* one who engages in or is guilty of barratry

**barratry** /'barətri/ *n* 1 the purchase or sale of church or state appointments 2 a fraudulent breach of duty by the master or crew of a ship to the prejudice of the owner of the ship or cargo 3 the practice of persistently inciting and maintaining quarrels or lawsuits [ME *barratrie*, fr MF *baraterie* deception, fr *barater* to deceive, exchange, prob deriv of Gk *prattein, prassein* to do, perform (cf BARTER)] – **barratrous** *adj*

**barre** /bah/ *n* a horizontal handrail used by ballet dancers to maintain balance while exercising [Fr, bar]

¹**barrel** /'barəl/ *n* 1 an approximately cylindrical container with bulging sides and flat ends, typically made from wooden staves held together with metal hoops 2 a barrelful; *esp* any of various units of volume that are fixed for a particular commodity (e g beer or oil) 3 a drum or cylindrical part: e g 3a the tube through

which a bullet, shell, etc leaves a gun **b** the cylindrical metal box enclosing the principal spring (MAINSPRING 1) of a watch or clock **c** the part of a fountain pen containing the ink **d** an (approximately) cylindrical case in a microscope, camera, etc, that contains the lenses 4 the trunk of a 4-legged animal 5 *informal* a great quantity or amount ⟨*it wasn't exactly a* ∼ *of fun*⟩ [ME *barel*, fr MF *baril*] – **over a barrel** *informal* at a disadvantage; in an awkward situation so that one is helpless [prob fr the state of a person held over a barrel to clear his lungs of water after being saved from drowning] – **scrape (the bottom of) the barrel** to resort to the weakest or worst resources at one's disposal, usu because they are the only ones available

²**barrel** *vb* **-ll-** (*NAm* **-l-**, **-ll-**) *vt* to put or pack in a barrel ∼ *vi, NAm informal* to move at a high speed

**barrel chair** *n* an upholstered chair with a high solid rounded back

,**barrel-'chested** *adj* having a large rounded chest

**barrelful** /'barəl(ə)l/ *n, pl* **barrelfuls, barrelsful** the amount contained in a barrel

**barrelhouse** /'barə/,hows/ *n* 1 a style of jazz characterized by a very heavy beat and simultaneous improvisation by each player 2 *NAm* a cheap rowdy drinking and usu dancing establishment

**barrel organ** *n* a musical instrument typically worked by turning a handle that causes a cylinder studded with pegs to revolve and open a series of valves that admit air from a bellows to a set of pipes

**barrel printer** *n* DRUM PRINTER (type of printer linked to a computer)

**barrel roll** *n* a manoeuvre in which an aeroplane moves in a spiral path by turning over sideways while continuing to fly in a straight line

**barrel vault** *n* an arched roof, ceiling, etc (VAULT 1a) having the form of a half cylinder unbroken by joins

**barren** /'barən/ *adj* 1 not reproducing: e g **1a** *of a female* incapable of producing offspring; sterile **b** not producing offspring ⟨*a* ∼ *mating*⟩ **c** habitually failing to produce fruit ⟨*a* ∼ *tree*⟩ 2 not productive: e g **2a** *of soil or land* lacking or unable to support normal growth of vegetation or crops; infertile **b** unproductive of results or gain; unprofitable ⟨*a* ∼ *scheme*⟩ 3 lacking, devoid *of* 4 lacking interest, information, or charm ⟨*a* ∼ *life-style*⟩ 5 lacking inspiration or ideas; dull, unresponsive ⟨∼ *minds*⟩ *synonyms* see ¹BARE, STERILE *antonyms* fertile, fecund [ME *bareine*, fr OF *baraine*] – **barrenly** *adv*, **barrenness** *n*

**barrette** /ba'ret/ *n, NAm* a hair-slide [Fr, dim. of *barre* bar]

¹**barricade** /'barikayd, --'-/ *vt* 1 to block off or stop up with a barricade ⟨∼d *the street*⟩ 2 to prevent access to (as if) by means of a barricade

²**barricade** /'barikayd/ *n* 1 a usu temporary obstruction or barrier placed across a passage, street, etc to prevent access 2 a barrier, obstacle [Fr, fr MF, fr *barriquer* to barricade, fr *barrique* barrel]

**barrier** /'bari-ə/ *n* 1 an object (e g a railing) or set of objects that separates, demarcates, or prevents access or passage 2 the part of the Antarctic ICE CAP that extends into the sea 3 something immaterial that separates or prevents or hinders communication, progress, etc ⟨∼s *of reserve*⟩ [ME *barrere*, fr MF *barriere*, fr *barre*]

**barrier cream** *n* any of various creams for protecting the skin (e g from intensive sunlight or chemicals that cause irritation)

**barrier reef** *n* a coral reef lying roughly parallel to a shore and separated from it by a lagoon

**barriers to entry** *n pl* factors which give rise to cost disadvantages for new entrants to an industry in relation to established firms

**barring** /'bahring/ *prep* excepting

**barrio** /'bahrioh, 'ba-/ *n, pl* **barrios** 1 a quarter or district of a city or town in Spanish-speaking countries 2 a Spanish-speaking neighbourhood in a US city or town, esp in the Southwest [Sp, fr Ar *barrī* of the open country, fr *barr* outside, open country]

**barrister** /'baristə/, ,**barrister-at-'law** *n* a lawyer who is qualified to practise in the superior courts (e g a CROWN COURT) in England and Wales and is entitled to represent the prosecution or defence – compare SOLICITOR [¹*bar* + *-i-* + *-ster*]

**barroom** /-,roohm, -room/ *n, chiefly NAm* a bar for the sale of alcoholic drinks

¹**barrow** /'baroh/ *n* a large mound of earth or stones over an

ancient grave or burial chamber [ME *bergh,* fr OE *beorg;* akin to OHG *berg* mountain, Skt *bṛhant* high]

²**barrow** *n* a male pig castrated before sexual maturity [ME *barow,* fr OE *bearg;* akin to OHG *barug* barrow, OE *borian* to bore]

³**barrow** *n* **1a** HANDBARROW (flat frame on which loads are carried) **b** a wheelbarrow **2** a cart, usu with two or four wheels, that can be pulled or pushed by hand and from which fruit, vegetables, flowers, etc are sold (eg in the street or a market) [ME *barew,* fr OE *bearwe;* akin to OE *beran* to carry – more at BEAR]

**barrow boy** *n* a man or boy who sells goods (eg fruit or vegetables) from a barrow

**barrowload** /'baroh‚lohd/ *n* as much as a barrow will hold

**bar sinister** *n* **1** an imaginary heraldic design or figure indicating illegitimate birth **2** the fact or condition of being of illegitimate birth

**bartender** /'bah‚tendə/ *n* one who serves drinks in a bar; a barman or barmaid

¹**barter** /'bahtə/ *vi* **1** to trade by exchanging one commodity for another without the use of money **2** to negotiate the terms of a sale or similar agreement; haggle ~ *vt* **1** to trade or exchange (as if) by bartering **2** to part with unwisely or for less than the true value – often + *away* [ME *bartren,* fr MF *barater* (cf BARRATRY)] – **barterer** *n*

²**barter** *n* the act or practice of carrying on trade by bartering

**Bartholin's gland** /'bahthəlinz/ *n* either of two oval glands lying one on each side of the lower part of the vagina, that secrete a lubricating mucus – compare COWPER'S GLAND [Kaspar *Bartholin* †1738 Dan physician]

**bartizan** /'bahtiz(ə)n, ‚bahti'zan/ *n* a small structure (eg a corner turret or parapet) projecting from a tower, castle, etc [ME *bretasinge,* fr *bretasce* parapet – more at BRATTICE]

**Baruch** /'bahrook, 'beə-/ *n – see* BIBLE table [*Baruch* (fr LL, fr Gk *Barouch,* fr Heb *Bārūkh*), companion of the prophet Jeremiah]

**baryon** /'bari‚on/ *n* any of a family of particles of matter (ELEMENTARY PARTICLES), including protons and neutrons, which are both HADRONS and FERMIONS [ISV *bary-* (fr Gk *barys* heavy) + ²-*on* – more at GRIEVE] – **baryonic** *adj*

**barysphere** /'bari‚sfiə/ *n* the dense inner part of the earth below the crust

**baryta** /bə'rietə/ *n* **1** barium oxide **2** barium hydroxide [NL, modif of Gk *barytēs* weight] – **barytic** *adj*

**barytes** /bə'rieteez/ *n* a whitish or colourless mineral consisting of naturally occurring BARIUM SULPHATE, $BaSO_4$ [Gk *barytēs* weight, fr *barys* heavy]

**baryton** /'baritohn/ *n* a bass VIOL (Renaissance stringed instrument) with extra strings that vibrate in sympathy with the six main strings

**basal** /'bays(ə)l/ *adj* **1a** of, situated at, or forming the base **b** *of a leaf* arising from the base of a stem **2** of or being the foundation, basis, or essence; fundamental – **basally** *adv*

**basal body** *n* a minute specialized cell part found at the base of a FLAGELLUM or CILIUM (hairlike structures used for movement)

**basal granule** *n* BASAL BODY

**basal metabolic rate** *n* the rate at which heat is given off by an animal at complete rest

**basal metabolism** *n* the amount of energy required by an animal at complete rest (eg during hibernation) using energy solely to maintain vital cellular activity, breathing, and circulation of the blood

**basalt** /'basawlt, 'bay-, bə'sawlt/ *n* a very common dark grey to black fine-grained rock that occurs typically in large sheets or sometimes hexagonal columns, is formed by the solidification of lava on the earth's surface, and that consists of a feldspar mineral of the PLAGIOCLASE group together with minerals, usu a PYROXENE and often OLIVINE, containing iron and magnesium [L *basaltes,* MS var of *basanites* touchstone, fr Gk *basanitēs* (*lithos*), fr *basanos* touchstone, fr Egypt *bḥnw*] – **basaltic** *adj*

**bascule** /'baskyool, 'baskyoohl/ *n* **1 bascule bridge, bascule** a bridge with a part that can be raised and lowered, in which one end is counterbalanced by the other either on the principle of the seesaw or by using weights **2** an apparatus or structure that works on the same principle as a bascule bridge [Fr, seesaw]

¹**base** /bays/ *n* **1a(1)** the lower part of a complete structure (eg a building) **a(2)** the bottom of something considered as its support; a foundation **b** the lower part of a wall, pillar, or column considered as a separate architectural feature **c** the side

or face of a geometric figure on which it is considered to stand **d** that part of a limb or other projecting body part by which it is attached to another structure nearer the centre of a living organism ⟨*the* ~ *of the thumb*⟩ **2a** a main or predominating ingredient ⟨*a drink with a rum* ~⟩ **b** a supporting or carrying ingredient ⟨*paint with a water* ~⟩ **3** the fundamental principle or part on which something is built up; a basis **4** the lower part of a heraldic shield **5a(1)** the point or line from which a start is made in an action, process, undertaking, etc; a starting point **a(2)** a centre from which operations or activities proceed or are coordinated ⟨*Windermere is an ideal* ~ *for exploring the Lake District*⟩ **b** base, baseline **b(1)** a level, line, etc that serves as a standard for comparison or from which measurements can be taken **b(2)** a line in surveying whose length and position are accurately calculated and that is used for determining the positions of remote points **c** the place or set of buildings from which a military force starts operations or on which it relies for supplies **d(1)** the number on which a system of counting is constructed ⟨*the decimal system uses the* ~ *10*⟩ **d(2)** a number with reference to which logarithms are calculated **e** ROOT **6** (core part of a word from which related words are derived) **6a** the starting place or goal in various games **b** any of the four stations at the corners of the square forming the inner part of a baseball field, to which a batter must run in turn in order to score a run **7a** any of various chemical compounds, including all alkalis, capable of reacting with an acid to form a salt; *specif* a compound capable of taking up a HYDROGEN ION from an acid or giving a pair of electrons to an acid **b** any of several compounds that are chemical bases occurring in the structure of the genetic material DNA and RNA, and whose order in the DNA or RNA chain constitutes the inheritable information contained in the genes – compare ADENINE, CYTOSINE, GUANINE, THYMINE, URACIL **8** the lowest price that a stock, share, etc reaches on the stock market **9** the middle region of a transistor that controls the flow of an electric current through the transistor – compare COLLECTOR, EMITTER **10** base, base component *linguistics* that part of a TRANSFORMATIONAL GRAMMAR that consists of a set of rules and vocabulary and that produces the sentences of a language by the application of the rules to the words [ME, fr Mf, fr L *basis,* fr Gk, step, base, fr *bainein* to go N more at COME] – **based** *adj,* **baseless** *adj*

synonyms **Base, basis, foundation, ground,** and **groundwork** all mean "that on which something else is built". A **base** is chiefly material, and suggests either a broad substructure or the lowest part of something ⟨*the* **base** *of a lamp/a tree/a triangle*⟩. A **basis** is chiefly abstract ⟨*the* **basis** *of their friendship*⟩. **Foundation** emphasizes firm and enduring support for something of some size ⟨*the* **foundations** *of a house*⟩ ⟨*a* **foundation** *for lifelong friendship*⟩. A rumour which has its **basis** in speculation may have no real **foundation**. **Ground** is that upon which something else is superimposed, and may extend vertically rather than horizontally ⟨*a blue pattern on a white* **ground**⟩. In the plural, it suggests a reasonable basis for action ⟨**grounds** *for complaint*⟩. **Groundwork** emphasizes the effort involved in laying a foundation, and is chiefly abstract ⟨*reading is the best* **groundwork** *for a career in publishing*⟩. **antonyms** top, summit, superstructure *usage* see BASIS

²**base** *vt* **1** to station, place, or establish ⟨*a salesman* ~d *in Leeds*⟩ **2** to use something specified as a base or basis for; found ⟨*the book is* ~d *on fact*⟩ – usu + *on* or *upon*

³**base** *adj* **1a** resembling or being a VILLEIN (peasant renting land from and owing allegiance to a feudal lord) ⟨*a* ~ *tenant*⟩ **b** held by a villein ⟨~ *tenure*⟩ **2a** *of a metal* not precious – compare NOBLE **b** *esp of a coin* containing a larger than usual proportion of base metals; counterfeit **3a** lacking or indicating the lack of moral values (eg honour, chivalry, or loyalty) ⟨*a* ~ *betrayal*⟩ **b** lacking higher values; degrading, menial ⟨*a drab* ~ *way of life*⟩ **4** of relatively little value; inferior **5** *archaic* of humble or illegitimate birth; baseborn synonyms see ¹MEAN antonym noble [ME *bas* short, low, bass, fr MF, fr ML *bassus* short, low] – **basely** *adv,* **baseness** *n*

**baseball** /'bays‚bawl/ *n* (the ball used in) a game played with a bat and a ball between two teams of nine players who are positioned on a large field having four bases arranged in a square that mark the course a batter must run to score

**baseboard** /'bays‚bawd/ *n, NAm* SKIRTING 3

**baseborn** /'bays‚bawn/ *adj* **1a** of humble birth; lowly **b** of illegitimate birth **2** mean, dishonourable

**base burner** *n, NAm* a stove in which coal, coke, etc is fed to the fire automatically as the lower layer is used up

**baselevel** /'bays,levəl/ n the lowest level to which a land surface can be eroded by running water

**baseline** /'bays,lien/ n 1 a line serving as a base; BASE 5b 2 the back line at each end of a court in various games (e g tennis)

**basement** /'baysmənt/ n 1 the storey of a building that is wholly or partly below ground level 2 the lowest or fundamental part of something [prob fr ¹base]

**basement membrane** n, anatomy a usu single-layered membrane of flat cells underlying the EPITHELIUM (tissue covering or lining surfaces) of many organs – called also LAMINA PROPRIA

**basenji** /bə'senji/ n, pl **basenjis** (any of) an African breed of small compact curly-tailed chestnut-brown dogs that seldom bark [of Bantu origin; akin to Lingala basenji, pl of mosenji native]

**base rate** n the rate of interest used by British CLEARING BANKS (major banks that issue cheques) as a basis for calculating charges on loans and interest on deposits

**base unit** n BASIC UNIT (unit of measurement on which a system of measurements is based)

¹**bash** /bash/ vt 1 to strike violently; hit; also to injure, damage, or smash in this way – often + in or up 2 informal to attack with criticism, abuse, etc ⟨he's always ~ing the unions⟩ [prob imit] – **basher** n

  **bash into** vt to collide violently with

²**bash** n 1 a forceful blow 2 NAm a festive social gathering; a party 3 chiefly Br informal a try, attempt ⟨have a ~ at it⟩

**bashaw** /bə'shaw/ n PASHA (person of high rank in Egypt or ancient Turkey)

**bashful** /'bashf(ə)l/ adj 1 socially shy, timid, or self-conscious 2 characterized by, showing, or resulting from extreme sensitiveness, self-consciousness, or shyness ⟨a ~ smile⟩ **synonyms** see ¹SHY **antonyms** forward, brazen [obs bash (to be abashed), fr ME basshen, short for abasshen, abaishen – more at ABASH] – **bashfully** adv, **bashfulness** n

¹**basic** /'baysik, -zik/ adj 1 of or forming the base or basis; fundamental ⟨a ~ principle⟩ 2 being or serving as the minimum or starting point ⟨on ~ salary⟩ ⟨a ~ education⟩ 3 designed for or used for teaching beginners ⟨~ readers⟩ 4a of, being, containing, or like a chemical BASE (compound that reacts with an acid to form a salt) b having an alkaline reaction; being an alkali 5 of a rock containing relatively little SILICA (silicon dioxide occurring as quartz, agate, etc) 6 of, being, used in, or made by a steelmaking process in which the furnace is lined with material (e g lime) that is basic as distinguished from acidic ⟨~ steel⟩ – **basically** adv, **basicity** n

  **usage** The use of **basic, basically** to mean no more than "essential(ly)" or "important(ly)" ⟨it's a **basic** fact that children need exercise⟩ ⟨**basically**, we'll have to wait and see⟩ is widely disliked.

²**basic** n 1 something (e g a principle) that is basic or fundamental ⟨the ~s of biology⟩ 2 **basic training, basic** the initial training of a military recruit

**BASIC** /'baysik/ n a HIGH-LEVEL computer language (language closer to English than the code recognized by a computer) for programming esp small computers [Beginner's All-purpose Symbolic Instruction Code]

**Basic English** n a simplified version of English with a vocabulary of 850 words designed for teaching and international communication

**basic rate** n 1 a standard rate or amount of pay exclusive of additional payments or allowances 2 the standard rate of income tax

**basic slag** n a SLAG (waste material containing impurities) produced as a by-product in steelmaking, that is rich in phosphates and is used as a fertilizer

**basic unit** n any of the units of measurement (e g the metre, kilogram, or second) on which all the other units of a particular system of measurement are based – compare DERIVED UNIT

**basidiomycete** /bə,sidioh'mieseet, -,----'-/ n any of a large class (Basidiomycetes) of fungi bearing basidiospores and including RUSTS, mushrooms, and puffballs [deriv of NL basidium + Gk mykēt-, mykēs fungus – more at MYC-] – **basidiomycetous** adj

**basidiospore** /bə'sidioh,spaw/ n a reproductive body (SPORE) produced by and borne on a basidium, that grows to form a new fungus [NL basidium + E -o- + spore] – **basidiosporous** adj

**basidium** /bə'sidi-əm/ n, pl **basidia** /-di-ə/ a specialized cell on a basidiomycete fungus that bears usu four basidiospores

produced by sexual reproduction [NL, fr L basis] – **basidial** adj

**basil** /'baz(ə)l/ n any of several plants of the mint family; esp SWEET BASIL [MF basile, fr LL basilicum, fr Gk basilikon, fr neut of basilikos]

**basilar** /'basila, 'bazilə/ also **basilary** /'basiləri/ adj, chiefly anatomy of or situated at the base ⟨~ artery of the brain⟩ [irreg fr basis]

**basilar membrane** n a membrane in the spiral bony structure (COCHLEA) of the innermost part of the ear, that vibrates in response to sound waves and transmits the resulting stimuli to the organ that converts them into nerve impulses which are received by the brain

**Basilian** /bə'zilian/ n a member of a monastic order of the Eastern Christian church following a rule laid down by St Basil in the fourth century – **Basilian** adj

**basilica** /bə'zilikə, bə'si-/ n 1 an oblong building, typically ending in a domed semicircular recess (APSE 1) that was used in ancient Rome as a place of public assembly and as a lawcourt 2 an early Christian church similar to a Roman basilica in shape, that has a wide central area (NAVE) flanked on each side by one or two aisles separated from the nave by columns, and a large raised platform surrounding the altar from which an apse usu projects 3 a Roman Catholic church given certain ceremonial privileges [L, fr Gk basilikē, fr fem of basilikos royal, fr basileus king] – **basilican** adj

**basilisk** /'basilisk, 'bazi-/ n 1 a mythical reptile whose breath and glance could kill 2 any of several tropical American lizards (genus Basiliscus) related to the iguanas that have a crest on the back or head [ME, fr L basiliscus, fr Gk basiliskos, fr dim. of basileus]

**basin** /'bays(ə)n/ n 1a a rounded open usu metal or ceramic vessel with a greater width than depth and sides that slope or curve inwards, that is used typically for holding water for washing b a bowl; esp a round bowl that has a greater depth than width and is used esp for holding, mixing, or cooking food ⟨a pudding ~⟩ c the contents of or quantity contained in a basin 2a a dock built in a river or harbour near the sea b an enclosed or partly enclosed water area 3a a depression in the surface of the land or in the ocean floor b the area of country that supplies a river and its tributaries with water 4 a broad area of the earth beneath which the rock strata dip, usu from the sides towards a centre [ME, fr OF bacin, fr LL bacchinon] – **basined** adj

**basinet** /'basinet, -nit/ n a light often pointed steel helmet formerly worn under a larger helmet [ME bacinet, fr OF, dim. of bacin]

**basipetal** /bay'sipitl/ adj, of flowers, leaves, etc developing from the top towards the base of a stem so that the oldest are at the top; also of or being the development or production of flowers, leaves, etc in this order – compare ACROPETAL [L basis + petere to go towards – more at FEATHER] – **basipetally** adv

**basis** /'baysis/ n, pl **bases** /'bayseez/ 1 a foundation or support 2 the principal component of something 3 something on which something else is constructed or established ⟨he has no ~ for his beliefs⟩ 4 a basic principle or way of proceeding [L – more at BASE]

  **usage 1** It is often shorter and neater to avoid the use of **basis** by using an adverb ⟨employed on a permanent **basis** (= permanently)⟩. **2** When **bases** is the plural, not of **basis** but of **base**, it is pronounced /'baysiz/. **synonyms** see ¹BASE

**bask** /bahsk/ vi 1 to lie in or expose oneself to pleasant warmth, esp from the sun 2 to take pleasure or derive enjoyment – usu + in [ME basken, fr ON bathask, refl of batha to bathe; akin to OE bæth bath]

**basket** /'bahskit/ n 1a a rigid or semirigid container made of interwoven strips of cane, wood, plastic, etc b any of various lightweight usu wood containers in which fruit, vegetables, etc are packed or sold c the contents of or quantity contained in a basket 2 something that resembles a basket, esp in having a perforated or open structure 3a a net open at the bottom and suspended from a metal ring that is the goal in basketball b a goal in basketball 4 Br informal a person of a specified type ⟨she's a nice old ~⟩ [ME, prob fr (assumed) ONF baskot; akin to OF baschoue wooden vessel; both fr L bascauda dishpan, of Celt origin; akin to MIr basc necklace – more at FASCIA; (4) euphemism for bastard] – **basketful** n, **basketlike** adj

**basketball** /'bahskit,bawl/ n (the ball used in) a usu indoor court game between two teams of five or six players who score by tossing a large ball through a net fixed to a high ring

**basket chair** n a wickerwork armchair

**basket hilt** *n* a sword hilt with a curved guard of metal strips to protect the hand – **basket-hilted** *adj*

**basketry** /'bahskitri/ *n* **1** the art or craft of making baskets or objects woven like baskets **2** objects produced by basketry; *specif* wickerwork

**basket weave** *n* a textile weave resembling the chequered pattern of a plaited or woven basket

**basketwork** /'bahskit,wuhk/ *n* basketry

**basking shark** /'bahsking/ *n* a very large species of shark (*Cetorhinus maximus*) that commonly lies at the surface of the sea, basking in the sun

**bas mitzvah** /,bas 'mitzvə/ *n, often cap B&M* **1** a Jewish girl who at about 13 years of age assumes adult religious obligations and responsibilities **2** the initiatory ceremony recognizing a girl as a bas mitzvah □ called also BAT MITZVAH [Heb *bath miṣwāh*, lit., daughter of the (divine) law]

**basophil** /'baysə,fil, 'bayzə-/, **basophile** /-,fiel/ *n* a basophilic cell, cell structure, etc; *esp* a WHITE BLOOD CELL with large basophilic granules – compare EOSINOPHIL, NEUTROPHIL

**basophilic** /,baysə'filik, ,bayzə-/ *also* **basophil** /'baysəfil/, **basophile** /-,fiel/ *adj* staining readily with BASIC dyes as distinguished from acidic dyes – compare ACIDOPHILIC [ISV *base* + *-o-* + *-philic*] – **basophilia** *n*

**Basotho** /bə'soohtooh, bə'sohtoh/ *n, pl* **Basothos**, *esp collectively* **Basotho** MOSOTHO (citizen of Lesotho) – not now used technically

**Basque** /bask, bahsk/ *n* **1** a member of a people of obscure origin inhabiting the W Pyrenees in NE Spain and SW France **2** the language of the Basques [Fr, fr L *Vasco*] – **Basque** *adj*

**bas-relief** /,bas ri'leef, ,bah, ,bahs, '- -,-/ *n* **1** a form of sculpture in which the design projects very slightly from the surrounding surface – compare HIGH RELIEF **2** sculpture executed in bas-relief □ called also BASSO-RILIEVO [Fr, fr *bas* low + *relief* raised work]

**¹bass** /bas/ *n, pl* **bass**, *esp for different types* **basses** any of numerous sea and freshwater spiny-finned fishes (esp families Centrarchidae and Serranidae) most of which are edible [ME *base*, alter of OE *bærs*; akin to OE *byrst* bristle – more at BRISTLE]

**²bass** /bays/ *adj* **1** deep or grave in tone **2a** of low pitch **b** relating to or having the range or part of a bass [ME *bas* base]

**³bass** /bays/ *n* **1a** the lowest part in written, sung, or played music; *esp* the lowest part in conventional 4-part harmony **b** the lower half of the whole range of pitches that a voice, instrument, etc can produce – compare TREBLE **2a** (a person with) the lowest adult male singing voice **b** a member of a family of instruments having the lowest range: e g **b(1)** DOUBLE BASS **b(2)** BASS GUITAR

**⁴bass** /bas/ *n* a coarse tough fibre from palm trees [alter. of *bast*]

**bass clef** /bays/ *n* **1** a symbol on a musical stave that designates a note written on the next to top line of the stave as the F below MIDDLE C **2** the musical stave that has a bass clef and on which the bass part of a musical composition is written □ called also F CLEF; compare TREBLE CLEF

**bass drum** /bays/ *n* a large drum with a taut sheet of plastic, animal skin, etc at each end that gives a low-pitched booming sound

**basse danse** /,bas 'donhs/ *n* a stately 14th- and 15th-century dance performed with small gliding steps [Fr *basse-danse, danse basse*, lit., low dance]

**basset** /'basit/, **basset hound** *n* (any of) an old French breed of short-legged slow-moving hunting dogs with very long ears and usu crooked front legs [Fr *basset*, fr MF, fr *basset* short, fr *bas* low – more at BASE]

**basset horn** *n* an early form of the clarinet having a range slightly lower than that of the modern clarinet [prob fr Ger *bassetthorn*, fr It *bassetto* (dim. of *basso* bass) + Ger *horn*, fr OHG]

**bass guitar** /bays/ *n* a usu electric guitar with four strings tuned like those of a DOUBLE BASS, that is used for playing the bass part

**bassinet** /,basi'net, '---/ *n* a baby's basketlike cradle (e g of wickerwork or plastic) often with a hood over one end [prob modif of Fr *barcelonnette*, dim. of *berceau* cradle]

**bassist** /'baysist/ *n* a player of a DOUBLE BASS or bass guitar

**basso** /'basoh/ *n, pl* **bassos, bassi** /'basi/ a bass singer; *esp* an operatic bass [It, fr ML *bassus*, fr *bassus* short, low]

**bassoon** /bə'soohn/ *n* a large woodwind instrument of low range that has a DOUBLE REED (two flat pieces of cane that when blown across vibrate to produce sound) connected by a thin metal tube to a long U-shaped tube with a moderately flared free end [Fr *basson*, fr It *bassone*, fr *basso*] – **bassoonist** *n*

**basso profundo** /prə'foondoh/ *n, pl* **basso profundos** (a person with) a deep heavy bass singing voice with an exceptionally low range [It, lit., deep bass]

**basso-ri'lievo** /ri'lyayvoh/ *n, pl* **basso-rilievos** BAS-RELIEF (sculpture with slightly raised design) [It, fr *basso* low + *rilievo* raised work]

**bass viol** /bays/ *n* **1** the bass member of the VIOL family (precursor of the violin family); VIOLA DA GAMBA **2** a cello – not used technically

**basswood** /'bas,wood/ *n* (the light-coloured wood of) any of several N American linden trees [⁴*bass* + *wood*]

**bast** /bast/ *n* **1** PHLOEM (type of plant tissue) – not used technically **2** a strong woody fibre obtained from various plants (e g jute and hemp) and used esp in ropes, matting, and fabrics [ME, fr OE *bæst*; akin to OHG & ON *bast*]

**¹bastard** /'bahstəd, 'ba-/ *n* **1** an illegitimate child **2** something that is irregular, inferior, or of questionable or mixed origin **3** *informal* **3a** an offensive or disagreeable person – often + *you* as a generalized term of abuse **b** a person, esp a man, of a usu specified type ⟨*poor old ~*⟩ **4** *informal* something difficult, trying, or unpleasant ⟨*the word is a ~ to define*⟩ [ME, fr OF, prob fr the phrase *fils de bast* (meaning either 'son of the packsaddle' or 'son of the barn')] – **bastardly** *adj*

**²bastard** *adj* **1** of a person illegitimate **2** of inferior breed or stock; mongrel **3** abnormal or irregular in size, shape, appearance, etc **4** of a kind similar to but inferior to or less typical than some standard ⟨*~ oats*⟩ **5** lacking genuineness or authority; false

**bastard-ize, -ise** /'bahstədiez, 'ba-/ *vt* **1** to declare or prove to be illegitimate or a bastard **2** to debase – **bastardization** *n*

**bastardry** /'bahstədri, 'bas-/ *n, chiefly Austr* malicious behaviour

**bastard wing** *n* the part of a bird's wing corresponding to the thumb of mammals and bearing a few short feathers – called also ALULA

**bastardy** /'bahstədi, 'ba-/ *n* the quality or state of being a bastard; illegitimacy

**¹baste** /bayst/ *vt* to sew with long loose temporary stitches; TACK 2b; *also* to sew by making large diagonal stitches worked in rows [ME *basten*, fr MF *bastir*, of Gmc origin; akin to OHG *besten* to patch; akin to OE *bæst* bast] – **baster** *n*

**²baste** *vt* to moisten (esp meat) with melted butter, dripping, etc at intervals during cooking, esp roasting [origin unknown] – **baster** *n*

**³baste** *vt* to beat severely or soundly; thrash [prob fr ON *beysta*; akin to OE *bēatan* to beat]

**bastille** /ba'steel/ *n* a prison, jail [Fr, fr the *Bastille*, tower in Paris used as a prison, fr MF *bastille* tower, fortress]

**Bastille Day** /ba'steel/ *n* July 14 observed in France as a national holiday in commemoration of the fall of the Bastille in 1789

**bastinade** /,basti'nahd/ *n* (a) bastinado

**¹bastinado** /,basti'naydoh/ *n, pl* **bastinadoes** **1** a blow or beating with a stick **2** a punishment in which the soles of the feet are beaten with a stick **3** a stick, cudgel [Sp *bastonada*, fr *bastón* stick, fr LL *bastum*]

**²bastinado** *vt* **bastinadoes; bastinadoing; bastinadoed** to subject to repeated blows; *esp* to beat repeatedly on the soles of the feet

**basting** /'baysting/ *n* a severe beating

**bastion** /'basti•ən/ *n* **1** a part of a wall or similar fortification round a fort, town, etc, that projects outwards forming a 5-sided figure **2** a fortified area, place, or position **3** one who or that which provides powerful defence or support; a stronghold [MF, fr *bastille* fortress, modif of OProv *bastida*, fr *bastir* to build, of Gmc origin; akin to OHG *besten* to patch] – **bastioned** *adj*

**Basuto** /bə'soohtoh/ *n, pl* **Basutos**, *esp collectively* **Basuto** MOSOTHO (citizen of Lesotho) – not now used technically

**¹bat** /bat/ *n* **1** a stout solid stick; a club **2** a sharp blow or stroke **3** any of various solid usu wooden implements used for hitting the ball in cricket, table tennis, baseball, etc **4a** a batsman **b** a turn at batting, esp in cricket ⟨*had a good ~ this morning*⟩ **5** bat, batt, bats *pl* BATTING 2 (packaging or stuffing material) **6** either of a pair of hand-held implements having a round flat shape and a short handle like a table-tennis bat, that are used by a man on the ground for guiding aircraft when landing or taxiing **7** *Br informal* rate of speed ⟨*travel at a fair* ~⟩ [ME, fr OE *batt*, prob of Celt origin; akin to Gaulish anda*bata*, a gladiator – more at BATTLE] – **carry one's bat** to open an innings in cricket and be the only remaining batsman when all the other batsmen are out – **off one's own bat** through one's own efforts, esp without being prompted

²**bat** *vb* **-tt-** *vt* **1** to strike or hit (as if) with a bat **2** *NAm* to produce in a casual, careless, or hurried manner – *usu* + *out* ~ *vi* **1** to strike or hit a ball with a bat **2** to take one's turn at batting ⟨*he* ~*s at number five for the England cricket team*⟩ – see also GO **to bat for**

³**bat** *n* any of an order (Chiroptera) of small furry flying mammals, that are active at night and have the forelimbs modified to form thin leathery wings [alter. of ME *bakke*, prob of Scand origin; akin to OSw natt*bakka* bat]

⁴**bat** *vt* **-tt-** to wink or flutter (eg one's eyes or eyelashes), esp in surprise or emotion [prob alter. of ²*bate*] – **not bat an eyelid/eye** *informal* to show no surprise or emotion

**batata** /bə'tahtə/ *n* SWEET POTATO [Sp, fr Taino]

¹**batch** /bach/ *n* **1** the quantity, esp of bread, baked at one time **2a** a quantity of material prepared, required for, or produced in one operation ⟨*a* ~ *of cement*⟩ **b** a group of programs or jobs to be run on a computer at one time ⟨~ *processing*⟩ **3** a group of people or things arriving, handled, etc together, or considered as a set ⟨*the latest* ~ *of school leavers*⟩ [ME *bache*; akin to OE *bacan* to bake]

²**batch** *vt* to bring together or process as a batch – **batcher** *n*

¹**bate** /bayt/ *vb* to abate, diminish, or lessen – see also **with bated** BREATH △ bait [ME *baten*, short for *abaten* to abate]

²**bate** *vi*, *of a falcon or other bird used for hunting* to beat the wings impatiently or flutter wildly while restrained (eg on a perch) [ME *baten*, fr MF *batre* to beat – more at DEBATE]

³**bate** *n*, *Br* a rage, temper [var of *bait*, perh back-formation fr *baited*, pp of ¹*bait*]

**bateau** /ba'toh/ *n*, *pl* **bateaux** /ba'toh(z)/ a light flat-bottomed river boat used in N America, esp Canada [CanF, fr Fr, fr OF *batel*, fr OE *bāt* boat – more at BOAT]

**bateleur** /ˌbatə'luh/, **bateleur eagle** *n* a small black, reddish-brown, and white eagle of Africa and Arabia that has a short tail and long pointed very wide wings [Fr *bateleur*, fr OF *bastelleur* juggler, puppet player, fr *baastel* puppet]

**Batesian mimicry** /'baytsi-ən/ *n* the resemblance of a harmless species of animal to another species having repellent qualities (e g unpalatability) that protect it from predators [Henry Walter *Bates* †1892 E naturalist]

¹**bath** /bahth/ *n*, *pl* **baths** /bahths; *sense 3 also* bahdhz/ **1** the act or an instance of washing or soaking all or part of the body ⟨*a mud* ~⟩ **2a** water used for bathing ⟨*run a* ~⟩ **b(1)** a liquid used for a special purpose (e g keeping something at a constant temperature or developing photographs) **b(2)** a vat, tank, or similar container holding such a liquid **3a baths** *taking sing or pl vb*, **bath 3a(1)** a building containing a room or series of rooms designed for bathing; a bathhouse **a(2)** SWIMMING BATH **b baths** *pl*, **bath** a spa **4** a large container (e g of enamelled metal or plastic) for taking a bath in; *esp* one that is permanently fixed in a bathroom **5** *NAm* a bathroom [ME, fr OE *bæth*; akin to OHG *bad* bath, OE *bacan* to bake]

²**bath** *vb*, *Br vt* to wash (e g a child) in a bath ~ *vi* to take a bath

*usage* In British English one **baths** in the bathroom to get clean, but **bathes** in the sea or a river or lake for pleasure.

³**bath** *n* an ancient Hebrew unit for measuring liquid of about 38 litres (about 8¹⁄₂ gallons) [Heb]

**bath-** – see BATHY-

**Bath bun** *n* a sweet bun made with yeast and containing dried fruit (e g raisins and sultanas) and topped with sugar crystals [*Bath*, town in England]

**bath chair** *n*, *often cap B* a wheelchair with a hood over one end, used esp by invalids; *broadly* a wheelchair [*Bath*, town in England]

**Bath chap** *n* the lower cheek or fleshy part of the lower jaw of a pig used as food

**bath cube** *n* a block of compressed powdered material that dissolves in bathwater to scent and soften it

¹**bathe** /baydh/ *vt* **1** to wash, soak, or immerse in a liquid (e g water) **2** to apply a liquid or a cleansing or soothing liquid to (e g a cut) **3** *of a lake, sea, wave, etc* to flow along the edge of **4** to suffuse (as if) with light, colour, etc ⟨*the mountains were* ~*d in golden light*⟩ ~ *vi* **1** to swim (e g in the sea or a river)

for pleasure **2** to bask **3** *chiefly NAm* to take a bath [ME *bathen*, fr OE *bathian;* akin to OE *bæth* bath]

²**bathe** *n*, *Br* an act of bathing, esp in the sea; a swim

**bather** /'baydhə/ *n* **1** one who bathes, esp in the sea **2** *pl*, *Austr* SWIMMING COSTUME

**bathetic** /bə'thetik/ *adj* characterized by bathos [*bathos* + -*etic* (as in *pathetic*)] – **bathetically** *adv*

**bathhouse** /'bahth,hows/ *n* a building equipped with baths for public use

**bathing beauty** /'baydhing/ *n* a woman in a swimming costume who is a contestant in a beauty contest

**bathing costume** *n* SWIMMING COSTUME

**bathing hut** *n* a hut for bathers to change their clothes in

**bathing machine** *n* a bathing hut on wheels that was pulled to the water's edge for the convenience of the bather

**bathing suit** *n* SWIMMING COSTUME

**bath mat** *n* **1** a usu washable mat often of absorbent material that is placed beside a bath to protect the floor from water dripping from the bather **2** a mat of nonslip material, esp rubber, placed in a bath to prevent the bather from slipping

**batho-** – see BATHY-

**batholith** /'batholith/ *n* a large dome-shaped mass of rock (e g granite) formed at a great depth below the earth's surface from molten rock material that forced its way into spaces between existing rocks and later solidified [ISV] – **batholithic** *adj*

**Bath Oliver** /'olivə/ *n* a large round unsweetened biscuit often eaten with cheese [William *Oliver* †1764 E physician employed at *Bath* in England]

**bathometer** /bə'thomitə/ *n* an instrument for measuring depths in water

**bathos** /'baythos/ *n* **1** a sudden descent from the sublime or elevated to the commonplace or absurd in writing or speech; an anticlimax, letdown **2** exceptional commonplaceness; triteness **3** insincere or overdone pathos; sentimentalism ☐ compare PATHOS [Gk, lit., depth, fr *bathys* deep]

**bathrobe** /'bahth,rohb/ *n* a loose robe made usu of an absorbent material (e g towelling) that is worn before and after having a bath and sometimes as a dressing gown

**bathroom** /'bahth,roohm, -room/ *n* **1** a room containing a bath or shower and usu a washbasin and toilet **2** *chiefly euph* a toilet

**bath salts** *n pl* a usu coloured preparation in the form of crystals, used for scenting and softening bathwater

**Bath stone** *n* building stone consisting of a type of limestone [*Bath*, town in England]

**bathtub** /'bahth,tub/ *n* a bath: **a** *chiefly Br* one not permanently fixed in a bathroom **b** *chiefly NAm* one permanently fixed in a bathroom

**bathy-** /bathi-/, **bath-**, **batho-** *comb form* **1** deep; depth ⟨*bathymetry*⟩ ⟨*batholith*⟩ **2** deep-sea ⟨*bathysphere*⟩ [ISV, fr Gk, fr *bathos* depth & *bathys* deep; akin to Skt *gāhate* he dives into]

**bathyal** /'bathiəl/ *adj* of, being, or living in that part of the ocean that extends downwards from the edge of the CONTINENTAL SHELF at about 180 metres (about 540 feet) below the surface to a depth of about 1800 metres (about 5400 feet)

**bathymetry** /bə'thimətri/ *n* the measurement of depths of water in oceans, seas, and lakes [ISV] – **bathymetric**, **bathymetrical** *adj*, **bathymetrically** *adv*

**bathyscape** /'bathiskayp/ *n* a bathyscaphe

**bathyscaphe** /'bathiskayf, -skaf/ *also* **bathyscaph** /-,skaf/ *n* a submarine used for deep-sea exploration, that often has a spherical observation cabin attached to its underside [ISV *bathy-* + Gk *skaphē* light boat]

**bathysphere** /'bathisfiə/ *n* a strongly built spherical vessel for deep-sea observation

**batik** /'batik/ *n* **1a** an Indonesian method of hand-printing textiles by coating the parts to be left undyed with wax **b** a design produced by batik **2** a fabric printed by batik [Malay, fr Jav, painted]

**batiste** /bə'teest/ *n* a fine soft fabric made originally of cotton and now of various fibres and used esp for clothing [Fr]

**batman** /'batmən/ *n* a British officer's personal servant [*bat* (pack-saddle, luggage), fr MF, deriv of Gk *bastazein* to carry]

**bat mitzvah** /ˌbaht 'mitsvə/ *n, often cap B&M* BAS MITZVAH (Jewish girl of 13 or ceremony recognizing her religious responsibilities)

**baton** /'bat(ə)n, 'ba,ton, bə'ton (*Fr* batɔ̃)/ *n* **1** a cudgel, truncheon **2** a staff carried as a symbol of office (e g by an army officer) **3** *heraldry* a narrow diagonal stripe running from top right to bottom left on a shield; *esp* one indicating illegitimacy **4** a thin stick or wand with which a conductor directs a band, orchestra, choir, etc **5** a stick or hollow cylinder that is carried in turn by each member of a relay-race team while he/she is running and is then passed to the next runner in the team **6** a hollow metal rod, usu with a knob at one end, that is carried and twirled by a drum major or drum majorette [Fr *bâton*, fr OF *baston*, fr LL *bastum* stick]

**baton charge** /'bat(ə)n/ *n* a charge by police or troops wielding truncheons or batons

**batrachian** /bə'trayki·ən/ *adj or n* (of or being) a tailless amphibian animal, esp a frog or a toad [deriv of Gk *batrachos* frog]

**bats** /bats/ *adj, chiefly Br informal* batty, crazy [prob fr the phrase *to have bats in the belfry* to be crazy]

**batsman** /'batsmən/ *n* **1** one who bats or is batting, esp in cricket **2** a cricketer who specializes in batting rather than bowling or fielding – **batsmanship** *n*

**batt** /bat/ *n* BATTING 2 (packaging or stuffing material)

**battalion** /bə'talyən/ *n taking sing or pl vb* **1** a large organized body of troops **2** a basic military unit composed of a headquarters and two or more companies organized to work and fight together **3** a large group ⟨*a ~ of relations arrived*⟩ [MF *bataillon*, fr OIt *battaglione*, aug of *battaglia* company of soldiers, battle, fr LL *battalia* combat – more at BATTLE]

**battels** /'batlz/ *n pl, Br* a bill for accommodation, food, or other expenses given to a member of an Oxford or Durham university college [perh fr obs *battle* to nourish, perh of Scand origin]

**¹batten** /'bat(ə)n/ *vi* **1** to grow fat (as if) by feeding **2** to feed gluttonously *on* or *upon* [prob fr ON *batna* to improve]
**batten on, batten onto** *vt* **1** to grow prosperous or thrive on; *esp* to prosper at the expense of ⟨*battened on his relatives*⟩ **2** to seize on (an excuse, argument, etc)

**²batten** *n* **1** a strip, bar, or support used in building: eg **1a** a thin narrow strip (eg of wood) used to seal or reinforce a joint **b** a wooden bar fastened across a structure (eg a door) composed of parallel boards, to hold the boards together or add strength **2a** a thin strip (eg of wood or plastic) inserted into a sail to keep it flat and taut **b** a metal or wooden slat used to fasten down the tarpaulin covering a ship's hatch **3** a strip holding a row of floodlights **4** *chiefly Br* a long narrow piece of wood used esp for flooring [Fr *bâton*]

**³batten** *vt* to provide, strengthen, or fasten (eg hatches) with battens – often + *down*

**¹batter** /'batə/ *vt* **1** to beat or hit persistently or hard so as to bruise, damage, or break **2** to subject to strong, overwhelming, or repeated attack, abuse, or criticism **3** to wear or damage by hard usage or blows ⟨*a ~ed old hat*⟩ ~ *vi* to strike heavily and repeatedly ; beat [ME *bateren*, prob freq of *batten* to bat, fr *bat*]

**²batter** *n* a mixture consisting of flour, egg, and milk or water that is thin enough to pour or drop from a spoon and that is used for pancakes, Yorkshire pudding, etc and as a coating for some foods; *also* cooked batter surrounding fried food (eg fish) – compare DOUGH [ME *bater*, prob fr *bateren*]

**³batter** *vb* to (cause to) slope upwards and backwards [origin unknown]

**⁴batter** *n* an upwards and backwards slope of a wall or similar structure

**⁵batter** *n* one who bats; *specif* the player whose turn it is to bat in baseball

**battering ram** /'batəring/ *n* a large wooden beam with a head of iron (eg in the shape of a ram's head) used in ancient times to beat down the walls of a besieged place

**battery** /'bat(ə)ri/ *n* **1** the act of battering; *specif, law* the unlawful use of any degree of force on a person without his/her consent ⟨*an unwanted kiss may be a ~ – Salmond on the Law of Tort* 16th ed⟩ – compare ASSAULT 2a **2a** a group of similar artillery guns (eg cannons) **b** the guns of a warship **3** *taking sing or pl vb* an artillery unit or subunit in the army equivalent to a company in an infantry regiment **4** a CELL (device that converts chemical energy into electrical energy) or series of connected cells that provides an electric current: eg **4a** STORAGE CELL (one or a series of rechargeable cells like those in a car battery) **b** DRY CELL (battery, as in an electric torch, that cannot be recharged); *also* a connected group of dry cells **5a** a number of similar articles, items, etc arranged, occurring, connected, or used together; a set, series, or array ⟨*a ~ of psycho-*

*logical tests*⟩ **b** a series of cages or compartments for raising or fattening animals; *specif* a large number of small cages in which egg-laying hens are kept **6** the position of readiness of a gun for firing **7** the PITCHER (person who throws the ball to the batter) and CATCHER (fielder standing behind the batter) of a baseball team [MF *batterie*, fr OF, fr *battre* to beat, fr L *battuere* – more at BATTLE]

**batting** /'bating/ *n* **1a** the act of one who bats **b** the use of or ability with a bat **2** layers or sheets of matted cotton or wool fibres used for lining quilts or for stuffing or packaging

**batting average** *n* the number of runs scored by a cricketer in a season, his/her career, etc divided by the number of times he/she has been out in the same period – compare BOWLING AVERAGE

**¹battle** /'batl/ *n* **1** a fight or hostile encounter between armies, warships, aircraft, etc **2** a fight or combat between two people **3** an extended contest, struggle, or controversy □ compare ENGAGEMENT, ACTION, COMBAT, FIGHT, CAMPAIGN [ME *batel*, fr OF *bataille* battle, fortifying tower, battalion, fr LL *battalia* combat, alter. of *battualia* fencing exercises, fr L *battuere* to beat, of Celt origin; akin to Gaulish anda*bata*, a gladiator; akin to L *fatuus* foolish, Russ *bat* cudgel] – **do/give/join battle** to fight or start fighting – see also HALF **the battle**

**²battle** *vi* **1** to take part in a battle; fight **2** to struggle, strive, or contend vigorously in order to win or achieve something, make progress, etc ⟨*~d against the wind*⟩ ⟨*~d for her rights*⟩ ~ *vt* **1** to force (eg one's way) by battling **2** *archaic or NAm* to fight against – **battler** *n*

**'battle-,axe** *n* **1** a large broad-bladed axe formerly used as a weapon of war **2** a quarrelsome domineering woman

**battle cruiser** *n* a large heavily armed warship that is faster than a battleship

**battle cry** *n* WAR CRY

**battledore** /'batl,daw/ *n* a small light racket used in the game of battledore and shuttlecock [ME *batyldore* wooden bat used in washing clothes, prob modif of OProv *batedor* beating instrument, fr *batre* to beat, fr L *battuere*]

**battledore and shuttlecock** *n* a game from which badminton evolved, that is played by two people, esp children, who attempt to hit a shuttlecock to and fro without letting it touch the ground

**battledress** /'batl,dres/ *n* the uniform worn by soldiers in battle

**battle fatigue** *n* SHELL SHOCK

**battlefield** /'batl,feeld, -,fiald/ *n* **1** a place where a battle is or was fought **2** an area of conflict

**battleground** /'batl,grownd/ *n* a battlefield

**battlement** /'batlmənt/ *n*, **battlements** *n pl* a parapet with open spaces, built on top of a wall and used for defence or decoration [ME *batelment*, fr MF *bataille*] – **battlemented** *adj*

**battler** /'batlə/ *n* **1** one who battles **2** *Austr* one willing to struggle to overcome hardship ⟨*that old Australian breed, the ~s – Australian Women's Weekly*⟩

**battle royal** *n, pl* **battles royal, battle royals** **1** a fight in which more than two people participate; *esp* one in which the last person in the ring or on his/her feet is declared the winner **2** a violent struggle or heated dispute

**battleship** /-,ship/ *n* **1** a warship of the largest and most heavily armed and armoured class **2** *pl but taking sing vb* a naval war game for two players, each of whom has a squared diagram on which he/she marks numbered squares to station his/her own fleet, and records shots made by both players in the effort to locate and sink the opponent's ships [short for *line-of-battle ship*]

**battue** /ba't(y)ooh/ *n* the beating of woodland and bushes to drive game in the direction of hunters; *also* a hunt in which this procedure is used [Fr, fr *battre* to beat]

**batty** /'bati/ *adj, informal* mentally unstable; crazy [³*bat* + ¹*-y* – more at BATS] – **battiness** *n*

**bauble** /'bawbl/ *n* **1** a trinket **2** a staff carried by a court jester **3** something of little value; a trifle [ME *babel*, fr MF]

**baud** /bawd, bohd/ *n, pl* **baud** *also* **bauds** any of several units for measuring the rate at which data is transmitted (eg between a computer and a printer); *specif* one equal to one unit of computer information (⁴BIT) per second [*baud* (telegraphic transmission speed unit), fr J M E Baudot †1903 Fr inventor]

**Bauhaus** /'bow,hows (*Ger* bauhaus)/ *adj* (characteristic) of a German school of architecture and design established in 1919 and noted esp for a programme that combined technology, craftsmanship, and design aesthetics [Ger *Bauhaus*, lit., architecture house, academy founded in Weimar, Germany]

**¹baulk** /bawk/ *vb or n, chiefly Br* BALK

**²baulk,** *NAm chiefly* **balk** *n* **1** the area behind the baulk line on a billiard table **2** any of the areas between the cushions round the edge of a billiard table and the baulk lines

**baulk line** *n* **1** a line across a billiard table near one end behind which the balls to be struck by the cue are placed in making opening shots in billiards and snooker **2** one of four lines parallel to the edges of a billiard table dividing it into nine compartments

**bauxite** /'bawksiet/ *n* an impure claylike mixture of water-containing aluminium oxides and HYDROXIDES that is produced by the weathering of certain rocks and is the principal source of aluminium [Fr, fr Les *Baux,* place near Arles in France] – **bauxitic** *adj*

**Bavarian** /bə'veəri·ən/ *n* **1** a native or inhabitant of Bavaria **2** the HIGH GERMAN dialect of Bavaria and Austria [*Bavaria,* region in S Germany] – **Bavarian** *adj*

**bawbee** /baw'bee/, **baubee** *n* **1** any of various former Scottish coins of small value **2** *Scot* something of little value; a trifle **3** *archaic Scot* an English halfpenny [prob fr Alexander Orrok, laird of Sille*bawby fl*1541 Sc master of the mint]

**bawd** /bawd/ *n* **1** a woman who runs a brothel; MADAM **3 2** a prostitute [ME *bawde,* perh fr MF *baude* bold, merry]

**bawdry** /'bawdri/ *n* bawdy [ME *bawderie,* fr *bawde*]

**¹bawdy** /'bawdi/ *adj* boisterously or humorously indecent ⟨*a* ~ *play*⟩ ⟨~ *language*⟩ [*bawd* + ¹-*y*] – **bawdily** *adv,* **bawdiness** *n*

**²bawdy** *n* suggestive, coarse, or obscene language or behaviour; *also* the use of this in writing or drama ⟨*Shakespeare's* ~⟩ [prob fr ¹*bawdy*]

**bawdy house** *n* a brothel

**¹bawl** /bawl/ *vb* **1** to cry out loudly and unrestrainedly; yell, bellow **2** to cry noisily; wail [ME *baulen,* prob of Scand origin; akin to Icel *baula* to low] – **bawler** *n*

**bawl out** *vt, informal* to reprimand loudly or severely

**²bawl** *n* a loud prolonged cry

**¹bay** /bay/ *adj, esp of a horse* of the colour bay [ME, fr MF *bai,* fr L *badius;* akin to OIr *buide* yellow]

**²bay** *n* **1** a horse with a bay-coloured body and black mane, tail, and lower legs – compare ¹CHESTNUT 4, ¹SORREL 1 **2** a reddish-brown colour

**³bay** *n* **1a** a laurel tree (*Laurus nobilis*) of S Europe with foliage used by the ancient Greeks to crown victors in the Pythian games and whose leaves are used extensively as a herb in cooking **b** any of several shrubs or trees (eg of the genus *Magnolia*) resembling the laurel **2a** an honorary garland or crown, esp of laurel, given for victory or excellence **b bays** *pl,* **bay** *chiefly poetic* honour, fame [ME, berry, fr MF *baie,* fr L *baca*]

**⁴bay** *n* **1** a vertical division of a wall or building between columns or buttresses **2a** a recess in a wall, often containing a window **b** BAY WINDOW **3** any of several compartments in the body of an aircraft ⟨*the bomb* ~⟩ **4** a compartment (eg in a service station) for a car, lorry, etc [ME, fr MF *baee* opening, fr OF, fr fem of *baé,* pp of *baer* to gape, yawn – more at ABEYANCE]

**⁵ba⊕** *vi* to bark with prolonged tones ~ *vt* **1** to bark at ⟨*to* ~ *the moon*⟩ **2** to utter in deep prolonged tones [ME *baien, abaien,* fr OF *abaiier,* of imit origin]

**⁶bay** *n* **1** the position of one unable to retreat and forced to face a foe or danger – + *to* or *at* ⟨*brought his quarry to* ~⟩ ⟨*turned to face them like a fox at* ~⟩ **2** the prolonged barking of dogs ⟨*in full* ~ *the hounds followed the trail*⟩ [ME *bay, abay,* fr OF *abai,* fr *abaiier*] – **hold/keep at bay** to keep off or repel with difficulty ⟨*police* held *the rioters* at bay⟩ ⟨kept *the infection* at bay⟩

**⁷bay** *n* (a land formation resembling) an inlet of a sea, lake, etc, usu smaller than a gulf [ME *baye,* fr MF *baie,* fr OSp *bahia,* perh fr LL *baia*]

**bayadere** /,bie·ə'diə, -'deə/ *n* a fabric with horizontal stripes in strongly contrasted colours [Fr *bayadère* Hindu dancing girl, fr Pg *bailadeira* female dancer, fr *bailar* to dance, fr LL *ballare* – more at BALL]

**bayberry** /'bayb(ə)ri/ *n* **1** a W Indian tree (*Pimenta acris*) of the eucalyptus family, from which a yellow aromatic oil used in BAY RUM is obtained **2** (the waxy grey-white berries of) any of several hardy N American shrubs [³*bay* + *berry*]

**Bayesian** /'bayziən/ *adj* being or relating to a statistical theory or method, often used in decision-making, in which new information can be incorporated into what is already known about the likelihood of an event occurring, thus allowing the refinement or alteration of a previous estimate or decision [Thomas *Bayes* †1761 E mathematician]

**bay leaf** *n* the leaf of the European bay tree (*Laurus nobilis*) used as a herb in cooking

**¹bayonet** /,bayə'net, '---/ *n* a steel blade attached at the muzzle end of a firearm and used in hand-to-hand combat [Fr *baïonnette,* fr *Bayonne,* city in SW France]

**²bayonet** *vt* **-t-** *also* **-tt-** to stab with a bayonet

**bayonet joint** *n* a joint (eg between a light bulb and its socket) in which two parts can be separated by pressing against a retaining spring and then twisting, thereby releasing the pins on one part from slots on the other

**bayou** /'bie·ooh, 'bie·oh/ *n* a sluggish marshy tributary of a river or lake, esp in the southern USA [LaF, fr Choctaw *bayuk*]

**bay rum** *n* a fragrant cosmetic and medicinal liquid originally distilled from the leaves of the W Indian bayberry tree using rum and now usu prepared by mixing the oil from these leaves with alcohol, water, and other oils

**bay salt** *n* common salt obtained by evaporating sea water – compare ROCK SALT [⁷*bay*]

**bay window** *n* a window or series of windows forming a bay or recess in a room and projecting outwards from the wall – compare BOW WINDOW [⁴*bay*]

**bazaar** /bə'zah/ *n* **1** a market, esp in an Oriental country, consisting of rows of shops or stalls selling miscellaneous goods **2** a fair for the sale of miscellaneous articles, esp for charitable purposes ⟨*a church* ~⟩ [Per *bāzār*]

**bazooka** /bə'zoohkə/ *n* a portable cylindrical rocket launcher that fires a rocket able to penetrate several inches of armour plate, and is used by infantrymen as a short range antitank weapon [*bazooka* (a crude musical instrument made of pipes and a funnel), prob of imit origin]

**BCG vaccine, BCG** *n* a vaccine used to protect people against tuberculosis [bacillus Calmette-Guérin, fr Albert *Calmette* † 1933 and Camille *Guérin* †1961 Fr bacteriologists]

**B complex** *n* VITAMIN B COMPLEX

**bdellium** /'deli·əm/ *n* a GUM RESIN similar to myrrh obtained from various trees (genus *Commiphora*) of the E Indies and Africa [ME, fr L, fr Gk *bdellion*]

**be** /bi, bee; *strong bee/ vb, pres 1 sing* **am** /(ə)m; *strong* am/; *2 sing* **are** /ə; *strong* ah/; *3 sing* **is** /z; *strong* iz/; *pl* **are;** *pres subjunctive* **be;** *pres part* **being** /'bee·ing/; *past 1 & 3 sing* **was** /wəz; *strong* woz/; *2 sing* **were** /wə; *strong* wuh/; *pl* **were;** *past subjunctive* **were;** *past part* **been** /bin, been; *strong* been/ *vi* **1a** to equal in meaning; have the same connotation as ⟨*January is the first month*⟩ ⟨*let x* ~ *10*⟩ **b** to represent, symbolize ⟨*God is love*⟩ ⟨*Olivier* was *Hamlet*⟩ ⟨*Valentino* was *romance*⟩ **c** to have identity with ⟨*the first person I met* was *my brother*⟩ ⟨*the difficulty is finding them*⟩ **d** to belong to the class of ⟨*this fish is a trout*⟩ **e** to occupy a specified position in space ⟨*the book is on the table*⟩ ⟨*where* are *the Grampians?*⟩ **f** to take place at a specified time; occur ⟨*the concert* was *last night*⟩ **g** to have a specified qualification ⟨*the leaves* are *green*⟩ ⟨~ *quick*⟩, destination ⟨~ *off*⟩, origin ⟨*she is from India*⟩, occupation ⟨*what's he up to?*⟩, function or purpose ⟨*it's for you*⟩ ⟨*it's to cut with*⟩, cost or value ⟨*the book is 5*⟩, or standpoint ⟨~ *against terrorism*⟩ **2** to have reality or actuality; exist ⟨*I think, therefore I* am⟩ ⟨*once upon a time there was a castle*⟩ ~ **va 1** – used with the past participle of transitive verbs as a passive-voice auxiliary ⟨*the money* was *found*⟩ ⟨*the house is* ~ing *built*⟩ **2** – used as the auxiliary of the present participle in progressive tenses expressing continuous action ⟨*he is reading*⟩ ⟨*I have been sleeping*⟩ or arrangement in advance ⟨*we are leaving tomorrow*⟩ **3** – used with the past participle of some intransitive verbs as an auxiliary forming archaic perfect tenses ⟨*my father* is *come* – Jane Austen⟩ **4** – used with *to* and an infinitive to express destiny ⟨*he was to become famous*⟩ ⟨*they were to have been married*⟩, arrangement in advance ⟨*I am to interview him today*⟩, obligation or necessity ⟨*you are not to smoke*⟩, or possibility ⟨*it was nowhere to be found*⟩ ⟨*you weren't to know*⟩ □ (*vi 1*) used regularly as the linking verb for stating or denying facts; used in the past SUBJUNCTIVE or often in the INDICATIVE to express unreal conditions ⟨*if I were you*⟩ ⟨*if I wasn't a Catholic* – Daily Mirror⟩; often in British English used of groups in the plural form ⟨*Somerset* were *28 for 2* – The Observer⟩ *usage* The combinations **being** *as,* **being** *as how,* and **being** *that* ⟨△ **being** *as how it's Sunday, he's still in bed*⟩ are nonstandard, and should be replaced by *be-*

*cause* or *as*. [ME *been*, fr OE *bēon;* akin to OHG *bim* am, L *fui* I have been, *futurus* about to be, *fieri* to become, be done, Gk *phynai* to be born, be by nature, *phyein* to bring forth] – **be oneself** to behave in a normal, unconstrained, or unpretentious manner

**be-** /bi-/ *prefix* 1 (*vb* → *vb*) on; round; all over ⟨be*daub*⟩ ⟨bes*mear*⟩ 2 (*vb* → *vb*) to a great or greater degree; thoroughly ⟨be*fuddle*⟩ ⟨be*rate*⟩ ⟨be*labour*⟩ 3a (*vb* → *vb*) excessively; ostentatiously **b** (*adj* → *adj*) wearing (a specified article of dress) ⟨be*wigged*⟩ ⟨be*ribboned*⟩ **4a** (*vb* → *vb*) about; to; at; upon; against; across ⟨be*stride*⟩ ⟨be*speak*⟩ 5 (*adj, n* → *vb*) make; cause to be; treat as ⟨be*little*⟩ ⟨be*fool*⟩ ⟨be*friend*⟩ 6 (*n* → *vb*) affect, afflict, provide, or cover with, esp excessively ⟨be*calmed*⟩ ⟨be*devil*⟩ [ME, fr OE *bi-, be-;* akin to OE *bī* by, near – more at BY]

¹**beach** /beech/ *n* a usu gently sloping seashore or lakeshore, usu covered by sand or pebbles; *esp* the part of this between the high and low water marks [origin unknown]

²**beach** *vt* to run or drive (a boat or ship) ashore

**beach ball** *n* a large light usu brightly coloured ball for use at the beach

**beach buggy** *n* a usu small sturdily built open car with very wide tyres, designed originally for travel over rough ground (e g beaches)

**beachcomber** /-,kohmə/ *n* a person who searches along a shore for useful or salable articles; *esp* a white man on the islands of the S Pacific who earns a living by doing this – **beachcomb** *vb*

**beach flea** *n* SANDHOPPER (tiny jumping animal)

**beachhead** /-,hed/ *n* an area on a shore that has been captured from the enemy and on which troops and supplies may be landed

**beach-la-mar** /,beech lə 'mah/ *n* BÊCHE-DE-MER 2 (form of pidgin English) [modif of Pg *bicho do mar*]

**beacon** /'beekən/ *n* 1 a guiding or warning fire commonly on a hill, tower, or pole; *also, Br* a high conspicuous hill suitable for or used in the past for such a fire 2a a lighthouse or similar signal used to guide shipping in dangerous waters **b** RADIO BEACON (radio transmitter that emits signals to guide aircraft) 3 a source of light or inspiration [ME *beken*, fr OE *bēacen* sign; akin to OHG *bouhhan* sign (cf BECKON)] – **beacon** *vb*

¹**bead** /beed/ *n* 1 a small ball (e g of wood or glass) pierced for threading on a string or wire 2 *pl* a rosary 3 a small ball-shaped body: e g **3a** a drop of liquid ⟨~s *of sweat stood on his forehead*⟩ **b** a bubble formed in or on a drink **c** a small metal knob on a firearm used as a front SIGHT (device that guides the eye in aiming) 4 a clear glassy drop of BORAX or a similar substance, that when melted with a metal oxide takes on a characteristic colour and that is used to test for the presence of certain metals in a sample of ore or other metal-containing mixture **5a** a projecting rim, band, or moulding (e g round the top of a glass jar or as a decoration on furniture) **b** the inner edge of a pneumatic tyre, that locks onto the wheel rim [ME *bede* prayer, prayer bead, fr OE *bed, gebed* prayer; akin to OE *biddan* to entreat, pray – more at BID] – **draw a bead on** 1 to take aim at 2 to single out for attention [*bead* 3c] – **say/tell one's beads** to pray using a rosary

²**bead** *vt* to supply or decorate with beads or beading ~ *vi, of a liquid* to form into beads

**beading** /'beeding/ *n* 1 material decorated with or consisting of beads 2 a narrow rounded ornamental moulding used on furniture, walls, etc 3 ornamental work in beads 4 a narrow lacy panel or trimming (e g on lingerie) having holes through which ribbon, elastic, etc can be threaded 5 BEAD 5b

**beadle** /'beedl/ *n* a minor parish official in former times, whose duties included ushering and keeping order in church [ME *bedel*, fr OE *bydel;* akin to OHG *butil* bailiff, OE *bēodan* to command – more at BID]

**beadroll** /'beed,rohl/ *n* a list of names; a catalogue [fr the reading in church of a list of names of people for whom prayers are to be said]

**beadsman** /'beedzmən/ *n* 1 a person in former times who prayed for another's soul, often in return for food or payment 2 *archaic* a resident of an almshouse

**beady** /'beedi/ *adj* 1 resembling or covered with beads 2 *esp of eyes* small, round, and shiny with interest or greed – **beadily** *adv*

**beagle** /'beegl/ *n* (any of) a breed of small hound with short legs and a smooth coat, often used for hunting rabbits and

hares [ME *begle*, perh fr MF *beegueule* noisy person, fr *beer* to open wide + *gueule* throat]

**beagling** /'beegling/ *n* the sport of hunting on foot with beagles – **beagler** *n*

**beak** /beek/ *n* **1a** the hard, often pointed, bill of a bird **b(1)** any of various rigid projecting mouth parts (e g of a turtle) **b(2)** the elongated sucking or piercing mouth of some insects (e g the bedbug); ROSTRUM 3b **c** *informal* the human nose 2 a pointed or projecting structure or formation: e g **2a** a metal-tipped beam projecting from the bow of an ancient galley for ramming an enemy ship **b** the pouring spout or lip of a container (e g a jug or bucket) **c** an architectural moulding resembling a bird's beak 3 *chiefly Br slang* **3a** a magistrate **b** a schoolmaster [ME *bec*, fr OF, fr L *beccus*, of Gaulish origin; (3) perh of different origin] – **beaked** *adj*

**beaked whale** /beekt/ *n* any of various TOOTHED WHALES (family Ziphiidae) with visible teeth usu only in the lower jaw

**beaker** /'beekə/ *n* 1 a large drinking cup with a wide mouth; a mug 2 a cylindrical flat-bottomed typically glass container usu with a pouring lip, that is used esp by chemists and pharmacists [ME *biker*, fr ON *bikarr*, prob fr OS *bikeri;* akin to OHG *behhari* beaker; both fr a prehistoric WGmc word borrowed fr ML *bicarius* beaker, fr Gk *bikos* earthen jug (cf PITCHER)]

**Beaker Folk** /'beekə/ *n taking pl vb* a group of prehistoric peoples living in Europe in the late Neolithic and early BRONZE AGE (in the centuries around 2000 BC), whose culture was characterized by finely decorated pottery beakers which they buried with their dead, esp in round burial mounds

**be-all and end-all** *n the* chief factor; *the* essential element

¹**beam** /beem/ *n* **1a** a long piece of heavy timber suitable for use in building **b** a wood or metal cylinder in a loom on which the yarns that run lengthways or the finished cloth are wound **c** the central shaft of a plough to which the handles, blade, etc are attached **d** the bar of a balance from which scales hang **e** any of the principal horizontal structural supports of a building or ship ⟨*a steel* ~ *supporting a floor*⟩ **f** the width of a ship at its widest part **2a** a ray or shaft of radiation, esp light **b** a collection of nearly parallel rays (e g X rays) or of particles (e g electrons) moving in nearly parallel paths **c** (the course indicated by) a radio signal transmitted continuously in one direction as a guide for aircraft or missiles 3 the main stem of a deer's antler 4 BALANCE BEAM (beam used for exercises in gymnastics) – usu + *the* 5 *informal* the width of the buttocks ⟨*broad in the* ~⟩ [ME *beem*, fr OE *bēam* tree, beam; akin to OHG *boum* tree] – **off (the) beam** wrong, irrelevant [*beam* 2c] – **on the beam** proceeding or operating correctly

²**beam** *vt* 1 to emit in beams or as a beam 2 to aim (a broadcast) in a particular direction ~ *vi* 1 to send out beams of light 2 to smile with joy

,**beam-'ends** *n pl, Br informal* the buttocks – **on her beam-ends** *of a ship* about to capsize – **on one's beam-ends** near the end of one's (financial) resources

**beam engine** *n* an early form of engine powered by steam, in which steam entering a large vertical cylinder causes one end of a pivoted horizontal metal bar to move up and down, this motion being transmitted to the other end of the bar which is attached to a pump or similar device

**beamer** /'beemə/ *n* a ball bowled in cricket that is designed to disconcert the batsman by passing or hitting him/her at above waist height before bouncing

**beamy** /'beemi/ *adj* 1 *of a ship* broad in the beam 2 *poetic* emitting beams of light; radiant ⟨*Day's* ~ *banner up the east is borne* – A E Housman⟩

¹**bean** /been/ *n* **1a** (the often edible seed of) any of various erect or climbing plants of the pea family (esp genera *Phaseolus* and *Vicia*) **b** a bean pod used when young as a vegetable – compare FRENCH BEAN, RUNNER 7 **c** (a plant producing) any of various seeds or fruits that resemble beans or bean pods ⟨*catalpa* ~⟩ 2 *informal* **2a** a valueless item ⟨*not worth a* ~⟩ **b** the smallest possible amount of money ⟨*gave up my job and haven't a* ~⟩ 3 *Br informal* a person, esp a man – not now in vogue; esp in *old bean* [ME *bene*, fr OE *bēan;* akin to OHG *bōna* bean] – **full of beans** lively, energetic – **spill the beans** to divulge a secret; GIVE THE GAME AWAY

²**bean** *vt, chiefly NAm slang* to strike (a person) on the head with an object [*bean* (head); fr its shape]

**bean aphid** *n* BLACK BEAN APHID (insect and garden pest)

**beanbag** /-,bag/ *n* 1 a small fabric bag that is filled with dried beans or peas and used in games or as a toy 2 a large loosely stuffed cushion usu containing granules or fragments of plastic foam, used as an informal low chair that moulds itself to support the sitter

**bean curd** *n* a soft cheeselike food that is much used in Eastern cooking and is prepared from soya-bean milk

**beanfeast** /-,feest/ *n, Br informal* a festivity, celebration – no longer in vogue

**beano** /'beenoh/ *n, pl* **beanos** *informal* a beanfeast [by shortening & alter.]

**beanpole** /-,pohl/ *n* **1** a pole for a climbing plant (eg a bean) to climb up **2** *informal* a very tall thin person

**bean shoot** *n* BEAN SPROUT

**bean sprout** *n* the sprout of a bean seed, esp that of a MUNG BEAN, used as a vegetable esp in Chinese dishes

**bean tree** *n* CATALPA (N American and Asian tree)

[1]**bear** /beə/ *n, pl* **bears**, (*1*) **bears**, *esp collectively* **bear 1** any of a family (Ursidae) of large heavy mammals having long shaggy hair and feeding largely on fruit and insects as well as on flesh **2** a surly, uncouth, or shambling person **3** a speculator on the STOCK EXCHANGE who sells shares, commodities, etc in expectation of a decline in prices, in order to buy them back more cheaply, thus making a profit – compare BULL [ME *bere*, fr OE *bera;* akin to OE *brūn* brown; (3) prob fr the proverbial phrase *selling the bearskin before catching the bear*]

[2]**bear** *vb* **bore** /baw/; **borne** *also* **born** /bawn/ *vt* **1a** to carry, transport ⟨~ *gifts*⟩ – often in combination ⟨*airborne troops*⟩ **b** to carry or own as equipment ⟨~ *arms*⟩ **c** to entertain mentally ⟨~ *malice*⟩ **d** to behave, conduct ⟨~ing *himself well*⟩ **e** to have or show as a feature ⟨~ *scars*⟩ ⟨~ *no relationship*⟩ **f** to give as testimony ⟨~ *false witness*⟩ **g** to have as an identification ⟨bore *the name of John*⟩ **2a** to give birth to – compare BORN **b** to produce as yield ⟨~ *apples*⟩ ⟨~ *interest*⟩ **c** to contain – often in combination ⟨*oil-bearing shale*⟩ **3a** to support the weight of **b** to accept the presence of; tolerate ⟨~ *pain*⟩ ⟨*couldn't ~ his wife's family*⟩ **c** to sustain, incur ⟨~ *the cost*⟩ ⟨~ *the responsibility*⟩ **d** to admit of; allow ⟨*it won't ~ repeating*⟩ **e** to provoke, invite ⟨*his odd behaviour* ~s *watching*⟩ ~ *vi* **1a** to become directed ⟨*bring guns to ~ on a target*⟩ **b** to go or extend in a usu specified direction ⟨~ *South*⟩ ⟨*the road* ~s *to the right*⟩ **2** to have relevance; apply ⟨*facts* ~ing *on the situation*⟩ **3** to support weight or strain **4** to produce fruit; yield [ME *beren*, fr OE *beran*; akin to OHG *beran* to carry, L *ferre*, Gk *pherein*] – **bearable, bearably** *adv* – **be borne in upon one** to become one's conviction – see also BRING **to bear, bear** FRUIT

*synonyms* Bear, suffer, and endure can all mean "put up with something unpleasant or trying". Bear and suffer have associations of difficulty or painfulness respectively, carried over from their other senses. Endure stresses length of time and not giving in ⟨she endured the noise as long as she could⟩. Stand and abide are usually found with can and a negative; bear and endure may be used like this too. *Not* bear and *not* endure suggest dislike and intolerance respectively, while *not* stand and *not* abide suggest repugnance and impatient intolerance. Stand used positively implies bearing something without flinching or giving in. Tolerate suggests overcoming one's repugnance to people or behaviour by an act of will. See [1]CARRY *usage* see BORNE

**bear down** *vt* to overcome, overwhelm ⟨borne down *by his troubles*⟩ ~ *vi, of a woman in childbirth* to exert a voluntary muscular pressure in order to force the baby downwards

**bear down on** *vt* **1** to weigh heavily on **2** to come towards purposefully or threateningly

**bear out** *vt* to confirm, substantiate ⟨*research* bore out his hypothesis⟩

**bear up** *vi* to endure hardship, esp with courage and cheerfulness ~ *vt* to support, encourage

**bear with** *vt* to show patience or indulgence towards ⟨bear with *the old bore for a while longer*⟩

**bearbaiting** /-,bayting/ *n* the practice of setting dogs on a captive bear, that was formerly a popular entertainment

**bearberry** /'beəb(ə)ri/ *n* a trailing evergreen plant (*Arctostaphylos uva-ursi*) of the heather family with astringent foliage and red berries [[1]bear + berry]

[1]**beard** /biəd/ *n* **1a** the hair that grows on the lower part of a man's face, usu excluding the moustache **2** a hairy or bristly appendage or tuft: eg **2a** a tuft of hair on the chin of a goat **b** the cluster of bristles at the base of the beak of certain birds **c** the gills of an oyster **d** the BYSSUS (strong threads used for attachment) of mussels and related animals **e** the tuft of bristly hairs (AWNS) on plants such as barley and wheat **3** the space beneath a letter on a page of type [ME *berd*, fr OE *beard;* akin

to OHG *bart* beard, L *barba*] – **bearded** *adj*, **beardedness** *n*, **beardless** *adj*

[2]**beard** *vt* **1** to confront and oppose boldly and often with effrontery; defy **2** to remove the beard of (eg a mussel or oyster)

**bearded tit** *n* a small long-tailed European bird (*Panurus biarmicus*) that frequents secluded reedy places

**bearer** /'beərə/ *n* one who or that which bears: eg **a** a porter; *esp* one who carries equipment on an expedition, safari, etc **b** a native servant of a European, esp in former times in India and Africa **c** a pallbearer **d** one holding an order for payment (eg a cheque or bank note), esp if marked payable to the bearer

**bear garden** *n* a scene of great noise or tumult [fr the rowdiness of places used for bearbaiting]

**bear hug** *n* a rough tight embrace

**bearing** /'beəring/ *n* **1** the manner in which one bears or conducts oneself ⟨a man of erect and soldierly ~⟩ – compare DEPORTMENT, DEMEANOUR, [1]AIR, MIEN, MANNER, CARRIAGE **2** the act, power, or time of bringing forth offspring or fruit **3a** an object, surface, or point that supports **b** **bearing, bearings** *pl* a machine part in which another part turns or slides **c** the part of a beam or post that rests on its supports **4** an emblem or figure on a heraldic shield **5a** the compass direction of one point as measured from another (eg one's present position) **b** a determination of position, esp one's own position ⟨take a ~⟩ **c** *pl* comprehension of one's position, environment, or situation ⟨lost his ~s⟩ **6** relevance, connection – usu + *on* ⟨has no ~ on the matter⟩

**bearing rein** *n* CHECKREIN 1 (rein from bit to saddle obliging the horse to hold its head up)

**bearish** /'beərish/ *adj* **1** resembling a bear in roughness, gruffness, or surliness **2** marked by, tending to cause, or fearful of falling prices (eg in a stock market) – **bearishly** *adv*, **bearishness** *n*

**béarnaise sauce** /,bayə'nayz/ *n* a rich sauce made with egg yolks and flavoured with wine, onion, and tarragon [Fr *béarnaise*, fem of *béarnais* of Béarn, fr *Béarn*, region & former province of France]

**bearskin** /-,skin/ *n* **1** an article made of the skin of a bear **2** a tall black fur hat worn by a member of the Brigade of Guards

**beast** /beest/ *n* **1a** an animal as distinguished from a plant **b** a 4-footed mammal as distinguished from human beings, lower VERTEBRATE animals, and INVERTEBRATE animals **c** an animal under human control (eg a cow) **2** a contemptible person; a brute [ME *beste*, fr OF, fr L *bestia*]

**beastings** /'beestingz/ *n taking sing or pl vb, NAm* BEESTINGS (first milk given by a cow after calving)

[1]**beastly** /'beestli/ *adj* **1** of or resembling a beast; bestial **2** *chiefly informal* abominable, disagreeable ⟨~ *weather*⟩ – **beastliness** *n*

[2]**beastly** *adv, chiefly informal* very ⟨a ~ cold day⟩

**beast of burden** *n* an animal employed to carry heavy loads or to perform other strenuous work (eg pulling a plough)

[1]**beat** /beet/ *vb* **beat; beaten** /'beet(ə)n/, **beat** *vt* **1** to strike repeatedly: **1a** to hit repeatedly so as to inflict pain – often + *up* **b** to dash or strike directly against (something) forcefully and repeatedly ⟨waves ~ing *the shore*⟩ **c** to flap or thrash at vigorously ⟨a trapped bird ~ing *the air*⟩ **d** to strike at (eg undergrowth) or range over (eg woodland) (as if) in order to rouse game **e** to mix (esp food) by stirring; whip ⟨~ *the egg whites until they are stiff*⟩ **f** to strike repeatedly in order to produce music or a signal ⟨~ *a drum*⟩ **2a** to drive or force by blows ⟨to ~ *off the savage dogs*⟩ **b** to pound into a powder, paste, or pulp **c** to make by repeated treading or driving over ⟨~ *a path*⟩ **d(1)** to dislodge by repeated hitting ⟨~ *the dust from the carpet*⟩ **d(2)** to lodge securely by repeated striking ⟨~ *a stake into the ground*⟩ **e** to shape by beating; *esp* to flatten thin by blows ⟨gold ~en *into strips*⟩ **f** to sound or express, esp by drumbeat **3** to cause to strike or flap repeatedly ⟨~ *his foot nervously on the ground*⟩ **4a** to overcome, defeat; *also* to surpass ⟨~ *his opponent in a straight fight*⟩ ⟨~ *her in the spelling test*⟩ **b** to prevail despite ⟨~ *the odds*⟩ ⟨~ *the system*⟩ **c** to leave dispirited, irresolute, or hopeless ⟨a failure at fifty, a ~en *man*⟩ **d** to be or to bowl a ball that is too good for (a batsman) to hit **5a** to reach a place or achieve an object ahead of ⟨wanted to make a bid, but the rival company ~ *them to it*⟩ ⟨~ *him to the finishing post*⟩ **b** to report a news item in advance of **6** to indicate by beating ⟨~ *time*⟩ **7** *informal* to bewilder, baffle ⟨it ~s *me how she does it*⟩ **8** *NAm informal* to cheat, swindle ⟨~ *them out of several million dollars*⟩ ~ *vi* **1a**

to dash, strike ⟨*the rain was* ~*ing on the roof*⟩ **b** to glare or strike with oppressive intensity ⟨*the sun was* ~*ing down*⟩ **2a** to pulsate, throb ⟨*the patient's heart was* ~*ing steadily once more*⟩ **b** to produce a sound on being struck ⟨*could hear the drums* ~*ing*⟩ **3** *of a vibration* to combine with another vibration of an only slightly different frequency to produce a regular pulsing sound, signal, etc **4a** to strike repeatedly – usu + *on* or *upon* ⟨*their air attack still* ~*ing upon us* – Sir Winston Churchill⟩ **b** to strike the air; flap ⟨*the bird's wings* ~ *frantically*⟩ **c** to strike bushes or undergrowth in order to rouse game **5** to progress with much difficulty; *specif, of a sailing vessel* to make way at sea against the wind by sailing in a zigzag line [ME *beten*, fr OE *bēatan*; akin to OHG *bōzan* to beat, L *-futare* to beat, *fustis* club; (5) perh of different origin] – **beat it** *informal* to hurry away; scram – see also **beat one's** BRAINS out, **beat the** CLOCK, **beat to the** PUNCH

**beat about** *vi* **1** to search anxiously ⟨beat about *for a solution to the problem*⟩ **2** *of a ship* to change direction

**beat down** *vt* **1** to reduce by argument or other influence ⟨*competition should* beat *the price* down⟩ **2** to persuade (someone) to reduce a price ⟨*she wanted £650 for the car but we managed to* beat *her* down *to £600*⟩

²**beat** *n* **1a** a single stroke or blow, esp in a series; *also* a pulsation, throb ⟨*her heart missed a* ~⟩ **b** a sound produced (as if) by beating ⟨*the* ~ *of the drums*⟩ **2** one swing of the pendulum or oscillation of the BALANCE (small wheel that turns to and fro) of a clock or watch **3** any of the regular pulsing sounds or signals produced by combining sound or radio waves or electric currents having slightly different frequencies **4a** a metrical or rhythmic stress in poetry or music or the rhythmic effect of these stresses **b** the tempo indicated (eg by a conductor) to a musical performer **c** the pronounced rhythm that is the characteristic driving force in jazz or rock music; *also* rock music **5** the route or area regularly patrolled by a policeman, sentry, etc ⟨*a constable on the* ~⟩ **6** the reporting of a news story ahead of competitors – compare SCOOP **7** the act or an instance of rousing game by beating; *also* the area of woodland, undergrowth, etc in which this takes place **8** *nautical* an instance of beating against the wind; *also* any stretch (TACK 3b) of the zigzag course involved in this **9** *NAm slang* a deadbeat, scrounger

³**beat** *adj* **1** of or being beatniks ⟨~ *poets*⟩ **2** *informal* exhausted [short for *beaten*, pp of ¹*beat*; (1) influenced by ²*beat* 4c]

⁴**beat** *n* a beatnik

**beaten** /'beet(ə)n/ *adj* **1** hammered into a desired shape ⟨~ *gold*⟩ **2** much trodden and worn smooth; *also* familiar, well-known ⟨*off the* ~ *track*⟩ **3a** exhausted **b** defeated

**beater** /'beetə/ *n* **1** one who or that which beats: eg **1a** any of various hand-held implements for whisking or beating ⟨*an egg* ~⟩ ⟨*a carpet* ~⟩ **b** a rotary blade attached to an electric mixer **c** a stick for beating a gong **2** one who strikes bushes, undergrowth, etc to rouse game

**beatific** /,bee·ə'tifik/ *adj* **1** of, possessing, or giving great happiness or blessedness **2** having a blissful or benign appearance; saintly, angelic ⟨*a* ~ *smile*⟩ [L *beatificus* making happy, fr *beatus* happy, fr pp of *beare* to bless; akin to L *bonus* good – more at BOUNTY] – **beatifically** *adv*

**beatific vision** *n*, *Christianity* the direct knowledge of God enjoyed by those in heaven

**beatify** /bee'atifie/ *vt* **1** to make supremely happy **2** to declare (a deceased person) worthy of being honoured by Catholics by conferring the title "Blessed" [MF *beatifier*, fr LL *beatificare*, fr L *beatus*] – **beatification** *n*

**beating** /'beeting/ *n* **1** an act of striking with repeated blows so as to injure, damage, or punish; *also* the injury or damage thus inflicted ⟨*gave the boys a* ~ *for stealing apples*⟩ **2** a throbbing **3** a defeat, setback ⟨*our plans took a real* ~⟩

**beating reed** *n* a thin flat piece of metal, cane, etc (REED 4a) in a musical instrument, that vibrates against the edges of an air opening (eg in a clarinet or organ pipe) to which it is attached – compare FREE REED

**beatitude** /bi'atityoohd, -choohd/ *n* **1a** a state of great happiness or blessedness **b** – used as a title for a bishop, esp of an Eastern church **2** *often cap* any of a series of sayings of Jesus beginning in the Authorized Version of the Bible with the words "Blessed are" [L *beatitudo*, fr *beatus*]

**beatnik** /'beetnik/ *n* a person, esp in the 1950s and 1960s, who rejected the moral attitudes of established society (eg by unconventional behaviour and dress) [³*beat* + *-nik*]

**beau** /boh/ *n*, *pl* **beaux**, **beaus** /bohz/ *archaic* **1** a dandy **2** a man who is a frequent escort of a girl or woman; a sweetheart, lover [Fr, fr *beau* beautiful, fr L *bellus* pretty]

**Beaufort scale** /'bohfawt/ *n* a scale that indicates the force of the wind by numbers from 0 to 12 [Sir Francis *Beaufort* †1857 E admiral]

**beau geste** /,boh 'zhest/ *n*, *pl* **beaux gestes** /~/, **beau gestes** /zhest(s)/ a graceful, magnanimous, or ingratiating gesture [Fr, lit., beautiful gesture]

**beau ideal** /,boh ie'deel/ *n*, *pl* **beau ideals** /ie'deelz/ the perfect type or model – often + *of* [Fr *beau idéal* ideal beauty]

**Beaujolais** /'bohzhəlay/ *n* a red table wine made in S Burgundy in France [Fr, fr *Beaujolais*, region of central France]

**beau monde** /,boh 'mond/ *n*, *pl* **beaux mondes** /~/, **beaux mondes** /mond(z)/ the world of high society and fashion [Fr, lit., fine world]

¹**beaut** /byooht/ *n*, *chiefly Austr & NZ informal* a brilliant or outstanding example; BEAUTY 3 [short for *beauty*]

²**beaut** *adj, chiefly Austr & NZ informal* fine, marvellous

**beauteous** /'byoohti·əs, -tyəs/ *adj, chiefly poetic* beautiful [ME, fr *beaute*] – **beauteously** *adv*, **beauteousness** *n*

**beautician** /byooh'tish(ə)n/ *n* a person who gives or specializes in beauty treatments (eg for the skin or nails) [*beauty* + *-ician*]

**beautiful** /'byoohtif(ə)l/ *adj* **1** having qualities of beauty; exciting aesthetic pleasure or keenly delighting the senses **2** generally pleasing; excellent – **beautifully** *adv*

**synonyms** Beautiful, lovely, comely, fair, pretty, handsome, and good-looking all describe what gives pleasure to the mind, spirit, or senses, and especially to the eyes. **Beautiful** conveys a closeness to perfection which gives intellectual and/or spiritual satisfaction as well as sensual pleasure ⟨*a* **beautiful** *sunset*⟩. **Lovely** suggests, rather, personal involvement and an emotional delight, with a lingering contemplation by the senses ⟨*her* **lovely** *eyes fascinated him*⟩. **Pretty**, in contrast to **beautiful** and **lovely**, suggests attractiveness of a less mature and more superficial kind. Used positively, it conveys grace and delicacy; charm rather than perfection, and daintiness rather than grandeur. Used disparagingly, it stresses the lack of intellectual or spiritual satisfaction gained from something which is merely pleasing to look at. **Comely** and **fair** are not used much now, but suggest a fresh and wholesome attractiveness of appearance. Of the above terms, **beautiful**, **lovely**, **fair**, and **pretty** are not usually applied to men, but **handsome** may be used for either men or women. More detached than either **beautiful** or **lovely**, it describes something which gives aesthetic rather than emotional or spiritual pleasure, by satisfying demands of form, taste or proportion, and suggests a certain dignity ⟨*a* **handsome**, *rather proud face*⟩ ⟨*a* **handsome** *town house in Bath*⟩. **Good-looking** is a modern expression which applies to either men or women. **antonym** ugly

**beautiful people** *n pl*, *often cap B&P* rich people associated with international society – compare JET SET

**beautify** /'byoohtifie/ *vt* to make beautiful; adorn **beautifier** *n*, **beautification** *n* synonyms see DECORATE

**beauty** /'byoohti/ *n* **1** the qualities in a person or thing that give pleasure to the senses or pleasurably exalt the mind or spirit; loveliness **2** a beautiful person or thing; *esp* a beautiful woman **3** a brilliant, extreme, or outstanding example or instance ⟨*that mistake was a* ~⟩ **4** a particularly advantageous or excellent quality ⟨*the* ~ *of my idea is that it costs so little*⟩ [ME *beaute*, fr OF *biauté*, fr *bel*, *biau* beautiful, fr L *bellus* pretty; akin to L *bonus* good – more at BOUNTY]

**beauty parlour** *n* BEAUTY SALON

**beauty queen** *n* a girl or woman who wins a beauty contest

**beauty salon** *n* an establishment where professional beauty treatment (eg hairdressing, treatments for the face, and manicures) is provided, esp for women

**beauty sleep** *n* sleep considered as being beneficial to a person's beauty; *also* sleep during the early part of the night, esp before midnight

**beauty spot** *n* **1** ¹PATCH 2 (small piece of dark silk formerly worn on the face); *also* a similar decorative mark painted on with make-up **2** a mole or any similar natural mark on the skin **3** a beautiful scenic area

**beaux arts** /,bohz 'ah (*Fr* boz ar)/ *n pl* FINE ARTS (painting, sculpture, etc) [Fr]

**beaux esprits** /,bohz e'spree (*Fr* boz ɛspri)/ *pl of* BEL ESPRIT (witty or clever person)

¹**beaver** /'beevə/ *n, pl* **beavers**, (*1a*) **beavers**, *esp collectively* **beaver 1a** either of two large rodents (genus *Castor*) that have webbed hind feet and a broad flat tail, build dams and homes

(LODGES) with underwater entrances, and are hunted for their valuable fur and CASTOR (secretion used in medicine and perfumes) **b** the fur or pelt of the beaver **2** a hat made of beaver fur or a fabric imitation **3** a heavy fabric of felted wool having a soft pile (NAP) on both sides **4** an energetic hardworking person – compare EAGER BEAVER [ME *bever*, fr OE *beofor*; akin to OHG *bibar* beaver, OE *brūn* brown]

²**beaver** *vi* to work energetically 〈~ing *away at the problem*〉

³**beaver** *n* a movable piece on a medieval helmet protecting the lower part of the face [ME *baviere*, fr MF]

**beaverboard** /-ˌbawd/ *n* a light board of compressed wood fibre used for partitions and ceilings [fr *Beaver Board*, a trademark]

**bebop** /'beeˌbop/ *n* BOP (form of jazz) [imit] – **bebopper** *n*

**becalm** /bi'kahm/ *vt* to keep (a sailing vessel) motionless by lack of wind

¹**because** /bi'koz, bə-, -kəz/ *conj* **1** for the reason that; since 〈*rested ~ he was tired*〉 **2** and the proof is that 〈*they must be in, ~ the light's on*〉 **3** the fact that; that – used in expressions of reason or cause 〈*the latter fact, we suggest, was ~ the world was ... particularly attentive at that moment to the subject of violence – TLS*〉 [ME *because that, because*, fr *by cause that*] – **because of 1** as a result of **2** for the sake of

   *usage* **1** The use of **because** in sentences like 〈**because** *he's old doesn't mean he's stupid*〉 or 〈*the importance of this rule is* **because** *it prevents cheating*〉 is disapproved of by some people, who prefer 〈*the fact that he's old doesn't mean he's stupid*〉 〈*the importance of this rule is that it prevents cheating*〉. See ¹REASON **2** Negative sentences with **because** may be ambiguous. Does 〈*she didn't marry her* **because** *he was poor*〉 mean that she renounced her on the grounds of his poverty, or that she married her for some other reason? **3** In sense **2**, where the main statement is more important than the reason, **for** or **since** may be preferable to **because** in formal writing 〈*they must be in,* **for** *the light is on*〉. See ¹COS, ¹DUE

²**because** *adv, informal* because of something forgotten or unmentionable 〈*I did it – well, just ~*〉

**beccafico** /ˌbekə'feekoh/ *n, pl* **beccaficos, beccaficoes** any of various songbirds that are sometimes eaten as a delicacy, esp in Italy [It, fr *beccare* to peck + *fico* fig, fr L *ficus*]

**béchamel** /'bayshəmel/ (*Fr* beʃameːl) *n* a white sauce made with a ROUX (mixture of fat and flour heated and blended together) and milk in which vegetables and herbs have been infused and that is sometimes enriched with cream – compare VELOUTÉ [Fr *sauce béchamelle*, fr Louis de *Béchamel* †1703 Fr courtier]

**bechance** /bi'chahns/ *vb, archaic* to befall

**bêche-de-mer** /ˌbesh də 'meə/ *n, pl* **bêches-de-mer, bêche-de-mer** /~/ **1** TREPANG (sea creature) **2** *cap B&M* a pidgin English used esp in the W Pacific [Fr, fr Pg *bicho do mar*, lit., sea grub; (2) fr the importance of the trepang in the commerce for which the language is chiefly used]

¹**beck** /bek/ *n* a brook, esp in N England; *esp* a mountain stream with a pebbly bed [ME *bek*, fr ON *bekkr*; akin to OE *bæc* brook, OHG *bah*, MIr *būal* flowing water]

²**beck** *n* [ME, nod, bow, gesture of command, fr *becken, beknen*] – **at somebody's beck and call** in continual readiness to obey any command from somebody

**becket** /'bekit/ *n, nautical* a device for holding something in place; *specif* a bracket, loop of rope, hook, etc for securing ropes, posts, etc supporting the sails of a ship [origin unknown]

**beckon** /'bekən/ *vi* **1** to summon or signal, typically with a wave or nod **2** to appear inviting; attract ~ *vt* to beckon to [ME *beknen*, fr OE *bīecnan*, fr *bēacen* sign – more at BEACON] – **beckon** *n*

**becloud** /bi'klowd/ *vt, formal* **1** to darken or obscure (as if) with a cloud **2** to confuse, muddle 〈*prejudices that ~ his judgment*〉

**become** /bi'kum/ *vb* **became** /bi'kaym/, **become** *vi* **1** to come into existence **2** to come to be 〈~ *sick*〉 〈*became party leader*〉 ~ *vt, formal* to suit or be suitable to 〈*her clothes ~ her*〉 [ME *becomen* to come to, become, fr OE *becuman*, fr *be-* + *cuman* to come] – **become of** *vt* to happen to 〈*what* became of *that girl who always came top at school?*〉

**becoming** /bi'kuming/ *adj* suitable, fitting; *esp* attractively suitable – **becomingly** *adv* **synonyms** see ³FIT

¹**bed** /bed/ *n* **1a** a piece of furniture on or in which one may lie and sleep and which usu includes a bedstead, mattress, and

**bedding** 〈*threw himself on the ~*〉 〈*an unmade ~*〉 **b** a place of sexual relations; *also* SEXUAL INTERCOURSE **c** a place for sleeping or resting **d** sleep; *also* a time for sleeping 〈*took a walk before ~*〉 **e** a mattress 〈*a feather ~*〉 **f** the use of a bed for the night – compare BED AND BREAKFAST **2** a flat or level surface: e g **2a** a plot of ground, esp in a garden, prepared for plants; *also* this ground together with the plants growing in it **b** the bottom of a body of water; *esp* an area of sea or lake bottom used for cultivating a particular plant or animal 〈*an oyster ~*〉 **3** a supporting surface or structure; *esp* the foundation of crushed rock, gravel, etc that supports a road or railway **4** STRATUM **1a** (layer of rock) **5a** the place or material (e g mortar) in which a brick or block is laid **b** the lower surface of a brick, slate, or tile **6** a mass or heap resembling a bed 〈*a ~ of ashes*〉; *esp* a heap on which something else is laid 〈*coleslaw on a ~ of lettuce*〉 [ME, fr OE *bedd;* akin to OHG *betti* bed, L *fodere* to dig] – **get out of bed on the wrong side** *informal* to be in a bad temper all day – **go to bed** *of a newspaper, magazine, etc* to go to press; be printed – **go to bed with somebody** to have sexual intercourse with somebody – **put to bed** to finalize work on (a newspaper, magazine, etc) so that it is ready for printing – **take to one's bed** to become ill and have to remain in bed

²**bed** *vb* **-dd-** *vt* **1a** to provide with a bed or bedding; settle in sleeping quarters **b** to go to bed with, usu for sexual intercourse **2a** to embed **b** to plant or arrange (seeds, young plants, etc) in beds – often + *out* **3** to lay flat or in a layer ~ *vi* **1a** to find or make sleeping accommodation **b** to go to bed **2** to form a layer **3** to lie flat or flush □ (*vt 1a; vi 1&2*) often + down

¹**bed and breakfast** *n* overnight sleeping accommodation and breakfast the following morning, as provided by a hotel, guest house, etc

²**bed and breakfast** *adj, of a stock exchange transaction* establishing a loss for tax purposes by selling shares late one day and buying them back the following morning 〈*Time seems to be fast running out for ~ operations – The Observer*〉 – **bed and breakfast** *vt*

**bedaub** /bi'dawb/ *vt* **1** to smear all over, esp with something sticky **2** to ornament in a gaudy or excessive manner

**bedazzle** /bi'daz(ə)l/ *vt* to dazzle – **bedazzlement** *n*

**bed board** *n* a stiff thin wide board inserted usu between the bedsprings and the mattress to give support to one's back

**bedbug** /-ˌbug/ *n* a wingless bloodsucking bug (*Cimex lectularius*) that sometimes infests houses, living esp in bedclothes, and that feeds on human blood

**bedchamber** /'bedˌchaymbə/ *n, archaic* a bedroom

**bedclothes** /-ˌklohdhz/ *n pl* the covers (e g sheets and blankets) used on a bed

**bedder** /'bedə/ *n* **1** a woman servant employed esp to make beds at a Cambridge University college – compare GYP, SCOUT **2** a bedding plant

¹**bedding** /'beding/ *n* **1** bedclothes **2** a bottom layer; a foundation **3** material (e g straw) to provide a bed for livestock **4** the arrangement or pattern of layers of rock within a mass of rock [ME, fr OE, fr *bedd*]

²**bedding** *adj, of a plant* suitable for growing in garden beds [fr gerund of ²*bed*]

**beddy-byes** /'bedi ˌbiez/ *n taking sing or pl vb* sleep; *also* a time for sleeping – used by or to children [blend of *bed* and *bye-byes*]

**bedeck** /bi'dek/ *vt* to clothe with finery; deck out **synonyms** see DECORATE

**bedevil** /bi'devl/ *vt* **-ll-** (*NAm* **-l-**, **-ll-**) **1** to possess (as if) with a devil; bewitch **2** to change for the worse; spoil, frustrate 〈~ed *all his plans*〉 **3** to torment maliciously; harass **4** to confuse utterly; bewilder – **bedevilment** *n*

**bedew** /bi'dyooh/ *vt, chiefly poetic* to wet (as if) with dew

**bedfast** /'bedˌfahst/ *adj, archaic* confined to bed; bedridden

**bedfellow** /-ˌfeloh/ *n* **1** one who shares a bed **2** a close associate; an ally 〈*political ~s*〉

**Bedford cord** /'bedfəd/ *n* a clothing fabric with lengthways raised ribs, that resembles corduroy [prob fr *Bedford*, town in Bedfordshire, England]

**bedim** /bi'dim/ *vt* **-mm-** *chiefly poetic* **1** to make less bright **2** to make indistinct; obscure

**bedizen** /bi'diez(ə)n, bi'diz(ə)n/ *vt, archaic* to dress or adorn with gaudy finery [*be-* + arch. *dizen* to dress gaudily, fr earlier *disen* to dress a distaff with flax, fr MD] – **bedizenment** *n*

**bed joint** *n* a horizontal joint in brickwork or stonework

**bedlam** /'bedləm/ *n* **1** a place, scene, or state of uproar and confusion 2 *archaic* a mental hospital [*Bedlam*, popular name for the Hospital of St Mary of Bethlehem, London, a lunatic asylum, fr ME *Bedlem* Bethlehem] – **bedlam** *adj*

**bedlamite** /'bedləmiet/ *n, archaic* a madman, lunatic – **bedlamite** *adj*

**bed linen** *n* the sheets and pillowcases used on a bed

**Bedlington terrier** /'bedlingtən/ *n* (any of) a breed of rough-coated terrier of light build, usu groomed to resemble a lamb [*Bedlington*, village in Northumberland, England]

**bedmaker** /-,maykə/ *n* BEDDER 1 (woman servant at a Cambridge college)

**bedmate** /-,mayt/ *n* one who shares one's bed; *esp* a sexual partner

**bed of roses** *n* a place or condition of agreeable ease

**bedouin, beduin** /'bedwin, 'bedooh·in/ *n, pl* **bedouins, beduins,** *esp collectively* **bedouin, beduin** *often cap* a nomadic Arab of the Arabian, Syrian, or N African deserts [Fr *bédouin*, fr Ar *badāwi, bidwān*, pl of *badawi* desert dweller]

**bedpan** /-,pan/ *n* a shallow vessel used for urination or defecation by a person confined to bed

**bedplate** /'bed,playt/ *n* a metal plate, platform, or frame to which a machine is attached

**bedpost** /-,pohst/ *n* any of the four upright posts at the corners of a bedstead

**bedraggle** /bi'dragl/ *vt* to wet thoroughly

**bedraggled** /bi'dragəld/ *adj* **1** left wet and limp (as if) by rain **2** soiled and stained (as if) by trailing in mud

**bedridden** /-,rid(ə)n/ *adj* confined to bed (e g by illness) [alter. of ME *bedrede, bedreden*, fr OE *bedreda*, fr *bedreda* one confined to bed, fr *bedd* bed + *-rida, -reda* rider, fr *rīdan* to ride]

**bedrock** /-,rok/ *n* **1** the solid rock underlying loose surface materials (e g soil) **2a** the lowest point **b** the basic facts or principles about something – **bedrock** *adj*

**bedroll** /'bed,rohl/ *n* bedding, esp that used for sleeping in the open, rolled up for carrying

¹**bedroom** /'bedroohm, -room/ *n* a room furnished with a bed and intended primarily for sleeping

²**bedroom** *adj* dealing with, suggestive of, or suggesting sexual relations ⟨a ~ *farce*⟩

**-bedroomed** /-bedroohmd, -roomd/ *comb form* (adj → adj) having (such or so many) bedrooms ⟨three-*bedroomed house*⟩

**bedsettee** /-se'tee/ *n, Br* an upholstered settee that can be converted into a single or double bed (e g by lowering a hinged back) – compare STUDIO COUCH

**bedside** /-,sied/ *adj* **1** of, relating to, or conducted at the bedside ⟨a ~ *diagnosis*⟩ **2** suitable for a person in bed ⟨~ *reading*⟩ – **bedside** *n*

**bedside manner** *n* the manner with which a doctor deals with his/her patients

**bed-sitter** /-'sitə/, **'bed-,sit** *n, Br* a single room serving as both bedroom and sitting room [*bed*room + *sit*ting room + *-er*]

**bed-'sitting-room** *n, Br* a bed-sitter

**bedsock** /'bed,sok/ *n* a loose-fitting sock for wearing in bed

**bedsore** /-,saw/ *n* a sore resulting from prolonged pressure on the body surface of an invalid as a consequence of lying in bed for a long time

**bedspread** /-,spred/ *n* a usu ornamental cloth cover for a bed

**bedspring** /-,spring/ *n* a spring supporting a mattress

**bedstead** /-,sted/ *n* the wooden, metal, etc framework of a bed [ME *bedstede*, fr *bed* + *stede* place – more at STEAD]

**bedstraw** /-,straw/ *n* any of a genus (*Galium*) of usu short-stemmed plants of the madder family having clusters of small white, pink, or yellow flowers [fr its use for mattresses]

**bed table** *n* a small table placed at the bedside; *esp* a table that fits over a bed and whose height can be adjusted

**bedtime** /'bed,tiem/ *n* time to go to bed

**bedtime story** *n* a simple story for young children

**beduin** /'bedwin, 'bedooh·in/ *n, pl* **beduins,** *esp collectively* **beduin** BEDOUIN (nomadic Arab)

**bed warmer** *n* WARMING PAN

'**bed-,wetting** *n* the involuntary discharge of urine occurring in bed during sleep – **bed wetter** *n*

**bee** /bee/ *n* **1** an insect (*Apis mellifera*) having a well-defined social organization, that is often kept in hives for the honey that it produces; *broadly* any of numerous insects (superfamily Apoidea) that differ from the related wasps esp by having a hairier body and legs, and sometimes a special body structure for carrying pollen **2** *NAm* a gathering of people for a usu specified purpose ⟨a *sewing* ~⟩ ⟨a *spelling* ~⟩ [ME, fr OE

*bēo;* akin to OHG *bīa* bee, Lith *bitis*] – **beelike** *adj* – **bee in one's bonnet** an obsession about a usu specified subject or idea

**Beeb** /beeb/ *n, Br humorous* the BBC [by shortening & alter.]

**beebread** /-,bred/ *n* bitter yellowish-brown pollen stored in honeycomb cells and used, mixed with honey, by bees as food

**beech** /beech/ *n, pl* **beeches, beech** (the wood of) any of a genus (*Fagus*) of the family Fagaceae, the beech family) of deciduous trees with smooth grey bark and small edible triangular nuts [ME *beche*, fr OE *bēce;* akin to OE *bōc* beech, OHG *buohha*, L *fagus*, Gk *phēgos* oak] – **beechen** *adj*, **beechy** *adj*

**beech marten** *n* a Eurasian MARTEN (mammal related to the weasel) (*Martes foina*) having a white patch on the chest and throat

**beech mast** *n* the nuts of the beech tree, esp when lying on the ground

**bee eater** *n* any of a family (Meropidae) of brightly coloured slender-billed insect-eating birds that live in warm or tropical regions of Europe, Africa, and Australasia

¹**beef** /beef/ *n, pl* (2) **beeves** /beevz/, *NAm chiefly* **beefs,** *esp collectively* **beef,** (4) **beefs** **1** the flesh of a bullock, cow, or other adult domestic bovine animal when killed for food **2** an ox, cow, or bull in a (nearly) full-grown state; *esp* a bullock or cow fattened for food ⟨a *herd of good* ~⟩ **3** muscular flesh; brawn **4** *informal* a complaint [ME, fr OF *buef* ox, beef, fr L *bov-, bos* head of cattle – more at COW]

²**beef** *vt* to add weight, strength, or power to – usu + *up* ~ *vi, informal* to complain

**beefburger** /'beef,buhgə/ *n* a hamburger [*beef* + ham*burger*]

**beefcake** /-,kayk/ *n, chiefly NAm* a photographic display of muscular male physique – compare CHEESECAKE

**beef cattle** *n* cattle with heavy well-fleshed bodies and rapid growth, developed primarily for the efficient production of meat

**beefeater** /'beefeetə/ *n* YEOMAN 1 (member of the bodyguard of the English sovereign in former times) – not used technically [*beef* + *eater;* orig sense, a well-fed servant]

**bee fly** *n* any of numerous flies (family Bombyliidae), many of which resemble bees

**beefsteak fungus** /'beef,stayk/ *n* a bright red edible fungus (*Fistulina hepatica*) that grows on dead trees

**beef tea** *n* a nourishing drink made from beef juice and prepared esp for invalids

**beefwood** /-,wood/ *n* any of several hard heavy reddish woods used esp for fine furniture; *also* any of various Australian or W Indian trees from which beefwood is obtained

**beefy** /'beefi/ *adj* **1** full of beef **2** brawny, powerful

**beehive** /'bee,hiev/ *n* **1** a hive for housing bees **2** a scene of crowded activity **3** a conically shaped hairstyle worn by a woman – **beehive** *adj*

**beekeeper** /'bee,keepə/ *n* one who looks after bees – **beekeeping** *n*

**beeline** /-,lien/ *n* a straight direct course – chiefly in *make a beeline for* [fr the belief that nectar-laden bees return to their hives in a direct line]

**Beelzebub** /bi'elzibub, 'beelzi-/ *n* the devil [*Beelzebub*, prince of devils, fr L, fr Gk *Beelzeboub*, fr Heb *Ba'al zĕbhūbh*, a Philistine god, lit., lord of flies]

**been** /bin, been/ *vb past* & *past part* **1** past part of BE **2** paid a visit ⟨never ~ *to Paris*⟩ ⟨has *the postman* ~?⟩

**bee orchid** *n* any of several European orchids (genus *Ophrys*) with velvety flowers resembling bees in colour and shape

¹**beep** /beep/ *n* a sound (e g from a horn or electronic device) that serves as a signal or warning [imit]

²**beep** *vi* **1** to sound a horn **2** to make a beep ~ *vt* to cause (e g a horn) to sound – **beeper** *n*

**beer** /biə/ *n* **1** an alcoholic drink brewed from fermented malt flavoured with hops; *also* a glass of this ⟨I'll *have a* ~⟩ **2** a fizzy nonalcoholic or fermented slightly alcoholic drink flavoured with roots or other plant parts – compare ROOT BEER, GINGER BEER [ME *ber*, fr OE *bēor;* akin to OHG *bior* beer]

**beer and skittles** *n taking sing vb, informal* a situation of agreeable ease ⟨*life isn't all* ~⟩

**beerenauslese** /'beərən,owslayzə/ (*Ger* be:rənauslezə)/ *n, often cap* a German and Austrian sweet white table wine made only from individually selected, very ripe grapes that have been attacked by a special mould [Ger, fr *beere* berry + *auslese* selection]

**beer gut** *n, informal* a potbelly due to habitual beer drinking

**beer parlour** *n, Can* a room in a hotel where beer is served

**beery** /'biəri/ *adj* 1 affected by beer ⟨~ *voices*⟩ 2 smelling or tasting of beer ⟨*a* ~ *tavern*⟩

**bee's knees** *n, informal the* best or most outstanding in a category or class ⟨*thinks he's the* ~ *when it comes to fashion*⟩

**beestings**, *NAm chiefly* **beastings** /'beestingz/ *n taking sing or pl vb* the first milk produced, esp by a cow, immediately after giving birth; COLOSTRUM [ME *bestynge*, fr OE *bȳsting*, fr *bēost* beestings]

**beeswax** /'beez,waks/ *n* a dull-yellow easily moulded substance produced by bees, that is used by the bees to make honeycomb and that can also be used as a wood polish

**beeswing** /'beez,wing/ *n* a thin sediment that forms in wine, esp port, after it has been bottled a long time [*bee's wing*; fr its appearance of shining scales]

**beet** /beet/ *n* 1 any of various plants (genus *Beta*) of the goosefoot family with thick long-stalked edible leaves and a swollen root used as a vegetable, as a source of sugar, or as food for animals 2 *NAm* a beetroot [ME *bete*, fr OE *bēte*, fr L *beta*]

**beet bug** *n* any of various bugs (family Piesmidae) that feed almost entirely on plants (e g beet and spinach)

¹**beetle** /'beetl/ *n* 1 any of an order (Coleoptera) of insects that have four wings of which the front pair are modified into stiff coverings that protect the inner pair 2 a game in which the players attempt to be the first to complete a stylized drawing of a beetle in accordance with the numbers obtained by throwing a dice [ME *betylle*, fr OE *bitula*, fr *bītan* to bite]

²**beetle** *vi, Br informal* to move swiftly ⟨~d *off down the road*⟩

³**beetle** *n* 1 a heavy wooden tool for hammering or ramming 2 a machine for giving fabrics a lustrous finish [ME *betel*, fr OE *bīetel*; akin to OE *bēatan* to beat]

⁴**beetle** *adj, esp of eyebrows* beetling [ME *bitel-browed* having overhanging brows, prob fr *betylle, bitel* beetle]

**beetling** /'beetling/ *adj* prominent and overhanging ⟨*to scale the* ~ *crags* – R L Stevenson⟩

**beetroot** /'beetrooht/ *n, pl* **beetroot**, **beetroots** *chiefly Br* 1 a cultivated beet (*Beta vulgaris*) with a red edible root that is a common salad vegetable; *also* this root 2 **beetroot**, **beetroot red** of the colour of a beetroot; deep red – **beetroot** *adj*

**beeves** /beevz/ *pl of* BEEF

**befall** /bi'fawl/ *vb, formal or poetic* **befell** /bi'fel/, **befallen** /bi'fawlən/ to happen (to), esp as if by fate *synonyms see* HAPPEN

**befit** /bi'fit/ *vt* -tt- to be proper or becoming to

**befitting** /bi'fiting/ *adj* suitable, appropriate – **befittingly** *adv*

**befog** /bi'fog/ *vt* -gg- 1 to make foggy; obscure 2 to confuse

¹**before** /bi'faw/ *adv* 1 so as to be in advance of others; ahead 2 on the front 3 earlier in time; previously ⟨*haven't we met* ~?⟩ ⟨*had left a week* ~⟩ [ME, adv & prep, fr OE *beforan*, fr *be-* + *foran* before, fr *fore*]

²**before** *prep* 1a IN FRONT OF b under the jurisdiction or consideration of ⟨*the case* ~ *the court*⟩ c in store for ⟨*the ordeal that lay* ~ *them*⟩ 2 preceding in time; earlier than ⟨~ *tea*⟩ ⟨*150 years* ~ *Christ*⟩ 3 in a higher or more important position than ⟨*put quantity* ~ *quality*⟩ 4 under the onslaught of ⟨*the tree fell* ~ *the force of the wind*⟩

³**before** *conj* 1 earlier than the time when ⟨*say goodbye* ~ *you go*⟩ 2 rather than ⟨*I'll resign* ~ *I give in*⟩

**beforehand** /bi'faw,hand/ *adv or adj* 1 in anticipation ⟨*prepared her talk* ~⟩ 2 ahead of time; IN ADVANCE

**beforetime** /bi'fawtiem/ *adv, archaic* formerly

**befoul** /bi'fowl/ *vt* to make foul (as if) with dirt or filth

**befriend** /bi'frend/ *vt* to become a friend of purposely; show kindness and understanding to ⟨~ *a helpless person*⟩

**befuddle** /bi'fudl/ *vt* 1 to muddle or stupefy (as if) with drink 2 to confuse, perplex – **befuddlement** *n*

**beg** /beg/ *vb* -gg- *vt* 1 to ask for as a charity ⟨~ged *alms*⟩ 2a to ask earnestly (for); entreat ⟨~ *a favour*⟩ ⟨~ged *her to stay*⟩ b to ask permission *to-* + *infin* ⟨~ *to differ*⟩ 3a to evade, sidestep ⟨~ged *the real problems*⟩ b to assume as established or proved without justification ⟨~ *the question*⟩ ~ *vi* 1 to ask for alms or charity 2 to ask earnestly ⟨~ged *for mercy*⟩ 3 *of a dog* to sit up and hold out the forepaws – see also GO **begging** [ME *beggen*, prob alter. of OE *bedecian*]

*synonyms* **Beg**, **entreat**, **beseech**, **implore**, **supplicate**, and **importune** all signify the making of an appeal which is likely to be refused or demurred at. A person **begs** for what he/she cannot claim as a right; **beg** suggests earnestness, insistence, and sometimes self-abasement. By **entreating** someone, one hopes to persuade him/her by earnest pleading and reasoning. **Beseech** and **implore** convey eager anxiety which seeks to inspire sympathy or pity. **Implore** may be stronger than **beseech**, with a suggestion of tearfulness or evident anguish. **Supplicate** adds to **entreat** a humble, prayerful attitude ⟨*invite,* **entreat, supplicate** *them to accompany you* – Lord Chesterfield⟩. **Importune** denotes persistence with one's requests to the point of annoyance or even harassment. See ASK

**beg off** *vi* to ask to be released from something (e g an obligation)

**beget** /bi'get/ *vt* -tt-; **begot** /bi'got/, *archaic* **begat** /bi'gat/; **begotten** /bi'gotn/ 1 to procreate as the father; sire 2 to produce as an effect; cause ⟨*economic dependency* ~s *a moral subserviency* – J M Morse⟩ [ME *begeten*, alter. of *beyeten*, fr OE *bigietan* – more at GET] – **begetter** *n*

¹**beggar** /'begə/ *n* 1 one who lives by asking for money, food, etc 2 a pauper 3 *informal* a person, esp a man, of a usu specified type ⟨*lucky* ~⟩ [ME *beggere, beggare*, fr *beggen* to beg + *-ere, -are* -er; (3) partly euphemism for *bugger*]

²**beggar** *vt* 1 to reduce to beggary 2 to exceed the resources or abilities of ⟨~s *description*⟩

**beggarly** /-li/ *adj* 1 marked by extreme poverty 2 contemptibly mean, scant, petty, or paltry – **beggarliness** *n*

**beggary** /'begəri/ *n* poverty, penury

**begin** /bi'gin/ *vb* -nn-; **began** /bi'gan/; **begun** /bi'gun/ *vi* 1a to do the first part of an action; start ⟨*if you're all ready, we'll* ~⟩ b to undergo initial steps ⟨*work on the project* began *in May*⟩ 2a to come into existence; arise ⟨*the war* began *in 1939*⟩ b to have a starting point ⟨*the alphabet* ~s *with* A⟩ ~ *vt* 1 to set about the activity of ⟨*the children* began *laughing*⟩ 2 to call into being; found ⟨~ *a dynasty*⟩ 3 to come first in ⟨A ~s *the alphabet*⟩ 4 to have the slightest degree of success in ⟨*can't* ~ *to describe her beauty*⟩ [ME *beginnen*, fr OE *beginnan*; akin to OHG *biginnan* to begin, OE *onginnan*]

*synonyms* **Begin, commence,** and **start** are closely related when they mean "take the first steps in an enterprise" or "set something in progress". **Begin**, opposed to "end", and the formal **commence**, opposed to "conclude", are interchangeable in meaning but not context. **Commence** in everyday contexts seems bookish or pedantic ⟨*things never* began *with Mr Borthrop Trumbull; they always* commenced – George Eliot⟩. **Start** may sometimes be interchangeable with **begin**, but has a more limited and specific use, too. Opposed to "stop", it emphasizes the fact of making a beginning, and so is used for action after inaction, as ⟨*the conversation stopped, and failed to* start *again*⟩. It also implies setting out from a specific point, as on a journey, a course of some kind, or a race ⟨*we* started *for the Pole at once*⟩. Used transitively, **start** can express indirect aid in setting up or beginning something in a way which **begin** cannot ⟨*It was her aunt who* started *her on the violin*⟩. See INITIATE *antonyms* end, conclude, stop

**beginner** /bi'ginə/ *n* a person who is just beginning to do or learn something

**beginning** /bi'gining/ *n* 1 the point at which something begins; the start 2 the first part 3 the origin, source 4 *usu pl* a rudimentary stage or early period

**begone** /bi'gon/ *vi* to go away; depart – in the infin and esp the imper [ME, fr *be gone* (imper)]

**begonia** /bi'gohni-ə/ *n* any of a large genus (*Begonia* of the family Begoniaceae, the begonia family) of tropical plants that have irregularly shaped leaves and are widely cultivated as ornamental garden and house plants [NL, genus name, fr Michel *Bégon* †1710 Fr governor of Santo Domingo]

**begorra, begorrah** /bi'gorə/ *interj, Irish* – used as a mild oath [euphemism for *by God*]

**begrime** /bi'griem/ *vt* to make dirty

**begrudge** /bi'gruj/ *vt* 1 to give or concede reluctantly ⟨*she* ~d *every minute taken from her work*⟩ 2 to envy the pleasure or enjoyment of ⟨*they* ~ *him his wealth*⟩ – **begrudger** *n*, **begrudgingly** *adv*

**beguile** /bi'giel/ *vt* 1 to deceive, hoodwink 2 to deprive by guile; cheat – usu + *of* ⟨~d *of sleep*⟩ 3 to while away, esp by some agreeable occupation 4 to please or persuade by the use of wiles; charm ⟨*her ways* ~d *him*⟩ ~ *vi* to deceive by wiles – **beguilement** *n*, **beguiler** *n*, **beguilingly** *adv*

**beguine** /bi'geen/ *n* a vigorous W Indian dance similar to the rumba [AmerF *béguine*, fr Fr *béguin* flirtation]

**begum** /'beegəm/ *n* an Indian Muslim woman of high rank [Hindi *begam*]

**begun** /bi'gun/ *past of* BEGIN

**behalf** /bi'hahf/ *n* [ME, benefit, support, fr *by* + *half* half, side] – **on behalf of**, *NAm* **in behalf of** in the interest of; as a representative of ⟨*writing* on behalf of *my client*⟩ – **on somebody's behalf** in somebody's interest or as his/her representative ⟨*wrote* on my behalf⟩

**usage** In modern British English, **behalf** is used with *on*. In American English, and formerly in British English too, some people have distinguished between ⟨*in your* **behalf** (= in your interest)⟩ and ⟨*on your* **behalf** (= as your representative)⟩. In any case, *on* **behalf** *of* should not be confused with *on the* **part** *of*.

**behave** /bi'hayv/ *vi* 1 to act, function, or react in a usu specified way ⟨*How does this chemical* ~ *when heated?*⟩ 2 to conduct oneself in a specified way ⟨*they have* ~d *very unfairly towards us*⟩ 3 to conduct oneself properly ⟨*you must learn to* ~ *in company*⟩ ~ *vt* to conduct (oneself) properly ⟨*be quiet and* ~ *yourself*⟩ [ME *behaven*, fr *be-* + *haven* to have, hold]

**behaviour** /bi'hayvyə/, *NAm chiefly* **behavior** *n* 1 the way in which a person conducts him-/herself 2a anything that any living animal or plant does involving action and response to stimulation b the response of an individual, group, or species to its environment 3 the way in which something (eg a machine) behaves [alter. of ME *behavour*, fr *behaven*] – **behavioural** *adj*, **behaviourally** *adv*

**synonyms** Behaviour, conduct, manners, and demeanour describe the way characteristic attitudes or qualities reveal themselves in our actions. **Behaviour** relates to social situations and social norms, while **conduct** sets a moral standard ⟨*his* conduct *left much to be desired*⟩. **Manners** refers specifically to the standards set by individual societies, or sets within societies ⟨*that child has the* manners *of a pig!*⟩. **Demeanour** describes outward appearance or behaviour expressing character or outlook ⟨*her meek* demeanour *concealed a stubborn wilfulness*⟩.

**behavioural science** /bi'hayvyərəl/ *n* a science (eg psychology, sociology, or anthropology) dealing with animal, esp human, action and seeking general principles and explanations of man's behaviour in society – compare BEHAVIOURISM

**behaviourism** /bi'hayvyə,riz(ə)m/ *n* (the branch of psychology based on) a theory holding that the proper concern of psychology is the objective study of observable behaviour and that data (eg feelings and opinions) that cannot be verified by observation is not valid psychological evidence – compare INTROSPECTION – **behaviourist** *adj or n*

**behaviour therapy** *n* therapy using conditioning techniques to change abnormal or maladaptive behaviour (eg a phobia) and establish normal behaviour

**behead** /bi'hed/ *vt* to cut off the head of; decapitate

**behemoth** /bi'heemoth/ *n* 1 *often cap* an animal, probably the hippopotamus, described in Job 40:15–24 2 something of oppressive or monstrous size or power [ME, fr L, fr Heb *bĕhēmōth*]

**behest** /bi'hest/ *n* an urgent prompting or insistent request ⟨*returned home at the* ~ *of his friends*⟩ [ME, promise, command, fr OE *behǣs* promise, fr *behātan* to promise, fr *be-* + *hātan* to command, promise]

**¹behind** /bi'hiend/ *adv* 1a in the place, situation, or time from which someone or something is departing or has departed ⟨*I've left the keys* ~ – *SEU S*⟩ b in, to, or towards the back ⟨*look* ~⟩ 2a unable to keep up with others, or with an established rate or schedule ⟨*I'm a bit* ~ *with work*⟩ ⟨*always* ~ *at school*⟩ b in arrears ⟨~ *in his payments*⟩ [ME *behinde*, fr OE *behindan*, fr *be-* + *hindan* from behind; akin to OE *hinder* behind – more at HIND]

**²behind** *prep* 1a(1) at or to the back or rear of ⟨*look* ~ *you*⟩ a(2) remaining after (someone who has departed) ⟨*left a great name* ~ *him*⟩ b obscured by ⟨*malice* ~ *the mask of friendship*⟩ 2 – used to indicate backwardness ⟨~ *his classmates in performance*⟩, delay ⟨~ *schedule*⟩, or deficiency ⟨*lagged* ~ *last year's sales*⟩ 3a in the background of ⟨*the conditions* ~ *the strike*⟩ b in a supporting position at the back of ⟨*solidly* ~ *their candidate*⟩

**³behind** *n*, *informal* the buttocks [¹*behind*]

**behindhand** /bi'hiend,hand/ *adj* 1 behind schedule; in arrears 2 lagging behind the times; backward **synonyms** see TARDY **antonym** beforehand

**be,hind-the-'scenes** *adj* kept, made, or held in secret

**behold** /bi'hohld/ *vb* **beheld** /bi'held/ *vt*, *chiefly poetic* to see, observe ~ *vi*, *archaic* – used in the imperative to call attention **synonyms** see ¹SEE [ME *beholden* to keep, behold, fr OE *behealdan*, fr *be-* + *healdan* to hold] – **beholder** *n*

**beholden** /bi'hohldn/ *adj* under obligation for a favour or gift; indebted – usu + *to* [ME, fr pp of *beholden*]

**behoof** /bi'hoof, bi'hoohf/ *n*, *archaic* advantage, profit [ME *behof*, fr OE *behōf*; akin to OE *hebban* to raise – more at HEAVE]

**behoove** /bi'hoohv/ *vb*, *NAm* to behove

**behove** /bi'hohv/ *vb* to be incumbent (on) or necessary, proper, or advantageous (for) ⟨*it* ~s *us to fight*⟩ [ME *behoven*, fr OE *behōfian*, fr *behōf*]

**beige** /bayzh, bayj/ *n* 1 cloth made of natural undyed wool 2 the colour of natural wool; a yellowish-grey colour [Fr] – **beige** *adj*, **beigy** *adj*

**beignet** /'baynyay, ˌ-'- (Fr bɛɲɛ)/ *n* a deep-fried puffed-up ball of choux pastry [Fr, fr MF *bignet*, *buignet*, fr *buigne* bump, bruise]

**being** /'bee·ing/ *n* 1a the quality or state of having existence ⟨*the scheme was in* ~ *three years ago*⟩ b conscious existence; life ⟨*the mother who gave him his* ~⟩ 2 the qualities that constitute an existent thing; the essence; *esp* personality 3 a living thing; *esp* a person ⟨*strange* ~s *from outer space*⟩ [ME, fr gerund of *been*, *beon* to be]

**bel** /bel/ *n* 10 DECIBELS (unit of the intensity of sound) [Alexander Graham *Bell* †1922 US inventor]

**belabour** /bi'laybə/ *vt* 1 to work on or at to absurd lengths ⟨~ *the obvious*⟩ 2 to beat soundly; thrash 3 to assail, attack

**belated** /bi'laytid/ *adj* delayed beyond the usual time ⟨~ *birthday greetings*⟩ [pp of arch. *belate* to make late] – **belatedly** *adv*, **belatedness** *n*

**¹belay** /bi'lay/ *vt* 1 to secure or make fast (esp a rope) by winding round a support (eg a pinnacle of rock or a post aboard a ship) 2 to stop 3 to secure (a person) at the end of a rope (eg in mountaineering) ~ *vi* 1 to be made fast ⟨*knows where each rope* ~s *on deck*⟩ 2 *nautical* to stop, leave off – in the imper ⟨~ *there*⟩ 3 to make a rope fast (eg by winding it round a support) [ME *beleggen* to beset, fr OE *belecgan*, fr *be-* + *lecgan* to lay]

**²belay** *n* 1 a method or the act of belaying a rope or person in mountain climbing 2 something (eg a pinnacle of rock) to which a mountain climber's rope is belayed

**bel canto** /ˌbel 'kantoh/ *n* operatic singing originating in 17th- and 18th-century Italy and stressing ease, purity, and evenness of tone [It, lit., beautiful singing]

**belch** /belch/ *vi* 1 to expel gas suddenly from the stomach through the mouth 2 to erupt, explode, or detonate violently 3 to issue forth spasmodically; gush ~ *vt* 1 to eject or emit violently ⟨*chimneys* ~ing *forth smoke*⟩ 2 to expel (gas) suddenly from the stomach through the mouth [ME *belchen*, fr OE *bealcian*] – **belch** *n*

**belcher** /'belchə/ *n* a coloured handkerchief worn as a neck scarf; *esp* a blue one with white and blue spots [James *Belcher* †1811 E boxer]

**beldam, beldame** /'beldəm, -dam/ *n* an old woman; *esp* a hag [ME *beldam* grandmother, fr MF *bel* beautiful + ME *dam*]

**beleaguer** /bi'leegə/ *vt* 1 to surround with an army so as to prevent escape; besiege 2 *formal* to beset, harass ⟨~ed *parents*⟩ [D *belegeren*, fr *be-* (akin to OE *be-*) + *leger* camp; akin to OHG *legar* bed – more at LAIR]

**belemnite** /'belemniet/ *n* a conical fossil shell of an extinct marine INVERTEBRATE animal (family Belemnitidae of the class Cephalopoda) related to the present-day octopus and squid [Fr *bélemnite*, fr Gk *belemnon* dart; akin to Gk *ballein* to throw – more at DEVIL] – **belemnitic** *adj*

**bel esprit** /ˌbel e'spree (Fr bɛl ɛspri)/ *n*, *pl* **beaux esprits** /ˌbohz e'spree (Fr boz ɛspri)/ a person with a fine and gifted mind [Fr, lit., fine mind]

**belfry** /'belfri/ *n* 1 the part of a tower, esp a church tower or steeple, in which one or more bells are hung 2 a framework (eg of stone or timber) that encloses a bell [ME *belfrey*, alter. of *berfrey*, fr MF *berfrei*, deriv of Gk *pyrgos phorētos* movable war tower]

**Belgian** /'belj(ə)n/ *n* a native or inhabitant of Belgium [*Belgium*, country in NW Europe] – **Belgian** *adj*

**Belgian endive** *n* chicory

**Belgian hare** *n* (any of) a breed of slender dark-red domestic rabbits

**Belgian sheepdog** *n* (any of) a breed of hardy black or grey dogs developed in Belgium, esp for herding sheep

**Belgo-** /belgoh-/ *comb form* Belgian and ⟨Belgo-*English*⟩ [*Belgian*]

**Belial** /'beeli·əl/ *n* worthlessness, wickedness – often personified in the Bible ⟨*children of* ~⟩ [Gk, fr Heb *bĕlīya'al*]

**belie** /bi'lie/ *vt* **belying** 1 to give a false impression of ⟨*his pleasant appearance* ~d *his true character*⟩ 2 to show (something) to be false

**belief** /bi'leef/ *n* **1** trust or confidence in some person or thing ⟨*destroyed her ~ in her father*⟩ **2** something believed; *specif* **belief, beliefs** *pl* a religious faith **3** conviction of the truth of some statement or the reality of some being, thing, or phenomenon, esp without conclusive proof ⟨*it's my ~ that he will succeed*⟩ ⟨*~ in the supernatural*⟩ **synonyms** see OPINION [ME *beleave*, prob alter. of OE *geléafa*, fr *ge-*, associative prefix + *léafa;* akin to OE *lýfan*]

**believe** /bi'leev/ *vi* **1a** to have a firm religious faith ⟨*~ in God*⟩ **b** to accept something trustfully and on faith ⟨*people who ~ in the natural goodness of man*⟩ **2** to have a firm conviction as to the reality or goodness of something **3** to hold an opinion; think ⟨*I ~ as you do*⟩ ~ *vt* **1a** to consider to be true, genuine, or honest ⟨*~ the reports*⟩ **b** to accept a statement made by (a person) as the truth ⟨*I don't ~ you*⟩ **2** to hold as an opinion; think ⟨*I ~ it will rain soon*⟩ □ *(1&2)* usu + *in* – see also MAKE **believe** [ME *beleven*, fr OE *beléfan*, fr *be-* + *lýfan, léfan* to allow, believe; akin to OHG *gilouben* to believe, OE *léof* dear – more at LOVE] – **believable** *adj*, **believer** *n*

**belike** /bi'liek/ *adv, archaic* most likely; probably

**Belisha beacon** /bə'leeshə/ *n* a flashing light in an amber globe mounted on a usu black and white striped pole, that marks a zebra crossing [Leslie Hore-*Belisha* †1957 E politician, responsible as Minister of Transport for the introduction of the beacon]

**belittle** /bi'litl/ *vt* to undermine the value of ⟨*~s her efforts*⟩ – **belittlement** *n*, **belittler** *n*

**¹bell** /bel/ *n* **1a** a hollow usu metal cup-shaped device with a flaring mouth, that produces a ringing sound when struck (e g by a metal clapper hanging inside it) **b** a hollow saucer-shaped device (e g in a telephone or alarm clock) that is operated mechanically and produces a ringing or buzzing sound **2a** the sound made by a bell, esp as a signal, warning (e g of fire), to tell the hour, or to mark the beginning or end of a period of activity (e g in a school) ⟨*the dinner ~*⟩ **b** the sound of a bell marking the start of the last lap in a running or cycling race or the start or end of a round in boxing, wrestling, showjumping, etc **3** a half hour subdivision of a WATCH (any of six periods of four hours reckoned from midnight) on board a ship, indicated by the strokes of a bell **4** something having the form of a bell: e g **4a** the flower of any of many plants (e g a bluebell) **b** the flared end of a WIND INSTRUMENT (e g a clarinet or trumpet) **5** a musical instrument that produces a clear ringing sound when struck; *esp, usu pl* CHIME 2b [ME *belle*, fr OE; akin to OE *bellan* to roar – more at BELLOW] – **bell, book, and candle 1** instruments used formerly in ceremonies of EXCOMMUNICATION (expelling somebody from the Catholic church) or in exorcising evil spirits **2** *informal* excessively elaborate or solemn ritual – used to cause a memory to stir in one's mind; be or sound familiar ⟨*Ponsonby-Smythe – yes, the name certainly rings a bell!*⟩

**²bell** *vt* **1** to provide with a bell or bells **2** to give the flaring shape of a bell to ~ *vi* to take the form of a bell; flare

**³bell** *vi, of a hound or male deer* to make a resonant bellowing or baying sound [ME *bellen*, fr OE *bellan*]

**⁴bell** *n* a bellow, roar; *esp* one made by a hound, or a male deer in RUT (period of sexual excitement)

**belladonna** /,belə'donə/ *n* **1** DEADLY NIGHTSHADE **2** a medicinal extract obtained from deadly nightshade or a related poisonous plant; *esp* one containing the drug ATROPINE [It, lit., beautiful lady; fr its use as a cosmetic]

**belladonna lily** *n* a plant (*Amaryllis belladonna*) of the daffodil family often cultivated for its fragrant usu white or pink flowers

**bell bird** *n* any of various unrelated songbirds (e g the HONEY EATER) of S America, Australia, and New Zealand, having a ringing bell-like call

**'bell-,bottoms** *n pl* trousers with wide flaring bottoms – **bell-bottom** *adj*

**bellboy** /-,boy/ *n, chiefly NAm* a messenger in a hotel, club, etc; ¹PAGE 2

**bell buoy** *n* a floating buoy fitted with a warning bell which is rung by the action of the waves

**belle** /bel/ *n* a popular and attractive girl or woman ⟨*bathing ~s*⟩ ⟨*the ~ of the ball*⟩ [Fr, fr fem of *beau* beautiful – more at BEAU]

**belles lettres** /,bel 'letrə, 'letə (Fr bɛl lɛtr)/ *n taking sing vb* literature that has no practical or informative function; *esp* light, entertaining, usu sophisticated literature [Fr, lit., fine letters]

**belletrist** /,bel 'letrist/ *n* a writer of belles lettres [*belles lettres*] – **belletristic** *adj*

**bellflower** /-,flowə/ *n* any of a genus (*Campanula*) of plants of the harebell family having usu showy bell-shaped flowers – called also CAMPANULA

**bell heather** *n* a W European heather (*Erica cinerea*) with whorls of usu crimson-purple flowers

**bellhop** /-,hop/ *n, NAm* a bellboy [short for *bell-hopper*]

**bellicose** /'belikohs/ *adj* inclined to fight; quarrelsome, warlike [ME, fr L *bellicosus*, fr *bellicus* of war, fr *bellum* war] – **bellicosely** *adv*, **bellicoseness, bellicosity** *n*

**-bellied** /-belid/ *comb form* (*adj → adj*) having (such) a belly ⟨*a big-bellied man*⟩

**belligerence** /bə'lij(ə)rəns/, **belligerency** /bə'lij(ə)rənsi/ *n* **1** an aggressive or hostile attitude, atmosphere, or disposition **2** the state of being at war; *specif* the status of a country, person, etc legally recognized as being at war

**belligerent** /bə'lij(ə)rənt/ *adj* **1** engaged in war; *specif* being a country, person, etc legally recognized as being at war **2** inclined to or displaying assertiveness, hostility, or aggressiveness [modif of L *belligerant-, belligerans*, prp of *belligerare* to wage war, fr *belliger* waging war, fr *bellum* + *gerere* to wage – more at CAST] – **belligerent** *n*, **belligerently** *adv*

**bell jar** *n* a bell-shaped usu glass vessel that is designed to cover objects or to contain gases or a vacuum

**,bell-'lyra** /'lie(ə)rə/, **bell lyre** *n* a GLOCKENSPIEL (musical instrument) mounted in a portable lyre-shaped frame [*lyra* fr L, lyre]

**bellman** /'belmən/ *n* a man (e g a town crier) who rings a bell

**bell metal** *n* bronze with a high tin content used for making bells

**bellow** /'beloh/ *vi* **1** to make the loud deep hollow sound characteristic of a bull **2** to shout in a deep voice ~ *vt* to bawl ⟨*~s the orders*⟩ [ME *belwen*, fr OE *bylgian;* akin to OE & OHG *bellan* to roar, Skt *bhāsate* he talks] – **bellow** *n*

**bellows** /'belohz/ *n taking sing or pl vb, pl* **bellows 1** a device that by alternate expansion and contraction draws in air through a valve and expels it through a tube and that is used to provide a stream of air (e g for making an organ pipe produce sound, or a fire burn at a higher temperature) **2** the pleated expandable part in some types of camera that allows the lens to move in and out [ME *bely, below, belwes* – more at BELLY]

**bellpull** /-,pool/ *n* (a handle or knob attached to) a cord by which one rings a bell

**bell push** *n* a button that is pushed to operate an electric bell

**bell tower** *n* a tower that supports or shelters a bell

**bellwether** /-,wedhə/ *n* a male sheep that leads the flock; *broadly* a leader who is followed blindly [ME, fr *belle* bell + *wether;* fr the practice of belling the leader of a flock]

**¹belly** /'beli/ *n* **1a** the abdomen of a person **b(1)** the undersurface of an animal's body **b(2)** a cut of pork consisting of this part of a pig's body **c** the stomach and associated organs (e g the intestines) **2** an internal cavity; the interior ⟨*the ~ of the ship*⟩ **3** appetite for food **4a** a surface or object curved or rounded like a human belly **b** the surface of a stringed musical instrument over which the strings pass **5** the enlarged fleshy part of a muscle **6** *chiefly poetic* the womb, uterus [ME *bely* bellows, belly, fr OE *belg* bag, skin; akin to OHG *balg* bag, skin, OE *blāwan* to blow]

**²belly** *vb* to swell, fill ⟨*the sails bellied*⟩

**¹bellyache** /-,ayk/ *n* pain in the abdominal region, esp in the bowels; colic

**²bellyache** *vi, informal* to complain whiningly or peevishly; FIND FAULT – **bellyacher** *n*

**bellyband** /'beli,band/ *n* a strap round the body of a draught horse holding the harness or the shafts of a vehicle in place

**belly board** *n* a short surfboard on which ones lies rather than stands

**belly button** *n, informal* the navel

**belly dance** *n* a sensuous dance of oriental origin, that is performed by a woman and involves undulating movements of the hips – **belly dance** *vi*, **belly dancer** *n*

**belly flop** *n* a dive into water in which the front of the body strikes flat against the surface – **belly flop** *vi*

**bellyful** /-f(ə)l/ *n, informal* an excessive amount ⟨*a ~ of advice*⟩

**'belly-,land** *vi* to land an aircraft on its undersurface without the use of the supporting undercarriage – **belly landing** *n*

**belly laugh** *n* a deep hearty laugh

**belong** /bi'long/ *vi* **1** to be in a proper situation (eg according to ability or social qualification), position, or place *⟨a man of his ability ∼s in teaching⟩ ⟨who put this book where it doesn't ∼?⟩* **2** to be an attribute, part, or function of a person or thing *⟨nuts and bolts ∼ to a car⟩ ⟨this cup ∼s with that saucer⟩* **3** to be properly classified *⟨whales ∼ among the mammals⟩* **4** chiefly NAm to be suitable, appropriate, or advantageous *⟨a telephone ∼s in every home⟩* [ME *belongen*, fr *be-* + *longen* to be suitable – more at LONG]

**belong to** *vt* **1** to be the property of **2** to be attached or bound to by birth, allegiance, dependency, or membership *⟨belong to Glasgow⟩ ⟨belongs to the cricket club⟩*

**belonging** /bi'long·ing/ *n* **1** *usu pl* a possession **2** close or intimate relationship *⟨a sense of ∼⟩*

**Belorussian** /,beloh-, ,byeloh-/ *n or adj* BYELORUSSIAN

**beloved** /bi'luvid, bi'luvd/ *n or adj, pl* **beloved** (somebody) dearly loved – usu in formal or religious use [ME, fr pp of *beloven* to love, fr *be-* + *loven* to love]

**¹below** /bi'loh/ *adv* **1** in or to a lower place, floor, or deck *⟨went ∼ to her cabin⟩ ⟨disturbed by the noise from the flat ∼⟩* **2a** on earth as contrasted with heaven *⟨all creatures here ∼⟩* **b** in or to Hades or hell **3** under the surface of the water or earth **4** UNDER 2a *⟨all those of 20 and ∼⟩* **5** lower on the same or a following page *⟨for further details see ∼⟩* [*be-* + *low*, adj]

**²below** *prep* **1a** in or to a lower place than; under **b** lower than the level of *⟨two inches ∼ the knee⟩* **2** inferior to (eg in rank) **3** not suitable to the rank or dignity of; unworthy of *⟨regarded talking to the servants as ∼ him⟩* **4** covered by; underneath *⟨hid ∼ the table⟩* **5** downstream from **6** UNDER 4 *⟨∼ the age of 18⟩ ⟨∼ average⟩*

**synonyms** Below, under, underneath, and beneath all mean "lower than" but with slightly different implications. Below is concerned chiefly with the comparison of levels *⟨any captain is below any general⟩*; under expresses a relationship, either of physical contact *⟨put a mat under a hot casserole⟩* or of direct subjection *⟨Captain Jones served under General Brown⟩*; underneath is strictly literal, stressing more strongly than under the closeness of what is directly overhead *⟨snuggled underneath the eiderdown⟩*; beneath is today confined chiefly to the sense "unworthy of" *⟨beneath my notice⟩* and is otherwise a somewhat literary synonym for under or underneath *⟨strolled beneath the ancient trees⟩*.

**³below** *interj* – used (eg by a climber) to warn others below that they should beware of falling stones, rocks, etc

**bel paese** /,bel pah'ayzay/ *n, often cap B&P* a mild soft creamy Italian cheese with a thin dark yellow rind [It, lit., beautiful country]

**¹belt** /belt/ *n* **1** a strip of material worn round the waist or hips or over the shoulder for decoration or to hold something (eg clothing or a weapon) in place *⟨a suspender ∼⟩ ⟨a sword ∼⟩* **2** an endless band of tough flexible material for transmitting motion and power in a machine or for conveying materials *⟨a fan ∼⟩ ⟨a conveyor ∼⟩* **3** an area characterized by some distinctive feature (eg of culture, geology, or life forms) *⟨a ∼ of trees⟩ ⟨stockbroker ∼⟩; also* one suited to a particular crop *⟨the corn ∼⟩* – compare GREEN BELT **4** SEAT BELT [ME, fr OE; akin to OHG *balz* belt; both fr a prehistoric WGmc-NGmc word borrowed fr L *balteus* belt] – **belted** *adj,* **beltless** *adj* – **(hit) below the belt** (to act) in an unfair way *⟨alluding to his past misdeeds in that way was really hitting below the belt⟩* – **under one's belt** as part of one's experience; having been attained *⟨got a few qualifications under her belt⟩*

**²belt** *vt* **1a** to encircle or fasten with a belt **b** to strap on **2a** to beat (as if) with a belt; thrash **b** *informal* to strike, hit ∼ *vi* to move or act in a vigorous or violent manner *⟨∼ing along the road⟩*

**belt out** *vt, informal* to sing, play, or produce (music) loudly or forcefully *⟨belting the songs out⟩*

**belt up** *vi, Br slang* SHUT UP

**³belt** *n, informal* a jarring blow; a whack

**Beltane** /'beltayn, -tən/ *n* the ancient Celtic May Day festival [ME, fr ScGael *beálltainn*]

**belted** /'beltid/ *adj, of an animal* marked with a band of colour about the body *⟨a ∼ pig⟩*

**¹belting** /'belting/ *n* **1** belts collectively **2** material for belts

**²belting** *n, informal* a beating, thrashing

**beltway** /-,way/ *n, NAm* RING ROAD

**beluga** /bi'loohgə/ *n* **1** a white sturgeon (*Acipenser huso*) of the Black sea, Caspian sea, and their tributaries **2 beluga, beluga whale** a whale (*Delphinapterus leucas*) that is about 3 metres

(about 10 feet) long and white when adult [Russ, fr *belyĭ* white; akin to Gk *phainein* to show – more at FANCY]

**belvedere** /'belvidiə/ *n* a structure (eg a summerhouse) placed to command an extensive view; *esp* a turret, dome, etc placed on the roof of a house [It, lit., beautiful view]

**bema** /'beemə/ *n* **1** the part of an early Christian church containing the altar **2** the speaker's platform at a public assembly in ancient Athens **3** a platform in a synagogue from which the scriptures are read [LL & LGk; LL, fr LGk *bēma*, fr Gk, step, tribunal, fr *bainein* to go – more at COME]

**bemire** /bi'mie·ə/ *vt, formal* **1** to soil with mud or dirt **2** to drag through or sink in mire

**bemoan** /bi'mohn/ *vt* to express regret, displeasure, or deep grief over; lament

**bemuse** /bi'myoohz/ *vt* to make confused; bewilder – **bemusedly** *adv,* **bemusement** *n*

**Bence-Jones protein** /,bens 'johnz/ *n* any of various proteins found in the blood and urine in some types of cancer of the bone marrow, esp MULTIPLE MYELOMA [Henry *Bence-Jones* † 1873 E physician & chemist]

**¹bench** /bench/ *n* **1a** a long often backless seat (eg of wood or stone) for two or more people **b** a seat for one or more oarsmen that runs across the width of a boat; ⁴THWART **c** a seat on which the members of a sports team sit when they are not playing **2a(1)** *often cap* a judge's seat in court **a(2)** the office of judge or magistrate *⟨appointed to the ∼⟩* **b** *taking sing or pl vb* the judges or magistrates **(1)** hearing a particular case **(2)** collectively **3a** a seat for an official **b** the office or dignity of such an official **c** the officials occupying such a bench *⟨the ∼ of bishops of the Church of England⟩* **4** any of the long seats on which members sit in the House of Commons and the House of Lords *⟨the opposition ∼es⟩* – compare BACK BENCH, FRONT BENCH **5a** a long worktable **b** a table forming part of a machine **6** a narrow ledge or shelf of land; *esp* one marking the former shoreline of a sea or lake, or the floodplain of a river – called also TERRACE **7a** a platform on which a dog or other domestic animal is displayed at a show **b** a dog show [ME, fr OE *benc;* akin to OHG *bank* bench]

**²bench** *vt* **1** to exhibit (eg a dog) at a show **2** *NAm* to remove from or keep out of a game

**bencher** /'benchə/ *n* a person who sits on or presides at a bench; *specif* a member of the governing body of the INNS OF COURT (legal societies with the exclusive right to admit people as barristers)

**benchmark** /-,mahk/ *n* **1** a point of reference (eg a mark on a permanent object indicating height above sea level) from which measurements may be made, esp in surveying **2** something that serves as a standard by which others may be measured [fr providing a base for a bracket or "bench" to support a surveying instrument]

**bench seat** *n* a single seat running the width of a car

**bench warrant** *n* a warrant issued by a judge ordering that an offender should be arrested

**¹bend** /bend/ *n* **1** a diagonal band that runs from the upper left to the lower right on a heraldic shield **2** any of various knots by which one rope is fastened to another or to some object – compare HITCH [ME, fr MF *bende*, of Gmc origin; akin to OHG *binta, bant* band; (2) ME, band, fr OE, fetter – more at BAND]

**²bend** *vb* **bent** /bent/ *vt* **1** to constrain or strain to tension by curving *⟨∼ a bow⟩* **2a** to turn or force from straight or even to curved or angular **b** to force back to an original straight or even condition **c** to force from a proper shape **3** to fasten – used nautically *⟨∼ a sail to its yard⟩* **4** to make submissive; subdue *⟨peoples unwilling to be bent by colonial power⟩* **5a** to cause to turn from a straight course; deflect **b** to guide or turn in a specified direction; direct *⟨they bent their steps homewards⟩* **c** to incline, dispose *⟨bent their minds to the Buddhist concept of eternity* – C Rand⟩ **6** to direct strenuously or with interest; apply *⟨bent themselves to the work at hand⟩* **7** to alter or modify to make more acceptable, esp to oneself *⟨∼ the rules⟩* ∼ *vi* **1** to move or curve out of a straight line or position; become curved, crooked, or bent **2** to incline the body, esp in submission; bow **3** to incline, tend **4** to apply oneself vigorously *⟨∼ing to their work⟩* – see also **bend over** BACKWARDS [ME *bendan*, fr OE *bendan;* akin to OE *bend* fetter]

**³bend** *n* **1** the act or process of bending; the state of being bent **2** a curved or bent part, esp of a road or stream **3** *pl but taking sing or pl vb* CAISSON DISEASE (condition caused by sudden

changes in pressure, as when a diver surfaces too quickly) –
**round the bend** *informal* mad, crazy ⟨*thought his friends must
have gone* round the bend⟩

**benday** /ben'day/ *adj, often cap* involving a printing process
for adding shaded or tinted areas made up of dots for reproduction by LINE ENGRAVING [*Benjamin Day* †1916 US printer]
– **benday** *vt*

**bender** /'bendə/ *n, informal* a drinking spree

**bend sinister** *n* a diagonal band that runs from the upper
right to the lower left of a heraldic shield, indicating bastardy
or a bastard branch of the family

**bendy** /'bendi/ *adj* 1 having many bends 2 PLIABLE 1a ⟨~ *toy*⟩

**¹beneath** /bi'neeth/ *adv* 1 in or to a lower position; below 2
directly under; underneath [ME *benethe*, fr OE *beneothan*, fr
*be-* + *neothan* below; akin to OE *nithera* nether]

**²beneath** *prep* 1a in or to a lower position than; below b
directly under, esp so as to be close or touching c at the foot
of 2 not suitable to; unworthy of ⟨~ *contempt*⟩ 3 under the
control, pressure, or influence of

**Benedicite** /ˌbeni'disitay, -tee/ *n* a hymn of praise to God,
used in Christian worship, beginning "All the works of the
Lord, bless ye the Lord" [ME, fr LL, bless ye, imper pl of
*benedicere* to bless; fr the first word of the hymn]

**benedick** /'benədik/ *n* a newly married man; *esp* one who has
long been a bachelor [*Benedick*, character in Shakespeare's
*Much Ado About Nothing*]

**Benedictine** /ˌbeni'dikteen, -tin/ *n* 1 a monk or nun of any of
the congregations following the rule of St Benedict and devoted
esp to scholarship 2 a brandy-based liqueur made by French
Benedictine monks – **Benedictine** *adj*

**benediction** /ˌbeni'diksh(ə)n/ *n* 1 the invocation of a blessing;
*esp* the short blessing with which public Christian worship is
concluded 2 *often cap* a Catholic ceremony in which a piece
of consecrated bread (⁴HOST) is shown to the people and the
people are blessed with the bread [ME *benediccioun*, fr LL *bene-
diction-, benedictio*, fr *benedictus*, pp of *benedicere* to bless, fr
L, to speak well of, fr *bene* well + *dicere* to say – more at
BOUNTY, DICTION]

**benedictory** /ˌbeni'dikt(ə)ri/ *adj* of or expressing benediction

**Benedictus** /ˌbeni'diktəs/ *n* either of two texts taken from the
Christian Bible: a one from Mt 21:9 beginning "Blessed is he
that comes in the name of the Lord", used in the Roman
Catholic Mass b one from Lk 1:68 beginning "Blessed be the
Lord God of Israel", sung as a hymn [LL, blessed, fr pp of
*benedicere*; fr its first word]

**benefaction** /ˌbeni'faksh(ə)n/ *n* 1 the act of doing good, esp
by generous donation 2 a benefit conferred; *esp* a charitable
donation [LL *benefaction-, benefactio*, fr L *bene factus*, pp of
*bene facere* to do good to, fr *bene* + *facere* to do – more at
DO]

**benefactor** /'beni,faktə/, *fem* **benefactress** /-tris/ *n* a person
who gives aid; *esp* one who makes a gift or bequest to a person,
institution, etc △ beneficiary

**benefice** /'benifis/ *n* 1 an ecclesiastical office to which an
income is attached 2 an estate held in medieval times in return
for feudal service (e g military services); FIEF [ME, fr MF, fr
ML *beneficium*, fr L, favour, promotion, fr *beneficus* beneficent, fr *bene* + *facere*] – **benefice** *vt*

**beneficence** /bi'nefis(ə)ns/ *n* 1 the quality or state of being
beneficent 2 (a) benefaction [L *beneficentia*, fr *beneficus*]

**beneficent** /bi'nefis(ə)nt/ *adj* 1 doing or producing good; *esp*
performing acts of kindness and charity 2 beneficial [back-for-
mation fr *beneficence*] – **beneficently** *adv*

**beneficial** /ˌbeni'fish(ə)l/ *adj* 1 conferring benefits; conducive
to personal or social well-being 2 receiving or entitling one to
receive personal advantage, use, or benefit ⟨*the* ~ *owner of an
estate*⟩ ⟨*a* ~ *legacy*⟩ [L *beneficium* favour, benefit] – **beneficially** *adv*, **beneficialness** *n*

**synonyms Beneficial, advantageous,** and **profitable** all mean
"bringing good or gain". **Beneficial** describes whatever promotes
personal or social well-being ⟨*tea is* **beneficial** *in a warm climate*⟩.
What is **advantageous** may confer a relative superiority or improve
one's chances of success ⟨*it is* **advantageous** *to have a private
income*⟩. What is **profitable** yields useful results or material profit
⟨*a* **profitable** *day's work/return on one's money*⟩. **antonyms** harmful, detrimental

**beneficiary** /ˌbeni'fish(ə)ri/ *n* 1 one who or that which
benefits from something ⟨*beneficiaries of government programmes*⟩ 2a the person receiving the income from a sum of
money, shares, etc held in trust for him/her b the person

entitled (e g in an insurance policy) to receive proceeds or
benefits △ benefactor – **beneficiary** *adj*

**beneficiate** /ˌbeni'fishi,ayt/ *vt* to treat (a raw material) so as
to improve properties; *esp* to prepare (iron ore) for smelting –
**beneficiation** *n*

**¹benefit** /'benifit/ *n* 1a something that promotes well-being;
an advantage b good, welfare ⟨*did it for their* ~⟩ 2a financial
help in time of need (e g sickness, old age, or unemployment) b
a payment or service provided for under an ANNUITY (yearly
grant), pension scheme, or insurance policy 3 an entertainment,
game, or social event to raise funds for a person or cause; *also*
a series of these ⟨*Boycott is having his* ~ *this year*⟩ 4 *archaic*
an act of kindness [ME, fr AF *benfet*, fr L *bene factum*, fr neut
of *bene factus*] – **give somebody the benefit of the doubt** to
consider or judge somebody innocent or correct without definite proof

**²benefit** *vb* **-t-** (*NAm* **-t-, -tt-**) *vt* to be useful or profitable to
⟨*medicines that* ~ *mankind*⟩ ~ *vi* to receive benefit – **benefiter** *n*

**benefit of clergy** *n* 1 the former privilege of members of the
clergy of being tried for serious crimes in an ecclesiastical, not
a civil, court 2 the official approval of the church ⟨*a couple
living together without* ~⟩

**Benelux** /'beniluks/ *n* (the economic union allowing free circu-
lation of people, goods, money, etc between) Belgium, the
Netherlands, and Luxembourg [*Belgium* + *Netherlands* +
*Luxembourg*]

**benevolence** /bi'nevələns/ *n* 1 disposition to do good; charitableness 2a an act of kindness b a generous gift 3 a compulsory and arbitrary levy forced by certain English kings in the
Middle Ages on their subjects

**benevolent** /bi'nevələnt/ *adj* 1a marked by or disposed to
doing good; charitable b organized for the purpose of doing
good ⟨*a* ~ *society*⟩ 2 showing or characterized by goodwill
⟨~ *smiles*⟩ **synonyms** see ²KIND **antonym** malevolent [ME, fr
L *benevolent-, benevolens*, fr *bene* + *volent-, volens*, prp of *velle*
to wish – more at WILL] – **benevolently** *adv*, **benevolentness** *n*

**Bengali** /ben'gawli, beng'gawli/ *n* 1 a native or inhabitant of
Bengal 2 a native or inhabitant of Bangladesh 3 the modern
Indic language of Bengal [Hindi *Baṅgālī*, fr *Baṅgāl* Bengal,
region of the Indian subcontinent] – **Bengali** *adj*

**bengaline** /'beng·gəleen, --'-/ *n* a fabric with a crosswise rib
made from textile fibres (e g rayon, nylon, cotton, or wool),
often in combination [Fr, fr *Bengal*]

**Bengal light** /beng'gawl/ *n* any of various coloured lights or
flares; *specif* a blue light or flare used, esp formerly, for signalling or illumination

**benighted** /bi'nietid/ *adj* 1 overtaken by darkness or night 2
intellectually, morally, or socially unenlightened – **benightedly**
*adv*, **benightedness** *n*

**benign** /bi'nien/ *adj* 1 of a gentle disposition; gracious 2a
showing kindness and gentleness ⟨~ *faces*⟩ b favourable, mild
⟨*a* ~ *climate*⟩ 3 of a tumour not cancerous – compare
MALIGNANT [ME *benigne*, fr MF, fr L *benignus*, fr *bene* well
+ *gigni* to be born, passive of *gignere* to beget – more at
BOUNTY, KIN] – **benignly** *adv*, **benignity** *n*

**benignant** /bi'nignənt/ *adj* 1 serenely mild and kindly; BENIGN
1,2a 2 favourable, beneficial ⟨*a* ~ *power*⟩ [*benign* + -*ant* (as
in *malignant*)] – **benignancy** *n*, **benignantly** *adv*

**benison** /'benizən, -sən/ *n, formal* a blessing, benediction [ME
*beneson*, fr OF *beneiçon*, fr LL *benediction-, benedictio*]

**benny** /'beni/ *n, slang* a tablet of BENZEDRINE (drug that stimulates the brain) [by shortening & alter. fr *Benzedrine*]

**¹bent** /bent/ *n* 1 an area of unenclosed grassland 2a(1) a reedy
grass a(2) a stalk of stiff coarse grass b bent, bent-grass any
of a genus (*Agrostis*) of grasses including important velvety or
wiry pasture and lawn grasses [ME, grassy place, bent grass, fr
OE *beonot-*; akin to OHG *binuz* rush]

**²bent** *adj* 1 changed from an original straight or even condition
by bending; curved, crooked ⟨~ *twigs*⟩ 2 strongly inclined;
determined – *+ on* or *upon* ⟨*was* ~ *on winning*⟩ 3 *Br slang* 3a
corrupt, dishonest ⟨*a* ~ *official*⟩ b stolen ⟨~ *watches*⟩ c
homosexual [ME, fr pp of *benden* to bend]

**³bent** *n* 1a a strong inclination or interest; a bias b a special
ability or talent ⟨*a* ~ *for painting*⟩ 2 a stiffening framework
(e g across a bridge) to carry horizontal as well as vertical loads
[irreg fr ²*bend*]

**Benthamism** /'benthə,miz(ə)m/ *n* the philosophy (UTILITARI-
ANISM) of Jeremy Bentham, based on the aim that legislation
should provide the greatest good for the greatest number of
people [Jeremy *Bentham* †1832 E philosopher] – **Benthamite** *n*

**benthos** /'benthos/ *n* organisms (e g animals or plants) that live on or in the bottom of lakes, seas, etc [NL, fr Gk, depth, deep sea; akin to Gk *bathys* deep – more at BATHY-] – **benthal, benthic, benthonic** *adj*

**bentonite** /'bentəniet/ *n* a clay that absorbs water easily and is used to give bulk to paper, drugs, etc [Fort *Benton* in Montana, USA] – **bentonitic** *adj*

**bentwood** /-,wood/ *n* wood that is steamed and bent into shape for use in furniture – **bentwood** *adj*

**benumb** /bi'num/ *vt* 1 to make inactive ⟨*their minds* ∼ed *by the tragedy*⟩ 2 to make numb, esp by cold; deaden [ME *benomen*, fr *benomen, benome*, pp of *benimen* to deprive, fr OE *beniman*, fr *be-* + *niman* to take – more at NIMBLE]

**benz-** /benz-/, **benzo-** *comb form* related to benzene or benzoic acid ⟨*benzophenone*⟩ ⟨*benzyl*⟩ [ISV, fr *benzoin*]

**benzaldehyde** /ben'zaldihied/ *n* an oily liquid chemical compound, $C_6H_5CHO$, found in ESSENTIAL OILS (e g in peach kernels) and used in flavouring and perfumery, as a solvent, and in the synthesis of dyes [Ger *benzaldehyd*, fr *benz-* + *aldehyd* aldehyde]

**Benzedrine** /'benzədrin, -dreen/ *trademark* – used for a type of AMPHETAMINE (drug that stimulates the brain)

**benzene** /'benzeen/ *n* an inflammable poisonous liquid hydrocarbon, $C_6H_6$, used in the synthesis of other organic chemical compounds and as a solvent – compare BENZINE [ISV *benz-* + *-ene*] – **benzenoid** *adj*

**benzene ring** *n* the molecular structure comprising a ring of six carbon atoms held together by a particular arrangement of chemical bonds that confers special properties, esp RESONANCE (phenomenon in which the molecular structure of a compound can be represented by a combination of two or more structures), on benzene and other AROMATIC chemical compounds in which it occurs

**benzidine** /'benzədeen, -din/ *n* a poisonous and cancer-producing chemical compound, $NH_2C_6H_4C_6H_4NH_2$, used esp in making dyes [prob fr Ger *benzidin*, fr *benzin* + *-idin* -idine]

**benzimidazole** /,ben,zimə'dayzohl/ *n* a chemical compound, $C_7H_6N_2$, that inhibits the growth of various organisms (e g some viruses); also a derivative of this [ISV *benz-* + *imidazole*]

**benzine** /'benzeen/ *n* any of various (mixtures of) volatile inflammable liquids distilled from petroleum and used esp as solvents or as motor fuels – compare BENZENE [Ger *benzin*, fr *benz-*]

**benzoate** /'benzoh·ayt, -ət/ *n* any of various chemical compounds (SALTS or ESTERS) formed by combination between BENZOIC ACID and a metal atom, an alcohol, or another chemical group

**benzocaine** /'benzəkayn, -zoh-/ *n* a synthetic chemical compound, $NH_2C_6H_4CO_2C_2H_5$, used as a local anaesthetic [ISV]

**benzodiazepine** /,benzohdie'ayzipin/ *n* any of several chemically related synthetic drugs (e g DIAZEPAM, CHLORDIAZEPOXIDE, and NITRAZEPAM) widely used as tranquillizers, sedatives, and hypnotics [*benz-* + *di-* + *az-* + *epoxide* + *-ine*]

**benzofuran** /,benzoh'fyooəran/ *n* COUMARONE (chemical compound used in the manufacture of plastics) [*benz-* + *furan*]

**benzoic acid** /ben'zoh·ik/ *n* an acid, $C_6H_5CO_2H$, found naturally (e g in benzoin or in cranberries) or made synthetically and used esp as a preservative of foods, in the treatment of fungous skin infections, and in the manufacture of other chemical compounds [ISV, fr *benzoin*]

**benzoin** /'benzoh·in, -'--, 'benzoyn/ *n* 1 a hard fragrant yellowish semisolid chemical compound obtained directly as exudations from trees (genus *Styrax*) of SE Asia, used esp in medicines to treat excessive catarrh 2 a chemical compound, $C_6H_5CH(OH)COC_6H_5$, that is a KETONE and has two linked benzene rings and is used in making other organic chemical compounds 3a a tree yielding benzoin b SPICEBUSH (yellow-flowered shrub) [MF *benjoin*, fr OCatal *benjui*, fr Ar *lubān jāwi*, lit., frankincense of Java]

**benzol** /'benzol/ *n* 1 a mixture of benzene and other chemical compounds (e g TOLUENE) 2 benzene – not now used technically [Ger, fr *benz-* + *-ol*]

**benzophenone** /,benzohfi'nohn/ *n* a chemical compound, $C_6H_5COC_6H_5$, that is a KETONE and is used esp in the manufacture of perfumes [ISV]

**benzopyrene** /,benzoh'pie(ə)reen/, **benzpyrene** /benz-'pie(ə)reen/ *n* a yellow cancer-producing chemical compound, $C_{20}H_{12}$, found in COAL TAR [ISV]

**benzoyl** /'benzoh·il/ *n* the chemical group, $C_6H_5CO$, derived

from benzoic acid [Ger, fr *benzoësäure* benzoic acid + Gk *hylē* matter, lit., wood]

**benzyl** /'benzil, -zeel/ *n* the chemical group, $C_6H_5CH_2$, with a VALENCY of one, derived from TOLUENE [ISV *benz-* + *-yl*] – **benzylic** *adj*

**bequeath** /bi'kweeth, bi'kweedh/ *vt* 1 to give or leave (something, esp personal property) in a will – compare DEVISE 2 2 to transmit; HAND DOWN ⟨*ideas* ∼ed *to us by the 19th century*⟩ [ME *bequethen*, fr OE *becwethan*, fr *be-* + *cwethan* to say – more at QUOTH] – **bequeathal** *n*

**bequest** /bi'kwest/ *n* 1 the act of bequeathing 2 something bequeathed; a legacy [ME, irreg fr *bequethen*]

**berate** /bi'rayt/ *vt, formal* to scold or condemn vehemently and at length *synonyms* see ²SCOLD [*be-* + *rate* (to chide), fr ME *raten*]

**Berber** /'buhbə/ *n* 1 a member of a CAUCASIAN (light-skinned) people of northern Africa west of Tripoli 2a a branch of the Afro-Asiatic language family comprising languages spoken by various tribal groups (e g the Tuareg or the Kabyle) in N Africa b any of these languages [Ar *Barbar*]

**berberine** /'buhbəreen/ *n* a bitter chemical compound, $C_{20}H_{19}NO_5$, that is an ALKALOID obtained from the roots of various plants (e g barberry) and used esp as a medicinal tonic [Ger *berberin*, fr NL *berberis*]

**berberis** /'buhbəris/ *n* any of several shrubs of the barberry family; *esp* the barberry [NL, genus name, fr ML *barberis*, fr Ar *barbārīs*]

**berceuse** /beə'suhz/ *n, pl* **berceuses** /∼/ (a musical composition in the style of) a lullaby [Fr, fr *bercer* to rock]

**bereave** /bi'reev/ *vt* **bereft** /bi'reft/, **bereaved** 1 to deprive of something or someone held dear, esp through death – usu + *of* 2 *archaic* to take away (a valued or necessary possession), esp by force [ME *bereven*, fr OE *berēafian*, fr *be-* + *rēafian* to rob; akin to OHG *roubōn* to rob, L *rumpere* to break, *ruere* to rush, dig up]

¹**bereaved** /bi'reevd/ *adj* suffering the death of a loved one ⟨∼ *parents*⟩

*synonyms* **Bereaved** is preferred to **bereft** in the emotional context "deprived by death" ⟨*a* **bereaved** *mother*⟩. One is usually **bereft** *of* something.

²**bereaved** *n, pl* **bereaved** one who is bereaved

**bereavement** /bi'reevmənt/ *n* the state or fact of being bereaved; *esp* the loss of a loved one by death

**bereft** /bi'reft/ *adj* 1 deprived or robbed *of*; completely without something ⟨∼ *of all hope*⟩ 2 bereaved

**beret** /'beray/ *n* a cap with a tight headband, a soft full flat top, and no peak [Fr *béret*, fr Prov *berret* – more at BIRETTA]

¹**berg** /buhg/ *n* an iceberg

²**berg** *n, SAfr* a mountain – often in place-names [Afrik, fr MD *bergh, berch*; akin to OHG *berg* mountain]

**bergamot** /'buhgəmot/ *n* 1 a pear-shaped orange of a tree (*Citrus bergamia*) whose rind yields an ESSENTIAL OIL used in perfumery 2 any of several plants of the mint family (genera *Mentha* or *Monarda*) [prob fr *Bergamo*, town in Italy; (2) fr its yielding an oil like that of the bergamot orange]

**bergschrund** /'beəg,shroont/ /(Ger berk∫rond)/ *n* a usu deep crevasse or series of crevasses frequently occurring near the top of a mountain glacier [Ger, fr *berg* mountain + *schrund* crack]

**berg wind** /buhg/ *n* a hot dry wind blowing from the north in coastal regions of S Africa

**beribboned** /bi'ribənd/ *adj* adorned with ribbons

**beriberi** /'beri,beri, ,--'--/ *n* a disease caused by a lack of or inability to absorb VITAMIN $B_1$ and marked by degeneration of the nerves causing pain and paralysis [Sinhalese *bæribæri*]

**berk** /buhk/ *n, Br slang* a burk

**Berkeleian, Berkeleyan** /bah'klee-ən, 'bahkli·ən/ *adj* (characteristic) of Bishop Berkeley or his theory that only what is immediately perceived has existence [George *Berkeley* †1753 Ir bishop & philosopher] – **Berkeleian** *n*, **Berkeleianism** *n*

**berkelium** /bə'keeli·əm/ *n* an artificially produced radioactive metallic chemical element [NL, fr *Berkeley*, city in California, USA]

**Berkshire** /'bahkshiə/ *n* (any of) a breed of medium-sized black pigs with white markings [*Berkshire*, county in England]

**berlin** /buh'lin/ *n* a four-wheeled 2-seat covered carriage with a hooded rear seat [Fr *berline*, fr *Berlin*, city in Germany]

**berm, berme** /buhm/ *n* 1 a narrow path or ledge between a ditch or moat and the base of a parapet in a fortification 2 a narrow path beside a road, canal, etc [Fr *berme*, fr D *berm* strip of ground along a dyke; akin to ME *brimme* brim]

**Bermuda grass** /bə'myoohdə/ *n* a trailing grass (*Cynodon dactylon*) native to southern Europe but now widely distributed in warm countries [*Bermuda* islands in the W Atlantic ocean]

**Bermuda rig** /bə'myoohdə/ *n* a sailing-boat rig with a tall mainmast to which a triangular FORE-AND-AFT mainsail pointing in the direction of the stern is directly attached rather than being suspended from a crosspiece

**Bermuda shorts** *n pl* knee-length shorts

**Bernoulli trial** /beə'nooh·i, -'nooh·yi, buh-/ *n* a statistical experiment that has two mutually exclusive outcomes, each of which has a constant probability of occurrence ⟨*tossing a coin for heads or tails is a* ∼⟩ [Jacques *Bernouilli* †1705 Swiss mathematician]

**berried** /'berid/ *adj* 1 having or bearing berries 2 *of a lobster or related animal* bearing eggs

**¹berry** /'beri/ *n* 1a a small, pulpy, and usu edible fruit (eg a strawberry or raspberry) b a simple fruit (eg a currant, grape, tomato, or banana) with a pulpy or fleshy PERICARP (ripened ovary wall enclosing the seeds) – used technically in botany c the dry seed of some plants (eg coffee) 2 an egg of a fish or lobster [ME *berye*, fr OE *berie*; akin to OHG *beri* berry] – **berrylike** *adj*

**²berry** *vi* 1 to bear or produce berries ⟨*a* ∼*ing shrub*⟩ 2 to gather or seek berries ⟨*go* ∼*ing*⟩

**bersagliere** /,beəsah'lyeəri/ *n, pl* **bersaglieri** /∼/ a member of a highly-trained crack Italian regiment [It, fr *bersaglio* target, deriv of OF *berser* to shoot, hit]

**¹berserk** /bə'zuhk, buh-/ *n* a pre-medieval and medieval Scandinavian warrior noted for fighting in a reckless insane fury and for brutality [ON *berserkr*, fr *björn* bear + *serkr* shirt]

**²berserk** *adj* frenzied, esp through anger, grief, etc; crazed – chiefly in **go berserk** – **berserk** *adv*

**berserker** /bə'zuhkə/ *n* a berserk

**¹berth** /buhth/ *n* 1 safe distance for manoeuvring maintained between a ship and another object 2 the (assigned) place where a ship lies when at anchor or at a wharf 3 a place (eg a bunk) to sleep, esp on a ship or train 4 *informal* a job, appointment [prob fr ²*bear* + -*th*] – **give a wide berth to** to remain at a safe distance from; avoid

**²berth** *vt* 1 to bring into a berth; dock 2 to allot a berth to ∼ *vi* to come into a berth

**bertha** /'buhthə/ *n* a wide round collar covering the shoulders [Fr *berthe*, fr *Berthe* (Bertha) †783 Queen of the Franks, famed for her modesty]

**-berther** /-buhthə/ *comb form* (→ *n*) something having berths of a specified kind or number

**Bertillon system** /'buhtilon (*Fr* bɛrtiːjɔ̃)/ *n* a system of identification of people, esp criminals, by a standardized detailed physical description and photographs [Alphonse *Bertillon* †1914 Fr criminologist]

**beryl** /'beril/ *n* a mineral, Be$_3$Al$_2$ Si$_6$O$_{18}$, that is a very hard SILICATE of beryllium and aluminium, occurs in green, bluish-green, yellow, pink, or white crystals, and is used as a gemstone – compare AQUAMARINE, EMERALD [ME, fr OF *beril*, fr L *beryllus*, fr Gk *bēryllos*, of Indic origin; akin to Skt *vaidūrya* cat's-eye]

**beryllium** /bə'rili·əm/ *n* a steel-grey light strong brittle metallic chemical element with a VALENCY of two, used chiefly as a hardening agent in alloys [NL, fr Gk *bēryllion*, dim. of *bēryllos*]

**beseech** /bi'seech/ *vt* **besought** /-sawt/, **beseeched** 1 to beg for urgently or anxiously ⟨*he besought a favour*⟩ 2 to request earnestly; implore ⟨*do not go, I* ∼ *you*⟩ **synonyms** see BEG [ME *besechen*, fr *be-* + *sechen* to seek] – **beseechingly** *adv*

**beseem** /bi'seem/ *vb, archaic vi* to be fitting or becoming ∼ *vt* to be suitable to [ME *besemen*, fr *be-* + *semen* to seem]

**beset** /bi'set/ *vt* -**tt**- 1 to trouble or assail constantly ⟨∼ *by fears*⟩ 2 to surround and attack ⟨∼ *by the enemy*⟩ 3 *archaic* to set or stud (as if) with ornaments [ME *besetten* to set round, encompass, fr OE *besettan*, fr *be-* + *settan* to set] – **besetment** *n*

**besetting** /bi'seting/ *adj* constantly causing temptation or difficulty; continuously present ⟨*a* ∼ *sin*⟩

**beshrew** /bi'shrooh/ *vt, archaic* to curse [ME *beshrewen*, fr *be-* + *shrewen* to curse, fr *shrewe* evil person – more at SHREW]

**¹beside** /bi'sied/ *adv, archaic* 1 nearby 2 besides [ME, adv & prep, fr OE *be sīdan* at or to the side, fr *be* at (fr *bī*) + *sīdan*, dat & acc of *sīde* side – more at BY]

**²beside** *prep* 1a by the side of ⟨*walk* ∼ *me*⟩ b in comparison

with **c** on a par with **d** unconnected with; wide of ⟨∼ *the point*⟩ 2 besides – **beside oneself** in a state of extreme agitation or excitement

**¹besides** /bi'siedz/ *adv* 1 as an additional factor or circumstance ⟨*has a wife and six children* ∼⟩ 2 moreover, furthermore

**²besides** *prep* 1 other than; unless we are to mention ⟨*who* ∼ *John would say that?*⟩ 2 as an additional circumstance to ⟨∼ *being old, she is losing her sight*⟩

**synonyms** Compare **besides**, **beside**, **except**: in modern English, **besides** is used rather than **beside** in the meaning "in addition to" ⟨**besides** *being old, she is losing her sight*⟩; while **beside** is the only one used in the literal sense ⟨*walk* **beside** *me*⟩. In the meaning "other than", **besides** is inclusive and **except** is exclusive. Compare ⟨*all of us passed* **besides** *John* (= he passed too)⟩ ⟨*all of us passed* **except** *John* (= he failed)⟩.

**besiege** /bi'seej/ *vt* 1 to surround with armed forces; lay siege to 2a to press with questions, requests, etc; importune b to crowd round; surround closely – **besieger** *n*

**besmirch** /bi'smuhch/ *vt* to sully, soil

**besom** /'beez(ə)m/ *n* BROOM 2; *esp* one made of twigs [ME *beseme*, fr OE *besma*; akin to OHG *besmo* broom]

**besotted** /bi'sotid/ *adj* 1 made foolish or confused, esp by infatuation 2 drunk, intoxicated [fr pp of *besot* (to make dull or foolish), fr *be-* + *sot* (to befool)]

**bespatter** /bi'spatə/ *vt* 1 to spatter 2 to render less attractive or valuable ⟨*the meaningless abstractions that* ∼ *history books* – *TLS*⟩

**bespeak** /bi'speek/ *vt* **bespoke** /bi'spohk/, **bespoken** *formal* 1 to hire, engage, or claim beforehand; arrange for in advance 2 to speak to; address 3 to indicate, signify ⟨*her performance* ∼*s considerable practice*⟩ 4 to order (goods)

**bespectacled** /bi'spektəkld/ *adj* wearing glasses

**bespoke** /bi'spohk/ *adj, Br* 1 made-to-measure; *broadly* made or arranged according to particular requirements 2 dealing in or producing articles that are made-to-measure [fr pp of *bespeak*]

**besprent** /bi'sprent/ *adj, archaic* sprinkled over [ME *bespreynt*, fr pp of *besprengen* to besprinkle, fr OE *besprengan*]

**besprinkle** /bi'springkl/ *vt* to sprinkle [ME *besprengeln*, freq of *besprengen*]

**Bessemer converter** /'besimə/ *n* the furnace used in the Bessemer process

**Bessemer process** *n* a steelmaking process in which air is blasted through molten unrefined iron (PIG IRON) to remove impurities [Sir Henry *Bessemer* †1898 E engineer & inventor]

**¹best** /best/ *adj, superlative of* GOOD 1 excelling all others (eg in ability, quality, or integrity) ⟨*the* ∼ *student*⟩ 2 most productive of good ⟨*what is the* ∼ *thing to do?*⟩ 3 most, largest ⟨*for the* ∼ *part of a week*⟩ 4 reserved for special occasions ⟨*got out the* ∼ *sherry glasses*⟩ [ME, fr OE *betst*; akin to OE *bōt* remedy – more at BETTER]

**²best** *adv, superlative of* WELL 1 in the best manner; to the best extent or degree ⟨*a Wednesday would suit me* ∼ – *SEU S*⟩ 2 BETTER 2 ⟨*is* ∼ *avoided*⟩ – **as best** in the best way ⟨*climbed over as best he could*⟩

**³best** *n, pl* **best** 1 the best state or part ⟨*never at my* ∼ *before breakfast*⟩ ⟨*that's the* ∼ *of living out of London*⟩ 2 somebody or something that is best ⟨*can ride with the* ∼ *of them*⟩ 3 the greatest degree of good or excellence ⟨*only the* ∼ *is good enough for me*⟩ 4 one's maximum effort ⟨*do your* ∼⟩ 5 best clothes ⟨*Sunday* ∼⟩ 6 a winning majority ⟨*the* ∼ *of three games*⟩ 7 the victory, advantage ⟨*had the* ∼ *of the argument*⟩ – **at best** even under the most favourable circumstances; seen in the best light – **make the best of** to cope with (an unfavourable situation) in the best and most optimistic manner possible – see also SIX **of the best**

**⁴best** *vt* to get the better of; outdo

**¹bestead** *also* **bested** /bi'sted/ *adj, archaic* situated [ME *bested*, fr *be-* + *sted*, pp of *steden* to place, fr *stede* place – more at STEAD]

**²bestead** *vt* **bestead** *archaic* to help, avail [*be-* + *stead*]

**best end, best end of neck** *n* a cut of lamb, veal, etc from between the lower end of the neck and the loin

**bestial** /'besti·əl/ *adj* 1 of beasts 2 marked by brutal or inhuman instincts or desires; *specif* sexually depraved [ME, fr MF, fr L *bestialis*, fr *bestia* beast] – **bestialize** *vt*, **bestially** *adv*

**bestiality** /,besti'aləti/ *n* 1 the condition or status of a lower animal 2 bestial behaviour; *specif* sexual relations between a human being and an animal

**bestiary** /'besti·əri/ n a medieval book containing both illustrations of real or imaginary animals and moralizing or allegorical tales about them [ML *bestiarium*, fr L, neut of *bestiarius* of beasts, fr *bestia*]

**bestir** /bi'stuh/ vt to stir up; rouse to action

**best man** n the principal attendant of a bridegroom at a wedding

**bestow** /bi'stoh/ vt 1 to present as a gift; *also* to confer as an honour 2 *formal* 2a to put to use b to put in a particular place c to provide with accommodation *synonyms* see ¹GIVE [ME *bestowen*, fr be- + *stowe* place – more at STOW] – **bestowal** n

**bestrew** /bi'strooh/ vt **bestrewed; bestrewed, bestrewn** /bi'stroohn/ 1 to strew 2 to lie scattered over

**bestride** /bi'stried/ vt **bestrode** /bi'strohd/; **bestridden** /bi'stridən/ 1 to ride, sit, or stand astride; straddle 2 to tower over; dominate

**best-'seller** n 1 something, esp a book, which has sold in very large numbers, usu over a given period 2 an author or performer whose works sell in very large numbers – **best-selling** adj

**¹bet** /bet/ n **1a** the act of risking a sum of money or other stake on the forecast outcome of a future event (eg a race or contest), esp in competition with a second party **b** a stake so risked **c** the predicted outcome of such an act 2 an opinion, belief ⟨*my ~ is it will pour with rain*⟩ 3 *informal* a plan of action ⟨*your best ~ is to call a plumber*⟩ [perh short for obs *abet* (abetment)]

**²bet** vb **-tt-; bet** *also* **betted** vt **1a** to stake on the outcome of an issue **b** to make a bet with (somebody) 2 *informal* to be convinced that ⟨*I ~ they don't come*⟩ ~ vi to lay a bet – **you bet** *informal* you may be sure; certainly – see also **bet one's bottom** DOLLAR

*usage* The usual past **bet** is used for definite transactions ⟨*she bet me £5 I couldn't do it*⟩. The rarer past **betted** is used in a more general sense, particularly with no object ⟨*they betted a lot in the 18th century*⟩.

**¹beta** /'beetə; *also* 'baytə/ n **1a** the 2nd letter of the Greek alphabet **b** ¹B 4 2 – used to designate the second brightest star of a constellation [Gk *bēta*, of Sem origin; akin to Heb *bēth* beth]

**²beta,** β- adj 1 of or being an atom or chemical group second in position from a particular major or conspicuous atom or group in the molecular structure of an organic compound 2 of or being the second of two or more chemical compounds closely related in structure and having the same number of each type of atom as a specified chemical compound ⟨β-*naphthol*⟩

**beta-adrenergic** /ˌadri'nuhjik/ adj relating to or being a beta-receptor ⟨~ *blocking action*⟩

**beta-adrenergic receptor** /ˌadri'nuhjik/ n a beta-receptor

**'beta-,blocker** n a drug (eg PROPRANOLOL) that inhibits the action of adrenalin and similar compounds and is used esp to treat high blood pressure – **beta-blocking** n or adj

**betake** /bi'tayk/ vt **betook** /bi'took/; **betaken** /bi'taykən/ *formal* to cause (oneself) to go

**beta-oxi'dation** n gradual breakdown of FATTY ACIDS, esp in MITOCHONDRIA (energy-producing body in a cell)

**beta particle** n an electron or POSITRON (positively charged electron) ejected from the nucleus of an atom during radioactive decay

**beta ray** n a stream of beta particles

**beta-re'ceptor** n a site (RECEPTOR) on the surface of a cell to which adrenalin and similar substances bind, causing the stimulation of those body actions (eg increased heart rate and output, dilation of small blood vessels, and relaxation of intestinal, uterine, and bronchial muscle) that are activated by the SYMPATHETIC NERVOUS SYSTEM – compare ALPHA-RECEPTOR; called also BETA-ADRENERGIC RECEPTOR

**betatron** /'beetətron/ n a machine for accelerating electrons to a very high speed using a rapidly varying magnetic field and used in research and to produce X-rays of very high energy [ISV]

**betel** /'beetl/ n a climbing pepper (*Piper betle*) whose leaves are chewed together with betel nut and lime, esp by SE Asians, to stimulate the flow of saliva [Pg, fr Tamil *verrilai*]

**betel nut** n the sharp-tasting seed of the betel palm [fr its being chewed with betel leaves]

**betel palm** n an Asian palm tree (*Areca catechu*) that has an orange-coloured fruit [*betel* nut]

**bête noire** /ˌbet 'nwah/ n, pl **bêtes noires** /~/ a person or thing strongly detested or avoided [Fr, lit., black beast]

**beth** /bayth, bayt, bays/ n the 2nd letter of the Hebrew alphabet [Heb *bēth*, fr *bayith* house]

**bethel** /'beth(ə)l/ n 1 a chapel for NONCONFORMISTS (members of Protestant Christian denominations who disagree with the established Church) 2 a place of worship for seamen [Heb *bēth' ēl* house of God]

**bethink** /bi'thingk/ vt **bethought** /bi'thawt/ *archaic* to cause (oneself) to call something to mind

**betide** /bi'tied/ vb, *formal or poetic* vt to happen to; befall ~ vi to happen, esp as if by fate □ used only in the 3rd person sing., pres subj, and infin *synonyms* see HAPPEN [ME *betiden*, fr be- + *tiden* to happen, fr OE *tīdan*; akin to MD *tiden* to go, come, OE *tid* time]

**betimes** /bi'tiemz/ adv, *formal* 1 in good time; early 2 in a short time

**bêtise** /be'teez/ n, pl **bêtises** /~/ 1 lack of good sense; stupidity 2 an act of foolishness or stupidity [Fr, fr *bête* foolish, fr *bête* fool, beast]

**betoken** /bi'tohkən/ vt 1 to give evidence of; show 2 to presage, portend

**betony** /'betəni/ n any of several plants of the mint family (genera *Betonica* or *Stachys*) [ME *betoine*, fr OF *betoine*, fr L *vettonica, betonica*, fr *Vettones*, an ancient Spanish people]

**betray** /bi'tray/ vt 1 to lead astray; deceive 2a to deliver to an enemy by treachery, disloyalty, or violation of trust **b** to be a traitor to ⟨~ed *the people*⟩ **3a** to fail or desert, esp in time of need **b** to disappoint the hopes, expectation, or confidence of **4a** to be a sign of (something one would like to hide) **b** to disclose, deliberately or unintentionally, in violation of confidence *synonyms* see ¹REVEAL [ME *betrayen*, fr be- + *trayen* to betray, fr OF *traīr*, fr L *tradere* – more at TRAITOR] – **betrayal** n, **betrayer** n

**betroth** /bi'trohth, -'trohdh/ vt to promise to marry or give in marriage [ME *betrouthen*, fr be- + *trouthe* truth, troth]

**betrothal** /bi'trohdhəl/ n 1 the act of betrothing or fact of being betrothed 2 a mutual promise or contract for a future marriage

**betrothed** /bi'trohdhd/ n, pl **betrothed** the person to whom one is betrothed

**¹better** /'betə/ adj, comparative of GOOD or of WELL 1 more than half ⟨*for the ~ part of a month*⟩ **2a** improved in health **b** cured, recovered ⟨*not quite ~ yet*⟩ 3 of higher quality ⟨*ladies' ~ dresses*⟩ [ME *bettre*, fr OE *betera*; akin to OE *bōt* remedy, Skt *bhadra* fortunate]

*usage* The common use of **better** in commercial and advertising language ⟨*the better class of customer*⟩, where there is no true comparison, is disapproved of by some people.

**²better** adv, comparative of WELL 1 in a better manner; to a better extent or degree ⟨*he knows the story ~ than you do*⟩ 2 more wisely or usefully ⟨*is ~ avoided*⟩ – often in *had better* ⟨*I'd ~ not go round at lunchtime* – SEU S⟩ 3 more ⟨*it is ~ than nine miles to the nearest shop*⟩ – disapproved of by some speakers

*usage* Had **better** is to be preferred to *would* **better** as a way of expressing a recommendation. *I'd* **better**, *he'd* **better**, etc may stand for either, and in informal use the form *I* / **better** is becoming common.

**³better** n, pl better, (1b) **betters 1a** something better ⟨*a change for the ~* ⟩ **b** usu pl one's superior, esp in merit or rank 2 *the* advantage, victory ⟨*get the ~ of him*⟩ – **for better or (for) worse** whatever the outcome – **get the better of** to overcome, defeat

**⁴better** vt 1 to make better: eg **1a** to make more tolerable or acceptable ⟨*trying to ~ the lot of slum dwellers*⟩ **b** to make more complete or perfect ⟨*looked forward to ~ing her acquaintance with the new neighbours*⟩ 2 to surpass in excellence; excel ~ vi to become better

**better half** n, *chiefly humorous* a spouse; *esp* a wife

**betterment** /'betəmənt/ n an improvement; *esp* the enhanced value of a building or land due to improvements or development in its immediate vicinity

**better-'off** adj being in comfortable economic circumstances ⟨*the ~ live in the older section of town*⟩

**betting shop** /'beting/ n Br a bookmaker's shop

**bettor, better** /'betə/ n one who bets

**¹between** /bi'tween/ prep **1a** through the common action of; jointly engaging ⟨*shared the work ~ the two of them*⟩ **b** in shares to each of ⟨*divided ~ his four grandchildren*⟩ **2a** in or into the time, space, or interval that separates ⟨~ meals⟩ ⟨in ~ the rafters⟩ **b** in intermediate relation to ⟨a colour ~ blue and grey⟩ **3a** from one to the other of ⟨travelling ~ London and Paris⟩ **b** serving to connect or separate ⟨air serves ~ the two capitals⟩ ⟨the line ~ fact and fancy⟩ **4** in point of comparison of ⟨the difference ~ bread and cake⟩ ⟨not much to choose ~ the two coats⟩ **5** taking together the total effect of; WHAT WITH ⟨kept very busy ~ cooking, writing, and gardening⟩ [ME betwene, prep & adv, fr OE betwēonum, fr be- + -twēonum (dat pl) (akin to Goth tweihnai two each); akin to OE twā two] – **between you and me** in confidence

*usage* **1** It is normal after **between** to use either a plural noun ⟨the distance **between** the two houses⟩ or else two or more nouns joined by and ⟨the distance **between** my house and hers⟩. It is common, but disapproved of by many people, to use a singular noun when **between** is followed by each or every ⟨⚠ the distance **between** each house⟩. **2** When two or more nouns follow **between**, they should properly be joined by and, and not by any other word ⟨⚠ choose **between** going on holiday or buying new clothes⟩. **3** In modern written English, a pronoun after **between** should correctly be in the objective case, although ⟨**between** you and I⟩ has long been common in speech, particularly in the meaning "confidentially" ⟨**between** you and I, he's not very reliable⟩ ⟨all debts are cleared **between** you and I – Shak⟩. See AMONG

²**between** adv in or into an intermediate space or interval

**betweentimes** /bi'tween,tiemz/ adv at or during intervals

**betweenwhiles** /bi'tween,wielz/ adv betweentimes

**betwixt** /bi'twikst/ adv or prep, archaic between [ME, fr OE betwux, fr be- + -twux (akin to Goth tweihnai)]

**betwixt and between** adv or adj in a midway position; neither one thing nor the other

**beurre manié** /,buh 'manyay, ,- -'- (Fr bœːr manje)/ n a thick paste made with equal weights of flour and butter kneaded together and used for thickening soups, sauces, and stews [Fr, kneaded butter]

¹**bevel** /'bevl/ adj oblique, bevelled

²**bevel** n **1a** the angle that one surface or line meeting another makes when they are not at right angles **b** a surface, line, or join so slanting **2** an instrument consisting of two straight rules or arms jointed together and opening to any angle for drawing angles or adjusting surfaces to be given a bevel **3** the part of printing type extending from the printing surface (FACE) to the bottom of the raised character (SHOULDER) [(assumed) MF, fr OF baïf with open mouth, fr baer to yawn – more at ABEYANCE]

³**bevel** vb **-ll-** (NAm **-l-, -ll-**) vt to cut or shape to a bevel to incline, slant

**bevel gear** n either of a pair of toothed wheels that rotate and work shafts inclined to each other; also a system of such gears

**beverage** /'bev(ə)rij/ n a liquid for drinking; esp one that is not water [ME, fr MF bevrage, fr beivre to drink, fr L bibere – more at POTABLE]

**bevvy** /'bevi/ n, dial Br informal an alcoholic drink; esp beer [by shortening & alter. fr beverage]

**bevy** /'bevi/ n **1** a large group or collection ⟨a ~ of girls⟩ **2** a group of animals, esp quail, together [ME bevey]

**bewail** /bi'wayl/ vt to express deep sorrow for, usu by wailing and lamentation ⟨wringing her hands and ~ing her fate⟩

**beware** /bi'weə/ vi to be on one's guard – often + of ⟨~ of the dog⟩ ~ vt to be wary of □ usu in imper and infin [ME been war, fr been to be + war careful – more at BE, WARE]

**bewigged** /bi'wigd/ adj wearing a wig

**bewilder** /bi'wildə/ vt to perplex or confuse, esp by a complexity, variety, or multitude of objects or considerations *synonyms* see ¹PUZZLE [be- + arch. wilder (to lead astray, perplex), prob irreg fr wilderness] – **bewilderedly** adv, **bewilderedness** n, **bewilderingly** adv

**bewilderment** /bi'wildəmənt/ n **1** the quality or state of being bewildered **2** a bewildering tangle or confusion

**bewitch** /bi'wich/ vt **1a** to influence or affect, esp harmfully, by witchcraft **b** to cast a spell over **2** to attract as if by the power of witchcraft; enchant ⟨~ed by her beauty⟩ ~ vi to bewitch someone or something □ compare CHARM – **bewitchery** n, **bewitchingly** adv

**bewitchment** /bi'wichmənt/ n **1a** the act or power of bewitching **b** a spell that bewitches **2** the state of being bewitched

**bewray** /bi'ray/ vt, archaic to divulge, betray [ME bewreyen, fr be- + wreyen to accuse, fr OE wrēgan]

**bey** /bay/ n **1a** a provincial governor in the Ottoman Empire **b** the former ruler of Tunis or Tunisia **2** – formerly used as a courtesy title in Turkey and Egypt ⟨Ali Bey⟩ [Turk, gentleman, chief]

¹**beyond** /bee'ond/ adv **1** on or to the farther side; farther **2** as an additional amount; besides [ME, prep & adv, fr OE begeondan, fr be- + geondan beyond, fr geond yond – more at YOND]

²**beyond** prep **1** on or to the farther side of; at a greater distance than **2a** out of the reach or sphere of ⟨~ my control⟩ ⟨~ repair⟩ **b** in a degree or amount surpassing ⟨~ my wildest dreams⟩ **c** out of the comprehension of **3** other than; ²BESIDES ⟨nothing ~ the clothes on her back⟩ **4** later than; past

³**beyond** n **1** something that lies beyond **2** something that lies outside the scope of ordinary experience; specif ²HEREAFTER

**bezant** /'bezənt, bə'zant/ n SOLIDUS 1 (ancient Roman gold coin) [ME besant, fr MF, fr ML Byzantius Byzantine, fr Byzantium, ancient name of Istanbul, city in Turkey]

**bezel** /'bez(ə)l/ n **1** a sloping edge or face, esp on a cutting tool (e g a chisel) **2** the oblique side or face of a cut gem; specif the upper faceted portion of a gem cut to have special brilliance that projects from the setting **3** a rim or groove that holds a transparent covering on a watch, clock, headlight, etc; also a rotatable ring with special markings round a watch face [prob Fr dial., alter. of Fr biseau]

**bezique** /bə'zeek/ n a card game for two people that is played with a double pack of 64 cards; also the combination of queen of spades and jack of diamonds in this game [Fr bésigue]

**bezoar** /'beezaw/ n any of various hard masses (e g hair balls) found chiefly in the stomachs and intestines esp of cattle, sheep, and other ruminants and formerly believed to be an antidote to poison [Fr bézoard, fr Sp bezoar, fr Ar bāzahr, fr Per pād-zahr, fr pād protecting (against) + zahr poison]

**Bhadon** /'bahdohn/ n – see MONTH table [Hindi bhādō, fr Skt bhādrapada, fr Bhādrapada, a constellation]

**Bhagavad Gita** /,bahgəvahd 'geetah/ n a Hindu religious text consisting chiefly of discourses of Krishna in poetic form and mentioning devotion to a particular god as a means of salvation [Skt Bhagavadgītā, lit., song of the blessed one (Krishna)]

**bhakti** /'bahkti/ n devotion to a particular god constituting a way to salvation in Hinduism [Skt, lit., portion]

**bhang, bang** /bang/ n **1** HEMP 1 **2** a mild form of cannabis used esp in India [Hindi bhãg]

**Bhojpuri** /'bojpoo,ree/ n the dialect of Bihari spoken in W Bihar and the E United Provinces in India [Hindi Bhojpurī, fr Bhojpur, village in Bihar]

**B-horizon** /bee/ n the subsurface layer of soil that is frequently enriched by substances (e g clay) from the layer above (A-HORIZON)

**bi** /bie/ n or adj, informal (a) bisexual

¹**bi-** /bie-/ prefix **1a** two ⟨biparous⟩ ⟨bilingual⟩ **b** appearing or occurring every two ⟨bimonthly⟩ ⟨biweekly⟩ **c** into two parts ⟨bisect⟩ **2a** twice; doubly; on both sides ⟨biconvex⟩ ⟨biserrate⟩ **b** appearing or occurring twice in ⟨biweekly⟩ – often disapproved in this sense because of the likelihood of confusion with sense 1b; compare SEMI- **3** located between, involving, or affecting two (specified) symmetrical parts ⟨biaural⟩ **4** DI- 2 ⟨biphenyl⟩ **5** acid salt ⟨bicarbonate⟩ [ME, fr L; akin to OE twi-]

²**bi-, bio-** comb form life ⟨biography⟩; living organisms or tissue ⟨biology⟩ [Gk, fr bios mode of life – more at QUICK]

**biannual** /-'anyooəl/ adj occurring twice a year – compare BIENNIAL – **biannually** adv

¹**bias** /'bie-əs/ n **1** a line diagonal to the grain of a fabric, often used in the cutting of garments for smoother fit – usu + the ⟨cut on the ~⟩ **2a** an inclination of temperament or outlook ⟨a strong liberal ~⟩; esp a personal and unreasoned distortion of judgment; a prejudice **b** a bent, tendency ⟨a man of antiquarian ~⟩ **c** a tendency of a statistical estimate to deviate from its EXPECTED VALUE (e g because of non-random sampling) **3** the property of the shape or weight of a bowl used in the game of bowls that causes it to take a curved path when rolled; also the tendency of a bowl to take such a path **4** a voltage applied to an electronic device (e g a transistor or valve) to enable it to function suitably [MF biais, fr OProv] – **on the bias** askew, obliquely

²**bias** adj, esp of fabrics and their cut diagonal, slanting – **biasness** n

³**bias** adv in a slanting manner; diagonally

⁴**bias** vt **-s-, -ss-** **1** to give a prejudiced outlook to; influence

unfairly ⟨*his background* ~es *him against foreigners*⟩ **2** to apply an electrical bias to

**bias binding** *n* a strip of material cut on the bias and used to finish hems, edges, etc

**biased, biassed** /'bie·əst/ *adj* **1** exhibiting or characterized by bias **2** tending to yield one outcome more frequently than others in a statistical experiment ⟨*a* ~ *coin*⟩

**biathlon** /bie'athlən/ *n* an athletic contest consisting of combined cross-country skiing and rifle shooting – compare DECATHLON, PENTATHLON [¹*bi*- + Gk *athlon* contest – more at ATHLETE]

**biaxial** /bie'aksyəl/ *adj* having two axes ⟨*a* ~ *crystal*⟩ – **biaxially** *adv*

¹**bib** /bib/ *vb* **-bb-** *formal* to drink [ME *bibben*, perh fr L *bibere*]

²**bib** *n* **1** a covering (eg of cloth or plastic) placed over a child's front to protect his/her clothes **2** a small rectangular section of a garment (eg an apron or dungarees) extending above the waist – **bibbed** *adj*, **bibless** *adj*

**bib and tucker** /'tukə/ *n, informal* an outfit of clothing – chiefly in *best bib and tucker*

**bibb** /bib/ *n* a timber support bolted to a ship's mast to support the TRESTLETREES (pieces of timber that support the upper section of a mast) [alter. of ²*bib*]

**bibber** /'bibə/ *n* a person who regularly drinks alcoholic beverages; a tippler – **bibbery** *n*

**bibcock** *also* **bibb cock** /'bib,kok/ *n* a tap with a nozzle that ejects the flow downwards [prob fr ²*bib* + *cock*]

**bibelot** /'bib(ə)loh/ *n, pl* **bibelots** /'bib(ə)loh, -lohz/ a small ornament or decorative object; a trinket [Fr]

**bible** /'biebl/ *n* **1a** *cap* the sacred book of Christians comprising the Old Testament and the New Testament **b** the sacred book of some other religion **2** *cap* a copy or an edition of the Bible **3** an authoritative book ⟨*the fisherman's* ~⟩ [ME, fr OF, fr ML *biblia*, fr Gk, pl of *biblion* book, dim. of *byblos* papyrus, book, fr *Byblos*, ancient Phoenician city from which papyrus was exported]

**Bible Belt** *n* an area characterized by ardent literal interpretation of the Bible; *esp* such an area in the southern USA

**biblical** /'biblikl/ *adj* **1** of or in accord with the Bible **2** suggestive of the Bible or Bible times [ML *biblicus*, fr *biblia*] – **biblically** *adv*

**biblicism** /'biblisiz(ə)m/ *n, often cap* narrow or exclusive use of the Bible – **biblicist** *n, often cap*

**biblio-** *comb form* book ⟨*bibliography*⟩ [MF, fr L, fr Gk, fr *biblion*]

**bibliography** /bibli'ogrəfi/ *n* **1** the history, identification, or description of writings and publications **2a** a list, often with descriptive or critical notes, of writings relating to a particular subject, period, or author **b** a list of works written by an author or issued by a publishing house **3** a list of the works referred to in a text or consulted by the author in its production [Fr *bibliographie* or NL *bibliographia*, fr Gk, the copying of books, fr *biblio-* + *-graphia* -graphy] – **bibliographer** *n*, **bibliographic, bibliographical** *adj*, **bibliographically** *adv*

**bibliolater** /bibli'olətə/ *n* **1** one excessively devoted to books **2** a person who has excessive reverence for the literal meaning of the Bible – **bibliolatrous** *adj*, **bibliolatry** *n*

**bibliomania** /biblioh'maynyə/ *n* extreme preoccupation with collecting books [Fr *bibliomanie*, fr *biblio-* + *manie* mania, fr LL *mania*] – **bibliomaniac** *n or adj*, **bibliomaniacal** *adj*

**bibliophile** /'bibli·ə,fiel/ *n* a lover or collector of books [Fr, fr *biblio-* + *-phile*] – **bibliophilic** *adj*, **bibliophilism** *n*, **bibliophilist** *n*, **bibliophily** *n*

**bibliotheca** /bibli·ə'theekə/ *n, pl* **bibliothecas, bibliothecae** /-kee, -see/ a collection of books [L, fr Gk *bibliothēkē*, fr *biblio-* + *thēkē* case; akin to Gk *tithenai* to put, place – more at DO ] – **bibliothecal** *adj*

**bibulous** /'bibyooləs/ *adj* inclined to overindulge in alcoholic drinks [L *bibulus*, fr *bibere* to drink – more at POTABLE] – **bibulously** *adv*, **bibulousness** *n*

**bicameral** /bie'kam(ə)r(ə)l/ *adj* having, consisting of, or based on two separate law-making bodies ⟨*a* ~ *legislature*⟩ [¹*bi*- + *cameral* (of a chamber), fr LL *camera* room – more at CHAMBER] – **bicameralism** *n*

**bicarb** /'bie,kahb/ *n, informal* SODIUM BICARBONATE

**bicarbonate** /bie'kahbənət/ *n* an acidic chemical compound derived from CARBONIC ACID; *esp* SODIUM BICARBONATE [ISV]

**bicarbonate of soda** *n* SODIUM BICARBONATE

**biccie, bickie, bikkie** /'biki/ *n, Br informal* a biscuit [by shortening alter.]

**bice** /bies/ *n* a dull blue or green pigment [ME *bis*, fr *bis* (adj) dark grey, fr MF]

**bicentenary** /biesen'teenəri, -'te-/ *n* a 200th anniversary or its celebration – **bicentenary** *adj*

**bicentennial** /biesen'teni·əl/ *n or adj* (a) bicentenary

**biceps** /'bieseps/ *n* the large muscle at the front of the upper arm that bends the arm when it contracts; *broadly* any muscle attached in two places at one end [NL *bicipit-, biceps,* fr L, two-headed, fr *bi-* + *capit-, caput* head – more at HEAD]

**bicipital** /bie'sipitl/ *adj* of or being a biceps muscle

**bicker** /'bikə/ *vi* to engage in petulant or petty argument *synonyms* see ²QUARREL [ME *bikeren*] – **bicker** *n*, **bickerer** *n*

**bicollateral** /biekə'lat(ə)ral/ *adj* of or being a VASCULAR BUNDLE (group of tubes transporting food and water through plants) that has the PHLOEM (food-transporting tissue) lying on both the inside and outside of the XYLEM (water-transporting tissue) – compare COLLATERAL

**bicolour** /'bie,kulə/ *adj* having two colours – **bicolouring** *n*

**biconcave** /bie'konkayv/ *adj* curving inwards on both sides [ISV] – **biconcavity** *n*

**biconditional** /biekən'dish(ə)nl/ *n* a link between two statements in logic that means *if and only if*

**biconvex** /bie'konveks, biekən'veks/ *adj* curving outwards on both sides [ISV] – **biconvexity** *n*

**biculturalism** /bie'kulchərəliz(ə)m/ *n* the existence of two distinct cultures in one nation ⟨*Canada's* ~⟩ – **bicultural** *adj*

¹**bicuspid** /bie'kuspid/ *also* **bicuspidate** /-ayt/ *adj* having or ending in two points or prominences ⟨~ *teeth*⟩ ⟨~ *leaves*⟩ [NL *bicuspid-, bicuspis,* fr *bi-* + L *cuspid-, cuspis* point]

²**bicuspid** *n* a human PREMOLAR (tooth between the eyetooth and the molars)

**bicuspid valve** *n* LEFT ATRIOVENTRICULAR VALVE (valve preventing backflow of blood in the heart)

¹**bicycle** /'biesikl/ *n* a vehicle with two wheels one behind the other, handlebars, saddle, and pedals by which it is propelled by the rider [Fr, fr *bi-* + *-cycle* (as in *tricycle*)]

²**bicycle** *vi* to ride a bicycle ~ *vt* to transport by bicycle – **bicycler** *n*, **bicyclist** *n*

**bicycle clip** *n* a clip for confining a cyclist's trouser leg to the ankle

**bicycle pump** *n* a pump for inflating bicycle tyres that is usu carried on the bicycle frame

**bicyclic** /bie'siklik, -'sie-/ *adj* **1** consisting of or arranged in two cycles or circles ⟨*a* ~ *flower with the petals in two whorls*⟩ **2** *of a chemical compound* containing atoms arranged in two rings with at least two atoms common to both [ISV]

¹**bid** /bid/ *vb* **-dd-;** **bade** /bad, bayd/, **bid,** (3) **bid;** **bidden** /'bidn/, **bid** *also* **bade** *vt* **1a** to issue an order to; tell ⟨*they* bade *him enter*⟩ **b** to request to come; invite **2** to give expression to ⟨bade *her a tearful farewell*⟩ **3a** to offer (a price) whether for payment or acceptance (eg at an auction) **b** to make a bid of or in (a suit at cards) **4** *obs* to beseech, entreat ~ *vi* to make a bid [partly fr ME *bidden* to request, entreat, fr OE *biddan;* akin to OHG *bitten* to entreat, Skt *bādhate* he harasses; partly fr ME *beden* to offer, command, fr OE *bēodan;* akin to OHG *biotan* to offer, Gk *pynthanesthai* to learn by inquiry] – **bidder** *n*

**bid up** *vt* to raise the price of (eg property at auction) by a succession of increasing offers

²**bid** *n* **1a** the act of one who bids **b** a statement of what one will give or take for something; *esp* an offer of a price **c** something offered as a bid **2** an opportunity to bid **3** (a declaration of) the amount of tricks a player will try to win in a card game, sometimes with the stipulation that a specified suit should be trumps **4** *chiefly journalistic* an attempt or effort to win, achieve, or attract ⟨*a* ~ *for power*⟩ ⟨*a rescue* ~⟩

*usage* The new sense of **bid** meaning "attempt", which originated in newspaper headlines, is now acceptable to most people.

**biddable** /'bidəbl/ *adj* **1** easily led, or controlled; docile **2** capable of being reasonably bid *synonyms* see OBEDIENT *antonym* naughty – **biddability** *n*, **biddably** *adv*

**bidding** /'biding/ *n* an order, command ⟨*they came at the minister's* ~⟩

¹**biddy** /'bidi/ *n, chiefly NAm informal* HEN 1a; *also* a young chicken [perh imit]

²**biddy** *n, derog* a woman ⟨*an eccentric old* ~⟩ [dim. of the name *Bridget*]

¹**biddy-,bid** *n* (the burr of) a grassland plant of New Zealand (*Acaera viridior*) of the rose family [modif of Maori *piripiri*]

¹**biddy-,biddy** *n* the biddy-bid

**bide** /bied/ *vb* **bode** /bohd/, **bided; bided** *vi, archaic or dial* to remain awhile; stay ~ *vt, archaic* to endure confidently or defiantly – see also **bide one's** TIME [ME *biden*, fr OE *bīdan*; akin to OHG *bītan* to wait, L *fidere* to trust, Gk *peithesthai* to believe] – **bider** *n*

**bidet** /'beeday/ *n* a usu plumbed fixture on which one sits esp to wash the external genitals and the anus [Fr, small horse, bidet, fr MF, fr *bider* to trot]

**bidonville** /ˌbeedonveel (*Fr* bidɔ̃vil)/ *n* a shanty town, built esp of old oil drums, in a French-speaking country [Fr, fr *bidon* tin can + *ville* town]

**Biedermeier, Biedermaier** /'beedəˌmie·ə/ *adj* **1** of or suggesting a conventional and unimaginative style of furniture and interior decoration popular among the middle classes in Germany in the 19th century **2** conventional or philistine in attitude [Gottlieb *Biedermeier*, fictitious simple German bourgeois, ostensible author of poems by Adolf Kussmaul †1902 & others]

**bield** /beeld/ *vt or n, chiefly Scot* (to) shelter [ME *belden* to encourage, protect, fr OE *bieldan* to encourage; akin to OE *beald* bold]

**biennial** /bie'eni·əl/ *adj* **1** occurring every two years – compare BIANNUAL **2** *of a plant* growing vegetatively during the first year and flowering, fruiting, and dying during the second – **biennial** *n*, **biennially** *adv*

**biennium** /bie'eni·əm/ *n, pl* **bienniums, biennia** /bie'eniə/ a period of two years [L, fr *bi-* + *annus* year – more at ANNUAL]

**bier** /biə/ *n* a stand on which a corpse or coffin is placed; *also* a coffin together with its stand [ME *bere*, fr OE *bǣr*; akin to OE *beran* to carry – more at BEAR]

**bifacial** /bie'faysh(ə)l/ *adj* **1** having opposite surfaces alike ⟨~ *leaves*⟩ **2** having two fronts or faces

**biff** /bif/ *n, informal* a whack, blow [prob imit] – **biff** *vt*

**bifid** /'biefid/ *adj* divided into two equal lobes or parts by a central cleft ⟨*a ~ petal*⟩ [L *bifidus*, fr *bi-* + *-fidus* -fid] – **bifidly** *adv*, **bifidity** *n*

**bifilar** /ˌbie'fielə/ *adj* **1** involving two threads or wires ⟨~ *suspension of a pendulum*⟩ **2** involving a single thread or wire doubled back on itself ⟨*a ~ resistor*⟩ [ISV *bi-* + L *filum* thread – more at FILE] – **bifilarly** *adv*

**bifocal** /bie'fohk(ə)l/ *adj* **1** having two FOCAL LENGTHS (distance between a lens or mirror and a focus) **2** having one part that corrects for near vision and one for distant vision ⟨*a ~ lens*⟩ [ISV]

**bifocals** /bie'fohk(ə)lz/ *n pl* glasses with bifocal lenses

**biform** /'bieˌfawm/ *adj* combining the qualities or forms of two distinct kinds of individuals (eg in the case of a mermaid) [L *biformis*, fr *bi-* + *forma* form]

**bifurcate** /'biefuhˌkayt, 'bi-, -fə-/ *vb* to divide into two branches or parts [ML *bifurcatus*, pp of *bifurcare*, fr L *bifurcus* two-pronged, fr *bi-* + *furca* fork] – **bifurcate** *adj*, **bifurcately** *adv*

**bifurcation** *n* **1** the act of bifurcating; the state of being bifurcated **2a** the point at which bifurcating occurs **b** a branch

[1]**big** /big/ *adj* **-gg- 1** of great force ⟨*a ~ storm*⟩ **2a** large in dimensions, bulk, or extent ⟨*a ~ house*⟩; *also* large in number or amount ⟨*a ~ fleet*⟩ **b** conducted on a large scale ⟨~ *business*⟩ **c** important in influence, standing, or wealth **3a** pregnant; *esp* nearly ready to give birth ⟨~ *with child*⟩ **b** full to bursting, swelling ⟨~ *with rage*⟩ ⟨*eyes* ~ *with tears*⟩ **4** *of the voice* loud and resonant **5a** elder ⟨*my ~ sister*⟩ **b** older, grown-up ⟨*I'll be a lexicographer when I'm* ~⟩ **6a** chief, outstanding ⟨*the ~ issue of the campaign*⟩ **b** outstandingly worthy or able ⟨*a truly ~ person*⟩ **c** of great importance or significance ⟨*the ~ moment*⟩ **7a** pretentious, boastful ⟨~ *talk*⟩ **b** magnanimous, generous ⟨*a ~ heart*⟩ **8** *informal* popular ⟨*she's very ~ in Las Vegas*⟩ **9** *obs* of great strength; powerful *synonyms* see [1]LARGE *antonym* little [ME, prob of Scand origin; akin to OE *bȳl* boil, Skt *bhūri* abundant] – **bigly** *adv*, **bigness** *n*

[2]**big** *adv, informal* **1a** outstandingly ⟨*made it ~ in London*⟩ **b** on a large scale ⟨*think ~!*⟩ **2** pretentiously, boastfully ⟨*he talks ~*⟩

**bigamous** /'bigəməs/ *adj* **1** guilty of bigamy **2** involving bigamy – **bigamously** *adv*

**bigamy** /'bigəmi/ *n* the crime of going through a marriage ceremony with one person while still legally married to another [ME *bigamie*, fr ML *bigamia*, fr L *bi-* + LL *-gamia* -gamy, fr Gk, fr *gamos* marriage; akin to L *gener* son-in-law] – **bigamist** *n*

**big bang theory** *n* a theory in cosmology: the universe originated from the explosion of a single mass of material so that the components are still flying apart – compare STEADY STATE THEORY

**Big Brother** *n* **1** the leader of an authoritarian state or movement **2** a ruthless and all-powerful government ⟨*proliferating data banks that tell* ~ *all about us* – Herbert Brucker⟩ [*Big Brother*, omnipotent head of state in the novel *Nineteen Eighty-four* by George Orwell †1950 E writer]

**big bud** *n* any of several diseases of plants (eg the black currant) characterized by abnormal swelling of the buds and caused by a GALL MITE

**big business** *n* large-scale commerce capable of exerting social and political pressures; *also* the businesses controlling large-scale enterprises

**big cat** *n* a large member of the cat family (eg a lion or a leopard)

**big dipper** /'dipə/ *n* **1** *often cap B&D*, *Br* ROLLER COASTER **2** *cap B&D, NAm* URSA MAJOR (constellation)

**big end** *n* the larger end of the rod connecting the piston to the crankshaft in an engine

**big game** *n* **1** large animals or fish killed for sport **2** an important objective; *esp* one involving risk

**biggie** /'bigi/ *n, informal* someone or something very important or well-known

**big gun** *n, informal* someone or something important or powerful

**bighead** /'bigˌhed/ *n* **1** any of several diseases of animals marked by swelling of the head **2** *informal* a conceited person

**big head** *n, chiefly NAm informal* conceit

**big-'headed** *adj, informal* conceited – **big-headedness** *n*

**bighearted** /ˌbig'hahtid/ *adj* generous and kindly – **bigheartedly** *adv*, **bigheartedness** *n*

**bighorn** /'bigˌhawn/ *n, pl* **bighorns, esp collectively bighorn** a wild sheep (*Ovis canadensis*) of mountainous western N America

**bight** /biet/ *n* **1a** the middle part of a slack rope **b** a loop in a rope **2a** a bend, esp in a river or a mountain chain **b** a bend in a coast forming an open bay; *also* a bay formed by such a bend [ME, bend, angle, fr OE *byht*; akin to OE *būgan* to bend – more at BOW]

**bigmouth** /'bigˌmowth/ *n, informal* **1** a loudmouth **2** an indiscreet person

**bigmouthed** /-ˌmowdhd, -ˌmowtht/ *adj, informal* loud-mouthed

**big name** *n* a very famous or important performer or personage – **big-name** *adj*

**big noise** *n, informal* BIG SHOT

**bignonia** /big'nohnyə/ *n* any of a family (Bignoniaceae, the jacaranda family) of tropical trees, shrubs, and vines, chiefly of northern S America [NL, genus name, fr J P Bignon †1743 Fr royal librarian]

**bigot** /'bigət/ *n* one who is obstinately or intolerantly devoted to his/her own religion, opinion, etc [MF, hypocrite, bigot] – **bigoted** *adj*, **bigotedly** *adv*

**bigotry** /'bigətri/ *n* **1** the state of mind of a bigot **2** acts or beliefs characteristic of a bigot

**big shot** *n, informal* an important person

**big stick** *n* a threat; *esp* the threat of military force

**big time** *n, informal* the highest rank, esp among entertainers – **big-time** *adj*, **big-timer** *n*

**big toe** *n* the innermost and largest toe of the foot

**big top** *n* **1** the main tent of a circus **2** CIRCUS 2a,b,c

**big tree** *n* a Californian evergreen tree (*Sequoiadendron giganteum*) of the pine family that often exceeds 100 metres (about 300 feet) in height

**big wheel** *n* an amusement device consisting of a large upright power-driven revolving wheel carrying seats that remain horizontal round its rim **2** *informal* BIG SHOT

**bigwig** /'bigˌwig/ *n, informal* an important person

**Bihari** /bee'hah·ri/ *n* **1** a native or inhabitant of Bihar **2** a group of Indic dialects spoken by the Biharis

**bijection** /bie'jeksh(ə)n/ *n* a mathematical function that is both INJECTIVE and SURJECTIVE [[1]*bi-* + *-jection* (as in *surjection*)] – **bijective** *adj*

[1]**bijou** /'beeˌzhooh/ *n, pl* **bijous, bijoux** /'beeˌzhooh(z)/ a small dainty usu ornamental piece of delicate workmanship (eg in the form of jewellery) [Fr, fr Bret *bizou* ring, fr *biz* finger; akin to W *bys* finger]

²**bijou** *adj, esp of a house* desirably elegant and usu small

**bijouterie** /bi'zhooht(ə)ri/ *n* a collection of trinkets or ornaments; jewellery [Fr, fr *bijou*]

¹**bike** /biek/ *n* **1** a bicycle **2** a motorcycle [by shortening & alter.] – **biker** *n* – **get off one's bike** *informal* to become annoyed

²**bike** *vi* to ride a bike

**bikini** /bi'keeni/ *n* a woman's brief two-piece swimming costume resembling bra and pants [Fr, fr *Bikini*, atoll of the Marshall islands] – **bikinied** *adj*

**bikky** /'biki/ *n, Br informal* a biscuit [by shortening & alter.]

¹**bilabial** /bie'laybiəl/ *adj* **1** *of a consonant* produced with both lips **2** of both lips [ISV]

²**bilabial** *n* a bilabial consonant (e g /b, p, m/)

**bilabiate** /ˌbie'laybiayt, -ət/ *adj* having two lips ⟨*the* ~ *corolla of many plants of the mint family*⟩

**bilateral** /bie'lat(ə)rəl/ *adj* **1** having two sides **2** bipartite ⟨*a* ~ *treaty*⟩ **3** having bilateral symmetry – **bilateralism** *n*, **bilaterally** *adv*, **bilateralness** *n*

**bilateral symmetry** *n* a pattern of symmetry (e g in animals) in which similar parts are arranged on opposite sides of a central axis so that one and only one plane can divide the individual into essentially identical halves

**bilberry** /'bilb(ə)ri/ *n* a dwarf bushy European shrub (*Vaccinium myrtillus*) of the heath family that grows on moorland; *also* its bluish edible fruit – called also BLUEBERRY [*bil-* (prob of Scand origin; akin to Dan *ḅolle* whortleberry) + *berry*]

**bilbo** /'bilboh/, **bilboa** /'bilboh(ə)/ *n, archaic* a sword, esp a rapier, with a finely tempered blade [*Bilboa, Bilbao*, town in Spain]

**bilboes** /'bilbohz/ *n pl* a long bar of iron with sliding shackles used to confine the feet of prisoners, esp on board ship ⟨*condemned to the* ~⟩ [perh fr *Bilboa*]

**bildungsroman** /'bildəngzroh,mahn/ (*Ger* bilduṇsrɔmɑːn)/ *n* a novel that deals with the usu early development of one person [Ger, fr *bildung* development + *roman* novel]

**bile** /biel/ *n* **1a** a yellow or greenish fluid secreted by the liver into the intestines to aid in the digestion of fats **b** either of two HUMOURS (body fluids) associated in medieval physiology with anger and melancholy **2** inclination to anger [Fr, fr L *bilis;* akin to W *bustl* bile]

**bile acid** *n* a STEROID acid (e g CHOLIC ACID) of or derived from bile

**bile duct** *n* a duct by which bile passes from the liver or GALL BLADDER to the DUODENUM (first part of the intestine)

**bile salt** *n* a chemical compound (SALT) formed by combination between a BILE ACID and a metal atom or another chemical group

¹**bilge** /bilj/ *n* **1** the bulging part of a cask or barrel **2a** the lowest usu rounded part of a ship's hull between the keel and the vertical sides **b bilge, bilges** the lowest part of the interior of a ship's hull **c bilge, bilge water** foul water that collects in the bilge of a ship **3** *informal* stale or worthless remarks or ideas [prob modif of MF *boulge, bouge* leather bag, curved part – more at BUDGET] – **bilgy** *adj*

²**bilge** *vi* to undergo damage (e g a fracture) in the bilge

**bilge keel** *n* a lengthways projection along a ship's hull near the turn of the bilge on either side to reduce rolling and support the weight of the vessel when grounded

**bilharzia** /bil'hahzi-ə/ *n* **1** SCHISTOSOME (parasitic worm of birds and mammals) **2** SCHISTOSOMIASIS (parasitic disease) [NL, fr Theodor *Bilharz* †1862 Ger zoologist] – **bilharzial** *adj*

**bilharziasis** /ˌbilhah'zie-əsis/ *n, pl* **bilharziases** /-seez/ SCHISTOSOMIASIS (parasitic disease) [NL, fr *bilharzia* + *-iasis*]

**biliary** /'bilyəri/ *adj* of or conveying bile; *also* affecting the bile-conveying structures ⟨~ *disorders*⟩ [Fr *biliaire*, fr L *bilis*]

**bilinear** /bie'liniə/ *adj, maths* of the first DEGREE (not squared, cubed, etc) with respect to each of two mathematical variables ⟨$x + y = 4$ *is a* ~ *equation*⟩

**bilingual** /bie'ling-gwəl/ *adj* **1** of, containing, or expressed in two languages **2** using or able to use two languages with the fluency characteristic of a native speaker [L *bilinguis*, fr *bi-* + *lingua* tongue – more at TONGUE] – **bilingual** *n*, **bilingualism** *n*, **bilingually** *adv*

**bilious** /'bili-əs/ *adj* **1a** of bile **b** marked by or suffering from disordered liver function, esp excessive secretion of bile **c** appearing as though affected by a bilious disorder **2** peevish, ill-natured **3** *of a colour* extremely distasteful [MF *bilieux*, fr L *biliosus*, fr *bilis*] – **biliously** *adv*, **biliousness** *n*

**bilirubin** /ˌbili'roohbin/ *n* a reddish yellow pigment,

$C_{33}H_{36}N_4O_6$, occurring in bile, blood, urine, and gallstones [L *bilis* + *ruber* red – more at RED]

**biliverdin** /ˌbili'vuhdin/ *n* a green pigment, $C_{33}H_{34}N_4O_6$, occurring in bile [Sw, fr L *bilis* + obs Fr *verd* green]

**bilk** /bilk/ *vt* **1** to block the free development of; frustrate ⟨*fate* ~s *their hopes*⟩ **2** to cheat out of what is due **3** to slip away from; elude ⟨~ *the pursuers*⟩ [perh alter. of ²*balk*] – **bilker** *n*

¹**bill** /bil/ *n* **1** the jaws of a bird together with variously shaped and coloured horny coverings, often specialized for a particular diet **2** a mouthpart (e g the beak of a turtle) that resembles a bird's bill **3** a projection of land like a beak [ME *bile*, fr OE; akin to OE *bill* (weapon)]

²**bill** *vi* **1** *of birds* (*e g doves*) to touch and rub bill to bill **2** to caress affectionately □ chiefly in *bill and coo*

³**bill** *n* **1** a weapon in use up to the 18th century that consists of a long staff ending in a hook-shaped blade **2** a billhook [ME *bil*, fr OE *bill;* akin to OHG *bill* pickaxe, Gk *phitros* log]

⁴**bill** *n* **1** a draft of a law presented to a law-making body for approval **2** a paper carrying a statement of particulars (e g a list of men and their duties as part of a ship's crew) **3a** (an itemized account of) charges due for goods or services **b** a statement of a creditor's claim **4a** a written or printed notice advertising an event of interest to the public (e g a theatrical entertainment) **b** an item (e g a film or play) in a programme of entertainment **5** *chiefly NAm* BANK NOTE [ME, fr ML *billa*, alter. of *bulla*, fr L, bubble, boss] – **clean bill of health** a statement or report declaring that a person or thing is in a healthy or acceptable condition ⟨*the authorities gave the rebuilt warehouse* a clean bill of health⟩ – **fill the bill** to answer a need; suffice

⁵**bill** *vt* **1** to submit a bill of charges to **2a** to advertise, esp by posters or placards **b** to arrange for the presentation of as part of a programme

**billabong** /'biləbong/ *n, Austr* **1a** a blind channel leading out from a river **b** a usu dry stream bed that is filled seasonally **2** a backwater forming a stagnant pool [native name in Australia]

¹**billboard** /'bil,bawd/ *n* a projection or ledge fixed on the bow of a vessel for the anchor to rest on [¹*bill* (the end of an anchor fluke) + *board*]

²**billboard** *n, chiefly NAm* an advertising hoarding [⁴*bill* + *board*]

**-billed** /-bild/ *comb form* (→ *adj*) having (such) a bill ⟨*hard-billed*⟩

¹**billet** /'bilit/ *n* **1a** an official order directing that a member of a military force be provided with board and lodging (e g in a private home) **b** quarters assigned (as if) by a billet **2** *informal* a position, job ⟨*a lucrative* ~⟩ [ME *bylet*, fr MF *billette*, dim. of *bulle* document, fr ML *bulla*]

²**billet** *vt* to assign lodging to (e g soldiers) by a billet – often + *on*

³**billet** *n* **1** a small thick piece of wood (e g for firewood) **2** a usu small bar of iron, steel, etc [ME *bylet*, fr MF *billette*, dim. of *bille* log, of Celt origin; akin to OIr *bile* sacred tree]

**billet-doux** /ˌbili 'dooh, ˌbeeyay/ /(*Fr* bije du)/ *n, pl* **billets-doux** /~/ a love letter [Fr *billet doux*, lit., sweet letter]

**billfold** /'bil,fohld/ *n, NAm* a wallet [short for earlier *billfolder*, fr ⁴*bill* 5]

**billhook** /'bil,hook/ *n* a cutting tool, used esp for pruning, that has a blade with a hooked point [³*bill* + *hook*]

**billiard** /'bilyəd/ *adj* used for playing billiards ⟨~ *ball*⟩ [back-formation fr *billiards*]

**billiards** /'bilyədz/ *n taking sing vb* any of several games played on an oblong table by driving small balls against one another or into pockets with a cue [MF *billard* billiard cue, billiards, fr *bille* log]

**billing** /'biling/ *n* **1** ADVERTISING **2** ⟨*advance* ~⟩ **2** the relative emphasis given to a name (e g of an actor) in advertising programmes ⟨*top* ~⟩ [⁵*bill*]

**billion** /'bilyən/ *n* **1a** a thousand millions ($10^9$) **b** *Br* a million millions ($10^{12}$) **2** *pl, informal* an indefinitely large number □ (*l*) see NUMBER table [Fr, fr *bi-* + *-illion* (as in *million*)] – **billion** *adj*, **billionth** *adj or n*

*usage* The older British sense of **billion**, "a million millions", is so large a number as to be useful only to astronomers. The British are now using **billion** increasingly in the sense "a thousand millions", which is standard not only in American but in international scientific English; but one must be careful to avoid ambiguity or misconception over these two senses. **Milliard**, which also means "a thousand millions", is not used technically in modern English.

**billionaire** /ˌbilyə'neə/ *n* a person whose assets are worth a billion or more monetary units (eg pounds or dollars) [*billion* + *-aire* (as in *millionaire*)]

**bill of exchange** *n* an unconditional written order from one person to another to pay a specified sum of money to a designated person at a given date

**bill of fare** *n* a menu

**bill of health** *n* a certificate given to the ship's captain at the time of leaving port that indicates the state of health of a ship's crew and of a port with regard to infectious diseases; *broadly* a usu satisfactory report about a condition or situation ⟨*getting a clean ~ in the investigation*⟩

**bill of indictment** *n* INDICTMENT 2 (legal charge)

**bill of lading** *n* a receipt signed usu by the agent or owner of a ship listing goods (to be) shipped

**bill of quantities** *n, Br* a statement of work and materials involved in a construction job

**bill of rights** *n, often cap B&R* a summary in law (eg the English statute of 1684) of fundamental rights and privileges guaranteed by the state

**bill of sale** *n* a formal document for the conveyance or transfer of title to goods and personal property

**billon** /'bilən/ *n* gold or silver heavily alloyed with a less valuable metal [Fr, fr MF, fr *bille* log – more at BILLET]

**¹billow** /'biloh/ *n* 1 a great wave or surge of water, esp in the open sea 2 a rolling swirling surging mass (eg of flame or smoke) [prob fr ON *bylgja;* akin to OHG *balg* bag – more at BELLY] – **billowy** *adj*

**²billow** *vb* to (cause to) rise, roll, bulge, or swell out (as if) in billows

**billposter** /'bil,pohstə/ *n* one who pastes up advertising bills or public notices on hoardings – **billposting** *n*

**billsticker** /'bil,stikə/ *n* a billposter

**¹billy** /'bili/, **'billy ,club** *n, NAm* a truncheon [prob fr *Billy,* nickname for *William*]

**²billy,** *chiefly Austr* **billycan** /'bili,kan/ *n* a can of metal or enamelware that has an arched handle and a lid, used for outdoor cooking or carrying food or liquid [prob fr the name *Billy*]

**billycock** /'bili,kok/ *n, Br* a stiff felt hat [perh fr William ("*Billy*") *Coke* fl1840 E sportsman, for whom such a hat was reputedly first made]

**billy goat** *n, informal* a male goat [fr the name *Billy*]

**bilobed** /'bie,lohbd/ *adj* divided into two lobes

**bilocular** /bie'lokyoolə/, **biloculate** /-lət, -layt/ *adj* divided into two cells or compartments ⟨*a ~ ovary*⟩ [*bi-* + NL *loculus*]

**biltong** /'biltong/ *n, chiefly SAfr* strips of lean meat dried in the sun [Afrik, fr *bil* buttock + *tong* tongue]

**bimanual** /,bie'manyooəl/ *adj* done with or requiring the use of both hands – **bimanually** *adv*

**bimestrial** /bie'mestriəl/ *adj* 1 lasting two months 2 bimonthly [L *bimestris,* fr *bi-* + *mensis* month – more at MOON]

**bimetallic** /,biemi'talik/ *adj* 1 of, based on, or using bimetallism 2 composed of two different metals, esp ones that expand by different amounts when heated – **bimetallic** *n*

**bimetallism** /,bie'metl,iz(ə)m/ *n* the use of two metals (eg gold and silver) jointly as a monetary standard with both constituting legal tender at a predetermined ratio [Fr *bimétallisme,* fr *bi-* + *métal* metal] – **bimetallist** *n,* **bimetallistic** *adj*

**bimillenary** /,biemi'lenəri/, **bimillenial** /-mi'leniəl/ *n* 1 a period of 2000 years 2 a 2000th anniversary – **bimillenary** *adj*

**bimodal** /,bie'mohdl/ *adj* having two statistical MODES (values more likely than any immediately adjacent ones) – **bimodality** *n*

**bimolecular** /biemə'lekyoolə/ *adj* 1 relating to or formed from two molecules 2 being two molecules thick [ISV] – **bimolecularly** *adv*

**bimonthly** /,bie'munthli/ *adj or adv* (occurring) every two months or twice a month – compare SEMIMONTHLY

**¹bin** /bin/ *n* 1 a container or enclosed place used for storage (eg of flour, grain, bread, or coal) 2 a partitioned case or stand for storing and aging bottles of wine 3 *Br* a wastepaper basket, dustbin, or similar container for rubbish [ME *binn,* fr OE, manger, basket, prob of Celtic origin]

**²bin** *vt* **-nn-** to put into a bin; *esp* to store and age (bottled wine) in a bin

**bin-** /bien-/ *comb form* ¹BI- ⟨*binaural*⟩ [ME, fr LL, fr L *bini* two by two; akin to OE *twin* twine]

**¹binary** /'bienəri/ *adj* 1 consisting of or marked by two things or parts 2 composed of two chemical elements, an element and a RADICAL (chemical group) that acts as an element, or two such radicals 3a of, being, or belonging to a system of numbers having 2 as its base ⟨*the ~ digits 0 and 1*⟩ b involving a choice or condition of two alternatives (eg *on* or *off, yes* or *no*) ⟨*~ logic*⟩ 4 relating or combining two mathematical elements ⟨*~ operation*⟩ 5 having two musical subjects or two complementary sections [LL *binarius,* fr L *bini*]

**²binary** *n* something made of two things or parts

**binary fission** *n* reproduction of a cell by division into two approximately equal parts ⟨*the ~ of amoebae*⟩

**binary star** *n* a system of two stars that revolve round each other

**binaural** /,bien'awrəl/ *adj* 1 of or used with two ears 2 stereophonically (recorded and) played to the hearer via headphones [ISV] – **binaurally** *adv*

**¹bind** /biend/ *vb* **bound** /bownd/ *vt* 1a to make secure by tying (eg with cord) b to confine, restrain, or restrict (as if) with bonds ⟨*they were bound and thrown into prison*⟩ ⟨*a sense of fair play ~s them*⟩ c to put under a (legal) obligation ⟨*we are all bound to keep the law*⟩ ⟨*bound by contract*⟩ 2a to wrap around with something (eg cloth) so as to enclose or cover b to bandage ⟨*~ the wound*⟩ 3 to fasten round about; encircle, gird 4 to tie together ⟨*~ the reaped grain into sheaves*⟩ 5a to cause to stick together ⟨*add an egg to ~ the mixture*⟩ b to take up and hold (eg by chemical forces); combine with ⟨*enzymes ~ their substances*⟩ 6 to make firm or sure; settle ⟨*a deposit ~s the sale*⟩ 7 to protect, strengthen, or decorate by a band or binding ⟨*a carpet bound with a yellow edging*⟩ 8 to apply a binding to (a book) 9 to set at work as an apprentice; indenture 10 to cause to be attached (eg by gratitude or affection) 11 to fasten together; unite ~ *vi* 1 to form a cohesive mass 2 to become hindered from free operation 3 to exert a restraining, compelling, or uniting influence ⟨*a promise that ~s*⟩ 4 *informal* to complain [ME *binden,* fr OE *bindan;* akin to OHG *bintan* to bind, Gk *peisma* cable]

**bind over** *vt* to impose a specific legal obligation on ⟨*bound over to keep the peace*⟩

**²bind** *n* 1a something that binds b binding or being bound 2 a tie joining written musical notes 3 *informal* a nuisance, bore – **in a bind** *chiefly NAm informal* in trouble; in an awkward situation

**binder** /'biendə/ *n* 1 a person who binds something (eg books) 2a something (eg rope or string) used for binding b a usu detachable cover (eg for holding sheets of paper) c the sheet of tobacco that binds the filler in a cigar 3 something (eg tar or cement) that produces or promotes cohesion in loosely assembled substances 4 a harvesting machine that binds straw into bundles

**bindery** /'biendəri/ *n* a place where books are bound

**¹binding** /'biending/ *n* 1 the action of someone who or something that binds 2 a material or device used to bind: eg 2a a covering that fastens the leaves of a book b a narrow strip of fabric used to finish raw edges c a set of ski fastenings for holding the boot firm on the ski

**²binding** *adj* 1 that binds 2 imposing an obligation ⟨*a ~ promise*⟩ – **bindingly** *adv,* **bindingness** *n*

**binding energy** *n* the energy required to break up a molecule, atom, or atomic nucleus completely into its constituent particles

**bindweed** /'biend,weed/ *n* any of various twining plants (esp genus *Convolvulus* of the family Convolvulaceae, the bindweed family) that have usu large showy trumpet-shaped flowers

**bine** /bien/ *n* a twining stem or flexible shoot (eg of the hop) [alter. of ²*bind*]

**'bin-,end** *n* any of the last few bottles of a parcel of wine, usu sold at a reduced price

**Binet-Simon scale** /,beenay see'mohn/ /(Fr binɛ simɔ̃)/ *n* an intelligence test consisting of graded tasks for children of successive ages [Alfred *Binet* †1911 & Théodore *Simon* †1961 Fr psychologists]

**binful** /'binf(ə)l/ *n, pl* **binfuls, binsful** as much as a bin will hold

**binge** /binj/ *n, informal* 1 a drunken revel; a spree 2 an unrestrained indulgence in something ⟨*a buying ~*⟩ ⟨*broke my diet with an eating ~*⟩ [E dial. *binge* (to drink heavily)]

**¹bingo** /'bing-goh/ *interj* 1 – used to express the suddeness or unexpectedness of an event 2 – used as an exclamation to show that one has won a game of bingo [alter. of *bing* (interj suggesting a sharp ringing sound), of imit origin]

**²bingo** *n, pl* **bingos** a game of chance played with cards having numbered squares corresponding to numbers drawn at random and won by covering or marking off a set number of such squares in a row

**binman** /'bin,man, -mən/ *n, pl* **binmen** /-,men, -mən/ *Br* a dustman

**binnacle** /'binəkl/ *n* a case, stand, etc containing a ship's compass and the lamp by which it is illuminated at night [alter. of ME *bitakle*, fr OPg or OSp; OPg *bitácola* & OSp *bitácula*, fr L *habitaculum* dwelling place, fr *habitare* to inhabit – more at HABITATION]

**binocular** /bi'nokyoolə/ *adj* of, using, or adapted to the use of both eyes ⟨*good ~ vision*⟩ – **binocularly** *adv*, **binocularity** *n*

**binoculars** /bi'nokyooləz/ *n pl* a binocular optical instrument; *esp* field glasses or opera glasses

**binomial** /bie'nohmyəl/ *n* **1** a mathematical expression consisting of two terms connected by a plus sign or minus sign **2** a biological species name consisting of two terms [NL *binomium*, fr ML, neut of *binomius* having two names, alter. of L *binominis*, fr *bi-* + *nomin-, nomen* name – more at NAME] – **binomial** *adj*, **binomially** *adv*

**binomial distribution** *n* a PROBABILITY DISTRIBUTION each of whose values corresponds to the probability that a specific combination of two types of possible event will occur in a given proportion of statistical trials

**binomial nomenclature** *n* a system of naming in which each species of animal or plant receives a name of two terms of which the first identifies the genus to which it belongs and the second the species itself

**binomial theorem** *n* a mathematical theorem in which a binomial $x + y$ raised to the $n$th power (eg if $n = 2$ the binomial is $(x + y)^2$) is written out in a series of $n + 1$ terms, the general term having the form, $[n!/k!(n - k)!]x^k y^{(n-k)}$

**binominal** /bie'nominl/ *adj, of a scientific naming system* consisting of or using two names ⟨*Canis lupus is a ~ name*⟩

**bins** /binz/ *n pl, Br informal* **1** binoculars **2** glasses

**bint** /bint/ *n, Br slang* a girl, woman [Ar, girl, daughter]

**binturong** /bin'tooərong/ *n* an Asiatic CIVET CAT (*Arctictis binturong*) with a tail that it uses for grasping [Malay]

**binuclear** /,bie'nyoohkliə/ *adj* having two chemical or atomic nuclei; *also* binucleate

**binucleate** /,bie'nyoohkliayt, -ət/ *also* **binucleated** *adj, of a cell* having two nuclei

**bio-** – see ²BI-

**bioactive** /,bie·oh'aktiv/ *adj* having an esp damaging or destructive effect on living things or something (eg blood or sweat) derived from living things ⟨*washing powder that has ~ ingredients*⟩

**bioassay** /,bie·oh'asay, -ə'say/ *n* the determination of the relative strength, effect, etc of a substance (eg a drug) by observing its effect on a living organism (eg a bacterium or mouse) and comparing this effect with that of a standard preparation [*biological assay*] – **bioassay** *vt*

**bioastronautics** /,bie·oh·astrə'nawtiks/ *n taking sing vb* the study of the effects of space travel on living beings

**bioavailability** /,bie·oh·ə,vaylə'biləti/ *n* the degree to which a chemical compound, esp a drug, administered (eg through the mouth) to a living organism is available in active form at an intended site of action (eg the liver)

**biocatalyst** /,bie·oh'katəlist/ *n* a substance (eg an enzyme) that activates or accelerates biological processes – **biocatalytic** *adj*

**biochemical** /,bie·oh'kemikl/ *adj* **1** of biochemistry **2** characterized by, produced by, or involving chemical reactions in living organisms [ISV] – **biochemical** *n*, **biochemically** *adv*

**biochemical oxygen demand** *n* BIOLOGICAL OXYGEN DEMAND (measure of pollution in water)

**biochemistry** /,bie·oh'keməstri/ *n* chemistry that deals with the chemical compounds and processes occurring in living things [ISV] – **biochemist** *n*

**biocide** /'bie·ə,sied/ *n* a substance (eg DDT) that kills many different living organisms – **biocidal** *adj*

**bioclimatic** /,bie·ohklie'matik, -klim-/ *adj* of or concerning the effects of the climate on living organisms

**biocoenosis** /,bie·ohsi'nohsis/ *n* BIOTIC COMMUNITY (type of ecological community) [NL, fr ²*bi-* + Gk *koinōsis* sharing, fr *koinos* common]

**biodegradable** /,bie·ohdi'graydəbl/ *adj* capable of being broken down, esp into simpler harmless products, by the action of living organisms (eg bacteria) ⟨*most plastics are not ~*⟩ [²*bi-* + *degrade* + *-able*] – **biodegradability** *n*, **biodegradation** *n*, **biodegrade** *vb*

**bioecology** /,bie·oh·ee'kolaji/ *n* ecology – **bioecologist** *n*, **bioecological** *adj*

**bioelectric** /,bie·oh·i'lektrik/, **bioelectrical** /-kl/ *adj* of or being electrical processes (eg the transmission of nerve impulses) in animals and plants – **bioelectricity** *n*

**bioenergetics** /-,enə'jetiks/ *n taking sing vb* the biology of energy transformations and exchanges (eg the conversion of light energy into chemical energy during photosynthesis) that occur within and between living things, esp within cells, and their environments

**bioengineering** /-,enji'niəring/ *n* the application to biological or medical science of engineering theories (eg the theory of control systems applied in making models of the nervous system) or of engineering equipment (eg in the construction of artificial limbs)

**bioenvironmental** /,bie·oh·in,vie·ərən'mentl/ *adj* concerned with the environment, esp with factors in the environment harmful to living organisms

**biofeedback** /-'feed,bak/ *n* the technique of making nonconscious or involuntary bodily processes (eg heartbeat or brain waves) perceptible to the senses (eg by the use of an oscilloscope) in order to affect them by conscious mental control

**bioflavonoid** /,bie·oh'flayvə,noyd/ *n* any of a group of water-soluble chemical compounds derived from FLAVONE, that occur in plants, esp in citrus fruits, rose hips, and blackcurrants and that decrease the fragility of the blood capillaries and reduce their permeability to RED BLOOD CELLS [*bi-* + *flavonoid* (derivative of *flavone*)]

**biogas** /'bie·oh,gas/ *n* (a) gas, esp methane that is obtained from processing manure or other biological waste and is used as a fuel

**biogenesis** /-'jenəsis/ *n* **1** the development of living things from preexisting living things – compare ABIOGENESIS **2** BIOSYNTHESIS [NL] – **biogenetic** *adj*

**biogenic** /,bie·oh'jenik/ *adj* produced by living organisms – **biogenicity** *n*

**biogeographical** /-jee·ə'grafikl/, **biogeographic** *adj* of, characteristic of, or being a geographical region viewed in terms of its animal and plant life

**biogeography** /,bie·ohji'ografi/ *n* a branch of biology that deals with the geographical distribution of animals and plants [ISV]

**biographer** /bie'ografə/ *n* a person who writes a biography or biographies

**biographical** /,bie·ə'grafikl/, **biographic** *adj* **1** of or being a biography **2** consisting of biographies or biographical matter ⟨*a ~ dictionary*⟩ – **biographically** *adv*

**biography** /bie'ografi/ *n* **1** a usu written account of a person's life by another **2** biographical writings in general **3** an account in biographical form of the life of something (eg an animal, coin, etc) ⟨*the ~ of the Commonwealth*⟩ [LGk *biographia*, fr Gk *bi-* + *-graphia* -graphy]

**biological** /,bie·ə'lojikl/ *adj* **1** of biology, life, or living processes ⟨*~ data*⟩ **2** acting on or by, or produced by living processes ⟨*~ action*⟩ ⟨*~ supplies*⟩ **3** containing a plant or animal product; *specif* being a detergent (eg a washing powder) containing an enzyme – **biologically** *adv*

**biological clock** *n* the natural inherent timing mechanism that controls various physiological processes (eg changes in hormone levels) that occur in cycles in living beings

**biological control** *n* the control of pests by biological means (eg by the introduction of species harmless to human beings or crops in order to reduce pests by predation, parasitism, or competition)

**biological oxygen demand** *n* the amount of oxygen used by microorganisms (eg bacteria) living in water, that is used as a measure of the amount of pollution in the water since the number of microorganisms present is proportional to the amount of organic matter (eg from pollution by sewage) present – called also BIOCHEMICAL OXYGEN DEMAND

**biological warfare** *n* warfare in which living organisms are used to poison, spread disease, etc; *also* warfare in which chemicals (eg defoliants) are used to destroy crops, forests, etc

**biology** /bie'oləji/ *n* **1** (a science that deals with) living organisms and life processes **2a** the plant and animal life of a particular region or environment **b** the properties and vital phenomena exhibited by an organism or group of organisms [Ger *biologie*, fr *bi-* + *-logie* -logy] – **biologist** *n*

**bioluminescence** /,bie·oh,loohmi'nes(ə)ns/ *n* the giving off of light by living organisms (eg a glowworm); *also* the light so produced [ISV] – **bioluminescent** *adj*

**biomass** /'bie·oh‚mas/ *n* **1** *ecology* the amount of living matter present in a region (eg in a square metre or cubic metre of habitat) **2** living matter cultivated esp for the purpose of producing energy

**biomaterial** /'bie·ohmə‚tiəriəl/ *n* material used for, or suitable for use in making, artificial body parts that are placed in direct contact with living tissues

**biomathematics** /‚bie·oh‚mathə'matiks/ *n taking sing or pl vb* the mathematics of biology

**biome** /'bie·ohm/ *n* a major type of ecological community ⟨*the grassland ∼*⟩ [²*bi-* + *-ome*]

**biomedicine** /'bie·oh‚medəsin/ *n* a branch of medical science concerned esp with the capacity of human beings to survive and function in environments (eg a spacecraft) that cause an abnormal amount of physiological or psychological stress, and also with how such environments can be modified to minimize stress – **biomedical** *adj*

**biometry** /bie'omətri/, **biometrics** /‚bie·ə'metriks/ *n taking sing or pl vb* the statistical analysis of observations made and experiments conducted in biology [ISV] – **biometric, biometrical** *adj*

**bionic** /bie'onik/ *adj* **1** concerning or involving bionics; *also* having or being a bionically designed part (eg a limb), liquid etc ⟨∼ *blood*⟩ **2** having exceptional abilities or powers – not used technically – **bionically** *adv*

**bionics** /bie·'oniks/ *n taking sing or pl vb* **1** a science that uses knowledge gained about biological systems in the creation of artificial systems (eg computers) **2** the use of artificial limbs, liquids (eg artificial blood), etc to replace or simulate the functions of damaged, diseased, or missing natural limbs, liquids, etc [²*bi-* + *-onics* (as in *electronics*)]

**bionomics** /‚bie·ə'nomiks, bie·oh-/ *n taking sing or pl vb* ecology [²*bi-* + *economics*] – **bionomic, bionomical** *adj*, **bionomically** *adv*

**-biont** /-bie·ont/ *comb form* (→ *n*) living organism having a (specified) mode of life ⟨*haplo*biont⟩ [deriv of Gk *biount-, biōn*, prp of *bioun* to live, fr *bios* life]

**biophysics** /bie·oh'fiziks/ *n taking sing vb* a branch of biology concerned with the application of principles and methods used in physics to biological problems – **biophysical** *adj*, **biophysicist** *n*

**biopic** /'bie·oh‚pik/ *n* a film about a nonfictional person's life *synonyms* see CINEMA [*biographical pic*ture]

**biopolymer** /‚bie·oh'polimə/ *n* a protein, DNA, or other POLYMER (large chemical compound consisting of many similar units) occurring in a living organism

**biopsy** /'bie‚opsi/ *n* the removal and examination of tissue, cells, or liquids from the living body in order to diagnose or determine the extent of a disease – compare NECROPSY [ISV *bi-* + Gk *opsis* appearance – more at OPTIC]

**biorhythm** /'bie·oh‚ridhəm/ *n usu pl* a supposed regular increase and decrease in the activity of the biological processes of a living thing that is held to affect and determine mood, behaviour, and performance – **biorhythmic** *adj*, **biorhythmically** *adv*

**bioscience** /'bie·oh‚sie·əns/ *n* biology – **bioscientist** *n*, **bioscientific** *adj*

**bioscope** /'bie·ə‚skohp/ *n, SAfr informal* a cinema; *also* the pictures [²*bi-* + *-scope*]

**-biosis** /-bie'ohsis/ *comb form* (→ *n*), *pl* **-bioses** /-bie'ohseez/ mode of life ⟨*sym*biosis⟩ [NL, fr Gk *biōsis*, fr *bioun* to live, fr *bios*] – **-biotic** *comb form* (→ *adj*)

**biosphere** /'bie·ə‚sfiə/ *n* **1** the part of the earth and its atmosphere on or in which life exists **2** living beings together with their environment

**biosynthesis** /‚bie·oh'sinthəsis/ *n, pl* **biosyntheses** /-seez/ the production of a chemical compound by a living organism [NL] – **biosynthetic** *adj*, **biosynthetically** *adv*

**biota** /bie'ohtə/ *n, ecology* the animal and plant life of a region [NL, fr Gk *biotē* life; akin to Gk *bios*]

**biotechnology** /‚bie·ohtek'noləji/ *n* **1** the use of living cells or microorganisms (eg bacteria) in industry and technology to manufacture drugs and chemicals, create energy, destroy waste matter, etc **2** *NAm* ERGONOMICS (study of the interaction between people and machines they use) – **biotechnologist** *n*, **biotechnological** *adj*, **biotechnologically** *adv*

**biotic** /bie'otik/ *adj* of life; *also* caused or produced by living organisms [Gk *biōtikos*, fr *bioun*]

**biotic community** *n* an ecological community (eg an oyster bed) dependent on a characteristic habitat that is modified and to some extent created by the activities of the organisms in it

**biotic index** *n, ecology* a ratio or other number that shows change (eg over several years) in the numbers of plant and animal species in an area and that is often used to monitor the effects of pollution (eg in rivers)

**biotic potential** *n, ecology* the highest possible rate of population increase (eg of an animal species) under conditions of maximum birthrate and minimum deathrate

**biotin** /'bie·ətin/ *n* a colourless growth-controlling vitamin, $C_{10}H_{16}N_2O_3S$, of the VITAMIN B COMPLEX, that is found esp in yeast, liver, and egg yolk, that functions in protein, fat, and carbohydrate metabolism, and the lack of which causes dermatitis and hair loss [ISV, fr Gk *biotos* life, sustenance; akin to Gk *bios*]

**biotite** /'bie·ə‚tiet/ *n* a black, brown, or dark green mineral, $K_2(Mg,Fe,Al)_6(Si,Al)_8O_{20}(OH)_4$, that is a variety of MICA and consists of a silicate of iron, magnesium, potassium, and aluminium [Ger *biotit*, fr Jean Baptiste *Biot* †1862 Fr physicist] – **biotitic** *adj*

**biotope** /'bie·ə‚tohp/ *n, ecology* a region in which the main environmental conditions and the populations of plants and animals adapted to them are uniform [²*bi-* + Gk *topos* place – more at TOPIC]

**biotransformation** /‚bie·oh‚transfə'maysh(ə)n, -‚trahns-/ *n* the transformation of chemical compounds into other chemical compounds within a living thing

**biotron** /'bie·ə‚tron/ *n* a chamber in which the climate can be controlled in order to study the effect of specific environmental factors on living beings [²*bi-* + *-tron* (as in *cyclotron*)]

**biotype** /'bie·ə‚tiep/ *n, chiefly genetics* a subgroup within a species that differs in some way from the rest of the species [ISV] – **biotypic** *adj*

**bipack** /'bie‚pak/ *n* a pair of films or plates, each sensitive to a different colour, that were used together in early colour photography in order to obtain COLOUR SEPARATION

**biparental** /‚biepə'rentl/ *adj* of or derived from two parents – **biparentally** *adv*

**bipartisan** /‚bie'pahtizn/ *adj* consisting of or involving members of two political parties ⟨*a ∼ commission*⟩ – **bipartisanism** *n*, **bipartisanship** *n*

**bipartite** /‚bie'pahtiet/ *adj* **1** being in two parts **2** *of a treaty, contract, etc between two parties* **2a** having two correspondent parts, one for each party **b** affecting both parties in the same way **3** divided into two parts almost to the base ⟨*a ∼ leaf*⟩ [L *bipartitus*, pp of *bipartire* to divide in two, fr *bi-* + *partire* to divide, fr *part-, pars* part] – **bipartitely** *adv*, **bipartition** *n*

**biped** /'bieped/ *n* a 2-footed animal [L *biped-, bipes*, fr *bi-* + *ped-, pes* foot – more at FOOT] – **biped, bipedal** *adj*, **bipedality** *n*

**biphenyl** /‚bie'feeniel/ *n* a white or colourless solid chemical compound, $C_6H_5C_6H_5$, used esp as a medium for the efficient transfer of heat and also for making dyes [ISV]

**bipinnate** /‚bie'pinayt/ *adj, of a compound leaf* having branches of PINNATE leaflets (being arranged in pairs, one on each side of a stalk) that branch pinnately from the main stem of the leaf – **bipinnately** *adv*

**biplane** /'bie‚playn/ *n* an aeroplane that has two pairs of wings, one pair of which is placed above and usu slightly forward of the other

**bipod** /'biepod/ *n* a 2-legged support or stand [*bi-* + *-pod* (as in *tripod*)]

**bipolar** /‚bie'pohlə/ *adj* **1** having or involving the use of two poles (eg north and south geographical or magnetic poles or positive and negative electrical poles) **2** of, being, or characterized by two opposed statements, views, natures, etc – **bipolarize** *vt*, **bipolarization** *n*, **bipolarity** *n*

**bipropellant** /‚bieprə'pelənt/ *n* a rocket propellant consisting of a fuel and an OXIDIZER (substance needed to make a fuel burn) that are stored separately and come together only in a combustion chamber

**biquadratic** /‚biekwo'dratik/ *n, maths* a quantity raised to the fourth POWER (eg $2^4$) or an equation that has at least one of its components raised to the fourth power (eg $2x + x^4 + 3 = 0$) – **biquadratic** *adj*

**biradial** /‚bie'raydiəl/ *adj, of* (a part of) *a plant* or *an animal* having both BILATERAL SYMMETRY and RADIAL SYMMETRY ⟨*some sea anemones are ∼*⟩

**biramous** /'birəməs/ *adj, of a plant or animal part* branching into two parts ⟨*a* ~ *antenna*⟩ [*bi-* + *ramous*, var of *ramose*]

¹**birch** /buhch/ *n* **1** any of a genus (*Betula* of the family Betulaceae, the birch family) of deciduous usu short-lived trees or shrubs that have separate male and female flowers that occur on the same plant and typically have a layered membranous outer bark that peels readily; *also* its hard pale close-grained wood **2** a birch rod or bundle of twigs for flogging [ME, fr OE *birce, beorc;* akin to OHG *birka* birch, L *fraxinus* ash tree, OE *beorht* bright – more at BRIGHT] – **birch, birchen** *adj*

²**birch** *vt* to beat (as if) with a birch

**birchbark** /'buhch,bahk/ *n, NAm* a canoe made from the bark of a birch tree

**Bircher** /'buhchə/, **Birchist, Birchite** *n* a member or supporter of the John Birch Society, a US right wing organization [John *Birch* †1945 US airforce officer] – **Birchism** *n*

**bird** /buhd/ *n* **1** any of a class (Aves) of warm-blooded VERTEBRATE animals that reproduce by means of eggs and that have the body usu completely covered with feathers and the forelimbs modified as wings **2** a bird hunted as game **3** *informal* a person; *esp* one who is in some way unusual ⟨*he's a very odd* ~⟩ **4** *informal* hissing or jeering expressive of disapproval or derision – chiefly in *give somebody the bird*/*get the bird* **5** *chiefly Br informal* a girl **6** *chiefly NAm informal* a manmade flying object **7** *NAm informal* dismissal from employment – + *the* **8** *Br slang* a prison sentence [ME, fr OE *bridd;* (4) fr the hissing of a goose; (8) rhyming slang *bird(lime)* time] – **birdlike** *adj* – **for the birds** trivial, worthless

**birdbath** /'buhd,bahth/ *n* a usu ornamental basin for birds to bathe in

**birdbrain** /-,brayn/ *n, informal* a silly or stupid person – **birdbrained** *adj*

**birdcall** /-,kawl/ *n* **1** the call or note of a bird; *also* an imitation of this **2** a device (e g a whistle) for imitating the call of a bird

**bird cherry** *n* a wild cherry tree (*Prunus padus*) with small black fruit [fr its fruit being eaten by birds]

**bird dog** *n NAm* **1** a dog trained to hunt or retrieve birds **2** a person who acts as a middleman or scout and seeks out potential customers, talent, or ideas for somebody else – **bird-dogging** *n*

**bird fancier** *n* one who is interested in birds; *esp* a collector or breeder of birds

**birdhouse** /'buhd,hows/ *n* an aviary

¹**birdie** /'buhdi/ *n* **1** a (little) bird – used by or to children **2** a golf score of one stroke less than PAR (standard number of strokes that a good player should need) on a hole

²**birdie** *vt* **birdieing** /'buhdi·ing/ to play (a hole in golf) in one stroke under PAR (standard number of strokes that a good player should need)

**birdlime** /-,liem/ *n* a sticky substance, usu made from the bark of a holly tree (*Ilex aquifolium*), that is smeared on twigs to snare small birds **2** the droppings of birds ⟨*a statue covered in* ~⟩ – **birdlime** *vt*

**bird louse** *n* any of numerous wingless insects (order Mallophaga) that can bite and are parasites, usu on birds

**birdman** /'buhd,man/ *n* **1** a person who deals with or studies birds **2** *humorous* an aviator

**bird of paradise** *n* a songbird (family Paradisaeidae) of the New Guinea area, the male of which has brilliantly coloured plumage

**bird of passage** *n* **1** a bird that migrates **2** a person who leads a wandering or unsettled life

**bird of prey** *n* a flesh-eating bird (e g a hawk, eagle, or vulture), usu with long sharp talons, that feeds chiefly on carrion or on meat taken by hunting and killing other animals

**birdseed** /-,seed/ *n* a mixture of seeds (e g of hemp, millet, and sunflowers) used for feeding caged and wild birds

¹'**bird's-,eye** *n* **1** any of numerous plants with small flowers of two contrasting colours – often in combination ⟨*the* ~ *pepper*⟩ **2a** an allover pattern for textiles consisting of a small diamond with a centre dot **b** a fabric woven with this pattern

²**bird's-eye** *adj* of or being wood (e g maple) with marks in the grain resembling bird's eyes

**bird's-eye primrose** *n* a usu small plant (*Primula farinosa*) of the primrose family, with small violet-pink flowers that form rosettes

**bird's-eye view** *n* **1** a view from above; an aerial view **2** a brief and general summary; an overview

**bird's-foot trefoil** *n* any of a genus (*Lotus*) of plants of the pea family having claw-shaped pods and usu yellow flowers;

*esp* a common European TREFOIL (*Lotus corniculatus*) with red-tipped yellow flowers

'**bird's-,nesting, 'bird-,nesting** *n* the practice of searching for birds' nests, esp in order to take the eggs

**bird's-nest soup** *n* a soup made from the edible gelatinous nest of any of several S Asian swifts

**birdstrike** /-,striek/ *n* a collision between one or more birds and an aircraft

**birdtable** /'buhd,taybl/ *n* a small raised platform on which food for wild birds is placed

'**bird-,watch** *vi* to observe or identify wild birds in their natural environment [back-formation fr *bird-watcher*] – **bird-watcher** *n*, **bird-watching** *n*

**birefringence** /,bieri'frinj(ə)ns/ *n* the REFRACTION of light (e g by a crystal) in two slightly different directions to form two rays of light waves that are POLARIZED (vibrating in only one direction) in directions opposite to one another – called also DOUBLE REFRACTION [ISV] – **birefringent** *adj*

**bireme** /'biereem/ *n* a galley with two rows of oars on each side [L *biremis*, fr *bi-* + *remus* oar – more at ROW]

**biretta** /bi'retə/ *n* a square cap with three ridges on top worn by clergy, esp of the Roman Catholic church [It *berretta*, fr OProv *berret* cap, irreg fr LL *birrus* cloak with a hood, of Celt origin; akin to MIr *berr* short]

**biriani** /,biri'ahni/ *n* a hot spicy Indian dish that consists of rice, usu coloured with saffron, mixed with meat, fish, etc [origin unknown]

¹**birk** /buhk/ *n, chiefly Scot & N Eng* a birch [ME *birch, birk*]

²**birk** *n, Br informal* a burk

**birkie** /'buhki/ *n, Scot* a smart swaggering person; *also* a fellow, man [origin unknown]

¹**birl, birle** /'buhl/ *vb, chiefly Scot vt* **1** to pour **2** to ply with drink ~ *vi* to have a good time, esp by getting rowdily drunk; carouse [ME *birlen*, fr OE *byrelian;* akin to OE *beran* to carry – more at BEAR] – **birler** *n*

²**birl** *vb, Scot* **1** to spin **2** to toss (a coin) [prob imit]

**Biro** /'bieroh/ *trademark* – used for a ball-point pen

¹**birr** /buh/ *vi & n, chiefly Scot* (to make) a whirring sound [prob imit]

²**birr** /buh, biə/ *n, pl* **birr** – see MONEY table [Ar]

**birse** /buhs, biəs/ *n, chiefly Scot* **1** a bristle or tuft of bristles **2** anger [(assumed) ME *birst*, fr OE *byrst* – more at BRISTLE]

**birth** /buhth/ *n* **1a** the emergence of a new individual from the body of its parent **b** the act or process of bringing forth young from within the body **2** the fact of being born, esp at a particular time or in a particular place ⟨*a Frenchman by* ~⟩ **3** lineage, descent ⟨*marriage between equals in* ~⟩ **4** the beginning, origin ⟨*the* ~ *of an idea*⟩ **5** natural or inherited tendency ⟨*an artist by* ~⟩ **6** *archaic* offspring **7** *archaic* high or noble birth ⟨*although a tramp he was a man of* ~⟩ [ME, fr ON *byrth;* akin to OE *beran*] – **give birth (to) 1** to bring forth as a mother **2** to cause the development or creation of; GIVE RISE TO

**birth certificate** *n* a copy of an official record of somebody's date and place of birth and their parentage

**birth control** *n* control of the number of children born, esp by lessening the frequency of or preventing conception; *broadly* contraception – compare FAMILY PLANNING

**birthday** /'buhthday, -di/ *n* **1a** the day of a person's birth **b** the day something originated ⟨*the* ~ *of gun powder*⟩ **2** an anniversary of a birth ⟨*her 21st* ~⟩

**birthday card** *n* a greetings card sent or given to somebody on their birthday

**Birthday Honours** *n pl* the HONOURS LIST published on the official birthday of the sovereign

**birthday suit** *n, humorous* nothing but bare skin; nakedness ⟨*a photograph of her at six months in her* ~⟩

**birthmark** /-,mahk/ *n* a usu red or brown blemish on the skin at birth; a naevus – **birthmark** *vt*

**birth pangs** *n pl* **1** disorder and distress caused esp by a major social change **2** *chiefly NAm* LABOUR PAINS

**birthplace** /'buhth,plays/ *n* the place of somebody's birth or something's origin

**birthrate** /-,rayt/ *n* the number of (live) births per unit of population (e g 1000 people) over a certain period of time (e g one year)

**birthright** /-,riet/ *n* something (e g a privilege or possession) to which a person is entitled by birth

**birthstone** /'buhth,stohn/ *n* a gemstone associated symbolically with the month of one's birth

**birthwort** /'buhth,wuht/ *n* any of several often woody climbing plants (genus *Aristolochia* of the family Aristolochiaceae, the birthwort family) with aromatic roots that were formerly believed to ease the pains of childbirth

**bis** /bis/ *adv* **1** again – used as a direction in music to repeat a passage **2** twice – used to point out that the same item occurs twice (eg in an account) [(1) Fr, fr L, fr OL *dvis;* akin to OHG *zwiro* twice, L *duo* two – more at TWO; (2) L]

**bis-** /bis-/ *comb form* containing two of the (specified) chemical group in the molecular structure ⟨bis(*methylphenyl*) *mercury*⟩ [L *bis*]

**biscuit** /'biskit/ *n* **1** earthenware or porcelain after the first firing and before glazing **2** a light yellowish brown colour **3** *Br* any of many variously-shaped typically flat thin dry crisp cakes that may be sweet (eg coated with chocolate) or savoury (eg tasting of cheese) **4** *NAm* a soft cake or bread (eg a scone) made without yeast – see also TAKE **the biscuit** [ME *bisquite* crisp dry bread, fr MF *bescuit,* fr (*pain*) *bescuit* twice-cooked bread]

**bise** /beez/ *n* a cold dry northerly or northeasterly wind of southern France, Switzerland, and Italy [ME, fr OF, of Gmc origin]

**bisect** /bie'sekt/ *vt* **1** *maths* to divide (eg an angle or line segment) into two equal parts **2** to cut or split into two ~ *vi* to cross, intersect – **bisection** *n,* **bisectional** *adj,* **bisectionally** *adv*

**bisector** /bie'sektə/ *n, maths* a straight line or plane that bisects an angle or a line

**bisexual** /bie'seksyoo(ə)l, -sh(ə)l/ *adj* **1a** possessing characteristics of both sexes; hermaphroditic **b** sexually attracted to both sexes **2** of or for both sexes – **bisexual** *n,* **bisexually** *adv,* **bisexuality** *n*

**bish** /bish/ *n, Br slang* a mistake [perh alter. of *bitch*]

**bishop** /'bishəp/ *n* **1a** an Anglican, Orthodox, or Roman Catholic clergyman ranking above a priest, having authority to ordain people as priests and administer the rite of CONFIRMATION, and usu governing a DIOCESE **b** any of various Protestant clerical officials who superintend other clergy **2** either of two pieces of each colour in a set of chessmen allowed to move diagonally across any number of consecutive unoccupied squares [ME *bisshop,* fr OE *bisceop,* fr LL *episcopus,* fr Gk *episkopos,* lit., overseer, fr *epi-* + *skeptesthai* to look – more at SPY]

**bishopric** /'bishəprik/ *n* **1** DIOCESE (district governed by a bishop) **2** the office of bishop [ME *bisshopriche,* fr OE *bisceoprīce,* fr *bisceop* + *rīce* kingdom – more at RICH]

**bishopweed** /'bishəp,weed/ *n* GROUND ELDER

**bismuth** /'bizməth/ *n* a heavy brittle greyish-white metallic chemical element, usu with a VALENCY of three, that is used in alloys and in the form of its compounds in certain medical preparations for soothing esp stomach disorders [obs Ger *bismut* (now *wismut*), modif of *wismut,* prob fr *wise* meadow + *mut* claim to a mine] – **bismuthic** *adj*

**bismuth glance** *n* bismuthinite

**bismuthinite** /biz'muthiniet/ *n* a grey mineral, consisting essentially of bismuth sulphide, $Bi_2S_3$, that is a source of bismuth [Fr *bismuthine,* fr *bismuth* bismuth]

**bismutite** /'bizmətiet/ *n* a mineral consisting essentially of bismuth carbonate, $(BiO)_2CO_3$ [Ger *bismutit,* fr *bismut* bismuth]

**bison** /'biesn/ *n, pl* **bison 1** any of several, now nearly extinct, large shaggy-maned European mammals (genus *Bison*) that are closely related to cattle and have a large head with short horns and heavy forequarters surmounted by a large fleshy hump **2** BUFFALO **b** (N American wild ox) [L *bisont-, bison,* of Gmc origin; akin to OHG *wisant* aurochs; akin to OPruss *wissambrs* aurochs] – **bisontine** *adj*

**¹bisque** /bisk/ *n* an advantage allowed to an inferior player: eg **a** a free point taken when desired in a set of tennis **b** an extra turn in croquet **c** one or more strokes subtracted from a golf score when desired [Fr]

**²bisque** *n* a thick cream soup made esp with shellfish or game [Fr]

**³bisque** *n* BISCUIT 1; *esp* a type of white unglazed ceramic ware [by shortening & alter.]

**bissextile** /bi'sekstiel/ *adj* of or being a month or year having the extra day of a leap year [ML *bissextilis,* fr LL *bissextus,* an extra day (after 24 February, the sixth day before the calends of March) in the Julian calendar, fr *bis-* + *sextus* sixth]

**bistable** /,bie'staybl/ *adj, of an electrical circuit* having two stable states (eg off or on)

**bistort** /bi'stawt/ *n* (any of several plants related to) a European plant (*Polygonum bistorta*) of the dock family with twisted roots and a spike of usu pink flowers [MF *bistorte,* fr (assumed) ML *bistorta,* fr L *bis-* + *torta,* fem of *tortus,* pp of *torquēre* to twist – more at TORTURE]

**bistre, NAm bister** /'beestə/ *n* (the dark yellowish-brown colour of) a pigment used in pen and ink drawings and made by boiling the soot of wood [Fr *bistre*]

**bistro** /beestroh/ *n, pl* **bistros** a small bar, restaurant, or tavern [Fr]

**bisulphate** /bie'sulfayt/ *n* any of various chemical compounds (SALTS or ESTERS) of SULPHURIC ACID, containing the group $HSO_4^-$; an acid sulphate [ISV]

**bisulphide** /bie'sulfied/ *n* DISULPHIDE (chemical compound containing two sulphur atoms) [ISV]

**bisulphite** /bie'sulfiet/ *n* any of various chemical compounds (SALTS or ESTERS) of SULPHUROUS ACID, containing the group $HSO_3^-$; an acid sulphite [Fr *bisulfite,* fr *bi-* + *sulfite* sulphite]

**¹bit** /bit/ *n* **1** a bar of metal or occasionally rubber to which the reins of a horse's bridle are attached and which is inserted in the mouth of a horse **2a(1)** the edge or part of a tool that bites or cuts **a(2)** a replaceable drilling, boring, etc part of a tool (eg a drill) **b** *pl* the gripping parts of tongs or pincers **3** something that curbs or restrains **4** the part of a key that enters the lock and acts on the bolt and tumblers [ME *bitt,* fr OE *bite* act of biting; akin to OE *bītan* to bite] – **on the bit** holding and accepting the bit correctly

**²bit** *vt* **-tt- 1a** to put a bit in the mouth of (a horse) **b** to curb, check **2** to form a bit on (a key)

**³bit** *n* **1a** a small piece or quantity of anything (eg food) ⟨*a ~ of cake*⟩ ⟨*a ~ of string*⟩ ⟨*a little ~ more*⟩ **b(1)** a usu specified small coin ⟨*a fivepenny ~*⟩ **b(2)** a monetary unit worth $\frac{1}{8}$ of a US dollar ⟨*four ~s*⟩ **c** a part, section ⟨*couldn't hear the next ~*⟩ **2** something small or unimportant of its kind: eg **2a** a brief period; a while **b(1)** an indefinite usu small degree, extent, or amount ⟨*a ~ of a rascal*⟩ ⟨*every ~ as powerful*⟩ **b(2)** an indefinite small fraction ⟨*3 inches and a ~*⟩ **c** BIT PART **3** everything caused, implied by, or associated with a given way of life, sphere of activity, role, etc ⟨*rejected the whole love and marriage ~*⟩ **4** *slang* a young woman [ME, piece bitten off, morsel of food, fr OE *bita;* akin to OE *bītan*] – **a bit** *informal* **1** somewhat, rather ⟨*a bit difficult*⟩ **2** to even the smallest or most insignificant amount or degree ⟨*not a bit sorry*⟩ – **a bit much** a little more than one wants to endure – **a bit of all right** *Br informal* somebody or something very pleasing; *esp* a sexually attractive person – **bit by bit** little by little; by degrees; gradually – **do one's bit** *Br* to make one's personal contribution, esp to a cause – **to bits** TO PIECES ⟨*fell to bits*⟩ ⟨*thrilled to bits*⟩ – see also **bit on the** SIDE

*usage* Some people feel that **bit** should be used only for solids ⟨*a bit of cake*⟩ rather than for liquids ⟨*a little bit of rain*⟩; but nobody objects to its use for abstractions ⟨*had a bit of trouble*⟩.

**⁴bit** *n* **1** a unit of computer information equivalent to the result of a choice between two alternatives (eg *on* or *off, yes* or *no*) **2** the physical representation (eg in a computer tape or electronic memory) of a bit by an electrical pulse, magnetized spot, or hole whose presence or absence indicates data [*binary digit*]

**¹bitch** /bich/ *n* **1** a female dog; *also* the female of certain other flesh-eating animals ⟨*a ~ otter*⟩ **2** *informal* a complaint **3** *slang* a malicious, spiteful, and domineering woman [ME *bicche,* fr OE *bicce;* akin to OE *bæc* back]

**²bitch** *vb, informal vt* to bungle, mess *up* ~ *vi* **1** to complain **2** to be spiteful or malicious

**bitchy** /'bichi/ *adj* characterized by malicious, spiteful, or arrogant behaviour – **bitchily** *adv,* **bitchiness** *n*

**¹bite** /biet/ *vb* **bit** /bit/; **bitten** /'bit(ə)n/ *also* **bit** *vt* **1a** to seize with teeth or jaws, so that they enter, grip, or wound **b** to remove or sever with the teeth ⟨*bit a piece out of the pear*⟩ **c** to wound or sting by puncturing or tearing the skin or flesh with a fang or other specially designed body part ⟨*the midges are biting me*⟩ **2** to cut or pierce (as if) with an edged weapon ⟨*the sword bit him to the bone*⟩ **3** to cause sharp pain or stinging discomfort to **4** to take strong hold of; grip ⟨*the wheels have difficulty in biting the road when it's icy*⟩ **5** to eat into; corrode **6** *archaic* to cheat; TAKE IN ~ *vi* **1** to bite or have the habit of biting something, esp in order to cause injury ⟨*does that dog ~?*⟩ **2** *of a weapon or tool* to cut, pierce **3** to have a sharp penetrating effect ⟨*the sauce is a bit too sharp; it really ~s*⟩ **4** *esp of fish* to take a bait **5** to take or maintain a firm hold [ME *biten,* fr OE *bītan;* akin to OHG *bīzan* to bite, L *findere* to split] – **biter** *n* – **bite off more than one can chew** to undertake more than one can perform – see also **bite the** DUST, **bite the** HAND **that feeds one, bite somebody's** HEAD **off**

**²bite** *n* **1** the act or manner of biting **2a** the amount of food taken with one bite; a morsel **b** the taking of or the nibbling at bait by a fish **3** a wound made (eg by an insect, snake, or dog) by biting or stinging **4a** the hold or grip that a machine or tool part (eg a cog or vice) gets on something (eg another cog on a piece of metal being worked on) **b** the cutting power of a tool **5** a surface (eg of a file) that creates friction **6a** a keen incisive quality ⟨the ~ of sharp analysis⟩ **b** a sharp penetrating effect ⟨the ~ of whisky⟩ **7** the way in which the upper and lower teeth meet when brought together naturally – used in dentistry **8** the corroding of an etcher's plate by acid **9** *informal* a small amount of food; a snack

**bitewing** /'biet,wing/ *n* a dental X-ray film that shows the crowns of both the upper and lower teeth

**biting** /'bieting/ *adj* **1** keen, penetrating ⟨a ~ wind⟩ **2** sarcastic, cutting ⟨the report is ~ in its intolerance of deceit⟩ – **bitingly** *adv*

**biting louse** *n* BIRD LOUSE (small parasitic biting insect)

**biting midge** *n* any of a family (Ceratopogonidae) of tiny bloodsucking flies

**bit of work** *n, pl* **bits of work** *derog* a person ⟨a nasty ~⟩

**bit part, bit** *n* a small acting part, usu with a few spoken lines, in a play, film, etc

**bit player** *n* a player of bit parts

**bits and bobs** /bobz/ *n pl* ODDS AND ENDS

**bits and pieces** *n pl* ODDS AND ENDS

**bitsy** /'bitsi/ *adj* tiny [*itsy-bitsy*]

**¹bitt** *n* either of a pair of posts of metal or wood fixed on the deck of a ship for securing cables, ropes, etc [perh fr ON *biti* beam; akin to OE *bōt* boat]

**²bitt** *vt* to secure (a cable, rope, etc) around a bitt

**¹bitter** /'bitə/ *adj* **1a** being or inducing an acrid, astringent, or disagreeable taste similar to that of QUININE (substance used to flavour tonic water) that is one of the four basic taste sensations – compare SALT, SOUR, SWEET **b** very distressing or intensely humiliating ⟨a ~ sense of shame⟩ ⟨~ truths⟩ **2** resentful, unforgiving ⟨he was still ~ about the unjust accusations made against him⟩ ⟨having lived through both wars and a depression she was now a very ~ old woman⟩ **3** marked by intensity or severity: eg **3a** accompanied by severe pain or suffering ⟨a ~ death⟩ **b** relentless, unswerving ⟨a ~ monarchist⟩ **c** marked by or exhibiting intense dislike or hostility ⟨~ enemies⟩ ⟨~ fighting⟩; *also* acrimonious, unfriendly ⟨a ~ argument⟩ **d** very cold; raw ⟨a ~ winter⟩ **4** expressive of severe pain, grief, or regret ⟨~ tears⟩ [ME, fr OE *biter;* akin to OHG *bittar* bitter, OE *bītan*] – **bitterish** *adj,* **bitterly** *adv,* **bitterness** *n*

**²bitter** *adv, NAm* bitterly

**³bitter** *n* **1** *pl but taking sing or pl vb* a usu alcoholic solution of bitter and aromatic plant products, used esp in preparing mixed drinks or as a mild tonic **2** *Br* a very dry beer heavily flavoured with hops that has a slightly bitter taste and is usu sold on draught

**⁴bitter** *vt* to make bitter

**bitter-cress** /'bit,kres/ *n* any of a genus (*Cardamine*) of flowering plants of the cabbage family

**¹bitter end** *n, nautical* the end of a rope, cable, etc that is fastened round the bitt on board a ship [*bitter* (a turn of cable round the bitts)]

**²bitter end** *n* the very end, no matter the pain or difficulties involved [prob fr ¹*bitter end;* influenced in meaning by ¹*bitter*] – **bitter-ender** *n*

**bitterling** /'bitəling/ *n* a small silvery freshwater fish (*Rhodeus amarus*) of central Europe that resembles the carp [Ger, fr *bitter* bitter + *-ling* -ling]

**¹bittern** /'bitən/ *n* any of various small or medium-sized marsh birds (*Botaurus* and related genera) that are active at night and resemble the heron but have a shorter neck, and the male of which makes a loud booming cry [ME *bitoure,* fr MF *butor,* deriv of L *butio*]

**²bittern** *n* the liquid that remains after common salt has been crystallized from brine and that is a commercial source of magnesium chemical compounds [irreg fr ¹*bitter*]

**bitter orange** *n* SEVILLE ORANGE

**bitter principle** *n* any of various chemically neutral very bitter-tasting substances (eg aloin) extracted from plants

**¹bittersweet** /-,sweet/ *n* **1** something that is bittersweet; *esp* pleasure mixed with pain **2** a rambling poisonous nightshade (*Solanum dulcamara*) of the potato family with purple flowers, conspicuous yellow ANTHERS (pollen-producing parts), and red berries

**²bittersweet** *adj* tasting or being both bitter and sweet ⟨~ chocolate⟩; *esp* pleasant but at the same time tinged with or causing sadness or regret ⟨a ~ ballad⟩ ⟨~ memories⟩ – **bittersweetly** *adv,* **bittersweetness** *n*

**bittock** /'bitək/ *n, chiefly Scot* a little bit [³*bit* + *-ock*]

**bitty** /'biti/ *adj* **1** made up of or containing bits; scrappy, disjointed **2** *dial Am* small, tiny – chiefly in *little bitty* – **bittily** *adv*

**Bitumastic** /,bityoo'mastik, ,bie-/ *trademark* – used for a protective bituminous paint (eg for metal)

**bitumen** /'bityoomin/ *n* any of various usu brown or black mixtures of HYDROCARBONS (eg asphalt, crude petroleum, or tar) that occur naturally or are obtained as residues after heating naturally occurring substances [ME *bithumen* mineral pitch, fr L *bitumin-, bitumen*] – **bituminize** *vt,* **bituminization** *n,* **bituminoid** *adj*

**bituminous** /bi'tyoohminəs/ *adj* resembling, containing, or impregnated with bitumen

**bituminous coal** *n* a soft black coal that contains a large amount of bituminous matter that evaporates when heated – called also SOFT COAL

**bivalent** /bie'vaylənt/ *adj* **1** having a VALENCY of two **2** of or being CHROMOSOMES (strands of gene-carrying material in cells) that are associated in pairs during MEIOSIS (cell division resulting in four new cells) – **bivalent** *n*

**¹bivalve** /'bie,valv/ *also* **bivalved** *adj* **1** having a shell composed of two valves ⟨a clam is a ~ mollusc⟩ **2** having or consisting of two corresponding movable pieces

**²bivalve** *n* an animal with a bivalve shell: eg **a** LAMELLIBRANCH **b** BRACHIOPOD

**bivariate** /bie'veəriət/ *adj, statistics* of, involving, or containing two variables ⟨~ distribution⟩

**bivoltine** /bie'vohlteen/ *adj, of an animal, esp an insect* laying eggs or giving birth twice a year ⟨a ~ silkworm⟩ – compare MULTIVOLTINE, UNIVOLTINE [Fr *bivoltin,* fr *bi-* + It *volta* time, instance]

**¹bivouac** /'bivoo·ak/ *n* a rough or improvised shelter or temporary camp [Fr, fr LG *biwake,* fr *bi* at + *wake* guard]

**²bivouac** *vi* **-ck-** to make a bivouac; camp

**bivvy** /'bivi/ *n, informal* a bivouac [by shortening & alter.]

**¹biweekly** /,bie'weekli/ *adj or adv* (issued or occurring) **a** every two weeks; fortnightly **b** twice a week – compare SEMIWEEKLY

**²biweekly** *n* a biweekly publication

**biyearly** /,bie'yiəli/ *adj or adv* (issued or occurring) **a** every two years **b** twice a year

**biz** /biz/ *n, informal* business [by shortening & alter.]

**bizarre** /bi'zah/ *adj* odd, incongruous, or eccentric, esp in a sensational or amusing way [Fr, fr It *bizzarro* capricious, fr Sp *bizarro* brave, perh fr Basque *bizarra* beard] – **bizarrely** *adv,* **bizarreness** *n*

**bizonal** /,bie'zohnl/ *adj* of the affairs of a zone governed or administered by two powers acting together ⟨the ~ currency existing in Germany after World War II⟩ – **bizone** *n*

**¹blab** /blab/ *n, informal* **1** one who blabs; ³BLABBER **2** ²BLABBER [ME *blabbe;* akin to ME *blaberen*] **blabby** *adj*

**²blab** *vb* **-bb-** *informal vt* to reveal (a secret), esp by talking thoughtlessly or indiscreetly ~ *vi* **1** to reveal a secret, esp by indiscreet or thoughtless chatter **2** to talk indiscreetly or thoughtlessly

**¹blabber** /'blabə/ *vb, informal vi* to talk foolishly or excessively ~ *vt* to say indiscreetly [ME *blaberen,* prob of imit origin]

**²blabber** *n, informal* indiscreet or idle chatter

**³blabber, blabbermouth** /'blabə,mowth/ *n, informal* one who talks too much or indiscreetly [²*blab* + ²*-er*]

**¹black** /blak/ *adj* **1a** of the colour black **b** very dark in colour ⟨his face was ~ with rage⟩ **2** often cap **2a** of a group or race having dark pigmentation; *esp* of the Negro race ⟨~ Americans⟩ – compare COLOURED **3 b** of black people or their culture ⟨~ literature⟩ ⟨~ power⟩ **3** dressed in black ⟨the ~ Prince⟩ **4** dirty, soiled ⟨hands ~ with dirt⟩ **5a** having or reflecting little or no light ⟨a ~ night⟩ ⟨~ water⟩ **b** of coffee served without milk or cream **6a** evil, wicked ⟨a ~ deed⟩ **b** of, using, or invoking evil or supernatural powers, esp the devil ⟨a ~ curse⟩ **7a** indicative of disapproval or discredit ⟨got a ~ mark for being late⟩ **b** indicative of hostility or resentment ⟨gave me ~

looks〉 **8a** very gloomy, dismal, or depressing 〈*the future looks* ~ *indeed*〉 **b** marked by the occurrence of misfortune or disaster 〈~ *Friday*〉 **9** showing a profit 〈*a* ~ *financial statement*〉 – compare ¹RED 6 **10** deriving humour out of the unpleasant aspects of life, esp in a grotesque or macabre manner 〈~ *comedy*〉 **11** *of propaganda* conducted so as to appear to originate within an enemy country and designed to weaken enemy morale **12** *of a ski run* for very good skiers; steep **13** bought, sold, or operating illegally and esp in contravention of official economic regulations 〈~ *economy*〉 〈~ *food*〉 **14** *chiefly Br* subject to boycott by trade-union members because of employing or favouring nonunion workers or operating under conditions considered unfair by the trade union 〈*declare a factory* ~〉 [ME *blak*, fr OE *blæc*; akin to OHG *blah* black, L *flagrare* to burn, Gk *phlegein*, OE *bæl* fire – more at BALD; (14) short for *blackleg*] – **blackish** *adj*, **blackly** *adv*, **blackness** *n*

synonyms **Black, coloured, Negro, Negress:** Black is now the form preferred by black people themselves, reflecting the pride in their African origins expressed in the concept of "negritude". **Coloured**, except in South Africa, where it has a technical meaning, may be used to differentiate people of African and Asian descent from Caucasians, but is disliked as a label for precisely this reason, and is considered extremely derogatory if used as a noun. It is better to use the so far neutral term **nonwhite**. **Negro** and **Negress** are considered insulting by black Americans because of their historical associations. Compare ASIATIC

²**black** *n* **1a** the absence or absorption of all light; complete darkness 〈*the* ~ *of night*〉 **b** the least light colour perceived to belong to objects that reflect and transmit almost no light **2** a black pigment or dye; *esp* one consisting largely of carbon **3** something black: eg **3a** black clothing 〈*looks good in* ~〉 **b** a black animal (eg a horse) **4** one who belongs to a dark-skinned race or descends in part from such a race; *esp* a Negro – compare COLOURED **5** (the player playing with) the dark-coloured pieces in a BOARD GAME (eg chess) for two players **6** the condition of being financially in credit or solvent or of making a profit – usu + *in the*; compare RED 4

³**black** *vt* **1** to make black **2** *chiefly Br* to declare (eg a business or industry) subject to boycott by trade-union members

**black out** *vt* **1** to extinguish or cover (lights) (eg as a precaution against an air raid or during a stage performance); *also* to extinguish or cover the lights of 〈*the electricity failure* blacked out *the city*〉 **2a** to suppress (news or information), esp by censorship **b** to erase 〈blacked out *the event from his mind*〉 ~ *vi* **1** to undergo a temporary loss of consciousness, memory, or sight **2** to extinguish or cover lights

**black up** *vi* to put on black makeup, esp in order to play a Negro role

**blackamoor** /'blakə,maw, -,mooə/ *n, archaic* a dark-skinned person, a Negro; *also* a small black boy used as a slave or servant [irreg fr *black* + *Moor*]

,**black-and-'blue** *adj* discoloured by blood that has leaked under the skin; bruised

,**black-and-'tan** *n* a drink consisting of porter or stout and ale

**black and tan** *n* **1** *cap B&T* a recruit enlisted in England in 1920–21 for service in support of the Royal Irish Constabulary against the armed movement for Irish independence **2** *NAm* a member of a political organization (eg in the S USA) that advocates proportional representation of whites and blacks in politics – compare LILY-WHITE [(1) fr the colour of his uniform]

,**black-and-'white** *adj* **1** characterized by the reproduction or transmission of visual images in black, white, and tones of grey rather than in colours 〈*a* ~ *photograph*〉 〈~ *television*〉 **2a** not allowing of degrees or alternatives; extreme 〈*she had very* ~ *views on love and marriage*〉 **b** simplified or made clear-cut to the extent of being inaccurate and ignoring complicating but relevant factors; *esp* evaluating things as all good or all bad 〈*he is so naive as to think there is a* ~ *solution to every problem in the world*〉

**black and white** *n* **1** a drawing or print done in black and white or in monochrome **2** (reproduction of visual images in) black, white, and tones of grey 〈~ *can be a good medium for portrait photography*〉 〈*the documentary was in* ~〉 **3** an oversimplified form 〈*he sees everything in* ~〉 – **in black and white** in writing or print 〈*get the terms of the agreement down in* black and white〉

**black art** *n* BLACK MAGIC

¹**blackball** /'blak,bawl/ *n* **1** a small black ball used as a negative vote in a ballot box **2** a negative vote or veto, esp against admitting someone to membership in an organization **3** *NZ* a round black and white BOILED SWEET

²**blackball** *vt* **1** to vote against; *esp* to exclude from membership of (a club, profession, etc) **2** to exclude socially; ostracize

¹**black ban** *n, Austr & NZ* a boycott by a trade union against a particular country, product, etc 〈*appealed to the ambulancemen's union to withdraw the* ~ – *The Sun (Melbourne)*〉

²**black ban** *vt, Austr & NZ* to boycott (a country, product, etc) 〈*postal workers may* ~ *mail* – *The Age (Melbourne)*〉

**black bean** *n* (the hard wood of) an Australian tree (*Castanospermum australe*) of the pea family with thin smooth bark

**black bean aphid, bean aphid** *n* a tiny insect (APHID) (*Aphis fabae*) that has a complex life cycle involving two forms of offspring, of which one form lives on trees (eg the SPINDLE TREE) and the other on beans, spinach, etc

**black bear** *n* a forest-dwelling bear (*Ursus americanus*, of the family Ursidae) that is the most common US bear, is much smaller than the grizzly bear, and breeds every other year

**blackbeetle** /'blak,beetl/ *n* ORIENTAL COCKROACH

**black belt** *n* **1** a rating of expert in judo, karate, etc **2** (the black belt worn by) one who has been rated expert in judo, karate, etc

**blackberry** /-,b(ə)ri/ *n* (the usu black or dark-purple juicy but seedy edible fruit of) any of various prickly shrubs (genus *Rubus*) of the rose family

**black bile** *n* the one of the four HUMOURS (bodily fluids believed to determine a person's disposition) in medieval physiology that was believed to be secreted by the kidneys or spleen and to cause melancholy – called also MELANCHOLY

**blackbird** /-,buhd/ *n* **1a** a common African and Eurasian thrush (*Turdus merula*) the male of which is black with an orange beak and eye rim and the female of which is brown **b** any of several American birds (family Icteridae) that are dark in colour **2** a Pacific islander kidnapped and sold, esp in Australia, as a slave labourer in former times

**blackboard** /-,bawd/ *n* a hard smooth usu dark surface used, esp in a classroom, for writing or drawing on with chalk

**black body** *n* a hypothetical ideal body or surface that would completely absorb all light or other ELECTROMAGNETIC RADIATION falling on it

**black book** *n* a book containing a blacklist

**black box** *n* **1** a usu electronic device (eg in a computer system) whose internal mechanism need not be known in order to use it; *esp* one that can be plugged in or removed as a unit **2** FLIGHT RECORDER (device that records the movements of an aircraft)

**black boy** *n* GRASS TREE

**black bread** *n* coarse dark bread made from rye flour; pumpernickel

**black bryony** *n* a European and Asian climbing plant (*Tamus communis*) of the yam family that bears red poisonous berries

**blackbuck** /-,buk/ *n* a common medium-sized Indian antelope (*Antilope cervicapra*) the male of which has long spiralling horns, a dark back, a white belly, and white circles around the eyes, and the female of which is hornless and yellowish-brown with the same white markings

**black bun** *n, Scot* a rich dark fruit cake or bread often encased in pastry

**black butt** *n* an Australian eucalyptus tree (*Eucalyptus piluloris*) with hard wood and with blackish bark on its lower trunk

**blackcap** /-,kap/ *n* a small African and Eurasian warbler (*Sylvia atricapilla*) the male of which has a black crown

**black cap** *n* a black head-covering formerly worn by a judge in Britain when passing the death sentence

,**black-'capped** *adj, of a bird* having the top of the head black

**blackcock** /-,kok/ *n* (the male of the) BLACK GROUSE

**black comedy** *n* comedy that derives humour out of the more unpleasant or unfortunate realities of life

**blackcurrant** /'blak,kurənt, ,-'--/ *n* the small black edible fruit of a widely cultivated European currant bush (*Ribes nigrum*), that is rich in vitamin C and is used esp for jams and jellies; *also* a bush that bears blackcurrants

**blackdamp** /-,damp/ *n* a nonexplosive gas containing CARBON DIOXIDE that occurs in mines, esp after an explosion, and is incapable of supporting animal life or a flame

**black death** *n, often cap B&D* the form of BUBONIC PLAGUE epidemic in Europe and Asia in the 14th century [fr the black patches formed on the skin of its victims]

**black diamond** *n* 1 *pl* coal 2 ³CARBONADO (hard impure form of diamond)

**blacken** /'blakən/ *vi* to become dark, black, or dirty ⟨*the sky* ~ed⟩ ~ *vt* 1 to make dark, black, or dirty 2 to defame, sully ⟨~ed *his name*⟩ – **blackener** *n*

**black eye** *n* a discoloration of the skin round the eye from bruising

**black-eyed pea** *n* a sprawling plant (*Vigna sinensis*) of the pea family widely cultivated in warm areas for food and green manure; *also* its edible seed – called also COWPEA

**blackface** /'blak,fays/ *n* makeup for a Negro role; *also* an actor who plays this role

**blackfellow** /-,feloh/ *n*, *chiefly derog* an Australian aborigine

**blackfish** /-,fish/ *n* 1 any of numerous dark-coloured fishes; *esp* a tautog 2 any of several small TOOTHED WHALES (genus *Globicephala*) related to the dolphins and found in warmer seas – called also PILOT WHALE 3 the female salmon just after spawning

**black flag** *n* a pirate's flag; *esp* JOLLY ROGER

**blackfly** /-,flie/ *n*, *pl* **blackflies**, *esp collectively* **blackfly** any of several small dark-coloured insects: e g a a bloodsucking fly (*Simulium* or related genera) whose larvae usu live in clear flowing streams b any of several tiny insects (APHIDS) that feed on plants; *also* an infestation of these

**Blackfoot** /'blak,foot/ *n*, *pl* (*l*) **Blackfeet**, *esp collectively* **Blackfoot** 1 a member of any of the three closely related American Indian tribes, the Piegan, the Kainah, and the Siksika, in Alberta and Montana that formed an alliance for mutual support against the white settlers 2 the ALGONQUIAN language of the Blackfeet

**black friar** *n* a Dominican friar [fr his black mantle]

**black gold** *n* crude oil [fr its value being compared to that of gold]

**black gram** *n* URD (bean plant)

**black grass** *n* an annual grass (*Alopecurus myosuroides*) of Europe and Asia that is a weed of cultivated ground

**black grouse** *n* a large Eurasian grouse (*Lyrurus tetrix*), the male of which is black with white stripes on the wings and has a lyre-shaped tail and the female of which is mottled with thin stripes on the wings and has a forked tail

¹**blackguard** /'blagəd,-,gahd/ *n* a coarse or unscrupulous person; a scoundrel [¹*black* + *guard*; orig sense, the kitchen servants of a large household] – **blackguardism** *n*, **blackguardly** *adj or adv*

²**blackguard** *vt* to ridicule or address in abusive terms

**black guillemot** *n* a small guillemot (*Cepphus grylle*) with bright red feet that is black with large white wing patches in summer and a mottled white colour in winter

**black gum** *n* a tree (*Nyssa sylvatica* of the family Nyssaceae) of the E USA with light and soft but tough wood

**black hand** *n*, *often cap B&H* a US secret society that engages in criminal activities (e g terrorism or extortion) [*Black Hand*, a Sicilian and Italian-American society of the late 19th and 20th centuries] – **blackhander** *n*

**blackhead** /-,hed/ *n* 1 a small usu dark-coloured plug of oily matter blocking a pore of the skin, esp on the face 2 an infectious often fatal disease of turkeys and related birds caused by a PROTOZOAN (single-celled organism) (*Histomonas meleagridis*) that invades the intestines and liver

**black-headed gull** *n* a small European gull (*Larus ridibundus*) that has a chocolate-brown head in summer and a mostly white head in winter, and is frequently seen inland

**blackheart** /'blak,haht/ *n* a plant disease (e g of potatoes) in which the central tissues blacken

**black hole** *n* 1 a hypothetical celestial body, probably formed from a collapsed star, with a very high density and an intense gravitational field from which no radiation (e g light) can escape 2 *informal* an overcrowded, uncomfortable, or confined place [(2) partly fr the *Black Hole of Calcutta*, a prison in Calcutta in India in which more than 100 people died of suffocation in one night in 1756]

**black ice** *n* thin transparent ice that forms esp on road surfaces

**blacking** /'blaking/ *n* 1 a substance that is applied to something (e g a metal or brown leather) to make it black 2 a substance used for cleaning and polishing black shoes or boots 3 a boycotting of business, industry, etc by trade-union members

¹**blackjack** /-,jak/ *n* 1 SPHALERITE (brownish to black zinc mineral) 2a the game of pontoon, esp when played in casinos

b the combination of an ace and a COURT CARD (e g a king), that is the highest possible combination in the game of blackjack 3 *NAm* a cosh [(1) ¹*jack* 1; (2) ¹*jack* 6a; (3) ¹*jack* 2]

²**blackjack** *vt*, *NAm* 1 to strike with a blackjack 2 to coerce with threats or pressure

**black kite** *n* a large brown KITE (bird of prey) (*Milvus migrans*) of Europe and Asia that feeds chiefly on carrion and is often seen over inland waters

**black knot** *n* a destructive disease of plum and cherry trees, esp in the USA, characterized by black knotty growths on the branches and caused by a fungus (*Dibotryon morbosa*)

**black lead** /led/ *n* graphite

**blackleg** /-,leg/ *n* 1 a bacterial disease, esp of young cattle, that is usu fatal 2 a gambler who cheats 3 *chiefly Br* a worker who acts in opposition to trade-union policies (e g by working during a strike)

**black letter** *n* GOTHIC 3A

**black light** *n* invisible ultraviolet or infrared radiation

**blacklight trap** *n* a trap for insects that uses a lamp emitting black light attractive to particular insects

¹**blacklist** /'blak,list/ *n* a list of people or organizations (e g strikebreakers or fraudulent business companies) that are under suspicion, held to be dishonest, disloyal, etc, or liable to be punished or boycotted

²**blacklist** *vt* to put on a blacklist – **blacklister** *n*

**black magic** *n* magic that invokes evil supernatural powers, esp the devil, and is used for evil purposes (e g to harm or kill somebody)

**blackmail** /-,mayl/ *n* 1 the extortion of money from somebody by threatening to disclose facts or spread rumours that would lead to prosecution, loss of reputation, etc; *also* money obtained in this way 2 the influencing of somebody's actions, esp against their will, by threats or by political, emotional, etc pressure [*black* + *mail* (tribute, payment), fr ME *male, maille*, fr OE *māl* agreement, pay, fr ON *māl* speech, agreement] – **blackmail** *vt*, **blackmailer** *n*

**Black Maria** /,blak mə'rie·ə/ *n* an enclosed motor vehicle used by police to carry prisoners [prob fr the forename *Maria*]

**black market** *n* illicit trade in goods, commodities, or currencies in violation of official regulations (e g rationing); *also* a place where such trade is carried on

**black marketeer** /,mahki'tiə/ *n* one who trades on a black market

**Black Mass** *n* a blasphemous travesty of the Christian Mass practised by worshippers of Satan

**Black Muslim** *n* a member of an exclusively black chiefly US Muslim group that advocate a strictly separate black community

**black nationalist** *n*, *often cap B&N* a member of a group of militant blacks who advocate separatism from the whites and the formation of self-governing black communities – **black nationalism** *n*

**black nightshade** *n* NIGHTSHADE 1a

**blackout** /-,owt/ *n* 1a the temporary extinguishing or covering of all visible lights enforced as a precaution against air raids b a temporary extinguishing of electric lights (e g in a city) caused by a failure or a cut of electric power c an extinguishing of all stage lighting (e g to separate scenes in a play) 2 a temporary loss of consciousness, memory, or sight ⟨*an alcoholic* ~⟩ 3 a usu temporary holding back or suppression of news or information (e g for political reasons) ⟨*a* ~ *of news about the invasion*⟩ 4 a usu temporary loss of radio signal communication (e g during the reentry of a spacecraft into the earth's atmosphere)

**Black Panther** *n* a member of a militant US organization fighting for Negro rights

**Black Paper** *n* any of a series of published critiques of the legislation that has been proposed by the British government; *esp* any of a series criticizing progressive education – compare WHITE PAPER

**black pepper** *n* a pungent aromatic condiment prepared from the dried black-husked berries of an E Indian plant (*Piper nigrum*), used either whole or ground – compare WHITE PEPPER

**black power** *n* a movement for the mobilization of the political, economic, and social power of Negroes, esp in N America and Australia, in order to gain racial equality

**black pudding** *n*, *chiefly Br* a very dark sausage made from suet and pigs' blood – compare WHITE PUDDING

**black rat** *n* a widely distributed agile European rat (*Rattus rattus*) that is a pest of granaries, warehouses, etc

149 **bla**

**black rhinoceros** *n* a greyish very large African rhinoceros (*Rhinoceros bicornis*) with two horns, a large one in front and a smaller one set behind

**Black Rod** *n* an officer of the HOUSE OF LORDS in Britain who is the chief usher and whose main duty is to summon the Commons to the Lords for the opening and official closing of parliamentary sessions [fr his staff of office]

**black rot** *n* a bacterial or fungal disease of plants causing dark brown discoloration and decay

**black salsify** *n* SCORZONERA (plant of the daisy family with a black edible root)

**black sheep** *n* a person who is thought by other members of his/her family, peer group, etc to be a failure or a disgrace

**Blackshirt** /-₁shuht/ *n* a member of a fascist organization having a black shirt as part of its uniform; *esp* a member of the Italian Fascist party before and during World War II

**blacksmith** /-₁smith/ *n* a person who works iron, esp at a forge [fr his working with iron, known as black metal] – **blacksmithing** *n*

**blacksnake** /'blak₁snayk/ *n, NAm* a long tapering braided whip of rawhide or leather

**black spot** *n* 1 any of several plant diseases characterized by black spots or blotches 2 *Br* a place on a road where accidents occur frequently

**black studies** *n pl, chiefly NAm* courses studying the history, literature, etc of black people

**black stump** *n, Austr & NZ* the edge of civilization; a remote or backward place – esp in *beyond the black stump*

**black tea** *n* tea that is dark in colour because of complete fermentation of the leaf before drying

**black tern** *n* any of several small TERNS (water birds) (genus *Chlidonias*); *esp* one (*Chlidonias niger*) that has dark-grey to black plumage in summer

**blackthorn** /-₁thawn/ *n* a European spiny shrub (*Prunus spinosa*) of the rose family with hard wood, small white flowers, and sour berries

**black-'tie** *adj* characterized by or requiring the wearing of formal evening dress (eg a dinner jacket and black bow tie for men) ⟨a ~ *dinner*⟩ – compare WHITE-TIE

**blacktop** /-₁top/ *n, NAm* a tarlike material used esp for surfacing roads; *also* a surface paved with blacktop – compare TARMAC – **blacktop** *vt*

**black velvet** *n* 1 a drink that is a mixture of stout and champagne or cider 2 *Austr & NZ slang* a dark-skinned woman

**black vomit** *n* (a condition characterized by) vomit that contains blood

**blackwater fever** /'blak₁wawtə/ *n* a severe form of malaria in which the urine becomes dark-coloured

**black widow** *n* a venomous American spider (*Latrodectus mactans*), the female of which is black with a red mark on its stomach

**blackwood** /'blakwood/ *n* a tall Australian acacia tree (*Acacia Melanoxylon*) valued for its dark wood

**bladder** /'bladə/ *n* 1a a membranous sac in animals that serves as the receptacle of a liquid or contains gas; *esp* the urinary bladder b a membranous pouch in a plant (eg a seaweed) filled with liquid or gas 2 a bag filled with a liquid or gas (eg the air-filled rubber one inside a football) [ME, fr OE *blædre*; akin to OHG *blātara* bladder, OE *blāwan* to blow] – **bladderlike** *adj*

**bladder campion** *n* a white-flowered plant (*Silene vulgaris*) of the pink family that has a large puffed-out CALYX (circle of leaflike structures) surrounding the base of the flower

**bladder fern** *n* any of several ferns (genus *Cystopteris*) with hooded or bladderlike INDUSIA (shields that cover developing spores)

**bladder worm** *n* a bladderlike larva of a tapeworm

**bladderwort** /-₁wuht/ *n* any of a genus (*Utricularia*) of chiefly aquatic plants of the butterwort family, with small hollow sacs that catch and digest insects

**bladder wrack** /rak/ *n* a common black seaweed (*Fucus vesiculosus*) with air bladders that is burnt for its iodine-containing ash and is used as a manure

**blade** /blayd/ *n* 1a a leaf, *esp* a long swordlike leaf (eg of a grass or iris) b the flat expanded part of a leaf as distinguished from the stalk 2a the broad flattened part of an oar, paddle, bat, etc b any of the radially projecting parts of an electric fan, ship's propeller, steam turbine, etc c the broad flat or concave part of a machine (eg a bulldozer or snowplough) that comes into contact with the material to be moved d a

broad flat body part; *specif* SCAPULA (shoulder blade) – used chiefly in naming cuts of meat e the flat part of the tongue immediately behind the tip; *also* this portion together with the tip 3a the cutting part of a knife, razor, etc b the runner of an ice skate c(1) *poetic* a sword c(2) *archaic or poetic* a swordsman c(3) *archaic or humorous* a dashing lively man [ME, fr OE *blæd*; akin to OHG *blat* leaf, L *folium*, Gk *phyllon*, OE *blōwan* to blossom – more at BLOW]

**bladed** /'blaydid/ *adj* 1 having blades – often in combination ⟨*broad*-bladed *leaves*⟩ 2 *of a mineral* composed of crystals flattened in one direction

**blae** /blay/ *adj, Scot* 1 dark blue or bluish grey 2 bleak [ME *bla, blo*, fr ON *blār*; akin to OHG *blāo* blue – more at BLUE]

**blaeberry** /'blayb(ə)ri/ *n, Scot & N Eng* (the fruit of) the bilberry

**blah** /blah/, **blahblah** /'--/ *n, informal* silly or pretentious chatter or nonsense [imit]

**blain** /blayn/ *n* an inflamed swelling or sore on the skin [ME, fr OE *blegen*; akin to MLG *bleine* blain, OE *blāwan* to blow]

**¹blame** /blaym/ *vt* 1 to find fault with; censure ⟨*the right to praise or* ~ *a literary work*⟩ 2a to hold responsible for something reprehensible ⟨~ *him for everything*⟩ b to place responsibility for (something reprehensible) – + *on* ⟨~s *it on me*⟩ [ME *blamen*, fr OF *blamer*, fr LL *blasphemare* to blaspheme, fr Gk *blasphēmein*, fr *blasphēmos* evil-speaking] – **blamable** *adj*, **blamably** *adv*, **blamer** *n*
**usage** The use of **blame** as in sense 2b, though disapproved of by some writers on usage, is well established in English ⟨*keep your head when all about you are losing theirs and blaming it on you* – Rudyard Kipling⟩. Available alternatives are ⟨**blame** *you for it*⟩ or ⟨*place the* **blame** *for it on you*⟩.

**²blame** *n* 1 an expression of disapproval or reproach; a censure 2 responsibility for something reprehensible ⟨*they must share the* ~ *for the crime*⟩ – **blameless** *adj*, **blamelessly** *adv*, **blamelessness** *n*, **blameful** *adj*, **blamefully** *adv*

**blameworthy** /-₁wuhthi/ *adj* being at fault; deserving blame – **blameworthiness** *n*

**blanc de blanc** /₁blong də 'blong (*Fr* blā də blā)/, **blanc de blancs** *n, often cap B&B* a white wine, esp champagne, made only from the juice of white grapes [Fr *blanc de blanc*, lit., white of white]

**blanc fixe** /₁blong 'feeks (*Fr* blā fiks)/ *n* BARIUM SULPHATE prepared as a heavy white powder and used esp as a filler in paper, rubber, and linoleum, or as a pigment [Fr, lit., fixed white]

**blanch** /blahnch/ *vt* 1 to take the colour out of: 1a to bleach (a growing plant) by excluding light b to scald or parboil (eg almonds or food for freezing) in water or steam in order to remove the skin, to whiten, or to stop enzyme action c to whiten (a metal) by treating with acid or covering with a layer of tin 2 to make ashen or pale ⟨*fear* ~es *the cheek*⟩ ~ *vi* to become white or pale ⟨~ed *when he heard the news*⟩ [ME *blaunchen*, fr MF *blanchir*, fr OF *blanche*, fem of *blanc*, adj, white] – **blancher** *n*

**blancmange** /blə'monj, -'monzh/ *n* a usu sweetened and flavoured dessert made from a gelatinous or starchy substance (eg cornflour) and milk [ME *blancmanger*, fr MF *blanc manger*, lit., white food]

**blanco** /'blangkoh/ *vt* **blancoes**; **blancoing**; **blancoed** to treat with Blanco

**Blanco** /'blangkoh/ *trademark* – used for a substance used esp in the armed forces to whiten or colour belts and webbing

**bland** /bland/ *adj* 1 gentle or soothing in manner ⟨a ~ *smile*⟩ 2 exhibiting no personal concern or embarrassment ⟨a ~ *confession of guilt*⟩ 3a not irritating or stimulating; mild ⟨a ~ *diet*⟩ b dull, insipid ⟨~ *stories with little plot or action*⟩ **synonyms** see SUAVE **antonyms** piquant, savoury (for 3) [L *blandus*] – **blandly** *adv*, **blandness** *n*

**blandish** /'blandish/ *vt* to coax or influence with flattery [ME *blandishen*, fr MF *blandiss-*, stem of *blandir*, fr L *blandiri*, fr *blandus* mild, flattering] – **blandisher** *n*

**blandishment** /'blandishmənt/ *n usu pl* a coaxing or flattering act or utterance

**¹blank** /blangk/ *adj* 1a devoid of covering or content; *esp* free from writing or marks ⟨~ *paper*⟩ b not filled in; empty, void ⟨a ~ *cheque*⟩ c lacking interest, variety, or change ⟨a ~ *prospect*⟩ 2a dazed, nonplussed ⟨*stared in* ~ *dismay*⟩ b expressionless ⟨a ~ *stare*⟩ 3 absolute, unqualified ⟨a ~ *refusal*⟩ 4a having a plain or unbroken surface where an opening is usual ⟨a ~ *arch*⟩ b made ready for stamping, cutting, punching, etc ⟨*a* ~ *key*⟩ [ME, white, fr MF *blanc*, of Gmc origin; akin to OHG *blanch* white; akin to L *flagrare* to burn – more at BLACK] – **blankly** *adv*, **blankness** *n*

²**blank** *n* 1 an empty space (eg on a form); *also* a form containing empty spaces 2a an empty place or space; a void ⟨*my mind was a complete ~ during the test*⟩ b an uneventful or featureless period or space ⟨*a long ~ in history*⟩ 3 a mark, esp a dash, substituted for an omitted word 4a a piece of material that is ready to be made into a key, coin, etc by a further operation (eg stamping, cutting, or punching) b a firearm cartridge loaded with powder but no projectile 5 VOID 3 (absence of cards of a particular suit) – **draw a blank** 1 to draw a raffle or lottery ticket that does not win 2 to obtain no positive results

³**blank** *vt* 1a to delete, blot, or obscure – usu + *out* ⟨~ *out a line*⟩ b to make (a piece of material) ready for stamping, cutting, punching, etc c to block, seal – usu + *off* ⟨~ *off a tunnel*⟩ 2 *NAm* to keep (an opposing team) from scoring ⟨*were ~ed for eight innings*⟩

**blank cheque** *n* 1 a signed cheque with the amount payable unspecified 2 complete freedom of action or control; CARTE BLANCHE

**blank endorsement** *n* an endorsement of a cheque, BILL OF EXCHANGE, etc that does not name the payee, thus making the sum specified payable to the bearer

¹**blanket** /'blangkit/ *n* 1 a large thick usu rectangular piece of fabric (eg woven from wool or acrylic yarn) used esp as a bed covering; *also* a similar piece of fabric used as a body covering (eg for a horse) 2 a thick covering or layer ⟨*a ~ of snow*⟩ 3 a rubber or plastic sheet wrapped round a cylinder in an offset printing press to transfer the inked impression from the printing surface to the paper [ME (orig a white or undyed woollen cloth), fr OF *blankete*, fr *blanc*]

²**blanket** *vt* 1 to cover (as if) with a blanket ⟨*new grass ~s the slope*⟩ 2 to cover so as to obscure, interrupt, suppress, or extinguish ⟨~ *a fire with foam*⟩

³**blanket** *adj* 1 applicable to all members of a group or class; across-the-board ⟨*a ~ wage increase*⟩ 2 effective or applicable in all instances ⟨~ *rules*⟩

**blanket bath** *n* a wash given to a bedridden person

**blanket finish** *n* a finish to a race in which many competitors cross the finishing line very close together

**blanket stitch** *n* a needlework stitch forming a series of widely spaced interlocking loops that is used esp round the edges of thick fabrics (eg blankets) instead of hemming, in order to prevent fraying – compare BUTTONHOLE STITCH – **blanket-stitch** *vt*

**blank verse** *n* unrhymed verse; *esp* unrhymed verse, each line of which consists of five IAMBS (pairs of syllables in which the first syllable is unstressed and the second stressed)

**blanquette** /blong'ket/ *n* a stew of WHITE MEAT (eg veal) in a WHITE SAUCE; *broadly* a fricassee [Fr, fr *blanc* white]

**blare** /blea/ *vi* to emit loud and harsh sound ⟨*radios blaring away*⟩ ~ *vt* 1 to sound loudly and usu harshly or vehemently ⟨*sat blaring the car horn*⟩ 2 to proclaim loudly or sensationally ⟨*headlines ~d his defeat*⟩ [ME *bleren*; akin to OE *blætan* to bleat] – **blare** *n*

**blarney** /'blahni/ *n* 1 smooth wheedling talk; flattery 2 nonsense, humbug ⟨*gave her some ~ about why he was late*⟩ [*Blarney stone*, a stone in Blarney Castle, near Cork, in Ireland, reputed to give skill in flattery to those who kiss it] – **blarney** *vb*

**blasé** /'blahzay, -'-/ *adj* indifferent to pleasure or excitement as a result of excessive indulgence or enjoyment; *also* sophisticated [Fr, fr pp of *blaser* to exhaust by indulgence, prob fr D *blasen* to swell]

**blaspheme** /blas'feem/ *vt* to speak of or address (God or something sacred or inviolable) with impiety or irreverence ~ *vi* 1 to utter or write something blasphemous or irreverent 2 to utter curses or profanities [ME *blasfemen*, fr LL *blasphemare* – more at BLAME] – **blasphemer** *n*

**blasphemy** /'blasfəmi/ *n* 1a (the act of showing) contempt or lack of reverence for God or something sacred or inviolable b the act of claiming the attributes of a deity 2 irreverent language, writing, or behaviour directed towards something sacred or inviolable *synonyms* see PROFANATION – **blasphemous** *adj*, **blasphemously** *adv*, **blasphemousness** *n*

¹**blast** /blahst/ *n* 1 a sudden violent gust of wind 2 the sound produced by air blown through a wind instrument or whistle ⟨*the trumpet's ~*⟩ 3a a stream of air or gas forced through a

hole b a vehement outburst ⟨*the speaker's ~ against special privileges*⟩ c the continuous draught forced through a blast furnace to maintain a high temperature 4a a sudden pernicious influence or effect ⟨*the ~ of a huge epidemic*⟩ b a disease that suggests the effects of a noxious wind; *esp* a plant disease that causes the foliage or flowers to wither 5a an explosion or violent detonation b the explosive charge used esp for shattering rock c the violent effect produced in the vicinity of an explosion, that consists of a wave of increased atmospheric pressure followed by a wave of decreased atmospheric pressure 6 *informal* speed, capacity ⟨*going full ~ down the road*⟩ 7 *informal* a riotous or exuberant occasion; *esp* an enjoyable party [ME, fr OE *blǣst*; akin to OHG *blāst* blast, OE *blāwan* to blow]

²**blast** *vi* 1 to produce loud harsh sounds ⟨*music ~ing from the radio*⟩ 2a to use an explosive b to shoot 3 to make a vigorous attack ⟨*he ~ed away at their false idealism*⟩ 4 *esp of a plant* to shrivel, wither ~ *vt* 1a to injure (as if) by the action of wind; blight ⟨*frost ~ed the blossoms*⟩ b to ruin, thwart 2a to shatter, remove, or open (as if) with an explosive ⟨~ed *a new course for the stream*⟩ b to kill or destroy by shooting or bombing 3 to apply a forced draught to (eg fuel in a furnace) 4 to cause to BLAST OFF ⟨*will ~ themselves from the moon's surface*⟩ 5 *informal* to defeat decisively ⟨*they ~ed the home team*⟩ 6 *informal* to curse, damn ⟨*I'm not making it up, ~ you*⟩ 7 *journalistic* to denounce, criticize, or attack vigorously and effectively ⟨*judge ~s police methods*⟩ – **blaster** *n*, **blasting** *n or adj*

**blast off** *vi, esp of rockets and rocket-propelled missiles* TAKE OFF 2d – see also BLAST-OFF

³**blast** *interj, chiefly Br informal* – used to express annoyance

**blast-** /blast-/, **blasto-** *comb form* bud; embryo; germ ⟨*blastocyst*⟩ ⟨*blastula*⟩ [Ger, fr Gk, fr *blastos*]

**-blast** *comb form* (→ *n*) formative cell; cell layer ⟨*splanchoblast*⟩ ⟨*erythroblast*⟩; *also* formative unit, esp of living matter [NL *-blastus*, fr Gk *blastos* bud, shoot; akin to OE *molda* top of the head, Skt *mūrdhan* head]

**blasted** /'blahstid/ *adj* 1a blighted, withered b damaged (as if) by an explosive, lightning, or the wind ⟨*a ~ apple tree*⟩ 2 *informal* confounded, detestable ⟨*this ~ weather*⟩

**blastema** /bla'steemə/ *n, pl* **blastemas, blastemata** /-mətə/ a mass of undifferentiated living cells that are capable of growth and differentiation (eg into an organ or tissue) and are present esp in a developing organism or in a lower animal (eg a salamander) at the place where a body part has been lost [NL, fr Gk *blastēma* offshoot, fr *blastos*] – **blastematic, blastemic** *adj*

**blast furnace** *n* a furnace, esp for converting iron ore into iron, in which combustion is forced by a current of air under pressure

**-blastic** /-'blastik/ *comb form* (→ *adj*) having (such or so many) buds, cells, or cell layers ⟨*megalo*blastic⟩ ⟨*diplo*blastic⟩ [ISV, fr *-blast*]

**blastie** /'blasti/ *n, Scot* an ugly little creature [Sc *blast* to wither, fr ²*blast*]

**blastocoel, blastocoele** /'blastə,seel/ *n* the cavity inside a BLASTULA (early form of an embryo consisting of a hollow ball of cells) [ISV] – **blastocoelic** *adj*

**blastocyst** /'blastəsist/ *n* the BLASTULA (early form of an embryo consisting of a hollow ball of cells) of a placental mammal

**blastoderm** /'blastə,duhm/ *n* a blastodisc after completion of the first series of cell divisions and formation of the fluid-filled blastocoel of the developing embryo [Ger, fr *blast-* + *-derm*] – **blastodermatic, blastodermic** *adj*

**blastodisc** /'blastə,disk/ *n* the embryo-forming portion of eggs which contain a lot of yolk that usu appears as a small disc on the upper surface of the yolk mass

¹**blast-,off** *n* a blasting off (eg of a rocket); *also* the time at which this occurs

**blastomere** /'blastə,miə/ *n* a cell produced during the first series of CELL DIVISIONS in an egg [ISV] – **blastomeric** *adj*

**blastomycete** /,blastə'mieseet/ *n* any of a group (Blastomycetes) of fungi that cause disease and are similar to yeasts [deriv of *blast-* + Gk *mykēt-, mykēs* fungus – more at MYC-]

**blastomycosis** /,blastəmie'kohsis/ *n* a disease caused by a blastomycete [NL] – **blastomycotic** *adj*

**blastopore** /'blastə,paw/ *n* the opening of the cavity (ARCHENTERON) that forms in an embryo at a very early stage in its development – **blastoporal, blastoporic** *adj*

**blastosphere** /'blastə,sfiə/ *n* a blastula – **blastospheric** *adj*

**blastula** /'blastyoolə/ *n, pl* **blastulas, blastulae** /-lie/ the embryo of an animal at the stage in its development succeeding the MORULA (solid ball of cells), typically having the form of a hollow fluid-filled rounded cavity bounded by a single layer of cells – compare GASTRULA, MORULA [NL, fr Gk *blastos*] – **blastular** *adj*, **blastulation** *n*

**blat** /blat/ *vb* **-tt-** *NAm vi* to bleat like a sheep ~ *vt* to utter loudly or foolishly [imit] – **blat** *n*

**blatancy** /'blayt(ə)nsi/ *n* 1 the quality or state of being blatant 2 something that is blatant

**blatant** /'blayt(ə)nt/ *adj* 1 noisy, esp in a vulgar or offensive manner 2 completely obvious, conspicuous, or obtrusive, esp in a crass or offensive manner *synonyms* see VOCIFEROUS *antonyms* decorous, reserved [perh irreg fr L *blatire* to chatter] – **blatantly** *adv*

**blate** /blayt/ *adj, chiefly Scot* timid, sheepish [ME, prob fr OE *blāt* pale]

[1]**blather** /'bladhə/ *vi* to talk foolishly at length [ON *blathra;* akin to MHG *blōdern* to chatter] – **blatherer** *n*

[2]**blather** *n* foolish loquacious talk

**blatherskite** /'bladhə,skiet/ *n* a person who blathers a lot [*blather* + Sc dial. *skate* a contemptible person]

**blaw** /blaw/ *vb* **blawn** /blawn/ *Scot & N Eng* to blow [ME (northern) *blawen*, fr OE *blāwan*]

[1]**blaze** /blayz/ *n* **1a** an intensely burning flame or a sudden fire **b** intense direct light, often accompanied by heat ⟨*the ~ of noon*⟩ **2a** a dazzling display ⟨*a ~ of flowers*⟩ **b** a sudden outburst ⟨*a ~ of fury*⟩ **c** brilliance ⟨*the ~ of the jewels*⟩ 3 *pl* HELL **2b** – usu as an interjection or as a generalized term of abuse ⟨*what the ~s!*⟩ ⟨*go to ~s*⟩ [ME *blase*, fr OE *blæse* torch; akin to OE *bǣl* fire – more at BALD]

[2]**blaze** *vi* **1a** to burn intensely ⟨*the sun ~d overhead*⟩ **b** to flare up ⟨*he suddenly ~d with anger*⟩ 2 to be conspicuously brilliant or resplendent ⟨*fields blazing with flowers*⟩ 3 to shoot rapidly and repeatedly ⟨*~ away at the target*⟩ – **blazingly** *adv*

[3]**blaze** *vt* to make public or conspicuous; proclaim – often + *abroad* [ME *blasen*, fr MD *blāsen* to blow; akin to OHG *blāst* blast]

[4]**blaze** *n* 1 a broad white mark down the face of an animal, esp a horse 2 a marker indicating a trail or path to be followed; *esp* a mark made on a tree by chipping off a piece of the bark [Ger *blas*, fr OHG *plas;* akin to OE *blæse*]

[5]**blaze** *vt* 1 to mark (e g a trail) with a blaze or blazes 2 to lead or be a pioneer in (some direction or activity) – chiefly in *blaze a/the trail*

**blazer** /'blayzə/ *n* a jacket, esp with PATCH POCKETS, that is for casual wear or is part of a school uniform [[2]*blaze* + [2]*-er*]

[1]**blazon** /'blayz(ə)n/ *n* 1 COAT OF ARMS 2 a proper formal description of heraldic arms or emblems [ME *blason*, fr MF]

[2]**blazon** *vt* 1 to proclaim loudly and publicly – often + *forth* or *out* **2a** to describe (heraldic arms or emblems) in technical terms **b** to inscribe or paint (heraldic arms or emblems) – **blazoner** *n*, **blazoning** *n*

**blazonry** /-ri/ *n* **1a** the art or activity of blazoning heraldic arms **b** BLAZON 1 2 a dazzling display

[1]**bleach** /bleech/ *vt* 1 to remove colour or stains from 2 to make whiter or lighter, esp by removing colour with chemical agents or by exposing to sunlight ~ *vi* to grow white or lose colour [ME *blechen*, fr OE *blǣcean*; akin to OE *blāc* pale, *bǣl* fire – more at BALD] – **bleachable** *adj*

[2]**bleach** *n* 1 a preparation used in bleaching 2 the degree of whiteness obtained by bleaching

**bleacher** /'bleechə/ *n usu pl, NAm* a usu uncovered stand of tiered planks providing inexpensive seating for spectators [[1]*bleach* + [2]*-er;* fr its being usu unprotected from the sun]

**bleaching powder** /'bleeching/ *n* a white powder that smells of chlorine, consists chiefly of the chemical compounds calcium hydroxide, CALCIUM CHLORIDE, and calcium hypochlorite, and is used as a bleach, disinfectant, or deodorant

[1]**bleak** /bleek/ *adj* 1 exposed, barren, and often windswept ⟨*a ~ landscape*⟩ 2 cold, raw ⟨*~ weather*⟩ **3a** lacking in warmth or kindness ⟨*a ~ welcome*⟩ **b** not hopeful or encouraging ⟨*a ~ outlook*⟩ **c** severely simple or austere [ME *bleke* pale; prob akin to OE *blāc*] – **bleakish** *adj*, **bleakly** *adv*, **bleakness** *n*

[2]**bleak** *n* a small European river fish (*Alburnus lucidus*) of the carp family with silvery-green scales from which a pigment used in making artificial pearls is obtained [ME *bleke*, prob fr ON *bleikja*]

[1]**blear** /bliə/ *vt* **1a** to make (the eyes) sore or watery **b** to make (the mind) dull or dim 2 to blur (e g the outline of something) [ME *bleren*]

[2]**blear** *adj, archaic* bleary – ,**blear-'eyed** *adj*

**bleary** /'bliəri/ *adj* 1 of the eyes or vision dull, dimmed, or blurred, esp from fatigue, sleep, or tears 2 poorly outlined or defined; blurred – **blearily** *adv*, **bleariness** *n*

[1]**bleat** /bleet/ *vi* 1 to make the cry characteristic of a sheep, goat, or calf, or a similar sound **2a** to talk complainingly or with a whine; whimper **b** to talk foolishly ~ *vt* to utter in a bleating manner [ME *bleten*, fr OE *blǣtan;* akin to L *flēre* to weep, OE *bellan* to roar – more at BELLOW] – **bleater** *n*

[2]**bleat** *n* 1 the characteristic plaintive cry of a sheep, goat, or calf; *also* a similar sound 2 a feeble complaint

**bleb** /bleb/ *n* 1 a small blister on the skin 2 a bubble (e g in glass) [perh alter. of *blob*] – **blebby** *adj*

[1]**bleed** /bleed/ *vb* **bled** /bled/ *vi* **1a** to emit or lose blood **b** to be wounded or die, esp for a cause ⟨*men who fought and bled for their country*⟩ 2 to feel anguish, pain, or sympathy ⟨*a heart that ~s at a friend's misfortune*⟩ 3 to ooze or flow out from or through something ⟨*sap ~ing from cracks in the bark*⟩ 4 to lose some constituent (e g sap or dye) by exuding it or by diffusion **5a** to pay out or give money **b** to have money extorted 6 to be printed so as to run off an edge of a printed page or sheet after trimming – often + *off* 7 to lose vitality or lifeblood ~ *vt* 1 to remove or draw blood from 2 to get or extort money from 3 to draw sap from (a tree) **4a** to extract or let out some or all of a contained substance from ⟨*~ the car's brakes*⟩ **b** to extract or cause to escape from a container, esp through a valve ⟨*~ air from the car's brakes*⟩ 5 to cause (e g a printed illustration) to bleed; *also* to trim (e g a page) so that some of the printing bleeds 6 to extract or drain the vitality or lifeblood from ⟨*high taxes ~ing private enterprise*⟩ – see also **bleed** WHITE [ME *bleden*, fr OE *blēdan*, fr *blōd* blood]

[2]**bleed** *n* 1 an act or instance of bleeding, esp by a haemophiliac 2 an illustration that bleeds; *also* the part trimmed off in bleeding or the corresponding area of the printing plate

**bleeder** /'bleedə/ *n* 1 a haemophiliac – not used technically 2 *slang* **2a** a person, esp a man, of a usu specified type ⟨*lucky ~*⟩ **b** a worthless person [[1]*bleed* + [2]*-er*]

**bleeding** /'bleeding/ *adj or adv, Br slang* – used as a meaningless intensive ⟨*~ idiot*⟩

**bleeding heart** *n* 1 any of various plants (genus *Dicentra*) of the fumitory family; *esp* a garden plant (*Dicentra spectabilis*) with usu red or pink drooping heart-shaped flowers 2 a person who shows extravagant sympathy, esp for an object of alleged persecution

[1]**bleep** /bleep/ *n* 1 a short high-pitched sound (e g from electronic equipment) 2 **bleeper, bleep** a small portable electronic device for carrying in a pocket, attaching to clothing, etc, that emits a bleep as a signal that the wearer is required [imit]

[2]**bleep** *vt* 1 to call (somebody) by means of a bleeper 2 to replace (recorded words) with a bleep or other sound so that there is an interruption in a radio or television broadcast – usu + *out* ⟨*all the obscenities were ~ed out*⟩ ~ *vi* to emit a bleep

**blellum** /'bleləm/ *n, Scot archaic* a lazy talkative person [perh blend of Sc *bleber* to babble and *skellum* rascal]

[1]**blemish** /'blemish/ *vt* to spoil the perfection of; flaw; [ME *blemisshen*, fr MF *blesmiss-*, stem of *blesmir* to make pale, wound, of Gmc origin; akin to Ger *blass* pale; akin to OE *blæse* torch – more at BLAZE]

[2]**blemish** *n* a noticeable imperfection; a flaw; *esp* one that seriously impairs appearance *synonyms* see IMPERFECTION *antonym* ornament

[1]**blench** /blench/ *vi* to draw back or flinch from lack of courage *synonyms* see [1]RECOIL △ blanch [ME *blenchen* to deceive, blench, fr OE *blencan* to deceive; akin to ON *blekkja* to impose on]

[2]**blench** *vb* to bleach, whiten [alter. of *blanch*]

[1]**blend** /blend/ *vb* **blended** *also* **blent** /blent/ *vt* 1 to mix; *esp* to combine or associate so that the separate constituents or the line of demarcation cannot be distinguished 2 to prepare (e g tea or whisky) by thoroughly intermingling different varieties or grades ~ *vi* **1a** to mix or intermingle thoroughly **b** to combine into an integrated whole 2 to produce a harmonious effect (e g of colour or sound) *synonyms* see [1]MIX [ME *blenden*, modif of ON *blanda;* akin to OE *blandan* to mix, Lith *blandus* thick (of soup)]

[2]**blend** *n* 1 an act or product of blending ⟨*our own ~ of tea*⟩ **2a** a word (e g *motel*) produced by combining other words or parts of words **b** a deviant sentence (e g "What are you teaching English?") produced by change of construction in mid-

stream (eg from "What are you teaching?" to "Are you teaching English?")

**blende** /blend/ *n* 1 SPHALERITE (brownish to black zinc mineral) 2 any of various minerals that are sulphides of metals and have a brightish but nonmetallic lustre [Ger, fr *blenden* to blind, deceive, fr OHG *blenten* (akin to OE *blind*); fr its deceptive resemblance to galena]

**blended whisky** /'blendid/ *n* whisky consisting of either a blend of two or more similar MALT WHISKIES that may be made by different distillers and in different periods or a blend of a malt whisky with a whisky (GRAIN WHISKY) that has no distinctive flavour

**blender** /'blendə/ *n* one who or that which blends; *esp* a liquidizer or similar electric appliance for mixing, grinding, etc food

**blenny** /'bleni/ *n* any of numerous usu slim and small and often scaleless sea fishes (Blenniidae and related families) that have long spiny fins and live around rocky shores in pools or shallow water [L *blennius*, a sea fish, fr Gk *blennos*]

**blephar-** /'blefə-/, **blepharo-** *comb form* eyelid ⟨blepharitis⟩ [NL, fr Gk, fr *blepharon*]

**blepharitis** /ˌblefəˈrietəs/ *n* inflammation of the eyelids [NL]

**blepharoplast** /'blef(ə)rəˌplast/ **n** BASAL BODY; *esp* one at the base of a FLAGELLUM (long whiplike structure used by a cell for movement)

**blesbok** /'blesˌbok/ *n* a Southern African antelope (*Damaliscus dorcas*) that has a large white spot on the face [Afrik, fr *bles* blaze + *bok* male antelope]

**bless** /bles/ *vt* **blessed** *also* **blest** /blest/ 1 to hallow or consecrate by religious rite or word 2 to make the sign of the cross on or over 3 to invoke divine care for 4a to praise, glorify ⟨~ His holy name⟩ **b** to speak gratefully of ⟨~ed *him for his kindness*⟩ 5a to confer prosperity or happiness on **b** to favour, endow ⟨~ed *with a happy nature*⟩ 6 to protect, preserve ⟨~ me from marrying a usurer⟩ – Shak⟩ 7 – used in exclamations chiefly to express mild or good-humoured surprise ⟨~ my soul, what's happened now?⟩ [ME *blessen*, fr OE *blētsian*, fr *blōd* blood; fr the use of blood in consecration]

**blessed** /'blesid/ *adj* 1a *often cap* holy or made holy by religious ceremony; venerated, hallowed ⟨*the* Blessed *Sacrament*⟩ ⟨*the* Blessed *Trinity*⟩ **b** *cap* – used as a title in the Roman Catholic Church for a BEATIFIED person (person declared worthy of veneration) ⟨Blessed *Oliver Plunket*⟩ 2 of or enjoying great happiness or good fortune; *specif* enjoying the bliss of heaven 3 bringing pleasure or contentment 4 – used as an intensive ⟨*no one gave us a* ~ *penny*⟩ 5 *of a plant* endowed with healing properties ⟨*the* ~ *thistle*⟩ – **blessedly** *adv*, **blessedness** *n*

**Blessed Sacrament** *n* SACRAMENT 2 (consecrated bread and wine used at Communion)

**blessing** /'blesing/ *n* 1a the act of blessing; *esp* the invoking of God's favour on a person ⟨*the congregation stood for the* ~⟩ **b** approval, encouragement ⟨*the project had the* ~ *of the British government*⟩ 2 something conducive to happiness or welfare ⟨*it's a* ~ *the rain's stayed away for our holiday*⟩ 3 a short prayer of thanksgiving said before or after a meal; GRACE 2

**blest** /blest/ *past of* BLESS

**blether** /'bledhə/ *vi or n* (to) blather

**blew** /blooh/ *past of* BLOW

**blewits** /'blooh·its/ *n, pl* **blewits** an edible mushroom (*Tricholoma saevum*) that is lilac-coloured when young [prob irreg fr *blue*]

**[1]blight** /bliet/ *n* 1a a disease or injury of plants resulting in withering, cessation of growth, and death of parts without rotting **b** an organism (eg the WOOLLY APHID) that causes blight 2 something that impairs, frustrates, or destroys 3 a condition of disorder or decay ⟨*urban* ~⟩ [origin unknown]

**[2]blight** *vt* 1 to affect (eg a plant) with blight 2 to have a deteriorating or destructive effect on; impair, frustrate ~ *vi* to suffer from or become affected with blight

**blighter** /'blietə/ *n chiefly Br informal* 1 a person, esp a man, of a usu specified type ⟨*you lucky* ~!⟩ 2 a worthless or contemptible person [[2]*blight* + [2]*-er*]

*usage* It is usually unsafe to use **blighter** in the sense "something that blights" ⟨*Spring ... bitter* **blighter** – Thomas Hood⟩ because of confusion with the sense "low fellow".

**blighty** /'blieti/ *n, often cap, Br informal* 1 one's native land, esp Britain ⟨*go home to* ~ *after duty abroad*⟩ 2 **blighty one, blighty** a wound forcing the recipient to return home to Britain 3 leave □ used esp by British soldiers serving abroad [modif

of Hindi *bilāyatī, wilāyatī* foreign country, England, fr Ar *wilāyat* province, country]

**blimey, blimy** /'bliemi/ *interj, chiefly Br informal* – used to express surprise or amazement [short for *gorblimey*, alter. of *God blind me*]

**blimp** /blimp/ *n* 1 a nonrigid airship; *esp* one used as a barrage balloon 2 *cap* COLONEL BLIMP (pompous reactionary or bigoted person) [prob based on [3]*limp*]

**blimpish** /'blimpish/ *adj, often cap* of or suggesting a COLONEL BLIMP; reactionary, bigoted ⟨*a* Blimpish *colonel*⟩ – **blimpishly** *adv*, **blimpishness** *n*, **blimpery** *n*

**blin** /blin/ *n, pl* **blini** /'blini/, **blinis** /'blinis/ a pancake, of a type traditional in Russia, made with yeast and often buckwheat flour [Russ]

**[1]blind** /bliend/ *adj* 1a(1) unable to see; sightless a(2) *law and medicine* having less than $1/_{20}$ of normal vision in the more efficient eye when defects that can be corrected by lenses have been accounted for **b** of or designed for sightless people 2a unable or unwilling to discern or judge ⟨~ *to all arguments*⟩ **b** not based on reason, evidence, or knowledge ⟨~ *faith*⟩ ⟨~ *choice*⟩ 3 completely insensible; lacking all awareness ⟨*a* ~ *stupor*⟩ 4a made or done without sight or knowledge of anything that could have served for guidance **b** achieved or performed solely by the use of instruments ⟨*a* ~ *landing of the aircraft*⟩ 5 *of a plant* lacking a growing point or producing only leaves instead of flowers or fruit 6a hidden from sight; concealed ⟨~ *stitch*⟩ ⟨*a* ~ *entrance*⟩ **b** *of a corner on a road* not able to be seen round 7 having only one opening or outlet ⟨*a* ~ *alley*⟩ 8 having no opening for light or passage; blank ⟨*a* ~ *wall*⟩ 9 impressed or tooled without gilding or colouring – usu in combination ⟨blind-*blocking*⟩ ⟨blind-*tooling*⟩; see also **turn a blind** EYE **to** [ME, fr OE; akin to OHG *blint* blind, OE *blandan* to mix – more at BLEND] – **blindly** *adv*, **blindness** *n*

**[2]blind** *vt* 1a to make blind **b** to dazzle 2 to rob of judgment or discernment 3a to withhold light from; darken ⟨*shrubbery* ~*ing all their windows*⟩ **b** to outshine, eclipse ⟨*torches that* ~*ed the candles*⟩ 4 to fill with admiration or awe; overwhelm ⟨~*ed by his eloquence*⟩ ~ *vi, Br informal* to swear ⟨*cursing and* ~*ing*⟩ – see also EFF **and blind, blind with** SCIENCE [(vi) fr such curses as *God blind me* (cf BLIMEY)] – **blindingly** *adv*

**[3]blind** *n* 1 something to hinder sight or keep out light: eg 1a a window shutter **b** a flexible screen (eg a strip of cloth) usu mounted on a roller for covering a window **c** a curtain **d** VENETIAN BLIND **e** *chiefly Br* an awning 2 one who or that which acts as a decoy or distraction; a cover, subterfuge 3 a screen to prevent cold air from reaching the radiator of a vehicle 4 *NAm* a place of concealment (eg a bush) from which game is shot at; a hide

**[4]blind** *adv* 1 to the point of insensibility ⟨~ *drunk*⟩ 2 without seeing outside an aircraft ⟨*to fly* ~⟩ 3 – used as an intensive ⟨*swore* ~ *he wouldn't try to escape*⟩ – **fly blind** to fly an aircraft solely by instruments

**blind alley** *n* a fruitless or mistaken course or direction

**blind date** *n* a social meeting between two people who have not previously met; *also* either of these people

**blinder** /'bliendə/ *n* 1 *NAm* BLINKER 3a (flap preventing sideways vision of a horse) 2 *Br informal* something outstanding; *esp* an outstanding piece of play in cricket or football 3 *Br informal* a drinking bout; a binge ⟨*went on a* ~⟩

**blindfish** /'bliendˌfish/ *n* any of several small fishes with much reduced and functionless eyes, that are found usu in the waters of caves

**[1]blindfold** /'bliendˌfohld/ *vt* 1 to prevent sight by covering the eyes of with a blindfold 2 to hinder from seeing or esp understanding [by folk etymology (influenced by [2]*fold*) fr ME *blindfellen, blindfelden* to strike blind, cover the eyes, fr *blind* + *fellen* to fell]

**[2]blindfold** *n* 1 a piece of material (eg a bandage) for covering the eyes to prevent sight 2 something that hinders or obscures sight, understanding, or mental awareness

**blinding** /'bliending/ *n* material (eg sand, gravel, ash, or concrete) used to fill crevices, esp in a new road [fr gerund of [2]*blind* (in sense "to fill gaps in")]

**blind man's buff** /ˌbliendˌmanz 'buf/ *n* a group game in which a blindfolded player tries to catch and identify any one of the other players [obs *buff* buffet, fr ME *buffe*, fr MF; fr the blows given to the blindfolded player]

**blind side** *n* 1 the side away from which one is looking 2 the side of a scrum in rugby that is nearest to a touchline – compare OPEN SIDE

**blind spot** *n* **1a** the point in the retina of an eye where the OPTIC NERVE enters and the eye is insensitive to light **b(1)** a direction in which vision is obstructed or impaired ⟨*the wide door pillar gives the car a bad* ∼⟩ **b(2)** an area or place where vision is restricted or obscured ⟨*there's a bad* ∼ *at the top of the hill*⟩ **2** an area in which one lacks knowledge, judgment, or discrimination **3** a locality in which radio reception is markedly poorer than in the surrounding area

**blindworm** /'bliend,wuhm/ *n* SLOWWORM (snakelike lizard)

¹**blink** /blingk/ *vi* **1a** to close and immediately reopen the eyes involuntarily (e g when dazzled); *also* to do this continuously **b** to look with half-shut eyes (e g because of strong sunlight) **2** to shine intermittently (e g as a signal) or dimly ∼ *vt* **1a** to cause (one's eyes) to blink **b** to remove (e g tears) from the eye by blinking **2** BLINK AT **1** [ME *blinken* to open one's eyes]

**synonyms** Compare **blink** and **wink**: To **blink** at something or, as some writers on usage advise one to say, to **blink** it, is to "ignore" it, perhaps from cowardice ⟨**blink** *the unpleasant facts*⟩. To **wink** *at* something is to "condone" it deliberately, perhaps as a sympathetic accomplice ⟨**wink** *at his small failings*⟩.

**blink at** *vt* **1** to ignore or deliberately evade ⟨blink at *the injustices*⟩ **2** to view with surprise, amazement, or dismay ⟨*a professional might* blink at *our methods*⟩

²**blink** *n* **1** a glimmer, sparkle ⟨*a* ∼ *of bright flame*⟩ **2** a usu involuntary shutting and opening of the eye **3a** ICEBLINK (glare in the sky over an ice field) **b** WATER SKY (darkness of the sky over open water) **4** *chiefly Scot* a glimpse, glance – **on the blink** *informal* not working properly ⟨*the light switch is on the* blink⟩

¹**blinker** /'blingkə/ *n* **1** one who or that which blinks; *esp* a warning or signalling light that flashes on and off **2** *pl* an obstruction to sight or discernment **3a** *chiefly Br* either of two flaps on a horse's bridle that allow forward vision only **b** *pl* a cloth hood with shades projecting at the sides of the eye openings used on racehorses to allow forward vision only

²**blinker** *vt* **1** to put blinkers on **2** to limit the discernment or understanding of ⟨∼-ed *attitudes to global inflation*⟩

**blinking** /'blingking/ *adj or adv, Br euph* – used as a meaningless intensive [euphemism for *bloody*]

**blintze** /'blintsə/, **blintz** /blintz/ *n* a thin folded filled pancake [Yiddish *blintse*, fr Russ *blinets*, dim. of *blin* pancake]

**blip** /blip/ *n* **1** a bleep **2** an image on a radar screen [imit]

**bliss** /blis/ *n* **1** complete happiness **2** paradise, heaven [ME *blisse*, fr OE *bliss*; akin to OE *blīthe* blithe] – **blissful** *adj*, **blissfully** *adv*, **blissfulness** *n*

¹**blister** /'blistə/ *n* **1** a raised area of the outer skin containing watery liquid, caused esp by friction or burning **2** an enclosed raised spot (e g in paint) resembling a blister **3** a disease of plants marked by large swollen patches on the leaves **4** any of various domelike structures (e g a gunner's compartment on an aircraft) [ME, modif of OF or MD; OF *blostre* boil, fr MD *bluyster* blister; akin to OE *blǣst* blast] – **blistery** *adj*

²**blister** *vi* to develop a blister or blisters ∼ *vt* **1** to raise a blister on **2** to attack harshly ⟨∼-ed *his opponent with charges of corruption*⟩

**blister beetle** *n* a beetle (e g the SPANISH FLY) used medicinally in a dried and powdered form to raise blisters on the skin; *broadly* any of numerous soft-bodied beetles (family Meloidae)

**blister copper** *n* metallic copper that has a black blistered surface, is 98.5 to 99.5 per cent pure, and occurs as an intermediate product in copper refining

**blistering** /'blistəring/ *adj* **1** extremely intense or severe **2** extremely fast – **blistering**, **blisteringly** *adv*

**blister rust** *n* any of several diseases of pines that are caused by rust fungi (genus *Cronartium*) and that affect the sapwood and inner bark and produce blisters externally

**blithe** /bliedh/ *adj* **1** of a happy lighthearted character or disposition; merry, cheerful ⟨*hail to thee,* ∼ *spirit* – P B Shelley⟩ **2** casual, heedless ⟨∼ *unconcern*⟩ [ME, fr OE *blīthe*; akin to OHG *blīdi* joyous, OE *bǣl* fire – more at BALD] – **blithely** *adv*

**blither** /'blidhə/ *vi* to blather [by alter.]

**blithesome** /'bliedhs(ə)m/ *adj, poetic* merry, lighthearted – **blithesomely** *adv*

**blitz** /blits/ *n* **1a** a blitzkrieg **b** an intensive bombardment from the air; *specif, often cap the* bombardment of British cities by the German air force in 1940 and 1941 **2** *chiefly journalistic* an intensive nonmilitary campaign ⟨*a* ∼ *against the unions*⟩ – **blitz** *vb*

**blitzkrieg** /-,kreeg/ *n* a violent swift surprise campaign conducted by coordinated air and ground forces [Ger, fr *blitz* lightning + *krieg* war] – **blitzkrieg** *vb*

**blizzard** /'blizəd/ *n* **1** a long severe snowstorm **2** an intensely strong cold wind filled with fine snow **3** an overwhelming rush or deluge ⟨*the* ∼ *of mail at Christmas*⟩ [origin unknown] – **blizzardy** *adj*

¹**bloat** /bloht/ *vb* to make or become turgid or swollen [*bloat,* adj (swollen), alter. of ME *blout,* perh fr ON *blautr* soft, soaked]

²**bloat** *n* a digestive disturbance of domestic animals, esp cattle, involving excessive accumulation of gas in the stomach and resultant bloating of the abdomen

**bloated** /'blohtid/ *adj* puffed up (e g with pride)

**bloater** /'blohtə/ *n* a large herring or mackerel cured by being lightly salted and briefly smoked [obs *bloat* to cure, fr ME *blote* soft and moist]

**blob** /blob/ *n* **1a** a small drop of liquid ⟨*a* ∼ *of ink*⟩ **b** a small drop or lump of something viscous or thick **2** something ill-defined or amorphous [ME]

**bloc** /blok/ *n* **1** a (temporary) combination of parties in a legislative assembly **2** a combination of people, groups, or nations forming a unit with a common interest or purpose ⟨*the Communist* ∼⟩ [Fr, lit., block]

¹**block** /blok/ *n* **1** a compact usu solid piece of substantial material (e g wood or stone), esp when specially shaped to serve a particular purpose: e g **1a** a mould or form on which articles are shaped or displayed **b** a rectangular building unit that is larger than a brick **c** a usu cubical and solid wooden or plastic building toy that is usu provided in sets **d** the metal casting that contains the cylinders of an INTERNAL-COMBUSTION ENGINE **2a** an obstacle **b** an obstruction of an opponent's manoeuvre in sports; *esp* a halting or impeding of the progress or movement of an opponent in American football by use of the body **c** interruption of the normal physiological function (e g transmission of nerve impulses) of a body tissue or organ; *esp* HEART BLOCK **3** a wooden or metal case enclosing one or more pulleys **4** (a ballet shoe with) a solid toe on which a dancer can stand on points **5a** a quantity, number, or section of things dealt with as a unit **b(1)** a large building divided into separate functional units ⟨*office* ∼⟩ **b(2)** a part of a building or integrated group of buildings devoted to a particular use **c** BLOCK SECTION (a length of railway track governed by block signals) **d** *chiefly NAm* (the distance along one side of) a usu rectangular space (e g in a town) enclosed by streets and usu occupied by buildings **6** a piece of material (e g wood or metal) having an engraved or etched design on its surface from which impressions are printed **7** *slang* HEAD **1** [ME *blok,* fr MF *bloc,* fr MD *blok;* akin to OHG *bloh* block, MIr *blog* fragment] – **do one's block** *Austr informal* to become excitedly irrational (e g because of anger) [*block* 7] – see also CHIP **off the old block**

²**block** *vt* **1a** to make unsuitable for passage or progress by obstruction **b** to hinder the passage, progress, or accomplishment of (as if) by interposing an obstruction ⟨∼ *a kick*⟩ **c** to shut off from view ⟨*canopy of leaves* ∼ing *the sun*⟩ **d** to obstruct or interfere usu legitimately with (e g an opponent) in various games or sports **e** to prevent the normal functioning of **f** to prohibit or limit conversion of (foreign-held funds) into foreign exchange; *also* to limit the use to be made of (such funds) within the country **2** to shape on, with, or as if with a block ⟨∼ *a hat*⟩ **3** to make (two or more lines of writing or type) flush at the left or at both margins **4** to secure, support, mount on, or provide with a block **5** to arrange (e g a school timetable) in long continuous periods **6** *archaic* to blockade ∼ *vi* to block an opponent in sports *synonyms* see ¹HINDER – **blocker** *n*

**block in** *vt* to sketch the outlines of in a design

**block out** *vt* BLOCK IN

¹**blockade** /blə'kayd, blo-/ *n* **1** the isolation by a warring nation of a particular enemy area (e g a port) by means of troops or warships to prevent passage of people or supplies; *broadly* a restrictive measure designed to obstruct the commerce and communications of an unfriendly nation **2** something that constitutes an obstacle; an obstruction

²**blockade** *vt* **1** to subject to a blockade **2** to block, obstruct – **blockader** *n*

**blo'ckade-,runner** *n* a ship or person that runs through a blockade – **blockade-running** *n*

**blockage** /'blokij/ *n* an act or instance of blocking; the state of being blocked ⟨*a* ∼ *in the saltcellar*⟩

**block and tackle** *n* an arrangement of pulley blocks with associated rope or cable for hoisting or hauling

**blockboard** /-ˌbawd/ *n* material made of parallel wooden strips glued edge to edge and finished on top and underneath with thin wooden sheets

**block-'booking** *n* a booking of a number of places (e g theatre seats or hotel rooms) at one time – **block-book** *vb*

**blockbuster** /-ˌbustə/ *n, informal* 1 a huge high-explosive demolition bomb 2 somebody or something particularly outstanding, effective, or violent; *specif* a highly successful film or book

**block diagram** *n* a diagram (e g of a system, process, or computer program) in which labelled figures (e g rectangles) and interconnecting lines represent the relationship of parts

**block grant** *n* a lump sum of money paid annually to a British university by the Treasury

**blockhead** /-ˌhed/ *n* an extremely slow-witted or stupid person – **blockheadedness** *n*

**blockhouse** /-ˌhows/ *n* 1 a structure of heavy timbers formerly used as a fort, having small openings through which weapons are fired and often a projecting upper storey 2 a strong building serving as an observation post and designed to withstand heat, blast, radiation, etc

**blocklaying** /'blokˌlaying/ *n, NZ* the building of foundations or walls using concrete blocks

**block letter** *n* an often hand-drawn simple capital letter

**block plane** *n* a small plane made with the blade set at a low pitch and used chiefly to smooth or shape end grains of wood

**block practice** *n* a continuous period of teaching practice for a trainee teacher

**block release** *n* a short course of full-time study for which a worker is released by his/her employer – compare DAY RELEASE

**block section** *n* a length of railway track of defined limits, the use of which is governed by block signals

**blockship** /'blokˌship/ *n* a ship intended to be run in a channel to block its use

**block signal** *n* a signal at the entrance of a block section to govern trains entering and using that block section

**block system** *n* a system by which a railway track is divided into short sections and trains are controlled by signals

**bloke** /blohk/ *n, chiefly Br informal* a man, fellow [perh fr Shelta]

**¹blond** /blond/ *adj* 1 blond, *fem* blonde 1a *of hair* of a flaxen, golden, light auburn, or pale yellowish brown colour b of a pale white or rosy white colour ⟨~ skin⟩ c being a blond ⟨a handsome ~ youth⟩ 2a of a light colour ⟨~ pelts⟩ b of the colour blond c *esp of wood* made light-coloured by bleaching ⟨a table of ~ walnut⟩ [Fr] – **blondish** *adj*

**²blond** *n* 1 a man or boy with blond hair and usu a light complexion and blue or grey eyes 2 a light yellowish brown to dark greyish yellow colour

**blonde** /blond/ *n* a woman or girl with blonde hair and usu a light complexion and blue or grey eyes ⟨gentlemen prefer ~s⟩ [Fr, fem of *blond*]

**¹blood** /blud/ *n* 1a the usu red liquid that circulates in the heart, arteries, capillaries, and veins of a VERTEBRATE animal, carrying nourishment, oxygen, etc to, and bringing away waste products from, all parts of the body b a comparable liquid in an INVERTEBRATE animal c a fluid resembling blood 2a lifeblood; *broadly* life b human stock or lineage; *esp* the royal lineage ⟨a prince of the ~⟩ c relationship by descent from a common ancestor; kinship d people related through common descent; kindred e descent from parents of recognized breed or pedigree 3 the shedding of blood; *also* the taking of life 4a blood regarded as the seat of the emotions; temper b the one of the four HUMOURS (bodily fluids believed to determine a person's disposition) in medieval physiology that was believed to cause optimism or cheerfulness 5 people or ideas of the specified, esp innovative, kind ⟨need some fresh ~ in the organization⟩ 6 *chiefly humorous* a dashing, lively, esp young man; a rake 7 *obs* lust [ME, fr OE *blōd;* akin to OHG *bluot* blood] – **in cold blood** with premeditation; deliberately – **sweat blood** to work or worry intensely

**²blood** *vt* 1 to stain or wet with blood; *esp* to mark the face of (an inexperienced fox hunter) with the blood of the fox 2 to expose (a hunting dog) to the sight, scent, or taste of the blood of prey in order to make eager for the chase 3 to initiate in an activity, esp warfare ⟨troops already ~ed in battle⟩

**blood-and-'thunder** *adj, informal* violently melodramatic

**blood bank** *n* a place for storage of blood or plasma until required for medical use

**bloodbath** /-ˌbahth/ *n* a great slaughter; a massacre

**blood brother** *n* either of two men pledged to mutual loyalty, esp by a ceremonial mingling of each other's blood – **blood brotherhood** *n*

**blood cell** *n* a cell normally present in blood

**blood count** *n* (the determination of) the number of BLOOD CELLS in a definite volume of blood

**bloodcurdling** /-ˌkuhdling/ *adj* arousing horror ⟨~ screams⟩ – **bloodcurdlingly** *adv*

**blooded** /'bludid/ *adj* being entirely or largely of superior breed ⟨a herd of ~ stock⟩

**-blooded** /-bludid/ *comb form* (→ *adj*) having (such) blood or (such) a temperament ⟨cold-blooded⟩ ⟨warm-blooded⟩

**blood feud** *n* a feud involving murder or injury between different clans or families; a vendetta

**blood fluke** *n* SCHISTOSOME (parasitic flatworm)

**blood group** *n* any of the classes into which human beings can be separated on the basis of the presence or absence of specific ANTIGENS (substances stimulating the production of antibodies) in their blood

**bloodguilt** /-ˌgilt/ *n* guilt resulting from bloodshed, esp murder – **bloodguilty** *adj*

**blood heat** *n* a temperature approximating to that of the human body; about 37°C (98°F)

**bloodhound** /-ˌhownd/ *n* 1 a large powerful hound of European origin remarkable for its acute sense of smell and poor sight 2 a person (e g a detective) who is keen in pursuing or tracking somebody or something down

**bloodless** /-lis/ *adj* 1 deficient in or free from blood 2 not accompanied by loss or shedding of blood ⟨a ~ victory⟩ 3 lacking in spirit or vitality 4 lacking in human feeling ⟨~ statistics⟩ – **bloodlessly** *adv*, **bloodlessness** *n*

**bloodletting** /-ˌleting/ *n* 1 the letting out of blood from a vein for the treatment of disease 2 bloodshed

**bloodline** /-ˌlien/ *n* a group of related individuals (e g direct ancestors), esp with distinctive characteristics; a pedigree

**blood money** *n* 1 money paid to a hired murderer or to somebody giving information about where a potential victim is to be found 2 money paid to the next of kin of a murdered person

**blood orange** *n* a type of eating orange that has red and orange flesh and a reddish skin

**blood platelet** /'playtlit/ *n* any of the minute discs that are present in large numbers in the blood of VERTEBRATE animals, have no cell nuclei in human beings, and assist in blood clotting – called also THROMBOCYTE

**blood poisoning** *n* SEPTICAEMIA (infection of the blood)

**blood pressure** *n* pressure that is exerted by the blood on the walls of the BLOOD VESSELS, esp arteries, and that varies with the muscular efficiency of the heart, the blood volume, the age and health of the individual, and the state of the blood-vessel walls

**blood pudding** *n* BLACK PUDDING

**bloodred** /'bludˌred/ *adj* having the colour of blood

**'blood-reˌlation** *n* a person related by birth rather than marriage

**blood serum** *n* blood PLASMA (yellowish liquid part of blood) from which substances aiding clotting (e g FIBRINOGEN) have been removed

**bloodshed** /-ˌshed/ *n* 1 the shedding of blood 2 the taking of life; slaughter

**bloodshot** /-ˌshot/ *adj, of an eye* having the white part tinged with red due to inflammation

**blood sport** *n* a field sport (e g foxhunting or beagling) in which animals are killed

**bloodstain** /-ˌstayn/ *n* a discoloration caused by blood

**bloodstained** /'bludˌstaynd/ *adj* 1 stained with blood 2 involved with slaughter; *esp* guilty of bloodshed

**bloodstock** /-ˌstok/ *n taking sing or pl vb* horses of Thoroughbred breeding, esp when used for racing

**bloodstone** /-ˌstohn/ *n* a translucent green quartz gemstone sprinkled with red spots resembling blood

**bloodstream** /-ˌstreem/ *n* the flowing blood in a circulatory system

**bloodsucker** /-ˌsukə/ *n* 1 an animal that sucks blood; *esp* a leech 2 *informal* a person who exploits another, esp by extorting money – **bloodsucking** *adj*

**blood sugar** *n* (the concentration of) the glucose in the blood

**blood test** *n* a test of the blood (e g to ascertain the nature of an infection or to detect leukaemia)

**bloodthirsty** /-ˌthuhsti/ *adj* 1 eager for bloodshed 2 marked by the shedding of blood; violent ⟨*a ~ film*⟩ – **bloodthirstily** *adv*, **bloodthirstiness** *n*

**blood type** *n* BLOOD GROUP – **blood typing** *n*

**blood vessel** *n* any of the vessels through which blood circulates in an animal

**bloodworm** /-,wuhm/ *n* 1 any of various reddish segmented worms (phylum Annelida) often used as bait for fish 2 the red aquatic larva of some midges (family Chironomidae)

**¹bloody** /'bludi/ *adj* **1a** containing or made of blood **b** of or contained in the blood 2 smeared or stained with blood 3 accompanied by or involving bloodshed; *esp* marked by great slaughter **4a** murderous **b** merciless, cruel 5 bloodred 6 *slang* – used as a meaningless intensive [(6) prob fr the oath *God's blood*] – **bloodily** *adv*, **bloodiness** *n*

> *usage* It is often unsafe to use **bloody** in the senses connected with blood, because of confusion with the slang sense ⟨*What* **bloody** *man is that?* – Shak⟩

**²bloody** *vt* to make bloody

**³bloody** *adv, slang* – used as a meaningless intensive ⟨*not ~ likely*⟩

**Bloody Mary** /'meəri/ *n, pl* **Bloody Marys** a cocktail consisting chiefly of vodka and tomato juice [prob fr *Bloody Mary*, nickname of Mary I of England †1558; fr its red colour]

**bloody-'minded** *adj* deliberately obstructive or unhelpful – **bloody-mindedness** *n*

**bloody-nosed beetle** *n* a large black beetle (*Timarcha tenebricosa*) which exudes a red liquid (HAEMOLYMPH) from various joints when disturbed

**¹bloom** /bloohm/ *n* a bar of iron or steel hammered or rolled from an ingot [ME *blome* lump of metal, fr OE *blōma*]

**²bloom** *n* **1a(1)** a flower ⟨*green leaves and large yellow ~s*⟩ **a(2)** the mass of flowers on a single plant, tree, etc **b** the flowering state ⟨*the roses are in ~*⟩ **c** a period of flowering ⟨*the spring ~*⟩ **d** an excessive growth of PHYTOPLANKTON 2 a state or time of beauty, freshness, and vigour ⟨*the ~ of youth*⟩ **3a** a delicate powdery coating on some fruits and leaves **b** a cloudiness on a film of varnish or lacquer **c** a mottled white coating that appears on chocolate, often caused by incorrect temperatures in manufacture or storage 4 rosy or healthy appearance of the cheeks or face [ME *blome*, fr ON *blōm*; akin to OE *blōwan* to blossom – more at BLOW] – **bloomy** *adj*

**³bloom** *vi* **1a** to produce or yield flowers **b** to support abundant plant life ⟨*make the desert ~*⟩ **2a** to flourish ⟨*~ing with health*⟩ **b** to reach full competence or maturity; blossom ⟨*their friendship ~ed over the weeks*⟩ 3 *of a body of water* to become densely populated with microorganisms, esp plankton **~** *vt* to give bloom to ⟨*while barred clouds ~ the soft-dying day* – John Keats⟩ *synonyms* see ²BLOSSOM *usage* see BLOOMING

**bloomer** /'bloohmə/ *n* 1 a plant that blooms, esp at a usu specified time ⟨*a late ~*⟩ 2 *chiefly Br* a large glazed loaf baked at the bottom of the oven and marked with diagonal cuts across the top 3 *informal* a stupid or embarrassing blunder; FAUX PAS

**bloomers** /'bloohməz/ *n pl* 1 a costume worn formerly by women and children consisting of a short skirt and long loose trousers gathered closely about the ankles **2a** full loose trousers gathered at the knee formerly worn by women, esp for athletics **b** an undergarment of similar design 3 *informal* knickers [Amelia *Bloomer* †1894 US feminist]

**bloomery** /'bloohməri/ *n* a furnace and forge where wrought-iron blooms were formerly made

**blooming** /'bloohming, 'blooh-/ *adj, chiefly Br euph* – used as a generalized intensive ⟨*that ~ idiot*⟩ [prob euphemism for *bloody*]

> *usage* It is usually unsafe to use **blooming** in the sense "in bloom" ⟨*Wan was her cheek, her* **blooming** *mantle torn* – Alfred Tennyson⟩ because of confusion with the sense "bloody".

**blooper** /'bloohpə/ *n, NAm informal* an embarrassing public blunder [*bloop* (a grating or howling sound), of imit origin]

**¹blossom** /'blosəm/ *n* **1a** the flower of a plant; *esp* a flower that produces edible fruits ⟨*apple ~s*⟩ **b** the mass of bloom on a single plant; *also* the state of bearing flowers ⟨*a plum tree in full ~*⟩ 2 a peak period or stage of development [ME *blosme*, fr OE *blōstm*; akin to OE *blōwan*] – **blossomy** *adj*

**²blossom** *vi* 1 to bloom 2 to come into one's own; develop ⟨*a ~ing talent*⟩

> *synonyms* **Blossom** is used particularly of plants whose flower produces edible fruits ⟨*the apple trees are* **blossoming**⟩ and **bloom** of plants whose flower is their main achievement ⟨*the roses* **bloomed**⟩. In figurative use, to **blossom** is to develop with further

promise ⟨*she's* **blossoming** *into a fine singer*⟩ and to **bloom** or be full-blown is to be in fullest development.

**¹blot** /blot/ *n* 1 a soiling or disfiguring mark; a spot 2 a mark of reproach; a blemish [ME]

**²blot** *vb* -tt- *vt* 1 to spot, stain, or spatter with a discolouring substance 2 to dry or remove with an absorbing agent (eg blotting paper) **~** *vi* 1 to make a blot 2 to become marked with a blot – see also **blot one's** COPYBOOK *synonyms* see ERASE

> **blot out** *vt* 1 to obscure, eclipse ⟨*this one good act* blots out *many bad ones*⟩ 2 to destroy; WIPE OUT ⟨*one such bomb can* blot out *a city*⟩

**³blot** *n* 1 a backgammon piece exposed to capture 2 *archaic* a weak or exposed point [perh fr Dan *blot* naked, exposed]

**blotch** /bloch/ *n* 1 an imperfection, blemish 2 an irregular spot or mark (eg of colour or ink) [prob partly alter. (influenced by ¹*blot*) of *botch* (swelling), & partly fr OF *bloche* clod of earth] – **blotch** *vt*, **blotchily** *adv*, **blotchy** *adj*

**blotter** /'blotə/ *n* something used for blotting; *esp* a piece of blotting paper

**blotting paper** /'bloting/ *n* a soft spongy unsized paper used to absorb ink

**blotto** /'blotoh/ *adj, Br slang* extremely drunk [prob irreg fr ²*blot*]

**¹blouse** /blowz/ *n* a usu loose-fitting woman's upper garment that resembles a shirt or smock and is waist-length or longer [Fr]

**²blouse** *vb* to (cause to) fall in folds

**blouson** /'bloohzon, 'blowzon/ *n* a short loose jacket or blouse usu gathered in at the waist and cuffs [Fr, fr *blouse*]

**¹blow** /bloh/ *vb* **blew** /blooh/; **blown** /blohn/ *vi* 1 *of air* to move with speed or force ⟨*it's ~ing hard tonight*⟩ 2 to send forth a current of gas, esp air ⟨*blew on his cold hands*⟩ **3a** to make a sound (as if) by blowing ⟨*the whistle* blew⟩ **b** *of a wind instrument* to sound **4a** to pant, gasp ⟨*the horse* blew *heavily*⟩ **b** *of a whale* to eject moisture-laden air from the lungs through the blowhole 5 to move or be carried (as if) by wind 6 *of an electric fuse* to melt when overloaded 7 *of a tyre* to loose the contained air through a spontaneous rupture – usu + *out* 8 *chiefly Austr & NAm informal* to boast **~** *vt* **1a** to set (gas or vapour) in motion **b** to act on with a current of gas or vapour; *specif* to force a strong current of air from the lungs through (the nose) in order to clear 2 to damn, disregard ⟨*~ the expense*⟩ 3 to produce or shape by the action of blown or injected air ⟨*~ing bubbles*⟩ ⟨*~ing glass*⟩ 4 *of an insect* to deposit eggs or larvae on or in 5 to shatter, burst, or destroy by explosion – compare BLOW UP **6a** to put (eg a horse) out of breath with exertion **b** to let (eg a horse) pause to catch the breath 7 to cause (a fuse) to blow 8 to rupture by too much pressure ⟨*blew a gasket*⟩ 9 *informal* to lose by failing to use an opportunity; muff ⟨*blew his chance*⟩ 10 *informal* to leave hurriedly ⟨*blew town*⟩ 11 *informal* to spend extravagantly; squander ⟨*blew £50 on a pair of shoes*⟩ – see also **blow one's** COOL/**the** GAFF, **blow** HOT **and cold, blow somebody's** MIND/**one's** TOP/**one's own** TRUMPET, **blow the** WHISTLE **on** [ME *blowen*, fr OE *blāwan*; akin to OHG *blāen* to blow, L *flare*, Gk *phallos* penis]

> **blow in** *vi, informal* to arrive casually or unexpectedly

> **blow off** *vi* 1 *of a gas* to gush out when pressure is relieved 2 *vulg* to emit air noisily from the anus

> **blow out** *vi* 1 to become extinguished by a breath or gust of air 2 *of an oil or gas well* to erupt out of control **~** *vt* 1 to extinguish by a breath or gust of air 2 *of a storm* to dissipate (itself) by blowing

> **blow over** *vi* to pass by without lasting effect

> **blow up** *vt* 1 to shatter or destroy by explosion 2 to build up or exaggerate to an unreasonable extent 3 to fill up with a gas, esp air ⟨*blow up a balloon*⟩ 4 to make a photographic enlargement of **~** *vi* **1a** to explode **b** to be disrupted or destroyed (eg by explosion) **c** to become violently angry **2a** to become filled with a gas, esp air **b** to become expanded to unreasonable proportions 3 to come into being; arise ⟨*a storm blew up*⟩

**²blow** *n* 1 a strong wind or windy storm 2 an act or instance of blowing ⟨*give your nose a good ~*⟩ 3 *chiefly Austr & NAm informal* a brag, boast

**³blow** *vi* **blew**; **blown** to flower, bloom ⟨*a full-blown rose*⟩ [ME *blowen*, fr OE *blōwan*; akin to OHG *bluoen* to bloom, L *florēre* to bloom, *flor-, flos* flower]

**⁴blow** *n, poetic* ²BLOOM 1b ⟨*lilacs in full ~*⟩

**⁵blow** *n* **1** a forceful stroke delivered with a part of the body or with an instrument **2** a hostile act or state; combat – esp in *come to blows* **3** a forcible or sudden act or effort; an assault ⟨*a ~ for freedom*⟩ **4** a shock or misfortune ⟨*failure to land the job came as a ~*⟩ [ME (northern) *blaw*]

**blowback** /-ˌbak/ *n* the action of a recoil-operated firearm in which no locking or inertia mechanism delays the rearward motion of the bolt or breechblock; *also* a firearm using such an action

**blow-by-ˈblow** *adj* minutely detailed ⟨*a ~ account*⟩

**¹blow-ˌdry** *n* an act of drying the hair, usu into a particular style, with a hairdrier ⟨*cut and ~*⟩

**²blow-ˈdry** *vt* to blow warm air over, through, or onto (eg the hair) until dry

**blower** /ˈbloh-ə/ *n* **1** somebody or something that blows or is blown **2** a device for producing a current of air or gas ⟨*snow ~*⟩ **3** *Br informal* the telephone **4** *Br informal* a whale

**blowfly** /-ˌflie/ *n* any of various flies (family Calliphoridae) that deposit their eggs or maggots esp on meat or in wounds; *esp* a bluebottle (*Calliphora vomitoria*) commonly found in houses

**blowgun** /-ˌgun/ *n* BLOWPIPE 3

**blowhard** /-ˌhahd/ *n* a braggart

**blowhole** /-ˌhohl/ *n* **1** a nostril in the top of the head of a whale, porpoise, or dolphin **2** a hole in the ice to which aquatic mammals (eg seals) come to breathe

**blowlamp** /-ˌlamp/ *n* a small portable burner that produces an intense flame usu by burning paraffin expelled from a pressurized fuel tank and that is used chiefly in plumbing and in stripping paint

**blown** /blohn/ *adj* **1** swollen; *esp* afflicted with BLOAT (digestive disturbance of animals) **2** FLYBLOWN **3** out of breath [ME *blowen*, fr pp of *blowen* to blow]

**blowout** /-ˌowt/ *n* **1** an uncontrolled eruption of an oil or gas well **2** a bursting of a container (eg a tyre) because of pressure of the contents on a weak spot **3** *informal* a large meal

**blowpipe** /-ˌpiep/ *n* **1** a tube for directing a jet of gas or mixture of gases (eg air) into a flame so as to concentrate and increase the heat **2** a tubular instrument used for revealing or cleaning a bodily cavity by forcing air into it **3** a tube from which a projectile (eg a dart) may be fired by blowing **4** a long metal tube on the end of which a glassblower gathers a quantity of molten glass and through which he/she blows to expand and shape it

**blowsy** *also* **blowzy** /ˈblowzi/ *adj* **1** having a coarse ruddy complexion **2** *esp of a woman* slovenly in appearance and usu fat [E dial. *blowse, blowze* wench, slattern]

**blowtorch** /-ˌtawch/ *n, chiefly NAm* a blowlamp

**blowup** /-ˌup/ *n* **1** an explosion **2** an outburst of temper **3** a photographic enlargement

**blow wave** *n* a method of styling the hair in which sections of it are curled round a brush and dried with a hand-held hairdrier; *also* a style so achieved – **blow wave** *vt*

**blowy** /ˈbloh-i/ *adj* windy ⟨*a ~ March day*⟩

**blub** /blub/ *vb* **-bb-** *informal* to blubber

**¹blubber** /ˈblubə/ *n* **1a** the fat of large marine mammals, esp whales **b** *informal* superfluous fat on the body **2** *informal* an act of blubbering [ME *bluber* bubble, foam, prob of imit origin] – **blubbery** *adj*

**²blubber** *vb, informal vi* to weep noisily ~ *vt* to utter while weeping [ME *blubren* to make a bubbling sound, fr *bluber*]

**³blubber** *adj* puffed out; thick ⟨*~ lips*⟩

**blubbery** /ˈblubəri/ *adj* ³BLUBBER

**blucher** /ˈbloohkə, ˈbloohchə/ *n, archaic* a strong laced leather shoe [G L von *Blücher* †1819 Prussian general]

**¹bludge** /bluj/ *vi, Austr & NZ informal* **1** to avoid work, responsibility, or duty; shirk **2** to impose on others **3** to scrounge [prob back-formation fr *bludger*, fr earlier *bludger* pimp, prob contr of *bludgeoner* pimp, bully, fr ²*bludgeon* + ²-*er*] – **bludger** *n*

**²bludge** *n, Austr & NZ informal* **1** an easy task; a doddle **2** a period of idleness

**¹bludgeon** /ˈblujən/ *n* **1** a short club that is used as a weapon **2** something used to attack or bully ⟨*the ~ of satire*⟩ [perh modif of OF *bougeon*, dim. of *bouge, bolge* club]

**²bludgeon** *vt* **1** to hit or beat with a bludgeon **2** to overcome by aggressive argument

**¹blue** /blooh/ *adj* **1** of the colour blue **2a** discoloured through cold, anger, bruising, or fear **b** bluish grey ⟨*a ~ cat*⟩ **3a** low in spirits; melancholy **b** depressing, dismal ⟨*things looked ~*⟩ **4** CONSERVATIVE 2 **5a** obscene, pornographic ⟨*a ~ film*⟩ **b** off-colour, risqué ⟨*~ jokes*⟩ **6** *of a ski run* for beginners – see also *until one is blue in the* FACE, *once in a blue* MOON, *cry blue* MURDER [ME, fr OF *blou*, of Gmc origin; akin to OHG *blāo* blue; akin to L *flavus* yellow, OE *bǣl* fire – more at BALD] – **bluely** *adv*, **blueness** *n*

**²blue** *n* **1** a colour whose hue is that of the clear sky and lies between green and violet in the spectrum **2a** a blue pigment or dye **b** a blue preparation used to whiten clothes in laundering **3** blue clothing ⟨*dressed in ~*⟩ **4a(1)** the sky **a(2)** the far distance **b** the sea **5** a blue object ⟨*the poker player bought a stock of ~s*⟩ **6** a bluestocking **7** any of numerous small chiefly blue butterflies (family Lycaenidae) **8** *often cap, Br* one who represents or has represented either of the two universities of Oxford and Cambridge in a major sport, esp against the other university; *also* a usu notional award given to him/her ⟨*got my ~ for rowing*⟩ **9** *Austr informal* a redhead **10** *Austr informal* a quarrel, row **11** *Austr informal* a faithful or reliable person ⟨*she's a real ~*⟩ – *out of the blue* without warning; unexpectedly ⟨*he just turned up out of the blue*⟩ [orig referring to thunder and lightning coming out of a clear blue sky] – see also a BOLT *from the blue*

**³blue** *vb* **blueing, bluing** *vt* **1** to make blue **2** to treat (laundry) with blue ~ *vi* to turn blue

**⁴blue** *vt* **blueing, bluing** *Br informal* to spend lavishly and wastefully [prob fr *blew*, pp of ¹*blow* (sense 11)]

**blue asbestos** *n* CROCIDOLITE (blue or green mineral)

**blue baby** *n* a baby with a bluish tint usu resulting from a CONGENITAL (existing at birth) defect of the heart in which mingling of blood from veins and arteries occurs

**bluebeard** /-ˌbiəd/ *n* a man who marries and kills one wife after another [*Bluebeard*, a folklore character]

**bluebell** /-ˌbel/ *n* **1** any of various plants (genus *Endymion*) of the lily family bearing blue bell-shaped flowers; *esp* WILD HYACINTH **2** *chiefly Scot* a harebell

**blueberry** /-b(ə)ri; *NAm* -ˌberi/ *n* the edible blue or blackish berry (eg a bilberry) of any of several shrubs (genus *Vaccinium*) of the heath family; *also* a shrub bearing blueberries

**bluebird** /-ˌbuhd/ *n* any of several small N American songbirds (genus *Sialia*) having (partly) blue plumage on their backs

**blue-ˈblack** *adj* very dark blue in colour

**blue blood** *n* high or noble birth [trans of Sp *sangre azul*; prob fr the comparatively blue veins of fair-skinned people] – **blue-blooded** *adj*

**bluebonnet** /ˈbloohˌbonit/ *n* **1** a wide round flat cap of blue wool formerly worn in Scotland **2** one who wears such a cap; *specif* a Scot

**blue book** *n* **1** an official government report or document bound in a blue cover **2** *NAm informal* a register, esp of socially prominent people

**Blue Book** *n* – used for the annual government publication "National Income and Expenditure" which sets out the national accounts of the UK

**bluebottle** /-ˌbotl/ *n* **1a** CORNFLOWER 1 **b** GRAPE HYACINTH (blue spring-flowering plant) **2** any of several blowflies of which the abdomen or the whole body is iridescent blue, that make a loud buzzing noise in flight **3** *Austr informal* PORTUGUESE MAN-OF-WAR **4** *Br slang* a policeman

**blue cheese** *n* cheese marked with veins of greenish-blue mould

**blue chip** *n* **1** a stock issue of high investment quality, usu from a substantial well-established company enjoying public confidence in its worth and stability **2** an outstandingly worthwhile or valuable property or asset – **blue-chip** *adj*

**bluecoat boy** /ˈbloohˌkoht/, *fem* **bluecoat girl** *n* a pupil at Christ's Hospital [fr the long blue gowns worn by pupils at Christ's Hospital at Horsham in England & (formerly) other charity schools]

**blue-ˈcollar** *adj* of or being the class of manual wage-earning employees whose duties call for the wearing of work clothes or protective clothing – compare WHITE-COLLAR

**blue devils** *n pl, informal* **1** low spirits; despondency **2** DELIRIUM TREMENS

**blue-eyed boy** *n, informal often derog* a favourite – used with reference to boys or men

**bluefin tuna** /ˈbloohˌfin/ *n* a very large tuna fish (*Thunnus thynnus*)

**bluefish** /-ˌfish/ *n* **1** an active voracious fish (*Pomatomus saltatrix*) that is found in all warm seas **2** any of various dark or bluish fishes (eg the pollack)

**blue fox** *n* a small arctic fox (*Alopex lagopus*) whose coat remains blue-grey in winter; *also* the pelt or fur of this fox, often imitated by dyeing white fox pelts

**bluegrass** /-,grahs/ *n* 1 a type of COUNTRY MUSIC played on unamplified stringed instruments (eg banjos, guitars, and fiddles) and usu characterized by free improvisation and close usu high-pitched harmony 2 *NAm* MEADOW GRASS [(1) *Bluegrass state*, nickname of Kentucky, USA, where such music prob originated]

**blue-green alga** *n* any of a class (Cyanophyceae) of algae that contain bluish green pigments in addition to chlorophyll

**blue gum** *n* any of several Australian eucalyptuses which have a bluish bark and are grown for their wood

**blueing** /'blooh·ing/ *n* BLUING (preparation used in laundering to whiten fabrics)

**bluejacket** /'blooh,jakit/ *n* a sailor

**blue john** /jon/ *n* a blue form of the mineral FLUORITE found only in Derbyshire and used esp for jewellery and ornaments [fr the name *John*]

**blue line** *n* either of two blue lines that divide an ice-hockey rink into three equal zones and that separate the offensive and defensive zones from the neutral zone in the middle

**blue mould** *n* 1 any of a genus (*Penicillium*) of fungi that form a bluish mildew on decaying food or other matter 2 a disease of tobacco seedlings caused by a fungus (*Peronospora tabacina*) and characterized by yellowish spots and bluish grey mildew on the undersides of the leaves

**bluenose** /'blooh,nohz/ *n, informal* 1 an inhabitant of Nova Scotia 2 *chiefly NAm* somebody who advocates a rigorous moral code [(1) fr an effect of the very cold winters in Nova Scotia]

**blue note** *n* a flattened third or seventh note used esp in jazz and blues in a chord where a major unflattened interval would be expected

**blue-'pencil** *vt* to edit by correcting or deleting

**blue peter** /'peetə/ *n* a blue signal flag with a white square in the centre, used to indicate that a merchant vessel is ready to sail [fr the name *Peter*]

**blue point** *n* a Siamese cat having a bluish body and dark grey markings on its extremities – compare SEAL POINT

**blue pointer** *n, chiefly Austr* MAKO (type of shark)

**blueprint** /-,print/ *n* 1 a photographic print in white on a bright blue ground used esp for maps, mechanical drawings, and architects' plans **2a** a detailed programme of action ⟨*a ~ for victory*⟩ **b** a plan, prototype ⟨*the new method of organization served as a ~ for future work*⟩ – **blueprint** *vt*

**blue ribbon** *n* 1 a blue ribbon worn as a symbol of honour, esp by members of the Order of the Garter 2 the greatest honour or award in a specified field

**blues** /bloohz/ *n taking sing or pl vb* 1 low spirits; melancholy – + *the* 2 (a song in) a melancholy style of music which originated among American blacks in the early 20th century and is characterized by usu 12-bar 3-line stanzas in which the words of the second line repeat those of the first and by BLUE NOTES in melody and harmony ⟨*singing the ~*⟩ – **bluesy** *adj*

**blue shark** *n* a voracious shark (*Prionace glauca*) that is found in all tropical and temperate seas and occasionally attacks human beings

**bluestocking** /-,stoking/ *n, chiefly derog* a woman having intellectual or literary interests [*Bluestocking* Society, 18th-c literary club]

**blue tit** *n* a common European tit (*Parus caeruleus*) that has a blue and white head and a mostly yellow underside

**bluetongue** /'blooh,tung/ *n* 1 a serious virus disease, esp of sheep, characterized by bluish discoloration of the skin due to lack of oxygen in the blood, haemorrhaging, and swelling and shedding of tissue, esp about the mouth and tongue 2 an Australian lizard (*Tiliqua scincoides*) with a cobalt-blue tongue 3 *Austr slang* a handyman who works on a cattle or sheep station

**blue vitriol** *n* a water-containing form of the chemical compound COPPER SULPHATE, $CuSO_4.5H_2O$

**blue whale** *n* a WHALEBONE WHALE (*Sibbaldus musculus*) that is the largest known animal and is found esp in N European waters

**bluey** /'blooh·i/ *n, Austr* 1 a bundle carried by a bushman; swag 2 BLUE 9 [fr the blue blanket commonly used to wrap the bundle]

**¹bluff** /bluf/ *adj* 1 rising steeply with a broad flat or rounded front ⟨*~ cliffs*⟩ 2 good-naturedly frank and outspoken; hearty [obs D *blaf* flat; akin to MLG *blaff* smooth] – **bluffly** *adv*, **bluffness** *n*

**²bluff** *n* a high steep bank; a cliff

**³bluff** *vt* 1 to deceive (an opponent) in cards by a bold bet on an inferior hand with the result that the opponent withdraws a winning hand 2 to deter or frighten by pretence or a show of strength, confidence, etc ~ *vi* to bluff somebody [prob fr D *bluffen* to boast, play a kind of card game] – **bluffer** *n*

**⁴bluff** *n* 1 an act or instance of bluffing 2 the practice of bluffing – **call somebody's bluff** to challenge somebody to prove his/her claims

**bluing, blueing** /'blooh·ing/ *n* a preparation used in laundering to counteract yellowing of white fabrics

**bluish** /'blooh·ish/ *adj* having a tinge of blue; rather blue – **bluishness** *n*

**¹blunder** /'blundə/ *vi* 1 to move unsteadily or confusedly 2 to make a mistake through stupidity, ignorance, or carelessness ~ *vt* to utter stupidly, confusedly, or thoughtlessly [ME *blundren*, prob of Scand origin] – **blunderer** *n*, **blunderingly** *adv*

**²blunder** *n* an error or mistake resulting usu from stupidity, ignorance, or carelessness

**blunderbuss** /'blundə,bus/ *n* 1 an obsolete short firearm with a large BORE (hollow part of the barrel) and usu a flaring muzzle 2 *informal* a blundering person [by folk etymology (influenced by *blunder*) fr obs D *donderbus*, fr D *donder* thunder + obs D *bus* gun]

**¹blunt** /blunt/ *adj* 1 insensitive, dull 2 having an edge or point that is not sharp **3a** abrupt in speech or manner; aggressively outspoken **b** direct, straightforward [ME] – **bluntly** *adv*, **bluntness** *n*

**²blunt** *vt* to make less sharp or definite

**¹blur** /bluh/ *n* 1 a smear or stain that obscures 2 something vague or lacking definite outline or distinct character [perh akin to ME *bleren* to blear]

**²blur** *vb* **-rr-** *vt* 1 to obscure or blemish by smearing 2 to make dim, indistinct, or confused in outline or character ~ *vi* to become vague, indistinct, or indefinite – **blurry** *adj*, **blurrily** *adv*

**blurb** /bluhb/ *n* a short promotional description (eg on a book jacket) [coined by Gelett Burgess †1951 US humorist]

**blurt out** /bluht/ *vt* to utter abruptly and impulsively [*blurt* prob imit] – **blurter** *n*

**¹blush** /blush/ *vi* 1 to become red in the face, esp from shame, modesty, or embarrassment 2 to feel shame or embarrassment [ME *blusshen* to shine, glance, redden, fr OE *blyscan* to redden, fr *blȳsa* flame; akin to OHG *bluhhen* to burn brightly] – **blushingly** *adv*

**²blush** *n* 1 a reddening of the face, esp from shame, modesty, or embarrassment 2 a red or rosy tint – **blushful** *adj* – **at first blush** when first seen or glimpsed

**blusher** /'blushə/ *n* a cream or powder for adding colour to the cheeks

**¹bluster** /'blustə/ *vi* 1 to blow in stormy gusts 2 to talk or act in a noisily self-assertive or boastful manner ~ *vt* 1 to utter noisily or boastfully 2 to drive or force *into* by blustering [ME *blustren*, prob fr MLG *blüsteren*] – **blusterer** *n*, **blusteringly** *adv*

**²bluster** *n* 1 a violent blowing of wind 2 violent commotion 3 loudly boastful or threatening talk – **blusterous** *adj*, **blustery** *adj*

**bo** /boh/ *n, chiefly NAm* a fellow – used chiefly in informal address [perh short for E dial. *bor* friend, neighbour]

**BO** /,bee 'oh/ *n* a disagreeable smell, esp of stale perspiration, given off by a person's body [*body odour*]

**boa** /'boh·ə/ *n* 1 a large snake (eg the BOA CONSTRICTOR, anaconda, or python) that crushes its prey 2 a long fluffy scarf of fur, feathers, or delicate fabric [L, a water snake]

**boab** *n, Austr* BAOBAB (broad-trunked tropical tree) [by alter.]

**boa constrictor** *n* a tropical American boa (*Constrictor constrictor*) that is light brown striped or mottled with darker brown and reaches a length of 3 metres (about 10 feet) or more; *broadly* BOA 1

**boar** /baw/ *n* **1a** an uncastrated male pig **b** the male of any of several mammals (eg a GUINEA PIG or badger) 2 a European and Asian wild pig (*Sus scrofa*) with a dark-brown bristly coat, the male of which has large tusks. Most domestic pigs derive from it. [ME *bor*, fr OE *bār*; akin to OHG & OS *bēr* boar] – **boarish** *adj*

**¹board** /bawd/ *n* 1 the distance that a sailing vessel makes on one TACK (course) in steering towards the direction from which the wind is blowing **2a** a usu long thin narrow piece of sawn timber **b** *pl* STAGE 2a(2),(3) **3a** a table spread with a meal **b** daily meals, esp when provided in return for payment ⟨*bed and* ~⟩ **4** *taking sing or pl vb* **4a** a group of people having managerial, supervisory, or investigatory powers ⟨~ *of directors*⟩ ⟨~ *of examiners*⟩ **b** an official body ⟨*the electricity* ~⟩ **5a** the exposed hands of all the players in a STUD POKER game **b** an exposed dummy hand in bridge **6a** a flat usu rectangular piece of material (eg wood) designed or marked for a special purpose (eg for playing chess, ludo, backgammon, etc) **b** SPRINGBOARD 1 **c** a surfboard **d** a blackboard **7a** any of various wood pulps or composition materials formed into stiff flat rectangular sheets **b** cardboard **c** the stiff foundation piece for the side of a book cover **8** a line across the front wall of a squash court at a height of 19 inches (48.3 centimetres), above which a return must be hit **9** *pl* the low wooden wall enclosing an ice-hockey rink **10** *NAm* a surface or frame on which notices or market quotations are posted **11** *NAm informal* an organized securities or commodities exchange **12** *archaic* TABLE 3a **13** *obs* a border, edge [ME *bord* piece of sawed lumber, border, ship's side, fr OE; akin to OHG *bort* ship's side, Skt *bardhaka* carpenter] – **boardlike** *adj* – **go by the board 1** to be carried over a ship's side **2** to be discarded – **on board** aboard – **sweep the board** to win convincingly; win everything – **take on board** *Br* to understand fully; grasp

²**board** *vt* **1** to come up against or alongside (a ship), usu to attack **2** to go aboard (eg a ship, train, aircraft, or bus) **3** to cover with boards – often + *over* or *up* ⟨~ *up a window*⟩ **4** to provide with regular meals and often also lodging, usu for a fixed price **5** to block the progress of (a player) against the wall surrounding an ice-hockey rink ~ *vi* to receive one's meals and lodging as a paying guest away from home

**boarder** /'bawdə/ *n* **1** a lodger **2** a resident pupil at a boarding school

**board foot** *n* a unit of quantity for timber equal to the volume of a board 12 x 12 x 1 inches

**board game** *n* a game of strategy (eg draughts, chess, or backgammon) played by moving pieces on a board

**boarding house** /'bawding/ *n* a LODGING HOUSE at which meals are provided

**boarding school** *n* a school at which meals and lodging are provided

**board measure** *n* measurement in BOARD FEET

**board of trade** *n* **1** *cap B&T* a British government department concerned with commerce and industry that in 1970 was absorbed into the Department of Trade and Industry **2** *NAm* CHAMBER OF COMMERCE

**boardroom** /-,roohm, -room/ *n* a room in which board meetings are held

**boardwalk** /-,wawk/ *n, NAm* a walk often constructed of planking, usu beside the sea

**boart** /'boh·ət, bawt/ *n* BORT (imperfectly crystallized diamond or diamond fragments)

¹**boast** /bohst/ *n* **1** the act or an instance of boasting **2** a cause for pride [ME *boost*] – **boastful** *adj*, **boastfully** *adv*, **boastfulness** *n*

²**boast** *vi* **1** to praise oneself **2** *archaic* to glory, exult ~ *vt* **1** to speak of or assert with excessive pride **2** to possess or contain, esp as something notable or a source of pride ⟨*their home* ~s *all the newest conveniences*⟩ – **boaster** *n*

**synonyms Boast, brag, crow,** and **vaunt: boast,** the most general term, implies self-praise which may be exaggerated, conceited, or ostentatious. **Brag,** more colloquial, suggests vulgar or crude boasting with a hint of swagger. **Crow,** also colloquial, suggests the exulting, triumphant crow of a cock. **Vaunt** is the most literary term, conveying more pomp and ceremony than **boast** ⟨*charity vaunteth not itself, is not puffed up* – I Cor 13:47⟩. **usage** Although it is perfectly correct to use **boast** in the sense "contain as a source of pride", some people prefer to avoid this use where it might be confused with the "self-praise" sense.

³**boast** *n* a usu defensive shot in squash made from a rear corner of the court and hitting a side wall before the front wall [prob fr Fr *bosse* protuberance, place where the ball hits the wall]

¹**boat** /boht/ *n* **1** a small open vessel or craft for travelling across water propelled by oars, paddles, sail, or an engine **2** a usu small ship ⟨*left England on the Calais* ~⟩ **3** a submarine **4** a boat-shaped utensil or device ⟨*a gravy* ~⟩ [ME *boot*, fr OE *bāt;* akin to ON *beit* boat] – **in the same boat** in the same

situation or predicament – **rock the boat** to disturb an otherwise harmonious situation; make trouble – see also BURN **one's boats**

²**boat** *vt* to place in or bring into a boat ⟨*catch and* ~ *a fish*⟩ ~ *vi* to go by or use a boat, esp for recreation – esp in *go boating*

**boatcloak** /'boht,klohk/ *n* a long black naval cloak

**boatel** /boh'tel/ *n* a waterside hotel with berths to accommodate people travelling by boat [blend of *boat* and *hotel*]

**boater** /'bohtə/ *n* **1** somebody who travels in a boat **2** a stiff straw hat with a shallow flat crown and a brim

**boathook** /-,hook/ *n* a pole with a hook at one end, used esp for fending off or holding boats alongside

**boathouse** /-,hows/ *n* a shed near to water for housing boats

**boatie** /'bohti/ *n, NZ informal* one who goes boating for pleasure

**boatman** /-mən/ *n* one who works on, deals in, or operates boats; *specif* one who hires out pleasure boats – **boatmanship, boatsmanship** *n*

**boat race** *n, often cap B&R the* annual rowing race held on the Thames between eights from the universities of Cambridge and Oxford

**boatswain, bosun** /'bohz(ə)n, 'bohs(ə)n/ *n* a PETTY OFFICER on a merchant vessel or WARRANT OFFICER in the navy who supervises all work done on deck and is responsible esp for routine maintenance of the ship's structure and equipment [ME *bootswein*, fr *boot* boat + *swein* boy, servant (cf COXSWAIN)]

**boatswain's chair** *n* a board or seat suspended by ropes and pulleys and used for work at a height (eg on the side of a ship or tall building)

**boat train** *n* an express train for transporting passengers to or from a ship

¹**bob** /bob/ *vb* -**bb-** *vt* **1** to move up and down in a short quick movement ⟨~ *one's head*⟩ **2** to perform (a respectful gesture, esp a curtsy) briefly **3** *obs* to strike with a quick light blow; rap ~ *vi* **1** to move down and up briefly or repeatedly ⟨*a cork* ~*bed in the water*⟩ **2** to curtsy briefly **3** to try to seize a suspended or floating object with the teeth ⟨~ *for apples*⟩ [ME *boben* to strike, move with a jerk, prob of imit origin]

²**bob** *n* **1** a short quick down-and-up motion **2** (a method of bell ringing using) a modification of the order in CHANGE RINGING **3** a small polishing wheel of solid felt or leather with rounded edges **4** *obs* a blow or tap esp with the fist

³**bob** *vt* -**bb-** *obs* **1** to deceive, cheat **2** to take by fraud; filch [ME *bobben*, fr MF *bober*, fr *bobe* deceit]

⁴**bob** *n* **1a** a knot, twist, or curl, esp of ribbons, yarn, or hair **b** a short haircut for a woman or girl, in which the hair hangs loose just above the shoulders **2** a fishing float **3** a hanging ball or weight (eg on a plumb line or on the tail of a kite) **4** *Scot* a nosegay **5** *informal* a small insignificant item; a trifle ⟨*bits and* ~s⟩ [ME *bobbe* bunch, cluster]

⁵**bob** *vt* -**bb-** **1** to cut shorter; crop ⟨~ *a horse's tail*⟩ **2** to cut (hair) in a bob

⁶**bob** *n, pl* **bob** *Br informal* a shilling; *also* the sum of five new pence [perh fr *Bob,* nickname for *Robert*]

⁷**bob** *n* **1** a bobsleigh **2** SKIBOB (small steerable sledge on skis)

⁸**bob** *n, often cap, Br* – **bob's your uncle** – used in triumph at overcoming an obstacle, carrying out a difficult task, etc ⟨*throw the pancake into the air, hold the pan out to catch it, and* bob's your uncle⟩ [fr the name *Bob*]]

**bobbery** /'bobəri/ *n, archaic informal* a noisy disturbance [Hindi *bāp re,* lit., oh father!]

**bobbin** /'bobin/ *n* **1a** any of various small round devices on which threads are wound for working handmade lace **b** a cylinder or spindle on which yarn or thread is wound (eg for use in spinning or sewing) **2** a coil of insulated wire or the reel on which it is wound [Fr *bobine*]

**bobbinet** /,bobi'net/ *n* a machine-made net of cotton, silk, or nylon, usu with a six-sided mesh [blend of *bobbin* and *net*]

**bobbin lace** *n* PILLOW LACE

¹**bobble** /'bobl/ *vi* to move jerkily down and up briefly or repeatedly ⟨*Denness . . . was able to recover his ground as the ball* ~d *in Taylor's gloves* – *Express & Star* [*Wolverhampton*]⟩ [freq of ¹*bob*]

²**bobble** *n* **1** a repeated bobbing movement **2** a small often fluffy ball (eg of wool) used for ornament or trimming ⟨*curtains with plush* ~s – H E Bates⟩ ⟨*a* ~ *hat*⟩

**bobby** /'bobi/ *n, Br informal* a policeman [*Bobby,* nickname for *Robert,* after Sir *Robert* Peel †1850 E statesman, who reorganized the London police force (cf PEELER)]

**bobby calf** *n, Austr* an unweaned calf killed a short time after birth [E dial. *bob* young calf, prob fr the name *Bob*]

**bobby-'dazzler** *n, informal* a remarkable or striking person or thing [prob fr the name *Bobby*]

**bobby pin** *n, NAm* a hairgrip [⁴*bob*]

**bobby socks, bobby sox** *n pl, chiefly NAm* socks reaching above the ankle worn esp by girls [fr the name *Bobby*]

¹**bobby-,soxer** /,soksə/ *n, NAm chiefly derog* an adolescent girl

**bobcat** /-,kat/ *n* a common N American lynx (*Felis rufus*) with rusty or reddish fur and usu dark spots [⁴*bob*; fr the stubby tail]

**boblet** /'boblit/ *n* a bobsleigh for two people

**bobsled** /'bob,sled/ *n* a bobsleigh – **bobsled** *vi*, **bobsledder** *n*

**bobsleigh** /-,slay/ *n* 1 a short sledge, usu used as one of a pair joined by a coupling 2 a large usu metal sledge used in racing and equipped with two pairs of runners in tandem, a long seat for usu two or four people, a steering rope or wheel, and a hand brake operated by the rear man [perh fr ⁴*bob*]

**bobstay** /'bob,stay/ *n* a chain, wire, or rod running from the end of a BOWSPRIT (spar projecting from the bow of a vessel) to the front edge of the bow so as to counteract the upward pull of the FORESTAY (rope running from the foremast to the deck) [prob fr ²*bob*]

**bobtail** /-,tayl/ *n* (a horse or dog with) a bobbed tail [⁴*bob*] – **bobtail, bobtailed** *adj*

**bobwig** /'bob,wig/ *n* a wig with short curls [⁴*bob*]

**boccie, bocci, bocce** /'bochi/ *n* an Italian game similar to bowls played on a long narrow green [It *bocce*, pl of *boccia* ball, fr (assumed) VL *bottia* boss]

**Boche** /bosh/ *n, pl* **Boches**, *esp collectively* **Boche** *chiefly derog slang* a German; *esp* a German soldier in World War I [Fr (slang), rascal, German, prob short for *alboche*, alter. of *allemand* German]

**bock** /bok/ *n* a strong dark German beer [Ger, short for *bockbier*, by shortening & alter. fr *Einbecker bier*, lit., beer from Einbeck, fr *Einbeck*, town in Germany]

**bod** /bod/ *n, informal* a person ⟨*an odd* ∼⟩ [short for *body*]

¹**bode** /bohd/ *vt* 1 to indicate by signs; presage ⟨*this controversy . . . will* ∼ *ill for both of us* – A H Lowe⟩ 2 *archaic* to announce beforehand; foretell *synonyms* see FORETELL [ME *boden*, fr OE *bodian*; akin to OE *bēodan* to proclaim – more at BID] – **bodement** *n*

²**bode** *past of* BIDE

**bodega** /boh'deegə, -'daygə/ *n* a storehouse for wine, esp sherry [Sp, fr L *apotheca* storehouse – more at APOTHECARY]

**bodge** /boj/ *vt, informal* to botch [by alter.]

**bodger** /'bojə/ *n, Br* a person who carves or turns wood; *specif* a turner who makes chairs of beech wood [origin unknown]

**bodgie** /'boji/ *n, Austr* TEDDY BOY [perh fr Austr *bodger* worthless, fr *bodge*]

**bodhisattva, boddhisattva** /,bohdi'satvə/ *n* 1 a being that according to MAHAYANA Buddhism has attained perfect enlightenment but compassionately refrains from entering NIRVANA (state of bliss) in order to save others and is worshipped as a deity 2 a being (e g Siddharta Gautama before his enlightenment) who according to THERAVADA Buddhism is destined to attain perfect enlightenment [Skt *bodhisattva* one whose essence is enlightenment, fr *bodhi* enlightenment + *sattva* being]

**bodice** /'bodis/ *n* 1 the part of a dress that is above the waist 2 *archaic* a corset, stays [alter. of *bodies*, pl of ¹*body* (sense 3a)]

**-bodied** /-bodid/ *comb form* (*adj, n* → *adj*) having (such) a body ⟨*full*-bodied⟩ ⟨*glass*-bodied⟩

¹**bodily** /'bodəli/ *adj* 1 having a body; physical 2 of the body ⟨∼ *comfort*⟩ ⟨∼ *organs*⟩

²**bodily** *adv* 1 IN THE FLESH, IN PERSON 2 as a whole; altogether

**bodkin** /'bodkin/ *n* 1a a small sharp slender instrument for making holes in cloth b a long ornamental hairpin 2 a blunt thick needle with a large eye for use in drawing tape or ribbon through a loop or hem 3 *archaic* a dagger, stiletto [ME]

¹**body** /'bodi/ *n* 1a(1) the organized physical substance of an animal or plant a(2) the material part or nature of human beings a(3) the dead organism; a corpse b a human being; a person 2a the main part of a plant or animal body, esp as distinguished from limbs and head; the trunk b the main, central, or principal part: e g b(1) the nave of a church b(2) the part of a vehicle on or in which the load is placed 3a the part of a garment covering the body or trunk b the central part of printed or written matter c the SOUND BOX (reverberating

chamber) or pipe of a musical instrument 4a a mass of matter distinct from other masses ⟨*a* ∼ *of water*⟩ b one of the seven planets of the old astronomy c something that embodies or gives concrete reality to a thing; *specif* a material object in physical space 5 *taking sing or pl vb* a group of people or things: e g 5a a fighting unit; a force b a group of individuals organized for some purpose ⟨*a legislative* ∼⟩ 6a viscosity, consistency – used esp with reference to oils and grease b compactness or firmness of texture; consistency c fullness or resonance of a musical tone d comparative richness of flavour in wine 7 the part of a printing type extending from bottom (FOOT 6b) to top (SHOULDER 5b) and underlying the raised character (BEVEL 3) [ME, fr OE *bodig*; akin to OHG *botah* body]

²**body** *vt* 1a to give material form or shape to; embody b to represent, symbolize – usu + *forth* 2 to increase the viscosity of (an oil)

**body blow** *n* 1 a usu hard blow in boxing that lands between the neck and waistline 2 a serious setback

**body brush** *n* a broad flat hard brush for grooming horses

**body cavity** *n* a cavity within an animal body; *specif* COELOM

**body check** *n* the legal obstruction of an opposing player with the body (e g in ice hockey or lacrosse)

**body corporate** *n* CORPORATION 2

**bodyguard** /-,gahd/ *n* an escort whose duty it is to protect a person from bodily harm

**bodyline bowling** /'bodilien/ *n* intimidatory fast bowling in cricket aimed persistently at the batsman's body

**body louse** *n* a louse that feeds primarily on the body; *esp* a sucking louse (*Pediculus humanus*) that feeds on the body and lives in the clothing of human beings

**body politic** *n* 1 a group of people politically organized under a single government 2 *archaic* CORPORATION 2

**body scanner** *n* a machine that rotates round the body taking cross-sectional X-ray photographs of it that can be used as aids to medical diagnosis

**body snatcher** *n* a person who formerly dug up corpses illegally for dissection

**body stocking** *n* a closely fitting usu nylon one-piece garment for the torso that often has sleeves and legs

**bodysurf** /-,suhf/ *vi* to surf without a surfboard by planing on the chest and stomach – **bodysurfer** *n*

**body wall** *n* the external surface of the body in animals, usu consisting of two of the original embryonic body tissues (ECTODERM and MESODERM) and enclosing the BODY CAVITY

**bodywork** /-,wuhk/ *n* the structure or form of a vehicle body

**boehmite** /'buhmiet/ *n* a mineral consisting of a chemical compound that is a form of aluminium oxide and hydroxide, AlO(OH), found in BAUXITE (substance that is the main source of aluminium) [Ger *böhmit*, fr J *Böhm* (*Boehm*), 20th-c Ger scientist]

**Boer** /'baw·ə, 'boh·ə/ *n* a S African of Dutch or Huguenot descent [Afrik, fr D, lit., farmer – more at BOOR]

**boerbull, boerboel, boerbul** /'booəbool/ *n* a breed of mastiff common in S Africa [Afrik *boerboel* mastiff]

**boerewors** /'booh·rə,vaws/ *n, SAfr* a heavily spiced sausage, usu made from a mixture of beef and pork [Afrik, fr *boere* country-style + *wors* sausage]

**boffin** /'bofin/ *n, chiefly Br informal* a scientific expert; *esp* one involved in technological research [origin unknown]

**Bofors gun** /'bohfəz/ *n* a light automatic antiaircraft gun [*Bofors*, munition works in Sweden]

**bog** /bog/ *n* 1 (an area of) wet spongy poorly-drained ground consisting largely of decaying vegetation 2 *Br slang* a toilet [of Celt origin; akin to OIr *bocc* soft; akin to OE *būgan* to bend – more at BOW; (2) short for *bog-house*, fr earlier *boggard*, perh of different origin] – **boggy** *adj*

**bog asphodel** /'asfə,del/ *n* either of two bog plants (genus *Narthecium*) of the lily family

**bogbean** /-,been/ *n* a bog plant (*Menyanthes trifoliata* of the family Menyanthaceae) that has pinkish white flowers – called also BUCKBEAN

**bog down** *vb* **-gg-** *vt* to cause to sink (as if) into a bog; impede ∼ *vi* to become impeded

¹**bogey** *also* **bogy, bogie** /'bohgi/ *n, pl* **bogeys** *also* **bogies** 1 a spectre, ghost 2 a source of fear, perplexity, or harassment 3 a golf score of one stroke more than the standard score for a hole 4 *chiefly NAm* an unidentified aircraft on a radar screen [prob alter. of *bogle*]

²**bogey** *vt* to play (a hole in golf) in one stroke more than the standard score

**bogeyman** /-ˌman/ *n* a terrifying person or thing; *esp* a monstrous imaginary figure used to threaten children

¹**boggle** /'bogl/ *vi* 1 to start with fright or amazement; be overwhelmed ⟨*the mind* ~s *at the amount of research yet to be done*⟩ 2 to hesitate because of doubt, fear, or scruples [perh fr *bogle*] – **boggle** *n*

²**boggle** *n* a bogle

**bogie** *also* **bogey, bogy** /'bohgi/ *n, pl* **bogies** *also* **bogeys** 1 a pair of closely-spaced axles designed as a single unit (e g on a 6- or 8-wheeled vehicle or on a single aeroplane undercarriage leg) 2 any of the weight-carrying wheels on the inside perimeter of the tread of a tank serving to keep the treads in line 3 *chiefly Br* a swivelling framework with one or more pairs of wheels and springs to carry and guide one end of a railway vehicle [origin unknown]

ˌ**bog-'Irish** *n, chiefly derog* (the accent used by) rural Irish people

**bogle** /'bohgl/ *n, dial Br* a goblin, spectre; *also* an object of fear or loathing [E dial. (Sc & northern), terrifying apparition; akin to ME *bugge* scarecrow – more at BUG]

**bog myrtle** /'muhtl/ *n* a densely branched deciduous shrub (*Myrica gale* of the family Myricaceae) that grows in boggy land and has aromatic leaves

**bogroll** /'bog,rohl/ *n, slang* a roll of toilet paper

**bog spavin** *n* a tumorous swelling of the HOCK (joint corresponding to the human ankle) in horses

**bogus** /'bohgəs/ *adj* not genuine; spurious, sham [*bogus* (a machine for making counterfeit money)] – **bogusness** *n*

**bohea** /boh'hee/ *n, often cap* a black tea [Chin (Pek) *wŭyi* (*wu³-i²*), hills in China where it was grown]

**bohemia** /boh'heemiə, bə-/ *n, often cap* a community of or district inhabited by unconventional people, esp artists, writers, etc [trans of Fr *bohème*, fr *Bohème* Bohemia, region (former kingdom) in Czechoslovakia]

**Bohemian** /boh'heemyən, -mi·ən/ *n* **1a** a native or inhabitant of Bohemia **b** the group of Czech dialects used in Bohemia **2** *often not cap* **2a** a vagabond, wanderer; *esp* a gipsy **b** a person (e g a writer or artist) living an unconventional life, usu in a community with others – **bohemian** *adj, often cap*

**Bohr theory** /'boh·ə/ *n* a theory in physical chemistry: an atom consists of a positively charged nucleus about which revolves one or more electrons [Niels *Bohr* †1962 Dan physicist]

**bohunk** /'boh,hungk/ *n, NAm chiefly derog* an immigrant worker from Central Europe [*Bohemian* + *Hunk* (worker from Central Europe), prob fr *Hungarian*]

¹**boil** /boyl/ *n* a localized pus-filled swelling of the skin resulting from infection in a skin gland [alter. of ME *bile*, fr OE *bȳl* – more at BIG]

²**boil** *vi* **1a** *of a liquid* to change into (bubbles of) a vapour, esp when heated **b(1)** to come to the BOILING POINT **b(2)** to contain a liquid that is at the boiling point ⟨*the kettle's* ~ing⟩ **2** to bubble or foam violently; churn **3** to be moved, excited, or angry ⟨*made his blood* ~⟩ **4** to undergo the action of a boiling liquid; *specif* to be cooked in boiling water ⟨*the eggs* ~ed *for three minutes*⟩ ~ *vt* **1** to subject to the action of a boiling liquid (e g in cooking) ⟨~ *eggs*⟩ **2a** to heat to the boiling point ⟨~ *water*⟩ **b** to bring (a vessel containing liquid) to the point at which the contents boil [ME *boilen*, fr OF *boillir*, fr L *bullire* to bubble, fr *bulla* bubble]

**boil down** *vt* **1** to reduce in bulk by boiling **2** to condense, summarize ⟨*boil down a report*⟩ ~ *vi* to amount to ⟨*her speech* boiled down *to a plea for more money*⟩

**boil off** *vb* to remove or be removed by boiling

**boil over** *vi* **1** to overflow while boiling **2** to become so incensed as to lose one's temper

**boil up** *vi* to rise towards a dangerous level (e g of unrest); ferment

³**boil** *n* the act or state of boiling; BOILING POINT ⟨*keep it on the* ~⟩

**boiled sweet** *n* a sweet made of boiled sugar

**boiler** /'boylə/ *n* **1** a vessel used for boiling **2a** the part of a steam generator in which water is converted into steam **b** a tank in which water is heated or hot water is stored **3** an old chicken which has to be boiled before it is tender enough to eat

**boilermaker** /'boylə,maykə/ *n* a workman who makes, assembles, or repairs boilers

**boiler suit** *n, chiefly Br* a one-piece outer garment combining shirt and trousers that is worn chiefly to protect clothing

¹**boiling** /'boyling/ *adj* suitable for boiling ⟨*a* ~ *fowl*⟩

²**boiling** *adv* to an extreme degree; very ⟨~ *mad*⟩ ⟨~ *hot*⟩

**boiling point** *n* **1** the temperature at which a liquid boils **2a** the point at which a person loses his/her self-control **b** the point at which decisive action becomes imperative; HEAD 18b ⟨*matters had reached* ~⟩

**boisterous** /'boyst(ə)rəs/ *adj* **1a** noisily turbulent; rowdy **b** marked by or expressive of exuberance and high spirits **2** stormy, wild **3** *obs* **3a** durable, strong **b** coarse **c** massive *synonyms* see VOCIFEROUS [ME *boistous* rough] – **boisterously** *adv*, **boisterousness** *n*

**Bokmål** /'bookmohl/ *n* a literary form of Norwegian developed by the gradual adaptation of written Danish – compare NYNORSK [Norw, lit., book language]

**bola** /'bohlə/ *n* a weapon of S American origin consisting of two or more stone or iron balls attached to the ends of a cord for hurling at and entangling an animal [AmerSp *bolas*, fr pl of Sp *bola* ball]

**bolas** /'bohləs/ *n* a bola

¹**bold** /bohld/ *adj* **1a** fearless in the face of danger; intrepid **b** showing or requiring a fearless adventurous spirit ⟨*a* ~ *plan*⟩ **2** impudent, presumptuous **3** sheer, steep ⟨~ *cliffs*⟩ **4** marked by a departure from tradition; unconventional ⟨*a* ~ *thinker*⟩ **5** standing out prominently; conspicuous ⟨~ *newspaper headlines*⟩ **6** (set) in boldface **7** *obs* assured, confident – see also put a bold FACE on *synonyms* see ¹ADVENTURE *antonyms* timid, unadventurous, fainthearted [ME, fr OE *beald*; akin to OHG *bald* bold] – **boldly** *adv*, **boldness** *n*

²**bold** *n* boldface

**boldface** /-ˌfays/ *n* (printing in) the thickened form of a typeface used to give prominence or emphasis

ˈ**bold-ˌfaced** *adj* bold in manner or conduct; impudent ⟨*a fine, gay,* ~ *ruffian* – Sir Walter Scott⟩

**bole** /bohl/ *n* the trunk of a tree [ME, fr ON *bolr*]

**bolection** /boh'leksh(ə)n/ *n* a moulding that projects beyond framing (e g from between panels on a wall) [origin unknown]

**bolero** /bə'leəroh; *sense 2* 'boləroh/ *n, pl* **boleros** 1 (music in 3 beats to the bar for) a Spanish dance characterized by sharp turns, stamping of the feet, and sudden pauses in a position with one arm arched over the head **2** a loose waist-length jacket open at the front [Sp, perh fr *bola* ball]

**boletus** /bə'leetəs, boh-/ *n, pl* **boletuses, boleti** /-ti/ any of a genus (*Boletus*) of fleshy fungi (class Basidiomycetes), some of which are edible [NL, genus name, fr L, a fungus, fr Gk *bōlitēs*]

**bolide** /'bohlied, -lid/ *n* an exploding or exploded meteor or meteorite; a fireball [Fr, fr L *bolid-, bolis* arrow-shaped meteor, fr Gk, lit., missile, javelin, fr *ballein* to throw – more at DEVIL]

**bolivar** /bo'leevah/ *n, pl* **bolivars, bolivares** /ˌboli'vahrays/ – see MONEY table [AmerSp *bolivar*, fr Simón *Bolivar* †1830 Venezuelan soldier & statesman]

**boliviano** /boh,livi'ahnoh (*Sp* boliβjano)/ *n, pl* **bolivianos** a former monetary unit of Bolivia replaced in 1963 by the peso [Sp, fr *boliviano* Bolivian, fr *Bolivia*, country in S America]

**boll** /bohl/ *n* the seed pod or capsule of a plant (e g cotton) [ME *bolle* bowl, bubble, fr MD]

**bollard** /'bolahd, -ləd/ *n* **1** a post of metal or wood on a wharf round which mooring lines are fastened **2** BITT (post on the deck of a ship for securing lines) **3** *Br* a short post (e g on a kerb or traffic island) to guide vehicles or forbid access [perh irreg fr *bole*]

**bollock** /'boluk/ *n, Br vulg* **1** usu pl a testicle **2** pl nonsense, rubbish – often used interjectionally [ME *ballock*, fr OE *bealluc* – more at BALL]

**bollocking** /'boluking/ *n, Br vulg* a harsh or severe reprimand

**boll weevil** /bohl/ *n* a greyish weevil (*Anthonomus grandis*) that infests the cotton plant and feeds on the unopened flowers and bolls both as a larva and an adult

**bollworm** /'bohl,wuhm/ *n* any of several moth larvae (family Noctuidae) that feed on cotton bolls

**bolo** /'bohloh/ *n, pl* **bolos** a long heavy single-edged knife of Philippine origin [Sp]

**bologna sausage** /bə'lonyə/ *n* a large smoked sausage made of beef, veal, and pork [*Bologna*, town in Italy]

**bolometer** /bə'lomitə, boh-/ *n* a very sensitive electronic device used in the detection and measurement of radiant energy and esp adapted to the study of the INFRARED part of the spectrum [Gk *bolē* beam of light + E *-o-* + *-meter*] – **bolometric** *adj*, **bolometrically** *adv*

**boloney** /bə'lohni/ *n* **1** baloney **2** *NAm* BOLOGNA SAUSAGE

**Bolshevik** /'bolshəvik/ *n, pl* **Bolsheviks** *also* **Bolsheviki**

/ˌbolshə'veeki/ **1** a member of the more radical wing of the Russian Social Democratic party that seized power in Russia in the Revolution of 1917 – compare MENSHEVIK **2** *chiefly derog* COMMUNIST 1 [Russ *bol'shevik*, fr *bol'she* larger; fr their forming the majority group of the party] – **Bolshevik** *adj*

**bolshevism** /'bolshəviz(ə)m/ *n, often cap* **1** the principles or practice of the Bolsheviks; *esp* the policy of advocating the violent overthrow of capitalism **2** *chiefly derog* Soviet communism

**Bolshevist** /'bolshəvist/ *n or adj* (a) Bolshevik

**bolshev·ize, -ise** /'bolshəviez/ *vt* to make Bolshevik – **Bolshevization** *n*

¹**bolshie, bolshy** /'bolshi/ *n, informal* a Bolshevik [by shortening & alter.]

²**bolshie, bolshy** *adj, Br informal* obstinate and argumentative; stubbornly uncooperative – **bolshiness** *n*

¹**bolster** /'bolstə/ *n* **1** a long pillow or cushion placed across the head of a bed, usu under other pillows **2** a pad, cushion, or other structural part (e g in machinery) designed to eliminate friction or provide support [ME, fr OE; akin to OE *belg* bag – more at BELLY]

²**bolster** *vt* **1** to support (as if) with a bolster; reinforce **2** to give a boost to ⟨*news that* ~ed *his spirits*⟩ – **bolsterer** *n*

¹**bolt** /bolt, bohlt/ *n* **1a** a short stout usu blunt-headed arrow shot from a crossbow **b** a lightning stroke; a thunderbolt **2a** a sliding bar or rod used to fasten a door **b** the part of a lock that is shot or withdrawn by the key **3** a roll of cloth or wallpaper of a standard length **4a** a metal rod or pin for fastening objects together **b** a screw-bolt with a head suitable for turning with a spanner **5** a rod or bar that closes the BREECH (part of a gun behind the barrel) of a breech-loading firearm [ME, fr OE; akin to OHG *bolz* crossbow bolt, Lith *beldėti* to beat] – **a bolt from the blue** a completely unexpected occurrence – **shoot one's bolt** to exhaust one's capabilities or resources

²**bolt** *vi* **1** to move rapidly; dash ⟨*she* ~ed *for the door*⟩ **2a** to dart off or away; flee **b** to break away from control or a set course **3** to produce seed prematurely, esp before a desired feature has developed ⟨*spinach may sometimes* ~⟩ **4** *NAm* to break away from or oppose one's political party ~ *vt* **1** to flush, start ⟨~ *rabbits*⟩ **2** to secure with a bolt **3** to attach or fasten with bolts **4** to swallow (e g food) hastily or without chewing **5** *NAm* to break away from, oppose, or refuse to support (one's political party) **6** *archaic* to shoot, discharge ⟨*she* ~ed *arrows at the target*⟩ – **bolter** *n*

³**bolt** *adv* in an erect or straight-backed position; rigidly ⟨*sat* ~ *upright*⟩

⁴**bolt** *n* the act or an instance of bolting: e g **a** a dash, run ⟨*she made a* ~ *for the door*⟩ **b** *NAm* a refusal to support one's usual political party

⁵**bolt** *vt* **1** to sift (e g flour), usu through a fine-meshed cloth **2** *archaic* SIFT 2b (study or investigate) [ME *bulten*, fr OF *buleter*, of Gmc origin; akin to MHG *biuteln* to sift, fr *biutel* bag, fr OHG *būtil*] – **bolter** *n*

'**bolt-·hole** *n* **1** a hole into which an animal runs for safety **2** a place of refuge ⟨*a favourite* ~ *from real life* – Basil Boothroyd⟩

**boltrope** /'bolt,rohp, 'bohlt-/ *n* a strong rope stitched to the edges of a sail to prevent it tearing or fraying

**bolus** /'bohləs/ *n* a rounded mass: e g **a** a large pill **b** a soft mass of food that has been chewed but not swallowed [LL, fr Gk *bōlos* lump]

¹**bomb** /bom/ *n* **1a** any of several explosive or incendiary devices that are typically detonated by impact or a timing mechanism and are usu dropped from aircraft, thrown or placed by hand, or fired from a mortar **b** ATOM BOMB; *broadly* nuclear weapons – + *the* **2** a vessel containing a compressed gas (e g for chemical experiments or for use as a fire extinguisher) **3** a rounded mass of lava exploded from a volcano **4** a lead-lined container for radioactive material, used esp in the treatment of cancer by radiation ⟨*a cobalt* ~⟩ **5** *NAm informal* a failure, flop ⟨*a terrible* ~ *of a play* – Paul Newman⟩ **6** *Austr & NZ* an old and dilapidated car **7** *Br slang* a large sum of money ⟨*the repairs cost a* ~⟩ [Fr *bombe*, fr It *bomba*, prob fr L *bombus* deep hollow sound, fr Gk *bombos*, of imit origin] – **a bomb** *Br informal* very successfully ⟨*the new act went down a bomb*⟩

²**bomb** *vt* to attack with bombs; bombard ~ *vi, informal* **1** to move quickly – usu + *along, down,* or *off* ⟨*came* ~ing *along the road towards me*⟩ **2** *NAm* to fall flat; fail

**bomb out** *vi, Austr* DROP OUT 1

¹**bombard** /'bombahd/ *n* a cannon used in late medieval times chiefly to hurl large stones [ME *bombarde*, fr MF, prob fr L *bombus*]

²**bombard** /bom'bahd/ *vt* **1** to attack with heavy artillery or bombers **2** to assail vigorously or persistently (e g with questions) **3** to subject to the impact of rapidly moving particles (e g electrons or ALPHA RAYS) *synonyms* see ¹ATTACK – **bombardment** *n*

**bombarde** /bom'bahd, '--/ *n* a powerful 16-foot or 32-foot reed STOP (set of vibrators) on an organ [Er]

**bombardier** /ˌbombə'diə/ *n* **1** a noncommissioned officer in the British artillery **2** a US bomber-crew member who aims and releases the bombs

**bombardon** /'bombəd(ə)n, bom'bahd(ə)n/ *n* **1** the bass member of the SHAWM (early musical instrument family) **2** a bass tuba **3** a bombarde [Fr, fr It *bombardone*]

**bombast** /'bombast/ *n* pretentious inflated speech or writing [MF *bombace* material used for padding, fr ML *bombac-, bombax* cotton, alter. of L *bombyc-, bombyx* silkworm, silk, fr Gk *bombyk-, bombyx*] – **bombast** *adj*, **bombaster** *n*, **bombastic** *adj*, **bombastically** *adv*

**Bombay duck** /bom'bay/ *n* a small fish (*Harpodon nehereus*) found off S Asiatic coasts and eaten dried and salted with curry – called also BUMMALO [*Bombay* (now *Mumbai*), city in India]

**bombazine** /'bombə,zeen, ,--'-/ *n* a silk fabric woven in twill weave and dyed black [MF *bombasin*, fr ML *bombacinum, bombycinum* silken texture, fr L, neut of *bombycinus* of silk, fr *bombyc-, bombyx*]

**bomb bay** *n* a bomb-carrying compartment in the underside of a combat aircraft

**bomb disposal** *n* the making safe of unexploded bombs (e g by defusing)

**bombe** /bomb/ *n* a frozen dessert usu containing ice cream and made in a round or cone-shaped mould; *also* the mould in which a bombe is made [Fr, lit., bomb]

**bombed** /bomd/ *adj, informal* affected by alcohol or drugs

**bomber** /'bomə/ *n* **1** an aircraft designed for bombing **2** somebody who throws or places bombs

**bomber jacket** *n* a short jacket with elasticated waistband and cuffs

**bombinate** /'bombinayt/ *vi, poetic* to buzz, drone [NL *bombinatus,* pp of *bombinare,* alter. of L *bombilare,* fr *bombus* – more at BOMB] – **bombination** *n*

**bombshell** /-,shel/ *n* **1** BOMB 1a **2** somebody or something that has a stunning or devastating effect ⟨*the book was a political* ~⟩

**bombsight** /-,siet/ *n* a sighting device for aiming bombs

**bombsite** /-,siet/ *n* an area of ground on which buildings have been destroyed by bombing, esp from the air

**bona fide** /ˌbohnə 'fiedi/ *adj* **1** made in good faith without fraud or deceit; sincere ⟨*a* ~ *offer to purchase a farm*⟩ **2** neither specious nor counterfeit; genuine ⟨*a* ~ *antique*⟩ *synonyms* see GENUINE *antonym* bogus [L, in good faith]

**bona fides** /'fiediz/ *n taking sing or pl vb* lack of fraud or deceit; sincerity ⟨*a man on whom suspicion had never rested and whose* ~ *was unshakeable* – Victor Canning⟩

*usage* The noun **bona fides** is not a plural, and should correctly take a singular verb ⟨*his* bona fides *was questioned*⟩. Bona fide, which looks like the singular, is not a noun but an adjective. [L, good faith]

**bonanza** /bə'nanzə/ *n* **1** an exceptionally large and rich mass of ore in a mine **2** something (unexpectedly) valuable, profitable, or rewarding ⟨*was a box-office* ~⟩ [Sp, lit., calm, fair weather, fr ML *bonacia*, alter. of L *malacia* calm at sea, fr Gk *malakia,* lit., softness, fr *malakos* soft]

**Bonapartism** /'bohnə,pah,tiz(ə)m/ *n* **1** support of the French emperors Napoleon I or Napoleon III or their dynasty **2** a political movement associated chiefly with authoritarian rule by a military leader claiming popular support [*Bonaparte, Buonaparte,* family name of the dynasty] – **Bonapartist** *n or adj*

**bona vacantia** /ˌbohnə və'kantiə/ *n* property without an apparent owner; *esp* property belonging to somebody who has died without leaving a will [L, ownerless goods]

**bonbon** /'bon,bon/ *n* a sweet; *specif* one with a chocolate or fondant coating and fondant centre that sometimes contains fruits and nuts [Fr (baby talk), redupl of *bon* good, fr L *bonus* –more at BOUNTY]

**bonce** /bons/ *n, Br informal* the head [E dial. *bonce* large marble]

**¹bond** /bond/ *adj, archaic* bound in slavery [ME *bonde*, fr *bonde* peasant, serf, fr OE *bōnda* householder, fr ON *bōndi*]

**²bond** *n* **1** something (eg a fetter) that binds or restrains **2** a binding agreement; a covenant **3a** a material or device for binding **b** (an imaginary line representing) a mechanism by means of which atoms, ions, or groups of atoms are held together in a molecule or crystal **c** an adhesive or cementing material that combines or strengthens **4** a uniting or binding element or force ⟨*the ~s of friendship*⟩ **5a** a legally enforceable agreement binding one person to pay a specified amount, fulfil a contract, etc **b** a certificate of intention to pay the holder a specified sum with or without other interest on a specified date that is sold either at a discount or at face value; *specif* a form of long-term fixed-interest security issued usu by central or local government **c** *NAm* an insurance policy covering losses suffered by the insured as the result of some contingency out of his/her control or of the actions of a third party **6** the system of overlapping bricks in a wall **7** a strong durable paper, now used esp for writing and typing [ME *band, bond* – more at BAND] – **in bond** *of goods* in storage in a bonded warehouse under the care of customs officers until excise duties are paid

**³bond** *vt* **1** to overlap (eg bricks) for solidity of construction **2** to put (goods) in bond until duties and taxes are paid **3a** to cause to stick firmly **b** to hold together in a molecule or crystal by chemical bonds ~ *vi* to hold together or solidify (as if) by means of a bond or binder; cohere – **bondable** *adj*, **bonder** *n*

**bondage** /'bondij/ *n* **1** the tenure or service of a villein, serf, or slave **2a** slavery, serfdom ⟨*the ~ of the Israelites in Egypt*⟩ **b** servitude or subjugation to a controlling person or force ⟨*young people in ~ to drugs*⟩ **c** a form of sexual gratification involving the physical restraint of one partner ⟨*~ fantasies*⟩ *synonyms* see SERVITUDE

**bonded** /'bondid/ *adj* **1** composed of two or more layers of the same or different fabrics held together by an adhesive; laminated ⟨*~ fabrics*⟩ **2** *of a debt* secured by bonds **3** *of imported goods* kept in bond

**bonded warehouse** *n* a warehouse in which imported goods are retained awaiting payment of duty or re-export

**bonder·ize, -ise** /'bondəriez/ *vt* to coat (steel) with a patented phosphate solution for protection against corrosion [back-formation fr *Bonderized*, a trademark]

**bondholder** /-,hohldə/ *n* one who holds a government or company bond

**bondman** /-mən/, *fem* **bondwoman** *n* a slave, serf

**bond servant** *n* one bound to service without wages; *also* a slave

**bondsman** /'bondzmən/, *fem* **bondswoman** *n* a bondman

**bondstone** /-,stohn/ *n* a stone long enough to extend through the full thickness of a wall to bind it together

**¹bone** /bohn/ *n* **1a** any of the hard parts of the skeleton of a VERTEBRATE animal **b** any of various hard animal substances or structures (eg baleen or ivory) akin to or resembling bone **c** the hard largely calcium-containing CONNECTIVE TISSUE of which the adult skeleton of most VERTEBRATE animals is chiefly composed **2** *the* essential part or level; *the* core ⟨*cut expenses to the ~*⟩ **3** *pl* the basic design or framework; *the* essentials ⟨*reduce the idea to its bare ~s*⟩ **4a** *pl* thin bars of bone, ivory, or wood held in pairs between the fingers and used to produce musical rhythms **b** a strip of whalebone or steel used to stiffen a corset, dress, etc **5** a domino **6** *pl, informal* a skeleton, body ⟨*sit down and rest your weary ~s*⟩; *also* a corpse **7** *pl, informal* dice [ME *bon*, fr OE *bān*; akin to OHG & ON *bein* bone] – **boned** *adj*, **boneless** *adj* – **close to/near the bone** indecent, risqué ⟨*his remarks were rather* close to the bone⟩ – **feel something in one's bones** to know or be aware of something intuitively – **have a bone to pick with somebody** to have a matter to argue about with somebody – **make no bones about** to do openly and without shame [prob fr the difficulties presented by bones in soups or stews] – **make old bones** to live to a great age

**²bone** *vt* **1** to remove the bones from ⟨*~ a fish*⟩ **2** to stiffen (a garment) with bones

    **bone up** *vi, informal* to try to master necessary information in a short time, esp for a special purpose; cram – + *on* ⟨*better bone up on those theories before the exam*⟩

**³bone** *adv* absolutely, utterly ⟨*~ dry*⟩ ⟨*~ idle*⟩

**bone ash** *n* the white porous residue, consisting chiefly of the chemical compound CALCIUM PHOSPHATE, that is produced from bones heated to a high temperature in air and that is used esp in making pottery and glass and in cleaning jewellery

**bone black** *n* the black residue, consisting chiefly of the chemical compound CALCIUM PHOSPHATE and carbon, that is produced from bones heated in closed vessels and that is used esp as a pigment or as a decolorizing agent in sugar manufacturing

**bone china** *n* a type of translucent and durable white hard-paste porcelain that is made from a mixture of bone ash and kaolin

**bonehead** /-,hed/ *n, informal* a slow-witted or stupid person; a blockhead – **boneheaded** *adj*

**bone meal** *n* fertilizer or feed made of crushed or ground bone

**bone of contention** *n* a subject or matter of dispute [fr dogs fighting each other to possess a bone]

**bonesetter** /-,setə/ *n* a person, usu with no formal medical qualifications, who sets broken or dislocated bones

**bone shaker** *n* an old vehicle; *esp* an early bicycle with solid tyres

**bone spavin** *n* a bony enlargement on the lower inside of a horse's HOCK (joint corresponding to the human ankle)

**bonfire** /'bonfie·ə/ *n* a large fire built in the open air [ME *bonefire* a fire of bones, fr *bon* bone + *fire*]

**Bonfire Night** *n* GUY FAWKES NIGHT

**bong** /bong/ *n* a deep resonant sound, esp of a large bell [imit] – **bong** *vi*

**¹bongo** /'bong·goh/ *n, pl* **bongos**, *esp collectively* **bongo** any of three large striped antelopes (genus *Tragelaphus*) of tropical Africa [of African origin]

**²bongo** *n, pl* **bongos** *also* **bongoes** either of a pair of small tuned Cuban drums played with the hands [AmerSp *bongó*] – **bongoist** *n*

**bonheur du jour** /,bo,nuh dooh 'zhooə (*Fr* bɔnœr dy ʒur)/ *n* a small desk or writing table with a cabinet top [Fr, lit., happiness of the day]

**bonhomie** /,bono'mee, bo'nomi/ *n* good-natured friendliness, geniality [Fr, fr *bonhomme* good-natured man, fr *bon* good + *homme* man]

**bonito** /bə'neetoh/ *n, pl* **bonitos**, *esp collectively* **bonito** any of various medium-sized tuna fish (esp genera *Sarda* and *Euthynnus*) [Sp, prob fr *bonito* pretty, fr L *bonus* good]

**bonkers** /'bongkəz/ *adj, chiefly Br informal* mad, crazy ⟨*it's enough to drive you ~*⟩ [origin unknown]

**bon mot** /,bon 'moh (*Fr* bɔ̃ mo)/ *n, pl* **bons mots, bon mots** /,bom 'moh(z) (*Fr* ~)/ a clever remark; a witticism [Fr, lit., good word]

**bonne** /bon (*Fr* bɔn)/ *n* a French nursemaid or maidservant [Fr, fr fem of *bon*]

**bonne bouche** /,bon 'boohsh (*Fr* bɔn buʃ)/ *n, pl* **bonnes bouches** a tasty morsel of food; a titbit [Fr, lit., good mouth]

**bonnet** /'bonit/ *n* **1** a cloth or straw hat tied under the chin and now worn chiefly by children or as part of a uniform **2** an additional piece of canvas laced to the foot of a jib or foresail to increase sail area **3** *chiefly Br* the hinged metal covering over the engine of a motor vehicle **4** *chiefly Scot* a soft brimless cap – see also BEE **in one's bonnet** [ME *bonet*, fr MF, fr ML *abonnis*]

**bonnet monkey** *n* a MACAQUE (type of monkey) (*Macaca radiata*) that lives in India and has tufts of hair on its head forming the shape of a bonnet

**bonny** /'boni/ *adj, chiefly Br* attractive, comely [ME *bonie*, prob fr OF *bon* good, fr L *bonus* – more at BOUNTY] – **bonnily** *adv*

**bonsai** /'bon'sie/ *n, pl* **bonsai** (the art of growing) a potted plant (eg a tree) dwarfed by special methods of culture [Jap]

**bonspiel** /'bon,speel, -spəl/ *n* a match or tournament between curling clubs [perh fr D *bond* league + *spel* game]

**bontebok** /'bontə,bok/ *n* a S African antelope (*Damaliscus pygargus*) that is very closely related to the BLESBOK and is now almost extinct [Afrik, fr *bont* pied + *bok* male antelope]

**bon ton** /,bon 'tonh (*Fr* bɔ̃ tɔ̃)/ *n* **1** the fashionable manner, style, or thing ⟨*it was considered ~ to go to the event*⟩ **2** fashionable society [Fr, lit., good tone]

**bonus** /'bohnəs/ *n* **1** something given in addition to what is usual or strictly due **2a** money or an equivalent given in addition to an employee's usual remuneration **b** a premium (eg of shares) given by a company to a purchaser of its securities, to a promoter, or to an employee **c** *Br* DIVIDEND 1b [L, good – more at BOUNTY]

**bon vivant** /(*Fr* bɔ̃ vivɑ̃)/ *n, pl* **bons vivants, bon vivants** /~/ a person having cultivated, refined, and sociable tastes, esp with regard to food and drink [Fr, lit., good liver]

**bon viveur** /(Fr vivœːr)/ *n, chiefly Br* BON VIVANT

**bon voyage** /ˌbon vwahˈyahj, -yahzh (Fr bɔ̃ vwajɑːʒ)/ *interj* – used to express farewell to a person undertaking a journey [Fr, lit., good journey]

**bonxie** /ˈbongksi/ *n, Scot* GREAT SKUA (large seabird) [perh of Scand origin]

**bony, boney** /ˈbohni/ *adj* **1a** consisting of bone **b** resembling bone **2a** full of bones ⟨*a ~ piece of fish*⟩ **b** having prominent bones ⟨*a rugged ~ face*⟩ **3** skinny, scrawny

**bony fish** *n* any of a major group (Teleostei) of fishes comprising all those with a bony rather than a cartilaginous skeleton and including the salmon, carp, herring, etc – called also TELEOST

**bony labyrinth** *n* the cavity in the TEMPORAL BONE (bone on the side of the human skull) that contains the MEMBRANOUS LABYRINTH of the ear

**bonze** /bonz/ *n* a Chinese or Japanese Buddhist monk [Fr, fr Pg *bonzo*, fr Jap *bonsō*]

**bonzer** /ˈbonzə/ *adj, Austr informal* extremely good; excellent – no longer in vogue [perh alter. of *bonanza*] – **bonzer** *n*

**¹boo** /booh/ *interj* – used to express contempt or disapproval or to startle or frighten [ME *bo*]

**²boo** *n, pl* **boos** a shout of disapproval or contempt

**³boo** *vb* to show scorn or disapproval (of) by uttering "boo"

**¹boob** /boohb/ *n, informal* a stupid mistake; a blunder [fr ¹*booby*]

**²boob** *n, slang* BREAST 1 [short for ²*booby*]

**³boob** *vi, informal* to make a stupid mistake

**boobialla, boobyalla** /ˌboohbiˈahlə/ *n, Austr* an Australian tree (*Acacia sophora*) with pliable branches [native name in Australia]

**¹boo-, boo** *n, pl* **boo-boos** *informal* ¹BOOB

**boobook** /ˈboohˌboohk/ *n,* a medium-sized Australian owl (*Ninox boobook*) with brown plumage – called also MOPOKE [imit]

**boob tube** *n, informal* a television

**¹booby** /ˈboohbi/ *n* **1** an awkward foolish person **2** any of several small gannets (genus *Sula*) of tropical seas **3** the poorest performer or lowest scorer in a group [modif of Sp *bobo*, fr L *balbus* stammering, prob of imit origin]

**²booby** *n, informal* a girl's or woman's breast [alter. of *bubby*]

**booby hatch** *n, NAm informal* MADHOUSE 1 [¹*booby*]

**booby prize** *n* **1** an award for the poorest performance in a game or competition **2** an acknowledgment of notable inferiority

**booby trap** *n* **1** a trap for the unwary or unsuspecting **2** a harmless-looking object concealing an explosive device that is set to explode by remote control if touched – **booby-trap** *vt*

**boodle** /ˈboohdl/ *n* **1** *NAm informal* a caboodle **2** *slang* money, esp when stolen or used for bribery [D *boedel* estate, lot, fr MD; akin to ON *būth* booth]

**¹boogie** /ˈboohgi/ *n* boogie-woogie

**²boogie** *vb* **boogieing; boogied** *vi* to dance to pop music; bop ~ *vt* to bop ⟨*~d the night away*⟩

**boogie-'woogie** /ˈwoohgi/ *n* **1** a style of playing blues on the piano characterized by a steady rhythmic bass with four beats to the bar and a simple, often improvised, melody **2** pop music with a strong regular beat suitable for dancing to in a disco [perh imit]

**¹book** /book/ *n* **1a** a set of written, printed, lined, or blank sheets bound together into a volume ⟨*a paperback ~*⟩ ⟨*an exercise ~*⟩ **b** a long written or printed (literary) composition ⟨*when is your ~ being published?*⟩ **c** a major division of a treatise or literary work **d** *pl* journals, ledgers, etc recording business accounts ⟨*their ~s show a profit*⟩ **2** *cap* the Bible **3a** something regarded as enlightening or revealing – chiefly in *open book* ⟨*her face was an open ~*⟩ **b** something regarded as unknown, impenetrable, or baffling – chiefly in *closed book* ⟨*maths was a closed ~ to him*⟩ **4** a libretto **5** a packet of paper, cardboard, etc commodities (eg tickets, stamps, or matches) bound together **6** the bets registered by a bookmaker **7** the number of tricks a card player or side must win before any trick can have scoring value **8** *informal* a magazine [ME, fr OE *bōc;* akin to OHG *buoh* book, OE *bōc* beech – more at BEECH; prob fr the early Germanic practice of carving runes on beechwood tablets] – **according to/by the book** by following previously laid down instructions and not using personal initiative ⟨*it is safer to go by the book than to risk making a mistake*⟩ – **bring somebody to book** to punish or reprimand somebody – **in one's book** in one's own opinion ⟨*in my book this is the*

*way to handle it*⟩ – **in somebody's good/bad books** in favour/disfavour with somebody – **one for the book** an act or occurrence worth noting – **throw the book at 1** to charge with all the offences that can be found **2** to reprimand severely or comprehensively – see also BELL, **book, and candle**

**²book** *vt* **1a** to reserve a seat or passage for (somebody) ⟨*~ed you on the 4:30 pm train to Edinburgh*⟩ **b** to reserve in advance ⟨*~ two seats at the theatre*⟩ ⟨*~ a table for noon*⟩ **c** to hire the services of in advance ⟨*~ the band for a week*⟩ ⟨*~ a taxi*⟩ **2a** to take the name of with a view to prosecution ⟨*~ed by the police for speeding*⟩ **b** to enter the name of (a rugby or soccer player) in a book for a violation of the rules, usu involving foul play ~ *vi* to reserve something in advance ⟨*~ through your travel agent*⟩ – often + *up* ⟨*should ~ up early*⟩ – **booker** *n*

**book in** *vb, Br vt* to make an appointment or reservation for ⟨*I'll book you in at 3:30 pm*⟩ ~ *vi* to register at a hotel

**book out** *vt* **1** *Br* to sign one's name to show that one has borrowed (something) **2** *Austr & NZ* BOOK UP – pass

**book up** *vt* to reserve all the seats, accommodation, etc for, or the services of – pass

**bookable** /ˈbookəbl/ *adj, chiefly Br* **1** that may be reserved in advance ⟨*all seats for the evening performance are ~*⟩ **2** that renders a player liable to be booked by a referee ⟨*a ~ offence*⟩

**bookbinding** /ˈbookˌbiending/ *n* the craft or trade of binding books – **bookbinder** *n*, **bookbindery** *n*

**bookcase** /ˈbookˌkays/ *n* a piece of furniture consisting of a set of shelves to hold books

**bookend** /ˈbookˌend/ *n* a support placed at the end of a row of books to hold them upright

**bookie** /ˈbooki/ *n* a bookmaker [by shortening & alter.]

**booking** /ˈbooking/ *n* **1** an engagement or scheduled performance ⟨*she has ~s for several concerts*⟩ **2** a reservation, esp for transport, entertainment, or lodging **3** an entry in a referee's book against a rugby or soccer player who has violated a rule

**booking office** *n, chiefly Br* an office where tickets are sold and bookings made, esp at a railway station

**bookish** /ˈbookish/ *adj* **1a** relating to books **b** fond of books and reading **2a** inclined to rely on theoretical knowledge rather than practical experience **b** literary and formal as opposed to colloquial and informal ⟨*many English words derived from Latin have a ~ flavour*⟩ **c** given to literary or scholarly pursuits; *also* pedantic – **bookishly** *adv*, **bookishness** *n*

**bookkeeper** /ˈbookˌkeepə/ *n* somebody who records the accounts or transactions of a business – **bookkeeping** *n*

**'book-ˌlearning** *n* knowledge derived from books or a formal education rather than from personal experience

**booklet** /ˈbooklit/ *n* **1** a little book; *esp* a pamphlet **2** a set of postage stamps bound together in the form of a small book

**book louse** *n* any of several minute wingless insects (order Psocoptera) that live esp under the bark of trees and sometimes in books

**book lung** *n* a breathing organ in many ARACHNIDS (spiders, scorpions, etc) that contains numerous thin folds of membrane arranged like the leaves of a book

**bookmaker** /ˈbookˌmaykə/ *n* somebody who determines odds and receives and pays off bets – **bookmaking** *n*

**bookman** /ˈbookˌman/ *n* a litterateur

**bookmark** /ˈbookˌmahk/, **bookmarker** /ˈbookˌmahkə/ *n* something (eg a strip of leather) used to mark a place in a book

**'book-ˌmatch** *vt* to match the grains of (eg two sheets of veneer) so that one sheet seems to be the mirror image of the other

**bookmobile** /ˈbookməˌbeel/ *n, chiefly NAm* a mobile library [*book* + auto*mobile*]

**book of account** *n* a book of business records (eg a ledger, journal, or register) that is an integral part of a system of accounts

**Book of Common Prayer** *n* a service book of the Anglican Communion

**book of original entry** *n* a book of account (eg a cashbook or register of sales) in which transactions are first recorded before being transferred (eg to a ledger)

**book of prime entry** *n* BOOK OF ORIGINAL ENTRY

**bookplate** /ˈbookˌplayt/ *n* an often decorative label that is placed inside the cover of a book to identify the owner

**bookrest** /ˈbookˌrest/ *n* an (adjustable) support for an open book

**bookseller** /'book,selə/ n somebody who sells books; *specif* the owner or manager of a bookshop

**bookshelf** /'book,shelf/ n an open shelf for holding books

**bookshop** /'book,shop/ n a shop where books are the main item offered for sale

**bookstall** /'book,stawl/ n 1 a stall where books are sold 2 *chiefly Br* a stall (eg at a railway station) where magazines and newspapers are sold

**book token** n a gift token for a certain value that can be exchanged for books

**book value** n the value of something as shown by the BOOKS OF ACCOUNT of the business owning it; *esp* the value of a company's buildings, machinery, vehicles, etc that is recognized by the government for accounting and tax purposes, allowing for depreciation – compare MARKET VALUE

**bookworm** /'book,wuhm/ n 1 any of various insect larvae (eg of a beetle) that feed on the binding and paste of books 2 a person unusually devoted to reading and study

**Boolean** /'boohli·ən/ adj of or being a type of algebra in which logical symbols are used to represent relations between sets, and which is used extensively in the theory of computer programming ⟨~ *expression*⟩ [George *Boole* †1864 E mathematician]

¹**boom** /boohm/ n 1 a long spar used to extend the foot of a sail or facilitate handling of cargo or mooring 2a a long beam projecting from the mast of a derrick to support or guide an object that is to be lifted or swung b a long movable arm used to manipulate a microphone 3 a barrier across a river or enclosing an area of water to keep logs together; *also* the enclosed logs 4 a chain cable or line of spars extended across a river or the mouth of a harbour as a barrier to navigation [D, tree, beam; akin to OHG *boum* tree – more at BEAM]

²**boom** /boom, boohm/ vi 1 to make a deep hollow sound or cry 2 to experience a sudden rapid increase in activity or importance ⟨*business was* ~ing⟩ ~ vt to cause to resound – usu + *out* or *forth* ⟨*his voice* ~s out the lyrics⟩ [imit]

³**boom** /boom, boohm/ n 1 a booming sound or cry 2a a rapid growth or expansion (eg in population) ⟨*the baby* ~⟩ b a rapid increase in public interest or participation 2 a rapid widespread expansion of economic activity 3 SONIC BOOM – **boomy** adj

**boomer** /'boohmə/ n, *Austr* a large male kangaroo [E dial. *boomer* something very large of its kind, fr ²*boom* + ²*-er*]

¹**boomerang** /'boohmərang/ n 1 a bent or angular piece of wood, designed in such a way that it can be thrown so as to return to the thrower, that is used by Australian aborigines as a hunting weapon 2 an act or utterance that backfires on its originator [native name in Australia]

²**boomerang** vi to recoil on the utterer or originator, esp with unpleasant effects

**boomslang** /'boohm,slang/ n a large venomous tree snake (*Dispholidus typus*) of southern Africa [Afrik, fr *boom* tree + *slang* snake]

¹**boon** /boohn/ n 1 a benefit, favour; *esp* one that is given in answer to a request 2 *informal* a timely benefit; a blessing [ME, prayer, request, favour, fr ON *bōn* petition; akin to OE *bēn* prayer, *bannan* to summon – more at BAN]

²**boon** adj close, intimate, and convivial – chiefly in *boon companion* [ME *bon*, fr MF, good – more at BONNY]

**boondocks** /'boohn,doks/ n pl, NAm 1 rough country filled with dense brush 2 a (remote) rural area [Tagalog *bundok* mountain]

**boondoggle** /'boohn,dogl/ n 1 a simple handicraft article that is of little practical use 2 *chiefly NAm informal* a trivial, useless, or wasteful project or activity [coined by Robert H Link †1957 US scoutmaster] – **boondoggle** vi, **boondoggler** n

**boor** /booə, baw/ n 1 a peasant 2 a coarse, ill-mannered, or insensitive person [D *boer;* akin to OE *būan* to dwell – more at BOWER] – **boorish** adj, **boorishly** adv

¹**boost** /boohst/ vt 1 to push or shove up from below 2 to increase, raise ⟨*plans to* ~ *production by 30 per cent next year*⟩ 3 to encourage, promote ⟨*extra pay to* ~ *morale*⟩ 4 to increase in force, pressure, or amount; *esp* to raise the voltage of or across (eg an electric circuit) **synonyms** see ¹LIFT **antonym** depress [origin unknown]

²**boost** n 1 a push upwards 2 an increase in amount 3 an act that brings help or encouragement

**booster** /'boohstə/ n 1 one who or that which boosts 2 a radio-frequency amplifier for intensifying a weak signal 3a the first stage of a multistage rocket that provides thrust for the

launching and the initial part of the flight b an auxiliary engine or device that assists (eg at take-off) by providing a large thrust for a short time 4 a substance that increases the effectiveness of a medicament; *esp* a supplementary dose of an immunizing agent to increase immunity

¹**boot** /booht/ n, *obs* avail, use [ME, fr OE *bōt* remedy; akin to OE *betera* better] – **to boot** *formal or humorous* besides

²**boot** vb, *archaic* to be of help, profit, or advantage (to) ⟨*it* ~s *not to look backwards* – Thomas Arnold⟩

³**boot** n 1a an outer covering for the human foot that extends above the ankle and that has a stiff or thick sole and heel b a stout shoe, esp for sports ⟨*football* ~s⟩ 2 an instrument of torture that crushes the leg and foot 3 a blow or kick delivered (as if) by a booted foot 4 *Br* the luggage compartment of a motor car 5 *slang* a rude discharge or dismissal – chiefly in *give/get the boot* [ME, fr MF *bote*] – **put/stick the boot in** *chiefly Br informal* 1 to kick somebody, esp when he/she is already on the ground 2 to treat somebody cruelly or unfairly, esp when he/she is already in a vulnerable position 3 to act with brutal decisiveness

⁴**boot** vt to kick

**boot out** vt, *informal* to eject or discharge summarily ⟨*was booted out of office*⟩

**bootblack** /'booht,blak/ n somebody who cleans and shines shoes

**booted** /'boohtid/ adj wearing boots

**bootee, bootie** /'booh,tee, -'-/ n 1 a short boot 2 an infant's sock worn in place of a shoe

**booth** /boohth/ n, pl **booths** /boohths, boohdhz/ 1a a stall or stand (eg at a fair) in which goods are sold or displayed or games are played b a small enclosed area or cubicle affording privacy (eg for telephoning or dining) 2 *archaic* a temporary shelter, esp made of tree branches [ME *bothe*, of Scand origin; akin to ON *būth* booth; akin to OE *būan* to dwell – more at BOWER]

**bootjack** /'booht,jak/ n a device (eg of metal or wood) shaped like the letter V and used in pulling off boots

**bootlace** /'booht,lays/ n, *Br* a long stout shoelace

**bootlace fungus** n HONEY FUNGUS

¹**bootleg** /-,leg/ adj or n, *chiefly NAm* (being) smuggled or illegally produced alcoholic drink [fr a former practice of carrying a concealed bottle of liquor in the top of a boot]

²**bootleg** vb **-gg-** *chiefly NAm* to manufacture, sell, or transport for sale (esp alcoholic drink) contrary to law

**bootless** /-lis/ adj, *formal* useless, unprofitable [¹*boot* + *-less*] – **bootlessly** adv, **bootlessness** n

**bootlick** /'booht,lik/ vi, *informal* to attempt to gain favour by a cringing or flattering manner – **bootlicker** n

**boots** /boohts/ n, pl boots *Br* a servant who polishes shoes and carries luggage, esp in a hotel [fr pl of ³*boot*]

¹**bootstrap** /'booht,strap/ n a looped strap sewn on a boot to help in pulling it on – **haul/pull oneself up by one's own bootstraps** to improve oneself or one's situation by means of one's own unaided efforts

²**bootstrap** adj or n (of or being) a computer operating technique that uses the input of a short sequence of instructions to make a computer receptive to a fuller set of instructions

³**bootstrap** vt **-pp-** to initiate a sequence of bootstrap instructions in (a computer)

**booty** /'boohti/ n 1 plunder taken (eg in war) 2 a rich gain or prize [modif of MF *butin*, fr MLG *būte* exchange]

¹**booze** /boohz/ vi, *slang* to drink alcohol to excess [ME *bousen*, fr MD or MFlem *būsen;* akin to MHG *būs* swelling] – **boozy** adj, **boozily** adv

²**booze** n, *slang* 1 alcoholic drink 2 a drinking spree ⟨*go on the* ~⟩

**boozed** /boohzd/ adj, *slang* drunk – usu + *up*

**boozer** /'boohzə/ n, *slang* 1 a habitual heavy drinker; a drunkard 2 *Br* a pub

**boozeroo** /,boohzə'rooh/ n, *NZ chiefly humorous* a booze-up [*booze* + *-eroo*, arbitrary slang suffix]

'**booze-,up** n, *slang* a drunken party or drinking spree

¹**bop** /bop/ vt or n **-pp-** *informal* (to strike with) a blow (eg of the fist) [imit]

²**bop** n jazz characterized by unusual chord structures, a syncopated rhythm, and harmonic complexity and innovation [short for *bebop*] – **bopper** n

³**bop** vb **-pp-** vi to dance (eg in a disco) in a casual and unrestricted manner, esp to popular music ~ vt to dance casually ⟨~ped *his way from party to party*⟩ – **bop** n, **bopper** n

**bora** /'bawrə/ n a violent cold northerly wind of the Adriatic [It dial., fr L *boreas* – more at BOREAL]

**boracic acid** /bə'rasik/ n BORIC ACID [ML *borac-, borax* borax]

**boracite** /'bawrə,siet/ n a mineral, $Mg_3B_7O_{13}Cl$, consisting essentially of a BORATE and chloride of magnesium [Ger *borazit*, fr ML *borac-, borax*]

**borage** /'borij, 'burij/ n a coarse hairy blue-flowered European herb (*Borago officinalis*) of the forget-me-not family that is used medicinally and as a food or flavouring (e g in salads or drinks) [ME, fr MF *bourage*, prob deriv of LL *burra* shaggy cloth]

**borane** /'bawrayn/ n a chemical compound of the elements boron and hydrogen or a derivative of such a compound [ISV, fr *boron*]

**borate** /'bawrayt/ n any of several chemical compounds (SALTS or ESTERS) formed by combination between BORIC ACID and a metal atom, an alcohol, or another chemical group

**borated** /'bawraytid/ adj mixed or impregnated with borax or BORIC ACID

**borax** /'bawraks/ n a white chemical compound, $Na_2B_4O_7.10H_2O$, that consists of a borate of sodium combined with water, that occurs naturally as a mineral or is prepared from other minerals, and that is used esp as a FLUX (substance promoting fusion of metals or minerals), cleansing agent, and water softener and as a preservative [ME *boras*, fr MF, fr ML *borac-, borax*, fr Ar *būraq*, fr Per *būrah*]

**borazon** /'bawrə,zon/ trademark – used for a substance that consists of a chemical compound of boron and nitrogen that is as hard as diamond but more resistant to high temperature and that is used in abrasives, drills, etc

**borborygmus** /,bawbə'rigməs/ n, pl **borborygmi, borborygmus** rumbling in the stomach or intestines [NL, fr Gk *borborygmos*, fr *borboryzein* to rumble, of imit origin]

**Bordeaux** /baw'doh/ n, pl **Bordeaux** /~/ a red or white wine of the Bordeaux region of France

**Bordeaux mixture** n a fungicide, used esp on fruit trees, that is made by mixing COPPER SULPHATE with lime and water [*Bordeaux*, city in SW France]

**bordel** /'bawd(ə)l/ n, archaic chiefly NAm a brothel [ME, fr MF, fr OF, fr *borde* hut, of Gmc origin; akin to OE *bord* board]

**bordello** /baw'deloh/ n, pl **bordellos** a brothel [It, fr OF *bordel*]

**¹border** /'bawdə/ n 1 an outer part or edge 2 a boundary, frontier ⟨crossed the ~ into Italy⟩ 3 a narrow bed of planted ground along the edge of a garden, lawn, path, etc ⟨a ~ of tulips⟩ 4 an ornamental design at the edge of something (e g printed matter, fabric, or a rug) [ME *bordure*, fr MF, fr OF, fr *border* to border, fr *bort* border, of Gmc origin; akin to OE *bord*] – **bordered** adj

**²border** vt 1 to add or attach a border to ⟨~ a bedspread with a fringe⟩ 2 to adjoin at the edge or boundary ⟨an airport ~s the city on the south⟩ – **borderer** n

**border on** vt 1 BORDER 2 ⟨the USA borders on Canada⟩ 2 to resemble closely ⟨his devotion to his dog borders on the ridiculous⟩

**Border collie** n (any of) a breed of rough-haired, often black-and-white, stocky collie dogs, that are used in Britain most commonly for herding sheep [fr its origin in the borderlands of England and Scotland]

**bordereau** /,bawdə'roh/ n, pl **bordereaux** /-'roh(z)/ a detailed note or memorandum of account; esp one containing a list of documents [Fr, fr MF, fr *bord* border, fr OF *bort*]

**borderland** /'bawdə,land/ n 1 territory at or near a border; a frontier 2 a vague intermediate state or region ⟨the ~ between fantasy and reality⟩

**borderline** /-,lien/ adj 1 situated at or near a border line 2a situated between two points or states b verging on one or other place or state without being definitely assignable to either one c not quite meeting accepted patterns (e g of morality or good taste) or an accepted standard; esp verging on the indecent ⟨a ~ joke⟩

**border line** n a line of demarcation

**Border terrier** n (any of) a breed of small terriers of British origin with a harsh dense coat [fr its origin in the borderlands of England and Scotland]

**bordure** /'bawdyooə/ n, heraldry a border surrounding a shield [ME – more at BORDER]

**¹bore** /baw/ vt 1 to pierce (as if) with a rotary tool 2 to form

or construct by boring ~ vi 1a to make a hole by boring b to sink a mine shaft, well, or borehole ⟨~ for coal⟩ 2 to make one's way laboriously ⟨we ~d through the jostling crowd⟩ [ME *boren*, fr OE *borian*; akin to OHG *borōn* to bore, L *forare* to bore, *ferire* to strike]

**²bore** n 1 a hole made (as if) by boring 2a an interior lengthwise cylindrical cavity ⟨the ~ of a thermometer⟩ b the inside tube of a gun; BARREL 3a **3a** the size of a hole b the diameter of the inside of a tube, esp a firearm; the calibre, gauge c the diameter of an engine cylinder

**³bore** past of BEAR

**⁴bore** n a tidal flood that moves swiftly as a steep-fronted wave in a channel, estuary, etc – called also EAGRE [(assumed) ME *bore* wave, fr ON *bāra*]

**⁵bore** n 1 a tedious person; somebody who induces boredom 2 something that is dull, uninteresting, or tiresome [perh fr *²bore*]

**⁶bore** vt to weary because dull or monotonous ⟨a good entertainer never ~s her audience⟩

**boreal** /'bawri-əl/ adj, often cap of or growing in northern and mountainous parts of the northern hemisphere [ME *boriall*, fr LL *borealis*, fr L *boreas* north wind, north, fr Gk, fr *Boreas*]

**Boreas** /'bawriəs/ n 1 the god of the north wind in Greek mythology 2 the north wind personified [L, fr Gk]

**boredom** /'bawd(ə)m/ n the state of being bored

**borehole** /'baw,hohl/ n a hole drilled in the earth to obtain water, gas, oil, etc

**borer** /'bawrə/ n one who or that which bores: e g a a tool used for boring b an insect that as larva or adult bores into the woody parts of plants

**boric** /'bawrik/ adj of or containing boron

**boric acid** n a white solid acid, $H_3BO_3$, used esp as a weak antiseptic

**boride** /'bawried/ n any of several chemical compounds of boron combined usu with a metal

**boring** /'bawring/ adj causing boredom – **boringly** adv

**born** /bawn/ adj 1a brought into existence (as if) by birth b by birth – usu in combination ⟨Chinese-born⟩ 2 having a specified character or situation from birth ⟨a ~ leader⟩ 3 destined or as if from birth ⟨~ to succeed⟩ – see also to the MANNER born usage see BORNE [ME, fr OE *boren*, pp of *beran* to carry – more at BEAR]

**born-a'gain** adj having undergone a conversion, esp to evangelical Christianity – compare TWICE-BORN

**borne** /bawn/ past part of BEAR

usage **Borne** is the past participle of **bear** in all senses except those connected with birth ⟨I've **borne** it as long as I could⟩. In the "birth" sense, **borne** is used when the female who gives birth is the subject ⟨she has **borne** two sons⟩ and in the passive with by ⟨children **borne** (= given birth to) by her⟩ and **born** in the passive without by ⟨her sons were **born** in Greece⟩ ⟨children **born** to her⟩.

**borneol** /'bawni,ol/ n a chemical compound, $C_{10}H_{17}OH$, that is an ALCOHOL chemically related to camphor, occurs in some ESSENTIAL OILS, and is used chiefly in the manufacture of perfumes [ISV, fr *Borneo*, island in the Malay archipelago]

**bornite** /'bawniet/ n a red-brown mineral, $Cu_5FeS_4$, consisting of a SULPHIDE of copper and iron and constituting an important source of copper [Ger *bornit*, fr Ignaz von *Born* †1791 Austrian mineralogist]

**boron** /'bawron/ n a solid non-metallic chemical element with a VALENCY of three, used in hardening steel and in the control rods of nuclear reactors [*borax* + *-on* (as in *carbon*)] – **boronic** adj

**boron nitride** n a chemical compound, BN, of boron and nitrogen that has a very high melting point and occurs in various forms: e g a a relatively soft form used in heat-resistant linings (e g for furnaces) and lubricants b BORAZON (man-made substance as hard as diamond)

**borosilicate glass** /,bawroh'silikət, -,kayt/ n glass containing more boron than usual, used esp to make heat-resistant casserole dishes, plates, laboratory flasks, etc [ISV *boron* + *silicate*]

**borough** /'burə/ n 1a a medieval fortified group of houses forming a town with special duties and privileges b an urban constituency in Britain that sends a member to Parliament c an urban area in Britain that had powers of local self-government granted to it by royal charter 2a any of the 32 local-government areas that together with the City of London comprise Greater London b a municipal corporation in certain states of the USA c any of the five political divisions of New

York City [ME *burgh*, fr OE *burg* fortified town; akin to OHG *burg* fortified place, OE *beorg* mountain – more at BARROW]

**borough English** *n* a custom, formerly existing in parts of England, by which the lands of a tenant who had not made a will descended to the youngest son [part trans of AF (*tenure en*) *Burgh Engloys* (tenure in an) English borough; fr its being prevalent in certain boroughs, and distinctively English (ie not French)]

**¹borrow** /'boroh/ *vt* **1** to take or receive with the implied or expressed intention of returning ⟨~ *a book*⟩ **2** to appropriate or adopt (for a temporary period) ⟨~ing *prestige from her predecessor*⟩ **3** to take (one) from the number of the next highest power of ten when the number being subtracted from is less than the number to be subtracted ⟨*if you subtract 9 from 43, you have to* ~ *one and take 9 from 13*⟩ – compare CARRY 5 **4** to introduce into one language from another ~ *vi* **1** to borrow something ⟨*English* ~s *from other languages*⟩ **2** *of a golf ball* to deviate from a straight line because of the slope of the green ⟨*it will* ~ *from the right*⟩ [ME *borwen*, fr OE *borgian;* akin to OE *beorgan* to preserve – more at BURY] – **borrower** *n*

*usage* One borrows things *from* other people. **Borrow** *of* is now old-fashioned, and **borrow** *off* or *off of* is nonstandard.

**²borrow** *n* the tendency of a golf ball to deviate from a straight line because of the slope of the green

**borrowing** /'boroh·ing/ *n* a word or phrase adopted from one language into another

**borsch** /bawsh/ *n* borscht

**borscht** /bawsht/ *n* a soup made primarily from beetroots and served hot or cold, often with sour cream [Russ *borshch*]

**borstal** /'bawstl/ *n*, *Br* a penal institution to which young offenders between the ages of 16 and 21 may be sent for reformative training [*Borstal*, village in Kent, England, where the first such institution was set up]

**bort, boart** /bawt/ *n* imperfectly crystallized diamond or diamond fragments used as an abrasive [prob fr D *boort*]

**bortsch** /bawch, bawshch/ *n* borscht

**borzoi** /'bawzoy, -'-/ *n* (any of) a breed of large long-haired dogs developed in Russia, esp for hunting wolves [Russ *borzoĭ*, fr *borzoĭ* swift; akin to L *festinare* to hasten]

**boscage** *also* **boskage** /'boskij/ *n*, *archaic* a growth of trees or shrubs; a thicket [ME *boskage*, fr MF *boscage*, fr OF, fr *bois*, *bosc* forest, perh of Gmc origin; akin to ME *bush*]

**bosh** /bosh/ *n*, *informal* nonsense [Turk *boş* empty, useless]

**bosh shot** *n*, *Br informal* an unsuccessful attempt [alter. of *boss shot*, prob fr E dial. *boss* to miss, bungle, perh fr *boss*- (as in *boss-eyed*)]

**bosie** /'bohzi/ *n*, *Austr* GOOGLY (bowled ball in cricket that turns the opposite way from expected) [B J T *Bos*anquet †1936 E cricketer who invented the googly]

**bosk** /bosk/ *n*, *archaic* a small wooded area [prob back-formation fr *bosky*]

**bosket, bosquet** /'boskit/ *n*, *archaic* a thicket [Fr *bosquet*, fr It *boschetto*, dim. of *bosco* forest, perh of Gmc origin; akin to ME *bush*]

**bosky** /'boski/ *adj*, *archaic* full of trees; wooded [E dial. *bosk* bush, fr ME *bush*, *bosk*]

**¹bosom** /'boozəm/ *n* **1** the front of the human chest; *esp* a woman's breasts **2a** the breast considered as the centre of secret thoughts and emotions **b** enclosing or protective relationship ⟨*lived in the* ~ *of her family*⟩ **3** the part of a woman's garment covering the chest [ME, fr OE *bōsm;* akin to OHG *buosam* bosom, Skt *bhūri* abundant – more at BIG]

**²bosom** *vt*, *archaic* **1** to enclose or carry in the bosom **2** to embrace

**³bosom** *adj* close, intimate ⟨~ *friends*⟩

**-bosomed** /-'boozəmd/ *comb form* (*adj→adj*) having (such) a bosom ⟨*big*-bosomed⟩

**bosomy** /'boozəmi/ *adj* having large breasts

**boson** /'bohson/ *n* an ELEMENTARY PARTICLE (minute particle of matter) (eg a photon or meson) that obeys relations stated by Bose and Einstein and whose SPIN (property of a particle causing an apparent rotation of itself about an axis) is either zero or a WHOLE NUMBER [Satyendranath *Bose* †1974 Indian physicist] – **bosonic** *adj*

**¹boss** /bos/ *n* **1a** a part or piece that sticks out ⟨*a* ~ *of granite*⟩ ⟨*a* ~ *on an animal's horn*⟩ **b** a raised ornamentation **c** a carved ornament concealing the intersection of the ribs of a vault or panelled ceiling **2a** the enlarged part of a shaft, esp on which a wheel is mounted **b** the hub of a propeller [ME *boce*, fr OF, fr (assumed) VL *bottia*]

**²boss** *vt* to ornament with bosses; emboss

**³boss** *n* **1** one who exercises control or authority; *specif* one who directs or supervises employees at a place of work **2a** an official with authority over an organization **b** *chiefly derog* a politician who exercises control over a party organization (eg in the USA) [D *baas* master; akin to Fris *baes* master]

**⁴boss** *vt*, *chiefly informal* **1** to act as director or supervisor of **2** ORDER 2a – often + *about* or *around*

**bossa nova** /,bosə 'nohvə/ *n* **1** a Brazilian dance similar to the samba **2** music resembling the samba with jazz interpolations [Pg, lit., new trend]

**boss-'eyed** *adj*, *Br informal* cross-eyed [perh fr ¹*boss*]

**bossism** /'bosiz(ə)m/ *n*, *NAm chiefly derog* the system under which party organizations are controlled by leading politicians

**boss shot** *n*, *Br informal* BOSH SHOT

**bossy** /'bosi/ *adj* somewhat dictatorial; domineering – **bossiness** *n*

**Boston** /'bostən/ *n* a card game for four players with two packs of cards, similar in some ways to SOLO, but with a more complicated system of bidding and scoring [Fr, fr *Boston*, city in Massachusetts, USA]

**Boston terrier** *n* (any of) a breed of small smooth-coated terriers originating as a cross between the bulldog and BULL TERRIER [*Boston* in Massachusetts]

**bosun** /'bohz(ə)n, 'bohs(ə)n/ *n* a boatswain

**botanical** /bə'tanikl/ *adj* **1** of plants or botany **2** derived from plants **3** *of a plant* occurring more or less unchanged from the original wild form [Fr *botanique*, fr Gk *botanikos* of herbs, fr *botanē* pasture, herb, fr *boskein* to feed; akin to Lith *gauja* herd] – **botanically** *adv*

**botanic garden** /bə'tanik/, **botanical garden** *n*, **botanic gardens, botanical gardens** *n pl* a place in which plant collections are grown for display and scientific study

**botan·ize, -ise** /'botəniez/ *vi* to collect plants for botanical investigation; *also* to study plants, esp on a field trip

**botany** /'botəni/ *n* **1** (a branch of biology that deals with) plants and plant life in the world **2a** the plant life of a particular region or environment **b** the properties and vital phenomena exhibited by a plant, plant type, or plant group [back-formation fr *botanical*] – **botanist** *n*

**botany wool** *n* a fine grade of wool from the MERINO sheep that comes esp from Australia [*Botany* Bay in New South Wales, Australia]

**¹botch** /boch/ *vt*, *informal* **1** to repair, patch, or assemble in a makeshift or inept way **2** to foul up hopelessly; bungle [ME *bocchen*] – **botcher** *n*

**²botch** *n*, *informal* something that is botched; a mess – **botchy** *adj*

**botel** /boh'tel/ *n* BOATEL (hotel with berths for boats)

**botfly** /'bot,flie/ *n* any of various heavy-bodied flies (esp families Oestroidea and Gasterophilidae) with larvae that live as parasites in the stomach, intestines, etc of various large mammals including cows and, rarely, human beings [*bot* (the larva of the botfly), perh modif of ScGael *boiteag* maggot]

**¹both** /bohth/ *adj* being the two; affecting or involving the one as well as the other ⟨~ *her feet*⟩ ⟨~ *eyes*⟩ [ME *bothe*, fr ON *bāthir;* akin to OHG *beide* both]

**²both** *pron taking pl vb* the one as well as the other ⟨~ *of the books*⟩ ⟨~ *refused to speak*⟩ ⟨*why not do* ~?⟩

**³both** *conj* – used to indicate and stress the inclusion of each of two or more things specified by coordinated words or word groups ⟨~ *London and New York*⟩ ⟨*she* ~ *speaks and writes Swahili*⟩

*usage* **1** In formal writing, **both** should be avoided where more than two items are involved ⟨⚠ **both** *useful, interesting, and inexpensive*⟩. **2** It is sometimes thought redundant to combine **both...and** with expressions such as *as well as, equal, equally, alike, at once,* or *together*, which themselves convey the idea of "two-ness" ⟨**both** *in France and in England alike*⟩. **3** When **both** is used to emphasize *and,* the two words should correctly link parallel constructions. Compare ⟨**both** *in France and in England* (joining two phrases)⟩ ⟨*in* **both** *France and England* (joining two nouns)⟩ ⟨⚠ **both** *in France and England* (joining a phrase to a noun)⟩. **4** In possessive constructions, it is more formally correct and usually clearer to choose the form ⟨*the fault of* **both**⟩ rather than ⟨**both** *their fault(s)*⟩. The latter pattern is ambiguous in ⟨**both** *their houses* (do they share two houses or have one each?)⟩ and impossible when a single possession or relationship is shared; here one must prefer ⟨*she's the mother of* **both** *of them*⟩ to ⟨⚠ *she's* **both** *their mother*⟩. **5** The use of **both** for **each** can lead to ambiguity ⟨**both** *houses cost £50,000*

(£50,000 each or £25,000 each?)⟩ or to absurdity ⟨there's a policeman on both sides of the road⟩.

¹**bother** /'bodhə/ vt **1a** to cause to be troubled or perplexed ⟨the complexities of life ~ him⟩ **b** to cause discomfort or pain to ⟨her hip ~s her a bit sometimes⟩ **2a** to annoy, esp by provocation; pester ⟨don't ~ your mother now⟩ **b** to disturb, irritate ⟨will the radio ~ you?⟩ **c** – used as a mild interjection of annoyance ⟨oh ~ it!⟩ ~ vi **1** to feel mild concern or anxiety **2** to take pains; take the trouble **synonyms** see ANNOY **antonym** comfort [perh fr IrGael bodhar deaf, bothered]

²**bother** n **1a** a state of petty discomfort, annoyance, or worry **b** something or someone that causes petty annoyance or worry **2** unnecessary fussing **3** a disturbance or fight; trouble ⟨there was a spot of ~ here today⟩ ⟨gangs of C-stream fifteen-year-old dropouts . . . were looking for ~ – George Melly⟩

**botheration** /,bodhə'raysh(ə)n/ n **1** bothering or being bothered **2** – used as a mild interjection of annoyance

**bothersome** /-s(ə)m/ adj causing bother; annoying

**bothy** /'bothi/ n, Scot **1** a small outbuilding on a farm which formerly provided accommodation for farmworkers **2** a small hut in the mountains which provides shelter for mountaineers and hill walkers [Sc, prob fr obs Sc both booth, fr ME bothe]

**bo tree** /boh/ n the PIPAL tree (large Indian fig tree) [Sinhalese bō, fr Skt bodhi, lit., enlightenment; fr the tradition that Buddha attained enlightenment while sitting beneath such a tree]

**botryoidal** /,botri'oydl/ also **botryoid** /'botri,oyd/ adj having the form of a bunch of grapes ⟨~ garnets⟩ [Gk botryoeidēs, fr botrys bunch of grapes]

**botrytis** /bə'trietəs/ n a plant disease caused by a fungus (Botrytis cinerea) in which large areas of the plant rot [NL, irreg fr Gk botrys]

¹**bottle** /'botl/ n **1a** a rigid or semirigid container, esp for liquids, that typically is made of glass or plastic and has a comparatively narrow neck or mouth and no handle **b** the contents of or quantity in a bottle **2a** a glass or plastic container with a teat, used for feeding esp milk to infants ⟨have you given him his ~?⟩ **b** bottled milk used to feed infants ⟨hasn't drunk her ~⟩ **3** slang alcoholic drink ⟨hit the ~⟩ **4** Br slang NERVE **3b** [ME botel, fr MF bouteille, fr ML butticula, dim. of LL buttis cask] – **bottleful** n

²**bottle** vt **1** to put into a bottle **2** Br to preserve (eg fruit) by storage in glass jars

**bottle out** vi, Br slang to withdraw or refuse to take part because of lack of nerve

**bottle up** vt to confine as if in a bottle; restrain ⟨bottling up their anger⟩

**bottlebrush** /'botl,brush/ n **1** a brush for cleaning bottles; specif one with a cylindrical head on a thin stem **2** any of various Australasian shrubs (esp genera Callistemon and Melaleuca) of the eucalyptus family with spikes of brightly coloured, esp red, flowers

**bottled gas** n gas under pressure in portable cylinders

¹**bottle-,feed** vt **bottle-fed** to feed (eg an infant) with milk by means of a bottle

**bottle glass** n tough dark green or amber glass used in making bottles

**bottle gourd** n a cultivated plant (Lagenaria siceraria) of the cucumber family whose fruit, of various shapes, is sometimes used as a container

**bottle green** adj or n very dark green

**bottleneck** /'botl,nek/ n **1a** a narrow stretch of road **b** a point or situation where free movement or progress is held up **2** a style of guitar playing using an object (eg a metal bar or the neck of a bottle) pressed against the strings to produce the effect (GLISSANDO) of one note sliding into another

*usage* Although **bottleneck** now often means "point of constriction", our sense of its literal meaning as the neck of a bottle makes it odd to speak of *curing* or *solving* a **bottleneck**, of making things better by *reducing* it, or of a *big* **bottleneck** as a specially serious one.

**bottle-nosed dolphin** n any of various moderately large stout-bodied TOOTHED WHALES (genus Tursiops and esp Tursiops truncatus) with a prominent beak and long curved fin on the back

**bottle party** n a private party to which guests bring their own drinks

**bottler** /'botlə/ n **1** one who or that which bottles **2** Austr informal something or someone exceptional

**bottle store** n, SAfr an off-licence

**bottle washer** n, chiefly Br humorous somebody employed to do all the work – in head/chief cook and bottle washer

¹**bottom** /'botəm/ n **1a** the underside of something **b** a surface on which something rests **c** the buttocks, rump **2** the ground beneath a body of water **3a** the part of a ship's hull lying below the water **b** archaic a boat, ship; esp a merchant ship **4a** the lowest, deepest, or farthest part or place **b** the lowest or last place in order of precedence ⟨started work at the ~⟩ **c** the transmission gear of a motor vehicle giving the lowest speed of travel **d bottoms** pl, **bottom** the lower part of a two-piece garment ⟨pyjama ~s⟩ **5 bottoms** pl, **bottom** low-lying grassland along a watercourse **6** a basis, source **7** a foundation colour applied to textile fibres before dyeing [ME botme, fr OE botm; akin to OHG bodam bottom, L fundus, Gk pythmēn] – **bottomed** adj – **at bottom** basically, really – **get to the bottom of** to find out the truth, source, or basis of

²**bottom** vt **1** to provide with a bottom **2** to provide a foundation for **3** to bring to the bottom **4** to get to the bottom of ~ vi **1** to become based **2** to reach the bottom **3** of a motor vehicle **3a** to bounce down so violently that the springs are fully compressed **b** to touch the ground while in motion – **bottomer** n **bottom out** vi to reach the lowest point and level out ⟨prices beginning to bottom out⟩

³**bottom** adj **1** of or situated at the bottom ⟨~ rock⟩ **2** living in or at the bottom ⟨~ fishes⟩ – see also **bet one's bottom DOLLAR**

**bottom drawer** n, Br (a place for storing) a woman's collection of clothes and esp household articles and furnishings (eg linen and tableware) kept in anticipation of her marriage

**bottomless** /-lis/ adj **1** extremely deep **2** boundless, unlimited – **bottomlessly** adv, **bottomlessness** n

**bottommost** /'botəm,mohst/ adj situated at the very bottom; lowest, deepest

**bottomry** /'botəmri/ n a contract by which a ship is pledged as security for a loan which is to be repaid at the end of a successful voyage [modif of D bodemerij, fr bodem bottom, ship; akin to OHG bodam]

**botty** /'boti/ n, informal the buttocks, rump [alter. of bottom]

**botulin** /'botyoolin, 'bochəlin/ n an extremely poisonous protein that is formed by botulinum bacteria and is the cause of botulism [prob fr NL botulinus]

**botulinum** /,botyoo'lienəm, ,bochə-/ n a spore-forming bacterium (Clostridium botulinum) that secretes botulin and whose growth (eg in badly canned food) causes botulism [NL, neut of botulinus] – **botulinal** adj

**botulinus** /,botyoo'lienəs, ,bochə-/ n botulinum [NL, fr L botulus sausage]

**botulism** /'botyoo,liz(ə)m, -chə-/ n acute, often fatal, food poisoning caused by botulin in food

**bouchée** /booh'shay/ n a very small vol-au-vent [Fr, lit., mouthful, fr (assumed) VL buccata, fr L bucca cheek, mouth – more at POCK]

**bouclé, boucle** /'boohklay/ n **1** an uneven yarn of three strands, one of which forms loops at intervals **2** a fabric made of bouclé yarn [Fr bouclé curly, fr pp of boucler to curl, fr boucle buckle, curl]

**boudoir** /'boohdwah/ n a woman's dressing room, bedroom, or private sitting room [Fr, fr bouder to pout]

**bouffant** /'boohfong/ adj puffed out (in shape) ⟨a ~ hairstyle⟩ ⟨~ sleeves⟩ [Fr, fr MF, fr prp of bouffer to puff]

**bougainvillaea**, chiefly NAm **bougainvillea** /,boohgən'vilyə/ n any of a genus (Bougainvillaea, family Nyctaginaceae) of ornamental tropical American woody climbing plants with brilliant purple or red petal-like leaves (BRACTS) [NL, fr Louis Antoine de Bougainville †1811 Fr navigator]

**bough** /bow/ n a branch of a tree; esp a main branch [ME, shoulder, bough, fr OE bōg; akin to OHG buog shoulder, Gk pēchys forearm] – **boughed** adj

**bought** /bawt/ past of BUY

**bougie** /'boozhi/ n **1** medicine a tapering cylindrical instrument for inserting into a tubular passage of the body (eg the urethra or anus) **2** archaic a wax candle [Fr, candle, fr Bougie, seaport in Algeria]

**bouillabaisse** /,booh·yə'bes (Fr bujabɛs)/ n a highly seasoned fish stew made with at least two kinds of fish [Fr, fr Prov bouiabaisso]

**bouillon** /'booh·yong (Fr bujɔ̃)/ n a thin clear soup made usu from lean beef △ bullion [Fr, fr OF boillon, fr boillir to boil

**boulangerite** /boo'lanzhəriet/ n a mineral, $Pb_5Sb_4S_{11}$, consisting of a sulphide of antimony and lead and occurring as thin flexible needles [Ger *boulangerit*, fr C L *Boulanger* †1849 Fr mining engineer]

**boulder** /'bohldə/ *n* a very large stone or mass of rock [short for *boulder stone*, fr ME *bulder ston*, part trans of a word of Scand origin; akin to Sw dial. *bullersten* large stone in a stream, fr *buller* noise + *sten* stone]

**boulder clay** *n* a glacial deposit consisting of pebbles, boulders, and rock fragments, embedded in clay

¹**boule** /boohl/ *n* 1 an orig French game similar to bowls in which usu metal balls are thrown or rolled in an attempt to place them nearer to a wooden jack than the opponent's balls 2 a pear-shaped mass of sapphire, SPINEL (hard mineral), etc, formed synthetically, with the atomic structure of a single crystal [Fr, ball – more at BOWL]

²**boule** /boohl, byoohl/, **boulework** *n* BUHL (inlaid brass, tortoiseshell, etc)

**boulevard** /'boohlə,vahd, -,vah/ *n* a broad avenue usu lined by trees [Fr, modif of MD *bolwerc* bulwark]

**boulevardier** /boohl'vahdi,ay/ *n* a worldly, fashionable city-dweller [Fr, fr *boulevard* + *-ier* *-er*]

**bouleversement** /bool'vuhsmənt (*Fr* bulversəmã)/ *n* an upset, disorder [Fr, fr MF, fr *bouleverser* to overturn, fr *boule* ball + *verser* to overturn]

**boulle** /boohl, byoohl/, **boullework** *n* BUHL (inlaid brass, tortoiseshell, etc)

¹**bounce** /bowns/ *vt* 1 to cause to spring back or up again from a hard surface ⟨~ *a ball*⟩ 2 to return (a cheque) as not good because of lack of funds in the payer's account 3 *NAm informal* to dismiss, fire 4 *obs* to beat, bump ~ *vi* 1 to spring back after being struck 2 to be returned by a bank as not good ⟨*will his cheque* ~?⟩ 3 to move exuberantly, violently, or with springing steps ⟨~d *into the room*⟩ [ME *bounsen* to beat, thump, prob of imit origin]

**bounce back** *vi* to recover quickly from a blow or defeat

²**bounce** *n* 1 a sudden leap or bound 2a an act of springing back (after hitting a hard surface) b the quality of bouncing well; springiness 3 exuberance, liveliness

**bouncer** /'bownsə/ *n* 1 a person employed in a public place to restrain or remove disorderly people 2 a fast intimidatory delivery of the ball in cricket that passes or hits the batsman at above chest height after it bounces

**bouncing** /'bownsing/ *adj* enjoying good health; robust ⟨*a bonny* ~ *baby*⟩

**bouncing bet** *n, often cap 2nd B* SOAPWORT (type of flowering plant) [*Bet*, nickname for *Elizabeth*]

**bouncy** /'bownsi/ *adj* 1 buoyant, exuberant 2 that bounces readily – **bouncily** *adv*

¹**bound** /bownd/ *adj* 1 going or intending to go ⟨~ *for home*⟩ 2 *archaic* ready – often in combination ⟨*college*-bound⟩ [ME *boun*, fr ON *būinn*, pp of *būa* to dwell, prepare; akin to OHG *būan* to dwell – more at BOWER]

²**bound** *n* 1 **bounds** *pl*, **bound** a limiting line; a boundary ⟨*her pleasure knew no* ~s⟩ 2 **bounds** *pl*, **bound** something that limits or restrains ⟨*beyond the* ~s *of decency*⟩ 3 *maths* a number which is greater than or less than all elements of a given set: 3a LOWER BOUND b UPPER BOUND [ME, fr OF *bodne*, fr ML *bodina*]

³**bound** *vt* 1 to set limits to 2 to form the boundary of; enclose

⁴**bound** *adj* 1a confined or limited, esp in a specified way or by a specified place or situation – often in combination ⟨*desk*-bound⟩ ⟨*house*-bound⟩ b certain, sure ⟨~ *to rain soon*⟩ 2 placed under legal or moral restraint or obligation ⟨*I'm* ~ *to say...*⟩ – often in combination ⟨*duty*-bound⟩ 3 of a book having the pages held securely together, esp between covers 4 held in chemical or physical combination ⟨~ *water in a molecule*⟩ 5 always occurring in combination with another linguistic form (eg *un*- in *unknown* and *-er* in *speaker*) – compare FREE 6 unable to function, esp for a specified reason – usu in combination ⟨*strike*-bound⟩ [ME *bounden*, fr pp of *binden* to bind]

⁵**bound** *n* 1 a leap, jump 2 a bounce [MF *bond*, fr *bondir* to leap, fr (assumed) VL *bombitire* to hum, fr L *bombus* deep hollow sound – more at BOMB]

⁶**bound** *vi* 1 to move by leaping 2 to rebound, bounce

**boundary** /'bownd(ə)ri/ *n* 1 something that indicates or fixes a limit or extent; *specif* a line that bounds or divides 2a the marked limits of a cricket field b (the score of four or six made by) a stroke in cricket that sends the ball over the boundary – compare SIX, FOUR

**boundary layer** *n* a region of liquid or gas near the surface of a body which is slowed down by the passage of the liquid or gas past that body

**bounden** /'bowndən/ *adj* 1 made obligatory; binding – usu in *bounden duty* 2 *archaic* being under obligation; beholden [ME]

**bounder** /'bowndə/ *n* 1 one who or that which bounds 2 a cad – not now in vogue

**boundless** /-lis/ *adj* limitless – **boundlessly** *adv*, **boundlessness** *n*

**bound up** *adj* closely involved or associated *with*

**bounteous** /'bowntyəs, -ti-əs/ *adj* giving or given freely and plentifully [ME *bountevous*, fr MF *bontif* kind, fr OF, fr *bonté* ] – **bounteously** *adv*, **bounteousness** *n*

**bountied** /'bowntid/ *adj* having the support or assistance of a bounty

**bountiful** /'bowntif(ə)l/ *adj* 1 generous, liberal 2 abundant, plentiful ⟨*a* ~ *harvest*⟩ – **bountifully** *adv*, **bountifulness** *n*

**bounty** /'bownti/ *n* 1 generosity 2 something given generously 3 a financial inducement or reward, esp when offered by a government: eg 3a a payment to encourage the killing of vermin or dangerous animals b a payment for the capture of an outlaw [ME *bounte* goodness, fr OF *bonté*, fr L *bonitat-, bonitas*, fr *bonus* good, fr OL *duenos*; akin to MHG *zwīden* to grant, L *bene* well]

**bounty hunter** *n* one who tracked down and captured outlaws for whom a reward was offered

**bouquet** /booh'kay/ *n* 1 a bunch of flowers fastened together (eg for presenting to somebody) 2 a compliment ⟨*didn't mean to throw* ~s *at him*⟩ – esp in *bouquets and brickbats* 3 a distinctive and characteristic fragrance (eg of wine) *synonyms* see ²SMELL [Fr, fr MF, thicket, fr ONF *bosquet*, fr OF *bosc* forest – more at BOSCAGE]

**bouquet garni** /'gahni/ *n* a small bunch of herbs (eg thyme, parsley, and a bay leaf) tied together or dried and enclosed in a muslin bag for use in flavouring stews and soups [Fr, lit., garnished bouquet]

**bourbon** /'buhbən, 'booəbən (*Fr* burbɔ̃)/ *n* 1 *cap* a member of a French dynasty founded in 1272 to which belonged some of the rulers of France, of Spain, of Naples, and of the Two Sicilies 2 a whisky distilled from a MASH (mixture of mashed grain and water) made up of not less than 51 per cent maize plus malt and rye – compare CORN WHISKEY 3 *often cap, chiefly NAm* a person who clings obstinately to the social and political ideas of the past [*Bourbon*, seigniory in France; (2) *Bourbon* county in Kentucky, USA] – **bourbonism** *n, often cap*

**bourbon biscuit** *n* an oblong chocolate-flavoured biscuit with a chocolate-cream filling [*Bourbon* in France]

**bourdon** /'booədn, 'bawdn/ *n* 1 a 16-foot organ stop that produces low notes 2 the one of the usu three pipes (DRONES) of a bagpipe that produces low notes [Fr, fr MF *bourdon* bass pipe, of imit origin]

**bourg** /booəg (*Fr* bu:r)/ *n* a French market town [ME, town, fr MF, fr OF *borc*, fr L *burgus* fortified place, of Gmc origin; akin to OHG *burg* fortified place – more at BOROUGH]

¹**bourgeois** /'booəzhwah, 'baw-/ *n, pl* **bourgeois** 1 a middle-class person 2 somebody whose behaviour and views are held to be influenced by bourgeois values or interests 3 *pl* the bourgeoisie [MF, burgher, fr OF *borjois*, fr *borc*]

²**bourgeois** *adj* 1 middle-class 2 marked by a narrow-minded concern for material interests and respectability 3 capitalist

**bourgeoisie** /,booəzhwah'zee/ *n taking sing or pl vb* 1 MIDDLE CLASS 2 the capitalist class [Fr, fr *bourgeois*]

**bourgeon** /'buhjən/ *vi* to burgeon

**bourkha** /'buhkə/ *n* BURKA (enveloping Muslim garment)

¹**bourn, bourne** /bawn/ *n* a small stream; a burn [ME *burn, bourne* – more at BURN]

²**bourn, bourne** *n, archaic* 1 a boundary, limit 2 a goal, destination [MF *bourne*, fr OF *bodne* – more at BOUND]

**bournonite** /'booənəniet, 'baw-/ *n* a mineral, $PbCuSbS_3$, consisting of a SULPHIDE of lead, copper, and antimony and occurring as wheel-shaped grains [Count J L de *Bournon* †1825 Fr mineralogist]

**bourrée** /'booray/ *n* 1 a 17th-century French dance usu to music with two beats in a bar; *also* a musical composition with the rhythm of this dance 2 PAS DE BOURRÉE (type of ballet step) [Fr]

**bourse** /booəs, baws/ *n* a continental stock exchange [Fr, lit., purse, fr ML *bursa* – more at PURSE]

**Boursin** /,booə'sanh, ,baw- (*Fr* bursɛ̃)/ *trademark* – used for a thick cream cheese of French origin that is flavoured with herbs, garlic, or pepper

**boustrophedon** /ˌboohstrə'feed(ə)n, -don, ˌbow-/ *adj* having alternate lines written in opposite directions (eg from left to right and from right to left); *also* of or using boustrophedon writing [Gk *boustrophēdon*, adv, lit., turning like oxen in ploughing, fr *bous* ox, cow + *strephein* to turn – more at COW, STROPHE]

**bout** /bowt/ *n* **1** a spell of activity ⟨*a* ∼ *of work*⟩ **2** an athletic match (eg of boxing or fencing) **3** an outbreak or attack, esp of something bad (eg illness) ⟨∼ *of fever*⟩ [E dial. *bout* a trip going and returning in ploughing, fr ME *bought* bend]

**boutique** /booh'teek/ *n* a small fashionable shop selling specialized goods, esp clothes; *also* a small shop within a large department store [Fr, shop]

**boutonniere** /ˌboohtoh'nyeə/ *n* BUTTONHOLE 2 [Fr *boutonnière* buttonhole, fr MF, fr *bouton* button]

**Bouvier des Flandres** /ˌboohvyay day 'flondrə, də 'flahndəz (*Fr* buvje de flãdr)/ *n* (any of) a breed of large powerfully built rough-coated dogs originating in Belgium and used esp for herding and guarding [Fr, lit., cowherd of Flanders]

**bouzouki** *also* **bousouki** /boo'zoohki/ *n* a long-necked stringed instrument of Greek origin that resembles a mandolin [NGk *mpouzouki*, prob fr Turk *büyük* large]

**¹bovine** /'bohvien/ *adj* **1** of oxen or cows **2** like an ox or cow (eg in being slow, stolid, or dull) [LL *bovinus*, fr L *bov-*, *bos* ox, cow – more at COW] – **bovinely** *adv*, **bovinity** *n*

**²bovine** *n* an ox (genus *Bos*) or a closely related animal

**Bovril** /'bovril/ *trademark* – used for a concentrated beef extract that is added to soups and stews to give flavour and is mixed with hot water to make a beverage – compare MARMITE

**bovver** /'bovə/ *n*, *Br slang* rowdy or violent disturbance; aggro ⟨∼ *boy*⟩ [alter. of *bother*]

**bovver boot** *n*, *Br* a laced boot with a steel toe cap (eg worn by a skinhead)

**¹bow** /bow/ *vi* **1** to submit, yield ⟨∼ *to the inevitable*⟩ **2** to bend the head, body, or knee in reverence or submission **3** to incline the head or body in greeting or agreement or to acknowledge applause ∼ *vt* **1** to cause to incline **2** to bend or incline (eg the head), esp in respect, submission, or shame **3** to crush (as if) with a heavy burden ⟨*whose heavy hand hath* ∼*ed you to the grave* – Shak⟩ **4a** to express by bowing ⟨∼*ed his thanks*⟩ **b** to usher in or out with a bow ⟨∼*ing them to the door*⟩ *synonyms* see ¹YIELD [ME *bowen*, fr OE *būgan*; akin to OHG *biogan* to bend, Skt *bhujati* he bends] – **bow and scrape** to act in an obsequious manner

**bow out** *vi* to retire, withdraw

**²bow** /bow/ *n* a bending of the head or body in respect, submission, agreement, or greeting, or as an acknowledgment of applause after a performance

**³bow** /boh/ *n* **1** something bent into a simple curve; a bend, arch **2** a strip of wood, fibreglass, or other flexible material held in a curved shape by a strong cord connecting the two ends that is used to shoot an arrow (eg at a target or enemy) **3** an archer **4a** a metal ring or loop forming a handle (eg of a key) **b** a slipknot, often ornamental, formed by doubling a shoelace, ribbon, etc into two or more loops **5a** a resilient wooden rod with horsehairs stretched from one end to the other used in playing an instrument of the viol or violin family **b** a stroke played on the strings of a musical instrument with such a bow **6** *NAm* a frame for the lenses of glasses; *also* the curved sidepiece of the frame passing over the ear [ME *bowe*, fr OE *boga*; akin to OE *būgan*] – **draw a bow at a venture** to make a random guess

**⁴bow** /boh/ *vb* **1** to (cause to) bend into a curve **2** to play a (stringed musical instrument) with a bow

**⁵bow** /bow/ *n* **1** bows *pl*, **bow** the front part of a ship **2** ²BOWMAN; *specif* somebody who rows in the front end of a boat [prob fr Dan *bov* shoulder, bow, fr ON *bōgr*; akin to OE *bōg* bough]

**bowdler·ize, -ise** /'bowdləriez/ *vt* to cut (eg a book) by omitting or changing parts considered vulgar; expurgate [Thomas Bowdler †1825 E editor of an expurgated edition of Shakespeare's plays] – **bowdlerization** *n*, **bowdlerizer** *n*

**¹bowed** /bowd/ *adj* **1** bent downwards and forwards ⟨*listened with* ∼ *heads*⟩ **2** having the back and head bent forwards [pp of ¹*bow*]

**²bowed** /bohd/ *adj* provided with or shaped like a bow

**bowel** /'bowəl/ *n* **1a** (a specified division of) the intestine or gut – usu *pl* except in medical use ⟨*the large* ∼⟩ **b** the passing of faeces ⟨*early* ∼ *training*⟩ ⟨*good* ∼ *habits*⟩ **2** *pl* the innermost parts ⟨∼*s of the earth*⟩ **3** bowels *pl*, **bowel** *archaic* feelings of tenderness or pity [ME, fr OF *boel*, fr MF *botellus*, fr L, dim. of *botulus* sausage] – **bowelless** *adj*

**¹bower** /'bowə/ *n* **1** an attractive dwelling or retreat **2** a shelter (eg in a garden) made with branches, vines, etc twined together; an arbour **3** *archaic or poetic* a lady's private apartment, esp a boudoir, in a medieval hall or castle [ME *bour* dwelling, fr OE *būr*; akin to OE & OHG *būan* to dwell, OE *bēon* to be] – **bowery** *adj*

**²bower** *n* a ship's principal anchor carried in the bows

**bowerbird** /'bowəˌbuhd/ *n* any of various songbirds (family Paradisaeidae) of Australia and New Guinea, the male of which builds a chamber or passage arched over with twigs and grasses, often adorned with bright-coloured objects, that are used esp to attract the female

**bowfront** /'bohˌfrunt/ *adj* having an outward curving front ⟨∼ *furniture*⟩

**bowhead** /'bohˌhed/ *n* GREENLAND RIGHT WHALE

**bowie knife** /'boh·i/ *n* a stout hunting knife with a sharpened part on the back edge curved concavely to the point [James Bowie †1836 US soldier]

**bowing** /'boh·ing/ *n* the technique of using the bow in playing a stringed musical instrument

**¹bowl** /bohl/ *n* **1** any of various round hollow usu hemispherical vessels used esp for holding liquids or food or for mixing food **2** the contents of a bowl **3a** the hollow of a spoon or tobacco pipe **b** the main bowl-shaped part of a toilet **4a** a natural formation or geographical region shaped like a bowl **b** *NAm* a bowl-shaped structure; *esp* a sports stadium [ME *bolle*, fr OE *bolla*; akin to OHG *bolla* blister, OE *blāwan* to blow] – **bowled** *adj*, **bowlful** *n*

**²bowl** *n* **1a** a ball used in bowls that is weighted or shaped to make it roll in a curve **b** *pl but taking sing vb* a game played typically outdoors on a green in which players roll bowls towards a target JACK (small white ball) in an attempt to get their bowl closer to the jack than their opponent's **2** a delivery of the ball in bowling; *also* a series of deliveries of the ball by one player in cricket ⟨*had a long* ∼⟩ [ME *boule*, fr MF, fr L *bulla* bubble]

**³bowl** *vi* **1a** to participate in a game of bowling or bowls **b** to roll a ball in bowls or bowling **c** to play as a bowler in cricket **2** to move smoothly and rapidly as in a vehicle or carriage with wheels – often + *along* ∼ *vt* **1a** to roll (a ball or bowl) in bowling or bowls **b** to score by bowling ⟨∼*s 150*⟩ **c** to hurl or roll (a round object) as if in bowling or cricket ⟨∼*ing hand grenades down the dockside* – The Guardian⟩ **2a** to deliver (a ball) to a batsman in cricket **b** *of a bowled ball or a bowler* to dismiss (a batsman in cricket) by breaking the wicket – often + *out*

**bowl out** *vt* to dismiss all the members of (the batting side) in cricket ⟨*bowled England out for a low score*⟩

**bowl over** *vt* **1** to strike or bump into (somebody) so that they fall down; KNOCK DOWN **2** to overwhelm with surprise; KNOCK OUT

**bowlegged** /'bohˌleg(i)d/ *adj* having legs that are bowed outwards at the knees and close together at the ankles

**¹bowler** /'bohlə/ *n* the person on the fielding side who bowls in a team sport; *specif* a cricketer who specializes in bowling rather than batting or fielding

**²bowler, bowler hat** *n* a stiff felt hat with a rounded crown and a narrow brim [*Bowler*, 19th-c family of E hatters]

**bowline** /'bohˌlien/ *n* **1** a rope used to keep the front edge of a sail taut and steady when a ship is sailing almost straight into the wind **2** a knot used to form a non-slipping loop at the end of a rope [ME *bouline*, perh fr *bowe* bow + *line*]

**bowling** /'bohling/ *n* any of several games in which balls are rolled on a green or down an alley at one or more target objects

**bowling alley** *n* a long narrow enclosure or lane with a smooth usu wooden floor for bowling or playing skittles; *also* a building or room having several of these

**bowling average** *n* the average number of runs scored off the bowling of a cricketer per number of wickets taken (eg in a season or his/her career) – compare BATTING AVERAGE

**bowling crease** *n* either of the lines drawn perpendicularly across a cricket pitch in line with each wicket

**bowling green** *n* a smooth close-cut area of turf for playing bowls

**¹bowman** /'bohmən/ *n*, *archaic* an archer [³*bow*]

**²bowman** /'bowmən/ *n* a boatman, oarsman, etc stationed in the front of a boat [⁵*bow*]

**Bowman's capsule** /'bohmənz/ *n* a thin membranous double-walled capsule surrounding each GLOMERULUS (network of blood capillaries) of a kidney tubule in a VERTEBRATE animal [Sir William *Bowman* †1892 E surgeon]

**bow saw** /boh/ *n* a saw having a narrow blade held under tension, esp by a light bow-shaped frame

**bowser** /'bowzə/ *n* 1 a tanker for refuelling aircraft; *broadly* any tanker delivering fuel 2 *Austr* a petrol pump [fr *Bowser*, trademark for a petrol pump]

**bowshot** /'boh,shot/ *n* the distance covered by an arrow shot from a bow

**bowsprit** /'boh,sprit/ *n* a spar projecting forwards from the bow of a ship [ME *bouspret*, prob fr MLG *bōchsprēt*, fr *bōch* bow + *sprēt* pole]

**bowstring** /'boh,string/ *n* the string that joins the ends of a bow for shooting arrows

**bow tie** /boh/ *n* a short tie fastened in a bow

**bow window** /boh/ *n* a curved BAY WINDOW

**bowwow** /'bow,wow/ *n* 1 the bark of a dog – often used imitatively 2 a dog – used esp by or to children [imit]

**bowyangs** /'bohyangz/ *n pl, Austr* strings tied below the knee round each leg of a pair of trousers [E dial. *bowy-yanks* leather leggings

**bowyer** /'bohyə/ *n* a person who makes or sells bows for shooting arrows

**¹box** /boks/ *n, pl* **box, boxes** any of several evergreen shrubs or small trees (genus *Buxus* of the family Buxaceae, the box family) that have small shiny leaves; *esp* a widely cultivated shrub (*Buxus sempervirens*) used for hedges, borders, and TOPIARY (hedges cut into shapes) [ME, fr OE, fr L *buxus*, fr Gk *pyxos*]

**²box** *n* **1a** a rigid container having four sides, a bottom, and usu a cover **b** the contents of a box **2a** a small compartment (e g for a group of spectators in a theatre) **b(1)** PENALTY AREA (area of a football pitch) **b(2)** PENALTY BOX (area of a hockey pitch) **3a** a boxlike protective case (e g for a bearing in machinery) **b** a shield to protect the genitals, worn esp by batsmen and wicketkeepers in cricket **c** a structure that contains a telephone for use by members of a specified organization ⟨*police* ~⟩ ⟨*AA or RAC* ~⟩ **d(1)** a horsebox **d(2)** *Br* LOOSE BOX (stall for an animal) **4** a square or oblong division or storage compartment **5** a square or oblong hollow space or recess **6** a small simple sheltering or enclosing structure **7** printed matter enclosed by lines, a white space, etc **8** POST-OFFICE BOX **9** *Br* a gift (e g money) given to tradesmen at Christmas **10** *Br informal* television – + *the* [ME, fr OE, fr LL *buxis*, fr Gk *pyxis*, fr *pyxos*] – **boxful** *n*, **boxy** *adj*, **boxiness** *n*

**³box** *vt* **1** to provide with a box **2a** to enclose in a box – often + *up* **b** to lead (a horse) into a horsebox; *also* to transport in a horsebox **3** BOXHAUL – see also **box the** COMPASS

**box in** *vt* **1** to enclose with boarding, lathing, etc, esp so as to hide something unsightly or to bring to a required shape ⟨*box the pipes in*⟩ ⟨*boxed in the bath*⟩ **2** to enclose or confine in a small place; hem in ⟨*felt boxed in*⟩

**⁴box** *n* a punch or slap, esp on the ear [ME]

**⁵box** *vt* **1** to slap (e g somebody's ears) with the hand **2** to engage in boxing with – ~ *vi* to engage in boxing

**Box and Cox** /koks/ *adv or adj, Br* alternating; IN TURN [*Box and Cox*, farce by J M Morton †1891 E dramatist, in which two men unknowingly rent the same room, one occupying it by day and one by night]

**box bed** *n* **1** a bed enclosed (e g by panels) or in an alcove **2** a bed that folds up into the form of a box

**box calf** *n* calfskin leather that has square markings on it

**box camera** *n* a box-shaped camera with a simple lens and shutter

**boxcar** /'boks,kah/ *n, NAm* a roofed railway freight wagon

**box coat** *n* a heavy overcoat formerly worn for driving (e g in a carriage) [fr its use by coachmen sitting on the box seat]

**box elder** *n* a N American maple (*Acer negundo*) cultivated for the shade it gives

**¹boxer** /'boksə/ *n* somebody who engages in the sport of boxing

**²boxer** *n* (any of) a breed of compact medium-sized short-haired dogs that originated in Germany and have a docked tail [Ger, fr E *¹boxer*]

**Boxer** *n* a member of a Chinese secret society that was opposed to foreign influence in China and whose rebellion was suppressed in 1900 [approx trans of Chin (Pek) *yìhéchúan* (*i⁴hé²ch'üan²*), lit., righteous harmonious fist]

**boxer shorts** *n pl* men's loosely fitting underpants

**boxfish** /'boks,fish/ *n* TRUNKFISH (fish with head and body enclosed in a bony boxlike cover)

**'box-,girder** *n* a hollow rectangular girder

**boxhaul** /'boks,hawl/ *vt* to bring (a ship with sails attached to the mast in the middle) into a position in which the opposite side faces the wind by a manoeuvre that swings the ship round rapidly with the bows turning away from the wind

**boxing** /'boksing/ *n* the art of attacking and defending with the fists practised as a sport

**Boxing Day** *n* December 26, observed as a public holiday in Britain (except Scotland) and elsewhere in the Commonwealth, on which service workers (e g postmen) were traditionally given Christmas gifts [*²box* 9]

**boxing glove** *n* a heavily padded leather mitten worn in boxing

**box iron** *n* an iron for ironing clothes that is heated by inserting a hot iron or hot charcoal into the hollow boxlike base

**box junction** *n, Br* a road junction at which a pattern of crosshatched yellow lines on the road warns the road-user not to enter until his/her exit is clear

**box kite** *n* a tailless kite consisting of two or more open-ended connected boxes

**box number** *n* the number of a box or pigeonhole at a newspaper or post office where arrangements are made for replies to advertisements or other mail to be sent

**box office** *n* **1** an office (e g in a theatre) where tickets of admission are sold **2** something that enhances ticket sales ⟨*the publicity is all good* ~⟩

**box pew** *n* a church pew enclosed like a box

**box pleat** *n* a pleat made by forming two folded edges, one facing right and the other left, leaving a wide band of material on the right side of the fabric

**boxroom** /-,roohm, -room/ *n, Br* a storeroom (e g for luggage or furniture) in a house

**box seat** *n* **1** the driver's seat on a horse-drawn coach **2** a seat in a box (e g in a theatre or grandstand)

**box spanner** *n* a spanner in the form of a tube that is shaped at one or both ends to fit over a nut, bolt-head, etc

**box spring** *n* any of a set of spiral bedsprings that are attached to a foundation and enclosed in a cloth-covered frame; *also* a set of box springs

**box stall** *n, NAm* LOOSE BOX (stall for an animal)

**boxwood** /'boks,wood/ *n* (the very close-grained heavy tough hard wood of) the box tree

**boxy** /'boksi/ *adj* **1** like a box **2** being or producing a sound in which the higher and lower frequencies are not accurately reproduced – **boxiness** *n*

**¹boy** /boy/ *n* **1a** a male child from birth to puberty **b** a son **c** an immature male; *broadly* a youth **d** a boyfriend **2** a lad, person ⟨*the* ~s *at the office*⟩ **3** a male servant – sometimes taken to be offensive [ME; prob akin to Fris *boi* boy] – **boyhood** *n*, **boyish** *adj*, **boyishly** *adv*, **boyishness** *n*

synonyms Boyish and girlish may refer to adult behaviour as well as to that of boys and girls. Boyish is usually appreciative ⟨*his* boyish *good looks*⟩. Girlish is less flattering ⟨*her coy* girlish *giggle gets on my nerves*⟩. See GENTLEMAN. Compare CHILDISH antonym girl

**²boy** *interj, chiefly NAm* – used to express esp excitement or surprise

**boyar** *also* **boyard** /'bohyah/ *n* a member of the pre-imperial Russian aristocracy [Russ *boyarin*, fr OSlav *boljarinŭ*]

**boycott** /'boykot/ *vt* to refuse to have dealings with (e g a person, shop, or organization) or to purchase, usu so as to express disapproval or to force acceptance of certain conditions [Charles *Boycott* †1897 E land agent in Ireland who was ostracized for refusing to reduce rents] – **boycott** *n*, **boycotter** *n*

**boyfriend** /'boy,frend/ *n* **1** a frequent or regular male companion of a girl or woman **2** a male lover

**boyo** /'boyoh/ *n, pl* **boyos** *Irish & Welsh* a boy, lad [*boy* + *-o*]

**boy scout** *n* SCOUT **4** – no longer used technically

**boysenberry** /'boyzənb(ə)ri/ *n* (the large raspberry-flavoured fruit of) a spring shrub (genus *Rubus*) of the rose family that was developed by crossing several varieties of blackberry and raspberry [Rudolph *Boysen* fl1923 US horticulturist + E *berry*]

**bozo** /'bohzoh/ *n, pl* **bozos** *NAm slang* a fellow, guy [origin unknown]

**'B-,picture** *n* a low-budget film, esp with stereotyped plot and characterization, usu shown as a supporting film

**bra** /brah/ *n* a woman's closely fitting undergarment with cups for supporting the breasts [short for *brassiere*]

**braai** /brie/ *vt or n*, *SAfr* (to) barbecue [short for *braaivleis*]

**braaivleis** /'brie‚flays/ *n*, *SAfr* BARBECUE 1,3 [Afrik, lit., grilled meat, fr *braai* to grill + *vleis* meat]

¹**brace** /brays/ *n*, *pl* **braces**, (*1*) **braces**, *after a number or other determiner* **brace 1** two of a kind; a pair ⟨*several ~ of quail*⟩ **2** something (eg a clasp) that connects or fastens **3** a crank-shaped instrument for turning a drilling bit **4a** a diagonal piece of structural material that serves to strengthen **b** a rope attached to the spar (YARD) from which a ship's sail is hung, that swings the yard horizontally to bring the sail into the right position to catch the wind **c** *pl* straps worn over the shoulders in order to hold up trousers **d** an appliance for supporting a weak back, leg, etc **e** a dental fitting worn to correct irregular teeth **5a** a punctuation mark { or } used to connect words or items to be considered together – called also BRACKET **b** (this mark connecting) two or more musical STAVES (sets of five lines on which music is written), the parts written on which are to be performed simultaneously **c** SQUARE BRACKET [ME, pair, clasp, fr MF, two arms, fr L *bracchia*, pl of *bracchium* arm, fr Gk *brachiōn*, fr compar of *brachys* short – more at BRIEF]

²**brace** *vt* **1a** to prepare for use by making taut **b** to prepare, steel ⟨*~ yourself for the shock*⟩ **2** to turn (the spar from which a sail is hung) by means of an attached rope (BRACE 4b) **3a** to provide or support with a brace **b** to make stronger; reinforce **4** to put or plant firmly, esp so as to resist impact, pressure, etc ⟨*~s her foot against the wall*⟩ **5** *archaic* to fasten tightly; bind

**brace up** *vb* to (cause to) have more courage, spirit, and cheerfulness

**bracelet** /'brayslit/ *n* **1** an ornamental band or chain worn round the wrist **2** *pl*, *slang* something (eg handcuffs) resembling a bracelet [ME, fr MF, dim. of *bras* arm, fr L *bracchium*]

¹**bracer** /'braysə/ *n* an arm or wrist protector, esp for use by an archer [ME, fr MF *braciere*, fr OF, fr *braz* arm, fr L *bracchium*]

²**bracer** *n* **1** one who or that which braces, binds, or makes firm **2** a drink (eg of an alcoholic beverage) taken as a stimulant

**brachi-** /bra(y)ki-/, **brachio-** *comb form* arm ⟨brachi*ate*⟩ ⟨brachio*pod*⟩ [L *brachi-* & NL *brachio-*, fr L *brachium*, *bracchium*]

**brachial** /'bra(y)ki·əl/ *adj* of or located in (a part like) an arm ⟨*a ~ artery*⟩

**brachiate** /'bra(y)ki·ət, -ayt/ *vi*, *zoology* to move by swinging from one hold to another by the arms – **brachiation** *n*

**brachiopod** /'bra(y)ki·ə‚pod/ *n* any of a phylum (Brachiopoda) of mostly extinct marine INVERTEBRATE animals with bivalve shells within which is a pair of arms bearing tentacles by which a current of water is made to bring microscopic food to the mouth – called also LAMPSHELL [deriv of L *brachium* + Gk *pod-*, *pous* foot – more at FOOT] – **brachiopod** *adj*

**brachiosaurus** /‚brakiə'sawrəs, ‚brayki-/ *n* any of a genus (*Brachiosaurus*) of huge plant-eating dinosaurs that were up to 30 metres (about 100 feet) long [NL, genus name, fr *brachi-* + Gk *sauros* lizard; fr its long forelegs]

**brachium** /'braykiəm, 'brakiəm/ *n*, *pl* **brachia** /-kiə/ *anatomy* **1** the upper part of the arm or forelimb from the shoulder to the elbow **2** a part of an INVERTEBRATE animal (eg a starfish) that corresponds to an arm [L *bracchium*, *brachium* arm] – **brachial** *adj*

**brachy-** /braki-, brayki-/ *comb form* short ⟨brachy*dactylous*⟩ [Gk, fr *brachys* – more at BRIEF]

**brachycephalic** /‚brakisi'falik/ *adj* having a relatively short or broad head – compare DOLICHOCEPHALIC, ORTHOCEPHALIC [NL *brachycephalus*, fr Gk *brachy-* + *kephalē* head – more at CEPHALIC] – **brachycephaly** *n*

**brachydactylous** /‚braki'daktiləs/ *adj* having abnormally short fingers or toes – **brachydactyly** *n*

**brachylogy** /bra'kiləji/ *n* conciseness or excessive conciseness of expression; *esp* the omission of a necessary word from a sentence [Gk *brachylogia*, fr *brachy-* + *-logia* -logy]

**brachypterous** /bra'kiptərəs/ *adj* having rudimentary or abnormally small wings ⟨*~ insects*⟩ [Gk *brachypteros*, fr *brachy-* + *pteron* wing – more at FEATHER]

**brachyuran** /‚braki'yooərən/ *n* any of a tribe or suborder (Brachyura of the class Crustacea) of INVERTEBRATE animals (eg the typical crabs) having the abdomen greatly reduced [deriv of Gk *brachy-* + *oura* tail – more at SQUIRREL] – **brachyuran** *adj*, **brachyurous** *adj*

**bracing** /'braysing/ *adj* refreshing, invigorating ⟨*a ~ breeze*⟩

**bracken** /'brakən/ *n* (a dense growth of) a common large coarse fern (*Pteridium aquilinum*), found esp on moorland, that is poisonous to grazing animals (eg sheep and horses) and is a serious pest in grasslands [ME *braken*, prob of Scand origin; akin to OSw *brækne* fern]

¹**bracket** /'brakit/ *n* **1** a projecting or overhanging (scroll-shaped) architectural part designed to support a vertical load or to strengthen an angle **2a** a shelf supported against a wall by props underneath **b** a fixture (eg for holding a lamp) projecting from a wall or column **3a** SQUARE BRACKET **b** ANGLE BRACKET **c** PARENTHESIS **3 d** BRACE 5a **4** (the distance between) a pair of shots fired usu in front of and beyond a target to aid in range-finding **5** any of a graded series of income groups ⟨*the upper income ~*⟩ [MF *braguette* codpiece, fr dim. of *brague* breeches, fr OProv *braga*, fr L *braca*, fr Gaulish *brāca*, of Gmc origin; akin to OHG *bruoh* breeches – more at BREECH]

²**bracket** *vt* **1** to place (as if) within brackets **2** to provide or fasten with brackets **3** to put in the same category; associate – usu + *together* **4a** to estimate the correct range by firing in front of and beyond (a target) **b** to establish a margin on either side of (eg an estimation)

**bracketed** /'brakitid/ *adj*, *of a serif of a printed letter* joined to the stroke by a curved line

**bracket fungus** *n* a BASIDIOMYCETE (type of fungus) that forms shelflike spore-bearing bodies (eg on tree trunks)

**brackish** /'brakish/ *adj* slightly salty ⟨*~ water*⟩ [D *brac* salty; akin to MLG *brac* salty] – **brackishness** *n*

**braconid** /'brakənid/ *n* any of a large family (Braconidae) of wasps which live as parasites on a wide range of insects [deriv of Gk *brachys* short]

**bract** /brakt/ *n* **1** a leaf which has a flower or flower stem growing from its AXIL (angle between leaf and stem) **2** a leaf borne on a flower stem; *esp* one growing just below and often enclosing a flower or flower cluster [NL *bractea*, fr L, thin metal plate] – **bracteal** *adj*, **bracteate** *adj*, **bracted** *adj*

**bracteole** /'braktiohl/ *n* a small or secondary bract, esp on a floral axis [NL *bracteola*, fr L, dim. of *bractea*] – **bracteolate** *adj*

**brad** /brad/ *n* a thin wedge-shaped nail having a slight projection at the top of one side instead of a head [ME, fr ON *broddr* spike; akin to OE *byrst* bristle – more at BRISTLE]

**bradawl** /'brad‚awl/ *n* AWL (piercing tool); *esp* one used by a woodworker

**bradycardia** /‚bradi'kahdi·ə/ *n* relatively slow heart action whether normal or associated with disease – compare TACHYCARDIA [NL, fr Gk *bradys* slow + NL *-cardia*]

**bradykinin** /‚bradi'kinin/ *n* a hormone that is a KININ, that is formed in injured tissue, that acts in the widening of the tiny blood vessels that link arteries to capillaries, and that is considered to play a part in inflammatory processes [Gk *bradys* slow]

**brae** /bray/ *n*, *chiefly Scot* a hillside, esp along a river [ME *bra*, fr ON *brā* eyelash; akin to OE *bregdan* to move quickly – more at BRAID]

¹**brag** /brag/ *n* **1** a boastful statement **2** boasting talk or manner **3** a very old card game from which poker was derived, and which in several modern forms is still popular [ME *brag* spirited, boastful; (3) fr the "brag" or challenge made by one player to another]

²**brag** *vb* **-gg-** to talk or assert boastfully *synonyms* see ²BOAST – **bragger** *n*

**braggadocio** /‚bragə'dochioh, -'dokioh/ *n*, *pl* **braggadocios 1** a braggart **2** empty boasting [*Braggadocchio*, personification of boasting in the poem *The Faerie Queene* by Edmund Spenser †1599 E poet]

**braggart** /'bragət/ *n* a loud arrogant boaster – **braggart** *adj*

**brahma** /'brahmə/ *n* (any of) an Asian breed of large domestic fowls with feathered legs [*Brahmaputra* river, India]

¹**Brahma** *n* **1** BRAHMAN 1b **2** the creator deity of the Hindu sacred trinity, the other members of which are Siva and Vishnu [Skt *brahman*]

²**Brahma** *n* BRAHMAN 2

**Brahman** /'brahmən/ *n* **1a** a Hindu of the highest caste traditionally assigned to the priesthood **b** the impersonal ground of all being in Hinduism **2** (any of) an Indian breed of humped cattle; ZEBU; *also* a large vigorous heat-resistant and tick-resistant animal developed in the USA by interbreeding Indian cattle [Skt *brāhmana*, lit., having to do with prayer, fr *brahman*, neut, prayer] – **Brahmanic** *adj*

# Bra
172

**Brahmanism** /'brahmə,niz(ə)m/ *n* orthodox Hinduism following the teachings of the VEDAS (ancient sacred writings), believing in several gods, and practising ancient sacrifices and family ceremonies

**Brahmin** /'brahmin/ *n* **1** (a) Brahman **2** *NAm* an intellectually and socially cultivated but aloof person – **Brahminism** *n*, **Brahminical** *adj*

¹**braid** /brayd/ *vt* **1** to ornament, esp with ribbon or braid **2** *chiefly NAm* to plait [ME *breyden*, lit., to move suddenly, fr OE *bregdan*; akin to OHG *brettan* to draw (a sword), Gk *phorkon* something white or wrinkled] – **braided** *adj*

²**braid** *n* **1** a narrow piece of fabric, esp a woven or plaited cord or ribbon used esp for trimming **2** *chiefly NAm* a length of plaited hair

¹**brail** /brayl/ *n* a rope fastened to the edge or end of a sail and used for hauling the sail up or in [ME *brayle*, fr AF *braiel*, fr OF, strap]

²**brail** *vt* to take in (e g a sail) by the brails

**braille** /brayl/ *n, often cap* a system of writing or printing for the blind that uses characters made up of raised dots [Louis *Braille* †1852 Fr teacher of the blind]

**braillewriter** /'brayl,rietə/ *n, often cap* a machine for writing in braille

¹**brain** /brayn/ *n* **1a** the portion of the CENTRAL NERVOUS SYSTEM of a VERTEBRATE animal that constitutes the organ of thought and nervous coordination, includes all the higher nerve centres receiving stimuli from the SENSE ORGANS and interpreting and correlating them to formulate the impulses that cause muscular movement, is made up of nerve cells (NEURONS) and supporting and nutritive structures, is enclosed within the skull, and is continuous with the SPINAL CORD **b** a nervous centre in INVERTEBRATE animals comparable in position and function to the brain of VERTEBRATE animals **2a**(1) an intellect, mind ⟨*has a good* ∼⟩ **a**(2) *pl* intellectual endowment; intelligence ⟨*she's definitely got* ∼s⟩ **b**(1) a very intelligent or intellectual person **b**(2) **brains** *pl but taking sing vb*, **brain** the chief planner of an organization or enterprise **3** an automatic device (e g a computer) that performs one or more of the functions of the human brain for control or computation [ME, fr OE *brægen*; akin to MLG *bregen* brain, Gk *brechmos* front part of the head] – **beat one's brains out** to try intently to resolve something difficult by thinking – **cudgel/rack one's brains** to make a great mental effort; think hard – **on the brain** as an obsession; continually in mind ⟨*I've got that tune* on the brain *again*⟩ – **pick somebody's brains** to get information or ideas from somebody more knowledgeable than oneself

²**brain** *vt, informal* **1** to kill by smashing the skull **2** to hit hard on the head

**brainchild** /-,chield/ *n* a product of one's creative imagination

**brain death** *n* the death of a human being determined by the assessment that his/her brain has irreversibly ceased to function – **brain dead** *adj*

**brain drain** *n* the loss of scientists, doctors, academics, and other highly trained or skilled people by emigration

**-brained** /-braynd/ *comb form* (*adj, n → adj*) having (such) a brain ⟨*featherbrained*⟩

**brain hormone** *n* a hormone that is secreted by specialized cells in the insect brain and that stimulates the PROTHORACIC GLANDS to secrete ECDYSONE (hormone that triggers moulting)

**brainish** /'braynish/ *adj, archaic* impetuous, hotheaded ⟨*and in this* ∼ *apprehension kills the unseen good old man* – Shak⟩

**brainless** /-lis/ *adj* devoid of intelligence; stupid – **brainlessly** *adv*, **brainlessness** *n*

**brainpan** /'brayn,pan/ *n* the skull

**brainpower** /-,powə/ *n* intellectual ability; intelligence

**brain stem** *n* the part of the brain that is composed of the MESENCEPHALON, PONS, and MEDULLA OBLONGATA, connects the SPINAL CORD with the forebrain and cerebrum, and controls many unconscious processes (e g the regulation of body temperature)

**brainstorm** /-,stawm/ *n* **1** a fit of insanity **2** *chiefly NAm* BRAIN WAVE 2

**brainstorming** /-,stawming/ *n, chiefly NAm* a problem-solving technique that involves the spontaneous contribution of ideas from all members of a group – **brainstorm** *vt*

**brains trust**, *NAm chiefly* **brain trust** *n taking sing or pl vb* a group of expert advisers assembled esp to answer questions of immediate or current interest

**brainteaser** /-,teezə/ *n* something (e g a mathematical puzzle) that demands mental effort and keenness for its solution

**brainwashing** /-,woshing/ *n* a systematic attempt to instil beliefs into somebody, often in place of beliefs already held [trans of Chin (Pek) *xǐ naǒ* (*hsi³ nao³*)] – **brainwash** *vt*, **brainwasher** *n*

**brain wave** *n* **1** rhythmic fluctuations of voltage between parts of the brain that vary with the state of arousal – compare ALPHA WAVE **2** a sudden bright idea

**brainy** /'brayni/ *adj, informal* intelligent, clever **synonyms** see INTELLIGENT – **braininess** *n*

**braise** /brayz/ *vt* to cook (e g meat) slowly by first sautéeing in hot fat and then simmering gently in very little liquid in a closed container [Fr *braiser*, fr *braise* live coals, fr OF *brese* – more at BRAZE]

¹**brake** /brayk/ *archaic past of* BREAK

²**brake** *n* **1** a device for arresting usu rotary motion, esp by friction **2** something that slows down or stops movement or activity ⟨*interest rates that act as a* ∼ *on expenditure*⟩ [ME, bridle, curb] – **brakeless** *adj*

³**brake** *vt* to slow or stop by a brake ∼ *vi* **1** to operate, manage, or apply a brake, esp on a vehicle **2** to become slowed by a brake

⁴**brake** *n* an area of rough or marshy land overgrown usu with one kind of plant [ME *-brake*] – **braky** *adj*

**brake horsepower** *n* the useful power of an engine or motor as calculated from the resistance to a brake or DYNAMOMETER (instrument for measuring power) applied to a power output

'**brake-,light** *n* a usu red light at the rear of a motor vehicle that is illuminated when the driver presses the brake pedal

**brakeman** /'braykmən/ *n* **1** the person in the rear in a bobsleigh team who operates the brake **2** *NAm* a goods or passenger train crew member who inspects the train and assists the guard

**brake van** *n, Br* GUARD'S VAN

**bramble** /'brambl/ *n* a rough prickly shrub, esp a blackberry [ME *brembel*, fr OE *brēmel*; akin to OE *brōm* broom] – **brambly** *adj*

**brambling** /'brambling/ *n* a brightly coloured African and Eurasian finch (*Fringilla montifringilla*) [prob fr *bramble* + -*ing*]

**Bramley** /'bramli/, **Bramley's seedling** *n* a large green variety of cooking apple [Matthew *Bramley fl*1850 E butcher & reputed first grower of the fruit]

**bran** /bran/ *n* the broken husk of cereal grain separated from the flour or meal by sifting [ME, fr OF]

¹**branch** /brahnch/ *n* **1** a natural division of a plant stem; *esp* a secondary shoot or stem (e g a bough) arising from a main stem or trunk (e g of a tree) **2a** a tributary to a stream or river **b** a side road or way **c** a slender projection (e g the tine of an antler) **d** a separate part of a mathematical curve ⟨*the two* ∼es *of the hyperbola*⟩ **e** a part of a computer program at which a choice is made to execute one of two or more alternative sequences of instructions **3a** a division of a family descending from a particular ancestor **b** an area of knowledge that may be considered apart from related areas ⟨*pathology is a* ∼ *of medicine*⟩ **c** a division or separate part of an organization ⟨*the store had opened three new* ∼es⟩ ⟨∼ *officer of the Union*⟩ **d** a language group less inclusive than a family ⟨*the Germanic* ∼ *of the Indo-European language family*⟩; *also* a single language (e g Greek) of analogous rank or importance – compare GROUP 3d [ME, fr OF *branche*, fr LL *branca* paw] – **branched** *adj*, **branchless** *adj*, **branchy** *adj*

²**branch** *vi* **1** to put forth branches **2** to spring out (e g from a main stem) **3** to be an outgrowth ⟨*poetry that* ∼ed *from religious prose*⟩ **4** to follow one of two or more branches (e g in a computer program)

**branch out** *vi* to extend activities ⟨*the business is* branching out *all over the country*⟩

**branchia** /'brangki-ə/ *n, pl* **branchiae** /-ki,ee/ ²GILL 1 [L (sing.), fr Gk, pl of *branchion* gill; akin to Gk *bronchos* trachea –more at CRAW] – **branchial** *adj*, **branchiate** *adj*

**branchiopod** /'brangki-ə,pod/ *n* any of a group (Branchiopoda of the class Crustacea) of aquatic INVERTEBRATE animals (e g a WATER FLEA) typically having a long body, a hard outer covering, and many pairs of leaflike limbs that are used for swimming, feeding, and breathing [deriv of Gk *branchia* gills + *pod-*, *pous* foot – more at FOOT] – **branchiopod** *adj*, **branchiopodan** *adj*, **branchiopodous** *adj*

**branchlet** /'brahnchlit/ *n* a small branch, usu coming at and forming the end of a larger branch

**branch line** *n* a minor railway line that joins a main line

**¹brand** /brand/ *n* **1** a charred piece of wood **2a** a mark made by burning with a hot iron to designate ownership (e g of cattle) **b** a mark formerly put on criminals with a hot iron **3a** a mark made with a stamp, stencil, etc to identify manufacture or quality **b** a class of goods identified by name as the product of a single firm or manufacturer **c** a characteristic or distinctive kind; a variety ⟨a *lively* ~ *of humour*⟩ **4** a tool used to produce a brand **5** *poetic* a sword [ME, torch, sword, fr OE; akin to OE *bernan* to burn]

**²brand** *vt* **1** to mark with a brand **2** to stigmatize **3** to impress indelibly ⟨~ *the lesson on his mind*⟩ – **brander** *n*

**branded** /'brandid/ *adj* labelled with the manufacturer's brand

**brandied** /'brandid/ *adj* preserved or flavoured with brandy

**brandish** /'brandish/ *vt* **1** to shake or wave (e g a weapon) menacingly **2** to exhibit in an ostentatious or aggressive manner [ME *braundisshen*, fr MF *brandiss-*, stem of *brandir*, fr OF, fr *brand* sword, of Gmc origin; akin to OE *brand*] – **brandish** *n*

**brand name** *n* TRADE NAME 1b

**,brand-'new** *adj* conspicuously new and unused

**brandy** /'brandi/ *n* **1** a spirit distilled from wine **2** a spirit distilled from fermented fruit juice ⟨*plum* ~⟩ **3** a spirit made by steeping fruit in alcohol ⟨*apricot* ~⟩ [short for *brandywine*, fr D *brandewijn*, fr MD *brantwijn*, fr *brant* burnt, distilled + *wijn* wine]

**brandy butter** *n* butter that has been sweetened and flavoured with brandy, usu served with sweet puddings – compare RUM BUTTER

**brandy glass** *n* BALLOON GLASS

**brandy snap** *n* a very thin cylindrical ginger biscuit sometimes flavoured with brandy

**bran mash** *n* a laxative feed for horses made by mixing bran with boiling water

**brant** /brant/ *n, pl* **brants**, *esp collectively* **brant** *n, chiefly NAm* BRENT GOOSE [origin unknown]

**¹brash** /brash/ *n* a mass of fragments (e g of ice) [obs *brash* to breach a wall, prob fr MF *breche* breach]

**²brash** *vt* to remove the lower branches of (a tree)

**³brash** *adj* **1** uninhibitedly energetic or demonstrative **2** aggressively self-assertive; impudent ⟨*a man* ~ *to the point of arrogance*⟩ [origin unknown] – **brashly** *adv*, **brashness** *n*

**brass** /brahs/ *n* **1** an alloy consisting essentially of copper and zinc in variable proportions **2a** *taking sing or pl vb* the brass instruments of an orchestra or band **b** a usu brass memorial tablet (e g set in the floor of a church) **c** bright metal fittings or utensils **d** used cartridge shells **3** *informal* brazen self-assurance **4** *taking sing or pl vb, informal* people in high-ranking positions (e g in a firm or industry) ⟨*the top* ~⟩ **5** *chiefly N Eng informal* money [ME *bras*, fr OE *bræs*; akin to MLG *bras* metal; (4) fr *brass hat*] – **brass** *adj*

**brassage** /'brasij (*Fr* brasaʒ)/ *n* a charge made by a mint for coining money [Fr, act of stirring, coining money, fr *brasser* to stir, fr OF *bracier* to brew]

**brassard** /'brasahd/ *n* a piece of armour for protecting the arm [Fr, fr MF *brassal*, fr OIt *bracciale*, fr *braccio* arm, fr L *bracchium* – more at BRACE]

**brass band** *n* a band consisting chiefly or solely of brass and percussion instruments

**'brass-,collar** *adj, NAm* invariably supporting the party line ⟨~ *Democrats*⟩

**brasserie** /'bras(ə)ri/ *n* a restaurant that serves beer and esp is open to sell food outside normal restaurant hours [Fr, fr MF *brasser* to brew, fr OF *bracier*, fr L *braces* spelt]

**brass farthing** *n* a trivial amount; PENNY 3

**brass hat** *n, informal* a high-ranking military officer [fr the gilt insignia on an officer's cap]

**brassica** /'brasikə/ *n* any of a large genus (*Brassica*) of temperate-zone plants of the mustard family that includes many important vegetables and crop plants (e g cabbage, turnip, mustard, and rape) [NL, genus name, fr L, cabbage]

**brassie, brassey** /'brasi, 'brahsi/ *n* a golf club that has a wooden head with a metal sole plate and is used esp for long shots from the FAIRWAY (area of mown grass between tee and green) – no longer in vogue [*brass* + *-ie, -ey*]

**brassiere** /'brazi-ə/ *n, formal* a bra [obs Fr *brassière* bodice, fr OF *braciere* ¹ bracer]

**brass instrument** *n* any of a group of wind instruments (e g a trombone, trumpet, or tuba) with a long usu curved cylindrical or conical metal tube, a mouthpiece against which the player's lips vibrate, and usu valves or a slide for producing all the notes within the instrument's range

**brass knuckles** *n taking sing or pl vb, NAm* a knuckle-duster

**brass off** *vt, Br informal* to cause to be fed up; make disgruntled

**brass tacks** *n pl* details of immediate practical importance – usu in *get down to brass tacks*

**brassy** /'brahsi/ *adj* **1** shamelessly bold; brazen **2** resembling brass, esp in colour **3** resembling the sound of a brass instrument – **brassily** *adv*, **brassiness** *n*

**brat** /brat/ *n, informal* an (ill-mannered or annoying) child [perh fr E dial. *brat* ragamuffin] – **brattish** *adj*, **bratty** *adj*, **brattiness** *n*

**brattice** /'bratis/ *n* an esp temporary partition of planks or cloth used to control ventilation in mine workings [ME *bretais*, *bretasce* parapet, fr OF *bretesche*, fr ML *breteschia*] – **brattice** *vt*

**bratwurst** /'braht,vooəst (*Ger* bra:tvʊəst)/ *n* a fresh usu pork sausage for frying [Ger, fr OHG *brātwurst*, fr *brāt* meat without waste + *wurst* sausage]

**bravado** /brə'vahdoh/ *n, pl* **bravadoes**, **bravados** **1** (a display of) blustering swaggering conduct **2** a pretence of bravery; an attempt to appear brave [MF *bravade* & OSp *bravata*, fr OIt *bravata*, fr *bravare* to challenge, show off, fr *bravo*]

**¹brave** /brayv/ *adj* **1** courageous, fearless **2** making a fine show; colourful ⟨~ *banners flying in the wind*⟩ ⟨*the first* ~ *daffodils of spring*⟩ **3** excellent, splendid ⟨*the business collapsed despite a* ~ *start*⟩ ⟨*oh* ~ *new world that hath such people in it* – Shak⟩ [MF, fr OIt & OSp *bravo* courageous, wild, fr L *barbarus* barbarous] – **bravely** *adv*

**synonyms** People or actions displaying firmness in the face of danger are **brave**. **Courageous** expresses the same ideas with some emphasis on mental or moral strength to confront difficulty ⟨*her* **courageous** *struggle against her disability*⟩. **Valiant** and **gallant** often apply to lost causes ⟨*a* **valiant**/**gallant** *attempt to rescue the survivors*⟩ with **gallant** carrying an extra suggestion of noble and dashing behaviour. **Valorous** is often more positive, suggesting success in the enterprise undertaken. **Intrepid** and **dauntless** emphasize the resolute absence of fear, with **dauntless** particularly suggesting the defying of intimidation. **Heroic** and the less formal **plucky** suggest spirited daring in action rather than passive resistance.

**²brave** *vt* to face or endure with courage ⟨*braving the winter gales*⟩ – **braver** *n*

**brave out** *vt* to react to (an accusation, charge, difficulty, etc) by feigning indifference or ignorance

**³brave** *n* **1** a N American Indian warrior **2** *archaic* a bully, assassin **3** *archaic* bravado

**bravery** /'brayv(ə)ri/ *n* **1** showy display ⟨*the chivalry of Europe in all its pomp and* ~⟩ **2** courage, valour

**¹bravo** /'brahvoh/ *n, pl* **bravos**, **bravoes** a villain, desperado; *esp* a hired assassin [It, fr *bravo*, adj]

**²bravo** /brah'voh/ *n, pl* **bravos** a shout of approval – often used interjectionally in applauding a performance [Fr, fr It, fr *bravo*, adj]

**³bravo** *vt* **bravoing**; **bravoed** to applaud by shouts of *bravo*

**Bravo** /'brah,voh/ – a communications code word for the letter *b*

**bravura** /brə'v(y)ooərə/ *n* **1** a florid brilliant style **2** a musical passage requiring exceptional agility and technical skill in execution **3** a show of daring or brilliance [It, lit., bravery, fr *bravare*]

**braw** /braw/ *adj, chiefly Scot* **1** good, fine **2** well dressed [modif of MF *brave*]

**¹brawl** /brawl/ *vi* **1** to quarrel or fight noisily **2** to make a loud confused bubbling sound ⟨*the river* ~*ing by*⟩ [ME *brawlen*] – **brawler** *n*

**²brawl** *n* **1** a noisy quarrel or fight **2** a brawling sound

**brawn** /brawn/ *n* **1a** strong muscles **b** muscular strength **2** (a meat loaf made of) pork trimmings, esp the meat from a pig's head, boiled, chopped and pressed into a mould ⟨*a hen, two cold fowls, and a large pink* ~ *came out of the hamper*⟩ [ME, fr MF *braon* muscle, of Gmc origin; akin to OE *brǣd* flesh]

**brawny** /'brawni/ *adj* **1** muscular, strong **2** *medicine, of body tissue* hard and swollen – **brawnily** *adv*, **brawniness** *n*

**¹bray** /bray/ *vi* to utter the loud harsh cry characteristic of a donkey ~ *vt* to utter or play loudly, harshly, or discordantly ⟨*transistors* ~*ing music all night long*⟩ [ME *brayen*, fr OF *braire* to cry, fr (assumed) VL *bragere*, of Celt origin; akin to MIr *braigid* he breaks wind; akin to L *frangere* to break – more at BREAK] – **bray** *n*

**²bray** *vt* **1** to crush or grind fine ⟨~ *seeds in a mortar*⟩ **2** to spread thinly ⟨~ *printing ink*⟩ [ME *brayen*, fr MF *broiier*, of Gmc origin; akin to OHG *brehhan* to break – more at BREAK]

**brayer** /'brayə/ *n* a printer's hand-inking roller

¹**braze** /brayz/ *vt, archaic* to harden [fr *brass*, by analogy to glass : *glaze*]

²**braze** *vt* to solder with a nonferrous alloy (e g of brass and silver) that melts on contact with the heated metals being joined [prob fr Fr *braser*, fr OF, to burn, fr *brese* live coals] – **brazer** *n*

¹**brazen** /'brayz(ə)n/ *adj* **1** made of brass **2a** sounding harsh and loud like struck brass **b** of the colour of polished brass **3** contemptuously bold; *broadly* outrageous ⟨*well, of all the ~ cheek!*⟩ [ME *brasen*, fr OE *bræsen*, fr *bræs* brass] – **brazenly** *adv*, **brazenness** *n*

²**brazen** *vt* to face with defiance or impudence – chiefly in *brazen it out*

'**brazen-,faced** *adj* insolently disrespectful; BRAZEN 3

¹**brazier** /'brayzi·ə, 'brayzhə/ *n* someone who works in brass [ME *brasier*, fr *bras* brass]

²**brazier** *n* a receptacle or stand for holding burning coals [Fr *brasier*, fr OF, fire of hot coals, fr *brese*]

**Brazil nut** /brə'zil/ *n* a tall S American tree (*Bertholletia excelsa* of the family Lecythidaceae) that bears large globular capsules each containing several closely packed roughly triangular oily edible nuts; *also* the nut of this tree [*Brazil*, country in S America (fr Sp *Brasil*, fr *brasil* brazilwood)]

**brazilwood** /brə'zil,wood/ *n* (the red or purple dye obtained from) the heavy wood of any of various tropical trees (esp genus *Caesalpinia*) of the pea family [Sp *brasil*, fr *brasa* live coals; fr its red colour]

¹**breach** /breech/ *n* **1** an infraction or violation (e g of a law, obligation, tie, or standard) ⟨~ *of contract*⟩ **2a** a broken, ruptured, or torn condition or area ⟨*a ~ in the canal bank*⟩ **b** a gap (e g in a wall) made by battering **3a** a break in accustomed friendly relations; a rift **b** a temporary gap in continuity; a hiatus **4** a leap, esp one made out of the water by a whale △ **breech** [ME *breche*, fr OE *bryce*; akin to OE *brecan* to break]

²**breach** *vt* **1** to make a breach in ⟨~ *the city walls*⟩ **2** to break, violate ⟨~ *an agreement*⟩ ~ *vi* to leap out of water ⟨*a school of whales* ~ing⟩

**breach of promise** *n* violation of a promise, esp to marry

**breach of the peace** *n* an instance of disorderly conduct (e g swearing in public, fighting, or doing something that may provoke retaliation) that disturbs the public peace

**breach of trust** *n* violation by a trustee of the terms of a trust; *broadly* any misuse of another's property by one who is legally responsible for it

¹**bread** /bred/ *n* **1** a food made from a baked dough consisting of flour or meal, water, and usu a raising agent, esp yeast **2** food, sustenance ⟨*our daily ~*⟩ **3a** livelihood ⟨*earns his ~ in the fleshpots of Fleet Street*⟩ **b** *informal* money [ME *breed*, fr OE *brēad*; akin to OHG *brōt* bread, OE *brēowan* to brew] – **break bread 1** to take a meal *with* **2** to celebrate or participate in Holy Communion

²**bread** *vt* to cover with breadcrumbs ⟨*a ~ed pork chop*⟩

,**bread-and-'butter** *adj* **1a** as basic or fundamental as the earning of one's livelihood ⟨*low wages, inadequate housing, and other ~ issues*⟩ **b** routine, day-to-day ⟨*the ~ repertoire of an orchestra*⟩ **2** sent or given as thanks for hospitality ⟨*a ~ letter*⟩

**bread and butter** *n* a means of sustenance or livelihood

**bread and circuses** *n pl* entertainment provided at public expense; *also* a palliative offered to avert potential discontent [trans of L *panis et circenses* (the only concerns of the Roman populace, according to Juvenal †*ab*140 Roman satiric poet)]

**breadbasket** /-,bahskit/ *n* **1** a basket for holding or serving bread **2** *informal* the stomach

**breadboard** /'bred,bawd/ *n* **1** a board on which bread is cut or dough is kneaded **2** a board on which electric or electronic components may be arranged and interconnected quickly and usu temporarily

¹**breadcrumb** /-,krum/ *n* a small fragment of bread

²**breadcrumb** *vt* ²BREAD

**breadfruit** /-,frooht/ *n* the large starchy fruit of a tropical tree (*Artocarpus incisa*) of the fig family, that has a white pulp of a breadlike texture which is often eaten roasted or baked; *also* the tree that bears this fruit

**breadline** /-,lien/ *n* **1** *Br* the level of income required for subsistence; the poverty level **2** *chiefly NAm* a line of people waiting to receive food given in charity

**bread sauce** *n* a savoury sauce of milk thickened with breadcrumbs and served esp with poultry

**breadth** /bret·th, bredth/ *n* **1** distance from side to side; width, broadness **2a** something of full width ⟨*a ~ of cloth*⟩ **b** a wide expanse ⟨~s *of grass*⟩ **3a** extent, scope ⟨*the remarkable ~ of his learning*⟩ **b** liberality of views or taste [obs *brede* breadth (fr ME, fr OE *brǣdu*, fr *brād* broad) + *-th* (as in *length*)]

**breadthways** /-,wayz, -wiz/, **breadthwise** /-wiez/ *adv or adj* in the direction of the breadth ⟨*a course of bricks laid ~*⟩

**breadwinner** /-,winə/ *n* the person in a family whose wages are the main source of the family's income – **breadwinning** *n*

¹**break** /brayk/ *vb* **broke** /brohk/; **broken** /'brohkən/ *vt* **1a** to separate into parts with suddenness or violence **b** to fracture ⟨~ *an arm*⟩ **c** to rupture ⟨~ *the skin*⟩ **2** to (deliberately) fail to observe; violate, transgress ⟨~ *the law*⟩ ⟨~ *the speed limit*⟩ **3a** to burst and force a way through ⟨~ing *the obstacles put in his path*⟩ ⟨*the river broke its banks and flooded the town*⟩ **b** to escape (by force) from ⟨*he broke jail*⟩ **4** to make or effect by cutting or forcing through ⟨~ *a trail through the woods*⟩ **5** to make ineffective as a binding or restraining force ⟨~ing *the bonds of ignorance and superstition*⟩ **6** to disrupt the order or compactness of ⟨~ *ranks*⟩ **7a** to defeat utterly; destroy **b** to crush the spirit of ⟨*long years of imprisonment could not ~ him*⟩ **c** to train (an animal, esp a horse) to adjust to the service or convenience of human beings; accustom (a horse, ox, etc) to perform some particular task or to tolerate some piece of equipment **d** to exhaust in health, strength, or capacity **8a** to ruin financially **b** to reduce in rank; cashier **9a** to reduce the force or intensity of ⟨*the bushes will ~ his fall*⟩ **b** to cause failure and discontinuance of (a strike) by measures outside bargaining processes (e g by bringing in ununionized labour) **10a** to exceed, surpass ⟨~ *a speed record*⟩ **b(1)** to score less than (a specified total) ⟨*golfer trying to ~ 90*⟩ **b(2)** to run a race in less than (a specified time) ⟨~ *4 minutes for the mile*⟩ **11** to ruin the prospects of ⟨*could make or ~ her career*⟩ **12** to demonstrate the falsity of ⟨~ *an alibi*⟩ ⟨*no amount of questioning could ~ his story*⟩ **13a** to stop or bring to an end suddenly; halt ⟨~ *a deadlock*⟩ ⟨*don't ~ my train of thought*⟩ **b** to interrupt, suspend ⟨~ *the silence with a cry*⟩ **c** to open and bring about suspension of operation ⟨~ *an electric circuit*⟩ **d** to destroy unity or completeness of ⟨*they must be bought together; I don't want to ~ the collection*⟩ **e** to destroy the uniformity of ⟨*a dormer ~s the line of the roof*⟩ **14** to cause to discontinue a habit ⟨*tried to ~ him of smoking*⟩ **15** to make known; tell ⟨~ *the bad news gently*⟩ **16** to solve or discover the principles of (a code or cipher system); crack **17** to split into smaller units, parts, or processes; divide ⟨~ *a £10 note*⟩ – often + *up* or *down* **18** to open the operating mechanism of (a gun) ~ *vi* **1a** to escape with sudden forceful effort – often + *out* or *away* ⟨*broke out of jail*⟩ ⟨*broke away from his captors*⟩ **b** of the liquid surrounding the unborn offspring to be released when the surrounding membrane (AMNION) ruptures ⟨*her waters broke*⟩ **2a** to come into being; become evident ⟨*day was ~ing*⟩ ⟨*the storm broke just as it was getting dark*⟩ **b** to show signs of emotion, esp with abruptness ⟨~ing *into tears*⟩ ⟨*his face ~s out into a smile*⟩ **c** of a news story to be released (e g by an official spokesman); happen ⟨*of a fish, esp a trout or salmon*⟩ to emerge through the surface of the water **3** to effect a penetration ⟨~ *through enemy lines*⟩ **4** to take a different course; depart ⟨~ *away from tradition*⟩ **5** to make a sudden dash ⟨~ *for cover*⟩ **6** to separate after a clinch in boxing **7** to come apart or split into pieces; burst, shatter **8** *of a wave* to curl over and disintegrate in surf or foam (e g against a rock or on a beach) **9** *of weather* to change, esp suddenly after a settled period **10** to give way in disorderly retreat **11a** to fail in health, strength, vitality, or control ⟨*may ~ under questioning*⟩ **b** to become inoperative because of damage, wear, or strain ⟨*the part may ~ if used outside the recommended temperature range*⟩ **12** to end a relationship, connection, accord, or agreement *with* **13** *of a ball, esp bowled in cricket* to change direction of forward travel (e g by moving towards or away from the batsman) on bouncing **14a** *of the voice or the tone of a wind instrument* to alter sharply in tone, pitch, or intensity; shift abruptly from one register to another **b** *of a voice* to deepen slowly at puberty **15** *of a horse* to fail to keep moving in a desired manner (e g by reverting to trotting when it should be at a canter) **16** to interrupt one's activity or occupation for a brief period ⟨~ *for lunch*⟩ **17** to make the opening shot of a game of snooker, billiards, or pool – often + *off* **18a** to fold, bend, lift, or come apart at a seam, groove,

or joint **b** *of cream* to separate during churning into liquid and fat **19** *chiefly NAm* to happen, develop ⟨*for the team to succeed, everything has to* ∼ *right*⟩ – see also **break one's** BACK/**the** BACK **of/the** BANK, **break** BREAD/CAMP/COVER/EVEN/(**new**) GROUND, **break one's/somebody's** HEART, **break one's** DUCK/**the** ICE/**a** LEG, **break** LOOSE, MAKE **or break, break somebody's** SERVICE, **break** STEP/WIND [ME *breken,* fr OE *brecan;* akin to OHG *brehhan* to break, L *frangere*]

**break down** *vt* **1a** to cause to fall or collapse by breaking or shattering **b** to make ineffective ⟨break down *legal barriers*⟩ **2a** to divide into parts or categories **b** to separate (e g a chemical compound) into simpler substances; decompose **c** to take apart, esp for storage or shipment and for later reassembly ∼ *vi* **1a** to become inoperative through breakage or wear **b** to become inapplicable or ineffective; deteriorate ⟨*relations began to* break down⟩ **2a** to be susceptible to analysis or subdivision ⟨*the outline* breaks down *into three parts*⟩ **b** to undergo decomposition **c** to lose one's composure completely ⟨broke down *in tears*⟩ – see also BREAKDOWN *usage* see BREAKDOWN

**break in** *vi* **1** to enter a house or building by force **2a** to interrupt a conversation **b** to intrude ⟨break in *on his privacy*⟩ ∼ *vt* **1** to accustom to a certain activity ⟨break in *a new reporter*⟩; *esp* to train (a horse) to carry a rider **2** to use or wear (a new article) so as to get rid of undesirable qualities (e g stiffness) – see also BREAK-IN

**break into** *vt* **1** to begin (as if) with a sudden throwing off of restraint ⟨*the horse* breaks into *a gallop*⟩ **2** to make entry or entrance into ⟨*trying to* break into *show business*⟩ **3** to interrupt ⟨*kept* breaking into *the conversation*⟩

**break off** *vi* **1** to become detached; separate **2** to stop abruptly ⟨break off *in the middle of a sentence*⟩ to discontinue, sever ⟨break off *diplomatic relations*⟩

**break out** *vi* **1** to become affected with a skin complaint (e g a rash) **2** to develop or emerge with suddenness and force ⟨*a riot* broke out⟩ **3** to escape *from* ∼ *vt* **1a** to take from stowage on board ship ready for use ⟨break out *the mainsail*⟩ **b** to make ready for action or use ⟨break out *the tents and make camp*⟩ **c** to produce for consumption ⟨break out *another bottle*⟩ **2** to unfurl (a flag) at the mast ⟨break out *the signal at my order*⟩ – see also BREAKOUT

**break up** *vt* **1** to disrupt; *esp* to disrupt the continuity or flow of ⟨*too many footnotes can* break up *a text*⟩ **2** to decompose ⟨break up *a chemical*⟩ **3** to end, close, or destroy as if by breaking ⟨*it* broke up *their marriage*⟩ **4a** to break into pieces (e g for salvage); scrap **b** to crumble ⟨break up *soil around growing plants*⟩ **5** to cause anguish to; distress ⟨*his wife's death really* broke *him* up⟩ **6** *chiefly NAm informal* to cause to laugh heartily ⟨*that joke* breaks *me* up⟩ ∼ *vi* **1a** to come to an end ⟨*the partnership* broke up⟩ **b** to end a love affair or marriage; separate ⟨*John and Mary have* broken up⟩ **2** to lose morale, composure, or resolution ⟨*he is likely to* break up *under attack*⟩; *also* to give way to (helpless) laughter ⟨*he* broke up *completely and dissolved into a paroxysm of laughter*⟩ **3** *Br, of a school* to disband for the holidays – see also BREAKUP

**[2]break** *n* **1a** an act or action of breaking **b** the opening shot in a game of snooker, billiards, or pool **2a** a condition produced (as if) by breaking; a gap ⟨*a* ∼ *in the clouds*⟩ **b** a discontinuation of previously good relations **c** a gap in an otherwise continuous electric circuit **3** the action or act of breaking in, out, or forth ⟨*a jail* ∼⟩ **4** a dash, rush ⟨*make a* ∼ *for it*⟩ **5** the act of separating after a clinch in boxing **6** a discontinuity in space or time: e g **6a** an abrupt or noteworthy departure from tradition in manners, morals, artistic production, etc **b** an abrupt or noteworthy change or interruption in a continuous process or trend ⟨*it makes a* ∼⟩ **c** a respite from work or duty; *specif, Br* a daily pause for play and refreshment at school ⟨*played rounders during* ∼⟩ **d** a planned interruption in a radio or television programme ⟨*a* ∼ *for the commercials*⟩ **7a** the change in direction of forward travel of a cricket ball on bouncing, usu resulting from spin imparted by the bowler; *also* the deviation of a pitched baseball from a straight line **b** a slow ball bowled in cricket that moves in a specified direction on bouncing ⟨*an off* ∼⟩ **8** failure of a horse to continue to move in a required manner **9a** the action or an instance of breaking an opponent's service at tennis **b** a sequence of successful shots or strokes; *also* a score thus made ⟨*a* ∼ *of 86 in snooker*⟩ **10** a marked change in the quality of the sound of a voice or musical instrument **11** a place, situ-

ation, or time at which a break occurs: e g **11a** the point where one musical register changes to another **b** a short ornamental passage between phrases in jazz **c** the place at which a word is divided, esp at the end of a line of print or writing **12a** a stroke of (good) luck ⟨*a bad* ∼⟩ **b** an opportunity, chance ⟨*give me a* ∼⟩ **13** an act of breaking away ahead of the main body of riders in a bicycle road race; *also* the group of riders who have broken away in this manner ⟨*the eight-man* ∼ – *Cycling*⟩ *synonyms* see [1]HOLIDAY

**breakable** /'braykəbl/ *n or adj* (something) capable of being broken

**breakage** /'braykij/ *n* **1a** the action of breaking **b** *usu pl* something that has been broken **2** allowance for things broken (e g in transit)

**[1]breakaway** /'braykə,way/ *n* **1a** one who or that which breaks away **b** an act or instance of breaking away (e g from a group or tradition); a secession, withdrawal **c** BREAK 13 **2** an object (e g part of a stage set) made to shatter or collapse under pressure or impact

**[2]breakaway** *adj* **1** favouring independence from an affiliation; seceding, withdrawing ⟨*a* ∼ *faction formed a new party*⟩ **2** made to break, shatter, or bend easily ⟨∼ *signs for improved road safety*⟩

**breakbone fever** /'brayk,bohn/ *n* DENGUE (infectious virus disease)

**breakdown** /-,down/ *n* the action or result of breaking down: e g **a** a failure to function **b** a physical, mental, or nervous collapse **c** failure to progress or have effect; a collapse ⟨*a* ∼ *of negotiations*⟩ **d** the process of decomposing ⟨∼ *of food during digestion*⟩ **e** a division into categories; a classification **f** a whole analysed into parts; *specif* a financial account in which the transactions are recorded under various categories **g** a failure of insulation; *esp* a sudden ability of an insulator to conduct electricity

*usage* The use of **breakdown** to mean "classification" and of **break down** to mean "classify" should be avoided where there is risk of confusion with the more literal senses, as in ⟨*demanded a complete* **breakdown** *of our exports*⟩ or ⟨*statistics of the adult population* **broken down** *by sex*⟩.

**breakdown lorry** *n* a lorry fitted with equipment suitable for repairing or towing motor vehicles which have broken down

**[1]breaker** /'braykə/ *n* **1** one who or that which breaks **2** a wave breaking into foam (e g against the shore) **3** a user of CITIZENS' BAND radio

**[2]breaker** *n* a small water cask [by folk etymology fr Sp *barrica*]

**break-'even** *adj* of or being the point at which profits equal losses ⟨*the* ∼ *point in a business venture*⟩

**breakfall** /'brayk,fawl/ *n* a potentially injurious fall (e g in judo) which is cushioned by beating an arm or leg against the surface onto which one falls

**breakfast** /'brekfəst/ *n* **1** the first meal of the day, esp when taken in the morning; *also* the food prepared for a breakfast **2** WEDDING BREAKFAST [ME *brekfast,* fr *breken* to break + [4]*fast*] – breakfast *vb,* breakfaster *n*

**breakfront** /'brayk,frunt/ *n or adj* (a piece of furniture) having a centre section that projects beyond the flanking end sections ⟨*a* ∼ *sideboard*⟩

**'break-,in** *n* an entry (e g to a building) made by force and usu for criminal purposes

**breaking point** /'brayking/ *n* **1** the point at which a person or thing gives way under stress **2** the point at which a situation becomes critical

**breakneck** /-,nek/ *adj* dangerous, esp because of excessive speed ⟨*her* ∼ *driving scares me stiff*⟩

**breakout** /-,owt/ *n* a violent or forceful break from a restraining condition or situation (e g prison or military encirclement)

**breakpoint** /'brayk,poynt/ *n* a point (e g in a computer program) at which an interruption can be made

**breakthrough** /-,throoh/ *n* **1** an act or point of breaking through an obstruction **2** an offensive thrust that penetrates and goes beyond enemy defensive lines **3** a sudden advance, esp in knowledge or technique ⟨*a* ∼ *in the treatment of cancer*⟩

**breakup** /-,up/ *n* **1** dissolution, disruption ⟨*the* ∼ *of a marriage*⟩ **2** a division into smaller units ⟨*the* ∼ *of the large estates*⟩ **3** *chiefly Can* the spring thaw, esp when ice on rivers and lakes breaks up

**breakwater** /-,wawtə/ *n* an offshore structure (e g a wall or line of piles driven into the shore) used to protect a harbour or beach from the force of waves

**¹bream** /breem/ *n, pl* **bream,** *esp for different varieties* **breams** 1 (any of various fishes related to) a silvery European freshwater fish (*Abramis brama*) that is related to the carp and has a body that is flattened from side to side 2 SEA BREAM (any of various sea fishes somewhat like the freshwater bream) [ME *breme,* fr MF, of Gmc origin; akin to OHG *brahsima* bream, *brettan* to draw (a sword) – more at BRAID]

**²bream** *vt* to clean (the tarred bottom of a wooden ship) by heating and scraping [prob fr D *brem* furze; fr the use of burning furze in the process]

**¹breast** /brest/ *n* **1a** either of two rounded protuberant organs consisting mainly of milk-producing glands that are situated on the front of the chest in mature human females and some other mammals (eg higher apes); *broadly* a separate milk-producing gland – compare UDDER **b** either of the two corresponding usu rudimentary and nonfunctional MAMMARY GLANDS of the human male and immature human female 2 the front or under part of the body between the neck and the abdomen; the front of the chest ⟨*a bird with an orange* ~⟩; *also* a cut of meat taken from this part of the body of a lamb, calf, chicken, etc 3 something (eg a swelling or curve) reminiscent of a breast ⟨*as we came over the* ~ *of the hill an astonishing sight met our eyes*⟩ 4 *formal* the seat of emotion and thought; the bosom ⟨*caused little concern in official* ~s⟩ [ME *brest,* fr OE *brēost;* akin to OHG *brust* breast, Russ *bryukho* belly]

**²breast** *vt* 1 to contend with resolutely, confront ⟨~ *the rush-hour traffic*⟩ **2a** to thrust the chest against ⟨*the sprinter* ~ed *the tape*⟩ **b** to meet or lean against with the breast or front ⟨*a ship* ~ing *the waves*⟩ 3 *chiefly Br* to climb, ascend

**'breast-,beating** *n* an ostentatious and noisy protestation of emotion

**breastbone** /-,bohn/ *n* STERNUM (central bone in the chest to which the ribs are joined)

**'breast-,feed** *vt* to feed (a baby) from a mother's breast rather than from a bottle

**breastplate** /-,playt/ *n* 1 a metal plate worn as defensive armour for the chest 2 a vestment covering the chest and bearing 12 precious stones symbolizing the tribes of Israel, worn in ancient times by a Jewish high priest at special ceremonies 3 a strap or straps which attach to the sides of a saddle across the horse's chest and keep the saddle from slipping backwards 4 PLASTRON 2 (underpart of the shell of a tortoise or turtle)

**breaststroke** /-,strohk/ *n* a swimming stroke in which the swimmer lies chest downwards in the water and extends the arms in front of his/her head while drawing the knees forwards and outwards and then sweeps the arms back with palms out while kicking outwards and backwards – **breaststroker** *n*

**breastsummer** /'bres(t)səmə/ *n* BRESSUMER (supporting beam set across an opening)

**'breast-,wheel** *n* a waterwheel to which the water is admitted on the same level as the wheel's axis

**breastwork** /-,wuhk/ *n* a temporary fortification, usu consisting of a low parapet

**breath** /breth/ *n* **1a** a fragrance, odour ⟨*the* ~ *of flowers*⟩ ⟨*a* ~ *of summer*⟩ **b** a slight indication; suggestion ⟨*the faintest* ~ *of scandal*⟩ **2a** the faculty of breathing ⟨*recovering his* ~ *after the race*⟩ **b** an act of breathing ⟨*fought to his last* ~⟩ 3 a slight movement of air 4 air inhaled and exhaled in breathing ⟨*bad* ~⟩ 5 spirit, animation ⟨*the heady* ~ *of a new age*⟩ 6 breathing out of air with the GLOTTIS (organ containing the vocal cords) wide open (eg in the formation of /f/ and /s/ sounds) [ME *breth,* fr OE *brǣth;* akin to OHG *brādam* breath, OE *beorma* yeast – more at BARM] – **catch one's breath** 1 to rest long enough to restore normal breathing 2 to stop breathing briefly, usu under the influence of strong emotion – **out of breath** breathing heavily (eg from strenuous exercise); unable to speak as a result of exertion – **take somebody's breath away** to astonish, surprise, or astound somebody ⟨*a performance that took the audience's breath away*⟩ – **under one's breath** in a whisper – **waste one's breath** to accomplish nothing by speaking – **with bated breath** anxiously, worriedly

**breathable** /'breedhəbl/ *adj* 1 suitable for breathing ⟨~ *air*⟩ 2 allowing air to pass through; porous ⟨*a* ~ *synthetic fabric*⟩ – **breathability** *n*

**breathalyse** *also* **breathalyze** /'bretha,liez/ *vt* to subject (a person) to testing by a breathalyser [back-formation fr *breathalyser*]

**breathalyser** *also* **breathalyzer** /-,liezə/ *n* a device used to measure the alcohol content of breath; *specif* one used to give an indication of the alcohol content in the blood of a motorist and typically consisting of a plastic bag into which the subject blows through alcohol-sensitive crystals which change colour if more than a certain level of alcohol is passed through them [*breath* + an*alyse* + ²*-er*]

**breathe** /breedh/ *vi* **1a** to draw air into and expel it from the lungs; respire; *also* to take in oxygen and give out carbon dioxide through natural processes that resemble or are analogous to breathing ⟨*fish cannot* ~ *out of water*⟩ **b** to inhale and exhale freely ⟨*the doctor listened to his* breathing⟩ 2 to live 3 to pause and rest before continuing 4 *of a wind* to blow softly 5 *of an internal-combustion engine* to use air to support combustion 6 *of wine* to be exposed to the beneficial effects of air after being kept in an airtight container 7 *obs* to emit a fragrance or aura ~ *vt* **1a** to send out by exhaling ⟨~d *whisky and pickled onions all over the other guests*⟩ – often + *out* **b** to instil (as if) by breathing ⟨~ *new life into the movement*⟩ **2a** to utter, express ⟨*don't* ~ *a word of it to anyone*⟩ **b** to make manifest; display ⟨*the novel* ~s *despair*⟩ 3 to allow (eg a horse) to rest after exertion 4 to take in in breathing; inhale ⟨~ *the scent of pines*⟩ [ME *brethen,* fr *breth*] – **breathe easily/freely** to enjoy relief (eg from pressure or danger) – see also **breathe down somebody's** NECK

**breathed** /breedhd/ *adj, linguistics* VOICELESS 2 (not involving vibration of the vocal cords)

**breather** /'breedhə/ *n* 1 one who or that which breathes 2 a small vent in an otherwise airtight enclosure (eg a crankcase) 3 *informal* a break in activity for rest or relief

**breathing** /'breedhing/ *n* either of the marks ' and ' used in writing Greek to indicate ASPIRATION (audible release of air accompanying a speech sound) or its absence

**breathing space** *n* a pause in a period of activity, esp for rest and recuperation

**breathless** /'brethlis/ *adj* 1 not breathing; *esp* holding one's breath (eg at a moment of tension) **2a** gasping; OUT OF BREATH **b** leaving one breathless ⟨*drove at a* ~ *speed*⟩ **c** gripping, intense ⟨~ *tension*⟩ 3 without any breeze ⟨*a* ~ *winter morning*⟩ 4 *poetic* dead – **breathlessly** *adv,* **breathlessness** *n*

**breathtaking** /-,tayking/ *adj* 1 making one breathless **2a** exciting, thrilling ⟨*a* ~ *stock-car race*⟩ **b** astonishing ⟨*his* ~ *ignorance and stupidity*⟩ – **breathtakingly** *adv*

**breath test** *n, Br* a test made with a breathalyser

**breathy** /'brethi/ *adj* characterized or accompanied by the audible passage of breath – **breathily** *adv,* **breathiness** *n*

**breccia** /'breki-ə, 'brechi-ə/ *n* a rock consisting of sharp fragments embedded in sand, clay, or a similar fine-grained substance [It, of Gmc origin; akin to OHG *brehhan* to break]

**brecciate** /'brekiayt, 'brechiayt/ *vt* 1 to break (rock) into fragments 2 to form (rock) into breccia – **brecciation** *n*

**Brechtian** /'brekhti-ən/ *adj* (suggestive) of Bertolt Brecht or his writings; *esp* using dramatic techniques aimed at getting an audience to distance itself emotionally from what is happening on the stage in order to stimulate a critical attitude towards the characters and events which are portrayed [Bertolt *Brecht* †1956 Ger dramatist]

**bred-in-the-'bone** *adj, chiefly NAm* inveterate, dyed-in-the-wool ⟨*a* ~ *gambler*⟩

**bree** /bree/ *n, chiefly Scot* a broth [ME *bre*]

**breech** /breech/ *n* 1 the rear end of the body; the buttocks, haunches 2 the part of a firearm at the rear of the barrel which can be opened to allow the insertion or ejection of a cartridge △ breach [ME, breeches, fr OE *brēc,* pl of *brōc* leg covering; akin to OHG *bruoh* breeches, OE *brecan* to break]

**breech birth** *n* a birth in which the lower part of the body of the baby appears first

**breechblock** /-,blok/ *n* the block that closes the rear of the barrel against the force of the charge in breech-loading firearms

**breech delivery** *n* BREECH BIRTH

**breeches** /'brichiz, 'breechiz/ *n pl* 1 knee-length trousers that are usu closely fitting or fastened at the lower ends 2 jodhpurs that are baggy at the thigh and close fitting and fastened from the knee to the ankle with buttons or laces 3 *dial or humorous* trousers [ME *breech*]

**breeches buoy** *n* a lifesaving apparatus in the form of loose canvas breeches hung from a life buoy running on a rope between one ship and another or between a ship and the shore

**breeching** /'breeching/ *n* 1 the part of a harness that passes round the haunches of a draught animal 2 the short coarse wool on the haunches and hind legs of a sheep or goat; *also* the hair on the corresponding part of a dog

**breechloader** /-,lohdə/ *n* a firearm that is loaded at the breech – **breech-loading** *adj*

¹**breed** /breed/ *vb* **bred** /bred/ *vt* 1 to produce (offspring) by hatching or GESTATION (development of an offspring within the mother's body) 2a to father, beget **b** to produce, engender ⟨*despair often* ~s *violence*⟩ 3 to propagate (plants or animals) sexually and usu under controlled conditions ⟨bred *several strains of corn together to produce a new variety*⟩ ⟨~s *pigs in Cornwall*⟩ 4a to rear; BRING UP ⟨*born and* bred *in the country*⟩ **b** to inculcate by training ⟨bred *to look after themselves*⟩ ⟨~ *respect for law or order* into *the young*⟩ 5 to mate with; inseminate 6 to produce (FISSILE material for use in nuclear reactors or bombs) by bombarding a nonfissile chemical element with neutrons in a BREEDER REACTOR ~ *vi* 1 to produce offspring by sexual union 2 to propagate animals or plants [ME *breden*, fr OE *brēdan*; akin to OE *brōd* brood]

²**breed** *n* 1 a group of animals or plants presumably related by descent from common ancestors and visibly similar in most characteristics; *esp* such a group differentiated from the WILD TYPE (typical form occurring in nature) by selective breeding 2 a race, lineage 3 a class, kind ⟨*a new* ~ *of radicals*⟩ 4 *chiefly Can & W US derog* the offspring of a white and a N American Indian; a half-breed

**breeder** /'breedə/ *n* one who or that which breeds: eg **a** an animal or plant kept for propagation **b** someone who is engaged in the breeding of a specified organism ⟨*dog* ~s⟩

**breeder reactor** /'breedə/ *n* a NUCLEAR REACTOR in which more material (eg plutonium) capable of acting as fuel for a nuclear reaction is produced than is consumed – compare FAST BREEDER REACTOR

**breeding** /'breeding/ *n* 1 the action or process of bearing young; the production of new members of a species ⟨*the* ~ *season*⟩ 2 ancestry 3 behaviour; *esp* that showing good manners 4 the sexual propagation of plants or animals; *esp* the development of new or improved varieties ⟨*took up* ~ *champion collies*⟩ 5 *archaic* education ⟨*she had her* ~ *at my father's charge* – Shak⟩

**breeding ground** *n* 1 the place to which animals go to breed 2 a place or set of circumstances considered favourable esp to the propagation of certain ideas or conditions

**breeks** /breeks/ *n pl, chiefly Scot* breeches [ME (northern) *breke*, fr OE *brēc*]

¹**breeze** /breez/ *n* 1 a light gentle wind; *also* a wind of between 6 and 50 kilometres per hour (4 and 31 miles per hour) 2 *informal* a slight disturbance or quarrel 3 *chiefly NAm* something easily done; a cinch *synonyms* see ¹WIND [MF *brise* NE wind, perh alter. of *bise* cold N wind] – **breezeless** *adj*

²**breeze** *vi* 1 to move swiftly and airily ⟨*she* ~d *in as if nothing had happened*⟩ 2 *informal* to make progress quickly and easily ⟨~ *through the books*⟩

³**breeze** *n* residue from the making of coke or charcoal [prob modif of Fr *braise* cinders]

'**breeze-,block** *n* a rectangular building block made of breeze mixed with sand and cement

**breezy** /'breezi/ *adj* 1 swept by breezes 2 brisk, lively 3 carefree, airy – **breezily** *adv*, **breeziness** *n*

**bregma** /'bregmə/ *n, pl* **bregmata** /-mətə/ the point on the top of the skull at which the bone forming the forehead and the bones forming the main dome of the skull meet [NL *bregmat-, bregma*, fr LL, front part of the head, fr Gk; akin to Gk *brechmos* front part of the head – more at BRAIN] – **bregmatic** *adj*

**bremsstrahlung** /'brem,s(h)trahləng/ *n* the ELECTROMAGNETIC RADIATION produced by the sudden slowing down of a charged particle (eg an electron) in an intense electric field [Ger, lit., braking radiation]

**Bren gun** /bren/ *n* a gas-operated magazine-fed light machine gun of .303 inch or 7.62 millimetre calibre [*Br*no, city in Czechoslovakia + *En*field, town in England]

**brent goose** /brent/, **brent** *n* any of several small dark geese (genus *Branta*, esp *Branta bernicla*) that breed in the Arctic and migrate southwards

**bressumer** /'bresəmə/ *n* a large supporting beam set across an opening (eg a fireplace) [alter. of *breastsummer*, fr ¹*breast* + ⁴*summer*]

**brethren** /'bredhrin/ *pl of* BROTHER – chiefly in formal or solemn address or in referring to the members of a profession, society, or sect

**Breton** /'bret(ə)n/ *n* 1 a native or inhabitant of Brittany 2 the Celtic language of the Bretons [Fr, fr ML *Briton-, Brito*, fr L, Briton] – **Breton** *adj*

**breve** /breev/ *n* 1 a curved mark ˘ used to indicate a short vowel or a short or unstressed syllable 2 a musical note equal in time value to two semibreves or four minims [L, neut of *brevis* brief – more at BRIEF]

¹**brevet** /'brevit/ *n* a commission giving a military officer higher nominal rank than that for which he/she receives pay ⟨*a* ~ *major*⟩ [ME, an official message, fr MF, fr OF, dim. of *brief* letter – more at BRIEF]

²**brevet** *vt* **-tt-, -t-** to confer a usu specified rank on by brevet

**breviary** /'brevi·əri, 'bree-, -yəri/ *n often cap* 1a a book containing the prayers, hymns, psalms, and readings for the various daily services of the Catholic church **b** DIVINE OFFICE 2 a brief summary; an abridgment [L *breviarium* summary, fr *brevis* – more at BRIEF]

**brevity** /'brevəti/ *n* 1 shortness of duration; the quality of being brief 2 expression in few words; conciseness [L *brevitas*, fr *brevis*]

¹**brew** /brooh/ *vt* 1 to prepare (eg beer or ale) by steeping, boiling, and fermentation or by infusion and fermentation 2a to foment; BRING ABOUT ⟨~ *trouble*⟩ **b** to contrive, plot – often + *up* 3 to prepare (eg tea) by infusion in hot water ~ *vi* 1 to brew beer or ale 2 to be in the process of formation ⟨*a storm is* ~ing *in the east*⟩ – often + *up* 3a *chiefly Br* to prepare (a beverage) by infusion in hot water; *specif* to make tea – usu + *up* **b** to undergo infusion ⟨*let the tea* ~ *for a few more minutes*⟩ [ME *brewen*, fr OE *brēowan*; akin to L *fervēre* to boil – more at BURN] – **brewer** *n*

²**brew** *n* 1a a brewed beverage **b(1)** an amount brewed at one time **b(2)** the quality of what is brewed ⟨*likes a nice strong* ~⟩ **c** a product of brewing 2 the process of brewing

**brewer's droop** /'brooh·əz/ *n, Br vulg* the inability to produce an erection when drunk

**brewer's yeast** *n* a yeast used in beer making which is also a source of many vitamins of the B complex

**brewery** /'brooh·əri/ *n* an establishment in which beer or ale is brewed

**Brewster sessions** /'broohstə/ *n pl* the annual sittings of magistrates at which licences to sell alcoholic drink are issued or renewed [arch. *brewster* brewer, fr ME]

¹**briar** /'brie·ə/ *n* ¹BRIER (thorny shrub)

²**briar** *n* 1 ²BRIER (type of heather) 2 a tobacco pipe made from the root of a briar

¹**bribe** /brieb/ *vt* to induce or influence (as if) by bribery ~ *vi* to practise bribery – **bribable** *adj*, **briber** *n*

²**bribe** *n* 1 something, esp money, given or promised to influence the judgment or conduct of a person in authority 2 something that serves to induce or influence ⟨*the children would only go to bed after we had offered them a trip to the zoo as a* ~⟩ [ME, something stolen, fr MF, bread given to a beggar]

**bribery** /'brieb(ə)ri/ *n* the act or practice of giving or taking a bribe

**bric-a-brac** /'brik ə ,brak/ *n* a miscellany of small articles, usu of ornamental or sentimental value; curios; *broadly* clutter [Fr *bric-à-brac*]

¹**brick** /brik/ *n* 1a a rectangular block of baked clay and sand that is used in the construction of buildings, is usu in Britain of a standard size of 215 x 102.5 x 65 millimetres (about 8 x 3³/₄ x 2¹/₄ inches), and ranges in colour from a deep bluish black through a rich red brown to a pale yellowish fawn; *also* a similar block made of some other hard material (eg concrete) **b** the material from which bricks are typically made **c** a brick slab used for paving 2 a rectangular compressed mass (eg of ice cream); *also* a briquette 3 *informal* a reliable stout-hearted person; a stalwart ⟨*Angela, you're a real* ~⟩ – see also DROP a brick [ME *bryke*, fr MF *brique*, fr MD *bricke*; akin to OE *brecan* to break]

²**brick** *vt* to face or pave with bricks

**brick up** *vt* to close with bricks or other masonry ⟨*discovered an Adam fireplace behind a* bricked-up *chimney*⟩

**brickbat** /-,bat/ *n* 1 **brickbat, bat** a piece of brick shorter than a whole brick; *esp* a half brick ⟨*in English bond the first course consists of whole bricks, while the second course starts and finishes with a* ~⟩ 2 a fragment of a hard material (eg a brick) used as a missile 3 an uncomplimentary remark

**brickfield** /-,feeld/ *n, Br* a site on which brickmaking takes place

**brickie** /'briki/ *n, informal* a bricklayer

**bricklayer** /-ˌlayə/ *n* one who lays bricks – **bricklaying** *n*

**brickle** /'brikl/ *adj, dial N Eng* brittle [ME *brekyl*, prob deriv of OE *brecan* to break]

**brick red** *n* a reddish brown colour

**brickwork** /'brik,wuhk/ *n* (the part of) a structure made from bricks and mortar

**brickworks** /'brik,wuhks/ *n taking sing vb, pl* **brickworks** a place where bricks are produced

**brickyard** /-ˌyahd/ *n* a brickworks

¹**bridal** /'briedl/ *n, archaic* a wedding feast or ceremony; a marriage [ME *bridale*, fr OE *brȳdealu*, fr *brȳd* + *ealu* ale – more at ALE]

²**bridal** *adj* of a bride or wedding; nuptial

**bridal wreath** *n* a plant (*Spiraea prunifolia*) of the rose family that is a type of SPIRAEA grown for the clusters of small white flowers it bears in spring

¹**bride** /bried/ *n* a woman at the time of her wedding [ME, fr OE *brȳd;* akin to OHG *brūt* bride]

²**bride** *n* a bar or link connecting patterns or parts of a pattern in lace or embroidery work [Fr, lit., reins, bridle]

**bridegroom** /-ˌgroohm, -ˌgroom/ *n* a man at the time of his wedding [alter. (influenced by *groom*) of ME *bridegome*, fr OE *brȳdguma;* akin to OHG *brūtigomo* bridegroom; both fr a prehistoric NGmc-WGmc compound whose constituents are represented by OE *brȳd* & by OE *guma* man – more at HOMAGE]

**bridesmaid** /-ˌmayd/ *n* **1** an unmarried girl or woman who attends a bride **2** someone who is never the centre of attraction or who always comes off second best

**bridewell** /'briedwel/ *n, Br archaic* a house of correction; a prison [*Bridewell*, former house of correction in London]

¹**bridge** /brij/ *n* **1a** a structure spanning a depression or obstacle and supporting a roadway, railway, canal, or path **b** a time, place, or means of connection or transition **2** something resembling a bridge in form or function: eg **2a** the upper bony part of the nose; *also* the part of a pair of glasses that rests on it **b** an arch serving to raise the strings of a musical instrument **c** a raised platform on a ship from which it is directed **d** the support for a billiards or snooker cue formed by the hand; *also* a device used as a cue rest **e** the position of a wrestler on his back with his body arched so that he is supported usu by his head and feet **3** something that fills a gap: eg **3a** one or more false teeth that are permanently fixed to the natural teeth on either side of them **b** a musical passage or phrase linking two unrelated SUBJECTS (themes or tunes) **4** *chemistry* a connection (eg an atom or chemical BOND) that joins two different parts of a molecule (eg opposite sides of a ring of atoms) **5** an electrical circuit or network for measuring or comparing RESISTANCES, INDUCTANCES, CAPACITANCES, or IMPEDANCES by balancing two opposing voltages so that no current flows in the circuit, thus demonstrating the equality of an unknown to a known ratio – see also BURN **one's bridges**, WATER **under the bridge** [ME *brigge*, fr OE *brycg;* akin to OHG *brucka* bridge, OSlav *brŭvŭno* beam] – **bridgeless** *adj*

²**bridge** *vt* to make a bridge over or across; *also* to cross (eg a river) by a bridge – **bridgeable** *adj*

³**bridge** *n* any of various card games for usu four players in two partnerships that bid for the right to name a TRUMP suit (suit that takes precedence over others), score points for TRICKS (winning combinations of cards) made in excess of six, and play with the hand of the declarer's partner exposed and played by the DECLARER (person who has named the trump suit); *esp* CONTRACT BRIDGE [alter. of earlier *biritch*, of unknown origin]

**bridgehead** /-ˌhed/ *n* **1** the arch around the end of a bridge; *esp* the fortified area protecting the end of a bridge nearest an enemy **2** an advanced position seized or to be seized in hostile territory as a foothold for further advance

**bridge roll** *n* a small finger-shaped soft bread roll [prob fr ¹*bridge* or ³*bridge*]

**bridgework** /-ˌwuhk/ *n* (the techniques and principles of making) dental bridges

**bridging loan** /'brijing/ *n* a short-term loan made to someone who is waiting for a long-term loan or mortgage to be agreed

**bridie** /'briedi/ *n, Scot & N Eng* a meat pasty [prob alter. of *bride's pie* (orig a pie for a wedding, made by the bride's friends)]

¹**bridle** /'briedl/ *n* **1** a head harness for a draught or riding animal, usu consisting of leather straps and having the bit and reins for controlling the animal attached to it **2** a Y-shaped arrangement of ropes, cables, chains, etc (eg used to tow or moor a boat) in which both ends of one rope are attached to the load and the moving or restraining force is applied to a second rope attached to the first **3** a curb, restraint ⟨*set a ~ on his power*⟩ [ME *bridel*, fr OE *brīdel;* akin to OE *bregdan* to move quickly – more at BRAID]

²**bridle** *vt* **1** to put a bridle on **2** to restrain, check, or control (as if) with a bridle; *esp* to get and keep under restraint ⟨*you must learn to ~ your tongue*⟩ ~ *vi* to show hostility or resentment (eg because of an affront to one's pride or dignity), esp by drawing back the head and chin **synonyms** see RESTRAIN

**bridle path** *n* a track or right-of-way suitable for horse riding

**bridleway** /-ˌway/ *n* BRIDLE PATH

**bridoon** /bri'doohn/ *n* a light jointed bit (SNAFFLE) with a thin mouthpiece, used esp as part of a DOUBLE BRIDLE – compare CURB [Fr *bridon*, fr *bride* bridle]

**Brie** /bree/ *n* a large round cream-coloured soft cheese which increases in flavour and becomes runny as it ripens [Fr, fr *Brie*, district in NE France]

¹**brief** /breef/ *adj* **1** short in duration or extent **2** concise ⟨*a ~ report*⟩ [ME *bref, breve*, fr MF *brief*, fr L *brevis;* akin to OHG *murg* short, Gk *brachys*] – **briefness** *n*

²**brief** *n* **1** a formal mandate (eg an official letter); *esp* a papal letter less formal than a BULL **2** a brief written item or document; a synopsis, summary **3a(1)** a concise statement of the facts of a client's case drawn up (eg by a solicitor) for the information of the barrister retained in the case; *also* a folder in which this is contained **a(2)** a case or piece of employment given to a barrister ⟨*hadn't had a ~ for years*⟩ **a(3)** *Br slang* a barrister or solicitor; a lawyer **b** a set of instructions outlining some purpose or objective, and often setting limits on an agent's freedom of action ⟨*she went beyond her ~ when she agreed to a 15% increase*⟩ **4** *pl* short close-fitting pants [ME *bref*, fr MF, fr ML *brevis*, fr LL, summary, fr L *brevis*, adj] – **hold a brief for 1** to be retained as legal counsel for **2** to advocate, champion – **in brief** in a few words; briefly

³**brief** *vt* **1** to provide with the necessary instructions and information, esp immediately prior to the activity for which they are needed ⟨*~ journalists on the state of negotiations*⟩ ⟨*~ a minister before question time*⟩ **2** *Br* to retain (a barrister) as legal counsel – **briefer** *n*

**briefcase** /-ˌkays/ *n* a flat rectangular case for carrying papers or books

**briefing** /'breefing/ *n* (a meeting to give out) final instructions or necessary information

**briefly** /'breefli/ *adv* **1a** in a brief way **b** IN BRIEF ⟨*~, he can't come because he's ill*⟩ **c** by way of digression **2** for a short time

¹**brier, briar** /'brie-ə/ *n* a plant (eg of the genera *Rosa, Rubus,* and *Smilax*) with a tough and woody stem bearing thorns or prickles; *also* a mass of brier plants or a twig of a brier [ME *brere*, fr OE *brēr*] – **briery** *adj*

²**brier, briar** *n* a heather (*Erica arborea*) of S Europe with a root used for making tobacco pipes [Fr *bruyère* heath, fr (assumed) VL *brucaria*, fr LL *brucus* heather, of Celt origin; akin to OIr *froech* heather; akin to Gk *ereikē* heather]

**brierroot** /'brie-əˌrooht/ *n* a root (eg of the brier *Erica arborea*) used for making tobacco pipes

¹**brig** /brig/ *n* a 2-masted sailing vessel with the sails on both the fore and main masts suspended at their midpoint and set at right angles to the keel [short for *brigantine*]

²**brig** *n* a prison (eg on a ship) in the US Navy [prob fr ¹*brig*]

³**brig** *n, dial N Eng & Scot* a bridge

¹**brigade** /bri'gayd/ *n* **1** a tactical and administrative military unit composed of a headquarters, one or more fighting units (eg of infantry battalions or armoured regiments), and supporting units **2** an organized or uniformed group of people: eg **2a** an organizational unit of firemen **b** a team of kitchen staff working under a chef [Fr, fr It *brigata*, fr *brigare*]

²**brigade** *vt* to form or unite into a brigade; combine

**brigadier** /ˌbrigə'diə/ *n* – see MILITARY RANKS table [Fr, fr *brigade*]

**brigadier general** *n* – see MILITARY RANKS table

**brigalow** /'brigəloh/ *n, Austr* (a thick scrub formed of) any of various species of acacia trees [native name in Australia]

**brigand** /'brigənd/ *n* one who lives by plunder, usu as a member of a band of thieves; a bandit [ME *brigaunt*, fr MF *brigand*, fr OIt *brigante*, fr *brigare* to fight, fr *briga* strife, of Celt origin; akin to OIr *brig* strength] – **brigandage** *n*, **brigandism** *n*

**brigandine** /'briganˌdeen, -din/ *n* medieval body armour of mail or plate [ME, fr MF, fr *brigand*]

**brigantine** /'brigən‚teen/ *n* a 2-masted sailing vessel with the sails on the foremast suspended from their midpoint and set at right angles to the keel, and those on the mainmast suspended at their front edge and set lengthways – compare ¹BRIG [MF *brigantin*, fr OIt *brigantino*, fr *brigante*]

**bright** /briet/ *adj* **1a** radiating or reflecting light; shining **b** radiant with animation, happiness, or good fortune ⟨~ *faces*⟩ **c** clear and sunny ⟨*a ~ windy April morning*⟩ **2** *of a colour* of high saturation or brilliance **3a** intelligent, clever ⟨*a ~ idea*⟩ ⟨*a class full of ~ children*⟩ **b** lively, charming ⟨*be ~ and jovial among your guests* – Shak⟩ **c** promising ⟨*a ~ career ahead of her*⟩ **4** *of tobacco* bright-coloured, esp because FLUE-CURED [ME, fr OE *beorht;* akin to OHG *beraht* bright, Skt *bhrājate* it shines] – **bright** *adv*, **brightly** *adv*, **brightish** *adj*

**synonyms** Bright, brilliant, radiant, luminous, lustrous, lambent, and incandescent describe something glowing or shining with light. Most also have figurative or technical meanings. **Brightness** varies in intensity and usually describes what may at other times be dim or dull ⟨**bright** sunshine, **brighter** than yesterday's⟩. **Brilliant** is more intense, and often has the suggestion of sparkle or glitter ⟨the **brilliant** blue of the sea⟩. **Radiant** is intense, too, and appears to radiate light ⟨**radiant** white flowers turn their faces to the sun⟩. **Lustrous**, a sensuous word, describes the sheen or glow of reflected light, while **luminous** portrays a steady glow often coming from within. With colours, **luminous** suggests translucency, or light seen through water. **Lambent** implies the gentle flickering light of candles, while **incandescent** describes the burning brilliance of white-hot heat. See INTELLIGENT **antonyms** dull, dim

**bright and early** *adv, informal* very early in the morning

**brighten** /'brietn/ *vb* to make or become bright or brighter – often + *up* – **brightener** *n*

**bright lights** *n pl* (the attractions of) a big city

**brightness** /'brietnis/ *n* **1** (an instance of) being bright ⟨*the ~ of the morning*⟩ **2** the subjective attribute of visual stimuli that is correlated with light intensity and that allows such stimuli to be ordered continuously from light to dark

**Bright's disease** /'briets/ *n* inflammation of the kidneys; NEPHRITIS [Richard *Bright* †1858 E physician]

**brightwork** /-‚wuhk/ *n* polished or plated metalwork

**brill** /bril/ *n, pl* **brill** a European flatfish (*Bothus rhombus*) related to the turbot; *broadly* a turbot [perh fr Corn *brÿthel* mackerel]

¹**brilliant** /'brilyənt, -li·ənt/ *adj* **1** very bright; glittering **2a** distinctive, exceptional ⟨*a ~ performance of a difficult piece*⟩ **b** having great intellectual ability ⟨*one of the most ~ minds of the decade*⟩ **3** *informal* of high quality; good ⟨*this spaghetti's ~*⟩ **synonyms** see BRIGHT, INTELLIGENT **antonym** subdued (of light, colour) [Fr *brillant*, prp of *briller* to shine, fr It *brillare*, prob fr *brillo* beryl, fr L *beryllus*] – **brilliance, brilliancy** *n*, **brilliantly** *adv*, **brilliantness** *n*

²**brilliant** *n* a gem, esp a diamond, cut with numerous facets so that as much light as possible is reflected back from inside it, giving it maximum brilliance

**brilliantine** /'brilyən‚teen/ *n* **1** a cosmetic preparation for making hair glossy and smooth **2** *chiefly NAm* a light lustrous fabric that is similar to ALPACA and is woven from cotton and mohair

¹**brim** /brim/ *n* **1a** an upper or outer margin; a brink **b** the edge or rim of a hollow vessel, a natural depression, or a cavity **2** the projecting rim of a hat [ME *brimme;* akin to MHG *brem* edge] – **brimless** *adj*

²**brim** *vi* **-mm-** to be full to the brim

**brim over** *vi* to become filled to overflowing

**brimful** /‚brim'fool/ *adj* full to the brim; ready to overflow ⟨*~ of confidence*⟩

**-brimmed** /-brimd/ *comb form* (→ *adj*) having (such) a brim ⟨*a wide-brimmed hat*⟩

**brimmer** /'brimə/ *n* a brimming cup or glass

**brimstone** /'brim‚stohn/ *n* **1a** sulphur – no longer used technically **b** a fiery substance that is a means of divine punishment (eg in Hell) **2** a sulphur-yellow butterfly (*Gonepteryx rhamni*) common in Britain and N Europe [ME *brinston*, prob fr *birnen* to burn + *ston* stone]

**brinded** /'brindid/ *adj, archaic* brindled [ME *brended;* prob akin to OE *brand* brand, fire]

**brindle** /'brindl/ *n* **1** a brindled colour **2** a brindled animal [*brindled, brindle,* adj]

**brindled** /'brind(ə)ld/ *adj* having dark streaks or flecks on a grey or tawny ground [alter. of *brinded*]

¹**brine** /brien/ *n* **1a** water saturated or strongly impregnated with common salt **b** a strong solution of a chemical SALT (eg calcium chloride) in water **2** *chiefly poetic* the water of a sea or salt lake [ME, fr OE *brÿne;* akin to MD *brīne* brine, L *fricare* to rub – more at FRICTION]

²**brine** *vt* to treat with brine (eg by soaking) – **briner** *n*

**Brinell hardness** /bri'nel/ *n* the hardness of a metal or alloy measured by pressing a hard ball under a standard load into a specimen of the material [Johann *Brinell* †1925 Sw engineer]

**Brinell number** *n* a number expressing BRINELL HARDNESS and denoting the load applied in testing in kilograms divided by the spherical area of indentation produced in the specimen in square millimetres

**bring** /bring/ *vt* **brought** /brawt/ **1a** to convey (something) to a place or person; come with or cause to come **b(1)** to attract ⟨*her screams* brought *the neighbours*⟩ **b(2)** to force, compel ⟨*cannot ~ myself to do it*⟩ **b(3)** to cause to achieve a particular condition ⟨*~ water to the boil*⟩ **2** to result in; produce ⟨*the tablets may ~ some relief*⟩ **3** to lay (a prosecution or civil action) before a court; open (a legal case) against someone **4** to be sold for (a price); fetch ⟨*the car should ~ £800*⟩ [ME *bringen*, fr OE *bringan;* akin to OHG *bringan* to bring, W *hebrwng* to accompany] – **bring to bear 1** to put to use ⟨*bring knowledge* to bear *on the problem*⟩ **2** to apply, exert ⟨*bring pressure* to bear *on the management*⟩ – see also **bring to** ACCOUNT, **bring somebody to** BOOK, **bring** HOME, **bring somebody to his/her** KNEES, **bring to** LIGHT/**to** TASK

**synonyms** Compare bring and take: while bring implies "come with", towards the speaker or writer, take implies "go with", either away from the speaker or writer or accompanying him/her. Either verb can be used where the point of view is irrelevant ⟨the obelisk was **brought/taken** from Egypt to London⟩.

**bring about** *vt* to cause to take place; effect

**bring down** *vt* **1** to cause to fall (eg from the sky) **2** to carry (a total) forward **3** to kill by shooting – see also **bring the** HOUSE **down**

**bring forth** *vt* **1** to bear ⟨brought forth *fruit*⟩ **2** to give birth to; produce **3** to advance, present ⟨brought forth *arguments to justify his conduct*⟩

**bring forward** *vt* **1** to produce to view; introduce ⟨*the next speaker was then* brought forward⟩ **2** to carry (a total) forward

**bring in** *vt* **1** to produce as profit or return ⟨*this will* bring in *the money*⟩ **2** to include, introduce **3** to pronounce (a verdict) in court **4** to cause (eg an oil well) to be productive **5** to earn ⟨*he* brings in *a good salary*⟩

**bring off** *vt* to carry to a successful conclusion; achieve, accomplish ⟨brought off *an astonishing business coup*⟩

**bring on** *vt* to cause to appear or occur ⟨bring on *the dancing girls!*⟩ ⟨*it* brought on *his asthma*⟩

**bring out** *vt* **1** to make clear **2a** to present to the public **b** to introduce (a young woman) formally to society **3** to utter ⟨brought out *his news in a kind of stutter*⟩ **4** *Br* to cause (a person) to be afflicted with a specified skin disorder ⟨brought *him* out *in spots*⟩ – usu + *in* **5** to encourage to be less reticent – esp in **bring somebody out of him-/herself 6** *chiefly Br* to instruct or cause (workers) to go on strike

**bring round** *vt* **1** to cause (someone) to adopt a particular opinion or course of action; persuade **2** to restore to consciousness; revive

**bring to** *vt* **1** to cause (a boat) to come to a standstill, esp facing into the wind **2** BRING ROUND 2

**bring up** *vt* **1** to educate, rear ⟨*his foster-parents* brought *him* up *as a Catholic*⟩ **2** to cause to stop suddenly ⟨*a new thought* brought *him* up *with a start*⟩ **3** to bring to attention; introduce ⟨*she* brought up *a new topic*⟩ **4** to vomit – see also **bring up the** REAR

**bring and buy sale** *n* a sale of goods donated by members of the community that is usu held to raise money for charity

**brinjal** /'brinjəl/ *n, Ind & Afr* an aubergine [Pg *bringella, beringela*, fr Ar *bādhinjān*, fr Per *bādingān*]

**brink** /bringk/ *n* **1** an edge; *esp* the edge at the top of a steep place ⟨*on the very ~ of the volcano's crater*⟩ **2** a bank, esp of a river **3** the verge, onset ⟨*on the ~ of war*⟩ [ME, prob of Scand origin; akin to ON *brekka* slope; akin to L *front-, frons* forehead]

**brinkmanship** /'bringkmən‚ship/ *also* **brinksmanship** /'bringksmən‚ship/ *n* the art or practice of going to the very brink of conflict or danger before drawing back [*brink* + *-manship* (as in *horsemanship*)]

**¹briny** /'brieni/ *adj* of or resembling brine or the sea; salty – **brininess** *n*

**²briny** *n, poetic* the sea

**brio** /'bree·oh/ *n* enthusiastic vigour; vivacity; verve – compare CON BRIO [It]

**brioche** /bree'osh/ *n* a light slightly sweet bread roll made with a rich yeast dough [Fr, fr MF dial., fr *brier* to knead, fr Gmc origin; akin to OHG *brehhan* to break – more at BREAK]

**briolette** /,breeoh'let/ *n* an oval or pear-shaped gem, esp a diamond, cut in long triangular facets [Fr, prob irreg fr *brillant* brilliant

**briquette, briquet** /bri'ket/ *n* a compacted block, usu of powdered material ⟨*a charcoal* ~⟩ [Fr *briquette*, dim. of *brique* brick] – **briquette** *vt*

**¹brisk** /brisk/ *adj* 1 keenly alert; lively 2 fresh, invigorating ⟨~ *weather*⟩ 3 sharp in tone or manner ⟨*many find her* ~ *tone standoffish*⟩ 4 energetic, quick ⟨*a* ~ *pace*⟩ **synonyms** see NIMBLE **antonyms** slow, lethargic [prob modif of MF *brusque* – more at BRUSQUE] – **briskly** *adv*, **briskness** *n*

**²brisk** *vb* to make or become brisk

**brisken** /'briskən/ *vb* to brisk

**brisket** /'briskit/ *n* 1 the breast or lower chest of a 4-legged animal 2 a cut of beef taken from the chest of the animal, that is usu boned and rolled and cooked by boiling or stewing [ME *brusket*; akin to OE *brēost* breast]

**brisling, bristling** /'brizling, 'bris-/ *n* a small herring (*Clupea sprattus*) that resembles and is processed like a sardine [Norw *brisling*, fr LG *bretling*, fr *bret* broad; akin to OE *brād* broad]

**¹bristle** /'brisl/ *n* 1 a short stiff filament or coarse hair ⟨*a toothbrush with nylon* ~s⟩ 2 a material consisting of natural bristles (e g from an animal) ⟨*a pure* ~ *toothbrush*⟩ [ME *bristil*, fr *brust* bristle, fr OE *byrst*; akin to OHG *burst* bristle, L *fastigium* top] – **bristlelike** *adj*

**²bristle** *vi* 1a to rise and stand stiffly erect ⟨*quills* bristling *in all directions*⟩ b to raise the bristles, hairs, quills, etc (e g in anger) ⟨*the angry dog* ~d *at our approach*⟩ 2 to take on an aggressive attitude or appearance (e g in response to a slight) 3 to be full of or covered with something suggestive of bristles ⟨*roofs* ~d *with chimneys*⟩ ~ *vt* 1 to furnish with bristles 2 to make bristly; ruffle

**bristletail** /-,tayl/ *n* any of various wingless insects (orders Thysanura and Entotrophi) with two or three slender bristles at the hind end of the body

**bristly** /'brisli/ *adj* 1a consisting of or resembling bristles b thickly covered with bristles 2 tending to bristle easily; belligerent ⟨*pay no attention, he's in one of his* ~ *moods*⟩

**Bristol board, bristol** /'bristl/ *n* fine cardboard with a smooth surface suitable for drawing, writing, or printing [*Bristol*, city & seaport in SW England]

**Bristol fashion** /'bristl/ *adj* in good order; spick and span – chiefly in *all shipshape and Bristol fashion*

**bristols** /'bristlz/ *n pl, often cap, Br vulg* a woman's breasts [rhyming slang *Bristol* (*city*) titty, breast]

**brit, britt** /brit/ *n* 1 the young of the herring or mackerel; *broadly* any small fish found together in schools or shoals 2 minute marine animals [Corn *brÿthel* mackerel]

**Brit** /brit/ *n, informal* a British person

**Britannia** /bri'tanyə/ *n* Great Britain or the British Empire personified in the form of a usu seated female figure wearing a helmet and carrying a trident, depicted on various British coins ⟨*rule* ~⟩ [*Britannia*, poetic name for Great Britain, fr L]

**Britannia metal** *n* a soft silver-white alloy consisting largely of tin, antimony, and copper that resembles pewter and is used for bearings and ornaments

**Britannia silver** *n* silver of at least 95.84 per cent purity – compare STERLING 2a

**Britannic** /bri'tanik/ *adj* British – used chiefly in diplomatic and governmental contexts ⟨*Her* ~ *Majesty's government*⟩

**britches** /'brichiz/ *n pl* breeches

**Brith Milah** /,brit 'meelah, ,brith, ,bris/ *n* the Jewish rite of circumcision [LHeb *bĕrīth mīlāh* covenant of circumcision]

**Briticism** /'briti,siz(ə)m/ *n* a characteristic feature of British English [*British* + *-icism* (as in *gallicism*)]

**British** /'british/ *n* 1a the Celtic language of the ancient Britons b BRITISH ENGLISH – used esp by those who speak another variety of English 2 *taking pl vb* the people of Great Britain [ME *Bruttische* of Britain, fr OE *Brettisc*, of Celt origin; akin to W *Brython* Briton] – **British** *adj*, **Britishness** *n*

*usage* The people of the United Kingdom are all **British**. They do not like to be called **English** unless they actually are so, though those who are **English** may find the word more emotionally appealing than **British**; the others prefer to be called **Irish**, **Scottish**, or **Welsh**. Nobody likes to be called a **Briton**, though it saves space in journalism ⟨*12* Britons *Die In Air Crash*⟩, and is the correct way of referring to the Ancient **Britons**. **Britisher** is an Americanism.

**British English** *n* English as spoken and written in Britain and in areas influenced by British culture – often taken to include that of parts of the Commonwealth

**Britisher** /'britishə/ *n, chiefly NAm* BRITON 2 *usage* see BRITISH

**British Summer Time, Summer Time** *n* time one hour ahead of GREENWICH MEAN TIME, used in Britain from late March to late October and corresponding to CENTRAL EUROPEAN TIME – compare DAYLIGHT SAVING TIME

**British thermal unit** *n* a unit of energy equal to the quantity of heat required to raise the temperature of 1 pound of water at or near 39.2° Fahrenheit by 1° Fahrenheit

**Briton** /'brit(ə)n/ *n* 1 a member of any of the peoples inhabiting Britain before the Anglo-Saxon invasions 2 a native, inhabitant, or subject of Britain *usage* see BRITISH [ME *Breton*, fr MF & L; MF, fr L *Briton-, Brito*, of Celt origin; akin to W *Brython*]

**britt** /brit/ *n* BRIT

**¹brittle** /'britl/ *adj* 1 easily broken, cracked, or snapped; *broadly* frail, fragile ⟨*a* ~ *friendship*⟩ ⟨*a* ~ *argument*⟩ 2 easily hurt or offended; sensitive ⟨*a* ~ *personality*⟩ 3 esp of a sound light and thin in tone; sharp ⟨*the* ~ *staccato of snare drums*⟩ 4 lacking warmth, depth, or generosity of spirit; cold ⟨*a brilliant but* ~ *comedy of manners*⟩ [ME *britil*; akin to OE *brēotan* to break, Skt *bhrūna* embryo] – **brittlely** *adv*, **brittleness** *n*

**²brittle** *vi* to become brittle; crumble, deteriorate ⟨*a plastic that* ~s *when exposed to extremes of heat and cold*⟩

**³brittle** *n* a sweet made with caramelized sugar and nuts ⟨*peanut* ~⟩

**brittle star** *n* any of a subclass or class (Ophiuroidea) of marine INVERTEBRATE animals related to the starfish that have a star-shaped body with slender flexible arms clearly marked off from a central disc – called also OPHIUROID

**Brittonic** /bri'tonik/ *adj* BRYTHONIC 2 [L *Britton-, Britto* Briton]

**¹broach** /brohch/ *n* any of various pointed or tapered tools, implements, or parts: e g a a spit for roasting meat b a tool for tapping casks c a metal-cutting tool used to smooth the inside of a hole which has already been cut out roughly △ **brooch** [ME *broche*, fr MF, fr (assumed) VL *brocca*, fr L, fem of *broccus* projecting]

**²broach** *vt* 1 to pierce (a container, esp a cask or bottle) prior to using the contents; tap 2a to make known for the first time b to open up (a subject) for discussion – **broacher** *n*

**³broach** *vi, of a sailing ship* to change direction dangerously, esp in a following sea, so as to lie broadside to the waves – usu + *to* [perh fr ²*broach*]

**¹broad** /brawd/ *adj* 1a having ample extent from side to side or between limits ⟨~ *shoulders*⟩ b having a specified extension from side to side; across ⟨*made the path 10 feet* ~⟩ 2 extending far and wide; spacious ⟨*the* ~ *plains*⟩ 3a open, full – esp in *broad daylight* b plain, obvious ⟨*a* ~ *hint*⟩ 4 marked by lack of restraint, delicacy, or subtlety; coarse ⟨*cracked rather too many* ~ *jokes for much of his audience*⟩ 5a liberal, tolerant b widely applicable or applied; general 6 relating to the main or essential points ⟨~ *outlines*⟩ 7 dialectal, esp in pronunciation ⟨*spoke* ~ *Somerset*⟩ 8 *of a vowel* open – used specif of *a* pronounced as /ah/ (e g in *father*) [ME *brood*, fr OE *brād*; akin to OHG *breit* broad] – **broadly** *adv*, **broadness** *n*

*synonyms* **Broad**, **wide**, and **deep** can all describe horizontal extent. **Broad** and **wide** are measured from side to side, **deep** from back to front ⟨*deep shelving*⟩. **Wide** is used rather than **broad** for specific measurements ⟨*a table one metre* wide⟩ and for emphasis ⟨*the road is* wide *here*⟩ while **broad** is preferred for general spaciousness ⟨**broad** *acres*⟩. **Wide**, but not **broad**, applies to openings ⟨*a* wide *doorway*⟩. **Deep** can stress great extent ⟨*a* deep *forest*⟩. Compare HUGE **antonym** narrow

**²broad** *adv* in a broad manner; fully ⟨~ *awake*⟩

**³broad** *n* 1 the broad part ⟨~ *of his back*⟩ 2 *often cap, Br* 2a a large area of shallow fresh water formed by a slow-flowing river ⟨*Hickling* Broad⟩ b *pl* an area, esp in Norfolk, whose rivers form broads ⟨*the Norfolk* Broads⟩ 3 a woman – slang in NAm, but strongly derog elsewhere

**broad arrow** *n* 1 an arrow with a flat barbed head 2 *Br* a mark shaped like a broad arrow that identifies government property, including clothing formerly worn by convicts

**broadband** /'brawd,band/ *adj* of, having, or involving operation with uniform efficiency over a wide band of frequencies ⟨*a ~ radio aerial*⟩

**broad bean** *n* 1 a widely cultivated Eurasian bean plant (*Vicia faba*) that bears large flat green or whitish edible seeds in long fleshy pods 2 the pod, together with its enclosed seeds, of a broad-bean plant 3 the edible seed of a broad-bean plant

[1]**broadcast** /'brawd,kahst/ *adj* cast or scattered in all directions

[2]**broadcast** *n* 1 the act of transmitting sound or images by radio or television 2 a single radio or television programme

[3]**broadcast** *vb* **broadcast** *also* **broadcasted** *vt* 1 to scatter or sow (seed) broadcast 2 to make widely known 3 to transmit as a broadcast, esp for widespread reception ~ *vi* 1 to transmit a broadcast 2 to speak or perform on a broadcast programme – **broadcaster** *n*

[4]**broadcast** *adv* to or over a broad area

**Broad Church** *adj* of a liberal school of thought in the Anglican church, esp in the later 19th century – **Broad Churchman** *n*

**broadcloth** /-,kloth/ *n* 1 a smooth lustrous fabric of dense texture made usu of wool or worsted 2 a fabric, usu of cotton, silk, or rayon made in plain and rib weaves with a soft semigloss finish

**broaden** /'brawdn/ *vb* to make or become broad

**broad jump** *n, NAm* LONG JUMP – **broad jumper** *n*

**broadleaf** *n* any of various cigar tobaccos having broad leaves

**'broad-,leaved, broad-leafed, broadleaf** *adj* having broad leaves; *specif, of a tree* not coniferous

[1]**broadloom** /'brawd,loohm/ *adj* woven on a wide loom; *also* so woven in one solid colour

[2]**broadloom** *n* a broadloom carpet

**broadly** /'brawdli/ *adv* in general terms; overall ⟨*the problem is ~ one of organization*⟩

,**broad-'minded** *adj* 1 tolerant of varied views; liberal 2 not easily shocked or offended, esp by the sexual behaviour or preferences of others; *broadly* permissive – **broad-mindedly** *adv*, **broad-mindedness** *n*

**broadsheet** /-,sheet/ *n* 1 large sheet of paper printed on one side only; *also* something (eg a ballad or advertisement) printed on a broadsheet 2 a newspaper whose page depth corresponds to the full size of a rotary press plate – compare TABLOID

[1]**broadside** /-,sied/ *n* 1 the side of a ship above the waterline 2 a broad or unbroken surface 3 a broadsheet 4a (the usu simultaneous firing of) all the major guns on one side of a ship **b** a strong, sometimes abusive, attack in speech or writing

[2]**broadside** *adv* 1 with the broad or broader side towards a given object or point 2 in one volley 3 *chiefly NAm* at random

,**broad-'spectrum** *adj* effective against a wide range of insects, microorganisms, weeds, etc ⟨*a ~ antibiotic*⟩

**broadsword** /-,sawd/ *n* a sword with a broad blade for cutting rather than thrusting

**broadtail** /'brawd,tayl/ *n* (the skin of) a very young KARAKUL lamb with fur that resembles moiré silk

**Broadway** /'brawdway/ *n* the New York commercial theatre and amusement world [*Broadway*, street in New York on or near which were once located most of the city's legitimate theatres] – **Broadway** *adj*, **Broadwayite** *n*

**broadways** /'brawdwayz/ *adv* breadthways

**broadwise** /'brawdwiez/ *adv* breadthways

**Brobdingnagian** /,brobding'nagi-ən/ *adj* gigantic, colossal [*Brobdingnag*, imaginary country inhabited by giants in *Gulliver's Travels* by Jonathan Swift †1745 Ir satirist] – **Brobdingnagian** *n*

**brocade** /brə'kayd/ *n* 1 a rich oriental silk fabric with raised patterns in gold and silver 2 a fabric having a raised woven design [Sp *brocado*, fr Catal *brocat*, fr It *broccato*, fr *broccare* to spur, brocade, fr *brocco* small nail, fr L *broccus* projecting] – **brocade** *vt*, **brocaded** *adj*

**brocatelle** /,brokə'tel/ *n* a stiff fabric with patterns in high relief [Fr, fr It *broccatello*, dim. of *broccato*]

**broccoli, brocoli** /'brokəli/ *n* 1 a cauliflower 2 any of various plants of the same species as the cabbage whose flower heads are eaten cooked as a vegetable before the flower buds have opened: eg 2a a variety of cauliflower with a tightly packed purple to white flower head similar to that of the cauliflower **b** a plant with a green to purple flower head that is looser and more branched than that of the cauliflower 3 the edible flower head of a broccoli [It *broccoli*, pl of *broccolo* flowering top of a cabbage, dim. of *brocco* small nail, sprout]

**broch** /brokh, brawkh/ *n* any of several ancient stone dwellings in the form of a fortified circular tower that are found in N and W Scotland [Sc, lit., borough, fr ME (Sc) *brugh*, alter. of ME *burgh*]

**brochette** /bro'shet, broh-/ *n* (food grilled on) a skewer [Fr, fr OF *brochete*, fr *broche* pointed tool – more at BROACH]

**brochure** /'brohshə, broh'shooə/ *n* a small pamphlet or booklet; *esp* one containing descriptive or advertising material [Fr, fr *brocher* to sew, fr MF, to prick, fr OF *brochier*, fr *broche*]

**brock** /brok/ *n, archaic* a badger – now used chiefly in stories as a proper name for a badger [ME, fr OE *broc*, of Celt origin; akin to W *broch* badger]

**brocket** /'brokit/ *n* 1 a male RED DEER two years old – compare PRICKET 2 any of several small S American deer (genus *Mazama*) with unbranched horns [ME *broket*, prob modif of ONF *brocard, brockart* fallow deer one year old]

**broderie anglaise** /,brohdəri 'ong-glez, ,--- -'-/ *n* (cloth decorated with) openwork embroidery consisting chiefly of designs composed of round and oval eyelets worked typically with white thread on white fine cloth (eg cotton lawn) [Fr, lit., English embroidery]

[1]**brogue** /brohg/ *n* a stout walking shoe characterized by decorative perforations on the uppers [IrGael & ScGael *brōg*, fr MIr *bróc*, fr ON *brók* leg covering; akin to OE *brōc* leg covering – more at BREECH]

[2]**brogue** *n* a dialect or regional pronunciation; *esp* an Irish accent [perh fr IrGael *barrōg* wrestling hold, bond (as in *barrōg teangan* lisp, lit., hold of the tongue)]

**broider** /'broydə/ *vt, archaic* to embroider [ME *broideren*, modif of MF *broder* – more at EMBROIDER] – **broidery** *n*

[1]**broil** /broyl/ *vt* to cook by direct exposure to radiant heat (eg over a fire); *specif, NAm* to grill ~ *vi* to become extremely hot [ME *broilen*, fr MF *bruler* to burn, modif of L *ustulare* to singe, fr *ustus*, pp of *urere* to burn]

[2]**broil** *n, archaic* a noisy disturbance; a tumult; *esp* a brawl [*broil*, vb (to entangle, brawl), fr ME *broilen*, fr MF *brouiller* to mix, confuse, fr OF *brooilier*, fr *breu* broth, of Gmc origin]

**broiler** /'broylə/ *n* 1 one who or that which broils 2 a bird suitable for broiling; *esp* a young chicken weighing up to about 1 kilogram (2½ pounds) when prepared for cooking

[1]**broke** /brohk/ *past of* BREAK

[2]**broke** *adj, informal* penniless [ME, alter. of *broken*]

**broken** /'brohkən/ *adj* 1 violently separated into parts; shattered 2a having undergone or been subjected to fracture ⟨*a ~ leg*⟩ **b** *of a land surface* being irregular, interrupted, or full of obstacles **c** not fulfilled or adhered to ⟨*a ~ promise*⟩ ⟨*a ~ treaty*⟩ **d** discontinuous, interrupted **e** *of a flower* having an irregular, streaked, or blotched pattern, esp from virus infection **f** no longer in working order ⟨*my watch is ~*⟩ **g** *of a marriage, home, or family* having been subject to or showing the effects of divorce, separation, or desertion 3a made weak or infirm **b** subdued completely; crushed ⟨*a ~ spirit*⟩ **c** reduced in rank 4a cut off; disconnected **b** imperfect ⟨*~ English*⟩ 5 *of a colour* mixed with grey so that the tone is dulled [ME, fr OE *brocen*, fr pp of *brecan* to break] – **brokenly** *adv*, **brokenness** *n*

,**broken-'down** *adj* 1 no longer working, esp as a result of age, overuse, neglect, or mechanical failure 2 extremely infirm; spiritually or physically exhausted

**brokenhearted** /-'hahtid/ *adj* overcome by grief or despair

,**broken-'mouthed** *adj, esp of a sheep* having lost some of the teeth, esp through old age

**broken wind** /wind/ *n* a lung disease of horses that results in breathing difficulty, heaving of the flanks, and a persistent cough – **broken-winded** *adj*

**broker** /'brohkə/ *n* 1 one who acts as an intermediary (eg in a business deal) 2 an agent who negotiates contracts of purchase and sale (eg of commodities or securities) [ME, negotiator, fr (assumed) AF *brocour*; akin to OF *broche* pointed tool, tap of a cask – more at BROACH]

**brokerage** /'brohk(ə)rij/ *n* 1 the business or establishment of a broker 2 the fee or commission for transacting business as a broker

**broking** /'brohking/ *n* BROKERAGE 1 [fr gerund of obs *broke* (to negotiate), prob back-formation fr *broker*]

**brolga** /'brolgə/ *n* a large Australian crane (*Grus rubicunda*) with grey plumage [native name in Australia]

**brolly** /'broli/ *n, chiefly Br informal* an umbrella [by shortening & alter.]

**brom-** /brohm-/, **bromo-** *comb form* bromine ⟨*bromobenzene*⟩ [prob fr Fr *brome*, fr Gk *brōmos* bad smell]

**¹bromate** /'brohmayt/ *n* a chemical compound (SALT) formed by combination between BROMIC ACID and a metal atom or other chemical group

**²bromate** *vt* to treat with a bromate; *broadly* to treat with bromine or one of its compounds

**bromegrass** /'brohm,grahs/ *n* any of a large genus (*Bromus*) of tall grasses often having drooping flower spikes [NL *Bromus*, genus name, fr L *bromos* oats, fr Gk]

**bromelain** /'brohmǝlin, -layn/, **bromelin** /-lin/ *n* an ENZYME obtained from the juice of the pineapple that breaks down proteins [*bromelain* by alter. (influenced by *papain*) of *bromelin*, fr NL *Bromelia*, genus name of the pineapple in some classifications + E *-in*]

**bromeliad** /broh'meeliad/ *n* any of a family (Bromeliaceae) of chiefly tropical American plants including the pineapple and various ornamental plants [NL *Bromelia*, genus of tropical American plants, fr Olaf *Bromelius* †1705 Sw botanist]

**bromic** /'brohmik/ *adj* of or containing bromine, esp with a VALENCY of 5

**bromic acid** *n* an unstable acid, $HBrO_3$, that is a strong OXIDIZING AGENT and is known only in solution or in the form of bromates

**bromide** /'brohmied/ *n* **1** a chemical compound of bromine with another chemical element or group; *esp* such a compound (e g potassium bromide) used formerly as a sedative **2a** a dull or tiresome person; a bore **b** a commonplace or hackneyed statement or notion; *esp* one calculated to avoid a critical response **3 bromide, bromide print** a photograph printed on photographic paper coated with silver bromide emulsion; *specif* one reproducing printed matter

**bromidic** /broh'midik/ *adj* dull, hackneyed

**brominate** /'brohminayt/ *vt* to treat or cause to combine with bromine or a compound of bromine – **bromination** *n*

**bromine** /'brohmeen, -min/ *n* a nonmetallic chemical element belonging to the same group in the PERIODIC TABLE as chlorine, fluorine, and iodine, that normally occurs as a deep red corrosive liquid giving off an irritating reddish-brown vapour of disagreeable smell [Fr *brome* bromine + E *-ine*]

**bromism** /'brohmiz(ǝ)m/ *n* abnormal lethargy and depression due to excessive or prolonged use of bromide sedatives

**bronch-** /brongk-/, **broncho-** *comb form* bronchial tube; bronchial ⟨bronch*itis*⟩ [deriv of Gk *bronchos* – more at CRAW]

**bronchi** /'bronki/ *pl of* BRONCHUS

**bronchi-** /brongki-/, **bronchio-** *comb form* bronchial tubes ⟨bronchi*ectasis*⟩ [NL, fr *bronchia*, pl, branches of the bronchi, fr Gk, dim. of *bronchos* bronchus]

**bronchia** *n pl* BRONCHIAL TUBES

**bronchial** /'brongki-ǝl/ *adj* of the bronchi or the smaller vessels branching off them in the lungs – **bronchially** *adv*

**bronchial asthma** *n* asthma resulting from the spasmodic contraction of bronchial muscles

**bronchial pneumonia** *n* bronchopneumonia

**bronchial tube** *n* (any of the branches or subdivisions of) a bronchus

**bronchiectasis** /,brongki'ektǝsis/ *n* an abnormal condition in which the air vessels in the lungs are permanently dilated [NL]

**bronchiole** /'brongkiohl/ *n* any of the minute thin-walled branches of a bronchus [NL *bronchiolum*, dim. of *bronchia*] – **bronchiolar** *adj*

**bronchitis** /brong'kietǝs/ *n* (a disease marked by) inflammation of the BRONCHIAL TUBES [NL] – **bronchitic** *adj*

**bronchogenic** /,brongkoh'jenik/ *adj* of or arising in or by way of the air passages of the lungs

**bronchopneumonia** /,brongkohnyoo'mohnyǝ, -ni-ǝ/ *n* pneumonia involving many relatively small areas of lung tissue [NL]

**bronchoscope** /'brongkǝ,skohp/ *n* a tubular usu flexible illuminated instrument used for inspecting or passing instruments into the bronchi [ISV] – **bronchoscopic** *adj*, **bronchoscopically** *adv*, **bronchoscopist** *n*, **bronchoscopy** *n*

**bronchus** /'brongkǝs/ *n, pl* **bronchi** /'brongki, -kie/ either of the two primary divisions of the wind pipe (TRACHEA) that lead respectively into the right and the left lung; *broadly* BRONCHIAL TUBE [NL, fr Gk *bronchos*]

**bronco** /'brongkoh/ *n, pl* **broncos** a wild horse of the ranges of western N America which has not been (fully) trained to carry a rider; *broadly* a mustang [MexSp, fr Sp, rough, wild]

**broncobuster** /'brongkoh,bustǝ/ *n* one who breaks wild horses for riding

**brontosaur** /'brontǝsaw/ *n* a brontosaurus

**brontosaurus** /,brontǝ'sawrǝs/ *n* any of various large four-footed and probably plant-eating dinosaurs (genus *Apatosaurus*) [deriv of Gk *brontē* thunder (akin to Gk *bremein* to roar) + *sauros* lizard – more at SAURIAN]

**Bronx cheer** /brongks/ *n, NAm* RASPBERRY 2 [*Bronx*, borough of New York City, USA]

**¹bronze** /bronz/ *vt* **1** to give the appearance of bronze to **2** to make brown or tanned ~ *vi* to become bronzed – **bronzer** *n*

**²bronze** *n* **1** any of various alloys consisting mainly of copper; *esp* one with a high proportion of tin **2a** a sculpture or artefact made of bronze **b bronze medal, bronze** a medal of bronze awarded to one who comes third in any of several competitions, esp in athletics ⟨*won a ~ in the 100 metres*⟩ – compare GOLD MEDAL, SILVER MEDAL **3** a yellowish brown colour [Fr, fr It *bronzo*, perh fr Per *birinj, pirinj* copper] – **bronze** *adj*, **bronzy** *adj*

**Bronze Age** *n* the period of human culture between the STONE AGE and IRON AGE, characterized by the use of bronze or copper tools and weapons

**brooch** /brohch/ *n* an ornament worn on clothing and fastened by means of a pin [ME *broche* pointed tool, brooch – more at BROACH]

**¹brood** /broohd/ *n taking sing or pl vb* **1** the young of an animal; *esp* the young (e g of a bird or insect) hatched or cared for at one time **2** a group having a common nature or origin *humorous* the children in one family [ME, fr OE *brōd;* akin to OE *beorma* yeast – more at BARM]

**²brood** *vt* **1a** to sit on or incubate (eggs) **b** to produce (as if) by incubation; hatch **2** *of a bird* to cover (young) with the wings **3** to think anxiously or gloomily about; ponder ~ *vi* **1** *of a bird* to sit on eggs in order to hatch them **2** to hover menacingly ⟨*the ~ing hills*⟩ **3a** to dwell gloomily on a subject; worry *over* or *about* **b** to be in a state of depression – **broodingly** *adv*

**³brood** *adj* kept for breeding ⟨*a ~ flock*⟩

**brooder** /'broohdǝ/ *n* **1** one who or that which broods **2** a heated structure used for raising young birds (e g chickens or pheasants)

**broodmare** /'broohd,meǝ/ *n* a mare kept for breeding

**broody** /'broohdi/ *adj* **1** *of a bird* in a state of readiness to brood eggs **2** given or conducive to introspection; contemplative, moody **3** *informal, of a woman* feeling a strong urge or desire for motherhood ⟨*her sister's new baby made her come over all ~*⟩ – **broodiness** *n*

**¹brook** /brook/ *vt* to tolerate; stand for ⟨*he would ~ no interference with his plans*⟩ [ME *brouken* to use, enjoy, fr OE *brūcan;* akin to OHG *brūhhan* to use, L *frui* to enjoy]

**²brook** *n* a small freshwater stream [ME, fr OE *brōc;* akin to OHG *bruoh* marshy ground]

**brookite** /'brookiet/ *n* a mineral composed of TITANIUM DIOXIDE, $TiO_2$, usu occurring as brown to black crystals [Henry *Brooke* †1857 E mineralogist]

**broom** /broohm, broom/ *n* **1** any of various shrubs (esp genus *Cytisus*) of the pea family that have long slender branches, small leaves, and bright usu yellow flowers **2** a brush for sweeping composed of a bundle of firm stiff twigs or bristles (e g of nylon) bound to or set on a long handle [ME, fr OE *brōm;* akin to OHG *brāmo* bramble, MF *brimme* brim]

**broomball** /'broohm,bawl, 'broom-/ *n* a variation of ice hockey played, esp in the USSR, without skates and with brooms and a soccer ball used instead of sticks and a puck – **broomballer** *n*

**broomrape** /-,rayp/ *n* any of various leafless plants (genus *Orobanche* of the family Orobanchaceae, the broomrape family) that grow as parasites on the roots of other plants [trans of ML *rapum genistae;* fr the parasitic growth of one species on the roots of broom]

**broomstick** /-,stik/ *n* the long thin handle of a broom

**brose** /brohz/ *n, chiefly Scot* an oatmeal porridge made with water, milk, or stock [perh alter. of Sc *bruis* broth, fr ME *brewes*, fr OF *broez*, nom sing. & acc pl of *broet*, dim. of *breu* broth, of Gmc origin]

**broth** /broth/ *n* **1a** the liquid in which meat, fish, cereal grains, or vegetables have been cooked; *broadly* a thin soup made from stock **2** a liquid in which microorganisms (e g bacteria) can be grown [ME, fr OE; akin to OHG *brod* broth, L *fervēre* to boil – more at BURN]

**brothel** /'broth(ǝ)l, 'brodh(ǝ)l/ *n* an establishment or premises where a number of prostitutes, usu working for the establishment's owner, are housed and where clients are entertained on the premises [ME, worthless fellow, prostitute, fr *brothen*, pp of *brethen* to waste away, go to ruin, fr OE *brēothan* to waste away; akin to OE *brēotan* to break – more at BRITTLE]

**brothel creeper** *n, Br informal* a usu suede man's shoe with a thick crepe sole [suggested by the silent footsteps it allows]

**brother** /'brudhə/ *n, pl* **brothers**, (3,4,& 5) **brothers** *also* **brethren** /'bredhrin/ **1a** a male having the same parents as another **b** a male having only one parent in common with another; HALF BROTHER **2a** a kinsman **b** one, esp a male, who shares with another a common national or racial origin **3** a fellow member – used as a title in some evangelical churches and trade unions **4** one, esp a male, who is related to another by a common tie or interest **5** a member of a men's religious order who is not in HOLY ORDERS ⟨*a lay ~*⟩ [ME, fr OE *brōthor*; akin to OHG *bruodor* brother, L *frater*, Gk *phratēr* member of the same clan]

**brotherhood** /'brudhəhood/ *n* **1a** the quality or state of being brothers **b** (an ideal of) fellowship between human beings ⟨*the ~ of the Commonwealth*⟩ **2** *taking sing or pl vb* an association (e g a religious body) for a particular purpose **3** *NAm* the whole body of people engaged in a business or profession [ME *brotherhede*, *brotherhod*, alter. of *brotherrede*, fr OE *brōthorrǣden*, fr *brōthor* + *rǣden* condition – more at KINDRED]

**'brother-in-,law** *n, pl* **brothers-in-law 1** the brother of one's spouse **2a** the husband of one's sister **b** the husband of one's spouse's sister

**brotherly** /'brudhəli/ *adj* **1** of, resembling, or appropriate between brothers; fraternal **2** based upon feelings of brotherhood with others; sympathetic, compassionate – **brotherliness** *n*, **brotherly** *adv*

**brougham** /'brooh(ə)m/ *n* a light closed four-wheeled horse-drawn carriage with the driving position outside and in front [Henry Peter *Brougham*, Baron Brougham and Vaux †1868 Sc jurist]

**brought** /brawt/ *past of* BRING

**brouhaha** /'brooh,hah,hah/ *n* a hubbub, uproar [Fr]

**brow** /brow/ *n* **1a** an eyebrow **b** the forehead **2** the top or edge of a hill, cliff, etc **3** *poetic* (the expression of) the face [ME, fr OE *brū*; akin to ON *brūn* eyebrow, Gk *ophrys*]

**brow antler** *n* the first branch of a stag's antler

**browband** /-,band/ *n* the strap on a horse's bridle that crosses the forehead and prevents the headpiece from slipping back behind the ears

**browbeat** /-,beet/ *vt* **browbeat; browbeaten** to intimidate or bully, esp by behaving or speaking in an arrogant or domineering manner ⟨*they were finally ~en into returning to work by management's refusal to improve its offer*⟩

**-browed** /-browd/ *comb form* (→ *adj*) having (such) a brow or brows ⟨*smooth-*browed⟩ ⟨*beetle-*browed⟩

**¹brown** /brown/ *adj* **1** of the colour brown; *esp* of dark or tanned complexion **2** (made with ingredients that are) partially or wholly untreated, unrefined, or unpolished ⟨*~ bread*⟩ ⟨*~ sugar*⟩ ⟨*~ rice*⟩ [ME *broun*, fr OE *brūn*; akin to OHG *brūn* brown, Gk *phrynē* toad]

**²brown** *n* **1** any of a range of dark colours between red and yellow in hue **2** a flock of game birds in flight ⟨*haphazardly firing into the ~*⟩ – **brownish** *adj*, **browny** *adj*

**³brown** *vb* to make or become brown (e g in cooking, sunbathing, etc)

**brown ale** *n* a sweet, dark, usu bottled beer

**brown alga** *n* any of a division (Phaeophyta) of mostly marine algae with chlorophyll masked by brown pigment

**brown bear** *n* any of several bears predominantly brown in colour; *esp* a European bear (*Ursus arctos*)

**brown bread** *n* bread made with flour which has not been bleached and has not had (all of) the wheat germ and bran removed from it

**brown china mark moth** *n* a delicate moth (*Nymphula nymphaeata*), the caterpillar of which is able to live under water and often damages aquatic plants [fr the resemblance of its wing-markings to potters' marks on china]

**brown coal** *n* LIGNITE

**brown earth** *n* any of a group of soils developed in temperate humid regions and characterized by a dark brown level rich in organic material (MULL) which grades through lighter coloured soil into parent material (e g sand)

**,browned-'off** *adj, chiefly Br informal* **1** bored **2** disheartened; FED UP [*browned* fr pp of ³*brown*]

**brown fat** *n* a heat-producing tissue that is present in significant amounts in hibernating mammals, human infants, and adults acclimatized to cold

**brown house moth** *n* a dull-coloured moth (*Hofmannophila pseudospretella*) with a flattened body, the caterpillar of which is often a pest in houses

**Brownian motion** /'browniən/ *n* a random movement of microscopic particles suspended in liquids or gases resulting from the impact of molecules of the liquid or gas surrounding the particles [Robert *Brown* †1858 Sc botanist]

**Brownian movement** *n* BROWNIAN MOTION

**brownie** /'browni/ *n* **1** a good-natured goblin believed to perform helpful household services at night **2 brownie guide, brownie** a member of the most junior section of the British Guide movement aged from 7 to 10; *broadly* a junior member of any national Guide movement **3** *chiefly NAm* a small square or rectangle of rich chocolate cake containing nuts [¹*brown* + *-ie*]

**browning** /'browning/ *n* **1** the process of becoming or causing to become brown **2** a substance (e g caramelized sugar) used to give a brown colour (e g to gravy)

**Browning automatic rifle** *n* a .30 inch calibre gas-operated air-cooled magazine-fed automatic rifle [John *Browning* †1926 US designer of firearms]

**Browning machine gun** *n* a .30 or .50 inch calibre recoil-operated air- or water-cooled machine gun fed by a cartridge belt

**brown lacewing** *n* any of a family (Hemerobiidae) of long-bodied insects (LACEWINGS) both the adults and larvae of which are predators on a variety of insect pests

**brown owl** *n* the woman leader of a brownie-guide pack

**brown rat** *n* the common widely distributed domestic rat (*Rattus norvegicus*)

**brown sauce** *n* a sauce usu made from a ROUX (mixture of flour and fat heated together) combined with a dark-coloured meat stock – compare WHITE SAUCE

**brownshirt** /'brown,shuht/ *n, often cap* a nazi; *specif* STORM TROOPER 1 [trans of Ger *braunhemd*; fr the uniform worn by Nazis]

**brownstone** /'brown,stohn/ *n, NAm* (a building, usu an apartment block, made of) a reddish brown sandstone ⟨*lived in an old ~ in the upper 70's*⟩

**brown study** *n* a state of serious absorption or abstraction; a reverie

**brown sugar** *n* **1** unrefined or partially refined sugar; *also* refined sugar whose crystals are covered with a film of brown syrup **2** *slang* heroin

**brown-tail moth** *n* a TUSSOCK MOTH (*Euproctis chrysorrhoea*) whose colourful larvae feed on foliage and are irritating to the skin

**brown trout** *n* a brownish speckled trout (*Salmo trutta*) which is the common native species in Europe and is usu caught using fly-fishing techniques

**¹browse** /browz/ *n* **1** tender shoots, twigs, and leaves of trees and shrubs that provide food for animals (e g deer) **2** an act or instance of browsing; *also* a period of time spent browsing ⟨*had a good ~ through the back numbers of the magazine*⟩ [prob modif of MF *brouts*, pl of *brout* sprout, fr OF *brost*, of Gmc origin; akin to OS *brustian* to sprout; akin to OE *brēost* breast]

**²browse** *vt* **1** *of an animal* to nibble at (vegetation, esp leaves or grass) **2** to graze ~ *vi* **1** to nibble at grass or other vegetation, esp in a leisurely manner ⟨*sheep that have the spent the summer browsing on the lush upland pastures*⟩ **2** to read or search idly through a book, a shop, or a mass of items in the hope of finding something interesting – **browser** *n*

**brucella** /brooh'selə/ *n, pl* **brucellae** /-'seli/, **brucellas** any of a genus (*Brucella*) of bacteria that cause disease, esp brucellosis, in humans and domestic animals [NL, genus name, fr Sir David *Bruce* †1931 Brit bacteriologist]

**brucellosis** /,broohsə'lohsis, -siz/ *n, pl* **brucelloses** /-'lohseez/ infection with or disease caused by brucellae; *specif* an often long-lasting infectious disease of farm animals and humans that may lead to abortion in pregnant cattle and in humans is marked by fever, pain and swelling in the joints, and great weakness [NL]

**brucine** /'broohseen, -sin/ *n* a poisonous chemical compound, $C_{23}H_{26}N_2O_4$, found with strychnine, esp in NUX VOMICA (poisonous seed of an Asian tree) [prob fr Fr, fr NL *Brucea* (genus name of *Brucea antidysenterica*, a shrub)]

**brucite** /'broohsiet/ *n* a mineral consisting essentially of MAG-

NESIUM HYDROXIDE, Mg(OH)₂ [Archibald *Bruce* †1818 US mineralogist]

**bruin** /'brooh·in/ *n* – used chiefly in stories as a name for the bear [D, name of the bear in the medieval poem *Reynard the Fox*]

¹**bruise** /broohz/ *vt* 1 to batter, dent 2 to inflict a bruise on 3 to break down (vegetable matter) by pounding; crush 4 to wound, injure; *esp* to inflict psychological hurt on ~ *vi* 1 to inflict a bruise 2 to undergo bruising ⟨*tomatoes ~ easily*⟩ [ME *brusen, brisen*, fr MF & OE; MF *bruisier* to break (of Celt origin; akin to OIr *brūu* I shatter) & OE *brȳsan* to bruise (akin to OIr *brūu*, L *frustum* piece)]

²**bruise** *n* 1a an injury involving rupture of small blood vessels and discoloration without a break in the overlying skin; a contusion **b** a similar injury to plant tissue 2 an abrasion, scratch 3 an injury, esp to the feelings

**bruiser** /'broohzə/ *n, informal* a big husky man; *specif* a prize-fighter

¹**bruit** /brooht, 'brooh·i/ *n* 1 any of several generally abnormal sounds (e g a heart murmur) heard on AUSCULTATION (listening to sounds in the body in medical diagnosis) 2 *archaic* 2a a noise, din **b** a report, rumour [(1) Fr, lit., noise, fr MF; (2) ME, fr MF, fr OF, noise]

²**bruit** /brooht/ *vt* to noise abroad; report – usu + *about* or *abroad*

**Brumaire** /'broohmeə (*Fr* brymɛːr)/ *n* the 2nd month of the French Revolutionary calendar, corresponding to 23 October–21 November [Fr, fr *brume*]

**brumal** /'broohml/ *adj, archaic* indicative of or occurring in the winter [L *brumalis*, fr *bruma* winter]

**brumby** /'brumbi/ *n, Austr & NZ* a wild or unbroken horse [prob native name in Queensland, Australia]

**brume** /broohm/ *n, poetic* mist, fog [Fr, mist, winter, fr OProv *bruma*, fr L, winter, fr *brevis* short – more at BRIEF] – **brumous** *adj*

**brummagem** /'bruməjim/ *adj* cheap or inferior, tatty [*Brummagem*, alter. of *Birmingham*, city in England formerly famed for cheap manufactured goods]

**Brummie, Brummy** /'brumi/ *n, Br informal* a native or inhabitant, or the dialect, of Birmingham in England [by shortening & alter. fr *Brummagem*] – **Brummie, Brummy** *adj*

**brunch** /brunch/ *n* a meal usu taken in the middle of the morning that combines a late breakfast and an early lunch [*breakfast* + *lunch*]

¹**brunette**, *NAm also* **brunet** /brooh'net/ *adj* 1 of a dark-brown or black colour ⟨~ *hair*⟩ 2 being a brunette ⟨*his ~ wife*⟩ [Fr *brunet* (masc), *brunette* (fem), fr OF, fr *brun* brown, fr ML *brunus*, of Gmc origin; akin to OHG *brūn* brown]

²**brunette**, *NAm also* **brunet** *n* a person, esp a young adult woman, with dark hair and usu a relatively dark complexion ⟨*gentlemen marry ~s* – Anita Loos⟩

**brunt** /brunt/ *n* 1 the principal force, shock, or stress (e g of an attack) 2 the greater part; the burden – esp in *bear the brunt of* [ME]

¹**brush** /brush/ *n* 1 brushwood 2 (land covered with) scrub vegetation [ME *brusch*, fr MF *broce*, fr OF]

²**brush** *n* 1 an implement composed of stiff strands (e g of hair, bristle, nylon, or wire) set into a firm piece of material (e g wood or plastic) and used esp for grooming hair, painting, sweeping, or scrubbing – often in combination ⟨*paint*brush⟩ 2 a bushy tail; *esp* the tail of a fox 3a a conductor (e g a piece of carbon or braided copper wire) that makes electrical contact between a stationary and a moving part of a generator or a motor **b** **brush discharge, brush** a faintly luminous electrical discharge that is of much lower intensity than a true spark 4a an act of brushing **b** a quick light touch or momentary contact in passing ⟨*felt the ~ of her coat*⟩ [ME *brusshe*, fr MF *broisse*, fr OF *broce*]

³**brush** *vt* 1a to apply a brush to **b** to apply with a brush 2a to remove with sweeping strokes (e g of a brush) – usu + *away* or *off* ⟨~ed *the dirt off his coat*⟩ **b** to dispose of in an offhand way; dismiss ⟨~ed *him off*⟩ ⟨~ed *her comments aside*⟩ 3 to pass lightly over or across; touch gently against in passing ~ *vi, of a horse* to hit and injure the FETLOCK (joint just above the hoof) of an opposite leg in movement – see also **brush something under the** CARPET – **brusher** *n*

**brush up** *vt* 1 to polish by eliminating small imperfections 2 to renew one's skill in; refresh one's memory of – see also BRUSHUP

**brush up on** *vt* BRUSH UP 2 ⟨*he'll have to* brush up on *his French before he goes to that conference in Lyon*⟩

⁴**brush** *vi* to move lightly or heedlessly – usu + *by* or *past* ⟨~ed *by well-wishers in his path*⟩ [ME *bruschen* to rush, fr MF *brosser* to dash through underbrush, fr *broce*]

⁵**brush** *n* a short sharp encounter or skirmish ⟨*a ~ with the law*⟩ [ME *brusche* rush, hostile collision, fr *bruschen*]

**brush border** *n* a layer of MICROVILLI (minute hairlike projections) on the surface of a cell that has an absorptive function (e g one forming part of the lining of the intestine)

**brushed** /brusht/ *adj* finished with a nap ⟨*a ~ fabric*⟩

**brush fence** *n* an obstacle for horses to jump consisting of a dense row of vertically bunched twigs

**brushfire** /'brush,fie·ə/ *adj* involving mobilization only on a small and local scale ⟨~ *border wars*⟩ [*brush fire* (a fire involving brush but not full-sized trees)]

**brushland** /'brush,land, -lənd/ *n* an area covered with brush vegetation

'**brush-,off** *n, informal* a quietly curt or disdainful dismissal; a rebuff

**brushup** /'brush,up/ *n, chiefly Br* an act of tidying up one's appearance – esp in *wash and brushup*

**brushwood** /'brush,wood/, **brush** *n* 1 twigs or small branches, esp when cut, broken, or near the ground 2 a thicket of shrubs and small trees

**brushwork** /'brush,wuhk/ *n* the technique of applying paint with a brush; *esp* a particular artist's characteristic style of applying paint with a brush

**brusque** /brusk, broosk, broohsk/ *adj* 1 short and abrupt 2 curt in manner or speech, often to the point of rudeness [Fr *brusque*, fr It *brusco*, fr ML *bruscus* butcher's-broom] – **brusquely** *adv*, **brusqueness** *n*

synonyms **Abrupt, brusque**, and **curt**: an **abrupt** manner departs from social norms by unexpected interjections or undue brevity. It may be due to social unease or simply ill temper ⟨*you were rather abrupt with Michael. He was only a little late*⟩ ⟨*Mr Darcy's* abrupt *manner did not endear him to the ladies*⟩. **Brusque** suggests a businesslike brevity, with little time or inclination for social niceties, which may as a result seem discourteous. A **curt** remark is one which is short and to the point. It is often intended as a snub. antonyms bland, unctuous

**brusquerie** /,bruskə'ree, ,broo-, ,brooh-, '---/ *n* abruptness of manner [Fr, fr *brusque*]

**Brussels carpet** /'bruslz/ *n* a carpet with a looped woollen pile fixed onto a strong linen base [*Brussels*, city in Belgium]

**Brussels griffon** *n* GRIFFON a (breed of toy dog)

**Brussels lace** *n* 1 any of various fine embroidered (NEEDLE-POINT) or bobbin-woven (PILLOW) laces with floral designs made originally in or near Brussels 2 a machine-made net of hexagonal mesh

**brussels sprout** *n, often cap B* 1 an edible small green bud that resembles a miniature cabbage head and is borne in large numbers on the stem of a plant (*Brassica oleracea gemmifera*) of the cabbage family 2 *pl* the plant that bears brussels sprouts

**brut** /brooht (*Fr* bryt)/ *adj, of champagne* very dry; *specif* containing less than 1.5 per cent sugar by volume [Fr, lit., rough]

**brutal** /'broohtl/ *adj* 1a grossly ruthless or unfeeling ⟨*a ~ slander*⟩ **b** cruel, cold-blooded ⟨*a ~ attack*⟩ **c** harsh, severe ⟨~ *weather*⟩ **d** unpleasantly accurate and incisive ⟨*the ~ truth*⟩ 2 *archaic* relating to beasts – **brutally** *adv*

**brutality** /brooh'taləti/ *n* 1 being brutal 2 a brutal act or course of action

**brutal·ize, -ise** /'brooht(ə)l,iez/ *vt* 1 to make brutal, unfeeling, or inhuman ⟨*people ~* d *by poverty and disease*⟩ 2 to treat brutally ⟨*an accord not to ~ prisoners of war*⟩ – **brutalization** *n*

¹**brute** /brooht/ *adj* 1 of beasts or animals ⟨*the ways of the ~ world*⟩ 2 INANIMATE 1a 3 characteristic of an animal in quality, action, or instinct: e g 3a cruel, savage **b** not working by reason; mindless ⟨~ *instinct*⟩ 4 purely physical ⟨~ *strength*⟩ 5 of unrelieved severity ⟨~ *necessity*⟩ [ME, fr MF *brut* rough, fr L *brutus* stupid, lit., heavy; akin to L *gravis* heavy – more at GRIEVE]

²**brute** *n* 1 a beast, animal 2 a brutal person

**brutish** /'broohtish/ *adj* 1 befitting beasts ⟨*lived a short and ~ life as a slave*⟩ 2a strongly and grossly sensual ⟨~ *gluttony*⟩ **b** showing little intelligence or sensibility ⟨*a ~ lack of understanding*⟩ – **brutishly** *adv*, **brutishness** *n*

**bruxism** /'bruksiz(ə)m/ *n* the habit of unconsciously gritting or grinding the teeth, esp in situations of stress or during sleep [irreg fr Gk *brychein* to gnash the teeth + E *-ism*]

**bryology** /brie'oləji/ *n* a branch of botany that deals with the bryophytes [Gk *bryon* moss + ISV *-logy*]

**bryony** /'brie·əni/ n any of a genus (*Bryonia*) of tendril-bearing climbing plants of the marrow family that have large leaves and red or black fruit [L *bryonia*, fr Gk *bryōnia*; akin to Gk *bryon*]

**bryophyte** /'brie·ə,fiet/ n any of a division (Bryophyta) of nonflowering plants comprising the mosses and liverworts [deriv of Gk *bryon* + *phyton* plant; akin to Gk *phyein* to bring forth – more at BE] – **bryophytic** adj

**bryozoan** /,brie·ə'zoh·ən/ n any of a phylum or class (Bryozoa) of aquatic mostly marine INVERTEBRATE animals that reproduce by budding and usu form branched or mossy colonies that live permanently attached to rocks, seaweed, etc [NL *Bryozoa*, class name, fr Gk *bryon* + NL -*zoa*] – **bryozoan** adj

**Brython** /'brith(ə)n/ n 1 a member of the British branch of Celts 2 a speaker of a Brythonic language [W – more at BRITON]

**¹Brythonic** /bri'thonik/ adj 1 (characteristic) of the Brythons 2 (characteristic) of the group of the Celtic languages comprising Welsh, Cornish, and Breton

**²Brythonic** n the Brythonic group of the Celtic languages

**B Special** n a member of a former part-time volunteer police force in N Ireland

**btm** /,bee tee 'em/ n, euph or humorous a person's bottom; the buttocks [*bottom*]

**¹bub** /bub/ n, slang a woman's breast [short for *bubby*]

**²bub** n, NAm – used as a familiar form of address to a boy or man [prob by shortening & alter. fr *brother*]

**bubal** /'byoohbl/ n a large HARTEBEEST (type of antelope) of N Africa that is now almost extinct [NL *bubalis*, fr Gk *boubalis*, an African antelope]

**¹bubble** /'bubl/ vi 1 to form or produce bubbles 2 to make a gurgling sound like that of bubbles forming and bursting in a liquid ⟨a brook *bubbling* over rocks⟩ 3 to be highly excited, animated, etc or overflowing with happiness or some other strong feeling – often + *over* ⟨*bubbling* over with good humour⟩ ~ vt to pass (a gas) through a liquid in the form of small bubbles [ME *bublen*, prob of imit origin] – **bubbler** n

**²bubble** n 1a a usu small body of gas (eg air) within a liquid (eg a fizzy drink) or a solid b a thin usu spherical and transparent film of liquid filled with a gas c something resembling a bubble; esp a representation of a bubble that encloses the words or thoughts of a character in a STRIP CARTOON d a transparent dome 2a something that lacks firmness, stability, or reality b an unreliable or risky business enterprise or scheme 3 a gurgling sound like that of bubbling

**bubble and squeak** n, chiefly Br a dish consisting of usu left-over potato, cabbage, and sometimes meat fried together [fr the noises of frying]

**bubble bath** n a usu perfumed and coloured liquid or preparation of granules or crystals that produces foam when added to water; also a bath to which this has been added

**bubble car** n, chiefly Br a small usu 3-wheeled car with a domed, often transparent, roof

**bubble chamber** n a device containing heated liquid (eg liquid hydrogen) in which the path of an ionizing particle (eg a neutron or proton) is made visible by a string of bubbles

**bubble gum** n 1 a chewing gum that can be blown into large bubbles 2 light bouncy popular music with repetitive musical phrases

**bubble memory** n a computer memory that permits a large amount of information to be stored as tiny areas of magnetization in a semiconductor

**¹bubbly** /'bubli/ adj 1 full of bubbles 2 overflowing with good spirits or liveliness; animated, vivacious ⟨a ~ *personality*⟩ 3 resembling a bubble or bubbles

**²bubbly** n, informal champagne; broadly any sparkling wine

**bubby** /'bubi/ n, slang a woman's breast [perh imit of the noise made by a sucking baby]

**Bube** /'booh,bay/ n, pl Bubes, esp collectively Bube a member, or the Bantu language, of the people of Bioko, island of Equatorial Guinea in the Bight of Biafra

**bubo** /'byoohboh/ n, pl buboes a swelling formed when a LYMPH NODE, esp in the groin, becomes inflamed [ML *bubon-*, *bubo*, fr Gk *boubōn* groin, swelling in groin] – **bubonic** adj

**bubonic plague** /byoo'bonik, byooh-/ n a highly infectious fatal type of plague in which the formation of buboes is a prominent feature

**buccal** /'bukl/ adj of or affecting the cheeks or the cavity of the mouth [L *bucca* cheek – more at POCK]

**buccaneer** /,bukə'niə/ n 1 a pirate; esp one who plundered Spanish ships and settlements, esp in the W Indies in the 17th century; 2 an unscrupulous adventurer, esp in politics or business [Fr *boucanier* (orig a 17th-c woodsman in the W Indies), fr *boucaner* to dry meat in a wooden frame over a fire, fr *boucan* wooden frame for drying meat, of Tupian origin] – **buccaneer** vi

**Büchner funnel** /'boohkhnə (Ger by:çnər)/ n a cylindrical usu ceramic funnel with a flat perforated base through which liquids are drawn and filtered by suction [Ernst *Büchner* fl 1888 Ger chemist]

**¹buck** /buk/ n, pl bucks, (1&4) bucks, esp collectively buck 1 the male of any of various animals (eg the deer, antelope, or rabbit) 2 VAULTING HORSE (block for gymnastic exercises) 3 NAm SAWHORSE (rack supporting wood during sawing) 4 chiefly SAfr an antelope 5a informal a man; esp a strong powerfully-built virile man b a dashing fellow; a dandy c NAm derog a male Negro 6 NAm & Austr informal a dollar [ME, fr OE *bucca* stag, he-goat; akin to OHG *boc* he-goat, MIr *bocc*; (3) short for *sawbucks*; (6) perh short for *buckskin* (fr the use of deerskins as a unit of exchange in early trade with American Indians)]

**²buck** vi 1 of a horse, mule, etc to spring into the air with the back curved and come down with the front legs stiff and the head lowered 2 chiefly NAm to move erratically or jerkily; jolt 3 chiefly NAm 3a to charge against something (eg an obstruction) b informal to refuse to submit or agree; balk ⟨~ *against* authority⟩ ~ vt 1 to throw (eg a rider) by bucking 2 chiefly NAm informal to fight against or refuse to comply with; oppose, resist ⟨~ *the system*⟩ – **bucker** n

**buck up** vb, informal vi 1 to become encouraged or more cheerful 2 to hurry up – usu in the imper ~ vt 1 to improve, smarten ⟨you'll have to *buck* your ideas up⟩ 2 to raise the morale or spirits of ⟨the news *bucked* her up no end⟩

**³buck** n the act or an instance of bucking; specif a plunging leap by a horse, mule, etc

**⁴buck** adj, NAm of the lowest grade within a military category ⟨~ *private*⟩ [prob fr ¹*buck* 5a]

**⁵buck** n 1 an object formerly used in poker to mark the next player to deal; broadly something used as a mark or reminder 2 the responsibility [short for earlier *buckhorn knife* (a knife with a handle made of a buck's horn)] – **pass the buck** to shift responsibility to someone else

**⁶buck** n, Br a basket for trapping eels [origin unknown]

**buckbean** /-,been/ n BOGBEAN (marsh plant)

**buckboard** /-,bawd/ n, chiefly NAm a 4-wheeled horse-drawn open vehicle having a springy platform with a seat mounted on it set between the front and back wheels [obs *buck* body of a waggon + E *board*]

**bucked** /bukt/ adj, informal pleased, encouraged [fr pp of *buck* (up)]

**¹bucket** /'bukit/ n 1a a large container open at the top, that has a roughly cylindrical shape, straight sides that slope slightly inwards to a flat base, and a semicircular handle, and that is used esp for holding or carrying liquids b the contents of or quantity contained in a bucket 2 something resembling a bucket, esp in shape or function: eg 2a the scoop of a digging or excavating machine b any of the scooped-out blades on the rim of a waterwheel into which the water rushes causing the wheel to rotate c any of the blades of the rotating part of a TURBINE, esp a water turbine 3 a large unit of storage area on a computer DISK (information storage device) 4 pl, informal a large quantity ⟨~s *of blood*⟩ [ME, fr AF *buket*, fr OE *būc* jug, belly; akin to OHG *būh* belly, Skt *bhūri* abundant – more at BIG] – **kick the bucket** informal DIE 1 – see also DROP in a **bucket** [perh fr *bucket* 1a, or perh fr E dial. *bucker*, *bucket* piece of wood on which slaughtered animals are hung]

**²bucket** vt 1 to lift or carry in buckets 2 Br 2a to ride (a horse) hard b to drive hurriedly, roughly, or jerkily 3 Austr informal to criticize, denigrate ⟨McGovern after he ~ed Eagleton – Nation Review (Melbourne)⟩ ~ vi 1 to move hurriedly, recklessly, or haphazardly 2 chiefly Br informal 2a of rain to fall heavily b to rain very hard ⟨it ~ed down all morning⟩ □ (vi 2) usu + down

**bucket brigade** n, NAm BUCKET CHAIN

**bucket chain** n, Br a chain of people who pass buckets of water from hand to hand esp to put out a fire

**bucketful** /-f(ə)l/ n, pl bucketfuls, bucketsful as much as a bucket will hold

**bucket seat** n a padded seat with a curved back for one person, in a car, aeroplane, etc

**bucket shop** *n* **1** a dishonest stockbroking firm that speculates and gambles on stocks and commodities using the funds of its clients **2** *chiefly Br* a small-scale business (e g a travel agent selling low-priced air tickets) that operates on the edge of the law and may default on its commitments to its customers [orig a shady establishment where small quantities of liquor were dispensed in buckets]

**buck fever** *n, chiefly NAm* nervous excitement or tension felt by a person exposed to a new situation or responsibility (e g a novice hunter at the sight of game)

**buckjumper** /'buk,jumpə/ *n, Austr & NZ* an often untamed horse given to bucking – compare BRONCO

**¹buckle** /'bukl/ *n* a fastening typically consisting of a rigid metal, plastic, etc rim, often with a hinged prong, through which an end of a belt, strap, etc is looped and pulled tight to join it with the other end or to fasten a bag, shoe, etc; *also* a similar object used as an ornament [ME *bocle*, fr MF, boss of a shield, buckle, fr L *buccula*, dim. of *bucca* cheek – more at POCK]

**²buckle** *vt* **1** to fasten with a buckle **2** to cause to bend, crumple, or become distorted ~ *vi* **1** to be fastened with a buckle **2** to bend or warp, esp so as to be permanently distorted or to crumple or collapse ⟨*the pavement* ~d *in the heat*⟩ ⟨*his knees* ~d⟩ **3** to yield; GIVE WAY ⟨*one who does not* ~ *under pressure*⟩

**buckle down** *vi* to apply oneself vigorously – often + *to* ⟨*about time he buckled down to some work*⟩

**buckle to** *vi* to brace oneself or gather up one's strength to put effort into work ⟨*we must buckle to and get on with the job*⟩

**³buckle** *n* a bulge or similar distorted formation due to buckling

**buckler** /'buklə/ *n* **1** a small round shield held by a handle at arm's length and used esp for parrying or stopping blows **2** a shield worn on the forearm, esp the left arm, to protect the front of the body [ME *bocler*, fr OF, shield with a boss, fr *bocle*]

**buckler fern** *n* any of various ferns (genus *Dryopteris*) that grow esp on mountains and in wet places [fr the shield-shaped outgrowths of its leaves]

**buckling** /'bukling/ *n* a herring smoked until lightly cooked – compare KIPPER [Ger *bückling*]

**bucko** /'bukoh/ *n, pl* **buckoes 1** a domineering swaggering person, esp a man **2** *chiefly Irish* a young fellow; a lad [¹*buck* + *-o*]

**buckra** /'bukrə/ *n, chiefly S US derog* a white man – used chiefly by Negroes [of Niger-Congo origin]

**¹buckram** /'buckrəm/ *n* **1** a cotton or linen fabric that has been stiffened (e g with size) and is used in bookbinding and as a stiffening material in cuffs, collars, hats, etc **2** *archaic* stiffness or rigidity in manner [ME *bukeram*, fr OF *boquerant*, fr OProv *bocaran*, fr *Bokhara*, city in central Asia (now Bukhara in the USSR)]

**²buckram** *vt* to give strength or stiffness to (e g with buckram)

**buck rarebit** *n* WELSH RAREBIT topped with a poached egg [¹*buck*]

**bucksaw** /'buk,saw/ *n* a saw set in a usu H-shaped frame that is used for sawing wood [¹*buck* 3]

**buckshee** /'bukshee, -'-/ *adj or adv, Br slang* without charge; free [Hindi *bakhšiš* gratuity, gift, fr Per *bakhshīsh* – more at BAKSHEESH]

**buckshot** /'buk,shot/ *n* a lead shot consisting of large pellets, that is used esp for shooting large animals

**buckskin** /-,skin/ *n* **1** a soft pliable greyish-yellow leather, usu with a suede finish, made from the skin of a deer; *also* a leather resembling buckskin made from the skin of a goat, sheep, etc **2** a thick heavy cotton or woollen fabric with a smooth finish **3** *NAm* **3a** *pl* breeches made of buckskin leather **b** *archaic* a person dressed in clothes made of buckskin leather; *esp* an early American living in an isolated country, esp wooded, area **4** *NAm* a horse of a light greyish-yellow colour, usu with a dark mane and tail – **buckskin** *adj*

**buckthorn** /-,thawn/ *n* any of a genus (*Rhamnus* of the family Rhamnaceae, the buckthorn family) of often thorny trees or shrubs

**bucktooth** /-'tooth/ *n, pl* **buckteeth** /-'teeth/ a large projecting front tooth [¹*buck*] – **buck-toothed** *adj*

**buckwheat** /-,weet/ *n* **1** any of a genus (*Fagopyrum*) of plants of the dock family that have clusters of pinkish white flowers and triangular seeds; *esp* either of two plants (*Fagopyrum es-*

*culentum* and *Fagopyrum tartaricum*) cultivated, esp in N America, for their edible seeds **2** the seed of a buckwheat plant used as animal fodder or ground for flour [D *boekweit*, fr MD *boecweit*, fr *boec-* (akin to OHG *buohha* beech tree) + *weit* wheat – more at BEECH; fr the resemblance of the seeds to beechnuts]

**¹bucolic** /byooh'kolik/ *adj* **1** of shepherds or herdsmen; pastoral **2** (typical) of the countryside or rural life *synonyms* see RURAL [L *bucolicus*, fr Gk *boukolikos*, fr *boukolos* cowherd, fr *bous* head of cattle + *-kolos* (akin to L *colere* to cultivate) – more at COW, WHEEL] – **bucolically** *adv*

**²bucolic** *n usu pl* a poem portraying rural life

**¹bud** /bud/ *n* **1** a small protuberance on the stem of a plant that may develop into a flower, leaf, or shoot **2** something not yet mature or at full development: e g **2a** an incompletely opened flower **b** an outgrowth of an organism (e g a yeast) that develops into a new individual **3** something that resembles a bud in shape ⟨*a cotton-wool* ~⟩ [ME *budde;* akin to OE *budda* beetle, Skt *bhūri* abundant – more at BIG] – **nip in the bud** to prevent the growth, development, or success of at an early stage ⟨*nipped the rebellion* in the bud⟩

**²bud** *vb* **-dd-** *vi* **1** of a plant to produce buds **b** to start growth from buds **2** to grow or develop from an immature stage **3** to reproduce asexually by forming buds that develop into new individuals ~ *vt* **1** to produce or develop (e g leaves) from buds **2** to graft a bud from a plant of one kind onto (a plant of another kind), usu in order to propagate a desired variety – **budder** *n*

**³bud** *n, NAm* – used as a familiar form of address, esp to a man [short for *buddy*]

**Buddha** /'boodə/ *n* **1** a person who has attained the state of ENLIGHTENMENT (freedom from desire and thus suffering) that is the ultimate state sought in Buddhism **2** a representation (e g a statue) of Gautama Buddha [Skt, enlightened; (2) Gautama *Buddha* †*ab*483 BC Indian philosopher who founded Buddhism]

**Buddhahood** /'boodəhood/ *n* the state attained by a Buddha

**buddha stick** *n, often cap B, NZ* a bundle of cannabis leaves or flowers wound round a small slender stick

**Buddhism** /'boodiz(ə)m/ *n* a religion of eastern and central Asia growing out of the teaching of Gautama Buddha that maintains that sorrow and suffering are inherent in life and that one can be released from them by ridding oneself of desire and self-delusion – **Buddhist** *n or adj*, **Buddhistic** *adj*

**budding** /'buding/ *adj* in an early and usu promising stage of development ⟨~ *novelists*⟩

**buddleia** /'budli-ə/ *n* any of a genus (*Buddleia* of the family Buddleiaceae, the buddleia family) of shrubs or trees of warm regions, with long showy clusters of usu yellow, mauve, or violet flowers that are attractive to butterflies – called also BUTTERFLY BUSH [NL, genus name, fr Adam *Buddle* †1715 E botanist]

**buddy** /'budi/ *n* **1** *chiefly NAm informal* a friend, colleague, or partner **2** *NAm* – used as a familiar form of address, esp to a man [prob baby talk alter. of *brother*]

**bud gall** *n* a disease of ornamental plants characterized by the formation of swellings (GALLS) on the buds and caused by any of various minute GALL MITES (spiderlike animals) (family Eriophyidae)

**budge** /buj/ *vb* **1** to (cause to) move or shift ⟨*the mule wouldn't* ~⟩ **2** to (persuade or cause to) yield or change an opinion, decision, etc ⟨*couldn't* ~ *her on the issue*⟩ [MF *bouger*, fr (assumed) VL *bullicare*, fr L *bullire* to boil – more at BOIL]

**budgerigar** /'buj(ə)ri,gah/ *n* a small Australian bird (*Melopsittacus undulatus*) that belongs to the same order as the parrots and is usu light green with black and yellow markings in the wild but is bred under domestication in many colours [native name in Australia]

**¹budget** /'bujit/ *n* **1a** a statement of a financial position (e g of an organization) for a definite period of time (e g the following year) based on estimates of expenditures and income during the period **b** *cap* a statement of the financial position of the country for the following year, that is presented annually to the British parliament by the CHANCELLOR OF THE EXCHEQUER and includes a set of proposals for financing government expenditure during this period **2** a plan of how money will be spent or allocated ⟨*the weekly family* ~⟩ **3** the amount of money that is available for, required for, or assigned to a particular purpose [ME *bowgette* leather pouch or wallet, fr MF *bougette*, dim. of *bouge* leather bag, fr L *bulga*, of Gaulish origin; akin to MIr *bolg* bag; modern senses fr an orig satiric reference to the Chancellor of the Exchequer "opening his budget"] – **budgetary** *adj* – **on a budget** having, using, or requiring only a small amount of money

**²budget** *vt* 1 to make provision for or put in a budget 2 to plan or provide for the use of (eg money, time, or manpower) ~ *vi* to arrange or plan a budget

**budget for** *vt* to allocate, set aside, or save money for ⟨budgeting for *a holiday*⟩

**³budget** *adj* designed or suitable for a limited income ⟨~ *holidays*⟩ ⟨~ *prices*⟩

**budget account** *n* 1 an account with a large shop that allows a customer to buy goods on credit up to an agreed limit and pay for them in monthly instalments 2 a bank account for the payment of household bills, being credited with regular or equal monthly payments from the customer's CURRENT AC-COUNT

**budgie** /'buji/ *n, informal* a budgerigar [by shortening & alter.]

**bud scale** *n* any of the hard usu small leaves resembling scales that form the protective sheath of a plant bud

**¹buff** /buf/ *n* 1 a strong supple cream to yellowish leather with a soft velvety surface, that is produced chiefly from cattle hides 2 a pale yellowish-brown colour 3 a device (eg a pad or wheel) having a soft surface (eg of suede) and used for polishing something 4 one who has a keen interest in and wide knowledge of a usu specified subject; an enthusiast ⟨*a film* ~⟩ – compare DEVOTEE, ADDICT, FAN, ENTHUSIAST 5 *informal the* bare skin – chiefly in *in the buff* [MF *buffle* wild ox, fr OIt *bufalo;* (4) earlier *buff* (an enthusiast about going to fires); fr the buff overcoats worn by volunteer firemen in New York City *ab* 1820] – **buff** *adj*

**²buff** *vt* 1 to polish, shine ⟨~ed *her fingernails*⟩ 2 to give a velvety surface like that of buff to (leather)

**buffalo** /'bufəloh/ *n, pl* **buffaloes** *also* **buffalos**, *esp collectively* **buffalo** any of several wild oxen: eg **a** WATER BUFFALO **b** a large shaggy-maned N American wild ox (*Bison bison*) with a large head, short horns, and heavy forequarters surmounted by a large muscular hump – called also BISON [It *bufalo* & Sp *búfalo,* fr LL *bufalus,* alter. of L *bubalus,* fr Gk *boubalos* African gazelle, irreg fr *bous* head of cattle – more at COW]

**buffalo robe** *n, chiefly NAm* the hide of an N American buffalo lined on the skin side with fabric and used esp as a rug

**¹buffer** /'bufə/ *n, informal* a silly or ineffectual person, esp a man – chiefly in *old buffer* [origin unknown]

**²buffer** *n* one who or that which buffs

**³buffer** *n* 1 any of various devices for reducing the effect of an impact; *esp* an apparatus on a railway vehicle or at the end of a railway track that absorbs the effect of the impact occurring when two vehicles are coupled or when a train hits the end of the track 2 a device, person, etc that serves to protect something or someone or to cushion against shock: eg **2a** BUFFER STOCK **b** BUFFER STATE **c** a person who shields another, esp from annoying routine matters **3a** a substance capable of neutralizing both acids and alkalis in a solution and thereby maintaining the original acidity or alkalinity of the solution **b** **buffer solution, buffer** a solution containing a buffer 4 a temporary information storage area, esp in a computer; *esp* one that accepts information at one speed and delivers it at another [obs *buff* to react like a soft body when struck, prob of imit origin]

**⁴buffer** *vt* 1 to lessen the shock of; cushion **2a** to add a buffer to (eg a solution) in order to keep the acidity or alkalinity constant; *also* to maintain (eg the acidity of a solution) with a buffer **b** to keep constant or at an unchanging level; stabilize

**buffer state** *n* a small neutral state lying between two larger potentially rival powers

**buffer stock** *n* a stock of a basic commodity (eg tin) that is built up when supply is plentiful and prices are relatively low, and distributed when the supply is less plentiful, thus offsetting fluctuations in the availability of the commodity and thereby stabilizing its price

**buffer zone** *n* a neutral area separating conflicting forces; *broadly* an area designed to separate

**¹buffet** /'bufit/ *n* 1 a blow, esp with the hand 2 something that strikes with telling force 3 **buffeting, buffet** the shaking or vibrating of an aircraft or part of an aircraft caused by irregular air currents [ME, fr MF, fr OF, dim. of *buffe*]

**²buffet** /'bufit/ *vt* 1 to strike sharply, esp with the hand; cuff **2a** to strike or knock against repeatedly; batter ⟨*the waves* ~ed *the shore*⟩ **b** to contend or battle against 3 to use roughly;

treat unkindly or harshly ⟨~ed *by life*⟩ ~ *vi* to make one's way, esp under difficult conditions

**³buffet** /'boofay/ *n* 1 a sideboard or cupboard often used for displaying china 2 a counter where refreshments are served 3 a meal at which diners help themselves to food set out on tables, a sideboard, etc and often eat standing up 4 *chiefly Br* a self-service restaurant or snack bar (eg in a railway station) [Fr]

**buffet car** *n, chiefly Br* a railway carriage with a counter at which snacks and drinks can be bought

**bufflehead** /'bufl,hed/ *n* a very small chiefly N American DIVING DUCK (*Bucephala albeola*) [arch. *buffle* buffalo + E head]

**buffo** /'bufoh/ *n, pl* **buffi** /'bufi/, **buffos** a clown, buffoon; *specif* a male singer of comic roles in opera [It, fr *buffone*]

**buffoon** /bə'foohn/ *n* 1 a person who appears ridiculous or ludicrous, often to amuse others; a clown 2 a rough noisy usu stupid person [MF *bouffon,* fr OIt *buffone,* prob fr *buffare* to puff, blow] – **buffoonery** *n,* **buffoonish** *adj*

**¹bug** /bug/ *n* **1a** a creeping or crawling insect; *esp* any of several insects commonly considered obnoxious **b** TRUE BUG (insect of the order Hemiptera) 2 a device concealed in a room, telephone, etc that is used to record or listen into private conversations 3 a disease-producing germ; *also* a disease caused by it ⟨*a stomach* ~⟩ 4 *informal* an unexpected defect, fault, flaw, or imperfection ⟨*we'll need to iron the* ~s *out*⟩ 5 *informal* a usu temporary enthusiasm; a craze □ (*1a*&*3*) not used technically [ME *bugge* scarecrow, spectre, goblin; akin to Norw dial. *bugge* important man – more at BIG]

**²bug** *vt* **-gg- 1a** to plant a concealed listening device in **b** to record or listen in to by means of bug ⟨*the conversation was* ~*ged*⟩ 2 *informal* to bother, annoy ⟨*don't* ~ *me with petty details*⟩

**bugaboo** /'bugə,booh/ *n, pl* **bugaboos** a bugbear [prob of Celt origin; akin to W *bwcibo* the Devil (fr *bwci* hobgoblin + *bo* scarecrow), Cornish *buccaboo*]

**bugbear** /'bug,beə/ *n* 1 a source of groundless fear or dread 2 an object or source of concern, anxiety, or difficulty ⟨*this national* ~ *of inflation*⟩ [prob fr ¹*bug* + ¹*bear*]

**,bug-'eyed** *adj* having bulging eyes

**¹bugger** /'bugə/ *n* 1 one who practises sodomy; a sodomite 2 *informal* a person, esp a man, of a usu specified type ⟨*poor* ~⟩ ⟨*cheeky little* ~⟩ 3 *slang* **3a** an offensive or disagreeable person, esp a man – often in *you bugger* as a generalized term of abuse **b** *chiefly Br* something difficult, trying, or unpleasant [ME *bougre* heretic, sodomite, fr MF, fr ML *Bugarus, Bulgarus,* lit., Bulgarian]

**²bugger** *vt* 1 to practise sodomy on 2 *slang* **2a** – used interjectionally to express contempt or annoyance ⟨~ *Tom! We'll go without him*⟩ **b** *chiefly Br* to damage or ruin, often because of incompetence – often + *up* **c** to exhaust; WEAR OUT ⟨*I felt absolutely* ~ed *after that meeting*⟩

**bugger about/around** *vb, Br slang* to cause problems or difficulties for, esp by being indecisive, evasive, or misleading ⟨*don't bugger me about*⟩ to fool or mess around; *also* to waste time by dithering or being indecisive

**bugger off** *vi, slang* to go away; depart – often in imper

**bugger all** *n, Br slang* nothing ⟨*there's* ~ *else to do*⟩

**buggery** /'bugəri/ *n* sodomy

**Buggins' turn** /'buginz/ *also* **Buggins's turn** *n, Br informal* the system or principle of awarding an appointment or promotion to the person next in line according to seniority, length of service, etc, regardless of his/her merit [fr the name *Buggins*]

**¹buggy** /'bugi/ *adj* infested with bugs

**²buggy** *n* 1 a light carriage for one or two people, drawn by one horse 2 BABY BUGGY 3 *chiefly informal* a small car; *broadly* any of various motorized vehicles (eg a moon buggy) [origin unknown]

**bughouse** /'bug,hows/ *n, chiefly NAm informal* a lunatic asylum

**¹bugle** /'byoohgl/ *n* any of a genus (*Ajuga*) of plants of the mint family; *esp* a European plant (*Ajuga reptans*) that has spikes of usu blue but occasionally white or pink flowers [ME, fr OF, fr LL *bugula*]

**²bugle** *n* a BRASS INSTRUMENT that resembles a trumpet but has no finger-operated valves for varying the pitch, and is used esp for military calls [ME, buffalo, instrument made of buffalo horn, bugle, fr OF, fr L *buculus,* dim. of *bos* head of cattle – more at COW]

**³bugle** *vi* to play or sound a bugle – **bugler** *n*

**⁴bugle** *n* a small cylindrical bead used esp as a decorative trimming on clothing [perh fr ²*bugle*]

**bugloss** /'byooh,glos/ *n* any of several coarse hairy plants (genera *Lycopsis* and *Echium*) of the forget-me-not family, that grow chiefly in dry and sandy areas [MF *buglosse,* fr L *buglossa,* irreg fr Gk *bouglōssos,* fr *bous* head of cattle + *glōssa* tongue – more at COW, GLOSS]

**buhl, boule, boulle** /'boohl/ *also* **buhlwork, boulework, boullework** *n* decorative work (eg on cabinets) consisting typically of inlaid pieces of tortoiseshell and brass, and often other metals (eg pewter or silver) [André Charles *Boulle* †1732 Fr cabinetmaker]

**buhr, burr** /buh/, **buhrstone, burrstone** *n* 1 a hard quartz-containing rock used for millstones 2 a millstone cut from buhr [prob fr ¹*burr*]

¹**build** /bild/ *vb* **built** /bilt/ *vt* 1 to construct or form by gradually putting together materials and parts into a composite whole ⟨~ *a house*⟩ ⟨~ *a road*⟩ 2 to cause to be constructed; *esp* to finance or be responsible for the building of 3a to develop or found according to a systematic plan, by a definite process, or on a particular base ⟨*an argument* built *on logic*⟩ 4 to increase, enlarge, or develop gradually ⟨~ ing *a business*⟩ ~ *vi* 1 to engage in building 2a to increase in intensity ⟨~ *to a climax*⟩ b to develop in extent ⟨*outside the arena a queue was already* ~ ing⟩ 3 to make or form for a specified purpose or in a specified way ⟨*a horse* built *for speed*⟩ [ME *bilden,* fr OE *byldan;* akin to OE *büan* to dwell – more at BOWER]
*usage* Some people feel that **build** in the literal sense should be confined to the meaning "put up" or "erect", and not used about things such as tunnels and canals which are dug or excavated.

**build in** *vt* to construct or develop as an integral part – see also BUILT-IN

**build up** *vt* 1 to develop gradually by increments or stages ⟨built up *a library*⟩ 2 to promote the esteem of; praise or publicize 3 to improve the health or strength of (esp a person), esp after an illness ~ *vi* to accumulate or develop appreciably ⟨*clouds* building up *on the horizon*⟩ – see also BUILDUP, BUILT-UP

²**build** *n* the physical form, structure, or proportions of something or somebody; *esp* a person's figure of a usu specified type ⟨*an athletic* ~ ⟩

**builded** /'bildid/ *archaic past of* BUILD

**builder** /'bildə/ *n* one who or that which builds; *esp* one who contracts to build a house, school, etc and supervises building operations

**building** /'bilding/ *n* 1 a permanent structure (eg a school or house) that usu has walls and a roof 2 the art, business, or act of assembling materials into a structure

**building block** *n* a part or unit that together with others forms a complete construction

**building line** *n* a line that marks the boundary beyond which the owner of a plot of land may not build; *esp* a line along a street beyond which houses may not project

**building society** *n* any of various British organizations in which people can invest money, and which makes loans in the form of mortgages to those wishing to buy a house, flat, etc

**buildup** /-,up/ *n* 1 the act or process of building up or increasing gradually 2 something produced by building up ⟨*deal with the* ~ *of traffic*⟩ 3 favourable publicity or praise, usu given in advance ⟨*sales were slow in spite of the* ~ *the product received*⟩

**built** /bilt/ *adj* having a specified physical build ⟨*a slightly* ~ *girl*⟩

**built-'in** *adj* 1 forming an integral part of a structure ⟨~ *cupboards*⟩ 2 inherent ⟨~ *safeguards*⟩

**built-'up** *adj* 1a made of several sections or layers fastened together b enlarged or made higher by the addition of extra parts ⟨*shoes with* ~ *heels*⟩ 2 covered with buildings ⟨*a* ~ *area*⟩

**bulb** /bulb/ *n* 1a the short rounded base of the stem of some plants (eg the lily, onion, hyacinth, or tulip), that consists of one or more buds enclosed in overlapping fleshy leaves and is usu formed underground as a resting stage in the plant's development b a fleshy plant structure (eg a tuber or corm) resembling a bulb in appearance c a plant having or developing from a bulb 2a a bulb-shaped part (eg of a thermometer) b LIGHT BULB 3 a rounded or swollen anatomical structure (eg in the brain) [L *bulbus,* fr Gk *bolbos* bulbous plant; akin to Arm *bolk* radish] – **bulbed** *adj*

**bulbar** /'bulbə/ *adj, chiefly anatomy* of a bulb; *specif* involving the MEDULLA OBLONGATA (rounded structure at the base of the brain)

**bulbil** /'bulbil/ *n* a small or secondary bulb; *esp* a bud that grows in the angle between the stem and the leaf or in place of flowers on some plants and that is capable of producing a new plant [Fr *bulbille,* dim. of *bulbe* bulb, fr L *bulbus*]

**bulbourethral gland** /,bulbohyoo(ə)'reethrəl/ *n* COWPER'S GLAND (gland in male animal associated with the production of semen)

**bulbous** /'bulbəs/ *adj* 1 having a bulb; growing from or bearing bulbs 2 resembling a bulb, esp in roundness ⟨*a* ~ *nose*⟩ – **bulbously** *adv*

**bulbul** /'bool,bool/ *n* 1 a Persian songbird frequently mentioned in poetry 2 any of a group of active noisy songbirds (family Pycnonotidae) of Asia and Africa [Per, fr Ar]

**Bulgarian** /bul'geəri·ən, bool-/ *n* 1 *also* **Bulgar** a native or inhabitant of Bulgaria 2 the Slavonic language of the Bulgarians [*Bulgaria,* country in SE Europe] – **Bulgarian** *adj*

¹**bulge** /bulj/ *n* 1 a swelling or rounded projection on a surface, usu caused by pressure from within or below 2 a sudden, usu temporary, expansion in numbers, volume, etc ⟨*a population* ~ ⟩ 3 *archaic* BILGE 2 (lowest, usu rounded, part of a ship's hull) [MF *boulge, bouge* leather bag, curved part – more at BUDGET] – **bulgy** *adv,* **bulginess** *n*

²**bulge** *vb* to (cause to) swell or curve outwards

**bulimia** /byooh'limi·ə/ *n* an abnormal and constant craving for food [NL, fr Gk *boulimia* great hunger, fr *bous* head of cattle + *limos* hunger – more at COW, LESS]

¹**bulk** /bulk/ *n* 1a thickness, volume, size, or extent, esp when great b indigestible fibrous food (eg bran); roughage 2a (a) large, heavy, or substantial mass – often used with reference to a fat person ⟨*hauled his great* ~ *out of the chair*⟩ b a structure, esp when viewed as a solid mass of material ⟨*the shrouded* ~ s *of snow-covered cars*⟩ 3 the main or greater part *of* something [ME, cargo, heap, belly, fr ON *bulki* cargo] – **in bulk** in large amounts or quantities
*usage* The **bulk** of means "the greater quantity of", not "the greater number of". One should avoid saying ⟨⚠ the **bulk** of the crowd are still waiting⟩. Compare MAJORITY

²**bulk** *vt* 1 to cause to swell or to be or seem thicker or fuller; pad – often + *out* or *up* 2 to gather into a mass or aggregate ~ *vi* 1 to swell, expand 2 to form into a cohesive mass – see also bulk LARGE

³**bulk** *adj* 1 in large quantities ⟨~ *cement*⟩ 2 of materials in large quantities ⟨~ *buying*⟩

**bulkhead** /-,hed/ *n* 1 an upright partition separating compartments (eg in an aircraft or ship) 2 a structure or partition built to resist pressure or to shut off water, fire, or gas [*bulk* (structure projecting from a building; perh fr ON *bālkr* partition) + *head*]

**bulky** /'bulki/ *adj* 1 having bulk; large in size, volume, etc; *esp* so large as to be unwieldy or cumbersome 2 *euph* fat, corpulent – **bulkily** *adv,* **bulkiness** *n*

¹**bull** /bool/ *n* 1a an adult male ox or other bovine animal; *esp* the uncastrated adult male of domestic cattle b the adult male of any of various large animals (eg the elephant or whale) ⟨~ *elephant*⟩ 2 one who buys shares, commodities, etc in expectation of, or to bring about a price rise, in order to sell them later at a profit – compare BEAR 3 one who resembles a bull (eg in brawny build, strength, or aggressive attitude) 4 (a shot that hits) the bull's-eye of a target 5 *cap the* constellation or zodiacal sign of Taurus 6 *NAm slang* a policeman, detective – see also red RAG to a bull [ME *bule,* fr OE *bula;* akin to OE *blāwan* to blow; (2) prob suggested by ¹*bear* 3]

²**bull** *adj* 1 suggestive of a bull; *esp* large or strong 2 characterized by rising prices of shares, commodities, etc ⟨*a* ~ *market*⟩

³**bull** *vt* to try to raise the price or prices of (eg stocks) or in (a market) by buying shares, commodities, etc

⁴**bull** *n* 1 a formal proclamation or letter on a subject of major importance, that is issued by the pope and is sealed with a bulla or stamped with a representation of the design on the bulla 2 an edict, decree [ME *bulle,* fr ML *bulla* seal, sealed document, fr L, bubble, amulet]

⁵**bull** *n* 1 IRISH 4 (ludicrously illogical or incongruous statement) 2 *NAm informal* a grotesque blunder or error [perh fr obs *bull* to mock]

⁶**bull** *n, slang* 1 empty, boastful, or insincere talk 2 nonsense 3 *Br* unnecessary or irksome tasks or discipline, esp in the army, navy, etc [short for *bullshit*]

⁷**bull** *vb, NAm slang vi* to talk boastfully or insincerely ~ *vt* to try to fool or impress by boastful or insincere talk

**bulla** /'boolə, 'bulə/ *n, pl* **bullae** /-lie/ 1 the round usu lead seal attached to a papal bull **2** a large blister [(1) ML, fr L; (2) NL, fr L]

**bullace** /'boolis/ *n* a European plum tree (*Prunus domestica insititia*) that bears clusters of small oval fruit and whose cultivated form is the damson; *also* the fruit of the bullace [ME *bolace*, fr MF *beloce*, fr ML *bolluca*]

**bulldog** /-,dog/ *n* **1** (any of) an English breed of dog with a thickset muscular short-haired body, widely separated forelegs, a short neck, and a large wide head with a projecting lower jaw **2** the assistant of a PROCTOR (official responsible for the students' conduct) at Oxford or Cambridge University **3** a courageous, stubborn, or tenacious person [fr its orig use for baiting bulls]

**bulldog ant, bull ant** *n* a large Australian ant (genus *Myrmecia*) with a vicious sting

**bulldog clip** *n* a large clip used esp to clamp sheets of paper together, that consists of two approx T-shaped metal bars attached to a solid cylindrical metal spring

**bulldoze** /'bool,dohz/ *vt* **1** to bully, intimidate **2** to move, clear, demolish, level off, etc with a bulldozer **3** to force insensitively or ruthlessly ⟨~d *his way to power*⟩ [perh fr ¹*bull* + alter. of *dose*]

**bulldozer** /-,dohzǝ/ *n* **1** a tractor-driven machine that has a broad blunt horizontal blade at the front for pushing earth, rubble, etc and is used esp for clearing or levelling land **2** *informal* one who bulldozes

**bullet** /'boolit/ *n* **1** a round or cylindrical missile (e g of lead) designed to be fired from a pistol, rifle, or similar firearm; *broadly* CARTRIDGE 1a (casing containing a bullet and explosive) **2** something resembling a bullet (e g in shape or speed) [MF *boulette* small ball & *boulet* missile, dims. of *boule* ball – more at BOWL] – **bulletproof** *adj*

**bulletin** /'boolǝtin/ *n* **1** a brief public notice issued usu from an authoritative source; *specif* a brief news item intended for immediate publication **2** a journal published at regular intervals; *esp* the journal of an institution or association **3** a short programme of news items on radio or television [Fr, fr It *bullettino*, dim. of *bulla* papal edict, fr ML]

**bulletin board** *n, chiefly NAm* NOTICE-BOARD

**bullfight** /-,fiet/ *n* a traditional spectacle of Spain, Portugal, Latin America, and SW France, that is held in an arena and in which men ceremonially excite, fight with, and often kill bulls for public amusement – **bullfighter** *n*

**bullfinch** /-,finch/ *n* (any of several finches related to) a European finch (*Pyrrhula pyrrhula*) of which the male has rosy-red underparts, a blue-grey back, and a black cap, chin, tail, and wings

**bullfrog** /-,frog/ *n* any of various large heavy-bodied deep-voiced frogs (e g of the genus *Rana*)

**bullhead** /-,hed/ *n* **1** any of various small river fishes (esp family Cottidae) with a big head; *esp* MILLER'S THUMB **2** any of several common freshwater large-headed catfishes (genus *Ictalurus*) of the USA

**bullheaded** /-'hedid/ *adj* stupidly stubborn; headstrong *synonyms* see OBSTINATE – **bullheadedly** *adv,* **bullheadedness** *n*

**bullhorn** /-,hawn/ *n, chiefly NAm* a hand-held combined microphone and loudspeaker; a megaphone or loud-hailer

**bullion** /'boolyǝn/ *n* gold or silver in bulk; *specif* gold or silver in bars or ingots before being worked on or made into coins △ **bouillon** [ME, fr AF, mint, prob fr MF *bouillir, boillir* to boil]

**bullish** /'boolish/ *adj* **1** suggestive of a bull (e g in brawniness) **2a** marked by, tending to cause, or hopeful of rising prices (e g in a stock market) **b** *informal* optimistic – **bullishly** *adv,* **bullishness** *n*

**bull mastiff** *n* (any of) a breed of powerful short-haired dog produced by crossing the bulldog with the mastiff

**bull neck** *n* a thick short powerful neck – **bullnecked** *adj*

**bullnose** /'bool,nohz/ *n* a brick with a rounded corner

**bullock** /'boolǝk/ *n* **1** a young bull **2** a castrated bull; a steer [ME *bullok*, fr OE *bulluc*, dim. of *bull*] – **bullocky** *adj*

**bullock's heart** *n* CUSTARD APPLE 1a (W Indian tree or its edible fruit)

**bullous** /'boolǝs/ *adj, medicine* resembling or characterized by large blisters [NL *bulla* + E *-ous*]

**bull pen** *n, NAm informal* a large detention cell where prisoners are held until brought into court

**bullring** /-,ring/ *n* an arena for bullfights

**'bull-,roarer** *n* a wooden slat tied to the end of a thong, that is whirled to make a roaring sound and is used esp by Australian aborigines in religious ceremonies

**bullrush** /'bool,rush/ *n* a bulrush

**bull session** *n, NAm* an informal group discussion [⁶*bull*]

**'bull's-,eye** *n* **1** a small thick disc of glass inserted (e g in a ship's deck) to let in light **2** a very hard round usu peppermint-flavoured sweet **3** the small lump of glass left at the centre of a sheet of blown glass by the end of the blowpipe **4a** the centre of a target; *also* something central or crucial **b(1)** a shot that hits the bull's-eye of a target **b(2)** something that precisely attains a desired end **5** (a lantern having) a lens or piece of glass that is flat on one side and curves outwards on the other **6** a small circular window or opening to let in light or air

**¹bullshit** /'bool,shit/ *n, slang* foolish or empty talk; nonsense [¹*bull* + *shit*]

**²bullshit** *vb* **-tt-** *slang vi* to talk loudly or confidently about something of which one has no knowledge ~ *vt* to try to deceive or impress by bullshitting

**bullswool** /'boolz,wool/ *n, Austr & NZ informal* nonsense

**bull terrier** *n* (any of) an English breed of short-haired terrier produced by crossing the bulldog with terriers

**bullwhip** /'bool,wip/ *n* a whip with a long plaited lash, esp of rawhide

**¹bully** /'booli/ *n* **1** a blustering browbeating person; *esp* one habitually cruel to others weaker than him-/herself **2** *archaic* **2a** the protector of a prostitute; a pimp **b** a hired ruffian **3** *obs* a sweetheart [prob modif of D *boel* lover, fr MHG *buole*]

**²bully** *adj or interj* excellent, first-rate – **bully for** – used as an expression of often ironic congratulation ⟨bully for *you*⟩

**³bully** *vt* to treat cruelly; persecute, intimidate ~ *vi* to behave purposely in a cruel or intimidating way

**⁴bully, 'bully-,off** *n* a procedure for starting or restarting play (e g after a goal) in a hockey match in which two opposing players face each other and alternately strike the ground and the opponent's stick three times before attempting to hit the ball [origin unknown]

**⁵bully** *vt* to put (a hockey ball) in play by means of a bully ~ *vi* to start or restart a hockey match with a bully □ usu + *off*

**bully beef** *also* **bully** *n* beef that has been preserved with salt and tinned; corned beef [prob modif of Fr (*boeuf*) *bouilli* boiled beef]

**bullyboy** /-,boy/ *n* a swaggering ruffian

**bullyrag** /'booli,rag/ *vt* **-gg-** to torment or bully, esp by mocking or playing cruel practical jokes [origin unknown]

**bulrush** *also* **bullrush** /'bool,rush/ *n* any of several tall reedlike plants growing in wet areas: e g a any of a genus (*Scirpus,* esp *Scirpus lacustris*) of grasslike sedges **b** *Br* either of two REED-MACES (*Typha latifolia* and *Typha angustifolia*) with a thick furry spike of densely packed brown flowers **c** the papyrus plant – used in the Bible [ME *bulrysche,* perh fr *bule* bull + *rysche, rusche* rush]

**bulwark** /'boolǝk/ *n* **1a** a solid wall-like structure built (e g round a fort) from defence **b** BREAKWATER (structure protecting a harbour or beach from the waves) **2** one who or that which acts as a strong support, protection, or defence ⟨a *pay rise of 30 per cent would be a* ~ *against inflation*⟩ **3** bulwark, **bulwarks** *pl* the side of a ship above the upper deck [ME *bulwerke,* fr MD *bolwerc,* fr MHG, fr *bole* plank + *werc* work]

**¹bum** /bum/ *n, chiefly Br informal* the buttocks [ME *bom*]

**²bum** *vt* **-mm-** *Br vulg* to have anal intercourse with

**³bum** *vb* **-mm-** *informal vi* to spend time being idle or unemployed and often travelling aimlessly – often + *around* ⟨~med *around Europe for a year*⟩ to obtain by begging; cadge ⟨can *I* ~ *a lift?*⟩ [prob back-formation fr ¹*bummer*]

**⁴bum** *n, chiefly NAm informal* **1a** one who sponges off others and avoids work; a loafer, idler **b** an incompetent, worthless, or contemptible person ⟨called *the umpire a* ~⟩ **c** one who devotes his/her time to a specified recreational activity ⟨a *beach* ~⟩ ⟨ski ~s⟩ **2** a vagrant, tramp *usage* see ²TRAMP [prob short for *bummer*]

**⁵bum** *adj, chiefly NAm informal* **1a** inferior, worthless ⟨~ *advice*⟩ **b** disagreeable ⟨a ~ *trip*⟩ **2** disabled, injured ⟨a ~ *knee*⟩

**bumbailiff** /bum'baylif/ *n, Br chiefly derog* BAILIFF 1 [¹*bum;* fr his close pursuit of debtors]

**¹bumble** /'bumbl/ *vi* to make a low humming or droning sound [ME *bomblen* to boom, of imit origin]

**²bumble** *vi* **1** to speak ineptly in a faltering or rambling manner **2** to move, act, or proceed in a clumsy, unsteady, or incompetent manner ~ *vt* to make (one's way) in an incompetent or clumsy manner [prob alter. of *bungle*] – **bumbler** *n*, **bumblingly** *adv*

**bumblebee** /-,bee/ *n* any of numerous large robust hairy bees (genus *Bombus*)

**bumbledom** /'bumbldəm/ *n* petty and pompous officiousness [Mr *Bumble*, pompous parish beadle in the novel *Oliver Twist* by Charles Dickens †1870 E writer]

**bumboat** /-,boht/ *n* a boat that brings provisions and goods for sale to larger ships in port or offshore [prob fr LG *bumboot*, fr *bum* tree + *boot* boat]

**bumf, bumph** /bumf/ *n*, *Br informal* pamphlets, forms, etc, esp when undesirable or superfluous [Brit slang *bumf* toilet paper, short for *bumfodder*, fr ¹*bum*]

**bumfreezer** /'bum,freezə/ *n*, *Br* a tight-fitting waist-length jacket, esp for a man

**bumkin** /'bumkin/ *n* ²BUMPKIN (pole projecting from the rear of a ship)

**bummalo** /'buməloh/ *n*, *pl* **bummalo** BOMBAY DUCK (small fish) [prob modif of Marathi *bombīl*]

**bummaree** /,bumə'ree/ *n*, *Br* a self-employed porter at Smithfield meat market in London [origin unknown]

¹**bummer** /'bumə/ *n*, *chiefly NAm informal* an indolent or idle person; a bum [prob modif of Ger *bummler* loafer, fr *bummeln* to dangle, loaf]

²**bummer** *n*, *informal* 1 an unpleasant or unfortunate experience (eg a bad reaction to a hallucinogenic drug) 2 something inferior or worthless [⁵*bum* + *-er*]

¹**bump** /bump/ *vt* 1 to strike or knock with force or violence 2 to collide with 3 to dislodge with a jolt 4 to catch up with and touch (a boat) in a BUMPING RACE 5 to subject (a person, esp a child) to the bumps ~ *vi* 1 to knock against something with a forceful jolt 2 to move or proceed in a series of bumps [imit]

  **bump into** *vt* to encounter, esp by chance

  **bump off** *vt*, *informal* to murder

  **bump up** *vt*, *informal* to raise or increase ⟨bumped *the price* up⟩; *also* to promote ⟨bumped *him* up *to sergeant*⟩

²**bump** *n* 1 a sudden forceful blow, impact, or jolt 2a the act or an instance of bumping a boat in a BUMPING RACE b *pl* BUMPING RACE 3a a rounded projection from or area of unevenness on a surface (eg a road) b a swelling of body tissue caused by a blow or knock c any of the natural protuberances of the skull, that are considered by some people to indicate a person's character 4 an act of thrusting the hips forward in an erotic manner – compare ²GRIND 4 5 *pl the* act of holding a person, esp a child, by his/her arms and legs and swinging him/her into the air and back to the ground ⟨gave her the ~s *on her birthday*⟩

¹**bumper** /'bumpə/ *n* 1 a cup or glass filled to the brim with wine, ale, etc 2 something unusually large [prob fr ¹*bump* (in obs sense, to bulge)]

²**bumper** *adj* unusually large or good ⟨a ~ *crop*⟩ ⟨the ~ *Christmas edition of a magazine*⟩

³**bumper** *n* 1 one who or that which bumps 2 a device for absorbing shock or preventing damage (eg in collision); *specif* a metal or rubber bar attached to the front or back of a motor vehicle 3 BOUNCER b (ball that passes a batsman in cricket at or above waist height)

,**bumper-to-'bumper** *adj or adv* with a minimal distance between cars ⟨*travelling* ~⟩

**bumph** /bumf/ *n*, *Br informal* bumf

**bumping race** *n* a rowing race, esp at the universities of Oxford and Cambridge, in which the boats start at fixed distances from each other and the object is to catch up with and touch the boat in front, thereby taking its place and eliminating it from the race

¹**bumpkin** /'bum(p)kin/ *n* an awkward and unsophisticated person, esp from the country [perh fr Flem *bommekijn* small cask, fr MD, fr *bomme* cask] – **bumpkinish** *adj*

²**bumpkin, bumkin** /'bumkin/ *n* a pole that projects from the rear of a ship, to which a rope is attached for holding a sail open or altering its position [prob fr Flem *boomken*, dim. of *boom* tree]

**bump start** *vt or n*, *chiefly Br* PUSH-START

**bumptious** /'bum(p)shəs/ *adj* self-assertive in a presumptuous and often noisy manner [¹*bump* + *-tious* (as in *fractious*)] – **bumptiously** *adv*, **bumptiousness** *n*

**bumpy** /'bumpi/ *adj* 1 having or covered with bumps; uneven ⟨a ~ *road*⟩ 2 marked by jolts ⟨a ~ *ride*⟩ – **bumpily** *adv*, **bumpiness** *n*

**bum's rush** *n*, *NAm slang* forcible eviction or dismissal – chiefly in *give/get the bum's rush*

**bun** /bun/ *n* 1 any of various usu sweet and round small bread rolls that may contain currants, spice, etc 2 a usu tight round knot of hair worn esp at the back of the head by women 3 *chiefly N Eng* a small round sweet cake often made from a sponge-cake mixture 4 *Scot* BLACK BUN (rich dark fruit cake) [ME *bunne*] – **bun in the oven** *slang* a child in the womb ⟨*she's got a* bun in the oven⟩

**Buna** /'b(y)oohnə/ *trademark* – used for any of several synthetic rubbers made from BUTADIENE

¹**bunch** /bunch/ *n* 1 a compact group formed by a number of things of the same kind, esp when growing or loosely held together; a cluster ⟨a ~ *of grapes*⟩; *broadly* a collection, lot 2 *taking sing or pl vb* 2a the main group (eg of cyclists) in a race ⟨soon caught up with the ~⟩ b *informal* a group of people 3 *pl*, *Br* a hairstyle in which the hair is divided into two lengths, usu one on each side of the head, and tied [ME *bunche* swelling, bundle] – **bunchy** *adj*, **bunchiness** *n*

²**bunch** *vb* to form (into) a group or cluster – often + *up*

**buncombe** /'bungkəm/ *n* bunkum

¹**bund** /bund/ *n* 1 an embankment or dyke, esp in India and the Far East, used to direct the flow of water or prevent flooding 2 a road, quay, etc along a river or the sea, that is protected or enclosed by an embankment [Hindi *band*, fr Per; akin to OE *binden* to bind]

²**bund** /boont, boond (Ger bʊnt)/ *n*, *often cap* a political association: eg a the Jewish Social Democratic Party of tsarist Russia b a pro-Nazi German-American organization of the 1930s [Ger, fr MHG *bunt;* akin to OE *byndel* bundle] – **bundist** *n*, *often cap*

¹**bundle** /'bundl/ *n* 1a a collection of things held loosely together b something or a number of things wrapped or held together for carrying; a package c a collection, conglomerate ⟨a ~ *of contradictions*⟩ 2a a small band of mostly parallel anatomical fibres (eg of nerve or muscle) b VASCULAR BUNDLE (mass or strand of water- and nutrient-conducting plant tissue) 3 *chiefly informal* a great deal or amount; a mass ⟨it *was hardly a ~ of fun*⟩ ⟨he's *a ~ of nerves*⟩ 4 *slang* a sizable sum of money [ME *bundel*, fr MD; akin to OE *byndel* bundle, *bindan* to bind] – **go a bundle on** to like very much

²**bundle** *vt* 1 to make into a bundle or package – often + *up* 2 to hustle or hurry unceremoniously ⟨~d *the children off to school*⟩ 3 to deposit or put away hastily and untidily ⟨~d *her clothes into the cupboard*⟩ ~ *vi* to practice bundling – **bundler** *n*

  **bundle up** *vb* to dress warmly

**bundling** /'bundling, 'bundl·ing/ *n* a former custom whereby an unmarried couple occupied the same bed without undressing, esp during courtship

**bundu** /'boondooh/ *n*, *SAfr* rugged open country away from towns; the bush [Bantu]

'**bun-,fight** *n*, *Br informal* 1 an informal often noisy gathering at which food is served 2 a confused gathering at which people are jostling and shoving, esp in a confined space

¹**bung** /bung/ *n* a rubber, cork, etc stopper (eg for the bunghole of a cask); *broadly* something used to plug an opening [ME, fr MD *bonne, bonghe*, prob fr LL *puncta* puncture, fr L, fem of *punctus*, pp of *pungere* to prick – more at PUNGENT]

²**bung** *vt* 1 to plug, block, or close (as if) with a bung – often + *up* 2 *chiefly Br informal* 2a to throw, toss ⟨~ *it over here*⟩ b to put ⟨~ *that record on*⟩

**bungalow** /'bung-gəloh/ *n* a usu detached or semidetached single-storeyed house [Hindi *baṅglā*, lit., (house) in the Bengal style]

**bunghole** /-,hohl/ *n* a hole through which a cask is emptied or filled

**bungle** /'bung-gl/ *vi* to act or work clumsily and awkwardly, esp so as to make mistakes ~ *vt* to perform or handle clumsily; mishandle, botch; *esp* to spoil or ruin thus [perh of Scand origin; akin to Icel *banga* to hammer] – **bungler** *n*, **bungling** *adj*

**bunion** /'bunyən/ *n* an inflamed swelling on the first joint of the big toe [prob irreg fr E dial. *bunny* swelling, fr ME *bony*, prob, fr MF *bugne* bump on the head]

¹**bunk** /bungk/ *n* 1a a built-in bed (eg on a ship) that is often one of a tier b **bunk bed, bunk** either of two single beds constructed so as to be one above the other 2 *chiefly informal* a sleeping place [prob short for *bunker*]

²**bunk** *vi* to occupy a bunk or bed; sleep; *esp* to sleep or bed

*down*, esp in a temporary or makeshift bed ~ *vt* to provide with a bunk or bed; PUT UP

**³bunk** *vi, chiefly Br informal* to depart or disappear hurriedly; DO A BUNK – often + *off* [origin unknown]

**⁴bunk** *n* – **do a bunk** *chiefly Br informal* to make a hurried departure, esp in order to escape

**⁵bunk** *n* nonsense, humbug ⟨*history is* ~ – Henry Ford⟩ [short for *bunkum*]

**¹bunker** /'bungkə/ *n* **1** a bin or compartment for storage ⟨a *coal* ~⟩; *esp* one on a ship for storing fuel **2a** a protective embankment or deep trench; *esp* a fortified shelter or chamber, often of reinforced concrete, that is built largely below ground and is often provided with openings for guns **b** an obstacle on a golf course that consists of an area of bare ground usu covered with sand and bordered by a ridge or bank on at least one side [Sc *bonker* chest, box]

**²bunker** *vt* **1** to place or store (esp fuel) in a bunker **2** to drive (the ball) into a bunker in golf

**bunkered** /'bungkəd/ *adj, of a golf player* having driven one's ball into a bunker

**bunkhouse** /'bungk,hows/ *n, NAm* a rough simple building providing sleeping quarters (e g for workers on a ranch)

**bunkum** *also* **buncombe** /'bungkəm/ *n* empty or foolish talk; nonsense [*Buncombe* county in North Carolina, USA, whose congressional representative in 1820 made a long irrelevant speech to impress his constituents]

**bunny** /'buni/ *n* **1** bunny, bunny rabbit a rabbit – used by or to children **2** bunny girl, bunny a nightclub hostess who wears a costume that includes a stylized rabbit's tail and ears [E dial. *bun* rabbit, rabbit's tail, fr ScGael *bun* root, stump, bottom]

**bun penny** *n* a penny minted between 1860 and 1894, showing Queen Victoria wearing her hair in a bun

**Bunraku** /boon'rahkooh/ *n* Japanese puppet theatre featuring large costumed wooden puppets, puppeteers who are onstage, and a chanter who speaks all the lines [Jap]

**Bunsen burner** /'buns(ə)n/ *n* a gas burner consisting typically of a straight tube with usu one or two adjustable small holes at the bottom where air enters and mixes with the gas to produce an intensely hot blue flame [Robert *Bunsen* †1899 Ger chemist]

**¹bunt** /bunt/ *n* **1a** the middle part of a SQUARE SAIL **b** the gathered or bunched part of a furled sail at the centre of the YARD (pole from which the sail is suspended) **2** the baggy part of a fishing net [perh fr LG, bundle, fr MLG; akin to OE *byndel* bundle]

**²bunt** *n* a destructive disease of wheat caused by either of two fungi (*Tilletia foetida* or *Tilletia caries*) and characterized by the presence of dark sooty masses of spores in the ears [origin unknown]

**³bunt** *vt* **1** to strike or push (as if) with the head; butt **2** to push or tap (a baseball) lightly without swinging the bat ~ *vi* to bunt a baseball [alter. of *butt*]

**⁴bunt** *n* an act or instance of bunting

**¹bunting** /'bunting/ *n* any of various songbirds (*Emberiza* and related genera) that have short strong beaks and are related to the finches [ME]

**²bunting** *n* **1** a lightweight loosely woven fabric used chiefly for flags and festive decorations (e g streamers) **2** flags, pennants, streamers, etc collectively [perh fr E dial. *bunt* to sift, fr ME *bonten*]

**buntline** /'buntlin, -,lien/ *n* any of the ropes attached to the bottom of a SQUARE SAIL to haul the sail up to the YARD (pole from which the sail is suspended) for furling

**bunyip** /'bunyip/ *n* a mythical monster that is supposed to inhabit swamps in remote parts of Australia [native name in Australia]

**¹buoy** /boy/ *n* **1** a distinctively shaped and marked float that is moored to the bottom of a body of water to mark a navigable channel or a hazard (e g a submerged wreck or sandbank); *also* a similar float to which a ship may be moored **2** LIFE BUOY [ME *boye*, fr (assumed) MF *boie*, of Gmc origin; akin to OE *bēacen* sign – more at BEACON]

**²buoy** *vt* **1** to mark (as if) with a buoy **2a** to keep afloat **b** to support, sustain ⟨*an economy* ~ed up by the dramatic postwar growth of industry⟩ **3** to raise the spirits of ⟨*hope* ~s him up⟩ □ (2&3) usu + *up* [(1) ¹*buoy*; (2, 3) prob fr Sp *boyar* to float, fr *boya* boy, fr (assumed) MF *boie*]

**buoyancy** /'boyənsi/ *n* **1a** the tendency of a body to float or to rise when submerged in a fluid **b** the power of a liquid or gas to exert an upward force on a body placed in it; *also* the

upthrust on a body placed in a liquid or gas **2** the ability to recover quickly from discouragement or disappointment; resilience, cheerfulness **3** the capacity (e g of prices or business activity) to maintain or return rapidly to a satisfactorily high level

**buoyant** /'boyənt/ *adj* having buoyancy: eg **a** capable of floating **b** cheerful, resilient – **buoyantly** *adv*

**buqsha** /'booksha/ *n* – see *rial* at MONEY table [Ar]

**¹bur** /buh/ *n* ¹BURR (except 5&7)

**²bur** *vt* -rr- ²BURR 2

**buran** /'booh,rahn/ *n* a violent storm, often accompanied by snow and intense cold, that occurs in the Russian steppes [Russ, of Turkic origin]

**Burberry** /'buhb(ə)ri/ *trademark* **1** – used for any of various fabrics used esp for coats for outdoor wear **2** – used for a raincoat

**burble** /'buhbl/ *vi* **1** to make a bubbling sound; gurgle **2** to speak rapidly and usu at length; babble, prattle **3** *of airflow* to become turbulent [ME *burblen*, prob of imit origin] – **burble** *n*

**burbot** /'buhbət/ *n, pl* **burbots**, *esp collectively* **burbot** a freshwater fish (*Lota lota*) of the cod family, that lives in cold rivers and lakes of Europe, Asia, and N America and has slender sensitive projections (²BARBELS) round the mouth [ME *borbot*, fr MF *bourbotte*, fr *bourbeter* to burrow in the mud, fr OF, fr *bourbe* mud]

**¹burden** /'buhd(ə)n/ *n* **1** something that is carried; a load **2** something (e g a duty or responsibility) oppressive, wearisome, or hard to bear **3** *nautical* capacity for carrying cargo ⟨a *ship of a 100 tons* ~⟩ [ME, fr OE *byrthen*; akin to OE *beran* to carry – more at BEAR]

**²burden** *vt* to load (as if) with something heavy; weigh down, oppress ⟨*I will not* ~ *you with a lengthy account*⟩

**³burden** *n* **1** the chorus or refrain of a song, poem, etc **2** a central or recurring topic or theme [alter. of earlier *bourdon* bass or accompanying part, fr ME *burdoun*, fr MF *bourdon* bass pipe, of imit origin]

**burden of proof** *n* the duty of proving a disputed assertion

**burdensome** /-səm/ *adj* imposing or constituting a burden; oppressive

**burdock** /'buhdok/ *n* any of a genus (*Arctium*) of sturdy plants of the daisy family that have round prickly purple flower heads like those of thistles [*burr* + *dock*]

**bureau** /'byooəroh/ *n, pl* **bureaus**, *also* **bureaux** /-rohz/ **1a** a specialized administrative unit; *esp* a subdivision of a government department **b** an office or agency where business is transacted, information or contacts are provided, etc; *esp* one providing a public service ⟨*an advice* ~⟩ **2a** *Br* WRITING DESK; *esp* one having drawers and a sloping top that pulls down to form a writing surface **b** *NAm* a low CHEST OF DRAWERS for use in a bedroom [Fr, desk, cloth covering for a desk, fr OF *burel* woollen cloth, fr (assumed) OF *bure*, fr LL *burra* shaggy cloth]

**bureaucracy** /byooə'rokrəsi/ *n* **1a** (a system of) government characterized by specialization of functions, adherence to fixed rules, and a hierarchy of authority **b** the body of government officials that are appointed rather than elected ⟨*the Civil Service* ~⟩ **2** an apparently inflexible and often infuriating system of administration marked by rigid adherence to rules and official procedures [Fr *bureaucratie*, fr *bureau* + *-cratie* -cracy]

**bureaucrat** /'byooərə,krat/ *n* a member of a bureaucracy; *esp* an official who rigidly follows a formal system of rules or procedures

**bureaucratic** /,byooərə'kratik/ *adj* of or having the characteristics of a bureaucracy or a bureaucrat ⟨~ *government*⟩ – **bureaucratically** *adv*

**bureaucrat·ize, -ise** /byooə'rokrətiez/ *vt* to make bureaucratic – **bureaucratization** *n*

**burette**, *NAm also* **buret** /byoo'ret/ *n, chemistry* a long glass tube graduated usu in millilitres, that has a small hole at the bottom that is opened and closed by a tap, and is used esp for dispensing measured amounts of a liquid [Fr *burette*, fr MF, cruet, fr *buire* jug, alter. of OF *buie*, of Gmc origin; akin to OE *būc* jug – more at BUCKET]

**burg** /buhg/ *n* **1** an ancient or medieval fortress or walled town **2** *NAm* a city, town [OE – more at BOROUGH]

**burgage** /'buhgij/ *n* a system by which land in an English or Scottish town was held under the king or a lord for a yearly rent or for performing services (e g watching for and guarding the town against enemies) [ME, property held by burgage, fr MF *bourgage*, lit., burgage, fr OF, fr *bourg*, *borc* town – more at BOURG]

burgee /'buhjee/ n a forked or triangular flag flown by a ship,
esp a racing yacht, for identification [perh fr Fr dial. *bourgeais*
shipowner]
burgeon /'buhj(ə)n/ vi 1a to send forth new growth (eg buds
or branches); sprout b to blossom, bloom 2 to grow and
expand rapidly; flourish ⟨~ing *cities*⟩ [ME *burjonen*, fr *burjon*
bud, fr OF, fr (assumed) VL *burrion-, burrio*, fr LL *burra*
shaggy cloth]
burger /'buhgə/ n 1a a savoury flat cake, usu of minced meat,
that is eaten grilled or fried ⟨*nut*burger⟩ ⟨*beef*burger⟩ b a
hamburger 2a a sandwich of a burger in a bread roll b a
sandwich containing a burger, esp a hamburger, topped with a
usu specified food ⟨*cheese*burger⟩ □ (*1a&2b*) usu in combination [back-formation fr *hamburger*]
burgess /'buhjis/ n 1 a Member of Parliament for a borough,
city, or university in former times 2 *archaic* a citizen of a British
borough [ME *burgeis*, fr OF *borjois*, fr *borc*]
burgh /'burə/ n a borough; *specif* a town in Scotland having a
written grant (CHARTER 2b) that originally gave it legal rights
and privileges, and that up to 1975 had distinct LOCAL
GOVERNMENT functions [ME – more at BOROUGH] –
burghal adj
burgher /'buhgə/ n an inhabitant of an esp medieval borough
or town
burglar /'buhglə/ n one who commits burglary [AF *burgler*, fr
ML *burglator*, prob alter. of *burgator*, fr *burgatus*, pp of *burgare*
to burgle, fr L *burgus* fortified place] – burglarize vb, *chiefly NAm*
burglary /'buhgləri/ n the act or offence of unlawfully entering
a building with the intent to commit a crime, esp to steal
burgle /'buhgl/ vb to commit burglary on (eg a house) or
against (eg a person) [back-formation fr *burglar*]
burgomaster /'buhgə,mahstə/ n the chief magistrate of a town
in certain European countries; a mayor [part modif & part
trans of D *burgemeester*, fr *burg* town + *meester* master]
burgoo /'buh,gooh, ,-'-/ n, pl burgoos 1 porridge – used, esp
formerly, by sailors 2 *NAm* a stew or thick soup of meat and
vegetables originally served at outdoor gatherings, esp in the S
USA [perh fr Ar *burghul*]
Burgundy /'buhgəndi/ n a red or white TABLE WINE from the
Burgundy region of France; *also* a similar wine made elsewhere
⟨*Spanish* ~⟩
burial /'beri·əl/ n the act, process, or ceremony of burying
somebody or something, esp a dead body [ME *beriel, berial*
tomb, interment, back-formation fr *beriels* (taken as a plural),
fr OE *byrgels* tomb; akin to OS *burgisli* tomb, OE *byrgan* to
bury – more at BURY]
burial mound n ¹BARROW
burin /'byooərin/ n 1 a steel cutting tool having a flat blade
ground to a sharp point at the tip and used for engraving
metal, marble, etc 2 a prehistoric flint tool with a sloping end
like that of a chisel [Fr]
burk, berk *also* birk /buhk/ n, *Br informal* an absurd or stupid
person; a fool ⟨*felt a right* ~⟩ [short for rhyming slang *Berkshire* (or perh *Berkeley*) *Hunt* cunt]
burka, burkha /,buhkə/ n a long loose concealing garment that
covers the body including the head and face and is worn by
Muslim women in public [Hindi *burqa', fr Ar *burqu'*]
burke /buhk/ vt 1 to suffocate or strangle in order to obtain a
relatively unmarked or undamaged body to be sold for dissection 2a to suppress quietly or indirectly; HUSH 3 ⟨~ *an
inquiry*⟩ b to bypass, avoid ⟨~ *an issue*⟩ [William *Burke* †
1829 Ir criminal executed for this crime]
¹burl /buhl/ n 1 a knot or lump in thread or cloth 2 ¹BURR 3
(hard rounded outgrowth on a tree or veneer made from this)
[ME *burle*, fr (assumed) MF *bourle* tuft of wool, fr (assumed)
VL *burrula*, dim. of LL *burra* shaggy cloth] – burled adj
²burl vt to finish (cloth) by removing burls and repairing loose
threads – burler n
³burl n, *Austr* a try, attempt – esp in *give it a burl* [E dial. *birl*
rapid twist or turn]
burlap /'buhlap/ n hessian [alter. of earlier *borelapp*]
¹burlesque /buh'lesk/ n 1 a literary or dramatic work that
uses grotesque exaggeration or imitation to ridicule 2 (a)
mockery, usu by caricature or imitation 3 a US stage show of
a broadly humorous and earthy character, that consists of
short turns, comic sketches, and frequently striptease acts –
compare MUSIC HALL, VAUDEVILLE [*burlesque*, adj (comic, droll),
fr Fr, fr It *burlesco*, fr *burla* joke, fr Sp] – burlesque adj
²burlesque vb to imitate in a humorous or derisive manner;
mock – burlesquer n

burletta /buh'letə/ n a COMIC OPERA with little spoken dialogue,
popular in England in the 18th century [It, dim. of *burla* joke]
burley /'buhli/ n, *often cap* a yellowish-brown tobacco grown
mainly in Kentucky [prob fr the name *Burley*]
burly /'buhli/ adj, *esp of a person* strongly and heavily built
[ME, comely, noble, well-built; prob akin to OE *borlīce* extremely, excellently, OHG *burlīh* lofty, excellent] – burliness n
bur marigold n any of a genus (*Bidens*) of plants of the daisy
family with yellow flowers and prickly flattened seeds that stick
to clothing
Burmese /buh'meez/ n, pl (1) Burmese 1 a native or inhabitant
of Burma 2 the TIBETO-BURMAN language of the Burmese
[*Burma*, country in SE Asia] – Burmese adj
Burmese cat n (any of) a breed of cat resembling the Siamese
cat but of solid and darker colour, typically dark brown or
grey, and usu with orange or yellow eyes
¹burn /buhn/ n, *chiefly Scot* a small stream [ME, fr OE; akin
to OHG *brunno* spring of water, L *fervēre* to boil]
²burn vb burned /buhnd, buhnt/, burnt /buhnt/ vi 1a to consume fuel and give off heat, light, and gases ⟨*a small fire* ~s
*in the grate*⟩ b to undergo combustion ⟨*this wood* ~s *well*⟩ c
to undergo nuclear fission or nuclear fusion and to give off light;
shine, glow ⟨*a light* ~*ing in the window*⟩ 2a to be hot ⟨*the
~ing sand*⟩ b(1) to feel uncomfortably or painfully hot b(2)
*of the ears or face* to become very red and usu feel hot c to
produce or undergo a painfully stinging or smarting sensation
⟨*iodine* ~s *so*⟩ ⟨*ears* ~*ing from the cold*⟩ d to become reddened
and painful from exposure to the sun; receive sunburn ⟨*she
~s easily*⟩ 3 to become emotionally excited or agitated: eg 3a
to long passionately; ¹DIE 3b ⟨~*ing to tell the story*⟩ b to be
filled *with* a strong emotion; feel something strongly ⟨~*ing
with anger*⟩ 4 to become charred, scorched, or destroyed by
fire or heat ⟨*the cake is* ~*ing*⟩ 5a to be executed by burning b
*NAm informal* to die in the ELECTRIC CHAIR 6 to force or make
a way (as if) by burning ⟨*her words* ~t *into his heart*⟩ ~ vt 1a
to cause to undergo combustion; *esp* to destroy by fire ⟨~ *the
rubbish*⟩ ⟨~t *the house down*⟩ b to use as fuel ⟨*this furnace
~s gas*⟩ 2a to transform by exposure to heat or fire ⟨~ *clay
to bricks*⟩ b to produce (as if) by burning ⟨*the acid* ~ed *a hole
in the sleeve*⟩ 3a to injure, damage, or mark by exposure to
fire, heat, radiation, or caustic chemicals ⟨~ed *his hand*⟩ b to
char or scorch by exposure to fire or heat c to cause to sting
or smart painfully 4a to execute by burning ⟨~ *heretics at the
stake*⟩ b *NAm informal* to electrocute in an ELECTRIC CHAIR 5
*informal* to cheat, exploit – often pass ⟨*got* ~t *over that deal*⟩
[ME *birnan*, fr OE *byrnan*, vi, & *bærnan*, vt; akin to OHG
*brinnan* to burn, L *fervēre* to boil] – burnable adj – burn one's
boats/bridges to cut off all one's means of retreat – see also
burn the CANDLE at both ends, burn one's FINGERS/get one's
fingers burnt, burn the midnight OIL
*usage* Burned is the commoner inflection in both British and
American English when the verb is intransitive ⟨*the fire* burned
brightly⟩ ⟨*he* burned *with desire*⟩; burnt is commoner than
burned in British English when the verb is transitive ⟨*she* burnt *her
boats*⟩ and is used in both British and American English as an adjective ⟨burnt *toast*⟩.
burn in vt to make (areas of photographic print) darker by
extra exposure to light during enlarging – compare DODGE 3
burn out vt 1 to destroy (eg a building) by fire, esp so as to
leave only a shell – usu pass 2 to cause to be no longer active,
having completed a course of development ⟨*the disease had
burnt itself out*⟩ 3 to cause to stop working or fail as a result
of heat, friction, excessive use, or the passage of too high an
electric current 4 to completely exhaust by excessive physical
activity or mental strain ⟨*burnt himself out by the age of 30*⟩
5 to lose detail from (a photograph) by overexposure to light
~ vi 1 to become inoperative as a result of excessive heat,
friction, etc ⟨*the clutch* burnt out *on the steep hill*⟩ 2 *of a fuse,
light-bulb filament, etc* to cease to conduct electricity when
the conducting wire has melted (eg as a result of too high an
electric current being passed) – see also BURNOUT
burn up vt 1 to obsess to the point at which nothing else is
important ⟨*jealousy was* burning *him* up⟩ 2 *informal* to
drive at high speed along ⟨*we* burned up *the motorway*⟩; *also*
to cover (a distance) by driving or travelling rapidly ⟨burning
up *the miles*⟩ – see also BURN-UP
³burn n 1 the act, process, or result of burning: eg 1a an
injury or damage resulting from exposure to fire, heat, caustic
chemicals, electricity, or radiation ⟨*a* ~ *on the
table top*⟩ c an abrasion (eg of the skin) having the appearance

of a burn ⟨*rope* ~s⟩ **d** a burning sensation ⟨*the* ~ *of iodine on a cut*⟩ **2** a firing of a spacecraft rocket engine during flight

**burner** /'buhnə/ *n* one who or that which burns; *esp* the part of a fuel-burning device (e g a gas cooker or furnace) where the flame is produced

**burnet** /'buhnit/ *n* **1** any of a genus (*Sanguisorba*) of plants of the rose family with red or purplish flowers arranged in spikes **2 burnet, burnet moth** any of various day-flying moths (family Zygaenidae) with bright metallic green or blue front wings marked with red, and red hind wings [ME *burnet* (adj) dark brown, fr OF *burnete*, fr *brun* brown – more at BRUNETTE]

**burning** /'buhning/ *adj* **1a** on fire **b** ardent, intense ⟨~ *enthusiasm*⟩ **2a** affecting (as if) with heat ⟨*a* ~ *fever*⟩ **b** resembling that produced by a burn ⟨*a* ~ *sensation on the tongue*⟩ **3** of fundamental importance; urgent ⟨*one of the* ~ *issues of our time*⟩ – **burningly** *adv*

**burning bush** *n* **1** any of several plants with red fruit, seeds, or leaves; *esp* SUMMER CYPRESS (plant with leaves that turn red in autumn) **2** FRAXINELLA (plant that gives out an inflammable gas)

**burnish** /'buhnish/ *vt* to make shiny or lustrous, esp by rubbing; polish [ME *burnischen*, fr MF *bruniss*-, stem of *brunir*, lit., to make brown, fr *brun*] – **burnish** *n*, **burnishing** *adj or n*

**burnous** /buh'noohs, -'noohz/ *n* a hooded cloak traditionally worn by Arabs and Moors [Fr, fr Ar *burnus*, fr Gk *birros* hodded cloak]

**burnout** /'buhnowt/ *n* the moment at which a jet or rocket engine uses up its fuel and ceases to operate

**burnsides** /'buhn,siedz/ *n pl, NAm* side-whiskers; *esp* long thick side-whiskers that are narrow at the temple and broad at the lower jaw [Ambrose E *Burnside* †1881 US general]

**burnt lime** /buhnt/ *n* QUICKLIME (caustic type of lime)

**burnt offering** *n* **1** a sacrifice offered to a deity and usu burnt on or at an altar **2** *humorous* a burnt or overcooked meal or piece of food

**burnt sienna** *n* SIENNA (natural brownish-yellow earthy substance) heated to give it a reddish or orange hue and used as a pigment; *also* the reddish-brown or deep reddish-orange colour of this – compare RAW SIENNA

**burnt umber** *n* UMBER (natural dark brown earthy substance) heated to give it a reddish hue and used as a pigment; *also* the dark reddish-brown colour of this – compare RAW UMBER

**burn-,up** *n, informal* the act or an instance of driving at high speed

¹**burp** /buhp/ *n, informal* a belch [imit]

²**burp** *vb, informal vi* to belch ~ *vt* to help (a baby) to expel gas from the stomach, esp by patting or rubbing the back

¹**burr** /buh/ *n* **1 bur, burr 1a** a rough or prickly covering of a fruit or seed; *also* a fruit or seed with such a covering **b** a plant that bears burs **2 bur, burr 2a** something that sticks or clings **b** a hanger-on **3** *also* **bur 3a** an irregular rounded mass; *esp* a hard woody often rounded and flattish outgrowth on a tree trunk or branch **b** an ornamental veneer, often with a mottled effect, obtained by slicing across a tree burr ⟨~ *walnut*⟩ **4** *also* **bur** a thin ridge or rough edge left on metal, plastic, etc after cutting or shaping **5a** a trilled /r/ made at the back of the throat, as used by some speakers of English, esp in N England and in Scotland **b** a trilled /r/ made at the front of the mouth, that is the usual Scottish /r/ **6a** *also* **bur** a small rotary cutting tool or file used esp for removing burrs from metal, plastic, etc **b** **bur, burr** a drilling or cutting part of a drill used by a surgeon (e g for cutting holes in the skull during brain operations) or a dentist **7** a rough whirring or humming sound [ME *burre;* akin to OE *byrst* bristle – more at BRISTLE] – **burred** *adj*, **burry** *adj*

²**burr** *vi* **1** to speak with a burr **2** to make a whirring sound ~ *vt* **1** to pronounce with a burr **2** *also* **bur 2a** to form a rough or projecting edge on **b** to remove rough or projecting edges from – **burrer** *n*

³**burr, burstone** /'buh,stohn/ *n* BUHR (quartz-containing rock or a millstone made from this)

**bur reed** *n* any of a genus (*Sparganium*, family Sparganiaceae) of plants that grow in water and wet ground and have long narrow leaves and round prickly fruits

**burro** /'booroh/ *n, pl* **burros** *chiefly NAm* a donkey; *esp* a small donkey used as a pack animal [Sp, irreg fr *borrico*, fr LL *burricus* small horse]

¹**burrow** /'buroh/ *n* a hole, tunnel, etc in the ground made by

an animal (e g a rabbit) for shelter, habitation, and as a place for the rearing of young [ME *borow*]

²**burrow** *vt* **1a** to construct (e g a hole or passage) by tunnelling or digging **b** to make (one's way) by tunnelling ⟨~ed *their way under the hill*⟩ **2** to make a motion suggestive of burrowing with; nestle ⟨*she* ~ed *her grubby hand into mine*⟩ ~ *vi* **1** to conceal oneself (as if) in a burrow **2a** to make a burrow **b** to progress (as if) by digging or tunnelling **3** to make a motion suggestive of burrowing; snuggle, nestle ⟨~ed *against his back for warmth*⟩ **4** to search or rummage for something as if by digging ⟨~ed *into her pocket for a handkerchief*⟩ – **burrower** *n*

**bursa** /'buhsə/ *n, pl* **bursas, bursae** /-si/ a body pouch or sac; *esp* a small sac filled with a watery liquid between a tendon and a bone [NL, fr ML, bag, purse – more at PURSE] – **bursal** *adj*

**bursar** /'buhsə/ *n* **1** an officer (e g of a monastery or college) in charge of funds **2** *chiefly Scot* a student who holds a bursary [ML *bursarius*, fr *bursa*]

**bursary** /'buhs(ə)ri/ *n* **1a** the treasury of a college, monastery, etc **b** a bursar's office (e g in a college) **2** a monetary grant awarded to a student [ML *bursaria*, fr *bursa*]

**burse** /buhs/ *n* a square cloth case used during Mass to carry the linen cloth (CORPORAL) on which the bread and wine used at Communion are placed [MF *bourse*, fr ML *bursa*]

**bursitis** /,buh'sietəs/ *n* inflammation of the bursa of the knee, shoulder, elbow, or other joint [NL]

¹**burst** /buhst/ *vb* **burst** *vi* **1** to break open, apart, or into pieces, usu from impact or from pressure from within **2** to give way from an excess of emotion ⟨*his heart will* ~ *with grief*⟩ **3** to emerge or spring suddenly ⟨~ *out of the house*⟩ ~ *vt* **1** to cause to break open, apart, or into pieces, usu by means of pressure from within ⟨~ *a balloon*⟩ ⟨~ *a blood vessel*⟩ **2** to force by vigorous action ⟨~ *his way through the door*⟩ ⟨~ *the door open*⟩ **3** to produce (as if) by bursting ⟨~ *a hole in the bag*⟩ – see also **burst at the** SEAMS ⚠ **bust** [ME *bersten*, fr OE *berstan;* akin to OHG *brestan* to burst, MIr *brosc* noise]

**burst into** *vt* **1** to give vent suddenly to ⟨burst into *song*⟩ ⟨burst into *tears*⟩ **2** to pass suddenly into (a state or condition) ⟨burst into *flames*⟩ ⟨*the tree* burst into *flower*⟩

**burst out** *vi* to begin suddenly ⟨burst out *laughing*⟩

²**burst** *n* **1a** a sudden outbreak or eruption ⟨*a* ~ *of thunder*⟩ ⟨*a* ~ *of applause*⟩ **b** a temporary marked increase or display ⟨*an uncharacteristic* ~ *of generosity*⟩ **c** a sudden usu brief intense effort or exertion; a spurt ⟨*a* ~ *of speed*⟩ **d** a rapid succession of shots from a (usu automatic) firearm **2** an act of bursting open or apart **3** a result of bursting; *esp* a break, rupture

**bursting** /'buhsting/ *adj* full to overflowing or breaking point ⟨~ *with joy*⟩: e g **a** longing, yearning ⟨~ *to tell you the news*⟩ **b** *informal* desperately needing to urinate

**burthen** /'buhdhən/ *vt or n, archaic* (to) burden

¹**burton** /'buht(ə)n/ *n* any of several arrangements of ropes and pulleys for lifting something used, esp formerly, on sailing ships [origin unknown]

²**burton** *n* – **go for a burton** *Br slang* **1** to be killed or go missing, esp while in action in the air force **2** to be broken, destroyed, ruined, etc **3** to fall over [prob fr *Burton* [*ale*], a type of strong beer, for *Burton upon Trent*, town in Staffordshire (hence prob with the orig sense "go for a drink", used euphemistically)]

**burweed** /'buh,weed/ *n* any of various plants (e g a burdock) having burs or prickly fruit or seeds

**bury** /'beri/ *vt* **1a** to place (a corpse) in the earth or a tomb, usu with the appropriate funeral rites; *also* to deposit (a corpse) in the sea **b** to perform the burial rites of **c** to lose by death ⟨*has* buried *three husbands*⟩ **2a** to dispose of or hide (as if) by covering with or depositing in the earth ⟨buried *the treasure*⟩ **b** to cover from view; conceal, hide ⟨*the report was* buried *under miscellaneous papers*⟩ ⟨buried *her face in her hands*⟩ **3a** to put completely out of mind; HAVE DONE WITH ⟨~ing *their differences*⟩ **b** to conceal in obscurity ⟨buried *himself in the country*⟩ **c** to submerge, engross – usu + *in* ⟨buried *himself in his books*⟩ – see also **bury the** HATCHET [ME *burien*, fr OE *byrgan;* akin to OHG *bergan* to shelter, Russ *berech'* to save]

**burying beetle** /'beri·ing/ *n* any of various usu dark coloured beetles (family Silphidae) that bury small dead animals (e g birds and mice) which they and their larvae later feed on

¹**bus** /bus/ *n, pl* **buses, busses 1** a large motor-driven passenger vehicle operating usu according to a timetable along a fixed

route 2 **busbar** *also* **bus** an electrical conductor or set of conductors for 2a distributing electric power at a constant voltage to a number of electrical circuits in a radio, television, etc or to a number of POWER POINTS (e g in a factory) **b** carrying information in a computer from one point to another 3 *informal* a car [short for *omnibus*]

²**bus** *vb* **-s-, -ss-** *vi* to travel by bus ~ *vt* to transport by bus; *esp, chiefly NAm* to transport (children) by bus from a residential area to a district where the pupils are of a different race, in order to establish racial balance in the schools – **busing, bussing** *n*

**busboy** /'bus,boy/ *n, NAm* a waiter's assistant [earlier *omnibus* assistant in a restaurant (prob suggesting "one who does all tasks")]

**busby** /'buzbi/ *n* **1** a military full-dress fur hat that has a small bag hanging on one side and is worn esp by hussars **2** the bearskin hat worn by the Brigade of Guards – not used technically [perh fr the name *Busby*]

¹**bush** /boosh/ *n* **1a** a shrub; *esp* a low densely branched shrub **b** a dense thicket of shrubs resembling a single plant **2a** a large uncultivated or sparsely inhabited area (e g in Africa or Australia) that is usu covered by scrub or forest; wilderness ⟨*a ~ fire*⟩ – often + *the* **b** *informal or humorous* the countryside as opposed to a town ⟨*living in the ~*⟩ **3a** a bushy tuft or mass ⟨*a ~ of black hair*⟩ **b** a bushy tail (e g of a fox); ²BRUSH 2 **c** *slang* the pubic hair **4** *archaic* a bunch of ivy hung up as a sign of a wine seller or a tavern [ME; akin to OHG *busc* forest]

²**bush** *vt* to support, mark, cover, or protect with bushes ~ *vi* to extend, branch, or grow thickly like a bush; resemble a bush – often + *out*

³**bush** *also* **bushing** *n* **1** a usu removable cylindrical sleeve that lines an opening through which a shaft passes (e g in a car's suspension) and serves to limit the size of the opening, restrict abrasion, or keep the shaft in the desired position **2** an electrically insulated lining for a hole (e g in a radio) through which a wire passes [D *bus*, lit., box, fr MD *busse* box, fr LL *buxis* – more at BOX]

⁴**bush** *vt* to fit with a bush

**bush baby** *n* a member of either of two genera (*Galago* and *Euoticus*) of small tree-dwelling African PRIMATES (group of mammals including monkeys and humans) that are active at night and have large eyes and ears, a long tail, and long hind limbs that enable them to leap with great agility – called also GALAGO

**bushbuck** /-,buk/ *n, pl* **bushbucks,** *esp collectively* **bushbuck** (any of several antelopes related to) a small striped antelope (*Tragelaphus scriptus*) that lives in forests of tropical Africa and the male of which has spirally twisted horns [trans of Afrik *bosbok*]

**bushcraft** /-,krahft/ *n* skill and experience in living in the bush

**bushed** /boosht/ *adj* **1** *chiefly Austr* **1a** lost, esp in the bush **b** perplexed, confused **2** *informal* tired, exhausted

¹**bushel** /'booshl/ *n* **1** any of various units of volume, esp of a dry substance (e g grain) **2** a container that holds a bushel **3** **bushels** *pl,* **bushel** a large quantity; lots [ME *busshel,* fr OF *boissel,* fr (assumed) OF *boisse* one sixth of a bushel, of Celt origin; akin to MIr *boss* palm of the hand]

²**bushel** *vb, NAm* to repair or renovate (clothing) [prob fr Ger *bosseln* to do poor work, to patch; akin to OE *bēatan* to beat] – **bushelman** *n*

**Bushido** /,boohshi'doh/ *n* the Japanese code of chivalry, valuing honour above life, and stressing loyalty to the feudal lord or emperor, that originated with the Samurai warriors [Jap *bushidō,* fr *bushi* warrior + *dō* doctrine]

**bush jacket** *n* a belted cotton jacket that has PATCH POCKETS and resembles a shirt [fr its orig use in rough country]

**bushland** /-lənd, -,land/ *n* uncultivated land covered with scrub or forest; the bush

**Bushman** /'booshmən/ *n* **1** a member of a race of nomadic hunters of southern Africa **2** the KHOISAN language of the Bushmen **3** *not cap, chiefly Austr* one who lives in the bush and is experienced in bushcraft modif of obs Afrik *boschjesman,* fr *boschje* (dim. of *bosch* forest) + *man;* (3) ¹*bush* + *man*

**bushmaster** /-,mahstə/ *n* a large tropical American venomous snake (*Lachesis muta*) of the PIT VIPER group

**bushpig** /'boosh,pig/ *n* a wild pig (*Potamochoerus porcus*) of southern Africa, that has long reddish-brown to blackish body hair, white face markings, and a white crest on the back [trans of D *bosvark*]

**bush pilot** *n, chiefly Can* a pilot who flies over uninhabited country, esp on routes other than the standard commercial ones

**bush plane** *n, chiefly Can* a light aircraft flown by a BUSH PILOT and usu equipped with runners for landing in snow and ice

**bushranger** /-,raynjə/ *n* **1** one who lives in a sparsely populated uncultivated or forested area away from civilization **2** *Austr* an outlaw living in the bush

**bush shirt** *n* a usu loosely fitting cotton shirt with PATCH POCKETS [fr its orig use in rough country]

**bush telegraph** *n* **1** a primitive system of communication (e g one using drumbeats) used by people living in the bush, jungle, etc **2** the unofficial means, usu WORD OF MOUTH, by which news, rumours, etc are rapidly spread; GRAPEVINE 2

**bushwalking** /'boosh,wawking/ *n, Austr* the act or activity of hiking through the bush for recreation – **bushwalker** *n*

**bushwhack** /'boosh,wak/ *vi* **1** to clear a path through thick woods, esp by chopping down bushes and low branches **2** to live or hide out in the woods or bushland **3** to fight as a guerrilla or bandit in or attack from the bush to ambush [back-formation fr *bushwhacker*] – **bushwhacker** *n,* **bushwhacking** *n*

¹**bushy** /booshi/ *adj* **1** full of or overgrown with bushes **2** resembling a bush; *esp* thick and spreading ⟨~ *eyebrows*⟩ – **bushily** *adv,* **bushiness** *n*

²**bushy** *n, Austr* one who lives in the bush; BUSHMAN 3

**business** /'biznis/ *n* **1a** a role, function ⟨*he certainly knows his ~*⟩ **b** an immediate task or objective; a mission ⟨*the ~ of the meeting*⟩ **c** a particular field of endeavour ⟨*the best in the ~*⟩ **2a** a usu commercial activity engaged in as a means of livelihood ⟨*in the ~ of supplying emergency services to industry*⟩ **b** one's regular employment, profession, or trade; one's occupation – compare PROFESSION, OCCUPATION, CALLING, VOCATION **c** a commercial or sometimes an industrial firm or enterprise ⟨*sold his ~ and retired*⟩; *also* such enterprises ⟨*the ~ centre of London*⟩ **d(1)** transactions or dealings, esp of an economic nature ⟨*can't do ~ with them*⟩ **d(2)** the volume or quantity of commercial activity or transactions ⟨~ *is slow during the summer*⟩ **d(3)** patronage ⟨*ready to take my ~ elsewhere unless service improves*⟩ **e** commercial procedures or techniques ⟨*a good ~ sense*⟩ **3a** an affair, matter ⟨*a strange ~*⟩ **b** a difficult, complicated, or tedious matter; a palaver ⟨*what a ~ seeing her off on the train*⟩ **4** the movement or action (e g lighting a cigarette) performed by an actor that helps to set the scene, establish or reveal character, etc **5a** personal concern ⟨*none of your ~*⟩ **b** proper motive; justification, right ⟨*you have no ~ hitting her*⟩ **6** serious activity ⟨*immediately got down to ~*⟩ **7** *archaic* purposeful activity [ME *bisinesse,* fr *bisy* busy] – **like nobody's business** extraordinarily well or rapidly

**business cycle** *n* TRADE CYCLE (cycle of fluctuations in business activity)

**business end** *n, informal* the end of a tool, machine, etc that performs the work or at which the intended action occurs

**businesslike** /-,liek/ *adj* **1** exhibiting qualities likely to be useful or advantageous in business; *esp* briskly efficient **2** serious, purposeful

**businessman** /-mən, -,man/, *fem* **businesswoman** /-,woomən/ *n* **1** somebody professionally engaged in buying, selling, and making deals; *esp* a business executive **2** somebody with financial flair ⟨*I'm not much of a ~*⟩

¹**busk** /busk/ *vt, chiefly Scot* to make ready; prepare [ME *busken,* fr ON *būask* to prepare oneself, refl of *būa* to prepare, dwell]

²**busk** *vi, chiefly Br* to sing or play a musical instrument in the street (e g outside a theatre) or in a pub in order to earn money [perh fr obs *busk* to seek after, prob fr obs Fr *busquer* to shift, filch] – **busker** *n*

**buskin** /'buskin/ *n* **1** a laced boot reaching halfway up the calf **2a** COTHURNUS (thick-soled boot worn by Greek or Roman actor) **b** tragic drama; *esp* tragedy resembling that of ancient Greek drama [perh modif of Sp *borcegui*]

**bus lane** *n, Br* a traffic lane from which private cars or lorries are excluded; *esp* one for buses only

**busman** /'busmən/ *n, chiefly Br* one who works on a bus

**busman's holiday** *n* a holiday spent doing what one normally does at work

**buss** /bus/ *vt or n, archaic* (to) kiss [prob imit]

'**bus-,shelter** *n* a covered structure at a bus-stop that gives protection from bad weather to people waiting for a bus

'**bus-,stop** *n* a place on a bus route, usu marked by a standardized sign, where people may board and alight from buses

¹**bust** /bust/ *n* 1 a sculpture of the upper part of the human figure including the head and neck and usu the shoulders 2 the upper part of the human body between the neck and waist; *esp* a woman's breasts [Fr *buste*, fr It *busto*, fr L *bustum* tomb]

²**bust** *vb* **busted** *also* **bust** *vt* 1 *informal* **1a** to break or smash, esp with force; *also* to make inoperative ⟨~ *my watch this morning*⟩ **b** to ruin financially; make bankrupt 2 *chiefly NAm informal* to hit, strike 3 *NAm chiefly informal* to tame ⟨*bronco* ~ing⟩ 4 *NAm informal* to demote ⟨~ed *him to private*⟩ 5 *slang* **5a** to arrest ⟨~ed *for drug smuggling*⟩ **b** to raid ⟨*police* ~ed *the flat below looking for heroin*⟩ ~ *vi* 1 to lose at cards by exceeding a limit (e g the count of 21 in pontoon) 2 *informal* **2a** to burst ⟨*laughing fit to* ~⟩ **b** to stop working or become inoperative through breakage or wear; BREAK DOWN 1a △ burst [alter. of *burst*]

    **bust up** *vb, informal* to disrupt or bring an end to; BREAK UP ⟨*bust up the meeting*⟩ to come to an end; *esp* to part ⟨*bust up after six years of marriage*⟩ – see also BUST-UP

³**bust** *n* 1 *informal* a complete failure; a flop 2 *informal* a spree; *esp* a hearty drinking session 3 *chiefly NAm informal* a punch 4 *slang* a police raid or arrest

⁴**bust** *adj, chiefly informal* 1 broken; *also* not working or functioning 2 bankrupt – chiefly in **go bust** [fr pp of ²*bust*]

**bustard** /'bustəd/ *n* any of a family (Otididae) of usu large Eurasian, African, and Australian game birds that build nests on the ground, have a slow stately walk, and are capable of powerful swift flight when alarmed [ME, modif of MF *bistarde*, fr OIt *bistarda*, fr L *avis tarda*, lit., slow bird]

**bustee** /'bustee/ *n, Ind* a shantytown, slum [Hindi *bastī*, fr *basnā* to dwell, fr Skt *vasati* he dwells]

**buster** /'bustə/ *n* 1 *chiefly NAm* – used as a familiar form of address, esp to a boy or man ⟨*thanks a million*, ~⟩ 2 *Austr* SOUTHERLY BUSTER (sudden violent wind) 3 *informal* **3a** one who or that which that breaks or breaks up something ⟨*crime* ~s⟩ **b** *NAm* one who tames or breaks horses; a broncobuster [²*bust* + ²-*er*]

¹**bustle** /'busl/ *vi* 1 to move briskly and often with an ostentatious show of activity 2 to be busily astir; *esp* ⟨*a town* bustling *with activity*⟩ [prob alter. of obs *buskle* to prepare, freq of ¹*busk*] – **bustling** *adj*, **bustlingly** *adv*

²**bustle** *n* noisy and energetic activity ⟨*the hustle and* ~ *of the big city*⟩ **synonyms** see ¹FUSS

³**bustle** *n* a pad or framework worn in former times to expand and support the fullness at the back of a woman's skirt [origin unknown]

'**bust-,up** *n, informal* 1 a breaking up or apart ⟨*the* ~ *of their marriage*⟩ 2 a quarrel

**busty** /'busti/ *adj, of a woman* having large breasts

**busulphan**, *NAm* **busulfan** /byooh'sulfən/ *n* a synthetic drug, (CH₂)₄(OSO₂CH₃)₂, used to treat cancer, esp some forms of leukaemia [*butane* + *sulph*onyl, *sulf*onyl]

¹**busy** /'bizi/ *adj* 1 engaged in action or an activity; occupied 2 full of activity ⟨*a* ~ *seaport*⟩ ⟨*a* ~ *afternoon*⟩ 3 foolishly or intrusively active; meddlesome 4 full or too full of detail ⟨*a* ~ *design*⟩ 5 *chiefly NAm, esp of a telephone line* in use [ME *bisy*, fr OE *bisig*; akin to MD & MLG *besich* busy] – **busily** *adv*, **busyness** *n*

    **synonyms** Busy, industrious, diligent, assiduous, sedulous: busy contrasts with "idle", and may describe habitual or temporary purposeful (or apparently so) activity ⟨*the busy bee*⟩ ⟨*a busy life*⟩. Industrious suggests habitual or continuing worthwhile activity, or a predisposition towards it. It stresses regular, steady application. Diligent emphasizes care and thoroughness, and often suggests keen and intense activity towards a goal of one's own choosing ⟨*a diligent seeker after truth*⟩. Assiduous and the formal sedulous put the accent on sustained application; earnest and persistent for the former, careful and painstaking for the latter. antonyms idle, unoccupied

²**busy** *vt* to make or keep (esp oneself) busy; occupy ⟨*busied himself with the ironing*⟩

**busybody** /-,bodi/ *n* an officious, meddlesome, or inquisitive person

**busy lizzie** /'lizi/ *n* a common house plant (*Impatiens balsamina*) of the balsam family that bears usu pink, scarlet, or crimson flowers almost continuously [*Lizzie*, nickname for *Elizabeth*]

¹**but** /bət; *strong* but/ *conj* **1a** were it not; save ⟨*would have protested* ~ *that he was afraid*⟩ ⟨*would collapse* ~ *for your*

*help*⟩ **b** THAT 1a(1) – used after a negative ⟨*there is no doubt* ~ *he won*⟩ **c** without the necessary accompaniment that – used after a negative ⟨*it never rains* ~ *it pours*⟩ **d** otherwise than; that . . . not ⟨*I'm not such a fool* ~ *I can tell the difference*⟩ ⟨*who knows* ~ *that you may succeed*⟩ ⟨*I don't know* ~ *what I'll go*⟩ **e** *substandard* than, when ⟨*no sooner started* ~ *it stopped*⟩ **2a** on the contrary; on the other hand – used to join sentence parts that are of the same kind and are used to express contrast ⟨*he didn't waste time,* ~ *worked hard*⟩ ⟨*not peace* ~ *a sword*⟩ ⟨*I meant to tell you* ~ *you weren't here*⟩ **b** and nevertheless; and yet ⟨*poor* ~ *proud*⟩ **c** – used to introduce an expression of protest or enthusiasm ⟨~ *that's ridiculous*⟩ ⟨~ *how lovely*⟩ or to embark on a new topic ⟨~ *to continue . . .*⟩ **d** – used to introduce an emphatic utterance, esp a repetition ⟨*lost everything,* ~ *everything*⟩ [ME, fr OE *būtan*, prep & conj, outside, without, except, except that; akin to OHG *būzan* without, except; both fr a prehistoric WGmc compound whose constituents are represented by OE *be* by and OE *ūtan* outside]

    **usage** 1 There are many occasions on which it is perfectly legitimate and very effective to begin a sentence with but. 2 The use of but in the same sentence as *however, still, yet,* or *nevertheless* should probably be avoided as redundant ⟨*the sky grew darker;* (but) nevertheless *they struggled on*⟩; and the use of but with what in sense 1d ⟨*I don't know but what I'll go*⟩ is widely disliked.

²**but** *prep* **1a** with the exception of; barring ⟨*we're all here* ~ *Mary*⟩ ⟨*anywhere* ~ *in Scotland*⟩ **b** other than ⟨*this letter is nothing* ~ *an insult*⟩ **c** not counting ⟨*the next house* ~ *two*⟩ 2 *Scot* **2a** without, lacking **b** outside

    **usage** Although but is a conjunction as well as a preposition, but me/him/her/them are legitimate in formal writing ⟨*we're all here* but *him*⟩. Where a verb follows of which the pronoun may be felt to be the subject, some writers prefer to use I/he/she/they ⟨*no one but* she *can tell you*⟩.

³**but** *adv* 1 only, merely ⟨*he is* ~ *a child*⟩ 2 *Scot* outside 3 *NE Eng & Austr* however, though ⟨*its pouring with rain, warm* ~⟩

⁴**but** *n* a doubt, objection ⟨*there are no* ~s *about it*⟩

⁵**but** *n, Scot* the kitchen or living quarters of a 2-room cottage [Sc *but*, adj, outer]

**butadiene** /,byoohtə'die·een, ,---'-/ *n* an inflammable gas, CH₂=CHCH=CH₂, used in making synthetic rubbers [ISV *butane* + *di-* + *-ene*]

**butane** /'byoohtayn/ *n* an inflammable gas, C₄H₁₀, that is a member of the ALKANE series of organic chemical compounds, is obtained usu from petroleum or natural gas, and is used as a fuel (e g in cigarette lighters) [ISV *butyric* + *-ane*]

**butanoic acid** /,byoohtə'noh·ik/ *n* BUTYRIC ACID (organic acid that gives rancid butter its unpleasant smell)

**butanol** /'byoohtənol/ *n* either of two forms of a liquid organic chemical compound, C₄H₉OH, derived from butane, that are used in varnishes, paint removers, etc – called also BUTYL ALCOHOL

¹**butch** /booch/ *n* a butch person; *esp* a lesbian who adopts the masculine role in a homosexual relationship [*Butch*, a nickname for boys, prob short for *butcher*]

²**butch** *adj* aggressively masculine in appearance or behaviour; tough – used, often derogatorily, of both women and esp homosexual men

¹**butcher** /'boochə/ *n* **1a** one who slaughters animals bred for meat or cuts up and prepares their carcasses for sale **b** a dealer in or seller of meat 2 one who kills ruthlessly or brutally [ME *bocher*, fr OF *bouchier*, fr *bouc* he-goat, prob of Celt origin; akin to MIr *bocc* he-goat – more at BUCK] – **butcherly** *adj*

²**butcher** *vt* 1 to slaughter and prepare (an animal) for sale 2 to kill in a barbarous manner 3 to make a mess of; spoil, ruin – **butcherer** *n*

'**butcher-,bird** *n* any of various SHRIKES (medium-sized birds) (esp genus *Lanius*) that often impale their prey on thorns

**butchers, butcher's** /'boochəz/ *n, pl* **butchers** *Br slang* the act or an instance of looking; a look [rhyming slang *butcher's* (*hook*) look]

'**butcher's-,broom** *n* a European shrub (*Ruscus aculeatus*) of the lily family that has flat green leaflike twigs with stiff pointed ends instead of normal leaves [fr its formerly being used to make brooms for butchers]

**butchery** /'booch(ə)ri/ *n* 1 the preparation of meat for sale 2 cruel and ruthless slaughter of human beings 3 the action of destroying or ruining something 4 *chiefly Br* a slaughterhouse

**butler** /'butlə/ *n* 1 a servant, esp a manservant, in charge of the wines and spirits 2 the chief, usu male, servant of a household, who has charge of other employees, directs the serving of meals, and is a personal attendant to the householder [ME *buteler,* fr OF *bouteillier* bottle-bearer, fr *bouteille* bottle – more at BOTTLE]

¹**butt** /but/ *vt* to strike or shove with the head or horns ~ *vi* to thrust or push with the head foremost; strike with the head or horns [ME *butten,* fr OF *boter,* of Gmc origin; akin to OHG *bōzan* to beat – more at BEAT]

**butt in** *vi* 1 to meddle, intrude 2 to interrupt

²**butt** *n* a blow or thrust, usu with the head or horns

³**butt** *n* 1a a backstop (eg a mound or bank) for catching bullets, arrows, etc shot at a target **b** a target; *esp* one for firing arrows or bullets at **c** *pl* RANGE 4c; *specif* one for archery or rifle practice **d** a low mound or wall from behind which sportsmen shoot at game birds **e** a covered gallery which houses the targets and target operators in a rifle range 2 an object of abuse or ridicule; a victim 3 *archaic* a goal, aim ⟨*here is my journey's end, here is my ~* – Shak⟩ [ME; partly fr MF *but* target, end, of Gmc origin (akin to ON *būtr* log, LG *butt* blunt); partly fr MF *bute* backstop, fr *but* target]

⁴**butt** *vi* to abut – usu + *against* or *onto* ~ *vt* 1 to place end to end or side to side without overlapping; place the end of (eg a plank) against a flat surface 2 to join by means of a BUTT JOINT (joint made without overlapping the joined parts) [partly fr ³*butt,* partly fr ⁵*butt*]

⁵**butt** *n* 1 the large or thicker part at the end of something: eg **1a** the end of a plant (eg the base of a tree trunk) from which the roots spread out or downwards **b** the thicker or handle end of a tool or weapon ⟨*the ~ of a rifle*⟩ 2 an unused remainder; *esp* the unsmoked remnant of a cigar or cigarette 3 the part of a hide or skin corresponding to the animal's back and sides 4 *NAm informal* the buttocks [ME; prob akin to ME *buttok* buttock, LG *butt* blunt, OHG *bōzan* to beat]

⁶**butt** *n* 1 a large cask or barrel for storing wine, beer, water, etc; *specif* one having a volume of 108 gallons (about 491 litres) 2 any of various units of liquid capacity; *esp* one equal to 108 imperial gallons (about 491 litres) [ME, fr MF *botte,* fr OProv *bota,* fr LL *buttis*]

**butte** /byooht/ *n, chiefly NAm* an isolated hill or small mountain with steep sides, usu having a smaller summit area than a MESA [Fr, knoll, fr MF *bute* mound of earth serving as a backstop]

¹**butter** /'butə/ *n* 1 a pale yellow solid substance that is used as food (eg in baking or for spreading on bread) and is made by churning milk or cream so as to form an EMULSION of fat globules, air, and water 2 a substance like butter: eg **2a** any of various vegetable oils that remains solid or semisolid at ordinary temperatures ⟨*cocoa ~*⟩ **b** any of various food spreads made with or having the consistency of butter ⟨*peanut ~*⟩ [ME, fr OE *butere;* akin to OHG *butera* butter; both fr a prehistoric WGmc word borrowed fr L *butyrum* butter, fr Gk *boutyron,* fr *bous* cow + *tyros* cheese] – **butterless** *adj*

²**butter** *vt* to spread or cook with butter

**butter up** *vt, informal* to charm or beguile with lavish flattery or praise; cajole

**butterball** /'butə,bawl/ *n, informal* a fat or chubby person

**butter bean** *n* LIMA BEAN (bean plant with large flat edible seeds, or a seed of this plant): eg **a** a large dried LIMA BEAN **b** SIEVA BEAN

**butterbur** /'butə,buh/ *n* a large Eurasian plant (*Petasites hybridus*) of the daisy family that grows esp in damp places and has very large leaves and reddish-purple flowers

**buttercream** /'butə,kreem/ *n* a soft creamy spread made with butter and icing sugar and used as a filling or icing for cakes

**buttercup** /'butə,kup/ *n* any of many plants (genus *Ranunculus* of the family Ranunculaceae, the buttercup family) with usu bright yellow flowers that commonly grow in fields and as weeds

**butterfat** /'butə,fat/ *n* the natural fat of milk and chief constituent of butter, consisting essentially of a mixture of different GLYCERIDES

**butterfingered** /'butə,fing·gəd/ *adj, informal* apt to let things fall or slip through the fingers; careless

**butterfingers** /'butə,fing·gəz/ *n, pl* **butterfingers** *informal* a butterfingered person

**butterfish** /'butə,fish/ *n* any of numerous usu small and elongated mostly spiny-finned fishes (esp family Stromateidae) that are covered with a slippery coating of mucus and live esp in warm seas; *also* GUNNEL (slippery fish of northern seas)

**butterfly** /'butə,flie/ *n* 1 any of numerous slender-bodied insects (order Lepidoptera) that fly by day and have large broad often brightly coloured wings and slender antennae with broad club-shaped ends 2 something that resembles or suggests a butterfly; *esp* a person chiefly occupied with the pursuit of pleasure 3 a swimming stroke executed on the front by moving both arms together forwards out of the water and then sweeping them back through the water while kicking the legs up and down together 4 *pl, informal* a queasiness caused esp by emotional or nervous tension or anxious anticipation [ME *butterflie,* fr OE *buterflēoge,* fr *butere* butter + *flēoge* fly; perh fr the yellow colour of a common species, or fr a former folklore belief that butterflies steal milk and butter]

**butterfly bush** *n* the buddleia [fr butterflies being greatly attracted to its flowers]

**butterfly fish** *n* a fish having either variegated colours, or large wide fins, or both: eg **a** a European blenny (*Blennius ocellaris*) **b** any of a family (Chaetodontidae) of small brilliantly coloured spiny-finned fishes of tropical seas with a body that is narrow from side to side but deep from upper surface to lower surface, and fins partly covered with scales

**butterfly nut** *n* WING NUT (nut with projections for turning by hand)

**butterfly valve** *n* 1 a valve that stops or controls the flow of gas or liquid along a pipe and that consists of two flat semicircular halves attached by their straight edges to opposite sides of a central rod that forms a hinge 2 a valve for restricting the flow of gas or liquid along a pipe that consists of a disc lying inside the pipe which turns about an axis on its diameter and is used esp as the throttle and choke valve in the carburettor of a petrol engine

**buttermilk** /'butə,milk/ *n* 1 the liquid left after butter has been made from milk or cream, used for making bread, scones, etc or for drinking 2 fermented slightly sour milk made by the addition of suitable bacteria to milk

**butternut** /'butə,nut/ *n* (the edible oily nut of) an American tree (*Juglans cinerea*) of the walnut family – called also WHITE WALNUT

**butterscotch** /'butə,skoch/ *n* 1 a brittle toffee made from brown sugar, syrup, butter, and water; *also* the flavour of such toffee 2 a yellowish-brown colour [prob fr *butter* + *Scotch;* perh orig manufactured in Scotland]

**butterwort** /'butə,wuht/ *n* any of a genus (*Pinguicula* of the family Lentibulariaceae, the butterwort family) of insect-eating plants of wet places that have fleshy usu light-green leaves which produce a sticky secretion that helps in capturing and digesting insects

¹**buttery** /'but(ə)ri/ *n* a storeroom for food and esp drink 2 a room, esp in a college, in which food and drink are served or sold to a restricted group of people [ME *boterie,* fr MF, fr *botte* cask, butt – more at ⁶BUTT]

²**buttery** *adj* 1 having the qualities, consistency, or appearance of butter 2 containing or spread with butter

**butt joint** *n* a joint between two pieces (eg planks) placed together end to end or side to side without overlapping, that does not require any special shaping of the pieces

**buttock** /'butək/ *n* the back of a hip that forms one of the two large fleshy parts on which a person sits; *also* the corresponding part of a cow or other mammal [ME *buttok* – more at ⁵BUTT]

¹**button** /'but(ə)n/ *n* 1a a small knob or disc sewed, riveted, etc to an article, esp of clothing, and used as a fastener by passing it through a buttonhole or loop **b** a usu circular badge bearing a design or slogan 2 something that resembles a button, esp in being small and round: eg **2a** a small whole mushroom **b** a small globule of metal remaining, esp in a crucible, after melting (eg to determine the purity of a sample of gold) **c** a guard that makes the tip of a FOIL (type of sword) blunt for use in fencing 3 PUSH BUTTON 4 a rivet 5 something of little value – chiefly in *not worth a button* 6 *pl, Br informal* a liveried page boy [ME *boton,* fr MF, fr OF, fr *boter* to thrust – more at ¹BUTT; (6) fr the buttons on his uniform] – **buttonless** *adj,* **buttony** *adj* – **on the button** precisely

²**button** *vt* to close or fasten (as if) with buttons – often + *up* ⟨*~ up your overcoat*⟩ ~ *vi* to have buttons for fastening ⟨*this dress ~s at the back*⟩ – **buttoner** *n*

¹**button-,down** *adj* 1 *of a collar, esp of a shirt* having the ends fastened to the garment with buttons 2 *of a garment* having a button-down collar

¹**buttonhole** /'but(ə)n,hohl/ *n* 1 a loop or a usu stitched or bound slit in the edge of a piece of material, through which a

button is passed **2** *chiefly Br* a flower worn in a buttonhole or pinned to the lapel, esp of a jacket

²**buttonhole** *vt* **1** to provide with buttonholes **2** to sew with buttonhole stitch – **buttonholer** *n*

³**buttonhole** *vt* to detain (a person) in conversation [alter. of arch. *buttonhold* (to detain somebody by holding the buttons on his clothes)]

**buttonhole stitch** *n* a closely worked sewing stitch formed from interlocking loops, used to make a firm or neat edge (eg on a buttonhole) or prevent fraying – compare BLANKET STITCH

**buttonhook** /'but(ə)n,hook/ *n* a hook for drawing small buttons through buttonholes – **buttonhook** *vi*

**button quail** *n* any of various small ground-living birds (family Turnicidae) of warm parts of Africa, Europe, and Asia that resemble quails and are related to the cranes and bustards

'**button-,through** *adj, of a garment* fastened from the top to the bottom with buttons ⟨*a* ~ *skirt*⟩

¹**buttress** /'butris/ *n* **1** a projecting structure built against a wall or building to provide support or reinforcement **2a** a projecting part of a mountain or hill **b** either of two horny projections that lie one at each side of the back of a horse's hoof **c** the broadened base of a tree trunk **3** something that supports or strengthens ⟨*a* ~ *of the cause of peace*⟩ [ME *butres*, fr MF *bouterez*, fr OF *boterez*, fr boter to thrust] – **buttressed** *adj*

²**buttress** *vt* to provide or shore up (as if) with a buttress; *also* to support, strengthen ⟨*arguments* ~ed *by solid facts*⟩

**buttstock** /'but,stok/ *n* the rear part of the stock of a rifle, shotgun, etc; the butt

**butt weld** *n* a BUTT JOINT (joint made without overlapping the joined parts) made by welding – **butt-weld** *vt*, **butt welding** *n*

¹**butty** /'buti/ *n, chiefly Br informal* **1** a fellow workman; a friend, mate **2** a middleman between a mine-owner and miners [origin unknown]

²**butty** *n, dial Br* a sandwich [¹*butter* + -*y*]

'**butty-,gang** *n taking sing or pl vb, Br* a gang of labourers in former times who shared a lump sum as wages

**butut** /booh'tooht/ *n* – see *dalasi* at MONEY table [native word in the Gambia]

**butyl** /'byooti/, -tiel/ *n* any of four chemical groups, $C_4H_9$, that have a VALENCY of one and can be derived from butane by the removal of a single hydrogen atom [ISV *butyric* + -*yl*]

**Butyl** /'byoohtil, -tiel/ *trademark* – used for any of various synthetic rubbers made from ISOBUTYLENE

**butyl alcohol** *n* any of four organic chemical compounds, $C_4H_9OH$: **a** BUTANOL (either of two liquid organic chemical compounds) **b** either of two derivatives of propane, one solid and one liquid, that are used in varnishes and in manufacturing flavourings

**butyr-** /byooti-/, **butyro-** *comb form* **1** butyric ⟨butyr*al*⟩ **2** butyric acid ⟨butyr*ate*⟩ [ISV, fr *butyric*]

**butyraceous** /,byoohti'rayshəs/ *adj* buttery – used technically [L *butyrum* butter – more at BUTTER]

**butyraldehyde** /,byoohti'raldihied/ *n* either of two pungent liquid organic chemical compounds, $CH_3(CH_2)_2CHO$, used esp in making plastics and solvents [ISV]

**butyrate** /'byoohtirayt/ *n* any of various chemical compounds (SALTS or ESTERS) formed by combination between BUTYRIC ACID and a metal atom, an alcohol, or another chemical group

**butyric** /byooh'tirik/ *adj* relating to or producing butyric acid ⟨~ *fermentation*⟩ [Fr *butyrique*, fr L *butyrum*]

**butyric acid** *n* a FATTY ACID, $CH_3(CH_2)_2COOH$, that gives rancid butter its unpleasant smell and taste and is used in making flavourings and varnishes

**buxom** /'buks(ə)m/ *adj* **1** *esp of a woman* attractively or healthily plump; *specif* having large breasts **2** *archaic* full of gaiety; blithe **3** *obs* offering little resistance; flexible, pliant ⟨*wing silently the* ~ *air* – John Milton⟩ [ME *buxsum* obedient, pliant, fr (assumed) OE *būhsum*, fr OE *būgan* to bend – more at BOW] – **buxomly** *adv*, **buxomness** *n*

¹**buy** /bie/ *vb* **bought** /bawt/ *vt* **1** to acquire possession or rights to the use of by payment, esp of money; purchase **2** to obtain, often by some sacrifice ⟨bought *peace with their lives*⟩ **3** to corrupt by bribery; bribe ⟨*we* bought *the chief of police*⟩ **4** to be the purchasing equivalent of ⟨*the pound* ~s *less today than it used to*⟩ **5** *slang* to believe, accept ⟨*OK, I'll* ~ *that*⟩ ~ *vi* to make a purchase [ME *byen*, fr OE *bycgan*; akin to Goth *bugjan* to buy]

**buy in** *vt* **1** to buy (a stock or supply of something) in anticipation of a need; stockpile **2** to buy (stocks, shares, etc that a

seller has failed to hand over at the agreed time) on the Stock Exchange, charging the extra cost involved to the defaulting or delaying seller **3** to buy (something offered for sale at an auction that has failed to exceed an agreed minimum price) back on behalf of a seller, so as to guarantee a minimum price ~ *vi* to buy in stocks, shares, etc on the Stock Exchange – **buy-in** /'- ,-/n

**buy off** *vt* to make a payment to in order to avoid some undesired course of action; *esp* to bribe

**buy out** *vt* **1** to purchase the share held in a business, enterprise, etc by (a person, company, etc) ⟨bought *his partner* out⟩ **2** to free (eg from military service) by payment ⟨bought *himself* out *of the army*⟩

**buy up** *vt* **1** to buy freely or extensively **2** to buy the entire available supply of

²**buy** *n* **1** an act of buying **2** something bought, esp when considered from the point of view of value for money ⟨*it was not a good* ~⟩

**buyer** /'bie·ə/ *n* one who buys; *esp* one whose occupation is selecting and buying stock to be sold in an esp large shop or chain of shops

**buyer's market** *n* a market in which the supply of goods exceeds demand, buyers have a wide range of choice, and prices tend to be low – compare SELLER'S MARKET

¹**buzz** /buz/ *vi* **1** to make the low continuous vibratory humming sound characteristic of a bee **2** to be filled with a confused murmur ⟨*the room* ~ed *with excitement*⟩; *also* to be full of gossip or rumours ⟨*oil-industry publications* ~ *with talk of further cutbacks – Time*⟩ **3** to make a signal with a buzzer **4** to move in a hurried, energetic, or busy manner **5** *archaic* to murmur, whisper ~ *vt* **1** to cause to buzz **2** to summon or signal with a buzzer **3** to fly over or close to ⟨*the airliner was* ~ed *by fighters during its approach*⟩ **4** *chiefly Br slang* to throw, fling [ME *bussen*, of imit origin]

**buzz off** *vi, informal* to go away quickly

²**buzz** *n* **1** a persistent vibratory sound **2a** a confused murmur or flurry of activity **b** rumour, gossip **3** *informal* a signal conveyed by a buzzer or bell; *specif* a telephone call **4** *informal* a pleasant stimulation; a kick

**buzzard** /'buzəd/ *n* **1** any of a genus (*Buteo*) of fairly large hawks with broad rounded wings and soaring flight; *esp* the common European one (*Buteo buteo*) **2** any of various usu large BIRDS OF PREY (eg the TURKEY BUZZARD) **3** a contemptible, greedy, or avaricious person [ME *busard*, fr OF, alter. of *buison*, fr L *buteon-*, *buteo*]

**buzzer** /'buzə/ *n* one who or that which buzzes; *specif* an electric device that makes a buzzing sound (eg for signalling)

**buzz saw** *n, chiefly NAm* CIRCULAR SAW

**buzzword** /'buz,wuhd/ *n* a usu technical word or phrase, often of little meaning, used to impress laymen

**bwana** /'bwahnə/ *n, chiefly E Africa* a master, boss – often used by a black man to a white man as a form of address corresponding to Sir [Swahili, fr Ar *abūna* our father]

¹**by** /bie/ *prep* **1a** in proximity to; near ⟨*standing* ~ *the window*⟩ **b** on the person or in the possession of ⟨*I keep a spare set* ~ *me*⟩ **2a** through or through the medium of; via ⟨*enter* ~ *the door*⟩ ⟨*go* ~ *sea*⟩ ⟨*delivered* ~ *hand*⟩ **b** in the direction of (another compass point); *specif* 11°15' towards (a cardinal point less than 90° away) ⟨*north* ~ *east*⟩ ⟨*southwest* ~ *south*⟩ **c** up to and then beyond; past ⟨*went right* ~ *him*⟩ ⟨*go round* ~ *Piccadilly*⟩ **3a** in the circumstances of; during ⟨*studied* ~ *night*⟩ ⟨*see it* ~ *daylight*⟩ **b** not later than ⟨*in bed* ~ *10 pm*⟩ **4a(1)** through the instrumentality or use of ⟨~ *force*⟩ ⟨~ *bus*⟩ ⟨*live* ~ *teaching music*⟩ ⟨*learn* ~ *rote*⟩ ⟨*what did he mean* ~ *that?*⟩ **a(2)** holding ⟨*seize it* ~ *the handle*⟩ **a(3)** through the action or creation of ⟨*a symphony* ~ *Mozart*⟩ **b(1)** sired by – compare OUT OF 2c **b(2)** with the participation of (the other parent) ⟨*his daughter* ~ *his first wife*⟩ **5** with the witness or sanction of ⟨*swear* ~ *Heaven*⟩ **6a** in conformity with; as a result of ⟨*acted* ~ *the rules*⟩ ⟨*opened it* ~ *mistake*⟩ **b** ACCORDING TO 2 ⟨~ *her I'm no writer*⟩ – used esp by Jews of European origin **c** IN TERMS OF ⟨*paid* ~ *the hour*⟩ ⟨*sold* ~ *the dozen*⟩ ⟨*called her* ~ *name*⟩ **d** from the evidence of ⟨*judge* ~ *appearances*⟩ **e** with the action of ⟨*began* ~ *scolding her*⟩ **7** with respect to ⟨*French* ~ *birth*⟩ ⟨*a doctor* ~ *profession*⟩ ⟨*do my duty* ~ *her*⟩ **8a** to the amount or extent of ⟨*win* ~ *a nose*⟩ ⟨*better* ~ *far*⟩ **b** *chiefly Scot* in comparison with; beside **9** in successive units or increments of ⟨~ *inches*⟩ ⟨~ *degrees*⟩ ⟨*day* ~ *day*⟩ ⟨*succeeded little* ~ *little*⟩ ⟨*walk two* ~ *two*⟩ **10** – used in division to show that the preceding number is to be

shared ⟨*divide 70 ~ 35*⟩, in multiplication ⟨*multiply 10 ~ 4*⟩, and in measurements ⟨*a room 15 feet ~ 20 feet*⟩ [ME, prep & adv, fr OE, prep, *be, bī;* akin to OHG *bī* by, near, L *ambi-* on both sides, round, Gk *amphi*] – **by oneself 1** in solitude; alone **2** without assistance

²**by** *adv* **1** close at hand; near ⟨*when nobody was ~*⟩ **2** past ⟨*saw him go ~*⟩ **3** aside, away; *esp* in or into reserve ⟨*keep a few bottles ~*⟩ **4** chiefly *NAm* to or at another's home ⟨*stop ~ for a chat*⟩ – **by and by** soon; in a short time

³**by, bye** *adj* **1** off the main route; side **2** incidental, secondary ⟨*a ~ effect*⟩ □ usu in combination

⁴**by, bye** *n, pl* **byes** – **by the by/bye** incidentally; BY THE WAY

'**by-,blow** *n* **1** an indirect blow **2** *archaic* an illegitimate child

¹**bye, by** /bie/ *n* **1** the pass to the next round of a tournament allowed to a competitor who has no opponent or whose opponent has withdrawn **2** a run that is scored in cricket off a ball that passes the batsman without striking his/her bat or body and that is credited to the batsman's side but not to his/her individual score – compare LEG BYE, EXTRA [alter. of ²*by*]

²**bye, by** *interj* – used to express farewell [short for *goodbye*]

'**bye-,bye, by-by** *interj* – used to express farewell [baby-talk redupl of *goodbye*]

'**bye-,byes, by-bys** *n pl,* **bye-bye, by-by** *n* bed, sleep – used esp by or to children ⟨*go to ~*⟩

'**by-e,lection** *also* **bye-election** *n* a special election held between regular elections in order to fill a vacancy that has arisen unexpectedly (eg from the death or resignation of a member of parliament)

**Byelorussian, Belorussian** /,b(y)eloh'rushən/ *n* **1** a native or inhabitant of Byelorussia **2** the Slavonic language of the Byelorussians [*Byelorussia, Belorussia,* region in E Europe (now a republic of the USSR)] – **Byelorussian** *adj*

¹**bygone** /'bie,gon/ *adj* earlier, past; *esp* outmoded

²**bygone** *n* something that is bygone; *specif* a domestic, industrial, etc implement or machine of an early and disused type – **let bygones be bygones** to forgive and forget past quarrels

**bylaw, byelaw** /'bie,law/ *n* **1** an enactment made by a local authority and having effect only within the area controlled by that authority **2** a standing rule controlling the affairs of a club, company, etc **3** a secondary law or regulation [ME *bilawe,* prob fr (assumed) ON *bȳlög,* fr ON *bȳr* town + *lög* law; (3) partly fr ²*by*]

¹**by-,line** *n* **1** a sideline **2** the author's name printed with a newspaper or magazine article **3** by-line, bye-line *informal* **3a** the GOAL LINE at either end of a soccer field **b** the touchline at either side of a rugby field

²**by-line** *vt* to write (a newspaper or magazine article) under a by-line – **byliner** *n*

**byname** /'bie,naym/ *n* **1** a secondary name **2** a nickname

**bypass** /-,pahs/ *n* **1** a passage to one side; *esp* a road built so that through-traffic can avoid a town centre **2a** a pipe, channel, etc carrying a flow of liquid or gas round a part that it would otherwise be directed through, then back to the main stream **b** an electrical circuit (eg in an amplifier) that diverts part of the

**bypath** /-,pahth/ *n* a byway

**byplay** /-,play/ *n* action engaged in on the side while the main action (eg of a play or film) proceeds

'**by-,product** *n* **1** something produced (eg during a manufacturing process) in addition to a principal or desired product **2** a secondary and sometimes unexpected or unintended result

**byre** /'bie-ə/ *n, chiefly Br* a cow shed [ME, fr OE *bȳre;* akin to OE *būr* dwelling – more at BOWER]

**byroad** /'bie,rohd/ *n* a byway

**Byronic** /bie'ronik/ *adj* (having the characteristics) of Byron or his writings, esp in displaying a self-conscious romanticism [George Gordon, Lord *Byron* †1824 E poet] – **Byronically** *adv,* **Byronism** *n*

**byssinosis** /,bisi'nohsis/ *n, pl* **byssinoses** /-'nohseez/ a long-lasting industrial disease of the lungs that is characterized esp by bronchitis and is associated with the inhalation of cotton dust over a long period of time [NL, fr L *byssinus* of fine linen, fr Gk *byssinos,* fr *byssos*]

**byssus** /'bisəs/ *n, pl* **byssuses, byssi** /-sie/ **1** a fine cloth of ancient times that was probably linen **2** a tuft of long tough filaments or threads by which mussels and related animals attach themselves to rocks or other hard surfaces [L, fr Gk *byssos* flax, of Sem origin; akin to Heb *būs* linen cloth] – **byssal** *adj*

**bystander** /'bie,standə/ *n* one present at but not involved in a demonstration, riot, sporting event, etc

**byte** /biet/ *n* a string of eight adjacent binary numbers (BITS) that is processed by a computer as a unit of information [perh alter. of ²*bite*]

**byway** /-,way/ *n* **1** a little-used road **2** a secondary or little-known aspect ⟨*the author takes us down the ~s of medieval literature*⟩

**bywoner** /'bie,vohnə, 'bay-/ *n* a poor white S African farmer who works part of someone else's land and gives a share of his profits or labour or both in return [Afrik, fr *by* with, at + *woner* dweller, fr *woon* to dwell]

**byword** /-,wuhd/ *n* **1** a proverb **2** somebody or something regarded as possessing or characterized by a specified or implied quality ⟨*he's a ~ for punctuality*⟩

,**by-your-'leave** *n* a request for permission – esp in *without so much as a by-your-leave*

¹**Byzantine** /bi'zantien, bie-, -teen/ *n* a native or inhabitant of Byzantium [LL *Byzantinus,* fr *Byzantium* (later called Constantinople, now Istanbul), city in Turkey]

²**Byzantine** *adj* **1** (characteristic) of the ancient city of Byzantium or the empire of which it was the capital **2a** of, being, or similar to a style of architecture developed in the Byzantine Empire, esp in the 5th and 6th centuries, featuring a central dome covering a square space, incrustation with marble slabs, and coloured mosaics on a gold background **b** of, being, or similar to the style of religious art that developed in the Byzantine Empire, featuring brightly coloured stylized figures on an often gold background **3** ORTHODOX 2a (of the Eastern Orthodox Christian churches) **4** intricately tortuous; complicated in an obscure manner ⟨*the ~ complexity of their politics*⟩

# C

c, C /see/ n, pl c's, cs, C's, Cs 1a the 3rd letter of the English alphabet b a graphic representation of or device for reproducing the letter c c a speech counterpart of printed or written c 2 one hundred 3 the keynote of the major scale that has no sharps or flats, having a pitch which is that of MIDDLE C multiplied or divided by 2, 4, 8, 16, 32, etc 4 one designated c, esp as the 3rd in order or class 5a a mark or grade rating a pupil's or student's work as fair or mediocre in quality b one who or that which is graded or rated with a C 6 something shaped like the letter C 7 slang cocaine 8 chiefly NAm slang a sum of $100

C-1 n a single-seater CANADIAN CANOE

C-2 n a 2-seater CANADIAN CANOE

ca' /kah, kaw/ vb or n, Scot (to) call

¹cab /kab/ n an ancient Hebrew unit of capacity equal to about 1.6 litres (about 3 pints) [Heb qabh]

²cab n 1a a CABRIOLET or a similar light closed two-wheeled one-horse carriage (e g a hansom) b a carriage for hire 2 a taxi 3 the usu enclosed part of a railway engine, lorry, crane, etc that houses the driver or operator [short for cabriolet; (3) prob influenced by cabin]

¹cabal /kə'bal/ n taking sing or pl vb a clandestine or unofficial group of people forming a faction, esp in political intrigue [Fr cabale cabala, intrigue, cabal, fr ML cabbala cabala, fr LHeb qabbālāh, lit., received (lore)]

²cabal vi -ll- to unite in or form a cabal

cabala, cabbala, cabbala also kabala, kabbala, kabbalah /kə'bahlə, 'kabələ/ n, often cap 1 a system of esoteric Jewish belief based on the extraction of hidden meanings and predictions from the Old Testament and other texts 2 a traditional, esoteric, occult, mysterious, or secret doctrine, art, or subject [ML cabbala] – cabalism n, cabalistic adj

cabaletta, cabbaletta /,kabə'letə/ n 1 an operatic song in a simple popular style characterized by an even rhythm 2 a song in RONDO form, sometimes with variations 3 a recurring passage in a song, appearing simply the first time and subsequently varied [It]

¹cabalist also kabalist, kabbalist /'kabəlist/ n 1 often cap an interpreter, devotee, or student of the Jewish cabala 2 one who is skilled in an esoteric doctrine or a mysterious art

²cabalist n a member of a cabal

caballero /,kabə'lyeəroh, kabə'yeəroh/ n, pl caballeros 1 a Spanish gentleman or knight 2 chiefly SW US a horseman [Sp, fr LL caballarius horseman – more at CAVALIER]

cabaret /'kabəray/ n a stage show or series of acts provided by singers, dancers, etc at a nightclub or similar establishment; also, chiefly NAm a restaurant providing such entertainment [Fr, lit., tavern, fr ONF, prob irreg fr LL camera chamber]

¹cabbage /'kabij/ n 1 a cultivated plant (Brassica oleracea capitata of the family Cruciferae, the cabbage family) of European origin that has a short stem and a dense round head of usu green leaves, eaten as a vegetable 2 a bud at the top of the stem of a cabbage palm tree that resembles a head of cabbage and is eaten as a vegetable 3 informal 3a one who has lost his/her mental faculties as a result of illness, brain damage, etc and is incapable of leading an independent life b an inactive or apathetic person 4 NAm slang paper money [ME caboche, fr ONF, head]

²cabbage vt, archaic to take surreptitiously; steal, filch [cabbage (a remnant of cloth taken as a perk by a tailor), perh fr MF cabas cheating, lit., basket]

cabbage palm n a palm tree with buds that resemble the heads of cabbages and are eaten as a vegetable

cabbage palmetto n a fan-leaved CABBAGE PALM (Sabal palmetto) of the Bahamas and coastal regions of the S USA

cabbage white n any of several largely white butterflies (family Pieridae), the caterpillar of which feeds on plants of the cabbage family; esp SMALL WHITE

cabbala, cabbalah /kə'bahlə, 'kabələ/ n CABALA (esoteric doctrine or system of beliefs)

cabby, cabbie /'kabi/ n, informal a taxi driver [²cab + -y]

caber /'kaybə/ n a roughly trimmed tree trunk that is thrown in the Scottish sport of TOSSING THE CABER in which the winner is the person who throws it furthest [ScGael cabar]

¹cabin /'kabin/ n 1a a (private) room on a ship for passengers or crew b a compartment below deck on a small boat for passengers or crew c a compartment in an aircraft, airship, or spacecraft for cargo, crew, or passengers 2 a small usu single-storeyed dwelling of simple construction 3 chiefly Br ²CAB 3 (driver's compartment in lorry, railway engine, etc) [ME cabane, fr MF, fr ML capanna hut, fr ML capanna]

²cabin vi, chiefly poetic to confine

cabin boy n a boy employed as a servant on board a ship

cabin class n a class of accommodation on a passenger ship superior to TOURIST CLASS and inferior to FIRST CLASS

cabin cruiser n a private motorboat with living accommodation

cabinet /'kab(ə)nit/ n 1a a case or cupboard usu with doors, shelves, and compartments for storing or displaying articles b an upright case housing a domestic radio, television, etc c a chamber in which samples (e g of bacteria) can be subjected to controlled conditions of humidity, temperature, etc 2a taking sing or pl vb, often cap a body of advisers of a head of state (e g a monarch or prime minister) or other senior official; specif a body consisting of the British prime minister and senior ministers who together formulate government policy ⟨a ~ reshuffle⟩ b Br a meeting of a cabinet 3 archaic 3a a small secluded room b the private council chamber used by the chief councillors or ministers of a sovereign [MF, small room, dim. of ONF cabine gambling house]

cabinetmaker /'kab(i)nit,maykə/ n a craftsman who makes fine furniture in wood – cabinetmaking n

cabinet minister n a senior government minister who is a member of the Cabinet

cabinetwork /-,wuhk/ n high-quality woodwork produced by a cabinetmaker

¹cable /'kaybl/ n 1a a strong rope, esp about 8 or more centimetres (3 or more inches) in thickness b a wire rope or metal chain of great strength; specif, nautical the rope or chain to which an anchor is attached 2 cable, cable length any of various nautical units of length: e g 2a Br a unit equal to one tenth of a NAUTICAL MILE; 185 metres or 202 yards b NAm a unit equal to 120 fathoms (219 metres or 240 yards) 3a an assembly of electrical conductors, esp wires, insulated from each other and surrounded by a sheath b cable, cablegram a telegram sent, esp to a foreign country, by telephone, underwater cable, communications satellite, etc 4 something resembling or made like a cable [ME, fr ONF, fr ML capulum lasso, fr L capere to take – more at HEAVE]

²cable vt 1 to fasten or provide with a cable or cables 2a to transmit (a message) by underwater cable, communications satellite, etc b to communicate with or inform (somebody) by means of a telegram transmitted in this way 3 to make into a cable or into a form resembling a cable ~ vi to communicate by means of a telegram transmitted as a cable

cable car n 1 a carriage that is pulled along a cable railway by a stationary motor 2 a carriage that is moved by an overhead cable from which it hangs

'cable-,laid adj, of a rope composed of three ropes twisted together, each containing three strands – compare HAWSER-LAID

cable railway n a railway along which the carriages are pulled by an endless cable operated by a stationary motor; esp FUNICULAR (railway in which a descending car is balanced by an ascending car)

**cablese** /ˌkaybl'eez/ n a style of writing characterized by the running together of words and phrases to save money when sending telegrams [*cable* + *-ese*]

**cable stitch** n a knitting stitch that produces a twisted ropelike pattern

**cable television** n cablevision

**cablevision** /'kaybl,vizh(ə)n/ n a system for receiving television signals in which domestic television receivers are connected by cable, rather than by a separate aerial, either directly to the transmitter to avoid use of the crowded airwaves, or to a large aerial feeding the whole of one area where the signal is weak

**cableway** /'kaybl,way/ n an overhead cable along which goods carriers or passenger carriers (e g cable cars) can be pulled

**cabman** /'kabmən/ n a taxi driver

**cabob** /kə'bob/ n a kebab

**Caboc** /'kabək/ n a rich soft esp Scottish cream cheese rolled in toasted oatmeal [ScGael *càbag*, or ME (Sc) *cabok*]

**cabochon** /'kabə,shon/ n a highly polished gem or bead cut in a rounded dome-shaped form without facets; *also* this style of cutting [MF, aug of ONF *caboche* head] – **cabochon** adv

**caboodle** /kə'boohdl/ n, informal a collection, lot ⟨*sell the whole* ~⟩ [prob fr *ca-* (intensive prefix, prob of imit origin) + *boodle*]

**caboose** /kə'boohs/ n 1 a ship's kitchen (GALLEY), esp when housed in a cabin attached to the deck 2 *NAm* a wagon attached to a goods train, usu at the rear, mainly for the train crew to eat and sleep in – compare GUARD'S VAN [prob fr D *kabuis*, fr MLG *kabūse*]

**cabotage** /'kabə,tahzh/ n 1 trade or transport in coastal waters or between two points within a country (e g by air) 2 the right to engage in cabotage [Fr, fr *caboter* to sail along the coast]

**'cab-,rank** n, Br TAXI RANK

**cabriole** /'kabri,ohl/ n 1 a curved furniture leg, often ending in an ornamental foot 2 a ballet leap in which one leg is extended to the side, front, or back in mid-air and the other struck against it [Fr, caper]

**cabriolet** /ˌkabrioh'lay/ n 1 a light two-wheeled one-horse carriage with a folding hood and upward-curving shafts 2 a convertible two-door motor car – not now used technically [Fr, fr dim. of *cabriole* caper, alter. of MF *capriole*]

**cabstand** /'kab,stand/ n TAXI RANK

**cac-** /kak-/, **caco-** *comb form* bad; unpleasant ⟨*cacogenics*⟩ ⟨*cacophony*⟩ [NL, fr Gk *kak-, kako-*, fr *kakos* bad]

**ca' canny** /ˌkah 'kani, ˌkaw/ n, Scot & N Eng 1 caution, wariness 2 GO-SLOW (slow working by employees as action against an employer) [E dial. & Sc *ca' canny* to proceed cautiously, fr *ca'* to call, drive + *canny* cautious(ly)] – **ca' canny** vi, Scot & N Eng

**cacao** /kə'kah·oh, -'kayoh/ n, pl **cacaos** COCOA 1 (cocoa tree or its edible seeds) [Sp, fr Nahuatl *cacahuatl* cacao beans]

**cacao bean** n COCOA 1b (seed of cocoa tree)

**cacao butter** n COCOA BUTTER

**cachalot** /'kashəlot/ n SPERM WHALE [Fr]

**¹cache** /kash/ n 1 a hiding place, esp for concealing and preserving provisions or weapons; *broadly* a secure place of storage 2 something hidden or stored in a cache [Fr, fr *cacher* to press, hide, fr (assumed) VL *coacticare* to press together, fr L *coactare* to compel, fr *coactus*, pp of *cogere* to compel – more at COGENT]

**²cache** vt to place, hide, or store in a cache

**cachectic** /kə'kektik/ adj affected by cachexia [Fr *cachectique*, fr L *cachecticus*, fr Gk *kachektikos*, fr *kak-* + *echein*]

**cache-sexe** /'kash ˌseks/ n a small garment worn to cover only the genitals [Fr, fr *cacher* to hide + *sexe* sex]

**cachet** /'kashay, kə'shay/ n 1a ³SEAL 1b (distinguishing mark stamped on document, or device for doing this); *esp* one used as a mark of official approval **b** a prestigious indication of approval 2 (a characteristic feature or quality conferring) prestige 3 a rice-paper or flour-paste case in which unpleasant-tasting medicine may be swallowed 4 a design or inscription other than the postmark that is stamped by hand on a letter or other item sent through the post [MF, fr *cacher* to press, hide]

**cachexia** /kə'keksi·ə/ *also* **cachexy** /kə'keksi, ka'keksi/ n general physical wasting and malnutrition, usu associated with long-lasting disease [LL *cachexia*, fr Gk *kachexia* bad condition, fr *kak-* cac- + *hexis* condition, fr *echein* to have, be disposed – more at SCHEME]

**cachinnate** /'kakinayt/ vi, formal to laugh loudly or immoder-

ately [L *cachinnatus*, pp of *cachinnare*, of imit origin] – **cachinnation** n

**cachou** /'kashooh, kə'shooh/ n 1 CATECHU (substance obtained from plants, used in tanning and dyeing) 2 a pill or lozenge used to sweeten the breath △ cashew [Fr, fr Pg *cachu*, fr Malayalam *kāccu*]

**cachucha** /kə'choohchə/ n a lively Andalusian solo dance in a tempo having three beats in the bar, done usu while clicking castanets [Sp, small boat, cachucha]

**cacique** /kə'seek/ n 1 an American Indian chief in areas dominated primarily by a Spanish culture 2 a local political leader in Spain and Latin America [Sp, of Arawakan origin; akin to Taino *cacique* chief] – **caciquism** n

**cack-handed** /kak/ adj, Br 1 informal awkward, clumsy 2 derog left-handed [perh fr E dial. *cack* excrement, muck, fr ME *cakken* to defaecate, fr L *cacare*]

**cackle** /'kakl/ vi 1 to make the sharp broken squawking noise or cry that a domestic hen makes, esp after laying 2 to laugh in a way suggestive of a hen's cackle 3 to chatter ~ vt to utter in a cackling manner ⟨*the witch* ~d *her spell*⟩ [ME *cakelen*, of imit origin] – **cackle** n, **cackler** n

**caco-** – see CAC-

**cacodemon** /ˌkakə'deemən/ n an evil spirit; a demon [Gk *kakodaimōn*, fr *kak-* cac- + *daimōn* spirit] – **cacodemonic** adj

**cacodyl** /'kakə,dil/ n 1 an arsenic-containing chemical group, $As(CH_3)_2$, with a VALENCY of one, whose compounds usu have a vile smell and are often poisonous 2 a colourless garlic-smelling liquid, $As_2(CH_3)_4$, consisting of two cacodyl groups joined together [ISV, fr Gk *kakōdēs* ill-smelling, fr *kak-* + *-ōdēs* (akin to Gk *ozein* to smell) – more at ODOUR] – **cacodylic** adj

**cacoëthes** /ˌkakoh'eetheez/ n, formal an insatiable desire for something [L, fr Gk *kakoëthes* wickedness, fr neut of *kakoëthēs* malignant, fr *kak-* cac-+ *ēthos* character]

**cacogenesis** /ˌkakə'jenəsis/ n the deterioration of a race of animals, plants, etc, esp when due to the retention of inferior breeding stock [NL] – **cacogenic** adj

**cacogenics** /ˌkakə'jeniks/ n taking sing or pl vb 1 DYSGENICS (study of deterioration of races) 2 cacogenesis [*cac-* + *-genics* (as in *eugenics*)]

**cacography** /kə'kogrəfi, ka-/ n 1 bad handwriting – compare CALLIGRAPHY 2 bad spelling – compare ORTHOGRAPHY – **cacographical** adj

**cacology** /ka'koləji, kə-/ n (an instance of) faulty pronunciation or use of words

**cacomistle** /'kakə,misl/ n a carnivorous tree-dwelling mammal (*Bassariscus astutus*) that occurs in the southern parts of N America and is related to and resembles the raccoon [MexSp, fr Nahuatl *tlacomiztli*, fr *tlaco* half + *miztli* mountain lion]

**cacophony** /kə'kofəni/ n harsh or discordant sound; dissonance; *specif* harshness in the sound of words or phrases [deriv of Gk *kakophōnia*, fr *kak-* cac- + *phōnē* voice, sound – more at BAN] – **cacophonous** adj, **cacophonously** adv

**cactus** /'kaktəs/ n, pl **cacti** /-tie/, **cactuses** any of a family (Cactaceae, the cactus family) of plants that have thick fleshy stems and scales or spines instead of leaves and occur in deserts and other very dry areas [NL, genus name, fr L, cardoon, fr Gk *kaktos*]

**cacuminal** /ka'kyoohminl/ adj, of a speech sound RETROFLEX 2 (made with the tip of the tongue curled back against the roof of the mouth) [ISV, fr L *cacumin-, cacumen* top, point]

**cad** /kad/ n an unscrupulous or dishonourable man ⟨"*You* ~!"⟩ – not now in vogue [E dial., unskilled assistant, short for Sc *caddie*] – **caddish** adj

**cadastral** /kə'dastrəl/ adj showing or recording the ownership, boundaries, and value of land and buildings, esp for the purposes of taxation ⟨*a* ~ *register*⟩ [Fr, fr *cadastre* register of property used in assessing taxes, fr It *catastro*, deriv of LGk *katastichon* notebook] – **cadastrally** adv

**cadaver** /kə'davə, -'dahvə, -'dayvə/ n a dead body, usu intended for dissection (e g by people studying anatomy) [L, fr *cadere* to fall] – **cadaveric** adj

**cadaverine** /kə'davəreen/ n a syrupy colourless poisonous liquid, $NH_2(CH_2)_5NH_2$, that is formed esp during the putrefaction of flesh and is sometimes responsible for FOOD POISONING

**cadaverous** /kə'dav(ə)rəs/ adj 1 of, like, or suggestive of a corpse, corpses, or tombs 2a unhealthily pale; pallid, livid **b** gaunt, emaciated – **cadaverously** adv

**caddie, caddy** /'kadi/ n 1 one who assists a golfer, esp by carrying his/her clubs 2 *Scot* one who seeks work (e g running errands) at a place where casual labour is often required [Fr *cadet* military cadet] – **caddie** *vi*

**caddie car** *n* GOLF CART

**caddie cart** *n* GOLF CART

**caddis fly** /'kadis/ *n* any of an order (Trichoptera) of insects with four membranous wings, long slender many-jointed antennae, and aquatic larvae that are caddis worms

**caddis worm** *n* the larva of a CADDIS FLY that lives in and carries round a protective case that it makes from silk covered with bits of debris (e g grains of sand) [prob alter. of obs *codworm*, fr *cod* bag, case, fr ME, fr OE *codd*]

**Caddo** /'kadoh/ *n*, *pl* **Caddos**, *esp collectively* **Caddo** a member of an American Indian people ranging from N Dakota south to Texas

**caddy** /'kadi/ *n* 1 a small box or tin used esp for keeping tea 2 a protective cover or container (e g for a video disc) △ caddie [Malay *kati*, a unit of weight (cf ¹CATTY)]

**cade** /kayd/ *adj*, *of an animal* left by its mother and reared by humans, esp as a pet; pet ⟨*a ~ lamb*⟩ [E dial. *cade* pet lamb, fr ME *cad*]

**-cade** /-kayd/ *comb form* (*n* → *n*) procession ⟨*motor*cade⟩ [*caval*cade]

**cadelle** /kə'del/ *n* a small black beetle (*Tenebroides mauritanicus*) found all over the world, that lives on stored grain [Fr, fr Prov *cadello*, fr L *catella*, fem of *catellus* little dog, dim. of *catulus* young animal]

**cadence** /'kayd(ə)ns/, **cadency** /-si/ *n* 1a the rhythmic sequence or flow of sounds or intonations in language b the beat, time, or measure of a rhythmical motion or activity (e g rowing or marching) 2a a falling inflection of the voice b a concluding sequence of sounds; *specif* a sequence of chords in a piece of music moving to a harmonic close or point of rest and giving the sense of harmonic completion at the end of a musical phrase, section, or composition 3 the modulated and rhythmic recurrence of a sound [ME, fr OIt *cadenza*, fr *cadere* to fall, fr L – more at CHANCE] – **cadenced** *adj*, **cadential** *adj*

**cadency** /'kayd(ə)nsi/ *n* the status of a branch of a family derived from a younger son or daughter

**cadent** /'kayd(ə)nt/ *adj* 1 having a rhythmic fall in pitch, tone, etc 2 *archaic* falling, dropping ⟨*with ~ tears fret channels in her cheeks* – Shak⟩ [L *cadent-, cadens*, prp of *cadere*]

**cadenza** /kə'denzə/ *n* 1 a flourish or other showy embellishment by a solo singer or instrumentalist, usu just before a cadence, that was common esp in 18th-century music 2 a technically showy sometimes improvised solo passage in a concerto [It, cadence, cadenza]

**cadet** /kə'det/ *n* 1a a younger brother or son b (a member of) a younger branch of a family 2a a young person who is training to be a policeman or an officer in the armed forces b a member of an organization of young people receiving some basic part-time military training, esp at school ⟨*the school ~ force*⟩ [Fr, fr Fr dial. *capdet* chief, fr LL *capitellum*, dim. of L *capit-, caput* head – more at HEAD] – **cadetship** *n*

**cadge** /kaj/ *vb, informal* to get (something) by imposing on someone's hospitality or good nature [back-formation fr Sc *cadger* carrier, huckster, fr ME *cadgear*, fr *caggen* to tie] – **cadger** *n*

**cadi** /'kahdi, 'kay-/ *n* QADI (Muslim judge)

**cadmium** /'kadmi·əm/ *n* a chemical element that is a soft bluish-white poisonous metal, used esp in protective platings and in alloys for making bearings [NL, fr L *cadmia* calamine; fr the occurrence of its ores together with calamine]

**cadmium yellow** *n* (a pigment of) a vivid yellow colour

**cadre** /'kahdə/ *n* 1 *taking sing or pl vb* 1a a permanent group of trained people forming the nucleus of a military force or other organization and capable of training other people and expanding rapidly if required b a group of activists working for the cause of the Communist party, esp in a Communist-controlled country 2 a member of a cadre 3 *archaic* a frame, framework [Fr, fr It *quadro*, fr L *quadrum* square – more at QUARREL]

**caduceus** /kə'dyoohsi·əs/ *n*, *pl* **caducei** /-si·,ie/ 1 the symbolic staff of an ancient Greek or Roman herald; *specif* a representation of a staff with two entwined snakes and two wings at the top 2 an insignia bearing a caduceus, used as a traditional symbol for the medical profession [L, modif of Gk *karykeion*, fr *karyx, kēryx* herald; akin to OE *hrēth* glory] – **caducean** *adj*

**caducity** /kə'dyoohsəti/ *n*, *formal* 1 the quality of being tran-

sitory or perishable 2 senility [Fr *caducité*, fr *caduc* transitory, fr L *caducus*]

**caducous** /kə'dyoohkəs/ *adj, esp of a petal or other flower part* falling off easily [L *caducus* tending to fall, transitory, fr *cadere* to fall – more at CHANCE]

**caecilian** /see'silyən/ *n* any of an order (Apoda) of chiefly tropical burrowing amphibian animals that resemble worms [deriv of L *caecilia*, a lizard, fr *caecus* blind] – **caecilian** *adj*

**caecum**, *NAm chiefly* **cecum** /'seekəm/ *n* a cavity open at one end; *esp* the blind pouch in which the LARGE INTESTINE begins and into which the ILEUM of the SMALL INTESTINE opens from one side [NL, fr L *intestinum caecum*, lit., blind intestine] – **caecal** *adj*, **caecally** *adv*

**caen-** /seen-/, **caeno-** – see CAIN-

**Caerphilly** /keə'fili, kah-, kə-/ *n* a mild white moist cheese [*Caerphilly*, town in Wales]

**Caesar** /'seezə/ *n* 1 – used as a title for any of the Roman emperors who succeeded Augustus Caesar 2a *often not cap* an emperor, dictator, or other powerful ruler b the civil government or ruler as contrasted with God [Gaius Julius *Caesar* †44 BC Roman general & statesman; (2b) fr the reference in Mt 22:21] – **Caesarean, Caesarian** *adj*

**caesarean, caesarian, caesarean section, caesarian section**, *NAm chiefly* **cesarean, cesarian, cesarean section, cesarian section** /si'zeəri·ən/ *n* surgical cutting of the walls of the abdomen and the womb for the delivery of offspring [fr the legend that Julius *Caesar* was born in this way]

**Caesarism** /'seezə,riz(ə)m/ *n* government by a single absolute ruler; dictatorship, imperialism – **Caesarist** *n*

**caesious** /'seezi·əs/ *adj* bluish or greyish green [L *caesius* bluish grey]

**caesium**, *NAm chiefly* **cesium** /'seezi·əm/ *n* a silver-white very soft metal that is a chemical element of the ALKALI METAL group and is used esp in PHOTOELECTRIC CELLS (devices converting light into an electric current) [NL, fr L *caesius*]

**caespitose** /'sespitohs/ *adj, of a plant* growing in thick tufts; forming a turf [NL *caespitosus*, fr L *caespit-, caespes* turf]

**caesura** /si'zyooərə, -'zhooərə/ *n, pl* **caesuras, caesurae** /-ri/ 1 a break in a line of classical Greek or Latin verse caused by the ending of a word 2 a pause in the middle of a line of verse [LL, fr L, act of cutting, fr *caedere* to cut – more at CONCISE] – **caesural** *adj*

**cafard** /'kafah/ *n* melancholy, depression [Fr, lit., cockroach]

**café** *also* **cafe** /'kafay/ *n* 1 *chiefly Br* a small restaurant or coffeehouse serving light meals and nonalcoholic drinks 2 *NAm* a bar for the sale of alcoholic drinks [Fr *café* coffee, café, fr Turk *kahve* – more at COFFEE]

**café au lait** /oh 'lay (*Fr* kafɛ o lɛ)/ *n* 1 coffee with milk in about equal parts 2 the colour of coffee with milk [Fr]

**café noir** /,kafay 'nwah (*Fr* kafe nwar)/ *n* black coffee [Fr]

**cafeteria** /,kafə'tiəri·ə/ *n* a restaurant in which the customers serve themselves or are served at a counter and take the food to tables to eat [AmerSp *cafetería* retail coffee shop, fr Sp *café* coffee]

**caff** /kaf/ *n, Br informal* a café; *esp* a cheap plain one [by shortening & alter.]

**caffeine** /'kafeen/ *n* a chemical compound, $C_8H_{10}N_4O_2$, that occurs naturally esp in tea, coffee, and KOLA NUTS and that acts as a stimulant and DIURETIC (substance that increases production of urine) [Ger *kaffein*, fr *kaffee* coffee, fr Fr *café*] – **caffeinic** *adj*

**caftan, kaftan** /'kaftan/ *n* a loose ankle-length garment with long sleeves, traditionally worn by Arabs [Russ *kaftan*, fr Turk, fr Per *qaftān*]

**¹cage** /kayj/ *n* 1 a box or enclosure with gates, bars, netting, etc for confining or carrying animals 2 an enclosure, room, device, etc resembling a cage in construction or use; *esp* the moving enclosed platform of a lift 3 a barred cell or fenced area for confining prisoners 4 a framework serving as support ⟨*the steel ~ of a skyscraper*⟩ 5 *NAm* 5a the goal in ice hockey b the basket in basketball; *also* a basketball court [ME, fr OF, fr L *cavea* cavity, cage, fr *cavus* hollow – more at CAVE]

**²cage** *vt* 1 to confine or keep (as if) in a cage 2 to put (e g an animal or the puck in ice hockey) into a cage

**cage bird** *n* a bird that is kept or is suitable for keeping in a cage

**cagey** *also* **cagy** /'kayji/ *adj, informal* 1 hesitant about committing oneself 2 wary of being trapped or deceived; shrewd [origin unknown] – **cagily** *adv*, **caginess** *also* **cageyness** *n*

**cagoule** /ka'goohl/ *n* a long outer garment, usu with a hood, that is made of very light waterproof material and is put on by pulling over the head rather than by closing with a zip [Fr, lit., hood, cowl, fr LL *cucula* monk's cowl]

**cahier** /'kah·yay (*Fr* kaje)/ *n* a report or memorandum concerning policy, esp that to be considered or adopted by a parliamentary body [Fr, fr MF *quaer*, *caier* quire – more at QUIRE]

**cahoots** /kə'hoohts/ *n pl, informal* partnership, league – chiefly in *in cahoots* ⟨*he's in* ~ *with organized crime*⟩ [perh fr Fr *cahute* cabin, hut]

**cailleach** /'kaylyəkh, 'kalyəkh, -lək/ *n, Scot* an old woman [ScGael & IrGael, fr OIr *caillech* nun, fr *caille* veil, fr L *pallium* cloak]

**caiman** /'kaymən/ *n, pl* **caimans**, *esp collectively* **caiman** CAYMAN (reptile similar to crocodile)

**Cain** *n* – **raise Cain** to act wildly; create a disturbance [*Cain* (Heb *Qayin*), eldest son of Adam & murderer of his brother Abel (Gen 4)]

**cain-** /kayn-/, **caino-**, **caen-**, **caeno-**, *chiefly NAm* **cen-**, **ceno-** *comb form* new; recent ⟨Cainozoic⟩ [Gk *kain-*, *kaino-*, fr *kainos* – more at RECENT]

**-caine** /-kayn/ *comb form* (→ *n*) synthetic local anaesthetic resembling cocaine ⟨lignocaine⟩ [Ger *-kain*, fr *kokain* cocaine]

**Cainozoic** /,kaynə'zoh·ik/ *adj* of or being an era of geological history that extends from the beginning of the TERTIARY period to the present time and is marked by a rapid evolution of mammals, birds, and higher flowering plants; *also* relating to the system of rocks formed in this era – **Cainozoic** *n*

**caïque** /kie'eek/ *n* **1** a light rowing boat used on the Bosphorus **2** any of various small sailing vessels used in the E Mediterranean [Turk *kayık*]

**caird** /keəd/ *n, Scot* a travelling tinker; *also* a tramp, gypsy [ScGael *ceard;* akin to Gk *kerdos* profit]

**cairn** /keən/ *n* a pile of stones built as a memorial or landmark (eg at the top of a mountain) [ME *carne*, fr ScGael *carn;* akin to OIr & W *carn* cairn] – **cairned** *adj*

**cairngorm** /'keən,gawm/ *n* a yellow or smoky-brown quartz [*Cairngorm*, mountain in Scotland]

**cairn terrier** *n* a small compactly built terrier of Scottish origin [fr its use in hunting among cairns]

**caisson** /'kays(ə)n, kə'soohn/ *n* **1** a chest or wagon for carrying ammunition, esp for use by large guns and cannons **2a** a watertight chamber, usu with a supply of compressed air, used to house people doing construction work under water (eg the laying of foundations for bridges); *also* such a chamber filled with concrete and used as an underwater foundation **b** a float for raising a sunken vessel **c** a hollow floating box or a boat used as a gate to keep water in or out of a dock, harbour, etc **3** COFFER **4** (recessed decorative panel) [Fr, aug of *caisse* box, fr OProv *caisa*, fr L *capsa* chest, case – more at CASE]

**caisson disease** *n* a sometimes fatal disorder suffered esp by deep-sea divers, in which there are often intense pains, esp in the joints, and paralysis, difficulty in breathing, and often collapse, and which is caused by the release of gas bubbles in tissue upon too rapid decrease in air pressure after a stay in a compressed atmosphere – called also BENDS, DECOMPRESSION SICKNESS

**caitiff** /'kaytif/ *n, archaic or poetic* a base, cowardly, or despicable person [ME *caitif* prisoner, wretched person, fr ONF (adj), captive, vile, fr L *captivus* captive] – **caitiff** *adj*

**cajole** /kə'johl/ *vt* to persuade with flattery or deception, esp in the face of reluctance to do or believe something; coax [Fr *cajoler* to chatter like a jay in a cage, cajole, alter. of MF *gaioler*, fr ONF *gaiole* birdcage, fr LL *caveola*, dim. of L *cavea* cage – more at CAGE] – **cajolement** *n*, **cajoler** *n*, **cajolery** *n*

**¹cake** /kayk/ *n* **1a** a breadlike food made from an often unleavened dough or batter typically fried or baked in small flat shapes – usu in combination ⟨oatcake⟩ **b** (a shaped mass of) any of various sweet baked foods made from a dough or thick batter usu containing flour and sugar and often fat, eggs, and a raising agent (eg baking powder or sometimes yeast) ⟨ginger ~⟩ **c** a flattened usu round mass of food that is baked or fried ⟨*a fish* ~⟩ **2** a block or coating of compacted or congealed matter ⟨*a* ~ *of ice*⟩ – see also TAKE **the cake** [ME, fr ON *kaka;* akin to OHG *kuocho* cake]

**²cake** *vt* to encrust ⟨*shoes* ~d *with mud*⟩ ~ *vi* to form or harden into a mass

**cakewalk** /'kayk,wawk/ *n* **1** an American Negro entertainment in which a cake is given as a prize for the most accomplished or stylish steps and figures in walking **2** a stage dance developed from walking steps and figures, typically involving

a high strutting movement **3** *informal* an easy task – **cakewalk** *vi*, **cakewalker** *n*

**Calabar bean** /'kalə,bah/ *n* the dark-brown very poisonous seed of a tropical African woody climbing plant (*Physostigma venenosum*) of the pea family, used as a source of PHYSOSTIGMINE (drug used to treat muscle weakness) [*Calabar*, city in Nigeria]

**calabash** /'kalə,bash/ *n* **1** GOURD (very hard-shelled fruit, or plant of marrow family that bears it); *esp* one whose hard shell is used as a container (eg a bottle) **2** a utensil (eg a tobacco pipe) made from the shell of a calabash [Fr & Sp; Fr *calebasse* gourd, fr Sp *calabaza*, prob fr Ar *qar'ah yābisah* dry gourd]

**calaboose** /'kalə,boohs, ,- - '-/ *n, dial NAm* a jail; *esp* a local jail [Sp *calabozo* dungeon]

**calabrese** /,kalə'brayzi, -'bree-/ *n* BROCCOLI 2b [It, of Calabria, fr *Calabria*, region in Italy]

**caladium** /kə'laydiəm/ *n* any of a genus (*Caladium*) of tropical American plants of the arum family, grown for their attractive green-and-white leaves [NL, genus name, fr Malay *kĕladi*, a plant of the arum family]

**calamander** /,kalə'mandə/ *n* the hard hazel-brown black-striped wood of an E Indian tree (genus *Diospyros*, esp *Diospyros quaesita*) of the ebony family that is used in making furniture [prob fr D *kalamanderhout* calamander wood]

**calamary** /'kaləməri, ,kalə'mahri/, **calamar** /'kaləmah/ *n* a squid [L *calamarius* of a pen, fr *calamus* reed; fr the shape of its inner shell]

**calamine** /'kaləmien/ *n* **1** a mixture of zinc carbonate with a small amount of FERRIC OXIDE that has a mild astringent action on the skin and is used in cooling or soothing lotions, liniments, and ointments **2** *archaic* **2a** *Br* SMITHSONITE (white or nearly white zinc mineral) **b** *NAm* HEMIMORPHITE (mineral that is major ore of zinc) ⚠ calomel [Fr, ore of zinc, fr ML *calamina*, alter. of L *cadmia*, fr Gk *kadmeia*, lit., Theban (earth), fr fem of *kadmeios* Theban, fr *Kadmos* Cadmus, legendary founder of Thebes]

**calamint** /'kaləmint/ *n* any of a genus (*Calamintha*) of pleasant-smelling purple-or pink-flowered plants of the mint family [ME *calament*, fr OF, fr ML *calamentum*, fr Gk *kalaminthē*]

**calamite** /'kaləmiet/ *n* any of various plants (esp genus *Calamites*), known only from fossils formed in the PALAEOZOIC era, that resemble a giant HORSETAIL plant [NL *Calamites*, genus of fossil plants, fr L *calamus*]

**calamity** /kə'laməti/ *n* **1** a state of deep distress or misery caused by misfortune or loss **2** an extremely grave event; a disaster [MF *calamité*, fr L *calamitat-*, *calamitas;* akin to L *clades* destruction – more at HALT] – **calamitous** *adj*, **calamitously** *adv*, **calamitousness** *n*

**calamus** /'kaləməs/ *n, pl* **calami** /-mie/ **1** (the aromatic root of) SWEET FLAG **2** the central shaft of a feather; a quill [L, reed, reed pen, fr Gk *kalamos* – more at HAULM]

**calandria** /kə'landri·ə/ *n* a closed vessel through which a set of tubes passes, used (eg in nuclear reactors) as a HEAT EXCHANGER (device for transferring heat from one body to another) [Sp, lit., lark]

**calash** /kə'lash/ *n* **1** a light horse-drawn carriage with a folding top and small wheels; *also* the folding top of such a carriage **2** a hood on a framework worn by women over high elaborate wigs in the 18th century [Fr *calèche*, fr Ger *kalesche*, fr Czech *kolesa* wheels, carriage; akin to Gk *kyklos* wheel – more at WHEEL]

**calc-** /kalk-, kals-/, **calci-**, **calco-** *comb form* calcium; calcium salt ⟨calcify⟩ ⟨calcareous⟩ [L *calc-*, *calx* lime – more at CHALK]

**calcaneum** /kal'kayniəm/ *n, pl* **calcanea** /-niə/ the calcaneus [L, heel – more at CALKIN]

**calcaneus** /kal'kayniəs/ *n, pl* **calcanei** /-niçie/ a bone of the TARSUS (ankle or corresponding part) that in human beings is the bone of the heel [LL, heel, alter. of L *calcaneum*] – **calcaneal** *adj*

**calcareous** /kal'keəri·əs/ *adj* **1a** containing, resembling, or consisting of compounds of calcium, esp CALCIUM CARBONATE ⟨~ *soils*⟩ **b** containing calcium **2** growing or living on limestone or in soil impregnated with lime or chalk [L *calcarius* of lime, fr *calc-*, *calx* lime] – **calcareously** *adv*, **calcareousness** *n*

**calceolaria** /,kalsi·ə'leəri·ə/ *n* any of a genus (*Calceolaria*) of tropical American plants of the foxglove family with brightly coloured pouch-shaped flowers [NL, genus name, fr L *calceolus* small shoe, dim. of *calceus* shoe, fr *calc-*, *calx* heel]

**calces** /'kal,seez/ *pl of* CALX

**calcic** /'kalsik/ *adj* derived from or containing calcium or lime; rich in calcium

**calcicole** /'kalsi,kohl/ *n* a plant that usually grows on soils that contain lime or other calcium compounds – compare CALCIFUGE [Fr, calcicolous, fr *calc-* + *-cole* -colous] – **calcicole, calcicolous** *adj*

**calciferol** /kal'sifə,rol/ *n* VITAMIN D₂ [blend of *calciferous* and *ergosterol*]

**calciferous** /kal'sif(ə)rəs/ *adj* producing or containing CALCIUM CARBONATE

**calcific** /kal'sifik/ *adj* involving or caused by calcification ⟨~ *lesions*⟩

**calcification** /,kalsifi'kaysh(ə)n/ *n* 1 the process of calcifying or becoming calcified; *specif* the laying down of solid calcium salts (eg in tissue) so as to cause hardening 2 a body part or other structure that has become hardened by calcification

**calcifuge** /'kalsifyoohj/ *n* a plant that does not normally grow on soils that contain lime or other calcium compounds – compare CALCICOLE [Fr, calcifugous, fr *calc-* + L *fugere* to flee – more at FUGITIVE] – **calcifuge, calcifugous** *adj*

**calcify** /'kalsifie/ *vb* 1a to convert or become converted into a solid compound of calcium, esp CALCIUM CARBONATE b to harden (eg body tissue) or become hard by the laying down of CALCIUM CARBONATE or other calcium compound 2 to make or become inflexible or unchangeable

**calcimine** /'kalsəmien/ *n* a thin white or light-coloured liquid that usu contains a white pigment made from powdered CALCIUM CARBONATE or ZINC OXIDE and is used for colouring esp plastered surfaces [alter. (influenced by *calc-*) of *kalsomine*, of unknown origin] – **calcimine** *vt*

¹**calcine** /'kalsin, -sien/ *vt* to heat (esp a metal ore or other inorganic substance) to a high temperature but without melting, usu in order to drive off matter that evaporates easily or to bring about combination with oxygen or powdering of the heated substance ~ *vi* to be calcined [ME *calcenen*, fr MF *calciner*, fr L *calc-, calx* lime – more at CHALK] – **calcination** *n*

²**calcine** *n* a solid substance (eg an oxide of a metal) left after calcining something

**calcite** /'kalsiet/ *n* a mineral that consists of a crystalline form of CALCIUM CARBONATE, CaCO₃, and occurs esp as limestone, chalk, and marble – **calcitic** *adj*

**calcitonin** /,kalsi'tohnin/ *n* a hormone produced by the THYROID GLAND that acts to reduce the amount of calcium present in the blood by lowering the rate at which it leaves bone – called also THYROCALCITONIN [*calci-* + ¹*tonic* + *-in*]

**calcium** /'kalsi·əm/ *n* a silver-white chemical element that is a metal of the ALKALINE-EARTH group, has a VALENCY of two, and occurs naturally only in the form of its compounds (eg CALCIUM CARBONATE) [NL, fr L *calc-, calx* lime]

**calcium carbide** *n* a usu dark-grey solid chemical compound, CaC₂, that produces acetylene when mixed with water and is used esp in acetylene lamps

**calcium carbonate** *n* a chemical compound, CaCO₃, that occurs naturally in the form of limestone, chalk, marble, etc and as a major constituent of shells and bone, and is used industrially in making lime and cement and in fertilizers and animal feed

**calcium chloride** *n* a white chemical compound, CaCl₂, used in its ANHYDROUS (water-free) state as a drying agent and in a HYDRATED (chemically combined with water) state for melting ice on roads

**calcium cyanamide** *n* a chemical compound, CaCN₂, that is made by heating CALCIUM CARBONATE in nitrogen and is used as a fertilizer and as a starting point from which to make other nitrogen-containing compounds

**calcium hydroxide** *n* a white chemical compound, Ca(OH)₂; LIME 2b

**calcium oxide** *n* a white chemical compound, CaO; LIME 2a

**calcium phosphate** *n* any of various chemical compounds formed by combination between calcium and PHOSPHORIC ACID: eg **a** a phosphate, Ca(H₂PO₄)₂, used in fertilizers and baking powder **b** a phosphate, CaHPO₄, used esp in medicines and animal feeds to increase the amount of calcium in the diet **c** a phosphate, Ca₃(PO₄)₂, used in fertilizers and animal feeds **d** the mineral APATITE that is the chief constituent of bones, teeth, and PHOSPHATE ROCK

**calco-** – see CALC-

**calcspar** /'kalk,spah/ *n* calcite [part trans of Sw *kalkspat*, fr *kalk* lime + *spat* spar]

**calculable** /'kalkyooləbl/ *adj* subject to or ascertainable by calculation – **calculability, calculableness** *n*, **calculably** *adv*

**calculate** /'kalkyoolayt/ *vt* 1 to determine (eg the answer to an arithmetical expression) by the principles and techniques of mathematics 2 to reckon by exercise of practical judgment; estimate ~ *vi* 1 to make a calculation 2 to count or rely *on* or *upon* [L *calculatus*, pp of *calculare*, fr *calculus* pebble (used in counting), dim. of *calc-, calx* stone used in gaming, lime – more at CHALK]

**calculated** /'kalkyoolaytid/ *adj* 1a worked out by mathematical calculation b engaged in, undertaken, or displayed after calculating or estimating the probability of success or failure ⟨*they took a* ~ *risk*⟩ 2a shrewdly planned or contrived to accomplish an often specified purpose ⟨*the speech was* ~ *to stir up emotion*⟩ b intended, deliberate ⟨*a* ~ *insult*⟩ 3 apt, likely *to* – **calculatedly** *adv*, **calculatedness** *n*

**calculating** /'kalkyoolayting/ *adj* 1 used for making calculations ⟨*a* ~ *machine*⟩ 2 marked by prudent and deliberate analysis or by shrewd consideration of self-interest; scheming – **calculatingly** *adv*

**calculation** /,kalkyoo'laysh(ə)n/ *n* 1 the process or an act of calculating; *also* the result of such an act 2 studied care in planning, esp to promote self-interest – **calculative** *adj*

**calculator** /'kalkyoolaytə/ *n* 1 one who or that which calculates; *specif* a mechanical or electronic device for performing mathematical calculations 2 a set or book of tables used in making calculations

**calculous** /'kalkyooləs/ *adj, medicine* caused or characterized by a stony calculus or several calculi

**calculus** /'kalkyooləs/ *n, pl* **calculi** /-lie/ *also* **calculuses** 1a a hard stony mass (eg of cholesterol) that forms abnormally in the kidney, GALL BLADDER, or other hollow organ or tube, may cause a severely painful blockage, and often requires removal by a surgical operation b ¹TARTAR 2 (hard material accumulating on teeth) 2a a method of computation or calculation (eg formal logic) using a special symbolic notation b a branch of mathematics that deals with the nature of functions as infinitesimally small changes are made in their variables and with the ideas of LIMITS, and that is basically composed of DIFFERENTIAL CALCULUS and INTEGRAL CALCULUS [L, pebble, stone in the bladder or kidney, stone used in counting]

*usage* The usual plural is **calculi** in the medical senses, **calculuses** in the mathematical ones.

**calculus of variations** *n* a branch of mathematics dealing with the finding of a function that when subjected to the process of INTEGRATION will result in a required maximum or minimum value (eg the minimum value for the area bounded by the curve defined by the function)

**caldera** /kal'deərə/ *n* a very wide crater formed by collapse of the central part of a volcano after the expulsion from the volcano of an underlying bed of molten rock [Sp, lit., cauldron, fr LL *caldaria*]

**caldron** /'kawldrən/ *n* a cauldron

**Caledonian** /,kalə'dohnyən, -ni·ən/ *adj* of (ancient) Scotland; *esp* of the Highlands of (ancient) Scotland [NL *Caledonia* Scotland, fr L, part of N Britain] – **Caledonian** *n*

**calefactory** /,kali'fakt(ə)ri/ *n* a heated room in a monastery, used as a sitting room [ML *calefactorium*, fr L *calefactus*, pp of *calefacere* to warm – more at CHAFE]

¹**calendar** /'kaləndə/ *n* 1 a system for fixing the beginning, length, and divisions of the year and arranging days and longer divisions of time (eg weeks and months) in a definite order 2 a tabular display of the days of one year 3 a list, schedule, etc of events or activities arranged in chronological order 4 *Br* a list of courses offered by a university in a particular year or term [ME *calender*, fr AF or ML; AF *calender*, fr ML *kalendarium*, fr L, moneylender's account book, fr *kalendae* calends]

²**calendar** *vt* to enter in a calendar

**calendar year** *n* a period of a year as recorded by a calendar; *esp* a normal year of 365 days or LEAP YEAR of 366 days as recorded in the GREGORIAN CALENDAR (calendar in general use throughout the world)

¹**calender** /'kaləndə/ *vt* to press (eg cloth, rubber, or paper) between rollers or plates, esp so as to produce a smooth glossy surface or to make into thin sheets [MF *calandrer*, fr *calandre* machine for calendering, modif of Gk *kylindros* cylinder – more at CYLINDER] – **calenderer** *n*

²**calender** *n* a machine for calendering cloth, rubber, paper, etc △ calendar

³**calender** *n* a member of a mystical Muslim sect (a SUFIC), esp in Turkey, Iran, or India, who travels around relying on gifts

# cal

204

from believers for food and lodging [Per *qalandar*, fr Ar, fr Per *kalandar* uncouth man]

**calendrical** /kə'lendrikl/, **calendric** *adj* (characteristic) of or used in a calendar

**calends** /'kalindz/ *n taking sing or pl vb* the first day of an ancient Roman month [ME *kalendes*, fr L *kalendae, calendae;* akin to L *calare* to call, proclaim]

**calendula** /kə'lendyoolə/ *n* a POT MARIGOLD or related orange- or yellow-flowered plant (genus *Calendula*) of the daisy family [NL, genus name, fr ML, fr L *calendae* calends]

**calenture** /'kalǝntyooǝ/ *n* a fever affecting somebody in a tropical country, supposedly caused by exposure to heat [Sp *calentura*, fr *calentar* to heat, fr L *calent-, calens*, prp of *calēre* to be warm – more at LEE]

**¹calf** /kahf/ *n, pl* **calves** /kahvz/ *also* **calfs**, (2) **calfs 1a** the young of the ox or other bovine animal (e g the bison or WATER BUFFALO) **b** the young of any of various large animals (e g the elephant or whale) **2** calfskin ⟨*the book was bound in fine* ~⟩ **3** a small mass of ice broken off from an iceberg or ICE FLOE or from a glacier that runs into the sea [ME, fr OE *cealf;* akin to OHG *kalb* calf, ON *kālfi* calf of the leg, L *galla* gallnut] – **calflike** *adj* – **in calf** *of a domestic cow* pregnant

**²calf** *n, pl* **calves** the fleshy back part of the leg below the knee [ME, fr ON *kālfi*]

**calf love** *n* PUPPY LOVE

**calf's-foot jelly** *n* a jelly made from the gelatine obtained by boiling calves' feet

**calfskin** /'kahf,skin/ *n* (a high-quality leather made from) the skin of a calf

**Calgon** /'kalgon/ *trademark* – used for a substance that is essentially a complex phosphate of sodium and is used as a water-softener

**calibrate** /'kali,brayt/ *vt* **1** to determine the diameter of (e g a gun barrel or thermometer tube) **2** to determine, adjust, or mark the graduations of (e g a thermometer) so as to obtain a correct reading **3** to determine the correct reading of (an arbitrary or inaccurate scale or instrument) by comparison with an accurate standard – **calibrator** *n*

**calibration** /,kali'braysh(ǝ)n/ *n* **1** calibrating or being calibrated **2** **calibrations** *pl*, **calibration** a set of graduations (e g on a thermometer or radio tuning dial) that indicate values or positions

**calibre**, *NAm chiefly* **caliber** /'kalibǝ/ *n* **1a** the diameter of a round body, esp a bullet, shell, or other projectile **b** the internal diameter of a hollow cylinder; *specif* the diameter of the hole in the barrel of a gun, usu expressed in millimetres or hundredths or thousandths of an inch **2a** degree of mental capacity or moral quality **b** degree of excellence or importance [MF *calibre*, fr OIt *calibro*, fr Ar *qālib* shoemaker's last]

**caliche** /kə'leechi/ *n* **1** a deposit of gravel or crumbly rock that occurs in Chile and Peru, contains a large amount of SODIUM NITRATE and other sodium salts, and is used esp as a source of nitrogen compounds (e g for fertilizers) **2** a crust of CALCIUM CARBONATE that forms on the stony soil of dry regions [AmerSp, fr Sp, flake of lime, fr *cal* lime, fr L *calx* – more at CHALK]

**calico** /'kalikoh/ *n, pl* **calicoes, calicos 1** white unprinted cotton cloth of medium weight, originally imported from India **2** an animal that is blotched or spotted with usu more than two different colours; *also, NAm* a horse blotched or spotted usu with white on a dark colour **3** *NAm* any of various cheap brightly printed cotton fabrics [*Calicut*, city in India] – **calico** *adj*

**calico printing** *n* the process of printing coloured patterns on cotton fabrics (e g calico)

**calid** /'kalid/ *adj, formal* warm [L *calidus* – more at CAULDRON]

**calidarium** /,kali'dahriǝm/ *n, pl* **calidaria** the chamber of a Roman bathhouse containing the hot bath – compare FRIGIDARIUM, LACONICUM, TEPIDARIUM [L, fr *calidus*]

**California condor** /,kali'fawniǝ/ *n* CONDOR b (large US vulture-like bird) [*California*, state of USA]

**California poppy** *n* ESCHSCHOLTZIA (garden plant of poppy family)

**californium** /,kali'fawnyǝm, -ni-ǝm/ *n* an artificially produced radioactive chemical element made by bombarding atoms of curium 242 with ALPHA PARTICLES [NL, fr *California*]

**caliginous** /kǝ'lijinǝs/ *adj, formal* misty, dark [MF or L; MF *caligineux*, fr L *caliginosus*, fr *caligin-, caligo* darkness; akin to Gk *kelainos* black – more at COLUMBINE]

**Calinago** /,kali'nahgoh/ *n* an Arawakan language of the Lesser Antilles and Central America

**calipash** /'kali,pash/ *n* a fatty jellylike dull-greenish edible substance found next to the upper shell of a turtle [perh native name in W Indies]

**calipee** /'kali,pee/ *n* a fatty jellylike light-yellow edible substance found next to the lower shell of a turtle [perh native name in W Indies]

**caliper** /'kalipǝ/ *vt or n, chiefly NAm* (to) calliper

**caliph, calif** /'kalif, 'kay-/ *n* a former leader of Islam who was regarded as a successor of Muhammad – used esp as a title ⟨*the* ~ *of Baghdad*⟩ [ME *caliphe*, fr MF *calife*, fr Ar *khalīfah* successor] – **caliphal** *adj*

**caliphate** /'kalifayt, -fǝt, 'kay-/ *n* the office or area of control of a caliph

**calisthenics** /,kalis'theniks/ *n taking sing or pl vb, chiefly NAm* callisthenics

**calix** /'kaliks, 'kay-/ *n, pl* **calices** /-li,seez/ a cup; *esp* one used in church [L *calic-, calix* – more at CHALICE]

**¹calk** /kawk/ *vt* CAULK (stop up seams or cracks in hull of boat) – **calker** *n*

**²calk, caulk** *n* a calkin [prob by alter.]

**calkin** /'kawkin, 'kalkin/ *n* a tapered piece projecting downwards from the shoe of a horse to prevent slipping [ME *kakun*, fr MD or ONF; MD *calcoen* horse's hoof, fr ONF *calcain* heel, fr L *calcaneum*, fr *calc-, calx;* akin to Gk *kōlon* limb, *skelos* leg]

**¹call** /kawl/ *vi* **1a** to speak loudly or distinctly so as to be heard at a distance; shout ⟨~ *for help*⟩ **b** to make a request or demand ⟨~ *for an investigation*⟩ **c** *of an animal* to utter a characteristic note or cry **d** to telephone – often + *up* **e** to make a demand in a card game (e g for a particular card to be played or for a player to show his/her hand) **f** to predict the result of tossing a coin ⟨*I'll toss the coin and you* ~⟩ **2** *of a batsman in cricket* to indicate vocally to one's batting partner, usu after a ball has been hit, whether one intends to take a run or not **3** to make a brief visit ⟨~ed *to pay his respects*⟩ – often + *in* or *by* ⟨~ed *in at the pub*⟩ **4** *Scot* to drive an animal, vehicle, etc ~ *vt* **1a** to utter in a loud distinct voice – often + *out* ⟨~ *out a number*⟩ **b** to read (e g a list of names) aloud ⟨~ *the roll*⟩ **2a** to command or request to come or be present ⟨*she was* ~ed *to court to testify as a witness*⟩ ⟨*we* ~ed *the police*⟩ **b** to cause to come; bring ⟨*it* ~s *to mind an old saying*⟩ **c** to summon to a usu specified activity, employment, or office ⟨*he was* ~ed *to active duty*⟩ **d** to invite or command people to meet at (a meeting, assembly, etc) **3** to rouse from sleep or summon to get up **4** to give the order for; bring into action ⟨~ *a strike against the company*⟩ **5a** to bid (e g a suit) in bridge **b** to require (a player in a game of poker) to show the hand of cards by making an equal bet **6** to attract (e g a game bird) by imitating a characteristic note **7a** to give an often specified ruling on the status of (e g a bouncing ball in tennis) ⟨*the linesman* ~ed *it out*⟩ **b** *of a cricket umpire* to pronounce the bowling delivery of (a bowler) to be illegal ⟨*Griffin was* ~ed *for throwing*⟩ **8** to call out the instructions (CALLS 8) for the dancers of (a SQUARE DANCE) **9a** to telephone – often + *up* **b** to transmit a message to (e g by radio) **10** to speak of or address (somebody or something) by a specified name; give a name to ⟨~ *her Kitty*⟩ **11a** to regard or characterize in a specified way or as a specified kind; consider ⟨*you wouldn't* ~ *them quick* – Clive James⟩ **b** to consider for purposes of an estimate or for convenience ⟨~ *it an even quid*⟩ **12** to name or specify in advance; predict, guess ⟨~ *the toss of a coin*⟩ **13** to demand payment of (e g a loan or a sum left unpaid when an issue of shares or securities was bought) esp by formal notice [ME *callen*, prob fr ON *kalla;* akin to OE *hildecalla* battle herald, OHG *kallōn* to talk loudly, OSlav *glasŭ* voice] – **call the tune/shots** to be in charge or control; determine the policy or procedure – see also **call to** ACCOUNT, **called to the** BAR, **call somebody's** BLUFF, **call it a** DAY, **call to** ORDER, **call in** QUESTION, **call it** QUITS, **call a** SPADE **a spade, call to** TASK, WHAT **do you call him/her/it**

**call down** *vt* to cause or entreat to descend; invoke ⟨call down *a blessing on the crops*⟩

**call for** *vt* **1** to call to get; collect **2** to require as necessary or appropriate ⟨*it* called for *all her strength*⟩ ⟨*didn't think her rude remarks were* called for⟩ **3** to demand, order ⟨*legislation* calling for *the establishment of new schools*⟩

**call in** *vt* **1** to order to return or to be returned: e g **1a** to withdraw (e g troops) from a position in advance of the main body ⟨call in *the outposts*⟩ **b** to withdraw (e g bank notes) from circulation 2 to summon to one's aid or for consultation ⟨call in *an arbitrator to settle the dispute*⟩

**call off** *vt* 1 to draw away; divert ⟨call *the dogs* off!⟩ 2 to cancel ⟨call *the trip* off⟩

**call up** *vt* 1 to bring to mind; evoke 2 to summon before an authority ⟨*I was* called up *before the magistrate*⟩ 3 to summon together or collect (eg for a united effort) ⟨*they* called *all their strength* up *for the attack*⟩ 4 to summon (esp somebody who does not serve regularly in the armed forces) for active military service

**call on, call upon** *vt* 1 to require, oblige ⟨*you may be* called on *to do several jobs*⟩ 2 to appeal to; request to do something ⟨*universities are* called upon *to meet the needs of a technological world*⟩

**call out** *vt* 1 to summon into action ⟨call *the army* out⟩ 2 to challenge to a duel 3 to order a strike of ⟨call *the steelworkers* out⟩

²**call** *n* 1a an act of calling with the voice b the cry of a bird or other animal c (an instrument used to produce) an imitation of an animal's cry made to attract the animal ⟨*a duck* ∼⟩ 2a a request or command to come or assemble b a summons or signal on a drum, bugle, pipe, etc c admission to the bar as a barrister of a law student who has passed the required examinations and fulfilled the required conditions d an invitation to accept a professional appointment or to become the minister of a church e a divine vocation or other strong inner prompting to a course of action f a summoning of actors to the stage (eg for rehearsal) g the attraction or appeal of a particular activity, place, etc ⟨*the* ∼ *of the wild*⟩ 3a (a) demand, request ⟨*there's not much* ∼ *for green bananas*⟩ b a need, justification ⟨*there was no* ∼ *for such rudeness*⟩ c a demand for repayment of a loan d an option to buy a certain amount of a share issue, security, commodity, etc at a fixed agreed price at or within an agreed time – compare ²PUT 2 4 a short usu formal visit ⟨*a courtesy* ∼⟩ 5 the name or thing (eg a suit in a card game) called ⟨*the* ∼ *was heads*⟩ 6 the act of calling in a card game 7 the act of telephoning 8 an instruction or series of instructions called out rhythmically to the dancers of a SQUARE DANCE 9 a usu vocal decision or ruling made by the umpire, referee, or other official at a sports contest – **on call** 1 available for use ⟨*the company car is always* on call *for you*⟩ 2 ready or waiting to respond to a summons or command ⟨*the doctor will be on call all night*⟩ – **within call** within hearing or reach of a call or summons – see also **at somebody's** BECK **and call**

**calla** /'kalə/, **calla lily** *n* any of several plants of the arum family; eg a any of a genus (*Zantedeschia*) of African plants with brightly coloured flowers; *esp* a plant (*Zantedeschia aethiopia*) grown commercially for its brilliant white flowers b a very poisonous European plant (*Calla palustris*) that grows in wet places [NL, genus name, modif of Gk *kallaia* cock's wattles]

**callable** /'kawləbl/ *adj* capable of being called; *specif, of a loan or debt* subject to payment or repayment on demand or at short notice

**callan** /'kahlən/ *n* a callant

**callant** /'kahlənt/ *n, chiefly Scot* a boy, lad [D or ONF; D *kalant* customer, fellow, fr ONF *calland* customer, fr L *calent-, calens*, prp of *calēre* to be warm – more at LEE]

**call box** *n, Br* a public telephone box

**callboy** /'kawl,boy/ *n* 1 a person who tells actors when it is time to go on stage 2 *NAm* a hotel page

**caller** /'kawlə/ *n* 1 one who or that which calls 2 *Austr* a person who gives a running commentary at a race meeting

**call girl** *n* a female prostitute who accepts appointments by telephone – compare STREETWALKER

**calligraphy** /kə'ligrəfi/ *n* (the art of) handwriting; *esp* (the art of producing) beautiful or elegant handwriting – compare CACOGRAPHY [Fr or Gk; Fr *calligraphie*, fr Gk *kalligraphia*, fr *kalli-* beautiful (fr *kallos* beauty) + *-graphia* -graphy; akin to Gk *kalos* beautiful, Skt *kalya* healthy] – **calligrapher, calligraphist** *n*, **calligraphic** *adj*, **calligraphically** *adv*

**calling** /'kawling/ *n* 1 a strong inner impulse towards a particular course of action, esp when accompanied by the conviction that the impulse is the result of God's influence 2 a vocation or profession – compare BUSINESS 3 the characteristic howling cry of a female cat during heat

**calling card** *n, NAm* VISITING CARD

**calliope** /kə'lieəpi/ *n* 1 *cap* the Greek Muse of epic poetry 2 *NAm* a keyboard musical instrument resembling an organ and

consisting of a series of whistles sounded by steam or compressed air [L, fr Gk *Kalliopē*]

¹**calliper,** *chiefly NAm* **caliper** /'kalipə/ *n* 1 **callipers** *pl*, **calliper** any of various measuring instruments with two arms that can be adjusted to determine thickness (eg of paper), diameter (eg of a log), or the distance between surfaces ⟨*a pair of* ∼s⟩ 2 a device that consists of two plates with heat-resistant linings which can be pressed against opposite sides of a disc that rotates between them and forms part of the DISC BRAKE system of a car or other vehicle 3 thickness; *specif* thickness of paper, cardboard, etc 4 a support for the human leg consisting of two metal rods extending between a plate under the foot and a band round the thigh or knee [alter. of *calibre*]

²**calliper** *vt* to measure (as if) by using a pair of callipers

**callipygous** /ˌkaliˈpiegəs/, **callipygian** /ˌkaliˈpijiən/ *adj* having well-shaped attractive buttocks [Gk *kallipygos*, fr *kalli-* beautiful + *pygē* buttocks]

**calisthenics,** *chiefly NAm* **calisthenics** /ˌkalisˈtheniks/ *n pl* 1 systematic rhythmic bodily exercises, performed usu without apparatus 2 *taking sing vb* the art or practice of callisthenics [Gk *kallos* beauty + *sthenos* strength] – **callisthenic** *adj*

**call loan** *n* a loan that is liable to be repaid whenever the lender wishes

**call number** *n* a combination of numbers, letters, etc assigned to a book to indicate its place in a library

**call of nature** *n, euph* the urge to urinate or defecate

**callose** /'kalohs/ *n* a carbohydrate that consists of many glucose molecules attached to each other and is present in plant calluses [L *callosus* callous]

**callosity** /kəˈlosəti/ *n* (an area on skin, bark, etc of) marked or abnormal hardness and thickness

¹**callous** /'kaləs/ *adj* 1 *esp of skin or bark* hardened and thickened; *also* having hardened or thickened areas 2 feeling no sympathy for others; unsympathetic, insensitive △ callus [MF *calleux*, fr L *callosus*, fr *callum*, *callus* callous skin; akin to Skt *kiṇa* callosity] – **callously** *adv*, **callousness** *n*

²**callous** *vb* to make or become callous

**callow** /'kaloh/ *adj* 1 *of a bird* not yet having enough feathers to fly 2 lacking adult attitudes; immature ⟨*a* ∼ *youth*⟩ [ME *calu* bald, fr OE; akin to OHG *kalo* bald] – **callowness** *n*

**call sign** *n* a combination of letters and numbers assigned to a radio operator, radio station, etc for identification of a radio broadcast

'**call-,up** *n* an order to report for military service

¹**callus** /'kaləs/ *n* 1 a thickening of or a hard thickened area on skin or bark 2 a mass of CONNECTIVE TISSUE that forms round a break in a bone and is converted into bone as the break heals 3 soft tissue that forms over a wounded or cut plant surface 4 a deposit of callose that forms a plug over a SIEVE PLATE (pore-filled end wall) in a SIEVE TUBE (sugar-conducting tube) of a VASCULAR PLANT esp during winter when plant growth ceases 5 a tumour of plant tissue that can usu be grown artificially away from the plant (eg in a laboratory) △ callous [L]

²**callus** *vb* to (cause to) form a callus

¹**calm** /kahm; *NAm* kah(l)m/ *n* 1a the absence of winds or rough water; stillness b complete absence of wind, or presence of wind having a speed no greater than 1 kilometre per hour (about ⁵⁄₈ mile per hour) 2 a state of repose free from turmoil or agitation [ME *calme*, fr MF, fr OIt *calma*, fr LL *cauma* heat, fr Gk *kauma*, fr *kaiein* to burn – more at CAUSTIC]

²**calm** *adj* 1 marked by calm; still ⟨*a* ∼ *sea*⟩ 2 free from agitation, excitement, or disturbance ⟨*a* ∼ *manner*⟩ – **calmly** *adv*, **calmness** *n*

synonyms **Calm** is contrasted with "stormy", and stresses real or apparent quietness as opposed to any kind of agitation ⟨*heard the news with a* **calm** *face but a beating heart*⟩. **Tranquil** suggests a deeper quietude and more settled and inherent composure ⟨*went about his work with a* **tranquil** *disregard of danger*⟩. **Serene** suggests complete and utter peace, often sublime ⟨*her face,* **serene** *in death, bore no sign of earthly torments*⟩. **Placid**, usually applied to people, stresses an absence of disturbance or excitement, and an equability of temperament which, if the term is used derogatorily, may imply stupidity ⟨*continued her* **placid** *munching without appearing to hear his remarks*⟩. **Peaceful** suggests rest, and undisturbed tranquillity ⟨*I am grown* **peaceful** *as old age tonight* – Robert Browning⟩. **Halcyon** conveys a sense of magical stillness and serenity ⟨*the* **halcyon** *skies of our youth, so bright, so blue*⟩.

antonyms stormy, agitated

³**calm** *vb* to make or become calm – often + *down*

**calmative** /'kahmətiv; NAm 'kah(l)mətiv/ n or adj (a) sedative – not now in technical use [³calm + -ative (as in sedative)]

**calomel** /'kalə,mel, -məl/ n MERCUROUS CHLORIDE (chemical formerly used as a laxative) △ calamine [prob fr (assumed) NL calomelas, fr Gk kalos beautiful + melas black – more at CALLIGRAPHY, MULLET]

**Calor gas** /'kalə/ trademark – used for butane gas in liquid form that is contained in portable metal cylinders and used as a fuel (e g for domestic heating)

¹**caloric** /kə'lorik/ n a hypothetical weightless fluid formerly held to be responsible for the phenomena of heat and burning [Fr calorique, fr L calor]

²**caloric** adj 1 of heat 2 of calories – **calorically** adv

**calorie** also **calory** /'kaləri/ n 1 any of several units for measuring amounts of energy, esp heat energy, that have now been superseded in the standardized SI system of units by the joule or the kilojoule: e g **1a calorie, small calorie** the amount of heat required to raise the temperature of 1 gram of water by 1°C (from 14.5°C to 15.5°C) under standard conditions of atmospheric pressure, that is equal to about 4.19 joules **b calorie, large calorie, kilocalorie** often cap the amount of heat required to raise the temperature of 1 kilogram of water by 1°C, that is equal to about 4.19 kilojoules; a thousand SMALL CALORIES **2a** a unit equivalent to the LARGE CALORIE expressing the heat-producing or energy-producing value of food when used in the body **b** an amount of food having an energy-producing value of one LARGE CALORIE [Fr calorie, fr L calor heat, fr calēre to be warm – more at LEE]

**calorific** /,kalə'rifik/ adj 1 caloric 2 relating to the production of heat [Fr or L; Fr calorifique, fr L calorificus, fr calor]

**calorimeter** /,kalə'rimitə/ n any of several devices for measuring quantities of heat given out or taken up (e g during a chemical reaction or the melting of a solid) [ISV, fr L calor] – **calorimetry** n, **calorimetric** adj, **calorimetrically** adv

**calotte** /kə'lot/ n a skullcap; esp one sometimes worn by Roman Catholic priests [Fr]

**caloyer** /'kal,oyə, ka'loyə/ n a monk of the Greek Orthodox church [It & Fr; Fr caloyer, fr obs It caloiero, fr MGk kalogēros venerable, fr kalos beautiful + gēras old age]

**calque** /kalk/ n LOAN TRANSLATION (word, phrase, etc introduced into one language by translation from another) [Fr, lit., copy, fr calquer to trace, fr It calcare to trample, trace, fr L, to trample – more at CAULK]

**calthrop** /'kalthrəp/ n a caltrop

**caltrap** n /'kaltrəp/ a caltrop

**caltrop** /'kaltrəp/ n 1 WATER CHESTNUT 1 (water plant or its spiny fruit) 2 a device used to hinder enemy horses, vehicles, etc, that has four metal points so arranged that when any three are on the ground the fourth projects upwards [ME calketrappe star thistle, fr OE calcatrippe, fr ML calcatrippa, prob fr L calc-, calx heel + ML trappa trap]

**calumet** /'kalyoo,met/ n a highly ornamented long-stemmed pipe of the N American Indians, smoked esp on ceremonial occasions as a symbol of peace – called also PEACE PIPE [AmerF, fr Fr dial., straw, fr LL calamellus, dim. of L calamus reed – more at CALAMUS]

**calumniate** /kə'lumniayt/ vt, formal to maliciously make false statements, charges, or imputations about; slander synonyms see ²MALIGN antonyms eulogize, vindicate – **calumniator** n, **calumniation** n

**calumny** /'kaləmni/ n (the act of uttering) a false charge or misrepresentation maliciously calculated to damage another's reputation ⟨a circle of false friends spending their time in calumnies⟩ [MF & L; MF calomnie, fr L calumnia, fr calvi to deceive; akin to OE hōl calumny, Gk kēlein to beguile] – **calumnious** adj, **calumniously** adv

**calvados** /'kalvədos/ n, often cap apple brandy made by distilling cider [Fr, fr Calvados, department of Normandy in France]

**calvaria** /kal'veəri·ə/ n the upper portion of the skull enclosing the brain – called also SKULLCAP [L, skull, fr calva bald head, skull, fr fem of calvus bald]

**calvary** /'kalvəri/ n 1 a representation of the crucifixion of Christ (e g in sculpture) 2 an experience of intense mental suffering △ cavalry [Calvary, the hill near Jerusalem where Christ was crucified]

**calve** /kahv/ vb 1 to give birth to (esp a calf) 2 of an ice mass to release (a smaller floating mass of ice) ⟨the glacier ∼d a large iceberg⟩ [ME calven, fr OE cealfian, fr cealf calf] – **calver** n

**calves** /kahvz/ pl of CALF

**Calvinism** /'kalviniz(ə)m/ n 1 the Christian doctrines of Calvin and his followers, marked by emphasis on God's control of events on Earth according to a predetermined plan 2 puritanism [Jean Calvin †1564 Fr theologian] – **Calvinist** n or adj, **Calvinistic** adj, **Calvinistically** adv

**calx** /kalks/ n, pl **calxes, calces** /'kalseez/ the crumbly residue left when an ore of a metal or other mineral has been subjected to intense heat [ME cals, fr L calx lime – more at CHALK]

**calyculate** /kə'likyoolayt, -lət/ adj having a calyculus

**calyculus** /kə'likyooləs/ n, pl **calyculi** /-lie/ a small cup-shaped structure (e g a TASTE BUD) [NL, deriv of L caliculus small cup, dim. of calic-, calix cup – more at CHALICE]

**calypso** /kə'lipsoh/ n, pl **calypsos** also **calypsoes** an improvised ballad usu satirizing current events in a style originating in the W Indies [perh fr Calypso, island nymph in Homer's Odyssey] – **calypsonian** n or adj

**calyptra** /kə'liptrə/ n 1 the ARCHEGONIUM (female sex organ) of a LIVERWORT (primitive type of plant) or moss; esp one forming a membranous hood over the spore-containing capsule in a moss 2 a covering (e g the calyx) of a flower or fruit suggestive of a cap or hood 3 ROOT CAP (protective cap of tissue over the growing tip of a root) [NL, fr Gk kalyptra veil, fr kalyptein to cover – more at HELL] – **calyptrate** adj

**calyptrogen** /kə'liptrəjən/ n the layer of cells from which a ROOT CAP (protective cap of tissue over the growing tip of a root) originates [calyptra + -gen]

**calyx** /'kaliks, 'kay-/ n, pl **calyxes, calyces** /'kali,seez, 'kay-/ 1 the outer usu green or waxy part of a flower or floret consisting of a ring of SEPALS that protect the developing flower bud 2 a cup-shaped bodily structure; esp any of several cavities in the kidney of a mammal through which urine passes before it reaches the bladder [L calyc-, calyx, fr Gk kalyx – more at CHALICE] – **calyceal** adj

**cam** /kam/ n a mechanical device (e g a wheel or shaft with a projecting part) that transforms circular motion into intermittent or back-and-forth motion [perh fr Fr came, fr Ger kamm, lit., comb, fr OHG kamb]

**camaraderie** /,kamə'rahdəri, -'radəri/ n a spirit of good humour and trust among friends [Fr, fr camarade comrade]

**camarilla** /,kamə'rilə/ n a group of unofficial often secret and scheming advisers; also a cabal [Sp, lit., small room]

¹**camber** /'kambə/ vi to curve upwards in the middle ∼ vt to give a camber to [Fr cambrer, fr MF cambre curved, fr L camur – more at CHAMBER]

²**camber** n 1 a slight arching, curvature, or upward sloping from the sides to the middle of a road, ship's deck, beam, etc 2 the degree to which an aircraft wing or other AEROFOIL curves upwards from its front edge and down again to its back edge 3 an arrangement of the wheels of a motor vehicle closer together at the bottom than at the top

**cambered** /'kambəd/ adj, of a pair of vehicle wheels closer together at the bottom than at the top

**Camberwell Beauty** /'kambəwəl/ n, Br a blackish-brown butterfly (Nymphalis antiopa) that has a broad yellow border on the wings and is found in temperate parts of Europe, Asia, and N America [Camberwell, district of London]

**cambium** /'kambi·əm/ n, pl **cambiums, cambia** /-biə/ a thin layer of tissue between the XYLEM (water-conducting tissue) and PHLOEM (food-conducting tissue) of many plants, that divides to form extra xylem and phloem and is responsible for SECONDARY THICKENING (increase in diameter of stems and roots) – compare PROCAMBIUM [NL, fr ML, exchange, fr L cambiare to exchange – more at CHANGE] – **cambial** adj

**Cambodian** /kam'bohdi·ən/ n a native or inhabitant or the official language of Cambodia (now Kampuchea) – **Cambodian** adj

**Cambrian** /'kambri·ən/ adj 1 Welsh 2 of or being the earliest geological period of the PALAEOZOIC era, or the corresponding system of rocks marked by fossils of every great animal type except the VERTEBRATE, fr and by scarcely recognizable plant fossils [ML Cambria Wales, fr W Cymry Welshmen] – **Cambrian** n

**cambric** /'kambrik/ n a fine thin white linen or cotton fabric [obs Flem Kameryk Cambrai, city in N France]

¹**came** /kaym/ past of COME

²**came** /kaym/ n a narrow grooved lead strip used to hold together panes of glass, esp in a stained-glass window [origin unknown]

**camel** /'kaməl/ n 1 either of two large RUMINANTS (cud-chewing mammals) used for riding or carrying goods in desert regions, esp of Africa and Asia: **1a** the Arabian camel (*Camelus dromedarius*), with a single large hump on its back – called also DROMEDARY **b camel, Bactrian camel** the camel (*Camelus bactrianus*) with two humps **2** a watertight float attached to a ship to increase its buoyancy **3** a light yellowish-brown colour [ME, fr OE & ONF, fr L *camelus,* fr Gk *kamēlos,* of Sem origin; akin to Heb & Phoenician *gāmāl* camel]

**camelback** /'kaməl‚bak/ *n* an inferior chemical compound chiefly of reclaimed or synthetic rubber used for retreading or recapping the pneumatic tyres of motor vehicles

**cameleer** /‚kamə'liə/ *n* a camel driver

**camel hair** *n* **1** cloth that is made of camel hair or a mixture of camel hair and wool and is usu light tan and of soft silky texture **2** the hair of the camel or a substitute for it (eg hair from squirrels' tails) used esp in paint brushes

**camellia, camelia** /kə'meelyə; *also* kə'melyə/ *n* any of several shrubs or trees (genus *Camellia* of the family Theaceae, the camellia family); *esp* an ornamental greenhouse shrub (*Camellia japonica*) with glossy evergreen leaves and showy roselike flowers [NL *Camellia,* genus name, fr Georgius *Camellus* (Georg Josef Kamel) †1706 Moravian Jesuit missionary]

**camelopard** /kə'melə‚pahd/ *n, archaic* a giraffe [LL *camelopardus,* alter. of L *camelopardalis,* fr Gk *kamēlopardalis,* fr *kamēlos* + *pardalis* leopard]

**Camembert** /'kaməmbeə (*Fr* kamãbɛːr)/ *n* a round pale yellow soft cheese that has a thin greyish-white rind and is ripened through bacterial action [Fr, fr *Camembert,* town in Normandy, France]

**cameo** /'kamioh/ *n, pl* **cameos 1a** a usu small piece of gemstone (eg onyx) having at least two differently coloured layers, carved in such a way that the background is of a contrasting colour to the raised design **b** a small medallion (eg on a ring or brooch) with a profiled head in relief **2** a short literary or dramatic piece that brings into delicate or sharp relief the character of a person, place, or event **3** a small theatrical role (eg in television or in a film) performed by a well-known actor and often limited to a single scene [NL, fr It] – **cameo** *adj,* **cameo** *vt*

**camera** /'kamrə/ *n* **1** the treasury department of the papal CURIA (court and government of the Catholic church) **2a** CAMERA OBSCURA **b** a lightproof box fitted with a lens which forms an image of an object on some light-sensitive material: eg **b(1)** one containing photographic film for producing a permanent record **b(2)** one containing a camera tube and electronic parts which convert the image into an electrical signal that is usu used for television transmissions [LL, room – more at CHAMBER]

**cameraman** /-‚man, -mən/ *n* a person who operates a camera

**camera obscura** /əb'skyooərə/ *n* a darkened box or room having an aperture usu fitted with a lens through which light from external objects enters to form an image of the objects on a prepared surface (eg a screen) [NL, lit., dark chamber]

**camera tube** *n* any of several devices, used esp in television cameras, that convert an optical image into an electrical signal by scanning a light-sensitive screen with a beam of electrons: eg a ICONOSCOPE **b** IMAGE ORTHICON **c** IMAGE ORTHICON **d** VIDICON

**camerlengo** /‚kamə'leng‚goh/ *n, pl* **camerlengos** a cardinal who heads the the papal treasury department [It *camarlingo,* of Gmc origin (cf CHAMBERLAIN)]

**camiknickers** /'kami‚nikəz/ *n pl, Br* a one-piece clcsely fitting undergarment worn by women that combines a camisole and knickers [*camisole* + *knickers*]

**camisado** /‚kami'sahdoh/ *n, pl* **camisados** *archaic* an attack by night [obs Sp *camisada,* fr *camisa* shirt; fr the attackers wearing shirts over their armour so that they could recognize one another]

**camisole** /'kami‚sohl/ *n* a short bodice worn as an undergarment by women [Fr, fr Sp *camisola* or OProv *camisolla,* dim. of *camisa* shirt, fr LL *camisia*]

**camlet** /'kamlit/ *n* a medieval Asian fabric of camel hair or angora wool [ME *cameloit,* fr MF *camelot,* fr Ar *ḥamlat* woollen plush]

**camomile** *also* **chamomile** /'kaməmiel/ *n* any of a genus (*Anthemis,* esp *Anthemis nobilis*) of herbs of the daisy family whose leaves and flowers are used medicinally ( ~ *tea*); *also* a similar plant of a related genus (*Matricaria*) [ME *camemille,* fr ML *camomilla,* modif of L *chamaemelon,* fr Gk *chamaimēlon,* fr *chamai* on the ground + *mēlon* apple]

**Camorra** /kə'morə/ *n* a secret organization formed about 1820

in Naples and practising extortion; *broadly, not cap* any similar group organized for criminal ends [It]

¹**camouflage** /'kamə‚flahzh, -‚flahj/ *n* **1** the disguising of esp military equipment or installations (eg with paint, nets, or foliage); *also* the disguise so applied **2a** concealment by means of disguise (eg by adaptation to a natural environment) ⟨*the chameleon's use of* ~ ⟩ **b** behaviour designed to deceive or hide [Fr, fr *camoufler* to disguise, fr It *camuffare*]

²**camouflage** *vt* to conceal or disguise by camouflage ~ *vi* to practise camouflage – **camouflageable** *adj*

¹**camp** /kamp/ *n* **1a** ground on which temporary shelters (eg tents) are erected by gipsies, travellers, etc **b** the group of shelters erected on a camping ground **c** a place where troops are housed or trained temporarily or permanently **d** a settlement newly sprung up (eg in a lumbering or mining region) **e** a place where prisoners or detainees are housed (eg in huts or cabins) **2** *taking sing or pl vb* **2a** a group of people encamped **b** a group of people, esp one engaged in promoting or defending a theory, doctrine, or position ⟨*liberal and conservative* ~s⟩ **3** military service or life **4** *chiefly Br* a prehistoric fortified site ⟨*Barbury* Camp⟩ [MF, deriv of L *campus* plain, field; akin to OHG *hamf* crippled, Gk *kampē* bend] – **break camp** to pack up and leave a camp

²**camp** *vi* **1** to pitch or live in a camp **2** *informal* **2a** to live for a short time, esp in uncomfortable or makeshift conditions – often + *out* **b** to settle down as if to a siege ⟨*reporters* ~ed *outside the house*⟩

³**camp** *adj, informal* **1** homosexual **2** exaggeratedly effeminate **3** being so outrageously artificial, affected, inappropriate, or exaggerated as to be considered amusing [origin unknown] – **campness** *n,* **campy** *adj*

⁴**camp** *n* something (eg a style) that is camp ⟨*a marvellous piece of high* ~⟩

⁵**camp** *vi, informal* to behave in a camp manner

**camp up** *vt, informal* to give a camp quality to – esp in *camp it up*

¹**campaign** /‚kam'payn/ *n* **1a** a connected series of military operations that forms a distinct phase of a war or takes place in a particular geographical area **b** military life in the field ⟨*six months on* ~⟩ **2** a connected series of operations designed to bring about a particular result ⟨*a highly successful political* ~⟩ □ compare ¹BATTLE [Fr *campagne,* fr It *campagna* level country, campaign, fr LL *campania* level country, fr L, the level country round Naples, fr *campus* field]

²**campaign** *vi* to go on, engage in, or conduct a campaign – **campaigner** *n*

**campanile** /‚kampə'neeli/ *n, pl* **campanili, campaniles** a usu freestanding bell tower, esp in Italy and the USA [It, fr *campana* bell, fr LL]

**campanology** /‚kampə'noləji/ *n* the art of bell ringing [NL *campanologia,* fr LL *campana* + NL *-o-* + *-logia* -logy] – **campanologist** *n*

**campanula** /kəm'panyoolə/ *n* a bellflower [NL, dim. of LL *campana*]

**campanulate** /kəm'panyoolət, -layt/ *adj, of a flower* shaped like a bell [NL *campanula* bell-shaped part, dim. of LL *campana*]

**Campari** /kam'pahri/ *trademark* – used for a type of Italian bitters that is drunk as an aperitif

**camp bed** *n* a small collapsible bed, usu of fabric stretched over a lightweight frame

**camp chair** *n* a lightweight portable folding chair

**Campden tablet** /'kamd(ə)n/ *n* a tablet containing the chemical compound POTASSIUM METABISULPHITE used as a sterilizing agent in winemaking and as a preservative for fruit [*Campden* Research Station, at Chipping Campden in Gloucestershire, England, where it was orig developed]

**camper** /'kampə/ *n* **1** one who camps **2** a motor vehicle equipped for use as temporary accommodation (eg while holidaying)

**campestral** /kam'pestrəl/ *adj, formal* of fields or open country; rural [L *campestr-, campester,* fr *campus*]

**camp follower** *n* **1** a civilian who provides goods and services for a military unit but is not officially attached to it; *esp* a prostitute **2** a follower who is not of the main body of members or adherents; *esp* a politician who joins a party or movement solely for personal gain

**campground** /'kamp‚grownd/ *n, NAm* **1** a campsite **2** a place where outdoor religious meetings are held

**camphene** /'kam‚feen/ *n* any of several chemical compounds

(TERPENES) related to camphor; *esp* one, $C_{10}H_{16}$, used in insecticides [ISV, fr *camph*or + *-ene*]

**camphor** /'kamfə/ *n* a gummy fragrant chemical compound, $C_{10}H_{16}O$, obtained esp from the wood and bark of the camphor tree and used as a liniment, insect repellent, and in making celluloid; *also* any of several similar chemical compounds [ME *caumfre*, fr AF, fr ML *camphora*, fr Ar *kāfūr*, fr Malay *kāpūr*] – **camphoric** *adj*, **camphorate** *vt*

**camphorated oil** /'kamfəraytid/ *n* a liniment containing camphor

**camphor tree** *n* a large evergreen tree (*Cinnamomum camphora*) of the laurel family grown in most warm countries, whose wood and bark yield camphor

**campion** /'kampi·ən/ *n* any of various plants (genera *Lychnis* and *Silene*) of the pink family: eg a RED CAMPION b WHITE CAMPION [perh fr obs *campion* champion]

**camp meeting** *n, chiefly NAm* a series of evangelistic meetings usu held outdoors or in a tent, attended by families who camp nearby

**campo** /'kampoh/ *n, pl* **campos** a type of grassland plain in S America [AmerSp, fr Sp, field, fr L *campus*]

**campodeiform** *adj, of an insect larva* having long true legs, a hardened body, and active predatory habits – compare APODOUS, ERUCIFORM, SCARABAEIFORM

**campsite** /'kamp,siet/, **camping site** /'kamping/ *n* a place suitable for or used as the site of a camp

**camp stool** *n* a small portable folding stool, typically with a canvas seat

**campus** /'kampəs/ *n, pl* **campuses** 1 a university; *esp* a geographically self-contained university out in the country considered in terms of its grounds and buildings 2 *NAm* a separate branch of a university [L, plain, field – more at CAMP]

**campylotropous** /,kampi'lotrəpəs/ *adj* of or being an OVULE (immature seed before fertilization) that is bent over so as to appear to be attached to the side of its stalk [Gk *kampylos* bent (akin to Gk *kampē* bend) + ISV *-tropous*]

**camshaft** /'kam,shahft/ *n* a shaft to which a cam is attached or of which a cam forms an integral part

**camwood** /'kam,wood/ *n* (the wood of) a W African hardwood tree yielding a red dye [Temne *k'am*]

**¹can** /kən; *strong* kan/ *vb* **can; could** /kəd; *strong* kood/ *vt* 1 *archaic* to be able to do, make, etc ⟨*Too scanty 'twas to die for you, The merest Greek could* that – Emily Dickinson⟩ 2 *obs* to know, understand ⟨*But I* ~ *rymes of Robyn Hood and Randolf erle of Chestre* – Piers Plowman 5.402⟩ ~ *vi, archaic* to have knowledge or skill ⟨*He who* ~, *does. He who cannot, teaches* – G B Shaw⟩ ~ *va* 1a know how to ⟨*he* ~ *read*⟩ b be physically or mentally able to ⟨*he* ~ *lift 200 pounds*⟩ ⟨*I can't think why*⟩ c may perhaps – chiefly in questions ⟨*do you think he* ~ *still be living?*⟩ ⟨*what* ~ *they want?*⟩ **d**(1) be permitted or possible to ⟨~ *hardly blame him*⟩ **d**(2) ¹WILL 1 – used in the question form with the force of a request ⟨~ *you hold on a minute, please?*⟩ **e** be logically inferred or supposed to – chiefly in negatives ⟨*he* ~ *hardly have meant that*⟩ – compare MUST 4 **f** be inherently able or designed to ⟨*everything that money* ~ *buy*⟩ **g** be (logically) able to ⟨*2 + 2* ~ *also be written 3 + 1*⟩ **h** be enabled by law, agreement, or custom to ⟨*you* ~ *if you want*⟩ 2 have permission to – used interchangeably with *may* ⟨*you* ~ *go now if you like*⟩; – compare MAY 1a 3 will have to ⟨*if you don't like it you* ~ *lump it*⟩ [ME (1 & 3 sing. pres indic), fr OE; akin to OHG *kan* (1 & 3 sing. pres indic) know, am able, OE *cnāwan* to know – more at KNOW]

*usage* The idea of "giving or refusing permission" is now more commonly expressed by **can/could/can't** than by **may/might/ mayn't** ⟨*can we go now?*⟩ ⟨*they asked if they could go*⟩ ⟨*you can't go yet*⟩. Many people now find it somewhat pompous to use **may/might** in such situations, except in formal writing ⟨*if the Minister is satisfied that it is reasonable to do so, he* **may** (= the regulation permits him to) *award a higher pension*⟩ or when one speaks of oneself ⟨**may** *I help you?*⟩ or in cases where **can** could be misunderstood as perhaps referring to "ability" ⟨*what right have we to tell someone in Germany what he* **may** *or* **may** *not do?* – SEU S⟩

**²can** /kan/ *n* 1 a usu cylindrical container: **1a** a vessel for holding liquids ⟨*petrol* ~⟩ **b** TIN 2a; *specif* a tin containing a beverage (eg beer) 2 a depth charge 3 *chiefly NAm* a typically cylindrical metal receptacle, often with a removable cover and sometimes with a spout or side handles, for holding milk, oil, ashes, refuse, etc; a bin, drum 4 *chiefly NAm slang* jail **5a** *NAm slang* TOILET 1 **b** *NAm slang* the buttocks [ME *canne*, fr OE; akin to OHG *channa* vessel] – **canful** *n* – **carry the can** *in-*

*formal* to bear the responsibility; accept the blame – **in the can** *of a film or videotape* completed and ready for release

**³can** *vt* **-nn-** 1 to pack or preserve in a tin 2 *informal* to record on discs or tape ⟨*they* ~ned *the music for the broadcast*⟩ 3 *chiefly NAm slang* to put a stop or end to ⟨~ *that racket* – Nathaniel Burt⟩ – **canner** *n*

**Canaanite** /'kaynə,niet/ *n* a member of a Semitic people who inhabited ancient Palestine and Phoenicia from about 3000 BC [Gk *Kananitēs*, fr *Kanaan* Canaan, ancient region in Palestine] – **Canaanite** *adj*

**Canada balsam** /'kanədə/ *n* a thick yellowish to greenish oily resin produced by the balsam fir (*Abies balsamea*) that becomes transparent on solidifying and is used as an adhesive, esp in microscopy [*Canada*, country in N America]

**Canada goose** *n* the common wild goose (*Branta canadensis*) introduced into Europe from N America that has chiefly grey and brownish plumage with a black head and neck and a white patch under the throat

**Canadian** /kə'naydi·ən/ *n* a native or inhabitant of Canada – **Canadian** *adj*

**Canadian canoe** *n* a long light narrow boat with sharp ends and curved sides that is usu propelled by hand-driven paddles

**Canadian football** *n* a game resembling American football that is played with teams of 12 players each

**Canadian French** *n* French as spoken or written in Canada

**Canadian pondweed** *n* a submerged plant of slow-moving water (*Elodea canadensis*) of the family Hydrocharitaceae) that was introduced into Europe from N America and is used in garden ponds to increase the oxygen content of the water

**canaille** /kə'nayəl, kə'nie/ *n taking sing or pl vb* the rabble, riffraff [Fr, fr It *canaglia*, fr *cane* dog, fr L *canis* – more at HOUND]

**Canajan** /kə'nayj(ə)n/ *n, Can informal* Canadian English [alter. of *Canadian*]

**¹canal** /kə'nal/ *n* 1 an artificial waterway for navigation, drainage, or irrigation 2 a tubular anatomical passage or channel; a duct ⟨*alimentary* ~⟩ 3 any of various faint narrow markings on a planet, esp Mars [ME, fr L *canalis* pipe, channel, fr *canna* reed – more at CANE]

**²canal** *vt* **-ll-** (*NAm* **-ll-, -l-**) to construct a canal through or across

**canal boat** *n* a boat for use on a canal

**canaliculate** /,kanə'likyoolət, -layt/ *adj* grooved or channelled longitudinally ⟨*a* ~ *leafstalk*⟩

**canaliculus** /,kanə'likyooləs/ *n, pl* **canaliculi** /-li/ a minute canal in a body structure (eg a bone or the liver) [L, dim. of *canalis*]

**canal·ize, -ise** /'kanəliez/ *vt* **1a** to provide with a canal or channel **b** to make into or similar to a canal 2 to direct into a preferred channel or outlet – **canalization** *n*

**canapé** /'kanəpay, -pi/ *n* an appetizer consisting of a piece of bread or toast or a biscuit topped with a savoury spread (eg caviar or cheese) – compare HORS D'OEUVRE [Fr, lit., sofa, fr ML *canopeum, canapeum* mosquito net – more at CANOPY]

**canard** /kə'nahd, 'kanahd/ *n* 1 a false or unfounded report or story; *esp* a fabricated report 2 a small surface providing stability or control mounted in front of the main supporting surface on an aeroplane or hydrofoil; *also* an aeroplane having its tail assembly (EMPENNAGE) located in front of the main wings [Fr, lit., duck; (1) Fr, fr MF *vendre des canards à moitié* to cheat, lit., to half-sell ducks]

**canary** /kə'neəri/ *n* 1 a sweet white wine of the Canary Islands 2 a small finch (*Serinus canarius*) of the Canary Islands that is usu greenish to yellow in colour and is widely kept as a cage bird [*Canary* Islands in the Atlantic Ocean, fr Sp *Islas Canarias*, lit., islands of dogs]

**canary creeper** *n* a climbing plant (*Tropaeolum peregrinum*) of the nasturtium family that has fragrant yellow flowers

**canary grass** *n* any of several grasses (genus *Phalaris*); *esp* one (*Phalaris canariensis*) that originated in the Canary Islands and is now native to most of Europe and whose seeds are used for feeding cage birds

**canary yellow** *n* a vivid yellow colour

**canasta** /kə'nastə/ *n* 1 a form of rummy using two full packs plus jokers, in which players or partnerships try to accumulate points for sets of three or more cards of the same rank and score bonuses for 7-card sets (MELDS) 2 a set (MELD) of seven cards of the same rank in canasta [Sp, lit., basket]

**canaster** /'kanəstə, kə'nastə/ *n* a smoking tobacco made of coarsely broken dried leaves and used esp in pipes [D *kanaster*, prob fr Sp *canastro* basket; fr its being imported from S America in baskets]

**cancan** /'kan‚kan/ *n* a dance of French origin performed by women and characterized by high kicking, usu with the skirt held up in front [Fr]

**¹cancel** /'kansl/ *vb* **-ll-** (*NAm* **-l-, -ll-**) *vt* **1** to mark or strike out for deletion **2a** to destroy the force, effectiveness, or validity of; annul ⟨∼ *a magazine subscription*⟩ ⟨∼ *a cheque*⟩ **b** to bring to nothingness; destroy ⟨∼ *all government sinecures*⟩ **c** to match in force or effect; offset – often + *out* ⟨*his irritability* ∼led *out his natural kindness* – Osbert Sitwell⟩ **d** to call off, usu without expectation of rescheduling at a later date ⟨*the match had to be* ∼led⟩ **3** *maths* **3a** to remove (a common divisor) from the numerator and denominator of a fraction **b** to remove (equal terms or values) on opposite sides of an equation or account **4** to deface (a postage or revenue stamp), esp with a set of parallel lines, so as to prevent reuse ∼ *vi* to neutralize each other's strength or effect; counterbalance *synonyms* see ABROGATE, ERASE [ME *cancellen*, fr MF *canceller*, fr LL *cancellare*, fr L, to make like a lattice, fr *cancelli* (pl), dim. of *cancer* lattice, alter. of *carcer* prison] **cancellable** *adj*, **canceller** *n*

**²cancel** *n* **1** a cancellation; *esp* a postal cancellation **2a** a deleted part or passage **b(1)** a leaf in a book containing printed matter to be deleted or corrected **b(2)** a new leaf or slip in a book substituted for matter already printed

**cancellate** /'kansilayt/, **cancellated** /'kansilaytid/ *adj* **1** having a netlike or reticular structure ⟨*an insect with* ∼ *wings*⟩ **2** cancellous [L *cancellatus*, pp of *cancellare*]

**cancellation** /‚kansə'laysh(ə)n/ *n* **1** the act or an instance of cancelling; something that has been cancelled ⟨*Do you want to see if there's a* ∼?⟩ **2** a mark made to cancel something (eg a postage stamp)

**cancellous** /'kansələs, kan'seləs/ *adj, of bone* having a porous structure [NL *cancelli* intersecting bony plates and bars in porous bone, fr L, lattice]

**cancer** /'kansə/ *n* **1a** a malignant tumour of potentially unlimited growth **b** an often fatal condition marked by such tumours **2** a spreading evil in a person, society, etc ⟨*the* ∼ *of hidden resentment – Irish Digest*⟩ [L, crab, cancer; akin to Gk *karkinos* crab, cancer] – **cancerous** *adj*, **cancerously** *adv*

**Cancer** *n* **1a** a small constellation of the ZODIAC (imaginary belt in the heavens) lying between Gemini and Leo and represented as a crab **b(1)** the 4th sign of the zodiac in astrology, held to govern the period June 22 – July 22 approx **b(2)** somebody born under this sign [ME, fr L, lit., crab] – **Cancerian** *n or adj*

**cancrinite** /'kangkriniet/ *n* a complex mineral, ($Na_{21}Ca)_4(AlSiO_2)_6CO_3.nH_2O$, consisting of a carbonate and combined ALUMINATE and silicate of sodium and calcium [Ger *cancrinit*, fr Count Georg *Cancrin* †1845 Russ statesman]

**¹cancroid** /'kangkroyd/ *adj* **1** resembling a crab **2** resembling a cancer [L *cancr-*, *cancer* crab, cancer]

**²cancroid** *n* any of various forms of slow-growing skin cancer

**candela** /kan'daylə, -'deelə/ *n* the basic SI unit of luminous intensity equal to the luminous intensity of $^1/_{600\,000}$ square metre of the surface of a black body at the temperature of freezing platinum and a pressure of 101 325 newtons per square metre (1 atmosphere) [L, candle]

**candelabrum** /‚kandl'ahbrəm/, **candelabra** /-brə/ *n, pl* **candelabra** *also* **candelabrums, candelabras** a candlestick or lamp with several branches [L *candelabrum* (pl *candelabra*), fr *candela*]

*synonyms* A candelabrum usually stands on a surface, but a chandelier hangs from the ceiling. *usage* The use of the plural form candelabra for the singular ⟨*a beautiful* candelabra⟩ ⟨*two* candelabras⟩ is now common but still disapproved of by some people.

**candescent** /kan'des(ə)nt/, **candent** /'kand(ə)nt/ *adj, formal* glowing or dazzling, esp because white-hot [L *candescent-*, *candescens*, prp of *candescere*, incho of *candēre*] – **candescence** *n*

**candid** /'kandid/ *adj* **1a** indicating or suggesting complete sincerity; frank, open **b** tending to criticize severely; blunt **2** relating to photography of subjects acting naturally or without being posed ⟨∼ *picture*⟩ **3** *archaic* free from bias, prejudice, or malice; fair ⟨*a* ∼ *observer*⟩ [Fr & L; Fr *candide*, fr L *candidus* bright, white, fr *candēre* to shine, glow; akin to LGk *kandaros* ember] – **candidly** *adv*, **candidness** *n*

**candida** /'kandidə/ *n* any of a genus (*Candida*) of parasitic IMPERFECT FUNGI that resemble yeasts and include the agent

that causes thrush [NL, genus name, fr L, fem of *candidus* white] – **candidal** *adj*

**candidate** /'kandidayt, -dət/ *n* a person who is nominated or qualified for or who applies for an office, post, award, etc [L *candidatus*, fr *candidatus* clothed in white, fr *candidus* white; fr the white toga worn by a candidate for office in ancient Rome] – **candidacy** *n*

**candidature** /'kandidəchə/ *n, chiefly Br* the state of being a candidate

**candid camera** *n* a usu small camera equipped with a fast lens that is used for taking informal photographs of unposed subjects, often without their knowledge

**candidiasis** /‚kandi'die-əsis/ *n, pl* **candidiases** /-seez/ a disease (eg thrush) caused by a candida [NL]

**¹candle** /'kandl/ *n* **1** a usu cylindrical piece of tallow or wax enclosing a wick that gives out light when burning **2** something resembling a candle in shape or use ⟨*a sulphur* ∼ *for fumigation*⟩ **3** a candela [ME *candel*, fr OE, fr L *candela*, fr *candēre*] – **burn the candle at both ends** to use one's resources or energies to excess; *esp* to be active at night as well as by day – **hold a candle to** to qualify for comparison with – used in a negative clause ⟨*can't* hold a candle to *him as far as experience is concerned. He's the expert*⟩ [lit., to (be worthy to) assist another person by holding a candle to give light while he/she works] – **not worth the candle** *chiefly Br* not worth the effort; not justified by the result – see also BELL, **book, and candle**

**²candle** *vt* to test (eggs) for staleness, blood clots, fertility, etc by holding up between the eye and a source of light

**candleberry** /'kandlb(ə)ri/ *n* WAX MYRTLE (tree yielding oil and wax)

**candleholder** /'kandl‚holdə/ *n* a candlestick

**candlelight** /'kandl‚liet/ *n* **1** the light of a candle **2** *archaic* the time for lighting up; twilight

**candlelighter** /'kandl‚lietə/ *n* a long-handled implement with a taper and a snuffer, used for the ceremonial lighting and extinguishing of candles

**Candlemas** /'kandlməs/ *n* February 2 observed as a church festival in commemoration of the presentation of Christ in the temple and the purification of the Virgin Mary [ME *candelmasse*, fr OE *candelmæsse*, fr *candel* + *mæsse* mass, feast; fr the candles blessed and carried to celebrate the feast]

**candlenut** /'kandl‚nut/ *n* a tropical tree (*Aleurites moluccana*) of the spurge family that is a source of oil used in paints and varnishes; *also* the seeds of this tree formerly used for making candles

**candlepin** /'kandl‚pin/ *n* **1** a slender pin used in some bowling games that tapers towards top and bottom **2** *pl but taking sing vb* a bowling game using candlepins

**candlepower** /-‚powə/ *n* luminous intensity expressed in candelas

**candlestick** /-‚stik/ *n* a holder with a socket for a candle

**candletree** /'kandl‚tree/ *n* WAX MYRTLE (tree yielding oil and wax)

**candlewick** /-‚wik/ *n* a very thick soft cotton yarn; *also* fabric made from this yarn, usu with a raised tufted pattern

**candlewood** /-‚wood/ *n* **1** any of several trees or shrubs that have resinous wood **2** slivers of resinous wood burned for light

**candour**, *NAm chiefly* **candor** /'kandə/ *n* **1** the quality of being frank and candid; forthrightness **2** *archaic* freedom from prejudice or malice; fairness *synonyms* see TRUTH [Fr & L; Fr *candeur*, fr L *candor* whiteness, fr *candēre* – more at CANDID]

**¹candy** /'kandi/ *n* **1** crystallized sugar formed by boiling down sugar syrup **2** *chiefly NAm* sweets, confectionery [ME *sugre candy*, part trans of MF *sucre candi*, part trans of OIt *zucchero candi*, fr *zucchero* sugar + Ar *qandī* candied, fr *qand* cane sugar]

**²candy** *vt* to encrust or coat with sugar; *specif* to cook (eg fruit or fruit peel) in a heavy syrup until glazed ∼ *vi* to become coated or encrusted with sugar; *also* to become crystallized into sugar

**candy floss** /flos/ *n, Br* **1** a sweet consisting of a light fluffy mass of spun sugar, usu wound round a stick **2** something attractive but insubstantial

**candytuft** /-‚tuft/ *n* any of a genus (*Iberis*) of plants of the cabbage family cultivated for their white, pink, or purple flowers [*Candy* (now *Candia*) Crete, Greek island + E *tuft*]

**¹cane** /kayn/ *n* **1a(1)** a hollow or pithy usu slender jointed stem (eg of a reed) **a(2)** any of various slender woody stems; *esp* an elongated flowering or fruiting stem (eg of a raspberry), usu growing directly out of the ground ⟨*it is important to keep*

~ *fruits free of pests and diseases*⟩ **b** any of various tall woody grasses or reeds: e g **b**(1) any of a genus (*Arundinaria*) of coarse grasses resembling bamboo **b**(2) sugarcane **b**(3) sorghum **2a** a cane walking stick; *broadly* WALKING STICK **b** a slender length of cane used for supporting flowers, shrubs, etc **c** a cane or rod for beating someone; *also* punishment by this means ⟨*abolition of the* ~⟩ **d** rattan; *esp* split rattan for use in basketry, wickerwork, etc [ME, fr MF, fr OProv *cana*, fr L *canna*, fr Gk *kanna*, of Sem origin; akin to Ar *qanāh* hollow stick, reed]

²**cane** *vt* **1** to beat with a cane; *broadly* to punish **2** to weave or repair with cane ⟨~ *the seat of a chair*⟩ **3** *chiefly Br* to defeat thoroughly; trounce

**canebrake** /'kayn,brayk/ *n, NAm* a thicket of canes

**canescent** /kə'nes(ə)nt/ *adj* growing white, whitish, or hoary; *esp* having a grey covering of hairs ⟨~ *leaves*⟩ [L *canescent-, canescens*, prp of *canescere*, incho of *canēre* to be grey, be white, fr *canus* white, hoary – more at HARE]

**cane sugar** *n* sugar obtained from sugarcane

**cangue** *also* **cang** /kang/ *n* a portable pillory formerly fastened round the neck of petty offenders in China [Fr *cangue*, fr Pg *canga* yoke]

¹**canine** /'kaynien/ *adj* **1** of dogs or the family (Canidae) of flesh-eating mammals that includes the dogs, wolves, jackals, and foxes **2** of or resembling a dog [L *caninus*, fr *canis* dog – more at HOUND]

²**canine** *n* **1** a conical pointed tooth; *esp* one situated between the last incisor and the first premolar **2** a dog

**canine distemper** *n* ²DISTEMPER 1 (virus disease of dogs)

**canister** /'kanistə/ *n* **1** a small, usu metal, box or tin for holding a dry product (e g tea or shot) **2** canister, canister shot CASE SHOT [L *canistrum* basket, fr Gk *kanastron*, fr *kanna* reed – more at CANE]

¹**canker** /'kangkə/ *n* **1** an ulcer or spreading sore attacking esp the mouth **2** an area of local dead tissue in a plant or tree **3a** a long-lasting inflammation of the ear in dogs, cats, and rabbits **b** a disease in horses that leads to the softening of the horny material on the underside of the hoof **4** a source of corruption or debasement perceived as spreading **5** *chiefly dial* DOG ROSE **6** *obs* GANGRENE 1 [ME, fr ONF *cancre*, fr L *cancer* crab, cancer] – **cankerous** *adj*

²**canker** *vt* **1** to undermine progressively ⟨*God help that country*, ~ed *deep by doubt* – Archibald MacLeish⟩ ~ **2** *obs* to infect with a spreading sore ~ *vi* **1** to become infested with canker **2** to become corrupted

**cankerworm** /'kangkə,wuhm/ *n* any of the larvae of various US moths (e g *Paleacrita vernata*) that injure trees, esp by feeding on buds and leaves

**canna** /'kanə/ *n* any of several tropical plants (genus *Canna* of the family Cannaceae) grown for their bright red or yellow flowers and decorative leaves [NL, genus name, fr L, reed, fr Gk *kanna*]

**cannabin** /'kanəbin/ *n* CANNABIS RESIN

**cannabis** /'kanəbis/ *n* the dried leaves and flowering tops of the female plants of the hemp that yield CANNABIS RESIN and are sometimes smoked or eaten for their intoxicating effect – compare HASHISH, MARIJUANA [L, hemp, fr Gk *kannabis*, fr the source of OE *hænep* hemp]

**cannabis resin** *n* a dark resin obtained from female hemp plants that contains the physiologically active ingredients of cannabis

**canned** /kand/ *adj* **1** *informal* recorded for mechanical or electronic reproduction; *esp* prerecorded for addition to a sound track or videotape ⟨~ *laughter*⟩ **2** *slang* drunk **3** *chiefly NAm* tinned

**cannel coal** *also* **cannel** /'kanl/ *n* a bituminous coal that burns brightly [prob fr E dial. *cannel* candle, fr ME *candel*]

**cannelloni** /,kanə'lohni/ *n taking sing or pl vb* pasta in the form of large tubular rolls filled with a savoury mixture (e g of meat and cheese) [It, pl of *cannellone* tubular noodle, aug of *cannello* piece of cane, small tube, fr *canna* cane, reed, fr L – more at CANE]

**cannery** /'kanəri/ *n* a factory for canning foods

**cannibal** /'kanibl/ *n* **1** a human being who eats human flesh **2** an animal that eats its own kind [NL *Canibalis* Carib, fr Sp *Canibal* (orig used by Columbus, referring to man-eating Caribs in the W Indies), fr Arawakan *Caniba*, Carib Carib – more at CARIB] – **cannibal** *adj*, **cannibalism** *n*, **cannibalistic** *adj*

**cannibal·ize, -ise** /'kanibl,iez/ *vt* **1a** to dismantle (a machine) for parts to be used as replacements in other machines **b** to

make use of parts of (e g a mechanism) in producing a new whole **2** to deprive of parts or men in order to repair or strengthen another unit – **cannibalization** *n*

**cannikin** /'kanikin/ *n* a small can or drinking vessel [prob fr obs D *kanneken*, fr MD *canneken*, dim. of *canne* can; akin to OE *canne* can]

¹**cannon** /'kanən/ *n, pl* **cannons**, *esp collectively* **cannon 1a** a usu large gun mounted on a carriage; a heavy artillery piece **b** an automatic shell-firing gun mounted esp in an aircraft **2** a heavy hollow cylinder able to rotate freely on its supporting shaft **3** the part of the leg in which the CANNON BONE is found [MF *canon*, fr It *cannone*, lit., large tube, aug of *canna* reed, tube, fr L, cane, reed – more at CANE] – **cannon** *vt*

²**cannon** *n, Br* a shot in billiards in which the CUE BALL strikes each of two balls in succession [alter. of *carom*]

³**cannon** *vi, Br* **1** to make a cannon in billiards **2** to run *into*; *also* to collide with and be deflected *off*

¹**cannonade** /'kanə'nayd/ *n* heavy continuous artillery fire

²**cannonade** *vt* to attack with artillery fire

**cannonball** /-,bawl/ *n* **1** a round solid missile made for firing from an old type of cannon **2** a jump into water made with the arms holding the knees tight against the chest **3** a hard straight tennis serve – **cannonball** *vi*

**cannon bone** *n* a bone in horses and other hoofed mammals that supports the leg from the hock joint to the fetlock [Fr *canon*, lit., cannon]

**cannon fodder** *n* soldiers regarded merely as material to be expended in battle

**cannonry** /-ri/ *n* **1** a cannonade **2** artillery

**cannot** /'kanot, -nət, kə'not/ **can not** – **cannot but/cannot choose/help but** to be bound to; must ⟨could not but *smile at the answer*⟩

*usage* **1** Some writers on usage accept either **cannot but** ⟨could not but *smile*⟩ or **cannot help** ⟨could not *help smiling*⟩, but advise one to avoid **cannot help but** in formal writing. **2** The use of **cannot** can lead to ambiguity in such sentences as ⟨*I* **cannot** *speak too highly of his contribution*⟩ or ⟨*his contribution* **cannot** *be overestimated*⟩. Was his contribution great, or only mediocre?

**cannula** /'kanyoolə/ *n, pl* **cannulas, cannulae** /-lie/ a small tube for insertion into a body cavity or into a duct or vessel [NL, fr L, dim. of *canna* reed – more at CANE]

**cannular** /'kanyoolə/ *adj* tubular

**cannulate** /'kanyoolayt/ *vt* to insert a tube or cannula into (a body cavity) – **cannulation** *n*

¹**canny** /'kani/ *adj* **1** cautious and shrewd; astute **2** *Scot* free from unnatural powers; normal **3** *Scot & NE Eng* careful, steady; *esp* thrifty **4** *Scot* quiet, snug **5** *NE Eng* agreeable, fine ⟨*a* ~ *lass*⟩ [¹can + ¹-y] – **cannily** *adv*, **canniness** *n*

²**canny** *adv, Scot* in a canny manner ⟨*ca'* ~⟩

¹**canoe** /kə'nooh/ *n, CANADIAN CANOE* **2** *chiefly Br* a kayak [Fr, fr NL *canoa*, fr Sp, fr Arawakan, of Cariban origin; akin to Galibi *canaoua*]

²**canoe** *vi* **canoed; canoeing 1** to paddle a canoe, esp for recreation or sport ⟨*goes* ~ing *every weekend*⟩ **2** to go or travel in a canoe – **canoeist** *n*

**can of worms** *n, informal* a potentially embroiled or complicated matter, situation, area

¹**canon** /'kanən/ *n* **1a** a decree or dogma issued by a church council **b** a provision of canon law **2** a series of prayers forming the set part of the Mass and including the consecration of the bread and wine **3a** an authoritative list of books accepted as Holy Scripture **b** the authentic works of a writer **4a** an accepted principle or rule **b** a criterion or standard of judgment **c** a body of principles, rules, standards, or norms **5** a CONTRAPUNTAL musical composition for two or more voices or instrumental parts in which the melody is repeated by the voices or instruments entering in succession, though not always at the same pitch △ cannon [ME, fr OE, fr LL, fr L, ruler, rule, model, standard, fr Gk *kanōn*; akin to Gk *kanna* reed – more at CANE; (2) ME, prob fr OF, fr LL, fr L; (3) ME, fr LL, fr L; (5) LGk *kanōn*, fr Gk]

²**canon** *n* **1** a clergyman belonging to the chapter or the staff of a cathedral or collegiate church **2** CANON REGULAR [ME *canoun*, fr AF *canunie*, fr LL *canonicus* one living under a rule, fr L, according to rule, fr Gk *kanonikos*, fr *kanōn*]

**cañon** /'kanyən/ *n* a canyon

**canoness** /'kanənəs, -,nes/ *n* **1** a woman living in a community under a religious rule but not under a perpetual vow **2** a member of a Roman Catholic congregation of women corresponding to CANONS REGULAR

**canonical** /kə'nonikl/, **canonic** /kə'nonik/ adj 1 relating to a canon 2 conforming to a general or accepted rule; orthodox 3 accepted as forming the canon of Scripture 4 maths reduced to the simplest or clearest equivalent mathematical form ⟨a ~ matrix⟩ – **canonically** adv, **canonicity** also **canonicality** n

**canonical form** n, maths the simplest form of a MATRIX (arrangement of numbers, letters, etc in rows and columns); specif the form of a square matrix that has zero elements everywhere except along the PRINCIPAL DIAGONAL (leading from upper left to lower right)

**canonical hour** n 1 a time of day appointed by canon law for religious service 2 any of the daily religious services that make up the Divine Office – see MATINS, LAUD, PRIME, TERCE, SEXT, NONE, VESPERS, and COMPLINE

**canonicals** /kə'noniklz/ n pl the vestments prescribed by canon law for an officiating clergyman

**canonist** /'kanənist/ n a specialist in canon law

**canon-ize, -ise** /'kanəniez/ vt 1 to declare (a deceased person) an officially recognized saint 2 to include in a canon, esp of Scripture 3 to sanction by ecclesiastical authority 4 to give authoritative sanction or approval to [ME canonizen, fr ML canonizare, fr LL canon catalogue of saints, fr L, standard] – **canonization** n

**canon law** n the usu codified law governing a church

**canon lawyer** n a canonist

**canon regular** n, pl **canons regular** a member of any of several Roman Catholic institutes of regular priests living in a community under a usu Augustinian rule

**canonry** /'kanənri/ n 1 the office of a canon 2 the endowment that financially supports a canon 3 the building in which a canon resides ⟨the North Canonry in Salisbury's Cathedral Close⟩

**canoodle** /kə'noohdl/ vi, informal to fondle someone or each other amorously; pet [prob fr E dial. canoodle donkey, fool, silly lover] – **canoodler** n, **canoodling** n

**canopic jar** /kə'nohpik/ n, often cap C a jar with detachable lid in which the ancient Egyptians preserved the viscera of an embalmed body [Canopus, city in ancient Egypt]

**canopy** /'kanəpi/ n 1a a cloth covering suspended over a bed b a cover (eg of cloth) fixed or carried above a person of high rank or a sacred object; a baldachin c the uppermost layer of a forest composed of spreading leafy branches d an ornamental rooflike structure; also an awning 2 the transparent enclosure over an aircraft cockpit 3 the lifting or supporting surface of a parachute [ME canope, fr ML canopeum mosquito net, fr L conopeum, fr Gk kōnōpion, fr kōnōps mosquito] – **canopy** vt

**canorous** /kə'nawrəs/ adj, formal sounding pleasantly; melodious [L canorus, fr canor melody, fr canere to sing – more at CHANT] – **canorously** adv, **canorousness** n

**canst** /kənst; strong kanst/ archaic pres 2 sing of CAN

**¹cant** /kant/ adj, N Eng & Scot cheerful, lively [ME, prob fr (assumed) MLG kant]

**²cant** n 1 an external angle (eg of a building) 2a a sudden thrust that produces some displacement b the displacement so caused 3 an oblique or slanting surface 4 an inclination from a given line; a slope [ME, edge, niche, prob fr MD or ONF; MD, edge, corner, fr ONF, fr L canthus, cantus iron tyre, perh of Celt origin; akin to W cant rim]

**³cant** vt 1 to give a cant or oblique edge to; bevel 2 to set at an angle; tip or tilt up or over ~ vi 1 to pitch to one side; lean 2 to slope

**⁴cant** n 1a the slang used by thieves, beggars, etc b the jargon used by members of a particular profession 2 a set or stock phrase 3 the expression or repetition of conventional, trite, or unconsidered opinions; esp the insincere and hypocritical use of pious phraseology 4 obs the speech used by a particular religious class or sect synonyms see DIALECT [cant (vb) to talk, speak whiningly like a beggar, deriv of L cantare to sing, chant] – **cant** vi, **canter** n

**can't** /kahnt/ can not

**cantabile** /kan'tahbili, -lay/ adv or adj in a singing manner – often used as a direction in music [It, fr LL cantabilis worthy to be sung, fr L cantare to sing]

**Cantabrigian** /,kantə'brijiən/ n 1 a native or inhabitant of Cambridge 2 a student or graduate of Cambridge University or Harvard University [ML Cantabrigia Cambridge, city in England; applied by extension to Cambridge, city in Massachusetts, USA, site of Harvard University] – **Cantabrigian** adj

**Cantal** /kon'tahl (Fr kãtal)/ n a hard strong-flavoured French cheese similar to Cheddar [Fr, fr Cantal, department in S France]

**cantala** /kan'tahlə/ n a hard fibre produced from the leaves of an AGAVE (Agave cantala) and used for making coarse twine [origin unknown]

**cantaloup, cantaloupe** /'kantə,loohp/ n any of several varieties of MUSKMELON (type of cultivated melon); esp one with a hard ridged or warty rind and reddish-orange flesh [Cantalupo, former papal villa near Rome in Italy]

**cantankerous** /,kan'tangkərəs/ adj ill-natured, quarrelsome [perh irreg fr obs contack contention, fr ME contak] – **cantankerously** adv, **cantankerousness** n

**cantata** /kan'tahtə/ n a usu sacred choral composition comprising choruses, solos, recitatives, and interludes [It, fr L, sung mass, ecclesiastical chant, fr fem of cantatus, pp of cantare]

**cantatrice** /'kantətrees (Fr kãtatris; It kantatritʃe)/ n, pl **cantatrices** /-treesiz (Fr ~)/, **cantatrici** /,kantə'treechi (It -tritʃi)/ a female singer; esp a female opera singer [It & Fr; Fr, fr It, fr LL cantatric-, cantatrix, fem of L cantator singer, fr cantatus, pp]

**cant dog** n CANT HOOK [²cant]

**canteen** /kan'teen/ n 1a a shop providing supplies (eg food or alcoholic drink) in a servicemen's camp b a dining hall in a school, factory, etc 2 a partitioned chest or box for holding cutlery 3 a soldier's mess kit 4 a usu cloth-covered flask for carrying liquids (eg drinking water) [Fr cantine, fr It cantina wine cellar, fr canto corner, fr L canthus iron tyre – more at CANT]

**¹canter** /'kantə/ vi 1 to move (as if) at a canter 2 to progress or ride at a canter ~ vt to cause to canter [short for obs canterbury, fr canterbury, n (canter), fr Canterbury, city in England; fr the supposed gait of the horses of pilgrims to Canterbury]

**²canter** n 1 a 3-beat gait of a horse, donkey, etc resembling but smoother and slower than the gallop – compare GALLOP, RUN, TROT, WALK 2 a ride at a canter

**canterbury** /'kantəb(ə)ri/ n a low partitioned stand used esp for holding sheet music or magazines [Canterbury in England]

**Canterbury bell** n any of several bellflowers (genus Campanula) of the harebell family cultivated for their showy flowers [fr the small bells on the horses of pilgrims to Canterbury]

**cantharid** /'kanthərid/ n any of a family (Cantharidae) of flesh-eating beetles [NL Cantharidae, family name, fr cantharis, type genus]

**cantharis** /'kanthəris/ n, pl **cantharides** /kan'tharideez/ 1 SPANISH FLY 1 (type of beetle) 2 pl but taking sing or pl vb a preparation of dried beetles, esp Spanish flies, formerly used as a counterirritant and aphrodisiac [ME & L; ME cantharide, fr L cantharid-, cantharis, fr Gk kantharid-, kantharis]

**cant hook** n a stout wooden lever with a metal-clad end used esp in handling logs [²cant]

**canthus** /'kanthəs/ n, pl **canthi** /'kanthi/ either of the angles formed where the upper and lower eyelids meet [LL, fr Gk kanthos – more at CANT]

**canticle** /'kantikl/ n a song; specif any of several liturgical songs (eg the Magnificat) taken from the Bible [ME, fr L canticulum, dim. of canticum song, fr cantus, pp of canere to sing]

**Canticles** /'kantiklz/, **Canticle of Canticles** n taking sing vb SONG OF SONGS

**cantilena** /,kanti'laynə/ n 1 a simple fluid style in vocal music 2 the part carrying the main tune in choral music [It, fr L, song, fr cantus]

**cantilever** /'kanti,leevə/ n a projecting beam or member supported at only one end: eg a a bracket-shaped member supporting a balcony or a cornice b either of the two beams or trusses that project from piers towards each other and that when joined directly or by a suspended connecting member form a span of a cantilever bridge [perh fr ²cant + -i- + lever]

**cantillate** also **cantilate** /'kantilayt/ vt to recite on usu improvised musical notes, esp in a Jewish liturgical service [L cantillatus, pp of cantillare to sing low, fr cantare to sing – more at CHANT] – **cantillation** n

**cantina** /kan'teenə/ n a small bar or wine shop, esp in SW USA or Central or South America [AmerSp, fr Sp, canteen, fr It, wine cellar – more at CANTEEN]

**canting** /'kanting/ adj 1 affectedly pious or righteous; hypocritical 2 heraldry expressing a name by means of a visual pun ⟨the branches of broom stand for Bromley ... an example of ~ heraldry⟩

**cantle** /'kantl/ *n* **1** the upward projecting rear part of a saddle **2** *archaic* a segment cut off or out of something [ME *cantel,* fr ONF, dim. of *cant* edge, corner – more at CANT]

**canto** /'kantoh/ *n, pl* **cantos** a major division of a long poem [It, fr L *cantus* song, fr *cantus,* pp of *canere* to sing – more at CHANT]

**canto fermo** /'feəmoh, 'fuhmoh/ *n* CANTUS FIRMUS [It]

**¹canton** /'kanton, -'-/ *n* **1** a small territorial division of a country: eg **1a** any of the states of the Swiss confederation **b** a division of a French arrondissement **2a** the top inner quarter of a flag **b** a rectangle in the top left corner of a heraldic field [MF, section, corner, fr L *cantone,* fr *canto* corner, fr L *canthus* iron tyre – more at CANT] – **cantonal** *adj*

**²canton** /kan'ton; *sense 2* kən'toohn/ *vt* **1** to divide into parts; *specif* to divide into cantons **2** to allot quarters to (eg a body of troops) – **cantonization** *n*

**canton crepe** /'kantən/ *n, often cap lst C* a soft thick dress crepe made in plain weave with fine crosswise ribs [*Canton,* city in SE China]

**Cantonese** /,kantə'neez/ *n, pl* **Cantonese** **1** a native or inhabitant of Canton **2** the dialect of Chinese spoken in and around Canton – **Cantonese** *adj*

**cantonment** /kən'toohnmənt/ *n* **1** the quartering of troops **2** more or less temporary accommodation for troops

**cantor** /'kantaw/ *n* **1** a singer who leads liturgical music **2** a synagogue official who sings or chants liturgical music and leads the congregation in prayer [L, singer, fr *cantus,* pp of *canere* to sing]

**cantorial** /kan'tawri•əl/ *adj* of the North side of the choir (eg in a cathedral) where the precentor sits – compare DECANAL

**cantrip** /'kantrip/ *n, chiefly Scot* **1** a witch's trick; a spell **2** a mischievous or whimsically playful act [origin unknown]

**cantus** /'kantəs/ *n, pl* **cantus** **1** CANTUS FIRMUS **2** the principal melody or voice in 16th- and 17th-century choral music [L, song – more at CHANT]

**cantus firmus** /'fiəməs, 'fuhməs/ *n, pl* **cantus firmi** /'fiəmi, 'fuhmi/ **1** the plainchant or simple Gregorian melody, originally sung in unison and with a prescribed form and use **2** a melodic theme or subject; *esp* one for contrapuntal treatment [ML, lit., fixed song]

**canty** /'kanti, 'kahnti/ *adj, chiefly Scot* cheerful, sprightly [¹*cant* + ¹-*y*]

**Canuck** /kə'nuk/ *n* **1** *chiefly NAm informal* a Canadian **2** *chiefly Can* slang FRENCH CANADIAN **3** *derog* the CANADIAN FRENCH language [prob alter. of *Canadian*]

**¹canvas,** *Br also* **canvass** /'kanvəs/ *n, pl* **canvases,** *Br also* **canvasses 1** a firm closely woven cloth, usu of linen, hemp, or cotton, used for clothing and sails **2** a set of sails; sail **3** a military or camping tent; *also* such tents collectively **4a** a cloth surface suitable for painting on in oils; *also* the painting on such a surface **b** the background against which events take place (*the crowded ~ of history*) **5** a coarse cloth so woven as to form regular meshes for working with the needle (eg in embroidery or tapestry work) **6** the floor of a boxing or wrestling ring [ME *canevas,* fr ONF, fr (assumed) VL *cannabaceus* hempen, fr L *cannabis* hemp – more at CANNABIS] – **canvaslike** *adj* – **under canvas 1** living in a tent; camping **2** *of a ship* UNDER SAIL

**²canvas** *vt* **canvassed,** *Br also* **canvassed; canvasing,** *Br also* **canvassing** to cover, line, or furnish with canvas

**canvasback** /-,bak/ *n* a N American wild duck (*Aythya valisineria*) characterized esp by the elongated sloping profile of its bill and head and closely related to the European pochard [fr its colour]

**¹canvass** /'kanvəs/ *vt* **1a** to examine in detail; *specif, NAm* to examine (votes) officially for authenticity **b** to discuss, debate **2** to visit (a district or person) in order to solicit (political) support or to ascertain opinions or feelings **3** *obs* to toss in a canvas sheet in sport or punishment ~ *vi* to seek orders or votes; solicit △ canvas – **canvasser** *n*

**²canvass** *n* **1** the act of canvassing (*a house-to-house ~*): eg **1a** the personal solicitation of votes **b** a survey to ascertain the probable vote before an election **2** *chiefly NAm* a scrutiny, esp of votes

**canyon, canon** /'kanyən/ *n* a deep narrow valley with steep sides, often with a stream flowing through it [AmerSp *canón,* fr Sp, tube, pipe, aug of *cana* cane]

**canzona** /kant'sohnə/ *n* a canzone

**canzone** /kant'sohni/ *n, pl* **canzoni** /~/ *also* **canzones 1** a medieval Provençal or Italian lyric poem **2** a musical polyphonic setting of a canzone; *broadly* such a work resembling a madrigal [It, fr L *cantion-, cantio* song, fr *cantus,* pp of *canere* to sing – more at CHANT]

**canzonet** /,kanzə'net/ *also* **canzonetta** /,kanzə'netə/ *n* **1** a part-song resembling but less elaborate than a madrigal **2** a light and graceful song [It *canzonetta,* dim. of *canzone*]

**caoutchouc** /'kow,choohk/ *n* ¹RUBBER 2a [Fr, fr obs Sp *cauchuc* (now *caucho*), fr Quechua]

**¹cap** /kap/ *n* **1a** a soft close-fitting head covering that has no brim and usu a peak **b** a head covering that denotes the rank or occupation of the wearer (eg a nurse) **c** a head covering awarded to a player selected for a special (eg a national) team in cricket, rugby, soccer, etc or as a mark of distinction to a regular member of a team (eg in English county cricket); *also* a player to whom such a cap has been awarded **2** a natural cover or top: eg **2a** an overlying rock layer that is usu hard to penetrate **b(1)** PILEUS (upper dome-shaped part of a mushroom) **b(2)** CALYPTRA (hood covering the spore-bearing capsule in a moss or liverwort) **c** (a patch of distinctively coloured feathers on) the top of a bird's head **3** something that serves as a cover or protection esp for the end or top of an object (*a lens ~*) **4** a mortarboard – chiefly in *cap and gown* **5** the uppermost part; top **6** a paper or metal container holding an explosive charge (eg for a toy pistol or for priming the charge in a firearm) **7** the mathematical symbol ∩ indicating an INTERSECTION (set of all elements common to two sets) – compare CUP **8** CROWN 3E (external part of a tooth) **9** *medicine* the accumulation of proteins on the surface of a cell that occurs during CAPPING **10** *Br* DUTCH CAP **11** *Br* the collection taken at a fox hunt [ME *cappe,* fr OE *cæppe,* fr LL *cappa* head covering, cloak, perh fr L *caput* head] – **have/put on one's thinking cap** to (begin to) ponder or reflect on something – **set one's cap at** to try to attract (a man) with a view to marriage – see also **a** FEATHER **in one's cap**

**²cap** *vt* **-pp-** **1a** to provide or protect with a cap; *specif* CROWN 5 (*have a tooth ~ped*) **b** to award a cap to as a symbol of honour or rank (*South Africa's most ~ped rugby forward*) **2** to form a cap over; crown (*the mountains were ~ped with mist* – John Buchan) **3a** to follow with something more noticeable, appropriate, or significant; outdo (*I can ~ that story with a better*) **b** to put the finishing touch to; end (*today's announcement that the treaty has been signed ~s three years of negotiations*) **4** *medicine* to form a cap

**³cap** *n, chiefly NAm slang* a capsule or tablet containing a small quantity of a drug (eg heroin) [short for *capsule*]

**capability** /,kaypə'biləti/ *n* **1** the quality or state of being capable **2** a feature or faculty capable of development; potential
*synonyms* Capability, capacity, ability, and potential all mean "power to do something". Capability implies the possession of the required qualities (*the capability of a good secretary to do several jobs at once*). Capacity suggests the power to receive or absorb (*a capacity for learning languages*). Ability often implies skill (*musical ability*). Potential applies to an inherent but untried power (*a site with excellent potential*). *antonyms* inability, incapability, incapacity

**capable** /'kaypəbl/ *adj* **1** susceptible – + *of* (*a remark ~ of being misunderstood*) **2** having the attributes or traits required to perform some deed or action – + *of* (*a man ~ of intense concentration*) (*~ of murder*) **3** having ability (*her ~ fingers*) [MF or LL; MF *capable,* fr LL *capabilis,* irreg fr L *capere* to take – more at HEAVE] – **capableness** *n,* **capably** *adv*

**capacious** /kə'payshəs/ *adj* able to contain a great deal [L *capac-, capax* capacious, capable, fr L *capere*] – **capaciously** *adv,* **capaciousness** *n*

**capacitance** /kə'pasit(ə)ns/ *n, physics* **1** the ability of an isolated conductor or system of conductors and insulators to store electric charge **2** the measure of capacitance equal to the ratio of the charge induced to the potential difference [*capacity*] – **capacitive** *adj,* **capacitively** *adv*

**capacitate** /kə'pasətayt/ *vt* **1** to make legally competent **2** *archaic* to make capable; qualify

**capacitor** /kə'pasətə/ *n* a component that is included in an electrical circuit to provide capacitance and that usu consists of an insulator (eg air, mica, or waxed paper) sandwiched between two opposing charged conductors (eg metal foil or plates)

**¹capacity** /kə'pasəti/ *n* **1a** the ability to receive, accommodate, or deal with **b** the measured ability to contain; volume (*a jug with a ~ of 2 litres*) **c** maximum production or output (*we are working at ~ already*) **d(1)** capacitance **d(2)** the quantity of electricity that a battery, motor, etc can deliver under particular conditions **2** legal qualification, competency, or fitness **3a** ability, talent **b** POTENTIAL 1 ⟨*a ~ for violence*⟩ **4** a position or role assigned or assumed ⟨*in his ~ as a judge*⟩ **synonyms** see CAPABILITY **antonym** incapacity [ME *capacite*, fr MF *capacité*, fr L *capacitat-, capacitas*, fr *capac-, capax*]

²**capacity** *adj* reaching or equalling maximum capacity ⟨*a ~ crowd at the match*⟩

**cap and bells** *n, pl* **caps and bells** a cap with bells attached worn by a professional jester

**cap and gown** *n taking sing or pl vb* formal academic dress worn by university staff and students

**cap-a-pie, cap-à-pie** /ˌkap ə 'pee/ *adv, archaic or humorous* from head to foot ⟨*armed ~*⟩ [MF (*de*) *cap a pé* from head to foot]

**caparison** /kə'paris(ə)n/ *n* **1a** an ornamental covering for a horse **b** a decorative harness, fittings, etc **2** rich clothing; adornment [MF *caparaçon*, fr OSp *caparazón*] – **caparison** *vt*

¹**cape** /kayp/ *n* a point or area of land jutting out into water as a peninsula or promontory [ME *cap*, fr MF, fr OProv, fr L *caput* head – more at HEAD]

²**cape** *n* **1** a sleeveless outer garment or outer part of a garment that fits closely at the neck and hangs loosely from the shoulders – compare CLOAK 1 **2** the short feathers covering the shoulders of a fowl below the hackle [Fr *cape* or Sp *capa* cloak, fr LL *cappa* head covering, cloak]

**Cape buffalo** *n* a large fierce buffalo (*Syncerus caffer*) of southern Africa with large curved horns [*Cape* of Good Hope, province of South Africa]

**Cape cart** *n, SAfr* a hooded two-wheeled horse-drawn cart [incorrect trans (influenced by *Cape* of Good Hope) of Afrik *kapkar*, fr *kap* hood + *kar* cart]

**Cape Coloured** *n* a person of mixed black and white ancestry in South Africa [*Cape* of Good Hope] – **Cape Coloured** *adj*

**Cape Doctor** *n* a strong southeasterly wind of South Africa [fr the belief that it blows away disease & germs]

¹**Cape Dutch** *n* **1** Afrikaans; *esp* the Afrikaans language considered as a dialect of Dutch **2** *pl* the early Dutch colonists of South Africa

²**Cape Dutch** *adj* of a style of architecture popular in the Cape of Good Hope in the 18th century characterized by high gables and whitewash

**Cape gooseberry** *n* a tropical plant (*Physalis peruviana*) of the potato family bearing yellow flowers and edible yellow fruit

**capelin** *also* **caplin** /'kap(ə)lin/ *n* a small fish (*Mallotus villosus*) related to the smelts that lives in northern seas [CanF *capelan*, fr Fr, codfish, fr OProv, chaplain, codfish, fr ML *cappellanus* chaplain – more at CHAPLAIN]

¹**caper** /'kaypə/ *n* **1** any of a genus (*Capparis* of the family Capparaceae, the caper family) of low prickly shrubs of the Mediterranean region; *esp* one (*Capparis spinosa*) cultivated for its buds and berries **2** any of the greenish flower buds or young berries of the caper pickled and used as a seasoning or garnish [back-formation fr earlier *capers* (taken as a plural), fr ME *caperis*, fr L *capparis*, fr Gk *kapparis*]

²**caper** *vi* to leap about in a playful way; prance ⟨*~s nimbly in a lady's chamber* – Shak⟩ [prob by shortening & alter. fr *capriole*]

³**caper** *n* **1** a playful leap **2** a capricious escapade; a prank **3a** *chiefly Br slang* an activity or occupation, esp one regarded as frivolous or disreputable **b** *chiefly NAm informal* an illegal enterprise; a crime

**capercaillie** /ˌkapə'kayli/ *n* the largest African and Eurasian grouse (*Tetrao urogallus*) [ScGael *capalcoille*, lit., horse of the woods]

**capercailzi** /-'kaylzi/ *n* a capercaillie

**capeskin** /'kaypˌskin/ *n* a light flexible leather made from sheepskins with the natural grain retained [*Cape* of Good Hope]

**Capetian** /kə'peesh(ə)n/ *n* a member of the dynasty that ruled France from 987 to 1328 [Fr *capétien*, fr Hugues *Capet* †996 Fr king, founder of the dynasty] – **Capetian** *adj*

**capework** /'kaypˌwuhk/ *n* the art of the bullfighter in making the bull follow the movements of the cape

**capful** /'kapf(ə)l/ *n* **1** as much as a cap will hold **2** a light puff ⟨*a ~ of wind*⟩

**capillarity** /ˌkapi'larəti/ *n* **1** the property or state of being capillary **2** the phenomenon in which the surface of a liquid where it is in contact with a solid (eg in a capillary tube) is

raised or lowered depending on the relative attraction of the molecules of the liquid for each other and for those of the solid

¹**capillary** /kə'piləri/ *adj* **1a** resembling a hair, esp in being slender and elongated **b** *of a tube* having a very fine bore **2** involving or due to the surface force that results when a liquid is confined in a narrow space (eg in a fine-bore tube) ⟨*~ action*⟩ **3** relating to capillaries or capillarity [Fr or L; Fr *capillaire*, fr L *capillaris*, fr *capillus* hair]

²**capillary** *n* a capillary tube; *esp* any of the smallest blood vessels connecting small arteries (ARTERIOLES) with small veins (VENULES) and forming networks throughout the body

,**cap in 'hand** *adv* in a deferential manner

¹**capital** /'kapitl/ *adj* **1a** punishable by death ⟨*a ~ crime*⟩ **b** involving execution ⟨*~ punishment*⟩ – compare CORPORAL **2** *of a letter* of or conforming to the series (eg A, B, C rather than a, b, c) used to begin sentences or proper names **3** of the greatest importance or influence ⟨*the ~ importance of criticism in the work of creation itself* – T S Eliot⟩ **4** being the seat of government ⟨*a ~ city*⟩ **5** relating to capital **6** excellent ⟨*a ~ book*⟩ [ME, fr L *capitalis*, fr *capit-, caput* head – more at HEAD] – **capitally** *adv*

²**capital** *n* **1a(1)** a stock of accumulated goods, esp considered at a specified time and in contrast to income received during a specified period; *also* the value of these accumulated goods **a(2)** accumulated goods set aside for or used in the production of other goods **a(3)** accumulated possessions calculated to bring in income **a(4)** a sum of money saved **b(1)** net worth **b(2)** CAPITAL STOCK **c** *taking sing or pl vb* people holding capital; the capitalist class **d** advantage, gain **2** a capital letter; *esp* an initial capital letter **3a** *often cap* a city serving as a seat of government **b** a city preeminent in some usu specified area ⟨*London, the antiques ~ of the world*⟩ [(1) Fr or It; Fr, fr It *capitale*, fr *capitale*, adj, chief, principal, fr L *capitalis*; (2,3) ¹*capital*]

³**capital** *n* the uppermost part of a column or pilaster crowning the shaft and in classical architecture taking the weight of the entablature [ME *capitale*, modif of ONF *capitel*, fr LL *capitellum* small head, top of column, dim. of L *capit-, caput*]

**capital assets** *n pl* tangible or intangible long-term business assets (eg machinery or goodwill)

**capital expenditure** *n* an expenditure for long-term additions or improvements to the value of a property, facility, etc that is properly chargeable to a capital assets account

**capital gain** *n* the profit from the sale of a capital asset (eg a house)

**capital gains tax** *n*, often cap *C, G, & T* tax levied on CAPITAL GAINS

**capital goods** *n pl* ²CAPITAL 1a(1)&(2)

,**capital-in'tensive** *adj* using or requiring proportionately large amounts of capital (eg buildings and machinery) relative to other inputs in the process of production. As labour costs rise relative to those of capital, processes may tend to become more capital-intensive. – compare LABOUR-INTENSIVE

**capitalism** /'kapitlˌiz(ə)m/ *n* an economic system characterized by the profit motive and the control of the means of production, distribution, and exchange of goods by private ownership

¹**capitalist** /'kapitl·ist/ *n* **1** a person who has capital, esp invested in business; *broadly, derog* a person of wealth **2** a person who favours capitalism

²**capitalist** /'kapitl·ist; *also* kə'pitl·ist USE *the last pron is disliked by some speakers*/ *also* **capitalistic** /ˌkapitl'istik/ *adj* **1** owning capital ⟨*the ~ class*⟩ **2a** practising or advocating capitalism ⟨*~ nations*⟩ **b** marked by capitalism ⟨*the modern ~ period of history from 1815 to 1914*⟩

**capitalization, -isation** /ˌkapitl·ie'zaysh(ə)n/ *n* **1a** the act or process of capitalizing **b** a sum resulting from a process of capitalizing **c** the total liabilities of a business including both ownership capital and borrowed capital **d** CAPITAL STOCK **2** the use of a capital letter in writing or printing

**capital·ize, -ise** /'kapitlˌiez/ *vt* **1** to write or print in capitals or esp with an initial capital **2** to convert into capital ⟨*~ the company's reserve fund*⟩ **3a** to calculate the present value of (an income extended over a period of time) **b** to convert (a periodic payment) into an equivalent capital sum ⟨*~d annuities*⟩ **4** to supply capital for ~ *vi* to gain by turning something to advantage; profit – usu + *on* ⟨*~ on an opponent's mistake*⟩

**capital levy** *n* a levy on personal or industrial capital in addition to income tax and other taxes; a general property tax

**capital profit** *n* profit arising from an increase in the value of assets rather than from economic activity – compare TRADING PROFIT

**capital ship** *n* a warship of the first rank in size and importance (e g an aircraft carrier or battleship)

**capital stock** *n* 1 the outstanding or outstanding and unissued shares of a company considered as an aggregate; *also* the total value of such shares 2 the total amount of goods used in the process of production that exist in a firm, industry, or country at any specified time

**capital structure** *n* the make-up of the capitalization of a business in terms of the amounts and kinds of equity and debt securities; the equity and debt securities of a business together with its surplus and reserves

**capital sum** *n* a lump sum of money, esp payable under an insurance policy

**capital transfer tax** *n*, often cap *C,T,&T* tax levied on transfers of capital (e g by gift or inheritance)

**capitate** /'kapitayt/ *adj* 1 *of the flowers of a plant* forming a head ⟨*a ~ inflorescence*⟩ 2 *of a plant or animal part* enlarged and spherical at the end ⟨*a ~ insect antenna*⟩ [L *capitatus* headed, fr *capit-, caput* head]

**capitation** /ˌkapi'taysh(ə)n/ *n* 1 a direct uniform tax imposed on each person; POLL TAX 2 a uniform per capita payment or fee; *specif, Br* expenditure by a local education authority on certain items (e g books) [LL *capitation-, capitatio*, fr L *capit-, caput*]

**capitol** /'kapitl/ *n* 1 a building in which a US state legislative body meets 2 *cap the* building in which the US Congress meets at Washington △ capital [L *Capitolium*, temple of Jupiter in Rome]

**Capitol Hill** *n* the legislative branch of the US government [*Capitol Hill*, Washington, site of the US Capitol]

**Capitoline** /kə'pitəlien, 'kapitəlien/ *adj* relating to the smallest of the seven hills of ancient Rome, the temple on it, or the gods worshipped there [L *capitolinus*, fr *Capitolium*]

**capitular** /kə'pityoolə, -choolə/ *adj* relating to a cathedral chapter [ML *capitularis*, fr *capitulum* chapter]

**capitulary** /kə'pityooləri, -choo-/ *n* a civil or ecclesiastical ordinance; *also* a collection of ordinances (e g that issued by the Frankish kings) [ML *capitulare*, lit., document divided into sections, fr LL *capitulum* section, chapter – more at CHAPTER]

**capitulate** /kə'pityoolayt, -choo-/ *vi* 1 to surrender, often after negotiation of terms 2 to cease resisting; acquiesce *synonyms* see [1]YIELD [ML *capitulatus*, pp of *capitulare* to distinguish by heads or chapters, fr LL *capitulum*]

**capitulation** /kəˌpityoo'laysh(ə)n, -choo-/ *n* 1 a set of terms or articles constituting an agreement between governments; *esp* a treaty by which in former times a Christian state was permitted to establish courts to judge its citizens living in a state that was not Christian 2 an act of capitulating; *esp* the act or agreement of an individual or state that surrenders on stipulated terms *synonyms* see [2]SURRENDER

**capitulum** /kə'pityoolǝm, -choolǝm/ *n, pl* **capitula** /-lə/ 1 a rounded enlarged part on the end of an anatomical structure (e g a bone) 2 a specialized flower head, esp of the chrysanthemum, dandelion, daisy, or other composite plant with the axis shortened and dilated to form a rounded or flattened cluster of stalkless flowers, often simulating one larger flower [NL, fr L, small head – more at CHAPTER]

**caplin** /'kaplin/ *n* a capelin

**capo** /'kapoh, 'kay-/ *n, pl* **capos** a movable bar attached to the fingerboard esp of a guitar to raise the pitch of all the strings uniformly [short for *capotasto*, fr It, lit., head of fingerboard]

**capon** /'kaypən, -pon/ *n* a castrated male chicken [ME, fr OE *capūn*, prob fr ONF *capon*, fr L *capon-, capo*; akin to Gk *koptein* to cut] – **caponize** *vt*

**capote** /kə'poht (*Fr* kapɔt)/ *n* a usu long hooded cloak or overcoat [Fr, fr *cape* cloak, fr LL *cappa*]

**capping** *n, medicine* a process by which proteins, esp those acting as ANTIGENS in a cell membrane, having combined with ANTIBODIES accumulate in clusters or patches at one site on the surface of the cell

**cappuccino** /ˌkapoo'cheenoh/ *n, pl* **cappucinos** coffee made with espresso coffee and hot milk or whipped cream [It, lit., Capuchin; fr its colour resembling that of a Capuchin's habit]

**capric acid** /'kaprik/ *n* a FATTY ACID, $CH_3(CH_2)_8COOH$, found in fats and oils and used in flavourings and perfumes [ISV, fr L *capr-, caper* goat; fr its odour]

**capriccio** /kə'prichioh/ *n, pl* **capriccios** an instrumental piece in free form, usu lively in tempo [It]

**capriccioso** /kəˌprichi'ohzoh/ *adv* in a free and lively manner – used as an instruction in music [It, fr *capriccio*]

**caprice** /kə'prees/ *n* 1a a sudden impulsive and seemingly unmotivated change of mind b a sudden change or series of changes hard to explain or predict ⟨*the ~s of the weather*⟩ 2 a tendency to change one's mind impulsively ⟨*he's a creature of ~*⟩ 3 a capriccio [Fr, fr It *capriccio*, lit., head with hair standing on end, shudder, fr *capo* head (fr L *caput*) + *riccio* hedgehog, fr L *ericius* – more at HEAD, URCHIN]

*synonyms* **Caprice, freak, whim, whimsy, fancy: caprice** stresses lack of apparent motivation, and implies wilfulness. **Freak** suggests an impulsive change of mind, as by a child or lunatic, for no apparent reason ⟨*sailed this way and that, as the freak took him*⟩. **Fancy** stresses imagination and liking in place of reason, and may include a suggestion of self-delusion ⟨*the harmless fancy that she had been a cavalier in an earlier existence*⟩. A **whim** is a humorous or fantastic notion ⟨*he had a sudden whim to throw his hat over the wall*⟩. **Whimsy** may be used like **whim**, but often stresses fancifulness where **whim** suggests capriciousness.

**capricious** /kə'prishəs/ *adj* governed or characterized by caprice; apt to change suddenly or unpredictably – **capriciously** *adv*, **capriciousness** *n*

**Capricorn** /'kaprikawn/ *n* 1 CAPRICORNUS 2a the 10th sign of the zodiac in astrology, held to govern the period December 23 – January 20 approx b somebody born under this sign [ME *Capricorne*, fr L *Capricornus*, fr *capr-* goat + *cornu* horn – more at HORN] – **Capricornian** *adj or n*

**Capricornus** /ˌkapri'kawnəs/ *n* a constellation of the ZODIAC (imaginary belt in the heavens) lying between Sagittarius and Aquarius and represented as a creature resembling a goat with the tail of a fish

**caprification** /ˌkaprifi'kaysh(ə)n/ *n* artificial pollination of figs that usu bear only female flowers by hanging male flowering branches of the caprifig tree in the trees of the edible fig to encourage pollen transfer by wasps [L *caprification-, caprificatio*, fr *caprificatus*, pp of *caprificare* to pollinate by caprification, fr *caprificus*]

**caprifig** /'kapriˌfig/ *n* the wild fig (*Ficus carica sylvestris*) of S Europe and Asia Minor, used for artificial pollination of the edible fig; *also* its fruit [ME *caprifige*, part trans of L *caprificus*, lit., goat's fig]

**caprine** /'kaprien/ *adj* of or being a goat [L *caprinus*, fr *capr-, caper*]

**capriole** /'kapriohl/ *n* a vertical leap made by a trained horse with a backward kick of the hind legs at the height of the leap [MF or OIt; MF *capriole*, fr OIt *capriola*, fr *capriolo* roebuck, fr L *capreolus* goat, roebuck, fr *capr-, caper* he-goat; akin to OE *hæfer* goat, Gk *kapros* wild boar] – **capriole** *vi*

**caproic acid** /kə'proh·ik/ *n* a liquid FATTY ACID, $CH_3(CH_2)_4CO_2H$, that is found in fats and oils or made synthetically and is used in flavourings and in medicine [ISV, fr L *capr-, caper*]

**caprylic acid** /kə'prilik/ *n* a FATTY ACID, $CH_3(CH_2)_6COOH$, with a rancid smell occurring in fats and oils and used to make perfumes [ISV *capryl*, a radical contained in it]

**caps** /kaps/ *n pl* capital letters

**capsaicin** /kap'sie·isin/ *n* a colourless chemical compound, $C_{18}H_{27}NO_3$, that is obtained from various capsicums [irreg fr NL *Capsicum*]

**Capsian** /'kapsi·ən/ *adj* relating to a Mesolithic culture of N Africa and S Europe with distinctive art forms [Fr *capsien*, fr L *Capsa* Gafsa, town in Tunisia]

**capsicum** /'kapsikəm/ *n* 1 any of a genus (*Capsicum*) of tropical plants and shrubs of the potato family widely cultivated for their many-seeded usu fleshy-walled fruit (e g RED PEPPERS and GREEN PEPPERS) 2 the dried ripe fruit of some capsicums (e g *Capsicum frutescens*) used as a condiment [NL, genus name, perh fr L *capsa* case]

[1]**capsid** /'kapsid/ *n* MIRID (type of bug) [deriv of Gk *kapsis* gulping, fr *kaptein* to gulp down]

[2]**capsid** *n* the outer protein shell of a virus particle [L *capsa* case + E [2]*-id* – more at CASE] – **capsidal** *adj*

**capsize** /kap'siez/ *vt* to cause to overturn ⟨*~ a canoe*⟩ *~ vi* to turn over; upset ⟨*the canoe ~d*⟩ [origin unknown]

**capstan** /'kapstən/ *n* 1 a machine for moving or raising heavy weights by winding cable round a drum that is rotated about a vertical axis manually or by a motor 2 a rotating shaft that drives tape at a constant speed in a tape recorder or similar electrical device [ME, fr OProv *cabestan*, fr *cabestre* halter, fr L *capistrum*, prob fr *capere* to seize, hold]

**capstone** /'kap,stohn/ *n* coping stone; coping [¹*cap*]

**capsular** /'kapsyoolə/ *adj* 1 of or resembling a capsule 2 capsulate

**capsulate** /'kapsyoolət, -layt/, **capsulated** /'kapsyoolaytid/ *adj* enclosed in a capsule

**capsule** /'kapsyoohl, -yool/ *n* 1a a membrane or sac enclosing a body part b either of two layers of WHITE MATTER in the forebrain 2 a closed plant receptacle containing spores or seeds: e g 2a a dry usu many-seeded fruit composed of two or more female reproductive organs (CARPELS) that burst open spontaneously when mature to release their seeds b the spore-producing sac of a moss 3 a usu gelatine shell enclosing a drug for swallowing 4 an envelope, often composed of POLYSACCHARIDES (complex sugars) surrounding a microorganism (e g a bacterium) 5 a compact usu rounded container 6 a detachable pressurized compartment, esp in spacecraft or aircraft, housing crew and controls and sometimes used for emergency escape; *also* a spacecraft 7 a usu metal, wax, or plastic covering that encloses the top of a bottle, esp of wine, and protects the cork [Fr, fr L *capsula*, dim. of *capsa* box – more at CASE]

**capsul·ize, -ise** /'kapsyoo,liez/ *vt* 1 to equip with or enclose in a capsule 2 to formulate in a brief or compact way

**¹captain** /'kaptin/ *n* 1a – see MILITARY RANKS table b a commander under a sovereign or general c(1) an officer in charge of a ship c(2) a commissioned officer in the navy ranking above a commander and below a rear admiral d a distinguished military leader e a leader of a side or team in a contest (e g in a sport or game) f *Br* the head boy or head girl at a school g *NAm* a fire or police officer usu ranking between a lieutenant and a chief h *NAm* a supervisor of waiters or bellboys in a hotel 2 a dominant figure ⟨~s of industry⟩ [ME *capitane*, fr MF *capitain*, fr LL *capitaneus*, adj & n, chief, fr L *capit-, caput* head – more at HEAD] – **captaincy** *n*, **captainship** *n*

**²captain** *vt* to be captain of; lead ⟨~ed *the first eleven*⟩

**¹caption** /'kapsh(ə)n/ *n* 1 a heading; *esp* the heading of an article or document 2 the explanatory comment or description accompanying a pictorial illustration 3 a film subtitle [*caption* (part of a legal document certifying its authority), fr ME *capcioun* seizure, arrest, fr L *caption-, captio* act of taking, fr *captus*, pp of *capere* to take – more at HEAVE; modern senses influenced by L *capit-, caput* head]

**²caption** *vt* to provide with a caption

**captious** /'kapshəs/ *adj* marked by an often ill-natured inclination to stress faults and raise objections [ME *capcious*, fr MF or L; MF *captieux*, fr L *captiosus*, fr *captio* act of taking, deception] – **captiously** *adv*, **captiousness** *n*

**captivate** /'kaptivayt/ *vt* to influence and dominate by some irresistible charm; fascinate *antonym* repel – **captivator** *n*, **captivation** *n*

**captive** /'kaptiv/ *adj* 1a taken and held as prisoner, esp by an enemy in war b kept within bounds; confined c held under control 2 relating to captivity 3 being in a situation that makes departure or inattention difficult ⟨a ~ *audience*⟩ [ME, fr L *captivus*, fr *captus*, pp of *capere* (cf CAITIFF)] – **captive** *n*

**captivity** /kap'tivəti/ *n* the state of being captive ⟨*some birds* thrive in ~⟩

**captor** /'kaptə/ *n* a person or animal that has captured another [LL, fr L *captus*]

**¹capture** /'kapchə/ *n* 1 the act of gaining control or possession 2 one who or that which has been taken; *esp* a ship captured at sea in time of war 3 a move in various board games (e g chess) that gains an opponent's man 4 any of several processes in which an atom, molecule, ion, or nucleus acquires an additional elementary particle, often with associated emission of radiation [MF, fr L *captura*, fr *captus*]

**²capture** *vt* 1a to take captive; win, gain ⟨~ *a city*⟩ b to preserve in a relatively permanent form ⟨*how well the scene* was ~d *on film*⟩ ⟨*data can be* ~d *on tape*⟩ 2 to take according to the rules of a game; remove from the playing board 3 *physics* to cause the capture of (an electron, neutron, or other ELEMENTARY PARTICLE) *synonyms* see ¹CATCH

**capuche** /kə'poohsh/ *n* a hood; *esp* the cowl of a Capuchin friar [It *cappuccio*, fr *cappa* cloak, fr LL]

**capuchin** /kə'pyoohchin, -shin/ *n* 1 *cap* a member of a strict branch of the first order of St Francis of Assisi engaged in missionary work and preaching 2 a hooded cloak formerly worn by women 3 any of a genus (*Cebus*) of S American monkeys; *esp* one (*Cebus capucinus*) with hair on its

crown resembling a monk's cowl [MF, fr OIt *cappuccino*, fr *cappuccio*]

**capybara** /,kapi'bahrə/ *n* a large tailless mainly aquatic S American rodent (*Hydrochoerus hydrochaeris*) that resembles a guinea pig [Pg *capibara*, fr Tupi]

**car** /kah/ *n* 1 a vehicle moving on wheels: 1a a vehicle (e g a carriage or wagon) built to run on rails ⟨*a buffet* ~⟩ b MOTOR CAR c *chiefly NAm* a railway carriage or van; *also* a tramcar d *poetic* a chariot of war or of triumph ⟨*whose body opposing the progress of the* ~ *of Juggernaut is crushed beneath its monstrous wheels* – F W Robertson⟩ 2 the passenger compartment of an airship or balloon 3 *chiefly NAm* the cage of a lift [ME *carre*, fr AF, fr L *carra*, pl of *carrum*, alter. of *carrus*, of Celt origin; akin to OIr & MW *carr* vehicle; akin to L *currere* to run]

**carabid** /'karəbid/ *n* any of a large family (Carabidae) of usu flesh-eating and often shiny black beetles [deriv of Gk *karabos* horned beetle] – **carabid** *adj*

**carabineer, carabinier** /,karəbi'niə/ *n* a soldier armed with a carbine [Fr *carabinier*, fr *carabine* carbine]

**carabiner** /,karə'beenə/ *n* an oblong ring with an openable side that is used in mountaineering to hold freely running rope (e g in attaching it to pitons) [Ger *karabiner*]

**carabiniere** /,karəbi'nyeəri/ *n, pl* **carabinieri** /~/ a member of the Italian national police force [It, fr Fr *carabinier*]

**caracal** /'karəkal/ *n* an African and Asian medium-sized cat (*Felis caracal*) with long legs and sharply pointed ears [Fr, fr Sp, fr Turk *karakulak*, lit., black-ear, fr *kara* black + *kulak* ear]

**caracara** /,kahrə'kahrə/ *n* any of various large long-legged mostly S American hawks resembling vultures in habits [Sp *caracara* & Pg *caracará*, fr Tupi *caracará*, of imit origin]

**caracole** /'karəkohl/ *n* a half turn to right or left executed by a mounted horse in dressage [Fr, fr Sp *caracol* snail, spiral stair, caracole] – **caracole** *vi*

**carafe** /kə'rahf, -'raf, 'karəf/ *n* a glass bottle, typically with a flaring lip, used to hold water or beverages and esp to serve wine at table [Fr, fr It *caraffa*, fr Ar *gharrāfah*, fr *gharafa* to draw water]

**caramba** /kə'rambə/ *interj* – used to express surprise, dismay, etc [Sp]

**caramel** /'karəməl, -mel/ *n* 1 a brittle brown slightly bitter substance obtained by heating sugar and used as a colouring and flavouring agent 2 a chewy usu soft and caramel-flavoured toffee, often made with milk or cream [Fr, fr Sp *caramelo*, fr Pg, icicle, caramel, fr LL *calamellus* small reed – more at SHAWM]

**caramel·ize, -ise** /'karəməliez/ *vt* to change (sugar or the sugar content of a food) into caramel ~ *vi* to change to caramel

**carangid** /kə'ranjid, kə'rang·gid/ *adj* relating to a large family (Carangidae) of marine spiny-finned fishes (e g the pilot fish) that include some important food fishes [deriv of Fr *carangue* shad, horse mackerel, fr Sp *caranga*] – **carangid** *n*

**carapace** /'karə,pays/ *n* 1 a case or shield made of bone or chitin covering (part of) the back of an animal (e g a turtle or crab) 2 a hard protective outer covering; *esp* an attitude or state of mind serving to protect or isolate from outside influence [Fr, fr Sp *carapacho*]

**carat** /'karət/ *n* 1 carat, *NAm chiefly* **karat** a unit of fineness for gold equal to ¹/₂₄ part of pure gold in an alloy 2 a unit of weight for precious stones equal to 200 mg △ caret [MF, deriv of Ar *qīrāt* bean pod, a small weight, fr Gk *keration* carob bean, a small weight, fr dim. of *kerat-, keras* horn – more at HORN]

**¹caravan** /'karə,van/ *n* 1 *taking sing or pl vb* 1a a company of travellers on a journey through desert or hostile regions; *also* a train of pack animals b a group of vehicles travelling together 2a a covered often gaily painted wagon capable of being pulled by a horse and providing permanent accommodation (e g for gipsies) b *Br* a covered vehicle designed to be towed by a motor car and to serve as a (temporary) dwelling; *also* one that is used as a permanent dwelling, often after connection to utilities [It *caravana*, fr Per *kārwān*]

**²caravan** *vi* **-nn-** (*NAm* **-n-, -nn-**) to travel in a caravan

**caravanner** /'karə,vanə/ *n* 1 *NAm* **caravaner** one who travels in a caravan 2 *Br* one who goes camping with a caravan

**caravanserai** /,karə'vansərie/ *also* **caravansary** /-'vansəri/ *n, pl* **caravanserai, caravanserais, caravansaries** a usu large unfurnished building surrounding a court found in eastern countries and used as a resting place for caravans by night [Per *kārwānsarāī*, fr *kārwān* caravan + *sarāī* palace, inn]

**caravan site** *n, chiefly Br* an area set aside for the temporary or permanent parking of caravans

**caravel** /'karə,vel/ *n* any of several sailing ships; *specif* a small 15th- and 16th-century ship with broad bows, a high narrow poop, and lateen sails [MF *caravelle*, fr OPg *caravela*]

**caraway** /'karəway/ *n* a usu white-flowered aromatic plant (*Carum carvi*) of the carrot family with pungent seeds used as flavouring in food [ME, prob fr ML *carvi*, fr Ar *karawyā*, fr Gk *karon*]

**carb-** /kahb-/, **carbo-** *comb form* carbon; carbonic; carbonyl; carboxyl ⟨carb*ide*⟩ ⟨carb*ohydrate*⟩ [Fr, fr *carbone*]

**carbachol** /'kahbəkol, -kohl/ *n* a synthetic drug, $C_6H_{15}ClN_2O_2$, that acts like ACETYLCHOLINE (substance that transmits nerve impulses) on the PARASYMPATHETIC NERVOUS SYSTEM and is used medicinally to treat conditions where abnormal quantities of fluids (e g urine) are retained [*carba*mic acid + *cho*line]

**carbamate** /'kahbə,mayt/ *n* any of various chemical compounds (SALTS OR ESTERS) formed by combination between CARBAMIC ACID and a metal atom, an alcohol, or another chemical group; *esp* one that is a synthetic insecticide

**carbamic acid** /kah'bamik/ *n* an acid, $NH_2COOH$, known only in the form of its chemical compounds (SALTS AND ESTERS) that occur in the blood and urine of mammals [ISV *carb-* + *am*ide + *-ic*]

**carbamide** /'kahbəmied/ *n* UREA (chemical compound occurring esp in urine) [ISV *carb-* + *amide*]

**carbamino** /,kahbə,meenoh/ *adj* relating to any CARBAMIC ACID derivative formed by the reaction of CARBON DIOXIDE with an AMINO ACID or a protein (e g haemoglobin)

**carbamyl** /'kahbəmil, -miel/, **carbamoyl** /kah'bamoh·il, -eel/ *n* the chemical group, $NH_2CO$, that is formed from CARBAMIC ACID by the loss of a hydrogen atom

**carbanion** /kah'ban,ie-ən/ *n* an ion carrying a negative electric charge at a carbon position – compare CARBONIUM

**carbazole** /'kahbə,zohl/ *n* a chemical compound, $C_{12}H_9N$, having a structure of two rings linked by nitrogen that is used in making dyes and photographic plates [ISV]

**carbide** /'kahbied/ *n* a chemical compound of carbon combined with another chemical element; *esp* CALCIUM CARBIDE [ISV]

**carbine** /'kahbien/ *n* 1 a short light rifle or musket originally carried by cavalry 2 a short light gas-operated magazine-fed semiautomatic or automatic rifle [Fr *carabine*, fr MF *carabin* carabineer]

**carbinol** /'kahbinol/ *n* methanol; *also* an alcohol derived from it [ISV, fr obs Ger *karbin* methyl, fr Ger *karb-* carb-]

**carbocyclic** /,kahboh'sieklik, 'siklik/ *adj* being or having a ring of carbon atoms in the molecular structure [ISV]

**carbohydrase** /,kahboh'hiedrayz/ *n* any of a group of ENZYMES (e g amylase) that promote the breakdown or synthesis of a carbohydrate [ISV *carbohydra*te + *-ase*]

**carbohydrate** /,kahbə'hiedrayt, -boh-/ *n* any of various chemical compounds of carbon, hydrogen, and oxygen (e g sugars, starches, and celluloses) some of which are formed by and often stored by all green plants and which constitute a major class of energy-providing animal foods

**carbolated** /'kahbəlaytid/ *adj* impregnated with PHENOL

**carbolic acid** /kah'bolik/ *n* PHENOL 1 △ carbonic acid [ISV *carb-* + L *oleum* oil – more at OIL]

**car bomb** *n* an explosive device concealed in a motor vehicle; *esp* one intended for use against people or property in the vicinity of the vehicle

**carbon** /'kahb(ə)n/ *n* 1 a nonmetallic chemical element having a VALENCY of four occurring naturally (e g in diamond and graphite) or as a constituent of coal, petroleum, and asphalt, of carbonates (e g limestone), and of organic chemical compounds or obtained artificially in varying degrees of purity, esp as CARBON BLACK, lampblack, ACTIVATED CARBON, charcoal, and coke 2a a sheet of carbon paper b CARBON COPY 3a a carbon rod used in an ARC LAMP b a piece of carbon used as an element in a battery [Fr *carbone*, fr L *carbon-*, *carbo* ember, charcoal] – **carbonless** *adj*

**carbon 14, carbon fourteen** *n* a radioactive ISOTOPE (form in which an atom can occur) of carbon of MASS NUMBER 14 used esp in biochemistry and medicine to trace the behaviour of molecules in chemical reactions and in dating archaeological and geological materials

**carbonaceous** /,kahbə'nayshəs/ *adj* 1 relating to, containing, or composed of carbon 2 CARBONOUS 2

**carbonade** *also* **carbonnade** /,kahbə'nayd, -'nahd/ *n* a rich beef stew made with beer [Fr *carbonnade* meat grilled over charcoal, fr It *carbonata*, fr *carbone* charcoal, fr L *carbon-*, *carbo*]

**¹carbonado** /,kahbə'naydoh, -'nahdoh/ *n, pl* **carbonados**, **carbonadoes** *archaic* a grilled piece of meat, fish, etc scored before cooking [Sp *carbonada*, fr *carbón* charcoal, coal]

**²carbonado** *vt* **carbonadoing**, **carbonadoed** *archaic* to make a carbonado of ⟨*how she long'd to eate Adders heads, and Toads* carbonado'd – Shak⟩

**³carbonado** *n, pl* **carbonados** an impure dark opaque diamond that is extremely hard and is used industrially as an abrasive [Pg, lit., carbonated, fr *carbone* carbon, fr Fr]

**Carbonari** /,kahbə'nahri/ *n pl* the members of a 19th-century revolutionary society operating in France, Spain, and esp Italy [It, pl of *Carbonaro*, fr It dial. *carbonaro* charcoal-burner]

**¹carbonate** /'kahbənət, -nayt/ *n* any of various chemical compounds (SALTS OR ESTERS) formed by combination between CARBONIC ACID and a metal atom, an alcohol, or another chemical group

**²carbonate** /'kahbənayt/ *vt* 1 to convert into a carbonate 2 to impregnate with CARBON DIOXIDE; aerate ⟨*a ~d beverage*⟩ – **carbonation** *n*

**carbon bisulphide** /bie'sulfied/ *n* CARBON DISULPHIDE

**carbon black** *n* any of various black substances consisting wholly or principally of very small particles of carbon that are obtained usu as soot and are used esp as pigments

**carbon copy** *n* 1 a copy made by carbon paper 2 an exact replica or repeat

**carbon cycle** *n* 1 a cycle of thermonuclear reactions in which four hydrogen atoms combine to form a helium atom with the release of nuclear energy, and which is held to be the source of most of the energy radiated by the sun and other stars 2 the cycle of carbon in living organisms in which CARBON DIOXIDE from the atmosphere is processed by plants during photosynthesis to form organic nutrients and is ultimately restored to the inorganic state by respiration and tissue decay

**carbon dating** *n* the determination of the age of ancient organic material (e g wood, food remains, or fossil bones) by recording the deterioration of carbon 14, which decays at a known rate

**carbon dioxide** *n* a heavy colourless gas, $CO_2$, that does not support combustion, dissolves in water to form CARBONIC ACID, is formed esp by the burning and decomposition of organic substances, is absorbed from the air by plants in photosynthesis, and is used in the carbonation of beverages

**carbon disulphide** *n* a colourless inflammable poisonous liquid, $CS_2$, used as a solvent for rubber and as an insect fumigant

**carbon fourteen** *n* CARBON 14

**carbonic** /kah'bonik/ *adj* of, containing, or derived from carbon, CARBONIC ACID, or CARBON DIOXIDE

**carbonic acid** *n* a weak acid, $H_2CO_3$, known only in solution, that reacts with metal atoms, alcohols, or other chemical groups to form carbonates △ carbolic acid

**carbonic acid gas** *n* CARBON DIOXIDE

**carbonic anhydrase** /,an'hiedrayz/ *n* a zinc-containing ENZYME that occurs in living tissues (e g RED BLOOD CELLS) and aids the transport of CARBON DIOXIDE from the tissues and its release from the blood in the lungs by catalysing the reversible reaction between carbon dioxide and water to form CARBONIC ACID [*carbonic* + *anhydr*ous + *-ase;* fr its causing dehydration]

**carboniferous** /,kahbə'nif(ə)rəs/ *adj* 1 producing or containing carbon or coal ⟨*~ fuels*⟩ 2 *cap* of or being the period of the PALAEOZOIC era between the DEVONIAN and the PERMIAN, or the corresponding system of rocks that includes coal deposits – **Carboniferous** *n*

**carbonium** /kah'bohni-əm/ *n* an ion carrying a positive electric charge at a carbon position – compare CARBANION [*carb-* + *-onium*]

**carbon-ize, -ise** /'kahb(ə)n,iez/ *vt* 1 to convert into carbon or a carbonic residue 2 CARBURIZE 1 ~ *vi* to become carbonized; char – **carbonization** *n*

**carbon monoxide** *n* a colourless odourless very toxic gas, CO, that burns to CARBON DIOXIDE with a blue flame and is formed as a product of the incomplete combustion of carbon

**carbonnade** /,kahbə'nayd/ *n* CARBONADE

**carbonous** /'kahbənəs/ *adj* 1 derived from, containing, or resembling carbon 2 brittle and dark

**carbon paper** *n* a thin paper coated with a waxy pigment so that when placed between two sheets of paper the pressure of writing or typing on the top sheet transfers the pigment to the bottom sheet

**carbon tetrachloride** /ˌtetrəˈklawried/ *n* a colourless non-inflammable poisonous liquid, CCl₄, that has a smell resembling that of chloroform and is used as an industrial solvent and a starting material for making other organic chemical compounds

**carbonyl** /ˈkahbənil/ *n* 1 a chemical group, CO, with a VALENCY of two that is the characteristic chemical group of KETONES and also occurs in aldehydes and CARBOXYLIC ACIDS 2 a chemical compound of the carbonyl group with a metal ⟨*nickel* ~⟩ – **carbonylic** *adj*

**Carborundum** /ˌkahbəˈroondəm/ *trademark* – used for various abrasives △ corundum

**carboxy-** /kahboksi-/, **carbox-** *comb form* carboxyl

**carboxyl** /kahˈboksil/ *n* a chemical group, COOH, with a VALENCY of one that is typical of acidic organic chemical compounds (e g acetic acid) [ISV] – **carboxylic** *adj*

**carboxylase** /kahˈboksilayz, -lays/ *n* an ENZYME that promotes the reaction in which a carboxyl group or CARBON DIOXIDE is introduced into or removed from another chemical compound [ISV]

¹**carboxylate** /kahˈboksilayt/ *n* any of various chemical compounds (SALTS or ESTERS) that are formed by combination between CARBOXYLIC ACID and a metal atom, an alcohol, or another chemical group

²**carboxylate** *vt* to introduce a carboxyl group or CARBON DIOXIDE into (a chemical compound) so as to produce a CARBOXYLIC ACID – **carboxylation** *n*

**carboxylic acid** /ˌkahbəkˈsilik/ *n* an organic chemical acid (e g acetic acid) containing one or more carboxyl groups

**carboxypeptidase** /kahˌboksiˈpeptidayz, -days/ *n* an ENZYME that promotes the breakdown of POLYPEPTIDES (sections of proteins) by splitting off the AMINO ACIDS containing free carboxyl groups

**carboy** /ˈkahˌboy/ *n* a large usu spherical container for transporting liquids that is often cushioned in a special frame [Per *qarāba*, fr Ar *qarrābah* demijohn]

**carbuncle** /ˈkahˌbungkl/ *n* 1 the garnet cut in the form of a CABOCHON (smooth rounded unfacetted stone) 2 a painful boil-like inflammation of the skin and deeper tissues with several openings for the discharge of pus 3 *obs* any of several red precious stones [ME, fr MF, fr L *carbunculus* small coal, carbuncle, dim. of *carbon-, carbo* charcoal, ember – more at CARBON] – **carbuncled** *adj*, **carbuncular** *adj*

**carburation** /ˌkahbyoo'raysh(ə)n/ *n* the process of mixing air with petrol or other fuel in the correct proportions to ensure proper combustion in an INTERNAL-COMBUSTION ENGINE

**carburet** /ˈkahbyooret/ *vt* -tt- (*NAm* -t- *also* -tt-) 1 to combine chemically with carbon 2 to enrich (e g gas) by mixing with readily vaporizing carbon compounds (e g hydrocarbons) [obs *carburet* carbide] – **carburetion** *n*

**carburettor**, *NAm* **carburetor** /ˌkahbyoo'retə, ˌkahbə'retə/ *n* an apparatus for supplying an INTERNAL-COMBUSTION ENGINE with a fixed quantity of vaporized fuel mixed with air in an explosive mixture

**carbur·ize, -ise** /ˈkahbyooriez, ˈkahbəriez/ *vt* 1 to combine or impregnate (e g metal) with carbon 2 CARBURET 2 [obs *carburet* carbide] – **carburization** *n*

**carcajou** /ˈkahkəˌjooh, -ˌzhooh/ *n, pl* **carcajous** WOLVERINE (type of carnivorous mammal) [CanF, of AmerInd origin]

**carcanet** /ˈkahkənet, -nit/ *n, archaic* an ornamental necklace or headband [MF *carcan*]

**carcass**, *Br also* **carcase** /ˈkahkəs/ *n* 1 a dead body; corpse; *esp* the dressed body of a meat animal 2 the decaying or worthless remains of something constructed ⟨*the half-submerged* ~ *of a wrecked vessel*⟩ 3 a framework; *esp* the framework of a tyre as distinct from the tread 4 *humorous or derog* a human body [MF *carcasse*, fr OF *carcois*]

**carcin-** /kahsin-/, **carcino-** *comb form* 1 crab ⟨carcinology⟩ 2 tumour; cancer ⟨carcinogenic⟩ [Gk *karkin-, karkino-*, fr *karkinos* – more at CANCER]

**carcinogen** /ˈkahsinəjən/ *n* something (e g a chemical compound) that causes cancer – **carcinogenesis** *n*, **carcinogenic** *adj*, **carcinogenically** *adv*, **carcinogenicity** *n*

**carcinoid** /ˈkahsinoyd/ *n* a usu mild nonlethal tumour arising esp from the MUCOUS MEMBRANE that lines the stomach, appendix, or other part of the digestive tract

**carcinoma** /ˌkahsiˈnohmə/ *n, pl* **carcinomas, carcinomata** /-mətə/ a cancerous tumour originating in the EPITHELIUM (tissue covering an external surface or lining a body cavity) [L, fr Gk *karkinōma* cancer, fr *karkinos*] – **carcinomatous** *adj*

**carcinomatosis** /ˌkahsinohmə'tohsis/ *n* a condition in which multiple carcinomas develop simultaneously, usu after spreading from a primary source [NL, fr L *carcinomat-, carcinoma*]

**car coat** *n* a three-quarter-length coat originally designed for car drivers

¹**card** /kahd/ *vt* to clean, disentangle, and collect together (e g fibres) with a carding machine or instrument before spinning – **carder** *n*

²**card** *n* 1 an implement for raising a nap on cloth 2 CARDING MACHINE [ME *carde*, fr MF, fr LL *cardus* thistle, fr L *carduus* – more at CHARD]

³**card** *n* 1a PLAYING CARD **b**(1) *pl but taking sing or pl vb* any game played with cards **b**(2) card playing 2 a valuable asset or right for use in negotiations ⟨*I still have one* ~ *up my sleeve*⟩ ⟨*Will America play the China* ~?⟩ 3 COMPASS CARD 4a a flat stiff usu small and rectangular piece of paper or thin paperboard: e g 4a(1) a postcard **a**(2) VISITING CARD **b** PROGRAMME 1a; *esp* one for a sporting event **c** GREETINGS CARD **d** *pl, informal* the official documents relating to an employee held by the employer 5 *chiefly Br informal* a joker, wag; *also* a person of a specified type ⟨*he's a bit of a* ~⟩ ⟨*a knowing* ~⟩ [ME *carde*, modif of MF *carte*, fr OIt *carta*, lit., leaf of paper, fr L *charta* leaf of papyrus, fr Gk *chartēs* (cf CHART)] – **lay/put one's cards on the table** to divulge or declare one's positions, plans, resources, etc – **on the cards** quite possible; likely to occur

⁴**card** *vt* 1 to score ⟨~ed 7 under par in the golf tournament⟩ 2 to place or fasten on or by means of a card

**cardamom, cardamum** /ˈkahdəməm/ *also* **cardamon** /-mən/ *n* the aromatic fruit of an East Indian plant (*Elettaria cardamomum*) of the ginger family whose seeds are used as a spice or condiment; *also* the plant itself [L *cardamomum*, fr Gk *kardamōmon*, blend of *kardamon* peppergrass and *amōmon*, an Indian spice plant]

¹**cardboard** /ˈkahdbawd, ˈkahbawd/ *n* a thick stiff material made from the same ingredients as paper and used esp for boxes and packaging

²**cardboard** *adj* 1 made of or as if of cardboard 2a flat, two-dimensional **b** unreal, stereotyped ⟨*the story has too many* ~ *characters*⟩

'**card-,carrying** *adj* 1 being a fully paid-up member of an organized group, esp the Communist party 2 dedicated, committed [fr the assumption that such a person carries a membership card]

**card catalogue** *n* a catalogue (e g of books) in which the entries are arranged systematically on index cards

**cardi-** /kahdi-/, **cardio-** *comb form* heart; cardiac ⟨cardiogram⟩; cardiac and ⟨cardiovascular⟩ [Gk *kardi-, kardio-*, fr *kardia* – more at HEART]

**-cardia** /-kahdi-ə/ *comb form* (→ *n*) heart action or location (of a specified type) ⟨dextrocardia⟩ ⟨tachycardia⟩ [NL, fr Gk *kardia*]

¹**cardiac** /ˈkahdiak/ *adj* 1a of, situated near, or acting on the heart **b** of the part of the stomach into which the oesophagus opens 2 of heart disease [L *cardiacus*, fr Gk *kardiakos*, fr *kardia*]

²**cardiac** *n* someone suffering from heart disease

**cardiac muscle** *n* muscle tissue that is found in the heart, is made up of cells united in a continuous mass, and is supplied with nerves but is not under voluntary control

**cardialgia** /ˌkahdiˈalj(y)ə/ *n* 1 heartburn 2 pain in the heart [NL, fr Gk *kardialgia*, fr *kardia* + *-algia*]

**cardie** /ˈkahdi/ *n, Br informal* a cardigan [by shortening & alter.]

**cardigan** /ˈkahdigən/ *n* a usu knitted sleeved garment for the upper body that opens the full length of the centre front and is usu fastened with buttons [James Thomas Brudenell, 7th Earl of *Cardigan* †1868 E soldier]

¹**cardinal** /ˈkahdinl/ *adj* of primary importance; fundamental [ME, fr OF, fr LL *cardinalis*, fr L, of a hinge, fr *cardin-, cardo* hinge; akin to OE *hratian* to rush, Gk *skairein* to gambol] – **cardinally** *adv*

²**cardinal** *n* 1 *often cap* a member of a body of officials of the Roman Catholic church who rank next below the pope, are appointed by him to act as his advisers, and elect his successor 2 CARDINAL NUMBER 3 a woman's short hooded cloak, origi-

nally made of scarlet cloth **4** any of several finches (genus *Richmondena*) of the USA, the male of which is bright red [ME, fr ML *cardinalis*, fr LL *cardinalis*, adj; (3,4) fr the scarlet colour of a cardinal's robes] – **cardinalship** *n*

**cardinalate** /'kahdinl-ət, -ayt/ *n* the office, rank, or dignity of a cardinal

**cardinal beetle** *n* any of a family (Pyrochroidae) of bright red beetles which usu live under bark

**cardinality** /,kahdi'naləti/ *n* the number of elements in a given mathematical set [²*cardinal* + *-ity*]

**cardinal number** *n* **1** a number (eg 4 or 15) that is used in the counting of WHOLE NUMBERS and that indicates how many elements there are in a set – compare ORDINAL NUMBER **2** the property common to all mathematical sets having the same number of elements

**cardinal point** *n* any of the four principal compass points north, south, east, and west

**cardinal virtue** *n* any of the four traditionally defined natural virtues, namely prudence, justice, temperance, and fortitude; *broadly* any important moral quality

**card index** *n, Br* a filing system in which each item is entered on a separate card – **card-index** *vt*

**carding machine** /'kahding/ *n* an instrument or machine for carding fibres, usu consisting of bent wire teeth set closely in rows in a thick piece of leather fastened to a board or roller

**cardiogram** /'kahdiəgram/ *n* the curve or tracing made by a cardiograph [ISV]

**cardiograph** /'kahdiə,grahf, -,graf/ *n* an instrument that registers movements of the heart in the form of a graph [ISV] – **cardiographer** *n*, **cardiography** *n*, **cardiographic** *adj*

**cardioid** /'kahdioyd/ *n* a heart-shaped curve traced by a point on the circumference of a circle that rolls completely round a fixed circle of equal radius

**cardiology** /,kahdi'oləji/ *n* the study of the heart and its diseases and their treatment [ISV] – **cardiologist** *n*, **cardiological** *adj*

**cardiomyopathy** /,kahdioh-mie'opəthi/ *n* a typically longlasting disorder of heart muscle that may involve enlargement and obstructive damage to the heart [*cardi-* + *my-* + *-pathy*]

**cardiopathy** /,kahdi'opəthi/ *n* a disease of the heart

**cardiopulmonary** /,kahdio'poolmən(ə)ri/ *adj* of the heart and lungs

**cardiorespiratory** /,kahdioh'resprit(ə)ri/ *adj* of the heart and the respiratory system

**cardiotonic** /,kahdioh'tonik/ *adj* tending to increase the TONE (condition of tension and elasticity) of heart muscle – **cardiotonic** *n*

**cardiovascular** /,kahdioh'vaskyoolə/ *adj* of or involving the heart and blood vessels [ISV]

**-cardium** /-kahdi-əm/ *comb form* (→ *n*) *pl* **cardia** /kahdiə/ heart ⟨*epicardium*⟩ [NL, fr Gk *kardia*]

**cardoon** /kah'doohn/ *n* a large plant (*Cynara cardunculus*) of the daisy family that is related to the GLOBE ARTICHOKE and cultivated for its edible root and leafstalks [Fr *cardon*, fr LL *cardon-*, *cardo* thistle, fr *cardus*, fr L *carduus* thistle, artichoke – more at CHARD]

**cardplayer** /'kahd,playə/ *n* one who plays cards

**card punch** *n* that part of a data processing system which transfers information from the central computer by punching a series of cards; *also* a machine with a keyboard that enables this to be done manually

**cardsharp** /-,shahp/, **cardsharper** /-,shahpə/ *n* one who habitually cheats at cards

¹**care** /keə/ *n* **1a** (a cause for) anxiety ⟨*the* ~s *of the world*⟩ ⟨*cast* ~ *aside!*⟩ **b** someone or something that is an object of attention, anxiety, or solicitude ⟨*the flower garden was her special* ~⟩ **2** painstaking or watchful attention ⟨*he performed the operation with great* ~⟩ **3a** a sense of loving responsibility ⟨*nothing can replace a mother's* ~⟩ ⟨*the* ~ *of the elderly is our first concern*⟩ **b** charge, supervision ⟨*under a doctor's* ~⟩; *specif, Br* legal responsibility placed on a local authority for the welfare and control of a child – chiefly in *in care* [ME, fr OE *caru;* akin to OHG *kara* lament, L *garrire* to chatter] – **take care** to be careful; exercise caution or prudence – usu imper – **take care of** to attend to or provide for the needs, operation, or treatment of

*synonyms* Care, concern, solicitude, anxiety, and worry, and their related adjectives can all describe a troubled or engrossed state of mind. **Care** implies involvement with what causes this because of responsibility or affection for others, while **concern**, more intellec-

tual and less emotional, expresses voluntary involvement arising from an absence of indifference ⟨*the Minister expressed her* **concern** *at the incident, and promised something would be done*⟩. **Solicitude** and **solicitous** suggest deep, caring **concern** allied to disinterested and kindly activity ⟨*tended the wounded with* **solicitude**⟩. **Anxiety** and **anxious**, and **worry** and **worried**, express greater agitation and distress. **Anxiety** stresses uncertainty and apprehension, even fear ⟨*her daughter's unusual lateness gave her* **anxiety**/*made her* **anxious**⟩. **Worry** suggests persistent and nagging mental perturbation, which is often futile or unnecessary ⟨*her* **worries** *about her husband's frequent absences were groundless*⟩. **antonym** unconcern

²**care** *vi* **1a** to feel trouble or anxiety **b** to feel interest or concern ⟨~ *about freedom*⟩ ⟨*I couldn't* ~ *less!*⟩ **2** to give care ⟨~ *for the sick*⟩ **3** to have a liking, inclination, or taste ⟨*don't* ~ *for her*⟩ ⟨*would you* ~ *for some pie?*⟩ ~ *vt* **1** to wish ⟨*if you* ~ *to go*⟩ **2** to be concerned about ⟨*nobody* ~s *what I do*⟩ – **carer** *n*

**careen** /kə'reen/ *vt* **1** to cause (eg a boat) to lean over on one side, esp so that work can be done on the parts which are normally underwater **2** to clean, caulk, or repair (a boat) in this position ~ *vi* **1** to careen a boat **2** to heel over **3** *chiefly NAm* to career [MF *carène* keel, fr OIt *carena*, fr L *carina*, lit., nutshell; akin to Gk *karyon* nut]

*usage* The "career" sense is now well established in American English. It appears to combine the idea of rapid motion with that of "heeling over" and hence of "swaying".

¹**career** /kə'riə/ *n* **1a** a history or course, often a headlong course ⟨*the runaway bull ran on a wild* ~ *through the streets*⟩ **b** the exercise of activity ⟨*shall quips and sentences. . . awe a man from the full* ~ *of his humour?* – *Shak*⟩ **2a** a series of achievements or posts of responsibility lying within some sphere of activity ⟨*Washington's* ~ *as a soldier*⟩ **b** a field or type of employment which offers a long-term series of opportunities for advancement; *esp* such a field which requires special qualifications or training ⟨*gave a talk on* ~ s⟩ [MF *carrière*, fr OProv *carriera* street, fr ML *carraria* road for vehicles, fr L *carrus* car]

²**career** *vi* to move swiftly in an uncontrolled fashion and usu beyond the normal limits of motion ⟨*a car* ~ed *off the road*⟩

³**career** *adj* of or engaging in a career in a usu specified occupation ⟨~ *diplomat*⟩ ⟨~ *girl*⟩

**careerist** /kə'riərist/ *n* someone who would advance his/her career often at the cost of integrity – **careerism** *n*

**carefree** /'keə,free/ *adj* **1** free from care ⟨*a* ~ *vacation*⟩ **2** irresponsible ⟨*is* ~ *with his money*⟩ *synonyms* see CARELESS

**careful** /-f(ə)l/ *adj* **1** exercising or taking care **2a** marked by attentive concern **b** marked by wary caution or prudence ⟨*be very* ~ *with knives*⟩ ⟨*be* ~ *of the horses*⟩ – often + *to* and an infinitive ⟨*be* ~ *to adjust the machine*⟩ – **carefully** *adv*, **carefulness** *n*

*synonyms* **Careful**, **meticulous**, **punctilious**, **conscientious**, and **scrupulous** may all mean "showing close attention to detail". **Careful** is the most general term: it may suggest painstaking effort, thoroughness, and cautiousness in avoiding errors. The other terms all imply different motives for taking care. **Meticulous** describes a fastidious attention to detail which may approach fussiness. It often implies a nervousness lest one should make a mistake or fail to reach the required standard ⟨*her* **meticulous** *planning paid off – the meal went off without a hitch*⟩. **Punctilious** suggests a knowledge of the finer points of etiquette, morality, law, and so on, and a desire to adhere to them rigorously. This attention to detail may be found excessive by others. **Scrupulous** and **conscientious** both suggest a carefulness based on a standard, usually moral but sometimes aesthetic or legal ⟨*a* **scrupulous** *regard for the truth*⟩ ⟨*a* **conscientious** *researcher*⟩. **antonyms** careless, negligent, remiss

**careless** /-lis/ *adj* **1a** free from care; untroubled ⟨~ *days*⟩ indifferent, unconcerned ⟨~ *of the consequences*⟩ **2** not taking care **3** not showing or receiving care: **3a** negligent, slovenly ⟨*writing that is* ~ *and full of errors*⟩ **b** unstudied, spontaneous ⟨~ *grace*⟩ – **carelessly** *adv*, **carelessness** *n*

*synonyms* Both **careless** and **carefree** can mean "free from care" in the "good" sense. When **carefree** is used to mean "irresponsible", it comes closer to the "bad" senses of **careless** but with a less censorious attitude on the part of the speaker.

¹**caress** /kə'res/ *n* **1** a caressing touch **2** a kiss [Fr *caresse*, fr It *carezza*, fr *caro* dear, fr L *carus* – more at CHARITY]

²**caress** *vt* **1a** to touch or stroke lightly and lovingly **b** to touch or affect as if with a caress ⟨*echoes that* ~ *the ear*⟩ **2** to treat

kindly or fondly □ compare FONDLE, ³PET, CUDDLE – **caresser** *n*, **caressingly** *adv*

**caret** /'karət/ *n* a mark ⟨ or ʌ or ⟩ used on written or printed matter to indicate an insertion to be made △ carat [L, there is lacking, fr *carēre* to lack, be without – more at CASTE]

¹**caretaker** /'keə,taykə/ *n* **1** one who takes care of the house or land of an owner who may be absent **2** *Br* one who keeps clean a large public building (eg a school), looks after the heating system, and does minor repairs

²**caretaker** *adj* temporarily installed in office ⟨*a ~ government*⟩

**careworn** /-,wawn/ *adj* showing the effect of grief or anxiety ⟨*a ~ face*⟩

**carex** /'kareks, 'kah-/ *n*, *pl* **carices** /'karəseez/ any of a genus (*Carex*) of sedges that have 1-seeded fruits enclosed in pouches in the angle between the BRACTS (tiny specialized leaves) and the stem [NL, genus name, fr L, sedge]

**Carey Street** /'keəri/ *n*, *Br informal* a state of financial ruin [*Carey Street* in London, former location of the Bankruptcy Department of the Supreme Court]

**carfare** /'kah,feə/ *n*, *NAm* passenger fare (eg on a bus)

**carfax** /'kahfaks/ *n*, *Br* a carrefour, crossroads [ME *carfouk*, *carfuks*, modif of AF *querrefoure*, fr LL *quadrifurcum* – more at CARREFOUR]

**carful** /'kahfool/ *n* as much or as many as a car will hold

**cargo** /'kahgoh/ *n*, *pl* **cargoes**, **cargos** the nonhuman load that is conveyed by a means of transport (eg an aircraft or ship); freight [Sp, load, charge, fr *cargar* to load, fr LL *carricare* – more at CHARGE]

**cargo cult** *n* a belief among certain Pacific islanders that divine benefactors bringing food and goods will imminently appear by ship and aircraft – **cargo cultism** *n*, **cargo cultist** *n*

**carhop** /'kah,hop/ *n*, *NAm* a waiter at a drive-in restaurant [*car* + *hop* (as in *bellhop*)]

**cariama** /,kari'ahmə, -'amə/ *n* SERIEMA [NL, genus name, fr Pg, modif of Tupi *çariama*]

**Carib** /'karib/ *n* **1** a member of an American Indian people of northern S America and the Lesser Antilles **2** the language of the Caribs [NL *Caribes* (pl), fr Sp *Caribe*, fr Arawakan *Carib*, of Cariban origin; akin to Carib *Galibi* Caribs, lit., strong men]

**Cariban** /'karəbən, kə'reebən/ *n* **1** a member of a group of American Indian peoples of northern S America, the Lesser Antilles, and the Caribbean coast of Honduras, Guatemala, and Belize **2** the language family comprising the languages of the Caribans – **Cariban** *adj*

**Caribbean** /,kari'bee-ən; *also* kə'ribiən USE *the last pron is disliked by some speakers*/ *adj* of the Caribs, the eastern and southern W Indies, or the Caribbean sea [NL *Caribbaeus*, fr *Caribes*]

**caribou** /'kari,booh/ *n*, *pl* **caribous**, *esp collectively* **caribou** any of several large deer (genus *Rangifer*) of northern N America that have broad branching antlers and are related to the reindeer [CanF, of Algonquian origin]

¹**caricature** /'karikəchə, -chooə, -tyooə/ *n* **1** exaggeration by distortion of parts or characteristics, often to a ludicrous extent **2** a representation, esp in literature or art, that has the qualities of caricature **3** a distortion so gross as to seem like caricature □ compare ¹BURLESQUE, ¹PARODY, ¹TRAVESTY, LAMPOON, ²SPOOF, TAKEOFF [Fr, fr It *caricatura*, lit., act of loading, fr *caricare* to load, fr LL *carricare*] – **caricatural** *adj*, **caricaturist** *n*

²**caricature** /'karikə,chooə, -,tyooə/ *vt* to make or draw a caricature of; represent in caricature ⟨*his face has often been ~d in the newspapers*⟩

**caries** /'keəreez, -riz/ *n*, *pl* **caries** a progressive destruction of bone or tooth by microorganisms; *esp* tooth decay [L, decay; akin to Gk *kēr* death]

**carillon** /kə'rilyən/ *n* **1a** a set of fixed chromatically tuned bells sounded by hammers controlled from a keyboard **b** an electronic instrument imitating a carillon **2** (the sound of) a tune played on a carillon; *also* the sound of bells [Fr, alter. of OF *quarregnon*, fr LL *quaternion-*, *quaternio* set of four – more at QUATERNION]

**carina** /kə'reenə, -'rienə/ *n*, *pl* **carinas**, **carinae** /-nie/ a keel-shaped anatomical or botanical part; *esp* the part of a flower of a bean, pea, etc plant that encloses the male and female reproductive structures (STAMENS and OVARY) [NL, fr L, keel – more at CAREEN] – **carinal** *adj*

**carinate** /'karinayt/ *also* **carinated** /-,naytid/ *adj*, *biology*

shaped like the keel or prow of a ship; keeled, ridged ⟨*a ~ sepal*⟩

**carioca** /,kari'ohkə/ *n* **1** *cap* a native or resident of Rio de Janeiro **2a** a variation of the samba **b** the music for this dance [Pg, fr Tupi, fr *cari* white + *oca* house]

**carious** /'keəri-əs/ *adj* affected with caries ⟨*a ~ tooth*⟩ [L *cariosus*, fr *caries*]

**carking** /'kahking/ *adj*, *archaic* burdensome, worrying – chiefly in *carking care* [fr prp of *cark* (to worry), fr ME *carken*, lit., to load, burden, fr ONF *carquier*, fr LL *carricare*]

**carl, carle** /kahl/ *n* **1** *Scot* a niggard, miser **2** *archaic* a man of the common people **3** *archaic* an uncouth fellow; a churl [ME, fr OE *-carl*, fr ON *karl* man; akin to OE *ceorl* churl – more at CHURL]

¹**carline, carlin** /'kahlin/ *n*, *chiefly Scot* a woman; *esp* an old woman or witch [ME *kerling*, fr ON, fr *karl* man]

²**carline** *n* a carling

³**carline, carline thistle** *n* any of a genus (*Carlina*) of Eurasian thistlelike plants of the daisy family; *esp* one (*Carlina vulgaris*) with spiny leaves and pale golden-yellow flower heads [MF *carline*, fr OIt *carlina*, prob deriv of L *carduus* thistle – more at CHARD]

**carling** /'kahling/ *n* a fore-and-aft timber supporting a deck of a ship or framing a deck opening [Fr *carlingue*, fr ONF *calingue*, fr ON *kerling*, lit., old woman]

**Carlist** /'kahlist/ *n* a supporter of Don Carlos or his successors as having the rightful title to the Spanish throne [Sp *carlista*, fr *Don Carlos* †1855 claimant to the Spanish throne under the Salic law] – **Carlist** *adj*

**carload** /,-lohd/ *n* the quantity, or number of people, that can be carried by a car

**Carlovingian** /,kahloh'vinjiən/ *adj or n* (a) Carolingian [Fr *carlovingien*, prob fr ML *Carl*us Charles + Fr *-ovingien* (as in *mérovingien* Merovingian)]

**carmagnole** /,kahmə'nyohl/ (*Fr* karmaɲɔl)/ *n* **1** a lively song popular at the time of the first French Revolution **2** a street dance in a meandering course to the tune of the carmagnole [Fr, fr Fr dial. *carmagniola* jacket worn by peasants, fr *Carmagnola*, town in NW Italy]

**Carmelite** /'kahmə,liet/ *n* a member of the Roman Catholic mendicant Order of Our Lady of Mount Carmel, founded in the 12th century [ME, fr ML *carmelita*, fr *Carmel* Mount Carmel in Palestine, where the order was founded] – **Carmelite** *adj*

**carminative** /kah'minətiv/ *adj* expelling or causing the expulsion of gas from the digestive tract so as to relieve colic or griping [Fr *carminatif*, fr L *carminatus*, pp of *carminare* to card, fr *carmin-*, *carmen* card, fr *carrere* to card – more at CHARD] – **carminative** *n*

**carmine** /'kahmin/ *n* **1** a rich crimson or scarlet pigment (LAKE) made from cochineal **2** a vivid red colour [Fr *carmin*, fr ML *carminium*, irreg fr Ar *qirmiz* kermes + L *minium* – more at MINIUM]

**carnage** /'kahnij/ *n* great and bloody slaughter (eg in battle) [MF, flesh of slain animals or men, fr ML *carnaticum* tribute consisting of animals or meat, fr L *carn-*, *caro*]

**carnal** /'kahnl/ *adj* **1a** marked by sexual desires; sexual **b** relating to or given to bodily pleasures and appetites **2** temporal, worldly *antonyms* spiritual, intellectual [ME, fr ONF or LL; ONF, fr LL *carnalis*, fr L *carn-*, *caro* flesh; akin to Gk *keirein* to cut – more at SHEAR] – **carnally** *adv*, **carnality** *n*

**carnal knowledge** *n*, *chiefly law* sexual intercourse – chiefly in *have carnal knowledge of*

**carnallite** /'kahnəliet/ *n* a mineral, $KMgCl_3.6H_2O$, consisting essentially of a chloride of potassium and magnesium chemically combined with water molecules, that is important as a source of potassium [Ger *carnallit*, fr Rudolf von *Carnall* † 1874 Ger mining engineer]

**carnassial** /kah'nassi-əl/ *adj* of or being those teeth of a carnivore that are larger and longer than adjacent teeth and are adapted for cutting rather than tearing [Fr *carnassier* carnivorous, deriv of L *carn-*, *caro*] – **carnassial** *n*

**carnation** /kah'naysh(ə)n/ *n* **1** a light red or pink colour **2** any of numerous cultivated usu double-flowered varieties of the CLOVE PINK (*Dianthus caryophyllus*) with fragrant typically red, pink, or white flowers [MF, flesh colour, fr OIt *carnagione*, fr *carne* flesh, fr L *carn-*, *caro*]

**carnauba** /kah'nowbə/ *n* a palm (*Copernicia cerifera*) of Brazil that has fan-shaped leaves and has an edible root, and yields a useful leaf fibre and CARNAUBA WAX [Pg]

**carnauba wax** *n* a hard brittle wax from the leaves of the carnauba palm, used chiefly in polishes

**carnelian** /kah'neelyən/ *n* CORNELIAN [alter. of *cornelian*, fr ME *corneline*, fr MF, perh fr *cornelle* cornel]

**carnet** /'kahnay, -'- (*Fr* karnɛ)/ *n* 1 a customs document permitting free movement (eg of a motor car) across a frontier or temporary duty-free import (eg of goods en route to another country) 2 a permit allowing entry (eg of campers to a campsite) ⟨*camping* ∼⟩ [Fr, lit., notebook, fr MF *quernet*, fr L *quaterni* set of four – more at QUATERNION]

**carnitine** /'kahnitien, -teen/ *n* a white chemical compound that is an essential vitamin for some insect larvae (eg mealworms) and that occurs in liver tissue and in the muscles of VERTEBRATE animals where it is associated with the transfer of fatty substances to sites of fat breakdown [ISV, deriv of L *carn-, caro* meat, flesh]

**carnival** /'kahnivl/ *n* 1 a period of merrymaking before Lent, esp in Roman Catholic countries 2 an instance of merrymaking or feasting 3a *chiefly NAm* a travelling circus or fun fair b an exhibition or organized programme of entertainment; a festival [It *carnevale*, alter. of earlier *carnelevare*, lit., removal of meat, fr *carne* flesh (fr L *carn-, caro*) + *levare* to remove, fr L, to raise]

**carnivore** /'kahni,vaw/ *n* 1 a flesh-eating animal; *esp* any of an order (Carnivora) of flesh-eating mammals 2 an insect-eating plant [deriv of L *carnivorus*]

**carnivorous** /kah'niv(ə)rəs/ *adj* 1 subsisting or feeding on animal tissues 2 *of a plant* living wholly or partly on nutrients obtained from the breakdown of animal tissue (eg by the capture and digestion of insects) 3 of the carnivores [L *carnivorus*, fr *carn-, caro* flesh + *-vorus* -vorous – more at CARNAL] – **carnivorously** *adv*, **carnivorousness** *n*

**carnotite** /'kahnətiet/ *n* a yellow radioactive mineral, $K_2(UO)_2(VO_4)_2.3H_2O$, that consists essentially of the chemical elements vanadium, uranium, and potassium chemically combined with water molecules, and is a source of radium and uranium [Fr, fr M A *Carnot* †1920 Fr inspector-general of mines]

**carob** /'karəb/ *n* a Mediterranean evergreen tree (*Ceratonia siliqua*) of the pea family that has red flowers and bears a pod with an edible pulp; *also* the pod of the carob [MF *carobe*, fr ML *carrubium*, fr Ar *kharrūbah*]

**¹carol** /'karəl/ *n* 1 an old round dance with singing 2 a song of joy or mirth ⟨*the* ∼ *of a bird* – Lord Byron⟩ 3 a popular seasonal usu religious song or ballad; *esp* a Christmas song or hymn [ME *carole*, fr OF, prob modif of LL *choraula* choral song, fr L, choral accompanist, fr Gk *choraulēs*, fr *choros* chorus + *aulein* to play a reed instrument, fr *aulos*, a reed instrument]

**²carol** *vb* -ll- (*NAm* -l-, -ll-) *vi* 1 to sing, esp in a joyful manner 2 to sing carols; *specif* to go about outdoors in a group singing Christmas carols ∼ *vt* 1 to praise (as if) in song 2 to sing, esp in a cheerful manner; warble – **caroller**, *NAm* **caroler** *n*

**Carolean** /,karə'lee·ən/ *adj* Caroline [by alter. (influenced by *Jacobean*)]

**Caroline** /'karəlien/ *adj* of Charles – used esp with reference to Charles I and Charles II of Britain [NL *carolinus*, fr ML *Carolus* Charles]

**Carolingian** /,karə'linji·ən/ *n* a member of a Frankish dynasty dating from about AD 613 and including among its members the rulers of France from 751 to 987, of Germany from 752 to 911, and of Italy from 774 to 961 [Fr *carolingien* (adj), fr ML *karolingi* French people, prob fr (assumed) OHG *karling, Karl* Charles] – **Carolingian** *adj*

**¹carom** /'karəm/ *n*, *NAm* a cannon in billiards or bagatelle [by shortening & alter. fr obs *carambole*, fr Sp *carambola*]

**²carom** *vi*, *NAm* 1 to make a carom; cannon 2 to rebound, glance ⟨*the car* ∼ed *off several trees*⟩

**carotene** /'karəteen/ *n* any of several forms of an organic chemical compound, $C_{40}H_{56}$, that occur as orange or red pigments in plants and in the fatty tissues of plant-eating animals and are convertible to vitamin A in the body [ISV, fr LL *carota* carrot]

**carotenoid** *also* **carotinoid** /kə'rotənoyd/ *n* any of various usu yellow to red pigments including the carotenes that are found widely in plants and animals – **carotenoid** *adj*

**carotid** /kə'rotid/ *adj or n* (of or being) the chief artery or pair of arteries that pass up the neck and supply blood to the head [Fr or Gk; Fr *carotide*, fr Gk *karōtides* carotid arteries, fr *karoun* to stupefy; akin to Gk *kara* head – more at CEREBRAL]

**carotid body** *n* a small body of tissue lying close to the CAROTID SINUS that is sensitive to changes in the oxygen content and acidity of blood and forms part of the system whereby these are kept stable

**carotid sinus** *n* a small enlargement of either carotid artery that is located at the point in the neck where the artery forms its main branches, is richly supplied with nerves, and functions in the regulation of heart rate and blood pressure

**carousal** /kə'rowzl/ *n* a drunken revel △ carousel

**¹carouse** /kə'rowz/ *n* 1 a carousal 2 *archaic* a large draught of an alcoholic beverage; a toast [MF *carrousse*, fr *carous*, adv, completely, all out (in *boire carous* to empty the cup), fr Ger *garaus*]

**²carouse** *vi* 1 to drink alcoholic beverages deeply or freely 2 to take part in a drinking spree – **carouser** *n*

**carousel** *also* NAm **carrousel** /,karə'sel, -'zel/ *n* 1 a tournament in which companies of liveried horsemen executed various manoeuvres 2 a rotating stand or delivery system ⟨*a luggage* ∼ *at the airport*⟩ 3 *chiefly NAm* MERRY-GO-ROUND 1,2 △ carousal [Fr *carrousel*, fr It *carosello*]

**¹carp** /kahp/ *vi* to find fault or complain querulously and often perversely [ME *carpen* to talk, of Scand origin; akin to Icel *karpa* to dispute; prob influenced in meaning by L *carpere* to pluck, slander] – **carper** *n*

**²carp** *n, pl* **carp**, *esp for different types* **carps** 1 a large Eurasian soft-finned freshwater fish (*Cyprinus carpio*) of sluggish waters that is often farmed for food; *also* any of various fishes of the same family 2 a fish (eg the European sea bream) resembling a carp [ME *carpe*, fr MF, fr LL *carpa*, prob of Gmc origin; akin to OHG *karpfo* carp]

**carp-** /kahp-/, **carpo-** *comb form* fruit ⟨*carpology*⟩ [Fr & NL, fr Gk *karp-, karpo-*, fr *karpos* – more at HARVEST]

**-carp** /-kahp/ *comb form* (→ *n*) part of a fruit ⟨*mesocarp*⟩; fruit ⟨*schizocarp*⟩ [NL *-carpium*, fr Gk *-karpion*, fr *karpos*]

**¹carpal** /'kahpl/ *adj* of or forming part of the CARPUS (wrist or corresponding structure) [NL *carpalis*, fr *carpus*]

**²carpal** *n* a carpal bone

**carpale** /kah'payli/ *n, pl* **carpalia** /-li·ə/ a carpal [NL, neut of *carpalis*]

**car park** *n, chiefly Br* an area or building set aside for the parking of motor vehicles

**carpe diem** /,kahpay 'dee·em/ *n* the enjoyment of the pleasures of the moment without concern for the future ⟨*thē* ∼ *theme in poetry*⟩ [L, enjoy (lit., pluck) the day]

**carpel** /'kahpl/ *n* the female reproductive organ of a flowering plant that either singly or together with others usu forms the innermost part of a flower and that consists usu of an ovary attached to a pollen-receiving structure (STIGMA) by a thin tubular STYLE [NL *carpellum*, fr Gk *karpos* fruit] – **carpellary** *adj*, **carpellate** *adj*

**¹carpenter** /'kahpintə/ *n* one who builds or repairs large-scale structural woodwork (eg that of a roof); *broadly* one who constructs woodwork – compare JOINER [ME, fr ONF *carpentier*, fr L *carpentarius* carriage-maker, fr *carpentum* carriage, of Celt origin; akin to OIr *carr* vehicle – more at CAR]

**²carpenter** *vi* to follow the trade of a carpenter ⟨∼ed *when he was young*⟩ ∼ *vt* 1 to make (as if) by carpentry 2 to put together often in a rough-and-ready manner ⟨∼ed *many television scripts*⟩

**carpentry** /'kahpintri/ *n* 1 the craft or trade of a carpenter 2 timberwork constructed by a carpenter 3 the form or manner of putting together the parts (eg of a literary or musical composition); structure, arrangement

**carpet** /'kahpit/ *n* 1 a heavy woven or felted fabric used as a floor covering; *also* a floor covering made of this fabric 2 a surface resembling or suggesting a carpet ⟨*a* ∼ *of leaves*⟩ [ME, fr MF *carpite*, fr OIt *carpita*, fr *carpire* to pluck, modif of L *carpere* – more at HARVEST] – **carpet** *vt*, **carpeter** *n* – **brush/sweep something under the carpet** to conceal something in the hope that it will be ignored – **on the carpet** before an authority for censure or reproof

**carpetbag** /-,bag/ *n* a bag made of carpet fabric and used by travellers, esp in the 19th century

**carpetbagger** /-,bagə/ *n* 1 a Northerner in the South after the American Civil War usu seeking private gain under the reconstruction governments 2 a nonresident who meddles in politics, esp for personal gain [fr their carrying all their belongings in carpetbags] – **carpetbaggery** *n*

**carpet beetle** *n* any of several small beetles (family Dermestidae, esp genus *Anthrenus*) whose larvae feed on fabrics and woollen goods

**carpet bomb** *vt* to drop bombs on (eg an area) so as to cover as if with a carpet

**carpeting** /'kahpiting/ *n* 1 material for carpets; *also* carpets 2 *informal* a severe reproof ⟨*he gave me a real* ~⟩

**carpet shark** *n* (any of various sharks related to) a shark (*Orectolobus barbatus*) of the W Pacific that has a flattened body and mottled skin

**-carpic** /-kahpik/ *comb form* (→ *adj*) -CARPOUS ⟨*poly*carpic⟩ [NL *-carpicus*, fr Gk *karpos* fruit]

**carping** /'kahping/ *adj* critical esp in a petty or querulous manner

**carpo-** – see CARP-

**carpogonium** /ˌkahpə'gohniəm/ *n*, *pl* **carpogonia** /-niə/ 1 the flask-shaped egg-bearing part of the female reproductive organ in RED ALGAE and some related plants 2 ASCOGONIUM (female reproductive structure in some fungi) [NL] – **carpogonial** *adj*

**carpology** /kah'poləji/ *n* a branch of plant anatomy dealing with fruit and seeds [ISV]

**car pool** *n* an arrangement by a group of private car owners by which each in turn conveys the others as passengers; *also*, *taking sing or pl vb* such a group itself

**carpophagous** /kah'pofəgəs/ *adj* fruit-eating [Gk *karpophagos*, fr *karp-* carp- + *-phagos* -phagous]

**carpophore** /'kahpəfaw/ *n* 1 the stalk of the spore-bearing structure in some fungi; *also* the entire spore-bearing structure 2 a prolongation of the main axis of a flower from which the female parts (CARPELS) are suspended [NL *carpophorum*, fr *carp-* + *-phorum* -phore]

**carport** /-ˌpawt/ *n* an open-sided shed built as a shelter for cars

**carpospore** /'kahpəˌspaw/ *n* a spore of a RED ALGA that is produced after fertilization of the egg in the carpogonium – **carposporic** *adj*

**-carpous** /-kahpəs/ *comb form* (→ *adj*) having (such) fruit or (so many) fruits ⟨*poly*carpous⟩ [NL *-carpus*, fr Gk *-karpos*, fr *karpos* fruit – more at HARVEST] – **-carpy** *comb form* (→ *n*)

**carpus** /'kahpəs/ *n*, *pl* **carpi** /'kahpi/ 1 (the bones of) the wrist – compare METACARPUS 2 (the bones of) the part of the fore-limb of a VERTEBRATE animal that corresponds to the carpus of a human being [NL, fr Gk *karpos* – more at WHARF]

**carr** *also* **car** /kah/ *n*, *Eng dial* a wet boggy area often colonized by alders, willows, etc [ME *ker*, of Scand origin; akin to Sw *kärr* marsh]

**carrack** /'karak/ *n* a large SQUARE-RIGGED trading vessel of the 14th to 17th centuries that was sometimes equipped for warfare [ME *carrake*, fr MF *caraque*, fr OSp *carraca*, fr Ar *qarāqīr*, pl of *qurqūr* merchant ship]

**carrageen** *also* **carragheen** /'karəgeen/ *n* 1 a dark purple branching edible seaweed (*Chondrus crispus*) found on the coasts of northern Europe and N America 2 carrageenan [*Carragheen*, town near Waterford (Port Láirge) in SE Ireland]

**carrageenan** /ˌkarə'geenən/, **carrageenin** *also* **carragheenin** /-nin/ *n* a carbohydrate extracted esp from carrageen and used esp as an EMULSIFYING agent (eg in foods), as a clarifying agent (eg for drinks), and in preventing crystal growth in ice cream and other frozen confections [*carrageen* + ³*-an* or *-in*]

**carrefour** /ˌkarə'fooə, -'faw/ *n* SQUARE 6; *esp* one where four ways meet ⟨*the farmers ... preferred the open* ~ *for their transactions* – Thomas Hardy⟩ [MF, fr LL *quadrifurcum*, neut of *quadrifurcus* having four forks, fr L *quadri-* + *furca* fork]

**carrel** /'karəl/ *n* a partitioned area or cubicle used for individual study, esp in a library [alter. of ME *carole* round dance, ring – more at CAROL]

**carriage** /'karij/ *n* 1 the act of carrying 2 manner of bearing the body; posture – compare BEARING 3 the price or expense of carrying – chiefly in *carriage paid*, *carriage forward* 4 a wheeled vehicle; *esp* a horse-drawn passenger-carrying vehicle designed for private use 5 a wheeled undercarriage for bearing a heavy weight ⟨*gun* ~⟩ 6 a movable part of a machine that supports some other part ⟨*a typewriter* ~⟩ 7 *Br* a railway passenger vehicle; a coach 8 *archaic* 8a the manner in which one conducts oneself; bearing b management [ME *cariage*, fr ONF, fr *carier* to transport in a vehicle – more at CARRY]

**carriage bolt** *n* COACH BOLT

**carriage clock** *n* a small robust clock enclosed in a glass-sided metal frame, usu with a handle at the top

**carriage dog** *n*, *archaic* a dalmatian – compare COACH DOG [fr its formerly being kept to run in attendance on a carriage]

**carriage trade** *n* trade from well-to-do people

**carriageway** /-ˌway/ *n*, *Br* a road for vehicular traffic; *specif* either of the two roadways of a dual carriageway

**carrick bend** /'karik/ *n* a knot used to join the ends of two large ropes [prob fr obs *carrick* carrack, fr ME *carrake*, *carryk*]

**carrier** /'kari·ə/ *n* 1 one who or that which carries; a bearer, messenger 2a COMMON CARRIER (transport organization) b a mobile HOLE (vacancy resulting from the absence of an electron from its normal position) or electron capable of carrying an electric charge in a SEMICONDUCTOR 3a a container or platform for carrying; *esp* a part of a cycle for carrying luggage b a device or machine that carries; a conveyer 4 AIRCRAFT CARRIER 5 a bearer and transmitter of a causative agent of disease; *esp* one who carries in his/her system the causative agent of a disease (eg typhoid fever) to which he/she is immune 6a a usu inactive accessory substance; a vehicle ⟨*a* ~ *for a drug or insecticide*⟩ b a substance (eg a catalyst) by whose agency an atom or chemical group is transferred from one chemical compound to another 7 **carrier, carrier wave** a radio or electrical wave of relatively high frequency that can be modulated (eg in frequency) by a signal (eg representing sound or vision information), esp in order to transmit that signal; that part of a transmitted signal that is necessary in order that a radio, television set, etc is able to receive the signal, but itself represents no sound or vision information 8 a strip or loop of material attached to a garment, through which a belt is threaded in order to hold it in position

**carrier bag** /'--- ˌ-, ˌ--- '-/ *n*, *Br* a simple bag of plastic or heavy paper, usu with a handhold on either side of the opening, used for carrying goods away from a shop

**carrier pigeon** *n* 1 a homing pigeon used to carry messages 2 any of a breed of large long-bodied show pigeons

**carrion** /'kari·ən/ *n* 1 dead and putrefying flesh; *broadly* flesh unfit for human consumption 2 something that is vile, corrupt, or rotten [ME *caroine*, fr AF, fr (assumed) VL *caronia*, irreg fr L *carn-*, *caro* flesh – more at CARNAL]

**carrion crow** *n* the common European black crow (*Corvus corone corone*)

**carronade** /ˌkarə'nayd/ *n* a short-barrelled muzzle-loaded large-calibred gun formerly used esp on ships [*Carron*, town in Scotland where it was first made]

**carrot** /'karət/ *n* 1 a plant (*Daucus carota* of the family Umbelliferae, the carrot family) with feathery leaves and a usu orange tapering or conical root; *also* this root eaten as a vegetable 2 a promised and often illusory reward or advantage [MF *carotte*, fr LL *carota*, fr Gk *karōton*; (2) fr the traditional method of urging a donkey forwards by holding a carrot in front of him]

'**carrot-ˌfly** *n* a small blue-black fly (*Psila rosae*) whose larvae cause damage by feeding on the roots of carrots, celery, and related plants

**carroty** /'karəti/ *adj* 1 like carrots in colour 2 having bright orange-red hair

**carrousel** /ˌkarə'sel, -'zel/ *n*, *NAm* a carousel, merry-go-round

¹**carry** /'kari/ *vt* 1 to support and move (a load); transport 2 to convey by direct communication ⟨~ *tales about a friend*⟩ 3 to lead or influence by appeal to the emotions ⟨*his oratory carried them all with him*⟩ 4 to gain possession or control of; win ⟨~ *a town by storm*⟩ 5 to transfer from one place to another; *esp* to transfer (a digit corresponding to a multiple of 10) in arithmetical addition to the next higher power of ten ⟨*when you add 6 to 37, you have to* ~ *one and add it to the 3*⟩ – compare BORROW 3 6 to bear as a load: 6a to convey, conduct ⟨*that drain carries the overflow*⟩ ⟨*his need for love carried him into her company*⟩ b to support ⟨*this beam carries the weight of the upper storeys*⟩ 7a to wear or have on one's person ⟨*I always* ~ *a gun*⟩ b to be pregnant with ⟨~*ing an unborn child*⟩ 8 to have as a mark, attribute, or property ⟨*I still* ~ *the scars of that episode*⟩ 9 to have as a consequence, esp in law; involve ⟨*the crime* carried *a heavy penalty*⟩ 10 to hold or bear (eg oneself) in a specified manner ⟨*he always* carried *himself upright*⟩ 11 to bear as a crop; support; *also* to provide sustenance for ⟨*that field just will not* ~ *that number of cattle*⟩ 12 to sing with reasonable correctness of pitch ⟨~ *a tune*⟩ 13 to keep in stock for sale ⟨*I'm afraid that's a line we no longer* ~⟩ 14 to maintain through financial support or personal effort ⟨*he* carried *the magazine single-handedly*⟩ 15 a to cause to be in a specified active state ⟨~ *the plan into effect*⟩ b to extend or prolong in space, time, or degree ⟨~ *the war into Africa*⟩ ⟨~ *a principle too far*⟩ 16 to gain victory for; *esp* to secure the

adoption or passage of (eg by winning a majority of votes)
**17a** to publish ⟨*newspapers ~ weather reports*⟩ **b** to broadcast
⟨*the new station will not ~ advertisements*⟩ **18a** to bear the
charges of holding (eg merchandise) from one time to another
⟨*you're ~*ing *far too much stock*⟩ **b** to keep on one's books as a
debtor ⟨*a merchant* carries *a customer*⟩ **19** to have (a sail)
hoisted ⟨*the danger of ~*ing *too much sail*⟩ **20** to cover (a
distance) or pass (an object) at a single stroke in golf **21a** to
allow (a teammate) to take a less active part in a game (eg
because of injury) ⟨*we can't afford to ~ anyone!*⟩ **b** to perform
with sufficient ability to make up for the poor performance of
(a partner or teammate) ~ *vi* **1** to act as a bearer **2a** to reach
or penetrate to a distance ⟨*voices ~ well*⟩ **b** to convey itself to
a reader or audience **3** to undergo or admit of carriage in a
specified way – see also **carry one's BAT/the CAN/the DAY/a
TORCH** [ME *carien,* fr ONF *carier* to transport in a vehicle, fr
*car* vehicle, fr L *carrus* – more at CAR]

**synonyms Bear, convey,** and **transport** may replace **carry** (sense
1) in certain circumstances. **Bear** stresses weightiness, or may be
used to give more importance or significance to what is carried ⟨*let
four captains* bear *Hamlet . . . to the stage* – Shak⟩. **Convey** replaces
**carry** for things which move continuously or by artificial means ⟨con-
vey *water to the valley in pipes*⟩. **Transport** is used for moving people
or things in bulk or large numbers or over long distances ⟨transporting
*troops to the continent*⟩. It can also be used where **carry** would be too
physical ⟨transported *us to the age of Elizabeth the First*⟩.

**carry away** *vt* **1** to carry off **2** to arouse to a high and often
excessive degree of emotion and enthusiasm
**carry forward** *vt* to transfer to the succeeding column, page,
or book relating to the same account
**carry off** *vt* **1** to cause the death of ⟨*the plague* carried off
*thousands*⟩ **2** to perform easily or successfully ⟨*the leading
lady* carried off *her part brilliantly*⟩ **3** to gain possession or
control of; capture ⟨carried off *the prize*⟩
**carry on** *vi* **1** to behave in a foolish, excited, or improper
way ⟨*embarrassed by the way he* carries on⟩ **2** to continue
one's course or activity in spite of hindrance or discouragement **3** *Br* to flirt; *also* to have a love affair – usu + *with;* see
also CARRYING-ON, CARRYON, CARRY-ON
**carry out** *vt* **1** to put into execution ⟨carry out *a plan*⟩ **2** to
bring to a successful conclusion; complete, accomplish ⟨*you
will be paid when you have* carried out *the assignment*⟩ – see
also CARRYOUT
**carry over 1a** to hold over (eg goods) for another season **b**
to carry forward **2** to deduct (a loss or an unused credit) for
taxable income of a subsequent period to persist from one
stage or sphere of activity to another – see also CARRY-OVER
**carry through** *vt* to carry out ~ *vi* to persist, survive ⟨*feelings that* carry through *to the present*⟩
²**carry** *n* **1** carrying power or range: esp **1a** the power of a
projectile to travel far; *also* the range of a gun or projectile **b**
the distance between the place from which a ball (eg a golf
ball) is struck and that where it first lands; *also* the trajectory
of a ball **2a** the act or a method of carrying **b** PORTAGE 1a
**carryall** /'kari,awl/ *n, NAm* **1** a passenger vehicle similar to an
estate car but usu with sideways-facing bench seats **2** a holdall
[(1) by folk etymology fr Fr *carriole* light carriage, deriv of L
*carrus* car; (2) ¹*carry + all*]
**carrycot** /-,kot/ *n, chiefly Br* a small lightweight boxlike bed,
usu having two handles, in which a baby can be carried
**carrying capacity** /'kari·ing/ *n* the population (eg of deer)
that an area will support without undergoing deterioration
**carrying charge** *n* **1** the cost of holding unrealized assets (eg
stock) **2** *chiefly NAm* a charge added to the price of merchandise sold on hire purchase
,**carrying-'on** *n, pl* **carryings-on,** *informal* foolish, excited, or
improper behaviour; *also* an instance of such behaviour ⟨*scandalous* carryings-on⟩
**carryon** /-,on/ *n, NAm* a piece of luggage suitable for a passenger to carry aboard an aeroplane
'**carry-,on** *n, informal* an instance of foolish, excited, or improper behaviour; *also* such behaviour; a to-do
**carryout** /-,owt/ *n, NAm & Scot* a take-away – **carryout** *adj*
'**carry-,over** *n* **1** the act or process of carrying over **2** something (eg an influence) carried over
**carse** /kahs/ *n, Scot* a stretch of low-lying land beside water
[ME *cars, kerss*]
**carsey** /'kahzi/ *n, Br informal* a karzy, toilet
**carsick** /'kah,sik/ *adj* affected with motion sickness, esp in a
motor car – **car sickness** *n*

¹**cart** /kaht/ *n* **1** a heavy usu horse-drawn two-wheeled or four-
wheeled vehicle used for transporting bulky or heavy loads (eg
on farms) **2** a lightweight two-wheeled passenger vehicle drawn
by a horse, pony, or dog **3** a small wheeled vehicle (eg a hand-
trolley) [ME, prob fr ON *kartr;* akin to OE *cræt* cart, OE *cradol*
cradle] – **in the cart** *chiefly Br slang* in an awkward position
[prob fr the cart in which criminals were formerly taken to
punishment or execution]
²**cart** *vt* **1** to carry in a cart; *also, informal* to convey as if in a
cart ⟨*buses to ~ the kids to school*⟩ **2** *informal* **2a** to carry
with difficulty ⟨*I've ~*ed *this all the way home and my arms
are killing me*⟩ **b** to take or drag away without ceremony or
by force – usu + *off* ⟨*they ~*ed *him off to jail*⟩ ~ *vi* to pull or
drive a cart – **carter** *n*
**cartage** /'kahtij/ *n* the act of carting; *also* the charge for this
**carte blanche** /,kaht 'blonh·sh (*Fr* kart blɑ̃ʃ)/ *n, pl* **cartes
blanches** full discretionary power ⟨*was given ~ to build, landscape and furnish the house*⟩ [Fr, lit., blank document]
**carte du jour** /dooh 'zhooə (*Fr* dy ʒuːr)/ *n, pl* **cartes du jour**
a menu; *esp* that of a particular day [Fr, lit., card of the day]
**cartel** /kah'tel/ *n* **1** a combination of independent commercial
enterprises designed to limit competition (eg by regulating
prices and output); *also* a formal agreement between firms in
an industry covering prices, output, etc **2** a combination of esp
French or Belgian political groups for common action [MF,
letter of defiance, fr OIt *cartello,* lit., placard, fr *carta* leaf of
paper – more at CARD]
**Cartesian** /kah'teezh(y)ən, -zyən/ *adj* of René Descartes or his
philosophy [NL *cartesianus,* fr Renatus *Cartesius* (René Descartes) †1650 Fr philosopher] – **Cartesian** *n*, **Cartesianism** *n*
**Cartesian coordinate** *n* **1** either of two numbers fixing a
point's position on a plane (eg on a graph or map) by its distance from each of two straight lines (AXES) drawn normally at
right angles to each other – compare POLAR COORDINATE **2** any
of three numbers fixing a point's position in space by its distance from each of three planes lying usu at right angles to
each other – compare SPHERICAL COORDINATE
**Cartesian plane** *n* a plane whose points are assigned CARTES-
IAN COORDINATES
**Cartesian product** *n*, *maths* a set that is constructed from
two given sets and comprises all pairs of elements such that
one element of the pair is from the first set and the other element is from the second set – called also DIRECT PRODUCT
**carthorse** /'kaht,haws/ *n* a large strong horse bred or used for
drawing heavy loads
**Carthusian** /kah'thyoohzh(y)ən, -zyən/ *n* a member of an austere contemplative religious order founded by St Bruno [ML
*cartusiensis,* irreg fr OF *Chartrouse* Chartreuse – more at
CHARTERHOUSE] – **Carthusian** *adj*
**cartilage** /'kahtilij/ *n* (a structure composed of) a translucent
firm somewhat elastic tissue that makes up most of the skeleton
of embryonic and very young VERTEBRATE animals and
becomes mostly converted into bone in adult higher vertebrates
(eg mammals) [L *cartilagin-, cartilago;* akin to L *cratis* wickerwork – more at HURDLE]
**cartilaginous** /,kahti'lajinəs/ *adj* composed of, relating to, or
resembling cartilage
**cartilaginous fish** *n* any of the fishes (eg the sharks) whose
skeletons are wholly or largely composed of cartilage;
ELASMOBRANCH; *also* a cyclostome
**cartload** /-,lohd/ *n* the quantity that a cart can hold
**cartogram** /'kahtə,gram/ *n* a map showing quantitative information diagrammatically [Fr *cartogramme,* fr *carte +
-gramme* -gram]
**cartography** /kah'togrəfi/ *n* **1** the art, science, or technology
of making maps or charts **2** the process of making a map as a
graphic image [Fr *cartographie,* fr *carte* card, map + -*graphie*
-graphy – more at CARD] – **cartographer** *n*, **cartographic,
cartographical** *adj*
**cartomancy** /'kahtə,mansi/ *n* the telling of fortunes by the
use of playing cards [Fr *cartomancie,* fr *carte* card + -*o*- +
-*mancie* -mancy]
¹**carton** /'kaht(ə)n/ *n* a plastic or cardboard container [Fr, fr It
*cartone* pasteboard]
²**carton** *vt* to pack or enclose in a carton
**cartoon** /kah'toohn/ *n* **1** a preparatory design, drawing, or
painting (eg for a fresco) **2a** a satirical drawing commenting
on public and usu political matters **b** STRIP CARTOON **c**
ANIMATED CARTOON [It *cartone* pasteboard, cartoon, aug of
*carta* leaf of paper – more at CARD] – **cartoon** *vb*, **cartoonist** *n*

**cartouche** also **cartouch** /kah'toohsh/ n 1 a gun cartridge with a paper case 2 an ornate or ornamental frame 3 an oval or oblong outline (e g on ancient Egyptian monuments) enclosing a ruler's name [Fr cartouche, fr It cartoccio, fr carta]

**cartridge** /'kahtrij/ n 1 an often cylindrical container of material for insertion into a larger mechanism or apparatus: e g 1a a tube of metal, paper, or plastic containing the primer, and often the bullet or shot, for a firearm b a case containing an explosive charge for blasting c a case containing a reel and an endless loop of magnetic tape or film 2 that part of a record deck containing the stylus and the device (e g a PIEZOELECTRIC crystal) which converts movements of the stylus into electrical signals [alter. of earlier cartage, modif of MF cartouche]

**cartridge belt** n a belt with a series of loops for holding cartridges

**cartridge brass** n a brass usu composed of 70 per cent copper and 30 per cent zinc

**cartridge clip** n 2CLIP 2

**cartridge paper** n a rough-surfaced close-grained often heavy paper used for book printing and for drawing

'**cart-,track** n a road fit only for carts

**cartulary** /'kahtyoolǝri/ n a collection of records or charters; also the room where these are kept [ML chartularium, fr chartula charter – more at CHARTER]

¹**cartwheel** /-,weel/ n 1 a sideways handspring with arms and legs extended 2 informal a large coin (e g a silver dollar)

²**cartwheel** vi to move like a turning wheel; specif to perform cartwheels – **cartwheeler** n

**cartwright** /-,riet/ n a maker and repairer of carts

**caruncle** /'karǝngkl/ n 1 a hairless fleshy outgrowth (e g the comb or wattle of a turkey, hen, etc) 2 a fleshy outgrowth near the MICROPYLE of a seed [obs Fr caruncule, fr L caruncula little piece of flesh, dim. of caro flesh – more at CARNAL] – **caruncular** adj, **carunculate, carunculated** adj

**carve** /kahv/ vt 1a to cut so as to shape ⟨he ~d a fine statue from Parian marble⟩ b to produce by cutting ⟨~d his initials in the soft sandstone⟩ c to cut designs in (e g leather or fabric) 2 to fashion, make, or get as if by cutting – usu + out ⟨~ out a fortune⟩ 3 to cut (food, esp meat) into pieces or slices ~ vi 1 to cut up (and serve) meat 2 to work as a sculptor or engraver [ME kerven, fr OE ceorfan; akin to MHG kerben to notch, Gk graphein to scratch, write]

**carve up** vt 1 to divide into parts ⟨the Allies carved up Germany after the War⟩ 2 Br informal, of a motorist to overtake (a vehicle) and cut in front of too soon; also to outperform esp in speed ⟨he carved me up down the motorway⟩ 3 slang to wound with a knife – see also CARVE-UP

**carvel** /'kahvl/ n CARAVEL (sailing ship) [ME carvile, fr MF caravelle, carvelle]

'**carvel-,built** adj, of a vessel built with the planks meeting flush at the seams – compare CLINKER-BUILT [prob fr D karveel-, fr karveel caravel, fr MF carvelle]

**carven** /'kahvǝn/ adj, archaic wrought or ornamented by carving; carved

**carver** /'kahvǝ/ n 1a one who or that which carves; specif a long sharp knife used for carving meat b pl a knife and fork set used for carving and serving meat 2 Br a chair with armrests in a set of dining-room chairs

'**carve-,up** n, slang a division into parts; esp the sharing-out of loot

**carving** /'kahving/ n 1 the act, art, or craft of one who carves 2 a carved object, design, or figure

**car wash** n an area or structure set aside for the washing of cars

**cary-, caryo-** comb form kary-, karyo-

**caryatid** /'kari-ǝ,tid, ,kari'atid, kǝ'rie-ǝtid/ n, pl caryatids, caryatides /,kari'atideez, kǝ'rie-ǝ'teediz/ a draped female figure used as a column to support an ENTABLATURE – compare ATLAS [L caryatides, pl, fr Gk karyatides priestesses of Artemis at Caryae, caryatids, fr Karyai Caryae, town in Greece]

**caryopsis** /,kari'opsis/ n, pl caryopses /-seez/, caryopsides /-sideez/ a small 1-seeded dry INDEHISCENT (nonopening) fruit (e g of grasses) in which the PERICARP (structure surrounding the seed) clings so closely to the seed coat that the fruit and seed fuse in a single grain [NL, fr Gk karyon nut + opsis appearance]

**casa** /'kahsǝ/ n, SW US a dwelling [Sp & It, fr L, cabin]

**casaba, cassaba** /kǝ'sahbǝ/ n any of several WINTER MELONS with yellow rind and sweet flesh [Kasaba (now Turgutlu), town in Turkey]

**Casanova** /kasǝ'nohvǝ/ n a man who is a promiscuous and often unscrupulous lover [Giacomo Girolamo (or Giovanni Jacopo) Casanova †1798 It adventurer]

**casbah, kasbah** /'kaz,bah/ n, often cap the older Arab section of a N African city; also a market held there [Fr, fr Ar dial. qaṣbah]

¹**cascade** /kas'kayd/ n 1 a steep usu small fall of water; esp one of a series 2a something arranged in a series or in a succession of stages so that each stage derives from or acts upon the product of the preceding stage ⟨a ~ amplifier⟩; also such an arrangement b an arrangement of fabric (e g lace) that hangs in a zigzag line 3 something falling or rushing forth in profusion ⟨a ~ of sound⟩ ⟨a ~ of roses and daisies⟩ [Fr, fr It cascata, fr cascare to fall, fr (assumed) VL casicare, fr L casus, pp of cadere to fall]

²**cascade** vi to fall or pour (as if) in a cascade ~ vt 1 to cause to fall like a cascade 2 to connect in a cascade arrangement

**cascara** /ka'skahrǝ/ n 1 CASCARA BUCKTHORN 2 CASCARA SAGRADA [Sp cáscara bark, fr cascar to crack, break, fr (assumed) VL quassicare to shake, break, fr L quassare – more at QUASH]

**cascara buckthorn** n a buckthorn (Rhamnus purshiana) of the Pacific coast of the US

**cascara sagrada** n the dried bark of CASCARA BUCKTHORN, used as a mild laxative [AmerSp cáscara sagrada, lit., sacred bark]

¹**case** /kays/ n 1 a circumstance or condition; a situation: 1a what actually exists or happens; a fact ⟨that is not the ~⟩ b an instance that directs attention to a situation or exhibits it in action; an example ⟨that's a ~ of having your cake and eating it!⟩ ⟨the only ~ known to me ...⟩ c an instance of disease or injury; also a patient ⟨I see many ~s of meningitis on my rounds⟩ d condition; specif condition of body or mind e informal a peculiar person; a character ⟨she's a real ~ and no mistake!⟩ 2 the object of investigation or consideration: 2a a situation requiring investigation or action (e g by the police) ⟨do you remember the Wokingham ~?⟩; also a report concerning such a case b a suit or action that reaches a court of law ⟨the ~ of Jones v Regina⟩ c(1) the arguments supporting a conclusion or judgment ⟨the ~ for bringing back hanging⟩ c(2) an argument; esp a convincing argument ⟨do we have a ~?⟩ 3a an inflectional form of a noun, pronoun, or adjective indicating its grammatical relation to other words b such a relation whether indicated by inflection or not [ME cas, fr OF, fr L casus fall, chance, fr casus, pp of cadere to fall – more at CHANCE] – **in any case** without regard to, or in spite of, other considerations; whatever else is done or is the case ⟨hardship is inevitable in any case⟩ – **in case 1** as a precaution (against the event that) ⟨take a towel anyway just in case you want to swim⟩ 2 chiefly NAm if – **in case of 1** in the event of ⟨in case of trouble, yell⟩ 2 for fear of; as a precaution against ⟨posted sentries in case of attack⟩

*usage* The excessive use of *the* case is disliked by many careful writers, who prefer to replace ⟨*in the* case *of cigars sold singly, they were made smaller*⟩ by ⟨*cigars sold singly were made smaller*⟩ and ⟨*is it the* case *that pigs have wings?*⟩ by ⟨*do pigs have wings?*⟩

²**case** n 1 a box or receptacle for holding something: e g 1a chiefly Br a suitcase b a glass-panelled box for the display of specimens (e g in a museum) 2a a box together with its contents ⟨a ~ of champagne⟩ b a pair – used chiefly with reference to pistols 3a an outer covering or housing ⟨pastry ~⟩ b a stiff book cover that is made apart from the book and glued onto it 4 a shallow divided tray for holding printing type 5 the frame of a door or window; CASING 1a [ME cas, fr ONF casse, fr L capsa chest, case, fr capere to take – more at HEAVE]

³**case** vt 1 to enclose in or cover with a case; encase 2 to pack (tobacco) in bulk with sufficient moisture to allow conditioning 3 slang to inspect or study (e g a house), esp with intent to rob

**caseation** /,kaysi'aysh(ǝ)n/ n NECROSIS (death of tissue) with conversion of adjacent damaged tissue into a soft cheesy substance [L caseus cheese] – **caseate** vi

**casebearer** /'kays,beǝrǝ/ n an insect larva that forms a protective case (e g of silk)

**case-bearing clothes moth** n a moth (Tinea pellionella) the larva of which causes serious damage to fabrics

**casebook** /-,book/ n 1 a book containing records of illustrative cases that is used for reference and instruction (e g in law or medicine) 2 a compilation of primary and secondary documents relating to a certain topic (e g a work of literature) and designed for educational purposes

**cased** /kayst/ *adj, of a book* being a hardback

**case goods** *n pl* products (eg alcohol or tinned milk) often sold by the case

**'case-ˌharden** *vt* 1 to harden (an iron-based alloy) so that the surface layer is harder than the interior 2 to make callous – **case-hardened** *adj*

**case history** *n* a record of history, environment, and relevant details (eg of individual behaviour or condition), esp for use in analysis, illustration, or diagnosis

**casein** /'kaysi·in, -seen/ *n* 1 a PHOSPHOPROTEIN (type of protein) of milk: eg 1a one that is precipitated from milk by heating with an acid or by the action of LACTIC ACID in souring and is used in making paints and adhesives **b** one that is produced when milk is curdled by rennet, is the chief constituent of cheese, and is used also in making plastics 2 a technique of painting using casein [deriv of L *caseus* cheese]

**caseinogen** /kay'seenajin/ *n* the principal protein of milk, that is converted into insoluble casein by the action of RENNIN

**case in point** *n* a relevant example

**case knife** *n, chiefly NAm* a knife with a fixed blade; SHEATH KNIFE

**case law** *n* law established by previous judicial decision in particular cases rather than by legislation

**case load** *n* the number of cases handled in a particular period (eg by a court or clinic)

**casemate** /'kays,mayt/ *n* a fortified position or chamber or an armoured enclosure on a warship from which guns are fired through embrasures [MF, fr OIt *casamatta*]

**casement** /'kaysmənt/ *n* a window that opens on hinges at the side [ME, hollow moulding, prob fr ONF *encassement* frame, fr *encasser* to enshrine, frame, fr *en-* + *casse*]

**case of conscience** *n* a moral dilemma difficult for conscience to resolve unaided

**caseous** /'kaysi·əs/ *adj* marked by CASEATION; *also* CHEESY [L *caseus* cheese]

**case shot** *n* an artillery projectile consisting of a number of balls or metal fragments enclosed in a case

**case stated** *n* an agreed statement of the facts in a legal case, submitted to a higher court for a decision on a point of law

**case study** *n* 1 an intensive analysis of an individual unit (eg a person or community) that stresses interacting factors (eg developmental factors in relation to environment) and is often used to provide generalized information about a class of entities of which this unit is a member 2 CASE HISTORY

**casette** /kə'set/ *n* a cassette

**casework** /-ˌwuhk/ *n* social work involving direct consideration of the problems, needs, and adjustments of the individual case (eg a person or family) – **caseworker** *n*

**'cash** /kash/ *n* 1 ready money 2 money or its equivalent paid promptly at time of purchase [MF or OIt; MF *casse* money box, fr OIt *cassa*, fr L *capsa* chest – more at CASE]

**'cash** *vt* 1 to pay or obtain cash for ⟨~ *a cheque*⟩ 2 to lead and win a bridge trick with (a card that is the highest remaining card of its suit) ⟨*he drew all the trumps and was then able to ~ the last spade*⟩ – **cashable** *adj*

**cash in** *vt* to convert into cash ⟨cashed in *all his bonds*⟩ ~ *vi* 1a to retire from a gambling game **b** to settle accounts and withdraw from an involvement (eg a business deal) 2 to obtain an advantage or financial profit – usu + *on* ⟨cashing in *on the success of recent peace initiatives*⟩

**'cash** *n, pl* **cash** 1 any of various coins of small value in China and India; *esp* a Chinese coin usu of copper alloy with a square hole in the centre 2 a monetary unit equivalent to one cash [Pg *caixa*, fr Tamil *kācu*, a small copper coin, fr Skt *karsa*, a weight of gold or silver]

**'cash-and-ˈcarry** *adj or adv* sold or provided for cash and usu without a delivery service ⟨*we bought it ~*⟩

**'cash-and-carry** *n* a shop selling goods on a cash-and-carry basis; *esp* a shop selling goods in bulk to the retail trade

**cashbook** /'kash,book/ *n* a book in which a record is kept of all money received and paid out

**cash card** *n* a card that is issued by a bank and allows the holder to operate a cash-dispensing machine – compare CHEQUE CARD, CREDIT CARD

**cash crop** *n* a readily salable crop (eg cotton, tobacco, or sugar beet) produced or gathered primarily for market rather than for consumption by the farmer

**cash desk** *n* a desk where money is received from customers, esp in a supermarket

**cash discount** *n* a discount granted in consideration of immediate payment or payment within a prescribed time

**cashew** /'kashooh, kə'shooh, ka'shooh/ *n* a tropical American tree (*Anacardium occidentale*) of the sumach family, grown for its edible kidney-shaped nut and the gum it yields; *also* the nut of the cashew △ cachou [Pg *acajú, cajú*, fr Tupi *acajú*]

**cash flow** *n* the aggregate of net income after taxation but before dividend distribution; *esp* the total money left available for investment after deductions for salaries, raw-material costs, and financial charges are made

**'cashier** /ka'shiə/ *vt* to dismiss from (military) service; *esp* to dismiss dishonourably [D *casseren*, fr MF *casser* to discharge, annul – more at QUASH]

**'cashier** *n* one who has charge of money: eg **a** a high officer in a bank or company, responsible for moneys received and expended ⟨*chief ~ of the Bank of England*⟩ **b** one who is employed to receive cash from customers, esp in a shop **c** *Br* a bank employee who receives and pays out money over the counter [D or MF; D *kassier*, fr MF *cassier*, fr *casse* money box] – **cashiering** *n*

**cashmere** /'kashmiə, -'-/ *n* 1 (a yarn of) fine wool from the undercoat of the Kashmir goat 2 a soft fabric made originally from cashmere [*Cashmere* (Kashmir), region of the Indian subcontinent]

**cash register** *n* a business machine that usu has a money drawer, indicates the amount of each sale, totals receipts, records the amount of money received, and often automatically gives change

**casing** /'kaysing/ *n* 1 something that encases; material for encasing: eg 1a an enclosing frame, esp round a door or window opening **b** a metal pipe used to case a well **c** a membranous case for processed meat, esp a sausage 2 a space formed between two parallel lines of stitching through at least two layers of cloth into which something (eg a rod or tape) may be inserted

**casino** /kə'seenoh/ *n, pl* **casinos** 1 a building or room used for gambling 2 CASSINO (card game) [It, fr *casa* house, fr L, cabin]

**'cask** /kahsk/ *n* 1 a wooden barrel-shaped vessel of staves, heads, and hoops, esp for alcoholic liquids; *broadly* a barrel 2 a cask and its contents; *also* the quantity contained in a cask [MF *casque* helmet, fr Sp *casco* potsherd, skull, helmet, fr *cascar* to break – more at CASCARA]

**'cask** *adj, Br* drawn from a traditional wooden cask (by hand) ⟨~ *beer knocks spots off keg!*⟩

**casket** /'kahskit/ *n* 1 a small chest or box (eg for jewels) 2 *NAm* a rectangular and usu fancy coffin [ME, modif of MF *cassette*] – **casket** *vt*

**casque** /kask/ *n* 1 a helmet 2 an anatomical structure suggestive of a helmet [MF – more at CASK]

**cassaba** /kə'sahbə/ *n* CASABA (type of melon)

**Cassandra** /kə'sahndrə, -'san-/ *n* one who predicts misfortune or disaster; *esp* one whose warnings are fated to be ignored [L, fr Gk *Kassandra*, daughter of King Priam of Troy in Gk legend]

**cassareep** /'kasəreep/ *n* the thickened and spiced juice of the rootstock of a bitter variety of cassava (*Manihot utilissima*) used esp in W Indian cookery as a condiment [alter. of earlier *casserepo*, of Cariban origin; akin to Galibi *kaseripu*]

**cassava** /kə'sahvə/ *n* any of several plants (genus *Manihot*) of the spurge family grown in the tropics for their fleshy edible rootstocks which yield a nutritious starch; *also* the rootstock of cassava [Sp *cazabe* cassava bread, fr Taino *caçábi*]

**Cassegrainian telescope** /ˌkasi'graynyən/, **Cassegrain telescope** /'kasigrayn/ *n* a REFLECTING TELESCOPE in which light that has been reflected from a secondary mirror passes through a perforation in the primary mirror to the eyepiece [N *Cassegrain* fl 1672 Fr physicist]

**casserole** /'kasərohl/ *n* 1 a heatproof dish (eg of stoneware or Pyrex) that usu has a cover and in which food may be baked slowly and served 2 the savoury food cooked and served in a casserole [Fr, saucepan, fr MF, irreg fr *casse* ladle, dripping pan, deriv of Gk *kyathos* ladle] – **casserole** *vt*

**cassette, casette** /kə'set/ *n* 1 a lightproof supply chamber for holding film for use in a camera 2 a small plastic container of MAGNETIC TAPE arranged on two spools so as not to need manual threading [Fr, *cassette* casket, fr MF, dim. of ONF *casse* case]

**cassia** /'kasi·ə/ *n* 1 a coarse cinnamon bark (eg from *Cinnamomum cassia*) 2 SENNA 1 (plant of warm regions) [ME, fr OE, fr L, fr Gk *kassia*, of Sem origin; akin to Heb *qĕṣī'āh* cassia]

**cassino, casino** /kə'seenoh/ *n* a card game in which each player wins cards by matching or combining cards in his/her hand with those exposed on the table [*casino*]

**cassis** /'kasees/ *n* a liqueur made from blackcurrants and used esp as a flavouring (e g in white wine) [Fr *cassis* blackcurrant, fr L *cassia*]

**cassiterite** /kə'sitəriet/ *n* a brown or black mineral that is a naturally occurring form of tin dioxide, $SnO_2$, and is the chief source of tin [Fr *cassitérite*, fr Gk *kassiteros* tin]

**cassock** /'kasək/ *n* an ankle-length garment with sleeves that is fastened the full length of the centre front, and is worn esp by the Roman Catholic and Anglican clergy and by laymen assisting in services [MF *casaque*, prob fr Per *kazhāghand* padded jacket, fr *kazh* raw silk + *āghand* stuffed]

**cassone** /ka'sohni/ *n, pl* **cassoni** /~/ a large usu carved or painted chest esp of the Italian Renaissance, originally made to hold the costume of a bride [It, aug of *cassa* box – more at CASH]

**cassoulet** /'kasə,lay/ *n* a stew of haricot beans and various meats (e g goose, duck, and pork) [Fr, fr Fr dial., lit., stone dish, deriv of Gk *kyathos* ladle]

**cassowary** /'kasə,weəri/ *n* any of several large flightless birds (genus *Casuarius*) found esp in New Guinea and Australia and closely related to the emu [Malay *kĕsuari*]

**¹cast** /kahst/ *vb* **cast** *vt* **1a** to cause to move by throwing ⟨~ *a fishing lure*⟩ **b** to direct ⟨~ *a glance*⟩ ⟨~ *one's mind back to last year*⟩ **c** to put forth ⟨*the fire* ~s *a warm glow*⟩ **d** to place as if by throwing ⟨~ *doubt on their reliability*⟩ **e** to deposit (a vote) formally ⟨*the total of votes* ~⟩ **f(1)** to throw off or away ⟨*the horse* ~ *a shoe*⟩ **f(2)** to get rid of; discard ⟨~ *off all restraint*⟩ ⟨*she* ~ *him aside like an old shoe*⟩ **f(3)** to shed, moult **g** *of animals* to bring forth; *esp* to give birth to prematurely **2a** to perform arithmetical operations on; add – no longer used technically **b** to calculate (e g a horoscope) by astrology **3a** to dispose or arrange into parts or into a suitable form or order **b(1)** to assign the parts of (a dramatic production) to performers **b(2)** to assign (a performer) to a role or part **4** to form or give a shape to (a substance) by pouring in liquid or plastic form into a mould and letting harden without pressure ⟨~ *steel*⟩ ⟨~ *machine parts*⟩ ~ *vi* **1** to throw something; *specif* to throw out a lure with a fishing rod **2** *of timber* to warp **3** *of a boat* to veer **4** to take form in a mould **5** to look, seek – + *about* or *around* ⟨*he* ~s *around uncertainly for somewhere to sit*⟩ – see also cast ANCHOR/LOTS/**to the** WINDS **synonyms** see ¹THROW [ME *casten*, fr ON *kasta*; akin to ON *kös* heap]

**cast away** *vt* to shipwreck; *also* to maroon – see also CASTAWAY

**cast down** *vt* **1** to throw down **2** to depress – see also DOWNCAST

**cast off** *vt* **1** to loose ⟨cast off *a hunting dog*⟩ **2** to unfasten (a boat) **3** to remove (a stitch or stitches) from a knitting needle in such a way as to prevent unravelling of the knitted work **4** to calculate the amount of space to be taken in print by (manuscript copy) ~ *vi* **1** to untie a mooring-line or anchor; *also, of a boat* to cast off moorings **2** to turn one's partner in a square dance and pass round the outside of the set and back **3** to finish knitted work by casting off all stitches – see also CAST OFF

**cast on** *vb* to place (stitches, esp the first row of stitches) on a knitting needle; *broadly* to begin (knitting) thus

**cast out** *vt* to drive out; expel ⟨cast out *devils*⟩

**²cast** *n* **1a** an act of casting **b** a throw of dice **c** a throw of a line (e g a fishing line) or net **2** the form in which a thing is constructed **3** *taking sing or pl vb* the set of performers in a dramatic production **4** the distance to which a thing can be thrown **5a** a turning of the eye in a particular direction **b** a slight squint in the eye **6** something that is cast or the amount cast: e g **6a** the number of hawks released by a falconer at one time **b** *Br* the leader of a fishing line **c** the quantity of metal cast at a single operation **7a** something that is formed by casting in a mould or form: e g **7a(1)** a reproduction (e g of a statue) in metal or plaster; a casting **a(2)** a fossil reproduction of the details of a natural object by mineral infiltration of a mould of the object (e g in a rock) **b** an impression taken from an object with a molten or plastic substance; a mould **c** PLASTER CAST **2 8a** an overspread of a colour or modification of the appearance of a substance by a trace of some added hue; a shade ⟨grey *with a greenish* ~⟩ **b** a tinge, suggestion **9** a ride on one's way in a vehicle; a lift **10a** shape, appearance ⟨*the delicate* ~ *of her features*⟩ **b** characteristic quality ⟨*modern science was in conflict with the humanist* ~ *of mind* – T F O'Dea⟩ **11** something that is shed, ejected, or thrown out or off: e g **11a** the excrement of an earthworm **b** a mass of soft matter formed in cavities of diseased organs and discharged from the body **c** the skin of an insect △ **caste**

**³cast** *adj, of an animal, esp a horse* unable to rise from the ground [fr pp of ¹cast]

**Castalian** /ka'staylyən/ *adj, of poetry* of or inspired (by the Muses) [*Castalia*, spring on Mount Parnassus sacred to the Muses]

**castanets** /,kastə'nets/ *n pl* a pair of small shells of ivory, hard wood, or plastic fastened to the thumb and clicked together by the other fingers and used esp by dancers as a rhythm instrument; *also, sing* either of these castanets [Sp *castaneta*, fr *castana* chestnut, fr L *castanea* – more at CHESTNUT]

**castaway** /'kahstə,way/ *n* a person who is left adrift or ashore as a result of a shipwreck or as a punishment; *broadly* a person rejected – **castaway** *adj*

**caste** /kahst/ *n* **1** *taking sing or pl vb* any of the hereditary social groups in Hinduism that restrict the occupation of their members and their association with the members of other castes **2a** a division of society based on differences of wealth, inherited rank or privilege, profession, or occupation **b** the position conferred by caste standing; prestige **3** a system of rigid social stratification characterized by hereditary status, marriage within one's group (ENDOGAMY), and social barriers sanctioned by custom, law, or religion **4** a specialized form (e g the soldier or worker among ants) of a social insect, adapted to carry out a particular function in the colony △ **cast** [Pg *casta*, lit., race, lineage, fr fem of *casto* pure, chaste, fr L *castus*; akin to L *carēre* to be without, Gk *keazein* to split, Skt *śasati* he cuts to pieces] – **casteism** *n*

**castellan** /'kastilən/ *n* a governor or warden of a castle or fort [ME *castelleyn*, fr ONF *castelain*, fr L *castellanus* occupant of a castle, fr *castellanus* of a castle, fr *castellum* castle]

**castellanus** /,kastə'lahnəs/ *adj, of a cloud* characterized by rounded projections like CUMULUS from the upper surface ⟨*nimbostratus* ~⟩ [L *castellanus* of or resembling a castle]

**castellated** /'kasti,laytid/ *adj* having battlements like a castle [ML *castellatus*, pp of *castellare* to fortify, fr L *castellum*]

**caster** /'kahstə/ *n* **1** one who or that which casts; *esp* a machine that casts type **2** **castor, caster 2a** a container with a perforated top for sifting, sprinkling, or dispensing powdered or granulated foods, esp sugar – compare SHAKER, SIFTER **b** any of a set of wheels in swivel frames mounted under something (e g a piece of furniture) to make it easier to move

**caster sugar, castor sugar** *n* finely granulated white sugar

**castigate** /'kastigayt/ *vt* to subject to severe punishment, reproof, or criticism **synonyms** see PUNISH [L *castigatus*, pp of *castigare* – more at CHASTEN] – **castigator** *n*, **castigation** *n*

**castile soap** /ka'steel/ *n, often cap C* a fine hard mild soap made from olive oil and SODIUM HYDROXIDE; *also* any of various similar soaps [*Castile*, region of Spain]

**Castilian** /ka'stilyən/ *n* **1** a native or inhabitant of Castile **2a** the dialect of Castile **b** the official and literary language of Spain based on this dialect – **Castilian** *adj*

**casting** /'kahsting/ *n* **1** the act of one who casts: e g **1a** the throwing of a fishing line by means of a rod and reel **b** the assignment of parts of a dramatic production to performers **2** something cast in a mould **3** something cast out or off (e g by an earthworm)

**casting vote** *n* a vote cast by a presiding officer to break a tie

**cast-'iron** *adj* **1** made of cast iron **2** resembling cast iron: e g **2a** capable of withstanding great strain **b** not admitting change, adaptation, or exception; rigid ⟨*a man of* ~ *will*⟩

**cast iron** *n* a hard brittle alloy of iron, carbon, and silicon that is shaped by being poured into a mould and allowed to harden

**¹castle** /'kahsl/ *n* **1a** a large fortified building or set of buildings **b** a large or imposing mansion **2** a stronghold, retreat **3** ³ROOK (piece in chess) [ME *castel*, fr OE, fr ONF, fr L *castellum* fortress, castle, dim. of *castrum* fortified place]

**²castle** *vt* to move (the chess king) in castling ~ *vi* to move a chess king two squares towards a rook and, in the same move, the rook to the next square beyond the king (ie the square passed over by the king in moving to its new position)

**castle in Spain** *n* CASTLE IN THE AIR

**castle in the air** *n* an impracticable project; a daydream

**¹cast-'off** *adj* given up or discarded, esp as outgrown or no longer wanted ⟨~ *clothes*⟩ ⟨*a* ~ *lover*⟩

²'**cast-,off** *n* **1** one who or that which has been given up or discarded; *esp* a garment that has been discarded and passed on to another ⟨*I don't want your old* ~s⟩ **2** an estimate of the space that will be required (eg in a book or newspaper) for a given amount of copy

¹**castor** /'kahstə/ *n* a bitter strong-smelling creamy orange-brown substance consisting of the dried PERINEAL glands of the beaver and their secretion and used esp by perfumers [ME, beaver, fr L, fr Gk *kastōr*, fr *Kastōr* Castor]

²**castor** /'kahstə/ *n* CASTER 2

**Castor** *n* one of the Dioscuri [L, fr Gk *Kastōr*]

**castor oil** *n* a pale viscous fatty oil from the seed of the castor-oil plant, used esp as a laxative [prob fr its former use as a substitute for castor in medicine]

**castor-oil plant** *n* a tropical plant (*Ricinus communis*) of the spurge family widely grown for its oil-rich beans

**castor sugar** *n* CASTER SUGAR

**castrate** /ka'strayt/ *vt* **1a** to deprive of the testes; geld **b** to deprive of the ovaries; spay **2** to deprive of vitality or effect; emasculate [L *castratus*, pp of *castrare*; akin to Skt *śasati* he cuts to pieces – more at CASTE] – **castrate** *n*, **castrater** *n*, **castration** *n*, **castratory** *adj*

**castrato** /ka'strahtoh/ *n, pl* **castrati** /-ti/ a singer castrated in boyhood to preserve the soprano or contralto range of his voice [It, fr pp of *castrare* to castrate, fr L]

**Castroism** /'kastroh,iz(ə)m/ *n* the political, economic, and social principles and policies of Fidel Castro [Fidel *Castro* b1927 Cuban premier] – **Castroite** *n*

¹**casual** /'kazh(y)ooəl, kazyooəl/ *adj* **1** subject to, resulting from, or occurring by chance **2** occurring without regularity; occasional **3** employed for irregular periods **4a** feeling or showing little concern; nonchalant **b(1)** informal, natural **b(2)** designed for informal use or wear *synonyms* see FORTUITOUS *antonym* deliberate [ME, fr MF & LL; MF *casuel*, fr LL *casualis*, fr L *casus* fall, chance – more at CASE] – **casually** *adv*, **casualness** *n*

²**casual** *n* **1** a casual or migratory worker **2** *pl* informal clothes or shoes

**casualty** /'kazh(y)ooəlti, -zyooəl-/ *n* **1** a serious or fatal accident; a disaster **2a** a military person lost (eg through death, sickness, or capture) in warfare **b** a person or thing injured, lost, or destroyed ⟨*small firms will be the first* casualties *of these policies*⟩ [ME *casuelte* chance, mischance, loss, fr ML *casualitas*, fr LL *casualis*]

**casuarina** /,kasyooə'rienə/ *n* any of a genus (*Casuarina* of the family Casuarinaceae) of chiefly Australian trees which yield a heavy hard wood [NL, genus name, fr Malay (*pohon*) *kěsuari*, lit., cassowary tree; fr the resemblance of its twigs to cassowary feathers]

**casuist** /'kazh(y)ooist, 'kazyooist/ *n* a person skilled in or given to casuistry [Fr *casuiste* or Sp *casuista*, fr L *casus* fall, chance – more at CASE] – **casuistic, casuistical** *adj*

**casuistry** /'kazh(y)oo,istri, 'kazyooistri/ *n* **1** a method or doctrine dealing with cases of conscience and the resolution of conflicting moral obligations **2** the false application of general principles to particular instances, esp with regard to morals or law ⟨*no* ~ *will convince us that this serious loss is really a victory*⟩

**casus belli** /,kahsoos 'beli/ *n, pl* **casus belli** /~/ an event or action that brings about a war or conflict [NL, occasion of war]

¹**cat** /kat/ *n* **1a** a flesh-eating mammal (*Felis catus*) long domesticated and kept by man as a pet or for catching rats and mice **b** any of a family (Felidae) of flesh-eating mammals including the domestic cat, lion, tiger, leopard, jaguar, cougar, lynx, and cheetah **2** a malicious woman **3** a strong tackle used to hoist an anchor to the CATHEAD (projection near the bow) of a ship **4** a cat-o'-nine-tails **5** *slang* **5a** a player or devotee of jazz **b** a person; *esp* a fellow [ME, fr OE *catt*; akin to OHG *kazza* cat; both fr a prehistoric NGmc-WGmc word prob borrowed fr LL *cattus, catta* cat]

²**cat** *vt* **-tt-** **1** to bring (an anchor) up to the CATHEAD **2** to flog with a cat-o'-nine-tails

³**cat** *n, informal* CATAMARAN 2

**cata-, cat-, cath-** *prefix* **1** down ⟨*catapult*⟩ ⟨*catarrh*⟩ **2** wrong ⟨*catachresis*⟩ [Gk *kata-, kat-, kath-*, fr *kata* down, in accordance with, by; akin to L *com-* with – more at CO-]

**catabolism** /kə'tabəliz(ə)m/ *n* destructive METABOLISM (life-supporting chemical reactions) involving the release of energy and resulting in the breakdown of complex materials (eg glucose) within the organism – compare ANABOLISM [Gk *katabolē* throwing down, fr *kataballein* to throw down, fr *kata-* + *ballein* to throw – more at DEVIL] – **catabolic** *adj*, **catabolically** *adv*

**catabolite** /kə'tabəliet/ *n* a substance (eg nectar or a waste product) produced in catabolism

**catabol·ize, -ise** /kə'tabəliez/ *vt* to subject to catabolism ~ *vi* to undergo catabolism

**catachresis** /,katə'kreesis/ *n, pl* **catachreses** /-seez/ **1** use of the wrong word for the context **2** use of a forced, esp a paradoxical, figure of speech (eg in "*change bulls in mid china shop*") [L, fr Gk *katachrēsis* misuse, fr *katachrēsthai* to use up, misuse, fr *kata-* + *chrēsthai* to use] – **catachrestic, catachrestical** *adj*, **catachrestically** *adv*

**cataclysm** /'katə,kliz(ə)m/ *n* **1** a flood, deluge **2** a violent geological change of the earth's surface **3** a momentous event marked by violent upheaval and destruction *synonyms* see CATASTROPHE [Fr *cataclysme*, fr L *cataclysmos*, fr Gk *kataklysmos*, fr *kataklyzein* to flood, fr *kata-* + *klyzein* to wash] – **cataclysmal, cataclysmic** *adj*

**catacomb** /'katə,koohm; -,kohm/ *n taking sing or pl vb*, **catacombs** *n pl* **1** a galleried subterranean cemetery with recesses for tombs ⟨*the early Christian* Catacombs *in Rome*⟩ **2** something resembling a catacomb: eg **2a** an underground passageway or group of passageways; an underground labyrinth **b** a tangled set of interrelated things △ hecatomb [MF *catacombe*, prob fr OIt *catacomba*, fr LL *catacumbae*, pl] – **catacombic** *adj*

**catadromous** /kə'tadrəməs/ *adj* living in fresh water and going to the sea to spawn ⟨~ *eels*⟩ – compare ANADROMOUS [*cata-* + *-dromous*]

**catafalque** /'katə,falk/ *n* **1** an ornamental structure sometimes used in funerals for the lying in state of the body **2** a coffin-shaped structure covered with a pall and used at requiem masses celebrated after burial △ catacomb, cenotaph [It *catafalco*, fr (assumed) VL *catafalicum* scaffold, fr *cata-* + L *fala* siege tower]

**Catalan** /'katə,lan, -lən/ *n* **1** a native or inhabitant of Catalonia **2** the Romance language of Catalonia, Valencia, and the Balearic islands [Sp *Catalán*, fr *Cataluna* Catalonia, region in NE Spain] – **Catalan** *adj*

**catalase** /'katə,layz/ *n* a red ENZYME that catalyses the decomposition of HYDROGEN PEROXIDE into water and oxygen [*catalysis*] – **catalatic** *adj*

**catalectic** /,katə'lektik/ *adj* lacking a syllable at the end or ending in an imperfect metrical unit (FOOT) [LL *catalecticus*, fr Gk *katalēktikos*, fr *katalēgein* to leave off, fr *kata-* + *lēgein* to stop – more at SLACK] – **catalectic** *n*

**catalepsy** /'katə,lepsi/ *n* a condition of loss of voluntary movement in which the limbs remain in whatever position they are placed [ME *catalempsi*, fr ML *catalepsia*, fr LL *catalepsis*, fr Gk *katalēpsis*, lit., act of seizing, fr *katalambanein* to seize, fr *kata-* + *lambanein* to take – more at LATCH] – **cataleptic** *adj or n*, **cataleptically** *adv*

**catalo** /'katəloh/ *n, pl* **cataloes, catalos** CATTALO (hybrid of buffalo and cattle)

¹**catalogue, NAm chiefly catalog** /'katəlog/ *n* **1** a list, register **2** (a pamphlet or book containing) a complete enumeration of items arranged systematically with descriptive details [ME *cateloge*, fr MF *catalogue*, fr LL *catalogus*, fr Gk *katalogos*, fr *katalegein* to list, fr *kata-* + *legein* to gather, speak – more at LEGEND]

²**catalogue, NAm chiefly catalog** *vt* **1** to make a catalogue of; *broadly* to list **2** to enter in a catalogue; *esp* to classify (books or information) descriptively ~ *vi* **1** to make or work on a catalogue **2** to be listed in a catalogue at a specified price ⟨*this stamp* ~s *at two pounds*⟩

**catalogue raisonné** /,katəlog ,rezo'nay (Fr katalɔg REZɔne)/ *n, pl* **catalogues raisonnés** /~/ a systematic descriptive catalogue (eg of paintings or books) [Fr, lit., reasoned catalogue]

**catalpa** /kə'talpə/ *n* any of a genus (*Catalpa*) of American and Asian trees of the jacaranda family with heart-shaped leaves and pale showy flowers [Creek *kutuhlpa*, lit., head with wings]

**catalyse, NAm catalyze** /'katəliez/ *vt* **1** to bring about the catalysis of (a chemical reaction) **2** to inspire; BRING ABOUT

**catalysis** /kə'taləsis/ *n, pl* **catalyses** /-seez/ **1** a modification, esp an increase in the rate of a chemical reaction that is induced by a catalyst **2** a stimulus, trigger [Gk *katalysis* dissolution, fr *katalyein* to dissolve, fr *kata-* cata- + *lyein* to dissolve, release – more at LOSE]

**catalyst** /'katəlist/ n 1 someone or something whose relatively limited action inspires a much wider-ranging series of events 2 a substance (eg an ENZYME) that modifies, esp increases, the rate of a chemical reaction and enables it to proceed under milder conditions (eg at a lower temperature) than otherwise possible but itself remains chemically unchanged at the end of the reaction [fr *catalysis*, by analogy to *analysis : analyst*]

**catalytic** /,katə'litik/ *adj* causing, involving, or relating to catalysis ⟨*a ~ reaction*⟩ ⟨*a ~ personality*⟩ – **catalytically** *adv*

**catalytic cracker** n the unit in a petroleum refinery in which CRACKING (breakdown of crude petroleum into petrol, diesel oil, etc) is carried out in the presence of a catalyst

**catamaran** /'katəmə,ran, -rahn, ,---'-/ n 1 a traditional raft consisting of logs or pieces of wood lashed together and propelled by paddles or sails 2 a modern sailing boat with twin hulls or planing surfaces side by side [Tamil *kaṭṭumaram*, fr *kaṭṭu* to tie + *maram* tree]

**catamite** /'katə,miet/ n a boy kept by a pederast [L *catamitus*, fr *Catamitus* Ganymede, fr Etruscan *Catmite*, fr Gk *Ganymēdēs*]

**catamount** /'katə,mownt/ n any of various wild cats: eg a the puma b the lynx [short for *cat-a-mountain*]

**cat-a-,mountain** n any of various wild cats: eg a the European wildcat b the leopard [ME *cat of the mountaine*]

**,cat-and-'mouse** *adj* consisting of watchful waiting for the best opportunity to attack ⟨*the ~ technique of handling an opponent*⟩

**cataphora** /kə'tafərə/ n the use of a grammatical form to refer to a following word or group of words (eg *the* in "*the* house with red shutters") [Gk *kataphora* carrying down, conveyance, fr *kataphorein* to carry down, fr *kata-* cata- + *pherein* to carry – more at BEAR] – **cataphoric** *adj*

**cataphoresis** /,katəfə'reesis/ n, pl **cataphoreses** /-seez/ ELECTROPHORESIS – not now used technically [NL] – **cataphoretic** *adj*, **cataphoretically** *adv*

**cataplexy** /'katə,pleksi/ n sudden temporary paralysis in animals and humans following a strong emotional stimulus (eg shock or fright) [Ger *kataplexie*, fr Gk *kataplēxis*, fr *kataplēssein* to strike down, terrify, fr *kata-* + *plēssein* to strike – more at PLAINT]

**¹catapult** /'katəpoolt, -pult/ n 1 an ancient military device for hurling missiles 2 a device for launching an aeroplane at flying speed (eg from an aircraft carrier) 3 *Br* a Y-shaped wooden stick or metal bar with elastic attached for firing small objects (eg stones) [MF or L; MF *catapulte*, fr L *catapulta*, fr Gk *katapaltēs*, fr *kata-* + *pallein* to hurl – more at POLEMIC]

**²catapult** *vt* to throw or launch (as if) by a catapult ~ *vi* to become catapulted

**cataract** /'katərakt/ n 1 a clouding of the lens of the eye or of its enclosing membrane, obstructing the passage of light 2a a waterfall; *esp* a large one over a precipice b steep rapids in a river c a downpour, flood [L *cataracta* waterfall, portcullis, fr Gk *kataraktēs*, fr *katarassein* to dash down, fr *kata-* + *arassein* to strike, dash; (1) ML *cataracta*, fr L, portcullis] – **cataractal**, **cataracted** *adj*

**catarrh** /kə'tah/ n inflammation of a MUCOUS MEMBRANE; *esp* one chronically affecting the human nose and air passages [MF or LL; MF *catarrhe*, fr LL *catarrhus*, fr Gk *katarrhous*, fr *katarrhein* to flow down, fr *kata-* + *rhein* to flow – more at STREAM] – **catarrhal** *adj*, **catarrhally** *adv*

**catarrhine** /'katərien/ *adj* of or being any of a division (Catarrhina) of primates that includes the Old World monkeys (eg the baboons), apes, and man and is characterized by having nostrils close together and directed downwards and 32 teeth – compare PLATYRRHINE [Gk *katarrhin* having a hooked nose, fr *kata-* cata- + *rhin-*, *rhis* nose]

**catastrophe** /kə'tastrəfi/ n 1 the final events of a play, esp of a tragedy; the denouement – compare EPITASIS, PROTASIS 2 a momentous and tragic event of extreme severity 3 a violent and sudden change in a feature of the earth [Gk *katastrophē*, fr *katastrephein* to overturn, fr *kata-* + *strephein* to turn – more at STROPHE] – **catastrophic** *adj*, **catastrophically** *adv*

**synonyms** **Catastrophe** and **cataclysm** both mean "momentous destructive event". **Catastrophe** stresses the idea of disaster, and **cataclysm** that of violent upheaval.

**catastrophism** /kə'tastrəfiz(ə)m/ n the theory that geological changes (eg in the earth's crust) have occurred in response to sudden violent stimuli, rather than by gradual processes – **catastrophist** n

**catatonia** /,katə'tohnyə, -ni-ə/ n 1 CATALEPSY (loss of voluntary movement) 2 a psychological disorder, esp schizophrenia, marked by catalepsy [NL, fr Ger *katatonie*, fr *kata-* cata- + NL *tonus*] – **catatonic** *adj or n*

**Catawba** /kə'tawbə/ n 1 a member of an American Indian people of N and S Carolina 2 the Siouan language of the Catawba people 3 (a dry white wine produced from) a native N American grape

**catbird** /'kat,buhd/ n a dark grey American songbird (*Dumetella carolinensis*) with a black cap and reddish feathers under the tail [fr one of its calls sounding like that of a cat]

**catboat** /-,boht/ n a sailing boat with one mast close to the bows and a single sail [perh fr *cat*, a former type of cargo ship]

**cat burglar** n, *Br* a burglar who enters buildings by skilful or daring feats of climbing

**catcall** /-,kawl/ n a loud or raucous cry made (eg at the theatre) to express disapproval – **catcall** *vb*

**¹catch** /kach/ *vb* **caught** /kawt/ *vt* **1a** to capture or seize, esp after pursuit **b** to take or entangle in or as if in a snare **c** to deceive ⟨*these clever forgeries have* caught *many people*⟩ **d** to discover unexpectedly; find ⟨caught *in the act*⟩ **e** to become suddenly aware of ⟨*I* caught *myself swearing*⟩ **f** to get entangled ⟨*~ a sleeve on a nail*⟩ **2a(1)** to take hold of; snatch; *esp* to receive and hold (a moving object) in the hands ⟨*~ the ball*⟩ ⟨caught *the bullet between his teeth*⟩ **a(2)** to dismiss (a batsman in cricket) by taking and holding the ball in esp the hands after it has been hit and before it has touched the ground – often + *out* **b** to affect suddenly ⟨*the idea* caught *his imagination immediately*⟩ **c** to intercept ⟨*they* caught *it just in time to prevent a major outbreak*⟩ **d** to avail oneself of; take ⟨*I try and ~ what sleep I can*⟩ **e** to obtain through effort; get **3** to become affected by ⟨*the grease* caught *fire*⟩: eg **3a** to contract ⟨*~ a cold*⟩ **b** to respond sympathetically to the point of being imbued with ⟨*~ the spirit of an occasion*⟩ **c** to be struck by **4a** to take in and retain ⟨*a barrel to ~ rainwater*⟩ **b** to fasten **5** to take or get momentarily or quickly ⟨*~ a glimpse of a friend*⟩ ⟨*~ sight of her*⟩ **6** to be in time for ⟨*~ the bus*⟩ ⟨*~ the last post*⟩ **7a** to grasp by the senses or the mind; apprehend ⟨*what was that? I didn't quite ~ it*⟩ **b** to capture a likeness of ⟨*the new portrait ~es her perfectly*⟩ ~ *vi* **1** to become caught; stick ⟨*the sugar* caught *on the bottom of the pan*⟩ **2a** *of a crop* to sprout and become established **b** *of a fire* to catch alight and become established **3** to play the position of catcher on a baseball team [ME *cacchen*, fr ONF *cachier* to hunt, fr (assumed) VL *captiare*, alter. of L *captare* to chase, fr *captus*, pp of *capere* to take – more at HEAVE] – **catchable** *adj* – **catch it** *informal* to incur blame, reprimand, or punishment – see also **catch one's** BREATH/a CRAB/FIRE/**somebody on the** HOP/**the** SUN, **be caught** SHORT

**synonyms** **Catch** in the sense of "taking" or "seizing" may be replaced by **capture** to express overcoming greater opposition or difficulty, or a more complete and final success ⟨*they finally* captured *the castle*⟩ ⟨*what artist can* capture *the charm of a child?*⟩ **Trap**, **entrap**, **snare**, **ensnare**, and **bag** are all terms from hunting. **Trap** and **snare** may be either literal or figurative, and suggest some kind of device that either, for **trap**, holds what is caught at one's mercy, or, for **snare**, suggests that struggles to escape only bind what is caught more tightly. **Entrap** and **ensnare** express these ideas figuratively, and all four suggest craft and trickery in the hunter, and lack of caution in the hunted. **Bag** has evolved from its original idea of catching and putting in a bag, to successfully hunting and killing or capturing ⟨bagged *fifty pheasants each*⟩ ⟨bagged *the film rights to her new novel*⟩. **antonym** miss

**catch at** *vt* to grasp or try to grasp hastily

**catch on** *vi* **1** to become popular ⟨*the kind of zany comedy that has already* caught on *in Britain*⟩ **2** *informal* to understand, learn – often + *to*

**catch out** *vt* to expose or detect in a mistake or instance of wrongdoing

**catch up** *vt* **1a** to pick up often abruptly ⟨*he* caught *his coat up and was gone*⟩ **b** to ensnare, entangle ⟨*wasn't he* caught up *with the Chelsea gang?*⟩ **c** to enthrall – usu + *in*; usu pass ⟨*the audience were obviously* caught up *in the play*⟩ **2** to travel fast enough to overtake ⟨*I'll* catch *you* up *at the crossroads*⟩ ~ *vi* **1** to travel fast enough to overtake an advance party – often + *with* **2** to complete or become informed about something belatedly – + *on* or *with* ⟨catch up *on the bookkeeping*⟩ ⟨catch up *with the news*⟩ – see also CATCH-UP

**catch up with** *vt* ARREST 2

**²catch** n **1** something caught; *esp* the total quantity caught at one time ⟨*a large* ~ *of fish*⟩ **2a** the act or action of catching ⟨*the batsman was finally dismissed after three dropped* ~es⟩ **b** a game in which a ball is thrown and caught **3** something that checks or fastens **4** a round for three or more unaccompanied voices written out as one continuous melody; *specif* such a round that is of a ludicrous or coarse nature **5** a fragment, snatch **6** a concealed difficulty ⟨*there must be a* ~ *to it somewhere*⟩ **7** the germination of a field crop to such an extent that replanting is unnecessary **8** *informal* one worth catching, esp as a spouse

¹**catchall** /'kach,awl/ *n* something to hold various odds and ends or cater for a variety of contingencies

²**catchall** *adj* designed to cover all situations; indiscriminately all-embracing

¹**catch-as-catch-'can** *n* a style of wrestling in which all mutually agreed holds are allowed and in which a fall is gained by pinning an opponent's shoulders to the ground

²**catch-as-catch-can** *adj* using any available means or method

**catch basin** *n* CATCH PIT

**catch crop** *n* an extra crop that is grown between the harvesting of one main crop and the planting of another, or that is planted between the rows of the main crop – **catch-cropping** *n*

**catchcry** /-,krie/ *n, Austr* a slogan; TAG 4a,b ⟨*resort to 1950s catchcries about red perils – The Australian*⟩

**catcher** /'kachə/ *n* one who catches; *specif* a baseball player who stands behind the batter to catch balls that the batter fails to hit

**catchfly** /-,flie/ *n* any of various plants (eg of the genera *Lychnis* and *Silene*) of the pink family with sticky stems to which small insects adhere

**catching** /'kaching/ *adj* **1** infectious, contagious **2** alluring, attractive

**catchment** /'kachmənt/ *n* **1** the catching of water **2** something that collects water; *also* the amount of water collected

**catchment area** *n* **1** the area from which water drains into a river, reservoir, etc **2** *chiefly Br* the officially designated area from which a school's pupils or a hospital's patients are drawn ⟨*if you live outside the* ~ *for a hospital, you take second place to those within it – Islington Gutter Press (London)*⟩; *broadly* an area from which people may be expected to be drawn ⟨*a huge* ~ *for skilled and semi-skilled labour – The Times*⟩

**catchpenny** /'kach,peni, 'kachpəni/ *adj* designed to appeal to the ignorant or unwary by cheap sensationalism; *broadly* rubbishy

**catchphrase** /-,frayz/ *n* an arresting phrase that is temporarily fashionable and much repeated

**catch pit** *n* a chamber to retain sediment that would otherwise clog a channel (eg a sewer or drain)

**catchpole, catchpoll** /'kach,pohl/ *n* **1** a sheriff's deputy in medieval England **2** *derog* a minor official [ME *cacchepol*, fr OE *cæcepol*, fr (assumed) ONF *cachepol*, lit., chicken chaser, fr ONF *cachier* to chase + *pol* chicken, fr L *pullus* – more at CATCH, PULLET]

**catch** *n, often cap C* a predicament from which a victim is unable to extricate him-/herself because the means of escape depends on mutually exclusive prior conditions [*Catch-22*, novel by Joseph Heller *b* 1923 US writer]

**catchup** /'kachəp/ *n* ketchup

'**catch-,up** *adj* designed to catch up (eg by overcoming an inequality or working through a backlog) – **catch-up** *n*

**catchword** /-,wuhd/ *n* **1a** a word under the right-hand side of the last line on a book page that repeats the first word on the following page **b** GUIDE WORD **2** a word or expression repeated in connection with some school of thought or political movement; a slogan

**catchy** /'kachi/ *adj* tending to catch the interest or attention ⟨*a* ~ *title*⟩

**cat distemper** *n* PANLEUCOPAENIA

**cate** /kayt/ *n usu pl, archaic* a dainty or choice food [ME, article of purchased food, short for *acate*, fr ONF *acat* purchase, fr *acater* to buy, fr (assumed) VL *accaptare*, fr L *acceptare* to accept]

**catechesis** /,katə'keesis/ *n, pl* **catecheses** /-seez/ oral instruction of catechumens [LL, fr Gk *katēchēsis*, fr *katēchein* to teach] – **catechetical** *adj*

**catechin** /'katəkin/ *n* a complex compound, $C_{15}H_{14}O_6$, that is related chemically to the FLAVONES (compounds occurring in

plants), is found in catechu, and is used in dyeing and tanning [ISV *catechu* + *-in*]

**catechism** /'katə,kiz(ə)m/ *n* **1** instruction by question and answer **2** a manual for catechizing; *specif* a summary of religious doctrine often in the form of questions and answers **3** a set of formal questions put as a test – **catechismal** *adj*, **catechistic** *adj*

**catechist** /'katəkist/ *n* one who catechizes: eg **a** a teacher of catechumens **b** a local Christian teacher in a missionary district – **catechistic** *adj*

**catech·ize, -ise** /'katə,kiez/ *vt* **1** to teach systematically, esp by asking questions, explaining, and correcting; *specif* to give religious instruction in such a manner to **2** to question systematically or searchingly [LL *catechizare*, fr Gk *katēchein* to teach, lit., to din into, fr *kata-* cata- + *ēchein* to resound, fr *ēchē* sound – more at ECHO] – **catechizer** *n*, **catechization** *n*

**catechol** /'katə,kohl, -,chohl/ *n* **1** catechin **2** PYROCATECHOL

**catecholamine** /,katə'kohləmeen, -'choh-/ *n* any of various chemical compounds (eg adrenalin, noradrenalin, and dopamine) that are AMINES, function as hormones or NEUROTRANSMITTERS (substances that transmit nerve impulses between nerves) or both, and are related to PYROCATECHOL

**catechu** /'katə,chooh/ *n* any of several dry, earthy, or resinous astringent substances obtained from tropical Asian plants: eg **a** an extract of the heartwood of an E Indian acacia (*Acacia catechu*) used for tanning and dyeing, and formerly in medicine **b** GAMBIER [prob fr Malay *kachu*, of Dravidian origin; akin to Tamil & Kannada *kācu* catechu]

**catechumen** /,katə'kyoohmin/ *n* a person receiving instruction in Christian doctrine and discipline before baptism or before admission to membership of a church [ME *cathecumyn*, fr MF *cathecumine*, fr LL *cathecumenus*, fr Gk *katēchoumenos*, prp passive of *katēchein* to teach]

**categorical** /,katə'gorikl/ *also* **categoric** /-'gorik/ *adj* **1** absolute, unqualified ⟨*a* ~ *denial*⟩ **2** of or being a category ⟨*I am in favour of* ~ *aid over general aid*⟩ [LL *categoricus*, fr Gk *katēgorikos*, fr *katēgoria* affirmation, category] – **categorically** *adv*

**categorical imperative** *n* a moral obligation that is unconditionally and universally binding

**categor·ize, -ise** /'katəgə,riez/ *vt* to put into a category; classify – **categorization** *n*

**category** /'katəg(ə)ri/ *n* **1a** a general logical class to which a predicate or that which it predicates belongs **b** any of the underlying forms to which an object of experience must conform **c** a fundamental or ultimate class or form (eg in philosophy or linguistics) **2** a division within a system of classification [LL *categoria*, fr Gk *katēgoria* predication, category, fr *katēgorein* to accuse, affirm, predicate, fr *kata-* + *agora* public assembly – more at GREGARIOUS]

**catena** /kə'teenə/ *n, pl* **catenae** /-nie/, **catenas** a connected series of related things; *specif* patristic comments on the Bible arranged in such a series [ML, fr L, chain – more at CHAIN]

¹**catenary** /'katən(ə)nri, kə'tee-/ *n* **1** the curve assumed by a perfectly flexible inextensible cord of uniform density and cross section hanging freely from two fixed points **2** something in the form of a catenary [NL *catenaria*, fr L, fem of *catenarius* of a chain, fr *catena*]

²**catenary** *adj* **1** of or being a catenary **2** being or belonging to a catena [L *catenarius*]

**catenate** /'katənayt/ *vt, formal* to connect in a series as a chain does; link [L *catenatus*, pp of *catenare*, fr *catena*] – **catenation** *n*

**catenulate** /kə'tenyoolayt, -lət/ *also* **catenuliform** /kə'tenyooli,fawm/ *adj* arranged in chains; chain-like [ISV, fr LL *catenula*, dim. of L *catena*]

**cater** /'kaytə/ *vi* **1** to provide a supply of food **2** to supply what is required or desired – usu + *for* or to ⟨*can't* ~ *for all tastes*⟩ [obs *cater* buyer of provisions, fr ME *catour*, short for *acatour*, fr AF, fr ONF *acater* to buy – more at CATE] – **caterer** *n*, **cateress** *n*

**cateran** /'katərən/ *n* a former irregular or brigand of the Scottish Highlands [ME *ketharan*, prob fr ScGael *ceathairneach* freebooter, robber]

**catercorner** /,kaytə'kawnə/, **cater-cornered** *adv or adj, NAm* in a diagonal or oblique position; on a diagonal or oblique line ⟨*the house stood* ~ *across the square*⟩ [obs *cater* a four on cards or dice (deriv of L *quattuor* four) + E *corner*]

**caterpillar** /'katə,pilə/ *n* the elongated wormlike larva of a butterfly or moth; *also* any of various similar larvae [ME *catyrpel*, fr ONF *catepelose*, lit., hairy cat]

**Caterpillar** *trademark* – used for a tractor made for use on rough or soft ground and moved on two endless metal belts

**caterwaul** /'katə,wawl/ *vi* 1 to make a harsh cry as of a cat 2 to quarrel noisily [ME *caterwawen*, prob fr *cat* + *-wawen*, of imit origin] – **caterwaul** *n*

**catfish** /-,fish/ *n* 1 any of numerous usu stout-bodied large-headed fishes (order Ostariophysi) with long sensitive whisker-like projections (BARBELS) round the mouth 2 *Br* WOLFFISH (N Atlantic food fish)

**cat flu** *n* PANLEUCOPAENIA

**catgut** /-,gut/ *n* a tough cord made usu from sheep intestines and used esp for the strings of musical instruments (e g violins), for the strings of tennis rackets, and for stitching wounds

**cath-** – see CATA-

**Cathar** /'ka,thah/ *n, pl* **Cathars, Cathari** /'kathə,rie/ a member of any of various ascetic and dualistic Christian sects flourishing in the later Middle Ages esp in Provence, teaching that the material world is evil, and professing faith in an angelic Christ who did not really undergo human birth or death [LL *cathari* (pl), fr LGk *katharoi*, fr Gk, pl of *katharos*, adj] – **Catharism** *n*, **Catharist, Catharistic** *adj*

**catharsis** /kə'thahsis/ *n, pl* **catharses** /-seez/ 1 purgation; *esp* evacuation of the bowels 2 purification or purgation of the emotions, esp of pity and fear, through art, esp tragic drama 3 the process of alleviating a complex by bringing it to consciousness and affording it expression [NL, fr Gk *katharsis*, fr *kathairein* to cleanse, purge, fr *katharos* pure]

<sup>1</sup>**cathartic** /kə'thahtik/ *adj* of or producing catharsis; purgative [LL or Gk; LL *catharticus*, fr Gk *kathartikos*, fr *kathairein*]

<sup>2</sup>**cathartic** *n* a medical purgative; a laxative

**Cathay** /ka'thay, kə-/ *n, archaic* China [ML *Cataya, Kitai*, of Turkic origin]

**cathead** /-,hed/ *n* a projecting piece of timber or iron near the bow of a ship, to which the anchor is hoisted and secured

**cathect** /kə'thekt, ka-/ *vt* to invest with mental or emotional energy [back-formation fr *cathectic*, fr *cathexis*]

**cathedra** /kə'theedrə/ *n* a bishop's throne [L, chair – more at CHAIR]

<sup>1</sup>**cathedral** /kə'theedrəl/ *adj* 1 of, containing, or being a bishop's throne or church 2 *formal* emanating from a chair of authority

<sup>2</sup>**cathedral** *n* a usu large church that is the official seat of a diocesan bishop

**cathepsin** /kə'thepsin/ *n* any of several ENZYMES that occur inside cells, esp LYSOSOMES, and that break down proteins and are important in AUTOLYSIS (self-destruction of the cell) in certain diseased conditions and after death [Gk *kathepsein* to digest (fr *kata-* cata- + *hepsein* to boil) + E *-in*]

**catherine wheel** /'kath(ə)rin/ *n, often cap C* 1 a firework in the form of a wheel that spins as it burns 2 CARTWHEEL 1 [St *Catherine* of Alexandria † *ab* 307 Christian martyr tortured on a spiked wheel]

**catheter** /'kathətə/ *n* a tubular device for insertion into a hollow body part (e g a blood vessel, passageway, or cavity) usu to permit injection or withdrawal of fluids or to keep a passage open [LL, fr Gk *kathetēr*, fr *kathienai* to send down, fr *kata-* cata- + *hienai* to send – more at JET]

**catheter·ize, -ise** /'kathətə,riez/ *vt* to introduce a catheter into – **catheterization** *n*

**cathexis** /kə'theksis/ *n, pl* **cathexes** /-seez/ investment of mental or emotional energy in a person, object, or idea [NL (intended as trans of Ger *besetzung*), fr Gk *kathexis* holding, fr *katechein* to hold fast, occupy, fr *kata-* + *echein* to have, hold – more at SCHEME] – **cathectic** *adj*

**cathode** *also* **kathode** /'ka,thohd/ *n* the ELECTRODE (wire, plate, etc that conducts an electric current) by which electrons leave an external circuit and enter a device: e g a the negative electrode of a chemical cell undergoing ELECTROLYSIS (chemical decomposition of a substance by an electric current) b the positive terminal of a PRIMARY CELL or of a STORAGE BATTERY that is delivering current c that electrode in a THERMIONIC VALVE or similar electronic device that emits electrons [Gk *kathodos* way down, fr *kata-* + *hodos* way] – **cathodic** *adj*, **cathodically** *adv*

**cathode ray** *n* a beam of high-speed electrons projected from the heated cathode of a VACUUM TUBE

**cathode-ray tube** *n* a usu glass VACUUM TUBE in which a controlled usu narrow beam of electrons from a heated cathode is projected onto a fluorescent screen (e g a television screen) to produce a visible spot of light

**catholic** /'kath(ə)lik/ *adj* 1 comprehensive, universal; *esp* broad in sympathies, tastes, or interests 2 *cap* **2a** of or forming the church universal **b** of or forming the ancient undivided Christian church or a church claiming historical continuity from it; *specif* ROMAN CATHOLIC [MF & LL; MF *catholique*, fr LL *catholicus*, fr Gk *katholikos* universal, general, fr *katholou* in general, fr *kata* by + *holos* whole – more at CATA-, SAFE] – **catholically** *adv*, **catholicize** *vb*

*usage* Except in specialized theological contexts, **Catholic** can be used everywhere today for **Roman Catholic** ⟨*a* **Catholic** *school*⟩

**Catholic** *n* 1 a person who belongs to the universal Christian church 2 a member of a Catholic church; *specif* ROMAN CATHOLIC

**Catholic Apostolic** *adj* of a Christian sect founded in 19th-century England in anticipation of Christ's Second Coming

**catholicate** /kə'tholikayt, -kət/ *n* the jurisdiction of a catholicos

**Catholic Epistles** *n pl* the five New Testament letters (James, I and II Peter, I John, and Jude) addressed to the early Christian churches at large

**Catholicism** /kə'tholə,siz(ə)m/ *n* 1 the faith, practice, or system of Catholic Christianity 2 ROMAN CATHOLICISM

**catholicity** /,kathə'lisəti/ *n* 1 *cap* the quality of being in conformity with a Catholic church **2a** liberality of sentiments or views **b** universality **c** comprehensive range

**catholicon** /kə'tholi,kon, -kən/ *n* a cure-all, panacea [Fr or ML; Fr, fr ML, fr Gk *katholikon*, neut of *katholikos*]

**catholicos** /kə'tholikəs, -kos/ *n, pl* **catholicoses** /kə'tholikəsəs, -,kosiz/, **catholicoi** /-koy/ *often cap* a primate of certain Eastern churches, esp the Armenian or the Assyrian church [LGk *katholikos*, fr Gk, general]

**cathouse** /'kat,hows/ *n, NAm slang* a brothel

**cation** /'kat,ie-ən/ *n* an ION (electrically charged atom or group of atoms) with a positive electrical charge; *esp* the ion in an ELECTROLYSED solution (one broken down into its constituents by an electric current) that is attracted towards the CATHODE (negative terminal) [Gk *kation*, neut of *katiōn*, prp of *katienai* to go down, fr *kata-* cata- + *ienai* to go – more at ISSUE]

**cationic** /,katie'onik/ *adj* 1 of cations 2 characterized by an active, esp a SURFACE-ACTIVE, cation ⟨*a* ~ *dye*⟩ – **cationically** *adv*

**catkin** /'kat,kin/ *n* a usu long flower cluster (e g in willow) densely crowded with BRACTS (tiny specialized leaves) and flowers without petals [obs D *katteken*, lit., kitten; fr its resemblance to a cat's tail] – **catkinate** *adj*

**catlike** /'kat,liek/ *adj* resembling a cat; *esp* stealthy

**catmint** /-,mint/ *n* a strong-scented plant (*Nepeta cataria*) of the mint family that has whorls of small pale purple-spotted flowers in spikes and contains a substance attractive to cats

**catnap** /-,nap/ *n* a very brief period of sleep, esp during the day – **catnap** *vi*

**catnip** /-,nip/ *n, NAm* catmint [<sup>1</sup>*cat* + obs *nep* catnip, fr ME, fr OE *nepte*, fr L *nepeta*]

**cat-o'-'nine-,tails** *n, pl* **cat-o'-nine-tails** a whip made of usu nine knotted lines or cords fastened to a handle and used for flogging offenders [fr the resemblance of the scars it makes to the scratches of a cat]

**catoptric** /ka'toptrik/ *adj* of a mirror or reflected light; *also* produced by reflection [Gk *katoptrikos*, fr *katoptron* mirror, fr *katopsesthai* to be going to observe, fr *kata-* cata- + *opsesthai* to be going to see – more at OPTIC] – **catoptrically** *adv*

**cat's cradle** *n* 1 a game in which a string looped in a pattern like a cradle on the fingers of one person's hands is transferred to the hands of another so as to form a different figure 2 intricacy ⟨*the socioreligious* ~ *of small Greek communities* – *TLS*⟩

**catsear** /-,iə/ *n* any of various European plants (genus *Hypochoeris*) of the daisy family with yellow flower heads resembling those of the dandelion

'**cat's-,eye** *n, pl* **cat's-eyes** 1 any of various gems (e g a chrysoberyl or a chalcedony) that reflect a narrow band of light from within 2 a small reflecting device that reflects beams from vehicle headlights and is set together with others, usu in a line to mark the centre or edge of a road

'**cat's-,foot** *n, pl* **cat's-feet** any of several plants (genus *Antennaria*, esp *Antennaria dioica*) of the daisy family with leaves whose undersurfaces are covered in fine woolly hairs and with small whitish or pink flower heads

**cat's meat** *n* meat that is fed to cats

'cat's-,paw *n, pl* cat's-paws 1 a light air that ruffles the surface of the water in irregular patches during a calm 2 one used by another as a tool; a dupe 3 a hitch in a rope onto which a tackle may be hooked [(2) fr the fable of a monkey that used a cat's paw to draw chestnuts from a fire]

'cat's-,tail *n* 1 TIMOTHY (type of grass) 2 REEDMACE (tall marsh plant)

catsuit /-,s(y)ooht/ *n* a tightly fitting one-piece garment combining top and trousers

catsup /'katsəp/ *n* ketchup

cat's whisker *n* 1 the fine wire that is the metallic electrode in a crystal detector 2 *pl* an excellent person or thing – + *the* ⟨*he thinks he's the* ~*s*⟩

cattail /'kat,tayl/ *n, NAm* REEDMACE (tall marsh plant)

cattalo *also* catalo /'katəloh/ *n, pl* cattaloes, cattalos; *also* cataloes, catalos a hybrid between the American buffalo and domestic cattle that is hardier than the latter [*cat*tle + buffalo]

cattery /'katəri/ *n* a place for the breeding, rearing, or care of cats

cattle /'katl/ *n taking pl vb* 1 domesticated 4-legged animals held as property or reared for use; *specif* bovine animals (e g cows) kept on a farm or ranch 2 human beings, esp en masse [ME *catel*, fr ONF, personal property, fr ML *capitale*, fr L, neut of *capitalis* of the head – more at CAPITAL]

cattle grid *n, Br* a set of parallel bars fixed into a road surface over a pit that prevent livestock but not wheeled vehicles from crossing

cattleman /-mən, -,man/ *n* a man who tends or raises cattle

cattlestop /-,stop/ *n, NZ* CATTLE GRID

cattletruck /'katl,truk/ *n* 1 a lorry or railway wagon used for transporting cattle 2 an overcrowded passenger vehicle

cattleya /'katliə, kat'lee·ə, kat'layə/ *n* any of a genus (*Cattleya*) of tropical American EPIPHYTIC orchids with showy hooded flowers [NL, genus name, fr William *Cattley* †1832 E patron of botany]

'catty /'kati/ *n* any of various units of weight of China and SE Asia of about 0.6 kilogram (about 1$\frac{1}{2}$ pounds); *also* a standard Chinese unit equal to 0.5 kilogram (about 1$\frac{1}{10}$ pounds) [Malay *kati*]

²catty *adj* 1 slyly spiteful; malicious 2 of or like a cat – cattily *adv*, cattiness *n*

,catty-'corner, ,catty-'cornered /'kati/ *adv or adj, NAm* CATERCORNER (on a diagonal)

catwalk /-,wawk/ *n* a narrow walkway

Caucasian /kaw'kayzh(y)ən/ *adj* 1 of the Caucasus or its inhabitants or languages 2 of the white race of mankind as classified according to physical features [*Caucasus, Caucasia*, region of USSR] – Caucasian *n*, Caucasoid *adj or n*
   *usage* It is better to avoid the second sense of Caucasian, and use white (not White) in general writing.

Cauchy sequence /'kowshi (Fr koʃi)/ *n, maths* a sequence of mathematical elements in which any two elements are arbitrarily close together if they are chosen far enough along in the sequence [Augustin-Louis *Cauchy* †1857 Fr mathematician]

'caucus /'kawkəs/ *n* a closed meeting of a group of people belonging to the same political party or faction, usu to select candidates or decide on policy [prob fr Algonquian origin]

²caucus *vi* to hold or meet in a caucus

caudad /'kawdad/ *adv* towards the tail or posterior end – compare CEPHALAD [L *cauda*]

caudal /'kawdl/ *adj* 1 of or being a tail 2 situated in or directed towards the hind part of the body [NL *caudalis*, fr L *cauda* tail – more at COWARD] – caudally *adv*

caudate /'kawdayt/ *also* caudated /-,daytid/ *adj* having a tail or a tail-like appendage – caudation *n*

caudate nucleus *n* either of two masses of nerve tissue that lie one at each side of the base of the brain and are involved in the control of the movement of the limbs, head, etc

caudex /'kawdeks/ *n, pl* caudices /'kawdiseez/, caudexes 1 the main axis including both stem and root of a plant, esp a palm or TREE FERN 2 the woody base of a perennial plant that persists for several years and from which new growth arises [L, tree trunk or stem – more at CODE]

caudillo /kaw'deelyoh, kow-, -'dheelyoh/ *n, pl* caudillos a Spanish or Latin-American military dictator [Sp, fr LL *capitellum* small head – more at CADET]

caudle /'kawdl/ *n* a drink (e g formerly given to invalids) usu of warm ale or wine mixed with bread or gruel, eggs, sugar, and spices [ME *caudel*, fr ONF, fr *caut* warm, fr L *calidus*]

'caught /kawt/ *past of* CATCH

²caught *adj, informal* pregnant – chiefly in *get caught*

caul /kawl/ *n* 1 a decorative net used for confining the hair and worn by women as part of a medieval headdress 2a the large fatty fold of membrane covering the intestines b the inner foetal membrane of higher VERTEBRATE animals (e g humans), esp when covering the head at birth [ME *calle*, perh fr MF *cale*]

cauldron, caldron /'kawldrən/ *n* 1 a large rounded open vessel or pot of metal (e g iron) used, esp formerly, over an open fire for baking or cooking 2 something that resembles a boiling cauldron ⟨*a* ~ *of intense emotions*⟩ [ME, alter. of *cauderon*, fr ONF, dim. of *caudiere*, fr LL *caldaria*, fr L, warm bath, fr fem of *caldarius* suitable for warming, fr *calidus* warm, fr *calēre* to be warm]

caulescent /kaw'les(ə)nt/ *adj, of a plant* having a stem evident above ground [ISV, fr L *caulis*]

caulicle /'kawlikl/ *n* a rudimentary stem (e g of an embryo or seedling) [L *cauliculus*, dim. of *caulis*]

cauliflower /'koli,flowə/ *n* a garden plant (*Brassica oleracea botrytis*) closely related to the cabbage and grown for its compact edible head of usu white undeveloped flowers; *also* the flower cluster eaten as a vegetable [modif of It *cavolfiore*, fr *cavolo* cabbage (fr LL *caulus*, fr L *caulis* stem, cabbage) + *fiore* flower, fr L *flor-, flos* – more at HOLE, BLOW]

cauliflower ear *n* an ear deformed from injury and excessive growth of reparative tissue

cauline /'kawleen, -lien/ *adj* of or growing on a stem; *specif, of a plant part* growing on the upper part of a stem ⟨~ *leaves*⟩ – compare RADICAL [NL *caulinus*, fr L *caulis*]

'caulk, calk /kawk/ *vt* 1 to stop up and make watertight the seams of (e g a boat) by filling them with a waterproofing compound or material 2 to stop up and make tight against leakage (e g the seams of a boat, the cracks in a window frame, or a joint in a pipe) [ME *caulken*, fr ONF *cauquer* to trample, fr L *calcare*, fr *calc-, calx* heel] – caulker *n*

²caulk' *n* CALK (projection on a horse's shoe)

cauri /'kow(ə)ri/ *n, pl* cauris – see *syli* at MONEY table [native name in Guinea]

causal /'kawzl/ *adj* 1 expressing or indicating cause; causative ⟨*a* ~ *clause that is introduced by* since *or* because⟩ 2 of or constituting a cause ⟨*the* ~ *agent of a disease*⟩ 3 arising from a cause ⟨*a* ~ *development*⟩ △ casual – causally *adv*

causality /kaw'zaləti/ *n* 1 a causal quality or agency 2 the relation between a cause and its effect

causation /kaw'zaysh(ə)n/ *n* 1a the act or process of causing b the act or agency by which an effect is produced 2 causality

causative /'kawzətiv/ *adj* 1 effective or operating as a cause or agent 2 expressing causation – causative *n*, causatively *adv*

'cause /kawz/ *n* 1a one who or that which brings about an effect or result b a reason for an action or condition; a motive 2a a ground for legal action b CASE 2b 3 a principle or movement worthy of defence or support [ME, fr OF, fr L *causa*] – causeless *adj*
   synonyms Cause, determinant, antecedent, reason, and occasion all denote things or conditions which bring about results. A cause produces a necessary effect, while a determinant is a factor contributing to an effect and determining its nature ⟨*malnutrition was* the cause *of the child's weakness*⟩ ⟨*malnutrition is a* determinant *of small size in an adult*⟩. A reason is a logical explanation for a certain effect; it can be interchangeable with cause if the latter is known ⟨*missing the bus was the* cause *of/*reason *for his lateness*⟩. An antecedent precedes in time, but does not necessarily have a causal relationship with what follows ⟨*the* antecedents *of the Welfare State were the Guardians of the Poor*⟩. An occasion is not itself a cause, but a time or situation which allows existing causes to come into operation ⟨*the* occasion *for open hostility came when Jones spilt beer all over him*⟩.

²cause *vt* 1 to serve as a cause or occasion of 2 to effect by command, authority, or force ⟨*the president* ~d *the ambassador to protest*⟩ – causer *n*
   usage Things and events cause, or are the cause of, other things and events. Constructions with due to or as a result, such as ⟨*the* cause *of the accident was due to icy roads*⟩ or ⟨*the delay was* caused *as a result of fog*⟩ are widely disliked, because people feel that the idea of "explanation" should not be expressed twice in the same sentence. See ¹BECAUSE

'cause, 'cos /kəz; strong koz/ *conj* BECAUSE – used in writing to represent a casual pronunciation

cause célèbre /,kohz say'leb(rə) (Fr ko:z selɛbr)/ *n, pl* causes

**célèbres** /~/ 1 a legal case that excites widespread interest 2 a notorious incident or episode [Fr, lit., celebrated case]

**cause list** *n*, *Br* a list of legal actions awaiting trial

**causerie** /'kohz(ə)ri/ *n* 1 an informal conversation; a chat 2 a short informal essay or article, esp on a literary subject [Fr, fr *causer* to chat, fr L *causari* to plead, discuss, fr *causa*]

**causeway** /'kawz,way/ *n* a raised road or pathway across wet ground or water [ME *cauciwey*, fr *cauci* causey + *wey* way] – **causeway** *vt*

**causey** /'kawzi/ *n*, *archaic or dial* a causeway [ME *cauci*, fr ONF *caucie*, fr ML *calciata* paved highway, fr fem of *calciatus* paved with limestone, fr L *calc-*, *calx* limestone – more at CHALK]

¹**caustic** /'kostik, 'kaw-/ *adj* 1 capable of destroying or eating away by chemical action; corrosive 2 bitter, sarcastic, or biting ⟨~ *wit*⟩ ⟨*a* ~ *satire on contemporary government*⟩ 3 of or being the curve formed by rays coming from a point and reflected or refracted by a curved surface **synonyms** see SARCASTIC [L *causticus*, fr Gk *kaustikos*, fr *kaiein* to burn; akin to Lith *kulė* smut of plants] – **caustically** *adv*, **causticity** *n*

²**caustic** *n* 1 a curve formed by rays of light from a point source that are reflected or refracted by a curved surface; *also* a surface having the shape of such a curve 2 a caustic substance or chemical; *esp* a strong alkali

**caustic lime** *n* ¹LIME 2a

**caustic potash** *n* POTASSIUM HYDROXIDE

**caustic soda** *n* SODIUM HYDROXIDE

**cauter·ization, -isation** /,kawtərie'zaysh(ə)n/ *n* the act or effect of cauterizing

**cauter·ize, -ise** /'kawtə,riez/ *vt* to sear (eg a wound) or destroy (eg infected body tissue) with a cautery or caustic chemical, esp to destroy infection

**cautery** /'kawtəri/ *n* 1 cauterization 2 an agent (eg a hot iron or caustic chemical) used to burn, sear, or destroy tissue [L *cauterium*, fr Gk *kautērion* branding iron, fr *kaiein*]

¹**caution** /'kawsh(ə)n/ *n* 1 a warning, admonishment; *specif* an official warning given to someone who has committed a minor offence that further action may be taken if the offence is repeated 2 prudent forethought to minimize risk; care 3 *informal* one who or that which arouses astonishment or commands attention ⟨*she's a proper* ~⟩ [L *caution-*, *cautio* precaution, fr *cautus*, pp of *cavēre* to be on guard – more at HEAR] – **cautionary** *adj*

²**caution** *vt* 1a to advise caution to; warn; *specif* to advise (a person under arrest) that answers to questions will be recorded and may be used as evidence in a prosecution b to admonish, reprove; *specif* to give an official warning to ⟨~ed *for disorderly conduct*⟩ 2 of a soccer referee to take the name of (a player) for any of several specific breaches of the rules ~ *vi* to urge, warn, or advise against ⟨*he* ~ed *against the use of excessive force in dealing with the rioters*⟩ **synonyms** see WARN

**caution money** *n*, *Br* money deposited (eg by a student) as security for possible damages (eg to laboratory equipment or to the furniture of a flat) [*caution* (security, bail), fr ME *caucion*, fr OF *caution*, fr L *caution-*, *cautio*]

**cautious** /'kawshəs/ *adj* careful, prudent ⟨*made a* ~ *move towards the barking dog*⟩ – **cautiously** *adv*, **cautiousness** *n*

**synonyms** Cautious, wary, chary, and circumspect all mean "paying prudent attention to possible dangers or harmful effects". Cautious implies tentativeness, even fear, in taking action, and carefulness in proceeding. ⟨*the cautious traveller tested the ground at every step until he was out of the bog*⟩. Wary adds a sense of watchfulness or alertness for danger; it also suggests suspicion, and so less real ground for fearfulness ⟨*she kept a* wary *eye on her purse, all the same*⟩. Circumspect deals mainly with social behaviour, and suggests extreme care in assessing the possible consequences of an action in order to avoid embarrassing or harmful consequences ⟨*the old politician was too* circumspect *to commit himself when lobbied on the matter*⟩. Chary suggests a cautiousness in making statements or taking action that is almost grudging in its hesitancy ⟨*she was as* chary *of thanks as she had been slow to ask for help*⟩. **antonyms** adventurous, foolhardy

**cavalcade** /'kavl,kayd, ,--'-/ *n* 1 a procession; *esp* one of riders or carriages 2 a dramatic sequence, esp of events; a series ⟨*the* ~ *of English naval history*⟩ [MF, ride on horseback, fr OIt *cavalcata*, fr *cavalcare* to go on horseback, fr LL *caballicare*, fr L *caballus* horse; akin to Gk dial. *kaballeion* horse-drawn vehicle]

¹**cavalier** /,kavə'liə/ *n* 1 a courtly gentleman of former times, esp one attending or escorting a lady; a gallant 2 *cap* an ad-

herent of the party of Charles I of England, esp during the Civil War ⟨*the confiscation of the estates of* Cavaliers *who had gone into exile with the young Charles II in France*⟩ 3 a fashionable young man – no longer in vogue 4 *archaic* a mounted soldier; a knight [MF, fr OIt *cavaliere*, fr OProv *cavalier*, fr LL *caballarius* horseman, fr L *caballus*]

²**cavalier** *adj* 1 debonair 2 given to or characterized by offhand dismissal of important matters ⟨*the report was dealt with in a very* ~ *manner*⟩ 3 *cap* of the party of Charles I of England during the Civil War or of his son, Charles II, during his exile – **cavalierism** *n*, **cavalierly** *adv*

**cavalletto** /,kavə'letoh/ *n*, *pl* **cavalletti** /-ti/ a low training rail for horses to jump [It, lit., little horse, dim. of *cavallo* horse, fr L *caballus*]

**cavalry** /'kavəlri/ *n taking sing or pl vb* 1 horsemen; *specif* soldiers trained, armed, and equipped to fight on horseback 2a the mounted part of an army b a branch of the army formerly mounted and now using armoured vehicles or carrying out reconnaissance roles [It *cavalleria* cavalry, chivalry, fr *cavaliere*]

**cavalryman** /'kavəlrimən/ *n* a cavalry soldier

**cavalry twill** *n* a strong fabric woven in a double TWILL and used originally for riding breeches

**cavatina** /,kavə'teenə/ *n* 1 an operatic solo simpler and briefer than an ARIA 2 a usu slow instrumental composition similar to an operatic cavatina [It, fr *cavata* production of sound from an instrument, fr *cavare* to dig out, fr L, to make hollow, fr *cavus*]

¹**cave** /kayv/ *n* 1 a natural underground chamber (eg in the side of a hill) having an often horizontal opening to the surface 2 *archaic Br* the withdrawal of an organized group from a political party; *also, taking sing or pl vb* the group withdrawing [ME, fr OF, fr L *cava*, fr *cavus* hollow; akin to ON *hūnn* cub, Gk *kyein* to be pregnant, *koilos* hollow, Skt *śvayati* he swells; (2) fr *cave of Adullam*, where David was joined by malcontents (I Sam 22:1, 2)]

²**cave** *vt* to form a cave in or under; hollow, undermine ~ *vi* to explore a cave system, esp for recreation; pothole – **caver** *n*

³**cave** *vi* 1 to fall in or down, esp from being undermined 2 to cease to resist; submit □ usu + *in* [prob alter. (influenced by ²*cave*) of E dial. *calve*, perh fr Flem *inkalven*]

⁴**cave** /'kay'vee/ *interj*, *Br* – used at school, esp public school, as a warning meaning "look out!" [L, beware, fr *cavēre* to beware, be on guard] – **keep cave** *Br* to act as a lookout at school

**caveat** /'kavi·at, 'kay-/ *n* 1 a cautionary statement or warning; *esp* one intended to prevent misinterpretation 2 *law* an official notice to a court to suspend a proceeding until the opposition has been heard [L, let him beware, fr *cavēre* – more at HEAR]

**caveat emptor** /'emptaw/ *n* a principle in commerce: without a guarantee the buyer takes the risk of quality upon him-/herself [NL, let the buyer beware]

**caveman** /'kayv,man/ *n* 1 someone who lives in a cave; *esp* a member of a STONE AGE society – not used technically 2 someone who acts in a rough primitive manner, esp towards women

**cavendish** /'kavəndish/ *n*, *often cap* a moistened usu sweetened tobacco pressed into flat cakes or bars [prob fr the name *Cavendish*]

**cavern** /'kavən/ *n* a usu large underground chamber or cave [ME *caverne*, fr MF, fr L *caverna*, fr *cavus*]

**cavernicolous** /,kavə'nikələs/ *adj* inhabiting caves ⟨~ *fauna*⟩

**cavernous** /'kavənəs/ *adj* 1 having caverns or cavities 2 constituting or suggesting a cavern 3 *of animal tissue* composed largely of spaces capable of filling with blood to bring about the erection of a body part – **cavernously** *adv*

**cavesson** /'kavəsən/ *n* 1 a stiff padded noseband for a horse 2 a bridle or halter with a cavesson [modif of It *cavezzone* halter with noseband, aug of *cavezza* halter, irreg fr L *capitium* opening for head in tunic, fr *capit-*, *caput* head]

**cavetto** /kə'vetoh/ *n*, *pl* **cavetti** /-ti/ a concave architectural moulding with a curve that roughly approximates to a quarter circle [It, fr *cavo* hollow, fr L *cavus*]

**caviar, caviare** /'kaviah/ *n* 1 the processed salted roe of large fish (eg sturgeon) eaten as a delicacy 2 something considered too delicate or lofty for mass appreciation – often + *to* ⟨*will be* ~ *to the multitude*⟩ [earlier *cavery*, *caviarie*, fr obs It *caviari*, pl of *caviaro*, fr Turk *havyar*, fr MGk *kabiari*]

**cavil** /'kavil, -vl/ *vi* -ll- (*NAm* -l-, -ll-) to raise trivial and frivolous objections; split hairs [L *cavillari* to jest, cavil, fr *cavilla* raillery] – **cavil** *n*, **caviler**, **caviller** *n*

**cavitary** /'kavit(ə)ri/ *adj* of or characterized by the formation of cavities in the body ⟨~ *tuberculosis*⟩

**cavitate** /'kavitayt/ *vb* to form cavities or bubbles (in) [backformation fr *cavitation*]

**cavitation** /,kavi'taysh(ə)n/ *n* the process of cavitating: eg **a** the formation of partial vacuums in a liquid by a swiftly moving solid body (eg a propeller) or by high-frequency sound waves; *also* the pitting and wearing away of solid surfaces (eg of metal or concrete) as a result of the collapse of these vacuums in surrounding liquid **b** the formation of cavities in an organ or tissue, esp in the course of a disease [*cavity* + *-ation*]

**cavity** /'kavəti/ *n* an empty or hollowed out space within a mass; *specif* a decaying hollow in a tooth [MF *cavité*, fr LL *cavitas*, fr L *cavus* hollow]

**cavity wall** *n* a wall built in two thicknesses with an air space in between which provides insulation

**cavort** /kə'vawt/ *vi* 1 to prance 2 to behave in an extravagant or exaggerated manner [perh alter. of *curvet*]

**cavy** /'kayvi/ *n* 1 any of several short-tailed roughhaired S American rodents (family Caviidae); *esp* a guinea pig 2 **cavy, spotted cavy** PACA (S American rodent) [NL *Cavia*, genus name, fr obs Pg *çavia* (now *savia*), fr Tupi *sawiya* rat]

**caw** /kaw/ *vi* to utter (a sound similar to) the harsh raucous cry characteristic of the crow [imit] – **caw** *n*

**cay** /kee, kay/ *n* a low island or reef of sand or coral, esp in the Caribbean [Sp *cayo* – more at ⁴KEY]

**cayenne pepper** /kay'en/ *n* 1 a pungent hot red condiment consisting of the ground dried pods and seeds of HOT PEPPERS – compare CHILLI, PAPRIKA 2 a plant bearing HOT PEPPERS; *esp* a cultivated variety with very long twisted red fruit-pods 3 the fruit of a cayenne pepper [alter. (influenced by *Cayenne*, town in French Guiana) of earlier *cayan*, modif of Tupi *kyinha*]

**cayman, caiman** /'kaymən, 'kie-/ *n* any of several Central and S American reptiles of the crocodile family closely related to the alligators [Sp *caimán*, prob fr Carib *caymán*]

**Cayuga** /kee'oohgə, kay-, kie-/ *n, pl* **Cayugas**, *esp collectively* **Cayuga** (a member of) an American Indian people of New York State; *also* their Iroquoian language

**Cayuse** /'kie,yoohs, -'-/ *n, pl* **Cayuses**, *esp collectively* **Cayuse** 1 a member of an American Indian people of Oregon and Washington 2 *not cap, NAm* an American Indian-bred pony

**C clef** *n* a symbol on a musical score indicating the position of MIDDLE C on the stave – compare ALTO CLEF, TENOR CLEF

**cease** /sees/ *vt* to bring to an end; terminate ⟨~ *this noise!*⟩ ⟨*the dying man soon* ~d *to breathe*⟩ ~ *vi* 1 to come to an end ⟨*when will this quarrelling* ~?⟩ 2 to bring an activity or action to an end; discontinue ⟨*cried for hours without* ceasing⟩ – see also cease FIRE [ME *cesen*, fr OF *cesser*, fr L *cessare* to delay, fr *cessus*, pp of *cedere*]

**'cease-,fire** *n* 1 a military order to cease firing 2 a usu temporary suspension of active hostilities ⟨*arranged a* ~ *so that details of a peace treaty could be discussed*⟩

**ceaseless** /'seeslis/ *adj* continuing endlessly; constant – **ceaselessly** *adv*, **ceaselessness** *n*

**cecity** /'seesəti/ *n, poetic* blindness [MF *cécité*, fr L *caecitas*, fr *caecus* blind]

**cecum** /'seekəm/ *n, pl* **ceca** /-kə/ *NAm* CAECUM (part of the intestine) – **cecal** *adj*

**cedar** /'seedə/ *n* any of a genus (*Cedrus*) of usu tall coniferous trees (eg the cedar of Lebanon) of the pine family; *also* their fragrant durable wood [ME *cedre*, fr OF, fr L *cedrus*, fr Gk *kedros*; akin to Lith *kadagys* juniper]

**cedarn** /'seedən/ *adj, archaic* made or suggestive of cedar

**cedar of Lebanon** /'lebənən/ *n* a long-lived tall evergreen tree (*Cedrus libani*) with short leaves in small bundles and upright cones that is native to Asia Minor [*Lebanon*, country in Asia Minor]

**cedarwood** /'seedə,wood/ *n* the wood of a cedar, which is esp repellent to insects

**cede** /seed/ *vt* to yield or grant (eg a territory), typically by treaty; relinquish [Fr or L; Fr *céder*, fr L *cedere* to go, withdraw, yield; prob akin to L *cis* on this side and to Gk *hodos* road, way, L *sedēre* to sit – more at HE, SIT] – **ceder** *n*

**cedi** /'saydi, 'sidi/ *n, pl* **cedi** – see MONEY table [Akan *sedie* cowrie]

**cedilla** /sə'dilə/ *n* a mark **,** placed under a letter (eg ç in French) to indicate an alteration or modification of its usual pronunciation (eg in the French word *façade*) [Sp, the obs letter ç (actually a medieval form of the letter z), cedilla, fr dim. of *ceda, zeda* the letter z, fr LL *zeta*, fr Gk *zēta*]

**Ceefax** /'see,faks/ *trademark* – used for a service provided by the BBC which transmits information (eg stock market results or subtitles for programmes for the hard of hearing) on usu special channels to viewers who have paid an additional fee

**ceiba** /'saybə/ *n* a large tropical tree (*Ceiba pentandra*) of the baobab family that bears large pods filled with seeds covered with a silky floss that yields the fibre kapok [Sp, prob fr Arawakan origin]

**ceilidh** /'kayli/ *n* an informal evening gathering for traditional Scottish or Irish dancing, singing, etc [IrGael *cēilidhe* & ScGael *cēilidh*, fr MIr *cēlide*, fr OIr *cēle, cēile* companion, husband; akin to L *civis* citizen]

**ceiling** /'seeling/ *n* 1 the overhead inside surface of a room 2 the height above the ground of the base of the lowest layer of clouds when over half of the sky is obscured 3 the actual (ABSOLUTE CEILING) or prescribed (SERVICE CEILING) maximum height at which an aircraft can fly 4 an upper usu prescribed limit ⟨*a* ~ *on prices, rents, and wages*⟩ [ME *celing*, fr *celen* to furnish with a ceiling, prob deriv of L *caelare* to carve, fr *caelum* chisel, fr *caedere* to cut] – **ceilinged** *adj*

usage Although **ceiling** is often used today to mean "upper limit", our sense of its literal meaning as the top of a room makes it odd to speak of *increasing, extending*, or *waiving* a ceiling, or of an *unrealistic* ceiling.

**ceilometer** /see'lomitə, si-/ *n* an instrument for determining the height above the ground of the base of a layer of cloud; CLOUD BASE RECORDER [*ceiling* + *-o-* + *-meter*]

**celadon** /'selədon, -dn/ *n* 1 a greyish-green colour 2 (a type of usu Chinese porcelain having) a greyish-green ceramic glaze [Fr *céladon*, fr *Céladon*, languid lover in the romance *L'Astrée* by Honoré d'Urfé †1625 Fr writer]

**celandine** /'selən,dien/ *n* 1 *also* **greater celandine** a yellow-flowered plant (*Chelidonium majus*) of the poppy family 2 *also* **lesser celandine** a common early-flowering European plant (*Ranunculus ficaria*) of the buttercup family [ME *celidoine*, fr MF, fr L *chelidonia*, fr fem of *chelidonius* of the swallow, fr Gk *chelidonios*, fr *chelidon-, chelidōn* swallow]

**-cele** /-seel/ *comb form* (→ *n*) hernia ⟨*meningo*cele⟩ [MF, fr L, fr Gk *kēlē*; akin to OE *hēala* hernia, OSlav *kyla*]

**celebrant** /'selibrənt/ *n* a person who performs a public ritual; *specif* the priest officiating at Communion

**celebrate** /'selibrayt/ *vt* 1 to perform (a religious ceremony) publicly and with appropriate rites ⟨~ *the mass*⟩ 2a to mark (eg a holy day or feast day) by solemn ceremonies or by refraining from ordinary business ⟨*Christmas is* ~d *on 25 December*⟩ **b** to mark (a special occasion) with festivities or suspension of routine activities ⟨~ *a royal wedding*⟩ 3 to hold up for public acclaim; extol ⟨*his poetry* ~s *the glory of nature*⟩ ~ *vi* 1 to officiate at a religious ceremony 2 to observe a special occasion, usu with festivities [L *celebratus*, pp of *celebrare* to frequent, celebrate, fr *celeber, celeber* much frequented, famous; akin to L *celer* swift] – **celebrator** *n*, **celebratory** *adj*, **celebration** *n*

**celebrated** /'selibraytid/ *adj* widely known and often referred to – **celebratedness** *n*

**celebrity** /sə'lebrəti/ *n* 1 the state of being famous 2 a well-known and widely acclaimed person

**celeriac** /sə'le(ə)riak/ *n* a type of celery grown for its turnip-like edible root [irreg fr *celery*]

**celerity** /sə'lerəti/ *n, formal* rapidity, esp of motion or action [ME *celerite*, fr MF *célérité*, fr L *celeritat-, celeritas*, fr *celer* swift – more at HOLD]

**celery** /'seləri/ *n* a European plant (*Apium graveolens*) of the carrot family; *specif* any of a cultivated variety (*Apium graveolens dulce*) with leafstalks that are usu kept white by excluding light during growth and that can be eaten raw or cooked [prob fr It dial. *seleri*, pl of *selero*, modif of LL *selinon*, fr Gk]

**celesta** /sə'lestə/ *n* a keyboard instrument with hammers that strike steel plates producing a soft tinkling tone [Fr *célesta*, alter. of *céleste*, lit., heavenly, fr L *caelestis*]

**celeste** /sə'lest/ *n* 1 a celesta 2 an organ and harmonium stop with a soft tremulous tone [Fr *céleste*, lit., heavenly]

**¹celestial** /sə'lestiəl/ *adj* 1 of or suggesting heaven or divinity; divine 2 of the sky or visible heavens ⟨*the sun, moon, and stars are* ~ *bodies*⟩ [ME, fr MF, fr L *caelestis*, fr *caelum* sky; akin to Skt *citra* bright] – **celestially** *adv*

**²celestial** *n* a heavenly or mythical being

**Celestial Empire** *n* Imperial China – used, esp in translations from the Chinese, to stress the divinity of the Emperor and his role in reproducing the divine harmony of the heavens in his earthly rule [trans of Chin *Tiān Cháo* (*T'ien*[1] *Ch'ao*[2])]

**celestial equator** *n* the GREAT CIRCLE on the CELESTIAL SPHERE midway between the CELESTIAL POLES

**celestial globe** *n* a globe showing the relative positions of the celestial bodies

**celestial hierarchy** *n* **1** a traditional hierarchy of angels ranked from lowest to highest into the nine orders of angels, archangels, principalities, powers, virtues, dominions, thrones, cherubim, and seraphim **2** a Chinese ranking of the heavenly bodies in which each star or constellation has a position paralleling the hierarchy of the Imperial Court

**celestial horizon** *n* HORIZON 1b(2)

**celestial navigation** *n* ASTRONAVIGATION

**celestial pole** *n* either of the two points on the CELESTIAL SPHERE around which the daily rotation of the stars appears to take place

**celestial sphere** *n* an imaginary sphere of infinite radius against which the celestial bodies appear to be projected and of which the apparent dome of the visible sky forms half

**celestine** /'selǝstien, -steen, sǝ'lestien, -stin/, **celestite** /'selǝstiet, sǝ'lestiet/ *n* a naturally occurring mineral consisting mainly of strontium sulphate, $SrSO_4$ [Ger *zölestin*, fr L *caelestis*]

**celiac** /'seeliak/ *adj, chiefly NAm* coeliac

**celibacy** /'selibǝsi/ *n* **1** the state of not being married **2a** abstention from sexual intercourse **b** abstention by vow from marriage

**celibate** /'selibǝt/ *n* someone who lives in celibacy (e g as the result of some religious vow) [L *caelibatus*, fr *caelib-, caelebs* unmarried; akin to Skt *kevala* alone and to OE *libban* to live] – **celibate** *adj*

**cell** /sel/ *n* **1** a small religious house dependent on a monastery or convent **2a** a one-roomed dwelling occupied by a solitary person (e g a hermit) **b** a sparsely furnished room for one person (e g in a convent or monastery) **c** a small room in a prison or police station for the confinement of one or more prisoners **3** a small compartment (e g in a honeycomb), cavity (e g in a plant ovary), bounded space (e g in an insect wing), or receptacle **4** a part that behaves as or is treated as a unit: e g **4a** a small and usu microscopic mass of jellylike living material surrounded by a membrane and forming the smallest structural unit of living matter capable of functioning either alone or with others in all fundamental life processes **b** the basic and usu smallest unit of an organization or movement; *esp* the primary unit of a Communist organization **c** a portion of the atmosphere that behaves as a unit **d** a basic subdivision of a computer memory that is addressable and can hold one unit (e g a word) of a computer's basic operating data **5a** a device that produces electricity by chemical action e g: **5a(1)** WET CELL **a(2)** DRY CELL (battery) **a(3)** an electrical cell in which the OXIDATION of a fuel produces electrical energy directly; FUEL CELL **b** a vessel in which a liquid is decomposed by passing an electrical current through it (e g so as to deposit a metal on one of the electrodes in electroplating) **c** a single unit in a device for converting radiant energy into electrical energy or for varying the intensity of an electrical current in accordance with radiation [ME, fr OE, religious house, & OF *celle* hermit's cell, fr L *cella* small room; akin to L *celare* to conceal – more at HELL]

**cella** /'selǝ/ *n* the principal chamber of an ancient temple containing the shrine to the divinity; *broadly* the main body of any classical building – compare NAOS [L, small room, cella]

[1]**cellar** /'selǝ/ *n* **1** an underground room; *esp* one used for storage **2** an individual's stock of wine (*kept a good* ~) [ME *celer*, fr AF, fr L *cellarium* storeroom, fr *cella*]

[2]**cellar** *vt* to store or place (e g wine) in a cellar

**cellarage** /'selǝrij/ *n* **1** cellar space, esp for storage **2** charge for storage in a cellar

**cellarer** /'selǝrǝ/ *n* an official (e g in a monastery) in charge of provisions [ME *celerer*, fr OF, fr LL *cellariarius*, fr L *cellarium*]

**cellaret, cellarette** /,selǝ'ret/ *n* a case or sideboard for holding bottles of alcoholic drink [*cellar* + *-et*]

**cell body** *n* the nucleus-containing central part of a NERVE CELL excluding its AXONS and DENDRITES

**cell cycle** *n* the complete series of events from one CELL DIVISION to the next

**cell division** *n* the process by which two daughter cells are formed from a parent cell – compare MEIOSIS, MITOSIS

**-celled** /-seld/ *comb form* (→ *adj*) having (such or so many) cells (*single*-celled *organisms*)

**cell membrane** *n* **1** a membrane surrounding a cell; *specif* PLASMA MEMBRANE **2** a cell wall

**cello** /'cheloh/ *n, pl* **cellos** a musical instrument of the violin family that is intermediate in range between the viola and the DOUBLE BASS and is played held between the knees, supported on the ground by an adjustable metal spike [short for *violoncello*] – **cellist** *n*

**cellobiose** /,selǝ'bie·ohs, -ohz/ *n* a faintly sweet sugar, $C_{12}H_{22}O_{11}$, obtained from the partial breakdown of cellulose [ISV *cellul*ose + *-o-* + *biose* (disaccharide), fr [1]*bi-* + *-ose*]

**cellophane** /'selǝ,fayn/ *n* thin transparent sheets of cellulose used esp for wrapping goods [Fr, fr *cellul*ose + *-phane* (as in *diaphane* diaphanous, fr ML *diaphanus*)]

**cell plate** *n* a disc formed in a dividing plant cell that eventually separates the daughter cells and forms the middle layer of the wall between them

**cell sap** *n* **1** the liquid contents of a plant cell vacuole **2** CYTOPLASM (jellylike material inside a cell)

**cellular** /'selyoolǝ/ *adj* **1** (consisting) of cells **2** containing cavities; having a porous texture (~ *rocks*) [NL *cellularis*, fr *cellula* living cell, fr L, dim. of *cella* small room] – **cellularity** *n*, **cellularly** *adv*

**cellulase** /'selyoolayz/ *n* an ENZYME that promotes the chemical breakdown of cellulose [ISV *cellul*ose + *-ase*]

**cellule** /'selyoohl/ *n* a small cell [L *cellula*]

**cellulite** /'selyoo,liet/ *n* a type of body fat held to be caused by water retention, and producing a dimpled effect on the skin (e g of the thigh) [Fr, fr *cellule* + *-ite* -itis]

**cellulitis** /,selyoo'lietǝs/ *n* inflammation of body tissue, esp below the surface of the skin [NL, fr *cellula*]

**celluloid** /'selyoo,loyd/ *n* cinematographic film (*a historic moment captured on* ~); *also* the world of motion pictures [fr *Celluloid*, a trademark] – **celluloid** *adj*

**Celluloid** *trademark* – used for a tough highly inflammable thermoplastic composed mainly of CELLULOSE NITRATE and CAMPHOR

**cellulolytic** /,selyoooh'litik/ *adj* breaking down or having the capacity to break down cellulose (~ *bacteria*) (~ *activity*) [*cellul*ose + *-o-* + *-lytic*]

**cellulose** /'selyoo,lohs/ *n* **1** a chemical compound ($C_6H_{10}O_5$), consisting of a POLYSACCHARIDE of glucose units that constitutes the chief part of the CELL WALLS of plants, occurs naturally in such fibrous products as cotton and kapok, and is the raw material of many manufactured goods (e g paper, rayon, and cellophane) **2** paint or lacquer of which the main constituent is CELLULOSE NITRATE or CELLULOSE ACETATE [Fr, fr *cellule* living cell, fr NL *cellula*] – **cellulose** *adj*

**cellulose acetate** *n* any of several chemical compounds insoluble in water that are formed esp by the action of ACETIC ACID, anhydride of acetic acid, and SULPHURIC ACID on cellulose and are used for making textile fibres, packaging sheets, photographic films, and varnishes *synonyms* see NYLON

**cellulose nitrate** *n* any of several chemical compounds formed by the action of NITRIC ACID on cellulose and used for making explosives, plastics, rayon, and varnishes

**cellulosic** /,selyoo'lohsik/ *n* a substance made from (a derivative of) cellulose – **cellulosic** *adj*

**cell wall** *n* the firm nonliving wall formed usu from cellulose that encloses and supports most plant cells

**Celsius** /'selsi·ǝs/ *adj* conforming to or being a scale of temperature on which water freezes at 0° and boils at 100° under standard conditions [Anders *Celsius* †1744 Sw astronomer]

**celt** /selt/ *n* a prehistoric chisel or axe head made of stone, bronze, or occasionally iron – no longer used technically [LL *celtis* chisel]

**Celt** /kelt/ *n* **1** a member of a division of the early Indo-European peoples distributed from the British Isles and Spain to Asia Minor **2** a Highland Scot, Irishman, Welshman, Cornishman, Manxman, or Breton; esp one speaking Celtic [Fr *Celte*, sing. of *Celtes*, fr L *Celtae*]

[1]**Celtic** /'keltik; *football team* 'seltik/ *adj* (characteristic) of the Celts or their languages

  *usage* An older pronunciation /'seltik/ is preserved in the name of **Celtic**, the Scottish football team.

[2]**Celtic** *n* a distinct branch of Indo-European languages which is usu subdivided into a BRYTHONIC group comprising Welsh, Cornish, and Breton and a GOIDELIC group comprising Irish, Scots Gaelic, and Manx

**Celtic cross** *n* a cross consisting of a LATIN CROSS with a ring centred on the intersection of the crossbar and upright shaft

**Celtic fringe** *n, often cap F* Cornwall, N & W Wales, Ireland, and the Highlands and Islands of Scotland considered as being different from, and marginal to, the rest of Britain, esp culturally and in their political characteristics – regarded as offensive by most Celts

**Celticist** /'keltisist/ *n* a specialist in Celtic languages, literature, or cultures

**cembalo** /'chembə,loh/ *n, pl* **cembali** /-bəli/, **cembalos** a harpsichord [It, short for *clavicembalo*, fr ML *clavicymbalum*, fr L *clavis* key + *cymbalum* cymbal]

**¹cement** /si'ment/ *n* **1a** a powder consisting of alumina, silica, lime, IRON OXIDE, and magnesia pulverized together and burnt in a kiln and used as the binding agent in mortar and concrete **b** concrete – not used technically **2** a binding element or agency: eg **2a** a substance (eg a glue or adhesive) used for sticking objects together **b** something serving to unite firmly ⟨*justice is the ~ that holds a political community together* – R M Hutchins⟩ **3** cementum **4** a pliable adhesive dental preparation used for filling or lining cavities or for attaching crowns or inlays **5** the fine-grained body of a PORPHYRY (type of rock) in which the larger crystals are suspended [ME *sement*, fr OF *ciment*, fr L *caementum* stone chips used in making mortar, fr *caedere* to cut – more at CONCISE]

**²cement** *vt* **1** to unite or make firm (as if) by cement **2** to overlay with concrete ~ *vi* to become cemented – **cementer** *n*

**cementation** /,semen'taysh(ə)n, ,see-/ *n* **1** the act or process of cementing; the state of being cemented ⟨*~ of sand into stone*⟩ **2** a process of surrounding a solid with a powder and heating the whole so that the solid is changed by chemical combination with the powder; *esp* the heating of iron surrounded by charcoal to make steel

**cementite** /si'mentiet/ *n* a hard brittle iron-containing chemical compound (CARBIDE), $Fe_3C$, occurring in steel, CAST IRON, and iron-carbon alloys [¹*cement*]

**cementum** /si'mentəm/ *n* a specialized thin bony layer enclosing the DENTINE of the root of a tooth [NL, fr L *caementum*]

**cemetery** /'semətri/ *n* a burial ground; *esp* one that is not in a churchyard [ME *cimitery*, fr MF *cimitere*, fr LL *coemeterium*, fr Gk *koimētērion* sleeping chamber, burial place, fr *koiman* to put to sleep; akin to L *cunae* cradle]

**cen-, ceno-** *comb form, chiefly NAm* cain-, caino-

**-cene** /-seen/ *comb form* (→ *adj*) recent – in names of geological periods ⟨*Eocene*⟩ [Gk *kainos*]

**cenobite** /'seenoh,biet/ *n, NAm* a coenobite – **cenobitic, cenobitical** *adj*

**cenospecies** /'seenoh,spees(h)iz/ *n, NAm* a coenospecies

**cenotaph** /'senə,tahf/ *n* a tomb or a monument erected in honour of a person or group of people whose remains are elsewhere; *specif, cap* that standing in Whitehall in London in memory of the dead of World Wars I and II △ catacomb, catafalque [Fr *cénotaphe*, fr L *cenotaphium*, fr Gk *kenotaphion*, fr *kenos* empty + *taphos* tomb – more at EPITAPH]

**Cenozoic** /,seenə'zoh·ik/ *adj, NAm* cainozoic – **Cenozoic** *n*

**cense** /sens/ *vt* to perfume, esp with a censer [ME *censen*, prob short for *encensen* to incense, fr MF *encenser*, fr LL *incensare*, fr *incensum* incense]

**censer** /'sensə/ *n* a vessel for burning incense; *esp* a covered incense burner swung on chains in a religious ritual △ censor

**¹censor** /'sensə/ *n* **1** either of two magistrates of early Rome who acted as census takers, assessors, and inspectors of morals and conduct **2** one who supervises conduct and morals: eg **2a** an official who examines publications or films with the power to suppress objectionable (eg obscene or libellous) matter **b** an official (eg in time of war) who scrutinizes communications for material considered harmful (eg useful to an enemy) **3** a hypothetical mental agency that represses certain ideas and desires before they reach consciousness [L, fr *censēre* to assess, tax; akin to Skt *śaṃṣati* he recites] – **censorial** *adj*

**²censor** *vt* to subject to censorship

**censorious** /sen'sawri·əs/ *adj* marked by or given to censure [L *censorius* of a censor, fr *censor*] – **censoriously** *adv*, **censoriousness** *n*

**censorship** /'sensə,ship/ *n* **1a** the institution, system, or practice of censoring **b** the actions, practices, or duties of a censor; *esp* censorial control exercised repressively **2** the office, power, or term of a Roman censor **3** the repression from consciousness of unacceptable ideas or desires

**¹censure** /'senshə/ *n* **1** a judgment involving condemnation **2** the act of blaming or condemning sternly **3** an official reprimand **4** *archaic* an opinion, judgment [L *censura*, fr *censēre*]

**²censure** *vt* **1** to find fault with and criticize as blameworthy **2** *obs* to estimate, judge – **censurable** *adj*, **censurer** *n*

**census** /'sensəs/ *n* **1** a count of the population together with a survey of property, held in early Rome **2** a usu complete enumeration of a population; *specif* a periodic counting of the population and gathering of related statistics (eg age, sex, occupation, or social class) necessary for planning, carried out by a government **3** a usu official count or tally [L, fr *censēre*] – **census** *vt*

**cent** /sent/ *n* (a coin or note representing) a monetary unit worth $1/100$ of a basic money unit of certain countries – see MONEY table [MF, hundred, fr L *centum* – more at HUNDRED]

**cental** /'sentl/ *n, chiefly Br* a unit of weight equal to 100 pounds (about 45.36 kilograms) – used formerly, esp for measures of grain [L *centum* + E *-al* (as in *quintal*)]

**centare** /'senteə/, **centiare** /'senti,eə/ *n* a metric unit of area equal to 1 square metre [Fr *centiare*, fr *centi-* hundred + *are*]

**centaur** /'sen,taw/ *n* any of a race of creatures who according to Greek mythology had the head, arms, and upper body of a man and the lower body and legs of a horse and lived in the mountains of Thessaly [ME, fr L *Centaurus*, fr Gk *Kentauros*]

**centaurea** /sen'tawriə/ *n* any of a large genus (*Centaurea*) of plants of the daisy family (eg knapweed) including several cultivated for their showy heads of tubular flowers [NL, genus name, fr ML]

**centaury** /'sen,tawri/ *n* any of a genus (*Centaurium*) of low plants of the gentian family △ century [ME *centaure*, fr MF *centaurée*, fr ML *centaurea*, fr L *centaureum*, fr Gk *kentaureion*, fr *Kentauros;* fr the reputed discovery of its medicinal qualities by a centaur]

**centavo** /sen'tahvoh/ *n, pl* **centavos** (a coin or note representing) a unit worth $1/100$ of the basic money unit of certain Spanish- or Portuguese-speaking countries (eg Chile, Cuba, Mexico, Portugal) – see MONEY table [Sp & Pg; Pg, fr Sp, lit., hundredth, fr L *centum* hundred]

**centenarian** /,sentə'neəri·ən/ *n* someone who is (more than) 100 years old – **centenarian** *adj*

**centenary** /sen'teenəri, -'tenəri/ *n* a 100th anniversary or its celebration [LL *centenarium*, fr L *centenarius* of a hundred, fr *centeni* one hundred each, fr *centum* hundred – more at HUNDRED] – **centenary** *adj*

*usage* The pronunciation /sen'teenəri/ is recommended for BBC broadcasters.

**centennial** /sen'teni·əl/ *n or adj, chiefly NAm* (a) centenary [L *centum* + E *-ennial* (as in *biennial*)] – **centennially** *adv*

**center** /'sentə/ *vb or n, NAm* (to) centre

**centesimal** /sen'tesiml/ *adj* marked by or relating to division into hundredths [L *centesimus* hundredth, fr *centum*]

**¹centesimo** /sen'tesimoh/ *n, pl* **centesimi** (a now obsolete coin representing) $1/100$ of an Italian LIRA – see *lira* at MONEY table [It, lit., hundredth, fr L *centesimus*]

**²centesimo** *n, pl* **centesimos** – see *balboa*, *peso* at MONEY table [Sp *centésimo*, fr L *centesimus*]

**centi-** /senti-/ *comb form* **1** hundred ⟨*centipede*⟩ **2** one hundredth ($10^{-2}$) part of (a specified unit) ⟨*centimetre*⟩ [Fr & L; Fr, hundredth, fr L, hundred, fr *centum* – more at HUNDRED]

**centigrade** /'senti,grayd/ *adj* Celsius [Fr, fr L *centi-* hundred + Fr *grade*]

**centigram** /'senti,gram/ *n* one hundredth of a gram (about $1\frac{1}{2}$ grains) [Fr *centigramme*, fr *centi-* + *gramme* gram]

**centilitre** /'senti,leetə/ *n* one hundredth of a litre (about $1/3$ fluid ounce) [Fr, fr *centi-* + *litre*]

**centillion** /sen'tiliən, -'tilyən/ *n* – see NUMBER table [L *centum* + E *-illion* (as in *million*)]

**centime** /'sonteem/ *n* (a note or coin representing) a unit worth $1/100$ of the basic money unit of certain French-speaking countries (eg Algeria, Belgium, France) – see MONEY table [Fr, fr *cent* hundred, fr L *centum*]

**centimetre** /'sentimeetə/ *n* one hundredth of a metre (about $2/5$ inch) [Fr *centimètre*, fr *centi-* + *mètre* metre]

**,centimetre-gram-'second** *adj* of or being a system of units based on the centimetre as the unit of length, the gram as the unit of mass, and the second as the unit of time

**centimetric** /,senti'metrik/ *adj* having a wavelength of between 1 and 10 centimetres

**centimo** /'sentimoh/ *n, pl* **centimos** (a coin or note representing) a unit worth $1/100$ of the basic money unit of Spain and certain South American countries – see MONEY table [Sp *céntimo*, fr Fr *centime*]

**centipede** /'senti,peed/ *n* any of a class (Chilopoda of the phylum Arthropoda) of long flattened many-segmented INVERTEBRATE animals with each segment bearing one pair of legs of which the foremost pair is modified into poison fangs [L *centipeda*, fr *centi-* + *ped-*, *pes* foot – more at FOOT]

**centner** /'sentnə/ *n* a unit of weight used in Germany and Scandinavia usu equal to 50 kilograms (about 110.23 pounds); *also* a unit used in the USSR equal to 100 kilograms (about 220.46 pounds) [prob fr LG, deriv of L *centenarius* of a hundred]

**cento** /'sentoh/ *n*, *pl* **centones** /sen'tohneez/, **centos** a literary work made up of parts from other works [LL, fr L, patchwork garment; akin to OHG *hadara* rag, Skt *kanthā* patched garment]

**centr-** /-sentr-/, **centri-**, **centro-** *comb form* centre ⟨centri*fugal*⟩ ⟨centr*oid*⟩ [Gk *kentr-*, *kentro-*, fr *kentron* centre – more at CENTRE]

**central** /'sentrəl/ *adj* 1 containing or constituting a centre 2 of primary importance; principal ⟨*the* ~ *character of the novel*⟩ 3a situated at, in, or near the centre ⟨*the plains of* ~ *N America*⟩ b easily accessible from outlying districts; convenient ⟨*a* ~ *location for a new theatre*⟩ 4 having overall power or control ⟨*decided by the* ~ *committee*⟩ ⟨~ *management*⟩ 5 maintaining a middle position between extremes; moderate 6 of or comprising the brain and spinal cord; *also* originating within the CENTRAL NERVOUS SYSTEM ⟨~ *deafness*⟩ [L *centralis*, fr *centrum* centre, fr Gk *kentron*] – **centrally** *adv*

**central angle** *n* an angle formed by two radii of a circle

**central bank** *n* the main banking institution of a country that usu acts as banker to the government and other banks and is often responsible for note issue, credit regulation, and holding the country's foreign reserves

**Central Criminal Court** *n* a special CROWN COURT having jurisdiction over all offences committed in Greater London

**Central European Time** *n* the standard time, one hour ahead of GREENWICH MEAN TIME, which is used by most countries of Western and Central Europe in the first time zone east of Greenwich

**central heating** *n* a system of heating a building in which heat produced at a single source (eg in a boiler) is distributed to individual outlets (eg radiators or air vents) situated throughout the building

**centralism** /'sentrə,liz(ə)m/ *n* (the principle of) the concentration of power and control in the central authority of an organization (eg a political or educational system) ⟨*the growing* ~ *of government and the declining powers of Local Authorities*⟩ – compare FEDERALISM – **centralist** *n or adj*, **centralistic** *adj*

**centrality** /sen'traləti/ *n* 1 the quality or state of being central 2 central situation 3 tendency to remain in or at the centre

**central·ize, -ise** /'sentrə,liez/ *vi* to come to or gather round a centre; *specif* to gather under the control of some central body (eg government) ~ *vt* 1 to bring to a centre; consolidate ⟨~ *all the data in one file*⟩ 2 to bring (power, authority, etc) under central control ⟨*Stalin's great achievement as Party Secretary was his* centralizing *of its organization*⟩ – **centralizer** *n*, **centralization** *n*

**central limit theorem** *n* any of several fundamental theorems of probability sampling and statistics that allow the distribution of independent RANDOM VARIABLES to be related to the NORMAL DISTRIBUTION curve; *esp* a special case of the central limit theorem which states that if MEANS (averages) of various samples of a variable are plotted on a graph, the curve obtained will approximate closely to the NORMAL DISTRIBUTION curve for that variable in the population as a whole, providing that the samples are sufficiently large

**central nervous system** *n* the part of the nervous system which in VERTEBRATE animals consists of the brain and spinal cord, to which sensory impulses are transmitted and from which motor impulses pass out, and which supervises and coordinates the activity of the entire nervous system

**central processing unit** *n* the vital part of a computer system that actually carries out all the arithmetical and logical operations

**central reservation** *n* a usu paved, tarred, or planted strip in the middle of a road and esp a motorway

**¹centre**, *NAm chiefly* **center** /'sentə/ *n* **1a** the point round which a circle or sphere is described; *broadly* CENTRE OF SYM

METRY **b** the centre of a circle inscribed in a regular polygon ⟨~ *of a square*⟩ **2a** a place, esp a collection of buildings, round or in which a usu specified activity is concentrated ⟨*a shopping* ~⟩ ⟨*the Lincoln* ~ *for the Performing Arts*⟩ **b** the topic round which interest is concentrated ⟨*the* ~ *of the debate*⟩ **c** a source from which something originates ⟨*a propaganda* ~⟩ **d** a region of concentrated population ⟨*an urban* ~⟩ **3** a group of nerve cells having a common function ⟨*respiratory* ~⟩ **4** the middle part (eg of a stage) **5** *often cap* **5a** a grouping of political figures holding moderate views esp between those of Conservatives and Labour **b(1)** the views of such politicians **b(2)** *taking sing or pl vb* the adherents of such views **6a** a player occupying a usu attacking position in the forward line of a team (eg in football, hockey, or basketball); *also* the position itself **b** an instance of passing the ball from a wing to the centre of a pitch or court (eg in football) **7** either of two tapered rods which support work in a lathe or grinding machine and about or with which the work revolves **8** a temporary wooden framework on which an arch is supported during construction [ME *centre*, fr MF, fr L *centrum*, fr Gk *kentron* sharp point, centre of a circle, fr *kentein* to prick; akin to OHG *hantag* pointed]

**²centre**, *NAm chiefly* **center** *vi* **1** to have a centre; focus – usu + *round* or *on* **2** to come to or towards a centre or central area **3** to centre a ball, puck, etc ~ *vt* **1** to place at or bring to a centre or central area ⟨~ *the picture on the wall*⟩ **2** to gather to a centre; concentrate ⟨~s *her hopes on her son*⟩ **3** to adjust (eg lenses in a microscope) so that the axes coincide **4** to pass (a ball or puck) from either side towards the middle of the playing area

*usage* Things **centre** or are **centred** *on*, *upon*, or *in* other things. A thing can be **centred** *at* a place ⟨*a nationwide organization* **centred** *at Tewkesbury*⟩. The use of **centre** with *about*, *round*, or *around* ⟨*many legends* **centre** *around him*⟩ is widely disliked but is now very common.

,**centre-'back** *n* a defensive player in soccer positioned in the middle of the defence; *also* the position itself

**centre bit** *n* a drilling tool with a central point for guidance and a lip for cutting away inside a scored circumference, usu used for boring holes in wood

**centreboard** /'sentə,bawd/ *n* a retractable keel used esp in dinghies and small yachts

**centred** /'sentəd/ *adj* having a centre – often in combination ⟨*a dark-centred flower*⟩

,**centre-'fold** *n* (a pictorial display covering) the two facing pages in the centre of a newspaper or magazine ⟨*a* ~ *portrait of the Crown Prince*⟩

,**centre-'forward** *n* a player in some games (eg hockey and soccer) positioned in the middle of the forward line; *also* the position itself

,**centre-'half** *n* a player in some games (eg hockey and soccer) positioned in the middle of the half-back line; *also* the position itself

**centreline** /'sentə,lien/ *n* a real or imaginary line that divides a symmetrical shape or cross-section into two equal parts

**centre of curvature** *n* the centre of the circle that has the same curvature as a curve at a given point

**centre of gravity** *n* **1** CENTRE OF MASS **2** the point at which the entire weight of a body may be considered as concentrated so that if supported at this point the body would remain in equilibrium in any position **3** the centre of main interest, involvement, or concern ⟨*the* ~ *of industrial strategy has shifted from control of the trade unions to the question of youth unemployment*⟩

**centre of mass** *n* the point in a body or system of bodies at which the whole mass may be considered as concentrated; *also* the point at which the application of a force will produce an acceleration but no rotation

**centre of symmetry** *n* the point about which a geometric figure displays symmetry

**centrepiece** /'sentə,pees/ *n* an object occupying a central position; *specif* an ornament or decoration in the centre of a table

**centreplate** /'sentə,playt/ *n* a centreboard

**centre punch** *n* a hand tool consisting of a short steel bar with a hardened conical point at one end, used to punch a mark showing the centres of holes to be drilled

,**centre-'spread** *n* a centre-fold

,**centre-three-'quarter** *n* either of the two players in rugby positioned in the middle of the three-quarter-back line; *also* the position itself

**centri-** /'sentri/ – see CENTR-

**centric** /'sentrik/, **centrical** /-kl/ *adj* **1** central **2** of a nerve centre **3** of or being a CHROMOSOME (strand of gene-carrying material in a cell) having a CENTROMERE [Gk *kentrikos* of the centre, fr *kentron*] – **centrically** *adv*, **centricity** *n*

**-centric** /-'sentrik/ *comb form* (→ *adj*) having (such) a centre or (such or so many) centres ⟨*poly*centric⟩; having (something specified) as a centre ⟨*helio*centric⟩ [ML *-centricus*, fr L *centrum* centre]

**centrifugal** /ˌsentri'fyoohg(ə)l, sen'trifyoog(ə)l/ *adj* **1** proceeding or acting in a direction away from a centre or axis **2** using or acting by centrifugal force ⟨*a* ~ *pump*⟩ **3** tending away from centralization; separatist ⟨ ~ *tendencies in modern society leading to greater local autonomy*⟩ [NL *centrifugus*, fr *centr-* + L *fugere* to flee – more at FUGITIVE] – **centrifugally** *adv*

*usage* The pronunciation /ˌsentri'fyoohg(ə)l/ is recommended for BBC broadcasters.

**centrifugal force** *n* the force that appears to act on an object moving along a circular path and that acts outwardly away from the centre of rotation

**¹centrifuge** /'sentriˌfyoohj, -ˌfyoohzh/ *n* a machine using CENTRIFUGAL FORCE for separating substances of different densities, for removing moisture, or for simulating gravitational effects [Fr, fr *centrifuge* centrifugal, fr NL *centrifugus*]

**²centrifuge** *vt* to subject to centrifugal action, esp in a centrifuge – **centrifugation** *n*

**centriole** /'sentriˌohl/ *n* either of a pair of ORGANELLES (specialized cell parts) that are adjacent to the nucleus, function in the formation of the apparatus that separates pairs of corresponding CHROMOSOMES (strands of gene-carrying material) during CELL DIVISION, and consist of a cylinder with nine MICROTUBULES (microscopic tubular structures) arranged peripherally in a circle [Ger *zentriol*, fr *zentrum* centre]

**centripetal** /sen'tripitl, ˌsentri'peetl/ *adj* **1** proceeding or acting in a direction towards a centre or axis **2** tending towards centralization; unifying [NL *centripetus*, fr *centr-* + L *petere* to go to, seek – more at FEATHER] – **centripetally** *adv*

*usage* The pronunciation /sen'tripitl/ is recommended for BBC broadcasters.

**centripetal force** *n* the force that is necessary to keep an object moving in a circular path and that is directed inwards towards the centre of rotation

**centrist** /'sentrist/ *n, often cap* a member of a centre party – **centrism** *n*

**centro-** – see CENTR-

**centroid** /'sentroyd/ *n* CENTRE OF MASS – **centroidal** *adj*

**centromere** /'sentrəˌmiə/ *n* the point on a CHROMOSOME (strand of gene-carrying material in a cell) by which it appears to attach to the SPINDLE (arrangement of fibres along which chromosomes are distributed) during CELL DIVISION [ISV] – **centromeric** *adj*

**centrosome** /'sentrəˌsohm/ *n* **1** the region of clear CYTOPLASM (jellylike material in a cell) that contains the centriole and is adjacent to the cell nucleus **2** a centriole [Ger *zentrosom*, fr *zentr-* centr-+ *-som* -some] – **centrosomic** *adj*

**centrosphere** /'sentrəˌsfiə/ *n* **1** the layer of CYTOPLASM (jellylike substance contained in a cell) surrounding the centriole within the centrosome **2** the central part of the earth, composed of very dense material [ISV]

**centrum** /'sentrəm/ *n, pl* **centrums, centra** /'sentrə/ **1** a centre **2** the body of a VERTEBRA (bone of the spine) [L – more at CENTRE]

**centurion** /sen'tyooəri·ən/ *n* **1** an officer commanding a century in the ancient Roman army **2** someone who scores a century in cricket [ME, fr MF & L; MF, fr L *centurion-, centurio*, fr *centuria*]

**century** /'senchəri/ *n* **1** *taking sing or pl vb* a subdivision of the Roman legion numbering between 80 and 100 men **2** *taking sing or pl vb* a group, sequence, or series of 100 like things **3** a period of 100 years, esp of the years reckoned forwards or backwards from the conventional date of the birth of Christ **4** 100 runs in cricket ⟨*a* ~ *fourth-wicket partnership*⟩; *esp* 100 runs scored by a batsman in a single innings ⟨*completed his half-*~ *in record time*⟩ [L *centuria*, irreg fr *centum* hundred]

*usage* Just as the 1900s are the 20th century, so the period 1801–1900 was the 19th century, 1301–1400 was the 14th century, and so on. Expressions such as ⟨*during this* century⟩ mean "since 1901", not "since 100 years ago".

**century plant** *n* a Mexican agave (*Agave americana*) with long lance-shaped leaves that matures and flowers only once in many years and then dies

**ceorl** /cheəl/ *n* a freeman of the lowest rank in Anglo-Saxon England [OE – more at CHURL]

**cep** /sep/ *n* any of several edible fungi (family Boletus) having a spongelike underside; *esp* one with a shiny brown cap and white underside (*Boletus edolis*) considered a delicacy esp in France and Germany [Fr *cèpe*, fr Fr dial. *cep* treetrunk, mushroom, fr L *cippus* stake, post]

**cephal-, cephalo-** *comb form* head ⟨*cephalad*⟩; head and ⟨*cephalothorax*⟩ [L, fr Gk *kephal-, kephalo-*, fr *kephalē*]

**cephalad** /'sefəˌlad/ *adv* towards the head or anterior end of the body – compare CAUDAD

**cephalic** /si'falik/ *adj* **1** of the head **2** directed towards or situated at, in, or near the head [MF *céphalique*, fr L *cephalicus*, fr Gk *kephalikos*, fr *kephalē* head; akin to OHG *gebal* skull, ON *gafl* gable] – **cephalically** *adv*

**cephalic index** *n* the ratio of the maximum breadth of the head to its maximum length multiplied by 100 – compare CRANIAL INDEX

**cephal·ization, -isation** /ˌsefəlie'zaysh(ə)n/ *n* an evolutionary tendency to specialization of the body with concentration of SENSE ORGANS and nerve centres in an anterior head

**cephalochordate** /ˌsefəloh'kawdayt/ *n* a small slender fishlike marine animal that has a NOTOCHORD (supporting skeletonlike rod) but no VERTEBRAL COLUMN; LANCELET [deriv of *cephal-* + L *chorda* cord]

**cephalometry** /ˌsefə'lomətri/ *n* the science of measuring the head [ISV] – **cephalometric** *adj*

**cephalopod** /'sefə(ə)ləˌpod/ *n* any of a class (Cephalopoda of the phylum Mollusca) of INVERTEBRATE animals that include the squids, cuttlefishes, and octopuses and have a tubular siphon, a group of muscular arms around the head which are usu furnished with suckers, and highly developed eyes [deriv of *cephal-* + Gk *pod-, pous* foot – more at FOOT] – **cephalopod** *adj*, **cephalopodan** *adj or n*

**cephaloridine** /ˌsefə'lorideen/ *n* an antibiotic drug, $C_{19}H_{17}N_3O_4S_2$, used esp in the treatment of infections of the respiratory and urinary tracts by penicillin-resistant bacteria [prob fr *cephalosporin* + *-idine*]

**cephalosporin** /ˌsef(ə)lə'spawrin/ *n* any of several antibiotics produced by an IMPERFECT FUNGUS (genus *Cephalosporium*) [*Cephalosporium*, genus of fungi + *-in*]

**cephalothorax** /ˌsef(ə)lə'thawraks/ *n* the united head and THORAX (central region of the body) of a spider, scorpion, crab, or related animal [ISV]

**Cepheid** /'sefi·id/ *n* any of a class of pulsating stars which show regular variation in the amount of light they give out [L *Cepheus*, a northern constellation (whose fourth star, Delta Cephei, varies in brightness), fr *Cepheus*, mythical king of Ethiopia & father of Andromeda, fr Gk *Kēpheus*]

**ceraceous** /sə'rayshəs/ *adj* resembling wax [L *cera* wax – more at CERUMEN]

**ceramal** /sə'rayməl/ *n* CERMET (alloy of a metal and some ceramic material) [*ceramic* alloy]

**¹ceramic** /sə'ramik/ *adj* of the manufacture of a product (eg earthenware, porcelain, or brick) made from a nonmetallic mineral (eg clay) by firing at high temperatures; *also* of or being such a product [Gk *keramikos*, fr *keramos* potter's clay, pottery]

**²ceramic** *n* **1** *pl but taking sing vb* the art or process of making ceramic articles **2** a product of ceramic manufacture – **ceramist** *n*, **ceramicist** *n*

**cerastes** /si'rasteez/ *n* a venomous viper (*Cerastes cornutus*) of the Near East that has a horny ridge over each eye – called also HORNED VIPER [ME, fr L, fr Gk *kerastēs*, lit., horned, fr *keras*]

**cerat-** /kerət-/, **cerato-, kerat-, kerato-** *comb form* **1** horn; horny ⟨*ceratodus*⟩ ⟨*keratin*⟩ **2** cornea ⟨*keratitis*⟩ [NL, fr Gk *kerat-, kerato-*, fr *keras* horn – more at HORN]

**ceratodus** /si'ratədəs, ˌserə'tohdəs/ *n* any of various recent or fossil lunged fishes (eg of the genus *Ceratodus*); *esp* a barramunda [NL, genus name, fr *cerat-* + Gk *odous* tooth – more at TOOTH]

**ceratopogonid** /ˌserətoh'pohgənid/ *n* any of a family (Ceratopogonidae) of biting midges [deriv of Gk *keras* horn + *pōgōn* beard]

**-cercal** /-'suhkl/ *comb form* (→ *adj*) -tailed ⟨*homo*cercal⟩ [Fr *-cerque*, fr Gk *kerkos* tail]

**cercaria** /suh'keəri·ə/ *n, pl* **cercariae** /-iˌee/ a usu tadpole-shaped larva of a parasitic flatworm (e g a LIVER FLUKE) that develops in an INTERMEDIATE HOST (e g a snail) [NL, fr Gk *kerkos* tail] – **cercarial** *adj*

**cercopid** /'suhkə,pid/ *n* FROGHOPPER (type of insect) [NL *Cercopis*, genus of insects]

**cercus** /'suhkəs, 'kuh–/ *n, pl* **cerci** /-see, -sie, 'kuhkee/ either of a pair of simple or segmented structures at the hind end of various insects (e g a cockroach) and other ARTHROPODS [NL, fr Gk *kerkos* tail]

**¹cere** /siə/ *vt* to wrap (as if) in an oiled or waxed shroud (CERE-CLOTH) [ME *ceren* to wax, fr MF *cirer*, fr L *cerare*, fr *cera*]

**²cere** *n* a usu waxy protuberance or swelling at the base of the bill of a bird [ME *sere*, fr MF *cere*, fr ML *cera*, fr L, wax]

**cereal** /'siəriəl/ *n* 1 a plant (e g a grass) yielding grain suitable for food; *also* its grain 2 a prepared foodstuff of grain; *esp* any of various processed foods usu eaten with milk and sugar at breakfast △ serial [Fr or L; Fr *céréale* of grain, fr L *cerealis* of Ceres, of grain, fr *Ceres*, goddess of grain & agriculture] – **cereal** *adj*

**cerebellum** /,serə'beləm/ *n, pl* **cerebellums, cerebella** /-'belə/ a large projecting part of the back of the brain that is concerned esp with the coordination of muscles and the maintenance of balance – compare CEREBRUM [ML, fr L, dim. of *cerebrum*] – **cerebellar** *adj*

**cerebr-** /serəbr-/, **cerebro-** *comb form* 1 brain; cerebrum 〈cerebr*ation*〉 2 cerebral and 〈cerebro*spinal*〉 [*cerebrum*]

**cerebral** /'serəbrəl/ *adj* 1a of the brain or the intellect b of or being the CEREBRUM (front region of the brain) 2a appealing to the intellect 〈~ *drama*〉 b primarily intellectual in nature 〈a ~ *society*〉 [Fr *cérébral*, fr L *cerebrum* brain; akin to Gk *kara* head, *keras* horn – more at HORN] – **cerebrally** *adv*

**cerebral cortex** *n* the surface layer of GREY MATTER of the CEREBRAL HEMISPHERES that functions chiefly in coordination of higher nervous activity

**cerebral hemisphere** *n* either of the two hollow convoluted lateral halves of the cerebrum of the brain

**cerebral palsy** *n* a disability caused by damage to the brain before or during birth and resulting in lack of muscular coordination and speech disturbances – compare SPASTIC PARALYSIS

**cerebrate** /'serəbrayt/ *vi, formal* to use the mind; think [back-formation fr *cerebration*, fr *cerebrum*] – **cerebration** *n*

**cerebroside** /,seri'broh,sied/ *n* any of various LIPIDS (complex fatlike chemical compounds) found esp in nerve tissue [*cerebrose* (galactose) + *-ide*]

**cerebrospinal** /,serəbroh'spienl/ *adj* of the brain and SPINAL CORD or these together with the nerves connecting them with the VOLUNTARY MUSCLES

**cerebrospinal fluid** *n* a liquid that is comparable to SERUM and is secreted from the blood into the VENTRICLES (spaces within the brain)

**cerebrospinal meningitis** *n* inflammation of the membranes surrounding both brain and SPINAL CORD; *specif* an infectious and often fatal form of this caused by the MENINGOCOCCUS (type of bacterium)

**cerebrovascular** /,seribroh'vaskyoolə/ *adj* of or involving the cerebrum and the blood vessels supplying it 〈~ *disease*〉

**cerebrum** /'seribrəm/ *n, pl* **cerebrums, cerebra** /-brə/ 1 BRAIN 1a 2 an enlarged front or upper part of the brain: 2a the forebrain and midbrain with their derivatives b FOREBRAIN 2a c the expanded front portion of the brain that in higher mammals overlies the rest of the brain, consists of CEREBRAL HEMISPHERES and connecting structures, and is considered to be the seat of conscious mental processes – compare CEREBELLUM [L]

**cerecloth** /-,kloth/ *n* cloth treated with melted wax or gummy matter and formerly used esp for wrapping a dead body [alter. of earlier *cered cloth* (waxed cloth)]

**cerements** /'siəmənts/ *n pl*, **cerement** *n* a shroud for the dead; *esp* a cerecloth

**¹ceremonial** /,serə'mohnyəl, -ni-əl/ *adj* marked by, involved in, or belonging to ceremony; stressing careful attention to form and detail *synonyms* see CEREMONIOUS – **ceremonialism** *n*, **ceremonialist** *n*, **ceremonially** *adv*

**²ceremonial** *n* 1a a ceremonial act or action b a usu prescribed set of formal or ritual actions for a particular occasion 〈altered the traditional ~ of the Trooping of the Colour〉 2 the order of service in the Roman Catholic church; *also* a book containing this

**ceremonious** /,serə'mohnyəs, -ni-əs/ *adj* 1 ceremonial 2 devoted to forms and ceremony; punctilious – **ceremoniously** *adv*, **ceremoniousness** *n*

*synonyms* Ceremonial is concerned with actual rituals 〈a cere-monial *occasion*〉 〈ceremonial *robes*〉 while the chief meaning of ceremonious is "observing established conventions" 〈ceremonious *politeness*〉 〈an ever precise, utterly proper, and extremely cere-monious *old gentleman*〉. People can be ceremonious but not ceremonial. *antonym* unceremonious

**ceremony** /'serəməni/ *n* 1 a formal act or series of acts prescribed by ritual, protocol, or convention 〈the marriage ~〉 2 (observance of) established conventions or procedures of civility or politeness 〈the door opened without ~ and a man strode in〉 [ME *ceremonie*, fr MF *cérémonie*, fr L *caerimonia*] – **stand on ceremony** to act in a formally correct manner 〈just come as you are, we aren't ones for standing on ceremony〉

**Cerenkov radiation** /chir'(y)engkəf, -kof/ *n* light produced by charged particles (e g electrons) passing through a transparent medium at a speed greater than that of light in the same medium [P A *Cherenkov* b 1904 Russ physicist]

**ceresin** /'serisin/ *n* a hard mineral wax used as a substitute for beeswax, esp in paints and polishes [deriv of L *cera* wax]

**cereus** /'siəriəs/ *n* any of various cacti (e g of the genus *Cereus*) of the western USA and tropical America [NL, genus name, fr L, wax candle, fr *cera* wax – more at CERUMEN]

**ceric** /'serik, 'siərik/ *adj* of or containing the chemical element cerium, esp when having a VALENCY of four

**cerise** /sə'rees, -'reez/ *n or adj* (a) light clear purplish red [Fr, lit., cherry, fr LL *ceresia* – more at CHERRY]

**cerium** /'siəri-əm/ *n* a metallic chemical element that can be easily worked and that is the most abundant of the RARE-EARTH ELEMENTS [NL, fr *Ceres*, an asteroid discovered just before the element]

**cerium metal** *n* any of a group of related metals that are RARE-EARTH ELEMENTS and include cerium, lanthanum, praseodymium, neodymium, promethium, samarium, and sometimes europium

**cermet** /'suhmit/ *n* a strong alloy of a heat-resistant usu ceramic chemical compound (e g titanium carbide) and a metal (e g nickel), used esp for turbine blades [*ceramic metal*]

**cernuous** /'suhnyooəs/ *adj, botany* pendulous, nodding 〈a ~ *flower*〉 [L *cernuus* with the face turned earthwards; akin to L *cerebrum*]

**cerograph** /'siərə,grahf, -,graf, -roh-/ *n* an engraving on wax [back-formation fr *cerography* (drawing with or on wax), fr Gk *kērographia*, fr *kēros* wax + *-graphia* -graphy]

**ceroplastic** /,si(ə)roh'plastik; *also* -'plah-/ *adj* 1 relating to modelling in wax 2 modelled in wax [Gk *kēroplastikos*, fr *kēros* + *plastikos* plastic]

**cerotic acid** /si'rotik, -'roh-/ *n* a solid FATTY ACID, $C_{26}H_{52}O_2$, occurring in waxes (e g beeswax) and some fats [L *cerotum*, a pomade, fr Gk *kērōton*, fr *kēros* wax – more at CERUMEN]

**cerous** /'siərəs/ *adj* of or containing the chemical element cerium, esp when having a VALENCY of three

**cert** /suht/ *n, Br informal* CERTAINTY 1; *esp* a horse that is sure to win a race – often + *dead* to emphasize the certainty 〈a dead ~ for the 4:30〉

**¹certain** /'suht(ə)n/ *adj* 1a proved to be true; indisputable 〈it is ~ that we exist〉 b dependable, reliable 〈no ~ remedy for this disease〉 c inevitable 〈the ~ advance of age and decay〉 d incapable of failing; destined – + a following infinitive 〈~ to happen〉 2a of a known but unspecified character, quantity, or degree; particular 〈the house has a ~ charm〉 〈guaranteed a ~ percentage of the profit〉 〈everyone has a ~ amount of success〉 b named but not otherwise known 〈a ~ Mrs Jones〉 3 assured in mind; confident 〈I'm ~ she saw me〉 *synonyms* see ¹SURE [ME, fr OF, fr (assumed) VL *certanus*, fr L *certus*, fr pp of *cernere* to sift, discern, decide; akin to Gk *krinein* to separate, decide, judge, *keirein* to cut – more at SHEAR] – **for certain** as a certainty; assuredly

**²certain** *pron taking pl vb* certain ones 〈~ of the people have no shoes〉

**certainly** /'suht(ə)nli/ *adv* 1 it is certain that 〈~ we shall come if we're not in France〉 2 in a confident manner 〈he dealt with the examiners' questions very ~〉 *usage* see ¹SURE

**certainty** /'suht(ə)nti/ *n* 1 something that is certain 2 the quality or state of being certain, esp on the basis of objective evidence

*synonyms* Certainty, certitude, assurance, and conviction all mean "freedom from doubt". The first two are often interchangeable, but certitude usually applies to subjective certainty approaching faith rather than to the rational objectivity of certainty. Assurance stresses confidence and sureness in something which cannot be proved or has yet to take place ⟨**assurance** *that the prize would be his*⟩. **Conviction** suggests that previous doubts have been overcome, and is connected with "convinced" ⟨*a* **conviction** *that she was, after all, telling the truth*⟩. **antonyms** uncertainty, doubt

**certes** /'suhtiz/ *adv, archaic* certainly; in truth [ME, fr OF, fr *cert* certain, fr L *certus*]

¹**certificate** /sə'tifikət/ *n* a document containing a certified statement, esp as to the truth of something; *esp* one attesting the status or qualifications of the holder ⟨*a ~ of vaccination*⟩ [ME *certificat*, fr MF, fr ML *certificatum*, fr LL, neut of *certificatus*, pp of *certificare* to certify]

²**certificate** /sə'tifikayt/ *vt* to testify to or authorize by a certificate – **certificatory** *adj*

**Certificate of Secondary Education** *n* a British examination in any of many subjects that is intended for the majority of children and is taken typically at about the age of 16

**certification** /,suhtifi'kaysh(ə)n/ *n* 1 the act of certifying; the state of being certified 2 a certified statement

**certified cheque** /'suhtified/ *n, chiefly NAm* a cheque that bears a guarantee of payment by the bank on which it is drawn

**certify** /'suhtifie/ *vt* 1a to confirm, esp officially in writing b to attest as being true or as represented or as meeting a standard ⟨*a* certified *copy of the document*⟩ c to declare officially to be insane 2 to give evidence of certification of; license 3 *chiefly NAm* to guarantee (a personal cheque) as to signature and amount by so indicating on the face 4 *archaic* to inform with certainty; assure [ME *certifien*, fr MF *certifier*, fr LL *certificare*, fr L *certus* certain – more at CERTAIN] – **certifiable** *adj*, **certifiably** *adv*, **certifier** *n*

**certiorari** /,suhtiaw'reəri, -shiaw-/ *n* an order of a superior court calling up for review the records of an inferior court or a body acting in a quasi-judicial capacity [ME, fr L, to be informed; fr the use of the word in the writ]

**certitude** /'suhti,tyoohd/ *n* 1 the state of being or feeling certain 2 certainty of act or event **synonyms** see CERTAINTY **antonym** doubt [ME, fr LL *certitudo*, fr L *certus*]

**cerulean** /si'roohli-ən/ *adj* resembling the deep blue of the sky [L *caeruleus* dark blue, prob fr *caelum* sky]

**ceruloplasmin** /,serəloh'plazmin/ *n* a blue-coloured protein that is found in the blood and is active in the biological storage and transport of copper [ISV *cerulo-* (fr L *caeruleus* dark blue) + *plasma* + *-in*]

**cerumen** /si'roohmən/ *n* the yellow waxy secretion from the glands of the outer ear [NL, irreg fr L *cera* wax, prob fr Gk *kēros*; akin to Lith *korys* honeycomb] – **ceruminous** *adj*

**ceruse** /'siə,roohs, si'roohs/ *n* white lead when used as a pigment [ME, fr MF *céruse*, fr L *cerussa*]

**cerussite** /'siərəsiet/ *n* a mineral consisting essentially of lead carbonate, $PbCO_3$, that occurs as colourless transparent crystals and also in massive form [Ger *zerussit*, fr L *cerussa*]

**cervelat** /'suhvəlat, -lah/ *n* a smoked sausage made of varying proportions of pork and beef [obs Fr (now *cervelas*)]

**cervic-** /suhvik-, səviek-/, **cervici-**, **cervico-** *comb form* neck; cervix ⟨*cervicitis*⟩; cervical and ⟨*cervicothoracic*⟩ [L *cervic-, cervex* neck]

**cervical** /'suhvikl; *tech usu* sə'viekl/ *adj* of a neck or cervix **usage** The pronunciations /sə'viekl/ and /'suhvikl/ are both recommended for BBC broadcasters.

**cervicitis** /,suhvi'sietəs/ *n* inflammation of the neck of the womb [NL]

**cervine** /'suhvien/ *adj* of or resembling deer [L *cervinus* of a deer, fr *cervus* stag, deer – more at HART]

**cervix** /'suhviks/ *n, pl* **cervices** /'suhviseez/, **cervixes** 1 the neck; *esp* the back part of the neck 2 a constricted portion of an organ or part; *esp* the narrow outer end of the womb [L *cervic-, cervix*]

**cesarean** *also* **cesarian** /si'zeəri-ən/ *n, NAm* a caesarean – **cesarean** *also* **cesarian** *adj*

**cesium** /'seezi-əm/ *n, NAm* caesium

**cess** /ses/ *n, chiefly Irish* luck – chiefly in *bad cess to you* [prob short for *success*]

**cessation** /si'saysh(ə)n/ *n* a temporary or final stop; an ending △ cession [ME *cessacioun*, fr MF *cessation*, fr L *cessation-, cessatio* delay, idleness, fr *cessatus*, pp of *cessare* to delay, be idle – more at CEASE]

**cesser** /'sesə/ *n* an ending or termination in law (e g of interest or liability) [MF, fr *cesser* to cease]

**cession** /'sesh(ə)n/ *n* an act or instance of renouncing or yielding rights, property, or esp territory △ cessation, session

[ME, fr MF, fr L *cession-, cessio,* fr *cessus,* pp of *cedere* to withdraw – more at CEDE]

**cesspit** /'ses,pit/ *n* 1 a pit for the collection and disposal of sewage; *esp* one in which waste matter is purified by bacterial action 2 a squalid or corrupt place or situation [*cesspool + pit*]

**cesspool** /'ses,poohl/ *n* a cesspit [alter. (influenced by *pool*) of earlier *cesperalle,* prob fr ME *suspiral* vent, fr MF *souspirail* ventilator, fr *soupirer* to sigh, fr L *suspirare,* lit., to draw a long breath – more at SUSPIRE]

**cesta** /'sestə/ *n* a narrow curved wicker basket used to catch and throw the ball in JAI ALAI and PELOTA [Sp, lit., basket, fr L *cista* box, basket]

**cestode** /'ses,tohd/ *n* any of a subclass (Cestoda) of internally parasitic flatworms comprising the tapeworms [deriv of Gk *kestos* girdle] – **cestode** *adj*

**cestus** /'sestəs/ *n* a hand covering of leather bands often loaded with lead or iron and used by boxers in ancient Rome [L *caestus,* fr *caedere* to strike – more at CONCISE]

**cesura** /si'zhooərə/ *n* a caesura

**cetacean** /si'taysh(ə)n/ *n* any of an order (Cetacea) of aquatic mostly marine mammals including the whales, dolphins, porpoises, and related animals which have a large head, a fishlike nearly hairless body, and paddle-shaped forelimbs [deriv of L *cetus* whale, fr Gk *kētos*] – **cetacean** *adj,* **cetaceous** *adj*

**cetane** /'see,tayn/ *n* a colourless oily chemical compound, $C_{16}H_{34}$, found in petroleum [*cetyl* (the radical $C_{16}H_{33}$; deriv of L *cetus* whale; fr its presence in spermaceti) + *-ane*]

**cetane number** *n* a measure of the ease with which a diesel fuel will ignite – compare OCTANE NUMBER

**cetane rating** *n* CETANE NUMBER

**ceteris paribus** /,ketəris 'paribəs, 'pah-/ *adv, formal* if all other relevant things, factors, or elements remain unaltered; all other things being equal [NL, other things being equal]

**cetyl alcohol** /'seetl, 'setl/ *n* a chemical compound, $C_{16}H_{33}OH$, found in the waxy SPERMACETI of certain whales and used in medical and cosmetic preparations and in making detergents [ISV *cetyl* (the radical $C_{16}H_{33}$), deriv of L *cetus* whale; fr its occurrence in spermaceti]

**cevitamic acid** /,seevie'tamik/ *n* VITAMIN C [*cee* (the letter *c*) + *vitam*in + *-ic*]

**cha** /chah/ *n* ⁵CHAR (tea)

**chabazite** /'kabə,ziet/ *n* a complex mineral, $(Ca,Na_2)(Al_2Si_4O_{12}).6H_2O$, consisting of sodium calcium aluminium silicate used in water softeners [Ger *chabasit,* fr Fr *chabasie,* deriv of Gk *chalaza* hailstone]

**Chablis** /'shabli/ *n, pl* **Chablis** /'shabliz, ~/ a very dry white table wine produced in northern Burgundy [Fr, fr *Chablis,* town in France]

**cha-cha** /'chah ,chah/, **cha-cha-cha** *n* a fast rhythmic ballroom dance of Latin-American origin with a basic pattern of three steps and a shuffle; *also* music intended for this dance or written to its rhythm [AmerSp *cha-cha-cha*]

**chacma** /'chakmə/ *n* a large grey-coated southern African baboon (*Papio* or *Chaeropithecus comatus*) [Hottentot]

**chaconne** /shə'kon/ *n* 1 an old Spanish dance tune resembling the PASSACAGLIA 2 a musical composition in moderate time with three beats to the bar and stress on the second beat and typically consisting of variations on a repeated succession of chords [Fr & Sp; Fr *chaconne,* fr Sp *chacona*]

**chad** /chad/ *n* small pieces of paper or cardboard produced as waste in punching paper tape or data cards; *also* a piece of chad [perh fr Sc, gravel] – **chadless** *adj*

**Chad** /chad/, **Chadic** *n* a branch of the Afro-Asiatic language family comprising numerous languages of N Nigeria and Cameroons [Lake *Chad,* central Africa] – **Chadic** *adj*

**chador, chadar, chuddar, chudder** /'chudə/ *n* a large cloth serving as a veil and head covering worn by women in India and Iran; *esp* one, usu black, worn by Islamic women in Iran as a sign of religious orthodoxy [Hindi *caddar,* fr Per *chaddar*]

**chaeta** /'keetə/ *n, pl* **chaetae** /'keeti/ a bristle or SETA, esp on the body of various worms [NL, fr Gk *chaitē* long flowing hair] – **chaetal** *adj*

**chaetognath** /'keetəg,nath/ *n* any of a class or phylum (Chaetognatha) of small free-swimming marine worms with movable curved bristles on either side of the mouth [deriv of Gk *chaitē* + *gnathos* jaw – more at GNATH-] – **chaetognath** *adj,* **chaetognathan** *adj or n*

¹**chafe** /chayf/ *vt* 1 to irritate, vex 2 to warm (a part of the body) by rubbing, esp with the hands 3a to rub so as to wear

away; abrade ⟨*the constant motion will soon ~ the paintwork*⟩ **b** to make sore (as if) by rubbing ~ *vi* **1** to feel irritation or discontent; fret ⟨*~s at his restrictive desk job*⟩ **2** to become sore, irritated, or worn as a result of rubbing △ chaff [ME *chaufen* to warm, fr MF *chaufer*, fr (assumed) VL *calfare*, alter. of L *calefacere*, fr *calēre* to be warm + *facere* to make – more at LEE, DO]

²**chafe** *n* **1** a state of vexation; a rage **2** (injury or wear caused by) friction

**chafer** /'chayfə/ *n* any of various large beetles (esp family Scarabaeidae) the fat white larvae of which live in the soil and do great damage to plant roots [ME *cheaffer*, fr OE *ceafor*; akin to OE *ceafl* jowl – more at JOWL]

¹**chaff** /chaf, chahf/ *n* **1** the seed coverings and other debris separated from the seed in threshing grain **2** chopped straw, hay, etc used for animal feed **3** something comparatively worthless – chiefly in *separate the wheat from the chaff* **4** the scales borne on the RECEPTACLE (enlarged tip of stem from which flower parts arise) among the individual flowers (FLORETS) in the flower heads of many plants of the daisy family **5** material (e g strips of foil or clusters of fine wires) ejected into the air for reflecting radar waves: **5a** to confuse enemy radar detection systems **b** to aid in the tracking of a descending spacecraft during the period when no radio communication is possible [ME *chaf*, fr OE *ceaf*; akin to OHG *cheva* husk] – **chaffy** *adj*

²**chaff** *n* light jesting talk; banter [prob alter. of *chafe*] – **chaff** *vb*

**chaffinch** /'chafinch/ *n* a common European finch (*Fringilla coelebs*) that has a reddish breast, a bluish head, white wing bars, and a cheerful song [ME, fr OE *ceaffinc*, fr *ceaf* + *finc* finch]

**chafing dish** /'chayfing/ *n* a serving dish usu incorporating a spirit burner for keeping food warm at table [ME *chafing*, prp of *chaufen, chafen* to warm]

**Chagas' disease** /'shahgəs(iz)/ *n* an often fatal tropical American disease that is marked by prolonged high fever, swelling, and enlargement of spleen, liver, and LYMPH NODES, and is caused by a parasitic microorganism (*Trypanosoma cruzi*) [Carlos *Chagas* †1934 Brazilian physician]

¹**chagrin** /'shagrin/ *n* mental distress caused by humiliation, disappointment, or failure [Fr, fr *chagrin* sad]

²**chagrin** *vt* to vex acutely through disappointment, failure, or humiliation

**Chaima** /'chiemə/ *n* a member, or the language, of a Cariban people of Venezuela

¹**chain** /chayn/ *n* **1a** a series of usu metal links or rings connected to one another and used for various purposes (e g support or restraint) ⟨*a ~ bridge*⟩ ⟨*an anchor ~*⟩ **b** an ornament or badge of office consisting of such a series of links ⟨*a locket on a ~*⟩ **c(1)** a measuring instrument of 100 links used in surveying **c(2)** a unit of length equal to 66 feet (about 20.12 metres) **2** chains *pl*, **chain** something that confines, restrains, or secures ⟨*the ~s of poverty and ignorance*⟩ **3a** a series of things linked, connected, or associated together ⟨*a ~ of events*⟩ ⟨*a mountain ~*⟩ **b** a group of associated establishments (e g shops or hotels) under the same ownership ⟨*a ~ of discount stores*⟩ **c** a number of atoms or chemical groups united like links in a chain [ME *cheyne*, fr OF *chaeine*, fr L *catena*; akin to L *cassis* net]

²**chain** *vt* to fasten, restrict, or confine (as if) with a chain – often + *up* ⟨*~ up that dog!*⟩

**chain armour** *n* CHAIN MAIL

**chaîné** /she'nay/ *n* a series of short regular usu fast turns by which a ballet dancer moves across the stage [Fr, fr pp of *chaîner* to chain]

**chain gang** *n taking sing or pl vb* a gang of convicts chained together, esp as an outside working party

**chain letter** *n* a letter containing a request that copies of it, sometimes together with money or goods, be sent to a specified number of people who should then repeat the process, and often containing threats of bad luck to those who fail to carry out the letter's instructions

**chain mail** *n* flexible armour of interlinked metal rings

**chainman** /'chaynmən/ *n* a surveyor's assistant; *esp* one taking measurements for him/her with a chain or tape measure

**chain printer** *n* a LINE PRINTER (one printing a whole line of text in a single operation) in which the type is carried on a continuous band past a line of hammers

**chain reaction** *n* **1** a series of events so related to each other that each one initiates the next **2** a self-sustaining chemical or nuclear reaction yielding energy or products that cause further reactions of the same kind – **chain-react** *vt*

**chain rule** *n* a mathematical rule concerning the differentiation of a function of a function (e g $f[u(x)]$) by which under suitable conditions of continuity and differentiability one function is differentiated with respect to the second considered as an INDEPENDENT VARIABLE and then the second function is differentiated with respect to the INDEPENDENT VARIABLE

**chain saw** *n* a portable power saw that has teeth linked together to form an endless chain

'**chain-,smoke** *vb* to smoke (esp cigarettes) continually, often by lighting one cigarette from the butt of the previous one

**chain stitch** *n* **1** an ornamental embroidery or crochet stitch that resembles a linked chain **2** a machine stitch forming a series of interlocking loops on the underside of the work

**chain store** *n* any of several usu retail shops under the same ownership and selling the same lines of goods

**chainwheel** /'chayn,weel/ *n* a toothed wheel (e g on a bicycle) that transmits power by means of a chain

¹**chair** /cheə/ *n* **1** a seat for one person, usu with four legs, a back, and sometimes arms **2a** an office or position of authority or dignity; *specif* a professorship ⟨*holds a university ~*⟩ **b** a chairperson **3** a sedan chair **4** a position of employment usu of one occupying a chair or desk ⟨*has a ~ on the board of directors*⟩; *specif* the position of a player in an orchestra or band **5** any of various devices that hold up or support; *esp* a deep-grooved metal block fastened to a sleeper to hold a rail in place [ME *chaiere*, fr OF, fr L *cathedra*, fr Gk *kathedra*, fr *kata-* cata- + *hedra* seat – more at SIT]

²**chair** *vt* **1** to install in office **2** to preside as chairperson of **3** *chiefly Br* to carry shoulder-high in acclaim ⟨*the time you won your town the race we ~ed you through the market place* – A E Housman⟩

**chair lift** *n* a ski lift with seats for passengers

**chairman** /-mən/ *n* **1** a usu male chairperson **2** a carrier of a sedan chair – **chairmanship** *n*

**chairperson** /-,puhs(ə)n/ *n* **1** someone presiding over or heading a meeting, committee, organization, or board of directors **2** a radio or television presenter; *esp* one who coordinates discussions or unscripted shows

**usage Chairperson** is used particularly when the sex is still unknown because the post has not yet been filled ⟨*a chairperson will be appointed*⟩. When it is filled, a woman is more likely than a man to call herself a **chairperson**. People who dislike the word **chairperson** say **chairman** of a man and **chairwoman** or **chairman** (*Madam* **Chairman**) of a woman, or avoid the problem by saying **chair** ⟨*address your remarks to the* **Chair**⟩. See PERSON

**chairwoman** /'cheə,woomən/ *n* a female chairperson

**chaise** /shez, shayz/ *n* **1** a light carriage usu with two wheels and a folding top **2** POST CHAISE [Fr, chair, chaise, alter. of OF *chaiere*]

**chaise longue** /long·g/ *n, pl* **chaise longues** *also* **chaises longues** /~ long·g, long·gz/ a chair the seat of which is elongated so that the legs of the sitter can be supported on it, and which typically has an upholstered back and a single low armrail *synonyms* see SOFA [Fr, lit., long chair]

**Chait** /chiet/ *n* – see MONTH table [Hindi *Cait*, fr Skt *Caitra*]

**chalaza** /kə'lahzə, -'la-/ *n, pl* **chalazae** /-zi/, **chalazas 1** either of a pair of spiral bands in the white of a bird's egg that extend from the yolk and are attached to opposite ends of the shell membrane **2** the point at the base of a plant OVULE (immature seed before fertilization) where the seed stalk is attached [NL, fr Gk, hailstone; akin to Per *zhāla* hail] – **chalazal** *adj*

**Chalcedonian** /,kalsi'dohnyən/ *adj* of Chalcedon or the ecumenical council held there in AD 451 declaring MONOPHYSITISM (the doctrine that Christ was divine rather than both divine and human in nature) heretical [*Chalcedon*, ancient city in Asia Minor (now *Kadikoy* in Turkey)] – **Chalcedonian** *n*

**chalcedony** /kal'sidəni, -'sedəni/ *n* a translucent quartz that is commonly pale blue or grey with a nearly waxlike lustre and is used as a gemstone [ME *calcedonie*, a precious stone, fr LL *chalcedonius*, fr Gk *Chalkēdōn* Chalcedon] – **chalcedonic** *adj*

**chalcid** /'kalsid/ *n* any of a large superfamily (Chalcidoidea) of very small insects which in their larval stage are parasites of the larvae or pupae of other insects [deriv of Gk *chalkos* copper; fr the insects' metallic colour] – **chalcid** *adj*

**chalcocite** /'kalkə,siet/ *n* a grey-black mineral consisting of copper sulphide, $Ca_2S$, that is an important source of copper [irreg fr Fr *chalcosine*, fr Gk *chalkos* copper]

**chalcopyrite** /ˌkalkə'pieriet/ *n* a brassy-yellow mineral consisting of copper-iron sulphide, $CuFeS_2$, and constituting an important source of copper [NL *chalcopyrites,* fr Gk *chalkos* + L *pyrites*]

**Chaldean** /kal'dee-ən/, *also* **Chaldaic** /kal'dayik/ *n* **1a** a member of an ancient Semitic people once dominant in Babylonia **b** the Semitic language of the Chaldeans **2** an adept or practitioner of the occult arts (eg astrology) [L *Chaldaeus* Chaldean, astrologer, fr Gk *Chaldaios,* fr *Chaldaia* Chaldea, region of ancient Babylonia] – **Chaldean** *adj*

**Chaldee** /'kal,dee, ,-'-/ *n* **1** the Aramaic original language of a few parts of the Old Testament **2** a Chaldean [ME *Caldey,* prob fr MF *chaldée,* fr L *Chaldaeus*]

**chaldron** /'chawldrən/ *n* any of various old units of measure varying from 32 to 72 imperial bushels (about 1164 to 2619 litres) [MF *chauderon,* fr *chaudere* pot, fr LL *caldaria* – more at CAULDRON]

**chalet** /'shalay/ *n* **1** a hut used by herdsmen on the upland summer pastures of the Alps **2a** a typically wooden house with a steeply pitched roof and overhanging eaves which is the traditional form of dwelling house in rural Switzerland **b** a small house or hut used esp for temporary accommodation (eg at a holiday camp) [Fr, fr Fr dial. (Swiss)]

**chalice** /'chalis/ *n* **1** a drinking cup; a goblet **2** a large usu gold or silver goblet used to hold the wine at Communion [ME, fr AF, fr L *calic-, calix;* akin to Gk *kalyx* calyx]

**¹chalk** /chawk/ *n* **1a** a soft white, grey, or buff limestone composed chiefly of the shells of small marine organisms **b** a geological area in which chalk is the main underlying formation; soil which is mainly chalk ⟨*azaleas will not grow on* ∼⟩ **c** a short rod formerly of chalk but now usu of calcium sulphate that is used for writing and drawing (eg on a blackboard); *also, pl* PASTELS **2a** a mark made with chalk **b** *Br* (a record of) a point scored in a game [ME, fr OE *cealc;* akin to OHG & MLG *kalk* lime; all fr a prehistoric WGmc word borrowed fr L *calc-, calx* lime, fr Gk *chalix* pebble; akin to Gk *skallein* to hoe – more at SHELL] – **chalky** *adj* – **by a long chalk** to a great extent; by far – often + *not* [fr the use of chalk to mark the score in games]

**²chalk** *vt* **1** to rub or mark with chalk **2** to write or draw with chalk **3** to set down or add up (as if) with chalk; tot – usu + *up* ⟨∼ *up the score*⟩ ∼ *vi, esp of paint* to become chalky

**chalk out** *vt* to delineate roughly; sketch

**chalk up** *vt* **1** to ascribe, credit ⟨chalk *that one* up *to me*⟩ **2** to attain, achieve ⟨chalk up *a record score for the season*⟩

**chalkboard** /'chawk,bawd/ *n, NAm* a blackboard

**¹challenge** /'chalinj/ *vt* **1** to order to halt and prove identity ⟨*the sentry* ∼d *the stranger at the gates*⟩ **2a** to dispute esp as being unjust, invalid, or outmoded; impugn ⟨*uncovered new data that* ∼s *old assumptions*⟩ ⟨*didn't* ∼ *the data, only the conclusions drawn from it*⟩ **b** to put (eg a theory) to the test ⟨*a view of the universe seriously* ∼d *by the recent findings of radio astronomy*⟩ **3** to object to (a prospective juror or jurors) either with or without cause being shown **4a** to defy boldly; dare **b** to call out to duel or combat **c** to invite into competition **5** to stimulate or excite, esp by a test of skill ⟨*maths* ∼s *him*⟩ **6** to administer infective (antigenic) material to (an experimental animal) in order to determine whether experimental immunization has been effective **7** *archaic* to demand as of right; require ⟨*an event that* ∼s *explanation*⟩ [ME *chalengen* to accuse, fr OF *chalengier,* fr L *calumniari* to accuse falsely, fr *calumnia* calumny] – **challenger** *n*

**²challenge** *n* **1a** a calling to account or into question; a protest **b** an exception taken to a juror before he/she is sworn **c** a command given by a sentry, watchman, etc to halt and prove identity, give a password, etc **d** a questioning of the right or validity of a vote or voter **2a** a summons that is threatening, provocative, or inciting; *specif* a summons to a duel **b** an invitation to compete in a sport **3a** (something having) the quality of being demanding or stimulating ⟨*the* ∼s *of the job were more organizational than practical*⟩ **b** a challenging effort, esp in a race or sporting contest ⟨*the horse's late* ∼ *just failed to win the race*⟩ **4** a test of immunity by re-exposure to infective (antigenic) material after specific immunization with it

**challenging** /'chalinjing/ *adj* stimulating interest, thought, or action ⟨*the curriculum should have* ∼ *intellectual content*⟩ – **challengingly** *adv*

**challis** /'shali, 'shalis/ *n* a lightweight soft clothing fabric made of cotton, wool, or synthetic yarns [prob fr the name *Challis*]

**chalone** /'ka,lohn/ *n* an internal secretion that depresses activity and inhibits the growth and differentiation of the cells in a tissue – compare HORMONE [Gk *chalōn,* prp of *chalan* to slacken] – **chalonic** *adj*

**chalybeate** /kə'libiət/ *adj* impregnated with iron-containing chemical compounds; *also* having a taste due to iron ⟨∼ *springs*⟩ [NL *chalybeatus,* irreg fr L *chalybs* steel, fr Gk *chalyb-, chalyps,* fr *Chalybes,* ancient people in Asia Minor]

**chamaephyte** /'kamə,fiet/ *n* a PERENNIAL plant that bears its overwintering buds just above the surface of the soil – compare GEOPHYTE, PHANEROPHYTE [Gk *chamai* on the ground + E *-phyte* – more at HUMBLE]

**¹chamber** /'chaymbə/ *n* **1** an enclosed space or cavity ⟨*a large underground* ∼ *filled with stalagmites*⟩ ⟨*the* ∼s *of the heart*⟩ ⟨*temperatures of over 1000°C in the combustion* ∼⟩ **2a** *pl* a room where a judge attends to private business or cases not heard in open court **b** *pl* a set of rooms occupied by a group of barristers, esp in one of the Inns of Court **3a** a room or hall used by a legislative, judicial, or administrative body for official business ⟨*a council* ∼⟩ **b** *taking sing or pl vb, often cap* a legislative body (eg either of the Houses of Parliament, a Senate, Congress, etc); HOUSE 6a – often + *Upper* or *Lower* ⟨*the amendments to the bill proposed by the Upper Chamber will probably be rejected in the Commons*⟩ **4** the hollow part of a firearm between the barrel and the breech that holds the charge or cartridge **5a** *archaic* a room; *esp* a bedroom **b** a room used esp by a sovereign for specified official purposes ⟨*an audience* ∼⟩ **6** *informal* a chamber pot [ME *chambre,* fr OF, fr LL *camera,* fr L, arched roof, fr Gk *kamara* vault; akin to L *camur* curved]

**²chamber** *vt* to place in or provide with a chamber; *esp* to accommodate (eg a cartridge) in the chamber of a firearm

**³chamber** *adj* of or designed for chamber music ⟨*a* ∼ *suite*⟩ ⟨*a* ∼ *concert*⟩ ⟨*a* ∼ *organ*⟩

**chambered** /'chaymbəd/ *adj* having a chamber ⟨*the* ∼ *nautilus*⟩

**chamberer** /'chaymb(ə)rə/ *n, archaic* a gallant, lover [ME, chamberlain, fr MF *chamberier,* fr LL *camerarius,* fr *camera*]

**chamberlain** /'chaymbəlin/ *n* **1** a chief officer of the household of a king or nobleman **2** a treasurer (eg of a corporation) [ME, fr OF *chamberlayn,* of Gmc origin; akin to OHG *chamarling* chamberlain, fr *chamara* chamber, fr LL *camera*]

**chambermaid** /'chaymbəmayd/ *n* a maid who makes beds and does general cleaning of bedrooms (eg in a hotel)

**chamber music** *n* **1** music formerly written for performance in a private household or at court **2** music written for small groups of instruments (eg a string quartet)

**Chamber of Commerce** *n* an association of businessmen to promote commercial and industrial interests in the community

**chamber of horrors** *n* a hall in which objects of macabre interest (eg instruments of torture) are exhibited; *also* a collection of such exhibits

**chamber orchestra** *n* a small orchestra, usu with a single player for each instrumental part

**chamber pot** *n* a bowl-shaped receptacle for urine and faeces that is used chiefly in the bedroom

**chambray** /'shambray/ *n* a lightweight clothing fabric with coloured warp and white weft yarns [irreg fr *Cambrai,* city in N France]

**chambré** /'shombray/ *(Fr* ʃãːbre) *adj, of wine* brought to room temperature before serving [Fr, fr *chambrer* to put in a room, fr *chambre* room] – **chambré** *vt*

**chameleon** /shə'meelyən, kə-/ *n* **1** any of a group (Rhiptoglossa) of African and Eurasian lizards with rough granular skin, a grasping tail, independently movable eyeballs, and the ability to change the colour of the skin **2** a fickle person; *specif* one who changes his/her opinions to suit the company [ME *camelion,* fr MF, fr L *chamaeleon,* fr Gk *chamaileōn,* fr *chamai* on the ground + *leōn* lion – more at HUMBLE] – **chameleonic** *adj*

**¹chamfer** /'chamfə/ *n* an edge which has been cut back to form a narrow surface with two oblique angles [MF *chanfreint,* fr pp of *chanfraindre* to bevel, fr *chant* edge (fr L *canthus* iron tyre) + *fraindre* to break, fr L *frangere* – more at CANT, BREAK]

**²chamfer** *vt* **1** to cut a furrow in (eg a column) **2** to make a chamfer on

**chammy** /'shami/ *n* CHAMOIS 2 [by shortening & alter.]

**chamois** /'shamwah/ *n, pl* **chamois** *also* **chamoix** /∼, 'shamwahz/ **1** a small goatlike antelope (*Rupicapra rupicapra*) of

Europe and the Caucasus 2 a soft pliant leather prepared from the skin of the chamois or sheep [MF, fr LL *camox*]

**chamomile** /'kaməˌmiel/ *n* camomile

¹**champ** /champ/ *vt* 1 to munch (food) noisily 2 to bite or gnash at 3 to mash, trample ⟨*the bank of the stream had been* ~ed *up by drinking cattle*⟩ ~ *vi* 1 to make biting or gnashing movements 2 to eat noisily 3 to show impatience or eagerness esp to start some action or activity – chiefly in *champ at the bit* ⟨*the children were* ~ing *at the bit to get on board*⟩ [perh imit]

²**champ** *n, informal* a champion

**champagne** /sham'payn/ *n* 1 a white SPARKLING WINE made in the old province of Champagne in France; *also* a similar wine made elsewhere; SPARKLING WINE 2 a pale greyish yellow [Fr, fr *Champagne*, region in NE France]

**champaign** /sham'payn/ *n* an expanse of level open country; a plain [ME *champaine*, fr MF *champagne*, fr LL *campania* – more at CAMPAIGN] – **champaign** *adj*

**champers** /'shampəz/ *n taking sing vb, Br informal* champagne [by shortening & alter.]

**champerty** /'champəti/ *n* the former offence of paying the costs of another's civil law suit (eg an action for damages or contesting a will) in the hope of sharing any benefits that the action may bring [ME *champartie*, fr MF *champart* field rent, fr *champ* field (fr L *campus*) + *part* portion – more at CAMP, PART]

**champignon** /'shompinˌyonh (*Fr* ʃãpiɲɔ̃)/ *n* an edible fungus; *esp* the common FIELD MUSHROOM (*Agaricus campestris*) [MF, fr *champagne* level country]

¹**champion** /'champi·ən/ *n* 1 a militant supporter of, or fighter for, a cause or person ⟨*an outspoken* ~ *of civil rights*⟩ 2 someone who does battle for another's rights or honour, esp in a tournament or trial by combat ⟨*God will raise me up a* ~ – Sir Walter Scott⟩ 3 one who or that which shows marked superiority; *specif* the winner of a competitive event ⟨*his leeks have been* ~s *at the last five shows*⟩ 4 *archaic* a warrior, fighter [ME, fr OF, fr ML *campion-*, *campio*, of WGmc origin]

²**champion** *vt* 1 to protect or fight for as a champion 2 to act as militant supporter of; uphold ⟨*always* ~s *the cause of the underdog*⟩ 3 *obs* to challenge, defy ⟨*come Fate into the lists and* ~ *me to the utterance* – Shak⟩ *synonyms* see ¹SUPPORT

³**champion** *adj, chiefly N Eng informal* superb, splendid – **champion** *adv*

**championship** /'champiənˌship/ *n* 1 the act of championing; defence ⟨*his* ~ *of freedom of speech*⟩ 2 a contest held to determine a champion ⟨*a national tiddlywinks* ~⟩

**champlevé** /'shomləˌvay, ˌ--'- (*Fr* ʃãləve)/ *n* a style of enamel decoration in which the enamel is applied and fired in shallow depressions that have been pressed or cut into a metal surface, thus leaving the higher parts of the metal visible often in irregular shapes – compare CLOISONNÉ [*champlevé*, adj, often fr Fr, fr *champ* field + *levé*, pp of *lever* to raise] – **champlevé** *adj*

¹**chance** /chahns/ *n* 1a an event without discernible human intention or observable cause ⟨*this is a strange* ~ *that throws you and me together* – Charles Dickens⟩ b the incalculable (assumed) element in existence that renders events unpredictable ⟨*we met by* ~⟩ ⟨*a* ~ *occurrence*⟩ 2 a situation favouring some purpose; an opportunity ⟨*the weekend gives him a* ~ *to relax*⟩ 3 an opportunity to dismiss a batsman in cricket ⟨*gave no* ~s *in his innings*⟩ 4a the possibility of a specified or favourable outcome in an uncertain situation ⟨*we have almost no* ~ *of winning*⟩ b *pl* the more likely indications ⟨~s *are he's already heard the news*⟩ 5 a risk, gamble ⟨*took a* ~ *on it*⟩ *synonyms* see FORTUITOUS [ME, fr OF, fr (assumed) VL *cadentia* fall, fr L *cadent-*, *cadens*, prp of *cadere* to fall; akin to Skt *śad* to fall] – **chanceless** *adj* – **stand a chance** to have a chance – see also **have an** EYE **to the main chance**

²**chance** *vi* 1 to take place or come about by chance; happen ⟨*it* ~d *that the street was empty*⟩ 2 to come or light *on* or *upon* by chance ⟨*just* ~d *on the idea*⟩ ~ *vt* to accept the hazard of; risk – see also **chance one's** ARM

**chancel** /'chahnsl/ *n* the part of a church containing the altar and seats for the clergy and choir [ME, fr MF, fr LL *cancellus* lattice, fr L *cancelli* – more at CANCEL; fr the latticework enclosing it]

**chancellery, chancellory** /'chahns(ə)ləri/ *n* 1a the position or department of a chancellor b the building or room where a chancellor has his office 2 the office or staff of an embassy or consulate □ compare CHANCERY

**chancellor** /'chahns(ə)lə/ *n* 1a the secretary of a nobleman, prince, or king in former times b LORD CHANCELLOR (British cabinet minister who presides over the House of Lords) c a Roman Catholic priest heading the chancery of a DIOCESE (district under the jurisdiction of a bishop) 2 the titular head of a British university who presides on ceremonial occasions but takes no part in the administration 3 a usu lay legal officer or adviser of an Anglican bishop 4 the chief MINISTER OF STATE in some European countries (eg the Federal Republic of Germany) 5 *often cap, Br* CHANCELLOR OF THE EXCHEQUER 6a the chief executive officer in some state systems of HIGHER EDUCATION b *NAm* the chief administrative officer of certain universities – compare VICE-CHANCELLOR [ME *chanceler*, fr OF *chancelier*, fr LL *cancellarius* doorkeeper, secretary, fr *cancellus*] – **chancellorship** *n*

**Chancellor of the Duchy of Lancaster** *n* a British government minister who has no direct responsibility for a government department but is usu a member of the cabinet

**chancellor of the exchequer** *n, often cap C&E* a member of the British cabinet in charge of public finances

**chancer** *n, Br informal* an unprincipled person; an opportunist

**chancery** /'chahnsəri/ *n* 1a *cap* Chancery, Chancery Division a division of the HIGH COURT having jurisdiction over lawsuits in EQUITY (legal system based on natural justice) b a court of EQUITY in the US judicial system 2 a record office for public archives or those of ecclesiastical, legal, or diplomatic proceedings 3a a chancellor's court or office or the building in which this office is sited b the office in which the business of a Roman Catholic DIOCESE (district under the jurisdiction of a bishop) is transacted and recorded c the office of an embassy; CHANCELLERY 2 [ME *chancerie*, alter. of *chancellerie* chancellery, fr OF, fr *chancelier*] – **in chancery 1a** *of a lawsuit* being heard in a court of chancery b under the superintendence of the lord chancellor ⟨*a ward in chancery*⟩ 2 *of a wrestler* with the head locked under the arm of one's opponent 3 in a hopeless predicament

**chancre** /'shangkə/ *n* an initial sore or ulcer of some diseases; *specif* the initial lesion of syphilis [Fr, fr L *cancer*] – **chancrous** *adj*

**chancroid** /'shangˌkroyd/ *n* a VENEREAL DISEASE caused by a bacterium (*Haemophilus ducreyi*) that thrives in blood – **chancroidal** *adj*

**chancy** /'chahnsi/ *adj* uncertain in outcome or prospect; risky – **chancily** *adv*, **chanciness** *n*

**chandelier** /ˌshandə'liə/ *n* a branched often ornate light suspended from a ceiling and holding several bulbs or candles *synonyms* see CANDELABRUM [Fr, lit., candlestick, modif of L *candelabrum*]

**chandelle** /shon'del (*Fr* ʃãdɛl)/ *n* an abrupt climbing turn of an aircraft in which the momentum of the craft is used to attain a higher rate of climb [Fr, lit., candle] – **chandelle** *vi*

**chandler** /'chahndlə/ *n* 1 a maker or seller of candles and usu soap 2 a retailer of provisions and supplies or equipment of a specified kind ⟨*a ship's* ~⟩ ⟨*a corn* ~⟩ [ME *chandeler*, fr MF *chandelier*, fr OF, fr *chandelle* candle, fr L *candela*]

**chandlery** /'chahndləri/ *n* 1 a place where candles are kept 2 the business or merchandise of a chandler

¹**change** /chaynj/ *vt* 1a to make different; alter b to give a different position, direction, status, or aspect to ⟨*we* ~d *our thinking on the matter*⟩ c to exchange, reverse – often + *over* or *round* ⟨*just* ~ *the speaker leads over*⟩ 2a to replace with another ⟨*let's* ~ *the subject*⟩ b to move from one to another ⟨~ *sides*⟩ c to exchange for an equivalent sum or comparable item; *specif* to exchange (money) for notes or coins of the same value but of a different denomination or currency – usu + *into* d to undergo a loss or modification of ⟨*foliage changing colour*⟩ e to put fresh clothes or covering on ⟨~ *a bed*⟩ ⟨~ *a baby*⟩ ~ *vi* 1 to become different ⟨*her mood* ~s *every hour*⟩ 2 *of the moon* to pass from one phase to another 3 to transfer from one bus, train, etc to another ⟨*if we take this train will we need to* ~ *at Derby?*⟩ 4 *of the voice* to shift to a lower register; BREAK 9a 5 to undergo transformation, transition, or conversion ⟨*winter* ~d *to spring*⟩ ⟨*most industries have* ~d *to the metric system*⟩ – often + *over* 6 to put on different clothes – often + *into* or *out of* 7 to engage in giving something and receiving something in return; exchange – usu + *with* – see also CHOP **and change**, **change** GEAR/HANDS/**one's** MIND/**one's** TUNE □ compare TRANSFORM [ME *changen*, fr OF *changier*, fr L *cambiare* to exchange, of Celt origin; akin to OIr *camm* crooked; akin to Gk *skambos* crooked] – **changer** *n*

*synonyms* Change, alter, vary, and modify all mean "make or become different". Change usually describes an essential difference or a complete substitution ⟨*can the leopard* change *his spots?*⟩. In contrast, alter usually refers to change in a particular aspect, rather than to total change ⟨*cutting down that tree has* altered *our view*⟩. Vary suggests a series of differences due to change ⟨*the weather* varies *from day to day*⟩; or it may suggest deviation from a norm or rule ⟨*a routine that never* varied⟩. Modify may suggest minor or major changes with some purpose in view, or it may involve changes that restrict or make less extreme ⟨*if you don't* modify *your views on hunting, you will have to resign from the party*⟩. Modify may also imply a contrast with change by suggesting only minor alterations ⟨*timid people only* modify *history, bold ones* change *it*⟩.

**change down** *vi* to engage a lower gear in a motor vehicle
**change up** *vi* to engage a higher gear in a motor vehicle
²**change** *n* **1** the act, process, or result of changing: eg **1a** an alteration ⟨*there was little* ~ *in her daily routine*⟩ **b** a transformation ⟨*has undergone a* ~ *since he was married*⟩ **c** a substitution, exchange ⟨*a* ~ *of players*⟩ **d** the passage of the moon from one phase to another; *specif* the coming of the new moon **2** an alternative set, esp of clothes **3a** money in smaller denominations received in exchange for an equivalent sum in larger denominations ⟨*have you got* ~ *for a pound?*⟩ **b** the money returned when a payment exceeds the amount due **c** coins of small denominations ⟨*a pocketful of* ~⟩ **4** an order in which a set of bells is struck in CHANGE RINGING **5** *Br archaic* EXCHANGE 6a (centre for trading in stocks and shares) – **changeful** *adj*, **changefully** *adv*, **changefulness** *n*, **changeless** *adj*, **changelessly** *adv*, **changelessness** *n* – **ring the changes** to vary the manner of doing or arranging something
**changeable** /'chaynjəbl/ *adj* **1** able or apt to vary ⟨~ *weather*⟩ **2** subject to change; alterable ⟨*a clause in the contract* ~ *at will*⟩ **3** fickle, capricious – **changeableness** *n*, **changeably** *adv*, **changeability** *n*
**changeling** /'chaynjling/ *n* **1** a child secretly exchanged for another in infancy; *specif* a half-witted or ugly elf-child left in place of a human child by fairies **2** *archaic* a turncoat – **changeling** *adj*
**change of heart** *n* a complete reversal in attitude
**change of life** *n* the menopause
¹**change-,over** *n* **1** a conversion to a different system, function, or method **2** the moving of a team or player from one end of a court or pitch to another, esp at halftime **3** the transfer of a baton from one person to another in a relay race; *also* the point at which this takes place
**change ringing** *n* the art or practice of ringing a set of tuned bells (eg in the bell tower of a church) in continually varying order
**changing room** /'chaynjing/ *n* a room in which one changes one's clothes (eg for sport), that usu also contains washing facilities, esp showers
¹**channel** /'chanl/ *n* **1a** the bed where a natural stream of water runs **b** the deepest part of a river, harbour, or strait **c** a narrow region of sea between two land masses or two larger areas of sea **d** a path along which data passes ⟨*the left* ~ *of the stereo was dead*⟩; *also* one along which data may be stored (eg on the tape used in a tape recorder) **e** channels *pl*, channel a usu fixed or official course of communication ⟨*used official military* ~s *to air his grievances*⟩ **f** a course or direction of thought or action ⟨*new* ~s *of exploration*⟩ **g(1)** a band of frequencies of sufficient width for a transmission (eg of a radio or television signal) **g(2)** a television or radio station ⟨*switch over to another* ~⟩ **2** a usu tubular enclosed passage, esp for liquids; a conduit **3** a long gutter, groove, or furrow [ME *chanel*, fr OF, fr L *canalis* pipe, channel – more at CANAL]
²**channel** *vt* -ll- (*NAm* -l-, -ll-) **1** to form, cut, or wear a channel or groove in **2** to convey into or through a channel; direct ⟨~ *his energy into constructive activities*⟩
**channel·ize, -ise** /'chanl,iez/ *vt* to channel – **channelization** *n*
**channel seam** *n* a decorative seam (eg on a dress yoke) made by turning under the two edges to be joined and sewing these to a piece of fabric underneath leaving the seam line open
**chanson** /'shans(ə)n (*Fr* ʃãsɔ̃)/ *n, pl* **chansons** /'shans(ə)nz (*Fr* ~)/ a song; *specif* a cabaret song in French [Fr, fr L *cantion-, cantio*, fr *cantus*, pp]
**chanson de geste** /ˌshonsonh də 'zhest (*Fr* ʃãsɔ̃ də ʒest)/ *n, pl* **chansons de geste** any of several Old French epic poems of the 11th to the 14th centuries that recount feats of heroism [Fr, lit., song of heroic deeds]
**chansonnier** /ˌshon'sonyay, ,--'- (*Fr* ʃãsɔnje)/ *n* a writer or singer of chansons; *esp* a cabaret singer [Fr, fr *chanson*]

¹**chant** /chahnt/ *vi* **1** to make melodic sounds with the voice; *esp* to sing a chant **2** to recite in a monotonous repetitive tone ~ *vt* **1** to utter as a chant ⟨~ *a psalm*⟩ **2** to celebrate or praise in song or chant [ME *chaunten*, fr MF *chanter*, fr L *cantare*, fr *cantus*, pp of *canere*; akin to OE *hana* cock, Gk *kanachē* ringing sound]
²**chant** *n* **1** a simple song **2a** a repetitive melody used for LITURGICAL singing (singing used in public services of worship) in which as many syllables are assigned to each note as required **b** a rhythmic monotonous utterance or song ⟨*the* ~ *of an auctioneer*⟩ **c** the music or performance of a chant
**chanter** /'chahntə/, *fem* **chantress** /'chahntris/ *n* **1a** a chorister **b** CANTOR (leader of singing or chanting, esp in a synagogue) **2** the chief singer in a chapel funded by a chantry **3** the REED PIPE (pipe producing sound by the vibration of a reed) of a bagpipe with finger holes on which the melody is played
**chanterelle** /ˌshantə'rel, ˌshon-/ *n* an edible mushroom (*Cantharellus cibarius*) that has a rich yellow colour and pleasant smell [Fr, fr NL *cantharella*, dim. of L *cantharus* drinking-vessel]
**chanteuse** /ˌshan'tuhz, ˌshon-/ *n, pl* **chanteuses** /~/ a female singer, esp in a cabaret or nightclub [Fr, fem of *chanteur* singer, fr *chanter*]
**chanticleer** /ˌchanti'kliə, '---/ *n* – used as a poetic name of the domestic cock [ME *Chantecleer*, name of the cock in narrative poems, fr OF *Chantecler*, the cock in the poem *Roman de Renart*]
**Chantilly** /shon'tili, shan-/, **Chantilly lace** *n* a delicate silk, linen, or synthetic lace having a background of 6-sided figures and a floral or scrolled design [*Chantilly*, town in N France]
**chantry** /'chahntri/ *n* **1** an ENDOWMENT (grant of money or other source of income) for the chanting of masses, usu for the founder's soul **2** a chapel or altar funded by a chantry [ME *chanterie*, fr MF, singing, fr *chanter*]
**Chanukah** /'hahnoo,kah/ *n* HANUKKAH (Jewish festival)
**chaos** /'kayos/ *n* **1a** *often cap* the confused unorganized state of original matter before the creation of distinct forms – compare COSMOS 1a **b** a state of utter confusion ⟨*the citywide blackout caused* ~⟩ **c** a confused mass ⟨*a* ~ *of television antennae*⟩ **2** *obs* a chasm, abyss ⟨*the Gulf of Tartarus . . . opens wide his fiery* Chaos *to receive their fall* – John Milton⟩ [L, fr Gk – more at GUM] – **chaotic** *adj*, **chaotically** *adv*
¹**chap** /chap/ *n, informal* a man, fellow [short for *chapman*]
²**chap** *vb* -pp- to (cause to) open in slits or cracks ⟨~ *ped lips*⟩ [ME *chappen*; akin to MD *cappen* to cut down]
³**chap** *n* a cracked patch on or sore roughening of the skin caused by exposure to wind or cold
⁴**chap** *n* **1** *usu pl* the fleshy covering of a jaw; *also* a jaw ⟨*the wolf's* ~s *were smeared with blood*⟩ **2** chaps *pl*, chap the lower front part of the face [prob fr ² *chap*]
**chaparajos** /ˌchapə'rah·khohs/, **chaparejos** /ˌchapə-'ray·khohs/ *n pl* CHAPS (leggings worn over trousers) [MexSp *chaparreras*]
**chaparral** /ˌshapə'ral/ *n* an area of dwarf evergreen oaks, esp in N America; *broadly* a dense impenetrable area of shrubs or dwarf trees [Sp, fr *chaparro* dwarf evergreen oak, fr Basque *txapar*]
**chapati, chapatti** /chə'pati, -'pahti/ *n, pl* **chapati, chapaties, chapatis, chapatti, chapatties, chapattis** a thin usu round bread made without yeast, that is eaten esp as part of an Indian meal [Hindi *capati*, fr Skt *carpaṭī* thin cake, fr *carpaṭa* flat]
**chapbook** /'chap,book/ *n* a small book formerly sold by pedlars, containing ballads, tales, or tracts [*chap*man + *book*]
**chape** /chayp/ *n* **1** the metal mounting or trimming of a scabbard or sheath and esp of its point **2** the part of a buckle by which it is fixed to a strap, belt, etc [ME, scabbard, fr MF, cape, fr LL *cappa*]
¹**chapel** /'chapl/ *n* **1a** a place of worship serving a residence or institution (eg a hospital) **b** a small house of worship usu related to a main church **c** a room or recess in a church for meditation and prayer or small religious services **2** a choir of singers belonging to a chapel **3** a chapel service or assembly ⟨*it's time for* ~⟩ **4** a place of worship used by a Christian group other than an established church ⟨*a Nonconformist* ~⟩ **5** *taking sing or pl vb* the body of members of a TRADE UNION in a printing office [ME, fr OF *chapele*, fr ML *cappella*, fr dim. of LL *cappa* cloak; fr the cloak of St Martin of Tours preserved as a sacred relic in a chapel built for that purpose]
²**chapel** *adj, chiefly Br* belonging to a Nonconformist church ⟨*we're strictly* ~⟩

**chapel of ease** *n* a chapel built to accommodate parishioners living in remote areas

**¹chaperon, chaperone** /'shapə,rohn/ *n* a married or older woman who accompanies a younger woman on social occasions to ensure propriety; *broadly* somebody responsible for supervising other, younger, people △ cicerone, chatelaine [Fr *chaperon*, lit., hood, fr MF, head covering, fr *chape*]

**²chaperon, chaperone** *vt* to act as chaperon to; escort *synonyms* see ACCOMPANY – **chaperonage** *n*

**chapfallen** /'chap,fawlən/ *adj* **1** having the lower jaw hanging loosely **2** depressed, dejected

**chaplain** /'chaplin/ *n* **1** a clergyman in charge of a chapel **2** a clergyman officially attached to a branch of the armed forces, to an institution (eg a university), or to a family or court **3** a clergyman appointed to assist a bishop [ME *chapelain*, fr OF, fr ML *cappellanus*, fr *cappella*] – **chaplaincy** *n*, **chaplainship** *n*

**chaplet** /'chaplit/ *n* **1** a wreath to be worn on the head **2a** a string of beads **b** a part of a rosary comprising five DECADES (parts at which ten HAIL MARYS are said) [ME *chapelet*, fr MF, fr OF, dim. of *chapel* hat, garland, fr ML *cappellus* head covering, fr LL *cappa*] – **chapleted** *adj*

**Chaplinesque** /,chapli'nesk/ *adj* resembling or suggesting the largely pantomime comedy of Charles Chaplin, esp in its blend of humour and pathos [Sir Charles *Chaplin* †1977 E actor]

**chapman** /'chapmən/ *n, archaic* an itinerant pedlar; a trader [ME, fr OE *cēapman*, fr *cēap* trade + *man*]

**chappal** /'chupl/ *n* an Indian sandal, usu with a strap attached to the sole at the sides and between the first and second toes [Hindi]

**chappati** /chə'pati, -'pahti/ *n* CHAPATI (round thin bread)

**chappie** /'chapi/ *n, informal* a man, fellow

**chaps** /chaps/ *n pl* leather leggings worn over the trousers, esp by N American ranch hands [modif of MexSp *chaparreras*]

**chaptal·ize, -ise** /'shaptl·iez/ *vt* to add sugar to (the juice of wine grapes) [Fr *chaptaliser*, fr Jean-Antoine *Chaptal* †1832 Fr chemist] – **chaptalization** *n*

**chapter** /'chaptə/ *n* **1a** a major division of a book **b** something resembling a chapter in being a significant specified unit ⟨*with his death a ~ in the history of the industry was closed*⟩ **2a** (a regular meeting of) the CANONS (clergymen) of a cathedral or COLLEGIATE CHURCH, or the members of a religious house **3** a local branch of a society or fraternity [ME *chapitre* division of a book, meeting of canons, fr OF, fr LL *capitulum* division of a book & ML, meeting place of canons, fr L, dim. of *capit-, caput* head – more at HEAD]

**chapter and verse** *n* (a full specification of the source of) a piece of information [fr the custom of citing passages in the Bible by chapter and verse number]

**chapter house** *n* the building or rooms where a chapter meets

**¹char, charr** /chah/ *n, pl* **chars, charrs,** *esp collectively* **char, charr** any of a genus (*Salvelinus*) of freshwater and sea fishes related to the trout and salmon [origin unknown]

**²char** *vb* **-rr-** *vt* **1** to convert to charcoal or carbon, usu by heat; burn **2** to burn slightly or partly; scorch ⟨*the fire ~ red the beams*⟩ ~ *vi* to become charred [back-formation fr *charcoal*]

**³char** *vi* **-rr-** to work as a cleaning woman [back-formation fr *charwoman*]

**⁴char** *n, Br informal* a charwoman

**⁵char, cha** *n, Br informal* tea as a drink [Hindi *cā*, fr Chin (Pek) *chá* (ch'a²)]

**charabanc** /'sharə,bang/ *n, Br* a motor coach used, esp formerly, for sightseeing or excursions [Fr *char à bancs*, lit., carriage with benches]

**characin** /'karəsin/ *n* any of a family (Characidae) of usu small brightly coloured tropical fishes [deriv of Gk *charak-, charax* pointed stake, a fish] – **characin** *adj*

**¹character** /'karəktə/ *n* **1a** a distinctive mark, usu in the form of a stylized graphic device **b** a graphic symbol (eg a hieroglyph, punctuation mark, or alphabet letter) used in writing or printing **c** a symbol (eg a letter or number) that represents information; *esp* a representation of such a symbol in a code that can be understood by a computer **2a** (any of) the mental or moral qualities that make up and distinguish the individual **b(1)** a feature used to separate distinguishable things into categories; *also* a group or kind so separated ⟨*people of this ~*⟩ ⟨*advertising of a very primitive ~*⟩ **b(2)** an inherited characteristic determined by a gene or group of genes **b(3)** the sum of all the distinctive qualities characteristic of a breed, strain, or

type ⟨*a wine of great ~*⟩ **c** the distinctive or essential nature of something ⟨*the building of new estates gradually changed the whole ~ of the town*⟩ **3a** a person marked by notable or conspicuous traits ⟨*one of the real ~s in Westminster today*⟩ **b** any of the people portrayed in a novel, play, film, etc **4** (good) reputation ⟨*~ assassination*⟩ **5** moral strength; integrity ⟨*a man of ~*⟩ **6** *archaic* REFERENCE 4b (statement about a person's qualifications) **7** *informal* a person ⟨*some ~ has just stolen her purse*⟩ *synonyms* see ¹TYPE [ME *caracter*, fr MF *caractère*, fr L *character* mark, distinctive quality, fr Gk *charaktēr*, fr *charassein* to scratch, engrave; akin to Lith *žerti* to scratch] – **characterful** *adj*, **characterless** *adj* – **in/out of character** in/not in accord with a person's usual qualities, traits, or behaviour

**²character** *vt, archaic* **1** to engrave, inscribe **2** to represent, portray

**character actor** *n* an actor capable of portraying unusual or eccentric personalities often markedly different (eg in age) from his/her own

**¹characteristic** /,karəktə'ristik/ *adj* serving to reveal and distinguish individual character; typical – **characteristically** *adv*
*synonyms* Characteristic, individual, peculiar, distinctive, and typical all refer to special or identifying qualities or traits. Typical has the widest, most general sense, suggesting what is broadly applicable to a particular person or class. Characteristic may mean something which distinguishes a thing, person, or group, or what is typical of them, or both ⟨*her* characteristic *generosity*⟩ ⟨*the camel's* characteristic *hump*⟩. Individual, unlike characteristic, stresses what makes a person or thing different from others ⟨*each member of the family had his or her own* individual *charm*⟩. Peculiar is similar to individual, but emphasizes that the distinguishing feature or trait belongs to that person, thing, or group alone, without any connotation of "oddness" from its other meanings ⟨*a sense of oneness with nature which was quite* peculiar *to him make these notebooks of more than scientific interest*⟩. Distinctive describes what distinguishes one thing from the rest of its class, and so is worthy of praise or admiration ⟨*Leonardo da Vinci's* distinctive *vision of the world sets him above his contemporaries*⟩.

**²characteristic** *n* **1** a distinguishing trait, quality, or property **2** the part of a COMMON LOGARITHM (logarithm whose base is 10) in front of the DECIMAL POINT ⟨*the logarithm of 20 is 1·3010 and the ~ is 1*⟩ – compare MANTISSA *synonyms* see ¹QUALITY

**characterization** /,karəktərie'zaysh(ə)n/ *n* the act, process, or result of characterizing; *esp* the artistic representation (eg in fiction or drama) of human character or motives

**character·ize, -ise** /'karəktə,riez/ *vt* **1** to describe the character or quality of; delineate ⟨*~d him as soft-spoken yet ambitious*⟩ **2** to be a characteristic of; distinguish ⟨*an awareness of injustice ~s all her works*⟩

**character sketch** *n* a brief description of a person's character

**character witness** *n* a person who gives evidence concerning the reputation, conduct, and moral nature of somebody involved in a legal action

**charactery** /'karikt(ə)ri/ *n, archaic* a system of written letters or symbols used to represent or express thoughts

**charade** /shə'rahd; *NAm* -'rayd/ *n* **1** *pl taking sing or pl vb* a game in which each syllable of a word or phrase is acted out by one team while the other team tries to guess the word or phrase **2** a ridiculous pretence [Fr, fr Prov *charrado* conversation]

**charas** /'chahrəs/ *n* HASHISH (cannabis drug) [Hindi *caras*]

**charcoal** /'chah,kohl/ *n* **1** a dark or black porous carbon prepared by partly burning vegetable or animal substances (eg wood or bone) **2a** fine charcoal used in pencil form for drawing **b** a charcoal drawing [ME *charcole*, fr *char* (perh fr *charen* to turn) + *cole* coal]

**charcuterie** /shah'koohtəri (*Fr* ʃarkytri)/ *n* cold meats (eg brawn and pâtés) prepared from a pig [Fr, fr MF *chaircuiterie*, fr *chaircuitier* seller of pork, fr *chair cuite* cooked meat]

**chard** /chahd/ *n* a beet (*Beta vulgaris cicla*) with large dark green leaves and succulent stalks that are often cooked as a vegetable – called also SPINACH BEET [Fr *carde*, fr OProv *cardo* thistle-like vegetable, fr L *carduus* thistle, artichoke; akin to MLG *harst* rake, L *carrere* to card]

**Charentais** /,sharon'tay (*Fr* ʃarɑ̃tɛ)/ *n* a small round melon with a yellowish-green rind and faintly scented orange flesh [Fr *charentais* of Charente, fr *Charente*, department of France]

**¹charge** /chahj/ *vt* **1a(1)** to place a charge (eg of powder) in (a firearm) **a(2)** to load or fill to capacity ⟨~ *the furnace with ore*⟩ **b(1)** to restore the active materials in (a car battery or other STORAGE BATTERY) by passing a current in the opposite direction to that in which it is given out – often + *up* **b(2)** to give an electric charge to **c** to place a heraldic charge on ⟨*a fess* ~d *with three royal crowns*⟩ **d** to fill *with* emotion, feeling, etc ⟨*a mind* ~d *with fancies*⟩ ⟨*the music is* ~d *with excitement*⟩ **2** to command, instruct, or exhort with right or authority ⟨*I* ~ *you not to leave*⟩ **3a** to blame ⟨~s *him as the instigator*⟩ **b** to make an assertion against, esp by ascribing guilt for an offence; accuse ⟨~d *him with armed robbery*⟩ **c** to place the guilt or blame for ⟨~ *her failure to negligence*⟩ **d** to assert as an accusation ⟨~s *that he distorted the data*⟩ **4a** to bring (a weapon) into position for attack; level ⟨~ *a lance*⟩ **b** to rush at or against or bear down on; attack; *also* to rush into (an opponent) usu illegally in various games or sports **5a(1)** to impose a monetary obligation on ⟨~ *his estate with debts incurred*⟩ **a(2)** to impose or record as a monetary obligation ⟨~ *debts to an estate*⟩ **b(1)** to fix or ask as fee or payment ⟨~s £10 *for a home visit*⟩ **b(2)** to ask payment of (a person) ⟨~ *a client for expenses*⟩ **c** to record (an item) as an expense, debt, obligation, or liability ⟨~ *a purchase to a customer*⟩ **6** *archaic* to lay or put a load on or in; load ~ *vi* **1** to rush forwards (as if) in assault; attack; *also* to charge an opponent in sports **2** to ask or set a price **3** *NAm* to charge an item to an account ⟨~ *now, pay later*⟩ [ME *chargen*, fr LL *carricare*, fr L *carrus* wheeled vehicle – more at CAR]

**usage** One **charges** somebody *with* a crime, but **accuses** him/her of it. **synonyms** see ACCUSE, ASCRIBE

**charge with** *vt* to impose a task or responsibility on (somebody) ⟨charged *her* with *writing a report on the meeting*⟩

²**charge** *n* **1** a shape, representation, or design depicted on a heraldic shield **2a** the quantity that an apparatus is intended to receive and equipped to hold; *esp* the quantity of explosive required for a gun, cannon, etc **b** power, force ⟨*the deeply emotional* ~ *of the drama*⟩ **c(1)** a basic property of matter that occurs in separate natural units, and is considered as negative (eg when belonging to an electron) or positive (eg when belonging to a proton) and that determines the strength of the electric force between any two particles having this property; *also* any of various similar properties possessed by ELEMENTARY PARTICLES **c(2)** a definite quantity of electricity; *esp* the charge that a STORAGE BATTERY (battery like that in a car) is capable of yielding **3a** an obligation, requirement ⟨*to maintain this readiness . . . is . . . a first* ~ *upon our military effort* – Sir Winston Churchill⟩ **b** control, supervision ⟨*has* ~ *of the home office*⟩ **c** somebody or something committed to the care of another **4a** an instruction, command **b** the instructions given by a judge to a jury concerning points of law and the proper way to consider the evidence **5a** the price demanded or paid for something ⟨*no admission* ~⟩ **b** a debit to an account ⟨*the purchase was a* ~⟩ **6** an accusation, indictment, or statement of complaint ⟨*pleaded guilty to all the* ~s⟩ **7** a violent rush forwards (eg to attack) **8** *slang* **8a** a thrill or pleasurable feeling **b** a cannabis drug; *specif* marijuana **9** *obs* a material load or weight – **chargeless** *adj* – **drunk in charge** (the official charge for the offence of) driving while intoxicated – **in charge** in a position of control or command (over) – **reverse the charges** *Br* to arrange for the recipient of a telephone call to pay for it – **take charge** to assume care, custody, command, or control

**usage** The expression *in charge of* ⟨*dogs* **in charge** *of children*⟩ leaves it undecided which of the two controls the other. It is clearer to write ⟨*dogs in the* **charge** *of children*⟩ if the child leads the dog.

**chargeable** /'chahjəbl/ *adj* **1** liable to be charged to a particular account ⟨*debts* ~ *on the estate*⟩ **2** liable to be the object of a legal charge ⟨*a* ~ *offence*⟩ – **chargeableness** *n*

**charge account** *n* CREDIT ACCOUNT

**charged** /chahjd/ *adj* capable of arousing strong emotion; intense, emotive ⟨*a highly* ~ *political theme*⟩

**chargé d'affaires** /ˌshahzhay da'feə/ *n, pl* **chargés d'affaires** /~/ **1** a diplomat who substitutes for an ambassador or minister in his absence **2** a diplomat who heads a minor diplomatic mission but is inferior in rank to an ambassador or minister [Fr, lit., one charged with affairs]

**chargehand** /'chahjˌhand/ *n, Br* a workman in charge of a group of workers or a piece of work; a foreman

**charge nurse** *n, Br* a usu male nurse in charge of a hospital ward – compare SISTER 4

¹**charger** /'chahjə/ *n* a large flat meat dish [ME *chargeour;* akin to ME *chargen* to charge]

²**charger** *n* a horse used in battle or on parade

**charge sheet** *n, Br* a police record of charges made and people to be tried in a MAGISTRATES' COURT

**chariot** /'chariət/ *n* **1** a light 4-wheeled horse-drawn carriage, used esp for state occasions **2** a 2-wheeled horse-drawn vehicle of ancient times used esp in warfare and racing [ME, fr MF, fr OF, fr *char* wheeled vehicle, fr L *carrus*]

**charioteer** /ˌchari·ə'tiə/ *n* the driver of a chariot

**charisma** /kə'rizmə/ *also* **charism** /'kariz(ə)m/ *n, pl* **charismata** /kə'rizmətə/ *also* **charisms 1** an extraordinary power (eg of healing) divinely given to a Christian **2** the special magnetic appeal, charm, or power of an individual (eg a political leader) that inspires popular loyalty and enthusiasm [Gk *charisma* favour, gift, fr *charizesthai* to favour, fr *charis* grace; akin to Gk *chairein* to rejoice – more at YEARN] – **charismatic** *adj*

**charitable** /'charitəbl/ *adj* **1a** liberal in giving to the poor; generous **b** concerned with or giving charity ⟨~ *institutions*⟩ **2** merciful or kind in judging others; lenient **synonyms** see ²KIND **antonym** uncharitable – **charitableness** *n*, **charitably** *adv*

**charity** /'charəti/ *n* **1** goodwill towards or love of humanity **2a** kindly generosity, esp towards the needy or suffering, in the form of help, money, etc ⟨*his* ~ *knew no bounds*⟩ ⟨*attended the* ~ *première*⟩ **b** an institution or organization engaged in relief of the poor, sick, etc **c** provision for the relief of the needy, esp in the form of money **3a** a gift for public benevolent purposes **b** an institution (eg a hospital) funded by such a gift **4** lenient judgment of others **synonyms** see MERCY **antonyms** malevolence, malice, ill will [ME *charite*, fr OF *charité*, fr LL *caritat-, caritas* Christian love, fr L, dearness, fr *carus* dear; akin to Skt *kāma* love]

**charivari** /ˌshahri'vahri/ *n* a noisy and raucous medley of sounds; a din [Fr, fr LL *caribaria* headache, fr Gk *karēbaria*, fr *kara, karē* head + *barys* heavy – more at CEREBRAL, GRIEVE]

**charka, charkha** /'chahkə/ *n* a domestic spinning wheel used in India chiefly for spinning cotton [Hindi *carkha*]

**charlady** /'chah,laydi/ *n, Br* a charwoman

**charlatan** /'shahlət(ə)n/ *n* **1** one who pretends to have medical knowledge or expertise; QUACK 1 **2** one who pretends, usu ostentatiously, to have special knowledge or ability; a fraud [It *ciarlatano*, alter. (influenced by *ciarlare* to babble, patter) of *cerretano*, lit., inhabitant of Cerreto, fr *Cerreto*, village in Italy] – **charlatanism, charlatanry** *n*

**Charles's Wain** /ˌchahlziz 'wayn/ *n* URSA MAJOR [ME *Charlewayn*, fr OE *Carles Wægn* the waggon of Charles (ie Charlemagne, 'Charles the Great' †814 Frankish king)]

**Charleston** /'chahlstən/ *vi or n* (to dance) a lively ballroom dance, popular in the 1920s, in which the knees are turned inwards and the heels are swung sharply outwards on each step [*Charleston*, city in South Carolina, USA]

**charley horse** /'chahli/ *n, NAm informal* muscle strain or bruising resulting from strenuous exercise [fr *Charley*, nickname for *Charles*]

**charlie** /'chahli/ *n, often cap, Br informal* an absurd or stupid person; a fool ⟨*felt a proper* ~⟩ [*Charlie*, nickname for *Charles*]

**Charlie** /'chahli/ – a communications code word for the letter *c*

**charlock** /'chah,lok/ *n* a wild mustard (*Sinapis arvensis*) that has yellow flowers and is a weed of cultivated ground [ME *cherlok*, fr OE *cerlic*]

**charlotte** /'shahlot, -lət/ *n* **1** a hot baked dessert consisting of fruit layered or covered with pieces of bread, sponge, etc **2** **charlotte russe** /roohs/, **charlotte** a cold dessert consisting of a mixture of whipped cream, custard, and sometimes fruit surrounded by sponge fingers and set in a mould [Fr, prob fr the name *Charlotte; charlotte russe* fr Fr, lit., Russian charlotte]

¹**charm** /chahm/ *n* **1** an act, expression or phrase believed to have magic power; *specif* an incantation **2** something that is worn to ward off evil or ensure good fortune; a talisman **3a** the quality of fascinating, alluring, or delighting others **b** a particular pleasing or attractive quality or feature **4** a small ornament worn on a bracelet or chain **5** *physics* a property of some ELEMENTARY PARTICLES (particles of matter), proposed to account for their unexpectedly long lifetimes compared with other elementary particles with which they are otherwise identical – compare STRANGENESS **6** *pl, euph* physical graces or attractions, esp of a woman [ME *charme*, fr OF, fr L *carmen* song, fr *canere* to sing – more at CHANT] – **charmless** *adj*

²**charm** *vt* **1a** to affect (as if) by magic; bewitch **b** to please,

soothe, or delight by compelling attraction ⟨∼s *the women with his suave manner*⟩ **2** to control (an animal) by the use of rituals held to have magical power (eg the playing of music) ⟨∼ *a snake*⟩ ∼ *vi* **1** to have the effect of a charm; fascinate **2** *archaic* to practise magic and enchantment □ compare CAPTIVATE, BEWITCH, FASCINATE, ENCHANT *antonym* disgust

**charmed** /'chahmd/ *adj, physics, of a particle* having charm

**charmer** /'chahmə/ *n* **1** a person who charms animals ⟨*a snake* ∼⟩ **2** *informal* an attractive or captivating person

**charming** /'chahming/ *adj* extremely pleasing or delightful; entrancing – **charmingly** *adv*

**charnel house** /'chahn(ə)l/ *n* a building or chamber in which bodies or bones are deposited [ME *charnel*, fr MF, fr ML *carnale*, fr LL, neut of *carnalis* of the flesh – more at CARNAL]

**Charolais** /'sharə,lay/ *n* (any of) a French breed of large white cattle used primarily for beef and crossbreeding [*Charolais*, district in E France]

**charpoy** /'chah,poy/ *n* a lightweight rope bedstead used esp in India [Hindi *cārpāi*]

**charqui** /'chahki/ *n* strips of meat, esp beef, that have been dried in the sun [Sp, fr Quechua *ch'arki* dried meat]

**charr** /chah/ *n, pl* **charrs**, *esp collectively* **charr** ¹CHAR (fish related to the trout)

**¹chart** /chaht/ *n* **1a** an outline map showing the geographical distribution of something (eg climatic or magnetic variations) **b** a map for the use of a navigator (eg on a ship) **2a** a sheet giving information in tabular form **b** *pl the* list of best-selling popular gramophone records, that is usu issued weekly **c** a graph **d** a schematic, usu large diagram **e** a sheet of paper ruled and graduated for use in an electrocardiograph or other instrument that traces a record (eg of heart beats) [MF *charte*, fr L *charta* piece of papyrus, document – more at CARD]

**²chart** *vt* **1** to make a chart of **2** to lay out a plan for **3** to display or mark (as if) on a chart △ **charter**

**¹charter** /'chahtə/ *n* **1** a formal written document or contract (eg a deed) **2a** a grant or guarantee of rights or privileges from the sovereign power of a state (eg to a city, company, or university) **b** an official document creating and defining the rights of a city, educational institution, or company **c** CONSTITUTION 5b (document embodying the rules and laws of a nation, organization, etc) **3** a special privilege, immunity, or exemption **4** a total or partial lease of a ship, aeroplane, etc for a particular use or group of people ⟨*low-cost travel on* ∼ *flights to Greece*⟩ **5** *chiefly NAm* an official document from the authorities of a society creating a LODGE (division of an organization) or branch [ME *chartre*, fr OF, fr ML *chartula*, fr L, dim. of *charta*]

**²charter** *vt* **1a** to establish, grant, or convey by charter **b** to certify as qualified ⟨*a* ∼ed *accountant*⟩ ⟨*a* ∼ed *surveyor*⟩ **2** to hire, rent, or lease for usu exclusive and temporary use ⟨∼ed *a boat for deep-sea fishing*⟩ *synonyms* see ²HIRE △ chart – **charterer** *n*

**chartered accountant** /'chahtəd/ *n, Br* an accountant who has passed all the official examinations of the Institute of Chartered Accountants

**charterhouse** /-,hows/ *n* a monastery of Carthusian monks [by folk etymology fr MF *chartrouse*, irreg fr *Chartosse* (now Saint-Pierre-de-*Chartreuse*), site in France of the first Carthusian monastery]

**charter member** *n* an original member of a society or corporation – **charter membership** *n*

**charterparty** /-,pahti/ *n* **1** a contract for the hire of all or part of a ship for the conveyance of cargo or passengers **2** a person or group that charters a ship [modif of Fr *charte partie*, fr ML *charta partita*, lit., divided charter]

**Chartism** /'chah,tiz(ə)m/ *n* the principles and practices of a body of 19th-century English political reformers demanding better social and industrial conditions for the working class [ML *charta* charter, fr L, document] – **Chartist** *n*

**chartreuse** /shah'truhz (*Fr* ʃartrǿz)/ *n* a brilliant yellowish-green colour [fr the colour of Chartreuse liqueurs]

**Chartreuse** /,shah'truhz/ *trademark* – used for an aromatic usu green or yellow liqueur

**charwoman** /'chah,woomən/ *n* a cleaning woman; *esp, Br* one employed in a private house [*chare* (chore) + *woman* – more at CHORE]

**chary** /'cheəri/ *adj* **1** cautious; *esp* wary of taking risks **2** slow to grant, accept, or expend ⟨*a man very* ∼ *of compliments*⟩ *synonyms* see CAUTIOUS [ME, sorrowful, dear, fr OE *cearig*

sorrowful, fr *caru* sorrow – more at CARE] – **charily** *adv*, **chariness** *n*

**¹chase** /chays/ *vt* **1a** to follow rapidly or persistently; pursue **b** to hunt **2** to cause to depart or flee; drive ⟨∼ *the dog out of the pantry*⟩ **3** *chiefly Br* to investigate (a matter) or contact (a person, company, etc) in order to obtain information or results – usu + *up* **4** *obs* to harass ⟨*though fortune, visible an enemy, should* ∼ *us* – Shak⟩ ∼ *vi* **1** to chase an animal, person, or thing – usu + *after* ⟨∼ *after material possessions*⟩ **2** to rush, hasten ⟨∼d *all over town looking for a place to stay*⟩ **3** *of a horse* to compete in a steeplechase [ME *chasen*, fr MF *chasser*, fr (assumed) VL *captiare* – more at CATCH]

**²chase** *n* **1a** the act of chasing; pursuit **b** *the* hunting of wild animals **2** something pursued; quarry **3a** a right to hunt within certain limits of land **b** a tract of unenclosed land set aside for the breeding of animals for hunting and fishing **4** a steeplechase – **give chase** to go in pursuit

**³chase** *vt* **1a** to ornament (metal) by indenting with a hammer and tools that have no cutting edge **b** to make by such ornamentation ⟨∼ *a monogram*⟩ **2a** to groove, indent **b** to cut (a thread on a screw) with a chaser [ME *chassen*, modif of MF *enchasser* to set (a jewel)]

**⁴chase** *n* **1a** a groove, furrow; *esp* one cut in a surface to allow piping or wiring to be set in **b** an opening made (eg in wood) in preparation for making a joint **2** the part of a large mounted gun (eg a cannon) enclosing the BORE (interior tube), between the TRUNNIONS (points on which the gun is swivelled) and the mouth of the muzzle [Fr *chas* eye of a needle, fr LL *capsus* enclosed space, fr L, cage, alter. of *capsa* box – more at CASE]

**⁵chase** *n* a rectangular steel or iron frame in which the metal type or blocks used in printing are arranged – compare FORME [prob fr Fr *châsse* frame, fr L *capsa*]

**¹chaser** /'chaysə/ *n* **1** a glass or swallow of a mild drink (eg beer) taken after spirits; *also* a drink of spirits taken after a mild drink (eg beer) **2** a horse that is a steeplechaser

**²chaser** *n* one who produces ornamented metal by indenting it with a hammer and other tools that have no cutting edge

**Chasid** /'hasid, 'khahsid/ *n, pl* **Chasidim** /'hasidim, khə'seedim/ HASID (member of a Jewish sect)

**chasm** /'kaz(ə)m/ *n* **1** a deep cleft in the earth; a gorge **2** an apparently unbridgeable gap ⟨*a political* ∼ *between the two countries*⟩ [L *chasma*, fr Gk; akin to L *hiare* to yawn – more at YAWN]

**chassé** /'shasay/ *vi or n* **chasséing** /'sha,saying/ (to make) a sliding dance step [Fr, n, fr pp of *chasser* to chase]

**chassepot** /'shas,poh, 'shasə,poh/ *n* a 19th-century rifle that is loaded at the BREECH (part of barrel furthest from the muzzle) which is then closed with a sliding bolt, and that fires bullets enclosed in paper cartridges [Fr, fr Antoine *Chassepot* †1905 Fr inventor]

**chasseur** /sha'suh (*Fr* ʃasœr)/ *n* **1** any of a body of cavalry or infantry soldiers in the French army, trained for rapid manoeuvring **2** a liveried attendant; a footman [Fr, fr MF *chasser*]

**chassis** /'shasi/ *n, pl* **chassis** /'shasiz/ **1** a supporting framework for the body of a vehicle (eg a car) **2** the frame on which the electrical parts of a radio, television, etc are mounted [Fr *châssis*, fr (assumed) VL *capsicum*, fr L *capsa* box – more at CASE]

**chaste** /chayst/ *adj* **1** innocent of unlawful or immoral sexual intercourse **2** abstinent from all sexual intercourse; celibate **3** pure in thought and act; modest **4** severely simple in design or execution; austere ⟨*the* ∼ *hospital corridor*⟩ ⟨∼ *poetry*⟩ *antonyms* lewd, wanton, immoral [ME, fr OF, fr L *castus* pure – more at CASTE] – **chastely** *adv*, **chasteness, chastity** *n*

**chasten** /'chays(ə)n/ *vt* **1** to correct by punishment or suffering; discipline **2** to subdue, restrain *synonyms* see PUNISH *antonym* pamper [alter. of obs *chaste* to chasten, fr ME *chasten*, fr OF *chastier*, fr L *castigare*, fr *castus* + *-igare* (fr *agere* to drive)] – **chastener** *n*

**chastise** /chas'tiez/ *vt* **1** to inflict punishment on, esp by whipping **2** to subject to severe reproof or criticism *synonyms* see PUNISH [ME *chastisen*, alter. of *chasten*] – **chastisement** *n*, **chastiser** *n*

**chastity belt** /'chastəti/ *n* a lockable device consisting of a belt with an attachment passing between the legs designed to prevent the woman wearing it from having sexual intercourse

**chasuble** /'chazyoobl/ *n* a sleeveless outer vestment worn by the officiating priest at mass [Fr, fr LL *casubla* hooded garment]

**¹chat** /chat/ *vi* **-tt-** **1** to talk in an informal or familiar manner

**2** *obs* to talk nonsense; prattle *synonyms* see SPEAK [ME *chatten*, short for *chatteren*]

**chat up** *vt, Br informal* to engage (somebody, esp a member of the opposite sex) in friendly conversation for ulterior, esp amorous motives

**²chat** *n* **1** idle or frivolous talk; chatter **2** (an instance of) light familiar talk; *esp* (a) conversation **3** any of several birds (e g the stonechat or whinchat) related to the thrushes (subfamily Turdinae) [(3) prob imit]

**château** /ˈshatoh/ *n, pl* **châteaus, châteaux** /ˈshatohz/ **1** a feudal castle or large country house in France **2** a French vineyard estate – used esp in the names of wines ⟨Château *Lafite*⟩ [Fr, fr OF *chastel*, fr L *castellum* castle]

**chateaubriand** /ˌshatohbreeˈonh (*Fr* ʃatobrijã)/ *n, often cap* a large thick fillet steak [François René de *Chateaubriand* †1848 Fr writer & statesman]

**Chateauneuf-du-Pape** /shatohˌnuhf dooh ˈpap (*Fr* ʃatonœf dy pap)/ *n* a full-bodied red table wine made near Avignon in the Rhône valley [*Châteauneuf-du-Pape*, commune near Avignon in France]

**chatelain** /ˈshatəˌlayn/ *n* CASTELLAN (keeper of a castle) [MF *châtelain*, fr L *castellanus* occupant of a castle]

**chatelaine** /ˈshatəˌlayn/ *n* **1a** the wife of a chatelain **b** the mistress of a château, castle, or large house **2** a clasp or hook with a short chain, formerly used to attach small articles (e g keys) to a woman's belt △ chaperon [Fr *châtelaine*, fem of *châtelain*]

**chatoyant** /shəˈtoyənt/ *n or adj* (a gem) having a changeable lustre or colour and reflecting an undulating narrow band of white light [*adj* Fr, fr prp of *chatoyer* to shine like a cat's eyes, fr *chat* cat; n fr adj] – **chatoyance, chatoyancy** *n*

**chat show** /chat/ *n* a radio or television programme in which people, esp celebrities, engage in discussion or are interviewed

**chattel** /ˈchatl/ *n* an item of movable personal property – chiefly in *goods and chattels* [ME *chatel* property, fr OF, fr ML *capitale* – more at CATTLE]

**¹chatter** /ˈchatə/ *vi* **1** to produce rapid successive inarticulate sounds suggestive of language ⟨*squirrels* ~ed *angrily*⟩ **2** to talk idly, incessantly, or fast; jabber **3a** *esp of teeth* to click repeatedly or uncontrollably (e g from cold) **b** *of a tool* to vibrate rapidly while cutting *synonyms* see SPEAK [ME *chatteren*, of imit origin] – **chatterer** *n*

**²chatter** *n* **1** the action or sound of chattering **2** idle talk; prattle

**chatterbox** /-ˌboks/ *n, informal* one who engages in much idle talk

**chatter mark** *n* a fine irregular mark formed on the surface of a piece of wood, metal, etc being worked on by a tool that chatters

**chatty** /ˈchati/ *adj* **1** fond of chatting; talkative ⟨*she's very* ~⟩ **2** having the style and manner of light familiar conversation ⟨*a* ~ *letter*⟩ *synonyms* see TALKATIVE – **chattily** *adv*, **chattiness** *n*

**chaudfroid** /ˌshohˈfwah (*Fr* ʃofrwa)/ *n* (an elaborate cold dish of meat, poultry, fish, etc cooked or coated with) a creamy sauce containing aspic that sets to a jelly [Fr, lit., hot-cold, fr *chaud* hot (fr L *calidus*) + *froid* cold (fr L *frigidus*)]

**¹chauffeur** /ˈshohˈfuh, ˈshohfə/, *fem* **chauffeuse** /shohˈfuhz/ *n* a person employed to drive a private passenger-carrying motor vehicle, esp a car [Fr, lit., stoker, fr *chauffer* to heat, fr MF *chaufer* – more at CHAFE]

**²chauffeur** *vi* to work as a chauffeur ~ *vt* **1** to transport in the manner of a chauffeur ⟨~s *the children to school*⟩ **2** to drive (e g a motor car) as chauffeur

**chaulmoogra** /ˌchawlˈmoohgrə/ *n* any of several E Indian trees (family Flacourtiaceae) that yield an acrid oil used in treating leprosy and skin diseases [Bengali *cāulmugrā*]

**chauvinism** /ˈshohvəˌniz(ə)m/ *n* **1** excessive or blind patriotism – compare JINGOISM **2** undue partiality or attachment to a group, cause, or place ⟨*male* ~⟩ [Fr *chauvinisme*, fr Nicolas *Chauvin* ƒ1815 Fr soldier of excessive patriotism and devotion to Napoleon] – **chauvinist** *n*, **chauvinistic** *adj*, **chauvinistically** *adv*

**¹chaw** /chaw/ *vb, dial* to chew [by alter.]

**²chaw** *n, dial* something for chewing; *esp* a quid of tobacco

**¹cheap** /cheep/ *n* [ME *chep* bargain, fr OE *cēap* trade; akin to OHG *kouf* trade; both from a prehistoric Gmc stem borrowed from L *caupo* tradesman] – **on the cheap** at minimum expense; cheaply ⟨*dresses produced* on the cheap⟩

**²cheap** *adj* **1a** (relatively) low in price; *esp* purchasable below the market price or the real value **b** charging a low price ⟨*a* ~ *supermarket*⟩ **c** depreciated in value (e g as a result of currency inflation) ⟨~ *dollars*⟩ **2** gained with little effort ⟨*a* ~ *victory*⟩; *esp* gained by contemptible means ⟨~ *laughs*⟩ ⟨*a* ~ *thrill*⟩ **3a** of inferior quality or worth; tawdry, sleazy **b** contemptible because of lack of any fine or redeeming qualities ⟨~ *election gimmickry*⟩ **4** *of money* obtainable at a low rate of interest **5** *NAm* stingy – **cheap, cheaply** *adv*, **cheapish** *adj*, **cheapishly** *adv*, **cheapness** *n*

*usage* Cheap as an adverb is used chiefly in contexts of buying and selling ⟨*get it for you* cheap⟩ and cannot replace cheaply, the usual adverb ⟨*the room was* cheaply *furnished*⟩.

**cheapen** /ˈcheep(ə)n/ *vt* **1a** to make cheap in price or value **b** to lower in general esteem **c** to make tawdry, vulgar, or inferior **2** *archaic* **2a** to ask the price of **b** to bid or bargain for ⟨*she would make a puritan of the Devil, if he should* ~ *a kiss of her* – Shak⟩ ~ *vi* to become cheap [(2) obs *cheap* (to price, bid for)]

**¹cheap-jack** /-jak/ *n, informal* somebody, esp a pedlar, who sells cheap wares [*cheap* + the name *Jack*]

**²cheap-jack** *adj, informal* **1** inferior, cheap, or worthless ⟨~ *film companies*⟩ **2** characterized by unscrupulous opportunism ⟨~ *speculators*⟩

**cheapo** /ˈcheepoh/ *adj, informal* inexpensive, cheap

**cheapskate** /ˈcheepˌskayt/ *n, chiefly NAm* a miserly or stingy person [*cheap* + *skate* (fellow, miser)]

**¹cheat** /cheet/ *n* **1** a fraudulent deception; a fraud **2** one who cheats; a pretender, deceiver [earlier *cheat* forfeited property, fr ME *chet* escheat, short for *eschete* – more at ESCHEAT]

**²cheat** *vt* **1** to deceive, trick; *esp* to deprive of something valuable by deceit or fraud ⟨~ed *me out of my inheritance*⟩ **2** to defeat the purpose or blunt the effects of ⟨~ *winter of its dreariness* – Washington Irving⟩ ~ *vi* **1a** to practise fraud or deception **b** to violate rules dishonestly (e g at cards or in an examination) **2** to be sexually unfaithful – often + *on* – **cheater** *n*

**¹check** /chek/ *n* **1** exposure of a chess king to an attack from which it must be protected or moved to safety – used interjectionally by a chess player who has put his/her opponent's king in this situation **2a** a sudden stoppage of a forward course or progress; an arrest **b** a checking of an opposing player (e g in ice hockey) **3** a sudden pause or break in a progression **4** one who or that which arrests, limits, or restrains; a restraint ⟨*against all* ~s, *rebukes, and manners, I must advance* – Shak⟩ **5a** a standard for testing and evaluation; a criterion **b** an inspection, examination **c** (a sample or unit used for) the act of testing or verifying **6a** (a square in) a pattern in squares, often of two alternating colours like a chessboard **b** a fabric woven or printed with such a design **7** a shallow crack or break (e g in wood or steel or on a painted surface) **8** RABBET (channel or groove, esp in wood) **9** *chiefly NAm* a ticket or token showing ownership or identity or indicating payment made ⟨*a baggage* ~⟩ **10a** *NAm* a slip indicating an amount due; *esp* a bill for food and drink consumed in a restaurant **11** *NAm* a counter in various games **12** *NAm* ²TICK 2 (marker used to show an item has been noted, examined, etc) **13** *obs* a reprimand, rebuke [ME *chek*, fr OF *eschec*, fr Ar *shāh*, fr Per, lit., king; (6) ME *chek*, short for *cheker* chequer] – **checkless** *adj* – **in check** under restraint or control ⟨*held the enemy* in check⟩

**²check** *vt* **1** to put (a chess opponent's king) in check **2a** to slow or bring to a stop, esp sharply **b** to block the progress of (e g an ice hockey player) **3a** to restrain or diminish the action or force of; control ⟨*hastily* ~ed *the impulse*⟩ **b** *chiefly nautical* to slack or ease off (e g a rope) and then secure again **4a** to compare with a source, original, or authority; verify **b** to inspect for satisfactory condition, accuracy, safety, or performance **5** to mark into squares; chequer – usu in past part **6** *chiefly NAm* to mark with a tick as examined, verified, or satisfactory – often + *off* ⟨~ed *off each item*⟩ **7** *NAm* CHECK IN 2 **8** *chiefly dial* to rebuke, reprimand ~ *vi* **1a** *of a dog* to stop in a chase, esp when the scent is lost **b** to halt through caution, uncertainty, or fear; stop **2** to investigate and make sure – often + *up* **3** to waive the right to initiate the betting in a round of poker **4** *chiefly NAm* to correspond point for point; tally ⟨*the description* ~s *with the photograph*⟩ – often + *out* ⟨*his story* ~ed *out*⟩ **5** *NAm* to draw a cheque on a bank – **checkable** *adj*

*usage* The use of check up on is widely disliked, and can sometimes be replaced by check alone ⟨check *the facts*⟩; but when check up on means "inquire about", the use of check alone ⟨*police* checked *her*⟩ might lead to confusion with one of its many other senses, such as "restrain". Another confusion arises over the American use of **check** in sense 7 ⟨**check** *your bag*⟩ which would be understood in Britain to mean "inspect". **synonyms** see RESTRAIN **antonyms** accelerate (eg speed), advance (eg a plan), release (eg feelings)

**check in** *vi* to report one's presence or arrival; *esp* to arrive and register at a hotel or airport ~ *vt* **1** to return or accept the return of ⟨check in *the equipment after using*⟩ **2** to deposit or accept (luggage) for transport, esp by air; *also, chiefly NAm* to leave or accept for safekeeping in a cloakroom or left-luggage office

**check into** *vt, chiefly NAm* to check in at ⟨check into *a hotel*⟩

**check out** *vi* to complete the formalities for leaving, esp at a hotel ~ *vt* **1** to have the removal of (something) recorded ⟨checked out *a library book*⟩ **2** *chiefly NAm* to find out about; investigate; *also; also* CHECK 4b ⟨check *the new product* out⟩ – see also CHECKOUT

**check up on, check on** *vt* **1** to examine for accuracy or truth, esp in order to corroborate information ⟨check up on *the facts*⟩ **2** to make thorough inquiries about ⟨*police* checked up on *her*⟩

¹**checker** /'chekə/ *n* **1** *chiefly NAm* a chequer; CHECK 6a **2** *NAm* DRAUGHTSMAN **4** (piece used in the game of draughts) [(2) back-formation fr *checkers*]

²**checker** *vt, chiefly NAm* to chequer

³**checker** *n* **1** one who or that which checks **2** *NAm* a cashier in a supermarket

**checkers** /'chekəz/ *n taking sing vb, NAm* the game of draughts [pl of *checker* (chessboard), fr ME *cheker*, fr OF *eschequier*, fr *eschec*]

**checking account** *n, NAm* CURRENT ACCOUNT

**checklist** /'chek,list/ *n* an inventory, catalogue; *esp* a list of checks to be made (eg on an aircraft before takeoff)

¹**checkmate** /,chek'mayt/ *vt* **1** to thwart or counter completely **2** to check (a chess opponent's king) so that escape is impossible [ME *chekmaten*, fr *chekmate*, interj used to announce checkmate, fr MF *eschec mat*, fr Ar *shāh māt*, fr Per, lit., the king is left helpless]

²**checkmate** *n* **1a** the act of checkmating **b** the situation of a checkmated king **2** complete defeat □ (1) used interjectionally by a chess player who has put his/her opponent's king in this situation

**checkout** /'chek,owt/ *n* a cash desk equipped with a cash register in a self-service shop

**checkpoint** /'chek,poynt/ *n* a location where inspection (eg of travellers) may take place ⟨*vehicles were stopped at various* ~s⟩

**check rail** *n* a rail placed alongside the inner edge of a rail on which a train runs to prevent derailment, esp on bends

**checkrein** /'chek,rayn/ *n* **1** a short rein attached to the bit of a bridle and looped over a hook on the saddle to prevent a horse from lowering its head **2** a rein connecting the driving rein of one horse of a pair with the mouthpiece of the other

**checkroom** /'chek,roohm, -room/ *n, NAm* a room in which luggage, parcels, or coats, jackets, etc may be left for safekeeping

**checkup** /'chek,up/ *n* an examination; *esp* a general physical examination

**checkweighman** /'chek,waymən, -man/ *n* a colliery worker employed on behalf of the miners to check the weighing of coal against company estimates

**cheddar** /'chedə/ *vt* to stack (slices of milk curd) so that whey will be drained off in the process of making cheese, esp Cheddar

**Cheddar** *n* a hard white, yellow, or orange smooth-textured cheese with a flavour that ranges from mild to strong as the cheese matures [*Cheddar*, village in Somerset, England]

**cheder** /'khaydə, 'khedə/ *n* HEDER (elementary Jewish school)

¹**cheek** /cheek/ *n* **1** the fleshy side of the face below the eye and above and to the side of the mouth **2** either of two paired parts which face one another (eg the jaws of a vice) **3** insolent boldness; impudence **4** *informal* either side of the buttocks [ME *cheke*, fr OE *cēace*; akin to MLG *kāke* jawbone] – **cheekful** *n* – **cheek by jowl** in close proximity – **turn the other cheek** to respond to injury or unkindness with patience; forgo retaliation (fr Christ's admonition in Matt 5:39 & Luke 6:29] – see also **with one's** TONGUE **in one's cheek**

²**cheek** *vt, informal* to speak rudely or impudently to

**cheekbone** /-,bohn/ *n* (the prominence below the eye that is formed by) the ZYGOMATIC BONE

**-cheeked** *comb form* (→ *adj*) having (such) cheeks ⟨*rosy-cheeked*⟩

**cheekpiece** /'cheek,pees/ *n* either of the two parts of a bridle connecting the bit to the headpiece

**cheek pouch** *n* a pouch in the cheeks of an animal (eg a monkey or hamster) for holding food

**cheeky** /'cheeki/ *adj* having or showing cheek; impudent – **cheekily** *adv*, **cheekiness** *n*

**cheep** /cheep/ *vi or n* (to utter) a faint shrill sound characteristic of a young bird [imit]

¹**cheer** /chiə/ *n* **1** state of mind or heart; spirit ⟨*be of good* ~ – Mt 9:2(AV)⟩ **2** happiness; gaiety **3** a shout of applause or encouragement **4** *archaic* facial expression **5** *archaic* food and drink for a feast; fare [ME *chere* face, cheer, fr OF, face, perh fr LL *cara*, fr Gk *kara* head] – **cheerless** *adj*, **cheerlessly** *adv*, **cheerlessness** *n*

²**cheer** *vt* **1a** to instil with hope or courage; comfort **b** to make glad or happy **2** to urge *on* or encourage, esp by shouts ⟨~ed *the team on*⟩ **3** to applaud with shouts ~ *vi* **1** to grow or be cheerful; rejoice **2** to utter a shout of applause or triumph **3** *obs* to be mentally or emotionally disposed ⟨*how* ~'st *thou, Jessica?* – Shak⟩ □ (*vt* 1; *vi* 1) usu + *up* – **cheerer** *n*

**cheerful** /-f(ə)l/ *adj* **1a** full of good spirits; merry **b** ungrudging ⟨~ *obedience*⟩ **2** conducive to happiness; likely to dispel gloom or worry ⟨*a* ~ *sunny room*⟩ **synonyms** see JOYFUL **antonyms** dejected, miserable – **cheerfully** *adv*, cheerfulness *n*

**cheerio** /,chiəri'oh/ *interj, chiefly Br* – used to express farewell [*cheery* + -*o*]

**cheerleader** /-,leedə/ *n* one, esp a female, who leads organized cheering (eg at a N American football game) – **cheerlead** *vt*

**cheers** /chiəz/ *interj* – used as a toast and sometimes as an informal farewell or expression of thanks

**cheery** /'chiəri/ *adj* marked by or causing good spirits; cheerful – **cheerily** *adv*, **cheeriness** *n*

¹**cheese** /cheez/ *n* **1a** a food consisting of coagulated, compressed, and usu ripened milk curds **b** an often cylindrical cake of this food **2** something resembling cheese in consistency or a cheese in shape **3** a fruit preserve with the consistency of cream cheese ⟨*damson* ~⟩ [ME *chese*, fr OE *cēse*; akin to OHG *kāsi* cheese; both fr a prehistoric WGmc word borrowed fr L *caseus* cheese; akin to OE *hwatherian* to foam, Skt *kvathati* he boils] – **cheesy** *adj*, **cheesiness** *n*

²**cheese** *n, slang* an important person; a boss – chiefly in *big cheese* [prob fr Urdu *chīz* thing, fr Per]

**cheesecake** /-,kayk/ *n* **1** a baked or refrigerated dessert consisting of a soft filling usu containing cheese, in a pastry or biscuit-crumb case **2** *informal* a photographic display of attractive and scantily clothed female figures – compare BEEFCAKE

**cheesecloth** /-,kloth/ *n* a lightweight loosely woven cotton gauze [fr its use in cheesemaking]

**cheesed off** *also* **cheesed** *adj, chiefly Br informal* annoyed or bored; FED UP [prob fr ²*cheese*]

**cheesehead** /'cheez,hed/ *adj, of a screw or bolt* having a squat cylindrical head

**cheese mite** *n* a small mite (*Tyroglyphus longior*) that breeds in cheese and lives esp in stored products (eg flour)

**cheesemonger** /'cheez,mung·gə/ *n* one who deals in cheese

**cheeseparing** /'cheez,peəring/ *n* miserly or petty economizing; stinginess – **cheeseparing** *adj*

**cheese skipper** *n* a small shiny fly (*Piophila casei*) whose larva infests stored cheese and bacon

**cheetah** /'cheetə/ *n* a long-legged spotted African and formerly Asian cat (*Acinonyx jubatus*) that is about the size of a small leopard, has blunt claws that cannot be drawn in, and is the fastest land animal [Hindi *cītā*, fr Skt *citrakāya* tiger, fr *citra* bright + *kāya* body]

**chef** /shef/ *n* a skilled cook; *esp* the chief cook in a restaurant or hotel [Fr, short for *chef de cuisine* head of the kitchen]

**chef d'oeuvre** /,shay 'duhvə (Fr ʃɛ dœːvr)/ *n, pl* **chefs d'oeuvre** /~/ a masterpiece, esp in art or literature [Fr *chef-d'oeuvre*, lit., chief piece of work]

**Chehalis** /chə'haylis/ *n, pl* **Chehalises**, *esp collectively* **Chehalis** a member, or the language, of an American Indian people of Washington in the NW USA

**cheka** /'chekə/ *n, often cap* the Soviet secret police organization between 1917 and 1922 [Russ, fr *che* + *ka*, names of initial letters of *Chrezvychainaya Kommissiya* extraordinary commission]

**chela** /'keelə/ *n, pl* **chelae** /'keelie/ a pincerlike claw on a limb of a CRUSTACEAN (eg a crab) or ARACHNID (eg a scorpion) [NL, fr Gk *chēlē* claw]

¹**chelate** /'kee,layt/ *adj* **1** resembling or having chelae **2** *chemistry* of, being, or having a molecular structure that contains a metal ION (electrically charged atom or group of atoms) held by one or more COORDINATE BONDS – **chelate** *n*

²**chelate** *vb, chemistry* to react (with) so as to form a chelate structure – **chelator** *n,* **chelatable** *adj,* **chelation** *n*

**chelicera** /ki'lisərə/ *n, pl* **chelicerae** /-rie/ either of the front pair of appendages on the heads of spiders and other ARACHNIDS, often modified as fangs [NL, fr Fr *chélicère,* fr Gk *chēlē* + *keras* horn – more at HORN] – **cheliceral** *adj*

**Chellean, Chellian** /'shelian/ *adj* ABBEVILLIAN (of an early Palaeolithic culture) [Fr *chelléen,* fr *Chelles,* town in France]

**chelonian** /ki'lohyən/ *adj or n* (of or being) a tortoise or turtle [Gk *chelōnē* tortoise]

**Chelsea bun** /'chelsi/ *n* a sweet bun made with yeast, that contains dried fruit (eg currants) and is shaped in a flat coil [*Chelsea,* district of London]

**Chelsea pensioner** *n* a veteran or disabled soldier living at the Chelsea Royal Hospital

**chem-** /kem-/, **chemo-** *also* **chemi-** *comb form* **1** chemical; chemistry ⟨chemo*therapy*⟩ ⟨chemo*taxis*⟩ **2** chemically ⟨chemi*sorb*⟩ [NL, fr LGk *chēmeia* alchemy, prob fr *chyma* fluid, fr *chein* to pour]

**chemic** /'kemik/ *adj* **1** chemical **2** *archaic* ALCHEMIC [NL *chimicus* alchemist, fr ML *alchimicus,* fr *alchymia* alchemy]

¹**chemical** /'kemikl/ *adj* **1** of, used in, or produced by chemistry **2a** acting, operated, or produced by chemicals **b** capable of detection by chemical means – **chemically** *adv*

²**chemical** *n* a substance (eg a chemical element or compound) obtained by a chemical process or used for producing a chemical effect

**chemical engineering** *n* engineering dealing with the application of chemistry to large-scale industrial processes (eg oil refining and plastics manufacture)

**chemical warfare** *n* warfare using harmful chemicals (eg poison gases) other than explosives

**chemical wood** *n* pulp from wood broken down by chemicals, that is used esp for making paper, rayon, and ACETATE fibres

**chemico-** /'kemikoh-/ *comb form* CHEM- 1 ⟨chemico*physical*⟩

**chemiluminescence** /,kemi,loohmi'nes(ə)ns/ *n* light produced by a chemical reaction occurring at a low temperature [ISV] – **chemiluminescent** *adj*

**chemin de fer** /shə,manh də 'fea (*Fr* ʃəmɛ̃ də fer)/ *n, pl* **chemins de fer** /~/ a card game resembling baccarat in which only two hands are dealt, any number of players may bet against the dealer, and the winning hand is the one that comes closer to but does not exceed a count of nine on two or three cards [Fr, lit., railway]

**chemise** /shə'meez/ *n* **1** a woman's one-piece undergarment **2** a usu loose straight-hanging dress [ME, fr OF, shirt, fr LL *camisia*]

**chemisorb** /,kemi'sawb/ *vt* to take up and hold, usu irreversibly, by chemical forces [*chem-* + *-sorb* (as in *adsorb*)] – **chemisorption** *n*

**chemist** /'kemist/ *n* **1** one who is trained in chemistry **2** *Br* (a pharmacist, esp in) a retail shop where medicines and miscellaneous articles (eg cosmetics and films) are sold **3** *obs* an alchemist [NL *chimista,* short for ML *alchimista* alchemist]

**chemistry** /'kemistri/ *n* **1** a science that deals with the composition, structure, and properties of substances and of the transformations that they undergo **2a** the composition and chemical properties of a substance ⟨the ~ *of iron*⟩ **b** chemical processes and phenomena (eg of an organism) ⟨blood ~⟩ **3** the nature of a specified relationship, feeling, etc, seen esp as something inexplicable and often instinctive ⟨the ~ *of our love affair*⟩

**chemmy** /'shemi/ *n* CHEMIN DE FER [by shortening & alter.]

**chemo-** /keemoh-/ – see CHEM-

**chemoautotrophic** /,keemoh,awtə'trohfik, ,kemoh-/ *adj, esp of a bacterium* AUTOTROPHIC (capable of making sugars, proteins, etc from carbon dioxide and other simple chemical compounds) and deriving energy from the reaction between a chemical and oxygen – compare PHOTOAUTOTROPHIC – **chemoautotrophically** *adv,* **chemoautotrophy** *n*

**chemoprophylaxis** /,keemoh,profi'laksis, ,kemoh-/ *n* the prevention of infectious disease (eg malaria) by the use of drugs – **chemoprophylactic** *adj*

**chemoreceptor** /'keemohri,septə, ke-/ *n* a SENSE ORGAN (eg a taste bud) that responds to chemical stimuli [ISV] – **chemoreception** *n,* **chemoreceptive** *adj,* **chemoreceptivity** *n*

**chemosphere** /'kemə,sfiə/ *n* THERMOSPHERE (layer of the earth's upper atmosphere)

**chemosterilant** /,keemoh'sterilənt, ,kemoh-/ *n* any of various substances that produce sterility (eg of an insect) without marked alteration of mating habits or length of life, and are often used as a means of controlling the numbers of crop pests [*chemosterilize* + *-ant*]

**chemosynthesis** /,keemoh'sinthəsis, ,kemoh-/ *n* the formation (eg in living cells) of organic chemical compounds (eg proteins) using energy derived from chemical reactions rather than that derived from light – compare PHOTOSYNTHESIS [ISV] – **chemosynthetic** *adj*

**chemotaxis** /,keemoh'taksis, ke-/ *n* the orientation or movement of cells or an organism (eg a bacterium) in response to a chemical stimulus [NL] – **chemotactic** *adj,* **chemotactically** *adv*

**chemotherapy** /,keemoh'therəpi, ,ke-/ *n* the use of drugs in the treatment or control of disease (eg cancer) [ISV] – **chemotherapist** *n,* **chemotherapeutic, chemotherapeutical** *adj,* **chemotherapeutically** *adv*

**chemotropism** /ki'motrə,piz(ə)m, ,keemə'trohpiz(ə)m/ *n* the movement or growth of cells or an organism, esp a plant, towards or away from a chemical stimulus [ISV] – **chemotropic** *adj*

**chenille** /shə'neel/ *n* **1** (a fabric made from) a soft wool, cotton, silk, or rayon yarn used esp for furniture trimmings **2** an imitation of chenille yarn or fabric [Fr, lit., caterpillar, fr L *canicula,* dim. of *canis* dog – more at HOUND; fr its hairy appearance]

**cheongsam** /'chong,sam/ *n* a dress with a slit skirt and a MANDARIN COLLAR worn esp by oriental women [Chin (Cant) *cheong shaam* (ch'eūng shaam), lit., long gown]

**cheque,** *NAm* **check** /chek/ *n* a written order for a bank to pay money as instructed; *also* a printed form on which such an order is usually written [*cheque* alter. of *check*]

**chequebook** /-,book/ *n* a book containing unwritten cheques

**chequebook journalism** *n* sensationalist journalism consisting of (the writing of) exclusive reports acquired by paying large amounts of money (eg to friends and relations of criminals)

**cheque card** *n* a card issued to guarantee that the holder's cheques up to a particular amount will be honoured by the issuing bank ⟨we accept cheques if you've got a ~⟩ – called also BANKER'S CARD; compare CREDIT CARD, CASH CARD

¹**chequer,** *chiefly NAm* **checker** /'chekə/ *n* (a square in) a pattern of squares, esp of two alternating colours; CHECK 6A [ME *cheker,* fr OF *eschequier* chessboard, fr *eschec* check]

²**chequer,** *chiefly NAm* **checker** *vt* **1** to variegate with different colours or shades; *esp* to mark with squares of usu two alternating colours **2** to vary with contrasting elements ⟨a ~ed *career*⟩ □ usu in pp

**cherish** /'cherish/ *vt* **1a** to hold dear; feel or show affection for **b** to keep or cultivate with care and affection; nurture **2** to entertain or harbour in the mind deeply and with affection ⟨still ~ es *that memory*⟩ [ME *cherisshen,* fr MF *cheriss-,* stem of *cherir* to cherish, fr OF, fr *chier* dear, fr L *carus* – more at CHARITY] – **cherishable** *adj,* **cherisher** *n*

**chernozem** /,chuhnə'zem, -'zhom, 'chuhnəzem, 'chawnəzyem/ *n* any of a group of dark-coloured humus-rich soils found in temperate to cool climates of rather low humidity [Russ, lit., black earth] – **chernozemic** *adj*

**Cherokee** /,cherə'kee/ *n, pl* (1) **Cherokees,** *esp collectively* **Cherokee 1** (a member of) a N American Indian people orig of Tennessee and N Carolina **2** the IROQUOIAN language of the Cherokee people [prob fr Creek *tciloki* people of a different speech]

**cheroot** /shə'rooht/ *n* a cigar cut square at both ends [Tamil *curuṭṭu,* lit., roll]

**cherry** /'cheri/ *n* **1** any of numerous trees and shrubs (genus *Prunus*) of the rose family, that bear pale yellow to deep red or blackish smooth-skinned fruits with a smooth stone, and that include some varieties cultivated for their fruits and some for their ornamental flowers; *also* the fruit or wood of a cherry **2** a light clear red colour **3** *slang* virginity [ME *chery,* fr ONF *cherise* (taken as a plural), fr LL *ceresia,* fr L *cerasus* cherry tree, fr Gk *kerasos* – more at CORNEL] – **cherry** *adj,* **cherrylike** *adj*

**cherry brandy** *n* a sweet liqueur in which cherries have been steeped

**cherry plum** *n* an Asiatic plum tree (*Prunus cerasifera*) used extensively in Europe as a STOCK onto which buds from domestic varieties are grafted

**chersonese** /'kuhsə,neez, -,nees/ *n, chiefly poetic* a peninsula [L *chersonesus*, fr Gk *chersonēsos*, fr *chersos* dry land + *nēsos* island]

**chert** /chuht/ *n* a rock resembling flint and consisting essentially of quartz [origin unknown] – **cherty** *adj*

**cherub** /'cherəb/ *n, pl* **cherubs**, (*I*) **cherubim** /'cherəbim/ **1a** a biblical attendant of God or of a holy place, often represented as a being with large wings, a human head, and an animal body **b** the second of the nine orders of angelic beings in the CELESTIAL HIERARCHY ranking immediately below SERAPHIM and above THRONES **2a** a beautiful usu winged child in painting and sculpture **b** an innocent-looking usu chubby and pretty person [L, fr Gk *cheroub*, fr Heb *kĕrūbh*] – **cherubic** *adj*, **cherubically** *adv*, **cherublike** *adj*

**chervil** /'chuhvil/ *n* (any of several plants related to) an aromatic plant (*Anthriscus cerefolium*) of the carrot family with leaves that are often used as a herb and in soups and salads [ME *cherville*, fr OE *cerfille*; akin to OHG *kervila*]

**Cheshire cheese** /'cheshiə, 'cheshə/ *n* a white or pinkish orange often crumbly cheese made originally in Cheshire [*Cheshire*, county of England]

**chesil** /'chezl/ *n* shingle, gravel – used esp in place names ⟨Chesil *Beach*⟩ [ME, fr OE *cisel, ceasel;* akin to OHG *kisil* pebble]

**chess** /ches/ *n* a game for two players each of whom moves his/her 16 chessmen according to fixed rules across a chessboard and tries to checkmate his/her opponent's king [ME *ches*, fr OF *esches*, acc pl of *eschec* check at chess – more at CHECK]

**chessboard** /-,bawd/ *n* a board used in various games (eg chess or draughts) that is divided into usu 64 equal squares of two alternating colours

**chessel** /'chesl/ *n* a vat or mould used in cheesemaking [prob fr ¹*cheese* + ¹*well*]

**chessman** /-,man/ *n* any of the 16 pieces used by each player in the game of chess – compare KING 4, QUEEN 4, ³ROOK, BISHOP 2, KNIGHT 2, ³PAWN 1

**chest** /chest/ *n* **1a** a container for storage or shipping; *esp* a box with a lid used esp for the safekeeping of belongings b a usu small cupboard used esp for the storing of medicines or first-aid supplies **2** a case in which a commodity (eg tea) is shipped **3** the part of the body enclosed by the ribs and breastbone [ME, fr OE *cest;* akin to OHG & ON *kista* chest, MD *kiste;* all fr a prehistoric NGmc-WGmc word borrowed fr L *cista* box, basket, fr Gk *kistē* basket] – **chestful** *n* – **get something off one's chest** to relieve the burden of a worry, problem, etc by talking about it

**-chested** /-chestid/ *comb form* (→ *adj*) having (such) a chest ⟨*flat*-chested⟩ ⟨*deep*-chested⟩

**chesterfield** /'chestə,feeld/ *n* **1** a semifitted overcoat with a velvet collar **2** a heavily padded usu leather sofa *synonyms* see SOFA [prob fr a 19th-c Earl of *Chesterfield*]

**Chester White** /'chestə/ *n* (any of) a breed of large white pigs [*Chester* County, in Pennsylvania, USA]

¹**chestnut** /'ches(t),nut/ *n* **1a** a tree or shrub (genus *Castanea*) of the beech family; *esp* SPANISH CHESTNUT **b** the nut of a chestnut that is edible when cooked **c** the wood of a chestnut **2** a greyish- to reddish-brown colour **3** HORSE CHESTNUT **4** a chestnut-coloured animal; *specif* a horse having a body colour of any shade of pure or reddish-brown with mane, tail, and ears of the same or a lighter shade – compare ²BAY 1, ¹SORREL 1 **5** a small callus on the inner side of the leg of a horse **6** an often repeated joke or story; *broadly* anything repeated excessively [ME *chasteine, chesten* chestnut tree, fr MF *chastaigne*, fr L *castanea*, fr Gk *kastanea*]

²**chestnut** *adj* of the colour chestnut

**chest of drawers** /drawz/ *n* a piece of furniture containing a set of drawers (eg for holding clothes)

**chest of viols** *n* a set of VIOLS (medieval stringed musical instrument) of different sizes for ensemble playing

**chesty** /'chesti/ *adj* **1** of, inclined to, symptomatic of, or suffering from disease of the chest ⟨*a ~ cough*⟩ – not used technically **2** *slang* having prominent breasts

**chetrum** /'cheetrəm, 'chet-/ *n, pl* **chetrums, chetrum** – see *ngultrum* at MONEY table [native name in Bhutan]

**cheval-de-frise** /shə,val də 'freez (*Fr* ʃəval də friz)/ *n*, **chevaux-de-frise** /shəvoh ~ (*Fr* ʃəvo ~)/ *n pl* **1** a defence, esp against a cavalry charge, consisting of an iron barrel or timber covered with projecting spikes and often strung with barbed wire **2** a security device (eg a line of spikes) set into the top of a wall [Fr, lit., horse from Friesland]

**cheval glass** /shə'val/ *n* a full-length mirror in a frame by which it may be tilted [Fr *cheval* horse, support]

**chevalier** /,shevə'liə/ *n* **1** a member of any of various orders of knighthood or of merit (eg the French Legion of Honour) **2** a member of the lowest rank of French nobility in former times [Fr, knight, horseman, fr MF, fr LL *caballarius* – more at CAVALIER]

**cheviot** /'cheevi·ət, 'che-/ *n* **1** *often cap* (any of) a breed of hardy hornless sheep that are a source of quality meat and thick wool and originated in the Cheviot hills **2** a heavy rough plain or twill fabric made from the wool of cheviot sheep [the *Cheviot* hills on the borders of England and Scotland]

**chevron** /'shevrən/ *n* a figure, pattern, or object having the shape of a V or an inverted V: eg **a** a heraldic design consisting of two diagonal stripes meeting at an angle, usu with the point uppermost **b** a sleeve badge that usu consists of one or more chevron-shaped stripes and that indicates the wearer's rank or length of service (eg in the armed forces) [ME, fr MF, rafter, chevron, fr (assumed) VL *caprion-, caprio* rafter; akin to L *caper* goat] – **chevroned** *adj*

**chevrotain** /'shevrətayn, -tin/ *n* any of several very small hornless RUMINANTS (animals that chew the cud) (family Tragulidae) of tropical Asia and W Africa [Fr, dim. of *chevrot* kid, fawn, fr MF, dim. of *chèvre* goat, fr L *capra* she-goat, fem of *capr-, caper* he-goat]

¹**chew** /chooh/ *vt* to crush, grind, or gnaw (eg food) (as if) with the teeth; masticate ~ *vi* to chew something [ME *chewen*, fr OE *cēowan;* akin to OHG *kiuwan* to chew, OSlav *živati*] – **chewable** *adj*, **chewer** *n*, **chewy** *adj* – **chew the fat/rag** to make friendly conversation; gossip – see also BITE **off more than one can chew**

**chew over** *vt, informal* to meditate on; think about reflectively ⟨*I'm not sure, I'll chew it over*⟩

²**chew** *n* **1** the act or an instance of chewing **2** something for chewing ⟨*a ~ of tobacco*⟩

**chewing gum** /'chooh·ing/ *n* a flavoured usu sweetened rubbery material (eg a preparation of CHICLE) for chewing

**Cheyenne** /,shie'an, -'en/ *n, pl* (*I*) **Cheyennes** /~/, *esp collectively* **Cheyenne 1** (a member of) an American Indian people of the western plains of the USA **2** the Algonquian language of the Cheyenne people [CanF, fr Dakota *Shaiyena*, fr *shaia* to speak unintelligibly]

**chez** /shay/ *prep* at or to the home of [Fr]

**chi** /kie/ *n* the 22nd letter of the Greek alphabet [Gk *chei*]

**chiack** /'chie·ək/ *vb, chiefly Austr* to make derisive remarks (about); tease [alter. of *chi-hike, chi-ike* (a shout of greeting or derision)] – **chiack** *n*

**Chianti** /ki'anti/ *n* a dry usu red Italian table wine [It, fr *Chianti*, district of Tuscany in Italy]

**chiao** /chow/ *n, pl* **chiao** – see *dollar* at MONEY table [Chin (Pek) *jiăo* (*chiao* ³)]

**chiaroscuro** /ki,ahrə'skooəroh/ *n, pl* **chiaroscuros 1** pictorial representation using light and shade without regard to colour **2** the arrangement or treatment of light and shade in a picture or painting [It, fr *chiaro* clear, light + *oscuro* obscure, dark]

**chiasm** /'kie,az(ə)m/ *n* a chiasma [NL *chiasma*]

**chiasma** /ki'azmə/ *n, pl* **chiasmata** /ki'azmətə/ a cross-shaped configuration formed by body structures or parts; *esp* one that forms between paired CHROMATIDS (strands of a chromosome) when a cell is dividing (undergoing MEIOSIS), and is considered to be the point where genetic material is exchanged [NL, X-shaped form, fr Gk, crosspiece, fr *chiazein* to mark with a chi, fr *chi* (x)] – **chiasmic, chiasmatic** *adj*

**chiasmus** /kie'azməs/ *n* inversion of the relationship between the elements of parallel phrases (eg in Goldsmith's "*to stop too fearful, and too faint to go*") [NL, fr Gk *chiasmos*, fr *chiazein*]

**Chibcha** /'chibchə/ *n, pl* (*I*) **Chibchas**, *esp collectively* **Chibcha 1** (a member of) a S American Indian people of central Colombia **2** the extinct language of the Chibcha people [Sp, of AmerInd origin]

**Chibchan** /'chibchən/ *adj* of or being a group of related languages of Colombia and Central America

**chibouk, chibouque** /chi'boohk/ *n* a long-stemmed Turkish tobacco pipe with a clay bowl [Fr *chibouque*, fr Turk *çibuk*]

**chic** /sheek, shik/ *adj or n* (having or showing) elegance and sophistication, esp of dress or manner ⟨*wears her clothes with superb* ∼⟩ [Fr] – **chicly** *adv*, **chicness** *n*

¹**chicane** /shi'kayn/ *vi* to use chicanery ⟨*a wretch he had taught to lie and* ∼ – George Meredith⟩ ∼ *vt* to trick, cheat [Fr *chicaner*, fr MF, to quibble, prevent justice]

²**chicane** *n* 1 chicanery 2 a series of tight usu narrow bends in opposite directions on an otherwise straight stretch of a racing course, esp a motor-racing circuit 3 a hand of cards containing no trumps

**chicanery** /shi'kayn(ə)ri/ *n* 1 deception by the use of untrue or irrelevant arguments 2 a piece of sharp practice or esp legal trickery

**chicano** /chi'kahnoh/ *n*, *NAm informal* an American originating from Mexico [modif of Sp *mejicano* Mexican]

¹**chichi** /'sheeshee/ *adj* 1 elaborately ornamented; showy, frilly ⟨*a* ∼ *dress*⟩ 2 unnecessarily elaborate or affected [Fr]

²**chichi** *n* 1 frilly or elaborate ornamentation 2 unnecessary elaboration; affectation

**chick** /chik/ *n* 1a a chicken; esp one newly hatched b the young of any bird 2 *slang* a young woman 3 *archaic* a child

**chickadee** /'chikə,dee/ *n* any of several crestless N American songbirds (genus *Penthestes* or *Parus*) related to the European tits [imit]

**chickaree** /'chikə,ree/ *n* a N American red squirrel (*Sciurus hudsonicus*) [imit]

**Chickasaw** /'chikə,saw/ *n*, *pl (1)* **Chickasaws**, *esp collectively* **Chickasaw** 1 a member of a N American Indian people of Mississippi and Alabama 2 a dialect of Choctaw spoken by the Chickasaw

¹**chicken** /'chikin/ *n* 1a the common DOMESTIC FOWL (*Gallus gallus*), esp when young; *also* its flesh used as food b any of various similar birds or their young 2 *informal* a young person – chiefly in *he/she's no* (*spring*) *chicken* 3 *informal* 3a a coward b any of various contests in which the participants risk personal safety in order to see who will give up first ⟨*she was hit by a car when running across a main road in a game of* ∼⟩ [ME *chiken*, fr OE *cicen* young chicken; akin to OE *cocc* cock]

²**chicken** *adj*, *informal* scared

**chicken feed** *n*, *informal* a small and insignificant amount, esp of money

**chickenhearted** /-'hahtid/ *adj* timid, cowardly

'**chicken-,livered** *adj* timid, cowardly

**chicken out** *vi*, *informal* to fail to do something because of losing one's nerve ⟨*chicken out of giving a speech*⟩

**chicken pox** /poks/ *n* a short-lasting contagious virus disease, esp of children, that is marked by mild fever and the formation of small blisters

**chicken wire** *n* a lightweight wire netting with a hexagonal mesh [fr its use for making enclosures for chickens]

**chick-pea** /'chik ,pee/ *n* a widely cultivated Asian plant (*Cicer arietinum*) of the pea family; *also* the hard edible seed of this plant [by folk etymology fr ME *chiche*, fr MF, fr L *cicer*]

**chickweed** /'chik,weed/ *n* any of various low-growing small-leaved plants of the pink family (esp genera *Arenaria*, *Cerastium*, and *Stellaria*) that occur commonly as weeds [fr its being eaten by chickens]

**chicle** /'chikl/ *n* a gummy substance from the milky sap of the sapodilla tree used as the chief ingredient of chewing gum [Sp, fr Nahuatl *chictli*]

**chicory** /'chik(ə)ri/ *n* a thick-rooted usu blue-flowered European plant (*Cichorium intybus*) of the daisy family, widely grown for its roots and as a salad plant; *also* the dried ground roasted root of chicory used as a coffee additive [ME *cicoree*, fr MF *cichorée*, *chicorée*, fr L *cichoreum*, fr Gk *kichoreia*]

**chide** /chied/ *vb* **chid** /chid/, **chided**; **chid**, **chidden** /'chid(ə)n/, **chided** *archaic* to rebuke (somebody) angrily; scold [ME *chiden*, fr OE *cīdan* to quarrel, chide, fr *cīd* strife] – **chidingly** *adv*

¹**chief** /cheef/ *n* 1 (a broad band across) the upper part of a heraldic FIELD (background of a shield) 2 the head of a body of people or of an organization; a leader ⟨∼ *of police*⟩ 3 *Br* – used as a familiar form of address to a man [ME, fr OF, head, chief, fr L *caput* head – more at HEAD] – **chiefdom** *n*, **chiefship** *n* – **in chief** most of all; primarily

²**chief** *adj* 1 accorded highest rank or office ⟨∼ *librarian*⟩ 2 of greatest importance, significance, or influence ⟨*the* ∼ *reasons*⟩

**chief constable** *n*, *often cap C&C* (the rank of) the principal officer of a British police force

**chief justice** *n* the presiding judge of a SUPREME COURT of justice (highest court of a nation or state); *esp* the presiding judge of the US Supreme Court

**chiefly** /'cheefli/ *adv* 1 most importantly; principally, especially 2 for the most part; mostly, mainly

**chief master sergeant** *n* – see MILITARY RANKS table

**chief of staff** *n*, *often cap C&S* the senior officer of an armed-forces staff who serves as principal adviser to a commander

**chief of state** *n*, *NAm* HEAD OF STATE

**chief petty officer** *n* – see MILITARY RANKS table

**chief superintendent** *n*, *often cap C&S* (the rank of) an officer in the British police ranking next above superintendent

**chieftain** /'cheeftən/, *fem* **chieftainess** /'cheeftənis, ,cheeftə'nes/ *n* a chief, esp of a band, tribe, or clan [ME *chieftaine*, fr MF *chevetain*, fr LL *capitaneus* chief – more at CAPTAIN] – **chieftainship** *n*

**chieftaincy** /'cheeftənsi/ *n* 1 the rank, dignity, office, or rule of a chieftain 2 a region or a people ruled by a chief

**chief technician** *n* – see MILITARY RANKS table

**chief warrant officer** *n* – see MILITARY RANKS table

**chiel** /cheel/, **chield** /cheel(d)/ *n*, *chiefly Scot* a fellow, lad [ME (Sc) *cheld*, alter. of ME *child* child]

**chiffchaff** /'chif,chaf/ *n* a small greyish European songbird (*Phylloscopus collybita*) that is a member of the warbler family and has a dull repetitive song [imit]

**chiffon** /'shifon, -'-/ *n* a sheer fabric, made esp of silk [Fr, lit., rag, fr *chiffe* old rag, alter. of MF *chipe*, fr ME *chip* chip]

**chiffonier** /,shifə'niə/ *n* a high narrow CHEST OF DRAWERS [Fr *chiffonnier*, fr *chiffon*]

**chigger** /'chigə/ *n* a chigoe [by alter.]

**chignon** /shi'nyon, 'shee-/ *n* a usu large smooth knot of hair worn at the back of the head, and usu at the nape of the neck [Fr, fr MF *chaignon* chain, collar, nape]

**chigoe** /'sheegoh/ *n* 1 a tropical flea (*Tunga penetrans*) the fertile female of which causes great discomfort by burrowing under the skin 2 HARVEST MITE (bloodsucking larva of a tiny spiderlike animal) [of Cariban origin; akin to Galibi *chico* chigoe]

**Chihuahua** /chi'wah•wə/ *n* (any of) a breed of very small round-headed large-eared dogs of Mexican origin [MexSp, fr *Chihuahua*, state & city in Mexico]

**chilblain** /'chil,blayn/ *n* an inflammatory swelling or sore, esp on the feet or hands, caused by exposure to cold [³*chill* + *blain*]

**child** /chield/ *n*, *pl* **children** /'childrən/ 1 an unborn or recently born person 2a a young person, esp between infancy and youth b a childlike or childish person c(1) a person not yet of (a legally specified) age c(2) somebody under the age of 14 – used in English law; compare YOUNG PERSON 3a a son or daughter of human parents ⟨*left the estate to her* ∼ren⟩ b a descendant ⟨*the Children of David*⟩ 4 one strongly influenced by another or by a place or state of affairs ⟨*a* ∼ *of the depression*⟩ 5 a product, result ⟨*dreams; which are the* ∼ren *of an idle brain* – Shak⟩ 6 *archaic* a youth of noble birth 7 *archaic & dial* a female infant [ME, fr OE *cild*; akin to Goth *kilthei* womb, Skt *jaṭhara* belly] – **childless** *adj*, **childlessness** *n* – **with child** *of a woman* pregnant

**childbearing** /'chield,beəring/ *n* the act or process of bringing forth children – **childbearing** *adj*

**childbed fever** /'chield,bed/ *n* PUERPERAL FEVER (serious fever occurring after childbirth)

**child benefit** *n* a usu weekly allowance paid through the post office for each child in a family

**childbirth** /-,buhth/ *n* the act of giving birth to a child

**childe** /chield/ *n*, *often cap*, *archaic* a youth or young man of noble birth ⟨Childe *Roland*⟩ [var of *child*]

**childhood** /'chield,hood/ *n* 1 the state or period of being a child 2 an early period in the development of something ⟨*there was a* ∼ *of religion as there was a* ∼ *of science* – TLS⟩

**childish** /'chieldish/ *adj* 1 of or befitting a child or childhood ⟨*a clear* ∼ *voice*⟩ ⟨*calling back* ∼ *memories*⟩ 2a marked by or suggestive of immaturity ⟨*a* ∼ *spiteful remark*⟩ b lacking complexity; simple ⟨*it's a* ∼ *device, but it works*⟩ □ compare BOYISH synonyms see CHILDLIKE – **childishly** *adv*, **childishness** *n*

**childlike** /'chield,liek/ *adj* of or resembling a child or childhood; *esp* marked by innocence, trust, and naivety – **childlikeness** *n*

*synonyms* Childlike is either neutral ⟨**childish** *ringlets*⟩ or suggestive of the unpleasant qualities, such as fretful impatience or undeveloped taste and mentality, that are appropriate to children but deplorable in adults ⟨a childish determination to excel⟩; childlike is either neutral or suggestive of the pleasant qualities of childhood such as innocence and simplicity ⟨played with childlike enthusiasm⟩. But an actual child can be only childish, not childlike ⟨the little boy's round childish face⟩.

**childly** /'chieldli/ adj, poetic childlike

**childminder** /'child,miendə/ n, chiefly Br one who looks after other people's children, esp when both parents are at work – **childminding** n

**childproof** /'child,proohf/ adj not liable to damage or misuse by children; specif designed to be impossible for children to open ⟨a ~ lock⟩

**Children of Israel** n pl the Jewish people

**child's play** n an extremely simple task or act

**Chile nitre** n CHILE SALTPETRE [Chile, country in S America]

**Chile pine** /'chili/ n the MONKEY-PUZZLE tree

**Chile saltpetre** /,sawlt'peetə/ n impure SODIUM NITRATE, esp when occurring naturally

**chiliad** /'kili,ad/ n 1 a group or series of 1000 2 a period of 1000 years; a millennium [LL chiliad-, chilias, fr Gk, fr chilioi thousand – more at MILE]

**chiliasm** /'kili,az(ə)m/ n, Christianity belief in the MILLENNIUM (future thousand year period during which Christ will reign on earth) [NL chiliasmus, fr LL chiliastes one who believes in chiliasm, fr chilias] – **chiliast** n, **chiliastic** adj

**¹chill** /chil/ vi 1 to become cold 2 to catch a chill 3 of a metal to become hardened on the surface by sudden cooling ~ vt 1a to make cold or chilly b to make (esp food or drink) cool, esp without freezing 2 to affect as if with cold; dispirit 3 to harden the surface of (a metal) by sudden cooling [ME chillen, fr chile cold, frost, fr OE cele; akin to OE ceald cold] – **chillingly** adv

**²chill** adj CHILLY 1, 3 – **chillness** n

**³chill** n 1a a (disagreeable) sensation of coldness b COMMON COLD ⟨caught a ~⟩ 2 a moderate but disagreeable degree of cold 3 coldness of manner ⟨felt the ~ of his opponent's stare⟩

**chilli, chili** /'chili/ n, pl **chillies, chilies** the red or green pod of a HOT PEPPER (type of capsicum) used either whole or ground as a pungent condiment – compare CAYENNE PEPPER [Sp chile, fr Nahuatl chilli]

**chilli con carne** /,chili kon 'kahni/ n a spiced Mexican stew of minced beef and beans strongly seasoned with chillies or chilli powder [Sp chile con carne chilli with meat]

**chillum** /'chiləm/ n the part of a WATER PIPE that contains the substance (eg tobacco or cannabis) which is smoked; also the quantity of tobacco, cannabis, etc in a chillum [Hindi cilam, fr Per chilam]

**chilly** /'chili/ adj 1 noticeably cold; chilling 2 sensitive to cold 3 lacking warmth of feeling; distant, unfriendly 4 tending to arouse fear or apprehension ⟨~ details⟩ – **chillily** adv, **chilliness** n

**chilopod** /'kielə,pod/ n a centipede [deriv of Gk cheilos lip + pod-, pous foot]

**Chiltern Hundreds** /'chiltən/ n pl a nominal office for which an MP applies in order to resign his/her seat [Chiltern Hundreds, district of Buckinghamshire in England, whose stewardship is a nominal office]

**chimaera** /ki'miərə, kie-/ n 1 any of a family (Chimaeridae) of marine fishes that have a skeleton made of cartilage and a tapering or threadlike tail 2 a chimera [(1) NL, genus name, fr L, chimera]

**¹chime** /chiem/ n 1 an apparatus for chiming a bell or set of bells 2a a musically tuned set of bells b a set of objects (eg hanging metal bars or tubes) that sound like bells when struck 3a chimes pl, chime the sound of a set of bells b a musical sound suggesting that of bells [ME, cymbal, fr OF chimbe, fr L cymbalum]

**²chime** vi 1a to make a musical, esp a harmonious, sound b to make the sounds of a chime 2 to be or act in accord ⟨the music and the mood ~d well together⟩ ~ vt 1 to cause to chime 2 to signal or indicate by chiming ⟨the clock ~d midnight⟩ – **chimer** n

**chime in** vi 1 to break into a conversation or discussion, esp in order to express an opinion 2 to combine harmoniously – often + with ⟨the artist's illustrations chime in perfectly with the text – Book Production⟩

**³chime** /chiem/, **chimb** /chim/ n the rim of a barrel formed esp by the projecting ends of the staves [ME chimbe, fr OE cimb-; akin to OE camb comb]

**chimera** /ki'miərə, kie-/ n 1a cap a fire-breathing female monster in Greek mythology, with a lion's head, a goat's body, and a serpent's tail b an imaginary monster made up of incongruous parts 2a an illusion or fabrication of the mind; esp an unrealizable dream b a terror that exists only in the mind; a bugbear 3 an individual, organ, or part consisting of tissues of different genetic makeup and occurring esp in plants and most frequently at a place where a plant of one type has been grafted onto a plant of a different type [L chimaera, fr Gk chimaira she-goat, chimera; akin to Gk cheimōn winter – more at HIBERNATE] – **chimeric, chimerical** adj, **chimerically** adv

**chimere** /ki'miə, kie-/ n a loose sleeveless robe (eg of black satin) worn by Anglican bishops [ME chimmer, chemeyr]

**chimerism** /ki'miə,riz(ə)m, kie-, 'kiemə,riz(ə)m/ n the state of being a genetic chimera

**chimney** /'chimni/ n 1a a vertical structure incorporated into a building and enclosing a flue or flues for carrying off smoke; esp the part of such a structure extending above a roof b CHIMNEY STACK 2 a structure through which smoke and gases (eg from a furnace or steam engine) are discharged 3 a tube, usu of glass placed round a flame (eg of an oil lamp) to serve as a shield and promote burning 4 something (eg a narrow cleft in rock) resembling a chimney 5 dial a fireplace, hearth [ME, fr MF cheminée, fr LL caminata, fr L caminus furnace, fireplace, fr Gk kaminos; akin to Gk kamara vault – more at CHAMBER]

**chimney breast** n a wall that encloses a chimney and projects into a room

**chimney corner** n a seat by or within a large open fireplace

**chimneypiece** /-,pees/ n a mantelpiece

**chimney pot** n a usu earthenware pipe at the top of a chimney

**chimney stack** n 1 a stone, brick, etc chimney rising above a roof and usu containing several flues 2 a tall, typically cylindrical, chimney serving a large or industrial building (eg a factory or power station)

**chimney sweep** n one whose occupation is cleaning soot from chimney flues

**chimo** /'chiemoh, 'cheemoh/ interj, Can – used as a greeting [Eskimo]

**chimp** /chimp/ n, chiefly informal a chimpanzee

**chimpanzee** /,chimpan'zee/ n an ANTHROPOID APE (Pan troglodytes) of equatorial Africa that is smaller and less fierce than the gorilla [Kongo dial. chimpenzi]

**¹chin** /chin/ n the lower portion of the face lying below the lower lip and including the prominence of the lower jaw [ME, fr OE cinn; akin to OHG kinni chin, L gena cheek, Gk genys jaw, cheek]

**²chin** vt **-nn-** 1 to bring to or hold with the chin ⟨~ned his violin⟩ 2 to raise one's chin to the level of (eg a bar) by pulling oneself up with the arms

**¹china** /'chienə/ n 1 porcelain; also porcelain ware (eg dishes, vases, or ornaments) with a smooth glassy finish, for domestic use 2 chinaware; broadly crockery ⟨set the table with the good ~⟩ 3 chiefly Br BONE CHINA [Per chīnī Chinese porcelain, fr China, country in Asia]

**²china** n, Cockney a close friend; a mate [rhyming slang china (plate) mate]

**chinaberry** /'chienəb(ə)ri/ n a small Asian tree (Melia azedarach) of the mahogany family that is often cultivated for shade or ornament

**china clay** n KAOLIN (fine white clay)

**Chinagraph** /'chienə,grahf, -,graf/ trademark – used for a pencil that will write on china or glass

**chinaman** /'chienəmən/ n 1 a slow ball bowled in cricket by a left-handed bowler that, when viewed by a right-handed batsman, deviates to the LEG SIDE after bouncing 2 cap, derog a native of China [(1)prob fr bowling of this type by Ellis Achong b 1904 Chinese-born West Indian cricketer]

**China rose** n any of numerous garden roses derived from a shrubby Chinese rose (Rosa chinensis)

**Chinatown** /-,town/ n the Chinese quarter of a city

**chinaware** /-,weə/ n tableware made of china

**chinchilla** /,chin'chilə/ n 1 (the soft pearly-grey fur of) a small rodent (Chinchilla laniger) that is the size of a large squirrel, is native to the mountains of Peru and Chile, and is extensively bred in captivity for its fur 2 (any of) a breed of domestic rabbit with long-haired white or greyish fur often tipped with a darker colour; also (any of) a breed of cat with similar fur 3 a heavy twilled woollen cloth used for making coats [Sp]

**chin-chin** /,chin 'chin/ interj, Br – used as an informal greeting, farewell, or toast [Chin (Pek) *qǐng, qǐngqǐng* (*ch'ing³, ch'ing³-ch'ing³*), an expression of courtesy]

**Chindit** /'chindit/ *n* a member of an Allied force fighting behind Japanese lines in Burma during World War II [Burmese *chinthé* fabulous lionlike animal]

¹**chine** /chien/ *n, Br* a steep-sided ravine – used chiefly with reference to such formations in Dorset or the Isle of Wight [ME *chin, chine* crack, chasm, – more at CHINK]

²**chine** *n* **1** (a cut of meat including the whole or part of) the backbone **2** a ridge, crest (e g of a mountain) **3** the intersection of the bottom and the sides of a boat [ME, fr MF *eschine*, of Gmc origin; akin to OHG *scina* shinbone, needle – more at SHIN]

³**chine** *vt* to separate the backbone from the ribs of (a joint of meat); *also* to cut through the backbone of (a carcass)

**Chinese** /,chie'neez/ *n, pl* **Chinese 1** a native or inhabitant of China **2** a group of related Sino-Tibetan TONE LANGUAGES (languages in which meaning is affected by tone) used by the people of China that are often mutually unintelligible in their spoken form but share a single system of writing; *specif* MANDARIN [*China*, country in Asia] – **Chinese** *adj*

**Chinese boxes** *n pl* a set of boxes graduated in size so that each fits into the next larger one

**Chinese burn** *n, Br* an act of seizing a person's wrist in both hands and twisting the flesh in opposite directions to cause severe pain

**Chinese cabbage** *n* either of two Asian varieties of cabbage (*Brassica pekinensis* and *Brassica chinensis*) widely used in oriental cookery

**Chinese chequers** *n* a game in which each player tries to be the first to transfer a set of pegs or marbles from a home point to the opposite point of a board in the form of a pitted 6-pointed star, by single moves or jumps

**Chinese copy** *n* an exact imitation or duplicate that includes defects as well as desired qualities

**Chinese cut** *n* an attacking shot in cricket played with the intention of hitting the ball on the OFF SIDE but inadvertently sending it behind the wicket on the LEG SIDE off the inside edge of the bat – called also HARROW DRIVE

**Chinese gooseberry** *n* KIWI 3

**Chinese lantern** *n* **1** a collapsible lantern of thin coloured paper **2** a widely cultivated plant (genus *Physalis*, esp *Physalis alkekengi*) related to the nightshade and petunia, that has thin-walled bulbous CALYXES which are a brilliant orange-red when mature

**Chinese leaves** *n pl* the long crisp edible pale-green leaves of a Chinese cabbage (*Brassica pekinensis*)

**Chinese puzzle** *n* **1** an intricate or ingenious puzzle **2** something intricate and obscure

**Chinese wall** *n* an apparently insurmountable barrier; *esp* a serious obstacle to understanding [*Chinese Wall*, a defensive wall built in the 3rd c BC between China and Mongolia]

**Chinese water deer** *n* a small Chinese and Korean deer (*Hydropotes inermis*) with no antlers that has become established in parts of Britain and France

**Chinese white** *n* a white zinc oxide pigment formerly used to make paints

¹**chink** /chingk/ *n* **1** a small cleft, slit, or fissure ⟨*a* ~ *in the curtain*⟩ **2** a means of evasion or escape; a loophole ⟨*a* ~ *in the law*⟩ [prob alter. of ME *chin* crack, fissure, fr OE *cine;* akin to OE *cīnan* to gape, crack OHG *chīnan* to split open]

²**chink** *n* **1** a short sharp sound (e g of coins striking together) **2** *archaic* coin, money [imit]

³**chink** *vb* to (cause to) make a sharp light metallic or ringing sound

**Chink, Chinkie, Chinky** *n, derog* a native of China [alter. of *Chinese*]

**Chinkie, Chinky** /'chingki/ *n, Br informal* (a shop where one can buy) a Chinese takeaway meal

**chinless** /'chinlis/ *adj* **1** lacking a chin **2** *Br informal* lacking courage or firmness of purpose; ineffectual

**chinless wonder** *n, Br informal* a person, esp a male of the upper-classes, who is weak and foolish

**Chino-** /chienoh-/ *comb form* Chinese and ⟨Chino-*Japanese*⟩ – compare SINO-

**chinoiserie** /shee'nwahzəri, ,---'-/ *n* (an object of decoration in) a style in art and interior design that copies Chinese features or motifs [Fr, fr *chinois* Chinese, fr *Chine* China]

**Chinook** /shə'nook; *also* chi'noohk, -'nook/ *n, pl* **Chinooks**, *esp collectively* **Chinook 1** a member or the language of an American Indian people of Oregon **2** *not cap* **2a** a warm moist southwesterly wind of the NW coast of the USA **b** a warm dry westerly wind of the E slopes of the Rocky mountains [Chehalis *Tsinúk*]

**Chinook Jargon** *n* a mixture of American Indian languages, French, and English, formerly used as a LINGUA FRANCA (language used between peoples whose native languages are different) in the NW USA and in W Canada and Alaska

**chinstrap** /'chin,strap/ *n* a strap that passes under the chin to hold a hat (e g a helmet) on the head

**chintz** /chints/ *n* **1** a printed calico from India **2** a usu glazed printed plain-weave fabric, esp of cotton, used for making curtains, furniture covers, etc [earlier *chints*, pl of *chint*, fr Hindi *chī̃t*]

**chintzy** /'chintsi/ *adj* **1a** decorated (as if) with chintz; *also* cosy, homely **b** typical of the kind of decor traditionally associated with country cottages **2** cheap, tawdry ⟨*compared to an old silver dollar, the* ~ *little coin is a more likely symbol of the decline of the American economy – Time*⟩ **3** mean, stingy ⟨*nor would the assistance be* ~. *The ... administration had decided to back a federal loan guarantee of $1.5 billion – Time*⟩

'**chin-,up** *n* PULL-UP (exercise in gymnastics)

'**chin-,wag** *n, informal* a conversation, chat

¹**chip** /chip/ *n* **1a** a small usu thin and flat piece (e g of wood or stone) cut, knocked, or flaked off **b** a flaw left when a small piece is broken off or knocked out of an object **2** a small piece of food, esp chocolate ⟨*chocolate* ~ *cookies*⟩ **3** any of the counters used as a token for money in poker and other games **4** INTEGRATED CIRCUIT; *also* the small piece of SEMICONDUCTOR material, typically silicon or sometimes sapphire, on which an integrated circuit is constructed **5** a thin strip of wood used for weaving baskets **6a** chip shot, chip a short stroke in golf that lofts the ball onto the green **b** a shot or kick in football, rugby, etc in which the ball is lofted into the air, esp over an obstacle, and travels only a short distance **7a** *chiefly Br* a strip of potato fried in deep fat **b** *NAm & Austr* CRISP 2 (potato crisp) [ME; prob akin to OE -*cippian* to cut] – **chip off the old block** a person who resembles one of his/her parents in character or appearance – **chip on one's shoulder** a belligerent or embittered attitude, usu resulting from a real or imagined grudge [fr a chip of wood placed on one's shoulder to challenge another person to knock it off and fight] – **have had one's chips** *informal* to have no hope of improvement or success; be defeated [*chip* 3] – **when the chips are down** when the crucial or critical point has been reached ⟨*when the chips are down you have only yourself to depend on*⟩ [*chip* 3]

²**chip** *vb* -**pp-** *vt* **1a** to cut or hew with an edged tool **b(1)** to cut or break (a small piece) from something ⟨~ *ped a piece out of the vase*⟩ **b(2)** to cut or break a fragment from ⟨~*ped one of the best plates*⟩ **2** to kick or hit (a ball, pass, etc) in a short high arc ~ *vi* **1** to break off in small pieces **2** to play a chip shot

**chip in** *vb, informal vi* **1** to contribute ⟨*everyone chipped in for the gift*⟩ **2** to add a comment to a conversation between other people ~ *vt* to contribute, give ⟨*chipped in £1 for the gift*⟩

**chip basket** *n* **1** a basket made of thin flat strips of wood woven together **2** a wire basket in which food (e g chips) is placed for deep frying

**chipboard** /'chip,bawd/ *n* an artificial board made from a mixture of wood chips and glue

**chipmunk** /'chip,mungk/ *n* any of numerous small striped American squirrels (genera *Tamias* and *Eutamias*); *esp* one (*Tamias striatus*) that lives in deciduous forests of N America [alter. of earlier *chitmunk*, of Algonquian origin; akin to Ojibwa *atchitamo* squirrel]

**chipolata** /,chipə'lahtə/ *n* a small thin sausage [Fr, fr It *cipollata*, fr fem of *cipollato* with onions, fr *cipolla* onion, fr LL *cepula*, dim. of L *cepa* onion]

**Chippendale** /'chipən,dayl/ *adj or n* (of or being) an 18th-century English furniture style characterized by graceful outline and often ornate ornamentation [Thomas *Chippendale* †1779 E cabinetmaker & designer]

**chipper** /'chipə/ *adj, NAm* sprightly, cheerful [prob alter. of E dial. *kipper* lively]

**Chippewa** /'chipi,wah/, **Chippeway** /-,way/ *n, pl* **Chippewas**, **Chippeways** *esp collectively* **Chippewa, Chippeway** OJIBWA (N American Indian people)

**chipping** /'chiping/ *n, usu pl* a fragment of stone used in surfacing roads

**chippy, chippie** /'chipi/ *n* **1** *informal* a carpenter **2** *slang* a promiscuous young woman **3** *Br informal* a shop selling ready-cooked fish and chips

**chip shot** *n* CHIP 6a (shot in golf)

**chir-** /-kir-/, **chiro-** *comb form* hand ⟨chiro*practic*⟩ [L, fr Gk *cheir-*, *cheiro-*, fr *cheir;* akin to Hitt *kesar* hand]

**chiral** /'kierəl/ *adj, esp of a crystal or molecule* not able to be superimposed on its mirror image [*chir-* + *-al;* lit., handed, ie asymmetric] – **chirality** *n*

**Chi-Rho** /ˌkie 'roh/ *n, pl* **Chi-Rhos** a Christian symbol formed from the first two letters X and P of the Greek word for *Christ* [*chi* + *rho*]

**chirography** /kie'rogrəfi/ *n* handwriting, penmanship – **chirographer** *n*, **chirographic, chirographical** *adj*

**chiromancy** /'kirəˌmansi/ *n* fortune-telling by the interpretation of the lines, bumps, etc on a person's hand; palmistry [deriv of ML *chiromantia*, fr Gk *cheir-* chir- + *-manteia* -mancy – more at -MANCY] – **chiromancer** *n*

**chironomid** /ki'ronəmid/ *n* any of a family (Chironomidae) of nonbiting midges [deriv of Gk *cheironomos* one who gestures with his hands]

**chiropody** /ki'ropədi, shi-/ *n* the care and treatment of the human foot in health and disease [*chir-* + *pod-;* fr its original concern with both hands and feet] – **chiropodist** *n*

**chiropractic** /'kirəˌpraktik/ *n* a system of healing based on the belief that disease results from a lack of normal nerve function and employing manipulation and adjustment of body structures (e g the spinal column) [*chir-* + Gk *praktikos* practical, operative – more at PRACTICAL] – **chiropractor** *n*

**chiropter** /ki'roptə/ *n* ³BAT △ chiropodist [deriv of Gk *cheir* hand + *pteron* wing – more at FEATHER] – **chiropteran** *adj or n*

**chirp** /chuhp/ *vb or n* (to make or speak in a tone resembling) the characteristic short shrill sound of a small bird or insect [imit]

**chirpy** /'chuhpi/ *adj, informal* lively or cheerful without affectation – **chirpily** *adv*, **chirpiness** *n*

**chirr** /chuh/ *vi or n* (to make) the trilled sound characteristic of certain insects (e g a grasshopper) [imit]

**chirrup** /'chirəp/ *vb or n* (to) chirp [imit]

**chirurgeon** /ki'ruhj(ə)n/ *n, archaic* a surgeon [ME *cirurgian*, fr OF *cirurgien*, fr *cirurgie* surgery]

**¹chisel** /'chizl/ *n* a metal tool with a cutting edge at the end of a blade used in dressing, shaping, or working wood, stone, metal, etc [ME, fr ONF, prob alter. of *chisoir* goldsmith's chisel, fr (assumed) VL *caesorium* cutting instrument, fr L *caesus*, pp of *caedere* to cut – more at CONCISE]

**²chisel** *vb* **-ll-** (*NAm* **-l-, -ll-**) *vt* **1** to cut or work (as if) with a chisel **2** *slang* **2a** to trick, cheat ⟨~led *me out of £5*⟩ **b** to obtain by cheating ~ *vi* to work with a chisel – **chiseller** *n*

**chiselled**, *NAm chiefly* **chiseled** /'chizəld/ *adj* **1** cut or wrought with a chisel **2** sharply defined, clear-cut

**chisel plough** *n* a plough fitted with spikes in place of a blade, used for breaking up compacted soil

'**chi-ˌsquare** /kie/ *n* a statistical value that is a sum of terms each of which is a quotient obtained by dividing the square of the difference between the observed and EXPECTED VALUES of a quantity by the expected value – **chi-squared** *adj*

**chi-square distribution, chi-squared distribution** *also* **chi-squared** *n* a FREQUENCY DISTRIBUTION that uses the properties of chi-square to test for statistical significance. The chi-square distribution can be used to determine how frequently a statistical distribution might arise by chance in an experiment.

**chi-square test, chi-squared test** *also* **chi-squared** *n* a statistical test based on the chi-square statistic that is widely used to test how well theoretical statistical frequencies match those of actual observed values

**¹chit** /chit/ *n* a spirited and often disrespectful woman or girl, typically of slight build [ME *chitte* kitten, cub]

**²chit** *n* a shoot, sprout [prob alter. of ME *chithe* sprout, fr OE *cīth*]

**³chit** *vb* **-tt-** *dial Br vi* to sprout ~ *vt* to remove shoots from (e g potatoes)

**⁴chit** *also* **chitty** *n* a small slip of paper with writing on it: e g a a signed note showing a sum of money owed **b** an order for goods [Hindi *ciṭṭhī*]

**chital** /'cheetl/ *n* AXIS DEER [Hindi *cītal*, fr Skt *citrala* variegated, fr *citra* spotted, bright]

**chitarrone** /ˌkeetə'rohni/ *n* a stringed musical instrument of the lute family, played by plucking with the fingers, and

corresponding in size to a modern DOUBLE BASS [It, aug of *chitarra* guitar, fr Gk *kithara* lyre]

**chitchat** /'chitˌchat/ *vi or n, informal* (to make) small talk; gossip [redupl of *chat*]

**chitin** /'kietin/ *n* a horny substance consisting of a complex carbohydrate (POLYSACCHARIDE) that forms part of the hard outer covering esp of insects and CRUSTACEANS (e g crabs and shrimps) [Fr *chitine*, fr Gk *chitōn* chiton, tunic] – **chitinous** *adj*

**chiton** /'kieton, -tn/ *n* **1** any of an order (Polyplacophora of the phylum Mollusca) of marine INVERTEBRATE animals related to the snails and limpets that have an elongated body and a shell consisting of usu eight overlapping plates covering the upper surface **2** a loose woollen tunic worn usu knee-length by men and full-length by women in ancient Greece [(1) NL, genus name, fr Gk *chitōn* tunic, of Sem origin; akin to Heb *kuttōneth* tunic; (2) Gk *chitōn*]

**chitterling** /'chitəˌling/ *n, usu pl* a section of the smaller intestines of pigs, esp when prepared as food [ME *chitirling*]

**chivalrous** /'shiv(ə)lrəs/ *adj* **1** having the characteristics (e g valour or knightly skill) of a knight **2** (characteristic) of chivalry and knight-errantry **3a** honourable, generous **b** graciously courteous and considerate, esp to women – **chivalrously** *adv*, **chivalrousness** *n*

**chivalry** /'shiv(ə)lri/ *n* **1** the system, spirit, or customs of medieval knighthood **2** the qualities (e g courage, integrity, and consideration for the weak or vanquished) of an ideal knight; chivalrous conduct **3** *archaic* knightly skill **4** *archaic, taking sing or pl vb* **4a** a body of heavily armed mounted soldiers **b** a body of knights or distinguished gentlemen [ME *chivalrie*, fr OF *chevalerie*, fr *chevalier*] – **chivalric** *adj*

**chive** /chiev/ *n*, **chives**, *n*, *pl* a plant (*Allium schoenoprasum*) related to the onion, leek, and garlic and used esp as a herb to flavour and garnish food [ME, fr ONF, fr L *cepa* onion]

**chivvy, chivy** /'chivi/ *vt, informal* **1** to tease or annoy with persistent petty attacks; harass **2** to rouse to activity – often + *up* or *along* [*chivy*, n (chase, hunt), prob fr E dial. *Chevy Chase* chase, confusion, fr the title of a ballad describing a battle in the Cheviot hills in 1388]

**chizz** /chiz/ *n or vt, slang* (to) swindle [by shortening & alter. fr *chisel*]

**chlamydomonas** /ˌklamidə'mohnəs/ *n* any of a genus (*Chlamydomonas*) of single-celled GREEN ALGAE that have two FLAGELLA (whiplike parts that are thrashed to produce movement) and are common in fresh water and damp soil [NL, genus name, fr L *chlamyd-, chlamys* + NL *monas* monad]

**chlamydospore** /kla'midəˌspaw/ *n* a thick-walled spore of some fungi, bacteria, and single-celled organisms that remains dormant or inactive for some time before developing into a new individual [L *chlamyd-, chlamys* + ISV *spore*] – **chlamydosporic** *adj*

**chlamys** /'klamis/ *n, pl* **chlamyses, chlamydes** a short cloak worn by men in ancient Greece and usu fastened on the right shoulder [L *chlamyd-, chlamys*, fr Gk]

**chlor-, chloro-** *comb form* **1** green ⟨chloro*phyll*⟩ ⟨chloro*sis*⟩ **2** chlorine; containing chlorine ⟨chlor*ic*⟩ ⟨chloro*promazine*⟩ [NL, fr Gk, fr *chlōros* greenish yellow – more at YELLOW]

**chloral** /'klawrəl/ *n* **1** a pungent liquid organic chemical compound, $CCl_3CHO$, used in making DDT and CHLORAL HYDRATE **2** **chloral, chloral hydrate** a synthetic drug, $Cl_3C(OH)CHOH$, used as a hypnotic [Fr, fr *chlor-* + *al*cool alcohol]

**chloralose** /'klawrəˌlohs, -ˌlohz/ *n* a hypnotic drug, $C_8H_{11}Cl_3O_6$, that is used chiefly as an anaesthetic for animals used in experiments [ISV]

**chlorambucil** /klaw'rambyoosil/ *n* a drug, $C_{14}H_{19}Cl_2NO_2$, that is a derivative of NITROGEN MUSTARD and is used esp to treat some types of cancer (e g leukaemia and HODGKIN'S DISEASE) [*chlor-* + *amin-* + *butyric* + *-cil* (of unknown origin)]

**chloramine** /'klawrəˌmeen/ *n* any of various chemical compounds that contain a nitrogen atom attached to a chlorine atom in the molecular structure and are used chiefly as antiseptics [ISV]

**chloramphenicol** /ˌklawram'fenikol/ *n* an antibiotic that was isolated originally from cultures of a soil bacterium (*Streptomyces venezuelae*) but is now mainly prepared synthetically and is used esp to treat typhoid fever [*chlor-* + *amid-* + *phen-* + *nitr-* + *glycol*]

**chlorate** /'klawrayt/ *n* a chemical compound (SALT) formed by combination between chloric acid and a metal atom or other chemical group and containing the group $ClO_3$ ⟨*potassium* ~⟩

**chlordan** /'klawdan/ *n* chlordane

**chlordane** /'klaw,dayn/ *n* a very poisonous liquid insecticide, $C_{10}H_6Cl_8$, that contains a large amount of chlorine [*chlor-* + in*dane*, in*dan* ($C_9H_{10}$)]

**chlordiazepoxide** /,klawdie,azi'poksied/ *n* a drug, $C_{16}H_{14}ClN_3O$, that has a molecular structure and actions similar to those of DIAZEPAM and is used as a tranquillizer and to treat the withdrawal symptoms of alcoholism – compare LIBRIUM [*chlor-* + *di-* + *az-* + *epoxide*]

**chlorella** /klə'relə/ *n* any of a genus (*Chlorella*) of single-celled GREEN ALGAE that do not have FLAGELLA (whiplike parts that are thrashed to produce movement) [NL, genus name, fr Gk *chlōros*]

**chlorenchyma** /klə'rengkimə/ *n* plant tissue that contains chlorophyll [NL]

**chloric** /'klawrik/ *adj* relating to, obtained from, or containing chlorine, esp with a VALENCY of five ⟨~ *acid*⟩

**chloride** /'klawried/ *n* a compound of chlorine with another chemical element or group; *esp* any of various compounds (SALTS or ESTERS) formed by combination between HYDROCHLORIC ACID and a metal atom, an alcohol, or another chemical group [Ger *chlorid*, fr *chlor-* + *-id* -ide]

**chlorinate** /'klawri,nayt/ *vt* to treat or cause to combine with chlorine or a chemical compound containing chlorine, esp for the purposes of disinfection – **chlorinator** *n*, **chlorination** *n*

**chlorine** /'klawreen/ *n* a chemical element that is isolated as a heavy poisonous greenish-yellow gas of pungent smell, has a VALENCY esp of one, and is used as a powerful bleaching agent and as a disinfectant in water purification

**chlorinity** /klaw'rinəti/ *n* a measure of the amount of chlorine, bromine, iodine, and fluorine present in seawater [*chlorine* + *-ity*]

¹**chlorite** /'klawriet/ *n* any of a group of usu green minerals associated with and resembling MICA (mineral that splits into thin sheets) [Ger *chlorit*, fr L *chloritis*, a green stone, fr Gk *chlōritis*, fr *chlōros*] – **chloritic** *adj*

²**chlorite** *n* a chemical compound (SALT) formed by combination between chlorous acid and a metal atom or other chemical group and containing the group $ClO_2$ ⟨*sodium* ~⟩ [prob fr Fr, fr *chlor-* + *-ite*]

**chloro-** – see CHLOR-

¹**chloroform** /'klorə,fawm/ *n* a colourless liquid, $CHCl_3$, that has a smell like that of ether, was used formerly as a general anaesthetic, and is now used esp as a solvent for other organic chemicals [Fr *chloroforme*, fr *chlor-* + *formyle* formyl; fr its having been regarded as a trichloride of this radical]

²**chloroform** *vt* to treat with chloroform, esp so as to produce unconsciousness or death

**chlorohydrin** /,klawroh'hiedrin/ *n* any of various organic chemical compounds containing one or more HYDROXYL groups together with one or more chlorine atoms in the molecular structure [ISV, fr *chlor-* + *hydr-*]

**Chloromycetin** /,klawrohmie'seetin/ *trademark* – used for CHLORAMPHENICOL (antibiotic)

**chlorophyll** /'klorəfil, 'klaw-/ *n* 1 any or a mixture of several closely related chemical substances that make up the green colouring matter in plants that absorbs the light energy used in PHOTOSYNTHESIS (process of making sugars and similar chemical compounds from carbon dioxide); *esp* the form of chlorophyll, $C_{55}H_{72}MgN_4O_5$, that occurs in nearly all plants and other living organisms that carry out photosynthesis 2 a waxy green chlorophyll-containing substance extracted from green plants and used as a colouring agent or deodorant [Fr *chlorophylle*, fr *chlor-* + Gk *phyllon* leaf – more at BLADE] – **chlorophyllose** *adj*, **chlorophyllous** *adj*

**chloropicrin** /,klawroh'pikrin/ *n* a heavy colourless liquid, $CCl_3NO_2$, that causes tears and vomiting and is used esp as an insecticide [Ger *chlorpikrin*, fr *chlor-* + Gk *pikros* bitter]

**chloroplast** /'klawroh,plast/ *n* a minute specialized body (PLASTID) that occurs inside the cells of green plants, contains chlorophyll, and is the site of photosynthesis [ISV]

**chloroprene** /,klawroh,preen/ *n* a colourless liquid chemical compound, $C_4H_5Cl$, used esp in making NEOPRENE rubber [*chlor-* + iso*prene*]

**chloroquine** /'klawroh,kween/ *n* a drug, $C_{18}H_{26}ClN_3$, that is used to treat malaria [*chlor-* + *quinoline*]

**chlorosis** /klaw'rohsis/ *n* 1 an anaemia, formerly common in girls and young women, caused by a lack of iron in the diet and characterized by a greenish colour of the skin 2 a diseased

condition of green plants in which chlorophyll fails to be produced and normally green parts become yellow or white [NL] – **chlorotic** *adj*, **chlorotically** *adv*

**chlorothiazide** /,klawroh'thie-əzied/ *n* a diuretic drug, $C_7H_6ClN_3O_4S_2$, used esp in the treatment of high blood pressure and OEDEMA (retention of excess water in the tissues)

**chlorous** /'klawrəs/ *adj* relating to, obtained from, or containing chlorine, esp with a VALENCY of three ⟨~ *acid*⟩

**chlorpromazine** /,klaw'prohmə,zeen/ *n* a drug, $C_{17}H_{19}ClN_2S$, that is used widely as a tranquillizer, esp to suppress disturbed behaviour (e g in the treatment of schizophrenia) – compare LARGACTIL [*chlor-* + *propyl* + *methyl* + phenothi*azine*]

**chlorpropamide** /,klaw'prohpəmied/ *n* a drug, $ClC_6H_4SO_2NHCONH(CH_2)_2CH_3$, that is given by mouth to lower the amount of sugar in the blood in the treatment of mild DIABETES MELLITUS [*chlor-* + *propane* + *amide*]

**chlortetracycline** /,klaw,tetrə'siekleen/ *n* an antibiotic, $C_{22}H_{23}ClN_2O_8$, produced by a bacterium (*Streptomyces aureofaciens*) and used in the treatment of various bacterial and viral infections [*chlor-* + *tetracycline*]

**choanocyte** /'koh-ənə,siet/ *n* COLLAR CELL (cell lining the inside of a living sponge) [ISV *choan-* (funnel-shaped; fr Gk *choanē* funnel) + *-cyte*]

**choc** /chok/ *n, informal* CHOCOLATE 3

**choc-ice** /'chok ,ies/ *n, Br* a bar of ice cream covered in chocolate

¹**chock** /chok/ *n* 1 a wedge or block for steadying a rounded object (e g a cask) and holding it motionless, for filling in an unwanted space, or for blocking the movement of a wheel 2 *chiefly NAm* a large metal ring (e g on the bow or stern of a ship) having an opening at the top through which a rope may be passed for mooring or towing [origin unknown]

²**chock** *vt* 1 to fit, stop, or make fast (as if) with chocks 2 to raise or support on chocks

³**chock** *adv* as close or as completely as possible [¹*chock*]

**chock-a-block** /,chok ə 'blok/ *adj or adv* 1 jammed close together ⟨*families living* ~⟩ 2 very full; crowded [¹*chock* + ¹*a-* on + *block*; orig referring to the position of a tackle when both blocks are together]

,**chock-'full** *adj* full to the limit; crammed [ME *chokkefull*, prob fr *choken* to choke + *full*]

**chocolate** /'choklət/ *n* 1 a food in the form of a paste, powder, or solid block prepared from ground roasted cacao seeds and often sweetened or flavoured 2 a drink made by mixing chocolate with usu hot water or milk 3 a sweet made with chocolate or with a chocolate coating 4 a dark brown colour [Sp, fr Nahuatl *xocoatl*] – **chocolate** *adj*

'**chocolate-,box** *adj* superficially pretty or sentimental ⟨*the picture on the wall was of a* ~ *farmhouse*⟩ [fr the pictures on some boxes of chocolates]

**Choctaw** /'choktaw/ *n, pl* **Choctaws**, *esp collectively* **Choctaw** 1 a member or the language of American Indian peoples of Mississippi, Alabama, and Louisiana 2 *not cap* a half turn in ice-skating from either edge of one foot to the opposite edge of the other foot – compare MOHAWK [Choctaw *Chahta*]

¹**choice** /choys/ *n* 1 the act of choosing; selection ⟨*what factors influenced you when you made your* ~?⟩ 2 the power of choosing; an option ⟨*you have no* ~ *but to obey orders*⟩ 3a a person or thing chosen ⟨*she is a good* ~ *as team leader*⟩ b the best part; the elite 4 a sufficient number and variety from which to choose ⟨*a wide* ~ *of dishes on the menu*⟩ [ME *chois*, fr OF, fr *choisir* to choose, of Gmc origin; akin to OHG *kiosan* to choose – more at CHOOSE]

*synonyms* Choice conveys the freedom to choose from a number of things or possible actions, while **option** stresses the power to choose, often an exclusive right, from two or more mutually exclusive possibilities ⟨*only sixth-formers have the* **option** *of wearing their own clothes*⟩. An **alternative** emphasizes that what is not chosen is necessarily rejected, and is often limited to two possible choices ⟨*the* **alternative** *to wearing your own clothes is school uniform*⟩. A **preference** is a choice influenced by one's likes or dislikes, or prejudices ⟨*I have no* **preference** *either way: take which one you like best*⟩. **Selection** suggests a wide range from which to choose, requiring the exercise of judgment and discrimination. The verbs **choose, select, prefer,** and **opt** have similar connotations to their related nouns. To **elect** is to choose formally for some given role, while **pick** means "choose the best". **Cull** adds the idea of collecting to **choosing**, and may mean to collect all the good things or all the rejects.

²**choice** *adj* **1** worthy of being chosen; *esp* of high quality **2** selected with care; well chosen ⟨*summed up the situation in a few ~ phrases*⟩ **antonyms** inferior, poor, ordinary – **choicely** *adv*, **choiceness** *n*

**choir** /kwie⋅ə/ *n* **1** *taking sing or pl vb* an organized group of singers; *esp* one reading or performing in the musical parts of church services **2** *taking sing or pl vb* a group of instruments of the same class playing together ⟨*a brass ~*⟩ **3** any of the nine divisions of angels in medieval theology **4** the part of a church occupied by the singers or by the choristers; *specif* the part of a church between the sanctuary, where the altar stands, and the NAVE (the main body of the church) **5** CHOIR ORGAN [ME *quer*, fr OF *cuer*, fr ML *chorus*, fr L, chorus]

**choirboy** /'kwie⋅ə‚boy/ *n* a boy member of a choir

**choirmaster** /'kwie⋅ə‚mahstə/ *n* the director of a choir (eg in a church) ⟨*served as organist and ~*⟩

**choir organ** *n* a division of an organ controlling a set of soft-toned pipes for accompanying singing

**choir school** *n* a school primarily intended for the choirboys of a cathedral or college choir

**choirstall** /'kwie⋅ə‚stawl/ *n* **1** one of a row of seats separated by armrests or small screens, for the use of the choir in a church **2** **choirstall, choirstalls** *pl* a bench or row of seats in a church, occupied by the choir

¹**choke** /chohk/ *vt* **1** to stop or interrupt the normal breathing of by compressing or obstructing the windpipe or by poisoning or adulterating available air **2** to stop or suppress expression of or by; silence **3a** to restrain the growth, development, or activity of ⟨*a lawn ~d with dandelions*⟩ **b** to obstruct by filling up or clogging – often + *up* ⟨*a path ~d with weeds*⟩ ⟨*leaves ~d up the drain*⟩ **4** to enrich the fuel mixture of (a petrol engine) by partially shutting off the air intake of the carburettor ~ *vi* **1** to become choked in breathing **2** to become speechless or incapacitated, esp from strong emotion ⟨*~d with rage when she read the announcement*⟩ ⟨*~d up and couldn't finish his speech*⟩ **3** *slang* to die [ME *choken*, alter. of *achoken*, fr OE *acēocian*; akin to OE *cēace* jaw, cheek]

²**choke** *n* **1** the act or sound of choking **2** something that obstructs passage or flow: eg **2a** a valve in the carburettor of a petrol engine for controlling the amount of air in the fuel-air mixture **b** a constriction in an outlet (eg of an oil well) that restricts flow **c choke, choke coil** INDUCTOR 2b (coil of wire in an electric circuit) **d** a narrowing towards the muzzle in the bore of a firearm, esp a shotgun

³**choke** *n* the central part of a GLOBE ARTICHOKE that is usu considered inedible [back-formation (influenced by ²*choke*) fr *artichoke*]

**chokeberry** /'chohkb(ə)ri/ *n* (the small astringent berry of) a shrub (genus *Aronia*) of the rose family that is cultivated chiefly for its brilliant autumn foliage

**choke collar** *n* a collar that may be tightened as a noose and is used esp in training and controlling powerful or stubborn dogs

**choked** /chohkt/ *adj, Br chiefly informal* angry, upset

**chokedamp** /'chohk‚damp/ *n* BLACKDAMP (air in a mine that is low in oxygen)

**choker** /'chohkə/ *n* **1** one who or that which chokes **2a** a high stiff collar **b** a short necklace or decorative band that fits closely round the throat

**chokey, choky** /'chohki/ *n, Br slang* prison [Hindi *caukī* shed, station, lockup, dim. of *cauk* market-place]

**choking** /'chohking/ *adj* **1** producing the feeling of being strangled **2** indistinct in utterance, esp because of strong emotion ⟨*a low ~ laugh*⟩ – **chokingly** *adv*

**choky** /'chohki/ *adj* tending to cause choking or to become choked

**chol-, chole-, cholo-** *comb form* bile; gall ⟨*cholate*⟩ ⟨*cholesterol*⟩ [Gk *chol-, cholē-, cholo-*, fr *cholē, cholos* – more at GALL]

**cholangiography** /kə‚lanji'ogrəfi/ *n* X-ray photography of the GALL BLADDER and the BILE DUCTS after the swallowing or injection of a substance that prevents the passage of X-rays [*chol- + angi- + -graphy*] – **cholangiographic** *adj*, **cholangiogram** *n*

**cholate** /'koh‚layt/ *n* any of various chemical compounds (SALTS or ESTERS) formed by combination between CHOLIC ACID and a metal atom, an alcohol, or another chemical group

**cholecalciferol** /‚kohlikal'sifərol/ *n* VITAMIN D₃ [ISV *chol- + calci- + -fer + -ol*]

**cholecystectomy** /‚kohləsi'stektəmi/ *n, pl* **cholecystectomies** surgical removal of the GALL BLADDER [NL *cholecystis* gallbladder (fr *chol-* + Gk *kystis* bladder) + ISV *-ectomy*]

**cholecystitis** /‚kohləsi'stietəs/ *n, pl* **cholecystitides** /-'sisti-deez/ inflammation of the GALL BLADDER [NL, fr *cholecystis*]

**cholecystokinin** /‚kohlə‚sistə'kienin/ *n* a hormone produced by the membrane lining the DUODENUM (first part of the SMALL INTESTINE) that regulates the emptying of bile from the GALL BLADDER and the release from the pancreas of ENZYMES that break down proteins [NL *cholecystis* + E *-o- + kinin*]

**cholelithiasis** /‚kohlili'thie⋅əsəs/ *n* the condition of suffering from gallstones; *also* the production of gallstones [NL *chol- + lithiasis*]

**choler** /'kolə, 'kohlə/ *n* **1** ill-temper; irritability **2a** *archaic* YELLOW BILE (body fluid formerly believed to cause irritability) **b** *obs* BILE 1a (liquid produced by the liver) **3** *obs* biliousness [ME *coler*, fr MF *colere*, fr L *cholera* bilious disease, fr Gk, fr *cholē*]

**cholera** /'kolərə/ *n* **1** a short-lasting often fatal infectious epidemic disease caused by a bacterium (*Vibrio comma*) and marked by severe diarrhoea, vomiting, abdominal pain, etc **2** any of several diseases of humans and domestic animals with similar symptoms to those of cholera [ME *colera* bile, fr L *cholera*] – **choleraic** *adj*

**cholera morbus** /'mawbəs/ *n* any of various digestive disorders marked by diarrhoea, vomiting, etc – not used technically [NL, lit., the disease cholera]

**choleric** /'kolərik/ *adj* bad-tempered

**cholesteric** /kə'lesterik/ *adj* of or being the form of a LIQUID CRYSTAL characterized by the arrangement of the molecules in layers with the long axes of the molecules parallel to the plane of the layers – compare SMECTIC, NEMATIC [Fr *cholestérique*, fr *cholestérine*]

**cholesterol** /kə'lestərol/ *n* a widely occurring chemical compound (STEROID), $C_{27}H_{45}OH$, present in animal and plant CELL MEMBRANES and most animal and plant tissues, that is important in biochemical processes (eg the formation of oestrogen and other SEX HORMONES) and is thought to contribute to heart disease when present in large quantities in the blood [Fr *cholestérine*, fr *chol-* + Gk *stereos* solid]

**choli** /'chohli/ *n* a usu short-sleeved closely fitting blouse that leaves the midriff bare and is worn under a sari [Hindi *colī*, fr Skt *cola, coḍa*]

**cholic acid** /'kohlik/ *n* an acid, $C_{24}H_{40}O_5$, found in bile, that helps in the digestion of fats [Gk *cholikos* bilious, fr *cholē*]

**choline** /'kohleen/ *n* a chemical compound, $(CH_3)_3N(OH)(CH_2)_2OH$, occurring in many animal and plant products that is a vitamin of the VITAMIN B COMPLEX, forms part of the fats in cell membranes, and is essential to the proper functioning of the liver by preventing the accumulation of fat [Ger *cholin*, fr *chol- + -in -ine*]

**cholinergic** /‚kohli'nuhjik/ *adj* **1** *of a nerve, esp in the* AUTONOMIC NERVOUS SYSTEM activated by ACETYLCHOLINE (chemical that transmits nerve impulses between nerves) or releasing acetylcholine in response to activation **2** resembling acetylcholine, esp in physiological action [ISV acetyl*choline* + Gk *ergon* work – more at WORK]

**cholinesterase** /‚kohli'nestə‚rayz, -‚rays/ *n* any of various ENZYMES that break down compounds containing choline; *esp* ACETYLCHOLINESTERASE

**cholinolytic** /‚kohlinoh'litik/ *adj* interfering with the action of ACETYLCHOLINE (chemical that transmits nerve impulses between nerves) or agents having an action like that of acetylcholine [*choline + -o- + -lytic*] – **cholinolytic** *n*

**chomp** /chomp/ *vb* to chew noisily [alter. of *champ*]

**chondr-, chondri-, chondro-** *comb form* cartilage ⟨*chondroblast*⟩ [NL, fr Gk *chondr-, chondro-*, fr *chondros* grain, cartilage]

**chondriosome** /'kondriə‚sohm/ *n* MITOCHONDRION (energy-producing body in cell) [Gk *chondrion* (dim. of *chondros*) + ISV *-some*]

**chondrite** /'kondriet/ *n* a meteoric stone containing chondrules [ISV, fr Gk *chondros* grain] – **chondritic** *adj*

**chondroblast** /'kondroh‚blahst/ *n* a cell that produces cartilage [ISV]

**chondrocranium** /‚kondroh'krayniəm/ *n* the skull, made of soft cartilage, of an embryo; *also* the part at the base of the adult human skull derived from this

**chondrocyte** /'kondroh‚siet/ *n* a cartilage cell

**chondroitin** /kən'droh⋅itin/ *n* a complex chemical compound (MUCOPOLYSACCHARIDE) that occurs in cartilage, tendons, and

# cho

256

other animal tissues [ISV *chondroitic* acid (an acid found in cartilage; fr *chondr-*) + *-in*]

**chondrule** /'kondroohl/ *n* a rounded stony granule often found embedded in meteorites and sometimes in marine sediments [Gk *chondros* grain]

**chook** /chook/ *n, Austr & NZ* a chicken, fowl [imit]

**choose** /choohz/ *vb* **chose** /chohz/; **chosen** /'chohz(ə)n/ *vt* **1a** to select freely and after consideration **b** to decide on; *esp* to elect ⟨*chosen as leader*⟩ **2a** to decide ⟨*chose to go by train*⟩ **b** to prefer ⟨*I ~ not to do it*⟩ ~ *vi* to make a selection – see also CANNOT **choose but** *synonyms* see [1]CHOICE *antonym* reject (for sense 1) [ME *chosen*, fr OE *cēosan*; akin to OHG *kiosan* to choose, L *gustare* to taste] – **chooser** *n*

**choosy, choosey** /'choohzi/ *adj* particular in making a choice; hard to please

[1]**chop** /chop/ *vb* **-pp-** *vt* **1a(1)** to cut into or sever usu by a blow or repeated blows of a sharp instrument ⟨*~ down a tree*⟩ ⟨*~ped off a piece and gave it to her*⟩ **a(2)** to produce by doing this *(went out to ~ firewood)* ⟨*had to ~ a path through the forest*⟩ **b** to cut into pieces – often + *up* ⟨*~ up the vegetables*⟩ **2a** to strike (a ball) with a sharp downward stroke (eg in tennis) **b** to strike (an opponent) with a short sharp blow, esp with the side of the hand (eg in karate) **3** to subject to the action of a chopper ⟨*~ a beam of light*⟩ **4** *informal* to dispense with or limit the scope of ⟨*forced to ~ the budget for this project*⟩ ~ *vi* to make a quick stroke or repeated strokes (as if) with a sharp instrument ⟨*I've been ~ping at this log for ages, but I can't split it*⟩ [ME *chappen, choppen* – more at CHAP]

[2]**chop** *n* **1a** a forceful usu slanting blow (as if) with an axe ⟨*a karate ~*⟩ **b** a sharp downward blow or stroke ⟨*made a ~ at the ball*⟩ **2** a small cut of meat often including part of a rib **3** the uneven motion of the sea, esp when wind and tide are opposed **4** *informal* dismissal from a job or position – + *the*; *esp in give/get the chop*

[3]**chop** *vi* **-pp-** *esp of the wind* to change direction [ME *chappen, choppen* to barter, fr OE *cēapian*] – **chop and change** to keep changing one's mind or one's plans – see also **chop** LOGIC

[4]**chop** *n* **1** a seal or official stamp such as was formerly used in China or India **2a** a mark on goods or coins to indicate nature or quality; a trademark, brand **b** a kind, brand, or lot of goods bearing the same chop **c** quality, grade ⟨*first-chop tea*⟩ [Hindi *chāp* stamp]

**chop-'chop** *adv* without delay; quickly – often used interjectionally [Pidgin E, redupl of *chop* fast – more at CHOPSTICK]

**chopfallen** /'chop,fawlən/ *adj* CHAPFALLEN (dejected)

**chophouse** /'chop,hows/ *n* a restaurant specializing in chops, steaks, etc

**chopine** /cho'peen/ *n* a shoe with a very high sole worn by women in the 16th and 17th centuries to protect the feet from dirt [MF *chapin*, fr OSp]

**chopper** /'chopə/ *n* **1** a short-handled axe; *also* an implement similar to this used by butchers to chop carcasses **2** a device that interrupts an electric current or a beam of radiation (eg light) at short regular intervals **3** a customized motorcycle; *esp* one with very high handlebars **4** *informal* a helicopter **5** *pl, slang* teeth **6** *NAm slang* a sub-machine gun

**Chopper** *trademark* – used for a bicycle with small wheels, the rear wheel being larger than the front wheel, an elongated saddle, and high handlebars

[1]**choppy** /'chopi/ *adj, of the wind* variable [3*chop*] – **choppiness** *n*

[2]**choppy** *adj* **1** *of the sea* rough with small waves **2** disconnected, erratic ⟨*short, ~ sentences*⟩ [2*chop*]

**chops** /chops/ *n pl* **1** the jaws, esp of an animal **2a** the mouth **b** the fleshy covering of the jaws ⟨*the hungry dog licked his ~*⟩ [alter. of 4*chap*]

**chopstick** /'chop,stik/ *n* either of a pair of slender sticks held between thumb and fingers and used chiefly in oriental countries to lift food to the mouth [Pidgin E, fr *chop* fast (of Chinese origin; akin to Cant *kap*) + E *stick*]

**chopsuey** /,chop'sooh·i/ *n* a Chinese dish of shredded meat or chicken, bean sprouts, and additional vegetable ingredients (eg onions, mushrooms, and bamboo shoots) commonly served with rice and soy sauce [Chin (Cant) *shap sui* odds and ends, fr *shap* miscellaneous + *sui* bits]

**choragus, choregus** /kaw'raygəs/ *n* the leader of an Ancient Greek chorus; *broadly* the leader of any group or movement [L & Gk; L *choragus*, fr Gk *choragos, chorēgos*, fr *choros* chorus + *agein* to lead – more at AGENT] – **choragic** *adj*

**choral** /'kawrəl/ *adj* **1a** of a chorus or choir ⟨*a ~ group*⟩ **b** accompanied with song ⟨*a ~ dance*⟩ **2** sung or designed for singing by a choir ⟨*a ~ arrangement*⟩ [Fr or ML; Fr *choral*, fr ML *choralis*, fr L *chorus*] – **chorally** *adv*

**chorale** *also* **choral** /ko'rahl/ *n* **1** (the music for) a usu German traditional hymn or psalm for singing in church, esp by the choir **2** *taking sing or pl vb, chiefly NAm* a chorus, choir [Ger *choral*, short for *choralgesang* choral song]

**chorale prelude** *n* a composition, usu for organ, based on a chorale

**choral speaking** *n* ensemble speaking of poetry or prose by a group, often using various voice combinations and contrasts

[1]**chord** /kawd/ *n* a combination of notes sounded together [alter. of ME *cord*, short for *accord*]

[2]**chord** *vt* to add notes to (a melody) to form chords; harmonize

[3]**chord** *n* **1** CORD 3a (nerve or other cordlike body structure) **2** a straight line joining two points on a curve; *specif* one joining two points on a circle that does not pass through the centre of the circle **3** *building* either of the two outside members of a TRUSS (framework of wood or metal used as a structural support) **4** the straight line joining the front and back edges of an aircraft wing or other AEROFOIL [alter. of [1]*cord*] – **strike a chord** to remind somebody of something [fr *chord* in arch. sense "string of a musical instrument"] – **touch the right chord** to produce a desired response by playing on somebody's emotions

*usage* Compare the spellings **chord** and **cord**. It is **chord** in the musical, mathematical, and aeronautical senses, **cord** for any kind of string, and either **cord** or **chord** for the anatomical senses associated with string ⟨*umbilical* cord⟩.

**chordal** /'kawdl/ *adj* **1** of or suggesting a chord **2** relating to music consisting principally of combinations of notes played together (HARMONY) rather than of two or more melodies or parts proceeding simultaneously (COUNTERPOINT 1b)

**chordamesoderm** /,kawdə'mesoh,duhm/ *n* the part of the middle layer of cells (MESODERM) in a developing embryo that forms the NOTOCHORD (supporting rod replaced in fully developed VERTEBRATE animals by the backbone) and induces the development of structures (eg the brain) that will form the CENTRAL NERVOUS SYSTEM [NL *chorda* cord + E *mesoderm*] – **chordamesodermal**

**chordate** /'kaw,dayt, -dət/ *n* any of a phylum or subkingdom (Chordata) of animals including the VERTEBRATES (eg reptiles, birds and mammals) and other less developed animals (eg the LANCELETS and TUNICATES), that have, at least at some stage of development, a NOTOCHORD (supporting rod replaced in vertebrates by the backbone), a CENTRAL NERVOUS SYSTEM along the back, and GILL SLITS [deriv of L *chorda* cord] – **chordate** *adj*

**chord organ** *n* an electronic organ or REED ORGAN with buttons to produce simple chords

**chore** /chaw/ *n* **1** a routine task or job **2** a difficult or disagreeable task *synonyms* see [1]TASK [alter. of *chare*, fr ME *char* turn, piece of work, fr OE *cierr*]

**-chore** /-kaw/ *comb form* (→ *n*) plant distributed by (a specified agency) ⟨*zoochore*⟩ [Gk *chōrein* to withdraw, go; akin to Gk *chēros* bereaved – more at HEIR] – **-chory** *comb form* (→ *n*), **-chorous** *comb form* (→ *adj*)

**chorea** /ko'ree·ə/ *n* a nervous disorder (eg of humans or dogs) marked by spasmodic movements of limbs and facial muscles and by lack of coordination [NL, fr L, dance, fr Gk *choreia*, fr *choros* chorus] – **choreic** *adj or n*

**choregus** *n* CHORAGUS

**choreograph** /'korio,grahf, -,graf/ *vb* to compose or arrange the steps and dances for (a ballet or piece of music) – **choreographer** *n*

**choreography** /,kori'ogrəfi/ *n* **1** the art of representing dancing by notation **2** stage dancing as distinguished from social or ballroom dancing **3** the composition and arrangement of dances for the stage [Fr *chorégraphie*, fr Gk *choreia* + Fr *-graphie* -graphy] – **choreographic** *adj*, **choreographically** *adv*

**choriamb** /'kori,amb/ *n* a unit of poetic metre (FOOT) consisting of two short syllables between two long syllables [LL *choriambus*, fr Gk *choriambos*, fr *choreios* of a chorus (fr *choros*) + *iambos* iambus] – **choriambic** *adj*

**choric** /'korik/ *adj* of or being in the style of an esp Greek chorus – **chorically** *adv*

**chorioallantois** /,korioh,alən'toh·is/ *n* ALLANTO-CHORION (membrane of a developing foetus) [NL, fr Gk *chorion* + NL *allantois*] – **chorioallantoic** *adj*

**choriocarcinoma** /ˌkorioh,kahsi'nohmə/ *n* a cancerous tumour developing in the uterus or, less commonly, in the testes [NL, fr *chorion* + *carcinoma*]

**chorion** /'kawri·ən/ *n* the outer membrane of the embryo of reptiles, birds, and mammals that contains many blood vessels and that in some mammals combines with another membrane (the ALLANTOIS) in the formation of the placenta [NL, fr Gk] – **chorionic** *adj*

**chorister** /'koristə/ *n* 1 a singer in a choir; *specif* a choirboy 2 *NAm* the singer in a church choir who leads the singing and in the absence of instrumental accompaniment sets the pitch and tempo [ME *querister*, fr AF *cueristre*, fr ML *chorista*, fr L *chorus*]

**chorizo** /chaw'reezoh, chə-/ *n, pl* **chorizos** a dried pork sausage that is highly seasoned with paprika, pimientos, garlic, and spices [Sp]

**'C-ho,rizon** *n* the layer of soil lying beneath the B-HORIZON and consisting of weathered rock

**choroid** /'kaw,royd/, **choroid coat** *also* **chorioid, chorioid coat** *n* the dark-coloured membrane of the eyeball, that contains many blood vessels and lies between the retina and the white firm outer coat (SCLERA) that encloses the back of the eyeball [NL *choroides* resembling the chorion, fr Gk *chorioeidēs*, fr *chorion*] – **choroid** *adj*, **choroidal** *adj*

**chortle** /'chawtl/ *vi* to laugh or chuckle esp in satisfaction or exultation ~ *vt* to say gleefully or triumphantly ⟨*"O frabjous day, calloo, callay!" he* ~ d *in his joy* – Lewis Carroll⟩ [blend of *chuckle* and *snort*] – **chortle** *n*, **chortler** *n*

**'chorus** /'kawrəs/ *n* **1a** *taking sing or pl vb* a group of singers and dancers in Athenian drama, esp those commenting on the action; *also* a similar group in later plays **b** the part of a drama sung or spoken by the chorus **2** a character in Elizabethan drama who speaks the prologue and epilogue and comments on the action **3a** *taking sing or pl vb* an organized company of singers who sing in concert; a choir; *specif* a body of singers who sing the choral parts of a work (eg in opera) **b** a composition to be sung by a number of voices in concert **4** *taking sing or pl vb* a group of dancers and singers supporting the featured players in a musical or revue **5a** a part of a song or hymn recurring at intervals **b** the main part of a popular song **6** something performed, sung, or uttered simultaneously by a number of people or animals; *also* sounds so uttered ⟨*the dawn* ~ ⟩ ⟨*the suggestion was met with a* ~ *of groans*⟩ [L, ring dance, chorus, fr Gk *choros*] – **in chorus** in unison

**'chorus** *vt* to sing or utter in chorus

**chorus girl** *n* a young woman who sings or dances in the chorus of a musical, cabaret, etc

**chose** /chohz/ *past of* CHOOSE

**chose in action** *n* a right to intangible property (eg debts or shares) that is enforceable by legal action; *also* the thing (eg a bond or bill) to which chose in action attaches [*chose* (piece of personal property, thing) fr Fr, fr L *causa* cause, reason]

**'chosen** /'chohz(ə)n/ *adj* selected or marked for favour or special privilege ⟨*granted to a* ~ *few*⟩ [ME, fr pp of *chosen* to choose]

**'chosen** *n, taking pl vb* those who are the objects of choice or of divine favour; *esp* those whom God has chosen for salvation – + *the*

**chota peg** /'chohtə/ *n* a small drink, esp of spirits [Hindi *choṭā* small + E *'peg* 8]

**chou** /shooh/ *n* CHOUX PASTRY

**Chou** /choh/ *n* a Chinese dynasty traditionally dated 1122 to about 256 BC and marked by the development of the philosophical schools of Confucius, Mencius, Lao-tzu, and Mo Ti [Chin (Pek) *Zhōu* (*Chou¹*)]

**chough** /chuf/ *n* a bird (*Pyrrhocorax pyrrhocorax*) of the crow family, found in parts of Europe, Asia, and Africa, that has glossy black plumage and red legs and bill, and that nests esp on cliffs [ME]

**choux pastry** /shooh/ *n* a light pastry made with an egg-enriched dough of piping consistency and used for sweet or savoury confections (eg éclairs) [Fr *choux*, pl of *chou*, lit., cabbage, fr L *caulis* stalk – more at HOLE]

**chow** /chow/ *n* **1** *slang* food **2** *Austr & NZ derog* a Chinese person [perh fr Chin (Pek) *jĭao* (*chiao³*) meat dumpling]

**'chow-,chow** *n* **1** a Chinese preserve of ginger, fruits, and peel in heavy syrup **2** a relish of chopped mixed pickles in mustard sauce [Pidgin E, mixture]

**chow chow, chow** *often cap both Cs* (any of) a breed of heavy-coated dog with a broad head and muzzle, a very full

ruff of long hair, and a distinctive blue-black tongue and black-lined mouth [fr a Chin dial. word akin to Cant *kaú* dog]

**chowder** /'chowdə/ *n* a thick soup or stew of seafood (eg clams or mussels) usu made with milk, bacon, onions, and additional vegetable ingredients (eg potatoes); *also* a soup resembling chowder ⟨*corn* ~ ⟩ [Fr *chaudière* kettle, contents of a kettle, fr LL *caldaria* – more at CAULDRON]

**chow mein** /ˌchow 'mayn/ *n* a Chinese dish of fried noodles usu mixed with diced or shredded meat or poultry and vegetables [Chin (Pek) *chǎo miàn* (*ch'ao³ mien⁴*), fr *chǎo* (*ch'ao³*) to fry + *miàn* (*mien⁴*) dough]

**chrestomathy** /kre'stomathi/ *n* an anthology of passages compiled as an aid to learning a language [NL *chrestomathia*, fr Gk *chrēstomatheia*, fr *chrēstos* useful + *manthanein* to learn; akin to Skt *hrasva* small – more at MATHEMATICAL]

**chrism** /'kriz(ə)m/ *n* consecrated oil used in GREEK ORTHODOX and ROMAN CATHOLIC churches, esp in the ceremonies of baptism, confirmation, and ordination [ME *crisme*, fr OE *crisma*, fr LL *chrisma*, fr Gk, ointment, fr *chriein* to anoint; akin to OE *grēot* grit, sand]

**chrisom** /'kriz(ə)m/ *n* a white cloth or robe put on a child at baptism as a symbol of innocence [ME *crisom*, short for *crisom cloth*, fr *crisom* chrism + *cloth*]

**chrisom child** *n* a child that dies in its first month

**Christ** /kriest/ *n* **1** MESSIAH (deliverer promised by God to the Jews) **2** Jesus [ME *Crist*, fr OE, fr L *Christus*, fr Gk *Christos*, lit., anointed, fr *chriein*]

**Christadelphian** /ˌkristə'delfiən/ *n* a member of a Christian sect originating in the USA in 1848 that claims to follow the practices of the earliest disciples, interprets the Bible literally, and holds that only the righteous will finally have eternal life, whilst the wicked are completely obliterated, and the ignorant and unconverted are not raised from the dead [*Christ* + Gk *adelphos* brother] – **Christadelphian** *adj*

**christen** /'kris(ə)n/ *vt* **1a** to baptize **b** to name at baptism **2** to name or dedicate (eg a ship or bell) by a ceremony suggestive of baptism **3** to give a nickname to **4** *informal* to use for the first time [ME *cristnen*, fr OE *cristnian*, fr *cristen* Christian, fr L *christianus*]

**Christendom** /'kris(ə)ndəm, 'krist-/ *n* **1** Christians collectively **2** the parts of the world in which Christianity is the most common religion [ME *cristendom*, fr OE *cristendōm*, fr *cristen*]

**christening** /'kris(ə)ning/ *n* the ceremony of baptizing and naming a child

**'Christian** /'kristi·ən/ *n* **1a** a person who acknowledges the divinity of Jesus Christ, who believes that, by his sacrificial death, he made possible the forgiveness of sins, and who attempts to follow his teachings as contained in the Bible **b** a member of a Christian denomination, esp by baptism **2** a good or kind person regardless of religion [L *christianus*, adj & n, fr Gk *christianos*, fr *Christos*]

**'Christian** *adj* **1a** of Christianity ⟨~ *scriptures*⟩ **b** based on or conforming with Christianity ⟨~ *ethics*⟩ **2a** of a Christian ⟨~ *responsibilities*⟩ **b** professing Christianity ⟨*a* ~ *affirmation*⟩ **3** commendably decent or generous ⟨*has a very* ~ *concern for others*⟩ – **Christianly** *adv*

**Christian Brother** *n* a member of a ROMAN CATHOLIC lay order founded in 1684 for the education of the poor

**Christian era** *n* the period dating from the birth of Christ

**christiania** /ˌkristi'ahnyə, -ni-ə/ *n* a christie [*Christiania*, former name of Oslo, city in Norway]

**Christianity** /ˌkristi'anəti/ *n* **1** the religion based on the teachings of Jesus Christ and his apostles, and on the Bible as sacred scripture **2** Christian beliefs or practices

**Christian-ize, -ise** /'kristiə,niez/ *vt* to make Christian – **Christianizer** *n*, **Christianization** *n*

**Christian name** *n* **1** a name given at christening or confirmation **2** a name that precedes a person's surname; *esp* FIRST NAME

*synonyms* There is a tendency today to avoid saying **Christian name** unless one knows that its possessor is a Christian. Alternatives are **forename** or (chiefly NAm) **given name**, or **first name** for the first or only name before the surname. People (eg Hungarians) whose surname comes first may prefer to use **given name**.

**Christian Science** *n* a religion, founded by Mary Baker Eddy in 1866, that includes the teaching that sin, sickness, and death will be destroyed by a full understanding of Jesus's teaching and healing – **Christian Scientist** *n*

**'christie, christy** /'kristi/ *n* a skiing turn used for stopping or for changing direction during descent, and executed, usu at high speed, by shifting the body weight forwards and swinging round with skis parallel [by shortening & alter. fr *christiana*]

²**christie, christy** *n often cap, Can* ²BOWLER (hat) [prob fr *Christy* & Co, E hatters]

**Christlike** /'kriest,liek/ *adj* resembling Christ in character, spirit, or action – **Christlikeness** *n*

**Christly** /'kriestli/ *adj* of or resembling Christ

**Christmas** /'krisməs/ *n* 1 a Christian festival observed by the Western Church on December 25, and by the Eastern Orthodox Church on January 6, that commemorates the birth of Christ and is usu observed as a public holiday 2 Christmastide [ME *Christemasse,* fr OE *Cristes mæsse,* lit., Christ's mass]

**Christmas box** *n, Br* a small gift of money given at Christmas to the milkman, the dustman, etc, for their services throughout the year

**Christmas cactus** *n* a branching S American cactus (*Zygocactus truncatus*) with flat stems, short joints, and showy red flowers commonly grown as a winter-flowering house plant

**Christmas card** *n* a greeting card traditionally sent at Christmas

**Christmas club** *n* a savings account in which regular deposits are made throughout the year to provide money for Christmas shopping

**Christmas Eve** *n* the evening or the whole day before Christmas Day

**Christmas pudding** *n* a rich steamed pudding containing dried fruit, candied peel, spices, brandy, etc, traditionally eaten at Christmas; PLUM PUDDING

**Christmas rose** *n* a European winter-flowering plant (*Helleborus niger*) of the buttercup family that has white or purplish flowers

**Christmassy** /'krisməsi/ *adj* having or showing the Christmas spirit of conviviality

**Christmastide** /'krisməs,tied/ *n* the festival season from CHRISTMAS EVE till after NEW YEAR'S DAY or till EPIPHANY (January 6th)

**Christmastime** /'krisməs,tiem/ *n* the Christmas season

**Christmas tree** *n* 1 an evergreen or artificial tree decorated with lights, tinsel, etc at Christmas 2 a device consisting of an assembly of fittings (e g valves) placed at the top of a well to control flow (e g of oil or gas)

**Christo-** *comb form* Christ ⟨*Christo*logy⟩ [LGk, fr Gk *Christos*]

**Christocentric** /'kriestə,sentrik, 'kris-/ *adj* centring theologically on Christ

**Christogram** /'kriestə,gram, 'kris-/ *n* a graphic symbol representing Christ; *esp* CHI-RHO (symbol formed by the first two letters of the Greek word for *Christ*)

**Christology** /krie'stoləji, kri-/ *n* the branch of theology concerned with the person, character, and role of Christ – **Christological** *adj*

**christy** /'kristi/ *n* CHRISTIE (turn in skiing)

**chrom-** /krohm-/, **chromo-** *comb form* 1 chromium ⟨*chromize*⟩ 2a colour; coloured ⟨*chromoprotein*⟩ b pigment ⟨*chromogen*⟩ [Fr, fr Gk *chrōma* colour]

**chroma** /'krohmə/ *n* 1 SATURATION 4 (degree to which a colour is mixed with black, grey, or white) 2 CHROMATICITY 2 [Gk *chrōma* colour]

**chromaffin** /'krohməfin/ *adj, esp of a cell or cell part* capable of being deeply coloured by compounds of chromium [ISV *chrom-* + L *affinis* bordering on, related – more at AFFINITY]

**chromat-, chromato-** *comb form* 1 colour ⟨*chromatophore*⟩ 2 chromatin ⟨*chromatolysis*⟩ [Gk *chrōmat-, chrōma*]

**chromate** /'kroh,mayt/ *n* any of various chemical compounds (SALTS or ESTERS) formed by combination between CHROMIC ACID and a metal atom, an alcohol, or another chemical group [Fr, fr Gk *chrōma*]

¹**chromatic** /kroh'matik, krə-/ *adj* 1 of, characterized by, or produced by colour 2a of or giving all the notes of the CHROMATIC SCALE b characterized by frequent use of intervals or notes outside the DIATONIC scale (musical scale having five tones and two semitones) [Gk *chrōmatikos,* fr *chrōmat-, chrōma* skin, colour, modified tone; akin to OE *grēot* sand – more at GRIT] – **chromatically** *adv*, **chromaticism** *n*

²**chromatic** *n* a chromatically altered musical note; ACCIDENTAL 2a

**chromatic aberration** /,abə'raysh(ə)n/ *n* distortion in an optical image caused by differences in the amount by which different colours of the spectrum undergo REFRACTION (bending of a light ray when entering or leaving a lens, prism, etc) and characterized by coloured outlines round the image

**chromaticity** /,krohmə'tisəti/ *n* 1 the quality or state of being chromatic 2 the property of the colour of an object or light that does not depend on the brightness and is defined in terms of the major light wavelength present (HUE) and the SATURATION (degree to which this is mixed with white or grey)

**chromatics** /kroh'matiks, krə-/, **chromatology** /,krohmə'toləji/ *n taking sing vb* the branch of physics or optics that deals with colour

**chromatic scale** *n* a musical scale that consists entirely of semitones. When its twelve notes are played consecutively on the piano, black as well as white keys must be used.

**chromatid** /'krohmətid/ *n* either of the two identical strands formed when a CHROMOSOME (length of gene-carrying material) divides during CELL DIVISION (splitting of a cell and its contents to form new cells), each strand becoming a chromosome in each of the new cells produced

**chromatin** /'krohmətin/ *n* the part of a cell nucleus that stains intensely with dyes that are chemical BASES; *specif* the material that makes up the gene-carrying chromosomes in the nucleus of a cell and consists of a complex compound between DNA and proteins – **chromatinic** *adj*

**chromatogram** /kroh'matəgram/ *n* the pattern formed on the adsorbent substance (e g paper or starch) by the layers of chemical compounds separated by chromatography; *also* a trace made on paper by an electronic recording instrument corresponding to this

**chromatography** /,krohmə'togrəfi/ *n* a technique for separating and usu identifying the chemical compounds present in a mixture (e g blood or milk) by dissolving the mixture in a liquid or gas and passing it over or through an adsorbent substance (e g paper or starch) so that each compound remains in the substance as a separate often coloured layer – **chromatograph** *vt*, **chromatographic** *adj*, **chromatographically** *adv*

**chromatolysis** /,krohmə'toləsis/ *n* the breaking up of cell material (e g chromatin) that stains easily with dyes [NL] – **chromatolytic** *adj*

**chromatophil** /kroh'matə,fil/ *adj* CHROMOPHIL

**chromatophore** /kroh'matəfaw/ *n* 1 a pigment-bearing cell; *esp* any of the cells found esp in the skin of an animal (e g a frog or chameleon), that, by expanding and contracting, cause the animal to change colour 2 CHROMOPLAST (coloured body inside plant cell) [ISV]

¹**chrome** /krohm/ *n* 1a chromium – not used technically in chemistry b a chromium pigment 2 something (e g the metal trimmings on a car) plated with chromium or an alloy of chromium; *also* the plating itself [Fr, fr Gk *chrōma;* fr the green, red, and yellow colours of chromium compounds]

²**chrome** *vt* to treat with a compound of chromium (e g in dyeing)

**-chrome** /-krohm/ *comb form* (→ *n or adj*) 1 coloured thing ⟨*helio*chrome⟩; coloured ⟨*poly*chrome⟩ 2 colouring matter ⟨*uro*chrome⟩ [ML *-chromat-, -chroma* coloured thing, fr Gk *chrōmat-, chrōma*]

**chrome alum** *n* an ALUM containing chromium; *esp* a dark-violet chemical compound, $KCr(SO_4)_2.12H_2O$, used in tanning, in photography, and as a MORDANT (substance used to fix colours) in dyeing

**chrome green** *n* any of various brilliant green pigments containing or consisting of chromium compounds

**chrome red** *n* a red pigment consisting of LEAD CHROMATE, $PbCrO_4.PbO$, in a form that is a chemical BASE

**chrome yellow** *n* a yellow pigment consisting essentially of LEAD CHROMATE, $PbCrO_4$, in a form that is chemically neither an acid nor a BASE

**chromic** /'krohmik/ *adj* of or derived from chromium, esp with a VALENCY of three

**chromic acid** *n* an acid, $H_2CrO_4$, that has a similar structure to SULPHURIC ACID but occurs only as a solution (e g in water)

**chrominance** /'krohminəns/ *n* 1 the measured difference between a colour and a particular reference colour of the same brightness 2 the part of a colour television signal that determines the colour to be displayed on the screen [*chrom-* + lum*inance*]

**chromite** *n* a mineral, $FeCr_2O_4$, that consists of a magnetic oxide of iron and chromium and is the major source of chromium [Ger *chromit,* fr *chrom-*]

**chromium** /'krohmyəm, -mi·əm/ *n* a blue-white metallic chemical element found naturally only in combination and used esp in alloys and as a shiny plating on other metals [NL, fr Fr *chrome*]

**chromo** /'krohmoh/ *n, pl* **chromos** a chromolithograph

**chromogen** /'krohmǝjǝn/ *n* **1** a chemical compound that is not itself a dye but contains a chromophore and is therefore capable of becoming a dye after undergoing a chemical reaction **2** a bacterium or other microorganism that produces a pigment [ISV] – **chromogenic** *adj*

**chromolithography** /ˌkrohmohli'thogrǝfi/ *n* a technique of colour printing, used esp in the 19th century, in which a colour picture is built up by superimposing impressions from several different LITHOGRAPHIC (printing from a flat rather than a raised surface) printing plates or stones, each of a different single colour – **chromolithographic** *adj*, **chromolithograph** *n*

**chromomere** /'krohmǝˌmiǝ/ *n* any of many small bead-shaped granules that form along the length of a cell's chromosomes during the early stages of CELL DIVISION (division of a cell and its contents to form new cells) [ISV] – **chromomeric** *adj*

**chromonema** /ˌkrohmǝ'neemǝ/ *n, pl* **chromonemata** /-mǝtǝ/ the thin complexly coiled filament that makes up the body of a chromosome [NL, fr *chrom-* + Gk *nēmat-, nēma* thread – more at NEMAT-] – **chromonemal, chromonematal, chromonematic** *adj*

**chromophil** /'krohmǝfil/, **chromatophil** /kroh'matǝfil/ *adj, esp of a cell or cell part* staining readily with dyes [ISV]

**chromophore** /'krohmǝˌfaw/ *n* a group of atoms that are responsible for colour in a chemical compound [ISV] – **chromophoric** *adj*

**chromoplast** /'krohmǝˌplast/ *n* a coloured PLASTID (small body inside some plant cells) containing no chlorophyll but usu containing a red or yellow chemical compound (e g carotene) [ISV]

**chromoprotein** /ˌkrohmoh'prohteen/ *n* any of various coloured compounds (e g haemoglobin) formed by combination between a noncoloured protein and a usu metal-containing nonprotein coloured part

**chromosome** /'krohmǝˌsohm, -ˌzohm/ *n* any of the tiny bodies in the nucleus of a cell that consist of protein molecules combined with the long strands of DNA that carry hereditary information in the form of genes, and appear during CELL DIVISION as typically rod-shaped structures that become intensely coloured when treated with dyes that have an affinity for acidic chemical compounds [ISV] – **chromosomal** *adj*, **chromosomally** *adv*, **chromosomic** *adj*

**chromosome number** *n* the usu constant number of chromosomes in the nucleus of a cell that is characteristic of a particular species of animal or plant

**chromosphere** /'krohmǝˌsfiǝ/ *n* (a part of the atmosphere of any star corresponding to) the lower layer of the sun's atmosphere that is several thousand kilometres thick, is immediately above the PHOTOSPHERE, and is composed chiefly of hydrogen gas – **chromospheric** *adj*

**chromous** /'krohmǝs/ *adj* of or derived from chromium, esp with a VALENCY of two

**chron-, chrono-** *comb form* time ⟨*chrono*logy⟩ [Gk, fr *chronos*]

**chronaxie, chronaxy** /'krohnaksi/ *n* the time taken by a muscle cell, nerve cell, etc to respond to stimulation by the passage of an electric current at a voltage with a value double that of the minimum voltage needed to produce any response [Fr *chronaxie*, fr *chron-* + Gk *axia* worthy]

**chronic** /'kronik/ *adj* **1a** *of a disease* marked by long duration or frequent recurrence ⟨~ *bronchitis*⟩ ⟨~ *leukaemia*⟩ – compare ACUTE **4a b** suffering from a chronic disease ⟨*the special needs of* ~ *patients*⟩ **2a** always present or encountered; *esp* constantly vexing, weakening, or troubling ⟨~ *border fighting*⟩ ⟨~ *unemployment*⟩ **b** habitual ⟨*a* ~ *grumbler*⟩ **3** *Br informal* bad, terrible [Fr *chronique*, fr Gk *chronikos* of time, fr *chronos*] – **chronic** *n*, **chronically** *adv*, **chronicity** *n*

¹**chronicle** /'kronikl/ *n* **1** a usu continuous and detailed historical account of events arranged chronologically without analysis or interpretation **2** a narrative [ME *cronicle*, fr AF, alter. of OF *chronique*, fr L *chronica*, fr Gk *chronika*, fr neut pl of *chronikos*]

²**chronicle** *vt* **1** to record (as if) in a chronicle **2** to list, describe – **chronicler** *n*

**chronicle play** *n* a play with a historical theme consisting usu of rather loosely connected episodes chronologically arranged

**Chronicles** /'kroniklz/ *n, taking sing vb* – see BIBLE table

**chronogram** /'krohnǝˌgram/ *n* **1** an inscription, sentence, or phrase in which the letters which are Roman numerals (e g C, L, M, X) express a date or epoch when added together **2** the record made by a chronograph – **chronogrammatic, chronogrammatical** *adj*

**chronograph** /'krohnǝˌgrahf, -ˌgraf/ *n* an instrument for measuring and recording usu very short time intervals: e g **a** an instrument having a revolving drum on which a stylus or pen makes marks **b** a watch with a sweep-second hand **c** an instrument for measuring the time of flight of bullets, shells, etc – **chronography** *n*

**chronological** /ˌkronǝ'lojikl, ˌkroh-/ *also* **chronologic** /-ik/ *adj* of or arranged in or according to the order of time ⟨~ *tables of British history*⟩ – **chronologically** *adv*

**chronolog·ize, -ise** /krǝ'nolǝˌjiez/ *vt* to arrange chronologically; establish the order in time of (e g events or documents)

**chronology** /krǝ'nolǝji/ *n* **1a** a system for setting past events in order of occurrence; *specif* such a system for recording historical events that has an epoch (e g the traditionally accepted date for the birth of Christ) and regular divisions of time (e g years) **b** the scientific study or use of such systems **2** an arrangement in order of occurrence; *specif* such an arrangement presented in tabular or list form [NL *chronologia*, fr *chron-* + *-logia* -logy] – **chronologer, chronologist** *n*

**chronometer** /krǝ'nomitǝ/ *n* an instrument for measuring time; *esp* one designed to keep time with great accuracy – **chronometric, chronometrical** *adj*, **chronometrically** *adv*

**chronometry** /krǝ'nomitri/ *n* the science of measuring time with great accuracy; HOROLOGY

**chronoscope** /'kronǝˌskohp/ *n* an instrument for precise measurement of small time intervals

**chrys-** /kris-/, **chryso-** *comb form* gold; yellow ⟨*chryso*lite⟩ [Gk, fr *chrysos* gold, of Sem origin]

**chrysalid** /'krisǝlid/ *n* a chrysalis – **chrysalid** *adj*

**chrysalis** /'krisǝlis/ *n, pl* **chrysalides** /kri'salǝˌdeez/, **chrysalises 1a** the PUPA (inactive stage of development between larva and adult) of an insect, esp a butterfly **b** a protective covering resembling a chrysalis **2** a sheltered state or stage of being or growth ⟨*ready to emerge from the* ~ *of adolescence*⟩ [L *chrysallid-, chrysallis* gold-coloured pupa of butterflies, fr Gk, fr *chrysos*]

**chrysanth** /kri'santh, -'zanth/ *n, informal* a chrysanthemum

**chrysanthemum** /kri'santhǝmǝm, -'zan-/ *n* any of a genus (*Chrysanthemum*) of plants of the daisy family that includes many varieties of garden plants grown for their brightly coloured often double flower heads [L, fr Gk *chrysanthemon*, fr *chrys-* + *anthemon* flower; akin to Gk *anthos* flower]

**chryselephantine** /ˌkriseli'fantin/ *adj, esp of classical Greek sculpture* made of, overlaid with, or decorated with gold and ivory [Gk *chryselephantinos*, fr *chrys-* + *elephantinos* made of ivory, fr *elephant-, elephas* ivory, elephant]

**chrysoberyl** /'krisǝˌberǝl, -ril/ *n* **1** a usu yellow or pale-green mineral, $BeAl_2O_4$, that consists of an oxide of the chemical elements beryllium and aluminium and is sometimes used as a gemstone **2** *obs* a yellowish variety of BERYL used as a gemstone [L *chrysoberyllus*, fr Gk *chrysobēryllos*, fr *chrys-* + *bēryllos* beryl]

**chrysolite** /'krisǝˌliet/ *n* a yellowish-green or brown OLIVINE used as a gemstone [ME *crisolite*, fr OF, fr L *chrysolithos*, fr Gk, fr *chrys-* + *-lithos* -lite]

**chrysom** /'kriz(ǝ)m/ *n* CHRISOM (white garment worn by child at baptism)

**chrysomelid** /ˌkrisǝ'melid/ *n* any of a large family (Chrysomelidae) of small usu oval shiny brightly coloured beetles that includes the COLORADO BEETLE [deriv of Gk *chrysomēlolonthē* golden cockchafer] – **chrysomelid** *adj*

**chrysophyte** /'krisǝˌfiet/ *n* any of a group (Chrysophyta) of algae (e g the DIATOMS) that contain yellowish-green to golden-brown pigments [deriv of Gk *chrysos* + *phyton* plant – more at PHYT-]

**chrysoprase** /'krisǝˌprayz/ *n* an apple-green variety of CHALCEDONY that is used as a gemstone [ME *crisopace*, fr OF, fr L *chrysoprasus*, fr Gk *chrysoprasos*, fr *chrys-* + *prason* leek; akin to L *porrum* leek]

**chrysotile** /'krisǝˌtiel/ *n* a green, grey, or white mineral that consists of a fibrous silky SERPENTINE and is an important variety of commercial asbestos [Ger *chrysotil*, fr *chrys-* + *-til* fibre, fr Gk *tillein* to pluck]

**chthonic** /'thonik/, **chthonian** /'thohnyǝn, -ni-ǝn/ *adj* of the underworld; infernal ⟨~ *deities*⟩ [Gk *chthon-, chthōn* earth – more at HUMBLE]

**chub** /chub/ *n, pl* **chubs**, *esp collectively* **chub** (any of several sea or freshwater fishes similar to) a European freshwater fish (*Leuciscus cephalus*) of the carp family [ME *chubbe*]

**chubby** /'chubi/ *adj* agreeably plump ⟨*a ~ baby*⟩ ⟨*~ cheeks*⟩ [*chub* + ¹-*y*] – **chubbiness** *n*

¹**chuck** /chuk/ *n, chiefly archaic or dial* – used as a term of endearment [prob alter. of *chick*]

²**chuck** *vt* **1** to pat, tap **2** *informal* **2a** to toss, throw ⟨*~ed his books down on the table*⟩ **b** to discard – often + *out* or *away* **3** *informal* HAVE DONE WITH – often + *in* or *up* ⟨*~ed in her job*⟩ ⟨*~ed his girlfriend*⟩ *synonyms see* ¹THROW [perh fr MF *chuquer, choquer* to knock] – **chuck it (in)** *informal* to stop it; quit ⟨*he got so tired of working he decided to chuck it all in*⟩ – **chuck it down** *informal* to rain heavily ⟨*it's chucking it down*⟩
**chuck out** *vt, informal* to force (a person) to leave ⟨*got chucked out of her job*⟩ ⟨*chucked him out of the pub for being violent*⟩

³**chuck** *n* **1** a pat or nudge under the chin **2** *informal* a throw, toss **3** *informal* dismissal – + *the*

⁴**chuck** *n* **1** a cut of beef that includes most of the neck and the area about the shoulder blade **2** a device for holding a tool or workpiece (eg a piece of metal being turned on a lathe); *esp* one that grips with three or more jaws set symmetrically round an axis [E dial. *chuck* lump, log, prob var of *chock*]

⁵**chuck** *n, Can* a large body of water [Chinook Jargon, water, river, sea]

,**chucker-'out** *n, Br* BOUNCER 1 (person employed to throw out troublemakers)

**chuckhole** /'chuk,hohl/ *n, NAm* a pothole; *also* a rut in a road [²*chuck* + *hole*]

**chuckle** /chukl/ *vi* **1** to laugh inwardly or quietly **2** to make a continuous gentle sound resembling suppressed mirth ⟨*a bright clear stream ~d over the stony ground*⟩ [prob freq of ¹*chuck* (to cluck, chuckle), fr ME *chukken*, of imit origin] – **chuckle** *n*

**chucklehead** /'chukl,hed/ *n, informal* a slow-witted or stupid person; a blockhead [*chuckle* (lumpish)] – **chuckleheaded** *adj*

**chuck wagon** *n, NAm* a wagon carrying a stove and provisions for cooking (eg on a ranch) [E dial. *chuck* food, prob fr ⁴*chuck*]

**chuff** /chuf/ *vi or n* (to produce or move with) a puffing sound, like that of a steam engine ⟨*the ~ing and snorting of switch engines* – Paul Gallico⟩ [imit]

**chuffed** /chuft/ *adj, Br informal* pleased [E dial. *chuff* fat, swollen, proud, satisfied]

**chug** /chug/ *vi or n* **-gg-** (to produce or move with) a short muffled sound, esp one which is rapidly repeated, like that made by a labouring engine [imit]

**chukar** /chu'kah/ *n, pl* **chukars**, *esp collectively* **chukar** a largely grey and black Indian partridge (*Alectoris graeca chukar*) with red legs and bill [Hindi *cakor*]

**chukka** /'chukə/, **chukka boot** *n* a usu ankle-length leather boot with two pairs of eyelets or a buckle and strap [*chukka*, alter. of *chukker*; fr its resemblance to a polo player's boot]

**chukker, chukkar, chukka** /'chukə/ *n* any of the playing periods of a polo game, each lasting 7¹/₂ minutes [Hindi *cakkar* circular course, fr Skt *cakra* wheel, circle – more at WHEEL]

¹**chum** /chum/ *n, informal* a close friend; mate – no longer in vogue [perh by shortening & alter. fr *chamber fellow* (room-mate)]

²**chum** *vi* **-mm-** *informal* to share a room – no longer in vogue
**chum up** *vi, informal* to form a friendship – often + *with* ⟨*the two boys* chummed up *and went fishing*⟩ ⟨*chummed up with another boy and went fishing*⟩

**chummy** /'chumi/ *adj, informal* friendly, intimate – **chummily** *adv*, **chumminess** *n*

**chump** /chump/ *n*, **1** a cut of meat taken from between the loin and hind leg of a lamb, mutton, or pork carcass; *broadly* the thick end of a loin **2** *informal* a fool, duffer [perh blend of *chunk* and *lump*]

**chunder** /'chundə/ *vi or n, Br slang* (to) vomit [origin unknown]

**chunk** /chungk/ *n* **1** a short thick piece or lump (eg of wood or meat) **2** *NAm* ¹COB 3 (short stocky horse) **3** *informal* a large amount ⟨*put a sizable ~ of money on the race*⟩ [perh alter. of E dial. *chuck* lump, log]

**chunky** /'chungki/ *adj* **1** stocky **2** filled with chunks ⟨*~ mar-*

*malade*⟩ **3** made of thick bulky material, esp wool ⟨*a ~ sweater*⟩ – **chunkily** *adv*

**Chunnel** *n, informal* a proposed tunnel under the English channel linking England and France [blend of *channel* and *tunnel*]

**chunter** /'chuntə/ *vi, Br informal* **1** to talk or mutter incessantly and usu irrelevantly – often + *on* **2** to move or go while making a noise reminiscent of chuntering [prob imit]

¹**church** /chuhch/ *n* **1a** a building for public Christian worship; *esp* a place of worship used by an ESTABLISHED CHURCH – compare CHAPEL **b** a place of worship of any religion **2** *often cap* institutionalized religion; *esp* the established Christian religion of a country **3** *taking sing or pl vb* the clergy or officials of a religious body **4** *taking sing or pl vb* **a** a body or organization of religious believers: eg **4a** the whole body of Christians throughout the world **b** DENOMINATION 3 (group having a distinctive interpretation of a religious faith, and usu its own organization) ⟨*the Methodist ~*⟩ **c** a congregation **5** an occasion for public worship ⟨*goes to ~ every Sunday*⟩ **6** *the* clerical profession ⟨*considered the ~ as a possible career*⟩ [ME *chirche*, fr OE *cirice*; akin to OHG *kirihha* church; both fr a prehistoric WGmc word derived fr LGk *kyriakon*, fr Gk, neut of *kyriakos* of the lord, fr *kyrios* lord, master, fr *kyros* power]

²**church** *adj* **1** of a church ⟨*~ government*⟩ **2** *chiefly Br* being a member of the ESTABLISHED CHURCH – compare CHAPEL

**Church Army** *n* an Anglican organization for social work founded in 1882 on the model of the Salvation Army

**Church Commissioner** *n* a member of a body of trustees responsible for overseeing and administering the finances, investments and properties of the Church of England

**church father** *n* FATHER 4 (early Christian writer)

**churchgoer** /'chuhch,goh-ə/ *n* a person who attends church regularly – **churchgoing** *adj or n*

**churching** /'chuhching/ *n* a ceremony of thanksgiving in which a woman who has recently had a baby is received and blessed in church – **church** *vt*

**churchly** /'chuhchli/ *adj* **1** of a church **2** suitable to or suggestive of a church **3** adhering to a church **4** CHURCHY 2a – **churchliness** *n*

**churchman** /'chuhchmən/ *n* **1** a clergyman **2** *fem* **churchwoman** a member of a church

**churchmanship** /'chuhchmən,ship/ *n* the attitude, belief, or practice of a churchman; *esp* a HIGH CHURCH or LOW CHURCH attitude to Anglican doctrine

**church mode** *n* any of several MODES (fixed arrangement of eight notes) prevalent in medieval music

**Church of England** *n* the Protestant ESTABLISHED CHURCH in England, governed by bishops and with the sovereign as its temporal head

**Church of Scotland** *n* the ESTABLISHED CHURCH in Scotland, which is CALVINIST in doctrine and PRESBYTERIAN in structure, each congregation being governed by an elected body of lay elders

**church school** *n* **1** a usu primary school controlled in part by a church **2** *chiefly NAm* an organization for moral and religious education supervised by a local church

**Church Slavic** *n* OLD CHURCH SLAVONIC (language used in Orthodox church services)

**churchwarden** /,chuhch'wawdən/ *n* **1** either of two lay parish officers in Anglican churches who are responsible for administering church property and money **2** a long-stemmed usu clay tobacco pipe

**churchy** /'chuhchi/ *adj* **1** of or suggesting a church **2a** marked by strict conformity or zealous adherence to the forms or beliefs of a church; *esp* obtrusively pious **b** involved in church affairs without necessarily having a personal spiritual commitment

**churchyard** /-,yahd/ *n* an enclosed piece of ground surrounding a church; *esp* one used as a burial ground

**churinga** /chə'ring-gə/ *n* a sacred stone amulet worn by Australian aborigines [native name in Australia]

**churl** /chuhl/ *n* **1** CEORL (Anglo-Saxon freeman of the lowest class); *broadly, archaic* someone of low birth **2a** a rude ill-bred person **b** a miserly person **3** *archaic* a countryman, rustic ⟨*the surly village ~s* – Tennyson⟩ [ME, fr OE *ceorl* man, ceorl; akin to Gk *gēras* old age – more at CORN]

**churlish** /'chuhlish/ *adj* **1** of, resembling, or befitting a churl; *esp* lacking refinement or sensitivity **2** rudely uncooperative; surly – **churlishly** *adv*, **churlishness** *n*

¹**churn** /chuhn/ *n* **1** a vessel used in the making of butter in

which milk or cream is agitated to separate the oily globules from the watery medium **2** *Br* a tall cylindrical metal container in which large quantities of milk are stored or carried (eg from the farm to the bottling plant) [ME *chyrne*, fr OE *cyrin;* akin to OE *corn* grain – more at CORN; fr the granular appearance of cream as it is churned]

²**churn** *vt* **1** to agitate (milk or cream) in a churn in order to make butter **2a** to stir or agitate violently (*motor boats* ~ing *the water of the bay*) (*the lorry's wheels* ~ed *up the path*) **b** to make (eg foam) by so doing ~ *vi* **1** to work a churn **2** to produce or be in violent motion (*my stomach started to* ~ *as soon as we left port*)

**churn out** *vt, chiefly informal* to produce prolifically and mechanically, usu without great concern for quality

**churr** /chuh/ *vi or n* (to make) the vibrant or whirring noise characteristic of certain insects and birds (eg the partridge); chirr [imit]

**churrigueresque** /ˌchooəriɡəˈresk/ *adj, often cap* of or being a Spanish baroque architectural style characterized by elaborate surface decoration [Sp *churrigueresco,* fr José *Churriguera* †1723 Sp architect]

**chute** /shooht/ *n* **1** a waterfall, rapid, etc **2a** an inclined plane, sloping channel, or passage down or through which things may pass (*a rubbish* ~) **b** a slide into a swimming pool **3** *informal* a parachute [Fr, fr OF, fr *cheoir* to fall, fr L *cadere* – more at CHANCE]

**chutist** /ˈshoohtist/ *n* a parachutist

**chutney** /ˈchutni/ *n* a thick saucelike condiment or relish of Indian origin that contains fruits, sugar, vinegar, and spices [Hindi *catṇī*]

**chutzpah, chutzpa** /ˈkhootspah, ˈhootspah/ *n, informal* brazen audacity, esp when springing from complete self-confidence; nerve [Yiddish, fr LHeb *ḥuṣpāh*]

**chyack** /ˈchieˌak/ *vt, Austr* CHIACK (tease) – **chyack** *n*

**chyle** /kiel/ *n* LYMPH that is milky from droplets of emulsified fat and is present in the LACTEALS esp during digestion and absorption of fats [LL *chylus,* fr Gk *chylos* juice, chyle, fr *chein* to pour – more at FOUND] – **chylous** *adj*

**chylomicron** /ˌkielohˈmiekron/ *n* any of the microscopic droplets of fat occurring in the blood during fat digestion and its incorporation into the tissues [Gk *chylos* + *mikron,* neut of *mikros* small]

**chyme** /kiem/ *n* the soft semifluid mass of partly digested food expelled by the stomach into the first part of the SMALL INTESTINE [NL *chymus,* fr LL, chyle, fr Gk *chymos* juice, fr *chein*] – **chymous** *adj*

**chymotrypsin** /ˌkiemohˈtripsin/ *n* an ENZYME that breaks down proteins and is released into the intestines from the pancreas during digestion [*chyme* + *-o-* + *trypsin*]

**chymotrypsinogen** /ˌkiemohtripˈsinəjən/ *n* an inactive protein that is converted by the enzyme TRYPSIN to its active form chymotrypsin

**ciao** /chow/ *interj* – used to express greeting or farewell [It, fr It dial., alter. of *schiavo* (I am your) slave, fr ML *sclavus*]

**ciborium** /siˈbawriəm/ *n, pl* **ciboria** /-riə/ **1** a goblet-shaped lidded vessel for holding consecrated waters used at communion **2** a freestanding vaulted canopy supported by four columns over a HIGH ALTAR (principal altar in a church) [ML, fr L, cup, fr Gk *kibōrion*]

**cicada** /siˈkahdə, -ˈkaydə/ *n* any of a family (Cicadidae) of insects with a stout body, wide blunt head, and large transparent wings, the males of which produce a shrill singing noise by means of a pair of drumlike organs at the base of the abdomen [NL, genus name, fr L, cicada]

**cicala** /siˈkahlə/ *n* a cicada [It, fr ML, alter. of L *cicada*]

**cicatrice** /ˈsikətrees/ *n* a cicatrix – **cicatricial** *adj*

**cicatricle** /ˈsikəˌtrikl/ *n* **1** CICATRIX **2a 2** BLASTODISC (part of an egg that forms the embryo) [L *cicatricula,* dim. of *cicatric-, cicatrix*]

**cicatrix** /ˈsikəˌtriks/ *n, pl* **cicatrices** /ˌsikəˈtrieseez, siˈkaytriˌseez/ **1** a scar resulting from the healing of a flesh wound **2** a mark resembling a scar, esp when caused by the previous attachment of a part or organ: eg **2a** a mark left on a stem after the fall of a leaf or BRACT **b** HILUM **1a** (scar on seed marking its point of attachment to the stalk) [L *cicatric-, cicatrix*]

**cicatr·ize, -ise** /ˈsikəˌtriez/ *vt* to scar ~ *vi* to heal by forming a scar – **cicatrization** *n*

**cicerone** /ˌsisəˈrohni, ˌchichə-/ *n, pl* **ciceroni** /~/ a person who acts as a guide to antiquities; *broadly* a guide, mentor

⚠ **chaperon** [It, fr *Cicerone* Cicero †43 BC Roman orator & statesman]

**cichlid** /ˈsiklid/ *n* any of a family (Cichlidae) of mostly tropical spiny-finned freshwater fishes including several kinds kept in tropical aquariums [deriv of Gk *kichlē* thrush, a kind of wrasse; akin to Gk *chelidōn* swallow] – **cichlid** *adj*

**cicisbeo** /ˌchichizˈbayoh/ *n, pl* **cicisbei** /-ˈbayˌee/ an escort or lover, esp of a married Italian woman [It]

**-cide** /-sied/ *comb form* (→ *n*) **1** killer (*insecti*cide) **2** killing (*sui*cide) [MF, fr L *-cida* (1) & *-cidium* (2), fr *caedere* to cut, kill – more at CONCISE] – **-cidal** *comb form* (→ *adj*)

**cider** /ˈsiedə/ *n* **1** *Br* fermented, often sparkling, apple juice **2** *NAm* unfermented apple juice [ME *sidre,* fr OF, fr LL *sicera* strong drink, fr Gk *sikera,* fr Heb *shēkhār*]

**ci-devant** /ˌsee dəˈvonh (*Fr* si dəvã)/ *adj* former [Fr] – **ci-devant** *adv*

**cig** /sig/ *n, informal* a cigarette

**cigala** /siˈgahlə/ *n* CICADA (insect) [Prov, fr ML *cicala,* alter. of L *cicada*]

**cigar** /siˈgah/ *n* a small roll of tobacco leaf for smoking [Sp *cigarro*]

**cigarette,** *NAm also* **cigaret** /ˌsigəˈret/ *n* a narrow cylinder of cut tobacco enclosed in thin paper for smoking; *also* a similar roll of a herbal or narcotic substance [Fr *cigarette,* dim. of *cigare* cigar, fr Sp *cigarro*]

**cigarillo** /ˌsigəˈriloh, -ˈreelyoh/ *n, pl* **cigarillos** a very small cigar open at both ends [Sp *cigarrillo* cigarette, dim. of *cigarro*]

**ciggie** /ˈsigi/ *n, informal* a cigarette [by shortening & alter.]

**ciliary** /ˈsilyəri/ *adj* **1** of cilia **2** of or being the CILIARY BODY

**ciliary body** *n* the ringlike muscular body supporting the lens of the eye

¹**ciliate** /ˈsiliət, -ˌayt/, **ciliated** /-ˌaytid/ *adj* having cilia (~ *protozoa*) (~d *epithelium*) – **ciliately** *adv*

²**ciliate** /ˈsiliət, -ayt/ *n* any of a subphylum (Ciliophora) of ciliate PROTOZOANS (tiny single-celled organisms)

**cilice** /ˈsilis/ *n* **1** haircloth **2** a garment made from haircloth esp as worn, esp formerly, by some religious orders [Fr, fr L *cilicium,* fr *Cilicius* of Cilicia, fr *Cilicia,* ancient region in Asia Minor]

**cilium** /ˈsiliˌəm/ *n, pl* **cilia** /ˈsiliə/ **1** an eyelash **2** a minute hairlike part; *esp* one that projects, usu together with many others, from a cell and that is capable of a lashing or vibratory movement that produces locomotion (eg in a single-celled organism) or a current of liquid over a surface (eg in the nose) [NL, fr L, eyelid]

**cimex** /ˈsiemeks/ *n, pl* **cimices** /ˈsimiˌseez/ a bedbug [L *cimic-, cimex*]

**Cimmerian** /siˈmiəriən/ *adj, poetic* gloomy, dark (*there under ebon shades . . . in dark* ~ *desert ever dwell* – John Milton) [the *Cimmerians* (fr L *Cimmerii,* fr Gk *Kimmerioi*), a mythical race living in a misty gloomy land]

¹**cinch** /sinch/ *n* **1** *NAm* a strong girth for a pack or saddle **2** *NAm* a tight grip **3** *informal* **3a** a task performed with ease **b** something certain [Sp *cincha,* fr L *cingula* girdle, girth, fr *cingere*]

²**cinch** *vt* **1** *NAm* to put a cinch on (a horse) **2** *NAm informal* to make certain; assure **3** *NAm informal* to take a tight grip of ~ *vi, NAm* to perform the act of cinching; tighten the cinch – often + *up*

**cinchona** /sinɡˈkohnə/ *n* **1** any of a genus (*Cinchona*) of S American trees and shrubs of the madder family **2** the dried bark of a cinchona (eg *Cinchona ledgeriana*) containing chemical compounds, esp quinine, that have a pharmacological effect [NL, genus name, fr the countess of *Chinchón* †1641 vicereine of Peru]

**cinchonine** /ˈsingkəneen/ *n* a bitter white chemical compound, $C_{19}H_{22}N_2O$, found esp in cinchona bark and used in medicine like quinine, esp in the treatment of malaria

**cincture** /ˈsingkchə/ *n* a girdle, belt; *esp* a cord or sash of cloth worn round an ecclesiastical vestment or the habit of a member of a religious order [L *cinctura* girdle, fr *cinctus,* pp of *cingere* to gird; akin to Skt *kāñcī* girdle]

**cinder** /ˈsində/ *n* **1** (a piece of) solid waste matter from the smelting of metal ores; slag **2** a fragment of ash **3** a piece of partly burned material (eg coal) that will burn further but will not flame **4** a fragment of solidified lava from an erupting volcano [ME *sinder,* fr OE; akin to OHG *sintar* dross, slag, OSlav *sędra* stalactite] – **cinder** *vt,* **cindery** *adj*

**Cinderella** /ˌsindəˈrelə/ *n or adj* **1** (someone or something) suffering undeserved neglect **2** (someone or something) suddenly raised from obscurity to honour or importance [*Cin-*

*derella*, heroine of a fairy-tale who is mistreated by her step-mother but, with the help of her fairy godmother, marries a prince]

**cine-** /sini-/ *comb form* relating to the cinema ⟨cine*camera*⟩ ⟨cine*film*⟩ [*cinema*]

**cineangiography** /ˌsiniˌanjiˈogrəfi/ *n* motion-picture photography of an X-ray image recording the passage of blood through the blood vessels [*cine-* + *angi-* + *-graphy*] – **cineangiographic** *adj*

**cineaste, cinéaste, cineast** /ˈsiniast/ *n* a devotee of films [Fr *cinéaste*, fr *ciné* (short for *cinéma*) + *-aste* (as in *enthousiaste* enthusiast)]

**cinecamera** /ˈsiniˌkamrə/ *n* a simple hand-held camera for making usu amateur films

**cinema** /ˈsinimə/ *n* **1a** films considered esp as an art form, entertainment, or industry **b** the art or technique of making films; *also* the effects appropriate to film ⟨*made good* ~⟩ **2** *chiefly Br* a theatre where films are shown – usu + *the* [short for *cinematograph*]

synonyms British people go to *the* cinema or *the* pictures to see a picture or film. Americans go to *the* movies, or more formally to *the* motion pictures or moving pictures, to see a movie. Devotees of the art form call it cinema or, in a newer usage, film ⟨*a student of film*⟩. *The* flicks is an informal expression, no longer in vogue except in the combination skin flick for a sexy film. A biographical film is a biopic. *The* talkies dates from the early 30s, when sound was a novelty.

**cinemagoer** /ˈsiniməˌgohˈə/ *n* one who frequently attends films – **cinemagoing** *n or adj*

**Cinemascope** /ˈsiniməˌskohp/ *trademark* – used for a method of film projection employing a cylindrical lens, an extra-wide screen, and usu stereophonic sound – compare CINERAMA

**cinematheque** /ˌsiniməˈtek/ *n* a small cinema specializing in avant-garde or classic films [Fr *cinémathèque* film library, fr *cinéma* cinema + *-thèque* (as in *bibliothèque* library)]

**cinematic** /ˌsiniˈmatik/ *adj* **1** made and presented as a film ⟨~ *fantasies*⟩ **2** of or suitable for films or the making of films ⟨~ *principles and techniques*⟩ – **cinematically** *adv*

**cinematograph** /ˌsiniˈmatəˌgrahf, -ˌgraf/ *n*, *chiefly Br* **1** a film camera or projector [Fr *cinématographe*, fr Gk *kinēmat-*, *kinēma* movement (fr *kinein* to move) + *-o-* + *-graphe* -graph]

**cinematography** /ˌsiniməˈtogrəfi/ *n* the art or science of cinema photography – **cinematographer** *n*, **cinematographic** *also* **cinematographical** *adj*, **cinematographically** *adv*

**cinema verité** /ˈveritay/ *n* the art or technique of film-making so as to convey documentary-style realism [Fr *cinéma-vérité*, lit., truth cinema]

**cineole** /ˈsiniohl/ *n* a liquid, $C_{10}H_{18}O$, with a camphor smell, contained in many ESSENTIAL OILS (e g that of eucalyptus) and used in inhalants and toothpastes and as an expectorant for animals [ISV, by transposition fr NL *oleum cinae* wormseed oil]

**Cinerama** /ˌsinəˈrahmə/ *trademark* – used for a method of film projection employing three projectors, an extra-wide concave screen, and stereophonic sound – compare CINEMASCOPE

**cineraria** /ˌsinəˈreəri·ə/ *n* any of several pot plants of the daisy family that are derived from a plant (*Senecio cruentus*) native to the Canary islands and have heart-shaped leaves and clusters of bright flower heads [NL, fr L, fem of *cinerarius* of ashes, fr *ciner-*, *cinis*; fr the ash-coloured down on the leaves]

**cinerarium** /ˌsinəˈreəri·əm/ *n*, *pl* **cineraria** /-riə/ a place in which the ashes of the dead are kept after cremation [L, fr *ciner-*, *cinis*] – **cinerary** *adj*

**cinereous** /siˈniəriəs/ *adj* **1** *esp of a bird or its plumage* grey tinged with black **2** resembling or consisting of ashes [L *cinereus*, fr *ciner-*, *cinis* ashes]

**cinerin** /ˈsinərin/ *n* either of two chemical compounds, $C_{20}H_{28}O_3$ or $C_{21}H_{28}O_5$, used as insecticides [L *ciner-*, *cinis* ashes]

**Cingalese** /ˌsing·gəˈleez/ *n*, *pl* **Cingalese** SINHALESE (native or language of Sri Lanka)

**cingulum** /ˈsing-gyooləm/ *n*, *pl* **cingula** /-lə/ a differentiated band or girdle (e g of colour) on an animal [NL, fr L, girdle, fr *cingere* to gird – more at CINCTURE] – **cingulate** *adj*

**cinnabar** /ˈsinəbah/ *n* **1** naturally occurring red mercuric sulphide, HgS, that is the only important source of mercury **2a** artificial red mercuric sulphide used esp as a pigment **b** bright red; vermilion **3** cinnabar, **cinnabar moth** a European moth (*Callimorpha jacobaeae*) with greyish-black fore wings marked

with red, and clear reddish-pink hind wings [ME *cynabare*, fr MF & L; MF *cenobre*, fr L *cinnabaris*, fr Gk *kinnabari*, of non-IE origin; akin to Ar *zinjafr* cinnabar]

**cinnamic** /səˈnamik/ *adj* of or obtained from cinnamon [Fr *cinnamique*, fr *cinname* cinnamon, fr L *cinnamon*]

**cinnamic acid** /səˈnamik/ *n* an odourless acid, $C_6H_5CH=CHCOOH$, found esp in cinnamon oil and STORAX (resinous substance obtained from an oriental tree) and used in making perfumes

**cinnamon** /ˈsinəmən/ *n* **1** the highly aromatic bark of any of several trees (genus *Cinnamomum*) of the laurel family used as a spice; *also* a tree that yields cinnamon **2** a light yellowish-brown [ME *cynamone*, fr L *cinnamomum*, *cinnamon*, fr Gk *kinnamōmon*, *kinnamon*, of non-IE origin; akin to Heb *qinnāmōn* cinnamon]

**cinnamon stone** *n* HESSONITE (brownish garnet)

**cinquecento** /ˌchingkwiˈchentoh/ *n* the 16th century in Italy, esp with reference to its literature and art [It, lit., five hundred, fr *cinque* five (fr L *quinque*) + *cento* hundred, fr L *centum* – more at HUNDRED] – **cinquecentist** *n*

**cinquefoil** /ˈsingkˌfoyl/ *n* **1** any of a genus (*Potentilla*) of plants (e g tormentil) of the rose family with 5-lobed leaves **2** a design enclosed by five joined arcs arranged in a circle [ME *sink foil*, fr MF *cincfoille*, fr L *quinquefolium*, fr *quinque* five + *folium* leaf – more at BLADE]

**Cinque Port** /singk/ *n* any of originally five and now seven towns on the SE coast of England that were granted special privileges in medieval times because of their importance in naval defence [back-formation fr *Cinque Ports*, pl, fr ME *sink pors*, fr OF *cinq ports* five ports, fr L *quinque portus*]

**cion** /ˈsie·ən/ *n*, *NAm* SCION

**¹cipher, *Br also* cypher** /ˈsiefə/ *n* **1a** ZERO **1a** (arithmetical symbol 0) **b** someone or something that has no weight, worth, or influence; a nonentity **2a** a method of transforming a text in order to conceal its meaning – compare CODE **3b b** a message in code **c** the key to a message in code **3** any of the ARABIC NUMERALS (0 to 9) **4** a design consisting of interwoven letters, esp the initials of a person, company, etc; a monogram **5** the continuous sounding of a note on an organ, owing to a mechanical defect *synonyms* see ¹ZERO [ME, fr MF *cifre*, fr ML *cifra*, fr Ar *sifr* empty, cipher, zero]

**²cipher, *Br also* cypher** *vi*, *archaic* to do arithmetic ~ *vt* **1** ENCIPHER (put into secret writing) **2** *archaic* to work out by arithmetic

**ciphertext** /ˈsiefəˌtekst/ *n* the version of a text that is in secret writing – compare PLAINTEXT

**ciphony** /ˈsiefəni/ *n* the electronic scrambling of voice transmissions [*cipher* + tele*phony*]

**circa** /ˈsuhkə/ *prep* at, in, or of approximately – used esp with dates expressed in years ⟨*born* ~ *1600*⟩ [L, fr *circum* around – more at CIRCUM-]

**circadian** /suhˈkaydi·ən/ *adj* being, having, characterized by, or occurring in approximately day-long periods or cycles ⟨~ *rhythms in hatching*⟩ ⟨~ *leaf movements*⟩ [L *circa* about + *dies* day + E *-an* – more at DEITY]

**Circassian** /suhˈkasi·ən/ *n* **1** a member of a group of peoples of the Caucasus who are white and not of Indo-European speech **2** the language of the Circassians [*Circassia*, region in Russia] – **Circassian** *adj*

**circinate** /ˈsuhsiˌnayt/ *adj* coiled; *esp* rolled in the form of a flat coil with the tip as a centre ⟨~ *fern fronds unfolding*⟩ [L *circinatus*, pp of *circinare* to round, fr *circinus* pair of compasses, fr *circus*] – **circinately** *adv*

**¹circle** /ˈsuhkl/ *n* **1a** a closed plane curve every point of which is equidistant from a fixed point within the curve **b** the plane surface bounded by such a curve **c** DISC **4a 2** the orbit or period of revolution of a planet, moon, etc **3** something in the form of a circle or arc of a circle: e g **3a** a part of an astronomical instrument (e g a telescope) used for setting direction **b** a balcony or tier of seats in a theatre **c** a circle formed on the surface of a sphere by the intersection of a plane ⟨~ *of latitude*⟩ **d** circle, **striking circle** the semicircular area in front of each goal within which an attacking player must be before he/she can score a goal in hockey **e** a ring of standing stones (e g Stonehenge) of the Neolithic or Bronze age **f** *NAm* a traffic roundabout **4** an area of action or influence; a realm **5a** a cycle ⟨*the year has come full* ~⟩ **b** an instance of circular reasoning ⟨*argue in a* ~⟩ **6** *taking sing or pl vb* a group of people sharing a common interest or activity ⟨*the gossip of* *court* ~s⟩ **7** a territorial or administrative division or district **8** something that binds, encloses, or surrounds ⟨*the* ~ *of hills dominating the town*⟩ – compare VICIOUS CIRCLE [ME *cercle*, fr OF, fr L *circulus*, dim. of *circus* ring, circus, fr or akin to Gk *krikos, kirkos* ring] – **go/run round in circles** to be frantically active without making any progress

²**circle** *vt* **1** to enclose (as if) in a circle **2** to move or revolve round ~ *vi* to move (as if) in a circle – **circler** *n*

**circlet** /'suhklit/ *n* a little circle; *esp* a circular ornament worn in the hair

**Circlip** /'suh,klip/ *trademark* – used for a clip that encircles a tubular fitting and is held in place by its natural springiness

**circs** /suhks/ *n pl, chiefly Br informal* circumstances [by shortening]

¹**circuit** /'suhkit/ *n* **1** a closed loop encompassing an area; *also* the space so enclosed **2a(1)** a course round a periphery **a(2)** a racetrack **b** a circuitous or indirect route **3a** a regular tour (e g by a travelling judge or preacher) round an assigned district or territory **b** the route travelled **c** a group of church congregations with one pastor (eg in the Methodist church) **4a** the complete path of an electric current, usu including the source of energy **b** an array of electrical components connected so as to allow the passage of current **c** a two-way communication path between points (e g in a computer) **5a** an association of similar groups, esp in sport; a league **b** a chain of theatres at which productions are presented successively [ME, fr MF *circuite*, fr L *circuitus*, fr pp of *circumire, circuire* to go round, fr *circum-* + *ire* to go – more at ISSUE] – **circuital** *adj*

²**circuit** *vt* **1** to make a circuit round **2** to provide with an electrical circuit ~ *vi* to make a circuit

**circuit breaker** *n* a switch that automatically interrupts an electric circuit under an infrequent abnormal condition

**circuitous** /suh'kyooh·itəs/ *adj* indirect in route or method; roundabout – **circuitously** *adv*, **circuitousness** *n*, **circuity** *n*

**circuitry** /'suhkitri/ *n* **1** a system of electrical circuits **2** the components of an electric circuit

**circuit training** *n* a system of athletic training in which several different exercises are performed in sequence

¹**circular** /'suhkyoolə/ *adj* **1** having the form of a circle; round **2** moving in or describing a circle or spiral **3** circuitous, indirect **4** having the fallacy of assuming something which is to be demonstrated ⟨~ *arguments*⟩ **5** marked by or moving in a cycle **6** intended for circulation [ME *circuler*, fr MF, fr LL *circularis*, fr L *circulus* circle] – **circularity** *n*, **circularly** *adv*

²**circular** *n* **1** a paper (e g a leaflet) intended for wide distribution **2** *cap, Br* RING ROAD – in names ⟨*the North* Circular⟩

**circular function** *n, maths* TRIGONOMETRIC FUNCTION (e g sine, cosine, or tangent)

**circular-ize, -ise** /'suhkyoolə,riez/ *vt* **1** to send circulars to **2** to publicize, esp by means of circulars – **circularization** *n*

**circular letter** *n* a letter of which many copies are made for distribution to a number of people

**circular measure** *n* the measurement of angles in RADIANS (one radian equals about 57°)

**circular saw** *n* a saw that has its teeth set on the edge of a steel disc which revolves on a spindle

**circulate** /'suhkyoo,layt/ *vi* **1** to move in a circle, circuit, or orbit; *esp* to follow a course that returns to the starting point ⟨*blood* ~s *through the body*⟩ **2** to pass from person to person or place to place: e g **2a** to flow without obstruction **b** to become well known or widespread ⟨*rumours* ~d *through the town*⟩ **c** to go from group to group at a social gathering **d** to come into the hands of readers; *specif* to become sold or distributed ~ *vt* to cause to circulate [L *circulatus*, pp of *circulare*, fr *circulus* circle] – **circulative** *adj*, **circulator** *n*, **circulatory** *adj*

**circulating capital** /'suhkyoolayting/ *n* WORKING CAPITAL

**circulating decimal** *n* RECURRING DECIMAL

**circulation** /,suhkyoo'laysh(ə)n/ *n* **1** flow **2** ordefly movement through a circuit; *esp* the movement of blood through the vessels of the body induced by the pumping action of the heart **3a** passage or transmission from person to person or place to place; *esp* the interchange of currency ⟨*coins in* ~⟩ **b** the extent of dissemination: e g **b(1)** the average number of copies of a publication sold over a given period **b(2)** the total number of items taken by borrowers from a library – **out of circulation** not participating in social life

**circulatory system** /'suhkyoolətri, ,suhkyoo'layt(ə)ri/ *n* the system of blood, blood vessels, lymph vessels, and heart concerned with the circulation of the blood and lymph

**circum-** /suhkəm-/ *prefix* round; about ⟨circum*navigate*⟩ [OF or L; OF, fr L, fr *circum*, fr *circus* circle – more at CIRCLE]

**circumambient** /,suhkəm'ambiənt/ *adj, formal* on all sides; encompassing [LL *circumambient-, circumambiens*, prp of *circumambire* to surround in a circle, fr L *circum-* + *ambire* to go round – more at AMBIENT] – **circumambience** *n*, **circumambiently** *adv*

**circumambulate** /-'ambyoolayt/ *vt, formal* to walk round, esp in a ritual fashion [LL *circumambulatus*, pp of *circumambulare*, fr L *circum-* + *ambulare* to walk]

**circumbendibus** /,suhkəm'bendibəs/ *n, humorous* a circumlocution [L *circum* + E *bend* + L *-ibus*, abl pl ending]

**circumcise** /'suhkəm,siez/ *vt* to cut off the foreskin of (a male) or the clitoris of (a female) [ME *circumcisen*, fr L *circumcisus*, pp of *circumcidere*, fr *circum-* + *caedere* to cut – more at CONCISE] – **circumciser** *n*

**circumcision** /-'sizh(ə)n/ *n* **1a** the act of circumcising, esp as a Jewish or Muslim rite or sanitary surgical measure **b** the condition of being circumcised **2** *cap* January 1 observed as a church festival in commemoration of the circumcision of Jesus

**circumference** /suh'kumfərəns/ *n* **1** (the length of) the perimeter of a circle **2** the external boundary or surface of a figure or object; the periphery [ME, fr MF, fr L *circumferentia*, fr *circumferre* to carry round, fr *circum-* + *ferre* to carry – more at BEAR] – **circumferential** *adj*

¹**circumflex** /'suhkəm,fleks/ *adj* **1a** characterized by the pitch, quantity, or quality indicated by a circumflex **b** being or marked with a circumflex **2** bending round ⟨*a* ~ *artery*⟩ [L *circumflexus*, pp of *circumflectere* to bend round, fr *circum-* + *flectere* to bend]

²**circumflex** *n* a diacritical mark ˆ, ˋ, or ˜, originally used in Greek over long vowels to indicate a rising-falling tone, and in other languages to mark length, contraction, or a particular vowel quality

**circumfluent** /sə'cumflooənt/ *also* **circumfluous** /-flooəs/ *adj, formal* flowing round or surrounding in the manner of a fluid [*circumfluent* fr L *circumfluent-, circumfluens*, prp of *circumfluere* to flow round, fr *circum-* + *fluere* to flow; *circumfluous* fr L *circumfluus*, fr *circum-* + *fluere*]

**circumfuse** /,suhkəm'fyoohz/ *vt, formal* to surround, envelop [L *circumfusus*, pp of *circumfundere* to pour round, fr *circum-* + *fundere* to pour – more at FOUND] – **circumfusion** *n*

**circumjacent** /,suhkəm'jays(ə)nt/ *adj, formal* lying adjacent on all sides; surrounding [L *circumjacent-, circumjacens*, prp of *circumjacēre* to lie round, fr *circum-* + *jacēre* to lie – more at ADJACENT]

**circumlocution** /-lə'kyoohsh(ə)n/ *n* **1** the use of an unnecessarily large number of words to express an idea **2** evasive speech [L *circumlocution-, circumlocutio*, fr *circum-* + *locutio* speech, fr *locutus*, pp of *loqui* to speak] – **circumlocutory** *adj*

**circumlunar** /-'loohnə/ *adj* revolving about or surrounding the moon

**circumnavigate** /-'navigayt/ *vt* to go completely round (e g the world), esp by water; *also* to go round instead of through; bypass ⟨~ *a congested area*⟩ [L *circumnavigatus*, pp of *circumnavigare* to sail round, fr *circum-* + *navigare* to navigate] – **circumnavigator** *n*, **circumnavigation** *n*

**circumnutation** /,suhkəmnyoo'taysh(ə)n/ *n* the movement of the growing portions of a climbing plant in usu irregular spirals – **circumnutate** *vi*

**circumpolar** /-'pohlə/ *adj* **1** continually visible above the horizon ⟨*a* ~ *star*⟩ **2** surrounding or found in the vicinity of one of the earth's poles

**circumscribe** /-,skrieb/ *vt* **1** to surround by a physical or imaginary line; bound **2** to restrict the range or activity of definitely and clearly **3** to draw or be drawn round in such a way that contact is made at as many points as possible ⟨*a polygon* circumscribing *a circle*⟩ [L *circumscribere*, fr *circum-* + *scribere* to write, draw – more at SCRIBE]

**circumscription** /-'skripsh(ə)n/ *n* **1** something that circumscribes: e g **1a** a limit, boundary **b** a restriction **2** the act of circumscribing: e g **2a** the act of setting a limit or boundary **b** the act of imposing a restriction [L *circumscription-, circumscriptio*, fr *circumscriptus*, pp of *circumscribere*]

**circumsolar** /,suhkəm'sohlə/ *adj* revolving about or found in the vicinity of the sun

**circumspect** /-,spekt/ *adj* careful to consider all circumstances and possible consequences; prudent *synonyms* see CAUTIOUS *antonym* audacious [ME, fr MF or L; MF *circonspect*, fr L *circumspectus*, fr pp of *circumspicere* to look round, be cautious, fr *circum-* + *specere* to look – more at SPY] – **circumspectly** *adv,* **circumspection** *n*

**circumstance** /'suhkəm,stahns, -stans, -stəns/ *n* **1a** a condition or event that accompanies, causes, or determines another; *also* the sum of such conditions or events ⟨*constant and rapid change in economic* ~ *– G M Trevelyan*⟩ **b** a detail **2a** **circumstance, circumstances** *pl* a state of affairs; an occurrence ⟨*open rebellion was a rare* ~⟩ ⟨*a victim of* ~ s⟩ **b** *pl* situation with regard to material or financial welfare ⟨*he was in easy* ~ s⟩ **3** attendant formalities and ceremony ⟨*pride, pomp, and* ~ *of glorious war* – Shak⟩ **4** an incident viewed as part of a narrative or course of events; a fact [ME, fr MF, fr L *circumstantia,* fr *circumstant-, circumstans,* prp of *circumstare* to stand around, fr *circum-* + *stare* to stand – more at STAND] – **in/under the circumstances** because of the conditions; considering the situation – **in/under no circumstances** on no account; never

usage **1** Some writers on usage have maintained that one should use *in,* rather than *under,* the **circumstances,** because **circumstance** is derived from the Latin *circum* = "around", and one is *in* whatever surrounds one; but the phrase **under the circumstances** has been established in English since the 17th century and is perfectly legitimate. **2** The pronunciations /'suhkəm,stahns, -stans/ are disliked by some people, who prefer /'suhkəmstəns/. **synonyms** see OCCURRENCE

**circumstanced** /'suhkəmstahnst, -stanst, -stənst/ *adj* placed in specified circumstances, esp in regard to property or income
**circumstantial** /,suhkəm'stansh(ə)l, -'stahnsh(ə)l/ *adj* **1** belonging to, consisting in, or dependent on circumstances **2** pertinent but not essential; incidental **3** abounding in factual details – **circumstantially** *adv,* **circumstantiality** *n*
**circumstantial evidence** *n* evidence that tends to prove a fact indirectly by proving other events or circumstances which afford a basis for a reasonable inference of the occurrence of the fact at issue ⟨*the presence of a suspect's fingerprints is* ~⟩
**circumstantiate** /,suhkəm'stanshi,ayt/ *vt* to supply with circumstantial evidence or support
**circumstellar** /,suhkəm'stelə/ *adj* surrounding or occurring in the vicinity of a star
**¹circumvallate** /,suhkəm'valayt/ *adj* surrounded (as if) by a rampart; *esp* enclosed by a ridge of tissue ⟨~ *papilla*⟩
**²circumvallate** *vt* to surround (as if) by a rampart [L *circumvallatus,* pp of *circumvallare,* fr *circum-* + *vallum* rampart – more at WALL] – **circumvallation** *n*
**circumvent** /-'vent/ *vt* **1** to check or evade, esp by ingenuity or stratagem **2** *formal* to make a detour round **3** *archaic* to trap by surrounding; hem in [L *circumventus,* pp of *circumvenire,* fr *circum-* + *venire* to come – more at COME] – **circumvention** *n*
**circumvolution** /,suhkəmvə'loohsh(ə)n, -'lyooh-/ *n, formal* an act or instance of turning round an axis [ME *circumvolucioun,* fr ML *circumvolution-, circumvolutio,* fr L *circumvolutus,* pp of *circumvolvere* to revolve, fr *circum-* + *volvere* to roll – more at VOLUBLE]
**circus** /'suhkəs/ *n* **1** a large arena partly or completely enclosed by tiers of seats and used esp for sports or spectacles (e g athletic contests, exhibitions of horsemanship, or, in ancient times, chariot racing) **2a** an entertainment in which a variety of performers (e g acrobats, jugglers, and clowns) and performing animals are involved in a series of unrelated acts; *also* the usu covered arena where a circus takes place **b** the physical plant, livestock, and personnel of such a circus **c** *informal* an activity suggestive of a circus (e g in being a busy scene of noisy or frivolous action) **3** *cap, Br* a road junction in a town partly surrounded by a circle of buildings – in proper names ⟨*Oxford* Circus⟩ ⟨*Piccadilly* Circus⟩ [L, circle, circus – more at CIRCLE] – **circusy** *adj*
**ciré** /'siray (*Fr* sire)/ *n or adj* (a fabric) having a highly glazed finish usu achieved by waxing and heating [Fr, fr pp of *cirer* to wax, fr *cire* wax, fr L *cera*]
**cire perdue** /,siə peə'dooh (*Fr* siːr pɛrdy)/ *n* a process used in the casting of metal, esp bronze, in which a clay impression of an object (e g a statue) is formed round an original wax model which is then melted away leaving a mould into which molten metal can be poured through a vent – called also LOST-WAX PROCESS [Fr (*moulage à*) *cire perdue,* lit., lost wax casting]
**cirl bunting** /suhl/ *n* a small European BUNTING (type of bird) (*Emberiza cirlus*) brightly marked in yellow, olive, and black [NL *cirlus,* specific epithet, fr It *cirlo,* of imit origin]
**cirque** /suhk/ *n* **1** a deep steep-walled basin on a mountain, shaped like a bowl **2** *poetic* a circle, circlet [Fr, fr L *circus*]

**cirr-, cirri-, cirro-** *comb form* cirrus ⟨cirriped⟩ ⟨cirrose⟩ ⟨cirrostratus⟩ [NL *cirrus*]
**cirrhosis** /si'rohsis/ *n, pl* **cirrhoses** /-seez/ the formation of fibrous tissue, esp in the liver, with hardening and distortion of the organ caused by excessive formation of CONNECTIVE TISSUE followed by contraction [NL, fr Gk *kirrhos* orange-coloured; fr the often yellowish appearance of a diseased liver] – **cirrhotic** *adj or n*
**cirriped** /'siri,ped/, **cirripede** /-peed/ *n* any of a subclass (Cirripedia of the class Crustacea) of specialized marine INVERTEBRATE animals (e g barnacles), free-swimming as larvae, but permanently attached or parasitic as adults [deriv of NL *cirr-* + L *ped-, pes* foot – more at FOOT] – **cirriped** *adj*
**cirrocumulus** /,siroh'kyoohmyooləs/ *n* a cloud form of small white rounded masses at a high altitude, usu in regular groupings forming a MACKEREL SKY [NL]
**cirrostratus** /,siroh'strahtəs/ *n* a fairly uniform layer of high veil-like stratus clouds that are darker than cirrus [NL]
**cirrus** /'sirəs/ *n, pl* **cirri** /'siri, -rie/ **1** a tendril **2** a slender usu flexible projecting structure of an animal: e g **2a** an arm of a barnacle **b** a filament of a CRINOID (primitive marine animal related to starfish) **c** a fused limblike group of CILIA (hairlike structures) on some minute single-celled organisms **d** the male copulatory organ of various INVERTEBRATE animals (e g snails and tapeworms) **3** a wispy white cloud, usu of minute ice crystals, formed at high altitudes [NL, fr L, curl]
**cirsoid** /'suhsoyd/ *adj* like a swollen vein; varicose [deriv of Gk *kirsos* swollen vein]
**cis** *adj* characterized by having identical atoms or chemical groups on the same side of a chemical DOUBLE BOND in a molecule – usu ital; often in combination ⟨*cis-dichloroethylene*⟩; compare TRANS
**cis-** /sis-/ *prefix* on this side ⟨cispontine⟩ ⟨cisatlantic⟩ [L, fr *cis* – more at HE]
**cisalpine** /sis'alpien/ *adj* situated on the south side of the Alps ⟨Cisalpine *Gaul*⟩ – compare TRANSALPINE [L *cisalpinus,* fr *cis-* + *Alpinus* of the Alps]
**cislunar** /sis'loohnə/ *adj* lying between the earth and the moon or the moon's orbit ⟨~ *space*⟩
**cissy, sissy** /'sisi/ *n, Br informal* **1** an effeminate boy or man **2** a cowardly person [by shortening & alter. fr *sister*]
**cist** /sist/ *also* **kist** /kist/ *n* a boxlike prehistoric or early medieval coffin constructed out of stone slabs or a hollowed-out tree trunk ⟨~ *grave*⟩ [W *cist* chest, fr L *cista*]
**Cistercian** /si'stuhsh(ə)n/ *n* a member of a monastic order founded by St Robert of Molesme in 1098 at Cîteaux in France observing an austere Benedictine rule [ML *Cistercium* Cîteaux] – **Cistercian** *adj*
**cistern** /'sist(ə)n/ *n* **1** an artificial reservoir for storing liquids, esp water: e g **1a** a water tank at the top of a house or building **b** a water reservoir for a toilet **c** *chiefly NAm* a usu underground tank for storing rainwater **2** a liquid-containing sac or cavity in an organism [ME, fr OF *cisterne,* fr L *cisterna,* fr *cista* box, chest]
**cisterna** /si'stuhnə/ *n, pl* **cisternae** /-nie/ CISTERN 2 [NL, fr L, reservoir]
**cistron** /'sistron/ *n* a gene consisting of a segment of DNA which codes for a single functional unit (e g a particular ENZYME) [*cis-* + *trans-* + *²-on*] – **cistronic** *adj*
**cistus** /'sistəs/ *n* any of a genus (*Cistus*) of shrubs of the rockrose family with large red or white flowers; a rockrose [NL, genus name, fr Gk *kistos* rockrose]
**citadel** /'sitədl, -,del/ *n* **1** a fortress; *esp* one that commands a city **2** a stronghold [MF *citadelle,* fr OIt *cittadella,* dim. of *cittade* city, fr ML *civitat-, civitas* – more at CITY]
**citation** /sie'taysh(ə)n/ *n* **1** a mention: e g **1a** a formal statement of the achievements of a person receiving an academic honour **b** specific reference in a military dispatch to meritorious performance of duty **c** *law* an official summons to appear before a court **2a** an act of citing or quoting legal authority **b** an excerpt, or quotation; *esp* one used to support an argument or as an illustration – **citational** *adj*
**cite** /siet/ *vt* **1** to quote by way of example, authority, or proof ⟨~ *Biblical passages*⟩ ⟨~ *a previous case*⟩ **2** to name in a citation: e g **2a** to refer to; *esp* to mention formally in commendation or praise **b** to call upon officially or authoritatively to appear (e g before a court) △ site [MF *citer* to cite, summon, fr L *citare* to put in motion, rouse, summon, fr *citus,* pp of *ciēre* to stir, move] – **citable** *adj*
**cithara** /'sithərə, 'ki-/ *n* an ancient Greek stringed musical

instrument of the lyre family with a wooden SOUNDING BOARD [L, fr Gk *kithara* (cf ZITHER)]

**cithern** /'sidhuhn/ *n* CITTERN (stringed musical instrument)

**citified** /'sitified/ *adj, often derog* having adopted city ways – **citify** *vt*, **citification** *n*

**citizen** /'sitiz(ə)n/ *n* **1** an inhabitant of a city or town; *esp* one entitled to the rights and privileges of a freeman **2** a member of a state; *specif* a native or naturalized person who owes allegiance to a government and is entitled to protection by it ⟨*UK* ~⟩ **3** *NAm* a civilian as distinguished from a specialized servant of the state [ME *citizein*, fr AF *citezein*, alter. (prob influenced by MF *denzein* denizen) of OF *citeien*, fr *cité* city] – **citizenly** *adj*, **citizenship** *n*

**citizenry** /-ri/ *n, taking sing or pl vb* the whole body of citizens

**citizens' band** *n, often cap C&B* a radio frequency for private communication (e g between motorists)

**citr-, citri-, citro-** *comb form* **1** citrus ⟨citri*culture*⟩ **2** citric acid ⟨citr*ate*⟩ [NL, fr *Citrus*, genus name]

**citral** /'sitrəl/ *n* a liquid chemical compound, $C_{10}H_{16}O$, contained in many ESSENTIAL OILS that has a strong lemon smell and is used esp in perfumery, as a flavouring, and in the synthesis of other organic chemical compounds (e g of vitamin A) [ISV]

**citrate** /'sitrayt, 'sie-/ *n* any of various chemical compounds (SALTS OR ESTERS) formed by combination between CITRIC ACID and a metal atom, an alcohol, or another chemical group [ISV]

**citric acid** /'sitrik/ *n* an acid, $CO_2HC(CH_2CO_2H)_2OH$, occurring in the KREBS CYCLE (final stage in the breakdown of sugars and fats inside a living cell), obtained esp from lemon and lime juices or by fermentation of sugars, and used as a flavouring because of its tart taste [ISV]

**citric acid cycle** *n* KREBS CYCLE (final stage in the breakdown of sugars and fats inside a living cell)

**citriculture** /'sitri,kulchə/ *n* the cultivation of citrus fruits – **citriculturist** *n*

**¹citrine** /'sitrin/ *adj* resembling a lemon, esp in colour [ME, fr MF *citrin*, fr ML *citrinus*, fr L *citrus* citron tree]

**²citrine** *n* a black quartz changed in colour by heating into a semiprecious yellow stone resembling topaz

**citron** /'sitrən/ *n* **1a** a fruit like the lemon in appearance and structure but larger and with a thicker rind; *also* a tree (*Citrus medica*) that bears citrons **b** the preserved rind of the citron used esp in cakes and puddings **2** a small hard-fleshed watermelon (*Citrullus vulgaris citroides*) used esp in pickles and preserves [ME, fr MF, fr OProv, modif of L *citrus* citron tree]

**citronella** /ˌsitrə'nelə/ *n* a fragrant grass (*Cymbopogon nardus*) of S Asia that yields an oil used in perfumery and as an insect repellent [NL, fr Fr *citronnelle* lemon balm, fr *citron*]

**citronellal** /ˌsitrə'nelal/ *n* a lemon-smelling liquid chemical compound, $C_{10}H_{18}O$, found in many ESSENTIAL OILS and used in perfumery [ISV, fr NL *citronella*]

**citrous** /'sitrəs/ *adj* of citrus trees or their fruit

**citrulline** /'sitrəleen/ *n* an AMINO ACID, $C_6H_{13}N_3O_3$, formed esp as an intermediate in the production of UREA (component of urine) in the living system [ISV, fr NL *Citrullus*, genus name of the watermelon]

**citrus** /'sitrəs/ *n, pl* **citruses**, *esp collectively* **citrus** any of several often thorny trees and shrubs (*Citrus* and related genera) of the orange family grown in warm regions for their edible fruit with firm usu thick rind and pulpy flesh [NL, genus name, fr L, citron tree] – **citrus** *adj*

**cittern** /'sitən/ *n* a plucked stringed instrument with a pear-shaped flat-backed body, popular esp in Renaissance England – compare ZITHER [blend of *cither* and *gittern*]

**city** /'siti/ *n* **1** an inhabited place of greater size, population, or importance than a town or village; *broadly* a large town: **1a** an incorporated British town usu of major size or importance that has a cathedral or has had civic status conferred on it by the crown **b** a usu large or important municipality in the USA governed under a charter granted by the state **c** an incorporated municipal unit of the highest class in Canada **2** the people living in a city ⟨*the* ~ *shivered in the cold*⟩ **3** *cap* **3a** *the* area of London in which financial and commercial activities are centred ⟨*I think he's something in the* City⟩ **b** *the* influential financial interests of the British economy **4** a city-state [ME *citie* large or small town, fr OF *cité* capital city, fr ML *civitat-, civitas*, fr L, citizenship, state, eity of Rome, fr *civis* citizen – more at HOME]

**City company** *n, Br* a corporation of businessmen developed from the ancient trade guilds of the City of London

**city editor** *n* **1** *Br* the editor of the financial section of a journal or newspaper **2** *NAm* a newspaper editor in charge of local news

**city father** *n* an important official or prominent citizen of a city

**city hall** *n, often cap C&H* **1** the chief administrative building of a city **2a** *NAm* a municipal government **b** *chiefly NAm* city officialdom or bureaucracy ⟨*you can't fight* ~⟩

**city manager** *n* an official employed by an elected council to direct the administration of a city government, esp in the USA

**city planner** *n, NAm* TOWN PLANNER – **city planning** *n*

**cityscape** /'siti,skayp/ *n* a view of a city; *also* its pictorial representation

**city slicker** *n* SLICKER 2b

**city-'state** *n* an autonomous state consisting of a city and its surrounding territory (e g in ancient Greece or medieval Italy)

**civet** /'sivit/ *n* **1a** civet cat, civet any of several flesh-eating mammals (family Viverridae); *esp* a long-bodied short-legged African animal (*Viverra civetta*) from which civet is obtained **b** the fur of the civet cat **2** a thick yellowish musky-smelling substance extracted from a pouch near the sexual organs of the civet cat and used in perfumery [MF *civette*, fr OIt *zibetto*, fr Ar *zabād* civet perfume]

**civic** /'sivik/ *adj* relating to a citizen, a city, or citizenship [L *civicus*, fr *civis* citizen] – **civically** *adv*

> **synonyms** Civic, civil, and civilian all apply to citizens, but in different ways. Civic implies a relation between the city or local community and its citizens ⟨civic *pride*⟩, or it may simply apply to the city itself ⟨civic **centre**⟩. Civil refers to citizens of the state ⟨civil *liberties*⟩. It may contrast with *religious* or *military* ⟨a civil *marriage* [= *in a registry office rather than in a church*]⟩ ⟨*the* Civil *Service*⟩. Civilian is contrasted with membership of the armed forces or some other uniformed public body ⟨civilian *personnel*⟩.

**civic centre** *n, Br* an area where a planned group of the chief public buildings of a town are situated

**civics** /'siviks/ *n, taking sing or pl vb* a social science dealing with the rights and duties of citizens

**civie** /'sivi/ *n* a civvy

**civil** /'sivl/ *adj* **1a** of or appropriate to citizens ⟨~ *liberties*⟩ **b** relating to the state or its citizenry **2** adequately courteous and polite; not rude **3** relating to private rights and to legal actions between individuals, as distinct from criminal, military, or ecclesiastical proceedings **4** *of time* based on the MEAN SUN (imaginary sun that moves at a constant rate equal to the average rate of the actual sun) and legally recognized for use in ordinary affairs ⟨*the* ~ *year*⟩ **5** relating to or involving the general public, their activities, needs, or interests, or civic affairs as distinguished from special (e g military or religious) affairs *synonyms* see CIVIC [ME, fr MF, fr L *civilis*, fr *civis*] – **civilly** *adv*

**civil commotion** *n, insurance* a stage of civil disturbance between riot and civil war

**civil death** *n, law* a loss of legal personality that in former times a living person could have (e g on banishment, on entering a monastery, or on committing a serious crime) that was equivalent in its legal consequences to natural death; *specif* deprivation of civil rights

**civil defence** *n, often cap C&D* the complex of protective measures and emergency relief activities conducted by and for civilians in case of hostile attack, esp by air, or natural disaster

**civil disobedience** *n* refusal to obey governmental demands (e g payment of tax) or commands, esp as a nonviolent and usu collective means of forcing concessions from the government

**civil engineer** *n* an engineer whose training or occupation is in the designing and construction of large-scale public works (e g roads or bridges) – **civil engineering** *n*

**civilian** /si'vilyən/ *n* one who is not a member of the armed forces; *also* one who is not a member of some other similarly organized body responsible to the state (e g the fire brigade or police force) *synonyms* see CIVIC – **civilian** *adj*

**civilian·ize, -ise** /si'vilyəniez/ *vt* to convert from military to civilian status or control – **civilianization** *n*

**civility** /si'viləti/ *n* **1** courtesy, politeness **2** *often pl* a polite act or expression

**civil·ization, -isation** /ˌsivilie'zaysh(ə)n, -li-/ *n* **1a** a relatively high level of cultural and technological development; *specif* the stage of cultural development at which writing and the keeping of written records is attained **b** the culture characteristic of a particular time or place **2** the process of becoming civilized **3** refinement of thought, manners, or taste **4** *often humorous* life in a place that offers the comforts of the modern world; *specif* life in a city

**civ·il·ize, -ise** /'siv(ə)l,iez/ *vt* **1** to cause to develop out of a primitive state; *specif* to bring to a technically advanced and rationally ordered stage of cultural development **2** to fit or train for a social environment **3** to educate, refine – **civilizable** *adj*, **civilizer** *n*

**civilized** /'siviliezd/ *adj* **1** of or being peoples or nations in a state of civilization **2** *informal* **2a** *of a place* congenial **b** *of a person* decent, enlightened

**civil law** *n, often cap C&L* **1** ROMAN LAW; *esp* Roman law as applied to private Roman citizens as distinct from that applicable to foreigners, and often also distinguished from that developed by the edicts of magistrates **2** the body of private law developed from Roman law as distinct from COMMON LAW **3** the law established by a nation or state for its own jurisdiction (eg as distinct from international law) **4** the law of civil or private rights

**civil liberty** *n* a right of freedom of the individual citizen in relation to the state (eg freedom of speech, assembly, and religion); *also* such rights or freedoms considered collectively – **civil libertarian** *n*

**civil list** *n* the annual grant of money by Parliament to the monarch for the expenses of the royal family

**civil marriage** *n, law* a marriage involving a civil contract but no religious rite or vow

**civil rights** *n pl* CIVIL LIBERTY; *esp* the rights of personal liberty and of status equality between races or minority and majority groups (eg black and white US citizens or Catholics and Protestants in N Ireland)

**civil servant** *n* a member of a CIVIL SERVICE

**civil service** *n taking sing or pl vb* the administrative service of a government or international agency exclusive of the armed forces; *esp* one in which appointments are determined by merit as opposed to patronage

**civil war** *n* a war between opposing groups of citizens of the same country

**civvy** *also* **civie** /'sivi/ *n, informal* **1** *pl* civilian clothes as distinguished from a military uniform **2** a civilian [by shortening & alter.]

**civvy street** /'sivi/ *n, often cap C&S, Br informal* civilian life as opposed to life in the services

**clachan** /'klak(h)ən, 'klah-/ *n, Scot & Irish* a small village; a hamlet [ME, fr ScGael]

**¹clack** /klak/ *vb, informal vi* **1** CHATTER 2 **2** to make an abrupt striking sound or series of sounds **3** *esp of chickens* to cackle, cluck ~ *vt* to cause to make a clatter [ME *clacken*, of imit origin] – **clacker** *n*

**²clack** *n, informal* **1** rapid continuous talk; chatter **2** a sound of clacking (*the* ~ *of a typewriter*)

**clack valve** *n* a valve usu hinged at one edge that permits flow of a liquid or gas in one direction only and that closes with a clacking sound

**Clactonian** /klak'tohnyən/ *adj* of an early PALAEOLITHIC (middle Stone Age) culture characterized by tools made from stone flakes with a half cone at the point of striking [*Clacton-on-Sea*, town in England where such tools were first discovered]

**¹clad** /klad/ *adj* **1** being covered or clothed (*ivy-clad buildings*) (~ *in Lincoln green*) **2** *of a coin* consisting of outer layers of one metal bonded to a core of a different metal *usage* see CLOTHE [fr pp of *clothe*]

**²clad** *vt* **-dd-; clad** to provide with cladding ; *specif* to cover (a metal) with another metal by bonding

**³clad** *n* **1** a composite material formed by cladding; *specif* a clad coin **2** something that overlays; cladding; *specif* the outer layer of a clad coin

**cladding** /'klading/ *n* something that covers or overlays (*stone* ~ *on the wall of a building*); *specif* metal coating bonded to a metal core

**clade** /klayd/ *n* a group of organisms (eg all animals with backbones) that includes all the descendants of a single common ancestor [Gk *klados* branch] – **cladistic** *adj*

**cladistics** /klə'distiks/ *n taking sing vb* a system for describing the relationship between types of organism based on the assumption that their sharing of a unique characteristic (eg the

mammary glands of mammals) possessed by no other organism indicates their descent from a single common ancestor

**cladode** /'kladohd/ *n* a branch assuming the form of and closely resembling an ordinary foliage leaf and often bearing leaves or flowers on its edges [NL *cladodium*, fr Gk *klados*] – **cladodial** *adj*

**cladogenesis** /kladoh'jenəsis/ *n* evolutionary change characterized by the treelike branching of groups of organisms to produce new types of organism [NL, fr Gk *klados* branch + L *genesis*] – **cladogenetic** *adj*, **cladogenetically** *adv*

**cladophyll** /'kladəfil/ *n* a cladode [NL *cladophyllum*, fr Gk *klados* branch + *phyllon* leaf – more at GLADIATOR, BLADE]

**claggy** /'klagi/ *adj, dial Eng* muddy [E dial. *clag* lump of dirt]

**¹claim** /klaym/ *vt* **1a** to ask for, esp as a right (~ed *Supplementary Benefit*) **b** to require, demand **2** to take as the rightful owner (*went to* ~ *his luggage at the station*) **3** to assert in the face of possible contradiction; maintain (~ed *that he'd been cheated*) **4** to put an end to; destroy (*the disaster* ~ed *hundreds of lives*) *synonyms* see ²DEMAND [ME *claimen*, fr OF *clamer*, fr L *clamare* to cry out, shout; akin to L *calare* to call – more at LOW] – **claimable** *adj*, **claimer** *n*

**²claim** *n* **1** a demand for something (believed to be) due (*insurance* ~) **2a** a right to something; *specif* a title to a debt, privilege, or other thing in the possession of another **b** an assertion open to challenge (*a* ~ *to fame*) **3** something that is claimed; *esp* a tract of land staked out – **lay claim (to)** to assert one's right or title (to) – **stake a/one's claim (to)** LAY CLAIM (TO)

**claimant** /'klaymənt/ *n* a person who asserts a right or entitlement (*a* ~ *to an estate*) (*social security* ~s)

**claiming race** /'klayming/ *n* a US horse race in which each horse is offered for sale for a specified price to a purchaser who pledges the selling price before the race

**clairaudience** /kleə'rawdiəns/ *n* the alleged power or faculty of mentally perceiving sound that is inaudible [*clair-* (as in *clairvoyance*) + *audience* (act of hearing)] – **clairaudient** *adj*, **clairaudiently** *adv*

**clairvoyance** /kleə'voyəns/ *n* **1** the alleged power or faculty of discerning objects not present to the physical senses **2** ability to perceive matters beyond the range of ordinary perception; penetration

**¹clairvoyant** /kleə'voyənt/ *adj* **1** of clairvoyance **2** unusually perceptive; discerning [Fr, fr *clair* clear (fr L *clarus*) + *voyant*, prp of *voir* to see, fr L *vidēre*] – **clairvoyantly** *adv*

**²clairvoyant** *n* one who has the power of clairvoyance

**¹clam** /klam/ *n* **1a** any of numerous edible marine shellfish (of the phylum Mollusca) (eg a scallop) that have a shell consisting of two halves hinged together and that live in sand or mud **b** a freshwater mussel **2** *informal* a stolid or taciturn person [*clam* (clamp), fr ME, fr OE *clamm* bond, fetter; fr the clamping action of the shells]

**²clam** *vi* **-mm-** to gather clams, esp by digging

**clam up** *vi, informal* to fall or remain silent; *also* to withhold information

**clamant** /'klaymənt/ *adj, formal* **1** demanding attention; urgent **2** clamorous, blatant [L *clamant-, clamans*, prp of *clamare* to cry out] – **clamantly** *adv*

**clambake** /-,bayk/ *n, NAm* **1** an outdoor party; *esp* a seashore outing where food is cooked on heated rocks covered by seaweed **2** a gathering characterized by noisy sociability; *esp* a political rally [¹*clam* + *bake*]

**clamber** /'klambə/ *vi* to climb using hands and feet; *also* to climb awkwardly or with difficulty [ME *clambren*; akin to OE *climban* to climb] – **clamber** *n*, **clamberer** *n*

**clammy** /'klami/ *adj* **1** damp, clinging, and usu cool (*a* ~ *and intensely cold mist* – Charles Dickens) **2** having qualities that cause unease or estrangement [ME, prob fr *clammen* to smear, stick, fr OE *clǣman*; akin to OE *clǣg* clay] – **clammily** *adv*, **clamminess** *n*

**clamorous** /'klamərəs/ *adj* **1** marked by confused din or outcry; tumultuous (*the busy* ~ *market*) **2** noisily insistent *synonyms* see VOCIFEROUS *antonym* taciturn – **clamorously** *adv*, **clamorousness** *n*

**¹clamour, *NAm chiefly* clamor** /'klamə/ *n* **1a** noisy shouting **b** a loud continuous noise **2** insistent public expression (eg of support or protest) (*the* ~ *for representation*) [ME *clamor*, fr MF *clamour*, fr L *clamor*, fr *clamare* to cry out – more at CLAIM]

**²clamour, *NAm chiefly* clamor** *vi* **1** to make a din **2** to become loudly insistent (~ed *for his impeachment*) ~ *vt* to utter or proclaim insistently and noisily

¹**clamp** /klamp/ *n* **1** a device designed to bind or constrict or to press two or more parts together so as to hold them firmly **2** any of various instruments or appliances having parts brought together for holding or compressing something [ME, prob fr (assumed) MD *klampe;* akin to OE *clamm* bond, fetter]

²**clamp** *vt* **1** to fasten (as if) with a clamp ⟨~ *an artery*⟩; *broadly* to hold tightly **2** to place by decree; impose
  **clamp down** *vi* to impose esp more stringent restrictions *on* – see also CLAMP-DOWN

³**clamp** *n, Br* **1** a heap of produce (eg potatoes or turnips) covered over usu with straw or earth so that it can be kept over the winter **2** a heap of wooden sticks for burning to form charcoal or of raw bricks for firing [prob fr D *klamp* heap]

⁴**clamp** *vt, Br* to heap (potatoes, turnips, etc) into a clamp

'**clamp-,down** *n* the esp sudden act or action of making regulations and restrictions more stringent

**clamshell** /'klam,shel/ *n, NAm* **1** a bucket or grapple (eg on a dredger) with two hinged jaws **2** an excavating machine with a clamshell

**clan** /klan/ *n* **1a** a Celtic group, esp in the Scottish Highlands, comprising a number of households whose heads claim descent from a common ancestor **b** a group of people descended from a common ancestor **2** *chiefly informal* a usu close-knit group united by a common interest or common characteristics [ME, fr ScGael *clann* offspring, clan, fr OIr *cland* plant, offspring, fr L *planta* plant]

**clandestine** /klan'destin, 'klandəstin/ *adj* held in or done with secrecy; surreptitious **synonyms** see ¹SECRET **antonym** open [MF or L; MF *clandestin,* fr L *clandestinus,* irreg fr *clam* secretly; akin to L *celare* to hide – more at HELL] – **clandestinely** *adv,* **clandestineness** *n*

¹**clang** /klang/ *vi* **1** to make a loud metallic ringing sound ⟨*anvils* ~ed⟩ **2** to go with a clang ⟨*the iron gate* ~ed *shut*⟩ ~ *vt* to cause to clang ⟨~ *a bell*⟩ [L *clangere;* akin to Gk *klazein* to scream, bark, OE *hlōwan* to low]

²**clang** *n* **1** a loud ringing metallic sound ⟨*the* ~ *of a fire alarm*⟩ **2** a harsh cry of certain birds (eg a crane or goose)

**clanger** /'klang-ə/ *n, chiefly Br informal* an embarrassing mistake; FAUX PAS – see also DROP a clanger

**clangour,** *NAm chiefly* **clangor** /'klang(g)ə/ *vi or n* (to make) a resounding clang or medley of clangs ⟨*the* ~ *of hammers*⟩ [n L *clangor,* fr *clangere;* vb fr n] – **clangorous** *adj*

¹**clank** /klangk/ *vi* **1** to make a clank or series of clanks ⟨*the engine hissed and* ~ed⟩ **2** to go with a clank ⟨*tanks* ~ing *through the streets*⟩ ~ *vt* to cause to clank [prob imit]

²**clank** *n* a sharp brief metallic sound (eg of a chain)

**clannish** /'klanish/ *adj* **1** of a clan **2** tending to associate only with a select group of similar background or status; cliquey – **clannishly** *adv,* **clannishness** *n*

**clansman** /'klanzmən/ *n* a member of a clan

¹**clap** /klap/ *vb* **-pp-** *vt* **1** to strike (eg two flat hard surfaces) together so as to produce a loud sharp percussive noise **2a** to strike (the hands) together repeatedly, usu in applause **b** to applaud **3** to strike with the flat of the hand in a friendly way ⟨~ped *his friend on the shoulder*⟩ **4** *informal* to place, put, or set, esp energetically ⟨~ *him into jail*⟩ ⟨*finest vessel I ever* ~ped *eyes on*⟩ ~ *vi* **1** to produce a loud sharp percussive noise **2** to applaud – see also clap EYES on [ME *clappen,* fr OE *clæppan;* akin to OHG *klaphōn* to beat, L *glēba* clod – more at CLIP]

²**clap** *n* **1** a part that is free to move for the purpose of causing vibration or noise, esp a clapping noise **2** a loud sharp percussive noise; *specif* a sudden crash of thunder **3** a friendly slap ⟨*a* ~ *on the shoulder*⟩ **4** the sound of clapping hands; *esp* applause

³**clap** *n, slang* VENEREAL DISEASE; *esp* gonorrhoea – often + *the* [MF *clapoir* bubo]

**clapboard** /'klabəd, 'klap,bawd/ *n, NAm* a weatherboard [part trans of D *klaphout* stave wood] – **clapboard** *vt*

**clapped out** /klapt/ *adj, Br informal* worn-out ⟨*a* ~ *old car*⟩ ⟨~ *notions of sex and power – Time Out*⟩

**clapper** /'klapə/ *n* someone or something that makes a clapping sound: eg **a** the tongue of a bell **b** a mechanical device that makes noise, esp by the banging of one part against another **c** a person who applauds – **go/run like the clappers** *Br informal* to go/run as fast as possible

'**clapper-,board** *n* a hinged board containing identifying details of the scene to be filmed that is held before the camera

and whose two parts are banged together to mark the beginning and end of each take

**clapper bridge** *n* a simple bridge; *specif* one consisting of stone slabs laid across from one pile of stones to another and found typically on Dartmoor and Exmoor and in Spain

**clapperclaw** /'klapə,klaw/ *vt, dial Eng or archaic* **1** to claw with the nails **2** to abuse verbally; scold [perh fr *clapper* + *claw* (vb)]

**claptrap** /'klap,trap/ *n* pretentious nonsense; rubbish [²*clap* + *trap;* fr its use to gain applause]

**claque** /klak/ *n taking sing or pl vb* **1** a group hired to applaud at a performance **2** a group of self-interested obsequious flatterers [Fr, fr *claquer* to clap, of imit origin]

**claqueur** /kla'kuh/ *n* a member of a claque [Fr, fr *claquer*]

**clarence** /'klarəns/ *n* a closed four-wheeled carriage for four passengers [Duke of *Clarence,* later William IV of England †1837]

**claret** /'klarit/ *n* **1** a dry red table wine from the Bordeaux district of France; *also* a similar wine produced elsewhere ⟨*Californian* ~⟩ **2** a dark purplish red colour [ME, fr MF (*vin*) *claret* clear wine, fr *claret* clear, fr *cler* clear] – **claret** *adj*

**clarify** /'klari,fie/ *vt* **1** to make (eg a liquid) clear or pure, usu by freeing from suspended matter **2** to make comprehensible or free from confusion ~ *vi* to become clear [ME *clarifien,* fr MF *clarifier,* fr LL *clarificare,* fr L *clarus* clear – more at CLEAR] – **clarifier** *n,* **clarification** *n*

**clarinet** /,klari'net/ *n* a woodwind instrument of middle range that has a SINGLE REED (flat piece of cane that when blown across vibrates to produce sound) and a cylindrical tube with a moderately flared free end [Fr *clarinette,* prob deriv of ML *clarion-, clario*] – **clarinettist,** *NAm* **clarinetist** *n*

**clarino** /kla'reenoh/ *n, pl* **clarinos, clarini** /-ni/ the trumpet played in its high register, esp in 17th- and 18th-century music [It, trumpet]

**clarion** /'klariən/ *n* **1** a medieval trumpet; *esp* one used for melody rather than military calls **2** the sound (as if) of a clarion [ME, fr MF & ML; MF *clairon,* fr ML *clarion-, clario,* fr L *clarus* clear]

**clarion call** *n* a direct and unambiguously clear prompting ⟨*a* ~ *to action*⟩

**clarity** /'klarəti/ *n* the quality or state of being clear **antonym** obscurity [ME *clarite,* fr L *claritat-, claritas,* fr *clarus*]

**clarkia** /'klahki·ə/ *n* a showy plant (genus *Clarkia*) of the fuchsia family that is grown in gardens in most parts of the world [NL, fr William *Clark* †1838 US explorer]

**claro** /'klahroh/ *n, pl* **claroes** *also* **claros** a light-coloured generally mild cigar [Sp, fr *claro* light, fr L *clarus*]

**clarsach** /'klahs(h)akh, -akh/ *n* the ancient small harp of Ireland and Scotland [ScGael *clārsach* & IrGael *clāirseach*]

**clarty** /'klahti/ *adj, dial chiefly Scot & NE Eng* dirty, mucky [E dial. *clart* clot of mud, mud]

**clary** /'kleəri/ *n* any of several plants (genus *Salvia*) of the mint family closely related to sage and often used as herbs in cookery [ME *clarie,* fr MF *sclaree,* fr ML *sclareia*]

**clash** /klash/ *vi* **1** to make a noisy usu metallic sound of collision ⟨*cymbals* ~ed⟩ **2a** to come into conflict ⟨*where ignorant armies* ~ *by night* – Matthew Arnold⟩ **b** to form a displeasing combination; not match ⟨*these colours* ~⟩ ~ *vt* to cause to clash [imit] – **clash** *n*

**clasmatocyte** /klaz'matəsiet/ *n* MACROPHAGE (large cell that can ingest harmful or unwanted material) [ISV, fr Gk *klasmat-, klasma* fragment (fr *klan* to break) + ISV *-cyte* – more at HALT] – **clasmatocytic** *adj*

¹**clasp** /klahsp/ *n* **1a** a device (eg a hook) for holding objects or parts together **b** a device (eg a bar) attached to a military medal ribbon to indicate the action or campaign at which the bearer was present **2** a holding or enveloping (as if) with the hands or arms [ME *claspe*]

²**clasp** *vt* **1** to fasten (as if) with a clasp **2** to enclose and hold with the arms; *specif* to embrace **3** to seize (as if) with the hand; grasp

**clasper** /'klahspə/ *n* a male copulatory structure: **a** either of a pair of projecting structures in the region of the anus of an insect **b** either of a pair of organs on the PELVIC FINS of ELASMOBRANCH fishes (eg sharks and rays)

**clasp knife** *n* a large single-bladed folding knife with a catch to hold the blade open

¹**class** /klahs/ *n* **1a** *taking sing or pl vb* a group sharing the same economic or social status in a hierarchically stratified society and possessing broadly similar cultural characteristics,

chances for achievement, social mobility, and aspirations ⟨*the working* ∼⟩ **b(1)** social rank; *esp, chiefly NAm* high social rank **b(2)** the system of differentiating society by classes based esp on occupation **c** high quality; elegance ⟨*the boy has* ∼*!*⟩ **2a** a course of instruction **b** *taking sing or pl vb* a body of students meeting regularly to study the same subject ⟨*the* ∼ *in philology meets in room 2*⟩ **c** the period during which such a body meets ⟨*who are you taking first* ∼ *after break?*⟩ **d** *chiefly NAm* YEAR 7 ⟨∼ *of '65*⟩ **3** a group, set, or kind sharing common attributes: eg **3a** a category in the classification of animals and plants ranking above the order and below the phylum or division **b** a group of adjacent values of a RANDOM VARIABLE **c** SET 19 (collection of mathematical elements) **d** a grammatical category **4a** a division or rating based on grade or quality **b** *Br* a level of university honours degree awarded to a student according to merit ⟨*What* ∼ *did she get?*⟩ [Fr *classe*, fr L *classis* group called to arms, class of citizens; akin to L *calare* to call – more at LOW]

**²class** *vt* to classify

**class action** *n* an action undertaken in US law by one or more people on behalf of themselves and all other people having an identical interest in the alleged wrong

**'class-ˌconscious** *adj* **1** actively aware of one's common status with others in a particular economic or social class **2** actively aware of one's class position as a prelude to believing in and taking part in class struggle – **class consciousness** *n*

**¹classic** /'klasik/ *adj* **1a** of recognized or historical value or merit; serving as a standard of excellence ⟨*these are* ∼ *recordings whose loss would be disastrous*⟩ **b** characterized by simply tailored and elegant lines that remain in fashion year after year ⟨*a* ∼ *suit*⟩ **2** CLASSICAL 2a **3** CLASSICAL 3a **4** noted because of special literary or historical associations ⟨*in Bath we are on* ∼ *ground*⟩ **5a** authoritative, definitive **b** being an example that shows clearly the characteristics of some group of things or occurrences; archetypal ⟨*the* ∼ *case of this motif is the Cinderella story*⟩ **6** CLASSICAL 4b(1) [Fr or L; Fr *classique*, fr L *classicus* of the highest class of Roman citizens, of the first rank, fr *classis*]

**²classic** *n* **1a** a literary work of ancient Greece or Rome **b** *pl but taking sing vb* ancient Greek and Latin literature, history, and philosophy considered as an academic subject ⟨*he read* ∼*s at university*⟩ **2** a work of enduring excellence; *also* its author – often + *the* ⟨*she will only read the* ∼*s*⟩ **3** a classic example; an archetype **4** an important long-established sporting event; *specif, Br* any of five flat races for horses (eg the Epsom Derby)

**classical** /'klasikl/ *adj* **1** standard, classic **2a** of the ancient Greek and Roman world, esp its literature, art, architecture, or ideals **b** expert in the classics ⟨*a* ∼ *scholar*⟩ **3a** *of a work of art, style, etc* adhering to traditional standards, derived ultimately from the works of ancient Greece and Rome, and characterized by such qualities as balance, restraint, and simplicity of form – compare ROMANTIC 4a, b **b(1)** of or being music of the late 18th and early 19th centuries characterized by an emphasis on simplicity, objectivity, and proportion; *also* of or being a composer of this music **b(2)** of or being music in the educated European tradition that includes such forms as chamber music, opera, and symphony as distinguished from folk or popular music or jazz **4a** being both authoritative and traditional **b(1)** of or being systems or methods that formerly constituted the accepted approach to a subject ⟨∼ *Mendelian genetics versus modern molecular genetics*⟩ **b(2)** based on longstanding theories of physics, esp those of Newton rather than more recent ones (eg QUANTUM THEORY) ⟨∼ *mechanics*⟩ **c** conforming to a pattern of usage sanctioned by a body of literature rather than by everyday speech ⟨∼ *Arabic*⟩ **5** concerned with or giving instruction in the humanities, the fine arts, and only the broadest aspects of science ⟨*a* ∼ *education*⟩ [L *classicus*]

**synonyms** Compare the various senses of **classic** and **classical**. The two words are partially interchangeable in meaning; but **classical** is normally used for the senses connected with ancient Greece and Rome (see ²CLASSIC 1) and also when **classical** *music* is contrasted with "romantic" or with "jazz", while **classic** is preferred when it means "of recognized and enduring excellence" ⟨*a* **classic** *sports event*⟩ (see ²CLASSIC 2, 3, & 4).

**classicality** /ˌklasi'kalɛti/ *n* the quality or state of being classic or classical

**classically** /'klasikli/ *adv* in a classic or classical manner

**classicism** /'klasiˌsiz(ə)m/ *also* **classicalism** /'klasiklˌiz(ə)m/ *n*

**1a** the principles or style embodied in the literature, art, or architecture of ancient Greece and Rome **b** scholarship in the classics **c** a classical idiom or expression **2** adherence to traditional standards (eg of simplicity, restraint, and proportion) that are universally and enduringly valid

**classicist** /'klasisist/ *also* **classicalist** /'klasiklˌist/ *n* **1** an advocate or student of classicism **2** a scholar or student of the classics – **classicistic** *adj*

**classic·ize, -ise** /'klasisiez/ *vt* to make classic or classical ∼ *vi* to follow classic style

**classification** /ˌklasifi'kaysh(ə)n/ *n* **1** the act or process of classifying **2a** systematic arrangement in groups or categories according to established criteria; *specif* the arrangement of animals and plants into species, genera, etc **b** a class, category – **classificatory** *adj*, **classificatorily** *adv*

**classified** /'klasiˌfied/ *adj* **1** divided into classes or placed in a class **2** withheld from general circulation for reasons of national or military security ⟨∼ *information*⟩

**classified ad, classified** *n* an advertisement in a newspaper or periodical, usu in small type and grouped according to subject

**classifier** /'klasifie·ə/ *n* **1** someone or something that classifies; *specif* a machine for sorting out the constituents of a substance (eg an ore) **2** a word or MORPHEME (meaningful segment of a word) used with numerals or with certain types of nouns ⟨*Bantu and Chinese* ∼*s*⟩

**classify** /'klasiˌfie/ *vt* to arrange in classes or assign to a category ⟨∼*ing books according to subject matter*⟩ – **classifiable** *adj*

**class interval** *n* CLASS 3b; *also* the width of a statistical class

**classless** /'klahslis/ *adj* **1** free from distinctions of social class ⟨*a* ∼ *society*⟩ **2** belonging to no particular social class – **classlessness** *n*

**'class-ˌlist** *n, Br* a university list assigning classes of degree to degree candidates

**classmate** /-ˌmayt/ *n* a member of the same class in a school or college

**classroom** /-room, -ˌroohm/ *n* a place where classes meet

**class struggle** *n* CLASS WAR

**class war** *n* the conflict between social classes; *esp* the struggle for political and economic power between workers and property owners assumed by Marxist theory to develop in a capitalist society of increasing polarization and class-consciousness

**classy** /'klahsi/ *adj, informal* elegant, stylish ⟨*coffins – anything from plain pine at R15 to* ∼ *mahogany at R45 – Fair Lady (S Africa)*⟩ – **classiness** *n*

**clast** /klast/ *n* a fragment of rock [Gk *klastos* broken]

**clastic** /'klastik/ *adj* made up of fragments of preexisting rocks ⟨*a* ∼ *sediment*⟩ [ISV, fr Gk *klastos* broken, fr *klan* to break – more at HALT] – **clastic** *n*

**clathrate** /'klathˌrayt/ *adj* **1** like a lattice **2** of or being a chemical compound formed by the inclusion of molecules of one kind in cavities of the crystal lattice structure of another [L *clathratus*, fr *clathri* (pl) lattice, fr Gk *klēithron* bar, fr *kleiein* to close – more at CLOSE] – **clathrate** *n*

**¹clatter** /'klatə/ *vi* **1** to make a clatter ⟨*the dishes* ∼*ed on the shelf*⟩ **2** to move or go with a clatter ⟨∼*ed down the stairs*⟩ **3** to prattle ∼ *vt* to cause to clatter [ME *clatren*, fr (assumed) OE *clatrian*, of imit origin] – **clatterer** *n*, **clatteringly** *adv*

**²clatter** *n* **1** a rattling sound (eg of hard bodies striking together) ⟨*the* ∼ *of pots and pans*⟩ **2** a commotion ⟨*the midday* ∼ *of the business district*⟩ – **clattery** *adj*

**claudication** /ˌklawdi'kaysh(ə)n/ *n, formal* the quality or state of being lame; ˌlimping [L *claudication-, claudicatio*, fr *claudicatus*, pp of *claudicare* to limp, fr *claudus* lame; akin to L *claudere* to close – more at CLOSE]

**clausal** /'klawzl/ *adj* of or being a clause

**clause** /klawz/ *n* **1** a distinct article or proviso in a formal document (eg a contract or treaty) **2** a group of words containing a subject and predicate and functioning either in isolation or as a member of a complex or compound sentence [ME, fr OF, clause, fr ML *clausa* close of a rhetorical period, fr L, fem of *clausus*, pp of *claudere* to close]

**claustral** /'klawstrəl/ *adj* of or like a cloister [ME, fr ML *claustralis*, fr *claustrum* cloister, fr L, bar, bolt]

**claustrophobia** /ˌklostrə'fohbi·ə, ˌklaw-/ *n* abnormal dread of being in closed or confined spaces [NL, fr L *claustrum* bar, bolt + NL *phobia* – more at CLOISTER] – **claustrophobic** *adj*

**clavate** /'klayˌvayt, -vət/ *adj, of an animal or plant part* gradually thickening near the end furthest from the point of attachment; shaped like a club [NL *clavatus*, fr L *clava* club, fr *clavus* nail, knot in wood] – **clavately** *adv*, **clavation** *n*

**clave** /klayv/ *past of* ¹CLEAVE

**claver** /'klayvə, 'klahvə/ *vi, chiefly Scot* to gossip, prattle [prob of Celt origin; akin to ScGael *clabaire* babbler] – **claver** *n*

**claves** /klayvz, klahvz/ *n pl* a pair of small wooden sticks struck together (eg in accompanying the rumba); *also, sing* either of these sticks [AmerSp *clave* (sing.), fr Sp, keystone, clef, fr L *clavis* key]

**clavichord** /'klavi,kawd/ *n* an early usu rectangular keyboard instrument having strings pressed by small metal pins (TANGENTS 4) attached to the key ends [ML *clavichordium*, fr L *clavis* key + *chorda* string – more at CORD] – **clavichordist** *n*

**clavicle** /'klavikl/ *n* a bone of the shoulder girdle typically serving to link the shoulder blade and breastbone – called also COLLARBONE [Fr *clavicule*, fr NL *clavicula*, fr L, dim. of *clavis* key; akin to Gk *kleid-, kleis* key, L *claudere* to close – more at CLOSE] – **clavicular** *adj*

**clavicorn** /'klavi,kawn/ *adj, of a beetle* having club-shaped antennae [L *clava* club + *cornu* horn]

**clavier** /'klavi-ə/ *n* **1** the keyboard of a musical instrument **2** a usu unspecified keyboard instrument [(1) Fr, fr OF, key-bearer, fr L *clavis* key; (2) Ger *klavier*, fr Fr *clavier*] – **clavierist** *n*

**claviform** /'klavi,fawm/ *adj* clavate [L *clava* club]

¹**claw** /klaw/ *n* **1a** a sharp usu slender and curved nail on the toe of an animal **b** any of various similar sharp curved parts of an animal, esp if at the end of a limb (eg of an insect); *also* a limb ending in such a claw **2** a pincerlike organ at the end of certain of the limbs of a crab, lobster, scorpion, etc **3** something that resembles a claw; *specif* the forked end of a tool (eg a claw hammer) [ME *clawe*, fr OE *clawu* hoof, claw; akin to ON *klō* claw, OE *cliewen* ball – more at CLEW] – **clawed** *adj*

²**claw** *vt* to rake, seize, dig, or progress (as if) with claws ~ *vi* to scrape, scratch, dig, or pull (as if) with claws

**claw back** *vt* to take back, esp by taxation ⟨*out of their gross gain of 150 millions, 125 millions is* clawed back *– The Guardian*⟩

**clawback** /'klaw,bak/ *n* recovery of an amount of money, esp by taxation; *also* the amount so recovered

**claw hammer** *n* a hammer with one end of the head forked for pulling out nails

¹**clay** /klay/ *n* **1a** an earthy material that is pliable when moist but hard when fired, is composed mainly of fine particles of aluminium SILICATES and other minerals, and is used for making bricks, tiles, and pottery; *also* soil composed chiefly of this material with particles less than 0.002 (in the USA 0.005) millimetres in diameter – compare SILT, SAND, LOAM **b** thick and clinging earth or mud **2** a substance that resembles clay in pliability and is used for modelling **3 clay pigeon, clay** a saucer-shaped target usu made of baked clay and pitch that is hurled into the air by a mechanical device (TRAP 3a) for people to shoot at **4** *archaic* the human body as distinguished from the spirit – compare FEET OF CLAY [ME, fr OE *clæg*; akin to OHG *klīwa* bran, LL *glut-, glus* glue, MGk *glia*] – **clayey** *adj*

²**clay** *vt* to treat or cover with clay; *also* to filter through clay

**clay mineral** *n* any of a group of water-containing SILICATES of aluminium and sometimes other metals formed chiefly in weathering processes and occurring esp in clay and shale

**claymore** /'klay,maw/ *n* **1** a large sword formerly used by Scottish Highlanders; *specif* a double- or often single-edged sword with a broad flat blade and an openwork guard covering the whole hand **2** a mine for use against people [ScGael *claidheamh mōr*, lit., great sword]

**claypan** /'klay,pan/ *n* HARDPAN (compacted layer of subsoil) consisting mainly of clay

**clay pipe** *n* a tobacco pipe made of esp white baked clay

¹**clean** /kleen/ *adj* **1a** free or relatively free from dirt or pollution ⟨*changed into* ~ *clothes*⟩ ⟨*the workshop floor was* ~⟩ **b** free from contamination or disease **c** relatively free from radioactive fallout ⟨*a* ~ *atomic explosion*⟩ **2** unadulterated or pure in various ways; eg **2a** relatively free from error or blemish; clear ⟨*turn over to a* ~ *page*⟩; *specif* legible ⟨~ *copy*⟩ **b(1)** ceremonially or spiritually pure ⟨*and all who are* ~ *may eat flesh – Lev 7:19* (RSV)⟩ **b(2)** not prohibited by dietary laws; lawful to eat **c(1)** free from illegal, immoral, or disreputable activities or connections ⟨*a* ~ *record*⟩ ⟨*you can start again with a* ~ *slate*⟩ **c(2)** *of a driving licence* free from endorsements or penalty points **d** free from offensive treatment of sexual subjects and from the use of obscenity ⟨*I just don't know any* ~ *jokes!*⟩ **e** free from growth that hinders the tilling of the soil **f** *of a precious stone* having no interior flaws visible **3a**

characterized by clarity, precision, or deftness ⟨*a* ~ *prose style*⟩ ⟨*architecture with* ~ *almost austere lines*⟩ **b** not jagged; smooth ⟨*a* ~ *edge*⟩ ⟨*a* ~ *break*⟩ **c** trim and streamlined ⟨*a* ~ *design for an aeroplane*⟩ **4** habitually neat **5** observing the rules; fair ⟨*a* ~ *fight*⟩ ⟨*a* ~ *catch*⟩ **6** thorough, complete ⟨*a* ~ *break with the past*⟩ **7** *chiefly NAm slang* carrying no concealed weapons, illegal drugs, etc [ME *clene*, fr OE *clæne*; akin to OHG *kleini* delicate, dainty, Gk *glainoi* ornaments] – **cleanness** *n* – **come clean** *informal* to confess all; OWN UP – see also **clean** BILL **of health, keep one's** NOSE **clean**

²**clean** *adv* **1a** so as to clean ⟨*a new broom sweeps* ~⟩ **b** in a clean manner ⟨*fight* ~⟩ **2a** all the way; completely ⟨*the bullet went* ~ *through his arm*⟩ ⟨*got* ~ *away*⟩ **b** without the ball touching the bat or batsman before hitting the stumps ⟨~ *bowled three batsmen*⟩

³**clean** *vt* **1** to make clean **2** to strip, empty ⟨*the tree was* ~ed *of fruit by the hurricane*⟩ ~ *vi* to undergo cleaning ⟨*how will this fabric* ~⟩ – **cleanable** *adj*

**synonyms** Cleanse is used in a more figurative sense than **clean**. Compare ⟨**clean** *the floor*⟩ ⟨**cleanse** *her of her sins*⟩. The use of **cleanser** rather than **cleaner**, therefore, for a cleaning substance suggests "purity" as well as mere cleanness. A person or thing that has been **cleaned** or **cleansed** is then **clean** but not necessarily cleanly. Cleanly and cleanliness imply habitual cleanness, and sometimes also "purity".

**clean out** *vt* **1** to make (eg the inside of a room, drawer, etc) clean and tidy, esp by removing unwanted things **2** to exhaust (eg stocks) totally; leave with nothing **3** *informal* to win or steal everything from

**clean up** *vi* **1** to make things clean and tidy **2** *informal* to make a large gain (eg in business or gambling) ~ *vt* to clean or remove by cleaning ⟨*cleaning up Soho*⟩ ⟨*clean that mess up at once!*⟩ – see also CLEANUP

⁴**clean** *n* **1** an act of cleaning away dirt, esp from the surface of something **2** a lift in weight lifting in which the weight is raised to shoulder height and held

,**clean-'cut** *adj* **1** cut so that the surface or edge is smooth and even; *also* of a streamlined design **2** unambiguously clear; definite **3** of wholesome appearance

**cleaner** /'kleenə/ *n* one who or that which cleans: eg **a(1)** one whose occupation is cleaning rooms or clothes **a(2) cleaners** *pl*, **cleaner's** a dry-cleaning establishment ⟨*took his suit to the* ~s⟩ **b** a substance for cleaning **c** an implement or machine for cleaning **synonyms** see ³CLEAN – **take to the cleaners** *informal* **1** to defraud thoroughly; fleece **2** to criticize strongly and damagingly

,**clean-'limbed** *adj* well proportioned; trim ⟨~ *youths*⟩

,**clean-'living** *adj* leading a life free from immorality or excess

¹**cleanly** /'klenli, 'kleenli/ *adj* **1** careful to keep clean; fastidious **2** habitually kept clean **synonyms** see ³CLEAN – **cleanliness** *n*

²**cleanly** /'kleenli/ *adv* in a clean manner

**clean room** *n* a room for the manufacture or assembly of objects (eg precision parts) that is maintained at a high level of cleanliness

**cleanse** /klenz/ *vb* to clean **synonyms** see ³CLEAN [ME *clensen*, fr OE *clǣnsian* to purify, fr *clǣne* clean]

**cleanser** /'klenzə/ *n* **1** one who or that which cleanses **2** a preparation (eg a scouring powder or skin cream) used for cleaning **synonyms** see ³CLEAN

,**clean-'shaven** *adj* having the beard and moustache shaved off; *also* having the hair shaved off

**cleanskin** /'kleen,skin/ *n, Austr informal* **1** a person who has no criminal record **2** an honest incorruptible person ⟨*whenever the police were on to him, Jack was always a complete, smiling* ~ *– The Sun (Melbourne)*⟩ [orig sense, an unbranded animal]

**clean sweep** *n* **1** a capture of all the prizes at stake in a contest or competition **2** a complete removal or purge ⟨*the new director made a* ~ *of the previous staff*⟩

**cleanup** /'kleen,up/ *n* **1** an act of cleaning up **2** *NAm informal* a large profit

¹**clear** /kliə/ *adj* **1a** bright, luminous **b** cloudless; *specif* less than one-eighth covered ⟨*a* ~ *sky*⟩ **c** free from mist, haze, or dust ⟨*a* ~ *day*⟩ **d** easily visible; plain **e(1)** free from obscurity or ambiguity; obvious ⟨*but it's perfectly* ~⟩ ⟨*a* ~ *case of nepotism*⟩ ⟨*it is* ~ *from his letter that he's very upset*⟩ – compare LUCID, LIMPID, PERSPICUOUS **e(2)** *of a message* not in code **e(3)** free from doubt; certain ⟨*we are not* ~ *as to how we should proceed*⟩ **f** untroubled, serene ⟨*a* ~ *gaze*⟩ **2a(1)** free from blemishes; pure ⟨*a* ~ *skin*⟩ ⟨~ *water*⟩ ⟨*a beautiful* ~ *red*⟩

**a(2)** free from the effects of an illness, disease, etc; recovered ⟨*he'd better stay in until he's ~*⟩ **a(3)** free from abnormal sounds when listened to through a stethoscope **b** free from guile or guilt ⟨*a ~ conscience*⟩ **c** easily seen through; transparent ⟨*~ glass*⟩ ⟨*crystal ~*⟩ **3a** easily heard; *also* unwavering ⟨*she has a good ~ voice*⟩ **b** pronounced with the quality of a FRONT vowel (vowel produced with the tongue towards the front of the mouth) ⟨*the ~ /l/ in French*⟩ **4** capable of sharp discernment; keen ⟨*a ~ intellect*⟩ **5** unhampered by restriction or limitation: eg **5a** unencumbered by debts or charges **b** net ⟨*a ~ profit*⟩ **c** free from obstruction or entanglement ⟨*~ of obstacles*⟩ **d** not close; away ⟨*stand ~ of the edge!*⟩ **e** being a round (eg in showjumping) in which no faults are committed **f** unqualified, absolute ⟨*a ~ majority*⟩ **g** complete and intervening ⟨*six ~ days*⟩ **6** empty ⟨*the hold is quite ~*⟩ – see also **the** COAST **is clear** □ (*1c,2a,5c,5d,6*) often *+ of synonyms* see EVIDENT *antonym* obscure [ME *clere*, fr OF *cler*, fr L *clarus* clear, bright; akin to L *calare* to call – more at LOW] – **clearly** *adv*, **clearness** *n*

²**clear** *adv* **1** in a clear manner ⟨*to cry loud and ~*⟩ **2a** out of the way; away ⟨*you over there! Stand ~!*⟩ ⟨*I managed to jump ~*⟩ **b** ²CLEAN 2a **3** *chiefly NAm* all the way ⟨*can see ~ to the mountains on a day like this*⟩ – **steer clear** to keep away – often *+ of*

*usage* The adverb **clear** is used particularly in the sense "without obstruction" ⟨*stand clear of the gates*⟩ ⟨*the burglar got clear away*⟩ and cannot replace **clearly** in the sense "unambiguously". ⟨*he's clearly wrong*⟩.

³**clear** *vt* **1a** to make transparent or translucent **b** to free from unwanted material ⟨*~ the land of trees and bushes*⟩ – often *+ out* ⟨*~ out that cupboard*⟩ **2** to free from accusation or blame; vindicate ⟨*the opportunity to ~ himself*⟩ **3** to free from obstruction: eg **3a** to rid (the throat) of phlegm; *also* to make a rasping noise in (the throat) **b** to erase accumulated totals or stored data from (eg a calculator or computer memory) **4a** to authorize, approve ⟨*the chairman ~ed the article for publication*⟩ ⟨*~ him for top secret work*⟩ **b** to successfully submit for approval ⟨*~ it with your superiors*⟩ **5a** to deal with until finished or settled ⟨*~ the backlog of work*⟩ ⟨*~ an account*⟩ **b** to free from obligation or encumbrance **c(1)** to free (a ship or shipment) by payment of duties or harbour fees **c(2)** to pass through (customs) **d** to gain without deduction; net ⟨*~ a profit*⟩ **e** to put through a clearinghouse **6a** to remove or get rid of; *also* to tidy ⟨*~ the plates from the table*⟩ – often *+ off, up*, or *away* ⟨*~ away the rubbish*⟩ **b** to kick or pass away from the goal, esp in soccer **7** to go over or past without touching ⟨*the horse ~ed the fence easily*⟩ **8** to be passed by ⟨*the bill ~ed the legislature*⟩ ~ *vi* **1a** to become clear – often *+ up* ⟨*it ~ed up quickly after the rain*⟩ **b** to go away; vanish ⟨*the symptoms ~ed gradually*⟩ – often *+ off, out, up* or *away* ⟨*told him to ~ out*⟩ ⟨*after the mist ~ed away*⟩ **2** to be processed in a bank or pass through a clearinghouse ⟨*the cheque will take three days to ~*⟩ **3a** to obtain permission to discharge cargo or passengers **b** to conform to regulations or pay requisite fees prior to leaving a port, airfield, etc – **clearable** *adj* – **clear the air/atmosphere** to remove elements of hostility, tension, confusion, or uncertainty from the mood or temper of the time – see also **clear the** DECKS

**clear up** *vt* to explain, solve ⟨*can you* clear up *the mystery?*⟩

⁴**clear** *n* **1** a clear space or part **2** a high long arcing shot in badminton **3** the position or colour of a signal when indicating that traffic may pass – compare DANGER **4** a form other than code or cipher ⟨*the message was in ~*⟩ – **in the clear** free from guilt or suspicion

**clear-air turbulence** *n* sudden severe turbulence occurring in cloudless regions that causes violent jarring or buffeting of aircraft

**clearance** /'kliərəns/ *n* **1** an act or process of clearing: eg **1a** the act of clearing a ship, aircraft, etc through customs; *also* the papers showing that a ship, aircraft, etc has cleared **b** the offsetting of cheques and other claims among banks through a clearinghouse **c** certification as clear of objection; authorization **d clearance sale** *also* **clearance** a sale to clear out stock **e** the act of removing something (eg buildings or people) from the space previously occupied by it ⟨*the Highland ~s*⟩ ⟨*slum ~*⟩ **f** an act of kicking or passing the ball away from the goal by a defender (eg in football) **2** the distance by which one object clears another or the clear space between them

**clearcole** /-,kohl/ *vt or n* (to paint with) a primer of SIZE (gluelike sealing agent) mixed with whiting or WHITE LEAD used

esp in house painting [part trans of Fr *claire colle*, fr *claire* clear + *colle* glue – more at COLLAGE]

,**clear-'cut** *adj* **1** sharply outlined; distinct **2** free from ambiguity or uncertainty; unambiguous

**clearer** /'kliərə/ *n* **1** one who or that which clears **2** CLEARING BANK

,**clear-'eyed** *adj* **1** having clear eyes **2** having no illusions about a state of affairs; realistic

,**clear-'fell** *vt* to cut down all the trees in (a group or area of trees)

**clearfilm** /'kliə,film/ *n* clingfilm

**clearheaded** /-'hedid/ *adj* **1** not confused; sensible, rational **2** CLEAR-EYED 2 – **clearheadedly** *adv*, **clearheadedness** *n*

**clearing** /'kliəring/ *n* **1** the act or process of making or becoming clear **2** an area of land cleared of trees and bushes **3a** a method of exchanging and offsetting commercial papers, cheques, or accounts with cash settlement only of the balances due after the clearing **b** *pl* the gross amount of balances so adjusted

**clearing bank** *n* a bank that is a member of a clearinghouse; *specif* any of several commercial banks of England and Wales that handle the finance of companies and individuals and are members of the London Bankers' Clearinghouse

**clearinghouse** /-,hows/ *n* **1** an establishment maintained by banks for settling mutual claims and accounts **2** an agency for collecting, classifying, and distributing something, esp information

**clearout** /'kliərowt/ *n, informal* a thorough removal of all unwanted material

,**clear-'sighted** *adj* **1** having clear vision **2** CLEAR-EYED 2; *esp* having perceptive insight – **clear-sightedly** *adv*, **clear-sightedness** *n*

**clearstory** /'kliəstəri, -stawri/ *n* CLERESTORY

**clearway** /-,way/ *n, Br* a road on which vehicles may only stop in an emergency

**clearwing** /'kliə,wing/ *n* any of several moths (esp family Sesiidae) that have largely transparent wings devoid of scales and often resemble wasps

¹**cleat** /kleet/ *n* **1a** a wedge-shaped piece fastened to or projecting from something and serving as a support or check **b** a wooden or metal fitting usu with two projecting horns to which a rope may be made fast **2** a small nail of triangular section used in glazing **3a** a strip fastened across something to give strength or hold it in position **b** a projecting piece (eg on the bottom of a shoe) that provides a grip [ME *clete* wedge, fr (assumed) OE *clēat*; akin to MHG *klōz* lump – more at CLOUT]

²**cleat** *vt* **1** to secure to or by a cleat **2** to provide with a cleat

**cleavage** /'kleevij/ *n* **1a** the quality of a crystallized substance or rock of splitting along definite planes that are parallel to actual or possible crystal faces **b** a fragment (eg of a diamond) obtained by splitting **2a** division or a division ⟨*a sharp ~ in society between rich and poor*⟩ **b** CELL DIVISION; *esp* the series of divisions of the egg that results in the formation of individual cells (the BLASTOMERES) and changes the ZYGOTE (fertilized egg) into a multicellular embryo **3** the splitting of a molecule into simpler molecules **4** the space between a woman's breasts, esp when exposed by a low-cut garment [²*cleave* + *-age*]

¹**cleave** /kleev/ *vi* **cleaved, clove** /klohv/ *also* **clave** /klayv/ to adhere firmly and closely or loyally and steadfastly ⟨*their tongue ~d to the roof of their mouth* – Job 29:10 (AV)⟩ [ME *clevien*, fr OE *clifian*; akin to ON *klīfa* to cling to, OE *clæg* clay]

²**cleave** *vb* **cleaved** *also* **cleft** /kleft/, **clove** /klohv/; **cleaved** *also* **cleft, cloven** /'klohv(ə)n/ *vt* **1** to divide, penetrate, or pass through (as if) by a cutting blow; split **2** to separate into distinct parts, esp into groups having divergent views ~ *vi* **1** to split, esp along the grain **2** to subject something to cleaving [ME *cleven*, fr OE *clēofan*; akin to ON *kljūfa* to split, L *glubere* to peel, Gk *glyphein* to carve]

*usage* The participles **cleft** and **cloven** are used in different fixed expressions: **cleft palate** but **cloven hoof**. *synonyms* see ²TEAR

**cleaver** /'kleevə/ *n* one who or that which cleaves; *esp* a butcher's implement for cutting animal carcases into joints or pieces

**cleavers** /'kleevəz/ *n taking sing or pl vb* **1** a plant (*Galium aparine*) of the madder family that has stems covered with curved prickles that make it stick to any surface it touches and that bears numerous small white flowers **2** any of several plants (genus *Galium*) closely related to cleavers [ME *clivre,* alter. of OE *clife* burdock, cleavers; akin to OE *clifian* to adhere]

**cleek** /kleek/ *n, chiefly Scot* a large hook (e g for hanging a pot over a fire) [ME (northern) *cleke,* fr *cleken* to clutch]

**clef** /klef/ *n* a symbol placed on the parallel horizontal lines of printed music to determine the position of the notes following it – compare ALTO CLEF, BASS CLEF, C CLEF, F CLEF, G CLEF, TENOR CLEF, TREBLE CLEF [Fr, lit., key, fr L *clavis* – more at CLAVICLE]

**¹cleft** /kleft/ *n* **1** a space or opening made by splitting; a fissure **2** a usu V-shaped indented formation; a hollow between ridges or protuberances ⟨*he had a ~ in his chin*⟩ [ME *clift,* fr OE *geclyft;* akin to OE *clēofan* to cleave]

**²cleft** *adj* partially split or divided ⟨*a ~ chin*⟩; *specif* divided about halfway to the midrib from the edge ⟨*a ~ leaf*⟩ [ME, fr pp of *cleven*]

**cleft palate** *n* a defect present at birth in which a longitudinal fissure exists in the roof of the mouth

**cleft stick** *n, chiefly Br* DILEMMA 2a ⟨*we were caught in a ~*⟩

**cleg** /kleg/ *n, Br* a dull grey fly (*Haematopota pluvialis*) that inflicts a painful bite; *broadly* a horsefly [ME, fr ON *kleggi*]

**cleidoic** /klie'doh·ik/ *adj, of an egg* isolated from free exchange with the environment by a more or less impervious shell ⟨*the eggs of birds are ~*⟩ [Gk *kleidoun* to fasten, lock up, fr *kleid-, kleis* key, bolt]

**cleistogamy** /klie'stogəmi/ *n* the production (e g in violets) of small inconspicuous closed self-pollinating flowers [Gk *kleistos* closed (fr *kleiein* to close) + ISV *-gamy* – more at CLOSE] – **cleistogamous, cleistogamic** *adj*

**clem** /klem/ *vb* **-mm-** *dial Eng* to starve – usu pass ⟨*'e was 'alf ~med*⟩ [ME *clemmen* to pinch]

**clematis** /klə'maytəs, 'klemətis/ *n* a usu climbing plant (genus *Clematis*) of the buttercup family with three leaflets on each leaf and usu white, pink, or purple flowers [NL, genus name, fr L, fr Gk *klēmatis* brushwood, clematis, fr *klēmat-, klēma* twig, fr *klan* to break – more at HALT]

**clemency** /'klemənsi/ *n* **1a** disposition to be merciful, esp to moderate the severity of punishment due **b** an act or instance of clemency **2** *formal* pleasant mildness of weather *synonyms* see MERCY *antonym* harshness

**clement** /'klemənt/ *adj, formal* **1** inclined to be merciful; lenient ⟨*a ~ judge*⟩ **2** *of weather* pleasantly mild [ME, fr L *clement-, clemens*] – **clemently** *adv*

**clementine** /'klemənteen/ *n* a small practically seedless citrus fruit that is a hybrid of an orange and a tangerine and has a stiff skin and a slightly acid pink-tinged flesh *synonyms* see TANGERINE [Fr *clémentine*]

**clench** /klench/ *vt* **1** CLINCH 1 **2** to hold fast; clutch ⟨*~ed the arms of his chair*⟩ **3** to set or close tightly ⟨*~ed his teeth*⟩ ⟨*~ed his fists*⟩ [ME *clenchen,* fr OE *-clencan;* akin to OE *clingan* to cling] – **clench** *n*

**clepe** /kleep/ *vt* **cleped** /kleept, klept/; **clept** /klept/, **ycleped, yclept** /i-/ *archaic* to name, call [ME *clepen,* fr OE *clipian* to speak, call; akin to OFris *kleppa* to ring, knock]

**clepsydra** /'klepsidrə/ *n, pl* **clepsydras, clepsydrae** /-drie/ WATER CLOCK [L, fr Gk *klepsydra,* fr *kleptein* to steal + *hydōr* water – more at WATER]

**clerestory** *also* **clearstory** /'kliəstəri, -stawri/ *n* **1** the part of an outside wall of a room or building, esp a church, that rises above an adjoining roof ⟨*~ windows*⟩ **2** *NAm* a ventilating section of a railway carriage roof [ME, fr *clere* clear + *story* storey]

**clergy** /'kluhji/ *n taking sing or pl vb* **1** the ordained ministers in a Christian church **2** the official or priestly class of a non-Christian religion [ME *clergie,* fr OF, knowledge, learning, fr *clerc* clergyman]

**clergyman** /-mən/, *fem* **clergywoman** /-ˌwoomən/ *n* a member of the clergy

**cleric** /'klerik/ *n* a member of the clergy; *specif* one below the grade of priest [LL *clericus*]

**clerical** /'klerikl/ *adj* **1** (characteristic) of the clergy, a clergyman, or a cleric **2** of a clerk or office worker – **clerically** *adv*

**clerical collar** *n* a narrow stiff upright white collar that is buttoned at the back of the neck and is worn by clergymen

**clericalism** /-ˌiz(ə)m/ *n* a policy of maintaining or increasing the power of a religious hierarchy – **clericalist** *n*

**clericals** /'klerikəlz/ *n pl* clerical clothes

**clerihew** /'kleriˌhyooh/ *n* a witty pseudo-biographical 4-line verse with lines of unequal length rhyming aabb [Edmund *Clerihew* Bentley †1956 E writer]

**clerisy** /'klerəsi/ *n taking sing or pl vb, chiefly archaic* learned or literary people viewed as a social class – compare INTELLIGENTSIA [Ger *klerisei* clergy, fr ML *clericia,* fr LL *clericus* cleric]

**¹clerk** /klahk; *NAm* kluhk/ *n* **1** a cleric ⟨*~ in holy orders*⟩ **2a** an official responsible for correspondence, records, and accounts **b** one whose occupation is keeping records or accounts or doing general office work ⟨*a filing ~*⟩ **3** *NAm* SHOP ASSISTANT **4** *archaic* a scholar ⟨*a ~ ther was of Oxenford* – Geoffrey Chaucer⟩ [ME, fr OF *clerc* & OE *cleric, clerc,* both fr LL *clericus,* fr LGk *klērikos,* fr Gk *klēros* lot, inheritance (in allusion to Deut 18:2); akin to Gk *klan* to break – more at HALT] – **clerkly** *adj or adv,* **clerkship** *n*

**²clerk** *vi* to act or work as a clerk ⟨*~ed in his father's office*⟩

**clerk of the course** *n* an official who has direct charge of the running of a horse-race or motor-race meeting

**clerk of the works** *n* the representative of an architect or engineering consultant on a large building site

**clerk regular** *n, pl* **clerks regular** a member of a Roman Catholic religious order who combines life in a monastic community with being a priest in a diocese

**Cleveland bay** /'kleevlənd/ *n* (any of) a breed of powerful reddish-brown riding horses adept at jumping [*Cleveland,* former district of Yorkshire, now a county of England]

**clever** /'klevə/ *adj* **1** skilful or adroit in using the hands or body; nimble **b** mentally quick and resourceful; intelligent **2** marked by wit or ingenuity; *also* witty or ingenious but lacking depth or soundness ⟨*a ~ but facile remark*⟩ ⟨*don't get ~ with me*⟩ **3** *informal* easy to use or handle ⟨*a ~ little gadget*⟩ **4** *dial* in good health; well – usu neg ⟨*not feeling very ~*⟩ [ME *cliver,* prob of Scand origin; akin to ON *kljūfa* to split – more at CLEAVE] – **cleverly** *adv,* **cleverness** *n*

**synonyms Clever, adroit, cunning,** and **ingenious** describe practical wit or skill in contriving things. **Clever** usually stresses mental quickness and resourcefulness as shown in physical dexterity ⟨*clever with his/her hands*⟩. **Adroit** suggests shrewdness in manipulation of things and circumstances, often to suit oneself ⟨*some adroit juggling with the figures in the account book*⟩. **Cunning** in this sense conveys an appreciation of skilful craftsmanship or creative work ⟨*a cunning use of lighting and stage effects*⟩. **Ingenious** stresses resourcefulness and inventiveness ⟨*an ingenious device for peeling potatoes without getting your hands wet*⟩ ⟨*ingenious market traders, who make sandals from old tyres to earn their living*⟩. See INTELLIGENT, compare SLY *antonym* stupid

**¹clever-, ¸clever** *adj, informal* anxious to appear clever or smart

**clever-dick** /dik/ *n, Br informal* SMART ALEC

**clevis** /'klevis/ *n* a usu U-shaped metal coupling projecting from the end of a beam, drawbar, etc and secured in position by means of a pin or bolt between the two arms [earlier *clevi,* prob of Scand origin; akin to ON *kljūfa* to split]

**¹clew** /klooh/ *n* **1a** either of the lower corners of a SQUARE SAIL attached to the mast at the centre, or the lower corner nearest the stern of a FORE-AND-AFT sail attached to the mast at one edge **b** a metal loop attached to the lower corner of a sail or to the corner nearest the stern **2** *archaic* a ball of thread, yarn, or cord [ME *clewe* ball of thread fr OE *cliewen;* akin to OHG *kliuwa* ball, Skt *glau* lump (cf CLUE)]

**²clew** *vt* to haul (a sail) up or down by ropes through the clews

**cliché** /'kleeˌshay/ *n* **1** a hackneyed phrase or expression; *also* the idea expressed by it **2** a hackneyed theme or situation [Fr, lit., stereotype, fr pp of *clicher* to stereotype, of imit origin] – **clichéd** *also* **cliché** *adj*

**¹click** /klik/ *n* **1a** a slight sharp sound **b** a speech sound found in certain southern African languages (e g Bantu) that is made by pressing the tongue against the teeth or the roof of the mouth and then suddenly pulling it away **2** a usu spring loaded locking mechanism (DETENT) [prob imit]

**²click** *vt* to strike, move, or produce with a click ⟨*~ed his heels together*⟩ ~ *vi* **1a** to make a click ⟨*the Geiger counter was ~ing furiously*⟩ **b** to operate with a click ⟨*the bolt ~ed into place*⟩ **2** *informal* **2a** *Br* to cause sudden insight or recognition ⟨*the name ~ed*⟩ – chiefly in *click into place* ⟨*the facts all ~ed into place*⟩ **b** to feel an immediately warm rapport with someone, esp a person of the opposite sex **c** to achieve popular success ⟨*I think this film will ~*⟩

**click beetle** *n* any of a family (Elateridae) of beetles able to right themselves with a click when turned on their backs

**clicker** /'klikə/ *n* **1** one who or that which clicks **2** *Br in-*

*formal* the foreman of a group of shoemakers or print workers

**,clickety-'click** /'klikəti/ *n* **1** a repeated slight short quick usu rhythmical sound **2** *Br informal* – used in calling the number sixty-six at bingo [irreg redupl of *click;* (2) rhyming]

**client** /'klie·ənt/ *n* **1** someone or something (eg a vassal or state) under the protection of another; *specif* a plebeian under the protection of an ancient Roman nobleman **2a** a person who engages or receives the advice or services of a professional person or organization ⟨*a lawyer's* ~s⟩ **b** a customer [ME, fr MF & L; MF *client,* fr L *client-, cliens;* akin to L *clinare* to lean – more at LEAN] – **clientage** *n,* **cliental** *adj*

**client-centred therapy** *n* a method of therapy designed to encourage clients to learn to take responsibility for their own actions and to solve their own problems

**clientele** /,klee·on'tel/ *n taking sing or pl vb* a body of clients ⟨*a shop that caters to an exclusive* ~⟩ [Fr *clientèle,* fr L *clientela,* fr *client-, cliens*]

**cliff** /klif/ *n* a very steep, vertical, or overhanging face of rock, earth, or ice; a precipice [ME *clif,* fr OE; akin to OE *clifian* to adhere to] – **cliffy** *adj*

**cliff dweller** *n* **1** *often cap C&D* a member of a prehistoric American Indian people of the SW USA who made their homes on rock ledges or in the natural recesses of canyon walls and cliffs **2** a member of any people who live on cliffs or in caves in cliffs – **cliff dwelling** *n*

**'cliff-,hanger** *n* **1** an adventure serial or melodrama; *esp* one presented in instalments, each ending in suspense **2** *informal* a situation (eg a contest) whose outcome is in doubt up to the very end

**'cliff-,hanging** *adj, informal* full of suspense

**climacteric** *n* /,klie'makterik, ,kliemak'terik/ **1** a major turning point or critical stage; *specif* one supposed to occur in life at intervals of seven years **2** the menopause; *also* a corresponding period in the male during which sexual activity and competence are reduced **3** the maximum to which the respiratory rate of fruit rises just prior to full ripening △ climatic, climactic [L *climactericus* of a climacteric fr Gk *klimaktērikos,* fr *klimaktēr* critical point, lit., rung of a ladder, fr *klimak-, klimax* ladder] – **climacteric** *adj*

**climactic** /klie'maktik/ *adj* of or being a climax △ climatic, climacteric [fr *climax,* by analogy to *syntax:syntactic*] – **climactically** *adv*

**climate** /'kliemət/ *n* **1** a region of the earth having specified weather conditions **2** the average course or condition of the weather at a place over a period of years as exhibited by temperature, wind speed, rainfall, etc **3** the prevailing state of affairs or mood of a group or period; atmosphere ⟨*a* ~ *of fear*⟩ [ME *climat,* fr MF, fr LL *climat-, clima,* fr Gk *klimat-, klima* inclination, latitude, climate, fr *klinein* to lean – more at LEAN] – **climatic** *adj,* **climatically** *adv*

**climatology** /,kliemə'toləji/ *n* the science that deals with climates and their phenomena – **climatologist** *n,* **climatological** *adj,* **climatologically** *adv*

**'climax** /'klie,maks/ *n* **1** a figure of speech in which a series of phrases or sentences is arranged in increasing order of rhetorical forcefulness **2a** the highest point; the culmination **b** the point of highest dramatic tension or a major turning point in some action (eg of a play) **c** an orgasm **3** a relatively stable final stage reached by a community, esp a plant community, in its ecological development that is characterized by equilibrium with natural environmental conditions *synonyms* see SUMMIT [L, fr Gk *klimax* ladder, fr *klinein* to lean]

**'climax** *vi* to come to a climax ~ *vt* to bring to a climax

**'climb** /kliem/ *vi* **1a** to go upwards with gradual or continuous progress; rise ⟨*watching the smoke* ~⟩ ⟨*the aeroplane* ~ed *slowly*⟩ **b** to slope upwards ⟨*the road* ~s *steadily*⟩ **2a** to go up, down, or about on a more or less vertical surface using the hands to grasp or give support ⟨~ed *upon her father's knee*⟩ ⟨~ *down the ladder*⟩ **b** *of a plant* to grow upwards (eg by twining) **3** to get into or out of clothing, usu with some haste or effort ⟨*the firemen* ~ed *into their clothes*⟩ ~ *vt* **1** to go up, to the top of, or over ⟨~ *a hill*⟩ **2** to draw or pull oneself up, over, or to the top of by using the hands and feet ⟨*children* ~ing *the tree*⟩ **3** *of a plant* to grow up or over – see also **climb on the** BANDWAGON *antonym* descend [ME *climben,* fr OE *climban;* akin to OE *clamm* bond, fetter] – **climbable** *adj*

**climb down** *vi* BACK DOWN

**'climb** *n* **1** a place where progress is impossible without climbing; a steep place or way **2** the act or an instance of climbing; ascent by climbing

**'climb-,down** *n, informal* an abandoning of a position, stance, etc

**climber** /'kliemə/ *n* **1** a person who climbs esp hills or mountains **2** a climbing plant **3** *chiefly Br* SOCIAL CLIMBER

**climbing frame** /'klieming/ *n, chiefly Br* an open structure usu made of wood or tubular metal on which children may climb

**climbing iron** *n* a steel framework with spikes attached that may be fastened to climbing boots; CRAMPON 2

**climbing perch** *n* a small Indian fish (*Anabas testudineus*) resembling the perch that travels overland by means of its spiny projecting fins, and has modified gills for breathing air

**clime** /kliem/ *n,* **climes** *n pl* a climate ⟨*travelled to sunnier* ~s⟩ [LL *clima*]

**clin-, clino-** *comb form* incline; slant ⟨clino*meter*⟩ [NL, fr Gk *klinein* to lean – more at LEAN]

**'clinch** /klinch/ *vt* **1** to turn over or flatten the protruding pointed end of (a driven nail, screw, rivet, etc); *also* to fasten in this way **2** to make final or irrefutable; settle ⟨*that* ~ed *the argument*⟩ ⟨~ *the deal*⟩ ~ *vi* **1** to hold an opponent (eg in boxing) at close quarters with one or both arms **2** *informal, esp of lovers* to embrace, hug [prob alter. of 'clench]

**'clinch** *n* **1** a fastening by means of a clinched nail, rivet, or bolt; *also* the clinched part of a nail, rivet, or bolt **2** an act or instance of clinching in boxing **3** *informal* a close embrace, esp between lovers; a hug ⟨*a tight* ~⟩

**clincher** /'klinchə/ *n, informal* a decisive fact, argument, act, or remark ⟨*the expense was the* ~ *that persuaded us to give up the enterprise*⟩

**'clincher-,built** *adj* CLINKER-BUILT (built with planks overlapping)

**cline** /klien/ *n* a graded series of differences in shape, form, or physiology exhibited by a group of related organisms (eg a species), usu along a line of environmental or geographical transition; *broadly* a continuum [Gk *klinein* to lean] – **clinal** *adj,* **clinally** *adv*

**-cline** /-klien/ *comb form* (→ *n*) slope ⟨mono*cline*⟩ [back-formation fr *-clinal,* fr Gk *klinein*] – **-clinal, -clinic** *comb form* (→ *adj*)

**cling** /kling/ *vi* **clung** /klung/ **1a** to stick as if glued firmly ⟨*the sweaty shirt* clung *to his back*⟩ **b** to hold or hold on tightly or tenaciously ⟨*they* clung *to their old beliefs*⟩ **2a** to have a strong or excessive emotional attachment or dependence ⟨*that child* ~s *too much*⟩ **b** to linger ⟨*the odour* clung *to the room for hours*⟩ [ME *clingen,* fr OE *clingan;* akin to OHG *klunga* tangled ball of thread, MIr *glacc* hand] – **clingy** *adj*

**clingfilm** /'kling,film/ *n* a thin transparent plastic film used to wrap foodstuffs in and keep them fresh

**cling peach** *n* a clingstone peach

**clingstone** /-,stohn/ *n* a fruit, esp a peach, whose flesh adheres strongly to the stone

**clinic** /'klinik/ *n* **1** a teaching class for medical students in which patients are examined and discussed (eg at the bedside in a hospital) **2a** a meeting held by an expert or person in authority, to which people bring problems for discussion and resolution ⟨*an MP's weekly* ~ *for his constituents*⟩ **b** a session at which skills or knowledge in a usu specified field are taught by an expert, esp remedially ⟨*a golf* ~⟩ **3a** a place for the diagnosis and treatment of outpatients, often part of a hospital; *also* one for treatment or advice in a specified area of medicine ⟨*antenatal* ~⟩ **b** *chiefly Br* a private hospital or sanatorium [Fr *clinique,* fr Gk *klinikē* medical practice at the sickbed, fr fem of *klinikos* of a bed, fr *klinē* bed, fr *klinein* to lean, recline – more at LEAN]

**clinical** /'klinikl/ *adj* **1** of or conducted (as if) in a clinic: eg **1a** involving direct observation of the patient ⟨~ *psychology*⟩ **b** apparent to or based on direct observation ⟨~ *tuberculosis*⟩ **2a** analytic, detached, or coolly dispassionate, esp to an excessive degree ⟨*a* ~ *attitude*⟩ **b** starkly bare or functional – **clinically** *adv*

**clinical thermometer** *n* a thermometer for measuring body temperature that has a constriction in the tube where the column of liquid (eg mercury) breaks and that continues to indicate the maximum temperature to which the thermometer was exposed until reset by shaking

**clinician** /kli'nish(ə)n/ *n* one qualified in the clinical practice of medicine, psychiatry, or psychology as distinguished from one specializing in laboratory or research techniques

**clinico-** *comb form* clinical and ⟨clinico*pathological*⟩

**¹clink** /klingk/ *vi* to make a slight sharp short metallic sound ~ *vt* to cause to clink [ME *clinken*, of imit origin] – **clink** *n*

**²clink** *n, slang* prison ⟨*he's still in* ~⟩ [*Clink*, a former prison in Southwark in London]

**¹clinker** /'klingkə/ *n* **1** a brick that has been burned too much in the kiln **2** (a mass of) stony matter (e g from impurities in coal) that has been fused together by fire (e g in a furnace); slag [alter. of earlier *klincard* (a hard yellowish Dutch brick), fr obs D *klinkaard*, fr *klinken* to clink]

**²clinker** *vt* **1** to cause to form clinker **2** to clear out the clinkers from ~ *vi* to turn to clinker under heat

**³clinker** *n, NAm informal* **1** a wrong note **2** a serious mistake or error **3** an utter failure; a flop [¹*clink* + ²-*er*]

**⁴clinker** *n* a clinker-built boat

**'clinker-,built** *adj, of a vessel* built with the lower edge of each external plank or plate overlapping the upper edge of the one below it – compare CARVEL-BUILT [*clinker*, n (clinch)]

**clino-** – see CLIN-

**clinometer** /kli'nomitə, 'klie-/ *n* any of various instruments used (e g by surveyors) for measuring slopes and other angles of elevation or inclination – **clinometry** *n*, **clinometric** *adj*

**¹clinquant** /'klingkənt/ *adj, archaic* glittering with gold or tinsel ⟨*the French, all* ~, *all in gold* – Shak⟩ [MF, fr prp of *clinquer* to glitter, clink, of imit origin]

**²clinquant** *n* imitation gold leaf; tinsel [Fr, fr *clinquant*, adj]

**clint** /klint/ *n* a flat block or ridge between vertical fissures in a horizontal limestone surface [ME, rocky cliff, perh fr MLG *klint* cliff, crag]

**¹clip** /klip/ *vt* **1** to clasp or fasten with a clip **2** *archaic* **2a** to hold in a tight grip; clutch **b** to embrace, encompass ⟨*yon fair sea, that* ~s *thy shore* – William Cowper⟩ [ME *clippen*, fr OE *clyppan;* akin to OHG *kläftra* fathom, L *gleba* clod, *globus* globe]

**²clip** *n* **1** any of various devices that grip, clasp, or hold **2** a device to hold cartridges for charging the magazines of some rifles; *also* a magazine from which ammunition is fed into the chamber of a firearm **3** a piece of jewellery held in position by a spring clip ⟨*tie* ~⟩

**³clip** *vt* -**pp**- **1** to cut or cut off (as if) with shears ⟨*she was* ~*ping the hedge*⟩ **b** to cut off the end or outer part of ⟨*his claws need to be* ~*ped*⟩ **c** to excerpt; *specif* to cut (passages) from a newspaper or periodical **d** *Br* to punch a hole in (esp a ticket) **2** *linguistics* to abbreviate in speech or writing ⟨*ad is a* ~*ped form of advertisement*⟩ **3** to trim the edge of (esp a coin) **4** *informal* to hit with a glancing blow; *also* to hit smartly ⟨~*ped him round the ear*⟩ [ME *clippen*, fr ON *klippa*]

**clip on** *vi* to be capable of being fastened with an attached clip

**⁴clip** *n* **1** *pl* **1a** a 2-bladed instrument for cutting esp the nails **b** *archaic or Scot* shears **2** something clipped: e g **2a** the product of a single shearing (e g of sheep) **b** an excerpt of filmed material **c** *chiefly NAm* a cutting, esp from a newspaper **d** *chiefly Austr* a crop of wool of a sheep, a flock, or a region **3** an act of clipping or the manner in which something is clipped **4** *informal* a sharp blow ⟨*a* ~ *round the ear*⟩ **5** *informal* a rate of motion; *esp* a rapid one ⟨*going at quite a* ~⟩

**clipboard** /-,bawd/ *n* a small writing board with a spring clip for holding papers

**clip-clop** /klop/ *vi or n* -**pp**- (to make) a rhythmic repeated sound characteristically produced by horses' hooves [imit]

**clip joint** *n, slang* a place of public entertainment, esp a nightclub, that makes a practice of defrauding patrons, usu by overcharging [³*clip* (to overcharge, swindle)]

**'clip-,on** *adj* of or being something that clips on ⟨*a* ~ *tie*⟩ ⟨~ *earrings*⟩

**clipped** /klipt/ *adj, of speech* tersely quick and distinct

**clipper** /'klipə/ *n* **1** one who or that which clips **2** *pl* an implement for cutting or trimming hair, fingernails, or toenails; *also* one for clipping hedges, wire, etc **3a** something (e g a horse) that moves swiftly **b** a fast sailing ship; *specif* one with long slender lines, a sharply raked bow, tall masts, and a large sail area ⟨*one of the old tea* ~s⟩

**clippie** /'klipi/ *n, Br informal* a conductor on a bus; *esp* a female one [³*clip* 1d + -*ie*]

**clipping** /'kliping/ *n* **1** something that is clipped from or out of something ⟨*nail* ~s⟩ **2** *chiefly NAm* PRESS CUTTING

**clique** /kleek/ *n taking sing or pl vb* a highly exclusive and often aloof group of people held together by the similarity of their interests, views, or purposes [Fr, fr MF *cliquer* to make a noise, of imit origin] – **cliquey, cliquy** *adj*, **cliquish** *adj*, **cliquishly** *adv*, **cliquishness** *n*

**clishmaclaver** /,klishmə'klayvə/ *n, Scot* gossip or rumour ⟨*after all the* ~ – *TLS*⟩ [Sc *clish* to gossip (of imit origin) + -*ma*-, connective affix + *claver* to gossip]

**clitellum** /kli'teləm/ *n, pl* **clitella** a thickened glandular section of the body wall of earthworms, leeches, and other ANNELIDS that secretes a thick sticky sac in which the eggs are deposited [NL, modif of L *clitellae* packsaddle]

**clitic** /'klitik/ *adj, linguistics* not capable of bearing the stress in a phrase or sentence, and pronounced as if part of the preceding or following word ⟨~ *pronoun*⟩ [back-formation fr *enclitic* & *proclitic*] – **cliticize** *vb*, **cliticization** *n*

**clitoridectomy** /,klitəri'dektəmi, ,klie-/ *n* surgical removal of the clitoris

**clitoris** /'klitəris, 'klie-/ *n* a small erectile organ at the front or top part of the vulva that is a centre of sexual sensation in females [NL, fr Gk *kleitoris*] – **clitoral, clitoric** *adj*

**cloaca** /kloh'aykə/ *n, pl* **cloacae** /-kie, -sie/ **1** ²SEWER **2** the common chamber into which the intestinal, urinary, and reproductive canals discharge in birds, reptiles, amphibians, and many fishes; *also* a comparable chamber of an INVERTEBRATE animal [L; akin to Gk *klyzein* to wash] – **cloacal** *adj*

**¹cloak** /klohk/ *n* **1** a sleeveless outer garment that usu fastens at the neck and hangs loosely from the shoulders – compare CAPE 1 **2** something that conceals; a pretence, disguise [ME *cloke*, fr ONF *cloque* bell, cloak, fr ML *clocca* bell; fr its shape]

**²cloak** *vt* to cover or hide (as if) with a cloak ⟨~*ed in secrecy*⟩

**,cloak-and-'dagger** *adj* dealing in or suggestive of melodramatic action or intrigue and usu involving espionage

**cloakroom** /-room, -,roohm/ *n* **1** a room in which outdoor clothing or luggage may be left during one's stay **2** *chiefly Br euph* a room with a toilet

**¹clobber** /'klobə/ *n, chiefly Br informal* **1** clothing; *esp* that for a specific activity **2** equipment [prob alter. of *clothes*]

**²clobber** *vt, informal* **1** to pound mercilessly; *also* to hit with force **2** to defeat overwhelmingly [origin unknown]

**clochan, clochán** /'klokhan/ *n, chiefly Irish* an esp early medieval Irish stone dwelling, usu circular and built using the technique of CORBELLING (use of projecting load-bearing ledges) [IrGael *clochán* fr *cloch* stone, rock]

**cloche** /klosh/ *n* **1** a translucent usu glass cover used, esp in small-scale gardening, for protecting outdoor plants **2** **cloche, cloche hat** a woman's usu soft closely fitting hat with a deeply rounded crown and narrow brim [Fr, lit., bell, fr ML *clocca*] – **cloche** *vb*

**¹clock** /klok/ *n* **1** a device other than a watch for indicating or measuring time **2** a recording or metering device with a dial and indicator attached to a mechanism: e g **2a** a speedometer **b** TIME CLOCK **c** *Br* a milometer **3** a synchronizing device (e g in a computer) that produces pulses at regular intervals. All activity in a computer is initiated or terminated with reference to pulses from the clock. **4** the head of a dandelion that has gone to seed **5** *Br informal* a face [ME *clok*, fr MD *clocke* bell, clock, fr ONF or ML; ONF *cloque* bell, fr ML *clocca*, of Celt origin; akin to MIr *clocc* bell] – **against the clock 1** so as to complete a usu specified task by a certain time ⟨*working against the clock*⟩ **2** timed by a stopwatch ⟨*a jump-off against the clock*⟩ – **beat the clock** to complete a specified task by or before a certain time – **put the clock back 1** to move the hands of a clock back; *esp* to make some retardation necessary to the maintenance of local time (e g by one hour in the autumn in conformity with BRITISH SUMMER TIME) **2** to be or take a retrogressive step ⟨*if passed, this bill will* put the clock back *fifty years*⟩ – **put the clock on/forward** to move the hands of a clock forward; *esp* to make some advancement necessary to the maintenance of local time (e g by one hour in the spring in conformity with BRITISH SUMMER TIME) – **round the clock 1** continuously for 24 hours; day and night without cessation **2** without relaxation and heedless of time

**²clock** *vt* **1** to time with a stopwatch or electric timing device ⟨*Coe was* ~ed *at 54 seconds for the first lap*⟩ – used chiefly in a sports context **2a** to register on a mechanical recording device ⟨*wind velocities were* ~ed *at 80 miles per hour*⟩ ⟨*Coe* ~ed *54 seconds for the first lap*⟩ – often + *up* ⟨*it's* ~ed *up hundreds of miles since then*⟩ **b** *Br informal* to put or have to one's credit; attain – often + *up* ⟨*the seventh victory he has* ~ed *up since March*⟩ **3** *Br slang* to hit ⟨*if you don't watch out, I'll* ~ *you one!*⟩ **4** *Br slang* to observe, notice – **clocker** *n*

**clock in/on** *vi* to record one's arrival at or time of starting work by pushing a card into a time clock; *broadly* to start work

**clock off/on** *vi* to record one's departure from or time of finishing work by pushing a card into a time clock; *broadly* to finish work

³**clock** *n* an ornamental pattern on the outside ankle or side of a stocking or sock [prob fr *clock* (bell); fr its original bell-like shape]

**clock golf** *n* a lawn game in which players putt a golf ball into a hole from twelve points in a circle round it

**clocklike** /'klok,liek/ *adj* 1 like a clock 2 unusually regular, undeviating, and precise

**clocktower** /'klok,towə/ *n* a usu square tower often forming part of a building (e g a church or market-hall) and having a clock face on each side at or near the top

**clock-watcher** /,wochə/ *n* a person (e g a worker or student) who keeps close watch on the passage of time in order not to work a single moment longer than he/she has to – **clock-watching** *n*

**clockwise** /-,wiez/ *adv or adj* in the direction in which the hands of a clock rotate as viewed from the front

**clockwork** /-,wuhk/ *n* **1a** the mechanism of a clock **b** machinery that operates in a manner similar to that of a mechanical clock; *specif* machinery that is powered by a coiled spring **2** something that seems to perform in response to clockwork or to be controlled by clockwork – **clockwork** *adj* – **like clockwork** with no trouble; smoothly

**clod** /klod/ *n* **1** a lump or mass, esp of earth or clay **2** a muscular gristly cut of beef taken from the neck **3a** *Br* a bumpkin **b** *chiefly NAm* an oaf, dolt **4** *poetic* soil, earth [ME, alter. of *clot*] – **cloddish** *adj*, **cloddishness** *n*, **cloddy** *adj*

**clodhopper** /'klod,hopə/ *n, informal* **1** a clumsy and uncouth rustic **2** *chiefly humorous* a large heavy shoe

**clodhopping** /-,hoping/ *adj, informal* **1** boorish, rude **2** *Br* awkward, clumsy

**clodpoll** *also* **clodpole** /'klod,pohl/ *n* CLOD 3

**clofibrate** /kloh'fiebrayt, -'fib-/ *n* a synthetic drug, $C_{12}H_{15}ClO_3$, used esp to lower abnormally high concentrations of fats and cholesterol in the blood [perh fr *chlor-* + *fibr-* + *propion*ate]

¹**clog** /klog/ *n* **1** a weight attached esp to an animal to hinder motion **2** a shoe, sandal, or overshoe with a thick typically wooden sole [ME *clogge* short thick piece of wood]

²**clog** *vb* **-gg-** *vt* **1a** to obstruct so as to hinder motion in or through ⟨*taxis* ~ged *the streets*⟩ **b** to fill or coat with extraneous matter ⟨*some creams only* ~ *the pores*⟩ **2a** to impede (as if) with a clog; encumber **b** to halt or retard the progress, operation, or growth of **3** *of a soccer player* to deliberately foul (another player), esp by kicking ~ *vi* to become filled with extraneous matter – often + *up* – **clogger** *n*

**clog dance** *n* a dance in which the performer wears clogs with which he/she beats out a clattering rhythm on the floor – **clog dancer** *n*, **clog dancing** *n*

**cloisonné** /,klwahzo'nay, '-,-/ *adj or n* (decorated in) a style of enamel decoration in which the enamel is fired in cells formed by a network of metal wires or strips that have been soldered to a metal base, thus leaving metal strips visible between the sections ⟨*the Sutton Hoo shoulder clasps represent the high point of Anglo-Saxon* ~ *work*⟩ – compare CHAMPLEVÉ [Fr, fr pp of *cloisonner* to partition, fr *cloison* partition]

¹**cloister** /'kloystə/ *n* **1a** a monastic establishment **b** monastic life ⟨*the* ~ *was not for him*⟩ **2** a covered passage on the side of an open court, esp in a monastery or convent, usu having one side walled and the other an open arcade or colonnade and used primarily for quiet thought and exercise [ME *cloistre*, fr OF, fr ML *claustrum*, fr L, bar, bolt, fr *clausus*, pp of *claudere* to close – more at CLOSE]

²**cloister** *vt* **1** to seclude from the world (as if) in a cloister ⟨*a scientist who* ~s *himself in a laboratory*⟩ **2** to surround with a cloister ⟨~ed *gardens*⟩

**cloistral** /'kloystral/ *adj* of or like a cloister

**clomiphene** /'kloməfeen, 'kloh-/ *n* a synthetic drug, $C_{26}H_{28}ClNO$, that is used to induce ovulation [*chlor-* + *amine* + *-phene* (fr *phenyl*)]

¹**clone** /klohn/ *n* **1** all the offspring of an individual that are asexually produced and therefore carry genetic information identical to that of the parent; *also* an individual offspring produced in this way **2** *informal* a near replica; a look-alike ⟨*an unruly throng of ... Buster Mottram* ~s, *dressed in pinstripe suits* – *Time Out*⟩ [Gk *klōn* twig, slip; akin to Gk *klan* to break] – **clonal** *adj*, **clonally** *adv*

²**clone** *vt* **1** to cause to reproduce so as to form a clone **2** to

make as a more or less exact copy ⟨*Somoza's national guard,* ~d *from the US Marine Corps* – *Time*⟩

**clonidine** /'klohnideen/ *n* a synthetic drug, $C_9H_9Cl_2N_3$, used esp to treat high blood pressure and in lower doses to treat migraine [*chlor-* + *ani*line + imid*azole* + *-ine*]

**clonk** /klongk/ *vi* to make a dull heavy thumping sound as if from the impact of a hard object on a hard but hollow surface ~ *vt, informal* to hit [imit] – **clonk** *n*

**clonus** /'klohnəs/ *n* rapid succession of alternating contractions and partial relaxations of a muscle occurring in some nervous diseases [NL, fr Gk *klonos* turmoil; akin to L *celer* swift] – **clonic** *adj*, **clonicity** *n*

**cloot** /klooht/ *n, Scot* **1** a cloven hoof **2** *pl, cap* Clootie [prob of Scand origin; akin to ON *klō* claw]

**Clootie** /'kloohti/ *n, chiefly Scot* – used as a name for the devil [dim. of *cloot*]

**clop** /klop/ *n* a hollow sound made (as if) by a hoof or shoe against a hard surface [imit] – **clop** *vi*

**cloqué** /'klohkay, -'-/ *n* a fabric with a surface raised in bosses or blisters [Fr, fr pp of *cloquer* to become blistered, fr Fr dial. *cloque* bell, blister, fr ML *clocca* bell]

¹**close** /klohz/ *vt* **1a** to move so as to bar passage through something; shut ⟨~ *the gate*⟩ **b** to deny access to ⟨~ *the park*⟩ **2a** to bring to an end; finish ⟨*wish to* ~ *my account*⟩ ⟨*she* ~d *her letter with best wishes*⟩ – compare SHUT **b** to conclude discussion or negotiation about ⟨*the question is* ~d⟩; *also* to bring to agreement, termination, or settlement ⟨~ *a deal*⟩ **3** to bring or bind together the parts or edges of; *also* to fill up or in ⟨*slowly he* ~d *his fist*⟩ ⟨*we must* ~ *that crack*⟩ **4** *archaic* to enclose, contain ~ *vi* **1a** to contract, fold, swing, or slide so as to leave no opening ⟨*the door* ~d *quietly*⟩ **b** to cease or discontinue operation ⟨*the shops* ~ *at 9pm*⟩ – often + *down* ⟨*the factory* ~d *down*⟩ **2a** to draw near – often + *on* or *with* ⟨*the ship was* closing *with the island*⟩ **b** to engage in a struggle at close quarters – often + *with* ⟨~ *with the enemy*⟩ **3a** to come to an end ⟨*and so the play* ~s⟩ – compare SHUT **b** to finish speaking or writing – often + *with* ⟨*I would like to* ~ *with this thought*⟩ **4** to bind or come together ⟨*that wound will never* ~⟩ – often + *on* ⟨*her jaws* ~d *ruthlessly on her kill*⟩ **5** *of commodities* to be worth a specified amount in the market at the close of the day's trading ⟨*softs generally* ~d *lower*⟩ **6** to finalize arrangements or settle a deal – usu + *with* ⟨*it's time we* ~d *with them*⟩ – see also close the DOOR on/to, close one's DOORS, close one's EYES to, close RANKS [ME *closen*, fr OF *clos-*, stem of *clore*, fr L *claudere*] – **closable, closeable** *adj*, **closer** *n*

*synonyms* **Close** in the sense of bringing or coming to a stopping point is often interchangeable with **end, conclude, finish, complete**, or **terminate. Close** may be contrasted with "open" ⟨**close** *a debate/a correspondence*⟩. **End** has a stronger sense of finality, and suggests a stop has been put to some process or development ⟨**end** *one's life*⟩ ⟨*the summer has* **ended** *that promised so much*⟩. **Conclude**, rather more formal, stresses the form or process of closing some proceeding ⟨**concluded** *their worship with a hymn*⟩. **Finish** suggests the end or last step in a process ⟨**finished** *sewing my dress last night*⟩ while **complete** stresses the successful finishing of a product or process, leaving no imperfections or deficiencies ⟨*at last I have* **completed** *my study of Robert Browning*⟩. **Terminate** suggests a limit in time or space ⟨*the examination will* **terminate** *in a quarter of an hour*⟩. *antonyms* **begin, commence, start, inaugurate**

**close down** *vi, Br* to cease broadcasting ~ *vt* to prevent (an opponent) from playing freely, esp in soccer, by close marking – see also CLOSEDOWN

**close in** *vi* **1** to gather in close all round with an oppressing or isolating effect ⟨*the fog* closed in⟩ – often + *on* ⟨*despair* closed in *on her*⟩ **2** to approach from various directions to close quarters, esp for an attack, raid, or arrest ⟨*at dawn the police* closed in⟩ – often + *on* **3a** to grow dark earlier ⟨*the nights are* closing in⟩ **b** to grow dark ⟨*the short November day was already* closing in – Ellen Glasgow⟩

**close out** *vi* **1** *chiefly NAm* to (attempt to) dispose of or sell off goods or a business, esp at a reduced price **2** to put an account in order for disposal or transfer (e g when the collateral deposited as security has run out) by buying or selling securities or commodities

**close up** *vi* **1** to draw closer together ⟨*ordered his troops to* close up⟩ **2** *of a wound* to heal completely

²**close** /klohz/ *n* **1** a conclusion or end in time or existence; a cessation ⟨*at the* ~ *of play*⟩ ⟨*by the* ~, *the market was 5 points down*⟩ **2** the conclusion of a musical phrase or section; a

cadence 3 the movement of the free foot in dancing towards or into contact with the supporting foot

³**close** /klohs; *sense 2 also* klohz/ *n* **1a** an enclosed area **b** *Br* an area beside or round a cathedral that is enclosed by buildings (e g the houses of clergy) **2a** *Br* a road closed at one end **b** *chiefly Scot* a narrow passage leading from a street to a court and the houses within or to the common stairway of tenements [ME *clos,* lit., enclosure, fr OF *clos,* fr L *clausum,* fr neut of *clausus,* pp]

⁴**close** /klohs/ *adj* **1a** confined or confining strictly ⟨*five days of ~ arrest*⟩ **b(1)** pronounced with some part of the tongue close to the palate ⟨feet *contains a ~ vowel*⟩ **b(2)** formed with the tongue in a higher position than for the other vowel of a pair **2** restricted to a privileged class or group; CLOSED **3a** **3a** hidden, secret – chiefly in *lie/keep close* **4** rigorous, strict ⟨*keep ~ watch*⟩ **5** hot and stuffy ⟨*it's very ~ in here*⟩ **6** having little space between items or units; *specif* compact, dense ⟨*~ texture*⟩ **7a** fitting tightly or exactly **b** very short or near to the surface ⟨*the barber gave him a ~ shave*⟩ **c** matching or blending without interval or gap ⟨*~ harmony*⟩ **8** near in time, space, effect, or degree ⟨*a ~ relative*⟩ **9** intimate, familiar ⟨*as children, we were very ~*⟩ **10a** marked by attention to detail ⟨*~ scrutiny*⟩ ⟨*a passage of ~ reasoning*⟩ **b** marked by fidelity to an original ⟨*a ~ copy of an old master*⟩ **11** being evenly contested or having a (nearly) even score ⟨*the match was far ~r than the score suggested*⟩ **12** difficult to obtain ⟨*money is ~*⟩ **13** *informal* reluctant to part with money or possessions **14** *informal* secretive ⟨*she could tell us something if she would... but she was as ~ as wax* – A Conan Doyle⟩ **15** *archaic* having no openings; closed ⟨*in a ~ carriage*⟩ **synonyms** see ³NEAR [ME *clos,* fr MF, fr L *clausus,* pp of *claudere* to shut, close; akin to Gk *kleiein* to close, OHG *sliozan*] – **closely** *adv,* **closeness** *n*

⁵**close** /klohs/ *adv* in a close position or manner; closely ⟨*a pretty ~ run thing*⟩ – **close by/to** at a small distance; nearby – **close on/to** almost ⟨close on 500 *people*⟩

**close call** /klohs/ *n* a narrow escape

**close company** /klohs/ *n* a company in which the majority of the shares are held by five or fewer people who are often those active in the management (e g directors)

,**close-'cropped** /klohs/ *adj* clipped short

**closed** /klohzd/ *adj* **1a** not open; shut **b** enclosed ⟨*a ~ porch*⟩ **2a** forming a self-contained unit allowing no additions ⟨*~ association*⟩ **b(1)** *of a curve* traced by a moving point that returns to its starting point without retracing its path ⟨*~ curve*⟩; *also* so formed that every cross section is a closed curve ⟨*a sphere is a ~ surface*⟩ **b(2)** characterized by mathematical elements that when subjected to an operation produce only elements of the same set ⟨*the set of whole numbers is ~ under addition and multiplication; you cannot get a fraction by adding or multiplying them*⟩ **b(3)** *of a mathematical set* containing all the LIMIT POINTS of every subset **c** characterized by continuous return and reuse of the working substance ⟨*a ~ cooling system*⟩ **3a(1)** confined to a few ⟨*~ membership*⟩ **a(2)** open only to members of a strictly defined group (e g a political party) ⟨*a ~ primary*⟩ **b** rigidly excluding outside influence or contact ⟨*a ~ economy*⟩ ⟨*a ~ mind*⟩ ⟨*a ~ prison*⟩ **4a** ending in a consonant ⟨*~ syllable*⟩ **b** ⁴CLOSE 1b **5** *of a wine* not revealing the bouquet to the full, esp because not yet fully matured

**closed book** *n, informal* **1** something which one does not or cannot understand; a mystery ⟨*lexicography is a ~ to me*⟩ **2** a subject concerning which no more consideration or discussion is permissible or possible

**closed chain** *n* RING 9 (circular arrangement of atoms)

**closed circuit** *n* a connected array of electrical components that will allow the passage of current; *specif* a television installation in which the signal is transmitted by wire to a limited number of receivers, usu in one location

**closed loop** *n* an automatic control system for an operation or process in which feedback in a closed path or group of paths acts to maintain output at a desired level

**closedown** /'klohz,down/ *n* the act or result of closing down; *esp* the end of a period of broadcasting

**closed scholarship** *n* a scholarship for which only candidates fulfilling certain preconditions are eligible – compare OPEN SCHOLARSHIP

**closed season** *n, chiefly NAm* CLOSE SEASON

**closed shop** *n* **1** an establishment in which the employer by agreement employs only union members – compare OPEN SHOP, UNION SHOP **2** something (e g an organization) that reserves membership to an exclusive category of people ⟨*even the private-eye game is no longer a "closed shop" for men* – Annabel⟩

**closed stance** *n* a preparatory position (e g in cricket batting or golf) in which the forward foot is closer to the line of play than the back foot

**closefisted** /,klohs'fistid/ *adj* stingy, tightfisted

,**close-'grained** *adj* having a closely compacted smooth texture; *esp* having narrow ANNUAL RINGS or small wood elements

**close-hauled** /klohs/ *adj or adv* with the sails set for sailing as near directly into the wind as possible

'**close-,in** /klohs/ *adj* of or operating at a small distance

**close-knit** /klohs/ *adj* bound together by intimate social or cultural ties or by close economic or political ties

,**close-'lipped** /klohs/ *adj* tight-lipped

**closemouthed** /,klohs'mowdhd/ *adj* cautious in speaking; uncommunicative; *also* secretive – **close-mouth** *n*

**close quarters** /klohs/ *n pl* immediate contact or close range ⟨*fought at ~*⟩

**close scholarship** /klohs/ *n* CLOSED SCHOLARSHIP

**close season** /klohs/ *n, Br* a period during which it is illegal to kill or catch certain game or freshwater fish

**close shave** /klohs/ *n, informal* a narrow escape

**closestool** /'klohs,stoohl/ *n* a stool with a removable seat covering a chamber pot, used in former times

¹**closet** /'klozit/ *n* **1** a small private room **2** WATER CLOSET **3** *chiefly NAm* a cupboard [ME, fr MF, dim. of *clos* enclosure] – **closetful** *n* – **come out of the closet** to declare oneself openly to be a homosexual (after leading an apparently heterosexual life) – see also SKELETON **in the closet**

²**closet** *adj* being privately but not overtly as specified; secret ⟨*a ~ romantic* – Punch⟩ **2** *chiefly NAm* working in or suited to the closet as the place of seclusion or study; theoretical

³**closet** *vt* **1** to shut up (as if) in a closet **2** to take into a small room for a secret interview or consultation ⟨*were ~ed in the office for hours*⟩

**close thing** *n, informal* **1** CLOSE SHAVE **2** *also* **close-run thing** something very nearly lost (e g a battle or election) but won in the end

**closet play** *n* a play more suitable for reading than performing

**closet queen** *n, informal* a man who secretly engages in homosexual activities while leading an ostensibly heterosexual life

**close-up** /klohs/ *n* **1** a photograph or film shot taken at close range **2** a close or personal view or examination of something

**closing time** /'klohzing/ *n, Br* a time set by law at which public houses must close and stop selling alcoholic drinks

**clostridium** /klo'stridi-əm/ *n, pl* **clostridia** /-diə/ *also* **clostridiums** any of various spore-forming soil or intestinal bacteria (esp genus *Clostridium*) that cause tetanus, GAS GANGRENE, and other diseases [NL, genus name, fr Gk *klōstēr* spindle, fr *klōthein* to spin; fr their being shaped like a rod or spindle] – **clostridial** *adj*

¹**closure** /'klohzhə/ *n* **1** an act of closing; the condition of being closed **2** something that closes ⟨*pocket with zip ~*⟩ **3** the closing or limitation of debate in a legislative body, esp by calling for a vote – compare GUILLOTINE **4** the property that a set has when it is mathematically CLOSED under an operation [ME, fr MF, fr L *clausura,* fr *clausus,* pp of *claudere* to close – more at CLOSE; (3) trans of Fr *clôture*]

²**closure** *vt* to close or limit (a debate) by closure

¹**clot** /klot/ *n* **1a** a roundish sticky lump formed by coagulation of a portion of liquid (e g cream) **b** a coagulated mass produced by clotting of blood **2** *Br informal* a stupid person; a fool [ME, fr OE *clott*; akin to MHG *klōz* lump, ball – more at CLOUT]

²**clot** *vb* **-tt-** *vi* **1** to become a clot; form clots **2** *of blood* to undergo a sequence of complex chemical and physical reactions that results in conversion from liquid form into a coagulated mass; coagulate ~ *vt* to cause to clot

**cloth** /kloth/ *n, pl* **cloths** /klodhz, kloths/ **1** a pliable material usu made by weaving, felting, or knitting together natural or synthetic fibres and threads **2** a piece of cloth adapted for a particular purpose: e g **2a** a tablecloth **b** a dishcloth **c** a duster **3** (the dress of) the clergy ⟨*a man of the ~*⟩ – + *the* [ME, fr OE *clāth*; akin to OE *clīthan* to adhere to, LL *glut-, glus* glue]

,**cloth-'cap** *adj informal* working-class [fr the cloth caps commonly worn, esp formerly, by working-class men in Britain]

**cloth cap** *n* **1** a soft flat woollen cap with a stiff peak **2** a symbol of the working class

**clothe** /klohdh/ *vt* **clothed,** *also chiefly archaic* **clad** /klad/ **1a** to cover (as if) with clothing; dress **b** to provide with clothes **2a** to invest or enhance ⟨*treaties* ∼d *in stately phraseology*⟩ **b** to disguise or conceal [ME *clothen,* fr OE *clāthian,* fr *clāth* cloth, garment]

   *usage* In the sense connected with actual clothes, **clothed** is to be preferred today to **clad.** In any case one can be **clad** only *in* something ⟨*silk-clad legs*⟩ ⟨*clad in armour*⟩ or in a particular way ⟨*warmly clad*⟩, so one must use **clothed** if one means simply "not naked".

'**cloth-**,**eared** /iəd/ *adj, informal* deaf or partially deaf

**clothes** /klohdhz/ *n pl* **1** articles of material (e g cloth) that are worn to cover the body (eg for warmth, protection, or decoration) **2** bedclothes [ME, fr OE *clāthas,* pl of *clāth*]

**clothes basket** *n* a basket used for storing dirty linen

**clothes brush** *n* a small stiff brush for removing dirt from clothes

**clotheshanger** /'klohdhz,hang-ə/ *n* COAT HANGER

**clotheshorse** /-,haws/ *n* **1** a frame on which to hang clothes, esp for drying or airing indoors **2** *informal* **2a** *derog* a conspicuously dressy person **b** a person who in wearing clothes displays them to advantage; a model

**clothesline** /-,lien/ *n* a line (eg of cord or nylon) on which clothes may be hung to dry, esp outdoors

**clothes moth** *n* any of several small yellowish or buff-coloured moths (family Tineidae) whose larvae eat wool, fur, hair, or feathers; *esp* the common clothes moth (*Tineola bisselliella*)

**clothespeg** /'klohdhz,peg/ *n, chiefly Br* a small forked device (e g of wood) or a small spring clip, esp of wood or plastic, used for fastening washing to a clothesline

**clothespin** /-,pin/ *n, NAm* a clothespeg

**clothesprop** /'klohdhz,prop/ *n, chiefly Br* a long pole for supporting a clothesline

**clothier** /'klohdhiə/ *n* one who makes or sells cloth or clothing [ME, alter. of *clother,* fr *cloth*]

**clothing** /'klohdhing/ *n* clothes or garments in general or collectively; *also* a covering – see also WOLF **in sheep's clothing**

**cloth yard** *n* a yard, esp for measuring cloth; *specif* a unit of 37 inches (0.94 metres) used as a length for arrows

**clotted cream** /,klotid/ *n* a thick cream made chiefly in Cornwall and Devon by slowly heating whole milk and then skimming the cooled cream from the top

**cloture** /'klohchə/ *n, NAm* CLOSURE 3 [Fr *clôture,* lit., closure, alter. of MF *closure*] – **cloture** *vt*

**clou** /klooh/ *n* that which is of chief interest, attraction, or importance [Fr, lit., nail, fr L *clavus*]

'**cloud** /klowd/ *n* **1a** a visible mass of particles of water or ice suspended usu at a considerable height in the air and varying from white to dark grey in colour ⟨*at 20,000 feet we ran into* ∼⟩ **b** a light filmy, puffy, or billowy mass (eg of smoke or dust) appearing suspended in the air **2a** a usu visible mass of minute particles suspended in the air or in a gas; *also* one of the masses of obscuring matter in interstellar space **b** an aggregate of electrically charged particles (eg electrons) **3** a great crowd or multitude; a swarm ⟨∼s *of mosquitoes*⟩ **4** something that has a dark or threatening aspect ⟨*a* ∼ *on the horizon*⟩ **5** something that obscures or blemishes ⟨*their reputation is under a* ∼⟩ **6** a dark or opaque vein or spot (eg in marble) [ME, rock, hill, cloud, fr OE *clūd* rock, hill; akin to Gk *gloutos* buttock] – **cloudlet** *n,* **cloudiness** *n,* **cloudless** *adj* – **in the clouds 1** out of touch with reality; unreal imaginary **2** lost in one's private thoughts or fantasies; daydreaming ⟨*he goes around with his head in the clouds*⟩

²**cloud** *vi* **1** to grow cloudy – usu + *over* **2a** of facial features to appear troubled, apprehensive, or distressed – often + *over* **b** to become blurred, dubious, or ominous ∼ *vt* **1a** to envelop or obscure (as if) with a cloud **b** to make opaque, esp by condensation of moisture **c** to make murky, esp with smoke or mist **2** to make unclear or confused ⟨*that will only* ∼ *the issue*⟩ **3** to taint or sully ⟨*a* ∼ed *reputation*⟩ **4** to cast gloom over ⟨*it* ∼ed *the whole day for them*⟩

**cloudbase recorder** /'klowd,bays/ *n* a photoelectric instrument for determining the height of the cloud ceiling

**cloudberry** /-b(ə)ri, -,beri/ *n* a creeping plant (*Rubus chamaemorus*) of the rose family that is closely related to the raspberry; *also* its pale amber-coloured edible fruit [¹*cloud* + *berry;* perh fr its shape]

**cloudburst** /-,buhst/ *n* a sudden very heavy fall of rain

**cloud chamber** *n* a vessel containing saturated water vapour

whose sudden expansion reveals the passage of an ionizing particle (e g a proton) by a trail of visible droplets

,**cloud-**'**cuckoo-**,**land** *n* a utopian world that exists only in the mind of someone who is resolutely idealistic and impractical [trans of Gk *nephelokokkygia,* imaginary realm in the play *The Birds* by Aristophanes †*ab*385 BC Gk dramatist]

**cloudland** /'klowd,land/ *n* **1** the realm of visionary speculation or poetic imagination **2** cloud-cuckoo-land

**cloudless** /'klowdlis/ *adj* free from clouds; clear – **cloudlessly** *adv,* **cloudlessness** *n*

**cloud nine** *n, informal* a feeling of extreme well-being or elation – usu + *on* ⟨*was on* ∼ *after her victory*⟩; compare SEVENTH HEAVEN [*nine* prob an arbitrary number; *seven* being sometimes used instead]

**cloudy** /'klowdi/ *adj* **1** relating to or resembling cloud **2** overcast with clouds; *specif* more than six tenths covered with clouds – **cloudily** *adv*

'**clout** /klowt/ *n* **1** a blow, esp with the hand; *also* a good strong hit with the bat in cricket or baseball ⟨*a* ∼ *round the ear*⟩ **2** a white cloth on a stake or frame used as a target in archery **3a** *dial chiefly N Eng & Scot* a piece of cloth or leather; a rag **b** *dial chiefly N Eng & Scot* CLOTH 2; *specif* a piece of cloth or rag used for polishing, cleaning, etc – often in combination ⟨*a* dishclout⟩ **4** *informal* influence; *esp* effective political power ⟨*carries a lot of* ∼ *with the PM*⟩ [ME, fr OE *clūt* patch, iron plate; akin to MHG *klōz* lump, Russ *gluda*]

²**clout** *vt* **1** *chiefly N Eng & Scot* to cover or patch with a clout **2** *informal* to hit forcefully

**clout nail** *n* a nail with a large flat head [¹*clout* (iron plate used to keep wood from wearing)]

'**clove** /klohv/ *n* any of the small individual bulbs (e g in garlic) developed as part of a larger bulb [ME, fr OE *clufu;* akin to OE *clēofan* to cleave]

²**clove** *past of* CLEAVE

³**clove** *n* the dried unopened flower bud of a tropical tree (*Eugenia aromatica*) of the eucalyptus family that is used as a spice and is the source of an oil; *also* this tree [alter. of ME *clowe,* fr OF *clou* (*de girofle*), lit., nail of clove, fr L *clavus* nail]

**clove hitch** *n* a knot used to secure a rope temporarily to a spar or another rope [ME *cloven, clove* divided, fr pp of *clevien* to cleave]

**cloven** /'klohv(ə)n/ *past part of* ²CLEAVE

**cloven foot** *n* a foot of an animal (e g of a sheep or goat) divided into two parts at the end farthest from the body – **cloven-footed** *adj*

**cloven hoof** *n* **1** CLOVEN FOOT **2** the sign of the devil or Satan [(2) fr the traditional representation of Satan as cloven-hoofed] – **cloven-hoofed** *adj*

**clove pink** *n* a pink (*Dianthus caryophyllus*) widely cultivated for its clove-scented flowers – compare CARNATION

**clover** /'klohvə/ *n* any of a genus (*Trifolium*) of plants of the pea family with 3-lobed leaves and flowers in dense heads, many of which are valuable for forage and attractive to bees [ME, fr OE *clāfre;* akin to OHG *klēo* clover] – **in clover** in prosperity or pleasant circumstances

**cloverleaf** /-,leef/ *n, pl* **cloverleaves** something that resembles a clover leaf in shape; *specif* a road junction that resembles a four-leaved clover, connects two roads at different levels, and merges traffic without the need for streams of traffic to cross – **cloverleaf** *adj*

'**clown** /klown/ *n* **1a** a jester in an entertainment (e g a play); *specif* a grotesquely dressed comedy performer in a circus **b** *informal* one who habitually plays the buffoon; a joker **c** *informal* an ineffectual or incompetent person; a fool **2a** a rude ill-bred person; a boor **b** *archaic* a farmer or countryman [perh fr MF *coulon* settler, fr L *colonus* colonist, farmer – more at COLONY] – **clownery** *n*

²**clown** *vi* to act as or like a clown – often + *about*

**clownish** /'klownish/ *adj* resembling or befitting a clown (e g in ignorance and lack of sophistication) – **clownishly** *adv,* **clownishness** *n*

**cloy** /kloy/ *vt* to satiate with an excess, usu of something originally pleasing ∼ *vi* to cause a feeling of satiety or excess *synonyms* see ²SATIATE [ME *acloien* to lame, fr MF *encloer* to drive in a nail, fr ML *inclavare,* fr L *in* + *clavus* nail] – **cloyingly** *adv*

'**club** /klub/ *n* **1a** a hand weapon consisting of a heavy stick that is thicker at one end than at the other **b** a stick or bat used to hit a ball in any of various games ⟨*a golf* ∼⟩ **c** INDIAN

CLUB **2a** a black trefoil-shaped figure marked on a playing card; *also* a card marked with one or more of these figures **b** *pl but taking sing or pl vb* the suit comprising cards identified by this figure **3a** *taking sing or pl vb* an association of people for a specified purpose usu jointly supported and meeting periodically ⟨*a sports* ∼⟩ **b** the meeting place or premises of a club **c** a group of people who agree to make regular payments or purchases in order to secure some advantage ⟨*book* ∼⟩ – compare CHRISTMAS CLUB, FRIENDLY SOCIETY **d** an often exclusive association of people, typically owning premises available as a congenial place of retreat or temporary residence **e** a nightclub – **in the club** *slang* pregnant [ME *clubbe*, fr ON *klubba;* akin to OHG *kolbo* club, OE *clamm* bond; (3) fr sense 'club-like mass, bunch']

²**club** *vb* **-bb-** *vt* **1** to beat or strike with or as if with a club ⟨*he* ∼*bed him to death with his rifle butt*⟩ **2a** to unite or combine for a common cause **b** to contribute to a common fund ∼ *vi* **1** to form a club; combine **2** to agree to share a joint expense – usu + *together*

**clubbable** *also* **clubable** /'klubəbl/ *adj* sociable

**clubbed** /klubd/ *adj* shaped like a club ⟨∼ *antennae*⟩

**clubfoot** /-'foot/ *n* a misshapen foot twisted out of position from birth; *also* this deformity – **clubfooted** *adj*

**club fungus** *n* any of a family (Clavariaceae) of BASIDIO-MYCETES (class of fungi) with a simple or branched often club-shaped SPOROPHORE (spore-bearing structure)

**clubhouse** /'klub,hows/ *n* **1** a house occupied by a club or used for club activities **2** a building having the changing rooms and social facilities of a sports club

**clubland** /'klub,land, -lənd/ *n, Br* the area or world of clubs: eg **a** the area around St James's in London **b** the area in esp N England containing a large number of working men's clubs

**clubman** /'klubmən/, *fem* **clubwoman** /-,woomən/ *n* a member of a club, esp of an exclusive social club

**club moss** *n* any of an order (Lycopodiales) of primitive VASCULAR PLANTS [trans of NL *muscus clavatus;* fr the club-shaped spore-producing vessels in some species]

**clubroot** /-,rooht/ *n* a disease of cabbages and related plants that is caused by a SLIME MOULD (*Plasmodiophora brassicae*) and produces swellings or distortions of the root

**club sandwich** *n, chiefly NAm* a sandwich of three slices of bread with two layers of filling (e g chicken or turkey and lettuce)

¹**cluck** /kluk/ *vi* **1** to make a cluck **2** to make a clicking sound with the tongue, esp to express disapproval; *also* to express an esp meddling interest or concern ⟨*critics* ∼*ed over the new developments*⟩ ∼ *vt* to express by clucking [imit]

²**cluck** *n* **1** the characteristic guttural sound made by a hen; *also* a similar sound **2** *NAm* a stupid or naive person

¹**clue** /klooh/ *n* **1** something that guides through an intricate procedure or maze of difficulties to the solution of a problem **2** a cryptic phrase, anagram, etc the solution of which enables a crossword answer to be filled in [var of *clew* ball of thread; fr the use of a ball of thread to find one's way out of a labyrinth] – **not have a clue 1** to know nothing; be ignorant **2** to be incompetent

²**clue** *vt*, **clued; clueing, cluing** *informal* to inform with the latest facts, news, etc – usu + *in* or *up* ⟨∼ *me in on how it happened*⟩ ⟨*not very* ∼*d up about buying a house*⟩

**clueless** /-lis/ *adj, Br informal* hopelessly ignorant or lacking in sense

**clumber spaniel, clumber** /'klumbə/ *n, often cap C&S* a large heavily built spaniel with a thick silky mainly white coat [*Clumber*, estate in Nottinghamshire in England]

¹**clump** /klump/ *n* **1** a compact group of things of the same kind; a cluster ⟨*a* ∼ *of bushes*⟩ **2** a compact mass (e g a blood clot) **3** a heavy tramping sound **4** a thick extra sole on a shoe or boot **5** *informal* a smart blow [prob fr LG *klump;* akin to OE *clamm* bond] – **clumpy** *adj*

²**clump** *vi* **1** to tread clumsily and noisily **2** to form clumps ∼ *vt* to arrange in or cause to form clumps ⟨*the serum* ∼*s the bacteria*⟩

**clumper** /'klumpə/ *n, Can* a large clump of ice piled up on a shoreline

**clumsy** /'klumzi/ *adj* **1a** lacking dexterity, nimbleness, or grace **b** lacking tact or subtlety ⟨*a* ∼ *attempt at sympathy*⟩ **2** awkwardly or poorly made; unwieldy ⟨*a* ∼ *fake*⟩ [prob fr obs E *clumse* benumbed with cold, of Scand origin] – **clumsily** *n*, **clumsiness** *n*

**synonyms Clumsy** and **awkward** are often interchangeable, but

**awkward** tends to be used for actions ⟨*an* **awkward** *gesture*⟩ while **clumsy** often describes an inherent condition or tendency ⟨*clumsy boy, to drop the plates!*⟩. **Gauche, maladroit**, and **inept** apply rather to behaviour than to actions. **Gauche** suggests the awkwardness that comes from ignorance of social conventions ⟨*a* **gauche** *lad skulking in the corner*⟩. A **maladroit** remark or action is one which is tactless or ill-timed; a **maladroit** person lacks skill in social situations requiring care ⟨*a* **maladroit** *messenger may spoil the effect of the message*⟩. **Inept** is the strongest word in this group and suggests a total lack of skill or competence ⟨*how could you be so* **inept** *as to forget the address I gave you?*⟩ An **inept** remark is one which is inappropriate, often so much so as to seem pointless. **antonyms** deft, graceful, adroit, dexterous, skilful

**clung** /klung/ *past or past part of* CLING

**clunk** /klungk/ *n* **1** a blow or the sound of a blow; a thump **2** a soft metallic sound [imit] – **clunk** *vi*

**clupeid** /'kloohpi·id/ *n* any of a large family (Clupeidae) of soft-finned BONY FISHES (e g herrings) that have a body flattened from side to side and a forked tail [deriv of L *clupea*, a small river fish] – **clupeid** *adj*

¹**cluster** /'klustə/ *n* **1** a compact group formed by a number of similar objects or people; a bunch **2** two or more consecutive consonants or vowels in a segment of speech **3** the group of four cups that connect the teats of a cow to a milking machine **4** a small metal insignia attached to a ribbon as an added distinction **5** a group of faint stars or galaxies that appear close together and have common properties (e g distance and motion) [ME, fr OE *clyster;* akin to OE *clott* clot] – **clustery** *adj*

²**cluster** *vt* to collect or arrange into a cluster ∼ *vi* to grow or assemble in a cluster – often + *about* or *around*

**cluster bomb** *n* a bomb that releases a number of smaller usu incendiary or fragmentation missiles on bursting

**cluster fly** *n* a fly (*Pollenia rudis*) that has furry golden hair on the THORAX (middle body region) and in the larval state is parasitic in earthworms [fr its habit of sheltering in large clusters in autumn]

¹**clutch** /kluch/ *vt* to grasp or seize (as if) with the hand or claws, esp strongly or tightly ∼ *vi* to seek to grasp and hold – often + *at* [ME *clucchen*, fr OE *clyccan;* akin to MIr *glacc* hand – more at CLING]

²**clutch** *n* **1a** the claws or a hand in the act of grasping or seizing firmly **b** *usu pl* control or possession ⟨*at last she was in his* ∼*es*⟩ **2** a device for gripping an object (e g attached to the end of a chain or tackle) **3a** a coupling used to connect and disconnect a driving and a driven part of a mechanism **b** a lever or pedal operating such a clutch, esp in a motor vehicle

³**clutch** *n* **1** a nest of eggs or a brood of chicks **2** a group or bunch [alter. of E dial *cletch* hatching, brood]

**clutch bag** *n* a small handbag with no handle

¹**clutter** /'klutə/ *vt* to fill or cover with scattered or disordered objects – often + *up* [ME *clotteren* to clot, fr *clot*]

²**clutter** *n* **1a** a crowded or confused mass or collection **b** scattered or disordered objects **2** interfering echoes visible on a radar screen caused by reflection from objects other than the target

**Clydesdale** /'kliedz,dayl/ *n* a powerfully built draught horse with heavily feathered legs of a breed originally from Clydesdale in Scotland

**clype** /kliep/ *vi, Scot* to tell tales [alter. of earlier *cleip*, fr ME *clepen* to call – more at CLEPE]

**clypeus** /'klipi·əs/ *n, pl* **clypei** /'klipi,ee, -ie/ a plate shaped like a shield on the front central part of an insect's head [NL, fr L, round shield] – **clypeate** *adj*

**clyster** /'klistə/ *n, archaic* ENEMA [ME, fr MF or L; MF *clistere*, fr L *clyster*, fr Gk *klystēr*, fr *klyzein* to wash out]

**,c·mi'tosis** *n* an artificially induced division of the nucleus of a cell (e g by treatment with colchicine) in which the number of CHROMOSOMES (strands of gene-carrying material) is doubled [colchicine + *mitosis*] – **c-mitotic** *adj*

**cnidoblast** /'niedə,blast/ *n* a cell (e g in a jellyfish or SEA ANEMONE) that develops (into) a NEMATOCYST (specialized stinging cell) [NL *cnida* nematocyst, fr Gk *knidē* nettle]

**co-** /koh-/ *prefix* **1** with; together; joint ⟨*coexist*⟩ ⟨*coheir*⟩ ⟨*coeducation*⟩ **2** in or to the same degree ⟨*coextensive*⟩ **3a** associate; fellow ⟨*coauthor*⟩ ⟨*co-star*⟩ **b** deputy; assistant ⟨*copilot*⟩ **4** of or constituting the angle which with a given angle makes 90° ⟨*cosine*⟩ ⟨*cotangent*⟩ [ME, fr L, fr *com-;* akin to OE *ge-*, perfective and collective prefix, Gk *koinos* common]

**coacervate** /koh'asəvayt/ n an aggregate of tiny droplets suspended in a liquid held together by electrostatic attractive forces [L *coacervatus*, pp of *coacervare* to heap up, fr *co-* + *acervus* heap] – **coacervate** adj, **coacervation** n

**¹coach** /kohch/ n **1a** a large usu closed four-wheeled carriage – compare STAGECOACH **b** a railway carriage **c** a usu single-deck bus used esp for long-distance or sight-seeing journeys that has all seats facing forwards **2a** a private tutor **b** one who instructs or trains a performer or sports players ⟨a *soccer* ∼⟩ [ME *coche*, fr MF, fr Ger *kutsche*, prob fr Hung *kocsi* (*szekér*) wagon from Kocs, fr *Kocs*, village in Hungary; (2) fr the notion that a tutor conveys or drives a student through examinations]

**²coach** vt **1** to train intensively by instruction, demonstration, and practice **2** to act as coach to (eg a sports team) ∼ vi **1** to travel in a coach **2** to instruct, direct, or prompt someone as a coach synonyms see TEACH

**coach bolt** n a large heavy-duty bolt for attaching woodwork to masonry

**coach box** n the coachman's seat in a horse-drawn carriage

**coachbuilt** /-,bilt/ adj, of a vehicle body built to individual requirements by craftsmen – **coachbuilder** n

**coach dog** n, archaic a dalmatian – compare CARRIAGE DOG

**coach house** n a building or outhouse for storing carriages

**coachman** /-mən/ n **1** the driver of a coach or carriage **2** an artificial fishing fly with white wings, peacock-feather body, and brown hackle

**coach screw** n a wood screw that has a square or hexagonal head

**coachwood** /'kohch,wood/ n an Australian tree (*Ceratopetalum apetalum*) having a light close-grained wood used esp in furniture making; also its wood [fr its orig use in coach-building]

**coachwork** /-,wuhk/ n the bodywork of a vehicle, esp a car

**coaction** /koh'aksh(ə)n/ n **1** joint action **2** the interaction between different organisms in an ecological community

**coadapted** /,koh-ə'daptid/ adj mutually adapted, esp by NATURAL SELECTION ⟨∼ *gene complexes*⟩

**coadjutor** /,koh'ajətə/ n an assistant; specif a bishop who assists a diocesan bishop and often has the right of succession [ME *coadjutour*, fr MF *coadjuteur*, fr L *coadjutor*, fr *co-* + *adjutor* aid, fr *adjutus*, pp of *adjuvare* to help – more at AID] – **coadjutant** n, **coadjutor** adj

**coadunate** /koh'adyoonət, -nayt/ adj, biology united; esp grown together [LL *coadunatus*, pp of *coadunare* to combine, fr L *co-* + *adunare* to unite, fr *ad-* +*unus* one – more at ONE] – **coadunation** n

**coagulant** /koh'agyoolənt/ n a substance that produces coagulation

**coagulase** /koh'agyoolayz/ n an ENZYME that promotes coagulation (eg of the blood)

**coagulate** /koh'agyoolayt/ vt **1** to cause to become viscous or thickened into a coherent mass; curdle, clot **2** to gather together or form into a mass or group ∼ vi to become coagulated [L *coagulatus*, pp of *coagulare* to curdle, fr *coagulum* curdling agent, fr *cogere* to drive together – more at COGENT] – **coagulable** adj, **coagulability** n, **coagulation** n

**coagulum** /koh'agyooləm/ n, pl **coagula** /-lə/, **coagulums** a coagulated mass or substance; a clot [L, coagulant]

**¹coal** /kohl/ n **1** a black or brownish-black mineral that is formed by the partial decomposition of vegetable matter under the influence of moisture and often of increased pressure and temperature within the earth. It is widely used as a natural fuel and is a source of various products (eg tar or gas). **2** a piece of glowing carbonized material (eg partly burned wood) **3** chiefly Br pieces of coal broken up to be used for burning [ME *col*, fr OE; akin to OHG & ON *kol* burning ember, IrGael *gual* coal] – **coaly** adj – **haul somebody over the coals** to reprove or reprimand somebody strongly [fr the burning of heretics in former times]

**²coal** vt **1** to burn to charcoal; char **2** to supply with coal ∼ vi to take in coal

**coal black** adj absolutely black; very black

**coaler** /'kohlə/ n a ship or train used to transport or supply coal

**coalesce** /,koh-ə'les/ vi **1** to grow together **2** to unite into a whole; fuse synonyms see ¹MIX [L *coalescere*, fr *co-* + *alescere* to grow – more at OLD] – **coalescence** n, **coalescent** adj

**coalface** /'kohl,fays/ n the exposed seam ready to be worked in a coalmine – **at the coalface** engaged in practical or hard

physical work, esp as opposed to theoretical or managerial work

**coalfield** /-,feeld/ n an area containing deposits of coal

**coalfish** /-,fish/ n any of several blackish or dark-backed fishes; esp a coley

**coal gas** n gas made from coal; esp gas made by carbonizing bituminous coal and used for heating and lighting

**coalhole** /-,hohl/ n **1** a hole or shute for receiving coal **2** Br a compartment for storing coal, esp on a ship

**coaling station** /'kohling/ n a port at which ships may take on coal

**coalition** /,koh-ə'lish(ə)n/ n **1a** the act of coalescing; a union **b** a body formed by the union of originally distinct elements; a combination **2** taking sing or pl vb a temporary alliance of distinct parties, individuals, or states for joint action ⟨a ∼ *government*⟩ [MF, fr L *coalitus*, pp of *coalescere*] – **coalitionism** n, **coalitionist** n

**coal measures** n pl beds of coal with the associated layers of rocks

**coalmine** /'kohl,mien/ n a mine from which coal is extracted

**coalmouse** /'kohl,mows/ n, pl **coalmice** /-,mies/ COAL TIT

**coal oil** n, chiefly NAm paraffin

**coal seam** n a bed of coal usu thick enough and of sufficient quality to be mined with profit

**coal tar** n tar obtained by distillation of bituminous coal and used esp in making dyes and drugs (eg ointments for the treatment of dermatitis)

**coal-tar creosote** n CREOSOTE 2

**coal tit** n a small European tit (*Parus ater*) with a black head and white patch on the neck

**coaming** /'kohming/ n a raised frame (eg round a hatchway in the deck of a ship) designed to keep out water [prob irreg fr comb]

**coarctate** /koh'ahktayt/ adj **1** constricted, compressed; esp having the abdomen separated from the THORAX (central body region) by a narrow constriction **2** of an insect larva or pupa enclosed in the skin of an earlier larval stage which forms a rigid protective case [L *coarctatus*, pp of *coartare* to press together, fr *co-* + *artus* narrow, confined; akin to L *artus* joint – more at ARTICLE] – **coarctation** n

**coarse** /kaws/ adj **1** of ordinary or inferior quality or value; common **2a(1)** composed of relatively large parts or particles; not fine ⟨∼ *sand*⟩ **a(2)** loose or rough in texture ⟨∼ *cloth*⟩ **b** adjusted or designed for heavy, fast, or less delicate work ⟨a ∼ *saw with large teeth*⟩ **c** not precise or detailed with respect to adjustment or discrimination ⟨the ∼ *control*⟩ **3** crude or unrefined in taste, manners, or language ⟨a very ∼ *joke*⟩ **4** harsh, raucous, or rough in tone [ME *cors*, prob fr *course*, (the common run of things)] – **coarsely** adv, **coarseness** n

synonyms **Coarse**, vulgar, gross, obscene, and ribald may describe people, their language, or their behaviour if it offends good taste or is contrary to moral principles. What is **coarse** is rough, crude, insensitive, or unrefined. **Vulgar**, stronger in condemnation, suggests boorishness and offensiveness to propriety, and often implies ill breeding ⟨*Burns is often* coarse, *but never* vulgar – Lord Byron⟩. **Gross** suggests materiality as opposed to spirituality, or coarseness more appropriate to animals than to people ⟨*merely* gross, *a scatological rather than a pornographic impropriety* – Aldous Huxley⟩. **Obscene** strongly suggests lewdness, immorality, or what is loathsome by any standard of decency ⟨the obscene system of slavery⟩ ⟨obscene literature⟩. **Ribald** describes the kind of laughter provoked by vulgar or indecent language or behaviour, or the behaviour and language itself. antonyms fine, refined, pure

**coarse fish** n, chiefly Br any freshwater fish not belonging to the salmon family (Salmonidae) – compare GAME FISH

**coarse-'grained** adj **1** having a coarse grain **2** crude

**coarsen** /'kaws(ə)n/ vb to make or become coarse

**¹coast** /kohst/ n **1** the land near a shore; the seashore **2** often cap, NAm the Pacific coast of the USA **3** NAm a slope suited to tobogganing; also an action of sliding down such a slope [ME *cost*, fr MF *coste*, fr L *costa* rib, side; akin to OSlav *kostĭ* bone] – **coastal** adj, **coastally** adv – **the coast is clear** the danger is past or absent

**²coast** vt to sail along the shore of ∼ vi **1** to sail along the shore **2a** to slide, run, or glide downhill by the force of gravity **b** to move along (as if) without further application of propulsive power (eg by momentum or gravity); freewheel **c** to proceed easily without special effort or concern ⟨she ∼ed through her exams⟩

**coaster** /'kohstə/ n **1** a small vessel trading from port to port

along a coast ⟨*dirty British ~ with a salt-caked smokestack –
John Masefield*⟩ **2a** a tray or stand, esp of silver, for a decanter
**b** a small mat used, esp under a drinks glass, to protect a surface (e g a table top) **3** *Br* a wooden stand for cheese **4** *NAm* a
small vehicle (e g a sledge) used in coasting

**coastguard, coast guard** /-ˌgahd/ *n taking sing or pl vb* **1** a
civil or naval force responsible for the safety of maritime traffic
along a coastline and for the enforcement of law and order in
neighbouring waters **2** *chiefly Br* a member of a coastguard

**coastguardsman** /'kohst,gahdzmən/ *also* **coastguardman**
/-ˌgahdmən/ *n, chiefly NAm* COASTGUARD 2

**coastland** /'kohstlənd/ *n* land bordering the sea

**coastline** /-ˌlien/ *n* **1** a line that forms the boundary between
land and water, esp the sea **2** the outline or shape of a coast

**coastwise** /'kohstwiez/ *adj or adv* (moving) along the coast
⟨*~ shipping*⟩

¹**coat** /koht/ *n* **1a** an outer garment that has sleeves and usu
opens the full length of the centre front **b** something resembling
a coat **2** the outer growth of wool, fur, etc on an animal **3** a
coating, covering ⟨*it just needs a ~ of paint*⟩ **4** COAT OF ARMS
[ME *cote,* fr OF, of Gmc origin; akin to OHG *kozza* coarse
mantle] – **coated** *adj*

²**coat** *vt* **1** to cover with a coat **2** to cover or spread with a
finishing, protecting, or enclosing layer

**coatdress** /'koht,dres/ *n* a dress styled like a coat

**coatee** /koh'tee, '--/ *n, chiefly Br* a short coat or jacket, esp
for a baby

**coat hanger** *n* a device that fits inside or round a garment for
hanging from a hook or rod; *specif* a slender arched device of
wood, metal, plastic, etc that is typically shaped somewhat like
a person's shoulders and over which garments may be hung

**coati** /koh'ahti/ *n* a tropical American mammal (genus *Nasua*)
related to the raccoon but with a longer body and tail and a
long flexible snout [Pg *coati,* fr Tupi]

**coatimundi** /-'moondi/ *n* a coati [Tupi]

**coating** /'kohting/ *n* **1** a layer of one substance covering
another **2** cloth suitable for making coats

**coat of arms** *n* **1** a tabard or surcoat decorated with armorial
bearings **2a** a set of distinctive heraldic insignia (e g of a
person), usu depicted on a shield **b** a similar symbolic emblem
[trans of Fr *cotte d'armes*]

**coat of mail** *n* a garment of overlapping metal scales or chain
mail worn as armour

**coatrack** /'koht,rak/ *n* a stand or rack fitted with pegs, hooks,
or hangers and used for the temporary storage of garments

**coat tails** *n pl* the skirts of a man's coat; *specif* two long
tapering skirts at the back of a coat – **on somebody's coat
tails** *chiefly NAm* thanks to the usu undeserved help of another
⟨*he came in* on *the President's* coat tails⟩

¹**coauthor** /'koh,awthə/ *n* a joint or associate author

²**coauthor** /koh'awthə, '-ˌ--/ *vt* to be coauthor of ⟨*the two ~ed
a novel*⟩

**coax** /kohks/ *vt* **1** to influence or persuade by tactful pleading,
flattery etc; wheedle ⟨*they ~ed him into agreeing*⟩ **2** to draw
or gain by means of gentle urging or flattery ⟨*~ed an answer
out of her*⟩ **3** to manipulate with great perseverance towards a
desired often specified condition ⟨*~ed the battered aircraft on
to the next airstrip*⟩ **4** *obs* to fondle or pet [earlier *cokes,* fr
*cokes,* n (simpleton)]

**coaxial** /koh'aksi·əl/ *adj* **1** having a common axis **2** mounted
on concentric shafts – **coaxially** *adv*

**coaxial cable** *n* a cable that consists of a tube of electrically
conducting material surrounding but insulated from a central
conductor and that is used to transmit high-frequency telegraph, telephone, and television signals

**coaxial line** *n* COAXIAL CABLE

¹**cob** /kob/ *n* **1** a male swan **2** CORNCOB 1 **3** (any of) a breed of
short-legged stocky horses of medium height **4a** a lump of coal
**b** a small rounded usu crusty loaf **c** a cobnut **5** *dial Eng* a
rounded mass, lump, or heap [ME *cobbe* leader; akin to OE
*cot* cottage – more at COT]

²**cob** *n, chiefly SW Eng* a type of building material usu consisting of natural clay or chalk mixed with straw as a binder; *also*
a house built of cob [prob fr ¹*cob* 5]

**cobalamin** *also* **cobalamine** /koh'baləmən, -'bawlə-/ *n* any
of several related chemical compounds that have the functions
of CYANOCOBALAMIN (vitamin essential for normal blood formation) and are vitamins of the VITAMIN B₁₂ group [*cobalt* +
vit*amin*]

**cobalt** /'koh,bawlt/ *n* a hard lustrous silver-white magnetic

metallic chemical element that is related to and occurs with
iron and nickel and is used esp in alloys [Ger *kobalt,* alter. of
*kobold,* lit., goblin, fr MHG *kobolt;* fr its occurrence in silver
ore, formerly believed to be due to goblins]

**cobalt 60, cobalt sixty** *n* a radioactive ISOTOPE (form in which
an atom can occur) of cobalt of the MASS NUMBER 60 produced
in nuclear reactors and used as a source of GAMMA RAYS (e g
for radiotherapy)

**cobalt blue** *n* a greenish-blue pigment consisting essentially of
cobalt oxide and alumina

**cobaltic** /koh'bawltik, '---/ *adj* relating to or containing cobalt,
esp when having a VALENCY of three

**cobaltite** /koh'bawltiet, '---/ *also* **cobaltine** /-teen, -tin/ *n* a
greyish to silver-white mineral, CoAsS, consisting of cobalt,
sulphur, and arsenic that is used in making SMALT (type of
glass) [*cobaltite,* alter. of *cobaltine,* fr Fr, fr *cobalt*]

**cobaltous** /koh'bawltəs, '---/ *adj* relating to or containing
cobalt, esp when having a VALENCY of two

**cobber** /'kobə/ *n, Austral informal* a man's male friend; a mate
[perh fr E dial. *cob* to take a liking to; or perh fr Yiddish
*chaber* comrade]

¹**cobble** /'kobl/ *vt* **1** to repair (esp shoes); *also* to make (esp
shoes) **2** to make or assemble roughly or hastily – usu + *together* **3** *chiefly Br* to mend or patch roughly [ME *coblen,* perh
back-formation fr *cobelere* cobbler]

²**cobble** *n* **1** a naturally rounded stone the size of a large
pebble; *esp* such a stone used in street paving or in construction
**2** *pl, chiefly Br* lump coal about the size of small cobblestones
[back-formation fr *cobblestone*]

³**cobble** *vt* to pave with cobblestones

**cobbler** /'koblə/ *n* **1** a maker or repairer of leather goods, esp
shoes **2** a tall iced drink consisting usu of wine, rum or whisky,
and sugar garnished with a slice of lemon or orange **3** *pl, Br
vulgar* nonsense, rubbish – often used interjectionally **4** a sweet
dish made of fruit covered with a thick scone-like crust ⟨*plum
~*⟩ **5** *archaic* a clumsy workman [ME *cobelere;* (3) rhyming
slang *cobblers' (awls)* balls]

**cobblestone** /-ˌstohn/ *n* COBBLE 1 [ME, fr *cobble-* (prob fr *cob*
rounded mass) + *stone*] – **cobblestoned** *adj*

**cobelligerent** /ˌkohbə'lijərənt/ *n* a country fighting with
another power against a common enemy – **cobelligerent** *adj*

**coble** /'kohbl, 'kobl/ *n* a flat-bottomed traditional type of fishing boat with a rudder extending below the keel and a single
mast, used in Scotland and NE England [ME, prob of Celt
origin]

**cobnut** /'kob,nut/ *n* the nut fruit of a European hazel (*Corylus
avellana grandis*); *also* the tree bearing this nut

**Cobol** *also* **COBOL** /'kohbol/ *n* a HIGH-LEVEL (having a form
that is easily understandable by humans) computer language
designed for business applications [*Common business-oriented
language*]

**cobra** /'kobrə, 'kohbrə/ *n* any of several venomous Asiatic and
African snakes (genus *Naja*) that have grooved fangs and when
excited expand the skin of the neck into a hood; *also* any of
several related African snakes [Pg *cobra (de capello),* lit.,
hooded snake, fr L *colubra* snake]

**cobweb** /'kob,web/ *n* **1** a disused and straggling web spun by
a house spider and found in the corners of rooms, windows,
etc **2** a single thread spun by a spider or insect larva; *also* the
material from which the web is spun **3** *usu pl* something undesirable that has arisen through neglect or inactivity ⟨*~s go
out of my mind as I write* – H J Laski⟩ [ME *coppeweb,* fr *coppe*
spider (fr OE ātor*coppe;* akin to MD *coppe* spider) + *web*] –
**cobwebbed** *adj,* **cobwebby** *adj*

**coca** /'kohkə/ *n* **1** any of several S American shrubs (genus
*Erythroxylon* of the family Erythroxylaceae, the coca family);
*esp* one (*Erythroxylon coca*) with leaves resembling those of
the tea plant **2** the dried leaves of a coca (e g *Erythroxylon
coca*) that contain cocaine and are chewed as a stimulant [Sp,
fr Quechua *kúka*]

**ˌCoca-'Cola** *trademark* – used for a brand of cola

**cocaine** /ˌkoh'kayn, kə-/ *n* a drug, C₁₇H₂₁NO₄, that is an
ALKALOID obtained from coca leaves, has been used as a
local anaesthetic, is commonly taken as a stimulant, and can
result in addiction [*coca* + *-ine*]

**cocainism** /koh'kayniz(ə)m, -kə-/ *n* habituation to cocaine

**cocainize, -ise** /koh'kayniez, kə-/ *vt* to treat or anaesthetize
with cocaine

**coccid** /'koksid/ *n* SCALE INSECT [NL *Coccus,* genus of scale
insects, fr Gk *kokkos* grain, kermes berry]

**coccidioidomycosis** /kok,sidioydohmie'kohsis/ *n* a disease affecting humans and lower animals caused by a fungus (*Coccidioides immitis*) and marked esp by fever and infection of the lungs [NL, fr *Coccidioides*, genus of fungi, (fr *coccidium*) + *mycosis*]

**coccidiosis** /kok,sidi'ohsis/ *n, pl* **coccidioses** /-seez/ infestation with or disease caused by coccidia; *specif* a disease of birds (eg poultry) and mammals (eg sheep) caused by coccidia [NL]

**coccidium** /kok'sidi•əm/ *n, pl* **coccidia** /-diə/ any of an order (Coccidia) of PROTOZOANS (single-celled microorganisms) that usu live as parasites in the lining of the digestive tract of VERTEBRATE animals [NL, dim. of *coccus*]

**coccinellid** /,koksi'nelid/ *n* a ladybird [NL *Coccinella*, genus of beetles, fr L *coccinus* scarlet, fr Gk *kokkinos*, fr *kokkos*]

**coccus** /'kokəs/ *n, pl* **cocci** /'koksi, -sie/ **1** any of the separable female reproductive organs (CARPELS) of a plant that split into one-seeded portions at maturity **2** a spherical bacterium [NL, fr Gk *kokkos*] – **coccal, coccic** *adj*, **coccoid** *n or adj*

**coccygeal** /kok'sijiəl/ *adj* relating to the coccyx [ML *coccygeus* fr Gk *kokkyk-, kokkyx*]

**coccyx** /'koksiks/ *n, pl* **coccyges** /'koksijeez/, **coccyxes** the end of the SPINAL COLUMN below the sacrum in human beings and tailless apes [NL, fr Gk *kokkyx* cuckoo, coccyx; fr its resemblance to a cuckoo's beak]

**Cochin** /'kohchin, 'kochin/, **Cochin China** *n, often cap both Cs* (any of) an Asian breed of large domestic fowl with thick plumage, small wings and tail, and densely feathered legs and feet [*Cochin China*, region in Vietnam]

**cochineal** /,kochi'neel/ *n* a red dyestuff consisting of the dried bodies of female cochineal insects, used esp as a colouring agent (eg in foods) and as a chemical indicator [MF & Sp; MF *cochenille*, fr OSp *cochinilla* wood louse, cochineal]

**cochineal insect** *n* a small bright red insect (*Dactylopius coccus*) that is related to and resembles the mealybug and feeds on cacti

**cochlea** /'kokli•ə/ *n pl* **cochleae** /-li,ie/ *also* **cochleas** a division of the INNER EAR of higher VERTEBRATE animals (eg mammals) that is usu coiled like a snail shell and is the seat of the hearing organ [NL, fr L, snail, snail shell, fr Gk *kochlias*, fr *kochlos* snail; akin to Gk *konchē* mussel] – **cochlear** *adj*

**cochleate** /'kokliayt, -ot/, **cochleated** /-,aytid/ *adj* having the spiral form typical of a snail shell

**¹cock** /kok/ *n* **1a** the adult male of the domestic fowl (*Gallus gallus*) **b** the male of birds other than the domestic fowl 〈*a ~ sparrow*〉 **c** the male of various mostly aquatic animals (eg fish or lobsters) **d** a woodcock **e** a weathercock **2** a device (eg a tap or valve) for regulating the flow of a liquid; a stopcock **3a** the hammer of a firearm **b** the position of the hammer or FIRING PIN when cocked ready for firing **4** *chiefly NEng & Cockney informal* PAL 2 **5** *Br slang* nonsense, rubbish **6** *vulgar* a penis **7** *archaic* the crowing of a cock; *also* cockcrow, dawn 〈*This is the foul fiend Flibbertigibbet: he begins at curfew, and walks till the first ~* – Shak〉 [ME *cok*, fr OE *cocc*, of imit origin]

**²cock** *vi* **1** to turn, stand, or stick upright 〈*your float will not ~ unless it is sufficiently weighted*〉 **2** to draw back and set the hammer or FIRING PIN of a firearm ready for firing *~ vt* **1a** to draw back and set the hammer or FIRING PIN of (a firearm) for firing; *also* to set (the trigger) for firing **b** to draw or bend back (eg the hand, arm, or wrist) in preparation for throwing or hitting **c** to set the trip mechanism of (eg a camera shutter) **2a** to set erect 〈*on hearing the noise the dog ~ed its ears*〉 **b** to turn, tip, or tilt 〈*she ~ed her hat at a jaunty angle*〉 **c** to lift and place high 〈*sat down and ~ed his feet up on the desk*〉 – see also **cock a** SNOOK

**³cock** *n* a tilt or slant 〈*a ~ of the head*〉

**⁴cock** *n* a small pile, esp of hay [ME *cok*, of Scand origin]

**⁵cock** *vt* to put (esp hay) into cocks

**cockade** /ko'kayd/ *n* a decoration (eg a rosette or knot of ribbon) worn on the hat as a badge [modif of Fr *cocarde*, fr fem of *cocard* vain, fr *coq* cock, fr OF *coc*, of imit origin] – **cockaded** *adj*

**cock-a-doodle-doo** /,kok ə ,doohdl 'dooh/ *interj* – used to represent the crowing of a cockerel [imit]

**cock-a-hoop** /,kok ə 'hoohp/ *adj* triumphantly boastful; exulting [fr the phrase *to set cock a hoop* to be festive]

**Cockaigne** *also* **Cockayne** /ko'kayn/ *n* an imaginary land of great luxury and ease [ME *cokaygne*, fr MF (*pais de*) *cocaigne* land of plenty]

**cock-a-leekie** /ə 'leeki/ *n* a soup made of chicken boiled with leeks [alter. of *cockie* (dim. of ¹*cock*) + *leekie*, dim. of *leek*]

**cockalorum** /,kokə'lawrəm/ *n* a self-important little man [prob modif of obs Flem *kockeloeren* to crow, of imit origin]

**,cock-and-'bull,story** *n* an incredible and apparently fabricated story

**cockatiel, cockateel** /,kokə'teel/ *n* a small crested grey Australian parrot (*Nymphicus hollandicus*) with a yellow head [D *kaketielje*, deriv of Malay *kakatua*]

**cockatoo** /,kokə'tooh/ *n, pl* **cockatoos 1** any of numerous large noisy chiefly Australasian parrots (esp genus *Kakatoe*), usu with crests and brightly coloured plumage **2** *Austr* COCKY (small farmer) **3** *Austr informal* LOOKOUT 1 [D *kaketoe*, fr Malay *kakatua*, fr *kakak* elder sibling + *tua* old; (3) fr the belief that a flock of cockatoos post a sentry while feeding]

**cockatrice** /'kokətris, -tries/ *n* a mythical serpent that was hatched by a reptile from a cock's egg and that had a glance that could kill – compare BASILISK [ME *cocatrice*, fr MF *cocatris* mongoose, cockatrice, fr ML *cocatric-, cocatrix* mongoose]

**cockboat** /'kok,boht/ *n* a small boat, esp one used as a tender to a larger boat [obs *cock* small boat, fr ME *cok*, fr OF *coque*, fr ML *caudica*, fr L *caudic-, caudex* tree-trunk]

**cockchafer** /'kok,chayfə/ *n* a large European beetle (*Melolontha melolontha*) destructive to roots as a larva and to vegetation as an adult; *also* any of various related beetles [¹*cock* + *chafer*]

**cockcrow** /-,kroh/ *n* dawn

**cocked hat** *n* **1** a hat with the brim turned up in three places to give a 3-cornered shape **2** a hat with the brim turned up on opposite sides to give an elongated shape carrying to a point at either end – **knock into a cocked hat** *informal* to defeat or surpass thoroughly 〈*he knocked all the other competitors* into a cocked hat〉

**¹cocker** /'kokə/ *vt* to indulge or pamper [ME *cokeren*]

**²cocker** *n, Cockney informal* PAL 2 [¹*cock* 4 + ²-*er*]

**cockerel** /'kok(ə)rəl/ *n* a young male domestic fowl [ME *cokerelle*, fr OF dial. *kokerel*, dim. of OF *coc*]

**cocker spaniel** /'kokə/ *n* a small spaniel with long ears, square muzzle, and a silky coat [*cocking* (woodcock hunting)]

**cockeye** /,kok'ie/ *n* a squinting eye

**cockeyed** /-'ied/ *adj* **1** having a cockeye **2a** *informal* askew or awry **b** somewhat foolish or mad 〈*a ~ scheme*〉 **c** drunk – **cockeyedness** *n*, **cockeyedly** *adv*

**cockfighting** /-,fieting/ *n* the setting of specially bred cocks, usu fitted with metal spurs, to fight each other for public entertainment – **cockfight** *n*

**cockhorse** /kok'haws/ *n* ROCKING HORSE [perh fr *cock*, adj, (male) + *horse*]

**¹cockle** /'kokl/ *n* any of several cornfield weeds; *esp* CORN COCKLE [ME, fr OE *coccel*]

**²cockle** *n* **1** a shellfish (family Cardiidae of the phylum Mollusca) having a hinged 2-part shell with convex radial ribs on each of the two halves; *esp* a common edible European shellfish (*Cardium edule*) **2** a cockleshell [ME *cokille*, fr MF *coquille* shell, modif of L *conchylia*, pl of *conchylium*, fr Gk *konchylion*, fr *konchē* conch]

**³cockle** *vi* to gather cockles for food 〈*the men were* cockling *in the hot sun* – Margaret Drabble〉

**⁴cockle** *n* a pucker or wrinkle (eg in fabric) [MF *coquille*] – **cockle** *vb*

**cocklebur** /'kokl,buh/ *n* any of a genus (*Xanthium*) of prickly-fruited plants of the daisy family; *also* any of its spiny fruits

**cockleshell** /-,shel/ *n* **1a** the hinged shell or one half of the shell of a cockle **b** a shell (eg of a scallop) resembling a cockleshell **2** a light flimsy boat

**cockles of the heart** *n* the core of one's being – chiefly in *to warm the cockles of one's heart* [perh fr ²*cockle;* fr the resemblance of the heart to a cockleshell]

**cockloft** /'kok,loft/ *n* a small garret [prob fr ¹*cock*]

**cockney** /'kokni/ *n, often cap* **1** a native of London and now esp of the working-class district in the East End of London **2** the dialect of London and esp of the East End of London [ME *cokeney*, pampered child, (effeminate) townsman lit., cocks' egg, fr *coken* (gen pl of *cok* cock) + *ey* egg, fr OE *ǣg*] – **cockney** *adj*, **cockneyism** *n*

**cock of the walk** *n, informal* a person who dominates or is self-assertive, esp overbearingly

**cockpit** /-,pit/ *n* **1a** a pit or enclosure for cockfights **b** a place noted for bloody, violent, or prolonged conflict **2a** the afterpart of the ORLOP (lowest) deck of a man-of-war formerly used as quarters for midshipmen and for treatment of the wounded in battle **b** a well or recess below deck level from which a small vessel (e g a yacht) is steered **c** a space in the fuselage of an aeroplane for the pilot and sometimes the crew or passengers **d** the driver's compartment in a racing car or sports car

**cockroach** /-,rohch/ *n* any of numerous omnivorous usu dark brown chiefly nocturnal insects (family Blattidae of the order Dictyoptera) that include some domestic pests; *esp* the common cockroach (*Periplaneta americana*) [by folk etymology fr Sp *cucaracha* irreg fr *cuca* caterpillar]

**cockscomb** /'kokskoom, -,kohm/ *n* 1 a coxcomb 2 a garden plant (genus *Celosia*) of the amaranth family grown for its red, yellow, or purple flowers

**cocksfoot** /'koks,foot/ *n* a tall hay and pasture grass (*Dactylis glomerata*) of Eurasian origin

**cockshut** /'kok,shut/ *n, dial Eng* evening twilight [fr the time poultry are shut in to rest]

**cockshy** /'kok,shie/ *n* SHY 4 [¹*cock* + *shy*, n]

**cocksucker** /'kok,sukə/ *n, chiefly NAm vulg* 1 an ingratiating and esp servile person; a toady 2 *derog* one, esp a male homosexual, who performs fellatio

**cocksure** /-'shooə, -'shaw/ *adj* 1 feeling perfect assurance, sometimes on inadequate grounds 2 *informal* cocky **synonyms** see ¹SURE **antonyms** doubtful [prob fr ¹*cock* + *sure*] – **cocksurely** *adv*, **cocksureness** *n*

**¹cocktail** /'kok,tayl/ *n* 1a a drink of two or more spirits mixed together or of spirits mixed with various flavourings **b** a mixture of diverse elements 2 an appetizer (e g tomato juice or a portion of shellfish) served as a first course at a meal ⟨*prawn* ~⟩ 3 a dish consisting of mixed esp fresh fruits [prob fr ²*cock* + *tail*]

**²cocktail** *adj* relating to, appropriate to, or set aside for cocktails or a cocktail party ⟨*the* ~ *hour*⟩ ⟨*a* ~ *dress*⟩

**cocktail stick** *n* a small pointed stick on which food (e g cubes of cheese or small sausages) may be served

**cockteaser** /'kok,teezə/ *n, derog slang* a sexually provocative woman who in the end refuses to have intercourse – **cocktease** *vb*

**'cock-,up** *n, chiefly Br slang* a mix-up, mess; *esp* one caused by bungling or incompetence

**¹cocky** /'koki/ *adj, informal* marked by overconfidence or presumptuousness [¹*cock* + ¹-*y*] – **cockily** *adv*, **cockiness** *n*

**²cocky** *n, Austr & NZ* one who owns and runs a small farm ⟨*little from the fruit* cockies. *They don't hire much labour* – Harold Lewis⟩ [by shortening & alter. fr *cockatoo*]

**coco** /'koh,koh/ *n, pl* cocos 1 COCONUT 1 2 COCONUT PALM [Sp & Pg; Sp, fr Pg *côco*, lit., bogeyman]

**cocoa** /'koh,koh/ *n* 1a an originally S American tree (*Theobroma cacao* of the family Sterculiaceae, the cocoa family) that bears fleshy yellow pods containing many seeds **b** cocoa, cocoa bean the dried partly fermented fatty seeds of the cocoa tree used in making chocolate, cocoa butter, etc 2a a powder prepared from ground roasted cocoa seeds from which some of the fat has been removed – compare CHOCOLATE **b** a drink made by mixing cocoa with usu hot water or milk 3 a light to mid-brown colour □ (1) called also CACAO [modif of Sp *cacao*]

**cocoa butter** *n* a pale vegetable fat with a low melting point obtained from cocoa beans and used esp in making soaps and cosmetics

**coconscious** /koh'konshəs/ *n* mental processes outside the main stream of consciousness but sometimes available to it – **coconscious** *adj*, **coconsciousness** *n*

**coconut** /'kohkə,nut/ *n* 1 the large oval fruit of the COCONUT PALM whose outer fibrous husk yields COIR and whose nut contains thick edible flesh and coconut milk 2 the edible flesh of the coconut

**coconut crab** *n* a large edible burrowing land crab (*Birgus latro*) widely distributed throughout the islands of the tropical Indian and Pacific oceans [fr its being reputed to feed on coconuts]

**coconut ice** *n* a sweet with the consistency of fudge that is made with sugar and desiccated coconut and is usu coloured pink or white

**coconut matting** *n* a coarse matting made from the outer fibrous husk (COIR) of the coconut and used esp for doormats

**coconut oil** *n* an almost colourless oil extracted from fresh coconuts and used esp in making soaps and cosmetics

**coconut palm** *n* a tall tropical palm (*Cocos nucifera*), probably of American origin, that bears coconuts

**coconut shy** *n* a stall at a fairground where balls are thrown at coconuts on stands to knock them off and win a prize

**¹cocoon** /kə'koohn/ *n* 1a an envelope, often mainly of silk, which an insect larva forms about itself and in which it passes the pupa stage **b** any of various other protective coverings produced by animals 2a a protective covering resembling a cocoon; *specif* one placed or sprayed over naval or military equipment in long-term storage **b** a sheltered or insulated state of existence ⟨*immersed in his own* ~ *of middle aged disillusionment* – *Nation Review* (*Melbourne*)⟩ [Fr *cocon*, fr Prov *coucoun*, fr *coco* shell, fr L *coccum* outgrowth on a tree, fr Gk *kokkos* grain, seed, kermes berry]

**²cocoon** *vt* to wrap or envelop, esp tightly, (as if) in a cocoon

**cocotte** /ko'kot, kə-/ *n* 1 a female prostitute 2 a small ovenproof dish in which a single course of a meal is cooked and served [Fr, fr (baby-talk) *cocotte* hen]

**cocultivate** /koh'kultivayt/ *vt* to cocultivate – **cocultivation** *n*

**coculture** /koh'kulchə/ *vt* to grow (living material or viruses) in a culture containing more than one type of living thing; *also* to grow (two types of living thing or viruses) together in a culture

**¹cod** /kod/ *n, pl* cods, *esp collectively* cod 1a a soft-finned fish (*Gadus morrhua*) of the colder parts of the N Atlantic that is a major food fish **b** a fish of the cod family (Gadidae); *esp* a Pacific fish (*Gadus macrocephalus*) closely related to the Atlantic cod 2 any of various spiny-finned fishes resembling the true cods 3 the flesh of the cod used as food [ME]

**²cod** *n, Br slang* nonsense – often used interjectionally in plural [short for *codswallop*]

**³cod** *vb* -dd- *Br informal* ³KID [origin unknown] – **cod** *n*

**coda** /'kohdə/ *n* 1 a concluding musical section that is formally distinct from the main structure of a piece 2 a concluding part, esp of a literary or dramatic work [It, lit., tail, fr L *cauda*]

**coddle** /'kodl/ *vt* 1 to cook (esp eggs) slowly and gently in a liquid just below boiling point 2 to treat with extreme care; pamper [perh fr *caudle*] – **coddler** *n*

**¹code** /kohd/ *n* 1 a systematic statement or collection of a body of laws; *esp* one given statutory force ⟨*the Justinian* Code⟩ 2 a system of principles or maxims ⟨*moral* ~⟩ 3a a system of signals for communication **b** a system of symbols (e g letters, numbers, or words) used to represent assigned and often secret meanings or to identify and retrieve information 4 GENETIC CODE [ME, fr MF, fr L *caudex, codex* trunk of a tree, tablet of wood covered with wax for writing on, book; akin to L *cudere* to beat – more at HEW]

**²code** *vt* 1 to put into the form or symbols of a code 2 to specify (an AMINO ACID, protein, or NUCLEIC ACID) in terms of the GENETIC CODE ~ *vi* to be or contain the GENETIC CODE *for* an AMINO ACID, protein, etc ⟨*isolate the messenger RNA that* ~ *s for insulin*⟩ – **codable** *adj*, **coder** *n*

**code book** *n* a book containing an alphabetic list of words or expressions with their coded equivalents

**codeclination** /,kohdekli'naysh(ə)n/ *n, astronomy* the COMPLEMENT of the MAGNETIC DECLINATION or the celestial declination

**codefendant** /,kohdi'fend(ə)nt/ *n* a joint defendant

**codeine** /'koh,deen/ *n* a drug (ALKALOID), $C_{18}H_{21}NO_3$, obtained from opium that is given orally to relieve pain and coughing [Fr *codéine*, fr Gk *kōdeia* poppy-head, fr *kōos* cavity; akin to Gk *koilos* hollow]

**code name** *n* a name that for secrecy or convenience is used in place of an ordinary name

**code of honour** *n* the unwritten rules forming a standard of conduct

**codetermination** /,kohdi,tuhmi'naysh(ə)n/ *n* the participation of the workforce with management in the determination of business policy

**codex** /'koh,deks/ *n, pl* codices /'kohdiseez/ a manuscript book, esp of Scriptural, Classical, or other ancient texts [L]

**codfish** /-,fish/ *n* cod; *also* its flesh used as food

**codger** /'kojə/ *n* an old and mildly eccentric man – chiefly in *old codger* [prob alter of *cadger*]

**codicil** /'kohdisil/ *n* 1 a clause added to a will to supplement, modify, or explain it 2 an appendix or supplement [MF *codicille*, fr L *codicillus*, dim. of *codic-, codex* book] – **codicillary** *adj*

**codify** /'kohdi,fie/ *vt* 1 to reduce to a code 2 to express or arrange in a systematic form – **codifier** *n*, **codification** *n*

**¹codling** /'kodling/ *n* a young cod

**²codling, codlin** /'kodlin/ *n* a small unripe apple; *also* any of several elongated greenish cooking apples [alter. of ME *querdlyng*]

**codling moth, codlin moth** *n* a small moth (*Cydia pomonella*) whose larva lives in apples, pears, quinces, and walnuts

**cod-liver oil** *n* an oil obtained from the liver of the cod and closely related fishes that is a source of VITAMIN A and VITAMIN D

**codominant** /ˌkoh'dominənt/ *adj* **1a** forming part of the main canopy of a forest ⟨∼ *trees*⟩ **b** being any of two or more dominant living organisms sharing in the controlling influence of an ecological community **2** *of two or more genes* being equally dominant so that when present together the organism shows a different characteristic from when each is present separately – **codominant** *n*

**codon** /'kohdon/ *n* a group of three adjacent NUCLEOTIDES in RNA or in the corresponding DNA that codes for a particular AMINO ACID in a section of a protein or starts or stops protein synthesis [¹*code* + ²-*on*]

**codpiece** /-ˌpees/ *n* a flap or bag in the front of men's breeches, esp in the 15th and 16th centuries, covering or protecting the genitals [ME *codpese*, fr *cod* bag, scrotum (fr OE *codd*) + *pese* piece]

**codswallop** /'kodzˌwoləp/ *n*, *chiefly Br informal* nonsense [origin unknown]

**coed** /ˌkoh'ed/ *n* **1** *NAm* a female student in a coeducational institution **2** *informal* a coeducational school ⟨*Bedales, the Hampshire* ∼ – *Private Eye*⟩ [short for *coeducational*] – **coed** *adj*

**¹co-eˌdition** *n* an edition of a book published simultaneously by more than one publisher, usu in different countries and in different languages

**coeditor** /'kohˌeditə/ *n* one who collaborates with another in editing a newspaper, magazine, or book – **coedit** *vt*

**coeducation** /ˌkoh·edyoo'kaysh(ə)n, -ejoo-/ *n* the education of pupils or students of both sexes at the same institution – **coeducational** *adj*, **coeducationally** *adv*

**coefficient** /ˌkoh·i'fish(ə)nt/ *n* **1** the number or mathematical quantity by which a VARIABLE is multiplied ⟨*the* ∼ *of 3x² is 3*⟩ ⟨*the* ∼ *of y in 4xyz² is 4xz²*⟩ **2** a measure or degree; *specif* a usu dimensioned number that serves as a measure of some property or characteristic (e g of a device or process) ⟨*the* ∼ *of expansion of copper*⟩ [NL *coefficient-*, *coefficiens*, fr L *co-* + *efficient-*, *efficiens* efficient]

**coefficient of correlation** *n* CORRELATION COEFFICIENT

**coefficient of viscosity** *n* VISCOSITY 3

**coel-** /seel-/, **coelo-**, *NAm also* **cel-, celo-**, *comb form* hollow; cavity ⟨*coelodont*⟩ ⟨*coelozoic*⟩ [NL, fr Gk *koil-*, *koilo-*, fr *koilos* hollow – more at CAVE]

**coelacanth** /'seelaˌkanth/ *n* any of a family (Coelacanthidae) of fishes that were known only from fossils until a living specimen (genus *Latimeria*) was caught in S African waters in 1938 [deriv of Gk *koilos* + *akantha* thorn, spine]

**-coele, coel** /-ˌseel/ *comb form* (→ *n*) cavity; chamber ⟨*blastocoele*⟩ ⟨*enterocoele*⟩ [deriv of Gk *-koilos*, fr *koilos*]

**coelenterate** /see'lentərayt, -rət/ *n* any of a phylum (Coelenterata) of INVERTEBRATE animals including the corals, SEA ANEMONES, and jellyfishes [deriv of Gk *koilos* + *enteron* intestine – more at INTER-] – **coelenterate** *adj*

**coelenteron** /see'lentəron/ *n*, *pl* **coelentera** /-rə/ the internal body cavity of a coelenterate [NL, fr Gk *koilos* + *enteron*]

**coeliac** /'seeliˌak/ *adj* relating to the abdominal cavity [L *coeliacus*, fr GK *koiliakos*, fr *koilia* cavity, fr *koilos*]

**coeliac disease** *n* a chronic nutritional disorder, esp of young children, characterized by faulty digestion of fats in the intestines

**coelom** /'seelm/ *n*, *pl* **coeloms, coelomata** /see'lohmətə/ a body cavity that develops secondarily as a space between the body wall and the digestive tract in multicellular animals above the lower worms [Ger, fr Gk *koilōma* cavity, fr *koilos*] – **coelomic** *adj*

**coelomate** /-ˌmayt/ *adj*, *of an animal* having a coelom – **coelomate** *n*

**coelostat** /'seeləˌstat/ *n* an astronomical instrument that incorporates an adjustable mirror capable of bending light from an observed planet, star, or other celestial body [ISV *coelo-* (fr ML *coelum* sky, heaven, fr L, heaven) + *-stat*]

**coemption** /koh'em(p)shən/ *n* the buying up of the whole supply of a commodity, esp in order to corner the market [L *coemption-*, *coemptio*, fr *coemptus*, pp of *coemere* to buy up, fr *co-* + *emere* to buy – more at REDEEM]

**coen-** /seen-/, **coeno-** *also chiefly NAm* **cen-, ceno-** *comb form* common; general ⟨*coenocyte*⟩ ⟨*coenobite*⟩ [NL, fr Gk *koin-*, *koino-*, fr *koinos* – more at CO-]

**coenobite,** *chiefly NAm* **cenobite** /'seenəˌbiet/ *n* a member of a religious order living in a monastic community – compare EREMITE [LL *coenobita*, fr *coenobium* monastery, fr LGk *koinobion*, deriv of Gk *kionos* + *bios* life] – **coenobitic, coenobitical** *adj*

**coenocyte** /'seenəˌsiet/ *n* SYNCYTIUM (tissue in which cells are not separated by cell walls) – **coenocytic** *adj* [ISV]

**coenospecies** /'seenohˌspeeshiz/ *n* a group (e g a subspecies or variety) of organisms that are closely related genetically and can interbreed to produce fertile offspring – compare ECOSPECIES

**coenurus** /see'nyooərəs/ *n*, *pl* **coenuri** /-ri, -rie/ a complex tapeworm larva consisting of a bladder from the inner wall of which numerous heads develop [NL, fr *coen-* + Gk *oura* tail]

**coenzyme** /ˌkoh'enziem/ *n* a nonprotein chemical compound that forms the active portion of an ENZYME system after combination with a protein portion (APOENZYME) – **coenzymatic** *adj*, **coenzymatically** *adv*

**coenzyme A** *n* a coenzyme, $C_{21}H_{36}N_7O_{16}P_3S$, that occurs in all living cells and is essential for the METABOLISM (biochemical processing) of carbohydrates, fats, and some AMINO ACIDS

**coenzyme Q** *n* UBIQUINONE (substance important in energy-producing reactions of living cells)

**coequal** /koh'eekwəl/ *adj* equal with one another – **coequally** *adv*, **coequality** *n*

**coerce** /koh'uhs/ *vt* **1** to dominate or restrain by authority or force **2** to compel to an act or choice ⟨*they could* ∼ *the citizens by threats but not persuade them to agree*⟩ – often + *into* + *into* ⟨∼d *into joining*⟩ [L *coercēre*, fr *co-* + *arcēre* to shut up, enclose – more at ARK] – **coercible** *adj*, **coercive** *adj*, **coercion** *n*

**coercive force** *n* the opposing magnetic intensity that must be applied to a magnetized material to demagnetize it

**coercivity** /ˌkoh·uh'sivəti/ *n* the property of a material determined by the value of the COERCIVE FORCE when the material has been fully magnetized

**coessential** /ˌkoh·i'senshəl/ *adj* having the same essence or nature ⟨*the persons of the Trinity are considered as* ∼⟩

**coetaneous** /ˌkoh·i'taynəs/ *adj* of the same age or epoch; coeval [L *coaetaneus*, fr *co-* + *aetas* age – more at AGE]

**coeternal** /ˌkoh·i'tuhnl/ *adj* equally or jointly eternal – **coeternally** *adv*, **coeternity** *n*

**coeval** /koh'eevl/ *adj* of the same or equal age or duration [L *coaevus*, fr *co-* + *aevum* age, lifetime – more at AGE] – **coeval** *n*, **coevality** *n*

**coexist** /ˌkoh·ig'zist/ *vi* **1** to exist together or at the same time **2** to live in peace with one another, esp as a matter of policy – **coexistence** *n*, **coexistent** *adj*

**coextensive** /ˌkoh·ik'stensiv/ *adj* having the same spatial or temporal scope or limits – **coextensively** *adv*

**cofactor** /ˌkoh'faktə, '-,--/ *n* **1** *maths* the MINOR of an element of a SQUARE MATRIX OR DETERMINANT, assigned to be positive or negative according to its position in the matrix or determinant **2** a substance that acts with another substance to bring about certain effects; *esp* COENZYME

**coffee** /'kofi/ *n* **1a** a beverage made by percolation, infusion, or decoction from the roasted and ground or pounded seeds of a coffee tree; *also* these seeds either green or roasted **b** COFFEE TREE 1 **2** a cup of coffee ⟨*two* ∼s⟩ **3** a time when coffee is drunk **4** a light brown colour [It & Turk; It *caffè*, fr Turk *kahve*, fr Ar *qahwa*]

**coffee bar** *n* an establishment where coffee and light refreshments are served; a cafe or snack bar

**coffeehouse** /-ˌhows/ *n* an establishment, esp in the 18th century, selling coffee and other refreshments and often serving as an important social and commercial meeting-place ⟨*women . . . during the 1790s, without the freedom men had in the university and* ∼s – Pamela Hansford Johnson⟩

**coffee morning** *n, Br* a morning social gathering at which coffee is served; *esp* one at which funds are raised for a charity

**coffeepot** /'kofiˌpot/ *n* a usu tall pot with a lid, spout or pouring lip, and handle, in which coffee is made or served

**coffee shop** *n, NAm* a small restaurant

**coffee table** *n* a low table usually placed in a living room or lounge

**coffee-table book** *n* an outsize and lavishly produced book (e g with extensive use of full-colour illustrations) [fr its suitability for display on a coffee table]

**coffee tree** *n* **1** a large evergreen shrub or small tree (*Coffea arabica*) of the madder family that is native to Africa but is now widely cultivated in warm regions for its seeds which are the commercial source of most coffee **2** KENTUCKY COFFEE TREE

**¹coffer** /'kofə/ *n* **1** a chest or box; a strongbox **2** *usu pl, chiefly humorous* treasury or exchequer ⟨*I'm afraid the* ~s *are empty*⟩ **3a** the chamber of a canal lock **b** CAISSON (watertight chamber used in construction work) **c** a cofferdam **4** a recessed decorative panel (e g in a vault, ceiling, or dome) [ME *coffre*, fr OF, fr L *cophinus* basket, fr Gk *kophinos*]

**²coffer** *vt* **1** to store or hoard up in a coffer **2** to ornament (e g a ceiling) with recessed panels

**cofferdam** /'kofə,dam/ *n* a watertight enclosure from which water is pumped to expose the bottom of a body of water and allow construction (e g of a pier)

**¹coffin** /'kofin/ *n* **1** a box or chest for the burial of a corpse **2** the horny part forming the hoof of a horse's foot [ME, basket, receptacle, fr MF *cofin*, fr L *cophinus*]

**²coffin** *vt* to enclose (as if) in a coffin

**coffin bone** *n* the bone enclosed within the hoof of the horse

**coffin nail** *n, slang* a cigarette

**coffle** /'kofl/ *n* a train of slaves or animals fastened together [Ar *qāfila* caravan]

**cofunction** /'koh,fungksh(ə)n/ *n* a TRIGONOMETRIC FUNCTION whose value for the COMPLEMENT (angle which with a given angle makes 90°) of an angle is equal to the value of a given TRIGONOMETRIC FUNCTION for the angle itself ⟨*the sine is the* ~ *of the cosine*⟩

**¹cog** /kog/ *n* **1** a tooth on the rim of a wheel or gear **2** a subordinate person or part [ME *cogge*, of Scand origin; akin to Norw *kug* cog; akin to OE *cycgel* cudgel] – **cogged** *adj*

**²cog** *vb* **-gg-** *vt* to direct the fall of (dice) fraudulently ~ *vi* to cheat, esp in throwing dice [*cog* (a trick)]

**³cog** *n* a tenon [prob alter. of *cock* (tenon), prob deriv of (assumed) ONF *coque* notch] – **cog** *vt*

**cogent** /'kohj(ə)nt/ *adj* **1** having power to compel or constrain ⟨~ *forces of nature*⟩ **2a** appealing strongly to the mind or reason; convincing ⟨~ *evidence*⟩ **synonyms** see VALID [L *cogent-*, *cogens*, prp of *cogere* to drive together, collect, fr *co-* + *agere* to drive – more at AGENT] – **cogency** *n*, **cogently** *adv*

**cogitable** /'kojitəbl/ *adj* capable of being conceived as a thought or idea; thinkable

**cogitate** /'kojitayt/ *vb* to ponder (on) usu intently and objectively; meditate (on) **synonyms** see PONDER [L *cogitatus*, pp of *cogitare* to think, think about, fr *co-* + *agitare* to drive, agitate – more at AGITATE] – **cogitative** *adj*, **cogitation** *n*

**cogito** /'kojitoh/ *n* **1** the philosophical principle that one's existence can be conclusively established by the fact that one thinks **2** the spontaneous intellectual processes of the self or ego [NL *cogito, ergo sum* I think, therefore I am (theorem stated by René Descartes †1650 Fr philosopher)]

**cognac** /'konyak/ *n* a brandy from the departments of Charente and Charente-Maritime distilled from white wine; *broadly* any French brandy [Fr, fr *Cognac*, town in W France]

**¹cognate** /'kog,nayt/ *adj* **1a** related by blood – compare AGNATE **b** related on the mother's side – used in some legal systems **2a** related by descent from the same ancestral language **b** *of a word or morpheme* related by derivation, borrowing, or descent ⟨*German* vater *is* ~ *with* father⟩ **c** *of a substantive* related in form and meaning to the verb of which it is the object ⟨*in "sing a song"* song *is the* ~ *object*⟩ **3** of the same or similar nature [L *cognatus*, fr *co-* + *gnatus*, *natus*, pp of *nasci* to be born; akin to L *gignere* to beget – more at KIN] – **cognately** *adv*, **cognateness** *n*, **cognation** *n*

**²cognate** *n* someone or something (esp a word) that is cognate with another

**cognition** /kog'nish(ə)n/ *n* the act or process of knowing that involves the processing of sensory information and includes perception, awareness, and judgment; *also* a product of this act [ME *cognicioun*, fr L *cognition-*, *cognitio*, fr *cognitus*, pp of *cognoscere* to become acquainted with, know, fr *co-* + *gnoscere* to come to know – more at KNOW] – **cognitional** *adj*

**cognitive** /'kognətiv/ *adj* **1** relating to cognition **2** based on or reducible to empirical knowledge – **cognitively** *adv*, **cognitivity** *n*

**cognitive dissonance** *n* psychological conflict resulting from incompatible beliefs and attitudes held simultaneously

**cogn·izable, -isable** /'kognizəbl, kog'niezəbl/ *adj* **1** capable of being known, perceived, or recognized; perceptible **2** capable of being judicially heard and determined – **cognizably** *adv*

**cogn·izance, -isance** /'kogniz(ə)ns/ *n* **1** a distinguishing mark or emblem (e g a heraldic bearing) **2a** knowledge **b** notice, heed

⟨*take* ~ *of a fault*⟩ **3** the right or power of a court to deal with a specific matter; jurisdiction; *also* judicial notice given to a specific matter [ME *conisaunce*, fr OF *conoissance*, fr *conoistre* to know, fr L *cognoscere*]

**cogn·izant, -isant** /'kogniz(ə)nt/ *adj, formal or technical* having cognizance; *esp* having special or certain knowledge, often from firsthand sources

**cognomen** /kog'nohmin/ *n, pl* **cognomina** /kog'nominə, -'noh-/, **cognomens 1** a surname; *esp* the family name and usu the third name of an ancient Roman (e g "Martialis" in Marcus Valerius Martialis) – compare NOMEN, PRAENOMEN **2** a name; *esp* a distinguishing nickname or epithet ⟨*Meirchion ab Owain's curious* ~, *Bawdfilwr or 'thumb-soldier'*⟩ [L, irreg fr *co-* + *nomen* name – more at NAME] – **cognominal** *adj*

**cognoscente** /,konyoh'shenti, ,kognə-/ *n, pl* **cognoscenti** /~/ a person having or claiming expert knowledge; a connoisseur [obs It (now *conoscente*), fr *cognoscente*, adj, wise, fr L *cognoscent-*, *cognoscens*, prp of *cognoscere*]

**cog railway, cogway** *n, NAm* RACK RAILWAY

**cogue** /kog, kohg/ *n, Scot* a round wooden vessel constructed barrel-fashion from staves and hoops [origin unknown]

**cogwheel** /-,weel/ *n* GEAR WHEEL

**cohabit** /koh'habit/ *vi* to live or exist together; *specif* to live together as husband and wife [LL *cohabitare*, fr L *co-* + *habitare* to inhabit, fr *habitus*, pp of *habēre* to have] – **cohabitant** *n*, **cohabitation** *n*

**cohere** /koh'hiə/ *vi* **1** to hold together firmly as parts of the same mass; *broadly*; stick or adhere **2** to consist of parts that cohere **3a** to become united in ideas or interests **b** to be logically or aesthetically consistent ⟨*a symphony that fails to* ~⟩ [L *cohaerēre*, fr *co-* + *haerēre* to stick – more at HESITATE]

**coherence** /koh'hiərəns/, *also* **coherancy** /-rənsi/ *n* the quality or state of cohering; *esp* logical connection or consistency in speech or writing

**coherent** /koh'hiərənt/ *adj* **1** having the quality of cohering **2** showing a unity of thought or purpose; logically consistent ⟨*a* ~ *argument*⟩ **3** relating to ELECTROMAGNETIC WAVES that have a definite relationship to each other: e g **3a** composed of WAVE TRAINS (succession of similar waves) in phase with each other ⟨~ *light*⟩ **b** producing coherent light ⟨*a laser is a* ~ *source*⟩ [MF or L; MF *cohérent*, fr L *cohaerent-*, *cohaerens*, prp of *cohaerēre*] – **coherently** *adv*

**coherer** /koh'hiərə/ *n* a radio detector in which an imperfectly conducting contact between pieces of conductive material loosely resting against each other is materially improved in conductance by the passage of high-frequency current

**cohesion** /koh'heezh(ə)n/ *n* **1** the act or process of cohering **2** union between similar plant parts or organs (e g the petals of a flower) **3** molecular attraction by which the particles of a body are united throughout the mass [L *cohaesus*, pp of *cohaerēre*] – **cohesionless** *adj*

**cohesive** /koh'heesiv, -ziv/ *adj* sharing or producing cohesion or coherence ⟨*a* ~ *social unit*⟩ ⟨~ *soils*⟩ – **cohesively** *adv*, **cohesiveness** *n*

**coho** *also* **cohoe** /'koh·hoh/ *n, pl* **coho, cohos** *also* **cohoes** a small N Pacific salmon (*Oncorhynchus kisutch*) having deep red flesh [origin unknown]

**cohort** /'koh,hawt/ *n* **1a** *taking sing or pl vb* any of 10 divisions of an ancient Roman legion; *broadly* a group of warriors or soldiers **b** a band or group; *specif* a group of individuals having a statistical factor (e g age or class membership) in common in a demographic study **2** *chiefly NAm* a companion or accomplice; *also* a follower or supporter [MF & L; MF *cohorte*, fr L *cohort-*, *cohors* – more at COURT]

*usage* The use of **cohort** for a single person, as in sense **2**, is widely disliked.

**¹coif** /koyf/ *n* a close-fitting cap: e g **a** a hoodlike cap worn by nuns under a veil **b** a protective usu metal skullcap formerly worn under a hood of mail [ME *coife*, fr MF, fr LL *cofea*]

**²coif** *vt* **-ff- 1** to cover or dress (as if) with a coif **2** to arrange (the hair) by combing, brushing, etc

**coiffeur** /kwah'fuh (*Fr* kwafœ:r)/, *fem* **coiffeuse** /kwah'fuhz (*Fr* kwafǿz)/ *n* a hairdresser [Fr, fr *coiffer*]

**coiffure** /kwah'f(y)ooə (*Fr* kwafy:r)/ *n* a hairstyle [Fr, fr *coiffer* to cover with a coif, arrange (hair), fr *coife*] – **coiffured** *adj*

**coign of vantage** /koyn/ *n, formal* an advantageous position [*coign*, earlier spelling of ¹*coin* 4 (corner)]

**¹coil** /koyl/ *n, archaic* turmoil or trouble [origin unknown]

**²coil** *vt* **1** to wind into rings or spirals **2** to roll or twist into a shape resembling a coil ~ *vi* **1** to move in a circular, spiral, or winding course **2** to form or lie in a coil [MF *coillir, cuillir* to gather – more at CULL]

**³coil** *n* **1a** a series of loops; a spiral; *specif* a length of flexible material (eg rope or cable) laid down in a series of loops **b** a single loop of a coil **2** a wire wound in a spiral through which an electric current is passed usu either to provide a MAGNETIC FIELD or to provide an electrical resistance **3** a series of connected pipes in rows, layers, or windings (eg in a condenser} **4** a roll of postage stamps; *also* a stamp from such a roll **5** INTRAUTERINE DEVICE (contraceptive device)

**¹coin** /koyn/ *n* **1a** a usu thin and often round piece of metal issued by governmental authority for use as money **b** metal money ⟨*I'd like to change all this ∼ for notes*⟩ **2** something accepted as having value or validity ⟨*good ∼*⟩ **3** something having two different and usu opposing aspects ⟨*consider the other side of the ∼*⟩ **4** *archaic* a corner or cornerstone [ME, fr MF, wedge, corner, fr L *cuneus* wedge] – **pay somebody back in his/her own coin** *informal* to treat somebody as he/she has treated others

**²coin** *vt* **1a** to make (a coin), esp by stamping; mint **b** to convert (metal) into coins **c** to shape (a piece of metal) in a mould or die **2** to create or invent ⟨*∼ a phrase*⟩ **3** *informal* to make or earn (money) rapidly and in large quantity – often + *in* ⟨*since she started up on her own she's really been ∼ing it in*⟩

**coinage** /'koynij/ *n* **1** the act or process of coining **2a** coins, esp in large numbers **b** something (eg a word) made up or invented

**'coin-,box** *n* a telephone whose operation is paid for by inserting coins; *also* the box on such a telephone that receives the coins

**coincide** /,koh·in'sied/ *vi* **1** to occupy the same place in space or time **2** to correspond in nature, character, function, or position **3** to be in accord or agreement; concur *synonyms* see AGREE *antonym* differ [ML *coincidere*, fr L *co-* + *incidere* to fall on, fr *in-* + *cadere* to fall – more at CHANCE]

**coincidence** /koh'insid(ə)ns; *sense 1 also* ,koh·in'sied(ə)ns/ *n* **1** the act or condition of coinciding; correspondence **2** the chance occurrence at the same time or place of two or more events that are seen as related or similar; *also* an example of such an occurrence

**coincident** /koh'insid(ə)nt/ *adj* **1** occupying the same space or time ⟨*∼ points*⟩ **2** of similar nature; harmonious ⟨*a theory ∼ with the facts*⟩ [Fr, fr ML *coincident-, coincidens*, prp of *coincidere*] – **coincidently** *adv*

**coincidental** /koh,insi'dentl, ,---'--/ *adj* resulting from a coincidence ⟨*similarity between the two texts is too consistent to be ∼*⟩

**coiner** /'koynə/ *n* one who coins; *esp, chiefly Br* a person who makes counterfeit coins

**coin-op** /op/ *n* a self-service laundry where the machines are operated by coins

**coinsurance** /,koh·in'shooərəns, -'shaw-/ *n* **1** joint assumption of risk (eg by two underwriters) **2** a system of insurance (eg against fire) in which the insured is required to maintain cover on a risk at a stipulated percentage of its total value or suffer a penalty in proportion to the deficiency in the event of loss – **coinsure** *vt*, **coinsurer** *n*

**Cointreau** /'kwontroh, 'kwun-/ *trademark* – used for a colourless liqueur flavoured with oranges

**coir** /'koyə/ *n* a stiff coarse fibre made from the outer husk of a coconut and used esp for ropes and matting [Tamil *kayịụu* rope]

**coition** /koh'ish(ə)n/ *n* coitus [LL, fr L *coition-, coitio* a coming together, fr coitus, pp of *coire* to come together, fr *co-* + *ire* to go – more at ISSUE] – **coitional** *adj*

**coitus** /'koytəs, 'koh·itəs/ *n* the natural conveying of semen to the female reproductive tract; *broadly* SEXUAL INTERCOURSE [L, fr *coitus*, pp] – **coital** *adj*, **coitally** *adv*

**coitus interruptus** /intə'ruptəs/ *n* coitus in which the penis is withdrawn before ejaculation as a contraceptive measure [NL, interrupted coitus]

**coitus reservatus** /rezuh'vahtəs/ *n* delayed ejaculation during intercourse; *also* COITUS INTERRUPTUS [NL, coitus held back]

**¹coke** /kohk/ *n* a solid porous fuel that remains after some gases have been driven off from coal by heating; *also* a similar solid residue left by other materials (eg petroleum) [ME; akin to Sw *kälk* pith, Gk *gelgis* bulb of garlic]

**²coke** *vt* to change into coke ∼ *vi* to become coked ⟨*the engine* ∼s *very quickly*⟩ – often + *up*

**³coke** *n, slang* cocaine [by shortening & alter.]

**Coke** *trademark* – used for Coca-Cola

**col** /kol/ *n* **1** a pass in a mountain range **2** a saddle-shaped depression in the crest of a ridge [Fr, fr MF, neck, fr L *collum*]

**¹col-** – see COM-

**²col-, coli-, colo-** *comb form* **1** colon ⟨*colitis*⟩ ⟨*colostomy*⟩ **2** colon bacillus ⟨*coliform*⟩ ⟨*coliphage*⟩ [NL, fr L *colon*]

**cola** /'kohlə/ *n* a carbonated soft drink flavoured with extract from coca leaves, KOLA NUT, sugar, caramel, and acid and aromatic substances [fr *Coca-Cola*, a trademark]

**colander** /'koləndə; *also* 'ku-/ *n* a perforated bowl-shaped utensil for washing or draining food [ME *colyndore*, prob modif of OProv *colador*, fr ML *colatorium*, fr L *colatus*, pp of *colare* to sieve, fr *colum* sieve]

**cola nut** *n* KOLA NUT

**colatitude** /,koh'latityoohd/ *n* the COMPLEMENT of the LATITUDE (angular distance from some specified circle or plane of reference) of a place on the earth or a star, moon, or other celestial body

**colcannon** /kol'kanən/ *n* an Irish dish of potatoes and cabbage boiled and mashed together usu with cream or buttermilk [IrGael *cál ceannan*, lit., white-headed cabbage]

**colchicine** /'kolchiseen, 'kolki-/ *n* a chemical compound, $C_{22}H_{25}NO_6$, that is an ALKALOID extracted from the corms or seeds of the MEADOW SAFFRON and used esp to inhibit division of the nucleus during MITOSIS (type of cell division) and so induce POLYPLOIDY (state of having several sets of genetic material in each cell) and in the treatment of gout

**colchicum** /'kolchikəm, 'kolki-/ *n* **1** any of a genus (*Colchicum*) of African and Eurasian corm-producing plants of the lily family with flowers that resemble crocuses – called also MEADOW SAFFRON **2** the colchicine-containing dried corm or dried ripe seeds of the MEADOW SAFFRON [NL, genus name, fr L, a kind of plant with a poisonous root, fr Gk *kolchikon*, lit., product of Colchis, ancient region in Asia]

**colcothar** /'kolkə,thah/ *n* a reddish-brown oxide of iron, $Fe_2O_3$, left as a residue when FERROUS SULPHATE is heated, and used as a glass polish and pigment [ML, fr MF or OSp; MF *colcotar*, fr OSp *cólcotar*, fr Ar dial. *qulquṭār*]

**¹cold** /kohld/ *adj* **1** having a low temperature, often below some normal temperature or below that compatible with human comfort **2a** marked by lack of warm feeling; unemotional; *also* unfriendly ⟨*a ∼ stare*⟩ **b** marked by deliberation or calculation ⟨*a ∼ act of aggression*⟩ **3a** previously cooked but served cold ⟨*∼ meats*⟩ **b** heated insufficiently ⟨*the soup was ∼*⟩ **c** not heated ⟨*stored in a ∼ cellar*⟩ ⟨*∼ cathode*⟩ **d** made cold ⟨*∼ drinks*⟩ **e** *of a process* performed on an unheated material ⟨*∼ conditioning of steel prior to rolling*⟩ **4a** depressing, cheerless **b** producing a sensation of cold; chilling ⟨*∼ blank walls*⟩ **c** COOL **5a 5a** dead **b** unconscious ⟨*knocked out ∼*⟩ **6** made uncomfortable by cold **7a** retaining only faint scents, traces, or clues ⟨*a ∼ trail*⟩ **b** far from a goal, object, or solution sought **c** stale, uninteresting ⟨*∼ news*⟩ **8** presented or regarded in a straightforward way; impersonal ⟨*the ∼ facts*⟩ **9** unprepared **10** intense yet without the usual outward effects ⟨*a ∼ fury*⟩ [ME, fr OE *ceald, cald*; akin to OHG *kalt* cold, L *gelu* frost, *gelare* to freeze] – **coldish** *adj*, **coldly** *adv*, **coldness** *n* – **knock cold** KNOCK OUT 2a,b ⟨*was knocked cold in the third round*⟩ – see also **in cold** BLOOD, **blow** HOT **and cold, give somebody the cold** SHOULDER

**²cold** *n* **1a** a condition of low temperature **b** cold weather **2** bodily sensation produced by relative lack of heat; chill **3** a bodily disorder popularly associated with chilling; *specif* COMMON COLD **4** a state of neglect or deprivation – esp in *come/bring in out of the cold*

**³cold** *adv* with utter finality ; absolutely ⟨*was turned down ∼*⟩

**,cold-'blood** *adj, of a horse or breed* lacking Thoroughbred or Arab blood

**,cold-'blooded** *adj* **1a** done or acting without consideration or compunction; ruthless ⟨*∼ murder*⟩ **b** concerned only with the facts; emotionless **2** having cold blood; *specif* having a body temperature that is not internally regulated but is close to and varies with that of the environment – compare WARM-BLOODED **3** noticeably sensitive to cold – **cold-bloodedly** *adv*, **cold-bloodedness** *n*

**cold chisel** *n* a chisel made of steel of a strength and temper suitable for chipping or cutting cold metal

**cold comfort** *n* scant consolation; quite limited sympathy or encouragement

**cold composition** *n* COLD TYPE

**cold cream** *n* a thick oily often perfumed cream for cleansing and soothing the skin of the neck, face, etc

**cold cuts** *n pl* sliced assorted cold cooked meats

**cold feet** *n pl* apprehension or doubt strong enough to prevent a planned course of action

**cold fish** *n* a cold aloof person

**cold frame** *n* a usu glass-covered frame without artificial heat used to protect plants and seedlings

**cold front** *n* an advancing edge of a cold air mass

**coldhearted** /ˌkold'hahtid/ *adj* marked by lack of sympathy, interest, or sensitivity – **coldheartedly** *adv*, **coldheartedness** *n*

**cold shoulder** *n* intentionally cold or unsympathetic treatment – usu + *the* – **cold-shoulder** *vt*

**cold sore** *n* a group of blisters appearing round or inside the mouth in HERPES SIMPLEX (virus disease) – called also HERPES LABIALIS

**cold storage** *n* 1 storage (eg of food) in a cold place for preservation 2 a condition of being held or continued without being acted on; abeyance

**cold store** *n* 1 a building for cold storage 2 COLD STORAGE 2

**cold sweat** *n* perspiration and chill occurring together, usu associated with fear, pain, or shock

**cold table** *n* a buffet offering a variety of cold foods and dishes (eg meats, salads, and cheese)

**cold turkey** *n* 1 *NAm* blunt language or procedure 2 *informal* (the shivering, nausea, feelings of fear, etc resulting from) the abrupt complete stopping of the use of an addictive drug by an addict

**cold type** *n* composition or typesetting (eg photocomposition) done without the casting of metal, esp produced directly by a typewriter mechanism

**cold war** *n* 1 a conflict, esp between nations, carried on by methods short of military action and usu without breaking off diplomatic relations – compare HOT WAR 2 a hostile but non-violent relationship – **cold warrior** *n*

**cold water** *n* depreciation of something as being ill-advised, unwarranted, or worthless ⟨poured ∼ *on our hopes*⟩

**cold wave** *n* 1 a period of unusually cold weather 2 a permanent wave in the hair set by a chemical preparation

**cole** /kohl/ *n* any of several usu edible plants (genus *Brassica*) of the cabbage family including broccoli, Brussels sprouts, cabbage, cauliflower, kohlrabi, and rape [ME, fr OE *cāl*, fr L *caulis* stem, cabbage – more at HOLE]

**colemanite** /'kohlmə,niet/ *n* a mineral, $Ca_2B_6O_{11}.5H_2O$, that consists of a BORATE of calcium chemically combined with water molecules and occurs in the form of brilliant colourless or white crystals [William *Coleman* †1893 US businessman & mine-owner]

**coleoptera** /ˌkoli'optərə/ *n pl* insects that are beetles [NL, deriv of Gk *koleon* sheath + *pteron* wing – more at FEATHER] – **coleopterist** *n*, **coleopterous** *adj*

**coleopteran** /ˌkoli'optərən/ *n* ¹BEETLE 1 – **coleopteran** *adj*

**coleoptile** /ˌkoli'optiel/ *n* the first leaf produced by a germinating seed of grasses and some related plants, that forms a protective sheath round the bud (PLUMULE) that develops into the shoot [NL *coleoptilum*, fr Gk *koleon* + *ptilon* down; akin to Gk *pteron*]

**coleorhiza** /ˌkoliə'riezə/ *n, pl* **coleorhizae** /-zi/ the protective sheath that in some plants (eg grasses) covers the part (RADICLE) of the seedling that develops into the first root [NL, fr Gk *koleon* + NL *-rhiza*]

**coleslaw** /'kohl,slaw/ *n* a salad of raw sliced or chopped white cabbage – compare SAUERKRAUT [D *koolsla*, fr *kool* cabbage + *sla* salad]

**coleus** /'kohli-əs/ *n, pl* **coleuses** any of a large genus (*Coleus*) of plants of the mint family that includes many species grown for their showy often variegated red and green leaves [NL, genus name, fr Gk *koleos, koleon* sheath]

**colewort** /'kohl,wuht/ *n* cole; *esp* one (eg kale) that forms no head

**coley** /'kohli/ *n, pl* **coley, coleys** *Br* a dark greenish-brown to blackish fish (*Pollachius virens*) of the N Atlantic, that is closely related to the cod and is an important food fish – called also COALFISH, SAITHE [prob by shortening & alter. fr *coalfish*]

**coli-** /koli/ – see ²COL-

**¹colic** /'kolik/ *n* a paroxysm of abdominal pain localized in the intestines or other hollow organ and caused by spasm, obstruction, or twisting [ME, fr MF *colique*, fr L *colicus* colicky, fr Gk *kōlikos*, fr *kōlon*, alter. of *kolon* colon]

**²colic** *adj* of the COLON (part of the LARGE INTESTINE) ⟨ ∼ *lymph glands*⟩

**colicin** /'kohləsin, 'ko-/ *also* **colicine** /-seen/ *n* any of various

antibacterial substances that are produced by some strains of bacteria that live in the intestines, and inhibit the production of DNA, proteins, etc by other bacteria [²colic + *-in* or *-ine*]

**colicky** /'koliki/ *adj* 1 relating to or associated with colic ⟨ ∼ *pain*⟩ 2 suffering from colic ⟨ ∼ *babies*⟩

**coliform** /'kolifawm, 'koh-/ *adj* of, like, or being the COLON BACILLUS (bacterium that lives in the intestines) [NL *Escherichia coli* colon bacillus + E *-form*] – **coliform** *n*

**colinear** /ˌkoh'liniə/ *adj* 1 collinear 2 having corresponding parts arranged in the same linear order ⟨a gene and the protein it determines are ∼⟩ – **colinearity** *n*

**coliseum** /ˌkolə'see-əm/ *n* 1 *cap* COLOSSEUM 1 2 coliseum, colosseum a large building (eg a stadium or theatre) used for public entertainments [ML *Colosseum, Colisseum*]

**colitis** /kə'lietəs, koh-/ *n* inflammation of the COLON (part of the LARGE INTESTINE) [NL]

**coll-** /kol-/, **collo-** *comb form* 1 glue ⟨collagen⟩ ⟨collodion⟩ 2 colloid ⟨collotype⟩ [NL, fr Gk *koll-, kollo-*, fr *kolla* – more at PROTOCOL]

**collaborate** /kə'labərayt/ *vi* 1 to work together or with another (eg in an intellectual endeavour) 2 to cooperate with or willingly assist an enemy of one's country, esp an occupying force [LL *collaboratus*, pp of *collaborare* to labour together, fr L *com-* + *laborare* to labour] – **collaborator** *n*, **collaborative** *adj*, **collaboration** *n*

**collaborationism** /kəˌlabə'rayshəniz(ə)m/ *n* collaboration with an enemy – **collaborationist** *adj or n*

**collage** /'kolahzh/ *n* 1 an often abstract composition made of various materials (eg paper, cloth, or wood) juxtaposed by the artist and fixed to a surface 2 the art of making collages 3 an assembly of diverse fragments ⟨a ∼ *of ideas*⟩ [Fr, gluing, fr *coller* to glue, fr *colle* glue, fr (assumed) VL *colla*, fr Gk *kolla*] – **collagist** *n*

**collagen** /'koləjən/ *n* a tough inelastic protein that occurs as the chief constituent of fibres of CONNECTIVE TISSUE making up tendons, the fibrous membrane surrounding bones, etc and that yields gelatin and glue on prolonged heating with water [Gk *kolla* + ISV *-gen*] – **collagenic** *adj*, **collagenous** *adj*

**collagenase** /'koləjənayz, kə'lajinayz, -nays/ *n* any of a group of ENZYMES that break down collagen and gelatin

**¹collapse** /kə'laps/ *vi* 1 to break down completely; disintegrate 2 to fall in or give way abruptly and completely (eg through compression) ⟨a blood vessel that ∼d⟩ 3 to lose force, value, or effect suddenly 4 to break down in energy, stamina, or self-control through exhaustion or disease; *esp* to fall helpless or unconscious 5 to fold down into a more compact shape ⟨a telescope that ∼s⟩ ∼ *vt* to cause to collapse [L *collapsus*, pp of *collabi*, fr *com-* + *labi* to fall, slide – more at SLEEP] – **collapsible** *adj*, **collapsibility** *n*

**²collapse** *n* 1a a breakdown in energy, strength, or stamina **b** a state of extreme physical weakness and depression of normal body functions (eg from heart failure or great loss of body fluids) **c** an airless state of (part of) a lung originating spontaneously or induced surgically 2 the act or an instance of collapsing; a breakdown

**¹collar** /'kolə/ *n* 1 a band, strip, or chain worn round the neck: eg 1a a band that serves to finish or decorate the neckline of a garment; *esp* one that is turned over **b** a short necklace **c** a band fitted round the neck of an animal **d** a part of the harness of draught animals that fits over the shoulders and takes the strain when a load is drawn **e** an indication of control; a token of subservience ⟨slyly slip off the ∼ *of their civil subjection* – Thomas Hobbes⟩ **f** a protective or supportive device worn round the neck 2 something resembling a collar in shape or use (eg a ring or round flange to restrain motion or hold something in place) 3 any of various animal structures or markings similar to a collar in appearance or form 4 a cut of bacon from the neck of a pig [ME *coler*, fr OF, fr L *collare*, fr *collum* neck; akin to ON & OHG *hals* neck, OE *hweol* wheel – more at WHEEL] – **collared** *adj*, **collarless** *adj*, **collarlike** *adj*

**²collar** *vt* 1 to put a collar on 2 *informal* **2a** to seize by the collar or neck **b** to apprehend, grab **c** to get control of ⟨with our machine . . . we can ∼ *nearly the whole of this market* – Roald Dahl⟩ **d** to stop and detain in conversation ⟨∼ed *the mayor at the reception*⟩

**collar beam** *n* a horizontal beam in a roof, that connects two opposite rafters at a place higher than their base – compare TIE-BEAM

**collarbone** /'kolə,bohn/ *n* CLAVICLE

**collar cell** *n* a cell that lines the internal cavity of a sponge and has a collarlike rim at the base of its FLAGELLUM (long whiplike structure) – called also CHOANOCYTE

**coll' arco** /kol 'ahkoh/ *adv* with the bow – usu used as a direction in music for stringed instruments; compare PIZZICATO [It]

**collared dove** /'koləd/ *n* a pinkish-grey European dove (*Streptopelia decaocto*) with a narrow black half-collar at the back of the neck

**collar of esses, collar of SS** *n* a chain of links shaped like the letter S that is worn round the neck as a badge of office and was formerly the badge of the House of Lancaster

**collate** /kə'layt/ *vt* **1a** to compare critically **b** to collect, compare carefully in order to verify, and often integrate or arrange in order **2** to appoint (a priest) to a Church of England office for which a bishop has the right of selection **3a** to verify the order of (printed sheets or sections of a book) **b** to assemble in proper order; *esp* to assemble (e g printed sheets) in order for binding [back-formation fr *collation*] – **collator** *n*

**1collateral** /kə'lat(ə)rəl/ *adj* **1** accompanying as secondary or subordinate ⟨*digress into ~ matters*⟩ **2** belonging to the same ancestral stock but not in a direct line of descent – usu contrasted with *lineal* **3** parallel or corresponding in position, time, or significance ⟨*~ states like Athens and Sparta*⟩ **4a** of or being collateral used as security (e g for repayment of a loan) **b** secured by collateral ⟨*a ~ loan*⟩ **5** of or being a VASCULAR BUNDLE (part of a plant's circulatory system) having PHLOEM (food-conducting tissue) only to the outside of the XYLEM (water-conducting tissue) – compare BICOLLATERAL [ME, prob fr MF, fr ML *collateralis*, fr L *com-* + *lateralis* lateral] – **collaterally** *adv*, **collaterality** *n*

**2collateral** *n* **1** a collateral relative **2** property pledged by a borrower to protect the interests of the lender **3** a branch of a body part (e g a vein)

**collation** /kə'laysh(ə)n/ *n* **1** a light meal; *esp* one allowed on fast days in place of lunch or supper **2** the act, process, or result of collating [(1) ME, fr ML *collation-, collatio*; fr LL, conference, fr L, bringing together, comparison, fr *collatus* (pp of *conferre* to bring together, bestow upon), fr *com* + *latus*, suppletive pp of *ferre* to carry; (2) ME, fr L *collation-, collatio*]

**colleague** /'koleeg/ *n* a fellow worker; *esp* an associate in a profession or in a civil or ecclesiastical office [MF *collegue*, fr L *collega*, fr *com-* + *legare* to appoint, depute – more at LEGATE] – **colleagueship** *n*

**1collect** /'kolikt/ *n* a short prayer comprising an invocation, petition, and conclusion; *specif, often cap* one preceding the Epistle read at Communion and varying with the day [ME *collecte*, fr OF, fr ML *collecta*, short for *oratio ad collectam* prayer upon assembly]

**2collect** /kə'lekt/ *vt* **1a** to bring together into one body or place; *specif* to assemble a collection of **b** to gather or exact from a number of sources ⟨*~ taxes*⟩ **2** to accumulate, gather ⟨*books ~ dust*⟩ **3** to gain or regain control of ⟨*~ his thoughts*⟩ **4** to claim as due and receive possession or payment of ⟨*~ social security*⟩ **5** to provide transport or escort for ⟨*~ the children from school*⟩ **6** *chiefly Br* to gain, obtain ~ *vi* **1** to come together in a band, group, or mass; gather ⟨*the troops ~ ed*⟩ ⟨*the dust ~ed*⟩ **2a** to assemble a collection **b** to receive payment ⟨*~ing on his insurance*⟩ **synonyms** see ¹GATHER **antonym** disperse [L *collectus*, pp of *colligere*, fr *com-* + *legere* to gather] – **collectible, collectable** *adj or n*

**3collect** /kə'lekt/ *adv or adj, NAm* to be paid for by the receiver ⟨*send the package ~*⟩ ⟨*a ~ telephone call*⟩

**collectanea** /ˌkolek'taynə/ *n pl* collected writings; *also* literary items forming a collection [L, neut pl of *collectaneus* collected, fr *collectus*, pp]

**collected** /kə'lektid/ *adj* **1** showing calmness and composure **2a** of a horse's gait performed or performable by a horse from a state of collection ⟨*a ~ canter*⟩ – compare EXTENDED **b** of a horse in a state of collection – **collectedly** *adv*, **collectedness** *n*

**collecting ring** /kə'lekting/ *n* an enclosure in which an animal waits before competing in a main ring (e g in showjumping)

**collection** /kə'leksh(ə)n/ *n* **1** the act or process of collecting **2** something collected; *esp* an accumulation of objects gathered for study, comparison, or exhibition **3** a range of similar products (e g garments) presented to the public ⟨*Christian Dior's spring ~*⟩ **4** a standard pose of a well-schooled riding horse in which it is responsive to the bit and has its head arched and the hocks well under the body so that the centre of gravity is towards the hindquarters **5** *pl* mid-year university examinations at Oxford and Durham

**1collective** /kə'lektiv/ *adj* **1** denoting a number of individuals considered as one group ⟨*flock is a ~ word*⟩ **2a** formed by collecting; aggregated **b** *of a fruit* formed from several flowers; MULTIPLE **5** **3** of, made by, or held in common by a group of individuals ⟨*~ opinion*⟩ ⟨*~ responsibility*⟩ **4** collectivized or characterized by collectivism – **collectively** *adv*

**2collective** *n* **1** *taking sing or pl vb* a collective body; a group **2a** a cooperative unit or organization ⟨*radical publishing ~ – Time Out*⟩ **b** COLLECTIVE FARM

**collective agreement** *n* an agreement between an employer and a union reached through collective bargaining

**collective bargaining** *n* negotiation between an employer and union representatives usu on wages, hours, and working conditions

**collective farm** *n* a farm, esp in a communist country, formed from many smallholdings collected into a single unit for joint operation under governmental supervision

**collective security** *n* the maintenance by common action of the security of all members of an association of nations

**collective unconscious** *n* that part of a person's unconscious which according to the analytical psychology of C G Jung is inherited and shared with all other people

**collectivism** /kə'lekti,viz(ə)m/ *n* a political or economic theory advocating collective control, esp over production and distribution – **collectivist** *adj or n*, **collectivistic** *adj*, **collectivistically** *adv*

**collectivity** /ˌkolek'tivəti, kəˌlek-/ *n* **1** the quality or state of being collective **2** a collective whole; *esp* the people as a body

**collectiv·ize, -ise** /kə'lektiviez/ *vt* to organize under collective control – **collectivization** *n*

**collector** /kə'lektə/ *n* **1** somebody who or something that collects: e g **1a** an official who collects funds, esp money **b** somebody who makes a collection ⟨*a stamp ~*⟩ **c** an object or device that collects ⟨*the statuette was a dust ~*⟩ **2** the chief administrative official of an Indian district **3** a conductor maintaining contact between moving and stationary parts of an electric circuit **4** a region in a transistor that collects carriers of current or electric charge (e g electrons) – **collectorship** *n*

**collector's item** *n* an item of such rarity or beauty that it warrants a place in a collection

**colleen** /ko'leen/ *n* **1** an Irish girl **2** *Irish* a girl [IrGael *cailīn*, dim. of *caile* girl, countrywoman]

**college** /'kolij/ *n* **1** a body of clergy living together and supported by a foundation **2** a building used for an educational or religious purpose **3a** a self-governing endowed constituent body of a university offering instruction and often living quarters but not granting degrees ⟨*Balliol and Magdalen Colleges at Oxford*⟩ **b** a small university **c** an independent American institution of higher learning offering a course of general studies leading to a bachelor's degree **d** an institution offering instruction usu in a professional, vocational, or technical field ⟨*business ~*⟩ ⟨*art ~*⟩ **e** *chiefly Br* a public school or private secondary school; *also* a state school for older pupils ⟨*a Sixth-form ~*⟩ **f** *taking sing or pl vb* the staff, students, or administration of a college **4** a company, group; *specif* an organized body of people engaged in a common pursuit or having common interests or duties **5** a group of people or a corporation having certain rights and privileges and considered by law to be a unit; *esp* one created for the promotion of learning **6** *slang* prison [ME, fr MF, fr L *collegium* society, fr *collega* colleague – more at COLLEAGUE] – **college** *adj*

**College of Advanced Technology** *n* any of 10 British institutions devoted to advanced technical studies that in 1966-67 were made universities or colleges of universities

**College of Education** *n* a college for the training of teachers

**College of Further Education** *n* a British college offering general or vocational adult non-degree courses

**College of Higher Education** *n* **1** COLLEGE OF EDUCATION **2** TECHNICAL COLLEGE

**collegial** /kə'leeji·əl, kə'leejyəl/ *adj* **1** COLLEGIATE 1,2 **2a** marked by power or authority vested equally in each of a number of colleagues **b** characterized by equal sharing of authority, esp by Roman Catholic bishops – **collegially** *adv*

**collegiality** /kəˌleej'aləti/ *n* the relationship of colleagues; *specif* equality of status among bishops sharing authority in the Roman Catholic church

**collegian** /kə'leejən/ *n* a member of a college

**collegiate** /kə'leeji·ət/ *adj* **1** of a collegiate church **2a** of or comprising a college **b** *of a university* having colleges **c** *of a* *university student* attached to a college **3** COLLEGIAL 2 [ML *collegiatus*, fr L *collegium*] – **collegiately** *adv*

**collegiate church** *n* **1** a church other than a cathedral that has a group (CHAPTER) of canons attached to it **2** *NAm & Scot* a church or corporate group of churches with two or more ministers of equal rank

**collembolan** /kə'lembələn/ *n* SPRINGTAIL (small wingless insect) [deriv of *coll-* + Gk *embolos* wedge, stopper – more at EMBOLUS; fr the structure on its abdomen, secreting a sticky substance] – **collembolan, collembolous** *adj*

**collenchyma** /kə'lengkimə/ *n* a plant tissue consisting of living usu elongated cells with irregularly thickened walls that occurs in growing stems, leaf veins and stalks, etc where it gives mechanical strength and support – compare PARENCHYMA, SCLERENCHYMA [NL] – **collenchymatous** *adj*

**collet** /'kolit/ *n* a metal band, collar, or flange: eg **a** a small collar pierced to receive the inner end of a balance spring on a timepiece **b** a circle or flange in which a gem is set [MF, dim. of *col* collar, fr L *collum* neck – more at COLLAR]

**collide** /kə'lied/ *vi* **1** to come together forcibly **2** to come into conflict [L *collidere*, fr *com-* + *laedere* to injure by striking (cf ELIDE)]

   *usage* Some people feel that **collide** and **collision** should be used only when two things are both in motion, rather than when one is stationary ⟨*car collided with a lamp post*⟩.

**collie** /'koli/ *n* a large dog of any of several varieties of a breed developed in Scotland, esp for use in herding sheep and cattle [prob fr E dial. *colly* (black), deriv of ME *col* coal]

**collier** /'kolyə/ *n* **1** a coal miner **2** a ship for transporting coal [ME *colier*, fr *col* coal]

**colliery** /'kolyəri/ *n* a coal mine and its associated buildings

**collieshangie** /'koli,shang·i/ *n*, *Scot* a squabble, disturbance [alter. of Sc *currieshangie* (uproar), fr *cur-*, *currie-* wrongly, bad + *shangie*, perh alter. of *shandy*, var of *shindy*]

**colligate** /'koligayt/ *vt* **1** to unite or group together **2** to subsume (isolated facts) under a general concept ~ *vi* to be or become a member of a group or unit [L *colligatus*, pp of *colligare*, fr *com-* + *ligare* to tie – more at LIGATURE] – **colligation** *n*

**colligative** /kə'ligətiv/ *adj*, *esp of a physical property* depending on the number rather than the nature of particles (e g atoms or molecules) ⟨*the pressure of a gas is a ~ property*⟩

**collimate** /'kolimayt/ *vt* **1** to make (e g rays of light) parallel **2** to adjust the line of sight of (a telescope, theodolite, etc) [L *collimatus*, pp of *collimare*, MS var of *collineare* to make straight, fr *com-* + *linea* line] – **collimation** *n*

**collimator** /'koli,maytə/ *n* **1** a device (e g in a telescope, spectroscope, or other optical instrument) for producing a beam of parallel rays of radiation (e g light) **2** a device for obtaining a beam of molecules, atoms, or nuclear particles of limited cross section

**collinear, colinear** /,koh'lini·ə/ *adj* lying on the same straight line ⟨*~ points*⟩ [ISV] – **collinearity** *n*

**collision** /kə'lizh(ə)n/ *n* **1** an act or instance of colliding; a clash **2** an encounter between particles (e g atoms, molecules, or neutrons) resulting in an exchange or transformation of energy *usage* see COLLIDE [ME, fr L *collision-*, *collisio* fr *collisus*, pp of *collidere*] – **collisional** *adj*

**collision course** *n* a course or approach that would result in collision or conflict if continued unaltered

**collo-** – see COLL-

**collocate** /'koləkayt/ *vt*, *formal* to set or arrange in a place or position; *esp* to set side by side ~ *vi*, *of a word or other linguistic element* to form part of a collocation *with* [L *collocatus*, pp of *collocare*, fr *com-* + *locare* to place, fr *locus* place – more at STALL]

**collocation** /,kolə'kaysh(ə)n/ *n* the act or result of placing or arranging together; *specif* a noticeable arrangement or joining together of words or other linguistic elements – **collocational** *adj*

**collodion** /kə'lohdi·ən/ *n* a sticky solution of PYROXYLIN used esp as a coating for wounds or for photographic films [modif of NL *collodium*, fr Gk *kollōdēs* glutinous, fr *kolla* glue]

**colloid** /'koloyd/ *n* **1a** a substance composed of particles that are too small to be seen with an ordinary microscope but too large to form a true solution, and that in suspension or solution fails to settle out but will typically scatter a beam of light – compare CRYSTALLOID **b** a system consisting of a colloid together with the gaseous, liquid, or solid medium in which it is dispersed ⟨*milk is a ~ composed of fat globules dispersed in*

*milk*⟩ **2** a gelatinous substance found in tissues, esp in disease [ISV *coll-* + *-oid*] – **colloidal** *adj*, **colloidally** *adv*

**collop** /'koləp/ *n* a small piece or slice, esp of meat; an escalope [ME, dish of fried or roasted meat]

**colloquial** /kə'lohkwi·əl/ *adj* **1** of conversation; conversational **2a** used in or characteristic of familiar and informal conversation **b** using conversational style – **colloquial** *n*, **colloquially** *adv*, **colloquiality** *n*

**colloquialism** /kə'lohkwi·ə,liz(ə)m/ *n* **1a** a colloquial expression **b** a local or regional dialect expression **2** colloquial style

**colloquium** /kə'lohkwi·əm/ *n*, *pl* **colloquiums, colloquia** /-kwi·ə/ a meeting at which one or more usu academic specialists deliver addresses on a topic and then answer questions relating it [L, colloquy]

**colloquy** /'koləkwi/ *n* a formal conversation or dialogue [L *colloquium*, fr *colloqui* to converse, fr *com-* + *loqui* to speak]

**collotype** /'kolə,tiep, 'koloh-/ *n* **1** a process for printing illustrations directly from a hardened film of gelatin **2** a print made by collotype [ISV]

**collude** /kə'loohd/ *vi* to conspire, plot ⟨*fined … for colluding to raise beer prices – Financial Times*⟩ [L *colludere*, fr *com-* + *ludere* to play, fr *ludus* game – more at LUDICROUS]

**collusion** /kə'loohzh(ə)n/ *n* secret agreement or cooperation for an illegal or deceitful purpose [ME, fr MF, fr L *collusion-*, *collusio*, fr *collusus*, pp of *colludere*] – **collusive** *adj*, **collusively** *adv*

**collyrium** /kə'liəri·əm/ *n*, *pl* **collyria** /-ri·ə/, **collyriums** an eye lotion [L, fr Gk *kollyrion* pessary, eye salve, fr dim. of *kollyra* bread roll]

**collywobbles** /'koli,woblz/ *n taking sing or pl vb*, *informal* **1** stomachache **2** qualms, butterflies □ usu + *the* [prob based on *colic* + *wobble*]

**colo-** – see ²COL-

**colobus monkey** /'koləbəs/ *n* any of various long-tailed slender-bodied African monkeys (genus *Colobus*) [NL *Colobus*, genus name, fr Gk *kolobos* docked, mutilated; fr its rudimentary thumb]

**cologne** /kə'lohn/ *n* a perfumed toilet water [*Cologne*, city in Germany] – **cologned** *adj*

**¹colon** /'koh,lon/ *n*, *pl* **colons, cola** /'kohlə/ the part of the LARGE INTESTINE that extends from the CAECUM (pouchlike beginning of the large intestine) to the rectum [L, fr Gk *kolon*] – **colonic** *adj*

**²colon** *n*, *pl* **colons, cola** **1** a punctuation mark : used chiefly to direct attention to matter (e g a list, explanation, or quotation) that follows, to introduce the words of a speaker (e g in a play), in various references (e g in John 4:10), and, esp in NAm, between the parts of an expression of time in hours and minutes (e g in 1:15) **2** the sign : used esp in a ratio where it is usu read as "to" (e g in 4:1 read "four to one"), or in a proportion, where it is usu read as "is to" or when doubled as "as" (e g in 2:1::8:4 read "two is to one as eight is to four") **3** a mark : used after a vowel in certain phonetic systems to indicate length [L, part of a poem, fr Gk *kōlon* limb, part of a strophe – more at CALK]

**³colon** *n*, *pl* **colones** /-nays/ – see MONEY table [Sp *colón*, fr *Cristóbal Colón* (Christopher Columbus) †1506 It navigator]

**colon bacillus** /'koh,lon/ *n* any of various bacteria (esp genera *Escherichia* and *Aerobacter*) that normally live in the intestines of VERTEBRATE animals; *esp* one (*Escherichia coli*) used extensively in genetic research

**colonel** /'kuhnl/ *n* **1** – see MILITARY RANKS table **2** – used as an American honorific title, esp in the southern and midland USA [alter. of earlier *coronel*, fr MF, modif of OIt *colonnello* column of soldiers, colonel, dim. of *colonna* column, fr L *columna*] – **colonelcy** *n*

**Colonel Blimp** /blimp/ *n* a pompous person with out-of-date or ultraconservative views; *broadly* a reactionary [*Colonel Blimp*, cartoon character created by David Low †1963 Brit cartoonist] – **Colonel Blimpism** *n*

**¹colonial** /kə'lohnyəl, -ni·əl/ *adj* **1** (characteristic) of a colony **2** possessing or composed of colonies ⟨*Britain's ~ empire*⟩ **3** *often cap, chiefly NAm* of the original 13 colonies forming the USA: e g **3a** made or prevailing in America during the colonial period, up to 1776 ⟨*~ architecture was a modification of English Georgian*⟩ **b** adapted from or reminiscent of an American colonial mode of design ⟨*~ furniture*⟩ – **colonialize** *vt*, **colonially** *adv*, **colonialness** *n*

**²colonial** *n* **1** a member or inhabitant of a (British Crown) colony **2** *NAm* a house built in colonial style

**colonialism** /kə'lohni·ə,liz(ə)m/ *n* **1** control by one power over a dependent area or people **2** a policy advocating or based on such control – **colonialist** *n or adj*, **colonialistic** *adj*

**colonist** /'kolənist/ *n* **1** a member or inhabitant of a colony **2** one who colonizes or settles in a new country

**colon·ize, -ise** /'koləniez/ *vt* to establish a colony in, on, or of ~ *vi* to make or establish a colony; settle – **colonizer** *n*, **colonization** *n*

**colonnade** /,kolə'nayd/ *n* a series of columns set at regular intervals and supporting an ENTABLATURE [Fr, fr It *colonnato*, fr *colonna* column] – **colonnaded** *adj*

**colonus** /kə'lohnəs/ *n, pl* **coloni** /-nie, -ni/ a free-born serf in the later Roman Empire who could sometimes own property but who was bound to the land and obliged to pay a rent, usu in produce [L, lit., farmer]

**colony** /'koləni/ *n* **1a** a body of people living in a new territory but retaining ties with the parent state **b** a territory that is inhabited by such a body and is typically subject to some degree of governmental control by the parent state **2a** a group of animals or plants of the same type, esp the same species, living or growing together and somewhat isolated from other groups **b** a localized population of animals within a species, forming a distinguishable organized society or community ⟨a ~ *of ants*⟩ **c** a mass of microorganisms (e g bacteria) grown from one or a small cluster of spores or cells, usu in or on a solid medium **d** all the interconnected units that together make up a compound animal (e g a coral or Portuguese man-of-war) and that function to a greater or lesser degree as a single individual **3a** *taking sing or pl vb* a group of individuals with common usu specified characteristics or interests living close together ⟨*an artists'* ~⟩ **b** the area occupied by such a group **4a** *taking sing or pl vb* a group of people segregated from the general public (e g for care or correction) ⟨*a leper* ~⟩ ⟨*a penal* ~⟩ **b** the land or buildings occupied by such a group [ME *colonie*, fr MF & L; MF, fr L *colonia*, fr *colonus* farmer, colonist, fr *colere* to cultivate – more at WHEEL]

**colophon** /'kolə,fon/ *n* **1** a statement that follows the end of the text of a book or manuscript and usu gives facts about its production **2** an identifying design used by a printer or publisher [L, fr Gk *kolophōn* summit, finishing touch

**colophony** /ko'lofəni/ *n* ROSIN [ME *colophonie*, deriv of Gk *Kolophōn* Colophon, an Ionian city]

**color** /'kulə/ *vb or n, chiefly NAm* (to) colour

**Colorado beetle** /,kolə'rahdoh/ *n* a black-and-yellow striped beetle (*Leptinotarsa decemlineata*) that feeds on the leaves of the potato – called also POTATO BEETLE [*Colorado*, state of USA]

**coloration**, *Br also* **colouration** /,kulə'raysh(ə)n/ *n* **1a** COLOURING 1c(2), COMPLEXION 1 ⟨*the dark* ~ *of his skin*⟩ **b** use or choice of colours (e g by an artist) ⟨*Millet's subdued* ~⟩ **c** arrangement of colours ⟨*the brilliant* ~ *of a butterfly's wing*⟩ **2a** characteristic quality **b** aspect suggesting an attitude; persuasion ⟨*only a hint of Marxist* ~⟩ **3** subtle variation of intensity or quality of musical tone

**coloratura** /,kolərə'tyooərə/ *n* **1** elaborate embellishment in vocal music **2** a soprano who has a light agile voice and specializes in coloratura [obs It, lit., colouring, fr LL, fr L *coloratus*, pp of *colorare* to colour, fr *color* colour]

**colorcast** /'kulə,kahst/ *n, NAm* a television broadcast in colour [*color* + tele*cast*] – **colorcast** *vb*

**colorcaster** /'kulə,kahstə/ *n, NAm* a broadcaster (e g commentating on a sports contest) who supplies vivid or picturesque details and often gives statistical or analytical information [*color* + broad*caster*]

**colorific** /,kulə'rifik/ *adj* producing or capable of giving colour

**colorimeter** /,kulo'rimitə/ *n* an instrument for determining and specifying colours; *specif* one used for chemical analysis of a solution (e g to determine the concentration of a coloured component) by comparison of the solution's colour with a standard colour [ISV] – **colorimetry** *n*, **colorimetric** *adj*, **colorimetrically** *adv*

**colossal** /kə'los(ə)l/ *adj* **1** of or like a colossus; *esp* of very great size or degree ⟨*a* ~ *building*⟩ ⟨*a* ~ *blunder*⟩ *synonyms* see HUGE *antonym* diminutive – **colossally** *adv*

**colosseum** /,kolə'see·əm/ *n* **1** Colosseum, Coliseum an amphitheatre built in Rome in the first century AD **2** COLISEUM 2 [ML, fr L, neut of *colosseus* colossal, fr *colossus*]

**Colossians** /kə'losh(ə)nz/ *n taking sing vb* – see BIBLE table [*Colossae*, ancient city in Asia Minor]

**colossus** /kə'losəs/ *n, pl* **colossuses, colossi** /-sie/ **1** a statue of gigantic size **2** somebody who or something that resembles a colossus in size or relative proportions; *specif* one remarkably preeminent over others ⟨*such an intellectual* ~ *as Leonardo da Vinci*⟩ [L, fr Gk *kolossos*]

**colostomy** /kə'lostəmi/ *n* surgical formation of an opening from the intestines to the body surface, that acts as an artificial anus [ISV ²*col-* + *-stomy*]

**colostrum** /kə'lostrəm/ *n* the milk that is secreted for a few days after giving birth and that differs from that secreted later in having a higher protein and antibody content [L, beastings] – **colostral** *adj*

**¹colour**, *NAm chiefly* **color** /'kulə/ *n* **1a** the visual sensation (e g red, brown, pink, or grey) resulting from the interpretation by the brain of the wavelength of perceived light, that enables one to differentiate between otherwise identical objects **b** the aspect of objects and light sources that may be described in terms of HUE (major light wavelength present), lightness, and SATURATION (degree of mixing with white, grey, or black) for objects and hue, brightness, and saturation for light sources **c** a hue, esp as contrasted with black, white, or grey ⟨~ *TV*⟩ **2a** an outward often deceptive show; an appearance ⟨*his story has the* ~ *of truth*⟩ **b** *law* an apparent right, authority, or office **c** a pretence offered as justification; a pretext ⟨*there have been received under the* ~ *of religion, a world of fables* – Bishop Berkeley⟩ **d** an appearance of authenticity; plausibility ⟨*lending* ~ *to this notion*⟩ **3a** the tint characteristic of good health **b** BLUSH 1 **4** colours *pl*, colour **4a** an identifying badge, pennant, or flag (e g of a ship or regiment) ⟨*a ship sailing under Swedish* ~s⟩ **b** coloured clothing distinguishing one as a member of a usu specified group or representative of a usu specified person or thing ⟨*a jockey riding in the* ~s *of his stable*⟩ **c** any of the five principal heraldic TINCTURES azure, vert, sable, gules, and purpure **5** colours *pl*, colour character, nature ⟨*showed himself in his true* ~s⟩ **6** the use or combination of colours (e g by painters) **7** *pl* **7a** a naval or nautical salute to a flag being hoisted or lowered **b** ARMED FORCES ⟨*was called to the* ~s⟩ **8** vitality, interest ⟨*the play had a good deal of* ~ *to it*⟩ **9** something used to give colour; a pigment **10** tonal quality in music **11** skin pigmentation other than white, characteristic of race **12** colours *pl*, colour *Br* the award made to a regular member of a team ⟨*got my cricket* ~s⟩ [ME *colour*, fr OF, fr L *color*; akin to L *celare* to conceal – more at HELL] – **troop the colour** to parade a military unit's flag ceremonially along the ranks of soldiers – **with flying colours** with complete or eminent success ⟨*passed the exam* with flying colours⟩

**²colour**, *NAm chiefly* **color** *vt* **1a** to give colour to **b** to change the colour of (e g by dyeing, staining, or painting) **2** to change as if by dyeing or painting: e g **2a** to misrepresent, distort **b** to disguise ⟨~ *a lie*⟩ **c** to influence, affect **to take on colour**; *specif* to blush – **colourant** *n*

**colourable** /'kul(ə)rəbl/ *adj, formal* **1** seemingly valid or genuine; plausible **2** intended to deceive; counterfeit ⟨~ *piety*⟩ – **colourably** *adv*

**colouration** /,kulə'raysh(ə)n/ *n, Br* coloration

**colour bar** *n* a social or legal barrier preventing coloured people from participating with whites in various activities or restricting their access to various places, amenities, or opportunities

**'colour-,blind** *adj* **1** partially or totally unable to distinguish one or more colours **2** insensitive, oblivious – **colour blindness** *n*

**colourbreed** /'kulə,breed/ *vt* to breed selectively for the development of particular colours ⟨~ing *canaries for red*⟩

**¹coloured** /'kuləd/ *adj* **1** having colour **2** marked by exaggeration or bias **3a** of a race other than the white; *esp* BLACK **2a b** of or for coloured people **c** *often cap* of mixed race – used esp of S Africans of mixed descent *synonyms* see ¹BLACK

**²coloured** *n, pl* **coloureds, coloured** *often cap* a coloured person

**colourfast** /'kulə,fahst/ *adj* having colour that will not fade or run – **colourfastness** *n*

**colour filter** *n* FILTER 3b

**colourful** /-f(ə)l/ *adj* **1** having striking colours **2** full of variety or interest – **colourfully** *adv*, **colourfulness** *n*

**colour guard** *n* a guard of honour for the colours of an organization

**colouring** /'kuləring/ *n* **1a** the act of applying colours **b** something that produces colour **c(1)** the effect produced by applying or combining colours **c(2)** natural colour **c(3)** COMPLEXION 1

⟨*her dark* ∼⟩ **d** change of appearance (e g by adding colour) **2** an influence, bias **3** COLOUR 8 **4** musical timbre or quality

**colourist** /'kulərist/ *n* a person who colours or deals with colour; *specif* an artist particularly concerned with effects of colour

**colourless** /'kuləlis/ *adj* lacking colour: e g **a** pallid, blanched **b** dull, uninteresting – **colourless** *adv*, **colourlessness** *n*

**colour line** *n* COLOUR BAR

**colour phase** *n* **1a** a genetic variant in which the skin or coat colour is unlike the WILD TYPE (typical form found in nature) of the animal group in which it appears **b** an animal with such a variant **2** a coat colour in a mammal (e g some weasels) that varies according to season

**colour scheme** *n* a systematic combination of colours ⟨*the* ∼ *of a room*⟩

**colour separation** *n* the usu photographic filtering of colours to produce a set of usu three negatives (e g in cyan, magenta, and yellow) from which, in addition to a black negative, plates are made for colour printing

**colour sergeant** *n* the senior sergeant in a British infantry company – see MILITARY RANKS table [fr his orig duty of guarding the colours of his regiment]

**colour supplement** *n*, *Br* an illustrated magazine printed in colour and published as a free supplement to a newspaper, esp on Sundays

**colour temperature** *n* the temperature at which a completely nonreflective surface emits RADIANT ENERGY of the same wavelength as that associated with a particular colour from a given source

**colourwash** /'kulə‚wosh/ *n* a coloured distemper

**colourway** /'kulə‚way/ *n* a set of colours chosen for use in a pattern or design (e g on a fabric)

**-colous** /-kələs/ *comb form* (→ *adj*) living or growing in or on ⟨*arenic*olous⟩ [L -*cola* inhabitant; akin to L *colere* to inhabit – more at WHEEL]

**colportage** /'kol‚pawtij (*Fr* kɔlpɔrta:z)/ *n* a colporteur's work

**colporteur** /'kol‚pawtə (*Fr* kɔlpɔrtœ:r)/ *n* a seller of religious books [Fr, alter. of MF *comporteur*, fr *comporter* to bear, peddle – more at COMPORT]

**colt** /kohlt, kolt/ *n* **1a** a foal **b** a young male horse that is either sexually immature or has not attained an arbitrarily designated age (e g three years) **2** a young untried person; a novice; *esp* a cricketer or rugby player in a junior team [ME, fr OE; akin to OE *cild* child]

**coltish** /'kohltish, 'kol-/ *adj* **1** frisky, playful **2** of or like a colt – **coltishly** *adv*, **coltishness** *n*

**coltsfoot** /'kohlts‚foot, 'kolts-/ *n*, *pl* **coltsfoots** a plant (*Tussilago farfara*) of the daisy family with yellow flower heads that appear early in spring before the large rounded heart-shaped leaves [fr the shape of its leaves]

**colubrid** /kə'loohbrid, -lyooh-/ *n* any of a large family (Colubridae) of nonvenomous snakes found in many parts of the world [deriv of L *coluber*, *colubra* snake] – **colubrid** *adj*

**colubrine** /kə'loohbrin, -brien, -lyooh-/ *adj* of or like a snake

**colugo** /kə'loohgoh/ *n*, *pl* **colugos** FLYING LEMUR [prob native name in Malaya]

**columbarium** /‚koləm'beəri·əm/ *n*, *pl* **columbaria 1** a structure of vaults (e g in a crematorium) lined with recesses for urns containing ashes of those who have been cremated **2** a recess in a columbarium [L, lit., dovecote, fr *columba* dove]

**Columbia** /kə'lumbiə/ *n*, *poetic* the United States of America [NL, fr Christopher *Columbus* †1506 It navigator & discoverer of America]

**Columbian** /kə'lumbiən/ *adj* of the USA or Christopher Columbus

**columbine** /'koləmbien/ *n* any of a genus (*Aquilegia*) of plants of the buttercup family that have showy flowers with five petals from which long spurs extend backwards [ME, fr ML *columbina*, fr L, fem of *columbinus* dovelike, fr *columba* dove; akin to OHG *holuntar* elder tree, Gk *kolymbos* a bird, *kelainos* black]

**columbite** /kə'lumbiet/ *n* a hard black mineral consisting essentially of an oxide of the metallic chemical elements iron, manganese, and niobium, (Fe, Mn)Nb$_2$O$_6$ [NL *columbium*]

**columbium** /kə'lumbi·əm/ *n* the chemical element niobium – not now used technically [NL, fr *Columbia*]

**columella** /‚kolyoo'melə/ *n*, *pl* **columellae** /-li/ **1a** the bony or partly cartilage rod connecting the eardrum with the INNER EAR in birds and in many reptiles and amphibians **b** the bony central axis of the COCHLEA (spirally coiled hearing organ) of the ear **2** the central column or axis of a spiral shell (e g of a snail) **3** the axis of the spore-bearing capsule in mosses and some LIVERWORTS **4** the central sterile portion of the SPORANGIUM (spore-producing case) in various fungi (*Mucor* and related genera) [NL, fr L, dim. of *columna*] – **columellar** *adj*, **columellate** *adj*

**column** /'koləm/ *n* **1a** a vertical arrangement of items printed or written on a page ⟨*adding up a* ∼ *of figures*⟩ **b** any of two or more vertical sections of a printed page separated by a line or blank space **c** an accumulation arranged vertically; stack **d** a special and usu regular feature in a newspaper or periodical **2** a pillar that usu consists of a round shaft, a CAPITAL (stylized top), and a base and is used either decoratively or as a support **3** something resembling a column in form, position, or function ⟨*a* ∼ *of water*⟩ **4** a long narrow formation of soldiers, vehicles, etc in rows [ME *columne*, fr MF *colomne*, fr L *columna*, fr *columen* top; akin to L *collis* hill – more at HILL] – **columned** *adj*

**columnar** /'koləmnə/ *adj* **1** of or characterized by columns **2** of, being, or made up of tall narrow cells; *esp* of or being EPITHELIUM (tissue covering external surfaces and lining internal cavities) composed of columnar cells

**columniation** /kə‚lumni'aysh(ə)n/ *n* the employment or arrangement of columns in a structure [modif. of L *columnation-*, *columnatio*, fr *columna*]

**column inch** *n* a unit of measure for printed matter one column wide and one inch deep

**columnist** /'koləmist, 'koləmnist/ *n* one who writes a newspaper or magazine column

**colure** /kə'lyooə, 'kohlyooə/ *n* the GREAT CIRCLE on the CELESTIAL SPHERE passing through the poles and either the EQUINOXES or SOLSTICES [LL *coluri*, pl, fr Gk *kolouroi*, pl of *kolouros* stump-tailed, fr *kolos* docked + *oura* tail; fr the lower part being cut off from sight by the horizon]

**colza** /'kolzə/ *n* **1** rape or another COLE (plant of the cabbage family) whose seed is used as a source of oil **2** rapeseed [Fr, fr D *koolzaad*, fr MD *coolsaet*, fr *coole* cabbage + *saet* seed]

**com-** /kom-/, **col-**, **con-** *prefix* with; together; jointly – usu *com-* before *b*, *p*, or *m* ⟨*com*mingle⟩, *col-* before *l* ⟨*col*linear⟩, and *con-* before other sounds ⟨*con*centrate⟩ [ME, fr OF, fr L, with, together, thoroughly – more at CO-]

**¹coma** /'kohmə/ *n* **1** a state of deep unconsciousness caused by disease, injury, or poison **2** a state of lethargy and sluggishness; torpor △ **comma** [NL, fr Gk *kōma* deep sleep]

**²coma** *n*, *pl* **comae 1** the head of a comet, usu containing a small bright dense portion (NUCLEUS) **2** an optical aberration in which the image of a tiny point of light (POINT SOURCE) is a comet-shaped blur [L, hair, fr Gk *komē*] – **comatic** *adj*

**Comanche** /kə'manchi/ *n*, *pl* **Comanches**, *esp collectively* **Comanche** a member of a N American Indian people ranging from Wyoming and Nebraska into New Mexico and NW Texas [Sp, of Shoshonean origin; perh akin to Hopi *kománči* scalp lock]

**Comanchean** /kə'manchiən/ *adj or n* (of or being) the geological period or system of rocks of the MESOZOIC era in N America that corresponds to the early part of the CRETACEOUS period [*Comanche*, town & county in Texas, USA] – **Comanchean** *n*

**comatose** /'kohmə‚tohs, -‚tohz/ *adj* **1** of or suffering from coma **2** characterized by lethargy and sluggishness; torpid ⟨*a* ∼ *economy*⟩ [Fr *comateux*, fr Gk *kōmat-*, *kōma*]

**comatulid** /kə'matyoolid/ *n* FEATHER STAR (marine animal related to starfish) [deriv of LL *comatulus* having hair neatly curled, fr L *comatus* hairy, fr *coma*]

**¹comb** /kohm/ *n* **1a(1)** a toothed implement for arranging or cleaning hair **a(2)** a similar usu curved implement worn in the hair by women for decoration or for holding the hair in place **b** a structure resembling such a comb; *esp* any of several toothed devices used in handling or ordering textile fibres **c** a currycomb **2a** a fleshy crest on the head of a DOMESTIC FOWL (e g a cock) or a related bird **b** something (e g the ridge of a roof) resembling the comb of a cock **3** a honeycomb [ME, fr OE *camb*; akin to OHG *kamb* comb, Gk *gomphos* tooth] – **combed** *adj*, **comblike** *adj*

**²comb** *vt* **1** to draw a comb through for the purpose of arranging or cleaning **2** to pass across with a scraping or raking action **3a** to eliminate (e g with a comb) by a thorough going over – usu + *out* **b** to search or examine systematically **4** to use with a combing action ∼ *vi*, *of a wave* to roll over or break into foam

¹**combat** /'kombat, kəm'bat/ *vb* -**tt**- (*NAm* -**t**-, -**tt**-) *vi* to engage in combat; fight ∼ *vt* **1** to fight with; battle **2** to struggle against; *esp* to strive to reduce or eliminate ⟨∼ *inflation*⟩ [MF *combattre*, fr (assumed) VL *combattere*, fr L *com*- + *battuere* to beat – more at BATTLE]

²**combat** /'kombat/ *n* **1** a fight or contest between individuals or groups **2** a conflict, controversy **3** active fighting in a war, action ⟨*casualties suffered in* ∼⟩ □ compare ¹BATTLE

³**combat** *adj* **1** relating to combat ⟨∼ *missions*⟩ **2** designed or destined for combat ⟨∼ *troops*⟩

**combatant** /'kombət(ə)nt; *also* kəm'bat(ə)nt USE *the last pron is disliked by some speakers*/ *n* a person, nation, etc that is or is ready to be an active participant in combat – **combatant** *adj*

**combat fatigue** *n* SHELL SHOCK

**combative** /'kombətiv, kəm'bativ/ *adj* marked by eagerness to fight or contend ⟨*the* ∼ *element in human nature*⟩ – **combatively** *adv*, **combativeness** *n*

**combe** /koohm/ *n*, *Eng* COOMB (valley)

**comber** /'kohmə/ *n* **1** somebody who or something that combs **2** a long curling wave; ¹BREAKER 2

**combinate** /'kombinayt/ *vt* to combine [L *combinatus*, pp of *combinare*]

**combination** /ˌkombi'naysh(ə)n/ *n* **1a** a result or product of combining **b** a group of people working as a team **2a** the sequence of letters or numbers that will open a COMBINATION LOCK **b** any of the different sets of a usu specified number of things that can be chosen from a group and are considered without regard to order within the set – compare PERMUTATION **3** *pl* any of various one-piece undergarments for the upper and lower parts of the body **4a** the act or process of combining; *esp* that of uniting to form a chemical compound **b** the quality or state of being combined **5** a single obstacle consisting of two or more elements (eg fences) for a horse to jump in succession – **combinational** *adj*

**combination lock** *n* a lock with a mechanism operated by the selection of a specific combination of letters or numbers

**combination room** *n* a college common room for students or fellows at Cambridge

**combinative** /'kombinətiv, -ˌnaytiv/, **combinatory** /'kombinət(ə)ri, ˌkombi'nayt(ə)ri/ *adj* **1** tending or able to combine **2** resulting from combination

**combinatorial** /ˌkombinə'tawri-əl/ *adj* **1** of or involving combinations **2** of the manipulation of mathematical elements within sets that have a finite number of elements ⟨∼ *mathematics*⟩ **3** *linguistics* of or for the combining of simple sentences ⟨∼ *rules*⟩

¹**combine** /kəm'bien/ *vt* **1a** to bring into such close relationship as to obscure individual characters; to merge **b** to cause to unite into a chemical compound **2** to cause to mix together **3** to possess in combination ∼ *vi* **1a** to become one **b** to unite to form a chemical compound **2** to act together *synonyms* see ¹JOIN *antonym* separate [ME *combinen*, fr MF *combiner*, fr LL *combinare*, fr L *com*- + *bini* two by two – more at BIN-] – **combinable** *adj*, **combinability** *n*, **combiner** *n*

²**combine** /'kombien/ *n* **1** a combination of people or organizations, esp in industry or commerce, to further their interests ⟨*L'Oréal, France's largest perfume and cosmetics* ∼ – *The Observer*⟩ **2 combine harvester**, **combine** a harvesting machine that cuts, threshes, and cleans grain while moving over a field

³**combine** *vt* to harvest with a combine harvester

**combined honours** /kəm'biend/ *n taking sing or pl vb*, Br a university first-degree course in which two subjects are studied concurrently and with equal weighting – compare SINGLE HONOURS

**combings** /'kohmingz/ *n pl* loose hair removed by a comb

**combing wool** /'kohming/ *n* wool with long strong fibres that is used esp in the manufacture of worsteds

**combining form** /kəm'biening/ *n* a linguistic form (eg *Franco-*) that cannot stand alone but forms compounds with other words, including prefixes and suffixes

**comb jelly** *n* CTENOPHORE (animal like a jellyfish)

**combo** /'komboh/ *n*, *pl* **combos** a usu small jazz or dance band [*combination* + *-o*]

**combust** /kəm'bust/ *vb* to burn [L *combustus*, pp of *comburere* to burn up, irreg fr *com*- + *urere* to burn]

**combustible** /kəm'bustəbl/ *adj* **1** capable of (easily) being set on fire **2** easily excited – **combustible** *n*, **combustibly** *adv*, **combustibility** *n*

**combustion** /kəm'buschən/ *n* **1** an act or instance of burning

**2a** a chemical process (eg a combining of a substance with oxygen) accompanied by the production of light and heat **b** a process (eg in the animal body) involving the slow reaction of a substance (eg a breakdown product of a food) with oxygen with the production of energy – **combustive** *adj*

**combustor** /kəm'bustə/ *n* a chamber (eg in a GAS TURBINE or a JET ENGINE) in which combustion occurs

¹**come** /kum/ *vb* **came** /kaym/; **come** *vi* **1a** to move towards something nearer, esp towards the speaker; approach ⟨∼ *here*⟩ ⟨*came running to her mother*⟩ **b** to move or journey nearer, esp towards or with the speaker, with a specified purpose ⟨*he came to see us*⟩ ⟨∼ *and see what's going on*⟩ ⟨∼ *skydiving*⟩ ⟨*the police came to their rescue*⟩ **c(1)** to reach a specified position in a progression ⟨*now we* ∼ *to the section on health*⟩ ⟨*came short of his goal*⟩ **c(2)** to arrive, appear, occur ⟨*the time has* ∼⟩ ⟨*the answer came to her*⟩ ⟨*the news came as a shock*⟩ ⟨*they came by train*⟩ ⟨*now* ∼s *the tricky bit*⟩ ⟨∼s *equipped with radio and heater*⟩ – used in the subjunctive before an expression of future time ⟨*a year ago* ∼ *March*⟩ **d(1)** to approach, reach, or fulfil a specified condition ⟨*this* ∼s *near perfection*⟩ ⟨*the artillery* came *into action*⟩ – often + *to* ⟨*came to his senses*⟩ ⟨*came to blows*⟩ ⟨∼ *to a decision*⟩ ⟨∼ *to the throne*⟩ ⟨*you'll* ∼ *to no harm*⟩ ⟨*what are things coming to?*⟩ **d(2)** – used with a following infinitive to express arrival at a condition ⟨*came to regard him as a friend*⟩ or chance occurrence ⟨*how did you* ∼ *to be invited?*⟩ **2a** to happen, esp by chance ⟨*no harm will* ∼ *to you*⟩ ⟨∼ *what may*⟩ ⟨*how* ∼s *it that you're at home?*⟩ **b(1)** to extend, reach ⟨*her dress came to her ankles*⟩ **b(2)** to amount ⟨*that* ∼s *to 75p exactly*⟩ **b(3)** to appear on a scene; make an appearance ⟨*children* ∼ *equipped to learn any language*⟩ **c** to originate, arise, or be the result *of* ⟨*wine* ∼s *from grapes*⟩ ⟨∼s *of sturdy stock*⟩ ⟨*this* ∼s *of not changing your socks*⟩ **d** to fall within the specified limits, scope, or jurisdiction ⟨*rabbits* ∼ *under rodents*⟩ ⟨*this* ∼s *within the terms of the treaty*⟩ **e** to issue *from* ⟨*a sob came from her throat*⟩ **f** to be available or turn out, usu as specified ⟨*this model* ∼s *in several sizes*⟩ ⟨*good clothes* ∼ *expensive*⟩ ⟨*learning new ways doesn't* ∼ *easy*⟩ ⟨*as good as they* ∼⟩ **g** to be or belong in a specified place or relation ⟨*the address* ∼s *above the date*⟩ ⟨*your family should* ∼ *first*⟩; *also* TAKE PLACE ⟨*Monday* ∼s *after Sunday*⟩ **h** to take form ⟨*the story won't* ∼⟩ **3** to pass to a person by lot, assignment, or inheritance **4** to become ⟨*it came untied*⟩ ⟨*the handle came off*⟩; *esp* to reach a culminating state ⟨*a dream that came true*⟩ ⟨*it all came right in the end*⟩ – compare GO 14c **5** *informal* to experience orgasm ∼ *vt* **1a** to move nearer by traversing ⟨*has* ∼ *several miles*⟩ **b** to reach some state after traversing ⟨*has* ∼ *a long way from humble beginnings*⟩ **2** *informal* to take on the aspect of; play the role of ⟨*don't* ∼ *the old soldier with me*⟩ [ME *comen*, fr OE *cuman*; akin to OHG *queman* to come, L *venire*, Gk *bainein* to walk, go] – **as it comes** without additions; *specif* NEAT 1a – **come and go** to exist or be present transiently – **come into one's own** to achieve one's potential; *also* to gain recognition – **come it** *chiefly Br slang* to act with bold disrespect ⟨*don't come it with me*⟩ – **come off it** *informal* to cease foolish or pretentious talk or behaviour – usu imper – **come to oneself 1** COME TO 1 **2** to regain self-control – **come to pass** *formal* HAPPEN **2** – **come to that** as a further consideration; actually ⟨*they still do*, come to that⟩ – **have coming** to deserve (something one gets, benefits by, or suffers) – **how come** *informal* how does it happen; why is it ⟨how come *we never meet?*⟩ – **to come** in the future; coming – **whether one is coming or going** – used to suggest frantic disorder and bewilderment ⟨*don't know* whether I'm coming or going⟩

*usage* The use of **come** as in sense 1c(2) with an expression of future time ⟨*a year ago* **come** *March*⟩ is to be avoided in formal writing.

**come about** *vi* **1** to occur; TAKE PLACE **2** to change direction ⟨*the wind has* come about *into the north*⟩ **3** *of a ship or her crew* to change direction by shifting the sails and rudder

**come across** *vt* to meet with or find by chance ⟨came across *an interesting problem*⟩ ∼ *vi* **1** to provide something demanded or expected, esp sex or money **2** to produce an impression ⟨comes across *as a persuasive speaker*⟩

**come across with** *vt* to provide (eg money or information) when needed

**come along** *vi* **1** to make an appearance ⟨*wouldn't just marry the first man that* came along⟩ **2** to hurry – usu imperative

**come around** *vi* COME ROUND 2

**come at** *vt* to accomplish an understanding or mastery of ⟨*art is not something to* come at *by dint of study* – Clive Bell⟩
**come back** *vi* **1** to return to memory ⟨*it's all* coming back *to me now*⟩ **2** to reply, retort **3** to regain a former condition or position – see also COMEBACK
**come between** *vt* to cause to be estranged ⟨*parents* came between *the lovers*⟩
**come by** *vt* to get possession of; acquire ⟨*cash may be tight and credit may be hard to* come by – *Sunday Times* (S Africa)⟩
**come down** *vi* **1** to pass by tradition ⟨*stories that have* come down *from medieval times*⟩ **2** *of an aircraft, missile, etc* to land; *esp* to crash **3a** to reduce itself; amount ⟨*it* comes down *to this*⟩ **b** to deal directly with ⟨*when you* come down *to it, we all depend on others*⟩ **4** to place oneself in opposition ⟨*the judge* came down *hard on gambling*⟩ **5** to formulate and express one's opinion or decision ⟨came down *in favour of abortion*⟩ **6** to become ill ⟨*they* came down *with measles*⟩ **7** to recover from the effects of a stimulant drug **8** *Br* to return from a university – compare GO DOWN, GO UP; see also COME-DOWN
**come from** *vt* to be or have been a native of or resident of
**come in** *vi* **1** to arrive ⟨*I was there when the train* came in⟩ **2** to finish as specified, esp in a competition ⟨came in *third*⟩ **3a** to function in a specified manner; be of use ⟨come in *handy*⟩ **b** to make reply to a signal or call ⟨came in *loud and clear*⟩ **4** to assume a role or function ⟨*that's where you* come in⟩
**come in for** *vt* to become subject to ⟨coming in for *increasing criticism*⟩
**come into** *vt* to acquire as a possession or inheritance ⟨came into *a fortune*⟩
**come off** *vi* **1** to finish or emerge from something in a specified condition ⟨came off *well in the contest*⟩ **2** to succeed ⟨*a visual effect that didn't quite* come off⟩ **3** to happen, occur **4** to become detached; *specif* to fall off a vehicle
**come on** *vi* **1a** to advance by degrees ⟨*as darkness* came on, *it got harder to see*⟩ **b** to begin by degrees ⟨*rain* came on *toward noon*⟩ **2** – used in cajoling, pleading, defiance, or encouraging ⟨come on, *you can do it*⟩ **3** COME ALONG **2 4** to appear on the radio, television, or stage – see also COME-ON **5** *chiefly NAm* to project a specified appearance ⟨comes on *as a Liberal in his speeches*⟩
**come out** *vi* **1** to come to public notice; be published **b** to become evident ⟨*this will* come out *in the full analysis*⟩ **2a** to declare oneself, esp in public utterance ⟨came out *in favour of the popular candidate*⟩ **b** to present oneself openly as homosexual **3** to end up; TURN OUT ⟨*everything will* come out *right*⟩ **4** to make a debut; *specif* to make one's first appearance in society as a debutante
**come out with** *vt* to utter or say, usu unexpectedly
**come over** *vt* to seize suddenly and strangely ⟨*what's* come over *you?*⟩ ~ *vi* **1a** to change from one side (eg of a controversy) to the other **b** to drop in casually ⟨come over *anytime; we're always in*⟩ **2** COME ACROSS **2** ⟨*she* comes over *as a very sincere person*⟩ **3** *Br* to become ⟨*she* came over *all queer*⟩
**come round** *vi* **1** COME TO **1 2** to accede to a particular opinion or course of action **3** COME ABOUT **2**
**come through** *vt* to survive (eg an illness) ~ *vi* **1** to survive something (eg an illness) **2** to do what is needed or expected **3** to become communicated
**come to** *vt* to be a question of ⟨*hopeless when it* comes to *arithmetic*⟩ ~ *vi* **1** to recover consciousness **2** *of a ship or her crew* **2a** to change course so as to sail as nearly as possible against the main force of the wind **b** to come to anchor or to a stop
**come up** *vi* **1** to rise in rank or status ⟨*an officer who* came up *from the ranks*⟩ **2a** to come to attention or consideration ⟨*the question never* came up *in discussion*⟩ **b** to occur in the course of time ⟨*any problem that* comes up⟩ **3** to appear before a magistrate ⟨*he* came up *for speeding*⟩ **4** to become, esp after cleaning ⟨*the table* came up *like new*⟩ – see also COME-UPPANCE
**come upon** *vt* COME ACROSS
**come up with** *vt* to provide, esp in dealing with a problem or challenge ⟨came up with *a better solution*⟩
**come with** *vt* to arrive or appear as a natural concomitant of ⟨*the increase in traffic that* comes with *new roads*⟩
²**come** *interj* – used to express encouragement or to urge reconsideration ⟨~, ~, *it's not as bad as that*⟩
,**come-at-'able** *adj* getatable

**comeback** /'kum‚bak/ *n* **1a** a means of redress **b(1)** REPERCUSSION **2 b(2)** a retrospective criticism of a decision **2** a return to a former state or condition **3** *informal* a sharp or witty reply; a retort
**Comecon** /'komi‚kon/ *n* an economic organization formed in 1949 by the socialist countries of the Soviet bloc to coordinate their economies, develop trading links between them, and promote mutual aid – compare COMINFORM, COMINTERN [*Council for Mutual Economic Assistance*]
**comedian** /kə'meedi‚ən/, *fem* **comedienne** /kə‚meedi'en/ *n* **1** an actor who plays comic roles **2** one, esp a professional entertainer, who aims to be amusing [*comedienne* fr Fr *comédienne*, fem of *comédien* comedian]
**comedic** /kə'meedik/ *adj* **1** of comedy **2** *NAm* COMICAL **2**
**comedo** /'komidoh/ *n, pl* **comedones** /‚komi'doneez/ BLACKHEAD **1** [NL, fr L, glutton, fr *comedere* to eat – more at COMESTIBLE]
**comedown** /-‚down/ *n, informal* a descent in rank or dignity
**comedy** /'komədi/ *n* **1a** a drama of light and amusing character, typically with a happy ending **b** the genre of dramatic literature that deals with comic or serious subjects in a light or satirical manner – compare TRAGEDY **2** a literary work written in a comic style or treating a comic theme **3** a ludicrous or farcical event or series of events **4** the comic aspect of something [ME, fr MF *comedie*, fr L *comoedia*, fr Gk *kōmōidia*, fr *kōmos* revel + *aeidein* to sing – more at ODE]
**comedy of manners** *n* comedy that portrays satirically the manners and fashions of a particular class or set
,**come-'hither** *adj* sexually inviting ⟨*that* ~ *look in her eyes*⟩
**comely** /'kumli/ *adj* having a pleasing appearance; not plain **synonyms** see BEAUTIFUL **antonym** homely [ME *comly*, alter. of OE *cȳmlic* glorious, fr *cȳme* lovely, fine; akin to OHG *kūmig* weak, Gk *goan* to lament] – **comeliness** *n*
'**come-‚on** *n* **1** *chiefly NAm* an attraction or enticement (e g in sales promotion) to induce an action **2** *informal* an instance of sexually provocative enticement
**comer** /'kumə/ *n* **1** someone who comes or arrives ⟨*all* ~s⟩ **2** *chiefly NAm* someone making rapid progress or showing promise
¹**comestible** /kə'mestəbl/ *adj, formal* edible [MF, fr ML *comestibilis*, fr L *comestus*, pp of *comedere* to eat, fr *com-* + *edere* to eat – more at EAT]
²**comestible** *n*, **comestibles** *n pl, formal* food
**comet** /'komit/ *n* a celestial body that follows a usu highly elliptical orbit, that consists of an indistinct head (COMA) usu surrounding a small bright dense part (NUCLEUS **1**), and that often when in the part of its orbit near the sun develops a long tail which points away from the sun [ME *comete*, fr OE *cometa*, fr L, fr Gk *kometes*, lit., long-haired, fr *koman* to wear long hair, fr *komē* hair] – **cometary** *adj*, **cometic** *adj*
**come-uppance** /'up(ə)ns/ *n* a deserved rebuke or penalty [*come up* + *-ance*]
**comfit** /'kumfit/ *n* a sweet consisting of a nut, seed (e g a caraway seed), piece of fruit, etc coated and preserved with sugar [ME *confit*, fr MF, fr pp of *confire* to prepare, fr L *conficere*, fr *com-* + *facere* to make – more at DO]
**comfiture** /'kumfichə/ *n, archaic* preserved or crystallized fruit [ME *confiture*, fr MF, fr *confit*]
¹**comfort** /'kumfət/ *n* **1a** assistance, support ⟨*accused of giving aid and* ~ *to the enemy*⟩ **b** consolation in time of trouble or worry; solace **2a** a feeling of relief or encouragement ⟨*you can take* ~ *from that*⟩ **b** contented well-being **3** someone who or something that provides comfort ⟨*the* ~s *of civilization*⟩ – **comfortless** *adj*
²**comfort** *vt* **1** to give strength and hope to; cheer up **2** to ease the grief or trouble of; console **synonyms** see RELIEVE **antonyms** afflict, bother [ME *comforten*, fr OF *conforter*, fr LL *confortare* to strengthen greatly, fr L *com-* + *fortis* strong] – **comfortingly** *adv*
**comfortable** /'kumftəbl/ *adj* **1a** providing or enjoying contentment and security ⟨*a* ~ *income*⟩ **b** providing or enjoying physical comfort ⟨*a* ~ *armchair*⟩ **2a** free from worry or doubt ⟨~ *assumptions that require no thought*⟩ **b** free from stress or tension ⟨*a* ~ *routine*⟩ **3** by a wide margin ⟨*the* ~ *winner*⟩ – **comfortableness** *n*, **comfortably** *adv*
**synonyms** Comfortable, cosy, snug, and restful all imply contentment, well-being, and tranquil ease. Comfortable implies the absence of any discomfort, pain, or distress. Cosy and snug suggest warmth, shelter, and sociability; both, but particularly snug, suggest intimacy or compactness ⟨*a* cosy *group by the fire*⟩ ⟨*a* snug *little*

*cottage*⟩. **Restful** stresses tranquillity and whatever induces it. *antonym* uncomfortable

**comforter** /'kumfətə/ *n* **1a** *cap* HOLY SPIRIT **b** someone who or something that gives comfort **2a** a scarf worn for warmth **b** *chiefly NAm* a large thin eiderdown or duvet

**comfort station** *n, NAm euph* a public toilet (eg at a petrol station)

**comfrey** /'kumfri/ *n* any of a genus (*Symphytum*) of usu tall plants of the forget-me-not family with coarse hairy leaves much used in herbal medicine and with white, pale yellow, pink to purple, or blue flowers that hang from one side of the main flower stem [ME *cumfirie*, fr OF, fr L *conferva*, a water plant, fr *confervēre* to boil together, heal, fr *com-* + *fervere* to boil]

**comfy** /'kumfi/ *adj, informal* comfortable [by shortening & alter.]

**¹comic** /'komik/ *adj* **1** of or marked by comedy **2** causing laughter or amusement; funny *synonyms* see COMICAL [L *comicus*, fr Gk *kōmikos*, fr *kōmos* revel]

**²comic** *n* **1** a comedian **2** a magazine consisting mainly of strip-cartoon stories **3** *pl, NAm* the part of a newspaper devoted to strip cartoons

**comical** /'komikl/ *adj* **1** of a kind to excite laughter, esp because of a startlingly or unexpectedly humorous impact ⟨*thought her hat was* ~⟩ **2** *obs* of comedy – **comically** *adv*, **comicality** *n*

*synonyms* Things that are unintentionally funny are **comical** rather than **comic**. Compare ⟨*a comic song*⟩ ⟨*the problem has its comical side*⟩.

**comic opera** *n* opera with humorous episodes and usu some spoken dialogue and a sentimental plot

**comic relief** *n* relief from the emotional tension of a drama that is provided by a comic episode

**comic strip** *n* STRIP CARTOON

**Cominform** /'komin,fawm/ *n* an organization operating from 1947 to 1956 to coordinate the activities of the Communist parties of Bulgaria, Czechoslovakia, France, Hungary, Italy, Poland, Romania, the USSR, and Yugoslavia – compare COMECON, COMINTERN [*Communist Information* Bureau]

**¹coming** /'kuming/ *n* an act or instance of arriving ⟨~s *and goings*⟩

**²coming** *adj* **1** immediately due in sequence or development; next ⟨*the* ~ *year*⟩ **2** gaining importance; up-and-coming ⟨*he's the* ~ *man*⟩

**Comintern** /'komin,tuhn/ *n* an international Socialist organization (²INTERNATIONAL 2) established in 1919 and dissolved in 1943 – compare COMECON, COMINFORM [Russ *Komintern*, fr *Kommunisticheskiĭ Internatsional* Communist International]

**comitia** /kə'mishiə/ *n, pl* **comitia** any of several public assemblies of the people in ancient Rome for the exercise of legislative, judicial, and electoral functions [L, pl of *comitium*, fr *com-* + *itus*, pp of *ire* to go – more at ISSUE] – **comitial** *adj*

**comity** /'komiti/ *n* **1** friendly quality of social atmosphere; social harmony **2** a loose widespread community **3 comity of nations, comity** the courtesy and friendship of nations, marked esp by recognition of each other's laws **4** the informal and voluntary recognition by courts of one jurisdiction of the laws and judicial decisions of another [L *comitat-, comitas*, fr *comis* courteous, fr OL *cosmis*, fr *com-* + *-smis* (akin to Skt *smayate* he smiles) – more at SMILE]

**comma** /'komə/ *n* **1** a punctuation mark , used esp as a mark of separation within the sentence **2** a butterfly (*Polygonia c-album*) with a silvery comma-shaped mark on the underside of the hind wing [LL, fr L, part of a sentence, fr Gk *komma* segment, clause, fr *koptein* to cut – more at CAPON]

**comma bacillus** *n* a curved or comma-shaped bacterium (*Vibrio comma*) that causes cholera

**¹command** /kə'mahnd/ *vt* **1** to direct authoritatively; order **2** to exercise a dominating influence over: eg **2a** to have at one's immediate disposal **b** to be able to ask for and receive ⟨~s *a high fee*⟩ **c** to overlook or dominate (as if) from a strategic position **d** to have military command of as senior officer ~ *vi* to be commander; be supreme [ME *comanden*, fr OF *comander*, fr (assumed) VL *commandare*, alter. (influenced by L *mandare* to order) of L *commendare* to commit to one's charge – more at COMMEND] – **commandable** *adj*

**²command** *n* **1** the act of commanding **2a** an order given **b** an electrical signal that actuates a device (eg a control mechanism in a spacecraft or one step in a computer); *also* the activation of a device by means of such a signal **3a** the ability or power

to control; mastery **b** the authority or right to command ⟨*the officer in* ~⟩ **c** facility in use ⟨*a good* ~ *of French*⟩ **4** taking *sing or pl vb* the personnel, area, or unit under a commander ⟨*aircraft of strike* ~⟩ **5** a position of highest usu military authority ⟨*had held several* ~s⟩

**³command** *adj* done on command or request ⟨*a* ~ *performance*⟩

**commandant** /,komən'dant, -'dahnt/ *n* COMMANDING OFFICER

**commandeer** /,komən'diə/ *vt* **1** to seize for military purposes **2** to take arbitrary or forcible possession of [Afrik *kommandeer*, fr Fr *commander* to command, fr OF *comander*]

**commander** /kə'mahndə/ *n* **1** one in a position of command or control: eg **1a** COMMANDING OFFICER **b** the presiding officer of a society or organization **2** – see MILITARY RANKS table – **commandership** *n*

**com,mander-in-'chief** *n* one who is in supreme command of an armed force

**commanding** /kə'mahnding/ *adj* **1** dominating or having priority ⟨*the castle's* ~ *position on the hilltop*⟩ ⟨*a* ~ *lead*⟩ ⟨*the* ~ *heights of the economy*⟩ **2** deserving or expecting respect and obedience ⟨*a* ~ *voice*⟩ – **commandingly** *adv*

**commanding officer** *n* an officer in command; *esp* an officer in the armed forces in command of a unit or installation

**commandment** /-mənt/ *n* something that is commanded; *specif* any of the biblical TEN COMMANDMENTS

**command module** *n* a part of a spacecraft designed to carry the crew, the main communication equipment, and the equipment for re-entry

**commando** /kə'mahndoh/ *n, pl* **commandos, commandoes 1** *taking sing or pl vb* a military unit trained and organized for surprise raids into enemy territory **2** a member of such a specialized raiding unit [Afrik *kommando*, fr D *commando* command, fr Sp *comando*, fr *comandar* to command, fr Fr *commander*]

**command paper** *n* a government report laid before Parliament at the command of the crown

**command post** *n* the headquarters of a military unit in the field

**commedia dell'arte** /kə,maydi-ə del 'ahti/ *n* Italian comedy of the 16th to 18th centuries improvised from standardized situations and stock characters [It, lit., comedy of art]

**comme il faut** /,kom eel 'foh/ *adj* conforming to accepted standards; proper [Fr, lit., as it should be]

**commemorate** /kə'memərayt/ *vt* **1** to call to formal remembrance **2** to mark by some ceremony or observation; observe **3** to serve as a memorial of [L *commemoratus*, pp of *commemorare*, fr *com-* + *memorare* to remind of, fr *memor* mindful – more at MEMORY] – **commemoration** *n*, **commemorator** *n*

**¹commemorative** /kə'memərətiv/ *adj* intended as a commemoration; commemorating – **commemoratively** *adv*

**²commemorative** *n* something commemorative; *esp* a commemorative postage stamp – compare DEFINITIVE

**commence** /kə'mens/ *vb, formal* to start, begin *synonyms* see BEGIN *antonym* conclude [ME *comencen*, fr MF *comencer*, fr (assumed) VL *cominitiare*, fr L *com-* + LL *initiare* to begin, fr L, to initiate] – **commencer** *n*

**commencement** /kə'mensmənt/ *n* **1** an act, instance, or time of beginning **2** *NAm* DEGREE DAY (day on which degrees are conferred)

**commend** /kə'mend/ *vt* **1** to entrust for care or preservation **2** to recommend as worthy of confidence or notice **3** to mention with approbation; praise [ME *commenden*, fr L *commendare*, fr *com-* + *mandare* to entrust – more at MANDATE] – **commendable** *adj*, **commendably** *adv*, **commender** *n*

**commendation** /,komən'daysh(ə)n/ *n* **1** an act of commending **2** something (eg a formal citation) that commends – **commendatory** *adj*

**commensal** /kə'mens(ə)l/ *adj* **1** of or for those who habitually eat together **2** living in a state of commensalism [ME, fr ML *commensalis*, fr L *com-* + LL *mensalis* of the table, fr L *mensa* table] – **commensal** *n*, **commensally** *adv*

**commensalism** /kə'mensə,liz(ə)m/ *n* an association between two kinds of organism whereby one or both obtain benefits (eg food or protection) without either organism being harmed

**commensurable** /kə'mensh(ə)rəbl/ *adj* having a common measure; *specif* divisible by a common unit a whole number of times – **commensurably** *adv*, **commensurability** *n*

**commensurate** /kə'menshərət/ *adj* **1** equal or approximately equal in measure or extent **2** corresponding in size, extent, amount, or degree proportionate ⟨*was given a job* ~ *with his abilities*⟩ 3 commensurable [LL *commensuratus,* fr L *com-* + LL *mensuratus,* pp of *mensurare* to measure, fr L *mensura* measure – more at MEASURE] – **commensurately** *adv,* **commensuration** *n*

¹**comment** /'koment/ *n* 1 a note explaining, illustrating, or criticizing the meaning of a piece of writing ⟨~s *printed in the margin*⟩ 2a an observation or remark expressing an opinion or attitude b a judgment expressed indirectly ⟨*this film is a ~ on current moral standards*⟩ [ME, fr LL *commentum,* fr L, invention, fr neut of *commentus,* pp of *comminisci* to invent, fr *com-* + *-minisci* (akin to *ment-, mens* mind) – more at MIND]

²**comment** *vi* to explain or interpret something by comment; *broadly* to make a comment – usu + *on*

**commentary** /'koment(ə)ri/ *n* 1 **commentary, commentaries** *pl* an explanatory treatise 2a a systematic series of explanations or interpretations (e g of a piece of writing) b a series of spoken remarks and comments used as a broadcast description of some event ⟨*a running* ~ *on the match*⟩ c COMMENT 2 3 something that serves to illustrate or explain

**commentary box** *n* an enclosed shelter used by commentators broadcasting about sports events

**commentate** /'komentayt/ *vi* to act as a commentator; *esp* to give a broadcast commentary ~ *vt, NAm* to give a commentary on [back-formation fr *commentator*]

**commentator** /'komən,taytə/ *n* a person who provides a commentary: e g a a broadcaster reporting on sports events b one who reports and discusses news on radio or television or in other media

**commerce** /'komuhs/ *n* 1 the exchange or buying and selling of commodities, esp on a large scale involving transport within a country or between countries 2 the principles and techniques of business and office practice ⟨*teaches* ~ *at the local poly*⟩ 3 *archaic* social intercourse; interchange of ideas, opinions, or sentiments 4 *archaic* SEXUAL INTERCOURSE [MF, fr L *commercium,* fr *com-* + *merc-, merx* merchandise (cf MARKET)]

¹**commercial** /kə'muhsh(ə)l/ *adj* 1a(1) engaged in work that is for sale ⟨*a* ~ *artist*⟩ a(2) (characteristic) of commerce ⟨~ *regulations*⟩ a(3) suitable, adequate, or prepared for commerce; having or being a good financial prospect ⟨*found oil in* ~ *quantities*⟩ b(1) *esp of a chemical* average or inferior in quality b(2) producing work to a standard determined only by market criteria 2a viewed with regard to profit ⟨*a* ~ *success*⟩ b designed for a large market 3 supported by advertisers ⟨~ *TV*⟩ – **commercially** *adv*

²**commercial** *n* an advertisement broadcast on radio or television

**commercial art** *n* graphic art put to commercial use, esp in advertising – **commercial artist** *n*

**commercial bank** *n* a bank including in its functions the acceptance of deposits subject to withdrawal by cheque without advance notice

**commercial bill** *n* a short-term negotiable BILL OF EXCHANGE (written order to pay money) arising out of commercial transactions

**commercialese** /kə,muhshə'leez/ *n* the language or vocabulary of the commercial world

**commercialism** /kə'muhshə,liz(ə)m/ *n* 1 commercial spirit, institutions, or methods 2 excessive emphasis on profit – **commercialist** *n,* **commercialistic** *adj*

**commercial-ize, -ise** /kə'muhshə,liez/ *vt* 1a to manage on a business basis for profit b to make commercial 2 to exploit for profit – **commercialization** *n*

**commercial paper** *n, chiefly NAm* short-term negotiable instruments (e g cheques and bills of exchange), usu sold by one company to another for immediate cash needs

**commercial traveller** *n, Br* SALES REPRESENTATIVE

**commie** /'komi/ *n, chiefly derog* a communist [by shortening & alter.] – **commie** *adj*

**commination** /,komi'naysh(ə)n/ *n, formal* a warning of vengeance; a denunciation [ME, fr MF or L; MF, fr L *commination-, comminatio,* fr *comminatus,* pp of *comminari* to threaten, fr *com-* + *minari* to threaten (cf MENACE)] – **comminatory** *adj*

**commingle** /ko'ming-gl/ *vt* 1 to combine (funds or properties) into a common fund or stock ⟨~ *accounts*⟩ 2 *poetic* to blend thoroughly into a harmonious whole ~ *vi* to become commingled

**comminute** /'kominyooht/ *vt* to reduce to minute particles; pulverize [L *comminutus,* pp of *comminuere,* fr *com-* + *minuere* to lessen] – **comminution** *n*

**commis** /kə'mee/ *n, pl* **commis** /~/ a junior or assistant in a hotel or catering establishment ⟨~ *waiter*⟩ ⟨~ *chef*⟩ [Fr, fr *commis,* pp of *committre* to commit, entrust, fr L *committere* to connect, entrust]

**commiserate** /kə'mizərayt/ *vi* to feel or express sympathy *with* someone [L *commiseratus,* pp of *commiserari,* fr *com-* + *miserari* to pity, fr *miser* wretched] – **commiserative** *adj,* **commiseration** *n*

**commissar** /,komi'sahr/ *n* 1a a Communist party official assigned to a military unit to teach party principles and policies and to ensure party loyalty b someone who attempts to control public opinion or its expression 2 the head of a government department in the USSR until 1946 [Russ *komissar,* fr Ger *kommissar,* fr ML *commissarius*]

**commissariat** /,komi'seəri-ət/ *n* 1 the department of an army that organizes food supplies 2 a government department in the USSR until 1946 [(1) NL *commissariatus,* fr ML *commissarius;* (2) Russ *komissariat,* fr Ger *kommissariat,* fr NL *commissariatus*]

**commissary** /'komis(ə)ri/ *n* 1 an officer in charge of military supplies 2 *NAm* 2a a store for supplying equipment and provisions, esp to military personnel b food supplies c a restaurant, esp in a film studio [ME *commissarie,* fr ML *commissarius,* fr L *commissus,* pp]

¹**commission** /kə'mish(ə)n/ *n* 1a a formal written warrant granting the power to perform various acts or duties b a certificate conferring military rank above a certain level; *also* the rank and authority so conferred 2 an authorization or command to act in a prescribed manner or to perform prescribed acts 3 authority to act as agent for another; *also* something to be done by an agent 4 *taking sing or pl vb* 4a a group of people directed to perform some duty b *often cap* a government agency having administrative, legislative, or judicial powers ⟨*the* Commission *for Racial Equality*⟩ 5 an act of committing something ⟨*charged with* ~ *of three murders*⟩ 6 a fee paid to an agent or employee for transacting a piece of business or performing a service; *esp* a percentage of the sum involved in such a transaction 7 an act of entrusting or giving authority [ME, fr MF, fr L *commission-, commissio* act of bringing together, fr *commissus,* pp of *committere*] – **in/into commission** 1 *of a ship* ready for active service 2 in use or in condition for use – **on commission** with commission serving as partial or full pay for work done – **out of commission** 1 out of active service or use 2 out of working order

²**commission** *vt* 1 to give a commission to: e g 1a to confer a formal commission on ⟨*was* ~ed *lieutenant*⟩ b to appoint or assign to a task or function ⟨*the writer who was* ~ed *to do the biography*⟩ 2 to order to be made ⟨*wealthy people who* ~ed *portraits of themselves*⟩ 3 to put (a ship) in commission

**commission agent** *n, Br* 1 one who buys or sells another's goods for a commission 2 a bookmaker

**commissionaire** /kə,mishə'neə/ *n, chiefly Br* a uniformed attendant at a cinema, theatre, office, etc [Fr *commissionnaire,* fr *commission*]

**commissioner** /kə'mishənə/ *n* a person with a commission: e g a a member or the head of a commission b the representative of the government in an administrative unit (e g a district or province) often having both judicial and administrative powers

**Commissioner for Oaths** *n, Br* a person, esp a solicitor, authorized to administer an oath or affirmation to someone swearing an AFFIDAVIT (written legal statement of facts)

**commission merchant** *n, NAm* COMMISSION AGENT 1

**commissure** /'komisyooə, -syə/ *n* 1 the place or line where two bodies or parts (e g leaf lobes) unite 2 a connecting band of nerve tissue in the brain or SPINAL CORD (e g one joining corresponding parts of the right and left halves of the brain) [ME, fr MF or L; MF, fr L *commissura* a joining, fr *commissus,* pp] – **commissural** *adj*

**commit** /kə'mit/ *vt* -tt- 1a to entrust b to place in a prison or mental institution c to send (an accused person) to a higher court for trial ⟨~ted *to the Crown Court on bail of £1000*⟩ d to transfer, consign ⟨~ *something to paper*⟩ e to refer (e g a legislative bill) to a committee 2 to carry out (a crime, sin, etc) 3a to obligate, bind; *esp* to bind (oneself) by giving a decided opinion or final judgment b to pledge or assign to some particular course or use ⟨*all available troops were* ~ted *to the attack*⟩ [ME *committen,* fr L *committere* to connect, entrust, fr *com-* + *mittere* to send] – **committable** *adj*

**commitment** /kə'mitmənt/ *n* 1a an act of committing to a charge or trust: eg **1a(1)** the consignment of a person to a prison or mental institution **a(2)** an act of referring a matter to a legislative committee **b** a written court order consigning a person to prison **2a** an agreement or pledge to do something in the future; *specif* an engagement to assume a financial obligation at a future date **b** something pledged **c** loyalty to a system of thought or action ⟨*his* ~ *to radical causes*⟩

*synonyms* There is some overlap of meaning between **commitment** and **committal**; but a pledge to something or to do something is a commitment ⟨*the firm's* commitment *to the policy of expansion*⟩ ⟨*make a firm* commitment *to fetch your children from school*⟩ and being delivered or transferred is usually **committal** ⟨*his* committal *to a mental hospital*⟩.

**committal** /kə'mitl/ *n* commitment or consignment (eg to prison or the grave)

**committal proceedings** *n pl* a preliminary review by a magistrates' court of the evidence against an accused person to decide whether he/she should be sent to a higher court for trial

**committee** /kə'miti/ *n taking sing or pl vb* a body of people delegated or elected **a** to consider, investigate, report on, or control some matter ⟨*a parliamentary* ~⟩ **b** to organize or administer a society, event, etc ⟨*the fête* ~⟩ [ME, one to whom a charge is committed, fr *committen*]

**committeeman** /kə'tmitimən, -,man/, *fem* **committeewoman** /-,woomən/ *n* a member of a committee

**committee of the whole house** *n, often cap C, W, & H* the whole membership of a legislative assembly sitting as a committee and operating under informal rules

**committee stage** *n* the stage in parliamentary procedure between the SECOND READING and the THIRD READING when a bill is discussed in detail in committee

**commix** /ko'miks/ *vb, poetic* to mingle, blend [back-formation fr ME *comixt* blended, fr L *commixtus*, pp of *commiscēre* to mix together, fr *com-* + *miscēre* to mix – more at MIX] – **commixture** *n*

**commo** /'komoh/ *n, pl* **commos** *Austr & NZ derog* a communist [by shortening & alter.] – **commo** *adv*

**commode** /kə'mohd/ *n* **1** a low CHEST OF DRAWERS **2** a movable washstand with a cupboard underneath **3** a boxlike structure or chair with a removable seat covering a chamber pot [Fr, fr *commode*, adj, suitable, convenient, fr L *commodus*, fr *com-* + *modus* measure – more at METE]

**commodious** /kə'mohdi•əs/ *adj* **1** *formal* comfortably or conveniently spacious; roomy ⟨*one* ~ *drawer held all his clothes*⟩ **2** *archaic* handy, serviceable [ME, useful, fr MF *commodieux*, fr ML *commodiosus*, irreg fr L *commodum* convenience, fr neut of *commodus*] – **commodiously** *adv*, **commodiousness** *n*

**commodity** /kə'modəti/ *n* **1** something useful or valuable **2** an article of trade or commerce, esp when delivered for shipment [ME *commoditee*, fr MF *commodité*, fr L *commoditat-*, *commoditas*, fr *commodus*]

**commodore** /'komədaw/ *n* **1** – see MILITARY RANKS table **2** the senior captain of a merchant shipping line **3** the chief officer of a yacht club or boating association [prob modif of D *commandeur* commander, fr Fr, fr OF *comandeor*, fr *comander* to command]

**¹common** /'komən/ *adj* **1** of a community at large; public ⟨*work for the* ~ *good*⟩ **2a** belonging to or shared by two or more individuals or by all members of a group **b** *maths* belonging equally to two or more quantities ⟨*triangles having a* ~ *side*⟩ **c** having two or more branches ⟨~ *carotid artery*⟩ **3a** occurring or appearing frequently; familiar ⟨*a* ~ *sight*⟩ **b** of the familiar kind ⟨~ *salt*⟩ **4a** widespread, general ⟨~ *knowledge*⟩ **b** characterized by a lack of privilege or special status ⟨*the* ~ *people*⟩ **c** simply satisfying accustomed criteria (and no more); elementary ⟨~ *decency*⟩ **5a** falling below ordinary standards; second-rate **b** lacking refinement ⟨*what a* ~ *voice!*⟩ **6a** either masculine or feminine in grammatical gender **b** denoting by a single word form relations that in a language with more forms for different grammatical cases might be denoted by two or more different word forms [ME *commun*, fr OF, fr L *communis* – more at MEAN] – **commonly** *adv*, **commonness** *n* – **common or garden** ordinary, commonplace ⟨common or garden *expression*⟩ [orig applied to the common horticultural variety of a plant]

*synonyms* Compare **common, ordinary, plain, familiar, popular,** and **commonplace. Common** implies frequency of occurrence ⟨common *error*⟩ ⟨*lacked* common *honesty*⟩ and sometimes also inferiority or coarseness ⟨*O hard is the bed...and* common *the blanket and cheap* – A E Housman⟩. **Ordinary** stresses conformity with

the regular order of things ⟨*an* ordinary *weekday*⟩ ⟨*a very* ordinary *sort of man*⟩. **Plain** suggests homely simplicity ⟨*the* plain *people everywhere...wish to live in peace* – F D Roosevelt⟩. **Familiar** is for things generally known and easily recognized ⟨*a* familiar *proverb*⟩. **Popular** is for what is accepted by people in general, sometimes in contrast to an élite ⟨*a* popular *song*⟩. **Commonplace** resembles **common** but is more likely to convey a derogatory meaning of inferiority or failure to be outstanding ⟨*a few* commonplace *remarks*⟩. see MUTUAL *antonyms* uncommon, exceptional

**²common** *n* **1** *pl* the common people – used chiefly in a historical context **2** *pl* the daily fare shared jointly by all members (eg of a college); *broadly* food, provisions – esp in *short commons* **3** *pl but taking sing or pl vb, often cap* **3a** the political group or estate made up of commoners **b** the parliamentary representatives of the common people **c** HOUSE OF COMMONS **4 common, right of common** a specific right allowing a person to take natural products from another's land (eg by fishing or pasturing one's animals) **5** a piece of land open to use by all: eg **5a** undivided land used esp for pasture **b** a more or less treeless expanse of undeveloped land available for recreation **6a** a religious service suitable for any of various festivals **b** the parts of the Mass that do not vary from day to day **7** *Br slang* COMMON SENSE – **in common** shared together ⟨*we had a lot in common*⟩ – **in common with** similarly to

**commonage** /'komənij/ *n* community land – used chiefly in a historical context

**commonality** /,komə'naliti/ *n* **1a** possession of common features or attributes or of some degree of standardization; commonness **b** a common feature or attribute **2** *taking sing or pl vb* the common people [ME *communalitie*, alter. of *communalte*]

**commonalty** /'komənəlti/ *n* **1a** *taking sing or pl vb* **1a(1)** the common people **a(2)** the political estate formed by the common people **b** a usage or practice common to members of a group **2** *taking sing or pl vb* a general group or body [ME *communalte*, fr OF *comunalté*, fr *comunal* communal]

**common carrier** *n* an individual or company undertaking to transport people or goods for payment

**common chord** *n, music* TRIAD 2

**common cold** *n* a short-lasting inflammation of the MUCOUS MEMBRANES lining the nose, throat, mouth, etc, caused by a virus

**common core** *n* the compulsory subjects in a British school curriculum

**common denominator** *n* **1** a COMMON MULTIPLE of the denominators of several fractions **2** a common trait or theme

**common divisor** *n* COMMON FACTOR

**Common Entrance examination** *n, often cap 2nd E* an examination taken, esp by boys between the ages of 12 and 14, in order to secure admission to a British public school

**commoner** /'komənə/ *n* **1** a member of the common people; someone not of noble rank **2** a student (eg at Oxford) whose fees are not paid by his/her college

**commonership** /'komənəship/ *n* the status of a college commoner

**common factor** *n* a number or combination of numbers that divides two or more numbers or combinations of numbers without remainder

**common fraction** *n, chiefly NAm* VULGAR FRACTION (fraction with numbers above and below the line)

**common ground** *n* a basis of mutual interest or understanding

**common-'law** *adj* **1** of or based on the COMMON LAW **2** recognized in law without marriage ⟨*his* ~ *wife*⟩

**common law** *n* the body of law that has been developed in England primarily from judicial decisions based on custom and precedent as distinct from STATUTE LAW and CIVIL LAW, and that constitutes the basis of the English legal system – compare EQUITY 2

**common-law marriage** *n* a union between a man and a woman based on the parties' cohabitation and agreement to regard themselves as man and wife without the performance of a marriage ceremony

**common logarithm** *n* a logarithm whose base is 10

**common market** *n* an economic unit formed to remove trade barriers among its members; *specif, often cap C&M* the European economic community

**common multiple** *n* a multiple of each of two or more numbers or combinations of numbers

**common noun** *n* a noun that designates any one of a class of beings or things and may occur with words (e g *a* or *an*, *some*, *every*, and *my*) that specify which one it is; a noun that does not designate a unique thing

¹**commonplace** /'komən,pleys/ *n* **1a** an obvious or trite observation **b** something taken for granted **2** *archaic* a striking passage entered in a COMMONPLACE BOOK [trans of L *locus communis* widely 'applicable argument, trans of Gk *koinos topos*]

²**commonplace** *adj* routinely found; ordinary, unremarkable – **commonplaceness** *n*

**commonplace book** *n* a notebook into which someone copies memorable writings or sayings

**common room** *n* a room or set of rooms in a college, school, etc for the recreational use of the staff or students

**common salt** *n* SALT 1a

**common sandpiper** *n* a small olive-brown sandpiper (*Tringa hypoleucos*)

**common seal** *n* the official seal of a corporation

**common sense** *n* sound and prudent but often unsophisticated judgment – **commonsense** *adj*, **commonsensical** *adj*

**common share** *n*, *NAm* ORDINARY SHARE

**common stock** *n*, *NAm* ORDINARY SHARES

**common time** *n* the musical metre marked by four crotchets per bar

**common touch** *n* the ability of some talented and exceptional people to appeal to the populace at large

**common vole** *n* a short-tailed European vole (*Microtus arvalis*) that is present in certain isolated areas in Britain (e g the Orkneys)

**commonweal** /'komən,weel/ *n* **1** the general welfare **2** *archaic* a commonwealth

**commonwealth** /-,welth/ *n* **1** a political unit, esp a nation or state: e g **1a** one founded on law and united by agreement of the people for the common good **b** one in which supreme authority is vested in the people **c** a republic **2** *cap* the English state from the death of Charles I in 1649 to the Restoration in 1660 **3** a state of the USA – used officially with reference to Kentucky, Massachusetts, Pennsylvania, and Virginia **4** *cap* a federal union of states – used officially with reference to Australia **5** *often cap* a loose association of self-governing states with a common allegiance; *specif* an association consisting of Britain and states that were formerly British colonies **6** *archaic* COMMONWEAL 1

**Commonwealth Day** *n* May 24 observed in Britain and the Commonwealth as the anniversary of Queen Victoria's birthday

**common year** *n* a year that is not a leap year

**commotion** /kə'mohsh(ə)n/ *n* **1** a state of civil unrest or insurrection **2** a disturbance, tumult **3** noisy confusion and bustle **4** *archaic* mental excitement or confusion *synonyms* see ¹FUSS [ME, fr MF, fr L *commotion-*, *commotio*, fr *commotus*, pp of *commovēre*]

**commove** /ko'moohv/ *vt*, *archaic* **1** to move violently; agitate **2** to rouse intense feeling in; excite to passion [ME *commoeven*, fr MF *commuev-*, present stem of *commovoir*, fr L *commovēre*, fr *com-* + *movēre* to move]

**communal** /'komyoonl/ *adj* **1** of a commune or communes **2** of a community **3a** characterized by collective ownership and use of property **b** participated in, shared, or used in common by members of a group or community ⟨~ *activity*⟩ ⟨*a ~ room*⟩ [Fr, fr LL *communalis*, fr L *communis*] – **communalize** *vt*, **communally** *adv*

**communalism** /'komyoonə,liz(ə)m/ *n* a principle or system of social organization on a communal basis – **communalist** *n* or *adj*

**communality** /,komyoo'naləti/ *n* **1** communal state or character **2** a feeling of group solidarity

**communard** /'komyoo,nahd/ *n* **1** *cap* one who supported or participated in the Commune of Paris in 1871 **2** one who lives in a commune [Fr]

¹**commune** /kə'myoohn/ *vi* **1** to communicate intimately *with* **2** *chiefly NAm* to receive Communion [ME *communen* to converse, administer Communion, fr MF *comunier* to converse, administer or receive Communion, fr LL *communicare*, fr L]

²**commune** /'ko,myoohn/ *n* **1** the smallest administrative district of many countries, esp in Europe **2** *taking sing or pl vb* a community: e g **2a** a medieval usu municipal corporation **b** MIR (village community in tsarist Russia) **c(1)** an often rural community organized on a communal basis in which the members share property and labour equally **c(2)** a group of usu un-

related individuals or families who live as members of a commune [Fr, alter. of MF *comugne*, fr ML *communia*, fr L, neut pl of *communis*]

**communicable** /kə'myoohnikəbl/ *adj* capable of being communicated; transmittable ⟨*a ~ disease*⟩ – **communicableness** *n*, **communicably** *adv*, **communicability** *n*

**communicant** /kə'myoohnikənt/ *n* **1** a church member who receives or is entitled to receive Communion; *broadly* a member of a fellowship **2** an informant – **communicant** *adj*

**communicate** /kə'myoohni,kayt/ *vt* **1** to convey knowledge of or information about; make known **2** to cause to pass from one to another ⟨*some diseases are easily ~*d⟩ ~ *vi* **1** to receive Communion **2** to transmit information, thought, or feeling so that it is satisfactorily received or understood **3** to give access to each other; connect ⟨*the rooms ~*⟩ [L *communicatus*, pp of *communicare* to impart, participate, fr *communis* common – more at MEAN] – **communicator** *n*, **communicatory** *adj*

**communication** /kə,myoohni'kaysh(ə)n/ *n* **1** an act or instance of communicating **2** a verbal or written message **3** a process by which information is exchanged between individuals through a common system of symbols, signs, or behaviour ⟨*insect ~*⟩; *also* exchange of information **4** *pl* **4a** a system (e g of telephones) for communicating **b** a system of routes for moving troops, supplies, and vehicles **5** *pl but taking sing or pl vb* techniques for the effective transmission of information, ideas, etc **6** *archaic* information communicated – **communicational** *adj*

**communication cord** *n*, *Br* a device (e g a chain or handle) in a railway carriage that a passenger may pull in an emergency to sound an alarm or stop the train

**communicative** /kə'myoohnikətiv/ *adj* **1** tending to communicate; talkative **2** of communication – **communicatively** *adv*, **communicativeness** *n*

**communion** /kə'myoohnyən, -ni-ən/ *n* **1** an act or instance of sharing **2a** *often cap* a Christian sacrament in which bread and wine are partaken of as a commemoration of the death of Christ **b** the act of receiving the sacrament ⟨*make one's ~*⟩ **c** *cap* the part of the Communion in which the sacrament is received **d** Communion, Communion Verse a variable verse of scripture said or sung at mass during the people's communion **3** intimate fellowship or rapport **4** a body of Christians having a common faith and organization [ME, fr L *communion-*, *communio* mutual participation, fr *communis*]

**communiqué** /kə'myoohni,kay/ *n* BULLETIN 1 [Fr, fr pp of *communiquer* to communicate, fr L *communicare*]

**communism** /'komyooniz(ə)m/ *n* **1a** a theory advocating elimination of private property **b** a system in which goods are held in common and are available to all as needed **2** *cap* **2a** a doctrine based on revolutionary Marxian socialism and Marxism-Leninism that is the official ideology of the USSR **b** a totalitarian system of government in which a single party controls state-owned means of production with the aim of establishing a classless society **c** a final stage of society in Marxist theory in which the state has withered away and economic goods are distributed equitably [Fr *communisme*, fr *commun* common]

**communist** /'komyoonist/ *n* **1** an adherent or advocate of communism **2a** *cap* a member of a Communist party or movement **b** *often cap* an adherent or advocate of a Communist government, party, or movement **3** *often cap* a left-wing revolutionary – **communist** *adj*, *often cap*, **communistic** *adj*, *often cap*, **communistically** *adv*

**communitarian** /kə,myoohni'teəri-ən/ *adj* of or based on social organization in small cooperative partly collectivist communities – **communitarian** *n*, **communitarianism** *n*

**community** /kə'myoohnəti/ *n* **1** *taking sing or pl vb* a unified body of individuals: e g **1a** a group of people living in a particular area **b** an ecological group comprising all the interacting populations of various living organisms in a particular area **c** a group of people with a common characteristic or interest living together within a larger society ⟨*a ~ of retired people*⟩ **d** a group who adopt common policies ⟨*the European Coal and Steel* Community⟩ **e** a body of people or nations having a common history or common social, economic, and political interests ⟨*the international ~*⟩ **2** society in general **3a** joint ownership or participation **b** common character; likeness ⟨*bound by ~ of interests*⟩ **c** social ties; fellowship **d** the state or condition of living in a society *synonyms* see ³RACE [ME *comunete*, fr MF *comuneté*, fr L *communitat-*, *communitas*, fr *communis*]

**community centre** *n* a building or group of buildings for the educational and recreational activities of a community

**community chest** *n, NAm* a general fund accumulated from individual subscriptions to pay for charity and social-welfare requirements in a community

**community college** *n* an American or Canadian nonresidential junior college that is usu government-supported

**community home** *n, Br* a local-authority centre replacing the APPROVED SCHOOL and the REMAND HOME for housing juvenile offenders and deprived children under the age of 17

**community school** *n* a school that is open outside school hours for community activities

**community service order** *n* a judicial order requiring a convicted person to perform a specified number of hours of unpaid work on behalf of the community

**commun·ize, -ise** /'komyooniez/ *vt* **1** to make into common or state-owned property **2** to subject to Communist principles of organization [back-formation fr *communization*] – **communization** *n*

**commutate** /'komyootayt/ *vt* to reverse the direction of (an electric current); *esp* to convert (ALTERNATING CURRENT) to DIRECT CURRENT [back-formation fr *commutation*]

**commutation** /ˌkomyoo'taysh(ə)n/ *n* **1** a replacement; *specif* a substitution of one form of payment or charge for another **2** the substitution by executive authority of a legal penalty less severe than that imposed judicially **3** an act or process of commuting **4** the action of commutating [ME, fr MF, fr L *commutation-, commutatio,* fr *commutatus,* pp of *commutare*]

**commutation ticket** *n, NAm* a ticket sold usu at a reduced rate for a fixed number of trips over the same route during a limited period – compare SEASON TICKET

**commutative** /kə'myoohtətiv/ *adj* **1** of or showing commutation **2a** of or being a mathematical operation (eg addition or multiplication) such that $x * y = y * x$, where $*$ denotes the operation **b** having all elements obeying a commutative operation ⟨$\sim$ *ring*⟩ – **commutativity** *n*

**commutator** /'komyoo,taytə/ *n* a device for reversing the direction of an electric current; *esp* a device on a motor or generator that converts ALTERNATING CURRENT to DIRECT CURRENT

**commute** /kə'myooht/ *vt* **1** to give in exchange for another; exchange **2** to convert (eg a payment) into another form **3** to exchange (a penalty) for another less severe ~ *vi* **1** to travel back and forth regularly (eg between home and work) **2** *of two mathematical quantities* to give a commutative result [L *commutare* to change, exchange, fr *com-* + *mutare* to change] – **commutable** *adj,* **commuter** *n*

**comose** /'kohmohs, -'-/ *adj, esp of a plant part* bearing a tuft of soft hairs [L *comosus* hairy, fr *coma* hair – more at ²COMA]

**comp** /komp/ *n* COMPOSITOR

¹**compact** /kəm'pakt/ *adj* **1** having parts or units closely packed or joined **2** succinct, terse ⟨*a* ~ *statement*⟩ **3** occupying a small volume because of efficient use of space ⟨*a* ~ *camera*⟩ [ME, firmly put together, fr L *compactus,* fr pp of *compingere* to put together, fr *com-* + *pangere* to fasten – more at PACT] – **compactly** *adv,* **compactness** *n*

²**compact** *vt* **1a** to knit or draw together; combine, consolidate **b** to press together; compress **2** to make up by connecting or combining – **compactible** *adj,* **compaction** *n,* **compactor** *n*

³**compact** /'kom,pakt/ *n* something compact or compacted: eg **a** a small slim case (eg for face powder), usu with a mirror inside the lid **b** a medium-sized US car

⁴**compact** /'kom,pakt/ *n* an agreement or contract between two or more parties [L *compactum,* fr neut of *compactus,* pp of *compacisci* to make an agreement, fr *com-* + *pacisci* to contract]

¹**companion** /kəm'panyən/ *n* **1** someone who accompanies another; a comrade **2** something belonging to a pair or set of matching things **3** someone, esp a woman, employed to live with and provide company and service for another [ME *compainoun,* fr OF *compagnon,* fr LL *companion-, companio,* fr L *com-* + *panis* bread, food] – **companionate** *adj,* **companionship** *n*

²**companion** *n* (a covering or hood at the top of) a companionway [by folk etymology fr D *kampanje* poop deck]

**companionable** /kəm'panyənəbl/ *adj* marked by, conducive to, or suggestive of companionship; sociable – **companionableness** *n,* **companionably** *adv*

**companionate marriage** /kəm'panyənət/ *n* a proposed form of marriage in which legalized birth control would be practised, the divorce of childless couples by mutual consent permitted,

and neither party would have any financial or economic claim on the other

**companion cell** *n* a living cell that is closely associated in origin, position, and probably function with a cell making up part of a SIEVE TUBE (long tubelike structure for the conduction of soluble foods) in the PHLOEM (food-conducting tissue) of a FLOWERING PLANT

**companion piece** *n* something (eg a literary work) that is associated with and complements something similar

**companionway** /kəm'panyən,way/ *n* a ship's stairway from one deck to another [²*companion*]

**company** /'kump(ə)ni/ *n* **1a** friendly association with another; fellowship **b** companions, associates ⟨*know a person by the* ~ *he keeps*⟩ **c** *taking sing or pl vb* visitors, guests ⟨*having* ~ *for dinner*⟩ **2** *taking sing or pl vb* **2a** a group of people or things ⟨*a* ~ *of horsemen*⟩ **b** a body of soldiers; *specif* a military unit (eg of infantry) composed usu of a headquarters and two or more platoons **c** an organization of musical or dramatic performers ⟨*an opera* ~⟩ **d** the officers and men of a ship **3a** *taking sing or pl vb* an association of people formed for carrying on a commercial or industrial enterprise and having a legal existence separate from the people so associated **b** those members of a partnership firm whose names do not appear in the firm name ⟨*John Doe and* Company⟩ [ME *companie,* fr OF *compagnie,* fr *compain* companion, fr LL *companio*] – **keep company 1** to go around together as frequent companions or in courtship **2** to provide with companionship ⟨*won't anyone stay and keep me* company⟩

**company officer** *n* a commissioned officer of the rank of captain or lower – compare FIELD OFFICER, GENERAL OFFICER

**company secretary** *n* a senior officer of a company who typically supervises its financial and legal requirements

**company sergeant major** *n* the senior noncommissioned officer of a company

**company union** *n, NAm* STAFF ASSOCIATION

**comparable** /'komp(ə)rəbl, kəm'peərəbl/ *adj* **1** capable of or suitable for comparison **2** approximately equivalent; similar ⟨*fabrics of* ~ *quality*⟩ – **comparability** *n,* **comparableness** *n,* **comparably** *adv*

*usage* The pronunciation /'komp(ə)rəbl/ rather than /kəm'peərəbl/ is recommended for BBC broadcasters.

¹**comparative** /kəm'parətiv/ *adj* **1** of or constituting the form of an adjective or adverb (eg slower) expressing increase in quality, quantity, or relation **2** considered as if in comparison to something else as a standard; relative ⟨*a* ~ *stranger*⟩ **3** characterized by the systematic comparison of phenomena ⟨~ *anatomy*⟩ – **comparatively** *adv,* **comparativeness** *n*

*usage* The use of **comparatively** and **relatively** to mean no more than "fairly" or "rather", where no true comparison is involved ⟨*a* **comparatively** *warm day*⟩, is widely disliked.

²**comparative** *n* the comparative degree or form (eg of an adjective or adverb) in a language

**comparator** /kəm'parətə/ *n* a device for comparing something with a similar thing or with a standard measure

¹**compare** /kəm'peə/ *vt* **1** to represent as similar; liken **2** to examine the character or qualities of, esp in order to discover resemblances or differences **3** to inflect or modify (an adjective or adverb) according to the degrees of comparison ~ *vi* **1** to bear being compared ⟨*it doesn't* ~⟩ **2** to be equal or alike – + with [ME *comparen,* fr MF *comparer,* fr L *comparare* to couple, compare, fr *compar* like, fr *com-* + *par* equal]

*usage* The constructions **compare** *to* and **compare** *with* are equally acceptable, but some writers recognize a difference in meaning. When the focus of interest is on one item which is to be put in the same class as another, they use *to* ⟨*shall I* **compare** *thee to a summer's day*? – Shak⟩. When two items are looked at together for a detailed comparison of resemblances and differences, they prefer *with* ⟨*an article* **comparing** *the human brain with that of the elephant*⟩ ⟨*Paris is small,* **compared** *with London*⟩. When **compare** is used intransitively it is always *with* ⟨*our garden can't* **compare** *with theirs*⟩.

²**compare** *n* COMPARISON 1 ⟨*beauty beyond* ~⟩

**comparison** /kəm'paris(ə)n/ *n* **1** the act or process of comparing: **1a** the representing of one thing or person as similar to or like another **b** an examination of two or more items to establish similarities and dissimilarities **2** identity or similarity of features ⟨*several points of* ~ *between the two authors*⟩ **3** the modification of an adjective or adverb to denote different levels of quality, quantity, or relation [ME, fr MF *comparaison,* fr L *comparation-, comparatio,* fr *comparatus,* pp of *comparare*]

¹**compartment** /kəm'pahtmənt/ *n* **1** any of the parts into which an enclosed space is divided **2** a separate division or section [MF *compartiment*, fr It *compartimento*, fr *compartire* to mark out into parts, fr LL *compartiri* to share out, fr L *com-* + *partiri* to share, fr *part-*, *pars* part, share] – **compartmental** *adj*

²**compartment** *vt* to compartmentalize – **compartmentation** *n*

**compartmental·ize, -ise** /,kompaht'ment(ə)l,iez/ *vt* to separate into isolated compartments; *also* to keep in isolated categories ⟨~d *knowledge* – H M McLuhan⟩ – **compartmentalization** *n*

¹**compass** /'kumpəs/ *vt, formal* **1** to devise or contrive often with craft or skill **2a** to encompass **b** to travel entirely round ⟨~ *the earth*⟩ **3a** to achieve; BRING ABOUT **b** to comprehend *synonyms* see ¹REACH [ME *compassen*, fr OF *compasser* to measure, fr (assumed) VL *compassare* to pace off, fr L *com-* + *passus* pace] – **compassable** *adj* – **box the compass** to name the 32 points of the compass in their order [perh for ³*box*, or perh for Sp *bojar, boxar* to sail round]

²**compass** *n* **1a** a boundary, circumference ⟨*within the* ~ *of the city walls*⟩ **b** a circumscribed space ⟨*within the narrow* ~ *of this short book*⟩ **c** range, scope ⟨*the* ~ *of a voice*⟩ **2a** an instrument for determining or indicating direction, typically by means of a freely-turning magnetic needle pointing to MAGNETIC NORTH **b** **compasses** *pl*, **compass** an instrument for drawing circles or transferring measurements that consists of two arms, at least one of which is pointed, joined at the top by a pivot **3** *archaic* a curved or roundabout route **b** any of various nonmagnetic devices (eg a gyrocompass) that serve the same purpose as the magnetic compass

³**compass** *adj* **1** forming a curve ⟨*a* ~ *timber*⟩ **2** *of a bow window* semicircular in plan

**compass card** *n* the circular card attached to the needles of a mariner's compass on which are marked 32 points of the compass and the 360° of the circle

**compassion** /kəm'pash(ə)n/ *n* sympathetic consciousness of others' distress together with a desire to alleviate it [ME, fr MF or LL; MF, fr LL *compassion-, compassio*, fr *compassus*, pp of *compati* to sympathize, fr L *com-* + *pati* to bear, suffer – more at PATIENT] – **compassionless** *adj*

**compassionate** /kəm'pash(ə)nət/ *adj* **1** having or showing compassion; sympathetic **2** granted because of unusual personal circumstances – used of special privileges (eg extra leave of absence) *synonyms* see ²KIND *antonym* pitiless – **compassionately** *adv*, **compassionateness** *n*

**compass rose** *n* a graduated often decorated circle printed on a chart, usu showing both magnetic and true directions

**compass saw** *n* a saw with a narrow blade for cutting curves

**compatible** /kəm'patəbl/ *adj* **1** capable of existing together in harmony **2** capable of being used without modification: eg **2a** being a television system in which colour transmissions may be received on unmodified black-and-white sets **b** of or being an audio system allowing stereo signals to be treated as mono by unmodified mono equipment ⟨~ *cartridge*⟩ **3** capable of forming a uniform mixture that neither separates nor is altered by chemical interaction **4** *of a plant* capable of self-fertilization or of uniting vegetatively (eg to form grafts) [MF, fr ML *compatibilis*, lit., sympathetic, fr LL *compati*] – **compatibility** *n*, **compatibleness** *n*, **compatibly** *adv*

**compatriot** /kəm'patri·ət/ *n* a fellow countryman [F *compatriote*, fr LL *compatriota*, fr L *com-* + LL *patriota* fellow countryman – more at PATRIOT] – **compatriotic** *adj*

**compeer** /'kompiə/ *n* **1** a companion, colleague **2** an equal, peer [(1) ME, fr OF *compere*, lit., godfather, fr ML *compater*, fr L *com-* + *pater* father – more at FATHER (2) modif of L *compar*, fr *compar*, adj, like – more at COMPARE]

**compel** /kəm'pel/ *vt -ll-* **1** to drive or urge forcefully or irresistibly *to* do something ⟨*poverty* ~led *him to work*⟩ **2** to cause to do or occur by overwhelming pressure ⟨*exhaustion of ammunition* ~led *their surrender*⟩ **3** *archaic* to drive together [ME *compellen*, fr MF *compellir*, fr L *compellere*, fr *com-* + *pellere* to drive – more at FELT] – **compellable** *adj*, **compeller** *n*

**compellation** /,kompe'laysh(ə)n/ *n, archaic* **1** an act or action of addressing someone **2** APPELLATION **1** (name or title) [L *compellation-, compellatio*, fr *compellatus*, pp of *compellare* to address, fr *com-* + *-pellare* (as in *appellare* to accost, appeal to)]

**compelling** /kəm'peling/ *adj* having an irresistible power of attraction – **compellingly** *adv*

**compendious** /kəm'pendi·əs/ *adj* comprehensive but relatively brief *synonyms* see CONCISE – **compendiously** *adv*, **compendiousness** *n*

**compendium** /kəm'pendi·əm/ *n, pl* **compendiums, compendia** /-di·ə/ **1** a brief summary of a larger work or of a field of knowledge; an abstract **2** *chiefly Br* a collection, esp of indoor games and puzzles sold together in one box [ML, fr L, saving, shortcut, fr *compendere* to weigh together, fr *com-* + *pendere* to weigh – more at PENDANT]

**compensable** /kəm'pensəbl/ *adj, chiefly NAm* that is to be or can be compensated – **compensability** *n*

**compensate** /'kompənsayt/ *vt* **1** to have an equal and opposite effect to; counterbalance **2** to make amends to, esp by appropriate payment ⟨~ *a neighbour for damage to his property*⟩ **3** to neutralize the effect of (variations) ~ *vi* **1** to supply an equivalent *for* **2** to counteract an error, defect, or undesired effect [L *compensatus*, pp of *compensare*, fr *compensus*, pp of *compendere*] – **compensative** *adj*, **compensator** *n*, **compensatory** *adj*

**compensation** /,kompen'saysh(ə)n, -pən-/ *n* **1a** correction of an organic defect by excessive development or by increased functioning of another organ or unimpaired parts of the same organ **b** a psychological mechanism by which a person attempts to alleviate feelings of inferiority, frustration, or failure in one field by endeavour in another **2** something that constitutes an equivalent or recompense ⟨*age has its* ~s⟩; *specif* payment to someone (eg an injured worker) for damage or loss – **compensational** *adj*

¹**compere** /'kompeə/ *n, Br* the presenter of a radio or television programme, esp a light entertainment programme [Fr *compère*, lit., godfather – more at COMPEER]

²**compere** *vb, Br* to act as compere (for)

**compete** /kəm'peet/ *vi* to strive consciously or unconsciously for an objective; *also* to be in a state of rivalry *synonyms* see ³RIVAL [LL *competere* to seek together, fr L, to come together, agree, be suitable, fr *com-* + *petere* to go to, seek – more at FEATHER]

**competence** /'kompit(ə)ns/ *also* **competency** /-si/ *n* **1** the quality or state of being competent: eg **1a** the properties of the tissue of an embryo that enable it to respond in a characteristic manner to an INDUCTOR (substance controlling development of tissues) **b** readiness of bacteria to undergo genetic TRANSFORMATION **2** the innate human capacity to acquire, use, and understand language – compare PERFORMANCE 6, LANGUE **3** *formal* sufficient income for the necessities and conveniences of life

**competent** /'kompit(ə)nt/ *adj* **1a** having requisite or adequate ability ⟨*a* ~ *workman*⟩ **b** showing clear signs of production by a competent agent (eg a workman or writer) ⟨*a* ~ *novel*⟩ **2** proper, appropriate **3** legally qualified ⟨*a wife is not a* ~ *witness against her husband*⟩ **4** having the capacity to function or develop in a particular way; *specif* having the capacity to respond (eg by producing an antibody) to a particular foreign substance (eg an antigen) ⟨*immunologically* ~ *cells*⟩ [ME, suitable, fr MF & L; MF, fr L *competent-, competens*, fr prp of *competere* to be suitable] – **competently** *adv*

**competition** /,kompə'tish(ə)n/ *n* **1** the act or process of competing; rivalry **2** a usu organized test of comparative skill, performance, etc ⟨*a high-diving* ~⟩; *also, taking sing or pl vb* the other competitors **3** the effort of two or more parties acting independently to secure the business of a third party **4** active demand by two or more (kinds of) organisms for some environmental resource in short supply [LL *competition-, competitio*, fr L *competitus*, pp of *competere*] – **competitory** *adj*

**competitive** /kəm'petətiv/ *adj* **1a** relating to, characterized by, or based on competition **b** suited to compete; *esp* being at least as good as the competitors ⟨*a* ~ *racing car*⟩ ⟨~ *prices*⟩ **2** inclined or desiring to compete **3** depending for effectiveness on the relative concentration of two or more substances ⟨~ *inhibition of an enzyme*⟩ – **competitively** *adv*, **competitiveness** *n*

**competitor** /kəm'petitə/ *n* one who or that which competes; a rival

**compilation** /,kompi'laysh(ə)n/ *n* **1** compiling **2** something compiled

**compile** /kəm'piel/ *vt* **1** to collect into one work **2** to compose out of materials from other documents [ME *compilen*, fr MF *compiler*, fr L *compilare* to snatch together, plunder]

**compiler** /kəm'pielə/ *n* **1** one who or that which compiles **2** a computer program that translates instructions written in a language (e g Cobol) easily understood by people into MACHINE CODE (language understood by the computer)

**complacency** /kəm'plays(ə)nsi/ *also* **complacence** *n* 1 self-satisfaction accompanied by unawareness of actual dangers or deficiencies 2 an instance of complacency ⟨*academic* complacencies *shattered by a barrage of counterexamples*⟩ 3 *archaic* complaisance

**complacent** /kəm'plays(ə)nt/ *adj* 1 self-satisfied ⟨*a ~ smile*⟩ 2 characterized by complacency 3 *archaic* COMPLAISANT 1 △ complaisant [L *complacent-, complacens,* prp of *complacēre* to please greatly, fr *com-* + *placēre* to please – more at PLEASE] – **complacently** *adv*

**complain** /kəm'playn/ *vi* 1 to express feelings of discontent, pain, etc, esp continually; speak in an unhappy, dissatisfied manner ⟨*~ed of toothache*⟩ ⟨*always ~*ing *about the neighbours*⟩ 2 to make a formal accusation or charge *~ vt* to state as a grievance ⟨*~ed that it was too hot*⟩ [ME *complaynen,* fr MF *complaindre,* fr (assumed) VL *complangere,* fr L *com- + plangere* to lament – more at PLAINT] – **complainer** *n,* **plainingly** *adv*

**complainant** /kəm'playnənt/ *n* one who makes a complaint; *specif* the party in a legal action or proceeding who makes a complaint

**complaint** /kəm'playnt/ *n* 1 an expression of discontent 2a something that is the cause or subject of protest or outcry b a bodily ailment or disease 3 a formal allegation by the plaintiff in a civil action [ME *compleynte,* fr MF *complainte,* fr OF, fr *complaindre*]

**complaisance** /kəm'plɑs(ə)ns/ *n* disposition to please or comply; affability

**complaisant** /kəm'plays(ə)nt/ *adj* 1 marked by an inclination to please or comply 2 tending to consent to others' wishes [Fr, fr MF, fr prp of *complaire* to gratify, acquiesce, fr L *complacēre* to please greatly] – **complaisantly** *adv*

synonyms **Complaisant** suggests that one graciously assents, compliant that one obeys or yields, willingly or otherwise. △ complacent

**compleat** /kəm'pleet/ *adj* having a complete range of relevant qualities or experience; COMPLETE 3 ⟨*the ~ conductor, excelling in both choral and symphonic works*⟩ [archaic variant of *complete,* popularized by *The Compleat Angler* by Izaak Walton †1683 E writer]

**complected** /kəm'plektid/ *adj, chiefly NAm* having a specified facial complexion; complexioned ⟨*a tall, thin man, fairly dark ~ – E J Kahn*⟩ [irreg fr *complexion*]

¹**complement** /'komplimənt/ *n* 1a something that fills up or completes b the quantity or number required to make something complete ⟨*had the usual ~ of eyes and ears*⟩; *specif* the total number of officers and men required to make up a ship's company c *taking sing or pl vb* the personnel of a ship d either of two parts that together make a whole; a counterpart 2a an angle or arc that when added to a given angle or arc equals 90° b *maths* the set of all things that do not belong to a given set c the number that must be added to a given number to obtain the least number containing one more digit ⟨*the ~ of 6 is 4 and that of 35 is 65*⟩ 3 a word or expression added to a verb to complete what is said of the subject ⟨*president and beautiful in "they elected him president" and "the house is beautiful" are ~*s⟩ 4 the heat-sensitive substance in normal blood that in combination with antibodies causes the destruction of antigens (e g bacteria and foreign blood cells) [ME, fr L *complementum,* fr *complēre*] – **complemental** *adj*

synonyms A **complement** completes the full quantity. A **supplement** is added as an extra to what might be thought to be already complete. △ compliment

²**complement** /'kompliment/ *vt* to be complementary to

**complementary** /,kompli'ment(ə)ri/ *adj* 1 serving to fill out or complete 2 mutually supplying each other's lack 3 of or constituting either of a pair of contrasting colours that produce a neutral colour when combined in suitable proportions 4 relating to the precise pairing of PURINE and PYRIMIDINE chemical bases between strands of DNA, strands of RNA, or between a single strand of DNA and messenger RNA (e g during protein synthesis) such that the sequence of bases on one strand determines that on the other 5 *of a pair of angles* having the sum of 90° – **complementarily** *adv,* **complementariness** *n,* **complementarity** *n,* **complementary** *n*

**complementation** /,komplimən'taysh(ə)n, -men-/ *n* 1 the determination of the complement of a given mathematical set 2 the production of a normal organism from the mating of two mutant organisms

**complement fixation** *n* (the action or natural process of) the absorption and binding of complement to the product of the union of an antibody and the antigen for which it is specific when added to a mixture of such antibody and antigen

**complement fixation test** *n* a test that uses COMPLEMENT FIXATION to detect specific antibodies in the presence of known antigens, esp for the diagnosis of disease (e g syphilis)

¹**complete** /kəm'pleet/ *adj* 1 having all necessary parts, elements, or steps 2 whole, concluded ⟨*after two ~ revolutions about the sun*⟩ 3 thoroughly competent; highly proficient 4a fully carried out; thorough ⟨*a ~ renovation*⟩ b total, absolute ⟨*~ silence*⟩ [ME *complet,* fr MF, fr L *completus,* fr pp of *complēre* to fill up, complete, fr *com-* + *plēre* to fill – more at FULL] – **completely** *adv,* **completeness** *n,* **completive** *adj*

usage Some people feel that when **complete** means "whole" or "total", things either are **complete** or are not, so that it is illogical to say ⟨△ *a more* **complete** *silence*⟩. This objection does not hold when **complete** means "thorough" ⟨*a more* **complete** *study of this subject*⟩.

²**complete** *vt* 1 to bring to an end; *esp* to bring into a perfected state ⟨*~ a painting*⟩ 2a to make whole or perfect ⟨*the church ~*s *the charm of this village*⟩ b to mark the end of ⟨*a rousing chorus ~*s *the show*⟩ c to execute, fulfil ⟨*~ a contract*⟩ synonyms see ¹CLOSE – **completion** *n*

**complete fertilizer** *n* a fertilizer that contains the three chief plant nutrients nitrogen, phosphate, and potassium

**complete metamorphosis** *n* a method of development (METAMORPHOSIS) in an insect (e g a butterfly or a beetle) in which the immature stages (e g caterpillars or larvae) differ markedly from the adult and include a resting stage, the pupa – compare INCOMPLETE METAMORPHOSIS

¹**complex** /'kompleks/ *adj* 1a composed of two or (many) more parts b(1) *of a word* having at least one part (e g *un-* or *-ly*) unable to be a word by itself ⟨*unmanly is a ~ word*⟩ b(2) *of a sentence* consisting of a main clause and one or more subordinate clauses 2 hard to separate, analyse, or solve 3 of or being a COMPLEX NUMBER ⟨*~ analysis*⟩; *also* taking on complex values ⟨*a ~ variable*⟩ [L *complexus,* pp of *complecti* to embrace, comprise (a multitude of objects), fr *com-* + *plectere* to braid – more at PLY] – **complexly** *adv,* **complexness** *n*

synonyms **Complex, complicated, intricate, tangled,** and **knotty**: complex usually implies a great number and variety of parts, requiring knowledge or study for their understanding ⟨*the* **complex** *mechanism of a clock*⟩. **Complicated** stresses the relationship between the parts, and the difficulty involved in understanding them ⟨*a* **complicated** *situation*⟩. Something which is **intricate** is formed of parts so closely intertwined that it is difficult to unravel or follow them through: ⟨**intricate** *embroidery*⟩. Where **intricate** invites admiration, what is **involved** implies confusion ⟨*a dreadfully* **involved** *story about a child, a dog, and a biscuit*⟩. **Tangled** suggests random disorder, and **knotty**, the most informal term, adds to the difficulty or unravelling constituent parts to that of solving additional problems (the knots), so that understanding may seem unattainable ⟨*the* **knotty** *problem of how to treat young offenders*⟩. **antonym** simple

²**complex** *n* 1 a whole made up of complicated or interrelated parts ⟨*a shopping ~*⟩ 2a a group of repressed related desires, feelings, memories, etc that usu adversely affects personality and behaviour b an exaggerated reaction to something ⟨*has a ~ about flying*⟩ – compare THING 10a 3 *chemistry* a complex substance or chemical compound in which the constituents are more intimately associated than in a simple mixture; COORDINATION COMPLEX

**complex fraction** *n* a fraction that itself has a further fraction above or below the line, or both – compare SIMPLE FRACTION

**complexion** /kəm'pleksh(ə)n/ *n* 1 the natural colour or appearance of the skin, esp of the face ⟨*a dark ~*⟩ 2 overall aspect or impression ⟨*that puts a different ~ on things*⟩ 3 *obs* the combination of the hot, cold, moist, and dry qualities held in medieval physiology to determine the quality of a body [ME, fr MF, fr ML *complexion-, complexio,* fr L, combination, fr *complexus,* pp] – **complexional** *adj,* **complexioned** *adj*

**complexity** /kəm'pleksəti/ *n* 1 being complex 2 something complex ⟨*the* complexities *of relativistic quantum mechanics*⟩

**complex number** *n* a number of the form $a + bi$ where $a$ and $b$ are REAL NUMBERS and $i$ is defined as the positive square root of minus one ($i = +\sqrt{-1}$)

**compliance** /kəm'plie-əns/ *n* 1 the act or process of complying (readily) with the wishes of others 2 a disposition to yield to others 3a (a measure of) the ability of an object to yield elastically when a force is applied; flexibility **b** the ease with which a loudspeaker cone moves in response to a force; *also* the ease of movement of a gramophone stylus with respect to the cartridge *synonyms* see COMPLAISANT – **compliant** *adj*, **compliantly** *adv*

**complicacy** /'komplikəsi/ *n* 1 complexity 2 something that is complicated [²*complicate*]

**complicate** /'komplikayt/ *vt* 1 to combine, esp in an involved or inextricable manner 2 to make complex or difficult 3 to make more complex or severe ⟨*a virus disease* ~d *by bacterial infection*⟩ ~ *vi* to become complicated [L *complicatus*, pp of *complicare* to fold together, fr *com-* + *plicare* to fold – more at PLY]

**complicated** /'kompli,kaytid/ *adj* 1 consisting of parts intricately combined 2 difficult to analyse, understand, or explain *synonyms* see ¹COMPLEX *antonym* simple – **complicatedly** *adv*, **complicatedness** *n*

**complication** /,kompli'kaysh(ə)n/ *n* 1a a complexity, intricacy; a situation or a detail of character complicating the main thread of a plot **b** an instance of making difficult, involved, or intricate **c** a complex or intricate feature or element **d** *usu pl* a factor or issue that occurs unexpectedly and changes existing plans, methods, or attitudes 2 a secondary disease or condition developing in the course of a primary disease

**complice** /'komplis, 'kum-/ *n*, *archaic* an associate [ME, MF, fr LL *complic-*, *complex*, fr L *com-* + *plicare* to fold]

**complicity** /kəm'plisəti/ *n* (an instance of) association or participation (as if) in a wrongful act [Fr *complicité*, fr *complice*]

¹**compliment** /'komplimənt/ *n* 1 an expression of esteem, respect, affection, or admiration; *esp* a flattering remark 2 *pl* best wishes; regards [Fr, fr It *complimento*, fr Sp *cumplimiento*, fr *cumplir* to be courteous]

²**compliment** /'kompli,ment/ *vt* 1 to pay a compliment to 2 to present with a token of esteem

**complimentary** /,kompli'ment(ə)ri/ *adj* 1 expressing or containing a compliment 2 given free as a courtesy or favour ⟨~ *tickets*⟩ – **complimentarily** *adv*

**compline** /'komplin/ *n*, *often cap* the last of the prescribed services of Christian worship that is traditionally said before retiring at night [ME *complie*, *compline*, fr OF *complie*, modif of LL *completa*, fr L, fem of *completus* complete]

**complot** /'komplot/ *vb or n*, *archaic* (to) plot [MF *complot* crowd, plot]

**comply** /kəm'plie/ *vi* 1 to conform or adapt one's actions to another's wishes, to a rule, or to necessity 2 *obs* to be ceremoniously courteous [It *complire*, fr Sp *cumplir* to complete, perform what is due, be courteous, fr L *complēre* to complete] – **complier** *n*

¹**compo** /'kompoh/ *n* a material made of a mixture of others ⟨*a board made of* ~⟩ [short for *composition*]

²**compo** *n*, *Austr informal* compensation (for an industrial injury) [by shortening & alter.]

¹**component** /kəm'pohnənt/ *n* 1 a constituent part; an ingredient 2 *maths* any of the VECTORS (quantities having both size and direction) added together to form a given vector [L *component-*, *componens*, prp of *componere* to put together – more at COMPOUND] – **componential** *adj*

²**component** *adj* serving or helping to constitute

**comport** /kəm'pawt/ *vb*, *formal vi* to be fitting; accord ⟨*acts that* ~ *with ideals*⟩ ~ *vt* to behave (oneself) in a manner conformable to what is right, proper, or expected ⟨~ed *himself well in the emergency*⟩ [MF *comporter* to bear, conduct, fr L *comportare* to bring together, fr *com-* + *portare* to carry – more at PORT]

**comportment** /kəm'pawtmənt/ *n*, *formal* bearing, demeanour

**compose** /kəm'pohz/ *vt* 1a to form by putting together ⟨~ *a collage with those pictures*⟩ **b** to form the substance of; MAKE UP – chiefly passive ⟨~d *of many ingredients*⟩ **c** SET 13d(1) (make ready for printing) 2 to create by mental or artistic labour ⟨~ *a sonnet*⟩; *esp* to formulate and write (a piece of music) 3 to settle (a point of disagreement) ⟨~ *their differences*⟩ 4 to arrange in proper or orderly form 5 to free from agitation; calm; settle ⟨~ *oneself*⟩ ~ *vi* to practise composition *synonyms* see COMPRISE [MF *composer*, fr L *componere* (perf indic *composui*) – more at COMPOUND]

**composed** /kəm'pohzd/ *adj* free from agitation; calm; COLLECTED 1 – **composedly** *adv*, **composedness** *n*

**composer** /kəm'pohzə/ *n* one who or that which composes; *esp* a person who writes music

**composing stick** /kəm'pohzing/ *n* a tray with an adjustable slide in which a compositor holds the type being set

¹**composite** /'kompəzit, 'kompəziet/ *adj* 1 made up of distinct parts: eg 1a a *cap* of or being a Roman order of architecture that combines angular Ionic scrolls with the acanthus-circled bell of the Corinthian **b** relating to a very large family (Compositae) of plants, shrubs, and trees including many familiar species (eg the dandelion and daisy), that are often considered to be the most highly evolved plants and are characterized by many small flowers (FLORETS) arranged in dense heads that resemble single flowers **c** *maths* having two or more factors; *esp*, *of a number* having two or more factors which are prime numbers; not prime ⟨*12, with factors of 2, 2, and 3, is a* ~ *number*⟩ 2 combining the typical or essential characteristics of individuals making up a group ⟨*a* ~ *portrait of mystics known to the painter*⟩ [L *compositus*, pp of *componere*] – **compositely** *adv*

*usage* The pronunciation /'kompəzit/ rather than /'kompəziet/ is recommended for BBC broadcasters.

²**composite** *n* 1 something composite; a compound 2 a composite plant

**composition** /,kompə'zish(ə)n/ *n* 1a the act or process of composing; *specif* arrangement into proper proportion or relation and esp into artistic form **b(1)** the arrangement of type for printing ⟨*hand* ~⟩ **b(2)** the production of type or typographic characters (eg in photocomposition) arranged for printing 2a the factors or parts which go to make something; *also* the way in which the parts or factors make up the whole **b** the qualitative and quantitative makeup of a chemical compound **c** makeup or composition (eg of coal sizes or a railroad train) by classes, types, or grades and arrangement 3 an agreement by which somebody who is owed money accepts partial payment 4 a product of mixing or combining various elements or ingredients 5 an intellectual creation: eg 5a a piece of writing; *esp* a school essay **b** a written piece of music, esp of considerable size and complexity 6 the quality or state of being compound [ME *composicioun*, fr MF *composition*, fr L *composition-*, *compositio*, fr *compositus*] – **compositional** *adj*, **compositionally** *adv*

**compositor** /kəm'pozitə/ *n* somebody who sets type

**compos mentis** /,kompəs 'mentis/ *adj*, *formal* of sound mind, memory, and understanding [L, lit., having mastery of one's mind]

¹**compost** /'kompost/ *n* 1 a mixture that consists largely of decayed organic matter and is used for fertilizing and conditioning land 2 *formal* a mixture, compound [MF, fr ML *compostum*, fr L, neut of *compositus*, *compostus*, pp of *componere* to put together]

²**compost** *vt* to convert (eg plant remains) to compost – **composter** *n*

**composure** /kəm'pohzhə/ *n* calmness or repose, esp of mind, bearing, or appearance [*compose* + *-ure*]

**compote** /'kompot/ *n* a dessert of fruit cooked in syrup and usu served cold [Fr, fr OF *composte*, fr L *composta*, fem of *compostus*, pp]

¹**compound** /kəm'pownd/ *vt* 1 to put together (parts) so as to form a whole; combine ⟨~ *ingredients*⟩ 2 to form by combining parts ⟨~ *a medicine*⟩ 3 to settle amicably; adjust by agreement ⟨~ *a debt*⟩ 4a to pay (interest) on both the accumulated interest and the amount borrowed **b** to add to; augment ⟨~ *to* ~ *an error*⟩ 5 to agree for a consideration not to prosecute (an offence) ⟨~ *a felony*⟩ ~ *vi* 1 to become joined in a (chemical) compound 2 to come to terms of agreement [ME *compounen*, fr MF *compondre*, fr L *componere*, fr *com-* + *ponere* to put – more at POSITION] – **compoundable** *adj*, **compounder** *n*

*usage* The legal sense of **compound** should not be confused with the others. To **compound** a crime is, legally, to condone it, not to make it worse.

²**compound** /'kompownd/ *adj* 1 composed of or resulting from union of separate elements, ingredients, or parts; *specif* composed of united similar elements esp of a kind usu independent ⟨*a* ~ *leaf consisting of several leaflets*⟩ 2 involving or used in a combination 3a *of a word* being a compound **b** *of a sentence* consisting of two or more main clauses [ME *compouned*, pp of *compounen*]

³**compound** /'kompownd/ *n* 1a a word consisting of components that are words (eg *houseboat*, *high school*, *devil-may-care*) **b** a word consisting of any of various combinations of words, combining forms, or affixes (eg *anthropology*, *kilocycle*,

*builder*) **2** something formed by a union of elements or parts; *specif* a distinct substance formed by chemical union of two or more ingredients (e g chemical elements) in definite proportion by weight

⁴**compound** /'kompownd/ *n* a fenced or walled-in area containing a group of buildings, esp residences [by folk etymology fr Malay *kampong* group of buildings, village]

**compound eye** *n* an eye (e g of an insect) made up of many separate visual units

**compound fracture** *n* a bone fracture produced in such a way as to form an open wound, through which bone fragments usu protrude

**compound interest** *n* interest computed on the original amount borrowed plus accumulated interest

**compound leaf** *n* a leaf which is divided to the midrib forming two or more leaflets on a common stalk

**compound lens** *n* LENS 1b

**compound microscope** *n* a microscope consisting of two lenses (the OBJECTIVE and the EYEPIECE) mounted at opposite ends of a tube of variable length

**comprehend** /ˌkompri'hend/ *vt* **1** to grasp the nature, significance, or meaning of; understand **2** *formal* to include ⟨*the park ~s all of the land beyond the river*⟩ [ME *comprehenden*, fr L *comprehendere*, fr *com-* + *prehendere* to grasp – more at PREHENSILE] – **comprehendible** *adj*

**comprehensible** /ˌkompri'hensəbl/ *adj* capable of being comprehended; intelligible △ comprehensive – **comprehensibleness** *n*, **comprehensibly** *adv*, **comprehensibility** *n*

**comprehension** /ˌkompri'hensh(ə)n/ *n* **1a** the act or process of comprising **b** the faculty or capability of including; comprehensiveness **2a** the act or action of grasping with the intellect; understanding **b** knowledge gained by comprehending **c** the capacity for understanding fully **3** CONNOTATION 3 **4** a school exercise testing understanding of a passage [MF & L; MF, fr L *comprehension-, comprehensio*, fr *comprehensus*, pp of *comprehendere*]

¹**comprehensive** /ˌkompri'hensiv/ *adj* **1** covering completely or broadly; inclusive ⟨*~ insurance*⟩ **2** having or exhibiting wide mental grasp ⟨*~ knowledge*⟩ **3** *chiefly Br* of or being the principle of educating in one unified school nearly all children above the age of 11 from a given area regardless of ability ⟨*~ education*⟩ △ comprehensible – **comprehensively** *adv*, **comprehensiveness** *n*

²**comprehensive** *n, Br* a comprehensive school

¹**compress** /kəm'pres/ *vt* **1** to press or squeeze together **2** to reduce in size or volume as if by squeezing ~ *vi* to be compressed; undergo compression *synonyms* see ²CONTRACT *antonyms* expand, stretch, spread [ME *compressen*, fr LL *compressare* to press hard, fr L *compressus*, pp of *comprimere* to compress, fr *com-* + *premere* to press] – **compressible** *adj*, **compressibility** *n*

²**compress** /'kompres/ *n* a folded cloth or pad applied so as to press upon a body part (e g to ease the pain and swelling of a bruise) [MF *compresse*, fr *compresser* to compress, fr LL *compressare*]

**compressed** /kəm'prest/ *adj* **1** pressed together; reduced in size or volume (e g by pressure) **2** *esp of a plant or animal part* flattened from side to side as though subjected to compression – **compressedly** *adv*

**compressed air** *n* air under pressure greater than that of the atmosphere

**compression** /kəm'presh(ə)n/ *n* **1** compressing or being compressed **2** (the quality of) the process of compressing the fuel mixture in a cylinder of an INTERNAL-COMBUSTION ENGINE (e g in a motor car) **3** a fossil plant flattened by the pressure of overlying rocks – **compressional** *adj*

**compressor** /kəm'presə/ *n* one who or that which compresses: e g **1** a muscle that compresses a part **2** a machine that compresses gases

**comprise** /kəm'priez/ *vt* **1** to include, contain **2** to be made up of **3** to constitute; MAKE UP [ME *comprisen*, fr MF *compris*, pp of *comprendre*, fr L *comprehendere*]

> *synonyms* Compare **comprise, consist, compose, constitute,** and **include**. When a whole is "made up of" several items which are all listed, it **comprises, consists of,** or *is composed of* them ⟨*a chess set comprises 32 chessmen*⟩; it is a common confusion to use comprise here like compose ⟨△ *a chess set is comprised of 32 chessmen*⟩. When several items which are all listed "make up" a whole, they **compose** or **constitute** it ⟨*32 chessmen constitute a chess set*⟩; the use of **comprise** in this second sense ⟨*32 chessmen comprise a chess set*⟩ is disapproved of by some people. When a whole is only partially "made up of" one or more items, it **includes** it or them ⟨*a chess set includes 4 bishops*⟩, and it is another common confusion to use **include** for the complete list ⟨△ *a chess set includes 32 chessmen*⟩.

¹**compromise** /'komprəmiez/ *n* **1a** the settling of differences through arbitration or through consent reached by mutual concessions **b** a settlement reached by compromise **c** something blending qualities of two different things **2** a concession to something disreputable or prejudicial ⟨*a ~ of principles*⟩ [ME, mutual promise to abide by an arbiter's decision, fr MF *compromis*, fr L *compromissum*, fr neut of *compromissus*, pp of *compromittere* to promise mutually, fr *com-* + *promittere* to promise – more at PROMISE]

²**compromise** *vt* **1** to adjust or settle by mutual concessions **2** to expose to discredit or scandal ~ *vi* **1** to come to agreement by mutual concession **2** to make a shameful or disreputable concession – **compromiser** *n*

**Comptometer** /komp'tomitə/ *trademark* – used for a calculating machine

**comptroller** /kən'trohlə; *also* ˌkom(p)'trohlə/ *n* CONTROLLER 1b – used esp as a title of a financial executive [ME, alter. (influenced by MF *compte* account) of *conterroller* controller] – **comptrollership** *n*

**compulsion** /kəm'pulsh(ə)n/ *n* **1a** compelling or being compelled **b** a force or agency that compels **2** a strong impulse to perform an irrational act [ME, fr MF or LL; MF, fr LL *compulsion-, compulsio*, fr L *compulsus*, pp of *compellere* to compel]

**compulsive** /kəm'pulsiv/ *adj* **1** having power to compel **2** of, caused by, or suggestive of psychological compulsion or obsession ⟨*~ actions*⟩; *also* suffering from a compulsion ⟨*~ gambler*⟩ – **compulsively** *adv*, **compulsiveness** *n*, **compulsivity** *n*

**compulsory** /kəm'puls(ə)ri/ *adj* **1** mandatory, enforced ⟨*~ arbitration*⟩ **2** involving compulsion or obligation; coercive – **compulsorily** *adv*

**compunction** /kəm'pungksh(ə)n/ *n* **1** anxiety arising from awareness of guilt; remorse **2** a twinge of misgiving; a scruple ⟨*cheated without ~*⟩ *synonyms* see ¹PENITENT, QUALM [ME *compunccioun*, fr MF *componction*, fr LL *compunction-, compunctio*, fr L *compunctus*, pp of *compungere* to prick hard, sting, fr *com-* + *pungere* to prick – more at PUNGENT] – **compunctious** *adj*

**compurgation** /ˌkompuh'gaysh(ə)n/ *n* a method of trial abolished in 1833 by which an accused person could be acquitted by making a sworn denial of the charge and having usu 12 witnesses swear to the truthfulness of his/her denial [LL *compurgation-, compurgatio*, fr L *compurgatus*, pp of *compurgare* to clear completely, fr *com-* + *purgare* to purge]

**compurgator** /'kompuhˌgaytə/ *n* a person who testified to the truthfulness of an accused in the procedure of compurgation

**computation** /ˌkompyoo'taysh(ə)n/ *n* **1a** computing, calculation **b** the use or operation of a computer **2** a system or reckoning **3** an amount computed – **computational** *adj*

¹**compute** /kəm'pyooht/ *n* computation – chiefly in *beyond compute*

²**compute** *vt* to determine, esp by mathematical means ⟨*~ your income tax*⟩; *also* to determine or calculate by means of a computer ~ *vi* **1** to make calculation; reckon **2** to use a computer [L *computare* – more at COUNT] – **computable** *adj*, **computability** *n*

**computer** /kəm'pyoohtə/ *n* one who or that which computes; *specif* a programmable electronic device that can store, retrieve, and process data, and that can also store programs that control its own action – **computerlike** *adj*

**computer·ize, -ise** /kəm'pyoohtəˌriez/ *vt* **1** to carry out, control, or conduct by means of a computer **2** to equip with computers ~ *vi* to install or begin to make use of computers – **computerizable** *adj*, **computerization** *n*

**computernik** /kəm'pyoohtəˌnik/ *n, chiefly NAm informal* a person who works with or has a deep interest in computers [*computer* + *-nik*]

**comrade** /'komrid, -rayd/ *n* **1a** an intimate friend or associate; a companion **b** a fellow soldier **2** a communist [MF *camarade* group sleeping in one room, roommate, companion, fr OSp *camarada*, fr *cámara* room, fr LL *camera, camara* – more at CHAMBER; (2) fr its use as a form of address by communists] – **comradely** *adj*, **comradeliness** *n*, **comradeship** *n*

**comsat** /'komˌsat/ *n* an artificial satellite in orbit round the earth, used for relaying radio, television, and telephone signals [*com*munications *satellite*]

**comstockery** /'kum,stokəri, 'kom-/ *n, chiefly NAm* strict censorship or censure of art, literature, or theatre containing alleged immorality or obscenity [Anthony *Comstock* †1915 US campaigner against the nude in art]

**¹con** /kon/ *vt* **-nn-** *chiefly formal* **1** to study or examine closely **2** to commit to memory [ME *connen* to know, learn, study, alter. of *cunnen* to know, infin of *can* – more at CAN]

**²con,** *NAm chiefly* **conn** *vt* **-nn-** to conduct or direct the steering of (eg a ship) [alter. of ME *condien* to conduct, fr MF *conduire*, fr L *conducere*]

**³con,** *NAm chiefly* **conn** *n* the control exercised by one who cons a ship

**⁴con** *adv* on the negative side; in opposition ⟨*so much has been written pro and* ∼⟩ [ME, short for *contra*]

**⁵con** *n* **1** an argument or evidence in opposition **2** (somebody holding) the opposing or negative position

**⁶con** *vt* **-nn-** *informal* **1** to swindle, trick **2** to persuade, cajole [*con* (*man, trick*), short for *confidence* (*man, trick*)] – **con** *n*

**⁷con** *n, informal* a convict

**⁸con** *prep* with – used in music ⟨∼ sordini⟩ [It]

**con-** – see COM-

**con amore** /,kon a'mawray/ *adv* **1** with love, devotion, or zeal **2** in a tender manner – used in music [It]

**conation** /koh'naysh(ə)n/ *n* an inclination (eg an instinct, drive, wish, or craving) to act purposefully [L *conation-, conatio* act of attempting, fr *conatus*, pp of *conari* to attempt – more at DEACON] – **conational** *adj,* **conative** *adj*

**conatus** /koh'naytəs/ *n, pl* **conatus** a natural tendency or striving (eg towards self-preservation) [NL, fr L, attempt, effort, fr *conatus*, pp]

**con brio** /kon 'breeoh/ *adv* in a vigorous or brisk manner – used in music [It, lit., with vigour]

**concanavalin** /konkə'navəlin, -,kanə'vaylin/ *n* either of two GLOBULINS (types of proteins) that occur in the JACK BEAN; *esp* one that causes AGGLUTINATION (clumping together) of blood cells and is also used to induce CELL DIVISION [*com-* + *canavalin* (a noncrystalline globulin found in the jack bean), fr NL *Canavalia*, genus name of the jack bean]

**concassé** /'konkasay/ *adj, of vegetables, esp tomatoes* roughly chopped [Fr, pp of *concasser* to break, crush, pound, fr L *conquassare* to shake, shatter, fr *com-* + *quassare* to shake, shatter – more at QUASH]

**concatenate** /kon'katənayt/ *vt, formal* to link together in a series or chain [LL *concatenatus*, pp of *concatenare*, fr L *com-* + *catena* chain – more at CHAIN] – **concatenation** *n,* **concatenate** *adj*

**concave** /,kon'kayv, '--/ *adj* hollowed or rounded inwards like the inside of a bowl – compare CONVEX [MF, fr L *concavus*, fr *com-* + *cavus* hollow – more at CAVE] – **concave** *n,* **concavely** *adv*

**concavity** /kon'kavəti, kən-/ *n* **1** a concave line or surface or the space included in it; a hollow **2** the quality of being concave

**concavo-concave** /kon,kayvoh kon'kayv/ *adj* concave on both sides

**concavo-convex** /kon,kayvoh kon'veks/ *adj* **1** concave on one side and convex on the other **2** having the concave side curved more than the convex

**conceal** /kən'seel/ *vt* **1** to prevent disclosure or recognition of **2** to place out of sight [ME *concelen*, fr MF *conceler*, fr L *concelare*, fr *com-* + *celare* to hide – more at HELL] – **concealable** *adj,* **concealer** *n,* **concealingly** *adv,* **concealment** *n*

**concede** /kən'seed/ *vt* **1** to grant as a right or privilege **2a** to accept as true, valid, or accurate **b** to acknowledge grudgingly or hesitantly **3** *chiefly journalistic* to allow involuntarily ⟨∼d *two more goals*⟩ to make concession; yield *synonyms* see ACKNOWLEDGE [Fr or L, Fr *concéder*, fr L *concedere*, fr *com-* + *cedere* to yield – more at CEDE] – **conceder** *n*

**¹conceit** /kən'seet/ *n* **1** excessively high opinion of oneself **2a** a fanciful idea **b** an elaborate, unusual, and cleverly-expressed figure of speech **c** use or presence of such conceits in poetry **3** *archaic* a result of mental activity; a thought *synonyms* see ¹PRIDE [ME, thought, opinion, fr *conceiven*]

**²conceit** *vt* **1** *dial Br* to take a fancy to **2** *obs* to conceive, understand

**conceited** /kən'seetid/ *adj* having an excessively high opinion of oneself – **conceitedly** *adv,* **conceitedness** *n synonyms* see ¹PRIDE *antonym* self-deprecating

**conceivable** /kən'seevəbl/ *adj* capable of being conceived; imaginable – **conceivableness** *n,* **conceivably** *adv,* **conceivability** *n*

**conceive** /kən'seev/ *vt* **1** to become pregnant with (young) **2a** to cause to originate in one's mind ⟨∼ *a prejudice against them*⟩ **b** to form a conception of; visualize **3** to understand **4** *formal* to be of the opinion ∼ *vi* **1** to become pregnant **2** to have a conception of ⟨*he* ∼s *of death as emptiness*⟩ [ME *conceiven*, fr OF *conceivre*, fr L *concipere* to take in, conceive, fr *com-* + *capere* to take – more at HEAVE] – **conceiver** *n*

**concelebrant** /kən'selibrənt, kon-/ *n* a person who concelebrates Mass or the Christian sacrament of the Eucharist

**concelebrate** /kən'selibrayt, kon-/ *vb* to celebrate or officiate at (Mass or the sacrament of the Eucharist) jointly with another priest or priests [L *concelebratus*, pp of *concelebrare* to celebrate in great numbers, fr *com-* + *celebrare* to celebrate] – **concelebration** *n*

**concent** /kən'sent/ *n, archaic* harmony (eg of voices or sounds) [L *concentus*, fr *concentus*, pp of *concinere* to sing together, fr *com-* + *canere* to sing]

**¹concentrate** /'kons(ə)ntrayt/ *vt* **1a** to bring or direct towards a common centre or objective; focus **b** to gather into one body, mass, or force ⟨*power was* ∼d *in a few able hands*⟩ **2a** to make less dilute **b** to express or exhibit in condensed form ⟨*the message is* ∼d *in the last paragraph*⟩ ∼ *vi* **1** to draw towards or meet in a common centre **2** to gather, collect **3** to concentrate one's powers, efforts, or attention ⟨∼ *on a problem*⟩ [*com-* + L *centrum* centre] – **concentrative** *adj,* **concentrator** *n*

**²concentrate** *n* something concentrated (eg a food or drink); *specif* a feed for animals rich in digestible nutrients

**concentration** /,konsən'traysh(ə)n/ *n* **1** concentrating or being concentrated; *specif* direction of attention to a single object **2** a concentrated mass or thing **3** the relative content of a (chemical) component; strength

**concentration camp** *n* a camp where political prisoners, refugees, or prisoners of war are confined; *esp* any of those used by the Nazis for the internment or mass execution of (Jewish) prisoners during World War II

**concentre** /kən'sentə, kon-/ *vb, formal* to draw, direct, or come to a common centre [MF *concentrer*, fr *com-* + *centre*]

**concentric** /kən'sentrik, kon-/ *adj* **1** having a common centre ⟨∼ *circles*⟩ **2** having a common axis; coaxial [ML *concentricus*, fr L *com-* + *centrum* centre] – **concentrically** *adv,* **concentricity** *n*

**concept** /'konsept/ *n* **1** something conceived in the mind; a thought, notion **2** a general idea covering many similar things derived from study of particular instances *synonyms* see IDEA [L *conceptum*, neut of *conceptus*, pp of *concipere* to take in, conceive]

**conceptacle** /kən'septəkl/ *n* an external cavity containing reproductive cells in algae (eg seaweeds of the genus *Fucus*) [NL *conceptaculum*, fr L, receptacle, fr *conceptus*, pp]

**conception** /kən'sepsh(ə)n/ *n* **1a(1)** the act of becoming pregnant or being fertilized; the state of being conceived **a(2)** an embryo, foetus **b** a beginning ⟨*joy had the like* ∼ *in our eyes* – Shak⟩ **2** a general idea; a concept **3** the originating of something in the mind *synonyms* see IDEA [ME *concepcioun*, fr OF *conception*, fr L *conception-, conceptio*, fr *conceptus*, pp] – **conceptional** *adj,* **conceptive** *adj*

**conceptual** /kən'septyooəl/ *adj* of or consisting of concepts [ML *conceptualis* of thought, fr LL *conceptus* act of conceiving, thought, fr L *conceptus*, pp] – **conceptuality** *n,* **conceptually** *adv*

**conceptual art** /kən'septyooəl/ *n* art in which the artist's intent is to convey a concept rather than create an art object

**conceptualism** /kən'septyooə,liz(ə)m, -choo-/ *n* a philosophical theory that is intermediate between REALISM and NOMINALISM and asserts that classes and universals exist as mental concepts but may be properly affirmed of reality – **conceptualist** *n,* **conceptualistic** *adj,* **conceptualistically** *adv*

**conceptual·ize, -ise** /kən'septyooəliez, -choo-/ *vt* to form a concept of – **conceptualization** *n,* **conceptualizer** *n*

**conceptus** /kən'septəs/ *n* a foetus [L, one conceived, fr pp of *concipere*]

**¹concern** /kən'suhn/ *vt* **1** to relate to; be about ⟨*the novel* ∼s *three soldiers*⟩ **2** to have an influence on; involve; *also* to be the business or affair of ⟨*the problem* ∼s *us all*⟩ **3** to be a care, trouble, or distress to ⟨*his ill health* ∼s *me*⟩ **4** to engage, occupy ⟨*he* ∼s *himself with trivia*⟩ [ME *concernen*, fr MF & ML; MF *concerner*, fr ML *concernere*, fr LL, to sift together, mingle, fr L *com-* + *cernere* to sift – more at CERTAIN]

²**concern** *n* **1** something that relates or belongs to one ⟨*it's not my* ~⟩ **2** matter for consideration **3a** marked interest or regard, usu arising through a personal tie or relationship **b** an uneasy state marked by interest, uncertainty, and apprehension **4** a business or manufacturing organization or establishment **5** a contrivance, thing ⟨*an odd-looking* ~⟩ *synonyms* see ¹CARE *antonym* unconcern

**concerned** /kən'suhnd/ *adj* **1** disturbed, anxious ⟨~ *for his safety*⟩ **2a** interestedly engaged ⟨~ *with books and music*⟩ **b** involved (illegally) ⟨*arrested all* ~⟩ **c** eager ⟨~ *to find the truth*⟩

**concerning** /kən'suhning/ *prep* relating to; with reference to

**concernment** /kən'suhnmənt/ *n, chiefly formal* **1** something in which one is concerned **2** importance, consequence **3** solicitude, anxiety

¹**concert** /'konsuht, -sət/ *vt* to settle or adjust by conferring and reaching an agreement ~ *vi* to act in harmony or conjunction [MF *concerter*, fr OIt *concertare*, fr LL, fr L, to contend, fr *com-* + *certare* to strive, fr *certus* decided, determined – more at CERTAIN]

²**concert** /'konsət/ *n* **1a** an instance of working together; an agreement **b** a concerted action ⟨*the sacrifice was hailed with a* ~ *of praise*⟩ **2** a public performance of music or dancing; *esp* a performance, usu by a group of musicians (e g a chorus, band, or orchestra), that is made up of several individual compositions [Fr, fr It *concerto*, fr *concertare*] – **in concert** together ⟨*he worked* in concert *with others*⟩

**concerted** /kən'suhtid/ *adj* **1a** planned or done together ⟨*a* ~ *effort*⟩ **b** performed in unison ⟨~ *artillery fire*⟩ **2** arranged in parts for several voices or instruments – **concertedly** *adv*, **concertedness** *n*

**concertgoer** /'konsət,goh·ə/ *n* one who frequently attends concerts – **concertgoing** *n*

**concert grand** /'konsət/ *n* a grand piano of the largest size, used esp in concerts

¹**concertina** /,konsə'teenə/ *n* a small hexagonal musical instrument of the accordion family [²*concert* + *-ina*]

²**concertina** *vi* **concertinaed** /-nəd/, **concertinaing** /-nə·ing/ to become compressed in the manner of a concertina being closed, esp in a crash

**concertino** /,konchə'teenoh/ *n, pl* **concertinos** **1** the solo instruments in a CONCERTO GROSSO **2** a short concerto [It, dim. of *concerto*]

**concertmaster** /'konsət,mahstə/ *n, chiefly NAm* LEADER 2d(2) [Ger *konzertmeister*, fr *konzert* concert + *meister* master]

**concertmeister** /'konsət,miestə/ *n* a concertmaster

**concerto** /kən'cheatoh, -'chuh-/ *n, pl* **concertos, concerti** /-ti/ a musical piece for one or more soloists and orchestra, usu with three contrasting sections (MOVEMENTS) [It, fr *concerto* concert]

**concerto grosso** /'grosoh/ *n, pl* **concerti grossi** /'grossi/ *also* **concerto grossos** a musical piece for a small group of solo instruments and full orchestra, typically written in a highly ornate (BAROQUE) style [It, lit., big concerto]

**concert pitch** /'konsət/ *n* **1** a musical tuning standard of usu 440 hertz for A above MIDDLE C **2** a high state of fitness, tension, or readiness

**concession** /kən'sesh(ə)n/ *n* **1a** conceding **2** something conceded: **2a** an acknowledgment, admission **b** a grant of land, property, or the right to undertake and profit by a specified activity made, esp by a government, in return for services or a particular use **c** *chiefly NAm* a lease of premises for a particular purpose; *also* the premises leased or the activities carried on **3** a reduction of demands or standards made, esp to accommodate shortcomings [Fr or L; Fr, fr L *concession-, concessio*, fr *concessus*, pp of *concedere* to concede] – **concessional** *adj*, **concessionally** *adv*, **concessionary** *adj*

**concessionaire** /kən,seshə'neə/ *n* the owner, operator, or beneficiary of a concession [Fr *concessionnaire*, fr *concession*]

**concessive** /kən'sesiv/ *adj* **1** making for or being a concession **2** denoting the yielding or admitting of a point ⟨*a* ~ *clause beginning with* "*although*"⟩ – **concessively** *adv*

**conch** /konch, kongk/ *n, pl* **conches** /'konchiz/ *also* **conchs** **1** any of various large spiral-shelled marine INVERTEBRATE animals (class Gastropoda of the phylum Mollusca) (e g of the genera *Strombus* and *Cassis*) that are related to snails and limpets; *also* its shell **2** a semicircular niche with a domed roof, esp in a church [L *concha* mussel, mussel shell, fr Gk *konchē*; (2) It *conca* semidome, apse, fr LL *concha*, fr L, shell]

**conch-** /kongk-/, **concho-** *comb form* shell ⟨*concho*logy⟩ ⟨*conchi*olin⟩ [Gk *konch-, koncho-*, fr *konchē*]

**concha** /'kongkə/ *n, pl* **conchae** /-ki/ something shaped like a shell; *esp* the largest and deepest cavity of the external ear [L, shell] – **conchal** *adj*

**conchiolin** /kong'kieəlin/ *n* a protein that forms the basis of shells of snails, mussels, and other MOLLUSCS [*conch-* + *-i-* + *-ol* + *-in*]

**conchoidal** /kong'koydl/ *adj, esp of a crystal or mineral fracture* shaped like the smooth curved inner surface of a mussel or oyster shell [Gk *konchoeidēs* like a mussel, fr *konchē*] – **conchoidally** *adv*

**conchology** /kong'koləji/ *n* a branch of zoology that deals with shells – **conchologist** *n*

**conchy, conchie** /'konchi/ *n, chiefly Br derog* CONSCIENTIOUS OBJECTOR (to war) [by shortening & alter.]

**concierge** /,konsi'eəzh/ *n* somebody who is employed as doorkeeper, landlord's representative, or caretaker, esp in France [Fr, deriv of L *conservus* fellow slave, fr *com-* + *servus* slave]

**conciliar** /kən'sili·ə/ *adj* of or issued by a council [L *concilium* council] – **conciliarly** *adv*

**conciliate** /kən'sili·ayt/ *vt* **1** to reconcile **2** to appease [L *conciliatus*, pp of *conciliare* to assemble, unite, win over, fr *concilium* assembly, council – more at COUNCIL] – **conciliative** *adj*, **conciliator** *n*, **conciliatory** *adj*, **conciliation** *n*

**concinnity** /kən'sinəti/ *n, formal* neatness and elegance, esp of literary style [L *concinnitas*, fr *concinnus* skilfully put together]

**concise** /kən'sies/ *adj* marked by brevity of expression or statement; free from all elaboration and superfluous detail [L *concisus*, fr pp of *concidere* to cut up, fr *com-* + *caedere* to cut, strike; akin to MHG *heie* mallet, Arm *xait'* to prick] – **concisely** *adv*, **conciseness** *n*

*synonyms* Concise, terse, laconic, pithy, succinct, summary, compendious, and epigrammatic all suggest conveying much in a few words. Concise implies that something is compact because all unnecessary details have been omitted ⟨*a* concise *report*⟩. Terse adds to this pointedness and cogency ⟨terse *headlines*⟩. What is laconic may be brief to the point of incivility or obscurity ⟨"*Maybe*" *was his* laconic *reply*⟩. Pithy suggests something full of meaning and substance, but expressed briefly and forcefully ⟨*a few* pithy *remarks about the economy*⟩. What is succinct is clear, compressed, and without elaboration, while summary conveys rather the main points of something ⟨succinct *directions*⟩ ⟨*a* summary *account of progress so far*⟩. Compendious suggests the condensation of much material into a small space, as in a *compendium*. What is epigrammatic is pointed, well-turned, and witty, like an *epigram*. *antonyms* diffuse, verbose, prolix, wordy Compare ²CONTRACT, ABRIDGMENT

**concision** /kən'sizh(ə)n/ *n* **1** conciseness ⟨*the commentary is exemplary in its* ~ *and lucidity*⟩ **2** *archaic* a cutting up or off [ME, fr L *concision-, concisio*, fr *concisus*, pp]

**conclave** /'kongklayv, 'kon-/ *n* a private meeting or secret assembly; *esp* the assembly of Roman Catholic cardinals having no outside contact while choosing a pope [ME, fr MF or ML; MF, fr ML, fr L, room that can be locked up, fr *com-* + *clavis* key – more at CLAVICLE]

**conclude** /kən'kloohd/ *vt* **1** to bring to an end, esp in a particular way or with a particular action ⟨~ *a meeting with a prayer*⟩ **2a** to reach as a logically necessary end by reasoning; infer on the basis of evidence ⟨~d *that the argument was sound*⟩ **b** to make a decision about; decide ⟨~d *he would wait a little longer*⟩ **c** to come to an agreement on; effect ⟨~ *a sale*⟩ **3** to bring about as a result; complete ~ *vi* **1** END 1 **2a** to form a final judgment **b** to reach a decision or agreement *synonyms* see ¹CLOSE [ME *concluden*, fr L *concludere* to shut up, end, infer, fr *com-* + *claudere* to shut – more at CLOSE] – **concluder** *n*

**conclusion** /kən'kloohzh(ə)n/ *n* **1a** a reasoned judgment; an inference **b** the necessary consequence of two or more propositions taken as true; *esp* the inferred proposition of a SYLLOGISM (specific type of reasoned argument) **2** the last part of something: e g **2a** a result, outcome **b** a final summing up (e g of an essay) **3** an act or instance of concluding [ME, fr MF, fr L *conclusion-, conclusio*, fr *conclusus*, pp of *concludere*]

**conclusive** /kən'kloohsiv, -ziv/ *adj* **1** of a conclusion **2** putting an end to debate or question, esp by reason of irrefutability *synonyms* see VALID *antonym* inconclusive – **conclusively** *adv*, **conclusiveness** *n*

**concoct** /kən'kokt/ *vt* **1** to prepare (a meal, story, etc) by combining diverse ingredients **2** to devise, fabricate [L *con-*

*coctus*, pp of *concoquere* to cook together, fr *com-* + *coquere* to cook] – **concocter** *n*, **concoction** *n*, **concoctive** *adj*

**¹concomitant** /kon'komit(ə)nt, kən-/ *adj, formal* accompanying, esp in a subordinate or incidental way [L *concomitant-*, *concomitans*, prp of *concomitari* to accompany, fr *com-* + *comitari* to accompany, fr *comit-*, *comes* companion – more at COUNT] – **concomitance** *n*, **concomitantly** *adv*

**²concomitant** *n, formal* something that accompanies, happens with, or goes with something else; an accompaniment

**concord** /'kongkawd, 'kon-/ *n* **1a** a state of agreement; harmony **b** a harmonious combination of simultaneously heard notes **2** a treaty, covenant **3** grammatical agreement – see "Ten Vexed Points" [ME, fr OF *concorde*, fr L *concordia*, fr *concord-*, *concors* agreeing, fr *com-* + *cord-*, *cor* heart – more at HEART]

**concordance** /kəng'kawd(ə)ns, kən-/ *n* **1** an alphabetical index of the principal words in a book or in the works of an author, with their immediate contexts **2** *formal* agreement [ME, fr MF, fr ML *concordantia*, fr L *concordans*]

**concordant** /kəng'kawd(ə)nt, kən-/ *adj* being in agreement or of the some regular pattern [ME, fr MF, fr L *concordant-*, *concordans*, prp of *concordare* to agree, fr *concord-*, *concors*] – **concordantly** *adv*

**concordat** /kon'kawdat, kən-/ *n* a compact, covenant; *specif* an agreement between a pope and a sovereign or government [Fr, fr ML *concordatum*, fr L, neut of *concordatus*, pp of *concordare*]

**concours d'elegance** /,kongkaw daylay'gonhs/ *n* a show or contest of vehicles and accessories in which the entries are judged chiefly on excellence of appearance [Fr, lit., competition of elegance]

**concourse** /'kongkaws, 'kon-/ *n* **1** a coming, gathering, or happening together ⟨*a large* ~ *of people*⟩ **2** a meeting produced by voluntary or spontaneous coming together **3a** an open space where roads or paths meet **b** an open space or main hall (e g in a station or shopping precinct) [ME, fr MF & L; MF *concours*, fr L *concursus*, pp of *concurrere* to run together – more at CONCUR]

**concrescence** /kəng'kres(ə)ns, kən-/ *n* **1** increase by the addition of particles **2** a growing together; a coalescence; *esp* the growing together of parts or organs (e g of an embryo) [L *concrescentia*, fr *concrescent-*, *concrescens*, prp of *concrescere*] – **concrescent** *adj*

**¹concrete** /'kongkreet, 'kon-/ *adj* **1** formed by coalition of particles into one solid mass **2** *of a noun* naming a thing rather than a quality, state, or action; not abstract ⟨*the word* poem *is* ~, poetry *is abstract*⟩ **3a** characterized by or belonging to immediate experience of actual things or events **b** specific, particular **c** real, tangible ⟨~ *proposals*⟩ **4** (made) of concrete [ME, fr L *concretus*, fr pp of *concrescere* to grow together, fr *com-* + *crescere* to grow – more at CRESCENT] – **concretely** *adv*, **concreteness** *n*

**²concrete** *n* **1** a mass formed by concretion or coalescence of separate particles of matter in one body **2** a hard strong building material made by mixing a cementing material (e g PORTLAND CEMENT) and a mineral aggregate (e g sand and gravel) with sufficient water to cause the cement to set and bind the entire mass

**³concrete** /kəng'kreet, kən-; *sense 2 usu* 'kongkreet, 'kon-/ *vt* **1** to form into a solid mass; solidify **2** to cover with, form of, or set in concrete ~ *vi* to become concreted

**concrete jungle** *n* a built-up urban area viewed as a hostile impersonal environment

**concrete music** /'kongkreet, 'kon-/ *n* MUSIQUE CONCRÈTE (modified recorded natural sounds)

**concrete poetry** *n* poetry whose effect depends partly on the way in which the words are printed and arranged

**concretion** /kəng'kreesh(ə)n, kən-/ *n* **1** concreting or being concreted **2** something concreted: e g **2a** a hard or solid mass of foreign material formed in a living body, organ, or blood vessel **b** a mass of mineral matter found generally in rock of a composition different from its own and produced by deposition from solution in the rock – **concretionary** *adj*

**concretism** /'kongkree,tiz(ə)m/ *n* representation of abstract things as concrete; *esp* the theory or practice of emphasizing graphic rather than linguistic effects in poetry – **concretist** *n*

**concret·ize, -ise** /'kongkree,tiez, 'kon-/ *vb* to make or become concrete, specific, or definite ⟨*tried to* ~ *his ideas*⟩ – **concretization** *n*

**concubinage** /'kongkyoobinij, kən'kyooh-/ *n* **1** the living together of people not legally married **2** being or having a concubine

**concubine** /'kongkyoobien, 'kon-/ *n* **1** a woman who lives with a man in addition to his lawful wife or wives in a society allowing a person to have many wives **2** a woman who lives with a man without being his wife; *broadly* MISTRESS **4** [ME, fr OF, fr L *concubina*, fr *com-* + *cubare* to lie – more at HIP]

**concupiscence** /kəng'kyoohpis(ə)ns, kən-/ *n* strong desire; *esp* lust [ME, fr MF, fr LL *concupiscentia*, fr L *concupiscent-*, *concupiscens*, prp of *concupiscere* to desire ardently, fr *com-* + *cupere* to desire – more at COVET] – **concupiscent** *adj*

**concupiscible** /kəng'kyoohpisəbl/ *adj* motivated by lust [ME, fr MF or LL; MF *concupiscibilis*, fr L *concupiscere*]

**concur** /kən'kuh/ *vi* **-rr-** **1** to happen together; coincide **2** to act together to a common end or single effect **3** to express agreement ⟨~ *with an opinion*⟩ **4** *obs* to come together; meet *synonyms* see ¹ASSENT [ME *concurren*, fr L *concurrere*, fr *com-* + *currere* to run]

**concurrence** /kən'kurəns/ *n* **1a** agreement or union in action; cooperation **b(1)** agreement in opinion or design **b(2)** consent **2** a coming together; conjunction

**concurrent** /kən'kurənt/ *adj* **1a** convergent; *specif* meeting or intersecting in a point **b** running parallel **2** operating or occurring at the same time or place **3** acting in conjunction; marked by agreement, harmony, etc **4** exercised over the same matter or area by two different authorities ⟨~ *jurisdiction*⟩ [ME, fr MF & L; MF, fr L *concurrent-*, *concurrens*, prp of *concurrere*] – **concurrent** *n*, **concurrently** *adv*

**concuss** /kən'kus/ *vt* to affect with concussion [L *concussus*, pp]

**concussion** /kən'kush(ə)n/ *n* **1** agitation, shaking **2a** a hard blow or collision **b** a stunning, damaging, or shattering effect from a hard blow; *esp* a jarring injury of the brain often resulting in loss of consciousness [MF or L; MF, fr L *concussion-*, *concussio*, fr *concussus*, pp of *concutere* to shake violently, fr *com-* + *quatere* to shake] – **concussive** *adj*, **concussively** *adv*

**condemn** /kən'dem/ *vt* **1** to declare to be utterly reprehensible, wrong, or evil, usu after considering evidence **2a** to prescribe punishment for (a convicted person); *specif* to sentence to death **b** to sentence, doom **c** to force (someone) into a usu unhappy state of affairs ⟨*the broken leg* ~ed *him to a wheelchair*⟩ **3** to declare unfit for use or consumption **4** *law* to declare to be taken for public use under the right of EMINENT DOMAIN [ME *condemnen*, fr OF *condemner*, fr L *condemnare*, fr *com-* + *damnare* to condemn – more at DAMN] – **condemnable** *adj*, **condemnatory** *adj*, **condemner, condemnor** *n*

**condemnation** /,kondəm'naysh(ə)n, -dem-/ *n* **1** censure, blame **2** the act of judicially convicting **3** the state of being condemned **4** a reason for condemning ⟨*speak, or thy silence . . . is thy* ~ *and thy death* – Shak⟩

**condemned cell** /kən'demd/ *n* a prison cell for people condemned to death

**condensate** /kən'densayt/ *n* a product of condensation; *esp* a liquid obtained by condensation of a gas or vapour ⟨*steam* ~⟩

**condensation** /,kondən'saysh(ə)n, -den-/ *n* **1** the act or process of condensing: e g **1a** a chemical reaction involving union between molecules often with elimination of a simple molecule (e g water) to form a new, more complex chemical compound **b** a change to a denser form (e g from steam to water) **c** compression of a written or spoken work into more concise form **2** a being condensed **3** a product of condensing; *specif* an abridgment of a literary work – **condensational** *adj*

**condense** /kən'dens/ *vt* to make denser or more compact; *esp* to subject to condensation ~ *vi* to undergo condensation *synonyms* see ²CONTRACT *antonyms* enlarge, amplify (e g a speech) [ME *condensen*, fr MF *condenser*, fr L *condensare*, fr *com-* + *densare* to make dense, fr *densus* dense] – **condensable** *also* **condensible** *adj*

**condensed** /kən'denst/ *adj* reduced to a more compact form; *specif* taking up less space than the normal printer's type

**condensed milk** *n* milk thickened by evaporation and sweetened

**condenser** /kən'densə/ *n* **1** one who or that which condenses: e g **1a** a lens or mirror used to concentrate light on an object **b** an apparatus for condensing gas or vapour **2** CAPACITOR (device for storing electric charge) – now used chiefly in the motor trade

**condescend** /,kondi'send/ *vi* **1** to waive the privileges of rank ⟨~ed *to eat with subordinates*⟩; *broadly* to descend to less formal or dignified action or speech **2** to adopt a patronizing attitude [ME *condescenden*, fr MF *condescendre*, fr LL *condescendere*, fr L *com-* + *descendere* to descend]

**condescending** /ˌkondiˈsending/ *adj* showing or characterized by condescension; patronizing – **condescendingly** *adv*

**condescension** /ˌkondiˈsensh(ə)n/ *n* **1** voluntary descent from one's rank or dignity in relations with an inferior **2** a patronizing attitude [LL *condescension-*, *condescensio*, fr *condescensus*, pp of *condescendere*]

**condign** /kənˈdien/ *adj, formal* deserved, appropriate ⟨~ *punishment*⟩ [ME *condigne*, fr MF, fr L *condignus* very worthy, fr *com-* + *dignus* worthy – more at DECENT] – **condignly** *adv*

**condiment** /ˈkondimənt/ *n* something used to enhance the flavour of food; *esp* seasoning [ME, fr MF, fr L *condimentum*, fr *condire* to pickle, fr *condere* to build, store up, fr *com-* + *-dere* to put – more at DO] – **condimental** *adj*

**¹condition** /kənˈdish(ə)n/ *n* **1a** something upon which the fulfilment of an agreement depends; a stipulation **b** a provision making the effect of a contract, will, etc dependent on the occurrence of a particular event; *also* that event itself **c** a fundamental term of a contract the breaking of which entitles the wronged party to cancel the contract **2** something essential to the appearance or occurrence of something else; a prerequisite: e g **2a** an environmental requirement ⟨*available oxygen is an essential ~ for animal life*⟩ **b** the subordinate clause of a conditional sentence; PROTASIS **3a** a restricting or modifying factor; a qualification **b** a favourable or unfavourable state of something ⟨*delayed by the ~ of the road*⟩ **4a** a state of being **b** social status; rank **c** a usu defective state of health or appearance ⟨*a serious heart ~*⟩ **d** a state of physical fitness or readiness for use ⟨*the car was in good ~*⟩ ⟨*exercising to get into ~*⟩ **e** *pl* attendant circumstances ⟨*under present ~*s⟩ **5a** *pl, archaic* manners, ways **b** *obs* temper of mind **synonyms** see ¹STATE [ME *condicion*, fr MF, fr L *condicion-*, *condicio* terms of agreement, condition, fr *condicere* to agree, fr *com-* + *dicere* to say, determine – more at DICTION]

**²condition** *vi, archaic* to make stipulations ~ *vt* **1** to agree by stipulating **2** to make conditional **3** to put into a proper or desired state for work or use ⟨*a shampoo that ~s the hair*⟩ **4** to give a certain condition to **5a** to adapt, modify, or mould so as to conform to a surrounding culture **b** to make (a stimulus) become associated with another stimulus, act, or response, or to modify so that an act or response previously associated with one stimulus becomes associated with another – **conditionable** *adj*, **conditioner** *n*

**conditional** /kənˈdish(ə)nl/ *adj* **1** subject to, implying, or dependent upon a condition ⟨*a ~ promise*⟩ **2** expressing, containing, or implying a supposition ⟨*the ~ clause* if he speaks⟩ **3a** true only for certain values of the variables or symbols involved ⟨*~ equations*⟩ **b** stating the case when one or more RANDOM VARIABLES are fixed or one or more events are known ⟨*~ frequency distribution*⟩ **4** CONDITIONED 3 ⟨*~ reflex*⟩ ⟨*~ response*⟩ – **conditional** *n*, **conditionality** *n*, **conditionally** *adv*

**conditional discharge** *n* a penalty involving merely compliance with some condition (e g to be of good behaviour) imposed by a court for a minor or technical offence – compare ABSOLUTE DISCHARGE

**conditioned** /kənˈdish(ə)nd/ *adj* **1** CONDITIONAL 1 **2** brought or put into a specified state determined or established by conditioning

**condole** /kənˈdohl/ *vi* to express sympathetic sorrow – usu + *with* ⟨*we ~ with you in your misfortune*⟩ [LL *condolēre*, fr L *com-* + *dolēre* to feel pain; akin to Gk *daidalos* ingeniously formed] – **condolatory** *adj*

**condolence** /kənˈdohləns/ *n* (an expression of) sympathy with another in sorrow

**condom** /ˈkondəm/ *n* a sheath, usu of rubber, worn over the penis (e g to prevent conception or venereal infection) during sexual intercourse [origin unknown]

**condominium** /ˌkondəˈminyəm, -niˈəm/ *n, pl* **condominiums** **1a** joint dominion or sovereignty **b** a government or territory operating under joint rule **2** *NAm* (individual ownership of) a unit in a multi-unit structure (e g a block of flats); *also* a flat [NL, fr L *com-* + *dominium* domain] – **condominial** *adj*

**condone** /kənˈdohn/ *vt* to pardon or overlook voluntarily; tacitly accept; *esp* to treat as if harmless or of no importance ⟨*~ corruption in politics*⟩ [L *condonare* to forgive, fr *com-* + *donare* to give – more at DONATE] – **condonable** *adj*, **condonation** *n*, **condoner** *n*

**condor** /ˈkondaw/ *n* either of two vultures that have a bare

head and neck and are the largest flying land birds: **a** a bird (*Vultur gryphus*) with a pink head and neck that nests in the high Andes **b** a nearly extinct bird (*Gymnogyps californianus*) with a yellowish head and red neck – called also CALIFORNIA CONDOR [Sp *cóndor*, fr Quechua *kúntur*]

**condottiere** /ˌkondoˈtyeəri/ *n, pl* **condottieri** /~/ **1** a leader of a band of mercenaries common esp in Italy between the 14th and 16th centuries **2** a member of the band of a condottiere; *broadly* a mercenary soldier [It, fr *condotta* act of hiring, troop of mercenaries, deriv of L *conductus*, pp of *conducere*]

**conduce** /kənˈdyoohs/ *vi, formal* to lead or tend *to* a particular and usu desirable result; to contribute [ME *conducen* to conduct, fr L *conducere* to conduct, bring together, hire, fr *com-* + *ducere* to lead – more at TOW]

**conducive** /kənˈdyoohsiv/ *adj* tending to promote or assist – **conduciveness** *n*

*usage* Things are **conducive** *to* results, not *of* them.

**¹conduct** /ˈkondukt/ *n* **1** the act, manner, or process of carrying on; management **2** a mode or standard of personal behaviour, esp as based on moral principles **synonyms** see BEHAVIOUR [alter. of ME *conduit*, fr OF, fr act of leading, escort, fr ML *conductus*, fr L *conductus*, pp of *conducere*]

**²conduct** /kənˈdukt/ *vt* **1** to bring (as if) by leading; guide ⟨*~ tourists through a museum*⟩ **2** to carry on or out, usu from a position of command or control ⟨*~ a siege*⟩ ⟨*~ an experiment*⟩ **3a** to convey in a channel, pipe, etc **b** to act as a medium for transmitting (e g heat or light) **4** to act or behave (oneself) in a particular and esp in a controlled or directed manner **5** to direct the performance or execution of (e g a musical work or group of musicians) ~ *vi* **1** to act as leader or director, esp of an orchestra **2** to have the property of transmitting heat, sound, electricity, etc **synonyms** see ACCOMPANY – **conductibility** *n*, **conductible** *adj*

**conductance** /kənˈdukt(ə)ns/ *n* **1** conducting power **2a** the readiness with which a conductor transmits an electric current **b** a measure of conductance being equal to the reciprocal of the electrical resistance

**conductimetric** /ˌkonˌduktiˈmetrik/ *adj* **1** relating to the measurement of conductivity **2** being or relating to TITRATION (chemical process for determining the strength of a solution) based on determination of changes in the electrical conductivity of the solution

**conduction** /kənˈduksh(ə)n/ *n* **1** the act of conducting or conveying **2** transmission through or by means of a conductor; *also* conductivity **3** the transmission of an electrical impulse through living (nerve) tissue

**conductive** /kənˈduktiv/ *adj* having conductivity; relating to conduction (e g of electricity)

**conductivity** /ˌkondukˈtivəti/ *n* the quality or power of conducting or transmitting: e g **a** a measure of the ease with which something may transmit electric current; the reciprocal of electrical resistivity **b** the quality of living matter responsible for the transmission of and progressive reaction to stimuli

**conductometric** /ˌkonˌduktəˈmetrik/ *adj* conductimetric

**conductor** /kənˈduktə/ *n* one who or that which conducts: e g **a** a guide or leader **b** a collector of fares on a public conveyance, esp a bus **c** one who directs the performance of musicians, esp by motions of the hands or of a baton **d** a substance or body capable of transmitting electricity, heat or sound, etc **e** *chiefly NAm* the guard on a train – **conductorial** *adj*

**conductor rail** *n* a rail for conducting current to an electric locomotive

**conductress** /kənˈduktris/ *n* a female bus conductor

**conduit** /ˈkondit, ˈkondwit, ˈkondyoo·it/ *n* **1** a natural or artificial channel through which something (e g water, gas, or other fluid) is conveyed **2** a pipe, tube, or tile for protecting electric wires or cables **3** *archaic* a fountain [ME, fr MF, lit., act of leading]

**conduplicate** /konˈd(y)oohplikət/ *adj, of a leaf or a petal in a bud* folded lengthways [L *conduplicatus*, pp of *conduplicare* to double, fr *com-* + *duplic-*, *duplex* double – more at DUPLEX] – **conduplication** *n*

**condyle** /ˈkondil/ *n* a projection of a bone forming part of a joint [Fr & L; Fr, fr L *condylus* knuckle, fr Gk *kondylos*] – **condylar** *adj*, **condyloid** *adj*

**condyloma** /ˌkondiˈlohmə/ *n* a warty growth on the skin or MUCOUS MEMBRANE, usu near the anus and genitals [NL, fr Gk *kondylōma*, fr *kondylos*] – **condylomatous** *adj*

**¹cone** /kohn/ *n* **1a** a mass of overlapping woody scales that, esp in trees of the pine family, are arranged on an axis and bear seeds between them **b** any of several flower or fruit clusters (eg those of the hop) suggesting a cone in shape **2a(1)** a solid consisting of the surface bounded by a straight line (the GENERATRIX) moving round a curved closed plane base (eg a circle or ellipse) at one end and terminating at a fixed point (the VERTEX) at the other end **a(2) cone, right circular cone** such a solid whose base is a circle, and that has the VERTEX lying directly above the centre of the circle **b** either of two surfaces generated by a moving straight line passing through a fixed point at its centre and intersecting a fixed curve **3** something that resembles a cone in shape: eg **3a** any of the relatively short light receptors in the light-sensitive membrane (the RETINA) of the eye of VERTEBRATE animals that are sensitive to bright light and function in colour vision – compare ROD **b** any of numerous somewhat conical tropical INVERTEBRATE animals (family Conidae of the class Gastropoda) related to snails, whelks, and limpets **c** the tip of a volcano built up from ejected material (eg lava) **d** a crisp cone-shaped wafer for holding a portion of ice cream **e** a cone-shaped package of yarn [MF or L; MF, fr L *conus*, fr Gk *kōnos* – more at HONE]

²**cone** *vt* **1** to shape like (the slanting surface of) a cone **2** to mark off or close (eg a road) with cone-shaped bollards ⟨*one lane of the motorway was ~d off*⟩

**coney** /'kohni/ *n* **1** CONY (rabbit) **2** rabbit fur

**confab** /'konfab/ *vi or n* **-bb-** *informal* (to have) a chat or discussion [short for *confabulate, confabulation*]

**confabulate** /kən'fabyoolayt/ *vi, humorous* **1** to chat **2** to hold a discussion [L *confabulatus*, pp of *confabulari*, fr *com-* + *fabulari* to talk, fr *fabula* story – more at FABLE] – **confabulator** *n*, **confabulatory** *adj*, **confabulation** *n*

**confect** /kən'fekt/ *vt* **1** to put together from varied material ⟨*writers ~ing best sellers*⟩ **2a** to prepare **b** to preserve [L *confectus*, pp of *conficere* to prepare – more at COMFIT] – **confect** *n*

**confection** /kən'feksh(ə)n/ *n* **1** the act or process of confecting **2** something confected: eg **2a** a fancy or rich dish (eg a cream cake or preserve) or sweetmeat **b** a medicinal preparation made with sugar, syrup, or honey – **confectionary** *adj*

**confectioner** /kən'fekshənə/ *n* a manufacturer of or dealer in confectionery

**confectionery** /kən'fekshənri/ *n* **1** confections, sweets **2** the confectioner's art or business **3** a confectioner's shop

**confederacy** /kən'fed(ə)rəsi/ *n* **1** a league or compact for mutual support or common action; an alliance **2** an unlawful association; a conspiracy **3** the body formed by persons, states, nations, etc united by a league; *esp, cap* the 11 southern states withdrawing from the USA in 1860 and 1861 – **confederal** *adj*, **confederalist** *n*

¹**confederate** /kən'fed(ə)rət/ *adj* **1** united in a league; allied **2** *cap* of the Confederacy [ME *confederat*, fr LL *confoederatus*, pp of *confoederare* to unite by a league, fr L *com-* + *foeder-, foedus* compact – more at FEDERAL]

²**confederate** *n* **1** an ally, accomplice **2** *cap* a supporter or follower of the Confederacy

³**confederate** /kən'fedə,rayt/ *vt* to unite in a confederacy ~ *vi* to band together – **confederative** *adj*

**confederation** /kən,fedə'raysh(ə)n/ *n* **1** confederating or being confederated **2** an alliance, league

**confer** /kən'fuh/ *vb* **-rr-** *vt* to bestow (as if) from a position of superiority ~ *vi* to come together to compare views or take counsel; consult *synonyms* see ¹GIVE [L *conferre* to bring together, fr *com-* + *ferre* to carry – more at BEAR] – **conferable** *adj*, **conferral** *n*, **conferrer** *n*

**conferee** /,konfə'ree/ *n* **1** one conferred with **2** one on whom something (eg a degree) is conferred

**conference** /'konf(ə)rəns/ *n* **1a** a usu formal interchange of views; a consultation **b** a meeting of two or more people for the discussion of matters of common concern **2** a representative assembly or administrative organization of an association, religious denomination, etc **3** *formal* the act of bestowing or conferring – **conferential** *adj*

**confess** /kən'fes/ *vt* **1** to make known (eg something wrong or damaging to oneself); admit **2a** to make (one's sins) known to God or to a priest **b** *of a priest* to receive the confession of (a person) **3** to declare faith in or adherence to **4** *poetic* to give evidence of ~ *vi* **1a** to disclose one's faults; *specif* to make one's sins or the state of one's conscience known to God or to a priest **b** to hear a confession **2** to admit (*to*) *synonyms* see ACKNOWLEDGE [ME *confessen*, fr MF *confesser*, fr OF, fr

*confes* having confessed, fr L *confessus*, pp of *confitēri* to confess, fr *com-* + *fatēri* to confess; akin to L *fari* to speak – more at BAN] – **confessable** *adj*

**confessedly** /kən'fesidli/ *adv* by confession; admittedly

**confession** /kən'fesh(ə)n/ *n* **1** an act of confessing; *specif* a disclosure of one's sins (eg to God or a priest) **2** a statement of what is confessed: eg **2a** a written acknowledgment of guilt by a party accused of an offence **b** a formal statement of religious beliefs **3** *taking sing or pl vb* an organized religious body having a common creed – **confessional** *adj*, **confessionalism** *n*, **confessionalist** *n*, **confessionally** *adv*

**confessional** /kən'fesh(ə)nl/ *n* **1** a place where a priest hears confessions **2** *the* practice of confessing to a priest

**confessor** /kən'fesə/ *n* **1** one who or that which confesses **2** a person who gives heroic evidence of religious faith but does not suffer martyrdom **3a** a priest who hears confessions **b** a priest who is one's regular spiritual guide

**confetti** /kən'feti/ *n* small bits of brightly coloured paper meant to be thrown (eg at weddings) [It, pl of *confetto* sweetmeat, fr ML *confectum*, fr L, neut of *confectus*, pp of *conficere* to prepare; fr the throwing of small sweets, or paper or plaster imitations of them, during Italian carnivals]

**confidant,** *fem* **confidante** /'konfi,dant, ,- -'-/ *n* one to whom secrets are entrusted; *esp* an intimate △ confident [Fr *confident* (fem *confidente*), fr It *confidente*, fr *confidente* confident, trustworthy, fr L *confident-, confidens*]

**confide** /kən'fied/ *vi* **1** to have confidence or trust *in* **2** to show confidence by imparting secrets *to* ~ *vt* **1** to tell confidentially **2** to entrust [ME *confiden*, fr MF or L; MF *confider*, fr L *confidere*, fr *com-* + *fidere* to trust – more at BIDE] – **confider** *n*

**confidence** /'konfid(ə)ns/ *n* **1** faith, trust ⟨*their ~ in God's mercy*⟩ **2** a feeling or consciousness of one's powers being sufficient or of reliance on one's circumstances **3** the quality or state of being certain ⟨*they had every ~ of success*⟩ **4a** a relationship of trust or intimacy ⟨*took his friend into his ~*⟩ **b** reliance on another's discretion ⟨*their story was told in strictest ~*⟩ **c** legislative support ⟨*vote of ~*⟩ **5** something said or written in confidence; a secret

**confidence interval** *n* a set of values within which there is a specified probability (eg 95 per cent) of including the true value of a statistical mean, average, variance, etc

**confidence limits** *n pl* the end points of a CONFIDENCE INTERVAL

**confidence man, con man** *n* a person who performs a CONFIDENCE TRICK; a swindler

**confidence trick** *n* a swindle performed by a person who pretends to be something that he/she is not

**confident** /'konfid(ə)nt/ *adj* **1** characterized by assurance; *esp* self-reliant **2** full of conviction; certain **3** *obs* trustful, confiding *synonyms* see ¹SURE [L *confident-, confidens*, fr prp of *confidere*] – **confidently** *adv*

**confidential** /,konfi'densh(ə)l/ *adj* **1** private, secret **2** marked by intimacy or willingness to confide ⟨*a ~ tone*⟩ **3** entrusted with confidences ⟨*a ~ secretary*⟩ – **confidentially** *adv*, **confidentialness** *n*, **confidentiality** *n*

**confiding** /kən'fieding/ *adj* tending to confide; trustful – **confidingly** *adv*, **confidingness** *n*

**configuration** /kən,figoo'raysh(ə)n, -,figyoo-/ *n* **1a** (relative) arrangement of parts **b** something (eg a figure, contour, pattern, or apparatus) produced by such arrangement **c** the relative positions in space of the atoms of a chemical compound **2** a set of separate psychological features (eg aspects of personality) that function as a single unit; GESTALT [LL *configuration-, configuratio* similar formation, fr L *configuratus*, pp of *configurare* to form from or after, fr *com-* + *figurare* to form, fr *figura* figure] – **configurational** *adj*, **configurationally** *adv*, **configurative** *adj*

**confine** /kən'fien/ *vt* **1** to keep within limits; restrict **2a** to shut up; imprison **b** to keep indoors or in bed, esp just before childbirth – **confiner** *n*

**confined** /kən'fiend/ *adj* **1** kept within confines **2** restricted to quarters; *esp* undergoing childbirth

**confinement** /-mənt/ *n* confining or being confined, esp in childbirth

**confines** /'konfienz/ *n* **1** bounds, borders **2** outlying parts; limits [MF or L; MF *confines*, pl, fr L *confine* border, fr neut of *confinis* adjacent, fr *com-* + *finis* end]

**confirm** /kən'fuhm/ *vt* **1** to make firm or firmer; strengthen **2** to give approval to; ratify **3** to administer the rite of confirmation to **4** to make certain of; remove doubt about by authoritative act or indisputable fact [ME *confirmen*, fr OF *confirmer*, fr L *confirmare*, fr *com-* + *firmare* to make firm, fr *firmus* firm] – **confirmability** *n*, **confirmable** *adj*

**synonyms** Confirm, corroborate, substantiate, verify, validate, and authenticate can all mean "show something to be true, genuine, or valid". Confirm implies making certain by removing any doubt, either by an authoritative statement or because of indisputable facts. Corroborate suggests additional evidence which supports that already given ⟨*her story was corroborated by another witness*⟩. Substantiate implies producing enough real evidence to back up a claim or strengthen a theory ⟨*the discovery of flint tools in the cave substantiated his suggestion that prehistoric people had lived there*⟩. Verify distinctively implies a comparison between what is claimed and established fact ⟨*verified her claim to be under age by producing her birth certificate*⟩. Validate may either imply official action to confirm something formally or in law (such as a stamp or signature), or simply suggest something which supports a contention, by demonstration or valid reasoning. Authenticate concerns genuineness and validity, and proof of these by testimony from experts or the authority involved ⟨*authenticated antiques*⟩ ⟨*a cheque authenticated by the bank*⟩. **antonyms** deny, contradict

**confirmation** /ˌkɒnfəˈmeɪʃ(ə)n/ *n* **1a** an act or process of confirming **b(1)** a Christian rite supplementing baptism and conferring the gift of the Holy Spirit **b(2)** a ceremony confirming Jewish youths in their ancestral faith **2a** something that confirms; corroboration **b** the process of supporting a statement by evidence – **confirmational** *adj*, **confirmatory** *adj*

**confirmed** /kənˈfɜːmd/ *adj* **1a** made firm; strengthened **b** being so fixed in habit as to be unlikely to change ⟨*a ~ bachelor*⟩ **c** marked by long continuance and likely to persist ⟨*a ~ habit*⟩ **2** having received the rite of confirmation – **confirmedly** *adv*, **confirmedness** *n*

**confiscable** /kənˈfɪskəbl, kɒn-/ *adj* liable to confiscation
**confiscatable** /ˌkɒnfɪˈskeɪtəbl/ *adj* confiscable

¹**confiscate** /ˈkɒnfɪskeɪt/ *adj* **1** seized, appropriated **2** deprived of property by confiscation [L *confiscatus*, pp of *confiscare* to appropriate to the public treasury, fr *com-* + *fiscus* treasury – more at FISCAL]

²**confiscate** *vt* to seize (as if) by authority, esp as a punishment or for public use – **confiscator** *n*, **confiscatory** *adj*, **confiscation** *n*

**confiteor** /kɒnˈfɪtiaw/ *n* a standardized form of confession of sins used esp in the Roman Catholic Church [ME, fr L, I confess, fr *confitēri* to confess – more at CONFESS]

**conflagrant** /kənˈfleɪɡrənt/ *adj*, *formal* burning, blazing [L *conflagrant-*, *conflagrans*, prp of *conflagrare* to burn, fr *com-* + *flagrare* to burn – more at BLACK]

**conflagration** /ˌkɒnfləˈɡreɪʃ(ə)n/ *n* **1** a (large disastrous) fire **2** a violent conflict [L *conflagration-*, *conflagratio*, fr *conflagratus*, pp of *conflagrare*]

**conflate** /kənˈfleɪt/ *vt* **1** to bring together; combine **2** to combine (e g two readings of a text) into a whole [L *conflare* to blow together, fuse, fr *com-* + *flare* to blow – more at BLOW] – **conflation** *n*

¹**conflict** /ˈkɒnflɪkt/ *n* **1a** a sharp disagreement or clash (e g between divergent ideas, interests, or people) **b** (distress caused by) mental struggle resulting from incompatible or opposing impulses **2** a hostile encounter (e g a fight, battle, or war) **3** a collision [ME, fr L *conflictus* act of striking together, fr *conflictus* pp of *confligere* to strike together, fr *com-* + *fligere* to strike – more at PROFLIGATE]

²**conflict** /kənˈflɪkt/ *vi* to be in opposition (to another or each other); disagree – **confliction** *n*, **conflictive** *adj*

**conflicting** /kənˈflɪktɪŋ/ *adj* being in conflict, collision, or opposition; incompatible ⟨*~ reports*⟩ – **conflictingly** *adv*

**conflict of interest** *n* a conflict between the private interests and the official responsibilities of a person in a position of trust

**confluence** /ˈkɒnflʊəns/, **confluency** /-si/ *n* **1** a coming or flowing together; a meeting or gathering at one point **2a** the flowing together of two or more streams **b** the place of meeting of two streams **c** the combined stream formed by conjunction

¹**confluent** /ˈkɒnflʊənt/ *adj* **1** flowing or coming together; *also* run together **2** characterized by confluent pimples, abscesses, or other lesions ⟨*a ~ rash*⟩ [L *confluent-*, *confluens*, prp of *confluere* to flow together, fr *com-* + *fluere* to flow – more at FLUID]

²**confluent** *n* a confluent stream; *broadly* a tributary
**conflux** /ˈkɒnˌflʌks/ *n* a confluence [ML *confluxus*, fr L *confluxus*, pp of *confluere*]

**confocal** /ˌkɒnˈfəʊkl/ *adj* having the same FOCI ⟨*~ ellipses*⟩ ⟨*~ lenses*⟩ – **confocally** *adv*

¹**conform** /kənˈfɔːm/ *vt* to give the same shape, outline, or contour to; bring into harmony or accord ~ *vi* **1** to be similar or identical **2** to be obedient or compliant; *esp* to adapt oneself to prevailing standards or customs [ME *conformen*, fr MF *conformer*, fr L *conformare*, fr *com-* + *formare* to form, fr *forma* form] – **conformer** *n*, **conformism** *n*, **conformist** *n*, **conformance** *n*

**usage** Correctly, one **conforms** *to*, rather than *with*, laws and requirements. **synonyms** see AGREE **antonym** diverge

²**conform** *adj*, *archaic* conformable

**conformable** /kənˈfɔːməbl/ *adj* **1** corresponding in form or character; similar – usu + *to* **2** submissive, compliant **3** *of layers of rock or other geological strata* following in unbroken sequence – **conformably** *adv*

**conformal** /kənˈfɔːml, kɒn-/ *adj* **1** *maths* leaving relative sizes and angles unchanged after transformation **2** *of a map* representing small areas in their true shape [LL *conformalis* having the same shape, fr L *com-* + *formalis* formal, fr *forma*]

**conformation** /ˌkɒnfɔːˈmeɪʃ(ə)n/ *n* **1** the act of conforming or producing conformity; adaptation **2** formation by appropriate arrangement of parts or elements; an assembling into a whole ⟨*the gradual ~ of the embryo*⟩ **3a** correspondence, esp to a model or plan **b** structure **c** the proportionate shape or contour, esp of an animal **d** any of the spatial arrangements of a molecule that can be obtained by rotation of the atoms about a single bond – **conformational** *adj*

**conformity** /kənˈfɔːməti/ *n* **1** correspondence in form, manner, or character; agreement ⟨*behaved in ~ with his beliefs*⟩ **2** an act or instance of conforming **3** action in accordance with a specified standard or authority; obedience ⟨*~ to social custom*⟩

**confound** /kənˈfaʊnd/ *vt* **1a** to put to shame; discomfit ⟨*a performance that ~ed his critics*⟩ **b** to refute ⟨*sought to ~ his arguments*⟩ **2** to damn – used as a mild interjection of annoyance ⟨*~ him!*⟩ **3** to throw into confusion or perplexity **4a** to fail to discern differences between; confuse **b** to increase the confusion of ⟨*confusion worse ~ed* – John Milton⟩ **5** *archaic* to bring to ruin; destroy **synonyms** see ¹PUZZLE [ME *confounden* to overthrow, ruin, fr OF *confondre*, fr L *confundere* to pour together, confuse, fr *com-* + *fundere* to pour – more at FOUND] – **confounder** *n*

**confounded** /kənˈfaʊndɪd/ *adj* **1** confused, perplexed **2** damned ⟨*that ~ dog*⟩ – **confoundedly** *adv*

**confraternity** /ˌkɒnfrəˈtɜːnəti/ *n* a society devoted to a religious or charitable cause [ME *confraternite*, fr MF *confraternité*, fr ML *confraternitat-*, *confraternitas*, fr *confrater* fellow, brother, fr L *com-* + *frater* brother – more at BROTHER]

**confrère** /ˈkɒnˌfreə/ *n* a colleague or comrade, esp in a profession [ME, fr MF, trans of ML *confrater*]

**confront** /kənˈfrʌnt/ *vt* **1** to face, esp in challenge; oppose ⟨*those who wish society to change must ~ it*⟩ **2a** to cause to meet; bring face to face with ⟨*~ a reader with statistics*⟩ **b** to be faced with; encounter ⟨*the problems that one ~s are enormous*⟩ [MF *confronter* to border on, confront, fr ML *confrontare* to bound, fr L *com-* + *front-*, *frons* forehead, front – more at BRINK] – **confrontal** *n*, **confronter** *n*

**confrontation** /ˌkɒnfrənˈteɪʃ(ə)n/ *n* a confronting or being confronted: e g **a** a face-to-face meeting **b** (an instance of) the clashing of forces or ideas; a conflict ⟨*'sit-ins'*, ~s *and riot* – Power & Authority in British Universities⟩ – **confrontational** *adj*, **confrontationism** *n*, **confrontationist** *n*

**Confucian** /kənˈfjuːʃ(ə)n/ *adj* of the Chinese philosopher Confucius, his teachings concerning respect for fellow humans, or his followers [*Confucius* †479 BC Chin philosopher] – **Confucian** *n*, **Confucianism** *n*

**confuse** /kənˈfjuːz/ *vt* **1a** to make embarrassed; abash **b** to disturb or muddle in mind or purpose **2a** to make indistinct; blur ⟨*stop confusing the issue*⟩ **b** to mix indiscriminately; jumble **c** to fail to see the difference from an often similar or related thing ⟨*~ Socialism with Communism*⟩ **3** *archaic* to bring to ruin [back-formation fr ME *confused* perplexed, fr MF *confus*, fr L *confusus*, pp of *confundere*] – **confusing** *adj*, **confusingly** *adv*

**confused** /kənˈfjuːzd/ *adj* **1** perplexed, disconcerted **2** indistinguishable, blurred **3** disordered, muddled – **confusedly** *adv*, **confusedness** *n*

**confusion** /kənˈfjuːʒ(ə)n/ *n* **1** an instance of confusing or being confused **2** (a) disorder, muddle – **confusional** *adj*

**confutation** /ˌkonfyoo'taysh(ə)n/ *n* **1** the act or process of confuting; a refutation **2** something (eg an argument or statement) that confutes – **confutative** *adj*

**confute** /kən'fyooht/ *vt* to overwhelm in argument; refute conclusively [L *confutare*, fr *com-* + *-futare* to beat – more at BEAT] – **confuter** *n*

**conga** /'kong-gə/ *n* **1** a Cuban dance of African origin involving three steps followed by a kick and performed by a group, usu in single file – compare SAMBA, RUMBA, MAMBO **2** a tall narrow bass drum beaten with the hands [AmerSp, fr Sp, fem of *congo* of the Congo, fr *Congo*, region in Africa]

**congé** /'konzhay/ *n* **1a** a formal permission to depart **b** dismissal **2** a ceremonious bow **3** a farewell **4** CORONA 1 (decorative architectural moulding) [Fr, fr L *commeatus* going back and forth, leave, fr *commeatus*, pp of *commeare* to go back and forth, fr *com-* + *meare* to go – more at PERMEATE]

**congeal** /kən'jeel/ *vt* **1** to bring from a fluid to a solid state (as if) by cold **2** to make (eg a liquid) thick or curdled; coagulate **3** to make rigid, inflexible, or immobile ~ *vi* to become congealed [ME *congelen*, fr MF *congeler*, fr L *congelare*, fr *com-* + *gelare* to freeze – more at COLD] – **congealment** *n*

**congelation** /ˌkonji'laysh(ə)n/ *n* the process or result of congealing

**congener** /kən'jeenə/ *n* **1** a member of the same genus as another plant or animal **2** a person or thing resembling another in nature or action **3** a chemical compound that is a secondary product present in an alcoholic beverage and significant in determining its flavour, colour, etc and in causing hangovers [L, of the same kind, fr *com-* + *gener-*, *genus* kind – more at KIN] – **congeneric** *adj*, **congenerous** *adj*

**congenial** /kən'jeenyəl, -ni·əl/ *adj* **1** having the same nature, disposition, or tastes **2a** existing or associated together harmoniously – often + *with* **b** pleasant; *esp* agreeably suited to one's nature, tastes, or outlook – often + *to* △ genial [*com-* + *genius*] – **congenially** *adv*, **congeniality** *n*

**congenital** /kən'jenit/ *adj* **1a** existing at or dating from birth ⟨~ *idiocy*⟩ **b** constituting an essential characteristic; inherent ⟨~ *fear of snakes*⟩ **c** acquired during development in the womb and not through heredity ⟨~ *drug addiction*⟩ **2** being such by nature ⟨*a* ~ *liar*⟩ – **congenitally** *adv* [L *congenitus*, fr *com-* + *genitus* pp of *gignere* to beget – more at KIN]

*synonyms* A **congenital** condition dates from one's birth ⟨**congenital** *brain damage*⟩; an inherited one is **genetic** or **genic**. **Inborn** and **innate** are imprecise nonscientific words which do not make this distinction ⟨*his* **innate** *shyness*⟩. **Inherent** is further removed from the idea of birth, and used chiefly for abstractions ⟨*the* **inherent** *weakness in your project*⟩.

**conger** /'kong-gə/, **conger eel** *n* any of various related eels (family Congridae); *esp* a large European edible one (*Conger conger*) [ME *congre*, fr OF, fr L *congr-*, *conger*, fr Gk *gongros;* akin to ON *kökkr* ball, L *gingiva* gum]

**congeries** /'konjəreez; *also* kən'jiəreez/ *n taking sing or pl vb*, *pl* **congeries** a (disordered) collection or aggregation [L, fr *congerere*]

**congest** /kən'jest/ *vt* **1** to cause an excessive fullness of the blood vessels of (eg an organ) **2** to clog ⟨*traffic* ~ed *the highways*⟩ **3** to concentrate in a small or narrow space ~ *vi* to become congested [L *congestus*, pp of *congerere* to bring together, fr *com-* + *gerere* to bear – more at CAST] – **congestion** *n*, **congestive** *adj*

**conglobate** /'kong-glohbayt, -'glo-/ *vt, formal* to form into a round compact mass [L *conglobatus*, pp of *conglobare*, fr *com-* + *globus* globe] – **conglobate** *adj*, **conglobation** *n*

¹**conglomerate** /kən'glomərət/ *adj* made up of parts from various sources or of various kinds ⟨*an ethnically* ~ *culture*⟩ [L *conglomeratus*, pp of *conglomerare* to roll together, fr *com-* + *glomerare* to wind into a ball, fr *glomer-*, *glomus* ball]

²**conglomerate** /kən'glomərayt/ *vt* to accumulate ~ *vi* to gather into a mass or coherent whole ⟨*numbers of dull people* ~d *round her* – Virginia Woolf⟩ – **conglomerative** *adj*, **conglomerator** *n*

³**conglomerate** /kən'glomərət/ *n* **1** a composite mass or mixture; *specif* (a) rock composed of rounded fragments varying from small pebbles to large boulders in a cement (eg of hardened clay) **2** a widely diversified business company – **conglomeratic** *adj*

**conglomeration** /kən,glomə'raysh(ə)n/ *n* **1** a conglomerating or being conglomerated **2** something conglomerated

**conglutinate** /kən'gloohtinayt/ *vb, formal vt* to unite (as if) by a sticky glue-like substance ~ *vi* to become conglutinated

⟨*blood platelets* ~ *in blood clotting*⟩ [L *conglutinatus*, pp of *conglutinare* to glue together, fr *com-* + *glutin-*, *gluten* glue] – **conglutination** *n*

**Congo dye** /'kong-goh/ *n* any of various AZO DYES that are derived from the chemical compound BENZIDINE [*Congo*, territory in Africa]

**Congo red** /'kong-goh/ *n* an AZO DYE, $C_{32}H_{22}N_6Na_2O_6S_2$, that is red in alkaline and blue in acid solution and that is used esp as an INDICATOR and as a stain for biological specimens

**congrats** /kən'grats/ *n pl*, *informal* congratulations

**congratulate** /kən'gratyoolayt, -choo-/ *vt* **1** to express pleasure to (a person) on account of success or good fortune **2** *archaic* to express pleasure at (an event) **3** *obs* to salute, greet [L *congratulatus*, pp of *congratulari* to wish joy, fr *com-* + *gratulari* to wish joy, fr *gratus* pleasing – more at GRACE] – **congratulator** *n*, **congratulatory** *adj*

*usage* The pronunciation of **congratulatory** as /kən'gratyoohlət(ə)ri/ rather than /-'layt(ə)ri/ is recommended for BBC broadcasters.

**congratulation** /kən,gratyoo'laysh(ə)n, -choo-/ *n* **1** the act of congratulating **2 congratulations** *pl*, **congratulation** a congratulatory expression

**congregant** /'kong-grigənt/ *n* a member of a congregation

**congregate** /'kong-gri,gayt/ *vb* to (cause to) gather together in a crowd, group, assembly, etc *synonyms* see ¹GATHER *antonym* scatter [ME *congregaten*, fr L *congregatus*, pp of *congregare*, fr *com-* + *greg-*, *grex* flock – more at GREGARIOUS] – **congregator** *n*

**congregation** /ˌkong-gri'gaysh(ə)n/ *n* **1a** an assembly of people; *esp* such an assembly for religious worship **b** a religious community; *esp* an organized body of believers in a particular locality **2** a congregating or being congregated **3** *taking sing or pl vb* a formal meeting of the resident senior members of an English university; *also* those eligible to participate therein – compare CONVOCATION 1b

**congregational** /ˌkong-gri'gaysh(ə)nl/ *adj* **1** of a congregation **2** *cap* of a body of Protestant churches believing in the importance and independence of the local congregation **3** of church government by the assembly of the local congregation – **congregationalism** *n, often cap*, **congregationalist** *n or adj, often cap*

**congress** /'kong-gres, -gris/ *n* **1** SEXUAL INTERCOURSE **2** *taking sing or pl vb* **2a** a formal meeting of delegates for discussion and usu action on some question **b** the supreme law-making body of a nation; *esp*, *cap* that of the USA **c** an association, usu made up of delegates from constituent organizations **d** a single meeting or session of a group **3** *formal* the act or action of coming together and meeting [L *congressus* meeting, fr *congressus*, pp of *congredi* to come together, fr *com-* + *gradi* to go – more at GRADE] – **congressional** *adj*, **congressionally** *adv*

**congressional district** /kən'gresh(ə)nl/ *n* a territorial division of a state from which a member of the US HOUSE OF REPRESENTATIVES is elected – compare SENATORIAL DISTRICT

**congressman** /'kong-gresmən, -gris-/, *fem* **congresswoman** /-,woomən/ *n* a member of a congress; *esp* a member of the US HOUSE OF REPRESENTATIVES

**congruence** /'kong-grooəns/, **congruency** /-si/ *n* **1** the quality or state of agreeing or coinciding; being congruent **2** a statement that two mathematical expressions are congruent with respect to a given number (the MODULUS)

**congruent** /'kong-grooənt/ *adj* **1** congruous **2** equal in size and shape ⟨~ *triangles*⟩ – compare SIMILAR 3 **3** having the difference divisible by a (multiple of a) specified number (the MODULUS) ⟨*12 is* ~ *to 2 (modulo 5) since* $12 \div 2 = 2 \times 5$⟩ [L *congruent-*, *congruens*, prp of *congruere*] – **congruently** *adv*

**congruity** /kən'grooh·əti/ *n* **1** being congruent or congruous **2** a point of agreement

**congruous** /'kong-grooəs/ *adj* **1** in agreement, harmony, or correspondence **2** marked or enhanced by harmonious agreement among constituent elements ⟨*a* ~ *theme in music*⟩ **3** *formal* conforming to the circumstances or requirements of a situation; appropriate ⟨*a* ~ *room to work in* – G B Shaw⟩ [L *congruus*, fr *congruere* to come together, agree, fr *com-* + *-gruere* (akin to Gk *zachrēēs* attacking violently)] – **congruously** *adv*, **congruousness** *n*

**conic** /'konik, 'kohnik/, **conic section** *n* **1** a plane curve, line, or point that is traced on the surface of a cone when an imaginary plane cuts through the cone in any of various ways **2** a mathematical curve generated by a point which moves so that the ratio of its distance from a fixed point (FOCUS) to its distance from a fixed line (DIRECTRIX) is constant

**conical** /'konikl/, **conic** /'konik, 'kohnik/ *adj* **1** resembling a cone in shape **2** of a cone – **conically** *adv*, **conicalness** *n*, **conicity** *n*

**conic projection** *n* a map projection of the earth's surface appearing as it would if projected onto the inside surface of a cone surrounding the globe and the cone being then unrolled and laid flat. This projection is only useful for sections of the globe since the distortion over a small area is almost negligible.

**conidiophore** /koh'nidi•əfaw/ *n* a structure that bears conidia; *specif* a specialized filamentous rootlike branch of a fungus that produces conidia usu by constriction and separation of its tip [NL *conidium* + ISV *-phore*] – **conidiophorous** *adj*

**conidium** /koh'nidi•əm/ *n*, *pl* **conidia** an asexual spore produced on a conidiophore [NL, fr Gk *konis* dust – more at INCINERATE] – **conidial** *adj*

**conifer** /'konifə, 'koh-/ *n* any of an order (Coniferales) of mostly evergreen trees and shrubs including pines, cypresses, and yews, that bear OVULES (immature seeds before fertilization) naked on the surface of scales (eg in cones) rather than enclosed in an ovary [deriv of L *conifer* cone-bearing, fr *conus* cone + *-fer*] – **coniferous** *adj*

**coniine** /'kohni•een, -in, 'koh,neen/ *n* a chemical compound, $C_8H_{17}N$, that is the principal poison in hemlock (*Conium maculatum*) [Ger *koniin*, fr LL *conium* hemlock, fr Gk *kōneion*]

**conjectural** /kən'jekch(ə)rəl/ *adj* **1** of the nature of or involving or based on conjecture **2** *archaic* given to conjectures – **conjecturally** *adv*

**¹conjecture** /kən'jekchə/ *n* **1a** the drawing of conclusions from inadequate evidence **b** a conclusion reached by surmise or guesswork **2** *obs* interpretation of omens [ME, fr MF or L; MF, fr L *conjectura*, fr *conjectus*, pp of *conicere*, lit., to throw together, fr *com-* + *jacere* to throw – more at JET]

**²conjecture** *vt* **1** to arrive at by conjecture **2** to make conjectures as to ∼ *vi* to form conjectures – **conjecturer** *n*

*synonyms* Conjecture, surmise, suppose, and guess all suggest the reaching of a conclusion on insufficient evidence. Conjecture acknowledges the lack of evidence, and usually deals with facts. Surmise suggests even less evidence, and the consequent use of imagination, intuition, or suspicion to corroborate what evidence there is, and to evaluate or interpret it ⟨*the general* conjectured *that the townspeople had seven days' supply of food, and* surmised *that they would have to surrender soon*⟩. One supposes what one expects to find true, and one guesses at what may be true, but which one lacks sufficient evidence to prove. Compare SPECULATE, INFER

*antonyms* know, ascertain, discover, prove

**conjoin** /kən'joyn/ *vb*, *formal* to (cause to) join together, esp for a common purpose [ME *conjoinen*, fr MF *conjoindre*, fr L *conjungere*, fr *com-* + *jungere* to join – more at YOKE]

**conjoint** /kən'joynt/ *adj*, *formal* (made up) of or carried on by two or more in combination; joint, united [ME, fr MF, pp of *conjoindre*] – **conjointly** *adv*

**conjugal** /'konjoogl, kən'joohgl/ *adj* of the married state or married people and their relationship [MF or L; MF, fr L *conjugalis*, fr *conjug-*, *conjux* husband, wife, fr *conjungere* to join, unite in marriage] – **conjugally** *adv*, **conjugality** *n*

*usage* The pronunciation /kən'joohgl/ rather than /kən'joohgl/ is recommended for BBC broadcasters.

**conjugal rights** *n pl* the sexual rights or privileges implied by and involved in the marriage relationship; the right of sexual intercourse between husband and wife

**conjugant** /'konjoogənt/ *n* either of a pair of conjugating GAMETES (reproductive cells) or organisms

**¹conjugate** /'konjoogət, -gayt/ *adj* **1a** joined together, esp in pairs; coupled **b** acting or operating as if joined **2** having features in common but opposite or inverse in some particular (eg having an opposite sign or lying on the opposite side of an axis) ⟨∼ *roots*⟩ ⟨∼ *focuses*⟩ **3** *of an acid or base* related by the difference of a proton ⟨*the acid* $NH_4$ *and the base* $NH_3$ *are* ∼ *to each other*⟩ **4** derived from the same root and therefore usu alike in meaning ⟨∼ *words*⟩ [ME *conjugat*, fr L *conjugatus*, pp of *conjugare* to unite, fr *com-* + *jugare* to join, fr *jugum* yoke – more at YOKE] – **conjugately** *adv*, **conjugateness** *n*

**²conjugate** /'konjoogayt/ *vt* **1** to give in prescribed order the various inflectional forms of (a verb) **2** to join together ∼ *vi* **1** *of a verb* to inflect **2** to become joined together **3** *of single-*

celled organisms, bacteria, reproductive cells, etc to pair (and fuse) in conjugation

**³conjugate** /'konjoogət, -gayt/ *n* **1** something conjugate; a product of conjugating **2** CONJUGATE COMPLEX NUMBER **3** an element of a mathematical group that is equal to a given element of the group multiplied on the right by another element and on the left by the INVERSE of the latter element

**conjugate complex number** *n* either of two COMPLEX NUMBERS (eg $a + bi$ and $a - bi$) which differ only in the sign connecting the two parts

**conjugated** /'konjoo,gaytid/ *adj* **1** formed by the union of two chemical compounds or united with another chemical compound ⟨∼ *bile acids*⟩ **2** of or containing a system of two chemical DOUBLE BONDS (forces which hold atoms together in molecules or crystals) separated by a single bond ⟨∼ *fatty acids*⟩

**conjugated protein** *n* a chemical compound of a protein portion combined with a nonprotein portion ⟨*haemoglobin is a* ∼ *consisting of haem* and *globin*⟩

**conjugation** /,konjoo'gaysh(ə)n/ *n* **1** conjugating or being conjugated **2a** (a diagrammatic arrangement of) the forms of a verb showing number, person, tense, etc **b** a class of verbs having the same type of such forms ⟨*the first* ∼ *in Latin*⟩ **3a** fusion of usu similar GAMETES (reproductive cells) with ultimate union of their nuclei that among lower plants (eg algae, fungi, and lichens) replaces the typical fertilization of higher forms **b** the one-way transfer of DNA between bacteria in cellular contact **c** the pairing of corresponding CHROMOSOMES (strands of gene-carrying material in the nucleus) during an early stage (SYNAPSIS) of MEIOSIS (type of cell division) – **conjugational** *adj*, **conjugationally** *adv*, **conjugative** *adj*

**¹conjunct** /kən'jungkt, 'konjungkt/ *adj* joint, united [ME, fr L *conjunctus*, pp of *conjungere*]

**²conjunct** *n* **1** something joined or associated with another; *specif* any of the components of a conjunction or coordinate structure **2** an adverbial linguistic form (eg *therefore* in "we must *therefore* refuse") that connects clauses and sentences – compare ADJUNCT, DISJUNCT

**conjunction** /kən'jungksh(ə)n/ *n* **1** a joining together; being joined together **2a** the apparent meeting or passing of two or more planets, stars, or other celestial bodies in the same part of the sky **b** a configuration in which two celestial bodies have their least apparent separation **3** a word (eg *and* or *when*) that joins together sentences, clauses, phrases, or words **4** a compound statement (eg in logic) true if and only if each of its components is true **5** *formal* occurrence together in time or space; concurrence – **conjunctional** *adj*, **conjunctionally** *adv*

**conjunctiva** /kən'jungktivə/ *n*, *pl* **conjunctivas, conjunctivae** /-vi/ the MUCOUS MEMBRANE that lines the inner surface of the eyelids and is continued over the front part of the eyeball [NL, fr LL, fem of *conjunctivus* conjoining, fr L *conjunctus*] – **conjunctival** *adj*

**conjunctive** /kən'jung(k)tiv/ *adj* **1** connective **2** meeting, joined **3** being or functioning like a conjunction or conjunct – **conjunctive** *n*, **conjunctively** *adv*

**conjunctivitis** /kən,jungkti'vietəs/ *n* inflammation of the conjunctiva [NL]

**conjuncture** /kən'jung(k)chə/ *n* a combination of circumstances or events, usu producing a crisis; a juncture

**conjuration** /,konjoo'raysh(ə)n/ *n* **1** the act or process of conjuring **2a** a magic spell **b** an expression or trick used in conjuring **3** a solemn appeal

**conjure** /'konjə, 'kun-; *vt sense 2* kən'jooə/ *vt* **1a** to summon by invocation or by uttering a spell, charm, etc **b**(1) to affect or effect (as if) by magical powers **b**(2) to imagine, contrive – often + *up* ⟨*to* ∼ *up imaginary dangers*⟩ **2** *archaic* to charge or entreat earnestly or solemnly ∼ *vi* **1a** to summon a devil or spirit by invocation or uttering a spell, charm, etc **b** to make use of magical powers **2** to use a conjurer's tricks [ME *conjuren*, fr OF *conjurer*, fr L *conjurare* to swear together, fr *com-* + *jurare* to swear – more at JURY]

**conjurer, conjuror** /'konjoorə, 'kun-/ *n* **1** one skilled in the use of magical powers; a wizard **2** one who performs tricks by sleight of hand or illusion

**¹conk** /kongk/ *n*, *slang* **1** the nose **2** the head [prob alter. of *conch*]

**²conk** *vi*, *informal* **1** BREAK DOWN 1a; *esp* to stall – usu + *out* ⟨*the motor suddenly* ∼ed *out*⟩ **2a** to faint – usu + *out* **b** to die ⟨*I caught pneumonia. I almost* ∼ed – Truman Capote⟩ – usu + *out* **c** *chiefly NAm* to go to sleep – usu + *off* or *out* ⟨∼ed *out for a while after lunch*⟩ [prob imit]

**conker** /'kongkə/ *n* **1** *pl but taking sing vb* a traditional game popular in Britain in which each player in turn swings a HORSE CHESTNUT on a string to try to break one held by its string by his/her opponent **2** the large inedible seed of the HORSE CHESTNUT which ripens in a thick spiky husk; *esp* this seed as used in playing conkers [E dial. *conker* snail shell, prob fr *conch* + ²-*er*; fr the orig use in the game of a snail shell on a string]

**conman** /'kon,man/ *n* one who engages in CONFIDENCE TRICKS

**con moto** /kon 'mohtoh/ *adv* with movement; in a spirited manner – used as a direction in music [It]

**conn** /kon/ *vt or n, NAm* ²,³CON

**connate** /'konayt/ *adj* **1** *of plant or animal parts* congenitally or firmly united ⟨*leaves* ~ *at their bases*⟩ **2** entrapped in sediments at the time of their deposition ⟨~ *water*⟩ **3** *formal* innate, inborn **4** *formal* akin, congenial **5** *formal* born or originated together [LL *connatus*, pp of *connasci* to be born together, fr L *com-* + *nasci* to be born – more at NATION] – **connately** *adv*

**connatural** /kə'nachərəl/ *adj, formal* **1** connected by nature; inborn **2** of the same nature [ML *connaturalis*, fr L *com-* + *naturalis* natural] – **connaturally** *adv*, **connaturality** *n*

**connect** /kə'nekt/ *vt* **1** to join or fasten together, usu by some intervening thing **2** to place or establish in relationship ~ *vi* **1** to become joined ⟨*the two rooms* ~ *through a hallway*⟩ **2** to make a successful hit or shot ⟨~ed *with a right to the jaw*⟩ **synonyms** see ¹JOIN **antonym** disconnect [L *conectere, connectere*, fr *com-* + *nectere* to bind] – **connectable** *also* **connectible** *adj*, **connector** *also* **connecter** *n*

**connected** /kə'nektid/ *adj* **1** joined or linked together **2** having a social, professional, or commercial relationship ⟨*for the well* ~*, there are elegantly overdone parties* – John Griffin⟩ **3** *of a set of mathematical points* not divisible into two subsets with no elements in common, neither of which contains a LIMIT POINT of the other – **connectedly** *adv*, **connectedness** *n*

**connecting rod** /kə'nekting/ *n* a rod that transmits power from a part of a machine that moves to and fro (eg a piston) to a part that rotates (eg a crankshaft)

**connection**, *chiefly Br* **connexion** /kə'neksh(ə)n/ *n* **1** connecting or being connected: eg **1a** a causal or logical relationship ⟨*the* ~ *between two ideas*⟩ **b** contextual relations or associations ⟨*in this* ~ *the word has a different meaning*⟩ **c** a relation of personal intimacy (eg of family ties) **d** coherence, continuity **2a** something that connects; a link ⟨*a loose* ~ *in the wiring*⟩ **b** an arrangement that assists communication or transport; *specif* a train, aeroplane, etc that one should transfer to at a particular airport, station, etc ⟨*missed their* ~ *at Crewe*⟩ **3a** a person connected with others, esp by marriage, kinship, or common interest ⟨*has powerful* ~s *in high places*⟩ **b** *pl* the owners, trainers, etc of a racehorse ⟨*her* ~s *say she does better in wet conditions*⟩ **4** a social, professional, or commercial relationship: eg **4a** an arrangement to execute orders or advance interests of another ⟨*a firm's foreign* ~s⟩ **b** a source of contraband (eg illegal drugs) **c** *chiefly NAm* a position, job **5** a religious denomination [L *connexion-, connexio*, fr *connexus*, pp of *connectere*] – **connectional** *adj* – **in connection with** with reference to; concerning

**¹connective** /kə'nektiv/ *adj* tending to connect – **connectively** *adv*, **connectivity** *n*

**²connective** *n* something that connects: eg **a** the tissue connecting the POLLEN SACS of an ANTHER (pollen-producing male part of a flower) **b** a linguistic form that connects words or word groups; a conjunction

**connective tissue** *n* any of various tissues (eg bone, cartilage, or fibrous tissue) that originate from the MESODERM (embryonic tissue layer) and that pervade, support, and bind together other tissues and organs

**Connemara pony** /,koni'mahrə/ *n* (any of) a breed of short-legged Irish ponies [*Connemara*, district in W Ireland]

**conning tower** /'koning/ *n* **1** an armoured control centre (eg on a battleship) **2** a raised structure on the deck of a submarine used as an observation tower and often as an entrance to the vessel [fr gerund of ¹*con*]

**conniption** /kə'nipsh(ə)n/ *n, NAm informal* a fit of rage, hysteria, or alarm [origin unknown]

**connivance** /kə'niev(ə)ns/ *n* the act of conniving; *esp* knowledge of and active or passive consent to wrongdoing

**connive** /kə'niev/ *vi* **1** to pretend ignorance of or fail to take action against something one ought to oppose **2a** to be indulgent or in secret sympathy **b** to cooperate secretly or have a secret understanding **3** to conspire, intrigue □ often + *at* [Fr or L; Fr *conniver*, fr L *coniuēre, connivēre* to close the eyes, connive, fr *com-* + -*nivēre* (akin to *nictare* to wink); akin to OE & OHG *hnigan* to bow, L *nicere* to beckon] – **conniver** *n*

**connivent** /kə'nievənt/ *adj* converging but not joined ⟨~ *stamens*⟩ [L *connivent-, connivens*, prp of *connivēre*]

**connoisseur** /,konə'suh, -'sooə/ *n* **1** an expert judge in matters of taste and appreciation (eg of art) **2** one who enjoys with discrimination and appreciation of subtleties ⟨*a* ~ *of fine wines*⟩ [obs Fr (now *connaisseur*), fr OF *connoisseor*, fr *connoistre* to know, fr L *cognoscere* – more at COGNITION] – **connoisseurship** *n*

**connotation** /,konə'taysh(ə)n/ *n* **1a** the suggesting of a meaning by a word apart from what it explicitly denotes **b** something suggested by a word or thing; an implication as distinct from a direct meaning (DENOTATION) ⟨*the* ~s *of comfort that surrounded that old chair*⟩ **2** *philosophy* the meaning of a word, term, symbol, etc ⟨*that abuse of logic which consists in moving counters about as if they were known entities with a fixed* ~ – W R Inge⟩ **3** *philosophy* the property or properties connoted by a concept or logical term ⟨*the* ~ *of the word "fir" is the set of characteristics (eg needle-shaped leaves and fir cones) that distinguish a fir from other trees*⟩ – called also INTENSION; compare DENOTATION – **connotational, connotative** *adj*

**connote** /kə'noht/ *vt* **1** to convey in addition to exact explicit meaning ⟨*all the misery that poverty* ~s⟩ **2** to be associated with or inseparable from as a consequence or concomitant ⟨*the remorse so often* ~d *by guilt*⟩ **3** to imply or indicate as a logically essential attribute of something denoted [ML *connotare*, fr. L *com-* + *notare* to note]

**synonyms** Although **connote** and **denote** can both mean "mean", they are complementary rather than synonymous. **Denote** makes a precise, explicit statement of primary meaning ⟨*"home" denotes the place where one lives*⟩: the definable class of things, ideas, acts, states, or qualities that are named. **Connote** conveys the ideas and associations that cling to a word or phrase, either as the result of one's personal experience or in the eyes of the community in general ⟨*for Jane, "home" connoted only misery, estrangement, and abuse*⟩.

**connubial** /kə'nyoohbi·əl/ *adj* of the married state; conjugal [L *connubialis*, fr *connubium* marriage, fr *com-* + *nubere* to marry – more at NUPTIAL] – **connubialism** *n*, **connubially** *adv*, **connubiality** *n*

**conodont** /'kohnə,dont, 'kon-/ *n* a PALAEOZOIC fossil that may consist of the teeth of an extinct CYCLOSTOME (type of jawless fish) or more probably the remains of an INVERTEBRATE animal [ISV *con-* (fr Gk *kōnos* cone) + -*odont*]

**conoid** /'koh,noyd/, **conoidal** /'koh,noydl/ *adj* shaped (nearly) like a cone – **conoid** *n*

**conquer** /'kongkə/ *vt* **1** to gain or acquire by force of arms; subjugate ⟨~ed *England*⟩ **2** to overcome by force of arms; vanquish ⟨~ed *Harold*⟩ **3** to gain mastery over ⟨~ed *the mountain*⟩ ⟨~ed *his fear*⟩ ~ *vi* to be victorious [ME *conqueren* to acquire, conquer, fr OF *conquerre*, fr (assumed) VL *conquaerere*, fr L *conquirere* to search for, collect, fr *com-* + *quaerere* to ask, search] – **conqueror** *n*

**conquest** /'kon(g)kwest/ *n* **1** the act or process of conquering **2a** *often pl* something conquered; *esp* territory gained in war **b** a person who has been won over, esp by love or sexual attraction **synonyms** see VICTORY [ME, fr OF, fr (assumed) VL *conquaesitus*, alter. of L *conquisitus*, pp of *conquirere*]

**conquian** /'kongkiən/ *n* a card game for two played with 40 cards (a normal 52-card pack lacking eights, nines, and tens) from which all games of rummy developed [MexSp *con quien*, fr Sp *con quién* with whom?]

**conquistador** /kon'k(w)istədaw/ *n, pl* **conquistadores, conquistadors** one who conquers; *specif* any of the Spanish conquerors of America, esp of Mexico and Peru in the 16th century [Sp, deriv of L *conquirere*]

**¹con-,rod** *n, Br* CONNECTING ROD (rod that transmits motive power) [by shortening]

**consanguine** /kon'sang-gwin/ *adj* consanguineous

**consanguineous** /,konsang'gwini·əs/ *adj* of the same blood or origin; *specif* descended from the same ancestor [L *consanguineus*, fr *com-* + *sanguin-, sanguis* blood – more at SANGUINE] – **consanguineously** *adv*

**consanguinity** /,konsang'gwinəti/ *n* **1** the quality or state of being consanguineous **2** a close relation or connection; an affinity

**conscience** /'konsh(ə)ns/ *n* 1 the consciousness of the moral quality of one's own conduct or intentions, together with a feeling of obligation to refrain from doing wrong 2 conformity to the dictates of conscience ⟨~ *argues against it*⟩ 3 sensitive regard for fairness or justice 4 *archaic* consciousness [ME, fr OF, fr L *conscientia*, fr *conscient-, consciens*, prp of *conscire* to be conscious, be conscious of guilt, fr *com-* + *scire* to know – more at SCIENCE] – **conscienceless** *adj* – **in all conscience** by any standard of fairness

**conscience clause** *n* a proviso in a law exempting those who have moral or religious convictions that prevent their complying with it

**conscience money** *n* money paid usu anonymously to relieve the conscience by restoring what has been wrongfully acquired

**conscientious** /ˌkonshi'enshəs/ *adj* 1 governed by or conforming to the dictates of conscience; scrupulous 2 meticulous or careful, esp in one's work; *also* hard-working *synonyms* see CAREFUL [Fr *conscientieux*, fr ML *conscientiosus*, fr L *conscientia*] – **conscientiously** *adv*, **conscientiousness** *n*

**conscientious objector** *n* one who refuses to serve in the armed forces or bear arms, esp on moral or religious grounds – **conscientious objection** *n*

¹**conscious** /'konshəs/ *adj* 1 perceiving or noticing with a degree of controlled thought or observation 2 personally felt 3 capable of or marked by thought, will, intention, or perception 4 self-conscious, affected 5 having mental faculties undulled by sleep, faintness, or stupor; awake ⟨*became ~ after the anaesthetic wore off*⟩ 6 done or acting with critical awareness ⟨*made a ~ effort to avoid the same mistakes*⟩ 7 marked by awareness of or concern for something specified ⟨*a bargain-conscious shopper*⟩ 8 *archaic* sharing another's knowledge or awareness of an inward state or outward fact [L *conscius*, fr *com-* + *scire* to know] – **consciously** *adv*

²**conscious** *n* CONSCIOUSNESS 3 – used in Freudian psychology

**consciousness** /'konshəsnis/ *n* 1a the quality or state of being aware of something within or outside oneself **b** concern, awareness ⟨*class ~*⟩ 2 all the conscious states of an individual 3 the upper level of mental life of which the person is aware, as contrasted with unconscious processes

**conscribe** /kən'skrieb/ *vt* 1 to limit, circumscribe ⟨*ill-health ... ~d the force of his intentions – TLS*⟩ 2 to enlist forcibly; conscript [L *conscribere* to enroll]

¹**conscript** /'konskript/ *adj* 1 enlisted into service by conscription 2 made up of conscripted people ⟨*a ~ army*⟩ [MF, fr L *conscriptus*, pp of *conscribere* to enrol, fr *com-* + *scribere* to write – more at SCRIBE]

²**conscript** /'konskript/ *n* a conscripted person (eg a military recruit)

³**conscript** /kən'skript/ *vt* to enlist by conscription

**conscription** /kən'skripsh(ə)n/ *n* compulsory enrolment of people, esp for military service

¹**consecrate** /'konsikrayt/ *adj, formal* dedicated to a sacred purpose; hallowed

²**consecrate** *vt* 1 to introduce (a person) into a permanent official position with a religious rite; *specif* to ordain to the office of bishop 2a to make or declare sacred; *specif* to devote irrevocably to the worship of God by a solemn ceremony **b** to prepare (bread and wine used at Communion) to be received as Christ's body and blood **c** to devote to a purpose with deep solemnity or dedication 3 to make inviolable or venerable ⟨*principles ~d by the weight of history*⟩ [ME *consecraten*, fr L *consecratus*, pp of *consecrare*, fr *com-* + *sacrare* to consecrate –more at SACRED] – **consecration** *n*, **consecrative** *adj*, **consecrator** *n*, **consecratory** *adj*

**consecution** /ˌkonsi'kyoohsh(ə)n/ *n, formal* a sequence [L *consecution-, consecutio*, fr *consecutus*, pp of *consequi* to follow closely – more at CONSEQUENT]

**consecutive** /kən'sekyootiv/ *adj* following one after the other in order without gaps – **consecutively** *adv*, **consecutiveness** *n*
*synonyms* Consecutive and successive both mean "following one after the other", but consecutive implies that there are no gaps. Monday, Tuesday, and Wednesday are consecutive, but Monday, Wednesday, and Friday are successive.

**consecutive course** *n* a course of professional education following after a degree in an academic subject

**consensual** /kən'sensyoool/ *adj* 1 involving or made by mutual consent; *esp* having validity by mere mutual consent, without a written agreement ⟨*a ~ contract*⟩ 2 relating to the simultaneous occurrence of an involuntary action with a voluntary action; *esp* of or being the contraction of the pupil of an eye

that is covered when the other eye is exposed to light [L *consensus* + E *-al*] – **consensually** *adv*

**consensus** /kən'sensəs/ *n* 1 solidarity of a group in feeling and belief 2a general agreement; unanimity; *also* an instance of this **b** the judgment arrived at by most of those concerned [L, fr *consensus*, pp of *consentire*]
*usage* Not spelt △ **concensus**. △ census

¹**consent** /kən'sent/ *vi* 1 to give assent or approval; agree *to* 2 *archaic* to be in agreement in opinion or feeling *synonyms* see ¹ASSENT *antonym* dissent [ME *consenten*, fr L *consentire*, fr *com-* + *sentire* to feel – more at SENSE] – **consentingly** *adv*

²**consent** *n* 1 agreement to or approval of what is done or proposed by another; acquiescence 2 agreement as to action or opinion; *specif* voluntary agreement by a people to organize a society and give authority to the government ⟨*government by ~*⟩ – **consenter** *n*

**consentaneous** /ˌkonsen'taynyəs/ *adj, formal* 1 expressing agreement; suited – often + *to* or *with* 2 done or made by the consent of all [L *consentaneus*, fr *consentire*] – **consentaneously** *adv*

**consenting adult** /kən'senting/ *n* an adult who consents to sexual, esp homosexual, acts

**consequence** /'konsikwəns/ *n* 1 something produced by a cause or necessarily following from a set of conditions 2a importance in terms of power to produce an effect; moment **b** social importance 3 *pl but taking sing vb* a game in which a story is made up consecutively by a group of people, each of whom is ignorant of what the previous player contributed, and which concludes with a contribution beginning "And the consequence was..." – **in consequence** as a result; consequently

¹**consequent** /'konsikwənt/ *n* 1 a logical deduction – used in philosophy 2 *philosophy* the conclusion of a conditional proposition (eg *then B* in "if A, then B") – compare ANTECEDENT

²**consequent** *adj, formal* 1 following as a result or effect – often + *on* 2 observing logical sequence; rational [MF, fr L *consequent-, consequens*, prp of *consequi* to follow closely, fr *com-* + *sequi* to follow – more at SUE]
*synonyms* Consequent, rather than **consequential**, is the usual word for "following as a result" ⟨*the expenses consequent to/on getting married*⟩ and must be distinguished from **subsequent**, which means merely "following in time" ⟨*the weeks subsequent to the wedding*⟩ with no idea of "result". Consequential is the only word of the three for "indirect result", as in consequential loss, and may now be best confined to that legal sense and to the more general sense "self-important" ⟨*a bustling consequential little man*⟩.

**consequential** /ˌkonsi'kwensh(ə)l/ *adj, formal* 1 consequent 2 having the nature of a secondary result; indirect 3 having significant consequences; important ⟨*a grave and ~ event*⟩ 4 self-important see ²CONSEQUENT – **consequentiality** *n*, **consequentially** *adv*, **consequentialness** *n*

**consequential loss** *n* an indirect or secondary loss brought about by a direct property loss (eg that caused by a fire or car crash), and often provided for by special provisions in insurance policies

**consequently** /'konsikwəntli/ *adv* as a result; in view of what has gone before

**conservancy** /kən'suhv(ə)nsi/ *n* 1a conservation **b** an organization designated to conserve and protect the environment from harmful influences, esp human activity; *also* an area protected by such an organization 2 *Br* a board regulating fisheries and navigation in a river or port [alter. of obs *conservacy* conservation, fr AF *conservacie*, fr ML *conservatia*, fr L *conservatus*, pp]

**conservation** /ˌkonsə'vaysh(ə)n/ *n* 1 careful preservation and protection, esp of a natural resource, the quality of the environment, or a plant or animal species, to prevent exploitation, destruction, or neglect 2 *chiefly physics* the conserving of a quantity ⟨*~ of momentum*⟩ [ME, fr MF, fr L *conservation-, conservatio*, fr *conservatus*, pp of *conservare*] – **conservational** *adj*

**conservationist** /ˌkonsə'vaysh(ə)n·ist/ *n* one concerned about or actively involved in conservation, esp of natural resources

**conservation law** *n* any of several principles in physics (eg the law of CONSERVATION OF MASS AND ENERGY) according to which a property (eg energy, charge, or momentum) of an isolated system remains constant during a change occurring in the system

**conservation of mass and energy** *n* a principle in physics:

in any system the sum of the total amount of mass and energy remains constant

**conservatism** /kən'suhvətiz(ə)m/ n **1a** disposition in politics to preserve what is established **b** a political philosophy based on tradition and social stability, stressing established institutions, and preferring gradual development to abrupt change **2** cap the principles and policies of a Conservative party **3** the tendency to prefer an existing situation rather than change

¹**conservative** /kən'suhvətiv/ adj **1** preservative **2a** of or advocating a philosophy of conservatism **b** cap of or being a political party that advocates the principles of conservatism; specif of or being a British political party associated with support of established institutions and opposed to radical change **3a** tending or disposed to maintain existing views, conditions, or institutions; traditional **b** moderate, cautious ⟨at a ~ estimate⟩ **c** marked by traditional norms of taste, elegance, style, or manners ⟨a ~ suit⟩ **4** often cap of or being Judaism as practised esp among some US Jews, with adherence to the TORAH and TALMUD (Jewish scriptures) but with allowance for some departures in keeping with circumstances – **conservatively** adv, **conservativeness** n

²**conservative** n **1a** an adherent or advocate of political conservatism **b** cap a member or supporter of a Conservative party **2** one who keeps to traditional methods or views

**conservat-ize, -ise** /kən'suhvə,tiez/ vb to make or become conservative

**conservatoire** /kən'suhvətwah/ n a school specializing in any one of the fine arts ⟨a ~ of music⟩ [Fr, fr It conservatorio home for foundlings, music school, fr L conservatus, pp]

**conservator** /kən'suhvətə, 'konsə,vaytə/ n **1a** one who or that which preserves from injury or violation; a protector **b** a museum official responsible for the care, restoration, and repair of exhibits **2** an official charged with the protection of something affecting public welfare and interests; esp a member of a conservancy – **conservatorial** adj

**conservatory** /kən'suhvət(ə)ri/ n **1** a greenhouse, usu forming a room of a house, for growing or displaying ornamental plants **2** chiefly NAm a conservatoire

¹**conserve** /kən'suhv/ vt **1a** to keep in a state of safety or wholeness ⟨~ wild life⟩ **b** to avoid wasteful or destructive use of ⟨~ natural resources⟩ **2** to preserve, esp with sugar **3** to maintain (mass, energy, momentum, etc) constant during a process of chemical or physical change [ME conserven, fr MF conserver, fr L conservare, fr com- + servare to keep, guard, observe; akin to OE searu armour, Avestan haurvaiti he guards (cf OBSERVE, PRESERVE, RESERVE)] – **conserver** n

²**conserve** /kən'suhv, 'konsuhv/ n a preserve of fruit boiled with sugar that is used like jam

**consider** /kən'sidə/ vt **1** to think about with care or caution **2** to give sympathetic or solicitous regard to ⟨~ed her every wish⟩ **3** to gaze on steadily or reflectively **4** to think of as specified; regard as being ⟨~ thrift essential⟩ ⟨their works are well ~ ed abroad⟩ **5** to have as an opinion ⟨~ed that he was wrong⟩ ~ vi to reflect, deliberate ⟨paused a moment to ~⟩ [ME consideren, fr MF considerer, fr L considerare, lit., to observe the stars, fr com- + sider-, sidus star – more at SIDEREAL] **usage** Since **consider** in sense 4 means "regard as being" writers on usage advise that it should not be used with another as ⟨⚠ **consider** thrift as essential⟩. **Consider** is used correctly with as when it means "think about carefully" ⟨we must **consider** the project both as (= in the role of) a training exercise and as a possible source of profit⟩.

**considerable** /kən'sid(ə)rəbl/ adj **1** worth consideration; significant **2** large in extent or degree ⟨a ~ number⟩ – **considerably** adv

**considerate** /kən'sid(ə)rət/ adj **1** marked by or given to consideration of the rights and feelings of others **2** archaic careful, circumspect – **considerately** adv, **considerateness** n

**consideration** /kən,sidə'raysh(ə)n/ n **1** continuous and careful thought ⟨after long ~⟩ **2a** something considered as a basis for thought or action; a reason **b** a taking into account **3** thoughtful and sympathetic or solicitous regard **4a** recompense, payment ⟨for a small ~⟩ **b** an element of benefit or loss that distinguishes a legally binding contract from a mere promise; broadly something of value given in return for a promise **5** formal respect, esteem ⟨became people of ~ – V S Pritchett⟩ – **in consideration of 1** in recompense or payment for **2** ON ACCOUNT OF, BECAUSE OF

**considered** /kən'sidəd/ adj matured by extended thought ⟨his ~ opinion⟩

¹**considering** /kən'sid(ə)ring/ prep taking into account ⟨he did well ~ his limitations⟩

²**considering** conj in view of the fact that ⟨~ he was new at the job, he did quite well⟩

**consign** /kən'sien/ vt **1** to give over to another's care **2** to give, transfer, or deliver into the hands or control of another; also to assign to something as a destination or end **3** to send or address to an agent to be cared for or sold [MF consigner, fr L consignare, to seal, vouch for, fr com- + signum sign, mark, seal] – **consignable** adj, **consignor** n, **consignation** n

**consignee** /,konsie'nee/ n one to whom something is consigned or shipped

**consignment** /kən'sienmənt/ n **1** the act or process of consigning **2** something consigned, esp in a single shipment – **on consignment** shipped to a dealer on a sale or return basis ⟨goods shipped on consignment⟩

**consist** /kən'sist/ vi **1** to lie, reside in ⟨liberty ~s in the absence of obstructions – A E Housman⟩ **2** to be made up or composed of ⟨breakfast ~ed of cereal, milk, and fruit⟩ **3** formal to be consistent with ⟨it ~s with the facts⟩ **synonyms** see COMPRISE [MF & L; MF consister, fr L consistere, lit., to stand together, fr. com- + sistere to take a stand; akin to L stare to stand – more at STAND]

**consistency** /kən'sist(ə)nsi/ also **consistence** n **1** degree of resistance of **1a** a liquid to movement ⟨boil the juice to the ~ of a thick syrup⟩ **b** a pliable solid to change of shape ⟨had the ~ of clay⟩ **2a** agreement or harmony of parts or features to one another or a whole; correspondence; specif ability to be asserted together without contradiction **b** harmony of conduct or practice with past performance or stated intent ⟨followed his own advice with ~⟩

**consistent** /kən'sist(ə)nt/ adj **1** marked by harmonious regularity or steady continuity; free from irregularity, variation, or contradiction ⟨a ~ style in painting⟩ **2** in agreement with ⟨a statement not ~ with his earlier ones⟩ **3** converging to the true value of a statistical quantity estimated as the sample becomes large ⟨a ~ estimator⟩ [L consistent-, consistens, prp of consistere] – **consistently** adv

**consistory** /kən'sist(ə)ri/ n a church tribunal or governing body: eg **a** a solemn meeting of Roman Catholic cardinals summoned and presided over by the pope **b** consistory court, consistory a bishop's court in the Church of England dealing with ecclesiastical matters [ME consistorie, fr MF, fr ML & LL; ML consistorium church tribunal, fr L, imperial council, fr L consistere to stand together] – **consistorial** adj

**consociate** /kon'sohshiayt, -si-/ vb, formal to bring or come into association [L consociatus, pp of consociare, fr com- + socius companion – more at SOCIAL]

**consociation** /kən,sohshi'aysh(ə)n, -si'aysh(ə)n/ n **1** an ecological community with a single dominant organism **2** formal association in fellowship or alliance – **consociational** adj

**consol** /kən'sol, 'kon,sol/ n usu pl an interest-bearing government bond that has no fixed date on which it becomes due for payment but can be cashed on call; specif one first issued by the British government in 1751 [short for Consolidated Annuities, British government securities]

**consolation prize** /,konsə'laysh(ə)n/ n a prize given to one who just fails to gain a major prize in a contest

¹**console** /kən'sohl/ vt to alleviate the grief or sense of loss of [Fr consoler, fr L consolari, fr com- + solari to console – more at SILLY] – **consolable** adj, **consolation** n, **consolatory** adj, **consolingly** adv

²**console** /'konsohl, 'konsl/ n **1** a carved bracket projecting from a wall to support a shelf or CORNICE (horizontal moulding) **2** a desk containing the keyboards, stops, etc of an organ **3a** CONTROL PANEL; also a cabinet in which a control panel is mounted **b** the part of a computer used for communication between the operator and the computer **4** a cabinet (eg for a radio or television set) designed to rest directly on the floor [Fr, fr MF, prob short for consolateur bracket in human shape, lit., one who consoles, fr L consolator, fr consolatus, pp. of consolari]

**console table** /'konsohl, 'konsl/ n a table fixed to a wall with its top supported by brackets or front legs; broadly a table designed to fit against a wall

**consolidate** /kən'solidayt/ vt **1** to join together into one whole; unite ⟨~ several small school districts⟩ **2** to make firm or secure; strengthen ⟨~ their hold on first place⟩ **3** to form into a compact mass ~ vi to become consolidated; specif to merge ⟨the two companies ~d⟩ [L consolidatus, pp of *consolidare* to make solid, fr *com-* + *solidus* solid] – **consolidator** *n*

**consolidated school** /kən'solidaytid/ *n* a US state school formed by merging other schools

**consolidation** /kən,soli'daysh(ə)n/ *n* 1 consolidating or being consolidated 2 uniting or being united; *esp* the unification of two or more companies by dissolution of existing ones and creation of a single new company – compare MERGER 2

**consommé** /kən'somay, ,konsə'may/ *n* a thin clear meat soup made from meat broth [Fr, fr pp of *consommer* to complete, boil down, fr L *consummare* to complete – more at CON-SUMMATE]

**consonance** /'kons(ə)nəns/ *n* 1a correspondence or recurrence of sounds, esp in words b a traditionally agreeable combination of musical notes in harmony 2 *formal* harmony or agreement among components

¹**consonant** /'kons(ə)nənt/ *n* 1 any of a class of speech sounds (eg /p/, /g/, /n/, /l/, /s/, /r/) characterized by constriction or closure at one or more points in the breath channel 2 a letter or other symbol representing a consonant; *esp* any letter of the English alphabet except *a, e, i, o,* and *u* [ME, fr L *consonant-, consonans,* fr prp of *consonare*] – **consonantal** *adj*

²**consonant** *adj* 1 marked by musical consonances 2 having similar sounds ⟨~ *words*⟩ 3 *formal* 3a in agreement or harmony; free from elements making for discord b in agreement *with;* CONSISTENT 2 [MF, fr L *consonant-, consonans,* prp of *consonare* to sound together, agree, fr *com-* + *sonare* to sound] – **consonantly** *adv*

¹**consort** /'konsawt/ *n, formal* 1 an associate 2 a spouse – compare PRINCE CONSORT [ME, fr MF, fr L *consort-, consors,* lit., one who shares a common lot, fr *com-* + *sort-, sors* lot, share]

²**consort** *n* 1 conjunction, association ⟨*he ruled in* ~ *with his father*⟩ 2a a group of musicians performing esp early music b a set of musical instruments of the same family (eg viols or recorders) played together; *also* a work composed for a consort [MF *consorte,* fr *consort*]

³**consort** /kən'sawt/ *vi, formal* 1 to keep company *with* ⟨~ing *with criminals*⟩ 2 to accord, harmonize *with* ⟨*the illustrations* ~ *admirably with the text* – *TLS*⟩

**consortium** /kən'sawti-əm/ *n, pl* **consortia** *also* **consortiums** an international business or banking agreement or combination for carrying out some operation, esp one requiring extensive financial backing [L, fellowship, fr *consort-, consors*]

**conspectus** /kən'spektəs/ *n, pl* **conspectuses** 1 a survey, summary; *esp* a brief one providing an overall view 2 an outline, synopsis [L, fr *conspectus,* pp of *conspicere*]

**conspicuous** /kən'spikyoo-əs/ *adj* 1 obvious to the eye or mind 2 attracting attention; striking ⟨*applause was* ~ *by its absence*⟩ [L *conspicuus,* fr *conspicere* to get sight of, fr *com-* + *specere* to look – more at SPY] – **conspicuously** *adv*, **conspicuousness** *n*

**conspicuous consumption** *n* lavish or wasteful spending thought to enhance social prestige

**conspiracy** /kən'spirəsi/ *n* 1 the act or an instance of conspiring together; *specif* the offence of agreeing with another to commit an unlawful act ⟨~ *to murder*⟩ 2a an agreement among conspirators b *taking sing or pl vb* a group of conspirators [ME *conspiracie,* fr L *conspiratus,* pp of *conspirare*]

**conspiracy of silence** *n* an agreement to keep silent, esp in order to promote or protect selfish interests

**conspirator** /kən'spirətə/ *n* one who conspires; a plotter

**conspiratorial** /kən,spirə'tawri-əl, ,kon-/ *adj* (suggestive) of a conspiracy or a conspirator – **conspiratorially** *adv*

**conspire** /kən'spie-ə/ *vi* 1a to join in an agreement to do an unlawful act or to use unlawful means to accomplish a lawful end b to scheme, plot 2 to act in harmony ⟨*circumstances* ~d *to defeat his efforts*⟩ [ME *conspiren,* fr MF *conspirer,* fr L *conspirare* to breathe together, agree, conspire, fr *com-* + *spirare* to breathe – more at SPIRIT]

**constable** /'konstəbl, 'kun-/ *n* 1 a high officer of a medieval royal or noble household 2 the warden or governor of a royal castle or a fortified town 3 *Br* a policeman; *specif* one ranking below sergeant [ME *conestable,* fr OF, fr LL *comes stabuli,* lit., officer of the stable]

¹**constabulary** /kən'stabyooləri/ *n taking sing or pl vb* 1 the police force of a particular district or country 2 an armed police force organized on military lines but distinct from the regular army ⟨*the Royal Ulster* Constabulary⟩ [ME *constabularie,* fr ML *constabularia,* fr *constabulus* constable, fr LL *comes stabuli*]

²**constabulary** *adj* of a constable or constabulary

**constancy** /'konstənsi/ *n* 1 fidelity, loyalty 2 freedom from change

¹**constant** /'konstənt/ *adj* 1 marked by steadfast resolution or faithfulness; exhibiting constancy of mind or attachment ⟨*his* ~ *friend for years*⟩ 2 invariable, uniform 3 continually occurring or recurring; regular ⟨*her* ~ *complaints*⟩ **synonyms** see CONTINUAL, ¹STEADY **antonyms** inconstant, fickle (for 1) fitful (for 2) [ME, fr MF, fr L *constant-, constans,* fr prp of *constare* to stand firm, be consistent, fr *com-* + *stare* to stand – more at STAND] – **constantly** *adv*

²**constant** *n* something invariable or unchanging: eg a *maths* a(1) a number that has a fixed value or is characteristic of some substance or instrument a(2) a number that is assumed not to change value in a given mathematical discussion b a term in logic with a fixed designation

**constantan** /'konstəntən/ *n* an alloy of copper and nickel used for RESISTORS (devices in electrical circuits that induce resistance to the flow of current) and in THERMOCOUPLES (electrical devices for measuring temperature) [¹*constant* + ¹-*on;* fr constancy of its resistance under change of temperature]

**constellate** /'konstəlayt/ *vt* 1 to unite in a cluster 2 to set or adorn (as if) with constellations ~ *vi* to cluster

**constellation** /,konstə'laysh(ə)n/ *n* 1 the astrological configuration of the planets, esp at one's birth 2a any of 88 arbitrary configurations of stars seen from the earth as being groups and generally named after the usu mythical figures their outlines suggest b an area of the CELESTIAL SPHERE covering such a configuration 3 a cluster, group; *esp* a large or impressive one 4 a pattern, arrangement [ME *constellacioun,* fr MF *constellation,* fr LL *constellation-, constellatio,* fr *constellatus* studded with stars, fr L *com-* + *stella* star – more at STAR] – **constellatory** *adj*

**consternate** /'konstənayt/ *vt* to fill with consternation

**consternation** /,konstə'naysh(ə)n/ *n* amazed dismay that hinders or throws into confusion **synonyms** see ¹FEAR **antonym** composure [Fr or L; Fr, fr L *consternation-, consternatio,* fr *consternatus,* pp of *consternare* to frighten, alter. of *consternere* to scatter, throw down, fr *com-* + *sternere* to spread out]

**constipate** /'konstipayt/ *vt* 1 to cause constipation in 2 to make turgid, dull, or immobile ⟨*a* ~d *writing style*⟩ [ML *constipatus,* pp of *constipare,* fr L, to crowd together, fr *com-* + *stipare* to press together – more at STIFF]

**constipation** /,konsti'paysh(ə)n/ *n* 1 abnormally delayed or infrequent passage of dry hardened faeces 2a impairment or blockage of proper functioning b turgidity, stultification

**constituency** /kən'stityoo-ənsi, -'stichoo-/ *n* 1a a body of citizens entitled to elect a representative to a public body, esp a legislature; *broadly* the residents in an electoral district b an electoral district 2a a group or body that patronizes or supports b the people involved in or served by an organization (eg a business or institution)

¹**constituent** /kən'stityoo-ənt, -choo-/ *n* 1 one who authorizes another to act for him/her 2 an essential part; a component 3 any of two or more linguistic forms that enter into a construction or a compound and are either IMMEDIATE (eg *he* and *writes reviews* in the construction "he writes reviews") or ULTIMATE (eg *he, write, -s, review,* and *-s* in the same construction) 4 any of the voters who elect someone to a public office; *broadly* a resident in a constituency [Fr *constituant,* fr MF, fr prp of *constituer* to constitute, fr L *constituere*]

²**constituent** *adj* 1 serving to form, compose, or make up a unit or whole; component 2 having the power to create a government or frame or amend a constitution ⟨*a* ~ *assembly*⟩ [L *constituent-, constituens,* prp of *constituere*] – **constituently** *adv*

**constitute** /'konstityooht, -chooht/ *vt* 1 to appoint to an often specified office, function, or dignity ⟨~d *authorities*⟩ ⟨~d *himself their representative*⟩ 2 to establish; set up: eg 2a to establish by a legal or formal act b ³FOUND 3 c to give legal form to 3 to form, make ⟨*12 months* ~ *a year*⟩ ⟨*unemployment* ~s *a major problem*⟩ **synonyms** see COMPRISE [L *constitutus,* pp of *constituere* to set up, constitute, fr *com-* + *statuere* to set up – more at STATUTE]

**constitution** /,konsti'tyoohsh(ə)n/ *n* 1 an established law or custom; an ordinance 2 the act of establishing, making, or setting up 3a the physical and mental make-up of an individual ⟨*she has a sturdy* ~⟩ b the factors or parts which go to make something; composition; *also* the way in which these parts or factors make up the whole 4 the way in which a state or society is organized; *esp* the manner in which sovereign power is distributed **5a** the fundamental principles and laws of a nation, state, or social group that guarantee certain rights to the people in it, determine the powers and duties of the government, and state how the government is appointed and what its structure shall be **b** a written document embodying the rules of a political or social organization – **constitutionless** *adj*

¹**constitutional** /ˌkonstiˈtyoohsh(ə)nl/ *adj* **1** relating to, inherent in, or affecting the constitution of body or mind **2** of or entering into the fundamental make-up of something; essential **3** in accordance with or authorized by the constitution of a state or society ⟨*a ~ government*⟩ **4** regulated by or ruling according to a constitution ⟨*a ~ monarchy*⟩ **5** of a constitution **6** loyal to or supporting an established constitution or form of government

²**constitutional** *n* a walk taken for one's health

**constitutionalism** /-iz(ə)m/ *n* adherence to or government according to constitutional principles; *also* a constitutional system of government – **constitutionalist** *n*

**constitutionality** /ˌkonstiˌtyoohsh(ə)nˈaləti/ *n* the quality or state of being constitutional; *esp* accordance with the provisions of a constitution ⟨*questioned the ~ of the law*⟩

**constitutional·ize, -ise** /ˌkonstiˈtyoohsh(ə)nl‚iez/ *vt* to provide with a constitution; *also* to organize in accordance with constitutional principles – **constitutionalization** *n*

**constitutional law** *n* a body of law dealing with the powers, organization, and responsibilities of local and central government

**constitutionally** /ˌkonstiˈtyoohsh(ə)nl‧i/ *adv* **1a** in accordance with one's mental or bodily constitution ⟨*~ unable to grasp subtleties*⟩ **b** in structure, composition, or physical constitution ⟨*despite repeated heatings the material remained ~ the same*⟩ **2** in accordance with a constitution ⟨*was not ~ eligible to fill the office*⟩

**constitutive** /kənˈstityootiv/ *adj* **1** having the power to enact or establish ⟨*a ~ assembly*⟩ **2** constituent, essential **3** relating to or dependent on constitution ⟨*a ~ property of all electrolytes*⟩ – **constitutively** *adv*

**constrain** /kənˈstrayn/ *vt* **1a** to force by imposed stricture or limitation ⟨*necessity ~s me to work*⟩ ⟨*the evidence ~s belief*⟩ **b** to restrict the motion of (a mechanical body) to a particular mode **2** to force or produce in an unnatural or strained manner ⟨*a ~ed smile*⟩ **3** to bring with narrow confines; *also* to clasp tightly **4** *archaic* to secure (as if) by bonds; confine ⟨*when winter frosts ~ the field with cold* – John Dryden⟩ [ME *constrainen*, fr MF *constraindre*, fr L *constringere* to constrict, constrain, fr *com-* + *stringere* to draw tight – more at STRAIN] – **constrainedly** *adv*

**constraint** /kənˈstraynt/ *n* **1a** constraining or being constrained **b** a constraining agency or force; a check ⟨*put legal ~s on the board's activities*⟩ **2a** repression of one's own feelings, behaviour, or actions **b** a sense of being constrained; embarrassment [ME, fr MF *constrainte*, fr *constraindre*]

**constrict** /kənˈstrikt/ *vt* **1a** to make narrow by compress, squeeze ⟨*~ a nerve*⟩ **2** to set or keep within limits ~ *vi* to become constricted **synonyms** see ²CONTRACT [L *constrictus*, pp of *constringere*] – **constriction** *n*, **constrictive** *adj*

**constrictor** /kənˈstriktə/ *n* **1** one who or that which constricts **2** a muscle that contracts a cavity or opening or compresses an organ **3** a snake (eg a BOA CONSTRICTOR) that kills prey by compressing it in its coils

¹**construct** /kənˈstrikt/ *vt* **1** to make or form by combining parts; build **2** to set in logical order **3** to draw (a geometrical figure) with suitable instruments and under given conditions [L *constructus*, pp of *construere*, fr *com-* + *struere* to build – more at STRUCTURE] – **constructible** *adj*, **constructor** *n*

²**construct** /ˈkonstrukt/ *n* something constructed, esp mentally

**construction** /kənˈstruksh(ə)n/ *n* **1** the arrangement and connection of MORPHEMES (parts of words), words, or groups of words ⟨*is this ~ possible in Finnish?*⟩ **2a** the process, art, or manner of constructing; *also* something constructed **b** a line or figure constructed in order to help solve a geometrical problem **3** the act or result of construing, interpreting, or explaining ⟨*put the wrong ~ on what I said*⟩ **4** a nonobjective sculptural creation that is put together out of separate pieces of often disparate materials – **constructional** *adj*, **constructionally** *adv*

**constructionist** *n*, *NAm* a person who construes a legal document (eg the US Constitution) in a specified way ⟨*a strict ~*⟩

**constructive** /kənˈstruktiv/ *adj* **1** inferred rather than explicit or directly expressed ⟨*~ permission*⟩ ⟨*~ dismissal*⟩; *specif* declared such by judicial construction or interpretation ⟨*~ fraud*⟩ **2** of or relating to construction **3** suggesting improvement or development ⟨*~ criticism*⟩ – **constructively** *adv*, **constructiveness** *n*

**constructivism** /kənˈstruktiˌviz(ə)m/ *n* **1** a nonobjective art movement originating in Russia about 1914 that was concerned with the aesthetic effect of the juxtaposition of (geometric) forms and various kinds of surface quality (eg colour, tone, texture, etc) and used modern industrial materials (eg glass and plastic) **2** an abstract style of stage setting that employs skeletal structures instead of realistic props – **constructivist** *adj or n*

¹**construe** /kənˈstrooh/ *vt* **1a** to analyse the grammatical structure of (eg a sentence part) **b** to translate closely **2** to understand or explain the sense or intention of, usu in a particular way or with respect to a given set of circumstances ⟨*~d my actions as hostile*⟩ ~ *vi* to construe a sentence or sentence part, esp in connection with translating [ME *construen*, fr LL *construere*, fr L, to construct] – **construable** *adj*

²**construe** *n* an act of construing, esp by close translation; *also* the translated version resulting from such an act

**consubstantial** /ˌkonsəbˈstansh(ə)l/ *adj, esp of the three persons of the Trinity* of the same substance [LL *consubstantialis*, fr L *com-* + *substantia* substance]

**consubstantiation** /ˌkonsəbˌstanshiˈaysh(ə)n, -siˈaysh(ə)n/ *n* (the Anglican doctrine of) the actual presence and combination of the body and blood of Christ with the bread and wine used at Communion, according to a teaching associated with Martin Luther – compare TRANSUBSTANTIATION

**consuetude** /ˈkonswityoohd/ *n, formal* social usage; custom [ME, fr L *consuetudin-, consuetudo* – more at CUSTOM] – **consuetudinary** *adj*

**consul** /ˈkons(ə)l/ *n* **1a** either of two annually elected chief magistrates of the Roman republic **b** any of three chief magistrates of the French republic from 1799 to 1804 **2** an official appointed by a government to live in a foreign country to look after the interests (eg commercial interests) of citizens of the appointing country [ME fr L, fr *consulere* to consult] – **consular** *adj*, **consulship** *n*

**consulate** /ˈkonsyoolət/ *n* **1** a government by consuls **2** the office, term of office, or jurisdiction of a consul **3** the residence or official premises of a consul

**consulate general** *n, pl* **consulates general 1** the office, term of office, or jurisdiction of a consul general **2** the residence or official premises of a consul general

**consul general** *n, pl* **consuls general** a senior diplomatic consul stationed in an important place or having jurisdiction in several places or over several consuls

**consult** /kənˈsult/ *vt* **1a** to ask the advice or opinion of ⟨*~ a doctor*⟩ **b** to refer to ⟨*~ a dictionary*⟩ **2** to have regard to; consider ⟨*resents always having to ~ her likes and dislikes*⟩ ~ *vi* **1** to consult an individual **2** to deliberate together; confer **3** to serve as a consultant [MF or L; MF *consulter*, fr L *consultare*, fr *consultus*, pp of *consulere* to discuss, consult] – **consulter, consultor** *n*

*usage* The use of **consult** as an intransitive verb followed by *with*, to mean "ask the advice of" ⟨**consult** *with my doctor*⟩ is disliked by some British people as an Americanism. Such people prefer to use the verb transitively in this sense ⟨**consult** *a lawyer*⟩.

**consultancy** /kənˈsult(ə)nsi/ *n* **1** an agency that provides consulting services **2** consultation

**consultant** /kənˈsult(ə)nt/ *n* **1** one who consults someone or something **2** an expert who gives professional advice or services **3** the most senior grade of British hospital doctor; *also* a doctor holding this post who has direct clinical responsibility for hospital patients – **consultantship** *n*

**consultation** /ˌkons(ə)lˈtaysh(ə)n/ *n* **1** a council, conference; *specif* a deliberation between doctors on a case or its treatment **2** the act of consulting or conferring

**consultative** /kənˈsultətiv/ *adj* of or intended for consultation; advisory ⟨*a ~ committee*⟩

**consulting** /kənˈsulting/ *adj* **1** providing professional or expert advice ⟨*a ~ architect*⟩ **2** of or for consultation or a consultant ⟨*the ~ room of a psychiatrist*⟩ [(1) fr prp of *consult;* (2) fr gerund of *consult*]

**consumables** /kənˈsyoohməblz/ *n pl* food, provisions

**consume** /kənˈsyoohm/ *vt* **1** to do away with completely; destroy ⟨*the fire ~d several buildings*⟩ **2a** to spend wastefully;

squander **b** to use or use up ⟨*furnaces* ~ *fuel*⟩ ⟨*work* ~s *time*⟩ **3** to eat or drink, esp in great quantity or eagerly **4** to obsess the thoughts and feelings of, usu detrimentally – usu pass ⟨*she was* ~d *with jealousy*⟩ ~ *vi* to waste or burn away; perish [ME *consumen*, fr MF or L; MF *consumer*, fr L *consumere*, fr *com-* + *sumere* to take up, take, fr *sub-* up + *emere* to take – more at SUB-, REDEEM] – **consumable** *adj*, **consumingly** *adv*

**consumedly** /kən'syoohmidli/ *adv, formal* very or too greatly; excessively

**consumer** /kən'syoohmə/ *n* one who or that which consumes: e g **a** one who utilizes economic goods; *broadly* one who purchases goods or services **b** an organism that obtains the complex organic material which it requires as food by preying on other organisms or by taking in particles of organic matter (e g plant tissue) – compare PRODUCER C, PRIMARY CONSUMER, SECONDARY CONSUMER – **consumership** *n*

**consumer credit** *n* credit granted to an individual, esp to finance the purchase of consumer goods or to defray personal or family expenses

**consumer goods** *n pl* goods (e g food, clothing, and domestic appliances) that directly satisfy human wants; goods not used in further production or manufacturing processes

**consumerism** /kən'syoohmə,riz(ə)m/ *n* **1** advocacy of the interests of consumers (e g in regulating the quality and price of products) **2** the theory that an increasing consumption of goods is economically desirable – **consumerist** *n*

**consumer society** *n* a society in which resources are chiefly allocated to the production, promotion, and consumption of material consumer goods which tend to be regarded as the ultimate means of satisfying human wants – compare ADMASS

**consumer surplus** *n* the difference between the maximum amount that a consumer would be prepared to pay for some quantity of a good and what is actually paid

¹**consummate** /kən'sumət, 'konsyoomət, -sə-, -su-/ *adj* **1** complete in every detail; perfect **2** extremely skilled and accomplished ⟨*a* ~ *liar*⟩ **3** of the highest degree ⟨~ *skill*⟩ ⟨~ *cruelty*⟩ [ME, fr L *consummatus*, pp of *consummare* to sum up, finish, fr *com-* + *summa* sum] – **consummately** *adv*

*usage* The pronunciation /kən'sumət/ is recommended for BBC broadcasters.

²**consummate** /'konsyoomayt, -sə-, -su-/ *vt* **1** to finish, complete ⟨~ *a business deal*⟩ **2** to make (a marriage) complete by sexual intercourse – **consummative** *adj*, **consummator** *n*

**consummation** /,konsə'maysh(ə)n, -su-, -syoo-/ *n* **1** the act of consummating ⟨*the* ~ *of a contract by mutual signature*⟩; *specif* the consummating of a marriage **2** the ultimate end; the goal

**consummatory** /kən'sumət(ə)ri/ *adj* **1** of consummation **2** of or being a response or act (e g eating or copulating) that terminates a period of behaviour usu directed at the achievement of a particular goal

**consumption** /kən'sumsh(ə)n, -'sumpsh(ə)n/ *n* **1** the act or process of consuming **2** the utilization of economic goods in the satisfaction of wants or in the process of production, resulting chiefly in their destruction, deterioration, or transformation **3a** a progressive wasting away of the body, esp from lung tuberculosis **b** tuberculosis [ME *consumpcioun*, fr L *consumption-*, *consumptio*, fr *consumptus*, pp of *consumere*]

¹**consumptive** /kən'sumptiv/ *adj* **1** tending to consume **2** of or affected with consumption – **consumptively** *adv*

²**consumptive** *n* someone suffering from consumption

¹**contact** /'kontakt/ *n* **1a** the state or act of touching; *also* an instance of this **b** the apparent touching of two stars, planets, or other celestial bodies or of the disc of one body with the shadow of another during an eclipse or similar phenomenon **c(1)** the junction of two electrical conductors through which a current passes **c(2)** a special part made for such a junction **2a** association, relationship ⟨*she needs human* ~⟩ **b** connection, communication ⟨*keep in* ~!⟩ **c** direct visual observation of the earth's surface made from an aircraft, esp as an aid to navigation **d** the act of establishing communication with someone or observing or receiving a significant signal from a person or object ⟨*radar* ~ *with Mars*⟩ **e** a reciprocal feeling between a horse's mouth and the hands of its rider through the bit and the reins **3** one serving as a carrier or source ⟨*our* ~ *in Berlin*⟩ [Fr or L; Fr, fr L *contactus*, fr *contactus*, pp of *contingere* to have contact with – more at CONTINGENT] – **fly contact** to fly an aircraft with the aid of visible landmarks or reference points

²**contact** /'kontakt, kon'takt, kən-/ *vt* **1** to bring into contact **2a** to enter or be in contact with; join **b** to get in communication with ⟨~ *your local agent*⟩ ~ *vi* to make contact

*usage* Although the use of **contact** as in sense **2b** to mean "get in communication with" was once disliked in Britain as an Americanism, it is now well established and very common in all except the most formal contexts, probably because it is so useful. It combines concisely the ideas of "write to", "telephone", "visit", and "send a message to".

³**contact** /'kontakt/ *adj* maintaining, involving, or activated or caused by contact ⟨~ *explosives*⟩

**contact flying** *n* navigation of an aircraft by means of direct observation of landmarks

**contact inhibition** *n* the stopping of movement and growth of a cell when it comes into contact with other cells, observed esp in tissue cultures

**contact lens** *n* a thin lens designed to fit over the cornea of the eye, esp for the correction of a visual defect

**contact poison** *n* any of various chemical pesticides that kill by penetrating the skin or other outer covering of the pest

**contact print** *n* a photographic print made with the negative in contact with the sensitized paper, plate, or film

**contagion** /kən'tayj(ə)n, -jyən/ *n* **1a** the transmission of a disease by direct or indirect contact **b** a contagious disease **c** a disease-producing agent (e g a virus) **2a** contagious influence, quality, or nature **b** corrupting influence or contact [ME, fr MF & L; MF, fr L *contagion-*, *contagio*, fr *contingere* to have contact with, pollute]

**contagious** /kən'tayjəs, -jyəs/ *adj* **1** communicable by contact; catching **2** bearing contagion **3** arousing similar emotions or conduct in others ⟨~ *enthusiasm*⟩ – **contagiously** *adv*, **contagiousness** *n*

**contagious abortion** *n* a contagious or infectious disease (e g brucellosis) of domestic animals that causes abortion

**contagium** /kən'tayj(y)əm/ *n, pl* **contagia** /-j(y)ə/ a virus or living organism capable of causing a communicable disease [L, contagion, fr *contingere*]

**contain** /kən'tayn/ *vt* **1** to keep within limits; hold back or down: e g **1a** to restrain, control ⟨*couldn't* ~ *himself*⟩ **b** to check, halt ⟨~ *the enemy's attack*⟩ **c** to follow successfully a policy of containment towards **d** to prevent (e g an enemy or opponent) from advancing or from making a successful attack **2a** to have within; hold **b** to comprise, include ⟨*the bill* ~s *several new clauses*⟩ **3a** to be divisible by, usu without a remainder **b** to enclose, bound [ME *conteinen*, fr OF *contenir*, fr L *continēre* to hold together, hold in, contain, fr *com-* + *tenēre* to hold – more at THIN] – **containable** *adj*

**container** /kən'taynə/ *n* **1** one who or that which contains **2** a receptacle or flexible covering for the packing or shipment of goods; *specif* a large usu metal packing case of standardized size in which goods are packed for transport by lorries, ships, etc and which is mechanically handled at all stages

**container·ization, -isation** /kən,taynərie'zaysh(ə)n/ *n* a shipping method in which a large amount of material (e g merchandise) is packaged together in one large container

**container·ize, -ise** /kən'taynəriez/ *vt* **1** to pack into containers for transport **2** to convert to the use of containers ⟨*plans to* ~ *the ports*⟩

**container ship** *n* a ship designed or equipped for carrying containerized cargo

**containment** /kən'taynmənt/ *n* **1** the act or process of containing **2** the policy, process, or result of preventing the expansion of a hostile power or ideology

**contaminant** /kən'taminənt/ *n* something that contaminates

**contaminate** /kən'taminayt/ *vt* **1a** to soil, stain, or infect by contact or association **b** to make inferior or impure by admixture ⟨*iron* ~d *with phosphorus*⟩ **2** to make unfit for use by the introduction of unwholesome or undesirable elements [L *contaminatus*, pp of *contaminare*; akin to L *contagio* contagion] – **contamination** *n*, **contaminative** *adj*, **contaminator** *n*

*synonyms* Contaminate, taint, pollute, and defile all suggest the sullying of something formerly pure with something external and offensive. **Contaminate** stresses the process, and **taint** the result. **Pollute** implies that the process of contamination is complete, and what was clean and pure is now foul or filthy ⟨*a polluted stream*⟩. **Defile** suggests wilfully befouling something which should be kept clean or sacred, and is strongly condemnatory ⟨*defiled the memory of his father*⟩. Compare INJURE

**contango** /kən'tang·goh/ *n, pl* **contangos** *Br* a premium paid by a buyer to a seller of shares to postpone delivery until a future day of settlement – compare BACKWARDATION [perh alter. of *continue*]

**conte** /konht, kawnt (*Fr* kɔ̃t)/ *n* a tale or short story, esp of adventure [Fr, fr *conter* to relate]

**contemn** /kən'tem/ *vt, formal* to view or treat with contempt; scorn △ condemn [ME *contempnen*, fr MF *contempner*, fr L *contemnere*, fr *com-* + *temnere* to despise – more at STAMP] – **contemner** *also* **contemnor** *n*

**contemplate** /'kontəmplayt/ *vt* 1 to view or consider with continued attention; meditate on 2 to have in view as contingent or probable or as an end or intention ⟨*what do you* ∼ *doing?*⟩ ∼ *vi* to ponder, meditate [L *contemplatus*, pp of *contemplari*, fr *com-* + *templum* space marked out for observation of auguries – more at TEMPLE] – **contemplator** *n*

**contemplation** /,kontəm'playsh(ə)n, -tem-/ *n* **1a** concentration on spiritual things as a form of private devotion **b** a state of mystical awareness of God's being **2** an act of considering with attention; a study **3** the act of regarding steadily **4** intention, expectation

¹**contemplative** /'kontəm,playtiv, -tem-, kən'templətiv/ *adj* marked by or given to contemplation; *specif* of a religious order devoted to prayer and penance – **contemplatively** *adv*, **contemplativeness** *n*

²**contemplative** *n* one who practises contemplation

**contemporaneous** /kən,tempə'raynyəs, kon-, -ni-əs/ *adj* CONTEMPORARY 1 [L *contemporaneus*, fr *com-* + *tempor-*, *tempus* time – more at TEMPORAL] – **contemporaneity** *n*, **contemporaneously** *adv*, **contemporaneousness** *n*

¹**contemporary** /kən'temp(ə)rəri, -pri/ *adj* 1 happening, existing, living, or coming into being during the same period of time 2 marked by characteristics of the present period; modern [*com-* + L *tempor-*, *tempus*] – **contemporarily** *adv*

   **usage** Both **contemporary** and **contemporaneous** mean "happening or existing at the same time" ⟨*Akbar was* contemporary/ contemporaneous *with Elizabeth I*⟩. In addition, **contemporary** means "happening at this time", "contemporary with ourselves", and therefore "modern". One should be careful to avoid ambiguity here ⟨*a production of* Hamlet *in* contemporary *dress* (= Shakespearian dress, or modern?)⟩. **synonyms** see ¹MODERN

²**contemporary** *n* one who or that which is contemporary with another; *specif* one of about the same age as another

**contempor·ize**, **-ise** /kən'tempəriez/ *vt* to make contemporary

**contempt** /kən'tem(p)t/ *n* **1a** the act of despising; the state of mind of one who despises **b** lack of respect or reverence for something **2** the state of being despised ⟨*he is held in* ∼⟩ **3** wilful disobedience to or open disrespect of a court, judge, or legislative body ⟨∼ *of court*⟩ [ME, fr L *contemptus*, fr *contemptus*, pp of *contemnere*]

**contemptible** /kən'tem(p)təbl/ *adj* 1 worthy of contempt 2 *obs* scornful, contemptuous △ contemptuous – **contemptibleness** *n*, **contemptibly** *adv*

**contemptuous** /kən'tem(p)choo·əs, -tyoo·əs/ *adj* manifesting, feeling, or expressing contempt [L *contemptus* contempt] – **contemptuously** *adv*, **contemptuousness** *n*

**contend** /kən'tend/ *vi* 1 to strive or vie in contest or rivalry or against difficulties ⟨∼*ing for the world title*⟩ 2 to strive in debate; argue ∼ *vt* to maintain, assert ⟨∼*ed that he was right*⟩ **synonyms** see ³RIVAL [MF or L; MF *contendre*, fr L *contendere*, fr *com-* + *tendere* to stretch – more at THIN] – **contender** *n*

¹**content** /kən'tent/ *adj* happy, satisfied ⟨∼ *to wait quietly*⟩ [ME, fr MF, fr L *contentus*, fr pp of *continēre* to hold in, contain] – **contentment** *n*

²**content** /kən'tent/ *vt* 1 to appease the desires of; satisfy 2 to limit (oneself) in requirements, desires, or actions ⟨∼*ed himself with two helpings*⟩

   **usage** One **contents** oneself *with* something. The use here of *by* ⟨**contented** *himself for the moment by shaking hands*⟩ is disapproved of by some writers on usage.

³**content** /kən'tent/ *n* being content; *esp* freedom from care or discomfort

⁴**content** /'kontent/ *n* 1 **contents** *pl*, **content 1a** that which is contained ⟨*the* ∼s *of the box*⟩ ⟨*the drawer's* ∼s⟩ ⟨*the bag's* ∼s⟩ **b** the topics or matter treated in a written work ⟨*table of* ∼s⟩ **2a** the substance, gist **b** essential meaning; significance **c** the events, physical detail, and information in a work of art – compare FORM 10c **3** the matter dealt with in a field of study **4** the amount of specified material contained; proportion ⟨*the*

*lead* ∼ *of paint*⟩ [ME, fr L *contentus*, pp of *continēre* to contain]

**contented** /kən'tentid/ *adj* marked by satisfaction with one's possessions, status, or situation; happy – **contentedly** *adv*, **contentedness** *n*

**contention** /kən'tensh(ə)n/ *n* 1 an act or instance of contending **2** a point advanced or maintained in a debate or argument **3** rivalry, competition [ME *contencioun*, fr MF, fr L *contention-*, *contentio*, fr *contentus*, pp of *contendere* to contend]

**contentious** /kən'tenshəs/ *adj* 1 exhibiting an often perverse and wearisome tendency to quarrels and disputes ⟨*a man of a most* ∼ *nature*⟩ 2 likely to cause disagreement and ill feeling ⟨*a* ∼ *argument*⟩ – **contentiously** *adv*, **contentiousness** *n*

**content word** *n* a word (e g *ship*, *dirty*, or *grumble*) that refers essentially to a thing or concept in the real world rather than to the relationship between other words – compare FUNCTION WORD

**conterminous** /kon'tuhminəs/ *adj* COTERMINOUS (having the same boundary or scope) [L *conterminus*, fr *com-* + *terminus* boundary – more at TERM] – **conterminously** *adv*

¹**contest** /kən'test/ *vt* to make the subject of dispute, contention, or legal action to strive, vie [MF *contester*, fr L *contestari* (*litem*) to bring an action at law, fr *contestari* to call to witness, fr *com-* + *testis* witness – more at TESTAMENT] – **contestable** *adj*, **contester** *n*

²**contest** /'kontest/ *n* 1 a struggle for superiority or victory 2 a competitive event; COMPETITION 2; *esp* one judged by a panel of specially chosen judges ⟨*Eurovision Song* Contest⟩

**contestant** /kən'test(ə)nt/ *n* 1 one who participates in a contest 2 one who contests an award or decision

**contestation** /,konte'staysh(ə)n/ *n, formal* controversy

**context** /'kontekst/ *n* 1 those parts of a piece of text that surround a word or passage and can throw light on its meaning 2 the interrelated conditions in which something exists or occurs; the environment [ME, weaving together of words, fr L *contextus* connection of words, coherence, fr *contextus*, pp of *contexere* to weave together, fr *com-* + *texere* to weave – more at TECHNICAL] – **contextual** *adj*, **contextually** *adv*

**contexture** /kən'tekschə/ *n, formal* the act, process, or manner of weaving parts into a whole; *also* a structure so formed ⟨*a* ∼ *of lies*⟩ [Fr, fr L *contextus*, pp]

**contiguous** /kən'tigyoo·əs/ *adj* 1 in actual contact; touching along a boundary or at a point 2 *of two angles* ADJACENT (having one of the lines making the angles in common) 3 next or near in time or sequence **synonyms** see ²NEXT △ contagious [L *contiguus*, fr *contingere* to have contact with – more at CONTINGENT] – **contiguity** *n*, **contiguously** *adv*, **contiguousness** *n*

**continence** /'kontinəns/ *n* 1 self-restraint from yielding to impulse or desire 2 ability to refrain from a bodily activity; the state of being continent **synonyms** see ABSTINENCE

¹**continent** /'kontinənt/ *adj* 1 exercising continence 2 not suffering from urinary or faecal incontinence [ME, fr MF, fr L *continent-*, *continens*, fr prp of *continēre* to hold in – more at CONTAIN] – **continently** *adv*

²**continent** *n* **1a** any of the seven great divisions of land on the globe **b** *cap* the continent of Europe **2** *archaic* a continuous extent or mass of land; *esp* the mainland [L *continent-*, *continens* continuous mass of land, mainland, fr *continent-*, *continens*, prp of *continēre*]

¹**continental** /,konti'nentl/ *adj* 1 (characteristic) of a continent ⟨∼ *waters*⟩; *specif* of the continent of Europe as distinguished from the British isles 2 *often cap* of the colonies later forming the USA ⟨Continental *Congress*⟩ – **continentally** *adv*

²**continental** *n* **1a** *often cap* an American soldier of the Revolution in the Continental army **b** a piece of paper currency issued by the Continental Congress at the time of the American Revolution **c** an inhabitant of a continent, esp the continent of Europe **2** *NAm informal* the least bit ⟨*not worth a* ∼⟩ [(2) fr the rapid depreciation of the continental currency]

**continental breakfast** *n* a light breakfast typically consisting of bread rolls, preserves (e g jam), and coffee

**continental drift** *n* a hypothetical slow movement of the continents on a deep-seated zone of molten rock within the earth

**continentalism** /,konti'nentl,iz(ə)m/ *n* the advocacy of strong economic and cultural links between Canada and the USA – **continentalist** *adj or n*

**continental quilt** *n, Br* a duvet

**continental shelf** *n* the gently sloping part of the ocean floor that borders a continent and typically ends in a steeper slope to the ocean depths

**contingency** /kən'tinj(ə)nsi/ *n* **1** the quality or state of being contingent **2** a contingent event or condition: e g **2a** an event that may occur; *esp* an undesirable one **b** an event that is liable to happen as an adjunct to another event

**contingency table** *n* a table that tabulates the FREQUENCY DISTRIBUTION of one variable in the rows and that of another variable in the columns and that is used esp in the study of correlation between the variables

¹**contingent** /kən'tinj(ə)nt/ *adj* **1** happening by chance or unforeseen causes **2** dependent *on* or conditioned by something else **3** not logically necessary; *esp* empirical, factual **4** *philosophy* not necessitated; free *synonyms* see ¹INCIDENTAL [ME, liable to happen, fr MF, fr L *contingent-, contingens,* prp of *contingere* to have contact with, befall, fr *com-* + *tangere* to touch – more at TANGENT] – **contingently** *adv*

²**contingent** *n* **1** something contingent **2** *taking sing or pl vb a* quota or share, esp of people supplied from or representative of an area, group, or military force

**continual** /kən'tinyoo·əl, -yool/ *adj* **1** continuing indefinitely without interruption 〈 ~ *fear*〉 **2** recurring in steady rapid succession [ME, fr MF, fr L *continuus* continuous] – **continually** *adv*
*synonyms* **Continual, continuous, constant, incessant, unremitting, perpetual,** and **perennial** may all mean "occurring or recurring over and over again". **Continual** suggests an unceasing succession which may go on and on, but is not without interruptions. **Continuous,** which may apply to time or space, suggests an uninterrupted continuity 〈*a* **continuous** *struggle against poverty is everyone's duty*〉 〈*their life is a* **continual** *struggle against poverty*〉. **Constant** stresses uniformity, steadiness, and persistence 〈*a* **constant** *flow of visitors*〉. What is **incessant** is ceaseless and without interruption 〈**incessant** *chattering*〉, while what is **unremitting** allows no slackening of effort, and no relief 〈**unremitting** *pain*〉. Something **perpetual** is lasting or unfailingly repeated 〈**perpetual** *friendship/outbursts of temper*〉. **Perennial** may imply self-renewal or that something is longlasting 〈*the* **perennial** *joys of spring*〉. *antonym* intermittent

**continuance** /kən'tinyoo·əns/ *n* **1** the act or process of continuing in a state, condition, or course of action **2** *NAm* adjournment of court proceedings
*synonyms* **Continuance** and **continuation** can both mean the "process of continuing"; but **continuance** is particularly used for the period for which something lasts 〈*the* **continuance** *of the fine weather*〉 and **continuation** for the active prolonging of something 〈*the government's* **continuation** *of the arms trade*〉.

**continuant** /kən'tinyoo·ənt/ *n* something that continues or serves as a continuation (e g a consonant, such as /l/or /f/, that may be prolonged like a vowel) – **continuant** *adj*

**continuate** /kən'tinyooayt/ *adj, obs* continuous

**continuation** /kən,tinyoo'aysh(ə)n/ *n* **1** the act or process of continuing in a state or activity **2** resumption after an interruption **3** something that continues, increases, or adds
*synonyms* see CONTINUANCE

**continuative** /kən'tinyooətiv/ *adj* relating to, causing, or being in the process of continuation

**continuator** /kən'tinyoo,aytə/ *n* one that continues; *esp* one who writes a continuation to the work of another

**continue** /kən'tinyooh/ *vi* **1** to maintain a condition, course, or action without interruption **2** to remain in existence; endure **3** to remain in a place or condition; stay **4** to resume an activity after interruption; *specif* to resume speaking 〈*pray* ~〉 ~ *vt* **1a** to maintain (a condition, course, or action) without interruption; CARRY ON 〈~s *walking*〉 **b** to prolong; *specif* to resume after interruption **2** to cause to continue **3** to say further 〈*"We must fight on for freedom",* ~d *the speaker*〉 **4** *NAm* to postpone (a legal proceeding) by a continuance [ME *continuen,* fr MF *continuer,* fr L *continuare,* fr *continuus*] – **continuer** *n*
*synonyms* **Continue, last, endure, abide,** and **persist** can all mean "remain or carry on, without ceasing or ending". **Continue** stresses the process and its lack of an end, and often suggests an unbroken course 〈*the river* **continues** *to the sea*〉. **Last** (and especially its derivative **lasting**) stresses unusual length of existence, though it may lose this if qualified 〈*the car should* **last** *three more years*〉. **Endure** suggests resistance to destructive forces 〈*an art which* **endures**〉. **Abide** and **abiding** strongly imply stability and constancy 〈*though much is taken, much* **abides** – *Tennyson*〉. **Persist** suggests something lasting longer than is usual, (as if) with stubbornness and resolution; it may also describe something which

continually recurs 〈*the idea of a universal remedy* **persists** *to this day*〉. *antonyms* stop, cease, desist

**continued fraction** /kən'tinyoohd/ *n* a fraction whose numerator is a WHOLE NUMBER and whose denominator is a whole number plus a fraction whose numerator is a whole number and whose denominator is a whole number plus a fraction and so on

**continuing education** /kən'tinyooing/ *n* an educational programme designed to update the knowledge and skills of its participants

**continuity** /,konti'nyooh·əti/ *n* **1a** uninterrupted connection, succession, or union **b** persistence without essential change **c** uninterrupted duration in time **2** something that has, displays, or provides continuity: e g **2a** a script or scenario in the performing arts; *esp* one giving the details of the sequence of individual shots **b** speech or music used to link parts of an entertainment, esp a radio or television programme **3** the property characteristic of a CONTINUOUS mathematical function; *also* an example of this property

**continuity girl** *n* the member of a film production team responsible for ensuring consistency between individual shots after a break in filming

**continuo** /kən'tinyoo,oh/ *n, pl* **continuos** a bass part for a keyboard or stringed instrument used esp in baroque ensemble music and written as a succession of bass notes with figures that indicate the required chords; *also* (the instruments playing) a continuo accompaniment [It, fr *continuo* continuous, fr L *continuus*]

**continuous** /kən'tinyoo·əs/ *adj* **1** marked by uninterrupted extension in space, time, or sequence **2** having the property that the difference in the values of a mathematical function at two points may be made as small as possible by choosing two points sufficiently close together *synonyms* see CONTINUAL *antonym* interrupted [L *continuus,* fr *continēre* to hold together – more at CONTAIN] – **continuously** *adv,* **continuousness** *n*

**continuous assessment** *n* appraisal of the value of a student's work throughout a course as a means of awarding his/her final mark or degree

**continuous spectrum** *n* a SPECTRUM that is produced by solids and liquids and consists of a continuous region of radiation – compare BAND SPECTRUM, LINE SPECTRUM

**continuum** /kən'tinyoo·əm/ *n, pl* **continua, continuums 1** something (e g duration or extension) absolutely continuous and homogeneous that can be described only by reference to something else (e g numbers) **2a** something in which a fundamental common character is discernible amongst a series of imperceptible or indefinite variations 〈*the* ~ *of experience*〉 **b(1)** *maths* an uninterrupted ORDERED sequence **b(2)** a series of ecological communities whose vegetation gradually changes along an environmental gradient; *also* SERE **3** a mathematical set having an infinite number of elements such that between any two elements of the set a further element can be found 〈*the* ~ *of real numbers*〉 [L, neut of *continuus*]

**contort** /kən'tawt/ *vi* to twist in a violent manner 〈*his features were* ~ed *with fury*〉 〈 ~ *spelling and grammar*〉 to twist into a strained shape or expression 〈*his features* ~ed *with fury*〉 [L *contortus,* pp of *contorquēre,* fr *com-* + *torquēre* to twist – more at TORTURE] – **contortion** *n,* **contortive** *adj*

**contortionist** /kən'tawsh(ə)nist/ *n* one who contorts something: e g **a** an acrobat who specializes in unnatural body postures **b** one who extricates him-/herself from a dilemma by complicated but dubious arguments – **contortionistic** *adj*

¹**contour** /'kon,tooə/ *n* **1** an outline, esp of a curving or irregular figure; a shape; *also* the line representing this outline **2** **contour, contour line** a line (e g on a map) connecting points of equal vertical distance above or below a zero point (DATUM) [Fr, fr It *contorno,* fr *contornare* to round off, sketch in outline, fr L *com-* + *tornare* to turn in a lathe, fr *tornus* lathe]

²**contour** *vt* **1a** to shape the contour of **b** to shape so as to fit contours **2** to construct (e g a road) in conformity to a contour

³**contour** *adj* following contour lines or forming furrows or ridges along them 〈 ~ *farming*〉

**contour feather** *n* any of the medium-sized feathers that form the general covering of a bird and determine the external contour

**contra-** /kontrə-/ *prefix* **1** against; contrary; contrasting 〈contra*distinction*〉 〈contra*ceptive*〉 **2** pitched below normal bass 〈contra*bass*〉 [ME, fr L, fr *contra* against, opposite – more at COUNTER]

**contraband** /'kontrə‚band/ *n* goods or merchandise whose importation, exportation, or possession is forbidden; *also* smuggled goods [It *contrabbando*, fr ML *contrabannum*, fr *contra-* + *bannus, bannum* decree, of Gmc origin; akin to OHG *ban* command] – **contraband** *adj*

¹**contrabass** /'kontrə‚bays/ *n* DOUBLE BASS

²**contrabass** *adj* pitched eight notes below the normal bass range

**contrabassoon** /-bə'soohn/ *n* a large woodwind instrument similar to but with a range lower than that of the bassoon – called also DOUBLE BASSOON

**contraception** /‚kontrə'sepsh(ə)n/ *n* voluntary prevention of conception or impregnation, esp by use of a contraceptive [*contra-* + *conception*] – **contraceptive** *adj*

**contraceptive** /‚kontrə'septiv/ *n* a method or device used in preventing conception; *esp* a condom

¹**contract** /'kontrakt/ *n* **1a** a legally binding agreement between two or more people or parties **b** a betrothal **2** a document containing the terms and conditions of a contract **3** the division or principles of law having to do with contracts **4** an undertaking in bridge made by the highest bidding partnership to win at least a specified number of TRICKS (winning combinations of cards) with a named suit as trumps or with no trumps [ME, fr L *contractus*, fr *contractus*, pp of *contrahere* to draw together, make a contract, reduce in size, fr *com-* + *trahere* to draw – more at DRAW]

²**contract** /kən'trakt/ *vt sense 1 and vi sense 1 usu* 'kontrakt/ *vt* **1a** to establish or undertake by contract ⟨~ed *to build the road in 18 months*⟩ **b** to transfer or convey by contract ⟨*the copyright was* ~ed *to the publisher*⟩ **c** to betroth **2a** to catch (a disease) ⟨~ *pneumonia*⟩ **b** to bring on oneself as an obligation; incur ⟨~ *a debt*⟩ **3** to knit, wrinkle ⟨*a frown* ~ed *his brow*⟩ **4** to reduce to smaller size (as if) by squeezing or forcing together **5** to shorten (eg a word) by omitting one or more sounds or letters ~ *vi* to draw together so as to become diminished in size ⟨*metal* ~s *on cooling*⟩; *also* to become less in range, duration, or length ⟨*muscle* ~s *in tetanus*⟩ [partly fr MF *contracter* to agree upon, fr L *contractus* n; partly fr L *contractus*, pp of *contrahere* to draw together] – **contractible** *adj*, **contractibility** *n*

**synonyms** Contract, shrink, condense, compress, constrict, and deflate all mean "make or become smaller". Contract suggests a drawing in of something by inner forces, or a limiting of scope ⟨*the market for our goods has* **contracted**⟩. Shrink contrasts the new size with the original one ⟨*my shirt/my income has* **shrunk**⟩. Condense suggests making something more compact, by removing parts of it ⟨**condense** *a novel into a radio play*⟩ or by changing it to a denser form (eg from gas into water). Compress implies squeezing from outside ⟨*waste paper* **compressed** *into bales*⟩. Constrict suggests a painful or difficult narrowing by squeezing ⟨*tight collar* **constricts** *my throat*⟩. Deflate implies the removal of air or something similarly insubstantial ⟨**deflate** *a balloon/a reputation*⟩. Compare ABRIDGMENT **antonym** expand

**contract in** *vb* to agree to inclusion (of) in a particular scheme

**contract out** *vb* to agree to exclusion (of) from a particular scheme ⟨*decided to* contract out *of the state pension scheme*⟩

**contract bridge** /'kontrakt/ *n* a form of bridge distinguished by the fact that tricks won above the number a partnership has undertaken to get (OVERTRICKS) do not count towards winning the game, although they add points to the final score

**contractile** /kən'traktiel/ *adj* having the power or property of contracting ⟨~ *muscles*⟩ ⟨~ *proteins*⟩ – **contractility** *n*

**contractile vacuole** *n* a small spherical sac in a single-celled organism (eg an amoeba) that contracts regularly to discharge surplus liquids from the body

**contraction** /kən'traksh(ə)n/ *n* **1a** contracting or being contracted **b** the shortening and thickening of a functioning muscle or muscle fibre **c** a reduction in business activity **2** a shortening of a word, syllable, or word group by omission of a sound or letter; *also* a form produced by such shortening – **contractional** *adj*, **contractive** *adj*

**contractor** /kən'traktə, 'kontraktə/ *n* **1** one who contracts to perform work or provide supplies usu on a large scale; *esp* one who contracts to build according to a customer's plans **2** something (eg a muscle) that contracts or shortens

**contractual** /kən'traktyoo‑əl, -choo‑əl/ *adj* of or constituting a contract – **contractually** *adv* [L *contractus* contract]

**contracture** /kən'trakchə/ *n* a permanent shortening of muscle, tendon, scar tissue, etc, producing deformity or distortion

**contra dance** /'kontrə ‚dahns/ *n* CONTREDANSE (a folk dance)

**contradict** /‚kontrə'dikt/ *vt* **1a** to state the contrary of (a statement or speaker) **b** to deny the truthfulness of (a statement or speaker) ⟨*dear Duff, prithee* ~ *thyself, and say it is not so* – Shak⟩ **2a** to be the contradictory of **b** to go counter to [L *contradictus*, pp of *contradicere*, fr *contra-* + *dicere* to say, speak – more at DICTION] – **contradictable** *adj*, **contradictor** *n*

**contradiction** /‚kontrə'diksh(ə)n/ *n* **1** contradicting or being contradicted **2** an expression or proposition containing contradictory parts **3a** logical inconsistency ⟨*a* ~ *in terms*⟩ **b** opposition of factors inherent in a system or situation

¹**contradictory** /‚kontrə'dikt(ə)ri/ *n* **1a** something that contradicts **b** *the* opposite, contrary **2** *philosophy* a proposition so related to another that if one is true the other must be false and if one is false the other must be true

²**contradictory** *adj* **1** given to or marked by contradiction **2** involving, causing, or constituting a contradiction – **contradictorily** *adv*, **contradictoriness** *n*

**contradistinction** /-di'stingksh(ə)n/ *n* distinction by contrast ⟨*painting in* ~ *to sculpture*⟩ – **contradistinctive** *adj*, **contradistinctively** *adv*

**contradistinguish** /-di'sting‑gwish/ *vt* to distinguish by contrast of qualities

**contraflexure** /'kontrə‚flekshə/ *n* **1** a point where contrary bending forces meet, that in a fixed beam is a point where no bending will take place **2** a bending in opposite directions, like the curve of an OGEE; *also* a point where contraflexure occurs

**contrail** /'kontrayl/ *n* the VAPOUR TRAIL of an aircraft or rocket [*condensation trail*]

**contraindicate** /-'indikayt/ *vt* to make (a treatment or procedure) inadvisable ⟨*this drug is* ~d *in pregnancy*⟩ – **contraindication** *n*, **contraindicative** *adj*

**contralateral** /-'lat(ə)rəl/ *adj, anatomy* occurring on or acting in conjunction with similar parts on an opposite side – compare IPSILATERAL [ISV]

**contralto** /kən'traltoh, kən'trahltoh/ *n, pl* **contraltos 1** the lowest female singing voice; *also* a person having this voice **2** the part sung by a contralto [It, fr *contra-* + *alto*]

**contraposition** /‚kontrəpə'zish(ə)n/ *n* **1** an opposition, antithesis **2** *philosophy* the relation between two propositions when the first term (SUBJECT) and second term (PREDICATE) of one negate respectively the predicate and the subject of the other [LL *contraposition-, contrapositio*, fr L *contrapositus*, pp of *contraponere* to place opposite, fr *contra-* + *ponere* to place]

**contrapositive** /‚kontrə'pozətiv/ *n, philosophy* a proposition resulting from an inference in which the terms of a given proposition are inverted and negated ⟨*"all not-P is not-S" is the* ~ *of "all* S *is* P"⟩

**contraption** /kən'trapsh(ə)n/ *n* a newfangled or complicated device; a gadget [perh blend of *contrivance, trap*, and *invention*]

**contrapuntal** /‚kontrə'puntl/ *adj* **1** of COUNTERPOINT **2** intermingling of melody and accompaniment) **2** POLYPHONIC □ compare HOMOPHONIC [It *contrappunto* counterpoint, fr ML *contrapunctus*] – **contrapuntally** *adv*

**contrapuntist** /‚kontrə'puntist/ *n* one who writes counterpoint

**contrariety** /‚kontrə'rie‑əti/ *n, formal* **1** the quality or state of being contrary; *esp* opposition, disagreement **2** something contrary [ME *contrariete*, fr MF *contrarieté*, fr LL *contrarietat-, contrarietas*, fr L *contrarius* contrary]

**contrariwise** /'kontrəri‚wiez, kən'treə-/ *adv* **1** ON THE CONTRARY **2** conversely; VICE VERSA

¹**contrary** /'kontrəri/ *n* **1** a fact or condition incompatible with another **2** either of a pair of opposites **3** *philosophy* **3a** a proposition so related to another that though both may be false, they cannot both be true **b** either of two terms (eg true and false) that cannot both simultaneously be said to be true of the same subject – **on the contrary** just the opposite; no – **to the contrary 1** to the opposite effect ⟨*if I hear nothing to the contrary I'll assume you're coming*⟩ **2** notwithstanding ⟨*his ill health* to the contrary, *he led a very active life*⟩

²**contrary** /'kontrəri; *sense 4 often* kən'treəri/ *adj* **1a** diametrically different ⟨*facts which point to a* ~ *conclusion*⟩ **b** opposite in character; tending to an opposing course ⟨*he remained firm in the* ~ *intention*⟩ **c** mutually opposed; antagonistic ⟨*they held* ~ *opinions*⟩ **2** opposite in position, direction, or nature **3** *of wind or weather* unfavourable **4** obstinately self-willed; inclined to oppose the wishes of others ⟨*a*

~ *child*⟩ [ME *contrarie*, fr MF *contraire*, fr L *contrarius*, fr *contra* opposite] – **contrarily** *adv*, **contrariness** *n* – **contrary to** in opposition to ⟨contrary to *orders, he set out alone*⟩

¹**contrast** /'kontrahst/ *n* **1a** juxtaposition of dissimilar elements (eg colour, tone, or emotion) in a work of art **b** degree of difference between the lightest and darkest parts of a picture **2** comparison of similar objects to set off their dissimilar qualities **3** a person or thing against which another may be contrasted

²**contrast** /kən'trahst/ *vi* to show contrast ~ *vt* **1** to put in contrast **2** to compare or appraise in respect to differences [Fr *contraster*, fr MF, to oppose, resist, alter. of *contrester*, fr (assumed) VL *contrastare*, fr L *contra-* + *stare* to stand – more at STAND] – **contrastable** *adj*

*usage* In modern use, **contrast** is followed by *with* ⟨*he* **contrasts** *the microscope with the telescope*⟩ ⟨*his reaction* **contrasted** *favourably with theirs*⟩.

**contrastive** /kən'trahstiv/ *adj* forming or consisting of a contrast; contrasting ⟨~ *analysis*⟩ – **contrastively** *adv*

**contrasty** /kən'trahsti, 'kontrahsti/ *adj* having or producing in photography great contrast between highlights and shadows

**contravene** /,kontrə'veen/ *vt* **1** to go or act contrary to ⟨~ *a law*⟩ **2** to oppose in argument; contradict ⟨*a proposition ... not likely to be* ~d – Robert Southey⟩ [MF or LL; MF *contrevenir*, fr LL *contravenire*, fr L *contra-* + *venire* to come – more at COME] – **contravener** *n*

**contravention** /,kontrə'vensh(ə)n/ *n* the act of contravening; (a) violation, infringement [MF, fr LL *contraventus*, pp of *contravenire*]

**contredanse, contra dance** /'kontrə,dahns/ *n* **1** a folk dance in which couples face each other in two lines or in a square **2** a piece of music for a contredanse [Fr *contredanse*, by folk etymology (influenced by *contre-* counter-) fr E *country-dance*]

**contretemps** /'kon(h)trə,tonh, 'kawntrə-, -tong (Fr kõtrətã)/ *n, pl* **contretemps** a minor setback, disagreement, or confrontation [Fr, fr *contre-* counter- + *temps* time, fr L *tempus* – more at TEMPORAL]

**contribute** /kən'tribyooht; *also* 'kontribyooht USE *the last pron is disliked by some speakers*/ *vt* **1** to give or supply in common with others **2** to supply (eg an article) for a publication ~ *vi* **1a** to give a part to a common fund or store **b** to play a significant part in bringing about an end or result **2** to supply articles to a publication [L *contributus*, pp of *contribuere*, fr *com-* + *tribuere* to grant – more at TRIBUTE] – **contributor** *n*

**contribution** /,kontri'byoohsh(ə)n/ *n* **1** a tax; *esp* one imposed for a special purpose – used in historical contexts **2** the act of contributing; *also* something contributed ⟨*her meagre* ~ *to the conversation*⟩ **3** a piece of writing for publication, esp in a periodical – **contributive** *adj*, **contributively** *adv*

¹**contributory** /kən'tribyoot(ə)ri/ *adj* **1** contributing to a common fund or enterprise **2** of or forming a contribution **3** financed by contributions; *specif, of an insurance or pension plan* contributed to by both employers and employees

²**contributory** *n* a person liable in British law to contribute towards meeting the debts of a bankrupt company

**contributory negligence** *n* partial legal responsibility of a wronged person for his/her injury, damage, or loss as a result of his/her carelessness or failure to take reasonable care

**contrite** /kən'triet/ *adj* **1** grieving and penitent for sin or shortcoming **2** showing contrition ⟨~ *sighs*⟩ [ME *contrit*, fr MF, fr ML, *contritus*, fr L, pp of *conterere* to grind, bruise, fr *com-* + *terere* to rub – more at THROW] – **contritely** *adv*, **contriteness** *n*

**contrition** /kən'trish(ə)n/ *n* the state of being contrite; repentance; *specif* sorrow for one's sins arising from the love of God rather than from fear of punishment – compare ATTRITION

*synonyms* see ¹PENITENT

**contrivance** /kən'triev(ə)ns/ *n* **1** contriving or being contrived **2** something contrived; *esp* a mechanical device

**contrive** /kən'triev/ *vt* **1a** to devise, plan ⟨~ *ways of handling the situation*⟩ **b** to form or create in an artistic or ingenious manner ⟨~d *household utensils from stone*⟩ **2** to bring about by stratagem or with difficulty; manage ⟨~d *to win the co-operation ... of Voltaire – TLS*⟩ ~ *vi* to make schemes [ME *controven, contreven*, fr MF *controver*, fr LL *contropare* to compare] – **contriver** *n*

**contrived** /kən'trievd/ *adj* somewhat clumsy and apparently produced by much effort; unnatural, forced

¹**control** /kən'trohl/ *vt* **-ll-** **1** to check, test, or verify by evidence or experiments **2a** to exercise restraining or directing influence over; regulate **b** to have power over; rule [ME *controllen*, fr MF *controller*, fr *controlle* copy of an account, audit, fr *contre-* counter-+ *rolle* roll, account] – **controllable** *adj*, **controllability** *n*

²**control** *n* **1a** an act or instance of controlling; *also* power or authority to control **b** skill in the use of a tool, instrument, technique, or artistic medium **c** direction, review, regulation, and coordination of business activities (eg production and administration) **2** restraint, reserve **3** one who or that which controls: eg **3a(1)** an experiment in which the subjects are treated as in a parallel experiment except for omission of the procedure or agent under test, and which is used as a standard of comparison in judging experimental effects **a(2)** something (eg an experimental organism or culture) that is part of a control **b controls** *pl*, **control** a mechanism used to regulate or guide the operation of a machine, apparatus, or system **c** *taking sing or pl vb* an organization that directs a space flight ⟨*mission* ~⟩ **d** a personality or spirit believed to be responsible for the utterances or performances of a spiritualistic medium at a séance

**control column** *n* a hand-operated lever in an aeroplane that controls the aeroplane's sideways and up-and-down movement

**controlled school** *n* a British VOLUNTARY SCHOOL which is financially maintained by the local education authority and whose managers do not have control over religious instruction

**controller** /kən'trohlə/ *n* **1a** a public-finance official **b** a chief financial officer, esp of a business enterprise **2** one who controls or has power or authority to control [ME *conterroller*, fr MF *contrerolleur*, fr *contrerolle*] – **controllership** *n*

**controlling interest** /kən'trohling/ *n* sufficient share ownership in a company or business to exert control over policy

**control panel** *n* a panel on which are mounted devices (eg dials and switches) used in the remote control and monitoring of electrified or mechanical apparatus

**control surface** *n* a part of an aircraft's wing or tail whose position can be altered to make the aircraft climb, descend, or turn to one side

**control tower** *n* a usu tall airport building from which movements of aircraft on the ground and in the air are controlled

**control unit** *n* (a prison installation providing) a special punitive regime of total isolation for especially violent prisoners

**controversial** /,kontrə'vuhsh(ə)l/ *adj* **1** of or arousing controversy ⟨*a* ~ *public figure*⟩ **2** given to controversy; argumentative – **controversialism** *n*, **controversialist** *n*, **controversially** *adv*

**controversy** /'kontrə,vuhsi, kən'trovəsi USE *the last pron is disliked by some speakers*/ *n* (a) debate or dispute, esp in public or in the media [ME *controversie*, fr L *controversia*, fr *controversus* disputable, lit., turned opposite, fr *contro-* (akin to *contra-*) + *versus*, pp of *vertere* to turn – more at WORTH]

*usage* The new chiefly British pronunciation /kən'trovəsi/ is widely disliked, and /'kontrə,vuhsi/ is recommended for BBC broadcasters.

**controvert** /'kontrə,vuht, ,--'-/ *vt, formal* to deny, dispute [back-formation fr *controversy*] – **controverter** *n*, **controvertible** *adj*

**contumacious** /,kontyoo'mayshəs/ *adj, formal* stubbornly disobedient; rebellious – **contumaciously** *adv*

**contumacy** /'kontyooməsi/ *n, formal* stubborn resistance to authority; *specif* wilful contempt of court [ME *contumacie*, fr L *contumacia*, fr *contumac-, contumax* insubordinate, fr *com-* + *tumēre* to swell, be proud – more at THUMB]

**contumelious** /,kontyoo'meelyəs/ *adj, formal* insolently abusive and humiliating – **contumeliously** *adv*

**contumely** /'kontyoomli, -mili, kən'tyoohmli, -mili/ *n, formal* rude language or treatment arising from haughtiness and contempt; *also* an instance of such language or treatment [ME *contumelie*, fr MF, fr L *contumelia*; perh akin to L *contumacia*]

*usage* The pronunciation /'kontyoomli/ is recommended for BBC broadcasters.

**contuse** /kən'tyoohz/ *vt, medicine* to injure (tissue), usu without breaking the skin; bruise [MF *contuser*, fr. L *contusus*, pp of *contundere* to crush, bruise, fr *com-* + *tundere* to beat – more at STINT] – **contusion** *n*

**conundrum** /kə'nundrəm/ *n* **1** a riddle; *esp* one whose answer is or involves a pun **2a** a question or problem having only a conjectural answer **b** an intricate and difficult problem

*synonyms* see ¹PROBLEM [origin unknown]

**conurbation** /,konuh'baysh(ə)n/ *n* a grouping of several towns that were previously separate, forming a single large community [*com-* + L *urb-, urbs* city]

**conus** /'kohnəs/ *n, pl* **coni** CONUS ARTERIOSUS

**conus arteriosus** /ˌkohnəs ahˌtiəri'ohsəs/ *n, pl* **coni arteriosi** /ˌkohnie ahˌtiəri'ohsie/ 1 a prolongation of the VENTRICLE (posterior chamber) of the hearts of amphibians and some fishes that has a spiral valve separating blood without oxygen that goes to the lungs or gills from blood with oxygen that goes to the aorta and arteries supplying the rest of the body 2 a conical prolongation of the right VENTRICLE (posterior chamber) of the hearts of mammals from which the arteries supplying the lungs emerge [NL, lit., arterial cone]

**convalesce** /ˌkonvə'les/ *vi* to recover health and strength gradually after sickness or weakness [L *convalescere,* fr *com-* + *valescere* to grow strong, fr *valēre* to be strong, be well – more at WIELD] – **convalescence** *n,* **convalescent** *adj* or *n*

**convect** /kən'vekt/ *vi* to transfer heat by convection ~ *vt* to circulate (warm air) by convection [back-formation fr *convection*]

**convection** /kən'veksh(ə)n/ *n* the circulatory motion that occurs in a gas or liquid at a nonuniform temperature owing to the variation of its density with temperature and the action of gravity; *also* the transfer of heat by this automatic circulation [LL *convection-, convectio* act of conveying fr L *convectus,* pp of *convehere* to bring together, fr *com-* + *vehere* to carry – more at WAY] – **convectional** *adj,* **convective** *adj*

**convector** /kən'vektə/ *n* a heating unit in which air heated by contact with a heating device in a casing circulates by convection

**convene** /kən'veen/ *vi* to come together in a body ~ *vt* 1 to summon before a tribunal 2 to cause to assemble ⟨~ *a meeting*⟩ [ME *convenen,* fr MF *convenir* to come together, fr L *convenire*]

**convenience** /kən'veenyəns, -ni·əns/ *n* 1 fitness or suitability for performing an action or fulfilling a requirement 2 an appliance, device, or service conducive to comfort 3 a suitable time; an opportunity ⟨*at your earliest* ~⟩ 4 personal comfort or advantage 5 *Br* PUBLIC CONVENIENCE

**convenience food** *n* (a) food (eg a cake mix, tinned meat, or a precooked frozen meal) that is commercially prepared and packaged and requires little or no further preparation before being eaten

**conveniency** /kən'veenyənsi/ *n, archaic* convenience

**convenient** /kən'veenyənt, -ni·ənt/ *adj* 1a suited to personal comfort or to easy use b suited to a particular situation; causing no difficulty or disturbance ⟨*you haven't come at a very* ~ *time*⟩ 2 near at hand; easily accessible ⟨*the shops are very* ~⟩ 3 *obs* suitable, proper [ME, fr L *convenient-, conveniens,* fr prp of *convenire* to come together, be suitable] – **conveniently** *adv*

**convenor, convener** /kən'veenə/ *n, chiefly Br* 1 a member of a group or esp committee responsible for calling meetings; *broadly* a chairperson 2 an elected union official responsible for coordinating the work of SHOP STEWARDS in an establishment [*convene* + *-or,* ²*-er*]

**convent** /'konv(ə)nt, -vent/ *n* a local community or house of a religious order or congregation; *esp* an establishment of nuns [ME *covent,* fr OF, fr ML *conventus,* fr L, assembly, fr *conventus,* pp of *convenire*]

**conventicle** /kən'ventikl/ *n* 1 an assembly, meeting; *specif* an irregular or unlawful one 2 an assembly for religious worship; *esp* a secret meeting for worship not sanctioned by law 3 a meetinghouse [ME, fr L *conventiculum,* dim. of *conventus* assembly] – **conventicler** *n*

**convention** /kən'vensh(ə)n/ *n* 1a an agreement, contract b an agreement between states that regulates matters affecting all of them c a compact between opposing military commanders, esp concerning prisoner exchange or armistice 2 a generally agreed principle or practice 3 an assembly of people met for a common purpose; *esp* a meeting of the delegates of a US political party for the purpose of formulating policies and selecting candidates for office 4a (an) accepted social custom or practice b an established artistic technique or practice ⟨*the* ~s *of the stream-of-consciousness novel*⟩ c an agreed system of bidding or playing that conveys information between partners in bridge or other card games [ME, fr MF or L; MF, fr L; MF, fr L *convention-, conventio,* fr *conventus,* pp of *convenire* to come together, be suitable, fr *com-* + *venire* to come – more at COME]

**conventional** /kən'vensh(ə)nl/ *adj* 1 formed by agreement or compact 2a conforming to, sanctioned by, or based on con-

vention b lacking originality or individuality 3 of traditional design 4 of, like, or for a convention, assembly, or public meeting 5 not making use of nuclear power ⟨~ *warfare*⟩ ⟨~ *weapons*⟩ – conventionalism *n,* conventionalist *n,* conventionality *n,* conventionally *adv*

**conventional·ize, ise** /kən'vensh(ə)nlˌiez/ *vt* to make conventional – **conventionalization** *n*

**conventual** /kən'ventyoo(ə)l, -choo(ə)l/ *adj* of or appropriate to a convent or monastic life; monastic [ME, fr MF or ML; MF, fr ML *conventualis,* fr *conventus* convent] – **conventually** *adv*

**converge** /kən'vuhj/ *vi* 1 *of two or more things* to move towards a single common point 2 to come together and unite in a common interest or focus 3 *of (the value of a term in) a mathematical series or sequence* to approach a limit; be convergent ⟨*the series* $1 + \frac{1}{2} + \frac{1}{4} + \frac{1}{8} + \dots$ ~s *to the limit* 2⟩ ~ *vt* to cause to converge [ML *convergere,* fr L *com-* + *vergere* to bend, incline – more at WRENCH]

**convergence** /kən'vuhj(ə)ns/, **convergency** /-si/ *n* 1 the act of converging, esp moving towards union or uniformity; *esp* coordinated movement of the two eyes that results in the image of what is observed being received at exactly corresponding areas of the retinas 2 the condition of converging; *esp* independent development of similar characters (eg of body structure or cultural traits) often associated with similarity of habits or environment 3 the property of mathematically converging

**convergent** /kən'vuhj(ə)nt/ *adj* 1 tending to move towards a single common point or to approach each other; converging ⟨~ *lines*⟩ 2 exhibiting convergence in form, function, or development 3 *maths* having the *n*th term or the sum of the first *n* terms approach a finite limit as *n* increases without bound ⟨*a* ~ *sequence*⟩ ⟨*a* ~ *series*⟩ [ML *convergent-, convergens,* prp of *convergere*]

**convergent evolution** *n* CONVERGENCE 2

**conversable** /kən'vuhssəbl/ *adj* 1 *formal* pleasant and easy to converse with 2 *archaic* relating to or suitable for social interaction

**conversant** /kən'vuhs(ə)nt/ *adj* 1 having knowledge or experience; familiar *with* ⟨~ *with the facts of the case*⟩ 2 *archaic* occupied, concerned 3 *archaic* having frequent, customary, or familiar association – **conversantly** *adv*

**conversation** /ˌkonvə'saysh(ə)n/ *n* 1a informal verbal exchange of opinions, ideas, or feelings b an instance of such exchange; a talk 2 **conversations** *pl,* **conversation** an informal discussion of an issue by representatives of governments, institutions, or groups 3 an exchange similar to conversation; *esp* interaction with a computer, esp through a keyboard [ME *conversacioun,* fr MF *conversation,* fr L *conversation-, conversatio,* fr *conversatus,* pp of *conversari* to live, keep company with] – **conversational** *adj,* **conversationally** *adv*

**conversationalist** /ˌkonvə'saysh(ə)nl·ist/ *n* one who converses a great deal or who excels in conversation

**conversation piece** *n* 1 a painting of a group of people (eg a family) in their customary surroundings 2 a new or striking object intended to stimulate conversation

**conversazione** /ˌkonvəsatsi'ohni/ *n, pl* **conversaziones** /-neez/, **conversazioni** /-ni/ a meeting for relatively informal discussion of intellectual or cultural matters [It, lit. conversation, fr L *conversation-, conversatio*]

¹**converse** /kən'vuhs/ *vi* 1a to exchange thoughts and opinions in speech; talk b to carry on an exchange similar to a conversation; *esp* to interact with a computer 2 *archaic* to have acquaintance or familiarity *synonyms* see SPEAK [ME *conversen,* fr MF *converser,* fr L *conversari* to live, keep company with, fr *conversus,* pp of *convertere* to turn round] – **converser** *n*

²**converse** /'konˌvuhs/ *n, formal* conversation

³**converse** /'konˌvuhs/ *adj* reversed in order, relation, or action; opposite [L *conversus,* pp of *convertere*] – **conversely** *adv*

⁴**converse** /'konˌvuhs/ *n* something converse to another; *esp* a proposition in logic obtained by interchange of the first term (SUBJECT) and the second term (PREDICATE) of another proposition ⟨*"no P is S" is the* ~ *of "no S is P"*⟩

**conversion** /kən'vuhsh(ə)n/ *n* 1 converting or being converted 2 (an experience associated with) a definite and decisive adoption of a religious faith 3 the operation of finding a converse in logic 4 something converted from one use to another 5 the unlawful exercising of rights of ownership over personal property belonging to another **6** the alteration of (part of) a building to a different purpose ⟨*a loft ∼* ⟩; *also* a (part of a) building so altered **7** a kick at goal that is awarded to the scoring team after a TRY (placing of the ball on the ground behind the opponents' goal) in rugby; *also* the score resulting from such a kick **8 conversion, conversion hysteria, conversion reaction** a process by which bodily symptoms (e g paralysis or anaesthesia) appear as a result of mental conflict without a physical cause [ME, fr MF, fr L *conversion-, conversio*, fr *conversus*, pp of *convertere*] – **conversional** *adj*

**conversion course** *n*, *Br* a course facilitating the switch from one subject of study to another

¹**convert** /kən'vuht/ *vt* **1a** to win over from one belief, view, or party to another **b** to bring about a religious conversion in **2a** to alter the physical or chemical nature or properties of, esp in manufacturing **b(1)** to change from one form or function to another; *esp* to make esp structural alterations to (a building or part of a building) ⟨*∼ed the loft into a bedroom*⟩ **b(2)** to alter for more effective utilization **b(3)** to take dishonestly or illegally ⟨*∼ed the money to his own use*⟩ **c** to exchange for an equivalent ⟨*∼ currency*⟩ **3** to subject to logical conversion **4** to complete (a TRY) in rugby by successfully kicking a conversion *∼ vi* to undergo conversion ⟨*this couch ∼s into a bed*⟩ [ME *converten*, fr OF *convertir*, fr L *convertere* to turn round, transform, convert, fr *com-* + *vertere* to turn – more at WORTH]

²**convert** /'konvuht/ *n* a person who is converted; *esp* one who has experienced a religious conversion

**converter** /kən'vuhtə/ *n* one who or that which converts: e g **a** the furnace used in the BESSEMER PROCESS of steel-making **b converter, convertor** a device employing mechanical rotation to change electrical energy from one form to another **c** an electronic device for converting signals from one frequency to another; *esp* one that adapts a television set to receive signals for which it was not originally designed **d** a device that accepts data in one form and converts it to another ⟨*analogue-digital ∼*⟩

¹**convertible** /kən'vuhtəbl/ *adj* **1** capable of being converted **2** *of a motor vehicle* having a top that may be lowered or removed ⟨*a ∼ sports car*⟩ **3** capable of being exchanged for a specified equivalent (e g another currency) ⟨*British currency is no longer ∼ to gold*⟩ – **convertibleness** *n*, **convertibility** *n*, **convertibly** *adv*

²**convertible** *n* something convertible; *esp* a convertible car

**convertiplane** /kən'vuhti,playn/ *n* an aircraft that takes off and lands like a helicopter and is convertible to a fixed-wing configuration for forward flight

**convex** /,kon'veks; *not attrib* kən'veks/ *adj* curved or rounded outwards like the outside of a bowl – compare CONCAVE [MF or L; MF *convexe*, fr L *convexus* vaulted, concave, convex, fr *com-* + *-vexus* (akin to OE *wōh* crooked, bent) – more at PREVARICATE] – **convexly** *adv*

**convexity** /kon'veksəti/ *n* **1** the quality or state of being convex **2** a convex line, surface, or part

**convexo-concave** /kən,veksoh kon'kayv/ *adj* **1** CONCAVO-CONVEX 1 **2** having the convex side curved more than the concave

**convey** /kən'vay/ *vt* **1a** to take or carry from one place to another; *esp* to move in a continuous stream or mass **b** to impart or communicate by statement, suggestion, gesture, or appearance ⟨*his glance ∼ed contempt*⟩ **c** to transfer or deliver to another; *specif* to transfer (property or the rights to property) legally to another, other than by a will **d** to cause to pass from one place or person to another; transmit **2** *archaic* to steal **3** *obs* to lead, conduct *synonyms* see ¹CARRY [ME *conveyen*, fr OF *conveier* to accompany, escort, fr (assumed) VL *conviare*, fr L *com-* + *via* way – more at VIA]

**conveyance** /kən'vayəns/ *n* **1** the action of conveying **2** a means or way of conveying: e g **2a** a legal document by which rights to property are transferred **b** *formal* a means of transport; a vehicle

**conveyancer** /kən'vayənsə/ *n* a person whose business is conveyancing

**conveyancing** /kən'vayənsing/ *n* the act or business of drawing up documents (e g deeds or leases) for transferring rights to property

**conveyer, conveyor** /kən'vayə/ *n* one who or that which conveys; *esp* a mechanical apparatus for carrying articles or bulk material (e g by an endless moving belt or a chain of receptacles)

¹**convict** /kən'vikt/ *vt* **1** to find or prove to be guilty **2** to convince of error or sinfulness [ME *convicten*, fr L *convictus*, pp of *convincere* to refute, convict]

²**convict** /'konvikt/ *n* **1** a person convicted of and under sentence for a crime **2** a person serving a prison sentence, usu for a long term

**conviction** /kən'viksh(ə)n/ *n* **1** an act or process of convicting or being convicted, esp of a crime after trial in a court of law **2a** a strong persuasion or belief **b** the state of being convinced *synonyms* see CERTAINTY, OPINION

**convince** /kən'vins/ *vt* to cause to believe; persuade ⟨*∼d them that they were wrong*⟩ [L *convincere* to refute, convict, prove, fr *com-* + *vincere* to conquer – more at VICTOR] – **convincer** *n* **usage** The use of **convince** to mean not only "persuade to believe" but, with an infinitive verb, "persuade into a course of action" ⟨*convinced them to leave the country*⟩ is disliked by some people.

**convincing** /kən'vinsing/ *adj* **1** satisfying or assuring by argument or proof ⟨*a ∼ test of a new product*⟩ **2** having power to convince of the truth, rightness, or reality of something; plausible ⟨*a very ∼ story*⟩ *synonyms* see VALID *antonym* unconvincing – **convincingly** *adv*, **convincingness** *n*

**convivial** /kən'vivi-əl/ *adj* occupied with or fond of feasting, drinking, and good company ⟨*a ∼ evening at the pub*⟩ [LL *convivialis*, fr L *convivium* banquet, fr *com-* + *vivere* to live – more at QUICK] – **conviviality** *n*, **convivially** *adv*

**convocation** /,konvə'kaysh(ə)n, -voh-/ *n* **1** an assembly of people called together: e g **1a** either of the two provincial assemblies of bishops and representative clergy of the Church of England ⟨*the ∼ of York*⟩ **b** a ceremonial assembly of graduates of a college or university – compare CONGREGATION **3 2** the act or process of calling together [ME, fr MF, fr L *convocation-, convocatio*, fr *convocatus*, pp of *convocare*] – **convocational** *adj*

**convoke** /kən'vohk/ *vt* to call together to a formal meeting [MF *convoquer*, fr L *convocare*, fr *com-* + *vocare* to call – more at VOICE]

¹**convolute** /'konvəlooht, -lyooht, ,--'-/ *vb* to twist, coil [L *convolutus*, pp of *convolvere*]

²**convolute** *adj*, *esp of a plant part or a shell* rolled or wound together with one part upon another; coiled – **convolutely** *adv*

**convoluted** /,konvə'loohtid, -'lyooh-/ *adj* **1** folded in curved or tortuous windings; *specif* having convolutions **2** involved, intricate ⟨*a ∼ argument*⟩

**convoluted tubule** *n* **1** PROXIMAL CONVOLUTED TUBULE **2** DISTAL CONVOLUTED TUBULE

**convolution** /,konvə'loohsh(ə)n/ *n* **1** any of the irregular ridges on the surface of the brain, esp of the CEREBRUM (anterior portion of the brain) of higher mammals **2** a convoluted form or structure – **convolutional** *adj*

**convolve** /kən'volv/ *vb* to roll or twist together [L *convolvere*, fr *com-* + *volvere* to roll – more at VOLUBLE]

**convolvulus** /kən'volvyoolǝs/ *n*, *pl* **convolvuluses, convolvuli** /-lie/ any of a genus (*Convolvulus*) of erect, trailing, or twining plants and shrubs (e g bindweed) of the bindweed family [NL, fr L *convolvere* to roll together, roll up]

¹**convoy** /'konvoy/ *vt* to accompany, guide; *esp* to escort for protection *synonyms* see ACCOMPANY [ME *convoyen*, fr MF *conveier, convoier* – more at CONVEY]

²**convoy** *n* **1** convoying or being convoyed ⟨*the ships were steaming in ∼*⟩ **2** taking sing or pl vb a group or formation organized for convenience or protection in moving: e g **2a** a formation of merchant ships accompanied by a protective naval escort **b** a group of esp military vehicles travelling together

**convulsant** /kən'vuls(ə)nt/ *adj* causing convulsions – **convulsant** *n*

**convulse** /kən'vuls/ *vt* **1** to shake or agitate violently, esp (as if) with irregular spasms **2** to cause to laugh helplessly *synonyms* see ¹SHAKE [L *convulsus*, pp of *convellere* to pluck up, convulse, fr *com-* + *vellere* to pluck – more at VULNERABLE]

**convulsion** /kən'vulsh(ə)n/ *n* **1** an abnormal violent and involuntary contraction or series of contractions of the muscles **2a** a violent disturbance **b** an uncontrolled fit; a paroxysm – **convulsionary** *adj*

**convulsive** /kən'vulsiv/ *adj* **1** constituting or producing a convulsion **2** attended or affected with convulsions – **convulsively** *adv*, **convulsiveness** *n*

**cony, coney** /'kohni/ *n* **1** a rabbit **2** PIKA (small animal related to the rabbit) **3** HYRAX (small rodentlike animal) [ME *conies* (pl), fr OF *conis*, plof *conil*, fr L *cuniculus*]

**¹coo** /kooh/ *vi* **cooed, coo'd 1** to make (a sound similar to) the low soft cry characteristic of a dove or pigeon **2** to talk lovingly or appreciatively ⟨~ed *over by the critics*⟩ [imit] – **coo** *n*

**²coo** *interj, Br informal* – used to express surprise [origin unknown]

**cooee** /'kooh•ee/ *interj, Br* – used to make one's presence known or to attract someone's attention at a distance [fr a native word in Australia] – **cooee** *vi*

**¹cook** /kook/ *n* one who prepares food for eating [ME, fr OE *cōc;* akin to OHG *koch;* both fr a prehistoric WGmc word borrowed fr L *coquus,* fr *coquere* to cook; akin to OE *āfigen* fried, Gk *pessein* to cook]

**²cook** *vi* **1** to prepare food for eating, esp by subjection to a heating process **2** to undergo the process of being cooked ⟨*the rice is* ~ing *now*⟩ **3** *informal* to occur, happen ⟨*what's* ~ing?⟩ ~ *vt* **1** to prepare (e g food) for eating by a heating process **2** to subject to the action of heat or fire

**cook up** *vt, informal* to concoct or devise, esp by way of improvisation ⟨cook up *a scheme*⟩

**cookbook** /'kook,book/ *n* COOKERY BOOK; *broadly* a book of detailed instructions (e g as used in statistics)

**cooker** /'kookə/ *n* **1** an apparatus, appliance, or vessel for cooking; *esp* a fixed cooking appliance, usu using gas, electricity, or solid fuel and typically consisting of an oven, hot plates or rings, and a grill – compare PRESSURE COOKER **2** a variety that is made more palatable by cooking – used chiefly with reference to fruit (e g apples)

**cookery** /'kook(ə)ri/ *n* **1** the art or practice of cooking **2** *NAm* an establishment for cooking

**cookery book** *n* a book of recipes and instructions for preparing and cooking food

**cook-'general** *n* a servant who performs the duties of a cook and housemaid

**cookhouse** /'kook,hows/ *n* a kitchen or kitchen building; *specif* a kitchen set up outdoors, at a campsite or military establishment

**cookie, cooky** /'kooki/ *n* **1a** *Scot* a plain bun **b** *NAm* a sweet flat or slightly leavened biscuit **2** *informal* **2a** *NAm* an attractive woman **b** *chiefly NAm* a person, esp of a specified type ⟨*a very tough* ~ *indeed* – John Crosly⟩ [D *koekje,* dim. of *koek* cake]

**cooking** /'kooking/ *adj* suitable for or used in cooking ⟨~ *apples*⟩ ⟨~ *sherry*⟩ ⟨~ *utensils*⟩

**cookout** /'kookowt/ *n, chiefly NAm* an outing at which a meal is cooked and served in the open; *also* the meal cooked

**Cook's tour** *n, informal* a quick tour in which attractions are viewed briefly and cursorily [Thomas *Cook* & Son, E travel agency]

**cooky** /'kooki/ *adj, chiefly NAm informal* eccentric, unconventional [alter. of *kooky*]

**¹cool** /koohl/ *adj* **1** moderately cold; lacking in warmth ⟨*warm days and* ~ *nights*⟩ **2a** dispassionately calm and self-controlled ⟨*a* ~ *and calculating approach to the problem*⟩ **b** lacking friendliness or enthusiasm **c** of or being an understated, restrained, and melodic style of jazz that became popular in the 1940s – compare HOT 2c **3** marked by deliberate effrontery or lack of due respect or discretion ⟨*a* ~ *reply*⟩ ⟨*that's pretty* ~ *of you, Marchbanks!*⟩ **4** bringing or suggesting relief from heat ⟨*a* ~ *dress*⟩ **5a** *of a colour* producing an impression of being cool; *specif* of a hue in the range violet through blue to green **b** *of a musical tone* relatively lacking in timbre or resonance **6** marked by sophistication or self-assured composure; displaying sophistication by restraint or detachment **7** *informal* – used as an intensive ⟨*made a* ~ *million on the deal*⟩ **8** *informal* – used as a generalized term of appreciation or approval [ME *col,* fr OE *cōl;* akin to OHG *kuoli* cool, OE *ceald* cold] – **coolish** *adj,* **coolly** *also* **cooly** *adv,* **coolness** *n*

**²cool** *vi* **1** to become cool; lose heat or warmth ⟨*placed the pie on the table to* ~⟩ – sometimes + *off* or *down* **2** to lose enthusiasm or passion ⟨*his anger* ~ed⟩ ⟨*she has noticeably* ~ed *towards him*⟩ ~ *vt* **1** to make cool; impart a feeling of coolness to ⟨~ed *the room with a fan*⟩ – often + *off* or *down* ⟨*a swim* ~ed *us off a little*⟩ **2a** to moderate the heat, excitement, or force of; calm ⟨~ed *her growing anger*⟩ **b** to slow or lessen the growth or activity of – usu + *off* or *down* – **cool it** *informal* to become calm or quiet; relax ⟨*just cool it, will you, so I can think*⟩ – see also **cool one's** HEELS

**cool down** *vi* to allow a violent emotion (e g anger) to pass

**³cool** *n* **1** a cool time, place, or situation ⟨*the* ~ *of the evening*⟩ **2** *informal* poise, composure ⟨*don't lose your* ~⟩ **3** *chiefly*

*NAm informal* self-assurance, sophistication – **blow one's cool** *informal* to lose one's composure

**⁴cool** *adv, informal* in a casual and nonchalant manner ⟨*play it* ~⟩

**coolabah, coolibah** /'koohlə,bah/ *n, Austr* any of several eucalyptuses or GUM TREES; *esp* one (*Eucalyptus microtheca*) with smooth bark and narrow leaves that grows near water

**coolant** /'koohlənt/ *n* a liquid or gas used in cooling, esp in an engine

**cooler** /'koohlə/ *n* **1** one who or that which cools: e g **1a** a container for cooling liquids **b** *NAm* a refrigerator **2** *slang* prison; *also* a prison cell

**coolgardie safe** /'koohl,gahdi/ *n, Austr* a container in which food is kept cool by the controlled evaporation of water [*Coolgardie,* town in SW Australia; prob partly intended as a pun on *cool* + *guard* + *-ie*]

**coolheaded** /-'hedid/ *adj* not easily excited or flustered

**coolie** /'koohli/ *n* an unskilled labourer or porter, usu in or from the Far East, hired for low or subsistence wages [Hindi *kulī*]

**coolie hat** *n* a conical-shaped usu straw hat worn esp to protect the head from the heat of the sun

**,cooling-'off** *adj* designed to allow passions to cool or to permit negotiation between parties ⟨*a* ~ *period*⟩

**coomb, coombe, combe** /koohm/ *n, Br* a valley or basin, esp on a hillside or running up from the coast [of Celt origin; akin to W *cwm* valley]

**coon** /koohn/ *n, chiefly NAm* **1** *informal* a raccoon **2** *derog* a negro [short for *raccoon*]

**cooncan** /'koohn,kan/ *n* **1** a card game for two players with a pack of 40 cards, being a variety of CONQUIAN **2** a game of rummy played by two players with two packs of cards **3** a game of rummy for more than six players, using two normal packs of cards and two jokers [modif of MexSp *con quien* – more at CONQUIAN]

**coonhound** /'koohn,hownd/ *n, NAm* a sporting dog trained to hunt raccoons

**coonskin** /-,skin/ *n* **1** the skin or pelt of the raccoon **2** a coat, cap, or other article made of coonskin

**¹coop** /koohp/ *n* **1** a cage or small enclosure or building, esp for housing poultry **2** a confined area [ME *cupe* basket; akin to OE *cȳpe* basket, *cot* cot]

**²coop** *vt* **1** to confine in a restricted and often crowded area – usu + *up* **2** to place or keep in a coop; pen – often + *up*

**co-op** /'koh ,op/ *n* a cooperative

**cooper** /'koohpə/ *n* one who makes or repairs wooden barrels, casks, or tubs – called also HOOPER [ME *couper, cowper,* fr MD *cūper* (fr *cūpe* cask) or MLG *kūper,* fr *kūpe* cask; MD *cūpe* & MLG *kūpe,* fr L *cupa;* akin to Gk *kypellon* cup – more at HIVE] – **cooper** *vb*

**cooperage** /'koohpərij/ *n* a cooper's work, products, or place of business

**cooperate** /koh'opərayt/ *vi* **1** to act or work with another or others for a common purpose; act together **2** to associate with another or others for mutual benefit [LL *cooperatus,* pp of *cooperari,* fr L *co-* + *operari* to work – more at OPERATE] – **cooperator** *n*

**cooperation** /koh,opə'raysh(ə)n/ *n* **1** the action of cooperating; common effort **2** association for common benefit **3** social interaction (e g division of labour) among individuals in communities of animals and plants, in which the mutual benefits of the association outweigh the disadvantages of crowding – **cooperationist** *n*

**¹cooperative** /koh'op(ə)rətiv/ *adj* **1a** marked by cooperation ⟨~ *efforts*⟩ **b** marked by a willingness and ability to work with others **2** of, or organized as, a cooperative – **cooperatively** *adv,* **cooperativeness** *n*

**²cooperative** *n* an enterprise (e g a shop) or organization (e g a society) owned by and operated for the benefit of those using its services ⟨*a housing* ~⟩

**Co-operative Party** *n* a political party that was formed in 1917 to promote social and economic cooperation and that is affiliated to the Labour Party

**co-opt** /,koh 'opt/ *vt* **1** to choose or elect as a member **2a** to take into a group (e g a faction, movement, or culture); absorb, assimilate **b** to take over; appropriate [L *cooptare,* fr *co-* + *optare* to choose] – **co-optation** *n,* **co-optative** *adj,* **co-option** *n,* **co-optive** *adj*

**¹coordinate** /koh'awd(ə)nət, -di-/ *adj* **1a** equal in rank, quality, or significance **b** of equal rank in a sentence ⟨~ *clauses*⟩ **2**

relating to or marked by coordination **3** *NAm* being a university in which men and women are taught in separate classes [L *co-* + *ordinatus*, pp of *ordinare* to arrange, fr *ordin-*, *ordo* order] – **coordinately** *adv*, **coordinateness** *n*

²**coordinate** *n* **1a** *maths* any of a set of numbers used to specify the location of a point on a line, in a plane, or in space – compare CARTESIAN COORDINATE, POLAR COORDINATE **b** *physics* any of a set of variables used in specifying the state of a substance (eg the temperature or pressure), or the motion of a particle (eg its position, velocity, or momentum) **2** *pl* outer garments, usu separates, in harmonizing colours, materials, and pattern designed to be worn together

³**coordinate** /koh'awd(ə)nayt, -di-/ *vi* **1** to bring into a common action, movement, or condition; harmonize **2** to bind with so as to form a COORDINATION COMPLEX ~ *vt* **1** to be or become coordinate, esp so as to act together in a harmonious way **2** to combine by means of a COORDINATE BOND [LL or L; LL *co-ordinatus*, pp of *coordinare*, fr L *co-* + *ordinare*] – **coordinative** *adj*, **coordinator** *n*

**coordinate bond** /koh'awd(ə)nət, -di-/ *n* a COVALENT BOND (type of chemical bond) formed between two atoms, in which only one atom provides the two electrons that are shared to make the bond

**coordinated** /koh'awd(ə)n,aytid, -di-/ *adj* able to move one's body efficiently and also gracefully in sports, gymnastics, etc

**coordinate geometry** /koh'awd(ə)nət, -di-/ *n* ANALYTICAL GEOMETRY (geometry using coordinates)

**coordinating conjunction** *n* a conjunction (eg *and*) that joins together elements of equal grammatical rank

**coordination** /koh,awdi'naysh(ə)n/ *n* **1** the act or action of coordinating **2** the state of being coordinate or coordinated [Fr or LL; Fr, fr LL *coordination-*, *coordinatio*, fr L *co-* + *ordination-*, *ordinatio* arrangement]

**coordination complex** *n* a chemical compound consisting of a central usu metal atom or ION (atom or group of atoms having electric charge) linked by COORDINATE BONDS to a definite number of surrounding ions, molecules, or chemical groups

**coordination number** *n* the number of attachments to the central atom or ION in a COORDINATION COMPLEX

**coot** /kooht/ *n* **1** any of various slow-flying slaty-black water birds (genus *Fulica*, esp *Fulica atra*) of the rail family that somewhat resemble ducks **2** *informal* a foolish person; *broadly* a fellow [ME *coote*; akin to D *koet* coot]

**cootie** /'koohti/ *n*, *NAm* BODY LOUSE – not used technically [perh modif of Malay *kutu*]

¹**cop** /kop/ *n* **1** a cylindrical or conical-ended mass of thread, yarn, or twisted strands of wool or cotton (ROVING) wound on a spindle; *also* a spindle on which the thread, yarn, etc is wound **2** *dial chiefly Eng* a top, crest (eg of a hill) [ME, top, head, fr OE *copp* top]

²**cop** *vt* **-pp-** **1** *dial Eng* to see, spot **2** *slang* to get hold of; catch, capture; *specif*, *Br* to arrest [perh fr D *kapen* to steal, fr Fris *kāpia* to take away; akin to OHG *kouf* trade – more at CHEAP] – **cop it** *Br slang* to be in serious trouble

**cop out** *vi*, *informal* to avoid an unwanted responsibility or commitment often + *of*; see also COP-OUT

³**cop** *n*, *informal* a policeman [short for ³*copper*]

⁴**cop** *n*, *Br slang* a capture, arrest – chiefly in *a fair cop* – **not much cop** *chiefly Br slang* fairly bad; worthless

**copacetic, copasetic** /,kohpə'setik, -'see-/ *adj*, *NAm informal* very satisfactory [origin unknown]

**copaiba** /koh'piebə, -'pay-, ,kohpə'eebə/ *n* an OLEORESIN (semisolid mixture of oil and resin) obtained from any of several S American trees (genus *Copaifera*) of the pea family and used esp in varnishes; *also* a tree that yields copaiba [Sp & Pg; Sp, fr Pg *copaiba*, of Tupian origin; akin to Guarani *cupaiba* copaiba]

**copal** /'kohp(ə)l/ *n* a resin from various tropical trees that is used esp in varnishes [Sp, fr Nahuatl *copalli* resin]

**coparcenary** /koh'pahsən(ə)ri/ *n* joint heirship or ownership of property; *specif* inheritance of land by joint, esp female, heirs in circumstances where an estate was not disposed of by will – called also PARCENARY

**coparcener** /koh'pahs(ə)nə/ *n* a person inheriting land as a joint heir; a joint, esp female, heir – called also PARCENER [*co-* + *parcener* (partner, joint heir), fr AF, fr OF *parçonier*, fr *parçon* portion, fr L *partition-*, *partitio* partition]

**copartner** /koh'pahtnə/ *n* a partner – **copartnership** *n*

¹**cope** /kohp/ *n* **1** a long semicircular cloak fastened with a band or clasp and worn by a member of the clergy at religious services **2a** something resembling a cope (eg because it conceals or covers) ⟨*the dark sky's starry* ~ – P B Shelley⟩ **b** *building* COPING (covering layer of bricks on top of a wall) [ME, fr OE *-cāp*, fr LL *cappa* head covering – more at ¹CAP]

²**cope** *vt* to cover or provide with a cope or coping

³**cope** *vi* **1** to maintain a contest or combat usu on even terms or with success **2** to deal with a problem or task effectively – usu + *with* [ME *copen*, fr MF *couper* to strike, cut, fr OF, fr *coup* blow, fr LL *colpus*, alter. of L *colaphus*, fr Gk *kolaphos* buffet]

⁴**cope** *vt* to cut or shape (the end of a brick, tile, moulding, etc) to fit a coping [prob fr F *couper* to cut]

**copeck** /'kohpek/ *n* KOPECK (Russian unit of money)

**copemate** /'kohp,mayt/, **copesmate** /'kohps-/ *n*, *obs* a partner, comrade [³*cope* + *mate*]

**copepod** /'kohpə,pod/ *n* any of a large subclass (Copepoda of the class Crustacea) of usu minute freshwater and marine INVERTEBRATE animals (eg of the genus *Cyclops*) that constitute the major part of the diet of fish such as herring and mackerel [deriv of Gk *kōpē* oar + *pod-*, *pous* foot] – **copepod** *adj*

**coper** /'kohpə/ *n*, *Br* a horse dealer; *esp* a dishonest one [E dial. *cope* to trade, fr ME *copen* to buy, fr MD]

**Copernican** /koh'puhnikən, kə'puh-/ *adj* of Copernicus or the belief that the earth rotates daily on its axis and the planets revolve in orbits round the sun – compare PTOLEMAIC [Nicolaus *Copernicus* †1543 Polish astronomer] – **Copernican** *n*, **Copernicanism** *n*

**copestone** /-,stohn/ *n* a copingstone

**copier** /'kopi-ə/ *n* one who or that which copies; *specif* a machine for making copies of graphic matter (eg printing, drawings, or pictures), esp by photocopying or xerography

'**co-,pilot** /koh/ *n* a qualified pilot who assists or relieves the pilot but is not in command

**coping** /'kohping/ *n* the final, usu sloping, course of brick, stone, tiles, etc on the top of a wall

**coping saw** *n* a narrow-bladed saw having a U-shaped frame for cutting curved outlines in thin wood [fr prp of ⁴*cope*]

**copingstone** /-,stohn/ *n*, *chiefly Br* a stone used in forming a coping

**copious** /'kohpi-əs, 'kohpyəs/ *adj* **1** yielding something abundantly; plentiful ⟨*a* ~ *harvest*⟩ **2** profuse in thought, words, or expression ⟨*a* ~ *talker* – W S Maugham⟩ **3** present in large quantity; taking place on a large scale ⟨ ~ *eating and still more* ~ *drinking* – Aldous Huxley⟩ [ME, fr L *copiosus*, fr *copia* abundance, fr *co-* + *ops* wealth – more at OPULENT] – **copiously** *adv*, **copiousness** *n*

**copita** /koh'peetə/ *n* a tulip-shaped glass used esp for sherry [Sp, dim. of *copa* cup]

**coplanar** /koh'playnə/ *adj* lying or acting in the same plane surface – **coplanarity** *n*

**copolymer** /koh'polimə/ *n* a POLYMER (large molecule composed of many repeating subunits) in which two or more chemically different subunits are present – **copolymeric** *adj*

**copolymer·ize, -ise** /koh'poliməriez/ *vb* to form a copolymer by combining (molecules of two or more different chemical compounds) – **copolymerization** *n*

'**cop-,out** *n* the act or an instance of copping out

¹**copper** /'kopə/ *n* **1** a common reddish metallic chemical element that is easily shaped, drawn out into wires, etc and is one of the best conductors of heat and electricity **2** articles made of copper **3** a coin or token made of copper or bronze and usu of low value **4** any of various small butterflies (family Lycaenidae) with usu copper-coloured wings **5** *chiefly Br* a large metal vessel used, esp formerly, for boiling clothes [ME *coper*, fr OE; akin to OHG *kupfar* copper; both fr a prehistoric WGmc-NGmc word borrowed fr LL *cuprum* copper, fr L (*aes*) *Cyprium*, lit., metal of Cyprus] – **coppery** *adj*

²**copper** *vt* **-pp-** to coat or sheathe (as if) with copper

³**copper** *n*, *informal* a policeman [²*cop* + ²*-er*]

**copperas** /'kopərəs/ *n* a green FERROUS SULPHATE, $FeSO_4.7H_2O$, used esp in making inks and pigments [alter. of ME *coperose*, fr MF, fr (assumed) VL *cuprirosa*, fr LL *cuprum* + L *rosa* rose]

**copper beech** *n* a variety of beech tree with copper-coloured leaves

,**copper-'bottomed** *adj*, *chiefly Br* completely safe; reliable ⟨*a* ~ *currency*⟩⟨*a* ~ *promise*⟩ [fr the durability of a ship which has its bottom sheathed with copper]

**copper glance** *n* CHALCOCITE (copper-containing mineral)

**copperhead** /'kopə,hed/ *n, NAm informal* a person in the northern states who sympathized with the grievances of the South during the American Civil War [*copperhead* (a venomous coppery-brown US snake)]

**copper nickel** *n* NICCOLITE (copper-coloured mineral)

**copperplate** /-,playt/ *n* 1 an engraved or etched copper printing plate; *also* a print made from such a plate 2 handwriting modelled on engravings in copper and characterized by lines of sharply contrasting thickness; *broadly* formal and ornate handwriting

**copper pyrites** *n* CHALCOPYRITE (yellow copper-containing mineral)

**coppersmith** /-,smith/ *n* one who works in, or produces articles of, copper

**copper sulphate** *n* a chemical compound, $CuSO_4$, that usu occurs chemically associated with water in the form of blue crystals but also occurs as a white powder when free from water, and that is used in fungicides, electroplating solutions, textile dyeing and as a timber preservative

**¹coppice** /'kopis/ *n* 1 a thicket, grove, or growth of small trees 2 forest originating mainly from shoots or root suckers rather than seed [MF *copeiz*, fr *couper* to cut – more at ³COPE]

**²coppice** *vt* to cut back (trees) to produce a dense growth of small trees ~ *vi* to form a coppice

**copr-, copro-** *comb form* dung; faeces ⟨copro*lite*⟩ [NL, fr Gk *kopr-, kopro-*, fr *kopros*; akin to Skt *śakṛt* dung]

**copra** /'koprə/ *n* dried coconut flesh yielding coconut oil [Pg, fr Malayalam *koppara*]

**coproduce** /,kohprə'dyoohs/ *vt* to produce in cooperation with each other or with another producer – **coproducer** *n*, **coproduction** *n*

**coprolite** /'koprəliet/ *n* fossilized excrement – **coprolitic** *adj*

**coprophagous** /ko'profəgəs/ *adj* feeding on dung ⟨*a* ~ *beetle*⟩ [Gk *koprophagos*, fr *kopr-* + *-phagos* -phagous] – **coprophagy** *n*

**coprophilia** /,koprə'fili·ə/ *n* a marked, esp sexual, interest in excrement [NL] – **coprophiliac** *n*

**coprophilous** /kə'profiləs, ko-/ *adj* growing on dung ⟨~ *fungi*⟩

**copse** /kops/ *n* COPPICE 1 [by alter.]

**cop shop** *n, Br humorous* POLICE STATION

**Copt** /kopt/ *n* 1 a member of a people descended from the ancient Egyptians 2 a member of the traditional Christian church originating and centring in Egypt that believes that Christ is of only one nature which is divine and not human [Ar *qubṭ* Copts, fr Coptic *gyptios* Egyptian, fr Gk *aigyptios*]

**¹Coptic** /'koptik/ *adj* of the Copts, their church, or the language of their worship

**²Coptic** *n* an Afro-Asiatic language descended from ancient Egyptian and used as the language of worship in the Coptic church

**copula** /'kopyoolə/ *n* something that connects: eg **a** a *philosophy* the link between subject and PREDICATE (property, characteristic, etc of the subject) of a PROPOSITION (statement that affirms or denies the predicate) **b** an intransitive verb (eg a form of *be, become, feel,* or *seem*) that links a subject with a property so as to state a relationship of identity ⟨*became is a* ~ *in* "She *became a film star*"⟩ [L, bond – more at COUPLE]

**copulate** /'kopyoolayt/ *vi* 1 to engage in sexual intercourse 2 *of gametes* (*eg sperm and egg*) to fuse permanently [L *copulatus*, pp of *copulare* to join, fr *copula*] – **copulation** *n*, **copulatory** *adj*

**¹copulative** /'kopyoolətiv/ *adj* **1a** joining together words or word groups that are equal in rank and expressing the sum of their meanings ⟨"*and*" *is a* ~ *conjunction*⟩ **b** functioning as a copula **2** of copulation ⟨~ *organs*⟩ **3** of coupling of chemical compounds or groups – **copulatively** *adv*

**²copulative** *n* a copulative word

**¹copy** /'kopi/ *n* 1 an imitation, transcript, or reproduction of an original work 2 any of a series of esp mechanical reproductions of an original impression; *also* an individual example of such a reproduction ⟨*a presentation* ~ *of a book*⟩ **3a** material ready to be printed or photoengraved **b** something considered to be printable or newsworthy ⟨*at the mercy of press reporters ... who found anything she did to be good* ~⟩ **4** *archaic* something to be imitated; a model [ME *copie*, fr MF, fr ML *copia*, fr L, abundance – more at COPIOUS]

**²copy** *vt* 1 to make a copy of 2 to model oneself on ~ *vi* 1 to

make a copy 2 to undergo copying ⟨*the document did not* ~ *well*⟩

**copybook** /'kopi,book/ *n* a book formerly used in teaching handwriting and containing models for imitation – **blot one's copybook** to mar one's previously good record or reputation

**'copy-,book** *adj* 1 trite, conventional 2 *Br* completely correct; proper

**copybook maxim** *n* a trite moral sentiment

**copycat** /-,kat/ *n* one who slavishly imitates the behaviour or practices of another – used chiefly by children

**'copy-,edit** *vt* to prepare (manuscript copy) for printing, esp by correcting errors and specifying style [back-formation fr *copy editor*] – **copy editor** *n*

**copyhold** /-,hohld/ *n* 1 a former tenure of land in England established by custom and evidenced by a written copy of the records kept for the lands attached to the manor house 2 land held by copyhold

**¹copyholder** /'kopi,hohldə/ *n* a person who has tenure of land by copyhold [*copyhold* + ²-*er*]

**²copyholder** *n* 1 a device for holding copy, esp for a typesetter in a printing house 2 one who reads copy aloud to a proofreader [¹*copy* + *holder*]

**copyist** /'kopi·ist/ *n* 1 one who makes copies 2 an imitator

**copyreader** /-,reedə/ *n* 1 a publishing-house editor who reads and corrects manuscript copy; COPY EDITOR 2 *NAm* one who edits and headlines newspaper copy; a subeditor

**¹copyright** /-,riet/ *n* the exclusive legal right to reproduce, publish, and sell an original literary, musical, dramatic, or artistic work – **copyright** *adj*

**²copyright** *vt* to secure a copyright on (a literary, musical, dramatic, or artistic work)

**copytaster** /-,taystə/ *n, Br* a journalist who selects potential COPY (material suitable for printing) from a range of news stories submitted by reporters

**copywriter** /-,rietə/ *n* a writer of advertising or publicity COPY (material suitable for printing)

**¹coquet** /ko'ket, kə-, koh-/ *n* 1 a coquette 2 *obs* a man who indulges in coquetry [Fr, dim. of *coq* cock]

**²coquet, coquette** *vi* -tt- 1 to play the coquette; flirt 2 to deal with something playfully rather than seriously; trifle

**coquetry** /'kokətri, 'koh-/ *n* flirtatious behaviour or attitude

**coquette** /ko'ket, kə-, koh-/ *n* a woman who tries to gain the attention and admiration of men without sincere affection; a flirt [Fr, fem of *coquet*]

**coquettish** /ko'ketish, kə-, koh-/ *adj* having the air or nature of a coquette – **coquettishly** *adv*, **coquettishness** *n*

**coquilla nut** /kə'kilə, koh'kee(l)yə/ *n* the nut of a Brazilian palm tree (*Attalea funifera*) having a hard brown shell used for carving articles and ornaments [Pg *coquilho*, dim. of *côco* coconut]

**coquina** /ko'keenə/ *n* 1 a small marine clam (genus *Donax*) used in thick seafood soups and stews (e g chowder) 2 a soft whitish limestone formed of broken shells and coral cemented together and used for building [Sp, prob irreg dim. of *concha* shell]

**cor** /kaw/ *interj, Br slang* – used to express surprise, incredulity, or enthusiasm [euphemism for *God*]

**coraciiform** /,korə'sieə,fawm, kə'raysiə-/ *adj* of an order (Coraciiformes) of tree-dwelling birds including the kingfishers and hornbills [deriv of Gk *korak-, korax* raven + L *forma* form – more at RAVEN]

**coracle** /'korəkl/ *n* a small boat of a traditional Welsh or Irish design that is circular or oval in shape and is made by covering a wicker frame with an animal skin or tarpaulin [W *corwgl*; akin to MIr *curach* coracle (cf CURRAGH)]

**coracoid** /'korəkoyd/ *adj* of or being a bone of many VERTEBRATE animals that extends from the SCAPULA (shoulder blade or its equivalent) to or towards the STERNUM (breastbone or its equivalent), and that in mammals is reduced to a small peg projecting from the scapula [NL *coracoides*, fr Gk *korakoeidēs*, lit., like a raven, fr *korak-, korax*] – **coracoid** *n*

**coral** /'korəl/ *n* **1a** any of a group (class Anthozoa) of marine INVERTEBRATE animals related to the SEA ANEMONES, that are POLYPS having a hollow cylindrical body with a ring of tentacles round the mouth and that secrete an external chalky or horny skeleton and usu occur united into branching, encrusting, or more or less solid colonies **b** the hard usu calcium-containing skeleton produced by a coral; *esp* a rich red precious one secreted by a GORGONIAN coral (*Corallium nobile*) **2a** a large mass of coral POLYPS and their skeleton that forms a rocklike ridge on the sea floor **b** a piece of coral, esp red coral **3a** a bright reddish mass of ovaries (e g of a lobster or scallop) **b** a deep orange-pink colour [ME, fr MF, fr L *corallium*, fr Gk *korallion*, perh of Sem origin] – **coral** *adj*, **coralloid, coral- loidal** *adj*

**coral fish** *n* any of various brightly coloured fishes living among coral reefs

¹**coralline** /'korəlien/ *adj* of or resembling coral or a coralline [F *corallin*, fr LL *corallinus*, fr L *corallium*]

²**coralline** *n* **1** any of a family (Corallinaceae) of chalky red seaweeds **2** an INVERTEBRATE animal that resembles a coral, esp in having a branching structure or appearance

**coral snake** *n* **1** any of several poisonous chiefly tropical American snakes (genus *Micrurus*) that have grooved fangs and are brilliantly banded in red, black, and yellow or white **2** any of several harmless snakes resembling the coral snakes

**cor anglais** /ˌkawr 'ong-glay, ˌ- -'- (*Fr* kɔr ãglɛ/ *n* a woodwind instrument resembling the oboe but having a slightly lower range and a longer tube with a somewhat globular free end [Fr, English horn]

**coranto** /ko'rantoh, koh-, -'rahn-/ *n, pl* **corantos, corantoes** COURANTE (Italian dance) [modif of Fr *courante*]

**corban** /'kawban/ *n* a sacrifice or offering to God made by the ancient Jews [Heb *qorbān* offering]

¹**corbel** /'kawbl/ *n, building* **1** a BRACKET (support) that projects from within a wall and supports a weight **2** a deeply embedded bracket of stone or wood that in medieval architecture is often elaborately carved [ME, fr MF, fr dim. of *corp* raven, fr L *corvus* – more at RAVEN]

²**corbel** *vt* **-ll-** (*NAm* **-l-, -ll-**) to furnish with or make into a corbel

**corbicula** /kaw'bikyoolə/ *n, pl* **corbiculae** /-lee/ POLLEN BASKET (part of a bee's hind leg where pollen is collected) [LL, basket, dim. of L *corbis* basket]

**corbie** /'kawbi/ *n, chiefly Scot* CARRION CROW; *also* a raven [ME, modif of OF *corbin*, fr L *corvinus* of a raven, fr *corvus* raven]

¹**cord** /kawd/ *n* **1a** a long slender flexible material usu consist- ing of several strands (e g of thread or yarn) woven or twisted together; *also* a length of this in the form of a usu thick string or thin rope **b** a hangman's noose **2** a moral, spiritual, or emotional bond **3a** an anatomical structure (e g a nerve) re- sembling a cord **b** an electric flex **4** a unit of volume of cut wood usu equal to 128 cubic feet (about 3.63 cubic metres) **5a** a rib like a cord on a textile **b(1)** a fabric made with such ribs **b(2)** *pl* trousers made of corduroy *usage* see ³CHORD [ME, fr OF *corde*, fr L *chorda* string, fr Gk *chordē* – more at YARN]

²**cord** *vt* **1** to provide, bind, or connect with a cord **2** to pile up (wood) in cords – **corder** *n*

**cordage** /'kawdij/ *n* **1** ropes or cords; *esp* the ropes in the rig- ging of a ship **2** the quantity (e g of pieces of wood) measured in cords, on a given area

**cordate** /'kawdayt/ *adj* heart-shaped ⟨*a* ~ *leaf*⟩ [NL *cordatus*, fr L *cord-, cor*] – **cordately** *adv*

**corded** /'kawdid/ *adj* **1** bound or fastened with cords **2** striped or ribbed (as if) with cord; twilled **3** made of cords or ridges; *specif* muscled in ridges

**cord grass** *n* any of a genus (*Spartina*) of robust grasses that grow in SALT MARSHES

¹**cordial** /'kawdi·əl/ *adj* **1** of medicines, food, or drinks tending to revive, cheer, or invigorate ⟨*for fainting age what* ~ *drop remains* – Alexander Pope⟩ **2a** warmly and genially affable ⟨*she received a most* ~ *welcome*⟩ **b** sincerely or deeply felt ⟨*a* ~ *and active dislike for both his parents* – Samuel Butler † 1902⟩ **3** *obs* of the heart; vital [ME, fr ML *cordialis*, fr L *cord-, cor* heart – more at HEART] – **cordially** *adv*, **cordialness** *n*, **cordiality** *n*

²**cordial** *n* **1** a stimulating medicine or drink **2** a nonalcoholic sweetened fruit drink; a fruit syrup

**cordia pulmonalia** /ˌkawdiə ˌpoolmo'nahliə, -'nayliə/ *pl of* COR PULMONALE (disease of the heart)

**cordierite** /'kawdiəˌriet/ *n* a blue mineral with a glassy lustre that consists of a SILICATE of aluminium, iron, and magnesium, $(MgFe)_2Al_4Si_5O_{18}$, and exhibits strong DICHROISM (property of appearing as two different colours when viewed from different directions) [Fr, fr Pierre *Cordier* †1861 Fr geologist]

**cordiform** /'kawdiˌfawm/ *adj* cordate [Fr *cordiforme*, fr L *cord-, cor* + Fr *-iforme* -iform]

**cordillera** /ˌkawdi'lyeərə/ *n* a system of mountain ranges, esp in western N America, consisting of a number of more or less parallel chains of mountain peaks [Sp, fr *cordilla*, dim. of *cuerda* cord, chain, fr L *chorda*] – **cordilleran** *adj*

**cordite** /'kawdiet/ *n* a smokeless explosive material used esp in firearms that consists chiefly of nitroglycerine and CELLULOSE NITRATE, often shaped into cords resembling brown twine [*cord* + *-ite*]

**cordless** /'kawdlis/ *adj, of an electrical device* containing an internal source of electrical power; *esp* battery-powered

**cordoba** /'kawdəbə/ *n* – see MONEY table [Sp *córdoba*, fr Fran- cisco Fernández de *Córdoba* †1526 Sp explorer]

¹**cordon** /'kawd(ə)n/ *n* **1a** an ornamental cord, esp worn as part of a costume **b** a ribbon worn as a badge of honour or as a decoration **c** STRING COURSE (band of bricks forming part of the design in a wall) **2** *taking sing or pl vb* **2a** a line of troops, police, etc enclosing an area **b** a line or ring of people or objects that surrounds something **3** a fruit tree made to fruit from a single horizontal shoot or two shoots growing horizontally in opposite directions by pruning all the side shoots [Fr, dim. of *corde* cord]

²**cordon** *vt* **1** to ornament with a cordon **2** to form a protective or restrictive cordon round – often + *off*

¹**cordon bleu** /ˌkawdonh 'bluh (*Fr* kɔrdõ blø)/ *n* **1** the highest distinction in cookery **2** a person with a high degree of skill or distinction in cookery, esp in classical French cuisine [Fr, lit., blue cordon]

²**cordon bleu** *adj* typical of or being a cordon bleu or the food prepared by a cordon bleu ⟨~ *cooking*⟩ ⟨*a* ~ *cook*⟩

**cordon sanitaire** /sani'teə (*Fr* ~ sanitɛːr)/ *n* **1** a boundary round an infected district or region that is policed to prevent the spread of infection **2** BUFFER ZONE (neutral area separating two hostile groups) [Fr, lit., sanitary cordon]

¹**cordovan** /'kawdəv(ə)n/ *adj* **1** *cap* of Córdoba in Spain **2** made of cordovan leather [OSp *cordovano*, fr *Córdova* (now *Córdoba*), city in Spain]

²**cordovan** *n* **1** a soft fine-grained coloured leather originally made in Córdoba **2** dense waterproof leather TANNED (prepared by special treatment) from the inner layer of horsehide

**corduroy** /'kawd(ə)roy/ *n* **1a** a durable usu cotton pile fabric with lengthways ribs **b** *pl* ¹CORDS 5b(2) **2** *chiefly NAm* a road built of logs laid side by side [perh fr ¹*cord* + obs *duroy* coarse woollen fabric]

**cordwain** /'kawdˌwayn/ *n, archaic* cordovan leather [ME *cordwane*, fr MF *cordoan*, fr OSp *cordovano, cordován*]

**cordwainer** /'kawdˌwaynə/ *n, archaic* **1** one who works in cordovan leather **2** a shoemaker – **cordwainery** *n*

**cordwood** /-ˌwood/ *n* wood piled or sold in CORDS (unit of volume of cut wood); *also* standing timber suitable for use as fuel

¹**core** /kaw/ *n* **1** a central or interior part that is usu distinct from an enveloping part: e g **1a** the usu inedible central part of some fruits (e g a pineapple); *esp* the papery parts encasing the seeds in fruit such as apples and pears **b** the part of a mould used for casting metal objects that shapes a depression, cavity, or hole in the object **c** a cylindrical portion removed from a mass for inspection; *specif* such a portion of rock obtained by boring **d** the central strand round which other strands twist in some types of rope **e(1)** a piece of iron or material having magnetic properties like those of iron that serves to concentrate and intensify the MAGNETIC FIELD resulting from passing an electric current through a surrounding coil **e(2)** a tiny ring- shaped piece of material capable of being magnetized in two directions corresponding to on and off, used formerly in com- puter memories **e(3) core, core memory, core storage** a com- puter memory consisting of an array of cores strung on fine wires **f** the central part of a planet, esp the earth, having physical properties (e g heat conductivity and density) that are different from those of the surrounding parts **g** a small rounded lump of stone (e g flint) from which flakes have been struck for making primitive weapons or tools **h** a conducting wire and its insulating material in an electric cable **i** a block of wood on which veneers are glued (e g in making plywood) **j** a subject which is central in a course of studies and to which minor related subjects may be linked **2a** the essential, basic, or central part (e g of an individual, class, or entity) **b** the inmost or most intimate part ⟨*he was honest to the* ~⟩ **3** the part of a NUCLEAR REACTOR that contains the rods of fuel (e g uranium) and in which the energy-producing reaction occurs [ME]

²**core** *vt* to remove a core from – **corer** *n*

³**core** *n taking sing or pl vb, chiefly Scot* a group of people [ME *chore* chorus, company, fr L *chorus*]

**coreferential** /ˌkoh·refəˈrensh(ə)l/ *adj* having the same referent

**corelate** /ˌkoh·riˈlayt/ *vt, chiefly Br* to correlate [back-formation fr *corelation*] – **corelation** *n*, **corelative** *adj*, **corelatively** *adv*

**coreligionist** /ˌkoh·riˈlijənist/ *n* a person of the same religion

**coremium** /koh'reemiəm, kə-/ *n, pl* **coremia** /miə/ a stalked club-shaped spore-producing body characteristic of certain ASCOMYCETE fungi (eg *Penicillium* and *Ceratocystis*), that consists of a clump of individual SPOROPHORES (fungal threads bearing spores) and measures about 1 centimetre in length [NL, fr Gk *korēma* broom, fr *korein* to sweep]

**coreopsis** /ˌkori'opsis, koh-/ *n* any of a genus (*Coreopsis*) of plants of the daisy family, widely grown for their showy yellow or yellow and red flowers [NL, genus name, fr Gk *koris* bedbug + NL *-opsis*]

**corepressor** /ˌkohri'presə/ *n* a substance that activates a particular genetic REPRESSOR (substance that indirectly inhibits the synthesis of a protein)

**co-respondent** /ˌkoh ri'spond(ə)nt/ *n* a person accused of adultery and cited in a divorce proceeding together with the RESPONDENT (husband or wife with whom the adultery has allegedly been committed) △ correspondent

**corf** /kawf/ *n, pl* **corves** /kawvz/ *Br* a basket formerly used in a mine to convey ore or coal; *also* a tub or truck now used as a corf [ME, basket, fr MD *corf* or MLG *korf*, fr L *corbis*]

**corgi** /'kawgi/ *n, pl* **corgis** WELSH CORGI

**coriaceous** /ˌkori'ayshəs, ˌkoh-/ *adj* resembling leather ⟨a ∼ leaf⟩ [LL *coriaceus* – more at CUIRASS]

**coriander** /ˌkori'andə/ *n* a European plant (*Coriandrum sativum*) of the carrot family that bears aromatic seeds; *also* the ripened dried seeds of coriander used as a flavouring in cooking [ME *coriandre*, fr OF, fr L *coriandrum*, fr Gk *koriandron*, *koriannon*]

**¹Corinthian** /kə'rinthiən/ *n* 1 a native or inhabitant of Corinth in Greece **2a** a shamelessly immoral man; a rake **b** a fashionable man-about-town **c** an amateur sportsman or yachtsman **3** *pl but taking sing vb* – see BIBLE table [L *Corinthiensis*, fr *Corinthus* Corinth, city in ancient Greece, fr Gk *Korinthos*; (2) fr the proverbial wealth & licentiousness of ancient Corinth]

**²Corinthian** *adj* **1** (characteristic) of Corinth or Corinthians **2** of the lightest and most ornate of the three Greek orders of architecture characterized esp by its bell-shaped CAPITAL (upper part of a column) enveloped with large spiny leaves modelled on the acanthus plant – compare DORIC 2, IONIC 2

**Coriolis force** /ˌkori'ohlis/ *n* a force that arises as a result of the earth's rotation and causes the deflection of moving objects (eg projectiles or air currents) to the right in the N hemisphere and to the left in the S hemisphere [Gaspard *Coriolis* †1843 Fr civil engineer]

**corium** /'kawriəm/ *n, pl* **coria** /'kawriə/ DERMIS (layer of the skin) [NL, fr L, leather – more at CUIRASS]

**¹cork** /kawk/ *n* **1a** the elastic tough outer tissue of the CORK OAK tree that is used esp for bottle stoppers and as an insulating material **b** PHELLEM (protective tissue round some plant stems) **2** a usu cork stopper, esp for a bottle **3** a float used in angling [ME, cork, bark, prob deriv of Ar *qurq*, fr L *cortic-*, *cortex*]

**²cork** *vt* **1** to provide or fit with (a) cork **2** to stop up with a cork **3** to blacken with burnt cork

**corkage** /'kawkij/ *n* a charge made for serving alcoholic drink, esp wine, in a restaurant; *esp* one made for serving drink bought elsewhere

**corkboard** /'kawk,bawd/ *n* a heat-insulating material made of compressed granulated cork

**corked** /'kawkt/ *adj, of wine* having an unpleasant smell and taste as a result of being kept in a bottle sealed with a faulty cork

**corker** /'kawkə/ *n, informal* something or someone astonishing or superlative [²*cork* + ²-er]

**corking** /'kawking/ *adj or adv* extremely good; excellent ⟨had a ∼ good time⟩ – not now in vogue

**cork oak** *n* an oak tree (*Quercus suber*) of S Europe and N Africa whose bark is the source of commercial cork used for insulation, bottle stoppers, etc

**¹corkscrew** /-ˌskrooh/ *n* an implement for removing cork stoppers from bottles, typically consisting of a pointed spiral piece of metal attached to a handle

**²corkscrew** *vt* to twist into a spiral ∼ *vi* to move in a winding course

**³corkscrew** *adj* resembling a corkscrew; spiral ⟨a ∼ staircase⟩

**corkwing** /'kawk,wing/ *n* a small colourful European WRASSE (type of marine fish) (*Crenilabrus melops*) that is found in shallow water and rock pools

**corkwood** /-ˌwood/ *n* any of several trees (eg the balsa) having light or corky wood

**corky** /'kawki/ *adj* resembling cork (eg in consistency)

**corm** /kawm/ *n* a rounded thick underground stem base with buds and scaly leaves that stores food and produces new shoots each year (eg in the crocus) – compare BULB, TUBER [NL *cormus*, fr Gk *kormos* tree trunk, fr *keirein* to cut – more at SHEAR]

**cormel** /'kawməl, kaw'mel/ *n* a small or secondary corm produced by a larger corm [dim. of *corm*]

**cormorant** /'kawmərənt/ *n* **1** a common dark-coloured web-footed European seabird (*Phalacrocorax carbo*) with a long neck, hooked bill, and white throat and cheeks; *broadly* any of various related seabirds (family Phalacrocoracidae) many of which are used in E Asia for catching fish **2** a gluttonous or greedy person [ME *cormeraunt*, fr MF *cormorant*, fr OF *cormareng*, fr *corp* raven + *marenc* of the sea, fr L *marinus*]

**¹corn** /kawn/ *n* **1** a small hard seed **2a** the grain of a cereal plant; *esp* the grain of the important cereal crop of a particular region (eg wheat and barley in Britain) **b** plants of a growing cereal crop **3a** maize, SWEET CORN **b** the kernels of sweet corn served as a vegetable while still soft and milky **4** *chiefly dial* a small hard particle **5** *informal* something corny ⟨the opening dance routine was pure ∼⟩ [ME, fr OE; akin to OHG & ON *korn* grain, L *granum*, Gk *gēras* old age]

**²corn** *vt* to preserve or season with salt or brine ⟨∼ed *beef*⟩ [orig sense, to granulate (hence, to preserve with granulated salt)]

**³corn** *n* **1** a hardening and thickening of skin usu on the toe, caused by friction (eg from ill-fitting shoes) **2** a bruise in the heel region of a horse's hoof – see also TREAD on somebody's corns [ME *corne*, fr MF, horn, corner, fr L *cornu* horn, point]

**¹cornball** /'kawn,bawl/ *n NAm informal* an unsophisticated person; a bumpkin [*corn ball* (ball of popcorn and molasses); influenced in meaning by ¹*corn* 5]

**²cornball** *adj, chiefly NAm* corny

**corn borer** *n* EUROPEAN CORN BORER (type of moth)

**corn bunting** *n* a large European bunting (*Emberiza calandra*) with streaky grey-brown plumage that frequents marshy fields and scrub

**corncob** /-ˌkob/ *n* **1** the core on which the edible kernels of sweet corn are arranged **2** an ear of sweet corn

**corncob pipe** *n* a tobacco pipe made from a corncob

**corn cockle** *n* a poisonous hairy plant (*Agrostemma githago*) related to the pink and carnation, that has purplish-red flowers and is a now rare weed of cornfields

**corncrake** /-ˌkrayk/ *n* a common Eurasian short-billed bird (*Crex crex*) of the rail family that frequents cornfields

**corn dodger** *n, chiefly S & Mid US* a cake of bread dough made with coarsely ground kernels of maize that is fried, baked, or boiled as a dumpling

**corn dolly** *n* an article of woven straw that originally had ritual significance but is now used for decoration

**cornea** /'kaw'nee·ə, 'kawni·ə/ *n* the hard transparent structure that forms the front part of the coat of the eyeball and covers the coloured iris and the pupil [ML, fr L, fem. of *corneus* horny, fr *cornu*] – **corneal** *adj*

**cornel** /'kawnl/ *n* dogwood or a related plant [deriv of L *cornus* cornel cherry tree; akin to Gk *kerasos* cherry tree]

**cornelian** /kaw'neelyən/ *n* a hard reddish CHALCEDONY (variety of quartz) used in jewellery [ME *corneline*, fr MF, perh fr *cornelle* cornel]

**cornelian cherry** *n* a deciduous shrub or small tree (*Cornus mas*) of the dogwood family that bears oval-shaped scarlet fruit [*cornel* + *-ian*]

**corneous** /'kawniəs/ *adj* HORNY 1a [L *corneus*]

**¹corner** /'kawnə/ *n* **1a** the point where converging lines, edges, or sides meet; an angle **b** the place of intersection of two streets or roads **c** a piece (eg a leather or metal cap) designed to form, mark, or protect a corner (eg of a book) **2** the angular space between meeting lines, edges, or borders: eg **2a** the area of a playing field or court near the intersection of the sideline and the goal line or baseline **b(1)** any of the four angles of a boxing ring; *esp* that in which a boxer rests between rounds **b(2)** *taking sing or pl vb* a contestant's group of supporters, adherents, etc **c** CORNER KICK; *also* CORNER HIT **3a** a private, secret, or remote place ⟨*a quiet* ∼ *of a small Welsh town*⟩ **b** a difficult or embarrassing situation; a position from which escape or retreat is difficult or impossible ⟨*talked himself into a tight* ∼⟩ **4** *economics* control or ownership of enough of the available supply of a commodity to allow manipulation of esp the price **5** a triangular cut of gammon or ham from the top of the hind leg **6** a point at which significant change occurs – often in *turn a corner* [ME, fr OF *cornere*, fr *corne* horn, corner] – **cut corners** to do or carry out something in the quickest, easiest, or cheapest way, often with bad results – **round the corner** imminent; AT HAND

²**corner** *vt* **1a** to drive into a corner **b** to catch and hold the attention of, esp so as to force into conversation ⟨∼ *the chairman after the match*⟩ **2** to get a corner on ⟨∼ *the wheat market*⟩ ∼ *vi* **1** to turn a corner ⟨*this car* ∼s *well*⟩ **2** *NAm* to meet or converge at a corner or angle

³**corner** *adj* **1** situated at a corner ⟨*a* ∼ *shop*⟩ **2** used or fitted for use in or on a corner ⟨*a* ∼ *cupboard*⟩ **3** of the corner (e g of a playing area or sports field)

**-cornered** /-kawnəd/ *comb form* (→ *adj*) **1** having such or so many corners **2** having so many participants or contestants ⟨*a* three-*cornered fight between Labour, the Tories, and the Liberals*⟩

**corner hit** *n* a free hit, esp in hockey or shinty, awarded to the attacking side when a member of the defending side has sent the ball over his/her own goal line

**corner kick** *n* a free kick in soccer that is taken from the corner of the field and is awarded to the attacking team when a member of the defending team has sent the ball behind his/her own goal line

**cornerman** /'kawnə,man/ *n, chiefly NAm* one (e g a basketball forward) who plays in or near the corner

**cornerstone** /-,stohn/ *n* **1** a block of stone forming a part of a corner or angle in a wall; *specif* FOUNDATION STONE **2** the most basic element; a foundation ⟨*a* ∼ *of foreign policy*⟩

**cornerwise** /-,wiez/, **cornerways** /-,wayz/ *adv* diagonally

¹**cornet** /'kawnit/ *n* **1** a brass instrument with finger-operated valves to vary the pitch that resembles the trumpet in design and range but has a shorter tube and less brilliant tone **2** something shaped like a cone: e g **2a** a piece of paper twisted for use as a container **b** *Br* an ice cream cone [ME, fr MF, fr dim. of *corn* horn, fr L *cornu*] – **cornetist, cornettist** *n*

²**cornet** *n* the former fifth commissioned officer of a British cavalry troop who carried the standard [MF *cornette* type of headdress, standard, standard-bearer, fr *corne* horn, fr L *cornu*]

**cornett** /kaw'net/ *n* a Renaissance woodwind instrument having a cup-shaped mouthpiece like a trumpet and a tapered tube with finger holes like a recorder [ME *cornette, cornet*]

**cornfield** /'kawn,feeld/ *n* a field in which corn is grown

**cornflakes** /-,flayks/ *n pl* toasted flakes of maize eaten as a breakfast cereal

**cornflour** /-,flowə/ *n* a finely ground flour made from grain, esp maize or rice, and used esp as a thickening agent in cooking

**cornflower** /-,flowə/ *n* **1** a European plant (*Centaurea cyanus*) of the daisy family that has bright-blue flowers and is a now rare weed of cornfields **2** CORN COCKLE (purple-flowered plant)

**cornflower blue** *n* a purplish-blue colour

**cornice** /'kawnis/ *n* **1** the ornamental projecting piece that forms the top edge of a building or pillar **2** a decorative band of metal or wood used to conceal curtain fixtures **3** an overhanging mass of snow, ice, or rock usu on a mountain ridge [MF, fr It, perh deriv of Gk *korōnis* copingstone] – **corniced** *adj*

**corniche** /kaw'neesh/ *n* a road built along a coast, esp along the face of a cliff [Fr *cornice, corniche*, lit., cornice]

**cornification** /,kawnifi'kaysh(ə)n/ *n* **1** formation of or conversion into horny tissue; KERATINIZATION **2** the conversion of the tall narrow cells lining the vagina into small scalelike cells [L *cornu* horn + E -*i-* + -*fication*] – **cornify** *vi*

¹**Cornish** /'kawnish/ *adj* of or characteristic of Cornwall, Cornishmen, or Cornish [*Corn*wall, county of England + E -*ish*]

²**Cornish** *n* **1** the ancient Celtic language of Cornwall **2** (any

of) an English breed of DOMESTIC FOWL much used in cross-breeding with popular commercial breeds for increased meat production

**Cornishman** /'kawnishmən/ *n* a native or inhabitant of Cornwall

**Cornish pasty** *n* a pasty consisting of a circular piece of pastry folded over a savoury filling typically of meat, potato, and onion and often other vegetables (e g carrot)

**Corn Laws** *n* a series of laws in force in Britain before 1846 restricting the import of foreign grain

**corn marigold** *n* an erect European plant (*Chrysanthemum segetum*) of the daisy family, that has golden-yellow flowers and is a weed of cornfields

**corn pone** /pohn/ *n, S & Mid US* a bread made with maize and baked or fried [¹*corn* + *pone* (bread), of Algonquian origin; akin to Delaware *äpân* baked]

**corn silk** *n* the silky tuft of long slender STYLES (female parts of the flower) at the top of the ear of a maize plant

**corn spurrey** *n* a European plant (*Spergula arvensis*) related to the pink and carnation, that has small white flowers and is a common weed of cultivated land

**cornstarch** /-,stahch/ *n, NAm* cornflour

**corn syrup** *n* a syrup containing sugar compounds (e g maltose and dextrose) that is obtained by partial chemical breakdown of maize meal

**cornu** /'kawnyooh/ *n, pl* **cornua** /'kawnyoohə/ a horn; *esp* a horn-shaped anatomical structure [L] – **cornual** *adj*

**cornucopia** /,kawnyoo'kohpi·ə/ *n* **1** a curved goat's horn overflowing with fruit and corn that is used as a decorative motif to symbolize abundance **2** an inexhaustible store; an abundance **3** a vessel shaped like a horn or cone [LL, fr L *cornu copiae* horn of plenty] – **cornucopian** *adj*

**cornuto** /kaw'nyoohtoh/ *n, pl* **cornutos** CUCKOLD (man with an unfaithful wife) [It, fr L *cornutus* having horns, fr *cornu*; fr the proverbial horn growing on the forehead of a cuckold]

**corn whiskey** *n, NAm* whiskey distilled from a mash made up of not less than 80 per cent maize – compare BOURBON

¹**corny** /'kawni/ *adj, informal* **1** tiresomely simple and sentimental; trite **2** hackneyed [¹*corn* + ¹-*y;* orig sense, rural, old-fashioned] – **cornily** *adv*, **corniness** *n*

²**corny** *adj* of or having corns on the feet

**corody, corrody** /'korədi/ *n* an allowance of provisions, esp food, for maintenance given in charity [ME *corrodie*, fr ML *corrodium*, deriv of OF *correer* to prepare – more at CURRY]

**corolla** /kə'rolə/ *n* the petals of a flower collectively [NL, fr L, dim. of *corona*] – **corollate** *adj*

**corollary** /kə'roləri/ *n* **1** *philosophy* a direct conclusion from a proved PROPOSITION (statement affirming or denying something) **2** something that naturally follows or accompanies [ME *corolarie*, fr LL *corollarium*, fr L, money paid for a garland, gratuity, fr *corolla*] – **corollary** *adj*

**corona** /kə'rohnə/ *n* **1** the decorative concave moulding on the upper part of a classical CORNICE (top edge of a wall or pillar) **2a** a usu coloured circle often seen round and close to a luminous body (e g the sun or moon) caused by DIFFRACTION (splitting of white light into coloured bands) produced by suspended droplets or occasionally particles of dust in the atmosphere **b** the outermost part of the atmosphere of the sun and other stars appearing as a halo round the moon's black disc during a total eclipse of the sun **c** a circle of light made by the apparent convergence of the streamers of light of the AURORA BOREALIS (light phenomenon seen in the night sky of arctic regions) **d** the upper portion of a body part (e g a tooth or the skull) **e** a circular appendage on the inner side of the corolla in some flowers (e g the daffodil or jonquil) **f** a faint glow near the surface of an electrical conductor which is at high voltage **3** a long straight-sided cigar of uniform thickness that has a straight-cut unsealed burning end and a roundly blunt sealed mouth end [L, garland, crown, cornice – more at CROWN; (3) fr *La Corona*, a trademark]

**coronach** /'korənəkh, -nək/ *n* a funeral dirge sung or played on the bagpipes in Scotland and Ireland [ScGael *corranach* & IrGael *corānach*, fr MIr *com-* together + (assumed) MIr *rānach* outcry, weeping]

**coronagraph** /kə'rohnəgrahf/ *n* CORONOGRAPH (telescope for observing the sun)

¹**coronal** *also* **coronel** /'korənl/ *n* a circlet for the head usu implying rank or dignity [ME *coronal*, fr AF, fr L *coronalis* of a crown, fr *corona*]

²**coronal** *adj* **1** of a corona or crown **2a** lying in the direction

of the CORONAL SUTURE **b** of or being the frontal plane that passes through the long axis of the body and divides it into front and back parts

**coronal suture** *n* a SUTURE (seamlike joint) extending across the top of the skull between the PARIETAL BONES (bones forming the sides of the skull) and the FRONTAL BONES (bones forming the front of the skull)

**corona radiata** /kə,rohnə raydi'ahtə/ *n, pl* **coronae radiatae** /kə,rohni raydi 'ahti/ the zone of small cells immediately surrounding the developing egg cell in the GRAAFIAN FOLLICLE (small sac in the mammalian ovary) and accompanying the egg cell on its discharge from the follicle [NL, lit., crown with rays]

**¹coronary** /'korən(ə)ri/ *adj* **1** of, resembling, or being a crown or coronal **2** of or being the CORONARY ARTERIES or CORONARY VEINS of the heart; *broadly* of the heart

**²coronary** *n* **1a** CORONARY ARTERY **b** CORONARY VEIN **2** CORONARY THROMBOSIS

**coronary artery** *n* either of two arteries, one on the right and one on the left of the heart, that arise from the AORTA (large artery carrying blood away from the heart) and supply blood to the tissues of the heart itself

**coronary occlusion** *n* the partial or complete blocking (e g by a blood clot, by spasm, or by hardening of tissue) of a CORONARY ARTERY

**coronary sinus** *n* a channel that carries blood from the veins in the walls of the heart into the right-hand ATRIUM (top chamber) of the heart

**coronary thrombosis** /throm'bohsis/ *n* the blocking of a CORONARY ARTERY of the heart by a blood clot, usu causing death of cells in the heart's muscle tissue

**coronary vein** *n* any of several veins that take blood from the tissues of the heart and empty into the CORONARY SINUS

**coronation** /,korə'naysh(ə)n/ *n* the act or ceremony of crowning a sovereign or his/her consort [ME *coronacion*, fr MF *coronation*, fr *coroner* to crown]

**coroner** /'korənə/ *n* a public officer (e g a barrister, solicitor, or doctor) whose principal duty is to investigate by an inquest the cause of any death for which there is reason to suspect that it might not be due to natural causes [ME, an officer of the crown, fr AF, fr OF *corone* crown, fr L *corona*]

**coronet** /'korənit/ *n* **1** a small crown signifying noble rank below that of a sovereign **2** an ornamental wreath or band for the head **3** the lower part of a horse's foot between the fetlock and hoof, where the horn ends in skin [MF *coronette*, fr OF *coronete*, fr *corone*]

**coronograph, coronagraph** /kə'rohnəgrahf/ *n* a telescope for observing the sun's CORONAS

**corotate** /kohroh'tayt/ *vi, astronomy* to rotate in conjunction with or at the same rate as another rotating body – **corotation** *n*

**corpora** /'kawpərə/ *pl of* CORPUS

**¹corporal** /'kawp(ə)rəl/ *n* a linen cloth on which the bread and wine are placed during a Communion service [ME, fr MF, fr ML *corporale*, fr L, neut. of *corporalis*; fr the doctrine that the bread of the Eucharist becomes or represents the body of Christ]

**²corporal** ·*adj* **1** of or affecting the body ⟨~ *punishment*⟩ – compare CAPITAL **2** *obs* corporeal, physical △ corporeal [ME, fr MF, fr L *corporalis*, fr *corpor-*, *corpus* body] – **corporality** *n*, **corporally** *adv*

**³corporal** *n* – see MILITARY RANKS table [MF, lowest non-commissioned officer, alter. of *caporal*, fr OIt *caporale*, fr *capo* head, fr L *caput* – more at HEAD]

**corporate** /'kawp(ə)rət/ *adj* **1a** *law* INCORPORATED **2 b** of a corporation ⟨*a plan to reorganize the* ~ *structure*⟩ **2** of or formed into a unified body of individuals **3** of corporatism ⟨*a* ~ *state*⟩ [L *corporatus*, pp of *corporare* to make into a body, fr *corpor-*, *corpus*] – **corporately** *adv*

**corporate planning** *n* the business function of formulating long-term objectives and plans relating to the total activities of a company

**corporation** /,kawpə'raysh(ə)n/ *n* **1** the civic authorities of a town or city, typically having the responsibility of administering local government and public services (e g housing, public health, and amenities and recreation) **2** a body made up of more than one person that is formed and authorized by law to act as a single person with a legal identity separate from that of its members and that is legally given various rights and duties including the capacity to continue in existence after the

death or withdrawal of individual members **3** an association of employers and employees in an industry or of members of a profession in a state exhibiting corporatism **4** *humorous* POTBELLY 1

**corporation tax** *n* a tax on a private company's profits

**corporatism** /'kawp(ə)rə,tiz(ə)m/ *also* **corporativism** /'kawp(ə)rəti,viz(ə)m/ *n* the organization of a society into corporations serving as subordinate groups for political representation and having some power to administer justice and exercise influence over people and activities within their area of control (e g in Fascist Italy) – **corporatist** *adj*

**corporative** /'kawp(ə)rətiv/ *adj* **1** of a corporation **2** of corporatism ⟨*a* ~ *state*⟩

**corporator** /'kawpəraytə/ *n* a corporation organizer, member, or shareholder

**corporeal** /kaw'pawri·əl/ *adj* **1** having or consisting of a physical body: e g **1a** not spiritual **b** not immaterial or intangible; substantial **2** *archaic* corporal *synonyms* see ¹MATERIAL *antonyms* spiritual, incorporeal [L *corporeus* of the body, fr *corpor-*, *corpus*] – **corporeality, corporealness** *n*, **corporeally** *adv*

**corposant** /'kawpəz(ə)nt/ *n* SAINT ELMO'S FIRE (electrical flaming phenomenon seen at prominent points on ships, aircraft, etc) [Pg *corpo-santo*, lit., holy body]

**corps** /kaw/ *n, pl* **corps** **1a** an organized branch of the military establishment ⟨*Royal Armoured* Corps⟩ **b** a tactical army unit usu consisting of two or more divisions and auxiliary arms and services **2a** a group of people associated together or acting under common direction; *esp* a body of people having a common activity or occupation ⟨*the press* ~⟩ **b** any of various associations of German university students **3** military training given as a subject in the school curriculum, typically in British schools; *also* the period of this training ☐ (*except* 3) *taking sing or pl vb* [Fr, fr L *corpus* body]

**corps de ballet** /,kaw də 'balay, *NAm* ba'lay/ *n taking sing or pl vb, pl* **corps de ballet** the supporting group of dancers in a ballet company [Fr]

**corps d'elite** /,kaw day'leet (*Fr* kɔːr delit)/ *n taking sing or pl vb, pl* **corps d'elite 2** an élite or select group [Fr *corps d'élite*]

**corpse** /kawps/ *n* **1** a dead body, esp of a human being **2** *obs* a human or animal body whether living or dead [ME *corps*, fr MF, fr L *corpus* – more at MIDRIFF]

**corpsman** /'kawmən, 'kawzmən/ *n, NAm* a member of the armed forces trained to give first aid and minor medical treatment

**corpulence** /'kawpyooləns/, **corpulency** /-si/ *n* the state of being excessively fat; obesity [ME, fr MF, fr L *corpulentin*, fr *corpulentus* large-bodied, fr *corpus*] – **corpulent** *adj*, **corpulently** *adv*

**cor pulmonale** /,kaw poolmo'nahli, -'nayli/ *n, pl* **cordia pulmonalia** /,kawdiə poolmo'nahliə, -'nayliə/ disease of the heart characterized by an increase in size and volume of the right-hand VENTRICLE (lower chamber of the heart) and following from disease of the lungs or their blood vessels [NL, lit., pulmonary heart]

**corpus** /'kawpəs/ *n, pl* **corpora** /'kawpərə/ **1a** the main part of a body structure or organ ⟨*the* ~ *of the uterus*⟩ **b** the main body or material substance of a thing; *specif* the sum of money in a fund or the sum at which an estate is valid as distinct from income or interest earned **2a** all the writings of a particular kind or on a particular subject; *esp* the complete works of an author **b** a collection of spoken and/or written language for scientific study of word formation, sentence structure, sounds, etc **3** *archaic* the body of a man or animal, esp when dead [ME, fr L]

**corpus allatum** /ə'laytəm/ *n, pl* **corpora allata** /,kawpərə ə'laytə/ either of a pair of separate or fused structures in many insects that lie behind the brain and that secrete hormones (e g JUVENILE HORMONE) [NL, lit., applied body]

**corpus callosum** /kə'lohs(ə)m/ *n, pl* **corpora callosa** /,kawpər, koəlohsə/ the wide band of nerve fibres joining the CEREBRAL HEMISPHERES (right and left halves of the main part of the brain) in humans and in the higher mammals [NL, lit., callous body]

**corpus cardiacum** /,kawpəs kah'dieəkəm/ *n, pl* **corpora cardiaca** /,kawpərə kah'dieəkə/ either of a pair of separate or fused bodies of nerve tissue in many insects that lie behind the brain and round the gullet and that function in the storage and secretion of BRAIN HORMONE [NL, lit., cardiac body]

**Corpus Christi** /'kristi/ *n* the Thursday after Trinity Sunday observed, esp by Roman Catholics, in honour of Communion, instituted for the commemoration of Christ's death [ME, fr ML, lit., body of Christ]

**corpuscle** /'kawpəsl, -pu-, kaw'pusl/ *n* **1** a minute particle **2a** a living cell, esp when not in continuous contact with others as part of a tissue; *esp* a blood cell **b** any of various small multicellular bodies – compare MALPIGHIAN CORPUSCLE [L *corpusculum*, dim. of *corpus*] – **corpuscular** *adj*

**corpus delicti** /di'likti/ *n, pl* **corpora delicti** /ˌkawpərə ~/ **1** the body of facts showing that a breach of the law has taken place **2** something (eg the body of a victim in a murder case) on which a crime has been committed

**corpus luteum** /'loohti-əm/ *n, pl* **corpora lutea** /ˌkawpərə 'loohti-ə/ a reddish-yellow mass of tissue that forms in the mammalian ovary after the release of an egg and produces a hormone (PROGESTERONE) that causes changes needed for pregnancy if the egg is fertilized but degenerates rapidly if the egg is not fertilized [NL, lit., yellowish body]

**corrade** /kə'rayd/ *vi, of land* to be worn away through abrasive action, esp the action of rock debris carried in rivers, ice, etc ~ *vt* to wear away (land) by abrasion [L *corradere* to scrape together, fr *com-* + *radere* to scrape – more at RAT] – **corrasion** *n*, **corrasive** *adj*

[1]**corral** /kə'rahl, ko-, kaw-, -ral/ *n, chiefly NAm* **1** a pen or enclosure for confining livestock **2** an enclosure made with covered wagons for the defence of a (military) camp [Sp, fr (assumed) VL *currale* enclosure for vehicles, fr L *currus* cart, fr *currere* to run – more at CAR]

[2]**corral** *vt* **-ll-** *chiefly NAm* **1** to enclose in a corral **2** to arrange (wagons) so as to form a corral **3** *informal* to collect, gather

[1]**correct** /kə'rekt/ *vt* **1a** to make or set right; amend **b** to counteract, neutralize **c** to alter or adjust so as to counteract some imperfection or failing ⟨~ *a lens for spherical aberration*⟩ **2a** to punish (eg a child) with a view to reforming or improving **b** to point out faults of ⟨*spent the whole day* ~ing *essays*⟩ [ME *correcten*, fr L *correctus*, pp of *corrigere*, fr *com-* + *regere* to lead straight – more at RIGHT] – **correctable** *adj*, **corrector** *n*

[2]**correct** *adj* **1** conforming to an approved or conventional standard **2** true, right [ME, corrected, fr L *correctus*, fr pp of *corrigere*] – **correctly** *adv*, **correctness** *n*

**correction** /kə'reksh(ə)n/ *n* **1** the action or an instance of correcting: eg **1a** amendment, rectification **b** rebuke, punishment **c** bringing into conformity with a standard **2** *economics* a decline in market price or business activity following and counteracting a rise **3a** something substituted, esp written, in place of what is wrong **b** a quantity applied by way of correcting (eg in adjusting an instrument) – **correctional** *adj*

**correctitude** /kə'rektiyoohd, -choohd/ *n* correctness or propriety of conduct [blend of *correct* and *rectitude*]

**corrective** /kə'rektiv/ *adj* tending to correct ⟨~ *lenses*⟩ ⟨~ *punishment*⟩ – **corrective** *n*, **correctively** *adv*, **correctiveness** *n*

[1]**correlate** /'korilayt, -lət/ *n* **1** *philosophy* either of two things so related that one directly implies the other (eg husband and wife) **2** a phenomenon (eg brain activity) that accompanies another phenomenon (eg behaviour), is usu parallel to it (eg in form, type, development, or distribution), and is in some way related to it [back-formation fr *correlation*] – **correlate** *adj*

[2]**correlate** /'korilayt/ *vi* to have a reciprocal or mutual relationship ~ *vt* **1** to establish a mutual or reciprocal relation of **2** *maths* to relate so that to each member of one set or series a corresponding member of another is assigned **3** to bring together in order to compare ⟨~ *the findings of research groups throughout Europe*⟩ – **correlatable** *adj*

**correlation** /ˌkori'laysh(ə)n/ *n* **1a** the act of correlating **b** the state of being correlated; *specif* a relation of phenomena as invariable accompaniments of each other **2** *biology* mutual or reciprocal relationship in the occurrence of different structures, characteristics, or processes in organisms **3** *statistics* an association between two variables such that a change in one implies a proportionate change in the other [ML *correlation-, correlatio*, fr L *com-* + *relation-, relatio* relation] – **correlational** *adj*

**correlation coefficient** *n* a number or function that indicates the degree of correlation between two sets of data or between two variables

**correlative** /kə'relətiv, ko-/ *adj* **1** mutually or reciprocally related; corresponding **2** *of words or word parts* regularly used together ⟨*the* ~ *conjunctions* either ... or⟩ ⟨-er *and* than *are*

~ *as in quicker than, sooner than*⟩ – **correlative** *n*, **correlatively** *adv*

**correspond** /ˌkori'spond/ *vi* **1a** to be in conformity or agreement; suit **b** to compare closely; match **c** to be equivalent or parallel **2** to communicate *with* a person by exchange of letters (*1a & b*) *usu* + *to* or *with* **synonyms** see AGREE [MF or ML; MF *correspondre*, fr ML *correspondēre*, fr L *com-* + *respondēre* to respond]

**correspondence** /ˌkori'spond(ə)ns/ *n* **1a** the agreement of things with one another **b** a particular similarity **c** *maths* an association of one or more members of one set with one or more members of another set **2a** (communication by) letters **b** the news, information, or opinion contributed by a correspondent to a newspaper or periodical

**correspondence college** *n* a college that teaches nonresident students by post

[1]**correspondent** /ˌkori'spond(ə)nt/ *adj, formal* **1** corresponding ⟨*each advantage having* ~ *disadvantages*⟩ **2** fitting, conforming – + *with* or *to* ⟨*the outcome was entirely* ~ *with my wishes*⟩ [ME, fr MF or ML; MF, fr ML *correspondent-, correspondens*, prp of *correspondēre*]

[2]**correspondent** *n* **1** something that corresponds **2a** one who communicates with another by letter **b** one who has regular commercial relations with another **c** one who contributes news or comment to a publication (eg a newspaper) or to a radio or television work, often from a distant place ⟨*a war* ~⟩ △ co-respondent

**corresponding** /ˌkori'sponding/ *adj* **1a** agreeing in some respect (eg kind, degree, position, or function) **b** related, accompanying **b** participating or serving at a distance and by post ⟨*a* ~ *member of the society*⟩ – **correspondingly** *adv*

**corresponsive** /ˌkori'sponsiv/ *adj* mutually responsive

**corrida** /ko'reedhə, -də/ *n* a bullfight [Sp, lit., act of running]

**corridor** /'koridaw, -də/ *n* **1** a passageway (eg in a hotel or railway carriage) onto which compartments or rooms open **2** a usu narrow passageway or route: eg **2a** a narrow strip of land through foreign-held territory; *esp* one that gives an inland country access to the sea **b(1)** a restricted path for air traffic **b(2)** a restricted path a spacecraft must follow to accomplish its mission; WINDOW 9 (passage for reentry into the earth's atmosphere) **3** a strip of land that by geographical characteristics is distinct from its surroundings [MF, fr OIt *corridore*, fr *correre* to run, fr L *currere* – more at CAR]

**corrie** /'kori/ *n, chiefly Scot* CIRQUE 1 (bowl-shaped depression on a mountain) [ScGael *coire*, lit., kettle]

**Corriedale** /'koriˌdayl/ *n* (any of) a breed of rather large usu hornless sheep developed in New Zealand for meat and wool [*Corriedale*, ranch in New Zealand]

**corrigendum** /ˌkori'jendəm/ *n, pl* **corrigenda** /-də/ an error in a printed work discovered after printing and shown with its correction on a sheet inserted into the publication [L, neut of *corrigendus*, gerundive of *corrigere* to correct]

**corrigible** /'korijəbl/ *adj* capable of being corrected [ME, fr MF, fr ML *corrigibilis*, fr L *corrigere*] – **corrigibly** *adv*, **corrigibility** *n*

**corroborant** /kə'robərənt/ *adj, archaic, of a medicine* having an invigorating effect [L *corroborant-, corroborans*, prp of *corroborare*]

**corroborate** /kə'robərayt/ *vt* to support with evidence or authority; make more certain **synonyms** see CONFIRM **antonym** contradict [L *corroboratus*, pp of *corroborare*, fr *com-* + *robor-, robur* strength (cf ROBUST)] – **corroborator** *n*, **corroborative** *adj*, **corroboratory** *adj*, **corroboration** *n*

**corroboree** /kə'robəri/ *n* **1** an Australian aboriginal festivity held at night with songs and symbolic dances to celebrate important events **2** *Austr* **2a** a noisy festivity **b** a tumult [native name in New South Wales, Australia]

**corrode** /kə'rohd/ *vt* **1** to eat or wear (esp metal) away gradually, esp by chemical action **2** to weaken or destroy by corrosion ~ *vi* to undergo corroding [ME *corroden*, fr L *corrodere* to gnaw to pieces, fr *com-* + *rodere* to gnaw – more at RAT] – **corrodible** *adj*

**corrody** /'korədi/ *n* CORODY (charitable allowance of provisions)

**corrosion** /kə'rohzh(ə)n/ *n* the action, process, or effect of corroding; *also* the product of such a process [ME, fr LL *corrosion-, corrosio* act of gnawing, fr L *corrosus*, pp of *corrodere*]

**corrosive** /kə'rohsiv, -ziv/ *adj* **1** tending or having the power to corrode ⟨~ *acids*⟩ ⟨~ *action*⟩ **2** bitingly sarcastic ⟨~ *satire*⟩ – **corrosive** *n*, **corrosively** *adv*, **corrosiveness** *n*

**corrosive sublimate** *n* MERCURIC CHLORIDE

**corrugate** /'korəgayt, -roo-/ *vb* to form or become formed into wrinkles or folds or into alternating ridges and grooves; furrow ⟨∼d *cardboard*⟩ [L *corrugatus*, pp of *corrugare*, fr *com-* + *ruga* wrinkle – more at ROUGH]

**corrugated iron** /'korəgaytid/ *n* usu GALVANIZED (treated with a protective coating of zinc) sheet iron or sheet steel shaped into straight parallel regular and equally curved alternate ridges and grooves

**corrugation** /ˌkorə'gaysh(ə)n/ *n* **1** the act of corrugating **2** a ridge or groove of a corrugated surface

**¹corrupt** /kə'rupt/ *vt* **1a** to change from good to bad in morals, manners, or actions; *also* to influence by bribery **b** to degrade with unsound principles or moral values **2** to make rotten; to spoil **3** to alter (a manuscript, text, etc) from the original or correct form or version ∼ *vi* **1a** to become tainted or rotten **b** to become morally debased **2** to cause disintegration or ruin [ME *corrupten*, fr L *corruptus*, pp of *corrumpere*, fr *com-* + *rumpere* to break – more at BEREAVE] – **corrupter, corruptor** *n*, **corruptible** *adj*, **corruptibly** *adv*, **corruptibility** *n*, **corruptive** *adj*

**²corrupt** *adj* **1a** morally degenerate and perverted; depraved **b** characterized by bribery, the selling of political favours, or other improper conduct ⟨∼ *judges*⟩ **2** having been debased (eg in aesthetic character) by mistakes or changes ⟨*a* ∼ *text*⟩ **3** *archaic* putrid, tainted [ME, fr MF or L; MF, fr L *corruptus*, fr pp of *corrumpere*] – **corruptly** *adv*, **corruptness** *n*

**corruption** /kə'rupsh(ə)n/ *n* **1** impairment of integrity, virtue, or moral principle; depravity **2** decay, decomposition **3** inducement to do wrong by unlawful or improper means, esp bribery **4** a departure from what is pure or correct

**corsage** /kaw'sahzh/ *n* **1** the bodice of a woman's evening dress **2** an arrangement of flowers in a small bouquet to be worn by a woman [Fr, bust, bodice, fr OF, bust, fr *cors* body, fr L *corpus*]

**corsair** /'kawseə/ *n* a pirate; *esp* a privateer of the Barbary coast [MF & OIt; MF *corsaire* pirate, fr OProv *corsari*, fr OIt *corsaro*, fr ML *cursarius*, fr L *cursus* course – more at COURSE]

**corse** /kaws/ *n*, *archaic* a corpse [ME *cors*, fr OF, body]

**corselette, corselet** /ˌkawsə'let/ *n* a one-piece undergarment combining girdle and bra [fr *Corselette*, a trademark]

**¹corset** /'kawsit/ *n* a boned supporting undergarment for women, extending from beneath the bust to below the hips, and designed to give shape to the figure; *also* a similar garment worn by men and women, esp in cases of injury [ME, fr OF, dim. of *cors*]

**²corset** *vt* to restrict closely (as if) with a corset; control rigidly

**corsetiere** /ˌkawseti'eə, kawˌse-/ *n* a person who makes, fits, or sells corsets, girdles, or bras [F *corsetière*, fem of *corsetier*, fr *corset*]

**corsetry** /'kawsitri/ *n* (women's) undergarments that give support or shape

**corslet, corselet** /'kawslit/ *n* a piece of armour (eg of metal or leather) covering the trunk of the body but usu not the arms or legs [MF *corselet*, dim. of *cors* body, bodice]

**cortege** /kaw'tayzh, -'teəzh/ *also* **cortège** /kaw'tezh/ *n* **1** a train of attendants; a retinue **2** a procession; *esp* a funeral procession [Fr *cortège*, fr It *corteggio*, fr *corteggiare* to court, fr *corte* court, fr L *cohort-*, *cohors* throng – more at COURT]

**cortex** /'kawteks/ *n*, *pl* **cortices, cortexes 1** a plant bark or rind (eg of the cinchona tree) used medicinally **2** the outer part of an organ or body structure (eg the kidney, ADRENAL GLAND, or a hair); *esp* the outer layer of GREY MATTER of the brain **3a** the layer of plant tissue, typically containing cells responsible for manufacturing sugars, which lies between the central VASCULAR tissue (containing vessels for conducting water and sugars) and the outer protective tissue layer of stems and roots **b** an outer or covering layer of various algae, lichens, or fungi [L *cortic-*, *cortex* bark – more at CUIRASS]

**cortical** /'kawtikl/ *adj* **1** of or consisting of cortex **2** involving or resulting from the action or condition of the CEREBRAL CORTEX of the brain – **cortically** *adv*

**corticate** /'kawtikət, -kayt/ *adj* having a cortex

**cortico-** /kawtikoh-/ *comb form* **1** cortex ⟨cortico*id*⟩ **2** cortical and ⟨cortico*spinal*⟩

**corticoid** /'kawtikoyd/ *n* a corticosteroid

**corticosteroid** /ˌkawtikoh'stiəroyd/ *n* any of several STEROID hormones produced by the cortex of the ADRENAL GLAND that regulate the synthesis and breakdown of proteins and reduce inflammation of tissues; *also* any synthetic drug with similar actions to these [ISV]

**corticosterone** /ˌkawtikoh'stiərohn, ˌkawti'kostərohn/ *n* a STEROID hormone, $C_{21}H_{30}O_4$, produced by the cortex of the ADRENAL GLAND that regulates the synthesis and breakdown of proteins and carbohydrates

**corticotrophin** /ˌkawtikoh'trohfin/, **corticotropin** /-'trohpin/ *n* ADRENOCORTICOTROPHIC HORMONE, esp when used medically to raise the concentration of the corticosteroid HYDROCORTISONE in the blood, in the treatment of some conditions (eg rheumatoid arthritis) [*cortico-* + *trophic* + *-in*]

**cortin** /'kawtin/ *n* the active ingredient involved in the production of hormones in the cortex of the ADRENAL GLAND

**cortisol** /'kawtisol, -zol, -sohl, -zohl/ *n* HYDROCORTISONE [*cortisone* + *-ol*]

**cortisone** /'kawtisohn, -zohn/ *n* a STEROID hormone, $C_{21}H_{28}O_5$, that is produced by the cortex of the ADRENAL GLAND and is used esp in the treatment of RHEUMATOID ARTHRITIS [alter. of *corticosterone*]

**corundum** /kə'rundəm/ *n* a very hard mineral consisting of an oxide of aluminium, $Al_2O_3$, that is used as an abrasive, can be made artificially, and that occurs naturally in various coloured varieties of which some (eg ruby and sapphire) are used as gemstones △ Carborundum [Tamil *kuruntam*, fr Skt *kuruvinda* ruby]

**coruscant** /kə'ruskənt, 'korəskənt/ *adj* shining, glittering

**coruscate** /'korəskayt/ *vi* **1** to give off or reflect light in bright beams or flashes; sparkle **2** to be brilliant or showy in technique or style [L *coruscatus*, pp of *coruscare*]

**coruscation** /ˌkorə'skaysh(ə)n/ *n* **1** glitter, sparkle **2** a flash of wit

**corvée** /'kaw,vay, ˌ-'-/ *n* **1** unpaid labour which under the FEUDAL system (arrangement in medieval Europe of land tenure in return for services) was due to a lord from a tenant on land under his control **2** labour exacted in lieu of taxes by public authorities (eg in France before the Revolution), esp for road construction or repair [ME *corvee*, fr MF, fr ML *corrogata*, fr L, fem of *corrogatus*, pp of *corrogare* to collect, requisition, fr *com-* + *rogare* to ask – more at RIGHT]

**corvette** /kaw'vet/ *n* **1** a small sailing warship with a single tier of guns, ranked in the old navies below a frigate **2** a highly manoeuvrable armed escort ship that is smaller than a destroyer [Fr]

**corvine** /'kawvien/ *adj* of the crows; resembling a crow [L *corvinus*, fr *corvus* raven – more at RAVEN]

**Corybant** /'koribant/ *n*, *pl* **Corybants, Corybantes** /ˌkori'banteez/ any of the attendants or priests of the goddess Cybele in classical mythology, noted for orgiastic processions and rites [Fr *Corybante*, fr L *Corybant-*, *Corybas*, fr Gk *Korybant-*, *Korybas*] – **corybantic** *adj*

**corydalis** /kə'ridəlis/ *n* any of a large genus (*Corydalis*) of plants of the fumitory family with a flower head in the shape of a spike [NL, genus name, fr Gk *korydallis* crested lark; akin to L *cornu* horn – more at HORN]

**corymb** /'korim(b)/ *n*, *pl* **corymbs** a flat-topped flower cluster; *specif* one in which the flower stalks arise at different levels on the main axis and reach approximately the same height and in which the outer flowers open first [F *corymbe*, fr L *corymbus* cluster of fruit or flowers, fr Gk *korymbos*] – **corymbed** *adj*, **corymbose** *adj*, **corymbosely** *adv*

**corynebacterium** /ˌkorinibak'tiəriəm/ *n* any of a large genus (*Corynebacterium*) of irregular or branching rod-shaped bacteria that require oxygen to live, including many (eg that causing diphtheria) that are important parasites of man, lower animals, and plants [NL, genus name, fr Gk *korynē* club; akin to L *cornu* horn] – **corynebacterial** *adj*

**coryphaeus** /ˌkori'fee-əs/ *n*, *pl* **coryphaei 1** the leader of a chorus, typically in ancient Greek drama **2** the leader of a party or school of thought [L, leader, fr Gk *koryphaios*, fr *koryphē* summit; akin to L *cornu*]

**coryphée** /ˌkawri'fay/ *n* a leading dancer in the corps de ballet of a ballet company [Fr, fr L *coryphaeus*]

**coryza** /kə'riezə/ *n* a short-lasting infection involving inflammation of the membranes lining the nose, mouth, etc; *esp* HEAD COLD [LL, fr Gk *koryza* nasal mucus; akin to OHG *hroz* nasal mucus, Skt *kardama* mud] – **coryzal** *adj*

**¹cos** /kəz; *strong* koz/ *conj* because – used in writing to represent a casual or childish pronunciation [by shortening & alter.]

*usage* This pronunciation of **because** should be avoided in careful speech.

²**cos** /koz/ *n* COS LETTUCE

**Cosa Nostra** /ˌkohsə 'nostrə/ *n* MAFIA 2; *specif* the N American branch of the Mafia organization [It, lit., our thing]

**cosecant** /koh'seekənt, -'se-/ *n* the mathematical function that is the reciprocal of SINE [NL *cosecant-, cosecans,* fr *co-* + *secant-, secans* secant]

¹**coseismal** /ˌkoh'siezməl/, **coseismic** /-ik/ *adj* (of or being points) simultaneously affected by the same phase of any particular vibration occurring during an earthquake

²**coseismal, coseismal line** *n* a line on a map joining coseismal points

**coset** /'koh,set/ *n* a subset of a mathematical GROUP that consists of all the products obtained by multiplying, either on the right or on the left, a fixed element of the group by each of the elements of a given SUBGROUP

¹**cosh** /kosh/ *n, chiefly Br* a hand weapon consisting typically of a short heavy rod enclosed in a softer material (e g leather) [perh fr Romany *kosh* stick]

²**cosh** *vt, chiefly Br* to strike or assault (as if) with a cosh

**cosignatory** /ˌkoh'signət(ə)ri/ *n* a joint signer (e g of a document)

**cosine** /'koh,sien/ *n* a fundamental and important mathematical function that for an angle is the ratio of the side adjacent to the angle to the hypotenuse in a right-angled triangle and that can be expressed algebraically as

$$\cos x = 1 + \frac{x^2}{2!} - \frac{x^4}{4!} + \frac{x^6}{6!} - \dots$$

– compare SINE, TANGENT [NL *cosinus,* fr *co-* + ML *sinus* sine]

**cos lettuce, cos** /koz/ *n* a crisp long-leaved variety of lettuce [*Kos, Cos,* Greek island]

¹**cosmetic** /koz'metik/ *n* a cosmetic preparation for external use

²**cosmetic** *adj* 1 of or designed to impart or improve beauty (e g of the skin, complexion, or hair) 2 correcting defects of appearance, esp on the face ⟨~ *surgery*⟩ [Gk *kosmētikos* skilled in adornment, fr *kosmein* to arrange, adorn, fr *kosmos* order] – **cosmetically** *adv*

**cosmetician** /ˌkozmi'tish(ə)n/ *n* a person who is professionally trained in the use of cosmetics

**cosmetology** /ˌkosmi'toləji/ *n* the cosmetic treatment of the skin, hair, and nails [Fr *cosmétologie,* fr *cosmétique* cosmetic (fr E *cosmetic*) + *-logie* -logy] – **cosmetologist** *n*

**cosmic** /'kozmik/ *also* **cosmical** /-kl/ *adj* 1 of the cosmos, the vastness of space beyond the earth's atmosphere, or the universe in contrast to the earth alone 2 great, esp in extent, intensity, or comprehensiveness [Gk *kosmikos,* fr *kosmos* order, universe] – **cosmically** *adv*

**cosmic dust** *n* very fine particles of solid matter suspended in space

**cosmic noise** *n* radiation having the same frequency as radio waves and originating from the Milky Way – called also GALACTIC NOISE

**cosmic ray** *n* a stream of high energy radiation that reaches the earth's atmosphere from space and that travels at speeds approaching that of light

**cosmochemistry** /ˌkozmə'keməstri/ *n* a branch of chemistry that deals with the chemical composition of, and changes in, the universe [Gk *kosmos* universe] – **cosmochemical** *adj*

**cosmodrome** /'kozmə,drohm/ *n* a site for launching esp Soviet spacecraft [Russ *kosmodrom,* fr *kosmo*navt cosmonaut + *-drom* -drome]

**cosmogenic** /ˌkozmə'jenik/ *adj* produced by the action of cosmic rays ⟨~ *carbon 14*⟩ [*cosmic ray* + *-o-* + *-genic*]

**cosmogony** /koz'mogəni/ *n* 1 the creation or origin of the universe 2 a theory or mythical account of the origin and development of the universe [NL *cosmogonia,* fr Gk *kosmogonia,* fr *kosmos* + *gonos* offspring] – **cosmogonist** *n,* **cosmogonic, cosmogonical** *adj*

**cosmography** /koz'mogrəfi/ *n, philosophy* a general description of the substance and interrelations of the world or of the universe 2 the branch of science that deals with the structure, composition, and physical makeup of the whole order of the universe [ME *cosmographie,* fr LL *cosmographia,* fr Gk *kosmographia,* fr *kosmos* + *-graphia* -graphy] – **cosmographer** *n,* **cosmographic, cosmographical** *adj,* **cosmographically** *adv*

**cosmology** /koz'moləji/ *n* 1 a branch of philosophy that deals with the universe as an ordered system 2 a theory or mythical account of the nature of the universe 3 a branch of astronomy that deals with the origin, structure, and space-time relationships of the universe [NL *cosmologia,* fr Gk *kosmos* + NL *-logia* -logy] – **cosmologist** *n,* **cosmologic, cosmological** *adj,* **cosmologically** *adv*

**cosmonaut** /'kozmə,nawt/ *n* an astronaut; *specif* a Soviet astronaut [part trans of Russ *kosmonavt,* fr Gk *kosmos* + Russ *-navt* (as in *aeronavt* aeronaut)]

¹**cosmopolitan** /ˌkozmə'polit(ə)n/ *adj* 1 having worldwide rather than provincial scope or relevance 2 marked by a sophistication that comes from wide and often international experience 3 composed of people, constituents, or elements from many parts of the world 4 *of a plant, animal, etc* found in most parts of the world and under varied environmental conditions; ubiquitous ⟨*shepherd's purse is a* ~ *plant*⟩ – **cosmopolitanism** *n*

²**cosmopolitan** *n* a cosmopolite

**cosmopolite** /koz'mopəliet/ *n* a cosmopolitan person or organism [NL *cosmopolites,* fr Gk *kosmopolitēs,* fr *kosmos* + *politēs* citizen] – **cosmopolitism** *n*

**cosmos** /'kozmos/ *n* 1a an orderly harmonious universe – compare CHAOS b order, harmony 2 a complex and orderly system (e g of ideas) that is complete in itself 3 any of a genus (*Cosmos*) of tropical American plants of the daisy family; *esp* a widely cultivated tall autumn-flowering plant (*Cosmos bipinnatus*) with showy yellow or red flowers [Ger *kosmos,* fr Gk; (3) NL, genus name, fr Gk]

**cossack** /'kosak/ *n, often cap* a member of a people of SE Russia noted for their skill as horsemen and formerly used as light cavalry in the Russian army [Russ *kazak* & Ukrainian *kozak,* fr Turk *kazak* free person]

¹**cosset** /'kosit/ *n* a pet lamb; *broadly* a pet [perh deriv of OE *cotsǣta* cottager]

²**cosset** *vt* to treat as a pet; pamper

**cossie** /'kozi/ *n, Br informal* a swimming costume [by shortening & alter. fr *costume*]

¹**cost** /kost/ *n* 1a the price paid or charged for something b the outlay or expenditure (e g of effort or sacrifice) made to achieve an object 2 loss or penalty incurred in gaining something 3 *pl* expenses incurred in carrying on a lawsuit; *esp* those ordered by the court to be paid to the successful party – **costless** *adj* – **at all costs** regardless of the price or difficulties – **to one's cost** to one's disadvantage or loss

²**cost** *vi* 1 to require a specified expenditure ⟨*the best goods* ~ *more*⟩ 2 to require the specified effort, suffering, or loss ~ *vt* 1 to have a price of 2 to cause to pay, suffer, or lose ⟨*frequent absences* ~ *him his job*⟩ ⟨*your suggestion would* ~ *us too much time*⟩ 3 to estimate or set the cost of [ME *costen,* fr MF *coster,* fr L *constare* to stand firm, to cost – more at CONSTANT]

**costa** /'kostə/ *n, pl* **costae** /'kosti/ 1 a rib 2 a part (e g the midrib of a leaf or the front vein of an insect wing) that resembles a rib [L – more at COAST] – **costal** *adj,* **costate** *adj*

**cost accounting** *n* the systematic recording and analysis of the costs of material, labour, and overheads that are incurred during production – **cost accountant** *n*

¹**co-,star** *n* a star who has equal billing with another leading performer in a film or play

²**co-star** *vi* to appear as a co-star in a film or play ~ *vt* to feature (an actor) as a co-star

**costard** /'kustəd/ *n, archaic* the head or brains [ME, large ribbed apple, prob fr OF *coste* rib, fr L *costa*]

**cost-benefit analysis** *n, economics* the evaluation of a project or undertaking in terms of its social advantages and disadvantages rather than of its economic viability

**,cost-ef'fective** *adj* achieving a given end at lowest cost; economically worthwhile ⟨~ *measures to combat a slump in sales*⟩ – **cost-effectiveness** *n*

**costermonger** /'kostə,mung-gə/, **coster** /'kostə/ *n, Br* one who sells articles, esp fruit or vegetables, from a street barrow or stall [alter. of obs *costardmonger,* fr *costard* (large apple) + *monger*]

**costive** /'kostiv/ *adj* 1 affected with or causing constipation 2 slow in action or expression 3 stingy, mean [ME, fr MF *costivé,* pp of *costiver* to constipate, fr L *constipare*] – **costively** *adv,* **costiveness** *n*

**costly** /'kostli/ *adj* 1 valuable, expensive ⟨~ *gems*⟩ 2 made at great expense or with considerable sacrifice – **costliness** *n*

**costmary** /'kost,meəri/ *n* a plant (*Chrysanthemum majus*) of the daisy family, that resembles the tansy and is used as a herb and a flavouring in cooking [ME *costmarie,* fr *coste* costmary (fr OE *cost*, fr L *costum*, fr Gk *kostos*, a fragrant root) + *Marie* the Virgin Mary]

**cost of living** *n* the cost of purchasing those goods and services (e g food, clothing, and fuel) which are included in an acceptable standard of living

**,cost-of-'living-,index** *n* RETAIL PRICE INDEX

**,cost-'plus** *adj, economics* calculated on the basis of a fixed fee or a percentage added to actual cost ⟨∼ *pricing*⟩

**cost price** *n* the price paid by a middleman or retailer for an article of merchandise to be resold; *also* the cost to the manufacturer of producing such an article

**'cost-,push, cost-push inflation** *n* an increase or upward trend in prices, resulting from increases in the cost of raw materials, production, etc – compare DEMAND-PULL – **cost-push** *adj*

**¹costume** /'kostyoohm, 'kostyoom/ *n* **1** a distinctive fashion in coiffure, jewellery, and apparel of a period, country, class, or group **2** a set of garments suitable for a specified occasion, activity, or season **3** a set of garments belonging to a specific time, place, or character, worn in order to assume a particular role (e g in a play or at a fancy-dress party) [Fr, fr It, custom, dress, fr L *consuetudin-, consuetudo* custom – more at CUSTOM] – **costumey** *adj*

**²costume** *vt* **1** to provide with a costume **2** to design costumes for ⟨∼ *a play*⟩

**³costume** *adj* characterized by the use of costumes ⟨*a* ∼ *ball*⟩ ⟨*a* ∼ *drama*⟩

**costume jewellery** *n* inexpensive jewellery designed for wear with current fashions

**costumier** /ko'styoohmi·ə/, **costumer** /'kostyoohmə, -yoo-, ko'styoohmə/ *n* one who deals in or makes costumes (e g for theatrical productions) [Fr]

**¹cosy,** *NAm chiefly* **cozy** /'kohzi/ *adj* **1** enjoying or giving warmth and ease; snug **2a** marked by the intimacy of the family or a close group **b** suggesting close association or connivance ⟨*a* ∼ *agreement*⟩; *also* self-satisfied, complacent ⟨∼ *morality*⟩ **3** marked by a discreet and cautious attitude or procedure *synonyms* see COMFORTABLE *antonyms* cavernous, draughty [prob of Scand origin; akin to Norw *koselig* snug, cosy] – **cosily** *adv,* **cosiness** *n*

**²cosy,** *NAm chiefly* **cozy** *adv* cautiously

**³cosy,** *NAm chiefly* **cozy** *n* a covering, esp for a teapot or boiled egg, designed to reduce the rate of cooling

**¹cot** /kot/ *n* **1** *dial* a cover, sheath; *esp* a protective sheath for a finger or toe **2** *poetic* a small house; a cottage [ME, cottage, fr OE; akin to ON *kot* small hut, L *guttur* throat]

**²cot** *n* **1** a lightweight bedstead **2** a swinging bed; *broadly* a hammock **3** a small bed with high enclosing sides, esp for a child **4** *chiefly NAm* CAMP BED [Hindi *khāṭ* bedstead, fr Skt *khaṭvā,* of Dravidian origin; akin to Tamil *kaṭṭil* bedstead]

**cotangent** /koh'tanj(ə)nt, '-,--/ *n* the mathematical function that is the reciprocal of TANGENT [NL *cotangent-, cotangens,* fr *co-* + *tangent-, tangens* tangent]

**cot death** *n* the sudden death of a young baby, typically while sleeping, from no apparent disease

**¹cote** /koht/ *n* **1** a shed or coop for small domestic animals, esp pigeons **2** *dial Eng* a cottage, ¹COT **2** [ME, fr OE]

**coterie** /'kohtəri/ *n taking sing or pl vb* an intimate and often exclusive group of people with a unifying common interest or purpose [Fr, fr MF, tenants, fr (assumed) MF *cotier* cottar, fr ML *cotarius*]

**coterminous** /koh'tuhminəs/ *adj* **1** having the same boundaries ⟨∼ *states*⟩ **2** extending over the same space or time in scope or duration ⟨∼ *interests*⟩ [alter. of *conterminous,* fr L *conterminus,* fr *com-* + *terminus* boundary – more at TERM] – **coterminously** *adv*

**cothurnus** /koh'thuhnəs/ *n, pl* **cothurni** /-nie/ **1** a high thick-soled laced boot worn by actors in Greek and Roman tragic drama **2** the dignified but somewhat stilted style of ancient Greek and Roman tragedy [L, fr Gk *kothornos*]

**cotidal** /,koh'tiedl/ *adj, esp of lines on a tidal chart* indicating equality in the tides or a coincidence in the time of high tide or low tide at two or more locations

**cotillion** *also* **cotillon** /kə'tilyən/ *n* **1** an elaborate French dance with frequent changing of partners carried out under the leadership of one couple at formal balls **2** *NAm* a ballroom SQUARE DANCE of five or more figures **3** *NAm* a formal ball [Fr *cotillon,* lit., petticoat, fr OF, fr *cote* coat]

**cotoneaster** /kə,tohni'astə/ *n* any of a genus (*Cotoneaster*) of N European flowering shrubs of the rose family [NL, genus name, fr L *cydonia, cotoneum* quince + NL *-aster*]

**cotquean** /'kot,kween/ *n, archaic* **1** a coarse masculine woman **2** a man who busies himself with women's work or affairs [¹*cot* + *quean* (woman); orig sense, cottar's wife]

**co-trimoxazole** /,koh trie'moksə,zohl, tree-/ *n* an antibacterial mixture of two drugs, sulphamethoxazole and trimethoprim, that is used against a wide range of bacteria, esp in the treatment of infections of the respiratory and urinary tracts and of the venereal disease, gonorrhoea [*co-* + *tri*methoprim + sulphameth*oxazole*]

**Cotswold** /'kots,wohld, -wəld/ *n (any of)* a breed of large long-woolled English sheep [*Cotswold* Hills in SW England]

**cotta** /'kotə/ *n* a waist-length surplice worn by choristers [ML, of Gmc origin; akin to OHG *kozza* coarse mantle – more at COAT]

**cottage** /'kotij/ *n* **1** the dwelling of a farm labourer or small farmer **2** a small country or suburban house, usu built in a traditional style **3** a small house for use in holidays or at weekends **4** *slang* a public lavatory considered esp as a venue for homosexual activity – used chiefly by homosexuals [ME *cotage,* fr (assumed) AF, fr ME *cot*] – **cottager** *n*

**cottage cheese** *n* a soft white mild cheese made from the curds of skimmed milk

**cottage hospital** *n, Br* a small hospital without resident doctors that is served by the doctors in general practice in the area

**cottage industry** *n* an industry that is carried on at home often by family units using their own equipment

**cottage loaf** *n* a loaf of bread having a distinctive shape formed by placing a small round mass of dough on top of a larger round dough mass

**cottage pie** *n* a shepherd's pie esp made with minced beef

**cottagey** /'kotəji/ *adj* reminiscent of a cottage, esp in small size or old-world charm

**cottar, cotter** /'kotə/ *n, Scot* a person who occupies a cottage and sometimes a small holding of land usu in return for services [ME *cottar,* fr ML *cotarius,* fr ME *cot*]

**cotter** /'kotə/ *n* a wedge-shaped or tapered piece used to fasten parts of a structure together [origin unknown]

**cotter pin** *n* (a pin for securing) a cotter; *also* SPLIT PIN

**¹cotton** /'kot(ə)n/ *n* **1a** a soft usu white fibrous substance composed of the hairs surrounding the seeds of various erect freely branching tropical plants (genus *Gossypium*) of the hollyhock family **b** a plant producing cotton; *esp* one grown for its cotton **c** a crop of cotton **2a** fabric made of cotton **b** yarn spun from cotton [ME *coton,* fr MF, fr Ar *quṭn*]

**²cotton** *vi* to come to understand; CATCH ON – + *on* or *onto* [orig sense, (of cloth) to rise with a nap (hence, to prosper, harmonize, agree)]

**cotton gin** *n* a machine that separates the seeds, hulls, and foreign material from cotton

**cotton grass** *n* any of a genus (*Eriophorum*) of sedges with a flower structure that resembles a tuft of wispy white cotton wool

**cottonmouth** /'kot(ə)n,mowth/ *n* WATER MOCCASIN (venomous snake) [fr the white streak along its lips]

**'cotton-,picking** *adj, chiefly NAm informal* damned [prob fr cotton picking being a hard menial task]

**cottonseed** /'kot(ə)n,seed/ *n* the seed of the cotton plant from which a yellow oil used chiefly in salad and cooking oils is obtained

**cottonseed cake** /'kot(ə)n,seed/ *n* a compressed mass of cottonseed used for feeding cattle

**cottontail** /'kot(ə)n,tayl/ *n* any of several rather small N American rabbits (genus *Sylvilagus*) that are sandy brown in colour and have a white fluffy tail

**cottonwood** /-,wood/ *n* a poplar tree (*Populus deltoides*) of the USA that has a tuft of cottony hairs on the seed and is often cultivated for its rapid growth and luxuriant foliage

**cotton wool** *n* **1** raw cotton; *esp* cotton pressed into layers or sheets and used for surgical dressings, swabs, etc **2** an overprotected comfortable environment

**cottony** /'kot(ə)ni/ *adj* **1** covered with (soft long) hairs **2** soft, fluffy

**cotyl-** /kotil-/, **cotyli-, cotylo-** *comb form* (organ or part like a) cup ⟨*cotyloid*⟩ ⟨*cotyliform*⟩ [Gk *kotyl-, kotylo-,* fr *kotylē*]

**-cotyl** /-'kotil/ *comb form* (→ *n*) cotyledon ⟨*dicotyl*⟩ [*cotyledon*]

**cotyledon** /,koti'leed(ə)n/ *n* **1** a small lobe of the placenta of a mammal **2** the first leaf or either of the first pair or first group of leaves developed by the embryo or germinating seed of a

SEED PLANT [NL, fr Gk *kotylēdōn* cup-shaped hollow, fr *kotylē* cup] – **cotyledonal** *adj*, **cotyledonary, cotyledonous** *adj*

**cotylosaur** /'kotilə,saw/ *n* any of an order (Cotylosauria) of extinct ancient reptiles with short legs and massive bodies [NL *Cotylosauria*, group name, deriv of Gk *kotylē* cup + *sauros* lizard]

¹**couch** /kowch/ *vt* **1** to lay (oneself) down for rest or sleep **2** to embroider (a design) by attaching a thread or cord to a fabric using small regularly spaced stitches **3** to lower and hold level in an attacking position ⟨∼ed *his lance*⟩ **4** to phrase in a specified manner ⟨∼ed *in warlike terms*⟩ **5** to treat (a cataract) by displacing the lens of the eye **6** to place in hiding or ambush ⟨*the cat* ∼ed *itself in readiness to spring*⟩ ∼ *vi*, *of an animal* to lie down to sleep; *also* to lie in ambush [ME *couchen*, fr MF *coucher*, fr L *collocare* to set in place – more at COLLOCATE]

²**couch** *n* **1** a piece of furniture for sitting or lying on **1a** with a back and usu armrests **b** with a low back and raised head-end **2** a long upholstered seat with a headrest for patients to lie on during medical examination or psychoanalysis **3** the den of an animal (e g an otter) *synonyms* see SOFA

**couchant** /'kowchənt/ *adj*, *of a heraldic animal* lying down, esp with the head up ⟨*a lion* ∼⟩ [ME, fr MF, fr prp of *coucher*]

**couchette** /kooh'shet/ *n* a bunk, esp one that converts from a seat, for sleeping on in a railway carriage [Fr, dim. of *couche* couch]

**couch grass** /'kowch, 'koohch/ *n* a European grass (*Agropyron repens*) that spreads rapidly by long creeping underground stems and is a troublesome weed; *also* any of several grasses that spread in the same way and are difficult to eradicate [alter. of *quitch grass*]

**coudé** /'koohday, -'-/ *adj* **1** *of a* REFLECTING TELESCOPE constructed so that, regardless of the direction in which the telescope is pointing, the light is reflected along a line parallel to the earth's axis to come to a focus at a fixed place where the holder for a photographic plate or a SPECTROSCOPE (instrument for separating light into a spectrum) may be mounted **2** of a coudé telescope [Fr *coudé* bent like an elbow, fr *coude* elbow, fr L *cubitum* – more at HIP]

**cougar** /'koohgə/ *n*, *pl* **cougars**, *esp collectively* **cougar** *chiefly NAm* a puma [Fr *couguar*, fr NL *cuguacuarana*, modif of Tupi *suasuarana*, lit., false deer, fr *suasú* deer + *rana* false]

¹**cough** /kof/ *vi* **1** to expel air from the lungs suddenly with an explosive noise **2** to make a noise like that of coughing [ME *coughen*, fr (assumed) OE *cohhian*; akin to MHG *kūchen* to breathe heavily]

**cough up** *vt* **1** to expel by coughing ⟨cough up *mucus*⟩ **2** *informal* to produce or hand over (esp money or information) unwillingly ∼ *vi*, *informal* to cough up esp money or information

²**cough** *n* **1** a condition marked by repeated or frequent coughing **2** an act or sound of coughing

**cough drop** *n* **1** a medicated sweet for relieving coughing and soothing a sore throat **2** *Br slang* CAUTION 3

**cough mixture** *n* any of various medicated liquids used to relieve coughing

**cough syrup** *n* any of various sweet usu medicated liquids used to relieve coughing

**could** /kəd; *strong* kood/ *verbal auxiliary* **1** *past of* CAN – used in the past ⟨*he found he* ∼ *go*⟩, in the past conditional ⟨*he said he would go if he* ∼⟩, as an alternative to *can* suggesting less force or certainty ⟨*you* ∼ *be right*⟩ or as a polite form in the present ⟨∼ *you do this for me?*⟩ ⟨*I* ∼ *come tomorrow if you like*⟩, as an alternative to *might* expressing purpose in the past ⟨*left the key under the mat so that I* ∼ *get in*⟩, and as an alternative to *ought* or *should* ⟨*you* ∼ *at least apologize*⟩ **2** feel impelled to ⟨*I* ∼ *wring her neck*⟩ *usage* see ¹CAN [ME *couthe*, *coude*, fr OE *cūthe*; akin to OHG *konda* could]

**couldest** /'koodist/ *archaic past 2 sing of* CAN

**couldn't** /'koodnt/ could not

**couldst** /koodst/ *archaic past 2 sing of* CAN

**coulee** /'koohli/ *also* **coulée** /'koohlay/ *n* **1** a thick sheet or stream of lava **2** *NAm* a steep-sided ravine [Fr *coulée* flowing, flow of lava, fr *couler* to flow, fr L *colare* to strain, fr *colum* sieve; (2) CanF *coulée*, fr Fr]

**coulisse** /kooh'lees/ *n* **1** a hallway **2** a piece of timber having a groove in which something (e g a portcullis or stage flat) slides [Fr, fr OF *couleïce* portcullis]

**couloir** /'koohlwah/ *n* a mountainside gorge, esp in the Alps [Fr, lit., strainer, fr LL *colatorium*, fr L *colatus*, pp of *colare*]

¹**coulomb** /'kooh,lom, -lohm, -'-/ *n* the SI unit of electric charge equal to the quantity of electricity transferred by a current of 1 amp in 1 second [Charles de *Coulomb* †1806 Fr physicist]

²**coulomb, coulombic** /kooh'lombik, -'lohm-/ *adj* of or being the force of attraction or repulsion between positively or negatively charged particles

**coulometry, coulombetry** /kooh'lomətri/ *n* **1** chemical analysis of a substance performed by determining the amount of its constituents that are released when it is broken down by ELECTROLYSIS using a known amount of electricity **2** VOLTAMETRY [*coulomb* + *-metry*] – **coulometric** *adj*, **coulometrically** *adv*

**coulter** /'kohltə/ *n* a blade or sharp disc attached to a plough, that makes a vertical cut in the ground before the PLOUGH-SHARE (cutting blade) cuts it horizontally [ME *colter*, fr OE *culter* & OF *coltre*, both fr L *culter* ploughshare, knife]

**coumarin** /'koohmərin/ *n* a white chemical compound, $C_9H_6O_2$, with a smell of new-mown hay, that is found in plants or made synthetically and is used esp in perfumery [Fr *coumarine*, fr *coumarou* tonka bean tree, fr Sp or Pg; Sp *coumarú*, fr Pg, fr Tupi]

**coumarone** /'koohmə,rohn/ *n* a chemical compound, $C_8H_6O$, obtained from coal tar and used to make resins that are used in varnishes, printing inks, etc [ISV *coumar*in + *-one*]

¹**council** /'kownsl, -sil/ *n* **1** an assembly or meeting for consultation, advice, discussion, etc **2** *taking sing or pl vb* **2a** an elected or appointed body having administrative, legislative, or advisory powers **b** *often cap* a locally elected body having administrative and some legislative power (e g to make bylaws) over a parish, district, county, etc **3** a meeting or the deliberation of a council **4** *often cap*, *taking sing or pl vb* an organization that has specialized responsibilities or interests ⟨*National* Council *for Civil Liberties*⟩ ⟨*Sports* Council⟩; *specif* a federation of or a central body uniting a group of organizations **5** *often cap* the chief executive body controlling esp the finances of a British university – compare SENATE 3 [ME *counceil*, fr OF *concile*, fr L *concilium*, fr *com-* + *calare* to call – more at LOW]

²**council** *adj* **1** used by a council ⟨*a* ∼ *chamber*⟩ **2** *Br* provided, maintained, or operated by local government ⟨*a* ∼ *house*⟩ ⟨∼ *flats*⟩

**councillor**, *NAm also* **councilor** /'kowns(ə)lə, -silə/ *n* a member of a council △ counsellor – **councillorship** *n*

**councilman** /'kownslmən, -sil-/, *fem* **councilwoman** /-,woomən/ *n*, *NAm* a member of a council (e g of a town or city)

**council of ministers** *n taking sing or pl vb*, *often cap C&M* CABINET 2a (advisors of a head of state)

¹**counsel** /'kownsl/ *n*, *pl* **counsels**, (3) **counsel 1a** advice; *esp* that given as a result of consultation **b** an advised policy or plan of action or behaviour **2** deliberation, consultation **3a**(1) a barrister or group of barristers engaged in the trial of a case in court **a**(2) a lawyer or group of lawyers appointed to advise and represent in legal matters an individual client or a corporate body **b** an expert adviser; CONSULTANT 2 [ME *conseil*, fr OF, fr L *consilium*, fr *consulere* to consult] – **keep one's own counsel** to keep one's thoughts and intentions to oneself

²**counsel** *vt* **-ll-** (*NAm* **-l-, -ll-**) to advise ⟨∼led *them to avoid rash actions* – George Orwell⟩

**counselee** /,kownsl'ee/ *n* one who is being counselled

**counselling**, *NAm chiefly* **counseling** /'kownsl·ing/ *n* professional guidance (e g by a psychologist or social worker) of the individual in personal and social matters ⟨*student* ∼⟩

**counsellor**, *NAm chiefly* **counselor** /'kownslə/ *n* **1** a person who gives esp professional advice or guidance ⟨*marriage guidance* ∼⟩ **2** a senior diplomatic officer **3** one who has supervisory duties at a US summer camp for children **4** **counselor-at-law, counselor** *NAm* a lawyer; *specif* a barrister △ councillor

**counsel of perfection** *n* a piece of excellent but impracticable advice

¹**count** /kownt/ *vt* **1a** to indicate or name by units or groups so as to find the total number of units involved – often + *up* **b** to name the numbers in order up to and including ⟨∼ *10*⟩ **c** to include in a tallying and reckoning ⟨*about 100 copies if you* ∼ *the damaged ones*⟩ – often + *in* **2** to consider to be ⟨∼ *yourself lucky*⟩ ∼ *vi* **1a** to recite or indicate numbers in order by units or groups ⟨∼ *by fives*⟩ ⟨∼ *down to zero*⟩ **b** to name or present numbers in order of increasing size ⟨*start* ∼ing *now*⟩ – often + *to* or *up to* ⟨∼ *up to ten*⟩ **c** to count the units

in a group 2 to add, total – often + *to* or *up to* ⟨*it* ~s *up to a sizable amount*⟩ 3 to have value or significance ⟨*these are the men who really* ~⟩ synonyms see RELY ON [ME *counten,* fr MF *compter,* fr L *computare,* fr *com-* + *putare* to consider – more at PAVE]

**count against** *vt* to be detrimental or disadvantageous to (in a given situation) ⟨*your previous record would* count against *you in a court of law*⟩

**count for** *vt* to be worth (something); have a value of ⟨*your experience should* count for *a lot*⟩

**count in** *vt* to include or take into account in plans or calculations ⟨*you can* count *us* in *for a picnic*⟩

**count on/upon** *vt* 1 to look forward to as certain; anticipate ⟨counted on *winning*⟩ 2 to rely or depend on or upon ⟨*you can* count on *me for help*⟩

**count out** *vt* 1 to pick out or take away by counting ⟨count out *three blue ones and burn the rest*⟩ 2 to complete a count of 10 seconds over (a floored boxer) 3 to exclude from plans or calculations ⟨count *me* out! *I hate parties*⟩ ~ *vi* 1 to count aloud ⟨count out *to one hundred*⟩ 2 to select a leader or reject a member by means of a COUNTING-OUT RHYME

²**count** *n* 1a the action or process of counting b a total obtained by counting 2a each separate and distinct charge in a legal declaration or indictment ⟨*guilty on all* ~s⟩ b a specific point under consideration; an issue ⟨*disagreed on several* ~s⟩ 3 the total number of individual things in a given unit or sample ⟨*blood* ~⟩ 4 the calling out of the seconds from one to ten when a boxer has been knocked down, during which he must rise or be defeated 5 any of various measures of the fineness of a yarn – compare HIGH-COUNT, TEX, DENIER, PICK 6 *chiefly NAm* the score ⟨*tied the* ~ *with a minute to play*⟩ 7 *archaic* 7a a reckoning, account b estimation, regard – **take the count** *of a boxer* to be counted out

³**count** *n* a European nobleman corresponding in rank to a British earl [MF *comte,* fr LL *comit-, comes,* fr L, companion, one of the imperial court, fr *com-* + *ire* to go – more at ISSUE]

**countable** /'kowntəbl/ *adj* capable of being counted: e g a *of a noun* capable of being used in the plural b *of a mathematical set* capable of having each member uniquely associated with one member of the set of NATURAL NUMBERS (1, 2, 3, 4, etc)

**countdown** /-,down/ *n* a continuous counting backwards to zero in fixed units (e g seconds) in order to mark exactly the time remaining before an event, esp the launching of a space vehicle; *also* preparations carried on during a countdown – **count down** *vi*

¹**countenance** /'kownt(ə)nəns/ *n* 1 mental composure or calmness; self-control – chiefly in *keep/lose one's countenance, out of countenance* 2 (an expression on) a face, esp as an indication of mood, emotion, or character ⟨*a pleasant* ~⟩ 3 moral support; sanction [ME *contenance,* fr MF, fr ML *continentia,* fr L, restraint, fr *continent-, continens,* prp of *continēre* to hold together – more at CONTAIN]

²**countenance** *vt* to extend approval or support to; tolerate ⟨*he never* ~d *violence*⟩ – **countenancer** *n*

¹**counter** /'kowntə/ *n* 1 a small disc of metal, plastic, etc used in counting or in games 2 something of value in bargaining; an asset 3 a level surface (e g a table) over which transactions are conducted or food is served or on which goods are displayed or work is conducted [ME *countour,* fr MF *comptouer,* fr ML *computatorium* computing place, fr L *computatus,* pp of *computare*] – **over the counter** 1 without a prescription ⟨*cough mixture available* over the counter⟩ 2 through a broker's office rather than through a stock exchange ⟨*stock bought* over the counter⟩ – **under the counter** by surreptitious, esp illegal, means

²**counter** *n* a device for indicating a number or amount; *esp* any device that detects and counts IONIZING particles (e g ALPHA PARTICLES) – compare GEIGER COUNTER [ME, fr MF *conteor,* fr *compter* to count]

³**counter** *vt* 1 to act in opposition to; oppose 2 to nullify the effects of; offset ⟨*tried to* ~ *the trend towards bureaucratization*⟩ ~ *vi* to resist or retaliate against attacks or arguments [ME *countren,* fr MF *contre*]

⁴**counter** *adv* 1 in an opposite or wrong direction 2 in a contrary or opposing manner ⟨*values that run* ~ *to those of established society*⟩ [ME *contre,* fr MF, fr L *contra* against, opposite; akin to L *com-* with, together – more at CO-]

⁵**counter** *n* 1 the contrary, opposite 2 an overhanging stern of a vessel 3a the act of making an attack while warding one off (e g in boxing or fencing); *also* a blow thus given in boxing b

something (e g a force) that offsets or opposes; a check 4 a stiffener giving shape to a boot or shoe round the heel 5 an area within the face of a letter (e g the middle of the letter O) that is less than type-high and so does not print

⁶**counter** *adj* 1 going in an opposite direction; *also* resulting in an opposite effect 2 given to or showing opposition, hostility, or antipathy 3 situated or lying opposite ⟨*the* ~ *side*⟩

**counter-** *prefix* 1a contrary; in the opposite direction ⟨counter*march*⟩ ⟨counter*current*⟩ b opposing, retaliatory ⟨counter*plot*⟩ ⟨counter*offensive*⟩ 2 complementary, corresponding ⟨counter*weight*⟩ ⟨counter*part*⟩ 3 duplicate, substitute ⟨counter*foil*⟩ [ME *contre-,* fr MF, fr *contre*]

**counteract** /,kowntə'rakt/ *vt* to restrain or neutralize the usu ill effects of by an opposing action – **counteraction** *n,* **counteractive** *adj*

**counterattack** /-ə'tak/ *vb* to make an attack (against) in response to an enemy's or an opponent's attack – **counterattack** *n,* **counterattacker** *n*

**counterattraction** /-ə,traksh(ə)n/ *n* an attraction that competes with another attraction

¹**counterbalance** /-,baləns/ *n* 1 a weight that balances another 2 a force or influence that offsets or checks an opposing force

²**counterbalance** *vt* 1 to oppose or balance with an equal weight or force 2 to equip with counterbalances

**counterblast** /-,blahst/ *n* an energetic and often vociferous reaction or response, esp to a verbal attack

**counterblow** /'kowntə,bloh/ *n* a retaliatory blow

**counter canter** *n* a canter in which the horse is bent away from the direction of travel (e g when swerving in one direction but with the other foreleg leading) – **counter-canter** *vb*

**counterchange** /-,chaynj/ *vt* 1 to interchange (e g parts or places); transpose 2 to variegate, chequer ~ *vi* to change places or parts

**countercharge** /-,chahj/ *n* a charge brought against an accuser by the accused

¹**countercheck** /'kowntə,chek/ *n* a check or restraint operating esp against something that is itself a check

²**countercheck** *vt* 1 to restrain, check 2 to check a second time for verification or accuracy

¹**counterclaim** /'kowntə,klaym/ *n* an opposing claim; *esp* such a claim in law made by a defendant against a person or people who are claiming against him/her

²**counterclaim** *vb* to claim in a counterclaim

**counterclockwise** /-'klokwiez/ *adj or adv, chiefly NAm* anticlockwise

**counterconditioning** /'kowntəkən,dishəning/ *n* psychological conditioning to replace an undesirable response (e g fear) to a stimulus (e g an engagement in public speaking) by a favourable response

**countercoup** /'kowntə,kooh/ *n* a coup directed towards overthrowing a government which seized power by a coup

**counterculture** /-,kulchə/ *n* a culture with values and habits that run counter to established social norms – **countercultural** *adj*

**countercurrent** /-,kurənt/ *adj* (involving interaction between materials) flowing in opposite directions ⟨~ *dialysis*⟩ – **countercurrent** *n*

**counterespionage** /-'espi-ənahzh/ *n* espionage directed towards detecting and thwarting enemy espionage

**counterexample** /-ig,zahmpl/ *n* an example that disproves a theorem, proposition, etc

¹**counterfeit** /'kowntəfit, -feet/ *vb* to imitate or copy (something) closely, esp with intent to deceive or defraud – **counterfeiter** *n*

²**counterfeit** *adj* 1 made in imitation of something else with intent to deceive or defraud ⟨~ *money*⟩ 2 insincere, feigned ⟨~ *sympathy*⟩ [ME *countrefet,* fr MF *contrefait,* fr pp of *contrefaire* to imitate, fr *contre-* + *faire* to make, fr L *facere* – more at DO]

³**counterfeit** *n* 1 something counterfeit; a forgery 2 something likely to be mistaken for something of higher value

**counterfoil** /-,foyl/ *n* a detachable part of a cheque, ticket, etc usu kept as a record or receipt

**counterfort** /'kowntə,fawt/ *n* a buttress that is bonded to and gives support to a retaining wall [part trans of MF *contrefort,* fr *contre-* counter- + *fort* force, strength, fr *fort* strong]

**counterinsurgency** /,kowntərin'suhj(ə)nsi/ *n* organized military activity designed to suppress rebellion – **counterinsurgent** *n*

**counterintelligence** /-in'telij(ə)ns/ *n* organized activity designed to block an enemy's sources of information, to deceive the enemy, to prevent sabotage, and to gather political and military information

**counterirritant** /-'irit(ə)nt/ *n* **1** something applied to an area of the skin to produce inflammation and reddening of the skin surface with the object of reducing inflammation in underlying tissue **2** an irritation or discomfort that diverts attention from another – **counterirritant** *adj*

'**counter-jumper** *n*, *derog* a salesperson in a shop – no longer in vogue [¹*counter* 3]

¹**countermand** /,kowntə'mahnd, '--,-/ *vt* **1** to revoke (a command) by a contrary order **2** to recall or order back (eg troops) by a superseding contrary order ⟨~ *reinforcements*⟩ [ME *countermaunden*, fr MF *contremander*, fr *contre-* counter- + *mander* to command, fr L *mandare* – more at MANDATE]

²**countermand** *n* (the giving of) a contrary order revoking an earlier one

**countermarch** /-,mahch/ *n* **1** a marching back along the same route **2** a movement in marching by which the front and rear or the left and right files of a unit of troops exchange places but still keep the order of the original files – **countermarch** *vb*

**countermeasure** /-,mezhə/ *n* a measure taken to counter another action or state of affairs

¹**countermine** /-,mien/ *n* **1a** a tunnel dug in order to intercept an enemy's tunnel **b** a mine, esp a submarine mine, laid in order to explode an enemy's mines by its own explosion **2** a plan for defeating an attack; a counterplot

²**countermine** *vt* **1** to thwart by secret measures **2** to intercept or blow up with a countermine ~ *vi* to make or lay down countermines

**countermove** /-,moohv/ *n* a move designed to counter another move – **countermovement** *n*

**counteroffensive** /-ə'fensiv/ *n* a large-scale military offensive undertaken by a force previously on the defensive

**counterpane** /-,payn/ *n* a bedspread [alter. of ME *countrepointe*, modif of MF *coute pointe*, lit., embroidered quilt]

**counterpart** /-,paht/ *n* **1** either of two corresponding copies of a legal document (eg a lease); a duplicate **2a** a thing that fits another perfectly **b** either of two parts that complete or complement one another **3** one who or that which has the same or similar characteristics as another; an equivalent

**counterplot** /'kowntə,plot/ *n* a plot designed to thwart an enemy's or an opponent's plot – **counterplot** *vi*

¹**counterpoint** /-,poynt/ *n* **1a** one or more independent melodies added above or below a given melody **b** the combination of two or more simultaneous independent melodies or voice-parts into a single harmonic texture; polyphony **2a** a complementing or contrasting item **b** the use of contrast or interplay of elements in a work of art [MF *contrepoint*, fr ML *contrapunctus*, fr L *contra-* counter- + ML *punctus* musical note, melody, fr L, act of pricking, fr *punctus*, pp of *pungere* to prick – more at POINT]

²**counterpoint** *vt* **1** to compose or arrange in counterpoint **2** to set off or emphasize by contrast or juxtaposition; set in contrast

**counterpoise** /'kowntə,poyz/ *n* **1** a counterbalance **2** a state of balance; equilibrium [alter. (influenced by *poise*) of ME *countrepeis*, fr MF *contrepeis*, fr *contre-* + *peis* weight – more at POISE] – **counterpoise** *vt*

**counterproductive** /-prə'duktiv/ *adj* tending to hinder the attainment of a desired end

**counter punch** *n* a return punch in boxing; *broadly* a blow or attack made in response to another blow or attack – **counterpunch** *vt*

**Counter-Reformation** /,kowntərefə'maysh(ə)n/ *n* the reform movement in the Roman Catholic church following the Reformation

**counterrevolution** /-,revə'loohsh(ə)n/ *n* a revolution directed towards overthrowing a government or social system established by a previous revolution; *also* activity intended to effect this – **counterrevolutionary** *adj or n*, **counterrevolutionist** *n*

**counterscarp** /-,skahp/ *n* the outer wall or slope of the ditch of a fort [MF *contrescarpe*, fr *contre-* counter- + *escarpe* scarp]

**countershading** /'kowntə,shayding/ *n* a pattern of coloration on an animal, serving as a means of concealment, in which the upper surface normally exposed to light is darker in colour than those parts normally in shadow, giving the body a uniform appearance

**countershaft** /-,shahft/ *n* an intermediate shaft that is driven by a main shaft and transmits motion to a working part

¹**countersign** /-,sien/ *n* a (secret) sign given in reply to another; *specif* a password or secret signal that must be given by one wishing to pass a military guard

²**countersign** *vt* to add one's signature to (a document) as a witness of another's signature – **countersignature** *n*

¹**countersink** /'kowntə,singk/ *vt* **countersunk** **1** to enlarge, esp by bevelling, the end of a (a hole) so that the head of a bolt, nail, screw, etc will fit below or level with the surface **2** to set the head of (eg a screw) below or level with the surface

²**countersink** *n* **1** a funnel-shaped enlargement at the outer end of a drilled hole made (as if) by countersinking **2** a part of a drill for making a countersink

**counterspy** /'kowntə,spie/ *n* a spy engaged in counterespionage

**countertenor** /-,tenə/ *n* an adult male singing voice higher than tenor; *also* a man with this voice [ME *countretenour*, fr MF *contreteneur*, fr *contre-* + *teneur* tenor]

**counterterrorism** /,kowntə'terərə(ə)m, '--,----/ *n* retaliatory terrorism – **counterterrorist** *adj*

**countervail** /-'vayl/ *vt* to counterbalance, offset ~ *vi* to exert force against an opposing and often bad or harmful force or influence – often + *against* [ME *countrevailen*, fr MF *contrevaloir*, fr *contre-* + *valoir* to be worth, fr L *valēre* – more at WIELD]

**counterweight** /-,wayt/ *n* a counterbalance – **counterweight** *vt*

**countess** /'kowntis, -tes/ *n* **1** the wife or widow of an earl or count **2** a woman having in her own right the rank of an earl or count

**countinghouse** /'kownting,hows/ *n* a building, room, or office used for keeping account books and transacting business

**counting-out rhyme** *n* a meaningless rhyme (eg "eeny, meeny, miney, mo") used for selecting a leader or rejecting a member in a children's game

**countless** /-lis/ *adj* too numerous to be counted; innumerable – **countlessly** *adv*

**count noun** *n* a noun (eg *bean* or *sheet*) that forms a plural and can be used with a number or the indefinite article – compare MASS NOUN

**count palatine** *n* **1a** a high judicial official in the HOLY ROMAN EMPIRE **b** a count of the Holy Roman Empire having imperial powers in his own domain **2** an earl or other lord of a COUNTY PALATINE in England or Ireland – called also EARL PALATINE

**countrified** *also* **countryfied** /'kuntrified/ *adj* **1** rural, rustic **2** unsophisticated [*country* + *-fied* (as in *glorified*)]

¹**country** /'kuntri/ *n* **1** an indefinite usu extended expanse of land; a region ⟨*the hill* ~ *is wild and inhospitable*⟩ **2a** the land of a person's birth, residence, or citizenship ⟨*fight for king and* ~⟩ **b** a political state or nation or its territory **3** *taking sing or pl vb* **3a** the people of a state or district; *the* populace **b** the electorate **4** rural as opposed to urban areas ⟨*let's get out into the* ~⟩ **5** COUNTRY AND WESTERN music [ME *contree*, fr OF *contrée*, fr ML *contrata*, lit., that which lies opposite, fr L *contra* against, on the opposite side] – **countryish** *adj* – **go to the country** *Br* to call a general election

²**country** *adj* of COUNTRY AND WESTERN music ⟨~ *singers*⟩

**country and western** *n* popular music in the style of the southern and western USA consisting of simple, esp sentimental or cowboy, folk songs sung esp to guitar

,**country-'bred** *adj* **1** brought up in the country rather than in a city or town **2** bred in the country rather than imported; indigenous

**country club** *n* a usu snobbishly select sporting or social club set in a rural area

**country cousin** *n* a person who is unused to or bewildered by the bustle and sophistication of city life

,**country-'dance** *n* any of various esp English folk dances for several pairs of dancers typically arranged in square or circular figures or in two long rows facing a partner – **country dancing** *n*

**country gentleman** *n* a member of the English landed gentry

**country house** *n* a house, mansion, or estate in the country

**countryman** /-mən/, *fem* **countrywoman** *n* **1** an inhabitant, esp from birth, of a specified country **2** a compatriot **3** a person who lives in the country or has country ways

**country music** *n* COUNTRY AND WESTERN

**country seat** *n* a mansion or estate in the country that is the hereditary property of one family

**countryside** /-,sied/ *n* a rural area

**country-'wide** *adj* nationwide

**'count-,up** *n* the act or an instance of counting

¹**county** /'kownti/ *n* **1a** any of the territorial divisions of Great Britain and Ireland constituting the chief units for administrative, judicial, and local government purposes **b** *taking sing or pl vb* the people of a county; *also, Br* the gentry of a county **2** the largest territorial division for local government in various countries (e g in the USA) **3** *archaic* the territory under the jurisdiction of a count or countess [ME *counte,* fr OF *conté* territory of a count, fr ML *comitatus,* fr LL, office of a count, fr *comit-, comes* count – more at ³COUNT]

²**county** *adj* **1** of a county ⟨~ *council*⟩ **2** *Br* characteristic of or belonging to the English landed gentry ⟨*a* ~ *accent*⟩

**county borough** *n* a town which until 1974 had the local government powers of a county

**county college** *n* a British college for the part-time education of students over the age of 16

**county court** *n, often cap 1st C* a local civil court in England which is presided over by a judge and deals with relatively minor claims

**county hall** *n* the chief administrative building of a county

**county palatine** *n, pl* **counties palatine** **1** the territory of a count palatine **2** a county in England or Ireland over which an earl or other lord formerly had many royal powers

**county school** *n* a school provided and entirely maintained by a local education authority

**county seat** *n, NAm* COUNTY TOWN

**county town** *n, chiefly Br* a town where the government of a county is based

¹**coup** /kohp/ *vb, chiefly Scot* to overturn, upset [ME *coupen* to strike, fr MF *couper* – more at COPE]

²**coup** /kooh/ *n, pl* **coups** /koohz/ **1** a brilliant, sudden, and usu highly successful stroke or act **2** COUP D'ÉTAT [Fr, blow, stroke – more at COPE]

**coup de grâce** /,kooh də 'grahs, 'gras *(Fr* ku də gras)/ *n, pl* **coups de grâce** /~ ~ ~/ **1** a fatal blow or shot administered to end the suffering of a mortally wounded person or animal **2** a decisive finishing blow, act, or event [Fr, lit., stroke of mercy]

**coup de main** /də 'manh *(Fr* də mẽ)/ *n, pl* **coups de main** /~ ~/ a very sudden forceful, esp military, attack [Fr, lit., stroke of the hand]

**coup d'état** /day'tah *(Fr* deta)/ *n, pl* **coups d'état** /~ ~/ a sudden violent overthrow or change of an existing government by a small group *synonyms* see REBELLION [Fr, lit., stroke of state]

**coup de théâtre** /,kooh də tay'ahtrə *(Fr* ku də teatr)/ *n, pl* **coups de théâtre** /~ ~ ~/ a sudden sensational turn of events, esp in a play; *also* a spectacular theatrical production or piece of staging [Fr, lit., stroke of theatre]

**coup d'oeil** /duh·i *(Fr* dœːj)/ *n, pl* **coups d'oeil** /~ ~/ a brief survey; a glance [Fr, lit., stroke of the eye]

**coupe** /koohp/ *n* a small goblet-shaped usu glass dish; *also* a cold dessert of fruit and ice cream served in such a dish [Fr, cup, fr LL *cuppa* – more at CUP]

**coupé** /'koohpay; *sense 2 also* koohp/, **coupe** /koohp/ *n* **1** a 4-wheeled closed horse-drawn carriage for two passengers with an outside seat for the driver in front **2** a 2-door motor car with a sloping back and a fixed roof [Fr *coupé,* fr pp of *couper* to cut]

¹**couple** /'kupl/ *vt* **1a** to fasten or link together (e g two hounds or railway carriages) **b** to fasten, link – + *to* or *with* ⟨*he* ~d *the dog to the cart*⟩ **2** to connect or associate in thought or speech, esp for joint consideration ⟨~d *his praise with a request*⟩ **3** to bring (two electrical circuits) into such close proximity as to permit mutual influence **4** to join in marriage or sexual union ~ *vi* **1** to copulate **2** to join **3** to combine together to form a chemical compound

²**couple** *n, pl* **couples, couple 1a** *taking sing or pl vb* two people paired together; *esp* two people who are married or engaged to each other or who live together **b** two things considered together; a pair **2** a pair of hounds in a hunting pack that are joined together by a leash attached to their collars; *also, pl* the pair of collars and the leash that are used for this **3** an indefinite small number; a few ⟨*a* ~ *of days ago*⟩ **4a** two equal and opposite forces that act along parallel lines and cause rotation **b** GALVANIC COUPLE **5** either of a pair of inclined

rafters that meet at the top and are joined at the bottom by a tie and form the principal support of a roof [ME, pair, bond, fr OF *cople,* fr L *copula* bond, fr *co-* + *apere* to fasten – more at APT]

³**couple** *adj* two – + *a* ⟨*a* ~ *more drinks*⟩

**couplement** /'kuplmənt/ *n, archaic* the act or result of coupling [MF, fr *coupler* to join, fr L *copulare,* fr *copula*]

**coupler** /'kuplə/ *n* **1** something that couples: e g **1a** a link, rotating rod, etc that transmits movement from one part to another of a mechanism **b** a device that connects two or more electrical circuits **2** a device on a keyboard instrument, esp an organ, by which keyboards, pedals, or notes on a keyboard are connected to play together

**couplet** /'kuplit/ *n* two successive lines of verse forming a unit, esp when rhyming and of the same length and metre [MF, dim. of *cople*]

**coupling** /'kupling/ *n* **1** the act of bringing or coming together; *specif* an act of copulation **2** an esp mechanical device that connects two things; *specif* a device for connecting two railway carriages or trucks together **3** the part of the body that joins the hindquarters to the forequarters of a 4-legged animal (e g a horse) **4** the means by which two electrical circuits are linked so that power passes between them, usu achieved by having a part (e g a transformer) common to both circuits

**coupon** /'koohpon/ *n* **1** a part of a bond, stating how much and when interest is due, that is detached and presented for the payment of this interest **2** a form handed over in order to obtain an article, service, or accommodation: e g **2a** a detachable part of a ticket or advertisement that entitles the holder to something (e g a free gift, discount, etc) **b** a voucher given with a purchase that can be exchanged for goods **c** any of a series of slips of paper that entitle the holder to a share in rationed food, clothing, etc **3** a part of a printed advertisement to be cut off for use as an order form or enquiry form **4** *Br* a printed entry form for a competition, esp the football pools [Fr, fr OF, piece, fr *couper* to cut – more at COPE]

**courage** /'kurij/ *n* mental or moral strength to confront and withstand danger, fear, or difficulty; bravery [ME *corage,* fr OF, fr *cuer* heart, fr L *cor* – more at HEART]

**courageous** /kə'rayjəs/ *adj* having or characterized by courage; brave *synonyms* see ¹BRAVE – **courageously** *adv,* **courageousness** *n*

**courante** /kooh'rahn(h)t *(Fr* kurãt)/ *n* **1** a dance of Italian origin consisting of quick running steps **2** a musical composition or movement (e g in a Baroque suite) in quick time with three or a mixture of three and six beats to the bar [MF, fr *courir* to run, fr L *currere*]

**courgette** /kaw'zhet, kooə-/ *n* a variety of small vegetable marrow cooked and eaten as a vegetable; *also* the plant that bears courgettes [Fr dial., dim. of *courge* gourd, fr L *cucurbita*]

**courier** /'koori·ə/ *n* **1** a messenger: e g **1a** a member of a diplomatic service who carries state or embassy papers **b(1)** an espionage agent transferring secret information **b(2)** the person who carries the goods in a smuggling operation **c** a member of the armed services whose duties include carrying mail, information, or supplies **2** a person employed by a travel agency to act as a tourist guide [MF *courrier,* fr OIt *corriere,* fr *correre* to run, fr L *currere*]

¹**course** /kaws/ *n* **1a** a movement or progression in space or time from point to point or through a series or period ⟨*the* ~ *of events*⟩ **b** a route or direction taken ⟨*the* ~ *of my career*⟩ **2** the path over which something moves: e g **2a** a racecourse **b(1)** the direction of travel, esp of an aircraft, usu measured as a clockwise angle from north **b(2)** a point of the compass ⟨*set her two* ~s *off to sea again* – Shak⟩ **c** a watercourse **d** GOLF COURSE **3a** usual procedure or normal action ⟨*the law must take its* ~⟩ ⟨*in the* ~ *of nature*⟩ **b** a chosen manner of conducting oneself; a plan of action ⟨*our wisest* ~ *is to retreat*⟩ **c** a duration ⟨*in the* ~ *of the year*⟩ **4** an ordered process or succession: e g **4a** a series of educational activities (e g lectures) relating to a subject, esp when constituting a curriculum ⟨*a management* ~⟩ **b** a particular medical treatment administered over a designated period **5a** a part of a meal served at one time **b** a row, layer; *esp* a continuous horizontal layer of brick or masonry throughout a wall **c** the lowest sail on the masts of a SQUARE-RIGGED vessel [ME, fr OF, fr L *cursus,* fr *cursus,* pp of *currere* to run – more at CAR] – **in due course** after a normal passage of time; in the expected or allotted time – **of course 1** as might be expected; naturally **2** admittedly; TO BE SURE

*usage* The disdainful use of **of course**, suggesting that a piece of out-of-the-way knowledge is commonplace ⟨*his last win*, **of course**, *was in 1977*⟩, and its dishonest use, to avoid defending an assumption ⟨*the committee are*, **of course**, *totally corrupt*⟩ are widely disliked. In general, **of course** should probably be used sparingly.

²**course** *vt* **1a** to hunt or pursue (eg hares) with dogs that follow by sight rather than scent **b** to use (dogs) to run after game (eg hares) **2** to follow close upon; pursue **3** to run or move swiftly through or over; traverse ⟨*jets coursed the area daily*⟩ ~ *vi, of a liquid* to flow rapidly (as if) along an indicated path ⟨*blood coursing through his veins*⟩

³**course** *adv, informal* OF COURSE

¹**courser** /'kawsə/ *n, poetic* a swift powerful horse; a charger [ME, fr OF *coursier*, fr *course* course, run]

²**courser** *n* any of various birds (subfamily Cursoriinae of the family Glareolidae) of Africa and S Asia, that are related to the plovers and are noted for their speed in running [²*course* + ²*-er*]

**course unit** *n* a recognized amount of academic work entitling a student to credit

**coursing** /'kawsing/ *n* the act or sport of hunting game, esp hares, with dogs that follow by sight instead of by scent

¹**court** /kawt/ *n* **1a** the residence or establishment of a dignitary, esp a sovereign **b** *taking sing or pl vb* the sovereign and his/her officers and councillors who make up the governing power **c** *taking sing or pl vb* the family and retinue or total body of courtiers of a sovereign **d** a state reception or formal assembly held by a sovereign **2a** a manor house or large building (eg a block of flats) surrounded by usu enclosed grounds – archaic except in proper names ⟨*Hampton Court*⟩ ⟨*Withdean Court*⟩ **b(1)** a space enclosed wholly or partly by buildings or circumscribed by a single building **b(2)** a college quadrangle at Cambridge University **b(3)** a yard surrounded by houses, with only one opening onto a street **c** (a division of) a rectangular space walled or marked off for playing lawn tennis, squash, basketball, etc **3** *law* **3a** (a session of) an official assembly of people authorized to adjudicate in civil, criminal, military, or ecclesiastical matters ⟨~ *is now adjourned*⟩ **b** a place in which a court of law is held **c** *taking sing or pl vb* judicial officers in session **4** *taking sing or pl vb* (the body of members of) an assembly or board with legislative or administrative powers **5** conduct or attention intended to win favour; homage ⟨*pay ~ to the king*⟩ [ME, fr OF, fr L *cohort-, cohors* enclosure, throng, cohort, fr *co- + -hort-, -hors* (akin to *hortus* garden) – more at YARD]

²**court** *vt* **1a** to seek to gain or achieve (honour, recognition, etc) **b** to act so as to invite or provoke ⟨~ s *disaster*⟩ **2a** to seek the affections of; woo **b** *of an animal* to perform actions in order to attract (a mate) **3** to seek to win the favour of ~ *vi* **1** *of two human beings* to be involved in a relationship that may lead to marriage **2** *of an animal* to engage in activity leading to mating

**court bouillon** /,kaw booh'yonh/ *n* a stock made with vegetables, herbs, and wine, in which fish is or has been cooked [Fr *court-bouillon*, fr *court* short + *bouillon*]

**court card** *n* a king, queen, or jack in a pack of cards – called also FACE CARD, PICTURE CARD [alter. of earlier *coat card*; fr the coats worn by the figures depicted]

**court cupboard** *n* a 16th- or 17th-century sideboard or cabinet with an open base and a closed top section with one or more doors

**court dance** *n* a grave and stately dance suitable for court functions

**Courtelle** /kaw'tel/ *trademark* – used for an acrylic fibre *synonyms* see NYLON

**courteous** /'kuhtyəs, -ti-əs, *also* 'kaw-/ *adj* **1** showing respect and consideration for others; polite in manner **2** *archaic* having the polished manners, gallantry, or ceremony of a court [ME *corteis*, fr OF, fr *court*] – **courteously** *adv*, **courteousness** *n*

**courtesan** /,kawti'zan, '--,-/ *n* a female prostitute; *esp* one with a courtly, wealthy, or upper-class clientele [MF *courtisane*, fr OIt *cortigiana* woman courtier, fem of *cortigiano* courtier, fr *corte* court, fr L *cohort-, cohors*]

¹**courtesy** /'kuhtəsi/ *n* **1a** courteous behaviour **b** a courteous act or expression **2** general allowance despite facts; favour as opposed to right – usu + *by* ⟨*hills called mountains by* ~ *only*⟩ [ME *corteisie*, fr OF, fr *corteis*] – **by courtesy of** through the kindness, generosity, or permission of (a person or organization) ⟨*flowers* by courtesy of *the local hospital*⟩

²**courtesy** *adj* granted, provided, or performed by way of courtesy ⟨*made a* ~ *call on the ambassador*⟩

**courtesy title** *n* a title (eg "Lord" preceding the Christian name of a peer's younger son) commonly accepted though without legal validity

**court game** *n* an athletic game (eg tennis, squash, or basketball) played on a court

**court hand** *n* a style of handwriting formerly used in legal documents

**courthouse** /'kawt,hows/ *n, chiefly NAm* **1** a building in which courts of law are regularly held **2** COUNTY TOWN

**courtier** /'kawtyə/ *n* one in attendance at a royal court

¹**courtly** /'kawtli/ *adj* **1** of a quality befitting a royal court; elegant **2** insincerely flattering; obsequious – **courtliness** *n*

²**courtly** *adv* in a courtly manner; politely

**courtly love** *n* a late medieval conventionalized code prescribing the conduct and emotions expected of ladies and their lovers

¹**court-'martial** *n, pl* **courts-martial** *also* **court-martials** (a trial by) a court that consists of commissioned officers and tries offences against military discipline by members of the armed forces and any civilians who may fall within its jurisdiction

²**court-martial** *vt* **-ll-** (*NAm* **-l-, -ll-**) to try by court-martial

**court of appeal** *n* a court hearing appeals from the decisions of lower courts; *specif, cap C&A* the higher branch of the SUPREME COURT in England and Wales, hearing both civil and criminal appeals – compare HIGH COURT

**court of cassation** *n, often cap both Cs* the highest court of appeal in various countries that deals only with points of law [*cassation* (abrogation), fr ME *cassacioun*, fr MF *cassation*, fr *casser* to annul]

**court of common pleas** *n* a former English superior court having civil jurisdiction

**court of inquiry** *n* **1** a military tribunal that inquires into and reports on some military matter (eg an officer's conduct), often as a preliminary to instituting legal or disciplinary proceedings **2** a board of people appointed to investigate a particular event; *esp* such a board appointed to ascertain the causes of an accident, disaster, etc

**court of law** *n* COURT 3

**court of record** *n* a court whose acts and proceedings are placed on an official permanent record that can be used as evidence, and which has power to fine or imprison for contempt of its authority

**Court of Session** *n* the supreme civil court in Scotland

**Court of St James's** *n* the court of the British sovereign [*St James's* Palace, London, former seat of the British Court]

**court order** *n* an order issuing from a court of law that requires a person to do or abstain from doing a specified act

**court plaster** *n* an adhesive plaster, esp of silk coated with ISINGLASS (type of gelatin) and glycerine [fr its former use for beauty spots by ladies at royal courts]

**court reporter** *n* a shorthand writer who records and transcribes a verbatim report of all proceedings in a court of law

**court roll** *n* a register of land holdings of a manor

**courtroom** /'kawt,roohm, -room/ *n* a room in which the sessions of a court of law are held

**courtship** /-,ship/ *n* the act, process, or period of courting

**court shoe** *n* a plain high-heeled woman's shoe with no fastenings [fr its use as part of dress at court]

**courtside** /'kawt,sied/ *n* the area outside the edge of the marked playing area of a court (eg for tennis or basketball)

**court tennis** *n, NAm* REAL TENNIS

**courtyard** /-,yahd/ *n* an open court or enclosure adjacent to a building

**couscous** /'koohs,koohs/ *n* a dish, originating in N Africa, consisting of crushed or coarsely ground wheat steamed over broth and served with meat, vegetables, and spices [Fr, fr Ar *kuskus*, fr *kaskasa* to pound, pulverize]

**cousin** /'kuzn/ *n* **1a** **cousin, first cousin** a child of one's uncle or aunt **b** a relative descended from one's grandparent or more remote ancestor in a different line **c** a kinsman, relative ⟨*a distant* ~⟩ ⟨*our American* ~ s⟩ **2** – formerly used as a title by a sovereign in addressing a nobleman [ME *cosin*, fr OF, fr L *consobrinus*, fr *com- + sobrinus* cousin on the mother's side, fr *soror* sister – more at SISTER] – **cousinhood** *n*, **cousinship** *n*

**cousinage** /'kuzn·ij/ *n* **1** the relationship of being cousins; kinship **2** *archaic* a collection of cousins; kinsfolk

**‚cousin-'german** *n, pl* **cousins-german** COUSIN 1a [ME *cosin germain*, fr MF, fr OF, fr *cosin* + *germain* german]

**couth** /koohth/ *adj* sophisticated, polished ⟨~ *and kempt in creaseless suits – Punch*⟩ [back-formation fr *uncouth*]

**couthie, couthy** /'koohthi/ *adj, chiefly Scot* 1 pleasant, kindly 2 cosy, snug [ME *couth* pleasant, familiar, fr OE *cūth* familiar]

**couture** /‚kooh'tyooə/ *n* HAUTE COUTURE (fashion design) [Fr, dressmaking, fr OF *cousture* sewing, fr (assumed) VL *consutura*, fr L *consutus*, pp of *consuere* to sew together, fr com- + *suere* to sew – more at SEW]

**couturier** /kooh'tyooəri·ə, -ri·ay/, *fem* **couturière** /kooh‚tyooəri'eə/ *n* (the proprietor of or designer for) an establishment engaged in couture [Fr, dressmaker, fr OF *cousturier* tailor's assistant, fr *cousture*]

**couvade** /kooh'vahd/ *n* a custom among some peoples by which a father retires to bed at the birth of his child as if bearing it himself [Fr, fr MF, cowardly inactivity, fr *cover* to sit on, brood over – more at COVEY]

**couverture** /'koohvəchə, ‚koohveə'tooə/ *n* chocolate used in cooking for coating, icing, or decorating confectionery [Fr, covering, fr *couvert*, pp of *couvrir* to cover, fr OF *covrir*]

**covalency** /koh'vaylənsi/, *chiefly NAm* **covalence** /koh'vayləns/ *n* a property of atoms whereby (pairs of) electrons are shared between combining atoms; *also* the number of such pairs of electrons an atom can share when forming COVALENT BONDS – compare ELECTROVALENCY – **covalent** *adj*, **covalently** *adv*

**covalent bond** /koh'vaylənt/ *n* a chemical bond formed by shared (pairs of) electrons between combining atoms

**covariance** /‚koh'veəri·əns/ *n, statistics* 1 the expected value (MEAN) of the product of the differences of two RANDOM VARIABLES from their respective means 2 the ARITHMETIC MEAN (average value) of the products of the differences of corresponding values of two RANDOM VARIABLES from their respective means

**covariant** /‚koh'veəri·ənt/ *adj* of or exhibiting covariance ⟨~ *distribution*⟩ [ISV]

**¹cove** /kohv/ *n* 1 *building* a concave MOULDING (shaped strip), esp at the point where a wall meets a ceiling or floor 2 a small sheltered inlet or bay, esp between rocky headlands 3a a (deep) recess or small valley in the side of a mountain or between cliffs **b** a level area sheltered by hills or mountains [ME, den, fr OE *cofa*; akin to OE *cot*]

**²cove** *vt, building* to make in a hollow concave form

**³cove** *n, Br informal* a man, fellow – no longer in vogue [prob fr Romany *kova* thing, person]

**covellite** /koh'veliet, 'kohvəliet/, **covelline** /koh'veleen, 'kohvə‚leen/ *n* a purple or indigo mineral consisting of copper sulphide, CuS, and occurring as thin flexible plates [Fr *covelline*, fr Niccolò *Covelli* †1829 It chemist]

**coven** /'kuvn, 'kovn/ *n taking sing or pl vb* an assembly or band of witches, esp of 13 witches [ME *covin* band, fr MF, fr ML *convenium* agreement, fr L *convenire* to agree – more at CONVENTION]

**¹covenant** /'kuv(ə)nənt, 'kov-/ *n* 1 a usu formal, solemn, and binding agreement; a contract 2 *law* 2a a written agreement or promise usu under seal between two or more parties, esp for the performance of some action **b** a particular clause or condition in a legal agreement, esp in a lease [ME, fr OF, fr prp of *covenir* to agree, fr L *convenire*] – **covenantal** *adj*

**²covenant** *vb* to promise by or enter into a covenant

**covenantee** /‚kuv(ə)nən'tee, ‚ko-/ *n* the party to whom a promise in the form of a covenant is made

**covenanter** /'kuv(ə)nəntə, 'ko-/ *n* 1 **covenanter, covenantor** a person who makes a covenant and is bound to perform the obligation expressed in it 2 *cap* a signer or adherent of the Scottish National Covenant of 1638

**Covenanting** /'kuv(ə)nənting, 'ko-/ *adj* of the adherents of the Scottish National Covenant ⟨~ *ancestry*⟩

**Coventry** /'kov(ə)ntri; *also* 'ku-/ *n* – **send somebody to Coventry** to exclude somebody from society; ostracize somebody [*Coventry*, city in England; perh fr the sending of Royalist prisoners to gaol in Coventry during the Civil War]

**¹cover** /'kuvə/ *vt* **1a** to guard from attack **b(1)** to protect by being in a position to fire at an attacker of the protected ⟨*you run for the trees while I* ~ *you*⟩ **b(2)** to hold within range of an aimed firearm **c(1)** to insure **c(2)** to provide protection against or compensation for (loss, risk, etc) **d(1)** to mark (eg a member of an opposing team or an opponent's piece in chess) in order to obstruct a play **d(2)** to protect (eg a team mate or a piece on a chess board) from attack by an opponent **e(1)** to make sufficient provision for (a demand or charge) by means of a reserve or deposit ⟨*his balance was insufficient to* ~ *his cheque*⟩ **e(2)** to maintain a check on, esp by patrolling ⟨*police* ~ing *the London area*⟩ **2a** to hide from sight or knowledge; conceal ⟨~ *up a scandal*⟩ **b** to lie or spread over; envelop ⟨*snow* ~ed *the ground*⟩ **3** to lay or spread something over **4** to extend thickly or conspicuously over the surface of ⟨~ed *in spots*⟩ **5** to place or set a cover or covering over **6a** *of a male animal* to copulate with (a female animal) **b** *of a bird* to sit on and incubate (eggs) **7** to invest with or bring upon (oneself) a large or excessive amount of something ⟨~s *himself with glory*⟩ **8** to play a higher-ranking card on (a previously played card) **9a** to include, consider, or take into account ⟨*this book* ~s *the whole Renaissance*⟩ **b** to deal with; treat ⟨*that book* ~s *complex numbers*⟩ **10a** to have as one's territory or field of activity ⟨*one salesman* ~s *the whole county*⟩ **b** to report news about ⟨*the only paper to* ~ *the strike*⟩ **11** to pass over; traverse ⟨~ed *five miles at great speed*⟩ **12** to place a stake equal with (the stake of one's opponent) in a bet **13** to buy securities or commodities to make up (an earlier short sale) and thus be able to meet obligations on the agreed delivery date ~ *vi* **1** to conceal something illicit, blameworthy, or embarrassing from notice – usu + *up* **2** to act as a substitute or replacement *for* during an absence; provide an alibi *for* – see also **cover the** GROUND/one's TRACKS [ME *coveren*, fr OF *covrir*, fr L *cooperire*, fr *co-* + *operire* to close, cover – more at WEIR] – **coverable** *adj*

**²cover** *n* **1** something that protects, shelters, or guards: eg **1a** natural shelter (eg undergrowth) for an animal; *also* the materials that provide such shelter **b(1)** a position or situation affording shelter from attack **b(2)** (the protection offered by) a force (eg of aircraft) supporting a military operation **b(3)** COVERAGE 4a **b(4)** COVERAGE 2 **2** something that is placed over or round another thing: **2a** a lid, top **b** (the front or back part of) a protective covering (eg a binding or jacket) for a book **c** an overlay or outer layer (eg for protection) ⟨*a chair* ~⟩ **d** a roof or shelter **e** a cloth (eg a blanket) used on a bed ⟨*threw back the* ~s⟩ **f** something (eg vegetation or snow) that covers the ground **g** the extent to which clouds obscure the sky **3a** something that conceals or obscures ⟨*under* ~ *of darkness*⟩ **b** a masking device; a pretext ⟨*the project was a* ~ *for intelligence operations*⟩ **4** an envelope or wrapper for postal use ⟨*under separate* ~⟩ **5** a single place setting, esp in a restaurant **6a** COVER-POINT, EXTRA COVER, or a fielding position in cricket between them **b** *pl* the fielding positions on the OFF SIDE of a cricket pitch that lie between point and mid-off ⟨*a brilliant fieldsman close to the bat or in the* ~s – John Arlott⟩; *also* the fieldsmen occupying these positions – **coverless** *adj* – **break cover** to emerge from a place of hiding or shelter

**coverage** /'kuv(ə)rij/ *n* **1** the act or fact of covering **2** the amount available to meet financial liabilities **3** news reporting, esp in terms of its extent, scope, or quality ⟨*the* ~ *of the trial*⟩ **4** the area or amount covered; the scope: eg **4a** the total range of risks covered by the terms of an insurance policy **b** the number or percentage of people reached by a communications medium

**'cover-‚all** *adj* COMPREHENSIVE ⟨~ *provisions*⟩

**cover charge** *n* a charge (eg for service) made by a restaurant or nightclub in addition to the charge for food and drink

**cover crop** *n* a crop (eg clover) planted in otherwise bare fields, esp between the planting of main crops, to enrich the soil and prevent erosion

**covered smut** /'kuvəd/ *n* a fungus disease (SMUT) of wheat and other cereal grasses in which a black mass of spores forms inside the ears, which appear intact from the outside

**covered wagon** *n* a horse-drawn wagon with a canvas top supported by bowed strips of wood or metal, esp as used by early settlers in the USA

**cover factor** *n* a measure of the compactness of a fabric

**cover girl** *n* a girl whose picture illustrates a magazine cover

**cover glass** *n* **1** a piece of very thin glass used to cover material on a glass microscope slide **2** a sheet of plain glass applied to a photographic transparency for protection

**¹covering** /'kuv(ə)ring/ *n* something that covers or conceals

**²covering** *adj* containing explanation ∗of or additional information about an accompanying item ⟨*a* ~ *letter*⟩

**coverlet** /-lit/ *n* a bedspread [ME, alter. of *coverlite*, fr AF *coverelyth*, fr OF *covrir* + *lit* bed, fr L *lectus* – more at LIE]

**cover note** *n, Br* a provisional insurance document providing temporary cover between acceptance of a risk and issue of a full policy

'cover-,point n a fielding position in cricket about halfway to the boundary on the OFF SIDE of the pitch, situated in front of the batsman's wicket between EXTRA COVER and a point in line with the stumps; *also* the fieldsman occupying this position

coverslip /'kuvə,slip/ n COVER GLASS 1

cover story n a story accompanying the illustration on the cover of a magazine

¹covert /'kuvət, -vuht, 'ko-/ adj 1 not openly shown; concealed or secret 2 *archaic* covered over; sheltered synonyms see ¹SECRET antonym overt [ME, fr OF, pp of *covrir* to cover] – covertly adv, covertness n

²covert /'kuvət, -vuht, 'ko-; esp senses 1a,1b also 'kuvə/ n 1a a hiding place; a shelter b a thicket affording cover for game c a masking or concealing device 2 any of a series of feathers covering the bases of the main shafts of a bird's wing or tail feathers 3 covert, covert cloth a firm durable TWILLED (woven to give an appearance of diagonal lines) sometimes water-proofed cloth usu of yarns of mixed colours

cover text n a text in plain language within which a ciphertext is concealed

coverture /'kuvəchə/ n shelter, concealment

'cover-,up n a device or course of action that conceals something (e g a crime)

covet /'kovit, 'ku-/ vt 1 to wish or crave for, esp enviously 2 to desire (the property of another) in an excessive or un-restrained manner [ME *coveiten*, fr OF *coveitier*, fr *coveitié* desire, modif of L *cupiditat-, cupiditas*, fr *cupidus* desirous, fr *cupere* to desire; akin to L *vapor* steam, vapour, Gk *kapnos* smoke] – covetable adj, covetingly adv

covetous /'kovitəs, 'ku-/ adj 1 showing an excessive or un-restrained desire for (esp another's) wealth or possessions 2 having a craving for possession ⟨~ of power⟩ – covetously adv, covetousness n

covey /'kuvi/ n taking sing or pl vb 1 a mature bird or pair of birds with a brood of young; *also* a small flock ⟨a ~ of partridges⟩ 2 a company, group [ME, fr MF *covee*, fr OF, fr *cover* to sit on, brood over, fr L *cubare* to lie – more at HIP]

coving /'kohving/ n, building COVE 1

¹cow /kow/ n 1 the mature female of cattle (genus *Bos*) or of any animal (e g the moose) the male of which is called *bull* 2 a domestic bovine animal regardless of sex or age ⟨bring home the ~s⟩ 3 *informal* a woman; *esp* one who is coarse or un-pleasant 4 *chiefly Austr slang* a cause of annoyance or diffi-culty [ME *cou*, fr OE *cū*; akin to OHG *kuo* cow, L *bos* head of cattle, Gk *bous*, Skt *go*] – cowy adj – till the cows come home forever

²cow vt to intimidate with threats or show of strength; daunt [prob of Scand origin; akin to Dan *kue* to subdue] – cowedly adv

cowage, cowhage /'kowij/ n a tropical woody climbing plant (*Mucuna pruritum*) of the pea family whose pods are covered with barbed hairs that cause severe itching [Hindi *kavãc*]

coward /'kowəd/ n one who lacks courage or resolve [ME, fr OF *coart*, fr *coe* tail, fr L *cauda*; prob fr an image of an animal with its tail between its legs] – coward adj

cowardice /'kowədis/ n lack of courage or resolve [ME *cowardise*, fr OF *coardise*, fr *coart*]

¹cowardly /-li/ adv in a cowardly manner

²cowardly adj resembling or befitting a coward ⟨a ~ retreat⟩ – cowardliness n

cowbane /-,bayn/ n any of several poisonous plants of the carrot family; *esp* a tall Eurasian plant (*Cicuta virosa*) that grows on marshy ground and bears clusters of small white flowers

cowbell /-,bel/ n a bell hung round the neck of a cow to make a sound by which it can be located

cowberry /'kow,beri/ n (the red edible fruit of) any of several low-growing shrubs (esp *Vaccinium vitis-idaea*) of the heather family that grow on open ground and are closely related to the bilberry

cowboy /-,boy/, *fem* cowgirl /-,guhl/ n 1 one who tends or drives cattle; *esp* a usu mounted cattle ranch hand in N America 2 *informal* one who uses irresponsible, irregular, or unscrupulous methods, esp in business ⟨ . . . *the 1972 legislation stopped the waste-disposal ~s doing as they pleased* . . . – *The Economist*⟩

cowboy boot n a boot with a high arch, a high thick heel, and usu fancy stitching

cowboy hat n a wide-brimmed hat with a large soft crown

cowcatcher /-,kachə/ n, chiefly NAm a frame on the front of a railway locomotive or tram for removing obstacles from the track or lessening injury to animals or pedestrians in case of collision – compare FENDER 3

cower /'kowə/ vi to shrink away or crouch down (e g in fear or distress) from something menacing or upsetting synonyms see ¹RECOIL [ME *couren*, of Scand origin; akin to Norw *kura* to cower; akin to Gk *gyros* circle, OE *cot*]

cowfish /-,fish/ n 1a any of various small porpoises or dol-phins b a MANATEE or DUGONG (whalelike plant-eating sea mammals) 2 any of various small brightly coloured fishes (family Ostraciidae) with projections resembling horns over the eyes

cowhage /'kowij/ n COWAGE (woody climbing plant)

cowhand /-,hand/ n a cowherd, cowboy, or cowgirl

'cow-,heel n a jelly obtained by stewing the foot of a cow or ox

cowherd /-,huhd/ n one who tends or herds cattle

cowhide /-,hied/ n 1 (leather made from) the hide of a cow 2 a coarse whip of rawhide or braided leather

¹cowl /kowl/ n 1a a hood or long hooded cloak, esp of a monk b COWL NECK 2a a hooded covering put on a chimney or ven-tilation shaft to improve ventilation b the part of a motor car body to which are attached the windscreen and instrument panel c a cowling [ME *cowle*, fr OE *cugele*, fr LL *cuculla* monk's hood, fr L *cucullus* hood]

²cowl vt to cover (as if) with a cowl

cowled /kowld/ adj shaped like a hood; hooded ⟨a ~ flower⟩

cowlick /-,lik/ n a lock or tuft of hair growing in a different direction from the rest of the hair; *esp* a tuft of hair that turns up from the forehead [fr its looking as if it had been licked by a cow]

cowling /'kowling/ n a removable metal covering over an engine, esp in an aircraft

cowl neck, cowl neckline, cowl n a draped neckline on a garment, that falls in loose folds at the front – cowl-necked adj

cowlstaff /'kowl,stahf/ n, archaic a stout stick from which a load can be suspended to be carried between two people [ME *cuvelstaff*, fr *cuvel* vessel (fr OE *cȳfel*, fr ONF *cuvele* small vat) + *staff*]

cowman /-mən/ n 1 a cowherd or cowboy 2 NAm a cattle owner or rancher

co-worker /,koh'wuhkə/ n a fellow worker

cow parsley n a coarse tall Eurasian and African plant (*Anthriscus sylvestris*) of the carrot family with clusters of tiny white flowers and with leaves that resemble those of parsley

cow parsnip n a tall coarse Eurasian plant (*Heracleum sphondylium*) of the carrot family with thick hairy stems, very large leaves, and broad clusters of white or pinkish flowers – called also HOGWEED

cowpat /-,pat/ n a small heap of cow dung

cowpea /-,pee/ n BLACK-EYED PEA

Cowper's gland /'koohpəz, 'kowpəz/ n either of two small glands in males that discharge into the URETHRA (canal carrying urine from the bladder) a liquid that makes up a small pro-portion of the semen – called also BULBOURETHRAL GLAND [William *Cowper* †1709 E surgeon]

cowpoke /'kow,pohk/ n, NAm informal a cowboy

cowpox /-,poks/ n a mild disease of the cow that when com-municated to humans gives protection against smallpox

cowpuncher /'kow,punchə/ n, NAm informal a cowboy

cowrie, cowry /'kowri/ n any of numerous marine INVERT-EBRATE animals (family Cypraeidae of the class Gastropoda, phylum Mollusca) related to the snail, whelk, etc that are widely distributed in warm seas and have thick glossy and often brightly coloured shells formerly used as money in parts of Africa and Asia [Hindi *kaurī*]

cowshot /'kow,shot/ n an inelegant shot in cricket in which the batsman hits, usu with a horizontal bat, a ball onto the LEG SIDE

cowslip /-,slip/ n a European meadow plant (*Primula veris*) of the primrose family with fragrant yellow or purplish flowers [ME *cowslyppe*, fr OE *cūslyppe*, lit., cow dung, fr *cū* cow + *slypa, slyppe* paste (cf OXLIP)]

cox /koks/ vb or n (to steer or command as) a coxswain – coxless adj

coxa /'koksə/ n, pl coxae /-si/ the first or upper segment of a limb of an insect, spider, etc [L, hip; akin to OHG *hāhsina* hock, Skt *kakṣa* armpit] – coxal adj

**coxcomb** /'koks,kohm, -kəm/ n 1 a conceited foolish person; a fop 2 obs a jester's cap adorned with a strip of red and resembling a cock's comb [ME cokkes comb, lit., cock's comb] – **coxcombical** adj

**coxcombry** /'koks,kohmri, -kəmri/ n conceited foolish behaviour; foppery

**coxed** /kokst/ adj provided with a coxswain – used esp of the crew of racing rowing boats ⟨won in the ~ pairs and fours⟩

**Coxsackie virus** /'kok,saki, 'kook,sahki/ n any of several viruses related to that of poliomyelitis and causing many human diseases, including meningitis and the common cold [Coxsackie, community in New York, USA, where the virus was first found]

**coxswain** /'koksn, -,swayn/ n 1 a sailor who commands and usu steers a ship's lifeboat 2 the steersman of a racing rowing boat who usu directs the crew and calls out the strokes [ME cokswayne, fr cok small boat + swain servant (cf BOATSWAIN)] – **coxswainless** adj

**coy** /koy/ adj 1a (affectedly) shy or demure b provocatively playful or coquettish 2 showing reluctance to make a definite commitment or face unpalatable facts **synonyms** see ¹SHY **antonym** pert [ME, quiet, shy, fr MF coi calm, fr L quietus quiet] – **coyly** adv, **coyness** n

**coyote** /'koyoht, -'-, -'ohti, kie'ohti/ n, pl coyotes, esp collectively coyote a fast intelligent predatory mammal (Canis latrans) of the dog family that is native to western N America, is smaller and lighter in build than the closely related wolf, and is noted for its nocturnal howling [MexSp, fr Nahuatl coyotl]

**coypu** /'koyp(y)ooh/ n, coypus, esp collectively coypu 1 a S American aquatic rodent (Myocastor coypus) with webbed feet, that is bred for its fur and now lives wild in E England and many other parts of the world [AmerSp coipú, fr Araucan coypu]

**coz** /kuz/ n cousin – used chiefly as a term of address [by shortening & alter.]

**cozen** /'kuz(ə)n/ vt 1 to win over, deceive, or beguile into doing something, esp by shrewd trickery ⟨tried to ~ his opponent's supporters⟩ 2 to gain by cozening someone ⟨~ed her supper out of the old man⟩ [prob fr obs It cozzonare, fr It cozzone horse trader, fr L cocion-, cocio trader] – **cozener** n, **cozenage** n

¹**cozy** /'kohzi/ adj, NAm cosy
²**cozy** n, chiefly NAm a cosy

**CQ** – communication code letters used at the beginning of radiograms of general information or safety notices, or by shortwave amateurs as an invitation to talk to other shortwave amateurs [abbr for call to quarters]

¹**crab** /krab/ n 1 any of numerous chiefly marine broadly built INVERTEBRATE animals related to shrimps and lobsters: 1a any of a tribe (Brachyura, of the class Crustacea) of animals with a short broad usu flattened CARAPACE (external shieldlike covering on the back) and the front pair of limbs usu modified as grasping pincers b any of various animals (tribe Anomura) (e g the hermit crab) resembling true crabs 2 cap CANCER 1 (sign of the zodiac) 3 pl infestation with CRAB LICE 4 the apparent sideways motion of an aircraft that is flying slightly into a crosswind in order to compensate for drift [ME crabbe, fr OE crabba; akin to OHG krebiz crab, OE ceorfan to carve] – **catch a crab** to fail to raise an oar clear of the water on recovery of a stroke in rowing; also to miss the water altogether when attempting a stroke

²**crab** vb -bb- vt 1 to cause to move sideways or in an indirect or diagonal manner 2 to steer (an aircraft) slightly into a crosswind in order to compensate for drift ~ vi 1a(1) to move sideways indirectly or diagonally a(2) to move at an angle to some natural direction of motion b to crab an aircraft 2 to fish for crabs – **crabber** n

³**crab** n CRAB APPLE [ME crabbe, perh fr crabbe ¹crab]

⁴**crab** vb -bb- vt 1 to make sullen; sour ⟨hard times have ~bed his nature⟩ 2 NAm to spoil, ruin – chiefly in crab one's act ~ vi, informal to complain, grouse ⟨always ~s about the weather⟩ [ME crabben, prob back-formation fr crabbed] – **crabber** n

⁵**crab** n, informal an ill-tempered person; a crosspatch

**crab apple** n 1 (a small sour wild apple that is the fruit of) a thorny tree (Malus silvestris) of the rose family 2 (a cultivated apple tree that bears) a small usu highly coloured sour fruit [³crab]

**crabbed** /'krabid/ adj 1 morose, peevish 2 difficult to read or understand ⟨~ handwriting⟩ [ME; partly fr crabbe ¹crab, partly fr crabbe ³crab] – **crabbedly** adv, **crabbedness** n

**crabbit** /'krabit/ adj, Scot ill-tempered, irritable [ME (Sc) crabyt, var of crabbed]

**crabby** /'krabi/ adj cross, ill-tempered [⁵crab]

**crabgrass** /-,grahs/ n a grass (esp Digitaria sanguinalis) with freely rooting creeping stems that grows as a weed on lawns, fields, and waste spaces in the USA and Europe

**crab louse** n a sucking louse (Phthirus pubis) that infests the pubic region of the human body

**crabwise** /-,wiez/ adv 1 sideways 2 in a sidling or cautiously indirect manner

¹**crack** /krak/ vi 1 to make a sudden sharp explosive noise ⟨the whip ~s through the air⟩ 2a to break, split, or snap apart ⟨the friendly atmosphere began to ~⟩ b to develop fissures ⟨the mirror ~ed⟩ 3a to lose control or effectiveness under pressure – often + up b to fail in tone, volume, etc ⟨his voice ~ed⟩ c to give in; yield ⟨he'll ~ in the end⟩ 4 esp of the components of crude oil to break up into simpler chemical compounds when heated, usu with a catalyst ~ vt 1a to break so that fissures appear on the surface ⟨~ a mirror⟩ b to break with a sudden sharp explosive sound ⟨~ nuts⟩ 2 to tell (a joke) 3 to strike with a sharp noise; rap ⟨then ~s him over the head⟩ 4a to puzzle out and expose, solve, or reveal the mystery of ⟨~ a code⟩ b to break into ⟨~ a safe⟩ c to break through (e g a barrier) so as to gain acceptance or recognition ⟨she ~ed my reserve⟩ 5a to destroy the tone, volume, etc of (a voice) b to destroy, ruin ⟨~ed his opponent's courage⟩ c to interrupt sharply or abruptly ⟨the criticism ~ed our complacency⟩ 6 to cause to make a sudden sharp noise ⟨~ one's knuckles⟩ 7 to break up (chemical compounds, esp the compounds of crude oil) into simpler compounds (e g petrol) by means of heat 8 informal 8a to open for drinking ⟨let's ~ a couple of cans⟩ b to achieve; get the better of ⟨I've ~ed this essay⟩ [ME crakken, fr OE cracian; akin to Skt jarate it crackles – more at CRANE] – **get cracking** to make a start; get going ⟨ought to get cracking on the washing up⟩

**crack down** vi to take positive regulatory or disciplinary action – usu + on; see also CRACKDOWN

**crack up** vt 1 informal to present in (excessively) favourable terms ⟨wasn't all that it was cracked up to be⟩ 2 chiefly NAm informal to cause much amusement to ⟨that joke really cracks him up⟩ ~ vi to undergo a physical or mental collapse – see also CRACK-UP

²**crack** n 1 a sudden sharp loud noise ⟨the ~ of rifle fire⟩ ⟨a ~ of thunder⟩ 2a a line or narrow opening that marks a break; a fissure ⟨a ~ in the ice⟩ b a narrow opening; a chink ⟨leave the door open a ~⟩ 3a a weakness or flaw that is likened to a crack ⟨~s appearing in the structure of contemporary society⟩ b a broken tone of the voice 4 a sharp resounding blow ⟨gave him a ~ on the head⟩ 5 chiefly Scot & Irish 5a lively or merry conversation; chatter b the latest or most current news or topic of conversation; gossip ⟨videos are all the ~ at the moment⟩ 6 informal a witty remark; a quip 7 informal an attempt, try ⟨her first ~ at writing a novel⟩

³**crack** adj, informal of superior quality or ability ⟨a ~ shot⟩

**crackdown** /-,down/ n an act or instance of cracking down

**cracked** /krakt/ adj 1a broken in such a way as to produce cracks b broken into coarse particles ⟨~ wheat⟩ c marked by harshness, dissonance, or failure to sustain a tone ⟨a ~ voice⟩ 2 informal mentally disordered; crazy

**cracker** /'krakə/ n 1a a firecracker b a brightly coloured paper and cardboard tube that makes a cracking noise when pulled sharply apart and usu contains a toy, paper hat, or other party item 2 pl a nutcracker 3 a thin often savoury biscuit 4 the equipment in which cracking, esp of petroleum, is carried out 5 Br informal somebody or something exceptional; esp an outstandingly attractive girl or woman

'**cracker-,barrel** adj, chiefly NAm homespun, rural ⟨a ~ philosopher⟩ [cracker barrel (a barrel of biscuits), once a feature of rural stores where customers lounged for informal conversation]

**crackerjack** also **crackajack** /'krakə,jak/ n, chiefly NAm informal somebody or something of marked excellence [¹crack + -er + jack] – **crackerjack** adj

**crackers** /'krakəz/ adj, chiefly Br informal mad, crazy ⟨it's enough to drive you ~⟩ [prob alter. of cracked]

¹**cracking** /'kraking/ adj, informal 1 very fast ⟨went at a ~ pace⟩ 2 chiefly Br outstanding, great ⟨~ party⟩ – no longer in vogue

²**cracking** adv, chiefly Br informal very, extremely ⟨a ~ good book⟩ – no longer in vogue

**³cracking** *n* a process in which relatively large molecules (e g those in crude oil) are broken up by heat into smaller molecules (e g those in petrol)

**¹crackle** /'krakl/ *vi* **1a** to make a crackle ⟨*the fire* ~s *on the hearth*⟩ **b** to show animation; sparkle ⟨*the essays* ~ *with wit*⟩ **2** to develop a surface network of fine cracks; craze ~ *vt* **1** to crush or crack with a snapping sound **2** to make minute cracks on the surface or glaze of (e g porcelain or pottery) [freq of ¹*crack*]

**²crackle** *n* **1a** the noise of repeated small cracks or reports **b** sparkle, effervescence **2** a network of fine cracks on an otherwise smooth surface

**crackleware** /'krakl,weə/ *n* porcelain or pottery with a decorative crackled glaze

**crackling** /'krakling/ *n* **1** the crisp brown skin of roast meat, esp pork **2** cracklings *pl*, crackling the crisp residue left after the rendering of animal fat, esp lard

**crackly** /'krakli, 'krakl·i/ *adj* inclined to crackle; crisp

**cracknel** /'krakn(ə)l/ *n* **1** a hard brittle biscuit **2** cracknels *pl*, cracknel *NAm* small pieces of crisp fried fat pork [ME *kraken-elle*, prob modif of MF *craquelin*, fr MD *crakelinc*, fr *cräken* to crack]

**crack of dawn** *n* the first light of dawn

**crack of doom** *n* the thunderclap that heralds the Day of Judgment

**crackpot** /-,pot/ *n, informal* somebody with eccentric ideas; a crank *synonyms* see LAUGHABLE [¹*crack* + *pot* (head)] – **crackpot** *adj*

**cracksman** /-mən/ *n, informal* a burglar; *esp* a safebreaker

**¹crack-,up** *n* **1** a mental collapse; NERVOUS BREAKDOWN ⟨*his wife's death brought on his* ~⟩ **2** a collapse; breakdown

**-cracy** /-krəsi/ *comb form* (→ *n*) **1** rule; form of government ⟨*demo*cracy⟩ **2** powerful or dominant social or political class ⟨*aristo*cracy⟩ **3** state having a (specified) government or ruling class ⟨*merito*cracy⟩ [MF & LL; MF *-cratie*, fr LL *-cratia*, fr Gk *-kratia*, fr *kratos* strength, power – more at HARD]

**¹cradle** /'kraydl/ *n* **1a** a baby's bed or cot, usu on rockers **b** a framework of wood or metal used as a support, scaffold, etc: e g **b(1)** the support for a telephone receiver or handset **b(2)** a low frame on castors on which a mechanic lies while working under a motor vehicle – called also CREEPER **b(3)** a framework on which a ship or boat rests when out of the water **b(4)** a scaffold hanging down the side of a ship or building on which people stand to do painting, repairs, etc **b(5)** a frame to keep the bedclothes from contact with an injured part of the body **2a** the earliest period of life; infancy ⟨*from the* ~ *to the grave*⟩ **b** a place of origin ⟨~ *of civilization*⟩ **3a** an implement with rods like fingers formerly attached to a scythe and used for gathering grain into bunches **b** cradle scythe, cradle a scythe with a cradle attached to it [ME *cradel*, fr OE *cradol*; akin to OHG *kratto* basket, Skt *grantha* knot]

**²cradle** *vt* **1a** to place or keep (as if) in a cradle **b** to shelter **c** to support or hold protectively **2** to cut (grain) with a scythe that has a cradle attached to it

**cradlesong** /'kraydl,song/ *n* a lullaby, berceuse

**¹craft** /krahft/ *n, pl* crafts, (5) craft *also* crafts **1** skill in planning, making, or executing; dexterity – often in combination ⟨*wine*craft⟩ **2** an activity or trade requiring manual dexterity or artistic skill; *broadly* a trade, profession ⟨*the carpenter's* ~⟩ **3** skill in deceiving to gain an end ⟨*used* ~ *and guile to get the contract*⟩ **4** *taking sing or pl vb* the members of a trade or trade association **5a** an esp small boat **b** an aircraft **c** a spacecraft [ME, strength, skill, fr OE *cræft;* akin to OHG *kraft* strength]

**²craft** *vt* to make (as if) by using skill and dexterity ⟨*a beautifully* ~ed *novel*⟩

**craftsman** /'krahftsmən/, *fem* craftswoman /-,woomən/ *n* **1** a person who practises a skilled trade or handicraft; an artisan **2** one who displays a high degree of manual dexterity or artistic skill – **craftsmanlike** *adj*, **craftsmanship** *n*

**craft union** *n* a trade union with membership limited to workers of the same trade or craft – compare INDUSTRIAL UNION, GENERAL UNION

**crafty** /'krahfti/ *adj* **1** showing or using subtlety and guile; cunning ⟨*a very* ~ *manoeuvre*⟩ **2** *archaic chiefly Br* skilful, clever *synonyms* see SLY – **craftily** *adv*, **craftiness** *n*

**¹crag** /krag/ *n* a steep rugged rock, cliff, or peak [ME, of Celt origin; akin to OIr *crec* crag]

**²crag** *n, chiefly Scot* the neck, throat [ME, fr MD *crāghe*]

**craggy** /'kragi/ *adj* **1** *NAm also* cragged having many crags

⟨~ *slopes*⟩ **2** rough, rugged ⟨*a* ~ *face*⟩ – **craggily** *adv*, **cragginess** *n*

**cragsman** /'kragzmən/ *n* somebody skilled in climbing crags or cliffs

**crake** /krayk/ *n* any of various RAILS (wading marsh birds); *esp* a short-billed rail (e g the corncrake) [ME, prob fr ON *krāka* crow or *krākr* raven; akin to OE *crāwan* to crow]

**cram** /kram/ *vb* **-mm-** *vt* **1** to pack tight; jam ⟨~ *a suitcase with clothes*⟩ **2** to feed (e g poultry) to excess **3** to thrust (as if) in a rough or forceful manner **4a** to prepare (students) hastily for an examination **b** to learn or prepare (work) hastily for examination **5** *informal* to eat voraciously; bolt ~ *vi* **1** to study hastily and intensively for an examination **2** *informal* to eat greedily or until uncomfortably full; stuff [ME *crammen*, fr OE *crammian;* akin to Gk *ageirein* to collect] – **cram** *n*

**crambo** /'kramboh/ *n, pl* **cramboes** a game in which a word to be guessed is chosen by one player, who offers as a clue another word that rhymes with it, and the other players each have three chances to hit on the secret word by suggesting rhymes to match the clue word [alter. of earlier *crambe*, fr L, cabbage, fr Gk *krambē*]

**cram-full** /kram/ *adj* as full as can be

**crammer** /'kramə/ *n, Br* a school or teacher that prepares students hastily and intensively for an examination – not used technically

**¹cramp** /kramp/ *n* **1** a painful involuntary spasmodic contraction of a muscle **2** a temporary paralysis of muscles from overuse – compare WRITER'S CRAMP **3** *pl* severe abdominal pain [ME *crampe*, fr MF, of Gmc origin; akin to LG *krampe* hook]

**²cramp** *n* **1a** cramp, cramp-iron a usu metal device bent at the ends and used in masonry to hold timbers or blocks of stone together **b** a clamp; *esp* one used for holding two planks together **2a** something that confines; a restraint **b** a confined state [LG or obs D *krampe* hook; akin to OE *cradol* cradle]

**³cramp** *vt* **1** to affect (as if) with cramp **2a** to confine, restrain **b** to restrain from free expression – chiefly in *cramp someone's style* **3** to fasten or hold with a cramp

**crampon** /'krampon/ *n* **1** crampons *pl*, crampon a hooked mechanical device for lifting heavy objects **2** a metal frame with spikes that is fixed to the sole of a climbing boot for climbing slopes of ice or hard snow [MF *crampon*, of Gmc origin; akin to LG *krampe*]

**cran** /kran/ *n, chiefly Scot* a unit of capacity used for measuring fresh herrings, equal to 170 litres ($37\frac{1}{2}$ gallons) [ScGael *crann* tree, lot, measure of herring; akin to OIr *crann* tree]

**cranberry** /'kranb(ə)ri/ *n* **1** any of various plants (e g *Vaccinium oxycoccos*) of the heather family that bear a red acid berry **2** the berry of a cranberry plant used in making sauces and jellies [part trans of LG *kraanbere*, fr *kraan* crane + *bere* berry]

**¹crane** /krayn/ *n* **1** any of a family (Gruidae) of tall long-legged long-necked WADING BIRDS superficially resembling the herons but structurally more closely related to the rails **2** a machine for raising, shifting, and lowering heavy weights by means of a projecting swinging arm or a hoisting apparatus supported on an overhead track **3** a movable platform with a long projecting arm for holding a film or television camera, thus allowing the camera to be moved easily up, down, and along [ME *cran*, fr OE; akin to OHG *krano* crane, Gk *geranos*, L *grus*, Skt *jarate* it crackles]

**²crane** *vt* **1** to raise or lift (as if) by a crane **2** to stretch (e g the neck), esp in order to see better ~ *vi* to stretch one's neck, esp in order to see better ⟨*I* ~d *out of the window*⟩

**crane fly** *n* any of numerous long-legged slender flies (family Tipulidae) that resemble large mosquitoes but do not bite – called also DADDY LONGLEGS

**cranesbill** /'kraynz,bil/ *n* GERANIUM 1

**crani-** /krayni-/, **cranio-** *comb form* **1** cranium ⟨*crani*ate⟩ **2** cranial and ⟨*cranio*sacral⟩ [ML *cranium*]

**cranial** /'krayni·əl/ *adj* of the skull or cranium – **cranially** *adv*

**cranial index** *n* the ratio of the maximum breadth of the skull to its maximum height multiplied by 100 – compare CEPHALIC INDEX

**cranial nerve** *n* any of the (10 or 12 pairs of) nerves that arise from the lower surface of the brain and pass through openings in the skull to connect with the body, esp the head

**craniate** /'krayni·ət, -,ayt/ *adj* having a skull; VERTEBRATE – **craniate** *n*

**craniofacial** /,kraynioh'faysh(ə)l/ *adj* of or involving both the skull and the face

**craniology** /ˌkrayniˈoləji/ *n* a science dealing with variations in size, shape, and proportions of the skull among the different races of human beings

**craniometry** /ˌkrayniˈomətri/ *n* a science dealing with the measurement of the skull [ISV]

**cranium** /ˈkrayni-əm/ *n, pl* **craniums, crania** /-ni-ə/ the skull; *specif* the part of the skull that encloses the brain [ML, fr Gk *kranion;* akin to Gk *kara* head – more at CEREBRAL]

**¹crank** /krangk/ *n* **1** a part of an axle or shaft bent at right angles by which backwards and forwards motion is changed into circular motion or vice versa **2** an eccentric person; *also* one who is excessively enthusiastic or fastidious about a particular subject or activity ⟨*a food ∼*⟩ **3** a clever turn of speech – chiefly in *quips and cranks* **4** *archaic* a bend, turn [ME *cranke*, fr OE *cranc-* (as in *crancstæf*, a weaving instrument); akin to OE *cradol* cradle]

**²crank** *vi* **1** to turn a crank (eg in starting an engine) **2** *archaic* to move with a winding course; zigzag ∼ *vt* **1** to bend into the shape of a crank **2** to attach a crank to **3a** to move or operate (as if) by a crank **b** to start by use of a crank – often + *up* **crank out** *vt* CHURN OUT ⟨cranked out *the story of his life again*⟩

**³crank** *adj, dial Br* merry, high-spirited [ME *cranke*, of unknown origin]

**⁴crank** *adj, of a boat* easily capsized [short for *crank-sided* (easily tipped)]

**crankcase** /ˈkrangkˌkays/ *n* the metal case enclosing a crankshaft

**crankle** /ˈkrangkl/ *vb, archaic vt* to break into turns, bends, or angles; crinkle ∼ *vi* to wind, zigzag [freq of ²*crank*]

**crankpin** /ˈkrangkˌpin/ *n* any of one or more cylindrical parts of a crankshaft that are offset from and parallel to the line of the main shaft and that are each attached to one end of a CONNECTING ROD that transmits movement from one of the pistons to the crankshaft

**crankshaft** /ˈkrangkˌshahft/ *n* a shaft (eg in a car engine) that is driven by or drives one or more cranks

**cranky** /ˈkrangki/ *adj* **1** *of machinery* working erratically; unpredictable ⟨*a ∼ old tractor*⟩ **2** eccentric, weird **3** full of twists and turns ⟨*a ∼ road*⟩ **4** *NAm, Austr, & NZ* easily angered or upset; crotchety ⟨*she is always ∼ in the mornings*⟩ [partly fr ¹*crank;* partly fr *crank* (maladjusted, loose), fr Sc, bent, distorted] – **crankily** *adv,* **crankiness** *n*

**crannog** /ˈkranəg/ *n* an artificial often fortified island dwelling constructed in a lake or marsh, orig in prehistoric and early medieval Ireland and Scotland [ScGael *crannag* & IrGael *crannōg*]

**cranny** /ˈkrani/ *n* a small crack or slit; a chink – often in *nooks and crannies* [ME *crany*, fr MF *cren, cran* notch – more at CRENEL] – **crannied** *adj*

**cranreuch** /ˈkranrookh/ *n, Scot* hoarfrost, rime [prob modif of ScGael *crannreotha*]

**¹crap** /krap/ *n* **1** *vulg* excrement **b** an act of defecation **2** *slang* nonsense, rubbish [ME *crappe* chaff, residue from rendered fat, fr MD, piece torn off, fr *crappen* to break off]

**²crap** *vi* **-pp-** *vulg* to defecate

**³crap** *n* a losing throw of 2, 3, or 12 in the game of craps – compare NATURAL 2 [back-formation fr *craps*]

**⁴crap** *adj* of or for craps ⟨*∼ game*⟩ ⟨*∼ table*⟩

**¹crape** /krayp/ *n* **1** CREPE 1 **2** a band of black crepe worn, esp on a hat, as a sign of mourning [modif of Fr *crêpe*]

**²crape** *vt* to cover or shroud (as if) with crape

**crap out** *vi* **1** *NAm* to make a losing throw in the game of craps **2** *NAm, Austr, & NZ* to fail, wear out; give up

**crapper** /ˈkrapə/ *n, vulg* a toilet [²*crap*]

**crappy** /ˈkrapi/ *adj, slang* very inferior in quality; lousy [¹*crap*]

**craps** /kraps/ *n taking sing or pl vb* a gambling game played with two dice in which players take turns to be the shooter, who bets against the rest of the players that he/she will throw certain set combinations and not others [LaF, fr Fr *crabs, craps*, fr E *crabs* (lowest throw at hazard), fr pl of ¹*crab*] – **shoot craps** *NAm* to play the game of craps

**crapshooter** /ˈkrapˌshoohtə/ *n, NAm* one who plays craps

**crapulent** /ˈkrapyoolənt/ *adj* crapulous [LL *crapulentus*, fr L *crapula*]

**crapulous** /ˈkrapyooləs/ *adj* **1** given to excessive indulgence, esp in alcohol **2** suffering the effects of or resulting from excessive drinking of alcohol [LL *crapulosus*, fr L *crapula* intoxication, fr Gk *kraipalē*]

**craquelure** /ˈkrakəl(y)ooə/ *n* a network of fine cracks that develops on the surface of old paintings, caused by the decay of pigment and varnish [Fr, fr *craqueler* to crack, crackle, fr *craquer*, of imit origin]

**¹crash** /krash/ *vt* **1a** to cause to collide violently and noisily ⟨∼ed *my head against the wall*⟩ **b** to cause to fall violently and noisily ⟨∼ *the vase to the floor*⟩ **c** to cause (an aircraft) to hit the land or sea or to collide with something, usu causing extensive damage **d** to collide (a vehicle) with a vehicle, wall, etc **2** to cause to make a loud smashing or clattering noise ⟨∼ *the cymbals together*⟩ **3** to force (eg one's way) loudly or violently ⟨∼ed *his way through the undergrowth*⟩ **4** to enter or attend without invitation or without paying; gate-crash ⟨∼ *the party*⟩ **5** to cause (eg a computer system or program) to crash ∼ *vi* **1a** to break or go to pieces (as if) with violence and noise **b** to collide with somebody or something noisily or violently ⟨*she ∼*ed *into the television set*⟩ **c** to fall (as if) with violence and noise ⟨*the stock marked ∼*ed⟩ **d** to crash an aircraft or vehicle **e** to be involved in a crash **2** to make a loud smashing or clattering noise **3** to move or force one's way loudly or violently ⟨∼es *into the room*⟩ ⟨∼ *through a roadblock*⟩ **4** *esp of a computer system or program* to become (suddenly) completely inoperative **5** *informal* to spend the night in a place; go to sleep – often + *out* ⟨*can I ∼ out on your floor tonight?*⟩ **6** *chiefly NAm informal* to return to a normal state after a drug-induced experience [ME *crasschen*, prob of imit origin]

**²crash** *n* **1** a loud, sudden, esp resounding, noise (eg of things smashing or clattering) ⟨*a ∼ of thunder*⟩ **2a** an act or instance of breaking to pieces **b** a noisy or violent collision (eg between two vehicles); *also* an instance of crashing ⟨*a plane ∼*⟩ **3** a sudden decline or failure (eg of a business) ⟨*the Wall Street ∼*⟩

**³crash** *adj* designed to achieve an intended result in the shortest possible time ⟨*a ∼ programme to deal with illiteracy*⟩ ⟨*a ∼ diet*⟩

**⁴crash** *n* a coarse fabric made originally of linen and used for draperies, towelling, clothing, etc [prob fr Russ *krashenina* coloured linen]

**crash barrier** *n* a barrier along the centre of a motorway, around a racetrack, etc to prevent vehicles from colliding or from leaving the road

**crash dive** *vi, esp of an aircraft or submarine* to descend or dive steeply and quickly (eg in an emergency or before crashing) – **crash dive** *n*

**crasher** /ˈkrashə/ *n, informal* a gate-crasher

**crash helmet** *n* a padded helmet that is worn (eg by motorcyclists) as protection for the head in the event of an accident

**crashing** /ˈkrashing/ *adj* utter, absolute ⟨*a ∼ bore*⟩

**crash-ˈland** *vb* to land (an aircraft) under emergency conditions, usu with damage to the craft – **crash landing** *n*

**crashpad** /ˈkrashˌpad/ *n, informal* a place where free temporary accommodation is available

**crasis** /ˈkraysis/ *n, pl* **crases** /-seez/ the contraction of two vowels or diphthongs into one long vowel or diphthong [NL, fr Gk *krasis* mixing, combination, fr *kerannynai* to mix]

**crass** /kras/ *adj* **1** insensitive and boorish; coarse ⟨*a ∼ remark*⟩ **2** gross, thick ⟨∼ *stupidity*⟩ *synonyms* see STUPID [L *crassus* thick, gross] – **crassly** *adv,* **crassitude, crassness** *n*

**-crat** /-krat/ *comb form* (→ *n*) **1** advocate or partisan of (a specified form of government) ⟨*democrat*⟩ **2** member of (a specified ruling class) ⟨*plutocrat*⟩ ⟨*technocrat*⟩ [Fr *-crate*, back-formation fr *-cratie* -cracy] – **-cratic** *comb form* (→ *adj*)

**cratch** /krach/ *n* **1** *dial Br* a rack, esp for holding fodder for cattle **2** *archaic* a manger [ME *cracche*, fr OF *creche* manger – more at CRÈCHE]

**¹crate** /krayt/ *n* **1** a container usu made of thin wooden slats for holding goods (eg fruit, bottles, etc), esp during transit **2** the contents of a crate ⟨*drank a whole ∼*⟩ **3** *informal* an old dilapidated car, aeroplane, etc [L *cratis* wickerwork – more at HURDLE]

**²crate** *vt* to pack in a crate

**¹crater** /ˈkraytə/ *n* **1** a (bowl-shaped) depression: eg **1a** one round the mouth of a volcano **b** one formed by the impact of a meteorite **2** a hole in the ground made by an explosion **3** **crater, krater** a large jar or vase used, esp by the ancient Greeks, for mixing wine and water [L, mixing bowl, crater, fr Gk *kratēr*, fr *kerannynai* to mix; akin to Skt *āsīrta* mixed]

**²crater** *vt* to form craters in

**craton** /ˈkrayton/ *n* a stable relatively immobile area of the earth's crust that forms the central mass of a continent or the central basis of an ocean [Ger *kraton*, modif of Gk *kratos* strength – more at HARD] – **cratonic** *adj*

**craunch** /krawnch/ *vb, dial Br* to crunch [prob imit] – **craunch** *n*

**cravat** /krə'vat/ *n* a long scarf worn round the neck, esp by men, usu folded across and tucked into a shirt or sweater [Fr *cravate*, fr *Cravate* Croatian; fr the linen scarves worn by 17th-c Croatian mercenaries]

**crave** /krayv/ *vt* 1 to have a strong or urgent desire for ⟨~ *a cigarette*⟩ 2 *formal* to ask for earnestly; beg ⟨*I ~ the court's indulgence*⟩ ~ *vi* to have a strong or inward desire; yearn ⟨~s *after affection*⟩ **synonyms** see ¹DESIRE [ME *craven*, fr OE *crafian*; akin to OHG *krāpfo* hook, OE *cradol* cradle] – **craver** *n*

**craven** /'krayv(ə)n/ *adj* completely lacking in courage; cowardly [ME *cravant* defeated, cowardly, perh fr OF *crevant*, prp of *crever* to burst, break, fr L *crepare*] – **craven** *n*, **cravenly** *adv*, **cravenness** *n*

**craving** /'krayving/ *n* a great desire or longing ⟨*a ~ for alcohol*⟩

**craw** /kraw/ *n* 1 the CROP of a bird or insect 2 the stomach of an animal, esp a lower animal [ME *crawe*, fr (assumed) OE *crawa*; akin to Gk *bronchos* windpipe, throat, L *vorare* to devour – more at VORACIOUS]

¹**crawfish** /'kraw,fish/ *n, chiefly NAm* a crayfish [by folk etymology fr ME *crevis*, *kraveys*]

²**crawfish** *vi, NAm* to retreat from a position; back out [fr the backward retreat of the crawfish to its lair in times of danger]

¹**crawl** /krawl/ *vi* 1a to move on hands and knees ⟨*the baby can ~ now*⟩ b to move slowly in a prone position (as if) without the use of limbs ⟨*the snake ~ed into its hole*⟩ 2 to move or progress slowly or laboriously ⟨*traffic ~s along at 10 miles an hour*⟩ 3 to behave in a servile manner ⟨*he'll just go ~ing to the boss as usual*⟩ 4 *of a plant* CREEP 3b (grow over a surface) 5a to be alive or swarming (as if) with creeping things ⟨*food ~ing with ants*⟩ b to have the sensation of insects creeping over one ⟨*the story made her flesh ~*⟩ 6 *of paint, varnish, or glaze* to fail to stay evenly spread ~ *vt* to move upon (as if) in a creeping manner ⟨*the meanest man who ever ~ed the earth*⟩ [ME *crawlen*, fr ON *krafla*; akin to OE *crabba* crab]

²**crawl** *n* 1a the act or action of crawling b slow or laborious motion or pace ⟨*traffic moving at a ~*⟩ c *chiefly Br* PUB CRAWL 2 the fastest swimming stroke, executed on the front and consisting of alternating overarm strokes combined with kicks with the legs

³**crawl** *n* an enclosure in shallow waters (eg for confining lobsters) [Afrik *kraal* pen –more at KRAAL]

**crawler** /'krawlə/ *n* 1a a heavy slow vehicle b a vehicle (eg a crane) that travels on caterpillar tracks 2 a servile obsequious person

**crawling peg** *n* a system of controlling exchange rates in which currencies are only allowed small changes in value against other currencies in a given period

**crayfish** /'kray,fish/ *n* 1 any of numerous edible freshwater INVERTEBRATE animals (esp genera *Austropotamobius* and *Astacus* of the tribe Astacura, class Crustacea) that resemble the related lobster but are usu much smaller 2 SPINY LOBSTER (edible spiny lobsterlike animal) [by folk etymology fr ME *crevis*, fr MF *crevice*, of Gmc origin; akin to OHG *krebiz* crab – more at CRAB]

¹**crayon** /'krayon, 'krayən/ *n* 1 a stick of white or coloured chalk or of coloured wax used for writing or drawing 2 a crayon drawing [Fr, crayon, pencil, fr dim. of *craie* chalk, fr L *creta*]

²**crayon** *vt* to draw or colour with a crayon – **crayonist** *n*

¹**craze** /krayz/ *vt* 1 to produce minute cracks on the surface or glaze of (glass or pottery) 2 to make (as if) insane ⟨~d *by pain and fear*⟩ 3 *obs* to shatter, break ~ *vi* 1 *esp of glaze or enamel* to develop a mesh of fine cracks 2 *archaic* to shatter, break [ME *crasen* to crush, crack, of Scand origin; akin to OSw *krasa* to crush]

²**craze** *n* 1 an exaggerated and often brief enthusiasm; a fad ⟨*skateboarding was the last ~*⟩ 2 fine cracks in a surface or coating (eg of glaze or enamel)

**crazy** /'krayzi/ *adj* 1 full of cracks or flaws; unsound 2 *informal* 2a mad, insane b impractical ⟨*a ~ scheme*⟩ c out of the ordinary; unusual, eccentric ⟨*a taste for ~ hats*⟩ d distracted with desire or excitement; extremely enthusiastic *about*; infatuated ⟨*he's ~ about her*⟩ ⟨*she's ~ about hang-gliding*⟩ **synonyms** see LAUGHABLE – **crazily** *adv*, **craziness** *n* – **like crazy** to an extreme degree ⟨*everyone dancing* like crazy⟩

**crazy bone** *n, NAm* FUNNY BONE

**crazy paving** *n, Br* a paved surface made up of irregularly shaped paving stones

**crazy quilt** *n* a patchwork quilt without a regular pattern

¹**creak** /kreek/ *vi* 1 to make a grating or squeaking noise, esp while moving ⟨*the wheelbarrow was ~*ing⟩ 2 *Br chiefly informal* to perform or function badly or ineffectively [ME *creken* to croak, of imit origin]

²**creak** *n* a prolonged rasping, grating, or squeaking noise (eg of an unoiled hinge)

**creaky** /'kreeki/ *adj* 1 marked by creaking; squeaky ⟨~ *shoes*⟩ 2 *esp of a play, novel, film, etc* badly made and often old-fashioned ⟨*a ~ old melodrama*⟩ – **creakily** *adv*, **creakiness** *n*

¹**cream** /kreem/ *n* 1 the yellowish part of milk containing from 18 to about 40 per cent butterfat, that forms a surface layer when milk is allowed to stand 2a a food (eg a sauce, mousse, or cake filling) prepared with cream or resembling cream in consistency, richness, etc ⟨~ *of mushroom soup*⟩ b a food (eg a biscuit or soft-centred chocolate) filled with (a soft preparation resembling) whipped cream ⟨~ *cake*⟩ ⟨*a box of coffee ~s*⟩ c something having the consistency of thick cream; *esp a* usu EMULSIFIED (containing a liquid suspended in droplets in an oily base) medicinal or cosmetic preparation ⟨*skin ~*⟩ 3 the choicest part ⟨*the ~ of the crop*⟩ 4 a pale yellowish-white colour [ME *creime*, *creme*, fr MF *craime*, *cresme*, fr LL *cramum*, of Celt origin; akin to W *cramen* scab] – **creamy** *adj*, **creamily** *adv*, **creaminess** *n*

²**cream** *vt* 1a SKIM 1c b to take (the choicest part of) – usu + *off* ⟨~ *off the brightest students*⟩ 2 to work, beat, or blend to the consistency of cream or creamy froth ⟨~ *butter and sugar together*⟩ 3 to provide, prepare, or treat with cream; *also* to prepare with a cream sauce 4 to cause to form a surface layer of or like cream ⟨~ *the milk*⟩ 5 *NAm informal* to defeat thoroughly ⟨*was ~ed in the first round*⟩ ~ *vi* 1 to form cream or a surface layer like the cream on standing milk 2 to break into a creamy froth

**cream cheese** *n* a mild white soft unripened cheese made from whole milk enriched with cream

**creamer** /'kreemə/ *n* 1 a can or pan for separating cream from milk 2 a small vessel (eg a jug) for serving cream

**creamery** /'kreeməri/ *n* an establishment where butter and cheese are made or where milk and milk products (eg cream) are prepared or sold – compare DAIRY

**cream of tartar** /'tahtə/ *n* a white chemical compound, $KHC_4H_4O_6$, used esp in baking powders or laxatives and for soldering metals

**cream puff** *n, chiefly NAm* an ineffectual person; a sissy [²*puff* 2]

**cream soda** *n* a soft drink containing CARBON DIOXIDE to make it fizzy, flavoured with vanilla, and sweetened with sugar

**cream tea** *n* a mid-afternoon refreshment at which scones accompanied by jam and whipped cream are served ⟨*a Cornish ~*⟩

¹**crease** /krees/ *n* 1 a line or mark made (as if) by folding a pliable substance 2a a specially marked area in various sports; *esp* an area surrounding the goal in lacrosse, hockey, etc into which an attacking player may not precede the ball or puck b the BOWLING CREASE or POPPING CREASE of a cricket pitch [prob alter. of earlier *creaste*, fr ME *creste* crest] – **creaseless** *adj*

²**crease** *vt* 1 to make a crease in or on; wrinkle 2 *chiefly Br informal* 2a to cause much amusement to – often + *up* ⟨*her hat was so small that it ~d me up*⟩ b to tire out ⟨*he was ~d when he reached home*⟩ ~ *vi* to become creased or wrinkled – **creaser** *n*

**create** /kri'ayt/ *vt* 1 to bring into existence ⟨*God ~d the heaven and the earth* – Gen 1:1 (AV)⟩ 2 to invest with a new form, office, or rank ⟨*was ~d a peer of the realm*⟩ 3 to produce, cause ⟨~ *problems*⟩ ⟨~ *a disturbance*⟩ 4 to produce (works of art, inventions, ideas, etc) through imaginative skill ~ *vi, Br slang* to make a fuss about something, esp vocally **synonyms** see ¹MAKE [ME *createn*, fr L *creatus*, pp of *creare*]

**creatine**, **creatin** /'kree-ə,teen/ *n* a white nitrogen-containing substance, $COOHCH_2N(CH_3)C(NH)NH_2$, that occurs esp in the muscles of VERTEBRATE animals either free or as CREATINE PHOSPHATE, and that is weakly alkaline [ISV, fr Gk *kreat-*, *kreas* flesh – more at RAW]

**creatine phosphate** *n* a chemical compound, $CO_2HCH_2N(CH_3)C(NH)NHPO_3H_2$, of creatine and PHOSPHORIC ACID that occurs esp in the muscles of VERTEBRATE animals, where it is an energy source for muscle contraction

**creatinine** /kree'atineen/ *n* a chemical compound, $C_4H_7N_3O$, formed naturally from the breakdown of creatine and found esp in muscle, blood, and urine [Ger *kreatinin,* fr *kreatin* creatine]

**creation** /kri'aysh(ə)n/ *n* 1 the act of creating; *specif, often cap* the act of bringing the world into ordered existence 2 something that is created: eg 2a the world b *taking sing or pl vb* creatures singly or collectively c an original work of art d a new usu striking article of clothing ⟨*a ~ in purple and gold stripes*⟩

**creative** /kri'aytiv/ *adj* 1 marked by the ability or power to create; given to creating 2 having the quality of something created imaginatively rather than imitated ⟨*the ~ arts*⟩ – **creatively** *adv,* **creativeness** *n*

**creator** /kri'aytə/ *n* a person who creates, usu by bringing something new or original into being; *esp, cap* God

**creature** /'kreechə/ *n* 1 something created ⟨*~s of fantasy*⟩ 2a an animate being; *esp* a non-human one b a human being; a person – used esp as a term expressing scorn or pity ⟨*poor ~*⟩ ⟨*the wicked ~!*⟩ 3 one who is the servile dependant or tool of another ⟨*he's the ~ of his boss; he does anything she asks*⟩ [ME, fr OF, fr LL *creatura,* fr L *creatus,* pp] – **creatural** *adj,* **creaturehood** *n,* **creatureliness** *n,* **creaturely** *adj*

**creature comfort** *n usu pl* something (eg food or warmth) that gives bodily comfort; a luxury

**crèche** /kresh/ *n* 1 a picture or model of the Nativity scene 2 a home for foundlings 3 *chiefly Br* a centre where children under school age are looked after while their mothers are at work; *broadly* DAY NURSERY [Fr, fr OF *creche* manger, crib, of Gmc origin; akin to OHG *krippa* manger – more at CRIB]

**credence** /'kreed(ə)ns/ *n* mental acceptance of or belief in something as true or real ⟨*give ~ to gossip*⟩ – compare LETTERS OF CREDENCE [ME, fr MF or ML; MF, fr ML *credentia,* fr L *credent-, credens,* prp of *credere* to believe, trust – more at CREED]

**credence table, credence** *n* 1 a Renaissance side table or sideboard used chiefly for gold or silver dishes, cutlery, etc 2 a small table or ledge where the communion bread and wine rest before consecration in many Christian churches, esp Roman Catholic and Anglican [(1) MF *credence,* fr OIt *credenza;* (2) Fr *crédence,* fr MF *credence*]

**credential** /kri'densh(ə)l/ *n* 1 *pl* something, esp a letter, that gives evidence of the status or authority of the bearer 2 a certificate, diploma

**credenza** /kri'denzə/ *n* 1 CREDENCE TABLE 1 2 a sideboard or bookcase patterned after a Renaissance credence table; *esp* one without legs [It, lit., belief, confidence, fr ML *credentia;* fr its being orig used for the tasting of food and drink to ensure they were not poisoned]

**credibility gap** /ˌkredə'bilati/ *n* a lack of credibility or trust, esp when caused by a discrepancy between what is claimed officially and what is seen to be true; *also* the discrepancy involved

**credible** /'kredəbl/ *adj* offering reasonable grounds for being believed or trusted [ME, fr L *credibilis,* fr *credere*] – **credibly** *adv,* **credibility** *n*

¹**credit** /'kredit/ *n* 1a the balance in a person's favour in a bank account b an amount or sum placed at a person's disposal by a bank and usu to be repaid with interest c time given for payment for goods or services provided but not immediately paid for ⟨*long-term ~*⟩ ⟨*bought it on ~*⟩ d(1) an entry on the right-hand side of an account constituting an addition to a revenue, net worth, or liability account d(2) a deduction from an expense or asset account or from an amount otherwise due 2 credence ⟨*too ready to give ~ to idle rumours*⟩ 3a influence, power, or recognition derived from enjoying the confidence, either deserved or undeserved, of another or others; standing ⟨*she brought ~ to her school*⟩ b good name; reputation, esteem; *also* financial or commercial trustworthiness 4 an acknowledgment by name of a contributor or performer, that appears at the beginning or end of a film or a television programme; *also, pl* the list of names giving this acknowledgment 5a the passing of an examination at a level well above the minimum though not necessarily with distinction; *also* a mark or certification of such passing b the recognition by a college that a student has fulfilled one of the requirements leading to a degree 6 *archaic* the quality of being credible; credibility [MF, fr OIt *credito,* fr L *creditum* something entrusted to another, loan, fr neut of *creditus,* pp of *credere* to believe, entrust – more at CREED]

²**credit** *vt* 1 to trust in the truth of; believe 2a to enter on the credit side of an account b to place to the credit of – compare DEBIT **synonyms** see ASCRIBE [partly fr ¹*credit;* partly fr L *creditus,* pp]

**credit to** *vt* to attribute to ⟨*they* credited *the invention* to *him*⟩

**credit with** *vt* 1 to consider as being responsible for ⟨*they* credited *him* with *the invention*⟩ 2 to consider as having (a specified favourable trait or characteristic) ⟨credit *me* with *some intelligence*⟩

**creditable** /'kreditəbl/ *adj* 1 worthy of esteem or praise 2 *NAm* capable of being attributed *to* 3 *archaic* credible – **creditably** *adv,* **creditableness** *n,* **creditability** *n*

**credit account** *n* an account (eg that of a customer with a shop) that allows the deferment of payments for the purchase of goods

**credit card** *n* a card, usu issued by a bank, authorizing the purchase without immediate cash payment of goods or services which are later charged to the holder's account – compare CASH CARD, CHEQUE CARD

**credit insurance** *n* insurance protecting commercial creditors from default by a debtor

**credit limit** *n* the maximum credit allowed a buyer or borrower

**creditor** /'kreditə/ *n* one to whom a debt is owed; *esp* a person who gives credit in business and to whom money or goods are due

**credit rating** *n* RATING 2b

**credit squeeze** *n* a restriction imposed on the lending of money, and usu entailing restrictions on bank overdrafts, raised interest rates, etc; *esp* one imposed on a country's money supply by a government as an anti-inflationary measure – compare SQUEEZE 3a

'**credit-,worthy** *adj* worthy of credit; *specif* qualifying for commercial credit – **credit-worthiness** *n*

**credo** /'kreedoh, 'kray-/ *n, pl* **credos** 1 a creed; *specif* the APOSTLES' CREED or the NICENE CREED 2 a musical setting of the Creed [ME, fr L, I believe]

**credulity** /kri'dyoohlati/ *n* undue readiness to believe; gullibility

**credulous** /'kredyoolas/ *adj* 1 ready to believe, esp on slight or uncertain evidence ⟨*foreigners were ready to be ~ about America* – Marcus Cunliffe⟩ 2 showing credulity ⟨*a ~ smile*⟩ [L *credulus,* fr *credere*] – **credulously** *adv,* **credulousness** *n*

**Cree** /kree/ *n, pl* **Crees,** *esp collectively* **Cree** 1 a member of a N American Indian people of Manitoba and Saskatchewan 2 the ALGONQUIAN language of the Cree [short for earlier *Christeno,* fr CanF *Christino,* prob modif of Ojibwa *Kenistenoag*]

**creed** /kreed/ *n* 1 a brief authoritative statement of religious belief; *specif, often cap* a statement recited or sung as part of a Christian service 2 a set of fundamental beliefs or principles [ME *crede,* fr OE *crēda,* fr L *credo* (first word of the Apostles' and Nicene Creeds), fr *credere* to believe, trust, entrust; akin to OIr *cretim* I believe, Skt *śrad-dadhāti* he believes] – **creedal, credal** *adj*

**creek** /kreek/ *n* 1 *chiefly Br* a small inlet or bay narrower, and extending farther inland, than a cove 2 *chiefly NAm & Austr* a brook 3 *archaic* a narrow or winding passage [ME *crike, creke,* fr ON -*kriki* bend; akin to ON *krōkr* hook – more at CROOK] – **up the creek** *informal* 1 in difficulties 2 wrong, mistaken

**Creek** *n, pl* **Creeks,** *esp collectively* **Creek** 1 a member of a N American Indian confederation of peoples of Alabama, Georgia, and Florida, now mainly living in Oklahoma 2 the MUSKOGEAN language of the Creek peoples – **Creek** *adj*

**creel** /kreel/ *n* 1 a wickerwork basket, esp for newly caught fish 2 a wickerwork trap for catching crabs, lobsters, etc 3 a framework consisting of a bar with skewers for holding bobbins in a spinning machine [ME *creille, crele,* prob fr (assumed) MF *creille* grill, fr L *craticula* – more at GRILL]

¹**creep** /kreep/ *vi* **crept** /krept/ **1a** to move along slowly with the body close to the ground **b** to crawl on all fours ⟨*mouse* crept *into its hole*⟩ **2a** to go very slowly ⟨*the hours* crept *by*⟩ **b** to go timidly or cautiously so as to escape notice **c** to enter, advance, or develop gradually ⟨*a note of irritation* crept *into her voice*⟩ ⟨*a period of ~*ing *inflation*⟩ **3a** CRAWL **5b** ⟨*the thought made his flesh ~*⟩ **b** *of a plant* to spread or grow over a surface, rooting at intervals, or clinging with tendrils, stems, or aerial roots **4a** to slip or gradually shift position **b** to change shape permanently because of prolonged stress or heat **5** *of paint, varnish, or glaze* to fail to stay evenly spread – see also

make one's FLESH **creep** [ME *crepen,* fr OE *crēopan;* akin to Gk *grypos* curved, bent]

²**creep** *n* **1** a movement of or like creeping **2** an enclosure that young animals (eg calves) can enter for feeding, and from which adults are excluded **3** the slow change of size of an object due to prolonged exposure to heat or stress **4** *pl, informal* a distressing sensation like that caused by the creeping of insects over one's flesh; a shudder; *esp* a feeling of revulsion, apprehension, or horror ⟨*gives me the* ∼s⟩ **5** *Br informal* a person who behaves in a cringingly servile way, esp to ingratiate him-/herself

**creepage** /'kreepij/ *n* gradual movement; creep

**creeper** /'kreepə/ *n* **1** one who or that which creeps: eg **1a** a creeping plant **b** a bird (eg a treecreeper) that creeps about on trees or bushes searching for insects **c** a creeping insect or reptile **2** a grapnel **3** a device (eg a conveyor belt) for supplying or moving material in a steady flow **4** *informal* a shoe with a thick crepe rubber sole **5** CRADLE 1b(2) (low frame on castors used for working under a motor vehicle)

**creeping jenny, creeping jennie** /ˌkreeping 'jeni/ *n* a yellow-flowered trailing plant (*Lysimachia nummularia*) of the primrose family, that grows in damp places throughout Europe – called also MONEYWORT [*Jenny,* nickname for *Jane*]

**creepy** /'kreepi/ *adj, informal* producing a nervous shivery apprehension or fear ⟨*a* ∼ *horror story*⟩ – **creepily** *adv,* **creepiness** *n*

¹**creepy-crawly** /ˌkreepi 'krawli/ *adj, Br informal* creepy

²**creepy-'crawly** *n, Br informal* a small creature (eg an insect or worm); *esp* one that does not fly

**cremaster** /kri'mastə, kree-/ *n* a usu hooked projection at the hind end of the pupa of butterflies and moths, that serves to suspend the pupa [NL, fr Gk *kremastēr* suspender, fr *kremannynai* to hang]

**cremate** /kri'mayt/ *vt* to reduce (a dead body) to ashes by burning [L *crematus,* pp of *cremare* to burn up, cremate] – **cremation** *n*

**crematorium** /ˌkremə'tawri-əm/ *n, pl* **crematoriums, crematoria** /-riə/ a place where cremation is carried out

**crematory** /'kremətəri/ *n, NAm* a crematorium – **crematory** *adj*

**crème** /krem (*Fr* krɛm)/ *n* CREAM 2a,b [Fr, fr OF *cresme* – more at CREAM]

**crème brulée** /ˌkrem brooh'lay/ *n* a thick custard made with eggs and cream and topped with caramelized sugar [Fr, lit., burnt cream]

**crème caramel** /ˌkrem karə'mel/ *n* a dessert made in a mould with eggs and milk and with sugar that caramelizes during cooking

**crème de la crème** /ˌkrem də lah 'krem/ *n* the very best [Fr, lit., cream of the cream]

**crème de menthe** /də 'mont (*Fr* də mãt)/ *n* a sweet green or white mint-flavoured liqueur [Fr, lit., cream of mint]

**crenate** /'kreenayt/, **crenated** /-aytid/ *adj* having the edge cut into rounded scallops ⟨*a* ∼ *leaf*⟩ [NL *crenatus,* fr ML *crena* notch] – **crenately** *adv*

**crenation** /kri'naysh(ə)n/ *n* **1** a crenate formation; *esp* one of the rounded projections on an edge (eg of a leaf) **2** the shrinkage of RED BLOOD CELLS in a solution that is HYPERTONIC (more concentrated than the solution inside the cells), resulting in scalloped edges

**crenel** /'krenl/ *n* a crenellation [MF *crenel,* fr OF, dim. of *cren* notch, fr *crener* to notch; akin to ML *crena* notch]

**crenellated** /'krenəˌlaytid/ *adj* having battlements

**crenellation** /ˌkrenə'laysh(ə)n/ *n* an indentation in a battlement

**crenelle** /krə'nel/ *n* a crenellation

**crenulate** /'krenyoolət, -layt/ *also* **crenulated** /-ˌlaytid/ *adj* having an irregularly wavy or serrated outline ⟨*a* ∼ *shoreline*⟩ ⟨*a* ∼ *leaf*⟩ [NL *crenulatus,* fr *crenula,* dim. of ML *crena*] – **crenulation** *n*

**creole** /'kree-ohl/ *adj* **1** *often cap* of Creoles or their language **2** of or being a domestic animal (eg a racehorse) of a native breed or strain, esp in Latin America **3** prepared with rice, OKRA (type of tropical vegetable), tomatoes, peppers, onions, and high seasoning ⟨*shrimp* ∼⟩

**Creole** *n* **1** a native-born person of European descent in the W Indies or Spanish America **2** a white descendant of early French or Spanish settlers of the Gulf States of the USA who retains their speech and culture **3** a person of mixed French or Spanish and Negro descent in the W Indies, speaking a dialect

of French or Spanish **4a** (one speaking) the French dialect of S Louisiana **b** (a) Haitian **c** *not cap* a language based on two or more languages that serves as the native language of its speaker, esp in the Caribbean area – compare PIDGIN [Fr *créole,* fr Sp *criollo,* fr Pg *crioulo* white person born in the colonies, fr *criar* to rear, breed, fr L *creare* to create, beget]

**creosol** /'kree-əsol, -sohl/ *n* an aromatic oily liquid chemical compound, $CH_2O(CH_2)C_6H_3OH$, that is one of the active constituents of creosote [ISV *creos*ote + *-ol*]

¹**creosote** /'kree-əˌsoht/ *n* **1** a clear or yellowish oily liquid mixture of chemical compounds obtained from WOOD TAR and used esp as an antiseptic or disinfectant **2** **creosote, coal-tar creosote** a brownish oily liquid consisting chiefly of aromatic chemical compounds obtained from COAL TAR and used esp as a wood preservative [Ger *kreosot,* fr Gk *kreas* flesh + *sōtēr* preserver, fr *sōzein* to preserve, fr *sōs* safe – more at RAW, THUMB; fr its antiseptic properties]

²**creosote** *vt* to treat with creosote

**crepe, crêpe** /krep, krayp/ *n* **1** a light crinkled fabric woven of any of various fibres, esp silk or cotton **2** CRAPE 2 (band worn as a sign of mourning) **3** a small very thin pancake, usu rolled round a sweet or savoury filling [Fr *crêpe,* fr MF *crespe,* fr *crespe* curled, fr L *crispus*] – **crepe** *adj,* **crepey, crepy** *adj*

**crepe de chine** /də 'sheen/ *n, often cap 2nd C* a soft fine clothing crepe, originally of silk [Fr *crêpe de Chine,* lit., China crepe]

**crepe paper** *n* thin paper with a crinkled or puckered texture, often used for gift wrapping

**crepe rubber** *n* crude or synthetic rubber in the form of usu colourless to brown crinkled sheets, used esp for shoe soles and in the making of medical and surgical goods

**crepe sole** *n* (a shoe with) a crepe rubber sole

**crêpe suzette** /sooh'zet/ *n, pl* **crêpes suzette** /∼/, **crêpe suzettes** /∼, -'zets/ a thin folded or rolled pancake in a hot orange-butter sauce that is sprinkled with a liqueur (eg cognac or curaçao) and set alight for serving [Fr *crêpe Suzette,* fr *crêpe* pancake + *Suzette,* dim of *Suzanne* Susan]

**crepitate** /'krepitayt/ *vi* to make a crackling sound; crackle – used chiefly in medicine [L *crepitatus,* pp of *crepitare* to crackle, fr *crepitus,* pp of *crepare* to rattle, crack – more at RAVEN] – **crepitant** *adj*

**crepitation** /ˌkrepi'taysh(ə)n/ *n* a crackling or grating sound: eg **a** one from the lungs that can be heard through a stethoscope and is characteristic of pneumonia **b** one produced by the fractured ends of a bone rubbing against each other

**crepitus** /'krepitəs/ *n* crepitation [L, fr *crepitus,* pp]

**crept** /krept/ *past of* CREEP

**crepuscular** /kri'puskyoolə/ *adj* **1** *esp of an animal* active in the twilight ⟨∼ *insects*⟩ **2** *formal* of or resembling twilight; dim [L *crepusculum* twilight, fr *creper* dusky]

¹**crescendo** /krə'shendoh/ *n, pl* **crescendos, crescendoes 1** a gradual increase; *esp* a gradual increase in volume of a musical passage **2** a crescendo musical passage **3** *informal* a climax – disapproved of by some people [It, lit., growing, fr L *crescendum,* gerund of *crescere* to grow] – **crescendo** *vi*

²**crescendo** *adv or adj* with an increase in volume – used as a direction in music

¹**crescent** /'krezənt/ *n* **1** (the curved shape of) the moon at any stage between new moon and first quarter, or between last quarter and the succeeding new moon **2** something shaped like a crescent with a convex and a concave curve **3** a curved street of usu terraced houses **4** *often cap* a crescent-shaped symbol that is the sign of the faith of Muslims [ME *cressant,* fr MF *creissant,* fr prp of *creistre* to grow, increase, fr L *crescere;* akin to OHG *hirsi* millet, L *creare* to create, Gk *koros* boy] – **crescentic** *adj*

²**crescent** /'kresənt/ *adj, formal* marked by an increase; growing [L *crescent-, crescens,* prp of *crescere*]

**cresol** /'kreesol, -sohl/ *n* any of three related poisonous colourless PHENOLS, $C_6H_4(CH_3)OH$, used esp as disinfectants and antiseptics and in the manufacture of plastics [ISV, irreg fr *creos*ote]

**cress** /kres/ *n* any of numerous plants (genera *Lepidium, Cardamine, Arabis,* etc) of the cabbage family usu with moderately pungent leaves, used raw in salads and garnishes; *esp* one (*Lepidium sativum*) cultivated throughout Europe and eaten when still a seedling ⟨*mustard and* ∼⟩ – compare WATERCRESS [ME *cresse,* fr OE *cærse, cressa;* akin to OHG *kressa* cress]

**cresset** /'kresit/ *n* an iron basket that is mounted on a pole or a wall and is used to hold material (eg pitch or wood) that is burnt for illumination or as a beacon [ME, fr MF, fr OF *craisset*, fr *craisse* grease – more at GREASE]

¹**crest** /krest/ *n* **1a** a showy tuft or growth of feathers, fur, or skin on the head of an animal, esp a bird **b** the plume or emblem worn on a knight's helmet; *also* the ridge of a helmet **c(1)** a symbol of a family, office, etc shown on the helmet above a coat of arms **c(2)** COAT OF ARMS 2a – not used in heraldry **d** the upper muscular ridge of a horse's neck from which the mane grows; *also* the mane **2** something suggesting a crest, esp in being an upper prominence, edge, or limit: e g **2a** a peak; *esp* the top line of a mountain or hill **b** the ridge or top of a wave or roof **3** a high point of an action or process; a climax, culmination ⟨*at the ~ of his fame*⟩ [ME *creste*, fr MF, fr L *crista*; akin to OE *hrisian* to shake, L *curvus* curved – more at CROWN] – **crestal** *adj*, **crestless** *adj*

²**crest** *vt* **1** to provide with a crest; crown **2** to reach the crest of ⟨*~ed the hill and looked about him*⟩ ~ *vi*, *esp of a wave* to rise to a crest

**crested** /'krestid/ *adj* **1** having a crest ⟨*a ~ bird*⟩ **2** marked or decorated with a crest or COAT OF ARMS ⟨*~ crockery*⟩

**crested newt** *n* a widely distributed European newt (*Triturus cristatus*) the male of which has a tall toothed crest on the back in spring

**crestfallen** /'krest,fawlən/ *adj* **1** having a drooping crest or hanging head **2** feeling shame or humiliation; dejected – **crestfallenly** *adv*, **crestfallenness** *n*

**cresylic** /kri'silik/ *adj* of cresol or creosote [ISV, fr *cresol* + *-yl* + *-ic*]

**cretaceous** /kri'tayshəs/ *adj* **1** resembling or containing chalk **2** *cap* of or being the (system of rocks formed in the) last period of the MESOZOIC era during which chalk deposits were formed and flowering plants first appeared [L *cretaceus*, fr *creta* chalk] – **cretaceous** *n*, **cretaceously** *adv*

**cretin** /'kretin/ *n* a person afflicted with cretinism; *broadly* an imbecile, idiot [Fr *crétin*, fr Fr dial. *cretin* Christian, human being, kind of idiot found in the Alps, fr L *christianus* Christian]

**cretinism** /'kretiniz(ə)m/ *n* a usu congenital abnormal condition marked by physical stunting and mental deficiency and caused by malfunctioning of the THYROID gland in infancy – **cretinoid** *adj*, **cretinous** *adj*, **cretinously** *adv*

**cretonne** /'kre,ton, 'kree-, -'-/ *n* a strong unglazed printed cotton or linen cloth used esp for curtains and upholstery [Fr, fr *Creton*, village in Normandy, France] – **cretonne** *adj*

**crevasse** /krə'vas/ *n* **1** a deep crevice or fissure (e g in a glacier or the earth) **2** *NAm* a breach in a river embankment [Fr, fr OF *crevace*]

**crevice** /'krevis/ *n* a narrow opening resulting from a split or crack; a fissure [ME, fr MF *crevace*, fr OF, fr *crever* to break, fr L *crepare* to crack – more at RAVEN]

¹**crew** /krooh/ *chiefly Br past of* CROW

²**crew** *n* **1** *taking sing or pl vb* a company of people temporarily associated; an assemblage **2** *taking sing or pl vb* a company of men working on one job or under one foreman, or operating a machine **3a** *taking sing or pl vb* the personnel of a ship (excluding the captain and officers) **b** *taking pl vb* members of a crew ⟨*the captain and 50 ~*⟩ **c** *taking sing or pl vb* the people who man an aircraft in flight **d** *taking sing or pl vb* the body of men or women manning a racing shell or other rowing boat **4** *taking sing or pl vb*, *archaic* a band or force of armed men [ME *crue*, lit., reinforcement, fr MF *creue* increase, fr *creistre* to grow – more at CRESCENT] – **crewless** *adj*, **crewman** *n*

³**crew** *vb* to serve as a member of a crew (on) ⟨*~ed on the winning yacht*⟩

**crew cut** *n* a very short bristly haircut, esp for a man [prob fr its adoption by crews of rowing boats] – **crew-cut** *adj*

**crewel** /'krooh·əl/ *n* slackly twisted worsted yarn used for embroidery and tapestry work [ME *crule*]

**crewel needle** *n* a relatively long needle with a large oval eye for use esp in embroidery

**crewelwork** /'krooh·əl,wuhk/ *n* embroidery design worked with crewel

**crew neck** *n* a round flat knitted neckline on a usu knitted garment [fr the pullovers worn by crews of rowing boats]

¹**crib** /krib/ *n* **1** a manger for feeding animals **2** an enclosure, esp of framework: e g **2a** a stall for a stabled animal **b** any of various constructions resembling a crate or framework **c** a bin for storage (e g of grain) **d** a heavy supporting or strengthening framework (e g for a shaft) **3** a small narrow room or dwelling; a hut, shack **4a** a set of cards contributed to equally by each

player in cribbage for the dealer to use in adding to his/her own score **b** the game of cribbage – used esp with reference to the 4-handed version **5** CRÈCHE 1 **6** a passage taken from another piece of writing or music without acknowledgment **7** *chiefly Br informal* **7a** a literal translation; *esp* one used surreptitiously by students **b** something used for cheating in an examination (e g a list of possible answers) **8** *chiefly Br informal* a building considered with a view to unlawful entry ⟨*crack a ~*⟩ **9** *chiefly NAm* a cradle, cot [ME, fr OE *cribb*; akin to OHG *krippa* manger, Gk *griphos* reed basket, OE *cradol* cradle]

²**crib** *vb* **-bb-** *vt* **1** to confine, cramp **2** to provide with or put into a crib; *esp* to line or support with a framework of timber **3** to pilfer, steal; *esp* to plagiarize ⟨*he ~bed the idea from his brother*⟩ ~ *vi* **1a** to steal, plagiarize ⟨*he was always ~bing*⟩ **b** to use a crib; cheat **2** to have the habit of crib biting – **cribber** *n*

**cribbage** /'kribij/ *n* a card game for two, three, or four players in which each player attempts to form various counting combinations of cards – used esp with reference to the 2-handed version [¹*crib*]

**crib biting** *n* a habit of horses in which they gnaw (e g at the manger) while slobbering and sucking in air – **crib biter** *n*

**crib death** *n*, *NAm* COT DEATH

**cribriform** /'kribri,fawm/ *adj*, *anatomy & botany* pierced with small holes [L *cribrum* sieve; akin to L *cernere* to sift – more at CERTAIN]

**cricetid** /krie'setid, -'see-/ *n* any of a family (Cricetidae) of small rodents including the hamsters [deriv of NL *Cricetus*, genus name, of Slav origin; akin to Czech *křeček* hamster] – **cricetid** *adj*

¹**crick** /krik/ *n* a painful spasmodic condition of the muscles (e g of the neck or back) [ME *cryk*]

²**crick** *vt* **1** to cause a crick in (e g the neck) **2** to turn or twist (e g the head), esp into a strained position

¹**cricket** /'krikit/ *n* a leaping insect (family Gryllidae) noted for the chirping sounds produced by the male rubbing together specially modified parts of the fore wings [ME *criket*, fr MF *criquet*, of imit origin]

²**cricket** *n* a game played, esp in the Commonwealth, by a bat and hard leather ball by two sides of 11 players each on a large field with two wickets near its centre, 22 yards (19.14 metres) apart, each of which in turn is defended against the bowling and fielding of the opposing side by a batsman who also attempts to score runs for his own side [MF *criquet* stake used as target in a game of bowls] – **cricketing** *adj* – **not cricket** against the dictates of fair play; not honourable

³**cricket** *n*, *NAm or dial* a low wooden footstool [origin unknown]

**cricketer** /'krikitə/ *n* one who plays cricket

**cricoid** /'kriekoyd/ *adj* of or being a ring-shaped cartilage of the LARYNX (voice box) [NL *cricoides*, fr Gk *krikoeidēs* ring-shaped, fr *krikos* ring – more at CIRCLE]

**cri de coeur** /,kree də 'kuh/ *n*, *pl* **cris de coeur** /~/ a passionate plea or protest [Fr, lit., cry from the heart]

**crier** /'krie·ə/ *n* a person or animal that cries: **a** an officer formerly employed to make announcements in a court of law **b** TOWN CRIER **c** someone who cries his/her wares in public

**crikey** /'krieki/ *interj*, *chiefly Br slang* – used for expressing surprise or amazement; no longer in vogue [euphemism for *Christ* (cf CRIPES, CRUMBS)]

**crime** /kriem/ *n* **1** an act or omission punishable by law; *also* such violations of law collectively ⟨*the pattern of ~*⟩ **2** a grave offence, esp against morality **3** criminal activity ⟨*a life of ~*⟩ **4** *informal* something reprehensible, foolish, or disgraceful ⟨*it's a ~ to waste good food*⟩ [ME, fr L *crimen* accusation, fault, crime]

**crime against humanity** *n* an atrocity (e g extermination or enslavement) that is directed esp against an entire population or part of a population regardless of the innocence or guilt of the victims

**crime passionel** /,kreem ,pasyon'nel/ *n* a crime, usu murder, prompted by sexual jealousy [Fr, lit., crime of passion]

¹**criminal** /'kriminl/ *adj* **1** involving or being a crime **2** relating to crime or its punishment ⟨*~ law*⟩ **3** guilty of crime **4** *informal* disgraceful [ME, fr MF or LL; MF *criminel*, fr LL *criminalis*, fr L *crimin-*, *crimen* crime] – **criminalistic** *adj*, **criminally** *adv*

²**criminal** *n* one who has committed or been convicted of a crime

**criminal court** *n* a court that has jurisdiction to try offenders against criminal law and to sentence them

**criminal damage** *n* the offence of wilfully damaging or destroying property belonging to another

**criminal law** *n* the law relating to crimes and their punishments

**criminate** /'kriminayt/ *vt, formal* 1 to accuse of a crime 2 to incriminate 3 to represent as criminal; condemn [L *criminatus*, pp of *criminari*, fr *crimin-*, *crimen* accusation] – **crimination** *n*

**criminology** /,krimi'noləji/ *n* the scientific study of crime as a social phenomenon, of criminals, and of penal treatment [It *criminologia*, fr L *crimin-*, *crimen* + It *-o-* + *-logia* -logy] – **criminologist** *n*, **criminological** *adj*, **criminologically** *adv*

**¹crimp** /krimp/ *vt* 1 to cause to become wavy, bent, or warped ⟨~ed *her hair*⟩: eg **1a** to form (eg leather or fabric) into a desired shape **b** to roll or curl the edge of (eg a steel panel) **c** to pinch or press together (eg the edges of a pie crust) in order to seal **d** to crush (the stems of a crop) between the rollers of a crimper 2 *NAm informal* to put a restriction on; inhibit [D or LG *krimpen* to shrivel; akin to LG *krampe* hook – more at CRAMP]

**²crimp** *n* 1 something produced (as if) by crimping: eg **1a** a section of artificially waved or curled hair; a wave ⟨*he put a* ~ *in her fringe*⟩ **b** a succession of waves (eg in wool fibre) 2 *NAm informal* something that cramps or inhibits

**³crimp** *n or vt, archaic* (a person employed in former times) to entrap or force (people) into military or sea service [perh fr ¹*crimp*]

**crimper** /'krimpə/ *n* 1 one who or that which crimps; *esp* a farm machine used to crimp the stems of a crop (eg hay) after cutting to make drying easier 2 *slang* a hairdresser

**crimple** /'krimpl/ *vt* to crumple, crinkle [ME *crymplen*]

**Crimplene** /'krimpleen/ *trademark* – used for a textured continuous-filament POLYESTER material which is crease-resistant

**¹crimson** /'krimz(ə)n/ *n or adj* (a) deep purplish red [ME *crimisin*, fr OSp *cremesin*, fr Ar *qirmizī*, fr *qirmiz* kermes]

**²crimson** *vb* to make or become crimson

**¹cringe** /krinj/ *vi* 1 to contract one's muscles involuntarily; wince 2 to shrink in fear or servility 3 to approach someone with fawning self-abasement; CRAWL 3 *synonyms* see ¹RECOIL [ME *crengen;* akin to OE *cringan* to yield, *cradol* cradle] – **cringer** *n*, **cringingly** *adv*

**²cringe** *n* a cringing act; *specif* a servile bow

**cringle** /'kring-gl/ *n* an eyelet or rope loop worked into or attached to the edge of a sail to which to secure a rope [LG *kringel*, dim. of *kring* ring; akin to OE *cradol* cradle]

**¹crinkle** /'kringkl/ *vi* **1a** to form many short bends or turns **b** to wrinkle, ripple 2 to make a thin crackling sound; rustle ⟨*crinkling silks*⟩ ~ *vt* to cause to crinkle [ME *crynkelen;* akin to OE *cringan* to yield]

**²crinkle** *n* 1 a wrinkle, fold 2 any of several plant diseases marked by crinkling of leaves ⟨*strawberry* ~⟩ – **crinkly** *adj*

**crinoid** /'krienoyd, 'kri-/ *n* any of a large class (Crinoidea of the phylum Echinodermata) of marine INVERTEBRATE animals related to the starfish, SEA URCHINS, etc and usu having a somewhat cup-shaped body with five or more feathery arms – called also SEA LILY [deriv of Gk *krinon* lily] – **crinoid** *adj*

**crinoline** /'krinəlin/ *n* 1 an open-weave fabric of horsehair or cotton that is usu stiffened and used esp for interlinings and millinery 2 a padded or hooped framework supporting a full skirt; *also* such a skirt worn by women in the mid 19th century [Fr, fr It *crinolino*, fr *crino* horsehair (fr L *crinis* hair; akin to L *crista* crest) + *lino* flax, linen, fr L *linum*] – **crinoline** *adj*

**criollo** /kri'oh(l)yoh/ *n, pl* **criollos** 1 a person born and usu raised in S America; *esp* one of Spanish descent 2 a domestic animal of a breed or strain developed in Latin America; *esp* a breed of strong hardy horses developed esp in Argentina [(1) Sp; (2) AmerSp, fr Sp – more at CREOLE] – **criollo** *adj*

**cripes** /krieps/ *interj, chiefly Br slang* – used for expressing surprise or amazement; no longer in vogue [euphemism for *Christ* (cf CRIKEY, CRUMBS)]

**¹cripple** /'kripl/ *n* 1 a lame or partly disabled person or animal 2 a person who is deficient in a specified way ⟨*an emotional* ~⟩ [ME *cripel*, fr OE *crypel;* akin to OE *crēopan* to creep – more at CREEP] – **cripple** *adj*

**²cripple** *vt* 1 to deprive of the use of a limb, esp a leg; disable 2 to deprive of strength, efficiency, wholeness, or capability for service ⟨*a crippling rate of interest*⟩ – **crippler** *n*

**crise** /kreez/ *n* 1 a sudden attack (as if) of a medical disorder – used chiefly in French phrases 2 *chiefly humorous* CRISIS 3b [Fr, crisis, fr L *crisis*]

**crise de nerfs** /də 'neəf/ *n, pl* **crises de nerfs** /~/ a fit of hysterical anxiety [Fr, lit., crisis of nerves]

**crisis** /'kriesis/ *n, pl* **crises** /'krieseez/ **1a** the turning point for better or worse in a short-lived and usu severe disease or fever **b** a sudden attack of pain, distress, or disordered function **c** an emotionally significant event or radical change of status in a person's life 2 the decisive moment (eg in a literary plot) **3a** an unstable or crucial time or state of affairs; *esp* one whose outcome will make a decisive difference for better or worse **b** a minor but annoying disruption of the smooth running of events ⟨*a* ~ *in the kitchen*⟩ [L, fr Gk *krisis*, lit., decision, fr *krinein* to decide – more at CERTAIN]

**¹crisp** /krisp/ *adj* **1a** curly, wavy; *also* having close stiff or wiry curls or waves **b** having the surface roughened into small folds or curling wrinkles **2a** easily crumbled; brittle, dry ⟨~ *snow*⟩ ⟨~ *bacon*⟩ **b** desirably stiff, fresh, or firm yet not very strong ⟨*a* ~ *apple*⟩ ⟨*the* ~ *pages of a new book*⟩ ⟨*a* ~ *pound note*⟩ **3a** sharp, clean-cut, and clear ⟨*a* ~ *illustration*⟩ **b** noticeably neat ⟨*a* ~ *white uniform*⟩ **c** sprightly, lively ⟨~ *banter between the debating opponents*⟩ **d** *of weather* briskly cold; frosty; *also* invigorating because of some slight degree of cold ⟨~ *autumn air*⟩ [ME, fr OE, fr L *crispus;* akin to L *curvus* curved – more at CROWN] – **crisply** *adv*, **crispness** *n*

**²crisp** *vt* 1 to curl, crimp 2 to make or keep crisp ⟨~ *the bread in the oven*⟩ ~ *vi* to become crisp – **crisper** *n*

**³crisp** *n* 1 something crisp or brittle ⟨*burnt to a* ~⟩ 2 *chiefly Br* a thin slice of potato that is fried crisp, usu salted, and sometimes flavoured and sold in small packets

**crispation** /kri'spaysh(ə)n/ *n* 1 curling or being curled 2 a slight spasmodic muscular contraction

**crispbread** /'krisp,bred/ *n* a plain dry unsweetened biscuit that is made from crushed grain (eg rye or wheat) which may have some portion of the starch removed and is often recommended as a food in a low-calorie diet

**crispen** /'krispən/ *vb* to make or become crisp

**crisper** /'krispə/ *n* one who or that which crisps or keeps crisp; *specif* a compartment at the bottom of a refrigerator for keeping vegetables, esp salad vegetables, cool

**crispy** /'krispi/ *adj* crisp – **crispiness** *n*

**¹crisscross** /'kris,kros/ *adj or n* (marked or characterized by) a crisscrossing pattern or network [partly fr obs *christcross*, *crisscross* (mark of a cross); partly redupl of ¹*cross*]

**²crisscross** *vt* 1 to mark with intersecting lines 2 to pass back and forth through or over ~ *vi* to go or pass back and forth

**crista** /'kristə/ *n, pl* **cristae** /'kristi/ any of the inwardly projecting folds of the inner membrane of a MITOCHONDRION (energy-producing structure in a cell) [NL, fr L, crest]

**cristobalite** /kri'stohbə,liet/ *n* a white silica, $SiO_2$, that is stable at high temperatures and is found in volcanic rocks [Ger *cristobalit*, fr Cerro San *Cristóbal*, site in Mexico]

**criterion** /krie'tiəri·ən/ *n, pl* **criteria** /-riə/ *also* **criterions** a standard on which a judgment or decision may be based ⟨*that is his* ~⟩ ⟨*he uses very rigorous* criteria⟩ [Gk *kritērion*, fr *krinein* to judge, decide – more at CERTAIN]

   *usage* The plural **criteria** is now sometimes treated as a singular noun ⟨*this* criteria⟩, but this usage is disapproved of by many people.

**cri'terion-,referenced** *adj* being a system of marking, esp of GCE O Level subjects, awarding marks for performance, skill, and knowledge, in contrast with NORM-REFERENCED marking in which each grade is awarded to a specified percentage of the entry

**criterium** /krie'tiəri·əm/ *n* a bicycle race consisting of several laps of a circuit on public roads (eg in a town centre) closed for the occasion [Fr *critérium*, lit., criterion, fr LL *criterium*, fr Gk *kritērion*]

**¹critic** /'kritik/ *n* one who criticizes: eg **a** one who engages, esp professionally, in the analysis, evaluation, or appreciation of works of art or literature **b** one who tends to judge harshly or to be overcritical of minor faults [L *criticus*, fr Gk *kritikos*, fr *kritikos* able to discern or judge, fr *krinein* to judge]

**²critic** *n, archaic* (a) criticism [Gk *kritikē* art of the critic, fr fem of *kritikos* able to discern]

**critical** /'kritikl/ *adj* **1a** inclined to criticize severely and unfavourably **b** consisting of or involving criticism ⟨~ *writings*⟩ **c** exercising or involving careful judgment or evaluation **d** including variant readings and scholarly emendations ⟨*a* ~ *edition*⟩ **2a** of or being a turning point or specially important juncture ⟨~ *phase*⟩ **b** of or being a state in which or a measurement, point, etc at which some quality, property, or phenomenon undergoes a definite change ⟨~ *temperature*⟩ **c** crucial, decisive ⟨~ *test*⟩ **d** in or approaching a state of crisis **3** *of a nuclear reactor* sustaining a chain reaction – chiefly in **go critical** – **critically** *adv*, **criticalness** *n*, **criticality** *n*

*synonyms* **Critical, crucial**, and **decisive** are all used of something that is a turning point, with attendant risk and suspense as to the outcome. **Critical** emphasizes the importance of the moment of crisis ⟨*a* **critical** *choice*⟩. **Crucial** expresses the effect on future events ⟨*a* **crucial** *decision*⟩. **Decisive** suggests that the crisis is resolved and the issue has been decided ⟨*scored a* **decisive** *goal*⟩.

**critical angle** *n* **1** the smallest angle of incident light reflected onto an interior surface at which TOTAL INTERNAL REFLECTION takes place **2** the ANGLE OF ATTACK at which the flow of air round an aerofoil changes abruptly or at which some important aerodynamic phenomenon occurs – called also STALLING ANGLE

**critical mass** *n* **1** the minimum mass of fissionable material that can sustain a nuclear chain reaction **2** an amount of something or number of items that is the necessary minimum for the beginning or continuance of a process

**critical path** *n* a sequence of activities that forms part of a complex activity, and whose timing determines the expected completion time of the complex activity

**critical region** *n* the set of outcomes of a statistical test for which the NULL HYPOTHESIS (hypothesis that a difference between two samples is due to chance) is to be rejected – used by some statisticians to denote the set of outcomes for which the null hypothesis is to be accepted

**criticism** /'kriti,siz(ə)m/ *n* **1a** the act of criticizing, usu unfavourably ⟨*the new manager was the victim of* ~⟩ **b** a critical observation or remark **c** a critique **2** the art or act of analysing and evaluating works of art or literature **3** the scientific investigation of literary documents (eg the Bible) with regard to such matters as origin, text, composition, character, or history – compare FORM CRITICISM, HIGHER CRITICISM, LOWER CRITICISM, TEXTUAL CRITICISM

**critic·ize, -ise** /'kriti,siez/ *vt* **1** to consider the merits and demerits of and judge accordingly; evaluate **2** to stress the faults of; cavil at ~ *vi* to criticize something or somebody – **criticizable** *adj*, **criticizer** *n*

**critique** /kri'teek/ *n* an act of criticizing; *esp* a critical estimate or discussion (eg an essay, article, or book) [alter. of ²*critic*]

**critter** /'kritə/ *n, dial* a creature [by alter.]

¹**croak** /krohk/ *vi* **1a** to make a croak **b** to speak in a hoarse throaty voice **2** *slang* to die ~ *vt* **1** to utter in a hoarse raucous voice **2** *slang* to kill [ME *croken*, of imit origin]

²**croak** *n* a deep hoarse cry characteristic of a frog or toad – **croaky** *adj*

**croaker** /'krohkə/ *n* **1** an animal that croaks **2** any of various tropical fishes (esp family Sciaenidae) that produce croaking or grunting noises

**Croat** /'kroh,at/ *n* a Croatian [NL *Croata*, fr Serbo-Croatian *Hrvat*]

**Croatian** /kroh'aysh(ə)n/ *n* **1** a native or inhabitant of Croatia **2** a south Slavonic language spoken by the Croatians and differing from Serbian only in being written in the Latin alphabet – **Croatian** *adj*

¹**crochet** /'krohshay/ *n* the act or process of crocheting; *also* crocheted work [Fr, hook, crochet, fr MF, dim. of *croche* hook, of Scand origin; akin to ON *krōkr* hook – more at CROOK]

²**crochet** *vt* to make (eg fabric, a garment, or a design) by drawing a single continuous yarn or thread into a pattern of interlocked loops using a hooked needle ~ *vi* to do or make crochet work – **crocheter** *n*

**crocidolite** /kroh'sidəliet/ *n* a fibrous blue or green mineral of the AMPHIBOLE group that occurs esp in asbestos [Ger *krokydolith*, fr Gk *krokyd-, krokys* nap on cloth + Ger *-lith* -lite]

¹**crock** /krok/ *n* **1** a thick earthenware pot or jar **2** a piece of broken earthenware used esp to cover the hole at the bottom of a flowerpot for drainage purposes **3** colouring matter that rubs off from cloth or dyed leather **4** *dial* soot, smut **5** *Can* a bottle of alcohol (eg whisky) [ME, fr OE *crocc*; akin to MHG *krūche* crock; (4) fr its formation on cooking pots]

²**crock** *vi* to transfer colour when rubbed ⟨*a suede that will not* ~⟩ ~ *vt, dial* to soil with crock; smudge

³**crock** *n, informal* **1** something (eg a vehicle) that is broken down, disabled, or impaired **2** an elderly disabled person [ME *crok* old disabled animal, prob of Scand origin; akin to Norw dial. *krokje* broken-down horse or person]

⁴**crock** *vb* to (cause to) become disabled or break down – sometimes + *up*

**crockery** /'krokəri/ *n* earthenware or china tableware, esp for everyday domestic use

**crocket** /'krokit/ *n* a carved ornament, usu in the form of curved foliage, placed at regular intervals on the edge of a gable, or spire, or canopy on Gothic buildings [ME *croket*, fr ONF *croquet* crook, dim. of *croc* hook, of Scand origin; akin to ON *krōkr* hook] – **crocketed** *adj*

**crock pot** *n* a deep round stoneware vessel with a removable inner bowl and a heating element that is used to cook food slowly

**crocodile** /'krokədiel/ *n* **1a** any of several large voracious thick-skinned long-bodied aquatic reptiles (eg of the genus *Crocodylus*) that live in tropical and subtropical waters; *broadly* a crocodilian **b** the skin or hide of a crocodile; *also* leather prepared from this **2** *archaic* one who hypocritically affects sorrow **3** *Br* a line of people (eg schoolchildren) walking in pairs [ME & L; ME *cocodrille*, fr OF, fr ML *cocodrillus*, alter. of L *crocodilus*, fr Gk *krokodilos* lizard, crocodile, fr *krokē* pebble + *drilos* worm; akin to Skt *śarkara* pebble – more at SUGAR]

**crocodile bird** *n* an African PLOVER (*Pluvianus aegypticus*) that alights on the crocodile and eats its insect parasites

**crocodile tears** *n pl* false or affected tears; hypocritical sorrow [fr an ancient belief that crocodiles shed tears over their prey]

**crocodilian** /,krokə'dili-ən/ *n* any of an order (Loricata) of reptiles including the crocodiles, alligators, caymans, and related extinct forms – **crocodilian** *adj*

**crocoisite** /'krokoh·i,siet/ *n* crocoite

**crocoite** /'krokoh,iet/ *n* a rare bright red or orange mineral consisting essentially of lead chromate, $PbCrO_4$ [Ger *krokoisit*, *krokoit*, fr Fr *crocoise*, fr Gk *krokoeis* saffron-coloured, fr *krokos*]

**crocus** /'krohkəs/ *n, pl* **crocuses 1** any of a large genus (*Crocus*) of usu early-flowering plants of the iris family that grow from bulbs and have a single yellow, blue, purple, or white flower and slender leaves **2a** a dark red FERRIC OXIDE used for polishing metals **b** SAFFRON **2** [NL, genus name, fr L, saffron, fr Gk *krokos*, of Sem origin]

**croft** /kroft/ *n, chiefly Br* **1** a small enclosed field, usu adjoining a house **2** a small farm on often poor land, esp in Scotland, worked by a tenant [ME, fr OE; akin to OE *crēopan* to creep – more at CREEP] – **crofter** *n*

**crofting** /'krofting/ *n, chiefly Br* the system of working the land as crofts

**croissant** /'kwahsong (*Fr* krwasõ)/ *n* a usu flaky rich crescent-shaped roll of bread or yeast-leavened pastry [Fr, lit., crescent, fr MF *creissant*]

**Croix de Guerre** /,krwa də 'geə (*Fr* krwa də ge:r)/ *n* the highest French military decoration [Fr, lit., war cross]

**Cro-Magnon** /,kroh 'manyən, 'magnən/ *n* a tall erect race of prehistoric human beings known from skeletal remains found chiefly in S France, having relatively large brains, and classified as the same species (*Homo sapiens*) as recent man [*Cro-Magnon*, a cave near Les Eyzies in France]

**cromlech** /'kromlək/ *n* **1** a megalithic burial chamber – no longer used technically **2** a circle of large MONOLITHS (standing stones), usu enclosing a mound or burial chamber [W, lit., bent stone]

**crone** /krohn/ *n* a withered old woman [ME, fr ONF *carogne*, lit., carrion, fr (assumed) VL *caronia* – more at CARRION]

**crony** /'krohni/ *n* **1** a close friend, esp of long standing; a chum **2** a member of a small group who share the same usu undesirable attitudes [alter. of obs *chrony*, prob fr Gk *chronios* long-lasting, fr *chronos* time]

¹**crook** /krook/ *n* **1** an implement or part of something having a bent or hooked form: eg **1a** a pothook **b(1)** a shepherd's staff **b(2)** a bishop's or abbot's crosier **2** a bend, curve **3** *informal* a person given to criminal practices [ME *crok*, fr ON *krōkr* hook; akin to OE *cradol* cradle]

²**crook** *vt* BEND **2a** ⟨*he* ~*ed his finger*⟩ ~ *vi* to curve, wind ⟨*the river* ~*ed behind the hill*⟩

³**crook** *adj, Austr & NZ informal* **1a** bad, unpleasant **b** not in correct working order; broken ⟨*this car is* ~⟩ **2** dishonest **3** ill ⟨*I feel* ~⟩ [perh alter. of Austr slang *cronk* (ill), fr Yiddish or Ger *krank*, fr MHG *kranc* weak] – **go crook** *Austr & NZ informal* to lose one's temper

**crookback** /'krook,bak/ *n, obs* a hunchback – **crookbacked** *adj*

**crooked** /'krookid; *sense 3* krookt/ *adj* **1** having or marked by a crook or curve; bent **2** not morally straightforward; *also* dishonest **3** *Austr informal* angry, irritable – **crookedly** *adv,* **crookedness** *n*

**Crookes tube** /krooks/ *n* a gas DISCHARGE TUBE used to demonstrate the properties of CATHODE RAYS (streams of electrons) [Sir William *Crookes* †1919 E physicist]

**croon** /kroohn/ *vi* **1** to sing usu sentimental popular songs in a low or soft voice while slurring the words **2** *chiefly Scot* **2a** to bellow, boom **b** to wail, lament **c** to make a continuous moaning sound ~ *vt* to sing in a crooning manner ⟨~ *a lullaby*⟩ [ME *croynen,* fr MD *cronen;* akin to OE *cran* crane] – **croon** *n*

**crooner** /'kroohnə/ *n* one who croons; *esp* a singer of popular songs who uses a soft-voice technique adapted to amplifying systems

¹**crop** /krop/ *n* **1** (the stock or handle of) a thonged riding whip **2** a pouched enlargement of the gullet of many birds in which food is stored and prepared for digestion; *also* an enlargement of the gullet of another animal (e g an insect) **3a** an earmark on an animal; *esp* one made by a straight cut squarely removing the upper part of the ear **b** a short haircut ⟨*an Eton* ~⟩ **4a** a plant or animal (product) that can be grown and harvested extensively for profit or subsistence ⟨*an apple* ~⟩ ⟨*a* ~ *of wool*⟩ **b** a batch or lot of something that resembles an agricultural crop ⟨*a new* ~ *of students*⟩ **5** the total yearly production from a specified area ⟨*India's cotton* ~ *had never been better*⟩ [ME, craw, head of a plant, yield of a field, fr OE *cropp* craw, head of a plant; akin to OHG *kropf* goitre, craw, OE *crēopan* to creep – more at CREEP]

²**crop** *vb* **-pp-** *vt* **1a** to remove the upper or outer parts of ⟨~ *a hedge*⟩ ⟨*sheep* ~ping *the new grass*⟩ **b** to harvest ⟨~ *trout*⟩ **c** to cut off short; trim ⟨~ *a photograph*⟩ **2** to cause (land) to bear a crop ⟨*planned to* ~ *another 40 acres*⟩; *also* to grow as a crop ~ *vi* **1** to feed by cropping something **2** to yield or make a crop

**crop out** *vi, of a rock* to appear or be exposed

**crop up** *vi* to appear unexpectedly or casually ⟨*problems crop up daily*⟩

'**crop-,eared** *adj* **1** having the ears cropped **2** having the hair cut short so that the ears are conspicuous

**cropland** /'krop,land/ *n* land that is suited to or used for crops

¹**cropper** /'kropə/ *n* **1** one who or that which crops; *esp* a plant that yields a crop of a usu specified quality ⟨*this apple is a fine* ~⟩ **2** *often cap* a domestic pigeon with a puffed-out crop

²**cropper** *n* [prob fr E dial. *crop* neck, fr ¹*crop*] – **come a cropper 1** *chiefly Br informal* to have a fall or accident **2** *slang* to fail completely

**crop rotation** *n* the practice of growing different crops in succession on the same land chiefly to preserve the productive capacity of the soil

**croquet** /'krohkay/ *n* **1** a game in which wooden balls are driven by mallets through a series of hoops set out on a lawn **2** the act of driving away an opponent's croquet ball by striking one's own ball placed against it [Fr dial., hockey stick, fr ONF, crook – more at CROCKET] – **croquet** *vt*

**croquette** /kroh'ket/ *n* a small (rounded) piece of minced meat, fish, or vegetable coated with egg and breadcrumbs and fried in deep fat ⟨*a chicken* ~⟩ ⟨~ *potatoes*⟩ [Fr, fr *croquer* to crunch, of imit origin]

**croquis** /kroh'kee/ *n, pl* **croquis** /kroh'kee(z)/ a rough draft; a sketch [Fr, fr *croquer* to crunch, sketch]

**crore** /kraw/ *n, pl* **crores** *also* **crore** *Ind* 10 million [Hindi *karor*]

**crosier, crozier** /'krohzhə/ *n* a staff resembling a shepherd's crook, carried by bishops and abbots as a symbol of office [ME *croser* crosier bearer, fr MF *crossier,* fr *crosse* crosier, of Gmc origin; akin to OE *crycc* crutch – more at CRUTCH]

¹**cross** /kros/ *n* **1a** a structure consisting of an upright with a transverse beam, used esp by the ancient Romans for execution by tying or nailing the victim to it **b** *often cap* the cross on which Jesus was crucified; *also* a representation of this used as the emblem of Christianity **c** a sign representing the Cross, made by tracing the shape in the air with a finger, or by touching the forehead, chest, and each shoulder **2a** the Crucifixion **b** an affliction that tries one's virtue, steadfastness, or patience ⟨*everyone has his* ~ *to bear*⟩ **3** *cap* the Christian religion **4** a structure (e g a monument) shaped like or sur-

mounted by a cross, often placed in the centre of a town ⟨*the market* ~⟩ **5** a figure or mark formed by two intersecting lines crossing at their midpoints; *esp* such a mark used as a signature by somebody illiterate, to indicate that a school exercise is wrong, or to indicate a kiss in a letter – compare ²TICK 2 **6** a badge, emblem, or decoration shaped like a cross ⟨*the Distinguished Flying* Cross⟩ **7** the intersection of two ways or lines; a crossing **8** an annoyance, thwarting ⟨*a* ~ *in love*⟩ **9a** an act of crossing dissimilar individuals **b** a crossbred individual or kind; a hybrid **c** somebody or something that combines characteristics of two different types of individuals **10** a movement from one side of a theatrical stage to another **11** a sideways punch delivered over the opponent's straight punch in boxing **12** the act of crossing the ball in soccer **13** *slang* a fraudulent or dishonest contest **14** *slang* a dishonest or illegal practice – esp in *on the cross* [ME, fr OE, fr ON or OIr; ON *kross,* fr (assumed) OIr *cross,* fr L *cruc-, crux* – more at RIDGE] – **on the cross** on the bias; diagonally ⟨*she cut the material* on the cross⟩

²**cross** *vt* **1a** to lie or be situated across **b** to intersect **2** to make the sign of the cross on or over **3** to cancel by marking a cross on or drawing a line through; strike out ⟨~ *names off a list*⟩ **4** to place or fold crosswise ⟨~ *one's arms*⟩ **5** to run counter to; oppose ⟨*gets very angry if he's* ~ed⟩ **6** to go across ⟨*the road* ~es *the railway here*⟩ ⟨*only two* ~ed *the finishing line*⟩ **7a** to draw a line across ⟨~ *one's t's*⟩ **b** to draw two parallel lines across (a cheque) so as to allow only direct payment into a bank account, not encashment **8** to cause (an animal or plant) to interbreed with one of a different kind; hybridize **9** to kick or pass (the ball) across the field in soccer ~ *vi* **1** to lie or be across each other **2** to pass simultaneously in opposite directions ⟨*our letters must have* ~ed⟩ **3** to interbreed, hybridize **4** to cross the ball in soccer – see also **keep one's** FINGERS **crossed, cross the** FLOOR/**one's** MIND, **cross** SWORDS, **get one's** WIRES **crossed** – **crosser** *n*

**cross over** *vi* to move, pass, or extend across something; *specif* to pass from one side of a theatrical stage to the other

³**cross** *adj* **1a** lying across **b** moving across ⟨~ *traffic*⟩ **2** mutually opposed ⟨~ *purposes*⟩ **3** involving mutual interchange; reciprocal **4a** marked by short-lived but recurrent bad temper; grumpy **b** angry, annoyed **5** extending over or treating several groups or classes ⟨*a* ~ *sample from 25 universities*⟩ **6** crossbred, hybrid – **crossly** *adv,* **crossness** *n*

⁴**cross** *prep* across

⁵**cross** *adv* not parallel; crisscross, crosswise

**crossable** /'krosəbl/ *adj* capable of being crossed

**cross action** *n* an action brought by a defendant in a lawsuit against the person who has sued him/her and on the same subject matter

**crossbar** /'kros,bah/ *n* a transverse bar or stripe: e g **a** a transverse bar between goalposts **b** a horizontal bar on a man's bicycle that joins the handlebar to the saddle support

**crossbeam** /'kros,beem/ *n* a transverse beam

**crossbearer** /'kros,beərə/ *n* CRUCIFER

,**cross-'bedded** *adj* having minor beds or LAMINAE (thin layers) lying obliquely to the main beds of stratified rock ⟨~ *sandstone*⟩ – **cross-bedding** *n*

**cross bench** *n usu pl* any of the benches in the House of Lords on which members who belong to neither government nor opposition parties sit [fr these benches being set at right angles to those occupied by the government and opposition] – **crossbencher** *n*

**crossbill** /'kros,bil/ *n* any of a genus (*Loxia,* esp *Loxia curvirostra*) of finches that have strongly curved beaks, the upper and lower parts of which cross each other at their tips, and that feed esp on the seeds of conifers

**crossbones** /'kros,bohnz/ *n pl* two human leg or arm bones placed or depicted crosswise, esp on a pirate flag or, with a skull, as a symbol of death – compare SKULL AND CROSSBONES

**crossbow** /'kros,boh/ *n* a weapon for discharging bolts and stones that consists chiefly of a short bow mounted crosswise near the end of a wooden stock – **crossbowman** *n*

**crossbred** /'kros,bred/ *adj* **1** hybrid; *specif* produced by interbreeding two pure but different breeds, strains, or varieties **2** of or being a type of wool that is coarser than MERINO – **crossbred** *n*

¹**crossbreed** /'kros,breed/ *vb* **crossbred** /-,bred/ *vt* to hybridize or cross (esp two varieties or breeds of the same species) ~ *vi* to engage in or undergo crossbreeding

²**crossbreed** *n* a hybrid

**,cross-'buttock** n a throw in which a wrestler places both legs across both legs of the opponent and rolls him/her forward

**,cross-'check** vt to check (information) for validity or accuracy by reference to more than one source – **cross-check** n

¹**,cross-'country** adj **1** proceeding over countryside and not by roads **2** of racing over the countryside instead of over a track or run ⟨∼ skiers⟩ – **cross-country** adv

²**cross-country** n cross-country sports; specif cross-country running, riding, etc

**crosscourt** /'kros,kawt/ adv or adj towards the diagonally opposite side of a court (eg in tennis or basketball)

**,cross-'cultural** adj dealing with or offering a comparison between different cultures or cultural groups

**crosscurrent** /'kros,kurənt/ n **1** a current in a river or sea running across the direction of another current **2** usu pl a conflicting tendency ⟨political ∼s⟩

¹**crosscut** /'kros,kut/ vt **1** to cut with a crosscut saw **2** to cut across the grain of (wood) **3** to intersperse (a length of film) with contrasting images

²**crosscut** adj made or used for cutting transversely or across the grain of wood ⟨a saw with ∼ teeth⟩ ⟨a ∼ incision⟩

³**crosscut** n something that cuts across or through; specif a mine passage driven through a body of ore or from a shaft to a body of ore

**crosscut saw** n a saw designed chiefly to cut across the grain of wood – compare RIPSAW

**'cross-,dresser** n a transvestite

**crosse** /kros/ n the long-handled netted stick used in lacrosse [Fr, lit., crosier – more at CROSIER]

**'crosse-,check** vi to hit an opponent's stick in lacrosse with one's own stick in order to knock the ball loose or to prevent the opponent from picking up the ball

**crossed** /krost/ adj, of a telephone line connected in error to two or more telephones

**,cross-ex'amine** vt to question (eg a witness in a law court) closely in order to test or check answers given previously or get new information – **cross-examination** n, **cross-examiner** n

**,cross-'eye** n **1** a squint in which the eye turns inwards toward the nose **2** pl eyes affected with cross-eye – **cross-eyed** adj

**'cross-,fade** vi a simultaneous fading out of one set of stage lighting and building up of another

**,cross-'fertile** adj fertile in a union of dissimilar individuals or types (CROSS 9) or capable of cross-fertilization – compare SELF-FERTILE

**,cross-,fertil·i·'zation, -i'sation** n **1a** fertilization in which the reproductive cells (GAMETES) are produced by different individuals (eg two individuals of the same kind or two of different kinds) – compare SELF-FERTILIZATION **b** cross-pollination **2** interchange or interaction, esp of a broadening or productive nature ⟨∼ of practical expertise with theoretical learning⟩ – **cross-fertilize** vt

**'cross-,file** vb to register as a candidate in the primary elections of more than one US political party

**cross fire** n **1** firing (eg in combat) from two or more points so that the lines of fire cross; also a situation in which the forces of opposing factions meet or cross **2** rapid or heated interchange of arguments or insults

**,cross-'gartered** adj having bands or thongs that cross over one another up the leg to function as a garter ⟨she did praise my leg being ∼ – Shak⟩

**'cross-,grained** adj **1** having the grain or fibres running diagonally, transversely, or irregularly **2** difficult to deal with, esp because obstinate and bad-tempered – **,cross-'grainedness** n

**cross hair** n any of the fine wires or threads in the focus of the eyepiece of an optical instrument used as a reference line

**crosshatch** /'kros,hach/ vt to shade with a series of intersecting parallel lines; specif to shade (a drawing) in this way – **crosshatch** n, **crosshatched** adj, **crosshatching** n

**crosshead** /'kros,hed/ n **1** a sliding metal block between a PISTON ROD and a CONNECTING ROD **2** a subhead centred in a column (eg of a newspaper or magazine) and dividing paragraphs

**,cross-'index** vt to provide (eg an item in a text) with a crossreference – **cross-index** n

**crossing** /'krosing/ n **1** the act or action of crossing: eg **1a** a traversing or travelling across ⟨the Dover/Calais ∼⟩ **b** an opposing, blocking, or thwarting, esp in an unfair or dishonest manner **2a** a place or structure (eg on a street or over a river) where pedestrians or vehicles may cross **b** LEVEL CROSSING **c** a place where railway lines cross each other

**,crossing-'over** n the interchange of genes or segments of genes between corresponding CHROMOSOMES (strands of genecarrying material in a cell) during MEIOSIS (process in which special cells divide to form sperm, eggs, etc)

¹**'cross-,kick** n a kick of a rugby ball across the field

²**cross-kick** vi to kick the ball across the field in rugby

**,cross-'legged** /'legid; also legd/ adv or adj **1** with legs crossed and knees spread wide apart ⟨sat ∼ on the floor⟩ **2** with one leg placed over and across the other

**'cross-,link** n a crosswise connecting part (eg an atom or chemical group) that connects parallel chains in a POLYMER or other complex chemical molecule – **cross-link** vb, **cross-link-able** adj, **cross-linkage** n

**cross multiply** vi to find the two products obtained by multiplying the numerator of each of two fractions by the denominator of the other fraction – **cross multiplication** n

**cross of Lorraine** /lə'rayn, lə'ren (Fr lɔrɛn)/ n a cross having one crossbar above the middle of the upright and a longer one below the middle [Lorraine, region of NE France]

**crossopterygian** /,krosoptə'rijiən/ n any of several fishes of a group (Crossopterygii) comprising mainly extinct lobe-finned fishes (eg the coelacanths) that are the probable ancestors of the amphibians [deriv of Gk krossoi tassels, fringe + pteryg-, pteryx wing, fin]

**crossover** /'kros,ohvə/ n **1** CROSSING 2a **2** an instance or product of genetic crossing-over

**crossover network** n a set of electronic components which divide up an audio signal into two or more frequency ranges (eg as used in a loudspeaker cabinet with a WOOFER and a TWEETER)

**crosspatch** /'kros,pach/ n, informal an ill-tempered person [³cross + patch (fool)]

**crosspiece** /'kros,pees/ n a horizontal beam, joist, etc

**crossply** /'kros,plie/ n or adj (a pneumatic tyre) with the cords bonded crosswise to strengthen the tread

**,cross-polli'nation** n the transfer of pollen from the ANTHER (pollen-producing part) of one flower to the STIGMA (pollen-receiving part) of another – compare SELF-POLLINATION – **,cross-'pollinate** vt

**,cross-'pollin·ize, -ise** vt to cross-pollinate

**cross product** n VECTOR PRODUCT

**,cross-'purposes** n pl – **at cross purposes** having a mutual misunderstanding or deliberately conflicting approach

**'cross-re,action** n reaction of one ANTIGEN (foreign substance activating antibody production) with antibodies developed against another antigen

**,cross-re'fer** vt **1** to direct (a reader) from one page or entry (eg in a book, list, or catalogue) to another **2** to refer from (eg a variant form) to a main entry ∼ vi to make a cross-reference

¹**,cross-'reference** n an indication at one place (eg in a book or filing system) of the existence of relevant information at another place

²**cross-reference** vt **1** to cross-refer **2** to provide (eg a book) with cross-references

**'cross-re,sistance** n tolerance (eg of an insect population) to a normally toxic substance (eg an insecticide) that is acquired not as a result of direct exposure but by exposure to a chemically related substance

**crossroad** /'kros,rohd/ n **1** a road that **1a** crosses a main road **b** runs transversely between main roads ⟨the ∼ connects the motorway with the A10⟩ **2** pl but taking sing or pl vb **2a** the place of intersection of two or more roads **b** a central meeting place ⟨the ∼s of the world⟩ **c** a crucial point, esp where a decision must be made ⟨defence policy at the ∼s⟩

**crossruff** /'kros,ruf/ n a series of plays in a card game, esp whist or bridge, in which partners (or in bridge the declarer playing both his/her own hand and his/her partner's) alternately trump different suits and lead to the other partner's hand for that purpose ⟨we set up a ∼ in hearts and diamonds⟩ – **crossruff** vb

**'cross-,section** n **1a** a cutting or piece of something cut off at right angles to an axis **b** the dimensions or plane shape revealed by a cutting at right angles to the length of something ⟨both girders are of the same length and ∼⟩; also a representation of this shape **2** physics a measure of the probability of an encounter between particles such as will result in a specified effect ⟨the ionization ∼⟩ **3** a composite representation typifying the relative parts of something; broadly a representative sample ⟨a ∼ of society⟩ – **cross-sectional** adj

**'cross-,stitch** *n* (needlework using) a stitch in the shape of an X formed by crossing one stitch over another – **cross-stitch** *vb*

**'cross-,talk** *n* **1** unwanted signals in a communications channel or storage location that come from another channel or storage location (eg signals in one track of a tape recording that come from another track) **2** *Br* rapid exchange of repartee (eg between comedians or members of different parties in Parliament)

**crosstown** /'kros,town/ *adv or adj, NAm* (in a manner) extending or running across a town ⟨*the bus ran ~ to the river*⟩ ⟨*a ~ street*⟩ ⟨*a ~ bus*⟩

**'cross-,trade** *n* trading by a shipping line carrying cargoes between countries other than its own – **cross-trader** *n*

**crosstree** /'kros,tree/ *n* either of a pair of horizontal crosspieces at the head of a lower mast to support the topmast and spread the shrouds

**crosswalk** /'kros,wawk/ *n, NAm* a specially paved or marked path for pedestrians crossing a street or road – compare ZEBRA CROSSING

**crossways** /'kros,wayz/ *adv* crosswise, diagonally

**crosswind** /'kros,wind/ *n* a wind blowing in a direction not parallel to a course (eg of an aircraft)

**¹crosswise** /'kros,wiez/ *adv* **1** so as to cross something; across ⟨*logs laid ~*⟩ **2** *archaic* in the form of a cross

**²crosswise** *adj* transverse, crossing ⟨*a ~ street*⟩

**crossword puzzle, crossword** /'kros,wuhd/ *n* a puzzle in which numbered often cryptic clues labelled "across" or "down" lead to the words to be written into a usu black and white symmetrically patterned grid of squares, each word starting in the square numbered to correspond with the clue and reading across or down

**crotch** /kroch/ *n* **1** a pole with a forked end used esp as a prop **2** an angle formed by the parting (eg from a trunk or body) of two legs, branches, or members **3** the area encompassed by the angle between the inner thighs where they meet the human body; the genital area [prob alter. of ¹*crutch*] – **crotched** *adj*

**crotchet** /'krochit/ *n* **1** a musical note with the time value of half a minim or two quavers **2** *informal* a highly individual and usu eccentric opinion or preference **3** *obs* a small hook or hooked instrument [ME *crochet*, fr MF – more at CROCHET]

**crotchet rest** *n* a musical REST (indicating silence) of the same time value as a crotchet

**crotchety** /'krochəti/ *adj, informal* subject to ill temper ⟨*a ~ old man*⟩ – **crotchetiness** *n*

**croton** /'kroht(ə)n/ *n* **1** any of a genus (*Croton*) of chiefly tropical plants and shrubs of the spurge family; *esp* an E Indian plant (*Croton tiglium*) yielding an oil formerly used as a strong laxative and now used, esp in physiological experiments, as an irritant **2** any of various tropical plants (genus *Codiaeum*) of the spurge family; *esp* a houseplant (*Codiaeum variegatum pictum*) with red and yellow leaves [NL, genus name, fr Gk *krotōn* castor-oil plant]

**Croton bug** *n* GERMAN COCKROACH [*Croton* river in New York state, USA, used as a water supply for New York City]

**crouch** /krowch/ *vi* **1** to lower the body by bending the legs **2** to bend or bow servilely; cringe ~ *vt* to bend (eg the knee), esp in humility or fear ⟨*he ~ed his back under the blows*⟩ [ME *crouchen*, perh fr MF *crochir* to become hook-shaped, fr *croche* hook] – **crouch** *n*

**¹croup** /kroohp/ *n* the rump of a horse, cow, or other 4-legged animal [ME *croupe*, fr OF, of Gmc origin; akin to OHG *kropf* craw – more at CROP]

**²croup** *n* a spasmodic laryngitis, esp of infants, marked by periods of difficult breathing and a hoarse metallic cough [E dial. *croup* to cry hoarsely, cough, prob of imit origin] – **croupous, croupy** *adj*

**croupier** /'kroohpi·ə, -ay/ *n* an employee of a gambling casino who collects and pays bets and assists at the gaming tables [Fr, lit., rider on the croup of a horse, fr *croupe* croup]

**crouse** /kroohs/ *adj, chiefly Scot & N Eng* brisk, lively [ME (northern), prob of LG origin]

**croute** /krooht/ *n* **1** a round slice of crisply fried, baked, or toasted bread on which savouries may be served **2** a pastry cover; a crust [Fr *croûte*, lit., crust]

**crouton** /'kroohton/ *n* a small cube of toasted or crisply fried bread served scattered over soup or used as a garnish [Fr *croûton*, dim. of *croûte* crust, fr MF *crouste*]

**¹crow** /kroh/ *n* **1** any of various large usu entirely glossy black birds (family Corvidae, esp genus *Corvus*) **2** a crowbar **3** *cap* a member of a N American Indian people of the region between the Platte and Yellowstone rivers; *also* their SIOUAN language [ME *crowe*, fr OE *crāwe*; akin to OHG *krāwa* crow, OE *crāwan* to crow; (3) trans of Dakota *Absaroka*, lit., crow people] – **as the crow flies** in a straight line ⟨*as the crow flies it's half a mile but by road it's two*⟩ – **eat crow** *NAm informal* to be forced to accept humiliation or defeat; EAT HUMBLE PIE

**²crow** *vi* **crowed**, (*1*) **crowed**, *chiefly Br* **crew 1** to make the loud shrill cry characteristic of a cock **2** *of an infant* to utter a joyful sound **3a** to exult gloatingly, esp over the distress of another **b** to brag exultantly or blatantly *synonyms* see ²BOAST [ME *crowen*, fr OE *crāwan*]

**³crow** *n* **1** the characteristic cry of the cock **2** a joyful sound; *esp* one made by an infant **3** a triumphant cry

**crowbar** /'kroh,bah/ *n* an iron or steel bar that is usu wedge-shaped at the working end for use as a lever [¹*crow* + *bar*; prob fr the forked end, like a crow's foot, it sometimes has]

**crowberry** /'krohb(ə)ri/ *n* **1** any of several low shrubby evergreen plants (family Empetraceae); *esp* a small low-growing shrub (*Empetrum nigrum*) of arctic and mountainous regions **2** the insipid black berry of the crowberry

**¹crowd** /krowd/ *vi* **1a** to press on; hurry ⟨*the ships ~ed northwards*⟩ **b** to press close ⟨*people ~ing through the narrow gates*⟩ **2** to collect in numbers; throng ~ *vt* **1a** to fill by pressing or thronging together ⟨*people ~ed the hall*⟩ **b** to press, force, or thrust into a small space ⟨*~ed books onto the shelves*⟩ **2** to push, force ⟨*~ed us off the pavement*⟩ **3** to put on (sail) in excess of the usual for greater speed – usu + *on* **4** *NAm informal* to put pressure on ⟨*~ing me with unreasonable demands for money*⟩ **5** *NAm informal* to press on; jostle ⟨*don't ~ me*⟩ [ME *crouden*, fr OE *crūdan*; akin to MHG *kroten* to crowd, OE *crod* multitude, MIr *gruth* curds]

**crowd out** *vt* **1** to exclude by depriving of space or time ⟨*news items being crowded out of the broadcast*⟩ **2** to fill to capacity by coming or collecting together ⟨*we crowded the hall out*⟩

**²crowd** *n taking sing or pl vb* **1** a large number of people, esp when collected temporarily into a compact body without order; a throng **2** *the* great body of the people; *the* populace **3** a large number of things close together and in disorder **4** a group of people having something in common ⟨*in with the wrong ~*⟩

**³crowd** *n* **1** an ancient Celtic stringed instrument played by plucking or with a short bow **2** *dial* a violin [ME *crowde*, fr (assumed) MW *crwth*]

**crowded** /'krowdid/ *adj* **1** filled with numerous people, things, or events ⟨*a very ~ hall*⟩ ⟨*a ~ programme*⟩ **2** pressed, forced, or thrust into a small space ⟨*~ spectators*⟩ – **crowdedness** *n*

**crowdie** /'krowdi, 'kroohdi, 'kroodi/ *n* a fine-grained COTTAGE CHEESE [Sc, of unknown origin]

**crowding out** *n* the reduction in either private consumption expenditure or private investment caused by an increase in government expenditure

**crowdpuller** /'krowd,poolə/ *n, chiefly Br informal* somebody or something that attracts crowds

**crowfoot** /'kroh,foot/ *n, pl (1)* **crowfoots**, *(2)* **crowfeet 1** any of numerous plants having lobed leaves shaped more or less like a crow's foot; *esp* any of several mostly white-flowered water plants of a genus (*Ranunculus*) of the buttercup family **2** *usu pl* CROW'S-FOOT 1

**¹crown** /krown/ *n* **1** a reward of victory or mark of honour; *esp* the title representing the championship in a sport ⟨*the world heavyweight ~*⟩ **2** a headdress that is worn by the monarch as a symbol of royal or imperial sovereignty on state occasions, and is typically made of gold and encrusted with jewels **3** the highest part: eg **3a** the topmost part of the skull or head **b** the summit of a mountain **c** the head of foliage of a tree or shrub **d** the part of a hat or cap that covers the crown of the head, excluding the brim **e** the part of a tooth external to the gum; *also* an artificial substitute for this **f** the highest part of a camber ⟨*~ of the road*⟩ **4** a wreath, band, or circular ornament for the head, esp worn as a symbol of victory; *also* something resembling this **5** *often cap* **5a(1)** the sovereign as head of state; *also* imperial or regal power; sovereignty **a(2)** the government under a constitutional monarchy **b** the prosecution in a criminal trial ⟨*the ~ began its case*⟩ ⟨*counsel for the ~*⟩ **6** something that imparts splendour, honour, or completion; a culmination **7a(1)** any of several former gold coins with a crown as part of the design on them **a(2)** a British coin worth 25 new pence (5 shillings) **b** a size of paper usu 20 × 15 inches (508 × 381 millimetres) **8a** KORUNA (Czech coin) **b** KRONA (Icelandic and Swedish coin) **c** KRONE (Danish, Norwegian, and former Austrian coin) **9a** the part of a FLOWERING PLANT at which stem and root merge **b** the thick arching end of the shank of an anchor where the arms join it [ME *coroune, crowne,* fr OF *corone,* fr L *corona* wreath, crown, fr Gk *korōnē;* akin to Gk *korōnos* curved, L *curvus,* MIr *cruind* round; (7b) fr its being orig watermarked with a crown] – **crowned** *adj*

²**crown** *vt* **1a** to place a crown or wreath on the head of, esp as a symbol of investiture with regal dignity and power ⟨~ed *him king*⟩ **b** to recognize, usu officially, as (the leader in a particular field) ⟨*they* ~ed *him athlete of the year*⟩ **2** to bestow something on as a mark of honour or recompense; adorn **3** to surmount, top; *esp* to put (a draughtsman) on top of another draughtsman to make a king **4** to bring to a successful conclusion **5** to put an artificial crown on (a tooth) **6** *informal* to hit on the head [ME *corounen,* fr OF *coroner,* fr L *coronare,* fr *corona*]

**crown canopy** *n* the cover formed by the topmost branches of trees in a forest

**crown cap** *n* a cork-lined metal cap for a bottle

**crown colony** *n, often cap both Cs* a colony of the Commonwealth over which the British government retains some control

**Crown Court** *n* a part of the SUPREME COURT in England and Wales having jurisdiction over serious criminal offences and hearing appeals from the MAGISTRATES' COURTS before a High Court judge, a circuit judge, or a RECORDER (barrister or solicitor appointed as a part-time judge)

**crown gall** *n* a plant disease that is destructive esp to fruit trees and roses and is caused by a bacterium (*Agrobacterium tumefaciens*) which forms tumorous enlargements just below the ground on the trunk or stem

**crown glass** *n* **1** a glass blown and whirled into the form of a disc with a centre lump left by the worker's rod, which was used esp formerly to make window panes **2** soda-lime silicate glass that has a relatively low REFRACTIVE INDEX and low DISPERSION (tendency to separate light into colours that form a spectrum) and is used in the construction of lenses

**crown green** *n* a bowling green which slopes downwards slightly from its centre to its circumference

**crown imperial** *n* a tall garden plant (*Fritillaria imperialis*) of the lily family, with usu orange bell-shaped flowers in a cluster of leaves at the top of the stem

**crown jewels** *n pl* the jewels (e g crown and sceptre) belonging to a sovereign's regalia

**crown land** *n* **1** land belonging to the crown and yielding revenue that the reigning sovereign is entitled to **2** public land in some British dominions or colonies

**crown lens** *n* the CROWN GLASS part of an ACHROMATIC LENS (lens designed to produce an image free from unwanted colours)

**crown of thorns** *n* a starfish (*Acanthaster planci*) of the Pacific region that is covered with long spines and is destructive to the coral of coral reefs

**crown prince** *n* a male heir to a crown or throne

**crown princess** *n* **1** the wife of a crown prince **2** a female heir to a crown or throne

**crown roast** *n* a roast of the rib-sections of pork or lamb arranged in a crown shape

**crown rust** *n* a leaf disease of grasses, esp oats, that is caused by a fungus (*Puccinia coronata*)

**crown saw** *n* a saw that has teeth at the edge of a hollow cylinder and is used to cut circular holes

**crown vetch** *n* a trailing European plant (*Coronilla varia*) of the pea family that has clusters of pink, purple, and white flowers and sharp-angled pods and is cultivated in N America

**crown witness** *n, often cap C* a witness for the crown in a criminal prosecution

'**crow's-foot** *n, pl* **crow's-feet** /'- ,-/ **1** *usu pl* any of the wrinkles round the outer corners of the eyes **2** CROWFOOT 1

**crow's nest** *n* a partly enclosed platform high on a ship's mast for use as a lookout; *also* a similar lookout ashore

**crozier** /'krohzhə/ *n* a crosier

**cru** /krooh (*Fr* kry)/ *n* a category in the classification of certain fine French wines (e g Bordeaux) ⟨*premier* ~⟩ [Fr, production, producing field, fr *crû,* pp of *croître* to grow]

**cruces** /'kroohseez/ *pl of* CRUX

**crucial** /'kroohsh(ə)l/ *adj* **1** important or essential to the resolving of a crisis; decisive **2** marked by or possessing importance or significance **synonyms** see CRITICAL [Fr, cross-shaped, fr L *cruc-, crux* cross – more at RIDGE] – **crucially** *adv*

**crucian carp, crucian** /'kroohsh(ə)n/ *n* a colourful European carp (*Carassius carassius*) often kept in aquariums [modif of LG *karuse,* fr MHG *karusse,* fr Lith *karušis*]

**cruciate** /'kroohshi,ayt/ *adj, biology* **1** cross-shaped ⟨~ *muscles*⟩ **2** *of a plant* having leaves or petals arranged in the form of a cross; cruciform [NL *cruciatus,* fr L *cruc-, crux*] – **cruciately** *adv*

**crucible** /'kroohsibl/ *n* **1** a vessel of a heat-resistant material (e g porcelain) used for melting and CALCINING (heating to drive off e g steam, or to oxidize or change in some other way) a substance that requires a high temperature **2** a severe test ⟨*tried in the* ~ *of adversity*⟩ [ME *corusible,* fr ML *crucibulum,* modif of OF *croiseul*]

**crucible steel** *n* hard cast steel made in pots that are lifted from the furnace before the metal is poured into moulds

**crucifer** /'kroohsifə/ *n* **1** a person who carries a cross, esp at the head of an ecclesiastical procession **2** a plant of the cabbage family (*Cruciferae*), that includes the mustard and numerous common weeds (e g SHEPHERD'S PURSE) [deriv of L *cruc-, crux* + *-fer*] – **cruciferous** *adj*

**crucifix** /'kroohsifiks/ *n* a representation of Christ on the cross, usu in the form of a model placed on an altar or elsewhere in a church, or worn on a chain round the neck [ME, fr LL *crucifixus* the crucified Christ, fr *crucifixus,* pp of *crucifigere* to crucify, fr L *cruc-, crux* + *figere* to fasten – more at DYKE]

**crucifixion** /,kroohsi'fiksh(ə)n/ *n* **1a** the act of crucifying **b** *cap* the crucifying of Christ **2** extreme and painful punishment, affliction, or suffering

**cruciform** /'kroohsi,fawm/ *adj* forming or arranged in a cross [L *cruc-, crux* + E *-form*] – **cruciform** *n,* **cruciformly** *adv*

**crucify** /'kroohsi,fie/ *vt* **1** to execute by nailing or binding the hands and feet to a cross and leaving to die **2** to treat cruelly; torture, persecute [ME *crucifien,* fr OF *crucifier,* fr LL *crucifigere*]

**cruck** /kruk/ *n, Br* either of a pair of curved timbers serving as wall and roof supports in a primitive cottage, and extending to the ground [ME *crokke,* prob var of *crok* crook]

**crud** /krud/ *n* **1** *informal* a deposit or incrustation of filth, grease, or refuse **2** *slang* a disagreeable or contemptible substance or person ⟨*you miserable* ~⟩ **3** *chiefly NAm slang* a usu ill-defined or imperfectly identified bodily disorder [ME *curd, crudd*] – **cruddy** *adj*

¹**crude** /kroohd/ *adj* **1** existing in a natural state and unaltered by processing ⟨~ *rubber*⟩ **2** primitive, elemental **3** vulgar, gross ⟨~ *jokes*⟩ **4** tabulated without being broken down into classes or otherwise processed ⟨~ *death rate*⟩ [ME, fr L *crudus* raw – more at RAW] – **crudely** *adv,* **crudeness** *n*

²**crude** *n* a substance in its natural unprocessed state; *esp* unrefined petroleum

**crudite, crudité** /'kroohditay/ *n usu pl* a small piece of raw carrot, onion, celery, etc cut into thin slices and served as an HORS D'OEUVRE with mayonnaise, vinaigrette, or other dressing [Fr *crudité,* lit., crudity, fr L *cruditas,* fr *crudus*]

**crudity** /'kroohdəti/ *n* **1** the quality or state of being crude **2** something crude

**cruel** /'krooh·əl/ *adj* -ll- (*NAm* -l-, -ll-) **1** disposed to inflict pain or suffering; pitiless **2a** causing injury, grief, or pain **b** unrelieved by leniency; harsh ⟨*a* ~ *regime*⟩ [ME, fr OF, fr L *crudelis,* irreg fr *crudus*] – **cruelly** *adv,* **cruelness** *n*

**cruelty** /'krooh·əlti/ *n* **1** the quality or state of being cruel **2** (an instance of) cruel behaviour [ME *cruelte,* fr OF *cruelté,* fr L *crudelitat-, crudelitas,* fr *crudelis*]

**cruet** /'krooh·it/ *n* **1** a vessel to hold wine or water for Communion **2a(1)** a small usu glass bottle or jug that holds oil or vinegar for use at table **a(2)** any of various small containers (e g a pot, shaker, or saltcellar) for holding or dispensing a condiment, specif salt, pepper, or mustard, at table **b** a set of cruets, usu on a stand [ME, fr AF, dim. of OF *crue,* of Gmc origin; akin to OE *crocc* crock]

¹**cruise** /kroohz/ *vi* **1** to travel on a ship or boat for pleasure rather than to reach a particular destination **2** to travel for the sake of travelling **3** to go or drive watchfully about the streets without any definite destination ⟨*a* cruising *taxi*⟩ **4** *of an aircraft* to fly at the most efficient operating speed **5** *of a vehicle* to travel at an economical speed that can be maintained for a long distance **6** to make progress easily ⟨*simply* ~d *through the exam*⟩ **7** *informal* to be on one's way; go ⟨*I'll* ~ *over to her house to see if she's in*⟩ **8** *NAm slang* to search (e g in public places) for a sexual partner, esp of the same sex ~ *vt* **1** to cruise over or about **2** to inspect (e g land) with reference to

possible timber yield [D *kruisen* to make a cross, cruise, fr MD *crucen*, fr *crūce* cross, fr L *cruc-*, *crux* – more at RIDGE]

²**cruise** *n* an act or an instance of cruising; *esp* a pleasure voyage by sea

**cruise missile** *n* a long-distance low-flying missile that is supported in flight by small wings, is guided by an inbuilt computerized navigation system, and typically carries a nuclear warhead

**cruiser** /'kroohzǝ/ *n* 1 a boat or vehicle that cruises; *specif* CABIN CRUISER 2 a large fast moderately armoured and gunned warship, usu weighing between 6000 and 15000 tons 3 *NAm* a police patrol car; *esp* one equipped with radio

**cruiserweight** /'kroohzǝ,wayt/ *n* a professional boxer who weighs not more than 13 stone 8 pounds (86.2 kilograms)

**cruller** /'krulǝ/ *n*, *NAm* a small sweet cake in the form of a twisted strip fried in deep fat [D *krulle*, a kind of twisted cake, fr *krul* curly, fr MD *crulle*]

¹**crumb** /krum/ *n* 1 a small fragment, esp of bread 2 a bit ⟨*not a ~ of comfort*⟩ 3 the soft part of bread inside the crust 4 loose crumbly soil 5 *slang* a worthless person [ME *crumme*, fr OE *cruma*; akin to MHG *krume* crumb] – **crumby** *adj*

²**crumb** *vt* 1 to break into crumbs 2 to cover or thicken with crumbs

¹**crumble** /'krumbl/ *vt* to break into small pieces ~ *vi* to fall into small pieces; disintegrate – often + *away* △ crumple [alter. of ME *kremelen*, freq of OE *gecrymian* to crumble, fr *cruma*]

²**crumble** *n* something that is crumbly or crumbled; *esp* a dessert of stewed fruit topped with a crumbly mixture of fat, flour, and sugar

**crumbly** /'krumbli/ *adj* easily crumbled; friable ⟨*~ soil*⟩ – **crumbliness** *n*

**crumbs** /krumz/ *interj*, *chiefly Br slang* – used to express surprise or mild annoyance [euphemism for *Christ* (cf CRIKEY, CRIPES)]

**crumhorn** /'krum,hawn/ *n* a Renaissance woodwind instrument of bass pitch with a slender hooked tube [Ger *krummhorn*, fr *krumm* crooked + *horn* horn]

**crummy, crumby** /'krumi/ *adj*, *slang* 1 miserable, filthy 2 having little merit; worthless [ME *crumme* crumb]

¹**crump** /krump/ *vi* 1 to crunch 2 to explode heavily [imit]

²**crump** *n* a crunching sound

³**crump** *adj*, *chiefly Scot* brittle [perh alter. of *crimp* (friable)]

**crumpet** /'krumpit/ *n* 1 a small round cake with a porous surface made from an unsweetened leavened mixture, cooked on a griddle, and eaten toasted and buttered 2 *taking sing or pl vb*, *Br slang* women as sexual objects [perh fr ME *crompid* (*cake*) wafer, lit., curled-up cake, fr *crumped*, pp of *crumpen* to curl up, fr *crump*, *crumb* crooked, fr OE]

¹**crumple** /'krumpl/ *vt* 1 to press, bend, or crush out of shape; rumple ⟨*~d up the paper*⟩ 2 to cause to collapse ~ *vi* 1 to become crumpled 2 to collapse ⟨*~d at the first blow*⟩ □ often + *up* △ crumble [(assumed) ME *crumplen*, freq of ME *crumpen*]

²**crumple** *n* a wrinkle or crease made by crumpling

¹**crunch** /krunch/ *vi* 1 to chew, press, or grind with a noisy crushing sound 2 to make one's way with a dry crisp brittle sound ⟨*~ed through the snow*⟩ ~ *vt* to chew (esp crisp food), press, or grind with a crunching sound [alter. (influenced by *munch*) of *craunch*, prob of imit origin]

²**crunch** *n* 1 an act or sound of crunching 2 *chiefly NAm* a severe economic squeeze (eg on credit) 3 *informal* a critical or decisive situation or time; *the crisis* ⟨*now we come to the ~*⟩

**cruncher** /'krunchǝ/ *n* 1 one who or that which crunches 2 *slang* a finishing blow

**crunchy** /'krunchi/ *adj*, *esp of food* crisp, brittle – **crunchiness** *n*

**crupper** /'krupǝ/ *n* 1 a leather loop passing under a horse's tail and buckled to the saddle to prevent the saddle from slipping forwards 2 ¹CROUP (animal's rump); *broadly* the buttocks [ME *cruper*, fr OF *crupiere*, fr *croupe* hindquarters]

**crural** /'krooǝrǝl/ *adj* of the thigh or leg; *specif* of the thigh or thigh bone [MF or L; MF, fr L *cruralis*, fr *crur-*, *crus* leg]

**crus** /kroohs, krus/ *n*, *pl* **crura** /'krooǝrǝ/ 1 the part of the hind limb between the femur or thigh and the tarsus or ankle 2 *usu pl* any of various parts that resemble a leg or a pair of legs [L *crur-*, *crus*; akin to Arm *srunk* shinbones]

¹**crusade** /krooh'sayd/ *n* 1 *cap* any of the military expeditions undertaken by Christian powers in the 11th, 12th, and 13th centuries to win the Holy Land from the Muslims 2 a campaign

or vigorous series of actions undertaken with zeal and enthusiasm for a specific cause or movement [blend of MF *croisade* & Sp *cruzada*; both derivs of L *cruc-*, *crux* cross]

²**crusade** *vi* to engage in a crusade or the Crusades ⟨*crusading for better prison conditions*⟩ – **crusader** *n*

**crusado** /krooh'sahdoh/ *n*, *pl* **crusadoes, crusados** a former gold or silver Portuguese coin having a cross on the back [Pg *cruzado*, lit., marked with a cross]

**cruse** /kroohz, kroohs/ *n* a small earthenware vessel (eg a jar or pot) for holding water, oil, etc [ME; akin to OE *crūse* pitcher]

¹**crush** /krush/ *vt* 1a to alter or destroy the structure of by pressure or compression ⟨*she ~ed the earwig*⟩ b to squeeze together into a mass ⟨*the cars were ~ed in the machine*⟩ 2 to hug or embrace strongly and closely 3 to reduce to particles by pounding or grinding 4a to suppress or overwhelm, esp completely, as if by pressure or weight ⟨*~ed all opposition*⟩ b to oppress or burden grievously ⟨*~ed by poverty*⟩ 5 to crowd, push ~ *vi* 1 to become crushed ⟨*eggshells ~ easily*⟩ 2 to advance (as if) with crushing ⟨*we ~ed through the snow*⟩ [ME *crusshen*, fr MF *cruisir*, of Gmc origin; akin to MLG *krossen* to crush] – **crushable** *adj*, **crusher** *n*

²**crush** *n* 1 an act of crushing 2 a crowding together, esp of many people 3 *informal* an intense and usu passing infatuation with someone ⟨*he had a ~ on his English teacher*⟩; *also* the human object of infatuation

**crush barrier** *n* a barrier erected to control crowds

**crushing** /'krushing/ *adj* 1 tending to crush 2 overwhelming ⟨*a ~ defeat*⟩ – **crushingly** *adv*

**crust** /krust/ *n* 1a the hardened exterior of bread b a piece of this or of dry hard bread c a bare living ⟨*impossible to earn a ~ from writing books – National Review (Melbourne)*⟩ 2 the pastry cover of a pie 3a a hard surface layer (eg of soil or snow) b the outer part of the earth, composed essentially of rocks c a deposit built up on the interior surface of a wine bottle during long aging d an encrusted deposit of dried secretions of exuded matter; *esp* a scab 4a a defensive hardness or coolness of behaviour ⟨*break through her ~ of reserve*⟩ b *informal* impudence, nerve ⟨*I like his ~!*⟩ [ME, fr L *crusta*; akin to OE *hrūse* earth, Gk *kryos* icy cold] – **crust** *vb*

**crustacean** /kru'staysh(ǝ)n/ *n*, *pl* **crustaceans, crustacea** /kru'staysh(y)ǝ/ any of a large class (Crustacea of the phylum Arthropoda) of mostly aquatic INVERTEBRATE animals that have a horny or bony outer shell, a pair of often much modified limbs or limblike structures on each segment, and two pairs of antennae, and that include the lobsters, shrimps, crabs, wood-lice, WATER FLEAS, and barnacles [NL *Crustacea*, group name, fr neut pl of *crustaceus*] – **crustacean** *adj*

**crustaceous** /kru'stayshǝs/ *adj* 1 having the characteristics of a crustacean 2 of, having, or forming a crust or shell; *esp* crustose [NL *crustaceus*, fr L *crusta* crust, shell]

**crustal** /'krustl/ *adj* of a crust, esp of the earth or the moon

**crusted** /'krustid/ *adj* 1 covered with or having formed a crust 2 having the accretion of age; fossilized ⟨*~ conservatism*⟩ 3 *of port* being a blend of ports from two or three different years that is matured in bottle and has the character of vintage port

**crustose** /'krustohs/ *adj*, *of a lichen or related plant* having a thin THALLUS (undifferentiated plant body) adhering closely to the substratum of rock, bark, or soil – compare FOLIOSE, FRUTICOSE [L *crustosus* crusted]

**crusty** /'krusti/ *adj* 1 having a hard well-baked crust 2 *esp of an old person* irritable and surly – **crustily** *adv*, **crustiness** *n*

¹**crutch** /kruch/ *n* 1a a wooden or metal support typically fitting under the armpit for use by the disabled in walking b a prop, stay 2 a forked leg rest constituting the pommel of a sidesaddle 3a the crotch of a human being or animal b the part of a garment that covers the human crotch 4 a forked support [ME *crucche*, fr OE *crycc*; akin to OHG *krucka* crutch, OE *cradol* cradle]

²**crutch** *vt* 1 to support on crutches; prop up 2 *Austr slang* to clip (a sheep or wool from a sheep) round the sheep's crutch

**crux** /kruks, krooks/ *n*, *pl* **cruxes** *also* **cruces** /'krooh,seez/ 1 a puzzling or difficult problem; an unsolved question 2 an essential or decisive point ⟨*the ~ of the problem*⟩ 3 a main or central feature (eg of an argument) [L *cruc-*, *crux* cross, torture – more at RIDGE]

**crux ansata** /an'saytǝ/ *n* ANKH (looped cross) [NL, lit., cross with a handle]

**cruzado** /krooh'zahdoh/ *n*, *pl* **cruzadoes, cruzados** CRUSADO (former Portuguese coin)

**cruzeiro** /krooh'zeəroh/ *n, pl* **cruzeiros** – see MONEY table [Pg, fr *cruz* cross]

**crwth** /kroohth/ *n* ³CROWD 1 (Celtic stringed instrument) [W]

¹**cry** /krie/ *vi* 1 to call loudly; shout ⟨cried *out in pain*⟩ 2 to weep, sob 3 *of a bird or animal* to utter a characteristic sound or call ∼ *vt* 1 to utter loudly; shout 2 to proclaim publicly; advertise ⟨∼ *their wares*⟩ 3 *archaic* to beg, beseech ⟨*I* ∼ *you mercy*⟩ – see also **cry** HAVOC, **for crying out** LOUD, **cry over spilt** MILK, **cry blue** MURDER, **cry** WOLF [ME *crien*, fr OF *crier*, fr L *quiritare* to cry out for help (from a citizen), to scream, fr *Quirit-, Quiris* Roman citizen]

**cry down** *vt* to disparage, depreciate ⟨*don't* cry *it* down⟩
**cry off** *vt* to call off (eg an agreement) ∼ *vi* to withdraw; BACK OUT ⟨*we had to* cry off *at the last minute*⟩
**cry out** *vi* to require or suggest strongly a remedy or other course of action ⟨*the whole system* cries out *for revision*⟩ ⟨*the room* cries out *to be painted white*⟩
**cry up** *vt* to praise highly; extol

²**cry** *n* 1 an instance of crying: eg **1a** an inarticulate utterance of distress, rage, or pain **b** an act or fit of weeping ⟨*feel better after a good* ∼⟩ **c** the characteristic sound or call of an animal or bird 2 *usu pl* an entreaty, appeal ⟨*ignored her* cries *for mercy*⟩ 3 a loud shout 4 a watchword, slogan ⟨*"death to the invader" was the* ∼⟩ 5 a general public demand or complaint ⟨*repeated droughts brought a* ∼ *for irrigation*⟩ 6 the baying of hounds pursuing a fox or other animal during a hunt; pursuit ⟨*in full* ∼⟩ 7 *pl, Scot* banns – **a far cry from** very different from

**cry-** /krie-/, **cryo-** *comb form* cold; low temperature; freezing ⟨*cryogen*⟩ ⟨*cryonics*⟩ [Ger *kryo-*, fr Gk, fr *kryos* – more at CRUST]

**crybaby** /'krie,baybi/ *n, informal* one who cries or complains too easily or often

**crying** /'krie·ing/ *adj* 1 calling for notice or immediate action ⟨*a* ∼ *need*⟩ 2 notorious, heinous ⟨*a* ∼ *shame*⟩

**crymotherapy** /'kriemoh,therəpi, ,--'---/ *n* CRYOTHERAPY (therapeutic use of cold) [Gk *krymos, kryos* icy cold + ISV *therapy*]

**cryobiology** /,krie·ohbie'oləji/ *n* the study of the effects of extremely low temperature on biological systems – **cryobiologist** *n*, **cryobiological** *adj*, **cryobiologically** *adv*

**cryogen** /'krie·əjən/ *n* a substance used for producing low temperatures; a refrigerant

**cryogenic** /,krie·ə'jenik/ *adj* 1 of, involving, or being (the production of) very low temperatures **2a** requiring or involving the use of a cryogenic temperature **b** requiring cryogenic storage **c** suitable for storage of a cryogenic substance – **cryogenically** *adv*

**cryogenics** /,krie·ə'jeniks/ *n taking sing or pl vb* a branch of physics that deals with the production and effects of very low temperatures

**cryolite** /'krie·ə,liet/ *n* a mineral consisting of sodium-aluminium fluoride, $Na_3AlF_6$, found in Greenland, usu in white masses, and used in making soda, aluminium, glass, and enamel [ISV, fr *cryo-* + *-lite*]

**cryonic suspension** /krie'onik/ *n* the freezing procedure by which a patient is preserved after his/her legal death in the hope of restoration to life and health at some future time when medical science will have advanced sufficiently to bring this about

**cryophilic** /,krie·ə'filik/ *adj, of an organism* thriving at low temperatures

**cryoscope** /'krie·ə,skohp/ *n* an instrument for determining FREEZING POINTS of substances

**cryoscopy** /krie'oskəpi/ *n* the determination of the MOLECULAR WEIGHT of a substance by observing the lowering of the FREEZING POINT produced when that substance is dissolved in a suitable solvent [ISV] – **cryoscopic** *adj*

**cryostat** /'krie·ə,stat/ *n* an apparatus for maintaining a constant low temperature [ISV]

**cryosurgery** /,krie·oh'suhj(ə)ri/ *n* surgery in which extreme chilling (eg by the application of liquid nitrogen) is used to destroy or cut tissue – **cryosurgeon** *n*, **cryosurgical** *adj*

**cryotherapy** /,krie·oh'therəpi, '--,---/ *n* the therapeutic use of cold (eg by the application of ice bags)

**cryotron** /'krie·ə,tron/ *n* a switch used in computer memories that is based on the principle that a magnetic field produced by a control current passing through a coil in a bath of liquid helium can cause a SUPERCONDUCTIVE element to become resistive [*cry-* + *-tron*]

**crypt** /kript/ *n* 1 a chamber (eg a vault) wholly or partly underground; *esp* a vault under the main floor of a church, often used as a chapel or for storing coffins 2 *anatomy* a simple gland, glandular cavity, or tube [L *crypta*, fr Gk *kryptē*, fr fem of *kryptos* hidden, fr *kryptein* to hide; akin to ON *hreysar* heap of stones, Lith *krauti* to pile up (cf GROTTO)] – **cryptal** *adj*

**crypt-** /kript-/, **crypto-** *comb form* 1 hidden; obscure ⟨*cryptogenic*⟩ 2 undeclared; secret ⟨*cryptofascist*⟩ 3 deciphering; cryptographic ⟨*cryptosystem*⟩ ⟨*cryptosecurity*⟩ [NL, fr Gk *kryptos*]

**cryptanalysis** /'kriptə,naləsis, ,--'---/ *n* the deciphering of cryptograms or cryptographic systems [*crypt*ogram + *analysis*] – **cryptanalyst** *n*, **cryptanalytic, cryptanalytical** *adj*, **cryptanalyse** *vt*

**cryptic** /'kriptik/ *adj* 1 secret, occult 2 intended to be obscure or mysterious ⟨*a* ∼ *remark*⟩ 3 serving to conceal ⟨∼ *coloration in animals*⟩ 4 *esp of a medical disorder* unrecognized 5 making use of cipher or code *synonyms* see ¹OBSCURE [LL *crypticus*, fr Gk *kryptikos*, fr *kryptos*] – **cryptically** *adv*

**crypto** /'kriptoh/ *n, pl* **cryptos** *informal* one who adheres or belongs secretly to a party, sect, or other group [*crypt-*]

**cryptococcosis** /,kriptəko'kohsis/ *n, pl* **cryptococcoses** /-'kohseez/ an infectious disease that is caused by a fungus (*Cryptococcus neoformans*) and is characterized by the production of lumps or abscesses in the lungs, the tissues under the skin, joints, and esp the brain and MENINGES (membranes enclosing the brain and spinal cord) [NL]

**cryptococcus** /,kriptə'kokəs/ *n, pl* **cryptococci** /-'kokie, -'koksie/ any of a genus (*Cryptococcus*) of budding IMPERFECT FUNGI that resemble yeasts and include a number of SAPROPHYTES (organisms living on dead or decaying matter) and a few serious disease-causing agents [NL, genus name, fr *crypt-* + *-coccus*] – **cryptococcal** *adj*

**cryptocrystalline** /,kriptə'kristl,ien/ *adj* having a crystalline structure so fine that no distinct particles are recognizable under the microscope [ISV]

**cryptogam** /'kriptə,gam/ *n* a plant (eg a fern, moss, alga, or fungus) reproducing by spores and not producing flowers or seed [deriv of Gk *kryptos* + *-gamia* -gamy] – **cryptogamic, cryptogamous** *adj*

**cryptogenic** /,kriptə'jenik/ *adj* of obscure or unknown origin ⟨*a* ∼ *disease*⟩

**cryptogram** /'kriptə,gram/ *n* 1 a communication in cipher or code 2 a figure or representation having a hidden significance [Fr *cryptogramme*, fr *crypt-* + *-gramme* -gram] – **cryptogrammic** *adj*

**cryptograph** /'kriptə,grahf, -,graf/ *n* 1 a cryptogram 2 a device for producing and interpreting cryptograms

**cryptography** /krip'togrəfi/ *n* 1 secret writing; cryptic symbolization 2 the preparation of cryptograms, ciphers, or codes 3 cryptanalysis [NL *cryptographia*, fr *crypt-* + *-graphia* -graphy] – **cryptographer** *n*, **cryptographic** *adj*, **cryptographically** *adv*

**cryptology** /krip'toləji/ *n* the scientific study of cryptography and cryptanalysis [NL *cryptologia*, fr *crypt-* + *-logia* -logy] – **cryptologic, cryptological** *adj*, **cryptologist** *n*

**cryptomeria** /,kriptə'miəriə/ *n* an evergreen tree (*Cryptomeria japonica*) of the cypress family with curved needle-like leaves and small cones that is a valuable timber tree of China and Japan [NL, genus name, fr *crypt-* + Gk *meros* part; fr the seeds of its cones being hidden within bracts]

**cryptorchid** /krip'tawkid/ *n* one affected with cryptorchidism [NL *cryptorchid-, cryptorchis*, fr *crypt-* + *orchid-, orchis* testicle, fr Gk *orchis* – more at ORCHIS] – **cryptorchid** *adj*

**cryptorchidism** /krip'tawki,diz(ə)m/ *n* a condition in which one or both of a boy's testes fail to descend normally

**cryptorchism** /krip'taw,kiz(ə)m/ *n* cryptorchidism

**cryptozoite** /,kriptə'zoh-iet/ *n* a malarial parasite that develops in the tissue cells of its host and gives rise to the forms that invade blood cells [*crypt-* + *-zoite* (as in *sporozoite*)]

¹**crystal** /'kristl/ *n* 1 quartz that is transparent or nearly so and that is either colourless or only slightly tinged 2 something resembling crystal in transparency and colourlessness **3a** a solid body that is formed by the solidification of a chemical substance (eg an element or compound) and has a regularly repeating internal arrangement of its atoms, molecules, etc and usu flat external faces at definite angles to each other **b** a piece of a substance composed of crystals 4 (objects made of) very clear colourless glass of superior quality 5 the glass or trans-

parent plastic cover over a watch or clock dial **6** an electronic component containing crystalline material that is used esp to control the frequency of an ALTERNATING CURRENT (eg in a radio) **7 crystal detector, crystal** an electronic device, esp in a CRYSTAL SET (early form of radio), that contains crystalline material which converts radio signals received from a transmitter into a varying electric current that corresponds to the sounds being broadcast [ME *cristal*, fr OF, fr L *crystallum*, fr Gk *krystallos* ice, crystal]

²**crystal** *adj* **1** consisting of or resembling crystal; clear, lucid **2** of or using a crystal ⟨*a ~ microphone*⟩

**crystal ball** *n* **1** a sphere, esp of quartz crystal, traditionally used by fortune-tellers as an object of concentration in crystal gazing **2** a means or method of predicting future events ⟨*have no ~ to forecast economic trends*⟩

**crystal clear** *adj* perfectly clear

**crystal gazing** *n* **1** the art or practice of concentrating on a glass or crystal ball to aid the discovery or perception of future or unknown events **2** the attempt to predict future events or make difficult judgments, esp without adequate data – **crystal gazer** *n*

**crystall-, crystallo-** *comb form* crystal ⟨crystall*iferous*⟩ [Gk *krystallos*]

**crystalliferous** /ˌkristlˈifərəs/ *adj* producing or bearing crystals [ISV]

**crystalline** /ˈkristlˌien/ *adj* **1** composed of crystals **2a** made of crystal **b** resembling crystal (eg in transparency) **3** being, relating to, or having the structure of a crystal [ME *cristallin*, fr MF & L; MF, fr L *crystallinus*, fr Gk *krystallinos*, fr *krystallos*] – **crystallinity** *n*

**crystalline lens** *n* the lens in the eye of VERTEBRATE animals

**crystallite** /ˈkristlˌiet/ *n* **1** a minute imperfectly formed crystal; *esp* one occurring in rocks formed from lava that has cooled rapidly before proper crystals could form and that marks the first step in crystallization **2** a single crystal or particle in something (eg a metal) composed of many crystals [Ger *kristallit*, fr Gk *krystallos*] – **crystallitic** *adj*

**crystall-ize, -ise** *also* **crystal-ize, -ise** /ˈkristlˌiez/ *vt* **1** to cause to form crystals or assume crystalline form **2** to cause to take a definite form ⟨*tried to ~ his thoughts*⟩ **3** to coat (eg fruit or flower petals) with crystals, esp of sugar ⟨*~d grapes*⟩ ~ *vi* to become crystallized – **crystallizable** *adj*, **crystallization** *n*, **crystallizer** *n*

**crystallography** /ˌkristlˈogrəfi/ *n* the science dealing with the formation, shapes, and structure of crystals – **crystallographer** *n*, **crystallographic, crystallographical** *adj*, **crystallographically** *adv*

**crystalloid** /ˈkristlˌoyd/ *n, chemistry* a substance that dissolves completely to form a solution and is capable of being crystallized – compare COLLOID 1a – **crystalloidal, crystalloidal** *adj*

**crystal set** *n* a simple form of radio receiver that has no amplifier or source of power and that uses a CRYSTAL DETECTOR to convert radio signals into a form that produces sound when passed through an earphone

**crystal system** *n* any of the six or, in some classifications, seven categories into which a crystal is placed according to the arrangement of its atoms

**csardas** /ˈchahdash/ *n* CZARDAS (Hungarian dance)

**CSE** *n* CERTIFICATE OF SECONDARY EDUCATION

**CS gas** *n* a greyish powder that causes irritation and watering of the eyes and that is dispersed in the air as a means of controlling riots [Ben Carson & Roger Staughton *fl*1920 US chemists]

**'C-ˌstream** *n* the third and often lowest stream in a school

**ctenoid** /ˈtenoyd, ˈtee-/ *adj* (having or consisting of scales) with a toothed edge ⟨*a ~ fish*⟩ ⟨*a ~ scale*⟩ [ISV, fr Gk *ktenoeidēs*, fr *kten-, kteis* comb – more at PECTINATE]

**ctenophore** /ˈtenəˌfaw/ *n* any of a phylum (Ctenophora) of transparent gelatinous sea animals that superficially resemble jellyfishes and move by means of eight bands of thin flat plates made up of hairlike filaments (CILIA) [deriv of Gk *kten-, kteis + pherein* to carry – more at ²BEAR] – **ctenophoran** *adj or n*

**cuadrilla** /kwahˈdree(l)yə/ *n taking sing or pl vb* the team helping the matador in a bullfight [Sp, dim. of *cuadra* square, fr L *quadra*]

**cub** /kub/ *n* **1** the young of any of various flesh-eating mammals (eg a bear, lion, or fox) **2** a rude or cheeky young person **3** a young or inexperienced person, esp a newspaper reporter **4 cub, wolf cub** *often cap W&C* CUB SCOUT [origin unknown]

**cuban heel** /ˈkyoohbən/ *n* a broad medium-high heel on a shoe or boot [*Cuba*, island in the W Indies]

**cubbing** /ˈkubing/ *n, Br* cubhunting [*cub + -ing*]

**cubbyhole** /ˈkubiˌhohl/, **cubby** *n* **1** a snug or cramped space or place **2** a pigeonhole or similar small compartment in a desk, cupboard, etc [obs *cub* cattle-pen, fr D *kub* thatched roof; akin to OE *cofa* den – more at COVE]

¹**cube** /kyoohb/ *n* **1a** a three-dimensional geometric shape having six equal square faces **b** a cube-shaped block of anything ⟨*a sugar ~*⟩ **2** the number resulting from multiplying a number by itself twice [ME, fr L *cubus*, fr Gk *kybos* cube, vertebra – more at HIP]

²**cube** *vt* **1** to multiply (a number) by itself twice; raise to the third POWER ⟨*3 ~d is 27*⟩ **2** to cut (eg meat for a casserole) into cubes – **cuber** *n*

**cubeb** /ˈkyoohˌbeb/ *n* the dried unripe berry of a tropical shrub (*Piper cubeba*) of the pepper family, formerly used in medicine, esp to treat infections of the bladder and urinary tract [MF *cubebe*, fr OF, fr ML *cubeba*, fr Ar *kubābah*]

**cube root** *n* a number that when cubed produces a particular number ⟨*3 is the ~ of 27*⟩

**cubhunting** /ˈkubˌhunting/ *n, Br* the hunting of young foxes

¹**cubic** /ˈkyoohbik/ *adj* **1** having the form of a cube; cube-shaped **2** of or being a crystal or CRYSTAL SYSTEM characterized by three axes of equal length at 90° to each other **3a** three-dimensional **b** denoting a volume equal to that of a cube whose edges are of the specified length ⟨*a ~ yard of sand*⟩ **4** of or involving (mathematical terms of) the third DEGREE, ORDER, or POWER – **cubicly** *adv*

²**cubic** *n, maths* a cubic curve, equation, etc

**cubical** /ˈkyoohbik/ *adj* **1** cubic; *esp* shaped like a cube **2** relating to volume – **cubically** *adv*

**cubicle** /ˈkyoohbikl/ *n* a small compartment or space partitioned off from a large room or area (eg in a dormitory, swimming pool, or public toilet) [L *cubiculum*, fr *cubare* to lie, recline – more at HIP]

**cubic measure** *n* a unit (eg cubic metre or cubic inch) for measuring volume

**cubiform** /ˈkyoohbiˌfawm/ *adj* having the shape of a cube [L *cubus* + E *-form*]

**cubism** /ˈkyoohˌbiz(ə)m/ *n* a 20th-century art movement or style that uses predominantly angular shapes and that stresses abstract form, esp by displaying several aspects of the same object simultaneously [Fr *cubisme*, fr *cube + -isme* -ism] – **cubist** *n*, **cubist, cubistic** *adj*

**cubit** /ˈkyoohbit/ *n* any of various ancient units of length based on the length of the forearm from the elbow to the tip of the middle finger and usu equal to about 0.46 metres (about 18 inches) [ME, fr L *cubitum* elbow, cubit – more at HIP]

¹**cuboid** /ˈkyoohboyd/, **cuboidal** /kyoohˈboydl, ˈ---/ *n* **1** cubic or approx cubic in shape **2** made up of approx cube-shaped parts ⟨*~ epithelial tissue*⟩ **3** of or being the cuboid bone

²**cuboid** *n* **1** a three-dimensional geometric shape having six rectangular faces **2 cuboid bone, cuboid** an approx cube-shaped bone that is the outermost of the bones of the ankle

**cub scout, cub** *n, often cap C&S* a member of the most junior section of the (British) Scout movement

**cucking stool** /ˈkuking/ *n* a seat to which offenders (eg dishonest traders) were tied in former times to be pelted, jeered at, or plunged into water – compare DUCKING STOOL [ME *cucking stol*, lit., defecating chair]

¹**cuckold** /ˈkukohld, ˈkookohld/ *n* a man whose wife commits adultery [ME *cokewold*, prob deriv of OF *cucuault*, fr *cucu* cuckoo]

²**cuckold** *vt* to make a cuckold of (a husband) – **cuckolder** *n*, **cuckoldry** *n*

¹**cuckoo** /ˈkookooh/ *n, pl* **cuckoos 1** a greyish-brown European bird (*Cuculus canorus*) that lays its eggs in the nests of other birds which hatch them and rear the offspring; *broadly* any of a large family (Cuculidae of the order Cuculiformes) to which this bird belongs **2** the characteristic call of the cuckoo **3** *informal* a silly or slightly erratic person [ME *cuccu*, of imit origin]

²**cuckoo** *vt* cuckoos; cuckooing; cuckooed to repeat monotonously as a cuckoo does its call

³**cuckoo** *adj, informal* deficient in sense or intelligence; silly

**cuckoo clock** *n* a clock that announces the hours by sounds resembling a cuckoo's call

**cuckooflower** /ˈkookoohˌflowə/ *n* **1** a European and American plant (*Cardamine pratensis*) of the cabbage family that

grows in damp places and has white, pink, or violet flowers –
called also LADY'S-SMOCK **2** RAGGED ROBIN (pink-flowered
plant)

**cuckoopint** /'kookooh,pient/ *n* a European plant (*Arum maculatum*) of the arum family that has a large pale green leaflike
structure (SPATHE) surrounding a spike of densely packed tiny
reddish-brown to purple flowers, and that bears a cluster of
bright red berries as fruit – called also LORDS AND LADIES [ME
*cuccupintel*, fr *cuccu* + *pintel* pintle; fr the shape of its spadix]

**cuckoo spit** *n* a frothy mass produced on plants by the larva
of a FROGHOPPER (small insect) and in which the larva lives to
protect itself from drying up; *also* a froghopper [fr a popular
belief that it is a cuckoo's spittle]

**cucullate** /'kyoohkə,layt, kyooh'kulayt, -ət/ *also* **cucullated**
/'kyoohkə,laytid/ *adj* having the shape of a hood; hooded ⟨*a
~ leaf*⟩ [ML *cucullatus*, fr L *cucullus* hood]

**cucumber** /'kyoohkumbə/ *n* the long green-skinned fruit of a
climbing plant (*Cucumis sativus*) of the marrow family, that is
cultivated as a garden vegetable and eaten esp in salads; *also*
the plant that bears cucumbers [ME, fr MF *cocombre*, fr L
*cucumer-, cucumis*]

**cucumber tree** *n* any of several American magnolias whose
fruit resembles a small cucumber

**cucurbit** /kyooh'kuhbit/ *n* **1** a vessel or flask used with or
forming part of an ALEMBIC (apparatus formerly used in distilling liquids) **2** any plant of the marrow family [ME *cucurbite*,
fr MF, fr L *cucurbita* gourd]

**cud** /kud/ *n* food that a cow, sheep, or other RUMINANT animal
with four stomach compartments brings up into the mouth
from its first stomach compartment to be chewed again [ME
*cudde*, fr OE *cwudu*; akin to OHG *kuti* glue, Skt *jatu* gum]

**cudbear** /'kud,beə/ *n* a reddish dye obtained from any of various lichens [irreg fr *Cuthbert* Gordon, 18th-c Sc chemist]

**¹cuddle** /'kudl/ *vt* to hold close for warmth or comfort, or in
affection ∼ *vi* **1** *of two people* to hold one another close; hug
**2** to lie close or snug; nestle, snuggle – often + *up* □ compare
CARESS [perh fr E dial. *cull, coll* to hug, fondle, fr ME *collen*,
fr OF *coler*, fr *col* neck, fr L *collum*]

**²cuddle** *n* an act of cuddling; a hug or close embrace

**cuddlesome** /'kudls(ə)m/ *adj* cuddly

**cuddly** /'kudli, 'kudl·i/ *adj* suitable for or inviting cuddling;
lovable

**¹cuddy** /'kudi/ *n* **1** a small cabin or shelter under the foremost
part of the deck of a small boat **2** a small room or cupboard
[perh deriv of Fr *cahute* hut, cabin]

**²cuddy, cuddie** *n, dial Br* **1** a donkey **2** a stupid person; a
blockhead [perh fr *Cuddy*, nickname for *Cuthbert*]

**¹cudgel** /'kuj(ə)l/ *n* a short heavy club [ME *kuggel*, fr OE
*cycgel*; akin to MHG *kugele* ball, OE *cot* hut – more at COT] –
**take up the cudgels** to act vigorously or take part in a dispute
in support or defence of somebody or something

**²cudgel** *vt* -ll- (*NAm* -l-, -ll-) to beat (as if) with a cudgel

**cudweed** /'kud,weed/ *n* any of several plants (esp genera
*Graphalium* and *Filago*) of the daisy family, with leaves or
leaflike parts covered in woolly or silky hairs

**¹cue** /kyooh/ *n* **1a** a signal (eg a word, phrase, or action) to a
performer in a play, film, etc to begin a specific speech or
action **b** something serving a comparable purpose; *esp* a signal
(eg to a stagehand) to begin a particular operation **2** *psychology* **2a** a signal to begin an action; a stimulus that produces a
response **b** a feature of something that determines the way in
which it is perceived ⟨*foreshortened lines in a picture are ∼s to
depth perception*⟩ **3** a hint or suggestion as to what course of
action to take or when to take it **4** *archaic* the part or function
one has or is expected to perform (as if) in a play ⟨*was it my
∼ to fight?* – Shak⟩ [prob fr *qu*, abbr (used as a direction in
actors' copies of plays) of L *quando* when]

**²cue** *vt* **cuing, cueing** to give a cue to; prompt

**³cue** *n* **1** QUEUE 1 (pigtail) **2** a leather-tipped tapering rod for
striking the ball in billiards, snooker, etc [Fr *queue*, lit., tail, fr
L *cauda*]

**⁴cue** *vb* **cuing, cueing** *vt* to strike (a ball) with a cue ∼ *vi* to
use a cue

**cue ball** *n* the ball in billiards, snooker, etc that is struck by a
cue

**cuesta** /'kwestə/ *n* a hill or ridge with a steep face on one side
and a gentle slope on the other [Sp, fr L *costa* side, rib – more
at COAST]

**¹cuff** /kuf/ *n* **1a** the part of a garment (eg a glove) that encircles
the wrist; *esp* a band or turned-back piece of material at the

end of a sleeve **b** an inflatable band that is placed round the
upper arm to apply pressure and is used when taking a person's
BLOOD PRESSURE **2** *chiefly NAm* the turn-up of a trouser leg **3**
*pl, informal* handcuffs [ME, glove, mitten] – **cuffless** *adj* – **off
the cuff** without preparation; spontaneous [fr notes written
on the shirt-cuff by a public speaker]

**²cuff** *vt* to strike (as if) with the palm of the hand [perh fr obs
*cuff* glove, fr ME]

**³cuff** *n* a blow with the hand, esp when unclenched; a slap

**cuff link** *n* a usu ornamental device typically consisting of two
linked parts that are threaded through buttonholes on either
side of a cuff in order to fasten the cuff

**cuffuffle** /kə'fufl/ *n, Br informal* KERFUFFLE (commotion, fuss)

**cui bono** /,kwee 'bonoh/ *n* **1** a principle that probable responsibility for an act or event lies with somebody having
something to gain **2** usefulness or utility as a criterion in
assessing the value of an act or course of action [L, to whose
advantage?]

**¹cuirass** /kwi'ras/ *n* **1** a piece of armour consisting of a breastplate and backplate joined together; *esp* the breastplate of such
a piece **2** something (eg bony plates covering an animal) resembling a cuirass [ME *curas*, fr MF *curasse, cuirasse*, fr LL
*coreacea*, fem of *coreaceus* leathern, fr L *corium* skin, leather;
akin to OE *heortha* deerskin, L *cortex* bark, Gk *keirein* to cut
– more at SHEAR]

**²cuirass** *vt* to cover or equip with a cuirass

**cuirassier** /,kwirə'siə/ *n* a cavalry soldier who wore a cuirass
[Fr, fr *cuirasse*]

**cuish** /kwish/ *n* a cuisse

**cuisine** /kwi'zeen/ *n* a manner or style of preparing or cooking
food; *also* the food prepared [Fr, lit., kitchen, fr LL *coquina* –
more at KITCHEN]

**cuisine minceur** /,kwizeen man'suh (*Fr* kчizin mɛ̃sœr)/ *n* a
style of cooking that is derived from NOUVELLE CUISINE but
puts greater emphasis on the lightness and delicacy of the food
and uses almost no fattening or rich ingredients (eg butter,
cream, flour, and sugar) – compare NOUVELLE CUISINE [Fr,
slimness cooking]

**cuisse** /kwis, kwees/ *n* a piece of armour for the front of the
thigh [ME *cusseis*, pl, fr MF *cuissaux*, pl of *cuissel*, fr *cuisse*
thigh, fr L *coxa* hip – more at COXA]

**cuittle** /'koohtl/ *vt, Scot* to coax, wheedle [origin unknown]

**culch** /kulch/ *n* CULTCH (material forming the base of an oyster
bed)

**cul-de-sac** /'kul di ,sak, 'kool/ *n, pl* **culs-de-sac, cul-de-sacs**
/saks/ **1** *anatomy* a body pouch or tube with an opening at
one end only **2** a usu residential street closed or blocked off at
one end [Fr, lit., bottom of the bag]

**culet** /'kyoohlit, 'kulet/ *n* **1** the small flat face at the bottom of
a cut gemstone **2** a piece of plate armour covering the buttocks
[Fr, fr dim. of *cul* backside, fr L *culus*; akin to OE *hȳdan* to
hide]

**culex** /'kyoo,leks/ *n* any of a large widely distributed genus
(*Culex*) of mosquitoes that includes the common house mosquito (*Culex pipiens*) of Europe and N America [NL, genus
name, fr L, gnat; akin to OIr *cuil* gnat] – **culicine** *adj or n*

**culinary** /'kulin(ə)ri/ *adj* of or used in the kitchen or cookery
[L *culinarius*, fr *culina* kitchen – more at KILN]

**¹cull** /kul/ *vt* **1a** to gather, pick ⟨*∼ flowers*⟩ **b** to select from a
group; choose ⟨*∼ed the best passages from the poet's work*⟩
**2a** to select (an animal) for slaughter because of age or condition **b** to identify and remove the rejects from (a flock, herd,
etc) **3** to control the size of a population of (animals) by killing
a limited number *synonyms* see ¹CHOICE [ME *cullen*, fr MF
*cuillir*, fr L *colligere* to bind together – more at COLLECT] –
**culler** *n*

**²cull** *n* **1** the act or process of culling **2** an animal that is culled

**cullender** /'kuləndə/ *n* a colander

**cullet** /'kulit/ *n* broken or waste glass added to new material
when making glass to increase the rate of melting and as a
means of recycling glass [perh fr Fr *cueillette* act of gathering,
fr L *collecta*, fr fem of *collectus*, pp of *colligere*]

**cullion** /'kulyən/ *n, archaic* a mean or base fellow [ME *coillon*
testicle, fr MF, fr (assumed) VL *coleon-, coleo*, fr L *coleus*
scrotum]

**¹cully** /'kuli/ *n* **1** *slang* a pal, mate **2** *archaic* a person who is
easily tricked or imposed on [perh alter. of *cullion*]

**²cully** *vt, archaic* to cheat, deceive

**¹culm** /kulm/ *n* **1** ⁴SLACK (coal particles) **2** *often cap* a rock
formation deposited during the Carboniferous period, that

consists of shale and sandstone together with an inferior type of hard coal (ANTHRACITE) [ME; prob akin to ME *col* coal]

²**culm** *n* the stem of a grass or similar plant [L *culmus* stalk – more at HAULM]

**culminant** /'kulmɪnənt/ *adj, of a planet, star, or other celestial body* at greatest ALTITUDE or on the MERIDIAN (imaginary circle passing overhead and through the north and south poles)

**culminate** /'kulmɪnayt/ *vi* 1 *of a planet, star, or other celestial body* to reach the highest ALTITUDE; be directly overhead 2a to rise to or form a summit b to reach the highest or a climactic or decisive point □ (2) usu + *in synonyms* see SUMMIT [ML *culminatus*, pp of *culminare*, fr LL, to crown, fr L *culmin-*, *culmen* top – more at HILL] – **culmination** *n*

**culottes** /koo'lots/ *n pl* a woman's garment consisting of wide flaring trousers shaped to look like a skirt [Fr *culotte* breeches, fr dim. of *cul* backside – more at CULET] – **culotte** *adj*

**culpable** /'kulpəbl/ *adj* deserving condemnation or blame ⟨~ negligence⟩ [ME *coupable*, fr MF, fr L *culpabilis*, fr *culpare* to blame, fr *culpa* guilt] – **culpably** *adv*, **culpableness, culpability** *n*

**culprit** /'kulprit/ *n* 1 *law* somebody awaiting trial who has pleaded not guilty 2 one guilty of a crime or a fault [AF *cul* (abbr of *culpable* guilty) + *prest*, *prit* ready (ie to prove it), fr L *praestus* – more at PRESTO]

**cult** /kult/ *n* 1 formal religious veneration; worship ⟨*the* ~ *of the Virgin Mary*⟩ 2 (the body of believers in or followers of) 2a a system of religious beliefs, practices, and ritual ⟨*the* ~ *of Apollo*⟩ b a religion regarded as unorthodox or false 3a great devotion to a person, idea, or thing; *esp* such devotion regarded as a fad or fetish ⟨*the Victorian* ~ *of self-help*⟩ b a usu small circle of people united by devotion to an artistic, intellectual, etc movement [Fr & L; Fr *culte*, fr L *cultus* care, adoration, fr *cultus*, pp of *colere* to cultivate – more at WHEEL ] – **cultic** *adj*, **cultism** *n*, **cultist** *n*

**cultch, culch** /kulch/ *n* material (e g oyster shells) that is laid down to form the base of an oyster bed and that provides points of attachment for the oyster eggs [perh fr a Fr dial. form of Fr *couche* couch]

**cultivar** /'kulti,vah, -,veə/ *n* an organism of a kind originating and kept under cultivation [*cultivated variety*]

**cultivate** /'kultivayt/ *vt* 1 to prepare or use (land, soil, etc) for the growing of crops; *also* to loosen or break up the soil about (growing plants) 2a to foster the growth of (a plant or crop) b CULTURE 2a c to improve by labour, care, or study; refine ⟨~ *the mind*⟩ 3 to further, encourage ⟨~ *a friendship*⟩ 4 to go out of one's way to seek the society of or make friends with, esp with the intention of personal gain ⟨ ~ *MPs who were sympathetic to the cause*⟩ [ML *cultivatus*, pp of *cultivare*, fr *cultivus* arable, fr L *cultus*, pp] – **cultivatable** *adj*

**cultivated** /'kulti,vaytid/ *adj* refined, educated

**cultivation** /,kulti'vaysh(ə)n/ *n* 1 the act or art of cultivating 2 culture, refinement

**cultivator** /'kulti,vaytə/ *n* one who or that which cultivates; *esp* an implement to break up the soil round growing crops

**cultural anthropology** *n* a branch of anthropology that deals with the study of culture rather than the evolution, physical characteristics, etc of human beings – compare PHYSICAL ANTHROPOLOGY – **cultural anthropologist** *n*

**Cultural Revolution** *n* a revolutionary movement launched in 1966 to develop the ideological consciousness and revolutionary potential of the Chinese masses

¹**culture** /'kulchə/ *n* 1 cultivation or tillage of the soil 2 the practice of raising animals or growing plants or crops, esp with the aim of improvement ⟨*bee* ~⟩ 3a the development and improvement of certain qualities or faculties of the body or esp mind, by education or training b professional or expert care and training 4a enlightenment and excellence of taste acquired by intellectual and aesthetic training; refinement in manners, taste, thought, etc ⟨*a man of* ~⟩ b (acquaintance with and interest or taste in) the arts, humanities, and broad aspects of science as distinguished from vocational and technical skills 5a the pattern of human behaviour and its products that includes thought, speech, action, institutions, and artefacts and that is taught to or is adopted by successive generations b the typical behaviour, customary beliefs, social forms, and material traits of a racial, religious, or social group ⟨*the Minoan* ~⟩ 6a the growth of living cells, bacteria, viruses, etc in an artificial medium containing all the nutrients necessary to sustain growth; *also* a product of such growth b a culture medium together with the bacteria, viruses, etc growing in it

[ME, fr MF, fr L *cultura*, fr *cultus*, pp] – **cultural** *adj*, **culturally** *adv*

²**culture** *vt* 1 to cultivate 2a to grow (bacteria, viruses, etc) in a culture medium b to start the growth of living cells, tissues, etc from ⟨ ~ *a specimen of urine*⟩

**cultured** /'kulchəd/ *adj* 1 cultivated 2 produced under artificial conditions ⟨ ~ *viruses*⟩

**cultured pearl** *n* a natural pearl grown under controlled conditions (e g in an oyster farm) and artificially started by inserting a piece of grit, tiny pearl, etc into the mouth of the oyster, round which the oyster deposits the mother-of-pearl

**culture shock** *n* psychological and social disorientation caused by confrontation with a new or alien culture

'**culture-,vulture** *n, humorous* somebody with an avid though uncritical interest in culture

**cultus** /'kultəs/ *n* the ritual part of a religion; a cult [L, adoration]

**culverin** /'kulvərin/ *n* 1 an early musket 2 a cannon of relatively light construction and with a long barrel, used both on land and at sea in the 16th and 17th centuries [ME, fr MF *couleuvrine*, fr *couleuvre* snake, fr L *colubra*]

**culvert** /'kulvət/ *n* 1 a construction (e g a drain or pipe) that allows water to pass over or under an obstacle (e g a road or canal) 2 a channel or conduit for an electric cable [origin unknown]

**cum** /kum/ *prep* with; combined with; along with ⟨*a lounge* ~ *dining room*⟩ [L; akin to L *com-* – more at CO-]

**Cumanagoto** /kooh,mahnə'gohtoh/ *n, pl* **Cumanagotos**, *esp collectively* **Cumanagoto** a member, or the language, of a Cariban people of Venezuela

¹**cumber** /'kumbə/ *vt, formal* 1 to hinder, hamper ⟨~ed *with heavy clothing*⟩ 2 to clutter up ⟨*luggage* ~ing *the doorway*⟩ 3 to burden, overload ⟨~ *the memory with trivial facts*⟩ [ME *cumbren, combren*, prob short for *encombren* to encumber]

²**cumber** *n, formal* something that cumbers; *esp* a hindrance

**cumbersome** /'kumbə(s)əm/ *adj* 1 unwieldy because of heaviness and bulk ⟨*trying to move a* ~ *old Victorian sideboard*⟩ 2 awkward or inelegant because of length or complexity ⟨*a* ~ *sentence*⟩ – **cumbersomely** *adv*, **cumbersomeness** *n*

**cumbrous** /'kumbrəs/ *adj* cumbersome – **cumbrously** *adv*, **cumbrousness** *n*

**cumin** /'kumin, 'kyoohmin/ *n* a low-growing plant (*Cuminum cyminum*) of the carrot family cultivated for its aromatic seeds that are used as a flavouring [ME, fr OE *cymen;* akin to OHG *kumīn* cumin; both fr a prehistoric WGmc word borrowed fr L *cuminum*, fr Gk *kyminon*, of Sem origin]

**cummer** /'kumə/ *n, Scot* 1 a godmother 2 a woman, girl [ME *commare*, fr MF *commere*, fr LL *commater*, fr L *com-* + *mater* mother]

**cummerbund** /'kumə,bund/ *n* a broad sash worn round the waist, esp with men's formal evening wear [Hindi *kamarband*, fr Per, fr *kamar* waist + *band*]

**cummingtonite** /'kumɪŋtə,niet/ *n* a dark green or brown mineral, $(Fe,Mg)_7Si_8O_{22}(OH)_2$, that is a member of the AMPHIBOLE group of minerals [*Cummington*, town in Massachusetts, USA]

**cumquat** /'kum,kwot/ *n* KUMQUAT (small orange fruit or a plant that bears this)

**cumshaw** /'kum,shaw/ *n* a present, gratuity [Chin (Amoy) *gam sia (kam sia)* grateful thanks (a phrase used by beggars)]

**cumul-** /kyoohmyool-/, **cumuli-, cumulo-** *comb form* cumulus and ⟨*cumulocirrus*⟩ [NL, fr L *cumulus*]

**cumulate** /'kyoohmyoolayt/ *vt* 1 to accumulate, amass 2 to combine (e g entries from previous issues of a catalogue or index) into one ~ *vi* to become massed; accumulate [L *cumulatus*, pp of *cumulare*, fr *cumulus* mass] – **cumulate** *adj*, **cumulation** *n*

**cumulative** /'kyoohmyoolətiv/ *adj* 1a made up of accumulated parts b increasing by successive additions 2a *of a dividend or interest* to be added to the next or a future payment if not paid when originally due to be paid b *of a share* bearing such a dividend and entitling the holder to receive payment before holders of ORDINARY SHARES are paid 3 formed by adding new material of the same kind ⟨ ~ *book index*⟩ 4 *statistics* including or considering together all values less than or less than and equal to a particular value ⟨ ~ *distribution*⟩ ⟨ ~ *frequency*⟩ – **cumulatively** *adv*, **cumulativeness** *n*

**cumuliform** /'kyoohmyooli,fawm/ *adj* resembling a cumulus cloud

**cumulonimbus** /,kyoohmyooloh'nimbəs/ *n, pl* **cumulonimbi**,

/-'nimbi/, **cumulonimbuses** a cumulus cloud that extends to a great height, often spreads out at the top in the shape of an anvil, and is characteristic of thunderstorm conditions [NL]

**cumulostratus** /,kyoohmyoohloh'strahtəs/ *n, pl* **cumulostrati** /-'strahti/ a cumulus cloud whose base extends horizontally [NL]

**cumulus** /'kyoohmyoohləs/ *n, pl* **cumuli** /-lie, -li/ a massive cloud formation with a flat base and rounded outlines often piled up like a mountain [NL, fr L]

**cunctation** /kungk'taysh(ə)n/ *n, formal* delay, procrastination [L *cunctation-, cunctatio,* fr *cunctatus,* pp of *cunctari* to hesitate; akin to Skt *śaṅkate* he wavers] – **cunctative** *adj*

**cuneate** /'kyoohni-ət, -ayt/ *adj* having a narrow triangular shape with the smallest angle towards the base ⟨*a* ~ *leaf*⟩ [L *cuneatus,* fr *cuneus* wedge; akin to Skt *śūla* spear] – **cuneately** *adv*

¹**cuneiform** /'kyoohni,fawm/ *adj* 1 having the shape of a wedge 2 composed of or written in the wedge-shaped characters used in ancient Assyrian, Babylonian, and Persian inscriptions ⟨~ *alphabet*⟩ [prob fr Fr *cunéiforme,* fr MF, fr L *cuneus* + MF *-iforme* -iform]

²**cuneiform** *n* 1 cuneiform writing 2 a cuneiform part; *specif* any of the three wedge-shaped bones of the ankle

**cunnilinctus** /,kuni'lingktəs/ *n* cunnilingus [NL, fr L *cunnus* vulva + *linctus* act of licking, fr *linctus,* pp of *lingere* to lick – more at LICK]

**cunnilingus** /,kuni'ling-gəs/ *n* oral stimulation of the female genitals [NL, fr L, one who licks the vulva, fr *cunnus* + *lingere*]

¹**cunning** /'kuning/ *adj* 1 characterized by cunning: **1a** ingenious, skilful **b** devious, crafty 2 *NAm* pretty, cute *synonyms* see CLEVER, SLY *antonym* simple [ME, fr prp of *can* know] – **cunningly** *adv,* **cunningness** *n*

²**cunning** *n* 1 ingenuity, skill, or resourcefulness (e g in devising or executing something) 2 cleverness or deviousness in deceiving or attaining an end; slyness, craftiness

**cunt** /kunt/ *n, vulg* 1 the female genitals 2 a woman regarded as a sexual object; *also* sexual intercourse with a woman 3 *Br* an offensive or unpleasant person [ME *cunte;* akin to MLG *kunte* female genitals, MHG *kotze* prostitute]

¹**cup** /kup/ *n* 1 a small open drinking vessel that is typically bowl-shaped, has a handle, and is used for hot drinks (e g tea or coffee) 2 the consecrated wine used in the Christian ceremony of Communion; *also* the CHALICE in which the wine is held 3 that which comes to a person in life (as if) by fate ⟨~ *of happiness*⟩ **4a** an ornamental usu metal cup offered as a prize **b** a competition or championship in which the winner is awarded a metal cup **5a** something (e g a plant or body part) shaped like a cup **b** either of two parts of a garment, esp a bra, that are shaped to fit over the breasts **c** (the metal case inside) a hole into which the ball must be played in golf 6 any of various usu alcoholic and cold drinks made from mixed ingredients ⟨*cider* ~⟩ – compare ⁴PUNCH **7a** the contents of a cup **b** the capacity of a cup; *specif* CUPFUL 2 8 the mathematical symbol ∪ indicating a UNION (set containing all the elements of two sets) – compare CAP 7 [ME *cuppe,* fr OE; akin to OHG *kopf* cup; both fr a prehistoric WGmc word borrowed fr LL *cuppa* cup, alter. of L *cupa* tub; akin to OE *hȳf* hive] – **cuplike** *adj* – **in one's cups** drunk – **one's cup of tea** *informal* something one likes or is suited to ⟨*hockey isn't* my cup of tea⟩

²**cup** *vt* **-pp-** 1 to treat by CUPPING (former method of drawing blood to the surface of the skin) 2 to form into the shape of a cup ⟨~ped *his hands*⟩

**cupbearer** /'kup,beərə/ *n* somebody who serves wine in a royal or noble household

**cupboard** /'kubəd/ *n* a shelved recess or freestanding piece of furniture with doors, used for storing food, clothes, utensils, etc – see also SKELETON **in the cupboard** [ME *cupbord,* fr *cuppe* cup + *bord* board, table]

**cupboard love** *n* insincere love shown with the intention of gaining something [implying love for the sake of food in a cupboard]

**cup cake** *n* a small round cake that is baked in a cup-shaped paper or foil container and is covered with a thick layer of icing

¹**cupel** /'kyoohpl, kyoo'pel/ *n* 1 a small shallow porous cup, esp of BONE ASH, that is used in separating out precious metals from a mixture of these metals and lead, as part of a process

to determine the amount of precious metal in an ore or the purity of a precious metal 2 a dish forming the floor of a furnace in which silver, gold, etc is refined [Fr *coupelle,* dim. of *coupe* cup, fr LL *cuppa*]

²**cupel** *vt* **-ll-** (*NAm* **-ll-, -l-**) to refine by means of a cupel – **cupeller** *n*

**cupellation** /,kyoohpl'aysh(ə)n/ *n* a method of refining gold, silver, or another precious metal by melting a mixture of the impure metal and lead in a cupel and directing a blast of air over the mixture. The lead and other unwanted metals become combined with oxygen and are either run off or partly sink into the porous cupel and are partly swept away in the blast.

**cupful** /'kupf(ə)l/ *n, pl* **cupfuls** *also* **cupsful** 1 as much as a cup will hold 2 any of various units of measure used esp in cookery: e g **2a** a British measure equal to 10 fluid ounces (about 0.28 litres) **b** a US measure equal to 8 fluid ounces (about 0.23 litres)

**cup fungus** *n* any of an order (Pezizales) of fungi that chiefly live on rotting wood and soil, and have a spore-containing body that is typically shaped like a cup, saucer, or disc

**cupid** /'kyoohpid/ *n* a representation of Cupid, as a winged naked boy often holding a bow and arrow [L *Cupido,* Cupid, Roman god of love, fr *cupido* desire, fr *cupere* to desire]

**cupidity** /kyooh'pidəti/ *n* strong desire, esp for wealth; avarice, greed [ME *cupidite,* fr MF *cupidité,* fr L *cupiditat-, cupiditas* – more at COVET]

**Cupid's bow** *n* the shape of a stylized archery bow having two convex curves – used in descriptions of the upper lip of a human mouth

**cupola** /'kyoohpələ/ *n* **1a** a small domed structure on top of a roof **b** a domed roof or ceiling 2 an upright cylindrical furnace used for melting iron in a foundry 3 a revolving armoured structure on a warship, housing one or more large guns; TURRET 3b [It, fr L *cupula,* dim. of *cupa* tub]

**cuppa** /'kupə/ *n, chiefly Br informal* a cup of tea [short for *cuppa tea,* pronunciation spelling of *cup of tea*]

**cupping** /'kuping/ *n* the former practice of applying a heated glass vessel to the skin in order to draw blood to the surface by suction (e g in preparation for bleeding the patient)

**cupr-** /kyoohpr-/, **cupri-, cupro-** *comb form* copper ⟨*cupri-ferous*⟩; copper and ⟨*cupro-nickel*⟩ [LL *cuprum* – more at COPPER]

**cuprammonium rayon** /,kyoohprə'mohnyəm, -ni-əm/ *n* a rayon made from CELLULOSE (constituent of woody or fibrous plant tissue) dissolved in an ammonia-containing solution of copper

**cupreous** /'kyoohpri-əs/ *adj* containing or resembling copper; coppery [LL *cupreus,* fr *cuprum*]

**cupric** /'kyoohprik/ *adj* of or containing copper, esp with a VALENCY of two

**cupriferous** /kyooh'prif(ə)rəs/ *adj* containing copper ⟨*a* ~ *ore*⟩

**cuprite** /'kyoohpriet/ *n* a red mineral that consists of copper oxide, $Cu_2O$, and is a source of copper [Ger *kuprit,* fr LL *cuprum*]

**cupro-nickel** /,kyoohproh 'nik(ə)l/ *n* an alloy of copper and nickel; *esp* one containing about 70 per cent copper and 30 per cent nickel used esp in British silver coins

**cuprous** /'kyoohprəs/ *adj* of or containing copper, esp with a VALENCY of one

¹**cup-,tie** *n* a match in a knockout competition for a cup

¹**cup-,tied** *adj* not allowed to play in a cup-tie ⟨*after his mid-season transfer he was* ~⟩

**cupulate** /'kyoohpyoolayt, -lət/ *also* **cupular** /'kyoohpyoolə/ *adj* shaped like, having, or bearing a cupule

**cupule** /'kyoohpyoohl/ *n* a cup-shaped anatomical or plant structure (e g a cup in which an acorn sits) [NL *cupula,* fr LL, dim. of L *cupa* tub – more at CUP]

**cur** /kuh/ *n* 1 a mongrel or inferior dog 2 a surly or cowardly person [ME, short for *curdogge,* fr (assumed) ME *curren* to growl + ME *dogge* dog]

**curable** /'kyooərəbl/ *adj* capable of being cured – **curably** *adv,* **curableness, curability** *n*

**curaçao** *also* **curaçoa** /,kyooərə'sow, -'soh, '---/ *n* a liqueur flavoured with the peel of bitter oranges [D *curaçao,* fr *Curaçao,* island in the Netherlands Antilles]

**curacy** /'kyooərəsi/ *n* (the term of) office of a curate

**curare, curari** /kyoo'rahri/ *n* a dried extract obtained esp from the bark of a woody climbing plant (e g *Strychnos toxifera* of the family Loganiaceae or *Chondodendron tomentosum* of the family Menispermaceae), that is used in arrow poisons by S American Indians and is the source of the drug tubocurarine used in medicine to relax the muscles [Pg & Sp *curare*, fr Carib *kurari*]

**curarine** /kyoo'rahrin, -reen/ *n* any of several chemical substances that are found in curare and act as muscle relaxants

**curar·ize, -ise** /kyoo'rahriez/ *vt* to treat (as if) with curare, esp so as to produce muscular relaxation (eg during major surgery) – **curarization** *n*

**curassow** /'kyooərə,soh/ *n* any of several large tree-dwelling game birds (esp genus *Crax*) of S and Central America related to the DOMESTIC FOWL [alter. of *Curaçao*]

**curate** /'kyooərət/ *n* 1 a clergyman in charge of a parish 2 a clergyman serving as assistant (eg to a rector) in a parish [ME, fr ML *curatus*, fr *cura* cure of souls, fr L, care]

**curate's egg** *n, Br* something that has both good and bad parts [fr a joke about a curate who, given a stale egg by his bishop, declared that parts of it were excellent]

**curative** /'kyooərətiv/ *n or adj* (one who or that which is) able or used to cure or remedy something, esp a disease – **curatively** *adv*

**curator** /kyoo'raytə/ *n* 1 somebody in charge of a place of exhibition (eg a museum or zoo) 2 the legal guardian of a child – used in Scots law [L, fr *curatus*, pp of *curare* to care, fr *cura* care] – **curatorship** *n*, **curatorial** *adj*

**¹curb** /kuhb/ *n* 1a **curb chain, curb** a chain of metal links that is attached to the side pieces of a horse's bit and passes under the horse's lower jaw to restrict movement of the bit and increase its restraining effect **b curb bit, curb** a bit, typically with long side pieces, that acts by leverage on the horse's mouth and is usu used in conjunction with a light simple mouthpiece (BRIDOON) and a curb chain in a DOUBLE BRIDLE (bridle with two sets of reins) – compare BRIDOON 2 a hard swelling just below a horse's hock that is usu caused by strain of a ligament 3 a check, restraint 4 an edge, border, or framework (eg of stone or metal) that strengthens or encloses a structure 5 *chiefly NAm* a kerb [MF *courbe* curve, curved piece of wood or iron, fr *courbe* curved, fr L *curvus*]

**²curb** *vt* 1 to put a curb on 2 to check or control (as if) with a curb ⟨*trying to ~ her curiosity*⟩ **synonyms** see RESTRAIN **antonym** spur

**curbstone** /'kuhb,stohn/ *n, chiefly NAm* a kerbstone

**curch** /kuhch/ *n, Scot* KERCHIEF 1 (headscarf) [ME]

**curcuma** /'kuhkyoomə/ *n* any of a genus (*Curcuma*) of tropical plants of the ginger family with short fleshy roots, including the plant from which turmeric is obtained [NL, genus name, fr Ar *kurkum* saffron]

**¹curd** /kuhd/ *n* 1 the thick part of coagulated milk that is rich in the protein CASEIN and is used as a food or made into cheese 2 something suggesting the curd of milk; *esp* a rich thick fruit preserve made with eggs, sugar, and butter ⟨*lemon ~*⟩ 3 the edible head of a cauliflower or similar related plant [ME] – **curdy** *adj*

**²curd** *vb* to coagulate, curdle

**curdle** /'kuhdl/ *vt* 1 to cause curds to form in; *specif* to cause to separate into solid curds and liquid ⟨*overheating ~d the milk*⟩ 2 to spoil, sour ~ *vi* 1a to form curds; coagulate **b** to separate out ⟨*add the eggs slowly to prevent the mixture curdling*⟩ 2 to go bad or wrong [freq of ²*curd*]

**¹cure** /kyooə/ *n* 1 *also* **cure of souls** spiritual and physical charge of a parish 2a recovery or relief from a disease **b** a drug, treatment, etc that cures a disease **c** a course or period of treatment ⟨*take the ~ for alcoholism*⟩ **d** (a resort with) water with health-giving qualities 3 something that corrects a harmful or troublesome situation 4 a process or method of curing [ME, fr OF, fr ML & L; ML *cura* cure of souls, fr L, care] – **cureless** *adj*

**²cure** *vt* 1a to restore to health, soundness, or normality **b** to bring about recovery from 2a to deal with in a way that rectifies **b** to free (a person) from something objectionable or harmful ⟨*~d him of excessive drinking*⟩ 3 to prepare for keeping or use by chemical or physical processing; *esp* to preserve (meat, fish, etc) by drying, smoking, or esp salting ~ *vi* 1 to undergo a curing process 2 to effect a cure – **curer** *n*

**curé** /'kyooəray/ *n* a French parish priest [OF, fr ML *curatus* – more at CURATE ]

**'cure-all** *n* a remedy for all ills; a panacea

**curettage** /kyoo'retij/ *also* **curettement** /kyoo'retmənt/ *n* the surgical scraping or cleaning (eg of the womb) by means of a curette

**¹curette, curet** /kyoo'ret/ *n* a scoop, loop, or ring used in curettage [Fr *curette*, fr *curer* to cure, clean, fr L *curare*, fr *cura*]

**²curette, curet** *vt* to perform curettage on

**curfew** /'kuhfyooh/ *n* 1 a regulation imposed on all or particular people, esp during times of civil disturbance, requiring their withdrawal from the streets by a stated time 2 a signal (eg the sounding of a bell) announcing the beginning of a time of curfew 3a the hour at which a curfew becomes effective **b** the period during which a curfew is in effect [ME, fr MF *covrefeu* signal given to bank the hearth fire, curfew, fr *covrir* to cover + *feu* fire, fr L *focus* hearth]

**curia** /'kyooəri·ə/ *n, pl* **curiae** /'kyooəri,ee/ **1a** a division of the people of ancient Rome made up of several families and constituting one tenth of a tribe **b** the place of assembly of one of these divisions 2 *often cap* the administration and governmental apparatus of the Roman Catholic church [L, prob fr *co-* + *vir* man – more at VIRILE] – **curial** *adj*

**curia regis** /,kyooəriə 'reejis/ *n, pl* **curiae regis** *often cap* a council of officers and advisers of a medieval king [ML, lit., king's curia]

**curie** /'kyooəri/ *n* a unit of radioactivity equal to the disintegration of $3.7 \times 10^{10}$ atomic nuclei per second; *also* a quantity of any radioactive substance with this rate of disintegration [Marie *Curie* †1934 Polish-Fr chemist]

**Curie point** *n* the temperature above which a FERROMAGNETIC material (material with strong magnetic properties like those of iron) loses its ferromagnetism and becomes PARAMAGNETIC (showing only the weak magnetic properties characteristic of most materials) [Pierre *Curie* †1906 Fr chemist]

**Curie temperature** *n* CURIE POINT

**curio** /'kyooərioh/ *n, pl* **curios** something considered novel, rare, or bizarre [short for *curiosity*]

**curiosa** /,kyooəri'ohzə, -sə/ *n pl* curiosities, rarities; *specif* unusual or pornographic books [NL, fr L, neut pl of *curiosus*]

**curiosity** /,kyooəri'osəti/ *n* 1 desire to know: **1a** inquisitive interest in others' concerns; nosiness **b** interest leading to inquiry ⟨*intellectual ~*⟩ **2a** a strange, interesting, or rare object, custom, etc **b** a curious trait or aspect 3 *archaic* undue fastidiousness

**curious** /'kyooəri·əs/ *adj* **1a** eager to investigate and learn **b** marked by inquisitive interest in others' concerns; nosy 2 strange, novel, or odd 3a *archaic* made carefully **b** *obs* abstruse [ME, fr MF *curios*, fr L *curiosus* careful, inquisitive, fr *cura* cure] – **curiousness** *n*

**curiously** /'kyooəriəsli/ *adv* 1 in a curious manner 2 as is or was curious ⟨*~, she's never been to Wales*⟩

**curium** /'kyooəri·əm/ *n* an artificially produced radioactive metallic chemical element with a VALENCY of three [NL, fr Marie & Pierre *Curie*]

**¹curl** /kuhl/ *vt* 1 to form into waves or coils ⟨*~ one's hair*⟩ 2 to form into a curved shape; twist ⟨*~ed his lip in a sneer*⟩ 3 to provide with curls ~ *vi* 1a to grow in coils or spirals **b** to form curls or twists ⟨*bacon ~ing in a pan*⟩ 2 to move or progress in curves or spirals ⟨*the path ~ed along the mountainside*⟩ 3 to play the game of curling [ME *curlen*, fr *crul* curly, prob fr MD; akin to OHG *krol* curly, OE *cradol* cradle]

**²curl** *n* 1 a curled lock of hair 2 something having a spiral or winding form; a coil 3 curling or being curled 4 a disease or abnormal condition of plants marked by rolling or curling of the leaves 5 a curved or spiral marking (eg in the grain of wood) 6 a function of a vector being the VECTOR PRODUCT of the function DIVERGENCE with a vector, and which can be used to find the ANGULAR VELOCITY at any point in a vector FIELD – compare DIVERGENCE 4, GRADIENT 3

**curler** /'kuhlə/ *n* 1 somebody or something that curls; *esp* a small cylinder on which hair is wound for curling 2 a player of curling

**curlew** /'kuhlyooh/ *n, pl* **curlews**, *esp collectively* **curlew** any of various largely greyish-brown to buff WADING BIRDS (genus *Numenius*, esp *Numenius arquata*) that chiefly inhabit heathland, shores, and other damp areas and have long legs and a long slender down-curved bill [ME, fr MF *corlieu*, of imit origin]

**curlicue** *also* **curlycue** /'kuhli,kyooh/ *n* a decorative curve or flourish (eg in handwriting) [*curly* + *cue* (a braid of hair)] – **curlicue** *vb*

**curling** /'kuhling/ *n* a game in which two teams of four players each slide heavy round flat-bottomed stones over ice towards a target circle marked on the ice [prob fr gerund of ¹*curl*]

**curling iron** *n* CURLING TONGS

**curling tongs** *n pl* a rod-shaped instrument that is heated and round which a lock of hair to be curled is wound

**curlpaper** /'kuhl,paypə/ *n* a piece of paper round which a lock of usu wet hair is wound to be curled

**curly** /'kuhli/ *adj* 1 tending to curl; *also* having curls 2 *of wood* having a wavy grain often with alternating light and dark lines ⟨∼ *maple*⟩ – **curliness** *n*

**curly kale** /kayl/ *n* KALE 1a (variety of cabbage)

**curly top** *n* a destructive virus disease of plants, esp beets, that kills young plants and causes curling and puckering of the leaves in older plants

**curmudgeon** /kə'mujən/ *n* 1 a crusty, ill-tempered, and usu old man 2 *archaic* a miser [origin unknown] – **curmudgeonly** *adj*

**curn** /kuhn/ *n, Scot* 1 GRAIN, CORN (small hard seed of a cereal plant) 2 an indeterminate usu small number; a few [ME *curn;* akin to ME *corn*]

**curragh, currach** /'kurə, 'kurəkh/ *n* 1 a small boat of design traditional in Ireland that is like a CORACLE in being constructed of hides stretched over a frame but is longer and narrower 2 *Irish* marshy wasteland [ScGael *curach* & IrGael *currach;* akin to MIr *curach* coracle]

**curran** /'kurən/ *n, Scot* (a) curn

**currant** /'kurənt/ *n* 1 a small seedless dried grape that is grown chiefly in the E Mediterranean and is used in cookery 2 the acid edible fruit (eg a redcurrant or blackcurrant) of any of several bushes or shrubs (genus *Ribes*) of the gooseberry family; *also* a plant bearing currants △ current [ME *raison of Coraunte*, lit., raisin of Corinth, fr *Corinth*, region & city of Greece]

**currency** /'kurənsi/ *n* 1a circulation as a medium of exchange ⟨*threepenny bits are no longer in* ∼⟩ **b** (the state of being in) general use, acceptance, or prevalence ⟨*the* ∼ *of these theories*⟩ 2 something (eg coins and bank notes) that is in circulation as a medium of exchange [ML *currentia* flowing, fr L *current-, currens*, prp of *currere* to run]

**¹current** /'kurənt/ *adj* 1a elapsing now; present ⟨*during the* ∼ *week*⟩ **b** occurring in or belonging to the present time 2 used as a medium of exchange 3 generally accepted, used, practised, or prevalent at the moment 4 *archaic* running, flowing **synonyms** see ¹MODERN **antonym** out-of-date [ME *curraunt*, fr OF *curant*, prp of *courre* to run, fr L *currere* – more at CAR] – **currently** *adv*, **currentness** *n*

**²current** *n* 1a a part of a volume of gas or liquid that flows continuously in a certain direction ⟨*a* ∼ *of air*⟩; *also* the rate of flow of a current **b** the swiftest part of a stream **c** a (tidal) movement of water in a lake, sea, or ocean **d** the condition of flowing 2 a tendency to follow a certain or specified course ⟨*an increasing* ∼ *of radicalism*⟩ 3 a flow of electricity round a circuit; a flow of electric charge; *also* the rate of such a flow **synonyms** see TENDENCY △ currant

**current account** *n, chiefly Br* a bank account against which cheques may be drawn and on which interest is not usu payable – compare DEPOSIT ACCOUNT

**current assets** *n pl* stocks, shares, money owed, etc that can readily be converted into cash

**curricle** /'kurikl/ *n* a 2-wheeled carriage, usu drawn by two horses [L *curriculum* running, chariot]

**curriculum** /kə'rikyoolǝm/ *n, pl* **curricula** /-lə/ *also* **curriculums** the courses offered by an educational institution or followed by an individual or group [NL, fr L, running, fr *currere*] – **curricular** *adj*

**curriculum vitae** /'veetie, 'vieti/ *n, pl* **curricula vitae** a summary of a person's career and qualifications, esp as relevant to a job application [L, course of (one's) life]

**currish** /'kuhrish/ *adj* 1 resembling a cur 2 ignoble, mean – **currishly** *adv*

**¹curry** /'kuri/ *vt* 1 to groom (eg a horse) with a currycomb 2 to treat (tanned leather), esp by beating, soaking, scraping, or colouring – see also curry FAVOUR [ME *currayen*, fr OF *correer* to prepare, curry, fr (assumed) VL *conredare*, fr L *com-* + a base of Gmc origin; akin to Goth *garaiths* arrayed – more at READY] – **currier** *n*

**²curry** *also* **currie** /'kuri/ *n* a food or dish seasoned with a mixture of hot strong-tasting or aromatic spices (eg chillies, turmeric, and cumin) [Tamil-Malayalam *kaṟi*]

**³curry** *vt* to flavour or cook with curry powder or sauce

**currycomb** /'kuri,kohm/ *n* a metal comb with rows of teeth or serrated ridges, used esp to clean grooming brushes or to curry horses – **currycomb** *vt*

**curry powder** *n* a condiment consisting of several hot and pungent ground spices (eg cayenne pepper, fenugreek, and turmeric)

**¹curse** /kuhs/ *n* 1a an utterance (of a deity) or a request (to a deity) that invokes harm or injury **b** an expression of anger, hate, etc 2 an evil or misfortune that comes (as if) in response to a curse or as retribution 3 a cause of great harm or misfortune 4 *informal* (a period of) menstruation – usu + *the* [ME *curs*, fr OE]

**²curse** *vt* 1a to call on divine or supernatural power to cause harm or injury to; *also* to doom, damn **b** to express great hate or distaste for in fervent and often profane terms 2 to use profanely insolent language against 3 to bring great evil on; afflict ∼ *vi* to utter curses; swear

**cursed** /'kuhsid, kuhst/ *also* **curst** /kuhst/ *adj* under or deserving a curse – **cursedly** *adv*, **cursedness** *n*

**¹cursive** /'kuhsiv/ *adj* running, flowing: eg **a** written in flowing, usu slanted, strokes with the characters joined in each word **b** of or being letters for printing imitating handwritten script [Fr or ML; Fr *cursif*, fr ML *cursivus*, lit., running, fr L *cursus*, pp of *currere* to run] – **cursively** *adv*, **cursiveness** *n*

**²cursive** *n* cursive writing; *also* a style of printed letter resembling this

**cursor** /'kuhsə/ *n* 1 a sliding part of an instrument; *esp* a transparent slide engraved with one or more fine reference lines that forms part of a SLIDE RULE 2 a movable pointer (eg a flashing square of light) on a VISUAL DISPLAY UNIT, radar screen, etc for indicating a specific position [obs *cursor* runner, fr ME, fr L, fr *cursus*, pp]

**cursorial** /kuh'sawri-əl/ *adj, of (a part of) an animal* adapted to running

**cursory** /'kuhsəri/ *adj* rapid and often superficial; hasty ⟨*a* ∼ *glance*⟩ **synonyms** see SUPERFICIAL **antonym** painstaking [LL *cursorius* of running, fr L *cursus* running, fr *cursus*, pp] – **cursorily** *adv*, **cursoriness** *n*

**cursus** /'kuhsəs/ *n, pl* **cursi** /-si/ a construction in earth consisting of two parallel banks with exterior ditches often of great length, closed at each end, dating from the later Neolithic period, of unknown use, and found only in Britain ⟨*the Dorset* ∼⟩ [L, course]

**curt** /kuht/ *adj* 1 sparing of words; terse 2 marked by rude or peremptory shortness; brusque **synonyms** see BRUSQUE **antonym** voluble [L *curtus* shortened – more at SHEAR] – **curtly** *adv*, **curtness** *n*

**curtail** /kuh'tayl/ *vt* to cut short; reduce, limit ⟨∼ *the conversation*⟩ ⟨∼ *expenditure*⟩ [alter. of obs *curtal* to dock an animal's tail, fr *curtal* animal with a docked tail, fr MF *courtault*] – **curtailer** *n*, **curtailment** *n*

**¹curtain** /'kuht(ə)n/ *n* 1 a hanging fabric screen, usu capable of being drawn back or up; *esp* one used at a window 2 a device or agency that conceals or acts as a barrier – compare IRON CURTAIN 3 **curtain, curtain wall** 3a the section of a wall of a castle or similar fortification between two neighbouring towers, bastions, etc **b** an exterior wall that carries no load; *specif* one consisting of panels attached to a light framework 4a the movable screen separating the stage from the area in which the audience sits in a theatre **b** the ascent or opening (eg at the beginning of a play) of a stage curtain; *also* its descent or closing **c** the final situation, line, or scene of an act, play, ballet, etc **d** **curtain call, curtain** an appearance by a performer after the finish of a play, ballet, etc in response to the applause of the audience **e** *pl, informal* the end; *esp* death ⟨*it was* ∼s *for him when his treachery was discovered*⟩ [ME *curtine*, fr OF, fr LL *cortina*, fr L *cohort-, cohors* enclosure, court – more at COURT] – **ring down the curtain 1** to lower the curtain at the end of a production in the theatre **2** to put an end to; conclude – usu + *on*

**²curtain** *vt* 1 to furnish (as if) with curtains 2 to veil or shut off (as if) with a curtain – often + *off*

**curtain lecture** *n* a private reproof or scolding given to a husband by his wife [fr its orig being given behind the curtains of a bed]

**curtain raiser** *n* 1 a short play presented before the main full-length drama 2 a usu short preliminary to a main event

**curtal** /'kuhtl/ *adj archaic* wearing a short frock – chiefly in *curtal friar* 2 *obs* brief, curtailed [MF *courtault* having a docked tail, fr *court* short, fr L *curtus*]

**curtal axe** *n, archaic* a cutlass [by folk etymology fr MF *coutelas* cutlass]

**curtana** /kuh'tahnə, -'taynə/ *n* a sword without a point, carried at the coronation of English monarchs as a symbol of mercy [ME, deriv of AF *curtain*, fr OF *cortain*, name of the broken sword of the legendary hero Roland, fr *cort* short]

**curtilage** /'kuhtəlij/ *n, law* a garden, yard, courtyard, etc belonging to a house [ME, fr OF *cortillage*, fr *cortil* courtyard, fr *cort* court]

**¹curtsy, curtsey** /'kuhtsi/ *n* an act of respect or reverence made mainly by women in which the knees are bent and the head and shoulders lowered [alter. of *courtesy*]

**²curtsy, curtsey** *vi* to make a curtsy

**curule** /'kyooəroohl/ *adj* 1 of a folding seat similar to a camp stool, reserved in ancient Rome for the use of the highest dignitaries 2 privileged to sit in a curule chair [L *curulis*, alter. of *currulis* of a chariot, fr *currus* chariot, fr *currere* to run]

**curvaceous** *also* **curvacious** /kuh'vayshəs/ *adj, informal, of a woman* having a pleasingly well-developed figure with attractive curves

**curvature** /'kuhvəchə/ *n* 1 curving or being curved 2 a measure or amount of curving; *specif* the rate of change of the angle through which the tangent to a curve turns in moving along the curve and which for a circle is equal to the reciprocal of the radius 3a an abnormal curving of a body part (e g the spine) b a curved surface of a body organ (e g the stomach) [L *curvatura*, fr *curvatus*, pp of *curvare*]

**¹curve** /kuhv/ *vi* to have or make a turn, change, or deviation from a straight line without sharp breaks or angles ~ *vt* to cause to curve [L *curvare*, fr *curvus* curved – more at CROWN]

**²curve** *n* 1 a curving line or surface 2 something curved (e g a curving line of the human body) 3 a representation on a graph of a varying quantity (e g speed varying with time) 4 *maths* a line that may be precisely defined by an equation in such a way that the coordinates of its points are functions of a single INDEPENDENT VARIABLE 5 a distribution indicating the relative performance of individuals measured against one another 6 **curve**, **curveball** a baseball thrown so as to deviate from a normal or expected course – **curvy** *adj*

**¹curvet** /kuh'vet/ *n* a prancing leap of a horse in which all legs are in the air at once, the forelegs being raised first [It *corvetta*, fr MF *courbette*, fr *courber* to curve, fr L *curvare*]

**²curvet** *vi* **-tt-** (*NAm* **-t-**, **-tt-**) to make a curvet; *also* to prance, caper

**curvilinear** /ˌkuhvi'linyə, -ni-ə/ *also* **curvilineal** /-nyəl, -ni-əl/ *adj* 1 consisting of or bounded by curved lines; represented by a curved line 2 characterized by flowing tracery ⟨~ *Gothic*⟩ [L *curvus* + *linea* line] – **curvilinearity** *n*, **curvilinearly** *adv*

**cuscus** /'kuskəs/ *n* any of several tree-dwelling PHALANGERS (marsupial mammals), esp of New Guinea, that have dense fine fur, a long tail, and large eyes [NL, fr a native name in New Guinea]

**cusec** /'kyooh,sek/ *n* a unit of flow equal to the flow of a volume of 1 cubic foot (about 28·3 litres) per second [*cubic foot per second*]

**cush** /koosh/ *n, informal* CUSHION 3b

**cushat** /'kushət/ *n, chiefly Scot* a woodpigeon [ME *cowschote*, fr OE *cūscote*]

**Cushing's disease** /'kooshingz/ *n* CUSHING'S SYNDROME

**Cushing's syndrome** *n* a condition characterized by fatness, esp of the face, and muscular weakness, that is caused by an excess of certain STEROID hormones (e g cortisone) resulting in the malfunctioning of the body's processing of proteins, fats, etc [Harvey *Cushing* †1939 US surgeon]

**¹cushion** /'kooshən/ *n* 1 a soft pillow or padded bag; *esp* one used for sitting, reclining, or kneeling on 2 a body part resembling a pad, esp in supporting a structure or protecting it against shock 3 something resembling a cushion: e g 3a PILLOW 3 (padded support used in lacemaking) b a pad of springy rubber along the inside of the rim of a billiard table off which the balls rebound c an elastic body (e g of air or steam) for reducing shock d the body of air on which a hovercraft rides 4 something serving to lessen the effects of disturbances or disorders [ME *cusshin*, fr MF *coissin*, fr (assumed) VL *coxinus*, fr L *coxa* hip – more at COXA] – **cushionless** *adj*, **cushiony** *adj*

**²cushion** *vt* 1 to seat or place on a cushion 2 to provide with a cushion or cushions 3a to lessen the effects of b to protect against force or shock 4 to slow gradually so as to minimize the shock or damage to moving parts

**Cushitic** /koo'shitik/ *n* a branch of the AFRO-ASIATIC language family comprising various languages of E Africa, esp Ethiopia and Somaliland [*Cush* (Kush), ancient country of NE Africa] – **Cushitic** *adj*

**cushy** /'kooshi/ *adj, informal* entailing little hardship or difficulty; easy ⟨*a ~ job with a high salary*⟩ [Hindi *khush* pleasant, fr Per *khūsh*] – **cushily** *adv*, **cushiness** *n*

**cusk** /kusk/ *n, pl* **cusks**, *esp collectively* **cusk** *NAm* TORSK (fish related to the cod) [prob alter. of *tusk*, var of *torsk*]

**cusp** /kusp/ *n* 1 a point, apex: e g **1a** either horn of a crescent moon b a fixed point on a mathematical curve at which a point tracing the curve would exactly reverse its direction of motion and begin to trace a MIRROR IMAGE of the curve c an ornamental pointed projection formed by or arising from the intersection of two curves (e g in an arch) d a point on the grinding surface of a tooth 2 a fleshy fold or flap of a heart valve 3 the initial point of an astrological house [L *cuspis* point] – **cuspate** *also* **cuspated** *adj*

**cuspid** /'kuspid/ *n* a pointed tooth; CANINE 1 [back-formation fr *bicuspid*]

**cuspidate** /'kuspidayt/, **cuspidated** /-aytid/ *adj* 1 having a cusp or cusps 2 *esp of a leaf* ending in a point [L *cuspidatus*, pp of *cuspidare* to make pointed, fr *cuspid-, cuspis* point]

**cuspidor** /'kuspidaw/ *n* SPITTOON (bowl for spitting in) [Pg *cuspidouro* place for spitting, fr *cuspir* to spit, fr L *conspuere*, fr *com-* + *spuere* to spit – more at SPEW]

**¹cuss** /kus/ *n, informal* 1 a curse 2 a fellow ⟨*a harmless old ~*⟩ [(1) by alter.; (2) partly alter. of *curse*, partly short for *customer*]

**²cuss** *vb, informal* to curse – **cusser** *n*

**cussed** /'kusid, kust/ *adj, informal* 1 cursed 2 obstinate, cantankerous – **cussedly** *adv*, **cussedness** *n*

**cussword** /'kus,wuhd/ *n, chiefly NAm* a swearword

**custard** /'kustəd/ *n* 1 a thick, usu sweetened, and often baked mixture made with milk and eggs 2 a sweet sauce made with milk and eggs or a commercial preparation of coloured cornflour [ME *custarde, crustade*, a kind of pie, prob deriv of OF *crouste* crust]

**custard apple** *n* 1 (the soft-fleshed edible fruit of) any of a genus (*Annona* of the family Annonaceae, the custard-apple family) of chiefly tropical American trees and shrubs: e g **1a** (the light green to yellow acid fruit of) a small W Indian tree (*Annona reticulata*) – called also BULLOCK'S HEART b SOURSOP c SWEETSOP 2 PAPAW 2 (N American tree or its yellow fruit) [fr the custard-like appearance & flavour of its pulp]

**custard pie** *n* a soft pie that is thrown at someone or applied forcefully to someone's face in slapstick comedy

**custodial** /ku'stohdi-əl/ *adj* 1 of guardianship or custody; *specif* marked by or given to watching and protecting rather than seeking to cure ⟨~ *care*⟩ 2 of or involving imprisonment or legal detention ⟨*a ~ sentence*⟩

**custodian** /ku'stohdi-ən/ *n* one who or that which guards and protects or maintains ⟨*a self-appointed ~ of public morals*⟩; *esp* the curator of a library, castle, museum, etc – **custodianship** *n*

**custody** /'kustədi/ *n* **1a** the state of being cared for or guarded b imprisonment, detention 2 the act or right of caring for somebody, esp when granted by a court of law; guardianship ⟨*the father gained ~ of the children after the divorce*⟩ [ME *custodie*, fr L *custodia* guarding, fr *custod-, custos* guardian]

**¹custom** /'kustəm/ *n* **1a** (an) established socially accepted practice b long-established practice having the force of law c the usual practice of an individual d the practices or conventions that regulate social life 2 *pl* **2a** duties, tolls, etc imposed by a country on imports or exports b *taking sing or pl vb* the agency, establishment, or procedure for collecting such customs 3 regular support given to a shop or business by people who buy their goods or services *synonyms* see ¹HABIT, ²TAX [ME *custume*, fr OF, fr L *consuetudin-, consuetudo*, fr *consuetus*, pp of *consuescere* to accustom, fr *com-* + *suescere* to accustom; akin to *suus* one's own – more at SUICIDE]

**²custom** *adj, chiefly NAm* 1 made or performed according to personal order ⟨~ *clothes*⟩ 2 specializing in custom work or operation ⟨*a ~ tailor*⟩

**customary** /'kustəm(ə)ri/ *adj* 1 based on or established by custom; usual 2 commonly practised, used, or observed *synonyms* see USUAL *antonym* occasional – **customariness** *n*, **customarily** *adv*

**custom-'built** *adj* built to individual specifications ⟨*a ~ car*⟩

**customer** /'kustəmə/ *n* 1 a person who (regularly) buys goods or services from a shop or trader 2 *informal* an individual, usu having some specified distinctive trait ⟨*a tough ~*⟩ [ME *customer*, fr *custume*]

**customhouse** /'kustəm,hows/ *n, NAm* CUSTOMS HOUSE
**custom·ize, -ise** /'kustəmiez/ *vt, chiefly NAm* to build, fit, or alter according to individual specifications – **customizer** *n*
,**custom-'made** *adj* made to individual specifications ⟨*a ~ suit*⟩
**customs house** *n* a building where customs and duties are paid or collected
**customs union** *n* an agreement between two or more states to allow free trade between themselves but to impose a common external tariff on imports from nonmember states
¹**cut** /kut/ *vb* **-tt-; cut** *vt* **1a** to penetrate (as if) with an edged instrument; make an incision **b** to castrate (a usu male animal) **c** to hurt the feelings of **d** to strike sharply with a cutting effect; slice or enter into with an effect like a sharp instrument ⟨*this wind ~s me to the bone*⟩ **e** to strike (a ball) with a glancing blow that imparts a reverse spin; ¹CHOP 2a **f** to play a cut shot in cricket at (a ball) or at the bowling of (a bowler) **g** to hit and propel (a ball in billiards, snooker, etc) at a marked angle by a fine contact with the ball struck by the cue **h** to experience the emergence of (a tooth) through the gum **2a** to trim, pare ⟨*~ one's nails*⟩ **b** to shorten by omissions ⟨*~ the script of the play*⟩; *also* EDIT 1b (put into final form by rearranging) **c** to dilute, adulterate ⟨*~ the whisky with water*⟩ **d** to reduce in amount ⟨*~ costs*⟩ **3a** to mow, reap ⟨*~ hay*⟩ **b(1)** to divide into parts with an edged instrument ⟨*~ bread*⟩; *also* to sever a part from ⟨*just going to ~ some flowers, dear*⟩ **b(2)** to fell, hew ⟨*~ timber*⟩ **c** to go across rather than round; go very near to **4a** to divide into segments or shares **b** to intersect, cross ⟨*this line ~s that one here*⟩ **c** to break, interrupt ⟨*~ our supply lines*⟩ **d(1)** to divide (a pack of cards) into ͏two portions **d(2)** to draw (a card) from the pack **5a** to stop, cease ⟨*~ the nonsense*⟩ **b** to refuse to recognize (an acquaintance) **c** to stop (a motor) by opening a switch; turn off **d** to end the filming of (a scene in a film, television show, etc) **6a** to make or give shape to (as if) with an edged tool ⟨*~ a diamond*⟩ ⟨*~ stone*⟩ **b** to shear or hollow out **c** to record sounds on (a gramophone record) **7a** to engage in (eg a mischievous action); perform, make ⟨*~ a caper*⟩ ⟨*~ a dash*⟩ **b** to give the appearance or impression of ⟨*~ a fine figure*⟩ **8** *informal* to absent oneself from (eg a class or function) ~ *vi* **1a** to function (as if) as an edged tool **b** to be able to be separated, divided, or marked with a sharp implement ⟨*cheese ~s easily*⟩ **c** to perform the operation of dividing, severing, incising, or intersecting **d** to make a stroke with a whip, sword, etc **e** to play a cut shot in cricket **f** to wound feelings or sensibilities **g** to cause constriction or chafing **h** to be of effect, influence, or significance ⟨*an analysis that ~s deep*⟩ **2a(1)** to divide a pack of cards, esp in order to decide who will deal or to settle a bet **a(2)** to draw a card from the pack **b** to divide spoils **3a** to proceed obliquely from a straight course ⟨*~ across the yard*⟩ **b** to move swiftly ⟨*a yacht ~ting through the water*⟩ **c** to follow an oblique or diagonal line **d** to change sharply in direction; swerve **e** to make an abrupt transition from one sound or image to another in film, radio, or television **f** to stop filming or recording – see also **cut** CORNERS, **cut it** FINE, **cut no** ICE, **cut off one's** NOSE **to spite one's face, cut** SHORT, **cut down to** SIZE [ME *cutten*]
 **cut across** *vt* **1** to take a shorter or easier way across (a field, corner, etc) **2** to go beyond or across the limits of ⟨*a new political group that* cuts across *old party loyalties*⟩ **3** to be opposed to ⟨*the decision* cut across *previous actions*⟩
 **cut along** *vi, informal* to go away; leave
 **cut back** *vt* **1** to shorten by cutting; prune ⟨cut back *the shrubs*⟩ **2** to reduce, decrease ⟨cut back *expenditure*⟩ ~ *vi* **1** to interrupt the sequence of a plot (eg of a film) by returning to events occurring previously **2** to reduce something in size or amount; economize – see also CUTBACK
 **cut down** *vt* **1** to bring down by cutting; fell ⟨cut down *the trees*⟩ **2** to strike down and kill or incapacitate ⟨cut down *in battle*⟩ ⟨*the disease* cut him down *in his prime*⟩ **3** to reduce or make smaller ⟨cut *the elder daughter's dress* down *to fit the younger*⟩ **4** to reduce, curtail ⟨cut down *expenses*⟩ ~ *vi* to reduce or curtail volume or activity ⟨cut down *on smoking*⟩
 **cut in** *vi* **1** to thrust oneself into a position between others or belonging to another; *esp* to drive into a gap in a line of traffic so as to nearly cause an accident **2** to join in something suddenly ⟨cut in *on the conversation*⟩ **3** to interrupt a dancing couple and take one of them as one's own partner **4** to become automatically connected or started in operation ⟨*the*

*fridge suddenly* cut in *as the temperature rose*⟩ ~ *vt* **1** to introduce into a number, group, or sequence **2** to include, esp among those benefiting or favoured ⟨cut *them* in *on the profits*⟩
 **cut off** *vt* **1** to strike off; sever **2** to bring to an untimely end ⟨cut off *in their prime*⟩ **3** to stop the passage of ⟨cut off *supplies*⟩ **4** to shut off; bar ⟨*the fence* cuts off *my view*⟩ **5** to separate, isolate ⟨cut *himself* off *from his family*⟩ **6** to disinherit ⟨cut *her* off *without a penny*⟩ **7a** to stop the operation of; turn off **b** to stop or interrupt while in communication ⟨*the operator* cut *me* off⟩ – see also CUTOFF
 **cut out** *vt* **1** to form or shape (as if) by cutting, erosion, etc ⟨cut out *a sewing pattern*⟩ ⟨cut out *a niche in politics*⟩ **2** to take the place of; supplant **3** to put an end to; desist from ⟨cut out *smoking*⟩ **4a** to remove or exclude (as if) by cutting; *esp* to intercept (a pass, shot, etc) in football **b** to make inoperative ~ *vi* **1** to drive suddenly to the other side of the road or into an adjacent lane, esp to overtake **2** to cease operating – see also CUTOUT, CUT OUT, **have one's** WORK **cut out**
 **cut up** *vt* **1** to cut into parts or pieces **2** to injure, damage, or destroy (as if) by cutting **3** to subject to hostile criticism; censure ~ *vi, NAm* to behave in a comic, boisterous, or unruly manner – see also CUT UP
²**cut** *n* **1** something that is cut or cut off: eg **1a** a length of cloth varying from 40 to 100 yards (44 to 109 metres) in length **b** the yield of products cut, esp during one harvest **c** a (slice cut from a) piece from a meat carcass or a fish **2** a product of cutting: eg **2a** a canal, channel, or inlet made by excavation or worn by natural action **b(1)** an opening made with an edged instrument **b(2)** a wound made by something sharp; a gash **c** a surface or outline left by cutting **d** a passage cut for a road, railway, etc **e** a pictorial illustration **3** the act or an instance of cutting: eg **3a** a gesture or expression that hurts the feelings **b** a straight or easy passage or course **c** a stroke or blow with the edge of a knife or other edged instrument, weapon, etc **d** a lash (as if) with a whip **e** the act of reducing size or amount or removing a part ⟨*a ~ in pay*⟩ ⟨*a ~ in a play*⟩ **f** an act or turn of cutting cards; *also* the result of such cutting **g** *the* reduction in the number of players in a golf tournament, made at the end of a day's play ⟨*beat the ~ with a score of 227*⟩ **4a** a sharp downward blow or stroke (eg of a racket or table-tennis bat; *also* backspin **b** an attacking stroke in cricket played towards the OFF SIDE with the bat held horizontally **5** an abrupt transition from one sound or image to another in films, radio, or television **6a** the shape and style in which a thing is cut, formed, or made ⟨*clothes of a good ~*⟩ **b** a pattern, type **7** a haircut **8** *informal* a share ⟨*took his ~ of the profits*⟩ – **a cut above** superior (to); of higher quality or rank (than)
³**cut** *adj* **1a** formed or fashioned by cutting **b** detached by cutting; *specif* cut from a growing plant ⟨*~ flowers*⟩ **c** sliced, chopped **d** castrated, gelded **2** indented, lobed ⟨*~ leaves*⟩ **3** *informal* drunk
 **cut and cover** *n* a method of tunnel construction in which the underground structure is built at the bottom of a CUTTING (excavation through high ground) that is then refilled to the previous ground level
,**cut-and-'dried** *also* ,**cut-and-'dry** *adj* **1** completely decided; not open to further discussion **2** being or done according to a simple, standard, or well-known plan, rule, method, etc [orig applied to herbs prepared for use, not growing or fresh]
 **cut and thrust** *n* purposeful, determined, and spirited action characteristic of a struggle ⟨*the ~ of the shopfloor – The Guardian*⟩
 **cutaneous** /kyooh'taynyəs, -ni·əs/ *adj* of or affecting the skin [NL *cutaneus*, fr L *cutis* skin – more at HIDE] – **cutaneously** *adv*
¹**cutaway** /'kutə,way/ *adj* having or showing parts cut away or absent (to reveal the interior)
²**cutaway** *n* **1** a man's coat, popular in the 19th century, that has skirts tapering from the front waistline to form tails at the back **2a** a cutaway picture or representation **b** a shot that interrupts the main action of a film or television programme to take up a related subject or to show action supposed to be going on at the same time as the main action
 **cutback** /'kut,bak/ *n* **1** something cut back **2** a reduction ⟨*~s in education due to lack of money*⟩
 **cute** /kyooht/ *adj* **1** clever, shrewd **2** attractive or pretty, esp in a dainty or delicate way **3** painfully arch; mawkish [short for *acute*] – **cutely** *adv*, **cuteness** *n*

**cut glass** *n* glass ornamented with patterns cut into its surface by an abrasive wheel and then polished

**cuticle** /'kyoohtikl/ *n* **1** a skin or outer covering: eg **1a** an often thick or horny layer forming the outer protective covering of many INVERTEBRATE animals (eg crabs, insects, and worms) **b** the outermost layer of the skin of humans and other vertebrate animals; EPIDERMIS **1a c** a thin waxy film of cutin coating the external surface of many plants **2** dead or horny skin; *esp* that surrounding the base and sides of a fingernail or toenail [L *cuticula*, dim. of *cutis* skin – more at HIDE] – **cuticular** *adj*

**cutie, cutey** /'kyoohti/ *n, informal* an attractive person; *esp* a pretty girl [*cute* + *-ie*]

**'cutie-,pie** *adj, informal* odiously sweet ⟨*child stars with ~ accents*⟩

**cutin** /'kyoohtin/ *n* a water-repellent substance containing waxes and fats, that becomes impregnated into plant cell walls and forms a continuous layer on the external surface of plants [ISV, fr L *cutis*]

**cutin·ization, -isation** /,kyoohtinie'zaysh(ə)n/ *n* the impregnation or coating of plant cell walls with cutin – **cutinized** *adj*

**cutis** /'kyoohtis/ *n, pl* **cutes** /'kyoohteez/, **cutises** DERMIS (inner layer of the skin) [L]

**cutlass** *also* **cutlas** /'kutləs/ *n* **1** a short curved sword, esp as formerly used by sailors on warships **2** MACHETE (broad heavy knife) [MF *coutelas*, aug of *coutel* knife, fr L *cultellus*, dim. of *culter* knife, ploughshare]

**cutler** /'kutlə/ *n* one who deals in, makes, or repairs cutlery [ME, fr MF *coutelier*, fr LL *cultellarius*, fr L *cultellus*]

**cutlery** /'kutləri/ *n* **1** edged or cutting tools; *esp* implements (eg knives, forks, and spoons) for cutting and eating food **2** the craft or business of a cutler

**cutlet** /'kutlit/ *n* **1** a small slice of meat from the neck of lamb, mutton, or veal; *also* a flat mass of minced food in the shape of a cutlet ⟨*nut ~*⟩ **2** a cross-sectional slice from between the head and centre of a large fish (eg cod) – compare STEAK [modif (influenced by *cut*) of Fr *côtelette*, fr OF *costelette*, dim. of *coste* rib, side, fr L *costa* – more at COAST]

**cutoff** /'kut,of/ *n* **1** (a device for) cutting off **2** something cut off **3** the point, date, or period for a cutoff **4** *chiefly NAm* SHORTCUT 1 (shorter route than usual) – **cutoff** *adj*

**cutout** /'kut,owt/ *n* **1** something cut out or off from something else **2** a device for interrupting or switching off an electric current; *esp* one that is operated automatically by an excessive current – **cutout** *adj*

**cut out** *adj* naturally fitted or suited ⟨*not ~ to be a lawyer*⟩

**,cut-'price** *adj* selling or sold at a discount

**cutpurse** /'kut,puhs/ *n, archaic* a pickpocket

**,cut-'rate** *adj, chiefly NAm* cut-price

**cutter** /'kutə/ *n* **1** one who or that which cuts: eg **1a** someone whose work is cutting or involves cutting (eg of cloth or film) **b** an instrument, machine, machine part, or tool that cuts **2a** a ship's boat for carrying stores or passengers **b** a FORE AND AFT rigged vessel with one mast, a mainsail, and two headsails set lengthways **c** a small armed boat in government service (eg as a coastguard vessel) **3** a category of FLUE-CURED tobacco consisting of the large leaves pulled from the centre of the plant stalk

**¹cutthroat** /'kut,throht/ *n* **1** someone likely to cut throats; a murderous thug **2 cutthroat, cutthroat razor** a razor with a rigid steel cutting blade hinged to a case that forms a handle when the razor is open for use

**²cutthroat** *adj* **1** murderous, cruel **2** unprincipled, ruthless ⟨*~ competition*⟩ **3** played with three players, esp instead of a usual four ⟨*~ bridge*⟩

**¹cutting** /'kuting/ *n* **1** something cut (off or out): eg **1a** a part of a stem or root or a leaf that is cut from a plant and is capable of developing into a new plant **b** a harvest **2** something made by cutting: eg **2a** a gramophone recording **b** *chiefly Br* an excavation through a hill or other area of high ground for a canal, road, railway, etc **c** *chiefly Br* an item (eg a photograph or advertisement) cut out of a publication

**²cutting** *adj* **1** given to or designed for cutting; *esp* sharp, edged **2** *of wind* marked by sharp piercing cold **3** intended or likely to wound the feelings of another; *esp* sarcastic ⟨*a ~ remark*⟩ **4** intense, piercing – **cuttingly** *adv*

**cuttlebone** /'kutl,bohn/ *n* the internal shell of the cuttlefish, used for supplementing the diet of CAGE BIRDS with minerals or in powdered form for polishing

**cuttlefish** /'kutl,fish/ *n* a 10-armed marine, INVERTEBRATE

animal (family Sepiidae of the class Cephalopoda, phylum Mollusca) related to the squids and octopuses and differing from the squids in having a hard internal shell [ME *cotul*, fr OE *cudele*]

**cutty** /'kuti/ *adj, chiefly Scot* (cut) short [²*cut* + *-y*]

**cutty stool** *n* a seat in a Scottish church where offenders formerly sat for public rebuke

**cut up** *adj* deeply distressed; grieved ⟨*he's very ~ about the engagement*⟩

**cutwater** /'kut,wawtə/ *n* the foremost part of a ship's bow

**cutworm** /'kut,wuhm/ *n* any of various caterpillars (family Noctuidae) active chiefly at night, many of which feed on plant stems near ground level

**cuvette** /kyooh'vet/ *n* a small often transparent laboratory vessel; *specif* one for holding samples to be investigated in a SPECTROPHOTOMETER [Fr, dim. of *cuve* tub, fr L *cupa* – more at CUP]

**cwm** /koohm/ *n* CIRQUE 1 (deep basin on a mountain) [W, valley]

**-cy** /-si/ *suffix* (*n, adj → n*) **1** action or practice of ⟨*mendicancy*⟩ ⟨*piracy*⟩ **2** rank or office of ⟨*baronetcy*⟩ ⟨*papacy*⟩ **3** body or class of ⟨*magistracy*⟩ **4** quality or state of ⟨*bankruptcy*⟩ – often replacing a final *-t* or *-te* of the base word ⟨*accuracy*⟩ [ME *-cie*, fr OF, fr L *-tia;* partly fr *-t-* (final stem consonant) + *-ia -y;* partly fr Gk *-tia, -teia*, fr *-t-* (final stem consonant) + *-ia, -eia -y*]

**cyan** /'sie,an, 'sieən/ *n* a greenish-blue colour – used in colour printing of one of the PRIMARY COLOURS; compare MAGENTA, YELLOW [Gk *kyanos*]

**cyan-, cyano-** *comb form* **1** dark blue; blue ⟨*cyanotype*⟩ ⟨*cyanosis*⟩ **2** cyanide ⟨*cyanogenetic*⟩; *also* containing the chemical group C≡N ⟨*cyanobenzene*⟩ [Ger, fr Gk *kyan-, kyano-*, fr *kyanos* dark blue enamel]

**cyanamide** /sie'anəmied/ *n* **1** a corrosive acidic chemical compound, $H_2NC≡N$ **2** any of various chemical compounds (SALTS or ESTERS) formed by combination between cyanamide and a metal atom, an alcohol, or another chemical group **3** CALCIUM CYANAMIDE (chemical used in the industrial production of fertilizer) [ISV]

**cyanate** /'sieənayt, -nət/ *n* any of various chemical compounds (SALTS or ESTERS) formed by combination between CYANIC ACID and a metal atom, an alcohol, or another chemical group [ISV]

**cyanic** /sie'anik/ *adj* **1** relating to or containing cyanide **2** of a blue or bluish colour [ISV]

**cyanic acid** *n* a strong acid, N≡COH, used to prepare cyanates

**cyanide** /'sie-ənied/ *n* **1** the chemical group or ION CN⁻ **2** a chemical compound containing the cyanide ion; *specif* any of several usu extremely poisonous SALTS formed by combination between HYDROCYANIC ACID and a metal atom **3** NITRILE – not now used technically [ISV] – **cyanide** *vt*, **cyanidation** *n*

**cyanide process** *n* a method of extracting gold and silver from ores by treatment with a solution containing cyanide

**cyanine** /'sieəneen, -nin/ *n* any of various dyes that cause photographic film to be sensitive to green, yellow, red, and infrared light [ISV]

**cyanite** /'sieəniet/ *n* KYANITE (usu blue mineral)

**cyano** /'sieənoh, sie'anoh/ *adj* being or containing the chemical group C≡N [*cyan-*]

**cyanoacrylate** /,sie-ənoh'akrilayt, sie,anoh-/ *n* any of several liquid compounds formed from ACRYLIC ACID, used as very rapidly setting strong adhesives in industry and medicine

**cyanocobalamin** *also* **cyanocobalamine** /,sie-ənohkoh'baləmin, sie,anoh-/ *n* a cobalt-containing water-soluble vitamin, $C_{63}H_{88}CoN_{14}P$, of the VITAMIN B COMPLEX that is found esp in liver, is essential for normal blood formation, nerve function, and growth in most animals, and whose lack or malabsorption from the intestines results in PERNICIOUS ANAEMIA – called also VITAMIN $B_{12}$ [*cyan- + cobalt + vitamin*]

**cyanogen** /sie'anəjin/ *n* **1** the chemical group C≡N – not now used technically **2** a colourless inflammable extremely poisonous gas, $(CN)_2$, with an almondlike smell [Fr *cyanogène*, fr *cyan- + gène -gen*]

**cyanogenesis** /,sieənoh'jenəsis, sie,anoh-/ *n* production of cyanide (eg by plants) – **cyanogenetic, cyanogenic** *adj*

**cyanophyte** /'sie'anəfiet/ *n* BLUE-GREEN ALGA

**cyanosed** /'sieə,nohzd, -nohst/ *adj* affected with cyanosis

**cyanosis** /,sie-ən'nohsis/ *n* a bluish or purplish discoloration of the skin, lips, etc due to lack of oxygen in the blood [NL, fr Gk *kyanōsis* dark blue colour, fr *kyan-* cyan-] – **cyanotic** *adj*

**cybernated** /'sieba,naytid/ *adj* characterized by or involving cybernation ⟨*a ~ bakery*⟩

**cybernation** /,sieba'naysh(a)n/ *n* the automatic control of a process or operation (eg in manufacturing) by means of machines, esp computers [*cybern*etics + *-ation*]

**cybernetics** /,sieba'netiks/ *n taking sing or pl vb* the science of communication and control theory that is concerned esp with the comparative study of automatic control systems (eg that formed by the nervous system and brain or mechanical-electrical communication systems) [Gk *kybernētēs* pilot, governor (fr *kybernan* to steer, govern) + E *-ics*] – **cybernetic** *also* **cybernetical** *adj*, **cybernetically** *adv*, **cyberneticist, cybernetician** *n*

**cyborg** /'sie,bawg/ *n* a usu unemotional fictional character that is part human and part machine [*cyb*ernetic *org*anism]

**cycad** /'siekad/ *n* any of an order (Cycadales) of primitive trees related to the conifers, that are represented by a single surviving family (Cycadaceae) of tropical palmlike plants having an unbranched trunk and a crown of large leaves [NL *Cycad-, Cycas,* genus name, prob deriv of Gk *koïkas,* acc pl of *koïx* doum palm]

**cycl-** /siekl-, sikl-/, **cyclo-** *comb form* 1 circle ⟨*cyclometer*⟩ 2 having a molecular structure consisting of a ring of atoms ⟨*cyclohexane*⟩ [NL, fr Gk *kykl-, kyklo-,* fr *kyklos*]

**cyclamate** /'sieklamayt, 'sik-, -mat/ *n* a synthetic chemical compound used, esp formerly, as a sweetener [*cyclohexyl* (fr *cyclohex*ane + *-yl*) + sulph*amate* (fr *sulpha*mic + *-ate*)]

**cyclamen** /'siklaman/ *n* any of a genus (*Cyclamen*) of plants of the primrose family having showy drooping usu pink or white flowers with petals that turn back [NL, genus name, fr Gk *kyklaminos*]

**cyclase** /'sieklayz/ *n* any of a group of enzymes that cause the formation of a ring of atoms in the molecular structure of a chemical compound [*cycl-* + *-ase*]

**cyclazocine** /sie'klazasin, -seen/ *n* a painkilling drug, $C_{18}H_{25}NO$, that inhibits the effect of morphine and related addictive drugs and is used in the treatment of drug addiction [*cycl-* + *az*ocine ($C_7H_7N$), of unknown origin]

¹**cycle** /'siekl/ *n* 1 (the time needed to complete) a series of related events or operations happening regularly and usu leading back to the starting point 2a one complete performance of a periodically recurring process (eg a vibration or electrical oscillation) b a permutation of a set of ordered mathematical elements (eg numbers) in which each element takes the place of the next and the last becomes first 3a a circular or spiral arrangement b an imaginary circle or orbit in the heavens 4 a long period of time; an age 5 a group of poems, plays, novels, or songs on a central theme 6 a bicycle, motorcycle, tricycle, etc [Fr or LL; Fr, fr LL *cyclus,* fr Gk *kyklos* circle, wheel, cycle – more at WHEEL]

²**cycle** *vi* 1a to pass through a cycle b to recur in cycles 2 to ride a cycle; *specif* to bicycle ~ *vt* to cause to go through a cycle – **cycler** *n*

**cycle track** *n* a path reserved for esp pedal cycles

**cycleway** /'siekl,way/ *n* CYCLE TRACK

**cyclic** /'sieklik, 'siklik/, **cyclical** /-kl/ *adj* 1 of, arranged in, or belonging to a cycle 2 of or containing a ring of atoms ⟨*benzene is a ~ compound*⟩ – **cyclically, cyclicly** *adv*

**cyclic AMP** *n* a chemical compound consisting of a NUCLEOTIDE containing ADENOSINE, that functions as a regulator of processes occurring inside cells (eg those caused by hormones)

**cyclic group** *n* a mathematical GROUP that contains an element from which every other element of the group can be derived by repeatedly applying an operation (eg addition) which is defined for the group

**cyclist** /'sieklist/ *n* one who rides a cycle

**cycl-ize, -ise** /'siek(a)l,iez, 'si-/ *vt* to make (a chemical compound) from one or more rings of atoms in the molecular structure ~ *vi* to undergo cyclization – **cyclization** *n*

**cyclo-** – see CYCL-

**cycloalkane** /,siekloh'alkayn/ *n* any of a group of SATURATED chemical compounds (eg cyclopropane) of the general formula $C_nH_{2n}$, that contain only carbon and hydrogen atoms arranged in a ring

**cyclo-cross** /'siekloh ,kros/ *n* the sport of racing bicycles on cross-country courses that usu require the contestant to carry the bicycle over obstacles, up steep banks, etc

**cyclodiene** /,siekloh'die-een, ,siekloh-, ,---'-/ *n* any of a group

of chlorine-containing insecticides (eg aldrin, dieldrin, or chlordane) with a characteristic molecular structure that includes two joined rings each containing five carbon atoms [*cycl-* + *diene*]

**cyclogenesis** /,siekloh'jenasis/ *n* the development or intensification of a cyclone [*cyclo*ne + *genesis*]

**cyclohexane** /,siekloh'heksayn/ *n* a liquid chemical compound, $C_6H_{12}$, having the six carbon atoms joined in a ring, that is found in petroleum and is used esp as a solvent for lacquers, resins, etc, as a paint and varnish remover, and in making other organic chemical compounds [ISV]

**cycloheximide** /,siekloh'heksamied, -mid/ *n* a fungicide, $C_{15}H_{23}NO_4$, that is used in the control and treatment of some plant diseases and is obtained from a soil bacterium (*Streptomyces griseus*) [*cyclohex*ane + *imide*]

**cyclohexylamine** /,siekloh-hek'sielamin, -'silamin, -meen/ *n* a chemical compound, $C_6H_{11}NH_2$, that is a possibly harmful product of the breakdown of cyclamate in the body [*cyclohex*ane + *-yl* + *amine*]

¹**cycloid** /'siekloyd, 'sikloyd/ *n* the curved path traced out by a point on the circumference of a circle rolling along a straight line [Fr *cycloïde,* fr Gk *kykloeidēs* circular, fr *kyklos*] – **cycloidal** *adj*

²**cycloid** *adj* 1 circular; *esp* arranged or progressing in circles 2 *esp of a fish scale* having a smooth edge and concentric lines of growth like those of a tree; *also* having or consisting of cycloid scales 3 of or marked by swings between elated and depressed moods

**cyclometer** /sie'klomita/ *n* a device for recording the revolutions of a wheel and often the distance traversed by a wheeled vehicle, esp a bicycle

**cyclone** /'sieklohn/ *n* 1a a storm or system of winds that rotates about a centre of low atmospheric pressure in a clockwise direction in the southern hemisphere and anticlockwise in the northern, advances at high speeds, and often brings abundant rain b a tornado c LOW 1b (region of low atmospheric pressure) 2 any of various devices for separating materials (eg solid particles from gases or liquids) by high-speed rotation *synonyms* see WHIRLWIND [modif of Gk *kyklōma* wheel, fr *kykloun* to go round, fr *kyklos* circle] – **cyclonic** *adj,* **cyclonically** *adv*

**cyclopean** /,siekla'pee-an, sie'klohpian/ *adj* 1 *often cap* (characteristic) of a Cyclops 2 huge, massive ⟨*~ architecture*⟩

**cyclopedia, cyclopaedia** /,siekla'peedya, -di-a/ *n* an encyclopedia – **cyclopedic** *adj*

**cyclophosphamide** /,siekloh'fosfamied/ *n* a synthetic drug, $C_7H_{15}Cl_2N_2O_2P$, that suppresses the action of the body's immune system and is used esp in the treatment of cancers (eg LYMPHOMAS and LEUKAEMIAS)

**cyclopropane** /,siekloh'prohpayn/ *n* a gas, $C_3H_6$, used esp as a general anaesthetic [ISV]

**cyclops** /'sieklops/ *n* 1 *cap* any of a race of giants in Greek mythology with a single eye in the middle of the forehead 2 any of a genus (*Cyclops* of the order Copepoda, class Crustacea) of minute freshwater 1-eyed animals that are a constituent of plankton – called also WATER FLEA [(1) L, fr Gk *Kyklōps,* fr *kykl-* cycl- + *ōps* eye; (2) NL, fr L]

**cyclorama** /,siekla'rahma/ *n* a curved curtain or wall used as a background of a stage set to suggest unlimited space; *broadly* the back wall of a stage [*cycl-* + *-orama* (as in *panorama*)] – **cycloramic** *adj*

**cycloserine** /,siekloh'sereen, -'searreen/ *n* an antibiotic, $C_3H_6N_2O_2$, produced by several species of bacteria (esp *Streptomyces orchidaceus*) that is used esp in the treatment of tuberculosis

**cyclosis** /sie'klohsis/ *n* the slow, usu circular, movement of the jellylike material (CYTOPLASM) inside a living cell [NL, fr Gk *kyklōsis* encirclement, fr *kykloun* to go round]

**cyclostome** /'siekla,stohm, 'si-/ *n* any of a class (Cyclostomata) of primitive fishlike VERTEBRATE animals having a large sucking mouth with no jaws and comprising the HAGFISHES and LAMPREYS [deriv of Gk *kykl-* + *stoma* mouth – more at STOMACH] – **cyclostome** *adj,* **cyclostomate, cyclostomatous** *adj*

¹**cyclostyle** /'siekla,stiel/ *n* a machine for making multiple copies that uses a stencil cut by a pen whose tip is a small spiked wheel [fr *Cyclostyle,* a trademark]

²**cyclostyle** *vt* to make multiple copies of by using a cyclostyle

**cyclothymia** /,siekloh'thiemi-a, ,si-/ *n* a condition marked by abnormal swings between elated and depressed moods – compare MANIC-DEPRESSIVE [NL, fr Ger *zyklothymie*, fr *zykl-* cycl- + *-thymie* -thymia] – **cyclothymic** *adj*

**cyclotron** /'sieklə,tron/ *n* a machine for producing high-energy particles in which minute particles (e g protons or ions) are accelerated by the action of an ALTERNATING CURRENT in a constant MAGNETIC FIELD [*cycl-* + *-tron;* fr the circular movement of the particles]

**cyder** /'siedə/ *n, Br* cider

**cygnet** /'signit/ *n* a young swan [ME *sygnett*, fr MF *cygne* swan, fr L *cycnus, cygnus*, fr Gk *kyknos*]

**Cygnus** /'signəs/ *n* a northern constellation of stars between Lyra and Pegasus in the MILKY WAY – called also *the* SWAN [L, lit., swan]

**cylinder** /'silində/ *n* **1** *maths* **1a** a surface or solid traced or bounded by a straight line moving in a circle or other closed curve round and parallel to a fixed straight line **b(1)** the space bounded by a cylinder and two parallel planes that cross it **b(2) cylinder, right circular cylinder** such a space having circles in the two parallel planes such that a straight line connecting their centres is perpendicular to the two planes **2** a hollow or solid object with the shape of a cylinder and a circular cross-section: e g **2a** the rotating chambered part (BREECH) of a revolver that lies behind the barrel and into which cartridges are loaded **b(1)** the hollow chamber in which the piston slides in an engine **b(2)** a hollow circular chamber in a pump from which the piston expels the liquid or gas **c** any of various rotating parts in printing presses; *esp* one that impresses paper on an inked FORME (case containing metal type) **d** CYLINDER SEAL [MF or L; MF *cylindre*, fr L *cylindrus*, fr Gk *kylindros*, fr *kylindein* to roll; akin to OE *sceol* squinting, L *scelus* crime, Gk *skelos* leg, *skolios* crooked] – **cylindered** *adj*

**cylinder seal** *n* an engraved cylinder (e g of stone) used, esp in ancient Mesopotamia, to roll an impression on wet clay

**cylindrical** /si'lindrikl/, **cylindric** *adj* having the form or properties of a cylinder – **cylindrically** *adv*

**cylindrical coordinate** *n, maths* any of the three coordinates r, $\theta$, or z used to define the location of a point in space where, in one of three planes, r is the distance on a line drawn from a fixed point to the point being defined, $\theta$ is the angle that this line makes with a fixed line originating from the fixed point, and z is the perpendicular distance of the point being defined from the fixed line

**cylindrical projection** *n* a map projection of the earth's surface appearing as it would if projected onto the inner surface of a cylinder surrounding the globe and the cylinder being then unrolled and laid flat; *also* this method of representing the earth's surface. This projection is not commonly used because areas lying near to the poles are grossly exaggerated in size.

**cyma** /'siemə/ *n, maths* a double curve formed by the union of a concave line and a convex line [Gk *kyma* wave, waved moulding]

**cymbal** /'simbl/ *n* a concave brass plate that produces a brilliant clashing tone when struck with a drumstick or against another cymbal △ symbol [ME, fr OE *cymbal* & MF *cymbale*, fr L *cymbalum*, fr Gk *kymbalon*, fr *kymbē* bowl – more at HUMP] – **cymbalist** *n*

**cymbidium** /sim'bidi·əm/ *n* any of a genus (*Cymbidium*) of tropical African and Eurasian orchids with showy boat-shaped flowers [NL, genus name, fr L *cymba* boat, fr Gk *kymbē* bowl, boat]

**cyme** /siem/ *n* a flower cluster in which all flower stems end in a single flower; *esp* one of this type in which the main flower stem bears the central and first-opening flower with subsequent flowers developing from side stems [NL *cyma*, fr L, cabbage sprout, fr Gk *kyma* swell, wave, cabbage sprout, fr *kyein* to be pregnant]

**cymophane** /'siemə,fayn/ *n* CHRYSOBERYL (usu yellow or pale-green mineral); *esp* chrysoberyl that reflects light in rainbow colours [Fr, fr Gk *kyma* wave + Fr *-phane*]

**cymose** /'siemohs/ *adj* of, being, or bearing a cyme – **cymosely** *adv*

**¹Cymric** /'kumrik, 'koom-, 'kim-/ *adj* (characteristic) of the southern group of Celts (BRYTHONS) or their language; *specif* Welsh

**²Cymric** *n* BRYTHONIC (southern group of Celtic languages); *specif* the Welsh language

**Cymry** /'kumri, 'koomri/ *n taking pl vb* the southern group of Celts (BRYTHONS); *specif* the Welsh [W, pl of *Cymro* Welshman]

**cynghanedd** /koong'hahnidh, kung-/ *n* a system of combining rhyme and ALLITERATION (repetition of consonant sounds) within a line of verse that is used in composing poetry in Welsh [W, fr *cym-* com- (akin to L *com-*) + *canu* to sing; akin to L *canere* to sing – more at CHANT]

**cynic** /'sinik/ *n* **1** *cap* an adherent of an ancient Greek school of philosophers who held that virtue is the highest good and that its essence lies in mastery over one's desires and wants **2** one who doubts the existence of human sincerity or of any motive other than self-interest; *esp* one who expresses these views sneeringly or sarcastically [MF or L; MF *cynique*, fr L *cynicus*, fr Gk *kynikos*, lit., like a dog, fr *kyn-, kyōn* dog – more at HOUND] – **cynic** *adj*

**cynical** /'sinikl/ *adj* **1** tending to find fault **2** having or showing the attitude or temper of a cynic; *esp* contemptuously distrustful of human nature and motives – **cynically** *adv*

**cynicism** /'sinisiz(ə)m/ *n* **1** *cap* the doctrine of the Cynics **2** (an expression of) cynical character or quality

**cynosure** /'sinə,zyooə, 'sie-, -,shooə/ *n* a centre of attraction or attention △ sinecure [MF & L; MF, Ursa Minor, guide, fr L *cynosura* Ursa Minor, fr Gk *kynosoura*, fr *kynos oura* dog's tail]

**Cynthia** /'sinthi·ə/ *n poetic* the moon personified [L, epithet of the moon goddess Artemis or Diana, fr fem of *Cynthius* of Cynthus, fr *Cynthus*, mountain on Delos, Greek island, where she was supposedly born]

**cypher** /'siefə/ *vb or n, chiefly Br* (to) cipher

**¹cypress** /'sieprəs/ *n* **1** any of a genus (*Cupressus* of the family Cupressaceae, the cypress family) of evergreen trees with aromatic overlapping leaves resembling scales; *also* the wood of this tree **2** branches of cypress used as a symbol of mourning △ Cyprus [ME, fr OF *ciprès*, fr L *cyparissus*, fr Gk *kyparissos*]

**²cypress** *n* a usu black silk or cotton gauze formerly used for mourning clothes [ME *ciprus, cipres*, fr *Cyprus*, Mediterranean island]

**cyprinid** /'siprənid/ *n* any of a family (Cyprinidae) of soft-finned freshwater fishes including the carps and minnows [deriv of L *cyprinus* carp, fr Gk *kyprinos*] – **cyprinid** *adj*

**cyprinodont** /si'prinə,dont/ *n* any of an order (Microcyprini) of soft-finned usu marine fishes having toothed jaws, and including the guppies and swordtails [deriv of L *cyprinus* + Gk *odont-, odous* tooth – more at TOOTH] – **cyprinodont** *adj*

**Cypriot** *also* **Cypriote** /'sipri·ət/ *n or adj* (a native or inhabitant) of Cyprus [Fr *cypriote*, fr *Cyprus*]

**cypripedium** /,sipri'peedi·əm/ *n* any of a genus (*Cypripedium* or *Paphiopedalum*) of leafy-stemmed orchids (e g LADY'S SLIPPER) having large usu showy drooping flowers [NL, genus name, fr LL *Cypris*, a name for the goddess Venus + Gk *pedilon* sandal]

**cyproterone acetate, cyproterone** /sie'protərohn/ *n* a synthetic STEROID drug that inhibits the secretion of male SEX HORMONES (e g testosterone) and is used esp to treat some male sexual disorders [prob fr *cycl-* + *progesterone*]

**cypsela** /'sipsələ/ *n, pl* **cypselae** /-li/ a 1-seeded fruit (e g that of the daisy) formed by fusion of two CARPELS (female reproductive organs) and surrounded by a tubular CALYX (circle of leaflike structures supporting a flower) [NL, fr Gk *kypselē* vessel, box]

**Cyrenaic** /,sirə'nayik, sie-/ *n* an adherent or advocate of the doctrine that pleasure is the sole or chief good in life; a hedonist [L *cyrenaicus*, fr Gk *kyrēnaikos*, fr *Kyrēnē* Cyrene, city in N Africa, birthplace of Aristippus † *ab* 356 BC, author of the doctrine] – **Cyrenaic** *adj*, **Cyrenaicism** *n*

**Cyrillic** /si'rilik/ *adj* of or constituting an alphabet used for writing OLD CHURCH SLAVONIC and for various modern Slavic languages (e g Russian) [St *Cyril* †869, apostle of the Slavs, reputed inventor of the Cyrillic alphabet]

**cyst** /sist/ *n* **1** a closed sac (e g of watery liquid) with a distinct membrane, developing abnormally in a cavity or structure of the body of an animal **2** a body resembling a cyst: e g **2a** a spore of many algae that is not undergoing CELL DIVISION **b** an air-filled vesicle (e g of the BLADDER WRACK seaweed) **c** a capsule formed about a microorganism in a dormant or spore stage; *also* this capsule with its contents **d** a resistant covering round a parasite produced by the parasite or the host [NL *cystis*, fr Gk *kystis* bladder, pouch]

**cyst-** /sist-/, **cysti-, cysto-** *comb form* bladder ⟨*cystitis*⟩; sac ⟨*cystocarp*⟩ [Fr, fr Gk *kyst-, kysto-*, fr *kystis*]

**-cyst** /-sist/ *comb form* (→ *n*) bladder; sac ⟨*blasto*cyst⟩ [NL *-cystis*, fr Gk *kystis*]

**cystathionine** /ˌsistəˈthieəneen/ *n* a sulphur-containing AMINO ACID, $C_7H_{14}N_2O_4S$, formed as an intermediate chemical compound in the synthesis of the amino acid cysteine from methionine in animal organisms [irreg fr *cyst*eine + me*thionine*]

**cysteamine** /siˈsteeˑəmin/ *n* a cysteine derivative, $HS(CH_2)_2NH_2$, used in medicine (eg in the prevention of radiation sickness) [*cyst*eine + *amine*]

**cysteine** /ˈsistiˌeen, ˈsistayn/ *n* a sulphur-containing AMINO ACID, $HSCH_2CH(NH_2)COOH$, that forms part of many proteins and is easily converted to cystine [ISV, fr *cystine* + -*ein*]

**cystic** /ˈsistik/ *adj* **1** composed of or containing cysts **2** of the URINARY BLADDER or the GALL BLADDER **3** enclosed in a cyst

**cysticercoid** /ˌsistiˈsuhkoyd/ *n* a tapeworm larva having the head inverted in a liquid-filled sac developed from a portion of the larval body and bearing a solid tail piece

**cysticercosis** /ˌsistisuhˈkohsis/ *n, pl* **cysticercoses** /-ˈkohseez/ infestation with or disease caused by cysticerci [NL]

**cysticercus** /ˌsistiˈsuhkəs/ *n, pl* **cysticerci** /-ˈsuhkie, -ˌsie/ a tapeworm larva having the head inverted in a liquid-filled sac developed from the whole of the larval body [NL, fr *cyst*- + Gk *kerkos* tail]

**cystic fibrosis** /fieˈbrohsis/ *n* a common often fatal hereditary disease that appears usu in early childhood and is marked esp by faulty digestion, difficulty in breathing and excessive loss of salt in the sweat

**cystine** /ˈsisteen, -in/ *n* an AMINO ACID, $HOOCCH(NH_2)$-$CH_2SSCH_2CH(NH_2)COOH$, that forms part of many proteins (eg keratins) and is a major source of sulphur for METABOLISM (life-supporting biochemical processes) [*cyst*- + -*ine*; fr its discovery in bladder stones]

**cystinuria** /ˌsistiˈnyooəriə/ *n* a hereditary defect of METABOLISM (life-supporting biochemical processes) that is characterized by excretion of excessive amounts of cystine in the urine [NL]

**cystitis** /siˈstietəs/ *n* inflammation of the URINARY BLADDER [NL]

**cysto-** – see CYST-

**cystocarp** /ˈsistəˌkahp/ *n* the fruiting structure, containing spores borne on filaments, produced in the RED ALGAE after fertilization [ISV]

**¹cystoid** /ˈsistoyd/ *adj* resembling a cyst [ISV]

**²cystoid** *n* a structure resembling a cyst but lacking a membrane

**cystolith** /ˈsistəˌlith/ *n* **1** a hard solid chalky mass occurring in cells on the surface of some plants (eg nettles) **2** a small hard stone found in the urinary tract [Ger *zystolith*, fr *zyst*- cyst- + -*lith*]

**cystoscope** /ˈsistəˌskohp/ *n* an instrument that is passed through the URETHRA (tube that discharges urine from the bladder) for the visual examination of the bladder and the introduction of instruments into the bladder under visual control [ISV] – **cystoscopic** *adj*

**cystoscopy** /siˈstoskəpi/ *n* the practice or act of investigating the bladder with a cystoscope

**cyt-** /siet-/, **cyto-** *comb form* **1** cell ⟨*cytology*⟩ **2** cytoplasm ⟨*cytokinesis*⟩ [Ger *zyt*-, *zyto*-, fr Gk *kytos* hollow vessel – more at HIDE]

**-cyte** /-siet/ *comb form* (→ *n*) cell ⟨*leucocyte*⟩ [NL -*cyta*, fr Gk *kytos* hollow vessel]

**Cytherean** /ˌsithəˈreeˑən, siˈthiəriən/ *adj* of the planet Venus [L *Cytherea*, epithet of the goddess Venus, fr Gk *Kythereia*, fr *Kythēra* Cythera, Greek island where she was supposedly born]

**cytidine** /ˈsietədeen, ˈsi-/ *n* a chemical compound (NUCLEOSIDE), $C_9H_{13}N_3O_5$, that forms part of RNA and contains CYTOSINE attached to the sugar RIBOSE [*cyt*osine + -*idine*]

**cytochemistry** /ˌsietohˈkemistri/ *n* **1** microscopical biochemistry **2** the chemistry of cells – **cytochemical** *adj*, **cytochemically** *adv*

**cytochrome** /ˈsietəˌkrohm/ *n* any of several iron-containing pigments related to haemoglobin that are ENZYMES and function during the energy-producing reactions of cell RESPIRATION as transporters of electrons, esp to oxygen, by undergoing successive OXIDATION and REDUCTION

**cytochrome c** *n, often cap 2nd C* the most abundant and stable of the cytochromes occurring in the cells of all oxygen-requiring organisms

**cytochrome oxidase** *n* a cytochrome ENZYME important in the energy-producing chemical reactions of cell RESPIRATION

because of its ability to promote the OXIDATION of CYTOCHROME in the presence of oxygen

**cytodifferentiation** /ˌsietohˌdifəˌrenshiˈaysh(ə)n/ *n* the development of specialized cells (eg muscle, blood, or nerve cells) from undeveloped and undifferentiated cells

**cytogenetics** /ˌsietohjəˈnetiks/ *n taking sing vb* a branch of biology that deals with the study of heredity and variation by the methods of both cytology and genetics [ISV] – **cytogenetic** *adj*

**cytokinesis** /ˌsietohkieˈneesis, -ki-/ *n* the changes in the CYTOPLASM (jellylike material within a cell) accompanying MITOSIS (process by which a cell divides); *specif* the separation of the cytoplasm into daughter cells following division of the nucleus [NL, fr *cyt*- + Gk *kinēsis* motion] – **cytokinetic** *adj*

**cytokinin** /ˌsietəˈkienin/ *n* any of various plant growth hormones that promote CELL DIVISION and are concerned with a variety of developmental processes (eg initiation of shoot formation and seed germination) [*cyt*- + *kinin*]

**cytology** /sieˈtoləji/ *n* **1** a branch of biology dealing with the structure, function, multiplication, pathology, and life history of cells **2** the cytological aspects of a process or structure [ISV] – **cytologist** *n*, **cytological, cytologic** *adj*, **cytologically** *adv*

**cytolysin** /ˌsietəˈliesin/ *n* a substance (eg an antibody that breaks down bacteria) producing cytolysis [ISV]

**cytolysis** /sieˈtoləsis/ *n* the dissolution or disintegration of cells usu associated with disease [NL] – **cytolytic** *adj*

**cytomegalic** /ˌsietohmiˈgalik/ *adj* characterized by or producing enlarged cells [NL *cytomegalia* condition of having enlarged cells (fr *cyt*- + *megal*- + -*ia*) + E -*ic*]

**cytomegalovirus** /ˌsietohˌmegəlohˈvie;ərəs/ *n* any of a large group of highly species-specific DNA-containing viruses that are widely distributed in human beings and that affect esp the salivary glands and kidney causing enlargement of the infected cells

**cytomegalovirus inclusion disease of the newborn, cytomegalovirus inclusion disease** *n* a severe often fatal disease of newborn babies caused by infection with a cytomegalovirus and characterized by enlargement of the cells of most of the body organs

**cytomembrane** /ˈsietohˌmembrayn/ *n* any of the internal or external membranes of a cell

**cyton** /ˈsieton/ *n* the nucleus-containing body of a nerve cell; CELL BODY

**cytopathic** /ˌsietəˈpathik/ *adj* of, characterized by, or producing abnormal changes in cells (eg those occurring in disease)

**cytopathogenic** /ˌsietohˌpathəˈjenik/ *adj* causing disease and abnormal changes in or destructive to cells [*cyt*- + *pathogenic*] – **cytopathogenicity** *n*

**cytopathology** /ˌsietohpəˈtholəji/ *n* a branch of pathology that deals with the effects of disease at the cellular level, esp of the structural and functional changes brought about by disease [ISV]

**cytopharynx** /ˈsietohˌfaringks/ *n, pl* **cytopharynges** /ˌsietohfaˈrinjeez/ *also* **cytopharynxes** a channel leading from the surface to the interior of certain single-celled organisms (eg paramecium) and functioning as a gullet

**cytophilic** /ˌsietəˈfilik/ *adj* having an affinity for cells ⟨~ *antibodies*⟩

**cytoplasm** /ˈsietəˌplaz(ə)m/ *n* the jellylike substance of a plant or animal cell enclosed by the CELL MEMBRANE including all the ORGANELLES (specialized cell structures) but excluding the nucleus [ISV] – **cytoplasmic** *adj*, **cytoplasmically** *adv*

**cytosine** /ˈsietəˌseen/ *n* a chemical compound, $C_4H_5N_3O$, that is a PYRIMIDINE and is one of the four BASES whose order in the molecular chain of DNA or RNA codes genetic information – compare ADENINE, GUANINE, THYMINE, URACIL [ISV *cyt*- + -*ose* + -*ine*]

**cytosol** /ˈsietohˌsol/ *n* that portion of the cytoplasm excluding the ORGANELLES (specialized cell structures)

**cytostatic** /ˌsietəˈstatik/ *adj* tending to retard cellular activity and multiplication – **cytostatic** *n*, **cytostatically** *adv*

**cytotechnologist** /ˌsietohtekˈnoləjist/ *n* a medical technician trained in the identification of cells and cellular abnormalities (eg in cancer)

**cytotoxic** /ˌsietəˈtoksik/ *adj* **1** of a cytotoxin **2** having a toxic effect on cells – **cytotoxicity** *n*

**cytotoxin** /ˌsietəˈtoksin/ *n* a chemical substance (eg a toxin or antibody) having a toxic effect on cells [ISV]

**cytotropic** /ˌsietəˈtrohpik, -ˈtropik/ *adj* attracted to cells ⟨*a ~ virus*⟩

**czar** /zah/ *n* a tsar

**czardas, csardas** /ˈchahdash/ *n, pl* **czardas, csardas** /~/ a

with a rapid whirl [Hung *csárdás*] Hungarian dance in which the dancers start slowly and finish

**Czech** /chek/ *n* **1** a native or inhabitant of Czechoslovakia; *specif* a member of a Slavonic people of W Czechoslovakia **2** the Slavonic language of the Czechs [Czech *Čech*] – **Czech** *adj*

# D

**d, D** /dee/ *n, pl* **d's, ds, D's, Ds 1a** the 4th letter of the English alphabet **b** a graphic representation of or device for reproducing the letter *d* **c** a speech counterpart of printed or written *d* **2** five hundred **3** the 2nd note of a C-major musical scale **4** one who or that which is designated *d*, esp as the 4th in order or class or as of a lesser quality than someone or something rated *a, b,* or *c* **5a** a mark or grade rating a pupil's or student's work as poor in quality **b** one who or that which is graded or rated with a D **6** something shaped like the letter D: e g **6a** a semicircular area marked on a billiard table with the central part of the BAULK LINE forming its diameter and its arc enclosing that part of the end of the table in which the CUE BALL is placed ready for the opening shot of a frame or after being potted **b** the metal loop on the cheek piece of the bit of a horse's bridle

**d-** *prefix* **1** dextrorotatory ⟨d-*tartaric acid*⟩ **2** having a similar CONFIGURATION (arrangement of atoms) at an optically active carbon atom to the configuration of dextrorotatory GLYCERALDEHYDE – usu printed as a small capital ⟨D-*fructose*⟩ [ISV, fr *dextr*-]

**¹-d** *suffix* **1** – used to form the past participle of regular weak verbs that end in *e* ⟨*loved*⟩ ⟨*faded*⟩; compare **¹-ED 1 2** – used to form adjectives of identical meaning from Latin-derived adjectives ending in -*ate* ⟨*crenulated*⟩ **3** **¹-ED 2** – used to form adjectives from nouns ending in *e* ⟨*brogued*⟩ ⟨*bow-tied*⟩

**²-d** *suffix* – used to form the past tense of regular weak verbs that end in *e*; compare **²-ED**

**³-d** *suffix* (→ *adj*, chiefly *NAm* – used after the figure 2 or 3 to indicate the ordinal number second or third ⟨2d⟩ ⟨53d⟩

**d'** *vb* do ⟨d'*you know*⟩

*usage* The pronunciation of *do you* as /dyooh/ or /djooh/, rather *than* as two words, should be avoided in careful speech.

**'d** *vb* **1** had **2** would **3** *informal* did – used in questions ⟨*when'd she go?*⟩ *usage* See SHOULD

**da** /dah/ *n, dial Br* a father, daddy [short for *dada*, of baby-talk origin]

**¹dab** /dab/ *n* **1** a sudden feeble blow or thrust; a poke **2** a gentle touch or stroke (e g with a sponge); a pat **3** a daub, patch **4** a small amount of something soft or moist ⟨*a ∼ of chutney*⟩ **5** *pl, Br informal* fingerprints [ME *dabbe* sharp blow, prob of imit origin; most senses influenced in meaning by *daub*]

**²dab** *vb* **-bb-** *vt* **1** to strike or touch lightly; pat ⟨*I ∼bed the blood from my nose* – Honor Tracy⟩ **2** to apply lightly or irregularly; daub ∼ *vi* to make a dab

**³dab** *n* a flatfish; *esp* any of several flounders (genus *Limanda*) [AF *dabbe*]

**dabber** /'dabə/ *n* **1** one who or that which dabs **2** a pad, brush, or ball used to ink type or engraving plates

**dabble** /'dabl/ *vt* to wet slightly or intermittently by dipping in a liquid ⟨*the fabric should be ∼d in warm water, but do not soak, scrub, or wring it*⟩ ∼ *vi* **1a** to paddle, splash, or play (as if) in water **b** *of a duck* to reach with the beak to the bottom of shallow water in order to obtain food **2** to work or concern oneself superficially ⟨*∼s in art*⟩ [perh freq of ²*dab*]

**dabbler** /'dablə/ *n* one who or that which dabbles: e g a someone not deeply engaged in or concerned with something **b** a duck (e g a mallard or shoveller) that feeds by dabbling

**dabbling** /'dabling/ *n* **1** a superficial or intermittent interest, investigation, or experiment ⟨*his ∼s in philosophy and art*⟩ **2** a smattering ⟨*has only a ∼ of French*⟩

**dabbling duck** *n* DABBLER b

**dabchick** /'dab,chik/ *n* **1** any of several small GREBES (water birds); *esp* LITTLE GREBE **2** *dial Eng* a moorhen [prob irreg fr obs *dop* to dive + E *chick*]

**dab hand, dab** /dab/ *n, chiefly Br informal* a skilful person; an expert ⟨*a ∼ at bridge*⟩ [*dab* perh alter. of *adept*]

**da capo** /dah 'kahpoh/ *adv or adj* from the beginning – used as a direction in music to repeat [It]

**dace** /days/ *n, pl* **dace** a small European freshwater fish (*Leuciscus leuciscus*) [ME, fr MF *dars*, fr ML *darsus*]

**dacha** /'dahchə/ *n* a Russian country cottage or villa used esp in the summer [Russ, lit., gift; fr its frequently being the gift of a ruler]

**dachshund** /'daksənd, 'daks,hoont/ *n* (any of) a breed of small dogs of German origin with a long body, short legs, long drooping ears, and either a short smooth or a long wiry coat [Ger, fr *dachs* badger + *hund* dog]

**dacoit** /də'koyt/ *n* a member of an armed gang of robbers in India and Burma [Hindi *ḍakait*]

**Dacron** /'dakron/ *trademark* – used for a synthetic polyester textile fibre *synonyms* see NYLON

**dactyl** /'daktil/ *n* **1** a unit of poetic metre FOOT consisting of one long followed by two short syllables or of one stressed followed by two unstressed syllables (e g in *tenderly*) **2** a finger or toe – often in combination ⟨*pterodactyl*⟩ [(1) ME *dactile*, fr L *dactylus*, fr Gk *daktylos*, lit., finger; fr the three syllables having the first one longest, like the joints of the finger; (2) NL *dactylus*, fr Gk *daktylos*] – **dactylic** *adj or n*

**-dactylous** /-daktiləs/ *comb form* (→ *adj*) having (such or so many) fingers or toes ⟨*didactylous*⟩ [Gk -*daktylos*, fr *daktylos*]

**dactylus** /'daktiləs/ *n, pl* **dactyli** /-lie/ a segment of the TARSUS (lower leg joint) of some insects following the enlarged and modified first segment [NL, fr Gk *daktylos* finger, toe]

**¹dad** /dad/ *n, informal* a father [prob baby talk]

**²dad** *vt* **-dd-** *Scot and N Eng* to hit, beat [prob imit]

**dada** /'dahdah/, **dadaism** /-iz(ə)m/ *n, often cap* an early 20th-century movement in art and literature that was active esp in Central Europe, was marked by anarchy, irreverence, and a rejection of traditional artistic values, and was one of the main influences upon SURREALISM [Fr, fr (baby talk) *dada* hobbyhorse] – **dada** *adj*, **dadaistic** *adj*

**daddy** /'dadi/ *n, informal* a father [*dad* + ⁴-*y*]

**daddy longlegs** /'long,legz/ *n taking sing vb, pl* **daddy longlegs 1** CRANE FLY; *esp* the common grey-bodied crane fly (*Tipula paludosa*) **2** *NAm* HARVESTMAN (spider with very long legs)

**¹dado** /'daydoh/ *n, pl* **dadoes 1a** the part of a pedestal or plinth between the base and the CORNICE (projecting part at the top) **b** the lower part of an interior wall when specially decorated or faced; *also* the decoration upon this part of a wall **2** a groove; *specif* a groove made across the grain of a piece of wood [It, die, plinth]

**²dado** *vt* **dadoes; dadoing; dadoed 1** to provide with a dado **2a** to set into a groove **b** to cut a rectangular groove in (e g a plank)

**daedal** /'deedl/ *adj, formal or poetic* **1a** intricate **b** skilful, artistic **2** adorned with many things, esp natural wonders [L *daedalus*, fr Gk *daidalos*]

**daemon** /'deemən/ *n* **1** an attendant power or spirit **2** a supernatural being or spirit of Greek mythology intermediate between gods and human beings **3** DEMON 1,2,4 [LL, evil spirit – more at DEMON]

**¹daff** /daf/ *vi, Scot* to play the fool; act foolishly [obs *daff* fool, coward, fr ME *daffe*; prob akin to ME *dafte* gentle, stupid]

**²daff** *vt* **1** *archaic* to thrust aside **2** *obs* to put off (e g with an excuse) [alter. of *doff*]

**³daff** *n, informal* a daffodil

**daffodil** /'dafədil/ *n* any of various bulb-producing plants (genus *Narcissus* of the family Amaryllidacea, the daffodil family); *esp* a plant whose flowers have a large typically yellow CORONA (central cup-shaped structure) elongated into a trumpet [prob fr D *de affodil* the asphodel, fr *de* the (fr MD) + *affodil* asphodel, fr MF *afrodille*, fr L *asphodelus*, fr Gk *asphodelos*]

**daffy** /'dafi/ *adj, informal* crazy, foolish [obs *daff* fool, coward]

[1]**daft** /dahft/ *adj, informal* **1a** silly, foolish **b** mad, insane **2a** *chiefly Br* fanatically enthusiastic 〈~ *about football*〉 **b** *Scot* frivolously merry [ME *dafte* gentle, stupid; akin to OE *gedæfte* mild, gentle, ME *defte* gentle, deft, L *faber* smith] – **daftly** *adv*, **daftness** *n*

[2]**daft** *adv, informal* foolishly 〈*don't talk so* ~〉

[1]**dag** /dag/ *n* **1** a hanging end or shred **2** *usu pl* a piece of matted or manure-coated wool [ME *dagge*]

[2]**dag** *vb* **-gg-** *vt* to cut off the dags from (sheep) ~ *vi* to remove dags

[3]**dag** *n, Austr & NZ* an unusual or entertaining person; a character [prob fr E cant *dagen* (artful criminal), fr *dagen*, *degen* (sword), fr Ger *degen*]

**dagga** /'dahgə, 'dah·khə/ *n, SAfr* cannabis, esp when prepared for smoking [Afrik, fr Hottentot *daga-b*]

**dagger** /'dagə/ *n* **1** a short sharp pointed weapon for stabbing **2** a sign † used as a reference mark or to indicate a death date [ME] – **at daggers drawn** in bitter conflict

**dago** /'daygoh/ *n, pl* **dagos, dagoes** *chiefly derog* a person of Italian, Spanish, or Portuguese birth or descent [alter. of earlier *diego*, fr *Diego*, a common Sp forename]

**daguerreotype** /də'ger(i)ə,tiep/ *n* an early photograph produced on a silver or a silver-covered copper plate; *also* the process of producing such photographs [Fr *daguerréotype*, fr L J M *Daguerre* †1851 Fr painter & inventor + Fr *-o-* + *type*] – **daguerreotype** *vt*, **daguerreotypy** *n*

**dah** /dah/ *n* [2]DASH 7 – used when articulating MORSE CODE [imit]

**dahl** /dahl/ *n* DHAL

**dahlia** /'dayli·ə, 'dah-/ *n* any of a genus (*Dahlia*) of American plants of the daisy family having tuberous roots, featherlike leaves, and showy flower heads and including many ornamental garden plants [NL, genus name, fr Anders *Dahl* †1789 Sw botanist]

**Dáil** /doyl, diel/, **Dáil Eireann** /~ 'eərən/ *n* the lower house of parliament in the Republic of Ireland [IrGael *Dáil Eireann* Irish assembly]

[1]**daily** /'dayli/ *adj* **1a** done or occurring every day **b** *of a newspaper* issued every day from Monday to Saturday **c** of or providing for every day **2** covering the period of or based on a day 〈~ *statistics*〉 [ME *dayly*, fr OE *dæglīc*, fr *dæg* day + *-līc* -ly] – **dailiness** *n*

[2]**daily** *adv* every day; once a day; by the day

[3]**daily** *n* **1** a daily newspaper **2** *also* **daily help** *Br informal* someone, usu a woman, employed to come into a home regularly, esp every weekday, to do domestic work; *esp* one employed by a Local Authority to do cleaning work, prepare meals, etc for someone who is handicapped or infirm

**daily dozen** *n* a series of physical exercises to be performed daily [fr its being orig a set of 12 exercises]

**daimon** /'diemohn/ *n, pl* **daimones** /'diemʒneez/, **daimons** DAEMON 1,2 [Gk *daimōn*] – **daimonic** *adj*

**daimyo, daimio** /'diemyoh/ *n, pl* **daimyos, daimios** a Japanese feudal baron [Jap *daimyō*, fr *dai* great + *myō* name]

[1]**dainty** /'daynti/ *n* **1** something delicious; a delicacy **2** something choice or pleasing [ME *deinte*, fr OF *deintié*, fr L *dignitat*, *dignitas* dignity, worth]

[2]**dainty** *adj* **1a** tasting good; tasty **b** attractively prepared and served **2** small and delicate 〈*a* ~ *Meissen figurine*〉 **3a** fastidious **b** showing avoidance of anything rough – **daintily** *adv*, **daintiness** *n*

**daiquiri** /'die'kiəri, də-, 'dakiri/ *n* a cocktail made of rum, lime juice, and sugar [*Daiquiri*, town in Cuba]

[1]**dairy** /'deəri/ *n* **1** a room, building, or establishment where milk is kept and butter or cheese is made **2** the section of farming or of a farm that is concerned with the production of milk, butter, and cheese **3** an establishment for the sale or distribution chiefly of milk and milk products – compare CREAMERY [ME *deyerie*, fr *deye* dairymaid, fr OE *dǣge* kneader of bread; akin to OE *dāg* dough – more at DOUGH]

[2]**dairy** *adj* of or concerned with (the production of) milk or milk products

**dairy cattle** *n pl* cattle bred or used for milk production

**dairy farm** *n* a farm chiefly devoted to milk production

**dairying** /'deəri·ing/ *n* the business of operating a dairy

**dairymaid** /'deəri,mayd/ *n* a woman employed in a dairy; *esp* a woman employed on a farm to milk the cattle and make butter, cheese, etc

**dairyman** /'deərimən/ *n* someone who operates a dairy farm or works in a dairy

**dais** /'day·is/ *n* a raised platform; *esp* one at the end of a hall [ME *deis*, fr OF, fr L *discus* dish, quoit – more at DISH]

**daishiki** /die'sheeki/ *n* DASHIKI (W African garment)

**daisy** /'dayzi/ *n* **1** any of several plants (genera *Bellis*, *Chrysanthemum*, etc of the family Compositae, the daisy family) having a flower head with well-developed RAY FLOWERS (outer strap-shaped flowers) usu arranged in one or a few whorls: e g **1a** a common short European plant (*Bellis perennis*) with white or pink RAY FLOWERS arranged round a central yellow disc **b** OXEYE DAISY **2** the flower head of a daisy **3** *informal* a first-rate person or thing – no longer in vogue [ME *dayeseye*, fr OE *dægesēage*, fr *dæg* day + *ēage* eye]

**daisy chain** *n* a string of daisies threaded together by their stalks

'**daisy-,cutter** *n, informal* a ball in cricket that is bowled along the ground or that keeps low on pitching

**Dakota** /də'kohtə/ *n, pl* **Dakotas,** *esp collectively* **Dakota** a member of an American Indian people of the N Mississippi valley; *also* their Siouan language

**Dalai Lama** /'dalie/ *n* the spiritual head of Tibetan Buddhism [Mongolian *dalai* ocean]

**dalasi** /dah'lahsi/ *n* – see MONEY table [native name in the Gambia]

**dale** /dayl/ *n* a vale, valley [ME, fr OE *dæl*; akin to OHG *tal* valley, Gk *tholos* rotunda]

**Dalek** /'dahlik/ *n* any of a race of ruthlessly aggressive fictional creatures protected by distinctive metallic shells containing their life-support systems [name of creatures in television science-fiction series 'Dr Who']

**dalesman** /'daylzmən/, *fem* **daleswoman** /-woomən/ *n, Br* someone (e g a Yorkshire farmer) living or born in a dale, esp in one of the dales in the Pennines

**Dales pony** /daylz/ *n* (any of) the largest and sturdiest breed of English native pony originating in the Pennines

**daleth** /'dahlid/ *n* the 4th letter of the Hebrew alphabet [Heb *dāleth*, fr *deleth* door]

**dalliance** /'dali·əns/ *n* an act of dallying: e g **a** amorous or flirtatious activity **b** frivolous action; trifling

**dally** /'dali/ *vi* **1a** to act playfully; *esp* to flirt **b** to deal lightly; toy 〈*accused him of* ~ing *with a serious problem*〉 **2** to waste time; dawdle [ME *dalyen*, fr AF *dalier*] – **dallier** *n*

**dalmatian** /dal'maysh(ə)n/ *n, often cap* (any of) a breed of medium-sized dogs having a white short-haired coat with black or brown spots [fr the supposed origin of the breed in *Dalmatia*, region of Yugoslavia]

**dalmatic** /dal'matik/ *n* a wide-sleeved overgarment with slit sides worn by a priest or deacon; *also* a similar robe worn by a British sovereign at his/her coronation [LL *dalmatica*, fr L, fem of *dalmaticus* Dalmatian, fr *Dalmatia*]

**dal segno** /dal 'senyoh/ *adv* – used as a direction in music to return to the sign that marks the beginning of a section to be repeated [It, from the sign]

**dalton** /'dawltən/ *n* ATOMIC MASS UNIT [John Dalton †1844 E chemist & physicist]

**Dalton plan** /'dawltən/ *n* a method of progressive education whereby the students assume responsibility for their own pace of work [*Dalton*, town in Massachusetts, USA, site of first school to use the method]

[1]**dam** /dam/ *n* a female parent – used esp with reference to domestic animals [ME *dam*, *dame* lady, dam – more at DAME]

[2]**dam** *n* **1a** a barrier built across a water course to hold back and raise the level of the water, esp to form a reservoir **b** a barrier to check the flow of liquid, gas, or air **2** a body of water confined by a dam [ME; akin to MHG *tam* dam]

[3]**dam** *vt* **-mm-** **1** to provide or restrain with a dam **2** to stop up; block *synonyms* see [1]HINDER

[1]**damage** /'damij/ *n* **1** loss or harm resulting from injury to person, property, or reputation **2** *pl* a sum of money ordered by a court to be paid as compensation for loss or injury **3** *informal* expense, cost 〈*what's the* ~?〉 *synonyms* see [1]RUIN [ME, fr OF, fr *dam* damage, fr L *damnum*]

[2]**damage** *vt* to cause damage to ~ *vi* to become damaged *synonyms* see INJURE – **damager** *n*

**damaging** /'damijing/ *adj* causing or able to cause damage; injurious 〈*has a* ~ *effect on wildlife*〉 – **damagingly** *adv*

**damar** /'damə/ *n* DAMMAR (type of plant resin)

[1]**damascene** /'damʒseen/ *n* **1** *cap* a native or inhabitant of Damascus **2** the characteristic wavy markings of DAMASCUS STEEL [ME, fr L *Damascenus*, adj & n, fr *Damascus*, city in Syria]

**²damascene** *adj* **1** *cap* (characteristic) of Damascus or its inhabitants **2** of damask or the art of damascening

**³damascene** *vt* to ornament (eg iron or steel) with wavy patterns like those of watered silk or with inlaid work of precious metals [MF *damasquiner*, fr *damasquin* of Damascus]

**Damascus steel** /dəˈmaskəs/ *n* a hard elastic steel developed in the Middle Ages that is suitable for sword blades and is made by forging strips of iron together, with the result that it has a characteristic wavy pattern on its surface

**¹damask** /ˈdaməsk/ *n* **1** a firm lustrous fabric (eg of linen, cotton, silk, or rayon) with a flat pattern woven into it and used esp for table linen – compare DIMITY **2a** DAMASCUS STEEL **b** the characteristic markings of this steel **3** a greyish-red colour [ME *damaske*, fr ML *damascus*, fr *Damascus*]

**²damask** *adj* **1** made of or resembling damask **2** of the colour damask

**damask rose** *n* a large hardy fragrant pink rose (*Rosa damascena*) that is cultivated in Asia Minor as a source of ATTAR (fragrant oil) of roses and is a parent of many varieties of cultivated rose [obs *Damask* of Damascus, fr obs *Damask* Damascus]

**dame** /daym/ *n* **1** *often cap* **1a** the wife or daughter of a lord **b** a female member of an order of knighthood – used as a title preceding the Christian name **2a** an elderly woman **b** a stock character in British pantomime who is a comic ill-tempered old woman usu played by a male actor **c** *chiefly NAm informal* a woman [ME, fr OF, fr L *domina*, fem of *dominus* master; akin to L *domus* house – more at TIMBER]

**dame school** *n* a small often rural school in which the rudiments of reading and writing were formerly taught to small children, usu by an elderly woman

**dame's violet** *n* a Eurasian plant (*Hesperis matronalis*) of the cabbage family widely cultivated for its spikes of showy fragrant white or purple flowers

**damfool** /ˌdamˈfoohl/ *adj, informal* extremely foolish or stupid [alter. of *damned fool*]

**dammar, damar** *also* **dammer** /ˈdamə/ *n* any of various resins obtained from SE Asian trees, esp an evergreen tree (genus *Agathis*) of the pine family and any of several other trees (family Dipterocarpaceae) and used in varnishes and inks [Malay *damar*]

**dammit** /ˈdamit/ *interj, informal* – used to express irritation [alter. of *damn it*] – **as near as dammit** almost exactly

**¹damn** /dam/ *vt* **1** to condemn to a punishment or fate; *esp* to condemn to hell **2a** to condemn vigorously and often irascibly for some real or fancied fault or defect ⟨~ed *the scheme out of hand*⟩ **b** to condemn as a failure by public criticism ⟨*a play* ~ed *by the critics*⟩ **3** to bring ruin on **4** to swear at; curse to swear, curse [ME *dampnen*, fr OF *dampner*, fr L *damnare*, fr *damnum* damage, loss, fine] – **I'll be damned** – used to express astonishment – **I'll be damned if** I emphatically do not or will not ⟨I'll be damned if *I'll go*⟩

**²damn** *n* **1** the utterance of the word *damn* as a curse **2** the slightest bit ⟨*I couldn't care a* ~⟩; *also* a least amount or degree of care or consideration ⟨*don't give a* ~ *what happens*⟩

**³damn** *adj or adv* damned ⟨*a* ~ *nuisance*⟩ ⟨*too* ~ *serious*⟩ – **damn well** beyond doubt or question; certainly ⟨*better* damn well *marry that boy* – *Dra Rib*⟩

**⁴damn** *interj* – used to express anger, annoyance, or frustration ⟨~ *it all!*⟩ ⟨~, *I've got no change for the coffee machine*⟩

**damnable** /ˈdamnəbl/ *adj* **1** liable to or deserving condemnation ⟨*a* ~ *crime*⟩ **2** very bad; detestable ⟨~ *weather*⟩ – **damnableness** *n*, **damnably** *adv*

**damn all** *n, slang* nothing at all ⟨*she told us* ~ *about the new project*⟩

**damnation** /damˈnaysh(ə)n/ *n* damning or being damned – often used as an interjection to express annoyance

**damnatory** /ˈdamnət(ə)ri/ *adj, formal* expressing, imposing, or causing condemnation; condemnatory

**¹damned** /damd/ *adj* **damnedest, damndest** /ˈdamdist/ **1** damnable **2** complete, utter ⟨~ *nonsense*⟩ ⟨*every* ~ *thing*⟩ **3** *chiefly NAm* extraordinary – in the superlative ⟨*the* ~est *contraption he ever saw*⟩

**²damned** *adv* extremely, very ⟨*a* ~ *good job*⟩

**damnedest, damndest** /ˈdamdist/ *n* utmost, best – chiefly in *do one's damnedest* ⟨*doing his* ~ *to succeed*⟩

**damnify** /ˈdamnifie/ *vt* to cause loss or damage to [MF *damnifier*, fr OF, fr LL *damnificare*, fr L *damnificus* injurious, fr *damnum* damage]

**damning** /ˈdaming/ *adj* **1** bringing damnation **2** causing or leading to condemnation or ruin; proving guilt ⟨*presented some* ~ *testimony*⟩ – **damningly** *adv*

**damosel, damozel** /ˈdaməzel/ *n, archaic* a damsel

**¹damp** /damp/ *n* **1** a foul air or poisonous gas, esp in a coal mine **2** moisture, humidity **3a** a discouragement, check; DAMPER 2 ⟨*no sentiment of shame gave a* ~ *to her triumph* – Jane Austen⟩ **b** *archaic* depression, dejection **4** *archaic* fog, mist [MD or MLG, vapour; akin to OHG *damph* vapour, OE *dim* dim]

**²damp** *vt* **1a** to affect with a poisonous gas; choke **b** to diminish the activity or intensity of ⟨~ed *the fire in the furnace*⟩ – often + *down* ⟨~ing *down the causes of inflation*⟩ **c** to reduce progressively the vibration or oscillation of (eg sound waves) **2** to make damp; dampen ~ *vi, of something vibrating or oscillating* to come gradually to rest

**³damp** *adj* **1** depressed, dull **2** slightly or moderately wet *synonyms* see ¹WET – **dampish** *adj*, **damply** *adv*, **dampness** *n*

**damp course, damp-proof course** *n* a horizontal layer of waterproof material near the ground in a masonry wall which prevents moisture from the ground rising above it

**dampen** /ˈdampən/ *vt* **1** to check or diminish the activity or vigour of; deaden ⟨*the heat* ~ed *our spirits*⟩ **2** to make damp ⟨*the shower barely* ~ed *the ground*⟩ **3** DAMP 1c ~ *vi* **1** to become damp **2** to become deadened or depressed – **dampener** *n*

**damper** /ˈdampə/ *n* **1** a device that damps: eg **1a** a valve or plate (eg in the flue of a furnace) for regulating the draft **b** a small felted block which prevents or stops the vibration of a piano string **c** a device (eg a shock absorber) designed to bring a mechanism to rest with minimum oscillation **2** a dulling or deadening influence ⟨*put a* ~ *on the celebration*⟩ **3** *chiefly Austr & NZ* a type of unleavened bread made with flour and water and often baked in the ashes of a fire

**damping-off** /ˈdamping/ *n* a diseased condition of seedlings or cuttings caused by fungi and marked by wilting or rotting

**damp squib** *n, Br informal* something that ends feebly, esp after a promising start

**damsel** /ˈdamzəl/ *n, archaic* a young unmarried woman, esp of noble birth [ME *damesel*, fr OF *dameisele*, fr (assumed) VL *domnicella* young noblewoman, dim. of L *domina* lady]

**damselfish** /ˈdamz(ə)l.fish/ *n* any of several small brightly coloured marine fishes (family Pomacentridae) of tropical and warm seas – called also DEMOISELLE

**damselfly** /ˈdamzəl.flie/ *n* any of numerous insects (suborder Zygoptera) distinguished from the related dragonflies by their smaller size, eyes that project from either side of the head, and stalked wings that are folded above the body when the insect is at rest

**damson** /ˈdamzən/ *n* an Asiatic plum tree cultivated for its fruit; *also* the small acid purple fruit of the damson used esp in jams [ME, fr L (*prunum*) *damascenum*, lit., plum of Damascus]

**dan** /dan/ *n* a level of expertise in an Oriental martial art (eg judo) [Jap]

**Dan** *n, archaic* master, sir – used esp as a title ⟨~ *Cupid*⟩ ⟨~ *Chaucer*⟩ [ME, title of members of religious orders, fr MF, fr ML *domnus*, fr L *dominus* master]

**dan buoy** *n* a small temporary buoy consisting of a spar passed through a float and having a flag fixed at the upper end, which is used as a marker in deep-sea fishing and minesweeping [origin unknown]

**¹dance** /dahns/ *vi* **1** to engage in or perform a dance **2** to move quickly up and down or about ~ *vt* **1** to perform or take part in as a dancer **2** to cause to dance; *esp* to dance with ⟨~d *her across the floor*⟩ **3** to bring into a specified condition by dancing ⟨~d *herself into a frenzy*⟩ ⟨~d *his way to fame*⟩ ⟨~ *the New Year in*⟩ [ME *dauncen*, fr OF *dancier*] – **danceable** *adj*, **dancer** *n*

**²dance** *n* **1** an act or instance of dancing **2** a series of rhythmic and patterned bodily movements, usu performed to music and involving movement of the feet **3** a social gathering for dancing **4** a piece of music which can be danced to **5** the art of dancing ⟨*modern* ~⟩ – **lead somebody a dance** to cause somebody a lot of (unnecessary) trouble

**dance hall** *n* a large room set aside or suitable for dances; *esp* a public hall offering facilities for dancing

**dance of death** *n* DANSE MACABRE

**D and C** *n* a common gynaecological procedure in which the womb is gently stretched open to allow its temporary lining to be scraped clean [dilatation *and* curettage]

**dandelion** /ˈdandi.lie-ən/ *n* any of a genus (*Taraxacum*) of yellow-flowered plants of the daisy family; *esp* a plant (*Taraxacum officinale*) that has a very widespread distribution as a weed [MF *dent de lion*, lit., lion's tooth; fr the shape of its leaves]

**¹dander** /'dandə/ *vi or n, Scot* (to) dawdle, stroll [origin unknown]

**²dander** *n* minute scales from hair, feathers, or skin that may cause allergies [alter. of *dandruff*]

**³dander** *n, informal* anger, temper – chiefly in such phrases as *have/get one's dander up* [perh fr *dander*, *dunder* (ferment)]

**Dandie Dinmont terrier** /ˌdandi 'dinmont/ *n* (any of) a breed of terrier characterized by short legs, a long body, hanging ears, a rough coat, and a full silky topknot [*Dandie Dinmont*, character owning such dogs in the novel *Guy Mannering* by Sir Walter Scott †1832 Sc writer]

**dandify** /'dandifie/ *vt* to cause to resemble a dandy – **dandification** *n*

**dandle** /'dandl/ *vt* **1** to move (e g a baby) up and down in one's arms or on one's knee in affectionate play **2** to pamper, pet [origin unknown]

**dandruff** /'dandruf, -drəf/ *n* a scurf that forms on the scalp and comes off in small white or greyish scales [prob fr *dand-* (origin unknown) + *-ruff*, of Scand origin; akin to ON *hrūfa* scab; akin to OHG *hruf* scurf, Lith *kraupus* rough] – **dandruffy** *adj*

**¹dandy** /'dandi/ *n* **1** a man who gives exaggerated attention to dress and manner **2** *chiefly NAm informal* something excellent in its class [perh fr *Dandy*, nickname for *Andrew*] – **dandyish** *adj*, **dandyishly** *adv*, **dandyism** *n*

**²dandy** *adj, NAm informal* very good; first-rate ⟨*a ~ place to stay*⟩

**dandy brush** *n* a stiff coarse brush used in grooming horses

**Dane** /dayn/ *n* a native or inhabitant of Denmark [ME *Dan*, fr ON *Danr*]

**danegeld** /'dayn,geld/ *n, often cap* an annual tax believed to have been imposed originally to buy off Danish invaders in England in the 9th century or to maintain forces to oppose them, but continued as a land tax [ME, fr *Dane* (gen pl of *Dan* Dane) + *geld* tribute, payment, fr OE *gield;* akin to OE *gieldan* to pay (for), reward – more at YIELD]

**Danelaw** /'dayn,law/ *n* (the law in force in) the part of England held by the Danes in pre-Conquest times

**danger** /'daynjə/ *n* **1** exposure to the possibility of injury, pain, or loss ⟨*a place where children could play without ~*⟩ **2** a case or cause of danger ⟨*the ~s of mining*⟩ **3** the position or colour of a signal when indicating that traffic must stop ⟨*the signals were at ~ but were overrun in the fog*⟩ – compare CLEAR [ME *daunger*, fr OF *dangier*, alter. of *dongier*, fr (assumed) VL *dominiarium*, fr L *dominium* ownership]

*synonyms* **Danger, peril, jeopardy, hazard, risk:** danger is the most general term, suggesting possible but not inescapable harm. Peril is stronger, suggesting greater harm, and more imminent danger ⟨*put in* **peril** *of my life by a rope breaking near the summit*⟩. **Jeopardy**, usually found in the form *in* jeopardy, implies putting something at present secure at unnecessary risk ⟨*why put your marriage in* **jeopardy** *for the sake of a casual relationship?*⟩. **Hazard** stresses danger from what is beyond one's control, and the role of chance ⟨*one of the* **hazards** *of playing rugby is the possibility of injury*⟩. **Risk** stresses chance, too, but weighed against possible gain. It therefore suggests willingness to face danger or the voluntary taking of unnecessary chances ⟨*always ask yourself "Is it worth the risk?"*⟩ ⟨*I'm a businesswoman. Taking* **risks** *is part of my job*⟩. *antonyms* security, safety

**danger list** *n* – **off/on the danger list** (no longer) critically ill

**'danger-,money** *n* money above a basic wage paid for doing a job that involves danger

**dangerous** /'daynj(ə)rəs/ *adj* **1** exposing to or involving danger **2** able or likely to inflict injury – **dangerousness** *n*

**dangerously** /'daynjərəsli/ *adv* **1** in a dangerous manner **2** to an alarming degree; perilously ⟨*~ near to a riot*⟩

**¹dangle** /'dang-gl/ *vi* **1** to hang loosely and usu so as to be able to swing freely **2** to occur in a sentence without proper syntactic connection ⟨*climbing in "Climbing the mountain the cabin came into view" is a* dangling *participle*⟩ – see "Ten Vexed Points" ~ *vt* **1** to cause to dangle; swing **2** to display enticingly ⟨*~d the possibility before them*⟩ [prob of Scand origin; akin to Dan *dangle* to dangle] – **dangler** *n*, **danglingly** *adv*

**²dangle** *n* **1** the action of dangling **2** something that dangles

**Daniel** /'danyəl/ *n* – see BIBLE table [*Daniel* (Heb *Dānī'ēl*), Heb hero & prophet (prob legendary)]

**¹Danish** /'daynish/ *adj* (characteristic) of Denmark, the Danes, or Danish

**²Danish** *n* **1** the Germanic language of the Danes **2** *NAm* DANISH PASTRY

**Danish blue** *n* a soft white blue-veined cheese, similar to Gorgonzola, produced in Denmark

**Danish pastry** *n* a piece of confectionery made in a variety of shapes from a rich yeast dough and with various sweet fillings

**dank** /dangk/ *adj* unpleasantly moist or wet ⟨*a cold ~ winter afternoon*⟩ *synonyms* see ¹WET [ME *danke*, prob of Scand origin] – **dankly** *adv*, **dankness** *n*

**danse macabre** /ˌdonhs mə'kahbrə, mə'kahb (*Fr* dɑ̃:s makaːbr)/ *n* a medieval theme occurring in art, literature, music, and dance in which death represented as a skeleton leads people to the grave; *also* a dance symbolizing this [Fr, lit., macabre dance]

**danseur** /donh'suh (*Fr* dɑ̃sœːr)/ *n* a male ballet dancer [Fr, *danser* to dance]

**danseuse** /donh'suhz (*Fr* dɑ̃søːz)/ *n* a female ballet dancer [Fr, fem of *danseur*]

**dap** /dap/ *vi* **-pp-** to fish by allowing the bait to touch the surface of the water lightly [perh alter. of ²*dab*]

**daphne** /'dafni/ *n* any of a genus (*Daphne* of the family Thymelaeaceae) of Eurasian shrubs with flowers that have no true petals but have coloured SEPALS that resemble petals [NL, genus name, fr L, laurel, fr Gk *daphnē*]

**daphnia** /'dafni·ə/ *n* any of a genus (*Daphnia* of the order Branchiopoda, class Crustacea) of minute freshwater INVERTEBRATE animals with two-branched antennae that are used as swimming organs – called also WATER FLEA [NL, genus name]

**dapper** /'dapə/ *adj* **1** *esp of a small man* neat and spruce as regards clothing and demeanour **2** alert and lively in movement and manners ⟨*the wren is a ~ little bird*⟩ *synonyms* see ²NEAT [ME *dapyr*, fr MD *dapper* quick, strong; akin to OHG *tapfar* heavy, OSlav *debelŭ* thick] – **dapperly** *adv*, **dapperness** *n*

**¹dapple** /'dapl/ *n* **1** any of numerous usu cloudy and rounded spots or patches of a colour or shade different from their background **2** the quality or state of being dappled **3** a dappled animal [ME *dappel-grey*, adj, grey variegated with spots of a different colour]

**²dapple** *vb* to mark or become marked with round patches of varying shades

**dapsone** /'dapsohn/ *n* a synthetic antibiotic drug, $(H_2NC_6H_4)_2SO_2$, that is used esp as the major treatment for leprosy [*di*aminodi*phenyl-sulph*one]

**darbies** /'dahbiz/ *n pl, Br slang* handcuffs [short for obs *Father Darby's* (*Derby's*) *bands* rigid bond binding a debtor]

**Darby and Joan** /ˌdahbi ənd 'john/ *n* a happily married elderly couple [prob fr *Darby & Joan*, couple in an 18th-c song]

**Dard** /dahd/ *n* a group of Indic languages spoken in the upper valley of the Indus – **Dardic** *adj*

**¹dare** /deə/ *vb* **dared**, *archaic* **durst** *va* to be sufficiently courageous to ⟨*no one ~*d *say a word*⟩ – used nonassertively *~ vi* to have sufficient courage ⟨*no one ~*d *to say a word*⟩ ⟨*try it if you ~*⟩ *~ vt* **1a** to challenge to perform an action, esp as a proof of courage ⟨*~d him to jump*⟩ **b** to confront boldly; defy ⟨*~d the anger of his family*⟩ **2** to have the courage to contend against, venture, or try ⟨*the actress ~*d *a new interpretation of this classic role*⟩ [ME *dar* (1 & 3 sing. pres indic), fr OE *dear;* akin to OHG *gitar* (1 & 3 sing. pres indic) dare, L in*festus* hostile] – **darer** *n*

*usage* **Dare** is used in two ways: either as a verbal auxiliary like *can* or *must*, followed by an infinitive without *to* ⟨*she* **daren't** *go*⟩ ⟨*it was an order which no soldier* **dare** *disobey*⟩ or as an ordinary verb, rather like *want*, which can be followed by an infinitive with *to* ⟨*she doesn't* **dare** *to go*⟩. Either of these constructions is perfectly correct, the former being on the whole preferred in British English and the latter in American English. The verbal auxiliary **dare** is used only in interrogatives, negatives, and subordinate clauses, and often without inflections or past tense forms (*he* **dare** rather than *he* **dares** or *he* **dared**).

**²dare** *n* a challenge to a bold act ⟨*foolishly took a ~*⟩

**daredevil** /'deə,devl/ *n* a recklessly bold person *synonyms* see ¹ADVENTURE – **daredevil** *adj*, **daredevilry** *n*

**daren't** /deənt/ dare not

**daresay** /ˌdeə'say/ *vb pres 1 sing* venture to say (so); think (it) probable; suppose (so) [ME (*I*) *dar sayen* I venture to say]

**darg** /dahg/ *n* **1** *Scot & N Eng* a day's work **2** *Austr* a definite amount of work [ME *dawerk, daywork*, fr OE *dægweorc*, fr *dæg* day + *weorc* work]

[1]**daring** /'deəring/ *adj* adventurously bold in action or thought ⟨~ *acrobats*⟩ ⟨~ *crimes*⟩ ⟨~ *ideas*⟩ ⟨~ *sex films*⟩ *synonyms* see [1]ADVENTURE *antonym* timid – **daringly** *adv*, **daringness** *n*

[2]**daring** *n* venturesome boldness

**dariole** /'dariohl/ *n* a small cup-shaped mould used in making baked or steamed cakes and puddings, creams, jellies, and aspics; *also* a dish cooked or set in a dariole [Fr, fr MF, a cream-filled pastry]

**Darjeeling** /dah'jeeling/ *n* a high-quality tea grown esp in the mountainous districts of northern India [*Darjeeling*, city in India]

[1]**dark** /dahk/ *adj* 1 (partially) devoid of light; receiving, reflecting, transmitting, or radiating little or no light 2a wholly or partially black b *of a colour* of (very) low lightness 3a arising from or showing evil traits or desires; evil b dismal, sad ⟨*took a ~ view of the future*⟩ c lacking knowledge or culture 4 not clear to the understanding 5 not fair; swarthy ⟨*her ~ good looks*⟩ 6 secret ⟨*kept his plans ~*⟩ 7a possessing depth and richness ⟨*the ~, voluminous abundance of his voice* – Irving Kolodin⟩ b *of a speech sound* pronounced with the quality of a BACK vowel (eg /ah/ or /aw/) ⟨*the ~ /l/ in* feel⟩ 8 *of a theatre* temporarily not presenting any production [ME *derk*, fr OE *deorc;* akin to OHG *tarchannen* to hide, Gk *thrassein* to trouble] – **darkish** *adj*, **darkly** *adv*, **darkness** *n*

[2]**dark** *n* 1a absence of light; darkness b a place or time of little or no light; night, nightfall ⟨*after ~*⟩ 2 a dark or deep colour – **in the dark** in ignorance ⟨*kept the public* in the dark *about the agreement*⟩ – **whistle in the dark** 1 to keep up one's courage (as if) by whistling 2 to make a guess at something about which one has no real knowledge – see also SHOT **in the dark**

**dark adaptation** *n* the processes by which the eye adapts to conditions of reduced illumination, that include dilation of the pupil and an increase in the sensitivity of the receptors of the retina to light due to the increased production of light-sensitive pigments, esp RHODOPSIN – compare LIGHT ADAPTATION – **dark-adapted** *adj*

**Dark Ages** *n pl* the period from about AD 476 to about 1000

**darken** /'dahkən/ *vb* to make or become darker – **darkener** *n*

**darkey** /'dahki/ *n* a darky

**dark horse** *n* 1 someone or something (eg a contestant) that is little known yet with a potential much greater than the evidence would suggest 2 *NAm* a political candidate unexpectedly nominated, usu as a compromise between factions

**dark lantern** *n* a lantern that can be closed to conceal the light

**darkle** /'dahk(ə)l/ *vi, formal or poetic* 1 to become concealed in the dark 2a to grow dark b to become clouded or gloomy [back-formation fr [2]*darkling*]

[1]**darkling** /'dahkling/ *adv, formal or poetic* in the dark [ME *derkelyng*, fr *derk* dark + *-lyng* -ling]

[2]**darkling** *adj, formal or poetic* 1 dark 2 done or taking place in the dark

**darkling beetle** *n* a black slow-moving ground-dwelling plant-eating usu hard-bodied beetle (family Tenebrionidae)

**dark reaction** *n* the phase of photosynthesis that does not require the presence of light and that involves the formation of sugars and other carbohydrates from CARBON DIOXIDE using the energy stored during the LIGHT REACTION

**darkroom** /'dahk,roohm, -room/ *n* a room with no light or with a SAFELIGHT for handling and processing light-sensitive photographic materials

**darksome** /'dahksəm/ *adj, poetic* dark

**darky, darkey** /'dahki/ *n, derog* a negro [[1]*dark* + [1]*-y*]

[1]**darling** /'dahling/ *n* 1a a dearly loved person b [3] DEAR 1b 2 a favourite ⟨*the critics' ~*⟩ [ME *derling*, fr OE *dēorling*, fr *dēore* dear]

[2]**darling** *adj* 1 dearly loved; favourite 2 very pleasing; charmingly attractive ⟨*a ~ little house*⟩ – used esp by women

[1]**darn** /dahn/ *vt* 1 to mend with interlacing stitches woven across a hole or worn part ⟨~ *a sock*⟩ ⟨~ *a hole*⟩ 2 to embroider by filling in with long running or interlacing stitches ~ *vi* to darn something [prob fr Fr dial. *darner*] – **darner** *n*

[2]**darn** *n* a place that has been darned ⟨*a sweater full of ~*s⟩

[3]**darn** *vb, informal* to damn [euphemism] – **darned** *adj or adv*

[4]**darn** *adj or adv* damned

[5]**darn** *n* a damn

**darned** /dahnd/ *adj or adv, informal* damned

**darnel** /'dahnl/ *n* any of several grasses (genus *Lolium*, esp *Lolium temulentum*) that often occur as weeds among growing corn [ME]

**darning needle** /'dahning/ *n* a long needle with a large eye for use in darning

[1]**dart** /daht/ *n* 1a a small projectile with a pointed shaft at one end and flights (eg of plastic or feathers) at the other b *pl but taking sing or pl vb* a game in which darts are thrown at a dartboard 2a something projected with sudden speed; *esp* a sharp glance b something causing sudden pain or distress ⟨~ s *of sarcasm*⟩ 3 something with a slender pointed shaft or outline; *specif* a stitched tapering fold put in a garment to shape it to the figure 4 a quick movement; a dash 5 *archaic* a light spear [ME, fr MF, of Gmc origin; akin to OHG *tart* dart]

[2]**dart** *vt* 1 to throw with a sudden movement 2 to thrust or move with sudden speed 3 to put a dart or darts in (a garment or part of a garment) ~ *vi* to move suddenly or rapidly ⟨~ed *across the street*⟩

**dartboard** /'daht,bawd/ *n* a circular target (eg of bristle or cork) in the game of darts that is divided usu by wire into different scoring areas

**darter** /'dahtə/ *n* any of several fish-eating birds (genus *Anhinga*) related to the cormorants but having a long slender neck – called also SNAKEBIRD [[2]*dart* + [2]*-er*]

**Dartmoor pony** /'dahtmaw, -mooə/ *n* (any of) an old breed of small shaggy English ponies [*Dartmoor*, region in SW England]

**Darwinian** /dah'winyən, -ni·ən/ *adj* of (the theories or followers of) Charles Darwin or Darwinism [Charles *Darwin* †1882 E naturalist] – **Darwinian** *n*

**Darwinism** /'dahwi,niz(ə)m/ *n* a theory of evolution asserting that widely divergent groups of plants and animals have arisen from the same ancestors as a result of NATURAL SELECTION of offspring showing slight variations that make them better adapted to their environment; *broadly* biological evolutionism – **Darwinist** *n*, **darwinist** *or* **darwinistic** *adj, often cap*

**Darwin's finch** /'dahwinz/ *n* any of a subfamily (Geospizinae) of finches that have great variation in beak shape and are confined mostly to the Galapagos islands [Charles *Darwin*]

[1]**dash** /dash/ *vt* 1 to strike or knock violently 2 to break by striking or knocking 3 to splash, spatter ⟨~ ed *water on the face of the unconscious man*⟩ 4a to destroy, ruin ⟨*the news* ~ ed *his hopes*⟩ b to depress, sadden 5 to affect by mixing in something different ⟨*milk* ~ ed *with brandy*⟩ ⟨*his delight was* ~ ed *with bitterness over the delay*⟩ 6 *Br euph* DAMN 4 ⟨~ *it all!*⟩ ~ *vi* 1 to move with sudden speed ⟨~ ed *through the rain*⟩ 2 to smash [ME *dasshen*, prob of imit origin; (6) euphemism]

**dash off** *vt* to complete, execute, or finish off (eg writing or drawing) hastily ⟨dash off *a letter*⟩

[2]**dash** *n* 1 (the sound produced by) a sudden burst or splash 2a a stroke of a pen b a punctuation mark – used esp to indicate a break in the thought or structure of a sentence 3 a small but significant addition ⟨*a ~ of salt*⟩ 4 liveliness of style and action; panache 5a a sudden onset, rush, or attempt b *chiefly NAm* a sprint ⟨*the 100 metres ~*⟩ 6 DASHBOARD 2 7 a signal (eg a flash or an audible tone) of relatively long duration that is one of the two fundamental units of MORSE CODE – compare [1]DOT 4 8 *Br* PRIME 7 (mathematical symbol) 9 *archaic* a blow

**dashboard** /'dash,bawd/ *n* 1 a screen on the front of a vehicle, esp a carriage, to intercept water, mud, or snow 2 a panel extending across a car, aeroplane, or motorboat below the windscreen and usu containing dials and controls

**dashed** /dasht/ *adj* marked with the symbol ′ ⟨f′(*x*) *is read* f ~ *of x*⟩

**dasheen** /da'sheen/ *n, chiefly WI* TARO (type of plant with edible roots) [origin unknown]

**dashiki** /də'sheeki/ *n* a usu brightly-coloured loosely fitting pullover garment traditionally worn in W Africa – called also DAISHIKI [modif of Yoruba *danshiki*]

**dashing** /'dashing/ *adj* 1 vigorously active; spirited 2 smart, esp in dress and manners – **dashingly** *adv*

**dashpot** /'dash,pot/ *n* a device for cushioning or damping a movement (eg of a mechanical part) to avoid shock

**dassie** /'dahsi/ *n* HYRAX (small rodentlike mammal); *esp* one (genus *Procavia*) of southern Africa [Afrik]

**dastard** /'dastəd/ *n, archaic* a coward; *esp* one who commits malicious acts [ME, perh fr ON *dæstr* exhausted]

**dastardly** /'dastədli/ *adj, archaic* despicably malicious or cowardly – **dastardliness** *n*

**dasyure** /'dasi,yooə/ *n* any of a genus (*Dasyurus*) of tree-dwelling flesh-eating marsupial mammals of Australia and Tasmania resembling large weasels [deriv of Gk *dasys* thick with hair + *oura* tail]

**data** /'daytə; *also* 'dahtə/ *n taking sing or pl vb* factual information (e g measurements or statistics) used as a basis for reasoning, discussion, or calculation ⟨*all the essential* ~ *... are here –* *TLS*⟩ ⟨*any* ~ *he could glean was valuable – TLS*⟩ [pl of *datum*] **usage 1** Although **data** is a Latin plural, it is now coming to be treated as an aggregate singular noun ⟨*all this* **data**⟩. This usage is widely disliked, especially in Britain, but is better established in American English and in the field of data processing. **2** The pronunciation /'daytə/ is recommended for BBC broadcasters.

**data bank** *n* a collection of data organized for rapid search and retrieval (e g by computer)

**data base** *n* the data that is accessible to a data-processing system (e g a computer); *esp* a large store of data that is made easily accessible to the user by a powerful computer

**data processing** *n* the conversion (e g by computer) of crude information into usable or storable form; *also* any manipulation of data by a computer – **data processor** *n*

**datary** /'daytəri/ *n* an office of the Roman Curia that investigates the fitness of candidates for papal benefices [NL *dataria*, deriv of LL *data* date of a letter; fr its orig function of dating papal documents]

¹**date** /dayt/ *n* (the oblong edible fruit of) a tall palm (*Phoenix dactylifera*) that has long featherlike leaves [ME, fr OF, deriv of L *dactylus*, fr Gk *daktylos*, lit., finger]

²**date** *n* **1a** the time, reckoned in days or larger units, at which an event occurs ⟨*the* ~ *of his birth*⟩ **b** a statement of such a time ⟨*the* ~ *on the letter*⟩ **2** the period of time to which something belongs **3a** an appointment for a specified time; *esp* a social engagement between two people of opposite sex **b** *NAm* a person of the opposite sex with whom one has a date **4** *archaic* duration [ME, fr MF, fr LL *data*, fr *data* (as in *data Romae* given at Rome), fem of L *datus*, pp of *dare* to give; akin to Gk *didonai* to give] – **it's a date** – used to express agreement on an arrangement for a meeting – **to date** up to the present moment

³**date** *vt* **1** to determine the date of ⟨~ *an antique*⟩ **2** to record the date of **3a** to mark with characteristics typical of a particular period **b** to show up plainly the age of ⟨*the way he always called the radio the "wireless"* ~d *him*⟩ **4** *chiefly NAm informal* to make or have a date with (a person of the opposite sex) ~ *vi* **1** to reckon chronologically **2** to bear a date **3** to have been in existence – usu + *from* ⟨*the castle* ~s *from the 13th century*⟩ **4** to become old-fashioned ⟨*clothes that never* ~⟩ **5** *chiefly NAm informal* GO OUT – **datable, dateable** *adj*, **dater** *n*

**dated** /'daytid/ *adj* **1** provided with a date ⟨*a* ~ *document*⟩ **2** out-of-date, old-fashioned ⟨*the* ~ *customs of an earlier generation*⟩ – **datedly** *adv*, **datedness** *n*

**dateless** /'daytlis/ *adj* **1** having no date **2** timeless ⟨*the play's* ~ *theme*⟩

**dateline** /'dayt,lien/ *n* **1** a line in a written document or printed publication giving the date and place of composition or issue **2** INTERNATIONAL DATE LINE – **dateline** *vt*

**datestamp** /'dayt,stamp/ *n* (the impression or mark made by) an implement or device for stamping a date – **datestamp** *vt*

**dative** /'daytiv/ *n* a grammatical case expressing typically the INDIRECT OBJECT of a verb, the object of some prepositions, or a possessor; *also* a form (e g French *lui*) in this case [ME *datif*, fr L *dativus*, lit., relating to giving, fr *datus*] – **dative** *adj*

**dative bond** *n* COORDINATE BOND (chemical bond between two atoms) [fr the donation of electrons by one of the atoms]

**datum** /'dahtəm, 'daytəm/ *n, pl* (*1*) **data** /'dahtə, 'daytə/, (*2*) **datums 1** something given or admitted, esp as a basis for reasoning or inference **2** something (e g a number, fixed point, or assumed value) used as a basis for calculating or measuring [L, fr neut of *datus*]

**datura** /də'tyooərə/ *n* any of a genus (*Datura*) of widely distributed and often very poisonous strong-scented plants, shrubs, or trees (e g the THORN APPLE) of the potato family [NL, genus name, fr Hindi *dhatūrā* jimsonweed]

¹**daub** /dawb/ *vt* **1** to cover or coat with soft adhesive matter; plaster **2** to coat with a dirty substance **3a** to apply colouring material crudely to ⟨*he* ~ed *the wall with cheap whitewash*⟩ **b** to apply (e g colouring material) crudely ⟨*he* ~ed *whitewash on the wall*⟩ ~ *vi* **1** to paint with little skill ⟨*though he* ~s *in his spare time, he doesn't see himself as a second Rousseau*⟩ **2** *archaic* to put on a false exterior [ME *dauben*, fr OF *dauber*, deriv of L *dealbare* to whiten, whitewash, plaster, fr *de-* + *albus* white] – **dauber** *n*

²**daub** *n* **1** material used to daub walls ⟨*cottages built of wattle*

*and* ~⟩ **2** a daubing **3** something daubed on; a smear **4** a crude picture

**daube** /dohb/ *n* a stew of meat, esp beef, braised in red wine; *also* this method of cooking [Fr]

¹**daughter** /'dawtə/ *n* **1a** a human female having the relation of child to parent; *broadly* any female offspring **b** a female adopted child **c** *usu pl* a female descendant **2a** a human female having a specified origin or affiliation ⟨*a* ~ *of the Church*⟩ **b** something considered as a daughter ⟨*invention must be the* ~ *of necessity*⟩ **3** a NUCLIDE (form of an atom characterized by the composition of its nucleus) that is produced by the radioactive decay of a given chemical element [ME *doughter*, fr OE *dohtor*; akin to OHG *tohter* daughter, Gk *thygatēr*] – **daughterless** *adj*

²**daughter** *adj* **1** having the characteristics or relationship of a daughter **2** belonging to the first generation of offspring, ORGANELLES (specialized cell structures), or molecules produced by reproduction, division, or replication ⟨~ *cell*⟩ ⟨~ *DNA molecules*⟩

¹**daughter-in-,law** *n, pl* **daughters-in-law** the wife of one's son

**daunomycin** /,dawnoh'miesin/ *n* daunorubicin [(assumed) It *daunomicina*, fr *Daunia*, ancient region of Apulia, Italy + It *-o-* + *-micina* (as in *streptomicina* streptomycin)]

**daunorubicin** /,dawnoh'roohbisin/ *n* an antibiotic, $C_{27}H_{29}NO_{10}$, that is used as an anticancer drug, esp in the treatment of leukaemia [(assumed) It *daunorubicina*, fr *Daunia* + It *-o-* + *rubi-* (deriv of L *rubidus* red) + *-micina*]

**daunt** /dawnt/ *vt* to lessen the courage of; inspire awe in [ME *daunten*, fr OF *danter*, alter. of *donter*, fr L *domitare* to tame, fr *domitus*, pp of *domare* – more at TAME]

**daunting** /'dawnting/ *adj* discouraging, disheartening ⟨*a* ~ *task*⟩ – **dauntingly** *adv*

**dauntless** /'dawntlis/ *adj* fearless, undismayed ⟨*a* ~ *hero*⟩ **synonyms** see ¹BRAVE – **dauntlessly** *adv*, **dauntlessness** *n*

**dauphin** /'dohfanh (*Fr* dofē)/ *n, often cap* the eldest son of a king of France [MF *dalfin*, fr OF, title of lords of the Dauphiné (region in SE France), fr *Dalfin*, a surname]

**dauphine** /'dohfeen (*Fr* dofin)/ *n, often cap* the wife of the dauphin [Fr]

**daven** /'dov(ə)n/ *vi* to make the prescribed daily prayers of Jewish worship [Yiddish *davnen*]

**davenport** /'davən,pawt/ *n* **1** a small compact writing desk **2** *chiefly NAm* a large upholstered sofa; *esp* one that can be converted into a bed **synonyms** see SOFA [prob fr the name *Davenport*]

**davit** /'davit/ *n* any of a pair or more of projecting usu metal arms on the side or stern of a ship or boat which are used as cranes, esp for lowering boats to the water [prob fr the name *David*]

**Davy Jones** /,dayvi 'johnz/ *n* the bottom of the sea personified

**Davy Jones's locker** /,dayvi 'johnziz/ *n* the bottom of the sea

**Davy lamp** /'dayvi/ *n* an early oil-burning safety lamp developed for use in mines, in which the flame is surrounded by a metal gauze that reduces the risk of setting alight any explosive gases which may be present [Sir Humphry *Davy* †1829 E chemist & inventor]

¹**daw** /daw, dah/ *vi, chiefly Scot* to dawn [ME *dawen*, fr OE *dagian*; akin to OHG *tagēn* to dawn, OE *dæg* day]

²**daw** *n, archaic or dial* a jackdaw [ME *dawe*; akin to OHG *taha* jackdaw]

**dawdle** /'dawdl/ *vi* **1** to spend time idly ⟨~ *over one's coffee*⟩ **2** to move lackadaisically ~ *vt* to spend (time) fruitlessly or lackadaisically; laze [origin unknown] – **dawdle** *n*, **dawdler** *n*

¹**dawn** /dawn/ *vi* **1** to begin to grow light as the sun rises **2** to begin to appear or develop **3** to begin to be perceived or understood ⟨*the truth finally* ~ed *on him*⟩ [ME *dawnen*, prob back-formation fr *dawning* daybreak, alter. of *dawing*, fr OE *dagung*, fr *dagian*]

²**dawn** *n* **1** the first appearance of light in the morning **2** a first appearance; a beginning ⟨*the* ~ *of the space age*⟩

¹**day** /day/ *n* **1** the time of light when the sun is above the horizon between one night and the next **2** the time taken by a celestial body, specif the earth, to turn once on its axis **3** the SOLAR DAY of 24 hours beginning at midnight **4** a specified day or date ⟨*wash* ~⟩ – often cap when used to name some specific festival, anniversary, or holiday ⟨*St Valentine's* Day⟩ ⟨*May* Day⟩ **5** day, days *pl* a specified time or period ⟨*in grand-*

*father's* ~⟩ ⟨*the last* ~s *of the Roman Empire*⟩ **6** the conflict or contention of the day ⟨*played hard and won the* ~⟩ **7** the time established by usage or law for work, school, or business ⟨*an eight-hour* ~⟩ **8** an era ⟨*dawn of a new* ~ *in industrial relations*⟩ [ME, fr OE *dæg*; akin to OHG *tag* day] – **call it a day** to call a (temporary) halt to an activity ⟨*since the fish weren't biting they decided to* call it a day *and go home*⟩ – **carry the day** to win, prevail – **day in, day out** for an infinite or seemingly endless number of days – **from day to day** ²DAILY – **make a day of it** to continue celebrations or social activities throughout the day – see also ORDER **of the day, pass the** TIME **of day**

²**day** *adj* **1** held in or operating during the daytime or weekdays ⟨*a* ~ *school*⟩ ⟨*a psychiatric* ~ *centre for patients recently released from institutional care*⟩ **2** attending in the daytime but not resident ⟨*a* ~ *patient*⟩

**day after day** *adv* for an indefinite or seemingly endless number of days

**Dayak** /'die,ak/ *n* DYAK (language or people of Borneo)

**daybed** /'day,bed/ *n* **1** CHAISE LONGUE **2** a bed which can be converted into a couch or sofa when not in use

**daybook** /'day,book/ *n* **1** a diary, journal **2** a book formerly used in accounting for recording the transactions of the day

**daybreak** /'day,brayk/ *n* dawn, sunrise

'**day-,care** *adj* of or providing supervision and facilities for those unable to look after themselves (eg preschool children, the elderly, or the handicapped) during the day ⟨~ *centres*⟩ – **day care** *n*

¹**daydream** /'day,dreem/ *n* **1** a state of mind in which one is withdrawn from one's immediate physical surroundings and indulges in pleasant thoughts and speculations; a reverie **2** an idle scheme or plan that is unlikely to be fulfilled and might form the subject of a daydream ⟨*a* ~ *of leaving the rat race and going to grow organic vegetables in Cornwall*⟩ – **daydreamlike** *adj*

²**daydream** *vi* to have daydreams; appear abstracted as if indulging in idle fantasies – **daydreamer** *n*

**dayglo** /'daygloh/ *adj* of a bright orange, green, or pink that appears to glow in natural daylight ⟨*punks in* ~ *socks with hair dyed to match*⟩ [fr *Day-Glo*, a trademark for a type of paint]

**daylight** /'day,liet/ *n* **1** the light of the sun during the day; sunshine ⟨*plants that should be protected from strong* ~⟩ **2** dawn **3** knowledge or understanding of something that has been obscure ⟨*began to see* ~ *with the problem*⟩ **4** *pl, informal* mental soundness or stability; wits ⟨*scared the* ~s *out of him*⟩

**daylight robbery** *n, Br informal* an instance of exorbitant pricing or charging

**daylight saving time** *n, chiefly NAm* time usu one hour ahead of STANDARD TIME and used esp during the summer – compare BRITISH SUMMER TIME

**day lily** *n* any of various American and Asian plants (genus *Hemerocallis*) of the lily family that are commonly cultivated for their short-lived flowers

**daylong** /'daylong/ *adj* lasting all day

,**day-'neutral** *adj, of a plant* having an ability to flower that is unaffected by length of daylight – compare LONG-DAY, SHORT-DAY

**day nursery** *n* a public centre for the care of young children

**Day of Atonement** *n* YOM KIPPUR

**day of reckoning** *n* a time when the results of mistakes or misdeeds are felt, or when offences are punished

**day release** *n* a system in Britain by which a usu young worker attends courses on one or more days a week without loss of pay – compare BLOCK RELEASE

,**day-re'turn** *n, Br* a ticket sold for a return journey on the same day and usu at a reduced rate if used outside rush hours

**days** /dayz/ *adv, chiefly NAm* by day repeatedly; on any day ⟨~ *you'd find him at work in the studio*⟩

**day shift** *n* a shift worked during the day; *also* the workers employed on this shift

**days of grace** *n pl* the time customarily allowed for payment of a BILL OF EXCHANGE or an insurance premium after it becomes legally due

**dayspring** /'day,spring/ *n, poetic* dawn

**daystar** /'day,stah/ *n* **1** MORNING STAR **2** SUN 1a

¹**daytime** /'day,tiem/ *n* the time during which there is daylight

²**daytime** *adj* taking place, existing, or presented during the daytime ⟨~ *flights*⟩

,**day-to-'day** *adj* **1** taking place, made, or done in the course

---

of successive days ⟨~ *problems*⟩ **2** providing for a day at a time with little thought for the future; routine ⟨*lived an aimless* ~ *existence*⟩

'**day-,tripper** *n* someone who takes a pleasure trip that does not last overnight – **day-trip** *n*

**daze** /dayz/ *vt* **1** to stupefy, esp by a blow; stun **2** to dazzle with light ⟨*a rabbit* ~d *by the headlights of the car*⟩ [ME *dasen*, fr ON *dasa* (in *dasask* to become exhausted)] – **daze** *n*, **dazedly** *adv*, **dazedness** *n*

**dazzle** /'dazl/ *vi* **1** to lose clear vision, esp from looking at bright light **2a** to shine brilliantly **b** to arouse admiration by an impressive display ~ *vt* **1** to blind for a short period with a bright light **2** to impress deeply, overpower, or confound with brilliance ⟨~d *the crowd with his oratory*⟩ [freq of *daze*] – **dazzle** *n*, **dazzler** *n*, **dazzlingly** *adv*

**D day** /dee/ *n* a day set for launching an operation; *specif* June 6, 1944, on which the invasion of France in World War II was begun by forces allied against Germany [*D*, abbr for *day*]

**DDD** *n* an insecticide, $(ClC_6H_4)_2CHCHCl_2$, closely related chemically and similar in properties to DDT [*di*chloro-*di*phenyl-*di*chloro-ethane]

**DDT** *n* a colourless odourless water-insoluble insecticide, $(ClC_6H_4)_2CHCCl_3$, that is not rapidly broken down in the environment and so tends to accumulate in FOOD CHAINS and has toxic effects on many VERTEBRATE animals [*di*chloro-*di*phenyl-*tri*chloro-ethane]

**DDVP** *n* an insecticide, $(CH_3)_2PO_4CH=CCl_2$, that is most commonly found in the form of solid strips from which the insecticide diffuses into the air as a gas [*di*methyl + *di*chlor- + *vinyl* + *phosphate*]

**de-** /dee-, di-/ *prefix* **1a** do the opposite of (a specified action) ⟨*depopulate*⟩ ⟨*decompose*⟩ **b** reverse of ⟨de-*emphasis*⟩ ⟨de-*industrialization*⟩ **2a** remove (something specified) from ⟨*delouse*⟩ ⟨*decapitate*⟩ **b** remove from (something specified) ⟨*dethrone*⟩ **3** reduce ⟨de*value*⟩ **4** derived from (a specified part of speech) ⟨*denominative*⟩ ⟨de*verbal*⟩ **5** alight from (a specified thing) ⟨de*train*⟩ **6** having a molecular structure characterized by the removal of one or more (specified atoms or chemical groups) ⟨de*oxy*-⟩ [ME, fr OF *de-, des-*, partly fr L *de-* from, down, away (fr *de*) and partly fr L *dis-*; L *de* akin to OIr *di* from, OE *tō* to – more at TO, DIS-]

**deacidify** /,dee-ə'sidifie/ *vt* to remove acid from; reduce the acidity of (eg by neutralization) – **deacidification** *n*

**deacon** /'deekən/ *n* **1** a holder of some minor office in a Christian church: eg **1a** a clergyman ranking next below a priest and in the Anglican and Roman Catholic churches usu being a candidate for ordination as priest **b** an assistant minister in a Lutheran parish **c** any of a group of laymen with administrative and sometimes pastoral duties in various Protestant churches **2** *Scot* the president of an association of craftsmen, often by virtue of his office a member of the town council [ME *dekene*, fr OE *dēacon*, fr LL *diaconus*, fr Gk *diakonos*, lit., servant, fr *dia-* + *-konos* (akin to en*konein* to be active); akin to L *conari* to attempt]

**deaconess** /,deekə'nes, '---/ *n* a woman assisting in the ministry of a Protestant church

**deactivate** /dee'aktivayt/ *vt* to make (chemically) inactive or ineffective – **deactivator** *n*, **deactivation** *n*

¹**dead** /ded/ *adj* **1** deprived of life; having died **2a(1)** having the appearance of death; deathly ⟨*in a* ~ *faint*⟩ **a(2)** lacking power to move, feel, or respond; numb **b(1)** incapable of being stirred emotionally or intellectually; unresponsive ⟨~ *to pity*⟩ **b(2)** grown cold; extinguished ⟨*a* ~ *fire*⟩ **3a** inanimate, inert ⟨~ *matter*⟩ **b** barren, infertile ⟨~ *soil*⟩ **4a(1)** no longer having power or effect ⟨*a* ~ *law*⟩ ⟨*a* ~ *battery*⟩ **a(2)** no longer having interest, relevance, or significance ⟨*a* ~ *issue*⟩ **b** no longer used; obsolete ⟨*a* ~ *language*⟩ **c** no longer active; extinct ⟨*a* ~ *volcano*⟩ **d** no longer existing ⟨*charity is* ~⟩ **e** lacking in gaiety or animation ⟨*a* ~ *audience*⟩ **f(1)** lacking in commercial activity; quiet **f(2)** commercially idle or unproductive ⟨~ *capital*⟩ **g** lacking elasticity, springiness, or resonance ⟨*the ball bouncing slowly on a* ~ *pitch*⟩ ⟨*a hall with* ~ *acoustics*⟩ **h** out of action or out of use ⟨*a* ~ *village*⟩ ⟨*are those beer glasses* ~?⟩; *specif* free from any connection to a source of voltage and free from electric charges **i(1)** temporarily out of play ⟨*a* ~ *ball*⟩ ⟨~ *cards*⟩ **i(2)** *Br, of a golf ball* on the green level with and near to the hole **5a** not running or circulating; stagnant ⟨~ *water*⟩ **b** not imparting motion or power although otherwise functioning ⟨*a* ~ *rear axle*⟩ **6** lacking warmth, odour, vigour, or taste **7a** absolutely uniform ⟨*a* ~ *level*⟩ **b(1)** unerring

⟨*a ~ shot with a catapult*⟩ **b(2)** exact ⟨*~ centre of the target*⟩ **c** abrupt ⟨*brought to a ~ stop*⟩ **d** complete, absolute ⟨*a ~ silence*⟩ ⟨*a ~ loss*⟩ ⟨*a ~ giveaway*⟩ **8 dead beat, dead** *informal* extremely tired; exhausted [ME *deed*, fr OE *dēad;* akin to ON *dauthr* dead, *deyja* to die – more at DIE] – **deadness** *n* – **drop dead 1** to die suddenly **2** *slang* to go away; SHUT UP – used in the imperative; see also **flog a dead** HORSE, **dead from the** NECK **up, dead to the** WORLD

 *usage* Since there can be no degrees in death, some people dislike expressions such as ⟨*very dead in spirit*⟩.

²**dead** *n* **1** *taking pl vb* dead people or animals ⟨*the ~ lay where they had fallen*⟩ **2** the state of being dead ⟨*raised him from the ~* – Col 2:12(RSV)⟩ **3** the time of greatest quiet or inactivity ⟨*the ~ of night*⟩

³**dead** *adv* **1a** absolutely, utterly ⟨*~ certain*⟩ **b** *Br* very, extremely ⟨*~ lucky*⟩ ⟨*it must all be ~ baffling* – *Punch*⟩ **2** suddenly and completely ⟨*stopped ~*⟩ **3** directly, exactly ⟨*~ ahead*⟩ ⟨*~ on time*⟩

**dead air** *n* a period of silence during a radio or television broadcast

**dead-air space** *n* a sealed or unventilated air space

**dead-ball line** *n* **1** a line at either end of a rugby field parallel to and from 5.5 to 23 metres (about 6 to 25 yards) beyond the GOAL LINE, beyond which no try can be scored **2** a soccer GOAL LINE

**dead bat** *n* a cricket bat held loosely, esp for defensive strokes, so that a ball striking it will not travel far through the air

¹**deadbeat** /'ded‚beet/ *adj* having a pointer that gives a reading with little or no oscillation ⟨*a ~ compass*⟩

²**deadbeat** *n, chiefly NAm* **1** one who persistently fails to pay his/her debts or his/her way **2** a loafer

**dead centre** *n* either of the two positions at the ends of a stroke in a crank and connecting rod when the crank is directly in line with the rod

**dead duck** *n, informal* something, or sometimes someone, that is unlikely to succeed; a nonstarter

**deaden** /'dedən/ *vt* **1** to impair in vigour or sensation; blunt ⟨*a shot of morphine to ~ the pain*⟩ **2** to reduce the resonance of; muffle – **deadener** *n*, **deadeningly** *adv*

‚**dead-'end** *adj* **1a** lacking opportunities for advancement ⟨*a ~ job*⟩ **b** lacking an exit ⟨*a ~ street*⟩ **2** made aggressively antisocial by a dead-end existence ⟨*~ kids*⟩

**dead end** *n* **1** an end (eg of a street) without an exit **2** a position, situation, or course of action that leads no further

**deadeye** /'ded‚ie/ *n* a circular or semicircular wooden block through which a rope may be secured

**deadfall** /'dedfawl/ *n* a type of trap in which the prey is killed or disabled by a heavy object (eg a log) falling on it

**dead ground** *n* terrain through which one can move without being seen by an enemy or by game which is being stalked (eg because of the slope of the ground)

**dead hand** *n* **1** MORTMAIN **2** the oppressive influence of the past

¹**deadhead** /‚ded'hed/ *n* **1** a dull or stupid person **2** *NAm* a person who has not paid for a ticket (eg for a train journey or theatre performance)

²**deadhead** *vt, Br* to remove dead flower heads from (a plant)

‚**dead-'heat** *vi* to finish in a dead heat with another competitor

**dead heat** *n* an inconclusive finish to a race or other contest, in which the fastest time, highest score, etc is achieved by more than one competitor

**dead letter** *n* **1** a law, custom, or convention that has lost its force or authority ⟨*dressing for dinner is now something of a ~*⟩ **2** an undeliverable and unreturnable letter

**deadlight** /'ded‚liet/ *n* **1** a metal cover or shutter fitted to a porthole to keep out light and water **2** a heavy glass pane set in a ship's deck or hull to admit light

**deadline** /'dedlien/ *n* **1** a line or boundary beyond which it is not possible or permitted to pass; *esp* a line drawn within or round a prison that a prisoner passes at the risk of being shot **2** a date or time before which something must be done; *specif* the time after which copy is not accepted for a particular issue of a publication

**dead load** *n* a static load or force on a structure resulting from the weight of that structure's component parts

**deadlock** /'dedlok/ *n* **1** a lock that can be opened and shut only by a key **2** a state of inaction or neutralization resulting from the opposition of equally powerful and uncompromising people or factions; a standstill

¹**deadly** /'dedli/ *adj* **1** likely to cause or capable of producing death ⟨*a ~ disease*⟩ ⟨*a ~ instrument*⟩ **2a** aiming to kill or destroy; implacable ⟨*a ~ enemy*⟩ **b** unerring ⟨*~ accuracy*⟩ **c** marked by determination or extreme seriousness ⟨*a remark made in ~ earnest*⟩ **3** lacking animation or sparkle; dull, boring ⟨*a ~ conversation*⟩ ⟨*a ~ man to spend a wet afternoon with*⟩ **4** intense, extreme ⟨*~ fear*⟩ – **deadliness** *n*

 *synonyms* Deadly is now commoner than **deathly** in the sense of actually "causing death" ⟨*a deadly blow*⟩, while **deathly** is the usual word for "suggestive of death" ⟨*a deathly pallor*⟩; but a **deathly** silence is sinister, while a **deadly** bore is merely extremely boring.

²**deadly** *adv* **1** suggesting death ⟨*~ pale*⟩ **2** extremely ⟨*~ serious*⟩

**deadly nightshade** /'niet‚shayd/ *n* a European plant (*Atropa belladonna*) of the potato family that is very poisonous, has dull purple bell-shaped flowers and shining black berries, and from the root and leaves of which the drug ATROPINE is produced

**deadly sin** *n* any of the seven sins of pride, covetousness, lust, anger, gluttony, envy, and sloth held to lead to damnation

**dead man's fingers** *n* DEAD MEN'S FINGERS

**dead man's handle** *n, Br* a fail-safe handle (eg on a train or tram) that if released disconnects the power supply

**dead march** *n* a piece of solemn funeral music intended to accompany or suggest a funeral procession

**dead men's fingers** *n* a fleshy soft coral (*Alcyonium digitatum*) of European coastal waters

**deadnettle** /'ded‚netl/ *n* any of various European and Asian plants (genus *Lamium*) of the mint family that resemble the STINGING NETTLE but have no stinging hairs

¹**deadpan** /ded'pan/ *adj* marked by an impassive matter-of-fact manner, style, or expression [*dead + pan*, n (face)]

²**deadpan** *adv* in a deadpan manner

**dead point** *n* DEAD CENTRE

**dead reckoning** *n* the calculation of the position of a ship or aircraft on the basis of its known movements (eg its course, speed, and drift) without the use of external navigational aids (eg observation of sun or stars or bearings taken on radio beacons) – **dead reckoner** *n*

**dead set** *n, Br* a determined effort to win or gain ⟨*made a ~ at him and married him*⟩

**deadweight** /'ded‚wayt/ *n* **1** the unrelieved weight of an inert mass **2** DEAD LOAD **3** a ship's total weight, including cargo, fuel, stores, crew, and passengers **4** *informal* something that deadens, depresses, or makes heavy ⟨*his presence was a real ~ on the spirits of the party*⟩

**deadwood** /'ded‚wood/ *n* **1** wood dead on the tree **2** superfluous personnel or material ⟨*a reshuffle to clear the ~ out of the Cabinet*⟩ **3** pins that have been knocked down but remain on the alley in bowling

**deaerate** /‚dee'eərayt/ *vt* to remove air or gas from – **deaeration** *n*

**deaf** /def/ *adj* **1** lacking or deficient in the sense of hearing; unable to hear (normally) ⟨*don't shout, I'm not ~*⟩ ⟨*tone ~*⟩ ⟨*after the concert we were all ~ for about an hour*⟩ **2** unwilling to hear or listen *to*; not to be persuaded ⟨*~ to reason*⟩ – see also **turn a deaf** EAR **(to), fall on deaf** EARS [ME *deef*, fr OE *dēaf*; akin to Gk *typhlos* blind, *typhein* to smoke, L *fumus* smoke – more at FUME] – **deafish** *adj*, **deafly** *adv*, **deafness** *n*

'**deaf-‚aid** *n* HEARING AID

**deafen** /'defən/ *vt* to make deaf ~ *vi* to cause deafness or stun someone with noise – **deafeningly** *adv*

‚**deaf-'mute** *n* someone who is both deaf and dumb – **deaf-mute** *adj*

¹**deal** /deel, diəl/ *n* **1** a usu large or indefinite quantity or degree; a lot ⟨*a great ~ of support*⟩ ⟨*a good ~ faster*⟩ ⟨*talked a ~ of good sense*⟩ **2a** the act or right of distributing cards to players in a card game ⟨*don't pick up your cards till the ~ is finished*⟩ ⟨*it's your ~ next*⟩ **b** HAND **9b 3** *obs* a part, portion [ME *deel*, fr OE *dǣl*; akin to OE *dāl* division, portion, OHG *teil* part]

²**deal** *vb* dealt /delt/ *vt* **1a** to give as someone's portion; apportion ⟨*tried to ~ justice to all men*⟩ **b** to distribute (playing cards) to players in a game **2** to administer, bestow ⟨*~t him a blow*⟩ ~ *vi* to distribute the cards in a card game – see also WHEEL **and deal**

**deal in** *vt* to sell or distribute as a business ⟨*they deal in insurance*⟩

**deal with** *vt* **1** to concern oneself or itself with ⟨*the work deals with education*⟩ **2** to trade with ⟨*they deal with all the* major breweries⟩ **3** to take action with regard to ⟨deal with an offender⟩ ⟨deal with last week's post⟩

**³deal** n **1** an act of dealing; a transaction **2** treatment received ⟨a raw ~⟩ **3** an arrangement for mutual advantage ⟨a by-election ~ between the Social Democrats and the Liberals⟩

**⁴deal** n **1** a piece of sawn fir or pine; esp one of standard dimensions **2** SOFTWOOD (fir, spruce, pine, etc) timber [MD or MLG dele plank; akin to OHG dili plank] – **deal** adj

**dealate** /ˌdeeˈaylayt, -lət/ n a dealated insect

**dealated** /ˌdeeˈaylaytid/ adj, of an adult insect (eg an ant) having dropped the wings after a mating flight [de- + alated having wings, fr L alatus, fr ala wing] – **dealation** n

**dealer** /ˈdeelə/ n one who or that which deals: eg **a** somebody who deals playing cards **b** a person or firm that deals in goods or services **c** one who deals in illegal drugs; a pusher

**dealing** /ˈdeeling, ˈdiəling/ n **1** pl business or personal relationships ⟨they had no further ~s with one another after their divorce⟩ **2** method of business; manner of conduct

**deaminase** /ˌdeeˈaminayz, -ays/ n an ENZYME that promotes the breakdown of AMINO ACIDS and related chemical compounds (AMINES) by the removal of the AMINO group [de- + amino + -ase]

**deaminate** /ˌdeeˈaminayt/ vt to remove an AMINO group from (a chemical compound) – **deamination** n

**¹dean, dene** /deen/ n a narrow wooded valley containing a stream – usu in place-names [ME dene, fr OE denu]

**²dean** n **1a** the head of the CHAPTER (body of canons) of a cathedral or COLLEGIATE CHURCH – often used as a title **b** RURAL DEAN **2a** the head of a division, faculty, or school of a university **b** chiefly NAm a college or secondary school administrator in charge of guiding and disciplining students ⟨~ of men⟩ **3** a doyen [ME deen, fr MF deien, fr LL decanus, lit., chief of ten, fr L decem ten – more at TEN] – **deanship** n

**deanery** /ˈdeenəri/ n the office, jurisdiction, or official residence of a clerical dean

**¹dear** /diə/ adj, archaic severe, grievous ⟨in our ~ peril – Shak⟩ [ME dere, fr OE dēor]

**²dear** adj **1** highly valued or esteemed; much loved ⟨a ~ friend⟩ – often used in address ⟨~ Sir⟩ **2** affectionate, fond **3** high or exorbitant in price; expensive ⟨eggs are very ~ just now⟩ **4** heartfelt ⟨her ~est wish⟩ **5** obs noble [ME dere, fr OE dēore; akin to OHG tiuri costly, ON dȳrr] – **dear** adv, **dearly** adv, **dearness** n

**usage** The adverb **dear** is today used chiefly in contexts of buying and selling, and cannot replace **dearly** in the meaning "fondly" ⟨love her **dearly**⟩ or "deeply" ⟨would **dearly** like to go⟩. **antonym** cheap

**³dear** n **1a** a loved one; a sweetheart **b** – used as a familiar or affectionate form of address **2** a lovable person

**⁴dear** interj – used typically to express annoyance or dismay ⟨oh ~!⟩ ⟨~ me!⟩ [prob short for dear God or dear Lord]

**Dear John, Dear John letter** n, chiefly NAm a letter (eg to a soldier) in which a wife asks for a divorce or a girl friend breaks off an engagement or friendship

**dearth** /duhth/ n an inadequate supply; a scarcity **synonyms** see ¹LACK [ME derthe, fr dere dear, costly]

**deary, dearie** /ˈdiəri/ n a dear person – used chiefly in address by women

**deasil** /ˈdesl, ˈdesh(ə)l/ adv clockwise – compare WIDDERSHINS [ScGael deiseil; akin to L dexter]

**death** /deth/ n **1** a permanent cessation of all the functions necessary for keeping (part of) an organism alive; the end of life **2** the cause or occasion of loss of life ⟨drinking was the ~ of him⟩ **3** cap death personified, usu represented as a skeleton with a scythe **4** the state of being dead **5** extinction, disappearance ⟨the ~ of the music hall⟩ ⟨the ~ of a species⟩ **6** slaughter ⟨keep ~ off the roads⟩ [ME deeth, fr OE dēath; akin to ON dauthi death, deyja to die – more at DIE] – **at death's door** seriously ill – **to death** beyond all acceptable limits; excessively ⟨bored to death⟩

**¹deathbed** /ˈdethˌbed/ n the bed in which a person dies – **on one's deathbed** near the point of death

**²deathbed** adj of or made in the last hours of life ⟨a ~ repentance⟩

**deathblow** /ˈdethˌbloh/ n a destructive or killing stroke or event

**death cap** n a very poisonous fungus (Amanita phalloides) having a pale olive-green cap and milky white gills that is found in most parts of the British isles, esp in beech and oak woodland

**death cell** n CONDEMNED CELL

**death duty** n, **death duties** n pl, chiefly Br a tax paid when property of more than a certain value changes hands by inheritance

**deathless** /ˈdethlis/ adj immortal, imperishable ⟨~ fame⟩ – **deathlessly** adv, **deathlessness** n

**deathly** /ˈdethli/ adj **1** fatal ⟨dealt him a ~ blow to the head⟩ **2** (suggestive) of death ⟨a ~ pallor⟩ **synonyms** see DEADLY – **deathly** adv

**death mask** n an impression (eg in plaster of paris) taken from the face of a dead person

**death rate** n the rate at which a given population is changing as the result of deaths of its members; the number of deaths per 1000 members of a population per annum; MORTALITY 4b

**death rattle** n a rattling or gurgling sound produced by air passing through mucus in the lungs and air passages of a dying person

**death row** n, chiefly NAm a part of a prison containing the cells of those condemned to death

**'death's-ˌhead** n a human skull symbolic of death

**death's-head hawkmoth** n a very large dark European hawkmoth (Acherontia atropos) having markings resembling a human skull on the back of the central body region

**death tax** n, NAm DEATH DUTY

**death trap** n something (eg a car or building) that is potentially lethal

**death warrant** n an official order to carry out a death sentence – **sign one's own death warrant** to do something which will lead to one's own destruction, detection, or disadvantage

**deathwatch** /ˈdethˌwoch/ n a vigil kept with the dead or dying [death + watch (vigil)]

**deathwatch beetle** n any of various small beetles (family Anobiidae and esp Xestobium rufovillosum) that are common in old buildings where they bore into woodwork and furniture making an ominous ticking sound

**death wish** n a usu unconscious desire for one's own death, or, occasionally, for the death of another

**deave** /deev/ vt, chiefly Scot **1** to deafen **2** to worry or bother, esp by making a noise [ME deven, deriv of OE dēaf deaf]

**deb** /deb/ n, Br informal a debutante – **debby** adj

**debacle** /diˈbahkəl/ n **1** a tumultuous breakup of ice in a river **2** a violent disruption (eg of an army); a rout **3** a complete failure; a fiasco △ debut [Fr débâcle, fr débâcler to unbar, fr MF desbacler, fr des- de- + bacler to bar, fr OProv baclar, fr (assumed) VL bacculare, fr L baculum staff – more at BACTERIUM]

**debag** /ˌdeeˈbag/ vt **-gg-** Br informal to remove the trousers from as a prank ⟨the new boy was ~ged and thrown into the fountain⟩ [de- + bags (trousers)]

**debar** /ˌdeeˈbah/ vt **-rr-** to bar from having, doing, or undergoing something; preclude ⟨his accepting a fee for an exhibition match ~red him from taking part in amateur events⟩ △ disbar [ME debarren, fr MF desbarrer to unbar, fr des- de- + barrer to bar] – **debarment** n

**¹debark** /ˌdeeˈbahk/ vb to disembark [MF debarquer, fr de- + barque bark] – **debarkation** n

**²debark** vt to remove the bark from (a tree) [de- + bark]

**debase** /diˈbays/ vt **1** to lower in status, esteem, quality, or character **2a** to reduce the amount of precious metal in (a coin) **b** to reduce the exchange value of (a monetary unit) **synonyms** see ²HUMBLE **antonym** enhance [de- + ⁴base] – **debasement** n, **debaser** n

**debatable** /diˈbaytəbl/ adj **1** claimed by more than one country ⟨~ border territory⟩ **2** open to debate; questionable ⟨a ~ conclusion⟩

**¹debate** /diˈbayt/ n **1** a formal discussion carried out under set rules ⟨the King and Country ~ in the Oxford Union⟩; esp a discussion of some topic, esp a proposed law, in some legislative body (eg parliament or a city council), usu brought to an end by a vote being taken ⟨a budget ~⟩ **2** public controversy on some issue of general concern ⟨the ~ on the virtues of comprehensive education⟩

**²debate** vi **1a** to contend in words **b** to discuss a question by considering opposed arguments **2** to participate in a debate **3** obs to fight, contend ~ vt **1a** to argue about **b** to engage (an opponent) in debate **2** to turn over in one's mind [ME debaten, fr MF debatre, fr OF, fr de- + batre to beat, fr L battuere – more at BATTLE] – **debatement** n, **debater** n

**usage** Correctly, one **debates** a topic, or **debates** whether something should happen, *where* to go, etc, rather than **debating** *on* or *about* something. **synonyms** see PONDER

**debating point** /di'bayting/ *n* an irrelevant, unimportant, or hair-splitting point made to gain a spurious advantage in debate

¹**debauch** /di'bawch/ *vt* **1** to lead away from virtue or excellence **2** to encourage a taste for vice or sensual pleasures in; *esp* to make unchaste; seduce [MF *debaucher*, fr OF *desbauchier* to scatter, rough-hew (timber), fr *des-* de- + *bauch* beam, of Gmc origin; akin to OHG *balko* beam – more at BALK] – **debaucher** *n*, **debauchery** *n*

²**debauch** *n* **1** an act or occasion of debauchery **2** an orgy

**debauchee** /di,baw'chee/ *n* one given to debauchery [Fr *débauché*, fr pp of *débaucher*]

**debenture** /di'bencha/ *n* **1** a voucher for refund of excise or import duty **2a** *Br* a loan secured on the assets of a company in respect of which the company must pay a fixed interest before any dividends are paid to its own shareholders **b** a bond backed by the general credit of a company rather than a specific claim on particular assets; *specif* a fixed-interest, long-term security issued by a limited liability company on which the interest is payable whether or not the company makes a profit [ME *debentur*, fr L, they are due, fr *debēre* to owe]

**debilitate** /di'bilitayt/ *vt* to impair the strength of; enfeeble [L *debilitatus*, pp of *debilitare* to weaken, fr *debilis*] – **debilitation** *n*

**debility** /di'bilati/ *n* weakness, infirmity [MF *debilité*, fr L *debilitat-*, *debilitas*, fr *debilis* weak]

¹**debit** /'debit/ *n* **1** a record of something, esp money, owed; *specif* an entry in an account recording an item of expenditure **2** the sum of the items so entered **3** a charge against a bank account **4** a drawback, shortcoming ⟨*one of the* ~s *of the plan was that the element of surprise would be lost*⟩ [L *debitum* debt]

²**debit** *vt* **1** to enter as a debit **2** to charge to the debit of ⟨~ *an account*⟩ – compare CREDIT

**debonair** /,deba'nea/ *adj* **1** suave, urbane **2** lighthearted, nonchalant **3** *archaic* gentle, courteous [ME *debonere*, fr OF *debonaire*, fr *de bonne aire* of good family or nature] – **debonairly** *adv*, **debonairness** *n*

**debouch** /di'bowch/ *vi* **1** *of troops* to march out from a place of concealment into open ground **2** to emerge or issue, esp from a narrow place into a wider place ⟨*a stream* ~ing *into a lake*⟩ [Fr *déboucher*, fr *dé-* de- + *bouche* mouth, fr L *bucca* cheek – more at POCK]

**debouchment** /di'bowchmant/ *n* **1** the act or process of debouching **2** a mouth or outlet, esp of a river

**debouchure** /,daybooh'shooa/ *n* DEBOUCHMENT 2

**debridement, débridement** /di'breedmant/ *n* the surgical removal from a wound of tissue that is dead or likely to die and that might provide an opportunity for a bacterial infection to develop [Fr *débridement*, fr *débrider* to remove unhealthy tissue, lit., to unbridle, fr MF *desbrider*, fr *des-* de- + *bride* bridle, fr MHG *brīdel*]

**debrief** /,dee'breef/ *vt* to interrogate (e g a pilot or diplomat) on return from a mission in order to obtain useful information

**debris** /'debri/ *n* **1** the remains of something broken down or destroyed; ruins ⟨*searching for survivors in the* ~ *of the bombed city*⟩ **2a** an accumulation of fragments of rock **b** accumulated rubbish or waste [Fr *débris*, fr MF, fr *debriser* to break to pieces, fr OF *debrisier*, fr *de-* + *brisier* to break, of Celt origin]

**debt** /det/ *n* **1** a state of owing ⟨*in* ~ *to the tune of £5000*⟩ **2** something owed; an obligation ⟨*a* ~ *of £500*⟩ ⟨*a* ~ *collector*⟩ [ME *dette, debte*, fr OF *dette* something owed, fr (assumed) VL *debita*, fr L, pl of *debitum* debt, fr neut of *debitus*, pp of *debēre* to owe, fr *de-* + *habēre* to have – more at GIVE] – **debtless** *adj* – **in somebody's debt** owing somebody gratitude; indebted to somebody

**debt of honour** *n* a debt which cannot be legally enforced but is nevertheless usu regarded as morally binding (e g a gambling debt)

**debtor** /'deta/ *n* someone who or something (e g a firm) that owes a debt

**debug** /,dee'bug/ *vt* **-gg-** **1** to eliminate errors in or malfunctions of ⟨~ *a computer program*⟩ **2** to remove a concealed microphone or wiretapping device from

**debunk** /,dee'bungk/ *vt* to expose the falseness of ⟨~ *the stories of the Loch Ness monster*⟩ [*de-* + ⁴*bunk*] – **debunker** *n*

**debus** /,dee'bus/ *vb* **-ss-** *vt* to unload (e g military stores or material) from a vehicle ~ *vi* to get out of a motor vehicle ⟨*the troops* ~sed⟩ [*de-* + *bus*]

**debut** /'dayb(y)ooh/ *n* **1** a first public appearance **2** a formal entrance into society [Fr *début*, fr *débuter* to begin, fr MF *desbuter* to play first, fr *des-* de- + *but* starting point, goal – more at BUTT] – **debut** *vi*
*usage* The use of **debut** as a verb ⟨*she debuts next week*⟩ is widely disliked. △ debacle

**debutant** /'debyoo,tont/ *n* someone making a debut [Fr *débutant*, fr prp of *débuter*]

**debutante** /'debyoo,tont/ *n* a woman making a debut; *esp* a young woman making her formal entrance into society by being presented at court [Fr *débutante*, fem of *débutant*]

**deca-** /deka-/, **dec-, deka-, dek-** *comb form* ten ⟨*decamerous*⟩ ⟨*decathlon*⟩ [ME, fr L, fr Gk *deka-, dek-*, fr *deka* – more at TEN]

**decade** /'dekayd; *also* di'kayd USE *the last pron is disliked by some speakers*/ *n* **1** a group, set, or sequence of 10 **2** a period of 10 years **3** a division of the rosary containing 10 Hail Marys [ME, fr MF *décade*, fr LL *decad-, decas*, fr Gk *dekad-, dekas*, fr *deka*]

**decadence** /'dekadans/ *n* (a period of) moral or cultural decay or decline [MF, fr ML *decadentia*, fr LL *decadent-, decadens*, prp of *decadere* to fall, sink – more at DECAY]

¹**decadent** /'dekadant/ *adj* **1a** marked by decline, esp in moral or cultural standards **b** tending to gratify one's desires, appetites, or whims in an excessive or unrestrained manner; self-indulgent **2** (having the characteristics) of the Decadents [back-formation fr *decadence*] – **decadently** *adv*

²**decadent** *n* **1** someone who is decadent **2** *often cap* any of a group of late 19th-century French and English writers whose work is characterized by subtlety, artificiality, and obscurity in style and subject matter – compare FIN DE SIÈCLE

**decaffeinated** /,dee'kafinaytid/ *adj, of coffee* having had most of the caffeine removed

**decagon** /'dekagon/ *n* a two-dimensional geometric figure having 10 sides; *esp* one that is REGULAR, having 10 equal sides and angles [NL *decagonum*, fr Gk *dekagōnon*, fr *deka-* deca- + *-gōnon* -gon]

**decahedron** /,deka'heedran/ *n* a three-dimensional geometric figure having 10 faces [ISV]

**decal** /'dee,kal, di'kal, 'dekal/ *n, chiefly NAm* a design or picture, esp on specially prepared paper, for transfer to another surface; TRANSFER 3 [short for *decalcomania*, fr Fr *décalcomanie*, fr *décalquer* to copy by tracing + *manie* mania]

**decalcification** /,dee,kalsifi'kaysh(a)n/ *n* the removal or loss of calcium or calcium chemical compounds (e g from bones or soil)

**decalcify** /,dee'kalsifie/ *vt* to remove calcium or calcium chemical compounds from [ISV]

**decalescence** /,deeka'les(a)ns/ *n* a decrease in the temperature of iron or a similar metal, that occurs as the metal is heated through a range of temperatures in which a change in crystal structure occurs [ISV *de-* + *-calescence* (as in *recalescence*)]

**Decalogue** /'dekalog/ *n* TEN COMMANDMENTS [ME *decaloge*, fr LL *decalogus*, fr Gk *dekalogos*, fr *deka-* + *logos* word – more at LEGEND]

**decametric** /,deka'metrik/ *adj* of or being a RADIO WAVE of high frequency [*decametre* (10 metres) + *-ic*; fr the wavelength range being between one and ten decametres]

**decamp** /,dee'kamp/ *vi* **1** to break up or leave a camp **2** to depart suddenly; abscond [Fr *décamper*, fr MF *descamper*, fr *des-* de- + *camper* to camp] – **decampment** *n*

**decanal** /di'kaynl/ *adj* **1** of a dean or deanery **2** of the south side of the choir (e g in a cathedral) where the dean sits – compare CANTORIAL [ML *decanus* dean, fr LL – more at ²DEAN]

**decane** /'dekayn/ *n* any of several liquids, $C_{10}H_{22}$, that are ISOMERIC (having the same molecular formula but a different structural arrangement of atoms) and belong to the ALKANE series of organic chemical compounds [ISV *deca-* + *-ane*]

**decanoic acid** /,deka'noh-ik/ *n* CAPRIC ACID [ISV, fr *decane*]

**decant** /di'kant/ *vt* **1** to pour from one vessel into another, esp a decanter **2** to draw off (a liquid) without disturbing the sediment or the lower liquid layers [NL *decantare*, fr L *de-* + ML *cantus* side, fr L, iron tyre – more at CANT] – **decantation** *n*

**decanter** /di'kanta/ *n* a vessel used to decant or to receive decanted liquids; *esp* an ornamental glass bottle used for serving an alcoholic drink (e g sherry)

**decapitate** /di'kapitayt/ *vt* to cut off the head of; behead [LL *decapitatus*, pp of *decapitare*, fr L *de-* + *capit-, caput* head – more at HEAD] – **decapitator** *n*, **decapitation** *n*

**decapod** /'deka,pod/ *n* **1** any of an order (Decapoda of the class Crustacea) of INVERTEBRATE animals including shrimps, lobsters, crabs, etc, with stalked eyes, five pairs of limbs, one or more of which are modified into pincers, and the head and upper segment of the body fused together and covered by a CARAPACE (thick hard outer covering) **2** any of an order (Decapoda of the class Cephalopoda, phylum Mollusca) of INVERTEBRATE animals including the cuttlefishes, squids, and related forms that have 10 arms [NL *Decapoda*, order name] – **decapod, decapodal** *adj*, **decapodan** *adj or n*, **decapodous** *adj*

**decarbonate** /ˌdeeˈkahbənayt/ *vt* to remove CARBON DIOXIDE or CARBONIC ACID from – **decarbonator** *n*, **decarbonation** *n*

**decarbon·ize, -ise** /ˌdeeˈkahbəniez/ *vt* to remove carbon from (eg the engine of a car) [ISV] – **decarbonizer** *n*

**decarboxylase** /ˌdeeˌkahˈboksilayz, -ays/ *n* any of a group of enzymes that speed up the rate of decarboxylation, esp of AMINO ACIDS

**decarboxylate** /ˌdeeˌkahˈboksilayt/ *vt* to remove a CARBOXYL group from – **decarboxylation** *n*

**decarbur·ize, -ise** /ˌdeeˈkahbyooriez, -bə-/ *vt* to decarbonize – **decarburization** *n*

**decasyllabic** /ˌdekəsiˈlabik/ *adj* **1** consisting of 10 syllables **2** *of a poem* composed of lines of 10 syllables each – **decasyllabic** *n*, **decasyllable** *n*

**decathlete** /diˈkathleet/ *n* somebody who competes in the decathlon [blend of *decathlon* and *athlete*]

**decathlon** /diˈkathlon/ *n* a men's athletic contest in which each competitor competes in 10 events, the 100-metre, 400-metre, and 1500-metre races, the 110-metre high hurdles, and the javelin, discus, shot put, pole vault, high jump, and long jump – compare BIATHLON, PENTATHLON [Fr *décathlon*, fr *déca-* + Gk *athlon* contest]

**¹decay** /diˈkay/ *vi* **1** to decline from a sound or prosperous condition **2** to decrease gradually in quantity, activity, or force; *specif* to undergo radioactive decay **3** to fall into ruin **4** to decline in health, strength, or vigour **5** to undergo decomposition; rot ~ *vt* **1** to destroy by decomposition **2** *obs* to cause to decay; impair ⟨*infirmity that* ~s *the wise* – Shak⟩ [ME *decayen*, fr ONF *decaïr*, fr LL *decadere* to fall, sink, fr L *de-* + *cadere* to fall – more at CHANCE]

**²decay** *n* **1** gradual decline in strength, soundness, prosperity, or quality ⟨*urban* ~⟩ **2** a wasting or wearing away; ruin **3a** rot; *specif* decomposition of organic matter (eg proteins) chiefly caused by bacteria in the presence of oxygen **b** the product of decay ⟨*remove* ~ *from a tooth*⟩ **4** a decline in health or vigour **5** decrease in quantity, activity, or force: eg **5a** spontaneous decrease in the number of radioactive atoms in radioactive material **b** spontaneous disintegration (eg of an atom or MESON) **6** *obs* destruction, death

**Decca** /ˈdekə/ *trademark* – used for a navigational aid that makes use of chains of long-wave radio transmitters to define position in terms of the relationships between the radio wave cycles – compare LORAN

**decease** /diˈsees/ *n, formal* death [ME *deces*, fr MF, fr L *decessus* departure, death, fr *decessus*, pp of *decedere* to depart, die, fr *de-* + *cedere* to go – more at CEDE] – **decease** *vi*

**¹deceased** /diˈseest/ *n, pl* **deceased** a deceased person ⟨*the will of the* ~⟩

**²deceased** *adj* no longer living; *esp* recently dead

**decedent** /diˈseed(ə)nt/ *n, NAm* a deceased person – used chiefly in law [L *decedent-, decedens*, prp of *decedere*]

**deceit** /diˈseet/ *n* **1** the act or practice of deceiving; deception **2** an attempt or device to deceive; a trick **3** the quality of being deceitful; deceitfulness [ME *deceite*, fr OF, fr L *decepta*, fem of *deceptus*, pp of *decipere*]

**deceitful** /-f(ə)l/ *adj* having a tendency or disposition to deceive; *specif* dishonest – **deceitfully** *adv*, **deceitfulness** *n*

**deceive** /diˈseev/ *vt* **1** to cause to accept as true or valid what is false or invalid; delude **2** to prove false to; *specif* to commit adultery against **3** *archaic* to fail to fulfil; disappoint ~ *vi* to practise deceit *usage* see UNDECEIVE [ME *deceiven*, fr OF *deceivre*, fr L *decipere*, fr *de-* + *capere* to take – more at HEAVE] – **deceivable** *adj*, **deceiver** *n*, **deceivingly** *adv*

**decelerate** /ˌdeeˈselərayt/ *vt* to reduce the speed or rate of progress of ~ *vi* to slow down; *specif* to take one's foot off the accelerator of a car gradually in order to make it move more slowly [*de-* + *accelerate*] – **decelerator** *n*, **deceleration** *n*

**December** /diˈsembə/ *n* the 12th month of the year according to the GREGORIAN CALENDAR (standard Western calendar) – see MONTH table [ME *Decembre*, fr OF, fr L *December* (tenth

month of the ancient Roman calendar(, fr *decem* ten – more at TEN]

**decemvir** /diˈsemvə/ *n* a member of a ruling body of 10; *specif* any of a body of 10 magistrates in ancient Rome [L, back-formation fr *decemviri*, pl, fr *decem* + *viri*, pl of *vir* man – more at VIRILE] – **decemviral** *adj*, **decemvirate** *n*

**decency** /ˈdeesənsi/ *n* **1** the quality or state of being decent; propriety, decorum **2** *pl the* standards of acceptable behaviour

**decennial** /diˈsenyəl, -niˈəl/ *adj* **1** consisting of or lasting for 10 years **2** occurring every 10 years – **decennial** *n*, **decennially** *adv*

**decennium** /diˈsenyəm, -niˈəm/ *n, pl* **decenniums, decennia** /diˈsenyə, -niə/ a period of 10 years; a decade [L, fr *decem* + *annus* year – more at ANNUAL]

**decent** /ˈdees(ə)nt/ *adj* **1** conforming to standards of propriety, good taste, or morality; *specif* clothed accordingly to standards of propriety **2** free from obscenity **3** adequate, tolerable ⟨~ *wages*⟩ ⟨~ *housing*⟩ ⟨*grow a* ~ *beard*⟩ **4** *chiefly Br informal* obliging, considerate ⟨*it was awfully* ~ *of you to help me out*⟩ [MF or L; MF, fr L *decent-, decens*, prp of *decēre* to be fitting; akin to L *decus* honour, *dignus* worthy, Gk *dokein* to seem, seem good] – **decently** *adv*

**decentral·ization, -isation** /deeˌsentrəlieˈzaysh(ə)n/ *n* **1** the distribution of functions and powers from a central authority to smaller units (eg regional authorities or departments of a business) **2** the redistribution of population and industry from urban centres to outlying areas – **decentralizationist** *n*

**decentral·ize, -ise** /ˌdeeˈsentrəliez/ *vt* to bring about the decentralization of ~ *vi* to undergo decentralization

**deception** /diˈsepsh(ə)n/ *n* **1a** the act of deceiving **b** the fact or condition of being deceived **2** something that deceives; a trick [ME *decepcioun*, fr MF *deception*, fr LL *deception-, deceptio*, fr L *deceptus*, pp of *decipere* to deceive] – **deceptional** *adj*

**deceptive** /diˈseptiv/ *adj* tending or having power to deceive; misleading – **deceptively** *adv*, **deceptiveness** *n*

**decerebrate** /ˌdeeˈserəbrayt/ *vt* to remove or inactivate the brain of – **decerebrate** *adj or n*, **decerebration** *n*

**decertify** /ˌdeeˈsuhtifie/ *vt* to withdraw or revoke the certification of – **decertification** *n*

**deci-** /ˈdesi-, desə/ *comb form* one tenth ($10^{-1}$) part of (a specified unit) ⟨*decilitre*⟩ [Fr *déci-*, fr L *decimus* tenth, fr *decem* ten – more at TEN]

**decibel** /ˈdesibel/ *n* **1** a unit for expressing the ratio of two amounts of electric or acoustic signal power equal to 10 times the COMMON LOGARITHM of this ratio **2** a unit for expressing the relative intensity of sounds on a scale from zero for the average least perceptible sound to about 130 for the average pain level [ISV *deci-* + *bel*]

**decide** /diˈsied/ *vt* **1** to arrive at a solution that ends uncertainty or dispute about ⟨~ *the borderline issues*⟩ **2** to bring to a definitive end or solution ⟨*that goal* ~d *the match*⟩ **3** to induce to come to a choice ⟨*her pleas* ~d *me*⟩ ~ *vi* to make a choice or judgment [ME *deciden*, fr MF *decider*, fr L *decidere*, lit., to cut off, fr *de-* + *caedere* to cut – more at CONCISE] – **decidable** *adj*, **decider** *n*, **decidability** *n*

**decided** /diˈsiedid/ *adj* **1** unquestionable ⟨*a* ~ *advantage*⟩ **2** free from doubt or hesitation ⟨*a woman of* ~ *opinions*⟩ *usage* see DECISIVE – **decidedly** *adv*, **decidedness** *n*

**deciding** /diˈsieding/ *adj* that decides; DECISIVE 1 ⟨*the* ~ *round in the contest*⟩

**decidua** /diˈsidyooˈə/ *n, pl* **deciduae** /-yooˈi/ a part of the lining of the womb that in higher placental mammals undergoes special changes in preparation for and during pregnancy and is cast off either during menstruation or childbirth [NL, fr L, fem of *deciduus*] – **decidual** *adj*

**deciduate** /diˈsidyooət/ *adj* having the tissues of the foetus and the mother firmly interlocked so that a layer of tissue from the mother is torn away during childbirth and forms a part of the afterbirth

**deciduous** /diˈsidyooˈəs/ *adj* **1** falling off or shed seasonally or at a certain stage of development; *also* having deciduous parts ⟨~ *teeth*⟩ ⟨*a* ~ *tree*⟩ – compare EVERGREEN **2** *formal* ephemeral, transitory [L *deciduus*, fr *decidere* to fall off, fr *de-* + *cadere* to fall – more at CHANCE] – **deciduously** *adv*, **deciduousness** *n*

**decigram** /ˈdesiˌgram/ *n* one tenth of a gram (.0035 ounce) [Fr *décigramme*, fr *déci-* + *gramme* gram]

**decile** /ˈdesil/ *n, statistics* any of nine values in a FREQUENCY DISTRIBUTION that divide it into 10 parts (INTERVALS) each containing ¹/₁₀ of the individuals, items, etc under consideration; *also* any of the 10 groups of individuals, items, etc comprising such an interval [L *decem* ten – more at TEN] – **decile** *adj*

**decilitre** /'desi,leetə/ *n* one tenth of a litre (approx ¹/₅ pint) [Fr *décilitre*, fr *déci-* + *litre*]

**decillion** /di'silyən/ *n* – see NUMBER table [L *decem* + E *-illion* (as in *million*)]

**¹decimal** /'desiməl/ *adj* 1 numbered or proceeding by tens: 1a based on the number 10; *specif* subdivided into units which are tenths, hundredths, etc of another unit b expressed as a decimal fraction 2 using a decimal system (e g of coinage) ⟨*when Britain went* ∼⟩ [(assumed) NL *decimalis*, fr ML, of a tithe, fr L *decima* tithe, fr fem of *decimus* tenth, fr *decem*] – **decimally** *adv*

**²decimal, decimal fraction** *n* a PROPER FRACTION (fraction having a value of less than one) that is expressed as a sum of multiples of powers of ¹/₁₀ by writing a dot followed by one digit for the number of tenths, one digit for the number of hundredths, and so on (e g $0.25 = {}^{25}/_{100}$) – compare COMMON FRACTION

**decimal-ize, -ise** /'desimə,liez/ *vt* to convert to a decimal system ⟨∼ *currency*⟩ – **decimalization** *n*

**decimal point** *n* the dot at the left of a decimal fraction

**decimate** /'desimayt/ *vt* 1 to select by lot and kill every tenth man of (e g mutinous soldiers) 2 to destroy or kill a large part of ⟨*the famine* ∼d *the population*⟩ [L *decimatus*, pp of *decimare*, fr *decimus* tenth] – **decimation** *n*

*usage* The use of **decimate** as in sense 2 "kill a large part of" is now well established in English ⟨*typhus fever* decimated *the school periodically* – Charlotte Brontë⟩, although it is disapproved of by some people. In any case, **decimate** does not mean either "kill 9 out of 10 of" or "exterminate completely", though its users should be aware that it may be so understood; nor should it be used where any proportion or degree is specified ⟨⚠ *seriously* decimated⟩ ⟨⚠ decimated *by 60 per cent*⟩ or in relation to a single creature ⟨⚠ *David* decimated *Goliath*⟩.

**decimetre** /'desi,meetə/ *n* one tenth of a metre (about 3.9 inches) [Fr *décimètre*, fr *déci-* deci- + *mètre* metre]

**decimetric** /,desi'metrik/ *adj* having a wavelength between 1 and 10 decimetres

**decipher** /di'siefə/ *vt* 1 to convert into intelligible form; *esp* to decode 2 to make out the meaning of despite indistinctness or obscurity ⟨*managed to* ∼ *his writing*⟩ – **decipherable** *adj*, **decipherer** *n*, **decipherment** *n*

**decision** /di'sizh(ə)n/ *n* 1a the act or process of deciding b a conclusion arrived at after consideration 2 promptness and firmness in deciding ⟨*a man of courage and* ∼⟩ [MF, fr L *decision-*, *decisio*, fr *decisus*, pp of *decidere* to decide]

**decisive** /di'siesiv/ *adj* 1 having the power or quality of deciding; conclusive 2 marked by or indicative of determination or firmness; resolute 3 unmistakable, unquestionable ⟨*a* ∼ *superiority*⟩ – **decisively** *adv*, **decisiveness** *n*

*usage* **Decisive** is now sometimes used, like **decided**, to mean "resolute" ⟨*a* decisive *person*⟩; but **decisively** should not replace **decidedly** to mean "unquestionably" ⟨⚠ *a* decisively *pleasant occasion*⟩. *synonyms* see CRITICAL

**¹deck** /dek/ *n* 1 a horizontal platform running from side to side and usu from end to end of a ship; *also* any of a number of such platforms which form the floors and ceilings for the compartments of a ship 2 something resembling the deck of a ship: e g 2a a level or floor of a bus with more than one floor b the roadway of a bridge c TAPE DECK d RECORD DECK 3 a group of PUNCHED CARDS used in computing or data processing 4 *chiefly NAm* a pack of playing cards [ME, covering, fr MD *dec* roof, covering, cloak, fr *decken* to cover; akin to OHG *decken*, *decchen* to cover – more at THATCH] – **decked** *adj* – **clear the decks** to remove all objects or obstacles (e g from a room or table), esp in order to prepare for another activity – **hit the deck** to fall or throw oneself to the ground

**²deck** *vt* to array, decorate – often + *out* ⟨∼ed *out in furs*⟩ ⟨*tree* ∼ed *with tinsel*⟩ *synonyms* see DECORATE [D *dekken* to cover; akin to OHG *decken*]

**deck chair** *n* a folding chair that has a fabric seat and back that are usu strung between interpenetrating rectangular frames (fr its use by passengers on a ship's deck)

**decker** /'dekə/ *n* something having a deck or a specified number of levels, floors, or layers – often in combination ⟨*triple*-decker *cheeseburger*⟩

**deckhand** /'dek,hand/ *n* a seaman who performs manual duties (e g cleaning the decks)

**deckhouse** /'dek,hows/ *n* a cabin built on a ship's upper deck

**decking** /'deking/ *n* a deck; *also* material for a deck

**deckle** /'dekl/ *n* 1 a detachable wooden frame round the outside edges of a hand mould used in making paper 2 either of the bands that run along the edges of the wire of a paper machine and determine the width of the WEB (continuous sheet of paper used in a printing machine) [Ger *deckel*, lit., cover, fr *decken* to cover, fr OHG]

**deckle edge** *n* the rough untrimmed edge of paper left by a deckle or produced artificially – **deckle-edged** *adj*

**deck tennis** *n* a game played esp on board ship in which participants toss a quoit or rubber ring back and forth over a net stretched across a small court

**declaim** /di'klaym/ *vi* 1 to speak rhetorically 2 to speak pompously or bombastically ∼ *vt* to deliver (e g a speech) rhetorically [ME *declamen*, fr L *declamare*, fr *de-* + *clamare* to cry out; akin to L *calare* to call – more at LOW] – **declaimer** *n*, **declamation** *n*

**declamatory** /di'klamət(ə)ri/ *adj* of or marked by declamation or rhetorical display

**declarant** /di'kleərənt/ *n* somebody who makes a legal declaration

**declaration** /,deklə'raysh(ə)n/ *n* 1 the act of declaring; announcement 2a something that is declared b a document containing such a declaration

**declarative** /di'klarətiv/ *adj* 1 constituting a statement rather than a command or a question ⟨∼ *sentence*⟩ 2 DECLARATORY 1 – **declaratively** *adv*

**declaratory** /di'klarət(ə)ri/ *adj* 1 serving to declare, set forth, or explain 2 declaring what is the existing law ⟨*a* ∼ *statute*⟩ ⟨*a* ∼ *judgment*⟩

**declare** /di'kleə/ *vt* 1 to make known formally or explicitly 2 to make evident; show 3 to state emphatically; affirm ⟨∼s *his innocence*⟩ 4 to make a full statement of (one's taxable or dutiable income or property) ⟨*all imported alcohol must be* ∼d⟩ 5a to announce (e g a TRUMP suit) in a card game b to MELD (show or announce a combination of playing cards) in canasta, rummy, etc 6 to make or judge (port or wine of a particular year) to be a vintage ∼ *vi* 1 to make a declaration 2 to avow one's support 3 *of a captain or team* to announce one's decision to end one's side's innings in cricket before all the batsmen are out ⟨*Cowdrey* ∼d *next morning at 362 for eight* – John Arlott⟩ – see also **declare an** INTEREST/WAR *synonyms* see ASSERT [ME *declaren*, fr MF *declarer*, fr L *declarare*, fr *de-* + *clarare* to make clear, fr *clarus* clear – more at CLEAR] – **declarable** *adj*

**declarer** /di'kleərə/ *n* one who declares; *specif* the player in a partnership in bridge who first named the TRUMP suit (suit that will win over any other) in the final contract successfully bid by his/her side, and who then plays both his/her own hand and that of the DUMMY (hand laid down on the table by the declarer's partner)

**declass** /,dee'klahs/ *vt* to remove from a class; *esp* to assign to a lower social status

**déclassé** /,day'klasay/ *adj* fallen or lowered in class, rank, social position, etc [Fr, fr pp of *déclasser* to declass]

**declassify** /,dee'klasifie/ *vt* to remove or reduce the security classification of ⟨∼ *a secret document*⟩

**declension** /di'klensh(ə)n/ *n* 1a (a diagrammatic arrangement of) the forms of a noun, adjective, or pronoun showing number, case, etc b a class of nouns or adjectives having the same type of such forms ⟨*the first* ∼ *in Latin*⟩ 2 *archaic* a falling off or away; *esp* a deterioration [prob alter. (influenced by *-ion*) of earlier *declenson*, modif of MF *declinaison*, fr LL *declination-*, *declinatio*, fr L, grammatical inflection, turning aside, fr *declinatus*, pp of *declinare* to inflect, turn aside] – **declensional** *adj*

**declinate** /'deklinayt/ *adj*, *esp of a plant part* bent or curved down or aside

**declination** /,dekli'naysh(ə)n/ *n* 1 angular distance north or south from the CELESTIAL EQUATOR measured along a GREAT CIRCLE passing through the CELESTIAL POLES 2 a bending downwards; an inclination 3 **declination, magnetic declination** the angle formed between a compass needle and the geographical MERIDIAN (one of many imaginary lines drawn from the N to the S pole and used to determine position) equal to the difference between magnetic and true north for that part of the earth 4 *archaic* a turning aside or swerving ⟨*his* ∼ *from virtue was tragic*⟩ 5 *archaic* deterioration ⟨*moral* ∼⟩ 6 *archaic* an esp formal refusal [ME *declinacioun*, fr MF *declination*, fr L *declination-, declinatio* turning aside, altitude of the pole] – **declinational** *adj*

¹**decline** /di'klien/ *vi* **1a** to slope downwards; descend **b** to bend down; droop **2a** *of a celestial body* to sink towards setting ⟨*the sun began to* ∼⟩ **b** to draw towards a close; wane **3** to withhold consent ∼ *vt* **1** to give in prescribed order the various inflected forms of (a noun, pronoun, or adjective) **2** to cause to bend or bow downwards **3a** to refuse to undertake, engage in, or comply with ⟨∼ *battle*⟩ **b** to refuse courteously ⟨∼ *an invitation*⟩ ⟨∼ *to answer*⟩ [ME *declinen*, fr MF *decliner*, fr L *declinare* to turn aside, inflect, fr *de-* + *clinare* to incline – more at LEAN] – **declinable** *adj*

²**decline** *n* **1** the process of declining: **1a** a gradual physical or mental decay **b** a change to a lower state or level **2** the period during which something is approaching its end **3** a downward slope **4** *archaic* a wasting disease; *esp* tuberculosis of the lungs

**declinometer** /,dekli'nomitə/ *n* an instrument for measuring astronomical or magnetic declination [ISV *declino-* (fr *declination*) + *-meter*]

**declivity** /di'klivəti/ *n, formal* **1** downward inclination **2** a descending slope – compare ACCLIVITY [L *declivitat-, declivitas*, fr *declivis* sloping down, fr *de-* + *clivus* slope, hill; akin to L *clinare*] – **declivitous** *adj*

**declutch** /,dee'kluch/ *vi* to disengage the clutch of a motor vehicle or other machine

**decoct** /di'kokt/ *vt* **1** to extract the essence of by boiling **2** to boil down; concentrate [L *decoctus*, pp of *decoquere*, fr *de-* + *coquere* to cook – more at COOK] – **decoction** *n*

**decode** /,dee'kohd/ *vt* to convert (a coded message) into intelligible language – **decoder** *n*

**decoke** /,dee'kohk/ *vt, Br* to remove carbon deposits from (an INTERNAL-COMBUSTION ENGINE) – **decoke** *n*

**decollate** /,dee'kolayt, 'dekəlayt/ *vt, archaic* to behead, decapitate [L *decollatus*, pp of *decollare*, fr *de-* + *collum* neck – more at COLLAR] – **decollation** *n*

**décolletage** /,daykol'tahzh (Fr dekɔlta:ʒ)/ *n* the low-cut neckline of a dress [Fr, action of cutting or wearing a low neckline, fr *décolleter*]

**décolleté** /,daykol'tay, -'-- (Fr dekɔlte)/ *adj* **1** wearing a strapless or low-necked dress **2** low-necked [Fr, fr pp of *décolleter* to give a low neckline to, fr *dé-* de- + *collet* collar, fr OF *colet*, fr *col* collar, neck, fr L *collum* neck]

**decolon·ize, -ise** /,dee'koləniez/ *vt* to free from colonial status; grant independence to – **decolonization** *n*

**decolor·ize, -ise** *also* **decolour·ize, -ise** /,dee'kuləriez/ *vt* to remove colour from – **decolorizer** *n*, **decolorization** *n*

**decommission** /,deekə'mish(ə)n/ *vt* to remove (e g a ship) from service

**decompensation** /,dee,kompən'saysh(ə)n, -pen-/ *n* loss of compensation; *esp* inability of the heart to maintain adequate circulation [ISV]

**decompose** /,deekəm'pohz/ *vt* **1** to separate into simpler chemical compounds ⟨∼ *water by electrolysis*⟩ **2** to rot ∼ *vi* to undergo chemical breakdown; decay, rot [Fr *décomposer*, fr *dé-* de- + *composer* to compose] – **decomposable** *adj*, **decomposability** *n*, **decomposition** *n*, **decompositional** *adj*

**decomposer** /,deekəm'pohzə/ *n* any of various organisms (e g many bacteria and fungi) that break down organic matter, esp dead tissue, into its constituent parts

**decompress** /,deekəm'pres/ *vt* to release from pressure or compression – **decompression** *n*

**decompression chamber** *n* a chamber in which air pressure can be gradually reduced until it reaches the level of atmospheric pressure and which is used esp for bringing deep-sea divers to the surface

**decompression sickness** *n* CAISSON DISEASE (disorder caused by a sudden change in atmospheric pressure)

**decondition** /,deekən'dish(ə)n/ *vt* **1** to cause to lose physical fitness ⟨∼ed *by idleness*⟩ **2** to cause (somebody) to forget a conditioned response, pattern of behaviour, etc

**decongest** /,deekən'jest/ *vt* to relieve the congestion of – **decongestion** *n*, **decongestive** *adj*

**decongestant** /,deekən'jest(ə)nt/ *n* something (e g a drug) that relieves congestion (e g of mucous membranes)

**deconsecrate** /,dee'konsikrayt/ *vt* to remove the sacred character of ⟨∼ *a church*⟩ – **deconsecration** *n*

**deconstruction** /,deekən'struksh(ə)n/ *n* a critical technique (e g in literary or film criticism) which claims that there is no single correct interpretation of a text, script, etc, derivable from the intentions of its producer, but that the task of the critic or reader is to deconstruct the implied unity of a work of art to reveal the variety of possible interpretations – **deconstructionist** *n*

**decontaminate** /,deekən'taminayt/ *vt* to rid of contamination (e g radioactivity) – **decontaminator** *n*, **decontamination** *n*

**decontrol** /,deekən'trohl/ *vt* **-ll-** to end control of (e g commodity prices) – **decontrol** *n*

**decor, décor** /'daykaw/ *n* **1** the style and layout of interior decoration and furnishings **2** a stage setting [Fr *décor*, fr *décorer* to decorate, fr L *decorare*]

**decorate** /'dekərayt/ *vt* **1a** to add something ornamental to **b** to apply new coverings of paint, wallpaper, etc to the interior or exterior surfaces of (a room, house, etc) **2** to award a mark of honour, esp a medal [L *decoratus*, pp of *decorare*, fr *decor-, decus* honour, ornament – more at DECENT]

*synonyms* Decorate, adorn, ornament, embellish, beautify, deck, bedeck, and garnish are often interchangeable, but all have slightly different emphases. Decorate suggests adding colour or design to relieve monotony or plainness, while adorn implies that what decorates is itself beautiful ⟨decorate *a room with flowers*⟩ ⟨*these lilies would* adorn *any garden*⟩. Beautify may describe enhancing something already beautiful, or counteracting something's plainness or ugliness ⟨beautify *a wall with a climbing rose*⟩. Ornament and embellish suggest adding something beautiful to set a thing off well ⟨*a straw hat* ornamented *with ribbons*⟩. It is usually people, rather than things that embellish, and what they add may be exaggerated, invented, or unnecessary ⟨embellished *his account with anecdotes of life in the jungle*⟩. Deck and bedeck aim to make a place, person, or thing look splendid or festive ⟨deck *the hall with boughs of holly*⟩ ⟨bedecked *with her finest jewels*⟩. Garnish suggests adding a final touch, especially when making food look attractive.

**Decorated** /'dekəraytid/ *adj or n* (of) a GOTHIC style of architecture prevalent in Britain from the late 13th to the mid 14th century that was characterized by OGEE arches (pointed arches with an S-shaped curve on either side at the top) and elaborate ornamentation – compare EARLY ENGLISH, PERPENDICULAR 3

**decoration** /,dekə'raysh(ə)n/ *n* **1** the act or process of decorating **2** an ornament ⟨*Christmas* ∼s⟩ **3** a badge of honour; *esp* a medal

**decorative** /'dek(ə)rətiv/ *adj* serving to decorate; *esp* purely ornamental rather than functional – **decoratively** *adv*, **decorativeness** *n*

**decorator** /'dekə,raytə/ *n* one whose occupation is decorating (e g painting and papering) buildings or their interiors or planning interior decoration schemes – compare INTERIOR DECORATOR

**decorous** /'dekərəs/ *adj* marked by propriety and good taste; correct [L *decorus*, fr *decor* beauty, grace; akin to L *decēre* to be fitting – more at DECENT] – **decorously** *adv*, **decorousness** *n*

**decorticate** /,dee'kawtikayt/ *vt* **1** to peel the husk, bark, or other outer covering from **2** to remove all or part of the CORTEX (outer layer of a plant or animal part) from (e g the brain) [L *decorticatus*, pp of *decorticare* to remove the bark from, fr *de-* + *cortic-, cortex* bark – more at CUIRASS] – **decorticator** *n*, **decortication** *n*

**decorum** /di'kawrəm/ *n* propriety and good taste in conduct or appearance [L, fr neut of *decorus*]

**decoupage, découpage** /,daykooh'pahzh (Fr dekupa:ʒ)/ *n* **1** the art of decorating surfaces by applying cutouts (e g of paper) and then coating with usu several layers of lacquer, varnish, etc **2** work produced by decoupage [Fr *découpage*, lit., act of cutting out, fr MF *decoupage*, fr *decouper* to cut out, fr *de-* + *couper* to cut – more at COPE]

**decouple** /,dee'kupl/ *vt, chiefly Br* to isolate (e g systems, esp oscillating electrical systems) one from another so that there is little interaction

¹**decoy** /'deekoy, di'koy/ *n* **1** a pond into which wild fowl are lured for capture **2** somebody or something used to lure or lead another into a trap; *esp* an artificial bird used to attract live birds within gunshot **3** somebody or something used to distract or divert the attention (e g of an enemy) [prob fr D *de kooi*, lit., the cage, fr *de*, masc def article + *kooi* cage, fr L *cavea* – more at CAGE]

*usage* The pronunciation /'deekoy/ is disliked by some people.

²**decoy** *vt* to lure (as if) by a decoy; entice *synonyms* see ²LURE

¹**decrease** /di'krees/ *vi* **1** to become progressively less (e g in size, amount, number, or intensity) **2** *of a mathematical*

*sequence, series, or function* to have each term less than the one preceding it ~ *vt* to cause to decrease [ME *decreessen*, fr (assumed) AF *decreistre*, fr L *decrescere*, fr *de-* + *crescere* to grow – more at CRESCENT] – **decreasingly** *adv*

²**decrease** /'dee,krees, di'krees/ *n* 1 the process of decreasing 2 an amount of diminution; a reduction

¹**decree** /di'kree/ *n* 1 an order usu having the force of law 2a a religious rule made by a council or by somebody in authority b the will of God, Providence, etc 3a a judicial decision of the Roman emperor b a judicial decision, esp in an EQUITY, PROBATE, or divorce court [ME, fr MF *decré*, fr L *decretum*, fr neut of *decretus*, pp of *decernere* to decide, fr *de-* + *cernere* to sift, decide – more at CERTAIN]

²**decree** *vt* to command or impose by decree ⟨~ *an amnesty*⟩ ⟨~ *a punishment*⟩ to ordain – **decreer** *n*

**decree absolute** *n* a decree making a divorce final

**decree nisi** /di,kree 'neezi, -zie, 'niesie/ *n* a provisional decree of divorce that is made absolute after a fixed period unless cause to the contrary is shown [L *nisi* unless, fr *ne- not* + *si* if]

**decrement** /'dekrimənt/ *n* 1 a gradual decrease in quality or quantity 2 the quantity lost by diminution or waste 3 a negative mathematical INCREMENT (small change in a variable) 4 *physics* a measure of the amount by which an OSCILLATOR damps the oscillation of the ALTERNATING CURRENT that it produces, expressed as a ratio of successive AMPLITUDES (maximum displacement of oscillations from a mean position) [L *decrementum*, fr *decrescere*] – **decremental** *adj*

**decrepit** /di'krepit/ *adj* 1 wasted and weakened (as if) by the infirmities of old age 2a impaired by use or wear; worn-out b fallen into ruin or disrepair *synonyms* see WEAK *antonym* sturdy [ME, fr MF, fr L *decrepitus*, fr *de-* + *crepitus*, pp of *crepare* to crack, creak] – **decrepitly** *adv*, **decrepitude** *n*

**decrepitate** /di'krepitayt/ *vt* to heat (e g a salt) so as to cause crackling or until crackling stops ~ *vi* to become decrepitated [prob fr (assumed) NL *decrepitatus*, pp of *decrepitare*, fr L *de-* + *crepitare* to crackle – more at CREPITATE] – **decrepitation** *n*

**decrescendo** /,deekrə'shendoh/ *n, adv, or adj, pl* **decrescendos** (a) DIMINUENDO [It, lit., decreasing, fr L *decrescendum*, gerund of *decrescere*]

**decrescent** /di'kres(ə)nt/ *adj, of the moon* decreasing, waning [alter. of earlier *decressant*, prob fr AF, prp of (assumed) AF *decreistre* to decrease]

**decretal** /di'kreetl/ *n* a decree; *esp* a papal letter giving an authoritative decision on a point of CANON LAW (organized body of laws governing the Church) [ME *decretale*, fr MF, fr LL *decretalis* of a decree, fr L *decretum* decree]

**decretory** /di'kreet(ə)ri/ *adj* of or fixed by a decree or decision [L *decretorius*, fr *decretus* – more at DECREE]

**decriminal·ize, -ise** /,dee'kriminəliez/ *vt* to legalize ⟨*attempts have been made to* ~ *prostitution*⟩ – **decriminalization** *n*

**decry** /di'krie/ *vt* 1 to depreciate (e g a coin) officially or publicly 2 to express strong disapproval of △ *descry* [Fr *décrier*, fr OF *descrier*, fr *des-* de- + *crier* to cry] – **decrier** *n*

**decrypt** /,dee'kript, di-/ *vt* to decode, esp without prior knowledge of the key [ISV *de-* + *crypto*gram, *crypto*graph] – **decryption** *n*

**decubitus ulcer** /di'kyoohbitəs/ *n* a bedsore – used technically [NL *decubitus* position of lying in bed, fr L, pp of *decumbere*]

**decumbent** /di'kumb(ə)nt/ *adj* 1 lying down 2 *of a plant* lying on the ground but with the tip growing upwards [L *decumbent, decumbens*, prp of *decumbere* to lie down, fr *de-* + *-cumbere* to lie down – more at SUCCUMB]

**decuple** /'dekyoopl/ *adj* 1 tenfold 2 taken in groups of 10 [Fr *décuple*, fr MF, fr LL *decuplus*, fr L *decem* ten + *-plus* multiplied by – more at TEN, DOUBLE]

**decurion** /di'kyooəriən/ *n* 1 an officer in command of 10 men in the ancient Roman cavalry 2 a member of a Roman senate [ME *decurioun*, fr L *decurion-, decurio*, fr *decuria* division of ten, fr *decem*]

**decurrent** /di'kurənt/ *adj* running or extending downwards; *specif, of a leaf* having a base that extends downwards on its stalk or on the plant stem [L *decurrent-, decurrens*, prp of *de-currere* to run down, fr *de-* + *currere* to run – more at CAR]

**decurved** /di'kuhvd, ,dee-/ *adj* curved downwards ⟨~ *beak*⟩ [part trans of LL *decurvatus*, fr L *de-* + *curvatus* curved]

¹**decussate** /di'kusayt/ *vb* to intersect, cross [L *decussatus*, pp of *decussare*, fr *decussis* the number ten, numeral X, intersection, irreg fr *decem* + *ass-, as* unit]

²**decussate** /di'kusayt, -sət/ *adj* 1 shaped like an X 2 *of leaves* arranged in pairs each at right angles to the next pair above or below – **decussately** *adv*

**decussation** /,deekə'saysh(ə)n/ *n* a crossing, intersection; *specif* a crossed group of nerve fibres passing between centres on opposite sides of the brain or spinal cord; COMMISSURE (connecting band of nerve tissue)

**dedicate** /'dedikayt/ *vt* 1 to devote to the worship of a divine being; consecrate; *specif* to set apart (a church) for sacred uses with solemn rites 2 to assign permanently to a goal or way of life ⟨*ready to* ~ *his life to public service*⟩ 3 to inscribe or address (a book, song, etc) *to* somebody or something as a mark of esteem or affection ⟨~ *a book to a friend*⟩ ⟨~d *the song to his wife*⟩ 4 *chiefly NAm* to set apart for a definite use ⟨*money* ~d *to their vacation fund*⟩ [L *dedicatus*, pp of *dedicare* to affirm, dedicate, fr *de-* + *dicare* to proclaim, dedicate – more at DICTION] – **dedicator** *n*

**dedicated** /'dedikaytid/ *adj* 1 devoted to a cause, ideal, or purpose; zealous ⟨*a* ~ *scholar*⟩ 2 *computers* given over to a particular purpose ⟨*a* ~ *process control computer*⟩ – **dedicatedly** *adv*

**dedication** /,dedi'kaysh(ə)n/ *n* 1 an act or rite of dedicating to a divine being or to a sacred use 2 a devoting or setting aside for a particular purpose 3 a phrase or sentence that dedicates a book, song, etc to a person or thing 4 self-sacrificing devotion – **dedicative** *adj*, **dedicatory** *adj*

**dedifferentiation** /,dee,difə,renshi'aysh(ə)n/ *n* reversion of specialized structures or cells to a more generalized or primitive condition often as a preliminary to major change

**deduce** /di'dyoohs/ *vt* 1 to establish by deduction; *specif* to infer from a general principle – compare INDUCE 2 *archaic* to trace the course of [L *deducere*, lit., to lead away, fr *de-* + *ducere* to lead – more at TOW] – **deducible** *adj*

**deduct** /di'dukt/ *vt* to take away (an amount) from a total; subtract [L *deductus*, pp of *deducere*] – **deductible** *adj*, **deductibility** *n*

**deduction** /di'duksh(ə)n/ *n* 1a an act of taking away; subtraction ⟨~ *of legitimate business expenses*⟩ b something that is or may be subtracted ⟨~s *from her taxable income*⟩ 2a the deriving of a necessary conclusion by reasoning; *specif* inference in which a particular conclusion is drawn from general premises b a conclusion reached by logical deduction

**deductive** /di'duktiv/ *adj* 1 of or employing mathematical or logical deduction ⟨~ *reasoning*⟩ – compare INDUCTIVE 1 2 capable of being deduced from premises; inferential – **deductively** *adv*

¹**deed** /deed/ *n* 1 something that is done ⟨*evil* ~s⟩ 2 a noble act or action; a feat, exploit 3 the act of performing or carrying out ⟨*never mistake the word for the* ~⟩ 4 a signed and usu sealed written document containing some legal settlement, transfer, bargain, or contract *synonyms* see ¹ACT [ME *dede*, fr OE *dǣd*; akin to OE *dōn* to do] – **deedless** *adj*

²**deed** *vt, NAm* to convey or transfer by deed

**deed poll** *n, pl* **deeds poll** a deed made and executed by one party only (e g to change his/her name) [¹*deed* + *poll*, adj (having the edges cut even rather than indented), fr ²*poll*]

**deejay** /'dee,jay/ *n* DISC JOCKEY [*disc jockey*]

**deem** /deem/ *vt, formal* to judge, consider ⟨*would* ~ *it an honour if you came*⟩ [ME *demen*, fr OE *dēman*; akin to OHG *tuomen* to judge, OE *dōm* judgment]

¹**deep** /deep/ *adj* 1 extending far from some surface or area: e g 1a extending far downwards ⟨*a* ~ *well*⟩ b(1) extending well inwards from an outer surface ⟨*a* ~ *gash*⟩ b(2) not located near the surface of the body ⟨~ *pressure receptors in muscles*⟩ c extending well back from a front surface ⟨*a* ~ *cupboard*⟩ d occurring or located near the outer limits of the playing area, esp in cricket or football ⟨*brought his* ~ *fielders in*⟩ 2 having a specified extension in an implied direction ⟨*shelf 20 inches* ~⟩ ⟨*cars parked three-*deep⟩ 3a difficult to penetrate or comprehend; recondite ⟨*may be true, but it's too* ~ *for me*⟩ b mysterious, obscure c capable of profound thought ⟨*a* ~ *thinker*⟩ d engrossed, involved ⟨*a man* ~ *in debt*⟩ ⟨~ *in thought*⟩ e intense, extreme ⟨*a* ~ *sleep*⟩ ⟨*in* ~ *disgrace*⟩ 4a *of a colour* intense and usu dark in hue b having a low musical pitch or pitch range ⟨*a* ~ *voice*⟩ 5 coming from or reaching very low in the chest ⟨*a* ~ *breath*⟩ – see also throw somebody in at the deep END, go off the deep END, in deep WATER *synonyms* see ¹BROAD *antonym* shallow [ME, fr OE *dēop*; akin to OHG *tiof* deep, OE *dyppan* to dip – more at DIP] – **deeply** *adv*, **deepness** *n*

²**deep** *adv* 1a to a great depth; deeply ⟨*still waters run* ~⟩ b

covered or filled to a specified degree – usu in combination ⟨*ankle*-deep *in mud*⟩ **2** far on; late ⟨*danced* ~ *into the night*⟩ **3** in a deep location ⟨*the wingers were playing* ~⟩ **4** well within the boundaries ⟨*a house* ~ *in the woods*⟩ **5** far back in space or time ⟨*had its roots* ~ *in the Dark Ages*⟩

   *usage* Deep as an adverb, but not **deeply**, can mean "far", or "well within". **Deeply**, but not **deep**, can mean "profoundly" ⟨*am* deeply *distressed*⟩.

³**deep** *n* **1** any of the points on a SOUNDING LINE (line used to measure the depth of water) that corresponds to a depth in whole fathoms but is not marked on the line – compare MARK 1b **2a** vast or immeasurable space, time, or extent ⟨*the black* ~ *of space*⟩ **b** *the* sea **3** the middle or most intense part ⟨*the* ~ *of winter*⟩ **4** any of the deep portions of a body of water; *specif* a generally long and narrow area in the ocean where the depth exceeds 3000 fathoms (approx 5500 metres)

**deep down** *adv* in one's inner self; deep in one's feelings, conscience, etc ⟨*I feel*, ~, *that he's untrustworthy*⟩

**deepen** /'deep(ə)n/ *vb* to make or become deeper or more profound

,deep-'freeze *vt* deep-froze /frohz/; deep-frozen /frohz(ə)n/ to freeze or store (e g food) in a freezer

**deep freeze** *n* a freezer

**deep-fry** /,- '-, '- ,-/ *vt* to fry (food) by complete immersion in hot fat or oil – **deep-fryer** *n*

**deep kiss** *n* FRENCH KISS

,deep-'rooted *adj* firmly established ⟨*a* ~ *loyalty*⟩

,deep-'sea *adj* of or occurring in the deeper parts of the sea ⟨~ *fishing*⟩

,deep-'seated *adj* **1** situated far below the surface ⟨*a* ~ *inflammation*⟩ **2** firmly established ⟨*a* ~ *tradition*⟩

**deep space** *n* space well beyond the limits of the earth's atmosphere including space outside the solar system – **deep-space** *adj*

**deep structure** *n, linguistics* a formal representation of the underlying meaning of a sentence; *also* the structure which such a representation specifies – compare SURFACE STRUCTURE

**deer** /diə/ *n, pl* deer *also* deers **1** any of several RUMINANTS (cud-chewing mammals) (family Cervidae, the deer family) that have two large and two small hoofs on each foot and antlers borne by the males of nearly all species and by the females of a few species **2** *archaic* an animal; *esp* a small mammal [ME, deer, animal, fr OE *dēor* beast; akin to OHG *tior* wild animal, Skt *dhvaṃsati* he perishes]

**deerfly** /'diə,fliə/ *n* a small fly (genus *Chrysops*) related to the horsefly that is parasitic esp on deer

**deer grass** *n* a European sedge (*Trichophorum caespitosum*) that forms dense tufts in boggy ground

**deerhound** /'diə,hownd/ *n* (any of) a breed of tall dogs that resemble the greyhound but are larger and have a rough coat

**deerstalker** /'diə,stawkə/ *n* a close-fitting hat with peaks at the front and the back and sometimes earflaps [fr its suitability to be worn by a person stalking deer]

,de-'escalate *vb* to (cause to) decrease in extent, volume, or scope – **de-escalation** *n*, **de-escalatory** *adj*

**deface** /di'fays/ *vt* to mar the external appearance of [ME *defacen*, fr MF *desfacier*, fr OF, fr *des*- de- + *face*] – **defacement** *n*, **defacer** *n*

¹**de facto** /di 'faktoh, day/ *adv* in reality; actually [NL]

²**de facto** *adj* existing in fact, though not necessarily legally; effective ⟨*a* ~ *state of war*⟩ ⟨*his* ~ *wife*⟩ – compare DE JURE

**defalcate** /'deefal,kayt/ *vi, formal* to embezzle [ML *defalcatus*, pp of *defalcare* to cut off, curtail, fr L *de*- + *falc*-, *falx* sickle] – **defalcation** *n*, **defalcator** *n*

**defame** /di'faym/ *vt* to injure the reputation of by libel or slander **synonyms** see ²MALIGN [ME *diffamen, defamen*, fr MF & L; ME *diffamen* fr MF *diffamer*, fr L *diffamare*, fr *dis*- + *fama* fame; ME *defamen* fr MF *defamer*, fr ML *defamare*, fr L *de*- + *fama*] – **defamation** *n*, **defamatory** *adj*, **defamer** *n*

**defat** /,dee'fat/ *vt* to remove fat from

¹**default** /di'fawlt/ *n* **1** failure to do something required by duty or law: eg **1a** failure to pay debts **b** failure to appear at the required time in a legal proceeding **2** failure to be present; absence ⟨*she won by* ~ *since her opponent refused to compete*⟩ [ME *defaute, defaulte*, fr OF *defaute*, fr (assumed) VL *defallita*, fr fem of *defallitus*, pp of *defallere* to be lacking, fail, fr L *de*- + *fallere* to deceive] – **in default of** in the absence of

²**default** *vi* **1** to fail to meet an esp financial obligation – often + *on* **2** to fail to appear in court **3** to fail to compete in or to finish an appointed contest; *also* to forfeit a contest by such

failure ~ *vt* **1** to fail to perform, pay, or make good **2** to lose (a legal case) because of failure to appear in court – **defaulter** *n*

**defeasance** /di'feez(ə)ns/ *n, law* **1** a rendering null or void **2** (a document containing) the conditions in accordance with which a deed is made void [ME *defesance*, fr AF, fr OF *deffesant*, prp of *deffaire*]

**defeasible** /di'feezəbl/ *adj, law* capable of being annulled or made void ⟨*a* ~ *claim to an estate*⟩ – **defeasibility** *n*

¹**defeat** /di'feet/ *vt* **1a** *law* to make null and void; nullify ⟨~ *an estate*⟩ **b** to frustrate ⟨~ *a hope*⟩ **2** to win victory over; beat ⟨~ *the opposing team*⟩ [ME *deffeten*, fr MF *deffait*, pp of *deffaire* to destroy, fr ML *disfacere*, fr L *dis*- + *facere* to do – more at DO]

²**defeat** *n* **1** a failure; *esp* a failure caused by something being rendered null and void ⟨*the Bill suffered a* ~ *in the House of Commons*⟩ **2** an overthrow, esp of an army in battle **3** the loss of a contest

**defeatism** /di'feetiz(ə)m/ *n* acceptance of or resignation to defeat, esp when too ready – **defeatist** *n or adj*

**defecate, defaecate** /'defəkayt/ *vb* **1** to free from impurity or corruption; refine **2** to discharge (esp faeces) from the bowels ~ *vi* to discharge faeces from the bowels [L *defaecatus*, pp of *defaecare*, fr *de*- + *faec-, faex* dregs] – **defecation** *n*

¹**defect** /'deefekt; *also* di'fekt/ *n* **1** an imperfection that impairs worth or utility; a shortcoming ⟨*the grave* ~s *in our foreign policy*⟩ ⟨*a hearing* ~⟩ **2** *physics* an irregularity (eg a foreign atom or the absence of an atom) in the lattice arrangement of atoms or molecules of a crystal [ME *defaicte*, fr MF *defect*, fr L *defectus* lack, fr *defectus*, pp of *deficere* to desert, fail, fr *de*- + *facere* to do]

   *usage* Some people dislike the pronunciation /'deefekt/. **synonyms** see IMPERFECTION

²**defect** /di'fekt/ *vi* to desert a cause or party, often in order to espouse another [L *defectus*, pp] – **defection** *n*, **defector** *n*

¹**defective** /di'fektiv/ *adj* **1** lacking something essential; faulty ⟨*a* ~ *pane of glass*⟩ ⟨~ *eyesight*⟩ **2** lacking one or more of the usual grammatical INFLECTIONS (changes in the form of a word indicating change in tense, person, etc) ⟨*must is a* ~ *verb*⟩ **3** markedly subnormal mentally or physically – **defectively** *adv*, **defectiveness** *n*

²**defective** *n* one who is subnormal physically or mentally

**defence**, *NAm chiefly* **defense** /di'fens/ *n* **1** the act or action of defending ⟨*to speak out in* ~ *of justice*⟩ **2** a means or method of defending; *also, pl* a defensive structure **b** an argument in support or justification; *specif* the collected facts and method adopted by a defendant to protect him-/herself against a plaintiff's action **3** *taking sing or pl vb* **3a** a defending party or group (eg in a court of law) ⟨*the* ~ *then rested its case*⟩ – compare PROSECUTION **b** defensive players, acts, or moves in a game or sport **4** the military resources of a country ⟨*the* ~ *budget*⟩ [ME *defens, defense*, fr OF, deriv of L *defensus*, pp of *defendere*] – **defenceless** *adj*, **defencelessly** *adv*, **defencelessness** *n*

**defence mechanism** *n* **1** a reaction by means of which a living organism defends itself against bacteria, viruses, and other disease-causing organisms **2** *psychology* an often unconscious mental process (eg REPRESSION, PROJECTION, or SUBLIMATION) that prevents the entry of unacceptable or painful thoughts into consciousness

**defend** /di'fend/ *vt* **1a** to counter or be prepared to counter an attack on; protect **b** to maintain by argument in the face of opposition or criticism **c** to attempt to prevent an opponent from scoring in or at (eg a goal) **2** to act as legal representative in court for (a defendant) **3** *archaic* to prevent, forbid ~ *vi* **1** to take action against attack or challenge **2** to play or be in defence ⟨*he* ~s *for Tottenham*⟩ [ME *defenden*, fr OF *defendre*, fr L *defendere*, fr *de*- + *-fendere* to strike; akin to OE *gūth* battle, war, Gk *theinein* to strike] – **defendable** *adj*

   **synonyms** Defend, protect, shield, guard, and safeguard all mean "make or keep safe from danger or attack". Defend implies the taking of measures to ward off an actual or likely attack ⟨defend *the castle with forty men*⟩ ⟨defend *our liberty against our enemies*⟩. Protect suggests providing a shelter from, or a bar to, what may harm or destroy ⟨protect *your eyes from strong sunlight*⟩ ⟨protect *your family with sufficient insurance*⟩. Shield suggests a protective interposition, as if by a shield, between the person threatened, and what is threatening him/her ⟨*she tried to* shield *her father from the truth*⟩. Guard implies constant vigilance in watching over something or someone ⟨*the president is* guarded *day and night*⟩. Safeguard usually describes the taking of preventive measures ⟨safeguard *your children against infection by means of vaccination*⟩.

**¹defendant** /di'fend(ə)nt/ *n* a party against whom a charge in CRIMINAL LAW (law concerned with crimes and their punishment) or a claim in CIVIL LAW (law concerned with the private rights of the individual) is made in legal proceedings – compare PLAINTIFF

**defender** /di'fendə/ *n* **1** one who or that which defends **2** a player in a sport (e g soccer) assigned to a defensive position **3** either of the two players in a game of bridge whose aim is to prevent the DECLARERS from fulfilling a contract to win a certain number of tricks **4** *Scot law* a defendant – compare PURSUER

**defenestration** /,dee,feni'straysh(ə)n/ *n, chiefly humorous* a throwing of a person or thing out of a window [*de-* + L *fenestra* window] – **defenestrate** *vt*

**defensible** /di'fensəbl/ *adj* capable of being defended [ME, fr LL *defensibilis*, fr L *defensus*] – **defensibly** *adv*, **defensibility** *n*

**¹defensive** /di'fensiv/ *adj* **1** serving to defend **2a** devoted to resisting or preventing aggression, attack, or criticism **b** of or constituting the attempt to keep an opponent from scoring in a game or contest ⟨~ *play*⟩ **3** designed to keep an opponent from being the highest bidder in a card game ⟨*a* ~ *bid*⟩ – **defensively** *adv*, **defensiveness** *n*

**²defensive** *n* – **on the defensive** prepared for expected aggression, attack, or criticism

**¹defer** /di'fuh/ *vt* **-rr-** to put off; delay [ME *deferren*, *differren*, fr MF *differer*, fr L *differre* to postpone, be different – more at DIFFER] – **deferrable** *adj*, **deferrer** *n*

**²defer** *vi* **-rr-** to submit *to* another's wishes, opinion, or control usu through deference or respect ⟨*a man who* ~red *only to God*⟩ [ME *deferren*, *differren*, fr MF *deferer*, *defferer*, fr LL *deferre*, fr L, to bring down, bring, fr *de-* + *ferre* to carry – more at ²BEAR]

**deference** /'def(ə)rəns/ *n* respect and esteem due to a superior or an elder – **in/out of deference to** because of respect for

**¹deferent** /'def(ə)rənt/ *adj* serving to carry down or out ⟨*a* ~ *duct*⟩ [L *deferent-*, *deferens*, prp of *deferre*]

**²deferent** *adj* deferential [back-formation fr *deference*]

**deferential** /,defə'rensh(ə)l/ *adj* showing or expressing deference ⟨~ *attention*⟩ – **deferentially** *adv*

**deferment** /di'fuhmənt/ *n* the act of delaying or postponing

**deferral** /di'fuhrəl/ *n* deferment

**deferred** /di'fuhd/ *adj* withheld for or until a fixed time ⟨*a* ~ *payment*⟩

**deferred share** *n, chiefly Br* a fixed-dividend share, now rarely issued, that ranks after an ORDINARY SHARE in the claim on dividends – compare PREFERENCE SHARE

**defiance** /di'fie·əns/ *n* **1** the act or an instance of defying **2** disposition to resist; contempt of opposition – **defiant** *adj*, **defiantly** *adv* – **in defiance of** with open disregard for; despite ⟨*he wilfully broke the speed limit in defiance of the law*⟩

**defibrillate** /,dee'fibrilayt/ *vt* to restore the normal regular beating and rhythm of (a heart) – **defibrillator** *n*, **defibrillative** *adj*, **defibrillatory** *adj*, **defibrillation** *n*

**defibrinate** /,dee'fiebrinayt/ *vt* to remove FIBRIN (white fibrous protein formed when blood clots) from (blood) – **defibrination** *n*

**deficiency** /di'fish(ə)nsi/ *n* **1** the quality or state of being deficient; inadequacy **2** a lack, shortage ⟨*vitamin* ~⟩ **3** the loss or absence of one or more genes from a chromosome

**deficiency disease** *n* a disease (e g scurvy) caused by a lack of essential vitamins, minerals, etc in the diet

**deficient** /di'fish(ə)nt/ *adj* **1** lacking in some necessary quality or element ⟨~ *in judgment*⟩ **2** not up to a normal standard or amount; inadequate [L *deficient-*, *deficiens*, prp of *deficere* to be wanting – more at DEFECT] – **deficient** *n*, **deficiently** *adv*

**deficit** /'defəsit/ *n* **1** a deficiency in amount or quality **2a** an excess of expenditure over revenue **b** an excess of LIABILITIES (financial obligations) over ASSETS (property or money owned) [Fr *déficit*, fr L *deficit* it is wanting, 3 sing. pres indic of *deficere*]

*usage* The pronunciation /'defəsit/ rather than /də'fisit/ is recommended for BBC broadcasters.

**deficit spending** *n* a deliberate policy on the part of a government of spending more money than is available from revenue and financing the excess expenditure by borrowing, usu in order to stimulate the economy and so alleviate unemployment

**de fide** /di 'fiedi/ *adj* held as an obligatory article of faith in the Roman Catholic church [NL, fr L, from faith]

**¹defilade** /,defi'layd/ *vt* to arrange (fortifications) so as to protect the lines from enemy fire [prob fr *de-* + *-filade* (as in *enfilade*)]

**²defilade** *n* the act or process of defilading

**¹defile** /di'fiel/ *vt* to make unclean or impure: e g **a** to deprive of virginity; deflower **b** to desecrate ⟨~ *a sanctuary*⟩ *synonyms* see CONTAMINATE [ME *defilen*, alter. (influenced by ME *filen* to befoul, fr OE *fȳlan*, fr *fūl* foul) of *defoulen* to trample, defile, fr OF *defouler* to trample, fr *de-* + *fouler* to trample, lit., to full – more at FULL] – **defilement** *n*

**²defile** *vi* to march off in a file [Fr *défiler*, fr *dé-* de- + *filer* to move in a column, fr OF, to spin – more at ⁵FILE]

**³defile** *n* a narrow passage or gorge [Fr *défilé*, fr pp of *défiler*]

**define** /di'fien/ *vt* **1a** to fix or mark the limits of; demarcate **b** to make clear or precise in outline ⟨*the issues aren't well* ~d⟩ **2a** to be the essential quality or qualities of; identify ⟨*whatever* ~s *us as human*⟩ **b** to set forth the meaning of ⟨~ *a word*⟩ ~ *vi* to make a definition [ME *definen*, fr MF & L; MF *definer*, fr L *definire*, fr *de-* + *finire* to limit, end, fr *finis* boundary, end] – **definable** *adj*, **definement** *n*, **definer** *n*

**definiendum** /di,fini'endəm/ *n, pl* **definienda** /-də/ a word or expression that is being defined [L, sthg to be defined, neut of *definiendus*, gerundive of *definire*]

**definiens** /di'fini·enz/ *n, pl* **definientia** /di,fini'ensh(y)ə/ a word or expression that defines; a definition [L, prp of *definire*]

**defining** /di'fiening/ *adj* limiting the reference of a word or phrase; RESTRICTIVE 2 ⟨~ *clause*⟩

**definite** /'definət/ *adj* **1** having distinct or certain limits ⟨*set* ~ *standards for pupils to meet*⟩ **2a** free of all ambiguity, uncertainty, or obscurity ⟨*demanded a* ~ *answer*⟩ **b** unquestionable, decided ⟨*a* ~ *advantage*⟩ **3** designating an identified or immediately identifiable person or thing ⟨*the* ~ *article* the⟩ **4a** *of flower parts* constant in number, usu less than 20, and occurring in multiples of the petal number **b** *of a flower cluster* CYMOSE (having a single flower at the end of each flower stem) [L *definitus*, pp of *definire*] – **definitely** *adv*, **definiteness** *n*, **definitude** *n*

*synonyms* Although they are close in meaning, **definite** and **definitive** are not synonymous. The chief meaning of **definite** is "free of ambiguity", so that a **definite** answer is one that is precise, not vague; the chief meaning of **definitive** is "conclusive" or "authoritative", so that a **definitive** answer is one that is final, not merely provisional. *usage* **Definite** and **definitely** are often used almost meaninglessly ⟨*a* **definite** *danger to health*⟩ ⟨*I'm* **definitely** *leaving*⟩ in situations where they might be better omitted in formal writing.

**definite integral** *n, maths* the difference between the values of an INTEGRAL at two given limits – compare INDEFINITE INTEGRAL, INTEGRAL

**definition** /,defi'nish(ə)n/ *n* **1a** a word or phrase expressing the essential nature of a person or thing; *also* a statement of the meaning of a word or phrase **b** the action or process of stating such a meaning **2a** the action or power of making definite and clear ⟨*the* ~ *of a telescope*⟩ **b** the state or condition of being definite and clear **c(1)** distinctness of outline or detail (e g in a photograph) **c(2)** clarity, esp of musical sound in reproduction – **definitional** *adj*

**¹definitive** /di'finətiv/ *adj* **1** serving to provide a conclusive solution ⟨*a* ~ *victory*⟩ **2** authoritative and apparently exhaustive ⟨*a* ~ *biography*⟩ **3** serving to define or specify precisely ⟨~ *laws*⟩ **4** fully differentiated or developed ⟨*the* ~ *form of an organ of the body*⟩ **5** *of a postage stamp* issued as one of the normal stamps of the country or territory of use – compare COMMEMORATIVE, PROVISIONAL *synonyms* see DEFINITE – **definitively** *adv*, **definitiveness** *n*

**²definitive** *n* a definitive postage stamp – compare COMMEMORATIVE, PROVISIONAL

**definitive host** *n* the host in which the sexual reproduction of a parasite takes place

**deflagrate** /'deflagrayt/ *vb* to (cause to) burn rapidly with intense heat and sparks being given off – compare DETONATE [L *deflagratus*, pp of *deflagrare* to burn down, fr *de-* + *flagrare* to burn – more at BLACK ] – **deflagration** *n*

**deflate** /di'flayt, ,dee-/ *vt* **1** to release air or gas from **2** to reduce in size or importance **3** to reduce (a price level) or cause (the availability of credit or the level of economic activity) to contract ~ *vi* to lose firmness (as if) through the escape of contained gas *synonyms* see²CONTRACT *antonym* inflate [*de-* + *-flate* (as in *inflate*)] – **deflator** *n*

**deflation** /di'flaysh(ə)n, ,dee-/ *n* **1** an act or instance of deflating; the state of being deflated **2** a contraction in the volume of available money and credit and thus in the level of economic activity, esp as a result of government policy; *also* a decline in the general level of prices and wages as a result of such a policy **3** the erosion of soil by the wind – **deflationary** *adj*

**deflect** /di'flekt/ *vt* to turn from a straight course or fixed direction to turn aside; deviate [L *deflectere* to bend down, turn aside, fr *de-* + *flectere* to bend] – **deflective** *adj*, **deflect-or** *n*

**deflection,** *Br also* **deflexion** /di'fleksh(ə)n/ *n* **1** (the amount or degree of) deflecting **2** the movement, usu as a departure from the zero reading, of an indicator or pointer on the scale of an (esp electrical) instrument

**deflexed** /di'flekst/ *adj* turned abruptly downwards ⟨*a ~ leaf*⟩ [L *deflexus,* pp of *deflectere*]

**deflocculate** /di'flokyoolayt/ *vb* to (cause to) disperse into fine particles ⟨*the soil ~*d⟩ – **deflocculant** *n,* **deflocculation** *n*

**defloration** /,deflaw'raysh(ə)n, ,dee-/ *n* the act of deflowering or condition of being deflowered; *specif* rupture of the HYMEN (membrane partly covering the entrance to the vagina) [ME *defloracioun,* fr LL *defloration-, defloratio,* fr *defloratus,* pp of *deflorare*]

**deflower** /,dee'flowə/ *vt* **1** to deprive of virginity **2** to take away the beauty of; spoil [ME *deflouren,* fr MF or LL; MF *deflorer,* fr LL *deflorare,* fr L *de-* + *flor-, flos* flower – more at BLOW] – **deflowerer** *n*

**defocus** /,dee'fohkəs/ *vb* **-ss-, -s-** to put or go out of focus

**defog** /,dee'fog/ *vt* **-gg-** *NAm* to demist – **defogger** *n*

**defoliant** /,dee'fohli-ənt/ *n* a chemical applied to plants (eg as a spray or dust) in order to cause the leaves to drop off prematurely

**defoliate** /dee'fohliayt/ *vt* to deprive of leaves, esp prematurely [LL *defoliatus,* pp of *defoliare,* fr L *de-* + *folium* leaf – more at BLADE] – **defoliate** *adj,* **defoliator** *n,* **defoliation** *n*

**deforest** /di'forist/ *vt* to clear of forests – **deforester** *n,* **deforestation** *n*

**deform** /di'fawm/ *vt* **1** to spoil the form or appearance of **2** to make hideous or monstrous **3** to alter the shape of by stress ~ *vi* to become misshapen or changed in shape [ME *deformen,* fr MF or L; MF *deformer,* fr L *deformare,* fr *de-* + *formare* to form, fr *forma* form] – **deformation** *n,* **deformational** *adj*

**deformed** /di'fawmd/ *adj* distorted or unshapely in form; misshapen

**deformity** /di'fawməti/ *n* **1** the state of being deformed **2a** a physical blemish or distortion; a disfigurement **b** an esp moral flaw or defect **3** a deformed person or thing [ME *deformite,* fr MF *deformité,* fr L *deformitat-, deformitas,* fr *deformis* deformed, fr *de-* + *forma*]

**defraud** /di'frawd/ *vt* to deprive of something by deception or fraud [ME *defrauden,* fr MF *defrauder,* fr L *defraudare,* fr *de-* + *fraudare* to cheat, fr *fraud-, fraus* fraud] – **defrauder** *n,* **defraudation** *n*

**defray** /di'fray/ *vt* to provide for the payment of (eg costs or expenses); pay [MF *deffrayer,* fr *des-* de- + *frayer* to expend, fr OF, fr *frai* expenditure, cost, prob fr L *fractum* sthg broken or damaged, neut of *fractus,* pp of *frangere* to break – more at BREAK] – **defrayable** *adj,* **defrayal** *n*

**defrock** /,dee'frok/ *vt* to deprive of clerical office; unfrock

**defrost** /,dee'frost/ *vt* **1** to thaw from a frozen state ⟨*~ meat*⟩ **2** to free from ice ⟨*~ the refrigerator*⟩ ~ *vi* to thaw out, esp from a deep-frozen state – **defroster** *n*

**deft** /deft/ *adj* marked by facility and skill [ME *defte* – more at DAFT] – **deftly** *adv,* **deftness** *n*

**defunct** /di'fungkt/ *adj* having finished the course of life, existence, or usefulness; *esp* dead [L *defunctus,* fr pp of *defungi* to finish, die, fr *de-* + *fungi* to perform – more at FUNCTION]

**defuse** /,dee'fyoohz/ *vt* **1** to remove the fuse from (eg a mine or bomb) **2** to make less harmful, potent, or tense ⟨*~ the crisis*⟩ △ diffuse

**defy** /di'fie/ *vt* **1** to challenge to do something considered impossible; dare **2** to resist or disregard openly ⟨*~ public opinion*⟩ **3** to resist attempts at ⟨*the paintings ~ classification*⟩ [ME *defyen* to renounce faith in, challenge, fr OF *defier,* fr *de-* + *fier* to entrust, fr (assumed) VL *fidare,* alter. of L *fidere* to trust – more at BIDE] – **defier** *n*

**dégagé** /,dayga'zhay/ *adj* **1** free from constraint; nonchalant **2** free and easy ⟨*clothes with a ~ look*⟩ **3** extended with toe pointed in preparation for a ballet step **4** politically uncommitted – compare ENGAGÉ [Fr, fr pp of *dégager* to redeem a pledge, free, fr OF *desgagier,* fr *des-* de- + *gage* pledge – more at GAGE]

**degas** /,dee'gas/ *vt* **-ss-, -s-** to remove gas from ⟨*~ an electron tube*⟩

**degauss** /,dee'gows, -'gaws/ *vt* to demagnetize; *esp* to demagnetize (a steel ship), esp as a protection against magnetic mines, by encircling the hull with a coil carrying an electric current which produces an opposing magnetic field – **degausser** *n*

**degeneracy** /di'jen(ə)rəsi/ *n* **1** the state of being degenerate **2** the process of becoming degenerate **3** the existence of more than one CODON (unit of three chemical BASES coding for a particular AMINO ACID) in the GENETIC CODE

¹**degenerate** /di'jen(ə)rət/ *adj* **1a** *esp of a plant or animal* having declined in nature, character, structure, function, etc from an ancestral or former state **b** having sunk to a condition below that which is normal to a type; *esp* having sunk to a lower and usu corrupt state; debased **2** mathematically simpler (eg by having a factor or constant equal to zero) than the typical case ⟨*two intersecting lines constitute a ~ hyperbola*⟩ **3** characterized by atoms stripped of their electrons and by very great density ⟨*~ matter*⟩; *also* consisting of degenerate matter ⟨*a ~ star*⟩ **4** *physics, of (a system of) particles* having two or more low and equal energy states **5** *of a gene* having more than one CODON (unit of three chemical BASES) representing a particular AMINO ACID; *also* being a codon in such a gene [ME *degenerat,* fr L *degeneratus,* pp of *degenerare* to degenerate, fr *de-* + *gener-, genus* race, kind – more at KIN] – **degenerately** *adv,* **degenerateness** *n*

²**degenerate** *n* one who or that which is degenerate

³**degenerate** /di'jenərayt/ *vi* **1** to pass from a higher to a lower type or condition; deteriorate ⟨*the road ~*d *into a bumpy track*⟩ **2** to sink into a low intellectual or moral state **3** to decline from a former thriving, advantageous, or healthy condition ⟨*dinosaurs ~*d *and disappeared*⟩ **4** to evolve or develop into a less autonomous or less functionally active form ⟨*~*d *into dependent parasites*⟩ ⟨*the digestive system ~*d⟩ – **degeneration** *n,* **degenerative** *adj*

**deglaze** /,dee'glayz/ *vt* to add wine, cream, stock, etc to (a pan in which food has been braised or cooked) in order to dilute the juices remaining and incorporate these and any food particles into a sauce

**deglutition** /,deeglooh'tish(ə)n/ *n* the act or process of swallowing [Fr *déglutition,* fr L *deglutitus,* pp of *deglutire* to swallow down, fr *de-* + *glutire, gluttire* to swallow – more at GLUTTON]

**degradable** /di'graydəbl/ *adj* capable of being chemically decomposed ⟨*~ detergents*⟩ – compare BIODEGRADABLE

**degrade** /di'grayd/ *vt* **1a** to lower in grade, rank, or status; demote **b** to strip of rank or honours **c** to deprive of standing or true function **d** to reduce the quality of; *specif* to impair with respect to some physical property **2** to bring to low esteem or into disrepute; disgrace **3** to wear down by erosion **4** to reduce the complexity of (a chemical compound); decompose ~ *vi* **1** to degenerate **2** *of a chemical compound* to decompose *synonyms* see ²HUMBLE *antonym* uplift [ME *degraden,* fr MF *degrader,* fr LL *degradare,* fr L *de-* + *gradus* step, grade] – **degradation** *n,* **degrader** *n*

**degrading** /di'grayding/ *adj* tending to degrade; debasing – **degradingly** *adv*

**degranulation** /,dee,granyoo'laysh(ə)n/ *n* the process of losing granules ⟨*~ of leucocytes*⟩

**degrease** /,dee'grees, -'greez/ *vt* to cleanse of grease or fat – **degreasant** *n*

**degree** /di'gree/ *n* **1** a step or stage in a process, course, or order of classification ⟨*advanced by ~*s⟩ **2** any of three measures of damage caused to tissue by burning – compare FIRST-DEGREE BURN, SECOND-DEGREE BURN, THIRD-DEGREE BURN **3** the extent or measure of an action, condition, or relation ⟨*the company's ~ of expansion was small*⟩ **4** any of the forms used in the comparison of an adjective or adverb, these being positive, comparative, and superlative **5** a rank or grade of official, ecclesiastical, or social position **6** a grade of membership attained in a ritualistic order or society **7a** an academic title conferred by a college, university, etc on students completing a programme of study and passing certain examinations **b** an academic title conferred honorarily **8** a division or interval of a scale of measurement; *specif* any of various units for measuring temperature **9** a 360th part of the circumference of a circle **10** *maths* **10a** the sum of the EXPONENTS of the variable factors of a MONOMIAL (mathematical expression consisting of a single term) ⟨*the ~ of $x^2yz^3$ is 6*⟩ **b** the sum of the exponents of the variable factors in the term of highest degree in a POLYNOMIAL (mathematical expression consisting of a sum of two or more terms) ⟨*the* ∼ *of* $4x^3y + zx + y^5$ *is 5*⟩ **c** the power of the DERIVATIVE of highest ORDER in a DIFFERENTIAL EQUATION

$$\langle the \sim of \left(\frac{d^2x}{dy^2}\right) + \frac{d^4x}{dy^4} = 0 \; is \; 2\rangle$$

**11** a note of a musical scale ⟨*the mediant is the third* ∼ *of the scale*⟩ **12** *NAm* any of several categories of criminal guilt or negligence ⟨*murder in the first* ∼⟩ **13a** *archaic* a member of a series arranged in steps **b** *obs* a step, stair **14** *archaic* a position or space on the earth or in the heavens as measured by degrees of latitude [ME, fr OF *degré*, fr (assumed) VL *degradus*, fr L *de-* + *gradus*] – **to a degree 1** to a remarkable extent **2** in a small way

**de'gree-,day** *n* a unit that represents one degree of deviation from a given point (e g 65°) in the average daily outdoor temperature and that is used to measure heat requirements

**degree day** *n, chiefly Br* a day when degrees and other academic honours are conferred by an educational establishment

**degree of freedom** *n* **1** *physics* any of a limited characteristic number of ways in which a body or system may move or change **2** the number of independent values or quantities which must be specified to completely define a statistical situation

**degressive** /di'gresiv/ *adj* tending to descend or decrease [*de-gres*sion (downward motion; fr ME, fr ML *degression-, degres-sio*, fr L *degressus*, pp of *degredi* to step down, fr *de-* + *gradi* to step) + *-ive* – more at GRADE] – **degressively** *adv*

**dégringolade** /,day,grang·go'lahd (*Fr* degrĕgɔlad)/ *n* a rapid decline or deterioration (e g in strength, position, or condition); a downfall [Fr, fr *dégringoler* to tumble down, fr *dé-* de- + *gringoler* to tumble]

**degust** /,dee'gust/ *vt, formal* to taste, relish [L *degustare*, fr *de-* + *gustare* to taste – more at CHOOSE] – **degustation** *n*

**de haut en bas** /də ,oh on(h) 'bah (*Fr* də o ã ba)/ *adj or adv* having a superior or condescending manner ⟨*there is a* ∼ *tone about such a judgment – TLS*⟩ [Fr, lit., from top to bottom]

**dehisce** /di'his/ *vi, botany* to split along a natural line; *also* to discharge contents by so splitting ⟨*seedpods* dehiscing *at maturity*⟩ [L *dehiscere* to split open, fr *de-* + *hiscere* to gape, incho of *hiare* to yawn – more at YAWN ] – **dehiscence** *n,* **dehiscent** *adj*

**dehorn** /,dee'hawn/ *vt* **1** to remove the horns of (e g cattle) **2** to prevent the growth of the horns of – **dehorner** *n*

**dehuman·ize, -ise** /,dee'hyoohməniez/ *vt* to divest of human qualities or personality – **dehumanization** *n*

**dehumidify** /,deehyooh'midifie/ *vt* to remove moisture from (e g air) – **dehumidifier** *n,* **dehumidification** *n*

**dehydr-** /deehiedr-/, **dehydro-** *comb form* **1** dehydrated **2** with hydrogen removed ⟨*dehydrocortisone*⟩

**dehydrate** /,deehie'drayt/ *vt* **1** to remove water, or hydrogen and oxygen in the proportion in which they form water, from (a chemical compound) **2** to remove water from (e g foods) ∼ *vi* to lose water or body fluids, esp to an abnormal degree – **dehydration** *n,* **dehydrator** *n*

**dehydrochlorinase** /,dee,hiedroh'klawrinăyz, -'klori-, -ays/ *n* an enzyme that dehydrochlorinates a chlorinated HYDRO-CARBON (e g DDT) and is found esp in some insects that are resistant to DDT

**dehydrochlorinate** /,dee,hiedroh'klawrinayt, -'klori-/ *vt* to remove hydrogen and chlorine or HYDROGEN CHLORIDE from (a chemical compound) [*de-* + *hydr-* + *chlorine*] – **dehydro-chlorination** *n*

**dehydrogenase** /,dee'hiedrəjə,nayz, ,deehie'drojənayz, -nays/ *n* an enzyme that accelerates the removal of hydrogen from metabolites and its transfer to other substances ⟨*succinic* ∼⟩ [ISV]

**dehydrogenate** /,dee'hiedrəjənayt, ,deehie'drojənayt/, **dehydrogen·ize, -ise** /-iez/ *vt* to remove hydrogen from – **dehydrogenation** *n*

**de-'ice** *vt* to keep free or rid of ice

**deicide** /'dayi,sied, 'dee-/ *n* **1** the act of killing a divine being or a symbolic substitute of such a being **2** the killer or destroyer of a god [deriv of L *deus* god + *-cidium, -cida* -cide]

**deictic** /'diektik/ *adj* showing or pointing out directly; DEMONSTRATIVE 2 ⟨this, that, *and* those *have a* ∼ *function*⟩ [Gk *deiktikos*, fr *deiktos*, verbal of *deiknynai* to show]

**deify** /'dayifie, 'dee-/ *vt* **1a** to make a god of **b** to take as an object of worship **2** to glorify as of supreme worth ⟨∼ *money*⟩

[ME *deifyen*, fr MF *deifier*, fr LL *deificare*, fr L *deus* god] – **deification** *n*

**deign** /dayn/ *vt* **1** to think it in accordance with one's dignity; condescend ⟨*he barely* ∼ed *to acknowledge their greeting*⟩ **2** *archaic* to condescend to give or offer [ME *deignen*, fr OF *deignier*, fr L *dignare, dignari*, fr *dignus* worthy – more at DECENT]

**deindustrial·ization, -isation** /,dee·in,dustriəlie'zaysh(ə)n/ *n* the tendency over time for the share of a country's GROSS DOMESTIC PRODUCT contributed by the manufacturing sector to fall relative to that contributed by the service sector

**deion·ize, -ise** /,dee'ie·əniez/ *vt* to remove IONS (electrically charged atoms or group of atoms) from ⟨∼ *water by ion exchange*⟩ – **deionization** *n*

**deism** /'dayiz(ə)m, 'dee-/ *n, often cap* a movement or system of thought advocating natural religion based on human reason rather than revelation; *specif* a chiefly 18th century doctrine asserting that although God created the universe he does not intervene in its functioning *synonyms* see THEISM [Fr *déisme*, fr L *deus* god + Fr *-isme* -ism] – **deist** *n, often cap,* **deistic, deis-tical** *adj,* **deistically** *adv*

**deity** /'dayəti, 'dee-/ *n* **1a** the rank or essential nature of a god; divinity **b** *cap the* Supreme Being; GOD 1 **2** a god or goddess ⟨*the* deities *of ancient Greece*⟩ **3** one exalted or revered as supremely good or powerful [ME *deitee*, fr MF *deité*, fr LL *deitat-, deitas*, fr L *deus* god; akin to OE *Tīw*, god of war, L *divus* god, *dies* day, Gk *dios* heavenly]

*usage* The pronunciation /'deeəti/ is recommended for BBC broad-casters.

**déjà vu** /,dayzhah 'vooh (*Fr* deʒa vy)/ *n* the illusion of remembering scenes and events when in fact they are being experienced for the first time [Fr, adj, already seen]

**dejecta** /di'jektə/ *n pl* excrement, faeces [NL, fr L, neut pl of *dejectus*]

**dejected** /di'jektid/ *adj* cast down in spirits; depressed [fr pp of *deject* (to throw down, depress), fr ME *dejecten* to throw down, fr L *dejectus*, pp of *deicere*, fr *de-* + *jacere* to throw – more at ²JET] – **dejectedly** *adv,* **dejectedness** *n*

**dejection** /di'jeksh(ə)n/ *n* lowness of spirits; melancholy

**de jure** /,di 'jooəri/ *adv or adj* by right; *esp* by full legal right ⟨*recognition extended* ∼ *to the new government*⟩ – compare DE FACTO [NL]

**deka-** /dekə-/, **dek-** – see DECA-

**dekko** /'dekoh/ *n, Br slang* a look, glance [Hindi *dekho* look!, imper pl of *dekhnā* to see, fr Skt *dṛś*; akin to Skt *dṛṣṭi* seeing, sight, eye]

**delaine** /də'layn/ *n* a lightweight, often print, woollen dress fabric [Fr (*mousseline*) *de laine* (muslin) of wool]

**delaminate** /,dee'laminayt/ *vb* to (cause to) undergo delamina-tion

**delamination** /,dee,lami'naysh(ə)n/ *n* **1** separation into constituent layers **2** the splitting off of the ENDODERM (inner layer of cells) from the inner surface of the BLASTODERM (inner layer of cells of the previous developmental stage) during development of the GASTRULA (double-layered cuplike stage in embryonic development)

**delate** /di'layt/ *vt, formal* to report (e g a malefactor or an offence) to the relevant authorities [L *delatus* (pp of *deferre* to bring down, report, accuse), fr *de-* + *latus*, suppletive pp of *ferre* to bear – more at TOLERATE, ²BEAR ] – **delator** *n,* **delation** *n*

**Delaware** /'deləweə/ *n, pl* **Delawares,** *esp collectively* **Delaware** a member, or the Algonquian language, of an American Indian people originally of the Delaware valley [*Delaware* river in E USA]

¹**delay** /di'lay/ *n* **1** the act of delaying; (an instance of) the state of being delayed **2** the time during which something is delayed

²**delay** *vt* **1** to put off; postpone **2** to stop, detain, or hinder for a time ∼ *vi* **1** to move or act slowly **2** to pause momentarily [ME *delayen*, fr OF *delaier*, fr *de-* + *laier* to leave, alter. of *laissier*, fr L *laxare* to loosen – more at RELAX] – **delayer** *n,* **delaying** *adj*

**delay line** *n* an electronic device that delays a transmitted signal by a desired amount

**del credere** /del 'kredəri/ *n* an agreement whereby an agent selling goods on credit guarantees the purchaser's solvency to the supplier, usu in return for an additional commission [It, of belief, of trust] – **del credere** *adj or adv*

¹**dele** /'deeli/ *vt* **deleing** to delete (e g a character) from typeset matter [L, imper sing. of *delēre*]

²**dele** n any of several proofreaders' marks (e g *dℓ*) indicating a deletion from a text

**delectable** /di'lektəbl/ adj 1 highly pleasing; delightful 2 delicious [ME, fr MF, fr L *delectabilis*, fr *delectare* to delight – more at DELIGHT] – **delectableness** n, **delectably** adv, **delectability** n

**delectation** /ˌdelek'taysh(ə)n, ˌdee-/ n 1 DELIGHT 1 2 enjoyment *synonyms* see ¹PLEASURE [ME *delectacioun*, fr MF or L; MF *delectation*, fr L *delectation-, delectatio*, fr *delectatus*, pp of *delectare*]

**delegable** /'deligəbl/ adj capable of being delegated

**delegacy** /'deligəsi/ n 1a the act of delegating b an appointment as delegate 2 *taking sing or pl vb* a body of delegates; a board

¹**delegate** /'deligət/ n a person delegated to act for another: e g a a representative to a convention or conference b a representative of a territory of the USA in the HOUSE OF REPRESENTATIVES [ME *delegat*, fr ML *delegatus*, fr L, pp of *delegare* to delegate, fr *de-* + *legare* to send as emissary – more at LEGATE]

²**delegate** /'deligayt/ vt 1 to entrust (e g a duty or responsibility) to another 2 to appoint as one's representative ~ vi to assign responsibility or authority

**delegation** /ˌdeli'gaysh(ə)n/ n 1 the act of empowering to act for another 2 *taking sing or pl vb* a group of people chosen to represent others

**delete** /di'leet/ vt to eliminate esp by blotting out, cutting out, or erasing ⟨~d *his name from the list*⟩ *synonyms* see ERASE [L *deletus*, pp of *delēre* to wipe out, destroy, fr *de-* + *-lēre* (akin to L *linere* to smear) – more at LIME]

**deleterious** /ˌdeli'tiəri-əs/ adj, *formal* harmful, detrimental [ML *deleterius*, fr Gk *dēlētērios*, fr *dēleisthai* to hurt] **deleteriously** adv, **deleteriousness** n

**deletion** /di'leesh(ə)n/ n 1 an act of deleting 2a something deleted b DEFICIENCY 3 (loss or absence of genes from a chromosome); *esp* a large deficiency not including either end of a chromosome [L *deletion-, deletio* destruction, fr *deletus*]

**delft** /delft/ n tin-glazed Dutch earthenware with blue and white or multicoloured decoration; *also* ceramic ware in this style [*Delft*, town in the Netherlands]

**deli** /'deli/ n, *pl* **delis** DELICATESSEN 2

¹**deliberate** /di'lib(ə)rət/ adj 1 characterized by or resulting from careful and thorough consideration ⟨*the council is taking* ~ *action to lower rates*⟩ 2 characterized by awareness of the consequences; wilful ⟨~ *disobedience*⟩ 3 slow, unhurried, and steady as though allowing time for decision on each individual action involved ⟨*walked with a* ~ *step*⟩ *synonyms* see ¹VOLUNTARY *antonym* impulsive [L *deliberatus*, pp of *deliberare* to weigh in mind, ponder, irreg fr *de-* + *libra* scale, pound] – **deliberately** adv, **deliberateness** n

²**deliberate** /di'libərayt/ vt to think about deliberately and often with formal discussion before reaching a decision ~ vi to ponder issues and decisions carefully *synonyms* see PONDER

**deliberation** /diˌlibə'raysh(ə)n/ n 1 the act of deliberating 2 careful discussion and consideration of an issue 3 the quality or state of being deliberate – **deliberative** adj, **deliberatively** adv, **deliberativeness** n

**delicacy** /'delikəsi/ n 1 something pleasing to eat that is considered rare or luxurious ⟨*oysters are a great* ~⟩ 2a the quality or state of being dainty; fineness ⟨*lace of great* ~⟩ b frailty, fragility 3 refinement or subtlety of expression (e g in painting or music) 4 precise and refined perception or discrimination 5a refined sensibility in feeling or conduct; tact ⟨*a certain* ~ *is required when talking about personal matters*⟩ b excessive sensibility; squeamishness 6 the quality or state of requiring sensitive treatment ⟨*the* ~ *of the current political situation*⟩ 7 *obs* the quality or state of being luxurious

¹**delicate** /'delikət/ adj 1a pleasing to the senses in a mild or subtle way ⟨~ *colours*⟩ b fine or exquisite in structure, quality, proportion, etc ⟨~ *silk*⟩ ⟨~ *handwriting*⟩ 2a marked by keen sensitivity or subtle discrimination ⟨~ *perception*⟩ b fastidious, squeamish 3a marked by extreme precision b having or showing extreme sensitivity ⟨*a* ~ *instrument*⟩ 4 requiring or involving sensitive treatment ⟨*the* ~ *balance of power*⟩ 5a easily torn or hurt; fragile ⟨*a* ~ *butterfly wing*⟩ b weak, sickly c marked by fine subtlety ⟨~ *irony*⟩ d marked by or requiring tact; sensitive ⟨*touches on a* ~ *subject*⟩ [ME *delicat*, fr L *delicatus* delicate, addicted to pleasure; akin to L *delicere* to allure] – **delicately** adv, **delicateness** n

²**delicate** n, *archaic* DELICACY 1

**delicatessen** /ˌdelikə'tes(ə)n/ n 1 *taking sing or pl vb* foods, esp delicacies and foreign foods (e g cooked meats and prepared salads), ready for eating 2 a shop where delicatessen are sold [obs Ger *delicatessen*), pl of *delicatesse* delicacy, fr Fr *délicatesse*, fr MF *delicatesse*, prob fr OIt *delicatezza*, fr *delicato* delicate, fr L *delicatus*]

**delicious** /di'lishəs/ adj 1 affording great pleasure; delightful, enchanting; *also* extremely amusing ⟨*a* ~ *story*⟩ 2 highly pleasing to one of the bodily senses esp of taste or smell [ME, fr OF, fr LL *deliciosus*, fr L *deliciae* (pl) delight, fr *delicere* to allure] – **deliciously** adv, **deliciousness** n

**delict** /di'likt, 'deelikt/ n a violation of law or improper act – used in Scottish law [L *delictum* fault, fr neut of *delictus*, pp of *delinquere* – more at ²DELINQUENT]

¹**delight** /di'liet/ n 1 great pleasure or satisfaction; joy 2 something that gives great pleasure ⟨*a* ~ *to behold*⟩ *synonyms* see ¹PLEASURE *antonym* pain

²**delight** vi 1 to take great pleasure *in* doing something ⟨~ed *in causing a stir*⟩ 2 to give keen enjoyment ⟨*a book certain to* ~⟩ ~ vt to give joy or satisfaction to ⟨~ed *the audience with his performance*⟩ [ME *deliten*, fr OF *delitier*, fr L *delectare*, fr *delectus*, pp of *delicere* to allure, fr *de-* + *lacere* to allure; akin to OE *lǣl* switch, L *laqueus* snare] – **delighter** n

**delighted** /di'lietid/ adj highly pleased – **delightedly** adv, **delightedness** n

**delightful** /di'lietf(ə)l/ adj highly pleasing – **delightfully**, adv, **delightfulness** n

**delightsome** /di'lietsəm/ adj, *poetic* delightful – **delightsomely** adv

**Delilah** /di'lielə/ n a treacherous and seductive woman [*Delilah* (Heb *Dělīlāh*), biblical woman who enticed Samson and betrayed him to his enemies (Judges 16)]

**delimit** /di'limit/, **delimitate** /-ayt/ vt to fix the limits of ⟨~ *a boundary*⟩ ⟨~ *a problem*⟩ *synonyms* see ²LIMIT [Fr *délimiter*, fr L *delimitare*, fr *de-* + *limitare* to limit, fr *limit-, limes* boundary, limit – more at LIMB] – **delimitation** n, **delimitative** adj

**delineate** /di'liniayt/ vt 1 to indicate by lines drawn in the shape of; portray 2 to describe in usu sharp or vivid detail [L *delineatus*, pp of *delineare*, fr *de-* + *linea* line] – **delineator** n, **delineative** adj, **delineation** n

**delinquency** /di'lingkwənsi/ n 1 (the practice of engaging in) antisocial or illegal conduct – used esp when emphasis is placed on social or psychological maladjustment, esp of young people, rather than on criminal intent 2 failure to fulfil one's obligations; *esp* (failure to pay) a debt

¹**delinquent** /di'lingkwənt/ n a delinquent person

²**delinquent** adj 1 guilty of wrongdoing or of neglect of duty 2 being overdue in payment ⟨*a* ~ *charge account*⟩ 3 marked by delinquency ⟨~ *behaviour*⟩ [L *delinquent-, delinquens*, prp of *delinquere* to fail, offend, fr *de-* + *linquere* to leave – more at LOAN] – **delinquently** adv

**deliquesce** /ˌdeli'kwes/ vi 1a to dissolve gradually and become liquid by attracting and absorbing moisture from the air b *of plant structures* (e g mushrooms) to become soft or liquid with age 2 *esp of the veins of a leaf* to divide repeatedly and so end in fine divisions [L *deliquescere*, fr *de-* + *liquescere*, incho of *liquēre* to be fluid – more at LIQUID] – **deliquescence** n, **deliquescent** adj

**delirious** /di'liəri-əs/ adj 1 (characteristic) of delirium 2 affected with or marked by delirium – **deliriously** adv, **deliriousness** n

**delirium** /di'liəri-əm/ n 1 a temporary mental disturbance characterized by confusion, disordered speech, and hallucinations 2 frenzied excitement [L, fr *delirare* to deviate, be crazy, fr *de-* + *lira* furrow – more at LEARN]

**delirium tremens** /'tremenz/ n a violent delirium characterized by tremors and terrifying visual hallucinations that is induced by alcoholism – called also DT's [NL, lit., trembling delirium]

**deliver** /di'livə/ vt 1 to set free ⟨*and lead us not into temptation, but* ~ *us from evil* – Mt 6:13 (AV)⟩ 2 to hand over; bring ⟨~ *the milk*⟩ 3a to aid in the birth of ⟨*they* ~ed *the child*⟩ b to give birth to ⟨*she* ~ed *her child at three in the morning*⟩ c to assist (a woman or female animal) in giving birth ⟨*successfully* ~ed *the ewe of twin lambs*⟩ 4 to utter, relate ⟨~ed *his speech effectively*⟩ 5 to send (something aimed or guided) to an intended target or destination ⟨~ed *a left hook to the jaw*⟩ ~ vi *informal* to produce the promised, desired, or expected results [ME *deliveren*, fr OF *delivrer*, fr LL *deliberare*, fr L *de-* + *liberare* to liberate] – **deliverer** n, **deliverable** adj, **deliverability** n – **be delivered of** *formal* to give birth to, esp with the assistance of a midwife, doctor, etc ⟨was delivered of *a fine daughter*⟩ – see also **deliver the** GOODS

**deliverance** /di'liv(ə)rəns/ *n* **1** liberation, rescue **2** something delivered or communicated; *esp* an opinion or decision (eg the verdict of a jury) expressed publicly

**delivery** /di'liv(ə)ri/ *n* **1** DELIVERANCE 1 **2a** the act of handing over or distributing ⟨*a* ~ *girl*⟩ **b** the act of putting something into the legal possession of another **c** something delivered ⟨*milk* deliveries⟩ **3** the act of giving birth **4** (manner or style of) utterance in speech or song ⟨*her* ~ *was clear and precise*⟩ **5** (an instance of) the act or manner of sending forth, throwing, or bowling a ball ⟨*played and missed at every* ~⟩

**deliveryman** /di'liv(ə)rimən, -,man/ *n* a person who delivers wholesale or retail goods to customers usu over a regular local route

**dell** /del/ *n* a small secluded hollow or valley, esp in a forest [ME *delle*; akin to MHG *telle* ravine, OE *dæl* valley – more at DALE]

**delocal·ize, -ise** /,dee'lohkəliez/ *vt* to free from the limitations of locality; *specif* to remove (electrons) from a particular position – **delocalization** *n*

**delouse** /,dee'lows/ *vt* to remove lice from

**Delphic** /'delfik/, **Delphian** /'delfi·ən/ *adj* **1** of ancient Delphi or its oracle **2** ambiguous, obscure [*Delphi*, town in ancient Greece; (2) fr the ambiguous statements made by the oracle] – **delphically** *adv*

**delphinium** /del'fini·əm/ *n* any of a large genus (*Delphinium*) of plants of the buttercup family that have large leaves which are each divided into five sections, and blue or purple spurred flowers borne in long spikelike clusters [NL, genus name, fr Gk *delphinion* larkspur, dim. of *delphin-, delphis* dolphin – more at DOLPHIN; fr the shape of its nectary]

**¹delta** /'deltə/ *n* **1a** the 4th letter of the Greek alphabet **b** ¹D **5a 2** something shaped like a capital delta; *esp* a triangular deposit of fine sand, silt, etc at the mouth of a river **3** *maths* an INCREMENT (positive or negative change) of a VARIABLE [ME *deltha*, fr Gk *delta*, of Sem origin; akin to Heb *dāleth* daleth] – **deltaic** *adj*

**²delta**, **δ-** *adj* fourth in position from a particular chemical group or atom in an organic molecule

**Delta** – a communications code word for the letter *d*

**delta ray** *n* an electron that acquires sufficient energy to eject from an atom as a result of the interaction of a charged particle with matter

**delta wing** *n* an approximately triangular backward-slanting aircraft wing with a (nearly) straight rearmost edge

**deltiology** /,delti'oləji/ *n* the hobby of collecting and studying picture postcards [Gk *deltion* small writing tablet (dim. of *deltos* writing tablet) + E *-logy*] – **deltiologist** *n*

**deltoid** /'deltoyd/ *n* a large triangular muscle that covers the shoulder joint and serves to raise the arm to the side [NL *deltoides*, fr Gk *deltoeidēs* shaped like a delta, fr *delta*]

**delude** /di'loohd/ *vt* **1** to mislead the mind or judgment of; deceive, trick **2** *obs* to frustrate, disappoint [ME *deluden*, fr L *deludere*, fr *de-* + *ludere* to play – more at LUDICROUS]

**¹deluge** /'delyoohj, -yoohzh/ *n* **1a** a great flood; *specif, cap* the Flood recorded in the Old Testament (Gen 6:8) **b** a heavy fall of rain **2** an overwhelming amount or number ⟨*a* ~ *of criticism*⟩ ⟨*a* ~ *of letters*⟩ [ME, fr MF, fr L *diluvium*, fr *diluere* to wash away, fr *dis-* + *lavere* to wash – more at LYE]

**²deluge** *vt* **1** to overflow with water; inundate **2** to overwhelm; swamp

**delusion** /di'loohzh(ə)n/ *n* **1** the act of deluding; the state of being deluded **2a** a false or misguided idea, belief, etc **b** (an abnormal mental state characterized by) a false belief regarding the self or people or objects outside the self that persists despite the facts and is common in certain types of severe mental disorder [ME, fr L *delusion-, delusio*, fr *delusus*, pp of *deludere*] – **delusional** *adj*, **delusionary** *adj*, **delusive** *adj*, **delusively** *adv*, **delusiveness** *n*, **delusory** *adj*

*synonyms* Compare **delusion** and **illusion**. An **illusion** is something that seems to exist, or seems true to the senses. It may be known to be false ⟨*the* **illusion** *that the sun goes round the earth*⟩ or may have no basis in reality ⟨*the happy* **illusions** *of childhood*⟩. An **illusion** is usually harmless and often pleasant, as compared with a **delusion**, which is a fixed false opinion such as that held by a mad person ⟨*his* **delusion** *that he is Napoleon I*⟩, and cannot be removed by any appeal to reason. In certain contexts, either word is equally appropriate ⟨*she's under the* **delusion/illusion** *that I'm brilliant*⟩.

**delustre** /,dee'lustə/ *vt* to reduce the sheen of (eg yarn or fabric)

**de luxe** /di 'luks/ *adj* notably luxurious or elegant [Fr, lit., of luxury]

**delve** /delv/ *vi* **1** to dig or burrow – usu + *in* or *into* ⟨~d *into his pockets*⟩ ⟨~d *into the ground*⟩ **2** to make a careful or detailed search for information – usu + *in* or *into* ⟨~d *into the past*⟩ [ME *delven*, fr OE *delfan*; akin to OHG *telban* to dig] – **delver** *n*

**demagnet·ize, -ise** /,dee'magnitiez/ *vt* to remove the magnetic properties of – **demagnetizer** *n*, **demagnetization** *n*

**demagogue**, *NAm also* **demagog** /'deməgog/ *n* **1** a leader of the common people in ancient times **2** a leader who makes use of popular prejudices and false claims and promises in order to gain power [Gk *dēmagōgos*, fr *dēmos* people (akin to Gk *daiesthai* to divide) + *agōgos* leading, fr *agein* to lead – more at TIDE, AGENT] – **demagogic, demagogical** *adj*, **demagogically** *adv*

**demagoguery** /'deməˌgogəri/, **demagoguism** /'deməgogˌiz(ə)m/, **demagogy** /'deməˌgogi/ *n* the principles or practices of a demagogue

**¹demand** /di'mahnd/ *n* **1a** an act of demanding or asking, esp with authority **b** something claimed as due ⟨*the workers made a ten per cent wage* ~⟩ **2a** willingness and ability to purchase a commodity or service **b** the quantities of goods and services wanted at specified prices at some period of time **3** a desire or need *for* ⟨*a great* ~ *for teachers*⟩ **4** the requirement of work or use; a claim ⟨*the structure was equal to the* ~s *made on it*⟩ ⟨*studying makes great* ~s *on my time*⟩ □ (2) compare SUPPLY 4 – **in demand** sought after or admired, esp because valuable, rare, or elusive ⟨*gold is in great demand*⟩ ⟨*computer programmers are in demand at present*⟩ – **on demand** whenever the demand is made ⟨*feed the baby* on demand⟩

**²demand** *vi* to make a demand; ask ~ *vt* **1** to ask or call for with authority; claim as due or just ⟨~ *payment of a debt*⟩ **2** to call for urgently, authoritatively, or insistently ⟨~ed *that the rioters disperse*⟩ **3** to ask authoritatively or earnestly to be informed of ⟨~ed *the reason for the intrusion*⟩ **4** to require ⟨*the work* ~s *great precision*⟩ [ME *demaunden*, fr MF *demander*, fr ML *demandare*, fr L *de-* + *mandare* to enjoin – more at MANDATE] – **demandable** *adj*, **demander** *n*

*synonyms* **Demand, claim, require,** and **exact**: **demand** stresses insistence and peremptoriness in a request, while **claim** suggests it is justified, or thought by the claimant to be justified. **Require** implies need or authority ⟨*the law* **requires** *you to wear a seat belt*⟩, but is often interchangeable with **demand**. **Exact** denotes not only asking but also obtaining one's request, usually with implication of exerting one's position or authority or using compulsion to obtain it ⟨*she* **exacted** *obedience in everything from all her pupils*⟩. *usage* One **demands** something of or from someone ⟨**demanded** *the time of a passerby*⟩; one **demands** to do something ⟨**demanded** *to see my passport*⟩, to have something done to one ⟨**demanded** *to be shaved*⟩, to be informed of something ⟨**demanded** *where we lived*⟩, or that something should happen ⟨**demanded** *that she should leave/that she left*⟩/(chiefly NAm) *that she leave*⟩. One makes a **demand** *for* something, *on* someone ⟨*constant* **demands** *on me for advice*⟩, to do something ⟨*her* **demand** *to see the documents*⟩ or to have something done to one ⟨*their* **demand** *to be allowed to vote*⟩ or that something should happen ⟨*his* **demand** *that she should tell him/that she tells him*⟩/(chiefly NAm) *that she tell him the truth*⟩.

**demandant** /di'mahndənt/ *n* one who makes a demand or claim

**demand deposit** *n* a bank deposit that can be withdrawn without advance notice – compare TIME DEPOSIT

**demanding** /di'mahndɪng/ *adj* exacting – **demandingly** *adv*

**demand note** *n* a note promising to pay a specified sum of money on demand

**de'mand-ˌpull, demand-pull inflation** *n* an increase or upward trend in prices resulting from an increase in aggregate demand or the money supply – compare COST-PUSH – **demand-pull** *adj*

**demantoid** /di'mantoyd/ *n* a green garnet [Ger, fr obs Ger *demant* diamond, fr MHG *diemant*, fr OF *diamant*]

**demarcate** /'deemahˌkayt/ *vt* **1** to mark the limits of **2** to set apart; separate [back-formation fr *demarcation*, fr Sp *demarcación* & Pg *demarcação*, fr *demarcar* to delimit, fr *de-* + *marcar* to mark, fr It *marcare*, of Gmc origin; akin to OHG *marha* boundary – more at MARK]

**demarcation** *also* **demarkation** /,deemah'kaysh(ə)n/ *n* the marking of limits or boundaries, esp between areas of work to be carried out by members of particular trade unions ⟨*a ~ dispute*⟩

**demarche** /'day,mahsh/ *n* **1** a course of action; a manoeuvre; *esp* a diplomatic move or manoeuvre **2** a diplomatic representation made to a foreign government [Fr *démarche*, lit., gait, fr MF *demarche*, fr *demarcher* to march, fr OF *demarchier*, fr *de-* + *marchier* to march]

**dematerial·ize, -ise** /,deemə'tiəri·əliez/ *vb* to deprive of or lose material form or qualities; (cause to) vanish – **dematerialization** *n*

**deme** /deem/ *n* **1** a unit of local government in ancient Attica **2** *biology* a local population of closely related organisms – usu in combination ⟨*gamo*deme⟩ [Gk *dēmos*, lit., people]

**demean** /di'meen/ *vt* to degrade, debase ⟨*such conduct ~s you in my eyes*⟩ ⟨*don't ~ yourself by acting like the others*⟩ **synonyms** see ²HUMBLE [*de-* + *mean*]

**demeanour**, *NAm chiefly* **demeanor** /di'meenə/ *n* behaviour toward others; outward manner – compare BEARING **synonyms** see BEHAVIOUR [*demean* (to conduct or behave )oneself(), fr ME *demenen*, fr OF *demener* to conduct, guide, fr *de-* + *mener* to lead, drive – more at AMENABLE]

**demented** /di'mented/ *adj* mad, insane [fr pp of arch. *dement* to drive mad, fr LL *dementare*, fr L *dement-, demens*] – **dementedly** *adv*, **dementedness** *n*

**dementia** /di'mensh(y)ə/ *n* **1** a state of mental deterioration due to brain damage or to natural change esp accompanying aging ⟨*senile ~*⟩ **2** madness, insanity [L, fr *dement-, demens* mad, fr *de-* + *ment-, mens* mind – more at MIND] – **demential** *adj*

**dementia praecox** /'preekoks/ *n* schizophrenia [NL, lit., premature dementia]

**demerara sugar** /,demə'reərə/ *n* brown crystallized unrefined CANE SUGAR from the W Indies [*Demerara*, region in Guyana]

**demerit** /,dee'merit, '-,--/ *n* **1** a quality that deserves blame or lacks merit; a fault, defect **2** *NAm* a mark usu entailing a loss of privilege given to somebody (eg a soldier) guilty of misconduct [ME, fr MF *demerite*, fr *de-* + *merite* merit]

**demersal** /di'muhsl/ *adj* of or living near the bottom of the sea ⟨*a ~ fish*⟩ – compare PELAGIC [L *demersus*, pp of *demergere* to sink, fr *de-* + *mergere* to dip, sink, plunge]

**demesne** /di'mayn, -'meen/ *n* **1** legal possession of land as one's own **2** land, esp surrounding a manor or other large house, actually occupied by the owner and not held by tenants **3a** landed property; an estate **b** a region or realm belonging to a sovereign or state [ME, alter. of *demeyne*, fr OF *demaine* – more at DOMAIN]

**demi-** /demi-/ *prefix* **1** half ⟨*demisemiquaver*⟩ **2** partly belonging to (a specified type or class) ⟨*demigod*⟩ [ME, fr *demi*, fr MF, fr L *dimidius*, prob back-formation fr *dimidiare* to halve, fr *dis-* + *medius* mid – more at MID]

**demi-glace** /dəmi 'glahs/ *n* a brown sauce reduced in volume by boiling until sufficiently thick to coat and give a glazed appearance to food [Fr, lit., half-glaze]

**demigod** /'demi,god/, *fem* **demigoddess** *n* **1a** a mythological superhuman being with less power than a god **b** a mythological being who is the offspring of a union between a mortal and a god **2** a person so outstanding that he/she seems to approach the divine

**demijohn** /'demi,jon/ *n* a narrow-necked large bottle of glass or stoneware, often having small handles at the neck [by folk etymology fr Fr *dame-jeanne*, lit., Lady Jane]

**demilitar·ize, -ise** /,dee'militəriez/ *vt* to strip of military forces, weapons, fortifications, etc ⟨*a ~d zone*⟩ – **demilitarization** *n*

**demimondaine** /,demimon'dayn/ *n* a woman of the demimonde [Fr *demi-mondaine*, fr fem of *demi-mondain*, fr *demi-monde*]

**demimonde** /-'mond/ *n taking sing or pl vb* **1** a class of women on the fringes of respectable society, esp in the 19th century, who were supported by wealthy lovers **2** a group engaged in activity of doubtful legality or propriety [Fr *demi-monde*, lit., half-world, fr *demi-* + *monde* world, fr L *mundus*]

**demineral·ize, -ise** /,dee'min(ə)rə,liez/ *vt* to remove the mineral matter from (eg water) – **demineralizer** *n*, **demineralization** *n*

**demirep** /'demi,rep/ *n* a demimondaine [*demi-* + *reputation* or *reputable*]

¹**demise** /di'miez/ *vt* **1** to transfer (an estate or other property) by will or lease **2** to transmit (eg a title) by succession or inheritance **3** *obs* to convey, give ~ *vi* **1** to pass by descent or bequest ⟨*the property ~d to the king*⟩ **2** *archaic* to die, decease

²**demise** *n* **1** the transfer of an estate, esp by the grant of a

lease **2** transfer of sovereignty (eg by the death or abdication of the sovereign) **3a** a cessation of existence or activity **b** *euph or formal* death [MF, fem of *demis*, pp of *demettre* to dismiss, fr L *demittere* to send down, fr *de-* + *mittere* to send]

**Demi-sel** /,demi 'sel/ *n* a soft very creamy cheese containing little salt [Fr, lit., half-salt]

**demisemiquaver** /,demisemi'kwayvə/ *n* a musical note with the time value of half a semiquaver

**demisemiquaver rest** *n* a musical rest of the same time value as a demisemiquaver

**demission** /di'mish(ə)n/ *n*, *formal* resignation, abdication [MF, fr L *demission-, demissio* lowering, fr *demissus*, pp of *demittere*]

**demist** /,dee'mist/ *vb*, *Br* to (cause to) become free of condensation or steam, esp by means of a heater or heated windscreen ⟨*~ed the car windows*⟩ – **demister** *n*

**demit** /di'mit/ *vb* **-tt-** *archaic vt* **1** to dismiss **2** to resign (an office, post, etc) ~ *vi* to withdraw from office or membership [MF *demettre*]

**demitasse** /'demi,tas/ *n* a small cup for serving coffee (eg after dinner); *also* the coffee, esp black coffee, served in a demitasse [Fr *demi-tasse*, lit., half-cup, fr *demi-* + *tasse* cup, fr MF, fr Ar *ṭass*, fr Per *tast*]

**demiurge** /-,uhj/ *n* **1** *cap* **1a** a deity who, according to the philosophy of Plato, is the creator of the material universe **b** a deity who, according to GNOSTIC philosophy, created the material universe but is inferior to the SUPREME BEING **2** something that is an autonomous creative force or decisive power [LL *demiurgus*, fr Gk *dēmiourgos*, lit., one who works for the people, fr *dēmios* of the people (fr *dēmos* people) + *-ourgos* worker (fr *ergon* work) – more at DEMAGOGUE, WORK] – **demiurgeous** *adj*, **demiurgic, demiurgical** *adj*, **demiurgically** *adv*

**demi-vierge** /vi'eəzh, 'vyeəzh/ *n* a woman who engages in sexual activity while still keeping her technical virginity [Fr, lit., half-virgin, fr *demi-* + *vierge* virgin, fr L *virgin-, virgo*]

**demo** /'demoh/ *n*, *pl* **demos 1** DEMONSTRATION **4 2** *cap*, *NAm* DEMOCRAT **2**

¹**demob** /,dee'mob/ *vt* **-bb-** *chiefly Br* to demobilize

²**demob** *n*, *chiefly Br* (a) demobilization

**demobil·ize, -ise** /,dee'mohbiliez/ *vt* **1** to disband **2** to discharge from military service ~ *vi* to disband, esp after having completed military service – **demobilization** *n*

**democracy** /di'mokrəsi/ *n* **1a** government by the people; *esp* rule of the majority **b** (a political unit with) a government in which the supreme power is vested in the people and exercised by them directly or indirectly through a system of representation usu involving periodically held free elections **2** control of an organization, group, etc by its own members, esp by participation in decision-making ⟨*How close are we to true industrial ~ ?*⟩ **3** the common people, esp when constituting the source of political authority **4** the absence of hereditary or arbitrary class distinctions or privileges; social equality [MF *democratie*, fr LL *democratia*, fr Gk *dēmokratia*, fr *dēmos* + *-kratia* -cracy]

**democrat** /'deməkrat/ *n* **1a** an adherent of democracy **b** one who practises social equality **2** *cap* a member of the Democratic party of the USA

**democratic** /,demə'kratik/ *adj* **1** of or favouring democracy **2** *often cap* of or being a political party of the USA associated with policies of broad social reform and internationalism – compare REPUBLICAN – **democratically** *adv*

,**Demo,cratic-Re'publican** *adj* of a major US political party of the early 19th century favouring a strict interpretation of the constitution to restrict the powers of the federal government, and emphasizing states' rights

**democrat·ize, -ise** /di'mokrətiez/ *vt* to make democratic – **democratizer** *n*, **democratization** *n*

**démodé** /,daymoh'day/ *adj* no longer fashionable; out-of-date [Fr, fr *dé-* de-+ *mode* fashion]

**demodulation** /,dee,modyoo'laysh(ə)n/ *n* the process of extracting information from a CARRIER wave (wave whose modulations are used as signals for radio, television, etc) that has been MODULATED (had the frequency, amplitude, or other characteristic of a modulating wave superimposed on it) so that the output wave has the characteristics of the original modulating wave – **demodulate** *vt*, **demodulator** *n*

**demography** /di'mogrəfi/ *n* the statistical study of human populations, esp with reference to size, density, and distribution [Fr *démographie*, fr Gk *dēmos* people + Fr *-graphie* -graphy] – **demographer** *n*, **demographic** *adj*, **demographically** *adv*

**demoiselle** /dəmwah'zel/ n 1 a small crane (*Anthropoides virgo*), found esp in Europe, with predominantly blue-grey plumage, characteristic tufts of white behind each eye, and elongated black breast feathers 2 DAMSELFLY (insect similar to the dragonfly) 3 DAMSELFISH (brightly coloured tropical fish) 4 *archaic or poetic* a young lady [Fr, fr OF *dameisele* – more at DAMSEL]

**De Moivre's theorem** /də 'mwahv(rə)z, 'moyvəz/ n, *maths* a theorem of COMPLEX NUMBERS: the *n*th power of a complex number has for its ABSOLUTE VALUE and its ARGUMENT respectively the *n*th power of the absolute value and *n* times the argument of the complex number [Abraham *De Moivre* †1754 E (Fr-born) mathematician]

**demolish** /di'molish/ vt 1 to destroy, smash, or tear down 2 to defeat, refute ⟨*she* ∼*ed my argument*⟩ 3 *informal* to eat up; devour ⟨∼*ed a plate of spaghetti*⟩ [MF *demoliss*-, stem of *demolir*, fr L *demoliri*, fr *de*- + *moliri* to construct, fr *moles* mass – more at ³MOLE] – **demolisher** n, **demolishment** n

**demolition** /ˌdemə'lish(ə)n/ n the act or an instance of demolishing 2 pl explosives for destruction in war ⟨*a* ∼*s expert*⟩ *synonyms* see ¹RUIN [MF & L; MF, fr L *demolition-*, *demolitio*, fr *demolitus*, pp of *demoliri*] – **demolitionist** n

**demolition derby** n a contest held chiefly in the USA in which drivers ram old cars into each other until only one car remains running

**demon** /'deemən/ n 1 an evil spirit; a devil 2 an evil or undesirable person, emotion, trait, etc 3 DAEMON 1,2 4 one who has unusual drive, enthusiasm, or effectiveness ⟨*a* ∼ *for work*⟩ [ME, fr LL & L; LL *daemon* evil spirit, fr L, divinity, spirit, fr Gk *daimōn*] – **demonize** vt, **demonization** n

**demonet·ize, -ise** /ˌdee'munitiez/ vt 1 to stop using (a metal) as a monetary standard 2 to deprive of value as a currency [Fr *démonétiser*, fr *dé*- de- + L *moneta* coin – more at MINT] – **demonetization** n

**demoniac** /di'mohniak/ *also* **demoniacal** /ˌdeemə'nie‑əkl/ *adj* 1 possessed or influenced by a demon 2 demonic [ME *demoniak*, fr LL *daemoniacus*, fr Gk *daimoniakos*, fr *daimon*-, *daimōn*] – **demoniac** n, **demoniacally** adv

**demonic** /di'monik/ *also* **demonical** /-kl/ *adj* of or suggestive of a demon; fiendish ⟨∼ *cruelty*⟩ – **demonically** adv

**demonism** /'deeməniz(ə)m/ n 1a belief in demons b the worship of demons 2 demonology

**demonolatry** /ˌdeemə'nolətri/ n the worship of demons – **demonolater** n

**demonology** /ˌdeemə'noləji/ n 1a the study of or belief in demons b a system of belief in or doctrine concerning demons 2 a catalogue of enemies

**demonstrable** /di'monstrəbl/ *adj* 1 capable of being demonstrated 2 apparent, evident – **demonstrably** adv, **demonstrability** n, **demonstrableness** n

**demonstrate** /'demənstrayt/ vt 1 to show clearly 2a to prove or make clear by reasoning or evidence b to illustrate and explain, esp with many examples 3 to show or prove the application, value, or efficiency of (eg a household implement) to a prospective buyer ∼ vi 1 to make or give a demonstration 2 to take part in a public demonstration or protest *synonyms* see ¹SHOW [L *demonstratus*, pp of *demonstrare*, fr *de*- + *monstrare* to show – more at MUSTER]

**demonstration** /ˌdemən'straysh(ə)n/ n 1 an outward expression or display 2 an act, process, or means of demonstrating to the intelligence: eg 2a(1) conclusive evidence; proof a(2) a proof in which the conclusion is the immediate sequence of reasoning from premises b a display and explanation of the merits of a product, implement, etc to a prospective buyer c a display of an action or process ⟨*a cooking* ∼⟩ 3 a show of armed force 4 a public display (eg a mass meeting or procession) of group feelings towards a person, cause, activity, etc – **demonstrational** adj, **demonstrationist** n

¹**demonstrative** /di'monstrətiv/ *adj* 1a demonstrating to be real or true ⟨*made noises* ∼ *of alarm*⟩ b characterized or established by demonstration 2 *grammar* pointing out the one referred to and distinguishing it from others of the same class ⟨∼ *pronouns*⟩ 3a marked by display of feeling b inclined to display feelings openly – **demonstratively** adv, **demonstrativeness** n

²**demonstrative** n a demonstrative word or MORPHEME (word-part)

**demonstrator** /'demənˌstraytə/ n one who demonstrates; *esp* a junior staff member who demonstrates experiments in a university science department

**demoral·ize, -ise** /di'morəˌliez/ vt 1 to corrupt the morals of 2a to weaken the morale of; discourage b to throw into disorder – **demoralization** n, **demoralizer** n

**demos** /'deemos/ n 1 the common people of an ancient Greek state 2 *often cap* the populace personified [Gk *dēmos* – more at DEMAGOGUE]

**demote** /di'moht/ vt to reduce to a lower grade, rank, or position [*de*- + -*mote* (as in *promote*)] – **demotion** n

¹**demotic** /di'motik/ *adj* 1 of the common people 2 of or written in a simplified form of the hieratic writing used by the ancient Egyptians 3 of the language commonly spoken in Modern Greece [Gk *dēmotikos*, fr *dēmotēs* commoner, fr *dēmos*]

²**demotic** n 1 demotic Egyptian script 2 demotic Greek

**demotivate** /ˌdee'mohtivayt/ vt to deprive of motivation – **demotivation** n

**demount** /ˌdee'mownt/ vt 1 to remove (eg a gun) from a mounting 2 to disassemble – **demountable** adj

**demulcent** /di'muls(ə)nt/ *adj, of a medicine or drug* soothing [L *demulcent*-, *demulcens*, prp of *demulcēre* to soothe, fr *de*- + *mulcēre* to soothe] – **demulcent** n

¹**demur** /di'muh/ vi -rr- 1 to take exception; object 2 *law* to put in a demurrer *synonyms* see ²OBJECT [ME *demeoren* to linger, fr OF *demorer*, fr L *demorari*, fr *de*- + *morari* to linger, fr *mora* delay – more at MEMORY] – **demurral** n, **demurrable** adj

**demur** n 1 hesitation ⟨*women who follow fashion without* ∼⟩ 2 objection, protest *synonyms* see QUALM

**demure** /di'myooə/ *adj* 1 reserved, modest 2 affectedly modest, reserved, or serious; coy *synonyms* see ¹SHY [ME, perh fr MF *demorer*, *demourer* to linger] – **demurely** adv, **demureness** n

**demurrage** /di'muhrij/ n 1 the detention of a ship or vehicle (eg for loading or unloading) beyond the time agreed upon between the owner and the charterer 2 a charge paid to the owner by the charterer for demurrage

¹**demurrer** /di'muhrə/ n 1 a pleading by a party to a legal action that accepts the truth of a point alleged by the opposite party but asserts that it is insufficient in law to support the opponent's claim or to allow the action to proceed further 2 an objection [MF *demorer*, vb]

²**demurrer** n someone or something that demurs [¹*demur* + ²-*er*]

**demy** /di'mie/ n a size of paper, usu 22½ × 17½ inches (572 × 444 millimetres) [ME *demi* half – more at DEMI-]

**demyelinate** /dee'mie‑iliˌnayt/ vt to remove or destroy the MYELIN (fatty substance forming an insulating sheath) of (a nerve fibre) – **demyelination** n

**demystify** /dee'mistifie/ vt to remove the mystifying features of; make clear or accessible ⟨∼ *the law*⟩ – **demystification** n

**demytholog·ize, -ise** /ˌdeemi'tholəjiez/ vt 1 to remove the mythological content of in order to uncover the underlying meaning ⟨∼ *the Gospels*⟩ 2 to remove the mythical elements or associations from ⟨*we should* ∼ *foreign aid* – *Saturday Night* (*Toronto*)⟩ – **demythologization** n, **demythologizer** n

¹**den** /den/ n 1 the lair of a wild usu predatory animal 2a a hollow or room used esp as a hideout or centre of illicit activity ⟨*an opium* ∼⟩ ⟨*a* ∼ *of thieves*⟩ b a small usu squalid dwelling 3 a comfortable usu secluded room [ME, fr OE *denn*; akin to OE *denu* valley, OHG *tenni* threshing floor, Gk *thenar* palm of the hand]

²**den** vb -nn- vi to live in or retire to a den (eg for hibernating) – often + *up* ∼ vt to drive (an animal) into a den

**denarius** /di'neəri‑əs/ n, pl **denarii** /di'neəri,ie/ a small silver coin of ancient Rome; *also* a gold coin of the Roman Empire equal to 25 silver denarii [ME, fr L – more at DENIER]

**denary** /'deenəri/ *adj* of, being, or belonging to a system of numbers having 10 as its base; decimal [L *denarius* containing ten]

**denational·ize, -ise** /dee'nashən(ə)lˌiez/ vt 1 to deprive of national status, character, or rights 2 to remove from ownership or control by the state ⟨∼d *industries*⟩ – **denationalization** n

**denatural·ize, -ise** /ˌdee'nachərəliez/ vt 1 to make unnatural 2 to deprive of the rights and duties of a citizen – **denaturalization** n

**denature** /dee'naychə/ vt 1 to deprive of natural qualities: eg 1a to make (alcohol) unfit for drinking (eg by adding an obnoxious substance) without impairing its usefulness for other purposes b to modify (eg a protein), esp by heat, acid, alkali, or ultraviolet radiation, so that some of the original structure of the molecule is lost and its properties are diminished or changed **c** to add nonfissile material to (fissile material) so as to make unsuitable for use in an atomic bomb **2** to dehumanize – **denaturant** *n*, **denaturation** *n*

**denazify** /ˌdeeˈnahtsiˌfie/ *vt* to rid of Nazism and its influence – **denazification** *n*

**dendr-** /dendr-/, **dendro-** *comb form* tree ⟨dendro*philous*⟩; branching like a tree ⟨dendr*ite*⟩ [Gk, fr *dendron*; akin to Gk *drys* tree – more at TREE]

**dendriform** /ˈdendriˌfawm/ *adj* resembling a tree in having a branched structure ⟨*a ~ sponge*⟩

**dendrite** /ˈdendriet/ *n* **1** a branching treelike figure produced on or in a mineral by a foreign mineral; *also* the mineral so marked **2** a branching form of a crystal **3a** any of the usu branching projections that conduct impulses toward the body of a NERVE CELL **b** any of the fine branches of a dendrite that constitute the place at which nerve impulses are passed from one NERVE CELL to another – **dendritic,** *also* **dendritical** *adj*, **dendritically** *adv*

**dendrochronology** /ˌdendrohkrəˈnoləji/ *n* the science of dating past events and variations in environment in former periods by comparative study of ANNUAL RINGS in trees and aged wood – **dendrochronological** *adj*, **dendrochronologically** *adv*

**dendroid** /ˈdenˌdroyd/ *adj* resembling a tree in form [Gk *dendroeidēs*, fr *dendron*]

**dendrology** /denˈdroləji/ *n* the study of trees – **dendrologic, dendrological** *adj*, **dendrologist** *n*

**dendron** *n* DENDRITE 3A

¹**dene** /deen/ *n* ¹DEAN

²**dene** *n*, *dial SEng* a bare sandy area or sand dune by the sea [ME *den, denne*; prob akin to OE *dūn* down]

**denegation** /deniˈgaysh(ə)n/ *n* a denial [ME *denegacioun*, fr MF or L; MF *denegation*, fr L *denegation-, denegatio*, fr *denegatus*, pp of *denegare* to deny – more at DENY]

**denervate** /ˈdeenuhˌvayt/ *vt* to deprive of a nerve supply (e g by cutting a nerve) – **denervation** *n*

**dengue** /ˈdengˈgi/ *n* an acute infectious viral disease characterized by headaches, severe joint pain, and a rash [Sp, prob of African origin]

**deniable** /diˈnie·əbl/ *adj* capable of being denied

**denial** /diˈnie·əl/ *n* **1** refusal to satisfy a request or desire **2a(1)** refusal to admit the truth or reality (e g of a statement or charge) **a(2)** assertion that an allegation is false **b** refusal to acknowledge a person or a thing; disavowal ⟨*Peter's ~ of Christ*⟩ **3** self-denial **4** negation in logic ⟨*a proposition whose ~ is self-contradictory*⟩

¹**denier** /diˈnie·ə/ *n* one who denies

²**denier** /ˈdeni·ə/ *n* **1** a small originally silver coin used in France and W Europe from the 8th to the 19th centuries **2** a unit of weight that is a measure of the fineness of silk, rayon, or nylon yarn and is equal to the weight in grams of 9000 metres of the yarn – compare TEX [ME *denere*, fr MF *denier*, fr L *denarius*, coin worth ten asses, fr *denarius* containing ten, fr *deni* ten each, fr *decem* ten – more at TEN]

**denigrate** /ˈdenigrayt/ *vt* **1** to cast aspersions on; defame **2** to deny the importance or validity of; belittle ⟨*they ~ a housewife's work*⟩ [L *denigratus*, pp of *denigrare*, fr *de-* + *nigrare* to blacken, fr *nigr-, niger* black] – **denigration** *n*, **denigrative** *adj*, **denigrator** *n*, **denigratory** *adj*

**denim** /ˈdenəm, ˈdenim/ *n* **1** a firm hard-wearing twilled fabric usu of cotton, woven with coloured, esp blue, warp threads and white weft threads **2** *pl* denim trousers or overalls; *esp* jeans [Fr (*serge*) *de Nîmes* serge of Nîmes, city in S France]

**denitrification** /ˌdeeˌnietrifiˈkaysh(ə)n/ *n* an act or the process of denitrifying; *specif* the conversion, (e g by bacteria in the soil) of nitrogen-containing compounds (e g nitrates or nitrites) to chemical compounds containing less oxygen or more hydrogen, usu resulting in the release of nitrogen gas into the atmosphere

**denitrify** /ˌdeeˈnietriˌfie/ *vt* **1** to remove nitrogen or a nitrogen-containing chemical compound from **2** to subject (a nitrogen-containing chemical compound, esp a nitrate or nitrite) to denitrification

**denizen** /ˈdeniz(ə)n/ *n* **1** an inhabitant **2** one allowed to reside in a foreign country; *esp* an alien admitted to rights of citizenship **3** a naturalized plant or animal **4** a person who frequents a place ⟨*~s of Soho nightclubs*⟩ [ME *denysen*, fr MF *denzein*, fr OF, inner, fr *denz* within, fr LL *deintus*, fr L *de-* + *intus* within]

**denominate** /diˈnominayt/ *vt* to give a name to; designate [L

*denominatus*, pp of *denominare*, fr *de-* + *nominare* to name – more at NOMINATE]

**denomination** /diˌnomiˈnaysh(ə)n/ *n* **1** an act of naming or designating **2** a name or designation; *esp* a general name for a category **3** a religious organization uniting a number of local congregations in a single legal and administrative body **4** any of the grades or degrees in a series of values or sizes (e g of money) – **denominational** *adj*, **denominationally** *adv*

**denominational** /diˌnomiˈnaysh(ə)nl/ *adj* relating to a denomination; *specif* offering or consisting of the form of worship of a particular religious denomination ⟨*a ~ school*⟩

**denominationalism** /diˌnominˈaysh(ə)n(ə)lˌiz(ə)m/ *n* **1** adherence to denominational principles or interests **2** the narrowly exclusive emphasizing of religious differences; sectarianism – **denominationalist** *n*

**denominative** /diˈnominətiv/ *adj* **1** conferring or constituting a name **2** *esp of verbs* derived from a noun or adjective [L *de* from + *nomin-, nomen* name] – **denominative** *n*

**denominator** /diˈnomiˌnaytə/ *n* the part of a fraction that is below the line and that indicates how many parts the numerator is divided into; the divisor

**denotation** /ˌdeenohˈtaysh(ə)n/ *n* **1** an act or process of denoting **2** a meaning; *esp* a direct specific meaning as distinct from a suggested or implied meaning (CONNOTATION) **3** a denoting term; a name **4** a sign or indication ⟨*visible ~s of divine wrath*⟩ **5** the totality of subjects to which a term is applicable esp in logic ⟨*the ~ of the word "fir" is the set of trees belonging to this family*⟩ – called also EXTENSION; compare CONNOTATION

**denotative** /diˈnohtətiv/ *adj* **1** denoting or tending to denote **2** relating to denotation

**denote** /diˈnoht/ *vt* **1** to serve as an indication of; signify ⟨*the swollen bellies that ~ starvation*⟩ **2** to serve as an arbitrary mark for; symbolize ⟨*red flares denoting danger*⟩ **3** to serve as a linguistic expression of the mental concept of; mean **synonyms** see CONNOTE [MF *denoter*, fr L *denotare*, fr *de-* + *notare* to note] – **denotement** *n*, **denotive** *adj*

**denouement, dénouement** /ˈday'noohmonh/ *n* **1** the resolution of the main plot in a literary work **2** the outcome of a complex sequence of events [Fr *dénouement*, lit., untying, fr MF *desnouement*, fr *desnouer* to untie, fr OF *desnoer*, fr *des-de-* + *noer* to tie, fr L *nodare*, fr *nodus* knot – more at NET]

**denounce** /diˈnowns/ *vt* **1a** to condemn, esp publicly, as blameworthy or evil **b** to inform against; accuse ⟨*we must ~ him to the authorities*⟩ **2** to announce formally the termination of (e g a treaty) [ME *denouncen*, fr OF *denoncier* to proclaim, fr L *denuntiare*, fr *de-* + *nuntiare* to report – more at ANNOUNCE] – **denouncement** *n*, **denouncer** *n*

**de novo** /di ˈnohvoh/ *adv* over again; anew ⟨*a case tried ~*⟩ [L]

**dens** /denz/ *n, pl* **dentes** /ˈdenteez/ a tooth or toothlike projection; *esp* ODONTOID PROCESS [L, tooth]

**dense** /dens/ *adj* **1** marked by high density, compactness, or crowding together of parts ⟨*~ undergrowth*⟩ **2** stupidly impervious to ideas or impressions; thickheaded **3** *of a mathematical set* having an element between any two elements ⟨*the rational numbers are ~*⟩ **4** demanding concentration to follow or comprehend ⟨*~ prose*⟩ **5** possessing relatively great retarding power upon light waves and consequently relatively high density ⟨*a ~ glass*⟩ **6** having high or relatively high opacity ⟨*a ~ fog*⟩ ⟨*a ~ photographic negative*⟩ **synonyms** see STUPID **antonyms** sparse, tenuous (for 1), subtle, bright (for 2) [L *densus*; akin to Gk *dasys* thick with hair or leaves] – **densely** *adv*, **denseness** *n*

**densify** /ˈdensiˌfie/ *vt* to make denser; *specif* to increase the density of (wood) by pressure, usu with impregnation of a resin – **densification** *n*

**densitometer** /ˌdensiˈtomitə/ *n* an instrument for determining optical or photographic density – **densitometric** *adj*, **densitometry** *n*

**density** /ˈdensəti/ *n* **1** the quality or state of being dense **2** the quantity per unit volume, unit area, or unit length: e g **2a** the ratio of the mass of a particular substance to its volume ⟨*osmium has the highest ~ of any metal*⟩ **b** the distribution of a quantity (e g mass, electricity, or energy) per unit, usu of space **c** the average number of individuals or units per unit of space ⟨*a population ~ of 500 people per square mile*⟩ **3** stupidity **4** the degree to which something (e g a liquid under test) obstructs the passage of light **5** the number of items occurring within a given statistical interval

¹**dent** /dent/ *n* **1** a depression or hollow made by a blow or by

pressure **2** an adverse effect, esp of reduction or diminution ⟨*made a ~ in the weekly budget*⟩ ⟨*a ~ in his pride*⟩ [ME, blow, alter. of *dint*]

*synonyms* Both **dent** and **dint** can mean "hollow made by a blow" ⟨*a* **dent** *in the wing of my car*⟩ or "adverse effect" ⟨*a* **dint** *in his reputation*⟩, but **dint** is the only one used in the phrase **by dint of**, which is connected with the older sense of **dint** "blow, stroke" ⟨*passed the exam* **by dint of** *hard work*⟩.

**²dent** *vt* **1** to make a dent in **2** to have a weakening or diminishing effect on ~ *vi* to form a dent by sinking inwards; become dented

**³dent** *n* TOOTH 3a [Fr, lit., tooth, fr L *dent-, dens*]

**dent-** /dent-/, **denti-, dento-** *comb form* **1** tooth; teeth ⟨*dentiform*⟩ ⟨*dentifrice*⟩ **2** dental and ⟨*dentosurgical*⟩ [ME *denti-*, fr L, fr *dent-, dens* tooth – more at TOOTH]

**¹dental** /'dentl/ *adj* **1** of the teeth or dentistry **2** *of a consonant* articulated with the tip or blade of the tongue against the back of the upper front teeth [L *dentalis*, fr *dent-, dens*] – **dentally** *adv*, **dentalize** *vt*

**²dental** *n* a dental consonant

**dental floss** /flos/ *n* a usu waxed thread used to clean between the teeth

**dental formula** *n* a formulaic expression of the number and kind of teeth of a mammal

**dentalium** /den'tayli-əm/ *n, pl* **dentalia** /-li-ə/ *also* **dentaliums** any of a genus (*Dentalium* of the phylum Mollusca) of widely distributed TOOTH SHELLS (class of burrowing marine IN-VERTEBRATE animals) related to the snails and mussels; *broadly* TOOTH SHELL [NL, genus name, fr L *dentalis*]

**dental technician** *n* a technician who makes dental appliances

**dentate** /'dentayt/, **dentated** *adj* having teeth or pointed conical projections ⟨*~ leaves*⟩ [L *dentatus*, fr *dent-, dens*] – **dentately** *adv*, **dentation** *n*

**dentex** /'denteks/ *n* a large mainly Mediterranean predatory fish (*Dentex dentex*) [NL, fr L *dentex, dentix*, a kind of fish]

**denticle** /'dentikl/ *n* a small tooth or other conical pointed projection [ME, fr L *denticulus*, dim. of *dent-, dens*]

**denticulate** /den'tikyoolət/, **denticulated** /den'tikyoo,laytid/ *adj* **1a** covered with small pointed projections ⟨*a ~shell*⟩ ; *esp* serrate ⟨*~ leaves*⟩ **b** having fine teeth or toothlike projections **2** cut into dentils ⟨*a ~ cornice*⟩ – **denticulately** *adv*, **denticulation** *n*

**dentiform** /'denti,fawm/ *adj* **1** shaped like a tooth **2** divided into dentate parts

**dentifrice** /'denti,fris/ *n* a powder, paste, or liquid for cleaning the teeth [MF, fr L *dentifricium*, fr *denti-* + *fricare* to rub – more at FRICTION]

**dentigerous** /den'tijərəs/ *adj* bearing teeth or toothlike structures

**dentil** /'dentil/ *n* any of a series of small projecting rectangular blocks, esp under a cornice [obs Fr *dentille*, fr MF, dim. of *dent* tooth]

**dentilingual** /,denti'lingwəl/ *adj, linguistics* DENTAL 2 – **dentilingual** *n*

**dentin** /'dentin/ *n, NAm* dentine

**dentine** /'denteen/ *n* a calcium-containing material that is similar to but harder and denser than bone and that composes the main part of a tooth – **dentinal** *adj*

**dentist** /'dentist/ *n* a person who is skilled in and licensed to practise the prevention, diagnosis, and treatment of diseases, injuries, and malformations of the teeth, jaws, and mouth and who makes and inserts false teeth [Fr *dentiste*, fr *dent*]

**dentistry** /'dentistri/ *n* the art or profession of a dentist

**dentition** /den'tish(ə)n/ *n* **1** cutting of teeth **2** the number, kind, and arrangement of teeth (e g of any animal including man) [L *dentition-, dentitio*, fr *dentitus*, pp of *dentire* to cut teeth, fr *dent-, dens*]

**dento-** – see DENT-

**dentulous** /'denchələs/ *adj* having teeth ⟨*a ~ jaw*⟩ [back-formation fr *edentulous*]

**denture** /'denchə, -chooə/ *n* **1** an artificial replacement for one or more teeth **2 dentures** *pl*, **denture** a set of false teeth [Fr *denture* set of teeth (cf Fr *dentier* set of false teeth), fr MF, fr *dent*]

**denuclear·ize, -ise** /,dee'nyoohkli-ə,riez/ *vt* to remove nuclear arms from; prohibit the use of nuclear arms in – **denuclearization** *n*

**denude** /di'nyoohd/ *vt* **1a** to strip of all covering; make bare or naked **b** to lay bare by erosion **c** to strip (land) of forests **2** to

take away something important from [L *denudare*, fr *de-* + *nudus* bare – more at NAKED] – **denudement** *n*, **denuder** *n*

**denumerable** /di'nyoohm(ə)rəbl/ *adj, maths* COUNTABLE b [*de-* + *numerable*] – **denumerability** *n*, **denumerably** *adv*

**denunciate** /di'nunsi,ayt/ *vt* to denounce; esp to condemn publicly [L *denuntiatus*, pp of *denuntiare* to denounce] – **denunciation** *n*, **denunciatory** *adj*

**deny** /di'nie/ *vt* **1** to declare untrue **2** to disclaim connection with or responsibility for **3a** to give a negative answer to **b** to refuse to grant ⟨*they will ~ her food*⟩ **c** to restrain (oneself) from self-indulgence **4** to refuse to accept the existence, truth, or validity of [ME *denyen*, fr OF *denier*, fr L *denegare*, fr *de-* + *negare* to deny – more at NEGATE] – **denyingly** *adv*

**deoch-an-doris** /'dokhən'dawris/ *n, Scot & Irish* DOCH-AN-DORRIS (parting drink)

**deodand** /'dee-oh,dand/ *n* something that had caused a person's death and was therefore in former times confiscated from its owner and given to the Crown for charitable use [AF *deodande*, fr ML *deodandum*, fr L *Deo dandum* that must be given to God]

**deodar** /'dee-ohdah, 'dee-ə-/ *also* **deodara** /,dee-oh'darə/ *n* an E Indian cedar (*Cedrus deodara*) [Hindi *deodār*, fr Skt *devadāru*, lit., timber of the gods, fr *deva* god + *dāru* wood]

**deodorant** /dee'ohdərənt/ *n* a preparation that destroys or masks unpleasant smells (e g on the body or in the air) – **deodorant** *adj*

**deodor·ize, -ise** /dee'ohdəriez/ *vt* **1** to eliminate or prevent the offensive smell of **2** to make (something felt to be unpleasant) more acceptable, esp by making bland – **deodorization** *n*, **deodorizer** *n*

**deontic** /,dee'ontik/ *adj* relating to duty or obligation; *also* being the branch of logic concerned with this area [Gk *deont-, deon* that which is obligatory, fr neut of prp of *dein* to lack, be needful – more at DEUTER-]

**deontology** /,dee-on'tolǝji/ *n* a theory or examination of the nature of moral obligation and duty – **deontological** *adj*, **deontologist** *n*

**Deo volente** /,day-oh vo'lenti/ *adv* God being willing [L]

**deoxid·ize, -ise** /,dee'oksidiez/ *vt* to remove oxygen from – **deoxidation** *n*, **deoxidizer** *n*

**deoxy-** /dee-oksi-/, **desoxy-** /desoksi-/ *comb form* containing fewer hydroxide groups in the molecule ⟨*deoxyribonucleic acid*⟩ [ISV]

**deoxycorticosterone** /,dee,oksi,kawti'kostə,rohn/ *n* a STEROID hormone, $C_{21}H_{30}O_3$, that is produced by the outer part (CORTEX) of the ADRENAL GLANDS and causes the retention in the body of water and sodium [ISV]

**deoxycortone** /,dee,oksi'kaw,tohn/ *n* deoxycorticosterone [by shortening]

**deoxygenate** /,dee'oksijinayt/ *vt* to deoxidize – **deoxygenation** *n*

**deoxygenated** /,dee'oksijin,aytid/ *adj, of blood* having little or no oxygen attached to the haemoglobin molecules; being the dark red blood normally found in the veins

**deoxyribonuclease** /,dee,oksi,rieboh'nyooklee,ayz/ *n* an ENZYME that promotes the breakdown of DNA into the separate NUCLEOTIDE molecules of which it is composed [*deoxyribonucleic acid* + *-ase*]

**deoxyribonucleic acid** /dee,oksi,riebohnyooh'klayik/ *n* DNA [*deoxyribose* + *nucleic acid*]

**deoxyribonucleoside** /,dee,oksi,rieboh'nyookli-əzied/ *n* any of several NUCLEOSIDES that contain deoxyribose

**deoxyribonucleotide** /dee,oksi,rieboh'nyoohkli-ə,tied/ *n* any of several NUCLEOTIDES that contain deoxyribose and some of which are constituents of DNA

**deoxyribose** /dee,oksi'riebohz/ *n* a sugar, $C_5H_{10}O_4$, that is part of the repeating structure that forms the long chains of a DNA molecule [ISV *deoxy-* + *ribose*]

**depart** /di'paht/ *vi* **1a** to go away; leave **b** *euph* to die **2** to turn aside; deviate – *+ from* ~ *vt, archaic & NAm* to go away from; leave ⟨*~ this life*⟩ ⟨*after* ~ing *Washington for his ranch*⟩ *synonyms* see ¹GO *antonyms* arrive, remain [ME *departen* to divide, go away, fr OF *departir*, fr *de-* + *partir* to divide, fr L *partire*, fr *part-, pars* part]

**¹departed** /di'pahtid/ *adj* **1** bygone **2** *euph* recently dead

**²departed** *n, pl* **departed** *euph* a person who has recently died

**department** /di'pahtmənt/ *n* **1** a functional or territorial division: e g **1a** a major administrative division of a government ⟨*the* Department *of Health and Social Security*⟩ **b** a major territorial administrative subdivision (e g in France) **c** a division of a university, college, or school giving instruction in a particular subject **d** a section of a department store **e** a territorial subdivision made for the administration and training of military units **f** a division of an institution (eg a hospital) or business that provides a specified service or deals with a specified subject ⟨*X-ray* ~⟩ ⟨*sales* ~⟩ **2** *informal* a distinct sphere or province (eg of activity or thought) ⟨*don't ask me about DIY – that's my wife's* ~⟩ [Fr *département*, fr MF, fr *departir*] – **departmental** *adj*, **departmentally** *adv*

**departmental·ize, -ise** /ˌdeepaht'mentəliez/ *vt* to divide into departments – **departmentalization** *n*

**department store,** *Br also* **departmental store** *n* a large shop selling a wide variety of goods arranged in several departments

**departure** /di'pahchə/ *n* **1a** the act of going away or setting out on a journey **b** a ship's position in latitude and longitude at the beginning of a voyage used as a basis for calculations of its subsequent position **c** a setting out (eg on a new course of action) **2** the distance due east or west travelled by a ship in its course **3** deviation or divergence **4** *archaic* death

**depasture** /ˌdee'pahschə/ *vt* **1** to graze (cattle) or put to graze; *also* to exhaust by grazing **2** to have sufficient grazing for; support ~ *vi* to graze – **depasturage** *n*

**depend** /di'pend/ *vi* **1** to be contingent **2** to be pending or undecided **3a** to place reliance or trust – + *on* or *upon* **b** to be dependent, *esp* for financial support – + *on* or *upon* **4** to hang down [ME *dependen*, fr MF *dependre*, modif of L *dependēre*, fr *de-* + *pendēre* to hang – more at PENDANT]

    **usage** In speech, **depend** is often used either alone ⟨"*what do they eat?*" "*It depends!*"⟩ or directly followed by an indirect question ⟨*it depends what you mean*⟩. In formal writing, writers on usage advise that **depend** should be followed by *on* or *upon* ⟨*it depends on what you mean*⟩. **synonyms** see RELY ON

**dependable** /di'pendəbl/ *adj* capable of being depended on; reliable – **dependability** *n*, **dependableness** *n*, **dependably** *adv*

**dependant,** *chiefly NAm* **dependent** /di'pendənt/ *n* someone who is dependent; *esp* a person who relies on another for support

**dependence,** *chiefly NAm* **dependance** /di'pendəns/ *n* **1** the quality or state of being dependent; *esp* the quality or state of being influenced by or subject to another **2** reliance, trust **3a** drug addiction **b** HABITUATION 2b

**dependency,** *chiefly NAm* **dependancy** /di'pend(ə)nsi/ *n* **1** DEPENDENCE 1 **2** something that is dependent on something else; *specif* a territorial unit under the jurisdiction of a nation but not formally annexed to it

**dependent** /di'pend(ə)nt/ *adj* **1a** determined or conditioned by another; contingent – often + *on* or *upon* **b** relying on another for support – often + *on* or *upon* **c** subject to another's jurisdiction **d** SUBORDINATE 3a ⟨*a* ~ *clause*⟩ **2** *formal or literary* hanging down [ME *dependant*, fr MF, prp of *dependre*] – **dependently** *adv*

**dependent variable** *n* a variable whose value is determined by that of one or more INDEPENDENT VARIABLES in a function ⟨*in* $z = x^2 + 3xy + y^2$, *z is the* ~⟩ – compare INDEPENDENT VARIABLE, DUMMY VARIABLE

**depersonal·ize, -ise** /ˌdee'puhsənl·iez/ *vt* **1** to deprive of the sense of personal identity ⟨*schools that* ~ *students*⟩ **2** to make impersonal – **depersonalization** *n*

**depict** /di'pikt/ *vt* **1** to represent by a picture **2** to describe [L *depictus*, pp of *depingere*, fr *de-* + *pingere* to paint – more at PAINT] – **depicter** *n*, **depiction** *n*

**depigmentation** /ˌdee,pigmən'taysh(ə)n/ *n* loss of normal pigmentation

**depilate** /'depilayt/ *vt* to remove hair from [L *depilatus*, pp of *depilare*, fr *de-* + *pilus* hair – more at PILE] – **depilation** *n*

**depilatory** /di'pilət(ə)ri/ *n* an agent (eg a cream or wax) for removing hair, wool, or bristles – **depilatory** *adj*

**deplane** /ˌdee'playn/ *vi, chiefly NAm* to get off an aircraft

**deplete** /di'pleet/ *vt* **1** to lessen markedly in quantity, content, power, or value **2** to empty wholly or partially [L *depletus*, pp of *deplēre*, fr *de-* + *plēre* to fill – more at FULL] – **depletable** *adj*, **depletion** *n*, **depletive** *adj*

**deplorable** /di'plawrəbl/ *adj* **1** fit to be deplored; lamentable **2** extremely bad or wretched – **deplorableness** *n*, **deplorably** *adv*

**deplore** /di'plaw/ *vt* **1a** to feel or express grief for **b** to regret strongly **2** to disapprove of strongly [MF or L; MF *deplorer*, fr L *deplorare*, fr *de-* + *plorare* to cry out (cf EXPLORE, IMPLORE)] – **deplorer** *n*, **deploringly** *adv*

**deploy** /di'ploy/ *vt* **1a** to extend (a military unit), esp in width **b** to place in battle formation or appropriate positions **2** to spread out, utilize, or arrange as if deploying troops ~ *vi* to move in being deployed [Fr *déployer*, fr L *displicare* to scatter – more at DISPLAY] – **deployable** *adj*, **deployment** *n*

**deplume** /ˌdee'ploohm/ *vt* **1** to pluck off the feathers of **2** to strip of possessions, honours, or attributes [ME *deplumen*, fr MF *deplumer*, fr ML *deplumare*, fr L *de-* + *pluma* feather – more at FLEECE]

**depolar·ize, -ise** /ˌdee'pohləriez/ *vt* **1** to prevent or remove POLARIZATION of (eg a dry battery or cell membrane) **2** to demagnetize – **depolarization** *n*, **depolarizer** *n*

**depolitic·ize, -ise** /ˌdeepə'litisiez/ *vt* to remove the political character of; take out of the realm of politics ⟨~ *foreign aid*⟩

¹**deponent** /di'pohnənt/ *adj* occurring with passive voice forms but with active voice meaning ⟨*the* ~ *verbs in Latin and Greek*⟩ [LL *deponent-, deponens*, fr L, prp of *deponere* to put down, fr *de-* + *ponere* to put – more at POSITION]

²**deponent** *n* **1** a deponent verb **2** a person who gives evidence, esp written evidence, under oath [(2) ML *deponent-, deponens*, prp of *deponere* to testify – more at DEPOSE]

**depopulate** /ˌdee'popyoolayt/ *vt* to reduce considerably the population of [ML *depopulatus*, pp of *depopulari* to reduce the population of, ravage, fr L, to ravage, fr *de-* + *populari* to ravage] – **depopulation** *n*, **depopulator** *n*

**deport** /di'pawt/ *vt* **1** to behave or conduct (oneself) in a specified manner **2a** to expel (eg an alien) from a country by legal deportation – compare BANISH **b** to transport (eg a convicted criminal) to a penal colony or place of exile [(1) MF *deporter*, fr L *deportare* to carry away, fr *de-* + *portare* to carry – more at FARE; (2) L *deportare*]

**deportation** /ˌdeepaw'taysh(ə)n/ *n* legal expulsion from a country of a person (eg an alien) whose presence is unlawful or deemed undesirable

**deportee** /ˌdeepaw'tee/ *n* a person who has been deported or is under sentence of deportation

**deportment** /-mənt/ *n* **1** the manner in which one conducts oneself; behaviour **2** the manner in which one stands, sits, or walks; posture ⟨*she was always slouching and had very poor* ~⟩ □ compare BEARING

**deposal** /di'pohz(ə)l/ *n* an act of deposing from office

**depose** /di'pohz/ *vt* **1** to remove from a position of authority (eg a throne) **2** *law* to testify to under oath or by affidavit; *broadly* to affirm, assert ~ *vi* to bear witness [(1) ME *deposen*, fr OF *deposer*, fr LL *deponere* (perf indic *deposui*), fr L, to put down; (2 & *vi*) ME *deposen*, fr ML *deponere*, fr LL]

¹**deposit** /di'pozit/ *vt* **1** to place, esp for safekeeping or as a pledge; *esp* to put in a bank **2a** to lay down; place **b** to let fall (eg sediment) ~ *vi* to become deposited; settle [L *depositus*, pp of *deponere*] – **depositor** *n*

²**deposit** *n* **1** the state of being deposited **2a** money deposited in a bank **b** money given as a pledge or down payment **3** a place of deposit; a depository **4** an act of depositing **5a** something laid down; *esp* material deposited by a natural process **b** a natural accumulation (eg of iron ore, coal, or gas)

**deposit account** *n, chiefly Br* an account (eg in a bank) on which interest is usu payable and from which withdrawals can be made usu only by prior arrangement or presentation of a bankbook or special form – compare CURRENT ACCOUNT

**depositary** /di'pozit(ə)ri/ *n* a person to whom something is entrusted

**deposition** /ˌdepə'zish(ə)n, ˌdee-/ *n* **1** an act of removing from a position of authority **2** a statement given as evidence; *esp* a written statement made under oath and presented as evidence in court **3** an act or process of depositing **4** something deposited; a deposit – **depositional** *adj*

**depository** /di'pozit(ə)ri/ *n* **1** a place where something is deposited, esp for safekeeping **2** a depositary **synonyms** see REPOSITORY

¹**depot** /'depoh/ *n* **1a** a place for the storage of military supplies **b** a place for the reception and training of military recruits **2** a place for storing goods; a warehouse **3a** *Br* a large garage or similar building used for the maintenance and storage of buses, trains, etc **b** *NAm* a station [Fr *dépôt*, fr ML *depositum*, fr L, neut of *depositus*]

²**depot** *adj, of a drug or a dose of a drug* designed to act over a long period ⟨*a* ~ *injection of penicillin*⟩

**deprave** /di'prayv/ *vt* to corrupt morally [ME *depraven*, fr MF *depraver*, fr L *depravare* to pervert, fr *de-* + *pravus* crooked, bad – more at PRAIRIE] – **depravation** *n*, **depravement** *n*, **depraver** *n*

**depraved** /di'prayvd/ *adj* marked by moral corruption or evil; *esp* perverted – **depravedly** *adv*, **depravedness** *n*

**depravity** /di'pravəti/ *n* **1** the quality or state of being depraved **2** a morally corrupt act or practice

**deprecate** /'deprikayt/ *vt* **1** to express disapproval of, esp mildly or regretfully **2** to disparage, depreciate [L *deprecatus*, pp of *deprecari* to avert by prayer, fr *de-* + *precari* to pray – more at PRAY ] – **deprecatingly** *adv*, **deprecation** *n*

*synonyms* From their different origins (**deprecate** from the Latin *de-* + "pray" and **depreciate** from the Latin *de-* + "price") and their earlier separate meanings (**deprecate** "express disapproval of" and **depreciate** "lower the worth of"), **deprecate** and **depreciate** have converged in meaning, so that they can now both mean "disparage" or "belittle". Writers on usage advise that only **depreciate** should be used in this sense ⟨*don't* **depreciate** *yourself – you can do it if you try*⟩; but the two words are now freely interchangeable in the sense "disparage oneself" ⟨*a shy* **self-deprecating** *manner*⟩.

**deprecatory** /'deprikayt(ə)ri/ *adj* **1** seeking to avert disapproval; apologetic **2** serving to deprecate; disapproving – **deprecatorily** *adv*

**depreciate** /di'prees(h)iayt/ *vt* **1** to lower the price or estimated value of **2** to represent as of little value, esp as of less value than usu assigned; disparage ~ *vi* to fall in value *synonyms* see DEPRECATE [LL *depretiatus*, pp of *depretiare*, fr L *de-* + *pretium* price – more at PRICE] – **depreciable** *adj*, **depreciatingly** *adv*, **depreciation** *n*, **depreciative** *adj*, **depreciator** *n*, **depreciatory** *adj*

**depreciation** /di,prees(h)i'aysh(ə)n/ *n* the reduction in the value of capital goods over time resulting from their use in production

**depredate** /'depridayt/ *vt* to lay waste; plunder, ravage ~ *vi* to engage in plunder [LL *depraedatus*, pp of *depraedari*, fr L *de-* + *praedari* to plunder – more at PREY] – **depredation** *n*, **depredator** *n*, **depredatory** *adj*

**depress** /di'pres/ *vt* **1a** to press down ⟨~ *a typewriter key*⟩ **b** to cause to sink to a lower position **2** to lessen the activity or strength of **3** to sadden, dispirit **4** to decrease the market value or marketability of [ME *depressen*, fr MF *depresser*, fr L *depressus*, pp of *deprimere* to press down, fr *de-* + *premere* to press – more at PRESS] – **depressible** *adj*, **depressingly** *adv*

**depressant** /di'pres(ə)nt/ *n* something that has the effect of depressing; *specif* a drug that reduces bodily activity or causes depression – compare STIMULANT – **depressant** *adj*

**depressed** /di'prest/ *adj* **1** low in spirits; sad, dejected; *specif* suffering from depression **2a** vertically flattened ⟨*a* ~ *cactus*⟩ **b** having the central part lower than the outside edge **c** lying flat or prostrate ⟨*a* ~ *plant*⟩ **d** flattened from front to back **3** suffering from economic depression ⟨*a* ~ *area*⟩ **4** being below the standard ⟨*his reading achievement is* ~⟩

**depressing** /di'presing/ *adj* that depresses; *esp* causing emotional depression ⟨*a* ~ *story*⟩ – **depressingly** *adv*

**depression** /di'presh(ə)n/ *n* **1a** the angular distance of a celestial object below the horizon **b** the size of an angle of depression **2** an act of depressing or a state of being depressed: e g **2a** a pressing down; a lowering **b(1)** a state of feeling sad; dejection **b(2)** a mental disorder marked by excessive sadness, lethargy, difficulty in thinking and concentration, and feelings of dejection and inadequacy **c(1)** a reduction in activity, amount, quality, or force **c(2)** a lowering of vitality or functional activity **3** a depressed place or part; a hollow **4** LOW 1b ⟨*a* ~ *over Iceland*⟩ **5** a period of low general economic activity marked esp by rising levels of unemployment: e g **5a** *cap* in the 1930s in Britain and the USA **b** in most Western nations in the late 1970s and early 1980s

**¹depressive** /di'presiv/ *adj* **1** tending to depress **2** relating to psychological depression – **depressively** *adv*

**²depressive** *n* one who is subject to periods of psychological depression

**depressor** /di'presə/ *n* something that depresses: e g **a** a muscle that draws down a body part – compare LEVATOR **b** a device or instrument for pressing a part down or aside **c** a nerve or nerve fibre that decreases the activity or the tone of the organ or part it supplies impulses to [LL, fr L *depressus*]

**deprivation** /,depri'vaysh(ə)n/ *n* **1** an act or instance of depriving; a loss **2** the state of being deprived; privation

**deprive** /di'priev/ *vt* **1** to take something away from ⟨*the accident* ~d *her of her eyesight*⟩ **2** to remove (e g a clergyman) from office **3** to withhold something from ⟨*he threatened to* ~ *them of their rights*⟩ [ME *depriven*, fr ML *deprivare*, fr L *de-*

+ *privare* to deprive – more at PRIVATE] – **deprival** *n*

**deprived** /di'prievd/ *adj* marked by deprivation, esp of the necessities of life or of beneficial environmental influences; underprivileged ⟨*culturally* ~ *children*⟩ *synonyms* see POOR

**de profundis** /'day prə'foondees/ *adv* out of the depths of grief, misery, etc [LL, out of the depths (the opening words of Psalm 130)]

**depth** /depth/ *n* **1a(1)** a deep place in a body of water – chiefly in *the depths of the ocean* **a(2)** a part that is far from the outside or surface ⟨*the* ~s *of the woods*⟩ **b(1)** a profound or intense state (e g of thought or feeling) ⟨*the* ~s *of despair*⟩; *also* a reprehensibly low condition ⟨*hadn't realized he would sink to such* ~s⟩ **b(2)** the part marked by the worst, the most intensive, or the severest degree ⟨*the* ~s *of winter*⟩ **2a** the perpendicular measurement downwards from a surface **b** the direct linear measurement from the point of viewing, usu from front to back **3** the quality of being deep **4** the degree of intensity ⟨~ *of a colour*⟩; *also* the quality of being profound (e g in insight) or full (e g of knowledge) [ME, prob fr *dep* deep] – **depthless** *adj* – **in depth 1** extending over a considerable distance ⟨*fortifications in depth*⟩ **2** with great thoroughness ⟨*haven't studied it in depth*⟩ – **out of one's depth 1** in water that is deeper than one's height **2** beyond one's ability to understand or cope – **plumb the depths (of)** to reach the lowest point (of) ⟨*this play plumbs the depths of nastiness*⟩

**depth bomb** *n* DEPTH CHARGE

**depth charge** *n* an explosive projectile for use underwater, esp against submarines

**depth finder** *n* an instrument for determining the depth of a body of water; *specif* ECHO SOUNDER

**depth psychology** *n* psychoanalysis; *broadly* psychological research or therapy based on the investigation of the unconscious

**depurate** /'depyooər,ayt/ *vt* to purify (e g the body) ~ *vi* to become free of impurities [ML *depuratus*, pp of *depurare*, fr L *de-* + *purare* to purify, fr *purus* clean, pure]

**deputation** /,depyoo'taysh(ə)n/ *n* **1** the act of appointing a deputy **2** *taking sing or pl vb* a group of people appointed to represent others

**¹depute** /di'pyooht/ *vt* to delegate [ME *deputen* to appoint, fr MF *deputer*, fr LL *deputare* to assign, fr L, to consider (as), fr *de-* + *putare* to consider – more at PAVE]

**²depute** *n*, *Scot* a deputy ⟨~ *procurator fiscal*⟩ [ME, fr MF *deputé*, *depute*, pp of *deputer*]

**deput-ize, -ise** /'depyoo,tiez/ *vt* to appoint as deputy ~ *vi* to act as deputy – often + *for* – **deputization** *n*

**deputy** /'depyooti/ *n* **1a** a person appointed as a substitute with power to act for another or others **b** a second-in-command or assistant who usu takes charge when a superior is absent **2** a member of the lower house of some legislative assemblies (e g the French Chamber of Deputies) [ME, fr MF *deputé*]

**deracinate** /,dee'rasinayt/ *vt*, *formal* to uproot [Fr *déraciner*, fr MF *desraciner*, fr *des-* de- + *racine* root, fr LL *radicina*, fr L *radic-*, *radix* – more at ROOT] – **deracination** *n*

**derail** /,dee'rayl/ *vt* **1** to cause (e g a train) to leave the rails **2** to throw off course ~ *vi* to leave the rails [Fr *dérailler*, fr *dé-* de- + *rail*, fr E] – **derailment** *n*

**derailleur** /di'raylə/ *n* a mechanism for changing gear on a bicycle that operates by moving the chain from one set of exposed gears to another; *also* a bicycle with such a mechanism [Fr *dérailleur*, fr *dérailler*]

**derange** /di'raynj/ *vt* **1** to disarrange ⟨*hatless, with tie* ~d – G W Stonier⟩ **2** to disturb the operation or functions of **3** to make insane [Fr *déranger*, fr OF *desrengier*, fr *de-* + *reng* place – more at RANK] – **derangement** *n*

**derate** /,dee'rayt/ *vt* to lower or abolish rates on (property)

**deration** /,dee'rash(ə)n/ *vt* to end rationing of (e g food)

**derby** /'dahbi/ *n* **1a** *cap* a flat race for 3-year-old horses over a distance of 1¹/₂ miles (2,400 metres) held annually at Epsom in England; *broadly*, *often not cap* any of several important flat races for horses **b** a usu informal race or contest for a specified category of contestant ⟨*donkey* ~⟩ **2** a sporting match against a major local rival (e g in soccer) **3** *chiefly NAm* a bowler hat [Edward Stanley, 12th Earl of *Derby* †1834]

**Derby** *n* a close-textured pale yellow cheese with a mild flavour that develops as the cheese matures ⟨*sage* ~⟩ [*Derby*, city & county in England]

**deregister** /,dee'rejistə/ *vt* to remove (e g one's name) from a register – **deregistration** *n*

**deregulate** /ˌdee'regyoolayt/ vt to remove from legal juris- diction by law – **deregulation** n

**¹derelict** /'derəlikt/ adj 1 abandoned, esp by the owner or occupant; run-down 2 *chiefly NAm* lacking a sense of duty; negligent [L *derelictus*, pp of *derelinquere* to abandon, fr *de-* + *relinquere* to leave – more at RELINQUISH]

**²derelict** n 1 something voluntarily abandoned; *specif* a ship abandoned on the high seas 2 a tramp, vagrant

**dereliction** /ˌderə'liksh(ə)n/ n 1a an intentional abandonment b the state of being abandoned 2 a recession of water leaving permanently dry land 3a intentional or conscious neglect ⟨~ *of duty*⟩ b a fault, shortcoming

**derepress** /ˌdeeri'pres/ vt to activate (a gene) by releasing from a blocked state – **derepression** n

**derestrict** /ˌdeeri'strikt/ vt to remove restrictions from; *esp* to remove or not apply a speed limit on vehicles in a particular road – **derestriction** n

**deride** /di'ried/ vt to subject to usu bitter or contemptuous ridicule; scorn **synonyms** see ²RIDICULE [L *deridēre*, fr *de-* + *ridēre* to laugh – more at RIDICULOUS] – **derider** n, **deridingly** adv

**de rigueur** /də ri'guh (*Fr* də rigœːr)/ adj prescribed or required by fashion, etiquette, or custom; proper ⟨*instructions as to when and where a dinner jacket is* ~⟩ [Fr, compulsory, lit., of strictness]

**derision** /di'rizh(ə)n/ n 1 an act of deriding 2 a state of being derided [ME, fr MF, fr LL *derision-, derisio*, fr L *derisus*, pp of *deridēre*]

**derisive** /di'riesiv, -ziv/ adj expressing or causing derision; mocking – **derisively** adv, **derisiveness** n

*usage* The pronunciation /di'riəsiv/ is recommended for BBC broad- casters.

**derisory** /di'riez(ə)ri/ adj 1 derisive ⟨*scornful* ~ *laughter*⟩ 2 worthy of derision; ridiculous; *specif* contemptibly small ⟨*a* ~ *pay offer*⟩

**derivation** /ˌderi'vaysh(ə)n/ n 1a(1) the formation of a word from another word or root form, esp by the addition of a word part (e g a prefix) often producing a different part of speech a(2) the history of a word; ETYMOLOGY 1 a(3) an act of ascertaining or stating the derivation of a word b the relation of a word to the word or root from which it has been derived ⟨*hardness is related to* hard *by* ~⟩ – compare INFLECTION 3c 2a a source or origin b descent ⟨*a family of Scottish* ~⟩ 3 something derived; a derivative 4 an act or process of deriving 5 a sequence of statements (e g in logic or mathematics) showing that a result (e g a formula) follows necessarily from accepted premises – **deri- vational** adj

**¹derivative** /di'rivətiv/ adj 1 formed by derivation 2 made up of or marked by derived elements; *esp, derog* not original; borrowing from other sources – **derivatively** adv, **derivative- ness** n

**²derivative** n 1 a word formed by derivation 2 something derived 3 the limit of the ratio of the change in a function to the corresponding change in its INDEPENDENT VARIABLE as the latter change approaches zero, that can be used to find the slope of a curve at any point, and is fundamental to the ideas of CALCULUS 4a a chemical substance related structurally to another substance and theoretically derivable from it b a sub- stance that can be made from another substance in one or more steps

**derive** /di'riev/ vt 1a to take or receive, esp from a specified source b to obtain from a specified source; *specif* to obtain (a chemical substance) actually or theoretically from a parent substance 2 to infer or deduce 3 to trace the derivation ~ 4 to form by derivation ~ vi to come as a derivative – usu + *from* [ME *deriven*, fr MF *deriver*, fr L *derivare*, fr *de-* + *rivus* stream – more at RISE] – **derivable** adj, **deriver** n

**derived unit** n a unit (e g newton, pascal, or watt) defined in terms of the basic units of a system (e g the SI system)

**derm** /duhm/ n 1 DERMIS (inside layer of skin) 2 SKIN 3a 3 CUTICLE 1a [NL *derma* & *dermis*]

**derm-, derma-, dermo-** *comb form* dermat- ⟨*dermal*⟩ ⟨*dermotropic*⟩ [NL, fr Gk *derm-, dermo-*, fr *derma*, fr *derein* to skin – more at TEAR]

**-derm** *comb form* (→ n) skin; layer ⟨*ecto*derm⟩ ⟨*pachy*derm⟩ [deriv of Gk *derma*]

**derma** /'duhmə/ n DERMIS (inner layer of skin) [NL, fr Gk]

**-derma** /-duhmə/ *comb form* (→ n) pl **-dermas, -dermata** /-duh'mahtə/ skin; skin ailment ⟨*sclero*derma⟩ [NL, fr Gk *dermat-, derma* skin]

**dermal** /'duhməl/ adj 1 of skin, esp the DERMIS (inner layer of skin(; cutaneous 2 EPIDERMAL

**dermat-** /duhmət-/, **dermato-** *comb form* skin ⟨*dermatitis*⟩ ⟨*dermatology*⟩ [Gk, fr *dermat-, derma*]

**dermatitis** /ˌduhmə'tietəs/ n a disease or inflammation of the skin [NL]

**dermatoglyphics** /ˌduhmətə'glifiks/ n pl 1 skin patterns; *esp* the patterns of the scale of the palms of the hand and the soles of the feet 2 *taking sing vb* the scientific study of skin patterns [*dermat-* + Gk *glyphein* to carve + E *-ics* – more at CLEAVE] – **dermatoglyphic** adj, **dermatoglyphicist** n

**dermatoid** /'duhmə,toyd/ adj resembling skin

**dermatology** /ˌduhmə'toləji/ n a branch of medicine dealing with the skin, its diseases, and their treatment – **derma- tological, dermatologic** adj, **dermatologist** n

**dermatome** /'duhmə,tohm/ n the side wall of a SOMITE (segment of an embryo) from which the dermis is produced [ISV *dermat-* + *-ome*] – **dermatomic** adj

**dermatophyte** /'duh'matəfiet/ n a fungus parasitic on the skin or skin derivatives (e g hair or nails) [ISV] – **dermatophytic** adj

**dermatosis** /ˌduhmə'tohsis/ n, pl **dermatoses** /-seez/ a disease of the skin [NL]

**-dermatous** /'duhmətəs/ *comb form* (→ adj) having (such) a type of skin ⟨*sclero*dermatous⟩ [Gk *dermat-, derma* skin]

**dermestid** /ˌduh'mestid/ n any of a family (Dermestidae) of beetles with clubbed antennae that are very destructive to dried meat, fur, fabrics, and insect collections [deriv of Gk *dermēstēs*, a leather-eating worm, lit., skin eater, fr *derm-* + *edmenai* to eat – more at EAT] – **dermestid** adj

**dermis** /'duhmis/ n the inner layer of the skin containing blood vessels and SENSE ORGANS [NL, fr LL *-dermis*]

**-dermis** /-duhmis/ *comb form* (→ n) layer of skin or tissue of an organism ⟨*epi*dermis⟩ [LL, fr Gk, fr *derma*]

**dermo-** /'duhmoh-, 'duhmə-/ – see DERM-

**dermoid** /'duh,moyd/ *also* **dermoidal** /ˌduh'moydl/ adj 1 made or derived from skin ⟨*a* ~ *tumour*⟩ 2 resembling skin

**dernier cri** /ˌdeənyay 'kree (*Fr* dɛrnje kri)/ n the newest fashion [Fr, lit., last cry]

**derogate** /'derəgayt/ vt, *formal* to disparage ~ vi 1 detract; take away a desirable part 2 to deviate or go astray from (e g a principle or standard) □ (vi 1 & 2) + *from* [LL *derogatus*, pp of *derogare*, fr L, to annul (a law), detract, fr *de-* + *rogare* to ask, propose (a law) – more at RIGHT] – **derogation** n, **derogative** adj

**derogatory** /di'rogət(ə)ri/ adj 1 tending to derogate from something; detracting 2 expressive of a low opinion; disparag- ing – **derogatorily** adv

**derrick** /'derik/ n 1 a hoisting apparatus employing a tackle rigged at the end of a beam 2 a framework or tower over a deep drill hole (e g of an oil well) for supporting boring tackle or for hoisting and lowering [obs *derrick* hangman, gallows, fr *Derick*, surname of 17th-c E hangman]

**derriere, derrière** /'deri-eə/ n, *euph* the buttocks [Fr *derrière*, fr *derrière*, adj, hinder, fr OF *deriere*, adv, behind, fr L *de retro*, fr *de* from + *retro* back]

**derring-do** /ˌdering 'dooh/ n daring action; daring ⟨*deeds of* ~⟩ [alter. of ME *dorring don* daring to do, fr *dorring* (gerund of *dorren* to dare) + *don* to do]

**derringer** /'derinjə/ n a short-barrelled pocket pistol of large calibre [Henry *Deringer* †1868 US inventor]

**derris** /'deris/ n 1 any of a large genus (*Derris*) of tropical Eura- sian and African shrubs and woody climbing plants of the pea family, including sources of poisons and esp commercial sources of the insecticide rotenone 2 a preparation of derris roots and stems used as an insecticide [NL, genus name, fr Gk, skin, fr *derein* to skin – more at TEAR]

**derry** /'deri/ n, *Austr* a dislike or prejudice – esp in *have a derry on someone* [perh suggested by *derry down*, a common refrain in old songs]

**derv** /duhv/ n fuel oil used by heavy road vehicles with diesel engines [*d*iesel-*e*ngined *r*oad *v*ehicle]

**dervish** /'duhvish/ n 1 a member of a Muslim religious order noted for its devotional practices (e g bodily movements leading to a trance) 2 someone who or something that whirls or dances in a way that suggests the abandonment of a dervish [Turk *derviş*, lit., beggar, fr Per *darvēsh*]

**desalinate** /ˌdee'salinayt/ vt to desalt – **desalination** n, **desalinator** n

**desalt** /ˌdee'sawlt/ vt to remove salt from – **desalter** n

**descale** /ˌdee'skayl/ vt to remove scale from ⟨*it's high time we* ~d *the kettle*⟩

**¹descant** /'des,kant/ *n* **1a** the art of composing or improvising music in which two or more independent melodic lines are combined; *also* the music so composed or improvised **b** a soprano or treble **c** an additional melodic line superimposed on a simple melody and usu sung by some or all of the sopranos **2** discourse or comment on a theme [ME *dyscant*, fr ONF & ML; ONF *descant*, fr ML *discantus*, fr L *dis-* + *cantus* song – more at CHANT]

**²descant** /des'kant, dis-/ *vi* **1a** to sing or play a descant **b** to sing or warble **2** to talk or write at considerable length; dilate ⟨*he* ~ed *to his heart's content on his favourite topic* – G B Shaw⟩

**descend** /di'send/ *vi* **1** to pass from a higher place or level to a lower one ⟨~ed *from the platform*⟩ **2** to pass in discussion from the general to the particular **3a** to come down from a stock (e g a family) or a source; derive – usu pass ⟨*man* ~s *from the apes*⟩ **b(1)** to pass by inheritance **b(2)** to pass by transmission ⟨*these songs* ~ed *from early ballads*⟩ **4** to incline, lead, or extend downwards ⟨*the road* ~s *to the river*⟩ **5a** to come down or make a sudden attack in the manner of an army – usu + *on* or *upon* ⟨*the plague* ~ed *upon them*⟩ **b** to make a sudden disconcerting visit or appearance – usu + *on* or *upon*; often humorous **6** to proceed from higher to lower in a sequence or gradation **7a** to sink in status or dignity; stoop ⟨*wouldn't* ~ *to such abusive language*⟩ **b** to worsen and sink in condition or estimation ⟨*they* ~ed *from prosperity to poverty*⟩ ~ *vt* to pass, move, or extend down or down along ⟨*he* ~ed *the steps*⟩ [ME *descenden*, fr OF *descendre*, fr L *descendere*, fr *de-* + *scandere* to climb – more at SCAN] – **descendible** *adj*

**descendant**, *NAm also* **descendent** /di'send(ə)nt/ *n* **1** one descended from another or from a common stock **2** one deriving directly from a precursor or prototype ⟨*the spinal column is the* ~ *of the notochord*⟩ [Fr & L; Fr *descendant*, fr LL *descendent-*, *descendens*, fr L, prp of *descendere*]

**descended** /di'sendid/ *adj* having an origin; sprung *from* ⟨*was* ~ *from an ancient family*⟩

**descendent** *also* **descendant** /di'send(ə)nt/ *adj* **1** moving or directed downwards **2** proceeding from an ancestor or source

**descender** /di'sendə/ *n* the part of a lower-case letter (e g p) that descends below the main body of the letter; *also* a letter that has such a part

**descendeur** /,deson'duh/ *n* any of several usu metal devices through which a mountaineer's or potholer's rope may be passed to allow a controlled descent in abseiling [Fr, fr *descendre* to descend]

**descent** /di'sent/ *n* **1** the act or process of descending **2** a downward step (e g in station or value); a decline ⟨~ *of the family to actual poverty*⟩ **3a** the fact or process of derivation from an ancestral stock; lineage ⟨*of French* ~⟩ **b** transmission or devolution of an estate by inheritance, usu in the descending line **c** a transmission from a usu earlier source that has had a shaping or developing effect; a derivation **4a** a downward inclination; a slope **b** a descending way (e g a stairway) **5a** a sudden disconcerting visit or appearance – often humorous **b** a hostile raid or predatory assault **6** a step downwards in a scale of gradation; *specif* one generation in an ancestral line or genealogical scale [ME, fr MF *descente*, fr *descendre*]

**describe** /di'skrieb/ *vt* **1** to represent or give an account of in words ⟨~ *a picture*⟩ **2** to trace or traverse the outline of ⟨~ *a circle*⟩ [L *describere*, fr *de-* + *scribere* to write – more at SCRIBE ] – **describable** *adj*, **describer** *n*

**description** /di'skripsh(ə)n/ *n* **1** an act or instance of describing; *specif* speech or writing intended to give a mental image of something experienced **2** kind, character ⟨*books of every* ~⟩ **synonyms** see ¹TYPE [ME *descripcioun*, fr MF & L; MF *description*, fr L *description-*, *descriptio*, fr *descriptus*, pp of *describere*]

**descriptive** /di'skriptiv/ *adj* **1** serving to describe ⟨*a* ~ *account*⟩ **2** characterized by description ⟨*the* ~ *basis of science*⟩ **3a** of a modifier expressing the quality, kind, or condition of what is denoted by the modified term; not limiting or demonstrative ⟨*hot in "hot water" is a* ~ *adjective*⟩ **b** nonrestrictive ⟨*a* ~ *clause*⟩ **4** serving to describe the structure of a language at a particular time without making value judgments and usu with exclusion of historical and comparative data ⟨~ *linguistics*⟩ – compare PRESCRIPTIVE 3 – **descriptively** *adv*, **descriptiveness** *n*

**descriptively adequate** *adj*, *of a grammar* presenting the grammatical phenomena of a language in full – compare EX-

PLANATORILY ADEQUATE, OBSERVATIONALLY ADEQUATE

**descriptor** /di'skriptə/ *n* a word, phrase, or symbol used to identify or describe (e g in an indexing system)

**descry** /di'skrie/ *vt* **1** to notice or see, esp at a distance **2** to find out; discover **synonyms** see ¹SEE ⚠ decry [ME *descrien*, fr OF *descrier* to proclaim, decry]

**desecrate** /'desikrayt/ *vt* **1** to violate the sanctity of; profane **2** to treat irreverently or contemptuously **synonyms** see PROFANATION [*de-* + *-secrate* (as in *consecrate*)] – **desecrater**, **desecrator** *n*, **desecration** *n*

**desegregate** /,dee'segrigayt/ *vt* to eliminate segregation in; *specif* to free of any law, provision, or practice that isolates the members of a particular racial group (e g black Americans) from the rest of the community ~ *vi* to end racial segregation – **desegregation** *n*

**desensit·ize, -ise** /,dee'sensotiez/ *vt* **1** to make (a sensitized or hypersensitive individual) insensitive, less sensitive, or nonreactive to a sensitizing agent **2** to make (a photographic material) less sensitive or completely insensitive to radiation **3** to make emotionally insensitive or callous – **desensitization** *n*, **desensitizer** *n*

**¹desert** /'dezət/ *n* **1** an arid barren region incapable of supporting much plant or animal life without an artificial water supply; *broadly* a lifeless region **2** a desolate or forbidding area ⟨*car parks are among the bleakest of modern urban* ~s⟩ ⟨*a cultural* ~⟩ ⚠ dessert [ME, fr OF, fr LL *desertum*, fr L, neut of *desertus*, pp of *deserere* to desert, fr *de-* + *serere* to join together – more at SERIES] – **desertic** *adj*

**²desert** /di'zuht/ *n* **1** the quality or fact of deserving reward or punishment **2** *usu pl* deserved reward or punishment – esp in *get one's just deserts* [ME *deserte*, fr OF, fr fem of *desert*, pp of *deservir* to deserve]

**³desert** /di'zuht/ *vt* **1** to withdraw from or leave, usu without intending to return **2a** to withdraw support for or attachment to ⟨~ *a friend in trouble*⟩ **b** to abandon (military duty) without permission ⟨*shot for* ~ing *his post*⟩ ~ *vi* to leave one's post, allegiance, or service without leave or justification; *esp* to absent oneself from military duty without leave and without intent to return **synonyms** see FORSAKE [Fr *déserter*, fr LL *desertare*, fr *desertus*] – **deserter** *n*

**desert boot** *n* an ankle-high laced suede boot with a rubber sole

**desertion** /di'zuhsh(ə)n/ *n* **1** an act of deserting; *esp* the abandonment without consent or legal justification of a person, post, or relationship and the associated duties and obligations ⟨*sued for divorce on grounds of* ~⟩ **2** a state of being deserted or forsaken; desolation

**desert island** *n* a remote tropical island; *esp* one that is uninhabited

**desert locust** *n* a destructive migratory locust (*Schistocerca gregaria*) of SW Asia and parts of N Africa

**desert rat** *n* **1** a JERBOA (long-tailed rodent) (*Jaculus orientalis*) found in the deserts of N Africa **2** *Br* a soldier of the British 7th Armoured Division who served in the N African desert campaign during World War II

**desert soil** *n* a soil that develops under sparse shrub vegetation in warm to cool arid climates and has a light-coloured surface soil usu underlain by chalky material and a hard compacted HARDPAN layer

**deserve** /di'zuhv/ *vt* to be worthy of; merit ⟨~s *another chance*⟩ ~ *vi* to be worthy, fit, or suitable for some reward or requital ⟨*have become recognized as they* ~ – T S Eliot⟩ [ME *deserven*, fr OF *deservir*, fr L *deservire* to serve zealously, fr *de-* + *servire* to serve] – **deserver** *n*

**deserving** /di'zuhving/ *adj* worthy; *specif* deserving financial aid ⟨*sponsorship for a* ~ *cause*⟩

**desex** /,dee'seks/ *vt* to desexualize

**desexual·ize, -ise** /,dee'seksyoo(ə)liez, -shəliez/ *vt* **1** to deprive of sexual characteristics or power, esp by surgical removal of the testes or ovaries **2** to divest of sexual quality – **desexualization** *n*

**deshabille** /,dayza'beel, dis-/, **déshabillé** /,dayza'bee,ay/ *n* the state of being only partially or carelessly dressed [Fr *déshabillé*, fr pp of *déshabiller* to undress, fr *dés-* dis- + *habiller* to dress – more at HABILIMENT]

**desiccant** /'desikont/ *n* a drying agent (e g CALCIUM CHLORIDE)

**desiccate** /'desikayt/ *vt* **1** to remove all or most of the moisture from; dry, dehydrate **2** to preserve (a food) by drying; dehydrate ⟨~d *coconut*⟩ **3** to drain of emotional or intellectual vitality ~ *vi* to become dried up [L *desiccatus*, pp of *desiccare* to dry

up, fr *de-* + *siccare* to dry, fr *siccus* dry – more at SACK] –
**desiccation** *n*, **desiccative** *adj*, **desiccator** *n*
**desiderate** /di'zidərayt/ *vt, formal* to entertain or express a
wish to have or attain [L *desideratus*, pp of *desiderare* to desire]
– **desideration** *n*, **desiderative** *adj*
**desideratum** /di͵zidə'raytəm, -'rah-/ *n, pl* **desiderata** /-'ahtə/
*formal* something desired as essential [L, neut of *desideratus*]
¹**design** /di'zien/ *vt* **1a** to conceive and plan out in the mind
⟨he ~ed *the perfect crime*⟩ **b** to have as a purpose; intend ⟨he
~ed *to excel in his studies*⟩ **c** to devise for a specific function
or end ⟨a *book* ~ed *primarily as a school textbook*⟩ **2a** to
draw the plans for **b** to create, fashion, execute, or construct
according to a plan, sketch, etc ~ *vi* **1** to conceive or execute
a plan **2** to draw, lay out, or prepare a design [MF *designer*, fr
L *designare*, fr *de-* + *signare* to mark, mark out – more at
SIGN] – **designedly** *adv*, **designer** *n*
²**design** *n* **1** a mental project, plan, or scheme **2a** a particular
purpose held in view by an individual or group ⟨my ~ *in writing
this preface is to forestall certain critics*⟩ **b** deliberate purposeful
planning ⟨battle was joined . . . more by accident than ~ – John
Buchan⟩ **3a** a deliberate undercover project or scheme; a plot **b**
*pl* aggressive or evil intent, often of a sexual nature – + *on* or
*against* ⟨he has ~s *on your daughter*⟩ **4** a drawing, plan, or
pattern showing the details of how something is to be constructed; *also* the art of producing such a drawing, plan, or
pattern **5** an underlying scheme that governs the functioning,
developing, or unfolding of something; a pattern ⟨the general ~
of the epic⟩ **6** the arrangement of elements or features of an
artistic or manufactured object **7** a decorative pattern
¹**designate** /'dezignət, -nayt/ *adj* chosen for an office but not
yet installed ⟨ambassador ~⟩ [L *designatus*, pp of *designare*]
²**designate** /'dezignayt/ *vt* **1** to serve as an indication of ⟨a
marker designating *the crest of the flood waters*⟩ **2** to specify,
stipulate **3** to call by a distinctive title, term, or expression **4**
to nominate or select for a specific purpose, office, or duty –
**designative** *adj*, **designator** *n*, **designatory** *adj*
**designation** /͵dezig'naysh(ə)n/ *n* **1** the act of indicating or
identifying **2** a distinguishing name, sign, or title **3** appointment to or selection for an office, post, or service
**designing** /di'ziening/ *adj* crafty, scheming
¹**desirable** /di'zie-ərəbl/ *adj* **1** arousing desire; attractive ⟨a ~
woman⟩ **2** worth seeking or doing as advantageous, beneficial,
or wise; advisable ⟨~ *legislation*⟩ ⟨a ~ *residence*⟩ – **desirability** *n*, **desirableness** *n*, **desirably** *adv*
²**desirable** *n usu pl* someone or something that is desirable
¹**desire** /di'zie-ə/ *vt* **1a** to long or hope for; *specif* to wish to
have sexual relations with **b** to wish for; want ⟨is there anything
you ~?⟩ ⟨I ~ *a clean napkin*⟩ **2a** to express a wish for; request
⟨~ *the pleasure of your company*⟩ **b** *formal* to express a wish
to; ask ⟨~ *him to wait*⟩ ~ *vi* to have or feel desire [ME *desiren*,
fr OF *desirer*, fr L *desiderare*, fr *de-* + *sider-*, *sidus* star]
  synonyms Desire, wish, and want are often interchangeable, but
  desire and wish are more dignified and formal ⟨this lady
  desires/wishes *to see you, Sir*⟩. Otherwise, they are chiefly distinguishable according to the feeling they express. Desire suggests
  ardour, and a strong intention of fulfilling one's desire ⟨desired
  above all things to be worthy of her⟩. Wish is less strong, and suggests that what is desired is or may be unattainable ⟨wished *herself*
  back at home⟩. Want is the least emphatic term, and may simply
  express a preference ⟨we all want to go home now⟩. Crave is
  stronger than all the others, in expressing a yearning which has the
  force of a physical appetite ⟨he craved her company⟩.
²**desire** *n* **1** a conscious impulse towards an object or experience that promises enjoyment or satisfaction **2a** a longing,
craving; *specif* a sexual longing **b** sexual attraction or appetite
**3** a *usu* formal request or petition **4** something desired ⟨it was
his heart's ~⟩
**desirous** /di'zie-ərəs/ *adj, formal* impelled or governed by
desire ⟨~ *of fame*⟩ – **desirously** *adv*, **desirousness** *n*
**desist** /di'zist/ *vi, formal* to cease to proceed or act – often +
*from* [MF *desister*, fr L *desistere*, fr *de-* + *sistere* to stand,
stop; akin to L *stare* to stand – more at STAND] – **desistance** *n*
**desk** /desk/ *n* **1a** a table, frame, or case with a sloping or horizontal surface, often with drawers and compartments, that is
used esp for writing and reading on **b** a reading table or lectern
supporting the book from which the liturgical service is read **c**
a table, counter, stand, or booth at which a clerk, cashier, etc
works **d** a music stand, esp as shared by two players in an
orchestra **2** a division of an organization, esp a newspaper
office, specializing in a *usu* specified phase of activity ⟨the for-

eign affairs ~⟩ [ME *deske*, fr ML *desca*, modif of OIt *desco*
table, fr L *discus* dish, disc – more at DISH]
**deskbound** /'desk͵bownd/ *adj* working or involving work in
an office rather than travelling
**desk research** *n* research conducted by examining existing
data (e g from records or published statistics)
**desm-** /desm-/, **desmo-** *comb form* bond; ligament ⟨desmo-
cyte⟩ [NL, fr Gk, fr *desmos*, fr *dein* to bind – more at DIADEM]
**desman** /'desmən/ *n, pl* **desmans** either of two semiaquatic
insect-eating mammals (*Desmana moschata* and *Galemys
pyrenaicus*) that resemble moles and have long snouts, dense
fur, and webbed hind feet [short for Sw *desmansråtta*, fr
*desman* musk + *råtta* rat]
**desmid** /'dezmid/ *n* any of numerous GREEN ALGAE (order
Zygnematales) that are typically single-celled but sometimes
occur united in colonies or as filaments [deriv of Gk *desmos*]
**desmosome** /'dezmə͵sohm/ *n* a small thickened area of a CELL
MEMBRANE by which a cell (e g in the skin) is anchored to a similar area on the membrane of an adjacent cell [*desm-* + *-some*]
¹**desolate** /'dezələt, 'des-/ *adj* **1** empty of inhabitants or visitors; deserted **2** joyless, disconsolate, or sorrowful (as if) through
the loss of hope, companionship, etc **3a** barren or lifeless ⟨a
~ landscape⟩ **b** devoid of warmth, comfort, or hope ⟨~
memories⟩ [ME *desolat*, fr L *desolatus*, pp of *desolare* to abandon, fr *de-* + *solus* alone – more at SOLE] – **desolately** *adv*,
**desolateness** *n*
²**desolate** /'dezəlayt, 'des-/ *vt* to make desolate: **a** to deprive
of inhabitants **b** to lay waste **c** to make wretched – **desolater**,
**desolator** *n*, **desolatingly** *adv*
**desolation** /͵dezə'laysh(ə)n, ͵des-/ *n* **1** the action of desolating
**2** the condition of being desolated; devastation, ruin ⟨the flood
left ~ *in its wake*⟩ **3** barren wasteland **4a** great grief or sadness **b** loneliness
**desorb** /͵dee'sawb/ *vt* to convert (a chemical compound) from
an absorbed or adsorbed state inside or on the surface of a
solid to a liquid or gaseous state – **desorption** *n*
**desoxy-** /desoksi-/ *comb form* deoxy-
¹**despair** /di'speə/ *vi* to lose all hope or confidence ⟨~ *of winning*⟩ [ME *despeiren*, fr MF *desperer*, fr L *desperare*, fr *de-* +
*sperare* to hope; akin to L *spes* hope – more at SPEED]
²**despair** *n* **1** utter loss of hope ⟨~, *which may find expression
in. . . suicide* – Rudyard Kipling⟩ **2** a cause of hopelessness or
extreme exasperation ⟨an incorrigible child is the ~ *of his
parents*⟩
**despairing** /di'speəring/ *adj* given to, arising from, or marked
by despair; hopeless – **despairingly** *adv*
**despatch** /di'spach/ *n or vb* (to) dispatch
**desperado** /͵despə'rahdoh/ *n, pl* **desperadoes, desperados** a
reckless or violent criminal; *esp* a bandit of the W USA in the
19th century [prob alter. (influenced by Sp *-ado*, as in *renegado*
renegade) of obs *desperate* desperate person]
**desperate** /'desp(ə)rət/ *adj* **1a** having lost hope ⟨a ~ *spirit
crying for relief*⟩ **b** giving no grounds for hope ⟨his situation
was ~⟩ **2a** moved, esp to recklessness, by despair ⟨a ~ *act*⟩ **b**
undertaken as a last resort **3** suffering extreme need or anxiety
⟨~ *for money*⟩ ⟨~ *for something to do*⟩ **4** fraught with extreme danger or impending disaster **5** *chiefly Irish* very bad
⟨this weather's ~⟩ [L *desperatus*, pp of *desperare*] – **desperately** *adv*, **desperateness** *n*
**desperation** /͵despə'raysh(ə)n/ *n* **1** despair **2** a state of hopelessness leading to rashness
**despicable** /di'spikəbl/ *also* 'despikəbl/ *adj* deserving to be
despised; morally contemptible [LL *despicabilis*, fr L *despicari*
to despise] – **despicableness** *n*, **despicably** *adv*
  usage The pronunciation /'despikəbl/ is recommended for BBC
  broadcasters.
**despise** /di'spiez/ *vt* **1** to look down on with contempt or
aversion ⟨~d *the weak*⟩ **2** to regard as negligible, worthless,
or distasteful [ME *despisen*, fr OF *despis-*, stem of *despire*, fr L
*despicere*, fr *de-* + *specere* to look – more at SPY] **despiser** *n*
¹**despite** /di'spiet/ *n* **1** *formal* **1a** active opposition ⟨my entire
life has been lived in its ~⟩ **b** harm or injury; disservice or
disadvantage ⟨I know of no government which stands to its
obligations, even in its own ~, more solidly – Sir Winston
Churchill⟩ **2** *archaic* the feeling or attitude of despising; contempt **3** *archaic* malice or spite [ME, fr OF *despit*, fr L *despectus*, fr *despectus*, pp of *despicere*]
²**despite** *prep* notwithstanding; IN SPITE OF ⟨ran ~ *his injury*⟩
**despiteous** /di'spitiəs/ *also* **despiteful** /di'spietf(ə)l/ *adj, archaic*
malicious

**despoil** /di'spoyl/ *vt* to strip of belongings or possessions; pillage △ spoil [ME *despoylen*, fr OF *despoillier*, fr L *despoliare*, fr *de-* + *spoliare* to strip, rob – more at SPOIL] – **despoiler** *n*, **despoilment** *n*

**despoliation** /di,spohli'aysh(ə)n/ *n* the act of plundering; the condition of being despoiled [LL *despoliation-*, *despoliatio*, fr *despoliatus*, pp of *despoliare*]

**despond** /di'spond/ *n* despondency – compare SLOUGH OF DESPOND

**despondent** /di'spond(ə)nt/ *adj* feeling extreme discouragement, dejection, or depression ⟨~ *about his health*⟩ [L *despondent-*, *despondens*, prp of *despondēre* to promise, give up, despair, fr *de-* + *spondēre* to promise – more at SPOUSE] – **despondence** *n*, **despondently** *adv*

**despot** /'despot/ *n* **1** an emperor, prince, or lesser ruler of the postclassical world **2a** a ruler with absolute power and authority; an autocrat ⟨*a benevolent* ~⟩ **b** a person exercising power oppressively or tyrannically [MF *despote*, fr Gk *despotēs* master, lord; akin to Skt *dampati* lord of the house; both fr a prehistoric IE compound whose constituents are akin to L *domus* house & to L *potis* able – more at TIMBER, POTENT] – **despotic** *adj*, **despotically** *adv*

**despotism** /'despə,tiz(ə)m/ *n* a system of government in which the ruler has unlimited power; absolutism; *broadly* the despotic exercise of power

**desquamate** /'deskwə,mayt/ *vi*, *esp of the outer layer of skin* to peel off in flakes or scales [L *desquamatus*, pp of *desquamare*, fr *de-* + *squama* scale – more at SQUALOR] – **desquamation** *n*

**dessert** /di'zuht/ *n* a hot or cold usu sweet course or dish (eg of pastry, pudding, or ice cream) served after the main course of a meal; *specif*, *Br* fresh fruit, nuts, etc as the final course of a meal, esp in former times △ desert [MF, fr *desservir* to clear the table, fr *des-* de- + *servir* to serve, fr L *servire*]

**dessertspoon** /-,spoohn/ *n* **1** a spoon intermediate in size between a teaspoon and a tablespoon, used for eating dessert **2** a dessertspoonful

**dessertspoonful** /-f(ə)l/ *n* **1** as much as a dessertspoon can hold **2** a unit of measure equal to about 8.9 cubic centimetres (about $2\frac{1}{2}$ fluid drachms)

**dessert wine** *n* a usu sweet wine, often served with dessert

**destabil·ize, -ise** /,dee'staybəliez/ *vt* to make (eg a government or the economy of a country) unstable – **destabilization** *n*

**destain** /,dee'stayn/ *vt* to remove a colouring stain selectively from (a specimen for microscopic study) so that only particular features remain coloured

**destalin·ize, -ise** /,dee'stahliniez, -stal-/ *vb* to dismantle the state apparatus, social structure, and cult of personality associated with Stalin and his rule in (a country) [Joseph *Stalin* † 1953 Russ political leader] – **destalinization** *n*

**destination** /,desti'naysh(ə)n/ *n* **1** the purpose for which something is destined **2** a place set for the end of a journey or to which something is sent ⟨*the honeymoon couple kept their* ~ *secret*⟩

**destine** /'destin/ *vt* **1** to designate, assign, or intend in advance ⟨*the younger son was* ~d *for the church*⟩ ⟨~d *for great things*⟩ **2** to direct, devise, or set apart for a specified purpose or end ⟨*freight* ~d *for English ports*⟩ □ usu pass [ME *destinen*, fr OF *destiner*, fr L *destinare* to fasten, determine, fr *de-* + *-stinare* (akin to L *stare* to stand) – more at STAND]

**destiny** /'destini/ *n* **1** the irresistible power or agency often held to determine the course of events **2** a predetermined course of events **3** something to which a person or thing is destined; fortune, fate △ destination [ME *destinee*, fr MF, fr fem of *destiné*, pp of *destiner*]

**destitute** /'destityooht/ *adj* **1** lacking something needed or proper – + *of* ⟨*a lake* ~ *of fish*⟩ **2** lacking possessions and resources; *esp* suffering extreme want or poverty ⟨*a* ~ *old man*⟩ synonyms see POOR [ME, fr L *destitutus*, pp of *destituere* to abandon, deprive, fr *de-* + *statuere* to set up – more at STATUTE] – **destitution** *also* **destituteness** *n*

**destrier** /'destri-ə/ *n*, *archaic* a war-horse; *also* a charger used esp in medieval tournaments [ME, fr OF, fr *destre* right hand (with which a squire led the horse), fr L *dextra*, fr fem of *dexter*]

**destroy** /di'stroy/ *vt* **1** to ruin or spoil ⟨*priceless art* ~ed *by water*⟩ **2a** to end the existence of; kill **b** to make ineffective; neutralize **c** to subject to a crushing defeat; annihilate ~ *vi* to cause destruction [ME *destroyen*, fr OF *destruire*, fr (assumed) VL *destrugere*, alter. of L *destruere*, fr *de-* + *struere* to build – more at STRUCTURE]

**destroyer** /di'stroyə/ *n* **1** someone who or something that des-

troys **2** a small fast warship usu armed with guns, depth charges, torpedoes, and sometimes guided missiles

**destroying angel** *n* either of two very poisonous toadstools (*Amanita phalloides* or *Amanita virosa*) of Europe and N America that vary in colour from pure white to olive or yellow and have a prominent VOLVA (cup-shaped sheath) at the base

**[1]destruct** /di'strukt/ *vt*, *NAm* to destroy [back-formation from *destruction*]

**[2]destruct** *n* the deliberate destruction of a rocket after launching, esp during a test; *also* the deliberate destruction of a military device (eg to prevent its falling into enemy hands)

*usage* Destroy and destruction are the usual words for **destruct** outside military and rocketry contexts. Compare SELF-DESTRUCT

**destructible** /di'struktəbl/ *adj* capable of being destroyed – **destructibility** *n*

**destruction** /di'struksh(ə)n/ *n* **1** the action or process of destroying something **2** the state or fact of being destroyed; ruin **3** a destroying agency; a cause of ruin ⟨*alcohol is likely to be his* ~⟩ synonyms see [1]RUIN [ME *destruccioun*, fr MF *destruction*, fr L *destruction-*, *destructio*, fr *destructus*, pp of *destruere*]

**destructive** /di'struktiv/ *adj* **1** causing destruction; ruinous ⟨*a* ~ *storm*⟩ **2** designed or tending to destroy ⟨~ *criticism*⟩ – **destructively** *adv*, **destructiveness** *also* **destructivity** *n*

*usage* Things are **destructive** *to* or *of* other things ⟨**destructive** *to antique furniture*⟩. △ destructible

**destructive distillation** *n* decomposition of a substance (eg wood, coal, or oil) by heating in a closed container and collecting the volatile products

**destructor** /di'struktə/ *n* **1** a furnace for burning refuse; an incinerator **2** a device for destroying a missile in flight [(1) L *destructor* destroyer, fr *destructus*, pp; (2) *destruct* (to destroy; back-formation fr *destruction*) + *-or*]

**desuetude** /'deswityoohd, di'syooh·i,tyoohd/ *n*, *formal* discontinuance from use or exercise; disuse ⟨*fallen into* ~⟩ [Fr or L; Fr *désuétude*, fr L *desuetudo*, fr *desuetus*, pp of *desuescere* to become unaccustomed, fr *de-* + *suescere* to become accustomed; akin to L *sui* of oneself – more at SUICIDE]

**desulphur·ize, -ise** /,dee'sulfəriez/ *vt* to remove sulphur or sulphur compounds from – **desulphurization** *n*

**desultory** /'desəlt(ə)ri, 'dez-/ *adj* marked by lack of cohesion, regularity, or purpose ⟨*wandered about in a* ~ *fashion*⟩ ⟨*their conversation became* ~⟩ [L *desultorius*, lit., of an acrobat on horseback, fr *desultor* acrobat on horseback, fr *desultus*, pp of *desilire* to leap down, fr *de-* + *salire* to leap – more at SALLY] – **desultorily** *adv*, **desultoriness** *n*

**detach** /di'tach/ *vt* **1** to separate, esp from a larger mass and usu without force or resulting damage; disengage **2** to separate from a parent organization for a special purpose or use; withdraw ⟨~ *a ship from the fleet*⟩ **3** to distance (oneself) from an emotional or involving situation [Fr *détacher*, fr OF *destachier*, fr *des-* de- + *-tachier* (as in *atachier* to attach)] – **detachability** *n*, **detachable** *adj*, **detachably** *adv*

**detached** /di'tacht/ *adj* **1** standing by itself; separate, unconnected; *specif* not sharing any wall with another building ⟨*a* ~ *house*⟩ **2** exhibiting an aloof objectivity, usu free from prejudice or emotional involvement ⟨*a* ~ *observer*⟩ synonyms see INDIFFERENT *antonym* involved – **detachedly** *adv*, **detachedness** *n*

**detachment** /-mənt/ *n* **1** the action or process of detaching; separation **2a** *taking sing or pl verb* a body of troops or part of a fleet separated from the main body for a special mission or service **b** the condition of being so separated – chiefly in *on detachment* **3a** indifference to worldly concerns; aloofness **b** freedom from bias or prejudice

**[1]detail** /'dee,tayl/ *n* **1** a part of a whole: eg **1a** a small and subordinate part considered in its own right; a particular; *specif* a part of a work of art considered or reproduced in isolation ⟨*pages of* ~s *of Leonardo's* Last Supper⟩ **b** the aggregate of the small elements that collectively constitute a work of art or photographic image ⟨*the* ~ *is unparalleled*⟩ **2** extended treatment of or attention to particular items ⟨*forget the* ~ *and concentrate on the broad outlines*⟩ **3** an instrument used for drawing enlargements and perspectives mechanically **4** *taking sing or pl vb* a person or body of people selected for a particular task (eg in military service); *also* the task in question [Fr *détail*, fr OF *detail* slice, piece, fr *detaillier* to cut in pieces, fr *de-* + *taillier* to cut – more at TAILOR] – **in detail** item by item; thoroughly

**[2]detail** *vt* **1** to report or list minutely and distinctly; specify ⟨~ed *his petty grievances*⟩ **2** to assign to a particular task or

place 3 to provide with the finer elements of design and finish ⟨*trimmings that ~ slips and petticoats*⟩
**detailed** /'deetayld/ *adj* marked by abundant detail or by thoroughness in treating small items or parts ⟨*the ~ study of history*⟩ – **detailedly** *adv*, **detailedness** *n*
**detain** /di'tayn/ *vt* 1 to hold or keep (as if) in custody ⟨*he was ~ed overnight for examination*⟩ 2 to restrain, esp from proceeding; delay *synonyms* see ¹KEEP *antonym* let go [ME *deteynen*, fr MF *detenir*, fr L *detinēre*, fr *de-* + *tenēre* to hold – more at THIN] – **detainment** *n*
**detainee** /ˌdeetay'nee/ *n* a person held in custody, esp for political reasons
**detainer** /di'taynə/ *n* 1 the act of keeping something in one's possession; *specif* the wrongful withholding from the rightful owner of something which has lawfully come into the possession of the holder 2 detention in custody 3 a writ authorizing the continued detention of a person [AF *detener*, fr *detener* to detain, fr L *detinēre*]
**detect** /di'tekt/ *vt* 1 to discover (a crime or criminal) 2 to discover or determine the existence, presence, or fact of ⟨*~ alcohol in the blood*⟩ 3 to extract information from (an electromagnetic wave or signal); DEMODULATE [ME *detecten*, fr L *detectus*, pp of *detegere* to uncover, fr *de-* + *tegere* to cover – more at THATCH] – **detectability** *n*, **detectable** *adj*
**detection** /di'teksh(ə)n/ *n* 1 the act of detecting; the fact of being detected 2 the extraction of audio, visual, etc information from an electromagnetic wave; DEMODULATION
¹**detective** /di'tektiv/ *adj* 1 fitted for or used in detecting something 2 of detectives or their work ⟨*a ~ novel*⟩
²**detective** *n* one employed or engaged in investigating crimes, detecting lawbreakers, or getting information that is not readily or publicly accessible; *specif* a member of the police force or a privately commissioned investigator engaged in this work
**detector** /di'tektə/ *n* something that detects: eg **a** a device used to detect the presence of electromagnetic waves **b** a part of an electronic circuit used in extracting the audio or visual information from a radio wave; DEMODULATOR **c** GEIGER COUNTER
**detent** /di'tent/ *n* a device that locks or unlocks one mechanical part in relation to another; *esp* a catch used to regulate the motion of a clock [Fr *détente*]
**détente, detente** /day'tonht/ *n* a relaxation of strained or hostile relations (eg between ideologically opposed nations) [Fr *détente* relaxation, fr MF *destente*, fr *destendre* to slacken, fr OF, fr *des-* de- + *tendre* to stretch, fr L *tendere* – more at THIN]
**detention** /di'tensh(ə)n/ *n* 1 the act or fact of detaining; *esp* a detention in custody 2 the state of being detained; *esp* a period of temporary custody 3 *chiefly Br* the keeping in of a pupil after school hours as a punishment [MF or LL; MF, fr LL *detention-, detentio*, fr L *detentus*, pp of *detinēre* to detain]
**detention centre** *n*, *Br* a highly disciplined penal institution to which young offenders may be sent for a 3-month or 6-month detention period
**detenu** *also* **détenu** /ˌdaytən'yooh (*Fr* detny)/ *n*, *chiefly Ind* a detainee [Fr *détenu*, fr pp of *détenir* to detain]
**deter** /di'tuh/ *vt* **-rr-** to inhibit, discourage, or prevent from acting (eg by fear) [L *deterrēre*, fr *de-* + *terrēre* to frighten – more at TERROR] – **determent** *n*
**deterge** /di'tuhj/ *vt* to wash off; cleanse [Fr or L; Fr *déterger*, fr L *detergēre*, fr *de-* + *tergēre* to wipe – more at TERSE]
**detergency** /di'tuhj(ə)nsi/ *n* cleansing quality or power
¹**detergent** /di'tuhj(ə)nt/ *adj* that cleans ; cleansing [Fr or L; Fr *détergent*, fr L *detergent-, detergens*, prp of *detergēre*]
²**detergent** *n* a cleansing agent: eg **a** SOAP 1 **b** any of numerous synthetic water-soluble or liquid preparations that are chemically different from soaps but have similar cleansing properties of being able to emulsify oils, hold dirt in suspension, and act as WETTING AGENTS ⟨*treated the oil spillage with ~*⟩ **c** an oil-soluble substance that holds insoluble foreign matter in suspension and is used in lubricating oils and dry-cleaning solvents
**deteriorate** /di'tiəri•ə,rayt/ *vt* to make inferior in quality or value; impair ~ *vi* to grow worse in quality or state; degenerate ⟨*allowed a tradition of academic excellence to ~*⟩ [LL *deterioratus*, pp of *deteriorare*, fr L *deterior* worse, fr *de-* + *-ter* (suffix, as in L *uter* which of two) + *-ior* (compar suffix)] – **deterioration** *n*, **deteriorative** *adj*
*usage* The pronunciation /di'tiəriə,rayt/ rather than /di'tiəri-ayt/ is recommended for BBC broadcasters.

**determinable** /di'tuhminəbl/ *adj* 1 capable of being determined 2 *law* terminable – **determinableness** *n*, **determinably** *adv*
**determinant** /di'tuhminənt/ *n* 1 an element that identifies or determines the nature of something or that fixes or conditions an outcome 2 a square array of numbers, bordered on either side by a vertical line, whose value is calculated by adding and multiplying the numbers according to a complex rule, and that is used in the study of matrices and to solve simultaneous equations ⟨*the ~* $\begin{vmatrix} a_1 & a_2 & a_3 \\ b_1 & b_2 & b_3 \\ c_1 & c_2 & c_3 \end{vmatrix}$

$= a_1(b_2c_3 - c_2b_3) - a_2(b_1c_3 - b_3c_1) + a_3(b_1c_2 - c_1b_2)$⟩ 3 something (eg a PLASMAGENE) that is inherited and produces a genetic effect; *esp* a gene *synonyms* see ¹CAUSE – **determinantal** *adj*
**determinate** /di'tuhminət/ *adj* 1 having defined limits; established 2 definitely settled; fixed 3 conclusively determined; definitive 4 *botany* CYMOSE 5 *of an egg* undergoing DETERMINATE CLEAVAGE [ME, fr L *determinatus*, pp of *determinare*] – **determinately** *adv*, **determinateness** *n*
**determinate cleavage** *n* cleavage of a fertilized egg in which each division irreversibly separates parts of the egg destined for development into specific tissues or organs – compare INDETERMINATE CLEAVAGE
**determination** /diˌtuhmi'naysh(ə)n/ *n* **1a** a judicial decision settling and ending a controversy **b** the resolving of a question by argument or reasoning **2a** the act of deciding definitely and firmly; *also* the result of such an act of decision **b** the power or habit of deciding definitely and firmly; resoluteness 3 a fixing of the position, amount, or character of something: eg **3a** the act, process, or result of an accurate measurement ⟨*the ~ of the salt in sea water*⟩ **b** the identification of the position of a plant or animal in a TAXONOMIC classification **c** the definition of a term or concept in logic by specifying its essential attributes 4 direction or tendency towards a particular end 5 the process by which the ultimate nature and development of undifferentiated embryonic tissue becomes irreversibly fixed
**determinative** /di'tuhminətiv/ *adj* that serves to determine ⟨*regard experiments as ~ of the principles from which deductions could be made* – S F Mason⟩ – **determinative** *n*, **determinatively** *adv*, **determinativeness** *n*
**determine** /di'tuhmin/ *vt* **1a** to fix conclusively or authoritatively **b** to decide by judicial pronouncement **c** to settle or decide by choosing between alternatives or possibilities **d** to resolve ⟨*he ~d to marry at all costs*⟩ **2a** to fix the form or character of beforehand ⟨*two points ~ a straight line*⟩ **b** to establish causally; regulate ⟨*demand ~s the price*⟩ **c** to limit in extent or scope ⟨*that hedge ~s the boundary*⟩ 3 *law* to put or set an end to; terminate ⟨*~ an estate*⟩ 4 to bring about the determination of (embryonic tissue) ~ *vi* 1 to come to a decision 2 *law* to come to an end or become void [ME *determinen*, fr MF *determiner*, fr L *determinare*, fr *de-* + *terminare* to limit, fr *terminus* boundary, limit – more at TERM]
**determined** /di'tuhmind/ *adj* 1 decided, resolved 2 firm, resolute – **determinedly** *adv*, **determinedness** *n*
**determiner** /di'tuhminə/ *n* something that determines: eg **a** a gene or genetic determinant **b** a word (eg *his* in "his new car") belonging to a group of words that refer to a noun and occur before descriptive adjectives modifying the same noun
**determinism** /di'tuhmi,niz(ə)m/ *n* 1 a doctrine that all phenomena are determined by preceding occurrences: eg **1a** the doctrine that all mental events are causally determined and that free will is illusory **b** economic determinism, determinism the theory that all human acts are ultimately determined by economic forces 2 a belief in predestination – **determinist** *n or adj*, **deterministic** *adj*, **deterministically** *adv*
**deterrence** /di'terəns/ *n* 1 the act or process of deterring 2 the discouragement of war by maintenance of vast military power and weaponry
¹**deterrent** /di'terənt/ *adj* 1 serving to deter 2 relating to deterrence [L *deterrent-, deterrens*, prp of *deterrēre* to deter] – **deterrently** *adv*
²**deterrent** *n* something that deters; *specif* an esp nuclear weapon or weapons system belonging to one state and considered as lessening the likelihood of attack from other hostile states
**detest** /di'test/ *vt* to feel intense and often violent dislike towards; loathe *synonyms* see ²HATE *antonym* adore [ME *detes-*

*ten,* fr L *detestari,* lit., to curse while calling a deity to witness, fr *de-* + *testari* to call to witness – more at TESTAMENT] – **detester** *n*

**detestable** /di'testəbl/ *adj* arousing or deserving intense dislike; hateful – **detestableness** *n,* **detestably** *adv*

**detestation** /,deete'staysh(ə)n/ *n, formal* 1 extreme hatred or dislike; abhorrence, loathing ⟨*had a* ∼ *of hypocrites*⟩ 2 an object of hatred or contempt

**dethrone** /,dee'throhn/ *vt* to remove from a throne or place of power or prominence; depose – **dethronement** *n,* **dethroner** *n*

**detinue** /'detinyooh/ *n* the unlawful detention of personal property belonging to another; *also* a common-law action for the recovery of such property or its value [ME *detenewe,* fr MF *detenue* detention, fr fem of *detenu,* pp of *detenir* to detain]

**detonate** /'detənayt/ *vi* to explode with sudden violence or great noise ∼ *vt* 1 to cause to detonate ⟨∼ *an atom bomb*⟩ – compare DEFLAGRATE 2 to set off in a burst of activity; activate ⟨*has* ∼d *a British tourist boom*⟩ [L *detonatus,* pp of *detonare* to thunder down, fr *de-* + *tonare* to thunder – more at THUNDER] – **detonatable** *also* **detonable** *adj,* **detonative** *adj*

**detonation** /,detə'naysh(ə)n/ *n* 1 the action or process of detonating 2 premature combustion in an INTERNAL-COMBUSTION ENGINE that results in knocking

**detonator** /'detənaytə/ *n* 1 a device or small quantity of explosive used for detonating a HIGH EXPLOSIVE 2 a device clipped onto a railway line, esp in fog or emergency, to explode as a warning signal when a train passes over it

**¹detour** /'dee,tooə/ *n* a deviation from a direct course or the usual procedure; *specif* a roundabout way temporarily replacing part of a route [Fr *détour,* fr OF *destor,* fr *destorner* to divert, fr *des-* de- + *torner* to turn – more at TURN]

**²detour** *vi* to make a detour ⟨∼ *to avoid road works*⟩ to send by a circuitous route

**detoxicate** /,dee'toksikayt/ *vt* to detoxify [*de-* + L *toxicum* poison – more at TOXIC] – **detoxicant** *n,* **detoxication** *n*

**detoxification centre** /di,toksifi'kaysh(ə)n/ *n* a place (eg a sanatorium) where patients are treated for alcoholism

**detoxify** /,dee'toksifie/ *vt* 1 to remove a poison (eg alcohol) or TOXIN from 2 to reduce the effect of (a poison or toxin), esp by chemical action to produce a less harmful substance – **detoxification** *n*

**detract** /di'trakt/ *vi* to take away something desirable, esp merit, praiseworthiness, or esteem – usu + *from* △ distract [ME *detracten,* fr L *detractus,* pp of *detrahere* to withdraw, disparage, fr *de-* + *trahere* to draw] – **detractive** *adj,* **detractively** *adv,* **detractor** *n*

**detraction** /di'traksh(ə)n/ *n* the lessening of reputation or esteem, esp by envious, malicious, or petty criticism; *also* an act or instance of this

**detrain** /,dee'trayn/ *vi* to alight from a railway train ∼ *vt* to remove from a railway train – **detrainment** *n*

**detribalize, -ise** /,dee'triebəliez/ *vt* to cause to give up tribal customs – **detribalization** *n*

**detriment** /'detrimənt/ *n* 1 injury, damage ⟨*did hard work without* ∼ *to his health*⟩ 2 a cause of injury or damage ⟨*the long strike was a* ∼ *to the industry*⟩ [ME, fr MF or L; MF, fr L *detrimentum,* fr *deterere* to wear away, impair, fr *de-* + *terere* to rub – more at THROW] – **detrimental** *adj,* **detrimentally** *adv*

**detrition** /di'trish(ə)n/ *n* a wearing off or away, esp by rubbing [ML *detrition-, detritis,* fr L *detritus*]

**detritus** /di'trietəs/ *n, pl* **detritus** 1 loose material (eg stones and silt) resulting from the wearing away or disintegration of rock 2 a product of disintegration or wearing away [Fr *détritus,* fr L *detritus,* pp of *deterere* – **detrital** *adj*

**de trop** /də'troh (Fr* də tro*)/ adj* too much or too many; superfluous ⟨*an overcoat is* ∼ *in such hot weather*⟩ ⟨*felt* ∼ *at the family gathering*⟩ [Fr]

**detumescence** /,deetyooh'mes(ə)ns/ *n* subsidence or diminution of swelling (eg of the penis) [L *detumescere* to cease swelling, fr *de-* + *tumescere* to swell up, fr *tumēre* to swell] – **detumescent** *adj*

**.deuce** /dyoohs/ *n* 1a the face of a dice that bears two spots b a playing card bearing the number two 2 a tie in a game (eg tennis) after which a player or team must score two consecutive clear points to win 3 *informal* – **the** devil, dickens – used as an interjection or intensive; not now in vogue ⟨*what the* ∼ *!*⟩ ⟨*the* ∼ *of a mess*⟩ [MF *deus* two, fr L *duos,* acc masc of *duo* two – more at TWO; (3) prob fr LG *duus* deuce (the worst throw at dice; hence, exclamation of dismay)]

**deuced** /dyoohst, 'dyoohsid/ *adj·* damned or confounded – **deuced, deucedly** *adv*

**deus ex machina** /'dayəs eks 'makinə/ *n* 1 an actor playing a god in ancient Greek and Roman drama who was introduced by means of a crane to decide the final outcome 2 a person or thing (eg in fiction or drama) introduced suddenly and unexpectedly to provide a contrived solution to an apparently insoluble difficulty [NL, a god from a machine, trans of Gk *theos ek mēchanēs*]

**deut-** /dyooht-/, **deuto-** *comb form* second; secondary ⟨*deutonymph*⟩ [ISV, fr *deuter-*]

**¹deuter-, deutero-** *comb form* second; secondary ⟨*deuterogenesis*⟩ ⟨*deuterogamy*⟩ [alter. of ME *deutro-,* modif of LL *deuter-,* fr Gk *deuter-, deutero-,* fr *deuteros;* prob akin to L *dudum* formerly, Gk *dein* to lack]

**²deuter-, deutero-** *comb form* deuterium; containing deuterium ⟨*deuterated*⟩ ⟨*deuteroalkanes*⟩ [ISV]

**deuteranope** /'dyoohtərənohp/ *n* a person with a type of COLOUR BLINDNESS in which the eye does not respond to green light, and greens and purplish-reds cannot be distinguished [ISV, fr NL *deuteranopia,* fr ¹*deuter-* + ²*a-* + *-opia;* fr green being regarded as the second primary colour] – **deuteranopia** *n*

**deuterate** /'dyoohtə,rayt/ *vt* to introduce deuterium into (a chemical compound) – **deuteration** *n*

**deuterium** /dyooh'tiəri-əm/ *n* the form (ISOTOPE) of hydrogen that is of twice the mass of ordinary hydrogen and that occurs in minute amounts in ordinary water and as the form of hydrogen present in HEAVY WATER [NL, fr Gk *deuteros* second]

**deuterium oxide** *n* water, $D_2O$, composed of deuterium and oxygen; HEAVY WATER

**deuterocanonical** /,dyoohtərohkə'nonikl/ *adj* of or constituting the books of the Old Testament contained in the Septuagint but not in the Hebrew canon [NL *deuterocanonicus,* fr ¹*deuter-* + LL *canonicus* canonical]

**deuterogamy** /,dyoohtə'rogəmi/ *n* a second marriage; digamy [LGk *deuterogamia,* fr Gk *deuter-* + *-gamia* -gamy]

**deuteron** /'dyoohtəron/ *n* the nucleus of the deuterium atom consisting of one proton and one neutron [*deuter*ium + *-on*]

**Deuteronomic** /,dyoohtərə'nomik/ *adj* relating to the book of Deuteronomy or its theology or style

**Deuteronomist** /,dyoohtə'ronəmist/ *n* any of the writers of a Deuteronomic body of source material often distinguished in the earlier books of the Old Testament – **Deuteronomistic** *adj*

**Deuteronomy** /,dyoohtə'ronəmi/ *n* – see BIBLE table [ME *Deutronomie,* fr LL *Deuteronomium,* fr Gk *Deuteronomion,* fr *deuter-* + *nomos* law – more at NIMBLE]

**deuterostome** /'dyoohtərə,stohm/ *n* any of a major division (Deuterostomia) of the ANIMAL KINGDOM consisting of all the animals (eg VERTEBRATES, starfish, and sea urchins) with mouths that, during the development of the embryo, do not arise from the BLASTOPORE (hole that forms in embryo at very early stage in its growth) [NL *Deuterostomia,* group name, fr *deuter-* + Gk *stoma* mouth – more at STOMACH]

**deutoplasm** /'dyoohtoh,plaz(ə)m/ *n* the nonliving nutritive material in the substance of a cell; *esp* the yolk or food reserves of an egg [ISV] – **deutoplasmic** *adj*

**Deutsche Mark** /'doych ,mahk (Ger* dɔɪtʃə mark*)/ n* – see MONEY table [Ger, German mark]

**deutzia** /'dyoohtsi-ə, 'doytsi-ə/ *n* any of a genus (*Deutzia*) of white- or pink-flowered ornamental shrubs of the saxifrage family [NL, fr Jean *Deutz* †1784? D patron of botany]

**devaluate** /,dee'valyooayt/ *vb* to devalue

**devaluation** /,dee,valyoo'aysh(ə)n/ *n* 1 a reduction in the exchange value of a currency by a lowering of its gold equivalency with gold or another currency 2 a lessening, esp of status or stature; a decline

**devalue** /,dee'valyooh/ *vt* 1 to reduce the exchange value of (money) 2 to cause or be responsible for a devaluation of (eg a person or a literary work) ∼ *vi* to institute devaluation

**Devanagari** /,dayvə'nahgəri/ *n* an alphabet usu employed for writing Sanskrit and also used for various modern languages of India [Skt *devanāgarī,* fr *deva* god + *nāgarī* script of the city]

· **devastate** /'devəstayt/ *vt* 1 to reduce to ruin; lay waste 2 to have a shattering effect on; overwhelm ⟨*utterly* ∼d *by the news of his mother's death*⟩ ⟨*a devastating attack on his incompetence*⟩ **synonyms** see ¹RUIN [L *devastatus,* pp of *devastare,* fr de- + *vastare* to lay waste – more at WASTE] – **devastatingly** *adv*, **devastation** *n*, **devastative** *adj*, **devastator** *n*

**develop** /di'veləp/ *vt* **1a** to unfold gradually or in detail; expound ⟨~ed *his argument*⟩ **b** to show signs of ⟨*fears he may be* ~ing *flu*⟩ **c** to treat (eg in dyeing) with an agent to cause the appearance of colour **d** to treat (exposed photographic film, plates, etc) with chemicals in order to produce a visible image; *also* to make visible by such a method **e** *music* to elaborate (a theme) by the unfolding of a musical idea and by the working out of rhythmic and harmonic changes **2** to bring out the possibilities of **3a** to promote the growth of ⟨~ed *her muscles*⟩ ⟨~ed *a new strain of bacteria*⟩ **b** to make available or usable ⟨*must* ~ *our natural resources*⟩ **c** to build on or change the use of (a piece of land) **4** to cause to grow, mature, or increase **5** to acquire gradually ⟨~ *a taste for good wine*⟩ **6** *maths* to unroll (a 3-dimensional surface that is curved in only one direction) onto a plane without stretching **7** to move (a chess piece) from its original position to one providing more opportunity for effective use ~ *vi* **1a** to go through a process of natural growth, differentiation, or evolution by successive changes ⟨*a blossom* ~s *from a bud*⟩ ⟨*studied the way in which the species had* ~ed⟩ **b** to acquire secondary sex characteristics; become mature **c** to evolve; *broadly* to grow **2** to become gradually manifest or apparent **3** to develop one's pieces in chess [Fr *développer*, fr OF *desvoloper*, fr *des-* de- + *voloper* to wrap (cf ENVELOP)] – **developable** *adj*

*usage* The use of **develop** to mean simply ''occur'' or ''arise'' where there is no idea of gradual evolving ⟨*a crisis has suddenly developed*⟩ is widely disliked.

**developer** /di'veləpə/ *n* **1** a chemical used to develop exposed photographic materials **2** a person who develops property; *esp* someone who improves and subdivides land and builds and sells houses on it

**developing** /di'veləping/ *adj* UNDERDEVELOPED **2** (having a low standard of living and little industrialization) ⟨*called for more aid for the* ~ *countries of the Third World*⟩

**development** /di'veləpmənt/ *n* **1** the act, process, or result of developing; *specif, music* the second of usu three parts of a movement written in SONATA FORM in which the main theme is divided up and elaborated upon – compare EXPOSITION 2b(1), RECAPITULATION 3 **2** the state of being developed – **developmental** *adj*, **developmentally** *adv*

**development area** *n*, *Br* an area of high unemployment where government encouragement is given to the development of new industries

¹**deviant** /'deevi·ənt/ *adj* deviating, esp from an accepted norm ⟨~ *behaviour*⟩ ⟨*a* ~ *child*⟩ – **deviance, deviancy** *n*

²**deviant** *n* someone or something whose behaviour differs markedly from what is regarded as normally occurring or socially acceptable; *esp* a person whose sexual behaviour differs from what is socially acceptable

¹**deviate** /'deevi·ayt/ *vi* **1** to turn aside, esp from an accepted norm **2** to stray, esp from a standard, principle, or topic ⟨*she never* ~d *from her first account*⟩ ~ *vt* to cause to turn from a previous course [LL *deviatus*, pp of *deviare*, fr L *de-* + *via* way – more at VIA] – **deviator** *n*, **deviatory** *adj*

²**deviate** /'deeviət, -ayt/ *n*, *chiefly NAm* a deviant

**deviation** /ˌdeevi'aysh(ə)n/ *n* **1** an act or instance of deviating ⟨*speak for one minute without hesitation, repetition, or* ~⟩ **2** deflection of the needle of a compass caused by local magnetic influences (eg on a ship) **3** the difference between a single value in a series of numbers and the average (MEAN) of those numbers **4** departure from an established ideology or party line **5** departure from accepted norms of behaviour ⟨*sexual* ~⟩ – **deviationism** *n*, **deviationist** *n*

**device** /di'vies/ *n* **1** a scheme to trick or deceive; a stratagem **2** something (eg a figure of speech or a dramatic convention) designed to achieve a particular artistic effect **3** a piece of equipment or a mechanism designed for a special purpose or function **4a** an ornamental design, drawing, or figure; *esp* one used as an emblem or in heraldry **b** a motto (eg on a COAT OF ARMS) ⟨*a banner with this strange* ~ *Excelsior! –* H W Longfellow⟩ **synonyms** see ¹TOOL [ME *devis, devise*, fr OF, division, intention, fr *deviser* to divide, regulate, tell – more at DEVISE] – **leave somebody to his/her own devices** to leave somebody free to do as he/she wishes, without supervision or interference

¹**devil** /'devl/ *n* **1** *often cap* the personal supreme spirit of evil in Jewish and Christian belief, the tempter of mankind, and the ruler of hell **2** a malignant spirit; a demon **3** an extremely cruel or wicked person; a fiend **4** a high-spirited, reckless, or

energetic person or animal ⟨*a* ~ *with the ladies*⟩ ⟨*be a* ~ *and have another drink!*⟩ **5a** PRINTER'S DEVIL (apprentice or errand boy) **b** a junior barrister working without payment to gain experience **6** any of various machines or devices (eg a paper shredder) **7** *informal* a person or animal of the specified type ⟨*cheeky* ~⟩ ⟨*her horse broke a leg and had to be put down, poor* ~⟩ **8** *informal* something very provoking, difficult, or trying ⟨*cleaning the carburettor is a* ~ *of a job*⟩ **9** *informal* – used as an interjection or intensive ⟨*what the* ~ *is that?*⟩ [ME *devel*, fr OE *dēofol*, fr LL *diabolus*, fr Gk *diabolos*, lit., slanderer, fr *diaballein* to throw across, slander, fr *dia-* + *ballein* to throw; akin to OHG *quellan* to well, gush] – **between the devil and the deep blue sea** faced with two equally unwelcome alternatives – **give the devil his due** to give deserved credit to an opponent or unpleasant person – **go to the devil 1** to fail completely; be ruined **2** to become depraved **3** leave immediately – used in the imperative – **like the devil** *informal* with great speed, intensity, etc ⟨*ran like the devil*⟩ – **speak/talk of the devil** – said when somebody appears who has just been mentioned [fr the folklore belief that the devil appears whenever his name is spoken] – **the very devil** very difficult or awkward ⟨*this car is the very devil to start in wet weather*⟩ – see also **the devil to** PAY

²**devil** *vb* -ll- (*NAm* -l-, -ll-) *vt* **1** to season (food) highly, esp with peppery condiments ⟨~led *kidneys*⟩ **2** *NAm informal* to tease, annoy ~ *vi* to serve as a printer's or lawyer's devil

**devilfish** /'devl·fish/ *n* **1** an octopus; *broadly* any large octopus, squid, or similar animal **2** *Br* ANGLER FISH (large predatory fish) **3** *chiefly NAm* MANTA RAY (extremely large fish with winglike fins)

**devilish** /'devl·ish/ *adj* **1** (characteristic) of a devil ⟨~ *tricks*⟩ **2** *informal* extreme, excessive – no longer in vogue ⟨*in a* ~ *hurry*⟩ – **devilish** *adv*, **devilishly** *adv*, **devilishness** *n*

**devil-may-'care** *adj* heedless of authority or convention; happy-go-lucky

**devilment** /'devlmənt/ *n* **1** devilish conduct or happenings **2** wild mischief

**devilry** /'devlri/ *n* **1a** actions performed with the help of the devil; witchcraft **b** gross or malignant cruelty; wickedness **2** (an act of) mischief

**devil's advocate** *n* **1** the Roman Catholic official who presents the possible objections to claims to CANONIZATION (being declared a saint), or to the title "Blessed" **2** a person who champions the less accepted or approved cause, esp for the sake of argument [trans of NL *advocatus diaboli*]

**devil's coach horse** *n* a large flesh-eating ROVE BEETLE (*Ocypus olens*)

**devils on horseback** *n taking sing or pl vb* prunes rolled in bacon, grilled, and served as an appetizer or as a savoury – compare ANGELS ON HORSEBACK

**deviltry** /'devltri/ *n, chiefly NAm* devilry

**devious** /'deevi·əs, -vyəs/ *adj* **1** deviating from a fixed or straight course; roundabout, circuitous ⟨*took a* ~ *route to avoid seeing him*⟩ **2a** deviating from a right, accepted, or common course; erring **b** not straightforward or wholly sincere ⟨*a thoroughly* ~ *person and not to be trusted*⟩ **c** tortuously underhand ⟨*obtained it by* ~ *means*⟩ [L *devius*, fr *de* from + *via* way – more at DE-, VIA] – **deviously** *adv*, **deviousness** *n*

¹**devise** /di'viez/ *vt* **1** to formulate in the mind; invent, contrive ⟨~d *a scheme for making greater profits*⟩ **2** to give (property, specif land) by will – compare BEQUEATH 1 [ME *devisen*, fr OF *deviser* to divide, regulate, tell, modif of (assumed) VL *divisare*, fr L *divisus*, pp of *dividere* to divide] – **devisable** *adj*, **devisal** *n*, **deviser** *n*

²**devise** *n* **1** the act of giving or disposing of property, specif land, by will **2** (a clause of) a will disposing of property **3** property devised by will △ device

**devisee** /diˌvie'zee, ˌdevi'zee/ *n* a person to whom a devise of property is made

**devisor** /di'viezə/ *n* a person who devises property in a will

**devital·ize, -ise** /ˌdee'vietl·iez/ *vt* to deprive of life, vigour, or effectiveness

**devitrify** /ˌdee'vitrifie/ *vt* to deprive of glassy lustre and transparency; *esp* to change (eg glass) from a clear to a crystalline condition [Fr *dévitrifier*, fr *dé-* de- + *vitrifier* to change into glass – more at VITRIFY] – **devitrifiable** *adj*, **devitrification** *n*

**devocal·ize, -ise** /ˌdee'vohkəliez/ *vt* to devoice

**devoice** /ˌdee'voys/ *vt* to pronounce (a normally VOICED sound, such as /b/ or /d/) without vibration of the vocal cords

**devoid** /di'voyd/ *adj* not having or using; lacking – + *of* ⟨*a* *book* ~ *of any literary merit*⟩ [ME, prob short for *devoided*, pp of *devoiden* to vacate, fr MF *desvuidier* to empty, fr OF, fr *des-* dis- + *vuidier* to empty – more at VOID]

**devoir** /'devwah, -'-/ *n, archaic* 1 duty, responsibility 2 *pl* respects, compliments [ME, alter. of *dever*, fr OF *deveir*, fr *devoir*, *deveir* to owe, be obliged, fr L *debēre* – more at DEBT]

**devolution** /ˌdeevə'loohsh(ə)n/ *n* 1a the passing of rights, powers, property, etc to a successor b delegation to a subordinate 2 the transfer of functions and powers to regional or local authorities by a central government; *specif* such a transfer of powers to Scottish and Welsh authorities by the UK government [ML *devolution-, devolutio*, fr L *devolutus*, pp of *devolvere*] – **devolutionary** *adj*, **devolutionist** *n*

**devolve** /di'volv/ *vt* 1a to transfer or delegate from one person to another b to surrender (power or a function) to a regional or local authority 2 *archaic* to cause to roll down ~ *vi* 1a to pass by inheritance or legal succession – usu + *to, on*, or *upon* b to fall or be passed, usu as an obligation or responsibility – + *on* or *upon* c to be centred *on*; depend *on* 2 to flow or roll onwards or downwards [ME *devolven*, fr L *devolvere*, fr *de-* + *volvere* to roll – more at VOLUBLE]

**devon** /'dev(ə)n/ *n, often cap* (any of) a breed of hardy red beef cattle that have their origin in Devonshire [*Devon*(shire), county of England]

**Devonian** /de'vohnyən, -iən/ *adj* 1 of Devon 2 of or being the prehistoric time period of the PALAEOZOIC era between the SILURIAN and the CARBONIFEROUS or the corresponding system of rocks – **Devonian** *n*

**devote** /di'voht/ *vt* 1 to set apart for a special purpose; dedicate *to* 2 to give (oneself) over wholly *to* [L *devotus*, pp of *devovēre*, fr *de-* + *vovēre* to vow]

**devoted** /di'vohtid/ *adj* loyally attached ⟨*a* ~ *friend*⟩ *synonyms* see LOVING – **devotedly** *adv*, **devotedness** *n*

**devotee** /ˌdevə'tee/ *n* 1 a deeply religious person 2 a keen follower or supporter; an enthusiast ⟨*a* ~ *of opera*⟩ – compare ADDICT, BUFF, FAN, ENTHUSIAST

**devotion** /di'vohsh(ə)n/ *n* 1a religious zeal; piety b *usu pl* an act of prayer or supplication ⟨*found her at her* ~s⟩ c a special religious exercise undertaken esp by Catholics and directed to a particular object of faith 2a the act of devoting or quality of being devoted b ardent love, affection, or dedication ⟨*assured her of his undying* ~⟩ ⟨~ *to duty*⟩ – **devotional** *adj*, **devotionally** *adv*

**devotional** /di'vohsh(ə)nl/ *n* a short religious service

**devour** /di'vowə/ *vt* 1 to eat up greedily or ravenously 2 to swallow up; consume ⟨~ ed *by fire*⟩ 3 to prey on; occupy or dominate the thoughts of ⟨*a man* ~ed *by jealousy*⟩ 4 to take in eagerly through the mind or senses ⟨~s *books*⟩ ⟨~ed *her with his eyes*⟩ [ME *devouren*, fr MF *devourer*, fr L *devorare*, fr *de-* + *vorare* to swallow – more at VORACIOUS] – **devourer** *n*

**devout** /di'vowt/ *adj* 1 devoted to religion; pious, reverent 2 sincere, heartfelt ⟨*a* ~ *hope*⟩ [ME *devot*, fr OF, fr LL *devotus*, fr L, pp of *devovēre*] – **devoutly** *adv*, **devoutness** *n*

**dew** /dyooh/ *n* 1 moisture that condenses on cool surfaces, esp at night 2 something resembling dew in freshness or power to refresh ⟨*the* ~ *of youth*⟩ 3 minute droplets of moisture (eg tears or sweat) [ME, fr OE *dēaw*; akin to OHG *tou* dew, Gk *thein* to run] – **dew** *vt*, **dewless** *adj*

**dewan** /di'wahn/ *n* an Indian official; *esp* the prime minister or finance minister of an Indian state [Hindi *dīwān*, fr Per, account book (cf DIVAN, DOUANE)]

**Dewar flask** /'dyooh-ə/ *n* a glass or metal VACUUM FLASK that is used esp in laboratories for storing liquefied gases [Sir James *Dewar* †1923 Sc chemist & physicist]

**dewberry** /'dyoohb(ə)ri/ *n* (the sweet edible berry of) any of several trailing prickly shrubs (genus *Rubus*) related to and resembling the blackberry

**dewclaw** /'dyooh,klaw/ *n* a functionless inner claw or small hoof on the foot of some mammals (eg dogs, goats, deer, etc) that corresponds to the underdeveloped first finger or toe – **dewclawed** *adj*

**dewdrop** /'dyooh,drop/ *n* a drop of dew

**Dewey decimal classification** /'dyooh-i/ *n* a system of book classification whereby main classes are shown by a 3-digit number and subdivisions by numbers after a decimal point [Melvil *Dewey* †1931 US librarian]

**dewfall** /'dyooh,fawl/ *n* 1 the formation of dew 2 the time when dew begins to form; evening

**dewlap** /'dyoohlap/ *n* a hanging fold of skin under the neck of an animal (eg a cow) – **dewlapped** *adj*

**deworm** /ˌdee'wuhm/ *vt* to rid (eg a dog) of worms; WORM 1

**dew point** *n* the temperature of the air at which dew begins to form

**dew pond** *n* a shallow usu artificial pond on the downs of S England formerly thought to be filled by the condensation of dew

**dewy** /'dyooh-i/ *adj* moist (as if) with dew – **dewily** *adv*, **dewiness** *n*

**dewy-'eyed** *adj* naively credulous or trusting

**dexamethasone** /ˌdeksə'methəzohn, -sohn/ *n* a synthetic STEROID drug, $C_{22}H_{29}FO_5$, that is widely used in the treatment of some blood disorders and to reduce inflammation (eg in arthritis) [perh fr *Dexa*myl, a trademark + *methyl* + *-sone* (as in *cortisone*)]

**Dexedrine** /'deksədrin/ *trademark* – used for a preparation of the stimulatory drug DEXTROAMPHETAMINE SULPHATE

**dexie** /'deksi/ *n, slang* a Dexedrine tablet [*Dex*edrine + *-ie*]

**dexiotropic** /ˌdeksiə'tropik, -'trohpik/, **dexiotropous** /ˌdeksi'otrəpəs/ *adj, of a plant or animal part* turning to the right; dextral [Gk *dexios* situated on the right + E *-tropic* or *-tropous*]

**dexter** /'dekstə/ *adj* of or being the side of a heraldic shield at the right of the person bearing it, and therefore at the left of the observer [L, of or on the right; akin to Gk *dexios* situated on the right, L *decēre* to be fitting – more at DECENT] – **dexter** *adv*

**dexterity** /dek'sterəti/ *n* 1 readiness and grace in physical activity; *esp* skill and ease in using one's hands 2 mental skill or quickness [MF or L; MF *dexterité*, fr L *dexteritat-, dexteritas*, fr *dexter*]

**dexterous, dextrous** /'dekstrəs/ *adj* 1 skilful and competent with one's hands 2 mentally adroit and skilful 3 done with dexterity ⟨*a* ~ *movement*⟩ [L *dextr-, dexter* dextral, skilful] – **dexterously** *adv*, **dexterousness** *n*

**dextr-** /dekstr-/ *comb form* 1 dextr-, dextro- on or towards the right; right ⟨*dextral*⟩ 2 DEXTRO- 2 (turning to the right) [LL, fr L *dextr-, dexter*]

**dextral** /'dekstrəl/ *adj* of or inclined to the right: eg a right-handed b *of a flatfish* having the right side uppermost c *of a snail shell* having whorls that turn in an anticlockwise direction from the top to the bottom as viewed with the top towards the observer – compare SINISTRAL – **dextrally** *adv*, **dextrality** *n*

**dextran** /'dekstrən/ *n* any of numerous POLYSACCHARIDES (complex sugars), $(C_6H_{10}O_5)_n$, that can be broken down to produce glucose: eg a any such chemical compound obtained by fermentation of sugar b any such chemical compound obtained by the breakdown of dextran and used as a substitute for the liquid portion of the blood in blood transfusions [*dextrose* + *-an*]

**dextranase** /'dekstrənayz/ *n* an ENZYME that breaks down dextran and is effective in attacking dental plaque

**dextrin** /'dekstrin/ *also* **dextrine** /~, 'dekstreen/ *n* any of various soluble gummy POLYSACCHARIDES (complex sugars), $(C_6H_{10}O_5)_n$, obtained from starch by the action of heat, acids, or ENZYMES and used as adhesives, as glazes for paper and textiles, and as thickening agents in foods [Fr *dextrine*, fr *dextr-*]

**dextro** /'dekstroh/ *adj* dextrorotatory [*dextr-*]

**dextro-** /dekstroh-/ *comb form* 1 DEXTR- 1 ⟨*dextrocardia*⟩ 2 **dextro-, -dextr-** dextrorotatory ⟨*dextro-tartaric acid*⟩

**dextroamphetamine sulphate, dextroamphetamine** *n* an AMPHETAMINE drug, $C_6H_5CH_2CH(NH_2)CH_3].H_2SO_4$, now used esp as a stimulant to treat sudden abnormal lapses into deep sleep – compare DEXEDRINE

**dextro-glucose** /ˌdekstroh 'gloohkohz, -ohs/ *n* dextrose

**dextrorotary** /ˌdekstroh'roht(ə)ri/ *adj* dextrorotatory

**dextrorotation** /ˌdekstrohroh'taysh(ə)n/ *n* right-handed or clockwise rotation – used with reference to the plane of POLARIZATION of light passing through a crystal or liquid; compare LAEVOROTATION

**dextrorotatory** /ˌdekstroh'rohtətri, -roh'taytəri/ *adj* turning clockwise or towards the right; *esp* rotating the plane of POLARIZATION of light towards the right ⟨~ *crystals*⟩ – compare LAEVOROTATORY

**dextrorse** /'dekstraws, -'-/ *adj* 1 *of a plant* twining spirally upwards round an axis from left to right – compare SINISTRORSE 2 DEXTRAL b (having the right side uppermost) [NL *dextrorsus*, fr L, towards the right, fr *dextr-* + *versus*, pp of *vertere* to turn – more at WORTH] – **dextrorsely** *adv*

**dextrose** /'dekstrohz, -ohs/ *n* dextrorotatory glucose

**dextrous** /'dekstrəs/ *adj* dexterous

**dey** /day/ *n* **1** the governor of Algiers in former times **2** a governor of part of the Ottoman empire (e g Tunis or Tripoli) in N Africa [Fr, fr Turk *dayı*, lit., maternal uncle]

**dhal** /dahl/ *n* a PULSE (plant of the pea family) cultivated in India; *also* a puree made esp from the seeds of this plant [Hindi *dāl*]

**dharma** /'dahmə/ *n* **1** *Hinduism* an individual's religious and moral duty fulfilled by the observance of social custom **2** *Buddhism* perfect truth as expounded in the teachings of Buddha **3** *Hinduism & Buddhism* **3a** the basic principles of cosmic or individual existence **b** conformity to one's duty and nature [Skt, fr *dhārayati* he holds; akin to L *firmus* firm] – **dharmic** *adj*

**dhobi** /'dohbi/ *n, pl* **dhobies** an Indian washerman or washer-woman [Hindi *dhobī*]

**dhole** /dohl/ *n* a fierce wild dog (*Cuon dukhunensis*) of India that hunts in packs [perh fr Kanarese *tōḷa* wolf]

**dhoti, dhootie** /'dohti/ *n, pl* **dhotis, dhooties 1** a loincloth worn by Hindu men **2** a fabric used for dhotis [Hindi *dhotī*]

**dhow** /dow/ *n* an Arab trading vessel usu having a large 4-sided sail, a long overhanging bow, and a high POOP (raised structure at the stern) [Ar *dāwa*]

**Dhu'l-Hijja** /‚dooəl 'hijah/ *n* – see MONTH table [Ar *Dhū-l-ḥijjah*, lit., the one of the pilgrimage]

**Dhu'l-Qa'dah** /‚dooəl kahdah/ *n* – see MONTH table [Ar *Dhū-l-qa'dah*, lit., the one of the sitting]

**¹di-** /die-/ *comb form* **1** twice; twofold; double ⟨dichromatic⟩ **2** containing two atoms, groups, or chemical equivalents in the molecular structure ⟨dichloride⟩ [ME, fr MF, fr L, fr Gk; akin to OE *twi-*]

**²di-** *prefix* dia-

**dia-** /die-ə/ *prefix* **1** through ⟨diapositive⟩ **2** across ⟨diameter⟩ [ME, fr OF, fr L, fr Gk, through, apart, fr *dia;* akin to L *dis-*]

**diabase** /'die‚bays/ *n* **1** *chiefly Br* any of various dark-coloured rocks with a composition similar to DOLERITE (rock formed by solidification of molten lava below the earth's surface) **2** *chiefly NAm* DOLERITE [Fr, fr Gk *diabasis* act of crossing over, fr *diabainein* to cross over, fr *dia-* + *bainein* to go – more at COME] – **diabasic** *adj*

**diabetes** /‚die-ə'beetis, -teez/ *n* any of various abnormal conditions characterized by the secretion and excretion of excessive amounts of urine; *specif* DIABETES MELLITUS [L, fr Gk *diabētēs*, fr *diabainein*]

**diabetes insipidus** /in'sipidəs/ *n* a disorder of the PITUITARY GLAND (gland close to the brain) in which there is a hormone deficiency characterized by intense thirst and by the excretion of large amounts of urine [NL, lit., insipid diabetes]

**diabetes mellitus** /'melitəs/ *n* a disorder of the process by which the body uses sugars and other carbohydrates, in which insufficient of the hormone INSULIN is produced, or the cells become resistant to its action. Diabetes is characterized by excessive urine production, by abnormally high levels of sugar in the blood and urine, and by thirst, hunger, and loss of weight. [NL, lit., honey-sweet diabetes]

**¹diabetic** /‚die-ə'betik/ *adj* **1** of diabetes or diabetics **2** affected with diabetes

**²diabetic** *n* a person affected with diabetes

**diablerie** /dee'ahbləri/ *n* **1** sorcery; BLACK MAGIC **2** demon lore; demonology **3** mischievous conduct; devilry [Fr, fr OF, fr *dïable* devil, fr LL *diabolus* – more at DEVIL]

**diabol-** /die-əbol-/, **diabolo-** *comb form* devil ⟨diabolism⟩ [ME *deabol-*, fr MF *diabol-*, fr LL, fr Gk, fr *diabolos* – more at DEVIL]

**diabolic** /‚die-ə'bolik/ *adj* **1** *also* **diabolical** /-kl/ (characteristic) of the devil; fiendish ⟨*a ~ laugh*⟩ **2 diabolical, diabolic** *chiefly Br informal* dreadful, appalling ⟨*it's the ~ way he treats his wife*⟩ ⟨*that meal was ~*⟩ [ME *deabolik*, fr MF *diabolique*, fr LL *diabolicus*, fr *diabolus*] – **diabolically** *adv*, **diabolicalness** *n*

**diabolism** /die'abəliz(ə)m/ *n* **1** dealings with, possession by, or worship of devils **2** evil character or behaviour – **diabolist** *n*

**diabol·ize, -ise** /die'abəliez/ *vt* to represent as or make diabolic

**diac** /'die‚ac/ *n* a SEMICONDUCTOR device used esp to provide pulses of electricity that activate a TRIAC (high speed electronic switch) [*di-* (fr its orig having two layers) + *-ac*]

**diachronic** /‚die-ə'kronik/ *adj* of or dealing with the historical development of phenomena, esp of language – compare SYN-CHRONIC – **diachronically** *adv*

**diachrony** /die'akrəni/ *n* **1** diachronic analysis **2** change extending through time [ISV *dia-* + *-chrony* (as in *synchrony*)]

**¹diacid** /die'asid/, **diacidic** /‚die-ə'sidik/ *adj* **1** *esp of a chemical* BASE having two HYDROXYL groups capable of reacting as bases in each molecule **2** *of an acid* DIBASIC 1

**²diacid** /'die‚asid/ *n* an acid with two acid hydrogen atoms [ISV]

**diaconal** /die'akənl, dee-/ *adj* of a DEACON (church officer) or deaconess [LL *diaconalis*, fr *diaconus* deacon – more at DEACON]

**diaconate** /die'akənit, -ayt/ *n* **1** the office or period of office of a DEACON (church officer) or deaconess **2** an official body of DEACONS

**diacritic** /‚die-ə'kritik/ *n* a mark placed over, under, or through a letter to denote a sound value different from that of the same letter when unmarked – compare ACCENT 4a

**diacritical** /‚die-ə'kritikl/ *also* **diacritic** *adj* **1** serving as a diacritic **2** serving to distinguish; distinctive [Gk *diakritikos* separative, fr *diakrinein* to distinguish, fr *dia-* + *krinein* to separate – more at CERTAIN]

**diadelphous** /‚die-ə'delfəs/ *adj, of the stamens of a flower* united so as to form two sets [*di-* + *-adelphous*]

**diadem** /'die-ə‚dem/ *n* **1** a crown; *specif* a headband worn as a badge of royalty **2** regal power or dignity [ME *diademe*, fr OF, fr L *diadema*, fr Gk *diadēma*, fr *diadein* to bind round, fr *dia-* + *dein* to bind; akin to Albanian *duai* sheaf, Skt *dāman* rope]

**diadromous** /die'adrəməs/ *adj, of a fish* migrating between salt and fresh waters

**diaeresis,** *chiefly NAm* **dieresis** /die'erəsis, -'irəsis/ *n, pl* **diaereses** /-əseez/ **1** a mark ¨ placed over a vowel to indicate that it is pronounced as a separate syllable (e g in *naïve* or *Brontë*) – compare UMLAUT 2 **2** the break in a line of verse which occurs when the end of a FOOT (unit of poetic rhythm) coincides with the end of a word [LL *diaeresis*, fr Gk *diairesis*, fr *diairein* to divide, fr *dia-* + *hairein* to take] – **diaeretic** *adj*

**diagenesis** /‚die-ə'jenəsis/ *n* **1** recombination or rearrangement of constituents (e g of a chemical or mineral) resulting in a new product **2** the conversion (e g by compaction or chemical reaction) of sediment into rock [NL] – **diagenetic** *adj*, **diagenetically** *adv*

**diageotropism** /‚die-əji'otrəpiz(ə)m/, **diageotropy** /-trəpi/ *n* the tendency of the growing organs of plants (e g branches or roots) to grow at right angles to the direction in which gravity operates – **diageotropic** *adj*

**diagnose** /‚die-əg'nohz, '--‚-/ *vt* to recognize (e g a disease) by signs and symptoms [back-formation fr *diagnosis*] – **diagnosable, diagnoseable** *adj*

**diagnosis** /‚die-əg'nohsis/ *n, pl* **diagnoses** /-'nohseez/ **1** the identification of a disease from its signs and symptoms **2** the investigation or analysis of the cause or nature of a problem or phenomenon ⟨*~ of engine trouble*⟩ **3** a statement or conclusion concerning the nature or cause of some phenomenon [NL, fr Gk *diagnōsis*, fr *diagignōskein* to distinguish, fr *dia-* + *gignōskein* to know – more at KNOW]

**¹diagnostic** /‚die-əg'nostik/ *also* **diagnostical** /-kl/ *adj* of or involving diagnosis – **diagnostically** *adv*

**²diagnostic** *n* **1 diagnostic, diagnostics** *pl but taking sing or pl vb* the art or practice of diagnosis **2** a distinguishing mark or characteristic; *esp* a symptom ⟨*the true ~ of modern gentility is parasitism* – G B Shaw⟩ – **diagnostician** *n*

**¹diagonal** /die'ag(ə)nl/ *adj* **1a** joining two nonadjacent angles or corners of a geometric figure having many sides or faces **b** passing through two nonadjacent edges of a 3-dimensional geometric figure **2a** running in an oblique direction from a reference line (e g the vertical) ⟨*wood with a ~ grain*⟩ **b** having diagonal markings or parts ⟨*a ~ weave*⟩ [L *diagonalis*, fr Gk *diagōnios* from angle to angle, fr *dia-* + *gōnia* angle – more at -GON] – **diagonally** *adv*

**²diagonal** *n* **1** a diagonal straight line or plane **2a** a diagonal direction **b(1)** a diagonal row, arrangement, or pattern **b(2)** a diagonal row of squares of the same colour on a chessboard **c** something placed or lying in a diagonal position **3** SOLIDUS 2 (punctuation mark /) **4** either of the two pairs of a horse's legs that includes one foreleg and the hindleg of the opposite side

**diagonal aid** *n* a signal given by a rider to guide his/her horse using hand movements on one side and leg pressure on the opposite side of the horse

**diagonal·ize, -ise** /die'agənəliez/ *vt, maths* to put (a SQUARE MATRIX) into the form of a DIAGONAL MATRIX – **diagonalizable** *adj*, **diagonalization** *n*

**diagonal matrix** *n* a SQUARE MATRIX (arrangement of numbers, letters, etc in rows and columns) in which all the elements are zero except those on the LEADING DIAGONAL (top left to bottom right)

**¹diagram** /'die-ə,gram/ *n* **1** a LINE DRAWING made for mathematical or scientific purposes **2** a drawing that shows arrangement and relations (e g of parts) [Gk *diagramma*, fr *diaphein* to mark out by lines, fr *dia-* + *graphein* to write – more at CARVE] – **diagrammable** *adj*, **diagrammatic** *also* **diagrammatical** *adj*, **diagrammatically** *adv*

**²diagram** *vt* **-mm-** (*NAm* **-m-**, **-mm-**) to represent by a diagram

**diagrammat·ize, -ise** /,die-ə'gramətiez/ *vt* to diagram

**diakinesis** /,die-əki'neesis, -kie-/ *n, pl* **diakineses** /-'neeseez/ the final stage of the first phase of MEIOSIS (process during which a nucleus divides to produce the sex cells) [NL, fr *dia-* + Gk *kinēsis* motion – more at –KINESIS] – **diakinetic** *adj*

**¹dial** /die-əl/ *n* **1** the face of a sundial **2** the graduated face of a clock, watch, etc **3a** a (circular) face on which some measurement is registered, usu by means of numbers and a pointer ⟨*the speedometer* ~ *registered 100 mph*⟩ **b** a esp circular panel on a radio on which the frequency, wavelength, or station is indicated by means of a pointer **4a** the dislike control on a radio or television set used to select the station or channel **b** a round numbered plate on a telephone, together with a movable disc with finger-holes which is rotated a set distance for every digit of a number being called **5** *Br slang* a person's face **6** *obs* a clock, watch, etc [ME, fr L *dies* day – more at DEITY]

**²dial** *vb* **-ll-** (*NAm* **-l-**, **-ll-**) *vt* to operate a dial so as to select ⟨~led *a wrong number*⟩ ⟨~-*a-disc*⟩ ~ *vi* **1** to manipulate a dial **2** to make a call on a telephone having a dial

**dialect** /'die-əlekt/ *n* **1** a regional or social variety of a language, usu transmitted orally and differing distinctively from the standard language ⟨*the Neapolitan* ~ *of Italian*⟩ ⟨*spoke a rough peasant* ~⟩ **2** any of a group of related languages ⟨*French and Italian are Romance* ~s⟩ **3** a variety of a language used by the members of an occupational group ⟨*the* ~ *of the atomic physicist*⟩ [MF *dialecte*, fr L *dialectus*, fr Gk *dialektos* conversation, dialect, fr *dialegesthai* to converse – more at DIALOGUE] – **dialectal** *adj*, **dialectally** *adv*

*synonyms* Dialect, vernacular, patois, jargon, cant, gobbledygook, slang, argot, lingo, and shop may all describe a form of language which differs from that accepted as standard. Dialect is the usual term for a variety of the language limited to a particular region or group, and established for generations. Vernacular is a neutral term which contrasts the language spoken by the people with learned, literary, or scientific language. It is sometimes loosely used to imply rusticity. Patois may be used for dialect or jargon, particularly among unlettered people in Romance-language areas ⟨*the patois of the peasantry round Carcassonne*⟩. Jargon, a much-needed word in today's English, is a word, usually derogatory, used by outsiders to describe ugly-sounding or unintelligible language, or to describe the technical, private vocabulary of particular professions or activities. These meanings overlap to a large extent, but jargon of the first kind, especially where it applies to official language, is now often known as gobbledygook. Cant may also be applied to the jargon of a small group, as in the phrase thieves' cant, but more often now means insincere, hypocritical talk about principles, religion, patriotism, etc. Argot is another word for underworld cant, but is often loosely used for slang. Slang describes the class of newly coined words, often picturesque or humorous, invented by particular groups for their own use, which are at first peculiar to them and unintelligible to outsiders, but which sometimes become more widely known, and adopted into standard English. Slang terms are usually ephemeral, being replaced by new terms as the old ones become either boring or too widely known to outsiders. Shop is a rather informal word for business talk outside working hours. Lingo is a term of contempt for any language or jargon the speaker does not understand. Compare LANGUAGE

**dialect atlas** *n* LINGUISTIC ATLAS (maps showing the distribution of speech variations)

**dialect geography** *n* LINGUISTIC GEOGRAPHY (study of regional variations of a language or dialect)

**dialectic** /,die-ə'lektik/ *n* **1** the practice of testing the truth of a theory or opinion by logical discussion **2** LOGIC 1a(1) (branch of philosophy) **3a** change involving stages of THESIS (a proposition or state), ANTITHESIS (its opposite), and SYNTHESIS (a blending of the two), in accordance with a process outlined by Hegel and developed by his followers; *also* the critical investigation of this process **b(1)** dialectics *pl but taking sing or pl vb*, **dialectic** development or change in real social conditions, through the stages of THESIS, ANTITHESIS, and SYNTHESIS, as described by the laws of DIALECTICAL MATERIALISM; *also* the critical investigation of this process **b(2)** the theoretical application of DIALECTICAL MATERIALISM, esp in Marxist investigation of economics and the SOCIAL SCIENCES **4** dialectics *pl but taking sing or pl vb*, **dialectic 4a** any systematic reasoning, exposition, or argument that juxtaposes opposed or contradictory ideas and usu seeks to resolve their conflict **b** an intellectual exchange of ideas **5** the dialectical tension or opposition between two interacting forces or elements [ME *dialetik*, fr MF *dialetique*, fr L *dialectica*, fr Gk *dialektikē*, fr fem of *dialektikos* of conversation, fr *dialektos*]

**dialectical** /,die-ə'lektikl/ *also* **dialectic** *adj* **1** of or being in accordance with dialectic ⟨~ *method*⟩ **2** (characteristic) of a dialect – **dialectically** *adv*

**dialectical materialism** *n* the philosophical theory outlined by Karl Marx which holds that only matter exists, so that the existence of the mind, social institutions, etc must be explained in material terms, and also holds that matter interacts according to dialectical laws – compare HISTORICAL MATERIALISM

**dialectician** /,die-əlek'tish(ə)n/ *n* **1** a person who is skilled in or practises dialectic **2** a student of dialects; a dialectologist

**dialectology** /,die-əlek'toləji/ *n* the study of dialect [ISV] – **dialectologist** *n*, **dialectological** *adj*, **dialectologically** *adv*

**diallel** /'die-ə,lel/ *adj* of or being the breeding of each of a group of individuals with two or more of the others in order to determine the relative importance of each parent in the transmission of certain characteristics to the offspring [Gk *diallēlos* reciprocating, confused, fr *di'allēlon* through or across one another]

**dialling tone**, *NAm* **dial tone** *n* an unbroken purring sound heard over a telephone indicating that a number may be dialled

**dialogic** /,die-ə'lojik/, **dialogical** /-kl/ *adj* of or characterized by dialogue ⟨~ *writing*⟩ – **dialogically** *adv*

**dialogist** /'die'aləjist/ *n* **1** a person who participates in a dialogue **2** a writer of dialogues – **dialogistic** *adj*

**dialogue**, *NAm also* **dialog** /'die-əlog/ *n* **1** a literary work in conversational form **2a** a conversation between two or more people; *also* a similar exchange between a person and something else (e g a computer) **b** an exchange of ideas and opinions **3** the conversational element of literary or dramatic composition **4** discussion or negotiation between two nations, factions, groups, etc with conflicting interests ⟨*East-West* ~⟩ [MF, fr OF, fr L *dialogus*, fr Gk *dialogos*, fr *dialegesthai* to converse, fr *dia-* + *legein* to speak]

**dialysate** /die'alisayt/, *NAm* **dialyzate** /-zayt/ *n* the material that passes through the membrane in dialysis; *also* the liquid into which this material passes [*dialysis* or *dialyse* + *-ate*]

**dialyse**, *NAm* **dialyze** /'die-ə,liez/ *vt* to subject to dialysis ~ *vi* to undergo dialysis – **dialysable** *adj*, **dialysability** *n*

**dialysis** /die'alosis/ *n, pl* **dialyses** /-əseez/ **1** a process whereby substances in solution can be separated by allowing them to filter slowly through a skin or membrane. Solutions containing small particles can diffuse through the membrane but COLLOIDS (solutions with large particles in suspension) cannot. **2** the purification of blood by dialysis (e g using a KIDNEY MACHINE) [NL, fr Gk, separation, fr *dialyein* to dissolve, fr *dia-* + *lyein* to loosen – more at LOSE] – **dialytic** *adj*

**diamagnet** /'die-ə,magnit/, **diamagnetic** /-'mag'netik/ *n* a diamagnetic substance [*diamagnet* back-formation fr *diamagnetic*, adj]

**diamagnetic** /,die-əmag'netik/ *adj* of or being a substance that has weak negative magnetic properties and in a MAGNETIC FIELD is attracted to points of lower intensity – compare FERROMAGNETISM, PARAMAGNETISM – **diamagnetism** *n*

**diamanté** /,dee-ə'manti, diə-/ *n* (cloth or other material decorated with) sparkling particles, esp powdered crystal [Fr, fr pp of *diamanter* to set with diamonds, fr *diamant* diamond]

**diamantiferous** /,dee-əman'tifərəs/ *adj* yielding diamonds [Fr *diamantifère*, fr *diamant*]

**diamantine** /,dee-ə'manteen/ *adj* of or resembling diamonds [Fr *diamantin*, fr *diamant*]

**diameter** /die'amitə/ *n* **1** a line passing through the centre of a geometric figure or body **2** the length of a straight line from one side of an object, esp a circle, to the other, passing through its centre – compare RADIUS 2 **3** a unit of magnification equal to the number of times the linear dimensions of an object are increased by a magnifying device ⟨*a microscope magnifying 60* ~s⟩ [ME *diametre*, fr MF, fr L *diametros*, fr Gk, fr *dia-* + *metron* measure – more at MEASURE] – **diametral** *adj*

**diametric** /ˌdie·ə'metrik/, **diametrical** /-kl/ *adj* **1** of, constituting, or located on a diameter **2** completely opposed or opposite – **diametrically** *adv*

**diamine** /'die·ə,meen, die'ameen/ *n* a chemical compound containing two AMINO groups [ISV]

**¹diamond** /'die·əmənd/ *n* **1** a (piece of) very hard usu colourless crystalline carbon occurring naturally or produced artificially, that is highly valued as a precious stone, esp when flawless and transparent, and that is used industrially as an abrasive powder and in rock drills **2** something resembling a diamond (e g in value or brilliance) **3** a figure with four equal sides (e g a square) orientated so that the diagonals are horizontal and vertical **4a** a red diamond-shaped figure marked on a playing card; *also* a card marked with one or more of these figures **b** *pl but taking sing or pl vb* the suit comprising cards identified by this figure **5** the entire playing field in baseball, or the area enclosed by the bases to which the batter must run in order to score [ME *diamaunde*, fr MF *diamant*, fr LL *diamant-, diamas*, alter. of L *adamant-, adamas* hardest metal, diamond, fr Gk (cf ADAMANT)]

**²diamond** *adj* of, marking, or being a 60th or 75th anniversary ⟨~ *wedding*⟩

**diamondback** /'die·əmənd,bak/ *n* a large and deadly rattlesnake (*Crotalus adamanteus*) of the southern USA [fr the diamond-shaped markings on its back]

**diamondback moth** *n* a common moth (*Plutella maculipennis*), the male of which has diamond-shaped yellow markings on the wings, and whose larva is a pest on certain crops (e g cabbage)

**diamondiferous** /ˌdie·əmən'difərəs/ *adj* diamantiferous

**diamorphine** /ˌdie·ə'mawfeen/ *n* heroin [*diacetyl morphine*]

**diandrous** /die'andrəs/ *adj, of a flower* having two STAMENS (male reproductive organs)

**dianthus** /die'anthəs/ *n* ³PINK 1 (flower) [NL, genus name, fr Gk *dios* heavenly + *anthos* flower – more at DEITY, ANTHOLOGY]

**diapason** /ˌdie·ə'payz(ə)n, -s(ə)n/ *n* **1a** a full deep burst of harmonious sound **b** a principal organ STOP (set of pipes which sound as a group to produce a certain kind of note) which operates through the complete range of the instrument **2a** the entire range of musical tones; *also* the range of an instrument or voice **b** the range, scope ⟨*the vast ~ of his poetic talent*⟩ **3a** TUNING FORK **b** a standard of pitch [ME, fr L, fr Gk (*hē*) *dia pasōn (chordōn symphōnia)* the concord through all the notes, fr *dia* through + *pasōn*, gen fem pl of *pas* all – more at DIA-, PAN-]

**diapause** /'die·ə,pawz/ *n* a period (e g in the life of an insect) of arrested development occurring between periods of activity and normal growth [Gk *diapausis* pause, fr *diapauein* to pause, fr *dia-* + *pauein* to stop – more at PAUSE]

**diapausing** /'die·ə,pawzing/ *adj* undergoing diapause

**diapedesis** /ˌdie·əpe'deesis/ *n, pl* **diapedeses** /-'deeseez/ the passage of blood cells through the walls of small BLOOD VESSELS into the surrounding tissues [NL, fr Gk *diapēdēsis* act of oozing through, fr *diapēdan* to ooze through, fr *dia-* + *pēdan* to leap] – **diapedetic** *adj*

**¹diaper** /'diepə, 'die·əpə/ *n* **1** a soft usu white linen or cotton fabric used for tablecloths or towels **2** an ornamental pattern consisting of one or more small repeated units of design (e g geometric figures); *also* fabric decorated with such a pattern **3** *chiefly NAm* a nappy [ME *diapre*, fr MF, fr ML *diasprum*, deriv of MGk *diapras* pure white, fr *dia-* + *aspros* white]

**²diaper** *vt* to ornament with diaper designs

**diaphaneity** /ˌdie,afə'nayəti, -'nee-/ *n* the quality or state of being diaphanous

**diaphanous** /die'afənəs/ *adj* **1** so fine in texture as to be almost transparent **2** characterized by extreme delicacy of form; ethereal ⟨*painted ~ landscapes*⟩ [ML *diaphanus*, fr Gk *diaphanēs*, fr *diaphainein* to show through, fr *dia-* + *phainein* to show – more at FANCY] – **diaphanously** *adv*, **diaphanousness** *n*

**diaphone** /'die·ə,fohn/ *n* a fog signal similar to a siren but producing a blast of two tones

**diaphoresis** /ˌdie·əfə'reesis/ *n* perspiration; *esp* profuse sweating brought about by artificial means [LL, fr Gk *diaphorēsis*, fr *diaphorein* to perspire, fr *dia-* + *pherein* to carry – more at ²BEAR]

**diaphoretic** /ˌdie·əfə'retik/ *adj, of a drug* causing sweating [LL *diaphoreticus*, fr Gk *diaphorētikos*, fr *diaphorētos*, verbal of *diaphorein*] – **diaphoretic** *n*

**¹diaphragm** /'die·ə,fram/ *n* **1** a body partition of muscle and CONNECTIVE TISSUE; *specif* the partition separating the chest and abdominal cavities in mammals **2** a dividing membrane or thin partition, esp in a tube **3** a partition in a plant or in the body or shell of an invertebrate animal **4** a device that controls the amount of light entering an optical instrument (e g a camera or telescope) – compare ¹IRIS 1b **5** a thin flexible disc in a telephone, microphone etc, that vibrates when receiving or producing sound waves and is used to convert sound signals to electrical signals and vice versa **6** DUTCH CAP (contraceptive device) [ME *diafragma*, fr LL *diaphragma*, fr Gk, fr *diaphrassein* to barricade, fr *dia-* + *phrassein* to enclose – more at FARCE] – **diaphragmatic** *adj*, **diaphragmatically** *adv*

**²diaphragm** *vt* to fit with a diaphragm

**diaphysis** /die'afəsis/ *n, pl* **diaphyses** /-əseez/ the shaft of a LONG BONE [NL, fr Gk, spinous process of the tibia, fr *diaphyesthai* to grow between, fr *dia-* + *phyein* to bring forth – more at BE] – **diaphyseal, diaphysial** *adj*

**diapositive** /ˌdie·ə'pozətiv/ *n* a transparent photographic positive (e g a transparency)

**diapsid** /die'apsid/ *adj* of or including reptiles (e g the crocodiles) with two pairs of openings in the bones of the skull that cover the temples [deriv of Gk *di-* + *hapsid-, hapsis* arch – more at APSIS]

**diarchy** /'die,ahki/ *n* DYARCHY (government by two rulers or authorities)

**diarist** /'die·ərist/ *n* a person who keeps a diary

**diarrhoea**, *NAm chiefly* **diarrhea** /ˌdie·ə'riə/ *n* an intestinal disorder characterized by abnormally frequent passing of more or less liquid faeces [ME *diaria*, fr LL *diarrhoea*, fr Gk *diarrhoia*, fr *diarrhein* to flow through, fr *dia-* + *rhein* to flow – more at STREAM] – **diarrhoeal, diarrhoeic** *also* **diarrhoetic** *adj*

**diarthrosis** /ˌdie·ah'throhsis/ *n, pl* **diarthroses** /-'throhseez/ a freely movable joint (e g the shoulder or hip joint) [NL, fr Gk *diarthrōsis*, fr *diarthroun* to joint, fr *dia-* + *arthroun* to fasten by a joint, fr *arthron* joint – more at ARTHR-]

**diary** /'die·əri/ *n* **1** (a book containing) a personal record of events, reflections, or observations kept daily or at frequent intervals; a journal **2** *chiefly Br* a book with dates marked in which memoranda (e g appointments) can be noted [L *diarium*, fr *dies* day – more at DEITY]

**diaspora** /die'aspərə/ *n* **1** *cap* **1a** the settling of scattered colonies of Jews outside Palestine after the Babylonian exile **b** the areas outside Palestine settled by Jews **c** *taking sing or pl vb* the Jews living outside Palestine or modern Israel **2** a dispersion or migration (e g of people originally coming from the same country or having a common culture) ⟨*the Armenian ~*⟩ [Gk, dispersion, fr *diaspeirein* to scatter, fr *dia-* + *speirein* to sow – more at SPROUT]

**diaspore** /'die·ə,spaw/ *n* a crystalline mineral, AlO(OH), consisting of aluminium hydrogen oxide [Fr, fr Gk *diaspora*]

**diastase** /'die·ə,stayz, -,stays/ *n* AMYLASE (enzyme that breaks down starch into sugars); *esp* a mixture of amylases obtained from malt [Fr, fr Gk *diastasis* separation, interval, fr *diistanai* to separate, fr *dia-* + *histanai* to cause to stand – more at STAND]

**diastasis** /die'astəsis; *also* ˌdie·ə'staysis/ *n, pl* **diastases** /-'staysees/ the rest phase of diastole in the heart which occurs between expansions and contractions of the chambers [NL, fr Gk, interval]

**diastatic** /ˌdie·ə'statik/ *adj* (having the properties) of diastase; *esp* converting starch into sugar

**diastema** /ˌdie·ə'steemə/ *n, pl* **diastemata** /-mətə/ a space between teeth in a jaw [NL, fr LL, interval, fr Gk *diastēma*, fr *diistanai*] – **diastematic** *adj*

**diastole** /die'astəli/ *n* a rhythmically recurrent expansion; *esp* the widening of the cavities of the heart during which they fill with blood – compare SYSTOLE [Gk *diastolē* expansion, fr *diastellein* to expand, fr *dia-* + *stellein* to send – more at STALL] – **diastolic** *adj*

**diastrophism** /die'astrəfiz(ə)m/ *n* the process of deformation of the earth's crust that produces continents, ocean basins, mountains, etc [Gk *diastrophē* twisting, fr *diastrephein* to distort, fr *dia-* + *strephein* to twist – more at STROPHE] – **diastrophic** *adj*, **diastrophically** *adv*

**diathermanous** /ˌdie·ə'thuhmənəs/ *adj* DIATHERMIC 1 [Gk *diatherman-*, stem of *diathermainein* to heat through]

**diathermic** /ˌdie·ə'thuhmik/ *adj* **1** transmitting infrared radiation **2** of or using diathermy ⟨~ *treatment*⟩

**diathermy** /'die·ə,thuhmi/ *n* the generation of heat in tissue by electric currents for medical or surgical purposes [ISV]

**diathesis** /die'athəsis/ *n, pl* **diatheses** /-əseez/ a natural susceptibility or tendency to a disease or abnormality [NL, fr Gk, lit., arrangement, fr *diatithenai* to arrange, fr *dia-* + *tithenai* to set – more at DO] – **diathetic** *adj*

**diatom** /'die·ətəm, -,tom/ *n* any of a class (Bacillariophyceae) of minute single-celled algae with hard shell-like skeletons composed of silica that form diatomite [deriv of Gk *diatomos* cut in half, fr *diatemnein* to cut through, fr *dia-* + *temnein* to cut – more at TOME]

**diatomaceous** /,die·ətə'mayshəs, die,atə-/ *adj* consisting of or containing diatoms or their fossil remains ⟨~ *silica*⟩

**diatomaceous earth** *n* diatomite

**diatomic** /,die·ə'tomik/ *adj* **1** consisting of two atoms; having two atoms in the molecule **2** having two replaceable atoms or chemical groups [ISV]

**diatomite** /die'atəmiet/ *n* a light crumbly silica-containing material derived chiefly from diatom remains and used esp as a filter and for thermal insulation – compare KIESELGUHR

**diatonic** /,die·ə'tonik/ *adj* relating to a MAJOR or MINOR musical scale of eight notes to the octave without ACCIDENTALS (notes raised or lowered by half a tone which do not belong to the scale) [LL *diatonicus*, fr Gk *diatonikos*, fr *diatonos* stretching, fr *diateinein* to stretch out, fr *dia-* + *teinein* to stretch – more at THIN] – **diatonically** *adv*

**diatribe** /'die·ə,trieb/ *n* a typically lengthy piece of bitter and abusive criticism [L *diatriba*, fr Gk *diatribē* pastime, discourse, fr *diatribein* to spend (time), wear away, fr *dia-* + *tribein* to rub]

**diatropism** /die'atrəpiz(ə)m/ *n* the tendency of some plant organs to grow at right angles to the direction in which an external stimulus (eg light) is operating [ISV] – **diatropic** *adj*

**diazepam** /die'azəpam/ *n* a synthetic tranquillizing drug, $C_{16}H_{13}ClN_2O$, that is also used as a sedative and muscle relaxant, esp before surgical operations – compare VALIUM [*di-* + *az-* + *epoxide* + *-am* (compound related to ammonia)]

**diazine** /'die·ə,zeen, die'azeen/ *n* any of three chemical compounds, $C_4H_4N_2$, containing four carbon atoms and two nitrogen atoms arranged in a ring [ISV *di-* + *az-* + *-ine*]

**diazo** /die'azoh/ *adj* **1** of or containing a chemical group composed of two nitrogen atoms united to a single carbon atom in another group **2** relating to or containing a diazonium ION **3** of a photograph or photocopy whose production involves the use of a coating of a diazo compound that is decomposed by exposure to light [ISV *diaz-, diazo-*, fr *di-* + *az-*]

**diazonium** /,die·ə'zohni·əm/ *n* an ION with a positive electric charge composed of two nitrogen atoms that are united to a carbon atom in another chemical group and that usu exists in the chemical compounds used in the manufacture of artificial dyes (AZO DYES) [ISV *di-* + *az-* + *-onium*]

**diazot·ize, -ise** /die'azətiez/ *vt* to convert (a compound) into a diazo compound [*di-* + *azote* + *-ize*] – **diazotization** *n*

**dibasic** /,die'baysik, -'bayzik/ *adj* **1** of an acid having two hydrogen atoms capable of reacting as acids in each molecule **2** of a chemical compound containing two atoms of a metal having a VALENCY of one **3** of a chemical BASE DIACID 1

**dibber** /'dibə/ *n* a dibble [by alter.]

¹**dibble** /'dibl/ *n* a small pointed tool used to make holes in the ground for plants, seeds, or bulbs [ME *debylle*]

²**dibble** *vt* **1** to plant with a dibble **2** to make holes in (soil) (as if) with a dibble

**dibranchiate** /,die'brangkiət/ *adj* of a group (Dibranchia of the class Cephalopoda, phylum Mollusca) of INVERTEBRATE animals including the squids and octopuses that have a single pair of gills and kidneys, an apparatus for emitting an inky fluid, and either eight or ten tentacles bearing suckers or hooks [deriv of Gk *di-* + *branchia* gill]

**dibs** /dibz/ *n pl, slang* money, esp in small amounts [prob short for *dibstones* (jacks), fr obs *dib* to dab]

**dicarboxylic** /,die,kahbok'silik/ *adj* containing two CARBOXYL groups in the molecule

**dicast** /'die,kast/ *n* any of the 6000 citizens chosen each year in ancient Athens to try legal cases, their role combining the functions of judge and jury [Gk *dikastēs*, fr *dikazein* to judge, fr *dikē* judgment – more at DICTION]

¹**dice** /dies/ *n, pl* **dice** **1a** a small cube marked on each face with from one to six spots, so that spots on opposite faces total seven, that is used in games of chance or in gambling to give random numbers; *also* a small cube bearing a different symbol or word on each face instead of a number ⟨*poker* ~⟩

**b** a gambling game played with dice **2** a small cubical piece (eg of food) [ME *dyce*, fr *dees, dyce*, pl of *dee* die – more at DIE] – **load the dice** to prearrange all the elements of a situation as if by fate – usu + *against* or *in favour of* ⟨*I will never get the job, the dice are loaded in favour of the other guy*⟩ – **no dice** *informal* of no avail; no use

²**dice** *vt* **1a** to cut (eg food) into small cubes **b** to ornament with square markings ⟨~ *d leather*⟩ **2** to gamble using dice ⟨~ *his money away*⟩ ⟨~ *d himself into debt*⟩ ~ *vi* **1** to play games with dice ⟨~ *for drinks in the bar* – Malcolm Lowry⟩ **2** to take a chance ⟨*the temptation to* ~ *with death* – Newsweek⟩ [ME *dycen*, fr *dyce*] – **dicer** *n*

**dicephalous** /,die'sef(ə)ləs/ *n* having two heads [Gk *dikephalos*, fr *di-* + *kephalē* head]

**dicey** /'diesi/ *adj, informal* risky, unpredictable [¹*dice* + *-y*]

**dich-** /diek-/, **dicho-** *comb form* in two; apart ⟨*dichogamous*⟩ ⟨*dichotomy*⟩ [LL, fr Gk, fr *dicha;* akin to Gk *di-*]

**dichasium** /,die'kayzyəm, -zh(y)əm/ *n, pl* **dichasia** an arrangement of the flowers on a stem consisting of a central stalked flower on each side of which develops another flower-bearing stalk [NL, fr Gk *dichasis* halving, fr *dichazein* to halve, fr *dicha*] – **dichasial** *adj*

**dichlamydeous** /,dieklə'midiəs/ *adj, of a flower* having both petals and SEPALS (leafy part supporting the flower head) [*di-* + Gk *chlamyd-, chlamys* mantle]

**dichlor-** /dieklaw-/, **dichloro-** *comb form* containing two atoms of chlorine in the molecular structure ⟨*dichloroethylene*⟩

**dichloride** /,die'klawried/ *n* a chemical compound containing two atoms of chlorine combined with an element or chemical group

**dichlorobenzene** /,die,klawroh'benzeen, -,kloroh-/ *n* any of a group of three chemical compounds, $C_6H_4Cl_2$; *esp* PARA-DICHLOROBENZENE

**dichlorodifluoromethane** /,die,klawroh,die,flawroh-'meethayn, -,kloroh-, -,flooəroh-, -'methayn/ *n* a nontoxic nonflammable easily liquefiable gas, $CCl_2F_2$, used as a refrigerant and as a propellant in aerosols and fire extinguishers [*dichlor-* + *di-* + *fluor-* + *methane*]

**dichlorvos** /,die'klawvos, -vəs/ *n* an insecticide used esp in houses, shops, etc [*dichlor-* + *vinyl* + *phosphate*]

**dichogamous** /die'kogəməs/ *adj, esp of a plant* having male and female reproductive parts that mature at different times, thus avoiding self-fertilization – **dichogamy** *n*

**dichotom·ize, -ise** /die'kotəmiez/ *vt* to divide into two esp mutually exclusive parts, classes, or groups ~ *vi* to display dichotomy [LL *dichotomos*] – **dichotomization** *n*

**dichotomous** /die'kotəməs/ *adj* **1** dividing into two parts **2** of, involving, or arising from dichotomy [LL *dichotomos*, fr Gk, fr *dich-* + *temnein* to cut – more at TOME] – **dichotomously** *adv*, **dichotomousness** *n*

**dichotomy** /die'kotəmi/ *n* **1** a division or the process of dividing into two esp mutually exclusive or contradictory groups **2** the phase of the moon, Mercury, or Venus in which half its disc appears illuminated **3a** *botany* a system of branching in which the main axis forks repeatedly into two branches **b** branching of an ancestral line into two equal diverging branches [Gk *dichotomia*, fr *dichotomos*]

*usage* The loose use of **dichotomy** to mean merely "difference" or "conflict" ⟨*the dichotomy between faith and reason*⟩ is disliked by some people.

**dichroism** /'diekroh,iz(ə)m/ *n* **1** the property of certain crystals of differing in colour when viewed from different angles **2a** the property of a solid of differing in colour according to the thickness of the transmitting layer or of a liquid according to the degree of concentration of the solution **b** the property of a surface of reflecting light of one colour and transmitting light of other colours **3** DICHROMATISM – **dichroic** *also* **dichroitic** *adj*

**dichromate** /die'krohmayt, -mət/ *n* a usu orange to red chemical compound containing chromium arranged in groups consisting of two atoms of chromium with seven of oxygen [ISV]

**dichromatic** /,diekroh'matik/ *adj* **1** having or using two colours **2** having two colour varieties or colour phases independent of age or sex ⟨*a* ~ *bird*⟩ **3** able to perceive only two colours [*di-* + *chromatic*] – **dichromatism** *n*

**dick** /dik/ *n* **1** *slang* a detective **2** *vulgar* a penis – compare CLEVER-DICK [*Dick*, nickname for *Richard;* (1) prob by shortening & alter.]

**dickens** /'dikinz/ *n, informal the* devil, deuce – used as an interjection or intensive [euphemism]

**Dickensian** /di'kenzi·ən/ *adj* (suggestive) of Charles Dickens or his writings: e g **a** (suggestive) of urban squalor in Victorian England ⟨*a ~ workhouse*⟩ **b** (suggestive) of the conviviality of Victorian amusements and customs ⟨*a real ~ Christmas*⟩ **c** vividly delineated in character or incident ⟨*a ~ personage*⟩ [Charles *Dickens* †1870 E novelist]

**dicker** /'dikə/ *vi* **1** to bargain **2** to hesitate, dither [NAm, perh fr *dicker* (a quantity of ten, esp of hides), fr ME *dyker;* fr the former use of hides in bartering on the NAm frontier]

**dickey, dicky** *also* **dickie** /'diki/ *n* **1** a false shirtfront **2** *chiefly Br* **2a** the driver's seat in a carriage **b** a folding seat at the back of a carriage or some early cars **3 dickey bow** *also* **dickey** *Br informal* BOW TIE [*Dicky*, nickname for *Richard*]

**dickeybird** /'diki,buhd/ *n, informal* **1** a small bird – used by or to children **2** so much as a single word ⟨*never said a ~*⟩ [*Dicky*, nickname for *Richard*]

**dicky** /'diki/ *adj, Br informal* in a weak or unsound condition ⟨*a ~ heart*⟩ [origin unknown]

**diclinous** /,die'klienəs/ *adj, of a plant* having the male reproductive parts (STAMENS) and female reproductive parts (OVARIES) in separate flowers – compare MONOCLINOUS – **dicliny** *n*

**dicot** /'die,kot/ *n* a dicotyledon

**dicotyl** /'die,kotil/ *n* a dicotyledon

**dicotyledon** /die,koti'leedn, ---'--/ *n* any of the group (Dicotyledoneae) of flowering plants that have two SEED LEAVES formed when the plant begins to grow – compare MONOCOTYLEDON [deriv of NL *di- + cotyledon*] – **dicotyledonous** *adj*

**dicoumarol** /,die'koohmərol/ *n* a drug that is taken by mouth to delay the clotting of blood, esp in the treatment of THROMBOSIS (blocking of blood vessels by blood clots) [fr *Dicumarol*, a trademark]

**dicrotic** /,die'krotik/ *adj, of the pulse* having a double beat (e g in certain feverish states) [Gk *dikrotos* having a double beat] – **dicrotism** *n*

**Dictaphone** /'diktə,fohn/ *trademark* – used for a DICTATING MACHINE

**¹dictate** /dik'tayt/ *vi* **1** to give dictation **2** to speak or act with authority, or in a domineering manner ~ *vt* **1** to speak or read (a letter, message, etc) for a person to write down or for a machine to record **2** to impose, pronounce, or specify authoritatively [L *dictatus*, pp of *dictare* to assert, dictate, fr *dictus*, pp of *dicere* to say – more at DICTION]

**²dictate** /'diktayt/ *n* **1** an authoritative rule, prescription, or command **2** *usu pl* a ruling principle ⟨*according to the ~s of his conscience*⟩

**dictating machine** /dik'tayting/ *n* a machine designed for the recording of dictated matter

**dictation** /dik'taysh(ə)n/ *n* **1a** the action of laying down authoritative rules **b** an arbitrary command **2a** the act or manner of uttering words to be written down ⟨*read it to them at ~ speed*⟩ **b** material that is dictated or written down as dictated ⟨*gave her class a French ~*⟩ ⟨*handed in their ~s to be corrected*⟩

**dictator** /dik'taytə, *fem* **dictatress** /-tris/ *n* **1** a person granted absolute emergency power; *esp* one appointed by the senate of ancient Rome **2** an absolute ruler; *esp* one who has seized power unconstitutionally and uses it oppressively **3a** a person who makes authoritative pronouncements (e g on fashion) **b** a domineering person [L, fr *dictatus*]

**dictatorial** /,diktə'tawri·əl/ *adj* **1** (characteristic) of a dictator ⟨*~ power*⟩ **2** arrogantly domineering – **dictatorially** *adv*, **dictatorialness** *n*

**dictatorship** /dik'taytəship/ *n* **1** the office or period of rule of a dictator **2** total or absolute control; leadership, rule **3** a state or form of government in which absolute power is concentrated in a dictator or a small clique

**dictatorship of the proletariat** *n* the assumption of absolute political power by the PROLETARIAT (industrial wage earners) held in Marxism to be an essential part of the transition from capitalism to communism

**diction** /'diksh(ə)n/ *n* **1** choice of words, esp with regard to correctness, clearness, or effectiveness **2** pronunciation and enunciation of words in speaking or singing [L *diction-, dictio* speaking, style, fr *dictus*, pp of *dicere* to say; akin to OE *tēon* to accuse, L *dicare* to proclaim, dedicate, Gk *deiknynai* to show, *dikē* judgment, right] – **dictional** *adj*, **dictionally** *adv*

**dictionary** /'diksh(ə)n(ə)ri/ *n* **1** a reference book containing words, usu alphabetically arranged, together with information

about them, esp their forms, pronunciations, PARTS OF SPEECH, meanings, origins, grammatical requirements, and idiomatic uses **2** a reference book listing alphabetically terms or names important to a specified subject or activity together with discussion of their meanings and applications ⟨*a sports ~*⟩ **3** a reference book giving for words of one language equivalents in another **4** a list (e g of synonyms or hyphenation instructions) stored in machine-readable form (e g on a computer disk) for reference by an automatic system (e g for computerized typesetting) [ML *dictionarium*, fr LL *diction-, dictio* word, fr L, speaking]

*usage* The pronunciation /'dikshənri/ is disliked by some people, who feel that **dictionary** should have four syllables.

**Dictograph** /'diktə,grahf, -,graf/ *trademark* – used for a telephonic device for recording sounds or for picking them up in one room and transmitting them to another

**dictum** /'diktəm/ *n, pl* **dicta** /'diktə/ *also* **dictums** **1** an authoritative statement on some topic; a pronouncement **2** a judicial opinion on a point other than the precise issue involved in determining a case; OBITER DICTUM [L, fr neut of *dictus*]

**dicty-** /dikti-/, **dictyo-** *comb form* net; network ⟨dictyo*stele*⟩ ⟨dictyo*some*⟩ [NL, fr Gk *dikty-, diktyo-*, fr *diktyon*, fr *dikein* to throw]

**dictyopteran** /,dikti'optərən/ *n* any of an order (Dictyoptera) of insects consisting of the cockroaches and mantises [deriv of Gk *diktyon* net + *pteron* wing]

**dictyosome** /'dikti·ə,sohm/ *n* GOLGI BODY (secretory structure inside a cell)

**dictyostele** /'diktiə,steel, ,diktiə'steeli/ *n* an arrangement of the central tissues in the roots and stems of some plants, esp ferns, in which the tissues that conduct water and food are broken up into a number of separate longitudinal strands, each having XYLEM (water-conducting tissue) surrounded by a ring of PHLOEM (food-conducting tissue) – compare PROTOSTELE

**dicyclic** /,die'sieklik, -'siklik/ *adj* having two peaks of population each year – **dicycly** *n*

**did** /did/ *past of* DO

**didactic** /die'daktik/ *adj* **1** designed or intended to teach; *esp* intended to convey instruction and information rather than entertainment **2** having a tendency to teach in an authoritarian manner [Gk *didaktikos*, fr *didaskein* to teach] – **didactically** *adv*, **didacticism** *n*

**diddle** /'didl/ *vt, informal* to cheat, swindle [prob fr Jeremy *Diddler*, character in the play *Raising the Wind* by James Kenny †1849 E dramatist] – **diddler** *n*

**diddums** /'didəmz/ *interj* – used to express commiseration to a child [baby-talk alter. of *did you/he/she*]

**didelphic** /die'delfik/ *adj* having or relating to a double womb [*di-* + Gk *delphys* womb – more at DOLPHIN]

**didgeridoo, didjeridoo** /,dijəri'dooh/ *n* an Australian WIND INSTRUMENT with a long wooden tube [imit]

**didicoi, didicoy, diddicoy** /'didi,koy/ *n, pl* **didicois, didicoys, diddicoys** *Br* a travelling tinker, scrap-metal dealer, etc, who lives like but is not truly a Gipsy; *broadly* a Gipsy [Romany]

**didn't** /'didnt/ did not

**didst** /didst/ *archaic past 2 sing of* DO

**didymium** /,die'dimi·əm, di-/ *n* a mixture of chemical elements, esp NEODYMIUM and PRASEODYMIUM of the RARE EARTH group, used chiefly for colouring glass for optical filters [NL, fr Gk *didymos* double, twin, testicle, fr *dyo* two – more at TWO]

**didynamous** /die'dinəməs/ *adj, of a plant* having two pairs of STAMENS (male reproductive parts) of unequal length [deriv of Gk *di- + dynamis* power – more at DYNAMIC] – **didynamy** *n*

**¹die** /die/ *vb* **dying** *vi* **1** to stop living; undergo physical death **2a** to pass out of existence; cease ⟨*their anger ~d at these words*⟩ ⟨*his secret ~d with him*⟩ **b** to diminish, subside – often + *down* or *away* ⟨*the final chord gradually ~d away*⟩ ⟨*the excitement took a long time to ~ down*⟩ ⟨*the fire has ~d down*⟩ **3a** to languish or pine (e g from love or exhaustion) **b** to long keenly or desperately ⟨*dying to go*⟩ ⟨*dying for a cigarette*⟩ **4** to stop ⟨*the engine spluttered and ~d*⟩ **5** *Christianity* to suffer spiritual death and separation from God; be damned ⟨*whoever lives and believes in me shall never ~* – Jn 11:26⟩ **6** to become indifferent *to;* be unaffected ⟨*~ to the world*⟩ ⟨*~ to sin*⟩ **7** *informal* to be overcome (e g by embarrassment or boredom) ⟨*my dear, I could have ~d!*⟩ ~ *vt* to undergo or endure (a death of a specified kind) ⟨*~d a heroic death*⟩ [ME *dien*, fr or akin to ON *deyja* to die; akin to OHG *touwen* to die, OIr *duine* human being] – **do or die** to make a supreme effort; make the best of a situation – see also **die** HARD *usage* Creatures die *of*, or less commonly *from*, causes ⟨*to* die *of thirst*⟩.

**die down/back** *vi, of a plant* to undergo death of the parts lying above ground

**die out** *vi* 1 to become extinct; disappear 2 **die off, die out** *of a species, family, etc* to die one by one until none remain

²**die** *n, pl* **dies** /diez/, (*1*) **dice** /dies/ 1 a dice 2 DADO 1a (part of a pedestal) 3 any of various tools or devices for imparting a desired shape, form, or finish to a material or for impressing an object or material: e g 3a (the larger of) a pair of cutting or shaping tools that, when moved towards each other, produce a desired form in or impress a desired pattern on an object by pressure or by a blow **b** a hollow internally threaded screw-cutting tool used for forming screw threads **c** a mould into which material (e g molten metal) is forced **d** a perforated block through which metal or plastic is forced or drawn for shaping [ME *dee*, fr MF *dé*, prob fr L *datum*, neut of *datus*, pp of *dare* to give, play] – **the die is cast** the irrevocable decision or step has been taken

³**die** *vt* **dieing** to cut or shape with a die

**dieback** /'die,bak/ *n* a condition in woody plants in which young shoots, branches, etc are killed, esp by parasites

'**die-,cast** *vt* to make by forcing molten material (e g plastic or metal) into a die – **die-cast** *adj*

**diecious** /die'eeshəs/ *adj* DIOECIOUS (having sexes separate)

**diehard** /'die,hahd/ *n* an irreconcilable opponent of change ⟨*party* ~s *who insisted that no concession of any kind be made*⟩ – **die-hard** *adj*, **die-hardism** *n*

**dieldrin** /'deeəl,drin/ *n* a long-lasting chlorine-containing insecticide, $C_{12}H_8Cl_6O$ [*Diels*-*Alder* reaction, fr Otto *Diels* †1954 & Kurt *Alder* †1958 Ger chemists]

**dielectric** /,die·i'lektrik/ *n* a substance in which an electric field can exist, but through which current cannot pass; an insulator [*dia-* + *electric*] – **dielectric** *adj*

**dielectric heating** *n* the rapid and uniform heating of a non-conducting material by means of a high-frequency ELECTROMAGNETIC field

**diencephalon** /,die·in'sef(ə)lon/ *n* the posterior subdivision of the FOREBRAIN [NL, fr *dia-* + *encephalon*] – **diencephalic** *adj*

**diene** /'die,een/ *n* a chemical compound containing two DOUBLE BONDS; *esp* any of a series of ALIPHATIC organic chemical compounds containing two double bonds between carbon atoms [*di-* + *-ene*]

**dieresis** /,die·ə'reesis/ *n, NAm* DIAERESIS (mark over a letter)

**diesel** /'deezl/ *n* 1 (a vehicle driven by) a DIESEL ENGINE 2 **diesel oil, diesel** a heavy MINERAL OIL used as a fuel in DIESEL ENGINES [Rudolph *Diesel* †1913 Ger mechanical engineer]

'**diesel-e,lectric** *adj* of or using the combination of a DIESEL ENGINE driving an electric generator ⟨*a* ~ *locomotive*⟩ – **diesel-electric** *n*

**diesel engine** *n* an INTERNAL-COMBUSTION ENGINE in which air is compressed to a sufficiently high temperature to ignite fuel sprayed into the cylinder where the combustion causes a piston to operate

**diesel·ize, -ise** /'deezl,iez/ *vt* to equip with a DIESEL ENGINE or with electric locomotives having electric generators powered by DIESEL ENGINES

**diesinker** /'die,singkə/ *n* a person or machine that makes dies for cutting and shaping metal and other substances – **die-sinking** *n*

**Dies Irae** /,dee·ayz 'iəray, 'iərie/ *n* a medieval Latin hymn describing the Day of Judgment, sung in masses for the souls of the dead [ML, day of wrath; fr the first words of the hymn]

**diester** /'die,estə/ *n* a compound containing two ESTER groupings

**diestock** /'die,stok/ *n* a piece of equipment to hold dies used for cutting threads

'**diet** /'die·ət/ *n* 1a the food and drink usu taken by an individual or group **b** the kind and amount of food prescribed for a person or animal for a special purpose (e g losing weight) 2 something habitually provided (e g for use or enjoyment) ⟨*a* ~ *of good drama*⟩ [ME *diete*, fr OF, fr L *diaeta* prescribed diet, fr Gk *diaita*, lit., manner of living, fr *dia-* + *-aita* (akin to Gk *aisa* share)]

²**diet** *vb* to (cause to) eat and drink sparingly or according to prescribed rules – **dieter** *n*

³**diet** *n* 1 any of various national or provincial legislatures 2a a session or sitting of a Scottish court or assembly **b** a date fixed by a Scottish court on which a party is to appear in that court

[ML *dieta* day's journey, assembly, fr L *dies* day – more at DEITY]

'**dietary** /'die·ət(ə)ri/ *n* an allowance or quantity of food provided for or eaten by an individual, group, or population in accord with medical orders, availability, economic controls, etc

²**dietary** *adj* of a diet or the rules of a diet

**dietetic** /,die·ə'tetik/ *adj* 1 of diet 2 adapted for use in special diets – **dietetically** *adv*

**dietetics** /,die·ə'tetiks/ *n taking sing or pl vb* the application of the principles of nutrition to the diets of people and animals

**diethyl ether** /die'ethl, -'eethl, -'eethiel/ *n* ETHER 3a (liquid chemical compound)

**diethylstilbestrol** /die,ethlstil'bestrol, -eethl-, -eethiel-/ *n, NAm* STILBOESTROL (synthetic drug) [ISV]

**dietitian, dietician** /,die·ə'tish(ə)n/ *n* a specialist in dietetics [*dietitian* irreg fr '*diet*]

**differ** /'difə/ *vi* 1a to be unlike in nature, form, or characteristics; be distinct *from* **b** to change from time to time; vary 2 to be of unlike or opposite opinion; disagree – often + *with* or *from* [ME *differen*, fr MF or L; MF *differer* to postpone, be different, fr L *differre*, fr *dis-* + *ferre* to carry – more at ²BEAR]

'**difference** /'difrəns/ *n* 1a the quality or state of being different **b** an instance of differing in nature, form, or quality **c** the element or factor that separates or distinguishes contrasting situations 2 distinction or discrimination in preference ⟨*avoided making a* ~ *between them*⟩ 3a disagreement in opinion; dissension **b** *usu pl* an instance or cause of disagreement ⟨*settle our* ~s⟩ 4 the degree or amount by which things differ in quantity or measure; *specif* REMAINDER 2b(1) (number left after one number has been subtracted from another) 5 a significant change in or effect on a situation ⟨*it makes no* ~ *whether you stay or go*⟩ – **split the difference** 1 to compromise 2 to take the average of two suggested amounts ⟨*he was asking £700 for the car, and I offered £650, so we finally agreed to* split the difference⟩

²**difference** *vt* 1 to differentiate, distinguish 2 to calculate the difference between

**difference equation** *n* a mathematical equation which defines successive members of a sequence in terms of differences between other members of the sequence

**different** /'difrənt/ *adj* 1 partly or totally unlike in nature, form, or quality; dissimilar ⟨*could hardly be more* ~⟩ – often + *from*, chiefly Br *to*, or chiefly NAm *than* ⟨*small, neat hand, very* ~ *from the captain's tottery characters* – R L Stevenson⟩ ⟨*a very* ~ *situation to the . . . one under which we live* – Sir Winston Churchill⟩ 2a distinct ⟨~ *age groups*⟩ **b** various ⟨~ *members of the class*⟩ **c** another ⟨*he switched to a* ~ *channel*⟩ 3 unusual, special [MF, fr L *different-*, *differens*, prp of *differre*] – **differently** *adv*, **differentness** *n*

**synonyms** Different, diverse, disparate, divergent, and various may all mean "not identical or alike". Different has the most general meaning, and may refer to distinctness, separateness, or contrast with something else ⟨*wears a* different *hat every day*⟩. Diverse suggests a marked difference between several things ⟨*though we hold* diverse *opinions on many matters, we all agree on this*⟩. Disparate implies not only essential and marked differences, but often incompatible ones ⟨*how can one person hold two such* disparate *views?*⟩ Divergent suggests that the difference between two things is widening, and there is no possibility of bringing them together ⟨*workers and management have* divergent *aims*⟩. Various stresses the number of kinds, or the variety within one whole ⟨*various strands to her personality*⟩. **antonyms** identical, alike, same *usage* 1 The use of different with either *to* or *than* has been long established in English ⟨*it's quite a* different *thing within to what it is without* – Henry Fielding⟩ ⟨*the consuls . . . had been elected for very* different *merits than those of skill in war* – Oliver Goldsmith⟩. Today, however, different *from* is the safest choice. Different *to* is a fairly acceptable mainly British alternative, although it has been censured by grammarians since the 18th century. Different *than*, a mainly American combination, has the convenience that it can introduce a clause ⟨*he wears* different *clothes on Sunday than he does on weekdays*⟩, but to avoid disapproval one may prefer to write ⟨*he wears* different *clothes on Sunday from those he wears on weekdays*⟩. 2 Different can be used with a singular noun to make a comparison with something else that may or may not be mentioned ⟨*you look* different (= from before) *with your hair short*⟩ ⟨*they each wanted to see a* different *film* (= from each other)⟩. This device is used with some dishonesty in advertising ⟨*the beer that's* **different**

( = from what?) ⟩ **3** The use of **different** with a plural noun to mean "various" or "separate" ⟨*visited them on three **different** occasions*⟩ is disapproved of by some people.

**differentia** /ˌdifə'renshyə/ *n, pl* **differentiae** /-shiˌee/ the mark or feature that distinguishes one member of a general class from another; *esp* a trait distinguishing species from other species of the same genus [L, difference, fr *different-*, *differens*]

**¹differential** /ˌdifə'renshəl/ *adj* **1a** of or constituting a difference; distinguishing **b** based on or resulting from a differential ⟨~ *freight charges*⟩ **c** functioning or proceeding differently or at a different rate **2** *maths* of or involving a differential or differentiation **3** *physics* **3a** of quantitative differences **b** producing effects by reason of quantitative differences ⟨~ *pulley*⟩ – **differentially** *adv*

**²differential** *n* **1** *maths* **1a** the product of the DERIVATIVE of a function of one variable with the increment of the INDEPENDENT VARIABLE **b** the sum of the products of each PARTIAL DERIVATIVE of a function of several variables with the increment of the corresponding variable **2** a difference between comparable individuals or classes; *specif* the difference between rates of pay for different jobs in the same industry **3a** **differential gear**, **differential** an arrangement of gears (eg in a vehicle) for connecting two shafts or axes in the same line, dividing the driving force equally between them and permitting one shaft to revolve faster than the other **b** a differential gear together with its case

**differential calculus** *n* a branch of mathematics that deals chiefly with the rate of change of functions with respect to their variables and is used to find the slope of a curve at any point and DERIVATIVES of functions

**differential equation** *n* an equation containing differentials or DERIVATIVES of functions

**differentiate** /ˌdifə'renshiayt/ *vt* **1** to obtain the mathematical DERIVATIVE of **2** to mark or show a difference in **3** to develop differential characteristics in **4** to cause differentiation of (the cells or tissues of a developing plant or animal) in the course of development **5** to express the specific difference between; discriminate ⟨~ *prose from poetry*⟩ ~ *vi* **1** to recognize a difference; distinguish ⟨*unable to* ~ *between red and green*⟩ **2** to become distinct or different in character **3** to undergo differentiation – **differentiability** *n*, **differentiable** *adj*

**differentiation** /ˌdifəˌrenshi'aysh(ə)n/ *n* **1** the act or process of differentiating **2** development into more complex, numerous, or varied forms ⟨~ *of Latin into vernaculars*⟩ **3a** modification of body parts for performance of particular functions **b** all the processes whereby apparently similar cells, tissues, and structures develop and attain their separate adult forms and functions **4** the processes by which various rock types are produced from a common molten form

**difficult** /'difik(ə)lt/ *adj* **1** hard to do, make, or carry out; arduous ⟨*a* ~ *climb*⟩ **2a** hard to deal with, manage, or overcome ⟨*a* ~ *child*⟩ **b** hard to understand; puzzling ⟨*a* ~ *text*⟩ **3** full of hardships or troubles ⟨*going through a very* ~ *time at present*⟩ **synonyms** see ¹HARD **antonyms** simple, facile [back-formation fr *difficulty*] – **difficultly** *adv*

**difficulty** /'difik(ə)lti/ *n* **1** the quality or state of being difficult **2a** something difficult; an obstacle, problem ⟨*his homework didn't present him with too many* difficulties⟩ **b** trouble ⟨*had great* ~ *in understanding him*⟩ ⟨*did it without much* ~⟩ **3** *usu pl* an objection, demur ⟨*she can be relied upon to make* difficulties⟩ **4** difficulties *pl*, **difficulty** a cause of (financial) trouble or embarrassment [ME *difficulte*, fr L *difficultas*, irreg fr *difficilis* difficult, fr *dis-* + *facilis* easy – more at FACILE]

**diffident** /'difid(ə)nt/ *adj* **1** lacking in self-confidence **2** reserved, unassertive **synonyms** see ¹SHY **antonyms** confident [L *diffident*, *diffidens*, prp of *diffidere* to distrust, fr *dis-* + *fidere* to trust – more at BIDE] – **diffidence** *n*, **diffidently** *adv*

**diffract** /di'frakt/ *vt* to cause to undergo diffraction [back-formation fr *diffraction*]

**diffraction** /di'fraksh(ə)n/ *n* a modification which light undergoes in passing the edges of opaque bodies or through narrow slits, or in being reflected from ruled surfaces, and in which the rays appear to be deflected and to produce patterns of parallel light and dark or coloured bands; *also* a similar modification of other waves (eg sound waves) [NL *diffraction-*, *diffractio*, fr L *diffractus*, pp of *diffringere* to break apart, fr *dis-* + *frangere* to break – more at BREAK]

**diffraction grating** *n* GRATING 3 (device used to diffract a beam of light)

**¹diffuse** /di'fyoohs/ *adj* **1** not concentrated or localized;

scattered **2** lacking conciseness; verbose [L *diffusus*, pp of *diffundere* to spread out, fr *dis-* + *fundere* to pour – more at FOUND] – **diffuseness** *n*, **diffusely** *adv*

**²diffuse** /di'fyoohz/ *vt* **1a** to cause to spread or mingle freely; disperse **b** to spread or scatter widely or thinly; disseminate **2** to subject to diffusion; *esp* to break up and distribute (light) by reflection ~ *vi* **1** to spread out or become transmitted **2** to undergo diffusion △ defuse [MF or L; MF *diffuser*, fr L *diffusus*, pp] – **diffusible** *adj*

**dif,fuse-'porous** *adj, of a woody plant* having water-conducting tubes more or less evenly distributed throughout an ANNUAL RING and not varying greatly in size – compare RING-POROUS [¹*diffuse*]

**diffuser** /di'fyoohzə/ *n* someone who or something that diffuses: eg **a** a device (eg a reflector) for distributing the light of a lamp evenly **b** a screen (eg of cloth or frosted glass) for softening lighting (eg in photography) **c** a device (eg slats at different angles) for deflecting air from an outlet in various directions **d** an irregularly-shaped structure used to break up the reflections of sound waves (eg in a recording studio) **e** a device for reducing the speed and increasing the pressure of a liquid or gas passing through a system, usu consisting of a chamber whose cross section increases in the direction of flow

**diffusion** /di'fyoohzh(ə)n/ *n* **1** diffusing or being diffused **2** longwindedness **3a** the process whereby particles of liquids, gases, or solids intermingle as the result of their spontaneous movement, and, in dissolved substances, move from a region of higher to one of lower concentration **b(1)** reflection of light by a rough reflecting surface **b(2)** transmission of light through a translucent material; scattering **4** the spread of a cultural characteristic (eg an artefact, building style, or custom) from one area or culture to another (eg by migration or trade) – **diffusional** *adj*

**diffusive** /di'fyoohziv/ *adj* tending to diffuse; characterized by diffusion ⟨~ *motion of atoms*⟩ – **diffusively** *adv*, **diffusiveness** *n*

**difunctional** /ˌdie'fungksh(ə)nl/ *adj* of or being a chemical compound with two sites in the molecule that are highly reactive

**¹dig** /dig/ *vb* **-gg-; dug** /dug/ *vi* **1** to turn up, loosen, or remove earth **2** to advance (as if) by removing or pushing aside material ⟨~ging *through a pile of papers in search of the letter*⟩ **3** to carry out an archaeological excavation **4** *chiefly NAm slang* to understand ~ *vt* **1a** to break up, turn, or loosen (earth) with an implement, the hands, etc **b** to prepare the soil of by digging – often + *over* ⟨~ *a garden*⟩ ⟨dug *over the flower bed*⟩ **2** to bring to the surface (as if) by digging; unearth – often + *up* ⟨~ging *potatoes*⟩ ⟨dug *up a vital piece of information*⟩ **3a** to hollow out or form by removing earth ⟨~ *a hole*⟩ **b** to excavate for archaeological purposes **4** to force or drive down into something; thrust ⟨dug *her spade into the soil*⟩ **5** to poke, prod ⟨~ *him in the ribs*⟩ **6** *slang* **6a** to pay attention to; notice ⟨~ *that fancy hat*⟩ **b** to understand, appreciate ⟨*what I don't* ~ *over there is the British money* – Jimmy Durante⟩ **c** to like, admire – see also **dig one's** HEELS **in** □ (*vi4; vt6*) no longer in vogue [ME *diggen*, perh deriv of OE *dīc* ditch – more at DYKE]

**dig in** *vt* to cover or mix thoroughly with the soil by digging ⟨dig *the compost well in*⟩ ~ *vi* **1** to dig defensive trenches **2** to hold stubbornly to a position; defend doggedly (eg in a tug-of-war or when batting in cricket) **3** *informal* to begin eating

**dig out** *vt* **1** to make hollow by digging **2** *informal* to find, unearth

**²dig** *n* **1a** a thrust, poke **b** a cutting or snide remark **2** *pl, chiefly Br* lodgings, accommodation **3** an archaeological excavation site; *also* the excavation itself [(2) short for *diggings*]

**digametic** /ˌdiegə'metik/ *adj* forming two kinds of reproductive cells (eg eggs and sperms)

**digamma** /die'gamə, '-,--/ *n* the original sixth letter (F, ͷ) of the Greek alphabet, which was pronounced like the English *w* and became extinct before the classical period [L, fr Gk, fr *di-* + *gamma*; fr its resemblance to two capital gammas, placed one above the other]

**digamy** /'digəmi/ *n* a second marriage after the termination of the first [LL *digamia*, fr LGk, fr Gk *digamos* married to two people, fr *di-* + *-gamos* -gamous]

**digastric** /ˌdie'gastrik/ *adj, of a muscle* having two enlarged fleshy parts at either end that are separated by a tendon [NL *digastricus*, fr *di-* + *gastricus* gastric]

**digenesis** /ˌdie'jenəsis/ *n* ALTERNATION OF GENERATIONS (successive reproduction by sexual and asexual methods) [NL]

**digenetic** /ˌdiejəˈnetik/ *adj* **1** of digenesis **2** of a subclass (Digenea) of flatworms (e g a LIVER FLUKE) in which sexual reproduction as an internal parasite of a VERTEBRATE animal (e g a sheep) alternates with asexual reproduction in an INVERTEBRATE animal (e g a snail)

¹**digest** /ˈdiejest/ *n* a collection or summary of information: e g **a** a systematic compilation of laws **b** a literary work in condensed form [ME *Digest* compilation of Roman laws ordered by the Emperor Justinian, fr LL *Digesta,* pl, fr L, collection of writings arranged under headings, fr neut pl of *digestus,* pp of *digerere* to arrange, distribute, digest, fr *dis-* + *gerere* to carry]

²**digest** /diˈjest, die-/ *vt* **1** to distribute or arrange systematically **2** to convert (food) into a form the body can use **3** to take into the mind or memory; *esp* to assimilate mentally ⟨*took her a long time to ~ this piece of information*⟩ **4** to soften or decompose or extract soluble ingredients from by heat and moisture or chemicals **5** to compress into a short summary [ME *digesten,* fr L *digestus*] – **digestible** *adj,* **digestibility** *n*

**digester** /diˈjestə, die-/ *n* **1** someone who or something that digests **2** an apparatus or vessel for digesting esp plant or animal materials

**digestif** /ˌdijeˈsteef/ *n* a drink taken after a meal as an aid to digestion [Fr, digestive, fr *digestif,* adj, fr L *digestivus,* fr *digestus*]

**digestion** /diˈjeschən, die-/ *n* the action, process, or power of digesting: e g **a** the process of making food chemically available to the body cells by breaking it down into simpler substances (e g through the action of digestive enzymes) and dissolving it **b** the process in sewage treatment by which organic matter in sludge is decomposed by bacteria **c** the process of treating substances with heat, moisture, or chemicals to cause softening or decomposition

¹**digestive** /diˈjestiv, die-/ *n* something that aids digestion

²**digestive** *adj* of, causing, or promoting digestion ⟨*~ enzymes*⟩ – **digestively** *adv*

**digestive biscuit** *n* a slightly sweet biscuit made from wholemeal flour

**digestive gland** *n* a gland producing digestive enzymes

**digger** /ˈdigə/ *n* **1** someone or something that digs **2** a tool or machine for digging; *specif* a vehicle fitted with a hydraulically-operated shovel for digging loose material (e g earth) **3** *cap* any of several N American Indian tribes (e g the PAIUTE) who dig up roots for food **4** *informal* a person from Australia or New Zealand **5** *often cap, informal* a private soldier from Australia or New Zealand, esp in World War I **6** *Austr & NZ informal* a fellow, man – often used as a term of address [(4) *digger* (gold miner, taken to be a typical Australian)]

**digger wasp** *n* a burrowing wasp; *esp* a wasp (superfamily Sphecoidea or Pompiloidea) that digs burrows in the soil, sand, etc and stocks them with live insects or spiders paralysed by stinging as food for the young

**diggings** /ˈdigingz/ *n pl* **1** material dug out **2** a place where mining has taken place, esp for ore, metals, or precious stones **3** *archaic Br informal* DIGS 2 (lodgings)

**dight** /diet/ *vt* **dighted, dight** *archaic* to dress, adorn [ME *dighten,* fr OE *dihtan* to arrange, compose, fr a prehistoric WGmc word borrowed fr L *dictare* to dictate, compose]

**digit** /ˈdijit/ *n* **1a** any of the ARABIC NUMERALS (0 to 9) **b** any of the elements that combine to form numbers in a system other than the decimal system **2** any of the divisions in which the limbs of amphibians and all higher vertebrates terminate, which are typically five in number but may be reduced (e g in the horse), and which typically have a series of small bones (PHALANGES) bearing a nail, claw, or hoof at the tip: e g **2a** a finger **b** a toe [ME, fr L *digitus* finger, toe – more at TOE]

¹**digital** /ˈdijitl/ *adj* **1** of the fingers or toes **2** done with a finger ⟨*a ~ examination of the rectum*⟩ **3** of calculation by numerical methods which use separate units **4a** of data in the form of numerical digits **b** of a DIGITAL COMPUTER **5** *of an automatic device* presenting information in the form of numerical digits rather than by a pointer moving round a dial ⟨*~ clock*⟩ – **digitally** *adv*

²**digital** *n* any of the keys, operated with the fingers, of an organ, piano, harpsichord, etc

**digital computer** *n* a computer that operates with numbers expressed as separate pulses representing digits – compare ANALOGUE COMPUTER

**digitalis** /ˌdijiˈtahlis/ *n* **1** a foxglove **2** the dried leaf of the common foxglove (*Digitalis purpurea*) containing several chemical compounds which are important as drugs used esp as powerful heart stimulants [NL, genus name, fr L, of a finger, fr *digitus;* fr its finger-shaped corolla]

**digital·ize,-ise** /ˈdijitlˌiez/ *vt* to digitize [¹*digital*]

**digitate** /ˈdijitayt/ *adj* **1** having fingers or toes **2** having divisions arranged like the fingers of a hand ⟨*a ~ leaf*⟩ – **digitately** *adv,* **digitation** *n*

**digiti-** /dijiti-/ *comb form* digit; finger; toe ⟨digiti*form*⟩ [Fr, fr L *digitus*]

**digitigrade** /ˈdijitiˌgrayd/ *adj, of a dog, cat, horse, etc* walking on the toes with the back of the foot more or less raised – compare PLANTIGRADE [Fr, fr *digiti-* + *-grade*] – **digitigrade** *n*

**digit·ize,-ise** /ˈdijitiez/ *vt* to put (data) into digital form ⟨*the analogue signal of the human voice has to be ~*d – *The Economist*⟩ – **digitizer** *n,* **digitization** *n*

**digitoxin** /ˌdijiˈtoksin/ *n* a chemical compound, $C_{41}H_{64}O_{13}$, that is the most active constituent of digitalis [ISV, blend of NL *Digitalis* and ISV *toxin*]

**diglot** /ˈdieˌglot/ *adj* bilingual [Gk *diglōttos,* fr *di-* + *glōtta* language – more at GLOSS]

**dignified** /ˈdignified/ *adj* showing or having dignity

**dignify** /ˈdignifie/ *vt* **1** to confer honour or distinction on; ennoble **2** to give the appearance of dignity to by the use of a high-sounding name [MF *dignifier,* fr LL *dignificare,* fr L *dignus* worthy – more at DECENT]

**dignitary** /ˈdignit(ə)ri/ *n* a person of high rank or holding a position of dignity or honour – **dignitary** *adj*

**dignity** /ˈdignəti/ *n* **1** the quality or state of being worthy, honoured, or esteemed **2a** high rank, office, or position **b** a high opinion of oneself; self-esteem – esp in *beneath one's dignity* and *stand on one's dignity* **3** formal reserve of manner or language; gravity, stateliness [ME *dignete,* fr OF *digneté,* fr L *dignitat-, dignitas,* fr *dignus*]

**digoxin** /diˈjoksin, diˈgoksin/ *n* a poisonous chemical compound, $C_{41}H_{64}O_{14}$, obtained from some foxgloves (e g *Digitalis lanata*) and used as a heart stimulant [ISV *dig-* (fr NL *Digitalis*) + *toxin*]

**digraph** /ˈdieˌgrahf, -ˌgraf/ *n* **1** a group of two successive letters that are pronounced as a single sound (e g *ea* in *bread* or *ng* in *sing*) or whose value is not the sum of a value borne by each in other occurrences (e g *ch* in *chin* where the value is /t/ + /sh/) **2** a group of two successive letters **3** LIGATURE **4** (character consisting of two or more joined letters) – **digraphic** *adj,* **digraphically** *adv*

**digress** /dieˈgres, di-/ *vi* to turn aside, esp from the main subject or line of argument in writing or speaking [L *digressus,* pp of *digredi,* fr *dis-* + *gradi* to step – more at GRADE] – **digressive** *adj,* **digressively** *adv,* **digressiveness** *n*

**digression** /dieˈgresh(ə)n, di-/ *n* the act or an instance of digressing – **digressional, digressionary** *adj*

**dihal-, dihalo-** *comb form* containing two atoms of a HALOGEN (e g chlorine, bromine, or iodine) in the molecular structure

¹**dihedral** /ˌdieˈheedrəl/ *adj* **1** having or contained by two flat surfaces **2a** *of an aeroplane* having wings that make with one another a dihedral angle, esp when the angle between the upper sides is less than 180° **b** *of aeroplane wing pairs* inclined at a dihedral angle to each other

²**dihedral** *n* **1 dihedral angle, dihedral** the angle formed by two intersecting planes **2** the angle between an upward- or downward-sloping aeroplane wing and a horizontal line – compare ANHEDRAL

**dihybrid** /dieˈhiebrid/ *adj* of or being an individual organism or a strain of organisms that is HETEROZYGOUS (having two different versions of one gene) for two different genetic characteristics [ISV] – **dihybrid** *n*

**dihydr-** /diehiedr-/, **dihydro-** *comb form* containing two atoms of hydrogen in the molecular structure

**dihydroxy-** /diehiedroksi-/ *comb form* containing two HYDROXYL groups in the molecular structure

**dihydroxyacetone** /ˌdiehieˌdroksiˈasitohn/ *n* a chemical compound, $(HOCH_2)_2CO$, that is used esp to produce artificial tanning of the skin when applied externally

**dik-dik** /ˈdikˌdik/ *n* any of several small E African antelopes (genus *Madoqua* or *Rhynchotragus*) [native name in E Africa]

**dike** /diek/ *n or vt* DYKE

**diktat** /dikˈtat/ *n* **1** a harsh settlement imposed (e g on a defeated nation) by a victor or authority **2** a categorical statement [Ger, lit., something dictated, fr NL *dictatum,* fr L, neut of *dictatus,* pp of *dictare* to dictate]

**dilapidated** /diˈlapidaytid/ *adj* falling to pieces, esp as a result of neglect or misuse ⟨*a scrapyard filled with ~ cars*⟩ [fr pp of *dilapidate* (to make or become decayed), fr L *dilapidatus*, pp of *dilapidare* to squander, destroy, fr *dis-* + *lapidare* to throw stones, fr *lapid-*, *lapis* stone – more at LAPIDARY] – **dilapidation** *n*

**dilatancy** /die'layt(ə)nsi/ *n* a property of some liquids, esp EMULSIONS or pastes, whereby they become thicker and more sticky the faster they move – compare THIXOTROPY – **dilatant** *adj*

**dilatation** /ˌdilə'taysh(ə)n, die-/ *n* **1** expanding or being expanded **2** *medicine* **2a** the condition of being stretched beyond normal dimensions, esp as a result of overwork or disease or of abnormal relaxation ⟨~ *of the bladder*⟩ **b** the action of stretching or enlarging an organ or part of the body **c** a dilated body part or formation **3** *formal* expansion or discursiveness in writing or speech – **dilatational** *adj*

**dilate** /die'layt, di-/ *vt* to enlarge or expand in bulk or extent; distend ~ *vi* **1** to become wide **2** *formal* to comment at length; discourse – + *on* or *upon* ⟨~ *on a topic*⟩ *synonyms* see EXPAND *antonyms* contract, constrict, circumscribe [ME *dilaten*, fr MF *dilater*, fr L *dilatare*, lit., to spread wide, fr *dis-* + *latus* wide – more at LATITUDE] – **dilatable** *adj*, **dilater** *n*, **dilative** *adj*, **dilatability** *n*

**dilated** /die'laytid, di-/ *adj* expanded, widened – **dilatedness** *n*

**dilation** /die'laysh(ə)n, di-/ *n* **1** dilating or being dilated **2** DILATATION 2b

**dilatory** /'dilət(ə)ri/ *adj* **1** tending or intended to cause delay **2** slow in action; tardy ⟨~ *in answering letters*⟩ *synonyms* see TARDY [LL *dilatorius*, fr L *dilatus* (pp of *differre* to postpone, differ), fr *dis-* + *latus*, suppletive pp of *ferre* to carry – more at DIFFER, TOLERATE] – **dilatorily** *adv*, **dilatoriness** *n*

**dildo**, also **dildoe** /'dildoh/ *n*, *pl* **dildos**, **dildoes** an object serving as an artificial penis for inserting into the vagina [perh modif of It *diletto* delight]

**dilemma** /di'lemə, die-/ *n* **1** an argument in which an opponent's position is refuted by being shown to lead to two or more unacceptable alternatives **2a** a choice or a situation involving choice between equally unsatisfactory alternatives **b** a problem seemingly incapable of a satisfactory solution – see also **on the** HORNS **of a dilemma** [LL, fr Gk *dilēmmat-*, *dilēmma*, prob back-formation fr Gk *dilēmmatos* involving two assumptions, fr *di-* + *lēmmat-*, *lēmma* assumption – more at LEMMA] – **dilemmatic** *adj*

*usage* **1** The pronunciation /di'lemə/ is recommended for BBC broadcasters. **2** Writers on usage advise that **dilemma** should not be used to mean merely a "problem", involving an open choice ⟨*the dilemma of where to go for one's holidays*⟩, but that its meaning should be restricted to that of a choice between two (because the word is ultimately derived from the Greek *di-* = "two"), or at any rate between a definite number, of equally unattractive alternatives ⟨*the dilemma of whether to lower prices or lose sales*⟩.

**dilettante** /ˌdili'tanti/ *n*, *pl* **dilettanti** /~/, **dilettantes** /-tiz/ **1** a person having a superficial interest in a branch of knowledge or one of the arts; a dabbler **2** an admirer or lover of the arts, esp the FINE ARTS [It, fr prp of *dilettare* to delight, fr L *delectare* – more at DELIGHT] – **dilettante** *adj*, **dilettantish** *adj*, **dilettantism** *n*

[1]**diligence** /'dilij(ə)ns/ *n* **1** steady application and effort **2** the attention and care legally expected or required of a person **3** a process in Scottish law by which people or property are seized in execution of a judgment [MF, fr L *diligentia*, fr *diligent-*, *diligens*]

[2]**diligence** *n* a stagecoach; *esp* one used in France [Fr, lit., haste, fr MF, persevering application]

**diligent** /'dilij(ə)nt/ *adj* showing steady application and effort *synonyms* see [1]BUSY *antonyms* negligent, indolent [ME, fr MF, fr L *diligent-*, *diligens*, fr prp of *diligere* to esteem, love, fr *di-* + *legere* to select – more at LEGEND] – **diligently** *adv*

**dill** /dil/ *n* any of several plants of the carrot family; *esp* a European plant (*Anethum graveolens*) with aromatic foliage and seeds both of which are used in flavouring foods (e g pickles) [ME *dile*, fr OE; akin to OHG *tilli* dill]

**dill pickle** *n* a small pickled cucumber seasoned with dill

**dilly** /'dili/ *n*, *NAm informal* a remarkable or outstanding person or thing [obs slang *dilly* delightful, alter. of *delightful*]

**dilly bag** *n* an Australian mesh bag of native grass or fibres [*dilli*, native name in Australia]

**dillydally** /'dili,dali/ *vi*, *informal* to waste time by loitering; dawdle [redupl of *dally*]

**diluent** /'dilyoo-ənt/ *adj* making thinner or less concentrated; diluting [L *diluent-*, *diluens*, prp of *diluere*] – **diluent** *n*

[1]**dilute** /die'looht, die'lyooht/ *vt* **1** to make thinner or more liquid by adding another liquid **2** to diminish the strength, flavour, or brilliance of by adding more liquid, light, etc **3** to attenuate [L *dilutus*, pp of *diluere* to wash away, dilute, fr *di-* + *lavere* to wash – more at LYE] – **diluter**, **dilutor** *n*, **dilutive** *adj*

[2]**dilute** *adj* weak, diluted ⟨~ *sulphuric acid*⟩ – **diluteness** *n*

**dilution** /die'loohsh(ə)n, die'lyoohsh(ə)n/ *n* **1** diluting or diluted **2** something (e g a solution) that is diluted

**diluvial** /di'loohvyəl/, **diluvian** /-yən/ *adj* of or brought about by a flood [LL *diluvialis*, fr L *diluvium* flood – more at DELUGE]

[1]**dim** /dim/ *adj* **-mm-** **1a** giving out a weak or insufficient light **b** dull, lustreless **2a** seen or perceived indistinctly or without clear outlines or details ⟨*a ~ shape loomed out of the fog*⟩ **b** not seeing clearly and distinctly ⟨*the old man's eyes were ~*⟩ **3** characterized by an unfavourable or pessimistic attitude – esp in *take a dim view of* **4** *informal* lacking intelligence; stupid [ME, fr OE; akin to OHG *timber* dark, Skt *dhamati* he blows] – **dimly** *adv*, **dimness** *n*

[2]**dim** *vb* **-mm-** *vt* **1** to make dim **2** *NAm* DIP **4** (switch headlights to lower beam) ~ *vi* to become dim

[3]**dim** *n*, *archaic* dusk

**dime** /diem/ *n* a coin worth $\frac{1}{10}$ of a US dollar [ME, tenth part, tithe, fr MF, fr L *decima* – more at DECIMAL]

**dime novel** *n*, *NAm* a usu paperback melodramatic novel – **dime novelist** *n*

[1]**dimension** /di'mensh(ə)n, die-/ *n* **1a(1)** measure in one direction; *specif* any of three or four coordinates determining a position in space or space and time **a(2)** *maths* any of a group of PARAMETERS (defining quantities or qualities) necessary and sufficient to determine uniquely each element of a system of usu mathematical entities ⟨*the surface of a sphere has two ~s*⟩ **b** *maths* the number of elements in a BASIS of a VECTOR SPACE **c** any of the fundamental quantities, specif mass, length, and time, in terms of which any physical quantity may be expressed ⟨*velocity has the ~s of length divided by time*⟩ **2** *pl* the range or area over which something extends; scope, size ⟨*a town of modest ~s*⟩ ⟨*confronted by a task of huge ~s*⟩ **3** any of the elements or factors making up a complete personality or entity; an aspect ⟨*a new ~ to the problem*⟩ [ME, fr MF, fr L *dimension-*, *dimensio*, fr *dimensus*, pp of *dimetiri* to measure out, fr *dis-* + *metiri* to measure – more at MEASURE] – **dimensional** *adj*, **dimensionally** *adv*, **dimensionality** *n*, **dimensionless** *adj*

[2]**dimension** *vt* **1** to shape or cut to the required dimensions **2** to indicate the dimensions on (a drawing)

**dimer** /'dimə/ *n* a chemical compound formed by the union of two chemical groups or two molecules of a simpler compound; *specif* one formed by the union of two identical groups [ISV *di-* + *-mer* (as in *polymer*)] – **dimerize** *vt*, **dimerization** *n*

**dimeric** /die'merik/ *adj* **1** consisting of two identical parts ⟨*a ~ chromosome*⟩ **2** involving or mediated by two factors **3** of a dimer [NL *dimerus*]

**dimerous** /'dimərəs/ *adj* consisting of two parts: e g **a** *of an insect* having two joints in the TARSUS (segment of leg) **b** *of a flower* having two parts in each WHORL (circle of flowers) [NL *dimerus*, fr L *di-* + NL *-merous* -merous] – **dimerism** *n*

**dimeter** /'dimitə/ *n* a line of verse consisting of two metrical FEET (units of poetic rhythm) [LL, fr Gk *dimetros*, adj, being a dimeter, fr *di-* + *metron* measure – more at MEASURE]

**dimethyl-** /diemethil-, -mee-, -thiel/ *comb form* containing two METHYL groups in the molecular structure

**dimethylhydrazine** /ˌdie,methil'hiedrəzeen, -ˌmeethiel-/ *n* an inflammable corrosive liquid, $(CH_3)_2NNH_2$, which is used in rocket fuels

**dimethylsulphoxide** /ˌdie,methilsul'foksied, -meethiel-/ *n* a compound, $(CH_3)_2SO$, obtained as a by-product in wood-pulp manufacture and used esp as a solvent (e g for drugs applied to the skin)

**dimethyltryptamine** /ˌdie,methil'triptəmeen, -meethiel-, -min/ *n* an easily prepared hallucinogenic drug, $C_{12}H_{16}N_2$, that is chemically similar to but acts for a shorter time than PSILOCYBIN [*dimethyl-* + *trypt*ophan + *amine*]

**dimidiate** /di'midiayt/ *adj* split into halves [L *dimidiatus*, pp of *dimidiare* to halve, fr *di-* (fr *dis-* apart) + *-midiare* (fr *medius* mid)]

**diminish** /di'minish/ *vt* **1** to make less or cause to appear less **2** to lessen the authority, dignity, or reputation of; belittle **3** to cause to taper ~ *vi* **1** to become gradually less (e g in size or importance); dwindle **2** to taper [ME *deminishen*, alter. of diminuen, fr MF diminuer, fr LL diminuere, alter. of L deminuere, fr de- + minuere to lessen – more at MINOR] – **diminishable** adj, **diminishment** n

**diminished** /di'minisht/ adj, of a musical interval made one semitone less than PERFECT or minor ⟨a ~ fifth⟩ – compare AUGMENTED, MAJOR 5c, MINOR 3c, PERFECT 5a

**diminished responsibility** n limitation of a person's criminal responsibility for the killing of another on the ground of mental abnormality

**diminishing returns** /di'minishing/ n pl a rate of yield that beyond a certain point fails to increase in proportion to additional quantities of a factor input (e g capital or labour)

¹**diminuendo** /di,minyoo'endoh/ adv or adj with a decrease in volume – used as a direction in music [It, lit., diminishing, fr LL diminuendum, gerund of diminuere]

²**diminuendo** n 1 a gradual decrease in volume of a musical passage 2 a diminuendo musical passage

**diminution** /,dimi'nyoohsh(ə)n/ n the act, process, or an instance of diminishing; decrease [ME diminucioun, fr MF diminution, fr ML diminution-, diminutio, alter. of L deminution-, deminutio, fr deminutus, pp of deminuere] – **diminutional** adj

¹**diminutive** /di'minyootiv/ n 1 a diminutive word, affix, or name 2 a diminutive individual or thing [ME diminutif, fr ML diminutivum, alter. of LL deminutivum, fr neut of deminutivus, adj, fr L deminutus]

²**diminutive** adj 1 indicating small size and sometimes lovableness or triviality – used in connection with affixes (e g -ette, -ling) and words formed with them (e g kitchenette, duckling), with clipped forms (e g Jim), and with altered forms (e g Peggy); compare AUGMENTATIVE 2 exceptionally or abnormally small; tiny synonyms see ¹SMALL – **diminutively** adv, **diminutiveness** n

**dimissory** /di'misəri/ adj granting leave to depart; dismissing [ML dimissorius dismissing and commending, fr LL, submitting a matter to a higher court, fr L dimissus, pp of dimittere to dismiss]

**dimity** /'dimiti/ n a corded cotton fabric of plain weave in checks or stripes – compare DAMASK [alter. of ME demyt, deriv of MGk dimitos of double thread, fr Gk di- + mitos warp thread]

**dimmer** /'dimə/ n a device for regulating the brightness of an electric lighting unit [²dim + ²-er]

**dimorphic** /,die'mawfik/ adj 1a DIMORPHOUS 1 2 having or occurring in two distinct forms ⟨humans are sexually ~⟩

**dimorphism** /,die'mawfiz(ə)m/ n the condition or property of being dimorphic or dimorphous: e g a(1) the existence of two different forms within a species, distinguished by colour, size, etc a(2) the existence of an organ (e g the leaves of a plant) in two different forms ⟨the floating and submerged leaves of an aquatic plant may exhibit considerable ~⟩ b crystallization of a chemical compound in two different forms [ISV]

**dimorphous** /,die'mawfəs/ adj 1 of a chemical compound crystallizing in two different forms 2 DIMORPHIC 2 [Gk dimorphos having two forms, fr di- + -morphos -morphous]

**dimout** /'dim,owt/ n, chiefly NAm a restriction limiting the use or showing of lights at night, esp during the threat of an air raid; also the condition of partial darkness produced (as if) by this restriction – compare BLACKOUT

¹**dimple** /'dimpl/ n 1 a slight natural indentation in the surface of some part of the human body; esp one that appears in the cheek when smiling 2 a depression or indentation on any surface (e g that of a golf ball) [ME dympull; akin to OHG tumphilo whirlpool, OE dyppan to dip – more at DIP] – **dimply** adj

²**dimple** vt to mark with dimples ~ vi to exhibit or form dimples

**dimwit** /'dim,wit/ n, informal a slow-witted or stupid person

,**dim-'witted** adj not mentally bright; stupid – **dim-wittedly** adv, **dim-wittedness** n

¹**din** /din/ n a loud continued noise; esp a confusion of discordant and noisy sounds [ME, fr OE dyne; akin to ON dynr din, Skt dhvanati it roars]

²**din** vb -nn- vt 1 to assail or deafen with loud continued noise 2 to impress (something upon someone) by insistent repetition ⟨it was ~ned into them⟩ ~ vi to make a din

**dinar** /'dee,nah/ n 1 – see MONEY table 2 – see rial at MONEY table [Ar dīnār, fr Gk dēnarion denarius, fr L denarius]

**dine** /dien/ vi 1 to eat dinner 2 to eat a specified food – + on, upon, or off to give a dinner to; feed ⟨wined and ~d his friends⟩ [ME dinen, fr OF diner, fr (assumed) VL disjejunare to

break one's fast, fr L dis- + LL jejunare to fast, fr L jejunus fasting]

**dine out on** vt to be socially in demand as a result of (e g an amusing or interesting story, or joke one has to tell) ⟨you'll be able to dine out on that story for years⟩

**diner** /'dienə/ n 1 someone who dines 2a DINING CAR b chiefly NAm a restaurant usu resembling a dining car in shape

**dinette** /,die'net/ n a small space, often off a kitchen, used for informal meals; also furniture for such a space [dine + -ette]

**ding** /ding/ vt DIN 2 ~ vi to make a ringing sound [prob imit]

**ding-a-ling** /'ding ə ,ling/ n, chiefly NAm informal a nitwit, fool [prob imit of the sound of bells (ie inside sby's head)]

**ding an sich** /ding ahn zikh (Ger dɪŋ an zɪç)/ n, pl **dinge an sich** /dingə (Ger dɪŋə)/ philosophy THING-IN-ITSELF (aspect of an object that is independent of sense-perception) [Ger]

**dingbats** /'ding,bats/ n pl, Austr & NZ an attack of nervous anxiety – + the [origin unknown]

¹**dingdong** /'ding,dong/ n 1 the ringing sound produced by repeated strokes esp on a bell 2 chiefly Br informal a noisy or heated argument [imit] – **dingdong,** vi

²**dingdong** adj 1 being or resembling the ringing sound made by a bell 2 informal marked by a rapid exchange or alternation esp of blows or words ⟨a real ~ argument⟩ 3 informal, of a race or contest with the advantage passing continually back and forth from one contestant to the other ⟨a ~ race between the two horses⟩

**dinghy** /'ding-gi/ n 1 a small boat propelled by oars, sails, or an engine that is often carried on a larger boat as a tender or lifeboat 2 a small open sailing boat used esp for racing 3 a rubber life raft △ dingy [Bengali ḍiṅgi & Hindi ḍiṅgī, dim. of ḍiṅgā boat]

**dingle** /'ding-gl/ n a small, narrow, and often wooded valley; a dell [ME, abyss]

**dingo** /'ding-goh/ n, pl **dingoes** 1 a reddish-brown wild dog (Canis dingo) of Australia 2 Austr informal a worthless person [native name in Australia]

**dingus** /'ding-gəs/ n, informal something (e g a gadget) whose common name is unknown or forgotten [D or Ger; D dinges, prob fr Ger dings, fr gen of ding thing, fr OHG – more at THING]

**dingy** /'dinji/ adj 1 dirty, discoloured 2 shabby, squalid; also gloomy and badly lit △ dinghy [perh alter. of dungy of dung, filthy, fr dung] – **dingily** adv, **dinginess** n

**dining car** /'diening/ n a railway carriage in which meals are served

**dining room** /'-- -, '-- ,-/ n a room where meals are eaten

**dinitro-** /,die'nietroh-/ comb form containing two NITRO groups in the molecular structure

**dinitrobenzene** /,die,nietroh'benzeen/ n any of three toxic chemical compounds, $C_6H_4(NO_2)_2$, having the same composition but different structural arrangements of atoms; esp the yellow form used chiefly in the manufacture of dyes [ISV]

**dinitrophenol** /,die,nietroh'feenol/ n any of six ISOMERIC (having the same composition but different arrangements of atoms) chemical compounds, $C_6H_4N_2O_5$, some of whose derivatives are pesticides; esp a highly poisonous compound that increases the rate at which fat is broken down and processed in the body and that was formerly given to reduce weight

¹**dinkum** /'dingkəm/ adj, Austr & NZ informal authentic, genuine – often in fair dinkum ⟨you've become a fair-dinkum Kiwi – Albert Wendt⟩ [prob fr E dial. dinkum, n work]

²**dinkum** adv, Austr & NZ informal truly, honestly

**dinky** /'dingki/ adj 1 chiefly Br informal neat and dainty 2 chiefly NAm derog small, insignificant [Sc dink neat]

**dinner** /'dinə/ n 1a the main meal of the day eaten either in the middle of the day or the evening; also the food prepared for a dinner b a formal feast or banquet 2 a packaged meal usu for quick preparation ⟨warmed up a frozen chicken ~⟩ [ME diner, fr OF, fr diner to dine] – **dinnerless** adj

'**dinner-,dance** n an entertainment at which a formal evening meal is followed by dancing

**dinner jacket** n a usu black jacket for men's semiformal evening wear – called also DJ

**dinoflagellate** /,dienoh'flajəlat, -ayt, -flə'jelət/ n any of a group of aquatic single-celled usu solitary organisms that propel themselves through the water by means of two FLAGELLA (whiplike appendages), are an important constituent of marine plankton, that include luminescent forms and forms causing RED TIDE. Dinoflagellates possess both animal and plant characteristics and can be classed as belonging to either an order (Dinoflagellata) of PROTOZOA (single-celled animals) or to a class (Dinophyceae) of algae. [deriv of Gk *dinos* rotation, eddy + NL *flagellum*] – **dinoflagellate** *adj*

**dinosaur** /'dienə,saw/ *n* any of a group (Dinosauria) of extinct chiefly ground-living flesh- or plant-eating reptiles; *broadly* any large extinct reptile or prehistoric monster [deriv of Gk *deinos* terrible + *sauros* lizard – more at DIRE, SAURIAN] – **dinosaurian** *adj or n*, **dinosauric** *adj*

**dinothere** /'dienə,thiə/ *n* any of a genus (*Deinotherium*) of extinct enormous elephantlike mammals with a pair of downward-directed tusks [NL *Deinotherium*, genus name, fr Gk *deinos* + NL *-therium* beast, animal, fr Gk *thērion*, dim. of *thēr*]

**¹dint** /dint/ *n* 1 ¹DENT 2 *archaic* a blow, stroke *synonyms* see ¹DENT [ME, fr OE *dynt*] – **by dint of** by MEANS OF

**²dint** *vt* 1 to make a dent in 2 to impress or drive in with force

**dinucleotide** /,die'nyoohkliə,tied/ *n* any of a class of compounds consisting of two chemically linked NUCLEOTIDES

**diocesan** /,die'osisən/ *n* a bishop having authority over a diocese

**diocese** /'dieəsis/ *n* the area over which a bishop has ecclesiastical authority [ME *diocise*, fr MF, fr LL *diocesis*, alter. of *dioecesis*, fr L, administrative division, fr Gk *dioikēsis* administration, administrative division, fr *dioikein* to keep house, govern, fr *dia-* + *oikein* to dwell, manage, fr *oikos* house – more at VICINITY] – **diocesan** *adj*

**diode** /'die,ohd/ *n* any of a number of electronic devices that have two terminals and that usu permit significant current flow in only one direction: eg **a** a THERMIONIC VALVE having only an ANODE (positive terminal) and a CATHODE (negative terminal) **b** a SEMICONDUCTOR device having only two terminals [ISV]

**dioecious**, *NAm also* **diecious** /,die'eeshəs/ *adj* 1 having male and female reproductive organs in different individuals 2 having male and female flowers borne on different plants □ compare MONOECIOUS [deriv of Gk *di-* + *oikos* house] – **dioeciously** *adv*, **dioecism** *n*

**dioestrous**, *NAm* **diestrous** /,die'eestrəs/ *adj or n* (of or having) a period of sexual inactivity that intervenes between two periods of OESTRUS (period when a female is capable of conceiving) [NL *dioestrus* period of sexual inactivity, fr *dia-* + *oestrus*]

**dioestrual**, *NAm* **diestrual** /,die'eestro_oəl/ *adj* dioestrous

**diol** /'die,ohl/ *n* a chemical alcohol (eg glycol) containing two HYDROXYL (alcohol) groups in each molecule [ISV *di-* + ¹*-ol*]

**Dionysia** /,dieə'niz(h)iə, ,dieə'nis(h)iə/ *n taking pl vb* ancient Greek festival observances held in seasonal cycles in honour of Dionysus, the Greek god of wine; *esp* such observances marked by dramatic performances [L, fr Gk, fr neut pl of *dionysios* of Dionysus, fr *Dionysos* Dionysus (also called Bacchus), god of wine]

**Dionysiac** /,dieə'niz(h)iak, ,dieə'nis(h)iak/ *adj* DIONYSIAN 2 [L *dionysiacus*, fr Gk *dionysiakos*, fr *Dionysos*] – **Dionysiac** *n*

**Dionysian** /,dieə'niz(h)yən, ,dieə'nis(h)yən/ *adj* 1 relating to Dionysus, the Greek god of wine 2a devoted to the worship of the god Dionysus **b** frenzied, orgiastic

**Diophantine equation** /,dieə'fantien, -tin/ *n* an indeterminate polynomial equation with integral coefficients for which it is required to find all integral solutions $\langle x = 3, y = 4, z = 5$ is one solution of the $\sim x^2 + y^2 = z^2 \rangle$ [*Diophantus* fl ab 275 Gk mathematician]

**diopside** /die'opsied/ *n* a green to white PYROXENE mineral consisting of a SILICATE of calcium and magnesium, $CaMgSi_2O_6$ [Fr, fr *di-* + Gk *opsis* appearance – more at OPTIC] – **diopsidic** *adj*

**dioptometer** /,die·op'tomitə/ *n* an instrument used in measuring the ACCOMMODATION (automatic adjustment for distance) of the eye and its ability to bring an image to a focus by REFRACTION – **dioptometry** *n*

**dioptre**, *NAm chiefly* **diopter** /,die'optə/ *n* a unit of measurement of the power of a lens to cause convergence or divergence of a beam of light, equal to the RECIPROCAL of the FOCAL LENGTH (distance between the lens centre and the point of convergence or divergence) in metres [*diopter* (an optical instrument), fr MF *dioptre*, fr L *dioptra*, fr Gk, fr *dia-* + *opsesthai* to be going to see]

**dioptric** /,die'optrik/ *adj* 1 causing or serving to cause the convergence or divergence of a beam of light; REFRACTIVE; *specif* assisting vision by refracting and focussing light 2 produced by means of REFRACTION [Gk *dioptrikos* of a diopter (instrument), fr *dioptra*]

**diorama** /,dieə'rahmə/ *n* 1 a representation of a scene in which a partly translucent painting, made more realistic by artificial lighting effects, is seen from a distance through an aperture 2a a representation of a scene in three dimensions, in which modelled figures, buildings, etc are displayed usu in miniature against a realistic painted background **b** a life-size museum exhibit of a wildlife specimen or scene with realistic natural surroundings and a painted background 3 a small-scale set used in films and television [Fr, fr *dia-* + *-orama* (as in *panorama*, fr E)] – **dioramic** *adj*

**diorite** /'dieəriet/ *n* a dark coarse-grained IGNEOUS rock that is formed by the solidification of molten lava below the earth's surface and consists of PLAGIOCLASE feldspar together with minerals (eg hornblende, pyroxene, or biotite) containing iron and magnesium [Fr, irreg fr Gk *diorizein* to distinguish, fr *dia-* + *horizein* to define – more at HORIZON] – **dioritic** *adj*

**dioxane** /die'oksayn/ *n* an inflammable poisonous chemical compound, $C_4H_8O_2$, used esp as a solvent [ISV *di-* + *ox-* + *-ane*]

**dioxide** /die'oksied/ *n* an OXIDE (compound of oxygen with one other chemical element or group) containing two atoms of oxygen in each molecule [ISV]

**¹dip** /dip/ *vb* **-pp-** *vt* 1a to plunge or immerse momentarily or partially under the surface (eg of a liquid) so as to moisten, cool, dye, or coat $\langle \sim candles \rangle$ **b** to thrust or move in a way that suggests immersion $\langle he \sim ped \ his \ hand \ into \ his \ pocket \rangle$ **c** to immerse (eg a sheep) in an antiseptic or parasite-killing solution 2 to lift up (eg milk or grain) by scooping or ladling 3 to lower and then raise again $\langle \sim a \ flag \ in \ salute \rangle$ 4 *chiefly Br* to lower (the beam of a vehicle's headlights) so as to reduce glare 5 *archaic* to baptize by total immersion $\sim vi$ 1a to plunge into a liquid and quickly emerge **b** to immerse something in a processing liquid or finishing material 2a to drop down suddenly, esp by a slight distance **b** *of an aircraft* to drop suddenly before climbing **c** to decline or decrease moderately and usu temporarily $\langle prices \sim ped \rangle$ 3 to reach down inside or below a surface, esp so as to take out part of the contents 4 to incline downwards from the plane of the horizon 5 COUNT OUT $\langle let's \sim for \ first \ go \rangle$ 6 *Br* to dip headlights [ME *dippen*, fr OE *dyppan*; akin to OHG *tupfen* to wash, Lith *dubus* deep] – **dippable** *adj*

**dip into** *vt* 1 to make inroads into for funds $\langle dipped \ into$ the family's savings$\rangle$ 2 to read superficially or in a random manner $\langle dipped \ into \ a \ book \ while \ he \ was \ waiting \rangle$

**dip out** *vi*, *Austr & NZ* 1 to fail 2 to miss an opportunity

**²dip** *n* 1 an act of dipping; *esp* a brief plunge into water for sport or exercise 2 a downward inclination: 2a a sharp downward course; a drop **b** the angle that a geological STRATUM (layer) or similar feature makes with a horizontal plane 3 **dip, magnetic dip** the angle formed with the horizon by a magnetic needle free to rotate in the vertical plane 4 a hollow, depression 5 something obtained by or used in dipping 6a a sauce or soft mixture into which food is dipped before being eaten $\langle cheese \sim \rangle$ **b** a liquid preparation into which an object or animal may be dipped (eg for cleansing or colouring) $\langle sheep- \sim \rangle$ 7 *Br* an electrical socket set in a theatre stage 8 *slang* a pickpocket

**dipeptidase** /,die'peptidayz/ *n* any of various ENZYMES that break down the linking bond in a dipeptide to form two AMINO ACIDS

**dipeptide** /,die'peptied/ *n* a compound consisting of two AMINO ACIDS linked by a chemical bond

**dip equator** *n* ACLINIC LINE

**diphase** /'die,fayz/, **diphasic** /,die'fayzik/ *adj*, *physics* TWO-PHASE

**diphenoxylate hydrochloride** /,diefe'noksilayt, -fee'noksi-/ *n* a drug, $C_{30}H_{32}N_2O_2 \cdot HCl$, derived from PETHIDINE (morphine-like drug) that is used to treat the symptoms of diarrhoea – compare LOMOTIL [*diphenoxylate* fr *di-* + *phen-* + *ox-* + *-yl* + *-ate*]

**diphenyl** /,die'feenl, -'fenl/ *n* BIPHENYL

**diphenylamine** /,die,feenl'amin, ,die,feenl·a'meen, -,fenl-/ *n* a pleasant-smelling chemical compound, $C_6H_5NHC_6H_5$, used chiefly in the manufacture of dyes and in stabilizing explosives [ISV]

**diphosgene** /,die'fosjeen/ *n* a liquid chemical compound, $ClCOOCCl_3$, used as a poison gas in World War I [ISV]

**diphosphate** /die'fosfayt/ *n* a PHOSPHATE containing two phosphate groups in each molecule

**diphosphoglyceric acid** /,die,fosfohgli'serik/ *n* a diphosphate of GLYCERIC ACID that occurs as an important intermediate compound in the processes of photosynthesis, GLY-COLYSIS (sequence of reactions whereby glucose is broken down in animals and plants), and fermentation

**diphosphopyridine nucleotide** /ˌdieˌfosfoh'pirədeen/ *n* NAD [*di-* + *phosph-* + *pyridine*]

**diphtheria** /dip'thiəriə, dif-/ *n* a severe short-lasting infectious disease marked by fever and the formation of a false membrane, esp in the throat, causing difficulty in breathing. The disease is caused by a bacterium which produces a poisonous substance (TOXIN) causing inflammation of the heart and nervous system. [NL, fr Fr *diphthérie*, fr Gk *diphthera* leather; fr the toughness of the false membrane] – **diphtherial, diphtherian, diphtheric** *adj*, **diphtheritic** *adj*, **diphtheroid** *adj*

   *usage* The pronunciation /dif'thiəri·ə/ is recommended for BBC broadcasters.

**diphtheroid** /'dipthəroyd, 'dif-/ *n* a bacterium that resembles that of diphtheria but does not produce the diphtheria TOXIN

**diphthong** /'dipthong, 'dif-/ *n* 1 a gliding vowel sound (e g /oy/ in *toy*) that is one syllable in length but composed of two elements 2 DIGRAPH (two letters representing one sound) 3 either of the LIGATURES (two letters written as one) æ or œ [ME *diptonge*, fr MF *diptongue*, fr LL *dipthongus*, fr Gk *diphthongos*, fr *di-* + *phthongos* voice, sound] – **diphthongal** *adj*

**diphthong·ize, -ise** /'dipthong·iez, 'dif-, -thong·giez/ *vi, of a simple vowel* to change into a diphthong ~ *vt* to pronounce as a diphthong – **diphthongization** *n*

**diphy-** /difi-/, **diphyo-** *comb form* double; consisting of two parts ⟨diphy*odont*⟩ [NL, fr Gk *diphy-*, fr *diphyēs*, fr *di-* + *phyein* to bring forth – more at BE]

**diphycercal** /ˌdifi'suhkəl/ *adj* 1 *of the tail fin of a fish* divided symmetrically into identical or very similar upper and lower parts by the SPINAL COLUMN which extends to the tip of the fin 2 having a diphycercal tail fin [*diphy-* + *-cercal*] – **diphycercy** *n*

**diphyletic** /ˌdiefie'letik/ *adj* derived from two lines of evolutionary descent ⟨~ *dinosaurs*⟩ [*di-* + *phyletic* (of a line of descent), deriv of Gk *phylē* tribe, clan]

**diphyodont** /ˌdie'fieə,dont/ *adj* having two successive sets of teeth; developing a set of permanent teeth after a first set of milk teeth ⟨*humans are* ~ *mammals*⟩ [ISV]

**dipl-, diplo-** *comb form* 1 double; twofold ⟨dipl*opia*⟩ 2 diploid ⟨dipl*ophase*⟩ [Gk, fr *diploos* – more at DOUBLE]

**diplegia** /die'pleej(y)ə/ *n* paralysis of corresponding parts on both sides of the body [NL]

**diplex** /'diepleks/ *adj* allowing or being the simultaneous transmission or reception of two telecommunications signals in the same direction – compare DUPLEX 2 [by alter. (influenced by *di-*)]

**diploblastic** /ˌdiploh'blastik/ *adj* (being or derived from an embryo) having two GERM LAYERS (primary differentiated layers of cells) ⟨*jellyfish are* ~ *animals*⟩ – compare TRIPLOBLASTIC

**diplococcus** /ˌdiploh'kokəs/ *n* any of a genus (*Diplococcus*) of parasitic bacteria that occur usu in pairs and include some serious disease-causing agents [NL, genus name] – **diplococcal, diplococcic** *adj*

**diplodocus** /di'plodəkəs/ *n* any of a genus (*Diplodocus*) of very large plant-eating dinosaurs [NL, genus name, fr *dipl-* + Gk *dokos* beam, fr *dekesthai, dechesthai* to receive; akin to L *decēre* to be fitting – more at DECENT]

**diploe** /'diploh,ee/ *n* porous bony tissue between the outer and inner layers of the skull [NL, fr Gk *diploē*, fr *diploos* double] – **diploic** *adj*

¹**diploid** /'diployd/ *adj* having or being double the basic (HAPLOID) number or single set of CHROMOSOMES (strands of gene-carrying material); having or being the number of chromosomes characteristic of the SOMATIC CELLS (all cells other than the egg and sperm cells) of mammals – compare HAPLOID, POLYPLOID [ISV] – **diploidy** *n*

²**diploid** *n* a diploid cell, individual, or generation

**diploma** /di'plohmə/ *n* 1 an official or state document; a charter 2 a writing usu under seal conferring some honour or privilege 3 a qualification usu in a more specialized subject or at a lower level than a degree; *also* a certificate proving the holder's possession of such a qualification [L, passport, diploma, fr Gk *diplōma* folded paper, passport, fr *diploun* to double, fr *diploos*]

**diplomacy** /di'plohməsi/ *n* 1 the art and practice of conducting international relations, esp negotiations between nations 2 skill in handling affairs without arousing hostility; tact

**diplomat** /'dipləmat/ *also* **diplomatist** /di'plohmətist/ *n* 1 one (e g an ambassador) employed in diplomacy 2 one skilled in dealing with people tactfully and adroitly [Fr *diplomate*, back-formation fr *diplomatique*]

   *synonyms* People in the profession of diplomacy were formerly called **diplomatists** in British English, but the American form **diplomat** is now standard.

**diplomate** /'dipləmayt/ *n* one who holds a diploma; *esp* the holder of a specialist qualification awarded by a professional body [*diploma* + ¹*-ate*]

**diplomatic** /ˌdiplə'matik/ *adj* 1a PALAEOGRAPHIC (of ancient writings) b exactly reproducing the original ⟨*a* ~ *edition*⟩ 2a concerned with or skilled in international relations b relating to those conducting international relations ⟨~ *corps*⟩ 3 employing tact and conciliation, esp in situations of stress *synonyms* see SUAVE [(1) NL *diplomaticus*, fr L *diplomat-, diploma*; (2, 3) Fr *diplomatique* connected with documents regulating international relations, fr NL *diplomaticus*] – **diplomatically** *adv*

**diplomatic immunity** *n* the exemption from local laws and taxes accorded to diplomatic staff abroad

**diplont** /'diplont/ *n* an organism whose SOMATIC CELLS (all cells other than the reproductive cells) have the diploid number of CHROMOSOMES (strands of gene-carrying material) – compare HAPLONT [ISV] – **diplontic** *adj*

**diplophase** /'diplə,fayz/ *n* a phase in the life cycle of an organism when the cells are diploid

**diplopia** /di'plohpiə/ *n* a disorder of vision in which two images of a single object are seen (e g because of unequal action of the eye muscles) – called also DOUBLE VISION [NL] – **diplopic** *adj*

**diplopod** /'diplə,pod/ *n* a millipede [deriv of Gk *dipl-* + *pod-, pous* foot – more at FOOT] – **diplopodous** *adj*

**diplotene** /'diploh,teen/ *n* the stage of MEIOSIS (division of a cell and its contents to form four new cells) during which the paired CHROMOSOMES (strands of gene-carrying material) begin to separate and sections of the chromosomes become interchanged [ISV] – **diplotene** *adj*

**dip net** *n* a small bag net with a handle that is used esp to scoop small fish from the water

**dipnoan** /'dipnoh-ən/ *adj* of or belonging to a group (Dipnoi) of fishes with a bony skeleton and both gills and lungs; *broadly* of the lungfish [deriv of Gk *dipnoos* having 2 apertures for breathing, fr *di-* + *pnoē* breath, fr *pnein* to breathe – more at SNEEZE] – **dipnoan** *n*

**dipole** /'die,pohl/ *n* 1a a pair of equal and opposite electric charges, or magnetic poles of opposite sign, separated by a small distance b a molecule having such charges 2 a radio aerial consisting of two horizontal rods in line with each other with their ends slightly separated [ISV] – **dipolar** *also* **dipole** *adj*

**dipper** /'dipə/ *n* 1 one who or that which dips: e g 1a a worker who dips articles into a processing solution (e g cleaner or dye) or a finishing solution (e g glaze or paint) b something (e g a long-handled cup) used for dipping 2 any of several diving birds (genus *Cinclus*); *specif* a European songbird (*Cinclus cinclus*) that has dark upper parts and a white front and is found esp in mountain streams 3 *cap, chiefly NAm* 3a **Dipper, Big Dipper** URSA MAJOR b **Dipper, Little Dipper** URSA MINOR 4 *Br slang* a pickpocket 5 *derog* a Baptist or Anabaptist – **dipperful** *n*

**dippy** /'dipi/ *adj, informal* crazy [perh alter. of *dipso*]

**dipropellant** /ˌdieprə'pelənt/ *n* BIPROPELLANT (rocket fuel)

**dipso** /'dipsoh/ *n, informal* a dipsomaniac

**dipsomania** /ˌdipsə'maynyə/ *n* an uncontrollable craving for alcoholic drinks; alcoholism [NL, fr Gk *dipsa* thirst + LL *mania*] – **dipsomaniac** *n*, **dipsomaniacal** *adj*

**dipstick** /'dip,stik/ *n* a measuring rod for indicating the depth of a liquid (e g of oil in a car's engine)

**dipswitch** /'dip,swich/ *n, chiefly Br* a switch that dips headlight beams

**dipteran** /'diptərən/ *n* TWO-WINGED FLY [deriv of Gk *dipteros*] – **dipteran** *adj*

**dipteron** /'diptəron/ *n, pl* **diptera** /-tərə/ *also* **dipterons** TWO-WINGED FLY [Gk, neut of *dipteros*]

**dipterous** /'diptərəs/ *adj* 1 having two wings or winglike appendages 2 of the TWO-WINGED FLIES [NL *dipterus*, fr Gk *dipteros*, fr *di-* + *pteron* wing – more at FEATHER]

**diptych** /'diptik/ *n* 1 a 2-leaved hinged writing tablet with waxed inner surfaces 2 a catalogue of living and dead people commemorated at the Communion service 3 a pair of paintings or carvings on two hinged panels used esp as an altarpiece [LL *diptycha*, pl, fr Gk, fr neut pl of *diptychos* folded in two, fr *di-* + *ptychē* fold; (2) ML *diptychum*, fr LL *diptycha* 2-leaved tablet]

**diquat** /'die͵kwot/ *n* a powerful weedkiller, $C_{12}H_{12}N_2Br_2$, that is used esp to kill water weeds (e g the water hyacinth), and that safely decomposes after a short interval rather than persisting in the environment [*di-* + *quaternary*]

**dirdum** /'diǝdǝm, 'duhdǝm/ *n, Scot* blame [ME (northern) *durdan*, fr ScGael, grumbling, hum, dim. of *durd* hum]

**dire** /dieǝ/ *adj* **1a** causing horror ⟨~ *suffering*⟩ **b** dismal, awful ⟨~ *days*⟩ **2** warning of disaster; ominous ⟨*a ~ forecast*⟩ **3a** desperately urgent ⟨~ *need*⟩ **b** extreme, grave ⟨~ *poverty*⟩ **synonyms** see SINISTER [L *dirus;* akin to Gk *deinos* terrible, Skt *dvesti* he hates] – **direly** *adv*, **direness** *n*

¹**direct** /di'rekt, die-/ *vt* **1a** to mark (e g an envelope) with the name and address of the intended recipient **b** to address, aim ⟨~ *ed his remarks to the gallery*⟩ **c** to adapt in expression so as to apply to a particular audience ⟨*a lawyer who* ~s *his appeals to intelligence and character*⟩ **2** to cause to turn, move, point without deviating, or follow a straight course ⟨*X rays are* ~ed *through the body*⟩ **3** to point, extend, or project in a specified line or course ⟨*the tusks of these mammoths are* ~ed *vertically upwards*⟩ **4** to show or point out the way for ⟨*I* ~ed *him to Woodborough*⟩ **5a** to regulate the activities or course of ⟨~ *the traffic*⟩ **b** to dominate and determine the course of ⟨*it is pride that* ~s *his every action*⟩ **c** to train and usu lead performances of ⟨*Peter Hall* ~s *the piece*⟩; *specif, chiefly NAm* to conduct ⟨~ed *the orchestra in a new work*⟩ **6** to request or order with authority ⟨*police* ~ed *the crowd to move back*⟩ ~ *vi* **1** to point out, prescribe, or determine a course or procedure **2** to act as director [ME *directen*, fr L *directus*, pp of *dirigere* to set straight, direct – more at DRESS]

²**direct** *adj* **1a** going from one point to another in time or space without deviation or interruption; straight **b** going by the shortest way ⟨*the ~ route*⟩ **2a** deriving immediately from a source ⟨~ *result*⟩ **b** being or passing in a straight line of descent from parent to offspring; lineal ⟨~ *ancestor*⟩ **3** having a close logical relationship with or being the immediate cause or consequence of ⟨~ *evidence*⟩ **4** frank, straightforward ⟨~ *manner*⟩ **5a** having no intervening agency or influence ⟨~ *observation*⟩ **b** brought about by the action of the people or the electorate and not by representatives ⟨~ *elections to the European Parliament*⟩ **c** consisting of or reproducing the exact words of a speaker or writer ⟨~ *speech*⟩ – compare INDIRECT **d** **6** capable of dyeing without the aid of a chemical fixative (MORDANT); SUBSTANTIVE **7** *of a celestial body* moving in the general planetary direction from west to east; not RETROGRADE [ME, fr L *directus*, fr pp of *dirigere*]

³**direct** *adv* in a direct way: e g **a** from point to point without deviation; by the shortest way ⟨*the bus goes* ~ *from London to Manchester*⟩ **b** from the source without interruption or diversion ⟨*the material must come* ~ *from life*⟩ **c** without an intervening agency or step ⟨*they are anxious to sell oil* ~ *to the Government*⟩ **synonyms** see DIRECTLY

**direct action** *n* action, esp that taken by organized workers against their employer, that seeks to achieve an end by the most immediately effective means (e g boycott or strike)

**direct current** *n* an electric current flowing in one direction only; *esp* such a current that is substantially constant in value – compare ALTERNATING CURRENT

**directed** /di'rektid, die-/ *adj* having a direction ⟨~ *line segment*⟩

**direct free kick** *n* a free kick in soccer that is awarded for any of several offences (e g an intentional foul) and from which a direct shot at goal may be made – compare INDIRECT FREE KICK, PENALTY KICK

**direct grant** *n, often cap D&G* money received direct from the Department of Education and Science, and not from the local education authority, by certain partially independent British grammar schools

**direction** /di'reksh(ǝ)n, die-/ *n* **1** guidance or supervision of action or conduct **2a** the art or technique of directing an orchestra, film, or theatrical production **b** a word, phrase, or sign indicating the appropriate tempo, mood, or intensity of a passage or movement in music **3a directions** *pl*, **direction** an explicit instruction or order ⟨*read the* ~s *on the bottle*⟩ **b** *pl* guidance as to a route to be followed ⟨*asked for* ~s *to King's Cross*⟩ **4** the line or course on which something is moving or is aimed to move or along which something is pointing or facing ⟨*drove off in the* ~ *of London*⟩ **5a** a channel or direct

course of thought or action; a tendency **b** a guiding, governing, or motivating purpose ⟨*he had a new sense of* ~⟩ **6** *archaic* an address on a letter or parcel – **directionless** *adj*

**directional** /di'reksh(ǝ)nl, die-/ *adj* **1a** of or indicating direction in space **b** of, using, or being an aerial that transmits or receives radio signals more efficiently in one or a limited number of directions than in others **c** operating most effectively in a particular direction; having greater sensitivity to waves, particles, etc coming from a particular direction ⟨*a* ~ *microphone*⟩ **d** concentrated in a particular direction ⟨*a* ~ *beam of electrons*⟩ **2** relating to direction or guidance, esp of thought or effort – **directionality** *n*

**direction finder** *n* a radio receiver designed to determine the direction of the received radio signal and typically having an aerial that is capable of being rotated freely

¹**directive** /di'rektiv, die-/ *adj* **1** serving or intended to guide, govern, or influence **2a** serving to indicate direction **b** *of an aerial* directional

²**directive** *n* something that serves to direct, guide, and usu impel towards an action or goal; *esp* an authoritative instruction issued by a high-level body or official

**direct labour** *n* **1** labour directly concerned with manufacture or with the provision of a service – compare INDIRECT LABOUR **2** labour that is employed directly rather than via a contractor ⟨*direct building labour forces of local authorities*⟩

¹**directly** /di'rektli, die-/ *adv* **1** in a direct manner ⟨~ *relevant*⟩ ⟨*the road runs* ~ *east and west*⟩ **2a** without delay; immediately **b** in a little while; shortly

> **synonyms** Either **direct** or **directly** can be used in the sense "in a straight line, by the shortest way" ⟨*the road runs* **direct(ly)** *to London*⟩ or in the sense "without intervention" ⟨*sell oil* **direct(ly)** *to the Government*⟩. Only **directly** can immediately precede a verb, adjective, adverb, or preposition that it modifies ⟨**directly** *relevant*⟩; and only **directly** can mean "in a straight line of descent" ⟨**directly** *descended from Francis Drake*⟩ or "as a close logical cause" ⟨*not* **directly** *affected by the changes*⟩ or "immediately" ⟨*left* **directly** *after lunch*⟩. One should be careful to avoid ambiguity where **directly** could either mean "immediately" or be used in one of the senses it shares with **direct**. ⟨*I communicated with him* **directly**⟩ has two meanings

²**directly** *conj, chiefly Br informal* immediately after; as soon as ⟨~ *I received the letter I rang them up*⟩

**direct method** *n* a method of teaching a foreign language without using the pupil's own language

**directness** /di'rektnis, die-/ *n* **1** the character of being accurate in course or aim **2** open frankness; straightforwardness

**direct object** *n* a grammatical object representing the primary goal or the result of the action of its verb ⟨*me in "he hit me" and house in "we built a house" are* direct objects⟩

**directoire** /͵direk'twah/ *adj, esp of furniture and women's clothes* in the style of the period of the French Directory [Fr, fr *Directoire* Directory (the ruling body in France from 1795–9), fr *directoire* directory (book), fr MF, fr ML *directorium*]

**director** /di'rektǝ, die-/, *fem* **directress** /-ris/ *n* one who directs: e g **a** the head of an organized group or administrative unit (e g a government department or college) **b** a member of a governing board entrusted with the overall direction of a company **c** one who has responsibility for supervising the artistic and technical aspects of a film or play – compare PRODUCER **d** *chiefly NAm* CONDUCTOR **c** – **directorship** *n*

**directorate** /di'rekt(ǝ)rǝt, die-/ *n* **1** the office of director **2** *taking sing or pl vb* a board of directors (e g of a company)

**directorial** /͵direk'tawriǝl/ *adj* **1** serving to direct **2** relating to a director or to theatrical direction **3** relating to or administered by a directory

**Director of Public Prosecutions** *n* a government legal official in Britain with responsibility for instituting, undertaking, or advising on prosecutions in important criminal cases

**director's chair** *n* a lightweight folding armchair with a usu canvas back and seat [fr its use by film directors on the set]

¹**directory** /di'rekt(ǝ)ri/ *adj* serving to direct; *specif* providing advisory but not compulsory guidance

²**directory** *n* **1a** a book or collection of directions, rules, etc **b** an alphabetical or classified list (e g of names and addresses) ⟨*telephone* ~⟩ **2** *taking sing or pl vb* a body of directors [ML *directorium*, fr neut of LL *directorius* directorial, fr L *directus*, pp; (2) Fr *Directoire*]

**direct primary** *n* a primary election in the USA in which nominations of candidates who will run for office are made by direct vote

**direct product** *n* 1 CARTESIAN PRODUCT (set of pairs of elements from two sets) 2 SCALAR PRODUCT (product of two vectors)

**direct proportion** *n* the relationship between two variables whose ratio is constant – **directly proportioned** *adj*

**directrix** /di'rektriks, die-/ *n, pl* **directrixes** /-triksiz/ *also* **directrices** /-tri,seez/ 1 a fixed curve with which a point, line, or surface maintains a given relationship in generating a geometric figure; *specif* a straight line that together with a fixed point (FOCUS) forms the reference system for generating a CONIC SECTION (eg an ellipse or parabola) in plane geometry 2 *archaic* a directress [ML, directress, fem of LL *director*, fr L *directus*, pp]

**direct tax** *n* a tax (eg income tax) exacted directly from the person, organization, etc on whom it is levied – compare INDIRECT TAX

**direct wave** *n* GROUND WAVE

**direful** /'dieəf(ə)l/ *adj, archaic* dreadful – **direfully** *adv*

**dirge** /duhj/ *n* 1 a song or hymn of grief or lamentation; *esp* one intended to accompany funeral or memorial rites 2 a slow, solemn, and mournful piece of music [ME *dirige* the Office of the Dead, fr the first word of a LL antiphon, fr L, imper of *dirigere*]

**dirham** /'dirəm, di'ram, diə'ham/ *n* 1 – see MONEY table 2 – see *dinar* at MONEY table [Ar, fr L *drachma* drachma]

¹**dirigible** /'dirijəbl, -'---/ *adj* capable of being steered [L *dirigere* to direct, make straight]

²**dirigible** *n* an airship [*dirigible (balloon)*]

**dirigisme** /,deeree'zheezm(ə)/ (*Fr* diriʒism)/ *n, chiefly derog* direct state control of the economy and of social institutions [Fr, fr *diriger* to direct, fr L *dirigere*] – **dirigiste** *adj*

**dirk** /duhk/ *n* a straight-bladed dagger; *esp* one formerly used by Scottish Highlanders [Sc *durk*]

**dirndl** /'duhndl/ *n* 1 a dress style with tight bodice, short sleeves, low neck, and gathered skirt 2 a full skirt with a tight waistband [short for Ger *dirndlkleid*, fr Ger dial. *dirndl* girl + Ger *kleid* dress]

**dirt** /duht/ *n* 1a excrement b a filthy or soiling substance (eg mud, dust, or grime) c somebody or something worthless or contemptible 2 EARTH 1, ³SOIL 2a 3a moral vileness; corruption b sexual unpleasantness or pornography in language or theme c scandalous or malicious gossip; *also* lowdown [ME *drit*, fr ON; akin to OE *drītan* to defecate, L *foria* diarrhoea] – **treat like dirt** *informal* to treat as though worthless (*he treated her like dirt*) – see also **one's/somebody's** NAME **is dirt**

**dirt cheap** *adj, informal* very inexpensive

**dirt road** *n, NAm* an unpaved road

**dirt track** *n* a track of earth, cinders, etc used for motorcycle races or flat races

**dirt wagon** *n, NAm* a dustcart

¹**dirty** /'duhti/ *adj* 1a not clean or pure; contaminated with dirt (~ *clothes*) b likely to make grimy or filthy (~ *jobs*) c contaminated with infecting organisms (~ *wounds*) 2a base, sordid (*war is a ~ business*) b unsportsmanlike, unfair (~ *players*) c low, despicable (~ *tricks*) 3a indecent, smutty (~ *language*) (~ *joke*) b involving an improper sexual relationship (~ *weekend*) 4 *of weather* rough, stormy 5a *of colour* not clear and bright; dullish (*drab dirty-pink walls*) b *of jazz music* characterized by a husky, rasping, or raw tonal quality 6 conveying resentment, disapproval, or disgust (*gave him a ~ look*) 7 producing considerable radioactive fallout (~ *bombs*) – **dirtily** *adv*, **dirtiness** *n* – **be dirty on** Austr to have a grudge against (*I was dirty on him for that*) – **do the dirty on** Br informal to treat in a mean or underhand way (*he's done the dirty on us*) – see also **wash one's dirty** LINEN **in public**

*synonyms* Dirty, filthy, foul, nasty, squalid, sordid: dirty, a neutral, factual term, is simply opposed to "clean" (*I'll do the dirty washing tomorrow*). Filthy adds a strong sense of offensiveness, and often suggests accumulated dirt (*a filthy floor that no one had cleaned for months*). Foul is even stronger, and implies something revolting because unwholesome, rotten, or smelly (*a foul refuse pit*). Nasty implies repugnance and contrasts with "nice" (*muckspreading is nasty work*). Squalid and sordid are closely related in suggesting a contrast with "decent"; the former connotes dirt due to neglect, and the latter suggests poverty or baseness as well as filth. All these terms may imply moral uncleanliness, too (*dirty work*) (*filthy barroom stories*) (*foul language*) (*a nasty mind*) (*squalid projects*) (*a sordid affair*). **antonym** clean

²**dirty** *vt* 1 to make dirty 2 to stain with dishonour; sully ~ *vi* to become soiled (*this jacket dirties easily*)

³**dirty** *adv* 1 in an unfair, underhand, or unsportsmanlike manner (*he fights ~*) 2 *slang* very – + *great* or *big* (*a ~ great explosion*)

**dirty linen** *n* private matters whose public exposure would bring distress and embarrassment (*I don't wash my ~ in public*)

**dirty old man** *n, slang* a lecherous older man

**dirty word** *n, informal* a word or expression that is offensive or unwelcome in a usu particular context (*capitalism is a ~ in Russia*)

**dirty work** *n, informal* behaviour or an act that is unfair, treacherous, or criminal (*sent her to do the ~*)

**dis-** /dis-/ *prefix* 1a do the opposite of (a specified action) (*disestablish*) (*disappear*) b deprive of; remove (something specified) from (*disarm*) (*dismember*) c exclude or expel from (*disbar*) 2 opposite or absence of (*disarray*) (*disbelief*) 3 not (*disagreeable*) (*dishonest*) 4 completely (*disannul*) (*disgruntled*) 5 DYS- (*disfunction*) [ME *dis-, des-*, fr OF & L; OF *des-, dis-*, fr L *dis-*, lit., apart; akin to OE *te-* apart, L *duo* two – more at TWO; (5) by folk etymology]

**disability** /,disə'biləti/ *n* 1a the condition of being disabled; *specif* inability to do something (eg pursue an occupation) because of physical or mental handicap b something that disables; a handicap 2 a legal disqualification

**disable** /dis'aybl/ *vt* 1 to deprive of legal right, qualification, or capacity; disqualify 2 to make incapable or useless; *esp* to deprive of physical soundness or strength – **disablement** *n*

**disabuse** /,disə'byoohz/ *vt* to free from a mistaken impression or judgment; undeceive [Fr *désabuser*, fr *dés-* dis- + *abuser* to abuse]

**disaccharidase** /,die'sakəridayz/ *n* any of various ENZYMES (eg maltase or lactase) that break down disaccharides to their constituent simpler sugars (eg glucose)

**disaccharide** /,die'sakəried/ *n* any of a class of sugars (eg sucrose or lactose), each molecule of which consists of two simpler sugar units (MONOSACCHARIDES) (eg two glucose units or one glucose and one fructose unit)

**disaccord** /,disə'kawd/ *vi* to clash, disagree [ME *disacorden*, fr MF *desacorder*, fr *desacort* disagreement, fr *des-* dis- + *acort* accord] – **disaccord** *n*

**disaccustom** /,disə'kustəm/ *vt, formal* to free from a habit [MF *desaccoustumer*, fr OF *desacostumer*, fr *des-* + *acostumer* to accustom]

¹**disadvantage** /,disəd'vahntij/ *n* 1 loss or damage, esp to reputation, credit, or finances 2a an unfavourable or inferior condition (*we were at a ~*) b a handicap (*his poor health is a great ~ to him*) [ME *disavauntage*, fr MF *desavantage*, fr OF, fr *des-* + *avantage* advantage]

²**disadvantage** *vt* to place at a disadvantage

**disadvantaged** /,disəd'vahntijd/ *adj* underprivileged; *esp* lacking basic resources, conditions, or social opportunities (eg standard housing, educational facilities, and civil rights) – **disadvantagedness** *n*

**disadvantageous** /,disadvan'tayjəs, -ədvən-/ *adj* 1 causing or being a disadvantage 2 unfavourable (*his action was viewed in a ~ light by many*) – **disadvantageously** *adv*, **disadvantageousness** *n*

**disaffect** /,disə'fekt/ *vt* to cause to lose affection or loyalty – **disaffection** *n*

**disaffected** /,disə'fektid/ *adj* discontented and resentful, esp towards authority; rebellious; *also* disenchanted

**disaffiliate** /,disə'filiayt/ *vt* to dissociate ~ *vi* to end an affiliation or connection – **disaffiliation** *n*

**disaffirm** /,disə'fuhm/ *vt* 1 to refuse to confirm (eg a legal settlement); annul, repudiate; *also* to reverse (a judicial decision) 2 *formal* to contradict – **disaffirmance, disaffirmation** *n*

**disafforest** /,disə'forest/ *vt, chiefly Br* DEFOREST

**disagree** /,disə'gree/ *vi* 1 to be unlike or at variance (*the two accounts ~*) 2 to differ in opinion (*he ~d with me on every topic*) 3 to have a bad effect; *specif* to cause illness – usu + *with* (*fried foods ~ with me*) [ME *disagreen*, fr MF *desagreer*, fr *des-* + *agreer* to agree]

**disagreeable** /disə'gree-əbl/ *adj* 1 unpleasant, offensive 2 bad-tempered, peevish – **disagreeableness, disagreeability** *n*, **disagreeably** *adv*

**disagreement** /,disə'greemənt/ *n* 1 the act of disagreeing 2a failure to match or correspond; disparity b *chiefly euph* a difference of opinion; a quarrel

**disallow** /ˌdisəˈlow/ vt 1 to refuse to allow; prohibit 2 formal to deny the force, truth, or validity of (eg an argument or opinion) – **disallowance** n

**disambiguate** /ˌdisamˈbigyooayt/ vt to make unambiguous; specif to establish a single meaning or grammatical interpretation for – **disambiguation** n

**disannul** vt, formal to annul, cancel

**disappear** /ˌdisəˈpiə/ vi 1 to pass from view suddenly or gradually; vanish 2 to cease to be or to be known ⟨politeness has all but ~ed⟩ 3 to leave, esp suddenly or secretly ⟨by the time the police got there he had ~ed⟩ – **disappearance** n

**disappoint** /ˌdisəˈpoynt/ vt to fail to meet the expectation or hope of; also to sadden by so doing ~ vi to fail to meet one's expectation or hope [MF desapointier, fr des- dis- + apointier to arrange – more at APPOINT]

**disappointed** /ˌdisəˈpoyntid/ adj defeated in expectation or hope; thwarted – **disappointedly** adv

**disappointing** /ˌdisəˈpoynting/ adj (unhappily) failing to meet expectations ⟨a ~ pupil⟩ – **disappointingly** adv

**disappointment** /ˌdisəˈpoyntmənt/ n 1 disappointing or being disappointed 2 one who or that which disappoints ⟨the concert was a ~⟩

**disapprobation** /ˌdisˌaprəˈbaysh(ə)n/ n, formal disapproval

**disapproval** /ˌdisəˈproohv(ə)l/ n unfavourable opinion; censure

**disapprove** /ˌdisəˈproohv/ vt to refuse approval to; also to pass unfavourable judgment on ~ vi to feel or express condemnation or lack of approval – often + of – **disapprover** n, **disapprovingly** adv

**disarm** /disˈahm/ vt 1a to deprive of a weapon or weapons b to deprive of a means of attack or defence c to make (eg a bomb) harmless, esp by removing a fuse or warhead 2a to deprive of the means, reason, or disposition to be hostile b to win over ~ vi 1 to lay aside weapons 2 to give up or reduce armed forces [ME desarmen, fr MF desarmer, fr OF, fr des- + armer to arm] – **disarmament** n, **disarmer** n

**disarming** /disˈahming/ adj tending to neutralize or dispel a critical or hostile attitude; winning ⟨a ~ smile⟩ – **disarmingly** adv

**disarrange** /ˌdisəˈraynj/ vt to disturb the arrangement or order of – **disarrangement** n

¹**disarray** /ˌdisəˈray/ n 1 a lack of order or sequence; disorder ⟨they fled in complete ~⟩ 2 disorderly dress

²**disarray** vt to throw into disorder [ME disarayen, fr MF desarroyer, fr OF desareer, fr des- + areer to array]

**disarticulate** /ˌdisahˈtikyoolayt/ vi to become disjointed ~ vt to disjoint – **disarticulation** n

**disassemble** /ˌdisəˈsembl/ vt to take (eg a machine) apart ⟨~ a watch⟩ ~ vi to disperse, scatter ⟨the crowd began to ~⟩ △ dissemble – **disassemblable** adj, **disassembly** n

**disassociate** /ˌdisəˈsohs(h)iayt/ vt to dissociate usage see DISSOCIATE – **disassociation** n

**disaster** /diˈzahstə/ n 1 a sudden or great misfortune; esp a sudden calamity bringing great damage, loss, or destruction 2 informal one who or that which falls calamitously short of the desired effect (eg through disorder or inappropriateness) ⟨my hair's a ~ this morning⟩ [MF & OIt; MF desastre, fr OIt disastro, fr dis- (fr L) + astro star, fr L astrum – more at ASTRAL]

**disaster area** n 1 an area officially declared to be the scene of an emergency created by a disaster and therefore qualified to receive certain types of government aid (eg emergency loans and relief supplies) 2 informal DISASTER 2

**disastrous** /diˈzahstrəs/ adj bringing or causing suffering or disaster; calamitous – **disastrously** adv

usage The pronunciation /diˈzahstrəs/ rather than /diˈzahstərəs/ is recommended for BBC broadcasters.

**disavow** /ˌdisəˈvow/ vt, formal 1 to refuse to acknowledge; disclaim 2 to deny knowledge of or responsibility for; repudiate [ME desavowen, fr MF desavouer, fr OF, fr des- dis- + avouer to avow] – **disavowable** adj, **disavowal** n

**disband** /disˈband/ vt to break up the organization of; dissolve ~ vi to become disbanded [MF desbander, fr des- + bande band] – **disbandment** n

**disbar** /disˈbah/ vt to expel from the bar; deprive (a barrister) of the right to practise △ debar – **disbarment** n

**disbelief** /ˌdisbiˈleef/ n the act of disbelieving; mental rejection of something as untrue

**disbelieve** /ˌdisbiˈleev/ vt to consider not to be true or real; reject or withhold belief in ~ vi to withhold or reject belief – usu + in – **disbeliever** n

**disbound** /disˈbownd/ adj no longer having or removed from a binding ⟨a ~ pamphlet⟩

**disbud** /disˈbud/ vt -dd- 1 to remove superfluous flower buds from in order to improve the quality of bloom 2 to dehorn (cattle) by destroying the undeveloped horn bud

**disburden** /disˈbuhd(ə)n/ vt 1 to unburden ⟨~ your conscience⟩ 2 to get rid of (a burden); unload ⟨~ed their merchandise in the town square⟩ ~ vi to discharge ⟨the vessels ~ed at the dock⟩ – **disburdenment** n

**disburse** /disˈbuhs/ vt, formal 1 to pay out; expend, esp from a fund 2 to make a payment in settlement of; defray △ disperse [MF desbourser, fr OF desborser, fr des- + borser to get money, fr borse purse, fr ML bursa – more at PURSE] – **disburser** n

**disbursement** /disˈbuhsmənt/ n the act of disbursing; also funds paid out

¹**disc**, NAm chiefly **disk** /disk/ n 1a the apparently flat circular shape of the sun, moon, or a planet ⟨the solar ~⟩ b CIRCLE 1b 2 the central part of the flower head of a plant such as the daisy, that is made up of many closely packed small tubular flowers 3 any of various rounded and flattened animal anatomical structures; esp any of the discs of cartilage between the spinal vertebrae ⟨suffering from a slipped ~⟩ 4a a thin circular object b a gramophone record c computers DISK 1 5 any of the sharp-edged concave circular steel cutting blades making up the working part of a harrow or plough; also an implement employing such blades [L discus dish, disc, quoit – more at dish]

²**disc**, NAm chiefly **disk** vt to cultivate with a harrow or plough that turns and loosens the soil with a series of discs

**discalced** /disˈkalst/ adj, of certain religious orders barefoot or wearing only sandals ⟨~ friars⟩ [part trans of L discalceatus, fr dis- + calceatus, pp of calceare to put on shoes, fr calceus shoe, fr calc-, calx heel – more at CALKIN]

¹**discard** /diˈskahd/ vt 1a to throw out (a playing card) from one's hand b to play (any card from a suit different from the one led except a trump) when unable to follow suit 2 to get rid of because useless or superfluous ~ vi to discard a playing card – **discardable** adj, **discarder** n

²**discard** /ˈdiskahd/ n 1a the act of discarding in a card game b a playing card when discarded 2 one who or that which is cast off or rejected

**disc brake** n a brake that operates by means of friction pads pressing against the sides of a rotating disc

**discern** /diˈsuhn/ vt 1 to detect with any of the senses, esp with the eyes 2 to perceive or recognize mentally 3 to recognize or identify as separate and distinct; discriminate ~ vi to see or understand the difference **synonyms** see ¹SEE [ME discernen, fr MF discerner, fr L discernere to separate, distinguish between, fr dis- apart + cernere to sift – more at DIS-, CERTAIN] – **discerner** n, **discernible** also **discernable** adj, **discernibly** adv

**discerning** /diˈsuhning/ adj showing insight and understanding; discriminating ⟨a ~ critic⟩ – **discerningly** adv

**discernment** /diˈsuhnmənt/ n 1 an act of discerning 2 skill in discerning; keen insight

**synonyms** Discernment, discrimination, perception, penetration, insight, and acumen all denote keen intellectual vision. **Discernment** suggests accuracy in aesthetic judgments and skill in assessing character, motives, etc ⟨she showed great **discernment** in her choice of friends⟩. **Discrimination** stresses the ability to distinguish between the good and the worthless or inappropriate. **Perception** suggests a keen mind quick to discern, and sensible to, the feelings, motives, and ideas of others. **Penetration** suggests a searching and subtle mind, able to penetrate beyond the obvious or superficial ⟨the **penetration** of his observations on London life⟩. **Insight** adds a sympathetic understanding ⟨showed an **insight** into her plight which astonished her⟩. **Acumen** suggests consistent penetration allied to shrewd judgment ⟨famous for his **acumen** in business matters⟩. See ¹REASON

**discerp** /diˈsuhp, diˈzuhp/ vt, formal to pull apart; dismember [ME discerpen, fr L discerpere, fr dis- apart + carpere to pick, pluck]

**discerptible** /diˈsuhptəbl, -ˈzuhptəbl/ adj, formal that can be plucked apart; not indivisible [L discerptus, pp of discerpere] – **discerptibility** n

**disc floret** n DISC FLOWER

**disc flower** n any of the small tubular flowers that make up the central part (DISC 2) of the flower head of a plant such as the daisy – compare RAY FLOWER

¹**discharge** /disˈchahj/ vt 1 to relieve of a charge, load, or

burden: **1a** to unload **b** to release from an obligation ⟨*a* ~d *bankrupt*⟩ **c** to remove (an) electric charge from or reduce the electric charge of **d** to cause (a battery) to lose stored electrical energy **2a** to fire ⟨~ *a gun*⟩ **b** to release from confinement, custody, or care ⟨~ *a prisoner*⟩ **c** to send or pour out; emit **3a** to dismiss or release from employment or service ⟨~ *a soldier*⟩ **b** to get rid of (eg a debt or obligation) by performing an appropriate action (eg payment); fulfil; *also* to carry out ⟨~ *a duty*⟩ **c** to set aside legally; annul **d** *NAm* to order (a committee) to end consideration of a bill in order to bring it before a lawmaking body for action **4** to bear and distribute (eg the weight of a wall above an opening) **5** to bleach out or remove (colour or dye) in dyeing and printing textiles ~ *vi* **1** to throw off or deliver a load, charge, or burden **2a** *of a gun* to fire; GO OFF **b** RUN 11c ⟨*some dyes* ~⟩ **c** to pour forth contents, esp fluid ⟨*his wound was discharging*⟩ **3a** to lose or reduce an electric charge **b** *of a battery* to lose stored electrical energy **synonyms** see PERFORM [ME *dischargen*, fr MF *descharger*, fr LL *discarricare*, fr L *dis-* + LL *carricare* to load – more at CHARGE] – **dischargeable** *adj*, **dischargee** *n*, **discharger** *n*

²**discharge** /'dischahj/ *n* **1a** the relieving of something (eg an obligation, accusation, or penalty) **b** something that discharges or releases; *esp* a proof of release or payment **2** the state of being discharged or relieved **3** the act of discharging or unloading **4a** legal release from confinement **b** an acquittal **5** a firing off; an expulsion of a charge ⟨*an artillery* ~⟩ **6a** a flowing or pouring out ⟨*a* ~ *of spores*⟩; *also* a rate of flow **b** something that is discharged or emitted ⟨*a* ~ *of pus*⟩ **7** the act of removing an obligation or liability **8** release or dismissal, esp from an office or employment (eg military service) **9a** a usu brief flowing or loss of an electric charge; *esp* that due to the total or partial equalization of a voltage difference between two parts of an electrically charged body or two points in an electric circuit **b** a brief or sustained flow of an electric current through a gas separating two electrically charged bodies or two points in a circuit between which there is a voltage difference, usu with associated emission of light – compare ARC, SPARK **c** the conversion of the chemical energy of a battery into electrical energy

**discharge lamp** *n* a lamp in which a DISCHARGE TUBE is used to produce a usu bright light

**discharge tube** *n* a tube which contains gas or vapour usu at very low pressure and in which a discharge of electricity, usu visible as light, occurs when a high voltage is applied to ELECTRODES (wires, plates, etc that conduct an electric current) in the tube

**disciform** /'disi,fawm, 'diski-/ *adj* round or oval in shape; disc-shaped

**disciple** /di'siepl/ *n* one who accepts and assists in spreading the teachings of another; a follower: eg **a** any of the 12 in the inner circle of Christ's followers according to the New Testament **b** a firm believer in the teaching of a particular school (eg in philosophy or art) or individual ⟨*a* ~ *of Kant*⟩ [ME, fr OE *discipul* & OF *desciple*, fr LL and L; LL *discipulus* follower of Jesus Christ in his lifetime, fr L, pupil] – **discipleship** *n*, **discipular** *adj*

**disciplinable** /'disi,plinəbl/ *adj* **1** capable of being disciplined or instructed; teachable **2** subject to or deserving discipline ⟨*a* ~ *offence*⟩

**disciplinarian** /,disipli'neəriən/ *n* one who enforces strict discipline or order – **disciplinarian** *adj*

**disciplinary** /,disi'plinəri/ *adj* **1a** relating to discipline **b** designed to correct or punish breaches of discipline ⟨*took* ~ *action*⟩ **2** relating to a particular field of study – **disciplinarily** *adv*, **disciplinarity** *n*

¹**discipline** /'displin/ *n* **1** a subject that is taught; a field of study **2** training and instruction that corrects, moulds, or perfects the mental faculties or moral character **3** punishment **4a** control gained by enforcing obedience (eg in a school or army) **b** orderly or prescribed conduct or pattern of behaviour **c** self-control **5** a rule or system of rules governing conduct or activity (eg of the members of a Church) [ME, fr MF & L; MF, fr L *disciplina* teaching, learning, fr *discipulus* pupil] – **disciplinal** *adj*

²**discipline** *vt* **1** to punish or penalize for the sake of discipline **2** to train or develop by instruction and exercise, esp in obedience and self-control **3a** to bring (a group) under control ⟨~ *troops*⟩ **b** to impose order on ⟨*the writer* ~s *and refines his style*⟩ **synonyms** see PUNISH, TEACH – **discipliner** *n*

**disciplined** /'disiplind/ *adj* marked by or possessing discipline ⟨*a* ~ *mind*⟩

**disc jockey** *n* one who introduces records of popular usu contemporary music (eg at a disco or on radio or TV programmes)

**disclaim** /dis'klaym/ *vi* to make a disclaimer ~ *vt* **1** to renounce a legal claim to (an interest or estate) **2** to deny, disavow [AF *disclaimer*, fr *dis-* + *claimer* to claim, fr OF *clamer*]

**disclaimer** /dis'klaymə/ *n* **1a** a denial or disavowal of legal responsibility **b** a renunciation of a legal claim to an interest or estate **2a** a denial, disavowal **b** a repudiation [AF, fr *disclaimer*, vb]

**disclamation** /,disklə'maysh(ə)n/ *n* a renunciation, disavowal

**disclose** /dis'klohz/ *vt* **1** to expose to view; enable to be seen **2** to make known; open up to general knowledge ⟨*demands that politicians* ~ *the sources of their income*⟩ **synonyms** see ¹REVEAL [ME *disclosen*, fr MF *desclos-*, stem of *desclore* to disclose, fr ML *disclaudere* to open, fr L *dis-* + *claudere* to close – more at CLOSE] – **discloser** *n*

**disclosure** /dis'klohzhə/ *n* **1** the act or an instance of disclosing; exposure **2** something disclosed; a revelation

**disco** /'diskoh/ *n, pl* **discos 1** a dance held mainly for young people to dance to suitable recorded popular music, usu introduced by a disc jockey and accompanied by special lighting effects; *also* the place, typically a nightclub, where such a dance is held **2** modern popular music that has a regular beat and is suitable for dancing to in a disco **3** modern dancing that is more or less free-form in style and is performed in time to music having a pronounced beat **4** the equipment (and operator) necessary for staging a disco ⟨*hiring a* ~ *for their party*⟩ [short for *discotheque*, fr Fr *discothèque*, fr *disque* disc, record + *-o-* + *-thèque* (as in *bibliothèque* library)] – **disco** *vi*

**discobolus** /di'skobələs/ *also* **discobolos** *n, pl* **discoboli** /-lie/ *also* **discoboloi** /-loy/ **1** a discus thrower, esp in classical Greece **2** a (classical) statue of a discus thrower ⟨*Myron's famous* Discobolus⟩ [L & Gk; L *discobolus*, fr Gk *diskobolos*, fr *diskos* discus + *ballein* to throw]

**discography** /di'skogrəfi/ *n* **1** a descriptive list of gramophone records; *also* an exhaustive list of the records of a performer, group, etc **2** the history of recorded music [Fr *discographie*, fr *disque* + *-graphie* -graphy] – **discographer** *n*, **discographical** *also* **discographic** *adj*, **discographically** *adv*

**discoid** /'diskoyd/ *adj* **1** resembling a disc or discus; flat and circular **2** relating to or having a disc: eg **2a** of or being a DISC FLOWER **b** *of the flower head of a plant* composed only of DISC FLOWERS [LL *discoides* quoit-shaped, fr Gk *diskoeidēs*, fr *diskos* disc]

**discoidal** /di'skoydl/ *adj* of, resembling, or producing a disc: eg **a** *of the shell of a snail or related animal* having whorls that form a flat coil **b** *of a placenta* having the VILLI restricted to one or more dislike areas

**discoloration** /dis,kulə'raysh(ə)n, ,---'--/ *n* **1** discolouring or being discoloured **2** a discoloured spot or formation; a stain

**discolour** /dis'kulə/ *vt* to change the colour of for the worse ~ *vi* to become discoloured; stain, fade [ME *discolouren*, fr MF *descolourer*, fr LL *discolorari*, fr L *discolor* of another colour, fr *dis-* + *color* colour]

**discombobulate** /,diskəm'bobyoolayt/ *vt, NAm humorous* to upset, confuse [prob alter. of *discompose*] – **discombobulation** *n*

**discomfit** /dis'kumfit/ *vt* **1** to frustrate the plans of; thwart **2** to put into a state of confusion and embarrassment; disconcert **3** *archaic* to defeat in battle [ME *discomfiten*, fr OF *desconfit*, pp of *desconfire*, fr *des-* + *confire* to prepare – more at COMFIT] – **discomfiture** *n*

¹**discomfort** /dis'kumfət/ *vt* to make uncomfortable or uneasy [ME *discomforten*, fr MF *desconforter*, fr OF, fr *des-* + *conforter* to comfort] – **discomfortable** *adj*, **discomforter** *n*

²**discomfort** *n* (something causing) mental or physical uneasiness ⟨*he gave every sign of intense* ~⟩

**discommode** /,diskə'mohd/ *vt, formal* to inconvenience; incommode [MF *discommoder*, fr *dis-* + *commode* convenient – more at COMMODE]

**discompose** /,diskəm'pohz/ *vt, formal* to destroy the composure or serenity of – **discomposure** *n*

**disconcert** /,diskən'suht/ *vt* **1** to throw into confusion; upset **2** to disturb the composure of; fluster [obs Fr *disconcerter*, alter. of MF *desconcerter*, fr *des-* + *concerter* to concert] – **disconcerting** *adj*, **disconcertingly** *adv*

**disconfirm** /,diskən'fuhm/ *vt* to disprove

**disconformable** /,diskən'fawməbl/ *adj* relating to a disconformity in rocks – **disconformably** *adv*

**disconformity** /ˌdiskən'fawməti/ *n* a break in a sequence of SEDIMENTARY rocks all of which have approximately the same angle of slope of strata from the horizontal, that corresponds to an interruption in the deposition of the rock as a result of a period of erosion of the older rock before more recent material was deposited in strata parallel to those already existing

**disconnect** /ˌdiskə'nekt/ *vt* 1 to sever the connection of or between 2 to cut off the supply of a public service (e g electricity or the telephone) ~ *vi* to become disconnected – **disconnection,** *Br also* **disconnexion** *n*, **disconnective** *adj*

**disconnected** /ˌdiskə'nekted/ *adj* 1 not connected 2 cut off from the supply of a public service (e g electricity or the telephone) ⟨*the* ~ *wires trailed uselessly*⟩ 3 disjointed, incoherent ⟨*his speech was* ~⟩ – **disconnectedly** *adv*, **disconnectedness** *n*

**disconsolate** /dis'konsələt/ *adj* 1 dejected, downcast ⟨*the team returned* ~ *after losing again*⟩ 2 cheerless ⟨*a clutch of* ~ *houses* – D H Lawrence⟩ [ME, fr ML *disconsolatus*, fr L *dis-* + *consolatus*, pp of *consolari* to console] – **disconsolately** *adv*, **disconsolateness** *n*, **disconsolation** *n*

¹**discontent** /ˌdiskən'tent/ *n* 1 discontent, discontentment lack of contentment; dissatisfaction 2 one who is discontented; a malcontent

²**discontent** *vt* to make discontented

**discontented** /ˌdiskən'tentid/ *also* **discontent** *adj* restlessly unhappy; dissatisfied

**discontinuance** /ˌdiskən'tinyooəns/ *n* 1 the act or an instance of discontinuing 2 the interruption or termination of a legal action because the PLAINTIFF (person bringing it) has either failed to observe the formalities necessary to keep it pending or has served notice voluntarily abandoning it

**discontinue** /ˌdiskən'tinyooh/ *vt* 1 to cease, stop; *specif* to cease production of ⟨*this line has been* ~d⟩ 2 to abandon or terminate by a legal discontinuance ~ *vi* to come to an end [ME *discontinuen*, fr MF *discontinuer*, fr ML *discontinuare*, fr L *dis-* + *continuare* to continue] – **discontinuance, discontinuation** *n*

**discontinuity** /ˌdis,konti'nyooh·əti/ *n* 1 lack of continuity or cohesion 2 a break, hiatus 3 a point in the DOMAIN of a mathematical function at which it is not CONTINUOUS 4 a zone below the earth's surface that represents a boundary separating parts of the earth with different physical properties – compare MOHOROVICIC DISCONTINUITY

**discontinuous** /ˌdiskən'tinyoo·əs/ *adj* 1a not continuous ⟨*a* ~ *series of events*⟩ b lacking sequence or coherence ⟨*this* ~ *style*⟩ 2 *of a mathematical function* having one or more discontinuities – **discontinuously** *adv*

**discophile** /'disko,fiel/ *n* one who studies and collects gramophone records

¹**discord** /'diskawd/ *n* 1a lack of agreement or harmony (e g between people, things, or ideas) b active quarrelling or conflict among people or factions; strife 2a a combination of musical sounds that strike the ear harshly; dissonance b a harsh or unpleasant sound

²**discord** /'diskawd, -'-/ *vi* to disagree, clash [ME *discorden*, fr OF *discorder*, fr L *discord-, discors* discordant, fr *dis-* + *cord-, cor* heart – more at HEART]

**discordance** /dis'kawd(ə)ns/ *also* **discordancy** /-si/ *n* 1 the state or an instance of being discordant 2 musical dissonance

**discordant** /dis'kawd(ə)nt/ *adj* 1a at variance; disagreeing b quarrelsome 2 relating to a discord ⟨ ~ *tones*⟩ – **discordantly** *adv*

**discotheque, discothèque** /'diskə,tek/ *n* a disco

¹**discount** /'diskownt/ *n* 1 a reduction made from the gross amount or value of something: e g 1a a reduction in the price of goods, accorded esp to special or trade customers or as part of a sales promotion b a reduction in the amount due on a BILL OF EXCHANGE, debt, etc when paid promptly or before the specified date c the amount by which one futures contract price is less than another – compare PREMIUM 1e 2 the act or practice of discounting 3 a deduction taken or allowance made – **at a discount 1** below the usual price **2** not valued or in demand ⟨*honesty seems to be rather* at a discount *today*⟩

²**discount** /'diskownt; *sense* 2 dis'kownt/ *vt* 1a to make a deduction from, usu for cash or prompt payment b to sell or offer for sale at a discount 2a to lend money on after deducting the discount or allowance for interest ⟨*a bank that* ~s *negotiable paper*⟩ b to buy or sell (a BILL OF EXCHANGE) before maturity at below the stated price 3a to leave out of

account; disregard; *also* to underestimate, minimize b to take into account beforehand, esp so as to reduce the effect of; anticipate [modif of Fr *décompter*, fr OF *desconter*, fr ML *discomputare*, fr L *dis-* + *computare* to count – more at COUNT] – **discountable** *adj*, **discounter** *n*

**discountenance** /dis'kownt(ə)nəns/ *vt, formal* 1 to abash, disconcert 2 to discourage by showing disapproval – **discountenance** *n*

**discount house** *n* 1 *chiefly Br* an organization whose business is discounting bills or notes not due 2 *chiefly NAm* a shop where goods (e g consumer durables) are sold at a discount from the recommended list price

**discount rate** *n* 1 the interest on an annual basis deducted in advance on a loan (e g a bank loan) 2 the charge levied by a central bank for advances and REDISCOUNTS

**discourage** /di'skurij/ *vt* 1 to deprive of courage or confidence; dishearten 2 to hinder by disapproval; dissuade *from* 3 to deter, prevent ⟨*will* ~ *clothes moths from breeding*⟩ [MF *descorager*, fr OF *descoragier*, fr *des-* dis- + *corage* courage]

**discouragement** /di'skurijmənt/ *n* 1 discouraging or being discouraged 2 something that discourages; a deterrent ⟨*there's no* ~ *shall make him once relent his first avowed intent to be a pilgrim* – John Bunyan⟩

**discouraging** /di'skurijing/ *adj* lessening confidence; disheartening – **discouragingly** *adv*

¹**discourse** /'diskaws/ *n* 1 a conversation, esp of a formal nature 2a formal and orderly expression of ideas in speech or writing; *also* such expression in the form of a sermon, treatise, etc b (a piece or unit of) connected speech or writing [ME *discours*, fr ML & LL *discursus*; ML, argument, fr LL, conversation, fr L, act of running about, fr *discursus*, pp of *discurrere* to run about, fr *dis-* + *currere* to run – more at CAR]

²**discourse** /dis'kaws, '--/ *vi* 1 to express one's ideas in speech or writing, esp formally and at length 2 to talk, converse *on* ~ *vt, archaic* to give forth (e g music) **synonyms** see SPEAK – **discourser** *n*

**discourteous** /dis'kuhtyəs/ *adj* lacking courtesy; rude – **discourteously** *adv*, **discourteousness** *n*

**discourtesy** /dis'kuhtəsi/ *n* 1 lack of politeness; incivility 2 an ill-mannered or impolite act ⟨*refusal to attend would be seen as a grave* ~⟩

**discover** /di'skuvə/ *vt* 1 to obtain sight or knowledge of for the first time; find ⟨ ~ *the solution of a puzzle*⟩ ⟨*Columbus did not* ~ *America*⟩ ⟨*I* ~ *I have not long to live*⟩ 2 *formal* to make known or visible; expose ~ *vi* to make a discovery **synonyms** see INVENT, ¹REVEAL [ME *discoveren*, fr OF *descovrir*, fr LL *discooperire*, fr L *dis-* + *cooperire* to cover – more at COVER] – **discoverable** *adj*, **discoverer** *n*

**discovery** /di'skuv(ə)ri/ *n* 1 the act or process of discovering 2 somebody or something discovered 3 a compulsory disclosure of documents or facts by a party to a legal action 4 *archaic* a disclosure

¹**discredit** /dis'kredit/ *vt* 1 to refuse to accept as true or accurate; disbelieve 2 to cause disbelief in the accuracy or authority of; deprive of credibility 3 to deprive of good repute; disgrace

²**discredit** *n* 1 loss of credit or reputation ⟨*I knew stories to the* ~ *of England* – W B Yeats⟩; *also* somebody or something causing disgrace 2 lack or loss of belief or confidence; doubt ⟨*contradictions cast* ~ *on his testimony*⟩

**discreditable** /dis'kreditəbl/ *adj* harmful to reputation; shameful – **discreditably** *adv*

**discreet** /di'skreet/ *adj* 1 judicious in speech or conduct; prudent; *esp* capable of maintaining a prudent silence 2 unobtrusive, modest ⟨*the house was furnished with* ~ *elegance*⟩ [ME, fr MF *discret*, fr ML *discretus*, fr L, pp of *discernere* to separate, distinguish between – more at DISCERN] – **discreetly** *adv*, **discreetness** *n*

**discrepancy** /di'skrep(ə)nsi/ *n* 1 the quality or state of being discrepant 2 an instance of being discrepant

**discrepant** /di'skrep(ə)nt/ *adj* at variance; disagreeing ⟨*widely* ~ *conclusions*⟩ [L *discrepant-, discrepans*, prp of *discrepare* to sound discordantly, fr *dis-* + *crepare* to rattle, creak – more at RAVEN] – **discrepantly** *adv*

**discrete** /di'skreet/ *adj* 1 constituting a separate item; individually distinct 2a consisting of distinct or unconnected elements; discontinuous b taking on or having a finite or COUNTABLE number of values ⟨*a* ~ *random variable*⟩ △ discreet [ME, fr L *discretus*] – **discretely** *adv*, **discreteness** *n*

**discretion** /di'skresh(ə)n/ *n* 1 the quality of being discreet 2 the ability to make responsible decisions **3a** individual choice or judgment ⟨*left the decision to his* ~⟩ **b** the power to manage one's own affairs and act on one's own freely taken decisions within certain legal bounds ⟨*reached the age of* ~⟩

**discretionary** /di'skresh(ə)nri/ *adj* **1** left to discretion; exercised at one's own discretion ⟨~ *powers*⟩ **2** subject to the discretion of another ⟨*a* ~ *grant*⟩

**discretionary account** *n* a security or commodity market account in which an agent (eg a broker) is allowed to make independent decisions and buy and sell for the account of a client

**discriminant** /di'skriminənt/ *n* a mathematical expression providing a criterion for the behaviour of another more complicated expression, relation, or set of relations

**discriminate** /di'skrimi,nayt/ *vt* **1** to serve to distinguish; differentiate **2** to distinguish (eg objects, qualities, or ideas) by discerning or exposing differences ⟨~ *good from bad*⟩ ~ *vi* **1a** to make a distinction ⟨~ *among the methods which should be used*⟩ **b** to use good judgment or discernment **2** to treat somebody differently and esp unfavourably on the grounds of race, sex, religion, etc – usu + *against* or *in favour of* ⟨~ *in favour of your friends*⟩ ⟨~ *against a certain nationality*⟩ [L *discriminatus*, pp of *discriminare*, fr *discrimin-, discrimen* distinction, fr *discernere* to distinguish between – more at DISCERN]

**discriminating** /di'skriminayting/ *adj* **1a** discerning, esp in matters of taste; judicious **b** discriminatory **2** *archaic* making a distinction; distinguishing □ compare INDISCRIMINATE *antonym* indiscriminating – **discriminatingly** *adv*

**discrimination** /di,skrimi'naysh(ə)n/ *n* **1a** the act of discriminating **b** the act or process of responding to different sensory stimuli in different ways **2** discernment and good judgment, esp in matters of taste **3** prejudiced or prejudicial outlook, action, or treatment *synonyms* see DISCERNMENT – **discriminational** *adj*

**discriminator** /di'skriminaytə/ *n* one who or that which discriminates; *specif* an electronic circuit that can be adjusted to accept or reject signals of different characteristics (eg amplitude or frequency)

**discriminatory** /di'skriminətri/ *also* **discriminative** /di'skriminətiv/ *adj* **1** showing esp unfavourable discrimination in treatment ⟨*a* ~ *law*⟩ **2** making distinctions – **discriminatorily** *adv*

**discursive** /di'skuhsiv, -ziv/ *adj* **1** passing usu unmethodically from one topic to another; digressive **2** proceeding by logical argument or reason; not intuitive ⟨*a* ~ *proof for the existence of God*⟩ [ML *discursivus*, fr L *discursus*, pp of *discurrere* to run about – more at DISCOURSE] – **discursively** *adv*, **discursiveness** *n*

**discus** /'diskəs/ *n, pl* **discuses** *also* **disci** /'diskie/ **1** a solid disc between 180 and 219 millimetres (about seven to nine inches) in diameter that is thicker in the centre than at the edge and is thrown as great a distance as possible by competitors in an athletic field event; *also* this event **2** DISC 2,3 **3** any of various aquarium fish (eg *Symphysodon discus*) of disclike appearance – not used technically [L – more at DISH]

**discuss** /di'skus/ *vt* **1** to investigate by reasoning or argument in speech or in writing **2** to present in detail for examination or consideration; *broadly* to talk about ⟨~ed *plans for the party*⟩ [ME *discussen*, fr L *discussus*, pp of *discutere*, fr *dis-* apart + *quatere* to shake – more at DIS-, QUASH] – **discussable**, **discussible** *adj*, **discussant**, **discusser** *n*

**discussion** /di'skush(ə)n/ *n* **1** the act or an instance of discussing; *esp* consideration of a question in open debate **2** a treatment of a topic, esp in a formal written work

**¹disdain** /dis'dayn/ *n* a feeling of contempt for something regarded as beneath one; scorn [ME *desdeyne*, fr OF *desdeign*, fr *desdeignier*]

**²disdain** *vt* **1** to regard with scorn **2** to refuse or abstain from because of disdain ⟨*she* ~ed *to answer him*⟩ **3** to treat disdainfully [ME *desdeynen*, fr MF *desdeignier*, fr (assumed) VL *disdignare*, fr L *dis-* + *dignare* to deign – more at DEIGN]

**disdainful** /dis'daynf(ə)l/ *adj* full of or expressing disdain *synonyms* see PROUD – **disdainfully** *adv*, **disdainfulness** *n*

**disease** /di'zeez/ *n* **1** an unhealthy condition of the living animal or plant body or of one of its parts that impairs the performance of a vital function; (a) sickness, malady **2** a harmful or corrupt development, situation, or condition (eg in a social institution) ⟨*the various* ~*s of civilization*⟩ [ME *disese* uneasiness, sickness, fr MF *desaise*, fr *des-* dis- + *aise* ease] – **diseased** *adj*

**diseconomy** /,disi'konəmi/ *n* **1** a lack of economy **2** a factor responsible for an increase in cost

**disembark** /,disim'bahk/ *vt* to put ashore from a ship ~ *vi* **1** to go ashore out of a ship **2** to get out of a vehicle (eg an aeroplane) [MF *desembarquer*, fr *des-* + *embarquer* to embark] – **disembarkation** *n*

**disembarrass** /,disim'barəs/ *vt, formal* to free from something troublesome or superfluous – usu + *of* – **disembarrassment** *n*

**disembodied** /,disim'bodid/ *adj* **1** of a soul existing apart from the body it inhabited **2** coming from an invisible source ⟨~ *voices*⟩

**disembody** /,disim'bodi/ *vt* to free from the body, physical existence, or reality

**disembogue** /,disim'bohg/ *vb, formal, of a stream, river, etc* to flow or pour (itself) forth (as if) from a channel [modif of Sp *desembocar*, fr *des-* dis- (fr L *dis-*) + *embocar* to put into the mouth, fr *en* in (fr L *in*) + *boca* mouth, fr L *bucca* – more at POCK]

**disembowel** /,disim'bowəl/ *vt* **1** to remove or rip out the bowels or entrails of **2** to remove the substance of – **disembowelment** *n*

**disembroil** /,disim'broyl/ *vt, formal* to free from a confused or entangled condition or situation

**disenchant** /,disin'chahnt/ *vt* to free from illusion or a particular passion, enthusiasm, etc; disillusion [MF *desenchanter*, fr *des-* + *enchanter* to enchant] – **disenchanter** *n*, **disenchanting** *adj*, **disenchantingly** *adv*, **disenchantment** *n*

**disencumber** /,disin'kumbə/ *vt, formal* to free from encumbrance or inconvenience; disburden [MF *desencombrer*, fr *des-* + *encombrer* to encumber]

**disendow** /,disin'dow/ *vt* to strip (eg a church) of an endowment – **disendower** *n*, **disendowment** *n*

**disenfranchise** /,disin'frahnchiez, -'fran-/ *vt* to disfranchise – **disenfranchisement** *n*

**disengage** /,dising'gayj/ *vt* **1** to release from something that engages or entangles **2** to withdraw (troops) from military engagement ~ *vi* **1** to release or detach oneself or itself; *specif, esp of troops* to withdraw **2** to move one's fencing sword to the other side of an opponent's sword in order to attack [Fr *désengager*, fr MF, fr *des-* + *engager* to engage] – **disengagement** *n*

**disengaged** /,dising'gayjd/ *adj* **1** *formal* free from social or official commitments ⟨*I should like to see the President if he is* ~⟩ **2** uncommitted; dégagé

**disentail** /,disin'tayl/ *vt, law* to free (an estate) from ENTAIL (restriction as to how landed estate shall be bequeathed) – **disentailment** *n*

**disentangle** /,disin'tang-gl/ *vb* to make or become free from entanglement; unravel – **disentanglement** *n*

**disenthral**, *chiefly NAm* **disenthrall** /,disin'thrawl/ *vt* -ll- to free from bondage; liberate – **disenthralment** *also* **disenthrallment** *n*

**disentitle** /disin'tietl/ *vt* to deprive of a title, claim, or right

**disentomb** /,disin'toohm/ *vt* to take out (as if) from a tomb; disinter – **disentombment** *n*

**disequilibrate** /,disee'kwilibrayt/ *vt* to put out of balance – **disequilibration** *n*

**disequilibrium** /,dis,eekwi'libriəm, -,ekwi-/ *n* loss or lack of equilibrium

**disestablish** /,disi'stablish/ *vt* to deprive of an established status; *esp* to deprive of the status and privileges of being an established church – **disestablishment** *n*

**disestablishmentarian** /,disi,stablishmən'teəriən/ *n, often cap* a person who opposes an established order – **disestablishmentarian** *adj, often cap*

**disesteem** /,disi'steem/ *vt, formal* to regard with disfavour; think little of – **disesteem** *n*

**diseuse** /dee'zuhz/, *masc* **diseur** /dee'zuh/ *n, pl* **diseuses**, *masc* **diseurs** /dee'zuhz/ a usu professional woman reciter [Fr, fr OF, fr *dire* to say, fr L *dicere* – more at DICTION]

**¹disfavour** /dis'fayvə/ *n* **1** disapproval, dislike ⟨*practices looked upon with* ~⟩ **2** the state or fact of being deprived of favour ⟨*fell into* ~⟩

**²disfavour** *vt* to withhold or withdraw favour from; *also* to regard with disfavour

**disfigure** /dis'figə/ *vt* to spoil the beauty of; deface, mar ⟨*a face* ~d *by smallpox*⟩ [ME *disfiguren*, fr MF *desfigurer*, fr *des-* + *figure*] – **disfigurement** *n*

**disforest** /dis'forist/ *vt, chiefly Br* to deforest

**disfranchise** /dis'frahnchiez, -'fran-/ *vt* to deprive of a

FRANCHISE (legal right, privilege, or immunity); *esp* to deprive of the right to vote – **disfranchisement** *n*
**disfrock** /ˌdisˈfrok/ *vt* to unfrock
**disfunction** /disˈfungksh(ə)n/ *n* impaired functioning; DYS-FUNCTION
**disgorge** /disˈgawj/ *vt* **1a(1)** to discharge via the throat and mouth; vomit **a(2)** to remove (a hook) from the mouth of a fish **b** to discharge violently, confusedly, or as a result of force ⟨the *dam-burst* ∼d *tons of mud and water*⟩ **c** to give up on request or under pressure ⟨*refused to* ∼ *his ill-gotten gains*⟩ **2** to discharge the contents of (eg one's stomach) ∼ *vi* to discharge contents ⟨*where the river* ∼s *into the sea*⟩; *also* to give up ill-gotten gains [MF *desgorger*, fr *des-* + *gorge* throat]
¹**disgrace** /disˈgrays/ *vt* **1** to bring reproach or shame to ⟨∼d *his family*⟩ **2** to cause to lose favour or standing ⟨*was* ∼d *by the hint of scandal*⟩ – **disgracer** *n*
²**disgrace** *n* **1a** loss of favour, honour, or respect; shame **b** the condition of being out of favour ⟨*he's in* ∼⟩ **2** one who or that which disgraces ⟨*that boy's manners are a* ∼⟩ ⟨*he's a* ∼ *to his regiment*⟩ [MF, fr OIt *disgrazia*, fr dis- (fr L) + *grazia* grace, fr L *gratia* – more at GRACE]
**disgraceful** /disˈgraysf(ə)l/ *adj* shameful, shocking – **disgracefully** *adv*, **disgracefulness** *n*
**disgruntled** /disˈgruntld/ *adj* aggrieved and dissatisfied [fr pp of *disgruntle* (to aggrieve), fr dis- + *gruntle* (to grumble), fr ME *gruntlen*, freq of *grunten* to grunt] – **disgruntlement** *n*
¹**disguise** /disˈgiez/ *vt* **1** to give a false appearance or an assumed identity to (eg oneself) ⟨∼d *himself as a tramp*⟩ **2** to hide the existence or true state of; conceal ⟨*he could not* ∼ *his true feelings*⟩ [ME *disgisen*, fr MF *desguiser*, fr OF, fr des- + *guise* manner] – **disguisedly** *adv*, **disguisement** *n*, **disguiser** *n*
²**disguise** *n* **1** something (eg clothing) that is used to conceal one's identity or imitate another's **2a** an outward appearance that misrepresents the true nature of something ⟨*blessings in* ∼⟩ **b** an artificial manner; pretence ⟨*threw off all* ∼⟩ **3** the act of disguising
¹**disgust** /disˈgust/ *n* strong loathing aroused by somebody or something highly distasteful; repugnance
²**disgust** *vt* to provoke to loathing, repugnance, or aversion; be offensive to ∼ *vi* to cause disgust [MF *desgouster*, fr des-dis- + *goust* taste, fr L *gustus*; akin to L *gustare* to taste – more at CHOOSE] – **disgusted** *adj*, **disgustedly** *adv*, **disgusting** *adj*, **disgustingly** *adv*
   *usage* One is **disgusted** *at* or *with* a person ⟨*I'm* **disgusted** *with you*⟩, **disgusted** *at* an action, quality, or event ⟨*I'm* **disgusted** *at what happened*⟩.
**disgustful** /disˈgustf(ə)l/ *adj* **1** disgusting **2** accompanied by disgust ⟨∼ *curiosity* – R L Stevenson⟩ – **disgustfully** *adv*
¹**dish** /dish/ *n* **1a** a more or less shallow usu concave vessel that is often circular or oval, and is used esp for holding or serving food; *broadly* a hollowed-out vessel from which food is eaten or served **b** a dishful ⟨*a* ∼ *of strawberries*⟩ **c** *pl* the utensils and tableware used in preparing, serving, and eating a meal ⟨*wash the* ∼es⟩ **2** (a) food prepared in a particular way ⟨*coq au vin, originally a French* ∼⟩ **3a(1)** any of various shallow concave vessels; *broadly* something shallowly concave **a(2)** an aerial, esp for receiving radio or television transmissions or microwaves, having a shallowly concave reflector **b(1)** a hollow, depression **b(2)** the concave appearance of a dished wagon or cart wheel **b(3)** the condition of being dished – used with reference to a pair of wagon wheels **4** *informal* an attractive person [ME, fr OE *disc* plate; akin to OHG *tisc* plate, table; both fr a prehistoric WGmc word borrowed fr L *discus* quoit, disc, dish, fr Gk *diskos*, fr *dikein* to throw]
²**dish** *vt* **1** to make concave like a dish **2** *chiefly Br informal* to ruin or spoil (a person or his/her hopes) ⟨*if he falls that'll completely* ∼ *his chances*⟩
   **dish out** *vt* **1** to serve (food) from a dish **2** *informal* to give or distribute freely ⟨*he dished out advice to numerous teenagers*⟩
   **dish it out** *vi*, *informal* to inflict punishment, criticism, etc often indiscriminately
   **dish up** *vt* **1** to put (a meal, food, etc) onto dishes; serve **2** *informal* to produce (facts or arguments) ⟨*our teacher has been dishing up the same old lessons for years*⟩ ∼ *vi* to put food onto dishes ready to be eaten ⟨*I'm just dishing up now*⟩
**dishabille** /ˌdisəˈbeel/ *n* deshabille
**disharmony** /disˈhahməni/ *n* lack of harmony; discord – **disharmonious** *adj*, **disharmoniously** *adv*, **disharmonize** *vt*
**dishcloth** /ˈdishˌkloth/ *n* **1** a cloth for washing dishes **2** TEA TOWEL

**dishearten** /disˈhaht(ə)n/ *vt* to cause to lose hope or morale; discourage – **dishearteningly** *adv*, **disheartenment** *n*
**dished** /disht/ *adj* **1** concave **2a** *of a wagon or cart wheel* having a concave appearance due to the spokes being angled slightly outwards from the hub **b** *of a pair of wagon or cart wheels* closer to one another at the bottom than at the top
**dishevel** /diˈshevl/ *vt* -ll- (*NAm* -l-, -ll-) to reduce (eg hair) to a state of disorder or disarray [back-formation fr *dishevelled*] – **dishevelment** *n*
**dishevelled**, *NAm chiefly* **disheveled** /diˈshev(ə)ld/ *adj*, *esp of a person's hair or appearance* unkempt, untidy [ME *discheveled*, part trans of MF *deschevelé*, fr pp of *descheveler* to disarrange the hair, fr des- + *chevel* hair, fr L *capillus*]
**dishful** /-f(ə)l/ *n* the amount a dish contains or will hold
**dishonest** /disˈonist/ *adj* not honest, truthful, or sincere [ME, fr MF *deshoneste*, fr des- + *honeste* honest] – **dishonestly** *adv*
**dishonesty** /disˈonisti/ *n* **1** lack of honesty or integrity; disposition to defraud or deceive **2** a dishonest act; a fraud
¹**dishonour** /disˈonə/ *n* **1** lack or loss of honour or reputation **2** the state of one who has lost honour or prestige; shame ⟨*would rather die than live in* ∼⟩ **3** a cause of disgrace ⟨*became a* ∼ *to his family*⟩ **4** the nonpayment or nonacceptance of COMMERCIAL PAPER (cheques, money orders, etc) by the party in whose name it was issued [ME, fr OF *deshonor*, fr des- + *honor* honour]
²**dishonour** *vt* **1** to treat without honour or respect ⟨*children should not* ∼ *their parents*⟩ **2** to bring shame on **3** to refuse to accept or pay (eg a draft, bill, or cheque)
**dishonourable** /disˈon(ə)rəbl/ *adj* **1** causing a loss of honour; shameful ⟨∼ *conduct*⟩ **2** lacking honour; unprincipled – **dishonourably** *adv*
**dishpan hands** /ˈdishpan/ *n pl* sore or reddened hands caused esp by doing the washing up
**dishwasher** /ˈdishˌwoshə/ *n* **1** a worker employed to wash dishes **2** a machine for washing dishes, cutlery, etc
**dishwater** /ˈdishˌwawtə/ *n* **1** water in which dishes have been or are being washed **2** something, esp a drink, that is repellently insipid – **dishwatery** *adj*
**dishy** /ˈdishi/ *adj*, *chiefly Br informal*, *esp of a man* attractive [¹dish 4 + ¹-y]
¹**disillusion** /ˌdisiˈloohzh(ə)n, -ˈlyooh-/ *n* the condition of being disenchanted; *also* an instance of this
²**disillusion** *vt* to free from illusion; *esp* to depress or cause to feel bitter by revealing the worthlessness of an object of admiration – **disillusionment** *n*
**disincentive** /ˌdisinˈsentiv/ *n* something that has a deterrent effect, esp financially
**disinclination** /ˌdisˌingkliˈnaysh(ə)n/ *n* a preference for avoiding something; a mild dislike of something
**disincline** /ˌdisingˈklien/ *vt* to make unwilling
**disinclined** /ˌdisingˈkliend/ *adj* unwilling because of mild dislike or disapproval
**disinfect** /ˌdisinˈfekt/ *vt* to free from infection, esp by destroying harmful microorganisms; *broadly* to cleanse [MF *desinfecter*, fr des- + *infecter* to infect] – **disinfection** *n*
**disinfectant** /ˌdisinˈfekt(ə)nt/ *n* something that frees from infection; *esp* a chemical that destroys harmful microorganisms
**disinfest** /ˌdisinˈfest/ *vt* to rid of small animal pests (eg insects or rodents) – **disinfestant** *n*, **disinfestation** *n*
**disinflation** /ˌdisinˈflaysh(ə)n/ *n* a reduction of inflation without the general reduction in economic activity associated with deflation – **disinflationary** *adj*
**disinformation** /ˌdisinfəˈmaysh(ə)n/ *n* deliberately false or misleading information supplied to an enemy
**disingenuous** /ˌdisinˈjenyooəs/ *adj* lacking in candour or sincerity; *also* giving a false appearance of simplicity, naivety, or frankness – **disingenuously** *adv*, **disingenuousness** *n*
**disinherit** /ˌdisinˈherit/ *vt* **1** to deprive (an heir) of an inheritance or of the right to inherit **2** to deprive of natural or human rights – **disinheritance** *n*
**disinhibition** /ˌdisˌinhiˈbish(ə)n/ *n* loss of a conditioned reflex (eg by the action of interfering stimuli)
**disintegrate** /disˈintigrayt/ *vt* **1** to break up into fragments or constituent elements **2** to destroy the unity or wholeness of **3** to cause (eg an atomic nucleus) to disintegrate ∼ *vi* **1** to break into fragments or constituent elements **2** to lose unity or wholeness (as if) by breaking into parts **3** to undergo a change in composition; *esp* to emit one or more particles or undergo splitting as a result of spontaneous radioactive decay or bombardment by a neutron, ALPHA PARTICLE, etc – used esp of an

atomic nucleus or an ELEMENTARY PARTICLE – **disintegration** *n*, **disintegrative** *adj*, **disintegrator** *n*

**disinter** /ˌdisin'tuh/ *vt* **-rr-** **1** to remove from a grave or tomb **2** to bring to light; unearth – **disinterment** *n*

**disinterest** /dis'intrest, -trast/ *n* **1** lack of interest; apathy, uninterestedness – disapproved of by some speakers **2** lack of self-interest; disinterestedness

**disinterested** /dis'intrestid, -əstid/ *adj* **1** uninterested – disapproved of by some speakers **2** free from selfish motive or interest; objective, unbiased ⟨*a* ~ *decision*⟩ – **disinterestedly** *adv*, **disinterestedness** *n*

*usage* After a long period of meaning only "impartial", **disinterested** is now reverting to its earlier meaning of "uninterested", which was first recorded in English in the 17th century. Since this trend arouses the strong disapproval of some people it is often wise to use **disinterested** only in the sense of "impartial" or indeed, where there may be danger of ambiguity, to avoid the word entirely, replacing it by **uninterested** or **impartial** according to the sense. *synonyms* See INDIFFERENT *antonym* interested

**disintoxicate** /ˌdisin'toksikayt/ *vt* to free (e g a drug user or an alcoholic) from an intoxicating agent in the body or from dependence on such an agent – **disintoxication** *n*

**disinvestment** /ˌdisin'vestmənt/ *n* reduction or ending of investment, esp by selling off assets or not replacing capital equipment – **disinvest** *vi*

**disjoin** /dis'joyn/ *vt* to end the joining of; separate ~ *vi* to become detached [MF *desjoindre*, fr L *disjungere*, fr *dis-* + *jungere* to join – more at YOKE]

**¹disjoint** /dis'joynt/ *adj* **1** having no elements in common ⟨~ *mathematical sets*⟩ **2** *obs* DISJOINTED 2a [ME *disjoynt*, fr MF *desjoint*, pp of *desjoindre*]

**²disjoint** *vt* **1** to disturb the orderly structure or arrangement of **2** to take (esp a meat carcass) apart at the joints ~ *vi* to come apart at the joints

**disjointed** /dis'joyntid/ *adj* **1** separated (as if) at the joint **2a** characterized by the disruption of orderly activity; dislocated ⟨*a* ~ *society*⟩ **b** lacking coherence or orderly sequence; disconnected ⟨*an incomplete and* ~ *history*⟩ – **disjointedly** *adv*, **disjointedness** *n*

**¹disjunct** /'disjungkt/ *adj* marked by separation of or from parts or individuals usu in contact: e g **a** discontinuous **b** relating to melody in which each successive note is at least two notes higher or lower in pitch than the preceding one **c** of an *insect* having the three body regions, the head, thorax, and abdomen, separated by deep constrictions [L *disjunctus*, pp of *disjungere* to disjoin]

**²disjunct** *n* **1** any of the alternatives in a logical disjunction **2** an adverbial linguistic form (e g *frankly* in "frankly, I'm annoyed") that expresses an evaluation of what is said – compare ADJUNCT, CONJUNCT

**disjunction** /dis'jungksh(ə)n/ *n* **1** (a) cleavage, separation ⟨*the* ~ *between theory and practice*⟩ **2a** INCLUSIVE DISJUNCTION **b** EXCLUSIVE DISJUNCTION

**¹disjunctive** /dis'jungktiv/ *n* a disjunctive conjunction or pronoun

**²disjunctive** *adj* **1a** being or belonging to a logical disjunction **b** expressing an alternative, or opposition between the meanings of the words connected ⟨*the* ~ *conjunction* or *in the question "Is he old or young?"*⟩ **c** expressed by mutually exclusive alternatives joined by *or* ⟨~ *pleading*⟩ **2** of a pronoun form stressed and not attached to the verb ⟨*French* moi, as in Donnez le moi *"Give it to me," is a* ~ *pronoun*⟩ **3** *formal* marked by breaks or disunity; DISJOINTED 2b ⟨*a* ~ *narrative sequence*⟩ – **disjunctively** *adv*

**disk** /disk/ *n* **1a** *Br also* **disc** a round flat plate coated with a magnetic substance on which data for a computer is stored – compare FLOPPY DISK **b** **disk, disk pack** a computer storage device consisting of a stack of disks rotating at high speed, each disk having its own HEAD to remove (READ) and enter (WRITE) data **2** a disc

**¹dislike** /dis'liek/ *vt* to regard with dislike; feel an aversion for – **disliker** *n*

*usage* Although one may **like** something, **like** doing it or **like** to do it, one cannot **dislike** to do it.

**²dislike** *n* a feeling of aversion or disapproval – + *for* or *of*

**dislocate** /'disləkayt/ *vt* **1a** to put out of place **b(1)** to displace (a bone) from normal connections with another bone at a joint **b(2)** to displace the bones of (a joint) ⟨~ *d his knee*⟩ **2** to disrupt [ML *dislocatus*, pp of *dislocare*, fr L *dis-* + *locare* to locate]

**dislocation** /ˌdislə'kaysh(ə)n/ *n* dislocating or being dislocated:

e g **a** displacement of one or more bones at a joint **b** a discontinuity in the otherwise regular geometrical arrangement of the atoms, ions, etc of a crystal **c** disruption of an established order

**dislodge** /dis'loj/ *vt* **1** to force out of a secure or settled position ⟨~ *d the rock with a spade*⟩ **2** to drive from a position of hiding, defence, or advantage [ME *disloggen*, fr MF *desloger*, fr *des-* + *loger* to lodge, fr *loge* lodge]

**disloyal** /dis'loyəl/ *adj* lacking in loyalty; untrue to personal obligations or allegiance ⟨*his* ~ *refusal to help his friend*⟩ [MF *desloial*, fr OF, fr *des-* + *loial* loyal] – **disloyally** *adv*, **disloyalty** *n*

**dismal** /'dizməl/ *adj* **1** showing or causing gloom or depression **2** marked by weakness or ineptness ⟨*a* ~ *failure*⟩ **3** *obs* disastrous, dreadful [ME, fr *dismal*, n, days marked as unlucky in medieval calendars, fr AF, fr ML *dies mali*, lit., evil days] – **dismally** *adv*, **dismalness** *n*

**dismantle** /dis'mantl/ *vt* **1** to strip of furniture and equipment **2** to take to pieces **3** *archaic* to strip of dress or covering; divest ~ *vi* to be able to be taken to pieces ⟨*it* ~ s *easily*⟩ [MF *desmanteler*, fr *des-* + *mantel* mantle] – **dismantlement** *n*

**dismast** /dis'mahst/ *vt* to remove or break off the mast of (a ship)

**¹dismay** /di'smay/ *vt* to deprive of courage and initiative through the pressure of sudden fear, anxiety, etc; discourage ⟨~ ed *at the size of his adversary*⟩ [ME *dismayen*, fr (assumed) OF *desmaiier*, fr OF *des-* + *-maiier* (as in *esmaiier* to dismay), fr (assumed) VL *-magare*, of Gmc origin]

**²dismay** *n* sudden loss of courage or resolution from alarm or fear *synonyms* see ¹FEAR *antonyms* satisfaction, relief

**dismember** /dis'membə/ *vt* **1** to cut or tear off the limbs, parts, etc of (e g a human body) **2** to break up or tear into pieces **3** to divide up (e g a territory) into parts [ME *dismembren*, fr OF *desmembrer*, fr *des-* + *membre* member] – **dismemberment** *n*

**dismiss** /dis'mis/ *vt* **1** to permit or cause to leave; send away ⟨~ ed *his visitor*⟩ **2** to remove from employment or service; discharge **3a** to refuse to give serious consideration or attention to ⟨~ ed *the thought*⟩ **b** to reject (e g a legal claim or charge); refuse to give further hearing or consideration to in court ⟨*the judge* ~ ed *all charges*⟩ **4** to cause (a batsman or side) to be out in cricket ⟨*he was* ~ ed *for a low score once more*⟩ [modif of L *dimissus*, pp of *dimittere*, fr *dis-* apart + *mittere* to send] – **dismissible** *adj*

**dismissal** /dis'misl/ *n* **1** dismissing or being dismissed **2** a discharge from employment or service

**dismissive** /dis'misiv/ *adj* **1** giving dismissal; serving to dismiss **2** disdainful, disparaging – **dismissively** *adv*

**dismount** /dis'mownt/ *vi* to get down from an elevated position (e g on a horse) ~ *vt* **1** to throw down or remove from a mount or an elevated position; *esp* to unhorse **2** to get down from or off (a horse, bicycle, etc) ⟨*he* ~ ed *his machine and walked away*⟩ **3** to remove from a mounting [prob modif of MF *desmonter*, fr *des-* + *monter* to mount] – **dismount** *n*

**disobedience** /ˌdisə'beediəns/ *n* **1** refusal or failure to obey **2** a refusal to jump a fence in showjumping

**disobedient** /ˌdisə'beediənt/ *adj* refusing or neglecting to obey [ME, fr MF *desobedient*, fr *des-* + *obedient*] – **disobediently** *adv*

**disobey** /ˌdisə'bay/ *vt* to fail to obey ~ *vi* to be disobedient [ME *disobeyen*, fr MF *desobeir*, fr *des-* + *obeir* to obey] – **disobeyer** *n*

**disoblige** /ˌdisə'bliej/ *vt* **1** to go against the wishes of; be unaccommodating towards **2** to inconvenience; PUT OUT; *also* to affront, offend [Fr *désobliger*, fr MF *desobliger*, fr *des-* + *obliger* to oblige]

**disomic** /ˌdie'sohmik/ *adj* having one or more of the set of CHROMOSOMES (strands of gene-carrying material) duplicated but not the entire set [*di-* + *-somic*]

**¹disorder** /dis'awdə/ *vt* **1** to disturb the order of **2** to upset the normal functions or health of

**²disorder** *n* **1** lack of order ⟨*clothes in* ~⟩ **2** breach of the peace or public order ⟨*troubled times marked by social* ~ s⟩ **3** a disturbance of the physical or mental condition; an ailment ⟨*suffering from a* ~ *of the bowel*⟩

**disordered** /dis'awdəd/ *adj* **1** marked by disorder **2** not functioning in a normal orderly healthy way

**disorderly** /-li/ *adj* **1** characterized by disorder ⟨*a* ~ *pile of clothes*⟩ **2** engaged in conduct likely to disturb the peace or violate public order; unruly ⟨*charged with being drunk and* ~⟩ – **disorderliness** *n*

**disorderly house** *n* a brothel or other establishment where activities tending to corrupt or deprave are carried on

**disorgan·ize, -ise** /dis'awgəniez/ *vt* to destroy or interrupt the orderly structure or function of [Fr *désorganiser*, fr *dés-* dis- + *organiser* to organize] – **disorganization** *n*

**disorgan·ized, -ised** /dis'awgəniezd/ *adj* lacking coherence, system, or a central guiding principle or agency; muddled ⟨~ *work habits*⟩

*usage* Besides meaning "unorganized" (= not having been organized) **disorganized** may mean "having been thrown into disorder" from the verb **disorganize**.

**disorientate** /dis'awriən,tayt/, *chiefly NAm* **disorient** /dis'awri·ent, -ənt/ *vt* **1a** to cause to lose bearings; displace from normal position or relationship **b** to cause to lose the sense of time, place, or identity **2** to confuse [*disorient* fr Fr *désorienter*, fr *dés-* dis- + *orienter* to orient, fr MF, fr *orient*, n; *disorientate* fr *dis-* + *orient* + *-ate*] – **disorientation** *n*

**disown** /dis'ohn/ *vt* **1** to refuse to acknowledge as one's own **2a** to reject any connection or identification with; repudiate **b** to deny the validity or authority of ⟨*they* ~ed *their king*⟩ – **disownment** *n*

**disparage** /di'sparij/ *vt* to speak slightingly of; depreciate [ME *disparagen* to degrade by marriage below one's class, disparage, fr MF *desparagier* to marry below one's class, fr OF, fr *des-* dis- + *parage* lineage, rank, fr *per* peer] – **disparagement** *n*, **disparager** *n*, **disparaging** *adj*, **disparagingly** *adv*

**disparate** /'dispərət/ *adj* **1** markedly distinct in quality or character **2** containing or made up of fundamentally different and often incompatible elements *synonyms* see DIFFERENT *antonyms* comparable, analogous [L *disparatus*, pp of *disparare* to separate, fr *dis-* + *parare* to prepare – more at PARE] – **disparately** *adv*, **disparateness** *n*

**disparity** /di'sparəti/ *n* **1** the state of being disparate; difference **2** lack of agreement; inequality [MF *disparité*, fr LL *disparitat*, *disparitas*, fr L *dis-* + LL *paritat-*, *paritas* parity]

**dispassion** /dis'pash(ə)n/ *n* absence of passion; coolness, detachment

**dispassionate** /dis'pash(ə)nət/ *adj* **1** not influenced by strong feeling; calm ⟨*a* ~ *nature*⟩ **2** not affected by personal or emotional involvement; impartial ⟨*a* ~ *critic*⟩ *synonyms* see ¹FAIR *antonym* involved – **dispassionately** *adv*, **dispassionateness** *n*

¹**dispatch, despatch** /di'spach/ *vt* **1** to send off or away with promptness or speed, esp on official business **2** to put to death, esp with quick efficiency; kill **3** to dispose of (e g a task) rapidly or efficiently ~ *vi*, *archaic* to hurry; MAKE HASTE *synonyms* see ¹KILL [Sp *despachar* or It *dispacciare*, fr Prov *despachar* to get rid of, fr MF *despeechier* to set free, fr OF, fr *des-* + *-peechier* (as in *empeechier* to hinder) – more at IMPEACH] – **dispatcher** *n*

²**dispatch, despatch** *n* **1** the act of dispatching: e g **1a** the act of killing **b** prompt settlement (e g of an item of business) **c** a sending off; a shipment **2a** a message sent with speed; *esp* an important official message sent by a diplomat or a military or naval officer ⟨*sent a* ~ *to the war department*⟩ **b** a news item sent in by a correspondent to a newspaper **3** promptness and efficiency in performance or transmission – **mention in dispatches** to give a favourable citation or commendation for bravery in military action ⟨*he was* mentioned *twice in dispatches*⟩

**dispatch box** *n* **1** a case or container for carrying esp official dispatches or documents **2** either of a pair of boxes before the Speaker's or Lord Chancellor's seat in the British parliament from which ministers or shadow ministers speak

**dispatch case** *n* DISPATCH BOX 1

**dispatch rider** *n* a motorcyclist or horseman carrying usu military dispatches

**dispel** /di'spel/ *vt* **-ll-** to drive away by scattering; dissipate *synonyms* see ¹SCATTER [L *dispellere*, fr *dis-* + *pellere* to drive, beat – more at FELT]

**dispensable** /di'spensəbl/ *adj* capable of being dispensed with; inessential – **dispensability** *n*

**dispensary** /di'spensəri/ *n* **1** a place where medical or dental aid is given **2** the part of a hospital or chemist's shop where drugs are dispensed **3** *NAm* a shop where alcoholic drinks are sold under state regulations

**dispensation** /,dispen'saysh(ə)n/ *n* **1a** a general state or ordering of things; *specif* a divine ordering and administration of world affairs **b** a particular arrangement or provision, esp of providence or nature **2a** an exemption from a law or from an impediment, vow, or oath ⟨*their marriage was annulled by special* ~⟩ **b** a formal authorization **3a** the act of dispensing **b** something dispensed or distributed – **dispensational** *adj*

**dispensatory** /di'spensət(ə)ri; *also* ,dispen'saytəri/ *n* a technical book listing the composition, preparation, and use of various drugs – compare PHARMACOPOEIA

¹**dispense** /di'spens/ *vt* **1a(1)** to deal out in portions; distribute **a(2)** to prepare and provide (medication available only on prescription), esp as a profession ⟨*a* dispensing *chemist*⟩ **b** to administer ⟨~ *justice*⟩ **2** to give dispensation to; exempt [ME *dispensen*, fr ML & L; ML *dispensare* to grant dispensation, fr L, to distribute, fr *dispensus*, pp of *dispendere* to weigh out, fr *dis-* + *pendere* to weigh – more at SPAN]
**dispense with** *vt* **1** DISCARD **2 2** to do without – compare DISPOSE OF

²**dispense** *n* a bar in a hotel or club which is for the staff's use only

**dispenser** /di'spensə/ *n* one who or that which dispenses: e g **a** a container that sprays or feeds something out in convenient units **b** a usu mechanical device for dispensing merchandise **c** a person who dispenses drugs

**dispeople** /dis'peepl/ *vt* to depopulate

**dispersal** /di'spuhsl/ *n* the act or result of dispersing; *specif* the process or result of the spreading of living organisms from one place to another ⟨~ *of seeds*⟩

**dispersant** /di'spuhs(ə)nt/ *n* a dispersing agent; *esp*, *chemistry* a substance for promoting the formation and stabilization of a dispersion of one substance in another – **dispersant** *adj*

**disperse** /di'spuhs/ *vt* **1a** to cause to break up ⟨*they* ~d *the meeting*⟩ **b** to cause to become spread widely **c** to cause to evaporate or vanish ⟨*sunlight* dispersing *the vapour*⟩ **2** to spread or distribute from a fixed or constant source: e g **2a** to subject (e g light) to dispersion **b** to distribute (e g fine particles) more or less evenly throughout a medium ~ *vi* **1** to break up in random fashion ⟨*the crowd* ~d *at the policeman's request*⟩ **2a** to become dispersed **b** to dissipate, vanish ⟨*the fog* ~d *towards morning*⟩ *synonyms* see ¹SCATTER △ disburse [ME *dysparsen*, fr MF *disperser*, fr L *dispersus*, pp of *dispergere* to scatter, fr *dis-* + *spargere* to scatter – more at SPARK] – **dispersedly** *adv*, **disperser** *n*, **dispersible** *adj*

**disperse system** *n* DISPERSION 5b

**dispersion** /di'spuhsh(ə)n/ *n* **1** *cap* DIASPORA 1a (dispersing of the Jews after the Babylonian exile) **2** dispersing or being dispersed **3** the (extent of the) scattering of the values of a FREQUENCY DISTRIBUTION from a MEAN (average) **4** the separation of light into colours by REFRACTION OR DIFFRACTION with formation of a spectrum; *also* the separation of radiation or a stream of particles into components in accordance with some characteristic (e g energy, wavelength, or mass) **5** *chemistry* **5a** a dispersed substance **b** a system consisting of a dispersed substance and the medium in which it is dispersed; COLLOID 1b

**dispersive** /di'spuhsiv, -ziv/ *adj* **1** of dispersion ⟨*a* ~ *medium*⟩ ⟨*the* ~ *power of a lens*⟩ **2** tending to disperse – **dispersively** *adv*, **dispersiveness** *n*

**dispersoid** /di'spuhsoyd/ *n*, *chemistry* DISPERSION 5

**dispirit** *also* **disspirit** /di'spirit/ *vt* to deprive of morale or enthusiasm [*dis-* + *spirit*] – **dispirited** *adj*, **dispiritedly** *adv*, **dispiritedness** *n*

**dispiteous** /di'spitiəs, -tyəs/ *adj*, *archaic* cruel [alter. (influenced by *dis-* & *piteous*) of *despiteous*, fr ME, alter. of *despitous*, fr MF *despiteus*, fr *despit* contempt, malice]

**displace** /dis'plays/ *vt* **1a** to remove from the usual or proper place or position **b** to remove from an office **2** to take the place of (e g in a chemical reaction); supplant **3** to cause a displacement of (esp a quantity of water) [prob fr MF *desplacer*, fr *des-* dis- + *place*] – **displaceable** *adj*

*synonyms* **Displace** often has more emotional colouring than **replace** in the sense "take the place of" ⟨*I don't want to be* **displaced** *by that young fool*⟩.

**displaced person** *n* a person forced to leave his/her country because of war or oppression; a refugee

**displacement** /dis'playsmənt/ *n* **1** displacing or being displaced **2a** the volume or weight of a liquid (e g water) displaced by a floating body (e g a ship) of equal weight **b** the difference between the initial position of a body and any later position **c** the volume displaced by a piston (e g in a pump or engine) in a single stroke; *also* the total volume so displaced by all the pistons in an INTERNAL-COMBUSTION ENGINE (e g in a car) **3** the transfer of emotions from the object that originally evoked them to a substitute (e g in dreams)

**displacement activity** *n* the substitution of another form of behaviour for what is normal or expected that arises esp when there is a conflict of impulses

¹**display** /di'splay/ *vt* 1 to expose to view (eg by spreading out) ⟨~ *the flag*⟩ 2 to make evident; show ⟨~ed *great skill*⟩ 3 to exhibit ostentatiously; show off ⟨*liked to* ~ *his erudition*⟩ ~ *vi, of an animal* to make a display ⟨*penguins* ~ed *and copulated*⟩ *synonyms* see ¹SHOW [ME *displayen*, fr AF *despleier*, fr L *displicare* to scatter, fr *dis-* + *plicare* to fold – more at PLY]

²**display** *n* **1a(1)** a setting or presentation of something in open view ⟨*a fireworks* ~⟩ **a(2)** a clear sign, show, or demonstration ⟨*a* ~ *of courage*⟩ **b** ostentatious show; showing-off ⟨*this is mere* ~⟩ **c** type, page design, or printing designed to catch the eye (eg in headlines and title pages) **d** an eye-catching arrangement by which something (eg goods for sale) is exhibited ⟨*window* ~⟩ **e** a device (eg a CATHODE-RAY TUBE) that gives information in visual form ⟨*a computer* ~⟩ ⟨*a radar* ~⟩ 2 a distinctive pattern of behaviour exhibited by an animal (eg in defending its territory) and designed to evoke a particular response in other animals, esp members of the same species; *esp* a pattern of courting behaviour exhibited esp by male birds in the breeding season to attract the attention of a female

**displease** /dis'pleez/ *vt* 1 to incur the disapproval of, esp when accompanied by annoyance or dislike ⟨*fired any employee who* ~d *him*⟩ 2 to be offensive to ⟨*abstract art* ~s *him*⟩ ~ *vi* to give displeasure ⟨*signs of inattention calculated to* ~⟩ [ME *displesen*, fr MF *desplaisir*, fr (assumed) VL *displacēre*, fr L *dis-* + *placēre* to please]

**displeasure** /dis'plezhə/ *n* 1 the feeling of one who is displeased; disapproval, disfavour 2 discomfort, unhappiness ⟨*the philosophical problem as to whether pleasure and* ~ *can be measured no longer interested her*⟩

¹**disport** /di'spawt/ *n, archaic* a pastime, sport

²**disport** *vt* 1 to divert or amuse (oneself) 2 to display (oneself) ~ *vi* to frolic, gambol [ME *disporten*, fr MF *desporter*, fr *des-* + *porter* to carry, fr L *portare* to carry, more at FARE] – **disportment** *n*

¹**disposable** /di'spohzəbl/ *adj* 1 subject to or available for disposal; *specif* remaining to an individual after deduction of taxes ⟨~ *income*⟩ 2 designed to be used once and then thrown away ⟨~ *plates*⟩ – **disposability** *n*

²**disposable** *n* something (eg a paper sheet) that is disposable

**disposal** /di'spohzl/ *n* 1 the act or process of disposing: eg **1a** orderly or systematic placement or distribution **b** regulation, management **c** bestowal **d** systematic destruction; *esp* destruction or transformation of waste matter 2 the power or authority to use freely ⟨*the car was at my* ~⟩

**dispose** /di'spohz/ *vt* 1 to put in place; set in readiness; arrange ⟨*disposing troops for withdrawal*⟩ 2 *formal* **2a** to give a tendency to; incline ⟨*faulty diet* ~s *one to sickness*⟩ **b** to give a feeling of a specified type to ⟨*he was favourably* ~d *to his secretary*⟩ 3 *archaic* to bestow ~ *vi* to control the course of events ⟨*man proposes, God* ~s⟩ □ (*vt* 2) usu + *to* or *towards* [ME *disposen*, fr MF *disposer*, fr L *disponere* to arrange (perf indic *disposui*), fr *dis-* + *ponere* to put – more at POSITION]

  **dispose of** *vt* 1 to transfer to the control of another ⟨*I have still to dispose of my property before I can leave*⟩ 2 to get rid of; throw away, esp as rubbish; *also, euph* to kill – compare DISPENSE WITH 3 to deal with conclusively; DEMOLISH 2b ⟨*the new evidence effectively disposes of his theory once and for all*⟩

**disposed** /di'spohzd/ *adj, formal* willing ⟨*I don't feel* ~ *to help you*⟩

**disposition** /,dispə'zish(ə)n/ *n* 1 the act or the power of disposing or the state of being disposed: eg **1a** final arrangement; settlement ⟨*the* ~ *of the case*⟩ **b** transfer of property to the possession of another; *esp* such a transfer made by will or deed **c** orderly arrangement **2a** prevailing tendency, mood, or inclination **b** temperamental make-up ⟨*a friendly* ~⟩ **c** the physical tendency of something to act in a certain manner under given circumstances [ME, fr MF, fr L *disposition-, dispositio*, fr *dispositus*, pp of *disponere*] – **dispositional** *adj*

**dispossess** /,dispə'zes/ *vt* to take away possession, occupancy, or use from [MF *despossesser*, fr *des-* dis- + *possesser* to possess] – **dispossession** *n*, **dispossessor** *n*

**dispossessed** /,dispə'zest/ *adj* deprived of homes, possessions, and security

**dispraise** /dis'prayz/ *vt, formal* to comment on with disapproval or censure [ME *dispraisen*, fr OF *despreisier*, fr *des-* dis- + *preisier* to praise] – **dispraise** *n*, **dispraiser** *n*, **dispraisingly** *adv*

**disproof** /dis'proohf/ *n* 1 the action of disproving 2 evidence that disproves

¹**disproportion** /,disprə'pawsh(ə)n/ *n* lack of proportion, symmetry, or proper relation; disparity; *also* an instance of such disparity – **disproportional** *adj*

²**disproportion** *vt* to make disproportionate

**disproportionate** /,disprə'pawshənət/ *adj* out of proportion – **disproportionately** *adv*

**disproportionation** /,disprə,pawshə'naysh(ə)n/ *n* the transformation of a substance into two or more dissimilar substances, usu by simultaneous OXIDATION (loss of one or more electrons from an atom, ion, etc) and REDUCTION (addition of one or more electron to another atom, ion, etc) – **disproportionate** *vi*

**disprove** /dis'proohv/ *vt* to prove to be false; refute [ME *disproven*, fr MF *desprover*, fr *des-* + *prover* to prove] – **disprovable** *adj*

**disputant** /di'spyooht(ə)nt, 'dispyoot(ə)nt/ *n* one who is engaged in a dispute

**disputation** /,dispyooh'taysh(ə)n/ *n* 1 the act of disputing; debate 2 an academic exercise in which a speaker defends a thesis by formal logic

**disputatious** /,dispyoo'tayshəs/ *also* **disputative** /di'spyoohtətiv/ *adj* 1 inclined to dispute 2 provoking debate; controversial – **disputatiously** *also* **disputatively** *adv*, **disputatiousness** *also* **disputativeness** *n*

¹**dispute** /di'spyooht/ *vi* to engage in argument; debate; *esp* to argue angrily and persistently ~ *vt* **1a** to make the subject of disputation **b** to call into question ⟨*the honesty of his intent was never* ~d⟩ **2a** to struggle against ⟨~d *the advance of the invaders*⟩ **b** to struggle over; contest ⟨*the defending troops* ~d *every inch of ground*⟩ [ME *disputen*, fr OF *desputer*, fr L *disputare* to discuss, fr *dis-* + *putare* to think – more at PAVE] – **disputable** *adj*, **disputably** *adv*, **disputer** *n*

²**dispute** /di'spyooht; *also* 'dispyooht USE *the last pron is disliked by some speakers*/ *n* 1 verbal controversy; debate ⟨*his honesty is beyond* ~⟩ **2a** an argument, quarrel **b** a state of disagreement between an employer and a trade union; *also* a strike

**disqualify** /dis'kwolifie/ *vt* 1 to make or declare unfit, unsuitable, or unable to do something – compare UNQUALIFIED 1 2 to make ineligible for a prize or for further competition because of violations of the rules ⟨*cheating will certainly* ~ *offending candidates*⟩ – **disqualification** *n*

¹**disquiet** /dis'kwieət/ *vt* to make uneasy or worried – **disquietedly** *adv*, **disquieting** *adj*, **disquietingly** *adv*

²**disquiet** *n* worry, anxiety

**disquietude** /dis'kwieətyoohd, -choohd/ *n, formal* disquiet

**disquisition** /,diskwi'zish(ə)n/ *n* a long or elaborate essay or discussion on a subject [L *disquisition-, disquisitio*, fr *disquisitus*, pp of *disquirere* to inquire diligently, fr *dis-* + *quaerere* to seek – more at QUEST]

**disrate** /dis'rayt/ *vt* to reduce (a sailor) in rank; demote

**disregard** /,disri'gahd/ *vt* to pay no attention to; treat as unworthy of regard or notice *synonyms* see ¹NEGLECT *antonym* heed – **disregard** *n*, **disregardful** *adj*

**disrelish** /dis'relish/ *vt, formal* to find unpalatable or distasteful – **disrelish** *n*

**disremember** /,disri'membə/ *vt, chiefly NAm or dial* to forget ⟨*I* ~ *rightly what I did* – Elizabeth Gaskell⟩

**disrepair** /,disri'peə/ *n* the state of being in need of repair ⟨*a building fallen into* ~⟩

**disreputable** /dis'repyootəbl/ *adj* 1 not reputable; of bad reputation 2 markedly worn, dirty, or tattered ⟨*a* ~ *old coat*⟩ – **disreputability** *n*, **disreputableness** *n*, **disreputably** *adv*

**disrepute** /,disri'pyooht/ *n* lack or decline of good reputation; a state of being held in low esteem ⟨*the hotel fell into* ~ *after the bar was added*⟩ ⟨*bringing the game into* ~⟩

¹**disrespect** /,disri'spekt/ *vt* to have disrespect for – **disrespectable** *adj*, **disrespectability** *n*

²**disrespect** *n* lack of respect or politeness – **disrespectful** *adj*, **disrespectfully** *adv*, **disrespectfulness** *n*

**disrobe** /dis'rohb/ *vt, formal* to strip of clothes or covering ~ *vi, formal or humorous* to take off one's clothes [MF *desrober*, fr *des-* dis- + *robe* garment – more at ROBE]

**disrupt** /dis'rupt/ *vt* 1 to break apart forcibly; rupture **2a** to throw into disorder ⟨*agitators trying to* ~ *the meeting*⟩ **b** to interrupt the continuity of [L *disruptus*, pp of *disrumpere*, fr *dis-* + *rumpere* to break – more at RUPTURE] – **disrupter** *n*, **disruption** *n*, **disruptive** *adj or n*, **disruptively** *adv*, **disruptiveness** *n*

**dissatisfaction** /di,satis'faksh(ə)n, ,---'--/ *n* the quality or state of being dissatisfied; discontent

**dissatisfactory** /di,satis'fakt(ə)ri, ,---'---/ *adj* causing dissatisfaction

**dissatisfy** /di'satisfie/ *vt* to cause to be displeased, discontent, or disappointed

**dissave** /di'sayv/ *vi* to use savings for current expenses after income has been exhausted

**dissect** /di'sekt, die-/ *vt* 1 to separate into pieces by incision; expose the different parts of (eg an animal) for scientific examination 2 to analyse and interpret in detail ~ *vi* to perform or make a dissection [L *dissectus*, pp of *dissecare* to cut apart, fr *dis-* + *secare* to cut – more at SAW] – **dissector** *n*

*usage* The pronunciation /di'sekt/ is recommended for BBC broadcasters.

**dissected** /di'sektid, die-/ *adj* 1 cut deeply into several fine lobes ⟨a ~ *leaf*⟩ 2 divided into hills and ridges (eg by gorges) ⟨a ~ *plateau*⟩

**dissection** /di'seksh(ə)n, die-/ *n* 1 dissecting or being dissected 2 an anatomical specimen prepared by dissecting 3 a thorough and detailed analysis

**disseise** *also* **disseize** /dis'seez/ *vt, law* to deprive, esp wrongfully, of SEISIN (possession of freehold land); dispossess [ME *disseisen*, fr ML *disseisiare* & AF *disseisir*, fr OF *dessaisir*, fr *des-* + *saisir* to put in possession of – more at SEIZE]

**disseisin** *also* **disseizin** /dis'seezin/ *n* disseising or being disseised [ME *dysseysyne*, fr AF *disseisine*, fr OF *dessaisine*, fr *des*-dis- + *saisine* seisin]

**dissemble** /di'sembl/ *vt* 1 to hide under a false appearance 2 to put on the appearance of; feign ~ *vi* to put on a false appearance; conceal facts, intentions, or feelings under some pretence □ compare ¹PRETEND *synonyms* see DISSIMULATE △ disassemble [alter. (influenced by MF *dessembler* to be unlike) of obs *dissimule*, fr ME *dissimulen*, fr MF *dissimuler*, fr L *dissimulare* – more at DISSIMULATE]

**disseminate** /di'seminayt/ *vt* 1 to spread freely or widely as though sowing seed ⟨~ *ideas*⟩ 2 to disperse throughout something ⟨~d *multiple sclerosis*⟩ ~ *vi* to spread widely [L *disseminatus*, pp of *disseminare*, fr *dis-* + *seminare* to sow, fr *semin-, semen* seed – more at SEMEN] – **dissemination** *n*, **disseminator** *n*

**disseminule** /di'seminyoohl, -yool/ *n* a part or organ (eg a seed or spore) produced by a plant to ensure propagation

**dissension** *also* **dissention** /di'sensh(ə)n/ *n* disagreement in opinion, esp leading to bigoted quarrelling; *also* an example of this [ME, fr MF, fr L *dissension-, dissensio*, fr *dissensus*, pp of *dissentire*]

¹**dissent** /di'sent/ *vi* 1 to withhold assent 2 to differ in opinion [ME *dissenten*, fr L *dissentire*, fr *dis-* + *sentire* to feel – more at SENSE]

²**dissent** *n* 1 difference of opinion 2 *often cap* refusal to accept the doctrines of the established national church, specif the Church of England; nonconformity ⟨is Dissent *stronger in Wales or in Cornwall?*⟩ 3 *chiefly NAm* a judge's opinion which does not agree with that of the majority of the other judges of a law case

**dissenter** /di'sentə/ *n* 1 one who dissents 2 *cap* an English Nonconformist

**dissentient** /di'sensh(y)ənt/ *adj, formal* expressing dissent, esp from a majority opinion [L *dissentient-, dissentiens*, prp of *dissentire*] – **dissentient** *n*

**dissenting** /di'senting/ *adj, often cap* Nonconformist

**dissepiment** /di'sepimənt/ *n* a dividing tissue; SEPTUM; *esp* a partition between parts of a plant OVARY (female reproductive part that contains seed) composed of two or more similar fused parts [L *dissaepimentum* partition, fr *dissaepire* to divide, fr *dis-* + *saepire* to fence in – more at SEPTUM]

**dissert** /di'suht/ *vi, archaic* to discourse [L *dissertus*, pp of *disserere*, fr *dis-* + *serere* to join, arrange – more at SERIES]

**dissertate** /'disətayt/ *vi, formal* to discourse [L *dissertatus*, pp of *dissertare*, freq of *disserere*]

**dissertation** /,disə'taysh(ə)n/ *n* an extended usu written treatment of a subject; *specif* a written treatise submitted as part of the requirements for a first degree in a British university or for a doctorate in an American university – compare THESIS

**disserve** /di'suhv/ *vt, archaic* to treat badly or falsely, sometimes unintentionally; harm

**disservice** /di'suhvis, ,dis'suhvis/ *n* a harmful action; harm ⟨you do yourself a ~ *to say that*⟩

**dissever** /di'sevə/ *vb, formal vt* to sever, separate ~ *vi* to come apart; disunite [ME *disseveren*, fr OF *dessevrer*, fr LL *disseparare*, fr L *dis-* + *separare* to separate] – **disseverance** *n*, **disseverment** *n*

¹**dissident** /'disid(ə)nt/ *adj* disagreeing, esp strongly or rebelliously, with an opinion or group [L *dissident-, dissidens*, prp of *dissidēre* to sit apart, disagree, fr *dis-* + *sedēre* to sit – more at SIT]

²**dissident** *n* a person who is known for his/her marked disagreement, esp with a political regime – **dissidence** *n*

**dissimilar** /di'similə, dis'si-/ *adj* unlike – **dissimilarly** *adv*, **dissimilarity** *n*

**dissimilate** /di'similayt/ *vt* to make dissimilar ~ *vi, esp of consonant sounds* to become dissimilar [*dis-* + *-similate* (as in *assimilate*)] – **dissimilative, dissimilatory** *adj*

**dissimilation** /di,simi'laysh(ə)n/ *n* the act of making or the process of becoming dissimilar: eg a CATABOLISM (breakdown in the body of complex molecules into simple ones) b the development of dissimilarity between two usu consonant sounds – compare ASSIMILATION

**dissimilitude** /,disi'milityoohd, -choohd/ *n, formal* lack of resemblance [L *dissimilitudo*, fr *dissimilis* unlike, fr *dis-* + *similis* like – more at SAME]

**dissimulate** /di'simyoolayt, dis'si-/ *vb, formal vt* to hide under a false appearance ~ *vi* to engage in pretence [L *dissimulatus*, pp of *dissimulare*, fr *dis-* + *simulare* to simulate] – **dissimulation** *n*, **dissimulator** *n*

*synonyms* One **dissimulates** or **dissembles** something that one has or is ⟨he **dissimulated/dissembled** *his boredom*⟩. One **simulates** something that one has not or is not ⟨he **simulated** *interest*⟩.

**dissipate** /'disipayt/ *vt* 1a to cause to disappear or scatter b to lose (eg heat or electricity) irrecoverably; dispel 2 to expend aimlessly or foolishly ~ *vi* 1 to separate and scatter or vanish 2 to be extravagant or debauched in the pursuit of pleasure; *esp* to drink alcohol to excess *synonyms* see ¹SCATTER *antonyms* accumulate, concentrate [L *dissipatus*, pp of *dissipare*, fr *dis-* + *supare* to throw; akin to ON *svāf* spear, Skt *svapū* broom] – **dissipater, dissipator** *n*

**dissipated** /'disipaytid/ *adj* given to or marked by dissipation; debauched – **dissipatedly** *adv*, **dissipatedness** *n*

**dissipation** /,disi'paysh(ə)n/ *n* dissipating or being dissipated: a dispersion, diffusion b wasteful expenditure c a debauched lifestyle; *esp* excessive drinking of alcohol

**dissipative** /'disipətiv/ *adj* relating to dissipation, esp of heat

**dissociable** /di'sohsh(y)əbl, dis'soh-/ *adj* separable – **dissociability** *n*

**dissociate** /di'sohshiayt/ *vt* 1 to separate from association or union with another; disconnect 2 to disunite; *specif* to subject to chemical dissociation ~ *vi* to undergo dissociation [L *dissociatus*, pp of *dissociare*, fr *dis-* + *sociare* to join, fr *socius* companion – more at SOCIAL]

*usage* **Dissociate** and **disassociate** mean exactly the same thing, but **dissociate** is the more usually recommended form.

**dissociation** /di,sohsi'aysh(ə)n, -,sohshi-/ *n* 1 dissociating or being dissociated: eg 1a the process by which a single chemical compound breaks up or separates into two or more simpler compounds or constituents; *esp* a reversible or temporary process that results from the action of energy, esp heat, on a compound (eg AMMONIUM CHLORIDE) or of a solvent (eg water) on a soluble substance (eg SODIUM CHLORIDE) b the separation of a more or less independent group of ideas or activities from the mainstream of consciousness, esp as a psychological defence mechanism 2 the property of some biological stocks (eg of certain bacteria) of differentiating into two or more distinct and relatively permanent strains; *also* such a strain – **dissociative** *adj*

**dissoluble** /di'solyoobl/ *adj* capable of being dissolved or disintegrated [L *dissolubilis*, fr *dissolvere* to dissolve] – **dissolubility** *n*

**dissolute** /'disəlooht, -lyooht/ *adj* unrestrained in conduct; *esp* loose in morals; debauched [L *dissolutus*, fr pp of *dissolvere* to loosen, dissolve] – **dissolutely** *adv*, **dissoluteness** *n*

**dissolution** /,disə'loohsh(ə)n, -'lyooh-/ *n* 1 the act or process of dissolving or breaking up: eg 1a separation into component parts b(1) disintegration, decay b(2) *euph* death c the termination or breaking up of an association, group, or partnership d liquefaction 2 debauchery, profligacy

¹**dissolve** /di'zolv/ *vt* 1a to cause to disperse or disappear; destroy b to bring to an end; terminate ⟨~ *Parliament*⟩ 2a to cause to pass into solution ⟨~ *sugar in water*⟩; *broadly* to melt, liquefy b to fade out (one film or television scene) while fading

in another ~ *vi* 1 to disperse; BREAK UP ⟨*the mist* ~d⟩ ⟨*Parliament* ~d⟩; *also* to fade away 2a to become fluid; melt b to pass into solution ⟨*will sugar* ~ *in water?*⟩ c to be overcome emotionally; collapse ⟨~ *into tears*⟩ [ME *dissolven*, fr L *dissolvere*, fr *dis-* + *solvere* to loosen – more at SOLVE] – **dissolvable** *adj*, **dissolver** *n*

²**dissolve** *n* an effect used in films and on television in which one scene is dissolved into the next

**dissolvent** /di'zolv(ə)nt/ *adj* able to act as a solvent; capable of dissolving another substance – **dissolvent** *n*

**dissonance** /'disənəns/ *n* 1 a mingling of discordant sounds; *specif* a discordant combination of musical notes 2 lack of agreement; discord; *specif* inconsistency between the beliefs one holds or between one's actions and one's beliefs ⟨*cognitive* ~⟩ 3 a musical note or chord that is not RESOLVED (sounds aesthetically incomplete); *specif* a combination of notes not included in a major or minor TRIAD

**dissonant** /'disənənt/ *adj* 1 marked by dissonance; discordant 2 incongruous, inappropriate 3 not harmonically RESOLVED (brought to an aesthetically pleasing completion) [MF or L; MF, fr L *dissonant-*, *dissonans*, prp of *dissonare* to be discordant, fr *dis-* + *sonare* to sound – more at SOUND] – **dissonantly** *adv*

**disspirit** /di'spirit/ *vt* to dispirit

**dissuade** /di'swayd/ *vt* to deter or discourage *from* a course of action by persuasion ⟨~ *a friend from joining the society*⟩ [MF or L; MF *dissuader*, fr L *dissuadēre*, fr *dis-* + *suadēre* to urge – more at SUASION] – **dissuader** *n*

**dissuasion** /di'swayzh(ə)n/ *n* the act of dissuading [MF or L; MF, fr L *dissuasion-*, *dissuasio*, fr *dissuasus*, pp of *dissuadēre*] – **dissuasive** *adj*, **dissuasively** *adv*, **dissuasiveness** *n*

**dissyllabic** /,diesi'labik/ *adj* DISYLLABIC

**dissyllable** /die'siləbl, '----/ *n* DISYLLABLE

**dissymmetry** /dis'simətri/ *n* absence or lack of symmetry – **dissymmetric, dissymetrical** *adj*

¹**distaff** /'distahf/ *n* 1 a staff for holding the flax, wool, etc in spinning 2 woman's work or domain [ME *distaf*, fr OE *distæf*, fr *dis-* (akin to MLG *dise* bunch of flax) + *stæf* staff]

²**distaff** *adj* 1 related to the mother; matrilineal, maternal ⟨*the* ~ *side of the family*⟩ – compare SPEAR 2 *chiefly NAm* female, feminine

**distal** /'distl/ *adj, anatomy* far from the centre or point of attachment or origin – compare PROXIMAL [*distant* + *-al*] – **distally** *adv*

**distal convoluted tubule** *n* the coiled tubular part of a NEPHRON (urine-secreting unit in a kidney) that forms the final portion of the nephron, is concerned esp with the concentration of urine, and opens into a duct that conveys urine away from the kidney

¹**distance** /'dist(ə)ns/ *n* 1a separation in time b the degree or amount of separation between two points, lines, surfaces, or objects measured along the shortest path joining them c(1) an extent of space or an advance along a route measured in a line ⟨*didn't know what* ~ *he'd walked*⟩; *specif* a usu particular length covered in a race ⟨*a world-class runner over all* ~s⟩ c(2) the extent of space over which the specified activity is possible ⟨*lived within walking* ~ *of the shops*⟩ d a distant point or place ⟨*in the* ~ *I could just make out the foothills*⟩ e an extent of advance away or along from a point considered primary or original ⟨*carried her Puritan morality to a ridiculous* ~⟩ f a large stretch (e g of landscape); an expanse ⟨*the great* ~s *of the Russian steppes*⟩ 2 the quality or state of being distant: e g 2a remoteness in space b reserve, coldness c difference, disparity – **go the distance** to complete a particular task or course of action – **keep one's distance** 1 to stay far enough away *from* 2 to behave with proper reserve towards another person – **keep somebody at a distance** to treat somebody with reserve and not in a friendly manner

²**distance** *vt* 1 to place or keep physically or emotionally at a distance 2 to leave far behind; outstrip

**distant** /'dist(ə)nt/ *adj* 1a separated in space or time by a specified distance; away ⟨*a few miles* ~⟩ b situated at a great distance; far-off ⟨*the* ~ *hills*⟩ c separated by a great distance from each other; far apart 2 not closely related ⟨*a* ~ *relative*⟩ 3 reserved or aloof in personal relationship; cold ⟨~ *politeness*⟩ 4a coming from or going to a distance ⟨~ *voyages*⟩ b concerned with or directed towards things at a distance ⟨~ *thoughts*⟩ 5 faraway, abstracted ⟨*but his voice was* ~, *his thoughts already elsewhere*⟩ [ME, fr MF, fr L *distant-*, *distans*, prp of *distare* to stand apart, be distant, fr *dis-* + *stare* to stand – more at STAND] – **distantly** *adv*, **distantness** *n*

**distant signal** *n* a preliminary railway signal that indicates how the next HOME SIGNAL (signal controlling a section of track) is set

¹**distaste** /dis'tayst/ *vt, archaic* to feel aversion to

²**distaste** *n* (an) aversion, dislike

**distasteful** /dis'taystf(ə)l/ *adj* 1a offensive to (an individual's sense of) good taste or proper or decent behaviour; disagreeable, unpleasant b uncongenial 2 *archaic* unpleasant to the taste – **distastefully** *adv*, **distastefulness** *n*

¹**distemper** /di'stempə/ *vt, archaic* to derange, unsettle [ME *distempren*, fr LL *distemperare* to temper badly, fr L *dis-* + *temperare* to temper, mingle]

²**distemper** /di'stempə/ *n* 1 distemper, canine distemper a highly contagious virus disease of dogs and some other animals (e g foxes, wolves, and badgers) that is marked by fever, catarrhal discharge from the nose and eyes, and in severe cases by pneumonia and disorder of the nervous system 2 any of various diseases or abnormal physical conditions of animals, esp 4-legged mammals, marked by fever and often catarrh: e g 2a PANLEUCOPAENIA b STRANGLES 3 *archaic* a mental or physical ailment; a malaise 4 *archaic* bad temper 5 *archaic* (a) disorder or disturbance ⟨*in the middle ages . . . resistance was an ordinary remedy for political* ~s – T B Macaulay⟩ □ (2) not now used technically [ME *distempren*, fr LL *distemperare* to temper badly, fr L *dis-* + *temperare* to temper, mingle] – **distemperate** *adj*

³**distemper** *vt* to paint in or with distemper [ME *distemperen* to mix with liquid, soak, fr MF *destemprer*, fr L *dis-* + *temperare*]

⁴**distemper** *n* 1 a process of painting in which the colouring matter is mixed with white or yolk of egg and SIZE (thin jellylike substance that binds) and which is used for mural decoration 2 the paint used in the distemper process; *broadly* any of numerous water-based paints for general, esp household, use

**distempered** /di'stempəd/ *adj* out of temper or order; upset, deranged

**distemperoid** /di'stempəroyd/ *adj* resembling distemper; *specif* relating to or being an ATTENUATED (made less damaging) distemper virus used to develop immunity to natural distemper infection in dogs

**distend** /di'stend/ *vt* 1 to extend, esp unduly or beyond normal limits 2 to enlarge from internal pressure; swell ~ *vi* to become expanded ⟨*the stomach has* ~ed⟩ **synonyms** see EXPAND **antonyms** contract, attenuate [ME *distenden*, fr L *distendere*, fr *dis-* + *tendere* to stretch – more at THIN] – **distensible** *adj*, **distensibility** *n*, **distension** *also* **distention** *n*

**distich** /'di,stik/ *n* two connected lines of verse, usu complete in sense; a couplet [L *distichon*, fr Gk, fr neut of *distichos* having two rows, fr *di-* + *stichos* row, line of verse; akin to Gk *steichein* to go – more at STAIR]

**distichous** /'distikəs/ *adj* 1 arranged in two vertical rows ⟨~ *leaves*⟩ 2 divided into two segments ⟨~ *antennae*⟩ [LL *distichus*, fr Gk *distichos*] – **distichously** *adv*

**distil**, *NAm chiefly* **distill** /di'stil/ *vb* **-ll-** *vt* 1 to exude or cause to fall in drops or in a fine mist 2a to subject to or transform by distillation b to obtain or extract (as if) by distillation c to separate *out* or *off* (as if) by distillation d to extract the essence of (e g an idea or subject); concentrate ~ *vi* 1a to fall or materialize in drops or in a fine moisture; drop b to appear slowly or in small quantities at a time 2a to undergo distillation b to condense or drop from a still after distillation [ME *distillen*, fr MF *distiller*, fr LL *distillare*, alter. of L *destillare*, fr *de-* + *stillare* to drip, fr *stilla* drop; akin to OE *stān* stone – more at STONE]

**distillate** /'distilət, -ayt/ *n* 1 a liquid product formed by the condensing of vapour during distillation 2 DISTILLATION 2

**distillation** /,disti'laysh(ə)n/ *n* 1 a process that consists of converting a liquid or solid into a gas or vapour by heating and condensing the gas or vapour back to a liquid, and that is used esp for purification, FRACTIONATION (separation into component chemicals), or the formation of new substances; *also* the product or products so obtained 2 something resembling a distillate in being a concentration, abstract, or essence ⟨*each paragraph is a* ~ *of the facts*⟩

**distiller** /di'stilə/ *n* a person or company that makes alcohol, esp spirits, by distilling

**distillery** /di'stiləri/ *n* the works where distilling (e g of spirits) is done

**distinct** /di'stingkt/ *adj* 1 distinguishable to the eye or mind as different or separate ⟨*things similar in effect but wholly* ~ *in* *motive* – Hilaire Belloc⟩ **2** readily perceptible to the senses or mind; presenting a clear unmistakable impression ⟨*a neat ~ handwriting*⟩ ⟨*the review gives a ~ idea of the book*⟩ **3a** notable ⟨*felt his sobriety a ~ achievement*⟩ **b** decided ⟨*there's a ~ possibility of snow*⟩ **synonyms** see DISTINCTIVE, ⟨EVIDENT **antonyms** indistinct, nebulous [ME, fr MF, fr L *distinctus*, fr pp of *distinguere*] – **distinctly** *adv*, **distinctness** *n*

**distinction** /di'stingksh(ə)n/ *n* **1a** the act of distinguishing or ability to distinguish a difference; discrimination, differentiation **b** the object or result of distinguishing; a contrast ⟨*a ~ well worth making*⟩ **2** a distinguishing mark **3** the quality or state of being distinguishable ⟨*there is no appreciable ~ between the twins*⟩ **4a** the quality or state of being distinguished ⟨*a man of some ~*⟩ **b** the passing of an examination at the highest level; *also* a mark or certification of such passing **c** the quality or state of being worthy

**distinctive** /di'stingktiv/ *adj* **1a** serving to distinguish **b** having or giving style or distinction **2** capable of making a segment of utterance different in meaning as well as in sound from an otherwise identical utterance ⟨*the ~ feature of plosion*⟩ – **distinctively** *adv*, **distinctiveness** *n*

**synonyms** A thing whose characteristics make it possible to "distinguish" it from others is either **distinct** *from* them, or **distinctive** ⟨*beer has a very* **distinctive** *smell; it's quite* **distinct** *from the smell of wine*⟩. A thing whose mere existence is clearly noticeable is **distinct**, not **distinctive** ⟨*there's a* **distinct** *smell of beer in the room*⟩. See [1]CHARACTERISTIC

**distinctive feature analysis** *n* description of a speech sound as a bundle of simultaneous positive or negative features

**distingué** /di'stang-gay (*Fr* distẽge)/ *adj* distinguished, esp in manner or bearing [Fr, fr pp of *distinguer*]

**distinguish** /di'sting-gwish/ *vt* **1** to perceive as being separate or different ⟨*~ the sound of a piano in an orchestra*⟩ **2a** to mark as separate or different; make a difference between – often + *from* **b** to separate into kinds, classes, or categories **c** to set above or apart from others; make eminent ⟨*~ed himself on the cricket field*⟩ ⟨*the translation by Father Oesterreicher ~es it further – The Commonweal*⟩ **d** to characterize **3** to discern ⟨*~ed a light in the distance*⟩ ~ *vi* to recognize the difference *between* [MF *distinguer*, fr L *distinguere*, lit., to separate by pricking, fr *dis-* + *-stinguere* (akin to L in*stigare* to urge on) – more at STICK] – **distinguishability** *n*, **distinguishable** *adj*, **distinguishably** *adv*

**distinguished** /di'sting-gwisht/ *adj* **1** marked by eminence, distinction, or excellence **2** befitting an eminent person

**distort** /di'stawt/ *vt* **1** to alter the true meaning of; misrepresent ⟨*~ed the news to make it sensational*⟩ **2** to twist out of a natural, normal, or original shape or condition ⟨*a face ~ed by pain*⟩ [L *distortus*, pp of *distorquēre*, fr *dis-* + *torquēre* to twist – more at TORTURE] – **distorter** *n*

**distortion** /di'stawsh(ə)n/ *n* **1** the act of distorting **2** the quality or state of being distorted; a product of distortion: e g **2a** a lack of proportion in an optical image resulting from defects in the optical system ⟨*the ~ from this lens is unacceptable*⟩ **b** faulty reproduction of radio sound, a television picture, etc caused by change in the wave form of the original signal – **distortional** *adj*

[1]**distract** /di'strakt/ *adj, archaic* insane, mad

[2]**distract** *vt* to draw or direct (eg one's attention) to a different object or in different directions at the same time ⟨*he ~ed me from my work*⟩ △ detract [ME *distracten*, fr L *distractus*, pp of *distrahere*, lit., to draw apart, fr *dis-* + *trahere* to draw – more at DRAW] – **distractible** *adj*, **distractingly** *adv*, **distractibility** *n*

**distracted** /di'straktid/ *adj* **1** confused, perplexed **2** agitated – **distractedly** *adv*

**synonyms** This is not such a strong word as **distraught**, but stronger than **distrait**.

**distraction** /di'straksh(ə)n/ *n* **1** distracting or being distracted; *esp* mental confusion ⟨*the children's shouting drives me to ~*⟩ **2** something that distracts; *esp* an amusement – **distractive** *adj*

**distrain** /di'strayn/ *vb, law* to levy a distress (upon); *also* to seize (goods, property, etc) by way of distress [ME *distreynen*, fr OF *destreindre*, fr ML *distringere*, fr L, to draw apart, detain, fr *dis-* + *stringere* to bind tight – more at STRAIN] – **distrainable** *adj*, **distrainer, distrainor** *n*

**distraint** /di'straynt/ *n, law* the act or action of distraining; DISTRESS 1a [fr *distrain*, by analogy to *constrain* : *constraint*]

**distrait** /di'stray (*Fr* distrɛ)/ *adj* **1** absentminded **2** inattentive or

mildly distraught because of anxiety or apprehension [Fr, fr L *distractus*]

**usage** The use of **distrait**, as in sense 2, to mean "anxious" is disliked by some.

**distraught** /di'strawt/ *adj* **1** agitated with doubt, mental conflict, or worry; distracted **2** *archaic* crazed **synonyms** see DISTRACTED [ME, fr L *distractus*] – **distraughtly** *adv*

[1]**distress** /di'stres/ *n* **1** *law* **1a** the seizure and detention of the goods of another as a security or in order to obtain satisfaction of a claim (eg for rent unpaid) by the sale of the goods seized; *broadly* an act of distraining **b** something that is distrained **2a** anguish of body or mind; trouble **b** a painful situation; a misfortune **3** a state of danger or desperate need ⟨*a ship in ~*⟩ [ME *destresse*, fr OF, fr (assumed) VL *districtia*, fr L *districtus*, pp of *distringere*] – **distressful** *n*, **distressfully** *adv*, **distressfulness** *n*

[2]**distress** *vt* **1** to subject to great strain or difficulties **2** to cause to worry or be troubled; upset **3** to damage (wood or furniture) deliberately to give an effect of age ⟨*~ed cherry*⟩ – **distressingly** *adv*

[3]**distress** *adj, NAm* **1** offered for sale at a loss ⟨*~ merchandise*⟩ **2** involving distress goods ⟨*a ~ sale*⟩

**distressed** /di'strest/ *adj* suffering distress; *specif, euph* impoverished ⟨*~ gentlefolk*⟩

**distressed area** *n, Br* an area of high unemployment and economic depression

**distributary** /di'stribyoot(ə)ri/ *n* a river branch flowing away from the main stream

**distribute** /di'stribyooht; *also* 'distribyooht/ *vt* **1** to divide among several or many; apportion **2a** to disperse or scatter over an area ⟨*the species is ~d throughout Britain*⟩ **b** to give out; deliver **c** to use (a term) so as to refer to every member of the class named ⟨*the proposition "all men are mortal" ~s "man" but not "mortal"*⟩ **3a** to divide or separate, esp into kinds **b** to return (eg used type) to the proper storage places [ME *distributen*, fr L *distributus*, pp of *distribuere*, fr *dis-* + *tribuere* to allot – more at TRIBUTE] – **distributee** *n*

**usage** The pronunciation /di'stribyooht/ rather than /'dis-/ is recommended for BBC broadcasters.

**distributed** /di'stribyootid; *also* 'distribyoohtid/ *adj* characterized by a specified statistical distribution ⟨*a normally ~ random variable*⟩

**distribution** /,distri'byoohsh(ə)n/ *n* **1** the act or process of distributing **2a** the position, arrangement, or frequency of occurrence (eg of the members of a group) over an area or throughout a space or unit of time **b** the natural geographical range of an organism **3a** something distributed **b(1)** FREQUENCY DISTRIBUTION **b(2)** PROBABILITY FUNCTION **b(3)** PROBABILITY DENSITY FUNCTION **2 4a** the means by which something (eg electric power) is distributed **b** (the area supplied by) the network of branches of a nerve, blood vessel, etc **5** the transport, marketing, and merchandising of goods – **distributional** *adj*

**distribution function** *n* a statistical FUNCTION representing the probability that a RANDOM VARIABLE has a value less than or equal to a given value

[1]**distributive** /di'stribyootiv/ *adj* **1** of or concerned with distribution **2** of a word referring singly and without exception to the members of a group ⟨*each, either, and none are ~*⟩ **3** of or being a mathematical law which relates the operations of addition and multiplication such that $x(y + z) = xy + xz$ – **distributively** *adv*, **distributiveness** *n*, **distributivity** *n*

[2]**distributive** *n* a distributive word

**distributor** /di'stribyootə/ *n* **1** one who or that which distributes **2** someone employed to manage the distribution of goods **3** an apparatus for directing current to the various SPARKING PLUGS of an INTERNAL-COMBUSTION ENGINE in the proper order

[1]**district** /'distrikt/ *n* **1** a territorial division (eg for administrative or local-government purposes) ⟨*a postal ~*⟩ ⟨*a ~ council*⟩ **2** an area, region, or section with a distinguishing character ⟨*a residential ~*⟩ ⟨*the Lake District*⟩ [Fr, fr ML *districtus* jurisdiction, district, fr *districtus*, pp of *distringere* to distrain – more at DISTRAIN]

[2]**district** *vt, chiefly NAm* to divide or organize into districts

**district attorney** *n* the prosecuting officer of a judicial district in the USA

**district court** *n* a federal court at which a case is first heard in the USA

**district heating** *n* the supply of heat or hot water from a central plant to several buildings

**district nurse** *n*, *Br* a qualified nurse employed by a local authority who visits and treats patients in their own homes

¹**distrust** /dis'trust/ *vt* to have no trust or confidence in

²**distrust** *n* the lack or absence of trust; suspicion, wariness – **distrustful** *adj*, **distrustfully** *adv*, **distrustfulness** *n*

**disturb** /di'stuhb/ *vt* **1a** to break in upon; interrupt **b** to alter the position or arrangement of **2a** to destroy the peace of mind or composure of **b** to throw into disorder **c** to alarm **d** to put to inconvenience ⟨*don't let me ~ you, please stay seated*⟩ [ME *disturben, destourben*, fr OF & L; OF *destourber*, fr L *disturbare*, fr *dis- + turbare* to throw into disorder – more at TURBID] – **disturber** *n*, **disturbingly** *adv*

**disturbance** /di'stuhbəns/ *n* **1a** disturbing or being disturbed **b** a sudden interruption, intrusion, or outburst **2** a local variation from the average or normal wind conditions **3** *law* an instance of interference with another person's rights or property

**disturbed** /di'stuhbd/ *adj* **1** showing symptoms of emotional or mental instability **2** designed for or occupied by disturbed patients ⟨*~ wards*⟩

**disubstituted** /ˌdie'substityoohtid, -chooh-/ *adj*, *of a chemical compound* having two of the atoms or chemical groups characteristically present in the molecule replaced by other atoms or groups

**disulfiram** /ˌdiesul'fiərəm/ *n* a chemical compound, $(C_2H_5)_2NC(S)SS(S)CN(C_2H_5)_2$, used in the treatment of alcoholism, that acts by causing severe nausea when alcohol is drunk [*disulf*ide (NAm var of *disulphide*) + thiourea + amyl]

**disulphide** /die'sulfied/ *n* **1** a chemical compound containing two atoms of sulphur in each molecule combined with another atom or chemical group **2** an organic chemical compound containing the group SS composed of two sulphur atoms

**disunion** /dis'yoohnyən, -iən/ *n* **1** the ending or destruction of union; separation **2** disunity

**disunionist** /dis'yoohnyənist, -iənist/ *n* one who favours disunion; *specif* an American SECESSIONIST (supporter of the South in the Civil War)

**disunite** /ˌdisyoo'niet/ *vt* to divide, separate

**disunited** /ˌdisyoo'nietid/ *adj*, *of a horse* cantering incorrectly with a diagonally opposite pair of legs leading; *also*, *of a canter* performed in this way

**disunity** /dis'yoohnəti/ *n* lack of unity; *esp* dissension

**disuse** /dis'yoohs/ *n* the state of no longer being in use ⟨*a custom long since fallen into ~*⟩

**disused** /dis'yoohzd/ *adj* no longer used or practised; discarded, abandoned

**disvalue** /dis'valyooh/ *vt* to consider of little value

**disyllable, dissyllable** /die'siləbl/ *n* a word, unit of metre, etc consisting of two syllables [part trans of MF *dissilabe*, fr L *disyllabus* having two syllables, fr Gk *disyllabos*, fr *di- + syllabē* syllable] – **disyllabic, dissyllabic** *adj*

**dit** /dit/ *n* ¹DOT 4 – used for the pronunciation of the short sound or symbol in MORSE CODE [imit]

¹**ditch** /dich/ *n* a long narrow channel dug in the earth (e g for defence, drainage, or irrigation) [ME *dich*, fr OE *dīc* dyke, ditch – more at DYKE]

²**ditch** *vt* **1a** to enclose with a ditch **b** to dig a ditch in **2** *informal* **2a** to drive (a car) into a ditch **b** to make a forced landing of (an aircraft) on water **3** *informal* to get rid of; discard ⟨*he ~ed her months ago*⟩ ~ *vi* **1** to dig or repair a ditch ⟨*we shall be hedging and ~ing on Sunday*⟩ **2** *informal* to make a forced landing on water – **ditcher** *n*

¹**dither** /'didhə/ *vi* **1** to act nervously or indecisively; vacillate **2** *dial or NAm* to shiver, tremble ⟨*the ~ing of grass* – Wallace Stevens⟩ [ME *didderen*, perh of imit origin] – **ditherer** *n*

²**dither** *n* a highly nervous, excited, or agitated state ⟨*he was all of a ~*⟩ – **dithery** *adj*

**dithi-** /diethie-/, **dithio-** *comb form* containing two atoms of sulphur, usu in place of two oxygen atoms, in the molecular structure [ISV *di- + thi-*]

**dithyramb** /'dithəˌram(b)/ *n* **1** a usu short poem in a rapturous irregular style; *specif* an ancient Greek choral hymn to the god Bacchus **2** a statement or writing in an exalted or passionate vein [Gk *dithyrambos*] – **dithyrambic** *adj*, **dithyrambically** *adv*

**ditransitive** /ˌdie'tranzətiv, -'trans-/ *adj* involving or governing two grammatical objects, esp an indirect and a direct object that do not refer to the same person or thing ⟨*"give her a kiss" is a ~ construction*⟩

**dittany** /'ditəni/ *n* a pink-flowered plant (*Origanum dictamnus*) of the mint family, that is native to Crete [ME *ditoyne*, fr MF

*ditayne*, fr L *dictamnum*, fr Gk *diktamnon*, perh fr *Diktē* Dicte, mountain in Crete]

¹**ditto** /'ditoh/ *n*, *pl* **dittos 1** a thing mentioned previously or above; the same – used to avoid repeating a word **2** *also* **ditto mark** a mark ,, or " used as a sign indicating repetition usu of a word directly above in a previous line [It dial., pp of It *dire* to say, fr L *dicere* – more at DICTION]

²**ditto** *vt* **dittos; dittoing; dittoed** to repeat the action or statement of; copy

³**ditto** *adv* as before or aforesaid; in the same manner

**dittography** /di'togrəfi/ *n* the unintentional repetition of letters in copying or printing (e g "literatature" for "literature") [Gk *dittographia, dissographia*, fr *dittos, dissos* twofold + *-graphia* -graphy] – **dittographic** *adj*

**dittology** /di'toləji/ *n* a double reading or twofold interpretation (e g of a biblical text) [Gk *dittologia, dissologia* repetition of a word, fr *dittos, dissos* + *-logia* -logy]

**ditty** /'diti/ *n* a short simple unaffected song [ME *ditee*, fr OF *ditié* poem, fr pp of *ditier* to compose, fr L *dictare* to dictate, compose]

**ditty bag** *n* a bag used esp by sailors to hold small articles of gear (e g thread, needles, and tape) [origin unknown]

**ditty box** *n* a box used for the same purpose as a ditty bag

**diuresis** /ˌdie·yoo'reesis/ *n*, *pl* **diureses** an increased excretion of urine [NL]

**diuretic** /ˌdie·yoo'retik/ *n or adj* (something, esp a drug) acting to increase the flow of urine [adj ME, fr MF or LL; MF *diuretique*, fr LL *diureticus*, fr Gk *diourētikos*, fr *diourein* to urinate, fr *dia- + ourein* to urinate – more at URINE; n fr adj] – **diuretically** *adv*

**diurnal** /die'uhnl/ *adj* **1a** recurring every day ⟨*~ tasks*⟩ **b** having a daily cycle ⟨*~ tides*⟩ **2a** relating to or occurring in the daytime ⟨*the city's ~ noises*⟩ **b** opening during the day and closing at night ⟨*~ flowers*⟩ **c** active during the day ⟨*~ animals*⟩ [ME, fr L *diurnalis* – more at JOURNAL] – **diurnally** *adv*

**diva** /'deevə/ *n*, *pl* **divas** *also* **dive** /'deevi/ PRIMA DONNA 1 [It, lit., goddess, fr L, fem of *divus* divine, god – more at DEITY]

**divagate** /'dievəˌgayt/ *vi*, *formal* to wander about or stray from one place or subject to another [LL *divagatus*, pp of *divagari*, fr L *dis- + vagari* to wander – more at VAGARY] – **divagation** *n*

**divalent** /ˌdie'vaylənt/ *adj*, *chemistry* having a VALENCY of two; BIVALENT

**divan** /di'van, 'dievan; *senses 2,3* di'van/ *n* **1a** the PRIVY COUNCIL of the Ottoman Empire **b** a council chamber in some Muslim countries, esp Turkey; *also* the council itself **2a** a long low couch, usu without arms or back, placed against a wall **b** a bed of a similar style without a headboard or footboard **3** a collection of poems in Persian or Arabic, usu by one author **4** *archaic* a smoking room ⟨*Craw had even attended an opium ~ with airconditioning* – John Le Carré⟩ [Turk, fr Per *dīwān* account book (cf DEWAN, DOUANE)]

**divaricate** /die'varikayt/ *vi*, *formal or biology* to spread apart; branch off; diverge [L *divaricatus*, pp of *divaricare*, fr *dis- + varicare* to straddle – more at PREVARICATE] – **divarication** *n*

¹**dive** /diev/ *vi* **1a** to plunge into water headfirst **b** to engage in the sport of diving ⟨*~s for the British team*⟩ **c** to submerge ⟨*the submarine ~d*⟩ **2a** to descend or fall quickly and steeply **b** to plunge one's hand quickly into ⟨*he ~d into the bag and brought out two apples*⟩ **c** *of an aircraft* to descend in a dive **3a** to plunge into some matter or activity – usu + *in* or *out* **b** to plunge or dash (e g for shelter) into some place or across some space ⟨*~d for cover*⟩ **c** to lunge ~ *vt* **1** to cause to descend ⟨*~d his plane through the sonic barrier*⟩ **2** to thrust or plunge *into* something ⟨*she ~d her arm into the drain*⟩ [ME *diven, duven*, fr OE *dyfan* to dip & *dūfan* to dive; akin to OE *dyppan* to dip – more at DIP]

**dive in** *vi* to begin or become involved in an action or activity with haste

²**dive** *n* **1** the act or an instance of diving: e g **1a(1)** a usu headlong plunge into water (e g one executed in a prescribed manner in diving) **a(2)** a submerging of a submarine **a(3)** a usu steep descent of an aircraft **b** *informal* a sharp decline **2** *informal* a disreputable bar or meeting place ⟨*a low ~*⟩ **3** *informal* **3a** a faked knockout in boxing – chiefly in *take a dive* **b** a ploy in soccer in which a player falls over deliberately or flamboyantly after being tackled in order to give the effect of having been fouled

'**dive-ˌbomb** *vt* to bomb from an aircraft by making a steep dive towards the target before releasing the bomb – **divebomber** n

**diver** /'dievə/ n 1 a person who dives 2 a person who works or explores underwater for long periods, either carrying a supply of air in cylinders or having it sent from the surface 3 any of several large fish-eating diving birds (genus *Gavia*) of the northern part of the northern hemisphere that have the legs placed far back under the body and as a result have a clumsy floundering gait on land; *broadly* any of various diving birds

**diverge** /die'vuhj, di-/ vi 1a to move or extend in different directions from a common point; draw apart ⟨diverging *rays of light*⟩ b to become or be different in character, form or opinion – often + *from* 2 to turn aside from a path or course; deviate – often + *from* 3 to be mathematically divergent ∼ vt to deflect *synonyms* see [1]SEPARATE [ML *divergere*, fr L *dis-* + *vergere* to incline – more at WRENCH]

**divergence** /die'vuhj(ə)ns, di-/ *also* **divergency** /-si/ n 1a a drawing apart (e g of lines extending from a common centre) b a difference, disagreement c the acquisition of dissimilar characteristics by related organisms living in different environments 2 a deviation from a course or standard 3 the condition of being mathematically divergent 4 a function of a vector that is the SCALAR PRODUCT of the function GRADIENT with a vector and can be used to find the rate of flow at any point in a vector field – compare CURL 6, GRADIENT 3

**divergent** /die'vuhj(ə)nt, di-/ adj 1a diverging from each other b differing from each other or from a standard ⟨the ∼ *interests of capital and labour*⟩ 2 *of a mathematical series* having a sum that does not converge to a limit as the number of terms in the series increases ⟨$1 + \frac{1}{2} + \frac{1}{3} + \frac{1}{4} + ...$ *is a* ∼ *series*⟩ 3 causing divergence of rays ⟨a ∼ *lens*⟩ *synonyms* see DIFFERENT *antonym* convergent [L *divergent-, divergens*, prp of *divergere*] – **divergently** adv

**divers** /'dievəz/ adj, archaic or formal sundry, various [ME *divers, diverse*]

**diverse** /'dievuhs, -'-/ adj 1 differing from one another; unlike 2 having various forms or qualities *synonyms* see DIFFERENT *antonyms* identical, selfsame [ME *divers, diverse*, fr OF & L; OF *divers*, fr L *diversus*, fr pp of *divertere*] – **diversely** adv, **diverseness** n

**diversify** /die'vuhsifie, di-/ vt 1 to make diverse; give variety to ⟨∼ *a course of study*⟩ 2 to divide (e g investment of funds) among different (types of) securities to reduce risk 3 to increase the variety of the products of (e g a company) ∼ vi 1 to produce variety 2 to engage in varied business operations in order to reduce risks ⟨if this company does not ∼ we are ruined⟩ – **diversifier** n, **diversification** n

**diversion** /die'vuhsh(ə)n, di-/ n 1 the act or an instance of diverting from a course, activity, or use; a deviation; *specif, chiefly Br* an alternative route for road traffic when the usual route is temporarily closed 2 something that diverts or amuses; a pastime 3 something (e g an attack or feint) that draws someone's attention away from the point of the principal operation – **diversionary** adj

**diversionist** /die'vuhsh(ə)nist, di-/ n one engaged in diversionary activities; *specif* a conspirator against a Communist state

**diversity** /die'vuhsəti, di-/ n 1 the condition of being different or having differences; variety 2 an instance or point of difference

**divert** /die'vuht/ vt 1a to turn from one course or use to another b to distract 2 to give pleasure to, esp by distracting the attention from what is wearisome or distressing [ME *diverten*, fr MF & L; MF *divertir*, fr L *divertere* to turn in opposite directions, fr *dis-* + *vertere* to turn – more at WORTH]

**diverticulitis** /,dievətikyoo'lietəs/ n inflammation of a diverticulum [NL]

**diverticulosis** /,dievətikyoo'lohsis/ n a disorder of the intestines characterized by the presence of many diverticula that probably results from a diet low in fibre [NL]

**diverticulum** /,dievə'tikyooləm/ n, pl **diverticula** /-lə/ 1 a pocket or closed branch opening off a main passage in the body 2 an abnormal pouch or sac opening from a hollow organ, esp the intestine [NL, fr L, bypath, prob alter. of *deverticulum*, fr *devertere* to turn aside, fr *de-* + *vertere*]

**divertimento** /di,vuhti'mentoh/ n, pl **divertimenti** /-'menti/, **divertimentos** 1a a piece of instrumental CHAMBER MUSIC in several movements b a lighthearted fantasia on airs from an opera 2 DIVERTISSEMENT 1 [It, lit., diversion, fr *divertire* to divert, amuse, fr Fr *divertir*]

**divertissement** /di'vuhtismənt (Fr divertismã)/ n, pl **divertisse-**

**ments** /-mənts (Fr ∼)/ 1 a ballet suite used as an INTERLUDE (brief piece played between sections of another performance) 2 DIVERTIMENTO 1 3 an amusing diversion or entertainment [Fr, lit., diversion, fr *divertiss-*, (stem of *divertir*)]

**divest** /die'vest/ vt 1a to deprive or dispossess *of* esp property, authority, or title b to rid or free (oneself) *of* c *formal* to undress or strip *of* esp clothing, ornament, or equipment 2 *formal* to take away (e g possessions or vested rights) from a person [alter. of *devest*, fr MF *desvestir*, fr ML *divestire*, fr L *dis-* + *vestire* to clothe – more at VEST] – **divestment** n

**divestiture** /die'vestichə/ n 1 the compulsory transfer of title or disposal of interests on government order 2 *formal* the act of divesting [*divest* + *-iture* (as in *investiture*)]

[1]**divide** /di'vied/ vt 1a to separate into two or more parts, areas, or groups b to separate into classes, categories, or divisions c to cleave, part 2a to give out in shares after separation into portions; distribute – often + *among* b to set aside for different purposes; apportion ⟨∼d his time between work and play⟩ 3a to cause to be separate, distinct, or apart from one another b to separate into opposing sides or parties c to cause (a parliamentary body) to vote by division 4a to mark divisions on; graduate ⟨∼ a sextant⟩ b(1) to determine how many times (a number or quantity) contains another number or quantity by means of a mathematical operation ⟨∼ 42 by 14⟩ b(2) of a number or quantity to be contained in (another number or quantity) a whole number of times ⟨14 ∼s 42⟩ ∼ vi 1 to perform mathematical division 2a(1) to become separated into parts a(2) to branch out b to become separated or disunited, esp in opinion or interest c to vote by division *synonyms* see [1]SEPARATE *antonym* unite [ME *dividen*, fr L *dividere*, fr *dis-* + *-videre* to separate – more at WIDOW] – **dividable** adj

**divide into** vt to use as a divisor of ⟨divide 14 into 42⟩

[2]**divide** n 1 a point or line of division 2 *chiefly NAm* a dividing ridge between drainage areas; a watershed

**divided** /di'viedid/ adj 1a separated into parts or pieces b *of a leaf* having distinct parts separated by cuts extending to the base or to the central vein 2a disagreeing with each other; disunited b directed or moved towards conflicting interests, states, or objects 3 separated by distance ⟨familiar objects from which she had never dreamed of being ∼ – James Joyce⟩

**divided highway** n, *NAm* DUAL CARRIAGEWAY

**dividend** /'dividend, -ənd/ n 1 an individual share of something distributed: e g 1a a share in a distribution (e g of profits) to shareholders in proportion to their holding b a share of surplus allocated to a policyholder by an insurance company 2 a reward, benefit ⟨her action will pay great ∼s⟩ 3a a number to be divided by another b a sum or fund to be divided and distributed [ME *divident*, fr L *dividendum*, neut of *dividendus*, gerundive of *dividere*]

**dividend yield** n the dividend paid per share expressed as a percentage of the market price of the share

**divider** /di'viedə/ n 1 one who or that which divides 2 pl a compasslike instrument for measuring or marking (e g in transferring dimensions) that consists of two pointed arms jointed together 3 a partition or screen used to separate parts of a room, hall, etc

**divi-divi** /,divi 'divi, ,deevi 'deevi/ n a small tropical American tree (*Caesalpinia coriaria*) of the pea family that bears twisted pods that contain a large proportion of tannin used in the tanning of leather; *also* the pods of this tree [Sp *dividivi*, of Cariban origin; akin to Cumanagoto *diwidiwi* divi-divi]

**divination** /,divi'naysh(ə)n/ n 1 the art or practice that seeks to foresee or foretell the future or discover hidden knowledge with the aid of supernatural powers or by interpretation of omens 2 unusual insight; intuitive perception [ME *divinacioun*, fr L *divination-, divinatio*, fr *divinatus*, pp of *divinare*] – **divinatory** adj

[1]**divine** /di'vien/ adj 1a relating to or proceeding directly from God or a god ⟨the ∼ right of kings⟩ b being a deity ⟨the ∼ Saviour⟩ c offered to a deity ⟨∼ worship⟩ 2a heavenly, godlike b *informal* supremely good; superb ⟨her pies were simply ∼⟩ [ME *divin*, fr MF, fr L *divinus*, fr *divus* god – more at DEITY] – **divinely** adv, **divineness** n

[2]**divine** n 1 a clergyman 2 a theologian [ME, fr ML *divinus*, fr L, soothsayer, fr *divinus*, adj]

[3]**divine** vt 1 to discover or perceive intuitively; infer, conjecture 2 to discover by inspiration or magic; *esp* to discover or locate (e g water) by means of a DIVINING ROD ∼ vi to practise divination; prophesy *synonyms* see [2]DOWSE [ME *divinen*, fr MF & L; MF *diviner*, fr L *divinare*, fr *divinus*, n] – **diviner** n

**Divine Liturgy** *n* the communion service in the Eastern Orthodox church

**Divine Office** *n* the OFFICE (prescribed religious rite) appropriate to any of the CANONICAL HOURS (services held at set times throughout the day) that is performed daily in the Roman Catholic church by persons in holy orders

**divine right** *n* **1** the right of a sovereign to rule as set forth by the theory that a monarch receives the right to rule directly from God **2** an undisputed right ⟨*thinks the Conservatives have a ~ to govern*⟩

**divine service** *n* a service of Christian worship; *esp* one that is not sacramental

**diving** /'dieving/ *n* the competitive sport of performing set gymnastic manoeuvres during a plunge into water from a board

**diving beetle** *n* any of various flesh-eating water beetles (family Dytiscidae) habitually living under water and rising to the surface to obtain air

**diving bell** /'dieving/ *n* a diving apparatus consisting of a container open only at the bottom and supplied with pressurized air by a tube

**diving duck** *n* any of various ducks (eg the pochard or goldeneye) that frequent deep waters and obtain their food by diving

**diving suit** *n* a waterproof diver's suit with a helmet that is supplied with a mixture of gases suitable for breathing pumped through a tube

**divining rod** /di'viening/ *n* a forked rod believed to indicate the presence of water, minerals, etc by dipping downwards when held over the precise spot where the desired material is hidden underground

**divinity** /di'vinəti/ *n* **1** the quality or state of being divine **2** *often cap* a divine being: eg **2a** GOD 1 **b** a male or female deity **3** theology

**divinity school** *n*, *chiefly NAm* THEOLOGICAL COLLEGE

**divisible** /di'vizəbl/ *adj* capable of being divided; *specif* capable of undergoing arithmetical division by a specified number without leaving a remainder – **divisibility** *n*

**division** /di'vizh(ə)n/ *n* **1a** dividing or being divided **b** the act, process, or an instance of distributing among a number; distribution **2** any of the parts, sections, or groupings into which a whole is divided or is divisible **3** *taking sing or pl vb* **3a** a major military unit that contains the necessary tactical and administrative services to function as a self-contained unit capable of independent action **b** an administrative military unit of infantry regiments of a similar background ⟨*the Guards Division*⟩ **c(1)** the basic unit of men for naval administration **c(2)** a subdivision of a squadron of ships considered as a tactical unit **4a** a portion of a territorial unit (eg for administrative or electoral purposes) **b** an administrative or operating unit of a government, business, or educational organization **5** a group of organisms forming part of a larger group; *specif* a primary category of the PLANT KINGDOM containing one or more classes and equivalent to a PHYLUM of the ANIMAL KINGDOM **6** a competitive class or category (eg in boxing or football) **7a** something that divides, separates, or marks off **b** the act, process, or an instance of separating or keeping apart; separation **8** the condition or an instance of being divided in opinion or interest; disagreement, disunity ⟨*exploited the ~s between the two countries*⟩ **9** (a means of registering a vote by) the physical separation into different LOBBIES (corridors) of the members of a parliamentary body voting for and against a question; *also* the vote so registered ⟨*they forced a ~ on the new bill*⟩ **10** an act, process, or instance of dividing one number by another **11** plant propagation by dividing parts and planting segments capable of producing roots and shoots **12** a part of an organ consisting of one MANUAL (keyboard) and the stops controlled by it [ME, fr MF, fr L *division-*, *divisio*, fr *divisus*, pp of *dividere* to divide] – **divisional** *adj*, **divisionalize** *vt*, **divisionally** *adv*

**division of labour** *n* the distribution of various parts of the process of production among different people, groups, or machines, each specializing in a particular job, to increase efficiency; *broadly* the carrying out of various processes and functions by (groups of) particular usu specialized individuals (eg in a colony of ants)

**division ring** *n* a mathematical RING in which every element that is not zero has an INVERSE under multiplication

**division sign** *n* **1** the symbol ÷ used to indicate division **2** the oblique stroke / used to indicate a fraction

**divisive** /di'viesiv/ *adj* creating disunity or dissension – **divisively** *adv*, **divisiveness** *n*

**divisor** /di'viezə/ *n* the number by which another number is to be divided

**¹divorce** /di'vaws/ *n* **1** (a decree declaring) a legal dissolving of a marriage **2** a separation, gap ⟨*the ~ between his version and the reality was almost total*⟩ [ME *divorse*, fr MF, fr L *divortium*, fr *divertere*, *divortere* to divert, leave one's husband]

**²divorce** *vt* **1a** to end marriage with (one's husband or wife) by divorce **b** to dissolve the marriage between (husband and wife) **2** to end the existing relationship or union of; separate – usu + *from* ⟨*~ church from state*⟩ ~ *vi* to obtain a divorce *synonyms* see ¹SEPARATE

**divorcee** /divaw'see/ *n* a divorced person

**divorcée** /divaw'see/, *masc* **divorcé** /divaw'say, -see/ *n* a divorced woman [Fr, fr *divorcé*, pp of *divorcer* to divorce, fr MF *divorse*]

**divot** /'divət/ *n* **1** a piece of turf dug out in making a golf shot **2** *Scot* a piece of turf [origin unknown]

**divulge** /die'vulj, di-/ *vt* to make known (eg a confidence or secret); disclose *synonyms* see ¹REVEAL [ME *divulgen*, fr L *divulgare*, fr *dis-* + *vulgare* to make known, fr *vulgus* common people – more at VULGAR] – **divulgence, divulgement** *also* **divulgation** *n*

**divulsion** /die'vulsh(ə)n/ *n* a tearing apart – now used chiefly in surgery [L *divulsion-*, *divulsio*, fr *divulsus*, pp of *divellere* to tear apart, fr *dis-* + *vellere* to pluck – more at VULNERABLE]

**¹divvy** /'divi/ *n*, *informal* DIVIDEND 1a; *esp* one paid by a Cooperative Wholesale Society [by shortening & alter.]

**²divvy** *vt*, *informal* to divide, share – usu + *up* ⟨*divvied up the sweets*⟩ [by shortening & alter. fr *divide*]

**dixie** /'diksi/ *n*, *Br* a metal, esp iron, pot in which food (eg stew) or drinks are made or carried (eg by soldiers) [Hindi *degcī*, dim. of *degcā* kettle, pot]

**Dixie** *n* the Southern states of the USA collectively; *specif* those formerly members of the Confederate States of America [name for the Southern states in the song *Dixie* (1859) by Daniel D Emmett †1904 US musician]

**Dixiecrat** /'diksi,krat/ *n*, *NAm informal* a rebellious member of the Democratic party in the southern USA; *specif* a supporter of a 1948 presidential programme opposing the civil-rights stand of the Democratic party – **Dixiecratic** *adj*

**dixieland** /'diksi,land/ *n*, *often cap* jazz music with a pronounced two-beat rhythm usu played by a small band and characterized by ensemble and solo improvisation [*Dixie* + *land*; fr its origin in the Southern states of the USA]

**DIY** *adj* do-it-yourself – **DIYer** *n*

**dizygotic** /,diezie'gotik/ *also* **dizygous** /,die'ziegəs/ *adj*, *of twins* produced from two separate eggs [*di-* + *zygotic*, *-zygous*]

**dizziness** /'dizinis/ *n* the condition of being or feeling dizzy; vertigo

**¹dizzy** /'dizi/ *adj* **1a** having a whirling sensation in the head and a tendency to lose one's balance **b** mentally confused or dazed **2a** causing giddiness or mental confusion ⟨*a ~ height*⟩ **b** extremely rapid ⟨*he drove at a ~ speed*⟩ **3** *informal* foolish, silly [ME *disy*, fr OE *dysig* stupid; akin to OHG *tusig* stupid, L *furere* to rage – more at DUST] – **dizzily** *adv*

**²dizzy** *vt* **1** to make dizzy or giddy **2** to bewilder ⟨*prospects so brilliant as to ~ the mind*⟩ – **dizzyingly** *adv*

**DJ** /'dee,jay/ *n* **1** DISC JOCKEY **2** DINNER JACKET

**djellaba** *also* **djellabah, jellaba** /jə'lahbə, 'jeləbə/ *n* a long loose outer garment with full sleeves and a hood traditionally worn by Arabs [Fr *djellaba*, fr Ar *jallabah*]

**djin, djinn** /jin/ *n* JINN (a Muslim spirit)

**djinni, djini** /ji'nee, 'jini/ *n*, *pl* **djinn, djinn** JINN (a Muslim spirit)

**dl-** *prefix* **1** *also* **d,l-** consisting of equal amounts of the DEXTROROTATORY and LAEVOROTATORY forms ⟨*dl-tartaric acid*⟩ **2** consisting of equal amounts of the D- and L- forms ⟨DL-*fructose*⟩

**D layer** *n* D REGION (layer of the atmosphere)

**DMSO** *n* DIMETHYLSULPHOXIDE

**DNA** *n* a chemical compound (NUCLEIC ACID) that occurs chiefly in the nuclei of cells, is the material that makes up genes, and consists of long strands of phosphate groups alternating with sugar (DEOXYRIBOSE) groups, from each of which projects an ADENINE, CYTOSINE, GUANINE, THYMINE, etc group (BASE 7b). The DNA chains typically occur as pairs in a DOUBLE HELIX (spiral of two parallel strands round the same central axis). [*deoxyribonucleic acid*]

**DNA polymerase** *n* an enzyme that promotes the synthesis of DNA

**DNase** /ˌdee 'en ayz/ *also* **DNAase** /ˌdee en 'ay ayz/ *n* DE-OXYRIBONUCLEASE (enzyme that breaks down DNA)

**'D-ˌnotice** *n, Br* an official request (eg to a newspaper) that certain information should be withheld from publication for reasons of national security [*Defence notice*]

**¹do** /dooh/ *vb* **does** /dəz; *strong* duz/; **doing** /'dooh·ing/; **did** /did/; **done** /dun/ *vt* **1** to carry out the task of; effect, perform ⟨~ *his bidding*⟩ ⟨~ *good*⟩ ⟨~ *some washing*⟩ ⟨~ *one's duty*⟩ ⟨~ *a vasectomy*⟩ ⟨~ *overtime*⟩ ⟨*crimes* done *deliberately*⟩ **2** to put into a specified condition ⟨~ *it into English*⟩ ⟨~ *him to death*⟩ **3** to have as a function ⟨*what's that book* ~ing *on the floor?*⟩ **4a** to cause, impart ⟨*sleep will* ~ *you good*⟩ ⟨*what have you* done *to your ear?*⟩ **b** to give freely; pay ⟨~ *honour to his memory*⟩ **5** to bring to an esp unwanted end; finish – used esp in the past participle ⟨*that's* done *it*⟩; compare ²DONE 2 **6** to expend, exert ⟨*did their damnedest to hog the game*⟩ **7** DO IN 2 **8a** to bring into existence; produce ⟨~ *a biography of the general*⟩ **b** to provide, sell ⟨~ *teas*⟩ ⟨*they* ~ *beds in moulded fibreglass* – *Home Beautiful (Australia)*⟩ **9a** to put on; perform ⟨*they're* ~ing *"The Merchant of Venice" tomorrow night*⟩ **b** to play the part of; act ⟨*did the main character in several films*⟩ ⟨*can* ~ *Harold Wilson very well*⟩ **c** to behave like ⟨*did a Houdini and escaped from his chains*⟩ **10** to treat or deal with in any way, typically with the sense of preparation or with that of care or attention: **10a(1)** to clean, wash ⟨~ *one's teeth*⟩ ⟨~ *the dishes*⟩ ⟨~ *the room out*⟩ **a(2)** to cook ⟨~ *an omelette*⟩ ⟨*likes his steak well* done⟩ **a(3)** to arrange ⟨~ *one's hair*⟩ ⟨~ *the flowers*⟩ **a(4)** to apply cosmetics to ⟨~ *one's face*⟩ **a(5)** to decorate, furnish ⟨*did the front bedroom in blue*⟩ **b** to execute an artistic representation of ⟨*did her in oils*⟩ **c(1)** to perform the appropriate professional service or services for ⟨*the barber will* ~ *you now*⟩ **c(2)** to feed and entertain ⟨*they* ~ *you quite well at the hotel*⟩ **11a** to work at, esp as a course of study or vocation ⟨~ *classics*⟩ ⟨~ *a PhD*⟩ ⟨~ *hockey*⟩ ⟨*what to* ~ *after college*⟩ **b** to work out or solve, esp by studying ⟨~ *a sum*⟩ ⟨~ *his homework*⟩ **c(1)** to have as a job; work at ⟨*what do you* ~?⟩ ⟨*what does he* ~ *for a living?*⟩ **c(2)** to have as an occupation ⟨*and what are you* ~ing *with yourself these days, Mr Noon?* – D H Lawrence⟩ **12a** to pass over traverse ⟨~ *30 miles to the gallon*⟩ **b** to travel at a speed of ⟨~ *80 on the motorway*⟩ **13** to see the sights of tour ⟨~ *12 countries in 12 days*⟩ **14** to suffice, suit ⟨*worms will* ~ *us for bait*⟩ **15** to approve, esp by custom, opinion, or propriety ⟨*you oughtn't to say a thing like that . . . it's not* done – Dorothy Sayers⟩ **16** – used as a substitute verb to avoid repetition ⟨*if you must make such a racket,* ~ *it somewhere else*⟩ **17** *informal* to serve out (a stint or period) ⟨*did two terms at the Birmingham School of Music* – *Express and Star (Wolverhampton)*⟩ **18a** *informal* to treat unfairly; *esp* cheat, deprive ⟨*we've been* done⟩ – compare DO OUT OF **b** *slang* to rob ⟨~ *a shop*⟩ **c** *chiefly Br slang* to arrest, convict ⟨*get* done *for kidnapping and attempted murder* – *Evening Mail (Birmingham)*⟩ **d** *chiefly Br slang* to attack, hurt ⟨*they'd* done *the Minister with a crowbar* – *Punch*⟩ **19** *slang* to have sexual intercourse with (a woman or passive partner) **20** *chiefly NAm slang* to take (an illegal drug) ⟨*two guys from the youth culture, who probably* ~ *dope* – *Time Out*⟩ ~ *vi* **1** to act, behave ⟨~ *as I say*⟩ **2a** to fare; GET ALONG ⟨~ *well at school*⟩ ⟨*how do you* ~?⟩ **b** to carry on business or affairs; manage ⟨*we can* ~ *without your help*⟩ ⟨*can't* ~ *with loud music*⟩ **c** to make good use ⟨*the C.I.A. . . . could* ~ *with a clean up* – *Sunday People*⟩ ⟨*I could* ~ *with a drink*⟩ **3** to be in progress; happen ⟨*what's* ~ing *across the street?*⟩ **4** to come to or make an end; finish – used in the past participle ⟨*have you* done *with the newspaper?*⟩; compare ²DONE 2 **5** to be active or busy ⟨*let us then be up and* ~ing – H W Longfellow⟩ **6** to suffice, serve ⟨*half of that will* ~⟩ ⟨*I said, that will* ~!⟩ **7** to be fitting; conform to custom or propriety ⟨*won't* ~ *to be late*⟩ **8a** – used as a substitute verb to avoid repetition ⟨*wanted to run and play as children* ~⟩ ⟨*you sing,* ~ *you?*⟩ and, esp in British English, after a modal auxiliary ⟨*haven't heard of her yet but you will* ~⟩ **b** – used as a substitute for verb and object ⟨*he likes it and so* ~ *I*⟩ **9** – used in the imperative after another imperative to add emphasis ⟨*be quiet,* ~⟩ ~ *va* – used with the infinitive without *to* **a** to form present and past tenses in legal and parliamentary language ⟨~ *hereby bequeath*⟩ and in poetry ⟨*gave what she* did *crave* – Shak⟩ **b** to form present and past tenses in declarative sentences with inverted word order ⟨*fervently* ~ *we pray* – Abraham Lincoln⟩ or in interrogative or negative sentences ⟨*did you hear that?*⟩ ⟨*we* don't *know*⟩ ⟨*don't go*⟩ **c** to form present and past tenses expressing emphasis ⟨*it does*

*hurt*⟩ ⟨~ *be careful*⟩ – used with the infinitive without *to* [ME *don*, fr OE *dōn*; akin to OHG *tuon* to do, L *-dere* to put, *facere* to make, do, Gk *tithenai* to place, set] – **do something for** to improve the appearance of ⟨*that new dress really does something for you*⟩ – **to do with** concerned with; of concern to ⟨*a job* to do with *plastics*⟩ ⟨*nothing* to do with *you*⟩

*usage* The British English use of an added **do**, **doing**, or **done** in such sentences as ⟨*we never go there now, but we used to* (**do**)⟩ ⟨*I don't know whether I'll come, but I might* (**do**)⟩ ⟨*John joined the union, and Ann may have* (**done**) *too*⟩ should probably be avoided in formal writing. See ²DONE, ¹HAVE

**do away with** *vt* **1** to put an end to; abolish **2** to put to death; kill

**do by** *vt* to deal with; treat ⟨*afraid you've been rather hard done by*⟩

**do down** *vt* **1** *chiefly Br informal* to cheat **2** to speak badly of (esp somebody not present) ⟨*he's always doing her down*⟩

**do for** *vt* **1** *chiefly Br* to keep house for ⟨*she did for the old man after his wife died*⟩ **2** *informal* to bring about the death or ruin of

**do in** *vt* **1** *informal* to bring about the death of; kill ⟨*tried to do him in with a club*⟩ **2** to exhaust; WEAR OUT **2** ⟨*waiting all day nearly did us in*⟩

**do out of** *vt, informal* to take away from or deprive of by swindling or unfair means ⟨*he did me out of a fiver*⟩

**do over** *vt* **1** to clean out and redecorate (esp a room) **2** *Br informal* to attack and injure

**do up** *vt* **1a(1)** to repair, restore ⟨do up *old furniture*⟩ **a(2)** to redecorate ⟨do up *the house*⟩ **b** to make more attractive; dress up ⟨*did herself* up *for the party*⟩ **2** to wrap up ⟨do up *a parcel*⟩ **3** to fasten (clothing or its fastenings) together ⟨*she did her blouse* up⟩

**²do** *n, pl* **dos**, **do's** /doohz/ **1** *usu pl* something one ought to do – chiefly in *dos and don'ts* ⟨*gave her a list of* ~s *and don'ts*⟩ **2** *chiefly Br informal* a festive party or occasion; broadly an organized event **3** *Br slang* a cheat, swindle – compare FAIR DOS

**³do** /doh/ *n, music* DOH

**doable** /'dooh·əbl/ *adj* capable of being done; practicable

**dobbin** /'dobin/ *n* – used chiefly as a familiar name for a farm horse or a quiet plodding horse [*Dobbin*, nickname for *Robert*]

**dobby** /'dobi/ *n* a loom attachment for weaving small geometric patterns in fabric [prob fr *Dobby*, nickname for *Robert*]

**Doberman pinscher** /ˌdohbəmən 'pinshə/, **Doberman** *n* (any of) a breed of short-haired medium-sized dog of German origin that has a docked tail and is frequently used as a guard dog [Ger *Dobermann-pinscher*, fr Ludwig *Dobermann*, 19th-c Ger dog breeder + Ger *pinscher*, a breed of hunting dog]

**dob in** /dob/ *vt, Austr* to inform against; betray ⟨*something the senator can use to* dob in *other members* – *The Age (Melbourne)*⟩ [*dob* (to set down sharply, throw down), var of *dab*]

**dobra** /'dohbrə, 'dob/ *n* – see MONEY table [Pg, deriv of L *duplus* double]

**doc** /dok/ *n* a doctor – often used as an informal term of address

**docent** /doh'sent, 'dohs(ə)nt/ *n, chiefly NAm* a college or university teacher or lecturer [obs Ger (now *dozent*), fr L *docent-*, *docens*, prp of *docēre*]

**Docetism** /doh'seetiz(ə)m, 'dohsəˌtiz(ə)m/ *n* a belief, regarded as a heresy in early Christianity, that Christ only seemed to have a human body and to suffer and die on the cross, but was in reality wholly and solely divine ⟨*theologians are agreed in wanting to be rid of* ~ *for good and all* – Don Cupitt⟩ [Gk *Dokētai* Docetists, fr *dokein* to seem – more at DECENT] – **docetic** *adj, often cap,* **Docetist** *n*

**doch-an-dorrach** /ˌdokh ən 'dawrəkh/ *n* a doch-an-dorris

**doch-an-dorris** /ˌdokh ən 'dawrəs/ *n, Scot & Irish* a drink taken before parting or setting out on a journey [ScGael & IrGael *deoch an doruis*, lit., drink of the door]

**docile** /'dohsiel/ *adj* **1** easily led or managed; tractable **2** *archaic* easily taught *synonyms* see OBEDIENT *antonyms* unruly, ungovernable [L *docilis*, fr *docēre* to teach; akin to L *decēre* to be fitting – more at DECENT] – **docilely** *adv,* **docility** *n*

**¹dock** /dok/ *n* any of a genus (*Rumex* of the family Polygonaceae, the dock family) of coarse plants that have long TAPROOTS (main roots that grow vertically downwards), are used as flavourings and in folk medicine (eg for the alleviation of nettle stings), and are common weeds [ME, fr OE *docce*; akin to MD *docke* dock, ScGael *dogha* burdock]

**²dock** *n* **1** the solid part of an animal's tail as distinguished from the hair **2** the cropped tail of an animal after clipping the hair or cropping the end [ME *dok,* fr OE *-docca* (as in *fingir-docca* finger muscle); akin to OHG *tocka* doll, ON *dokka* bundle]

³**dock** *vt* **1a** to cut off the end of a body part of; *specif* to remove part of the tail of **b** to cut (eg ears or a tail) short **2a** to take away a part of; abridge **b** to subject (eg wages) to a deduction **3** to deprive of a benefit ordinarily due (eg a point), esp as a penalty for a fault ⟨~ed *for lateness*⟩ – **docker** *n*

⁴**dock** *n* **1a** a usu artificially enclosed area of water in a port or harbour, where a ship can moor to be loaded, unloaded, or repaired **b** *pl the* total number of such enclosures in a harbour, together with their wharves, sheds, etc **2** a platform from which goods are loaded and unloaded **3** *NAm* a wharf, pier [MD *docke* dock, ditch, perh deriv of L *duction-, ductio* act of leading – more at DOUCHE] – **in dock** in a garage or repair shop ⟨*my car's* in dock *at the moment*⟩

⁵**dock** *vt* **1** to haul or guide into a dock **2** to join (eg two space-craft) mechanically while in space ~ *vi* **1** to come or go into dock **2** *of spacecraft* to join together while in space

⁶**dock** *n* the enclosure in a criminal court where a prisoner stands or sits during trial [Flem *docke* cage] – **in the dock** on trial ⟨*always found himself* in the dock *for his opinions*⟩

**dockage** /'dokij/ *n* **1** a charge for the use of a dock **2** docking facilities

**docker** /'dokə/ *n* one who loads and unloads ships, esp in a port [⁴*dock*]

¹**docket** /'dokit/ *n* **1** a brief written summary of a document; an abstract **2a** a document recording the contents of a shipment or the payment of customs duties **b** a label attached to goods bearing identification or instructions **c** (a copy of) a receipt **3** *chiefly NAm* a list of business matters to be acted on; an agenda **4** *NAm* **4a(1)** a formal abridged record of the proceedings in a legal action **a(2)** a register of such records **b** a list of legal cases to be tried [ME *doggette*]

²**docket** *vt* **1** to put an identifying statement or label on (eg a document) **2** to make a brief summary of (eg a legal matter) as part of a list of such summaries **3** *NAm* to place on the docket for legal action

**dockland** /'dokland/ *n, chiefly Br* the district around the docks in a large port

**dockside** /'doksied/ *n* the shore or area neighbouring a dock

**dockworker** /'dok,wuhkə/ *n* a docker

**dockyard** /'dok,yahd/ *n* **1** a shipyard **2** *Br* NAVY YARD

¹**doctor** /'doktə/ *n* **1a** a doctor, doctor of the church an eminent THEOLOGIAN (student of religion) whose doctrines the Roman Catholic church considers as authoritative **b** a person who has earned one of the highest academic degrees (eg a PhD) conferred by a university **c** a person awarded an honorary doctorate (eg an LLD or DLitt) by a college or university **2a(1)** one qualified to practise medicine; a physician or surgeon **a(2)** *NAm* a licensed dentist or vet **b** one skilled in repairing or treating a usu specified type of thing ⟨*a tree* ~⟩ ⟨*a car* ~⟩ **3a** material added (eg to food) to produce a desired effect **b** a blade (eg of metal) for spreading a coating or scraping a surface **4** a usu makeshift and emergency mechanical device or attachment for remedying a particular difficulty **5** any of several brightly coloured artificial flies used by fisherman **6** *archaic* a learned or authoritative teacher [ME *doctour* teacher, doctor, fr MF & ML; MF, fr ML *doctor,* fr L, teacher, fr *docēre* to teach – more at DOCILE] – **doctoral** *also* **doctorial** *adj,* **doctorship** *n*

usage In Britain, licensed physicians are called **doctor** whether or not they hold a doctorate in medicine, but qualified surgeons usually call themselves *Mr* (or *Miss, Mrs,* or *Ms*). The habitual use of the title **doctor** by the holder of a PhD may be thought ostentatious, and sometimes leads to confusion with medical **doctors**.

²**doctor** *vt* **1a** to give medical treatment to **b** to restore to good condition; repair; *also* to patch up ⟨~ *an old clock*⟩ **2a** to adapt or modify for a desired end by alteration or special treatment ⟨~ed *the play to suit the audience*⟩ **b** to alter in a dishonest way; interfere with ⟨*accused of* ~ing *the election returns*⟩ **3** *euph* to castrate, spay ~ *vi, informal* to practise medicine

**doctorate** /'doktərət/ *n* the degree, title, or rank of a doctor

¹**doctrinaire** /,doktri'neə/ *n* one who attempts to put into effect an abstract doctrine or theory with little or no regard for practical difficulties or alternative methods [Fr, fr *doctrine*]

²**doctrinaire** *adj* (characteristic) of a doctrinaire; dogmatic, hidebound – **doctrinairism** *n*

**doctrinal** /dok'trienl/ *adj* of or preoccupied with doctrine – **doctrinally** *adv*

**doctrine** /'doktrin/ *n* **1** something that is taught **2** a principle or the body of principles in a branch of knowledge or system of belief; a dogma [ME, fr MF & L; MF, fr L *doctrina,* fr *doctor*]

'**docu-,drama** /'dokyooh/ *n* a play, film, etc in which factual incidents are presented in dramatized form ⟨*Shakespeare's scurrilously inaccurate* ~ Richard III – *The Listener*⟩ [*documentary* + *drama*]

¹**document** /'dokyoomənt/ *n* an original or official paper that gives information about or proof or support of something [ME, fr MF, fr LL & L; LL *documentum* official paper, fr L, lesson, proof, fr *docēre* to teach – more at DOCILE] – **documental** *adj*

²**document** /'dokyooment/ *vt* **1** to provide documentary evidence of **2** to provide with documents **3a** to provide with factual support for statements made or a hypothesis proposed; *esp* to equip with exact references to authoritative supporting information ⟨*the thesis was well* ~ed *with footnotes on every page*⟩ **b** to construct or produce (eg a film or novel) with a high proportion of details closely reproducing real situations or events **c** to be or provide a documentary account of ⟨*his film* ~ed *the living conditions in the ghetto*⟩ **4** to provide (a ship) with ship's papers for the listing of ownership, cargo, and other details required by law – **documenter** *n,* **documentable** *adj*

**documentalist** /,dokyoo'mentl·ist/ *n* a specialist in documentation

¹**documentary** /,dokyoo'mentəri/ *adj* **1** being or consisting of documents; contained or certified in writing ⟨~ *evidence*⟩ **2** presenting or based on factual material ⟨*a* ~ *film of the war*⟩ – **documentarily** *adv*

²**documentary** *n* a broadcast, film, etc that presents a factual account of some topic, often concerning a social or political issue, using a mixture of techniques (eg narrative, interview, recordings, or dramatized reconstructions) – compare FEATURE 3a, c, SEMIDOCUMENTARY – **documentarist** *n*

**documentation** /,dokyoomən'taysh(ə)n, -men-/ *n* **1** the act or an instance of providing or authenticating with documents **2a** the provision of documents as proof; *also* documentary evidence **b(1)** the use of historical documents **b(2)** agreement with historical or objective facts **b(3)** the provision of footnotes, appendices, or addenda referring to or containing documentary evidence **3** INFORMATION SCIENCE – **documentational** *adj*

¹**dodder** /'dodə/ *n* any of a genus (*Cuscuta*) of leafless yellow, pinkish, or white flowered plants of the bindweed family that have no chlorophyll and therefore cannot manufacture their own food, and that live wholly as parasites on other plants to which they are attached by means of suckers [ME *doder;* akin to OE *dydring* yolk, Norw *dudra* to tremble, L *fumus* smoke – more at FUME]

²**dodder** *vi* **1** to tremble or shake from weakness or age **2** to progress feebly and unsteadily ⟨*an old man* ~ing *down the path*⟩ [ME *dadiren*] – **dodderer** *n*

**doddered** /'dodəd/ *adj* deprived of branches through age or decay ⟨*a* ~ *oak*⟩ [prob alter. of *dodded,* fr pp of E dial. *dod* (to lop), fr ME *dodden*]

**doddery** /'dodəri/ *adj* weak, shaky, and slow, esp because of old age

**doddle** /'dodl/ *n, chiefly Br informal* a very easy task [prob fr ²*dodder*]

**dodeca-** /dohdekə-/, **dodec-** /dohdek-/ *comb form* twelve ⟨do-decaphonic⟩ ⟨dodecasyllable⟩ [L, fr Gk *dōdeka-, dōdek-,* *dōdeka, dyōdeka,* fr *dyō, dyo* two + *deka* ten]

**dodecagon** /,doh'dekəgən/ *n* a two-dimensional geometric figure having 12 sides; *esp* one that is REGULAR, having 12 equal sides and angles [Gk *dōdekagōnon,* fr *dōdeka-* + *-gōnon* -gon] – **dodecagonal** *adj*

**dodecahedron** /,dohdekə'heedrən/ *n, pl* **dodecahedrons,** **dodecahedra** /-drə/ a three-dimensional geometric figure having 12 faces; *esp* one that is REGULAR, having 12 equal 5-sided faces [Gk *dōdekaedron,* fr *dōdeka-* + *-edron* -hedron] – **dodecahedral** *adj*

**dodecaphonic** /,dohdekə'fonik/ *adj* of or using the TWELVE-TONE musical scale [*dodeca-* + *phon-* + *-ic*] – **dodecaphonically** *adv,* **dodecaphonist** *n,* **dodecaphony** *n*

¹**dodge** /doj/ *vi* **1** to avoid a responsibility or duty, esp by trickery or deceit **2a** to move to and fro, usu in an irregular course ⟨~d *through the crowd*⟩ **b** to make a sudden move-

ment in a new direction (e g to avoid a blow) ⟨~d *behind the door*⟩ ~ *vt* **1** to avoid (e g a duty), usu indirectly and by trickery ⟨~d *the call-up by leaving the country*⟩ **2a** to avoid by a sudden or repeated shift of position **b** to avoid an encounter with **3** to reduce the intensity of (portions of a photographic print) by selectively shading during printing – compare BURN IN [origin unknown]

²**dodge** *n* **1** an act of avoiding by sudden movement of the body **2** a cunning device to avoid, deceive, or trick ⟨*a tax* ~⟩

**dodgem car** *n* a car used in dodgems [¹*dodge* + *'em*]

**dodgems** /'dojəmz/ *n taking sing or pl vb* a fairground amusement in which small electric cars may be driven about and bumped into one another in an enclosed arena

**dodger** /'dojə/ *n* **1** one who dodges; *esp* one who uses clever and often dishonest methods, esp to avoid payment (e g taxes) or responsibility **2** a canvas screen on a ship or boat that provides protection against the weather **3** *dial* food; *esp* bread or a sandwich

**dodgy** /'doji/ *adj, chiefly Br informal* **1** shady, dishonest **2** risky and possibly dangerous **3** liable to collapse, fail, or break down ⟨*a ~ knee*⟩ ⟨*don't sit on that chair, it's a bit* ~⟩

**dodo** /'doh₁doh/ *n, pl* **dodoes, dodos 1** an extinct heavy flightless bird (*Raphus cucullatus*) that formerly lived on the island of Mauritius **2a** a person or thing hopelessly out of date **b** a stupid person [Pg *doudo*, fr *doudo* silly, stupid]

**doe** /doh/ *n, pl* **does,** *esp collectively* **doe** the adult female FALLOW DEER; *broadly* the adult female of any of various mammals (e g the rabbit) or birds (e g the GUINEA FOWL) of which the male is called a buck [ME *do*, fr OE *dā;* akin to Ger dial. *tē* doe]

**doek** /dook/ *n, SAfr informal* a cloth; *esp* a head cloth worn by African women [Afrik, fr D – more at ³DUCK]

**doer** /'dooh·ə/ *n* one who takes an active part in something, rather than theorizing ⟨*a thinker or a* ~⟩

**does** /daz; *strong* duz/ *pres sing of* DO

**doeskin** /'doh₁skin/ *n* **1** the skin of a doe; *also* leather made from this **2** a closely woven woollen fabric treated to give a smooth surface **3** a soft leather made from sheepskins or lambskins

**doesn't** /'duznt/ does not

**doest** /'dooh·ist/ *archaic pres sing of* DO

**doeth** /'dooh·ith/ *archaic pres 3 sing of* DO

**doff** /dof/ *vt* **1** to take off (an article of clothing) **2** to take off (the hat) in greeting or as a sign of respect [ME *doffen*, fr *don* to do + *cf* off (cf DON)]

¹**dog** /dog/ *n* **1a** a 4-legged flesh-eating domesticated mammal (*Canis familiaris*) probably descended from the common wolf and existing in many different breeds **b** any of a family (Canidae, the dog family) of flesh-eating mammals to which the dog belongs **c** a male dog **2** a worthless person **3a** any of various usu simple mechanical devices for holding, gripping, or fastening that consist of a spike, rod, bar, or hook **b** ANDIRON (metal support for firewood) **4a** SUN DOG (luminous spot on each side of the sun) **b** FOGBOW (arc of light seen in fog) **5** *pl* ruin ⟨*go to the* ~s⟩ – + *the* **6** *informal* a fellow, chap ⟨*a lazy* ~⟩ **7** *pl, Br informal* greyhound races ⟨*"I come to the* ~s *to get away from me old woman"* – The Listener⟩ – usu + *the* **8** *NAm informal* **8a** an investment (e g a stock or bond) not worth its price **b** a slow-moving or undesirable piece of merchandise **9** *chiefly NAm slang* something inferior of its kind ⟨*the party was a real* ~⟩ **10** *pl, humorous* feet [ME, fr OE *docga*] – **doglike** *adj* – **dog in the manger** a person who selfishly deprives others of something that is of no use to him-/herself [fr the fable of the dog who prevented an ox from eating hay which he himself did not want] – **give a dog a bad name** to cause somebody to gain a bad reputation by slandering him/her [fr the phrase *give a dog a bag name and hang him,* ie a dog reputed to be mad or vicious is effectively condemned to death]

²**dog** *vt* -**gg**- **1** to hunt or track like a dog **2** to pursue and worry as if by dogs; hound

>*usage* When **dogged** is the past tense or past participle of **dog**, it is pronounced /dogd/. As an adjective meaning "determined" it is pronounced /'dogid/.

³**dog** *adj* **1** male ⟨*a ~ fox*⟩ **2** spurious; *esp* unlike that used by native speakers or writers ⟨*~ Latin*⟩

**dogan** /'dohgən/ *n, Can informal* an Irish Roman Catholic [prob fr *Dogan*, an Irish surname (cf DOOLAN)]

**dogbane** /'dog₁bayn/ *n* any of a genus (*Apocynum*) of chiefly

tropical and often poisonous plants of the periwinkle family with milky juice and usu showy flowers

**dogberry** /'dog₁beri/ *n* the inedible fruit of any of several plants; *esp* the fruit of the European dogwood

**dog biscuit** *n* a hard dry biscuit for dogs

**dogcart** /'dog₁kaht/ *n* a light horse-drawn 2-wheeled carriage with two seats set back to back, one of which faces forwards [fr its being orig designed to carry sportsmen's dogs]

**dog clutch** *n* a clutch in which slots in one plate are engaged by teeth in the other

**dog collar** *n, informal* CLERICAL COLLAR

**dog days** *n pl* the hottest days in the year [fr their being reckoned from the heliacal rising of the Dog Star (Sirius)]

**doge** /dohj/ *n* the chief magistrate of the former republics of Venice and Genoa [It dial., fr L *duc-, dux* leader – more at DUKE]

'**dog-₁ear** *n* the turned-down corner of a page of esp a book – **dog-ear** *vt*

'**dog-₁eared** *adj* having dog-ears; *broadly* shabby, worn

₁**dog-eat-'dog** *adj* marked by ruthless self-interest; cutthroat ⟨*~ competition*⟩

'**dog-₁end** *n, informal* **1** a cigarette end **2** something left over and considered of little value

**dog fennel** *n* STINKING MAYWEED (plant of the daisy family)

**dogfight** /'dog₁fiet/ *n* **1** a fight between dogs; *broadly* a fiercely disputed contest **2** a fight between two or more fighter aircraft, usu at close quarters – **dogfight** *vi*

**dogfish** /'dog₁fish/ *n* any of various small sharks (e g of the families Squalidae, Carcharhinidae, and Scyliorhinidae) important as food

**dogged** /'dogid/ *adj* stubbornly determined; tenacious **synonyms** see OBSTINATE *usage* see ²DOG [ME, doglike, cruel, spiteful, fr *dog, dogge* dog + -*ed*] – **doggedly** *adv,* **doggedness** *n*

¹**dogger** /'dogə/ *n* a 2-masted Dutch fishing boat [ME *doggere,* perh fr MD *dogge* fishing boat]

²**dogger** /'dogə/ *n, Austr* a hunter of dingoes [¹*dog* + ²-*er*]

¹**doggerel** /'dog(ə)rəl/ *adj* **1** *of verse* loosely styled and irregular in metre, esp for comic effect **2** crude, inferior [ME *dogerel,* perh fr *dog* + -*erel, -rel,* dim. & derog suffix (as in *cockerel, mackerel, mongrel*)]

²**doggerel** *n* verse in doggerel style; *also* an example of this

**doggie bag** *n* a bag used for carrying home leftover food from a meal eaten away from home [²*doggy;* fr the giving of such food to a pet dog]

**doggo** /'dogoh/ *adv, Br informal* in hiding and without moving – chiefly in *lie doggo* [prob fr ¹*dog*]

**doggone** /dog'gon/, **doggoned** /dog'gond/ *adj or adv, chiefly NAm euph* damned [euphemism for *God damn* or *God damned*]

¹**doggy** /'dogi/ *adj, informal* **1** resembling or suggestive of a dog ⟨*a ~ odour*⟩ **2** concerned with or fond of dogs ⟨*a book for ~ experts*⟩

²**doggy, doggie** /'dogi/ *n* a dog – used esp by or to children

**doghouse** /'dog₁hows/ *n, chiefly NAm* a kennel – **in the doghouse** in a state of disfavour or disgrace

**dogie** *also* **dogey, dogy** /'dohgi/ *n, W US* a motherless calf [origin unknown]

¹**dogleg** /'dog₁leg/ *n* a sharp bend (e g in a road or in a fairway on a golf course)

²**dogleg, doglegged** *adj* crooked or bent like a dog's hind leg

**dogma** /'dogmə/ *n* **1** a principle, belief, or tenet that is looked upon as authoritative and definite; *also* a code of such principles, beliefs, or tenets ⟨*communist* ~⟩ **2** a doctrine or body of doctrines concerning faith or morals formally and authoritatively stated by a church **3** a point of view or tenet put forth, esp arrogantly, as authoritative without adequate grounds [L *dogmat-, dogma,* fr Gk, fr *dokein* to seem – more at DECENT]

**dogmatic** /dog'matik/ *also* **dogmatical** /-kl/ *adj* **1** characterized by or given to the assertion of opinion in a very positive, usu arrogant, manner as if expressing established fact ⟨*a ~ supporter of apartheid*⟩ **2** of dogma or dogmatics – **dogmatically** *adv,* **dogmaticalness** *n*

**dogmatics** /dog'matiks/ *n taking sing or pl vb* a branch of theology that seeks to interpret the dogmas and doctrines of a religious faith

**dogmatism** /'dogmə₁tiz(ə)m/ *n* **1** positiveness and arrogance in assertion of opinion or point of view, as if expressing established fact **2** a viewpoint or system of ideas based on assumption or speculation rather than on experience or observation – **dogmatist** *n*

**dogmat·ize, -ise** /'dogmə,tiez/ vi to speak or write dogmatically ~ vt to state or write as a dogma or in a dogmatic manner [Fr *dogmatiser*, fr LL *dogmatizare*, fr Gk *dogmatizein*, fr *dogmat-*, *dogma*] – **dogmatization** n, **dogmatizer** n

**do-gooder** /,dooh 'goodə/ n an earnest usu impractical and often naive and ineffectual humanitarian or reformer – **do-gooding** n or adj

**dog paddle** n an elementary form of swimming (e g for learners) executed lying on the front, in which the arms paddle up and down like the front paws of a swimming dog and the legs kick – **dog-paddle** vi

**dog rose** n a common European wild rose (*Rosa canina*) that has pale pink flowers [trans of NL *rosa canina*, fr Gk *kynorodon;* prob fr its root supposedly curing the bite of a mad dog]

**dogsbody** /-,bodi/ n, chiefly Br a person who does very routine or menial work for others; esp a person who is expected to do other people's boring chores [Br naval slang *dogsbody* (pudding made of peas, junior officer)]

**dog's chance** n, informal any chance at all ⟨didn't have a ~⟩

**dog's dinner** n, chiefly Br informal one who is vulgarly overdressed ⟨got up like a ~⟩

**dogsled** /'dog,sled/ n a sledge drawn by a team of dogs (e g huskies)

**dog's life** n a miserable drab existence

**dog's mercury** n a woodland plant (*Mercurialis perennis*) of the spurge family that has inconspicuous green single-sex flowers

**dogstooth check** /'dogz,toohth/ n HOUNDSTOOTH CHECK (textile pattern)

**dog tag** n, NAm 1 an identity disc for a dog 2 informal an identification disc for military personnel worn round the neck

**,dog-'tired** n, informal extremely tired

**dogtooth** /'dog,toohth/ n 1 CANINE 1 (conical pointed tooth) 2 an Early English architectural ornamentation consisting of a series of four leaves radiating from a raised centre

**dog-tooth spar** n a mineral that is a variety of CALCITE and forms pointed crystals shaped like a dog's canine tooth

**dogtooth violet** n any of a genus (*Erythronium*) of small spring-flowering plants of the lily family that form bulbs

**dogtrot** /'dog,trot/ n a quick easy gait suggesting that of a dog – **dogtrot** vi

**dog violet** n either of two European wild violets (*Viola canina* and *Viola riviniana*) that have blue flowers with usu yellow backwards-pointing spurs [trans of NL *viola canina*]

**dogwatch** /'dog,woch/ n either of two watches of two hours on board ship that extend from 4 to 6 and 6 to 8 pm

**dogwhelk** /'dog,welk/ n (any of several whelks related to) the common British whelk (*Nucella lapillus*)

**dogwood** /'dog,wood/ n any of several trees and shrubs (genus *Cornus* of the family Cornaceae, the dogwood family) that bear heads of small usu white flowers

**doh, do** /doh/ n the 1st note of the scale in the SOL-FA method of representing the musical scale [It *do*]

**doily, doyley, doyly** /'doyli/ n 1 a small napkin 2 a small decorative mat, esp of paper, cloth, or plastic openwork, often placed under food, esp cakes, on a plate or stand [*Doily* or *Doyley* fl *ab* 1700 London draper]

**doing** /'dooh·ing/ n 1a the act or result of performing; action ⟨this must be your ~⟩ b effort, exertion ⟨that will take a great deal of ~⟩ 2 pl things that are done or occur; activities ⟨the daily ~ of the bank⟩ 3 chiefly Br informal a scolding, thrashing ⟨the cops gave me a ~⟩

**doings** /'dooh·ings/ n, pl **doings** also **doingses** chiefly Br informal a small object, esp one the name of which is forgotten or not known ⟨screw up that little ~ on the top⟩

**doited** /'doytid/ adj, chiefly Scot senile, confused [ME (Sc), prob alter. of *doted*, pp of *doten* to dote]

**,do-it,your'self** adj of or designed for use by an amateur, esp an amateur handyman – **do-it-yourselfer** n

**dojo** /'doh,joh/ n, pl **dojos** a school for training in various arts of self-defence (e g judo and karate) [Jap *dōjō*, fr *dō* way, art + *-jō* ground]

**¹Dolby** /'dolbi/ trademark – used for a sound recording technique or system that reduces unwanted noise by electronic processing

**²Dolby** vt to process (a recording) using a Dolby system

**dolce** /'dolchay, 'dolchi/ adj or adv in a soft smooth manner – used as a direction in music [It, lit., sweet, fr L *dulcis*]

**dolce far niente** /,dolchi fah 'nyenti/ n pleasant relaxation in carefree idleness [It, lit., sweet doing nothing]

**dolce vita** /'veetah/ n a life of indolence and self-indulgence [It, lit., sweet life]

**doldrums** /'doldrəmz/ n pl 1 a depressed or sad state of mind; *the* blues 2 a part of the ocean near the equator where calms, squalls, and light shifting winds prevail 3 a state of inactivity, stagnation, or slump [prob akin to OE *dol* foolish]

**¹dole** /dohl/ n 1 a distribution of food, money, or clothing to the needy 2 a portion or share of something (e g money or food) distributed at intervals to the needy 3 Br informal a grant of government funds to the unemployed; *specif the* government unemployment benefit [ME, fr OE *dāl* portion; akin to OE *dæl* part, lot] – **on the dole** Br informal receiving the government unemployment benefit

**²dole** n, archaic grief, sorrow [ME *dol*, fr OF, fr LL *dolus*, alter. of L *dolor* grief]

**doleful** /'dohlf(ə)l/ adj 1 causing grief; sad ⟨a ~ loss⟩ 2 full of grief; mournful ⟨a ~ face⟩ – **dolefully** adv, **dolefulness** n

**dole out** vt to give or distribute, esp in small portions

**dolerite** /'doləriet/ n any of various fine- to medium-grained dark IGNEOUS rocks (rocks formed by the solidification of molten lava); esp one formed by the solidification of lava below the earth's surface and consisting chiefly of FELDSPAR and AUGITE or another PYROXENE [Fr *dolérite*, fr Gk *doleros* deceitful, fr *dolos* deceit – more at TALE; fr its being easily mistaken for diorite] – **doleritic** adj

**dolich-, dolicho-** /dolik-/ comb form long ⟨dolichocranic⟩ [Gk, fr *dolichos* – more at LONG]

**dolichocephalic** /,dolikohsi'falik, -ki-/ adj having a head that is very long relative to its width; esp having a CEPHALIC INDEX of less than 75 ⟨the excavation revealed numerous ~ human remains⟩ – compare BRACHYCEPHALIC, ORTHOCEPHALIC [NL *dolichocephalus* dolichocephalic person, fr *dolich-* + *-cephalus* (fr Gk *kephalē* head) – more at CEPHALIC] – **dolichocephalism** n, **dolichocephaly** n

**dolichocranial** /,dolikoh'kraynyəl/ also **dolichocranic** /-'kraynik/ adj having a relatively long skull; esp having a CRANIAL INDEX of less than 75 [ISV] – **dolichocrany** n

**doll** /dol/ n 1 a small-scale figure of a human being used esp as a child's toy 2 informal 2a a (pretty but often silly) young woman b a very likable person [prob fr *Doll*, nickname for *Dorothy*] – **dollish** adj, **dollishly** adv, **dollishness** n

**dollar** /'dolə/ n 1 TALER (former European coin) 2a the standard monetary unit, divided into 100 cents, of the USA, Canada, Australia, etc – see MONEY table b a coin, note, or token representing one dollar 3 Br five shillings (25 pence) [D or LG *daler*, fr Ger *taler*, short for *joachimstaler*, fr Sankt *Joachimsthal*, town in Bohemia where talers were first made] – **bet one's bottom dollar** informal to be virtually certain

**dollar diplomacy** n the use by a country, esp the USA, of (the threat of) financial sanctions to ensure that another country adopts policies favourable to it (e g grants it trade advantages or follows its lead in relationship to other powers)

**dollar sign** n a mark $ placed before a number to indicate that it stands for dollars

**¹dollop** /'doləp/ n 1 a small soft shapeless blob; esp a serving of mushy or semiliquid food ⟨a ~ of mashed potato⟩ 2 informal a small amount or admixture ⟨prose without one ~ of humour⟩ [perh of Scand origin; akin to Norw dial. *dolp* lump]

**²dollop** vt to serve out carelessly or clumsily

**doll's house**, NAm dollhouse n a child's small-scale toy house

**doll up** vt to dress or decorate prettily or showily ⟨he was dolling himself up for the first night of her new opera when the phone rang⟩

**¹dolly** /'doli/ n 1 a child's doll – used chiefly by or to children 2 a wooden-pronged instrument for beating and stirring clothes in the process of washing them in a tub 3a a renewable pad placed on the head of a pile to prevent damage to the pile driver b a heavy bar with a cupped head for holding against the head of a rivet while the other end is being hammered flat 4a a platform on a roller or on wheels or castors for moving heavy objects b a wheeled platform for a film or television camera often running on tracks 5 a catch in cricket that is very simple to take

**²dolly** vi 1 to move a film or television camera on a dolly towards or away from a subject while shooting a scene – usu + in or out 2 of a camera to undergo dollying – compare ⁴PAN, TRACK 2

**dolly bird** n, chiefly Br a pretty young woman, esp one who wears fashionable or showy clothes and makeup and is not regarded as very intelligent

**dolly mixture** *n* tiny usu square brightly coloured mixed sweets; *also* one such sweet

**dolma** /'dohlmə, -mah/ *n, pl* **dolmas, dolmades** /dohl'mahdiz/ a vine leaf or cabbage leaf stuffed with a savoury filling (eg of minced lamb and rice) [*dolma* fr Turk, lit., sthg stuffed, fr *dolma* stuffed; *dolmades* fr NGk, pl of *dolmas*, fr Turk *dolma*]

**dolman** /'dolmən/ *n* 1 an outer robe traditionally worn by Turks 2 a wrap or coat made with dolman sleeves [Fr *doliman*, fr Turk *dolama*]

**dolman sleeve** *n* a sleeve very wide at the armhole and usu tight at the wrist, often cut in one piece with the bodice

**dolmen** /'dolmən/ *n* a prehistoric structure consisting of two or more upright stones supporting a horizontal slab found esp in Britain and France and often housing a burial chamber [Fr, fr Bret *tolmen*, fr *tol* table (fr L *tabula* board, plank) + *men* stone]

**dolomite** /'doləmiet/ *n* (a limestone rock composed of) a mineral, $CaMg(CO_3)_2$, consisting of a calcium magnesium carbonate [Fr, fr Déodat de *Dolomieu* †1801 Fr geologist] – **dolomitic** *adj*

**dolomit·ize, -ise** /'doləmietiez, -mitiez/ *vt* to convert into dolomite – **dolomitization** *n*

**dolorous** /'dolərəs/ *adj* causing or expressing misery or grief – **dolorously** *adv*, **dolorousness** *n*

**dolos** /'doləs/ *n, pl* **dolosse** /də'losə/ *SAfr* the knucklebone [Afrik]

**dolour,** *NAm chiefly* **dolor** /'dohlə/ *n* mental suffering or anguish; sorrow [ME *dolour*, fr MF, fr L *dolor* pain, grief, fr *dolēre* to feel pain, grieve – more at CONDOLE]

**dolphin** /'dolfin/ *n* 1 any of various small TOOTHED WHALES (family Delphinidae) that are usu larger than porpoises and usu have the snout elongated into a beak 2 **dolphin, dolphin fish** either of two large spiny-finned edible fishes (genus *Coryphaena*) of warm seas 3 a spar or buoy for mooring boats; *also* a group of posts set closely together in the water and used as a fender for a wharf or as a mooring or guide for boats [ME, fr MF *dophin, daufin*, fr OF *dalfin*, fr OProv, fr ML *dalfinus*, alter. of L *delphinus*, fr Gk *delphin-, delphis*; akin to Gk *delphys* womb, Skt *garbha*]

**dolphinarium** /,dolfi'neəriəm/ *n* (a place with) a large pool in which dolphins perform for the public

**dolt** /dohlt/ *n* an extremely dull or stupid person [prob akin to OE *dol* foolish] – **doltish** *adj*, **doltishly** *adv*, **doltishness** *n*

**Dom** /dom/ *n* 1 – used as a title for Benedictine, Carthusian, and Cistercian monks and members of certain enclosed Roman Catholic orders 2 – used formerly as a title preceding the Christian name of a Portuguese or Brazilian man of rank [(1) L *dominus* master; (2) Pg, fr L *dominus*]

**-dom** /-d(ə)m/ *suffix* (→ *n*) 1a rank or office of ⟨*duke*dom⟩ **b** realm or jurisdiction of ⟨*king*dom⟩ ⟨*Christen*dom⟩ 2 state or fact of being ⟨*free*dom⟩ ⟨*bore*dom⟩ 3 group or class of people having (a specified office, occupation, interest, or character) ⟨*official*dom⟩ ⟨*film*dom⟩ [ME, fr OE -*dōm*; akin to OHG *-tuom* -dom, OE *dōm* judgment – more at DOOM]

**domain** /də'mayn/ *n* 1 a territory over which control is exercised 2 a region distinctively marked by some physical feature ⟨*the ~ of rushing streams, tall trees, and lakes*⟩ 3 a sphere of influence or activity ⟨*the ~ of art*⟩ 4 the set of values to which a mathematical or logical variable is limited; *esp* the set of values that the independent variable of a function may take on ⟨*the ~ of Cos γ is all real numbers*⟩ – compare RANGE 5 any of the small randomly oriented regions of uniform magnetization in a FERROMAGNETIC substance (eg iron) [MF *domaine, demaine*, fr L *dominium*, fr *dominus*]

**domaine** /do'men, -'mayn/ (*Fr* dɔmɛn)/ *n* a French vineyard estate; *esp* one in Burgundy [Fr, lit., domain]

**domboek** /'dombook/ *n, SAfr* DOMPASS (identity document) [Afrik, fr *dom* stupid + *boek* book]

**¹dome** /dohm/ *n* 1 a (nearly) hemispherical roof or vault 2 a structure or natural formation that is shaped like the dome or cupola of a building 3 a form of crystal composed of two similar faces that slope equally in opposite directions and meet to produce a straight edge like the ridge of a pitched roof 4 *archaic* a stately building; a mansion [Fr, It, & L; Fr *dôme* dome, cathedral, fr It *duomo* cathedral, fr ML *domus* church, fr L, house – more at TIMBER] – **domal, domical** *adj*

**²dome** *vt* to cover with or form into a dome ~ *vi* to swell upwards or outwards like a dome

**Domesday Book** /'doohmz,day, -di/ *n* a record of a survey of English lands made, for tax purposes and to establish owner-

ship, by order of William the Conqueror about 1086 [ME, fr *domesday* doomsday; fr its being considered a final & irrevocable authority]

**¹domestic** /də'mestik/ *adj* 1 (characteristic) of the household or the family 2a very capable in matters relating to the management of a household **b** devoted to the pleasures of home and family life ⟨*in spite of his rather glamorous job he's a very ~ sort of person at heart*⟩ 3 of one's own country or some particular country; not foreign ⟨*~ politics*⟩ ⟨*~ wines*⟩ **c** tame, domesticated 4a living near or about the habitations of human beings ⟨*~ pigeons*⟩ **b** *of an animal* living with or kept by human beings ⟨*a ~ cat*⟩ [MF *domestique*, fr L *domesticus*, fr *domus*] – **domestically** *adv*

**²domestic** *n* a household servant

**domestic animal** *n* any of various animals (eg the horse or sheep) bred or tamed by human beings for some specific purpose (eg for food, companionship, or to carry loads)

**¹domesticate** /də'mestikayt/ *vt* 1 to bring (an animal or species) under human control for some specific purpose (eg for carrying loads, hunting, food, etc); tame 2 to cause to perform household tasks or duties with skill or pleasure – **domestication** *n*

**²domesticate** /də'mestikət, -kayt/ *n* a domesticated animal or plant

**domesticated** /də'mestikaytid/ *adj, chiefly Br* ready to undertake and able to perform household tasks

**domestic fowl** *n, pl* **domestic fowl, domestic fowls** a chicken, turkey, duck, or other bird kept for meat or egg production; *specif* one of a breed developed from the jungle fowl (*Gallus gallus*)

**domesticity** /,domə'stisəti/ *n* 1 the quality or state of being domestic or domesticated 2 home or family life 3 *pl* domestic affairs

**domestic science** *n* instruction and training in household skills and arts (eg cooking and sewing)

**¹domicile** /'domisiel/ *also* **domicil** /-s(i)l/ *n* 1 a place of residence; a home 2 a person's fixed, permanent, and principal home for legal purposes [MF, fr L *domicilium*, fr *domus*]

**²domicile** *vt* to establish in or provide with a domicile ⟨*at present ~*d *in the USA for tax purposes*⟩

**domiciliary** /,domi'silyəri/ *adj* 1 of or being a domicile 2 taking place in or going to the home ⟨*~ visit*⟩ ⟨*~ occupational therapist*⟩

**domiciliate** /,domi'siliayt/ *vb, formal vt* to domicile ~ *vi* to reside [L *domicilium*] – **domiciliation** *n*

**dominance** /'dominəns/ *n* the fact or state of being dominant: eg **a** a dominant position in a (social) hierarchy; ascendancy **b** the quality that a genetically dominant gene or characteristic possesses **c** the degree of influence or control over an ecological community exerted by a certain animal or esp a plant (DOMINANT 1b) **d** the tendency for one of a pair of bodily structures or organs to be preferred for or more involved in the performance of certain tasks or functions than the other member of the pair

**¹dominant** /'dominənt/ *adj* 1 commanding, controlling, or prevailing over all others 2 overlooking and commanding from a superior height 3 of or exerting ecological dominance 4 being the one of a pair of bodily structures that is the more effective or predominant in action ⟨*the ~ eye*⟩ ⟨*the ~ half of the brain*⟩ 5a being the one of a pair of alternative genes (ALLELES) that produce different states of a particular hereditary characteristic (eg eye colour) that predominates when both versions of the gene are present together – compare RECESSIVE **b** of or being a hereditary characteristic determined by a dominant gene [MF or L; MF, fr L *dominant-, dominans*, prp of *dominari*] – **dominantly** *adv*

**²dominant** *n* 1a a genetically dominant gene or characteristic **b** an organism (eg a species) in an ecological community that exerts a controlling influence on the environment and on the other kinds of organisms living in it **c** a dominant individual in a social hierarchy 2 the fifth note of a DIATONIC scale (ordinary 8-note musical scale), represented in sol-fa by *soh* – called also FIFTH

**dominate** /'dominayt/ *vt* 1 to exert controlling influence or power over; rule ⟨*the family financial houses that ~*d *Japan's industry*⟩ 2 to put in a subordinate position by exerting control; hold in subjection ⟨*~s his wife*⟩ 3 to overlook from a superior height or command because of superior height ⟨*the cathedral ~s the city*⟩ 4 to occupy a commanding or preeminent place or position in ⟨*name brands ~ the market*⟩ ~ *vi* 1 to have or exert mastery or control 2 to occupy a higher or superior position [L *dominatus*, pp of *dominari*, fr *dominus* master – more at DAME] – **dominative** *adj*, **dominator** *n*

**domination** /ˌdomiˈnaysh(ə)n/ *n* **1** ascendancy, control, or preeminence over another **2** the act or state of dominating or of being dominated **3** *pl* the fourth of the nine orders of angelic beings in the CELESTIAL HIERARCHY, ranking immediately below THRONES and above VIRTUES

**dominee** /ˈdoohmini/ *n, SAfr* a minister of the Dutch Reformed Church – used esp as a title of address [D, fr L *domine*, voc of *dominus*]

**domineer** /ˌdomiˈniə/ *vi* to exercise arbitrary or overbearing control; tyrannize ⟨*a ~ing husband*⟩ ~ *vt* to tyrannize over [D *domineren*, fr Fr *dominer*, fr L *dominari*] – **domineeringly** *adv*, **domineeringness** *n*

**dominical** /dəˈminikl/ *adj* **1** of Jesus Christ **2** of Sunday, the Lord's day [LL *dominicalis*, fr *dominicus* (*dies*) the Lord's day, fr L *dominicus* of a lord, fr *dominus*]

**dominical letter** *n* any of the first seven letters of the alphabet that are used to denote Sundays in a given year in order to determine the dates of various festivals (e g Easter) in the church calendar

**Dominican** /dəˈminikən/ *n* a member of a MENDICANT (living off alms) order of preaching friars founded by St Dominic in 1215 [St *Dominic* (Domingo de Guzman) †1221 Sp priest] – **Dominican** *adj*

**dominie** /ˈdomini/ *n* **1** *chiefly Scot* a teacher, schoolmaster **2** *archaic* a clergyman or minister [L *domine*, voc of *dominus*]

**dominion** /dəˈminyən, -niˈən/ *n* **1** the power or right to rule; sovereignty **2** *pl* DOMINATIONS **3** *often cap* a self-governing nation of the Commonwealth other than the United Kingdom that acknowledges the British monarch as head of state **4** *law* absolute ownership; right of possession [ME *dominioun*, fr MF *dominion*, modif of L *dominium*, fr *dominus*]

**Dominion Day** *n* July 1 observed as a public holiday in Canada in commemoration of the proclamation of dominion status in 1867

**dominium** /dəˈminiˑəm/ *n, law* DOMINION 4

**domino** /ˈdominoh/ *n, pl* **dominoes, dominos 1a(1)** a long loose hooded cloak worn with a half mask as a masquerade costume **a(2)** a half mask worn with a masquerade costume **b** somebody wearing a domino **2a** a flat rectangular block (e g of bone or plastic) whose face is divided into two equal parts that are blank or bear from one to usu six dots arranged as on dice faces **b** *pl but usu taking sing vb* any of several games played with a set of usu 28 dominoes [Fr (orig sense, a monk's hood), prob fr L (in the ritual formula *benedicamus Domino* let us bless the Lord), dat of *dominus*; (2) Fr, fr It, prob fr *domino* master, lord (exclamation of the winner), fr L *dominus*]

**domino theory** *n* a theory that if one vulnerable nation in an area, specif SE Asia, becomes Communist-controlled then this will lead to the neighbouring nations eventually also becoming Communist-controlled [fr the fact that if several dominoes are stood on end one behind the other with slight spaces between, a push on the first will make all the others topple]

**dompass, dompas** /ˈdom.pahs/ *n* an identity document containing personal information (e g details of domicile and a certificate of employment) that must be carried by non-whites in S Africa and produced on demand for examination – compare PASS LAW [Afrik *dompas*, fr *dom* stupid + *pas* pass]

**¹don** /don/ *n* **1a** *cap* – used as a title preceding the Christian name of a Spanish nobleman or gentleman ⟨Don *Quixote*⟩ **b** *archaic* a Spanish nobleman or gentleman **2** a head, tutor, or fellow at a college in Oxford University or Cambridge University; *broadly* a college or university teacher **3** *archaic* a person of consequence or rank [Sp, fr L *dominus* master – more at DAME]

**²don** *vt* **-nn-** PUT ON 1a,b [contr of *do* + *on* (cf DOFF)]

**dona** /ˈdonə/ *n* **1** a Portuguese or Brazilian woman of rank **2** *cap* – used in former times as a title preceding the Christian name of a Portuguese-speaking woman of rank [Pg, fr L *domina*]

**doña** /ˈdonyə/ *n* **1** *cap* – used as a title preceding the Christian name of a Spanish-speaking woman of rank **2** *archaic* a Spanish-speaking woman of rank [Sp, fr L *domina* lady]

**donate** /dohˈnayt/ *vt* **1** to make a gift or donation of, esp to a public or charitable cause ⟨~ *a site for a car park*⟩ **2** to give off or transfer (e g electrons) ~ *vi* to make a donation *synonyms* see ¹GIVE [back-formation fr *donation*] – **donator** *n*

**donation** /dohˈnaysh(ə)n/ *n* **1** the act of donating **2** something, esp money, that is donated; a gift [ME *donatyowne*, fr L *dona-*

*tion-, donatio*, fr *donatus*, pp of *donare* to present, fr *donum* gift; akin to L *dare* to give – more at DATE]

**Donatism** /ˈdonətiz(ə)m, ˈdoh-/ *n* the doctrines of a Christian sect that originated in N Africa in 311 and held that a sacrament administered by a priest not of blameless life was not efficacious [*Donatus*, 4th-c bishop of Carthage] – **Donatist** *n*

**¹donative** /ˈdohnətiv/ *n* a special gift or donation

**²donative** *adj* **1** of a donation **2** capable of being donated or subject to donation ⟨*a ~ trust*⟩ [L *donativus*, fr *donatus*]

**¹done** /dun/ **1** *past part of* DO **2** *chiefly dial & NAm past of* DO

**²done** *adj* **1** conformable to social convention ⟨*it's not ~ to eat peas off your knife*⟩ **2** arrived at or brought to an end; completed **3 done, done in/up** physically exhausted; spent **4** no longer involved; through ⟨*I'm ~ with the Army*⟩ **5** doomed to failure, defeat, or death **6** cooked sufficiently **7** *informal* arrested, imprisoned ⟨*robbed a bank and got ~ for ten years*⟩ – **done for** *informal* **1** dead or close to death **2** left with no capacity or opportunity for recovery; ruined

**³done** *interj* – used in acceptance of a bet or transaction

**donee** /ˌdohˈnee/ *n* a recipient of a gift or donation [*donor* + *-ee*]

**Donegal** /ˌdoniˈgawl/, **Donegal tweed** *n* a heavy woollen fabric with colourful flecks in the yarn [*Donegal* county in NW Ireland]

**¹dong** /dong/ *vt, Austr & NZ* to strike or hit (somebody) [imit] – **dong** *n*

**²dong** *n, vulg* the penis [perh fr ¹*dong*]

**³dong** *n* – see MONEY table [Annamese]

**donga** /ˈdong·gə/ *n, SAfr* a narrow steep-sided ravine usu conducting water in the rainy season [Afrik, fr Zulu]

**donjon** /ˈdunj(ə)n, ˈdon-/ *n* a massive central tower in a medieval castle [ME – more at DUNGEON]

**Don Juan** /don ˈjooh·ən, (*Sp* don Xwan)/ *n* a man who attempts to seduce many women; a lady-killer [*Don Juan*, legendary Sp nobleman featured in many works of literature]

**donkey** /ˈdongki/ *n* **1** a domesticated animal (*Equus asinus*) of the horse family that is smaller than the related horse and has long ears and is used to carry loads, pull carts, etc **2** a stupid or obstinate person ⟨*dun + -key* (as in *monkey*)⟩ – see also **talk the hind** LEG **off a donkey**

**donkey engine** *n* **1** a small usu portable auxiliary engine **2** a small locomotive used in shunting

**donkey jacket** *n* a thick hip-length hard-wearing jacket which is usu blue in colour and often has a strip of (imitation) leather across the shoulders

**donkey's years** *n pl, informal* a very long time ⟨*I haven't seen him for ~*⟩ [prob suggested by the length of *donkey's ears*]

**donkeywork** /-ˌwuhk/ *n* hard, monotonous, and routine work; drudgery

**donna** /ˈdonə/ *n, pl* **donne** /ˈdonay/ **1** *cap* – used as a title preceding the Christian name of an Italian woman, esp of rank **2** an Italian woman, esp of rank [It, fr L *domina*]

**donnée** /ˈdonay/ *n, pl* **données** /-nayz/ a basic fact or assumption essential to the action of a work of fiction or drama [Fr, fr fem of *donné*, pp of *donner* to give, fr L *donare* to donate]

**donnish** /ˈdonish/ *adj* characteristic of a university don; pedantic – **donnishly** *adv*, **donnishness** *n*

**donnybrook** /ˈdonibrook/ *n, often cap* an uproarious brawl; a free-for-all [*Donnybrook* Fair, former annual Irish event known for its brawls]

**donor** /ˈdohnə/ *n* **1** a person who or group or organization that gives, donates, or presents **2** an animal, plant, or person used as a source of biological material ⟨*a blood ~*⟩ **3a** a compound, molecule, atom, etc capable of giving up a part (e g an atom, chemical group, or electron) for combination with an ACCEPTOR in a chemical or nuclear reaction **b donor, donor impurity** an impurity that is added to a SEMICONDUCTOR (e g a silicon chip) to increase the number of mobile electrons and hence increase its ability to conduct electricity – compare ACCEPTOR 3b [MF *doneur*, fr L *donator*, fr *donatus*, pp of *donare*]

**¹don't** /dohnt/ **1** do not **2** *nonstandard* does not

*usage* The use of **don't** for "does not" was very common in educated informal speech until well into the 20th century ⟨*I only hope that this letter will reach you, though your loss will not be very great if it* **don't** – Aldous Huxley⟩ but is now regarded as nonstandard in British English. It still has some currency in educated American usage.

**²don't** *n usu pl* a command or entreaty not to do something; a prohibition ⟨*a long list of ~s*⟩

**don't know** *n* a person without a definite opinion, esp in response to a questionnaire ⟨*a few people ticked it but most of them were* don't knows⟩

**donut** /'dohnut/ *n, chiefly NAm* a doughnut

**doocot** /'doohkət/ *n, Scot* a dovecot [ME (Sc) *dow* dove, var of *douve, dove*]

**doodad** /'dooh,dad/ *n, chiefly NAm* **1** a doodah **2** a small trivial decorative article ⟨*a mantelpiece cluttered up with all kinds of* ∼s⟩ [origin unknown]

**doodah** /'dooh,dah/ *n, Br informal* a small article whose name is unknown or forgotten [origin unknown]

¹**doodle** /'doohdl/ *vi* to sketch or scribble in a bored or aimless manner ∼ *vt* to produce by doodling [perh fr *doodle* (to ridicule), fr *doodle* (fool, simpleton), fr LG *dudeltopf*] – **doodler** *n*

²**doodle** *n* an aimless scribble, design, or sketch

**doodlebug** /-,bug/ *n* **1** *NAm* the larva of an ANT LION **2** *NAm* a device (e g a divining rod) used in attempting to locate underground minerals **3** *informal* FLYING BOMB [prob fr *doodle* (fool) + *bug*]

**doohickey** /'dooh,hiki/ *n, NAm informal* a doodah [prob fr *doodad* + *hickey* (device, gadget), of unknown origin]

**doolan** /'doohlən/ *n, NZ informal* ROMAN CATHOLIC [prob fr *Doolan*, a common Irish surname (cf DOGAN)]

¹**doom** /doohm/ *n* **1** a law or ordinance in Anglo-Saxon England **2a** a judgment or decision; *also, archaic* a judicial condemnation or sentence **b(1)** LAST JUDGMENT **b(2)** JUDGMENT DAY **3a** an (unhappy or terrible) destiny **b** unavoidable death or destruction; *also* environmental disaster [ME, fr OE *dōm;* akin to OHG *tuom* condition, state, OE *dōn* to do]

²**doom** *vt* **1** to give judgment against; condemn **2** to destine, esp to failure, a terrible fate, or destruction

**doomful** /'doohmf(ə)l/ *adj* presaging doom; ominous – **doomfully** *adv*

**doomsday** /'doohmz,day, -di/ *n* JUDGMENT DAY

**doomster** /'doohmstə/ *n, informal* a person given to forebodings and predictions of impending calamity

**door** /daw/ *n* **1a** a usu hinged or sliding panel that fits into an entrance to a room or building and which can be opened to allow people in or out or closed for privacy, protection against the weather, etc – compare GATE **b** a part of a closed structure (e g a piece of furniture, motor car, or aircraft) which can be opened or closed to allow access to its inside **2** a doorway **3** a means of access ⟨∼ *to success*⟩ [ME *dure, dor*, fr OE *duru* door & *dor* gate; akin to OHG *turi* door, L *fores*, Gk *thyra*] – **doorless** *adj* – **at somebody's door** as a charge against somebody as being responsible ⟨*laid the blame* at our door⟩ – **close one's doors 1** to refuse admission ⟨*the nation* closed its doors *to immigrants*⟩ **2** to go out of business ⟨*after nearly 40 years he had to* close his doors *for lack of trade*⟩ – **close the door on/to** to make impossible, esp by being obstructive; preclude ⟨*his attitude* closed the door to *further negotiations*⟩ – see also **get a** FOOT **in the door, keep the** WOLF **from the door**

,**do-or-'die** *adj* requiring or having the determination to face a danger or challenge without flinching ⟨*it is a* ∼ *chance that you are taking*⟩

**doorframe** /-,fraym/ *n* **1** a frame round the opening in which a door is fitted **2** the framework in which the panels of a door are fitted

**doorjamb** /'daw,jam/ *n* either of the upright posts forming the side of a door opening

**doorkeeper** /'daw,keepə/ *n* a person who guards or is employed to stand at the main door of a building and let people in and out

**doorknob** /'daw,nob/ *n* a knob that when turned releases a door latch

**doorknock** /'daw,nok/ *n, Austr* a political or charitable campaign in which helpers make door-to-door calls – **door-knocking** *n*

**doorman** /'dawmən/ *n* a (uniformed) person who stands at the entrance to a hotel, theatre, etc and assists people (e g by calling taxis)

**doormat** /'daw,mat/ *n* **1** a mat (e g of bristles) placed before or inside a door for wiping dirt from the shoes **2** *informal* an uncomplaining person who submits to bullying and indignities

**doornail** /'daw,nayl/ *n* a large-headed nail formerly used for the strengthening or decoration of doors – chiefly in *dead as a doornail*

**doorplate** /'daw,playt/ *n* a nameplate on a door

**doorpost** /'daw,pohst/ *n* a doorjamb

**doorsill** /'daw,sil/ *n* a horizontal sill, ledge, or low step forming the bottom of a doorframe

**doorstep** /'daw,step/ *n* **1** a step in front of an outer door **2** *Br informal* a very thick slice of bread

**doorstop** /'daw,stop/ *n* **1** a device (e g a wedge or weight) for holding a door open **2** a projection attached to a wall or floor to prevent a door opening too far, hitting a wall or piece of furniture, etc

¹,**door-to-'door** *adj* **1** being or making a usu unsolicited call (e g for selling, canvassing, etc) at every residence in an area ⟨*a* ∼ *salesman*⟩ **2** providing delivery to a specific address ⟨*direct* ∼ *service*⟩

²**door-to-door** *adv* from the precise point of departure to the final point of arrival ⟨*a journey of two hours* ∼⟩

**doorway** /'daw,way/ *n* **1** an entrance into a building or room that is closed by means of a door **2** a means of gaining access ⟨*exercise is a* ∼ *to good health*⟩

**dooryard** /'daw,yahd/ *n, NAm* a yard outside the door of a house

**dopa** /'dopə/ *n* a chemical compound, $(HO)_2C_6H_3CH_2CH(NH_2)COOH$, one form of which is the drug L-DOPA [*di*hydroxy*p*henyl*a*l*a*nine]

**dopamine** /'dopə,meen/ *n* a chemical compound, $(HO)_2C_6H_3(CH_2)_2NH_2$, that occurs esp as a NEUROTRANSMITTER (substance that transmits electrical impulses from one nerve to another) in the brain and as an intermediate compound in the synthesis of adrenalin in body tissue [*dopa* + *amine*]

**dopant** /'dohp(ə)nt/ *n* an impurity added, usu in minute amounts, to a pure substance to alter its properties [²*dope* + *-ant*]

¹**dope** /dohp/ *n* **1a** a thick liquid or pasty preparation **b** a preparation for giving a desired quality to a substance; *specif* an antiknock added to petrol **c** a coating (e g a cellulose varnish) applied to a surface or fabric (e g of an aeroplane or balloon) to improve strength, impermeability, or tautness **2** absorbent or adsorbent material used in various manufacturing processes (e g the making of dynamite) **3a** a preparation given illegally to a racehorse, greyhound, etc to make it run faster or slower **b** *informal* marijuana, opium, or another narcotic or addictive drug **4** *informal* a stupid person; a dolt **5** *informal* information, esp from a reliable source ⟨*inside* ∼ *on the scandal*⟩ [D *doop* sauce, fr *dopen* to dip; akin to OE *dyppan* to dip – more at DIP]

²**dope** *vt* **1** to treat or affect with dope; *esp* to give a drug to **2** to add an impurity to (a semiconductor) so as to give the required electrical properties (e g in the manufacture of microchips) ∼ *vi* to take dope – **doper** *n*

**dopey, dopy** /'dohpi/ *adj* **1** under the (weak) influence of a drug (e g an anaesthetic) or sleep; not wholly awake or fully alert **2** *informal* dull, stupid – **dopiness** *n*

**doppelgänger** /'dopl,gengə/, **doppelganger** /-,gangə/ *n* the ghost of a living person [Ger *doppelgänger*, fr *doppel-* double + *-gänger* goer, walker]

**Doppler** /'doplə/ *adj* of or using a shift in frequency in accordance with the Doppler effect

**Doppler effect** *n* a change in the apparent frequency of sound, light, or other waves when there is relative motion between the source and the observer [Christian *Doppler* †1853 Austrian scientist & mathematician]

**dorbeetle** /'daw,beetl/ *n* any of various beetles (family Geotrupidae) that fly with a buzzing sound; *specif* a common European DUNG BEETLE (*Geotrupes stercorarius*) [*dor* (buzzing insect), fr ME *dorre, dore*, fr OE *dora* bumblebee]

**Dorian** /'dawri-ən/ *n* a member of an ancient Hellenic race that completed the overthrow of MYCENAEAN civilization and settled chiefly in the Peloponnesus and Crete [L *dorius* of Doris, fr Gk *dōrios*, fr *Dōris*, region of ancient Greece] – **Dorian** *adj*

**dorian mode** *n, often cap D* a MODE (fixed arrangement of eight notes) which may be represented on the white keys of the piano on a scale from D to D [trans of Gk *dōria harmonia*]

¹**Doric** /'dorik/ *adj* **1** of the Dorians or their dialect of ancient Greek **2** of the oldest and simplest of the three Greek orders of architecture – compare CORINTHIAN 2, IONIC 2

²**Doric** *n* **1** a dialect of ancient Greek spoken esp in the Peloponnesus, Crete, Sicily, and southern Italy **2** a broad rustic dialect of English; *esp* a Scots one

**dorm** /dawm/ *n, informal* DORMITORY 1

**dormant** /'dawmənt/ *adj* **1** *of a heraldic animal* lying with the head on the forepaws **2** marked by a suspension of activity: e g **2a** temporarily showing no signs of external activity ⟨*a* ∼ *volcano*⟩ **b** temporarily in suspended or put on one side yet capable of being activated or resumed ⟨*the report lay ~ for several years until the new administration came into power*⟩ **3a** (appearing to be) asleep or inactive **b** having the faculties suspended; sluggish **c** having biological activity suspended: e g **c(1)** in a state of hibernation or total inactivity **c(2)** *of a plant part* not actively growing but protected (e g by bud scales) from the environment **4** associated with, carried out, or applied while dormant ⟨*~ grafting*⟩ *synonyms* see INACTIVE [ME, fixed, stationary, fr MF, fr prp of *dormir* to sleep, fr L *dormire;* akin to Skt *drāti* he sleeps] – **dormancy** *n*

**dormer** /'dawmə/ *n* **1 dormer, dormer window** a window set vertically on a sloping roof and joined to it by a small projecting roofed structure **2** a roofed structure containing a dormer window [MF *dormeor* dormitory, fr L *dormitorium*]

**dormie, dormy** /'dawmi/ *adj* having a lead in a game of golf of as many holes as remain to be played [origin unknown]

**dormin** /'dawmin/ *n* ABSCISIC ACID (plant hormone that causes leaves to fall off) [*dormancy* + *-in*]

**dormitory** /'dawmət(ə)ri/ *n* **1** a large room containing a number of beds, esp in a boarding school or hostel **2** a residential community from which the inhabitants commute to their places of employment **3** *chiefly NAm* a HALL OF RESIDENCE, esp of a university [L *dormitorium*, fr *dormitus*, pp of *dormire*]

**Dormobile** /'dawmə,beel/ *trademark* – used for a small motorized caravan

**dormouse** /'daw,mows/ *n* any of numerous small African and Eurasian rodents (family Gliridae) that resemble mice with long bushy tails; *esp* a common European rodent (*Muscardinus avellanarius*) [ME *dormowse*, perh fr MF *dormir* + ME *mous* mouse]

**dorp** /dawp/ *n, SAfr* a village [D, fr MD; akin to OHG *dorf* village]

**dorper** /'dawpə/ *n* (any of) a breed of sheep with white bodies and black faces bred, esp in southern Africa, for their mutton [*Dorset* Horn + Blackhead *Persian* (a breed of sheep)]

**dors-** /daws-/, **dorsi-, dorso-** *comb form* **1** back ⟨*dorsad*⟩ **2** dorsal and ⟨*dorso*lateral⟩ [LL *dors-*, fr L *dorsum*]

**¹dorsal** /'dawsl/ *adj* **1** of, being, or situated near or on the back or upper surface of an animal or of a body part; *also* of, being, on, or near a top or upper surface (e g of an aircraft) – compare VENTRAL **2** of, being, or situated on the surface of a plant structure that faces away from the centre or axis; ABAXIAL [LL *dorsalis*, fr L *dorsum* back] – **dorsally** *adv*

**²dorsal** *n* **1** a dorsally located part **2** DOSSAL (cloth hung behind an altar)

**dorsal fin** *n* a vertical fin that extends lengthways along the midline of the back of a fish, dolphin, etc

**dorsal lip** *n* (the part of the embryo of a bird or mammal corresponding to) the rear edge of the opening (BLASTOPORE) that forms in the wall of the embryo of an amphibian at a very early stage in its development, containing cells that control further development of the embryo and cause the formation of nerve tissue

**dorsal root** *n* the one of the two ROOTS of a SPINAL NERVE that passes into the SPINAL CORD from the back part of the body and consists of fibres carrying information from the sense organs – compare VENTRAL ROOT

**dorset horn** /'dawsit/ *n, often cap* (any of) an English breed of sheep that have very large horns [*Dorset*, county of England]

**dorsiventral** /,dawsi'ventrəl/ *adj* **1** *esp of a leaf* having distinct upper and lower surfaces **2** DORSOVENTRAL 1 – **dorsiventrally** *adv*, **dorsiventrality** *n*

**dorsolateral** /,dawsoh'lat(ə)rəl/ *adj* of or involving both the back and the sides – **dorsolaterally** *adv*

**dorsoventral** /,dawsoh'ventrəl/ **1** extending from the dorsal side (e g the back) to the ventral side (e g the belly) **2** DORSIVENTRAL 1 [ISV] – **dorsoventrally** *adv*, **dorsoventrality** *n*

**dorsum** /'dawsəm/ *n, pl* **dorsa** /-sə/ **1** the back; *specif* the entire dorsal surface of an animal **2** the upper surface of an appendage or part [L]

**dorter** /'dawtə/ *n* the dormitory of a medieval monastery [ME, fr OF *dortoir*, fr L *dormitorium* – more at DORMITORY]

**¹dory** /'dawri/ *n* JOHN DORY (edible sea fish)

**²dory** *n* a flat-bottomed boat with high flaring sides and a sharp bow [Miskito *dóri* dugout]

**dos-à-dos** /,doh za 'doh/ *n* a seat (e g in a carriage) designed for sitting back to back – compare TÊTE-À-TÊTE **2** [Fr, fr *dos-à-dos* back to back]

**dosage** /'dohsij/ *n* **1** (the regulation or determination of) the amount of a therapeutic agent (e g a drug or electric shock)

given; *also* the act of giving a single dose or instalment of such an agent **2a** the addition of an ingredient or the application of an agent in a measured dose **b** the presence and relative representation or strength of a gene or genetic characteristic

**¹dose** /dohs/ *n* **1a** the measured quantity of a therapeutic agent (e g medicine or electric shock) to be taken or given at one time **b** the quantity of radiation administered or absorbed or to which somebody or something is or has been exposed **2** a measured portion of a substance; *esp* one added to affect a chemical process **3** a period of exposure to something unpleasant ⟨*a ~ of hard work*⟩ ⟨*a ~ of flu*⟩ **4** *informal* a venereal disease ⟨*caught a ~*⟩ [Fr, fr LL *dosis*, fr Gk, lit., act of giving, fr *didonai* to give – more at DATE]

**²dose** *vt* **1** to divide (e g a medicine) into doses **2** to give a dose, esp of medicine, to

**dosimeter** /doh'simitə/ *n* a device for measuring the amount of X-rays or of radioactivity to which somebody or something has been exposed [LL *dosis* + ISV *-meter*] – **dosimetric** *adj*, **dosimetry** *n*

**¹doss** /dos/ *n, chiefly Br informal* **1** a crude or makeshift bed, esp one in a dosshouse **2** a short sleep; a snooze **3** a very easy 'task; a pushover [perh fr obs *dorse, doss* back, fr L *dorsum*]

**²doss** *vi, chiefly Br informal* to sleep or bed down in a makeshift bed – often + *down* ⟨*we can ~ down here*⟩

**dossal, dossel** /'dosl/ *n* an ornamental cloth hung behind and above an altar – called also DORSAL [ML *dossale, dorsale,* neut of LL *dorsalis* dorsal]

**dosser** /'dosə/ *n, chiefly Br informal* a person with no fixed address and little or no money who sleeps where he/she can; a down-and-out; *esp* one who is forced to sleep in dosshouses

**dosshouse** /-,hows/ *n, chiefly Br* a cheap hostel, esp one used by tramps or derelicts

**dossier** /'dosi-ə, 'dosiay/ *n* a file of papers containing a detailed report or detailed information [Fr, bundle of documents labelled on the back, dossier, fr *dos* back, fr L *dorsum*]

**dost** /dust/ *archaic pres 2 sing of* DO

**¹dot** /dot/ *n* **1** a small spot; a speck **2a(1)** a small point, made with a pointed instrument ⟨*a ~ on the chart marked the ship's position*⟩ **a(2)** a small round mark used in spelling or punctuation ⟨*put a ~ over the* i⟩ **b** a point placed between two values as a multiplication sign **c(1)** a point after a note or rest in music indicating increase of the time value by one half of its original value **c(2)** a point over or under a musical note indicating that it is to be played STACCATO **3** a precise point, esp in time ⟨*arrived at six on the ~*⟩ **4** a signal (e g a flash or an audible tone) of relatively short duration that is one of the two fundamental units of MORSE CODE – compare ²DASH 7; see also **since the** YEAR dot [(assumed) ME, fr OE *dott* head of a boil; akin to OHG *tutta* nipple] – **dotty** *adj*

**²dot** *vb* **-tt-** *vt* **1** to mark with a dot **2** to intersperse with dots or objects scattered at random ⟨*boats ~ting the lake*⟩ ⟨*~ted with butter*⟩ ~ *vi* to make a dot – **dotter** *n*

**³dot** *n* DOWRY **1** [Fr, fr L *dot-, dos* dowry]

**dotage** /'dohtij/ *n* a state or period of senile mental decay resulting in feeblemindedness [ME, fr *doten* to dote]

**dotard** /'dohtəd/ *n* a person in his/her dotage

**dote** /doht/ *vi* **1** to exhibit mental feebleness of or like that of old age **2** to show excessive or foolish affection or fondness – usu + *on* ⟨*~d on her only grandchild*⟩ *synonyms* see LOVING [ME *doten;* akin to MLG *dotten* to be foolish] – **doter** *n*, **dotingly** *adv*

**doth** /duth/ *archaic pres 3 sing of* DO

**dot product** *n, maths* SCALAR PRODUCT (product of two vectors) [¹*dot;* fr its being commonly written *A·B*]

**dotterel** /'dotrəl/ *n* (any of various Australasian and S American birds related to) a Eurasian plover (*Eudromias morinellus*) that breeds on tundra and high stony ground and was formerly common in Britain [ME *dotrelle*, fr *doten* to dote + *-erelle* (as in *cokerelle* cockerel); fr its alleged foolishness in allowing itself to be caught]

**dottle** /'dotl/ *n* (partially) unburnt tobacco caked in the bowl of a pipe after smoking [ME *dottel* plug, fr (assumed) ME *dot*]

**dotty** /'doti/ *adj, informal* **1** mentally unbalanced; crazy ⟨*thought the man was ~ for paying the boys so much money*⟩ **2** amiably eccentric or absurd ⟨*an absentminded ~ old man*⟩ ⟨*some sublimely ~ exchanges of letters*⟩ **3** fond or infatuated, esp to excess – + *about* ⟨*she is completely ~ about animals*⟩ [alter. of Sc *dottle* fool, fr ME *dotel*, fr *doten*] – **dottily** *adv*, **dottiness** *n*

**douane** /dooh'ahn, dwahn (*Fr* dwan)/ *n* a customs house on the

Continent [Fr, fr MF, fr OIt *doana*, fr Ar *dīwān*, fr Per, account book (cf DEWAN, DIVAN)]

**Douay Version** /'dooh,ay/ *n* an English translation of the Bible from the Latin Vulgate version, published in 1582 and 1609 and used by Roman Catholics [*Douay, Douai*, city in France]

¹**double** /'dubl/ *adj* **1** having a twofold relation or character; dual **2** consisting of two, usu combined, similar members or parts ⟨*an egg with a ~ yolk*⟩ **3a** twice as great or as many ⟨*~ the number of applicants*⟩ **b** *of a coin* worth two of the specified amount ⟨*~ eagle*⟩ ⟨*~ crown*⟩ **4** marked by duplicity; deceitful ⟨*he was our most trusted man and yet all the time he was playing a ~ game*⟩ **5** folded in two **6** of twofold or extra size, strength, or value ⟨*a ~ Scotch*⟩ ⟨*a ~ room*⟩ **7** *of a (cultivated) plant or flower* having more than the normal number of petals or SEPALS (petal-like parts) – compare SINGLE [ME, fr OF, fr L *duplus*, fr *duo* two + *-plus* multiplied by; akin to Gk di*ploos* double, OE *fealdan* to fold – more at TWO, FOLD] – **doubleness** *n*

usage Double is used in British but not in American English for saying letters and telephone numbers. Compare ⟨*(Br) one oh double six*⟩ ⟨*(NAm) one zero six six*⟩.

²**double** *n* **1** something twice the usual size, strength, speed, quantity, amount, or value; *esp* a double measure of spirits **2** the counterpart of another; a duplicate ⟨*I haven't got exactly the same model but I have its ~*⟩: e g **2a** a living person who closely resembles another living person **b** a wraith, doppelgänger **c(1)** an understudy **c(2)** one who resembles an actor and takes his/her place in scenes calling for special skills **c(3)** an actor who plays more than one role in a production **3** a sharp turn or reversal **4a** a bet involving two selections in different events (e g horse races) such that, if the first selection is successful, the stake and winnings are bet on the second **b** two wins in or on horse races (e g by a jockey or punter), esp in a single day's racing **5** an act of doubling in a card game **6** the outermost narrow ring on a dartboard that counts as double the stated score; *also* a throw in darts that lands there **7** a set of two obstacles for a horse to jump consecutively – **at/on the double 1** at a rate between running and walking; *specif, of a military order* to move in double time **2** at a fast rate; immediately

³**double** *adv* **1** to twice the extent or amount **2** two together ⟨*see ~*⟩ – see also **double or** QUITS

⁴**double** /'dubling, 'dubl·ing/ *vt* **1** to make twice as great or as many: e g **1a** to increase by adding an equal amount **b** to amount to twice the number of ⟨*this list ~s the previous one*⟩ **c** to make a call in bridge that increases the value of tricks won or lost on (an opponent's bid) **2a** to make two thicknesses of; fold **b** to clench ⟨*~d his fist*⟩ **c** to cause to stoop or bend over – usu + *up* or *over* **3** to cause (a billiard or snooker ball) to rebound from the cushioned edge of the table **4** to reinforce (a musical note or part) with another either at the same pitch or at an octave above or below **~** *vi* **1a** to become twice as much or as many ⟨*the population ~d in ten years*⟩ **b** to double a bid (e g in bridge) **2a(1)** to turn sharply and suddenly; *esp* to turn back on one's course – usu + *back* **a(2)** to follow a circuitous course – often + *back* **3** to become bent or stooped usu in or from the middle – usu + *up* or *over* ⟨*he ~d up in pain*⟩ **4** to serve an additional purpose or perform an additional duty – usu + *as* ⟨*the bed ~s as a couch during the day*⟩ **5** to hurry along; *esp, of troops* to move at the double **6** *of a billiard or snooker ball* to rebound from the cushioned edge of the table – **doubler** *n*

**double up** *vi* to share a room or bed designed for one

'**double-,acting** *adj* acting or effective in two directions or ways; *esp, of an engine* having a piston that is moved backwards and forwards by pressure (e g from steam) that is applied alternately to each side of the piston

**double agent** *n* a spy pretending to serve one government while actually serving another

**double bar** *n* two adjacent vertical lines or a heavy single line on a stave marking the end of a musical composition or a section within it

,**double-'barrelled** *adj* **1** *of a firearm* having two barrels **2** having or serving a double purpose ⟨*asked a ~ question*⟩ **3** *of a surname* having two parts

**double bass** /bays/ *n* the largest and lowest-ranged instrument of the violin family – called also BASS, CONTRABASS – **double bassist** *n*

**double bassoon** *n* CONTRABASSOON (bassoon of very low range)

**double bed** *n* a bed designed for two people to sleep in

**double bill** *n* a programme (e g at a theatre or cinema) offering two principal attractions

**double bind** *n* (a psychological dilemma provoked by) a situation in which a person receives conflicting cues as to the behaviour expected of him/her towards another, usu a parent or other family member, so that anything he/she does will be considered wrong; *broadly* a situation where any choice a person makes will have unpleasant consequences

,**double-'blind** *adj* of or being an experimental procedure which is designed to eliminate false results due to the expectations of the experimenters or to PLACEBO EFFECTS, and in which neither the subjects nor the experimenters know the make-up of the test groups and control groups during the actual course of the experiments – compare SINGLE-BLIND

**double boiler** *n, chiefly NAm* DOUBLE SAUCEPAN

**double bond** *n* a chemical bond consisting of two COVALENT BONDS (chemical bonds, each consisting of a shared pair of electrons) between two atoms in a molecule – compare TRIPLE BOND

,**double-'breasted** *adj* having a front fastening with one half of the front overlapping the other and usu a double row of buttons and a single row of buttonholes ⟨*a ~ coat*⟩ – compare SINGLE-BREASTED

**double bridle** *n* a bridle that consists of two bits, each with a pair of reins, that work independently and that is used esp on show horses

**double check** *n* a careful check to determine accuracy, condition, or progress, esp of something already checked – **double-check** *vb*

**double chin** *n* a chin with a fleshy fold under it

**double counterpoint** *n, music* two-part COUNTERPOINT so constructed that either part may be played above or below the other

**double cream** *n* thick heavy cream that contains 48 per cent butterfat and is suitable for whipping – compare SINGLE CREAM

,**double-'cross** *vt* to deceive by double-dealing; betray – **double-crosser** *n*

**double cross** *n* **1** an act of betraying or cheating an associate **2** a cross between the first generation of organisms that result from the cross of four separate pure lines (e g in the production of hybrid seed corn)

**double dagger** *n* a sign ‡ used in printing as a (third) cross reference mark, esp to a footnote

,**double-'dashed** *adj, Br* marked with a double dash (e g to indicate that a mathematical function is to be differentiated twice)

¹,**double-'dealing** *n* underhand or deceitful action; duplicity – **double-dealer** *n*

²**double-dealing** *adj* given to or marked by deceit or duplicity

**double-decker** /'dekə/ *n* something that has two decks, levels, or layers: e g **a** a bus with seats on two floors **b** a sandwich made with three slices of bread enclosing two separate layers of filling

**double declutch** /dee'kluch/ *vi, Br* to change gear in a motor vehicle by disengaging the gear twice, first to pass to neutral, then to pass to the desired gear

**double decomposition** *n* a chemical reaction in which two different chemical compounds exchange parts to form two new compounds

**double doors** *n pl* an opening with two vertical doors that meet in the middle of the opening when closed – compare DUTCH DOOR

**double dutch** *n, often cap 2nd D, informal* speech or writing that is unintelligible or nonsensical; gibberish

,**double-'edged** *adj* **1** having two cutting edges **2a** having a dual purpose or effect ⟨*a spy with a ~ mission*⟩ **b** capable of being understood or interpreted in two different ways; *specif, of a remark* seeming innocent but capable of being interpreted as malicious

,**double-'ended** *adj* similar at both ends ⟨*a ~ bolt*⟩

**double entendre** /,doohbl on'ton(h)dr (*Fr* dubl ãtãdr)/ *n, pl* **double entendres** /~/ an ambiguous word or phrase, one of whose meanings usu has a risqué connotation [obs Fr, lit., double meaning]

**double entry** *n* a method of bookkeeping that recognizes both the receiving and the giving sides of a business transaction by debiting the amount of the transaction to one account and crediting it to another account so that the total debits equal the total credits

,**double-'faced** *adj* **1** having two faces or sides designed for use ⟨*a ~ bookshelf*⟩ **2** two-faced, hypocritical

**double fault** *n* two consecutive service faults in tennis, squash, etc resulting in the loss of a point or of the service – **double-fault** *vi*

**double feature** *n* a cinema programme consisting of two full-length films

**double fertil·ization, -isation** *n* fertilization characteristic of FLOWERING PLANTS in which one of the two sperm nuclei from a pollen cell fuses with the nucleus of the egg to form an embryo, and the other sperm nucleus fuses with an adjacent nucleus to form ENDOSPERM for nourishing the developing embryo

**double first** *n, Br* first-class honours gained either in two parts of a university course or in two university subjects

**double flat** *n* a character on the musical stave indicating a drop in pitch of two semitones

**double glazing** *n* a system of glazing in which two panes of glass are separated by an air space providing heat and sound insulation; *also* the two panes of glass so used – **double-glaze** *vt*

**Double Gloucester** /'glostə/ *n* a rich golden-orange coloured cheese with a firm smooth texture and a flavour that ranges from mellow to sharp as the cheese matures [*Gloucester*shire, county of England]

**doubleheader** /-'hedə/ *n* **1** a train pulled by two locomotives **2** *NAm* two games, contests, or events held consecutively during the same programme

**double helix** *n* two parallel HELICES that spiral round the same central axis; *specif* this arrangement of two COMPLEMENTARY (fitting together exactly) strands of DNA in which the BASES of each strand point inwards and are linked by HYDROGEN BONDS

,**double-'hung** *adj, of a window sash* supported on each side by a counterweighted sash cord to facilitate raising, lowering, and holding position

**double hyphen** *n* a punctuation mark = used in place of a hyphen at the end of a line to indicate that the word so divided is normally hyphenated

**double indemnity** *n* a provision in a life or accident insurance policy whereby the company agrees to pay twice the sum specified on the face of the contract in case of accidental death

**double jeopardy** *n* the putting of a person on trial for an offence for which he/she has already been validly tried

,**double-'jointed** *adj* having or being a joint that permits an exceptional degree of flexibility of the parts joined

**double knit** *n* a knitted fabric (e g wool) made with a double set of needles to produce a double thickness of fabric with each thickness joined by interlocking stitches

**double meaning** *n* DOUBLE ENTENDRE

**double negative** *n* a now substandard syntactic construction containing two negatives and having a negative meaning ⟨*"I didn't hear nothing" is a ~*⟩ – see "Ten Vexed Points"

,**double-'park** *vb* to park (a vehicle) beside a row of vehicles already parked parallel to the curb

**double precision** *n* the use of two computer WORDS (units of computer memory) rather than one to represent a number in order to allow more accurate calculations to be made

,**double-'quick** *n* very quick – **double-quick** *adv*

**double reed** *n* two cane reeds bound and vibrating against each other and used as the mouthpiece of woodwind instruments of the oboe family

**double refraction** *n* BIREFRINGENCE (splitting of a ray of light into two)

**doubles** /'dublz/ *n, pl* **doubles** a game (e g of tennis) between two pairs of players

**double salt** *n* **1** a chemical SALT (e g alum) containing two negative or positive chemical groups or atoms combined with one oppositely charged chemical group or atom **2** a chemical SALT regarded as a molecular combination of two simpler salts

**double saucepan** *n, Br* a cooking utensil consisting of two saucepans fitting into each other, the contents of the upper being cooked or heated by boiling water in the lower

**double sharp** *n* a character on the musical stave indicating a rise in pitch of two semitones

'**double-,space** *vt* to type (copy) leaving alternate lines blank ~ *vi* to type on every other line

**doublespeak** /-,speek/ *n* DOUBLE-TALK 2

**double standard** *n* **1** BIMETALLISM (use of two metals simultaneously as a monetary standard) **2** a principle or code that is

applied differently and usu more rigorously to one group of people or circumstances than to another

**double star** *n* **1** BINARY STAR (system of two stars rotating round each other) **2** two stars in very nearly the same line of sight but seen as physically separate by means of a telescope

**double stopping** *n* the simultaneous playing of two strings of a bowed instrument (e g a violin)

**double sugar** *n* DISACCHARIDE (sugar whose molecules consist of two simple sugar molecules combined)

**doublet** /'dublit/ *n* **1** a man's close-fitting jacket, with or without sleeves, worn in Europe, esp in the 15th to 17th centuries **2** something consisting of two identical or similar parts: e g **2a** a compound lens consisting of two simple lenses **b** a pair of lines of colour in a spectrum that are very close together **c** a domino with the same number of spots on each end **3** a set of two identical or similar things; *specif* two thrown dice showing the same number on the upper face **4** either of a pair; *specif* either of two words (e g *poison* and *potion*) in the same language having the same original derivation but different meanings [ME, fr MF, fr *double*]

**double take** *n* a delayed reaction to a surprising or significant situation, esp after an initial failure to notice anything unusual – chiefly in *do a double take*

'**double-,talk** *n* **1** language that appears to be earnest and meaningful but in fact is a mixture of sense and nonsense **2** inflated, involved, and often deliberately ambiguous language – **double-talk** *vi*, **double-talker** *n*

,**double-'team** *vt, chiefly NAm* to block or guard (an opponent) with two players at one time

**doublethink** /-,think/ *n* a simultaneous belief in two contradictory ideas

**double time** *n* **1** a US rate of marching of 180 36-inch (about 0·9 m) steps per minute **2** payment of a worker at twice his/her regular wage rate

,**double-'tongue** *vi* to move the tongue alternately between the positions for *t* and *k* so as to produce a fast succession of detached notes on a wind instrument

**double twill** *n* a TWILL weave with intersecting diagonal lines going in opposite directions

**double vision** *n* DIPLOPIA (condition in which each eye forms a separate image)

**doubloon** /dub'loohn/ *n* a former gold coin of Spain and Spanish America [Sp *doblón*, aug of *dobla*, an old Spanish coin, fr L *dupla*, fem of *duplus* double – more at DOUBLE]

**doubly** /'dubli/ *adv* **1** to twice the degree ⟨*~ pleased*⟩ **2** in two ways; on two counts ⟨*~ mistaken*⟩

¹**doubt** /dowt/ *vt* **1** to be in doubt about ⟨*he ~s everyone's word*⟩ **2a** to lack confidence in; distrust ⟨*find myself ~ing him even when I know that he is honest* – H L Mencken⟩ **b** to consider unlikely ⟨*I ~ that it is authentic*⟩ ~ *vi* to be uncertain [ME *douten* to fear, be uncertain, fr OF *douter* to doubt, fr L *dubitare*; akin to L *dubius* dubious – more at DUBIOUS] – **doubtable** *adj*, **doubter** *n*, **doubtingly** *adv*

²**doubt** *n* **1** (a state of) uncertainty of belief or opinion **2** a lack of confidence; distrust **3** an inclination not to believe or accept; a reservation – **in doubt** uncertain – **no doubt** DOUBTLESS **1** – see also **give somebody the** BENEFIT **of the doubt**

    **synonyms** Without **doubt** and **undoubtedly** express a stronger sense of certainty than do **no doubt** or **doubtless**, either of which may mean no more than "probably" or "I think". See UNCERTAINTY **antonyms** certitude, confidence **usage** In positive sentences, **doubt** (both verb and noun) and **doubtful** are correctly followed by *whether* or less formally by *if* ⟨*I* doubt *whether/if she'll come*⟩ ⟨*there's some* doubt *whether/if she'll come*⟩ ⟨*it's* doubtful *whether/if she'll come*⟩. The use of *that* in such situations is fairly well established in American English, particularly where **doubt** means "think it unlikely" ⟨*I* doubt *that he stole it*⟩. The noun **doubt** is also used with *about* ⟨*there's no* doubt *about it*⟩ and *as to* ⟨*there's some* doubt *as to her sanity*⟩. In negative sentences and questions, **doubt** and **doubtful** are followed by *that* or *but that* ⟨*I don't* doubt *[but] that she'll come*⟩ ⟨*is there any* doubt *[but] that he stole it?*⟩ Some writers on usage advise against using *but* here.

**doubtful** /-f(ə)l/ *adj* **1** giving rise to doubt; open to question ⟨*it is ~ that they ever knew what happened*⟩ ⟨*a ~ proposition*⟩ **2a** lacking a definite opinion or conviction; hesitant, unconvinced ⟨*they were ~ about the advantages of the new system*⟩ **b** uncertain in outcome; not settled ⟨*the outcome of the election remains ~*⟩ **3** of questionable worth, honesty, or validity *usage* see ²DOUBT – **doubtfully** *adv*, **doubtfulness** *n*

**doubting Thomas** /'toməs/ *n* a habitually doubtful person

[*Thomas*, apostle of Jesus who doubted Jesus' resurrection until he had proof of it (Jn 20:24–29)]

**doubtless** /-lis/ *adv* 1 without doubt 2 probably *synonyms* see ²DOUBT

**douce** /doohs/ *adj, chiefly Scot* sober, sedate ⟨*mourners with ~ faces*⟩ [ME, sweet, pleasant, fr MF, fr fem of *douz*, fr L *dulcis*] – **doucely** *adv*

**douceur** /dooh'suh (*Fr* dusœːr)/ *n* a conciliatory gift; a tip or bribe [Fr, pleasantness, fr LL *dulcor* sweetness, fr L *dulcis* sweet]

**douche** /doohsh/ *n* 1a a jet or current, esp of water, directed against a part or into a cavity of the body, esp the vagina b an act of cleansing with a douche 2 a device for giving douches [Fr, fr It *doccia*, fr *docciare* to douche, fr *doccia* water pipe, prob back-formation fr *doccione* conduit, fr L *duction-*, *ductio* action of leading, fr *ductus*, pp of *ducere* to lead – more at TOW] – **douche** *vb*

**dough** /doh/ *n* 1 a mixture that consists essentially of flour or meal and milk, water, or another liquid and is stiff enough to knead or roll – compare BATTER 2 something resembling dough, esp in consistency 3 *slang* money [ME *dogh*, fr OE *dāg*; akin to OHG *teic* dough, L *fingere* to shape, Gk *teichos* wall] – **doughlike** *adj*

**doughboy** /'doh,boy/ *n, informal* an American infantryman, esp in World War I [*doughboy* (a dumpling or piece of fried bread dough); prob fr the large round buttons on US infantry uniform in the Civil War]

**doughnut** /'doh,nut/ *n* 1 a small round or ring-shaped cake that is often made with a yeast dough, filled with jam, and deep-fried 2 something that is ring-shaped; *specif, maths* TORUS 4 (ring-shaped surface)

**doughty** /'dowti/ *adj, poetic* valiant, bold [ME, fr OE *dohtig*; akin to OHG *toug* is useful, Gk *teuchein* to make] – **doughtily** *adv*, **doughtiness** *n*

**doughy** /'doh·i/ *adj* 1 not thoroughly baked 2 unhealthily pale; pasty ⟨*a ~ complexion*⟩

**Douglas fir** /'duglas/ *n* a tall evergreen US tree (*Pseudotsuga menziesii*) of the pine family with large hanging cones, that is extensively grown for its wood [David *Douglas* †1834 Sc botanist]

**Douglas spruce** *n* DOUGLAS FIR

**Doukhobor** /'doohkohbaw/ *n* a member of a Christian sect originating in Russia in the 18th century that emphasizes obedience to the INNER LIGHT and rejection of church and civil authority [Russ *dukhoborets*, fr *dukh* spirit + *borets* wrestler]

**dour** /dooə, dowə/ *adj* 1 stern, harsh 2 obstinate, unyielding 3 gloomy, sullen [ME, prob fr Gael *dur* dull, obstinate, perh fr L *durus* hard] – **dourly** *adv*, **dourness** *n*

    *usage* The pronunciation /dooə/ is recommended for BBC broadcasters.

**douroucouli** /,doohrooh'koohli/ *n* any of several nocturnal S American monkeys (genus *Aotus*) [native name in S America]

¹**douse, dowse** /dows, dowz/ *vt* 1a to take (a sail) in or down b to slacken ⟨*~ a rope*⟩ 2 *archaic* to doff ⟨*~d my cap on entering the porch* – W M Thackeray⟩ [*douse*, n (blow, stroke), of unknown origin]

²**douse, dowse** /dowz/ *vt* 1 to plunge into water 2 to drench (as if) with liquid, esp water, in order to clean 3 to extinguish ⟨*~ the lights*⟩ [prob fr obs *douse* to smite, fr *douse*, n]

    *usage* Neither of the two **douse** verbs should be confused with the verb **dowse** that means "search for water".

¹**dove** /duv/ *n* 1 any of numerous pigeons (eg a COLLARED DOVE or ROCK DOVE) that are usu smaller and slenderer than the domestic pigeon 2 one who takes a conciliatory attitude (eg in a dispute) and advocates negotiations and compromise; *esp* an opponent of war – usu contrasted with *hawk synonyms* see PIGEON [ME, fr (assumed) OE *dūfe*; akin to OHG *tūba* dove] – **dovish** *adj*, **dovishness** *n*

²**dove** /dohv/ *NAm* past of DIVE

**dove-colour** /duv/ *n* a warm grey colour with a slight pinkish tint – **dove-coloured** *adj*

**dovecot, dovecote** /'duv,kot/ *n* a small compartmented raised house or box for domestic pigeons

**dovekie** /'duvki/ *n* LITTLE AUK (small seabird) [dim. of *dove*]

**doven** /'dovən/ *vi* DAVEN (utter Jewish prayers)

**Dover sole** /'dohvə/ *n* a European sole (*Solea solea*) highly valued for food [prob fr *Dover*, town in SE England]

**Dover's powder** *n* a powder of IPECACUANHA and opium used, esp formerly, to relieve pain and stimulate sweating [Thomas *Dover* †1742 E physician]

¹**dovetail** /'duv,tayl/ *n* 1 **dovetail, dovetail tenon** a TENON that widens towards its end 2 **dovetail, dovetail joint** a joint using dovetail tenons (eg to fit two pieces of wood together at right angles)

²**dovetail** *vt* 1a to join by means of dovetails b to cut to a dovetail 2 to fit skilfully together to form a whole ~ *vi* to fit together into a whole

**dowager** /'dowəjə/ *n* 1 a widow holding property or a title received from her deceased husband 2 a dignified elderly woman [MF *douagiere*, fr *douage* dower, fr *douer* to endow, fr L *dotare*, fr *dot-*, *dos* gift, dower – more at DOWRY]

¹**dowdy** /'dowdi/ *n, archaic* a dowdy woman [dim. of *dowd* (dowdy person), fr ME *doude*]

²**dowdy** *adj* 1 not smart or becoming in appearance; dull 2 old-fashioned, frumpy – **dowdily** *adv*, **dowdiness** *n*, **dowdyish** *adj*

¹**dowel** /'dowəl/ *n* 1 a usu metal or wooden headless pin fitting into holes in abutting or jointed pieces to keep them from coming apart; *also* material (eg wood) in the form of a cylindrical rod used esp for cutting up into dowels 2 a piece of wood driven into a wall so that other pieces can be nailed to it [ME *dowle*; akin to OHG *tubili* plug, LGk *typhos* wedge]

²**dowel** *vt* -**ll**- (*Nam* -**l**-, -**ll**-) to fasten by or provide with dowels

¹**dower** /'dowə/ *n* 1 a widow's legal share during her life of her deceased husband's property – no longer used technically 2 *archaic* a dowry [ME *dowere*, fr MF *douaire*, modif of ML *dotarium* – more at DOWRY]

²**dower** *vt* to supply with a dower or dowry; endow

**dower house** *n* a house provided for a widow, often on the estate of her deceased husband; *broadly* any small house on a country estate

**Dow-Jones average** *n* a daily index of the relative prices of shares on the New York stock exchange based on the daily average prices of a selected number of ordinary shares [Charles H *Dow* †1902 & Edward D *Jones* †1920 US financial statisticians]

**Dow-Jones index** *n* DOW-JONES AVERAGE

**dowlas** /'dowləs/ *n* 1 a rough linen fabric used for clothing in former times 2 a strong cotton fabric of coarse yarn used esp for household cloths and towels [*Daoulas*, town in Brittany, France]

¹**down** /down/ *n* 1 **downs** *pl*, **down** an undulating treeless usu chalk upland, esp in S England 2 *often cap* a sheep of any breed originating in the downs of S England [ME *doun* hill, fr OE *dūn*; akin to ON *dūnn* down of feathers]

²**down** *adv* 1a at or towards a relatively low level; *specif* towards the centre of the earth ⟨*~ into the cellar*⟩ ⟨*the river is ~*⟩ b downwards from the surface of the earth or water c below the horizon d downstream e in or into a lying or sitting position ⟨*lie ~*⟩ f to or on the ground, surface, or bottom ⟨*house burnt ~*⟩ ⟨*telephone wires are ~*⟩ g so as to conceal a particular surface ⟨*turned it face ~*⟩ h within the body as the result of swallowing ⟨*keep the medicine ~*⟩ i downstairs 2 in cash on the spot; *esp* as an initial payment ⟨*paid £10 ~*⟩ 3a(1) in or into a relatively low condition or status ⟨*family has come ~ in the world*⟩ – sometimes used interjectionally to express opposition or distaste ⟨*~ with the oppressors!*⟩ a(2) to prison – often + *go* or *send* b(1) in or into a state of relatively low intensity or activity ⟨*calm ~*⟩ ⟨*settle ~*⟩ ⟨*turn the radio ~*⟩ b(2) into silence ⟨*shouted him ~*⟩ b(3) into a slower pace or lower gear ⟨*changed ~ into second*⟩ c lower in amount, price, figure, or rank ⟨*prices are coming ~*⟩ ⟨*bacon's ~*⟩ d behind an opponent ⟨*we're three points ~*⟩ 4a so as to be known, recognized, or recorded, esp on paper ⟨*had it ~ pat*⟩ ⟨*scribbled it ~*⟩ ⟨*you're ~ to speak next*⟩ – compare SET DOWN, PUT DOWN b in or into storage; by – compare LAY DOWN c so as to be firmly held in position ⟨*stick ~ the flap of the envelope*⟩ ⟨*don't like to feel tied ~*⟩ d to the moment of catching or discovering ⟨*track the criminal ~*⟩ 5 in a direction conventionally the opposite of up: eg 5a toward b in or towards the south c *chiefly Br* away from the capital of a country or from a university city ⟨*~ in Wiltshire*⟩ d to or at the front of a theatrical stage 6 DOWNWARDS 3,4 ⟨*jewels handed ~ in the family*⟩ 7a to a concentrated state ⟨*got his report ~ to three pages*⟩ – compare BOIL DOWN b so as to be flattened, reduced, eroded, or diluted ⟨*water ~ the gin*⟩ ⟨*heels worn ~*⟩ c completely from top to bottom ⟨*hose the car ~*⟩ [ME *doun*, fr OE *dūne*, short for *adūne*, *of dūne*, fr a- (fr *of*), *of* off, from + *dūne*, dat of *dūn* hill] – **down to** – used to indicate a downward

limit or boundary ⟨*from the President* down to *the office boy*⟩ – **take something lying down** to accept something without protest or resistance

³**down** *adj* **1a** directed or going downwards ⟨*the ~ escalator*⟩ **b** behind an opponent (eg in points scored) ⟨*~ by two goals*⟩ **2a** depressed, dejected **b** ill ⟨*~ with flu*⟩ **3** having been finished or dealt with ⟨*eight ~ and two to go*⟩ **4** with the rudder to windward – used with reference to a ship's helm **5** *chiefly Br* bound in a direction conventionally regarded as down ⟨*the ~ train from London*⟩ – compare UP – **down for** on the list to enter (eg a race or school) – **down on** having a low opinion of or grudge against ⟨*always been* down on *him*⟩ – **down to 1** reduced to ⟨down to *my last penny*⟩ **2** – used to indicate a downward limit or boundary ⟨*I've sold everything*, down to *the teapot*⟩ **3a** to be attributed to ⟨*murders are* down to *the Kray gang*⟩ **b** being the responsibility of; UP TO **5** – **down under** (in or into) Australia or New Zealand

⁴**down** *prep* **1a** down along, round, through, towards, in, into, or on **b** at the bottom of ⟨*the bathroom is ~ those stairs*⟩ **2** *Br nonstandard* down to; to ⟨*going ~ the shops*⟩

⁵**down** *n* a grudge, prejudice – often in *have a down on*

⁶**down** *vt* **1** to cause to go or come down **2** *informal* to swallow quickly ⟨*he ~ed his pint of beer*⟩ **3** *informal* to defeat – see also **down** TOOLS

⁷**down** *n* a covering of soft fluffy feathers [ME *doun*, fr ON *dūnn*]

,**down-and-'out** *adj* destitute, impoverished – **down-and-out** *n*

¹**downbeat** /'down,beet/ *n* **1** the downward stroke of a conductor indicating the principally accented note of a bar of music; *also* the principally accented (eg the first) note of a bar **2** a decline in activity or prosperity

²**downbeat** *adj, informal* **1** pessimistic, gloomy **2** relaxed, informal

'**down-,bow** /boh/ *n* a stroke in playing a stringed instrument (eg a violin) in which the bow is drawn across the strings from the handle (NUT 4b) to the tip

**down calver** *n, Br* a cow that is nearly ready to calve – **down-calving** *adj*

¹**downcast** /'downkahst/ *adj* **1** dejected, depressed **2** directed downwards ⟨*with ~ eyes*⟩

²**downcast** *n* a ventilation shaft in a mine – compare UPCAST

**downdraught** /'down,drahft/ *n* a downward movement of gas, esp air (eg in a chimney)

**down east** *adv or adj, often cap D&E, NAm* in or into the northeast coastal section of the USA and parts of the Maritime Provinces of Canada; *specif* in or into coastal Maine

**downer** /'downə/ *n, informal* **1** a depressant drug; *esp* a barbiturate **2** a depressing experience or situation

**downfall** /'down,fawl/ *n* **1a** a sudden fall (eg from high rank or power); ruin **b** a fall (eg of rain or esp of snow) esp when sudden or heavy **2** something that causes a downfall (eg of a person) ⟨*drink was his ~*⟩ – **downfallen** *adj*

**downfield** /,down'feeld/ *adv or adj* in or into the part of the field towards which the attacking team is playing ⟨*kicked the ball ~*⟩

¹**downgrade** /'down,grayd/ *n* **1** a downward slope (eg of a road) **2** a descent towards a lower or inferior state or level

²**downgrade** *vt* **1** to lower in rank, value, or importance **2** to alter the status of (a job) so as to lower the rate of pay

**downhaul** /'downhawl/ *n* a rope or line for hauling down or holding down a sail or spar

**downhearted** /,down'hahtid/ *adj* downcast, dejected – **downheartedly** *adv*, **downheartedness** *n*

¹**downhill** /'down,hil/ *n* **1** a descending gradient **2** a skiing race downhill against time – compare SLALOM

²**downhill** /,down'hil/ *adv* **1** towards the bottom of a hill **2** towards a lower or inferior state or level – chiefly in *go downhill*

³**downhill** *adj* **1** sloping downhill **2** of skiing downhill **3** not difficult; easy ⟨*had solved the biggest problems and the rest was ~*⟩

**Downing Street** /'downing/ *n* the British government; *also* (a spokesman for) the British prime minister ⟨*talks between Dublin and ~*⟩ ⟨*~ is expected to announce cabinet changes soon*⟩ [*Downing Street*, London, location of the British Foreign & Commonwealth Office and of the prime minister's official residence]

**downland** /'down,land, -lənd/ *n* (countryside resembling) the downs

,**down-'market** *n* being, producing, using, or characteristic of goods designed to appeal to the lower social end of a market – **down-market** *adv*

**down payment** *n* a deposit paid at the time of purchase or delivery with the balance to be paid later

**downpipe** /'down,piep/ *n, Br* a pipe for carrying rainwater from the roof to the ground or drain

**downplay** /down'play/ *vt* to play down, de-emphasize

**downpour** /'down,paw/ *n* a heavy fall of rain

**downrange** /'down,raynj/ *adv* away from a launching site and along the course of a test range ⟨*a missile landing 8000 kilometres ~*⟩ – **downrange** *adj*

¹**downright** /'down,riet/ *adv* thoroughly, outright ⟨*~ nasty*⟩

²**downright** *adj* **1** absolute, thorough ⟨*a ~ lie*⟩ **2** plain, blunt ⟨*a ~ man*⟩ – **downrightly** *adv*, **downrightness** *n*

**downriver** /down'rivə/ *adv or adj* towards or at a point nearer the mouth of a river

**downshift** /down'shift/ *vi, NAm* to change down ⟨*~ from third gear*⟩ – **downshift** *n*

**Down's syndrome** /downz/ *n* a condition of mental deficiency present from birth that is typically accompanied by the physical characteristics of slanting eyes, a broad short skull, and broad hands with short fingers and that is associated with the presence in each cell of three rather than two copies of a particular CHROMOSOME (strand of gene-carrying material) [J L H *Down* †1896 E physician]

**downstage** /,down'stayj/ *adv or adj* at the front of a theatrical stage; *also* towards the audience or camera

¹**downstairs** /,down'steəz/ *adv* down the stairs; on or to a lower floor

²**downstairs** *adj* situated on the main, lower, or ground floor of a building

³**downstairs** *n, pl* **downstairs 1** a lower or ground floor of a building **2** *pl, Br informal* the people occupying the lower part of a building; *esp* the servants of a household collectively

**downstate** /'down,stayt/ *adj* in or relating to the (southerly) part of a US state that is away from metropolitan areas – compare UPSTATE – **downstate** *adv*, **downstater** *n*

**downstream** /,down'streem/ *adv or adj* in the direction of the flow of a stream

**downstroke** /'down,strohk/ *n* a stroke made in a downward direction

**downswing** /'down,swing/ *n* **1** a downward swing, esp of a golf club ⟨*having trouble with his ~*⟩ **2** a downward trend, esp in business activity

**downtime** /'down,tiem/ *n* time during which a machine (eg a computer) is inoperative during normal operating hours; *also*, *chiefly NAm* time during which a factory or department is inoperative during working hours

,**down-to-'earth** *adj* practical, realistic ⟨*a ~ appraisal of the situation*⟩

**downtown** /'down,town/ *adv or n, chiefly NAm* (to, towards, or in) the lower part or main business district of a town or city – **downtown** *adj*

**downtrend** /'down,trend/ *n* a downturn, esp in business and economic activity

**downtrodden** /'down,trod(ə)n/ *adj* oppressed or subjugated, esp by those in power ⟨*the ~ peasants*⟩

**downturn** /'down,tuhn/ *n* a downward turn, esp towards a decline in business activity

**downward** /'downwood/ *adj* **1** moving or extending downwards ⟨*the ~ path*⟩ **2** descending to a lower pitch **3** descending from a head, origin, or source – **downwardly** *adv*, **downwardness** *n*

**downwards** /'downwoodz/ *adv* **1a** from a higher to a lower place or level; in the opposite direction from up ⟨*sun sank ~*⟩ **b** downstream **c** so as to conceal a particular surface ⟨*turned it face ~*⟩ **2a** from a higher to a lower condition **b** going down in amount, price, figure, or rank ⟨*from the fourth form ~*⟩ **3** from an earlier time **4** from an ancestor or predecessor

**downwind** /,down'wind/ *adv or adj* in the direction that the wind is blowing

**downy** /'downi/ *adj* **1** resembling a bird's down, esp to the touch **2** covered with down **3** made of down **4** soft, soothing ⟨*shake off this ~ sleep, death's counterfeit* – Shak⟩

**downy mildew** *n* any of various simple fungi (family Peronosporaceae) that are parasitic on plants and produce fine whitish masses of spores on the undersurface of the leaves of the plant that they infest; *also* a plant disease caused by a downy mildew

**dowry** /'dowri/ *n* 1 the money, goods, or estate that a woman brings to her husband in marriage; *also* similar property given to a convent by a woman intending to join certain orders of nuns – compare DOWER 2 something given (eg by nature or fortune) ⟨*beauty should be the ~ of every man and woman* – R W Emerson⟩ [ME *dowarie*, fr AF, irreg fr ML *dotarium*, fr L *dot-, dos* gift, marriage portion; akin to L *dare* to give – more at DATE]

**¹dowse** /dows, dowz/ *vt* to douse

**²dowse** /dowz/ *vi* to search for hidden water or minerals with a divining rod ~ *vt* to find by dowsing [origin unknown]
*synonyms* To **dowse** *for* something is merely to search for it, but to **dowse** it or **divine** it is to actually find it.

**dowser** /'dowsə, -zə/ *n* a person who dowses; *also* DIVINING ROD (forked twig which reacts to the presence of hidden water or minerals)

**doxology** /dok'soləji/ *n* a text (eg a hymn) giving praise to God, usu forming part of a Christian service of worship [ML *doxologia*, fr LGk, fr Gk *doxa* opinion, glory (fr *dokein* to seem, seem good) + *-logia* -logy – more at DECENT]

**doxorubicin** /,doksoh'roohbisin/ *n* an anticancer drug, $C_{27}H_{29}ON_{11}$, used esp in the treatment of leukaemia [prob fr *deoxy-* + *ox-* + *-rubicin* (as in *daunorubicin*)]

**doxy** /'doksi/ *n, derog* 1 a woman; *esp* one who is promiscuous, of loose morals, etc 2 *archaic* MISTRESS 4 [perh modif of obs D *docke* doll, fr MD]

**doyen** /'doyən (*Fr* dwajɛ̃)/, *fem* **doyenne** /doy'en (*Fr* dwajɛn)/ *n* 1 the senior or most experienced member of a body or group 2 the oldest or most distinguished example or member of a category or group ⟨*the ~ of the country's newspapers*⟩ [Fr, fr LL *decanus* dean – more at DEAN]

**doyley, doyly** /'doyli/ *n* a doily

**¹doze** /dohz/ *vi* 1 to sleep lightly 2 to fall into a light sleep – usu + *off* [prob of Scand origin; akin to ON *dūsa* to doze] – **doze** *n*, **dozer** *n*
**doze away** *vt* to pass (time) drowsily ⟨*nothing can be pleasanter than to doze away a Sunday afternoon with a good crossword*⟩

**²doze** *vt* BULLDOZE 2 [prob back-formation fr *dozer* (bulldozer)] – **dozer** *n*

**dozen** /'duzən/ *n, pl* **dozens, dozen** 1 a group of 12 2 **dozens** *pl*, **dozen** an indefinitely large number ⟨*I've a ~ things to do*⟩ ⟨*there are ~s of people I should send my new address to*⟩ – see also **talk** NINETEEN **to the dozen** [ME *dozeine*, fr OF *dozaine*, fr *doze* twelve, fr L *duodecim*, fr *duo* two + *decem* ten – more at TWO, TEN] – **dozen** *adj*, **dozenth** *adj*

**dozy** /'dohzi/ *adj* 1 drowsy, sleepy 2 *chiefly Br informal* stupid and slow-witted; lacking understanding – **doziness** *n*

**DP** *n, pl* **DP's, DPs** DISPLACED PERSON (refugee)

**DPN** /,dee pee 'en/ *n* NAD – not now used technically [*di*-phosphopyridine *n*ucleotide]

**¹drab** /drab/ *n, archaic derog* a slovenly or morally loose woman [perh from LG *drabbe* mire, dirt]

**²drab** *n* 1 any of various cloths of a dull brown or grey colour; *esp* a thick woollen or heavy cotton cloth used for making coats 2 a light olive-brown colour [MF *drap* cloth, fr LL *drappus*]

**³drab** *adj* **-bb-** 1 of a dull olive-brown colour 2 dull and monotonous; cheerless – **drably** *adv*, **drabness** *n*

**⁴drab** *n* – see DRIBS AND DRABS [prob alter. of *drib*]

**drabble** /'drabl/ *vb* to make or become wet and muddy [ME *drabelen*, fr MLG *drabbeln* to paddle in water or mud]

**drachm** /dram/ *n* 1 a drachma 2a a unit of weight equal to ¹/₈ ounce apothecary (about 3.89 grams) **b** FLUID DRACHM
*synonyms* see ²GRAM [alter. of ME *dragme* – more at DRAM]

**drachma** /'drakmə/ *n, pl* **drachmas, drachmae, drachmai** 1a any of various ancient Greek units of weight **b** any of various modern units of mass; *esp* DRAM 1a 2a an ancient Greek silver coin equivalent to six OBOLS **b** – see MONEY table [L, fr Gk *drachmē* – more at DRAM]

**draconian** /dray'kohnyən, -ni·ən, drə-/, **draconic** /dray'konik/ *adj often cap* 1 (characteristic) of Draco or the severe code of laws held to have been framed by him 2 extremely harsh, cruel, or severe ⟨*the time has come to take ~ measures to beat inflation*⟩ [*Draco* (Gk *Drakōn*) *fl*621 BC Athenian lawgiver]

**draconic** /dray'konik, drə-/ *adj* of a dragon [L *dracon-, draco* serpent, dragon]

**draff** /draf/ *n* the remains of malt left after brewing [ME *draf* dregs, draff, fr (assumed) OE *dræf* or ON *draf*; akin to OE *deorc* dark]

**¹draft** /drahft/ *n* 1 a drawing, design, or plan esp of something to be constructed (eg a building) 2 a preliminary sketch, outline, or version ⟨*a ~ of the new abortion legislation*⟩ ⟨*submitted a ~ of the first five chapters of her novel*⟩ 3 an allowance paid to a buyer for loss in weight 4 an order for the payment of money, esp by a bank, to a person, firm, or other bank 5 (an instance of) drawing from or making demands upon something 6 an angle, taper; *specif* the taper given to a pattern or die so that the work cast in it can be easily withdrawn 7 a narrow border along the edge of a stone or across its face serving as a stonecutter's guide 8 an act or process of selection: eg 8a an act or process of selecting certain animals from a herd or flock; *also* a group of individuals so selected ⟨*the first ~ of lambs*⟩ **b** *chiefly NAm* conscription – + *the* 9 *NAm* a draught [var of *draught*]
*usage* Compare the spellings **draft** and **draught**. In British English, a preliminary version is a **draft**, and one **drafts** it. A money order is a **draft**. One drinks a **draught** of **draught** beer, and drives **draught** horses. A current of air is a **draught**, and the game is **draughts**. In American English **draft** is the preferred spelling for all these, but the game is called **checkers**.

**²draft** *adj* 1 constituting a preliminary or tentative version, sketch, or outline ⟨*a ~ treaty*⟩ 2 chosen from a group – used chiefly of livestock 3 *NAm* draught

**³draft** *vt* 1 to detach or select for some purpose: eg 1a *NAm* to conscript for military service **b** to select and detach (an animal) from a group for a special purpose 2 to draw or draw up the preliminary sketch, version, or plan of 3 to mark (eg a stone) with a draft in masonry ~ *vi* to drive close behind another car while racing at high speed in order to take advantage of the reduced air pressure created by the leading car – **draftable** *adj*, **draftee** *n*, **drafter** *n*

**draftsman** /'drahftsmən/ *n* 1 someone who draws up (legal) documents 2 *chiefly NAm* a draughtsman – **draftsmanship** *n*

**¹drag** /drag/ *n* 1 something that is dragged, pulled, or drawn along or over a surface: eg 1a **drag harrow, drag** an agricultural implement consisting of a heavy beam, often with spikes attached, that is used for levelling ground after ploughing and before seed is sown **b** a sledge for moving heavy loads 2 something used to drag with; *esp* a device for dragging under water to detect or obtain objects ⟨*three policemen with a ~ searched the pond for the body*⟩ 3a something that retards motion, action, or progress **b**(1) the retarding force that acts on a body (eg an aircraft) moving through a liquid or gas (eg air) in a direction parallel and opposite to the direction of motion **b**(2) (slowing due to) friction between engine parts **c** a burden, encumbrance ⟨*the ~ of population growth on living standards*⟩ 4 an object drawn over the ground to leave a scented trail (eg for foxhounds to follow) 5a a drawing along or over a surface with effort or pressure **b** slow or difficult motion **c** *informal* a drawing into the mouth of smoke from a pipe, cigarette, or cigar 6a *informal* clothing **b** *informal* clothing of one sex worn by the other; *esp* women's dress worn by a man ⟨*the ~ Miss World competition*⟩ – usu in *in drag* 7 *informal* one who or that which is dull or boring ⟨*school is a ~ for some youngsters*⟩ ⟨*don't ask them, they're a real ~ at parties*⟩ 8 *chiefly NAm informal* a street, road ⟨*the main ~*⟩ 9 *chiefly NAm slang* influence securing special favour

**²drag** *vb* **-gg-** *vt* 1a to draw slowly or heavily; haul **b** to cause to move with painful or undue slowness or difficulty ⟨*~ging the musical tempo*⟩ **c** to cause to trail along a surface ⟨*~ged his feet in the water*⟩ 2 to bring by force or compulsion ⟨*had to ~ her husband to the opera*⟩ 3a to explore (a body of water) with a drag ⟨*~ged the river for the child's body*⟩ **b** to catch with a dragnet or trawl ~ *vi* 1 to hang or lag behind 2 to fish or search with a drag 3 to trail along on the ground 4 to move on or proceed laboriously or tediously ⟨*the book ~s*⟩
*synonyms* see ¹PULL [ME *draggen*, fr ON *draga* or OE *dragan* – more at DRAW] – **draggingly** *adv* – **drag one's feet/heels** to act in a deliberately slow, dilatory, or ineffective manner
**drag down** *vt* to depress; lower in spirits ⟨*the divorce really dragged her down*⟩
**drag in** *vt* to introduce (eg into a conversation) unnecessarily ⟨*I wish he wouldn't keep dragging in the names of all the famous people he claims to have met*⟩
**drag on** *vi* to continue for an unreasonable length of time ⟨*negotiations dragged on into the New Year*⟩ ~ *vt* to inhale from (a pipe, cigarette, etc)
**drag out** *vt* to protract or lengthen unnecessarily ⟨*there was material for a short article, but he dragged it out into a rather thick book*⟩

**drag out of** *vt* to obtain (a statement or confession) with force or difficulty from ⟨*no one will ever know how confessions were* dragged out of *the victims of Stalin's show trials*⟩

**drag up** *vt* 1 to bring up (a child) badly or carelessly, esp without good manners 2 to mention (an unpleasant topic) unnecessarily ⟨*the book* drags up *all the gossip about his years in South Africa*⟩

**drag anchor** *n* SEA ANCHOR (device for keeping a ship's bows to the wind)

**dragée** /'drazhay *(Fr* draʒe)/ *n* 1 a sugar-coated nut or fruit 2 a small silver-coloured sugar ball for decorating cakes [Fr, fr MF *dragie* – more at DREDGE]

**draggle** /'dragl/ *vt* to make wet and dirty by dragging ~ *vi* 1 to trail on the ground 2 to straggle [freq of *drag*]

**draggled** /'dragld/ *adj* bedraggled

**draggy** /'dragi/ *adj, informal* sluggish, dull, or boring ⟨*a ~ party*⟩

**dragline** /'drag,lien/ *n* 1 a line used in or for dragging 2 an excavating machine in which the bucket is attached by cables and operates by being drawn towards the machine

**dragnet** /'drag,net/ *n* 1a a net drawn along the bottom of a body of water; a trawl b a net used on the ground (e g to capture small game) 2 a network of measures designed to lead to capture or discovery (e g of a criminal)

**dragoman** /'dragohman/ *n, pl* **dragomans, dragomen** /-mən/ an interpreter chiefly of Arabic, Turkish, or Persian employed esp in the Near East △ dragoon [ME *drogman*, fr MF, fr OIt *dragomanno*, fr MGk *dragomanos*, fr Ar *tarjumān*, fr Aram *tŭrgĕmānā*]

**dragon** /'dragən/ *n* 1 a mythical animal usu represented as a monstrous winged and scaly reptile with a crested head, enormous claws, and often the power to breathe fire 2 a violent, combative, or very strict person 3 any of numerous small brilliantly coloured tree-dwelling lizards (genus *Draco*) of the E Indies and southern Asia, that have the hind ribs on each side prolonged and covered with a web of skin [ME, fr OF, fr L *dracon-, draco* serpent, dragon, fr Gk *drakōn* serpent; akin to OE *torht* bright, Gk *derkesthai* to see, look at] – **dragonish** *adj*

**dragonet** /'dragənit/ *n* any of various small often brightly coloured scaleless marine fishes (family Callionymidae); *esp* a European fish (*Callionymus lyra*) sometimes used as food [*dragon* + *-et*]

**dragonfly** /'dragən,flie/ *n* any of a suborder (Anisoptera) of long slender-bodied slow-flying often brightly coloured insects that are larger and stouter than the related damselflies, have two pairs of intricately veined wings held outspread when at rest, and have larvae that live in water; *broadly* ODONATE

**dragon lizard** *n* KOMODO DRAGON (very large Indonesian lizard)

**dragonnade** /,dragə'nayd/ *n* persecution using troops; *specif* any of a series of persecutions of French Protestants during the reign of Louis XIV by soldiers who were quartered on them [Fr, fr *dragon* dragoon]

**dragon's blood** *n* any of several resinous mostly dark-red plant products; *specif* a resin from the fruit of a palm tree (genus *Daemonorops*) used esp for colouring varnishes

**dragon's teeth** *n pl* wedge-shaped concrete antitank barriers laid in multiple rows resembling teeth

π**dragoon** /drə'goohn/ *n* a member of a military unit formerly composed of mounted infantrymen armed with carbines [Fr *dragon* dragon, musket, dragoon, fr MF]

²**dragoon** *vt* 1 to persecute by harsh use of troops 2 to (attempt to) force into submission by persecution

**drag race** *n* an acceleration contest between cars, motorcycles, etc usu over ¹/₄ mile (about 402 metres) – **drag racing** *n*

**dragster** /'dragstə/ *n* (the driver of) a vehicle, esp a car, specially built or modified for use in a drag race

**drag strip** *n* the site of a drag race; *specif* the narrow strip on which the vehicles run

**drail** /drayl/ *n* a heavy fishhook used in TROLLING (method of fishing in which a baited hook is drawn through the water) [obs *drail* to drag, trail, perh alter. of *trail*]

¹**drain** /drayn/ *vt* 1a to draw off (liquid) gradually or completely ⟨~ed *all the water out*⟩ b to exhaust physically or emotionally ⟨*felt* ~ed *after the interview*⟩ 2a to make gradually dry ⟨~ *a swamp*⟩ b to carry away the surface water of ⟨*the river that* ~s *the valley*⟩ c to deplete or empty (as if) by drawing off by degrees or in increments ⟨*war that* ~s *a nation of youth and wealth*⟩ d to empty by drinking the contents of ⟨~ *a glass of beer*⟩ ~ *vi* 1a to flow off gradually b to disappear gradually;

**dwindle** ⟨*money* ~ing *away in expenses*⟩ 2 to become emptied or freed of liquid by its flowing or dropping; discharge surplus water [ME *draynen*, fr OE *drēahnian*] – **drainer** *n*

²**drain** *n* 1 a means (e g a pipe) by which usu liquid matter is drained away 2 a gradual outflow or withdrawal; a depletion 3 something that causes depletion; a burden ⟨*a ~ on the national resources*⟩ – **down the drain** utterly lost, wasted, or brought to nothing ⟨*any hope of being there on time went* down the drain *when the car ran out of petrol*⟩

**drainage** /'draynij/ *n* 1 the act, process, or method of draining; *also* something drained off 2 a system of drains 3 an area or district drained

**draining board** /'drayning/ *n, Br* a usu grooved and often slightly sloping surface at the side of a sink unit on which washed dishes are placed to drain

**drainpipe** /'drayn,piep/ *n* a pipe for drainage; *esp* a pipe that carries waste or liquid sewage or carries rainwater from a roof guttering to a drain

**drainpipe trousers, drainpipes** *n pl* tight trousers with narrow legs

**drain rod** *n, Br* a rod that when coupled to other similar rods may be pushed along drains to clear blockages

¹**drake** /drayk/ *n* a mayfly; *also* an artificial fly, resembling a mayfly, used in angling [ME, dragon, fr OE *draca*; akin to ON *dreki* dragon; both fr a prehistoric WGmc-NGmc word borrowed fr L *draco* dragon – more at DRAGON]

²**drake** *n* a male duck [ME; akin to OHG an*trahho* drake]

**Dralon** /'draylon/ *trademark* – used for an acrylic fibre used chiefly for upholstery *synonyms* see NYLON

**dram** /dram/ *n* 1a a unit of mass equal to ¹/₁₆ ounce avoirdupois (about 1.77 grams) b DRACHM 2a 2 *chiefly Scot* a tot of spirits, usu whisky *synonyms* see ²GRAM [ME *dragme*, fr MF & LL; MF, dram, drachma, fr LL *dragma*, fr L *drachma*, fr Gk *drachmē*, lit., handful, fr *drassesthai* to grasp]

**drama** /'drahmə/ *n* 1 a composition in verse or prose intended for performance by actors; a play 2 dramatic art, literature, or affairs 3 a state, situation, or group of events involving forces in opposition to each other and perceived as dramatic or having the qualities of a play [LL *dramat-, drama*, fr Gk, deed, drama, fr *dran* to do, act; prob akin to Lith *daryti* to do]

**dramatic** /drə'matik/ *adj* 1 of drama 2a like something which could appear or happen in drama; vivid b striking in appearance or effect 3 *of a singer* having a powerful voice and a clear pronounced operatic style – compare LYRIC – **dramatically** *adv*

**dramatic irony** *n* incongruity between a situation developed in a play and the words or actions of the characters, that is understood by the audience but not by the characters themselves

**dramatic monologue** *n* a poem or other literary work in which dramatic events are described by one of the characters involved in them, who is the only speaker

**dramatics** /drə'matiks/ *n pl taking sing or pl vb* the study or practice of theatrical arts (e g acting and stage management) 2 dramatic behaviour or expression; *esp* an exaggerated display of emotion

**dramatic unities** *n pl* the three principles of dramatic structure that are observed in classical drama, which require a play to have a single plot occurring in one place and within one day

**dramatis personae** /,drahmətis puh'sohnie/ *n* 1 *taking pl vb* the characters or actors in a drama 2 a list of the characters or actors in a drama [NL]

**dramatist** /'drahmətist, 'dra-/ *n* a playwright

**dramat-ization, -isation** /,drahmətie'zaysh(ə)n, dra-/ *n* 1 the act or process of dramatizing 2 a dramatized version (e g of a novel)

**dramat-ize, -ise** /'drahmətiez, dra-/ *vt* 1 to adapt (e g a novel) to a form suitable for acting 2 to present or represent in a dramatic manner ~ *vi* 1 to be suitable for dramatization 2 to behave dramatically; put on an act – **dramatizable** *adj*

**dramaturgy** /'dramə,tuhji/ *n* the art or technique of dramatic writing and theatrical presentation [Ger *dramaturgie*, fr Gk *dramatourgia* dramatic composition, fr *dramatourgos* dramatist, fr *dramat-, drama* + *-ourgos* worker, fr *ergon* work – more at WORK] – **dramaturgic, dramaturgical** *adj*, **dramaturgically** *adv*

**Drambuie** /dram'byooh·i/ *trademark* – used for a liqueur based on Scotch whisky and flavoured with honey

**drank** /drangk/ *past of* DRINK

¹**drape** /drayp/ *vt* 1 to cover or adorn (as if) with folds of cloth

**2** to cause to hang or stretch out loosely or carelessly ⟨~d his legs over the chair⟩ **3** to arrange in flowing lines or folds ⟨a cleverly ~d dress⟩ **4** to cover (a patient) with a drape in preparation for an operation ~ vi to become arranged in folds ⟨this silk ~s beautifully⟩ [ME drapen to weave, fr MF draper, fr drap cloth, fr LL drappus] – **drapable** also **drapeable** adj, **drapability** also **drapeability** n

²**drape** n **1** an arrangement in or of folds **2** the way in which clothing fabric hangs **3** something that is draped: **3a** a sterile covering for the parts of a patient's body surrounding an area to be operated on **b** usu pl, chiefly NAm a curtain

**draper** /'draypǝ/ n, chiefly Br a dealer in cloth and sometimes also in clothing, soft furnishings, or dressmaking accessories [ME, maker of cloth, fr MF drapier, fr OF, fr drap]

**drapery** /'drayp(ǝ)ri/ n **1** cloth or textile fabrics used esp for clothing or soft furnishings **2** the draping or arrangement of cloth or clothing **3** Br **3a** the business of a draper **b** the goods sold by a draper **4a** cloth or clothing arranged or hung gracefully, esp in loose folds; also a piece of cloth or clothing arranged in this manner **b** NAm hangings of heavy fabric for use as a curtain

**drastic** /'drastik/ adj **1** acting rapidly or violently ⟨a ~ purgative⟩ **2** radical in effect or action; severe ⟨~ measures⟩ [Gk drastikos, fr dran to do] – **drastically** adv

**drat** /drat/ vb -tt- informal – used as an oath to express mild irritation [prob euphemism for God rot]

¹**draught**, NAm chiefly **draft** /drahft/ n **1** the act of drawing a net; also the quantity of fish taken at one drawing **2a** the act of moving loads by drawing or pulling **b** a team of animals together with what they draw **3a** the force required to pull an implement **b** the maximum load or load-pulling capacity of an implement **4a** the act or an instance of drinking or inhaling; also the portion drunk or inhaled in one such act **b** a portion poured out or mixed for drinking; a dose **5a** the act of drawing (e g from a cask) **b** a portion of liquid so drawn ⟨a ~ of beer⟩ **6** the depth of water a ship requires to float in, esp when loaded **7a** a current of air in a closed-in space **b** a device for regulating the flow of air (e g in a fireplace) **8** DRAUGHTSMAN 4 [ME draght; akin to OE dragan to draw – more at DRAW] – **on draught** of beer or cider ready to be served from the cask or barrel with or without the use of added gas in serving

²**draught**, chiefly NAm **draft** adj **1** used for drawing loads ⟨~ animals⟩ **2** being on draught ⟨~ beer⟩

**draughtboard** /'drahft,bawd/ n a chessboard which is used for playing draughts

'**draught-,proof** vt to plug gaps round or cracks in to prevent a draught blowing through ⟨~ your house for the winter⟩ ⟨~ the windows⟩ – **draught-proofing** n

**draughts** /drahfts/ n taking sing or pl vb, Br a game for two players each of whom moves his/her usu twelve draughtsmen diagonally across usu the black squares of a draughtboard in order to jump over and thus capture his/her opponent's pieces [ME draghtes, fr pl of draght draught, move in chess]

**draughtsman** /'drahftsmǝn/ n **1** DRAFTSMAN **2** fem **draughts-woman** one who draws plans and sketches (e g of machinery or structures) **3** fem **draughtswoman** an artist who excels in drawing **4** Br a disc-shaped piece used in the game of draughts – **draughtsmanship** n

**draughty** /'drahfti/ adj having a cold draught blowing through

**Dravidian** /drǝ'vidi·ǝn, -dyǝn/ n **1** a member of any of the peoples of S India and Sri Lanka who speak Dravidian languages **2** DRAVIDIAN LANGUAGES [Skt Drāviḍa] – **Dravidian** adj

**Dravidian languages** n pl a non-Indo-European language family of S India, Sri Lanka, and to a smaller extent, Pakistan that includes Tamil, Telugu, Gondi, and Malayalam

¹**draw** /draw/ vb **drew** /drooh/; **drawn** /drawn/ vt **1** to pull, haul **2** to cause to go in a certain direction (e g by leading) ⟨drew him aside⟩ **3** to pull so as to cover something (e g a window) ⟨~ the curtains⟩ **4a** to bring, by inducement or allure; attract ⟨honey ~s flies⟩ **b** to bring, gather, or derive from a specified source ⟨a college that ~s its students from many towns⟩ ⟨drew inspiration from his teacher⟩ **c** to bring on oneself ⟨drew enemy fire⟩ **d** to bring out by way of response; elicit ⟨drew cheers from the audience⟩ **e** to cause (blood, pus, etc) to come to the surface of a wound, abscess, etc **f** to drive game out of ⟨~ a covert⟩ **5** to inhale ⟨drew a deep breath⟩ **6a** to bring or pull out, esp by effort ⟨~ a tooth⟩ ⟨~ a sword⟩ **b** to extract the essence from ⟨~ tea⟩ **c** to remove the entrails of; disembowel

⟨plucking and ~ing a goose before cooking⟩ **d** to cause (blood) to flow **e** DRAW OFF 2 **7** to require (a specified depth) to float in ⟨a ship that ~s 12 feet of water⟩ **8a** to accumulate, gain ⟨~ing interest⟩ **b** to take (money) from a place of deposit – often + out **c** to use in making a cash demand ⟨~ing a cheque on his account⟩ **d** to receive regularly or in due course ⟨~ a salary⟩ **9a** to take (cards) from a dealer or pack **b** to receive or take at random ⟨drew a winning number⟩ **10** to bend (a bow) by pulling back the string **11** to cause to shrink or tighten **12a** of a golfer to hit (a ball) so as to impart a leftward curve (when hit by a right-handed player) **b** NAm SCREW 4 (put backward spin on a billiard ball) **13** to leave (a contest) undecided, specif because of an equality in scores; also to have equal scores in ⟨England were ~ing the match 0-0 at halftime⟩ **14a(1)** to produce a likeness of by making lines on a surface **a(2)** to give a portrayal of; delineate ⟨a writer who ~s his characters well⟩ **b** to write out in due form ⟨~ a will⟩ **c** to design or describe in detail; formulate ⟨~ comparisons⟩ **15** to formulate or arrive at by reasoning ⟨~ a conclusion⟩ **16** to spread, stretch, or shape (e g metal) by hammering or by pulling through DIES; also to produce (e g a metal wire) by drawing through a perforated die ~ vi **1a** to come or go steadily or gradually ⟨night ~s near⟩ **b** to advance as far as a specified position ⟨drew level⟩ ⟨drew up to the front door⟩ ⟨the train drew into the station⟩ **2a** to move something by pulling ⟨~ing at the well⟩ **b** to exert an attractive force **3a** to pull back a bowstring **b** to bring out a weapon ⟨drew, aimed, and fired⟩ **4a** to produce or allow a draught of air ⟨the chimney ~s well⟩ **b** of a sail to swell out in a wind **5a** to cause blood or pus to localize at one point **b** to steep, infuse ⟨give the tea time to ~⟩ **6** to create a likeness or a picture in outlines; sketch **7** to finish a competition or contest without either side winning **8a** to make a written demand for payment of money on deposit **b** to obtain resources (e g of information) ⟨~ing from a common fund of knowledge⟩ **9** to start a game of lacrosse with a draw **10** to suck in something, esp tobacco smoke – usu + on ⟨~ing on his pipe⟩ – see also **draw a** BEAD **on, draw a** BLANK, **draw a** BOW **at a venture, at** DAGGERS **drawn, draw a/the** LINE, **draw** LOTS, **draw** REIN, **draw** STRAWS, **draw** STUMPS, **draw a** VEIL **over synonyms** see ¹PULL [ME drawen, dragen, fr OE dragan; akin to ON draga to draw, drag] – **drawable** adj

**draw away** vi to move ahead (e g of an opponent in a race) gradually

**draw back** vi to avoid an issue or commitment; retreat

**draw in** vt **1** to cause or entice to enter or participate ⟨heard the argument but would not be drawn in⟩ **2** to sketch roughly ⟨drawing in the first outlines⟩ ~ vi **1a** to draw to an end ⟨the day drew in⟩ **b** to shorten seasonally ⟨the evenings are already drawing in⟩ **2** of a train to come into and stop at a station – see also **draw in one's** HORNS

**draw off** vt **1** to remove, withdraw **2** to cause (liquid) to flow from a vessel by means of a tap or a siphon ⟨the wine was drawn off from the lees⟩ ~ vi to move apart; regroup ⟨the enemies' losses forced them to draw off⟩

**draw on** vi to approach ⟨night draws on⟩ ~ vt **1** to bring on; cause **2** to put on ⟨she drew on her gloves⟩ **3 draw on, draw upon** to use as source of supply ⟨drawing on the whole community for support⟩

**draw out** vt **1** to remove, extract **2** to extend beyond a minimum in time; protract **3** to cause to speak freely ⟨a reporter's ability to draw a person out⟩ ~ vi, of a train to leave a station

**draw up** vt **1** to bring (e g troops) into array **2** to draw or prepare a draft of; DRAFT 2 ⟨draw up a contract⟩ **3** to straighten (oneself) to an erect posture, esp as an assertion of dignity or resentment **4** to bring to a halt ~ vi to come to a halt

²**draw** n **1** the act or process of drawing: e g **1a** a sucking pull on something held with the lips ⟨take a ~ on his pipe⟩ **b** a removal of a handgun from its holster ⟨the sheriff was quicker on the ~⟩ **2** something that is drawn: e g **2a** a card drawn to replace a discard in poker **b** a lot or chance drawn at random **c** a raffle **d** the movable part of a drawbridge **3** a contest left undecided or deadlocked; specif one in which both sides make equal scores; a tie **4** someone who or something that draws a large audience **5a** the distance from the string to the back of a drawn bow **b** the force required to draw a bow fully **6** the usu random assignment of starting positions in a competition, esp a competitive sport **7** a shot in bowls that is intended to place the bowl next to or touching the jack **8** the start of play in a

game of lacrosse, in which two players from opposing sides stand holding their sticks (CROSSES) back to back with the nets overlapping and the ball held between them, and push to try to propel the ball towards their own team's forwards **9** *NAm* SCREW (backward spin put on a billiard ball) **10** *NAm* a gully shallower than a ravine

**drawback** /'draw,bak/ *n* **1** a refund of duties, esp on an imported product subsequently exported or used to produce a product for export **2** an objectionable feature; a hindrance

**drawbar** /'draw,bah/ *n* **1** a railway vehicle coupling **2** a beam across the rear of a tractor to which implements are hitched

**drawbridge** /'draw,brij/ *n* a bridge made to be raised up, let down, or drawn aside so as to permit or hinder passage

**drawcard** /'draw,kahd/ *n, Austr* ²DRAW 4

**drawee** /draw'ee/ *n* the person on whom an order or BILL OF EXCHANGE is drawn

**drawer** /*sense 1* 'draw-ə; *senses 2,3* draw/ *n* **1** one that draws: eg **1a** DRAFTSMAN **b** one who draws a BILL OF EXCHANGE or order for payment or makes a PROMISSORY NOTE **2** a sliding box or receptacle opened by pulling out and closed by pushing in **3** *pl, chiefly humorous* an undergarment for the lower body – **drawerful** *n*

**'draw-,frame** *n* a machine for reducing the thickness of slivers of a textile fibre

**draw gear** *n, Br* apparatus for joining railway cars together

**draw hoe** *n* a hook-shaped hoe with a blade at a right angle to the handle which the user pulls towards himself to pile up soil, make a drill, etc – compare DUTCH HOE

**drawing** /'draw-ing/ *n* **1** an act or instance of drawing **2** the art or technique of representing an object or outlining a figure, plan, or sketch by means of lines **3** something drawn or subject to drawing: eg **3a** an amount drawn from a fund **b** a representation formed by drawing; a sketch

*usage* A pronunciation /'drawring/ is widely disliked.

**drawing board** *n* **1** a rigid board used as a base to which paper is fixed while a drawing is made **2** a planning stage ⟨*a project still on the* ~⟩ ⟨*back to the* ~⟩

**drawing card** *n, NAm* ²DRAW 4

**drawing pin** *n, Br* a pin that has a broad flat head for pressing into a surface with the thumb and is used esp for fastening sheets of paper to boards

**drawing room** *n* **1a** *Br formal* LIVING ROOM **b** a formal reception room **2** *NAm* a private room on a railway passenger car with three berths and an enclosed toilet *synonyms* see SITTING ROOM [short for *withdrawing room*]

**drawknife** /'draw,nief/ *n* a woodworker's tool that has a blade with a handle at each end and is used for shaving off surfaces

**'drawl** /drawl/ *vi* to speak slowly and often affectedly with vowels greatly prolonged ~ *vt* to utter in a slow lengthened tone [prob freq of *draw*] – **drawler** *n*, **drawlingly** *adv*

**²drawl** *n* a drawling manner of speaking – **drawly** *adj*

**¹drawn** /drawn/ *past of* DRAW

**²drawn** *adj* **1** *esp of the face* changed as if by pulling or stretching ⟨*her face was* ~ *with sorrow*⟩ **2** *of a game, competition, etc* ended in a draw

**drawn butter** /drawn/ *n* melted butter often with seasoning

**drawn work** *also* **drawn-thread work** *n* decoration on cloth made by drawing out threads according to a pattern

**drawplate** /'draw,playt/ *n* a die with holes through which wires are drawn

**drawsheet** /'draw,sheet/ *n* a narrow sheet used esp in hospitals that is stretched across a bed lengthways underneath a patient's body and can be changed without remaking the bed

**drawstring** /'draw,string/ *n* a string, cord, or tape inserted into hems or casings or laced through eyelets for use in closing a bag or controlling fullness in garments or curtains

**¹dray** /dray/ *n* **1** a strong low cart or wagon without sides used esp by brewers **2** a brewer's lorry [ME *draye*, a wheelless vehicle, prob fr OE *dræge* dragnet; akin to OE *dragan* to pull – more at DRAW]

**²dray** *n* DREY (squirrel's nest)

**drayage** /'drayij/ *n, chiefly NAm* the work or cost of hauling by dray

**dray horse** /'dray,haws/ *n* a large and powerful horse used esp to pull drays

**drayman** /'drayman/ *n* one whose work is haulage by dray: eg **a** one who drives a vehicle for a brewery **b** one who travels with a brewer's dray or lorry in order to load and unload it

**¹dread** /dred/ *vt* **1** to fear greatly **2** to be extremely appre-

hensive about **3** *archaic* to regard with awe [ME *dreden*, fr OE *drǣdan;* akin to OHG int*rātan* to fear]

**²dread** *n* **1a** great fear, esp in the face of impending evil **b** extreme uneasiness in the face of a disagreeable prospect ⟨*his* ~ *of paperwork*⟩ **2** one causing dread ⟨*fire was an omnipresent* ~ *–* F W Saunders⟩ **3** *archaic* awe *synonyms* see ¹FEAR *antonym* confidence

**³dread** *adj, chiefly poetic* causing or inspiring dread [ME *dred*, fr pp of *dreden*]

**dreadful** /'dredf(ə)l/ *adj* **1** inspiring dread; causing great and oppressive fear **2** extremely disagreeable, unpleasant, or shocking **3** extreme ⟨~ *disorder*⟩ – **dreadfully** *adv*, **dreadfulness** *n*

**dreadlocks** /'dred,loks/ *n pl* long matted locks of hair that are often dyed with henna and are worn by male Rastafarians

**dreadnought** /'dred,nawt/ *n* **1** (the cloth used to make) a type of heavy esp 19th-century overcoat **2** a battleship whose main armament consists of big guns of uniform calibre **3** *archaic* a person who fears nothing [*Dreadnought*, Br battleship, the first of this type, launched in 1906]

**¹dream** /dreem/ *n* **1** a series of related thoughts, pictures, or emotions occurring during sleep **2** an experience of waking life having the characteristics of a dream: eg **2a** a daydream, reverie **b** an object seen in a dreamlike state; a vision **3** something notable for its beauty, excellence, or enjoyable quality ⟨*the new car goes like a* ~⟩ ⟨*it's a* ~ *of a car*⟩ **4a** a strongly desired goal; an ambition ⟨*his* ~ *of becoming president*⟩ **b** something that fully satisfies a wish; an ideal ⟨*a meal that was a gourmet's* ~⟩ [ME *dreem*, fr OE *drēam* noise, joy] – **dreamful** *adj*, **dreamfully** *adv*, **dreamless** *adj*, **dreamlessly** *adv*, **dreamlessness** *n*, **dreamlike** *adj*

**²dream** *vb* **dreamed** /dreemd, dremt/, **dreamt** /dremt/ *vi* **1** to have a dream **2** to indulge in daydreams or fantasies ⟨~*ing of a better future*⟩ **3** to appear tranquil or dreamy ⟨*that sweet city with her* ~*ing spires* – Matthew Arnold⟩ ~ *vt* **1** to have a dream of **2** to consider as a possibility; imagine **3** to pass (time) in reverie or inaction – usu + *away* ⟨~*ing the hours away*⟩

*usage* Dreamed and dreamt are equally common in British English, but dreamed is the commoner American form.

**dream of** *vt* to consider even the possibility of – in neg constructions ⟨*wouldn't dream of disturbing you*⟩

**dream up** *vt* to devise, invent

**³dream** *adj* like something occurring in a dream; *esp* having a quality of unreality or perfection ⟨*he lives in a* ~ *world*⟩ ⟨*build your* ~ *home*⟩ ⟨*this is turning into a* ~ *final* – David Vine⟩

**dreamboat** /'dreem,boht/ *n, informal* a highly attractive person of the opposite sex

**dreamer** /'dreemə/ *n* **1** one who dreams **2a** one who lives in a world of fantasy and imagination **b** one who has ideas or thinks up projects regarded as impractical; a visionary

**dreamland** /'dreem,land/ *n* an unreal delightful region existing only in imagination or in fantasy; NEVER-NEVER LAND

**dreamtime** /'dreem,tiem/ *n* a GOLDEN AGE recorded in the legends of certain Australian aboriginal peoples and held to be the time when their first ancestors were created

**dreamy** /'dreemi/ *adj* **1** pleasantly removed from reality **2** given to dreaming or fantasy ⟨*a* ~ *child*⟩ **3a** suggestive of a dream in vague or visionary quality **b** quiet and soothing **c** delightful, pleasing – **dreamily** *adv*, **dreaminess** *n*

**drear** /driə/ *adj* dreary

**dreary** /'driəri/ *adj* causing feelings of cheerlessness or gloom; dull [ME *drery*, fr OE *drēorig* sad, bloody, fr *drēor* gore; akin to OHG *trūrēn* to be sad, Goth *driusan* to fall, Gk *thrauein* to shatter] – **drearily** *adv*, **dreariness** *n*

**dreck** /drek/ *n, chiefly NAm slang* crap [Yiddish *drek* & Ger *dreck*, fr MHG *drec;* akin to OE *threax* rubbish, L *stercus* excrement]

**¹dredge** /drej/ *n* **1** an oblong iron frame with a bag net attached for gathering fish and shellfish from a river or sea bottom **2** a machine for removing earth, usu by buckets on an endless chain or by a suction tube [prob fr Sc *dreg-* (in *dregbot* dredge boat)]

**²dredge** *vt* **1a** to dig, gather, or pull out with a dredge – often + *up* or *out* **b** to deepen (eg a waterway) with a dredging machine **2** to bring to light by deep searching – usu + *up* ⟨*dredging up memories*⟩ ~ *vi* to use a dredge

**³dredge** *vt* to coat (food) by sprinkling with flour, sugar, etc [obs *dredge*, n, sweetmeat, fr ME *drage, drege*, fr MF *dragie*, prob modif of L *tragemata* sweetmeats, fr Gk *tragēmata*, pl of *tragēma* sweetmeat, fr *trōgein* to gnaw – more at TERSE] – **dredger** *n*

**dredger** /'drejə/ *n* a barge with an apparatus for dredging harbours, waterways, etc

**dree** /dree/ *vt, chiefly Scot* to endure, suffer [ME *dreen*, fr OE *drēogan* – more at DRUDGE]

**dreg** /dreg/ *n* 1 *pl* sediment contained in a liquid or precipitated from it; lees 2 *pl* the most undesirable part ⟨*the ~s of society*⟩ 3 the last remaining part; vestige 4 *Br slang* a contemptible or inept person [ME, fr ON *dregg;* akin to L *fraces* dregs of oil, Gk *thrassein* to trouble]

**D region** *n* the lowest part of the IONOSPHERE (upper part of the earth's atmosphere) occurring between about 40 and 65 kilometres (25 and 40 miles) above the surface of the earth

**dreich** /dreekh/ *adj, chiefly Scot* dreary [ME, of Scand origin; akin to ON *drjūgr* lasting]

**dreidel** *also* **dreidl** /'draydl/ *n* 1 a 4-sided toy marked with Hebrew letters and spun like a top 2 a children's game of chance played with a dreidel, esp at HANUKKAH (Jewish holiday) [Yiddish *dreidl,* fr *dreien* to turn, fr MHG *drǣjen,* fr OHG *drāen* – more at THROW]

**¹drench** /drench/ *n* 1 a poisonous or medicinal drink; *specif* a large dose of medicine mixed with liquid and put down the throat of an animal (e g a horse) 2a something that drenches b a quantity sufficient to drench or saturate

**²drench** *vt* 1 to administer a drench to (an animal) 2 to wet thoroughly (e g by soaking or immersing in liquid); saturate ⟨*desserts ~ed with brandy*⟩ 3 to soak or cover thoroughly with liquid that falls or is precipitated ⟨*~ed with rain*⟩ ⟨*~ed with sweat*⟩ 4 *archaic* to force to drink [ME *drenchen,* fr OE *drencan;* akin to OE *drincan* to drink] – **drencher** *n*

**Dresden** /'drezd(ə)n/ *n* an ornate delicately coloured porcelain made at Meissen near Dresden; MEISSEN [*Dresden,* city in Saxony, Germany]

**¹dress** /dres/ *vt* 1 to arrange (e g troops) in a straight line and at proper intervals 2a to put clothes on b to provide with clothing 3a to add decorative details or accessories to; embellish ⟨*~ a Christmas tree*⟩ b to arrange goods on a display in (e g a shop window) 4 to prepare for use or service; *esp* to prepare for cooking or eating by plucking, trussing, garnishing, etc ⟨*~ a chicken*⟩ ⟨*~ the salad with oil and vinegar*⟩ 5a to apply dressings or medicaments to ⟨*~ a wound*⟩ b(1) to arrange (the hair) by combing, brushing, or curling b(2) to groom (an animal) c to prepare (a slaughtered animal) for market by bleeding and cleaning – often + *out* d to cultivate, tend; *esp* to apply manure or fertilizer to e(1) to put through a finishing process; *specif* to give (textiles, wood, stone, etc) a smooth or finished surface e(2) to convert (animal hides) into leather ~ *vi* 1a to put on clothing b to put on or wear formal or evening clothes ⟨*guests were expected to ~ for dinner*⟩ 2 of a food animal to weigh after being dressed ⟨*the chicken ~ed four pounds*⟩ 3 to align oneself with the next soldier in a line to make the line straight 4 *of a man* to have one's genitals lying on a specified side of the trouser crutch ⟨*do you ~ to the right or left, sir?*⟩ – see also **dressed up to the** NINES, **dress** SHIP [ME *dressen,* fr MF *dresser,* fr (assumed) VL *directiare,* fr L *directus* direct, pp of *dirigere* to direct, fr *dis- + regere* to lead straight – more at RIGHT]

**dress down** *vt* to reprove severely – see also DRESSING-DOWN

**dress up** *vt* 1a(1) to clothe in best or formal clothes a(2) to make suitable for a formal occasion (e g by adding accessories) ⟨*dressing up a smock with a gilt belt and scarves*⟩ b to dress in clothes suited to a particular assumed role 2 to present or cause to appear in a certain light (e g by distortion or exaggeration) ⟨*dressed up his story to make himself appear a hero*⟩ ~ *vi* to get dressed up

**²dress** *n* 1 everyday or ornamental covering for the human body; *esp* clothing suitable for a particular purpose or occasion 2 a 1-piece outer garment for a woman or girl, including both top and skirt 3 covering, adornment, or appearance appropriate or peculiar to a specified time ⟨*18th-century ~*⟩ 4 a particular form of appearance or presentation; a guise ⟨*trees in their autumn ~*⟩

**³dress** *adj* of, being, or suitable for an occasion requiring or permitting formal dress ⟨*a ~ affair*⟩

**dressage** /'dresahzh, -'-/ *n* the performance by a trained horse of precise movements in response to barely perceptible movements of its rider's hands, legs, and weight; *also* the art of training a horse to carry out such a performance [Fr, preparation, straightening, training, fr *dresser* to prepare, make straight, train]

**dress circle** *n* the first or lowest curved tier of seats in a theatre [fr the evening dress formerly required to be worn by occupants]

**¹dresser** /'dresə/ *n* 1 a piece of kitchen furniture resembling a sideboard with a high back and having compartments and shelves for holding dishes and cooking utensils 2 *chiefly NAm* a chest of drawers or bureau with a mirror [ME, fr MF *dresseur,* fr OF *dreçor,* fr *drecier* to arrange]

**²dresser** *n* 1 one who or that which dresses ⟨*a fashionable ~*⟩ 2 a person who looks after stage costumes and helps actors to dress 3 a person who assists a surgeon during an operation (e g by passing instruments or dressings)

**dressing** /'dresing/ *n* 1 a sauce for adding to food ⟨*salad ~*⟩ 2 material applied to cover a wound 3 fertilizing material (e g manure or compost) to improve the growth of plants 4 *chiefly NAm* a seasoned mixture usu used as a stuffing (e g for poultry)

**,dressing-'down** *n* a severe scolding

**dressing gown** *n* a loose robe worn esp over nightclothes, when not fully dressed, or when resting

**dressing room** *n* a room used chiefly for dressing: e g a a room in a theatre for changing costumes and make-up b a room at a sports ground or centre for changing clothes

**dressing station** *n* a station for giving first aid to the wounded

**dressing table** *n* a table typically fitted with drawers and a mirror for use whilst dressing, applying make-up, combing one's hair, etc

**dressing-table set** *n* a set of toilet articles including a hairbrush, comb, and mirror for use at a dressing table

**dress length** *n* a piece of material large enough to be made into a dress

**dressmaker** /'dres,maykə/ *n* a person who does dressmaking

**dressmaking** /'dres,mayking/ *n* the process or occupation of making dresses and other clothes, esp for women and children

**dress rehearsal** *n* 1 a full rehearsal of a play in costume and with stage props shortly before the first performance 2 DRY RUN

**dress shield** *n* a waterproof shield worn to protect part of a garment

**dress shirt** *n* a man's formal shirt, esp for wear with evening dress

**dress uniform** *n* a uniform for formal wear

**dressy** /'dresi/ *adj* 1 *of a person* showy in dress 2 *of clothes* stylish, smart 3 overly elaborate in appearance – **dressiness** *n*

**drew** /drooh/ *past of* DRAW

**drey, dray** /dray/ *n* a squirrel's nest [origin unknown]

**Dreyfusard** /'drayfoo,sahd, 'drie-, ,--'-/ *n* a defender or partisan of Alfred Dreyfus [Fr, fr Alfred *Dreyfus* †1935 Fr army officer wrongly convicted of espionage]

**drib** /drib/ *n* – see DRIBS AND DRABS [prob back-formation fr *dribble & driblet*]

**¹dribble** /'dribl/ *vi* 1 to fall or flow in drops or in a thin intermittent stream; trickle 2 to let saliva trickle from the mouth; drool 3 to come or issue piece by piece or in disconnected fashion 4a to dribble a ball or puck b to proceed by dribbling c *of a ball* to move with short bounces ~ *vt* 1 to let or cause to fall in drops little by little 2 to issue sporadically and in small bits 3 to propel (a ball or puck) by successive slight taps or bounces with foot, hand, or stick (e g in soccer or hockey) [freq of *drib* (to dribble), prob alter. of *drip*] – **dribbler** *n*

**²dribble** *n* 1a a small trickling stream or flow b a drizzling shower 2 a tiny or insignificant bit or quantity 3 an act or instance of dribbling a ball or puck

**driblet** /'driblit/ *n* 1 a trifling sum or part 2 a drop of liquid [*drib* (to dribble) + *-let*]

**dribs and drabs** /,dribz ən 'drabz/ *n pl* small usu scattered amounts

**,dried-'up** *adj* no longer productive; wizened, shrivelled

**drier, dryer** /'drie-ə/ *n* 1 something that dries (e g by extracting or absorbing moisture) 2 a substance that accelerates drying (e g of oils, paints, and printing inks) 3 any of various machines for drying something (e g the hair or clothes), usu with warm air or by spinning

**¹drift** /drift/ *n* 1a the act of driving something along b the flow or the velocity of the current of a river or ocean stream 2 something driven or propelled along or drawn together in a clump (as if) by a natural force: e g 2a wind-driven snow, rain, cloud, dust, or smoke usu at or near the ground surface b(1) a mass of sand, snow, etc deposited together (as if) by wind or water b(2) rock debris deposited by wind, water, etc; *specif* a deposit of clay, sand, gravel, and boulders transported by (running water from) a glacier **3** a general underlying tendency or meaning, esp of what is spoken or written ⟨*do you get my* ∼?⟩ **4** a tool that is driven into or against something; *specif* a pin for stretching and aligning rivet holes **5** the motion or action of drifting, esp spatially and usu under external influence: e g **5a** the distance that a ship or aircraft deviates from its course due to the action of wind or current **b** a slow-moving ocean current **c** an easy moderate more or less steady flow or sweep along a spatial course **d** a gradual shift in attitude, opinion, or emotion **e** an aimless course with no attempt at direction or control **f** a deviation from a true reproduction, representation, or reading or from a set adjustment, esp of a measuring or receiving instrument **6a** a nearly horizontal mine passage bored on or parallel to the course of a vein or rock stratum **b** a small CROSSCUT (passage through a body of ore) in a mine connecting two larger tunnels **7a** an assumed trend towards a general change in the structure of a language over a period of time **b** GENETIC DRIFT **c** a gradual change in the zero reading of an instrument or in any measurement standard that is supposed to remain constant **8** *SAfr* a ford **synonyms** see TENDENCY [ME; akin to OE *drīfan* to drive – more at DRIVE]

²**drift** *vi* **1a** to become driven or carried along by a current of water, wind, or air **b** to move or float smoothly and effortlessly **2a** to move in a random or casual way **b** to become carried along aimlessly ⟨*the conversation* ∼ed *from one topic to another*⟩ **3** to accumulate in a mass or become piled up in heaps by wind or water **4** to vary or deviate from a set adjustment ∼ *vt* **1a** to pile up in a drift **b** to cover with drifts ⟨*slopes heavily* ∼ed *during winter*⟩ **2a** to cause to be drifted **b** *W US* to drive (livestock) slowly, esp to allow grazing **3** to insert a special pin (DRIFT 4) into – **driftingly** *adv*

**driftage** /'driftij/ *n* **1** a drifting of some object, esp through the action of wind or water **2** drifted material ⟨*seaweed and other* ∼⟩

**drifter** /'driftə/ *n* **1** one who or that which drifts; *esp* a person who travels or moves about aimlessly **2** a coastal fishing boat equipped with DRIFT NETS

**drift net** *n* a long shallow fishing net buoyed along its top edge by cork, glass, or plastic floats and weighted along its bottom edge so as to hang vertically and drift with the tide

**driftweed** /'drift,weed/ *n* a seaweed (e g of the genus *Laminaria*) that tends to break free and drift ashore

**driftwood** /'drift,wood/ *n* wood drifted or floated by water and often washed ashore on a beach

¹**drill** /dril/ *vt* **1a(1)** to bore or drive a hole in (as if) by the piercing action of a drill **a(2)** to make (e g a hole) by piercing action **b** to hit with piercing effect ⟨∼ed *the ball through the crowded goalmouth*⟩ **2a** to fix something in the mind or behaviour of by repetitive instruction ⟨∼ *pupils in the Highway Code*⟩ **b** to impart or communicate by repetition ⟨*impossible to* ∼ *the simplest idea into some people*⟩ **c** to train or exercise in military drill ∼ *vi* **1** to make a hole (as if) with a drill **2** to engage in esp military drill **synonyms** see TEACH [D *drillen;* akin to OHG *drāen* to turn – more at THROW] – **drillable** *adj,* **driller** *n*

²**drill** *n* **1a** a tool with an edged or pointed end for making a hole in a solid substance by revolving or by a succession of blows **b** a device or machine for rotating a drilling bit; *also* the bit itself **2** the act or exercise of training soldiers in marching and formalized parade movements with the accompanying handling of weapons **3a** a physical or mental exercise aimed at improving facility and skill by regular practice **b** a formal exercise by a team of marchers **4** (any of several INVERTEBRATE animals related to) a marine snail (*Urosalpinx cinerea*) that bores through the shells of oysters and feeds on the soft flesh **5** a drilling sound ⟨*the prolonged* ∼ *of the night insects*⟩ **6** *chiefly Br informal* the approved or correct procedure for accomplishing something efficiently

³**drill** *n* a W African baboon (*Mandrillus leucophaeus*) closely related to the typical MANDRILLS [prob native name in W Africa]

⁴**drill** *n* **1a** a shallow furrow or trench into which seed is sown **b** a row of seed sown in such a furrow **2** a planting implement that makes holes or furrows, drops in the seed and sometimes fertilizer, and covers them with earth [perh fr arch. *drill* (rill)]

⁵**drill** *vt* **1** to sow (seeds) by dropping along a shallow furrow **2a** to sow with seed or set with seedlings inserted in drills **b** to distribute seed or fertilizer in by means of a drill

⁶**drill** *n* a durable cotton fabric in twill weave [short for *drilling,*

modif of Ger *drillich,* fr MHG *drilich* fabric woven with a threefold thread, deriv of L *tri-* + *licium* thread]

**drillmaster** /'dril,mahstə/ *n* **1** an instructor in military drill **2** an instructor with a strict manner, often one who stresses trivial points

**drily** /'drieli/ *adv* dryly

¹**drink** /dringk/ *vb* **drank** /drangk/; **drunk** /drungk/ *vt* **1a** to swallow (a liquid); *also* to swallow the liquid contents of (e g a cup) **b** to take in or suck up; absorb ⟨∼ing *air into his lungs*⟩ **c** to take in or receive avidly – usu + *in* ⟨drank *in every word of the lecture*⟩ **2** to propose or join in (a toast); *also* to drink a toast to **3** to bring to a specified state by taking drink ⟨drank *himself into oblivion*⟩ ⟨∼ing *his troubles away*⟩ ∼ *vi* **1a** to swallow liquid **b** to receive something into one's consciousness – usu + *of* or *from* **2** to drink alcoholic beverages; *esp* to do this habitually or to excess **3** to drink a toast – + *to* [ME *drinken,* fr OE *drincan;* akin to OHG *trinkan* to drink]

²**drink** *n* **1** (a) liquid suitable for swallowing; a beverage; *esp* an alcoholic beverage **2** a draught or portion of liquid for drinking **3** excessive consumption of alcoholic beverages ⟨drove *him to* ∼⟩ **4** *informal* the sea; *broadly* any sizable body of water

**drinkable** /'dringkəbl/ *adj* suitable or safe for drinking – **drinkable** *n,* **drinkability** *n*

**drinker** /'dringkə/ *n* **1** one who drinks; *esp* one who drinks alcoholic beverages to excess **2** a device that provides water for domestic animals or poultry

**drinking fountain** /'dringking/ *n* a fixture with a nozzle that delivers a stream of water for drinking

**drinking-up time** *n, Br* a period allowed (e g in a public house) after the legal closing time during which drinks already bought may be finished

**drinking water** *n* water that is fit for humans to drink

**drinks** /dringks/ *adj* of, involving, or being for alcoholic drinks ⟨*a* ∼ *party*⟩ ⟨*a* ∼ *cupboard*⟩

¹**drip** /drip/ *vb* **-pp-** *vt* **1** to let fall in drops **2** to spill or let out copiously ⟨*her voice* ∼ping *sarcasm*⟩ ∼ *vi* **1a** to let fall drops of moisture or liquid **b** to overflow (as if) with moisture ⟨*a uniform* ∼ping *with gold braid*⟩ ⟨*a novel that* ∼s *with sentimentality*⟩ **2** to fall (as if) in drops [ME *drippen,* fr OE *dryppan;* akin to OE *dropa* drop] – **dripper** *n*

²**drip** *n* **1a** the action of falling in drops **b** liquid that falls, overflows, or is forced out in drops **2** the sound made (as if) by falling drops **3** a part of a cornice or other member that projects to deflect rainwater from the structure beneath; *also* an overlapping metal strip serving the same purpose **4a** a device for the administration of a liquid at a slow rate, esp into a vein **b** a substance administered by means of a drip ⟨*a saline* ∼⟩ **5** the liquid that exudes from frozen tissue (e g of meat, fruit, and vegetables) on thawing, owing to incomplete reabsorption of cell fluid **6** *informal* a dull, weak, or insipid person – **dripless** *adj,* **drippy** *adj,* **drippiness** *n*

¹**drip-'dry** *vb* to dry with few or no wrinkles when hung dripping wet

²**drip-dry** *adj* made of a washable fabric that drip-dries

'**drip-,feed** *n* ²DRIP 4A – **drip feed** *vt*

**drip mat** *n* a small mat placed under a glass, mug, etc to protect the surface on which it stands; a coaster

**dripping** /'driping/ *n* the fat that runs out from meat during roasting

**dripstone** /'drip,stohn/ *n* **1** a drip made of stone (e g over a window) **2** CALCIUM CARBONATE formed by dripping water in limestone areas and occurring as stalactites or stalagmites

**drip tray** *n* a tray for catching drips (e g of water from the freezing compartment of a refrigerator during defrosting)

¹**drive** /driev/ *vb* **drove** /drohv/; **driven** /'driv(ə)n/ *vt* **1a** to impart a forward motion to by physical force **b** to put into a specified position by physical force ⟨*waves* drove *the boat against the shore*⟩ ⟨∼ *the stake into the ground*⟩ **c** to repulse, remove, or cause to go by force, authority, or influence ⟨∼ *the enemy back*⟩ ⟨drove *the thought from my mind*⟩ **d** to set or keep in motion or operation ⟨∼ *machinery by electricity*⟩ **2a** to direct the motions and course of (a draught animal) **b** to control the mechanism and direct the course of (e g a motor vehicle) **c** to transport in a vehicle **3** to carry on or through energetically ⟨driving *a hard bargain*⟩ **4a** to exert inescapable or persuasive pressure on; force **b** to compel to undergo or suffer a change (e g in situation, awareness, or emotional state) ⟨drove *him crazy*⟩ **c** to urge relentlessly to continuous exertion ⟨*the sergeant* drove *his recruits to the point of exhaustion*⟩ **d** to press or force into an activity, course, or

direction ⟨*the expensive drug habit that* ∼s *addicts to steal*⟩ **5a** to cause (e g game or cattle) to move in a desired direction **b** to search (a district) for game **6** to bore (e g a tunnel or passage) **7a** to propel (a ball, puck, shuttlecock, etc) swiftly ⟨*drove the ball towards the goal*⟩ **b** to play a drive in cricket at (a ball) or at the bowling of (a bowler) **c** to hit (a golf ball) from the tee, esp with a driver **8** *NAm & NZ* to float (logs) down a stream ∼ *vi* **1a** to rush or dash rapidly or with force against an obstruction ⟨*rain driving against the windscreen*⟩ **b** to progress or rush along with strong momentum ⟨*the rain was driving hard*⟩ **2a** to operate a vehicle; *also* to be proficient in operating a vehicle **b** to drive or travel in a motor vehicle **3** to drive an object of play (e g a ball) [ME *driven*, fr OE *drīfan*; akin to OHG *trīban* to drive] – **drivable** *also* **driveable** *adj*

**drive at** *vt* to imply as an ultimate meaning or conclusion ⟨*couldn't work out what she was driving at*⟩

**drive off** *vi* to tee off in golf

²**drive** *n* **1** an act or instance of driving: e g **1a** a trip in a motor car or carriage **b** a collection and driving together of animals; *also, taking sing or pl vb* the animals gathered **c** a shoot in which the game is driven within the range of the guns **d** *NAm & NZ* the guiding of logs downstream to a mill; *also* the floating logs amassed in a drive **e(1)** a hard-hit long attacking shot in a racket game **e(2)** a stroke in cricket that is designed to send the ball in front of the batsman's wicket and that is conventionally played with a free swing of a straight bat ⟨*square* ∼⟩ **e(3)** a long golf shot, played esp with a driver from the tee **e(4)** a shot in bowls that is intended to hit an opponent's bowl or the jack with enough force to move it some distance along the green **2a** a private road giving access from a public way to a building on private land **b** a public road for leisure driving (e g in a park) **3** an offensive, aggressive, or expansionist move; *esp* a strong military attack against enemy-held terrain **4** the state of being hurried and under pressure **5** a strong systematic group effort; a campaign **6a** a basic or instinctual need; a motivating physiological condition (e g a state of hunger or thirst) ⟨*a strong sexual* ∼⟩; *also* an impelling or motivating force or desire that is acquired ⟨*enslaved by a* ∼ *for perfection*⟩ **b** great zeal in the pursuance of one's ends **7a** the means for giving motion to a machine or machine part ⟨*a shaft* ∼⟩ **b** the means by which the propulsive power of a motor vehicle is applied to the road ⟨*front-wheel* ∼⟩ **c** the position from which a motor vehicle is controlled and directed ⟨*right-hand* ∼⟩ **8** a device including a transport and heads for reading information from or writing information onto a tape, esp magnetic tape, or disk **9** *Br* a gathering of people to play a specified indoor game ⟨*a whist* ∼⟩ ⟨*a beetle* ∼⟩ ⟨*a bingo* ∼⟩ – **drive** *adj*

¹**drive-,in** *adj or n* (being) a place (e g a bank, cinema, or restaurant) that people can use while remaining in their cars

¹**drivel** /'drivl/ *vb* -ll- (*NAm* -l-, -ll-) *vi* **1** to let saliva dribble from the mouth or mucus run from the nose **2** to talk stupidly and childishly or carelessly ∼ *vt* **1** to utter in a childish or imbecilic manner **2** to fritter away in a childish fashion [ME *drivelen*, fr OE *dreflian*; akin to ON *draf* malt dregs, OE *deorc* dark] – **driveller** *n*

²**drivel** *n* foolish or childish nonsense

**driven** /'driv(ə)n/ *past part of* DRIVE

**driver** /'drievə/ *n* one who or that which drives: e g **a** a coachman **b** a person who drives a motor vehicle **c** a mechanical piece (e g a wheel) for imparting motion to another piece **d** an electronic circuit whose output provides the input of another circuit **e** a golf club that has a wooden head with a nearly vertical face and is used in driving – **driverless** *adj*

**driver ant** *n* ARMY ANT; *specif* any of various African and Asian ants (*Dorylus* or related genera) that are nomadic hunters and move in vast armies

**driver's seat** *n* DRIVING SEAT

**drive shaft** *n* PROPELLER SHAFT

**driveway** /'drievway/ *n* **1** a road or way along which animals are driven **2** DRIVE 2a

**driving** /'drieving/ *adj* **1** that communicates force ⟨*a* ∼ *wheel*⟩ **2a** having great force ⟨∼ *rain*⟩ **b** acting with vigour; energetic **3a** relating to a person's ability or suitability to drive a motor vehicle ⟨∼ *test*⟩ ⟨*a* ∼ *licence*⟩ **b** for use while driving a motor vehicle ⟨∼ *gloves*⟩ ⟨*a* ∼ *mirror*⟩ [(1, 2) fr prp of ¹*drive*; (3) fr gerund of ¹*drive*]

**driving range** *n* an area equipped with distance markers, clubs, balls, and tees for practising golf drives

**driving seat** *n* the position of top authority and control

¹**drizzle** /'driz(ə)l/ *vi* to rain in very small drops or very lightly ∼ *vt* to shed or let fall in minute drops or particles [perh alter. of ME *drysnen* to fall, fr OE -*drysnian* to disappear; akin to Goth *driusan* to fall] – **drizzlingly** *adv*

²**drizzle** *n* a fine misty rain – **drizzly** *adj*

**drogue** /drohg/ *n* **1** a cylindrical canvas device used as a SEA ANCHOR to reduce the drifting of a ship **2a** a cylindrical or funnel-shaped device towed as a target by an aeroplane **b** a small parachute for stabilizing or slowing down something (e g an astronaut's capsule) or for pulling a larger parachute out of stowage **3** a funnel-shaped device attached to the end of the refuelling hose of a tanker aircraft to receive the probe of another aircraft, thus enabling refuelling while both are in flight [prob alter. of ¹*drag*]

**droit** /droyt (*Fr* drwa)/ *n* a legal right or due ⟨∼s *of admiralty*⟩ [MF, fr ML *directum*, fr LL, neut of *directus* just, fr L, direct]

**droit du seigneur** /,drwah də se'nyuh (*Fr* drwa də sɛnœːr)/ *n* a supposed legal or customary right of a feudal lord to have sexual relations with a vassal's bride on her wedding night [Fr, right of the lord]

¹**droll** /drohl/ *adj* humorous, whimsical, or odd [Fr *drôle*, fr *drôle* scamp, fr MF *drolle*, fr MD, imp] – **drollness** *n*, **drolly** *adv*

²**droll** *n* one who amuses or diverts; a jester, comedian

**drollery** /'drohləri/ *n* **1** the act or an instance of jesting or of droll behaviour **2** droll humour

**-drome** /-,drohm/ *comb form* (→ *n*) **1** something that runs in (such) a direction ⟨*palindrome*⟩ ⟨*loxodrome*⟩ **2** racecourse ⟨*motor*-drome⟩ ⟨*hippo*drome⟩ **3** large place specially prepared for ⟨*aerodrome*⟩ [Gk -*dromos* running, fr *dromos* course, racecourse, act of running; akin to Gk *dramein* to run; (2, 3) MF, fr L -*dromos*, fr Gk *dromos*] – **dromous** *comb form* (→ *adj*)

**dromedary** /'droməd(ə)ri, 'drum-/ *n* **1** a camel of unusual speed bred and trained esp for riding **2** the 1-humped camel (*Camelus dromedarius*) of W Asia and N Africa [ME *dromedarie*, fr MF *dromedaire*, fr LL *dromedarius*, fr L *dromad*-, *dromas*, fr Gk, running; akin to Gk *dramein* to run, *dromos* racecourse, OE *treppan* to tread]

**dromond** /'dromənd, 'drum-/ *n* a large fast-sailing galley of medieval times [ME, fr MF *dromont*, fr LL *dromon*-, *dromo* light ship, fr Gk *dromōn*, fr *dramein* to run]

¹**drone** /'drohn/ *n* **1** a male bee in a colony of social bees that has no sting and gathers no honey and whose function is to mate with the queen **2** one who lives on the efforts or labours of others; a parasite **3** a pilotless aircraft, missile, or ship controlled by radio signals [ME, fr OE *drān*; akin to OHG *treno* drone]

²**drone** *vi* **1a** to make a sustained deep murmuring, humming, or buzzing sound **b** to talk in a persistently dull or monotonous tone **2** to pass, proceed, or act in a dull, drowsy, or indifferent manner ⟨*the trial* ∼d *on for months*⟩ ∼ *vt* **1** to utter or pronounce with a drone **2** to pass or spend in dull or monotonous activity or in idleness ⟨∼d *away the precious years of youth*⟩ – **droner** *n*, **droningly** *adv*

³**drone** *n* **1** any of the usu three pipes on a bagpipe that sound fixed continuous notes **2** a droning sound **3** an unvarying sustained bass note, usu the first or fifth note of the key of a piece of music

¹**drongo** /'drong·goh/ *also* **drongo shrike** *n, pl* **drongos** any of various insect-eating song birds (family Dicruridae) of tropical India, Africa, and Australia that typically have glossy black plumage and a long forked tail [Malagasy]

²**drongo** *n, pl* **drongos** *chiefly Austr informal* a worthless person; a fool [perh fr *Drongo*, name of an unsuccessful Austr racehorse]

¹**drool** /droohl/ *vi* **1a** to secrete saliva in anticipation of food **b** to drivel **2** to make a foolishly effusive show of pleasure ∼ *vt* to express sentimentally or effusively [perh alter. of *drivel*]

²**drool** *n* drivel

¹**droop** /droohp/ *vi* **1** to hang or incline downwards (as if) in weariness **2** to become depressed or weakened; languish **3** *esp of the sun, poetic* to sink gradually ∼ *vt* to let droop [ME *drupen*, fr ON *drūpa*; akin to OE *dropa* drop – more at DROP] – **droopingly** *adv*

²**droop** *n* the condition or appearance of drooping – **droopy** *adj*

¹**drop** /drop/ *n* **1a(1)** the quantity of liquid that forms, falls, or clings to a surface in one round, hemispherical, or pear-shaped mass **a(2)** *pl* a dose of medicine measured by drops; *esp* a solution for dilating the pupil of the eye **b** a minute quantity or

degree (eg of an emotion or feeling) ⟨*not a ~ of pity in him*⟩ **c** a small quantity of drink, esp alcohol **d** the smallest practical unit of liquid measure **2** something that resembles a liquid drop: eg **2a** an ornament that hangs from a piece of jewellery (eg an earring) **b** a small globular often medicated sweet or lozenge ⟨*pear ~*⟩ ⟨*cough ~*⟩ **3** the act or an instance of dropping; a fall **b** a decline in quantity or quality **c** a descent by parachute; *also* the personnel or equipment dropped by parachute **4a** the distance from a higher to a lower level or through which something drops **b** a difference in voltage between two points (eg of a circuit) **c** a steep slope **5** something that drops, hangs, or falls: eg **5a** an unframed piece of cloth stage scenery; *also* DROP CURTAIN **b** a hinged platform on a gallows **c** a fallen fruit **d** DROP SHOT **6a** *NAm* a central point or depository to which something (eg mail) is brought for distribution or transmission – compare MAIL DROP **b** *informal* a secret place used for the deposit and distribution of stolen or illegal goods; *also* the goods themselves [ME, fr OE *dropa*; akin to Goth *driusan* to fall – more at DREARY] – **droplet** *n* – **at the drop of a hat** without hesitation; promptly – **drop in a bucket/the ocean** something too small to have the desired effect – **have/get the drop on** *NAm slang* to have or get at a disadvantage

²**drop** *vb* -pp- *vi* **1** to fall in drops **2a(1)** to fall, esp unexpectedly or suddenly **a(2)** to descend from one level to another ⟨*his voice ~ped*⟩ **b** to fall in a state of collapse or death ⟨*he'll work until he ~s*⟩ ⟨*I'm ready to ~*⟩ **c** *of a card* to become played by reason of the obligation to follow suit **d** *of a ball* to roll into a hole, pocket, or basket **3** to move with a favouring wind or current – usu + *down* **4** to enter as if without conscious effort of will into some specified state, condition, or activity ⟨*~ped into sleep*⟩ **5a** to cease to be of concern; lapse ⟨*let the matter ~*⟩ **b** to become less ⟨*production ~ped*⟩ – often + *off* **6** to come or go unexpectedly or informally – usu + *in, by, over,* or *round* ⟨*~ in for a cup of tea*⟩ ⟨*~ round to see us sometime*⟩ ~ *vt* **1a** to let fall; cause to fall **b** to drop a catch offered by (a batsman) **2a** to lower or cause to descend from one level or position to another **b** to cause to lessen or decrease; reduce ⟨*~ped his speed*⟩ ⟨*~ped his voice*⟩ **3a** to set down from a ship or vehicle; unload; *also* to airdrop **b** to perform (a curtsy) **4a** to bring down with a shot or blow **b** to cause (a high card) to drop **c** to toss or roll (a ball) into a hole or basket **d** to score (a goal) with a dropkick **5a** to give up (eg an idea) **b** to leave incomplete; cease ⟨*~ped what he was doing*⟩ **c** to break off an association or connection with; dismiss ⟨*~ped his old friends*⟩; *also* to leave (eg a player) out of a team or group **6a** to leave (a letter representing a speech sound) unsounded ⟨*~ the g in running*⟩ **b** to leave out in writing **7a** to utter or mention in a casual way ⟨*~ a hint*⟩ **b** to send through the post ⟨*~ us a line soon*⟩ **8** *of an animal* to give birth to **9** to lose ⟨*~ped two games*⟩ ⟨*~ped £500 on the stockmarket*⟩ – compare LET DROP **10** *informal* to take (a drug, esp a narcotic) orally; swallow ⟨*~ acid*⟩ – compare SNORT – **drop a brick/clanger** *informal* to make an embarrassing error or mistaken remark – see also **drop DEAD/in somebody's LAP/off one's PERCH, LET drop, the PENNY drops**

**drop back** *vi* to move into a more backward position; *specif* to move towards the rear of an advancing line or column

**drop behind** *vb* to fail to keep up (with)

**drop off** *vi* **1** to fall asleep **2** to decline; *also* to dwindle – see also DROP-OFF

**drop out** *vi* **1** to withdraw from participation or membership; *esp* to withdraw from conventional society because of disenchantment with its values and customs **2** to make a drop-out in rugby **3** *of an electronic device* to cease operating for a short period of time – see also DROPOUT, DROP-OUT

**drop curtain** *n* a stage curtain that can be lowered and raised

'**drop-forging** *n* a method of forging metal between two DIES using a DROP HAMMER or similar weight dropped onto hot metal – **drop forge** *vt*, **drop forger** *n*

**drop front** *n* a hinged cover on the front of a desk that may be lowered to provide a surface for writing

**drop goal** *n* a score in rugby made with a dropkick

**drop hammer** *n* a power hammer to which a DIE is attached that is dropped onto hot metal resting on an anvil or a second die in the process of DROP-FORGING

**drop handlebars** *n pl* lowered curving handlebars, esp on a racing bicycle

**drophead** /'drop,hed/ *n, Br* the usu canvas roof of a convertible car

**dropkick** /'drop,kik/ *n* a kick made (eg in rugby or American football) by dropping a ball to the ground and kicking it at the moment it starts to rebound

'**drop-kick** *vi* to make a dropkick ~ *vt* to score (a goal) with a dropkick – **dropkicker** *n*

**drop leaf** *n* a hinged flap on the side or end of a table that can be folded down – **drop-leaf** *adj*

'**drop-off** *n* **1** a marked dwindling or decline ⟨*a ~ in attendance*⟩ **2** *NAm* a very steep or perpendicular descent

**dropout** /'dropowt/ *n* **1** one who drops out; *esp* one who drops out of conventional society or an educational institution **2a** a spot on a MAGNETIC TAPE from which data has disappeared **b** an instance of an electronic device ceasing to operate for a short time

'**drop-out** *n* a dropkick awarded to the defending team in rugby

**droppage** /'dropij/ *n* the part of a fruit crop that falls from the tree before it is ready for picking

**dropper** /'dropə/ *n* **1** one who or that which drops **2** a short glass tube that is fitted with a rubber bulb and used to measure or administer liquids, esp medications, by drops – **dropperful** *n*

**dropping** /'droping/ *n* **1** something dropped **2** *pl* animal dung

**drop scone** *n* a small round scone made by dropping a spoonful of batter onto a hot griddle

**drop shot** *n* a delicate shot (eg in tennis, badminton, or squash) that drops quickly after crossing the net or dies after hitting a wall

**dropsonde** /'drop,sond/ *n* a RADIOSONDE (radio transmitter used for relaying meteorological data) that is dropped by parachute from a high-flying aircraft [*drop* + *radiosonde*]

**dropsy** /'dropsi/ *n* OEDEMA; *esp* a condition in which an accumulation of excess liquid causes widespread swelling in the tissues of the body [ME *dropesie*, short for *ydropesie*, fr OF, fr L *hydropisis*, modif of Gk *hydrōps*, fr *hydōr* water – more at WATER] – **dropsical** *adj*

**drop tank** *n* an auxiliary fuel tank usu carried under the wing or fuselage of an aircraft, which can be detached and dropped in flight

**dropwort** /'drop,wuht/ *n* a Eurasian plant (*Filipendula vulgaris*) of the rose family that resembles the related meadowsweet and has fine leaflets arranged in pairs and small whitish flowers in dense clusters – compare WATER DROPWORT

**drop zone** *n* the area in which troops, supplies, or equipment are to be air-dropped; *also* the target on which a parachutist lands

**drosera** /'drosərə/ *n* SUNDEW (insect-eating bog plant) [NL, genus name, fr Gk, fem of *droseros* dewy, fr *drosos* dew]

**droshky** /'droshki/ *also* **drosky** /'droski/ *n* any of various 2-wheeled or 4-wheeled open carriages used esp in Russia in former times [Russ *drozhki*, fr *droga* shaft of a waggon]

**drosophila** /dro'sofilə/ *n* any of a genus (*Drosophila*) of small FRUIT FLIES extensively used in genetic research [NL, genus name, fr Gk *drosos* + NL *-phila*, fem of *-philus* -phil]

**dross** /dros/ *n* **1** the scum that forms on the surface of molten metal **2** waste, rubbish, or foreign matter; impurities [ME *dros*, fr OE *drōs* dregs] – **drossy** *adj*

**drought** /drowt/ *n* **1** a prolonged period of dryness **2** a prolonged shortage or lack of something [ME, fr OE *drūgath*, fr *drūgian* to dry up; akin to OE *drȳge* dry – more at DRY] – **droughtiness** *n*, **droughty** *adj*

**drouth** /drowt, drowth/ *n, Scot, Irish, or NAm* a drought – used poetically in other forms of English

¹**drove** /drohv/ *n* **1** taking sing or pl vb a large group of animals driven or moving in a body **2** **drove** taking sing or pl vb, **droves** *pl* a crowd of people moving or acting together **3a** a chisel used to form a groove or roughly shaped surface on stone **b** the grooved surface so formed [ME, fr OE *drāf*, fr *drīfan* to drive – more at DRIVE]

²**drove** *vt, chiefly Austr* to drive (cattle) ~ *vi* to work as a drover

³**drove** *past of* DRIVE

**drover** /'drohvə/ *n* one who drives cattle or sheep

**drown** /drown/ *vi* to become drowned ~ *vt* **1a** to suffocate by submergence, esp in water **b** to submerge, esp by a rise in the water level **c** to wet thoroughly; drench ⟨*~ed the chips with ketchup*⟩ **2** to engage (oneself) deeply and strenuously ⟨*~ed* *himself in work* 3 to cause (a sound) not to be heard by making a louder noise *⟨his speech was ~ed out by ... boos – New Yorker⟩* 4 to drive out (eg a sensation or an idea) as if by drowning *⟨~ed his sorrows in drink⟩* – see also **like a drowned RAT** [ME *drounen*]

**¹drowse** /drowz/ to doze 1 to make drowsy or inactive 2 to pass (time) drowsily or in drowsing; doze – usu + *away* [prob akin to Goth *driusan* to fall – more at DREARY]

**²drowse** *n* the act or an instance of drowsing; a doze

**drowsy** /'drowzy/ *adj* 1a sleepy b tending to induce sleepiness *⟨a ~ summer afternoon⟩* c lazy, lethargic 2 giving the appearance of peaceful inactivity – **drowsily** *adv*, **drowsiness** *n*

**drub** /drub/ *vb* -bb- *vt* 1 to beat severely (as if) with a stick or cudgel 2 to attack with words; berate *⟨the book was ~bed by every critic⟩* 3 to defeat decisively ~ *vi* to stamp, (eg with the feet); drum [prob deriv of Ar *ḍaraba*] – **drubber** *n*

**¹drudge** /druj/ *vi* to do hard, menial, routine, or monotonous work **synonyms** see ¹WORK [ME *druggen;* prob akin to OE *drēogan* to work, endure, L *firmus* firm] – **drudger** *n*, **drudgery** *n*

**²drudge** *n* someone who drudges

**¹drug** /drug/ *n* 1a a synthetic or natural substance used as, or in the preparation of, a medication **b(1)** a substance recognized in an official book or list of medicinal preparations, specif a pharmacopoeia or formulary **b(2)** a substance intended for use in the diagnosis, cure, treatment, or prevention of disease 2 a substance that has an effect on the body; esp an often poisonous substance taken internally to affect the structure or function of the body (eg to cause pleasant feelings, relaxation, or sleep) 3 a substance that causes addiction or habituation [ME *drogges, drouges,* pl, fr OF *drogue*] – **drug on the market** a commodity that will not sell, usu owing to a glut

**²drug** *vb* -gg- *vt* 1 to affect or adulterate with a drug *⟨ ~ his tea⟩* 2 to administer a drug to 3 to lull or stupefy as if with a drug *⟨~ged with exhaustion⟩* ~ *vi* to take drugs for narcotic effect

**drugget** /'drugit/ *n* a coarse durable cloth used chiefly as a floor covering [MF *droguet,* dim. of *drogue* trash, drug]

**druggist** /'drugist/ *n* 1 one who deals in or dispenses drugs and medicines; a pharmacist 2 NAm the owner or manager of a drugstore

**drugstore** /'drug,staw/ *n, chiefly NAm* a chemist's shop; *esp* one which also sells sweets, magazines, and refreshments

**druid** /'drooh·id/, *fem* **druidess** /'drooh·idis/ *n, often cap* 1 a member of an ancient Celtic priesthood appearing in Irish and Welsh sagas and Christian legends as magicians and wizards 2 an officer of the Welsh GORSEDD (institution of poets) 3 MANDARIN 1c [L *druides, druidae,* pl, fr Gaulish *druides;* akin to OIr *druī* wizard, W *derwen* oak tree, OE *trēow* tree] – **druidic, druidical** *adj, often cap*

**druidism** /'drooh·i,diz(ə)m/ *n, often cap* the system of religion, philosophy, and instruction of the druids; *also* a modern system in imitation of this

**¹drum** /drum/ *n* 1 a percussion instrument that usu consists of a hollow cylinder with a drumhead stretched over each end and is played by beating with a stick, a pair of sticks, or the hands; *broadly* a nonmetallic hollow instrument or device beaten to produce a deep-toned rumbling or booming sound 2 the TYMPANIC MEMBRANE of the ear; the eardrum 3 the sound made by striking a drum; *also* any similar sound 4 something resembling a drum in shape: **4a** a cylindrical machine or mechanical device or part; *esp* a metal cylinder coated with magnetic material on which data (eg for a computer) may be recorded **b** a cylindrical container; *specif* a large usu metal container for liquids **c** a disc-shaped magazine for holding ammunition for an automatic weapon 5 **drum, drumfish** any of various spiny-finned fishes (family Sciaenidae) that make a drumming noise **6a** *slang* a house, flat, or other dwelling place; PAD **6 b** *Austr informal* a brothel [prob fr D *trom;* akin to MHG *trumme* drum] – **drumlike** *adj*

**²drum** *vb* -mm- *vi* 1 to beat a drum 2 to make a succession of strokes, taps, or vibrations that produce drumlike sounds; *esp, of a bird or insect* to make a hollow rhythmic sound by continuous fast beating of the wings 3 to throb or sound rhythmically *⟨blood ~med in his ears⟩* 4 *chiefly NAm* to stir up interest; solicit *⟨~ming for business⟩* ~ *vt* 1 to summon or enlist (as if) by beating a drum *⟨~med them into service⟩* 2 to drive or force (eg an idea or lesson) by persistent effort or reiteration – usu + *into* or *out of ⟨~med the idea into them⟩* **3a** to strike or tap repeatedly **b** to produce (rhythmic sounds) by such action

**drum out** *vt* to dismiss ignominiously; expel *⟨drummed him out of the army⟩*

**drum up** *vt* 1 to bring about by persistent effort *⟨drum up some business⟩* 2 to invent, originate *⟨drum up a new time-saving method⟩*

**³drum** *n* 1 a drumlin 2 *chiefly Scot* a long narrow hill or ridge [ScGael *druim* back, ridge, fr OIr *druimm*]

**drumbeat** /'drum,beet/ *n* 1 (the sound of) a stroke on a drum 2 a cause which is vociferously supported – **drumbeater** *n*

**drum brake** *n* a brake that operates by the friction of pads pressing against a rotating drum

**drumfire** /'drum,fie·ə/ *n* 1 continuous artillery fire that sounds like a drumroll 2 something suggestive of drumfire in intensity *⟨a ~ of publicity⟩*

**drumhead** /'drum,hed/ *n* 1 the material (eg skin or plastic) stretched over the end of a drum 2 the top part of a capstan into which the bars used in turning it are inserted

**drumhead court-martial** *n* a court-martial that is convened at short notice to try offences committed during military action [fr the use of a drumhead as a table]

**drumlin** /'drumlin/ *n* an elongated or oval hill formed from debris transported and deposited by a glacier [IrGael *druim* back, ridge (fr OIr *druimm*) + E *-lin* (alter. of *-ling*)]

**drum major** *n* the marching leader of a band; *esp* a non-commissioned officer in charge of the corps of drums in a military band

**drum majorette** *n* 1 a female drum major 2 a girl who twirls a baton while accompanying a procession or marching band

**drummer** /'drumə/ *n* 1 someone who plays a drum 2 *chiefly NAm* SALES REPRESENTATIVE

**drum printer** *n* a LINE PRINTER (high-speed printing device used esp for computer data) in which the printing element is a revolving drum

**drumstick** /'drum,stik/ *n* 1 a stick for beating a drum 2 the lower part of a fowl's leg between the thigh and foot when cooked as food

**¹drunk** /drungk/ *past part of* DRINK

**²drunk** *adj* 1 having the faculties impaired by alcohol 2 overcome by an intense feeling *⟨ ~ with power⟩* 3 of, characterized by, or resulting from alcoholic intoxication; drunken – see also **drunk in** CHARGE **synonyms** see DRUNKEN [ME *drunke,* alter. of *drunken*]

**³drunk** *n* 1 a drunkard 2 *informal* a period of excessive drinking

**drunkard** /'drungkəd/ *n* a person who is habitually drunk

**drunken** /'drungkən/ *adj* 1 DRUNK 1 **2a** given to habitual excessive use of alcohol **b** of, characterized by, or resulting from alcoholic intoxication *⟨ ~ behaviour⟩ ⟨a ~ brawl⟩ ⟨ ~ homes⟩* 3 unsteady or lurching as if from alcoholic intoxication 4 *obs* saturated with liquid; drenched [ME, fr OE *druncen,* fr pp of *drincan* to drink] – **drunkenly** *adv*, **drunkenness** *n*

**synonyms Drunk** is used chiefly after a verb *⟨she got drunk⟩* while **drunken** is used chiefly before a noun *⟨drunken merriment⟩*. But since **drunken**, rather than **drunk**, is the word for habitual intoxication, **drunk** can be used before a noun *⟨a pub full of drunk sailors⟩* and **drunken** after a verb *⟨his habits were both drunken and lecherous⟩* to distinguish between the two meanings.

**drupaceous** /drooh'payshəs/ *adj* 1 of or being a drupe 2 bearing drupes

**drupe** /droohp/ *n* a fruit (eg a cherry, plum, or almond) having usu a single seed enclosed in a hard stony coat and surrounded by juicy flesh and a thin flexible or stiff skin [NL *drupa,* fr L, overripe olive, fr Gk *dryppa* olive]

**drupel** /'droohpl/, **drupelet** /'droohplit/ *n* a small drupe; *specif* any of the individual parts of an aggregate fruit (eg the raspberry)

**Druze, Druse** /droohz/ *n* a member of a religious sect originating among Muslims and centred in the mountains of Lebanon and Syria [Ar *Durūz,* pl, fr Muḥammed ibn-Ism'aīlal-Darazīy †1019 Muslim religious leader]

**¹dry** /drie/ *adj* **1a** free or relatively free from a liquid, esp water **b** not in or under water, esp the sea *⟨ ~ land⟩* **c** lacking precipitation or humidity *⟨a ~ climate⟩* **2a** characterized by exhaustion of a supply of water or liquid *⟨a ~ well⟩ ⟨the barrel ran ~⟩* **b** devoid of running water *⟨a ~ ravine⟩* **c** devoid of natural moisture *⟨ ~ mouth⟩; also* thirsty **d** no longer sticky or damp *⟨the paint is ~⟩* **e** of a mammal not giving milk *⟨a ~ cow⟩* **f** lacking freshness; stale **g** *chemistry* free from WATER OF CRYSTALLIZATION (water essential for maintenance of a crystal structure); ANHYDROUS **3a** marked by the absence or scantiness of secretions ⟨*a ~ cough*⟩ **b** not shedding or accompanied by tears ⟨*no ~ eyes*⟩ **4a** prohibiting the manufacture or distribution of alcoholic drink ⟨*a ~ county*⟩ **b** marked by the absence of alcoholic drinks ⟨*a ~ party*⟩ **5** served or eaten without butter, jam, etc ⟨*~ toast*⟩ **6a** lacking sweetness **b** having all or most sugar fermented to alcohol ⟨*a ~ wine*⟩ **7** solid as opposed to liquid ⟨*~ groceries*⟩ **8** functioning without lubrication ⟨*a ~ clutch*⟩ **9a** built or constructed without a process which requires water: **9a(1)** using no mortar ⟨*~ masonry*⟩ **a(2)** using prefabricated materials (e g plasterboard) rather than a construction involving plaster or mortar ⟨*~ wall construction*⟩ **b** requiring no liquid in preparation or operation ⟨*a ~ photocopying machine*⟩ **10a** not showing or communicating warmth, enthusiasm, or tender feeling; severe ⟨*a ~ style of painting*⟩ **b** wearisome, uninteresting ⟨*~ passages of description*⟩ **c** lacking descriptive detail, bias, or emotional concern; plain ⟨*the ~ facts*⟩ **11** not yielding what is expected or desired; unproductive ⟨*a ~ oil field*⟩ **12** marked by a matter-of-fact, ironic, or terse manner of expression ⟨*~ wit*⟩ **13** lacking smooth sound qualities ⟨*a ~ rasping voice*⟩ [ME, fr OE *drȳge;* akin to OHG *truckan* dry] – **dryish** *adj,* **dryly** *adv,* **dryness** *n*

**²dry** *vt* to make dry; desiccate ~ *vi* **1** to become dry **2** DRY UP 4b □ (*vt; vi1*) often + *out* – **dryable** *adj*

 **dry out** *vb* to (cause to) undergo treatment for alcoholism or drug addiction

 **dry up** *vi* **1** to disappear or cease to yield (as if) by evaporation, draining, or the cutting off of a source of supply **2** to wither or die through gradual loss of vitality **3** *Br* to dry washed-up dishes by hand **4** *informal* **4a** to stop talking; shut up **b** to forget one's lines when acting in a play ~ *vt* **1** to end the existence of (as if) by drying up **2** to dry (washed-up dishes) after a meal

**³dry** *n, pl* **drys 1** something dry: e g **1a** a dry place **b** *chiefly Austr* the dry season **2** *NAm* someone who supports a ban on the sale of alcoholic drinks; a prohibitionist

**dryad** /'drie·ad, -əd/ *n* a nymph of woods and trees in Greek mythology [L *dryad-, dryas,* fr Gk, fr *drys* tree – more at TREE]

**dryasdust** /,drie·əz'dust/ *adj* boring, pedantic – **dryasdust** *n*

**dry battery** *n* an electric battery consisting of a DRY CELL or group of two or more dry cells connected together

**dry-bulb** *adj* of, being, or recorded by the thermometer in a PSYCHROMETER (device for measuring atmospheric humidity) that has an unmoistened bulb and that measures the temperature of the surrounding air – compare WET-BULB

**dry cell** *n* a battery cell whose ELECTROLYTE (substance that conducts an electric current) is not a liquid – compare WET CELL

**,dry-'clean** *vb* to (cause to) undergo dry cleaning – **dry-cleanable** *adj*

**dry cleaning** *n* **1** the cleansing of fabrics or garments without the use of water, usu using an organic chlorine-containing chemical compound (e g 1,1,1 trichloroethylene) as a solvent **2** that which is dry-cleaned

**dry dock** *n* a dock from which the water can be pumped to allow the part of a ship that floats beneath the waterline to be examined or repaired – **dry-dock** *vt*

**dryer** /'drie·ə/ *n* a drier

**dry farming** *n* a system of farming in dry regions without using irrigation, that relies on methods of conserving moisture in the soil and on drought-resistant crops – **dry farm** *n,* **dry-farm** *vt,* **dry farmer** *n*

**dry fly** *n* an artificial angling fly designed to float on the surface of the water

**dry goods** *n pl, chiefly NAm* textiles, ready-to-wear clothing, and dressmaking accessories as distinguished esp from hardware and groceries

**dry ice** *n* solidified carbon dioxide, usu in the form of blocks, that does not melt into a liquid form but above −78.5° Celsius changes directly to a gas and is used chiefly as a refrigerant

**drying oil** /'drie·ing/ *n* an oil (e g linseed oil) that hardens to a tough elastic film when a thin layer is exposed to the air, and is used esp in paints and varnishes

**dry kiln** *n* a heated chamber for drying and seasoning cut timber

**dry martini** *n* a cocktail made from gin and dry vermouth

**dry measure** *n* a series of units for measurement of the capacity of dry goods

**dry nurse** *n* a nurse who takes care of but does not breast-feed another woman's baby – compare WET NURSE – **dry-nurse** *vt*

**dryopithecine** /,drie·ohpi'theesin, 'pithəsin, -seen/ *n* any of a subfamily (Dryopithecinae) of extinct manlike apes that lived in Europe, N Africa, and N India in the MIOCENE and PLIOCENE times and are sometimes regarded as ancestors of both man and modern apes [deriv of Gk *drys* tree + *pithēkos* ape] – **dryopithecine** *adj*

**drypoint** /'drie,poynt/ *n* **1** an engraving made with a pointed tool (e g a needle) directly into a metal plate without the use of acid as in etching; *also* a print made from such an engraving **2** the needle used for drypoint engraving

**dry riser** *n* a system of pipes in a building with outlets at certain points for distributing a fire-extinguishing fluid

**dry rot** *n* **1a** a decay of seasoned timber (e g in floorboards, door frames, etc) caused by any of various fungi that consume the CELLULOSE of the wood, leaving it brittle and crumbly **b** a fungous rot of plant tissue in which the affected areas are dry and often firmer than normal, or more or less mummified **2** a fungus (e g *Serpula lacrymans*) causing dry rot **3** moral or social decay from within caused esp by resistance to new forces ⟨*art ... infected by the ~ of formalism* – D G Mandelbaum⟩

**dry run** *n* **1** a firing practice without ammunition **2** a practice exercise; a rehearsal, trial

**drysalter** /'drie,sawltə/ *n, Br* a dealer in certain dry chemicals (e g dyes) – **drysaltery** *n*

**'dry-,shod** *adj* having or keeping dry shoes or feet

**dry socket** *n* an exposed painful tooth socket in which there is delayed healing after an extraction

**drystone** /'drie,stohn/ *adj, esp of a wall* constructed of usu local undressed stone without the use of mortar

**dry well** *n* a hole made in porous ground and filled with gravel or rubble to catch water (e g drainage from a roof) and allow it to seep away

**dt's** /,dee 'teez/ *n pl, often cap D&T* DELIRIUM TREMENS (nervous disorder resulting from alcoholism)

**duad** /'dyooh·ad/ *n* a pair [irreg fr Gk *dyad-, dyas* – more at DYAD]

**dual** /'dyooh·əl/ *adj* **1** of grammatical NUMBER (*whether singular, plural, etc*) denoting reference to two **2a** consisting of two (like) parts or elements **b** having a double character or nature △ **duel** [L *dualis,* fr *duo* two – more at TWO] – **dual** *n,* **duality** *n,* **dualize** *vt,* **dually** *adv*

**dual carriageway** *n, chiefly Br* a road that has traffic travelling in opposite directions separated by a central reservation

**dual citizenship** *n* the status of an individual who is a citizen of two or more nations

**,dual-con'trol** *adj, esp of a vehicle or aircraft* able to be controlled by two people, usu an instructor and a trainee

**dual fuel engine** *n* an engine that is capable of running on two types of fuel (e g petrol or gas) and can be switched from one fuel to the other

**dualism** /'dyooh·ə,liz(ə)m/ *n* **1** a theory that considers reality to consist of two independent and fundamental principles (e g mind and matter) **2** the quality or state of being dual **3a** a doctrine that the universe is ruled by two opposing principles, one of which is good and the other evil **b** a view of man as composed of two fundamental elements (e g mind and body) □ compare MONISM, PLURALISM – **dualist** *n,* **dualistic** *adj,* **dualistically** *adv*

**,dual-'purpose** *adj* intended for or serving two purposes ⟨*~ cleaning and polishing fluid*⟩ ⟨*~ cattle bred for milk and meat*⟩

**¹dub** /dub/ *vt* **-bb- 1a** to confer knighthood on, esp by a ceremonial touching on the shoulder with a sword **b** to call by a descriptive name or epithet; nickname **2** to trim or remove the comb and WATTLES (fleshy lobes hanging beneath the throat) of (e g a domestic fowl) **3** *Br* to prepare (a fishing fly or bait) for use on a hook [ME *dubben,* fr OE *dubbian;* akin to ON *dubba* to dub, OHG *tubili* plug] – **dubber** *n*

**²dub** *n, chiefly NAm informal* a clumsy person; a duffer [prob fr ¹*dub* (in the sense "to beat flat")]

**³dub** *n, chiefly Scot* a pool, puddle [ME (Sc) *dubbe*]

**⁴dub** *vt* **-bb- 1a(1)** to provide (a film) with a new or altered soundtrack, esp one in a different language ⟨*the film was ~bed in French*⟩ **a(2)** to provide (a film) with a soundtrack; *specif* to match the soundtrack to the pictures of (a film) **b** to match (a soundtrack) to the pictures of a film **c** *chiefly Br* to construct (a soundtrack) out of two or more different tracks (e g music, sound effects, or commentary); MIX **3 2** to add (sound effects) to a film or to a radio or television production – usu + *in* **3** to transpose (a previous recording) to a new record [by shortening & alter. fr *double*] – **dubber** *n*

**dubbin** /'dubin/ *n* a grease made of oil and tallow for softening and waterproofing leather [*dubbing*, gerund of *dub* (to dress leather)] – **dubbin** *vt*

**dubbing** /'dubing/ *n* dubbin

**dubbing mixer** *n* a person whose work is dubbing films

**dubiety** /dyooh'bie·əti/ *n, formal* **1** the state of being doubtful **2** a matter of doubt *synonyms* see UNCERTAINTY *antonym* decision [LL *dubietas*, fr L *dubius*]

**dubiosity** /ˌdyoohbi'osəti/ *n, formal* doubt

**dubious** /'dyoohbi·əs/ *adj* **1** giving rise to doubt; uncertain ⟨*they felt our scheme a little ∼*⟩ **2** unsettled in opinion; undecided ⟨*they were a little ∼ about our plan*⟩ **3** of doubtful promise or uncertain outcome ⟨*a rather ∼ experiment*⟩ **4** of questionable value, quality, or origin; *also, euph* dishonest ⟨*won by ∼ means*⟩ [L *dubius*, fr *dubare* to vacillate; akin to L *duo* two – more at TWO] – **dubiously** *adv*, **dubiousness** *n*

**dubitable** /'dyoohbitəbl/ *adj, formal* open to doubt or question [L *dubitabilis*, fr *dubitare* to doubt – more at DOUBT]

**dubitation** /ˌdyoohbi'taysh(ə)n/ *n, archaic* doubt

**Dublin Bay prawn** /ˌdublin 'bay/ *n* a large prawn, often eaten as scampi [*Dublin Bay*, inlet in E Ireland]

**Dubonnet** /dooh'bonay/ *trademark* – used for an aperitif wine

**ducal** /'dyoohkl/ *adj* of a duke or duchy [MF, fr LL *ducalis* of a leader, fr L *duc-, dux* leader – more at DUKE] – **ducally** *adv*

**ducat** /'dukət/ *n* a usu gold coin formerly used in many European countries [ME, fr MF, fr OIt *ducato* coin with the doge's portrait on it, fr *duca* doge, fr LGk *douk-, doux* leader, fr L *duc-, dux*]

**duce** /'doohchi/ *n* a leader – used chiefly with reference to the leader of the Italian Fascists [It (*Il*) *Duce*, lit., the leader, title of Benito Mussolini †1945 It dictator, fr L *duc-, dux*]

**duchess** /'duchis/ *n* **1** the wife or widow of a duke **2** a woman having in her own right the rank of a duke **3** *Br informal* a wife, woman – used affectionately [ME *duchesse*, fr MF, fr *duc* duke]

**duchy** /'duchi/ *n* the territory of a duke or duchess; dukedom [ME *duche*, fr MF *duché*, fr *duc*]

¹**duck** /duk/ *n, pl* **ducks**, (1a&2) **ducks**, *esp collectively* **duck** **1a** any of various swimming birds (family Anatidae) that have a short neck, short legs, webbed feet, and a broad flat beak, and the sexes of which are almost always different from each other in plumage **b** the flesh of any of these birds used as food **2** a female duck – compare DRAKE **3** *Br informal* **3a ducks** *pl taking sing vb*, **duck** a dear ⟨*cheer up, ∼ s!*⟩ ⟨*be a ∼ and help me with this*⟩ **b** a person, creature ⟨*she's a dear old ∼*⟩ [ME *doke*, fr OE *dūce*]

²**duck** *vt* **1** to thrust momentarily under water **2** to lower (e g the head), esp quickly as a bow or to avoid being hit **3** to avoid, evade ⟨*∼ the issue*⟩ ∼ *vi* **1** to plunge at least one's head under the surface of water, usu briefly **2a** to move the head or body suddenly downwards; dodge **b** to bow, bob **3** to evade a duty, question, or responsibility – often + *out* [ME *douken*; akin to OHG *tūhhan* to dive, OE *dūce* duck] – **duck** *n*, **ducker** *n*

³**duck** *n* a durable closely woven usu cotton fabric [D *doek* cloth; akin to OHG *tuoh* cloth]

⁴**duck** *n* an amphibious vehicle designed during World War II [*DUKW*, its code designation]

⁵**duck** *n* a score of nought, esp in cricket [short for *duck's egg*; fr the egg-shaped number 0] – **break one's duck** to make one's first score in a game; *esp* to score one's first runs in a cricket innings

**duckbilled platypus** /'duk,bild/, **duckbill platypus** /'dukbil/ *n* PLATYPUS (aquatic egg-laying mammal)

**duckboard** /'duk,bawd/ *n usu pl* a usu wooden board or slat used to make a path over wet or muddy ground

**ducking stool** /'duking/ *n* a seat attached to a plank, which was fixed in a seesaw-like arrangement at the edge of water, used in former times to duck culprits tied to it – compare CUCKING STOOL

**duckling** /'dukling/ *n* a young duck

**duckpin** /'duk,pin/ *n* **1** a small pin shorter and squatter than a tenpin, used in some bowling games **2** *pl but taking sing vb* a bowling game using duckpins [fr its short squat appearance]

**ducks and drakes** *n taking sing vb* the pastime of skimming flat stones or shells along the surface of calm water – **play ducks and drakes with** to use (e g money) recklessly; squander

**duck's arse** *n, informal* a hairstyle, often worn by TEDDY BOYS, in which the hair is swept back and cut so as to droop at the nape of the neck in the shape of a duck's tail

**duck soup** *n, chiefly NAm informal* something easy to do; a cinch

**duckweed** /'duk,weed/ *n* any of several small free-floating stemless plants (genus *Lemna* of the family Lemnaceae, the duckweed family), that have small rounded leaves and grow, often in profusion, on the surface of still water

¹**ducky, duckie** /'duki/ *n, informal* DEAR 1b

²**ducky** *adj, informal* **1** satisfactory, fine ⟨*everything is just ∼*⟩ **2** darling, sweet ⟨*a ∼ little tearoom*⟩

**Duco** /'dyoohkoh/ *trademark* – used in Australia for a lacquer applied to the bodywork of cars

¹**duct** /dukt/ *n* **1** a body tube or vessel, esp when carrying a secretion produced by a gland **2a** a pipe, tube, or channel that conveys a substance **b** a pipe or tubular channel for carrying an electric power line, telephone cables, etc **3a** a continuous tube formed in plant tissue by a row of elongated cells that have lost their intervening cross walls **b** an elongated cavity (e g a resin canal of a coniferous tree) formed in plant tissue by disintegration or separation of cells **4** a layer (e g in the atmosphere or the ocean) which occurs under usu abnormal conditions and in which radio or sound waves are confined to a restricted path [NL *ductus*, fr ML, aqueduct, fr L, act of leading, fr *ductus*, pp of *ducere* to lead – more at TOW] – **ductless** *adj*

²**duct** *vt* to convey (e g a gas) through a duct; *also* to propagate (e g radio waves) through a duct

**ducted** /'duktid/ *adj* situated or operating in a duct

**ductile** /'duktiel/ *adj* **1** capable of being easily fashioned into a new form **2** *of a metal* capable of being drawn out into wires, rods, etc or hammered thin – compare MALLEABLE 1 **3** *formal* easily led or influenced; tractable ⟨*the ∼ masses*⟩ *synonyms* see ¹PLASTIC [MF & L; MF, fr L *ductilis*, fr *ductus*, pp] – **ductility** *n*

**ducting** /'dukting/ *n* **1** a system of ducts **2** the material composing a duct

**ductless gland** /'duktlis/ *n* ENDOCRINE GLAND (gland that secretes hormones directly into the bloodstream)

**ductule** /'duktyoohl, -yool/ *n* a small duct

**ductus arteriosus** /ˌduktəs ahtiəri'ohsəs/ *n* a short broad blood vessel found normally only in a foetus, that connects the PULMONARY ARTERY (artery carrying blood from the heart to the lungs) with the AORTA (main artery carrying blood from the heart to the body) and conducts most of the blood directly from the right side of the heart to the aorta, bypassing the lungs, which are not yet in use [NL, lit., arterial duct]

¹**dud** /dud/ *n, informal* **1** *pl* personal belongings; *esp* clothes **2** something or someone of little use or value or that fails to serve its purpose: e g **2a** a bomb, missile, etc that fails to explode **b** a failure ⟨*the movie proved a box-office ∼*⟩ **c** an ineffectual person ⟨*a ∼ at cricket*⟩ **d** a counterfeit, fake [(1) ME *dudde* coarse cloak; (2) E dial. *dud* weak or spiritless person, perh fr *duds* clothes, rags]

²**dud** *adj, informal* of little use or no worth; valueless ⟨*∼ cheques*⟩

**duddie, duddy** /'dudi/ *adj, Scot* ragged, tattered [¹*dud* (rag)]

**dude** /d(y)oohd/ *n, chiefly NAm informal* **1** a man who is extremely fastidious in dress and manner; a dandy **2** a city-dweller; *esp* a man from the E USA who is holidaying, usu on a ranch, in the W USA **3** a fellow, guy [perh fr Ger dial., fool] – **dudish** *adj*, **dudishly** *adv*

**dudeen** /dooh'deen/ *n* a short tobacco pipe made of clay [IrGael *dúidín*, dim. of *dúd* pipe]

**dude ranch** *n* an American holiday centre offering activities (e g camping and riding) typical of western ranches

**dudgeon** /'dujən/ *n* a fit or state of angry indignation – esp in **in high dudgeon** [origin unknown]

¹**due** /dyooh/ *adj* **1** owed or owing as a debt **2a** owed or owing as a natural or moral right ⟨*got his ∼ reward*⟩ **b** according to accepted notions or procedures; appropriate ⟨*with all ∼ respect*⟩ ⟨*with ∼ regard for the niceties of form*⟩ **3a** (capable of) satisfying a need, obligation, or duty; adequate – compare IN DUE COURSE **b** regular, lawful ⟨*∼ proof of loss*⟩ – compare DUE PROCESS **4** capable of being attributed; ascribable – + *to* ⟨*this advance is partly ∼ to a few men of genius* – A N Whitehead⟩; compare DUE TO **5** having reached the date at which payment is required; payable **6** required or expected in the prescribed, normal, or logical course of events; scheduled ⟨*∼ to arrive at any time*⟩ [ME, fr MF *deu*, pp of *devoir* to owe, fr L *debēre* – more at DEBT] – **dueness** *n* – **due to** BECAUSE OF – compare DUE 4; see also **in due** COURSE

**usage** Since **due** is an adjective, it would appear that **due to** should

# due

be attached to a noun; "something" must be **due** to something else; and some people feel that **due to** should not be used like **because of** or **owing to** at the beginning of a sentence ⟨**due to** *the extreme cold, we were unable to plant the tomatoes*⟩ or after an ordinary verb ⟨*we were delayed* **due to** *the fog*⟩ but only after a linking verb such as *be* or *seem* ⟨*the delay was* **due to** *the fog*⟩ or directly after a noun ⟨*rheumatism* **due to** *bad housing was very common*⟩. The use of **due to** for **because of** seems now thoroughly established in English, and is used by many educated speakers and writers ⟨**due to** *inability to market their grain, prairie farmers have been faced for some time with a serious shortage* – Queen Elizabeth II (speech from the Throne)⟩; but as this usage still arouses the strong disapproval of some people it may be wise either to confine **due to** to adjectival constructions or, if in doubt, to replace it by **because of** or **owing to**.

²**due** *n* something due or owed: eg **a** something esp non-material that rightfully belongs to one ⟨*I don't like him, but to give him his* ∼, *he's a good singer*⟩ **b** *usu pl* a payment or obligation required by law or custom; a debt **c** *pl* fees, charges *synonyms* see ²TAX

³**due** *adv* directly, exactly – used before points of the compass ⟨∼ *north*⟩

¹**duel** /'dyooh·əl/ *n* **1** a combat between two people; *specif* a formal combat with weapons fought between two people in the presence of witnesses in order to settle a quarrel **2** a conflict between usu evenly matched antagonistic people, ideas, or forces △ dual [ML *duellum*, fr OL, war (whence L *bellum*)]

²**duel** *vb* **-ll-** (*NAm* **-l-, -ll-**) *vi* to fight a duel ∼ *vt* to encounter (an opponent) in a duel – **dueller, duellist** *n*

**duello** /dyooh'eloh/ *n*, *pl* **duellos** the rules or practice of duelling [It, fr ML *duellum*]

**duenna** /dyooh'enə/ *n* **1** an older woman serving as governess and companion to the younger ladies in a Spanish or Portuguese family **2** a chaperon [Sp *dueña*, fr L *domina* mistress] – **duennaship** *n*

**due process** *n* a course of legal proceedings carried out in accordance with established rules and principles

**duet** /dyooh'et/ *n* a musical composition for two performers; *also* the performers or performance of such a composition [It *duetto*, dim. of *duo*] – **duettist** *n*

¹**duff** /duf/ *n* **1** a boiled or steamed pudding, often containing dried fruit ⟨*plum* ∼⟩ **2** the partly decayed organic matter on the forest floor; LITTER 2b **3** fine coal; slack [E dial., alter. of *dough*]

²**duff** *adj*, *Br informal* not working; worthless, useless [perh back-formation fr *duffer*]

³**duff** *vt*, *informal* **1** *Br* to mishit (a golf ball) by hitting the ground before the ball **2** *Austr* to steal and change the brands on (cattle) [*duff* (to fake, cheat), perh back-formation fr *duffer*] **duff up** *vt*, *Br slang* to beat up ⟨*duffed him up a treat*⟩

**duffel, duffle** /'duf(ə)l/ *n* **1** a coarse heavy woollen material with a thick nap **2** *NAm* transportable personal belongings, equipment, and supplies [D *duffel*, fr *Duffel*, town in Belgium]

**duffel bag** *n* a cylindrical fabric bag, usu closed by a drawstring, that is used for carrying personal belongings

**duffel coat** *n* a coat made of duffel that is usu thigh- or knee-length, hooded, and fastened with toggles

**duffer** /'dufə/ *n*, *informal* **1** an incompetent, ineffectual, or clumsy person **2** *Austr* a cattle rustler [perh fr Sc *doofart* stupid person]

¹**dug** /dug/ *past of* DIG

²**dug** /dug/ *n* an udder; *also* a teat – usu used with reference to a suckling animal but derog when used of a woman [perh of Scand origin; akin to OSw *dæggia* to suckle; akin to OE *delu* nipple]

**dugong** /'dooh,gong/ *n* a large aquatic plant-eating mammal (*Dugong dugon*) that has flippers, a broad crescent-shaped tail, and tusks in the male and lives in shallow tropical waters, usu around the Indian Ocean – compare MANATEE [NL, genus name, fr Malay & Tagalog *duyong* sea cow]

**dugout** /'dug,owt/ *n* **1** a boat made by hollowing out a large log **2a** a shelter dug in the ground or in a hillside, esp for troops **b** a shelter, esp in the side of a trench, for quarters, storage, or protection on a battlefield **3** a shelter at the side of a sportsground; *esp* one from which football managers, trainers, etc watch a game

**duiker** /'diekə/ *n* any of several small African antelopes (*Cephalophus* or related genera) that have short backward-pointing horns and can weave and plunge through thick bush-

land [Afrik, lit., diver, fr *duik* to dive, fr MD *dūken;* akin to OHG *tūhhan* to dive – more at DUCK]

**duke** /dyoohk/ *n* **1** a sovereign ruler of a European duchy **2** a nobleman of the highest hereditary rank; *esp* a member of the highest grade of the British peerage **3** *pl, slang* fists, hands [ME, fr OF *duc*, fr L *duc-, dux,* fr *ducere* to lead – more at TOW; (3) rhyming slang *Duke* (*of Yorks*) forks, fingers, hands] – **dukedom** *n*

**Duke of Edinburgh's award** /'edinb(ə)rə/ *n* any of various medals awarded to young people in Britain for proficiency in a variety of leisure activities [HRH The Prince Philip, *Duke of Edinburgh b* 1921]

**dulcet** /'dulsit/ *adj* sweetly pleasing to the senses, esp to the ear; agreeable, soothing [ME *doucet*, fr MF, fr *douz* sweet, fr L *dulcis*] – **dulcetly** *adv*

**dulcimer** /'dulsimə/ *n* **1** a stringed instrument which has strings of graduated length stretched over a soundboard and is played with light hammers held in the hands **2** APPALACHIAN DULCIMER (dulcimerlike instrument played by plucking) [ME *dowcemere*, fr MF *doulcemer*, fr OIt *dolcimelo*, perh deriv of L *dulce melos* sweet song]

**dulcinea** /,dulsi'niə, dul'siniə/ *n* a man's idealized sweetheart [Sp, fr *Dulcinea del Toboso*, beloved of Don Quixote – more at QUIXOTIC]

¹**dull** /dul/ *adj* **1** mentally slow; stupid **2a** slow in perception or sensibility; insensible **b** lacking zest or vivacity; listless **3a** slow in action; sluggish **b** marked by little business activity ⟨*a* ∼ *season*⟩ **4** lacking sharpness of cutting edge or point; blunt **5** lacking brilliance, brightness, lustre, or intensity ⟨*a* ∼ *yellowish colour*⟩ ⟨*a* ∼ *light*⟩ **6** not resonant or ringing ⟨*a* ∼ *booming sound*⟩ **7** cloudy, overcast **8** boring, uninteresting *synonyms* see STUPID [ME *dul;* akin to OE *dol* foolish] – **dullish** *adj*, **dullness** *n*, **dully** *adv*

²**dull** *vb* to make or become dull ⟨*eyes and ears* ∼ed *by age*⟩

**dullard** /'duləd/ *n* a stupid or insensitive person

**dulse** /duls/ *n* any of several coarse edible red seaweeds (esp *Rhodymenia palmata*) found esp in northern latitudes [ScGael & IrGael *duileasg;* akin to W *delysg* dulse]

**duly** /'dyoohli/ *adv* in a due manner, time, or degree; properly ⟨*your suggestion has been* ∼ *noted*⟩

**duma** /'dooh,mah/ *n* a representative council in Russia; *specif* the principal legislative assembly in Russia from 1906 to 1917 [Russ, of Gmc origin; akin to OE *dōm* judgment – more at DOOM]

¹**dumb** /dum/ *adj* **1** lacking the power of speech ⟨*deaf and* ∼ *from birth*⟩ **2** naturally incapable of speech ⟨∼ *animals*⟩ **3** not expressed in uttered words ⟨∼ *grief*⟩ ⟨∼ *insolence*⟩ **4a** not willing to speak **b** temporarily unable to speak (eg from astonishment) ⟨*struck* ∼⟩ **5** lacking some usual attribute or accompaniment: eg **5a** devoid of speech or sound ⟨*a* ∼ *mute piano*⟩ **b** having no means of self-propulsion ⟨*a* ∼ *barge*⟩ **6** markedly lacking in intelligence; stupid ⟨*Miss World is certainly no* ∼ *blonde, she's a student of mathematics*⟩ [ME, fr OE; akin to OHG *tumb* mute, OE *dēaf* deaf – more at DEAF] – **dumbly** *adv*, **dumbness** *n*

*usage* Since dumb can mean "stupid", people who congenitally lack the power of speech may prefer to be called **mute. synonyms** see STUPID

²**dumb** *vt* to make silent; deaden ⟨*would lie around,* ∼ed *by the drugs* – Norman Mailer⟩

**dumbbell** /'dum,bel/ *n* **1** a short bar with two identical spheres or with adjustable weighted discs attached to each end and used usu in pairs for weight training **2** *NAm informal* DUMMY 8

**dumbfound, dumfound** /dum'fownd/ *vt* to strike dumb with astonishment; amaze *synonyms* see ²SURPRISE [*dumb* + -*found* (as in *confound*)]

**dumbhead** /'dum,hed/ *n*, *NAm slang* a blockhead

**dumb show** *n* (a play or part of a play presented by) movement, signs, and gesture without words

**dumbstruck** /'dum,struk/ *adj* made silent by astonishment; dumbfounded

**dumb waiter** *n* **1** a movable table or stand often with revolving shelves for holding food or dishes **2** a small lift for conveying food and dishes (eg from the kitchen to the dining area of a restaurant)

**dumdum** /'dum,dum/ *n* a bullet (eg one with a soft core or vertical cuts made in its point) that expands on impact and inflicts a severe wound [*Dum-Dum*, arsenal near Calcutta in India]

**dumka** /'doomkə, 'doohmkə/ *n, pl* **dumky** /-ki/ a Slavonic folk ballad, usu melancholy but often alternately melancholy and gay [Czech, *elegy*, of Gmc origin; akin to Goth *dōms* judgment, OE *dōm* doom]

**¹dummy** /'dumi/ *n* **1** one who is habitually silent or incapable of speaking **2** the exposed hand in bridge played by the DECLARER in addition to his/her own hand; *also* the player whose hand is a dummy **3** an imitation, copy, or likeness of something used to reproduce some of the attributes of the original: eg **3a** a large puppet in usu human form used by a ventriloquist **b** a model of the human figure, esp the torso, used for fitting in dressmaking or tailoring, or for display (eg in a shop window) **4** a person or corporation that seems to act independently but is in reality acting for or at the direction of another **5** a pattern for a printing job showing the position of typographic elements (eg text and illustrations) **6** an act or instance of dummying an opponent – esp in *sell a dummy* ⟨*he sold the All Blacks' fullback a beautiful ~*⟩ **7** *chiefly Br* a rubber teat for babies to suck in order to soothe them **8** *informal* a dull or stupid person [¹*dumb* + *-y*]

**²dummy** *adj* resembling or being a dummy: eg **a** sham, artificial **b** existing in name only; fictitious ⟨*bank accounts held in ~ names*⟩

**³dummy** *vt* **1** to make a dummy of (eg a book or page of a publication) **2** to deceive (an opponent) by dummying ~ *vi* **1** to deceive an opponent (eg in rugby or soccer) by pretending to pass or release the ball while still retaining possession of it **2** *NAm slang* to refuse to talk – usu + *up*

**dummy run** *n* a rehearsal; TRIAL RUN

**dummy variable** *n* a mathematical VARIABLE chosen at random whose choice does not affect the meaning of the expression in which it occurs ⟨*the variable of integration in a definite integral is a ~*⟩ – compare DEPENDENT VARIABLE, INDEPENDENT VARIABLE

**dumortierite** /dyooh'mawtiəriet, ,--'--/ *n* a bright blue or greenish-blue mineral consisting of a SILICATE of aluminium and used esp for jewellery [Fr *dumortiérite*, fr Eugène *Dumortier* †1876 Fr palaeontologist]

**¹dump** /dump/ *vt* **1a** to unload or let fall in a heap or mass **b** to get rid of unceremoniously or irresponsibly; abandon ⟨*~ed her lover*⟩ **c** to jettison ⟨*the tanker ~ed its load at sea*⟩ **2** to sell in quantity at a very low price; *specif* to sell abroad at less than the marginal cost of producing the goods **3** to copy (data in a computer's internal storage) onto an external medium (eg printout, a VDU screen, or magnetic tape) for viewing or storage ~ *vi* **1** to fall abruptly; plunge **2** to dump refuse [perh fr D *dompen* to immerse, topple; akin to OE *dyppan* to dip – more at DIP]

**²dump** *n* **1a** an accumulation of discarded materials (eg refuse) **b** a place where such materials are dumped **2a** a quantity of esp military reserve materials accumulated in one place **b** a place where such materials are stored; *esp* a place for the temporary storage of military supplies in the field ⟨*ammunition ~*⟩ **3** an instance of dumping data stored in a computer; *also* the data that has been dumped **4** *informal* a disorderly, slovenly, or dilapidated place

**dumper** /'dumpə/ *n* **1** one who or that which dumps **2** DUMPER TRUCK **3** *chiefly Austr* a powerful wave that breaks suddenly and erratically, and is impossible for a surfer to ride

**dumper truck** /'dumpə/, **dump truck** *n* a small lorry whose body may be tilted to empty the contents, used esp for transporting and dumping loose material (eg earth)

**dumping** /'dumping/ *n* the act of one who or that which dumps; *esp* the selling of goods in quantity at below marginal costs of production (eg to dispose of a surplus or to break down competition), esp in international trade

**dumpling** /'dumpling/ *n* **1a** a small usu rounded mass of dough cooked by boiling or steaming, often in a stew **b** a usu baked dessert of fruit wrapped in dough ⟨*apple ~*⟩ **2** *chiefly humorous* one who or that which has a fat and rounded shape like a dumpling; *esp* a short fat person or animal [perh alter. of *lump*]

**dumps** /dumps/ *n pl, informal* a gloomy state of mind; despondency – esp in *in the dumps* [prob fr D *domp* haze, fr MD *damp*]

**dumpy** /'dumpi/ *adj* short and thick in build; squat [E dial. *dump* lump] – **dumpily** *adv*, **dumpiness** *n*

**dumpy level** *n* a LEVEL (instrument used by a surveyor to establish a horizontal plane) with a short rigidly fixed telescope that can be rotated horizontally

**¹dun** /dun/ *adj* **1a** of the colour dun **b** *of a horse* of a variable

colour between mouse grey and yellow and usu having black POINTS (lower legs, tail, etc) **2** marked by dullness and drabness [ME, fr OE *dunn* – more at DUSK] – **dunness** *n*

**²dun** *n* **1** a dun horse **2** a nearly neutral slightly brownish dark grey colour **3** a mayfly that has not yet acquired all the typical adult characteristics; *also* a dark artificial fishing fly used to imitate such an insect

**³dun** *vt* **-nn-** to make persistent demands on for payment; *broadly* to plague or pester constantly [perh short for obs *dunkirk* privateer, fr *Dunkirk, Dunkerque,* port in France]

**⁴dun** *n* **1** one who duns **2** an urgent request; *esp* a demand for payment

**⁵dun** /dun, doohn/ *n* a prehistoric or early medieval Irish or Scottish stronghold protected usu by one or more earthen or stone ramparts; *esp* one sited on a promontory and taking advantage of natural cliff defences [ScGael & IrGael *dūn*]

**dunce** /duns/ *n* a dull or stupid person [John *Duns* Scotus †1308 Sc theologian, whose once accepted writings were ridiculed in the 16th c]

**dunce's cap** *also* **dunce cap** *n* a conical hat, usu made of paper, formerly used to humiliate slow learners at school

**Dundee cake** /dun'dee/ *n* a fairly rich fruit cake usu decorated on top with skinned almonds [*Dundee,* city in Scotland]

**dunderhead** /'dundə,hed/ *n* a dunce, blockhead [perh fr D *donder* thunder (akin to OHG *thonar* thunder – more at THUNDER) + E *head*] – **dunderheaded** *adj*

**dundrearies** /dun'driəriz/ *n pl, often cap* long flowing side-whiskers worn without a beard [Lord *Dundreary,* character in the play *Our American Cousin* by Tom Taylor †1880 E dramatist]

**dune** /dyoohn/ *n* a hill or ridge of sand piled up by the wind [Fr, fr OF, fr MD; akin to OE *dūn* down – more at DOWN] – **dunelike** *adj*

**duneland** /'dyoohnlənd/ *n* an area having many dunes

**¹dung** /dung/ *n* the excrement of an animal; manure [ME, fr OE; akin to ON *dyngja* manure pile, Lith *dengti* to cover] – **dungy** *adj*

**²dung** *vt* to fertilize or dress with manure ~ *vi, of an animal* to excrete dung

**¹dungaree** /,dung·gə'ree, '---/ *n* a heavy coarse durable cotton TWILL woven from coloured yarns; *specif* blue denim [Hindi *dūgrī*]

**²dungaree** *adj* of dungarees ⟨*my right ~ strap has come undone*⟩

**dungarees** /,dung·gə'reez/ *n pl* **1** a workman's 1-piece suit or overalls made of dungaree **2** a 1-piece outer garment consisting of trousers and a bib with shoulder straps attached or fastened to the waist at the back

**dung beetle** *n* a beetle (eg a dorbeetle or scarab) that rolls balls of dung in which to lay eggs and on which the larvae feed

**dungeon** /'dunjən/ *n* **1** DONJON (inner tower of a medieval castle) **2** a dark usu underground prison or vault, esp in a castle [ME *donjon,* fr MF, fr (assumed) ML *dominion-, dominio,* fr L *dominus* lord – more at DAME]

**dung fly** *n* any of various TWO-WINGED FLIES (subfamily Cordilurinae); *specif* the yellow dung fly (*Scatophaga stercoraria*) that breeds and finds its prey in dung

**dungheap** /'dung,heep/ *n* a dunghill

**dunghill** /'dung,hil/ *n* **1** a heap of dung (eg in a farmyard) **2** something (eg a place or condition) that is repulsive or degraded

**duniwassal** /'doohniwosəl/ *n* a lesser-ranking Highland gentleman [ScGael *duine-uasal,* fr *duine* man + *uasal* noble, well-born]

**¹dunk** /dungk/ *vt* **1** to dip (eg a piece of bread) into tea, soup, etc before eating **2** to dip or submerge temporarily in liquid ⟨*~ed her in the swimming pool*⟩ [PaG *dunke,* fr MHG *dunken,* fr OHG *dunkōn*]

**²dunk** *n* a small piece of food (eg bread) for dipping into a liquid or soft food mixture

**dunlin** /'dunlin/ *n, pl* **dunlins,** *esp collectively* **dunlin** a small widely distributed sandpiper (*Calidris alpina*) with chiefly reddish-brown upper parts and a white breast marked with a large black patch in summer [¹*dun* + *-lin,* alter. of *-ling* (cf DUNNOCK)]

**Dunlop** /'dunlop/ *n* a moist Scottish cheese similar to Cheddar but with a softer texture and usu a milder flavour [*Dunlop,* town in Strathclyde, Scotland]

**dunnage** /'dunij/ *n* **1** loose materials used round a cargo to prevent damage; *also* padding in a shipping container to protect the contents from breakage **2** baggage or personal effects, esp of a sailor [origin unknown]

**dunno** /də'noh/ don't know – used in writing to represent nonstandard speech [by alter.]

**dunnock** /'dunək/ *n* a small dull-coloured European bird (*Prunella modularis*) common in gardens, hedges, and bushy places – called also HEDGE SPARROW [ME *dunoke*, fr ¹*dun* + *-oc, -oke* *-ock* (cf DUNLIN)]

**dunny** /'duni/ *n, chiefly Austr & NZ informal* a toilet [by shortening & alter. fr *dunnaken, dannaken* (toilet), fr *danna* (human excrement)]

**dunt** /dunt, doont/ *n, Scot* a blow, thump ⟨*I gave him a right* ∼⟩ [ME, var of *dint*] – **dunt** *vt*, **dunter** *n*

**duo** /'dyooh,oh/ *n, pl* **duos 1** a duet **2** a pair [It, fr L, two – more at TWO]

**duo-** *comb form* two [L *duo*]

**duodecillion** /,dyooh-ohdə'silyən/ *n* – see NUMBER table [L *duodecim* twelve + E *-illion* (as in *million*)]

**duodecimal** /,dyooh-oh'desim(ə)l/ *adj* of, being, or belonging to a system of numbers having 12 as its base [L *duodecim* – more at DOZEN] – **duodecimal** *n*

**duodecimo** /,dyooh-oh'desimoh/ *n, pl* **duodecimos 1** the size of a piece of paper cut 12 from a sheet **2** a book format in which a folded sheet forms 12 leaves; *also* a book in this format [L, abl of *duodecimus* twelfth, fr *duodecim*]

**duoden-, duodeno-** *comb form* duodenum ⟨duoden*itis*⟩ ⟨duodeno*gram*⟩ [NL, fr ML *duodenum*]

**duodenary** /,dyooh-ə'denəri, -'dee-/ *adj* duodecimal [L *duodenarius*, fr *duodeni* twelve each, fr *duodecim*]

**duodenum** /,dyooh-ə'deenəm/ *n, pl* **duodena** /-'deenə/, **duodenums** the first part of the SMALL INTESTINE, extending from the stomach to the JEJUNUM [ME, fr ML, fr L *duodeni* twelve each; fr its length, about 12 fingers' breadth] – **duodenal** *adj*

**duologue** /'dyooh-ə,log/ *n* a dialogue between two people, esp in a play

**duomo** /dooh'ohmoh/ *n, pl* **duomos** an Italian cathedral [It – more at DOME]

**duopoly** /dyooh'opəli/ *n* a market situation which is controlled by two sellers [*duo-* + *-poly* (as in *monopoly*)] – **duopolistic** *adj*

**duotone** /'dyooh-oh,tohn, 'dyooh-ə-/ *adj* of or in two colours

**dup** /dup/ *vt* **-pp-** *Br archaic* to open [contr of *do up*]

**¹dupe** /dyoohp/ *n* someone who is easily deceived or cheated [Fr, fr MF *duppe*, prob alter. of *huppe* hoopoe]

**²dupe** *vt* to make a dupe of; deceive – **duper** *n*, **dupery** *n*

**³dupe** *vt or n, informal* (to) duplicate [by shortening & alter.]

**dupion** /'dyoohpiən, dyooh'pee-ən/ *n* a rough silk fabric [Fr *doupion*, fr It *doppione* double cocoon made by two silkworms, aug of *doppio* double, fr L *duplus*]

**duple** /'dyoohpl/ *adj* **1** having two elements; twofold **2** marked by two or a multiple of two beats per bar of music ⟨∼ *time*⟩ [L *duplus* double – more at DOUBLE]

**¹duplex** /'dyooh,pleks/ *adj* **1** double, twofold; *specif* having two parts that operate at the same time or in the same way ⟨*a* ∼ *lathe*⟩ **2** allowing telecommunication in opposite directions simultaneously [L, fr *duo* two + *-plex* -fold – more at TWO, SIMPLE]

**²duplex** *n* something duplex: eg **a** a double strand of a NUCLEIC ACID (eg DNA or RNA) consisting of two single complementary strands (eg of DNA or RNA, or one of DNA and one of RNA) **b** *NAm* a 2-family house **c** *NAm* a flat on two floors

**³duplex** *vt* to make (eg a communications line) duplex

**duplexer** /'dyooh,pleksə/ *n* a switching device that allows alternate transmission and reception with the same radio aerial

**¹duplicate** /'d(y)oohplikət/ *adj* **1a** consisting of or existing in two corresponding or identical parts or examples ⟨∼ *invoices*⟩ **b** being the same as another ⟨*a* ∼ *key*⟩ **2** being a card game in which different players play identical hands in order to compare scores ⟨∼ *bridge*⟩ [ME, fr L *duplicatus*, pp of *duplicare* to double, fr *duplic-, duplex*]

**²duplicate** *n* **1** either of two things that exactly resemble or correspond to each other; *specif* a legal document that is essentially identical with another and has equal validity as an original **2** a copy – **in duplicate** with an original and one copy ⟨*typed* in duplicate⟩; *also* with two identical copies

**³duplicate** /'d(y)oohpli,kayt/ *vt* **1** to make double or twofold **2a** to make an exact copy of ⟨∼ *the document*⟩ **b** to repeat, equal ⟨*a feat that can never be* ∼d⟩ ∼ *vi* to become duplicate; produce a replica; *specif* REPLICATE ⟨*DNA in chromosomes* ∼s⟩ – **duplicative** *adj*

**duplication** /,doohpli'kaysh(ə)n, ,dyooh-/ *n* **1** duplicating or being duplicated **2** a duplicate **3** an aberration of a CHROMOSOME (strand of gene-carrying material) in which a segment of genetic material is repeated △ duplicity

**duplicator** /'d(y)oohpli,kaytə/ *n* something that duplicates; *specif* a machine for making copies, esp by means other than photocopying or xeroxing

**duplicity** /dyooh'plisəti/ *n* **1** malicious deception in thought, speech, or action **2** the quality or state of being double or twofold △ duplication – **duplicitous** *adj*, **duplicitously** *adv*

**duppy** /'dupi/ *n* a usu malevolent ghost or spirit in W Indian folklore [Bube *dupe* ghost]

**dura** /'dyooərə/ *n* DURRA (type of cereal grass)

**durable** /'dyooərəbl/; *also* j-/ *adj* able to exist or be used for a long time without significant deterioration [ME, fr MF, fr L *durabilis*, fr *durare* to last, endure – more at DURING] – **durableness** *n*, **durably** *adv*, **durability** *n*

**durable press** *n* **1** the process of treating a fabric with a chemical and heat in order to make the fabric crease-resistant or to set a permanent pleat or crease in a garment **2** (the condition of) fabric treated by durable press

**durables** /'dyooərəblz/ *n pl* goods (eg cars, fridges, and cookers) that are typically used repeatedly over a period of years without being replaced

**Duralumin** /dyoo'ralyoomin; *also* joo-/ *trademark* – used for an alloy of aluminium, copper, manganese, and magnesium comparable in strength and hardness to soft steel

**dura mater** /,dyooərə 'mahtə, 'may-/ *n* the tough membrane that is the outermost of the three membranes surrounding the brain and SPINAL CORD – compare ARACHNOID, PIA MATER [ME, fr ML, lit., hard mother]

**duramen** /dyoo(ə)'rahmin, -'ray-; *also* j-/ *n* HEARTWOOD (dense hard wood in the centre of a tree trunk) [NL, fr L, hardness, fr *durare* to harden – more at DURING]

**durance** /'dyooərəns; *also* j-/ *n, archaic* **1** endurance **2** imprisonment – often in *durance vile* ⟨*a convict . . . suffered "*∼ *vile" - Irish Digest*⟩ [MF, fr *durer* to endure]

**duration** /dyoo(ə)'raysh(ə)n/ *n* **1** continuance in or length of time ⟨*a play of short* ∼⟩ **2** the time during which something exists or lasts ⟨*was in the army for the* ∼ *of the war*⟩ [ML *duration-, duratio*, fr L *duratus*, pp of *durare* to last]

**durative** /'dyooərətiv/ *adj, linguistics* of or being a verb or form of a verb expressing continuing action – **durative** *n*

**durbar** /'duh,bah/ *n* **1** a court of an Indian prince **2** a formal reception held in former times by an Indian prince or a British governor in India (eg to mark the visit of the British monarch) [Hindi *darbār*, fr Per, fr *dar* door + *bār* admission, audience]

**duress** /dyoo(ə)'res; *also* j-/ *n* **1** forcible restraint or restriction **2** compulsion by threat, violence, or imprisonment; *esp* the illegal use of coercion [ME *duresse*, fr MF *duresce* hardness, severity, fr L *duritia*, fr *durus*]

**Durex** /'dyooəreks/ *trademark* – used for a condom

**Durham** /'durəm/ *n* SHORTHORN (breed of English cattle) [*Durham*, county in N England]

**durian** /'dyooəri-ən/ *n* a large oval tropical fruit with a prickly rind and pleasant-tasting but foul-smelling flesh; *also* an E Indian tree (*Durio zibethinus*) that bears durians [Malay, fr *duri* thorn]

**during** /'dyooəring; *also* j-/ *prep* **1** throughout the whole duration of ⟨*swims every day* ∼ *the summer*⟩ **2** at some point in the course of ⟨*takes his holiday* ∼ *July*⟩ [ME, fr prp of *duren* to last, fr OF *durer*, fr L *durare* to harden, endure, fr *durus* hard; perh akin to Skt *dāru* wood – more at TREE]

**durmast** /'duh,mahst/ *n* a European oak tree (*Quercus petraea*) valued esp for its dark heavy tough springy wood [perh alter. of *dun mast*, fr ¹*dun* + ³*mast*]

**durn** /duhn/, **durned** /duhnd/ *adj or adv, chiefly NAm* damn, damned [euphemism]

**duroc** /'dyooərok/ *n, often cap* (any of) a breed of large red N American pigs [*Duroc*, 19th-c US stallion living on the farm where this breed of pigs was developed]

**durra** *also* **dura** /'durə/ *n* any of various SORGHUMS (cereal grasses) widely grown in warm dry areas, esp for their grain [Ar *dhurah*]

**dursn't** /'duhs(ə)nt/ durst not

**durst** /duhst/ *archaic past of* DARE

**durum** /'dyooərəm; *also* j-/, **durum wheat** *n* a wheat (*Triticum durum*) with a high protein content whose flour is used esp to make pasta [NL *durum* (specific epithet of *Triticum durum*), fr L, neut of *durus* hard]

**¹dusk** /dusk/ *adj, poetic* dusky [ME *dosk*, alter. of OE *dox; akin to L *fuscus* dark brown, OE *dunn* dun, *dūst* dust]

**²dusk** *vb, poetic* to make or become dark or dim; darken

**³dusk** *n* **1** (the darker part of) twilight **2** darkness or semi-darkness caused by the lack of light; gloom

**dusky** /'duski/ *adj* **1** somewhat dark in colour; *esp, chiefly poetic or euph* dark-skinned **2** marked by dim or deficient light; shadowy, gloomy – **duskily** *adv*, **duskiness** *n*

**¹dust** /dust/ *n* **1a** fine dry powdery particles of any solid matter, esp earth **b** the fine particles of ash, fluff, etc that settle, esp on household surfaces **2** the particles into which something, esp the human body, disintegrates or decays **3** something worthless ⟨*worldly success was ~ to him*⟩ **4a** the earth, esp as a place of burial **b** the surface of the ground – compare BITE THE DUST **5a** a cloud of dust ⟨*the cars raised quite a ~*⟩ **b** confusion, disturbance – chiefly in *kick up a dust* and *raise a dust* **6** the act or an instance of dusting ⟨*gave the house a quick ~*⟩ [ME, fr OE *dūst*; akin to L *furere* to rage, Gk *thyein*] – **dustless** *adj*, **dustlike** *adj* – **bite the dust 1** to fall dead, esp in battle **2** to be defeated; fail ⟨*another of his schemes has bitten the dust*⟩

**²dust** *vt* **1** to make free of dust (eg by wiping or brushing) **2a** to sprinkle with fine particles or a powdery substance ⟨*~ the cake with icing sugar*⟩ **b** to sprinkle (something in the form of a fine powder) ⟨*~ sugar over the cake*⟩ **3** *archaic* to make dusty ~ *vi* **1** *of a bird* to work dust into the feathers **2** to remove dust (eg from household articles), esp by wiping or brushing – **dusting** *n*

**dust down/off** *vt* to prepare to use again ⟨dusting off *the old jokes*⟩

**dustbin** /-,bin/ /'dus(t),bin/ *n, Br* a large container for holding household rubbish until collection

**dust bowl** *n* a region that suffers from prolonged droughts and dust storms

**dustcart** /-,kaht/ /'dust,kaht/ *n, Br* a vehicle for collecting household rubbish

**dustcoat** /'dust,koht/ *n, chiefly Br* **1** a lightweight washable garment shaped like a coat that is worn to protect clothing **2** **duster coat, dustcoat** a loose casual lightweight coat for indoor or summer wear

**dustcover** /'dust,kuvə/ *n* **1** a dustsheet **2** DUST JACKET **3** a cover (eg of plastic) that fits over and protects a record, equipment, etc from dust

**dust devil** *n* a small sand- or dust-laden whirlwind

**duster** /'dustə/ *n* **1** one who or that which removes dust; *specif* a cloth for dusting furniture, surfaces, etc **2** one who or that which scatters fine particles or a powder; *specif* a device or machine for scattering powdered insecticides or fungicides over crops **3** *NAm* a dustcoat

**dust jacket** *n* a removable paper cover for a book

**dustman** /'dus(t)mən/ *n, Br* one employed to remove household rubbish

**dustpan** /'dust,pan/ *n* a shovel-like utensil into which household dust and litter is swept

**dustsheet** /'dust,sheet/ *n* a large sheet (eg of cloth) used as a cover to protect something, esp furniture, from dust

**dust shot** *n* the smallest size of shot for a shotgun

**dust storm** *n* a strong wind or whirlwind carrying clouds of dust; *esp* one moving across a dry region

**'dust-,up** *n, informal* a quarrel, row, or fight ⟨*having a little ~ with that pudgy young thruster* – Punch⟩

**dust wrapper** *n* DUST JACKET

**dusty** /'dusti/ *adj* **1** covered with or full of dust **2** consisting of dust or fine particles; powdery **3a** resembling dust, esp in consistency or dull grey colour **b** *of a colour* tinged with grey ⟨*~ pink*⟩ **4** lacking vitality or interest; dry, dull ⟨*a ~ treatise*⟩ – **dustily** *adv*, **dustiness** *n*

**dusty miller** *n* any of several plants with ashy-grey or white leaves covered in dense white hairs

**¹dutch** /duch/ *adv, often cap* [¹*Dutch*] – **go dutch** to pay one's own share; divide expenses

**²dutch** *n, Cockney* one's wife [by shortening & alter. fr *duchess*]

**¹Dutch** *adj* of the Dutch or any of their Germanic languages; *specif* (characteristic) of the Netherlands, its inhabitants, or their language [ME *Duch* German, fr MD *duutsch;* akin to OHG *diutisc* German, Goth *thiudisko* as a gentile, *thiuda* people, Oscan *touto* city]

**²Dutch** *n* **1a** the Germanic language of the Netherlands **b** *taking pl vb* the people of the Netherlands **2** *chiefly NAm*

**PENNSYLVANIA DUTCH** (German-speaking people of E Pennsylvania or their dialect) **3** *archaic* **3a(1)** any of the Germanic languages of Germany, Austria, Switzerland, and the Low Countries **a(2)** the official German language **b** *taking pl vb* **b(1)** the German peoples of Germany, Austria, Switzerland, and the Low Countries **b(2)** people of Germanic descent

**Dutch auction** *n* an auction in which the auctioneer gradually reduces the bidding price until a bid is received

**Dutch barn** *n* a large structure with a typically curved roof and open sides, used esp for storing hay

**Dutch bond** *n* ENGLISH CROSS BOND (way in which bricks are laid)

**Dutch cap** *n* a cap, usu of thin rubber, that is shaped to fit over the cervix of the womb to act as a mechanical contraceptive barrier [fr its resemblance to a type of cap worn by Dutch women]

**Dutch clover** *n* WHITE CLOVER

**Dutch courage** *n* false courage induced by drinking alcohol [fr the former reputation of the Dutch for heavy drinking]

**Dutch door** *n* STABLE DOOR (door with upper and lower parts that can be shut separately)

**Dutch elm disease** *n* a disease of elm trees that is caused by a fungus (*Ceratostomella ulmi*), spread from tree to tree by a beetle that bores into the wood, and is characterized by yellowing and withering of the leaves and finally death of the tree

**Dutch hoe** *n* a garden hoe that is pushed forwards rather than pulled

**Dutchman** /'duchmən/, *fem* **Dutchwoman** /-,woomən/ *n* **1** a native or inhabitant of the Netherlands **2** *archaic* **2a** a member of any of the Germanic peoples of Germany, Austria, Switzerland, and the Low Countries **b** a German

**'Dutch-,metal** *n* an imitation GOLD LEAF consisting of thin sheets of copper turned yellow by exposure to the fumes from molten zinc

**Dutch oven** *n* **1** a 3-walled metal box used for roasting (eg meat) by placing the open side to face an open fire **2** a brick oven in which cooking is done by the preheated walls **3** a heavy pot (eg of cast iron) with a tight-fitting often domed cover, that is used for cooking (eg braising)

**Dutch Reformed Church** *n* the Calvinist Church to which the majority of Afrikaans-speaking S Africans belong

**Dutch treat** *n* a meal or entertainment for which each person pays for him/herself

**Dutch uncle** *n* one who criticizes or admonishes sternly and bluntly – chiefly in *talk to like a Dutch uncle*

**duteous** /'dyoohti·əs, -tyəs/ *adj, formal* dutiful, obedient [irreg fr *duty* + *-ous*]

**dutiable** /'dyoohti·əbl, -tyəbl/ *adj* subject to a duty ⟨*~ imports*⟩

**dutiful** /'dyoohtif(ə)l/ *adj* **1** filled with or motivated by a sense of duty ⟨*a ~ son*⟩ **2** resulting from or expressing a sense of duty ⟨*~ affection*⟩ – **dutifully** *adv*, **dutifulness** *n*

**duty** /'dyoohti/ *n* **1** respectful or obedient conduct due to parents and superiors **2** a task, service, or function that is assigned or that arises from one's position or job; *also* these collectively ⟨*do one's ~*⟩ **3a** (a task or action resulting from) a moral or legal obligation **b** the force of moral or legal obligation ⟨*~ bound*⟩ **4** a tax; *esp* a tax on imports **5a** a measure of the efficiency of a machine expressed in terms of the amount of work done in relation to the energy consumed **b** the service required of something (eg a machine), esp under given conditions *synonyms* see ¹TASK, ²TAX [ME *duete*, fr AF *dueté*, fr OF *deu* due] – **do duty** to act as a substitute – usu + *for* – **on/off duty** at/not at work

**,duty-'free** *adj* **1** *of goods* exempt from duty ⟨*bought ~ drinks on board the boat*⟩ **2** *esp of a shop* selling duty-free goods

**duumvir** /dyooh'umvə, 'dyooh·əmvə/ *n* either of two officers or magistrates of ancient Rome who together constituted a board or court [L, fr *duum* (gen of *duo* two) + *vir* man]

**duumvirate** /dyooh'umvərət/ *n* **1** an association of two people in high office **2** government or control by two people

**duvet** /'doohvay/ *n* a large quilt filled with a thick mass of insulating material (eg down, feathers, or a man-made fibre), that is usu placed inside a removable cover before use and is used on top of the bed in place of bedclothes – called also CONTINENTAL QUILT [Fr, lit., down]

**dux** /duks/ *n* the leading pupil in a class or school [L, leader – more at DUKE]

**¹dwarf** /dwawf/ *n, pl* **dwarfs, dwarves** /dwawvz/ **1** a person of unusually small stature; *esp* one whose bodily proportions

# dwa

are abnormal 2 an animal or plant much below normal size 3 a small legendary manlike being, esp in Norse and Germanic mythology, who was usu a skilled craftsman, and often ugly 4 **dwarf star, dwarf** a star of ordinary or low luminosity and relatively small size but high density – compare WHITE DWARF [ME dwerg, dwerf, fr OE dweorg, dweorh; akin to OHG twerg dwarf] – **dwarfish** adj, **dwarfishly** adv, **dwarfishness** n

**²dwarf** vt 1 to restrict the growth of; stunt ⟨children ~ed by malnutrition⟩ 2 to cause to appear smaller ⟨the other buildings are ~ed by the skyscraper⟩ ~ vi to become smaller

**dwarfism** /'dwaw,fiz(ə)m/ n the condition of stunted growth

**¹dwell** /dwel/ vi **dwelt** /dwelt/, **dwelled** 1 to exist or be present or inherent in a specified condition or thing 2 formal to live as a resident [ME dwellen, fr OE dwellan to go astray, hinder; akin to OHG twellen to tarry] – **dweller** n

**dwell on/upon** vt to keep the attention directed towards, esp in speech or writing ⟨dwelt on the weaknesses in his opponent's arguments⟩

**²dwell** n a short pause in the action of a machine

**dwelling** /'dweling/ n, formal a place (e g house or flat) in which people live

**dwelling house** n, chiefly law a building used as a dwelling

**dwindle** /'dwindl/ vb to (cause to) become steadily less in quantity or quality; shrink [prob freq of E dial. dwine to waste away, fr ME dwinen, fr OE dwīnan]

**DX, Dx** /,dee'eks/ n long-range radio transmissions ⟨when some of the best ~ may be heard – Radio & Electronics World⟩ ⟨~ listeners⟩ [DX, abbr for distance]

**DXer, Dxer** /,dee'eksə/ n someone whose hobby is listening to DX transmissions

**DXing, Dxing** /,dee'exing/ n the hobby of listening to DX

**dy-** /die-/, **dyo-** comb form two ⟨dyarchy⟩ [LL, fr Gk, fr dyo – more at TWO]

**dyad** /'die,ad/ n 1 a mathematical process indicated by writing the symbols of two VECTORS (quantities that have size and specified direction) without a dot or cross between them (e g AB) 2 formal a pair; specif a married couple [LL dyad-, dyas, fr Gk, fr dyo] – **dyadic** adj, **dyadically** adv

**Dyak, Dayak** /'die,ak/ n 1 (a member of) any of several Indonesian peoples of the interior of Borneo 2 the language of the Dyaks [Malay dayak up-country]

**dyarchy, diarchy** /'die,ahki/ n a government in which power is vested in two rulers or authorities

**dybbuk** /'dibək/ n, pl **dybbukim** /'dibəkim/ also **dybbuks** an evil spirit (e g the soul of a dead sinner) believed in Jewish folklore to enter the body of a living person [LHeb dibbūq]

**¹dye** /die/ n 1 a colour or tint produced by dyeing 2 **dye, dyestuff** a substance (e g a liquid or powder) used for colouring, staining, etc [ME dehe, fr OE dēah, dēag; akin to L fumus smoke – more at FUME]

**²dye** vb **dyeing** vt 1 to give a new and often permanent colour to, esp with a dye ⟨~d her hair black⟩ 2 to impart (a colour) by dyeing ⟨~ing blue on yellow⟩ ~ vi to take up or impart colour in dyeing – **dyeable** adj, **dyer** n

**,dyed-in-the-'wool** adj 1 of a material dyed before being woven 2 thoroughgoing, uncompromising ⟨a ~ conservative⟩

**dyer's broom** n, chiefly NAm dyer's-greenweed

**,dyer's-'greenweed** n a Eurasian shrub (Genista tinctoria) of the pea family that has yellow flowers yielding a yellow dye and grows in woods, grassland, etc

**dyer's rocket** n a Eurasian plant (Reseda luteola) of the mignonette family that has spiky pale yellow-green flowers, grows mainly in wasteland, sands, gravel, etc, and was formerly much cultivated as the source of a yellow dye

**dyer's weed** n any of various plants yielding dyes

**dyewood** /'diewood/ n any of various woods (e g FUSTIC) from which colouring matter is extracted for dyeing

**¹dying** /'die·ing/ pres part of DIE

**²dying** adj made or occurring at the point of death; final, last ⟨a ~ wish⟩ ⟨his ~ breath⟩

**¹dyke** /diek/, **dike** n 1 a man-made ditch or watercourse 2 a bank, usu of earth, constructed to control or confine water 3 a barrier 4 a raised path or road for crossing water or marshland 5 a wall-like body of rock that has flowed while molten into a fissure and that runs across layers of other rocks 6 chiefly Br a natural watercourse 7 dial Br a wall of turf or stone 8 slang a toilet [ME, fr OE dic ditch, dike; akin to MHG tīch pond, dike, L figere to fasten, pierce]

**²dyke, dike** vt 1 to surround or protect with a dyke 2 to drain by the use of a dyke

**³dyke, dike** n, derog a female homosexual [origin unknown]

**¹dynamic** /die'namik, di-/ adj 1a of physical force or energy in motion b of dynamics 2a marked by continuous activity or change ⟨a ~ population⟩ b energetic, forceful ⟨a ~ personality⟩ 3 of a computer memory using devices that require periodic renewal to preserve the stored information – compare STATIC synonyms see LIVELY [Fr dynamique, fr Gk dynamikos powerful, fr dynamis power, fr dynasthai to be able] – **dynamically** adv

**²dynamic** n 1 a dynamic force 2 DYNAMICS 2

**dynamics** /die'namiks, di-/ n taking sing or pl verb 1 a branch of physics that deals with forces and their relation to the motion of bodies 2 the pattern of change or growth of an object or phenomenon ⟨personality ~⟩ ⟨population ~⟩ ⟨group ~⟩ 3 variation and contrast in force or intensity (in music)

**dynamism** /'dienə,miz(ə)m/ n 1a a philosophical system that describes the universe in terms of the interplay of forces – compare MECHANISM, VITALISM b DYNAMICS 2 2 the quality of being energetic or forceful – **dynamist** n, **dynamistic** adj

**¹dynamite** /'dienə,miet/ n 1 a powerful blasting explosive that is made of nitroglycerine mixed with an absorbent material and that sometimes contains other explosive substances (e g AMMONIUM NITRATE) 2 informal someone or something that has a potentially dangerous or spectacular effect ⟨this letter is ~ – Erle Stanley Gardner⟩ [Gk dynamis + ISV -ite (formed by Alfred Nobel, inventor of the explosive)] – **dynamitic** adj

**²dynamite** vt 1 to blow up or destroy with dynamite 2 informal to cause the complete failure or destruction of – **dynamiter** n

**dynamo** /'dienəmoh/ n, pl **dynamos** 1 a machine by which mechanical energy is converted into electrical energy; specif such a device that produces DIRECT CURRENT (e g in a car) 2 a forceful energetic individual [short for dynamoelectric machine]

**dynamometer** /,dienə'momitə/ n an instrument for measuring the power exerted or generated (e g by an engine or animal) [Fr dynamomètre, fr Gk dynamis power + Fr -mètre -meter] – **dynamometry** n, **dynamometric** adj

**dynast** /'dinəst, -nast/ n a usu hereditary ruler [L dynastes, fr Gk dynastēs, fr dynasthai to be able, have power]

**dynasty** /'dinəsti, die-/ n 1 a succession of hereditary rulers; also the time during which such a dynasty rules 2 a powerful group or family that maintains its position for a considerable time – **dynastic** adj, **dynastically** adv

**dynatron** /'dienə,tron/ n a THERMIONIC VALVE having four ELECTRODES (plates, wires, etc to which a voltage is applied) and used esp to generate oscillations (e g for transmission of a radio signal) [Gk dynamis power]

**dyne** /dien/ n a unit of force in the CENTIMETRE-GRAM-SECOND system equal to the force that would give a mass of 1 gram an acceleration of 1 centimetre per second per second, equivalent to $10^{-5}$ newtons [Fr, fr Gk dynamis]

**dynode** /'die,nohd/ n an ELECTRODE (electrical conductor) that emits electrons by SECONDARY EMISSION when bombarded by a stream of particles and is used esp in a PHOTOMULTIPLIER (device for detecting low levels of light) to amplify a low-level signal [Gk dynamis]

**dyo-** – see DY-

**dys-** /dis-/ prefix 1 abnormal; impaired ⟨dysfunction⟩ ⟨dysplasia⟩ 2 difficult; painful ⟨dysuria⟩ ⟨dysmenorrhoea⟩ 3 bad ⟨dysphoria⟩ □ (2&3) compare EU- [ME dis- bad, difficult, fr MF & L dys-, MF dis-, fr L dys-, fr Gk; akin to OE tō-, te- apart, Skt dus- bad, difficult]

**dyscrasia** /dis'krayzi-ə, -zh(y)ə/ n an abnormal condition of the body or of one of its parts ⟨a blood ~⟩ [NL, fr ML, bad mixture of humours, fr Gk dyskrasia, fr dys- + krasis mixture, fr kerannynai to mix]

**dysentery** /'dis(ə)ntri/ n any of several infectious diseases characterized by severe diarrhoea, usu with passing of mucus and blood [ME dissenterie, fr L dysenteria, fr Gk, fr dys- + enteron intestine – more at INTER-] – **dysenteric** adj

**dysfunction, disfunction** /dis'fungksh(ə)n/ n impaired or abnormal functioning, esp of an organ of the body – **dysfunctional** adj

**dysgenesis** /dis'jenəsis/ n, pl **dysgeneses** /-'jenəseez/ defective development, esp of the sex glands (e g in KLINEFELTER'S SYNDROME OF TURNER'S SYNDROME) [NL]

**dysgenic** /dis'jenik/ adj 1 detrimental to the hereditary qualities of a race or stock 2 of dysgenics

**dysgenics** /dis'jeniks/ n taking sing vb the study of the degeneration of the hereditary qualities of a race or stock, esp the human race – called also CACOGENICS; compare EUGENICS

**dyslexia** /dis'leksi·ə/ *n* a maldevelopment of reading ability in otherwise normal children due to a neurological disorder; *broadly* any reading maldevelopment in people of normal intelligence, not resulting from a defect of the senses [NL, fr *dys-* + Gk *lexis* word, speech] – **dyslexic** *adj*

**dyslogistic** /ˌdislə'jistik/ *adj, of a remark, comment, or other utterance* uncomplimentary – compare EULOGISTIC [*dys-* + *-logistic* (as in *eulogistic*)] – **dyslogistically** *adv*

**dysmenorrhoea,** *chiefly NAm* **dysmenorrhea** /ˌdismenə'riə, -ˌ--'-/ *n* painful menstruation [NL] – **dysmenorrhoeal, dysmenorrheic** *adj*

**dyspepsia** /dis'pepsi·ə/ *n* indigestion [L, fr Gk, fr *dys-* + *pepsis* digestion, fr *peptein, pessein* to cook, digest – more at COOK]

¹**dyspeptic** /dis'peptik/ *adj* **1** relating to or having indigestion **2** ill-tempered – **dyspeptically** *adv*

²**dyspeptic** *n* a person suffering from indigestion

**dysphagia** /dis'fayjyə/ *n* difficulty in swallowing [NL] – **dysphagic** *adj*

**dysphasia** /-'fayzyə, -zh(y)ə/ *n* loss of or deficiency in the power to use or understand language as a result of injury to or disease of the brain; APHASIA [NL] – **dysphasic** *n or adj*

**dysphonia** /dis'fohnyə/ *n* impairment of voice quality and the ability to form proper speech sounds principally caused by malfunction of the vocal chords [NL, fr *dys-* + *-phonia* -phony] – **dysphonic** *adj*

**dysphoria** /dis'fawri·ə/ *n* a state of feeling unwell or unhappy –compare EUPHORIA [NL, fr Gk, fr *dysphoros* hard to bear, fr *dys-* + *pherein* to bear – more at BEAR] – **dysphoric** *adj*

**dysplasia** /-'playzi·ə, -zh(y)ə/ *n* abnormal growth, development or absence of organs, cells, etc [NL] – **dysplastic** *adj*

**dyspnoea,** *chiefly NAm* **dyspnea** /disp'nee·ə/ *n* difficult or laboured breathing [L *dyspnoea,* fr Gk *dyspnoia,* fr *dyspnoos* short of breath, fr *dys-* + *pnein* to breathe – more at SNEEZE] – **dyspnoeic** *adj*

**dysprosium** /dis'prohzi·əm, -si-/ *n* a soft silvery-white chemical element of the RARE EARTH group of elements that forms highly magnetic compounds and is used to absorb neutrons in the control rods of a nuclear reactor [NL, fr Gk *dysprositos* hard to get at, fr *dys-* + *prositos* approachable, fr *prosienai* to approach, fr *pros-* + *ienai* to go – more at ISSUE]

**dystopia** /dis'tohpi·ə/ *n* an imaginary place which is as depressingly wretched as possible – compare UTOPIA [NL, fr *dys-* + *-topia* (as in *utopia*)] – **dystopian** *adj*

**dystrophic** /dis'trohfik/ *adj* **1** relating to or caused by faulty nutrition **2** *of a lake* brownish with much dissolved undecomposed organic matter, a scarcity of oxygen and nutrients, and usu little plant or animal life

**dystrophy** /'distrəfi/ *n* **1** the state of being dystrophic **2** any of various disorders of the body characterized by wasting of organs or tissues (e g muscles or bones)

**dysuria** /dis'yooəri·ə/ *n* difficult or painful urination [NL, fr Gk *dysouria,* fr *dys-* + *-ouria* -uria]

**dytiscid** /die'tisid/ *n* DIVING BEETLE [deriv of Gk *dytikos* able to dive, fr *dyein* to enter, dive in, sink]

**dzo** /zoh, dzoh/, **zo** /zoh/ *n pl* **dzo, dzos, zos, zo** (any of) a breed of Tibetan cattle that is a cross between the yak and domestic cattle [Tibetan *wdzo*]

# E

**e, E** /ee/ *n, pl* **e's, es, E's, Es** **1a** the 5th letter of the English alphabet **b** a graphic representation of or a device for reproducing the letter *e* **c** a speech counterpart of printed or written *e* **2** the 3rd note of a C-major musical scale **3** one designated *e*, esp as the 5th in order or class **4** the base of the system of NATURAL LOGARITHMS that can be expressed as the sum of the infinite series, $e = 1 + 1 + \frac{1}{2}, + \frac{1}{3}, + \frac{1}{4}, + \ldots$, and that has the approximate numerical value 2.71828 **5a** a mark or grade rating a pupil's work as poor and usu constituting a low pass **b** one who or that which is graded or rated with an E **6** something shaped like the letter E

**e-** *prefix* **1a** deprive of; remove (a specified quality or thing) ⟨*emasculate*⟩ ⟨*eviscerate*⟩ **b** lacking; without ⟨*edentate*⟩ ⟨*e-caudate*⟩ **2** on the outside ⟨*evert*⟩ **3** thoroughly ⟨*evaporate*⟩ **4** out ⟨*emanate*⟩ ⟨*ejaculate*⟩ **5** away ⟨*eluvium*⟩ [ME, fr OF & L; OF, out, forth, away, fr L, fr *ex-*]

**¹each** /eech/ *adj* being one of two or more distinct individuals considered separately and often forming a group ⟨~ *foot in turn*⟩ ⟨*they* ~ *want something different*⟩ [ME *ech*, fr OE *ǣlc*; akin to OHG *iogilīh* each; both fr a prehistoric WGmc compound whose constituents are represented by OE *ā* always & OE *gelīc* alike]

**²each** *pron* each one ⟨~ *of us*⟩ ⟨~ *is equally attractive*⟩ – **each other** each of two or more in reciprocal action or relation – not used as subject of a clause ⟨*wore* each other's *shirts*⟩ ⟨*looked at* each other *in surprise*⟩

*usage* **1** When **each** is the subject of a sentence it is traditionally followed by a singular verb and pronoun ⟨**each** *must do his best*⟩; but plural verbs and pronouns are increasingly used today, in writing as well as in speech, in cases where **each** is followed by *of* and a plural noun, and particularly where one wishes to avoid using either *he* for both sexes or the awkward *he or she* ⟨**each** *of the members must clean their own equipment*⟩. When **each** follows a plural subject, the following verb and pronoun are normally plural ⟨*we* **each** *clean our own equipment*⟩. **2** There seems no foundation for the advice given by some former writers on usage that one should use **each other** for each of two and **one another** for more than two. The two expressions are now used interchangeably ⟨*the whole team helped* **each other**⟩ ⟨*he and his wife hate* **one another**⟩.

**³each** *adv* to or for each; apiece ⟨*tickets at £1* ~⟩

**each way** *adj or adv, Br, of a bet* placed so as to return a profit if the horse, dog, etc that is bet on finishes in the first three ⟨*an* ~ *bet*⟩ ⟨*backed it* ~⟩

**eager** /'eegə/ *adj* **1** marked by keen, enthusiastic, or impatient desire or interest ⟨*always* ~ *to help*⟩ **2a** *archaic* sharp, biting **b** *obs* sour [ME *egre*, fr OF *aigre*, fr L *acer* – more at EDGE] – **eagerly** *adv*, **eagerness** *n*

**eager beaver** *n, informal* an extremely diligent person, esp one who volunteers for extra work

**eagle** /'eegl/ *n* **1** any of various large birds of prey (family Accipitridae) that hunt by day and are noted for their strength, size, gracefulness, keenness of vision, and powers of flight **2** any of various emblematic or symbolic figures or representations of an eagle: eg **2a** the standard of the ancient Romans **b** the seal or standard of a nation (eg the USA) having an eagle as its emblem **3** a former 10-dollar gold coin of the USA bearing an eagle on the reverse **4** a golf score of two strokes less than PAR (standard score) on a hole – compare BIRDIE [ME *egle*, fr OF *aigle*, fr L *aquila*]

**eagle eye** *n* the ability to see or observe with exceptional keenness; *also* one with such ability

**eagle owl** *n* a large Eurasian owl (*Bubo bubo*) with prominent ear tufts and large orange eyes

**eagle ray** *n* any of several large active RAYS (family Myliobatidae) that are widely distributed in warm coastal waters and have broad side fins (PECTORAL FINS) like wings and a very long slender tail usu having one or more spines at its base

**eaglet** /'eeglit/ *n* a young eagle

**eagre** /'aygə/ *n* ⁴BORE (large wave in a river) [origin unknown]

**ealdorman** /'awldəmən/ *n* the chief officer in a district (eg a shire) in Anglo-Saxon England [OE – more at ALDERMAN]

**-ean** /-iən/ – see -AN

**¹ear** /iə/ *n* **1a** the organ of hearing and balance in VERTEBRATE animals that, in the typical mammal, consists of a sound-collecting OUTER EAR separated by a thin membrane from a sound-transmitting MIDDLE EAR, which in turn is separated from a sensory INNER EAR **b** any of various organs capable of detecting vibratory motion **2** the external visible part of the ear of humans and most mammals **3a** the sense or act of hearing **b** sharpness of hearing ⟨*has a keen* ~⟩ **c** sensitivity to musical tone and pitch **4** something resembling the mammalian external ear in shape or position: eg **4a** a projecting part (eg a handle) **b** either of a pair of tufts of lengthened feathers on the head of some birds **5a** sympathetic attention ⟨*gained the* ~ *of the managing director*⟩ **b** *pl* notice, awareness ⟨*it has come to my* ~*s that you are discontented*⟩ **6** a space in the upper corner of a newspaper, magazine, etc, usu containing an advertisement [ME *ere*, fr OE *ēare*; akin to OHG *ōra* ear, L *auris*, Gk *ous*] – **be all ears** to listen very attentively – **fall on deaf ears** to be ignored or unheeded – **get/give a thick ear** to receive or give a blow on the ear – **have/keep an/one's ear to the ground** to keep oneself informed about news, gossip, etc – **in one ear and out the other** through one's mind without making an impression – **out on one's ear** thrown out of a job, home, etc with no possibility of returning – **play by ear 1** to play music from memory of the sound without having seen it written **2** to do something without rehearsal or preparation; improvise – **prick up one's ears** to start listening closely – **turn a deaf ear (to)** to refuse to listen (to) – **wet behind the ears** naive, inexperienced – see also **with a FLEA in one's ear, make a PIG's ear of, UP to one's ears**

**²ear** *n* the cluster of seeds at the top of a stalk of a cereal grass, together with their protective structures [ME *er*, fr OE *ēar*; akin to OHG *ahir* ear, OE *ecg* edge – more at EDGE]

**earache** /'iə,rayk/ *n* an ache or pain in the ear

**eardrum** /'iədrum/ *n* TYMPANIC MEMBRANE

**eared** /iəd/ *adj* having ears, esp of a specified kind ⟨*a big-eared man*⟩ ⟨*golden-eared corn*⟩

**eared seal** *n* any of a family (Otariidae) of seals, including the SEA LIONS and FUR SEALS, that are characterized by independent mobile hind limbs, that enable movement on land, and small well-developed external ears – compare EARLESS SEAL

**earflap** /'iə,flap/ *n* **1** an extension on the lower edge of a hat that may be folded down to keep the ears warm **2** OUTER EAR

**earful** /'iəf(ə)l/ *n, informal* **1** an outpouring of news or gossip **2** a sharp verbal reprimand

**earhole** /'iə,hohl/ *n, slang* the ear, esp of a person

**earing** /'iəring/ *n* a line used to fasten a corner of a sail, or to reduce the area of a sail (eg by folding) [perh fr ¹*ear*]

**earl** /uhl/ *n* a member of the British peerage ranking below a marquess and above a viscount [ME *erl*, fr OE *eorl* warrior, nobleman; akin to ON *jarl* warrior, nobleman] – **earldom** *n*

**earless seal** /'iəlis/ *n* any of a family (Phocidae) of seals including the HAIR SEALS, that are characterized by having the hind limbs reduced to swimming flippers and no external ears – compare EARED SEAL

**earl marshal** *n* an officer of state in England serving chiefly as head of the College of Arms, and who performs various duties on ceremonial occasions and state processions

**earlobe** /'iə,lohb/ *n* the fleshy lower part of the external ear, esp of humans but also of some fowl

**earlock** /'iə,lok/ *n* a curl of hair hanging in front of the ear

**earl palatine** *n* COUNT PALATINE 2 (lord with royal powers in a county)

¹**early** /'uhli/ *adv* **1** at or near the beginning of a period of time or of a process or series – often + *on* ⟨earlier *on in the experiment*⟩ **2a** before the usual or proper time ⟨*got up* ~⟩ **b** sooner than related forms ⟨*these apples bear* ~⟩ **c** *archaic* soon [ME *erly*, fr OE *ǣrlīce*, fr *ǣr* early, soon – more at ERE]

²**early** *adj* **1a** of or occurring near the beginning of a period of time, a development, or a series **b(1)** distant in past time **b(2)** primitive **2a** occurring before the usual time **b** occurring in the near future **c** maturing or producing sooner than related forms ⟨*an* ~ *peach*⟩ – **earliness** *n*

³**early** *n* one who or that which arrives, produces, or is ready early; *esp* a plant (e g a potato) that matures more rapidly than average

**early bird** *n* **1** an early riser **2** one who or that which arrives early, esp before possible competitors [fr the proverb "the early bird catches the worm"]

**early closing** *n* the practice of closing the shops in a British town or district on one afternoon a week; *also* the day of the week on which this practice is observed

**Early English** *adj or n* (of) an early GOTHIC style of architecture prevalent in Britain from the late 12th to the late 13th century that was characterized by LANCET WINDOWS and pointed arches – compare DECORATED, PERPENDICULAR 3

**early leaver** *n* DROPOUT 1

**earlywood** /'uhli,wood/ *n* SPRINGWOOD (wood produced in the early part of a plant's growing season)

¹**earmark** /'iə,mahk/ *n* **1** a mark of identification on the ear of an animal **2** a distinguishing or identifying characteristic ⟨*all the* ~s *of poverty*⟩

²**earmark** *vt* **1a** to mark (livestock) with an earmark **b** to mark in a distinguishing manner, esp as one's property **2** to designate (e g funds) for a specific use or owner

**earmuffs** /'iə,mufs/ *n pl* a pair of ear coverings connected by a flexible band and worn as protection against cold or noises; *also, sing* either of these coverings

¹**earn** /uhn/ *vt* **1** to receive (e g money) as return for effort, esp for work done or services rendered **2** to bring in as income ⟨*my shares* ~ed *nothing last year*⟩ **3a** to come to be duly worthy of or entitled or suited to ⟨*he had* ~ed *a promotion by his devotion to duty*⟩ **b** to make worthy of or obtain for ⟨*his devotion to duty had* ~ed *him a promotion*⟩ – see also **earn one's** SALT *synonyms see* ¹WIN [ME *ernen*, fr OE *earnian*]

²**earn** *vi, obs* to grieve [prob alter. of *yearn*]

**earner** /'uhnə/ *n* **1** one who or that which earns **2** *Br slang* something profitable

¹**earnest** /'uhnist/ *n* [ME *ernest*, seriousness, fr OE *eornost*; akin to OHG *ernust* seriousness] – **in earnest** seriously, sincerely

²**earnest** *adj* **1** characterized by or proceeding from an intense and serious state of mind **2** grave, important *synonyms see* SERIOUS *antonym* frivolous – **earnestly** *adv*, **earnestness** *n*

³**earnest** *n* **1** something of value, esp money, given by a buyer to a seller to bind a bargain **2** a token of what is to come; an omen [ME *ernes*, *ernest*, fr OF *erres*, pl of *erre* pledge, fr L *arra*, short for *arrabo*, fr Gk *arrhabōn*, fr Heb *'ērābhōn*]

**earnings** /'uhningz/ *n pl* **1** something earned, esp money **2** the balance of revenue after deduction of costs and expenses

**earphone** /'iə,fohn/ *n* a device that converts electrical energy into sound waves and is worn over or inserted into the ear

**earpiece** /'iə,pees/ *n* **1** the part of an instrument (e g a stethoscope, telephone, or hearing aid) put next to the ear for listening; *esp* an earphone **2** either of the two sidepieces that support glasses by passing over or behind the ears

**earpiercing** /'iə,piəsing/ *adj* earsplitting

**earplug** /'iə,plug/ *n* a device inserted into the outer opening of the ear for protection against esp water or loud noise

**earring** /'iə,ring/ *n* an ornament for the ear that is attached to the earlobe

**ear rot** *n* a disease of maize that is characterized by the growth of mould on and decay of the ears and is caused by fungi (genera *Diplodia*, *Fusarium*, or *Gibberella*)

**ear shell** *n* ABALONE

**earshot** /'iə,shot/ *n* the range within which something, esp the unaided voice, may be heard

**earsplitting** /'iə,spliting/ *adj* distressingly loud or shrill

¹**earth** /uhth/ *n* **1** the loose material making up part of the surface of the globe; soil **2** the sphere of mortal life as distinguished from spheres of spirit life – compare HEAVEN, HELL **3a** areas of land as distinguished from sea and air **b** the solid surface of the ground composed of soil, rock particles, etc

⟨*good to feel the* ~ *under his feet again*⟩ **4** *often cap* the planet on which we live that is third in order from the sun **5** the people of the planet earth **6** the lair of a burrowing animal, esp a fox or badger **7** a metallic oxide (e g magnesia or alumina) formerly classed as a chemical element – compare ALKALINE EARTH, RARE EARTH **8** *chiefly Br* **8a** an electrical connection with the earth **b** a large conducting body (e g the planet earth) arbitrarily considered as having an electric POTENTIAL of zero **9** a huge amount of money – + *the* ⟨*it will cost you the* ~⟩ [ME *erthe*, fr OE *eorthe*; akin to OHG *erda* earth, Gk *eraze* to the ground] – **earthlike** *adj*, **earthward** *adj or adv*, **earthwards** *adv* – **like nothing on earth 1** unhealthy, esp as a result of tiredness **2** grotesque, outlandish – **on earth** – used to intensify an interrogative pronoun ⟨*where* on earth *is it?*⟩; – see also RUN **to earth**, SALT **of the earth**

²**earth** *vt* **1** to force (an animal) to hide in an earth ⟨~ed *the fox*⟩ **2** to cover the roots of (a plant) with soil – often + *up* **3** *chiefly Br* to connect electrically with the earth ~ *vi, chiefly Br, of a hunted animal* to hide in the ground

**earthborn** /'uhth,bawn/ *adj, chiefly poetic* **1** born on the earth; mortal **2** associated with earthly life ⟨~ *cares*⟩

**earthbound** /'uhth,bownd/ *adj* **1a** restricted to land or to the surface of the earth **b** heading or directed towards the planet earth ⟨*an* ~ *spaceship*⟩ **2a** bound by earthly interests; lacking spiritual quality ⟨~ *desires*⟩ **b** pedestrian, unimaginative

**earth closet** *n* a toilet in which earth is used to cover excreta

**earthen** /'uhdh(ə)n, -th(ə)n/ *adj* made of earth or baked clay

**earthenware** /'uhdhən,weə, 'uhthən-/ *n* articles (e g pots and vessels) made of opaque clay that is baked at a low temperature – compare STONEWARE – **earthenware** *adj*

**earthlight** /'uhth,liet/ *n* earthshine

**earthling** /'uhthling/ *n* an inhabitant of the earth, esp as contrasted with inhabitants of other planets

¹**earthly** /'uhthli/ *adj* **1a** characteristic of or belonging to this earth **b** relating to human beings' actual life on this earth; worldly **2** possible – usu + neg or interrog ⟨*there is no* ~ *reason for such behaviour*⟩`– **earthliness** *n*

²**earthly** *n, informal* a chance of success – usu + neg or interrog

**earthman** /'uhth,man/ *n* an earthling

**earth mother** *n, often cap E&M* **1** the earth viewed (e g in primitive religion) as the divine source of life **2** a female goddess of fertility **3** *informal* a sensual or maternal woman who embodies the earth mother

**earthnut** /'uhth,nut/ *n* PIGNUT

**earthquake** /'uhth,kwayk/ *n* a usu violent shaking or trembling of the earth caused by volcanic action or movements of the earth's crust

**earth science** *n* any of the sciences (e g geology, meteorology, or oceanography) that deal with the structure and features of the earth or one or more of its parts

**earthshaking** /'uhth,shayking/ *adj, chiefly informal* having tremendous importance or a widespread and usu violent effect – **earthshaker** *n*, **earthshakingly** *adv*

**earthshine** /'uhth,shien/ *n* sunlight reflected by the earth that illuminates the dark part of the moon

**earthstar** /'uhth,stah/ *n* a spherical fungus (genus *Geastrum*) with a double wall whose outer layer splits into the shape of a star

**earthwork** /'uhth,wuhk/ *n* **1 earthwork, earthworks** *pl* an embankment or other construction made of earth; *esp* one used as a military fortification **2** the operations connected with excavations and embankments of earth

**earthworm** /'uhth,wuhm/ *n* a ground-living segmented worm (class Oligochaeta of the phylum Annelida); *esp* any of a family (Lumbricidae) of numerous soil-dwelling widely distributed hermaphroditic worms

**earthy** /'uhthi/ *adj* **1** consisting of, resembling, or suggesting earth ⟨*an* ~ *flavour*⟩ **2a** unrefined, direct **b** crude, coarse ⟨~ *humour*⟩ **3** *archaic* earthly, worldly – **earthily** *adv*, **earthiness** *n*

**ear trumpet** *n* a trumpet-shaped device held to the ear to improve hearing

**earwax** /'iə,waks/ *n* CERUMEN

¹**earwig** /'iə,wig/ *n* any of numerous typically elongated brownish insects (order Dermaptera) that have slender many-jointed antennae, short leathery fore wings and thin membranous hind wings, and a pair of curved pincerlike structures at the rear end of the body [ME *erwigge*, fr OE *ēarwicga*, fr *ēare* ear + *wicga* insect – more at VETCH; fr a former belief that the insects creep into people's ears]

EFG

²**earwig** *vt* -gg- to annoy or attempt to influence by private talk

**earwitness** /'iə,witnis/ *n* one who can give a report on what he/she has heard – compare EYEWITNESS

¹**ease** /eez/ *n* 1 the state of being comfortable: e g 1a freedom from pain or discomfort **b** freedom from care **c** freedom from labour or difficulty **d** freedom from embarrassment or constraint; naturalness 2 relief from discomfort or obligation 3 facility, effortlessness 4 an act of easing or a state of being eased; *esp* a lowering trend in prices [ME *ese,* fr OF *aise* convenience, comfort, fr L *adjacent-, adjacens* neighbourhood, fr neut of prp of *adjacēre* to lie near – more at ADJACENT] – **easeful** *adj,* **easefully** *adv* – **at ease** 1 free from pain or discomfort 2 free from restraint or formality ⟨*he's quite at his ease in any kind of company*⟩ 3 standing silently with the feet apart and usu one or both hands behind the body – used esp as a military command

²**ease** *vt* 1 to free from something that pains, disquiets, or burdens ⟨*~d you of your troubles*⟩ 2 to make less painful; alleviate ⟨*~ his suffering*⟩ 3a to lessen the pressure or tension of, esp by slackening, lifting, or shifting **b** to moderate or reduce, esp in amount or intensity 4 to manoeuvre gently or carefully in a specified way ⟨*~d the heavy block into position*⟩ 5 to make less difficult ⟨*~ credit*⟩ 6 to steer the helm of a ship into the wind ~ *vi* 1 to decrease in activity, intensity, or severity – often + *off* or *up* ⟨*the rain is easing off*⟩ 2 to manoeuvre oneself gently or carefully ⟨*~d through a hole in the fence*⟩

**easel** /'eezl/ *n* an adjustable frame for supporting something (e g a blackboard or an artist's canvas) at a desired height and angle [D *ezel* ass; akin to OE *esol* ass; both fr a prehistoric EGmc-WGmc word borrowed fr L *asinus* ass]

**easement** /'eezmənt/ *n* 1 an act or means of easing or relieving 2 a right (e g a right of way) that entitles its holder to a specific limited use or enjoyment of a neighbour's land

**easily** /'eezəli/ *adv* 1 in an easy manner ⟨*my car will do a hundred ~*⟩ 2 without doubt; BY FAR ⟨*~ the best*⟩ **usage** see ²EASY

¹**east** /eest/ *adv* to, towards, or in the east **synonyms** see ¹NORTH [ME *est,* fr OE *ēast;* akin to OHG *ōstar* to the east, L *aurora* dawn, Gk *ēōs, heōs*]

²**east** *adj* 1 situated towards or at the east ⟨*an ~ window*⟩ 2 coming from the east ⟨*an ~ wind*⟩

³**east** *n* 1a the direction 90° to the right of north that is the general direction of sunrise; *also* the compass point that corresponds to this direction and is directly opposite to west **b** the place on the horizon where the sun rises 2a *often cap* regions or countries lying to the east of a specified or implied point of orientation; *also, taking sing or pl vb* the inhabitants of these regions **b** *cap* regions having a culture derived from ancient non-European, esp Asian areas **c** *cap* the part of the USA lying north of the Ohio river and east of the Mississippi **d** *cap* the countries of Eastern Europe and Asia which are under Communist government ⟨East-*West dialogue*⟩ 3 the altar end of a church 4 *often cap* 4a the one of the four positions at 90-degree intervals that lies to the east or to the right of South **b** a person (e g a bridge player) occupying the East in the course of a specified activity □ (2) usu + *the*

**East Anglian** *adj* (characteristic) of East Anglia

**eastbound** /'eest,bownd/ *adj* travelling, heading, or leading east ⟨*the ~ carriageway*⟩

**east by north** *adj, adv, or n* (from, towards, or in the direction of) the compass point that is one point north of due east; 78° 45′ clockwise from north

**east by south** *adj, adv, or n* (from, towards, or in the direction of) the compass point that is one point south of due east; 101° 15′ clockwise from north

**East End** *n the* densely populated INNER CITY area of east London containing industrial areas and docks – **East Ender** *n*

**Easter** /'eestə/ *n* a feast that commemorates Christ's resurrection and is observed, with variations of date due to different calendars, on the first Sunday after the full moon on or next after March 21 or one week later if the full moon falls on Sunday [ME *estre,* fr OE *ēastre;* akin to OHG *ōstarun* (pl) Easter; both fr the prehistoric WGmc name of a pagan spring festival, akin to OE *ēast* east]

**Easter egg** *n* an egg given as a present at Easter: e g **a** a decorated hard-boiled hen's egg **b** a usu chocolate confectionery egg

¹**easterly** /'eestəli/ *adj or adv* situated towards, belonging to,

or coming from the east; east [obs *easter* eastern]

²**easterly,** *NAm also* **easter** *n* a wind from the east

**Easter Monday** *n* the Monday after Easter observed as a public holiday (e g in Britain and elsewhere in the Commonwealth)

**eastern** /'eest(ə)n/ *adj* 1 *often cap* (characteristic) of a region conventionally designated East; e g 1a steeped in or stemming from Oriental traditions in contrast with those of Europe or America ⟨*~ philosophies*⟩ **b** of the communist countries of Eastern Europe and Asia ⟨*the ~ bloc*⟩ 2 **Eastern, Eastern Orthodox** or being the Christian churches originating in the church of the Eastern Roman Empire 3a lying or directed towards the east **b** coming from the east ⟨*an ~ wind*⟩ **synonyms** see ¹NORTH [ME *estern,* fr OE *ēasterne;* akin to OHG *ōstrōni* eastern, OE *ēast* east] – **easternmost** *adj*

**Easterner** /'eest(ə)nə/ *n* a native or inhabitant of the East; *esp, chiefly NAm* a native or inhabitant of the eastern part of the USA

**eastern hemisphere** *n* the half of the earth to the east of the Atlantic ocean including Europe, Asia, and Africa – compare WESTERN HEMISPHERE

**East Germanic** *n* a group of the Germanic languages that includes GOTHIC

**easting** /'eesting/ *n* 1 the distance due east in longitude from the preceding point of measurement 2 easterly progress

**east-north'east** *adj, adv, or n* (from, towards, or in the direction of) the compass point midway between east and northeast; 67° 30′ clockwise from north

**east-south'east** *adj, adv, or n* (from, towards, or in the direction of) the compass point midway between east and southeast; 112° 30′ clockwise from north

¹**eastward** /'eestwəd/ *adj* moving or extending eastwards

²**eastward** *n* eastward direction or part

**eastwards** /'eestwədz/ *adv* towards the east

¹**easy** /'eezi/ *adj* 1 causing or involving little difficulty or discomfort ⟨*an ~ problem*⟩ 2a not severe; lenient **b** not steep or abrupt ⟨*~ slopes*⟩ **c** readily prevailed on; compliant **d** not difficult to deceive or take advantage of ⟨*~ prey*⟩ **e**(1) plentiful in supply at low or declining interest rates ⟨*~ money*⟩ **e**(2) less in demand and usu lower in price ⟨*bonds were easier*⟩ 3a marked by peace and comfort ⟨*the ~ course of his life*⟩ **b** not hurried or strenuous ⟨*an ~ pace*⟩ 4a free from pain, annoyance, or anxiety ⟨*did all she could to make him easier*⟩ **b** marked by social ease ⟨*~ manners*⟩ 5a not burdensome or restricted ⟨*bought on ~ terms*⟩ ⟨*living in ~ circumstances*⟩ **b** fitting comfortably ⟨*an ~ shoe*⟩ **c** marked by ready facility and freedom from constraint ⟨*an ~ flowing style*⟩ **d** felt or attained to readily, naturally, and spontaneously ⟨*~ emotions*⟩ 6 *informal* readily persuaded to have sexual relations 7 *chiefly Br informal* not having marked preferences on a particular issue ⟨*I'm ~*⟩ [ME *esy,* fr OF *aisié,* pp of *aaisier* to ease, fr *a-* ad- (fr L *ad-*) + *aise* ease]

²**easy** *adv* 1 easily ⟨*promises come ~*⟩ 2 without undue speed or excitement; slowly, cautiously ⟨*take it ~*⟩ – **go easy on** to treat leniently

*usage* **Easy** as an adverb is used only in certain fixed phrases ⟨**easy** *does it*⟩ ⟨**easy** *come,* **easy** *go*⟩ ⟨*stand* **easy**⟩ and cannot replace **easily,** the usual adverb ⟨*the door opened* **easily**⟩.

**easy chair** *n* a large comfortable upholstered armchair

**easygoing** /,eezi'goh·ing/ *adj* 1 taking life easily: e g 1a placid **b** indolent and careless ⟨*his inertia, his laziness, his ~ ways* – *TLS*⟩ 2 unhurried, comfortable ⟨*an ~ pace*⟩ – **easygoingness** *n*

**easy meat** *n, chiefly Br* one easily duped, imposed upon, or mastered

**easy street** *n, informal* a state of affluence – often + *on* ⟨*on easy street in that good job*⟩

**easy virtue** *n* sexually promiscuous behaviour or habits

**eat** /eet/ *vb* **eating;** ate /et, ayt/; **eaten** /'eet(ə)n/ *vt* 1 to take in (esp solid food) through the mouth and swallow usu after chewing 2 to destroy, use up, or waste (as if) by eating; devour ⟨*locusts* ate *the country bare*⟩ 3a to consume gradually; corrode ⟨*the acid has ~en away the battery terminals*⟩ **b** *informal* to consume with vexation; bother ⟨*what's ~ing her now?*⟩ ~ *vi* 1 to take food or a meal 2 to be eatable in a specified way ⟨*perhaps it will ~ better than it looks* – Patrick White⟩ – see also **eat** CROW/**out of somebody's** HAND/**one's** HAT/**one's** HEART **out**/HUMBLE PIE/**one's** WORDS [ME *eten,* fr OE *etan;* akin to OHG *ezzan* to eat, L *edere,* Gk *edmenai*] – **eatable** *adj,* **eater** *n,* **eating** *n*

**eat out** *vi* to eat away from home, esp in a restaurant

**eat up** *vt* **1** to consume completely or very rapidly ⟨eaten up *with vanity*⟩ **2** *informal* to exhibit avid interest in or enjoyment of ⟨*really* ate up *those stories of hers*⟩

**eatables** /'eetablz/ *n pl* food

**eath** /eeth/ *adv or adj, Scot* easy [ME *ethe*, fr OE *ēathe*; akin to OHG *ōdi* easy]

**eating** /'eeting/ *adj* **1** used for eating ⟨*an* ~ *house*⟩ **2** suitable for eating raw ⟨*makes a better cooking than* ~ *apple*⟩

**eats** /eets/ *n pl, informal* food [ME *et* food, fr OE *ǣt*; akin to OE *etan* to eat]

**eau de cologne** /‚oh də kə'lohn/ *n, pl* **eaux de cologne** /~/ cologne [Fr, lit., Cologne water]

**eau-de-nil** /‚oh də 'neel/ *adj or n* (of) a dull green colour [Fr, lit., Nile water, fr *Nil* Nile, river in NE Africa]

**eau-de-vie** /‚oh də 'vee/ *n, pl* **eaux-de-vie** /~/ brandy [Fr, lit., water of life, trans of ML *aqua vitae*]

**eaves** /eevz/ *n pl* the lower border of a roof that overhangs the wall [ME *eves* (sing.), fr OE *efes*; akin to OHG *obasa* portico, OE *ūp* up – more at UP]

**eavesdrop** /'eevz‚drop/ *vi* to listen secretly to what is said in private [prob back-formation fr *eavesdropper*, lit., one standing under the drip from the eaves] – **eavesdropper** *n*

¹**ebb** /eb/ *n* **1** the flowing out of the tide towards the sea **2** a point or condition of decline ⟨*relations were at a low* ~⟩ [ME *ebbe*, fr OE *ebba*; akin to MD *ebbe* ebb, OE *of* from – more at OF]

²**ebb** *vi* **1** *of tidal water* to recede from the flood state or highest level **2** to decline from a higher to a lower level or from a better to a worse state

**ebb tide** *n* the tide while ebbing or at its lowest point

**ebon** /'ebən/ *adj, poetic* ebony

**ebonite** /'ebəniet/ *n* a hard black VULCANIZED (treated with sulphur) rubber

**ebon·ize, -ise** /'ebəniez/ *vt* to stain black in imitation of ebony

¹**ebony** /'ebəni/ *n* a hard heavy wood yielded by any of various tropical trees (genus *Diospyros* of the family Ebenaceae, the ebony family); *also* a tree yielding ebony [ME *eban*, fr L *ebenus*, fr Gk *ebenos*, fr Egypt *hbnj*]

²**ebony** *adj* **1** made of or resembling ebony **2** *chiefly apprec* black, dark

**ebracteate** /i'braktiət, -ayt/ *n, botany* without BRACTS (specialized leaflike parts) [NL *ebracteatus*, fr *e-* + *bracteatus* bracteate, fr *bractea* bract]

**ebullience** /i'buli·əns, -yəns/, **ebulliency** /-si/ *n* the quality of lively or enthusiastic expression of thoughts or feelings; exuberance

**ebullient** /i'buli·ənt, -yənt/ *adj* **1** boiling, agitated **2** characterized by ebullience [L *ebullient-, ebulliens*, prp of *ebullire* to bubble out, fr, *e-* + *bullire* to bubble, boil – more at BOIL] – **ebulliently** *adv*

**ebullition** /‚ebə'lish(ə)n/ *n, formal* **1** the act, process, or state of boiling or bubbling up **2** a sudden violent outburst or display

**ec-, eco-** *comb form* **1** habitat; environment ⟨*ecospecies*⟩ ⟨*ecophysiology*⟩ **2** ecological ⟨*ecosystem*⟩ [LL *oeco-* household, fr Gk *oik-, oiko-*, fr *oikos* house – more at VICINITY]

**Ecce homo** /‚ekay 'hohmoh/ *n* a representation of Christ crowned with thorns [LL, behold the man; fr the words (in the Vulgate Bible) spoken by Pilate when presenting Christ crowned with thorns (John 19:5)]

¹**eccentric** /ik'sentrik/ *adj* **1** not having the same centre ⟨~ *spheres*⟩ **2** deviating from an established pattern or from accepted usage or conduct; odd ⟨~ *behaviour*⟩ **3a** deviating from a circular path ⟨*an* ~ *orbit*⟩ **b** located elsewhere than at the geometrical centre; *also* having the axis or support so located ⟨*an* ~ *wheel*⟩ **synonyms** see STRANGE [ML *eccentricus*, fr Gk *ekkentros*, fr *ex* out of + *kentron* centre] – **eccentrically** *adv*

²**eccentric** *n* **1** a mechanical device (e g a cam) using eccentrically mounted parts to transform circular motion into motion alternately backwards and forwards along a straight line **2** an eccentric person

**eccentricity** /‚eksen'trisəti/ *n* **1** the quality, state, or an instance of being eccentric **2** a number that for a given geometric figure is the ratio of the distances from any point on the curve to the FOCUS (fixed point) and the DIRECTRIX (specified straight line)

**ecchymosis** /‚eki'mohsis/ *n, pl* **ecchymoses** /'mohseez/ (a bruise or other discoloration of the skin caused by) the escape of blood into the tissues from ruptured blood vessels [NL, fr Gk *ekchymōsis*, fr *ekchymousthai* to make blood escape, fr *ex-* + *chymos* juice – more at CHYME] – **ecchymotic** *adj*

**Eccles cake** /'ek(ə)lz/ *n* a small round cake of rich flaky pastry filled with currants [*Eccles*, town near Manchester in NW England]

**ecclesi-** /ikleezi-/, **ecclesio-** *comb form* church ⟨*ecclesiography*⟩ [ME *ecclesi-*, fr LL *ecclesia*, fr Gk *ekklēsia* assembly of citizens, church, fr *ekkalein* to call forth, summon, fr *ex-* + *kalein* to call]

**ecclesial** /i'kleezyəl/ *adj* of a church

**Ecclesiastes** /i‚kleezi'asteez/ *n* – see BIBLE table [Gk *Ekklēsiastēs*, lit., preacher (trans of Heb *Qōheleth*), fr *ekklēsiastēs* member of an assembly]

**ecclesiastic** /i‚kleezi'astik/ *n* a clergyman

**ecclesiastical** /i‚kleezi'astikl/, **ecclesiastic** /-ik/ *adj* **1** of a church, esp as a formal and established institution ⟨~ *law*⟩ **2** suitable for use in a church ⟨~ *vestments*⟩ [*ecclesiastical* fr ME, fr LL *ecclesiasticus; ecclesiastic* fr MF *ecclesiastique*, fr LL *ecclesiasticus*, fr LGk *ekklēsiastikos*, fr Gk, of an assembly of citizens, fr *ekklēsiastēs* member of an assembly, fr *ekklēsia*] – **ecclesiastically** *adv*

**ecclesiasticism** /i‚kleezi'astisiz(ə)m/ *n* excessive attachment to ecclesiastical forms and practices

**Ecclesiasticus** /i‚kleezi'astikus/ *n* – see BIBLE table [LL, fr *ecclesiasticus* ecclesiastic]

**ecclesiology** /i‚kleezi'oləji/ *n* **1** the study of church architecture and decoration **2** the study of the doctrine, theology, etc of churches – **ecclesiological** *adj*

**eccrine** /'ekrin, -ien, -een/ *adj* producing a liquid secretion without the loss of CYTOPLASM (jellylike material inside a cell) from the secreting cells ⟨*an* ~ *gland*⟩; *also* of or produced by an eccrine gland [ISV *ec-* (fr Gk *ex* out) + Gk *krinein* to separate – more at CERTAIN]

**eccrinology** /‚ekri'noləji/ *n* the branch of medical science that deals with (eccrine) secretions

**ecdysis** /'ekdisis/ *n, pl* **ecdyses** /-seez/ the act of moulting or shedding an outer skin or layer (e g in insects and crustaceans) [NL, fr Gk *ekdysis* act of getting out, fr *ekdyein* to take off, strip off]

**ecdysone** /ek'diesohn/ *also* **ecdyson** /-son/ *n* any of several hormones produced by insects and CRUSTACEANS (e g crabs and lobsters) that stimulate growth and trigger moulting and METAMORPHOSIS [ISV *ecdysis* + hormon*e*]

¹**echelon** /'eshəlon, 'ay-/ *n* **1a(1)** an arrangement of units (e g of troops or ships) with each successive unit behind and to one side of those ahead like a series of steps **a(2)** a formation of units or individuals resembling or in an echelon **b** a particular division of a headquarters or supply organization in warfare ⟨*the B* ~ *vehicles were mixed with the rear* ~ *headquarters vehicles*⟩ **2** any of a series of levels or grades (e g of authority or responsibility) in any organized field of activity; *also, taking sing or pl vb* the people occupying such a level or grade **3** **echelon, echelon grating** a DIFFRACTION GRATING that consists of a step-like array of glass plates and that is used for distinguishing between closely spaced lines of light in a spectrum that have very similar frequencies [Fr *échelon*, lit., rung of a ladder, fr OF *eschelon*, fr *eschele, eschiele* ladder, fr LL *scala* – more at SCALE]

²**echelon** *vt* to form or arrange in an echelon ~ *vi* to take position in an echelon

**echidna** /i'kidnə/ *n* an egg-laying spiny-coated toothless burrowing nocturnal mammal (*Tachyglossus aculeatus*) of Australia, Tasmania, and New Guinea that has a long extendable tongue and long heavy claws and that feeds chiefly on ants – called also SPINY ANTEATER [NL, fr L, viper, fr Gk]

**echin-** /ikien-/, **echino-** *comb form* **1** prickle; spine ⟨*echinodermata*⟩ **2** sea urchin ⟨*echinite*⟩ [L, fr Gk, fr *echinos* sea urchin]

**echinococcus** /i'kienoh‚kokəs, 'ekinoh-/ *n, pl* **echinococci** /‚kok(s)ie/ any of a genus (*Echinococcus*) of tapeworms that as adults live in the intestines of carnivores (e g dogs) without causing injury, and in the larval stage as BLADDER WORMS live as parasites in the tissues, esp the liver of cattle, sheep, pigs, and humans [NL, genus name]

**echinoderm** /i'kienoh‚duhm, 'ekinoh-/ *n* any of a phylum (Echinodermata) of widespread marine INVERTEBRATE animals, usu having five body parts radiating from a central axis of symmetry, and including the starfishes, sea urchins, and related forms [NL *Echinodermata*, phylum name, fr *echin-* + *-dermata* (fr Gk *derma* skin)] – **echinodermatous** *adj*

**echinoid** /i‚kienoyd, 'ekinoyd/ *n* any of a class (Echinoidea) of echinoderms having spherical or flattened bodies enclosed in a rigid chalky case and including the SEA URCHINS, HEART URCHINS, and SAND DOLLARS

**echinus** /i'kienəs/ *n, pl* **echini** /-nie/ 1 any of various SEA URCHINS (genus *Echinus*); *esp* the common European one (*Echinus esculentus*) 2 a rounded moulding projecting beneath the more substantial slabs at the top of a column [ME, fr L, fr Gk *echinos* hedgehog, sea urchin, architectural echinus]

**echiuroid** /‚eki'yooəroyd/ *n* any of a group (Echiuroidea) of marine worms that have cylindrical unsegmented bodies and a nonretractile PROBOSCIS capable of great extension that is situated above the mouth and is used for obtaining food [NL *Echiuroidea*, group name, deriv of Gk *echis* viper + *oura* tail]

**¹echo** /'ekoh/ *n, pl* **echoes** 1 the repetition of a sound caused by the reflection of sound waves (e g from a mountain side); *also* the repeated sound due to such reflection 2a a repetition, imitation; a reflection b a repercussion, result c a trace, vestige d a sympathetic response 3 one who closely imitates or repeats another's words, ideas, or acts 4 a soft repetition of a musical phrase 5a the reflection of transmitted radar signals by an object b a blip on a radar screen 6 a type of card-signalling (e g in bridge or whist) indicating which suit is preferred [ME *ecco*, fr MF & L; MF *echo*, fr L, fr Gk *ēchō*; akin to L *vagire* to wail, Gk *ēchē* sound] – **echoey** *adj*

**²echo** *vb* **echoed; echoing** *vi* 1 to resound with echoes 2 to produce an echo 3 to play an echo in a card game ~ *vt* 1 to repeat, imitate 2 to send back or repeat (a sound) as an echo

**Echo** – a communications code word for the letter *e*

**echo chamber** *n* a room with walls which reflect sound used (e g in sound recording) to produce hollow or echoing sound effects

**echoencephalography** /‚ekoh‚in‚sef(ə)l'ogrəfi/ *n* the examination and measurement of the internal structures of the skull and the diagnosis of its abnormalities by analysis of the echoes produced when the skull is scanned using ULTRASOUND (sound of high frequency) – **echoencephalograph, echoencephalogram** *n*

**echoic** /e'koh·ik/ *adj* 1 of an echo 2 formed in imitation of some natural sound; ONOMATOPOEIC – **echoism** *n*

**echolalia** /‚ekoh'layli·ə, -lyə/ *n* the automatic and meaningless repetition of what has just been said by other people, occurring usu as a symptom of mental disorder [NL] – **echolalic** *adj*

**echolocation** /'ekohlohkaysh(ə)n/ *n* the location of objects (e g prey) that cannot be detected visually by means of sound waves reflected back to the sender (e g a bat or submarine) by the objects ⟨*bats use* ~ *to catch moths*⟩

**echo sounder** *n* an instrument used to determine the depth of a body of water or of an object below the surface by means of sound waves

**echovirus** /'ekoh‚vie·ərəs/ *n* any of a group of viruses that are found in the stomach and intestines and are sometimes associated with respiratory illnesses and MENINGITIS (inflammation of the membranes surrounding the brain) [enteric *cytopathogenic human orphan* + *virus*]

**echt** /ekht (Ger εçt)/ *adj* genuine, authentic [Ger]

**éclair** /i'kleə, ay-/ *n* a small light oblong cake of CHOUX PASTRY that is split and filled (e g with whipped cream or custard) and usu topped with icing [Fr, lit., lightning]

**eclampsia** /i'klampsi·ə/ *n* a convulsive state; *esp* a dangerous condition occurring during pregnancy or while giving birth and characterized by convulsions and sometimes coma – compare PRE-ECLAMPSIA [NL, fr Gk *eklampsis* sudden flashing, fr *eklampein* to shine forth, fr *ex* out + *lampein* to shine] – **eclamptic** *adj*

**éclat** /ay'klah (Fr ekla)/ *n* 1 dazzling effect; brilliance 2 ostentatious display; publicity 3a brilliant or conspicuous success b acclaim, applause c social distinction; fame 4 *archaic* notoriety □ compare ÉLAN [Fr, splinter, burst, ostentation]

**¹eclectic** /e'klektik, i-/ *adj* 1 selecting or using elements from various doctrines, methods, or styles; not following just one system or set of ideas 2 composed of elements drawn from various sources [Gk *eklektikos*, fr *eklegein* to select, fr *ex* + *legein* to gather – more at LEGEND] – **eclectically** *adv*, **eclecticism** *n*

**²eclectic** *n* one who uses an eclectic method or approach

**¹eclipse** /i'klips/ *n* 1a the total or partial obscuring of one celestial body by another b the passage of one celestial body

(e g a planet or moon) into the shadow of another – compare OCCULTATION, TRANSIT 2 a falling into obscurity or decay; a decline 3 the state of being in ECLIPSE PLUMAGE [ME, fr OF, fr L *eclipsis*, fr Gk *ekleipsis*, fr *ekleipein* to omit, fail, suffer eclipse, fr *ex* + *leipein* to leave – more at LOAN]

**²eclipse** *vt* to cause an eclipse of: e g a to obscure, darken b to reduce in importance or repute; cause to decline c to surpass

**eclipse plumage** *n* a comparatively dull plumage that occurs usu seasonally in certain birds (e g ducks) that exhibit a distinct colourful plumage in the breeding season, and that lasts usu for only a short time after mating has occurred

**eclipsing binary** /i'klipsing/ *n* a BINARY STAR (two stars revolving round each other) whose mutual eclipses cause variations in its observed brightness – compare VARIABLE STAR

**eclipsing variable** *n* ECLIPSING BINARY

**¹ecliptic** /i'kliptik/ *n* 1 the GREAT CIRCLE (circle whose plane passes through the centre of the earth) that is the apparent path of the sun among the stars or of the earth as seen from the sun; the plane of the earth's orbit extended to meet the CELESTIAL SPHERE (imaginary sphere bounded by the sky and stars) 2 a GREAT CIRCLE drawn on any of a class of planets similar to the earth (e g in density and composition) making an angle of about 23° 27' with the equator and used for illustrating and solving astronomical problems [ME *ecliptik*, fr LL *ecliptica linea*, lit., line of eclipses]

**²ecliptic** *adj* of the ecliptic or an eclipse

**eclogue** /'ek‚log/ *n* a short pastoral poem, usu in the form of dialogue (e g between shepherds) [ME *eclog*, fr L *Eclogae*, title of Vergil's pastorals, lit., selections, pl of *ecloga*, fr Gk *eklogē*, fr *eklegein* to select]

**eclosion** /e'klozh(ə)n/ *n* the emergence of an insect from the cocoon or similar protective covering or of a larva from the egg [Fr *éclosion*, fr *éclore* to hatch, deriv of L *excludere* to hatch out, exclude]

**eco-** – see ECO-

**ecology** /i'koləji, ee-/ *n* 1 a science concerned with the interrelationship of living organisms and their environments 2 the whole pattern of relations between living organisms and their environment 3 HUMAN ECOLOGY [Ger *ökologie*, fr *ök-* ec- + *-logie* -logy] – **ecological** *adj*, **ecologically** *adv*, **ecologist** *n*

**econometrics** /i‚konə'metriks/ *n taking sing vb* the application of statistical methods to the study of economic data and problems [blend of *economics* and *metric*] – **econometric** *adj*, **econometrically** *adv*, **econometrician**, *n*, **econometrist** *n*

**economic** /‚ekə'nomik *or* ‚eekə-/ *adj* 1 economical, economic marked by careful or efficient use of resources without waste; thrifty 2a of economics b of or based on the production, distribution, and consumption of goods and services c of an economy 3 having practical or industrial significance or uses; affecting material resources ⟨~ *pests*⟩ 4 profitable ⟨~ *deposits of coal*⟩ – **economically** *adv*

**usage** 1 The pronunciations /‚ekə'nomik/ and /‚eekə'nomik/ are recommended as equally acceptable for BBC broadcasters. 2 **Economical** can mean only "thrifty", and writers on usage advise that **economic** should not be used in that sense, but should be confined to the other senses given. **synonyms** see SPARING

**economics** /‚ekə'nomiks, ‚ee-/ *n taking sing or pl vb* 1 a SOCIAL SCIENCE concerned chiefly with description and analysis of the production, distribution, and consumption of goods and services 2 economic significance or viability

**economist** /i'konəmist/ *n* 1 a specialist in economics 2 *archaic* one who practises economy

**econom·ize, -ise** /i'konə‚miez/ *vi* to practise economy; be frugal – usu + *on* ⟨~ *on oil*⟩ to use more economically; save ⟨~ *oil*⟩ – **economizer** *n*

**¹economy** /i'konəmi/ *n* 1a thrifty and efficient use of material resources; frugality in expenditures; *also* an instance or means of economizing b efficient and sparing use of nonmaterial resources (e g effort, language, or motion) 2 the arrangement or mode of operation of something; organization ⟨*the* ~ *of the mammalian cell*⟩ 3 the structure of economic life in a country, area, or period; *specif* an economic system 4 *archaic* the management of household or private affairs, esp expenses [MF *yconomie*, fr ML *oeconomia*, fr Gk *oikonomia*, fr *oikonomos* household manager, fr *oikos* house + *nemein* to manage – more at VICINITY, NIMBLE]

**²economy** *adj* designed to save money ⟨~ *cars*⟩ ⟨~ *measures*⟩

**economy of scale** *n* a lowering of average production costs resulting from the increased scale of production

**ecophysiology** /ˌeekoh‚fizi'oləji, ‚ekoh-/ *n* the science of the interrelationships between the physiology of living organisms and their ecology – **ecophysiological** *adj*

**écorché** /'aykaw‚shay/ *n* an anatomical diagram showing the muscles and muscular structure of the body stripped of skin [Fr, fr pp of *écorcher* to skin, deriv of LL *excorticare* to peel, fr L *ex-* + *cortic-, cortex* bark]

**ecospecies** /'eekoh‚speeshiz, 'ekoh-/ *n, pl* **ecospecies** a group of organisms associated with a particular ecological habitat that can interbreed without significant loss of fertility and that more or less corresponds to a species – compare COENOSPECIES – **ecospecific** *adj*

**ecosphere** /'eekoh‚sfiə, 'ekoh-/ *n* the parts of the universe habitable by living organisms; *esp* BIOSPHERE 1 (habitable parts of the earth)

**ecossaise** /ˌayko'sez, eko-/ *n* (the music for) a lively folk dance in DUPLE time (with two beats to the bar) [Fr *écossaise*, fr fem of *écossais* Scottish, fr *Ecosse* Scotland]

**ecosystem** /'eekoh‚sistəm, 'ekoh-/ *n* an ecological system (e g a lake) consisting of a community of interacting organisms and its environment functioning as a reasonably self-sustaining unit in nature

**ecotone** /'eekə‚tohn, 'ekə-/ *n* a border area between two adjacent ecological communities, usu exhibiting competition between organisms common to both [*ec-* + Gk *tonos* tension – more at TONE]

**ecotype** /'eekə‚tiep, 'ekə-/ *n* a subdivision of an ecospecies that more or less corresponds to a subspecies and is maintained as a distinct population by ecological and geographical factors (e g environmental selection and isolation) – **ecotypic** *adj*, **ecotypically** *adv*

**ecru** /'aykrooh, 'ek-, -'-/ *n* the colour beige [Fr *écru* unbleached, fr OF *escru*, fr *es-* completely (fr L *ex-*) + *cru* raw, fr L *crudus* – more at RAW]

**ecstasy** /'ekstəsi/ *n* **1** a state of overwhelming emotion or feeling, often to the point of loss of self-control; *esp* rapturous delight **2** a trance; *esp* a mystic or prophetic trance **3** *archaic* a swoon [ME *extasie*, fr MF, fr LL *ecstasis*, fr Gk *ekstasis*, fr *existanai* to derange, fr *ex* out + *histanai* to cause to stand – more at EX-, STAND]

¹**ecstatic** /ik'statik/ *adj* of, subject to, or causing ecstasy [ML *ecstaticus*, fr Gk *ekstatikos*, fr *existanai*] – **ecstatically** *adv*

²**ecstatic** *n* one who is subject to ecstasies

**ect-** /ekt-/, **ecto-** *comb form* outside, external [NL, fr Gk *ekto-*, fr *ektos*, fr *ex* out – more at EX-]

**ectoblast** /'ektoh‚blast/ *n* EPIBLAST (outer layer of tissue in an early embryo) [ISV] – **ectoblastic** *adj*

**ectocommensal** /ˌektohkə'mens(ə)l/ *n* an organism that lives harmlessly as a COMMENSAL on the body surface of another (e g for the purpose of obtaining food)

**ectoderm** /'ektoh‚duhm/ *n* **1** the outermost of the three primary layers of cells (GERM LAYERS) of an animal embryo, that is the source of EPIDERMIS (outer layer of the skin), hair, nails, and nerve tissue; *broadly* tissue derived from this germ layer – compare ENDODERM, MESODERM **2** the outer cellular membrane of a DIPLOBLASTIC (having two primary tissue layers) animal (e g a jellyfish) [ISV *ect-* + Gk *derma* skin – more at DERM-] – **ectodermal, ectodermic** *adj*

**ectogenous** /ek'tojinəs/, **ectogenic** /ˌektə'jenik/ *adj, esp of disease-causing bacteria* capable of development outside the body of the host

**ectomere** /'ektəmiə/ *n* a BLASTOMERE (cell produced by division of an egg) destined to form ectoderm – **ectomeric** *adj*

**ectomorph** /'ektə‚mawf/ *n* an ectomorphic person [*ecto*derm + *-morph*]

**ectomorphic** /ˌektə'mawfik/ *adj* having or being a light body build – compare ENDOMORPHIC, MESOMORPHIC [*ecto*derm + *-morphic;* fr the predominance in such types of structures developed from the ectoderm]

**-ectomy** /-'ektəmi/ *comb form* (→ *n*) surgical removal ⟨gastr*ectomy*⟩ [NL *-ectomia*, fr Gk *ektemnein* to cut out, fr *ex* out + *temnein* to cut – more at TOME]

**ectoparasite** /ˌektoh'parəsiet/ *n* a parasite (e g a flea) that lives on the exterior of its host – compare ENDOPARASITE [ISV] – **ectoparasitic** *adj*

**ectopic** /ek'topik/ *adj, anatomy* occurring in an abnormal position or in an unusual manner or form ⟨~ *lesions*⟩ ⟨~ *heartbeat*⟩ – compare ENTOPIC [Gk *ektopos* out of place, fr *ex*-out + *topos* place – more at TOPIC] – **ectopically** *adv*

**ectopic pregnancy** *n* the development of a foetus occurring

elsewhere than in the uterus (e g in a FALLOPIAN TUBE)

**ectoplasm** /'ektə‚plaz(ə)m, 'ektoh-/ *n* **1** the outer relatively rigid granule-free layer of the CYTOPLASM (jellylike material outside the nucleus) of a cell – compare ENDOPLASM **2** a form of spirit materialization held to emanate from a spiritualistic medium when in a trance – **ectoplasmic** *adj*

**ectotherm** /'ektə‚thuhm/ *n* a cold-blooded animal; POIKILOTHERM – **ectothermic** *adj*

**ectotrophic** /ˌektə'trohfik/ *also* **ectotropic** /-'tropik/ *adj* of or being a MYCORRHIZA (association between a fungus and the roots of a plant) in which the fungus forms a close web on the surface of the associated root – compare ENDOTROPHIC

**ecu** /'aykooh, -'-/ (*Fr* eky)/ *n, pl* **ecus** any of various former French coins [MF, lit., shield, fr OF *escu*, fr L *scutum;* fr the device of a shield on the coin]

**ecumenical** *also* **oecumenical** /ˌekyoo'menikl, ‚eek-/ *adj* **1** worldwide or general in extent, influence, or application **2a** of or representing the whole of a body of churches ⟨an ~ *council*⟩ **b** promoting or tending towards worldwide Christian unity or cooperation ⟨~ *discussions*⟩ [LL *oecumenicus*, fr LGk *oikoumenikos*, fr Gk *oikoumenē* the inhabited world, fr fem of *oikoumenos*, prp passive of *oikein* to inhabit, fr *oikos* house – more at VICINITY] – **ecumenically** *adv*, **ecumenicalism** *n*

**ecumenical patriarch** *n* the bishop of Constantinople as the dignitary given first honour in the Orthodox church

**ecumenics** /ˌekyoo'meniks, ‚ee-/ *n taking sing vb* the study of the worldwide nature, mission, problems, and strategy of the Christian church

**ecumenism** /'ekyooməniz(ə)m, i'kyoohməniz(ə)m/, **ecumenicism** /ˌekyoo'menəsiz(ə)m/ *n* ecumenical principles and practices, esp as exemplified among religious groups (e g Christian denominations) – **ecumenist, ecumenicist** *n*

**eczema** /'eks(i)mə/ *n* an inflammatory condition of the skin characterized by redness, itching, and oozing blisters which become scaly, crusted, or hardened [NL, fr Gk *ekzema*, fr *ekzein* to erupt, fr *ex* out + *zein* to boil – more at EX-, YEAST] – **eczematous**

¹**-ed** /-d *after vowels and* m,n,ng,v,z,zh,j,dh,r,l,b,g; -id *after* d,t; -t *after all others. Exceptions are given at their own entry*/ *suffix* **1** – used to form the past participle of regular weak verbs that end in a consonant ⟨end*ed*⟩ ⟨dropp*ed*⟩, a vowel other than *e* ⟨halo*ed*⟩, or a final *y* that changes to *i* ⟨cri*ed*⟩; compare ¹-D **1 2a** having; characterized by; provided with ⟨polo-neck*ed*⟩ ⟨two-legg*ed*⟩ **b** wearing; dressed in ⟨bowler-hatt*ed*⟩ ⟨jodhpur*ed*⟩ **c** having the characteristics of ⟨bigot*ed*⟩ □ (2) used to form adjectives from nouns that end in a consonant, a vowel other than *e*, or a final *y* that changes to *i*; compare ¹-D **2** [ME, fr OE *-ed, -od, -ad;* akin to OHG *-t*, pp ending, L *-tus*, Gk *-tos*, suffix forming verbals]

²**-ed** *suffix* – used to form the past tense of regular weak verbs that end in a consonant, a vowel other than *e*, or a final *y* that changes to *i*; compare ²-D [ME *-ede, -de*, fr OE *-de, -ede, -ode, -ade;* akin to OHG *-ta*, past ending (1 sing.), & prob to OHG *-t*, pp ending]

**edacious** /i'dayshəs/ *adj* **1** *formal* extremely hungry; voracious **2** *archaic* of eating [L *edac-, edax*, fr *edere* to eat – more at EAT] – **edacity** *n*

**Edam** /'eedam/ *n* a mild-flavoured yellow cheese of Dutch origin that is made from partly skimmed milk and usu shaped into slightly flattened balls which are coated with red wax [*Edam*, town in NW Netherlands]

**edaphic** /i'dafik/ *adj* of, resulting from, or influenced by the conditions of the soil rather than the climate ⟨an ~ *desert*⟩ [Gk *edaphos* bottom, ground] – **edaphically** *adv*

**edaphic climax** *n* an ecological CLIMAX (mature and stable stage reached by an ecological community) resulting from soil conditions – compare PHYSIOGRAPHIC CLIMAX

**Eddic** /'edik/, **Eddaic** /e'dayik/ *adj* of or resembling the Old Norse *Edda*, a 13th century collection of mythological and heroic poems [ON *Edda*, prob fr *Edda*, name of a great-grandmother in a poem]

¹**eddy** /'edi/ *n* **1** a current of water or air running contrary to the main current; *esp* a small whirlpool **2** something moving in the manner of an eddy or whirlpool ⟨little eddies *of dust kicked up by the galloping horses*⟩ [ME (Sc) *ydy*, prob fr ON *itha;* akin to OHG *ith-* again, L *et* and]

²**eddy** *vb* to (cause to) move in (the manner of) an eddy ⟨the crowd eddied *about in the marketplace*⟩

**eddy current** *n* a usu unwanted electric current that often causes a loss of energy and that is induced by a varying magnetic field

**edelweiss** /'aydl,vies/ *n* a small plant (*Leontopodium alpinum*) of the daisy family, that grows high in the Alps and has clusters of yellowish flower heads surrounded by woolly white lance-shaped leaves arranged in the form of a star [Ger, fr *edel* noble + *weiss* white]

**edema** /i'deemə/ *n, chiefly NAm* OEDEMA – **edematous** *adj*

**Eden** /'eedn/ *n* PARADISE 2 [*Eden*, the garden where Adam & Eve lived before the Fall (Gen 2:8), fr LL, fr Heb *'Edhen*] – **Edenic** *adj*

¹**edentate** /ee'dentayt/ *adj* **1** lacking teeth **2** of or being an edentate mammal [L *edentatus*, pp of *edentare* to make toothless, fr *e-* + *dent-, dens* tooth – more at TOOTH]

²**edentate** *n* any of an order (Edentata) of mammals having few or no teeth and including the sloths, armadillos, and American anteaters and formerly also the PANGOLINS (Asian and African anteaters) and the aardvark

**edentulous** /ee'dentyooləs/ *adj* toothless – used technically ⟨*an ~ area of the mouth*⟩ [L *edentulus*, fr *e-* + *dent-, dens*]

**Edgar** /'edgə/ *n* a statuette awarded annually by a professional organization in the USA for notable achievement in mystery-novel writing [*Edgar Allan Poe* †1849 US writer, regarded as father of the detective story]

¹**edge** /ej/ *n* **1a** the cutting side of a blade **b** the (degree of) sharpness of a blade **c** penetrating power; keenness ⟨*an ~ of sarcasm in his voice*⟩ ⟨*took the ~ off the proposal*⟩ **2a** the extreme verge or brink (e g of a cliff or precipice) **b** the crest of a hill or ridge **3a** the line where an object or area begins or ends; a border ⟨*the town stands on the ~ of a plain*⟩ **b** the narrow part adjacent to a border ⟨*walk on the ~ of the deck*⟩ **c** a point that marks a beginning or transition; a threshold – esp in *on the edge of* ⟨*she felt herself to be on the ~ of insanity*⟩ **d** a favourable margin; an advantage ⟨*had the ~ on the competition*⟩ **4** a line where two planes or two plane faces of a solid body meet or cross **5** the act or an instance of edging a cricket ball [ME *egge*, fr OE *ecg*; akin to L *acer* sharp, Gk *akmē* point] – **on edge** anxious, nervous – see also **set somebody's** TEETH **on edge** (at TOOTH)

²**edge** *vt* **1** to give or supply an edge to **2** to move or force gradually or with difficulty in a specified way ⟨*~d him off the road*⟩ ⟨*~d her out of the leadership*⟩ **3** to incline (a ski) sideways so that one edge cuts into the snow **4** *NAm* to defeat by a small margin – usu + *out* ⟨*~d out the opposing team by one point*⟩ **5** to hit (a ball) or the bowling of (a bowler) in cricket with the edge of the bat, esp so as to give a catch ~ *vi* to advance, esp gradually and obliquely, in a specified way ⟨*the climbers ~d along the cliff*⟩

**edged** /ejd/ *adj* **1** having a specified kind of edge, boundary, or border or a specified number of edges – usu in combination ⟨*rough-edged*⟩ ⟨*two-edged*⟩ **2** sharp, cutting ⟨*an ~ knife*⟩ ⟨*an ~ remark*⟩

**edge effect** *n* the result of the presence of two adjoining plant communities on the numbers and kinds of animals present in the immediate area

**edger** /'ejə/ *n* one who or that which edges; *esp* a tool used to trim the edge of a lawn

**edge tool** *n* a tool with a sharp cutting edge

**edgeways** /'ejwayz, -wiz/, **edgewise** /-,wiez/ *adv* **1** with the edge foremost; sideways ⟨*they shuffled ~ past each other*⟩ **2** on, by, with, or towards the edge ⟨*balanced the coins ~*⟩

**edging** /'ejing/ *n* something that forms an edge or border

**edgy** /'eji/ *adj* **1** having an edge; sharp **2** tense, irritable; ON EDGE – **edgily** *adv*, **edginess** *n*

**edh** /edh/ *n* ETH (letter used in old English)

**edible** /'edəbl/ *adj* fit to be eaten as food; eatable [LL *edibilis*, fr L *edere* to eat – more at EAT] – **edible** *n*, **edibleness** *n*, **edibility** *n*

**edict** /'eedikt/ *n* **1** an official public proclamation having the force of law **2** the order or command of an authority ⟨*we obeyed Grandmother's ~*⟩ [L *edictum*, fr neut of *edictus*, pp of *edicere* to decree, fr *e-* + *dicere* to say – more at DICTION] – **edictal** *adj*, **edictally** *adv*

**edification** /,edifi'kaysh(ə)n/ *n, formal* an act or process of edifying; instruction – **edificatory** *adj*

**edifice** /'edifis/ *n* **1** a building; *esp* a large or massive structure **2** a large abstract structure or organization ⟨*the keystone which holds together the social ~* – R H Tawney⟩ [ME, fr MF, fr L *aedificium*, fr *aedificare*]

**edify** /'edi,fie/ *vt* **1** to instruct and improve, esp in moral and

spiritual knowledge **2** *archaic* **2a** to build **b** to establish [ME *edifien*, fr MF *edifier*, fr LL & L; LL *aedificare* to instruct or improve spiritually, fr L, to erect a house, fr *aedes* temple, house; akin to OE *ād* funeral pyre, L *aestas* summer]

**edit** /'edit/ *vt* **1a** to prepare an edition of ⟨*~ed Pope's works*⟩ **b** to assemble (e g a film or tape recording) by cutting and rearranging **c** to alter, adapt, or refine (e g written or spoken words), esp to bring about conformity to a standard or to suit a particular purpose ⟨*carefully ~ed his speech*⟩ **2** to direct the publication of ⟨*~s the daily newspaper*⟩ **3** to delete – usu + *out* [back-formation fr *editor*] – **editable** *adj*

**edition** /i'dish(ə)n/ *n* **1a** the form in which a text (e g a printed book) is published ⟨*paperback ~*⟩ ⟨*abridged ~*⟩ **b(1)** the whole number of copies published at one time ⟨*an ~ of 50,000*⟩ **b(2)** the issue of a newspaper or periodical for a specified day, time of day, or month ⟨*the late ~*⟩ **b(3)** the issue of a newspaper or periodical published or circulated in a specified place ⟨*the Manchester ~*⟩ **2a** the form in which something is presented, esp on a particular occasion ⟨*this year's ~ of the annual charity ball*⟩ **b** the whole number of articles of one style put out at one time ⟨*a limited ~ of collectors' pieces*⟩ **3** a copy, version ⟨*she's a friendlier ~ of her mother*⟩ [MF, fr L *edition-, editio* publication, edition, fr *editus*, pp of *edere* to bring forth, publish, fr *e-* + *-dere* to put or *-dere* (fr *dare* to give) – more at DO, DATE]

**editio princeps** /i,dishio 'prinseps, ay,ditioh 'prinkeps/ *n, pl* **editiones principes** /idishi,ohneez 'prinsipeez, aydishi,ohneez 'prinkipeez/ the first printed edition, esp of an ancient or medieval text [NL, lit., first edition]

**editor** /'editə/, *fem* **editress** /-tris/ *n* **1** a person who edits, esp as an occupation; *esp* a person responsible for the editorial policy and content of the whole or a particular part of a newspaper or magazine ⟨*sports ~*⟩ **2** a person who writes editorials – **editorship** *n*

¹**editorial** /,edi'tawri-əl/ *adj* **1** of an editor ⟨*an ~ office*⟩ **2** being or resembling an editorial ⟨*an ~ statement*⟩ – **editorially** *adv*

²**editorial** *n* a newspaper or magazine article that gives the opinions of the editors or publishers

**editorial-ize, -ise** /,edi'tawriəliez/ *vi* **1** to express an opinion in the form of an editorial **2** to introduce opinion into an apparently factual report (e g by direct comment or hidden bias) **3** to express an opinion (e g on a controversial issue) – **editorializer** *n*, **editorialization** *n*

**editor-in-'chief** *n, pl* **editors-in-chief** an editor who is in charge of an editorial staff or of a group or series of publications

**Edomite** /'eedəmiet/ *n* a member of a Semitic people living south of the Dead sea in biblical times [*Edom* (Esau), ancestor of the Edomites (Gen 36)]

**EDTA** *n* an acid, $C_{10}H_{16}N_2O_8$, used in chemistry esp as a CHELATING agent, in medicine as an anticoagulant, and in the treatment of lead poisoning [ethylenediaminetetraacetic acid]

**educable** /'edyookəbl, 'ejə-/ *adj* capable of being educated; *specif* capable of some degree of learning – **educability**

**educate** /'edyoo,kayt, 'ejoo-/ *vt* **1** to provide schooling for **2** to cause to develop mentally, morally, or physically, esp by instruction **3** to train or improve (facilities, judgments, skills, etc) *synonyms* see TEACH [ME *educaten* to rear, fr L *educatus*, pp of *educare* to rear, educate] – **educatable, educative** *adj*

**educated** /'edyookaytid, 'ejə-/ *adj* **1** having an education; *esp* having an education beyond the average **2a** giving evidence of training or practice; skilled ⟨*an ~ palate*⟩ **b** befitting one who is educated ⟨*~ conversation*⟩ **c** based on some knowledge of fact ⟨*an ~ guess*⟩ – **educatedly** *adv*, **educatedness** *n*

**education** /,edyoo'kaysh(ə)n, -joo-/ *n* **1a** the action or process of educating or of being educated; *also* a stage of such a process **b** the knowledge and development resulting from an educational process ⟨*a man of little ~*⟩ **2** the field of study that deals mainly with methods of teaching and learning in schools – **educational** *adj*, **educationally** *adv*

**educationalist** /,edyoo'kaysh(ə)nl·ist, -joo-/ *also* **educationist** /,edyoo'kayshənist, ,ejə-/ *n* a specialist in educational theories or methods

**educational psychology** *n* psychology concerned with school learning, teaching methods, and evaluation of aptitude and progress (e g by standardized tests) – **educational psychologist** *n*

**educational television** *n* television that provides instruction esp for students

**educator** /'edyookaytə, -joo-/ *n* **1** one skilled in teaching; a teacher **2** an educationalist

**educe** /i'dyoohs; *also* ij-/ *vt, formal* **1** to elicit, develop **2** to arrive at through a consideration of the facts and evidence; infer [L *educere* to draw out, fr *e-* + *ducere* to lead – more at TOW] – **educible** *adj*

**educt** /'eedukt/ *n, chemistry* a substance separated from another substance or mixture in which it already existed – compare PRODUCT [L *eductus*, pp of *educere*]

**eduction** /i'duksh(ə)n/ *n* **1** an instance of educing; *also* something educed **2** the exhaust stroke of a steam or internal-combustion engine in which the steam or burnt gas is expelled –**eductor** *n*

**edulcorate** /i'dulkərayt, ee-/ *vt* **1** to remove soluble impurities from by washing; purify **2** to free from harshness; make pleasant [NL *edulcoratus*, pp of *edulcorare*, fr L *e-* + *dulcor* sweetness, fr *dulcis* sweet]

**Edwardian** /ed'wawdi•ən, ed'wahdi•ən/ *adj* (characteristic) of Edward VII or his age: e g **a** characterized by opulence and a complacent sense of material security **b** *of clothing* marked by the hourglass silhouette for women, and long narrow fitted suits for men [*Edward VII* †1910 King of Britain (reigned 1901–1910)]

**Edwardian car** *n, Br* an old motor car; *specif* one built after 1904 and before 1919 – compare VETERAN 2, VINTAGE 5

**ee** /ee/ *n, pl* **een** /een/ *Scot* an eye [ME (northern), fr OE *ēage* – more at EYE]

**¹-ee** /-ee/ *suffix* **1** (*vt → n*) one to whom (a specified action) is done ⟨*appointee*⟩ ⟨*trainee*⟩ **2** (*n, adj, vb → n*) one who acts (in a specified way) ⟨*escapee*⟩ ⟨*absentee*⟩ [ME *-e*, fr MF *-é*, fr *-é*, pp ending, fr L *-atus*]

**²-ee** *suffix* (*n → n*) **1** one associated with ⟨*bargee*⟩ ⟨*townee*⟩ **2** a particular, esp small, kind of ⟨*bootee*⟩ [prob alter. of *-ie*]

**eel** /eel/ *n* **1a** any of numerous voracious snakelike fishes (order Apodes) that have a smooth slimy skin, no PELVIC FINS, and long fins which run along the back and underside of the fish, meeting at the tip of the tail **b** any of numerous other elongated fishes (e g of the order Symbranchii) **2** *informal* an elusive or evasive person [ME *ele*, fr OE *ēl*; akin to OHG *āl* eel] – **eel-like**, **eely** *adj*

**eelgrass** /'eel,grahs/ *n* (any of various plants related to) a submerged marine plant (*Zostera marina* of the family Zosteraceae) that has very long narrow leaves

**eelpout** /'eel,powt/ *n* any of various eel-like sea fishes resembling BLENNIES (family Zoarcidae); *esp* the VIVIPAROUS (producing live young, not eggs) blenny (*Zoarces viviparus*)

**eelworm** /'eel,wuhm/ *n* any of various small NEMATODES (unsegmented round-bodied worms); *esp* one living free in the soil or as a plant parasite

**-een** /-een/ *suffix* (*n → n*) inferior fabric resembling (a specified fabric); imitation ⟨*velveteen*⟩ ⟨*sateen*⟩ [prob fr *ratteen*]

**e'en** /een/ *adv, poetic* even

**-eer** /-iə/ *suffix* person engaged in (a specified occupation or activity) ⟨*auctioneer*⟩ ⟨*buccaneer*⟩ – often derog ⟨*profiteer*⟩ ⟨*racketeer*⟩ [MF *-ier*, fr L *-arius* – more at -ARY]

**e'er** /eə/ *adv, chiefly poetic* ever

**eerie** *also* **eery** /'iəri/ *adj* **1** frightening because of strangeness or gloominess; weird **2** notably strange and mysterious; baffling ⟨*the eeriest mystery in modern court records – a persistent riddle – Life*⟩ *synonyms* see ²WEIRD [ME *eri* afraid, fr OE *earg* cowardly, wretched] – **eerily** *adv*, **eeriness** *n*

**eff** /ef/ *vi, Br slang* to say "fuck" ⟨*~ing and swearing*⟩ [euphemism for *fuck*] – **eff and blind** *euph* to curse, swear

**eff off** *vi, Br euph* FUCK OFF 1 – usu in imper

**efface** /i'fays/ *vt* **1** to eliminate or make indistinct (as if) by wearing away a surface; obliterate ⟨*coins with dates ~d by wear*⟩ ⟨*he could never ~ the memory*⟩ **2** to make (oneself) modestly or shyly inconspicuous *synonyms* see ERASE [MF *effacer*, fr *ex-* + *face*] – **effaceable** *adj*, **effacement** *n*, **effacer** *n*

**¹effect** /i'fekt/ *n* **1a** the result of a cause or agent **b** the result of purpose or intention ⟨*employed her knowledge to good ~*⟩ **2** the basic meaning; intent – esp in *to that effect* ⟨*he called me a fool or words to that ~*⟩ **3** power to bring about a result; efficacy **4** *pl* personal movable property; goods ⟨*personal ~*s⟩ **5a** a distinctive impression on the human senses ⟨*the use of colour produces a very striking ~*⟩ **b** the creation of an often false desired impression ⟨*her tears were purely for ~*⟩ **c** something designed to produce a distinctive or desired impression ⟨*special lighting ~*s⟩ **6** the quality or state of being operative; operation ⟨*the law goes into ~ next week*⟩ **7** an experimental

scientific phenomenon named usu after its discoverer [ME, fr MF & L; MF, fr L *effectus*, fr *effectus*, pp of *efficere* to bring about, fr *ex-* + *facere* to make, do – more at DO] – **in effect** for all practical purposes; actually although not appearing so – **take effect 1** to become operative **2** to be effective – **to the effect** with the meaning ⟨*issued a statement to the effect that he would resign*⟩

**²effect** *vt* **1** to bring about, often by surmounting obstacles; accomplish ⟨*~ a settlement of a dispute*⟩ **2** to put into effect; CARRY OUT ⟨*the duty of the legislature to ~ the will of the citizens*⟩ *synonyms* see OBTAIN, PERFORM *usage* see AFFECT

**¹effective** /i'fektiv/ *adj* **1a** producing a decided, decisive, or desired effect **b** impressive, striking **2** ready for service or action ⟨*~ manpower*⟩ **3** actual, real ⟨*the ~ strength of the army*⟩ **4** in effect; operative ⟨*the tax becomes ~ next year*⟩ – **effectiveness** *n*

*synonyms* Effective, effectual, efficient, and efficacious all mean "capable of producing results". Effective stresses the ability to produce an effect or its actual production ⟨*take effective measures*⟩ ⟨*make an effective speech*⟩ ⟨*an effective public speaker*⟩. Effectual applies only to the action taken and suggests it was completely successful and decisive ⟨*his remark put an effectual end to the conversation*⟩. Efficient describes people or measures that achieve results with the minimum of fuss and the best use of resources ⟨*an efficient worker/manager/unit/machine*⟩. Efficacious stresses that something has the power to achieve the desired result, and is usually used of medicines or remedies ⟨*a lotion efficacious against freckles*⟩. antonyms ineffective, ineffectual, inefficient

**²effective** *n* one who or that which is effective; *esp* a soldier equipped and fit for duty

**effectively** /i'fektivli/ *adv* **1** in an effective manner **2** for all practical purposes; IN EFFECT ⟨*~, she is the real force behind the throne*⟩

**effector** /i'fektə/ *n* **1** (a nerve supplying) a gland, muscle, or other body organ that becomes active in response to stimulation **2** a substance that combines with and affects the activity of a genetic REPRESSOR (substance that indirectly prevents protein synthesis by a gene): **2a** INDUCER (substance that inactivates a repressor) **b** COREPRESSOR (substance that makes a repressor fully operative)

**effectual** /i'fektyooəl, -chooəl/ *adj* producing or able to produce a desired effect; adequate, effective *synonyms* see ¹EFFECTIVE *antonym* ineffectual – **effectualness** *n*, **effectuality** *n*

**effectually** /i'fectyooəli, -choo-/ *adv* **1** in an effectual manner **2** for all practical purposes; in effect

**effectuate** /i'fektyoo,ayt, -choo-/ *vt, formal* to effect – **effectuation** *n*

**effeminate** /i'feminət/ *adj* **1** *of a man* having qualities or attributes usu thought of as feminine; not manly in appearance or manner **2** marked by an unbecoming delicacy or lack of vigour *synonyms* see ²FEMALE *antonyms* masculine, virile [ME, fr L *effeminatus*, fr pp of *effeminare* to make feminine, fr *ex-* + *femina* woman – more at FEMININE] – **effeminate** *n*, **effeminacy** *n*

**effendi** /e'fendi/ *n, pl* **effendis** a man of property, authority, or education in an E Mediterranean country [Turk *efendi* master, fr NGk *aphentēs*, alter. of Gk *authentēs* – more at AUTHENTIC]

**efferent** /'efərənt/ *adj* conducting outwards from a part or organ; *specif* carrying nerve impulses from a NERVE CENTRE (e g in the brain or spinal cord) to an effector – compare AFFERENT [Fr *efférent*, fr L *efferent-, efferens*, prp of *efferre* to carry outwards, fr *ex-* + *ferre* to carry – more at BEAR] – **efferent** *n*, **efferently** *adv*

**effervesce** /,efə'ves/ *vi* **1** *of a liquid* to bubble, hiss, and foam as gas escapes **2** to show liveliness or exhilaration [L *effervescere*, fr *ex-* + *fervescere* to begin to boil, incho of *fervēre* to boil – more at BURN] – **effervescence** *n*, **effervescent** *adj*, **effervescently** *adv*

**effete** /i'feet/ *adj* **1** *of animals or plants* no longer fertile **2a** worn out; exhausted **b** marked by weakness or decadent overrefinement ⟨*an ~ civilization*⟩ **3** effeminate ⟨*a good humoured, ~ boy brought up by maiden aunts* – Herman Wouk⟩ [L *effetus*, fr *ex-* + *fetus* fruitful – more at FEMININE] – **effetely** *adv*, **effeteness** *n*

**efficacious** /,efi'kayshəs/ *adj* having the power to produce a desired effect *synonyms* see ¹EFFECTIVE *antonyms* inefficacious, powerless [L *efficac-, efficax*, fr *efficere*] – **efficaciously** *adv*, **efficaciousness** *n*, **efficacy** *n*, **efficacity** *n*

**efficiency** /i'fish(ə)nsi/ *n* **1** the quality or degree of being efficient **2a** efficient operation **b** the ratio of the useful energy produced by an engine, machine, etc to the energy supplied to it

**efficiency apartment** *n, NAm* a small usu furnished flat with minimal kitchen and bath facilities; a bed-sitter

**efficient** /i'fish(ə)nt/ *adj* **1** of a person able and practical; briskly competent **2** producing desired effects, esp with minimum waste ⟨*an ~ method of generating electricity*⟩ *synonyms* see ¹EFFECTIVE *antonym* inefficient [ME, fr MF or L; MF, fr L *efficient-, efficiens*, fr prp of *efficere* to bring about] – **efficiently** *adv*

**effigy** /'efəji/ *n* an image or representation, esp of a person; *specif* a crude figure representing a hated person [L *effigies*, fr *effingere* to form, fr *ex-* + *fingere* to shape – more at DOUGH]

**effing** /'efing/ *adj or adv, Br slang* – used as a meaningless intensive

**effloresce** /,eflaw'res/ *vi* **1** to burst forth (as if) into flower; bloom **2a** *chemistry* to change from crystals to a powder on exposure to air due to loss of water **b** to form or become covered with a powdery covering ⟨*bricks may ~ owing to the deposition of soluble salts*⟩ [L *efflorescere*, fr *ex-* + *florescere* to begin to blossom – more at FLORESCENCE]

**efflorescence** /,eflaw'res(ə)ns/ *n* **1** the period or state of flowering **2** the action, process, period, or result of developing and unfolding as if coming into flower; blossoming ⟨*periods of... intellectual and artistic ~* – Julian Huxley⟩ **3** the process or product of efflorescing chemically **4** a redness of the skin; an eruption – **efflorescent** *adj*

**effluence** /'efloo⋅əns/ *n* **1** something that flows out **2** an action or process of flowing out

¹**effluent** /'efloo⋅ənt/ *adj* flowing out; emanating ⟨*an ~ river*⟩ [L *effluent-, effluens*, prp of *effluere* to flow out, fr *ex-* + *fluere* to flow – more at FLUID]

²**effluent** *n* something that flows out: e g **a** an outflowing branch of a main stream or lake **b** smoke, liquid industrial refuse, sewage, etc discharged into the environment, esp when causing pollution

**effluvium** /e'floohvi⋅əm, -vyəm/ *n, pl* **effluvia** /-viə/ *often taking sing vb,* **effluviums** **1** an offensive, gas, vapour or smell given off by something (e g rotting vegetation) **2** a by-product, esp in the form of waste [L, act of flowing out, fr *effluere*]

**efflux** /'efluks/ *n* an effluence, esp of liquid or gas [L *effluxus*, pp of *effluere*] – **effluxion** *n*

**effort** /'efət/ *n* **1** conscious exertion of physical or mental power **2** a serious attempt; a try **3** something produced by exertion or trying ⟨*the novel was his most ambitious ~*⟩ **4** the force applied to a simple machine (e g a lever) as distinguished from the force (LOAD) exerted by the machine to overcome external resistance **5** the total work done to achieve a particular end ⟨*the war ~*⟩ [MF, fr OF *esfort*, fr *esforcier* to force, fr *ex-* + *forcier* to force] – **effortful** *adj*, **effortless** *adj*, **effortlessly** *adv*, **effortlessness** *n*

**effrontery** /i'frunt(ə)ri/ *n* the quality of being shamelessly bold; insolence ⟨*the ~ to propound three such heresies* – TLS⟩ [Fr *effronterie*, deriv of LL *effront-, effrons* shameless, fr L *ex-* + *front-, frons* forehead – more at BRINK]

**effulgence** /i'fulj(ə)ns/ *n, formal* radiant splendour; brilliance [LL *effulgentia*, fr L *effulgent-, effulgens*, prp of *effulgēre* to shine forth, fr *ex-* + *fulgēre* to shine – more at FULGENT] – **effulgent** *adj*

¹**effuse** /i'fyoohz/ *vb, formal* *vt* **1** to pour out (e g a liquid) **2** to radiate; GIVE OFF ~ *vi* to flow out; radiate [L *effusus*, pp of *effundere*, fr *ex-* + *fundere* to pour – more at FOUND]

²**effuse** /i'fyoohs/ *adj* spread out flat without definite form ⟨*~ lichens*⟩

**effusion** /i'fyoohzh(ə)n/ *n* **1** an act of effusing **2** (an) unrestrained expression of words or feelings **3a(1)** the escape of a liquid or gas from its container; *esp* the escape of a body fluid (e g blood) from an anatomical vessel by rupture, exudation, etc **a(2)** the flow of a gas through an opening whose diameter is small as compared with the distance between the molecules of the gas **b** the liquid or gas which escapes in these ways

**effusive** /i'fyoohsiv/ *adj* **1** unduly emotionally demonstrative; gushing **2** characterized or formed by an outpouring of lava ⟨*~ rocks*⟩ **3** *archaic* pouring freely *synonyms* see TALKATIVE – **effusively** *adv*, **effusiveness** *n*

**eft** /eft/ *n* a newt [ME *evete, ewte*, fr OE *efete*]

**eftsoons** /eft'soohnz/ *adv, archaic* soon after [ME *eftsones*, fr *eft* after (fr OE) + *sone* soon + *-s*, adv suffix]

**egad** /,ee'gad, i-/ *interj, archaic* – used as a mild oath [prob euphemism for *oh God*]

**egalitarian** /i,gali'teəri⋅ən/ *adj* marked by or advocating egalitarianism [Fr *égalitaire*, fr *égalité* equality, fr L *aequalitat-, aequalitas*, fr *aequalis* equal] – **egalitarian** *n*

**egalitarianism** /-,iz(ə)m/ *n* a belief in or a philosophy advocating social, political, and economic equality among human beings

**Egeria** /i'jiəriə/ *n* a woman adviser or companion [L, a nymph who advised the legendary Roman king Numa Pompilius]

**egest** /ee'jest/ *vt* to rid the body of (waste material) [L *egestus*, pp of *egerere* to carry outside, discharge, fr *e-* + *gerere* to carry – more at CAST] – **egestion** *n*, **egestive** *adj*

**egesta** /ee'jestə/ *n pl* waste material egested [NL, fr L, neut pl of *egestus*]

¹**egg** /eg/ *vt* to incite to action – usu + *on* ⟨*~ed the mob on to riot*⟩ [ME *eggen*, fr ON *eggja*, fr or akin to *egg* edge; akin to OE *ecg* edge – more at EDGE]

²**egg** *n* **1a** the hard-shelled reproductive body produced by a bird; *esp* that produced by domestic poultry and used as a food **b** an animal reproductive body consisting of an OVUM together with its nutritive and protective envelopes which, usu on fusion with a male sperm, has the capacity to develop into a new individual capable of independent existence **c** egg, **egg cell** OVUM **2** something resembling an egg **3** *informal* a fellow, guy ⟨*he's a good ~*⟩ – no longer in vogue [ME *egge*, fr ON *egg*; akin to OE *ǣg* egg, L *ovum*, Gk *ōion*]

³**egg** *vt* **1** to coat (food) with beaten raw egg **2** *NAm informal* to pelt with eggs

**egg and dart** *n* architectural ornamentation consisting of alternate egg-shaped figures and arrowheads

**eggar, egger** /'egə, 'ay-/ *n* any of various large moths (family Lasiocampidae) with brown bodies and wings [*eggar* alter. of *egger*, fr ²*egg* + ²*-er;* fr the egg-shaped cocoon]

**eggbeater** /'eg,beetə/ *n, NAm slang* a helicopter [fr its rotor blades resembling those of a device used for beating eggs]

**eggbutt** /'eg,but/ *n* a SNAFFLE (simple bit) for a horse's bridle with oval cheekpieces fixed rigidly to the mouthpiece

**egg capsule** *n* EGG CASE

**egg case** *n* a protective case enclosing eggs; OOTHECA

**eggcup** /-,kup/ *n* a small cup without a handle that is used for holding a boiled egg that is to be eaten from the shell

**egghead** /-,hed/ *n, derog or humorous* an intellectual, highbrow ⟨*practical men who disdain the schemes and dreams of ~*s – W L Miller⟩ [fr the popular notion that intellectuals have bald domed heads] – **eggheaded** *adj*

**eggnog** /-,nog/ *n* a drink consisting of eggs beaten up with sugar, milk, or cream, and often spirits (e g rum or brandy) [*egg* + *nog* (strong beer), of unknown origin]

**eggplant** /-,plahnt/ *n* **1** a widely cultivated plant (*Solanum melongera*) of the potato family whose fruit is the aubergine **2** *chiefly NAm* the aubergine [fr the shape of the fruit]

¹**eggshell** /-,shel/ *n* **1** the hard exterior covering of an egg **2** something resembling an eggshell, esp in fragility

²**eggshell** *adj* **1** *esp of china* thin and fragile **2** *esp of paint* having a slight sheen

**egg timer** *n* an instrument like a small hourglass that runs for about three minutes and is used for timing the boiling of eggs

**egg tooth** *n* a hard sharp prominence on the beak of an unhatched bird or the nose of an unhatched reptile that is used to break through the eggshell

**egis** /'eejis/ *n* AEGIS

**eglantine** /'eglantien, -teen/ *n* SWEETBRIER (type of wild rose) [ME *eglentyn*, fr MF *aiglent*, fr (assumed) VL *aculentum*, fr L *acus* needle; akin to L *acer* sharp – more at EDGE]

**ego** /'eegoh, 'egoh/ *n, pl* **egos** **1** *philosophy* the self, esp as contrasted with another self or the world **2a** egotism **b** SELF-ESTEEM 1 **3** *psychology* the one of the three divisions of the mind in psychoanalytic theory that serves as the organized conscious mediator between the person and reality, esp in the perception of and adaptation to reality – compare ID, SUPEREGO [NL, fr L, I – more at I]

**egocentric** /-'sentrik/ *adj* **1** taking the ego as the starting point in philosophy **2** limited in outlook or concern to one's own activities or needs; self-centred, selfish – **egocentric** *n*, **egocentrically** *adv*, **egocentrism** *n*, **egocentricity** *n*

**ego ideal** *n* the positive standards, ideals, and ambitions that according to psychoanalytic theory form a person's conscious goals

**egoism** /-,iz(ə)m/ *n* **1** a doctrine in philosophy stating that all the elements of knowledge are in the ego **2** a doctrine in ethics stating that individual self-interest is the actual motive of and the best goal of all conscious action; *also* moral conduct based on such a doctrine **3** egotism

**egoist** /-ist/ *n* **1** a believer in egoism **2** an egocentric or egotistic person – **egoistic** *also* **egoistical** *adj*, **egoistically** *adv*

**egomania** /-'maynyə, -ni·ə/ *n* the quality or state of being extremely egocentric – **egomaniac** *n*

**egotism** /'eegə,tiz(ə)m, 'egə-/ *n* **1** the practice of talking or writing about oneself too much, with excessive use of *I* and *me* **2** an extreme sense of self-importance; self-centredness [L *ego* + E *-tism* (as in *idiotism*)] – **egotist** *n*, **egotistic**, **egotistical** *adj*, **egotistically** *adv*

'**ego-,trip** *vi* **-pp-** *informal* to engage in an activity solely in order to enhance one's self-esteem – **ego-tripper** *n*

**ego trip** *n, informal* an act or series of acts that enhances one's self-esteem

**egregious** /i'greej(y)əs/ *adj* **1** *formal* conspicuously or shockingly bad; flagrant ⟨*an* ∼ *mistake*⟩ **2** *archaic* distinguished [L *egregius* extraordinary, distinguished, fr *e-* + *greg-, grex* flock, herd – more at GREGARIOUS] – **egregiously** *adv*, **egregiousness** *n*

**egress** /'eegres/ *n* **1** the emergence of a celestial body into sight after being hidden by passing behind or in front of a larger celestial body **2** *formal* **2a** the act or right of going or coming out **b** a place or means of going out; an exit [L *egressus*, fr *egressus*, pp of *egredi* to go out, fr *e-* + *gradi* to go – more at GRADE] – **egress** *vi*, **egression** *n*

**egret** /'eegrit, -gret/ *n* any of various herons that bear long plumes during the breeding season [ME, fr MF *aigrette*, fr OProv *aigreta*, of Gmc origin; akin to OHG *heigaro* heron]

¹**Egyptian** /ee'jipsh(ə)n/ *adj* (characteristic) of Egypt or the Egyptians [*Egypt*, country in NE Africa]

²**Egyptian** *n* **1** a native or inhabitant of Egypt **2** the Afro-Asiatic language of the ancient Egyptians from earliest times to about the third century AD **3** Arabic as spoken in modern Egypt

**Egyptian cotton** *n* a fine long-fibred often somewhat brownish cotton, grown chiefly in Egypt

**Egyptian vulture** *n* a small S European, African, and Asian vulture (*Neophron percnopterus*) with white and black plumage and a weak slender beak

**Egypto-** *comb form* Egypt ⟨*Egypto*logy⟩ [prob fr Fr *Egypto-*, fr Gk *Aigypto-*, fr *Aigyptos*]

**Egyptology** /,eejip'toləji/ *n* the study of Egyptian antiquities – **Egyptologist** *n*

**eh** /ay/ *interj* – used to ask for confirmation or to express inquiry [ME *ey*]

**eider** /'iedə/ *n* **1** EIDER DUCK **2** EIDERDOWN **1** [D, Ger, or Sw, fr Icel *æthur*, fr ON *æthr*]

**eiderdown** /-,down/ *n* **1** the down of the EIDER DUCK **2** a thick warm quilt filled with eiderdown or other insulating material

**eider duck** *n* any of several large northern sea ducks (*Somateria* or related genera) having fine soft down that is used by the female for lining the nest

**eidetic** /ie'detik/ *adj* marked by or involving extraordinarily accurate and vivid recall of visual images ⟨*an* ∼ *memory*⟩ [Gk *eidētikos* of a form, fr *eidos* form; akin to Gk *eidōlon*] – **eidetically** *adv*

**eidolon** /ie'dohlon/ *n, pl* **eidolons, eidola** /-lə/ **1** a phantom, image **2** an ideal or idealized figure [Gk *eidōlon* – more at IDOL]

**eigenvalue** /'ieg(ə)n,valyooh/ *n, maths* the number by which an eigenvector is multiplied under its rotational, reflectional, expanding, or shrinking operation in one dimension [part trans of Ger *eigenwert*, fr *eigen* own, peculiar, characteristic (fr OHG *eigan*) + *wert* value – more at OWN]

**eigenvector** /-,vektə/ *n, maths* a vector that in one dimension under a given rotational, reflectional, expanding, or shrinking operation becomes a number that is a multiple of itself [ISV *eigen-* (fr Ger *eigen*) + *vector*]

**eight** /ayt/ *n* **1** – see NUMBER table **2** the eighth in a set or series **3** something having eight parts or members or a denomination of eight: eg **3a** an 8-person racing boat or its crew **b** an 8-cylinder engine or motor car [ME *eighte*, fr *eighte*, adj, fr OE *eahta*; akin to OHG *ahto* eight, L *octo*, Gk *oktō*] – **eight** *adj or pron*, **eightfold** *adj or adv* – **one over the eight** *informal* too much to drink

**eighteen** /,ay'teen/ *n* – see NUMBER table [ME *eightetene*, adj,

fr OE *eahtatīene*, fr *eahta* eight + *tīen* ten] – **eighteen** *adj or pron*, **eighteenth** *adj or n*

**18** *n or adj* (a film) certified in Britain as suitable only for people over 18 – compare U, PG, 15

**eighteenmo** /-moh/ *n, pl* **eighteenmos** the size of a piece of paper cut 18 from a sheet of standard size; *also* a book, a page, or paper of this size

**eighteens** /ay'teenz/ *n taking sing vb* a book format in which a folded sheet forms 18 leaves

**eighth** /ayt·th/ *n* **1** – see NUMBER table **2** *music* OCTAVE **3** – **eighth** *adj or adv*

**eighth note** *n, NAm* QUAVER **1** (short musical note)

**eighth rest** *n, NAm* a musical REST (indicating silence) of the same time value as a quaver

**eightsome** /'ayts(ə)m/, **eightsome reel** *n* a Scottish reel for eight dancers

**Eights Week** *n* an Oxford university festival period in June with boat races between the colleges and special balls at some colleges – compare MAY WEEK [*eight* 3a]

**eightvo** /'aytvoh/ *n* OCTAVO (size of paper) [*8vo*, abbr of *octavo*]

**eighty** /'ayti/ *n* **1** – see NUMBER table **2** *pl* the numbers 80 to 89; *specif* a range of temperatures, ages, or dates within a century characterized by those numbers [ME *eighty*, adj, fr OE *eahtatig*, short for *hundeahtatig*, n, group of eighty, fr *hund* hundred + *eahta* eight + *-tig* group of ten; akin to OE *tīen* ten] – **eightieth** *adj or n*, **eighty** *adj or pron*, **eightyfold** *adj or adv*

**einkorn** /'ien,kawn/ *n* a wheat (*Triticum monococcum*) having only one grain in each row of the ear, that is sometimes considered the most primitive wheat and is grown esp in poor soils in central Europe [Ger, fr OHG, fr *ein* one + *korn* grain – more at ONE, CORN]

**Einsteinian** /,ien'stieni·ən/ *adj* of Albert Einstein or his theories, esp the theory of relativity

**einsteinium** /,ien'stieni·əm/ *n* a radioactive chemical element produced artificially [NL, fr Albert *Einstein* †1955 US (German-born) physicist & mathematician]

**eirenic** /ie'reenik, ie'renik/ *adj* IRENIC (peace-making)

**eirenicon** /ie'reenikən/ *n* a statement that attempts to harmonize conflicting religious doctrines [LGk *eirēnikon*, fr neut of Gk *eirēnikos* peace-making – more at IRENIC]

**eisegesis** /,iesə'jeesis/ *n, pl* **eisegeses** /-seez/ the interpretation of a text (eg of the Bible) by reading one's own ideas into it – compare EXEGESIS [Gk *eis* into (akin to Gk *en* in) + E *exegesis*]

**eisteddfod** /ie'stedhvod, ay-/ *n, pl* **eisteddfods, eisteddfodau** /ie,stedh'vodie, ,aystedh-/ a Welsh-language competitive festival of the arts, esp music and poetry [W, lit., session, fr *eistedd* to sit + *bod* being] – **eisteddfodic** *adj*

**eiswein** /'iesvien (Ger* AISVAIN)/ *n, often cap* a German sweet golden-coloured table wine made from grapes which were frozen during the harvest and pressing [Ger, fr *eis* ice + *wein* wine]

¹**either** /'iedhə, 'ee-/ *adj* **1** being the one and the other of two; each ⟨*flowers blooming on* ∼ *side of the path*⟩ **2** being the one or the other of two ⟨*take* ∼ *road*⟩ [ME, fr OE *æghwæther* both, each, fr *ā* always + *ge-*, collective prefix + *hwæther* which of two, whether]
  *usage* The use of **either** for "each", though objected to by some writers on usage, is well established in English ⟨*on* **either** *side the river lie Long fields of barley and of rye* – Lord Tennyson⟩

²**either** *pron* the one or the other ⟨*could be happy with* ∼ *of them*⟩ ⟨*don't want* ∼⟩

³**either** *conj* – used before two or more sentence elements of the same class or function joined usu by *or* to indicate that what immediately follows is the first of two or more alternatives ⟨∼ *sink or swim*⟩ ⟨∼ *coffee, tea, or whisky*⟩
  *usage* **1** As a subject, **either** and **neither** are traditionally followed by a singular verb or pronoun ⟨*here are two books*; **either** *is perfectly suitable*⟩; but plural verbs and pronouns are increasingly used today, in writing as well as in speech, in cases where a plural noun follows ⟨**neither** *of the books are really suitable*⟩ and especially when **either…or** or **neither…nor** is followed by a plural noun next to the verb. Compare ⟨**either** *my father* or *my brothers are coming*⟩ ⟨**either** *my brother* or *my father is coming*⟩. The same principle holds where there is a change of grammatical person between the two items. Compare ⟨**neither** *you nor he has answered*⟩ ⟨**neither** *he nor you have answered*⟩. Plural verbs and pronouns are also used informally where one wishes to avoid using either *he* for both sexes or the awkward *he or she* ⟨*if* **either** *David* or *Janet come, they will want a drink*⟩. **2** In formal writing, **either** and **neither** should be placed next to the

part of the sentence that they concern. Compare 〈either *you must improve your work* or *you will be dismissed*〉 〈*you must improve* either *your work* or *your appearance*〉. 3 The use of either and neither as adjectives for more than two is perfectly legitimate 〈*come on* either *Friday, Saturday, or Sunday*〉 〈neither *beer* nor *wine* nor *spirits*〉; when they function as pronouns, either should be replaced by *any* for more than two and neither by *none* 〈either/ neither *of the twins*〉 〈any/none *of the triplets*〉.

⁴**either** *adv* likewise; FOR THAT MATTER – used for emphasis after a negative or implied negation or after an alternative following a question 〈*not wise or handsome* ~〉 〈*I can't swim,* ~〉 〈*who answers for the Irish parliament? or army* ~*?* – Robert Browning〉

,**either-'or** *adj or n* (involving) an unavoidable choice between only two alternatives 〈*never a matter of knowledge versus proficiency, never a simple* ~ – H J Muller〉

¹**ejaculate** /i'jakyoo,layt/ *vt* 1 to eject or discharge from a living body; *specif* to eject (semen) in orgasm 2 *formal* to utter suddenly and vehemently ~ *vi* to eject a fluid, specif semen [L *ejaculatus,* pp of *ejaculari* to throw out, fr *e-* + *jaculari* to throw, fr *jaculum* dart, fr *jacere* to throw – more at JET] – **ejaculatory** *adj*

²**ejaculate** /i'jakyoolət/ *n* the semen released by one ejaculation

**ejaculation** /i,jakyoo'laysh(ə)n/ *n* 1 an act of ejaculating; *specif* a sudden discharging of semen in orgasm 2 something ejaculated; *esp* a short sudden exclamation or emotional utterance

**ejaculatory duct** /i'jakyoolətri, *also* i,jakyoo'layt(ə)ri/ *n* a duct through which semen is ejaculated; *specif* either of the paired ducts in man that are formed by the junction of the duct from the SEMINAL VESICLE (pouch where semen is temporarily stored) with the VAS DEFERENS (duct carrying semen from the testicle)

**eject** /i'jekt/ *vt* 1a to drive out, esp by physical force 〈*the hecklers were* ~ed〉 b to evict from property 2 to throw out or off from within 〈~s *the empty cartridges*〉 ~ *vi* to escape from an aircraft by using the ejector seat [ME *ejecten,* fr L *ejectus,* pp of *eicere,* fr *e-* + *jacere*] – **ejectable** *adj,* **ejection** *n,* **ejective** *adj,* **ejector** *n*

**ejecta** /i'jektə/ *n taking sing or pl vb* material thrown out (e g from a volcano) [NL, fr L, neut pl of *ejectus*]

**ejectment** /i'jektmənt/ *n* a former legal action, based on judicial decisions, for recovering possession of property

**ejector seat, ejection seat** *n* an emergency escape seat that propels an occupant out and away from an aircraft by means of an explosive charge

**eka-** /'ekə-, aykə-/ *comb form* standing or assumed to stand next in order beyond (a specified chemical element) in the same family of chemical elements of the PERIODIC TABLE – used in names of chemical elements, esp when not yet discovered or synthesized 〈eka*silicon (now called germanium)*〉 〈eka*tantalum*〉 [Skt *eka* one – more at ONE]

**eke** /eek/ *adv, archaic also* [ME, fr OE *ēac;* akin to OHG *ouh* also, L *aut* or, Gk *au* again]

**eke out** /eek/ *vt* 1a to make up for the deficiencies of; supplement 〈*eked out his income by getting a second job*〉 b to make (a supply) last by economy 2 to make (e g a living) by laborious or precarious means [ME *eken* to increase, fr OE *īecan, ēcan;* akin to OHG *ouhhōn* to add, L *augēre* to increase, Gk *auxein*]

**ekistics** /i'kistiks/ *n taking sing vb* a science dealing with human settlements and their evolution [NGk *oikistikē,* fr fem of *oikistikos* relating to settlement, deriv of Gk *oikos* house – more at VICINITY] – **ekistic** *adj*

**ektexine** /ek'tekseen, -sien/ *n* the structurally variable outer layer of the EXINE (double-layered outer skin) of a POLLEN GRAIN – compare ENDEXINE [Gk *ekto-* outside + E *exine* – more at ECT-]

**ekuele** /ay'kwaylay/ *also* **ekpwele** /ek'pway-/ *n, pl* **ekuele** *also* **ekpweles** – see MONEY table [native name in Equatorial Guinea]

**el** /el/ *n, often cap, NAm* OVERHEAD RAILWAY [short for *elevated* (*railroad*)]

¹**elaborate** /i'lab(ə)rət/ *adj* 1 planned or carried out with great care and attention to detail 〈~ *preparations*〉 2 marked by complexity, fullness of detail, or ornateness; intricate 〈*a highly* ~ *coiffure*〉 [L *elaboratus,* fr pp of *elaborare* to work out, acquire by labour, fr *e-* + *laborare* to work – more at LABORATORY] – **elaborately** *adv,* **elaborateness** *n*

²**elaborate** /i'labə,rayt/ *vt* 1 to produce by labour 2 *of a living organism* to build up (complex organic compounds) from simpler substances 3 to work out in detail; develop ~ *vi* to go into detail; add further information 〈*need I* ~*?*〉 – often + on

〈*urged him to* ~ *on his scheme*〉 – **elaboration** *n,* **elaborative** *adj*

**Elamite** /'eeləmiet/ *n* a dead language having no known relationship with other languages, that was used in Elam, an ancient kingdom at the head of the Persian Gulf

**élan** /ay'lon, -'lan (*Fr* elã)/ *n* vigorous spirit or enthusiasm, typically shown by poise, verve, or liveliness of imagination – compare ÉCLAT [Fr, fr MF *eslan* rush, fr (s')*eslancer* to rush, fr *ex-* + *lancer* to hurl – more at LANCE]

**eland** /'eelənd/ *n* either of two large African antelopes (*Taurotragus oryx* and *Taurotragus derbianus*) that resemble the ox and have short spirally twisted horns in both sexes [Afrik, elk, fr D, fr obs Ger *elend,* fr Lith *elnis;* akin to OHG *elaho* elk – more at ELK]

**élan vital** /vee'tal (*Fr* vital)/ *n* a vital force; *specif* the creative urge, esp for improved and superior evolutionary development, held by the philosopher Henri Bergson to be inherent in all living organisms [Fr]

**elapid** /'eləpid/ *n* any of a family (Elapidae) of venomous snakes (e g the cobra) with grooved fangs [NL *Elap-, Elaps,* genus of snakes, fr MGk, a fish, alter. of Gk *elops*]

¹**elapse** /i'laps/ *vi, of a period of time* to slip away; pass 〈*four years* ~d *before he returned*〉 [L *elapsus,* pp of *elabi,* fr *e-* + *labi* to slip – more at SLEEP]

²**elapse** *n* a lapse, interruption, or interval 〈*went back to university after an* ~ *of 15 years*〉

**elapsed time** *n* the time taken (e g by a boat or motor vehicle) to travel over a course

**elasmobranch** /i'lasmə,brangk, i'laz-/ *n, pl* **elasmobranchs** any of a class (Chondrichthyes) of fishes having a skeleton wholly or largely composed of cartilage, and including the sharks, rays, skates, and various extinct related fishes [deriv of Gk *elasmos* metal plate (fr *elaunein*) + L *branchia* gill] – **elasmobranch** *adj*

**elastase** /i'lastayz, -ays/ *n* an ENZYME occurring esp in the digestive juice secreted by the pancreas that breaks down elastin

¹**elastic** /i'lastik, i'lah-/ *adj* 1a *of a solid* capable of recovering size and shape after deformation b *of a gas* capable of indefinite expansion 2 capable of recovering or rebounding quickly, esp from depression or disappointment; buoyant, resilient 3 capable of being easily stretched and resuming its former shape 〈*an* ~ *fabric*〉 4 capable of ready change or easy expansion or contraction; flexible, adaptable 〈*an* ~ *conscience*〉 〈~ *rules*〉 〈~ *demand for goods*〉 [NL *elasticus,* fr LGk *elastos* ductile, beaten, fr Gk *elaunein* to drive, beat out; akin to OIr *luid* he went] – **elastically** *adv*

²**elastic** *n* 1 an elastic fabric, usu made of yarns containing rubber 2 easily stretched rubber, usu prepared in cords, strings, or bands

**elasticated** /i'lastikaytid, i'lah-/, **elasticized** /i'lastisiezd, -i'lah-/ *adj* 1 *of fabric* made stretchy by the insertion or interweaving of elastic 2 incorporating elasticated material 〈~ *boots*〉

**elastic band** *n, Br* RUBBER BAND

**elastic collision** *n, physics* a collision in which the total KINETIC ENERGY of the colliding particles or bodies remains unchanged – compare INELASTIC COLLISION

**elasticity** /i,la'stisəti, ,ela'stisəti, -lah-/ *n* the quality or state of being elastic: e g a the capability of a material or body to recover its original size and shape after deformation b resilience c the quality of being adaptable d a measure of the responsiveness of one economic variable to a change in another

**elastic scattering** *n* a scattering of particles as the result of ELASTIC COLLISION

**elastin** /i'lastin/ *n* a protein that is the chief constituent of the fibres of the stretchy elastic tissue of ligaments, artery walls, etc [ISV, fr NL *elasticus*]

**elastomer** /i'lastəmə/ *n* any of various elastic materials resembling rubber 〈*polyvinyl* ~s〉 [*elastic* + *-o-* + Gk *meros* part – more at MERIT] – **elastomeric** *adj*

**Elastoplast** /i'lastə,plahst/ *trademark* – used for an elastic adhesive plaster

**elate** /i'layt/ *vt* to fill with joy or pride; put in high spirits [L *elatus* (pp of *efferre* to carry out, elevate), fr *e-* + *latus,* suppletive pp of *ferre* to carry – more at TOLERATE, BEAR] – **elation** *n*

**elated** /i'laytid/ *adj* marked by high spirits; exultant – **elatedly** *adv,* **elatedness** *n*

**elater** /'elətə/ *n* 1 CLICK BEETLE 2 a plant structure (e g in the spore-bearing capsule of a LIVERWORT) that functions in the distribution of spores [NL, genus of beetles, fr Gk *elatēr* driver, fr *elaunein*]

**E layer** *n* a layer of the IONOSPHERE (upper part of the earth's atmosphere) that occurs at about 95 kilometres (about 60 miles) above the earth's surface and is capable of reflecting RADIO WAVES – called also HEAVISIDE LAYER, KENNELLY-HEAVISIDE LAYER

**¹elbow** /'elboh/ *n* **1a** the joint between the human forearm and upper arm **b** a corresponding joint in the forelimb of a VERTEBRATE animal (e g a dog) **2** something resembling an elbow; *specif* an angular pipe fitting **3** the part of a garment that covers the elbow [ME *elbowe*, fr OE *elboga*; akin to OHG *elinbogo* elbow; both fr a prehistoric NGmc-WGmc compound whose constituents are akin to OE *eln* ell & OE *boga* bow – more at ELL, BOW] – **out at elbows 1** shabbily dressed **2** impoverished

**²elbow** *vt* **1** to push or shove aside (as if) with the elbow; jostle **2** to force (e g one's way) rudely or roughly (as if) by pushing with the elbow ⟨~ing *our way through the crowd*⟩ ⟨~ed *his way into the best circles*⟩ ~ *vi* **1** to advance by elbowing one's way **2** to make an angle; turn ⟨*here the passage* ~s *and we are in another room*⟩

**elbow grease** *n, informal* hard, esp repetitive, physical effort ⟨"*you need* ~ *to clean that silver. Rub it hard!*"⟩

**elbowroom** /-,roohm, -room/ *n* adequate space or scope for movement, work, or operation ⟨*the large kitchen gives plenty of* ~⟩

**eld** /eld/ *n, archaic* **1** old age **2** olden times [ME, fr OE *ieldo*; akin to OE *eald* old – more at OLD]

**¹elder** /'eldə/ *n* any of several shrubs or small trees (genus *Sambucus*, esp *Sambucus nigra*) of the honeysuckle family that bear flat clusters of small white or pink flowers and elderberries [ME *eldre*, fr OE *ellærn*; prob akin to OE *alor* alder – more at ALDER]

**²elder** *adj* **1** of earlier birth or greater age, esp than another related person or thing ⟨*his* ~ *brother*⟩ **2** of earlier times; former **3** *archaic* prior or superior in rank, office, or validity **4** *obs* of a more advanced time of life [ME, fr OE *ieldra*, compar of *eald* old]

    *synonyms* Elder and eldest cannot be used of things, apart from
    the now somewhat rare sense 2 "former" ⟨*writes in an* elder *tradi-*
    *tion*⟩. They describe particularly people within a family ⟨*my* elder
    *brother*⟩ or similar close group ⟨*the* eldest *partner*⟩. Older and
    oldest can be used of either things or people and older, but not
    elder, can be followed by *than* ⟨*she's* older *than I am*⟩.

**³elder** *n* **1** one who is older; a senior ⟨*the child trying to please his* ~s⟩ **2** one having authority by virtue of age and experience ⟨*the* ~s *of the tribal village*⟩ **3** any of various church officers: e g **3a** a member of the governing body of an early Christian church **b** a permanent officer elected by a Presbyterian congregation to serve on the governing body and assist at communion **c** a Mormon ordained to the higher order of priesthood **4** *archaic* an aged person – **eldership** *n*

**elderberry** /-b(ə)ri, -,beri/ *n* the edible black or red berry of an elder; *also* an elder shrub or tree

**elderly** /-li/ *adj* **1** rather old; *specif, of a person* past middle age **2** (characteristic) of later life *synonyms* see ¹OLD *antonyms* young, youthful – **elderliness** *n*

**elder statesman** *n* an eminent senior member of a group or organization; *esp* a retired statesman whose advice is often sought unofficially by current leaders

**eldest** /'eldist/ *adj* of the greatest age or seniority; oldest *synonyms* see ²ELDER

**eldest hand** *n* the card player who first receives cards in the deal

**El Dorado** /,el də'rahdoh, do'rah-/ *n* **1** a city or country of fabulous riches held by 16th-century explorers to exist in S America **2** a place of fabulous wealth, abundance, or opportunity [Sp, lit., the gilded one]

**eldritch** /'eldrich/ *adj, poetic* weird, uncanny *synonyms* see ²WEIRD [perh fr (assumed) ME *elfriche* fairyland, fr ME *elf* + *riche* kingdom, fr OE *rīce* – more at RICH]

**Eleatic** /,eli'atik/ *n or adj* (a member) of a school of Greek philosophers founded by Parmenides and continued by Zeno that stressed the unity of being and denied the existence of change [L *Eleaticus*, fr Gk *Eleatikos*, fr *Elea* (Velia), ancient town in S Italy where Parmenides and Zeno were born] – **Eleaticism** *n*

**elecampane** /,elikam'payn, --'--/ *n* a large coarse European plant (*Inula helenium*) of the daisy family with large yellow flower heads [ME *elena campana*, fr ML *enula campana*, lit., field elecampane, fr *inula*, *enula* elecampane (modif of Gk *helenion*) + *campana* of the field]

**¹elect** /i'lekt/ *adj* **1** SELECT 1,2 **2** chosen for salvation through divine mercy **3** chosen for office or position but not yet installed ⟨*the president*-elect⟩ □ compare ÉLITE [ME, fr L *electus* choice, fr pp of *eligere* to select, fr e- + *legere* to choose – more at LEGEND]

**²elect** *n, pl* **elect**, (2) **elects 1** a person chosen or set apart (e g by divine favour) **2** *usu taking pl vb* a select or exclusive group of people; an elite

**³elect** *vt* **1** to select by vote for an office, position, or membership ⟨~ed *him president*⟩ **2** *of God* to choose or predestine (someone) to receive salvation **3** *chiefly NAm* to make a selection of **4** *formal* to choose, decide ⟨*might* ~ *to sell the business*⟩ *synonyms* see ¹CHOICE – **electable** *adj,* **electability** *n*

**election** /i'leksh(ə)n/ *n* **1a** an act or process of electing **b** the fact of being elected **2** divine choice; *specif* God's marking out of individuals for salvation **3** *formal* the right, power, or privilege of making a choice

**election day** *n* **1** a day legally established for a political election **2** *cap E&D* the first Tuesday after the first Monday in November in an even year designated for national elections in the USA and observed as a public holiday in many states

**electioneer** /i,leksh(ə)n'iə/ *vi* **1** to work for a candidate or party in an election **2** to introduce party-political points into what ought to be a nonpolitical discourse, esp so as to gain votes; *broadly* to attempt to gain unfair electoral advantage for one's party ⟨*claimed the chancellor's tax cuts were blatant* ~*ing*⟩ [*election* + *-eer* (as in *auctioneer*, vb)] – **electioneer, electioneerer** *n*

**¹elective** /i'lektiv/ *adj* **1a** chosen or filled by popular election ⟨*the presidency is an* ~ *office*⟩ **b** of or based on election **2** permitting a choice; optional ⟨*an* ~ *year of study abroad*⟩ **3** tending to operate on one substance rather than another ⟨~ *fermentation*⟩ – **electively** *adv,* **electiveness** *n*

**²elective** *n* an elective course or subject

**elector** /i'lektə/ *n* **1** one qualified to vote in an election **2** one entitled to participate in an election: e g **2a** *often cap* any of the German princes entitled to elect the Holy Roman Emperor **b** a member of the ELECTORAL COLLEGE in the USA

**electoral** /i'lekt(ə)rəl/ *adj* **1** of an elector or electors ⟨*the* ~ *register*⟩ **2** of election ⟨*an* ~ *system*⟩

**electoral college** *n taking sing or pl vb* **1** a body of electors chosen in each state to elect the president and vice-president of the USA **2** any body of electors

**electorate** /i'lekt(ə)rət/ *n* **1** *often cap* the territory, jurisdiction, etc of a German elector **2** *taking sing or pl vb* a body of people entitled to vote

**electr-** /ilektr-/, **electro-** *comb form* **1a** (caused by) electricity ⟨electro*magnetism*⟩ ⟨electro*chemistry*⟩ **b** electric ⟨electro*de*⟩; electric and ⟨electro*chemical*⟩ ⟨electro*mechanical*⟩; electrically ⟨electro*positive*⟩ **2** electrolytic ⟨electro*analysis*⟩ ⟨electro*deposition*⟩ **3** electron ⟨electro*phile*⟩ [NL *electricus*]

**Electra complex** /i'lektrə/ *n, psychology* a sexual desire expressed by a female child for her father – compare OEDIPUS COMPLEX [*Electra*, figure in Gk mythology who incited her brother to kill their mother Clytemnestra, the murderer of their father Agamemnon]

**electret** /i'lektrət, -tret/ *n* a body usu made of plastic that can permanently retain a static electric charge and which is used in electrical devices such as microphones [*electr*icity + *magn*et]

**¹electric** /i'lektrik/ *adj* **1a** of, being, supplying, producing, or produced by electricity ⟨~ *currents*⟩ ⟨*an* ~ *plug*⟩ **b** operated by or using electricity ⟨*an* ~ *motor*⟩ **2** producing an intensely stimulating effect; thrilling ⟨*an* ~ *performance*⟩ **3a** generating music by electronic means ⟨*an* ~ *organ*⟩ **b** *of a musical instrument* electronically amplifying sound ⟨*an* ~ *guitar*⟩ [NL *electricus* produced from amber by friction, electric, fr ML, of amber, fr L *electrum* amber, electrum, fr Gk *ēlektron*; akin to Gk *ēlektōr* beaming sun, Skt *ulkā* meteor]

**²electric** *n* **1** *pl* electrical parts; electric circuitry **2** electric *also* **electrics** *pl, informal* electricity, electric power **3** *informal* something (e g a car or train) operated by electricity **4** *archaic* a nonconductor of electricity used to excite or accumulate electricity

**electrical** /i'lektrikl/ *adj* **1** of or connected with electricity ⟨~ *output*⟩ ⟨~ *engineering*⟩ **2** ELECTRIC 1 ⟨~ *appliances*⟩ – **electrically** *adv*

    *synonyms* Electric or electrical describes systems in which the
    electric current is used simply as a source of power (e g for heating,
    lighting, or producing a magnetic field). In electronic systems, one
    electric current is used to control another by way of an active device
    (e g a transistor or thermionic valve).

**electric blanket** *n* a blanket containing an electric heating element that is used to warm a bed

**electric blue** *n* a harsh bright slightly greenish-blue colour – **electric-blue** *adj*

**electric chair** *n* 1 an electrified chair used in certain states of the USA as the instrument of capital punishment for legal electrocution 2 the penalty of death by electrocution

**electric charge** *n* CHARGE 2c

**electric eel** *n* a large eel-shaped fish (*Electrophorus electricus*) of the Orinoco and Amazon rivers that is capable of giving a severe electric shock

**electric eye** *n* 1 PHOTOELECTRIC CELL 2 MAGIC EYE 2

**electric field** *n* a portion of space (e g that surrounding an electric charge) in which a perceptible force is exerted on an electric charge

**electrician** /,elək'trish(ə)n, i,lek-/ *n* 1 a specialist in the phenomena of electricity – not used technically 2 one who installs, maintains, operates, or repairs electrical equipment

**electricity** /,elək'trisəti, i'lek-, ,eelek-/ *n* 1a the phenomena caused by stationary or moving positively and negatively charged particles (e g protons and electrons) b electric current; *also* electric charge 2 a science that deals with the phenomena and laws governing the behaviour of electric charges 3 keen contagious excitement

**electric organ** *n* a specialized tract of tissue (e g in the ELECTRIC EEL) in which electricity is generated

**electric ray** *n* any of various round-bodied short-tailed rays (family Torpedinidae) found in warm seas, that are capable of giving electric shocks

**electric shock** *also* **shock** *n* a sudden stimulation of the nerves accompanied by convulsive contraction of the muscles caused by the passage of electricity through the body

**electric storm** *n* a violent atmospheric disturbance usu accompanied by thunder and lightning

**electrify** /i'lektrifie/ *vt* 1 to charge (a body) with electricity 2a to equip for use of electric power ⟨~ *the railway system*⟩ b to supply with electric power c to amplify (music) electronically – **electrification** *n*

**electro-** /i'lektroh-/ – see ELECTR-

**electroanalysis** /i,lektroh·ə'naləsis/ *n* chemical analysis using ELECTROLYSIS (passage of an electric current through a solution) – **electroanalytic, electroanalytical** *adj*

**electrocardiogram** /i,lektroh'kahdi·ə,gram/ *n* the tracing made by an electrocardiograph

**electrocardiograph** /-,grahf, -,graf/ *n* an instrument for recording the changes in electrical activity occurring during the heartbeat, used esp in diagnosing abnormalities of heart action – **electrocardiographic** *adj*, **electrocardiographically** *adv*, **electrocardiography** *n*

**electrochemistry** /i,lektroh'keməstri/ *n* a science that deals with the relation of electricity to chemical changes (e g in solutions conducting an electric current) and with the interconversion of chemical and electrical energy – **electrochemical** *adj*, **electrochemically** *adv*

**electroconvulsive** /i,lektroh·kən'vulsiv/ *adj* of or involving convulsive response to electric shocks ⟨*impaired learning ability in rats due to* ~ *shocks*⟩

**electroconvulsive therapy** /i,lektrohkən'vulsiv/ *n* a treatment for serious mental disorder, esp severe depression, in which a fit is induced by passing an electric current through the brain

**electrocute** /i'lektrə,kyooht/ *vt* 1 to execute (a criminal) by administering electric shock 2 to kill by electric shock [*electr-* + *-cute* (as in *execute*)] – **electrocution** *n*

**electrode** /i'lektrohd/ *n* an electrical conductor that is used to establish electrical contact with a nonmetallic part of a circuit (e g the acid in a car battery, the gas or vacuum in a valve, or the solid semiconductor material of a transistor) and by means of which electrons or other charge carriers enter and leave the circuit or are emitted, collected, or have their flow controlled

¹**electrodeposit** /i'lektrohdi,pozit/ *n* a deposit, esp of a metal, formed on or at an electrode in contact with a solution by ELECTROLYSIS

²**electrodeposit** /i,lektrohdi'pozit/ *vt* to deposit (e g a metal) by ELECTROLYSIS – **electrodeposition** *n*

**electrodialysis** /i,lektrohdie'aləsis/ *n* DIALYSIS (separation of substances in solution, by their unequal diffusion through a membrane) accelerated by applying a voltage to electrodes on either side of the membrane – **electrodialytic** *adj*, **electrodialyse** *vt*, **electrodialyser** *n*

**electrodynamics** /i,lektrohdie'namiks, -di-/ *n taking sing vb* a branch of physics that deals with the effects arising from the interactions between charged objects, magnets, and electric currents – **electrodynamic** *adj*

**electrodynamometer** /i,lektroh,dienə'momitə/ *n* an instrument that measures electric current by indicating the strength of the magnetic forces between a current flowing in fixed coils and one flowing in movable coils [ISV]

**electroencephalogram** /i,lektrohin'sef(ə)lə,gram/ *n* the tracing of BRAIN WAVES made by an electroencephalograph [ISV]

**electroencephalograph** /i,lektrohin'sef(ə)lə,grahf, -,graf/ *n* an instrument for detecting and recording the electrical activity of the brain [ISV] – **electroencephalographic** *adj*, **electroencephalography** *n*

**electrofishing** /i'lektroh,fishing/ *n* the taking of fish by a system based on their tendency to be attracted to a source of electric current

**electroform** /i'lektrə,fawm/ *vt* to form (shaped metal articles) by electrodeposition of a layer of metal on a mould

**electrogenesis** /i,lektroh'jenəsis/ *n* the production of electrical activity, esp in living tissue

**electrogram** /i'lektrə,gram/ *n* a tracing of the electrical activity of a tissue or organ (e g the brain or heart) made by means of electrodes placed directly in the tissue instead of on the surface of the body

**electrohydraulic** /i,lektroh·hie'drolik/ *adj* involving or produced by the action of very brief but powerful pulse discharges of electricity through a liquid, resulting in the generation of shock waves and highly reactive chemical groups ⟨*an* ~ *effect*⟩ – **electrohydraulically** *adv*

**electrokinetic** /i,lektroh·ki'netik, -kie-/ *adj* of or being the motion of a liquid or the motion of particles with respect to a gas or esp liquid in which the particles are suspended, that results from or produces a difference of electric POTENTIAL

**electrokinetics** /i,lektrohki'netiks/ *n taking sing vb* a branch of physics that deals with electrokinetic phenomena (e g electrophoresis)

**electrologist** /,elek'trolǝjist, i,lek-/ *n* one who removes hair, warts, moles, and birthmarks by means of an electric current applied to the body with a needle-shaped electrode [blend of *electrolysis* and *-logist* (fr *-logy* + *-ist*)]

**electroluminescence** /i,lektroh,loohmi'nes(ə)ns/ *n* emission of light resulting from the application of an ELECTRIC FIELD produced by an ALTERNATING CURRENT to a layer of PHOSPHOR (substance that emits light when bombarded by electrons or radiation) – **electroluminescent** *adj*

**electrolyse,** *NAm chiefly* **electrolyze** /i'lektrəliez/ *vt* to subject to electrolysis

**electrolysis** /,elek'trolǝsis, i,lek-/ *n* 1 the producing of chemical changes by passing an electric current through an electrolyte, causing the IONS (electrically charged atoms) present in the electrolyte to migrate towards the oppositely charged electrodes where reactions take place by the transfer of electrons between the ions and electrodes resulting in the formation of atoms or molecules; *esp* the decomposition of a substance (e g the decomposition of water into hydrogen and oxygen) by the process, typically resulting in the deposition of a metal on an electrode or the release of a gas 2 the destruction of hair roots, warts, moles, birthmarks, etc by means of an electric current

**electrolyte** /i'lektrə,liet/ *n* an electrically conducting liquid, solution (e g of an acid), or molten substance in which current is carried by the movement of IONS (positively and negatively charged atoms or groups of atoms) rather than by the movement of electrons; *also* a substance that when dissolved in a suitable solvent or when melted becomes an electrolyte

**electrolytic** /i,lektrə'litik/ *adj* of or being electrolysis or an electrolyte – **electrolytically** *adv*

**electromagnet** /i,lektroh'magnit/ *n* a core of magnetizable material surrounded by a coil of wire through which an electric current is passed that sets up a MAGNETIC FIELD, thus magnetizing the core

**electromagnetic** /i,lektroh·mag'netik/ *adj* of or produced by electromagnetism – **electromagnetically** *adv*

**electromagnetic force** *n* ELECTROMAGNETIC INTERACTION

**electromagnetic interaction** /i,lektrohmag'netik/ *n* a fundamental interaction that occurs between electrically charged particles (e g protons or electrons) and is responsible for the emission and absorption of PHOTONS (particles of electromagnetic radiation) and for electric and magnetic forces

**electromagnetic radiation** *n* radiation consisting of a series of ELECTROMAGNETIC WAVES

**electromagnetic spectrum** *n* the entire range of wavelengths or frequencies of ELECTROMAGNETIC RADIATION extending from GAMMA RAYS having the shortest wavelengths to the RADIO WAVES having the longest wavelengths and including visible light

**electromagnetic unit** *n* any of a series of electrical units in the CENTIMETRE-GRAM-SECOND system based primarily on the magnetic properties of electric currents

**electromagnetic wave** *n* any of the waves including RADIO WAVES, infrared, visible light, ultraviolet, X RAYS, and GAMMA RAYS that are propagated by the simultaneous periodic variation in the intensity of an ELECTRIC FIELD and a MAGNETIC FIELD acting at right angles to each other and to the plane of propagation

**electromagnetism** /iˌlektrohˈmagnǝtiz(ǝ)m/ *n* **1** magnetism developed (e g in an electromagnet) by a current of electricity **2** a branch of physics dealing with the relations between and the effects resulting from the interaction of electricity and magnetism

**electromechanical** /iˌlektroh·miˈkanikl/ *adj* of or being a mechanical process or device that is put into action or controlled electrically; *specif* being a device for converting mechanical energy to electrical energy or vice versa – **electromechanically** *adv*

**electrometallurgy** /iˌlektrohmiˈtalǝji, ˈmetǝluhji/ *n* a branch of metallurgy dealing with processes, specif the extraction and refining of metals and ELECTROPLATING (coating of objects with metals), involving the passage of an electric current through solutions containing metal ions; *broadly* metal manufacturing processes (e g steelmaking) in which electricity is used as a source of heat

**electrometer** /ˌelekˈtromitǝ, iˌlek-/ *n* any of various instruments for detecting or measuring esp voltages or very low currents by means of the forces of attraction or repulsion between two electrically charged bodies

**electromotive force** /iˌlektrǝˈmohtiv/ *n* that which causes or tends to cause an electric current to flow round a circuit; the amount of energy required from an electrical source (e g a cell or generator) to drive each unit of charge round a circuit and through the source – compare POTENTIAL DIFFERENCE

**electromyogram** /iˌlektrǝˈmie·ǝgram/ *n* a tracing made with an electromyograph

**electromyograph** /iˌlektrǝˈmie·ǝgrahf, -graf/ *n* an instrument for the recording of the electric waves associated with the activity of muscle under voluntary control, used esp in diagnosing disorders of the nerves and muscles [*electr-* + *my-* + *-graph*] – **electromyographic, electromyographical** *adj*, **electromyographically** *adv*, **electromyography** *n*

**electron** /iˈlektron/ *n* an ELEMENTARY PARTICLE (minute particle of matter) that carries a single negative electrical charge and occurs in atoms outside the nucleus and the mass movement of which constitutes an electric current in a metal – compare PROTON [*electr-* + *-on*]

**electron camera** *n* a device that converts optical images into electrical signals; CAMERA TUBE

**electronegative** /iˌlektrohˈnegǝtiv/ *adj* **1** carrying a negative electric charge **2** capable of acting as the electrode which emits electrons in an electric cell converting chemical energy to electrical energy **3** *of an atom, molecule, etc* having a tendency to gain or attract electrons □ compare ELECTROPOSITIVE – **electronegativity** *n*

**electron gas** *n* a mass of free electrons in a vacuum or in a metal acting as a conductor

**electron gun** *n* a device (e g in a CATHODE-RAY TUBE) for generating a beam of electrons that consists of an electron-emitting terminal and its surrounding assembly that controls and focusses the stream of electrons to produce a beam of desired size

**¹electronic** /ˌelǝkˈtronik, iˌlek-, ˌeelek-/ *adj* **1** of electrons **2** relating to, using, or involving the methods and principles of electronics **3** of, being, or using devices (e g a THERMIONIC VALVE or transistor) in which a flow of electrons through a gas, vacuum, or semiconductor is controlled by a voltage **4a** generating music electronically; ELECTRIC 3A **b** of or being music that consists of sounds electronically generated or modified *synonyms* see ELECTRICAL – **electronically** *adv*

**²electronic** *n* an electronic circuit or device

**electronic countermeasure** *n* an action taken to counter enemy signals (e g radar) electronically; *also, pl* electronic apparatus carried by combat aircraft for countering enemy signals

**electronics** /iˌlekˈtroniks, ˌeelek-/ *n taking sing vb* a branch of physics and technology that deals with the emission, behaviour, and effects of electrons in valves, transistors, and other electronic devices and with the development and use of such devices

**electron lens** *n* a device (e g in an ELECTRON MICROSCOPE) for focussing a beam of electrons by means of an ELECTRIC FIELD or a MAGNETIC FIELD

**electron microscope** *n* an instrument in which a beam of electrons focussed by means of an ELECTRON LENS is used to produce an enormously enlarged image of a minute object (e g a chromosome or bacterium) on a fluorescent screen or photographic plate – **electron microscopist** *n*, **electron microscopy** *n*

**electron multiplier** *n* a device for amplifying a current of electrons by means of SECONDARY EMISSION of electrons from a series of electrodes, each electrode emitting electrons in increasingly greater numbers when bombarded by electrons emitted by the preceding electrode – **electron multiplication** *n*

**electron optics** *n taking sing vb* a branch of electronics that deals with (the control and use of) those properties of beams of electrons (e g their ability to be focussed by a magnetic or electric field and form images) that are analogous to the properties of rays of light

**electron spin resonance** *n* the change in the SPIN and transition between different ENERGY LEVELS of unpaired electrons when placed in a strong MAGNETIC FIELD and subjected to microwave radiation of a particular frequency; the MAGNETIC RESONANCE of electrons; *also* a technique for identifying chemical compounds (e g in living tissue) by observation of this phenomenon

**electron transport** *n* the sequential transfer of electrons from one chemical compound to another in a living cell; *esp* a process occurring in most living cells as a part of cell RESPIRATION, in which electrons from the breakdown of compounds (e g sugars) are transferred from one chemical compound to another by a series of OXIDATION-REDUCTION reactions that involve the release of energy for the fuelling of other processes (e g growth, reproduction, and excretion of waste materials)

**electron tube** *n* an electronic device (e g a THERMIONIC VALVE or television tube) that consists of a sealed glass or metal container containing a vacuum or gas through which a controlled flow of electrons takes place

**electron volt** *n* a unit of energy equal to the energy gained by an electron in passing between two points between which there is a voltage difference of 1 volt

**electrooculogram** /iˌlektrohˈokyoolǝgram/ *n* a record of the voltage between the front and back of the eye that is correlated with eyeball movement (e g in sleep) and is obtained by placing electrodes on the skin near the eye [*electr-* + *ocul-* + *-gram*]

**eˌlectro-ˈoptics** *n taking sing vb* a branch of physics that deals with the effects of an ELECTRIC FIELD on light crossing it – **electro-optic, electro-optical** *adj*, **electro-optically** *adv*

**electrophile** /iˈlektrohˌfiel/ *n* an electrophilic substance (e g a chlorine or fluorine molecule)

**electrophilic** /iˌlektrohˈfilik/ *adj* involving or having an affinity for electrons; readily accepting electrons ⟨~ *reagents*⟩

**electrophoresis** /iˌlektrohfǝˈreesis/ *n* (the separation and identification of chemical compounds using) the movement of suspended particles through a liquid or gas in which the particles are suspended under the action of a voltage applied to electrodes in contact with the liquid or gas [NL] – **electrophoretic** *adj*, **electrophoretically** *adv*

**electrophoretogram** /iˌlektrohfǝˈretǝgram/ *n* a record of the separated components of a mixture (e g of proteins) produced by electrophoresis of esp a liquid absorbed in a supporting medium (e g filter paper) [*electrophoretic* + *-o-* + *-gram*]

**electrophorus** /iˌlekˈtrofǝrǝs, ˌeelek-/ *n, pl* **electrophori** /-ri/ an instrument for repeatedly generating electrostatic charges, that consists of a plate made of an insulating material (e g ebonite) and a metal plate with an insulating handle. The insulating plate is charged by friction and used to induce a charge in the metal plate. [NL, fr *electr-* + *-phorus* -phore (fr Gk *-phoros*)]

**electrophotography** /iˌlektroh-fǝˈtogrǝfi/ *n* photography in which images are produced by electrical means (e g in photocopying processes such as xerography) – **electrophotographic** *adj*

**electrophysiology** /i,lektroh-fizi'oləji/ *n* **1** a branch of physiology that is concerned with the electrical aspects (e g electrical activity of muscle and nerve fibres) of physiological processes and functions **2** electrical phenomena associated with the function of a particular body part ⟨~ *of the eye*⟩ – **electrophysiological** *also* **electrophysiologic** *adj*, **electrophysiologically** *adv*, **electrophysiologist** *n*

**electroplate** /i'lektroh,playt/ *vt* **1** to coat (a metal or metal object) with a thin continuous layer of esp a different metal by ELECTRODEPOSITION **2** ELECTROTYPE

**electropositive** /i,lektroh'pozətiv/ *adj* **1a** carrying a positive electric charge **b** capable of acting as the electrode which attracts electrons in an electric cell converting chemical energy to electrical energy **2** *of an atom, molecule, etc* having a tendency to release or lose electrons □ compare ELECTRONEGATIVE – **electropositivity** *n*

**electroretinogram** /i,lektroh'retinəgram/ *n* a tracing made by an electroretinograph

**electroretinograph** /i,lektroh'retinəgrahf, -graf/ *n* an instrument for recording electrical activity in the retina of the eye, used esp in diagnosing abnormal conditions of the retina – **electroretinographic** *adj*, **electroretinography** *n*

**electroscope** /i'lektrə,skohp/ *n* any of various instruments for detecting the presence of an electric charge on a body, for determining whether the charge is positive or negative, or for indicating and measuring the intensity of IONIZING radiation (e g GAMMA RAYS and ALPHA RAYS)

**electroshock therapy** /i,lektrə'shok/ *n* ELECTROCONVULSIVE THERAPY

**electrostatic** /i,lektrə'statik/ *adj* **1a** of, being, involving, or associated with stationary electric charges ⟨*an* ~ *field*⟩ **b** producing or produced by stationary electric charges or static electricity ⟨*an* ~ *generator*⟩ **c** of electrostatics **2** of or being a process (e g xerography) for printing or copying in which electrostatic forces are used to attract ink (e g carbon powder) to an image on a printing surface [ISV] – **electrostatically** *adv*

**electrostatic generator** *n* any of various machines (e g a VAN DE GRAAFF GENERATOR) for generating electrostatic charge at a high voltage

**electrostatics** /i,lektrə'statiks/ *n taking sing vb* a branch of physics dealing with stationary electric charges, esp the phenomena due to attractions between opposite charges and repulsions between identical charges

**electrostatic unit** *n* any of a series of electrical units in the CENTIMETRE-GRAM-SECOND system based primarily on forces of interaction between electric charges

**electrosurgery** /i,lektroh'suhjəri, -'--,---/ *n* surgery involving the use of electricity, esp the use of a high-frequency ALTERNATING CURRENT of electricity to cut through tissue – **electrosurgical** *adj*

**electrotherapy** /i,lektrə'therəpi, -troh-/ *n* treatment of disease involving the use of electricity (e g to generate heat in tissue)

**electrothermal** /i,lektrə'thuhməl/, **electrothermic** /-'thuhmik/ *adj* relating to or combining electricity and heat; *specif* relating to the generation of heat by electricity – **electrothermally** *adv*

**electrotonus** /i,lek'trotənəs, ,eelek/ *n* the altered sensitivity of a nerve to stimuli when a constant current of electricity passes through any part of it [NL] – **electrotonic** *adj*

**¹electrotype** /i'lektrə,tiep/ *n* **1** a duplicate printing surface made from a plastic mould of the surface to be reproduced on which a thin shell of typically copper is deposited by ELECTROPLATING and then backed with lead **2** a copy of a coin made by an ELECTROPLATING process

**²electrotype** *vt* to make an electrotype from (a printing surface) ~ *vi* to be reproducible by electrotyping – **electrotyper** *n*

**electrovalency** /i,lektroh'vaylənsi/, *chiefly NAm* **electrovalence** *n* the ability of an atom to lose or gain one or more electrons to form an ION (electrically charged atom) that can be linked to another by an ELECTROVALENT BOND; *also* the number of positive or negative charges possessed by an atom following the loss or gain of electrons – **electrovalent** *adj*

**electrovalent bond** /i,lektroh'vaylənt/ *n* a chemical bond formed by the attraction between IONS (electrically charged atoms or groups of atoms) having opposite electric charges – called also IONIC BOND

**electrowinning** /i'lektroh,wining/ *n* the recovery of esp a metal from a solution by ELECTROLYSIS (passage of an electric current through the solution)

**electrum** /i'lektrəm/ *n* a natural pale yellow alloy of gold and silver [ME, fr L – more at ELECTRIC]

**eleemosynary** /,eli·i'mosin(ə)ri/ *adj, formal* of, supported by, or giving charity [ML *eleemosynarius*, fr LL *eleemosyna* alms – more at ALMS]

**elegant** /'elig(ə)nt/ *adj* **1** gracefully refined or dignified (e g in manners, taste, or style) **2** tastefully rich or luxurious, esp in design or ornamentation ⟨~ *furnishings*⟩ **3** *of ideas* neat and simple ⟨*an* ~ *piece of reasoning*⟩ ⟨*an* ~ *mathematical proof*⟩ [MF or L; MF, fr L *elegant-, elegans*; akin to L *eligere* to select – more at ELECT] – **elegantly** *adv*, **elegance** *n*

**elegiac** /,eli'jie·ək/ *also* **elegiacal** /-ikal/ *adj* **1** written in or consisting of elegiac couplets **2** of or comprising (an) elegy; *esp* expressing sorrow, often for something now past ⟨*an* ~ *lament for departed youth*⟩ [LL *elegiacus*, fr Gk *elegeiakos*, fr *elegeion*] – **elegiac** *n*, **elegiacally** *adv*

**elegiac couplet** /,eli'jie·ək/ *n* a verse form from Greek and Roman poetry consisting of a line made up of six units followed by one made up of five units, each unit of which has a rhythm of one stressed syllable and two unstressed syllables

**elegiac stanza** *n* a group of four lines of verse, each of which is made up of five units that have a rhythm of one unstressed syllable followed by one stressed syllable, and of which the first and third and the second and fourth lines rhyme

**eleg·ize**, **-ise** /'eləjiez/ *vi* to lament or celebrate someone or something in an elegy ~ *vt* to write an elegy on – **elegist** *n*

**elegy** /'eləji/ *n* **1a** a song, poem, or other work expressing sorrow or lamentation, esp for one who is dead **b** a pensive or reflective poem that is usu nostalgic or melancholy **c** a short pensive musical composition **2** a poem in elegiac couplets □ compare EULOGY [L *elegia* poem in elegiac couplets, fr Gk *elegeia, elegeion*, fr *elegos* song of mourning]

**element** /'eləmənt/ *n* **1a** any of the four substances air, water, fire, and earth formerly believed to compose the physical universe **b** *pl* forces of nature; *esp* violent or severe weather ⟨*exposed to the* ~ *s*⟩ **c** the state or sphere natural or suited to someone or something ⟨*at school she was in her* ~⟩ **2** a constituent part e g **2a** *pl* the simplest principles of a subject of study; the rudiments **b** *maths* **b(1)** an expression (e g $dx$ in $_0\int^1 x^2 dx$) that is regarded as a quantity which is too small to be measured **b(2)** a shape that when subjected to one or more mathematical operations yields a shape formed of regular lines, curves, and angles ⟨*lines, points, and surfaces are geometrical* ~s⟩ **b(3)** a member of a set of objects, numbers, words, etc (e g a chair in a row of chairs) **b(4)** any of the numbers or symbols in a mathematical array (e g a matrix) **c element** *taking sing or pl vb*, **elements** *pl* a specified group within a human community ⟨*the criminal* ~ *in the city*⟩ ⟨*the smart* ~⟩ **d(1)** any of the necessary data or values on which calculations or conclusions are based **d(2)** any of the factors determining an outcome **e** *chemistry* any of more than 100 fundamental substances that consist of atoms of only one kind and that singly or in combination constitute all matter **f** a distinct part of a composite device; *esp* the part of an electric device (e g a heater or kettle) that contains the heating wire through which an electric current passes **g** MEMBER 4d **3** something present in a small quantity; a hint ⟨*there is an* ~ *of truth in what he said*⟩ **4** *pl* the bread and wine used in Communion [ME, fr OF & L; OF, fr L *elementum*]

**elemental** /,eli'mentl/ *adj* **1a** of or being an element; *specif* existing as an uncombined chemical element **b** of or being the basic or ultimate constituent of something; essential **2** of or resembling a great force of nature ⟨*the rains came with* ~ *violence*⟩ ⟨~ *passions*⟩ **3** *chiefly NAm* ELEMENTARY 1a,b – **elemental** *n*, **elementally** *adv*

**elementary** /,eli'ment(ə)ri/ *adj* **1a** of or dealing with the simplest elements or principles of something; simple ⟨*can't handle the most* ~ *decision-making*⟩ **b** of an elementary school ⟨*an* ~ *curriculum*⟩ **2** ELEMENTAL 1 – **elementarily** *adv*, **elementariness** *n*

**elementary body** *n* a distinguishable unit occurring in a cell in some virus infections that is probably the infective particle of the virus

**elementary particle** *n* any of the minute constituents of all matter and energy (e g the electron, proton, or photon) that are smaller and less complex than atoms; *esp* one whose nature has not yet been proved to be due to the combination of other more basic entities

**elementary school** *n* a state school that took children from the age of five to 13 or 14

**elemi** /'eləmi/ *n* any of various fragrant semisolid oils and resin mixtures obtained from tropical trees (family Burseraceae) and used chiefly in varnishes, lacquers, and printing inks [NL *elimi*]

**elenchus** /i'lengkəs/ *n, pl* **elenchi** /-ki/ *philosophy* a proof that a theory, argument, etc is wrong; *esp* one derived by deductive reasoning that has progressed from a general to a particular statement [L, fr Gk *elenchos* cross-examination, refutation, fr *elenchein* to shame, cross-examine, refute]

**elephant** /'elifənt/ *n* any of various very large nearly hairless mammals that constitute, with related extinct forms, a family (Elephantidae, the elephant family) and have the snout prolonged into a muscular trunk and two teeth in the upper jaw developed, esp in the male, into long ivory tusks; *broadly* any living or extinct animal of the elephant family [ME, fr OF & L; OF *olifant* elephant, ivory, fr L *elephantus*, fr Gk *elephant-, elephas*]

**elephant grass** *n* a tall tropical reedlike marsh plant (*Typha elephantina*) of the reedmace family used esp in making baskets

**elephantiasis** /,elifən'tie·əsis/ *n, pl* **elephantiases** /-seez/ enlargement and swelling of tissues; *specif* the enormous enlargement of a limb or the scrotum caused by obstruction, esp by FILARIAL worms (parasitic round-bodied worms), of the vessels carrying LYMPH [NL, fr L, a kind of leprosy, fr Gk, fr *elephant-, elephas*]

**elephantine** /,eli'fantien/ *adj* **1a** huge, massive **b** clumsy, ponderous **2** of an elephant *synonyms* see HUGE *antonyms* petite, dainty, elfin

**elephant seal** *n* a nearly extinct large seal (*Mirounga angustirostris*) that has a long trunklike snout and was formerly abundant along the coast of California; *also* a related seal (*Mirounga leonina*) formerly abundant on coasts of the S hemisphere

**elephant shrew** *n* any of several long-legged long-nosed African shrews (family Macroscelididae)

**Eleusinian mysteries** /,elyoo'sini·ən/ *n pl* secret religious rites believed to give long-lasting happiness that were celebrated at ancient Eleusis in worship of the Greek goddess Demeter and her daughter Persephone [*Eleusis*, city in ancient Greece]

**¹elevate** /'elivayt/ *adj, archaic* elevated

**²elevate** *vt* **1** to lift up; raise **2** to raise in rank or status; exalt **3** to improve morally, intellectually, or culturally **4** to raise the spirits of; elate *synonyms* see ¹LIFT *antonym* lower [ME *elevaten*, fr L *elevatus*, pp of *elevare*, fr *e-* + *levare* to raise – more at LEVER]

**¹elevated** /'elivaytid/ *adj* **1** raised, esp above a surface (e g the ground) ⟨*an* ~ *road*⟩ **2a** morally or intellectually on a high plane; lofty ⟨~ *thoughts*⟩ **b** formal, dignified ⟨~ *prose*⟩ **3** exhilarated in mood or feeling **4** slightly tipsy – no longer in vogue

**²elevated** *n, NAm* OVERHEAD RAILWAY

**elevation** /,eli'vaysh(ə)n/ *n* **1** the height to which something is elevated: e g **1a** the angle at which a gun is aimed above the horizon **b** the height above sea level; altitude **2** a ballet dancer's or a skater's leap and seeming suspension in the air; *also* the ability to achieve such an elevation **3** an act or instance of elevating **4** something elevated: e g **4a** an elevated place **b** a swelling, esp on the skin **5** the quality or state of being elevated **6** a representation drawn to scale of the front, back, or sides of a building **7** *often cap* the lifting up of one or both of the consecrated bread and wine during Communion in the view of the congregation – **elevational** *adj*

**elevator** /'eli,vaytə/ *n* **1** one who or that which raises or lifts something up: e g **1a** an endless belt or chain conveyor with scoops or buckets for raising grain, liquids, etc **b** *chiefly NAm* a lift **c** *NAm* a building for elevating, storing, discharging, and sometimes processing grain **2** a movable horizontal surface usu attached to the small winglike part (TAILPLANE) at the rear of an aircraft for controlling climb and descent

**eleven** /i'lev(ə)n/ *n* **1** – see NUMBER table **2** the 11th in a set or series **3** *taking sing or pl vb* something having 11 parts or members or a denomination of 11; *esp* a cricket, soccer, or hockey team [ME *enleven*, fr *enleven*, adj, fr OE *endleofan;* akin to OHG *einlif* eleven; both fr a prehistoric Gmc compound whose first element is akin to OE *ān* one, and whose second is prob akin to OE *lēon* to lend] – **eleven** *adj or pron,* **elevenfold** *adj or adv,* **eleventh** *adj or n*

**e,leven-'plus, 11-plus** *n* an examination taken, esp formerly, at the age of 10-11 to determine which type of British state secondary education a child should receive

**elevenses** /i'levənziz/ *n taking sing or pl vb, Br* light refreshment (e g a snack or hot drink) taken in the middle of the morning, traditionally around 11 am [irreg pl of *eleven* (o'clock)]

**eleventh hour** /i'levənth/ *n the* latest possible time ⟨*won his reprieve at the* ~⟩ [fr Christ's parable of labourers in a vineyard (Mt 20)] – **eleventh-hour** *adj*

**elevon** /'elivon/ *n* a movable surface on the wing of esp a delta-winged aircraft that combines the functions of an elevator controlling climb and descent and an AILERON giving lateral control [*elevat*or + *aileron*]

**elf** /elf/ *n, pl* **elves** /elvz/ **1** a fairy; *esp* a mischievous one **2** a small creature (e g a mischievous child) [ME, fr OE *ælf;* akin to ON *alfr* elf] – **elfish** *adj,* **elfishly** *adv*

**¹elfin** /'elfin/ *adj* **1** of or resembling an elf, esp in being small, sprightly, or impish **2** having an otherworldly or magical quality or charm; fey [irreg fr *elf*]

**²elfin** *n, archaic* an elf, dwarf

**'elf-,lock** *n usu pl* a matted lock of hair [fr the former belief that it was caused by elves]

**elicit** /i'lisit/ *vt* **1a** to draw forth or bring out (something latent or potential) **b** to derive (e g a truth) by logical processes **2** to call forth or draw out (a response or reaction); evoke △ illicit [L *elicitus*, pp of *elicere*, fr *e-* + *lacere* to allure – more at DELIGHT] – **elicitor** *n,* **elicitation** *n*

**elide** /i'lied/ *vt* **1** to suppress or alter (e g a vowel or syllable) by elision **2** to strike out (e g a written word or passage) [L *elidere* to strike out, fr *e-* + *laedere* to injure by striking (cf COLLIDE)]

**eligible** /'elijəbl/ *adj* **1** qualified to be chosen; *also* entitled ⟨~ *for promotion*⟩ ⟨~ *to retire*⟩ **2** worthy or desirable, esp as a marriage partner ⟨*an* ~ *young bachelor*⟩ △ illegible [ME, fr MF & LL; MF, fr LL *eligibilis*, fr L *eligere* to choose – more at ELECT] – **eligibility** *n,* **eligible** *n,* **eligibly** *adv*

**eliminate** /i'limi,nayt/ *vt* **1a(1)** to cast out or get rid of completely; eradicate ⟨*the need to* ~ *poverty*⟩ **a(2)** to set aside as unimportant; ignore **b** to expel (e g waste) from the living body **c** to remove (a competitor, team, etc) from a competition, usu by defeat **2** *maths* to cause (a quantity) to not appear in an equation by combining two or more equations **3** *euph* to kill (a person), esp so as to remove as an obstacle [L *eliminatus*, pp of *eliminare* to put out of doors, fr *e-* + *limin-, limen* threshold] – **eliminator** *n,* **eliminative** *adj,* **elimination** *n*

**Elinvar** /'elin,vah/ *trademark* – used for an iron alloy containing nickel and chromium and showing only a very small degree of expansion when subjected to heat

**elision** /i'lizh(ə)n/ *n* **1** omission of a vowel or syllable in pronunciation or in writing (e g *I'm* for *I am*) **2** the act or an instance of eliding; omission [LL *elision-, elisio*, fr L *elisus*, pp of *elidere*]

**élite, elite** /i'leet, ay-/ *n* **1** *taking sing or pl vb* a relatively small intellectually, professionally, or socially superior group that has a power out of proportion to its size; *broadly* the choice part of a group – compare ELECT **2** a typewriter type providing 12 characters to the inch [Fr *élite*, fr OF *eslite*, fr fem of *eslit*, pp of *eslire* to choose, fr L *eligere* – more at ELECT] – **élite** *adj*

**élitism, elitism** /-,tiz(ə)m/ *n* **1** (advocacy of) leadership or rule by an élite **2** consciousness of being or belonging to an élite – **élitist** *n or adj*

**elixir** /i'liksə, -siə/ *n* **1** an alchemist's substance supposedly capable of changing inferior metals into gold **2a elixir, elixir of life** a substance held capable of prolonging life indefinitely **b** a cure-all **3** a sweetened liquid (e g a syrup), containing a drug or medicine [ME, fr ML, fr Ar *al-iksīr* the elixir, fr *al* the + *iksīr* elixir, prob fr Gk *xērion* powder for drying wounds, fr *xēros* dry]

**Elizabethan** /i,lizə'beeth(ə)n/ *adj* (characteristic of) (the age of) Elizabeth I [*Elizabeth* I †1603 Queen of England] – **Elizabethan** *n*

**elk** /elk/ *n, pl* **elks**, *esp collectively* **elk** **1** the largest existing deer (*Alces alces*) of Europe and Asia that resembles but is smaller than the moose of N America, which belongs to the same species **2** *NAm* WAPITI (large American deer) [ME, prob fr OE *eolh;* akin to OHG *elaho* elk, Gk *elaphos* deer]

**elkhound** /-,hownd/ *n* (any of) a Norwegian breed of medium-sized hunting dogs with a very heavy grey coat tipped with black

**¹ell** /el/ *n* (any of various units of length similar in use to) a former English unit of length equal to 45 inches (about 1.14 metres) that was used chiefly for cloth [ME *eln*, fr OE; akin to ON *eln* forearm, ell, L *ulna* elbow, arm]

**²ell** *n* **1** an elbow in a pipe, channel, or tube **2** *NAm* an extension at right angles to the length of a building [alter. of *el* (the letter *l*)]

**ellipse** /i'lips/ *n* **1** a two-dimensional closed curve generated by a point moving such that the sum of its distances from two fixed points (FOCUSES) is constant; the intersection of a plane cutting obliquely through a cone – compare HYPERBOLA, PARABOLA 2 an ellipsis [Gk *elleipsis*]

**ellipsis** /i'lipsis/ *n*, *pl* **ellipses** /-seez/ 1 the omission of one or more words that are obviously understood but that must be supplied to make a construction grammatically complete ⟨*"the man that he sees" may be changed by* ∼ *to "the man he sees"*⟩ – see "Ten Vexed Points" 2 marks or a mark (eg ... or *** or m) indicating the omission of letters or words [L, fr Gk *elleipsis* ellipsis, ellipse, fr *elleipein* to leave out, fall short, fr *en* in + *leipein* to leave – more at IN, LOAN]

**ellipsoid** /i'lipsoyd/ *n* 1 a closed solid or surface obtained by rotating an ellipse about one of its axes: 1a OBLATE b PROLATE 2 something shaped roughly like an ellipsoid; a somewhat flattened sphere ⟨*the earth is an* ∼⟩ – compare HYPERBOLOID, PARABOLOID – **ellipsoid, ellipsoidal** *adj*

**elliptic** /i'liptik/, **elliptical** *adj* 1a of or shaped like an ellipse b of or being a geometry or space in which there are no lines parallel to some given line 2a of or marked by ellipsis or an ellipsis b(1) *of speech or writing* extremely or excessively concise b(2) consciously obscure in literary style [Gk *elleiptikos* defective, marked by ellipsis, fr *elleipein*] – **elliptically** *adv*, **ellipticity** *n*

**elm** /elm/ *n* 1 any of a genus (*Ulmus* of the family Ulmaceae, the elm family) of large graceful deciduous trees with serrated leaves and small light disc-shaped fruit each having a single usu off-centre seed 2 the wood of an elm [ME, fr OE; akin to OHG *elme* elm, L *ulmus*]

**elm bark beetle** *n* either of two European beetles (*Scolytus multistriatus* and *Scolytus scolytus*) that, by boring into the bark of elm trees, spread the fungus causing DUTCH ELM DISEASE

**elm blight** *n* DUTCH ELM DISEASE

**elocute** /'eləkyooht/ *vb*, *humorous* to deliver (words) rhetorically; *specif* to recite (something) in elocution [back-formation fr *elocution*]

**elocution** /,elə'kyoohsh(ə)n/ *n* 1 the art of effective public speaking 2 the cultivation of good diction [ME *elocucioun*, fr L *elocution-, elocutio*, fr *elocutus*, pp of *eloqui*] – **elocutionary** *adj*, **elocutionist** *n*

**elodea** /i'lohdiə/ *n* any of a small genus (*Elodea* of the family Hydrocharitaceae) of submerged aquatic plants; *esp* CANADIAN PONDWEED [NL, genus name, fr Gk *helōdēs* marshy, fr *helos* marsh; akin to Skt *saras* pond]

**eloign** /i'loyn/ *vt*, *archaic* 1 to take (oneself) far away 2 to remove to a distant or unknown place; conceal [ME *eloynen*, fr MF *esloigner*, fr OF, fr *es-* ex- (fr L *ex-*) + *loing* (adv) far, fr L *longe*, fr *longus* long]

¹**elongate** /'elong,gayt, 'ee-/ *vt* to extend the length of ∼ *vi* to grow in length [LL *elongatus*, pp of *elongare* to remove, withdraw, lengthen, fr L *e-* + *longe* far, or (in the last sense) *longus* long]

²**elongate, elongated** *adj* 1 stretched out; lengthened 2 *biology* long in proportion to width; slender

**elongation** /,elong'gaysh(ə)n, ,ee-/ *n* 1a the distance, measured in degrees, of a planet, moon, etc from a body round which it revolves or from a particular point in the sky b the daily extreme east or west position of a star with reference to the north CELESTIAL POLE (one of two points round which stars appear to rotate) 2a the state of being elongated b something elongated

**elope** /i'lohp/ *vi* 1a to run away from one's husband with a lover b to run away secretly with the intention of getting married or cohabiting, usu without parental consent 2 to slip away; escape, abscond [AF *aloper*] – **elopement** *n*, **eloper** *n*

**eloquence** /'eləkwəns/ *n* discourse marked by fluency, force, and persuasiveness; *also* the art or power of using such discourse

**eloquent** /'eləkwənt/ *adj* 1 marked by eloquence ⟨*an* ∼ *exposition of the subject*⟩ 2 vividly or movingly expressive or revealing ⟨*put his arm round her in an* ∼ *gesture of reassurance*⟩ ⟨*a gesture* ∼ *of his true feelings*⟩ [ME, fr MF, fr L *eloquent-, eloquens*, fr prp of *eloqui* to speak out, fr *e-* + *loqui* to speak] – **eloquently** *adv*

**Elsan** /'el,san/ *trademark* – used for a type of esp portable toilet in which chemicals are used to kill bacteria and mask the smell

**else** /els/ *adv* 1a apart from the person, place, manner, or time mentioned or understood ⟨*how* ∼ *could he have acted*⟩ ⟨*everybody* ∼ *but me*⟩ b also, besides ⟨*who* ∼ *did you see*⟩ ⟨*there's nothing* ∼ *to eat*⟩ 2 if the facts are or were different; if not; otherwise ⟨*do what you are told or* ∼ *you'll be sorry*⟩ ⟨*must be coming; they'd have phoned* ∼⟩ – used absolutely to express

a threat ⟨*do what I tell you or* ∼⟩ □ (1) used after question words and some pronouns and adverbs [ME *elles*, fr OE; akin to L *alius* other, *alter* other of two, Gk *allos* other]

**usage** 1 The usual possessive forms are *anybody/everybody/nobody/somebody* **else's**, but there is a choice between *who* **else's** and the more formal *whose* **else** ⟨*who* **else's**/*whose* **else** *can I borrow?*⟩ 2 Some writers on usage, advise that **else** should be followed by *than* rather than by *but*, or that **else** *than* should be replaced by *other than*, but all constructions are common ⟨*nothing* **else** *than/but a change of government*⟩ ⟨*anybody other than Peter*⟩.

**elsewhere** /-'weə/ *adv* in or to another place ⟨*took his business* ∼⟩

**eluant, eluent** /'elyoo·ənt/ *n* a solvent used in eluting [L *eluent-, eluens*, prp of *eluere*]

**eluate** /'elyoo·ət, -,ayt/ *n* the washings obtained by eluting [L *eluere* + E *-ate*]

**elucidate** /i'loohsi,dayt/ *vt* to make lucid, esp by explanation ∼ *vi* to give a clarifying explanation [LL *elucidatus*, pp of *elucidare*, fr L *e-* + *lucidus* lucid] – **elucidative** *adj*, **elucidator** *n*, **elucidation** *n*

**elucubrate** /i'loohk(y)əbrayt/ *vt*, *formal* to work out or express by studious effort [L *elucubratus*, pp of *elucubrare* to compose by lamplight, fr *e-* + *lucubrare* to work by lamplight – more at LUCUBRATION ] – **elucubration** *n*

**elude** /i'l(y)oohd/ *vt* 1 to avoid cunningly or adroitly 2 to escape the memory, understanding, or notice of *synonyms* see ¹ESCAPE [L *eludere*, fr *e-* + *ludere* to play – more at LUDICROUS] – **elusion** *n*

**Elul** /e'loohl/ *n* – see MONTH table [Heb *Elūl*]

**elusive** /i'loohsiv/ *adj* tending to elude: eg a tending to evade grasp or pursuit ⟨*an eligible though* ∼ *bachelor*⟩ b hard to comprehend, define, isolate, or identify ⟨*an* ∼ *concept*⟩ ⟨*an* ∼ *aroma*⟩ □ compare ILLUSIVE [L *elusus*, pp of *eludere*] – **elusively** *adv*, **elusiveness** *n*

**elute** /ee'l(y)ooht/ *vt* to extract; *specif* to remove (ADSORBED material) from the surface of a liquid or solid by means of a solvent [L *elutus*, pp of *eluere* to wash out, fr *e-* + *lavere* to wash – more at LYE] – **elution** *n*

**elutriate** /ee'l(y)oohtri,ayt/ *vt* to purify, separate, or remove by washing [L *elutriatus*, pp of *elutriare*, irreg fr *elutus*] – **elutriator** *n*

**eluvial** /i'l(y)oohviəl, ee-/ *adj* 1 (composed) of eluvium 2 of eluviation or eluviated materials or areas

**eluviate** /i'l(y)oohviayt, ee-/ *vi* to undergo eluviation

**eluviation** /i,l(y)oohvi'aysh(ə)n, ee-/ *n* the transportation of dissolved or suspended material within the soil by the action of rainwater when the amount of rainfall exceeds the quantity of water evaporating from the soil surface

**eluvium** /ee'l(y)oohvi·əm, i-, -vyəm/ *n* rock debris produced by the weathering and disintegration of rock in situ [NL, fr L *eluere* to wash out]

**elver** /'elvə/ *n* a young eel [alter. of *eelfare* (migration of eels)]

**elves** /elvz/ *pl of* ELF

**elvish** /'elvish/ *adj* 1 of elves 2 elfish

**elysian** /i'liziən/ *adj*, *often cap* 1 of Elysium 2 blissful, delightful

**elysian fields** /i'liziən/ *n pl*, *often cap* E Elysium

**Elysium** /i'lizi·əm/ *n*, *pl* **Elysiums, Elysia** /-ziə/ 1 the home of the blessed after death in Greek mythology 2 a place of bliss, happiness, or delight; a paradise [L, fr Gk *Elysion*]

**elytr-, elytri-, elytro-** *comb form* elytron ⟨*elytroid*⟩ ⟨*elytriferous*⟩ [NL *elytron*]

**elytron** /'elitron/ *n*, *pl* **elytra** /-trə/ either of the modified stiffened front pair of wings in certain insects (eg beetles and cockroaches) that cover and protect the hind pair of functional wings when at rest [NL *elytron, elytrum*, fr Gk *elytron* sheath, wing cover, fr *eilyein* to roll, wrap – more at VOLUBLE]

**elytrum** /'elitrəm/ *n*, *pl* **elytra** /-trə/ an elytron

**em, m** /em/ *n* 1 the width of the body of a piece of type bearing the letter M, used as a unit of measure of printed matter 2 ¹PICA 2 (unit of measure in typeset material)

**em-** /im-, em-/ – see EN-

**'em** /(ə)m/ *pron* them – used in writing to suggest casual speech

**emaciate** /i'maysi,ayt/ *vt* 1 to cause to become excessively thin 2 to make feeble ∼ *vi* to waste away physically [L *emaciatus*, pp of *emaciare*, fr *e-* + *macies* leanness, fr *macer* lean – more at MEAGRE] – **emaciation** *n*

**emalangeni** /,emələn'geni/ *pl of* LILANGENI

**emanate** /'emə,nayt/ *vi* to come out from a source ⟨*a foul smell* ∼d *from the sewer*⟩ ⟨*rumours emanating from high* *places*⟩ ~ *vt* to send out; emit; GIVE OFF ⟨*some radioactive substances* ~ *dangerous radiation for many centuries*⟩ ⟨~d *serenity*⟩ [L *emanatus*, pp of *emanare*, fr *e-* + *manare* to flow]

**emanation** /ˌemə'naysh(ə)n/ *n* **1a** the action of emanating **b** a philosophical theory that views the creation of all things as being through a series of outpourings of beings of descending perfection from God **2a** something that emanates or is produced by emanating; an effluence **b** a heavy gaseous product of radioactive disintegration; *specif* RADON – not now used technically – **emanational** *adj*, **emanative** *adj*

**emancipate** /i'mansi,payt/ *vt* to free from restraint, control, or the power of another; *esp* to free from slavery [L *emancipatus*, pp of *emancipare*, fr *e-* + *mancipare* to transfer ownership of, fr *mancip-, manceps* purchaser, fr *manus* hand + *capere* to take – more at MANUAL, HEAVE] – **emancipation** *n*, **emancipationist** *n*, **emancipator** *n*

**emarginate** /i'mahjinayt/ *adj, botany* having the edge notched, esp at the tip ⟨*an* ~ *leaf*⟩ [L *emarginatus*, pp of *emarginare* to deprive of a margin, fr *e-* + *margin-, margo* margin] – **emargination** *n*

**emasculate** /i'maskyoo,layt/ *vt* **1** to castrate **2** to deprive of strength, vigour, or spirit; weaken **3** to remove the male reproductive organs of (a flower) to prevent self-pollination and allow artificial pollination by a selected plant [L *emasculatus*, pp of *emasculare*, fr *e-* + *masculus* male – more at MALE] – **emasculate** *adj*, **emasculator** *n*, **emasculation** *n*

**embalm** /im'bahm/ *vt* **1** to treat (a dead body) so as to give protection against decay **2** to protect from decay or oblivion; preserve **3** *poetic* to fill with sweet odours; perfume [ME *embaumen*, fr MF *embaumer*, fr OF *embasmer*, fr *en-* + *basme* balm – more at BALM] – **embalmer** *n*, **embalmment** *n*

**embank** /im'bangk/ *vt* to enclose or confine by an embankment

**embankment** /im'bangkmənt/ *n* **1** the action of embanking **2** a raised structure to hold back water or to carry a roadway or railway

**¹embargo** /im'bahgoh/ *n, pl* **embargoes** **1** an order of a government prohibiting the departure of commercial ships from its ports **2** a legal prohibition on commerce ⟨*an* ~ *on arms shipments*⟩ **3** a stoppage, impediment; *esp* a prohibition ⟨*I lay no* ~ *on anybody's words* – Jane Austen⟩ [Sp, fr *embargar* to bar, fr (assumed) VL *imbarricare*, fr L *in-* + (assumed) VL *barra* bar]

**²embargo** *vt* to place an embargo on (e g ships or commerce)

**embark** /im'bahk/ *vt* **1** to cause to go on board a boat or aircraft **2** to engage, enlist, or invest (e g people or funds) in an enterprise ~ *vi* **1** to go on board a boat or aircraft for transportation **2** to make a start; commence – usu + *on* or *upon* ⟨~ *ed on a new career*⟩ [MF *embarquer*, fr OProv *embarcar*, fr *em-* (fr L *im-*) + *barca* ⁵bark] – **embarkment** *n*, **embarkation** *n*

**embarrass** /im'barəs/ *vt* **1a** to place in doubt, perplexity, or difficulties **b** to involve in financial difficulties, esp debt **c** to cause to experience a state of self-conscious distress; disconcert ⟨*bawdy stories* ~ed *her*⟩ **2** to impair the activity of (a body function) or the function of (a body part) ⟨*the blood supply to the brain was* ~ed⟩ **3** *archaic* to hamper the movement of; hinder, impede [Fr *embarrasser*, fr Sp *embarazar*, prob deriv of L *in-* + (assumed) VL *barra* bar] – **embarrassable** *adj*, **embarrassedly** *adv*

**embarrassingly** /im'barəsingli/ *adv* **1** to an embarrassing degree **2** in an embarrassing manner

**embarrassment** /im'barəsmənt/ *n* **1** the state of being embarrassed **2** difficulty in functioning as a result of disease **3a** something that embarrasses; an impediment **b** an excessive quantity from which to select – chiefly in *embarrassment of riches*

**embassage** /'embəsij/ *n, archaic* an embassy

**embassy** /'embəsi/ *n* **1a** the function or position of an ambassador **b** an ambassador's official mission abroad **2** a body of diplomatic representatives; *specif* one headed by an ambassador **3** the official residence and offices of an ambassador [MF *ambassee*, of Gmc origin; akin to OHG *ambaht* service]

**¹embattle** /im'batl/ *vt* **1** to prepare (an army) for battle **2** to fortify (a town, position, etc) against attack [ME *embatailen*, fr MF *embatailler*, fr *en-* + *batailler* to battle]

**²embattle** *vt* to provide (a building) with battlements ⟨*an* ~d *facade*⟩ [ME *embatailen*, fr *en-* + *batailen* to fortify with battlements]

**embattled** /im'batəld/ *adj* hemmed in by adversaries, difficulties, etc

**embay** /im'bay/ *vt* to enclose or shelter (as if) in a bay ⟨*an* ~ed *fleet*⟩

**embayed** /im'bayd/ *adj* formed into bays ⟨*an* ~ *shoreline*⟩

**embayment** /im'baymənt/ *n* **1** the formation of a bay **2** a bay or a geographical conformation resembling a bay

**embed** /im'bed/ *vb* **-dd-** *vt* **1a** to enclose closely (as if) in a matrix ⟨*pebbles* ~ded *in silt*⟩ **b** to make (something) an integral part of a whole ⟨*the tales of his courage that have become* ~ded *in folk lore*⟩ **c** to prepare (a microscope specimen) for cutting into very thin slices suitable for examination under the microscope, by infiltrating with and enclosing in a supporting substance (e g paraffin wax) **2** to place or fix firmly (as if) in surrounding matter ⟨*a splinter was* ~ded *in his finger*⟩ ⟨*hate was* ~ded *in their hearts*⟩ ~ *vi* to become embedded – **embedment** *n*

**embellish** /im'belish/ *vt* **1** to make beautiful by adding ornaments; decorate **2** to make (speech or writing) more interesting by the addition of fictitious or exaggerated detail ⟨*events in his life, heavily* ~ed *by his biographers* – Marvin Reznikoff⟩ *synonyms* see DECORATE [ME *embelisshen*, fr MF *embeliss-*, stem of *embelir*, fr *en-* + *bel* beautiful – more at BEAUTY] – **embellisher** *n*

**embellishment** /im'belishmənt/ *n* **1** the act or process of embellishing **2** one who or that which embellishes **3** ORNAMENT **3** (musical note included as ornamentation)

**ember** /'embə/ *n* **1** a glowing fragment (e g of coal or wood) in a fire; *esp* one smouldering in ashes **2** *pl* the smouldering remains of a fire **3** *pl* slowly cooling emotions, memories, ideas, or responses still capable of being enlivened [ME *eymere*, fr ON *eimyrja*; akin to OE *æmerge* ashes]

**ember day** *n* a day set aside for fasting and prayer in Anglican and Roman Catholic churches, that falls on the Wednesday, Friday, or Saturday following the first Sunday in Lent, Whitsunday, September 14, or December 13 [ME, fr OE *ymbrendæg*, fr *ymbrene* circuit, anniversary + *dæg* day]

**embezzle** /im'bezl/ *vt* to appropriate (e g property entrusted to one's care) fraudulently to one's own use [ME *embesilen*, fr AF *embeseiller*, fr MF *en-* + *besillier* to destroy] – **embezzlement** *n*, **embezzler** *n*

**embiopteran** /ˌembi'optərən/ *n* WEB SPINNER (type of small slender insect) [deriv of GK having life + *pteron* wing]

**embitter** /im'bitə/ *vt* **1** to make bitter **2** to cause bitter feelings in – **embitterment** *n*

**emblaze** /im'blayz/ *vt* **1** *poetic* to embellish, adorn ⟨*with gems and golden lustre rich* ~d – John Milton⟩ **2** *archaic* EMBLAZON 2a(2) [*en-* + *blaze* (to blazon)]

**emblazon** /im'blayz(ə)n/ *vt* **1** to display conspicuously **2a(1)** to deck in bright colours **a(2)** to inscribe, adorn, or decorate with heraldic arms, signs, or emblems **a(3)** to depict (heraldic arms) **b** to celebrate, extol ⟨*have his . . . deeds* ~ed *by a poet* – Thomas Nashe⟩ – **emblazoner** *n*, **emblazonment** *n*, **emblazonry** *n*

**¹emblem** /'embləm/ *n* **1** an object or a typical representation of an object symbolizing and suggesting another object or idea; a symbol **2** a design, symbol, or figure adopted and used as an identifying mark [ME, fr L *emblema* inlaid work, fr Gk *emblēmat-, emblēma*, fr *emballein* to insert, fr *en-* + *ballein* to throw – more at DEVIL]

**²emblem** *vt* to emblematize

**emblematic** /ˌemblə'matik/ *also* **emblematical** /-tikl/ *adj* of or being an emblem; symbolic – **emblematically** *adv*

**emblemat·ize, -ise** /em'blemə,tiez/ *vt* to represent (as if) by an emblem; symbolize

**emblements** /'embləmənts, 'emblmənts/ *n pl* crops from annual cultivation that used legally to belong to the tenant [ME *emblayment*, fr MF *emblaement*, fr *emblaer* to sow with grain, fr *en-* + *blee* grain]

**embodiment** /im'bodimənt/ *n* **1** embodying or being embodied **2** one who or that which embodies something ⟨*the* ~ *of all our hopes*⟩

**embody** /im'bodi/ *vt* **1** to give a body to (a spirit); incarnate **2** to make (e g ideas or concepts) concrete and perceptible ⟨*a chapter which embodies his new theory*⟩ **3** to make (e g connected ideas or principles) a part of a body or system; incorporate, include – usu + *in* ⟨*their way of life is embodied in their laws*⟩ **4** to represent in human or animal form; personify ⟨*men who embodied the idealism of the revolution*⟩ – **embodier** *n*

**embol-, emboli-, embolo-** *comb form* embolus ⟨*embolectomy*⟩ [NL, fr *embolus*]

**embolden** /im'bohld(ə)n/ *vt* to make bold or courageous

**embolectomy** /ˌembə'lektəmi/ *n* surgical removal of an embolus

**embolic** /em'bolik/ *adj* of an embolus or embolism

**embolism** /'embəliz(ə)m/ *n* **1** the insertion of one or more days in a calendar **2a** the sudden obstruction of a blood vessel by an embolus **b** an embolus [(1) ME *embolisme*, fr ML *embolismus*, fr Gk *embol-* (fr *emballein* to insert, intercalate) – more at EMBLEM; (2) NL *embolismus*, fr ML] – **embolismic** *adj*

**embol·ization, -isation** /ˌembəlie'zaysh(ə)n/ *n* the process or state in which a blood vessel or organ is obstructed by the lodging of a mass of material (e g an embolus)

**embolus** /'embələs/ *n, pl* **emboli** /-li, -lie/ a blood clot, air bubble, or other particle circulating abnormally in the blood and likely to become lodged in and cause obstruction of a blood vessel – compare THROMBUS [NL, fr Gk *embolos* wedge-shaped object, stopper, fr *emballein*]

**emboly** /'embəli/ *n* INVAGINATION 2 [Gk *embolē* insertion, fr *emballein*]

**embonpoint** /ˌombom'pwanh/ (*Fr* ãbɔ̃pwɛ̃)/ *n, euph* plumpness of person; stoutness [Fr, fr MF, fr *en bon point* in good condition]

**embosom** /im'booz(ə)m/ *vt* **1** *poetic* to enclose, shelter, envelop ⟨*his house* ~ed *in the grove* – Alexander Pope⟩ **2** *archaic* to take into or place in the bosom

**emboss** /im'bos/ *vt* **1** to raise the surface of (e g metal, leather cloth, or paper) into circular rounded projections; *esp* to ornament with raised work **2** to raise (e g lettering) from a surface in relief printing [ME *embosen*, fr MF *embocer*, fr *en-* + *boce* ¹boss] – **embossable** *adj*, **embosser** *n*, **embossment** *n*

**embouchure** /ˌombooh'shooə/ *n* the position and use of the lips in playing a musical wind instrument [Fr, fr (*s'*)*emboucher* to flow into, fr *en-* + *bouche* mouth – more at DEBOUCH]

**embourgeoisement** /ombooə'zhwahzmonh, -mənt (*Fr* ãburzwazmã)/ *n* the adjusting of the working class to middle-class life-styles and society; the convergence of nonmanual and manual classes in terms of affluence, social relationships, aspirations, values, and styles of life [Fr, fr (*s'*)*embourgeoiser* to become bourgeois, fr *en-* + *bourgeois*]

**embowed** /im'bohd/ *adj* shaped like a bow: e g **a** arched, vaulted ⟨*an* ~ *ceiling*⟩ **b** curved outward to form a projecting recess ⟨*an* ~ *window bay*⟩

**embowel** /im'bowəl/ *vt* **-ll-** (*NAm* **-l-, -ll-**) **1** to disembowel **2** *obs* to enclose

**embower** /im'bowə/ *vt* to shelter or enclose (as if) in a bower ⟨*like a rose* ~ed *in its own green leaves* – P B Shelley⟩

**¹embrace** /im'brays/ *vt* **1** to take or hold closely in the arms as a sign of affection; hug **2** to encircle, enclose **3a** to take up, esp readily or eagerly; adopt ⟨~ *a cause*⟩ **b** to avail oneself of; welcome ⟨~d *the opportunity to study further*⟩ **4** to take in or include as a part, item, or element of a more inclusive whole ⟨*charity* ~s *all acts that contribute to human welfare*⟩ ~ *vi* to join in an embrace; hug one another [ME *embracen*, fr MF *embracer*, fr OF *embracier*, fr *en-* + *brace* two arms – more at BRACE] – **embracer** *n*, **embracingly** *adv*, **embracive** *adj*

**²embrace** *n* an act of embracing or gripping ⟨*a loving* ~⟩ ⟨*helpless in the* ~ *of terror*⟩

**embranchment** /im'brahnchmənt/ *n* **1** a branching off or out (e g of a valley) **2** a branch [Fr *embranchement*, fr (*s'*)*embrancher* to branch out, fr *en-* + *branche* branch]

**embrangle** /im'brang·gl/ *vt* to entangle, confuse [*en-* + E dial. *brangle* squabble, blend of *brawl* and *wrangle*] – **embranglement** *n*

**embrasure** /im'brayzhə/ *n* **1** a door or window aperture, esp with splayed sides that increase the width of the opening on the inside **2** an opening with sides flaring outwards in a wall or parapet of a fortification, usu for allowing the firing of cannon [Fr, fr obs *embraser* to widen an opening]

**embrittle** /im'britl/ *vb* to make or become brittle – **embrittlement** *n*

**embrocate** /'embrəkayt, -broh-/ *vt* to moisten and rub (a part of the body) with a lotion or liniment [LL *embrocatus*, pp of *embrocare*, fr Gk *embrochē* lotion, fr *embrechein* to embrocate, fr *en-* + *brechein* to wet]

**embrocation** /ˌembrə'kaysh(ə)n/ *n* a liniment

**embroider** /im'broydə/ *vt* **1a** to ornament (e g cloth or a garment) with decorative stitches made by hand or machine **b** to form (e g a design or pattern) in ornamental needlework **2** to elaborate on (a narrative); embellish with usu exaggerated or fictitious details ~ *vi* **1** to do or make embroidery **2** to provide embellishments; elaborate – + *on* or *upon* [ME *embroderen*, fr MF *embroder*, fr *en-* + *broder* to embroider, of Gmc origin; akin to OE *brord* point, *byrst* bristle] – **embroiderer** *n*

**embroidery** /im'broyd(ə)ri/ *n* **1a** the art or process of embroidering designs **b** embroidered work **2** the act, process, or result of embroidering **3** unnecessary addition or ornament ⟨*considered the humanities mere educational* ~⟩

**embroil** /im'broyl/ *vt* **1** to throw (e g a person or affairs) into disorder or confusion **2** to involve in conflict or difficulties [Fr *embrouiller*, fr MF, fr *en-* + *brouiller* to broil] – **embroilment** *n*

**embrown** /im'brown/ *vt* to cause to turn dark or brown

**embry-** /embri-/, **embryo-** *comb form* embryo ⟨embryo*logist*⟩ [LL, fr Gk, fr *embryon*]

**embryo** /'embrioh/ *n, pl* **embryos 1a** a VERTEBRATE animal at any stage of development prior to birth or hatching – not now used technically **b** an animal in the early stages of growth and differentiation before birth or hatching; *esp* the developing human individual from the time of IMPLANTATION (embedding of fertilized egg in lining of the womb) to the end of the eighth week after conception – compare FOETUS **2** a young SEED PLANT that usu comprises a rudimentary plant with developing stem (PLUMULE), root (RADICLE), and leaves (COTYLEDONS) **3a** something as yet undeveloped ⟨*nursed his kids' wear firm from an* ~ *to a lusty youngster* – *Women's Wear Daily*⟩ **b** a beginning or undeveloped state of something ⟨*productions seen in* ~ *during their out-of-town tryout period* – Henry Hewes⟩ [ML *embryon-, embryo*, fr Gk *embryon*, fr *en-* + *bryein* to swell; akin to Gk *bryon* moss]

**embryogenesis** /ˌembrioh'jenəsis/ *n* the formation and development of the embryo [NL] – **embryogenetic** *adj*

**embryogeny** /ˌembri'ojəni/ *n* embryogenesis – **embryogenic** *adj*

**embryology** /ˌembri'oləji/ *n* **1** a branch of biology dealing with embryos and their development **2** the features and phenomena associated with the formation and development of an embryo [Fr *embryologie*, fr *embry-* + *logie* -logy] – **embryologist** *n*, **embryologic, embryological** *adj*, **embryologically** *adv*

**embryon-, embryoni-** *comb form* embry- ⟨embryon*ic*⟩ [ML *embryon-, embryo*]

**embryonated** /'embriəˌnaytid/ *adj* having or containing an embryo ⟨*an* ~ *egg*⟩

**embryonic** /ˌembri'onik/, **embryonal** /em'brie-ənl/ *adj* **1** of an embryo **2** in an early stage of development; incipient, rudimentary – **embryonically** *adv*

**embryonic disc** *n* **1a** BLASTODISC (layer of cells that will form the embryo) **b** BLASTODERM (blastodisc in which a cavity has formed) **2** the part of the inner cell mass of a BLASTOCYST (group of cells derived from a fertilized egg) from which the embryo of a mammal having a placenta develops

**embryonic layer** *n* GERM LAYER (primary layer of cells)

**embryonic membrane** *n* a structure (e g the amnion) that derives from the fertilized egg but does not form a part of the embryo

**embryonic shield** *n* EMBRYONIC DISC 2

**embryophyte** /'embri-əˌfiet/ *n* a plant (e g a fern or a FLOWERING PLANT) that produces an embryo and develops VASCULAR TISSUES (circulatory and transporting tissues)

**embryo sac** *n* the female GAMETOPHYTE (reproductive cell) of a SEED PLANT consisting of a thin-walled sac containing the egg nucleus and other nuclei which give rise to ENDOSPERM (nutritive tissue of a seed) on fertilization

**embryotic** /ˌembri'otik/ *adj* EMBRYONIC 2 [*embryo* + *-tic* (as in *patriotic*)]

**embus** /im'bus/ *vb* **-ss-** to board or put on board a bus

**¹emcee** /ˌem'see/ *n, informal* a compere; MASTER OF CEREMONIES [*M C*]

**²emcee** *vb* emceed; emceeing *informal* to act as emcee (of)

**-eme** /-eem/ *suffix* (→ *n*) significantly distinctive unit of (a specified feature of language structure) ⟨*taxeme*⟩ ⟨*lexeme*⟩ [Fr *-ème* (fr *phonème* speech sound, phoneme)]

**emend** /i'mend/ *vt* **1** to correct, usu by textual alterations ⟨*decided that the terms of the agreement should be* ~ed *to take the new conditions into account*⟩ **2** *archaic* to free from defects [ME *emenden*, fr L *emendare* – more at AMEND] – **emendable** *adj*, **emender** *n*

**emendate** /'eemenˌdayt/ *vt* to emend (a text or document) – **emendator** *n*, **emendatory** *adj*

**emendation** /ˌeemen'daysh(ə)n/ *n* **1** the act of emending **2** an alteration resulting from emending something (e g a text)

**emerald** /'em(ə)rəld/ *n* **1** a rich green variety of the mineral BERYL prized as a gemstone **2** any of various green gemstones (e g synthetic CORUNDUM or DEMANTOID) **3** the bright green colour of an emerald [ME *emerallde*, fr MF *esmeralde*, fr (assumed) VL *smaralda*, fr L *smaragdus*, fr Gk *smaragdos*, prob of Sem origin] – **emerald** *adj*

**emerge** /i'muhj/ *vi* **1** to rise (as if) from an enveloping fluid; come out into view ⟨*Venus emerging from the waves*⟩ **2** to become manifest or known ⟨*it* ~d *that he'd been married twice before and had wives living in Manchester and Glasgow*⟩ **3** to rise from an obscure or inferior condition; *esp* to undergo the socioeconomic and political processes characteristic of the rise to nationhood, esp from colonial status **4** to come into being by a process of evolution [L *emergere*, fr *e-* + *mergere* to plunge – more at MERGE]

**emergence** /i'muhj(ə)ns/ *n* **1** the act or an instance of emerging **2** any of various superficial outgrowths of plant tissue (e g the thorn of a rose) usu formed from both EPIDERMIS (outer protective layer) and immediately underlying tissues

**emergency** /i'muhj(ə)nsi/ *n* **1** an unforeseen event or series of events that will have harmful consequences unless acted upon immediately; a crisis **2** a pressing need; an exigency **3** a patient requiring immediate treatment **4 emergency, state of emergency** a grave state of affairs (e g civil unrest or a natural disaster) in which a government takes on special powers, declares martial law, etc

[1]**emergent** /i'muhj(ə)nt/ *adj* **1** emerging; *esp* in the early stages of formation or development ⟨*the growing infant's* ~ *personality*⟩ **2** being an emergency; urgent **3** newly formed ⟨*the* ~ *nations of Africa*⟩ [ME, fr L *emergent-, emergens*, prp of *emergere*]

[2]**emergent** *n* **1** something emergent **2a** a tree that rises above the surrounding forest **b** a plant rooted in shallow water and having most of the vegetative growth above water

**emergent evolution** *n* a biological and philosophical theory of evolution: the emergence of new qualities or properties is associated with the evolutionary development of more complex forms of organization of units that are not new in themselves, and the properties of new and more complex entities, while depending on the properties of their component subunits, cannot be predicted from a knowledge of these alone (e g life develops only when chemical substances become organized in the form of a cell, whose properties, although dependent upon the properties of its component chemicals, cannot be fully predicted from these alone)

[1]**emeritus** /i'meritəs/, *fem* **emerita** /i'meritə/ *adj* **1** holding after retirement an honorary title corresponding to that held last during active service **2** retired from an office or position ⟨*professor* ~⟩ – converted to *emeriti* after a plural noun ⟨*professors* emeriti⟩ [L, pp of *emereri* to serve out one's term, fr *e-* + *mereri, merere* to earn, deserve, serve – more at MERIT]

[2]**emeritus,** *fem* **emerita** *n, pl* **emeriti** /-itie/, *fem* **emeritae** /~/ someone having an emeritus rank or title

**emersed** /i'muhst/ *adj, of a plant* standing out of or rising above a surface (e g of a liquid) ⟨~ *aquatic weeds*⟩

**emersion** /i'muhsh(ə)n/ *n* emergence [L *emersus*, pp of *emergere*]

**emery** /'em(ə)ri/ *n* a dark granular mineral that consists mainly of CORUNDUM and is used for grinding and polishing; *also* a hard abrasive powder [ME, fr MF *emeri*, fr OIt *smiriglio*, fr ML *smiriglum*, fr Gk *smyrid-, smyris* – more at SMEAR]

**emery board** *n* a nail file made of cardboard or wood covered with powdered emery

**emery paper** *n* paper or cloth to which a thin layer of emery powder has been glued for use as an abrasive

**emesis** /'emәsis/ *n, pl* **emeses** /-seez/ an act or instance of vomiting – used technically [NL, fr Gk, fr *emein*]

**emetic** /i'metik/ *n* something that induces vomiting [L *emetica*, fr Gk *emetikē*, fr fem of *emetikos* causing vomiting, fr *emein* to vomit – more at VOMIT] – **emetic** *adj*, **emetically** *adv*

**emetine** /'emәteen, -tin/ *n* a chemical compound (ALKALOID), $C_{29}H_{40}N_2O_4$, extracted from the root of the ipecacuanha plant and used as an emetic and EXPECTORANT (substance that helps clear mucus from the lungs) [Fr *émétine*, fr *émétique* emetic, fr L *emetica*]

**émeute** /ay'muht (*Fr* emøt)/ *n, pl* **émeutes** /ay'muht(s) (*Fr* ~)/ an outbreak of disorder or violence; *esp* a popular uprising [Fr, fr OF *esmuete* act of starting up, motion, fr fem of *esmuet*, pp of *esmovoir* to start out, incite – more at EMOTION]

**-emia** /-'eemyə, -'eemi-ə/ *comb form* (→ *n*) *NAm* -aemia

**emigrant** /'emigrant/ *n* **1** one who emigrates **2** a migrant plant or animal – **emigrant** *adj*

*synonyms* An **emigrant migrates** or **emigrates** from his/her home or country, and the practice is **emigration** ⟨*a ship full of emigrants leaving Liverpool*⟩ ⟨*to emigrate to Canada*⟩. An **immigrant** (who may be the same person as an **emigrant** at a different stage on the journey) **migrates** or **immigrates** into another country, and the practice is **immigration** ⟨*language classes for immigrants*⟩ ⟨*Immigration Control at the airport*⟩. Migrants are people or birds that **migrate** between countries, and the practice is **migration** ⟨*migrant workers*⟩ ⟨*the spring migration of the wild ducks*⟩, but an **immigrant** into Australia may also be called a **migrant**.

**emigrate** /'emi,grayt/ *vi* to leave one's home or country for life or residence elsewhere *synonyms* see EMIGRANT [L *emigratus*, pp of *emigrare*, fr *e-* + *migrare* to migrate] – **emigration** *n*

**émigré, emigré** /'emigray (*Fr* emigre)/ *n* an emigrant; *esp* a person forced to emigrate for political reasons [Fr *émigré*, fr pp of *émigrer* to emigrate, fr L *emigrare*]

**eminence** /'eminəns/ *also* **eminency** /'eminənsi/ *n* **1** prominence, superiority – used as a title for a cardinal ⟨*Your Eminence*⟩ **2** one who or that which is high, prominent, or lofty: e g **2a** a person of high rank or attainments **b** a naturally formed geographical high place; a peak or ridge

**éminence grise** /aymi,nonhs 'greez (*Fr* eminãs griz)/ *n, pl* **éminences grises** /~/ someone who exercises power through his/her often unsuspected influence on another person or group of people who have apparent authority [Fr, lit., grey eminence, nickname of Père Joseph (François du Tremblay) †1638 Fr monk & diplomat, confidant of Cardinal Richelieu †1642 Fr statesman who was known as *Eminence Rouge* red eminence; fr the colours of their respective habits]

**eminent** /'eminənt/ *adj* **1** standing out so as to be readily seen or noted; conspicuous, notable **2** having or showing eminence, esp in position, fame, or achievement; distinguished △ imminent [ME, fr MF or L; MF, fr L *eminent-, eminens*, prp of *eminēre* to stand out, fr *e-* + *-minēre* (akin to L *mont-, mons* mountain)] – **eminently** *adv*

**eminent domain** *n* a right of a government to take private property for public use, subject to making reasonable compensation

**emir** /'emiə, -'-/ *n* a Muslim chieftain or prince: e g **a** a male descendant of Muhammad **b** a ruler of any of various Muslim states, esp in former times **c** a high-ranking Turkish official of former times [Ar *amīr* commander (cf ADMIRAL)]

**emirate** /'emirət/ *n* the position, state, power, etc of an emir

**emissary** /'emis(ə)ri/ *n* **1** an agent or negotiator sent on a mission to represent a government or head of state; an envoy ⟨*the US special* ~ *to the Middle East*⟩ **2** someone sent on a secret or spying mission [L *emissarius*, fr *emissus*, pp of *emittere*]

**emission** /i'mish(ə)n/ *n* **1** an act or instance of emitting **2a** something sent forth by an emitting agent: e g **2a(1)** electrons discharged from a surface **a(2)** ELECTROMAGNETIC WAVES (e g RADIO WAVES or X rays) radiated by an aerial or a star **a(3)** substances discharged into the air (e g by a factory chimney or car exhaust) **a(4)** a bodily secretion or discharge; *esp* an involuntary discharge of semen during sleep **b** an unpleasant by-product – **emissive** *adj*

**emissivity** /,emi'sivəti, imi-/ *n* the relative power of a surface to emit heat by radiation; the ratio of the RADIANT (travelling in waveform) energy emitted by a surface to that emitted by a BLACK BODY (body that completely absorbs the energy falling on it) at the same temperature

**emit** /i'mit/ *vt* **-tt-** **1a** to throw or give off or out (e g light) **b** to send out; eject **2** to issue with authority; *esp* to put (e g money) into circulation **3** to give utterance or voice to ⟨~ted *a groan*⟩ **4** *obs* to publish [L *emittere* to send out, fr *e-* + *mittere* to send]

**emitter** /i'mitə/ *n* one who or that which emits; *specif* a region of a TRANSISTOR (device for varying the strength and frequency of an electric current) that produces carriers of electrical charge (e g electrons)

**emmenagogue** /i'menəgog, i'mee-/ *n* something (e g a drug) that promotes the menstrual discharge [Gk *emmēna* menses (fr neut pl of *emmēnos* monthly, fr *en-* + *mēn* month) + E *-agogue* – more at MOON]

**Emmentaler, Emmenthaler** /'emən,tahlə (*Ger* emɛnta:lər)/ *n* Emmenthal [Ger, fr *Emmenthal*]

**Emmenthal, Emmental** /'emən,tahl (*Ger* emɛnta:l)/ *n* a pale yellow Swiss cheese with a rubbery texture, distinctive nutty flavour, and many holes that form during ripening [*Emmenthal*, region in Switzerland]

**emmer** /'emə/ *n* 1 a wild wheat (*Triticum turgidum* var *dicoccoides*) grown in the E Mediterranean 2 a cultivated wheat (*Triticum turgidum* var *dicoccum*) grown in the E Mediterranean and S Asia that has two grains in each flower (SPIKELET) of the ear that remain in the GLUMES (chaffy membranes) after threshing, and that is the ancestor of several modern wheats [Ger, fr OHG *amari*]

**emmet** /'emit/ *n* 1 *chiefly dial* an ant 2 *Cornwall* a visitor who is not Cornish [ME *emete* – more at ANT]

**Emmy** /'emi/ *n, pl* **Emmys** an award in the form of a statuette conferred annually by a US professional organization for notable achievement in television – compare OSCAR [alter. of *Immy*, nickname for *image orthicon* (a camera tube used in television)]

**¹emollient** /i'moliənt, i'moh-/ *adj* making soft or supple; *also* giving soothing relief, esp to the skin or a MUCOUS MEMBRANE [L *emollient-, emolliens*, prp of *emollire* to soften, fr *e-* + *mollis* soft – more at MELT]

**²emollient** *n* an emollient substance (e g lanolin)

**emolument** /i'molyoomənt/ *n* 1 **emoluments** *pl,* emolument the returns arising from office or employment; a salary 2 *archaic* an advantage [ME, fr L *emolumentum*, lit., miller's fee, fr *emolere* to grind up, fr *e-* + *molere* to grind – more at MEAL]

**emote** /i'moht/ *vi* to give expression to emotion, esp theatrically [back-formation fr *emotion*]

**emotion** /i'mohsh(ə)n/ *n* 1 excitement 2 a strong feeling (e g anger, fear, or joy) usu involving physiological changes (e g a rise in the pulse rate) [MF, fr *emouvoir* to stir up, fr L *exmovēre* to move away, disturb, fr *ex-* + *movēre* to move] – **emotionless** *adj*

**emotional** /i'mohsh(ə)nl/ *adj* 1 of the emotions ⟨an ~ disorder⟩ 2a inclined to show (excessive) emotion ⟨an ~ person⟩ b markedly aroused or agitated in feeling or sensibilities ⟨gets ~ if you argue with him⟩ 3 EMOTIVE 2 ⟨an ~ speech⟩ – **emotionalism** *n*, **emotionalist** *n*, **emotionalize** *vt*, **emotionality** *n*, **emotionally** *adv*

**emotive** /i'mohtiv/ *adj* 1 EMOTIONAL 1 2 appealing to, expressing, or arousing emotion rather than reason ⟨executions were an ~ issue⟩ ⟨the ~ use of language⟩ – **emotively** *adv*, **emotivity** *n*

**empanel** /im'panl/ *vt* -ll- (*NAm* -l-, -ll-) to enrol in or on a list or panel, esp for jury service

**empathetic** /ˌempə'thetik/ *adj* marked by empathy; empathic [fr *empathy*, by analogy to *sympathy* : *sympathetic*] – **empathetically** *adv*

**empathy** /'empəthi/ *n* 1 the capacity for imaginatively sharing in another's feelings or ideas ⟨while a degree of ~ is essential to any effective counselling, one must be careful not to identify too closely with the client⟩ 2 a method or technique in the appreciation of a work of art involving the imaginative recreation of a mood, feeling, or emotional state suggested by the work of art in order to understand it better [²en- + -pathy] – **empathic** *adj*, **empathize** *vi*

synonyms Although **sympathy** and **empathy** both mean "sharing in another's feelings", **sympathy** lays emphasis on the idea of compassion for distress, while **empathy** involves imaginative identification with the other person.

**empennage** /im'penij/ *n* the stabilizing assembly (e g fin, rudder, and tailplanes) of an aircraft [Fr, feathers of an arrow, empennage]

**emperor** /'emp(ə)rə/ *n* the supreme ruler of an empire [ME, fr OF *empereor*, fr L *imperator*, lit., commander, fr *imperatus*, pp of *imperare* to command, fr *in-* ²in- + *parare* to prepare, order – more at PARE] – **emperorship** *n*

**emperor moth** *n* a large moth (*Saturnia pavonia*) with eyespots on the wings

**emperor penguin** *n* the largest known penguin (*Aptenodytes forsteri*), that is found only south of the antarctic circle

**empery** /'empəri/ *n, poetic* empire, dominion [ME *emperie*, fr OF, fr *emperer* to command, fr L *imperare*]

**emphasis** /'emfəsis/ *n, pl* **emphases** /-seez/ 1a force or intensity of expression that gives special impressiveness or importance to something ⟨writing with ~ on the need for reform⟩ b a particular prominence given in speaking or writing to one or more words or syllables 2 special consideration of or stress or insistence on something ⟨the school's ~ on examinations⟩ ⟨... her Russian eye is underlined for ~ –T S Eliot⟩ [L, fr Gk, exposition, emphasis, fr *emphainein* to indicate, fr *en-* + *phainein* to show – more at FANCY ]

**emphas·ize, -ise** /'emfəˌsiez/ *vt* to give emphasis to; place emphasis or stress on ⟨~d the need for reform⟩

**emphatic** /im'fatik/ *adj* 1 spoken with or marked by emphasis 2 tending to express oneself in forceful speech or to take decisive action 3 attracting special attention [Gk *emphatikos*, fr *emphainein*] – **emphatically** *adv*

**emphysema** /ˌemfi'seemə/ *n* a disorder characterized by air-filled expansions of body tissues; *specif* such a condition of the lung in which lung and often heart function is impaired [NL, fr Gk *emphysēma* bodily inflation, fr *emphysan* to inflate] – **emphysematous** *adj*

**empire** /'empie-ə/ *n* 1a (the territory of) a large group of countries, colonies, or peoples under a single governing authority; *esp* one having an emperor as head of state b something that resembles a political empire; *esp* an extensive territory or enterprise under single domination or control ⟨the beautiful heiress to a meat-packing ~ – Punch⟩ 2 imperial sovereignty, rule, or dominion [ME, fr OF *empire, empirie*, fr L *imperium* absolute authority, empire, fr *imperare* to command]

**Empire** *adj* (characteristic) of a style (e g of interior decoration or furniture) popular in early 19th century France; *specif, of a style of women's dress* having a high waistline [Fr, fr (le premier) *Empire* the first Empire of France (1804-14)]

**Empire Day** *n* COMMONWEALTH DAY – used before the official adoption of *Commonwealth Day* in 1958

**empiric** /em'pirik/ *n* 1 one who relies on practical experience rather than theory 2 *archaic* a quack, charlatan [L *empiricus* doctor relying on experience alone, fr Gk *empeirikos*, fr *empeiria* experience, fr *en-* + *peiran* to attempt – more at FEAR]

**empirical** /em'pirikl/ *also* **empiric** *adj* originating in, based on, or relying on observation or experience rather than theory ⟨~ data⟩ ⟨~ laws⟩ – **empirically** *adv*

**empirical formula** *n* a chemical formula showing the simplest ratio of chemical elements in a compound rather than the total number of atoms in the molecule ⟨$CH_2O$ is the ~ for glucose⟩

**empiricism** /em'pirisiz(ə)m/ *n* 1a a former school of medical practice founded on experience without the aid of science or theory b quackery, charlatanism 2a the practice of working by empirical methods, esp those depending upon observation and experiment, to gain new knowledge or to develop scientific theories b a tenet arrived at empirically 3 a theory that all knowledge originates in or is dependent upon experience of the external world – compare RATIONALISM – **empiricist** *n*

**emplacement** /im'playsmənt/ *n* 1 the situation or location of something 2 a prepared position for weapons or military equipment ⟨radar ~s ⟩ 3 a putting into position; a placement [Fr, fr MF *emplacer* to emplace, fr *en-* + *place*] – **emplace** *vt*

**emplane** /im'playn/ *vb* to board or put on board an aircraft

**¹employ** /im'ploy/ *vt* 1a to make use of in a specified way or for a specific purpose ⟨~ a fine pen to fill in the details⟩ b to occupy (e g time) advantageously ⟨his evenings were mostly ~ed in the construction of a new greenhouse⟩ 2a to use or engage the services of ⟨he ~s a gardener for the heavy digging⟩ b to provide with a job that pays wages or a salary ⟨the firm ~s over 40000 worldwide⟩ 3 to devote to or direct towards a particular activity or person; use as a means to an end ⟨~ed all her wiles to get him to propose⟩ [ME *emploien*, fr MF *emploier*, fr L *implicare* to enfold, involve, implicate, fr *in-* + *plicare* to fold – more at PLY] – **employer** *n*

**²employ** *n, formal* the state of being employed, esp for wages or a salary ⟨in the government's ~⟩

**employable** /im'ployəbl/ *adj* capable of being employed – **employability** *n*

**employee, employé,** *NAm also* **employe** /im'ployee, imˌploy'ee, ˌemploy'ee/ *n* one employed by another, esp for wages or a salary and in a position below executive level [Fr *employé*, fr pp of *employer* to employ]

**employers' association** /im'ployəz/ *n* an organization of employers for dealing with problems of industrial relations

**employment** /im'ploymənt/ *n* 1 (an) activity in which one engages or is employed; (an) occupation ⟨suitable ~ was hard to find⟩ 2 employing or being employed

**employment agency** *n* an agency whose business is to find jobs for people seeking them or to find people to fill jobs that are vacant

**employment exchange** *n* LABOUR EXCHANGE

**empodium** /em'pohdiəm/ *n* a bristle or pod-shaped outgrowth between the claws on the last segment of the TARSUS (section of the leg furthest from the body) of a fly [NL, fr ²en- + -podium]

**empoison** /im'poyz(ə)n/ *vt* 1 to embitter ⟨a look of ~ed acceptance – Saul Bellow⟩ 2 *archaic* to poison [ME *empoysonen*, fr MF *empoisoner*, fr *en-* + *poison*] – **empoisonment** *n*

**emporium** /im'pawri•əm/ *n, pl* **emporiums** *also* **emporia** /-riə/ **1** a place of trade; a commercial centre **2** *formal or humorous* a usu large shop 〈*a product seldom found in West End* emporia〉 [L, fr Gk *emporion*, fr *emporos* traveller, trader, fr *en* in + *poros* passage, journey – more at IN, FARE]

**empower** /im'powə/ *vt* to give official authority or legal power to – **empowerment** *n*

**empress** /'empris/ *n* **1** the wife or widow of an emperor **2** a woman having in her own right the rank of emperor [ME *emperesse*, fr OF, fem of *empereor* emperor]

**empressement** /om'presmonh (*Fr* ãpresmã)/ *n* demonstrative warmth or cordiality [Fr, fr (*s'*)*empresser* to hurry, be eager, fr *en-* + *presser* to press]

**emprise** /em'priez/ *n, archaic* an undertaking, enterprise; *esp* an adventurous, daring, or chivalric enterprise [ME, fr MF, fr OF, fr *emprendre* to undertake, fr (assumed) VL *imprehendere*, fr L *in-* + *prehendere* to seize]

**¹empty** /'empti/ *adj* **1a** containing nothing; *esp* lacking typical or expected contents **b** not occupied, inhabited, or frequented 〈~ *house*〉 〈~ *streets*〉 **c** not pregnant 〈~ *heifer*〉 **d** *of a mathematical set* having no elements; NULL 4a 〈*the solution set of x* + 1 = *x is* ~〉 **2** lacking one or more desirable qualities: e g **2a** lacking reality or substance; hollow 〈*an* ~ *pleasure*〉 **b** lacking effect, force, value, or sincerity 〈~ *threats*〉 〈*an* ~ *gesture*〉 **c** lacking sense; foolish 〈*his* ~ *ideas*〉 **d** lacking purpose, result, or activity; idle 〈*an* ~ *day*〉 **3** *informal* **3a** hungry **b** without physical or emotional energy; limp – see also **on an empty** STOMACH [ME, fr OE *æmettig* unoccupied, fr *æemetta* leisure, fr ãe- without + *-metta* (fr *mōtan* to have to) – more at MUST] – **emptily** *adv*, **emptiness** *n*

**²empty** *vt* **1a** to make empty; remove the contents of **b** to deprive, divest 〈*acting* emptied *of all emotion*〉 **c** to discharge (itself) of contents **2** to remove from what holds, encloses, or contains **3** to transfer by emptying 〈emptied *the biscuits onto the plate*〉 ~ *vi* **1** to become empty **2** to discharge contents 〈*the river* empties *into the ocean*〉 – **emptier** *n*

**³empty** *n* something that is empty; *esp* an empty usu returnable container (e g a milk bottle)

**empty-'handed** *adj* **1** having or bringing nothing **2** having acquired or gained nothing 〈*came back* ~〉

**empty-'headed** *adj* foolish, silly

**empurple** /im'puhpl/ *vb* to make or become purple

**empyema** /ˌempie'eemə/ *n, pl* **empyemata** /-'eemətə/, **empyemas** the presence of pus in a body cavity, esp in the chest [LL, fr Gk *empyēma*, fr *empyein* to form or discharge pus, fr *en* in + *pyon* pus] – **empyemic** *adj*

**empyreal** /ˌempie'ree•əl/ *adj* of the empyrean; celestial [LL *empyrius, empyreus*, fr LGk *empyrios*, fr Gk *en* in + *pyr* fire]

**empyrean** /ˌempie'ree•ən/ *adj or n* **1** (of) the highest heavenly sphere in ancient and medieval cosmology, usu consisting of fire or light and sometimes identified as the true heaven or paradise **2** (of) the firmament, heavens

**em quad** *n* a type-metal space (QUAD) that is the same width as an EM (letter *M*); a quad with a square or almost square body [fr the casting of the capital letter *M* on a square body in some early founts]

**emu** /'eemyooh/ *n, pl* **emus 1** a swift-running Australian flightless bird (*Dromiceius novae-hollandiae*) that is related to and smaller than the ostrich [modif of Pg *ema* rhea]

**¹emulate** /'emyoolayt/ *vt* **1** to rival; strive to do as well as or better than **2** to imitate closely; approach equality with; *specif* to imitate (a piece of computer equipment) so closely as to be electronically indistinguishable **synonyms** see ³RIVAL [L *aemulatus*, pp of *aemulari*, fr *aemulus* rivalling] – **emulation** *n*, **emulative** *adj*

**²emulate** /'emyoolət/ *adj, obs* EMULOUS 1a 〈*pricked on by a most* ~ *pride* – Shak〉

**emulator** /'emyoo,laytə/ *n* a piece of HARDWARE or SOFTWARE (computer machinery or programs) that permits programs written for one computer to be run on another usu newer computer

**emulous** /'emyooləs/ *adj* **1a** ambitious or eager to emulate **b** inspired by or deriving from a desire to emulate **2** *obs* jealous – **emulously** *adv*, **emulousness** *n*

**emulsible** /i'mulsəbl/ *adj* capable of being emulsified [L *emulsus*, pp + E *-ible*]

**emulsifier** /i'mulsifie•ə/ *n* one who or that which emulsifies; *esp* a substance (e g a soap) that acts on the properties at the surface of contact between liquids, thus promoting the formation and stabilization of an emulsion

**emulsify** /i'mulsifie/ *vt* to convert (e g an oil) into an emulsion – **emulsifiable** *adj*, **emulsification** *n*

**¹emulsion** /i'mulsh(ə)n/ *n* **1** (the state of) a material consisting of a mixture of liquids that do not dissolve in each other and having droplets of one liquid dispersed throughout the other 〈*an* ~ *of fat in milk*〉 〈~ *paint*〉 **2** SUSPENSION 2b(3); *esp* a suspension of a light-sensitive silver-containing chemical compound or mixture of compounds, usu in a gelatin solution, forming a coating on photographic plates, film, or paper [NL *emulsion-, emulsio*, fr L *emulsus*, pp of *emulgēre* to milk out, fr *e-* + *mulgēre* to milk; akin to OE *melcan* to milk, Gk *amelgein*]

**²emulsion** *vt* to paint (e g a wall) with emulsion paint

**emulsoid** /i'mulsoyd/ *n* **1** a SOL (mixture of substances not forming a true solution) consisting of a liquid dispersed in a liquid – compare SUSPENSION 2 a SOL (e g a gelatin solution) containing particles that are LYOPHILIC (readily dispersible in the liquid medium) – **emulsoidal** *adj*

**emunctory** /i'mungktəri/ *n* an organ (e g a kidney) or part of the body (e g the skin) that carries away body wastes [NL *emunctorium*, fr L *emunctus*, pp of *emungere* to wipe or blow the nose, fr *e-* + *-mungere* (akin to *mucus*)]

**en, n** /en/ *n* the space taken up by a piece of type bearing the letter *n* that is used in printing as a measure of how much type of a particular kind will fit in a given space; one half of an EM

**¹en-** *also* **em-** *prefix* (→ *vb*) **1** put into or onto 〈*embed*〉 〈*enthrone*〉; go into or onto 〈*embus*〉 〈*entram*〉 **2** cause to be 〈*enslave*〉 〈*enrich*〉 **3** provide with 〈*empower*〉 〈*enfranchise*〉 **4** so as to cover 〈*engulf*〉; thoroughly 〈*entangle*〉 □ usu *em-* before *b, m*, or *p* [ME, fr OF, fr L *in-, im-*, fr *in*]

**²en-** *also* **em-** *prefix* in; within 〈*energy*〉 – usu *em-* before *b, m*, or *p* 〈*empathy*〉 [ME, fr L, fr Gk, fr *en* in – more at IN]

**¹-en** *also* **-n** /-(ə)n/ *suffix* (*n* → *adj*) made of; consisting of 〈*earthen*〉 〈*silvern*〉 [ME, fr OE; akin to OHG *-īn* made of, L *-īnus* of or belonging to, Gk *-inos* made of, of or belonging to]

**²-en** *suffix* (*n, adj* → *vb*) **1a** cause to be 〈*sharpen*〉 〈*embolden*〉 **b** cause to have 〈*heighten*〉 **2a** become 〈*steepen*〉 **b** come to have 〈*lengthen*〉 [ME *-nen*, fr OE *-nian*; akin to OHG *-inōn* *-en*]

**enable** /in'aybl/ *vt* **1a** to provide with the means or opportunity 〈*training that* ~s *people to earn a living*〉 **b** to make possible, practical, or easy **2** to give legal power, capacity, or sanction to 〈*legislation* enabling *a change in personal taxation*〉

*usage* The use of **enable** to mean not only "make able" 〈**enable** *them to evade taxation*〉 but also "make possible" 〈**enable** *tax evasion*〉 is now well established, though still disliked by some people.

**enact** /in'akt/ *vt* **1** to establish by legal and authoritative act; *specif* to make (e g a bill) into law 〈~ *legislation increasing the penalties for drunken driving*〉 **2** to play; ACT OUT 〈~ *a scene*〉 – **enaction** *n*, **enactor** *n*

**enactment** /i'naktmənt/ *n* **1** the act of enacting; the state of being enacted **2** something (e g a law) that has been enacted

**¹enamel** /i'naml/ *vt* **-ll-** (*NAm* **-l-, -ll-**) **1** to cover, inlay, or decorate with enamel **2** to form a glossy surface like enamel on (e g paper, leather, or cloth) [ME *enamelen*, fr MF *enamailler*, fr *en-* + *esmail* enamel, of Gmc origin; akin to OHG *smelzan* to melt – more at SMELT] – **enameller** *n*, **enamellist** *n*

**²enamel** *n* **1** a usu opaque glassy coating melted onto the surface of metal, glass, or pottery **2** a surface or outer covering that resembles enamel, esp in its hard and glossy properties **3** something that is enamelled; *esp* enamelware **4** a hard white substance, consisting mainly of calcium, that forms a thin layer capping the teeth of many VERTEBRATE animals including most mammals (e g humans) **5** a paint that dries to give a tough glossy finish **6** *chiefly NAm* NAIL VARNISH

**enamelware** /i'naml,weə/ *n* metal household or kitchen utensils coated with enamel

**enamoured,** *NAm chiefly* **enamored** /i'naməd/ *adj* fond *of* – formal when positive, but negative with humorous intention 〈*I am not* ~ *of the way you stub your cigarettes out in your saucer*〉 [fr pp of *enamour* (to inflame with love), fr ME *enamouren*, fr OF *enamourer*, fr *en-* + *amour* love – more at AMOUR]

**enantiomer** /i'nanti-əmə/ *n* an enantiomorph [Gk *enantios* + E *-mer*] – **enantiomeric** *adj*

**enantiomorph** /i'nanti-ə,mawf/ *n* either of a pair of chemical compounds or crystals whose molecular structures have a mirror-image relationship to each other [Gk *enantios* opposite (fr *enanti* facing, fr *en* in + *anti* against) + ISV *-morph*] –

enantiomorphic *adj*, enantiomorphism *n*, enantiomorphous *adj*

**enantiosis** /i,nanti'ohsis/ *n* a FIGURE OF SPEECH in which the meaning is the opposite of what is stated; *broadly* irony [NL, fr Gk *enantiōsis* opposition, contradiction, fr *enantios*]

**enargite** /i'nahjiet, 'enah,jiet/ *n* a black metallic mineral, $Cu_3AsS_4$, consisting of copper arsenic sulphide [Ger *enargit*, fr Gk *enargēs* visible, fr *en* in + *argēs* bright

**enarthrosis** /,enah'throhsis/ *n, pl* **enarthroses** /-'throhseez/ BALL-AND-SOCKET JOINT 2 [NL, fr Gk *enarthrōsis*, fr *en*- ²*en*- + *arthrōsis* jointing – more at ARTHROSIS]

**enation** /ee'naysh(ə)n/ *n* an outgrowth from the surface of an organ ⟨*a plant virus forming* ~s *on leaves*⟩ [L *enatus*, pp of *enasci* to rise out of, fr *e*- + *nasci* to be born – more at NATION]

**en bloc** /,om 'blok (*Fr* ã blɔk)/ *adv or adj* as a whole; in a mass ⟨*the eight could not be treated* ~ – THES⟩ [Fr]

**en brosse** /,om 'bros (*Fr* ã brɔs)/ *adv or adj, of a man's hair* cut short and standing erect; crew-cut [Fr, lit., in the manner of a brush]

**Encaenia** /en'seeni-ə, -nyə/ *n taking sing or pl vb* an annual university ceremony (eg at Oxford) of commemoration, with recital of poems and essays and conferring of degrees [NL, fr L, dedication festival, fr Gk *enkainia*, fr *en* in + *kainos* new – more at IN, RECENT ]

**encage** /in'kayj/ *vt* to place or confine in a cage

**encamp** /in'kamp/ *vt* to place or establish in a camp ~ *vi* to set up or occupy a camp

**encampment** /in'kampmənt/ *n* **1** the act of encamping; the state of being encamped **2** the place where a group (eg a body of troops) is encamped; a camp

**encapsulate** /in'kapsyoo,layt/ *also* **encapsule** /in'kapsyool/ *vt* **1** to enclose (as if) in a capsule **2** to epitomize, condense ⟨~ *a period of history*⟩ ~ *vi* to become encapsulated – **encapsulation** *n*

**encapsulated** /in'kapsyoo,laytid/ *adj* surrounded by a usu gelatinous or membranous capsule ⟨~ *water bacteria*⟩

**encase** /in'kays/ *vt* to enclose (as if) in a case – **encasement** *n*

**encash** /in'kash/ *vt, Br formal* to obtain cash for (a cheque or bond) – **encashment** *n*

**encaustic** /en'kawstik, -'kos-/ *n* **1** a paint which is made from pigment mixed with melted beeswax and resin and in which the colour is fixed by heat after application **2** (a work produced by) a method involving the use of encaustic; *broadly* any method involving the use of heat to fix or burn a colour onto or into a surface ⟨*tiles produced by* ~⟩ [*encaustic*, adj, fr L *encausticus*, fr Gk *enkaustikos*, fr *enkaiein* to burn in, fr *en*- + *kaiein* to burn – more at CAUSTIC]

**-ence** /n(ə)ns/ *suffix (vb → n)* **1** action or process of ⟨*emerg*ence⟩; *also* instance of (a specified action or process) ⟨*reference*⟩ ⟨*reminisc*ence⟩ **2** quality or state of ⟨*depend*ence⟩ ⟨*somnol*ence⟩ [ME, fr OF, fr L *-entia*, fr *-ent-*, *-ens*, prp ending + *-ia* *-y*] – **-ent** *suffix (vb → adj or n)*

¹**enceinte** /on'sant (*Fr* ãsẽt)/ *adj, of a woman* PREGNANT **1** [MF, fr (assumed) VL *incienta*, alter. of L *incient-*, *inciens* being with young, fr *in* + *-cient-*, *-ciens* (akin to Gk *kyein* to be pregnant) – more at CAVE]

²**enceinte** *n* a line of fortification enclosing a castle or town; *also* the area or town so enclosed [Fr, fr OF, enclosing wall, fr *enceindre* to surround, fr L *incingere*, fr *in*- + *cingere* to gird – more at CINCTURE]

**encephal-**, **encephalo-** *comb form* brain ⟨*encephalitis*⟩ ⟨*en*cephal*ocele*⟩ [Fr *encéphal*-, fr Gk *enkephal*-, fr *enkephalos*]

**encephalic** /,ensi'falik/ *adj* of the brain; *also* lying within the part of the skull enclosing the brain

**encephalitis** /in,sefə'lietəs/ *n, pl* **encephalitides** /-'litə,deez/ inflammation of the tissue of the brain, usu caused by infection [NL] – **encephalitic** *adj*

**encephalitogenic** /in,sefə,lietə'jenik/ *adj* tending to cause encephalitis ⟨*an* ~ *strain of a virus*⟩

**encephalogram** /en'sef(ə)lǝgram/ *n* an X-ray picture of the brain made by encephalography [ISV]

**encephalograph** /in'sef(ə)lə,grahf, -,graf/ *n* **1** an encephalogram **2** ELECTROENCEPHALOGRAPH (instrument recording the electrical activity of the brain)

**encephalography** /in,sef(ə)l'ogrəfi/ *n* X-ray photography of the brain after the CEREBROSPINAL FLUID (liquid in the spaces within the brain) has been replaced by a gas (eg air) [ISV]

**encephalomyelitis** /in,sef(ə)loh,mie-ə'lietəs/ *n* inflammation of both the brain and the SPINAL CORD, usu due to infection by a virus [NL]

**encephalon** /en'sef(ə)lon/ *n, pl* **encephala** /-lə/ the brain of a VERTEBRATE animal [NL, fr Gk *enkephalos*, fr *en* in + *kephalē* head – more at IN, CEPHALIC]

**encephalopathy** /in,sef(ə)l'opathi/ *n* a disease of the brain; *esp* one involving alterations of brain structure – **encephalopathic** *adj*

**enchain** /in'chayn/ *vt* to hold or bind (as if) with chains [ME *encheynen*, fr MF *enchainer*, fr OF, fr *en*- + *chaeine* chain]

**enchaînment** /on'shenmonh, --'- (*Fr* ãʃɛnmã)/ *n* a short series of steps in ballet (eg linking two held poses) which can be repeated or varied [Fr, fr MF *enchainement* chain, fr *enchainer*]

**enchant** /in'chahnt/ *vt* **1** to influence by charms and incantation; bewitch **2** to attract and move deeply; delight ⟨*the scene* ~*ed her to the point of tears* – Elinor Wylie⟩ – **enchantment** *n* □ compare CHARM **antonym** disenchant [ME *enchanten*, fr MF *enchanter*, fr L *incantare*, fr *in*- + *cantare* to sing – more at CHANT] – **enchantment** *n*

**enchanter** /in'chahntə/, *fem* **enchantress** /-tris/ *n* **1** someone with power to cast spells; a sorcerer **2** a particularly charming or delightful person; *esp* one with great powers of sexual attraction

**enchanter's nightshade** *n* any of several slender European plants (genus *Circaea*, esp *Circaea lutetiana*) of the fuchsia family that bear spikelike clusters of small whitish-pink flowers at the end of the stems

**enchanting** /in'chahnting/ *adj* charming – **enchantingly** *adv*

**enchase** /in'chays/ *vt* **1** to fix (a gem) in a setting **2** to ornament with raised or incised work (eg by engraving, embossing, inlaying, or carving) [ME *enchasen* to emboss, fr MF *enchasser* to enshrine, set, fr *en*- + *chasse* reliquary, fr L *capsa* case – more at CASE]

**enchilada** /,enchi'lahdə/ *n* a common Mexican dish consisting of a TORTILLA (maize pancake) spread with a meat filling, rolled up, and covered with chilli-seasoned tomato sauce [AmerSp]

**enchiridion** /,enkie'ridi-ən/ *n, pl* **enchiridia** /-'ridiə/ *formal* a handbook, manual [LL, fr Gk *encheiridion*, fr *en* in + *cheir* hand – more at IN, CHIR-]

**-enchyma** /-'engkimə/ *comb form (→ n), pl* **-enchymata** /-in-'kimətə/, **-enchymas** cellular tissue ⟨*collenchyma*⟩ [NL, fr *parenchyma*]

**encipher** /in'siefə/ *vt* to rewrite (a message) in code; encode – **encipherer** *n*, **encipherment** *n*

**encircle** /in'suhkl/ *vt* **1** to form a circle round; surround **2** to move or pass completely round – **encirclement** *n*

**enclasp** /in'klahsp/ *vt* to seize and hold; embrace

**enclave** /'enklayv/ *n* **1** a territorial or culturally distinct unit enclosed within foreign territory ⟨*ethnic* ~s⟩ **2** a small community of one kind of plant, often of a kind no longer generally found because of climatic or other changes, within a larger plant community [Fr, fr MF, fr *enclaver* to enclose, fr (assumed) VL *inclavare* to lock up, fr L *in*- + *clavis* key – more at CLAVICLE]

**enclitic** /in'klitik/ *adj, of a word or particle* without independent accent and forming part of the preceding word ⟨*thee in* prithee *and* not *in* cannot *are* ~⟩ [LL *encliticus*, fr Gk *enklitikos*, fr *enklinesthai* to lean on, fr *en*- + *klinein* to lean – more at LEAN] – **enclitic** *n*, **enclitically** *adv*

**enclose** /in'klohz/ *also* **inclose** *vt* **1a(1)** to close in completely; surround ⟨~d *the field with a high fence*⟩ **a(2)** to fence off (common land) for individual use **b** to hold in; confine **2** to include in a package or envelope, esp along with something else ⟨*a cheque is* ~d *herewith*⟩ [ME *enclosen*, prob fr *enclos* enclosed, fr MF, pp of *enclore* to enclose, fr (assumed) VL *inclaudere*, alter. of L *includere* – more at INCLUDE]

**enclosed order** *n taking sing or pl vb* a Christian religious community that avoids or forbids contacts with the outside world

**enclosure** /in'klohzhə/ *n* **1** enclosing or being enclosed; *specif* the act of enclosing common land for individual use ⟨*the numerous* ~s *contributed to the rural unrest of the 1790s*⟩ **2** something that encloses **3** something enclosed: eg **3a** something included in the same envelope or package as a letter **b** an area of enclosed ground; *esp* such an area reserved for a certain class of spectator in a sports ground

**encode** /in'kohd/ *vt* **1** to convert (eg a body of information) from one system of communication into another; *esp* to rewrite (a message) in code **2** CODE 2 (contain the necessary information for reproducing an AMINO ACID, protein, etc) ~ *vi* to code for an AMINO ACID, protein, etc – **encoder** *n*

**encomiast** /en'kohmi,ast/ *n, formal* one who praises in encomiums; a eulogist [Gk *enkōmiastēs*, fr *enkōmiazein* to praise, fr *enkōmion*] – **encomiastic** *adj*

**encomium** /en'kohmi-əm, -myəm/ *n*, *pl* **encomiums, encomia** /-miə/ *formal* a usu formal expression of warm or high praise; a eulogy [L, fr Gk *enkōmion*, fr *en* in + *kōmos* revel, celebration – more at IN, COMEDY]

**encompass** /in'kumpəs/ *vt* **1** to form a circle about; enclose **2a** to envelop **b** to include ⟨*a plan that* ∼es *a number of aims*⟩ **3** *formal* to cause to occur; BRING ABOUT ⟨*plans laid to* ∼ *his downfall*⟩ – **encompassment** *n*

**¹encore** /'ong,kaw/ *n* (an audience's appreciative demand for) a performer's reappearance to give a repeated or additional performance – often used interjectionally [Fr, still, again]

**²encore** *vt* to call for an encore of or by

**¹encounter** /in'kowntə/ *vt* **1a** to meet as an adversary or enemy **b** to engage in conflict with **2** to meet or come across, esp unexpectedly [ME *encountren*, fr OF *encontrer*, fr ML *incontrare*, fr LL *incontra* towards, fr L *in-* + *contra* against – more at COUNTER]

**²encounter** *n* **1** a meeting or clash between hostile factions or people **2** a chance meeting

**encounter group** *n* (a meeting of) a group of people who try to improve their social skills by means of activities (e g physical contact, describing personal problems, or criticizing the behaviour of other group members) designed to increase their insight into their own feelings and behaviour, reduce their inhibitions, and make them more sensitive to the thoughts and feelings of other group members

**encourage** /in'kurij/ *vt* **1** to inspire with courage, spirit, or hope **2** to spur on; stimulate ⟨*the bushes should be pruned back to the ground to* ∼ *the production of new fruiting wood*⟩ **3** to give help or patronage to (a person, process, or action); promote ⟨*many companies* ∼ *union membership*⟩ ⟨*Arts Council grants to* ∼ *young film directors*⟩ [ME *encoragen*, fr MF *encoragier*, fr OF, fr *en-* + *corage* courage] – **encourager** *n*, **encouragement** *n*, **encouragingly** *adv*

**encrimson** /in'krimz(ə)n/ *vt* to make or dye crimson

**encroach** /in'krohch/ *vi* **1** to enter gradually or by stealth into the possessions or rights of another; intrude, trespass ⟨*he* ∼ed *on my time*⟩ **2** to advance beyond the usual or proper limits □ usu + *on* or *upon* [ME *encrochen* to get, seize, fr MF *encrochier*, fr OF, fr *en-* + *croc, croche* hook – more at CROCHET] – **encroacher** *n*, **encroachment** *n*

**en croûte** /ong 'krooht (*Fr* ã krut)/ *adj* wrapped in pastry ⟨*fillet of beef* ∼⟩ [Fr]

**encrust** /in'krust/ *vt* to cover, line, or overlay with a hard or decorative layer, esp of jewels or precious metal ∼ *vi* to form a crust [partly fr *en-* + *crust*; partly fr L *incrustare*, fr *in-* + *crusta* crust]

**encrustation** /,enkru'staysh(ə)n/ *n* an incrustation

**encrypt** /in'kript/ *vt*, *formal* to rewrite (a message) in code; encode – **encryption** *n*

**encumber** /in'kumbə/ *vt* **1** to weigh down; burden **2a** to fill inconveniently full ⟨*a room* ∼ed *with heavy furniture*⟩ ⟨*an argument* ∼ed *with pointless examples*⟩ **b** to impede or hamper the function or activity of; hinder **3** to burden with a legal claim (e g a mortgage) ⟨∼ *an estate*⟩ [ME *encombren*, fr MF *encombrer*, fr OF, fr *en-* + (assumed) OF *combre* barricade, obstacle]

**encumbrance** /in'kumbrəns/ *n* **1** something that encumbers; an impediment **2** a claim (e g a mortgage) against property

**-ency** /n(ə)nsi/ *suffix* (→ *n*) quality or state of ⟨*despond*ency⟩ [ME *-encie*, fr L *-entia* – more at *-ENCE*]

**¹encyclical** /in'siklikl/ *adj* addressed to all the individuals of a group; general [LL *encyclicus*, fr Gk *enkyklios* circular, general, fr *en* in + *kyklos* circle, wheel]

**²encyclical** *n* an encyclical letter; *specif* a papal letter to the bishops of the church as a whole or to those in one country

**encyclopedia, encyclopaedia** /in,sieklə'peedi-ə, -dyə/ *n* a reference work that contains information on all branches of knowledge or treats comprehensively a specified branch of knowledge, usu in articles arranged in alphabetical order of subjects either in a single list or within each of several large subsections [ML *encyclopaedia* course of general education, fr Gk *enkyklios paideia* general education]

**encyclopedic, encyclopaedic** /in,sieklə'peedik/ *adj* (suggestive) of an encyclopedia or its methods of treating or covering a subject; comprehensive ⟨*an* ∼ *memory*⟩ – **encyclopedically** *adv*

**encyclopedism, encyclopaedism** /in,sieklə'peediz(ə)m/ *n* encyclopedic knowledge

**encyclopedist, encyclopaedist** /in,sieklə'peedist/ *n* **1** one who compiles or contributes to an encyclopedia **2** *often cap* any of the contributors to a French encyclopedia (1751-80) which embodied many of the central ideas of the ENLIGHTENMENT (18th-century movement opposed to superstition and traditional ideas and stressing the ability of human reason and empirical science to discover truth)

**encyst** /en'sist/ *vt* to enclose (as if) in a cyst ∼ *vi* to form or become enclosed in a cyst – **encystation** *n*, **encystment** *n*

**¹end** /end/ *n* **1a** the part of an area that lies at the boundary ⟨*the N* ∼ *of the village*⟩; *also* the farthest point from where one is ⟨*it's at the other* ∼ *of the garden*⟩ **b(1)** the point that marks the extent of something in space or time; the limit ⟨*at the* ∼ *of the day*⟩ **b(2)** the point at which something ceases to exist ⟨*world without* ∼⟩ **c** either of the extreme or last parts lengthways of an object that is appreciably longer than it is broad ⟨*a pencil with a point at each* ∼⟩ **2a** the cessation, action, activity, or existence ⟨*the* ∼ *of the war*⟩ ⟨*met a tragic* ∼⟩; *also* the events, parts, or sections that just precede such a cessation; the conclusion ⟨*the* ∼ *of the film was the weakest part*⟩ **b** the final condition; *esp* death ⟨*the* ∼ *being oblivion*⟩ **3** something left over; a remnant – esp in *odds and ends* **4** an aim, goal, or purpose ⟨*the* ∼ *justifies the means*⟩ **5a** either half of a games pitch, court, etc ⟨*change* ∼*s at halftime*⟩ **b** a period of action or turn to play in bowls, curling, etc; *specif* a period of play in bowls during which the bowls are all bowled in one direction and after which scores are judged **6** *informal* a particular part of an undertaking or organization ⟨*the advertising* ∼ *of a business*⟩ **7** *informal* something or someone extreme of a kind; *esp* something or someone particularly unpleasant – + *the* ⟨*I found his rudeness yesterday the absolute* ∼⟩ [ME *ende*, fr OE; akin to OHG *enti* and, L *ante* before, Gk *anti* against] – **ended** *adj* – **at a loose end** without any work or useful occupation; *broadly* bored – **end on 1** with the end towards one **2** END TO END – **get the wrong end of the stick** to misunderstand – **go off the deep end 1** to enter recklessly on a course of action **2** to become very excited, perturbed, or annoyed [fr the deep end of a swimming pool, where diving-boards are placed] – **in the end** ultimately; AT LAST – **make (both) ends meet** to cope financially ⟨*by giving up their second car they just managed to* make ends meet⟩ – **no end 1** exceedingly **2** an endless amount; a huge quantity – **on end 1** upright ⟨*turned the table* on end *to get it through the door*⟩ **2** without a stop ⟨*it rained for days* on end⟩ – **throw somebody in at the deep end** to confront somebody with a new task, job, etc without allowing time for preparation [fr the traditional method of teaching people to swim willy-nilly by throwing them into the deep end of a swimming pool] – see also **burn the** CANDLE **at both ends, at one's** WITS' **end**

**²end** *vt* **1** to bring to an end **2** to destroy **3** to make up the end of ⟨*a lingering shot of the sunset* ∼s *the film*⟩ ∼ *vi* **1** to come to an end **2** to reach a specified ultimate rank, condition, or situation – often + *up* ⟨∼ed *up as a colonel*⟩ **synonyms** see ¹CLOSE **antonym** begin

**³end** *vt*, *dial Eng* to put (grain or hay) into a barn or stack [prob alter. of E dial. *in* to harvest, fr *²in*]

**⁴end** *adj* final, ultimate ⟨∼ *results*⟩ ⟨∼ *markets*⟩ ⟨∼ *user*⟩

**end-** /end-/, **endo-** *comb form* **1** within; inside ⟨*endoskeleton*⟩ – compare ECT-, EXO- **2** taking in; absorbing ⟨*endothermal*⟩ [Fr, fr Gk, fr *endon* within, fr *en* in + *-don* (akin to L *domus* house) – more at IN, TIMBER]

**endamoeba** /,endə'meebə/ *n*, *NAm* ENTAMOEBA (parasitic microorganism) [NL, genus name, fr *end-* + *amoeba*] – **endamoebic** *adj*

**endanger** /in'daynjə/ *vt* to bring into or expose to danger or peril – **endangerment** *n*

**endangered** /in'daynjəd/ *adj* threatened with extinction ⟨∼ *species*⟩

**endarch** /'end,ahk/ *adj*, *botany* formed or taking place from the centre outwards; *specif* having the first-formed and oldest XYLEM (plant water-conducting tissue) internal to that formed later and nearest to the centre (e g of a stem) – compare EXARCH – **endarchy** *n*

**endarterectomy** /,end,ahtə'rektəmi/ *n* surgical removal of the inner layer of an artery when it is thickened or blocked (e g in arteriosclerosis), esp for the treatment of thrombosis [NL *endarter*ium inner layer of an artery (fr *end-* + *arteria* artery) + E *-ectomy*]

**endbrain** /'end,brayn/ *n* the foremost subdivision of the FOREBRAIN (front region of the brain)

**endear** /in'diə/ *vt* **1** to cause to become beloved or admired – often + *to* ⟨*so* ~ed *himself to the old woman that she left him her cat when she died*⟩ **2** *obs* to make higher in cost, value, or estimation – **endearingly** *adv*

**endearment** /in'diəmənt/ *n* **1** the act or process of endearing **2** a word or an act (eg a caress) expressing affection

¹**endeavour**, *NAm chiefly* **endeavor** /in'devə/ *vt* **1** to attempt (eg the fulfilment of an obligation) by exertion of effort; TRY **2a** –usu + infin ⟨~ing *to control her disgust*⟩ **2** *archaic* to strive to achieve or reach ~ *vi* to make an effort to do something [ME *endeveren* to exert oneself, fr *en-* + *dever* duty, fr OF *deveir*, fr *devoir, deveir* to owe, be obliged, fr L *debēre* – more at DEBT]

²**endeavour**, *NAm chiefly* **endeavor** *n* serious determined effort ⟨*fields of* ~⟩ ; *also* an instance of this

¹**endemic** /en'demik/ *adj* **1** belonging or native to a particular people or region; not introduced or naturalized ⟨~ *diseases*⟩ ⟨*an* ~ *species of plant*⟩ – compare EPIDEMIC, PANDEMIC **2** regularly occurring in or associated with a particular topic or sphere of activity ⟨*accidents or incidents* ~ *in steeplechasing*⟩ *synonyms* see ¹NATIVE *antonym* exotic [Fr *endémique*, fr *endémie* endemic disease, fr Gk *endēmia* action of dwelling, fr *endēmos* endemic, fr *en* in + *dēmos* people, populace – more at DEMAGOGUE] – **endemically** *adv*, **endemicity** *n*, **endemism** *n*

²**endemic** *n* NATIVE 4b

**endergonic** /ˌenduh'gonik/ *adj* requiring expenditure of energy ⟨~ *biochemical reactions*⟩ [*end-* + Gk *ergon* work – more at WORK]

**endermic** /en'duhmik/ *adj* acting through the skin or by direct application to the skin – **endermically** *adv*

**endexine** /en'dekseen/ *n* the inner membranous layer of the EXINE (double-layered outer skin) of pollen – compare EKTEXINE

**end game** *n* the last stage in various games; *esp* the stage of a chess game when only a few pieces remain on the board

**ending** /'ending/ *n* something that constitutes an end: eg **a** the last part of a book, film, etc **b** one or more letters or syllables added at the end of a word, esp as an inflection

**endive** /'en,diev/ *n* **1** a plant (*Cichorium endivia*) of the daisy family that resembles a lettuce and has bitter leaves used in salads **2** *NAm* the developing crown of chicory when blanched for use as a salad plant by growing in darkness or semidarkness – compare BELGIAN ENDIVE [ME, fr MF, fr LL *endivia*, fr LGk *entubion*, fr L *intubus*]

**endleaf** /'end,leef/ *n* an endpaper (eg of a book)

**endless** /'endlis/ *adj* **1** being or seeming without end **2** extremely numerous **3** joined to itself at its ends ⟨*an* ~ *belt*⟩ – **endlessly** *adv*, **endlessness** *n*

**end line** *n* a line marking an end or boundary, esp of a playing area

**endlong** /'end,long/ *adv, archaic* lengthways [ME *endelong*, alter. (influenced by *ende* end) of *andlong*, fr OE *andlang* along, fr *andlang*, prep – more at ALONG]

**endmost** /'end,mohst/ *adj* situated at the very end; farthest

**endo-** *comb form* **1** – see END- **2** forming a bridge between two atoms in a cyclic system

**endobiotic** /ˌendohbie'otik/ *adj* living within the tissues of a HOST (organism harbouring a parasite) [ISV]

**endoblast** /'endoh,blast/ *n* HYPOBLAST (inner layer of tissue in an early embryo) – **endoblastic** *adj* [ISV]

**endocardial** /ˌendoh'kahdiəl/ *adj* **1** situated within the heart **2** of the endocardium

**endocarditis** /ˌendohkah'dietəs/ *n* inflammation of the lining and valves of the heart [NL]

**endocardium** /ˌendoh'kahdi-əm/ *n, pl* **endocardia** /-'kahdiə/ a thin SEROUS MEMBRANE (membrane secreting a watery liquid) lining the cavities of the heart [NL, fr *end-* + Gk *kardia* heart]

**endocarp** /'endə,kahp, -doh-/ *n* the inner layer of the PERICARP (ripened ovary wall enclosing the seeds) of a fruit (eg an apple or orange) [Fr *endocarpe*, fr *end-* + *-carpe* -carp] – **endocarpal** *adj*

**endocentric** /ˌendoh'sentrik/ *adj, of a phrase* having the same role in grammar as the word of central importance ⟨*hot bath is an* ~ *construction, since it can be used in a sentence in the same way as* bath *itself*⟩ – compare EXOCENTRIC

**endocranial cast** /ˌendoh'krayniəl/ *n* a cast of the cavity within the CRANIUM (part of skull enclosing the brain) showing the approximate shape of the brain

¹**endocrine** /'endohkrin, -krien, -də-/ *adj* **1a** producing secretions that are discharged directly into the bloodstream ⟨~ *system*⟩ – compare EXOCRINE **b** of or being an ENDOCRINE GLAND or its secretions ⟨~ *hormone*⟩ **2** hormonal [ISV *end-* + Gk *krinein* to separate – more at CERTAIN]

²**endocrine** *n* **1** a hormone – no longer used technically **2** ENDOCRINE GLAND

**endocrine gland** *n* a gland (eg the thyroid or the pituitary) that produces an endocrine secretion

**endocrinologic** /ˌendohkrinə'lojik, -krie-, -də/, **endocrinological** /-kl/ *adj* of or involving the ENDOCRINE GLANDS or secretions, or endocrinology

**endocrinology** /ˌendohkri'noləji, -krie-/ *n* physiology and medicine dealing with (diseases of) the ENDOCRINE GLANDS [ISV] – **endocrinologist** *n*

**endocytosis** /ˌendohsie'tohsis/ *n* the uptake and incorporation of substances into a cell by PHAGOCYTOSIS (process of flowing round and engulfing a solid particle) or PINOCYTOSIS (process of folding inwards to surround a drop of liquid) – compare EXOCYTOSIS [NL, fr *end-* + *-cytosis* (as in *phagocytosis*)] – **endocytic** *adj*, **endocytically** *adv*, **endocytotic** *adj*, **endocytotically** *adv*, **endocytose** *vb*

**endoderm** /'endoh,duhm/ *n* **1** the innermost of the three primary layers of cells (GERM LAYERS) of an embryo that is the source of the EPITHELIUM (surface lining tissue) of the digestive tract and its derivatives; *broadly* any tissue that is derived from this germ layer – compare ECTODERM, MESODERM **2** the inner cellular membrane of a DIPLOBLASTIC (having two primary tissue layers) animal (eg a jellyfish) [Fr *endoderme*, fr *end-* + Gk *derma* skin – more at DERM-] – **endodermal** *adj*, **endodermally** *adv*

**endodermis** /ˌendoh'duhmis/ *n* the innermost tissue of the CORTEX (outer layer of tissue surrounding the transporting and circulatory structures) in many roots and stems [NL]

**endodontia** /ˌendoh'donsh(y)ə/ *n* a branch of dentistry concerned with diseases of the soft sensitive tissue (PULP) within teeth [NL, fr *end-* + *-odontia*] – **endodontic** *adj*, **endodontically** *adv*, **endodontist** *n*

**endodontics** /ˌendoh'dontiks/ *n taking sing vb* endodontia

**endoenzyme** /'endoh,enziem/ *n* an ENZYME (substance that speeds up a biochemical reaction) that functions within a cell [ISV]

**endoergic** /ˌendoh'uhjik/ *adj* absorbing energy; ENDOTHERMIC ⟨~ *nuclear reactions*⟩ [*end-* + *erg-* + *-ic*]

**endoerythrocytic** /ˌendoh·i,rithrə'sitik/ *adj* occurring within RED BLOOD CELLS – used chiefly of stages in the life cycle of parasites causing malaria

**endogamy** /en'dogəmi/ *n* **1** INTERMARRIAGE **2** – compare EXOGAMY **2** SEXUAL REPRODUCTION between near relatives; *esp* pollination of a flower by pollen from another flower of the same plant – compare AUTOGAMY – **endogamous, endogamic** *adj*

**endogenous** /en'dojinəs/ *also* **endogenic** /ˌendoh'jenik/ *adj* **1a** growing from or on the inside; developing within the cell wall **b** originating within the body ⟨*an* ~ *rhythm*⟩ **2** constituting or relating to METABOLISM (biochemical processing) of the nitrogen-containing constituents of cells and tissues **3** occurring without an immediate causal factor or event ⟨~ *depression*⟩ – **endogenously** *adv*

**endogeny** /en'dojəni/ *n* growth from within or from a deep-seated layer

**endolymph** /'endoh,limf/ *n* the watery liquid in the sensory structures of the INNER EAR [ISV] – **endolymphatic** *adj*

**endometriosis** /ˌendoh,meetri'ohsis/ *n* the presence of functioning endometrial tissue in places where it is not normally found (eg the ovary), often causing pain and malfunction [NL]

**endometrium** /ˌendoh'meetri-əm/ *n, pl* **endometria** /-'meetriə/ the MUCOUS MEMBRANE lining the uterus [NL, fr *end-* + Gk *metra* uterus, fr *mētr-, mētēr* mother – more at MOTHER] – **endometrial** *adj*

**endomixis** /ˌendoh'miksis/ *n* a periodic reorganization of the nucleus in CILIATES (single-celled organisms bearing small hairlike structures) [NL, fr *end-* + Gk *mixis* act of mixing, fr *mignynai* to mix – more at MIX]

**endomorph** /'endoh,mawf/ *n* **1** a crystal enclosed in another of a different type **2** an endomorphic person [(1) ISV, fr *end-* + *-morph*; (2) *endoderm* + *-morph*]

**endomorphic** /ˌendoh'mawfik, ˌendə-/ *adj* **1a** of an endomorph **b** of or produced by endomorphism **2** having or being a heavy rounded body build, often with a marked tendency to become fat – compare ECTOMORPHIC, MESOMORPHIC [(2)*endo*derm

+ *-morphic*; fr the predominance in such types of structures developed from the endoderm – **endomorphy** *n*

**endomorphism** /ˌendoh'mawfiz(ə)m/ *n* 1 a change produced in an INTRUSIVE rock (one formed from molten rock forced between existing layers) by reaction with the WALL ROCK in which it lies 2 a HOMOMORPHISM (mathematical function that maps one set onto another) that maps a set of mathematical elements into itself

**endonuclease** /ˌendoh'nyoohkliayz/ *n* an ENZYME that breaks down the chain of NUCLEOTIDES (chemical subunits) in a NUCLEIC ACID (e g DNA) at points away from the end of the chain and thereby produces two or more shorter nucleotide chains – compare EXONUCLEASE

**endoparasite** /ˌendoh'parəsiet/ *n* a parasite (e g a tapeworm) that lives in the internal organs or tissues of its host – compare ECTOPARASITE [ISV] – **endoparasitism** *n*

**endopeptidase** /ˌendoh'peptidayz/ *n* any of a group of ENZYMES that break down PEPTIDE BONDS (chemical bonds between carbon and nitrogen atoms) inside the long chains of protein molecules; PROTEINASE – compare EXOPEPTIDASE

**endophyte** /'endoh,fiet/ *n* a plant (e g a parasitic fungus) that lives within another plant [ISV] – **endophytic** *adj*

**endoplasm** /'endoh,plaz(ə)m/ *n* the inner relatively liquid part of the CYTOPLASM (inner jellylike material) of a cell – compare ECTOPLASM [ISV] – **endoplasmic** *adj*

**endoplasmic reticulum** /ˌendo,plazmik ri'tikyoolǝm/ *n* a system of interconnected double membranes in the CYTOPLASM (jellylike material) of a cell that functions esp in the transport of materials within the cell and that is studded with RIBOSOMES (specialized cell parts where proteins are synthesized) in some places

**endopodite** /en'dopədiet/ *n* the middle or internal branch of a typical two-branched limb of a crab, lobster, shrimp, or related animal – compare EXOPODITE [ISV] – **endopoditic** *adj*

**endopolyploid** /ˌendoh'poliployd/ *adj* of a POLYPLOID (having more than the typical amount of genetic material) state in which the CHROMOSOMES (strands of gene-carrying material) have divided repeatedly without subsequent division of the nucleus or cell – **endopolyploidy** *n*

**endopterygote** /ˌendoh'terigot/ *n* any of a major division (Endopterygota) of insects (e g butterflies and beetles) whose wings develop inside the body and which have a pupal stage in their life cycle – compare EXOPTERYGOTE [deriv of Gk *end-* + *pterygōtos* winged, fr *pteryx* wing]

**endoradiosonde** /ˌendoh'raydioh,sond/ *n* a tiny electronic device introduced into the body to record physiological data not otherwise obtainable

**end organ** *n* a structure (e g a muscle or a SENSE ORGAN) at the end of a nerve path

**endorphin** /en'dawfin/ *n* a natural painkiller secreted by the brain that resembles opium derivatives (e g morphine and heroin) [*end-* + *morphine*]

**endorse** /in'daws/ *vt* **1a** to write on the back of; *esp* to sign one's name as payee on the back of (a cheque) in order to obtain the cash or credit represented on the face **b** to write (one's signature) on a cheque, bill, or note **c** to inscribe (e g an official document) with a title or memorandum **d** to make over to another (the value represented in a cheque, bill, or note) by inscribing one's name on the document **e** to acknowledge receipt of (a sum specified) by one's signature on a document **2** to express approval of; support; *specif, chiefly NAm* to express support for (e g a political candidate) publicly **3** *Br* to record details of a motoring offence on (the driver's licence) [alter. of obs *endoss*, fr ME *endosen*, fr MF *endosser*, fr OF, to put on the back, fr *en-* + *dos* back, fr L *dorsum*] – **endorsable** *adj*, **endorser** *n*, **endorsee** *n*

**endorsement** /in'dawsmənt/ *n* **1** the act or process of endorsing ⟨*his ~ of all their plans was more than they had expected*⟩ **2** something that is written in the process of endorsing: e g **2a** a provision added to an insurance contract altering its scope or application **b** *Br* a record of a motoring offence entered on a driving licence

**endoscope** /'endǝ,skohp/ *n* an instrument for looking inside a hollow organ (e g the intestine) [ISV] – **endoscopic** *adj*, **endoscopically** *adv*, **endoscopy** *n*

**endoskeleton** /ˌendoh'skelitn/ *n* an internal skeleton or supporting framework in an animal (e g a fish, crocodile, or human) – **endoskeletal** *adj*

**endosmosis** /ˌendoz'mohsis/ *n* OSMOSIS (passage of a solvent, esp water, through a membrane) from the outside to the inside

(e g of a cell) – compare EXOSMOSIS [deriv of Gk *end-* + *ōsmos* act of pushing, fr *ōthein* to push; akin to Skt *vadhati* he strikes] – **endosmotic** *adj* **endosmotically** *adv*

**endosperm** /'endoh,spuhm/ *n* a tissue in SEED PLANTS that is formed within the seed and provides nutrition for the developing embryo [Fr *endosperme*, fr *end-* + Gk *sperma* seed – more at SPERM] – **endospermic** *adj*, **endospermous** *adj*

**endosperm nucleus** *n* the TRIPLOID (containing three sets of genetic material) nucleus formed in the seed of a plant by fusion of a SPERM NUCLEUS with two POLAR NUCLEI or with a single nucleus formed by the prior fusion of the polar nuclei

**endospore** /'endǝ,spaw/ *n* an asexual spore developed within the cell, esp in bacteria [ISV] – **endosporic** *adj*, **endosporous** *adj*

**endosteal** /en'dostiǝl/ *adj* **1** of the endosteum **2** located within bone or cartilage – **endosteally** *adv*

**endosternite** /ˌendoh'stuhniet/ *n* a segment of the endoskeleton of a spider, insect, crab, or related animal [ISV *end-* + *sternum* + *-ite*]

**endosteum** /en'dostiǝm/ *n, pl* **endostea** /en'dostiǝ/ the layer of fibrous CONNECTIVE TISSUE lining the cavities of bone [NL, fr *end-* + Gk *osteon* bone – more at OSSEOUS]

**endostyle** /'endǝ,stiel/ *n* a structure in lower CHORDATES (large group of animals including those with backbones and lower forms without a proper skeleton) consisting of a pair of parallel longitudinal folds projecting into the cavity of the PHARYNX (muscular tube forming front portion of digestive tract) and bounding a groove lined with glandular cells bearing CILIA (hairlike structures) [ISV *end-* + Gk *stylos* pillar – more at STEER]

**endosulfan** /ˌendoh'sulfǝn/ *n* an insecticide, $C_9H_6Cl_6O_3S$, used against crop pests [*endo-* + *sulf-* + *-an*]

**endothecium** /ˌendoh'theesyǝm, -sh(y)ǝm/ *n, pl* **endothecia** /-'theesyǝ, -sh(y)ǝ/ the inner lining of a mature ANTHER (pollen-producing structure) in a flower [NL]

**endothelioma** /ˌendoh,theeli'ohmǝ/ *n* a tumour that develops from endothelial tissue [NL]

**endothelium** /ˌendoh'theeli·ǝm/ *n, pl* **endothelia** /-'theelyǝ/ **1** an EPITHELIUM (surface lining tissue) that is derived from the MESODERM (middle embryonic tissue layer), is composed of a single layer of thin flattened cells, and lines internal body cavities **2** the inner layer of the SEED COAT of some plants [NL, fr *end-* + epi*thelium*] – **endothelial** *adj*, **endotheloid** *adj*

**endotherm** /'endoh,thuhm/ *n* a warm-blooded animal – **endothermy** *n*

**endothermic** /ˌendoh'thuhmik/, **endothermal** /-'thuhml/ *adj* **1** characterized by or formed with absorption of heat ⟨*an ~ chemical reaction*⟩ **2** warm-blooded [ISV]

**endotoxin** /ˌendoh'toksin/ *n* a toxin of internal origin; *specif* a poisonous substance present in bacteria (e g of typhoid fever) but separable from the CELL BODY only on its disintegration [ISV] – **endotoxic** *adj*

**endotracheal** /ˌendohtrǝ'kee·ǝl/ *adj* **1** placed within the TRACHEA (windpipe) ⟨*an ~ tube*⟩ **2** applied or effected through the trachea

**endotrophic** /ˌendoh'trofik, -'trohfik/ *also* **endotropic** /-'tropik/ *adj* of or being a MYCORRHIZA (association between a fungus and the roots of a plant) in which the fungus penetrates the associated root and branches out between the cells – compare ECTOTROPHIC

**endow** /in'dow/ *vt* **1** to furnish with an income; *specif* to furnish with a permanent source of funds (e g from investments) ⟨*an ~ed school*⟩ **2a** to provide or equip gratuitously, esp with an ability or attribute ⟨*~ed with a natural grace*⟩ **b** CREDIT WITH 2 **3** *obs* to furnish with a DOWER (income from the estate of a dead husband) or dowry □ (2) usu + *with* [ME *endowen*, fr AF *endouer*, fr MF *en-* + *douer* to endow, fr L *dotare*, fr *dot-*, *dos* gift, dowry – more at DOWRY]

**endowment** /in'dowmənt/ *n* **1** the act or process of endowing **2** something that is endowed; *specif* the part of an institution's income derived from donations **3** natural capacity, power, or ability; talent

**endowment insurance** *n* LIFE INSURANCE under which a certain sum is paid to the insured at the end of an agreed period or to a specified beneficiary if the insured dies within that period

**endowment policy** *n* an insurance policy that provides for the payment of an agreed sum to the person insured at the end of a specified period or to another designated person should the insured person die before the policy's expiry date

**endozoic** /ˌendəˈzoh·ik/ *adj* living within or involving passage through an animal ⟨∼ *dispersal of seeds*⟩ [ISV]

**endpaper** /ˈend͵paypə/ *n* a once-folded sheet of paper having one leaf pasted flat against the inside of the front or back cover of a book and the other pasted at the base to the first or last page to form the flyleaf

**end plate** *n* a flat plate or structure at the end of something; *specif* a complex branching structure at the end of a NERVE FIBRE that conveys impulses away from the brain

**end point** *n* a point marking the completion of a (stage of a) process

**end product** *n* the final product of a series of processes or activities

**'end-͵stopped** *adj, of verse* having a break in sense, or requiring a pause in delivery, at the end of a line – compare RUN-ON

**end to end** *adv* with ends (nearly) touching; in a row

**endue** /inˈdyooh/ *vt, formal* 1 to provide or endow with some quality or attribute; *also* to imbue **2a** to don; PUT ON **b** to clothe □ *(1&2b)* usu pass + *with* [ME *enduen*, fr MF *enduire* to bring in, introduce, fr L *inducere* – more at INDUCE; (2) ME *enduen*, fr L *induere*, fr *ind-* in (fr OL *indu*) + *-uere* to put on – more at EXUVIAE]

**endurable** /inˈdyooərəbl/ *adj* capable of being endured; bearable – **endurably** *adv*

**endurance** /inˈdyooərəns/ *n* the ability to withstand hardship, adversity, or stress

**endure** /inˈdyooə/ *vi* 1 to continue in the same state; last 2 to remain firm under suffering or misfortune without yielding ∼ *vt* 1 to undergo (e g a hardship), esp without giving in; suffer 2 to tolerate, permit **synonyms** see ²BEAR, CONTINUE [ME *enduren*, fr MF *endurer*, fr (assumed) VL *indurare*, fr L, to harden, fr *in-* + *durare* to harden, endure – more at DURING]

**enduring** /inˈdyooəring/ *adj* lasting, durable – **enduringly** *adv*, **enduringness** *n*

**endways** /ˈendwayz/, **endwise** /ˈendwiez/ *adv or adj* 1 with the end forwards (e g towards the observer) 2 in or towards the direction of the ends; lengthways 3 upright; ON END ⟨*boxes set* ∼⟩ 4 end to end ⟨*put the tables together* ∼⟩

**¹-ene** /-een/ *suffix* (→ *n*) inhabitant of ⟨*Slovene*⟩ ⟨*Nazarene*⟩; *also* language of [deriv of GK *-ēnos*] – **ene** *suffix* (→ *adj*)

**²-ene** *suffix* (→ *n*) unsaturated carbon-containing chemical compound ⟨*benzene*⟩; *esp* ALIPHATIC (consisting of chains of atoms) carbon-containing compound with one DOUBLE BOND ⟨*ethylene*⟩ [ISV, fr Gk *-ēnē*, fem of *-ēnos*, adj suffix] – **-ene** *suffix* (→ *adj*)

**enema** /ˈenimə/ *n, pl* **enemas** *also* **enemata** /͵eniˈmahtə/ 1 the injection of liquid into the intestine by way of the anus (e g to ease constipation) 2 material for injection as an enema [LL, fr Gk, fr *enienai* to inject, fr *en-* + *hienai* to send – more at JET]

**enemy** /ˈenəmi/ *n* 1 one who is antagonistic to another; *esp* one seeking to injure, overthrow, or confound an opponent 2 something harmful or deadly 3 *taking sing or pl vb* **3a** a military adversary ⟨*the* ∼ *resorted to guerrilla warfare*⟩ **b** a hostile body, tank, etc [ME *enemi*, fr OF, fr L *inimicus*, fr *in-* ¹in- + *amicus* friend – more at AMIABLE]

**energetic** /͵enəˈjetik/ *adj* 1 marked by energy, activity, or vigour 2 operating with power or effect; forceful 3 of energy ⟨∼ *equation*⟩ **synonyms** see LIVELY [Gk *energētikos*, fr *energein* to be active, fr *energos*] – **energetically** *adv*

**energetics** /͵enəˈjetiks/ *n taking sing vb* 1 a branch of MECHANICS that deals primarily with energy and its transformations 2 the total energy relations and transformations of a system (e g a chemical reaction or an ecological community) ⟨∼ *of muscular contraction*⟩

**energid** /ˈenəjid/ *n* a nucleus and the body of CYTOPLASM (jelly-like material in a cell) with which it interacts [ISV, fr. Gk *energos*]

**energ·ize, -ise** /ˈenəˌjiez/ *vi* to put forth energy; act ∼ *vt* 1 to give energy to; make energetic or vigorous 2 to apply voltage to (e g the windings of an electric motor) △ **enervate**

**energ·izer, -iser** /ˈenəjiezə/ *n* something that energizes; *esp* an antidepressant drug

**energy** /ˈenəji/ *n* 1 the capacity of acting or being active ⟨*great intellectual* ∼⟩ 2 **energies** *pl*, **energy** natural power vigorously exerted ⟨*devoted all his energies to it*⟩ 3 the capacity for doing work ⟨*solar* ∼⟩ [LL *energia*, fr Gk *energeia* activity, fr *energos* active, fr *en* in + *ergon* work – more at WORK]

**energy level** *n* 1 any of the stable states of constant energy that may be assumed by a physical system – used esp of the positions of electrons in atoms and of nuclei 2 any of the divi-

sions of a FOOD CHAIN defined by the method of obtaining food – compare TROPHIC

**enervate** /ˈenəˌvayt/ *vt* to lessen the mental or physical strength or vitality of; weaken [L *enervatus*, pp of *enervare*, fr *e-* + *nervus* sinew – more at NERVE] – **enervative** *adj*, **enervation** *n*

*usage* This word has nothing to do with "nervousness". △ energize

**en famille** /on faˈmee *(Fr* ã famiːj)/ *adv* all together as a family; *also* among the family [Fr]

**enfant terrible** /͵onfonh teˈreeblə *(Fr* ãfã teribl)/ *n, pl* **enfants terribles** /∼/ a person whose inopportune outspokenness or unconventional actions cause embarrassment but also often a sneaking admiration [Fr, lit., terrifying child]

**enfeeble** /inˈfeebl/ *vt* to make feeble [ME *enfeblen*, fr MF *enfeblir*, fr OF, fr *en-* + *feble* feeble] – **enfeeblement** *n*

**enfeoff** /inˈfeef/ *vt* to invest with possession of a freehold estate in land, esp in exchange for service or homage to a feudal lord [ME *enfeoffen*, fr AF *enfeoffer*, fr OF *en-* + *fief*] – **enfeoffment** *n*

**enfetter** /enˈfetə/ *vt* to bind in fetters; chain up

**¹enfilade** /͵enfiˈlayd/ *n* 1 an arrangement (e g of rooms) in opposite and parallel rows 2 gunfire directed along the length of an enemy position or battle line [Fr, fr *enfiler* to thread, enfilade, fr OF, to thread, fr *en-* + *fil* thread – more at FILE]

**²enfilade** *vt* (to be in a position) to direct gunfire along

**enfleurage** /͵onfluhˈrah *(Fr* ãflœraːʒ)/ *n* a process of extracting perfumes by allowing the scents of flowers to be absorbed in some other substance [Fr]

**enfold** /inˈfohld/ *vt* **1a** to cover with folds; envelop **b** to surround with a covering; contain 2 to clasp in the arms; embrace

**enforce** /inˈfaws/ *vt* 1 to give greater force to (e g an argument); reinforce 2 to impose, compel ⟨∼d *good behaviour upon them*⟩ ⟨∼ *obedience from them*⟩ 3 to ensure obedience to (a rule or law) 4 *obs* to effect or gain by force [ME *encorcen*, fr MF *enforcier*, fr OF, fr *en-* + *force*] – **enforceable** *adj*, **enforcement** *n*, **enforcer** *n*, **enforceability** *n*

**enfranchise** /inˈfranchiez/ *vt* 1 to set free (e g from slavery) 2 to endow with a franchise: e g **2a** to admit to the privileges of a citizen; *specif* to admit to the right of voting **b** to admit (a municipality) to political privileges or rights; *esp* to invest with the right of having a representative in Parliament [ME *enfranchisen*, fr MF *enfranchiss-*, stem of *enfranchir*, fr OF, fr *en-* + *franc* free – more at FRANK] – **enfranchisement** *n*

**engage** /inˈgayj/ *vt* 1 to offer (e g one's word) as security for a debt or cause **2a** to attract and hold (someone's attention, thoughts, etc) **b** to come into contact or interlock with; *also* to cause )mechanical parts) to mesh 3 to bind (e g oneself) to do something ⟨*he* ∼d *himself to discharge his brother's debts*⟩; *esp* to bind (oneself) by a pledge to marry **4a** to provide occupation for; involve ⟨*a new project which will* ∼ *her talents to the full*⟩ **b** to arrange to obtain the use or services of; employ ⟨*decided to* ∼ *an English nanny and sack the au pair*⟩ **c** to reserve (a hotel room, opera box, etc) **5a** to hold the attention of; engross ⟨*her work* ∼s *her completely*⟩ **b** to induce to participate ⟨∼d *the shy boy in conversation*⟩ **c** to cause to participate; bring into play ⟨*the horse will* ∼ *his hocks before making a movement* – *Riding*⟩ **6a** to enter into contest with ⟨∼ *the enemy fleet*⟩ **b** to bring together or interlock (e g weapons) ⟨*the stags* ∼d *their antlers*⟩ ∼ *vi* **1a** to pledge oneself; promise **b** to guarantee – usu + *for* ⟨*he* ∼s *for the honesty of his brother*⟩ **2a** to begin and carry on an enterprise ⟨*he* ∼d *in trade for a number of years*⟩ **b** to occupy one's time; participate ⟨*at university he* ∼d *in gymnastics*⟩ ⟨*they* ∼ *in earnest discussion for several hours*⟩ 3 to enter into conflict ⟨*the fleets* ∼d *in the Atlantic*⟩ 4 to be or become interlocked or meshed [ME *engagen*, fr MF *engagier*, fr OF, fr *en-* + *gage* gage]

**engagé** /͵ong·gaˈzhay *(Fr* ãgaʒe)/ *adj* actively involved in or committed to something, esp a political cause [Fr, pp of *engager* to engage, fr MF *engagier*]

**engaged** /inˈgayjd/ *adj* 1 involved in activity; fully occupied ⟨*the chairman is* ∼ *all next week*⟩ 2 pledged to be married; betrothed 3 involved esp in a hostile encounter 4 partly embedded in a wall ⟨*an* ∼ *column*⟩ 5 in gear; meshed 6 engagé ⟨*an* ∼ *writer*⟩ 7 *chiefly Br* **7a** *of a toilet or telephone line* in use ⟨*the number was* ∼⟩ **b** reserved, booked ⟨*this table is* ∼⟩

**engagement** /inˈgayjmənt/ *n* **1a** the act of engaging; the state of being engaged **b** an agreement to marry; a betrothal 2 something that engages; a pledge **3a** a promise to be present at a certain time and place; *broadly* a meeting ⟨*an* ∼ *book*⟩ **b**

employment, esp as a performer and for a stated time **4** the state of being in gear **5** a hostile encounter between military forces – compare ¹BATTLE

**engaging** /in'gayjing/ *adj* tending to draw favourable attention; attractive, pleasing ⟨*a sweet child with most ~ manners*⟩ – **engagingly** *adv*

**engarland** /in'gahlənd/ *vt* to adorn (as if) with a garland

**Engelmann spruce** /'eng·g(ə)lmən/ *n* (the light-coloured wood of) a large N American spruce (*Picea engelmannii*) of British Columbia and the Rocky Mountain region [George *Engelmann* †1884 US botanist]

**engender** /in'jendə/ *vt* **1** to cause to exist or develop; produce ⟨*angry words ~ strife*⟩ **2** *archaic* to beget, procreate ~ *vi* to assume form; originate [ME *engendren*, fr MF *engendrer*, fr L *ingenerare*, fr *in-* + *generare* to generate]

**engine** /'enjin/ *n* **1** a mechanical tool or appliance; *esp* an instrument of torture or machine of war **2** a machine for converting any of various forms of energy into mechanical force and motion ⟨*a jet ~*⟩ **3** a railway locomotive **4** *archaic* something used to effect a purpose; an agent, instrument ⟨*mournful and terrible ~ of horror and of crime* – E A Poe⟩ **5** *obs* evil contrivance; wile [ME *engin* ingenuity, contrivance, machine, fr OF, fr L *ingenium* natural disposition, talent, fr *in-* + *gignere* to beget – more at KIN] – **engineless** *adj*

**-engined** /-enjind/ *comb form* (→ *adj*) having (such or so many) engines ⟨*front*-engined *cars*⟩ ⟨*twin*-engined *planes*⟩

**¹engineer** /,enji'niə/ *n* **1** a soldier formerly engaged in siege work, but now having the job of ensuring that military vehicles can move quickly and easily across country by building roads, bridges, etc **2a** a designer or builder of engines **b** a person who is trained in or follows as a profession a branch of engineering **c** a person who starts or carries through an enterprise, esp by skilful or artful contrivance ⟨*the ~ of the agreement*⟩ **3** a person who runs or supervises an engine or an apparatus **4** *obs* a crafty schemer; a plotter

**²engineer** *vt* **1** to lay out, construct, or manage as an engineer **2** to contrive, plan, or guide, usu with more or less subtle skill and craft

**engineering** /,enji'niəring/ *n* **1** the art of managing engines **2** the application of science and mathematics by which the properties of matter and the sources of energy in nature are made useful to human beings in structures, machines, products, systems, and processes

**enginery** /'enjinri/ *n* machines and tools; machinery

**engirdle** /in'guhdl/ *vt* to encircle (as if) with a girdle

**englacial** /in'glaysyəl, -shyəl/ *adj* embedded in a glacier

**¹English** /'ing·glish/ *adj* (characteristic) of England, its people, or the English language [ME, fr OE *englisc*, fr *Engle* (pl) Angles] – **Englishness** *n*, **Englishman** *n*, **Englishwoman** *n*

    *usage* A sports commentator may speak of ⟨*the* **England** *team*⟩, perhaps because **English** would suggest "English people" rather than "representing England". See BRITISH

**²English** *n* **1a** the Germanic language of the people of Britain, the USA, and most Commonwealth countries **b** English language, literature, or composition as a subject of academic study **2** *taking pl vb* the people of England

**English bond** *n* a method of bricklaying in which each layer of brickwork (COURSE) consists either of bricks with their long sides parallel to the direction in which the brickwork is running (STRETCHERS) or of bricks at right angles to it (HEADERS) and in which courses of headers and stretchers usu alternate

**English cross bond** *n* a modification of the ENGLISH BOND in which the stretcher courses break joint

**English garden wall bond** *n* a masonry bond in which three courses of stretchers alternate with one of headers

**English horn** *n*, *chiefly NAm* COR ANGLAIS (musical instrument of the oboe family) [trans of It *corno inglese*]

**English setter** *n* (any of) a breed of gundogs characterized by a moderately long flat silky coat of white with tan or greyish flecks or markings

**English sonnet** *n* SHAKESPEAREAN SONNET (rhyme scheme *abab cdcd efef gg*)

**English toy spaniel** *n*, *NAm* KING CHARLES SPANIEL

**English walnut** *n* a Eurasian walnut (*Juglans regia*) valued for its large edible nut and its hard richly figured wood

**Eng Lit** *n* English literature as a subject of academic study ⟨*another ~ quarterly*⟩ – often used attrib to suggest mere second-hand experience in contrast with real life ⟨*took an infuriatingly ~ view of his friend's problems*⟩

**engorge** /in'gawj/ *vt* to gorge, glut; *specif* to fill (eg an organ of the body) with blood to an excess ~ *vi, esp of an insect* to suck blood to the limit of body capacity [MF *engorgier*, fr OF, to devour, fr *en-* + *gorge* throat – more at GORGE] – **engorgement** *n*

**engrailed** /in'grayld/ *adj* **1** *heraldry* indented with small concave curves ⟨*an ~ heraldic bordure*⟩ **2** made of or bordered by a circle of raised dots ⟨*an ~ coin*⟩ [ME *engreled*, fr MF *engreslé*, fr *en-* + *gresle* slender, fr L *gracilis*]

**engrain** /in'grayn/ *vt* to ingrain

**engram** *also* **engramme** /'engram/ *n* a supposed alteration in the tissue of the brain which is held in some theories to be the physical basis of memory – compare MEMORY TRACE [ISV] – **engrammic** *adj*

**engrave** /in'grayv/ *vt* **1a** to cut (a design or lettering) on a hard surface (eg metal or glass) with a sharp tool **b** to impress deeply, as if by engraving ⟨*the incident was ~d in his memory*⟩ **2a** to cut a design or lettering on (a hard surface) for printing; *also* to print from an engraved plate **b** PHOTOENGRAVE (reproduce by photographing and then etching on a plate) [MF *engraver*, fr *en-* + *graver* to grave, of Gmc origin; akin to OE *grafan* to grave] – **engraver** *n*

**engraving** /in'grayving/ *n* **1** the act or process of one who engraves **2** something that is engraved: eg **2a** an engraved printing surface **b** engraved work **3** an impression from an engraved printing surface

**engross** /in'grohs/ *vt* **1a** to copy or write in a large hand **b** to prepare the usu final handwritten or printed text of (an official document) **2a** to buy large quantities of (eg as a commercial speculation) **b** to occupy the whole of (eg a person's mind or attention; absorb ⟨*a scholar ~ed in research*⟩ ⟨*an ~ing problem*⟩ [ME *engrossen*, fr AF *engrosser*, prob fr ML *ingrossare*, fr L *in* + ML *grossa* large handwriting, fr L, fem of *grossus* thick] – **engrosser** *n*, **engrossment** *n*

**engulf** /in'gulf/ *vt* **1** to flow over and enclose; overwhelm ⟨*the mounting seas threatened to ~ the island*⟩ **2** *of a cell, an amoeba, etc* to take in (food) (as if) by flowing over and enclosing – **engulfment** *n*

**enhalo** /in'hayloh/ *vt* **enhaloed; enhaloing** to surround (as if) with a halo

**enhance** /in'hahns/ *vt* to increase the value, desirability, or attractiveness of; improve ⟨*a hillside location ~d by a broad vista*⟩ [ME *enhauncen*, fr AF *enhauncer*, alter. of OF *enhaucier*, fr (assumed) VL *inaltiare*, fr L *in* + *altus* high – more at OLD] – **enhancement** *n*

    *usage* One **enhances** a quality ⟨**enhance** *his prestige*⟩, or a thing, but not its possessor ⟨⚠ **enhance** *him*⟩. **synonyms** see INTENSIFY **antonym** detract (from)

**enharmonic** /,enhah'monik/ *adj* of or being musical notes that have different names when played in different musical scales (eg A flat in the key of E flat and G sharp in the key of A) but are produced identically (eg by depressing the same key on the piano) [Fr *enharmonique*, fr MF, of a scale employing quarter tones, fr Gk *enarmonios*, fr *en* in + *harmonia* harmony, scale] – **enharmonically** *adv*

**enigma** /i'nigmə/ *n* **1** intentionally obscure speech or writing; a riddle **2** something or someone hard to understand or explain; a puzzle **synonyms** see ¹OBSCURE, ¹PROBLEM [L *aenigma*, fr Gk *ainigmat-, ainigma*, fr *ainissesthai* to speak in riddles, fr *ainos* fable] – **enigmatic** *adj*

**enisle** /in'iel/ *vt* **1** to make an island of **2** *poetic* to isolate

**enjambment, enjambement** /in'jam·mənt (*Fr* ãʒãbmã)/ *n* the running over of a sentence from one verse or couplet into another so that there is no natural pause at the end of the line – compare RUN-ON [Fr *enjambement*, fr MF, encroachment, fr *enjamber* to straddle, encroach on, fr *en-* + *jambe* leg – more at JAMB]

**enjoin** /in'joyn/ *vt, formal* **1** to command (someone) to do something; order **2** to impose (a condition or course of action) on someone ⟨*she ~ed obedience on the children*⟩ **3** to forbid (as if) by law; prohibit ⟨*was ~ed by conscience from telling a lie*⟩ [ME *enjoinen*, fr OF *enjoindre*, fr L *injungere*, fr *in-* + *jungere* to join – more at YOKE]

    *usage* To **enjoin** something may mean either to "command" it or to "forbid" it ⟨*his religion* **enjoins** *fasting*⟩. It is therefore clearer to use the verb in some other construction. Compare ⟨*he was* **enjoined** (= commanded) *to fast*⟩ ⟨*he was* **enjoined** (= forbidden) *from fasting*⟩.

**enjoy** /in'joy/ *vt* **1** to take pleasure or satisfaction in **2a** to have the use or benefit of ⟨*the house ~s a clear view over the Downs to the South*⟩ **b** to experience (something good); undergo

⟨*he* ~s *the best of health*⟩ ⟨*she* ~ed *a liberal education at a continental university*⟩ **synonyms** see PLEASURE [MF *enjoir*, fr OF, fr *en-* + *joir* to enjoy, fr L *gaudēre* to rejoice – more at JOY] – **enjoyable** *adj*, **enjoyableness** *n*, **enjoyably** *adv*, **enjoyment** *n* – **enjoy oneself** to have a good time

**enlace** /in'lays/ *vt* 1 to encircle, enfold 2 to entwine, interlace [ME *enlacen*, fr MF *enlacier*, fr OF, fr *en-* + *lacier* to lace] – **enlacement** *n*

**enlarge** /in'lahj/ *vt* 1 to make larger 2 to reproduce in a larger form; *specif* to make a photographic enlargement of 3 to give greater scope to ⟨~d *his interests*⟩ 4 *archaic* to set free (e g a captive) ~ *vi* 1 to grow larger 2 to speak or write at length; elaborate – often + *on* or *upon* ⟨*let me* ~ *on that point*⟩ **synonyms** see ¹INCREASE **antonym** diminish [ME *enlargen*, fr MF *enlargier*, fr OF, fr *en-* + *large*] – **enlargeable** *adj*, **enlarger** *n*

**enlargement** /in'lahjmənt/ *n* 1 an act or instance of enlarging; the state of being enlarged 2 a photographic print that is larger than the negative and is made by projecting an image of the negative onto a photographic printing surface (e g sensitized paper)

**enlighten** /in'liet(ə)n/ *vt* 1a to give knowledge to and so free from ignorance or prejudice; cause to understand ⟨*a people* ~ed *by experience*⟩ ⟨*an* ~ed *ruling*⟩ **b** to give spiritual insight to ⟨*divine mercy can* ~ *the soul*⟩ 2 *archaic* to shed light on; illuminate

**enlightenment** /in'liet(ə)nmənt/ *n* 1 the act or means of enlightening; the state of being enlightened 2 *cap* an 18th-century movement marked by a belief in universal human progress and the sovereignty of reason and an emphasis on empirical research in the sciences – + *the* 3 *Hinduism & Buddhism* a final blessed state marked by the absence of desire or suffering – called also NIRVANA

**enlist** /in'list/ *vt* 1 to engage (a person) for duty in the armed forces 2 to secure the support and aid of; employ in advancing an interest ⟨~ *all the available resources*⟩ ⟨~ *you in a good cause*⟩; *broadly* to attract ⟨*failed to* ~ *much support*⟩ ~ *vi* to enrol oneself in the armed forces; *broadly* to join a movement ⟨~ed *in the local environment group*⟩ – **enlistee** *n*, **enlistment** *n*

**enlisted man** /in'listid/ *n* a person in the US armed forces ranking below a commissioned or warrant officer

**enliven** /in'liev(ə)n/ *vt* to give life, action, spirit, or interest to; animate – **enlivenment** *n*

**en masse** /,om 'mas (*Fr* ã mas)/ *adv* in a body; as a whole [Fr]

**enmesh** /in'mesh/ *vt* to catch or entangle (as if) in a net or mesh – **enmeshment** *n*

**enmity** /'enmiti/ *n* positive, active, and typically mutual hatred or ill will (e g between rivals) [ME *enmite*, fr MF *enemité*, fr OF *enemisté*, irreg fr *enemi* enemy]

**synonyms** Enmity, hostility, antipathy, antagonism, animosity, rancour, and animus describe feelings of intense ill will, or its expression. Enmity contrasts with "friendship", and suggests the hatred that exists between enemies, and which may be either latent or overt. Hostility is stronger, and often openly expressed ⟨*regarded the newcomers with* hostility⟩. Antipathy and antagonism express dislike on temperamental grounds: antipathy suggests a strong aversion to people or things ⟨*had an* antipathy *for cats*⟩. Antagonism implies a clash of temperaments and active, often mutual, hostility ⟨*the* antagonism *between Jane and her mother did not diminish with time*⟩. Animosity and rancour are violently felt emotions: the former suggests vindictive anger which may desire to cause actual harm, the latter describes the bitter ill will which comes from nursing a grievance. Animus stresses the personal nature of an irrational or prejudiced ill will which seeks expression ⟨*cherished an* animus *against the State because he could not go to university*⟩. Compare ¹HATE **antonyms** friendship, friendliness, charity

**ennead** /'eniad/ *n* a group or series of nine [Gk *ennead-*, *enneas*, fr *ennea* nine – more at NINE]

**ennoble** /in'nohbl/ *vt* 1 to make noble; elevate ⟨*believes that hard work* ~s *the human spirit*⟩ 2 to raise to the rank of the nobility [ME *ennobelen*, fr MF *ennoblir*, fr OF, fr *en-* + *noble*] – **ennoblement** *n*, **ennobler** *n*

**ennui** /on'wi (*Fr* ãnɣi)/ *n* a feeling of weariness, dissatisfaction, and lack of interest [Fr, fr OF *enui* annoyance, fr *enuier* to annoy]

**enol** /'eenol, 'eenohl/ *n* a carbon-containing chemical compound that contains a HYDROXYL group bonded to a carbon atom having a DOUBLE BOND and that is usu characterized by the grouping C=C(OH) [ISV *ene-* (fr *-ene*) + *-ol*] – **enolic** *adj*

**enolase** /'eenəlayz/ *n* an ENZYME that is found esp in muscle and yeast and is important in the METABOLISM (biochemical processing) of carbohydrates [ISV *enol* + *-ase*]

**enology** /,ee'noləji/ *n* OENOLOGY (science of wine making) – **enologist** *n*

**enophile** /'eenoh,fiel/, **enophilist** /ee'nofi,list/ *n* OENOPHILE (wine lover)

**enormity** /i'nawməti/ *n* 1 the quality or state of being immoderate, monstrous, or outrageous; *esp* great wickedness ⟨*the utter* ~ *of the crime*⟩ 2 a terribly wicked or evil act 3 the quality or state of being enormous; immensity

**usage** The now very common use of **enormity** to mean "enormousness" is still widely disliked.

**enormous** /i'nawməs/ *adj* 1 marked by extraordinarily great size, number, or degree; *esp* exceeding usual bounds or expectations 2a exceedingly wicked; shocking ⟨*an* ~ *sin*⟩ **b** *archaic* abnormal, inordinate **synonyms** see HUGE **antonyms** puny, tiny [L *enormis*, fr *e*, *ex* out of + *norma* rule] – **enormously** *adv*, **enormousness** *n*

**enosis** /'enohsis/ *n* the union of Cyprus and Greece, which is the aim of various groups of Greek nationalist Cypriots [NGK *henōsis*, fr Gk, union, fr *henoun* to unite, fr *hen-*, *heis* one]

¹**enough** /i'nuf/ *adj* fully adequate in quantity, number, or degree ⟨*not* ~ *beer*⟩ ⟨*chairs* ~ *for so many*⟩ ⟨*was fool* ~ *to believe him*⟩ **synonyms** see SUFFICIENT [ME *ynough*, fr OE *genōg*; akin to OHG *ginuog* enough; both fr a prehistoric Gmc compound whose first constituent is represented by OE *ge-* (perfective prefix) and whose second is akin to L *nancisci* to get, Gk *enenkein* to carry]

²**enough** *adv* 1 to a fully adequate degree; sufficiently ⟨*not cooked long* ~⟩ 2 to a tolerable degree ⟨*he understands well* ~⟩

**usage** The construction **enough** that ⟨*he's old* **enough** *that he can go to the theatre*⟩ is now common, especially in American English, but disliked by some people, who prefer **enough** to ⟨*he's old* **enough** *to go to the theatre*⟩.

³**enough** *pron*, *pl* **enough** a sufficient quantity or number ⟨~ *were present to constitute a quorum*⟩ ⟨*had* ~ *of their foolishness*⟩

**enounce** /i'nowns/ *vt* to pronounce formally; enunciate [Fr *énoncer*, fr L *enuntiare* to report – more at ENUNCIATE]

**enow** /i'now/; *formerly* i'noh/ *adv* or *adj*, *archaic* enough [ME *inow*, fr OE *genōg*]

**en passant** /,on pa'sonh (*Fr* ã pasã)/ *adv* in passing – used in chess of the capture of a pawn as it makes a first move of two squares, by an enemy pawn in a position to threaten the first of these squares [Fr]

**enphytotic** /,enfie'totik/ *adj*, *of a plant disease* occurring regularly in a district but only in moderate severity [²*en-* + *phyt-* + *-otic*] – **enphytotic** *n*

**enplane** /en'playn/ *vb*, *chiefly NAm* to board or put on an aircraft; emplane

**en prise** /,om 'preez (*Fr* ã priz)/ *adj*, *of a chess piece* exposed to capture [Fr]

**en quad** *n* a type-metal space (QUAD) that is the same length as an EN (letter *n*); one half of an EM QUAD [fr its being based on the width of the letter *n*]

**enquire** /in'kwie-ə/ *vb* to inquire

**usage** Some British writers distinguish between **enquire** ("ask about") and **inquire** ("conduct an investigation"); and between an **enquiry** (a "question") and **inquiry** (an "investigation"). In American English the two spellings are not distinguished in meaning.

**enquiry** /in'kwie-əri/ *n* an inquiry

**enrage** /in'rayj/ *vt* to fill with rage; anger [MF *enrager* to become mad, fr OF *enragier*, fr *en-* + *rage*]

**en rapport** /,onh ra'paw (*Fr* ã rapɔːr)/ *adj* in a state of harmony or agreement ⟨*we became so* ~ *that speaking was unnecessary*⟩ [Fr]

**enrapture** /in'rapchə/ *vt* to fill with delight

**enrich** /in'rich/ *vt* 1 to make rich or richer, esp in some desirable quality ⟨*the experience greatly* ~ed *his life*⟩ 2 to adorn, ornament ⟨~ing *the ceiling with frescoes*⟩ 3a to make (soil) more fertile **b** to improve (a food) in nutritive value by adding nutrients (e g vitamins or minerals), esp by restoring part of the nutrients lost in processing **c** to increase the proportion of a valuable or desirable ingredient in ⟨~ *uranium with uranium 235*⟩; *also* to add a desirable substance to ⟨~ *natural gas*⟩ [ME *enrichen*, fr MF *enrichir*, fr OF, fr *en-* + *riche* rich] – **enricher** *n*, **enrichment** *n*

**enrobe** /in'rohb/ *vt* to invest or adorn (as if) with a robe

**enrol**, *NAm also* **enroll** /in'rohl/ *vb* **-ll-** *vt* **1** to insert, register, or enter in a list, catalogue, or roll ⟨*the school* ~s *about 800 pupils*⟩ **2** to prepare a final perfect copy of (a bill passed by a legislature) in written or printed form **3** to roll or wrap up ~ *vi* to enrol oneself or cause oneself to be enrolled ⟨*he* ~*led in the history course*⟩ – **enrollee** *n*, **enroller** *n*, **enrolment** *n* [ME *enrollen*, fr MF *enroller*, fr *en-* + *rolle* roll, register]

**enroot** /in'rooht/ *vt* to fix or implant (as if) by roots; establish

**en route** /ˌon 'rooht (*Fr* ã rut)/ *adv or adj* on or along the way ⟨*soon they were* ~ *to the border*⟩ ⟨*civil* ~ *services – Principles of Transport*⟩ [Fr]

**ens** /enz/ *n, pl* **entia** /'enshiə/ the most abstract or undifferentiated form of being; being considered independently of any other incidental properties [ML, fr L, existing thing – more at ENTITY]

**ensample** /in'sahmpl/ *n, archaic* an example, instance [ME, fr MF *ensample, example*]

**ensanguine** /in'sang·gwin/ *vt, formal* to bloody

**ensconce** /in'skons/ *vt* to settle (e g oneself) comfortably or snugly ⟨*the cat* ~d *herself in her basket*⟩ [¹*en-* + ² *sconce*]

**ensemble** /on'sombl (*Fr* ãsã:bl)/ *n* **1** *taking sing or pl vb* a group that works together as a whole or produces a single effect: e g **1a** *music* a combination of two or more performers or players; *esp* a musical group having only one instrument playing each instrumental part and used chiefly to perform chamber music ⟨*the Philip Jones Brass* Ensemble⟩ **b** a complete outfit of matching or coordinated clothes and accessories **c(1)** a theatrical company **c(2)** a group of supporting players, singers, or dancers; *esp* CORPS DE BALLET **2** the quality of togetherness in performance ⟨*the quartet's* ~ *was poor*⟩ [Fr, fr *ensemble* together, fr L *insimul* at the same time, fr *in-* + *simul* at the same time – more at SAME]

**ensheathe** /in'sheedh/ *vt* to cover (as if) with a sheath

**enshrine** /in'shrien/ *vt* **1** to enclose (as if) in a shrine **2** to preserve or cherish, esp as sacred ⟨*they* ~d *their leader's memory in their hearts*⟩ – **enshrinement** *n*

**enshroud** /in'shrowd/ *vt* to shroud ⟨~ed *in mystery*⟩

**ensiform** /'ensi,fawm/ *adj* having sharp edges and tapering to a slender point ⟨~ *leaves of the gladiolus*⟩ [Fr *ensiforme*, fr L *ensis* sword + Fr *-forme* -form]

**ensign** /'ensien; *sense 1 naval* 'ensən/ *n* **1** a flag that is flown (e g by a ship) as the symbol of nationality and that may also be flown with a distinctive badge added to its design (e g by an organization having nautical associations) **2a** a badge of office, rank, or power **b** an emblem, sign **3a** *archaic* a standard-bearer **b** – see MILITARY RANKS table [ME *ensigne*, fr MF *enseigne*, fr L *insignia* insignia, flags]

**ensilage** /'ensilij/ *n* **1** the process of preserving fodder by ensiling **2** fodder produced by ensiling; silage

**ensile** /en'siel, '--/ *vt* to prepare and store (fodder made from grass and other green crops) in a silo or pit; convert (fodder) into silage [Fr *ensiler*, fr *en-* + *silo*, fr Sp]

**enslave** /in'slayv/ *vt* to reduce (as if) to slavery; subjugate – **enslavement** *n*, **enslaver** *n*

**ensnare** /in'sneə/ *vt* to take (as if) in a snare *synonyms* see ¹CATCH – **ensnarement** *n*, **ensnarer** *n*

**ensnarl** /in'snahl/ *vt* to entangle

**ensoul** /in'sohl/ *vt, formal or poetic* to endow or imbue with a soul

**ensphere** /in'sfiə/ *vt, chiefly formal* to enclose (as if) in a sphere

**ensue** /in'syooh/ *vt, poetic* to pursue ⟨*I wander, seeking peace, and ensuing it* – Rupert Brooke⟩ ~ *vi* **1** to take place afterwards; follow immediately **2** to happen as a result [ME *ensuen*, fr MF *ensuivre*, fr OF, fr *en-* + *suivre* to follow – more at SUE]

**en suite** /ˌon 'sweet (*Fr* ã syit)/ *adv or adj* in a set or series, esp so as to form a unit ⟨*rooms arranged* ~⟩ [Fr]

**ensure** /in'shooə, -'shaw/ *vt* to make sure or certain; guarantee [ME *ensuren*, fr AF *enseurer*, prob alter. of OF *aseürer* – more at ASSURE]

*usage* Ensure and insure have the same pronunciation.

**enswathe** /in'swaydh/ *vt* to enfold or enclose (as if) with a covering; swathe

**ent-** /ent-/, **ento-** *comb form* inner; within ⟨ento*blast*⟩ ⟨ent*amoeba*⟩ [NL, fr Gk *entos* within; akin to L *intus* within, Gk *en* in – more at IN]

**entablature** /en'tabləchə/ *n* the upper part of the facade of a classical building that is usu supported on columns or PILASTERS (columns attached to a wall) and consists of a projecting CORNICE at the top, a FRIEZE in the middle, and an ARCHITRAVE at the base; *also* any similar structure (e g an

elevated support for a machine part( [obs Fr, modif of It *intavolatura*, fr *intavolare* to put on a board or table, fr *in-* )fr L) + *tavola* board, table, fr L *tabula* – more at TABLE]

**entablement** /in'tayblmənt/ *n* a platform that supports a statue and that is placed above the DADO [Fr, fr OF, fr *en-* + *table*]

¹**entail** /in'tayl/ *vt* **1** to arrange for the future disposal of (esp land) in such a way that sale or bequeathal is not permitted and inheritance is limited to a specified category of the owner's heirs **2** to confer, assign, or transmit unalterably; fasten ⟨~ed *on them indelible disgrace* – Robert Browning⟩ **3** to impose, involve, or imply as a necessary accompaniment or result ⟨*the project will* ~ *considerable expense*⟩ **4** *obs* to fix (a person) permanently in some condition or status ⟨~ *him and his heirs unto the crown* – Shak⟩ [ME *entailen, entaillen*, fr ¹*en-* + *taile, taille* limitation, fr MF *taille*, fr OF, fr *taillier* to cut, limit – more at TAILOR] – **entailer** *n*, **entailment** *n*

²**entail** *n* **1a** an instance of entailing, esp of lands **b** something (e g an estate) that is entailed **c** the order of inheritance for an entailed property **2** something, esp an attribute, attitude, or behaviour, transmitted as if by entail

**entamoeba** /ˌentə'meebə/ *n* any of a genus (*Entamoeba*) of amoebas parasitic in the intestines of animals and including the amoeba (*Entamoeba histolytica*) that causes AMOEBIC DYSENTERY in humans

**entangle** /in'tang·gl/ *vt* **1** to make tangled, complicated, or confused ⟨*his explanation only served to* ~ *the question further*⟩ **2** to involve in a tangle; ensnare ⟨*become* ~d *in a ruinous lawsuit*⟩ – **entangler** *n*

**entanglement** /in'tang·glmənt/ *n* **1a** entangling or being entangled **b** **entanglements** *pl*, **entanglement** something that entangles, confuses, or ensnares ⟨*barbed-wire* ~s⟩ **2** the condition of being deeply involved

**entasis** /'entəsis/ *n* a slight convexity in the shaft of a column that is introduced to correct the visual illusion of concavity created by a straight shaft [Gk, lit., distension, stretching, fr *enteinein* to stretch tight, fr *en-* ²en- + *teinein* to stretch – more at THIN]

**entelechy** /en'teliki/ *n* **1** the (coming to) actuality of something that was potential **2** a hypothetical agency held in some VITALIST (believing life depends on a vital principle distinct from physico-chemical forces) doctrines to be inherent in living organisms and to regulate or direct their vital processes [LL *entelechia*, fr Gk *entelecheia*, fr *en telei echein* to be complete or perfect, fr *en* in + *telos* end, perfection + *echein* to have]

**entellus** /en'teləs/ *n* HANUMAN (monkey sacred to Hindus) [NL, prob fr L *Entellus*, a mythical Sicilian boxer]

**entente** /on'tont (*Fr* ãtã:t)/ *n* **1** an informal international agreement; *broadly* an agreement, understanding **2** *taking sing or pl vb* the parties to an entente [Fr, fr OF, intent, understanding – more at INTENT]

**entente cordiale** /ˌkawdi'al, -'dyal (*Fr* kɔrdjal)/ *n* ENTENTE 1; *specif* one concluded between Britain and France in 1904 or between Britain, France, and Russia in 1908 [Fr, cordial entente]

**enter** /'entə/ *vi* **1a** to go or come in **b** to pierce, penetrate ⟨*the bullet* ~ed *above the heart*⟩ **2** to come or gain admission into a group; join **3** to register as candidate in a competition ⟨*decided to* ~ *for the race*⟩ **4** to make a beginning ⟨~ing *upon a career*⟩ **5** to play a part; be a factor – usu + *in or into* ⟨~ *into a conversation*⟩ ~ *vt* **1a** to go or come into ⟨~ *a room*⟩ ⟨~ing *her early thirties*⟩ **b** to penetrate (e g flesh) **2** to inscribe, register ⟨~ *the names of qualified voters in the rolls*⟩ **3** to cause to be received, admitted, or considered – often + *for* ⟨~ *a child for a public school*⟩ **4** to put in; insert **5** to become a member of or an active participant in ⟨~ *university*⟩ ⟨~ *a race*⟩ ⟨~ *politics*⟩ **6** to report (a ship or her cargo) to customs authorities **7** to place in proper form before a court of law or upon record ⟨~ *a writ*⟩ **8** to go into or upon and take actual possession of (as land) **9** to put formally on record ⟨~ing *a complaint against his business partner*⟩ [ME *entren*, fr OF *entrer*, fr L *intrare*, fr *intra* within; akin to L *inter* between – more at INTER-] – **enterable** *adj*

**enter into** *vt* **1** to make oneself a party to or in ⟨enter into *an important agreement*⟩ **2** to form a constituent part of ⟨*tin* enters into *the composition of pewter*⟩ **3** to participate or share in ⟨*cheerfully* entering into *the household tasks*⟩

**enter-** /entə-/, **entero-** *comb form* intestine ⟨enter*itis*⟩ [Gk, fr *enteron*]

**enteric** /en'terik/ *adj* **1** of the intestines; *broadly* ALIMENTARY **2**

of or being a medicinal preparation treated to pass through the stomach unaltered and to disintegrate in the intestines

**enteritis** /ˌentə'rietəs/ n inflammation of the intestines, esp the lower part of the SMALL INTESTINE (part of intestine leading from the stomach), usu marked by diarrhoea [NL]

**enterobacterium** /ˌentərohbak'tiəriəm, '----,--/ n any of a family (Enterobacteriaceae) of straight rod-shaped bacteria (e g a salmonella or a COLON BACILLUS) that ferment the sugar glucose, including some that feed on dead or decaying matter and some that cause serious disease in humans, lower animals, and plants – **enterobacterial** adj

**enterobiasis** /ˌentero'bie-əsis/ n, pl **enterobiases** /-seez/ infestation with or disease caused by pinworms (genus Enterobius) that occurs esp in children [NL, fr Enterobius, genus name + -iasis]

**enterococcus** /'enterohˌkokəs/ n, pl **enterococci** /-ˌkokie, -ˌkoksie, -see/ STREPTOCOCCUS (chainlike bacterium); esp one (e g Streptococcus faecalis) normally present in the intestine [NL, genus name] – **enterococcal** adj

**enterocoele, enterocoel** /'entəroh,seel/ n a COELOM (body cavity between the body wall and gut) originating as an outgrowth from the ARCHENTERON (central cavity of an early animal embryo) – **enterocoelic** adj, **enterocoelous** adj

**enterocolitis** /ˌentərohko'lietəs/ n enteritis affecting both the SMALL INTESTINE (upper part of the intestine leading from the stomach) and the COLON (division of the lower intestine) [NL]

**enterogastrone** /ˌentəroh'gastrohn/ n a hormone produced by the MUCOUS MEMBRANE lining the DUODENUM (part of intestine leading from the stomach) that inhibits the secretion of digestive juice by the stomach and muscular movement of the stomach and intestines [enter- + gastr- + hormone]

**enterokinase** /ˌent(ə)roh'kienayz, -nays/ n an ENZYME esp of the upper intestine that converts TRYPSINOGEN (inactive substance secreted into the intestine) into the active protein-digesting enzyme TRYPSIN [ISV]

**enteron** /'entəron/ n 1 ALIMENTARY CANAL (digestive tract from mouth to anus); gut; esp the incompletely developed alimentary canal of an embryo 2 COELENTERON (body cavity of jellyfish, sea anemone, etc) [NL, fr Gk, intestine – more at INTER-]

**enteropathogenic** /ˌentəroh,pathə'jenik/ adj tending to produce disease in the intestinal tract ⟨~ bacteria⟩

**enteropathy** /ˌentə'ropəthi/ n a disease of the intestinal tract

**enterostomy** /ˌentə'rostəmi/ n the surgical formation of an opening into the intestine through the abdominal wall for the purpose of artificial feeding or to act as an artificial anus [ISV]

**enterotoxin** /ˌentəroh'toksin, '---,--/ n a poisonous substance that is produced by microorganisms (e g some STAPHYLOCOCCI bacteria) and is responsible for the gastrointestinal symptoms (e g vomiting and diarrhoea) of some forms of food poisoning

**enterovirus** /ˌentəroh'vie(ə)rəs, '--,--/ n any of a group of small RNA-containing viruses (PICORNAVIRUSES) that typically occur in the stomach and intestines and include viruses (e g the Coxsackie viruses, echoviruses, and polioviruses) associated with various respiratory ailments, MENINGITIS (inflammation of the membranes surrounding the brain), polio, and disorders of the nervous system [NL] – **enteroviral** adj

**enterprise** /'entə,priez/ n 1 an often complicated, difficult, or risky project or undertaking 2 a unit of economic organization or activity; esp a business organization 3 readiness to engage in enterprises; initiative [ME, fr MF entreprise, fr entreprendre to undertake, fr entre- inter- + prendre to take – more at PRIZE] – **enterpriser** n

**enterprising** /'entə,priezing/ adj ready to engage in enterprises; showing initiative

**entertain** /entə'tayn/ vt 1 to show hospitality to 2a to have in one's mind; HARBOUR 3 ⟨I ~ grave doubts about their sincerity⟩ b to consider ⟨she refused to ~ his plea⟩ 3 to hold the attention of, usu pleasantly or enjoyably; DIVERT 2 4 to play against (an opposing team) on one's home ground 5 archaic to maintain 6 obs to receive (a person) ~ vi to provide entertainment, esp at one's home, for guests ⟨they don't ~ much⟩ [ME entertinen, fr MF entretenir, fr entre- inter- + tenir to hold – more at TENABLE] – **entertainer** n

**entertainment** /ˌentə'taynmənt/ n 1 the act of entertaining ⟨his serious ~ of my idea was a surprise⟩ 2 something entertaining, diverting, or engaging ⟨this book is excellent ~⟩ 3 a public performance 4 archaic maintenance, provision 5 obs employment

**enthalpy** /'enthəlpi, en'thalpi/ n a THERMODYNAMIC property

of a system equal to the sum of its internal energy and the product of its volume and pressure [en- + Gk thalpein to heat]

**enthral, NAm chiefly enthrall** /in'thrawl/ vt -ll- 1 to hold the complete interest and attention of; fascinate, captivate 2 archaic to reduce to slavery [¹en- + thrall] – **enthralment** n

**enthrone** /in'throhn/ vt 1 to seat, esp ceremonially, (as if) on a throne in token of assigning high authority ⟨~ a king⟩ 2 to assign supreme virtue or value to; exalt – **enthronement** n

**enthuse** /in'thyoohz/ vt to make enthusiastic ⟨proposals which ... shocked the orthodox and ~d the rebellious – TLS⟩ ~ vi 1 to show enthusiasm ⟨he ~d about her obvious talents⟩ 2 to say with enthusiasm ⟨"a terrific performance by the Birmingham player," Ted Lowe ~d – Richard Boston⟩ [back-formation fr enthusiasm]

usage Some people disapprove of the use of **enthuse** in formal writing.

**enthusiasm** /in'thyoohzi,az(ə)m/ n 1 eager or intense interest or admiration; fervour – usu + for or about 2 something inspiring enthusiasm ⟨butterfly-collecting is one of his ~s⟩ 3 archaic excessive display of religious emotion synonyms see PASSION antonym indifference [Gk enthousiasmos, fr enthousiazein to be inspired, fr entheos inspired, fr en- + theos god] – **enthusiastic** adj, **enthusiastically** adv

**enthusiast** /in'thyoohzi,ast/ n 1 a person filled with enthusiasm; esp one who is ardently attached to a usu specified cause, object, or pursuit ⟨a rugby football ~⟩ ⟨he's a real ale ~⟩ ⟨an impassioned ~ for both literature and painting – TLS⟩ – compare DEVOTEE, ADDICT, BUFF, FAN 2 one who tends to give him-/herself completely to whatever engages his/her interest 3 archaic one who is excessively zealous in his/her religious views

**enthymeme** /enthi,meem/ n a SYLLOGISM (formal argument) in which one of the premises is implicit rather than stated [L enthymema, fr Gk enthymēma, fr enthymeisthai to keep in mind, fr en- + thymos mind, soul – more at FUME]

**entice** /in'ties/ vt to tempt or persuade by arousing hope or desire synonyms see ²LURE [ME enticen to incite, allure, fr OF enticier, fr (assumed) VL intitiare, fr L in- + titio firebrand] – **enticement** n, **enticingly** adv

**¹entire** /in'tie-ə/ adj 1 having no element or part left out ⟨was alone the ~ day⟩ 2 complete in degree; total ⟨his ~ devotion to his family⟩ 3a consisting of one piece; homogenous ⟨the book is ~ in mood⟩ b intact ⟨strove to keep the collection ~⟩ 4 not castrated 5 having the edge continuous or free from indentations ⟨~ leaves⟩ 6 heraldry 6a without a mark that serves to identify otherwise identical coats of arms b extending to the edges of the shield [ME, fr MF entir, fr L integer, lit., untouched, fr in- ¹in- + tangere to touch – more at TANGENT] – **entire** adv, **entireness** n

**²entire** n 1 the uncastrated male animal; esp a stallion 2 archaic the whole; the entirety

**entirely** /in'tie-əli/ adv 1 wholly, completely ⟨agreed with me ~⟩ ⟨you are ~ welcome⟩ 2 solely ⟨it is his fault ~⟩

**entirety** /in'tie-ərəti/ n 1 the state of being entire or complete ⟨perfect in its ~⟩ 2 an entire thing; a whole, total

**entitle** /in'tietl/ vt 1 to give (somebody or something) a title 2 to give the right to (do or have) something ⟨this ticket ~s the bearer to free admission⟩ [ME entitlen, fr MF entituler, fr LL intitulare, fr L in- ²in- + titulus title] – **entitlement** n

**entity** /'entəti/ n 1a being, existence; esp independent, separate, or self-contained existence b the existence of a thing as contrasted with its attributes 2 something that has separate and distinct existence [ML entitas, fr L ent-, ens existing thing, fr irreg prp of esse to be – more at IS]

**ento-** /entoh-/ – see ENT-

**entoblast** /'entəblast/ n HYPOBLAST (innermost layer of cells of an early embryo) – **entoblastic** adj

**entoderm** /'entə,duhm/ n ENDODERM – **entodermal, entodermic** adj

**entoil** /in'toyl/ vt, archaic to entrap, enmesh

**entom-** /entəm-/, **entomo-** comb form insect ⟨entomophagous⟩ [Fr, fr Gk entomon]

**entomb** /in'toohm/ vt 1 to place (as if) in a tomb; bury 2 to serve as a tomb for ⟨the sea ~s the lost ship⟩ [ME entoumben, fr MF entomber, fr en- + tombe tomb] – **entombment** n

**entomofauna** /'entəmoh,fawnə/ n the insects of an environment or region [NL]

**entomology** /ˌentə'moləji/ n a branch of zoology that deals with insects △ etymology [Fr entomologie, fr Gk entomon insect (fr neut of entomos cut up, fr en- + temnein to cut) + Fr

*-logie* -logy – more at TOME] – **entomologist** *n*, **entomological** *adj*, **entomologically** *adv*

**entomophagous** /ˌentəˈmofəgəs/ *adj* feeding on insects

**entomophilous** /ˌentəˈmofiləs/ *adj* normally pollinated by insects – compare ZOOPHILOUS – **entomophily** *n*

**entomostracan** /ˌentəˈmostrəkən/ *n* any of numerous simple typically small INVERTEBRATE animals including WATER FLEAS, barnacles, and other CRUSTACEANS sometimes placed together in a group (Entomostraca) [deriv of *entom-* + Gk *ostrakon* shell – more at OYSTER] – **entomostracan, entomostracous** *adj*

**entopic** /enˈtopik/ *adj, anatomy* occurring in the usual place or position – compare ECTOPIC [Gk *entopos* in a place, fr *en-* ²*en-* + *topos* place]

**entoproct** /ˈentəˌprokt/ *n* any of a small phylum (Entoprocta) of mainly marine animals lacking a true COELOM (secondary body cavity between the body wall and digestive tract) and having the anus near the mouth [deriv of *ent-* + Gk *prōktos* anus] – **entroproct, entoproctous** *adj*

**entourage** /ˈontooˌrahzh (Fr ãtura:ʒ)/ *n* 1 *taking sing or pl vb* a group of attendants or associates, esp of someone of high rank 2 *chiefly formal* surroundings [Fr, fr MF, fr *entourer* to surround, fr *entour* round, fr *en* in (fr L *in*) + *tour* circuit – more at TURN]

**en-tout-cas** /on ˌtooh ˈkah (Fr ã tu ka/ *n, pl* **en-tout-cas** 1 a combination umbrella and sunshade 2 a hard all-weather lawn-tennis court [Fr, lit., in any case; (2) fr *En-Tout-Cas*, a trademark]

**entozoa** /ˌentəˈzohˌə, ˌentoh-/ *n pl, sing* **entozoon** animal parasites living within the host's body; *esp* the intestinal worms [NL] – **entozoan** *adj or n*

**entozoic** /ˌentəˈzohˌik, ˌentoh-/ *adj* 1 of or being entozoa 2 *of an animal or plant* living within the body of an animal

**entrácte** /ˈontrakt, -ˈ- (Fr ãtrakt)/ *n* (a dance, piece of music, or dramatic entertainment performed in) the interval between two acts of a play [Fr, fr *entre-* inter- + *acte* act]

**entrails** /ˈentraylz/ *n pl* 1 the internal organs of a person or animal; the guts; *esp* the intestines 2 the interior or inner parts of something; the core ⟨~ *of the earth*⟩ [ME *entrailles*, fr MF, fr ML *intralia*, alter. of L *interanea*, pl of *interaneum* intestine, fr neut of *interaneus* interior]

¹**entrain** /inˈtrayn/ *vt* 1 to draw along with or after oneself 2 *of a liquid or gas* to draw in and transport (e g solid particles) by high speed flowing 3 to incorporate (air bubbles) into concrete in order to make it frost-resistant 4 to regulate or modify the cycle of ⟨*circadian rhythms* ~ed *by a light cycle*⟩ [MF *entrainer*, fr *en-* + *trainer* to draw, drag – more at TRAIN] – **entrainer** *n*, **entrainment** *n*

²**entrain** *vb* to put (esp troops) or go aboard a train

**entrammel** /inˈtraml/ *vt* -ll- (*NAm* -l-, -ll-) to entangle, hamper

¹**entrance** /ˈentrəns/ *n* 1 the act of entering ⟨*she made a stunning* ~⟩ 2 the means or place of entry ⟨*the* ~ *was a small green door*⟩ ⟨*such books gave the child* ~ *to a world of fantasy*⟩ 3 the right or permission to enter; admission ⟨*he passed the school* ~ *examination*⟩ 4 an arrival of a performer onto the stage or before cameras

²**entrance** /inˈtrahns/ *vt* 1 to put into a trance 2 to fill with wonder or rapture; overwhelm with joy – **entrancement** *n*

**entrant** /ˈentrənt/ *n* one who or that which enters or is entered; *esp* one who enters a contest

**entrap** /inˈtrap/ *vt* -pp- 1 to catch (as if) in a trap 2 to lure into a compromising statement or act ⟨~ped *into making a confession*⟩ *synonyms* see ¹CATCH [MF *entraper*, fr *en-* + *trape* trap] – **entrapment** *n*

**entreat** /inˈtreet/ *vt* 1 to ask earnestly or plead with; beg ⟨~ed *the judge for another chance*⟩ 2 *archaic* to deal with; treat ~ *vi* 1 to make an earnest request; plead 2 *obs* 2a to negotiate b to intercede *synonyms* see BEG [ME *entreten*, fr MF *entraitier*, fr *en-* + *traitier* to treat – more at TREAT] – **entreatingly** *adv*, **entreatment** *n*

**entreaty** /inˈtreeti/ *n* an act of entreating; a plea

**entrechat** /ˈontrəshah (Fr ãtrəʃa)/ *n* a vertical leap in which a ballet dancer repeatedly crosses one foot in front of the other and vice versa [Fr, modif of It (*capriola*) *intrecciata* intertwined leap]

**entrecote** /ˈontrəkot (Fr ãtrəko:t)/ *n* a steak cut from a boned sirloin [Fr *entrecôte*, fr *entre-* + *côte* rib, fr L *costa* – more at COAST]

**entrée, entree** /ˈontray (Fr ãtre)/ *n* 1a the act or manner of entering; an entrance ⟨*made a very grand* ~⟩ b freedom of

entry or access ⟨*had* ~ *into the highest circles*⟩ 2a *chiefly Br* a dish served between the main (fish and meat) courses of a dinner b the principal dish of the meal [Fr *entrée*, fr OF]

**entremets** /ˈontrəˌmay (Fr ãtrəmɛ)/ *n taking sing or pl vb* a dish served in addition to the main course of a meal; SIDE DISH [Fr, fr OF *entremes*, fr *entre-* + *mes* dish – more at MESS]

**entrench, intrench** /inˈtrench/ *vt* 1a to surround with a (defensive) trench b to place (oneself) in a strong defensive position 2 to establish solidly, esp so as to make change difficult; confirm ⟨*pity only* ~es *him in his misery*⟩ 3 to cut into; furrow; *specif* to erode downwards so as to form a trench ⟨*the hillside was* ~ed *with little streams*⟩ ~ *vi* 1 to dig or occupy a (defensive) trench 2 to enter upon or take over something unfairly, improperly, or unlawfully; encroach – + *on* or *upon* ⟨*she resented his* ~ *upon her privacy*⟩ – **entrenchment** *n*

**entre nous** /ˌontrə ˈnooh (Fr ãtr nu)/ *adv* between you and me; confidentially [Fr, between us]

**entrepôt** /ˈontrəˌpoh/ *n* a seaport, warehouse, or other intermediary centre of trade and transshipment ⟨*Singapore, the* ~ *of the Orient*⟩; *also* a centre to which goods are sent for subsequent distribution [Fr, fr *entreposer* to put in a warehouse, fr *entre-* inter- + *poser* to place]

**entrepreneur** /ˌontrəprəˈnuh (Fr ãtrəprɑnœ:r)/ *n* one who organizes, manages, and assumes the risks of a business or enterprise in the hope of profit [Fr, fr OF, fr *entreprendre* to undertake] – **entrepreneurial** *adj*, **entrepreneurship** *n*

**entresol** /ˈontrəˌsol (Fr ãtrəsɔl)/ *n* a low-ceilinged storey between the ground and first floors of a building; MEZZANINE [Fr, fr *entre-* + *sol* ground]

**entrism** /ˈentriz(ə)m/ *n* entryism

**entropy** /ˈentrəpi/ *n* 1 a property of a THERMODYNAMIC system (one viewed in terms of the interchange of heat and other forms of energy) for which there is no exchange of energy with the surroundings, that corresponds to a a measure of the amount of wasted energy or energy that is unavailable for doing work in the system, that is related to the state of the system in such a way that numerical change in the measure is equal to the heat energy absorbed divided by the ABSOLUTE TEMPERATURE of the system in undergoing reversible change b the degree to which the particles (e g atoms or molecules) of the system are randomly arranged, that gives a measure of the amount of disorder in the system and can be expressed statistically in terms of the NATURAL LOGARITHM of the probability of occurrence of a particular arrangement of the particles of the system 2a (the process by which the universe reaches) an ultimate state of inert uniformity – not used technically b (decay leading to) absence of form, pattern, or differentiation ⟨*cultural* ~⟩ [Ger *entropie*, fr Gk *en-* + *trepein* to turn, change – more at TROPE] – **entropic** *adj*

**entrust, intrust** /inˈtrust/ *vt* to confer a trust on; *esp* to deliver something in trust to – usu + *with* ⟨~ed *the bank with his savings*⟩ – **entrustment** *n*

    **entrust to** *vt* to commit to (another) with confidence ⟨*entrusted his savings to the bank*⟩

**entry** /ˈentri/ *n* 1 the act of entering; entrance 2 the right or privilege of entering; ENTRÉE 1b 3a a door, gate, hall, vestibule, or other place of entrance b the mouth of a river 4a(1) the act of registering a record a(2) the act of introducing a piece of information into computer storage b a record or notation (e g in a diary, account book or index) of an occurrence, transaction, or proceeding c a dictionary headword, often together with its definition 5a a person, thing, or group entered in a contest; an entrant b the aggregate of those entered or admitted ⟨*double the annual* ~ *to our medical schools*⟩ 6 *law* the act of entering or going on land with the intention of taking or declaring possession 7 the point at which a voice or instrumental part begins in ensemble music 8 (a card providing) the winning of a trick and hence the gaining of the lead [ME *entre*, fr OF *entree*, fr fem of *entré*, pp of *entrer* to enter]

**entryism** /ˈentriˌiz(ə)m/ *n* the practice of infiltrating a political party in order to influence that party's policy from within

**entryway** /ˈentriˌway/ *n*, *chiefly NAm* a passage for entrance

**entwine** /inˈtwien/ *vt* to twine together or round; interweave ⟨*the brambles were thickly* ~d⟩ ⟨*her fate was closely* ~d *with mine*⟩ ~ *vi* to become (as if) twisted or twined

**entwist** /inˈtwist/ *vt* to entwine

**enucleate** /iˈnyoohkliayt/ *vt* 1 to remove a nucleus from (a cell) 2 to remove surgically (e g a tumour or an eyeball) esp from a surrounding capsule or cover without cutting into or rupturing 3 *archaic* to explain [L *enucleatus*, pp of *enucleare*, lit., to remove the kernel from, fr *e-* + *nucleus* kernel – more at NUCLEUS] – **enucleation** *n*

**enumerable** /i'nyoohm(ə)rəbl/ *adj, maths* COUNTABLE b – **enumerability** *n*

**enumerate** /i'nyoohmərayt/ *vt* **1** to ascertain the number of; count **2** to specify one after another; list [L *enumeratus*, pp of *enumerare*, fr *e-* + *numerare* to count, fr *numerus* number – more at NIMBLE] – **enumerator** *n*, **enumeration** *n*, **enumerative** *adj*

**enunciate** /i'nunsi,ayt/ *vt* **1a** to make a definite or systematic statement of; formulate **b** to announce, proclaim ⟨~d *the principles to be followed by the new administration*⟩ **2** to articulate, pronounce ⟨~ *your words clearly*⟩ ~ *vi* to pronounce words; *esp* to do so clearly [L *enuntiatus*, pp of *enuntiare* to report, declare, fr *e-* + *nuntiare* to report – more at ANNOUNCE] – **enunciator** *n*, **enunciable** *adj*, **enunciation** *n*

**enure** /i'nyooə/ *vb* to inure

**enuresis** /,enyoo'reesis/ *n* involuntary urination; *esp* bed-wetting [NL, fr Gk *enourein* to urinate in, wet the bed, fr *en-* + *ourein* to urinate, fr *ouron* urine] – **enuretic** *adj or n*

**envelop** /in'veləp/ *vt* **1** to enclose or enfold completely (as if) with a covering ⟨*she* ~ed *him in her arms*⟩ ⟨*the matter was* ~ed *in mystery*⟩ **2** to surround so as to cut off communication or prevent retreat ⟨~ *the enemy*⟩ [ME *envolupen*, fr MF *envoluper*, *enveloper*, fr OF *envoloper*, fr *en-* + *voloper* to wrap (cf DEVELOP)] – **envelopment** *n*

**envelope** /'envəlohp, 'on-/ *n* **1** something that envelops; a wrapper, covering ⟨*the* ~ *of air around the earth*⟩ **2** a flat container usu of folded and gummed paper (e g for a letter) **3** the gas-containing bag in a balloon or airship **4** the sealed container of glass, metal, etc that encloses the gas or vacuum and working elements (e g a filament or ELECTRODES) of an electric light bulb, valve, etc **5** a natural enclosing covering (e g a membrane or shell) **6** the performance limits (e g of an aircraft or missile) ⟨*the flight* ~ *of the prototype fighter was explored*⟩ **7** a curve that touches each of a group of related curves at one point only [Fr *enveloppe*, fr MF *envelope*, fr *enveloper*]
*usage* The pronunciation /'envəlohp/ is recommended for BBC broadcasters.

**envenom** /in'venəm/ *vt* **1** to taint or fill (as if) with poison ⟨~ *a weapon*⟩ ⟨~ *an argument*⟩ **2** to embitter ⟨*jealousy* ~ing *his mind*⟩ [ME *envenimen*, fr OF *envenimer*, fr *en-* + *venim* venom]

**envenom·ization, -isation** /in,venəmie'zaysh(ə)n/ *n* a poisoning caused by a bite or sting

**enviable** /'envi·əbl/ *adj* worthy of envy; highly desirable – **enviableness** *n*, **enviably** *adv*

**envious** /'envi·əs/ *adj* **1** feeling or showing envy ⟨~ *looks*⟩ ⟨~ *of a neighbour's wealth*⟩ **2** *archaic* **2a** emulous **b** enviable – **enviously** *adv*, **enviousness** *n*

**environ** /in'vie(ə)rən/ *vt, formal, of people or things* to encircle or surround, sometimes protectively or hostilely ⟨*ladies-in-waiting* ~ed *the queen*⟩ ⟨*made light of the dangers that* ~ed *him*⟩ [ME *envirounen*, fr MF *environner*, fr *environ* round, fr *en* in (fr L *in*) + *viron* circle, fr *virer* to turn, fr (assumed) VL *virare*, prob alter. of L *vibrare* to shake or *gyrare* to turn round]

**environment** /in'vie(ə)rənmənt/ *n* **1** the circumstances, objects, or conditions by which one is surrounded **2a** the complex of climatic, soil, and biological factors that act on an organism or an ecological community **b** the social, physical, and cultural conditions that influence the life of an individual or community **3** an example of environmental art – **environmental** *adj*, **environmentally** *adv*

**environmental art** *n, often cap E&A* a form of art that encompasses or involves the spectator with three-dimensional creations instead of confronting him/her with a fixed image or object – compare HAPPENING

**environmental determinism** *n* environmentalism

**environmentalism** /in,vie(ə)rən'mentl,iz(ə)m/ *n* a theory that views environment rather than heredity as the important factor in human development, *esp* cultural and intellectual development

**environmentalist** /in,vie(ə)rən'mentl·ist/ *n* **1** an advocate of environmentalism **2** somebody concerned about the problems (e g air and water pollution) related to the protection of the environment – **environmentalist, environmentalistic** *adj*

**environs** /in'vie(ə)rənz/ *n pl* immediate surroundings or neighbourhood; *esp* the districts or suburbs round a city

**envisage** /in'vizij/ *vt* to have a mental picture of, esp in advance of an expected or hoped-for realization ⟨~s *an entirely new system of education*⟩ [Fr *envisager*, fr *en-* + *visage*]

**envision** /in'vizh(ə)n/ *also* **vision** /'vizh(ə)n/ *vt, chiefly NAm* to envisage

¹**envoy, envoi** /'envoy/ *n* the concluding remarks to a poem, essay, or book; *specif* a short final stanza of a BALLADE (fixed-form 3-versed poem) serving as a summary or dedication [Fr *envoi*, lit., message, fr OF *envei*, fr *envoier* to send on one's way, fr (assumed) VL *inviare*, fr L *in-* + *via* way]

²**envoy** *n* a messenger, representative; *esp* an agent sent by a government to transact diplomatic business [Fr *envoyé*, fr pp of *envoyer* to send, fr OF *envoier*]

**envoy extraordinary** *n* a diplomatic agent who ranks immediately below an ambassador

¹**envy** /'envi/ *n* **1** painful, resentful, or admiring awareness of an advantage enjoyed by another accompanied by a desire to possess the same advantage **2** an object of envy ⟨*his success with women made him the* ~ *of his friends*⟩ **3** *obs* malice [ME *envie*, fr OF, fr L *invidia*, fr *invidus* envious, fr *invidēre* to look askance at, envy, fr *in-* + *vidēre* to see – more at WIT]

²**envy** *vt* **1** to feel envy towards or on account of **2** *obs* to begrudge ~ *vi, obs* to feel or show envy – **envier** *n*, **envyingly** *adv*

**enwheel** /in'weel/ *vt, obs* to encircle

**enwind** /in'wiend/ *vt* **enwound** /-'wownd/ to wind in or around; enfold

**enwomb** /in'woohm/ *vt* to enclose or hide as if in a womb ⟨*he* ~ed *himself in words*⟩

**enwrap** /in'rap/ *vt* **-pp-** **1** to wrap, enfold **2a** to envelop ⟨*the coldness of the empty house* ~ped *her* – Edith Sitwell⟩ **b** ENGROSS 2b

**enwreathe** /in'reedh/ *vt* to wreath, envelop

**Enzedder** /,en'zedə/ *n, Austr & NZ informal* an inhabitant of New Zealand [New Zealand + ²-*er*]

**enzootic** /,enzoh'otik/ *n or adj* (a disease) affecting animals within a particular or restricted locality – compare EPIZOOTIC [*en-* + *zo-* + *-otic*] – **enzootic** *n*, **enzootically** *adv*

**enzygotic** /,enzie'gotik, -zi-/ *adj, of twins* identical [*en-* + *zyg-* + *-otic*]

**enzymatic** /,enzie'matik, -zi-/ *also* **enzymic** /en'ziemik/ *adj* of or produced by an enzyme – **enzymatically** *adv*

**enzyme** /'enziem/ *n* any of numerous proteins that are produced by living cells and that promote specific biochemical reactions at cell temperatures without undergoing change themselves in the process. Enzymes will also act outside living organisms and at other temperatures, being useful in some industrial processes. [Ger *enzym*, fr MGk *enzymos* leavened, fr Gk *en-* + *zymē* leaven]

**enzymology** /,enzie'moləji/ *n* a branch of science that deals with enzymes, their nature, activity, and significance [ISV] – **enzymologist** *n*

**eo-** /eeoh-/ *comb form* earliest; oldest ⟨*eolithic*⟩ [Gk *ēō-* dawn, fr *ēōs*]

**Eocene** /'eeoh,seen/ *adj or n* (of or being) an epoch of the TERTIARY geological period between the PALAEOCENE and the OLIGOCENE epochs or the corresponding system of rocks

**eohippus** /,eeoh'hipəs/ *n* any of a genus (*Eohippus*) of extinct small primitive 4-toed ancestors of the horse [NL, genus name, fr *eo-* + Gk *hippos* horse – more at EQUINE]

**Eoka** /ay'ohkə/ *n* a secret Greek Cypriot organization aiming for the union of Cyprus with Greece [NGk *Ethnikē Organōsis Kypriakou Agōnas* National Organization of Cypriot Struggle]

**eolian** /ee'ohli·ən, -lyən/ *adj, NAm* AEOLIAN 3 (borne, deposited, etc by the wind)

**eolith** /'eeoh,lith, 'ee-ə,lith/ *n* a very crudely chipped flint assumed to be the earliest form of stone tool

**Eolithic** /,ee-ə'lithik/ *adj* of the early period of the STONE AGE, characterized by the supposed use of eoliths by early human beings

**eon** /'eeon, 'ee-ən/ *n* an aeon

**eo nomine** /,ayoh 'nominay/ *adv* by or under that name [L]

**eosin** /'eeoh,sin, 'ee-ə-/ *also* **eosine** /-sin, -seen/ *n* **1** a red fluorescent chemical compound, $C_{20}H_8Br_4O_5$, derived from FLUORESCEIN (yellow to red dye) by the action of bromine and used in the form of its compounds (SALTS) as a dye (e g for wool and silk and in cosmetics); *also* the red to brown sodium or potassium salt of eosin used esp to stain biological specimens for examination under the microscope **2** any of several dyes chemically related to eosin [ISV, fr Gk *ēōs* dawn]

**eosinophil** /,ee-ə'sinəfil/ *also* **eosinophile** /-,fiel/ *n* an eosinophilic cell, tissue, etc; *specif* a WHITE BLOOD CELL with granules in the CYTOPLASM (jellylike material outside the nucleus of the cell) that are readily stained by eosin – compare BASOPHIL, NEUTROPHIL

**eosinophilia** /ˌee·ə‚sinəˈfiliə/ *n* abnormal increase in the number of eosinophils in the blood that is characteristic of allergic states and some parasitic infections

**eosinophilic** /ˌee·ə‚sinəˈfilik/ *also* **eosinophil, eosinophile** *adj* 1 staining readily with eosin 2 of or characterized by eosinophilia

**Eozoic** /ˌee·əˈzoh·ik/ *adj or n* 1 (of, being, or formed in) the PRECAMBRIAN era (earliest era of geological history) or the part of the Precambrian in which life first appeared 2 PROTEROZOIC

**EP** *n* a 45-revolutions-per-minute gramophone record with a playing time greater than normal [*Extended Play*]

**ep-** – see EPI-

**epact** /ˈeepakt/ *n* a period of time added to harmonize the lunar with the solar calendar [MF *epacte*, fr LL *epacta*, fr Gk *epaktē*, fr *epagein* to bring in, intercalate, fr *epi-* + *agein* to drive – more at AGENT]

**eparch** /ˈepahk/ *n* a governor or bishop of a diocese in the EASTERN ORTHODOX church [Gk *eparchos*]

**eparchy** /ˈepahki/ *n* a diocese of an EASTERN ORTHODOX church [Gk *eparchia* province, fr *eparchos* prefect, fr *epi-* + *archos* ruler – more at ARCH-]

**epaulette, NAm chiefly epaulet** /ˌepəˈlet/ *n* 1 an ornamental (fringed) strip or pad attached to the shoulder of a garment, esp of a military uniform 2 a 5-sided style of cut for a gem [Fr *épaulette*, dim. of *épaule* shoulder, fr LL *spatula* shoulder blade, spoon, dim. of L *spatha* spoon, sword – more at SPADE]

**épée** /ˈepay (*Fr* epe)/ *n* 1 a fencing or duelling sword having a bowl-shaped handle guard and a rigid blade of triangular longitudinal cross-section with no cutting edge but with a sharp point that is blunted for fencing – compare FOIL, SABRE 2 the art or sport of fencing with the épée, in which the whole body is allowed as target [Fr, fr L *spatha*]

**épéeist** /ˈepayist/ *n* one who fences with an épée

**epeirogeny** /ˌepieˈrojən/, **epeirogenesis** /eˌpie(ə)rohˈjenəsis/ *n* the slow large-scale deformation of the earth's crust by which continents and their broader features are produced [Gk *epeiros* mainland, continent + E *-geny* or L *genesis*] – **epeirogenic, epeirogenetic** *adj*, **epeirogenically** *adv*

**epenthesis** /eˈpenthəsis/ *n, pl* **epentheses** /-seez/ the insertion of an extra sound or letter in the original body of a word; *also* the sound or letter thus added (e g *b* in *nimble*, formerly *nimel*) [LL, fr Gk, fr *epentithenai* to insert a letter, fr *epi-* + *entithenai* to put in, fr *en-* + *tithenai* to put – more at DO] – **epenthetic** *adj*

**epergne** /iˈpuhn/ *n* a (tiered or branched) centrepiece for a dinner table having holders for fruit, flowers, sweets, etc [prob fr Fr *épargne* saving, fr *épargner* to spare]

**epexegesis** /iˌpeksiˈjeesis/ *n, pl* **epexegeses** /-seez/ the addition of a word or words to clarify, or provide additional information to, preceding text; *also* material thus added [Gk *epexēgēsis*, fr *epi-* + *exēgēsis* exegesis] – **epexegetic, epexegetical** *adj*, **epexegetically** *adv*

**ephah** /ˈeefə/ *n* an ancient Hebrew unit of dry measure equal to about 36.37 litres (1 bushel) [Heb *ēphāh*, fr Egypt *ipt*]

**ephedra** /iˈfedrə, ˈefədrə/ *n* any of a large genus (*Ephedra* of the family Gnetaceae) of jointed nearly leafless desert shrubs [NL, genus name]

**ephedrine** /iˈfedrin; *chem* ˈefidrin, -dreen/ *n* a drug, HOCH ($C_6H_5$)CH(CH$_3$)NHCH$_3$, obtained from Chinese ephedras or made synthetically that has the physiological actions of adrenalin and is used esp to relieve hay fever, asthma, and nasal congestion [NL *Ephedra*, genus of shrubs, fr L, horsetail plant, fr Gk, fr *ephedros* sitting upon, fr *epi-* + *hedra* seat – more at SIT]

**ephemera** /iˈfemərə/ *n, pl* **ephemeras, ephemerae** /-ie/ 1 a mayfly 2 *taking pl vb* things (e g writings) of short-lived duration or interest [NL, genus name, fr Gk *ephēmerē*, fem of *ephēmeros;* (2) partly fr (1), partly fr pl of *ephemeron*]

**¹ephemeral** /iˈfemə(rə)l/ *adj* 1 lasting one day only ⟨*an ~ fever*⟩ 2a lasting a very short time; transitory ⟨*~ pleasures*⟩ **b** *of a plant or animal* having a very brief life or life cycle *synonyms* see ¹TRANSIENT [Gk *ephēmeros* lasting a day, daily, fr *epi-* + *hēmera* day] – **ephemerally** *adv*, **ephemerality** *n*

**²ephemeral** *n* something ephemeral; *specif* an ephemeral organism (e g a plant that grows, flowers, and dies in a few days)

**ephemerid** /iˈfemərid/ *n* a mayfly [deriv of Gk *ephēmeron*] – **ephemerid** *adj*

**ephemeris** /iˈfemərise/ *n, pl* **ephemerides** /ˌefiˈmerideez/ a table showing the predicted position of a celestial body at regular intervals; *also* an astronomical almanac [L, diary, ephemeris, fr Gk *ephēmeris*, fr *ephēmeros*]

**ephemeris time** *n* a uniform measure of time defined by the orbiting motions of the planets

**ephemeron** /iˈfemə‚ron/ *n, pl* **ephemera, /-rə/ ephemerons** 1 a mayfly 2 an ephemeral [NL, fr Gk *ephēmeron* mayfly, fr neut of *ephēmeros*]

**ephemeropteran** /iˌfeməˈroptərən/ *n* any of an order (Ephemeroptera) of short-lived insects with large membranous forewings and reduced hindwings; a mayfly [deriv of Gk *ephēmeros* + *pteron* wing]

**Ephesians** /iˈfeezh(y)ənz/ *n taking sing vb* – see BIBLE table [*Ephesus*, ancient city in Asia Minor]

**ephod** /ˈeefod/ *n* 1 an apronlike garment formerly worn in religious rites by Jewish priests, esp the High Priest 2 an Old Testament instrument of priestly divine insight [Heb *ēphōdh*]

**ephor** /ˈefaw/ *n* 1 any of five magistrates of ancient Sparta having power over the king 2 a government official in modern Greece; *esp* one who supervises public works [L *ephorus*, fr Gk *ephoros*, fr *ephoran* to oversee, fr *epi-* + *horan* to see – more at WARY] – **ephorate** *n*

**Ephraimite** /ˈeefrayi‚miet/ *n* 1 a member of the Hebrew tribe of Ephraim 2 a native or inhabitant of the northern kingdom of the Israel of biblical times [*Ephraim*, younger son of Joseph (Gen 41:50–52)]

**epi-** /epi-/, **ep-** /ep-/ *prefix* 1 on; upon ⟨*epiphyte*⟩ 2 outer; external ⟨*epidermis*⟩ 3 besides; IN ADDITION ⟨*epilogue*⟩ ⟨*epiphenomenon*⟩ 4 after; later ⟨*epigone*⟩ 5 over; above ⟨*epigraph*⟩ 6a chemical entity related to another ⟨*epicholesterol*⟩ **b** chemical entity distinguished from a similar one by having chemical bonding such that a bridge is formed between two parts of the molecule ⟨*epichlorohydrin*⟩ [ME, fr MF & L; MF, fr L, fr Gk, fr *epi* on, at, besides, after; akin to OE *eof*ot crime]

**epibiotic** /ˌepibiˈotik/ *adj* living on the surface of another organism, usu without causing harm – **epibiotically** *adv*, **epibiosis** *n*, **epibiont** *n*

**epiblast** /ˈepi‚blast/ *n* the outer layer of cells of an embryo at a very early stage in its development; the cells that give rise to ECTODERM – **epiblastic** *adj*

**epiboly** /iˈpibəli/ *n* growth of one part or layer of an animal organism so as to cover another part; *esp* such growth occurring during the formation of a GASTRULA (early stage in the development of an animal embryo) in which the small cells in the relatively yolk-free side of the developing egg multiply and grow over the larger cells in the yolk region [Gk *epibolē* addition, fr *epiballein* to throw on, fr *epi-* + *ballein* to throw – more at DEVIL] – **epibolic** *adj*

**¹epic** /ˈepik/ *adj* 1 (having the characteristics) of an epic 2a extending beyond the usual or ordinary, esp in size or scope ⟨*his genius was ~ – TLS*⟩ **b** heroic ⟨*the ~ defence of Stalingrad*⟩ [L *epicus*, fr Gk *epikos*, fr *epos* word, speech, poem – more at VOICE] – **epically** *adv*

**²epic** *n* 1 a long formally structured classical narrative poem with a dignified style recounting the deeds of a legendary or historical hero 2 a novel, play, etc that resembles or suggests a classical epic in construction but that deals with different subject matter 3 a series of events or body of legend or tradition fit to form the subject of an epic ⟨*that great environmental ~, the wreck of the Torrey Canyon – The Guardian*⟩ △ epoch

**epicalyx** /ˌepiˈkayliks, -kaliks/ *n* a ring of usu small modified leaflike structures (BRACTS) lying outside and usu resembling the CALYX of some flowers (e g those of potentillas)

**epicanthic fold** /ˌepiˈkanthik/ *n* an extension of a fold of the skin of the upper eyelid covering the inner or sometimes both corners of the eye and found among Mongolian peoples [NL *epicanthus*, fr *epi-* + *canthus*]

**epicanthus** /ˌepiˈkanthəs/ *n* EPICANTHIC FOLD

**epicardium** /ˌepiˈkahdi·əm/ *n, pl* **epicardia** /-diə/ the innermost part of the PERICARDIUM (membranous sac) that closely covers the heart [NL, fr *epi-* + Gk *kardia* heart] – **epicardial** *adj*

**epicarp** /ˈepikahp/ *n* EXOCARP (outermost layer of a fruit) [Fr *épicarpe*, fr *épi-* epi + *-carpe* -carp]

**epicene** /ˈepi‚seen/ *adj* 1 *of a noun* having only one form to indicate either sex 2a being of one sex but having characteristics typical of the other sex; hermaphrodite **b** effeminate 3 *formal* lacking characteristics typical of either sex; sexless [ME, fr L *epicoenus*, fr Gk *epikoinos*, fr *epi-* + *koinos* common – more at CO-] – **epicene** *n*, **epicenism** *n*

**epicentre** /'epi,sentə/ *n* **1** the part of the earth's surface directly above the place of origin of an earthquake **2** CENTRE 2a [NL *epicentrum*, fr *epi-* + L *centrum* centre] – **epicentral** *adj*

**epichlorohydrin** /,epi,klawrə'hiedrin, -,klorə-/ *n* a volatile liquid toxic EPOXY chemical compound, $C_3H_5ClO$, having an odour like chloroform and used esp in making EPOXY RESINS and rubbers

**epicontinental** /,epi,konti'nentl/ *adj* lying on a continent or a CONTINENTAL SHELF ⟨~ *seas*⟩

**epicotyl** /,epi'kotil/ *n* the part of the stem of a plant embryo or seedling above the COTYLEDON (first leaf produced by a germinating seed) [*epi-* + *cotyl*edon]

**epicranial** /,epi'kraynyəl/ *adj* situated on the skull

**epicritic** /,epi'kritik/ *adj* **1** being or relating to the accurate discrimination between small degrees of sensation by RECEPTORS (cells or groups of cells that receive stimuli) in the skin or the nerves supplying such receptors **2** of or being a nerve or RECEPTOR in the skin that responds to and allows accurate discrimination of fine variations in touch, temperature, etc □ compare PROTOPATHIC [Gk *epikritikos* determinative, fr *epikrinein* to decide, fr *epi-* + *krinein* to judge – more at CERTAIN]

**epicure** /'epikyooə/ *n* **1** someone with sensitive and discriminating tastes, esp in food or wine **2** *archaic* someone devoted to sensual pleasure; SYBARITE [*Epicurus* †270 BC Gk philosopher] – **Epicurism** *n*

**Epicurean** /,epikyoo'ree•ən, -'kyooəri•ən/ *n or adj* **1** (a follower) of the doctrine of the Greek philosopher Epicurus who considered calmness of mind the highest good, held intellectual pleasures superior to all others, and advocated the renunciation of transient pleasures in favour of more enduring ones **2** *often not cap* (of or suited to) an epicure □ compare HEDONIST – **Epicureanism** *n*

**epicuticle** /'epi,kyoohtikl, ,--'---/ *n* the outermost waxy layer of the insect EXOSKELETON (external hard protective covering) – **epicuticular** *adj*

**epicycle** /'epi,siekl/ *n* **1** a circle that, according to Ptolemaic astronomy, is the path along which a planet moves. The centre of this circle itself moves uniformly round the circumference of a larger circle, which is the planet's orbit, so that the planet progresses in a series of loops. **2** a process or activity going on within the context of a larger one ⟨*an ~ of land erosion*⟩ [ME *epicicle*, fr LL *epicyclus*, fr Gk *epikyklos*, fr *epi-* + *kyklos* circle – more at WHEEL] – **epicyclic** *adj*

**epicyclic train** /,epi'sieklik/ *n* a system of gears designed to have one or more wheels travelling round the circumference of another wheel whose centre is fixed

**epicycloid** /,epi'siekloyd/ *n* a curve traced by a point on the circumference of a circle that rolls on the outside of a fixed circle – compare HYPOCYCLOID

**epideictic** /,epi'diektik/ *adj* intended for effect or display; *esp* designed to display the rhetorical skill of a speaker [Gk *epideiktikos*, fr *epideiknynai* to display, show off, fr *epi-* + *deiknynai* to show – more at DICTION]

**¹epidemic** /,epi'demik/ *adj* **1** affecting or tending to affect many individuals within a population, community, or region at the same time ⟨*typhoid was ~*⟩ – compare ENDEMIC, PANDEMIC **2** of or constituting an epidemic; *broadly* prevalent to an excessive degree ⟨*the practice had reached ~ proportions*⟩ [Fr *épidémique*, fr MF, fr *epidemie* epidemic disease, fr LL *epidemia*, fr Gk *epidēmia* visit, epidemic, fr *epidēmos* visiting, epidemic, fr *epi-* + *dēmos* people] – **epidemical** *adj*, **epidemically** *adv*, **epidemicity** *n*

**²epidemic** *n* **1** an outbreak of epidemic disease **2** an outbreak or product of sudden rapid spread, growth, or development

**epidemiology** /,epi,deemi'oləji/ *n* **1** a branch of medical science that deals with the occurrence, distribution, and control of disease in a population **2** the factors controlling the presence or absence of a disease or a disease-causing agent ⟨*the ~ of the common cold*⟩ [LL *epidemia* + ISV *-logy*] – **epidemiologist** *n*, **epidemiologic, epidemiological** *adj*, **epidemiologically** *adv*

**epiderm-** /epiduhm-/, **epidermo-** *comb form* epidermis ⟨*epidermal*⟩ [*epidermis*]

**epidermal** /,epi'duhml/ *also* **epidermic** /,epi'duhmik/ *adj* of or arising from the epidermis ⟨~ *cells*⟩

**epidermatic** /,epiduh'matik/ *adj* **1** *of an ointment* acting only on the outer surface of the skin **2** epidermal

**epidermis** /,epi'duhmis/ *n* **1a** the thin outer layer of the external covering of the animal body that is derived from ECTODERM (outermost of the three layers of cells of an embryo) and consists of EPITHELIAL tissue; *specif* the outer insensitive layer of the skin of a VERTEBRATE animal that contains no blood vessels and that covers the DERMIS **b** any of various covering layers of INVERTEBRATE animals resembling the epidermis **2** a thin protective surface layer of cells in higher plants [LL, fr Gk, fr *epi-* + *derma* skin]

**epidermoid** /,epi'duhmoyd/ *also* **epidermoidal** /,epiduh-'moydl/ *adj* resembling epidermis or epidermal cells; made up of elements like those of epidermis ⟨~ *cancers*⟩

**epidiascope** /,epi'die•ə,skohp/ *n* an optical projector for producing images of both opaque objects and transparencies [ISV]

**epididymis** /,epi'didimis/ *n, pl* **epididymides** /-meez/ a mass of coiled tubes, leading from the back of the testis, in which sperm is stored [NL, fr Gk, fr *epi-* + *didymos* testicle – more at DIDYMIUM] – **epididymal** *adj*

**epidote** /'epidoht/ *n* a yellowish-green to greenish-black mineral, $Ca_2(Al,Fe)_3Si_3O_{12}OH$, that is a complex SILICATE of calcium, aluminium, and iron, occurs most abundantly in METAMORPHIC rocks (rocks formed from others by heat, pressure, etc) and is sometimes used as a gem [Fr *épidote*, fr Gk *epididonai* to give in addition, fr *epi-* + *didonai* to give – more at DATE]

**¹epidural** /,epi'dyooərəl/ *adj* situated on or administered outside the DURA MATER (tough outermost membrane covering the brain and spinal cord) ⟨~ *anaesthesia*⟩ ⟨~ *structures*⟩ – **epidurally** *adv*

**²epidural** *n* an epidurally administered injection of a local anaesthetic into the lower portion of the canal housing the spinal nerve cord (e g to anaesthetize the lower part of the body in a painful childbirth)

**epifauna** /,epi'fawnə/ *n* aquatic animals living on a solid surface, esp a hard sea floor – compare INFAUNA [NL] – **epifaunal** *adj*

**epigastric** /,epi'gastrik/ *adj* **1** lying above or in front of the stomach **2a** of the front walls of the abdomen **b** of the epigastrium

**epigastrium** /,epi'gastri•əm/ *n, pl* **epigastria** /-ri-ə/ the middle region of the upper part of the abdomen above the navel – compare HYPOGASTRIUM [NL, fr Gk *epigastrion*, fr *epi-* + *gastrion*, dim. of *gastr-*, *gaster* stomach]

**epigeal** /,epi'jee•əl/, **epigeous** /,epi'jee•əs/ *adj* **1** growing, living, or occurring on or above the surface of the ground ⟨*an ~ insect*⟩ ⟨*an ~ stem*⟩ ⟨~ *germination of plants*⟩ **2a** *of a* COTYLEDON (*first leaf produced by a germinating seed*) forced above the ground by the elongation of the HYPOCOTYL (part of seedling stem above the cotyledon) during the germination of a seed **b** of or being plant germination characterized by the production of epigeal COTYLEDONS □ compare HYPOGEAL [Gk *epigaios* upon the earth, fr *epi-* + *gē* earth, produced]

**epigene** /'epi,jeen/ *adj* **1** *of rock* formed or occurring on or not far below the surface of the earth – compare HYPOGENE **2** *of a crystal* altered chemically since its formation [*epi-* + Gk *-genēs* born, produced]

**epigenesis** /,epi'jenəsis/ *n* **1** (the theory of) development of an organism by gradual production and organization of its different parts from a single undifferentiated fertilized egg cell – compare PREFORMATION **2** change in the mineral character of a rock owing to outside influences [NL] – **epigenesist** *n*

**epigenetic** /,epijə'netik/ *adj* **1** of or produced by epigenesis **2** *epigenetic, epigenic of a mineral structure or ore deposit* formed after the laying down of the enclosing rock – compare SYNGENETIC – **epigenetically** *adv*

**epiglottal** /,epi'glotl/, **epiglottic** /,epi'glotik/ *adj* (produced with the aid) of the epiglottis

**epiglottis** /,epi'glotis/ *n* a thin plate of flexible cartilage in front of the GLOTTIS (space between vocal chords) and at the root of the tongue that folds back over and protects the glottis during swallowing [NL, fr Gk *epiglōttis*, fr *epi-* + *glōttis* glottis]

**epigone** /'epi,gohn/ *n* a usu inferior imitator or follower of a creative thinker or artist of an often earlier generation [Ger, fr L *epigonus* successor, fr Gk *epigonos*, fr *epigignesthai* to be born after, fr *epi-* + *gignesthai* to be born – more at KIN] – **epigonic, epigonous** *adj*, **epigonism** *n*

**epigram** /'epi,gram/ *n* **1** a short poem with a witty or satirical point **2** a pointed witty statement, often with a paradoxical twist **3** epigrammatic expression *synonyms* see CONCISE △ epigraph, epitaph, epithet [ME *epigrame*, fr L *epigrammat-*, *epigramma*, fr Gk, fr *epigraphein* to write on, inscribe, fr *epi-*

+ *graphein* to write – more at CARVE] – **epigrammatic, epigrammatical** *adj*, **epigrammatically** *adv*, **epigrammatism** *n*, **epigrammatist** *n*, **epigrammatize** *vb*, **epigrammatizer** *n*

**epigraph** /'epi,grahf, -,graf/ *n* **1** an engraved inscription on a building, statue, coin, etc **2** a motto or quotation set at the beginning of a (division of a) literary work to suggest its theme △ epigram, epitaph, epithet [Gk *epigraphē*, fr *epigraphein*]

**epigraphy** /i'pigrəfi/ *n* **1** epigraphs collectively **2** the study of inscriptions; *esp* the deciphering, interpreting, and classifying of ancient inscriptions – **epigrapher, epigraphist** *n*, **epigraphic** *also* **epigraphical** *adj*, **epigraphically** *adv*

**epigynous** /i'pijinəs/ *adj* **1** *of a floral organ* (*e g a petal or sepal*) attached to the upper surface of the ovary **2** *of a flower* having epigynous floral organs □ compare HYPOGYNOUS, PERIGYNOUS – **epigyny** *n*

**epilate** /'epilayt/ *vt* to remove hair from by the roots; depilate [back-formation fr *epilation*, fr Fr *épilation*, fr *épiler* to remove hair, fr *é- e- + L pilus* hair – more at PILE] – **epilation** *n*

**epilepsy** /'epi,lepsi/ *n* any of various disorders marked by sudden disturbance of the electrical rhythms of the brain and typically manifested by convulsive attacks of varying severity and sometimes loss of consciousness – compare GRAND MAL, PETIT MAL [MF *epilepsie*, fr LL *epilepsia*, fr Gk *epilēpsia*, fr *epilambanein* to seize, fr *epi- + lambanein* to take, seize – more at LATCH]

**epilept-** /epilept-/, **epilepti-, epilepto-** *comb form* epilepsy ⟨epileptogenic⟩ [Gk *epilēpt-*, fr *epilēptos* seized by epilepsy, fr *epilambanein*]

**epileptic** /,epi'leptik/ *adj* of, affected with, or having the characteristics of epilepsy – **epileptic** *n*, **epileptically** *adv*

**epileptiform** /,epi'leptifawm/ *adj* resembling epilepsy ⟨an ~ convulsion⟩

**epileptogenic** /,epi,leptə'jenik/ *adj* inducing or tending to induce an attack of epilepsy

**epileptoid** /,epi'leptoyd/ *adj* **1** epileptiform **2** exhibiting symptoms resembling those of epilepsy ⟨the ~ person⟩

**epilimnion** /,epi'limnion, -ni·ən/ *n* the warm upper lighter oxygen-rich layer of water in a lake – compare HYPOLIMNION [NL, fr *epi- +* Gk *limnion*, dim. of *limnē* marshy lake – more at LIMNETIC]

**epilogist** /i'pilǝjist/ *n* the writer or speaker of an epilogue

**epilogue** /'epi,log/ *n* **1** a concluding part or appendix of a literary work or scene of a drama that comments on or summarizes the main action or plot **2** a speech or poem addressed to the audience by an actor at the end of a play; *also* the actor speaking such an epilogue – compare PROLOGUE **3** a brief programme devoted to spiritual matters at the end of the day's broadcasting [ME *epiloge*, fr MF *epilogue*, fr L *epilogus*, fr Gk *epilogos*, fr *epilegein* to say in addition, fr *epi- + legein* to say – more at LEGEND]

**epimer** /'epimə/ *n* either of the STEREOISOMERS (forms of a compound having the same order but different spatial arrangements of atoms) of a sugar or a compound derived from a sugar that differ only in the arrangement of atoms or groups of atoms attached to the final carbon atom in the chain of carbon atoms of the sugar molecule [*epi- + isomer*] – **epimeric** *adj*

**epimerase** /i'pimərayz/ *n* any of various ENZYMES that promote the interchange of two of the four different atoms or groups of atoms joined to the last carbon atom in a chemical compound containing more than one such carbon atom and that thus create epimers

**epimere** /'epi,miə/ *n* the upper part of a segment of MESODERM (middle layer of tissue) in the embryo of a VERTEBRATE animal, that gives rise to the muscles [ISV]

**epimer·ize, -ise** /i'piməriez/ *vt* to change (a molecule) into an epimer – **epimerization** *n*

**epimorphic** /,epi'mawfik/ *adj* of or being epimorphosis

**epimorphosis** /,epimaw'fohsis/ *n* regeneration of an organism or one of its parts (*e g* an amputated insect limb) involving extensive production of new cells followed by differentiation – compare MORPHALLAXIS [NL, fr *epi- +* Gk *morphōsis* formation, fr *morphoun* to form, fr *morphē* form – more at FORM]

**epimysium** /,epi'mizi·əm, -zhyəm/ *n, pl* **epimysia** /-zyə, -zhyə/ the sheath of CONNECTIVE TISSUE that surrounds a muscle [NL, fr *epi- +* Gk *mys* mouse, muscle – more at MOUSE]

**epinasty** /'epi,nasti/ *n* an occurrence of stronger or more rapid growth of the upper surface of a plant part (*e g* a flower petal) than of the lower surface, causing the part to bend outwards and often downwards – compare HYPONASTY [ISV *epi- + -nasty*] – **epinastic** *adj*

**epinephrine** /,epi'nefrin, i'pinəfrin, -freen/ *also* **epinephrin** /-frin/ *n, chiefly NAm* adrenalin [ISV *epi- +* Gk *nephros* kidney – more at NEPHRITIS]

**epineurium** /,epi'nyooəriəm/ *n* the sheath of CONNECTIVE TISSUE that encloses a bundle of nerve fibres, thus forming a NERVE TRUNK [NL]

**epipelagic** /,epipə'lajik/ *adj* of or being the zone of an ocean into which enough light penetrates for photosynthesis; EUPHOTIC

**epiphany** /i'pifəni/ *n* **1** *cap* January 6 observed as a church festival in commemoration **a** of the coming of the Magi to be the first Gentiles to witness the infant Christ **b** in the Eastern church, of the baptism of Christ **2** an appearance or manifestation, esp of a divine being **3** a usu sudden manifestation or perception of the essential nature or meaning of something, sometimes through a simple striking thing (*e g* an event) **4** a literary representation of an epiphany [(1) ME *epiphanie*, fr MF, fr LL *epiphania*, fr LGk, pl, prob alter. of Gk *epiphaneia* appearance, manifestation; (2-4) Gk *epiphaneia*, fr *epiphainein* to manifest, fr *phainein* to show – more at FANCY] – **epiphanic, epiphanous** *adj*

**epiphenomenalism** /,epifə'nominl,iz(ə)m/ *n* the theory that mental processes are merely epiphenomena of physical brain processes

**epiphenomenon** /,epifə'nominən/ *n, pl* **epiphenomena** /-nə/ a secondary phenomenon accompanying another and caused by it – **epiphenomenal** *adj*, **epiphenomenally** *adv*

**epiphragm** /'epifram/ *n* a membrane or plate that closes an opening (*e g* of a snail shell or spore-containing capsule of a moss) [Gk *epiphragma* covering]

**epiphysis** /i'pifisis/ *n, pl* **epiphyses** /-seez/ **1** a part of a bone that OSSIFIES (develops into bone tissue from cartilage) separately from the rest and later becomes united with the main part of the bone; *esp* an end of a LONG BONE of a limb **2** PINEAL GLAND (gland in the brain) [NL, fr Gk, growth, fr *epiphyesthai* to grow on, fr *epi- + phyesthai* to grow, passive of *phyein* to bring forth – more at BE] – **epiphyseal, epiphysial** *adj*

**epiphyte** /'epi,fiet/ *n* a plant (*e g* a moss or lichen) that grows on another plant or sometimes an object for support but derives its moisture and nutrients from the air and rain – **epiphytic** *adj*, **epiphytically** *adv*

**epiproct** /'epi,prokt/ *n* a plate above the anus in lower insects comprising the upper part of the 11th abdominal segment [*epi- +* Gk *prōktos* anus]

**episcopacy** /i'piskəpəsi/ *n* **1** government of the church by bishops or by a hierarchy **2** an episcopate

**episcopal** /i'piskəpl/ *adj* **1** of a bishop **2** of, having, or constituting government by bishops **3** *cap* founded on the principle of episcopacy; Anglican; *esp* of an Anglican church that is not the official national church (*e g* in the USA) [ME, fr LL *episcopalis*, fr *episcopus* bishop – more at BISHOP] – **episcopally** *adv*

**Episcopal** *n, informal* an Episcopalian

**Episcopalian** /i,piskə'paylyən/ *n* **1** an adherent of the episcopal form of church government **2** a member of an Episcopal church – **Episcopalian** *adj*, **Episcopalianism** *n*

**episcopate** /i'piskəpət, -,payt/ *n* **1** the position, office, or tenure of a bishop **2** a diocese **3** *taking sing or pl vb* the (national) body of bishops

**episcope** /'epi,skohp/ *n* an optical projector for producing images of opaque objects (*e g* photographs) [ISV *epi- + -scope*]

**episiotomy** /i,peezi'otəmi/ *n* surgical enlargement of the opening of the vulva when it does not stretch enough during childbirth [NL *episio-* vulva, fr Gk *epision* pubic region]

**episode** /'episohd/ *n* **1** the part of an ancient Greek tragedy between two songs from the CHORUS **2a** a developed situation or incident that is integral to but separable from a continuous narrative (*e g* a play or novel) **b** any of a series of loosely connected stories or scenes **3** an instalment of a serialized literary work or drama **4** an event that is distinctive and separate although usu part of a larger series (*e g* in history or in somebody's life) ⟨a coronary ~⟩ **5** a digressive subdivision or passage introducing a new theme in a musical composition *synonyms* see OCCURRENCE [Gk *epeisodion*, fr neut of *epeisodios* coming in besides, fr *epi- + eisodios* coming in, fr *eis* into (akin to Gk *en* in) + *hodos* road, journey – more at IN, CEDE]

**episodic** /,epi'sodik/ *also* **episodical** /-kl/ *adj* **1** made up of separate, esp loosely connected, episodes ⟨an ~ narrative⟩ **2** having the form of an episode; *specif* having the form of a RONDO ⟨an ~ musical passage⟩ **3** of or limited in duration or significance with respect to a particular episode; temporary ⟨*may be able to establish whether the sea-floor spreading is continuous or* ~ – A I Hammond⟩ **4** occasional, sporadic ⟨~ *care of his patients*⟩ – **episodically** *adv*

**episome** /'epi,sohm/ *n* any of various particles containing DNA that are found esp in bacteria and can reproduce either independently in the cell or as an integral part of the cell's CHROMOSOMES (strands of genes composed of DNA) – **episomal** *adj*, **episomally** *adv*

**epistasis** /i'pistəsis/ *n, pl* **epistases** /-seez/ the suppression of the effect of a gene by another gene that is not its allele – compare HYPOSTASIS [NL, fr Gk, act of stopping, fr *ephistanai* to stop, fr *epi-* + *histanai* to cause to stand – more at STAND] – **epistatic** *adj*

**epistasy** /i'pistəsi/ *n* epistasis

**epistaxis** /,epi'staksis/ *n, pl* **epistaxes** /-seez/ nosebleed [NL, fr Gk, fr *epistazein* to drip on, to bleed at the nose again, fr *epi-* + *stazein* to drip – more at STAGNATE]

**epistemic** /,epi'steemik/ *adj* of knowledge; cognitive – **epistemically** *adv*

**epistemology** /i,pistə'moləji/ *n* the study or theory of the nature, grounds, methods, and limits of experience, belief, and knowledge [Gk *epistēmē* knowledge, fr *epistanai* to understand, know, fr *epi-* + *histanai* to cause to stand] – **epistemologist** *n*, **epistemological** *adj*, **epistemologically** *adv*

**episternum** /'epi,stuhnəm/ *n* **1** a bone or cartilage element of or associated with the front or upper part of the STERNUM (breastbone or equivalent structure): eg **1a** INTERCLAVICLE **b** MANUBRIUM a **2** the main foremost subdivision of the side wall of a segment of the THORAX (middle body region) of an insect, lobster, or other ARTHROPOD [NL]

**epistle** /i'pisl/ *n* **1** *cap* (a reading at a church service from) any of the letters (e g of the apostle Paul) adopted as books of the New Testament **2a** a composition, usu in verse, in the form of a letter **b** *humorous* a letter; *esp* a long formal letter [ME, letter, Epistle, fr OF, fr L *epistula, epistola* letter, fr Gk *epistolē* message, letter, fr *epistellein* to send to, fr *epi-* + *stellein* to send – more at STALL] – **epistler** *n*

**epistle side** *n, often cap E* the right side of an altar or CHANCEL (part of church near the altar) as one faces it [fr the custom of reading the Epistle from this side]

¹**epistolary** /i'pistəl(ə)ri/ *adj* **1** of or suitable to a letter **2** contained in or carried on by letters ⟨*an endless sequence of . . .* ~ *love affairs – TLS*⟩ **3** written in the form of a series of letters ⟨*an* ~ *novel*⟩

²**epistolary** *n* a book containing the Epistles, used by the epistoler at a church service

**epistoler** /i'pistələ/ *n* the reader of the Epistle, esp in Anglican churches

**epistrophe** /i'pistrəfi/ *n* repetition of the same word or expression at the end of successive phrases, clauses, or sentences for rhetorical effect (e g in Abraham Lincoln's "of the people, by the people, for the people") – compare ANAPHORA [Gk *epistrophē*, lit., turning about, fr *epi-* + *strophē* turning – more at STROPHE]

**epitaph** /'epi,tahf, -taf/ *n* **1** a commemorative inscription on a tombstone or monument **2** a brief statement commemorating a deceased person or past event △ epigram, epigraph, epithet [ME *epitaphe*, fr MF, fr ML *epitaphium*, fr L, funeral oration, fr Gk *epitaphion*, fr *epi-* + *taphos* tomb, funeral] – **epitaphial, epitaphic** *adj*

**epitasis** /i'pitəsis/ *n, pl* **epitases** /-,seez/ the part of a classical drama that develops the main action – compare PROTASIS, CATASTROPHE [Gk, increased intensity, fr *epiteinein* to stretch tighter, fr *epi-* + *teinein* to stretch – more at THIN]

**epitaxy** /'epi,taksi/ *n* the growth of a usu thin layer of a substance on a crystal of a different substance whose crystal structure provides the orientation for that of the overlying layer [*epi-* + *-taxy* (fr Gk *-taxia* -taxis)] – **epitaxial** *adj*, **epitaxially** *adv*

**epithalamion** /,epithə'laymiən/ *n, pl* **epithalamia** /-myə/ an epithalamium [Gk]

**epithalamium** /,epithə'laymi-əm, -myəm/ *n, pl* **epithalamiums, epithalamia** a song or poem in praise or honour of a bride and bridegroom [L, fr Gk *epithalamion*, fr *epi-* + *thalamos* room, bridal chamber]

**epitheli-** /epitheeli-/, **epithelio-** *comb form* epithelium ⟨epithelioma⟩ [NL *epithelium*]

**epithelial·ize, -ise** /,epi'theelyəliez/ *vt* to cover with or convert to epithelium ⟨~d lesions⟩

**epithelioid** /,epi'theelioyd/ *adj* resembling epithelium ⟨~ cells⟩

**epithelioma** /,epi,theeli'ohmə/ *n* a tumour derived from epithelial tissue [NL] – **epitheliomatous** *adj*

**epithelium** /,epi'theeli-əm, -lyəm/ *n, pl* **epithelia** /-lyə/ **1** an animal tissue composed of closely bound cells that form a continuous sheet covering external surfaces or lining tubes or cavities of the body and serving esp to enclose and protect body parts, to produce secretions, or to function in absorption **2** a usu thin layer of cells that lines a cavity or tube of a plant [NL, fr *epi-* + Gk *thēlē* nipple – more at FEMININE] – **epithelial** *adj*

**epithel·ize, -ise** /,epi'theeliez/ *vt* to epithelialize

**epithet** /'epithet/ *n* **1a** a characterizing word or phrase accompanying or occurring in place of the name of a person or thing **b** a disparaging or abusive word or phrase **2** *obs* an expression [L *epitheton*, fr Gk, fr neut of *epithetos* added, fr *epitithenai* to put on, add, fr *epi-* + *tithenai* to put – more at DO] – **epithetic, epithetical** *adj*

*usage* The use of **epithet** to mean "term of abuse" ⟨*hurling epithets at the other driver*⟩, though still disliked, is now quite as prevalent as the earlier senses of the word. △ epigram, epigraph, epitaph

**epitome** /i'pitəmi/ *n* **1** a summary or condensed account, esp of a literary work; an abstract **2** a typical or ideal example; the embodiment ⟨*the British monarchy itself is the* ~ *of tradition* – Richard Joseph⟩ ⟨*very much . . . the* ~ *of a pop performer* – The Age (*Melbourne*)⟩ **3** brief or miniature form – often + *in* ⟨*man, the world in* ~⟩ [L, fr Gk *epitomē*, fr *epitemnein* to cut short, fr *epi-* + *temnein* to cut – more at TOME]

*usage* Epitome can mean a "typical example" of something bad, as well as an "ideal example" of something good ⟨*he's the* **epitome** *of selfishness*⟩.

**epitomist** /i'pitəmist/, **epitomizer, -iser** /i'pitəmiezə/ *n* a writer of an epitome

**epitom·ize, ise** /i'pitəmiez/ *vt* **1** to make or give an epitome of; summarize ⟨*his life's work is* ~d *in this book*⟩ **2** to serve as the typical or ideal example of; embody ⟨*she* ~s *an enthusiastic young dancer*⟩

**epizoic** /,epi'zoh·ik/ *adj* **1** living on or attached to the body of an animal ⟨*an* ~ *plant*⟩ **2** *of a plant* having seeds or fruits dispersed by being carried on the body of an animal – **epizoically** *adv*, **epizoism** *n*, **epizoite** *n*

**epizoon** /,epi'zoh·on/ *n, pl* **epizoa** /-ə/ an animal that lives on the body of another animal; ECTOPARASITE – **epizoan** *adj*

**epizootic** /,epizoh'otik/ *n or adj* (a disease) temporarily affecting many animals of one kind at the same time – compare ENZOOTIC [*epi-* + *zo-* + *-otic*] – **epizootically** *adv*

**epizootiology** /,epizoh,oti'oləji/, **epizootology** /,epi,zoh·o'toləji/, **epizoology** /,epizoh'oləji, -zooh-/ *n* **1** a science that deals with the occurrence, character, and causes of outbreaks of animal diseases **2** the factors controlling the presence or absence of a disease or a disease-causing agent of animals – **epizootiological** *also* **epizootiologic** *adj*, **epizootiologically** *adv*

**epoch** /'eepok/ *n* **1** a date or instant of time selected as a point of reference (e g in astronomy) **2** a memorable event or date; *esp* TURNING POINT **3a** an extended period of time usu characterized by a distinctive development or by a memorable series of events **b** a division of geological time less than a period and greater than an age, during which a series of rocks is formed **4** the displacement of a vibrating body from its resting position at the selected zero of time △ epic [ML *epocha*, fr Gk *epochē* cessation, fixed point, fr *epechein* to pause, hold back, fr *epi-* + *echein* to hold – more at SCHEME] – **epochal** *adj*, **epochally** *adv*

**'epoch-,making** *adj* uniquely or highly significant; momentous ⟨*the steam engine was an* ~ *invention*⟩

**epode** /'eepohd/ *n* **1** a LYRIC poem in which a long line is followed by a shorter one **2** the last part of a Greek LYRIC ode following the two parts of the choral ode and dance (the STROPHE and ANTISTROPHE) [L *epodos*, fr Gk *epōidos*, fr *epōidos* sung or said after, fr *epi-* + *aidein* to sing – more at ODE]

**eponym** /'epoh,nim, 'epə-/ *n* **1** the (name of a) real or mythical person after whom something, esp a place, is (believed to be) named **2** a name (e g of a drug or a disease) based on or derived from an eponym [Gk *epōnymos*, fr *epōnymos* eponymous, fr *epi-* + *onyma* name – more at NAME]

**eponymous** /i'ponimǝs/ *also* **eponymic** /ˌepǝ'nimik/ *adj* of or being the eponym ⟨*played the* ∼ *hero of* Hamlet⟩ – **eponymously** *adv*

**eponymy** /i'ponǝmi/, **eponymism** /i'ponǝmism/ *n* the derivation of a proper name (e g of a town or tribe) from a (fictitious) eponym

**epopee** /'epǝˌpee/ *n* 1 an EPIC poem 2 EPIC poetry generally [Fr *épopée*, fr Gk *epopoiia*, fr *epos* + *poiein* to make – more at POET]

**epos** /'epos/ *n* 1 an (early unwritten) body of poems on an EPIC theme that are not formally united 2 an EPIC poem [Gk, word, epic poem – more at VOICE]

**epoxide** /i'poksied/ *n* an epoxy compound

**epoxid·ize, ise** /i'poksiˌdiez/ *vt* to convert into an epoxide ⟨∼d oils⟩

¹**epoxy** /i'poksi/ *adj* 1 containing an oxygen atom attached in a 3-membered ring to two other atoms or groups; *specif* containing a 3-membered ring of atoms consisting of one oxygen and two carbon atoms 2 of an epoxide or EPOXY RESIN

²**epoxy** *vt* epoxied, epoxyed to glue with EPOXY RESIN

**epoxy resin** *n* any of various tough resistant THERMOSETTING (becoming rigid on heating) resins made from an epoxide and used chiefly in surface coatings and adhesives

**epsilon** /'epsilon/ *n* the 5th letter of the Greek alphabet [Gk *e psilon*, lit., simple e]

**Epsom salts** /'eps(ǝ)m/ *n taking sing or pl vb* MAGNESIUM SULPHATE chemically combined with water molecules, $MgSO_4.7H_2O$; *specif* a medicinal preparation of this used as a laxative [*Epsom*, town in Surrey, England]

**epulis** /i'pyoohlis/ *n* a tumour of the gums [NL, fr Gk *epoulis*, fr *epi-* + *oulon* gum]

**epyllion** /i'pilyǝn/ *n* a miniature EPIC poem [Gk, dim. of *epos*]

**equable** /'ekwǝbl/ *adj* 1 even, uniform; *esp* free from extremes or sudden changes ⟨*an* ∼ *climate*⟩ 2 even-tempered, placid ⟨*he was of an* ∼ *nature*⟩ **synonyms** see ¹STEADY **antonyms** variable, changeable △ equitable [L *aequabilis*, fr *aequare* to make level or equal, fr *aequus*] – **equably** *adv*, **equability** *n*, **equableness** *n*

¹**equal** /'eekwǝl/ *adj* 1a of the same quantity, amount, or number as another b identical in mathematical value or logical DENOTATION; EQUIVALENT 2a like in quality, nature, or status ⟨*bored with work not* ∼ *to his abilities*⟩ b like for each member of a group, class, or society ⟨*provide* ∼ *employment opportunities*⟩ ⟨∼ *rights*⟩ 3 evenly balanced or matched ⟨*the two opponents were* ∼⟩ 4 equable ⟨*an* ∼ *temperament*⟩ 5 not varying; similar throughout 6 capable of meeting the requirements of something (e g a situation or task) – + *to* ⟨*he is quite* ∼ *to the job*⟩ [ME, fr L *aequalis*, fr *aequus* level, equal] *usage* 1 One is **equal** *to* a task, or *to* performing it, but not *to* perform it ⟨△ *he's quite* **equal** *to find his own way home*⟩. 2 Since there can be no degrees in equality, some people dislike expressions such as ⟨*a more* **equal** *distribution of income*⟩. **synonyms** see ¹SAME **antonym** unequal

²**equal** *n* somebody or something that is equal to another ⟨*she is anyone's* ∼⟩

³**equal** *vb* **-ll-** (*NAm* **-l-, -ll-**) *vt* 1 to be equal to or indistinguishable from; *esp* to be exactly equivalent in value to 2 to make or produce something equal to 3 *archaic* to equalize ∼ *vi* to become equal or level – usu + *out* ⟨*our debts to each other* ∼ led *out*⟩

ˌ**equal-'area** *adj, of a map projection* showing the true size of areas relative to one another but distorting shape and direction

**equalitarian** /iˌkwoli'teǝri·ǝn/ *n or adj* (an) egalitarian – **equalitarianism** *n*

**equality** /i'kwolǝti/ *n* 1 the quality or state of being equal 2 EQUATION 3a

**equal·ize, -ise** /'eekwǝˌliez/ *vt* 1 to make equal 2 to make uniform; *esp* to distribute evenly or uniformly ⟨∼ *the tax burden*⟩ 3 to adjust or correct the frequency characteristics of (an electronic signal) by restoring to their original level frequencies, esp high frequencies, that have been reduced (e g in recording or transmission) ∼ *vi*, *chiefly Br* to make something equal; *esp* to bring the scores level (e g in a football match) – **equalization** *n*

**equal·izer, -iser** /'eekwǝˌliezǝ/ *n* 1 one who or that which equalizes: e g 1a a device to balance opposing forces or effects b an electronic device in a transmission system (e g a stereo system or radio) that is designed to reduce distortion by making the frequency response the same for a wide range of frequencies

c a score that ties a game ⟨*scored the* ∼ *in the 89th minute*⟩ 2 *NAm slang* a weapon; *esp* a gun

**equally** /'eekwǝli/ *adv* 1 in an equal or uniform manner; evenly 2 to an equal degree; alike ⟨*respected* ∼ *by young and old*⟩
*usage* 1 Some people dislike the combination **equally** *as* ⟨*X is* **equally** *as important as Y*⟩, and prefer to write ⟨*X is* **equally** *important with Y*⟩, or ⟨*X is (just) as important as Y*⟩, or ⟨*X and Y are* **equally** *important*⟩. 2 When two or more items follow **equally**, they should properly be joined by *and*, and not by any other word ⟨△ *she paid attention* **equally** *to X as to Y*⟩.

**equal pay** *n* equal payment of men and women for equal work

**equals sign** *also* **equal sign, equality sign** *n* a sign = indicating mathematical or logical equivalence

**equal temperament** *n* the division of the musical OCTAVE into 12 equal SEMITONES

**equanimity** /ˌeekwǝ'nimǝti, ˌekwǝ-/ *n* evenness of mind or temper, esp under stress; composure [L *aequanimitas*, fr *aequo animo* with even mind] – **equanimous** *adj*, **equanimously** *adv*

**equate** /i'kwayt/ *vt* 1 to make or set equal; equalize 2 to treat, represent, or regard as equal, equivalent, or comparable ⟨∼s dissension with disloyalty⟩ ∼ *vi* to be equal; correspond [ME *equaten*, fr L *aequatus*, pp of *aequare*]

**equation** /i'kwayzh(ǝ)n; *sense 1* i'kwaysh(ǝ)n/ *n* 1 equating or being equated 2 a complex of variable factors ⟨*the whole social* ∼⟩ 3a a statement of the equality of two mathematical or logical expressions b an expression representing a chemical reaction quantitatively by means of chemical symbols

**equational** /i'kwaysh(ǝ)nl/ *adj* 1 of, using, or involving an equation 2 dividing into two equal parts; *esp* being or involving the division of CHROMOSOMES (strands of gene-carrying material) in a cell undergoing MEIOSIS (splitting of a cell and its contents into four new cells), that occurs after REDUCTION DIVISION (division of a cell into two, each with half the chromosomes of the original cell) and results in the production of two chromosomes of equal size and form from each original chromosome – **equationally** *adv*

**equation of time** *n* the difference between a fictitious average standard time (MEAN TIME) and the actual time (APPARENT TIME), usu expressed as a correction, maximal in February (over 14 minutes) and November (over 16 minutes), which when added to the apparent time gives the local mean time

**equator** /i'kwaytǝ/ *n* 1 GREAT CIRCLE (circle on the surface of and having the same radius as a sphere); *specif* the great circle of the earth that is everywhere equally distant from the two poles and that divides the earth's surface into the northern and southern hemispheres 2 CELESTIAL EQUATOR 3 a circle or circular band dividing the surface of a body into two equal and symmetrical parts ⟨*the* ∼ *of a dividing cell*⟩ [ME, fr ML *aequator*, lit., equalizer, fr L *aequatus;* fr its containing the equinoxes] – **equatorward** *adj or adv*, **equatorwards** *adv*

¹**equatorial** /ˌekwǝ'tawrial/ *adj* 1 of, located at, or in the plane or region of an equator, esp the earth's equator ⟨*an* ∼ *orbit of a satellite*⟩ 2 *of the climate* characterized by consistently high temperatures and rainfall throughout the year – **equatorially** *adv*

²**equatorial** *n* (the mounting of) an EQUATORIAL TELESCOPE

**equatorial plane** *n* the plane perpendicular to, and midway between the poles of, the SPINDLE (spindle-shaped bundle of fibres) of a dividing cell

**equatorial plate** *n* the assembly of CHROMOSOMES (strands of gene-carrying material) on the EQUATORIAL PLANE during METAPHASE (stage of the process in which a cell nucleus divides)

**equatorial telescope** *n* as astronomical telescope that is mounted on two axes at right angles to each other, one being parallel to the earth's axis, and that allows a celestial body to be kept in view as the earth rotates

**equerry** /i'kweri, 'ekwǝri/ *n* 1 an officer of a prince or noble charged with the care of horses 2 an officer of the British Royal Household in personal attendance on a member of the royal family, esp the sovereign [obs *escuirie, equerry* stable, fr MF *escuirie* office of a squire, stable, fr *escuier* squire – more at ESQUIRE]

¹**equestrian** /i'kwestri·ǝn/ *adj* 1a of or featuring horses, horsemen, or horsemanship ⟨∼ *sports*⟩ b representing a person on horseback ⟨*an* ∼ *statue*⟩ 2a (composed) of knights; *esp* of the free knights of the Holy Roman Empire b (composed) of Roman EQUITES (members of cavalry order) 3 *archaic* riding on horse-

back; mounted [L *equestr-*, *equester* of a horseman, fr *eques* horseman, fr *equus* horse – more at EQUINE]

²**equestrian**, *fem* **equestrienne** /i‚kwestri'en/ *n* someone who (skilfully) rides or performs on horseback [*equestrienne* fr *equestrian* + *-enne* (as in *tragedienne*)]

**equestrianism** /i'kwestriəniz(ə)m/ *n* the art or practice of horsemanship or of equestrian sports

**equi-** /ekwi-, ekwi-/ *comb form* equal 〈equi*poise*〉; equally 〈equi*probable*〉 [ME, fr MF, fr L *aequi-*, fr *aequus* equal]

**equiangular** /‚eekwi'ang‚gyoolə, ‚ekwi-/ *adj* having all or corresponding angles equal 〈*an* ~ *triangle*〉 〈~ *polygons*〉

**equidistant** /‚eekwi'dist(ə)nt, ‚ekwi-/ *adj* equally distant from two or more places [MF or LL; MF, fr LL *aequidistant-*, *aequidistans*, fr L *aequi-* + *distant-*, *distans*, prp of *distare* to stand apart] – **equidistance** *n*, **equidistantly** *adv*

¹**equilateral** /‚eekwi'lat(ə)rəl, ‚ekwi-/ *adj* having all sides equal 〈~ *triangle*〉 [LL *aequilateralis*, fr L *aequi-* + *later-*, *latus* side – more at LATERAL] – **equilaterally** *adv*

²**equilateral** *n* (a side of) a geometric figure in which all the sides are of equal length

**equilibrant** /i'kwilibrənt/ *n* a force or system of forces capable of balancing another force or system of forces to produce equilibrium

**equilibrate** /‚eekwi'liebrayt, ‚ekwi-, -'lib-, i'kwili‚brayt/ *vt* to bring into or keep in equilibrium; balance ~ *vi* to bring about, come to, or be in equilibrium – **equilibrator** *n*, **equilibratory** *adj*, **equilibration** *n*

**equilibrist** /i'kwilibrist/ *n* someone who performs balancing tricks, esp on a high wire

**equilibrium** /‚eekwi'libri‚əm, ‚ekwi-/ *n, pl* **equilibriums, equilibria** /-briə/ **1** a state of balance between opposing forces or actions affecting a system that results either in a state of rest or uniform motion (e g when a body is acted on by forces whose resultant force is zero) or of dynamic balance (e g when a chemical reaction and its reverse reaction take place at equal rates) **2a** a state of balance between opposing or divergent influences or elements 〈*the introduction of a new and mighty force had disturbed the old* ~ *and had turned one limited monarchy after another into an absolute monarchy* – T B Macaulay〉 **b** a state of intellectual or emotional balance; equanimity **c** the economic condition in which supply and demand are matched **3** the normal balanced state of the animal body in relation to its environment that involves adjustment to changing orientation of the body with respect to gravity [L *aequilibrium*, fr *aequilibris* being in equilibrium, fr *aequi-* + *libra* weight, balance]

**equimolal** /‚eekwi'mohləl, ‚ekwi-/ *adj* **1** having equal MOLAL concentration **2** EQUIMOLAR 1

**equimolar** /‚eekwi'mohlə, ‚ekwi-/ *adj* **1** of or containing an equal number of MOLES (units of amount of a substance) 〈*an* ~ *mixture of chlorine and sulphur dioxide*〉 **2** having equal MOLAR concentration

**equimolecular** /‚eekwiməlekyoolə, ‚ekwi-/ *adj* **1** of or containing an equal number of molecules **2** EQUIMOLAR 1

**equine** /'ekwien/ *adj* of or resembling the horse (family) [L *equinus*, fr *equus* horse; akin to OE *eoh* horse, Gk *hippos*] – **equine** *n*, **equinely** *adv*

**equine influenza** *n* a contagious virus disease of horses marked by coughing

¹**equinoctial** /‚eekwi'noksh(ə)l, ‚ekwi-/ *adj* **1** of or occurring at or near the time of either or both equinoxes **2** of the regions or climate of the equinoctial line or equator **3** *of a plant* having flowers that open and close at definite times

²**equinoctial** *n* **1** an equinoctial storm **2** *also* **equinoctial circle, equinoctial line** CELESTIAL EQUATOR

**equinoctial point** *n* EQUINOX 2

**equinoctial year** *n* YEAR 1 (year of 365¼ days)

**equinox** /'ekwi‚noks/ *n* **1** either of the two times each year that occur about March 21st and September 23rd when the sun crosses the equator and day and night are of equal length everywhere on earth **2** either of the two points where the apparent path of the sun crosses the CELESTIAL EQUATOR [ME, fr MF or ML; MF *equinoxe*, fr ML *equinoxium*, alter. of L *aequinoctium*, fr *aequi-* equi- + *noct-*, *nox* night – more at NIGHT]

**equip** /i'kwip/ *vt* **-pp-** **1** to make ready for service, action, or use; provide with appropriate supplies **2** to dress, array **3** to provide with abilities, intellectual capabilities, etc 〈*he was amply* ~ped *to deal with the demanding degree course*〉 [MF *equiper*, of Gmc origin; akin to OE *scip* ship] – **equipper** *n*

**equipage** /'ekwipij/ *n* **1** material or articles used in the equipment and stores of an organized group, esp a military unit **2** an elegant horse-drawn carriage with its servants **3** *archaic* **3a** a set of small articles (e g for table service) **b** a small ornamental case **c** trappings **4** *archaic* a group of attendants; a retinue [MF, fr *equiper*]

**equipartition** /‚eekwipah'tish(ə)n, ‚ekwi-/ *n* the equal distribution of the available energy in a system (e g a gas) in thermal equilibrium among the DEGREES OF FREEDOM (limited number of possibilities for motion or change) possessed by the molecules, atoms, and ions present in the system

**equipment** /i'kwipmənt/ *n* **1** equipping or being equipped **2** the set of articles, apparatus, or physical resources serving to equip a person, thing, enterprise, expedition, etc **3** mental or emotional traits or resources

¹**equipoise** /'ekwipoyz/ *n* **1** a state of equilibrium of forces **2** a counterbalance

²**equipoise** *vt* **1** to serve as a counterbalance to **2** to put or hold in equipoise

**equipollent** /‚eekwi'polənt, ‚ekwi-/ *adj* **1** equal in force, power, validity, or effect **2** *of two propositions* able to be deduced logically from each other [ME, fr MF, fr L *aequipollent-*, *aequipollens*, fr *aequi-* equi- + *pollent-*, *pollens*, prp of *pollēre* to be able] – **equipollence, equipollency** *n*, **equipollent** *n*, **equipollently** *adv*

**equiponderate** /‚eekwi'pondərayt, ‚ekwi-/ *vb, archaic vi* to be equal in weight or force ~ *vt* to equal or make equal in weight or force; counterbalance [ML *aequiponderatus*, pp of *equiponderare*, fr L *aequi-* + *ponderare* to weigh, ponder] – **equiponderance, equiponderancy** *n*, **equiponderant** *adj or n*

**equipotent** /‚eekwi'pohtənt, ‚ekwi-/ *adj* **1** having equal effects or capacities for development 〈~ *genes*〉 〈~ *regions of an egg*〉 **2** EQUIPOTENTIAL 2 **3** *of a mathematical set* having the same CARDINAL NUMBER as another set

¹**equipotential** /‚eekwipə'tensh(ə)l, ‚ekwi-/ *adj* **1** having the same (electrical) potential or uniform (electrical) potential throughout 〈~ *points*〉 〈*an* ~ *surface*〉 **2** equal in power or effect – **equipotentiality** *n*

²**equipotential** *n* an equipotential line or surface

**equiprobable** /‚eekwi'probəbl, ‚ekwi-/ *adj* having the same degree of logical or mathematical probability 〈~ *alternatives*〉

**equisetum** /‚ekwi'seetəm/ *n, pl* **equisetums, equiseta** /-'seetə/ HORSETAIL [NL, genus name, fr L *equisaetum* horsetail (plant), fr *equus* horse + *saeta* bristle]

**equitable** /'ekwitəbl/ *adj* **1** fair and just **2** valid in equity as distinguished from COMMON LAW or STATUTE LAW *synonyms* see ¹FAIR *antonyms* inequitable, unfair △ equable – **equitableness** *n*, **equitably** *adv*, **equitability** *n*

**equitant** /'ekwitənt/ *adj, of leaves arranged in rows on opposite sides of an axis* folded inwards in a lengthways direction and overlapping each other at their base (e g in an iris) [L *equitant-*, *equitans*, prp of *equitare* to ride on horseback, fr *equit-*, *eques* horseman – more at EQUESTRIAN]

**equitation** /‚ekwi'taysh(ə)n/ *n* the act or art of riding on horseback

**equites** /'ekwiteez/ *n taking pl vb* members of a Roman order between the senatorial order and the ordinary citizens, serving originally as the cavalry, having entry requirements based on wealth, and having certain privileges [L, pl of *equit-*, *eques*]

**equity** /'ekwiti/ *n* **1a** justice according to natural law or right; fairness **b** something that is equitable **2** a system of justice originally developed in the Chancery courts on the basis of conscience and fairness to supplement or override the more rigid system of COMMON LAW **3a** a right, claim, or interest existing or valid in equity **b** the money value of (an interest in) a property in excess of claims against it **c** the value of shares issued by a company **4** *usu pl* a share that does not bear fixed interest – called also ORDINARY SHARE **5** *cap, Br* the trade union representing the interests of actors and performers [ME *equite*, fr MF *equité*, fr L *aequitat-*, *aequitas*, fr *aequus* equal, fair]

**equity capital** *n* capital (e g retained corporate earnings or individual savings) invested or available for investment in the ownership element of a new enterprise

**equity of redemption** *n* the equitable right of a mortgagor to redeem a mortgaged property on payment of the sum owed, even after the right of redemption at COMMON LAW has gone

**equivalence** /i'kwivələns/, **equivalency** /-si/ *n* **1a** the state or property of being equivalent **b(1)** the relation between two statements which are either both true or both false such that each implies the other **b(2)** a logical function of two statements, which takes the value true if both statements are true or both false, and the value false otherwise **2** a presentation of terms as equivalent **3** the state of having the same chemical combining capacities; *also* the state of having the same VALENCY □ (*1b*) compare BICONDITIONAL

**equivalence class** *n* a mathematical set in which an EQUIVALENCE RELATION holds between every pair of members of the set

**equivalence relation** *n* a relation between elements of a mathematical set that is SYMMETRIC, REFLEXIVE, and TRANSITIVE

**¹equivalent** /i'kwivələnt/ *adj* **1** equal or interchangeable in force, amount, importance, or value **2** corresponding or virtually identical, esp in effect, function, or meaning **3** having the same chemical combining capacity ⟨~ *quantities of two elements*⟩ **4** related by an EQUIVALENCE RELATION: eg **4a** having the same set of solutions ⟨~ *equations*⟩ **b** capable of being placed in BIJECTIVE correspondence ⟨~ *sets*⟩ **c** equal in area ⟨*a square* ~ *to a triangle*⟩ **5** *obs* equal in might or authority *synonyms* see ¹SAME *antonym* different [ME, fr MF or LL; MF, fr LL *aequivalent-, aequivalens,* prp of *aequivalēre* to have equal power, fr L *aequi-* + *valēre* to be strong – more at WIELD] – **equivalently** *adv*

**²equivalent** *n* **1** something that is equivalent **2 equivalent weight, equivalent** the weight of a substance in grams that combines with, displaces, or is otherwise chemically equivalent to 8 grams of oxygen or 1.00797 grams of hydrogen; the atomic or molecular weight of a substance divided by its VALENCY

**equivalent circuit** *n* an electrical circuit made up of simple basic components that is electrically equivalent to, and is used to represent, a more complicated circuit

**equivalent projection** *n* an EQUAL-AREA map projection

**equivocal** /i'kwivəkl/ *adj* **1** subject to two or more interpretations; ambiguous ⟨~ *evidence*⟩ **2** deliberately misleading or evasive; of uncertain nature **3** *of a person* questionable, suspicious *synonyms* see ¹OBSCURE *antonym* unequivocal [LL *aequivocus,* fr *aequi-* equi- + *voc-, vox* voice – more at VOICE] – **equivocally** *adv,* **equivocalness** *n,* **equivocality** *n*

**equivocate** /i'kwivə‚kayt/ *vi* to use equivocal language, esp with intent to deceive or avoid committing oneself; prevaricate – **equivocatingly** *adv,* **equivocator** *n,* **equivocation** *n*

**equivoque, equivoke** /'ekwi‚vohk, 'eekwi-/ *n* **1** a play on words or phrases; *specif* a pun **2** an ambiguity; DOUBLE ENTENDRE [Fr *équivoque,* fr *équivoque* equivocal, fr LL *aequivocus*]

**er, ur** /uh/ *interj* – used to express hesitation or doubt

**¹-er** /-ə/ *suffix* (*adj* → *adj, adv* → *adv*) – used to form the comparative of adjectives and adverbs of one syllable, and of some adjectives and adverbs of two or more syllables, that end in a consonant ⟨*hotter*⟩, a vowel other than *e,* or a final *y* that changes to *i* ⟨*drier*⟩; compare ¹-R [ME -*er, -ere, -re,* fr OE -*ra* (in adjectives), -*or* (in adverbs); akin to OHG -*iro,* adj compar suffix, L -*ior,* Gk -*iōn*]

**²-er, -ar** /ə/, **-ier** /yə/ *suffix* (→ *n*) **1a** a person engaged in the occupation of ⟨*hatter*⟩ ⟨*furrier*⟩ ⟨*lawyer*⟩ **b** person or thing belonging to or associated with ⟨*header*⟩ ⟨*oldtimer*⟩ **c** native of; resident of ⟨*cottager*⟩ ⟨*New Yorker*⟩ **d** something that has ⟨*three-decker*⟩ ⟨*four-poster*⟩ **2a** one who or that which does or performs (a specified action) ⟨*reporter*⟩ ⟨*eye-opener*⟩ – sometimes added to both elements of a compound ⟨*builder-upper*⟩ **b** something that is a suitable object of (a specified action) ⟨*broiler*⟩ ⟨*cooker*⟩ **3** one who or that which is ⟨*foreigner*⟩ □ *-yer* in a few words after *w, -ier* in a few words after other letters, otherwise *-er;* compare ²-R *usage* see ¹-OR [ME -*er, -ere, -are, -ier, -iere;* partly fr OE -*ere* (akin to OHG -*āri;* both fr a prehistoric Gmc suffix borrowed fr L -*arius*); partly fr OF -*ier, -iere,* fr L -*arius, -aria, -arium* -ary; partly fr MF -*ere,* fr L -*ator* -or – more at -ARY, -OR]

**era** /'iərə/ *n* **1** a fixed point in time from which an extended period of years is reckoned **2a** a usu historical period begun or typified by some distinctive figure or characteristic feature; EPOCH 3a ⟨*the* ~ *of space flight*⟩ **b** a stage in the development of a person or thing; *esp* any of the five major divisions of geological time ⟨*Palaeozoic* ~⟩ [LL *aera,* fr L, counters, pl of *aer-, aes* copper, money – more at ORE]

**eradiate** /i'raydiayt/ *vt* to irradiate [*e-* + *radiate*]

**eradicate** /i'radi‚kayt/ *vt* **1** to pull up by the roots **2** to eliminate; DO AWAY WITH ⟨~ *ignorance by better teaching*⟩ [L *eradicatus,* pp of *eradicare,* fr *e-* + *radic-, radix* root – more at ROOT] – **eradicator** *n,* **eradicative** *adj,* **eradicable** *adj,* **eradication** *n*

**erase** /i'rayz/ *vt* **1a** to obliterate or rub out (eg written, painted, or engraved letters) **b** to remove (recorded matter) from a MAGNETIC TAPE **c** to delete from a computer storage device **2** to remove from existence or memory as if by erasing ~ *vi* to yield to being erased ⟨*this mark is easily* ~d⟩ [L *erasus,* pp of *eradere,* fr *e-* + *radere* to scratch, scrape – more at RAT] – **erasable** *adj,* **erasibility** *n*

*synonyms* Erase, expunge, cancel, efface, obliterate, blot out, and delete may all mean "remove completely an impression, memory or inscription". Their abstract meaning is influenced by their literal meaning: **erase,** for instance, with its idea of "rubbing out" stresses the fact of removal and may imply a blank surface freed for future use ⟨*needed to* **erase** *sad memories, that happier ones might take their place*⟩. **Expunge,** falsely influenced by its likeness to "sponge", suggests completely wiping something out, as if it had never been ⟨*irrelevant testimony* **expunged** *from the court record*⟩. **Cancel,** coming from the practice of drawing lines through writing to show it is no longer valid, means "negative the effect of". **Efface** stresses the complete, though often gradual, process of wearing away somthing originally impressed or imprinted ⟨**efface** *the inscription on a tombstone*⟩ ⟨*time* **effaced** *her impressions of the holiday far too soon*⟩. **Blot out** suggests covering or smearing something to make it invisible ⟨*the fog* **blotted out** *the view*⟩ ⟨*she* **blotted out** *the memory with an effort of will*⟩. **Delete** is now used almost exclusively for crossing out material in a manuscript. The strongest of all these terms is **obliterate,** whch stresses complete removal of every trace of something, though it may be used only in the sense of "render indecipherable". Compare ABOLISH

**erase head** *n* a tape-recorder head used for erasing previously recorded material – compare MAGNETIC HEAD

**eraser** /i'rayzə/ *n* one who or that which erases; *esp* a device (eg a piece of rubber or a felt pad) used to erase marks (eg of pencil or chalk); ¹RUBBER 1b

**Erastian** /i'rasti‚on, -tyən/ *adj* of, characterized by, or advocating the doctrine of state supremacy in ecclesiastical affairs [Thomas *Erastus* †1583 Ger-Swiss physician & Zwinglian theologian] – **Erastian** *n,* **Erastianism** *n*

**erbium** /'uhbi‚əm/ *n* a metallic chemical element of the RARE-EARTH group that occurs with the element yttrium in various minerals [NL, fr *Ytterby,* town in Sweden]

**¹ere** /eə/ *prep, poetic* ²BEFORE 2 ⟨*contrived* ~ *the beginning of the world* – Norman Douglas⟩ [ME *er,* fr *ær,* fr *ǣr,* adv, early, soon; akin to OHG *ēr* earlier, Gk *ēri* early]

**²ere** *conj, poetic* ³BEFORE ⟨*I will be thrown into Etna* ... ~ *I will leave her* – Shak⟩

**¹erect** /i'rekt/ *adj* **1a** vertical in position; upright **b** characterized by firm or rigid uprightness (eg in bodily posture) ⟨*an* ~ *bearing*⟩ **2a** standing up or out from the body owing to a (temporary) muscle contraction ⟨~ *hairs*⟩ **b** in a state of physiological erection due to dilation with blood, as a result of usu sexual stimulation **c** *of a plant part* growing vertically or at right angles to a main stem or other part **3** *of an optical image* having the same orientation as the object; not inverted **4** *archaic* directed upwards **5** *obs* alert, watchful [ME, fr L *erectus,* pp of *erigere* to erect, fr *e-* + *regere* to lead straight, guide – more at RIGHT] – **erectly** *adv,* **erectness** *n*

**²erect** *vt* **1a** to put up by the fitting together of materials or parts; build **b** to fix in an upright position ⟨~ed *a statue*⟩ **c** to cause (a body part) to become erect ⟨~ed *his tail*⟩ **2** to hold up as an ideal; elevate in status ⟨~s *a few odd notions into a philosophy*⟩ **3** to establish; SET UP 7a **4** to draw or construct (eg a perpendicular) on a given base **5** to make (an inverted optical image) upright **6** *archaic* to direct upwards **7** *obs* to encourage, embolden ~ *vi, of a body part* to become erect – **erectable** *adj*

**erectile** /i'rektil/ *adj* **1a** capable of being erected; *esp, of animal tissue* capable of becoming swollen with blood to bring about the erection of a body part **b** *of a sexual organ* containing erectile tissue and capable of erection **2** of or involving the erection of the penis – **erectility** *n*

**erection** /i'reksh(ə)n/ *n* **1** the act or process of erecting; construction **2** something erected; a construction **3** (an occurrence of) the dilation with blood and resulting firmness of a previously limp sexual body part containing erectile tissue; *esp* (an occurrence of) such a state in the penis

**erector, erecter** /i'rektə/ *n* one who or that which erects; *esp* a muscle that raises or keeps a body part erect

**E region** *n* the part of the IONOSPHERE (upper part of the earth's atmosphere) occurring between about 65 and 145 kilometres (about 40 and 90 miles) above the earth's surface and containing a layer (E LAYER) capable of reflecting medium wavelength radio waves

**erelong** /ˌeə'long/ *adv, archaic or poetic* before long; soon

**eremite** /'erəmiet/ *n* a usu Christian hermit or recluse – compare COENOBITE [ME – more at HERMIT] – **eremitism** *n*, **eremitic, eremitical** *adj*

**erenow** /ˌeə'now/ *adv, archaic or poetic* before now; heretofore

**erepsin** /i'repsin/ *n* a mixture of protein-digesting ENZYMES present in the intestinal juice [ISV *er-* (prob fr L *eripere* to sweep away, fr *e-* + *rapere* to sweep) + *pepsin* – more at RAPID]

**erethism** /'erithiz(ə)m/ *n* **1** abnormal responsiveness, sensitivity, or irritability of a body part or system to stimulation **2** abnormal responsiveness to verbal or psychic stimulation, esp that of a sexual nature [Fr *éréthisme*, fr Gk *erethismos* irritation, fr *erethizein* to irritate; akin to Gk *ornynai* to rouse – more at RISE] – **erethismic, erethistic, erethitic** *adj*

**erewhile** /ˌeə'wiel/ *also* **erewhiles** *adv, archaic or poetic* some time ago; heretofore ⟨*I am as fair now as I was* ~ – Shak⟩

**erf** /eəf/ *n, pl* **erven** /'eəvən/ *SAfr* a plot of urban building land, usu large enough for one house [Afrik, fr D, plot of land, inheritance]

**¹erg** /uhg/ *n* a cgs unit of work or energy that is equal to the work done by a force of 1 dyne moving its point of application through 1 centimetre and that is equivalent to $10^{-7}$ joules [Gk *ergon* work – more at WORK]

**²erg** *n, pl* **ergs, areg** /ə'reg/ an area of shifting sand dunes in a desert, esp the Sahara [Fr, of Hamitic origin]

**erg-** /uhg-/, **ergo-** *comb form* work ⟨*ergonomics*⟩ [Gk, fr *ergon*]

**ergative** /'uhgətiv/ *adj* of or being the grammatical relationship between two sentences (e g "the prisoners marched" and "John marched the prisoners") such that the subject of the first corresponds to the object of the second, the new subject of which causes rather than performs the action [ISV *ergat-* worker (fr Gk, fr *ergatēs*, fr *ergazesthai* to work) + *-ive*] – **ergativity** *n*

**ergo** /'uhgoh/ *adv* therefore, hence [L, fr OL, because of, fr (assumed) OL *e rogo* from the direction (of)]

**ergo-** *comb form* ergot ⟨*ergosterol*⟩ [Fr, fr *ergot*]

**ergodic** /uh'godik/ *adj* of a statistical system in which the fraction of time each subsystem spends in a given statistical state equals the fraction of subsystems in that state at any given time [Ger *ergodenhypothese*, lit., hypothesis of the path of energy, fr *erg-* + Gk *hodos* path, road] – **ergodicity** *n*

**ergograph** /'uhgəˌgrahf, -ˌgraf/ *n* an apparatus for measuring the work capacity of a muscle [ISV]

**ergometer** /uh'gomitə/ *n* an apparatus for measuring the work performed by a group of muscles – **ergometric** *adj*

**ergometrine** /ˌuhgə'metreen, -'mee, -trin/ *n* a drug, $C_{19}H_{23}N_3O_2$, obtained from ergot that is less toxic and causes a more powerful contraction of the womb than ergot, and that is used esp to produce rhythmic contractions of the womb and to treat bleeding after childbirth [*ergo-* + *metr-* + *-ine*]

**ergonomics** /ˌuhgə'nomiks/ *n taking sing verb* a science that is concerned with the relationship between human beings, the machines and equipment they use, and their working environment, and that involves the application of physiological, anatomical, and psychological data to the design of efficient working systems [*ergo-* + *economics*] – **ergonomic** *adj*, **ergonomist** *n*

**ergonovine** /ˌuhgə'nohveen, -vin/ *n* ergometrine [*ergo-* + L *novus* new – more at NEW]

**ergosterol** /uh'gostərol/ *n* a STEROID, $C_{28}H_{43}OH$, that occurs esp in yeast, moulds, and ergot and that is ultimately converted into VITAMIN $D_2$ by ultraviolet light [ISV]

**ergot** /'uhgət, -got/ *n* **1** the black or dark purple club-shaped SCLEROTIUM (compact mass of hardened fungal threads) of some fungi (genus *Claviceps*) that develops in the OVARY (seedbearing structure) of a grass (e g rye), replacing the grass seed, and is used when dried as a source of various drugs; *also* a fungus bearing ergots **2** a disease of rye and other cereals caused by the replacement of the cereal's seeds by the SCLEROTIA of an ergot fungus **3a** the dried SCLEROTIA of an ergot fungus grown on rye, that contains several compounds, including ergometrine and ergotamine, used as drugs **b** any of such compounds used medicinally (e g to treat bleeding or migraine) for their contractile effect on SMOOTH MUSCLE, esp of the small arteries and womb [Fr, lit., cock's spur] – **ergotic** *adj*

**ergotamine** /uh'gotəmeen/ *n* a drug, $C_{33}H_{35}N_5O_5$, obtained from ergot that is used esp in treating migraine [ISV]

**ergotism** /'uhgəˌtiz(ə)m/ *n* a condition, characterized by gangrene of the fingers, toes, and other extremities or by muscular twitching and convulsions, that is produced by eating cereals or the grain or grain products (e g rye bread) of cereals infected with ergot fungus or by excessive use of an ergot drug over a long time

**erica** /'erikə/ *n* any of a large genus (*Erica*) of low many-branched evergreen shrubs including several species of heather and heaths [NL, genus name, fr L *erice* heather, fr Gk *ereikē*]

**ericaceous** /ˌeri'kayshəs/ *adj* of or being a member of the heather family that includes the heaths, heathers, and rhododendrons

**Erie** /'iəree/ *n* a member of a N American Indian people of the region south of Lake Erie; *also* their language, which belongs to the IROQUOIAN family of languages

**erigeron** /i'rijərən, -'rig-/ *n* any of a widely distributed genus (*Erigeron*) of plants of the daisy family with flower heads that resemble asters [NL, genus name, fr L, groundsel, fr Gk *ērigerōn*, fr *ēri* early + *gerōn* old man; fr the hoary down of some species]

**Erin** /'erin/ *n, chiefly poetic* Ireland [OIr *Erinn*, dat of *Eriu* Ireland]

**Erinys** /i'rinis, i'rienis/ *n usu pl, pl* **Erinyes** FURY 2a (Greek avenging goddess) [Gk]

**eriophyid** /ˌeri'ofiˌid/ *n* any of a large family (Eriophyidae) of minute plant-eating mites that have two pairs of legs placed at the front and lack a respiratory system [deriv of Gk *erion* wool + *phyē* growth; akin to Gk *physis* growth – more at PHYSICS] – **eriophyid** *adj*

**¹eristic** /e'ristik/ *also* **eristical** /-kl/ *adj* of or employing subtle, logical, controversial, and usu specious disputation [Gk *eristikos* fond of wrangling, fr *erizein* to wrangle, fr *eris* strife] – **eristically** *adv*

**²eristic** *n* (someone skilled in) the art or practice of logical controversial argument

**erk** /uhk/ *n, Br slang* **1** someone holding the lowest rank in the air force or navy; unpopular person **2** a stupid person; a fool [alter. of *airc*, short for *aircraftman*]

**Erlang** /'uhlang/ *n* a unit for measuring traffic intensity in esp telephone communications systems that is equivalent to maximum capacity usage [A K *Erlang* †1929 Dan mathematician]

**Erlenmeyer flask** /'eələnˌmieˌə/ *n* a narrow-necked flat-bottomed conical laboratory flask [Emil *Erlenmeyer* †1909 Ger chemist]

**ermine** /'uhmin/ *n, pl* **ermines,** *esp collectively* **ermine 1a** any of several weasels that have a white winter coat usu with more or less black on the tail; *esp* a stoat **b** the white winter fur of the ermine **2** (a rank or office having) a ceremonial or official robe ornamented with ermine **3** an animal (e g a horse) with black spots on a white coat **4** a heraldic fur consisting of black spots of any of various conventional shapes representing black ermine tails placed on a white field – compare VAIR 2 [ME, fr OF, of Gmc origin; akin to OHG *harmo* weasel; akin to Lith *šarmuo* weasel]

**erne, ern** /uhn/ *n* an eagle; *esp* WHITE-TAILED EAGLE [ME, fr OE *earn*; akin to OHG *arn* eagle, Gk *ornis* bird]

**Ernie** /'uhni/ *n* an electronic device that chooses at random the winning numbers of Premium Bonds [*Electronic random number indicator equipment*]

**erode** /i'rohd/ *vt* **1a** *of water, wind, glacial ice, etc* to eat into or wear away slowly; corrode **b** to cause to deteriorate or disappear as if by eroding ⟨*his quality has been* ~ d *by the years* – The Observer⟩ **2** to produce or form by eroding ⟨*glaciers* ~ *U-shaped valleys*⟩ **3** to eat away (tissue) by ulceration ~ *vi* to undergo erosion [L *erodere* to eat away, fr *e-* + *rodere* to gnaw – more at RAT] – **erodible** *adj*, **erodibility** *n*

**erogenous** /i'rojənəs/ *also* **erogenic** /ˌerə'jenik/ *adj* **1** of or producing sexual excitement when stimulated; sensitive to sexual stimulation ⟨~ *zones*⟩ **2** of or arousing sexual feelings [Gk *erōs* + E *-genous, -genic*] – **erogeneity** *n*

**Eros** /'iəros, 'eros/ *n, often not cap* the esp sexual life instincts that are directed towards self-preservation and uninhibited enjoyment; LIBIDO – compare THANATOS [Gk *Erōs*, god of sexual love, fr *erōs* love; akin to Gk *erasthai* to love, desire]

**erose** /i'rohs/ *adj* irregular, uneven; *specif* having an irregularly notched edge ⟨*an* ~ *leaf*⟩ [L *erosus*, pp of *erodere*] – **erosely** *adv*

**erosion** /i'rohzh(ə)n/ *n* **1** eroding or being eroded **2** an instance or product of erosive action – **erosional** *adj*, **erosionally** *adv*

**erosive** /i'rohsiv, -ziv/ *adj* tending to erode or to induce or permit erosion – **erosiveness** *n*, **erosivity** *n*

**erot-** /irot-/, **eroto-** *comb form* eroticism ⟨erot*ica*⟩ ⟨eroto-*genic*⟩ [Gk *erōto*, fr *erōt-*, *erōs*]

**erotic** /i'rotik/ *adj* 1 of, concerned with, or tending to arouse sexual desire; giving sexual pleasure ⟨∼ *art*⟩ 2 strongly affected by sexual desire △ esoteric, exotic [Gk *erōtikos*, fr *erōt-*, *erōs*] – **erotically** *adv* **eroticize** *vt*

**erotica** /i'rotikə/ *n taking sing or pl vb* literature or art with an erotic theme or quality [NL, fr Gk *erōtika*, neut pl of *erōtikos*]

**eroticism** /i'rotə,siz(ə)m/ *n* 1 an erotic theme, quality, or character 2 sexual arousal or excitement 3 (insistent) sexual impulse or desire – **eroticist** *n*

**erotism** /'erə,tiz(ə)m/ *n* eroticism

**erotogenic** /i,rotə'jenik, i,roh-/ *adj* erogenous

**erotology** /,erə'toləji/ *n* the study and description of sexual stimuli and behaviour

**erotomania** /i,rotə'maynyə, -roh-/ *n* (abnormally) excessive sexual desire [NL] – **erotomaniac** *n*

**err** /uh/ *vi* **1a** to make a mistake; be inaccurate or incorrect **b** to do wrong; sin 2 *archaic* to stray [ME *erren*, fr OF *errer*, fr L *errare*; akin to OE *ierre* wandering, angry, ON *rās* race – more at RACE]

**errancy** /'erənsi; *also* 'uhrənsi/ *n* 1 the state or an instance of erring 2 the holding of views deviating from accepted standards, esp of Christian doctrine

**errand** /'erənd/ *n* 1 (the object or purpose of) a short trip taken to attend to some business, esp for another ⟨*ran* ∼*s for pocket money*⟩ 2 *archaic* **2a** an oral message entrusted to a person **b** an embassy, mission [ME *erend* message, business, fr OE *ǣrend*; akin to OHG *ārunti* message]

**errant** /'erənt/ *adj* 1 (given to) travelling, esp in search of adventure – compare KNIGHT-ERRANT 2 going astray or deviating from expected course ⟨*an* ∼ *calf*⟩; *esp* doing wrong; erring ⟨*an* ∼ *child*⟩ 3 *obs* ARRANT [ME *erraunt*, fr MF *errant*, prp of *errer* to err & *errer* to travel, fr ML *iterare*, fr L *iter* road, journey – more at ITINERANT] – **errant** *n*, **errantly** *adv*

**errantry** /'erəntri/ *n* knight-errantry

**errata** /i'rahtə/ *n taking pl vb* a list of printing errors; *also* a page bearing such a list [pl of *erratum*]

> *usage* Although **errata** is a plural, it is sometimes used as a singular noun ⟨*this* errata⟩, but this usage is widely disliked.

¹**erratic** /i'ratik/ *adj* 1 having no fixed course; wandering ⟨*an* ∼ *comet*⟩ 2 of a boulder, rock, *etc* transported from an original resting place, esp by a glacier 3 characterized by lack of consistency, regularity, or uniformity, esp in behaviour; eccentric, unpredictable 4 *archaic* nomadic [ME, fr MF or L; MF *erratique*, fr L *erraticus*, fr *erratus*, pp of *errare*] – **erratically** *adv*, **erraticism** *n*

²**erratic** *n* someone or something that is erratic; *esp* an erratic boulder or block of rock

**erratum** /i'rahtəm/ *n, pl* **errata** CORRIGENDUM [L, fr neut of *erratus*]

**erroneous** /i'rohnyəs, -ni-əs/ *adj* 1 containing or characterized by error; mistaken, incorrect ⟨∼ *assumptions*⟩ 2 *archaic* wandering [ME, fr L *erroneus*, fr *erron-*, *erro* wanderer, fr *errare*] – **erroneously** *adv*, **erroneousness** *n*

**error** /'erə/ *n* **1a** a mistake or inaccuracy, esp in speech or action ⟨*a typing* ∼⟩ **b** the state of being wrong in behaviour or beliefs ⟨*he realized the* ∼ *of his ways*⟩ **2a** *maths & statistics* the difference between an observed or calculated value and a true value; *specif* variation in measurements, calculations, or observations of a quantity due to mistakes or to uncontrollable factors **b** the amount of deviation from a standard or specification [ME *errour*, fr OF, fr L *error*, fr *errare*] – **errorless** *adj* – **in error** 1 by mistake ⟨*I caught this train* in error⟩ 2 mistaken ⟨*I was* in error *when I called you a thief*⟩

**ersatz** /'eəzatz, 'uh-/ *adj* being a usu artificial and inferior substitute ⟨*margarine can no longer be called* ∼ *butter*⟩ [Ger *ersatz-*, fr *ersatz*, n, substitute] – **ersatz** *n*

**Erse** /uhs/ *n* 1 SCOTTISH GAELIC 2 IRISH 2 □ no longer used technically [ME (Sc) *Erisch*, adj, Irish, alter. of *Irish*] – **Erse** *adj*

**erst** /uhst/ *adv, archaic* in the past; formerly [ME *erest* earliest, formerly, fr OE *ǣrest*, superl of *ǣr* early – more at ERE]

**erstwhile** /'uhst,wiel/ *adj* former, previous ⟨*his* ∼ *students*⟩ – **erstwhile** *adv*

**erubescent** /,eroo'bes(ə)nt/ *adj* becoming or tending to red [L *erubescent-*, *erubescens*, prp of *erubescere* to grow red, fr *e-* + *rubescere* to grow red, incho of *rubēre* to be red] – **erubescence** *n*

**erucic acid** /i'roohsik/ *n* a FATTY ACID, $CH_3(CH_2)_7CH=$

$CH(CH_2)_{11}COOH$, found in many seed oils (e g those of rapeseed and nasturtium seeds) [NL *Eruca*, genus of plants, fr L, caterpillar, the plant rocket]

**eruciform** /i'roohsi,fawm/ *adj, of an insect larva* having well-developed abdominal limbs (PROLEGS) and a soft segmented body – compare APODOUS, CAMPODEIFORM, SCARABAEIFORM [L *eruca* caterpillar]

**eruct** /i'rukt/ *vi* to belch ∼ *vt*, *esp of a volcano* to pour or throw out (e g lava) [L *eructare*, fr *e-* + *ructare* to belch, fr *-ructus*, pp of *-rugere* to belch; akin to L *rugire* to roar] – **eructation** *n*

**erudite** /'eroodiet/ *adj* possessing or displaying extensive or profound knowledge, esp from books; learned ⟨*an* ∼ *scholar*⟩ synonyms see KNOWLEDGE [ME *erudit*, fr L *eruditus*, fr pp of *erudire* to instruct, fr *e-* + *rudis* rude, ignorant] – **eruditely** *adv*, **erudition** *n*

**erupt** /i'rupt/ *vi* **1a**, *esp of a volcano* to release lava, steam, etc suddenly and usu violently **b(1)** to burst violently from limits or restraint **b(2)** *of a tooth* to emerge through the gum **c** to become suddenly active or violent; explode ⟨*will terrorism* ∼ *again?*⟩ **d** *informal* to become violently angry ⟨*I* ∼*ed when he told me he had crashed my car*⟩ 2 to break out (e g in a skin rash) ∼ *vt* to force out or release usu suddenly and violently [L *eruptus*, pp of *erumpere* to burst forth, fr *e-* + *rumpere* to break – more at BEREAVE] – **eruptible** *adj*, **eruption** *n*, **eruptive** *adj*, **eruptively** *adv*

> synonyms Although the chief meaning of **erupt** is "break out", and that of **irrupt** is "break in", the two words have become almost interchangeable in the sense "become suddenly violent" ⟨*violence* erupted/irrupted *in the ghetto*⟩.

**-ery** /-(ə)ri/, **-ry** *suffix* (→ *n*) 1 quality or state of having (a specified trait or mode of behaviour) ⟨*snobb*ery⟩ ⟨*treach*ery⟩ 2 art or practice of ⟨*cook*ery⟩ ⟨*arch*ery⟩ 3 place of doing, keeping, producing, or selling (a specified thing) ⟨*fish*ery⟩ ⟨*bak*ery⟩ **4a** collection or body of ⟨*fin*ery⟩ ⟨*green*ery⟩ **b** class of (specified goods) ⟨*ironmong*ery⟩ ⟨*confection*ery⟩ 5 state or condition of ⟨*slav*ery⟩ 6 *chiefly derog* all that is concerned with or characteristic of ⟨*pop*ery⟩ ⟨*tomfool*ery⟩ □ *-ry* often after *d*, *t*, *l*, or *n*; otherwise *-ery* [ME *-erie*, fr OF, fr *-ier* + *-ie* *-y*]

**eryngo** /i'ring-goh/ *n, pl* **eryngoes**, **eryngos** any of a genus (*Eryngium*) of plants of the carrot family that have long spiny leaves and dense flower clusters; *specif* SEA HOLLY [modif of L *eryngion* sea holly, fr Gk *ēryngion*]

**erysipelas** /,eri'sipələs/ *n* a feverish disease characterized by intense deep red local inflammation of the skin, caused by a STREPTOCOCCUS bacterium – called also SAINT ANTHONY'S FIRE [ME *erisipila*, fr L *erysipelas*, fr Gk, fr *erysi-* (akin to Gk *erythros* red) + *-pelas* (akin to L *pellis* skin)]

**erythema** /,eri'theemə/ *n* abnormal redness of the skin, usu occurring in patches, caused by widening of the blood vessels (e g after injury) [NL, fr Gk *erythēma*, fr *erythainein* to redden, fr *erythros*] – **erythematous** *adj*

**erythr-**, **erythro-** *comb form* 1 red ⟨*erythro*cyte⟩ 2 erythrocyte ⟨*erythr*oid⟩ [Gk, fr *erythros* – more at RED]

**erythraemia** /,eri'threemyə/ *n* POLYCYTHAEMIA VERA (abnormal blood condition) [NL]

**erythrism** /'eri,thriz(ə)m/ *n* a condition marked by abnormally red pigmentation (e g in skin or hair) – **erythrismal** *adj*, **erythristic** *adj*

**erythrite** /'erithriet/ *n* a reddish mineral consisting of cobalt ARSENATE, $Co_3(AsO_4)_2.8H_2O$

**erythroblast** /i'rithroh,blast/ *n* a bone-marrow cell, with a nucleus, that is the first specifically identifiable stage in the formation of a RED BLOOD CELL – compare RETICULOCYTE [ISV] – **erythroblastic** *adj*

**erythroblastosis** /i,rithrohblə'stohsis/ *n, pl* **erythroblastoses** /-seez/ abnormal presence of erythroblasts in the circulating blood; *esp* ERYTHROBLASTOSIS FOETALIS [NL]

**erythroblastosis foetalis** /fee'tahlis/ *n* an abnormal condition of a foetus or newborn baby that is characterized by destruction of circulating RED BLOOD CELLS, increase in circulating erythroblasts, and jaundice, and that is usu associated with incompatibility between the blood type of the mother and that of the foetus [NL, foetal erythroblastosis]

**erythrocyte** /i'rithrə,siet/ *n* RED BLOOD CELL [ISV] – **erythrocytic** *adj*

**erythrocytometer** /i,rithrohsie'tomitə/ *n* HAEMOCYTOMETER (instrument for counting blood cells)

**erythroid** /'erithroyd, i'rithroyd/ *adj* relating to (stages in the development of) erythrocytes

**erythromycin** /i,rithrə'miesin/ *n* an antibiotic, $C_{37}H_{67}NO_{13}$, that is produced by a bacterium (*Streptomyces erythreus*) and is effective against many types of bacteria and some PROTOZOANS (single-celled organisms)

**erythropoiesis** /i,rithrohpoy'cesis/ *n* the formation of RED BLOOD CELLS [NL, fr *erythr-* + Gk *poiēsis* creation, fr *poiein* to make, create] – **erythropoietic** *adj*

**erythropoietin** /i,rithroh'poyitin, -poy'eetin/ *n* a hormone that is formed, esp in the kidney, in response to reduced oxygen concentration and that stimulates RED BLOOD CELL formation [*erythropoietic* + *-in*]

**erythrosin** /i'rithrəsin/ *also* **erythrosine** /-seen/ *n* any of several dyes made by combining FLUORESCEIN (red dye) with iodine, that yield reddish shades [ISV *erythr-* + *eosin*]

¹**-es** /-əz, -iz *after* s,z,sh,ch; -z *after* v *or a vowel*/ *suffix* (→ *n pl*) 1 – used to form the plural of most nouns that end in *s* ⟨*glas-ses*⟩, *z* ⟨*fuzz*es⟩, *sh* ⟨*bush*es⟩, *ch* ⟨*peach*es⟩, or a final *y* that changes to *i* ⟨*ladi*es⟩ and some nouns ending in *f* that changes to *v* ⟨*loav*es⟩; compare ¹-s 1 2 ¹-s 2 [ME *-es, -s* – more at ¹-s]

²**-es** *suffix* (→ *vb*) – used to form the third person singular present of most verbs that end in *s* ⟨*bless*es⟩, *z* ⟨*fizz*es⟩, *sh* ⟨*hush*es⟩, *ch* ⟨*catch*es⟩, or a final *y* that changes to *i* ⟨*defi*es⟩; – compare ²-s [ME – more at ²-s]

**escadrille** /'eskə,dril/ *n* 1 a small unit of the French air force 2 a small group of ships [Fr, flotilla, escadrille, fr Sp *escuadrilla*, dim. of *escuadra* squadron, squad – more at SQUAD]

**escalade** /,eskə'layd/ *n* an act of scaling something, esp the walls of a fortification [Fr, fr It *scalata*, fr *scalare* to scale, fr *scala* ladder, fr LL – more at SCALE] – **escalade** *vt*, **escalader** *n*

**escalate** /'eskəlayt/ *vi* 1 EXPAND 1 ⟨*the matter has* ~d *into something like a major scandal* – *Sunday Times Magazine*⟩ ⟨*local fighting threatens to* ~ *into full-scale war*⟩ 2 RISE 10b ⟨escalating *prices*⟩ ~ *vt* EXPAND 1 [back-formation fr *escalator*] – **escalation** *n*, **escalatory** *adj*

*usage* This verb is now well established in modern English, though some writers on usage advise that it should be confined to the meaning "increase step by step". *antonym* de-escalate

¹**escalator** /'eskəlaytə/ *n* 1 a power-driven set of stairs arranged like an endless belt that ascend or descend continuously 2 an escalator clause or provision [fr *Escalator*, orig a trademark, fr *escal*ating elev*ator*]

²**escalator** *adj* providing for a periodic proportional upward or downward adjustment (e g of prices or wages) ⟨*an* ~ *arrangement relating pay to the level of inflation*⟩ ⟨*an* ~ *clause*⟩

**escallop** /e'skoləp, e'skal-/ *n* SCALLOP 1,2

**escalope** /'eskə,lop/ *n* a thin boneless slice of meat (e g veal or pork); *esp* a slice cut from the leg, beaten flat, coated with egg and breadcrumbs, and fried [Fr, fr MF, shell – more at SCAL-LOP]

**escapade** /'eskəpayd/ *n* a wild or mischievous reckless adventure usu involving the flouting of rules or conventions [Fr, fr MF, fr OIt *scappata*, fr *scappare* to escape, fr (assumed) VL *excappare*]

¹**escape** /i'skayp/ *vi* 1a to get away, esp from confinement or restraint ⟨~d *from the burning building*⟩ ⟨*fantasy allows us to* ~ *from reality*⟩ **b** *of a gas, liquid, etc* to leak out gradually; seep **c** *of a cultivated plant* to run wild 2 to avoid threatening evil, danger, etc ~ *vt* 1 to get or stay out of the way of; avoid ⟨~ *death*⟩ 2 to fail to be noticed or remembered by ⟨*his name* ~s *me*⟩ 3 to come out from or be uttered by, esp involuntarily ⟨*a sigh* ~d *him*⟩ [ME *escapen*, fr ONF *escaper*, fr (assumed) VL *excappare*, fr L *ex-* + LL *cappa* head covering, cloak] – **escapable** *adj*, **escaper** *n*, **escapee** *n*

*synonyms* Escape, avoid, evade, and elude all mean "get away or keep away from". Escape, although it implies imminent danger, does not necessarily mean taking conscious action ⟨escaped *the family tendency to early grey hair*⟩. Avoid, on the other hand, stresses action consciously taken to keep away, rather than get away, from possible danger or harm. It often suggests forethought or caution ⟨*by* avoiding *human habitation, he managed to* escape *detection for several months*⟩. Evade stresses ingenuity, adroitness, and sometimes dishonesty in avoiding or escaping ⟨evaded *her pursuers by climbing a tree*⟩. Elude is used of something difficult or impossible to catch; it may connote bafflement, abstruseness, or even slyness ⟨*the exact meaning* eluded *him*⟩.

²**escape** *n* 1 an act or instance of escaping 2 a means or way of escape ⟨*an* ~ *hatch*⟩ ⟨*reading provides an* ~ *from reality*⟩ 3 a cultivated plant run wild

**escapement** /i'skaypmənt/ *n* 1a a device in a watch or clock

that controls the motion of the cogwheels and through which the energy of the power source (e g the spring) is delivered to the regulatory mechanism (e g the pendulum) **b** a ratchet device (e g the spacing mechanism of a typewriter) that permits motion in one direction only in equal steps **c** a space left between the hammer and the strings of a piano which allows the strings to vibrate 2a *archaic* the act of escaping; *also* the number (e g of spawning salmon) that escape and survive **b** a way of escape; a vent

**escape velocity** *n* the minimum velocity that a moving body (e g a rocket) must have to escape from the gravitational field of the earth, moon, etc and move outwards into space

**escapism** /i'skay,piz(ə)m/ *n* habitual diversion of the mind to purely imaginative activity or entertainment as an escape from reality or routine – **escapist** *adj or n*

**escapology** /,eskə'poləji/ *n* the art or practice of escaping, esp as a theatrical performance – **escapologist** *n*

**escargot** /e'skahgoh (*Fr* ɛskargo)/ *n, pl* **escargots** /e'skahgoh(z) (*Fr* ~)/ a snail, esp when prepared for use as food [Fr, fr MF, fr OProv *escaragol*]

**escarole** /'eskərohl/ *n* ENDIVE 1 (plant used for salads) [Fr, fr LL *escariola*, fr L *escarius* of food, fr *esca* food, fr *edere* to eat – more at EAT]

**escarp** /i'skahp/ *vt or n* (to cut) a slope or ditch; SCARP [n Fr *escarpe*, fr It *scarpa*; vt fr n]

**escarpment** /i'skahpmənt/ *n* 1 a steep usu artificial slope in front of a fortification 2 a long cliff or steep slope separating two comparatively level or more gently sloping surfaces and resulting from erosion or faulting

**-escence** /-'es(ə)ns/ *suffix* (→ *n*) process of becoming ⟨*obsol-*escence⟩; state or condition of being ⟨*alkal*escence⟩ ⟨*effer-*vescence⟩ [MF, fr L *-escentia*, fr *-escent-, -escens* + *-ia* -y]

**-escent** /-'es(ə)nt/ *suffix* (→ *adj*) 1 being or beginning to be; slightly ⟨*liqu*escent⟩ ⟨*conval*escent⟩ ⟨*incand*escent⟩ 2 reflecting or emitting light (in a specified way) ⟨*fluor*escent⟩ ⟨*opal*escent⟩ 3 having the properties of; resembling ⟨*arbor-*escent⟩ [MF, fr L *-escent-, -escens*, prp suffix of incho verbs in *-escere*]

¹**eschar** /'eskah/ *n* a scab formed esp after a burn [ME *escare* – more at SCAR]

²**eschar** *n* ESKER (ridge of sand, gravel, etc)

**escharotic** /,eskə'rotik/ *n or adj* (a corrosive or caustic agent) producing or capable of producing an eschar [Fr or LL; Fr *escharotique*, fr LL *escharoticus*, fr Gk *escharōtikos*, fr *esch-aroun* to form an eschar, fr *eschara* eschar]

**eschatology** /,eskə'toləji/ *n* a branch of theology or religious belief concerned with the ultimate destiny of the universe or of mankind; *esp* the Christian doctrine concerning death, judgment, heaven, and hell – compare LAST THINGS [Gk *eschatos* last, farthest] – **eschatological** *adj*, **eschatologically** *adv*

¹**escheat** /is'cheet/ *n* 1 the reversion of property to a government or sovereign as a result of the owner dying without having made a will and without heirs 2 the reversion of lands to the feudal lord either in the absence of legal heirs on the owner's death, or as a result of the owner breaking the feudal bond 3 escheated property [ME *eschete*, fr OF, reversion of property, fr *escheoir* to fall, devolve, fr (assumed) VL *excadēre*, fr L *ex-* + (assumed) VL *cadēre* to fall, fr L *cadere* – more at CHANCE]

²**escheat** *vb* to (cause to) revert by escheat – **escheatable** *adj*

**eschew** /is'chooh/ *vt, formal* to avoid habitually, esp on moral or practical grounds; shun ⟨*has always* ~ed *alcohol*⟩ [ME *es-chewen*, fr MF *eschiuver*, of Gmc origin; akin to OHG *sciuhen* to frighten off – more at SHY] – **eschewal** *n*

**eschscholtzia** /is'kolshə, e'shohltzi-ə/ *n* any of a genus (*Eschscholtzia*) of plants of the poppy family; *esp* one (*Eschscholtzia californica*) widely cultivated for its yellow to red flowers [NL, genus name, fr J F *Eschscholtz* †1831 Ger naturalist]

¹**escort** /'eskawt/ *n* 1 one or more people, cars, ships, etc accompanying somebody or something to give protection or show courtesy ⟨*a police* ~⟩ 2 a man or woman who accompanies another socially, esp in return for a fee ⟨*was her* ~ *for the evening*⟩ ⟨*an* ~ *agency*⟩ [Fr *escorte*, fr It *scorta*, fr *scorgere* to guide, fr (assumed) VL *excorrigere*, fr L *ex-* + *corrigere* to make straight, correct – more at CORRECT]

²**escort** /i'skawt/ *vt* to accompany as an escort *synonyms* see ¹ACCOMPANY

**escot** /i'skot/ *vt, obs* to support, maintain [MF *escoter*, fr *escot* contribution, of Gmc origin; akin to ON *skot* contribution]

**escritoire** /,eskri'twah/ *n* a writing table or desk; *specif*

SECRETAIRE [obs Fr, writing desk, scriptorium, fr ML *scriptorium*]

**escrow** /'eskroh, -'-/ *n* 1 a deed, a bond, money, or a piece of property deposited with a third person to be delivered by him/her to a designated person only upon the fulfilment of some condition 2 a written agreement to hand over money, property, etc on fulfilment of a condition [MF *escroue* scroll] – **in escrow** in trust as an escrow ⟨*have over £1000 in escrow to pay taxes*⟩

**escudo** /es'koohdoh/ *n, pl* **escudos** /es'koohdohz, -doohs/ 1 any of various gold or silver coins formerly used in Hispanic countries 2 – see *peso* at MONEY table [Sp & Pg, lit., shield, fr L *scutum*]

**esculent** /'eskyooələnt/ *n or adj, formal* (something that is) edible [adj L *esculentus*, fr *esca* food, fr *edere* to eat – more at EAT; n fr adj]

**escutcheon** /i'skuchən/ *n* 1 a shield on which a coat of arms is displayed 2 a protective or ornamental shield (e g round a keyhole) 3 the part of a ship's stern on which the name is displayed [ME *escochon*, fr MF *escuchon*, fr (assumed) VL *scution-, scutio*, fr L *scutum* shield – more at ESQUIRE]

**Esdras** /'ezdras/ *n* – see BIBLE table [LL, Ezra]

[1]**-ese** /-eez/ *suffix* (*n → adj*) of or originating in (a certain place or country) ⟨*Japan*ese⟩ ⟨*Vienn*ese⟩ [Pg *-ês* & It *-ese*, fr L *-ensis*]

[2]**-ese** *suffix* (*n → n*), *pl* **-ese** 1 inhabitant of ⟨*Chin*ese⟩ 2a language of ⟨*Portugu*ese⟩ ⟨*Canton*ese⟩ b *chiefly derog* speech, literary style, or diction peculiar to (a specified place, person, or group) ⟨*journal*ese⟩ ⟨*official*ese⟩

**esemplastic** /,esem'plastik/ *adj* shaping or having the power to shape disparate things into a unified whole ⟨*On the imagination, or ~ power* – S T Coleridge⟩ [irreg fr Gk *es, eis* into + *hen-, heis* one + *plastikos* moulding, fr *plassein* to mould, shape; formed by S T Coleridge †1834 E poet]

**eserine** /'esəreen/ *n* PHYSOSTIGMINE (chemical compound) [Fr *ésérine*, fr a native name in Africa]

**esker** *also* **eskar** /'eskə/ *n* a long narrow ridge or mound of sand, gravel, and boulders deposited by a stream flowing on, within, or beneath a glacier [IrGael *eiscir* ridge]

**Eskimo** *also* **Esquimau** /'eskimoh/ *n, pl* **Eskimos** *also* **Esquimaux,** *esp collectively* **Eskimo** *also* **Esqumau** 1 (a member of) any of a group of peoples of N Canada, Greenland, Alaska, and E Siberia 2 the language of the Eskimo people [Dan *Eskimo* & Fr *Esquimau*, of Algonquian origin; akin to Cree *askimowew* he eats it raw] – **Eskimoan** *adj*

**Eskimo dog** *n* (any of) a breed of broad-chested powerful sledge dogs native to Greenland and Labrador and characterized by a shaggy outer coat and a dense woolly inner coat

**Eskimo roll** *n* a manoeuvre to right a capsized canoe without leaving it

**esophag-, esophago-** *comb form, NAm* oesophag-, oesophago-

**esoteric** /,eesə'terik, ,esoh-/ *adj* 1 designed for, understood by, or restricted to a small group, esp of the specially initiated ⟨*~ knowledge*⟩ ⟨*~ pursuits*⟩ – compare EXOTERIC 2 private, confidential ⟨*an ~ purpose*⟩ △ erotic, exotic [LL *esotericus*, fr Gk *esōterikos*, fr *esōterō*, compar of *eisō, esō* within, fr *eis* into, fr *en* in – more at IN] – **esoterically** *adv*, **esotericism** *n*

**ESP** *n* EXTRASENSORY PERCEPTION [extrasensory perception]

**espadrille** /,espə'dril/ *n* a flat sandal that usu has a canvas upper and a rope sole and is sometimes tied round the ankle or leg with laces [Fr, deriv of L *spartum* esparto]

**espagnole** /,espanyohl/ *n* a rich thick brown sauce that is made with a MIREPOIX (mixture of sautéed chopped vegetables) and forms the basis for many other brown sauces [Fr *sauce espagnole*, lit., Spanish sauce]

[1]**espalier** /i'spalyay, -yə/ *n* 1 a plant (e g a fruit tree) trained to grow flat against a support (e g a wall or trellis) 2 a railing or trellis on which fruit trees or shrubs are trained to grow flat [Fr, deriv of It *spalla* shoulder, fr LL *spatula* shoulder blade – more at EPAULETTE]

[2]**espalier** *vt* to train (e g a fruit tree) to grow flat (as if) on an espalier

**esparto** /i'spahtoh/ *n, pl* **espartos** either of two Spanish and Algerian grasses (*Stipa tenacissima* and *Lygeum spartum*) used esp to make rope, shoes, and paper [Sp, fr L *spartum*, fr Gk *sparton* – more at SPIRE]

**especial** /i'spesh(ə)l/ *adj* distinctively or particularly special: e g **a** unusually or additionally great or significant ⟨*a decision of ~ relevance*⟩ **b** distinctly or distinctively particular or personal ⟨*his ~ friend*⟩ ⟨*had an ~ dislike of poetry*⟩ *usage* see [1]SPECIAL [ME, fr MF – more at SPECIAL] – **especially** *adv*

**esperance** /'espərəns/ *n, obs* hope, expectation [ME *esperaunce*, fr MF *esperance*, deriv of L *sperare* to hope]

**Esperanto** /,espə'rantoh/ *n* an artificial international language devised in 1887 and largely based on words common to the chief European languages [Dr *Esperanto* (deriv of L *sperare* to hope), pseudonym of L L Zamenhof †1917 Polish oculist, its inventor] – **Esparantist** *n or adj*

**espial** /i'spie-əl/ *n* 1 (an act of) espying or observing 2 the fact or state of being noticed; discovery

**espionage** /'espi-ənahzh, ,---'-, -nij, i'spie-/ *n* the practice of spying or the use of spies to obtain information about the plans and activities esp of a foreign government or a competing company ⟨*international ~*⟩ ⟨*industrial ~*⟩ [Fr *espionnage*, fr MF, fr *espionner* to spy, fr *espion* spy, fr OIt *spione*, fr *spia*, of Gmc origin; akin to OHG *spehōn* to spy – more at SPY]

**esplanade** /,esplə'nahd, -nayd/ *n* 1 a level open stretch of paved or grassy ground; *esp* one designed for walking or driving along a shore 2 an area of clear ground in front of a castle or other fortification [Fr, fr It *spianata*, fr *spianare* to level, fr L *explanare* – more at EXPLAIN]

**espousal** /i'spowzl/ *n* 1 the adoption or support of a cause or belief 2 **espousals** *pl*, **espousal** *archaic* a betrothal; *also* a marriage

**espouse** /i'spowz/ *vt* 1 to take up and support as a cause; become attached to ⟨*~ the problems of minority groups*⟩ 2 *archaic* to marry [ME *espousen*, fr MF *espouser*, fr LL *sponsare* to betroth, fr L *sponsus*, pp of *spondēre* to promise, betroth – more at SPOUSE] – **espouser** *n*

**espresso** /i'spresoh/ *n, pl* **espressos** (an apparatus for making) coffee brewed by forcing steam through finely ground darkly roasted coffee beans [It (*caffè*) *espresso*, lit., pressed-out coffee]

*usage* The pronunciation of **espresso** as /ik'spresoh/ is a common confusion.

**esprit** /e'spree/ *n* vivacious cleverness or wit [Fr, fr L *spiritus* spirit]

**esprit de corps** /də 'kaw/ *n* the spirit of loyalty, devotion, and common purpose existing among the members of a group [Fr]

**espy** /i'spie/ *vt* to catch sight of ⟨*espied a small figure in the distance*⟩ *synonyms* see [1]SEE [ME *espien*, fr OF *espier* – more at SPY]

**-esque** /-'esk/ *suffix* (*n → adj*) in the manner or style of; like ⟨*statu*esque⟩ ⟨*Kafka*esque⟩ ⟨*roman*esque⟩ [Fr, fr It *-esco*, of Gmc origin; akin to OHG *-isc* -ish – more at -ISH]

**Esquimau** /'eskimoh/ *n, pl* **Esquimaux** /'eskimoh(z)/, *esp collectively* **Esquimau** (an) Eskimo

**esquire** /i'skwie-ə/ *n* 1 a member of the English gentry ranking below a knight 2 a candidate for knighthood serving as shield bearer and attendant to a knight 3 – used instead of Mr as a man's courtesy title and usu placed in its abbreviated form after the surname ⟨*J R Smith,* Esq⟩ 4 *archaic* a landed proprietor [ME, fr MF *esquier* squire, fr LL *scutarius*, fr L *scutum* shield; akin to OHG *sceida* sheath]

*usage* The use of the abbreviation **Esq** in addressing letters is much commoner in Britain, where it may be applied to anyone who would otherwise be addressed as *Mr*, than in the USA, where it is now rare except when one is writing to lawyers.

**-ess** /-is, -əs, -es/ *suffix* (*n → n*) female ⟨*actr*ess⟩ ⟨*lion*ess⟩ – often derog ⟨*Negr*ess⟩ ⟨*poet*ess⟩ [ME *-esse*, fr OF, fr LL *-issa*, fr Gk]

*usage* In female titles ⟨*count*ess⟩ and certain traditional names for professions ⟨*seamstr*ess⟩ ⟨*waitr*ess⟩ the ending **-ess** is perfectly acceptable; but a serious woman writer does not like to be called an *auth*oress, and today even *instruct*resses and *actr*esses may prefer to think of themselves as *instructors* and *actors*, while *Jew*ess and *Negr*ess are apt to cause offence and should be avoided.

[1]**essay** /e'say/ *vt* 1a [2]ASSAY 1a (analyse ore) **b** *formal* to put to a test 2 *formal* to make an often tentative or experimental effort to perform; attempt △ assay – **essayer** *n*

[2]**essay** /'esay/ *n* 1a a short piece of prose writing usu dealing with its subject from a limited or personal point of view **b** something resembling such a composition ⟨*a photographic ~*⟩ 2 *formal* an esp initial or tentative effort or attempt [MF *essai*, fr LL *exagium* act of weighing, fr *ex-* + *agere* to drive – more at AGENT] – **essayist** *n*, **essayistic** *adj*

**essay question** *n* an examination question that requires an answer in a paragraph or usu a short essay

**essence** /'es(ə)ns/ *n* **1a** the real or ultimate nature of an individual being or thing, esp as opposed to its existence or its accidental qualities **b** the properties or attributes by means of which something can be categorized or identified **2** something that exists, esp in an abstract or immaterial form; an entity **3a** (an alcoholic solution or other preparation of) an extract, ESSENTIAL OIL, etc possessing the special qualities of a plant, drug, etc in concentrated form **b** an odour, perfume **c** somebody or something embodying the fundamental nature of an idea, characteristic, etc ⟨*was the very* ~ *of courtesy*⟩ ⟨*the* ~ *of the matter*⟩ [ME, fr MF & L; MF, fr L *essentia*, fr *esse* to be – more at IS] – **in essence** in or by its very nature; essentially ⟨*accusations which* in essence *are well-founded – TLS*⟩ – **of the essence** of the utmost importance; essential ⟨*time was* of the essence⟩

**Essene** /'eseen, -´-/ *n* a member of a monastic brotherhood of Jews in Palestine from the 2nd century BC to the 2nd century AD [Gk *Essēnos*] – **Essenism** *n*, **Essenian, Essenic** *adj*

¹**essential** /i'sensh(ə)l/ *adj* **1** of or being (an) essence; inherent **2** of the utmost importance; basic, necessary ⟨~ *foods*⟩ ⟨*an* ~ *requirement for admission to university*⟩ **3** *of a disease* IDIOPATHIC (arising from an unknown cause) *synonyms* see ²NECESSARY *antonym* inessential – **essentially** *adv*, **essentialness** *n*, **essentiality** *n*

²**essential** *n* something basic, necessary, indispensable, or fundamental ⟨*the* ~s *of astronomy*⟩

**essential amino acid** *n* any of various AMINO ACIDS that are required for normal health and growth, are manufactured in the body in insufficient quantities or not at all, and are usu supplied by dietary protein

**essentialism** /-ˌiz(ə)m/ *n* **1** an educational theory which maintains that ideas and skills fundamental to the prevailing culture should be taught to all by traditional methods – compare PROGRESSIVISM **2** *philosophy* a theory that regards the essence of something as different from and more important than its attributes or existence – compare EXISTENTIALISM – **essentialist** *adj or n*

**essential oil** *n* any of several oils that can readily vaporize, impart characteristic odours to plants, and are used esp in perfumes and flavourings – compare FIXED OIL

**essonite** /'esəniet/ *n* HESSONITE (type of garnet)

¹**-est** /-ist/ *suffix* (*adj or adv → adj or adv*) – used to form the superlative degree of adjectives and adverbs of one and sometimes two or more syllables that end in a consonant ⟨*fattest*⟩ ⟨*dearest*⟩, in a vowel other than *e*, or a final *y* that changes to *i* ⟨*dreariest*⟩ ⟨*beggarliest*⟩; compare ¹-ST [ME, fr OE *-st*, *-est*, *-ost*; akin to OHG *-isto* (adj superl suffix), Gk *-istos*]

²**-est** /-ist/-, **-st** *suffix* (→ *vb*) – used to form the archaic second person singular of English verbs (with *thou*) that end in a consonant ⟨*gettest*⟩, a vowel other than *e* ⟨*goest*⟩, or a final *y* that changes to *i* ⟨*liest*⟩; compare ¹-ST [ME, fr OE *-est*, *-ast*, *-st*; akin to OHG *-ist*, *-ōst*, *-ēst*, 2 sing. ending]

**establish** /i'stablish/ *vt* **1** to make firm, stable, or secure **2** to enact or cause to be accepted permanently ⟨~ *a law*⟩ ⟨~ *a precedent*⟩ **3a** to bring into existence; found ⟨~ed *a republic*⟩ **b** to bring about; effect ⟨~ed *friendly relations*⟩ **4** to set on a firm basis; place in a stable and usu favourable position ⟨~ *his son in business*⟩ **5** to gain full recognition or acceptance of ⟨~ed *herself as a leading politician*⟩ **6** to make (a church or religion) a national institution supported by civil authority **7** to put beyond doubt; prove ⟨~ed *his innocence*⟩ **8** to cause (a plant) to grow and multiply in a place where previously absent **9** *obs* SETTLE 7b ~ *vi, of a plant* to become established ⟨*a grass that* ~es *on poor soil*⟩ [ME *establissen*, fr MF *establiss-*, stem of *establir*, fr L *stabilire*, fr *stabilis* stable] – **establishable** *adj*, **establisher** *n*

**established church** *n, often cap E&C* a church recognized by law as the official church of a nation and supported by civil authority

**establishment** /-mənt/ *n* **1** something established: e g **1a** a usu large organization or institution **b** a place of business or residence with its furnishings and staff **2** *taking sing or pl vb, often cap* **2a** *the* group of institutions and people (e g the government, the established church, the armed forces, and their leaders) held to control public life and to support the existing order **b** a controlling group ⟨*the literary* ~⟩ **3** the act of establishing; the state of being established

**establishmentarian** /iˌstablishmən'teəri·ən/ *adj* of or favouring the social or political establishment or esp the established religion – **establishmentarian** *n*, **establishmentarianism** *n*

**estaminet** /e'staminay (*Fr* ɛstaminɛ)/ *n, pl* **estaminets** /~/ a small café or bar [Fr, prob fr Fr dial. *staminet* manager, cowshed]

**estate** /i'stayt/ *n* **1** a social or political class; *specif* any of the great classes (e g the nobility, the clergy, and the commons) formerly having distinct political powers **2a** the nature and extent of one's interest in land or other property **b(1)** possessions, property; *esp* a person's property in land and other holdings ⟨*a man of small* ~⟩ **b(2)** the assets and liabilities left by a person at death or to be disposed of in bankruptcy **c** a large landed property, usu in the country and with a large house on it **3** *Br* an area devoted to a particular type of development ⟨*an industrial* ~⟩; *specif* one devoted to housing ⟨*a council* ~⟩ **4** *Br* ESTATE CAR **5** *formal* a state or condition, esp with regard to social status ⟨*men of low* ~⟩ [ME *estat*, fr MF – more at STATE]

**estate agent** *n, Br* **1** an agent who is involved in the buying and selling of land and property (e g houses) **2** one who manages an estate; a steward

**estate car** *n, Br* a large motor car designed to carry passengers and bulky luggage, and having a rear door opening onto the luggage compartment and seats which may be folded down to create more space

**estate duty** *n, Br* DEATH DUTY

¹**esteem** /i'steem/ *n* **1** favourable regard ⟨*held in high* ~ *by his colleagues*⟩ **2** *archaic* worth, value **3** *archaic* opinion, judgment

²**esteem** *vt* **1** to consider, esp favourably; deem ⟨~ *it a privilege*⟩ **2** to set a high value on; regard or prize highly **3** *archaic* to appraise *synonyms* see ²REGARD [ME *estemen* to estimate, fr MF *estimer*, fr L *aestimare*]

**ester** /'estə/ *n* an often fragrant chemical compound formed by the reaction between an acid and an alcohol, usu with elimination of water [Ger, fr *essigäther* ethyl acetate, fr *essig* vinegar + *äther* ether]

**esterase** /'estərayz, -ays/ *n* an ENZYME that accelerates the breakdown or formation of esters

**esterify** /e'sterifie/ *vt* to convert into an ester – **esterification** *n*

**Esther** /'estə/ *n* – see BIBLE table [*Esther* (fr L, fr Heb *Ester*), Jewish heroine]

**esthesia** /ˌes'theezhyə, -zyə; *also* ˌes-/ *n, NAm* AESTHESIA (capacity for feeling)

**esthesio-** *comb form, NAm* aesthesio-

**esthesis** /ees'theesis; *NAm* es-/ *n, NAm* AESTHESIS (capacity for feeling)

**esthete** /'eestheet/ *n, NAm* an aesthete – **esthetic** *adj*, **esthetics** *n*

**estimable** /'estiməbl/ *adj* **1** worthy of esteem **2** capable of being estimated **3** *archaic* valuable – **estimableness** *n*

¹**estimate** /'estimayt/ *vt* **1a** to judge tentatively or approximately the value, worth, or significance of **b** to determine roughly the size, extent, or nature of **c** to produce a statement of the approximate cost of **2** to judge, conclude **3** *obs* **3a** to esteem **b** to appraise [L *aestimatus*, pp of *aestimare* to value, estimate] – **estimative** *adj*

²**estimate** /'estimət/ *n* **1** the act of appraising or valuing; a calculation **2** an opinion or judgment of the nature, character, or quality of somebody or something ⟨*what's your* ~ *of his character?*⟩ **3** (the numerical value of) a rough or approximate calculation **4** a statement of the expected cost of a certain job (e g building or repairs)

**estimation** /ˌesti'maysh(ə)n/ *n* **1** ESTIMATE 2 ⟨*in my* ~ *he's a good worker*⟩ **2a** the act of estimating **b** the value, amount, or size arrived at in an estimate **3** ESTEEM 1

**estimator** /'estimaytə/ *n* **1** one who or that which estimates **2** a statistical function whose value for a sample of a population provides an estimate of a particular variable quantity for the total population

**Estonian** /e'stohnyən, -ni·ən/ *n* a native or the Finno-Ugric language of Estonia [*Estonia*, country in N Europe (now a republic of the USSR)] – **Estonian** *adj*

**estop** /i'stop/ *vt* **-pp-** to stop, bar; *specif* to impede by estoppel [ME *estoppen*, fr MF *estouper*]

**estoppel** /i'stop(ə)l/ *n* the legal principle which precludes a person from denying or disproving facts he/she has previously stated to be true [prob fr MF *estoupail* bung, fr *estouper*]

**estr-, estro-** *comb form, NAm* oestr-, oestro-

**estrange** /i'straynj/ *vt* to arouse enmity or indifference in (somebody) in place of affection; alienate – usu + *from* ⟨~d *from her husband*⟩ [MF *estranger*, fr ML *extraneare*, fr L *extraneus* strange – more at STRANGE] – **estrangement** *n*, **estranger** *n*

**estuarine** /'estyooə,rin, -,rien/, **estuarial** /,estyoo'eəriəl/ *adj* of, living in, or formed in an estuary ⟨~ *currents*⟩ ⟨~ *animals*⟩ ⟨~ *environment*⟩

**estuary** /'estyooəri, 'estyoori/ *n* a water passage where the tide meets a river; *esp* a sea inlet at the mouth of a river [L *aestuarium*, fr *aestus* boiling, tide; akin to L *aestas* summer – more at AESTIVAL]

**esurient** /i'syooəri·ənt/ *adj, formal* hungry, greedy [L *esurient-, esuriens*, prp of *esurire* to be hungry, fr *edere* to eat] – **esurience, esuriency** *n*, **esuriently** *adv*

**-et** /-it, -et/ *suffix* (→ *n*) **1** small or lesser kind of ⟨*baron*et⟩ ⟨*isl*et⟩ **2** group of (a specified number) ⟨*oct*et⟩ [ME, fr OF *-et*, masc, & *-ete*, fem, fr LL *-itus* & *-ita*]

**eta** /'eetə/ *n* **1** the 7th letter of the Greek alphabet **2** *physics* an ELEMENTARY PARTICLE (minute particle of matter) that has no electric charge and has a mass about 1074 times that of an electron [LL, fr Gk *ēta*, of Sem origin; akin to Heb *lohēth* heth]

**et al** /,et 'al/ *adv* and others *usage* see ET CETERA [L *et alii* (masc), *et aliae* (fem), *et alia* (neut)]

**etalon** /'etəlon/ *n, physics* an instrument used for studying the fine structure of lines in a spectrum that are produced by the multiple reflection of a beam of light between two semi-silvered surfaces of high quality a few millimetres apart [Fr *étalon* standard of weights and measures, fr MF *estalon, estelon*]

**etatism** /ay'tatiz(ə)m/ *n* STATE SOCIALISM [Fr *étatisme*, fr *état* state, fr OF *estat*] – **etatist** *adj*

**etc** /et 'setrə/ *adv* ET CETERA

**et cetera** /et 'setrə/ *adv* and other things, esp of the same kind; *broadly* and so forth [L]

   *usage* **1** A new pronunciation /ek'setrə/ is not recommended for BBC broadcasters. **2** Et cetera is normally written etc or &c. None of these, however, should be used in formal continuous prose, though they are useful in footnotes and in works of reference. A list of items in formal writing can instead be preceded by *such as* or *for example*, or followed by *and so on* or *and so forth* (for things) or *and others* (for people). Et cetera is in any case somewhat offensive when applied to people; in condensed "footnote" style it can be replaced by et al. **3** Writers on usage advise against *and* etc, and against using etc at the end of a list of items that begins with *such as* or *for example*. A comma should precede etc unless only one item has been mentioned. Compare ⟨*cats, dogs,* etc⟩ ⟨*cats* etc⟩.

**etceteras** /et'setrəz/ *n pl* unspecified additional items; ODDS AND ENDS

**¹etch** /ech/ *vt* **1a** to produce (e g a picture or lettering) esp on metal or glass by the action of an acid or other corrosive chemical **b** to subject (e g metal or glass) to such etching **2** to delineate or imprint clearly ⟨*scenes that are indelibly* ~ed *on our minds*⟩ ~ *vi* to practise etching [D *etsen*, fr Ger *ätzen*, lit., to feed, fr OHG *azzen;* akin to OHG *ezzan* to eat – more at EAT] – **etcher** *n*

**²etch** *n* (the action or effect of) an acid or other chemical used in etching

**etching** /'eching/ *n* **1** the art, act, or process of producing pictures or designs by printing from an etched metal plate **2a** an etched design **b** an impression from an etched plate

**¹eternal** /i'tuhnl/ *adj* **1** having infinite duration; everlasting ⟨~ *life*⟩ **2** valid or existing at all times; timeless ⟨~ *truths*⟩ **3** *informal* incessant, interminable ⟨*your* ~ *arguments annoy me*⟩ [ME, fr MF, fr LL *aeternalis*, fr L *aeternus* eternal; akin to L *aevum* age, eternity – more at AYE] – **eternalize** *vt*, **eternally** *adv*, **eternalness** *n*, **eternize** *vt*

**²eternal** *n* **1** *cap* GOD 1 – + *the* **2** something eternal

**eternal triangle** *n* a situation of conflict resulting from the sexual and emotional involvement of two people with one other person

**eterne** /i'tuhn/ *adj, archaic* eternal [ME, fr MF, fr L *aeternus*]

**eternity** /i'tuhnəti/ *n* **1** the quality or state of being eternal **2** infinite time **3** the state after death, held to be outside or not subject to time **4** a seemingly endless or immeasurable time ⟨*we waited an* ~ *for the train*⟩ [ME *eternite*, fr MF *eternité*, fr L *aeternitat-, aeternitas*, fr *aeternus*]

**etesian winds** /i'teezhyən, -zhən/ *n pl, often cap E* annually recurring summer winds that blow over the E Mediterranean from the North [L *etesius* recurring annually, fr Gk *etēsios*, fr *etos* year – more at WETHER]

**eth** /eth/ *n* a character ð used in Old English and Icelandic to represent either of the sounds /th/ or /dh/ (e g in *thin* and *then*)

and in some phonetic alphabets to represent /dh/; *also* its capitalized form Ł – compare THORN 4 [Icel]

**eth-, etho-** *comb form* ethyl ⟨eth*aldehyde*⟩ ⟨etho*chloride*⟩ [ISV]

**¹-eth** /-ith/, **-th** *suffix* (*vb* → *vb*) – used to form the archaic third person singular present of verbs ⟨go*eth*⟩ ⟨do*th*⟩ [ME, fr OE *-eth, -ath, -th;* akin to OHG *-it, -ōt, -ēt*, 3 sing. ending, L *-t, -it*]

**²-eth** /-ith/ – see ¹,²-TH

**ethambutol** /e'thambyootol, -tohl/ *n* a synthetic antibacterial drug, $(CH_3CH_2CH)CH_2OH(NHCH_2)_2$, used esp in treating tuberculosis [*ethylene* + *amine* + *butanol*]

**ethane** /'eethayn/ *n* a colourless odourless gas, $C_2H_6$, that is a member of the ALKANE series of organic chemical compounds, is obtained usu from petroleum or NATURAL GAS, and is used esp as a fuel [ISV, fr *ethyl*]

**ethanol** /'ethə,nol, 'eeth-/ *n* a colourless liquid, $C_2H_5OH$, that vaporizes readily, is the intoxicating agent in beer, wine, etc and is also used as a solvent – called also ALCOHOL, ETHYL ALCOHOL

**ethanolamine** /,ethə'noləmeen, eethə-/ *n* any of three colourless liquid AMINO alcohols derived from ethanol and used esp as solvents and in removing acidic gases from gas streams

**ethene** /'etheen/ *n* ETHYLENE (type of gas)

**ether** /'eethə/ *n* **1 ether, aether** (the rarefied element formerly believed to fill) the upper regions of space **2 ether, aether** a medium formerly held to permeate all space and transmit electromagnetic waves (e g light) and heat **3a** a light inflammable liquid, $C_2H_5OC_2H_5$, that vaporizes readily and is used chiefly as a solvent and formerly as a general anaesthetic – called also DIETHYL ETHER, ETHYL ETHER **b** any of various organic chemical compounds characterized by an oxygen atom attached to two carbon atoms [ME, fr L *aether*, fr Gk *aithēr*, fr *aithein* to ignite, blaze] – **etherish** *adj*, **etherlike** *adj*

**ethereal** /i'thiəri·əl; *sense 3* ,ethə'ree·əl/ *adj* **1** of the regions beyond the earth **2a** lacking material substance; immaterial, intangible ⟨*an* ~, *rather disembodied chorus* – *Nation Review (Melbourne)*⟩ **b** unusually delicate, light, or refined **3** of, containing, or resembling a chemical ether **4** *poetic* celestial, heavenly – **etherealize** *vt*, **ethereally** *adv*, **etherealness** *n*, **etherealization** *n*, **ethereality** *n*

**ether extract** *n* the part of a complex organic material that is soluble in ether and consists chiefly of fats and FATTY ACIDS

**ether·ize, -ise** /'eethə,riez/ *vt* to treat or anaesthetize (as if) with ether – **etherizer** *n*, **etherization** *n*

**ethic** /'ethik/ *n* **1** *pl but taking sing vb* the study of the nature and basis of moral principles and judgments **2** a set of moral principles or values ⟨*the present-day materialistic* ~⟩ **3** *pl* the principles of conduct or morality governing an individual or a group ⟨*professional* ~s⟩ **4** *pl* the moral uprightness of an action, judgment, etc ⟨*I'm not sure of the* ~s *of your statement*⟩ [ME *ethik*, fr MF *ethique*, fr L *ethice*, fr Gk *ēthikē*, fr *ēthikos*] – **ethicist** *n*

**ethical** /'ethikl/ *also* **ethic** *adj* **1** of ethics **2** conforming to accepted, esp professional, standards of conduct or morality **3** *of a drug* available to the general public only on a doctor's or dentist's prescription [ME *etik*, fr L *ethicus*, fr Gk *ēthikos*, fr *ēthos* character] – **ethically** *adv*, **ethicalness** *n*, **ethicality** *n*

**ethic dative** *n* the dative case expressing a person's indirect interest ⟨me *in "buy me a drink" is in the* ~⟩

**ethinyl** /'ethənil, i'thienil, -niel/ *n* ETHYNYL (chemical group)

**ethionine** /i'thie·əneen, -nin/ *n* an AMINO ACID, $C_2H_5(CH_2)_2$ $CH(NH_2)COOH$, that induces cancer and is related to the amino acid METHIONINE whose biological function it reduces or prevents [eth- + *thion-* + *-ine*]

**¹Ethiopian** /,eethi'ohpiən/ *n* **1** a native or inhabitant of Ethiopia **2** *archaic* a Negro [*Ethiopia*, country in NE Africa]

**²Ethiopian** *adj* **1** (characteristic) of the inhabitants or the country of Ethiopia **2** of or being the biogeographic region that includes Africa south of the Sahara, S Arabia, and sometimes Madagascar and the adjacent islands

**¹Ethiopic** /,eethi'opik, -'ohpik/ *adj* **1** Ethiopian **2** of or constituting Ethiopic

**²Ethiopic** *n* **1** a Semitic language formerly spoken in Ethiopia and still used there in Christian services of worship **2** the group of Semitic languages spoken in Ethiopia

**ethmoid** /'ethmoyd/, **ethmoidal** /eth'moydl/ *adj* of, adjoining, or being one or more bones of the walls and SEPTUM (partition) of the nasal cavity [Fr *ethmoïde*, fr Gk *ēthmoeidēs*, lit., like a strainer, fr *ēthmos* strainer] – **ethmoid** *n*

# eth

ethnarch /'ethnahk/ n the governor of a province or people (e g of the Byzantine Empire) [Gk *ethnarchēs*, fr *ethnos* nation, people + *archos* ruler]

¹ethnic /'ethnik/, ethnical /'ethnikl/ adj 1 of or being human races or large groups of people classed according to common traits and customs ⟨~ *minorities*⟩ ⟨~ *groups*⟩ 2 (characteristic) of a traditional, esp peasant, culture ⟨~ *music*⟩ ⟨*the* ~ *look in fashion*⟩ 3 *archaic* heathen synonyms see ³RACE [ME, fr LL *ethnicus*, fr Gk *ethnikos* national, gentile, fr *ethnos*] – ethnicity n

²ethnic n, *chiefly NAm* a member of an ethnic group; *esp* a member of a minority group who retains the customs, language, or social views of his/her group

ethnical /'ethnikl/ adj 1 ethnic 2 of ethnology; ethnological – ethnically adv

ethno- *comb form* race; people; cultural group ⟨ethno*centric*⟩ [Fr, fr Gk *ethno-*, *ethn-*, fr *ethnos*]

ethnocentric /,ethnoh'sentrik/ adj 1 having race as a central interest 2 characterized by or based on the attitude that one's own race, culture, etc is superior – ethnocentrically adv, ethnocentrism n, ethnocentricity n

ethnography /eth'nografi/ n ethnology; *specif* descriptive ANTHROPOLOGY (study of human races) [Fr *ethnographie*, fr *ethno-* + *-graphie* -graphy] – ethnographer n, ethnographic, ethnographical adj, ethnographically adv

ethnology /eth'noləji/ n 1 a science that deals with races and peoples and their origin, distribution, relations, and characteristics 2 the comparative and analytical study of cultures; CULTURAL ANTHROPOLOGY – ethnologist n, ethnologic, ethnological adj, ethnologically adv

ethnomusicology /,ethnoh,myoohzi'koləji/ n the study of the music of non-European cultures – ethnomusicologist n, ethnomusicological adj

ethology /i'tholəji/ n 1 the study of the formation and evolution of human customs and beliefs 2 the scientific study of the behaviour of animals, esp in their natural environment – ethologist n, ethological adj

ethos /'eethos/ n the distinctive character, moral nature, or guiding beliefs of a person, group, institution, or culture ⟨*the* ~ *of hard work and thrift*⟩ [NL, fr Gk *ēthos* custom, character]

ethoxy /e'thoksi/ adj relating to or containing ethoxyl

ethoxyl /e'thoksil/ n a chemical group, $C_2H_5O$, with a VALENCY of one that is composed of ethyl united with oxygen [ISV *eth-* + *ox-* + *-yl*]

ethyl /'ethil, 'eethil, -thiel/ n a chemical group , $C_2H_5$, which has a VALENCY of one and is derived from the gas ETHANE [ISV *ether* + *-yl*] – ethylic adj

ethyl acetate n a colourless fragrant inflammable liquid ESTER (compound formed from a reaction between an acid and an alcohol), $CH_3COOC_2H_5$, that vaporizes readily and is used esp as a solvent and in flavourings

ethyl alcohol n ETHANOL

ethylate /'ethilayt, 'ee-/ vt to introduce the ethyl group into (a chemical compound) – ethylation n

ethyl chloride n a colourless pungent inflammable gas or readily vaporizing liquid, $C_2H_5Cl$, used esp as a local surface anaesthetic

ethylene /'ethi,leen/ n 1 a colourless inflammable gas, $H_2C=CH_2$, found in COAL GAS and used esp in the synthesis of other organic chemical compounds 2 a chemical group, $C_2H_4$, with a VALENCY of two, that is derived from the gas ETHANE – ethylenic adj, ethylenically adv

ethylene glycol n a thick liquid chemical alcohol, $HOCH_2CH_2OH$, used esp as an antifreeze

ethylene oxide n a colourless inflammable gas or readily vaporizing liquid, $C_2H_4O$, used esp in the manufacture of solvents and detergents and in sterilization and fumigation

ethyl ether n ETHER 3a

ethynyl, ethinyl /'ethənil, e'thienil, -niel/ n a chemical group, HC≡C, with a VALENCY of one, derived from the gas ACETYLENE by removal of one hydrogen atom [*ethyne, ethine* (acetylene; fr *ethyl* + *-ine*) + *-yl*]

-etic /-'etik/ suffix (→ adj) ¹-IC ⟨*ascetic*⟩ – often in adjectives corresponding to nouns ending in *-esis* ⟨*genetic*⟩ ⟨*synthetic*⟩ [L & Gk; L *-eticus*, fr Gk *-etikos, -ētikos*, fr *-etos, -ētos*, ending of certain verbals]

etiolate /'eeti·ə,layt, -tioh-/ vt 1 to bleach and alter the natural development of (a green plant) by excluding sunlight 2a to make weak, pale, or sickly b to make wishy-washy ⟨*an* ~d *child's*

*version of a barbaric old legend*⟩ [Fr *étioler*, fr ONF *étieuler* to turn to stubble, fr *éteule* stubble, deriv of L *stipula* straw] – etiolation n

etiology /,eeti'oləji/ n, NAm AETIOLOGY – etiologic, etiological adj, etiologically adv

etiquette /'eti,ket/ n the conventionally accepted standards of proper social, professional, or official behaviour ⟨*medical* ~⟩ [Fr *étiquette*, lit., ticket – more at TICKET]

Eton collar /'eetn/ n a large stiff white collar worn turned over the edge of a jacket [*Eton* College, public school in SW England]

Eton crop n a very short haircut for women, popular esp in the 1920s

Etonian /ee'tonhnyən, -ni·ən/ n or adj (a pupil) of Eton College

etrier /'aytriay (Fr etrje)/ n a short rope ladder with two or three rungs used esp in mountaineering or potholing [Fr *étrier*, lit., stirrup]

Etrurian /i'trooəriən/ adj or n Etruscan [*Etruria*]

¹Etruscan /i'truskən/ adj (characteristic) of Etruria, the Etruscans, or Etruscan [L *etruscus;* akin to L *Etruria*, ancient country in Italy]

²Etruscan n 1 a native or inhabitant of ancient Etruria 2 the language used by the Etruscans, which does not belong to any known language group

-ette /-'et/ suffix (n → n) 1 small or lesser kind of ⟨*kitchen*ette⟩ ⟨*cigar*ette⟩ 2 female ⟨*suffrag*ette⟩ ⟨*usher*ette⟩ 3 imitation; substitute ⟨*leather*ette⟩ ⟨*flannel*ette⟩ [ME, fr MF, fem dim. suffix, fr OF *-ete* – more at -ET]

étude /ay'tyoohd (Fr ety:d)/ n a piece of music written chiefly for the practice of a technique but often also played for its artistic value [Fr, lit., study, fr MF *estude, estudie*]

etui /e'twee/ n, pl etuis /e'twee(z)/ a small ornamental case, esp for holding needles [Fr *étui*, fr OF *estui* prison, container, fr *estuier* to shut up, keep, preserve]

etymolog·ize, -ise /,eti'moləjiez/ vt to discover, formulate, or give an etymology for ~ vi to study or formulate etymologies

etymology /,eti'moləji/ n 1 the history of the origin and development of a word or other linguistic form 2 a branch of language study concerned with etymologies 9 entomology [ME *ethimologie*, fr L *etymologia*, fr Gk, fr *etymon* + *-logia* -logy] – etymologist n, etymological adj, etymologically adv

etymon /'eti,mon/ n, pl etyma /-mə/ also etymons an earlier native or foreign linguistic form from which derivatives are formed [L, fr Gk, literal meaning of a word according to its origin, fr *etymos* true; akin to Gk *eteos* true]

eu- /yooh-, yoo-/ comb form 1a well; easily ⟨*euplastic*⟩ ⟨*euphonious*⟩ b good ⟨*eupepsia*⟩ 2 true ⟨*euchromatin*⟩ □ (1) compare DYS- 2,3 [ME, fr L, fr Gk, fr *ey, eu*, fr neut of *eys* good; akin to Hitt *asus* good]

eucalypt /'yoohkə,lipt/ n a eucalyptus

eucalyptol /,yoohkə'liptol/, eucalyptole /-tol, -tohl/ n CINEOLE (colourless liquid contained esp in eucalyptus oil)

eucalyptus /,yoohkə'liptəs/ n, pl eucalyptuses, eucalypti /-ti, -tie/ any of a genus (*Eucalyptus*) of the family Myrtaceae, the eucalyptus family) of mostly Australian evergreen trees and sometimes shrubs that have rigid leaves and flowers in clusters and are widely cultivated for their gums, resins, oils, and wood [NL, genus name, fr *eu-* + Gk *kalyptos* covered, fr *kalyptein* to conceal; fr the conical covering of the buds]

eucaryote /yooh'karioht, -ət/ n EUKARYOTE (organism with clearly defined nuclei controlling its cells) – eucaryotic adj

Eucharist /'yoohkərist/ n COMMUNION 2a [ME *eukarist*, fr MF *eucharistе*, fr LL *eucharistia*, fr Gk, Eucharist, gratitude, fr *eucharistos* grateful, fr *eu-* + *charizesthai* to show favour, fr *charis* favour, grace, gratitude – more at YEARN] – eucharistic adj, often cap

¹euchre /'yoohkə/ n a US card game in which a player must take at least 3 out of 5 TRICKS to win [origin unknown]

²euchre vt 1 to prevent from winning three TRICKS in euchre 2 NAm informal to cheat, trick ⟨*they* ~d *him into an agreement*⟩

euchromatin /yooh'krohmətin/ n the major portion of the CHROMOSOMES (threadlike genetic material in a cell) that contains the active genes – compare HETEROCHROMATIN [Ger, fr *eu-* + *chromatin*] – euchromatic adj

euclidean also euclidian /yooh'klidi·ən/ adj, often cap of or being the geometry of Euclid or a geometry based on Euclid's assumptions regarding space; *specif* being a geometry in which there is only one line through a point which is parallel to some other line – compare ELLIPTIC, HYPERBOLIC [*Euclid fl ab* 300 BC Gk mathematician]

**euclidean space** *n, often cap E* three-dimensional space in which euclidean geometry applies

**eucrite** /'yoohkriet/ *n* **1** any of a class of stony meteorites composed mainly of the minerals ANORTHITE and AUGITE **2** a rock composed mainly of the minerals OLIVINE, PLAGIOCLASE, and PYROXENE that is formed by slow cooling and solidification below the earth's surface [Ger *eukrit*, fr Gk *eukritos* easily discerned] – **eucritic** *adj*

**eudemonism, eudaemonism** /yooh'deemə,niz(ə)m/ *n, philosophy* the doctrine that the basis of moral and rational action should be its capacity to bring about personal well-being and happiness [Gk *eudaimonia* happiness, fr *eudaimōn* having a good attendant spirit, happy, fr *eu-* + *daimōn* spirit] – **eudemonist** *n*, **eudemonistic, eudemonistical** *adj*, **eudemonistically** *adv*

**eudiometer** /,yoohdi'omitə/ *n* a graduated glass tube used for the analysis and measurement of volumes of gases during chemical reactions [It *eudiometro*, fr Gk *eudia* fair weather (fr *eu-* + *-dia* weather; akin to L *dies* day) + It *-metro* -meter, fr Gk *metron* measure] – **eudiometric** *adj*, **eudiometrically** *adv*

**eugenic** /yooh'jenik/ *adj* **1** relating to or fitted for the production of good offspring ⟨*a ~ marriage*⟩ **2** of eugenics [Gk *eugenēs* wellborn, fr *eu-* + *-genēs* born – more at -GEN] – **eugenically** *adv*

**eugenics** /yooh'jeniks/ *n taking sing vb* a science that deals with the improvement of the hereditary qualities of the human race, esp by careful selection of future parents

**eugenol** /'yoohjinol/ *n* a colourless liquid chemical compound, $C_{10}H_{12}O_2$, that is a PHENOL found esp in clove oil and used chiefly in flavourings and perfumes [Fr *eugénol*, fr NL *Eugenia*, genus of tropical trees]

**euglena** /yooh'gleenə/ *n* any of a genus (*Euglena*) of green freshwater PROTOZOANS (single-celled microorganisms) having a combination of plant and animal characteristics. They manufacture food by PHOTOSYNTHESIS and move by means of a long FLAGELLUM (whiplike appendage). [NL, genus name, fr *eu-* + Gk *glēnē* eyeball, socket of a joint]

**euglenoid** /yooh'gleenoyd/ *n* any of a group (Euglenida of the phylum Protozoa) of single-celled solitary organisms (e g a euglena) that are usu green or colourless and have one or two FLAGELLA (whiplike appendages used for movement) – **euglenoid** *adj*

**euglobulin** /yooh'globyoolin/ *n* a simple protein that does not dissolve in pure water [ISV *eu-* + *globulin*]

**euhemerism** /yooh'hemə,riz(ə)m/ *n* the theory that the gods portrayed in myths are in fact heroes of history who have been accorded divine status [*Euhemerus*, 4th-c BC Gk mythographer] – **euhemerist** *n*, **euhemerize** *vt*, **euhemeristic** *adj*, **euhemeristically** *adv*

**eukaryote, eucaryote** /yooh'karioht, -ət/ *n* any of a large group of organisms characterized by possessing cells in which the nucleus is clearly defined and highly organized and that includes most living things except some minute forms (e g bacteria and viruses) – compare PROKARYOTE [*eu-* + *kary-* + *-ote* (as in *zygote*)] – **eukaryotic** *adj*

**eulogium** /yoo'lohjiəm/ *n, pl* **eulogia** /-jiə/, **eulogiums** a eulogy [ML]

**eulog·ize, -ise** /'yoohlə,jiez/ *vt* to praise highly in speech or writing; extol – **eulogizer** *n*

**eulogy** /'yoohləji/ *n* **1** an esp formal speech or piece of writing in praise of a person or thing **2** high praise □ compare ELEGY [ME *euloge*, fr ML *eulogium*, fr Gk *eulogia* praise, fr *eu-* + *-logia* -logy] – **eulogist** *n*, **eulogistic** *adj*, **eulogistically** *adv*

**Eumenides** /yooh'meni,deez/ *n pl* the snake-haired goddesses of Greek mythology who were held to pursue and punish criminals – called also FURIES [L, fr Gk, lit., the well-disposed ones]

**eunuch** /'yoohnək/ *n* **1** a castrated man employed, esp formerly, in a harem or as a chamberlain in a palace **2** a man or boy deprived of the testes or external genitals **3** *informal* a man lacking effectiveness or vitality [ME *eunuk*, fr L *eunuchus*, fr Gk *eunouchos*, fr *eunē* bed + *echein* to have, have charge of – more at SCHEME] – **eunuchism** *n*

**eunuchoid** /'yoohnəkoyd/ *n* a sexually deficient individual; *esp* one lacking in sexual differentiation and tending towards the intersex state – **eunuchoid** *adj*

**euonymus** /yooh'oniməs/ *n* SPINDLE TREE [NL, genus name, fr L *euonymos* spindle tree, fr Gk *euōnymos*, fr *euōnymos* having an auspicious name, fr *eu-* + *onyma* name – more at NAME]

**eupatrid** /yooh'patrid/ *n, pl* **eupatridae** /-die/ *often cap* any of the hereditary aristocrats of ancient Athens [Gk *eupatridēs*, fr *eu-* + *patr-, patēr* father – more at FATHER]

**eupepsia** /yooh'pepsi·ə/ *n* **1** good digestion **2** happiness, optimism [NL, fr *eu-* + *-pepsia* (as in *dyspepsia*)] – **eupeptic** *adj*

**euphausiid** /yooh'fawzi·id/ *n* any of an order (Euphausiacea of the class Crustacea) of small usu luminescent shrimplike INVERTEBRATE animals that form an important element in marine plankton [NL *Euphausia*, genus of crustaceans] – **euphausiid** *adj*

**euphemism** /'yoohfə,miz(ə)m/ *n* the substitution of a mild, vague, or indirect expression for one that may offend or suggest something unpleasant; *also* the expression so substituted ⟨*"fall asleep" is a ~ for "die"*⟩ **9** euphuism [Gk *euphēmismos*, fr *euphēmos* auspicious, sounding good, fr *eu-* + *phēmē* speech, fr *phanai* to speak – more at BAN] – **euphemistic** *adj*, **euphemistically** *adv*

**euphem·ize, -ise** /'yoohfə,miez/ *vt* to express by a euphemism ⟨*many people ~ death*⟩ ~ *vi* to make use of euphemistic expressions – **euphemizer** *n*

**euphenics** /yoo'feniks/ *n taking sing vb* a science that deals with the biological improvement of human beings after birth – compare EUGENICS [*eu-* + *phen-* (fr *phenotype*) + *-ics*] – **euphenic** *adj*

**euphonious** /yooh'fohnyəs, -ni·əs/ *adj* pleasing to the ear – **euphoniously** *adv*, **euphoniousness** *n*, **euphonize** *vt*

**euphonium** /yooh'fohnyəm, -ni·əm/ *n* a BRASS INSTRUMENT smaller than but resembling a tuba and having a higher range than that of the tuba [Gk *euphōnos* + E *-ium* (as in *harmonium*)]

**euphony** /'yoohfəni/ *n* (a) pleasing or sweet sound, esp in speech – compare CACOPHONY [Fr *euphonie*, fr LL *euphonia*, fr Gk *euphōnia*, fr *euphōnos* sweet-voiced, musical, fr *eu-* + *phōnē* voice – more at BAN] – **euphonic** *adj*, **euphonically** *adv*

**euphorbia** /yooh'fawbiə/ *n* any of a genus (*Euphorbia*) of plants of the spurge family that have a milky juice and usu green flowers; *broadly* spurge [NL, genus name, alter. of L *euphorbea* euphorbia, fr *Euphorbus*, 1st-c AD physician]

**euphoria** /yooh'fawri·ə/ *n* an esp exaggerated feeling of well-being or elation [NL, fr Gk, fr *euphoros* healthy, fr *eu-* + *pherein* to bear – more at BEAR] – **euphoric** *adj*, **euphorically** *adv*

**euphotic** /yooh'fohtik/ *adj* of or being the upper layers of a body of water into which sufficient light penetrates to permit growth of green plants [ISV]

**euphuism** /'yoohfyooh,iz(ə)m/ *n* an artificial and ornate style of writing or speaking; *specif* such a style fashionable in England in the late 16th and early 17th centuries **9** euphemism [*Euphues*, character in prose romances by John Lyly †1606 E writer] – **euphuist** *n*, **euphuistic** *adj*, **euphuistically** *adv*

**euploid** /'yoohployd/ *adj, biology* having a CHROMOSOME NUMBER (normal amount of genetic material in a cell) that is an exact multiple of the HAPLOID number (amount of genetic material in a reproductive cell) – compare ANEUPLOID [ISV] – **euploid** *n*, **euploidy** *n*

**eupnoea**, *NAm chiefly* **eupnea** /yoohp'nee·ə/ *n* normal respiration – compare DYSPNOEA [NL, fr Gk *eupnoia*, fr *eupnous* breathing freely, fr *eu-* + *pnein* to breathe – more at SNEEZE] – **eupnoeic** *adj*

**Eur-** /yooər-/, **Euro-** *comb form* **1** European ⟨Euro*communism*⟩ European and ⟨Eur*asian*⟩ **2** European Economic Community ⟨Euro*crat*⟩

**Eurasian** /yooə'rayzh(ə)n, yoo'ray-/ *adj* **1** of, growing in, or living in Europe and Asia **2** of mixed European and Asian origin – **Eurasian** *n*

**eureka** /yoo(ə)'reekə/ *interj* – used to express triumph at a discovery [Gk *heurēka* I have found, fr *heuriskein* to find; fr the exclamation attributed to Archimedes †212 BC Gk mathematician & inventor on finding a method for determining the purity of gold]

**eurhythmic, eurythmic** /yoo(ə)'ridhmik/ **1** harmonious **2** of eurhythmy or eurhythmics

**eurhythmics, eurythmics** /yoo(ə)'ridhmiks/ *n taking sing or pl vb* (the art of) harmonious body movement, esp in the form of expressive timed movements in response to music

**eurhythmy, eurythmy** /yoo(ə)'ridhmi/ *n* a system of harmonious body movement to the rhythm of spoken words [Ger *eurhythmie*, fr L *eurhythmia* rhythmical movement, fr Gk, fr *eurhythmos* rhythmical, fr *eu-* + *rhythmos* rhythm]

**euro** /'yooəroh/ *n, pl* **euros** *Austr* a large reddish grey kangaroo (*Macrobus robustus*) [native name in Australia]

**Eurobond** /'yooəroh‚bond/ *n* a BOND sold outside the country in whose currency it is issued

**Eurocommunism**/‚yooəroh'komyooniz(ə)m/*n*Communism as it manifests itself in W Europe (e g in Italy), most of the adherents of which seek to take a policy line independent of that of the Soviet Communist party – **Eurocommunist** *adj or n*

**Eurocrat** /'yooərəkrat/ *n, informal* an esp high-ranking staff member of the administration of the European Economic Community [blend of *Euro-* and *bureaucrat*]

**Eurocurrency** /'yooəroh‚kurənsi/ *n, sometimes not cap* a common currency for all countries in the European Economic Community ⟨*favours monetary union based on a standard* ∼⟩

**Eurodollar** /'yooəroh‚dolə/ *n, sometimes not cap* a US dollar held (e g by a bank) outside the USA, esp in Europe

¹**European** /‚yooərə'pee∙ən/ *adj* **1** native to Europe **2** of European descent or origin; *specif* white **3** concerned with or affecting the whole of Europe **4** advocating European unity or alliance [L *Europaeus,* fr Gk *Eurōpaios,* fr *Eurōpē* Europe] – **Europeanize** *vt,* **Europeanization** *n*

  *usage* A journalist may be referred to as ⟨*our East Europe correspondent*⟩ because *East* **European** would suggest that he/she was "native to Eastern Europe".

²**European** *n* a native or inhabitant of (the mainland of) Europe – **European** *adj,* **Europeanize** *vt,* **Europeanization** *n*

**European bison** *n* a bison (*Bison bonasus*) that is found in E Europe and is nearly extinct

**European corn borer** *n* a moth (*Ostrinia nubilalis*) that is widespread in eastern N America where its larva is a major pest, esp of maize, dahlias, and potatoes

**Europeanism** /‚yooərə'pee∙ə‚niz(ə)m/ *n* **1** the traditions or customs characteristic of Europeans **2** the advocacy of European unity

**European plan** *n, NAm* a system of payment in a hotel whereby the daily rates cover the cost of the room only – compare PENSION, AMERICAN PLAN

**European red mite** *n* a small bright or brownish red oval mite (*Panonychus ulmi*) that is a destructive orchard pest

**europium** /yooə'rohpi∙əm, -pyəm/ *n* a silvery-white metallic chemical element having a VALENCY of two or three and belonging to the RARE-EARTH group of elements [NL, fr *Europa* Europe]

**Eurovision** /'yooərə‚vizh(ə)n/ *trademark* – used for a television service enabling several chiefly W European broadcasting organizations to exchange programmes

**eury-** /yooəri-/ *comb form* broad; wide ⟨eury*haline*⟩ ⟨eury*therm*⟩ [NL, fr Gk, fr *eurys;* akin to Skt *uru* broad, wide]

**eurybathic** /‚yooəri'bathik/ *adj, of an animal* capable of living in both deep and shallow water ⟨∼ *gastropods*⟩ [*eury-* + Gk *bathos* depth]

**euryhaline** /‚yooəri'haylien, -'ha-, -lin/ *adj, of a marine animal* able to live in waters that have a wide range of salt concentrations [ISV *eury-* + Gk *halinos* of salt, fr *hals* salt – more at SALT]

**eurypterid** /yoo'riptərid/ *n* any of an order (Eurypterida) of extinct usu large aquatic scorpionlike animals that are related to the KING CRABS [deriv of Gk *eury-* + *pteron* wing – more at FEATHER] – **eurypterid** *adj*

**eurytherm** /'yooəri‚thuhm/ *n* an organism that tolerates a wide range of temperature [deriv of Gk *eury-* + *thermē* heat] – **eurythermal, eurythermic, eurythermous** *adj*

**eurythmic** /yoo(ə)'ridhmik/ *adj* EURHYTHMIC

**eurythmics** /yoo(ə)'ridhmiks/ *n taking sing or pl vb* EURHYTHMICS (art of harmonious body movement)

**eurythmy** /yoo(ə)'ridhmi/ *n* EURHYTHMY (body movements to the rhythm of words)

**eurytopic** /‚yooəri'topik/ *adj* tolerant of wide variation in one or more physical factors of the environment (e g altitude) [deriv of Gk *eury-* + *topos* place] – **eurytopicity** *n*

**eustachian tube** /yooh'stayshyən, -shən/ *n, often cap E* a tube consisting of bone and cartilage that connects the MIDDLE EAR with the throat and allows the air pressure on both sides of the eardrum to be equalized [Bartolommeo *Eustachio* †1574 It anatomist]

**eustasy** /'yoohstəsi/ *n* worldwide change of sea level brought about esp by movements of the sea bed [back-formation fr ISV *eustatic,* fr *eu-* + *static*] – **eustatic** *adj*

**eutectic** /yooh'tektik/ *adj* **1** of or being an alloy or other mixture in which the constituents are in such proportions that the melting point is the lowest possible for a mixture of these substances **2** of a eutectic alloy or solution or its melting or freez-

ing point [Gk *eutēktos* easily melted, fr *eu-* + *tēktos* melted, fr *tēkein* to melt – more at THAW] – **eutectic** *n,* **eutectoid** *adj or n*

**euthanasia** /‚yoohthə'nayzyə, -zhə, -zi∙ə/ *n* the act or practice of killing individuals who are incurably ill or injured, for reasons of mercy [Gk, easy death, fr *eu-* + *thanatos* death – more at THANATOS] – **euthanasic** *adj*

**euthenics** /yoo'theniks/ *n taking sing or pl vb* a science that deals with the development of human well-being by improvement of living conditions [Gk *euthenein* to thrive, fr *eu-* + *-thenein* (akin to Skt *āhanas* swelling)] – **euthenist** *n*

**eutherian** /yooh'thiəri∙ən/ *adj or n* (of or being) a mammal of a major division (Eutheria) comprising those mammals whose young are nourished in the womb via a placenta and are born in an advanced stage of development – compare MARSUPIAL, MONOTREME [deriv of NL *eu-* + Gk *thērion* beast – more at TREACLE]

**euthyroid** /yooh'thie(ə)‚royd/ *adj* characterized by normal functioning of the THYROID (gland in the neck that controls healthy growth)

**eutrophic** /yooh'trohfik/ *adj, of a body of water* rich in dissolved nutrients (e g phosphates) but often shallow and seasonally deficient in oxygen – compare MESOTROPHIC, OLIGO-TROPHIC [deriv of Gk *eutrophos* well nourished, nourishing, fr *eu-* + *trephein* to nourish – more at ATROPHY] – **eutrophication** *n,* **eutrophy** *n*

**evacuate** /i'vakyoo‚ayt/ *vt* **1** EMPTY 1a **2** to discharge from the body as waste **3** to remove gas, water, etc from, esp by pumping; *esp* to produce a vacuum in **4a** to remove, esp from a military zone or dangerous area **b** to withdraw from military occupation of **c** to vacate ⟨*rapidly* ∼d *the burning building*⟩ ∼ *vi* **1** to withdraw from a place in an organized way, esp for protection **2** to pass urine or faeces from the body [L *evacuatus,* pp of *evacuare,* fr *e-* + *vacuus* empty – more at VACUUM] – **evacuation** *n,* **evacuative** *adj*

**evacuee** /i‚vakyoo'ee/ *n* a person evacuated from a dangerous place

**evade** /i'vayd/ *vi* to take refuge by evading something ∼ *vt* **1** to get away from or avoid, esp by skill or deception ⟨∼ *punishment*⟩ **2a** to avoid facing up to ⟨∼d *the real issues*⟩ **b** to avoid the consideration or performance of ⟨∼d *the question*⟩; *esp* to fail to pay, esp in violation of the law ⟨∼ *taxes*⟩ **3** to baffle, foil ⟨*the problem* ∼s *all efforts at solution*⟩ *synonyms* see ¹ESCAPE [MF & L; MF *evader,* fr L *evadere,* fr *e-* + *vadere* to go, walk – more at WADE] – **evadable** *adj,* **evader** *n*

**evaginate** /i'vajinayt/ *vt* to turn (an organ or other body part) inside out; evert [LL *evagination-, evaginatio* act of unsheathing, fr L *evaginatus,* pp of *evaginare* to unsheathe, fr *e-* + *vagina* sheath] – **evagination** *n*

**evaluate** /i'valyoo‚ayt/ *vt* to determine the amount, value, or significance of, esp by careful appraisal and study [back-formation fr *evaluation,* fr Fr *évaluation,* fr *évaluer* to evaluate, fr *e-* + *value* value] – **evaluator** *n,* **evaluative** *adj,* **evaluation** *n*

**evanescent** /‚evə'nes(ə)nt/ *adj* tending to dissipate or vanish like vapour ⟨∼ *fame as a pop star*⟩ *synonyms* see ¹TRANSIENT [L *evanescent-, evanescens,* prp of *evanescere* – more at VANISH] – **evanescence** *n,* **evanesce** *vi*

¹**evangel** /i'vanj(ə)l/ *n, archaic* (the) gospel [ME *evangile,* fr MF, fr LL *evangelium,* fr Gk *euangelion* good news, gospel, fr *euangelos* bringing good news, fr *eu-* + *angelos* messenger]

²**evangel** *n* an evangelist

**evangelical** /‚eevan'jelikl/ *also* **evangelic** /‚eevan'jelik/ *adj* **1** of or being in agreement with the Christian message, esp as it is presented in the four Gospels **2** *often cap* Protestant; *specif* of the German Protestant church **3** *often cap* (of or being a usu Protestant denomination) emphasizing salvation by faith in the atoning death of Jesus Christ, personal conversion, the authority of Scripture, and the importance of preaching as contrasted with ritual **4a** of, adhering to, or marked by fundamentalism **b** LOW CHURCH **5** evangelistic, zealous ⟨∼ *ardour*⟩ – **Evangelical** *n,* **Evangelicalism** *n,* **evangelically** *adv*

**evangelism** /i'vanjə‚liz(ə)m/ *n* **1** the spreading of the Christian gospel in an effort to bring about personal conversion **2** militant or crusading zeal – **evangelistic** *adj,* **evangelistically** *adv*

**evangelist** /i'vanjəlist/ *n* **1** *often cap* a writer of any of the four Gospels **2** one who evangelizes; *specif* a Protestant minister or layman who spreads the Gospel by preaching outside as well as inside the Church

**evangel∙ize, -ise** /i'vanjə‚liez/ *vt* to preach the Christian gospel to, esp with the intention of converting ∼ *vi* **1** to preach the gospel **2** to advocate a cause strongly or insistently, esp in an effort to convince others ⟨*he's always* evangelizing, *trying to make me join his party*⟩ – **evangelization** *n*

**evanish** /i'vanish/ *vi, poetic* to vanish [ME *evanisshen*, fr MF *evaniss-*, stem of *evanir*] – **evanishment** *n*

**evaporate** /i'vapərayt/ *vi* **1a** to pass off in vapour or in invisible minute particles **b** to pass off or away; disappear, fade ⟨*his fears* ∼d⟩ **2** to give out vapour ∼ *vt* **1** to convert into vapour; *also* to dissipate or draw off in vapour or fumes **2a** to expel moisture, esp water, from **b** to expel ⟨∼ *electrons from a hot wire*⟩ **3** to cause to disappear or fade [ME *evaporaten*, fr L *evaporatus*, pp of *evaporare*, fr *e-* + *vapor* steam, vapour] – **evaporatable** *adj*, **evaporation** *n*, **evaporative** *adj*, **evaporatively** *adv*, **evaporativity** *n*, **evaporator** *n*

**evaporated milk** /i'vapəraytid/ *n* unsweetened milk concentrated by partial evaporation

**evaporite** /i'vapəriet, ee-/ *n* a SEDIMENTARY rock formed by the evaporation of sea water in an enclosed basin [*evaporation* + *-ite*] – **evaporitic** *adj*

**evapotranspiration** /i,vapoh,transpi'raysh(ə)n, ee-, -trahns-/ *n* the total loss of water from an area made up of that lost from the soil by evaporation and that lost from the leaves of plants growing there by transpiration [*evaporation* + *transpiration*]

**evasion** /i'vayzh(ə)n/ *n* an act, instance, or means of evading ⟨*suspected of tax* ∼⟩ [ME, fr MF or LL; MF, fr LL *evasion-, evasio*, fr L *evasus*, pp of *evadere* to evade]

**evasive** /i'vaysiv, -ziv/ *adj* tending or intended to evade; equivocal ⟨∼ *answers*⟩ – **evasively** *adv*, **evasiveness** *n*

**eve** /eev/ *n* **1** *often cap* the evening or the day before a special day, esp a religious holiday ⟨*Christmas* Eve⟩ **2** the period immediately preceding an event, new development, etc ⟨*on the* ∼ *of war*⟩ **3** *poetic* the evening [ME *eve, even*]

**evection** /i'veksh(ə)n/ *n* perturbation of the moon's orbital motion due to the attraction of the sun [L *evection-, evectio* rising, fr *evectus*, pp of *evehere* to carry out, raise up, fr *e-* + *vehere* to carry – more at WAY]

**¹even** /'eev(ə)n/ *n, archaic or poetic* the evening [ME *even, eve*, fr OE *æfen*]

**²even** *adj* **1a** having a horizontal surface; flat, level ⟨∼ *ground*⟩ **b** without break or irregularity; smooth **c** in the same plane or line – usu + *with* ⟨∼ *with the ground*⟩ **2a** without variation; uniform ⟨*an* ∼ *disposition*⟩ ⟨*an* ∼ *grey sky*⟩ **b** LEVEL **4** **3a** equal ⟨*we were* ∼ *after the fourth game, having won two each*⟩; *also* fair ⟨*an* ∼ *exchange*⟩ **b** in equilibrium; balanced; *specif* showing neither profit nor loss **4a** exactly divisible by two ⟨*an* ∼ *number*⟩ – compare ODD **3a** **b** marked by an even number **c** *of a mathematical function* not changing in value when the INDEPENDENT VARIABLE changes its sign ⟨*squaring is an* ∼ *function since* $(+x)^2 = (-x)^2 = x^2$⟩ **5** exact, precise ⟨*an* ∼ *pound*⟩ **6** fifty-fifty ⟨*she stands an* ∼ *chance of winning*⟩ **7** *obs* candid **synonyms** see ³LEVEL, ¹STEADY **antonym** uneven [ME, fr OE *efen*; akin to OHG *eban* evan] – **evenly** *adv*, **evenness** *n* – **be/get even with somebody** to have exacted or to exact revenge on somebody – **break even** to make neither profit nor loss

**³even** *adv* **1** at the very time – + *as* ⟨*she entered* ∼ *as we spoke*⟩ **2a** – used as an intensive to emphasize contrast with a less strong possibility ⟨*he looked content,* ∼ *happy*⟩ ⟨*can't* ∼ *walk, let alone run*⟩ ⟨*danger of injury or* ∼ *death*⟩ **b** – used as an intensive to emphasize the comparative degree ⟨∼ *better than last time*⟩ **c** – used to express nonfulfilment of expectation ⟨∼ *when I explained it, they didn't understand*⟩ **3** *archaic* – emphasizing identity ⟨*let us now go* ∼ *unto Bethlehem* - Lk 2:15 (AV)⟩ [ME, fr OE *efne*, fr *efen*, adj] – **even if** in spite of the possibility or fact that – **even now 1** at this very moment **2** in spite of what has happened – **even so** in spite of that

*usage* In formal writing, **even** should be placed next to the word it modifies. Compare ⟨**even** John (= so certainly everyone else) *works on Sundays*⟩ ⟨*John* works **even** *on Sundays* (= so certainly on weekdays)⟩; but the natural place for **even** is often next to the verb ⟨*John* even *works on Sundays*⟩ and such an arrangement is usually clear enough in speech, where the stress of the sentence helps to convey the meaning.

**⁴even** *vb* to make or become even – often + *up* or *out* – **evener** *n*

**evenfall** /'eev(ə)n,fawl/ *n, archaic* the beginning of evening; dusk

**evenhanded** /-'handid/ *adj* fair, impartial – **evenhandedly** *adv*, **evenhandedness** *n*

**evening** /'eevning/ *n* **1a** the latter part and close of the day

and the early part of the night **b** the time between sunset and bedtime **c** *dial* the afternoon **2** a late period (e g of time or life); the end ⟨*the* ∼ *of my life*⟩ **3** the period of an evening's entertainment [ME, fr OE *æfnung*, fr *æfnian* to grow towards evening, fr *æfen* evening; akin to OHG *āband* evening]

**evening dress** *n* **1** clothes for formal or semiformal evening occasions, usu including a black dinner jacket and bow tie for men **2** a dress, esp with a floor-length skirt, for wear on formal or semiformal occasions ⟨*she wore a grey* ∼⟩

**evening prayer** *n, often cap E&P* the daily evening service of the Anglican church

**evening primrose** *n* any of several plants (*Oenothera* and related genera) of the fuchsia family; *esp* a coarse plant (*Oenothera biennis*) with yellow flowers that open in the evening

**evenings** /'eevningz/ *adv, chiefly NAm* in the evening repeatedly; on any evening ⟨∼ *I work in the coffee bar*⟩

**evening star** *n* a bright planet, esp Venus, seen in the western sky at or just after sunset; *broadly* any planet that rises before midnight – compare MORNING STAR

**evening up** *n* buying or selling to offset an existing market position

**evensong** /-,song/ *n, often cap* **1** VESPERS 1 (Roman Catholic evening service) **2** EVENING PRAYER [ME, fr OE *æfensang*, fr *æfen* even + *sang* song]

**¹event** /i'vent/ *n* **1a** a (noteworthy or important) happening or occurrence **b** *philosophy* a qualitative or quantitative change or complex of changes located in a restricted portion of time and space **c** a social occasion or activity **2** a contingency, case – esp in *in the event of* ⟨*in the* ∼ *of my death*⟩ and (*chiefly NAm*) *in the event that* ⟨*in the* ∼ *that I die*⟩ **3a** any of the contests in a sporting programme ⟨*long jump is my* ∼⟩ **b** an equestrian contest usu involving DRESSAGE (various manoeuvres by horse and rider), cross-country, and showjumping ⟨*a three-day* ∼⟩ **4** any of the possible outcomes of an experiment ⟨*7 is an* ∼ *in the throwing of two dice*⟩ **5** *archaic* outcome **synonyms** see OCCURRENCE [MF or L; MF, fr L *eventus*, fr *eventus*, pp of *evenire* to happen, fr *e-* + *venire* to come – more at COME] – **eventful** *adj*, **eventfully** *adv*, **eventfulness** *n*, **eventless** *adj* – **in any event, at all events** whatever may happen; ANYWAY **1** ⟨*I'll probably see you next week but* in any event *I'll write*⟩ – **in the event** *Br* when it actually happens or happened ⟨*I was very frightened beforehand but* in the event *I didn't fall*⟩

**²event** *vi, of a horse or rider* to take part in an equestrian event ∼ *vt* to enter (a horse or rider) in an equestrian event – **eventer** *n*

**event horizon** *n, astronomy* the boundary of a BLACK HOLE (region in space from which neither matter nor light can escape)

**eventide** /'eev(ə)n,tied/ *n, poetic* the evening [ME, fr OE *æfentīd*, fr *æfen* evening + *tīd* time]

**eventide home** *n* a home for old people

**eventual** /i'ventyooəl, -chəl, -chooəl/ *adj* **1** taking place at an unspecified later time; ultimately resulting ⟨*they counted on his* ∼ *success*⟩ **2** *archaic* contingent, conditional – **eventually** *adv*

**eventuality** /i,ventyoo'aləti, -choo-/ *n* a possible, esp unwelcome, event or outcome; a possibility

**eventuate** /i'ventyooayt, -choo-/ *vi, formal* to result

**ever** /'evə/ *adv* **1** always – now chiefly in certain phrases and in combination ⟨∼ *yours, John*⟩ ⟨*an ever-growing need*⟩ **2** at any time ⟨*faster than* ∼⟩ – chiefly in negatives and questions ⟨*have you* ∼ *met?*⟩ ⟨*he won't* ∼ *do it*⟩ **3a** – used as an intensive ⟨*looks* ∼ *so angry*⟩ ⟨*as quick as* ∼ *I can*⟩ ⟨∼ *since Monday*⟩ ⟨*why* ∼ *not?*⟩ ⟨*my first* ∼ *anonymous letter* – The Bookseller⟩ **b** *NAm informal* – used to turn questions into exclamations ⟨*is it* ∼ *big!*⟩ [ME, fr OE *æfre*] – **ever so/such** *chiefly Br informal* – used as an intensive ⟨*ever such a nice girl*⟩ ⟨*thanks* ever so⟩

*usage* **1** The intensive **ever** is sometimes combined informally with an interrogative, such as *how* or *where*, to form one word ⟨*whoever can it be?*⟩ but it should remain a separate word in formal writing ⟨*who* ever *can it be?*⟩. **2 Ever so often** (= very often) should not be confused with **every so often** (= at intervals).

**ever and again** *adv, poetic* EVER AND ANON

**ever and anon** *adv, poetic* sometimes

**Everest** /'ev(ə)rist/ *n* the highest point or level, esp of achievement [Mount *Everest* in the Himalayas, the highest mountain in the world]

**¹evergreen** /-,green/ *adj* **1** *of a tree or shrub* having leaves that remain green and functional throughout the year – compare DECIDUOUS **2** always retaining freshness, interest, or popularity; enduring ⟨*the* ∼ *items of the American popular repertoire* – Benny Green⟩

²**evergreen** *n* **1** an evergreen tree or shrub; *also* a conifer **2** something evergreen in freshness, interest, or popularity

**evergreen oak** *n* any of various oaks (eg a holm oak) with foliage that lasts for two years so that the plant is more or less continuously green

¹**everlasting** /-'lahsting/ *adj* **1** lasting or enduring through all time; eternal **2a(1)** continuing long or indefinitely; perpetual **a(2)** *of a plant* retaining its form or colour for a long time when dried **b** tediously persistent; ETERNAL **3** ⟨*your ~ quarrels drive me mad*⟩ **3** lasting or wearing for a long time; durable – **everlastingly** *adv*, **everlastingness** *n*

²**everlasting** *n* **1** *cap* GOD **1** – + *the* **2** eternity ⟨*from ~ to ~*⟩ **3** any of several plants, chiefly of the daisy family, with flowers that can be dried without loss of form or colour

**evermore** /-'maw/ *adv* always, forever

**evert** /i'vuht/ *vt* to turn (eg an organ of the body) outwards or inside out [L *evertere*, fr *e-* + *vertere* to turn – more at WORTH] – **eversible** *adj*, **eversion** *n*

**every** /'evri/ *adj* **1** being each member without exception of a group larger than two ⟨*~ word counts*⟩ ⟨*enjoyed ~ minute*⟩ ⟨*his ~ action*⟩ **2** being each or all possible ⟨*was given ~ chance*⟩ ⟨*have ~ confidence in him*⟩ **3** being once in each ⟨*go ~ third day*⟩ ⟨*change the oil ~ 5,000 miles*⟩ – compare OTHER **1c** [ME *everich, every*, fr OE *æfre ælc*, fr *æfre* ever + *ælc* each] – **every bit** as just as; equally ⟨*he's every bit as lazy as she is*⟩ – **every now and again/then, every so often** at intervals; occasionally

*usage* **1** Since **every** is used with a singular noun, it seems logical that it should be followed by singular verbs and pronouns ⟨*every one of the employees was a union member*⟩ and this singular construction should be preferred for formal writing. The plural construction ⟨*every one of the employees were union members*⟩ is often used today, however, where a plural noun *(employees) is involved, and especially where one wishes to avoid using either he* for both sexes or the awkward *he or she* ⟨*I saw every student before they went away* – SEU S⟩. **2** Writers on usage recommend ⟨*there's a dishwasher in every kitchen*⟩ rather than ⟨*there are dishwashers in every kitchen*⟩. See EVER, EVERYDAY, EVERYONE

**everybody** /-,bodi/ *pron* every person; everyone ⟨*~ decides they're a bit hungry* – SEU S⟩

*usage* Since **everybody** and **everyone** are used with a singular verb, it seems logical that they should be followed by a singular pronoun ⟨*everybody decides he's a bit hungry*⟩ and this plural construction should be preferred for formal writing. The plural pronoun ⟨*everybody decides they're a bit hungry*⟩ is often used today, however, to avoid using either *he* for both sexes or the awkward *he or she*. See ELSE

**everyday** /-,day/ *adj* encountered or used routinely or typically; ordinary ⟨*clothes for ~ wear*⟩ – **everydayness** *n*

*usage* Compare ⟨*clothes for everyday* (= ordinary) *wear*⟩ ⟨*I wear it every day*⟩.

**everyman** /-,man/ *n* the typical or ordinary human being; MAN IN THE STREET [*Everyman*, allegorical character in *The Summoning of Everyman*, 15th-c E morality play]

**everyone** /-,wun/ *pron* everybody

*usage* Compare ⟨*invite everyone* (= everybody) *to the party*⟩ ⟨*eat every one of the biscuits*⟩; see EVERYBODY

**everyplace** /'evri,plays/ *adv, NAm* everywhere

*usage* In informal American English, **everyplace** is used for "everywhere" as an adverb but not as a noun. Compare ⟨*I looked for it everyplace*⟩ ⟨*I looked for it in every place*⟩.

**everything** /-,thing/ *pron* **1a** all that exists **b** all that relates or is necessary to something ⟨*my new car has ~*⟩ **c** all one's possessions ⟨*they lost ~ in the fire*⟩ **2** something of the greatest importance; all that counts ⟨*he meant ~ to her*⟩ ⟨*money is not ~*⟩

¹**everywhere** /'evriweə/ *adv* in, at, or to every place

²**everywhere** *n* **1** every place **2** the whole place ⟨*~ looks so dirty*⟩

**evict** /i'vikt/ *vt* **1a** to recover (property or the title to property) from a person by a legal process **b** to remove (a tenant) from rented accommodation or land by a legal process **2** to force out; expel [ME *evicten*, fr LL *evictus*, pp of *evincere* fr L, to vanquish, win a point – more at EVINCE] – **evictor** *n*, **eviction** *n*

¹**evidence** /'evid(ə)ns/ *n* **1** an outward sign; an indication ⟨*the broken window was ~ that all was not well*⟩ **2** something, esp a fact, that gives proof or reason for believing or agreeing with something; *specif* information used by a court to decide a point at issue or arrive at the truth – **evidential** *adj*, **evidentially**

*adv*, **evidentiary** *adj* – **in evidence 1** to be seen; conspicuous ⟨*the police were very much* in evidence *at the demonstration*⟩ **2** as evidence ⟨*anything you say may be taken down and used* in evidence⟩ – **turn King's/Queen's/(NAm) State's evidence** *of a criminal* to become a witness for the prosecution of one's fellow criminals, esp in order to obtain a lighter sentence for oneself

²**evidence** *vt* to offer evidence of; show *synonyms* see ¹SHOW

**evident** /'evid(ə)nt/ *adj* clear to the vision or understanding [ME, fr MF, fr L *evident-, evidens*, fr *e-* + *vident-, videns*, prp of *vidēre* to see – more at WIT]

*synonyms* **Evident, manifest, patent, distinct, obvious, apparent, palpable, plain,** and **clear** are closely related and often interchangeable. **Evident** may suggest the existence of visible signs pointing to a conclusion about something unseen ⟨*his* evident *pleasure at showing us round*⟩. **Manifest** describes something openly displayed without thought of concealment ⟨*his joy in the prospect of departure ... was more* manifest *than she could bear* – Arnold Bennett⟩. **Patent**, too, describes what is easily perceived, but its implied contrast with "latent" leads to its use with things not invariably evident, such as imperfections ⟨*a* patent *flaw in her argument*⟩. **Obvious**, likewise, is often contrasted with "subtle", though it also stresses facility of perception ⟨*her* obvious *manoeuvres to get a seat on the board*⟩. **Apparent** is very close to **evident**, but additionally suggests a conclusion reached by reasoning from the evidence ⟨*it became* apparent *that they would not reach home before dark*⟩. **Distinct** things are so sharply defined that they are easily perceived by the eyes, ears, or senses, while **palpable** suggests something so obvious one could touch it. **Plain** and **clear** both apply to what is immediately recognizable or unmistakable. **Clear** suggests the absence of confusion and **plain** distinctness or the absence of complexity. *antonyms* obscure, veiled, latent

**evidently** /-li/ *adv* **1** in an evident manner; clearly, obviously ⟨*any style that is ... so ~ bad or second-rate* – T S Eliot⟩ **2** on the basis of available evidence; as seems evident ⟨*~, he was born in Leeds*⟩

¹**evil** /'eevl/ *adj* **-ll-** (*NAm* **-l-, -ll-**) **1a** not good morally; sinful, wicked ⟨*a thoroughly ~ doctrine*⟩ **b** arising from bad character or conduct ⟨*a man of ~ reputation*⟩ **2a** causing discomfort or repulsion; offensive ⟨*an ~ smell*⟩ **b** disagreeable ⟨*an ~ temper*⟩ **3a** pernicious, harmful **b** marked by misfortune; unlucky, disastrous ⟨*an ~ day*⟩ **4** *archaic* inferior *synonyms* see ¹BAD *antonyms* exemplary, salutary [ME, fr OE *yfel*; akin to OHG *ubil* evil] – **evil** *adv, archaic*, **evilly** *adv*, **evilness** *n*

²**evil** *n* **1** something evil; something that brings sorrow, distress, or calamity **2a** the fact of suffering, misfortune, or wrongdoing **b** wickedness, sin

**evildoer** /,eevl'dooh·ə/ *n* one who does evil – **evildoing** *n or adj*

**evil eye** *n* **1** (a spell put on somebody or something by means of) a look believed to be capable of inflicting harm **2** (a person believed to have) the power of casting a spell with an evil eye

**evince** /i'vins/ *vt, formal* to show clearly; reveal *synonyms* see ¹SHOW [L *evincere* to vanquish, win a point, fr *e-* + *vincere* to conquer – more at VICTOR] – **evincible** *adj*

**eviscerate** /i'visərayt/ *vt* **1a** to take out the internal organs of; disembowel **b** to remove an organ from (a patient); *also* to remove the contents of (an organ) **2** *formal* to deprive of vital content or force [L *evisceratus*, pp of *eviscerare*, fr *e-* + *viscera* entrails] – **evisceration** *n*

**evocation** /,evə'kaysh(ə)n/ *n* **1** the act or fact of evoking eg **1a** the summoning of a spirit **b** imaginative, esp artistic, suggestion or portrayal (eg of other times or places) **2** INDUCTION **3e** (process determining the development of cells in an embryo) [L *evocation-, evocatio*, fr *evocatus*, pp of *evocare*]

**evoke** /i'vohk/ *vt* **1** to call forth or up ⟨*her speech ~d a lively response*⟩ **2** CONJURE **1a** ⟨*~ evil spirits*⟩ **3** to cite, esp with approval or for support; invoke **4** to bring to mind or recollection, esp imaginatively or poignantly ⟨*this place ~s memories of happier years*⟩ [Fr *évoquer*, fr L *evocare*, fr *e-* + *vocare* to call – more at VOCATION] – **evocable** *adj*, **evocative, evocatory** *adj*, **evocatively** *adv*, **evocativeness** *n*, **evocator** *n*

**evolute** /'eevəl(y)ooht/ *n, maths* a curve that is made up of the collection of points that are the CENTRES OF CURVATURE (centres of circles that determine the amount of curvature) of some given curve (the INVOLUTE) – compare INVOLUTE [L *evolutus*, pp of *evolvere*]

**evolution** /,eevə'loohsh(ə)n, -'lyooh- ,evə-/ *n* **1a** a process of change and development, esp from a lower or simpler state to a higher or more complex state **b** the action or an instance of forming and giving off something (e g heat or a gas); emission **c** a process of gradual and relatively peaceful social, political, and economic advance **d** something evolved **2** the process of working out or developing **3a** (one of) a set of prescribed movements (e g in a dance) **b** a military exercise following a set plan **4** *maths* an operation in algebra whereby the ROOT (e g the square root) of a number is extracted – compare INVOLUTION 2 **5a** the historical development of a biological group (e g a race or species); phylogeny **b** a theory that the various types of animals and plants have their origin in other preexisting types and that the distinguishable differences are due to NATURAL SELECTION of variations that arise (e g by mutation) in successive generations [L *evolution-, evolutio* unrolling, fr *evolutus*, pp of *evolvere*] – **evolutionarily** *adv*, **evolutionary** *adj*, **evolutionism** *n*, **evolutionist** *n or adj*

**evolve** /i'volv/ *vt* **1** EMIT 1 **2a** to work out, develop ⟨*a definite technique which they* ∼d, *elaborated and codified* – *The Dancer's Heritage*⟩ **b** to produce by natural evolutionary processes – *vi* **1** to develop gradually **2** to undergo evolutionary change [L *evolvere* to unroll, fr *e-* + *volvere* to roll – more at VOLUBLE] – **evolvable** *adj*, **evolvement** *n*

**evulsion** /i'vulsh(ə)n/ *n, medicine* extraction by force [L *evulsion-, evulsio*, fr *evulsus*, pp of *evellere* to pluck out, fr *e-* + *vellere* to pluck – more at VULNERABLE]

**evzone** /'ev,zohn/ *n* a member of an elite Greek infantry unit [NGk *euzōnos*, fr Gk, active, lit., well-girt, fr *eu-* + *zōnē* girdle – more at ZONE]

**ewe** /yooh/ *n* the female of the sheep, esp when mature; *also* the female of various related animals [ME, fr OE *ēowu*]

**Ewe** /'ewe/ *n* a Kwa language of Ghana and Togo

**'ewe-,neck** /yooh/ *n* a thin neck having an insufficient, faulty, or concave arch and occurring as a defect in dogs and horses; *also* a dog or horse with such a neck – **ewe-necked** *adj*

**ewer** /'yooh-ə/ *n* a wide-mouthed pitcher or jug; *esp* one used, esp formerly, to hold water for washing or shaving [ME, fr AF, fr OF *evier*, fr (assumed) VL *aquarium*, fr L, neut of *aquarius* of water, fr *aqua* water – more at ISLAND]

**'ex** /eks, egz/ *prep* **1** out of; from: e g **1a** from a specified place or source **b** from a specified mother ⟨*a promising calf by Eric XVI* ∼ *Heatherbell*⟩ **2** free from; without: e g **2a** *esp* of shares, bonds, *etc* without an indicated value or right ⟨*he bought the shares* ∼ *rights*⟩ **b** free of charges until the time of removal from (a place) ⟨∼ *dock*⟩ [L]

**²ex** *n, informal* a former spouse or girl/boy friend [¹*ex-*]

**¹ex-** /eks-, egz-/ *prefix* **1** out of; outside ⟨*exclude*⟩ ⟨*exodus*⟩ **2** cause to be ⟨*exacerbate*⟩ ⟨*exalt*⟩ **3** not ⟨*exanimate*⟩ **4** deprive of ⟨*expropriate*⟩ ⟨*excommunicate*⟩ **5** former ⟨*ex-president*⟩ ⟨*ex-convict*⟩ – compare ¹LATE 2a [ME, fr OF & L; OF, fr L (also, intensive prefix), fr *ex* out of, from; akin to Gk *ex, exout* of, from, OSlav *iz;* (5) ME, fr LL, fr L]

**²ex-** – see EXO-

**exa-** *comb form* million million million (10¹⁸)

**exacerbate** /eks'asəbayt, igz-/ *vt* to make (something bad) worse; aggravate [L *exacerbatus*, pp of *exacerbare*, fr *ex-* + *acerbus* harsh, bitter, fr *acer* sharp – more at EDGE] – **exacerbation** *n*

**¹exact** /ig'zakt/ *vt* to demand and obtain by force, threats, etc; require ⟨*from them has been* ∼ed *the ultimate sacrifice* – D D Eisenhower⟩ **synonyms** see ²DEMAND [ME *exacten*, fr L *exactus*, pp of *exigere* to drive out, demand, measure, fr *ex-* + *agere* to drive – more at AGENT] – **exactable** *adj*, **exactor** *also* **exacter** *n*

**²exact** *adj* **1** exhibiting or marked by strict, particular, and complete accordance with fact **2** marked by thorough consideration or minute measurement of small factual details ⟨*mathematics is an* ∼ *science*⟩ [L *exactus*, fr pp of *exigere*] – **exactness** *n*

**exact differential** *n* a mathematical expression that is the sum of the products of the PARTIAL DERIVATIVES of a function of several variables and the increment in their respective variables

**exacting** /ig'zakting/ *adj* making rigorous demands; *esp* requiring careful attention and precise accuracy – **exactingly** *adv*, **exactingness** *n*

**exaction** /ig'zaksh(ə)n/ *n* **1a** the act or process of exacting **b** extortion **2** something exacted; *esp* a fee, reward, or contribution demanded or levied with severity or injustice

**exactitude** /ig'zaktityoohd/ *n* the quality or an instance of being exact; exactness

**exactly** /ig'zaktli/ *adv* **1a** in an exact manner; precisely **b** altogether, entirely ⟨*not* ∼ *what I had in mind*⟩ **2** quite so – used to express agreement

**exaggerate** /ig'zajərayt/ *vt* **1** to say or believe more than the truth about ⟨*a friend* ∼s *a man's virtues* – Joseph Addison⟩ **2** to make greater or more pronounced than normal; overemphasize ⟨*he* ∼s *his limp to gain sympathy*⟩ ∼ *vi* to make an overstatement [L *exaggeratus*, pp of *exaggerare* to heap up, fr *ex-* + *agger* heap, fr *aggerere* to carry towards, fr *ad-* + *gerere* to carry – more at CAST] – **exaggeratedly** *adv*, **exaggeratedness** *n*, **exaggerative** *adj*, **exaggerator** *n*, **exaggeratory** *adj*, **exaggeration** *n*

**exalt** /ig'zawlt, ig'zolt/ *vt* **1** to raise high, esp in rank, power, or character **2** to praise highly; glorify **3** to enhance the activity of; intensify ⟨*rousing and* ∼ing *the imagination* – George Eliot⟩ **4** *obs* to elate ∼ *vi* to produce exaltation **9** *exult* [ME *exalten*, fr MF & L; MF *exalter*, fr L *exaltare*, fr *ex-* + *altus* high – more at OLD] – **exaltedly** *adv*, **exalter** *n*

**exaltation** /,egzawl'taysh(ə)n, ,egzol-/ *n* **1** exalting or being exalted **2** an excessively intensified sense of well-being, power, or importance

**exam** /ig'zam, ik'sam/ *n* EXAMINATION 2

**examen** /ig'zahmen/ *n* an examination of the conscience [L, tongue of a balance, examination, fr *exigere* – more at EXACT]

**examinable** /ig'zaminəbl/ *adj* being a subject in respect of which a student's progress can be assessed by examination

**examinant** /ig'zaminənt/ *n* **1** one who examines; an examiner **2** *archaic* one (e g a witness or a candidate for ordination) who is examined

**examination** /ig,zami'naysh(ə)n/ *n* **1** examining or being examined ⟨*a medical* ∼⟩ **2** an exercise designed to assess progress or test qualification or knowledge; *specif* a set of printed or oral questions on one subject **3** a formal interrogation (in a law court) – **examinational** *adj*

**exami,nation-in-'chief** *n* an examination of a witness in court by the party (e g prosecution or defence) calling him/her to give evidence

**examination paper** *n* **1** a paper on which a set of examination questions is printed **2** a candidate's written answers to an examination

**examinatorial** /ig,zaminə'tawri-əl/ *adj* of an examiner or examination

**examine** /ig'zamin/ *vt* **1a** to inspect closely **b** to test the condition of **c** to inquire into carefully; investigate ⟨∼ *the evidence*⟩ **2a** to interrogate closely ⟨∼ *a prisoner*⟩ **b** to test by questioning in order to determine progress, fitness, or knowledge [ME *examinen*, fr MF *examiner*, fr L *examinare*, fr *examin-, examen*] – **examiner** *n*

**examinee** /ig,zami'nee/ *n* a person who is examined

**¹example** /ig'zahmpl/ *n* **1** a particular single item, fact, incident, or aspect that is representative of all of a group or type to which it belongs **2** one who or that which may be copied by other people ⟨*a good or bad* ∼⟩ ⟨*set an* ∼⟩ **3** a parallel or closely similar case, esp when serving as a precedent or model ⟨*such temperate order in so fierce a cause doth want* ∼ – Shak⟩ **4** a punishment inflicted on someone as a warning to others; *also* an individual so punished ⟨*make an* ∼ *of them*⟩ **5** an instance (e g a mathematical problem to be solved) serving to illustrate a rule or to act as an exercise in the application of a rule [ME, fr MF, fr L *exemplum*, fr *eximere* to take out, fr *ex-* + *emere* to take – more at REDEEM] – **for example** as an example ⟨*there are many sources of air pollution; exhaust fumes,* for example⟩

**synonyms** Example, sample, and specimen can all mean an "item showing the quality of a group". **Example** is the most general word ⟨*an* **example** *of her handwriting*⟩. **Sample** is used particularly in commerce ⟨**samples** *of furnishing fabrics*⟩, and **specimen** in science and medicine ⟨*a urine* **specimen**⟩. See ¹INSTANCE

**²example** *vt* **1** to serve or use as an example of **2** *archaic* to be or set an example to

**exanimate** /ig'zanimət, -mayt/ *adj* LIFELESS a,d [L *exanimatus*, pp of *exanimare* to deprive of life or spirit, fr *ex-* + *anima* breath, soul – more at ANIMATE]

**exanthema** /,egzan'theemə, ,eks-/ *n, pl* **exanthemata** /-'theemətə/, **exanthemas** a disease (e g measles) that is accompanied by a skin rash; *also* its characteristic skin rash [NL, fr LL, skin rash, fr Gk *exanthēma*, fr *exanthein* to bloom, erupt fr *ex-* + *anthos* flower]

**exarate** /'eksərayt/ *adj, of a pupa* having the wings, legs, etc free and capable of movement – compare OBTECT [L *exaratus*, pp of *exarare* to plough up, fr *ex-* + *arare* to plough]

**¹exarch** /'ek,sahk/ *n* **1** a viceroy in the Byzantine empire **2** a bishop in the E Orthodox Church ranking below a PATRIARCH (head of the Church) and above a METROPOLITAN (bishop of a province); *specif* the head of a national Church (eg in Bulgaria) that is independent of patriarchal authority [LL *exarchus*, fr LGk *exarchos*, fr Gk, leader, fr *exarchein* to begin, take the lead, fr *ex-* + *archein* to rule, begin – more at ARCH-] – **exarchal** *adj*, **exarchate** *n*, **exarchy** *n*

**²exarch** *adj*, *botany* formed or taking place from the outer region towards the centre; *specif* having the first-formed and oldest XYLEM (water-conducting tissue in plants) external to that formed later and furthest from the centre (eg in a root) – compare ENDARCH [*exo-* + *-arch*]

**exasperate** /ig'zahspə,rayt, ig'zas-/ *vt* **1a** to excite or inflame the anger of; enrage **b** to cause irritation or annoyance to **2** *obs* to make (more) grievous or more malicious *synonyms* see IRRITATE [L *exasperatus*, pp of *exasperare*, fr *ex-* + *asper* rough] – **exasperatedly** *adv*, **exasperatingly** *adv*, **exasperation** *n*

**excardination** /eks,kahdi'naysh(ə)n/ *n* the transfer of a clergyman from one diocese to another [¹*ex-* + *-cardination* (as in *incardination*)]

**ex cathedra** /,eks kə'theedrə/ *adv or adj* by virtue of or in the exercise of one's official authority ⟨~ *pronouncements*⟩ [NL, lit., from the chair]

**excavate** /'ekskəvayt/ *vt* **1** to form a cavity or hole in **2** to form by hollowing **3** to dig out and remove **4** to expose to view by digging away a covering ~ *vi* to make excavations [L *excavatus*, pp of *excavare*, fr *ex-* + *cavare* to make hollow, fr *cavus* hollow – more at CAVE]

**excavation** /,ekskə'vaysh(ə)n/ *n* **1** the action or process of excavating **2** a hole formed by cutting, digging, or scooping – **excavational** *adj*

**excavator** /'ekskə,vaytə/ *n* one who or that which excavates; *esp* a power-operated excavating machine

**exceed** /ik'seed/ *vt* **1** to extend beyond ⟨*the new road will* ~ *this point*⟩ **2** to be greater than or superior to **3** to act beyond the limits of ⟨~ *the speed limit*⟩ ~ *vi* **1** to predominate **2** *obs* to go to extremes [ME *exceden*, fr MF *exceder*, fr L *excedere*, fr *ex-* + *cedere* to go – more at CEDE]

**exceeding** /ik'seeding/ *adj*, *archaic* exceptional in amount, quality, or degree ⟨*the* ~ *darkness surrounding our existence*⟩ – **exceeding** *adv*

**exceedingly** /ik'seedingli/ *adv* EXTREMELY **2** *usage* see EXCESSIVE

**excel** /ik'sel/ *vb* **-ll-** to be superior (to); surpass (others) in accomplishment or achievement – often + *at* or *in* ⟨~ *in mathematics*⟩ [ME *excellen*, fr L *excellere*, fr *ex-* + *-cellere* to rise, project; akin to L *collis* hill – more at HILL]

**excellence** /'eks(ə)ləns/ *n* **1** the quality of being excellent **2** an excellent or valuable quality; a virtue **3** EXCELLENCY **2**

**excellency** /'eksələnsi/ *n* **1** **excellencies** *pl*, **excellency** excellence; *esp* an outstanding or valuable quality ⟨*so crammed, as he thinks, with* excellencies – Shak⟩ **2** – used as a title for certain high dignitaries of state (eg a governor or ambassador) and church (eg a Roman Catholic archbishop or bishop)

**excellent** /'eksəl(ə)nt/ *adj* **1** very good of its kind; outstandingly good **2** *archaic* SUPERIOR 2,4 [ME, fr MF, fr L *excellent-, excellens*, fr prp of *excellere*] – **excellently** *adv*

**excelsior** /ik'selsi·aw/ *n*, *chiefly NAm* fine curled wood shavings used esp for packing fragile items [trade name, fr L, higher, compar of *excelsus* high, fr pp of *excellere*]

**¹except** /ik'sept/ *vt* to take or leave out from a number or a whole; exclude ~ *vi*, *chiefly law* to take exception; object – usu + *to* or *against* △ accept *synonyms* see EXCEPTING [ME *excepten*, fr MF *excepter*, fr L *exceptare*, fr *exceptus*, pp of *excipere* to take out, fr *ex-* + *capere* to take – more at HEAVE]

**²except** *prep* with the exclusion or exception of ⟨*daily* ~ *Sundays*⟩ ⟨*can do everything* ~ *cook*⟩ – **except for 1** with the exception of; except ⟨*all here except for Mary*⟩ **2** but for; were it not for ⟨*couldn't have done it except for your help*⟩

**³except** *conj* **1** only, but ⟨*would go* ~ *it's too far*⟩ ⟨*would have protested* ~ *that he was afraid*⟩ **2** *archaic or dial* unless ⟨~ *you repent*⟩

**excepting** /ik'septing/ *prep or conj* except

*synonyms* The prepositions **excepting** and **except** are not synonymous in modern English. **Excepting** is used after *always*, *not*, or *without* and before a noun. Compare ⟨*they were all saved* **except** *the captain*⟩ ⟨*they were all saved*, *not* **excepting** *the captain*⟩; while **excepted**, from the verb **except**, is used similarly but after a noun ⟨*they were all saved*, *the captain not* **excepted**⟩.

**exception** /ik'sepsh(ə)n/ *n* **1** the act of excepting; exclusion **2** one who or that which is excepted; *esp* a case to which a rule does not apply **3** question, objection ⟨*witnesses whose authority is beyond* ~ – T B Macaulay⟩ – **take exception (to)** to object (to) ⟨*took exception to his critic's remarks*⟩

**exceptionable** /-əbl/ *adj* likely to cause objection; objectionable – **exceptionably** *adv*, **exceptionability** *n*

**exceptional** /ik'sepsh(ə)nl/ *adj* **1** forming an exception; unusual ⟨*an* ~ *number of rainy days*⟩ **2** not average; *esp* superior ⟨*a student of* ~ *ability*⟩ – **exceptionally** *adv*, **exceptionality** *n*

**exceptive** /ik'septiv/ *adj* **1** *of a word or phrase* expressing exception ⟨*excluding*, *apart from*, *and not counting are* ~⟩ **2** *archaic* apt to find fault or raise objections

**¹excerpt** /ek'suhpt/ *vt* **1** to select (a passage) for quoting, copying, or performing **2** to take excerpts from (eg a book) [L *excerptus*, pp of *excerpere*, fr *ex-* + *carpere* to gather, pluck – more at HARVEST] – **excerpter** *also* **excerptor** *n*, **excerption** *n*,

**²excerpt** /'ek,suhpt/ *n* a passage (eg from a book or musical composition) selected, performed, or copied

**¹excess** /ik'ses/ *n* **1a** the state or an instance of exceeding usual, proper, or specified limits **b** the amount or degree by which one thing or quantity exceeds another **2** **excesses** *pl*, **excess** undue or immoderate indulgence; intemperance **3** an amount an insured person agrees to pay him-/herself out of each claim made on an insurance policy in return for a lower premium △ access [ME, fr MF or LL; MF *exces*, fr LL *excessus*, fr L, departure, projection, fr *excessus*, pp of *excedere* to exceed] – **in excess of** more than; over

**²excess** /'ekses, ik'ses/ *adj* more than the usual, proper, or specified amount; extra ⟨*charges for* ~ *baggage*⟩

**excessive** /ik'sesiv, ək-/ *adj* exceeding the usual, proper, or normal – **excessively** *adv*, **excessiveness** *n*

*usage* In modern English, **excessively** means "too much" and **exceedingly** means "very much", so one should say ⟨*I am* **exceedingly** (not △ **excessively**) *grateful*⟩.

**¹exchange** /iks'chaynj/ *n* **1** the act of exchanging one thing for another; a transaction ⟨*an* ~ *of prisoners*⟩ **2** a usu brief interchange of words or blows ⟨*had a short sharp* ~ *with the manager*⟩ **3** something offered, given, or received in an exchange ⟨*the book was a fair* ~ *for the record*⟩ **4** a reciprocal visit between school or college students of two countries, usu for the purpose of studying the language of the host country **5a** the system of settling debts payable currently, esp in a foreign country, usu by BILLS OF EXCHANGE rather than money **b(1)** change or conversion of one currency into another **b(2) exchange rate, exchange** the price at which one currency may be exchanged for another **b(3)** the difference in value between two currencies or between values of a particular currency at two places **c** documents (eg cheques, drafts, or BILLS OF EXCHANGE) presented by banks in a central institution (CLEARINGHOUSE) for settlement **6** a place where things or services are exchanged: eg **6a** an organized market for trading in shares or commodities **b** a centre or device controlling the connection of telephone calls between many different lines [ME *exchaunge*, fr MF *eschange*, fr *eschangier* to exchange, fr (assumed) VL *excambiare*, fr L *ex-* + *cambiare* to exchange – more at CHANGE]

**²exchange** *vt* **1a** to part with, give, or transfer in return for something received as an equivalent ⟨*where can I* ~ *my dollars for pounds?*⟩ ⟨*John* ~*d books with Peter*⟩ **b** *of two parties* to give and receive (things of the same type) ⟨*they* ~*d blows*⟩ ⟨*the two armies* ~*d prisoners*⟩ **2** to replace by other goods ⟨*will they* ~ *clothes that don't fit?*⟩ **3** to part with for a substitute ⟨*exchanging freedom for security*⟩ ~ *vi* **1** to pass or become received in exchange **2** to engage in an exchange – **exchangeable** *adj*, **exchangeability** *n*, **exchanger** *n*

**exchequer** /iks'chekə/ *n* **1** *cap* a department or office of state in medieval England charged with the collection and management of the royal revenue **2** *cap* a former civil court having jurisdiction in England and Wales primarily over revenue matters and now merged with the QUEEN'S BENCH DIVISION of the HIGH COURT **3** *often cap* the department of state in charge of the national revenue **4** the (national or royal) treasury **5** *humorous* money, funds [ME *escheker*, fr AF, fr OF *eschequier* chessboard, counting table, fr *eschec* check – more at CHECK]

**excide** /ik'sied/ *vt* ³EXCISE [L *excidere*]

**excipient** /ik'sipiant/ *n* an inert substance (eg gum or starch) that provides a medium in which a medicinally active substance (eg a drug) can be administered [L *excipient-, excipiens*, prp of *excipere* to take out, take up – more at EXCEPT]

**exciple** /'eksipl/ *n* a saucer-shaped rim round the spore-bearing layer of various lichens [NL *excipulum*, fr L, receptacle, fr *excipere*]

**excisable** /ik'siezəbl/ *adj* subject to excise

¹**excise** /'ek,siez, ,-'-/ *n* **1** an internal tax levied on the manufacture, sale, or consumption of a commodity within a country **2** any of various taxes on privileges that must be bought, often levied in the form of a licence **3** a former government department in Britain for collecting excise **synonyms** see ²TAX [obs D *excijs* (now *accijus*), fr MD, prob modif of OF *assise* session, assessment – more at ASSIZE]

²**excise** /ek'siez/ *vt* to impose an excise on

³**excise** *vt* to remove (as if) by cutting out [L *excisus*, pp of *excidere*, fr *ex-* + *caedere* to cut – more at CONCISE] – **excision** *n*

**exciseman** /'eksiez,mən/ *n* an officer who inspects and rates articles liable to excise

**excitable** /ik'sietəbl/ *adj* **1** capable of being readily activated or roused into a state of excitement; easily excited **2** *of a nerve, tissue, etc* capable of being activated by and reacting to stimuli; *esp* responding rapidly to stimuli – **excitableness, excitability** *n*

**excitant** /ik'sietənt/ *adj* tending to excite or stimulate ⟨~ *drugs*⟩ – **excitant** *n*

**excitative** /ik'sietətiv/ *adj* tending or able to excite

**excitatory** /ik'sietət(ə)ri/ *adj* **1** excitative **2** exhibiting or marked by excitement or excitation

**excite** /ik'siet/ *vt* **1a** to provoke or stir up (action) ⟨~ *a rebellion*⟩ **b** to rouse to strong, esp pleasurable, feeling ⟨~d *by her caresses*⟩ **c** to arouse (eg an emotional response) ⟨*the plight of the refugees* ~d *their pity*⟩ ⟨*her late arrival* ~d *much curiosity*⟩ **2a** to activate, esp by passing an electric current through; energize ⟨~ *an electromagnet*⟩ **b** to produce a magnetic field or electric current in; *also* to induce (eg a magnetic field or the flow of an electric current) **3** to increase the activity of or produce a response in (an organ, tissue, etc); stimulate **4a** to raise (eg an electron, atom, or molecule) to a higher ENERGY LEVEL **b** to excite the particles (eg atoms) in (a substance) so that the characteristic SPECTRUM (pattern of electromagnetic radiation of different wavelengths) is emitted; *also* to cause the emission of (a spectrum) thus [ME *exciten*, fr MF *exciter*, fr L *excitare*, fr *ex-* + *citare* to rouse – more at CITE] – **excitedly** *adv*, **excitement** *n*, **excitation** *n*

> **synonyms** Although **excitement** and **excitation** are both formed from **excite**, **excitation** is the usual word in scientific contexts. Compare ⟨*the* **excitation** *of atoms by electron impact*⟩ ⟨*opened their Christmas presents with shrieks of* **excitement**⟩.

**exciter** /ik'sietə/ *n* **1** a generator or battery that supplies the electric current used to produce the MAGNETIC FIELD in another generator or a motor **2** an electrical device (OSCILLATOR) that generates a CARRIER WAVE (eg for a radio transmitter) [*excite* + ²*-er*]

**exciting** /ik'sieting/ *adj* producing excitement – **excitingly** *adv*

**exciton** /'eksi,ton/ *n* a mobile combination of an excited electron bound to the HOLE caused by the absence of the electron in a crystal (eg of silicon or another semiconductor) [ISV *excit-ation* + *-on*] – **excitonic** *adj*

**excitor** *n* something that excites or induces activity; *specif* a nerve that produces increased activity of the organ or part it supplies

**exclaim** /ik'sklaym/ *vi* **1** to cry out or speak in strong or sudden emotion ⟨~ed *in delight*⟩ **2** to speak loudly or vehemently, esp in opposition – *usu* + *against* ⟨~ed *against immorality*⟩ ~ *vt* to utter sharply, passionately, or vehemently; proclaim [MF *exclamer*, fr L *exclamare*, fr *ex-* + *clamare* to cry out – more at CLAIM] – **exclaimer** *n*

**exclamation** /,eksklə'maysh(ə)n/ *n* **1** the act of exclaiming or the words exclaimed **2** a vehement expression of protest or complaint – **exclamatory** *adj*

**exclamation mark** *n* a punctuation mark ! used esp after an exclamation, assertion, or command to indicate forceful utterance, strong feeling, or irony

**exclamation point** *n, chiefly NAm* EXCLAMATION MARK

**exclave** /'eks,klayv/ *n* a portion of a country separated from the main part and surrounded by foreign territory [¹*ex-* + *-clave* (as in *enclave*)]

**enclosure** /iks'klohzhə/ *n* an area from which intruders (eg wild animals) are excluded, esp by fencing [¹*ex-* + *-closure* (as in *enclosure*)]

**exclude** /ik'skloohd/ *vt* **1a** to shut out **b** to bar from partici-

pation, consideration, or inclusion **2** to expel, esp from a place or position previously occupied [ME *excluden*, fr L *excludere*, fr *ex-* + *claudere* to close – more at CLOSE] – **excludable** *adj*, **excluder** *n*, **exclusion** *n*, **exclusionary** *adj*

**exclusionist** /iks'kloohzh(ə)nist/ *n* one who would exclude another from some right or privilege – **exclusionist** *adj*

**exclusion principle** /iks'kloohzh(ə)n/, **Pauli exclusion principle** *n* a principle in physics: no two electrons in any system (eg an atom or molecule) will be exactly equivalent in terms of their QUANTUM states

¹**exclusive** /ik'skloohsiv, -ziv/ *adj* **1a** excluding or having power to exclude **b** limiting or limited to possession, control, use, publication, etc by a single individual, group, or organization ⟨*an* ~ *contract*⟩ ⟨*an* ~ *interview*⟩ **2a** excluding others, esp those held to be inferior, from participation, membership, or entry ⟨*an* ~ *club*⟩ **b** snobbishly aloof **3** stylish and expensive **4a** SOLE 3,4 ⟨~ *jurisdiction*⟩ **b** whole, undivided ⟨*his* ~ *attention*⟩ **5** not inclusive ⟨*Monday to Friday* ~⟩ [MF *exclusif*, fr ML *exclusivus*, fr L *exclusus*, pp of *excludere*] – **exclusivley** *adv*, **exclusiveness, exclusivity** *n*

²**exclusive** *n* something exclusive: eg **a** a newspaper story released to or printed by only one newspaper **b** an exclusive right (eg to sell a particular product in a certain area)

**exclusive disjunction** *n* a compound statement in philosophy that is true when at least one but not both of its constituent statements is true

**excogitate** /eks'kojitayt/ *vt, formal* to think out; devise [L *excogitatus*, pp of *excogitare*, fr *ex-* + *cogitare* to think – more at COGITATE] – **excogitation** *n*, **excogitative** *adj*

¹**excommunicate** /,eksə'myoohni,kayt/ *vt* **1** to deprive officially of the rights of church membership **2** to exclude from fellowship in a group or community [ME *excommunicaten*, fr LL *excommunicatus*, pp of *excommunicare*, fr L *ex-* + LL *communicare* to communicate] – **excommunicator** *n*

²**excommunicate** /,eksə'myoohnikət, -,kayt/ *adj* excluded from the rites of the church; excommunicated – **excommunicate** *n*

**excommunication** /,eksə,myoohni'kaysh(ə)n/ *n* an ecclesiastical condemnation and judgment depriving a person of the rights of church membership – **excommunicative** *adj*

**excoriate** /ik'skawriayt/ *vt* **1** to wear off the skin of; abrade **2** *formal* to criticize severely and scathingly [ME *excoriaten*, fr LL *excoriatus*, pp of *excoriare*, fr L *ex-* + *corium* skin, hide – more at CUIRASS] – **excoriation** *n*

**excrement** /'ekskrəmənt/ *n* waste matter discharged from the body; *specif* faeces [L *excrementum*, fr *excernere*] – **excremental** *adj*, **excrementitious** *adj*

**excrescence** /ik'skres(ə)ns/, **excrescency** /-si/ *n* an esp excessive or abnormal outgrowth or enlargement

**excrescent** /ik'skres(ə)nt/ *adj* **1** forming an abnormal, excessive, or useless outgrowth **2** *linguistics* of or constituting the insertion of a sound or letter in a word [L *excrescent-, excrescens*, prp of *excrescere* to grow out, fr *ex-* + *crescere* to grow – more at CRESCENT] – **excrescently** *adv*

**excreta** /ik'skreetə/ *n* waste matter eliminated from an organism; EXCRETION 2; *esp* faeces [NL, fr L, neut pl of *excretus*] – **excretal** *adj*

**excrete** /ik'skreet/ *vt* to separate and eliminate or discharge (unwanted or harmful waste matter) from the body, cell, or tissue [L *excretus*, pp of *excernere* to sift out, discharge, fr *ex-* + *cernere* to sift – more at CERTAIN] – **excreter** *n*

**excretion** /iks'kreesh(ə)n/ *n* **1** the act or process of excreting **2** something excreted; *esp* useless, superfluous, or harmful material (eg the breakdown products of proteins) that is eliminated from the body and that differs from a SECRETION in not being produced to perform a useful function

**excretory** /iks'kreetəri/ *adj* of or functioning in excretion ⟨~ *ducts*⟩

**excruciating** /ik'skroohshi,ayting/ *adj* **1** causing great pain or anguish; agonizing, tormenting ⟨*an* ~ *migraine*⟩ **2** very intense; extreme ⟨~ *pain*⟩ **3** *humorous* of extremely poor quality; inferior ⟨*an* ~ *pun*⟩ [fr prp of *excruciate*, vb, fr L *excruciatus*, pp of *excruciare* to torture, fr *ex-* + *cruciare* to torture, crucify, fr *cruc-, crux* cross] – **excruciate** *vt*, **excruciatingly** *adv*, **excruciation** *n*

**exculpate** /'ekskul,payt, ik'skul,payt/ *vt* to clear from alleged fault, blame, or guilt [(assumed) ML *exculpatus*, pp of *exculpare*, fr L *ex* + *culpa* blame] – **exculpation** *n*, **exculpatony** *adj*

**excurrent** /,eks'kurənt/ *adj* running or flowing out: eg **a** *of a* *leaf* having the main central vein projecting beyond the tip **b** *botany* having the stem prolonged to form an undivided main stem or trunk (e g in conifers) **c** *of an anatomical duct, channel, etc* carrying an outwardly flowing current of liquid (e g water) ⟨~ *canals of a sponge*⟩ – compare INCURRENT [L *excurrent-, excurrens,* prp of *excurrere* to run out, extend, fr *ex-* + *currere* to run – more at CAR]

**excursion** /ik'skuhsh(ə)n/ *n* **1 a** (brief) pleasure trip, usu at reduced rates **2** a deviation from a direct, definite, or proper course; *esp* a digression ⟨*needless* ~s *into abstruse theory*⟩ **3** an exploration of a subject or area ⟨*an* ~ *into medieval history*⟩ **4a** a movement outwards and back or from a central position, point, or axis; *also* the distance moved or travelled ⟨*the* ~ *of a piston*⟩ **b** (the extent of) one complete movement of expansion and contraction of the lungs and their membranes in an act of breathing in and out [L *excursion-, excursio,* fr *excursus,* pp of *excurrere*]

**ex·cursion ticket** *n* a return ticket for off-peak travel at a reduced rate

**excursive** /ik'skuhsiv/ *adj* digressive – **excursively** *adv,* **excursiveness** *n*

**excursus** /ek'skuhsəs/ *n, pl* **excursuses** /-seez/ *also* **excursus** an appendix or digression that contains further discussion of some point or topic [L, digression, fr *excursus,* pp]

**excusatory** /iks'kyoohzətri/ *adj* making or containing an excuse

[1]**excuse** /ik'skyoohz/ *vt* **1a** to make apology for ⟨*quietly* ~d *his clumsiness*⟩ **b** to try to remove blame from ⟨~d *himself for being so careless*⟩ **2** to forgive entirely or overlook as unimportant ⟨*she graciously* ~d *his thoughtlessness*⟩ **3** to allow to leave; dismiss ⟨*the class was* ~d⟩ **4** to be an acceptable reason for; justify – usu neg ⟨*nothing can* ~ *his cruelty*⟩ **5** *Br* to free from (a duty) ⟨*the class was* ~d *homework*⟩ [ME *excusen,* fr OF *excuser,* fr L *excusare,* fr *ex-* + *causa* cause, explanation] – **excusable** *adj,* **excusably** *adv,* **excuser** *n* – **be excused** *euph* to go out to the toilet – **excuse me** – used to attract somebody's attention, to apologize for an interruption or mistake, or to ask to be allowed to pass

[2]**excuse** /ik'skyoohs/ *n* **1** the act of excusing **2a** something offered as grounds for being excused ⟨*he had a good* ~ *for being late*⟩ **b** *pl* an expression of regret for failure to do something or esp for one's absence ⟨*make my* ~s *at the party tomorrow*⟩ **3** justification, reason ⟨*such beauty needs no* ~⟩

**synonyms Apology, excuse,** and **plea** all seek to turn away anger or avoid punishment for admitted wrongdoing. An **apology** expresses regret for what is usually a minor offence ⟨*offered an apology for his lateness*⟩ while a **plea** seeks to enlist sympathy and elicit mercy by claiming mitigating circumstances ⟨*her only plea was that she did it for the sake of her husband*⟩. An **excuse** gives reasons, while a **pretext** is an excuse given as a cover for some other, unacknowledged activity ⟨*he left the room with the excuse that he had some work to do. But this was just a pretext; he simply wanted to be alone*⟩. In modern English, an **alibi** may mean a plausible excuse.

**ex-di·rectory** *adj, Br* intentionally not listed in a TELEPHONE DIRECTORY; unlisted [L *ex* out of – more at EX-]

**exeat** /'eksi,at/ *n* a formal leave of absence granted esp to a student [L, let him go out, fr *exire* to go out]

**execrable** /'eksikrəbl/ *adj, formal* deserving to be execrated; detestable, appalling ⟨~ *behaviour*⟩ ⟨~ *taste*⟩ – **execrably** *adv*

**execrate** /'eksi,krayt/ *vt, formal* **1** to declare to be evil or detestable; denounce **2** to detest utterly; abhor [L *exsecratus,* pp of *exsecrari* to put under a curse, fr *ex-* + *sacr-, sacer* sacred] – **execrative** *adj,* **execrator** *n,* **execration** *n*

**executant** /ig'zekyoot(ə)nt/ *n, formal* one who executes or performs; a performer, esp of musical pieces

**execute** /'eksi,kyooht/ *vt* **1** to carry out fully; put completely into effect ⟨*your orders have been* ~d⟩ **2** to do what is provided or required by ⟨~ *a decree*⟩ **3** to put to death, esp as a punishment, in compliance with a legal sentence **4** to make or produce (e g a work of art), esp by carrying out a design **5** to (do what is required to) make valid ⟨~ *a deed*⟩ **6** to play, perform ⟨~ *a piece of music*⟩ **synonyms** see [1]KILL, PERFORM [ME *executen,* fr MF *executer,* back-formation fr *execution*] – **executable** *adj*

**execution** /,eksi'kyoohsh(ə)n/ *n* **1** the act or process of executing **2** an act of putting to death, esp as a legal punishment **3** a judicial writ directing the enforcement of a judgment **4** the

act, mode, or result of performance ⟨*the* ~ *was perfect but the piece lacked expression*⟩ **5** *archaic* effective or destructive action ⟨*his brandished steel, which smoked with bloody* ~ – Shak⟩ – usu + *do* ⟨*as soon as day came, we went out to see what* ~ *we had done* – Daniel Defoe⟩ [ME, fr MF, fr L *exsecution-, exsecutio,* fr *exsecutus,* pp of *exsequi* to execute, fr *ex-* + *sequi* to follow – more at SUE]

**executioner** /,eksi'kyoohshənə/ *n* one who puts to death; *specif* one legally appointed to inflict capital punishment **9** executor

[1]**executive** /ig'zekyootiv/ *adj* **1** concerned with making and carrying out laws, decisions, etc; *specif, Br* of or concerned with the detailed application of policy or law rather than to its formulation – compare JUDICIAL, LEGISLATIVE **2** of or for the use of an executive ⟨*the* ~ *offices are on the top floor*⟩ ⟨*an* ~ *jet*⟩

[2]**executive** *n* **1** the executive branch of a government, esp the US government **2** an individual or group that controls or directs an organization **3** one who holds a position of administrative or managerial responsibility

**executive officer** *n* the officer who is second in command of a military or naval unit

**executive order** *n* an order, enforceable by law, that is issued by the executive of a government

**executive secretary** *n* a secretary having administrative duties

**executive session** *n* a usu closed session (e g of a legislative body) that functions as an executive council (e g of the US Senate when considering appointments or the confirmation of treaties)

**executor** /ig'zekyootə/, *fem* **executrix** /-,triks/ *n, pl* **executors,** *fem* **executrices, executrixes** one appointed to carry out the provisions of a will **9** executioner [ME, fr OF, fr L *exsecutor,* fr *exsecutus*] – **executorial** *adj*

**executory** /ig'zekyoot(ə)ri/ *adj* **1** administrative **2** remaining to be carried out ⟨*an agreement to sell is an* ~ *contract*⟩

**exedra** /'eksidrə, ek'sedrə/ *n, pl* **exedrae** /-ri/ **1** a room in an ancient Greek or Roman building formed by an open or columned recess that is often semicircular in shape and has seats **2** a large outdoor nearly semicircular seat with a solid back [L, fr Gk, fr *ex-* + *hedra* seat – more at SIT]

**exegesis** /,eksi'jeesis/ *n, pl* **exegeses** /-seez/ an explanation or critical interpretation of an esp biblical text; *broadly* an exposition [NL, fr Gk *exēgēsis,* fr *exēgeisthai* to explain, interpret, fr *ex-* + *hēgeisthai* to lead – more at SEEK]

**exegete** /'eksi,jeet/ *n* one who practises exegesis [Gk *exēgētēs,* fr *exēgeisthai*]

**exegetic** /,eksi'jetik/, **exegetical** /-kl/ *adj* of exegesis; explanatory

**exegetist** /,eksi'jeetist/ *n* an exegete

**exemplar** /ig'zemplə, -,plah/ *n* something that serves as a model or example: e g **a** a typical or ideal example **b** a copy of a book or writing **c** *philosophy* an incomprehensible entity that is the original pattern of which existing things are imperfect representations [ME, fr L *exemplum* example]

**exemplary** /ig'zempləri/ *adj* **1** deserving imitation; commendable ⟨*his conduct was* ~⟩ **2** serving as a warning ⟨~ *punishments*⟩ **3** serving as an exemplar, example, instance, or illustration – **exemplarily** *adv,* **exemplariness** *n,* **exemplarity** *n*

**exemplify** /ig'zemplifie/ *vt* **1** to show or illustrate by example **2** to be an instance of or serve as an example of; typify, embody [ME *exemplifien,* fr MF *exemplifier,* fr ML *exemplificare,* fr L *exemplum*] – **exemplification** *n*

**exemplum** /ig'zempləm/ *n, pl* **exempla** /-plə/ *chiefly informal* **1** an example, model **2** an anecdote or short story that illustrates a moral point or supports an argument [L]

[1]**exempt** /ig'zempt/ *adj* **1** freed from some liability or requirement to which others are subject ⟨*was* ~ *from jury service*⟩ **2** *obs* set apart; excluded [ME, fr L *exemptus,* pp of *eximere* to take out – more at EXAMPLE]

[2]**exempt** *n* one exempted, esp from duty

[3]**exempt** *vt* **1** to make exempt; excuse **2** *obs* to set apart; exclude

**exemption** /ig'zempsh(ə)n/ *n* one who or that which exempts or is exempted; *esp* a source or amount of income exempted from taxation

**exenterate** /eks'entərayt/ *vt, medicine* to remove the contents of (a body cavity) [L *exenteratus,* pp of *exenterare* to disembowel, modif of Gk *exenterizein,* fr *ex-* + *enteron* intestine – more at INTER-] – **exenteration** *n*

**exequies** /'eksikwiz/ *n pl,* **exequy** *n, formal* funeral ceremony

[ME *exequies*, fr MF, fr L *exequine*, fr *exequi*, *exsequi* to follow, perform]

¹**exercise** /'eksə,siez/ *n* **1** the use of a specified power or right ⟨*the ~ of his authority*⟩ **2a** regular or repeated use of a part of the body, the senses, or the powers of the mind (e g reason and memory) **b** physical exertion for the sake of developing and maintaining body fitness **3** something performed or practised in order to develop, improve, or display a specific power or skill ⟨*arithmetic ~s*⟩ **4** a book, play, speech, etc having a strongly marked secondary or ulterior aspect ⟨*a biography that is in truth an ~ in character assassination*⟩ **5** a manoeuvre, operation, or drill carried out for training and discipline, esp of military units [ME, fr MF *exercice*, fr L *exercitium*, fr *exercitus*, pp of *exercēre* to drive on, keep busy, fr *ex-* + *arcēre* to enclose, hold off – more at ARK]

²**exercise** *vt* **1a** to make effective in action; use ⟨*didn't ~ good judgment*⟩ **b** to bring to bear; exert ⟨*~ influence*⟩ **2a** to use repeatedly in order to strengthen or develop **b** to train (e g troops) by drills and manoeuvres **c** to give exercise to ⟨*~ the horses*⟩ **3a** to engage the attention and effort of ⟨*the problem greatly ~*d *his mind*⟩ **b** to cause anxiety, alarm, or indignation in ⟨*citizens ~*d *about pollution*⟩ *~ vi* to take exercise; *esp* to train △ exorcise – **exercisable** *adj*, **exerciser** *n*

**exercise book** *n* a booklet of blank pages used esp for written work in schools

**exergonic** /,eksuh'gonik/ *adj* liberating energy ⟨*an ~ biochemical reaction*⟩ [*exo-* + Gk *ergon* work – more at WORK]

**exergue** /ek'suhg/ *n* a space on a coin, token, or medal usu on the reverse side below the central part of the design [Fr, fr NL *exergum*, fr Gk *ex* out of + *ergon* work]

**exert** /ig'zuht/ *vt* **1** to bring (e g strength or authority) to bear, esp with sustained effort or lasting effect; employ, wield **2** to take upon (oneself) the effort of doing something ⟨*he never ~s himself to help anyone*⟩ [L *exsertus*, pp of *exserere* to thrust out, fr *ex-* + *serere* to join – more at SERIES] – **exertion** *n*

**exeunt** /'eksi,oont/ *vi pres 3 pl* – used as a stage direction to specify that all or certain named characters leave the stage [L, they go out, fr *exire* to go out – more at EXIT]

**exfoliate** /eks'fohliayt/ *vt* **1** to shed or cast off (e g skin or bark) in scales, layers, etc **2** to remove the surface of in scales or layers **3** to cause to separate and split into thin layers or flakes **4** to spread or extend ⟨*an ~ siphon of a clam*⟩ *~ vi* **1** to shed scales, an outer layer, surface body cells, a tooth, etc **2** to come off in a thin piece **3** to separate into thin flakes **4** to grow (as if) by producing or unfolding leaves [LL *exfoliatus*, pp of *exfoliare* to strip of leaves, fr L *ex-* + *folium* leaf – more at BLADE] – **exfoliation** *n*, **exfoliative** *adj*

**ex gratia** /,eks 'graysh(i)ə/ *adj or adv* as a favour; not compelled by legal right ⟨*~ payments*⟩ [NL, by favour]

**exhalant, exhalent** /eks'hayl(ə)nt, ig'zayl(ə)nt/ *adj* emitting vapour; exhaling, emissive; *also* carrying liquid or vapour from the interior outwards ⟨*an ~ siphon of a clam*⟩

**exhalation** /,eksə'laysh(ə)n, ,eks-hə-/ *n* **1** (an) exhaling **2** something exhaled or given off; an emanation

**exhale** /eks'hayl, ig'zayl/ *vt* **1a** to breathe out from the lungs ⟨*~ carbon dioxide*⟩ **b** to give off (gas or vapour); emit **2** *archaic* to cause to be emitted in vapour *~ vi* **1** to rise or be given off as vapour **2** to emit breath or vapour; breathe out [ME *exalen*, fr L *exhalare*, fr *ex-* + *halare* to breathe; akin to L *anima* breath – more at ANIMATE]

¹**exhaust** /ig'zawst/ *vt* **1a** to draw off or let out completely **b** to empty by drawing off the contents; *specif* to create a vacuum in **2a** to consume entirely; USE UP ⟨*~ed our funds in a week*⟩ **b** to tire out ⟨*~ed by their efforts*⟩ **c** to deprive of a valuable quality or constituent ⟨*~ a soil of fertility*⟩ **3a** to develop or deal with (a subject) to the fullest possible extent **b** to try out the whole number of ⟨*~ed all the possibilities*⟩ **c** to discharge, empty ⟨*the engine ~s through a silencer*⟩ [L *exhaustus*, pp of *exhaurire*, fr *ex-* + *haurire* to draw; akin to MHG *æsen* to empty, Gk *auein* to take] – **exhauster** *n*, **exhaustible** *adj*, **exhaustibility** *n*

²**exhaust** *n* **1** (the escape of) used gas or vapour from an engine **2a** exhaust, **exhaust pipe** the pipe through which used gases escape from an engine **b** an fan for withdrawing fumes, dust, or odours from a room (e g a laboratory or kitchen)

**exhaustion** /ig'zawschən/ *n* exhausting or being exhausted; *esp* extreme tiredness

**exhaustive** /ig'zawstiv/ *adj* **1** serving or tending to exhaust **2** testing all possibilities or considering all elements; comprehensive, thorough ⟨*conducted an ~ investigation*⟩ – **exhaustively** *adv*, **exhaustiveness** *n*, **exhaustivity** *n*

**usage** **Exhaustive** does not mean "tiring".

¹**exhibit** /ig'zibit/ *vt* to present to view: e g **a** to show or display outwardly, esp by visible signs or actions; reveal, manifest ⟨*~ed no fear*⟩ **b** to show publicly, esp for purposes of competition or demonstration *~ vi* to display something for public inspection **synonyms** see ¹SHOW [ME *exhibiten*, fr L *exhibitus*, pp of *exhibēre*, fr *ex-* + *habēre* to have, hold – more at GIVE] – **exhibitive** *adj*, **exhibitor** *n*, **exhibitory** *adj*

²**exhibit** *n* **1** something exhibited **2** a document or object produced as evidence in a court of law **3** *chiefly NAm* EXHIBITION 1

**exhibition** /,eksi'bish(ə)n/ *n* **1** an act or instance of exhibiting **2** a public showing (e g of works of art, objects of manufacture, or athletic skill) **3** *Br* a grant or scholarship awarded by a school or university to a student, usu on merit for performance in entrance examinations – **make an exhibition of oneself** to behave foolishly in public

**exhibitioner** /,eksi'bish(ə)nə/ *n*, *Br* a student who holds an exhibition △ exhibitor, exhibitionist

**exhibitionism** /-iz(ə)m/ *n* **1** a perversion marked by a tendency to indecent exposure **2** the act or practice of behaving so as to attract attention to oneself – **exhibitionist** *n or adj*, **exhibitionistic** *adj*

**exhilarate** /ig'zilə,rayt/ *vt* **1** to make cheerful **2** to enliven, invigorate [L *exhilaratus*, pp of *exhilarare*, fr *ex-* + *hilarare* to gladden, fr *hilarus* cheerful – more at HILARIOUS] – **exhilaration** *n*, **exhilarative** *adj*

**exhort** /ig'zawt/ *vt* to urge or advise strongly ⟨*~ed them to behave well*⟩ *~ vi* to give warnings or advice; make urgent appeals [ME *exhorten*, fr MF *exhorter*, fr L *exhortari*, fr *ex-* + *hortari* to urge – more at YEARN] – **exhorter** *n*

**exhortation** /,egzaw'taysh(ə)n/ *n* **1** an act or instance of exhorting **2** language intended to incite and encourage

**exhortative** /ig'zawtətiv/ *adj* exhortatory

**exhortatory** /ig'zawtətri/ *adj* using exhortation; serving to exhort

**exhume** /eks'hyoohm, ek'syoohm, ik-/ *vt* **1** to disinter **2** to bring back from neglect or obscurity [F or ML; F *exhumer*, fr ML *exhumare*, fr L *ex* out of + *humus* earth – more at EX-, HUMBLE] – **exhumer** *n*, **exhumation** *n*

**ex hypothesi** /,eks hie'pothə,sie/ *adj or adv* according to the hypothesis [NL]

**exigency** /'eksij(ə)nsi, ig'zij(ə)nsi/ *also* **exigence** /'eksij(ə)ns, 'egz-/ *n*, *formal* **1a** the quality or state of being exigent **b** an exigent state of affairs; an emergency ⟨*the cabinet must be free to act in any ~*⟩ **2 exigencies** *pl*, **exigency** such need or necessity as belongs to the occasion; a requirement

**exigent** /'eksij(ə)nt, 'egz-/ *adj*, *formal* **1** requiring immediate aid or action **2** exacting, demanding [L *exigent-, exigens*, prp of *exigere* to demand – more at EXACT] – **exigently** *adv*

**exiguous** /ig'zigyoo-əs/ *adj*, *formal* excessively scanty; inadequate, meagre [L *exiguus*, fr *exigere*] – **exiguously** *adv*, **exiguousness** *n*, **exiguity** *n*

¹**exile** /'eksiel, 'egziel/ *n* **1** enforced or voluntary absence from one's country or home **2** one who is expelled from his/her country or home voluntarily or by authority [ME *exil*, fr MF, fr L *exilium*, fr *exul* banished person]

²**exile** *vt* to send into exile, esp by force – compare BANISH

**exilic** /ek'silik/ *adj* of exile, esp that of the Jews in Babylon

**exine** /'eksin, 'eksien/ *n* the outer of the two major layers forming the wall of a POLLEN GRAIN or spore – compare INTINE [prob fr Ger, fr *ex-* + NL *in-* fibrous tissue, fr Gk *in-, is* tendon]

**exist** /ig'zist/ *vi* **1a** to have being in the real world; be ⟨*do unicorns ~?*⟩ **b** to have being in a specified place or with respect to understood limitations or conditions ⟨*strange ideas ~ed in his mind*⟩ ⟨*some chemical compounds ~ only in solution*⟩ **2** to continue to be ⟨*Nazism still ~s*⟩ **3a** to have life or the functions of vitality ⟨*man cannot ~ without water*⟩ **b** to live at an inferior level or under adverse circumstances ⟨*starving people ~ing from one day to the next*⟩ [L *exsistere* to come into being, exist, fr *ex-* + *sistere* to stand; akin to L *stare* to stand – more at STAND]

**existence** /ig'zist(ə)ns/ *n* **1a(1)** the totality of existent things **a(2)** a particular being ⟨*all the fair ~s of heaven* – John Keats⟩ **b** living, being, life ⟨*death is an elementary fact of ~*⟩ **2a** the state or fact of having being, esp independently of human consciousness ⟨*the ~ of other worlds*⟩ **b** manner of living or being ⟨*pursued a solitary ~*⟩ **3** *philosophy* the condition of a person who positively asserts him-/herself in the face of death, meaninglessness, or chance – used in the theory of existentialism

**existent** /ig'zist(ə)nt/ *adj* **1** having being; existing **2** currently or still existing; extant [L *existent-, exsistens,* prp of *exsistere*] – **existent** *n*

**existential** /,egzi'stensh(ə)l/ *adj* **1** of or affirming existence ⟨~ *propositions*⟩ **2** grounded in existence or the experience of existence; empirical **3** concerned with or involving human existence or its nature; existentialist [LL *existentialis,* fr *existentia* existence, fr L *existent-, existens;* (3) trans of Dan *eksistentiel* & Ger *existential*] – **existentially** *adv*

**existentialism** /-,iz(ə)m/ *n* a chiefly 20th-century philosophical movement characterized by inquiry into human beings' experience of themselves in relation to the world, esp with reference to their freedom, responsibility, and isolation and the experiences (e g of anxiety and despair) in which these are revealed

¹**existentialist** /,egzi'stenshəlist/ *n* an adherent of existentialism

²**existentialist** *adj* dealing with, subscribing to, or based on existentialism or existentialists ⟨*an ~ critique*⟩ – **existentialistic** *adj,* **existentialistically** *adv*

**existential quantifier** *n* a symbol stating that there exists at least one value of a variable

¹**exit** /'eksit, 'egzit/ *vi pres 3 sing* – used as a stage direction to specify who goes off stage [L, he goes out, fr *exire* to go out, fr *ex- + ire* to go – more at ISSUE]

²**exit** *n* **1** a departure of a performer from a scene in a play, opera, etc **2** the act of going out or going away **3** a way out of an enclosed place or space **4** *euph* a death [partly fr ¹*exit;* partly fr L *exitus,* fr *exitus,* pp of *exire*] – **exit** *vi*

**ex libris** /,eks 'leebris/ *n, pl* **ex libris** a bookplate [NL, from the books; used before the owner's name on bookplates]

**Exmoor** /'eks,mooə, -,maw/ *n* **1** (any of) a breed of horned Devonshire sheep valued esp for meat **2** (any of) a breed of hardy heavy-maned ponies native to the Exmoor district [*Exmoor,* district in SW England]

**ex nihilo** /,eks 'neehiloh/ *adv or adj* from or out of nothing ⟨*creation ~*⟩ [L]

**exo-** /eksoh-/, **ex-** *comb form* **1** outside ⟨exo*gamy*⟩; outer ⟨exo*skeleton*⟩ – compare ECT-, END- **2** giving off; releasing ⟨exo*crine*⟩ [Gk *exō* out, outside, fr *ex* out of – more at EX-]

**exobiology** /,eksohbie'oləgi/ *n* the study of plants and animals originating or existing outside the planet earth – **exobiologist** *n,* **exobiological** *adj*

**exocarp** /'eksoh,kahp/ *n* the outermost layer (e g the skin of a cherry) of the tissue (PERICARP) surrounding the seeds in a fruit – called also EPICARP [ISV]

**exocentric** /,eksoh'sentrik/ *adj, of a phrase* not fulfilling the same role in grammar as the word of central importance ⟨in the bath *is an ~ construction, since it is a prepositional phrase while* bath *is a noun*⟩ – compare ENDOCENTRIC

**exocrine** /'eksə,kreen, -krin, -,krien/ *adj* **1** secreting externally; *specif* producing secretions that are discharged through a duct – compare ENDOCRINE **2** of or being an EXOCRINE GLAND or its secretions [ISV *exo-* + Gk *krinein* to separate – more at CERTAIN]

**exocrine gland** *n* a gland (e g a sweat gland or a kidney) that releases a secretion external to or at the surface of an organ by means of a canal or duct

**exocytosis** /,eksohsie'tohsis/ *n* the release of substances (e g secretory or waste products) contained within a VESICLE (membrane-surrounded cavity or pouch) in a cell by fusion of the vesicle membrane and cell membrane and subsequent formation of an opening at the site of the fusion through which the vesicle contents are discharged to the outside – compare ENDOCYTOSIS [NL, fr *exo- + -cytosis* (as in *phagocytosis*)] – **exocytic** *adj,* **exocytose** *vb,* **exocytotic** *adj*

**exodermis** /,eksoh'duhmis/ *n* a layer of living cells lying inside the EPIDERMIS (outer protective layer) of plant roots and having a protective function when the epidermis is destroyed [NL]

**exodontia** /,eksoh'donshə, -tiə/ *n* a branch of dentistry that deals with the extraction of teeth [NL, fr *ex- + -odontia*] – **exodontist** *n*

**exodus** /'eksədəs/ *n* **1** *cap* – see BIBLE table **2** a mass departure; an emigration [L, fr Gk *Exodos,* lit., road out, fr *ex- + hodos* road – more at CEDE]

**exoenzyme** /,eksoh'enziem/ *n* an ENZYME (protein that promotes a biochemical reaction) that functions outside the cell [ISV]

**exoergic** /,eksoh'uhjik/ *adj* releasing energy; EXOTHERMIC ⟨~ *nuclear reactions*⟩

**exoerythrocytic** /,eksohi,rithroh'sitik/ *adj* occurring outside the RED BLOOD CELLS – used chiefly of stages in the life cycle of parasites causing malaria

**ex officio** /,eks ə'fis(h)ioh/ *adv or adj* by virtue or because of an office ⟨*the president is an ~ member of the committee*⟩ [LL]

**exogamy** /ek'sogəmi/ *n* **1** marriage outside a specific group (e g a tribe or village), esp as required by custom or law – compare ENDOGAMY **2** sexual reproduction between organisms that are not closely related – **exogamous, exogamic** *adj*

**exogenous** /ek'sojinəs/ *adj* originating from the outside; due to external causes: e g **a** growing from or on the outside ⟨~ *spores*⟩ **b** caused by something (e g bacteria) from outside a living organism ⟨~ *infection*⟩ **c** of or produced by the METABOLISM (biochemical processing) of nitrogen-containing substances obtained from food rather than of those forming part of cells and tissues [Fr *exogène,* fr *exo- + -gène* (fr Gk *-genēs* born) – more at -GEN] – **exogenously** *adv*

**exon** /'ekson/ *n* any of four officers of the YEOMEN OF THE GUARD who act as resident commanders [modif of Fr *exempt* cavalry officer exempt from normal duties]

**exonerate** /ig'zonərayt/ *vt* **1** to relieve of a responsibility, obligation, or hardship **2** to free from blame; exculpate ⟨~d *him from a charge of corruption*⟩ □ usu + *from* [ME *exoneraten,* fr L *exoneratus,* pp of *exonerare* to unburden, fr *ex- + oner-, onus* load]

**exonuclease** /,eksoh'nyoohkli,ayz/ *n* an ENZYME that breaks down a NUCLEIC ACID (e g DNA or RNA) by removing its constituent units (NUCLEOTIDES) one by one from the end of the chain of nucleotides – compare ENDONUCLEASE [*exo- + nucle- + -ase*]

**exopeptidase** /,eksoh'pepti,dayz/ *n* any of a group of ENZYMES that act in the removal of terminal AMINO ACIDS from a short chain of amino acids by breaking the bond (PEPTIDE BOND) linking one amino acid to the next; PEPTIDASE – compare ENDOPEPTIDASE

**exophthalmos** /,eksof'thalmos, -məs/ *also* **exophthalmus** /-məs/ *n* abnormal protrusion of the eyeball [NL, fr Gk *exophthalmos* having prominent eyes, fr *ex* out + *ophthalmos* eye] – **exophthalmic** *adj*

**exopodite** /ek'sopədiet/ *n* the external branch of a typical two-branched limb of a WATER FLEA, shrimp, or other CRUSTACEAN – compare ENDOPODITE

**exopterygote** /'eksoh,terigoht, -got/ *n* any of a major division (Exopterygota) of insects (e g the dragonfly and mayfly) that do not have an intermediate pupal form in their life cycle but instead gradually develop by successive moults from the juvenile nymph to the adult form as wings develop on the outside of the body – compare ENDOPTERYGOTE [deriv of Gk *exo- + pterygōtos* winged, fr *pteryx* wing]

**exorbitant** /ig'zawbit(ə)nt/ *adj* greatly exceeding in amount, intensity, quality, or size what is the customary, reasonable, or expected limits ⟨*an ~ price*⟩ [ME, irregular, not coming within the scope of the law, fr MF, fr LL *exorbitant-, exorbitans,* prp of *exorbitare* to deviate, fr L *ex- + orbita* track, rut – more at ORB] – **exorbitantly** *adv,* **exorbitance** *n*

**exorc·ise, -ize** /'eksaw,siez/ *vt* **1a** to expel (an evil spirit) by solemn command (e g in a religious ceremony) **b** to get rid of (e g an unpleasant thought or emotion) as if by exorcism **2** to free (e g a person or place) of an evil spirit **9** exercise [ME *exorcisen,* fr MF *exorciser,* fr LL *exorcizare,* fr Gk *exorkizein,* fr *ex- + horkizein* to bind by oath, adjure, fr *horkos* oath; akin to Gk *herkos* fence, L *sarcire* to mend] – **exorciser** *n*

**exorcism** /'eksaw,siz(ə)m/ *n* **1** the act or practice of exorcising **2** a spell or formula used in exorcising – **exorcist** *n*

**exordium** /ek'sawdi·əm, -dyəm/ *n, pl* **exordiums, exordia** /-di·ə, -dyə/ a beginning or introduction, esp to a formal speech or literary work [L, fr *exordiri* to begin, fr *ex- + ordiri* to begin – more at ORDER] – **exordial** *adj*

**exoskeleton** /,eksoh'skelitn/ *n* **1** an external supportive covering of an animal (e g a lobster, earwig, or beetle) **2** bony or horny parts of a VERTEBRATE animal (e g fingernails, hooves, and fish scales) produced from the outer layer of living skin tissues – **exoskeletal** *adj*

**exosmosis** /,eksoz'mohsis/ *n* OSMOSIS (movement of a liquid, esp water, through a membrane) from the inside (e g of a cell) to the outside – compare ENDOSMOSIS [alter. of obs *exosmose,* fr Fr, fr *ex- + Gk *ōsmos* act of pushing – more at ENDOSMOSIS] – **exosmotic** *adj*

**exosphere** /'eksoh‚sfiə/ *n* the outer region of a planet's atmosphere [ISV] – **exospheric** *adj*

**exospore** /'eksoh‚spaw/ *n* a spore formed asexually without fusion of reproductive cells by the growth of a dividing wall across a parent cell [ISV]

**exostosis** /‚eksoʻstohsis/ *n, pl* **exostoses** /-seez/ a spur or bony outgrowth from a bone or the root of a tooth [NL, fr Gk *exostōsis*, fr *ex* out of + *osteon* bone – more at OSSEOUS]

**exoteric** /‚eksoh'terik/ *adj* **1a** designed for, understood by, or suitable to be imparted to the public – compare ESOTERIC 1 **b** not admitted or belonging to the inner circle of initiated or enlightened members **2** *formal* of the outside; external [L & Gk; L *exotericus*, fr Gk *exōterikos*, lit., external, fr *exōterō*, compar of *exō* outside – more at EXO-] – **exoterically** *adv*

**exothermic** /‚eksoh'thuhmik/, **exothermal** /‚eksoh'thuhml/ *adj* characterized by or formed with the evolution or release of heat ⟨*an ~ chemical reaction*⟩ [ISV] – **exothermically** *adv*

**exotic** /ig'zotik/ *adj* **1** introduced from another country; not native to the place where found ⟨*an ~ plant*⟩ **2** strikingly or excitingly different or unusual ⟨*an ~ dish*⟩ **3** *archaic* outlandish, alien **9** erotic, esoteric [L *exoticus*, fr Gk *exōtikos*, fr *exō*] – **exotic** *n*, **exotically** *adv*, **exoticism** *n*

**exotica** /ig'zotikə/ *n taking pl vb* things excitingly different or unusual; *esp* literary or artistic items having an exotic theme or nature [NL, fr L, neut pl of *exoticus*]

**exotoxin** /‚eksoh'toksin/ *n* a soluble poisonous substance released by a microorganism (eg a bacterium) into the surrounding medium during its growth [ISV]

**expand** /ik'spand/ *vt* **1a** to increase the size, extent, number, volume, or scope of ⟨*the company has ~ed its interests overseas*⟩ **b** to introduce gas into (a plastic or resin) ⟨*~ed vinyl*⟩ **2a** to express in detail or in full ⟨*~ an argument*⟩ ⟨*~ the abbreviations*⟩ **b** to express in fuller mathematical form, esp as the sum of many terms of a series *~ vi* **1** to become expanded ⟨*iron ~s when heated*⟩ **2** to speak or write at length; enlarge **3** to become more sociable; open up ⟨*~s only among friends*⟩ [ME *expaunden*, fr L *expandere*, fr *ex-* + *pandere* to spread – more at FATHOM] – **expandable** *adj*

*synonyms* Expand, amplify, swell, distend, inflate, and dilate all mean "make or become bigger". **Expand** is the most general, suggesting a spreading or unfolding by inner or outer forces ⟨*roses* **expanding** *in the sun*⟩. **Amplify** implies the adding to or expansion of something otherwise inadequate ⟨**amplify** *sound/a statement*⟩. **Swell** can refer to volume or intensity ⟨**swell** *the chorus*⟩ but more often suggests expansion beyond the proper limits ⟨*a* **swollen** *river*⟩. **Distend** suggests internal pressure ⟨*a* **distended** *stomach*⟩. To **inflate** something is to distend it artificially with something insubstantial ⟨**inflate** *a balloon*⟩, and the word is often used figuratively ⟨**inflated** *ideas of his own importance*⟩. **Dilate** often applies to the two-dimensional expansion of a circumference ⟨*eyes* **dilated** *in terror*⟩. *antonym* contract

**expanded metal** *n* sheet metal cut and expanded into an open lattice framework and used esp as a backing for plaster or rendering

**expander** /-də/ *n* one who or that which expands; *specif* any of several substances (eg DEXTRAN) used as a blood or plasma substitute for increasing the blood volume

**expanse** /ik'spans/ *n* **1** something spread out, esp over a wide area: eg **1a** the heavens **b** expanses *pl*, **expanse** an extensive stretch of land or sea ⟨*the vast ~ of the ocean*⟩ **2** the extent to which something is spread out [NL *expansum*, fr L, neut of *expansus*, pp of *expandere*]

**expansible** /-səbl/ *adj* capable of being expanded – **expansibility** *n*

**expansile** /ik'spansiel/ *adj* of or capable of expansion

**expansion** /ik'spansh(ə)n/ *n* **1** the act or process of expanding ⟨*territorial ~*⟩ **2** the quality or state of being expanded **3** an expanse **4** the increase in volume of WORKING FLUID (eg steam) in an engine cylinder **5** something expanded: eg **5a** an expanded part **b** a fuller treatment of an earlier theme or work ⟨*the book is an ~ of a lecture series*⟩ **6** the result of expanding a mathematical expression or function – **expansional** *adj*, **expansionary** *adj*

**expansionism** /-‚iz(ə)m/ *n* a policy or practice of usu territorial expansion by a nation – **expansionist** *n*, **expansionist, expansionistic** *adj*

**expansive** /ik'spansiv/ *adj* **1** having a capacity or a tendency to expand or to cause expansion **2a** freely communicative; genial, effusive **b** *psychology* unrestrained in expression of feelings; *specif* marked by or indicative of exaggerated euphoria and delusions of self-importance **3** having wide expanse or extent **4** characterized by largeness or magnificence of scale ⟨*~ living*⟩ – **expansively** *adv*, **expansiveness** *n*, **expansivity** *n*

**ex parte** /‚eks 'pahti, -tay/ *adv or adj* **1** of legal proceedings on behalf of or in the presence of one side or party only **2** from a one-sided or partisan point of view [ML]

**expatiate** /ik'spayshi‚ayt, ek-/ *vi* **1** to wander in thought or imagination without restraint **2** to speak or write at length or in detail usu on a single subject – usu + *on* or *upon* ⟨*was* expatiating *upon the value of the fabric* – Thomas Hardy⟩ [L *exspatiatus*, pp of *exspatiari* to wander, digress, fr *ex-* + *spatium* space, course – more at SPEED] – **expatiation** *n*

¹**expatriate** /eks'patriayt/ *vt* **1** to exile, banish **2** to withdraw (oneself) from residence in or allegiance to one's native country [ML *expatriatus*, pp of *expatriare* to leave one's own country, fr L *ex-* + *patria* native country, fr fem of *patrius* of a father, fr *patr-, pater* father – more at FATHER] – **expatriation** *n*

²**expatriate** /‚eks'patri-ət/ *n* one who lives in a foreign country; *specif* one who has renounced his/her native country – **expatriate** *adj*

**expect** /ik'spekt/ *vi* **1** to look forward with anticipation **2** to be pregnant **3** *archaic* to wait, stay *~ vt* **1** to suppose, think ⟨*I ~ that's true*⟩ **2** to anticipate or look forward to the coming or occurrence of ⟨*~ed a telephone call*⟩ **3a** to consider (an event) probable or certain ⟨*~ to be forgiven*⟩ **b** to consider reasonable, due, or necessary ⟨*he ~ed respect from his children*⟩ **c** to consider bound in duty or obligated ⟨*they ~ed him to pay his dues*⟩ **4** *archaic* to wait for [L *exspectare* to look forward to, fr *ex-* + *spectare* to look at, fr *spectus*, pp of *specere* to look – more at SPY] – **expectable** *adj*, **expectably** *adv*, **expectedly** *adv*, **expectedness** *n*

**expectancy** /ik'spekt(ə)nsi/ *n* **1** expectancy, expectance EXPECTATION 1,2a,3 **2** the expected amount or number (eg of years of life) based on statistical probability

¹**expectant** /ik'spekt(ə)nt/ *adj* **1** characterized by expectation **2** expecting the birth of one's child; *specif, of a woman* pregnant – **expectantly** *adv*

²**expectant** *n* one who is expectant

**expectation** /‚ekspek'taysh(ə)n/ *n* **1** the act or state of expecting; anticipation ⟨*had given rise to a general ~ of their marriage* – Jane Austen⟩ **2a** something expected **b** expectations *pl*, **expectation** prospects of inheritance **3** the state of being expected **4a** EXPECTANCY 2 **b** EXPECTED VALUE

**expected value** *n, statistics* the mean value of a RANDOM VARIABLE

**expectorant** /ik'spektərənt/ *adj, of a drug or other agent* promoting expectoration – **expectorant** *n*

**expectorate** /ik'spektərayt/ *vb* **1** to eject (phlegm or similar matter) from the throat or lungs by coughing or spitting **2** to spit [L *ex-* + *pector-, pectus* breast, soul – more at PECTORAL] – **expectoration** *n*

**expediency** /ik'speedi-ənsi, -dyənsi/ *n* **1** expediency, expedience the quality or state of being expedient; suitability, fitness **2** development of or holding fast to expedient means and methods **3** an expedient **4** *obs* quickness in action; haste – **expediential** *adj*

¹**expedient** /-ənt/ *adj* **1** suitable for achieving a particular end **2** characterized by concern with what is opportune rather than what is right or just; *specif* governed by self-interest, rather than by concern with what is moral **9** expeditious [ME, fr MF or L; MF, fr L *expedient-, expediens*, prp of *expedire* to extricate, arrange, be advantageous, fr *ex-* + *ped-, pes* foot – more at FOOT] – **expediently** *adv*

²**expedient** *n* **1** something expedient; a means to an end **2** a means devised or used in case of urgent need; a makeshift

**expedite** /'ekspi‚diet/ *vt, formal* **1** to execute promptly **2** to hasten the process or progress of; facilitate **3** to send out; dispatch [L *expeditus*, pp of *expedire*]

**expediter** *also* **expeditor** /'ekspe‚dietər/ *n* one who expedites; *specif* one employed to ensure adequate supplies of raw materials and equipment or to coordinate the flow of materials, tools, parts, and processed goods within a manufacturing plant

**expedition** /‚ekspi'dish(ə)n/ *n* **1** a journey or excursion undertaken for a specific purpose (eg for war or exploration); *also, taking sing or pl vb* the group of people making such an expedition **2** *formal* efficient promptness; speed

**expeditionary** /-ri/ *adj* of or constituting an expedition; *also* sent on military service abroad ⟨*an ~ force*⟩

**expeditious** /-shəs/ *adj, formal* speedy *synonyms* see ¹FAST *antonyms* slow, tardy **9** expedient – **expeditiously** *adv*, **expeditiousness** *n*

**expel** /ik'spel/ *vt* -**ll**- **1** to drive or force out ⟨~led *air from the lungs*⟩ **2** to drive away; *esp* to deport **3** to cut off from membership ⟨~led *from school*⟩ [ME *expellen*, fr L *expellere*, fr *ex*- + *pellere* to drive – more at FELT] – **expellable** *adj*, **expeller** *n*

**expellee** /ˌekspe'lee, ikˌspe'lee/ *n* one who is expelled; *specif* one transferred from the country of residence for resettlement in the country with which he/she is ethnically associated

**expend** /ik'spend/ *vt* **1** to pay out (e g large amounts of money) ⟨*the new roads on which so much public money is* ~ed⟩ **2** to consume (e g time, care, or attention) by use; USE UP ⟨*projects on which he* ~ed *great energy*⟩ [ME *expenden*, fr L *expendere* to weigh out, pay, fr *ex*- + *pendere* to weigh – more at SPAN] – **expender** *n*

¹**expendable** /ik'spendəbl/ *adj* that may be expended: e g **a** normally used up or consumed in service; not intended to be kept or reused ⟨~ *supplies like pencils and paper*⟩ **b** regarded as available for sacrifice or destruction in order to accomplish an objective ⟨~ *troops*⟩ – **expendability** *n*

²**expendable** *n usu pl* one who or that which is expendable

**expenditure** /ik'spendichə/ *n* **1** the act or process of expending ⟨*renovations required an* ~ *of several thousand pounds*⟩ **2** the amount expended ⟨*his income only just covered his* ~⟩ [irreg fr *expend*]

**expense** /ik'spens/ *n* **1a** something expended to secure a benefit or bring about a result **b** financial burden or outlay; cost ⟨*he built the monument at his own* ~⟩ **c** *pl* the charges (e g for travelling) incurred by an employee in connection with performing his/her duties **d** an item of business outlay chargeable against revenue in a specific period **2** a cause or occasion of usu relatively high expenditure ⟨*a car is a great* ~⟩ **3a** *archaic* the act or practice of expending money; spending **b(1)** *archaic* the act or process of using up; consumption **b(2)** *obs* loss [ME, fr AF or LL; AF, fr LL *expensa*, fr L, fem of *expensus*, pp of *expendere*] – **at somebody's expense** in a manner that causes somebody to be ridiculed ⟨*made a joke* at my expense⟩ – **at the expense of** to the detriment of ⟨*develop a boy's physique* at the expense of *his intelligence* – Bertrand Russell⟩

**expense account** *n* a list or record of expenses reimbursable to an employee

**expensive** /ik'spensiv/ *adj* **1** involving great expense ⟨*an* ~ *hobby*⟩ **2** commanding a high price, esp that which is relatively high compared with a prospective buyer's means – **expensively** *adv*, **expensiveness** *n*

¹**experience** /ik'spiəri·əns/ *n* **1a** direct participation in, observation of, or acquaintance with events ⟨*learn by* ~⟩; *also* the knowledge, skill, or practice derived from such experience ⟨*get some* ~ *before you settle down*⟩ **b** the state or result of being engaged in a specified activity ⟨*ten years' teaching* ~⟩ **2** the sum total of conscious events that make up an individual life or the past of a community, nation, or mankind generally **3** *philosophy* the totality of one's perceptions and understanding of the material world and psychic phenomena as gained through one's senses; *also* the facts or events so perceived or understood **4** something personally encountered, undergone, or lived through ⟨*an unpleasant* ~⟩ [ME, fr MF, fr L *experientia* act of trying, fr *experient-, experiens*, prp of *experiri* to try, fr *ex*- + *-periri* (akin to *periculum* attempt) – more at FEAR]

²**experience** *vt* **1** to have experience of ⟨~d *severe hardships as a child*⟩ **2** to learn by experience ⟨*I have* ~d *that a landscape and the sky unfold the deepest beauty* – Nathaniel Hawthorne⟩

**experienced** /ik'spiəri·ənst/ *adj* skilful or wise as a result of experience of a particular activity or of life as a whole ⟨*an* ~ *driver*⟩

**experiencialism** /ikˌspiəri'enshəˌliz(ə)m/ *n* a doctrine in philosophy that all knowledge is derived from experience

**experiential** /ikˌspiəri'ensh(ə)l/ *adj* derived from or based on experience; empirical – **experientially** *adv*

¹**experiment** /ik'sperimənt/ *n* **1a** a tentative procedure or policy that is on trial **b** an operation carried out under controlled conditions in order to test or establish a hypothesis or to illustrate a known law ⟨*a scientific* ~⟩ **2** the process of experimenting; experimentation **3** *archaic* a test, trial ⟨*make another* ~ *of his suspicion* – Shak⟩ **4** *obs* experience [ME, fr MF, fr L *experimentum*, fr *experiri*]

²**experiment** /ik'speriˌment/ *vi* to carry out an experiment – **experimenter** *n*, **experimentation** *n*

**experimental** /ikˌsperi'mentl/ *adj* **1** experiential, empirical **2** based on or derived from experiment ⟨*the heart of the* ~ *method is the direct control of the thing studied* – B F Skinner⟩ **3** used as a means of or having the characteristics of experiment ⟨*an* ~ *school*⟩ ⟨*still in the* ~ *stage*⟩ – **experimentally** *adv*

**experimentalism** /ikˌsperiˈmentəˌlizem/ *n, philosophy* reliance on or active support for experimental or experiential principles and procedures; *specif* INSTRUMENTALISM (doctrine that ideas are instruments to be used for action)

**experimentalist** /ikˌsperi'mentəlist/ *n* one who experiments; *specif* a person conducting scientific experiments

¹**expert** /'ekspuht/ *adj* **1** having, involving, or displaying special skill or knowledge derived from training or experience ⟨~ *at disguising his feelings*⟩ **2** *obs* experienced **synonyms** see PROFICIENT **antonym** amateurish [ME, fr MF & L; MF, fr L *expertus*, fr pp of *experiri*] – **expertly** *adv*, **expertness** *n*

²**expert** *n* one who is expert at a particular subject [Fr, fr *expert*, adj]

**expertise** /ˌekspuh'teez/ *n* **1** expert opinion or commentary **2** skill in a particular field; know-how ⟨*technical* ~⟩ [Fr, fr MF, expertness, fr *expert*]

**expiable** /'ekspi·əbl/ *adj* capable of being expiated

**expiate** /'ekspiˌayt/ *vt* **1a** to extinguish the guilt incurred by (e g a sin) **b** to pay the penalty for (e g a crime) **c** to make amends for ⟨*permission to* ~ *their offences by their assiduous labours* – Francis Bacon⟩ **2** *obs* to put an end to [L *expiatus*, pp of *expiare* to atone for, fr *ex*- + *piare* to atone for, appease – more at PIOUS] – **expiator** *n*, **expiation** *n*, **expiatory** *adj*

**expiration** /ˌekspie·ə'raysh(ə)n, -spi-/ *n* **1** an act or the process of releasing air from the lungs through the nose or mouth **2** the fact, act, or process of expiry; termination **3** *archaic* the last emission of breath; death

**expiratory** /ik'spie·ərət(ə)ri/ *adj* of, used, or involved in the expiration of air from the lungs

**expire** /ik'spie·ə/ *vi* **1** to come to an end ⟨*his term of office* ~s *this year*⟩ **2** to breathe out; exhale **3** *formal* to die ~ *vt* **1** to breathe out (as if) from the lungs **2** *obs* to conclude [ME *expiren*, fr MF or L; MF *expirer*, fr L *exspirare*, fr *ex*- + *spirare* to breathe – more at SPIRIT]

**expiry** /-ri/ *n* **1** a termination; *esp* a time or period fixed by law, contract, or agreement **2** *archaic* expiration, death

**explain** /ik'splayn/ *vt* **1** to make plain or understandable ⟨*a commentary that* ~s *the wider implications of the theory*⟩ **2** to give the reason for or cause of ⟨*unwilling to* ~ *his conduct*⟩ **3** to show the logical development or relationships of, esp according to natural laws ⟨~ *the weather*⟩ ~ *vi* to make something plain or understandable [ME *explanen*, fr L *explanare*, lit., to make level, fr *ex*- + *planus* level, flat – more at FLOOR] – **explainable** *adj*, **explainer** *n* – **explain oneself** to clarify one's statements or the reasons for one's conduct

**explain away** *vt* **1** to get rid of (e g difficulties or unpleasant facts) (as if) by explanation **2** to minimize the significance of (e g errors or unpleasant facts) by making excuses ⟨*tried to* explain away *the corruption in his department*⟩

**explanation** /ˌeksplə'naysh(ə)n/ *n* **1** the act or process of explaining; something, esp a statement, that explains ⟨*the* ~ *offered was unconvincing*⟩ **2** a mutual discussion designed to correct a misunderstanding or reconcile differences

**explanative** /ik'splanətiv/ *adj* explanatory – **explanatively** *adv*

**explanatorily adequate** *adj, of a linguistic theory* selecting the most economical descriptively and observationally adequate grammar of a language

**explanatory** /ik'splanət(ə)ri/ *adj* serving to explain ⟨~ *notes*⟩ – **explanatorily** *adv*

¹**explant** /eks'plahnt/ *vt* to remove (living tissue) from an organism, esp to an artificial nourishing medium for experimental growth [*ex*- + *-plant* (as in *implant*)] – **explant** *n*, **explantation** *n*

²**explant** *n* a piece of living tissue removed from an organism and placed in an artificial nourishing medium for growth

¹**expletive** /ek'spleetiv/ *adj* **1** serving to fill up ⟨~ *phrases*⟩ **2** marked by the use of expletives [LL *expletivus*, fr L *expletus*, pp of *explēre* to fill out, fr *ex*- + *plēre* to fill – more at FULL]

²**expletive** *n* **1** a syllable, word, or phrase inserted to fill a space (e g in a sentence or a line of poetry having a rhythmical pattern) without adding to the sense **2** a usu meaningless exclamatory word or phrase; *specif* one that is obscene or profane

**expletory** /ek'spleet(ə)ri/ *adj* expletive

**explicable** /'eksplikəbl, ek'splikəbl/ *adj* capable of being explained – **explicably** *adv*

**explicate** /'eksplikayt/ *vt* **1** to give a detailed explanation of **2** to develop the implications of; analyse logically [L *explicatus*, pp of *explicare*, lit., to unfold, fr *ex-* + *plicare* to fold – more at PLY] – **explication** *n*, **explicative** *adj*, **explicator** *n*, **explicatory** *adj*

**explication de texte** /ˌekspli'kasionh də tekst/ *n*, *pl* **explications de texte** /~/ a method of literary criticism involving a detailed analysis of each part of a work [Fr, lit., explanation of text]

**explicit** /ik'splisit/ *adj* **1** clear, unambiguous ⟨~ *instructions*⟩; *also* graphically frank ⟨~ *sex scenes*⟩ **2** fully developed or formulated ⟨*an* ~ *statement of his objectives*⟩ **3** involving direct payment ⟨~ *costs*⟩ □ compare ¹EXPRESS, IMPLICIT [Fr or ML; F *explicite*, fr ML *explicitus*, fr L, pp of explicare] – **explicitly** *adv*, **explicitness** *n*

**explicit function** *n* a mathematical function defined by an expression containing only INDEPENDENT VARIABLES ⟨*in the expression* $3x^2 + 2x + 1 = y$, y *is an* ~ *of* x⟩ – compare IMPLICIT FUNCTION

**explode** /ik'splohd/ *vt* **1** to bring (eg a belief or theory) into disrepute or discredit by demonstrating falsity ⟨~ *a rumour*⟩ **2** to cause to explode or burst noisily ⟨~ *dynamite*⟩ ⟨~ *a bomb*⟩ ~ *vi* **1** to give expression to sudden, violent, and usu noisy emotion ⟨~ *with anger*⟩ **2a** to undergo a rapid chemical or nuclear reaction with the production of noise, heat, and violent expansion of gases ⟨*dynamite* ~s⟩ ⟨*an atomic bomb* ~s⟩ **b** to burst or expand violently (as if) as a result of pressure from within ⟨*the boiler* ~d⟩ ⟨*the exploding population*⟩ [L *explodere* to drive off the stage by clapping, fr *ex-* + *plaudere* to clap (cf APPLAUD)] – **exploder** *n*

**exploded** /ik'splohdid/ *adj, of a drawing, photograph, etc* showing the parts separated but in correct relationship to each other ⟨*an* ~ *view of a carburettor*⟩

¹**exploit** /'eksployt/ *n* a deed, act; *esp* a notable or heroic act **synonyms** see ¹ACT [ME, outcome, success, fr OF, fr L *explicitum*, neut of *explicitus*, pp]

²**exploit** /ik'sployt/ *vt* **1** to use or develop fully, esp for profit or advantage ⟨~ *a mine*⟩; *also* to utilize **2** to take unfair advantage of for financial or other gain ⟨~s *his friends*⟩ ⟨~s *the workers by paying low wages*⟩ – **exploitive** *adj*, **exploitively** *adv*, **exploitable** *adj*, **exploiter** *n*, **exploitability** *n*

**exploitation** /ˌeksploy'taysh(ə)n/ *n* **1** exploiting or being exploited **2** cashing in on a topical theme ⟨~ *movie*⟩ **3** interaction between organisms in which one benefits at the expense of the other – **exploitative** *adj*, **exploitatively** *adv*

**exploration** /ˌeksplə'raysh(ə)n/ *n* the act or an instance of exploring – **explorational** *adj*

**explorative** /ik'splorətiv/ *adj* exploratory – **exploratively** *adv*

**exploratory** /ik'splorət(ə)ri/ *adj* of or being exploration ⟨~ *surgery*⟩

**explore** /ik'splaw/ *vt* **1a** to examine or inquire into thoroughly ⟨~ *the possibilities of reaching an agreement*⟩ **b** to examine minutely (eg by surgery or with a probe), esp for diagnostic purposes **c** to travel into or through for purposes of geographical discovery **2** *obs* to seek for or after ~ *vi* to explore an area [L *explorare*, fr *ex-* + *plorare* to cry out (cf DEPLORE, IMPLORE); prob fr the outcry of hunters on sighting game]

**explorer** /iks'plawər/ *n* one who or that which explores; *esp* one who travels in search of geographical or scientific information

**explosible** /ik'splohsəbl/ *adj* capable of being exploded – **explosibility** *n*

**explosion** /ik'splohzh(ə)n/ *n* **1** the act or an instance of exploding: eg **1a** a rapid large-scale expansion, increase, or upheaval ⟨*the population* ~⟩ **b** a sudden violent outburst of emotion **2** production of a PLOSIVE consonant; PLOSION [L *explosion-*, *explosio* act of driving off by clapping, fr *explosus*, pp of *explodere*]

¹**explosive** /ik'splohsiv, -ziv/ *adj* **1** of, characterized by, or operated by explosion ⟨*an* ~ *engine*⟩ **2** tending to explode; *esp* tending or threatening to burst forth with sudden violence or noise ⟨*an* ~ *person*⟩ ⟨*an* ~ *situation*⟩ **3** tending to arouse strong reactions; controversial ⟨*the play's* ~ *topicality*⟩ – **explosively** *adv*, **explosiveness** *n*

²**explosive** *n* **1** an explosive substance **2** a PLOSIVE consonant

**expo** /'ekspoh/ *n, pl* **expos** a public exhibition or show; an exposition [short for *exposition*]

**exponent** /ik'spohnənt/ *n* **1** a symbol written above and to the right of a mathematical expression to indicate the number of times that a quantity is multiplied by itself ⟨*in the expression* $a^3$, *the* ~ **3** *indicates that* a *is cubed*⟩ **2a** one who or that which expounds or interprets **b** one who or that which champions, advocates, or exemplifies □ (*2*) usu + *of* [L *exponent-*, *exponens*, prp of *exponere* – more at EXPOSE]

**exponential** /ˌekspə'nensh(ə)l/ *adj* **1** of an exponent **2** *maths* involving a variable in an exponent ⟨$10^x$ *is an* ~ *expression*⟩ **3** expressed in terms of exponential functions ⟨*an* ~ *growth rate*⟩ – **exponentially** *adv*

**exponential function**, **exponential** *n* a mathematical function in which an INDEPENDENT VARIABLE appears in an exponent, esp of a constant BASE ⟨*in the* ~ $2x^2 + y = e^x$, x *is an independent variable and* e *is the constant base*⟩

**exponentiation** /ˌekspənenshi'aysh(ə)n/ *n, maths* the action or process of multiplying a quantity by itself the number of times specified by an exponent [*exponent* + *-iation* (as in *differentiation*)]

¹**export** /ik'spawt/ *vt* **1** to carry away; remove **2** to carry or send (eg a commodity) abroad for purposes of trade **3** to take or spread (an idea, custom, etc) abroad ~ *vi* to export something abroad [L *exportare*, fr *ex-* + *portare* to carry – more at FARE] – **exportable** *adj*, **exportability** *n*

²**export** /'ekspawt/ *n* **1** something exported; *specif* a commodity or service produced by one country to be sold to another – compare VISIBLE 4, INVISIBLE 2C **2** an act of exporting; exportation ⟨*the* ~ *of wheat*⟩

³**export** /'ekspawt/ *adj* of export or exports ⟨~ *duties*⟩

**exportation** /-'taysh(ə)n/ *n* an act of exporting; *also, chiefly NAm* a commodity exported

**exporter** /ik'spawtər/ *n* one who exports; *specif* a wholesaler who sells to merchants or industrial consumers in foreign countries

**expose** /ik'spohz/ *vt* **1a** to deprive of shelter, protection, or care; lay open to attack or distressing influence ⟨~ *troops needlessly*⟩ ⟨~s *himself to ridicule*⟩ **b** to submit or subject to an action or influence; *specif* to subject (a sensitive photographic film, plate, or paper) to the action of radiant energy **c** to abandon (an infant) in an unsheltered place **2** to lay open to view; display: eg **2a** to offer for sale openly and in a place that is accessible to the public **b** to exhibit (eg the bread and wine at communion) for the public esp a congregation in a Roman Catholic church, to look upon with reverence **c** to reveal the face of (a playing card) **d** to engage in indecent exposure of (oneself) **3** to bring (something shameful) to light; disclose ⟨~d *their sordid plan*⟩ ⟨~ *a tax evasion*⟩ **synonyms** see ¹SHOW [ME *exposen*, fr MF *exposer*, fr L *exponere* to set forth, explain (perf indic *exposui*), fr *ex-* + *ponere* to put, place – more at POSITION] – **exposer** *n*

**exposé**, **expose** /ek'spohzay (*Fr* εkspoze)/ *n* **1** a formal recital or exposition of facts; statement **2** an exposure of something discreditable ⟨*a newspaper* ~ *of organized crime*⟩ [Fr *exposé*, fr pp of *exposer*]

**exposed** /ik'spohzd/ *adj* open to view, to inclement weather conditions, etc; not shielded

**exposit** /ek'spozit/ *vt, formal* to expound [L *expositus*, pp of *exponere*]

**exposition** /ˌekspə'zish(ə)n/ *n* **1** the art or practice of expounding or explaining the meaning or purpose of something (eg a text) **2a** a detailed explanation or elucidation, esp of something that is difficult to understand ⟨*a brilliant* ~ *of existentialism*⟩ **b** *music* **b(1)** the first of usu three parts of a movement written in SONATA FORM in which the main musical material is introduced – compare DEVELOPMENT 1, RECAPITULATION 3 **b(2)** the opening section of a FUGUE in which the main theme is stated typically in each of the voice parts **3** an act or instance of exposing; *esp* a usu international public exhibition or show (eg of industrial products) – **expositional** *adj*

**expositive** /ik'spozətiv/ *adj* descriptive, explanatory

**expositor** /ik'spozitə/ *n* one who expounds; a commentator – **expository** *adj*

**ex post facto** /ˌeks ˌpohst 'faktoh/ *adj or adv* **1** (done, made, or formulated) after the fact ⟨~ *approval*⟩ **2** applied retrospectively ⟨~ *laws*⟩ [LL, from a thing done afterwards]

**expostulate** /ik'spostyoolayt, -chəlayt/ *vi, obs* to discuss, examine ~ *vi, formal* to reason earnestly with someone in order to dissuade or remonstrate – often + *with* **synonyms** see ²OBJECT [L *expostulatus*, pp of *expostulare* to demand, dispute, fr *ex-* + *postulare* to ask for – more at POSTULATE] – **expostulation** *n*

**exposure** /ik'spohzh(ə)/ *n* **1** the act or an instance of exposing: eg **1a** disclosure to view; display **b(1)** a disclosure, esp of a weakness or something shameful or criminal; an exposé, unmasking ⟨*continued his ~ of electoral frauds*⟩ **b(2)** presentation or exposition; *esp* to the public by means of the MASS MEDIA **c** abandoning an infant in an unsheltered place **d(1)** the act of exposing a sensitized photographic film, plate, or paper; *also* the duration of such an exposure **d(2)** a section of a film for an individual picture **2a** a condition or instance of being exposed; *specif* the condition arising from heat loss due to being without protection from cold weather ⟨*he died of ~*⟩ **b** the position of a building, room, etc with respect to the direction in which it faces or to climatic or weather influences; aspect ⟨*a house with a western ~*⟩

**exposure factor, factor** *n* the number by which a given time is multiplied in photography to give the complete time for exposure or development

**exposure meter** *n* a device for indicating correct photographic exposure under various light conditions

**expound** /ik'spownd/ *vt* to set forth, esp in careful or elaborate detail; state, explain ~ *vi* to make a statement – usu + *on* [ME *expounden*, fr MF *expondre*, fr L *exponere* to explain – more at EXPOSE] – **expounder** *n*

¹**express** /ik'spres/ *adj* **1** directly, firmly, and explicitly stated ⟨*he disobeyed my ~ orders*⟩ **2** of a particular sort; specific ⟨*she came for that ~ purpose*⟩ **3a** travelling at high speed; *specif* travelling with few or no stops along the way ⟨*~ train*⟩ **b** adapted or suitable for travel at high speed ⟨*an ~ highway*⟩ **c** *Br* designated to be delivered without delay by special messenger ⟨*~ mail*⟩ **4** arch exact, precise ⟨*he was the ~ image of his father*⟩ [ME, fr MF *expres*, fr L *expressus*, pp of *exprimere* to press out, express, fr *ex-* + *premere* to press – more at PRESS; (3) fr *express train*, orig a 'special' train provided for a particular occasion, or stopping only at particular stations]

²**express** *adv* **1** by express ⟨*send a parcel ~*⟩ **2** *obs* expressly

³**express** *n* **1** an express vehicle **2** *Br* express mail

⁴**express** *vt* **1a** to show or represent, esp in words; state, reflect **b** to make known or show the opinions, feelings, abilities, or creative impulses of (oneself) ⟨*~ed himself very strongly on that subject*⟩ ⟨*~es himself through his painting*⟩ **c** to represent by a sign or symbol **2a** to force out (eg the juice of a fruit) by pressure **b** to subject to pressure so as to extract something **3** to send by express **4** *archaic* to delineate, depict [ME *expressen*, fr MF & L; MF *expresser*, fr OF, fr *expres*, adj, fr L *expressus*, pp] – **expresser** *n*, **expressible** *adj*

**expressage** /ik'spresij/ *n* a carrying of parcels by express; *also* a charge for such carrying

**expression** /ik'spresh(ə)n/ *n* **1a** expressing, esp in words; utterance ⟨*freedom of ~*⟩ **b(1)** an outward manifestation or symbol ⟨*this gift is an ~ of my admiration for you*⟩ **b(2)** a significant word or phrase **b(3)** a mathematical or logical symbol or combination of symbols serving to express something **b(4)** the visible or detectable effect of a gene; *also* expressivity **2a** a means or manner of expressing something ⟨*read the poem with ~*⟩ **b(1)** the quality or fact of being expressive ⟨*a wonderful portrait: the eyes are full of light and ~*⟩ **b(2)** facial aspect or vocal intonation indicative of feeling **3** an act or product of squeezing out a liquid – **expressional** *adj*, **expressionless** *adj*, **expressionlessly** *adv*, **expressionlessness** *n*

**expressionism** /-,iz(ə)m/ *n* a mode of artistic expression that attempts to depict the artist's subjective emotions and responses to objects and events – **expressionist** *n or adj*, **expressionistic** *adj*, **expressionistically** *adv*

**expressive** /ik'spresiv/ *adj* **1** of expression ⟨*the ~ function of language*⟩ **2** serving to express, utter, or represent ⟨*he used foul and novel terms ~ of rage* – H G Wells⟩ **3** full of expression; significant ⟨*an ~ silence*⟩ – **expressively** *adv*, **expressiveness** *n*

**expressivity** /,ekspre'sivəti/ *n* **1** the relative capacity of a gene to affect the visible or detectable characteristics of an organism; the degree to which a gene produces an observable effect in a particular individual **2** the quality of being expressive

**expressly** /ik'spresli/ *adv* **1** in an express manner; explicitly ⟨*he ~ rejected capitalism*⟩ **2** for the express purpose; particularly, specially ⟨*needed a clinic ~ for the treatment of drug addicts*⟩

**expressway** /ik'spres,way/ *n*, chiefly *NAm* a motorway

**expropriate** /ek'sprohpri,ayt/ *vt* **1** to deprive of possession, occupancy, or owner's rights **2** to transfer (the property of another) to one's own possession ⟨*~d all the land within a 10 mile radius*⟩ [ML *expropriatus*, pp of *expropriare*, fr L *ex-* + *proprius* own] – **expropriator** *n*, **expropriation** *n*

**expulsion** /ik'spulsh(ə)n/ *n* expelling or being expelled [ME, fr L *expulsion-*, *expulsio*, fr *expulsus*, pp of *expellere* to expel] – **expulsive** *adj*

**expunge** /ik'spunj/ *vt, formal* **1** to strike out, rub out, or obliterate; erase **2** to efface completely; destroy ⟨*nothing can ~ his shame*⟩ **synonyms** see ERASE [L *expungere* to mark for deletion by dots, fr *ex-* + *pungere* to prick – more at PUNGENT] – **expunger** *n*, **expunction** *n*

**expurgate** /'ekspuh,gayt/ *vt* to rid of something morally harmful, offensive, or erroneous; *esp* to remove objectionable parts from, before publication or presentation ⟨*~ a book*⟩ [L *expurgatus*, pp of *expurgare*, fr *ex-* + *purgare* to purge] – **expurgator** *n*, **expurgation** *n*, **expurgatorial** *adj*, **expurgatory** *adj*

¹**exquisite** /ik'skwizit, 'ekswizit/ *adj* **1** of meat, drink, etc carefully selected; choice **2a** marked by flawless, beautiful, and usu delicate craftsmanship **b** keenly sensitive, esp in feeling; discriminating ⟨*~ taste*⟩ **3a** extremely beautiful; delightful ⟨*an ~ white blossom*⟩ **b** acute, intense ⟨*~ pain*⟩ ⟨*~ pleasure*⟩ **4** *archaic* accurate **5** *archaic* accomplished ⟨*an ~ gentleman*⟩ [ME *exquisit*, fr L *exquisitus*, fr pp of *exquirere* to search out, fr *ex-* + *quaerere* to seek] – **exquisitely** *adv*, **exquisiteness** *n*
**usage** The pronunciation /'ekskwizit/ is recommended for BBC broadcasters.

²**exquisite** *n*, *archaic* a dandy, fop

**exsanguinate** /ik'sang-gwi,nayt/ *vt* to drain of blood – used technically [L *exsanguinatus* bloodless, fr *ex-* + *sanguin-*, *sanguis* blood] – **exsanguination** *n*

**exscind** /ek'sind/ *vt, formal* to cut off or out; excise [L *exscindere*, fr *ex-* + *scindere* to cut, tear – more at SHED]

**exsert** /ek'suht/ *vt, biology* to thrust out; cause to extrude or project [L *exsertus*, pp of *exserere* – more at EXERT] – **exsertile** *adj*, **exsertion** *n*

**exserted** /ek'suhtid/ *adj, botany* projecting beyond an enclosing organ or part ⟨*anthers ~*⟩

**exsiccate** /'eksi,kayt/ *vt, formal* to remove moisture from; dry – usu pass [L *exsiccatus*, pp of *exsiccare*, fr *ex-* + *siccare* to dry, fr *siccus* dry – more at SACK] – **exsiccation** *n*

**exstipulate** /ek'stipyoolət, -,layt/ *adj*, of a plant or leaf having no STIPULES (small paired leaflike parts at the base of the leaf stalk)

**extant** /ek'stant/ *adj* **1** still or currently existing; not destroyed or lost ⟨*~ manuscripts*⟩ **2** *archaic* standing out or above **þ** extent [L *exstant-*, *exstans*, prp of *exstare* to stand out, be in existence, fr *ex-* + *stare* to stand – more at STAND]

**extemporaneous** /ik,stempə'raynyəs, -ni-əs/ *adj* **1a** done, spoken, performed, etc on the spur of the moment; impromptu ⟨*gave a witty ~ speech*⟩ **b** skilled at or given to extemporaneous speech **2** provided, made, or put to use as an expedient; makeshift [LL *extemporaneus*, fr L *ex tempore*] – **extemporaneously** *adv*, **extemporaneousness** *n*, **extemporaneity** *n*

**extemporary** /ik'stemp(ə)rəri/ *adj* extemporaneous – **extemporarily** *adv*

**extempore** /ik'stempəri/ *adv* in an extemporaneous manner ⟨*speaking ~*⟩ [L *ex tempore*, fr *ex* + *tempore*, abl of *tempus* time]

**extempor·ize, -ise** /ik'stempə,riez/ *vi* to speak, or perform something, extemporaneously; improvise ~ *vt* to compose, perform, or utter extemporaneously **þ** temporize – **extemporizer** *n*, **extemporization** *n*

**extend** /ik'stend/ *vt* **1** to spread or stretch forth; unfold ⟨*~ed both her arms*⟩ **2a** to stretch out to fullest length ⟨*~ed the sail*⟩ **b** to exert (eg a horse or oneself) to full capacity ⟨*won the race without ~ing himself*⟩ **c** to increase the bulk of (a product), esp by the addition of a cheaper substance or a modifier; *also* to adulterate **3** to give or offer, usu in response to need; proffer ⟨*~ing aid to the needy*⟩ ⟨*~ing credit to customers*⟩ **4a** to cause to reach (eg in distance or scope) ⟨*national authority was ~ed over new territories*⟩ ⟨*~ed the road to the coast*⟩ **b** to make longer; prolong in time ⟨*~ed their visit by another day*⟩ ⟨*~ed the period over which payment was to be made*⟩ **c** to advance, further ⟨*~ing human knowledge*⟩ **5a** to enlarge ⟨*~ the kitchen*⟩ **b** to increase the scope, meaning, or application of; broaden ⟨*beauty, I suppose, opens the heart, ~s the consciousness* – Algernon Blackwood⟩ **c** *archaic* to exaggerate ~ *vi* **1** to stretch out in distance, space, time, consideration, or coverage ⟨*his jurisdiction ~ed over the whole area*⟩ **2** to reach in scope or application ⟨*his concern ~s beyond mere business to real* *service to his customers*⟩ [ME *extenden*, fr MF or L; MF *esten-dre*, fr L *extendere*, fr *ex-* + *tendere* to stretch – more at THIN] – **extendable, extendible** *adj*

*usage* The use of **extended** rather than **extensive** to mean merely "long" ⟨*an* **extended** *tour of Scotland*⟩ is disliked by some people, who feel that **extended** should mean "lengthened".

**extended** /ik'stendid/ *adj, of a gait or horse* performed or performing with lengthened stride and extended neck ⟨*an ~ trot*⟩ – compare COLLECTED – **extendedly** *adv*, **extendedness** *n*

**extended family** *n* a family unit that includes three or more generations of near relatives in addition to parents and children in one household – compare NUCLEAR FAMILY

**extender** /-də/ *n* one who or that which extends; *esp* a substance (e g a diluting agent, modifier, or adulterant) added to a product to increase its bulk or improve its physical properties; a filler

**extensible** /ik'stensəbl/, **extensile** /-siel/ *adj* capable of being extended – **extensibility** *n*

**extension** /ik'stensh(ə)n/ *n* **1a** extending or being extended **b** an enlargement in scope ⟨*tools are ~s of human hands*⟩ **2a** extent, scope b DENOTATION 2 **3** *medicine* **3a** the stretching of a fractured or dislocated limb so as to restore it to its natural position **b** a straightening of (a limb at) a joint in such a way that the angle between the bones connected by the joint is increased – compare FLEXION 4 **4** *philosophy* the property whereby something occupies space **5** an increase in length of time, specif allowing extra time to fulfil an obligation **6** a programme of instruction by special arrangements (e g correspondence courses) for nonresident students of a university **7a** a part added (e g to a building) **b** an extra telephone connected to the principal line **8** a mathematical set (e g a FIELD or GROUP) that includes a given and similar set as a subset [ME, fr MF or LL; MF, fr LL *extension-*, *extensio*, fr L *extensus*, pp of *extendere*]

**extensional** /ik'stensh(ə)nl/ *adj, philosophy* **1** of or marked by extension; *specif* DENOTATIVE ⟨*the ~ meaning of* cat *is the group of all cats*⟩ **2** concerned with objective reality – **extensionally** *adv*, **extensionality** *n*

**extension lead** *n* an electric flex with suitable fittings (e g a plug or a socket) at either end, used to extend the length of another flex

**extensive** /ik'stensiv, -ziv/ *adj* **1** extensional **2** having wide or considerable extent ⟨*~ reading*⟩ **3** of or being farming in which large areas of land are utilized with minimum expenditure and labour *usage* see EXTEND – **extensively** *adv*, **extensiveness** *n*

**extensometer** /,eksten'somitə/ *n* an instrument for measuring minute deformations of materials (e g metals) resulting from tension, compression, bending, or twisting [*extension* + *-o-* + *-meter*]

**extensor** /ik'stensə, -saw/ *n* a muscle (e g the triceps along the back of the upper arm) that extends or straightens a body part (e g a limb) – compare FLEXOR

**extent** /ik'stent/ *n* **1** the range or distance over which something extends; the scope ⟨*the ~ of his knowledge*⟩ ⟨*the ~ of the forest*⟩ **2** the point, degree, or limit to which something extends ⟨*the ~ of our patience*⟩ [ME, land valuation, seizure of land, fr AF & MF; AF *extente* land valuation, fr MF, area, surveying of land, fr *extendre* to extend]

**extenuate** /ik'stenyoo,ayt/ *vt* **1a** to (try to) lessen the seriousness or extent of (e g a crime) by finding excuses **b** *archaic* to make light of **2** *archaic* **2a** to make thin or emaciated **b** to dilute, weaken **3** *obs* to disparage [L *extenuatus*, pp of *extenuare*, fr *ex-* + *tenuis* thin – more at THIN] – **extenuator** *n*, **extenuation** *n*, **extenuatory** *adj*

¹**exterior** /ik'stiəri-ə/ *adj* **1** on the outside or an outside surface; external **2** suitable for use on outside surfaces ⟨*~ paint*⟩ [L, compar of *exter, exterus* on the outside, foreign, fr *ex*] – **exteriorly** *adv*

*synonyms* **Exterior, external, extraneous,** and **extrinsic** all mean "outside". **Exterior** and **external** are used of things that have a corresponding **interior** or **internal** part or aspect ⟨*an* **exterior**/ **external** *door*⟩. A football, being hollow, has an **exterior** surface, but an apple has not. **External** is used particularly of a surface as seen by an outsider ⟨*the* **external** *appearance of the house*⟩ ⟨*medicine for* **external** *use*⟩. Something **extraneous** has been brought in from outside ⟨**extraneous** *light*⟩ ⟨*an* **extraneous** *body in my eye*⟩. **Extrinsic** applies particularly to qualities which are not essential: the **extrinsic** value of a £1 note can be contrasted with its **intrinsic** value as a piece of paper.

²**exterior** *n* **1a** an exterior part or surface; an outside **b** an

outward manner or appearance ⟨*a deceptively friendly ~*⟩ **2** a representation of an outdoor scene (e g in a film) – **exteriority** *n*

**exterior angle** *n, maths* **1** the angle outside a polygon formed between a line extending from a side and the adjacent side **2** an angle between a line and the two parallel lines that it crosses and that lies outside the parallel lines

**exterior·ize, -ise** /ik'stiəri-ə,riez/ *vt* **1** to externalize **2** *medicine* to move (e g an organ) temporarily outside the abdomen, esp in order to reach a part requiring surgery – **exteriorization** *n*

**exterminate** /ik'stuhmi,nayt/ *vt* to destroy completely; *esp* to kill all of ⟨*~d the mice*⟩ [L *exterminatus*, pp of *exterminare* to drive out, banish, fr *ex-* + *terminus* boundary – more at TERM] – **extermination** *n*, **exterminator** *n*, **exterminatory** *adj*

**extermine** /ik'stuhmin/ *vt, obs* to exterminate

**extern** /ik'stuhn/ *adj, archaic* external [MF or L; MF *externe*, fr L *externus*]

¹**external** /ik'stuhnl/ *adj* **1a** capable of being perceived outwardly ⟨*~ signs of a disease*⟩ ⟨*~ reality*⟩ **b(1)** superficial ⟨*it's just an ~ show of aggression; he's really an affectionate animal*⟩ **b(2)** not intrinsic or essential ⟨*~ circumstances*⟩ **2a** of, connected with, or intended for the outside or an outer part **b** applied or applicable to the outside ⟨*a medication for ~ use only*⟩ **3a(1)** *biology* situated outside, apart, or beyond; *specif* situated away from the central plane that divides an animal, plant, etc into right and left halves **a(2)** arising or acting from outside ⟨*an ~ force*⟩ **b** of dealings or relationships with foreign countries ⟨*the BBC's ~ services*⟩ **c** *philosophy* having existence independent of the mind ⟨*~ reality*⟩ *synonyms* see ¹EXTERIOR [ME, fr L *externus*, fr *exter*] – **externally** *adv*, **externality** *n*

²**external** *n* something that is external: e g **a** *pl* an external feature or aspect **b** *archaic* an outer part

**external-combustion engine** *n* an engine (e g a steam engine) that converts heat energy derived from fuel consumed outside the engine cylinder into mechanical energy

**external degree** *n* a degree taken without actually attending the university that awards it

**external examiner** *n* a visiting examiner who ensures impartiality and equality of standards in an examination

**external-ize, -ise** /ik'stuhnl,iez/ *vt* **1** to make (e g an emotion) external or externally visible **2** *psychology* to attribute to causes outside the self; rationalize ⟨*~s his failure*⟩ – **externalization** *n*

**external respiration** *n* exchange of gases between the external environment and a distributing system of the animal body (e g the lungs) – compare INTERNAL RESPIRATION

**exteroceptive** /,ekstəroh'septiv/ *adj* of, activated by, or being stimuli (e g light or heat) received by an organism from outside the body [L *exter* + E *-o-* + *-ceptive* (as in *receptive*)]

**exteroceptor** /'ekstəroh,septə/ *n* a SENSE ORGAN (e g the eye) that receives and transmits exteroceptive stimuli [NL, fr L *exter* + NL *-o-* + *-ceptor* (as in *receptor*)]

**exterritorial** /,eks,teri'tawri-əl/ *adj* EXTRATERRITORIAL (outside the boundaries of legal control) – **exterritoriality** *n*

¹**extinct** /ik'stingkt/ *adj* **1a** no longer burning **b** no longer active ⟨*an ~ volcano*⟩ **2** no longer existing as a species ⟨*an ~ animal*⟩ **3** having no qualified claimant ⟨*an ~ title*⟩ [ME, fr L *exstinctus*, pp of *exstinguere*]

²**extinct** *vt, archaic* to extinguish

**extinction** /ik'stingksh(ə)n/ *n* **1** making extinct or causing to be extinguished **2** being extinct or extinguished **3** the elimination or reduction of a conditioned or learned response by withdrawing the reward (REINFORCER) that usu follows and helps to establish the response

**extine** /'ekstin, 'ekstien, 'eksteen/ *n* EXINE

**extinguish** /ik'sting-gwish/ *vt* **1a** to cause (a fire, flame, etc) to cease burning; quench **b(1)** to bring to an end ⟨*hope for their safety was slowly ~ed*⟩ **b(2)** to reduce (e g an opponent) to silence or ineffectiveness **c** to cause extinction of (a conditioned response) **d** to dim the brightness of by overshadowing; eclipse **2** *law* **2a** to make void; nullify ⟨*~ a claim*⟩ **b** to abolish (a debt) by payment *synonyms* see ABOLISH [L *exstinguere* (fr *ex-* + *stinguere* to extinguish) + E *-ish* (as in *abolish*); akin to L *instigare* to incite – more at STICK] – **extinguishable** *adj*, **extinguisher** *n*, **extinguishment** *n*

**extirpate** /'ekstuh,payt/ *vt* **1** to destroy completely (as if) by uprooting; annihilate **2** *medicine* to cut out by surgery [L *exstirpatus*, pp of *exstirpare*, fr *ex-* + *stirp-, stirps* trunk, root – more at TORPID] – **extirpator** *n*, **extirpation** *n*, **extirpative** *adj*

**extol,** *NAm also* **extoll** /ik'stohl, -'stol/ *vt* **-ll-** to praise highly;

glorify ⟨~ling *its virtues*⟩ [ME *extollen,* fr L *extollere,* fr *ex-* + *tollere* to lift up – more at TOLERATE] – **extoller** *n,* **extolment** *n*

**extort** /ik'stawt/ *vt* to obtain from a person by force or threats ⟨~ *money*⟩ ⟨~ *a confession*⟩ [L *extortus,* pp of *extorquēre* to wrench out, extort, fr *ex-* + *torquēre* to twist – more at TORTURE] – **extorter** *n,* **extortive** *adj*

**extortion** /ik'stawsh(ə)n/ *n* 1 extorting; *specif* the unlawful extorting of money 2 something extorted; *esp* a gross overcharge – **extortioner** *n,* **extortionist** *n*

**extortionary** /ik'stawshən(ə)ri/ *adj, archaic* EXTORTIONATE 1

**extortionate** /ik'stawsh(ə)nət/ *adj* 1 characterized by extortion 2 excessive, exorbitant – **extortionately** *adv*

¹**extra** /'ekstrə/ *adj* 1 more than is due, usual, or necessary; additional ⟨~ *work*⟩ 2 subject to an additional charge ⟨*room service is* ~⟩ [prob short for *extraordinary*]

²**extra** *n* 1 something extra or additional: eg **1a** an added charge **b** a specified edition of a newspaper ⟨*late night* ~⟩ **c** an additional worker; *specif* one hired to act in a group scene in a film or stage production **d** a run in cricket (e g a bye, LEG BYE, no-ball, or wide) that is not scored by a stroke of the bat and is not credited to a batsman's individual score 2 *NAm* something of superior quality or grade

³**extra** *adv* beyond or above the usual size, extent, or amount ⟨~ *large*⟩ ⟨*to work* ~ *hard*⟩

**extra-** /ekstrə-/ *prefix* outside; beyond ⟨extra*judicial*⟩ ⟨extra*mural*⟩ [ME, fr L, fr *extra,* adv & prep, outside, except, beyond, fr *exter* on the outside – more at EXTERIOR]

**extracellular** /,ekstrə'selyoolə/ *adj* situated or occurring outside a cell or the cells of the body ⟨~ *digestion*⟩ ⟨~ *enzymes*⟩ – **extracellularly** *adv*

**extrachromosomal** /,ekstrə-/ *adj, genetics* situated or controlled by factors outside the CHROMOSOMES (strands of gene-carrying material) of a cell

**extra cover** *n* a fielding position in cricket about halfway to the boundary on the OFF SIDE of the pitch, situated in front of the batsman's wicket between cover-point and mid-off; *also* the fieldsman occupying this position

**extracranial** /ekstrə'krayni·əl/ *adj, anatomy* situated or occurring outside the skull

¹**extract** /ik'strakt/ *vt* 1 to draw forth or pull out, esp against resistance or with effort ⟨~ *data*⟩ ⟨~ed *a wisdom tooth*⟩ ⟨~ed *a confession*⟩ 2 to withdraw (e g a juice) or separate from a mixture by physical or chemical process (e g distillation or treatment with a solvent so as to remove a soluble substance) 3 to separate (a metal) from an ore 4 to find (a mathematical ROOT) by calculation 5 to select (excerpts) [ME *extracten,* fr L *extractus,* pp of *extrahere,* fr *ex-* + *trahere* to draw] – **extractable, extractible** *adj,* **extractor** *n,* **extractability** *n*

²**extract** /'ekstrakt/ *n* 1 an excerpt 2 a product (e g an essence or concentrate) prepared by extracting; *esp* a solution of the essential or active constituents of a complex material (e g meat or an aromatic plant) ⟨*beef* ~⟩ ⟨*lemon* ~⟩

**extraction** /ik'straksh(ə)n/ *n* 1 the act or process of extracting 2 ancestry, origin 3 something extracted

¹**extractive** /ik'straktiv/ *adj* **1a** of or involving extraction ⟨~ *processes*⟩ **b** tending towards or resulting in the depletion of natural resources by extraction with no provision for replenishment ⟨~ *agriculture*⟩ 2 capable of being extracted – **extractively** *adv*

²**extractive** *n* something extracted or extractable; an extract

**extractor fan** *n* a ventilator, usu electrically driven, designed to expel fumes, stale air, etc

**extracurricular** /,ekstrəkə'rikyoolə/ *adj* 1 not falling within the scope of a regular school or college curriculum ⟨~ *activities such as attendance of clubs and societies*⟩ 2 lying outside one's required or expected activities ⟨*worked extra hours on* ~ *tasks*⟩

**extraditable** /'ekstrə,dietəbl/ *adj* 1 subject or liable to extradition 2 warranting extradition ⟨*an* ~ *offence*⟩

**extradite** /'ekstrə,diet/ *vt* 1 to hand over for extradition – compare BANISH 2 to obtain the extradition of (a criminal suspect or fugitive) [back-formation fr *extradition*]

**extradition** /,ekstrə'dish(ə)n/ *n* the surrender of an alleged criminal, usu under the provisions of a treaty or statute, by one state to another having the power by law to try the charge [Fr, fr *ex-* + L *tradition-, traditio* act of handing over – more at TRADITION]

**extrados** /ek'straydos, -dohz/ *n, pl* **extrados, extradoses** the convex upper surface of an arch – compare INTRADOS [Fr, fr L *extra* + Fr *dos* back – more at DOSSIER]

**extragalactic** /,ekstrəgə'laktik/ *adj* situated or coming from outside the MILKY WAY [ISV]

**extrahepatic** /,ekstrəhe'patik/ *adj, anatomy* situated or originating outside the liver

**extrajudicial** /,ekstrəjooh'dish(ə)l/ *adj* **1a** not forming part of regular legal proceedings ⟨*an* ~ *investigation*⟩ **b** *of an opinion* not given in the speaker's judicial capacity 2 done in contravention of the law ⟨*an* ~ *execution*⟩ – **extrajudicially** *adv*

**extralimital** /,ekstrə'limitl/ *adj* not present in a given area – used of kinds of organisms (e g species)

**extralinguistic** /,ekstrəlin'gwistik/ *adj* lying outside the province of linguistics – **extralinguistically** *adv*

**extramarital** /,ekstrə'maritl/ *adj* of sexual relations with other than one's spouse; adulterous

**extramundane** /,ekstrə'mundayn, ---'-/ *adj* of or situated in a region beyond the material world [LL *extramundanus,* fr L *extra* + *mundus* the world]

**extramural** /,ekstrə'myooərəl/ *adj* 1 being or functioning outside or beyond the walls, boundaries, or precincts of a place or organization (e g a town or fortress) 2 *chiefly Br* of or taking part in extension courses or facilities ⟨*university* ~ *department*⟩ – **extramurally** *adv*

**extraneous** /ik'straynyəs, -ni·əs/ *adj* 1 existing on or coming from the outside ⟨~ *influences*⟩ 2 not forming an essential or vital part; irrelevant ⟨*an* ~ *scene that added nothing to the play*⟩ 3 *maths* being a number obtained in solving an equation that is not a solution of the equation ⟨~ *roots*⟩ *synonyms* see ¹EXTERIOR [L *extraneus* – more at STRANGE] – **extraneously** *adv,* **extraneousness** *n*

**extranuclear** /,ekstrə'nyoohkliə/ *adj* 1 situated or occurring in or affecting the parts of a cell outside the nucleus; CYTOPLASMIC 2 situated outside the nucleus of an atom

**extraocular muscle** /,ekstrə'okyoolə/ *n* any of six small VOLUNTARY MUSCLES that pass between the eyeball and the eye socket and control the movement of the eyeball in relation to the socket

**extraordinary** /ik'strawdin(ə)ri/ *adj* **1a** going beyond what is usual, regular, or customary ⟨*an Act that gave him* ~ *powers*⟩ **b** highly exceptional; remarkable ⟨~ *beauty*⟩ 2 being for a special function or service ⟨*an ambassador* ~⟩ ⟨*an* ~ *general meeting*⟩ [ME *extraordinarie,* fr L *extraordinarius,* fr *extra ordinem* out of course, fr *extra* + *ordinem,* acc of *ordin-, ordo* order] – **extraordinarily** *adv,* **extraordinariness** *n*

**extrapolate** /ek'strapə,layt/ *vt* 1 *maths* to predict (a value of a variable at a given point) by extending a line or curve plotted on a graph from known values at previous points – compare INTERPOLATE 3 **2a** to use or extend (known data or experience) in order to surmise or work out something unknown ⟨~s *present trends to construct an image of the future*⟩ **b** to predict by considering past experience or known data; infer ⟨~ *future energy demands*⟩ ~ *vi* to perform the act or process of extrapolating [L *extra* outside + E *-polate* (as in *interpolate*)] – **extrapolator** *n,* **extrapolation** *n,* **extrapolative** *adj*

**extrasensory** /,ekstrə'sens(ə)ri/ *adj* residing beyond or outside the ordinary physical senses ⟨*instances of* ~ *perception*⟩

**extrasensory perception** *n* (the faculty of) perception by means (e g telepathy and clairvoyance) other than the known senses

**extrasystole** /,ekstrə'sistəli/ *n, medicine* a premature beat of any of the chambers of the heart that leads to momentary change in rhythm of the heartbeat [NL] – **extrasystolic** *adj*

**extraterrestrial** /,ekstrətə'restriəl/ *adj* originating or existing outside the earth or its atmosphere ⟨~ *life*⟩; *also* of extraterrestrial space ⟨~ *exploration*⟩

**extraterritorial** /,ekstrə,teri'tawri·əl/ *adj* existing or taking place outside the territorial limits within which the authority of the law may be exercised

**extraterritoriality** /-,teri,tawri'aləti/ *n* exemption from the application or authority of local law or tribunals – used esp of the privileges granted to diplomats serving in a foreign country

**extra time** *n* a period of usu 30 minutes added to the end of a soccer match in certain competitions to resolve a draw

**extrauterine** /,ekstrə'yoohtə,rien/ *adj, anatomy* situated or occurring outside the uterus ⟨~ *pregnancy*⟩ [ISV]

**extravagance** /ik'stravəgəns/, **extravagancy** /-si/ *n* **1a** an extravagant act; *specif* an excessive outlay of money **b** something extravagant 2 the quality or fact of being extravagant

**extravagant** /-gənt/ *adj* **1a** lacking in moderation, balance, and restraint; excessive ⟨~ *praise*⟩ **b** excessively elaborate or showy **2a** wasteful, esp of money **b** profuse **3** unreasonably high in price; exorbitant **4a** *archaic* wandering **b** *obs* strange, curious [MF, wandering, irregular, fr ML *extravagant-, extravagans*, fr L *extra-* + *vagant-, vagans*, prp of *vagari* to wander about – more at VAGARY] – **extravagantly** *adv*

**extravaganza** /ik,stravə'ganzə/ *n* **1** a literary or musical work marked by extreme freedom of style and structure and usu by elements of comic imitation, mockery, or ridicule **2** a lavish or spectacular show or event [It *estravaganza*, lit., extravagance, fr *estravagante* extravagant, fr ML *extravagant-, extravagans*]

**extravagate** /ik'stravə,gayt/ *vi, archaic* to go beyond proper limits (e g of standards of acceptable conduct)

¹**extravasate** /ik'stravə,sayt/ *vt* to force out or cause (e g blood) to escape from the proper vessel, duct, or channel in the body ~ *vi* **1** to pass by permeating or pouring out from a vessel, duct, or channel (e g a blood vessel) into surrounding tissue **2** to pour out or erupt from a vent ⟨*lava* ~d *from the fissure*⟩ [L *extra* + *vas* vessel – more at VASE] – **extravasation** *n*

²**extravasate** *n* an extravasated liquid (e g blood)

**extravascular** /,ekstrə'vaskyoolə/ *adj* not contained in or not having vessels ⟨~ *plant fibres*⟩ ⟨~ *tissue fluids*⟩

**extravehicular** /,ekstrəvee'ikyoolə/ *adj* taking place outside a spacecraft in flight ⟨~ *activity*⟩

**extravert** /'ekstrə,vuht/ *n or adj* (an) extrovert

¹**extreme** /ik'streem/ *adj* **1a** existing in a very high degree ⟨~ *poverty*⟩ ⟨~ *cold*⟩ **b** going to great or exaggerated lengths; not moderate ⟨*an* ~ *right-winger*⟩ **c** exceeding the ordinary, usual, or expected; severe ⟨*took* ~ *measures*⟩ **2** situated at the farthest possible point from a centre or the nearest to an end ⟨*the country's* ~ *north*⟩ **3a** most advanced or thoroughgoing; utmost ⟨*the* ~ *avant-garde*⟩ **b** maximum ⟨*the* ~ *penalty*⟩ **4** *archaic* last [ME, fr MF, fr L *extremus*, superl of *exter, exterus* on the outside – more at EXTERIOR] – **extremeness** *n*

²**extreme** *n* **1a** something situated at or marking one or other extreme point of a range ⟨~s *of heat and cold*⟩ **b** the first term or the last term of a mathematical proportion (e g 4 or 5 in the proportion 4/2 = 10/5) **2** a very pronounced or extreme degree ⟨*his enthusiasm was carried to an* ~⟩ **3** an extreme measure or expedient ⟨*going to* ~s⟩ – **in the extreme** to the greatest possible extent ⟨*boring in the extreme*⟩

**extremely** /ik'streemli/ *adv* **1** in an extreme manner **2** to an extreme extent ⟨~ *rude*⟩

**extremely high frequency** *n* a radio frequency in the range between 30 000 and 300 000 megahertz

**extremely low frequency** *n* a radio frequency in the range between 30 and 300 hertz

**extreme unction** *n* ANOINTING OF THE SICK

**extremism** /ik'stree,miz(ə)m/ *n* the quality or state of being extreme; *esp* advocacy of extreme political measures; radicalism – **extremist** *n or adj*

**extremity** /ik'streməti/ *n* **1a** the most extreme part, section, point, or degree **b** a (human) limb or the part of a limb furthest from the body (e g a hand or foot) **2** (a moment marked by) extreme misfortune and esp danger of destruction or death – compare IN EXTREMIS **3 extremities** *pl*, **extremity** a drastic or desperate act or measure

**extremum** /ik'streeməm/ *n, pl* **extrema** /-mə/ a maximum or a minimum variable of a mathematical function in which a variable in one set corresponds to a variable in the same or another set [NL, fr L, neut of *extremus*]

**extricate** /'ekstri,kayt/ *vt* **1** to disentangle, esp with considerable effort ⟨*manage to* ~ *oneself from a tricky situation*⟩ **2** *archaic* to unravel [L *extricatus*, pp of *extricare*, fr *ex-* + *tricae* trifles, perplexities] – **extricable** *adj*, **extrication** *n*

**extrinsic** /ek'strinsik, -zik/ *adj* **1a** not forming part of or belonging to a thing; extraneous **b** *anatomy* originating from or on the outside; *esp* originating outside a part and acting on the part as a whole **2** external *synonyms* see ¹EXTERIOR *antonym* intrinsic [Fr & LL; Fr *extrinsèque*, fr LL *extrinsecus*, fr L, adv, from without; akin to L *exter* outward & to L *sequi* to follow – more at EXTERIOR, SUE] – **extrinsically** *adv*

**extrinsic factor** *n* VITAMIN B₁₂ – compare INTRINSIC FACTOR

**extro-** *prefix* outwards ⟨extro*vert*⟩ – compare INTRO- [alter. of L *extra-*]

**extrorse** /ek'straws/ *adj* of or being an ANTHER (pollen-bearing flower structure) opening on the side turned away from the centre of the flower [LL *extrorsus* outwards, fr L *extra-* + *-orsus* (as in *introrsus*) – more at INTRORSE] – **extrorsely** *adv*

**extrovert**, *also* **extravert** /'ekstrə,vuht/ *n* one whose attention and interests are directed wholly or predominantly towards what is outside the self – compare INTROVERT [deriv of L *extra-* + *vertere* to turn] – **extrovert** *adj*, **extroverted** *adj*, **extroversion** *n*

**extrude** /ik'stroohd/ *vt* **1** to force, press, or push out **2** to shape (e g metal or plastic) by forcing through a perforated block (DIE 3d) ~ *vi* to become extruded [L *extrudere*, fr *ex-* + *trudere* to thrust] – **extrudable** *adj*, **extruder** *n*, **extrudability** *n*

**extrusion** /ik'stroohzh(ə)n/ *n* **1** the act or process of extruding; *also* a form or product produced by this process **2a** the flowing out of lava onto the earth's surface through vents and fissures in the earth's crust during volcanic eruption **b** a mass of rock formed by extrusion; an extrusive rock [ML *extrusion-, extrusio*, fr L *extrusus*, pp of *extrudere*]

**extrusive** /ik'stroohsiv, -ziv/ *adj, of a rock* formed by the cooling and solidification of lava poured out at the earth's surface by volcanic action

**exuberant** /ig'zyoohb(ə)rənt/ *adj* **1a** joyously unrestrained and enthusiastic ⟨~ *high spirits*⟩ **b** lavish and flamboyant ⟨~ *metaphors*⟩ **2** great or extreme in degree, size, or extent **3** produced in extreme abundance; plentiful, luxuriant ⟨~ *vegetation*⟩ *synonyms* see PROFUSE *antonyms* restrained, austere [ME, fr MF, fr L *exuberant-, exuberans*, prp of *exuberare* to be abundant, fr *ex-* + *uber* fruitful, fr *uber* udder – more at UDDER] – **exuberance** *n*, **exuberantly** *adv*

**exuberate** /ig'zyoohbə,rayt/ *vi* **1** to become exuberant; show exuberance ⟨~d *over his victory*⟩ **2** *archaic* to have something in abundance; overflow

**exudate** /'eksyoo,dayt/ *n* exuded matter

**exude** /ig'zyoohd/ *vi* to ooze out ⟨*moisture* ~d *from the damp wall*⟩ ~ *vt* **1** to allow or cause to ooze or spread out in all directions ⟨~ *sweat*⟩ **2** to radiate an air of ⟨~s *charm*⟩ [L *exsudare*, fr *ex-* + *sudare* to sweat – more at SWEAT] – **exudation** *n*

**exult** /ig'zult/ *vi* **1a** to be extremely joyful; rejoice openly ⟨~ing *in their victory*⟩ – usu + *in, at,* or *over* **b** to revel in the defeat, humiliation, frustration, etc of a person or group of people ⟨~ed *over their vanquished foes*⟩ – usu + *over* **2** *obs* to leap for joy △ **exalt** [MF *exulter*, fr L *exsultare*, lit., to leap up, fr *ex-* + *saltare* to leap – more at SALTIRE] – **exultance** *n*, **exultancy** *n*, **exultant** *adj*, **exultantly** *adv*, **exultation** *n*, **exultingly** *adv*

**exurb** /'eksuhb, 'egzuhb/ *n* a prosperous district outside a city and usu beyond its suburbs [*ex-* + *-urb* (as in *suburb*)] – **exurban** *adj*, **exurbanite** *n*

**exurbia** /ek'suhbi·ə, egz-/ *n* exurbs collectively – compare SUBURBIA

**exuviae** /ig'zyoohvi,ee/ *n taking pl vb* the natural coverings of animals (e g the skins of snakes) after they have been shed [L, fr *exuere* to take off, fr *ex-* + *-uere* to put on; akin to ORuss *izuti* to take off footwear] – **exuvial** *adj*

**exuviate** /ig'zyoohvi,ayt/ *vb* to moult or shed (e g skin) – **exuviation** *n*

¹**ex-voto** /eks'vohtoh/ *n, pl* **ex-votos** an offering given in fulfilment of a vow or in gratitude or devotion [L *ex voto* according to a vow]

²**ex-voto** *adj* undertaken in accordance with a vow; votive

**-ey** /-i/ – see -Y

**eyas** /'ee·əs/ *n* a young hawk in the nest [ME, alter. (by incorrect division of *a neias*) of *neias*, fr MF *niais* fresh from the nest, fr (assumed) VL *nidax* nestling, fr L *nidus* nest – more at NEST]

¹**eye** /ie/ *n* **1a** any of various usu paired organs of sight; *esp* a nearly spherical liquid-filled organ that is lined with a light-sensitive retina and housed in a bony socket in the skull **b** all the visible parts of the eye with its surrounding structures (e g eyelids, eyelashes, and eyebrows) **c(1)** the faculty of seeing with eyes ⟨*a keen* ~ *for detail*⟩ **c(2)** the faculty of intellectual or aesthetic perception or appreciation ⟨*an* ~ *for beauty*⟩ **d** a gaze; glance ⟨*peering with an eager* ~⟩ ⟨*caught his* ~⟩ **e** an attentive watch ⟨*kept an* ~ *on his valuables*⟩ **f** view, attention ⟨*in the public* ~⟩ **2** something suggestive of an eye: e g **2a** the hole through the head of a needle **b** a (nearly) circular mark (e g on a peacock's tail) **c** a loop; *esp* one of metal or thread into which a hook is inserted (e g for fastening a skirt) – compare HOOK AND EYE **d** an undeveloped bud (e g on a potato) **e** an area in the centre of a tropical cyclone marked by only light winds or complete calm with no rain **f** the centre of a flower, esp when differently coloured or marked; *specif* the central part (DISC 2) of the flower head of a daisy or related plant **g(1)** a triangular piece of beef cut from the thigh **g(2)** the chief muscle of a pork, lamb, or veal chop **g(3)** a compact mass of muscular

tissue usu embedded in fat in a rib or loin cut of meat **3** the centre, nub ⟨*the ~ of the problem* – Norman Mailer⟩ **4** the direction from which the wind is blowing **5** the extreme forward end of a ship **6** the loop of an EYE SPLICE **7** a ring (e g of metal) through which a rope, rod, etc is passed [ME, fr OE *ēage;* akin to OHG *ouga* eye, L *oculus,* Gk *ōps* eye, face] – **eyeless** *adj,* **eyelike** *adj* – **close one's eyes to** to ignore deliberately – **do somebody in the eye** *slang* to trick or cheat somebody – **get/keep one's eye in 1** *chiefly Br* to get into or keep in practice; *specif* to gain or retain ability **2** to judge the speed and direction of a moving ball – **have an eye to the main chance** to look for opportunities for personal advancement, often at others' expense – **have one's eye on 1** to watch, esp constantly and attentively **2** to have as an objective – **in the eye/eyes of** in the judgment or opinion of ⟨*beauty is* in the eye of *the beholder*⟩ – **keep one's eyes open/peeled,** *Br* skinned to be on the alert; be watchful – **more than meets the eye** more than is at first obvious or apparent ⟨*there's* more *to this business* than meets the eye⟩ – **my eye** *informal* – used to express mild disagreement or sometimes surprise ⟨*a diamond,* my eye! *That's glass*⟩ – no longer in vogue – **one in the eye for** a disappointment or setback for – **see eye to eye (with)** to have the same opinion (as); agree (with) ⟨*we* saw eye to eye *over the problem*⟩ ⟨*I* saw eye to eye with *him over that matter*⟩ – **set/clap eyes on** to catch sight of – **turn a blind eye (to)** to overlook or disregard (something) deliberately ⟨*we* turned a blind eye *to his criminal record as he seemed so suitable for the job*⟩ – **with an eye to** having as an aim or purpose – **with one's eyes open** in a state of full awareness of the problems, difficulties, etc that a situation will present ⟨*I went into the army* with my eyes open⟩ – see also APPLE **of one's eye,** not BAT **an eye,** SIGHT **for sore eyes,** UP **to one's eyes,** pull the WOOL **over somebody's eyes**

**²eye** *vt* **eyeing, eying** to fix the eyes on; *esp* to watch closely *synonyms* see ¹GAZE – **eyer** *n*
   **eye up** *vt, informal* to look at (somebody) in order to assess sexual attractiveness ⟨*he was* eyeing up *the talent*⟩ ⟨*he was* eyeing *her* up⟩

**¹eyeball** /'ie,bawl/ *n* the more or less globular capsule of the eye of a VERTEBRATE animal, that is formed by the SCLERA (dense fibrous opaque white outer coat) and the transparent CORNEA at the front of the eye together with the structures they contain
**²eyeball** *vt, NAm informal* to look at intently
**,eyeball-to-'eyeball** *adj, informal* face-to-face and hostile ⟨*an ~ confrontation*⟩ – **eyeball-to-eyeball** *adv*
**eye bank** *n* a place where human CORNEAS (transparent membranes covering the front of the eye) are stored for transplanting to the eyes of those who are blind through corneal defects
**eyebath** /'ie,bahth/ *n* a small oval cup specially shaped for applying typically antiseptic solutions to the eye; *broadly* any object for rinsing the eyes
**eyebolt** /'ie,bohlt/ *n* a bolt with a looped head
**eyebright** /'ie,briet/ *n* any of a genus (*Euphrasia*) of tiny plants of the foxglove family with very small typically white or whitish-violet flowers [fr its former use as a remedy for eye ailments]
**eyebrow** /'ie,brow/ *n* (the line of hair growing on) the ridge over the eye – **raise an eyebrow/eyebrows** to cause or show surprise or astonishment – see also UP TO **one's eyebrows**
**eyebrow pencil** *n* a cosmetic pencil for colouring the eyebrows
**'eye-,catching** *adj* strikingly visually attractive – **eye-catchingly** *adv,* **eye-catcher** *n*
**eyed** /ied/ *adj* having an eye or eyes, esp of a specified kind or number – often in combination ⟨*an almond-eyed girl*⟩
**eye dialect** *n* the use of pronunciation-based spellings (e g *sez* for *says*) in a written representation of speech, esp to convey an impression of illiteracy

**eyeful** /-f(ə)l/ *n, informal* a pleasing sight; *specif* an attractive woman
**eyeglass** /'ie,glahs/ *n* **1a** an eyepiece **b** a lens worn to aid vision; *specif* a monocle **c** *pl* glasses, spectacles **2** an eyebath
**eyehole** /'ie,hohl/ *n* **1** the bony socket of the eye **2** a peephole
**eyelash** /'ie,lash/ *n* (a single hair of) the fringe of hair edging the eyelid
**eyelet** /'ielit/ *n* **1a** a small usu reinforced hole, either designed for a cord, lace, etc to be passed through it or used in embroidery **b** a small typically metal ring to reinforce an eyelet; a grommet **2** a peephole [ME *oilet,* fr MF *oillet,* dim. of *oil* eye, fr L *oculus*]
**eyelid** /'ie,lid/ *n* a movable lid of skin and muscle that can be closed over the eyeball – see also not BAT **an eyelid**
**eyeliner** /'ie,lienə/ *n* a cosmetic for emphasizing the contours of the eyes
**eyen** /'ie·ən/ *archaic pl of* EYE
**'eye-,opener** *n* **1** *chiefly NAm* a drink intended to stop one feeling sleepy on waking up **2** *informal* something startling or surprising, esp when revelatory ⟨*his behaviour was a real ~ to me*⟩ – **eye-opening** *adj*
**eyepiece** /'ie,pees/ *n* the lens or combination of lenses at the eye end of an optical instrument (e g a telescope)
**eye rhyme** *n* a rhyme in which two words (e g *move* and *love*) appear from text spelling to rhyme but are pronounced differently
**eyeshade** /'ie,shayd/ *n* a small shield, usu shaped like the peak of a cap, that shades the eyes from strong light and is fastened to the head with a headband
**eye shadow** *n* a coloured cream or powder that is applied to the eyelids to accentuate the eyes
**eyeshot** /'ie,shot/ *n* the range to which one can see; the view
**eyesight** /'ie,siet/ *n* the power or function of seeing; sight
**eyesore** /'ie,saw/ *n* something offensive to the sight
**eye splice** *n* a loop formed in a rope by bending back one end and interweaving the strands with the main body of the rope
**eyespot** /'ie,spot/ *n* **1** a simple visual organ consisting of a small area or body of light-sensitive pigment or pigmented cells; OCELLUS **2** a coloured eyelike marking (e g on the wings of moths and butterflies)
**eyestalk** /'ie,stawk/ *n* either of the movable stalks bearing an eye at the tip in a crab or related CRUSTACEAN
**eyestrain** /'ie,strayn/ *n* tiredness or a strained state of the eye caused by overuse of the eyes (e g with continual close work in poor light) or by neglecting to treat faulty vision
**Eyetie** /'ietie, -ti/ *n or adj, chiefly Br derog* (an) Italian [by shortening & alter.]
**eyetooth** /'ie,toohth/ *n* a CANINE tooth of the upper jaw
**eyewash** /'ie,wosh/ *n, informal* misleading or deceptive statements, actions, or procedures; rubbish, claptrap
**eyewink** /'ie,wingk/ *n, obs* a look, glance
**eyewitness** /'ie,witnis/ *n* one who sees an occurrence and can bear witness to it (e g in court)
**eyot** /ayt, 'ay·ət/ *n* AIT (small island)
**eyre** /eə/ *n* a circuit made by royal justices who travelled round in medieval times; *also* a court held on this circuit [ME *eire,* fr AF, fr OF *erre* trip, fr *errer* to travel – more at ERRANT]
**eyrie, aerie, aery** /'iəri, 'eəri, 'ie·əri/ *n* **1** the nest of a bird, esp a bird of prey (e g an eagle), on a cliff or a mountain top **2** a room or dwelling situated high up ⟨*sat in his 7th-floor ~ in Mayfair*⟩ [ML *aeria, aerea,* fr OF *aire,* fr L *area* area, feeding place for animals]
**eyrir** /'ayriə/ *n, pl* **aurar** /'aw,rah/ – see *krona* at MONEY table [Icel, fr ON, money (in pl)]
**Ezekiel, Ezechiel** /i'zeeki·əl, -kyəl/ *n* – see BIBLE table [*Ezekiel,* 6th-c BC Hebrew priest & prophet, fr LL *Ezechiel,* fr Heb *Yĕḥezqēl*]
**Ezra** /'ezrə/ *n* – see BIBLE table [*Ezra,* 5th-c BC Heb priest, fr LL, fr Heb *'Ezrā*]

# F

**f, F** /ef/ *n, pl* **f's, fs, F's Fs 1a** the 6th letter of the English alphabet **b** a graphic representation of or device for reproducing the letter *f* **2** the 4th note of a C-major musical scale **3** one designated *f*, esp as the 6th in order or class **4a** a mark or grade rating a pupil's or student's work as failing **b** one who or that which is graded or rated with an F **5** something shaped like the letter *f*

**fa** /fah/ *n, music* FAH

**FA** /,e'fay/ *n, Br euph* fuck all – often in *sweet FA*

**fab** /fab/ *adj, Br informal* – used as a generalized term of approval ⟨*had a ~ time at the disco*⟩; no longer in vogue [short for *fabulous*]

**Fabian** /'faybi·ən, -byən/ *adj* of or being a society founded in England in 1884 to work for the gradual establishment of socialism [Quintus *Fabius* Maximus †203 BC Roman general who wore down his enemies while avoiding open battles] – **Fabian** *n*, **Fabianism** *n*

¹**fable** /'faybl/ *n* **1** a fictitious narrative or statement: eg **1a** a legendary story of supernatural happenings **b** a story intended to convey a moral; *esp* one in which animals speak and act like human beings **c** a fictitious account; a lie **2** myths or legendary tales collectively ⟨*often found in Greek ~*⟩ *synonyms* see ALLEGORY [ME, fr OF, fr L *fabula* conversation, story, play, fr *fari* to speak – more at BAN]

²**fable** *vb, archaic vi* to tell fables ~ *vt* to talk or write about as if true – **fabler** *n*

**fabled** /'faybld/ *adj* **1** fictitious **2** told or celebrated in fables; legendary

**fabliau** /'fablioh/ *n, pl* **fabliaux** /'fablioh(z)/ a short usu coarsely satirical verse story popular in the 12th and 13th centuries [Fr, fr OF, dim. of *fable*]

**fabric** /'fabrik/ *n* **1a** a structure; *esp* the basic structure of a building ⟨*the ~ of the theatre*⟩ **b** an underlying structure; a framework ⟨*the ~ of society*⟩ **2** an act of constructing; an erection; *specif* the construction and maintenance of a church building **3a** structural plan or style of construction **b** texture, quality – used chiefly with reference to textiles **4a** cloth **b** a material that resembles cloth **5** the appearance or pattern produced by the shapes and arrangement of the crystal grains in a rock [MF *fabrique*, fr L *fabrica* workshop, structure, fr *fabr-*, *faber* smith]

**fabricate** /-kayt/ *vt* **1** to construct, manufacture; *specif* to construct from diverse and usu standardized parts **2** to invent or create, esp in order to deceive ⟨*he ~d the story in order to justify his actions*⟩ *synonyms* see ¹MAKE [ME *fabricaten*, fr L *fabricatus*, pp of *fabricari*, fr *fabrica*] – **fabricator** *n*, **fabrication** *n*

**fabulist** /'fabyoolist/ *n* **1** one who composes fables **2** a liar

**fabulous** /'fabyoolas/ *adj* **1** resembling things told of in fables, esp in incredible, marvellous, or exaggerated quality; extraordinary ⟨*~ wealth*⟩ **2** told in or based on fable **3** *informal* – used as a generalized term of approval ⟨*a ~ hairdo*⟩ [L *fabulosus*, fr *fabula*] – **fabulously** *adv*, **fabulousness** *n*

**facade, façade** /fə'sahd/ *n* **1** the front or principal face of a building; *also* any other face (eg on a street or court) of a building given special architectural treatment **2** a false or superficial appearance or effect ⟨*maintaining a ~ of contentment*⟩ [Fr *façade*, fr It *facciata*, fr *faccia* face, fr (assumed) VL *facia*]

¹**face** /fays/ *n* **1a** the front part of the human head including the chin, mouth, nose, cheeks, eyes, and usu the forehead **b** the part of an animal (eg the forehead, eyes, nose, and part of the muzzle of a horse) that corresponds to the human face **2a** a facial expression ⟨*a sad ~*⟩ **b** a grimace ⟨*he pulled a ~*⟩ **c** MAKE-UP 2a ⟨*she put her ~ on*⟩ **3a** an outward appearance ⟨*looks suspicious on the ~ of it*⟩ ⟨*put a good ~ on it*⟩ **b** effrontery, impudence ⟨*had the ~ to ask for his money back*⟩ **c** dignity, prestige ⟨*afraid to lose ~*⟩ ⟨*we must save ~ at all

costs*⟩ **4a(1)** a front, upper, or outer surface **a(2)** the front of something with two or four sides **a(3)** a facade **a(4)** an exposed surface of rock **a(5)** any of the 2-dimensional surfaces of a solid formed of regular lines, curves, and angles ⟨*the six ~s of a cube*⟩ **b** a surface specially prepared: eg **b(1)** the right side (eg of cloth or leather) **b(2)** an inscribed, printed, or marked side (eg of a certificate, document, or playing card) **c(1)** the surface (eg of type) that receives the ink and transfers it to the paper **c(2)** a style of type **5** the exposed working surface of a mine or excavation ⟨*coal ~*⟩ **6** *archaic* presence, sight [ME, fr OF, fr (assumed) VL *facia*, fr L *facies* make, form, face, fr *facere* to make, do – more at DO] – **faceless** *adj*, **facelessness** *n* – **in (the) face of** in opposition to; despite ⟨*succeed in the face of great difficulties*⟩ – **put a bold/good face on** to represent (a matter) or confront (an ordeal) as if all were well – **set one's face against** to oppose staunchly – **show one's face** to make an appearance ⟨*didn't think she'd have the audacity to show her face here*⟩ – **stare one/somebody in the face 1** to be very evident **2** to be imminent – **to somebody's face** candidly in somebody's presence so that he/she is fully aware of what is going on; frankly ⟨*told her exactly how I felt to her face*⟩ – **until one is blue in the face** unsuccessfully for ever ⟨*you can complain until you're blue in the face but no one will listen*⟩ – see also FLY **in the face of,** cut off one's NOSE **to spite one's face,** SLAP **in the face**

²**face** *vt* **1** to confront defiantly or impudently ⟨*~d out the opposition*⟩ – usu + *out* **2a** to apply a facing to (eg a dress neckline) **b** to cover the front or surface of ⟨*~ the building with marble*⟩ **3** to bring face-to-face *with;* confront ⟨*~d him with the evidence*⟩ **4** to have the face towards ⟨*~ the wall*⟩; *also* to front on ⟨*a house facing the park*⟩ **5** to meet or deal with firmly and without evasion ⟨*~ the facts*⟩ **6** to turn (eg a playing card) face-up **7** to make the surface of (eg a stone) flat or smooth **8** to cause (troops) to face in a particular direction on command ~ *vi* **1** to have the face or front turned in a specified direction ⟨*the house ~s to the east*⟩ **2** to turn the face in a specified direction – see also **face the** MUSIC

**face down** *vt* to master by defiant confrontation ⟨*faced down his critics*⟩

**face up to** *vt* to confront without shrinking

*usage* The expression **face up to** ⟨*we must face up to the situation*⟩ is disliked by some people, who prefer to use the verb *face* alone in this sense.

**face card** *n* COURT CARD

**facecloth** /'fays,kloth/ *n* a small cloth (eg of flannel) used in washing oneself, esp one's face

**-faced** /-fayst/ *comb form* (*adj, n → adj*) having (such) a face or (so many) faces ⟨*two-faced*⟩ ⟨*rosy-faced*⟩

**face flannel** *n, Br* a facecloth

'**face-,harden** *vt* to harden the surface of (a metal, esp steel) (eg by adding carbon at high temperatures)

**faceless** /-lis/ *adj* having no individuality, human traits, or distinguishing characteristics; anonymous ⟨*~ bureaucrats telling us what to do*⟩ – **facelessness** *n*

'**face-,lift** *n* **1** an operation involving PLASTIC SURGERY of the face or neck to remove signs of aging (eg wrinkles) **2** an often superficial alteration intended to improve; a change that alters only what can be immediately seen ⟨*a plan that would give the inner-city areas a ~ without tackling the real roots of urban blight*⟩ – **face-lift** *vt*

'**face-,off** *n* a method of putting a ball or puck in play in lacrosse or ice hockey in which two opposing players stand facing each other and, on a signal, attempt to gain control of the ball or puck dropped between them

'**face-,pack** *n* a cosmetic preparation (eg a cream or paste) that is applied to the face to tauten and clean the skin and to improve the complexion

**faceplate** /'fays,playt/ n 1 a disc fixed with its face at RIGHT ANGLES to the driven spindle of a lathe to which the article to be worked on is attached 2 a protective cover for the human face; *specif* the glass panel at the front of a diving helmet

**facer** /'faysə/ n 1 one who or that which faces; *specif* a cutter for facing or smoothing a surface 2 *informal* an unexpected situation or difficulty with no immediately apparent solution

**'face-,saving** n or adj (an act or instance of) preserving one's reputation, pride, or dignity – **face-saver** n

**facet** /'fasit/ n 1 a small flat surface (eg on a cut gem) 2 any of several aspects from which a specified subject or object may be considered ⟨*another ~ of his genius*⟩ 3 the external transparent surface of any of the visual units (OMMATIDIA) making up the COMPOUND EYE of an insect, lobster, etc, that functions as a lens 4 a small smooth area on a hard anatomical structure (eg a bone) that provides a surface for articulation [Fr *facette*, dim. of *face*] – **faceted, facetted** adj

**facetiae** /fə'seeshi,ee/ n pl 1 obscene or pornographic books – used as a technical euphemism by booksellers and collectors 2 *formal* humorous witticisms or pleasantries [L, pl of *facetia* jest, fr *facetus* witty]

**facetious** /fə'seeshəs/ adj 1 inappropriately unserious in manner; flippant ⟨*a ~ question*⟩ 2 intended to be amusing [MF *facetieux*, fr *facetie* jest, fr L *facetia*] – **facetiously** adv, **facetiousness** n

**,face-to-'face** adj in each other's presence; being a confrontation ⟨*a ~ meeting between the two leaders*⟩

**face to face** adv 1 in or into the presence of (one) another ⟨*they met ~ for the first time*⟩ 2 in or into confrontation *with* something which calls for immediate action ⟨*come ~ with the problem*⟩

**face value** n 1 the value indicated on the face (eg of a postage stamp, a coin, or a share certificate) 2 the apparent value or significance ⟨*it would be dangerous to take this survey of voting intentions at its ~, since governments are usually unpopular mid-term*⟩

**facia** /'fashi-ə/ n FASCIA

**'facial** /'faysh(ə)l/ adj 1 of the face 2 concerned with or used in improving the appearance of the face 3 of or being an outer surface ⟨*the ~ surface of a bone*⟩; *esp* of or being the surface of a tooth facing towards the lip or cheek – **facially** adv

**'facial** n a facial beauty treatment

**facial nerve** n either of the 7th pair of CRANIAL NERVES that supply the muscles of the face and jaw and receive stimuli from and transmit stimuli to the salivary glands, the TASTE BUDS of the front part of the tongue, and the LACHRYMAL glands of the eyes

**-facient** /-faysh(ə)nt/ comb form (→ adj) making; causing ⟨*somni*facient⟩ [L *facient-, faciens*, prp of *facere* to make, do – more at DO]

**facies** /'fayshi-eez/ n, pl **facies** /~/ 1 *medicine* an appearance and expression of the face characteristic of a particular (abnormal) condition 2 the general appearance or make-up of a particular plant, animal, or group of animals or plants ⟨*a plant species with a particularly distinct ~*⟩ 3 the sum of the characteristics (eg composition, fossil content, and texture) of a rock or group of rocks that distinguish it from comparable rocks [NL, fr L, face]

**facile** /'fasiel/ adj 1a easily or readily accomplished, attained, or performed ⟨*a ~ victory*⟩ ⟨*~ prose*⟩; *also* able to produce or perform in a facile manner ⟨*a ~ writer*⟩ b specious, superficial, or glib ⟨*I am not concerned with offering any ~ solution for so complex a problem* – T S Eliot⟩ 2 used, done, or comprehended with ease 3 readily manifested and often insincere or shallow ⟨*~ tears*⟩ [MF, fr L *facilis*, fr *facere* to do] – **facilely** adv, **facileness** n

**facilitate** /fə'silitayt/ vt, *formal* to make easier – **facilitator** n, **facilitative** adj

usage Correctly, one **facilitates** something that is done ⟨*used torches to facilitate our search*⟩ but not the people doing it ⟨△ we were facilitated in our search by torches⟩.

**facilitation** /fə,sili'taysh(ə)n/ n 1 *physiology* the increase in the ease with which a nerve impulse is conducted along a particular nerve resulting esp from previous stimulation of that nerve 2 *formal* facilitating or being facilitated

**facility** /fə'siləti/ n 1 the quality of being performed 2 the ability to perform something easily; aptitude ⟨*has considerable ~ on the penny whistle*⟩ 3 *usu pl* something that promotes the ease of an action, operation, or course of conduct ⟨*provide books and other* facilities *for independent study*⟩ 4 something

that is built, installed, or established to perform a (public) service; *broadly* a (public) utility ⟨*in times of economic difficulty the Social Service ~ is often the hardest hit*⟩ △ faculty

**facing** /'faysing/ n 1a a lining at the edge of something, esp a garment, for stiffening or ornament b pl the collar, cuffs, and trimmings of a uniform coat 2 an ornamental or protective layer (eg on the front of a building) ⟨*a ~ of white marble*⟩ 3 material for facing

**facsimile** /fak'siməli/ n 1 an exact copy, esp of printed material 2 the transmission and reproduction of graphic material (eg typescript or pictures) by wire or radio [L *fac simile* make similar] – **facsimile** vt

**fact** /fakt/ n 1 a thing done: eg 1a a criminal act – compare ACCESSORY AFTER THE FACT, ACCESSORY BEFORE THE FACT b *obs* a feat c *archaic* an action 2 the quality of having actual existence in the real world; actuality ⟨*a question of ~*⟩; *also* something that has such existence ⟨*space travel is now a ~*⟩ 3 an actual event or occurrence; *also* an actual or alleged event or state as distinguished from its legal effect ⟨*questions of ~ are for the jury and questions of law for the judge*⟩ 4 a piece of information presented as having objective reality ⟨*I hate it, and that's a ~*⟩ 5 *archaic* a performance, doing [L *factum*, fr neut of *factus*, pp of *facere*] – **factless** adj, **facticity** n – **in fact** 1 really; AS A MATTER OF FACT 2 briefly; IN SHORT

**'fact-,finding** n the looking into or determining of the facts of a case, situation, dispute, etc ⟨*a ~ tour of the riot area*⟩ – **fact finder** n

**'faction** /'faksh(ə)n/ n 1 a minority party or group within a larger body (eg a political party) that is often seen as divisive by the majority; a clique ⟨*the pro-Common Market ~ within the Labour Party*⟩ 2 (a spirit of) dissension within a group or party [MF & L; MF, fr L *faction-, factio* act of making, faction – more at FASHION] – **factional** adj, **factionalism** n, **factionally** adv

**'faction** n the dramatized reconstruction of some real historical situation or event ⟨*Shakespeare was the first great ~ writer in his history plays* – The Guardian⟩ [blend of *fact* and *fiction*] – **factionalize** vb

**-faction** /-'faksh(ə)n/ comb form (→ n) 1 making; -fication ⟨*lique*faction⟩ 2 state ⟨*satis*faction⟩ [ME -*faccioun*, fr MF & L; MF -*faction*, fr L -*faction-*, -*factio* (as in *satisfaction-, satisfactio* satisfaction)] – **-factive** comb form (→ adj)

**factious** /'fakshəs/ adj of faction: eg a caused by faction ⟨*~ disputes*⟩ b inclined to faction or the formation of factions ⟨*the ~ parties of the left*⟩ c seditious, treasonable △ fractious [MF or L; MF *factieux*, fr L *factiosus*, fr *factio*] – **factiously** adv, **factiousness** n

**factitious** /fak'tishəs/ adj 1 produced by human beings rather than by natural forces 2 produced artificially or by special effort; sham, unreal ⟨*created a ~ demand by spreading rumours of shortage*⟩ △ fictitious [L *facticius*, fr *factus*, pp of *facere* to make, do – more at DO] – **factitiously** adv, **factitiousness** n

**factitive** /'faktətiv/ adj or n (of) a transitive verb (eg *paint* in "*paint* the town *red*") that in some constructions requires an objective complement (*red*) as well as an object (*the town*) [NL *factitivus*, irreg fr L *factus*] – **factitively** adv

**fact of life** n, pl **facts of life** 1 pl the fundamental physiological processes and behaviour involved in sex and reproduction 2 something that is viewed as fundamental and unchangeable ⟨*it's a ~ that the rich just go on getting richer*⟩

**'factor** /'faktə/ n 1 one who acts or transacts business for another; an agent 2 a condition, force, or fact that actively contributes to the production of a result ⟨*the ~s determining the rate of unemployment*⟩ 3 a gene **4a(1)** any of the numbers or mathematical expressions that are multiplied together to form a product **a(2)** an integer or mathematical expression that exactly divides another ⟨5 is a ~ of 10⟩ ⟨(x÷y) is a ~ of $x^2 ÷ y^2$⟩ b a quantity by which a given measurement is multiplied or divided in order to produce a measurement in terms of a different system of units c *photography* EXPOSURE FACTOR [ME, fr MF *facteur*, fr L *factor* doer, fr *factus*] – **factorship** n

**'factor** vt to factorize ~ vi to work as a factor – **factorable** adj

**factorage** /'fakt(ə)rij/ n 1 the charges made by a factor for his/her services; COMMISSION 6 2 the commission paid to one who buys and sells goods for others

**factor analysis** n a method of analysing a body of statistical data that allows the identification of the various usu unrelated factors or causal elements that have contributed to the measurements obtained and the assessment of their respective contributions to these measurements – **factor analytic** adj

¹**factorial** /fak'tawri·əl/ *n* a mathematical function of a positive integer, *n*, that is denoted in *n!* or **n** and is equal to the result of multiplying together all the integers from 1 to *n*. Where the integer is zero, factorial zero, *0!*, is given the value 1. ⟨*n* ∼⟩ ⟨∼ *3 is 1* × *2* × *3*⟩

²**factorial** *adj* of or involving a factor or a factorial

**factor·ize, -ise** /'faktəriez/ *vt* to express (a number or mathematical expression) in terms of its component factors – **factorization** *n*

**factory** /'fakt(ə)ri/ *n* **1** a trading settlement or depot; *esp* one maintained by a European country in Asia or Africa before the establishment of true colonies ⟨*the East India Company* ∼ *at Bombay controlled the export of cotton to Europe*⟩ **2a** a building or set of buildings where the production of goods or processing of raw materials takes place **b** the seat or centre of a specified kind of production ⟨*the dream* ∼ *of Hollywood cinema*⟩ [MF *factorie*, fr *facteur* factor]

**factory farming** *n* a system of agriculture, esp in milk, egg, or meat production, that uses intensive production methods and in which animals usu live in a wholly man-made environment

**factory ship** *n* the base ship of a fishing or hunting fleet; *esp* the base ship of a whaling fleet on board which carcasses are processed and by-products stored

**factotum** /fak'tohtəm/ *n* someone employed to carry out many diverse activities or responsibilities; *esp* a general servant [NL, lit., do everything, fr L *fac* do + *totum* everything]

**factual** /'faktyooəl, -chooəl/ *adj* **1** of facts **2** restricted to or based on fact – **factuality** *n*, **factually** *adv*, **factualness** *n*

**facture** /'fakchə/ *n, formal* the manner in which something (e g an artistic work) is made; execution, style ⟨*his modelling of faces . . . his delicate yet firm* ∼ – J C Vandyke⟩ [ME, fr MF, fr L *factura* action of making, fr *factus*]

**facula** /'fakyoolə/ *n, pl* **faculae** /-lie/ any of the bright regions of the sun's PHOTOSPHERE (luminous surface layer) seen most easily near the sun's edge [NL, fr L, dim. of *fac-, fax* torch]

**facultative** /'fakəltətiv/ *adj* **1** of the grant of permission, authority, or privilege ⟨*though the members of the commission have already been appointed, they cannot begin work until* ∼ *legislation has spelt out its exact powers*⟩ **2** not bound to occur under particular conditions; optional **3** of a mental faculty **4a** *of an organism* able to live under more than one set of environmental conditions; *specif* able to live as an organism of the kind specified when environmental conditions require it, but not normally doing so ⟨*a* ∼ *parasite is a saprophyte that is capable of living as a parasite*⟩ **b** *of a process or activity* taking place when environmental conditions are unsuitable for an alternative, esp usual, process or activity to occur ⟨∼ *parasitism*⟩ ☐ (4) compare OBLIGATE – **facultatively** *adv*

**faculty** /'fakəlti/ *n* **1a** an inherent or acquired capability, power, or function of the mind or body ⟨*the* ∼ *of hearing*⟩ ⟨*in possession of all her* faculties *though well into her nineties*⟩ **b** a natural aptitude; a talent ⟨*he has a* ∼ *for saying the right things*⟩ **2** an administrative grouping of related university departments ⟨*the* Faculty *of Medicine*⟩ **3** *taking sing or pl vb* the members of a profession **4** power, authority, or prerogative given or conferred by law or a superior; *esp* a licence or permit from an ecclesiastical authority **5** *NAm* the teaching and administrative staff in an educational institution **6** *archaic* something in which one is trained or qualified △ facility [ME *faculte*, fr MF *faculté*, fr ML & L; ML *facultat-, facultas* branch of learning or teaching, fr L, ability, abundance, fr *facilis* facile]

**fad** /fad/ *n* **1** a practice or interest followed usu for a short time with exaggerated zeal; a craze **2** a peculiar or finicky taste or habit ⟨*cats that have* ∼s *about feeding*⟩ [origin unknown] – **faddy** *adj*, **faddish** *adj*, **faddishness** *n*, **faddism** *n*, **faddist** *n*

**FAD** *n* a chemical compound, $C_{27}H_{33}N_9O_{15}P_2$, containing the vitamin riboflavin in its molecular structure, that is the essential active nonprotein part (COENZYME) of several FLAVO-PROTEIN enzymes and acts esp as a carrier of hydrogen in the breakdown of fats, carbohydrates, etc and as a transporter of electrons in energy-producing reactions inside living cells

¹**fade** /fayd/ *vi* **1** to lose freshness, vigour, or vitality; wither **2** *of a motor car brake or brake lining* to lose braking power gradually, esp as a result of prolonged use **3** to lose freshness or brilliance of colour **4** to disappear gradually; vanish – often + *away* ⟨*the crowd* ∼d *away*⟩ ⟨*the smile* ∼d *from his face*⟩ **5** to change gradually in loudness, strength, or visibility – used

of recorded images or sounds; usu + *in* or *out;* see also FADE-IN, FADE-OUT ∼ *vt* to cause to fade [ME *faden*, fr MF *fader*, fr *fade* feeble, insipid, fr (assumed) VL *fatidus*, alter. of L *fatuus* fatuous, insipid]

²**fade** *n* **1a** an effect consisting of a fade-out or a fade-in or a combination of both **b** a gradual reduction in the brightness of stage lighting **2** a fading of a motor-car brake

**fadedly** /'faydidli/ *adv* in the manner of somebody or something that has faded ⟨*a* ∼ *handsome woman*⟩

'**fade-,in** *n* the gradual appearance of a sound or picture, usu in broadcasting or on film

**fadeless** /'faydlis/ *adj* not susceptible to fading – **fadelessly** *adv*

'**fade-,out** *n* the gradual disappearance of a sound or picture, usu in broadcasting or on film

**fado** /'fəedhooh, 'fadooh/ *n, pl* **fados** a plaintive Portuguese folk song [Pg, lit., fate, fr L *fatum*]

**faeces, ** *NAm chiefly* **feces** /feeseez/ *n pl* bodily waste discharged through the anus; excrement [ME *feces*, fr L *faec-, faex* (sing.) dregs] – **faecal** *adj*

**faena** /fah'enə/ *n* the final phase of a bullfight leading up to the kill, during which the matador works unassisted [Sp, lit., task, fr obs Catal, fr L *facienda* things to be done, fr *facere* to do – more at DO]

**faerie** *also* **faery** /'fayəri, 'feəri/ *n, poetic* **1** fairyland **2** a fairy [MF *faerie* – more at FAIRY] – **faery** *adj*

**Faeroese, Faroese** /,feəroh'eez/ *n, pl* **Faeroese, Faroese** **1** a member of the Germanic people inhabiting the Faeroes **2** the Germanic language of the Faeroese [*Faeroes, Faroes*, islands in the N Atlantic] – **Faeroese** *adj*

**faff** /faf/ *vi, Br informal* to waste time over trifles; fuss – usu + *about* or *around* ⟨*stop* ∼ing *about*⟩ [imit]

¹**fag** /fag/ *vb* **-gg-** *vi* **1** to work hard; toil **2** to act as a fag, esp in an English public school ⟨∼ging *for older boys during his first year*⟩ ∼ *vt, informal* to tire by strenuous activity; exhaust – usu + *out* ⟨*the walk really* ∼ged *me out*⟩; often pass [obs *fag* to droop, perh fr *fag* (fag end)]

²**fag** *n* **1** a junior pupil at a British public school who performs menial tasks (e g bed-making or shoe-cleaning) for a senior schoolmate **2** *chiefly Br informal* a tiring or boring task ⟨*it's a real* ∼⟩; *also* someone who habitually performs such tasks; a drudge

³**fag** *n, informal* a cigarette [*fag end*]

⁴**fag** *n, chiefly NAm derog* a usu male homosexual [short for *faggot*]

**fag end** *n* **1a** the last part or coarser end of a web of cloth **b** the untwisted end of a rope **2** *informal* **2a** a poor or worn-out end; a remnant **b** the usu stubbed-out end of a cigarette; a dog-end **c** the extreme end ⟨*the* ∼ *of one quarrel* – William Golding⟩ [earlier *fag*, fr ME *fagge* flap]

¹**faggot** /'fagət/ *n* **1** *NAm chiefly* **fagot** a bundle: e g **1a** a bundle of sticks ⟨*as the* ∼s *beneath her started to blaze, Joan gazed up to heaven*⟩; *also* a stick, esp for firewood ⟨*a woodcutter with a bundle of* ∼s *on his back*⟩ **b** a bundle of pieces of WROUGHT IRON to be shaped by rolling or hammering at high temperature **c** a bunch of herbs tied together; BOUQUET GARNI **d** *Br* a round mass of minced meat (e g pig's liver) mixed with herbs and usu breadcrumbs **2a** *derog* a woman or female animal ⟨*that old* ∼ *Mrs Riordan* – James Joyce⟩ **b** *chiefly NAm derog* a usu male homosexual [ME *fagot*, fr MF]

²**faggot, ** *NAm chiefly* **fagot** *vt* **1** to make a faggot of; bind together into a bundle ⟨∼ed *sticks*⟩ **2** to ornament with faggoting

**faggoting, ** *NAm chiefly* **fagoting** /'fagəting/ *n* **1** embroidery made by pulling out horizontal threads from a woven fabric and tying the remaining groups of cross threads in the middle to form hourglass shapes **2** a decorative joining, esp of openwork stitch, for edges of cloth or lace

**faghook** /'fag,hook/ *n, dial SEng* a long-handled BILLHOOK used esp for cutting and layering hedges [E dial. *fag, vag* to reap with a sickle and hooked stick]

**fagin** /'faygin/ *n* an adult who instructs others (e g children) in crime, esp theft, or who receives stolen goods, esp from children [*Fagin*, character in the novel *Oliver Twist* by Charles Dickens †1870 E novelist]

**fah, fa** /fah/ *n* the 4th note of the scale in the SOL-FA method of representing the musical scale [ME *fa*, fr ML – more at GAMUT]

**Fahrenheit** /'farən,hiet/ *adj* of, conforming to, or being a scale of temperature on which water freezes at 32° and boils at 212°

under standard conditions (e g of atmospheric pressure) [Gabriel *Fahrenheit* †1736 Ger physicist]

**faience, faïence** /fie'ahns, -'onhs (*Fr* fajã:s)/ *n* earthenware decorated with a glaze consisting mainly of compounds of tin – compare MAJOLICA, DELFT [Fr, fr *Faenza*, town in N Italy]

¹**fail** /fayl/ *vi* **1a** to lose strength; weaken ⟨*her health was ~*ing⟩ **b** to fade or die away ⟨*until the light ~*s⟩ **c** to stop functioning ⟨*the patient's heart ~*ed⟩ **2a** to fall short ⟨*~*ed *in his duty*⟩ **b** to be or become absent or inadequate ⟨*the water supply ~*ed⟩ **c** to be unsuccessful (e g in passing an examination) **d** to become bankrupt or insolvent *~ vt* **1a** to disappoint the expectations or trust of ⟨*his friends ~*ed *him*⟩ **b** to prove inadequate for or incapable of carrying out an expected service or function for ⟨*for once his wit ~*ed *him*⟩ **2** to be deficient in, lack ⟨*our youth . . . never ~*ed *an invincible courage* – Douglas MacArthur⟩ **3** to leave undone; neglect ⟨*~*ed *to shut the door behind him*⟩ **4a** to be unsuccessful in passing (e g a test) ⟨*~*ed *his oral*⟩ **b** to grade (e g a student) as not passing ⟨*~*ed *her on her practical*⟩ [ME *failen*, fr OF *faillir*, fr (assumed) VL *fallire*, alter. of L *fallere* to deceive, disappoint; prob akin to Gk *phēlos* deceitful] – **failingly** *adv*

²**fail** *n* **1** failure – usu in *without fail* **2** a failure in an examination **3** a failure (e g by a dealer in stocks) to deliver or receive stocks within a prescribed period after purchase or sale

¹**failing** /'fayling/ *n* a usu slight or insignificant defect in character, conduct, or behaviour ⟨*one of the ~*s *of the car is its stiff clutch*⟩

²**failing** *prep* in absence or default of ⟨*~ specific instructions, use your own judgment*⟩

**faille** /fayl/ *n* a somewhat shiny closely woven silk, rayon, or cotton fabric with faint crosswise ribs [Fr]

'**fail-,safe** *adj*, *of a machine, engine, etc* designed to return automatically to a safe condition (e g to switch itself off) in the event of failure or breakdown

**failure** /'faylyə/ *n* **1a** a failing to perform a duty or expected action ⟨*his ~ to turn up to the meeting*⟩ **b** a state of inability to perform a normal function ⟨*heart ~*⟩ **2a** lack of success **b** a failing in business; bankruptcy ⟨*the ~ of the bank left them with all their savings gone*⟩ **3a** a falling short; a deficiency ⟨*a ~ in the supply of raw materials*⟩ **b** deterioration, decay **4** someone or something unsuccessful ⟨*their scheme was a ~*⟩ ⟨*he's a good scriptwriter, but an utter ~ as a director*⟩ [alter. of earlier *failer*, fr AF, fr OF *faillir* to fail]

¹**fain** /fayn/ *adj*, *archaic* **1** happy, pleased, glad – usu + *of* **2** inclined, desirous, willing **3a** glad or willing under the circumstances ⟨*I must be ~ to pawn my plate* – Shak⟩ **b** obliged or constrained; having no alternative ⟨*Ascham . . . was ~ to apologise for having written in English* – Benjamin Disraeli⟩ □ (*2 & 3*) usu + infin [ME *fagen, fayn*, fr OE *fægen*; akin to ON *fegiun* happy, OE *fæger* fair]

²**fain** *adv*, *archaic* **1** with pleasure **2** rather ⟨*I would ~ die a dry death* – Shak⟩

**fainéant, faineant** /'fayni·ont/ *adj* idle and ineffectual; indolent [Fr *fainéant*, is, fr MF *fait-nient*, lit., (he) does nothing, by folk etymology fr *faignant*, fr prp of *faindre, feindre* to feign, shirk] – **fainéant** *n*

¹**faint** /faynt/ *adj* **1** cowardly, timid – chiefly in *faint heart* **2** weak, dizzy, and likely to faint ⟨*felt ~*⟩ **3** performed, offered, or accomplished weakly or languidly; feeble ⟨*made a ~ attempt at a smile*⟩ **4** of low intensity; indistinct, dim ⟨*a ~ hissing sound* – H G Wells⟩ ⟨*a ~ light in their window*⟩ [ME *faint, feint*, fr OF, fr pp of *faindre, feindre* to feign, shirk – more at FEIGN] – **faintish** *adj*, **faintishness** *n*, **faintly** *adv*, **faintness** *n*

²**faint** *vi* **1** to lose consciousness because of a temporary decrease in the blood supply to the brain (e g through exhaustion or shock) **2** to become weak **3** *archaic* to lose courage or spirit

³**faint** *n* (an instance or condition of) fainting

**fainthearted** /,faynt'hahtid/ *adj* lacking courage or resolution; timid – **faintheartedly** *adv*, **faintheartedness** *n*

¹**fair** /feə/ *adj* **1** attractive, esp because of fresh, charming, or flawless quality; beautiful **2** superficially pleasing; specious ⟨*she trusted his ~ promises*⟩ **3** clean, clear ⟨*a ~ copy*⟩ **4** not stormy or foul; fine ⟨*a ~ sky*⟩ ⟨*~ weather*⟩ **5a** free from self-interest, prejudice, or favouritism; honest ⟨*a very ~ man to do business with*⟩ **b** conforming with the established rules; allowed ⟨*a ~ tackle*⟩ **c** open to legitimate pursuit or attack ⟨*~ game*⟩ **6** promising, likely ⟨*he was in a ~ way to win*⟩ **7** favourable to a ship's course ⟨*a ~ wind*⟩ **8** light in colour; blond **9** moderately good, large, or fine; adequate ⟨*a ~ understanding of the work*⟩

⟨*a ~ income*⟩ **10** *informal* being such to a full degree or extent; real, perfect ⟨*a ~ treat to watch him – New Republic*⟩ – compare FAIR AND SQUARE **11** *archaic* free of obstacles [ME *fager, fair*, fr OE *fæger*; akin to OHG *fagar* beautiful] – **fairness** *n* – **bid fair** to seem likely; show promise – **say fairer** to make a more generous offer ⟨*can't say fairer than that*⟩

**synonyms** Fair, just, equitable, impartial, unbiased, dispassionate, objective: **fair** is the most general term in this group, which conveys lack of prejudice, of favouritism, or of self-interest in making judgments. **Just** stresses strict adherence to a moral or legal standard ⟨*a just judge*⟩. **Equitable** suggests a similar sense of right and wrong, but one applied less in accordance with a rigid set of rules than in accordance with reason and common sense ⟨*an equitable distribution of wealth*⟩. **Impartial** stresses an absence of favouritism or prejudice, and **unbiased** is even stronger in claiming lack of prejudice ⟨*an impartial witness*⟩ ⟨*an unbiased account of his trial*⟩. **Dispassionate** stresses the absence of strong feeling or emotion which might colour one's judgment, and may even connote coldness, while **objective** suggests a completely uncommitted stance, distanced from what is being judged, and thus the ability to judge something on its merits or according to the facts ⟨*took an objective view of his arrest*⟩. see BEAUTIFUL **antonyms** unfair, unjust, prejudiced, biased, foul

²**fair** *n* **1** good fortune – chiefly in *come fair or foul* **2** *archaic* a woman; *esp* a sweetheart

³**fair** *adv* fairly ⟨*it ~ makes you sick*⟩

**usage** Fair as an adverb is used chiefly in certain fixed phrases ⟨*fight fair*⟩ ⟨*play fair*⟩. It cannot replace **fairly**, the usual adverb ⟨*a fairly good book*⟩ except in some dialects where it means "completely" ⟨*it fair makes you sick*⟩.

⁴**fair** *vi*, *of the weather* to clear *~ vt* to join so that the external nal surfaces blend smoothly

⁵**fair** *n* **1** a gathering, esp formerly, of buyers and sellers at a particular place and time for trade or a competitive exhibition, often with accompanying entertainment and amusements ⟨*a sheep ~*⟩ **2** an exhibition usu designed to acquaint prospective buyers or the general public with a product ⟨*the Frankfurt Book* Fair⟩ **3** a sale of a collection of articles usu for a charitable purpose; FETE **2 4** *chiefly Br* FUN FAIR [ME *feire, faire, fayre*, fr OF *feire*, fr ML *feria* weekday, fair, fr LL, festal day, fr L *feriae* (pl) holidays – more at FEAST]

**fair and square** *adv* **1** in an honest or aboveboard manner ⟨*won the match ~*⟩ **2** exactly, directly ⟨*hit him ~ on the nose*⟩ – **fair and square** *adj*

**fair dos** /'dooz/ *n pl*, *chiefly Br informal* fair shares [*dos* (treatment, shares), fr pl of ²*do*]

**fairfaced** /'feə,fayst/ *adj*, *of brickwork* not plastered

**fair game** *n* a legitimate object for pursuit, criticism, or ridicule ⟨*thought that anyone with a posh accent was ~ and teased them mercilessly*⟩

**fairground** /'feə,grownd/ *n* an area where outdoor fairs, circuses, or exhibitions are held

¹**fairing** /'fearing/ *n*, *Br* **1** a present bought or given at a fair **2** *archaic* ²DESERT 2 [⁵*fair*]

²**fairing** *n* a structure whose main function is to produce a smooth outline and to reduce drag or air resistance (e g on a car or aircraft) [fr gerund of ⁴*fair*]

**fairish** /'feərish/ *adj*, *informal* fairly good ⟨*a ~ wage for those days*⟩ – **fairishly** *adv*

**Fair Isle, Fairisle** *n or adj* (a style of knitting or a knitted garment) having horizontal bands of traditional motifs worked in several colours against a plain background [*Fair Isle*, one of the Shetland islands, where the style originated]

**fairlead** /-,leed/ *n* a block, ring, or metal fitting with two arms that serves as a guide for a rope or chain and keeps it from fraying in use

**fairly** /-li/ *adv* **1** completely, quite ⟨*~ bursting with pride*⟩ **2a** in a proper or legal manner ⟨*~ priced stocks*⟩ **b** impartially, honestly ⟨*a story told ~ and objectively*⟩ **3** to a full degree or extent; plainly, distinctly ⟨*had ~ caught sight of him*⟩ **4** for the most part; quite ⟨*a ~ easy job*⟩ **usage** see ³FAIR

,**fair-'minded** *adj* just, unprejudiced – **fair-mindedness** *n*

**fair play** *n* **1** play that is according to the (spirit of the) rules of a game; *also* behaviour in accord with the unwritten conventions of social behaviour **2** equitable or impartial treatment; justice

,**fair-'spoken** *adj* pleasant and courteous in speech ⟨*a ~ youth*⟩

**fairway** /'feəway/ *n* **1** a navigable channel in a river, bay, or harbour **2** the mown part of a golf course between a tee and a green

'fair-,weather *adj* 1 suitable for, done during, or made in fair weather ⟨*a ~ voyage*⟩ 2 present, active, or loyal only in untroubled times – esp in *fair-weather friend*

fairy /'feəri/ *n* 1 a small creature of legend and folklore having magic powers and usu human form 2 *derog* an effeminate male or male homosexual [ME *fairie* fairyland, fairy people, fr OF *faerie*, fr *feie, fee* fairy, fr L *Fata*, goddess of fate, fr *fatum* fate] – fairy *adj*, fairylike *adj*

fairy godmother *n*, *informal* a benefactor

fairyland /'feəri,land/ *n* 1 the land of fairies; a place where magical things happen 2 a place of delicate beauty or magical charm

fairy lights *n pl* small coloured electric lights for decoration, esp outdoors or on a Christmas tree

fairy ring *n* 1a a ring of dark vegetation on the surface of the ground that corresponds to the outer edge of a body of MYCELIUM (underground network of filaments that make up most of the body of a fungus) which has grown outwards in a circle from an initial growth point **b** a ring of mushrooms or toadstools produced along the line of a fairy ring 2 a mushroom or toadstool (eg *Marasmius oreades*) that commonly forms fairy rings [fr the folk belief that such rings were dancing places of the fairies]

fairy shrimp *n* any of several delicate transparent freshwater INVERTEBRATE animals (order Anostraca of the class Crustacea) related to the WATER FLEAS, that typically swim on their backs propelling themselves by means of numerous flattened hair-fringed structures

fairy story *n* FAIRY TALE

'fairy-,tale *adj* characteristic of or suitable to a fairy tale: eg **a** marked by unusual grace or beauty **b** marked by apparently magical success or good fortune ⟨*a ~ start to his Test career*⟩

fairy tale *n* 1 a story which features supernatural or imaginary forces and beings (eg fairies) 2 a made-up story usu designed to mislead ⟨*told us some ~ about having to visit a sick aunt*⟩

fait accompli /,fayt ə'kompli, ,fet əkom'pli (*Fr* fɛt akɔ̃pli)/ *n, pl* faits accomplis /~/ a thing already accomplished and considered irreversible [Fr, accomplished fact]

faith /fayth/ *n* 1a allegiance to duty or a person; loyalty – esp in *good/bad faith* **b** fidelity to one's promises – esp in *keep/break faith* 2a(1) belief and trust in and loyalty to God **a(2)** belief in the traditional doctrines of a religion **b(1)** firm belief in something for which there is no proof ⟨*~ in the essential goodness of human nature*⟩ **b(2)** complete confidence ⟨*a ~ in whisky and hot lemon as a cure for a cold*⟩ 3a something that is believed with strong conviction; esp a system of religious beliefs ⟨*the ~ of our fathers*⟩ **b** *cap* – the Roman Catholic Church ⟨*returned to the Faith on his death bed*⟩ [ME *feith*, fr OF *feid, foi*, fr L *fides*; akin to L *fidere* to trust – more at BIDE]

¹faithful /-f(ə)l/ *adj* 1 showing faith; loyal, steadfast ⟨*a ~ friend*⟩; *specif* sexually loyal; having sexual relations only with an established partner (eg one's wife or husband) 2 firm in adherence to promises or in observance of duty; conscientious ⟨*a ~ worker*⟩ 3 true to the facts or to an original; accurate ⟨*the portrait is a ~ likeness*⟩ ⟨*a true and ~ account of his hero's early life*⟩ 4 *obs* full of (religious) faith – faithfully *adv*, faithfulness *n*

   usage Yours faithfully, or more rarely Yours truly, ends a formal letter to a stranger that begins *Dear Sir, Dear Madam, Dear Sirs*, etc. Compare SINCERELY

²faithful *n pl, pl* faithful, faithfuls 1 *the* full members of a church 2 *the* body of adherents of a religion (eg Islam) 3 faithful, faithfuls loyal followers or members

faith healing *n* the treatment of illness by prayer and exercise of faith in God rather than by conventional medical techniques – faith healer *n*

faithless /'faythlis/ *adj* 1a not true to allegiance or duty; treacherous, disloyal **b** without (religious) faith; lacking strong convictions 2 not to be relied on; untrustworthy ⟨*a ~ friend*⟩ – faithlessly *adv*, faithlessness *n*

faitour /'faytə/ *n, archaic* a cheat, impostor [ME, fr AF, fr OF *faitor* perpetrator, fr L *factor* doer – more at FACTOR]

¹fake /fayk/ *vt* to coil (eg a fire hose) in fakes [ME *faken*]

²fake *n* any of the loops of a coiled rope or cable

³fake *vt* 1 to alter, manipulate, or treat so as to impart a false character or appearance; falsify ⟨*~d all the results to suit his theories*⟩ – often + *up* 2 to counterfeit, simulate ⟨*has a business faking old family portraits for rich Americans*⟩ ⟨*~d a nervous breakdown* – Michael Billington⟩ ~ *vi* 1 to engage in faking something; pretend ⟨*she's not ill, only faking*⟩ 2 *NAm*

to make a movement in a game with the intention of deceiving or misleading an opponent; dummy synonyms see ¹PRETEND [prob fr Ger *fegen* to sweep, thrash] – faker *n*, fakery *n*

⁴fake *n* 1 an often worthless imitation passed off as genuine 2 an impostor, charlatan

⁵fake *adj* counterfeit, phoney ⟨*a ~ Picasso*⟩

fakir, faqir *also* fakeer /'faykiə, fə'kiə, 'fahkiə, -kə/ *n* a wandering Muslim or Hindu preacher, holy man, or ascetic ⚠ faker [Ar *faqīr*, lit., poor man]

Falangist /fə'lanjist/ *n* a member of any of various fascist parties: eg **a** a member of the Spanish fascist party founded in 1933 by José Antonio Primo de Rivera that ruled Spain after the civil war of 1936-39 and was the only legal political party in Spain until the death of Franco in 1975 **b** a member of a right-wing Christian faction in the Lebanon [Sp *Falangista*, fr *Falange española* Spanish Phalanx, a fascist organization]

falcate /'falkayt/ *also* falcated /fal'kaytid/ *adj, esp of a plant or animal part* hooked or curved like a sickle [L *falcatus*, fr *falc-, falx* sickle, scythe]

falchion /'fawlchən, -sh(ə)n/ *n* 1 a broad-bladed slightly curved medieval sword 2 *archaic* a sword [ME *fauchoun*, fr OF *fauchon*, fr *fauchier* to mow, fr (assumed) VL *falcare*, fr L *falc-, falx*]

falciform /'falsi,fawm/ *adj* falcate [L *falc-, falx* + E *-iform*]

falcon /'faw(l)kən/ *n* 1a any of various hawks trained for use in falconry; *esp* a peregrine – used technically with reference only to a female; compare TIERCEL **b** any of various hawks (family Falconidae) distinguished by long pointed wings and a notch on the edge of the upper part of the beak; *broadly* a hawk 2 a light cannon used from the 15th to the 17th centuries [ME, fr OF, fr LL *falcon-, falco*, prob of Gmc origin; akin to OHG *falcho* falcon]

falconer /'fawkənə, 'fawl-/ *n* 1 someone who hunts with hawks 2 a breeder or trainer of hawks for hunting

falconet /,falkə'net/ *n* 1 a very small cannon used in the 16th and 17th centuries 2 any of a genus (*Microhierax*) of very small Asian falcons

,falcon-'gentle *n* the female peregrine falcon – used esp technically in falconry [ME *faucon gentil* peregrine falcon, fr MF, lit., noble falcon]

falconry /'fawkənri, 'fawl-/ *n* 1 the art of training falcons to pursue game 2 the sport of hunting with falcons

falderal /'faldə,ral/ *n* (a) folderol

faldstool /'fawld,stoohl/ *n* 1 a folding stool or chair; *specif* one used by a bishop 2 a folding stool or small desk at which one kneels during devotions; *esp* one used by the sovereigns of England at their coronations 3 the desk from which the litany is read in church [ML *faldistolium*, of Gmc origin; akin to OHG *faltistuol* folding chair, fr a prehistoric WGmc compound whose constituents are represented by OHG *faldan* to fold and OHG *stuol* chair – more at FOLD, STOOL]

fale /'falay/ *n, pl* fale *Austr & NZ* a Samoan house [Samoan]

Faliscan /fə'liskən/ *n* the Latin dialect of the ancient Falisci of Italy

¹fall /fawl/ *vi* fell /fel/; fallen /'fawlən/ 1a to descend freely by the force of gravity **b** to hang freely ⟨*her hair ~s over her shoulders*⟩ **c** to come as if by descending ⟨*a hush fell on the audience*⟩ 2 *of a lamb* to become born 3a to become less or lower in degree, level, pitch, or volume ⟨*the temperature fell 10°*⟩ ⟨*their voices fell to a whisper*⟩ **b** to be uttered; issue ⟨*let ~ a remark*⟩ **c** *of the eyes* to become lowered 4a to come down from an erect to a usu prostrate position suddenly and esp involuntarily ⟨*slipped and fell on the ice*⟩ **b** to enter an undesirable state unintentionally; stumble, stray ⟨*fell into bad ways*⟩ ⟨*fell ill*⟩ **c** *euph* to drop because wounded or dead; *esp* to die in battle **d** to suffer military capture ⟨*after a long siege the city* fell⟩ **e** to lose office ⟨*hoping for the government to ~*⟩ **f** to suffer ruin, defeat, or failure ⟨*we must stand or ~ together*⟩ 5 to yield to esp sexual temptation; sin; *esp, euph* to lose one's virginity outside marriage 6a to move or extend in a downward direction – often + *off* or *away* ⟨*the land ~s away to the east*⟩ **b** to decline in quality, activity, or quantity; abate, subside – often + *off* or *away* ⟨*production fell off because of the strike*⟩ **c** to assume a look of disappointment, dejection, or dismay ⟨*his face* fell⟩ **d** to decline in financial value or price ⟨*shares fell sharply after the miners' vote*⟩ 7a to occur at a specified time or place ⟨*the accent ~s on the second syllable*⟩ ⟨*Christmas ~s on a Monday this year*⟩ **b** to come (as if) by chance -- + *in* or *into* ⟨*it fell into my mind to write to you*⟩ ⟨*fell in with bad company*⟩ **c** to come or pass by lot, assignment, or

inheritance; devolve – usu + *on, to,* or *upon* ⟨*it* fell *to me to break the news*⟩ **8** to come within the limits, scope, or jurisdiction of something ⟨~s *within our borders*⟩ **9** to pass, esp involuntarily and suddenly, into a new state or condition ⟨~ *asleep*⟩ ⟨~ *in love*⟩ ⟨*the book* fell *apart*⟩ **10** to begin heartily or actively ⟨fell *a-laughing*⟩ – usu + *to* ⟨fell *to work*⟩ **11** to impinge, strike ⟨*her glance* fell *on me*⟩ ⟨*music* ~ing *on the ear*⟩ [ME *fallen,* fr OE *feallan;* akin to OHG *fallan* to fall] – **fall over oneself** to display almost excessive eagerness – see also **fall on deaf** EARS/FLAT/**on one's** FEET (at FOOT)/**in** LOVE **with/off one's** PERCH/**between two** STOOLS, LET **fall**

**fall about** *vi* to laugh uncontrollably

**fall away** *vi* **1a** to withdraw friendship or support ⟨*gradually all his friends* fell *away*⟩ **b** to lapse in a faith **2a** to diminish gradually in size **b** to lose weight **3** to drift off course

**fall back** *vi* to retreat, recede – see also FALL BACK

**fall back on/upon** *vt* to have recourse to ⟨*when facts were scarce he* fell *back on his imagination*⟩

**fall behind** *vb* to lag behind

**fall below** *vt* to fail to reach ⟨*his performance* fell *well below his best*⟩

**fall down** *vi, informal* to fail to meet expectations or requirements; be inadequate ⟨*he* fell *down on the job*⟩

**fall for** *vt* **1** to fall in love with **2** to become a victim of ⟨fell *for the same old trick*⟩

**fall in** *vi* **1** to sink or collapse inwards ⟨*the roof* fell *in*⟩ **2** to take one's proper place in a military formation

**fall in with** *vt* to concur or harmonize with ⟨*had to* fall *in with her wishes*⟩

**fall off** *vi* **1** to decline ⟨*exports* fell *off sharply in May*⟩ **2** of *a ship* to deviate or have a tendency to deviate to leeward – see also FALLOFF

**fall on/upon** *vt* **1** to descend upon; attack ⟨fell *hungrily* upon *the pie*⟩ **2** to meet with ⟨fell *on hard times*⟩

**fall out** *vi* **1** to have a disagreement; quarrel ⟨*friends who have* fallen *out*⟩ **2** to leave one's place in the ranks of a military formation **3** *poetic* to happen; TURN OUT ⟨*as it* fell *out upon a day*⟩ – see also FALLOUT

**fall over** *vi* to overbalance – see also **fall over** BACKWARDS

**fall through** *vi* to fail to be carried out successfully ⟨*in the end the plan* fell *through*⟩

**fall to** *vi* to begin doing something (e g working or eating), esp vigorously – often imper

²**fall** *n* **1** the act of falling by the force of gravity **2a** a falling out, off, or away; a dropping ⟨*the* ~ *of leaves*⟩ ⟨*a* ~ *of snow*⟩ **b** a thing or quantity that falls or has fallen ⟨*a* ~ *of rock at the base of the cliff*⟩; *specif* one or more meteorites or their fragments that have fallen together **c** the quantity born – usu used with reference to lambs ⟨*a good* ~ *of lambs*⟩ **3** a hoisting-tackle rope or chain; *esp* the part of it to which the power is applied **4a** a loss of greatness or power; a collapse ⟨*the* ~ *of the Roman Empire*⟩ **b** the surrender or capture of a besieged place ⟨*the* ~ *of Troy*⟩ **c** lapse or departure from innocence or goodness, *specif, cap* the fall of mankind through the disobedience of Adam and Eve **5a** the downward slope (e g of a hill); a declivity **b** falls *pl taking sing or pl vb,* **fall** a precipitous descent of water; a usu large and steep waterfall **c** a musical cadence **d** a falling-pitch intonation in speech **6** a decrease in size, quantity, or degree; *esp* a decrease in price or value **7a** the distance which something falls ⟨*a* ~ *of five points in share prices*⟩ **b** inclination, pitch ⟨*the* ~ *of a sloping roof*⟩ **8a** the act of felling trees **b** the quantity of trees cut down **c(1)** an act of forcing a wrestler's shoulders to the mat for a prescribed time (e g one second) **c(2)** a bout of wrestling **9** *chiefly NAm* autumn

**fallacy** /ˈfaləsi/ *n* **1** deceptive appearance or nature; deception, delusiveness **2** a false idea ⟨*the popular* ~ *that scientists are illiterate*⟩ **3** an argument failing to satisfy the conditions of valid inference **4** *obs* guile, trickery [L *fallacia,* fr *fallac-, fallax* deceitful, fr *fallere* to deceive – more at FAIL] – **fallacious** *adj,* **fallaciously** *adv,* **fallaciousness** *n*

**fallback** /ˈfawlˌbak/ *n* **1** something on which one can fall back; a reserve **2** a falling back; a retreat

**fall guy** *n, informal* **1** someone who is easily cheated or tricked **2** a scapegoat

**fallible** /ˈfaləbl/ *adj* capable of making or containing a mistake; liable to be wrong ⟨*generals are never more* ~ *then when they are winning*⟩ ⟨*this statistical technique is highly* ~ *when samples are small*⟩ [ME, fr ML *fallibilis,* fr L *fallere*] – **fallibly** *adv,* **fallibility** *n*

**falling diphthong** /ˈfawling/ *n* a diphthong in which the first element is more prominent than the second (e g /oy/ in noise)

**falling star** *n* SHOOTING STAR

**fall line** *n* the natural slope of a hill (e g one used for skiing) straight down from top to bottom

**falloff** /ˈfawlˌof/ *n* a decline, esp in quantity or quality ⟨*a* ~ *in exports*⟩

**fallopian tube** /fəˈlohpi·ən, -pyən/ *n, often cap F* either of the pair of tubes in a female mammal along which eggs pass from either of the ovaries to the uterus [Gabriel *Fallopius* †1562 It anatomist]

**fallout** /ˈfawlˌowt/ *n* **1a** the radioactive particles that result from a nuclear explosion and descend through the atmosphere to fall on the ground; *also* other polluting particles (e g volcanic ash) that descend in a similar way **b** descent of fallout through the atmosphere ⟨*the* ~ *continued for many days and contaminated a wide area*⟩ **2** a set of secondary results or products ⟨*the war ... produced its own literary* ~ – *a profusion of books – Newsweek*⟩

¹**fallow** /ˈfaloh/ *adj* of a light yellowish brown colour [ME *falow,* fr OE *fealu;* akin to OHG *falo* pale, fallow, L *pallēre* to be pale, Gk *polios* grey]

²**fallow** *n* **1** (ploughed and harrowed) land, ordinarily used for crop production, that is left unsown and allowed to lie idle during the growing season **2** the state or period of being fallow **3** the practice of allowing land to lie fallow **4** *obs* ploughed land [ME *falwe, falow,* fr OE *fealg*]

³**fallow** *vt* to plough, harrow, and break up (land) without sowing, esp so as to destroy weeds and conserve soil moisture

⁴**fallow** *adj* **1** of *land* left unsown after ploughing **2** dormant, inactive – esp in *to lie fallow* – **fallowness** *n*

**fallow deer** *n* a small European deer (*Dama dama*) with broad antlers and a pale yellow coat that in summer is spotted with white

¹**false** /fawls/ *adj* **1a** not genuine ⟨~ *modesty*⟩ ⟨~ *documents*⟩ **b(1)** artificial ⟨~ *teeth*⟩ ⟨*a* ~ *leg*⟩ **b(2)** intended to disguise ⟨*a* ~ *nose*⟩ ⟨*a* ~ *beard*⟩ **2a** intentionally untrue; lying ⟨~ *testimony*⟩ ⟨~ *promises*⟩ **b** adjusted, made, or fabricated so as to deceive or mislead ⟨~ *scales*⟩ ⟨*a suitcase with a* ~ *bottom*⟩ **3** not true ⟨~ *premises*⟩ **4** not faithful or loyal; treacherous ⟨*a* ~ *friend*⟩ **5a** fitting over a main part to strengthen or protect it or to disguise its appearance ⟨*a* ~ *keel*⟩ ⟨*a* ~ *ceiling*⟩ **b** appearing forced or artificial; unconvincing ⟨*a* ~ *scene in a play*⟩ ⟨*a* ~ *smile*⟩ **6** *esp of a plant* resembling or related to the specified, usu more widely known, kind ⟨~ *acacia*⟩ **7** inaccurate in pitch or in vowel length ⟨*a* ~ *note*⟩ **8** inconsistent with or inappropriate to the true situation ⟨*a* ~ *position*⟩ ⟨*a* ~ *sense of security*⟩ ⟨~ *pride*⟩ ⟨*a* ~ *alarm*⟩ **9** imprudent, unwise ⟨*a* ~ *move*⟩ [ME *fals,* fr OF & L; OF, fr L *falsus,* fr pp of *fallere* to deceive] – **falsity** *n,* **falsely** *adv,* **falseness** *n*

²**false** *adv* in a false or faithless manner; treacherously – usu in *play someone false;* see also RING **false**

**false acacia** *n* LOCUST 2a(2) (N American tree)

**false alarm** *n* an occurrence that raises but fails to meet expectations; *esp* a groundless warning ⟨*it was a* ~: *Aunt Augusta isn't coming for Christmas*⟩ ⟨*we thought the twins had chicken pox, but it was a* ~⟩

**falsehood** /-hood/ *n* **1** an untrue statement; a lie **2** absence of truth or accuracy; falsity **3** the practice of telling lies

**false horizon** *n* HORIZON 1c (level mirror for observing altitudes)

**false imprisonment** *n* imprisonment of a person without legal justification

**false pregnancy** *n* **1** PSEUDOPREGNANCY (physiological state resembling pregnancy) **2** a PSYCHOSOMATIC state in which some of the signs of pregnancy (e g hormonal changes) occur in spite of the fact that conception has not taken place – called also PSEUDOCYESIS

**false pretences** *n pl* **1** *law* false representation, esp untrue statements, concerning past or present facts made with the intention of defrauding – no longer used technically **2** acts or appearances intended to deceive – chiefly in *under false pretences*

**false quantity** *n* an incorrect length given to a vowel sound in scanned verse

**false rib** *n* a rib whose cartilages are joined indirectly or not at all with the breastbone – compare FLOATING RIB

**false start** *n* **1** an incorrect start, esp an illegally early start, by a competitor in a race (e g in athletics or horse racing) **2** an unsuccessful beginning to an activity or course of action that requires the venture to be restarted from the beginning ⟨*after several* false starts *the computer program finally started to give the results we wanted*⟩

**falsetto** /fawl'setoh/ *n, pl* **falsettos 1** an unnaturally high speaking or singing voice ⟨*answered in a quavering* ~⟩ **2** (a singer who uses) an unnatural strained or artificial male singing voice produced by contraction of the vocal cords and having a higher range than the singer's normal voice; *broadly* COUNTERTENOR [It, fr dim. of *falso* false, fr L *falsus*] – **falsetto** *adv*

**false vampire bat** *n* either of two bats (genera *Megaderma* and *Macroderma*) that eat insects and small animals but do not, as is wrongly thought, suck blood

**falsework** /-,wuhk/ *n* a temporary erection (eg a framework supporting an arch) on which a main work is supported during construction

**falsie** /'fawlsi/ *n usu pl, informal* a pad in the cup of a bra which when worn makes the breasts appear larger; *also* an artificial breast (eg one worn after a breast has been removed in surgery)

**falsify** /'fawlsi,fie/ *vt* **1** to prove or declare false ⟨*an experiment which* falsifies *the theory*⟩ **2** to make false: eg **2a** to make false by fraudulent alteration ⟨*his accounts were* falsified *to conceal a theft*⟩ **b** to represent falsely; misrepresent ⟨*the newspaper report distorted and* falsified *his views*⟩ **3** to prove unsound by experience ⟨*the turn of events* falsified *his expectations*⟩ ~ *vi, NAm* [3]LIE 1 [ME *falsifien*, fr MF *falsifier*, fr ML *falsificare*, fr L *falsus*] – **falsifier** *n*, **falsification** *n*

[1]**falter** /'fawltə, 'foltə/ *vi* **1** to walk or move unsteadily or hesitatingly; stumble **2** to speak brokenly or weakly; stammer **3a** to hesitate in purpose or action; waver **b** to lose strength, purpose, or effectiveness; fail, weaken ⟨*the business was* ~ing⟩ ~ *vt* to utter hesitatingly or brokenly [ME *falteren*] – **falterer** *n*, **falteringly** *adv*

[2]**falter** *n* an act or instance of faltering ⟨*recited "To be or not to be" without a* ~⟩ – **falterless** *adj*

[1]**fame** /faym/ *n* **1a** public estimation; reputation **b** popular acclaim; renown **2** *archaic* rumour ⟨*as the* ~ *hath it*⟩ [ME, fr OF, fr L *fama* report, fame; akin to L *fari* to speak – more at BAN]

[2]**fame** *vt, archaic* to report, repute – usu pass

**famed** /faymd/ *adj* well-known, famous

**familial** /fə'mili·əl, -yəl/ *adj* **1** (characteristic) of a family or its members **2** tending to occur in more members of a family than expected by chance alone ⟨*a* ~ *disorder*⟩ [Fr, fr L *familia*]

[1]**familiar** /fə'mili·ə, -yə/ *n* **1** an intimate associate; a companion **2** a member of the household of a high official **3** FAMILIAR SPIRIT **4** someone who frequents a usu specified place

[2]**familiar** *adj* **1** closely acquainted; intimate ⟨*a subject I am* ~ *with*⟩ **2a** casual, informal **b** too intimate and unrestrained; presumptuous **c** moderately tame ⟨~ *animals*⟩ **3** frequently seen or experienced; common ⟨*the old tramp was a* ~ *sight in our part of the town*⟩ **4** FAMILIAL 1 **5** *obs* affable, sociable [ME *familier*, fr OF, fr L *familiaris*, fr *familia*] – **familiarly** *adv*, **familiarness** *n*

*usage* Well-known things are **familiar** *to* people, and the people are **familiar** *with* the things.

**familiarity** /fə,mili'arəti/ *n* **1a** the quality or state of being familiar **b** a state of close relationship; intimacy ⟨*the* ~ *grew between the two friends*⟩ **2a** absence of ceremony; informality **b** an unduly informal act or expression; an impropriety **c** *euph* (unwelcome) sexual intimacy ⟨*and then* ~ *occurred between the witness and the defendant*⟩ **3** close acquaintance with or knowledge of something ⟨*his* ~ *with the rules of cricket*⟩

**familiar·ize, -ise** /fə'mili·ə,riez, -yə,riez/ *vt* **1** to make known or familiar ⟨*Shakespeare* ~s *the wonderful* – Samuel Johnson⟩ **2** to make well acquainted ⟨~ *yourselves with the rules*⟩ – **familiarization** *n*

**familiar spirit** *n* a spirit or demon that serves an individual (eg a witch)

[1]**family** /'faməli/ *n taking sing or pl vb* **1a** a group of people united by their common convictions (eg of religion or philosophy); a fellowship, brotherhood **b** the staff of a high official, esp the US president **2a** a group of people of common ancestry or deriving from a common stock; a race **b** a group of things related by common characteristics or properties ⟨*a* ~ *of reference books*⟩ **3a** a group of people living under one roof; *esp* a group comprising one set of parents and their own or adopted children **b** a social group comprising one or more parents and

(representatives of) one or more generations of their offspring ⟨*a one-parent* ~⟩ ⟨*an extended* ~⟩ **4a** a closely related series of chemical elements or compounds **b** a group of related languages descended from a single ancestral language ⟨*a language* ~ (*the language taxonomic group usually recognised*) – H A Gleason⟩; *also* a single language (e g Quechua) of analogous rank of importance **5** a category in the biological classification of living things ranking above a GENUS and below an ORDER **6a(1)** the descendants or line of a particular individual, esp of some outstanding female **a(2)** an identifiable strain within a breed **b** an ecological community consisting of a single kind of organism **7** *maths* a set of curves, surfaces, etc that differ only by the constants appearing in the equations that describe them ☐ (*6a*) used in livestock breeding [ME *familie*, fr L *familia* household (including servants as well as kin of the householder), fr *famulus* servant; perh akin to Skt *dhāman* dwelling place]

[2]**family** *adj* of or suitable for a family or all of its members ⟨~ *entertainment*⟩

**family allowance** *n* CHILD BENEFIT

**family Bible** *n* a large Bible usu with special pages for recording births, marriages, and deaths

**Family Division** *n* a division of the HIGH COURT that deals with divorce, custody of children, etc

**Family Grouping** *n* the practice of teaching children of various ages in the same class

**family income supplement** *n* a social-security payment made to a family whose income is below the officially recognized minimum

**family law** *n* a body of law dealing with domestic matters (eg adoption and divorce)

**family man** *n* **1** a man with a wife and children dependent on him **2** a man of domestic habits

**family name** *n* a surname

**family planning** *n* contraception; *esp* contraception applied to the regulation of family size, interval between births of children, etc – compare BIRTH CONTROL

**family tree** *n* (a diagram of) a genealogy

**famine** /'famin/ *n* **1** an extreme scarcity of food; *broadly* any great shortage ⟨*the mortgage* ~ – *The Times*⟩ **2** *archaic* starvation **3** *archaic* a ravenous appetite [ME, fr MF, fr (assumed) VL *famina*, fr L *fames* hunger]

**famish** /'famish/ *vt* **1** to cause to suffer severely from hunger – usu pass ⟨*I'm* ~ed⟩ **2** *archaic* to cause to starve to death ~ *vi* to suffer for lack of something necessary ⟨*this invention of language, at a moment when French poetry in particular was* ~ing *for such invention* – T S Eliot⟩ [ME *famishen*, prob alter. of *famen*, fr MF *afamer*, fr (assumed) VL *affamare*, fr L *ad-* + *fames*] – **famishment** *n*

**famous** /'fayməs/ *adj* **1** widely known, esp for some special achievement; well-known ⟨*one of the most* ~ *women of her age*⟩ ⟨*the garden is* ~ *for its mulberry trees*⟩ **2** *informal* excellent, first-rate ⟨~ *weather for a walk*⟩ – no longer in vogue [ME, fr MF *fameux*, fr L *famosus*, fr *fama* fame] – **famously** *adv*, **famousness** *n*

**famulus** /'famyooləs/ *n, pl* **famuli** /-li/ a private secretary or attendant [Ger, assistant to a professor, fr L, servant]

[1]**fan** /fan/ *n* **1** any of various devices for winnowing grain **2** any of various instruments or devices for producing a current of air: eg **2a** an often folding circular or semicircular piece of fabric or paper mounted on thin slats that is held in the hand and waved to and fro to cool somebody **b** a series of radiating vanes rotated by a motor **c** *slang* an aircraft propeller **3** something resembling an open fan – see also **when the** SHIT **hits the fan** [ME, fr OE *fann*, fr L *vannus* – more at WINNOW] – **fanlike** *adj*

[2]**fan** *vb* **-nn-** *vt* **1a** to drive away the chaff of (grain) by means of a current of air **b** to eliminate (eg chaff) by winnowing **2** to move or impel (air) with a fan **3** to blow or breathe on ⟨*the breeze* ~ning *her hair*⟩ **4a** to direct a current of air on with a fan **b** to stir up to activity as if by fanning a fire; stimulate ⟨*he was* ~ning *the mob's fury with an emotive speech*⟩ **5** to spread like a fan ⟨~ned *the pack of cards*⟩ **6** to fire a series of shots from (a revolver) by holding the trigger back and successively striking the hammer backwards with the free hand **7** *archaic* to wave ~ *vi* **1** to move like a fan; flutter **2** to spread *out* like a fan ⟨*tanks* ~ning *out across the plain*⟩ – **fanner** *n*

[3]**fan** *n* **1** an enthusiastic devotee (e g of a sport, pursuit, or performing art) ⟨*a football* ~⟩ ⟨*a science-fiction* ~⟩ **2** an ardent admirer (e g of a celebrity or star) – compare DEVOTEE, ADDICT, BUFF, ENTHUSIAST [short for *fanatic*]

**Fanagalo** /'fanəgəloh/ *n* the BANTU pidgin language of southern Africa [Zulu *fana ka lo* be like this]

**fanatic** /fə'natik/ *n* someone who is excessively and often uncritically enthusiastic [L *fanaticus* inspired by a deity, frenzied, fr *fanum* temple – more at FEAST] – **fanatic, fanatical** *adj*, **fanatically** *adv*, **fanaticalness** *n*

**fanaticism** /fə'natisiz(ə)m/ *n* the outlook or behaviour of a fanatic

**fanatic·ize, -ise** /fə'natisiez/ *vt* to cause to become fanatical

**fan belt** *n* a continuous belt driving a fan to keep an engine cool

**fancier** /'fansi·ə/ *n* someone who has a special liking or interest; *esp* one who breeds or grows a usu specified animal or plant for competitive showing ⟨*a pigeon* ~⟩

**fanciful** /'fansif(ə)l/ *adj* 1 given to or guided by fancy or unrestrained imagination rather than by reason and experience 2 existing in fancy only; imaginary 3 marked (as if) by fancy or whim; *specif* elaborate, contrived ⟨*gave* ~ *names to their children*⟩ – **fancifully** *adv*, **fancifulness** *n*

**fancily** /'fansəli/ *adv* in an elaborate or ornate manner ⟨~ *dressed*⟩

**¹fancy** /'fansi/ *n* 1 a liking based on whim rather than reason; an inclination ⟨*took a* ~ *to the strange little animal*⟩ 2a a notion, whim b a mental image or representation of something 3a imagination, esp of a capricious or delusive sort b the power of mental conception and representation displayed in a work of art; *broadly* imagination 4 taste, judgment 5a *taking sing or pl vb* – *the* group of fanciers or of devotees of a particular sport, esp boxing b the object of such a fancy; *esp* boxing 6 a small iced and decorated cake 7 *informal* someone or something considered likely to do well (e g in a race) 8 *archaic* fantastic quality or state **synonyms** see CAPRICE, IMAGINATION [ME *fantasie, fantsy* fantasy, fancy, fr MF *fantasie*, fr L *phantasia*, fr Gk, appearance, imagination, fr *phantazein* to present to the mind (middle voice, to imagine), fr *phainein* to show; akin to OE *gebōned* polished, Gk *phōs* light]

**²fancy** *vt* 1 to believe without evidence or any great degree of certainty ⟨*I* ~ *the sun will be out before long*⟩ 2 *informal* 2a to have a fancy for; like, desire ⟨*I really* ~ *blond men*⟩ ⟨*I rather* ~ *an evening at home in front of the telly*⟩ b to consider as likely to do well ⟨*which horse do you* ~*?*⟩ 3 *informal* to form a conception of; imagine – often imper ⟨*just* ~ *that!*⟩ – **fanciable** *adj*

**fancy up** *vt, informal* to add superficial adornment to ⟨*fancy up an old dress with ruffles*⟩

**³fancy** *adj* 1 dependent or based on fancy or the imagination; whimsical 2a not plain or ordinary ⟨~ *cakes*⟩; *esp* fine, quality b ornamental or ornamented ⟨*a* ~ *hat*⟩ ⟨*a hat with* ~ *trimmings*⟩ c of an animal or plant bred for esp bizarre or ornamental qualities d parti-coloured ⟨~ *carnations*⟩ 3 executed with or requiring refined technical skill and grace ⟨~ *diving*⟩ ⟨*ruined by attempts at* ~ *camera work in the location shots*⟩ 4 *informal* extravagant, exorbitant ⟨~ *prices*⟩ – **fancily** *adv*, **fanciness** *n*

**fancy dress** *n* unusual or amusing costume (e g representing a historical character or a vegetable) worn to a party or for some other special occasion

**fancy-'free** *adj* free to do what one wants, esp because not loved or in love

**fancy goods** *n pl* small usu decorative goods or novelties

**fancy man** *n, derog informal* 1 a woman's lover 2 a pimp

**fancy woman** *n, informal* 1 *derog* a girlfriend or mistress; *esp* the girlfriend or mistress of a married man 2 a prostitute

**fancywork** /'fansi,wuhk/ *n* decorative needlework

**fan dance** *n* a solo dance performed by a woman in or appearing to be in the nude, who uses large fans to partially cover herself

**fandango** /fan'dang·goh/ *n, pl* **fandangos** 1 a lively Spanish or Spanish-American dance with three beats to the bar that is usu performed by a man and a woman to the accompaniment of guitar and castanets; *also* the music for this dance 2 tomfoolery [Sp]

**fane** /fayn/ *n, archaic* a church, temple [ME, fr L *fanum* – more at FEAST]

**fanfare** /'fan,feə/ *n* 1 a ceremonial flourish played on brass instruments, esp trumpets 2 a showy outward display [Fr, prob of imit origin]

**fanfaronade** /,fanfərə'nahd/ *n, formal* empty boasting; bluster [Fr *fanfaronnade*, fr Sp *fanfarronada*, fr *fanfarrón* braggart]

**fang** /fang/ *n* 1 a long sharp tooth or toothlike part: e g 1a a

tooth by which an animal seizes and holds or tears its prey b any of the long hollow or grooved teeth of a venomous snake c any of the clawlike structures (CHELICERAE) round the mouth of a spider, at the tip of which is an opening through which poison is ejected 2 the root of a tooth or any of the parts or prongs into which a root divides 3 a projecting tooth or prong (e g on a tool) [ME, fr OE; akin to OHG *fang* seizure, OE *fōn* to seize – more at PACT] – **fanged** *adj*

**'fan-,jet** *n* 1 a jet engine with a large fan that operates in a duct and draws extra air into the engine to provide extra thrust 2 an aircraft powered by a fan-jet engine

**fan letter** *n* a letter sent to a famous person (e g in entertainment) by a fan

**fanlight** /'fan,liet/ *n* a semicircular window with radiating divisions, placed over a door or another window; *broadly* any window over a door

**fan mail** *n* FAN LETTERS

**fanny** /'fani/ *n, vulg* 1 *Br* the external female genitals 2 *NAm* the buttocks [*Fanny*, nickname for *Frances*]

**fantail** /'fan,tayl/ *n* 1 a fan-shaped tail or end 2 a domestic pigeon having a broad rounded tail often with 30 or 40 feathers 3 ⁵COUNTER 2 (back overhang of a ship)

**'fan-,tan** *n* 1 a Chinese gambling game in which the banker divides a pile of objects (e g beans) into fours and players bet on what number will be left at the end of the count 2 a card game in which players must build in sequence upon sevens and attempt to be the first one with no cards left [Chin *fāntān* (*fan¹-t'an¹*)]

**fantasia** /fan'tayzhə, -zhyə; *also* -zyə/ *n* 1a a free instrumental composition not in strict form b a potpourri of operatic arias or familiar airs 2 a work (e g a poem or play) in which the author's imagination ranges freely and is unrestricted by a fixed plan [It, lit., fancy, fr L *phantasia* – more at FANCY]

**fantasied** /'fantəsid/ *adj* 1 existing only in the imagination; imagined, fantasized 2 *obs* full of fancies or strange whims

**fantasist** /'fantəsist/ *n* a creator of fantasias or fantasies

**fantas·ize, -ise** /'fantəsiez/ *vb* to indulge in reverie (about); create or develop imaginative and often fantastic views or ideas (about) ⟨~d *about winning the pools*⟩ ⟨*likes to* ~ *herself as very wealthy*⟩

**fantasm** /'fan,taz(ə)m/ *n* a phantasm

**fantast** /'fantast/ *n* a visionary, fantasist [Ger, fr ML *fantasta*, prob back-formation fr LL *phantasticus*]

**¹fantastic** /fan'tastik/ *adj* 1a (seemingly) conceived by unrestrained fancy; unreal, imaginary b so extreme as to challenge belief; incredible, amazing; *specif* exceedingly large or great 2 marked by extravagant fantasy or eccentricity ⟨*the* ~ *loops and curls of the baroque design*⟩ 3 – used as a generalized term of approval ⟨*looked* ~ *in his velvet jacket*⟩ [ME *fantastic, fantastical*, fr MF & LL; MF *fantastique*, fr LL *phantasticus*, fr Gk *phantastikos* producing mental images, fr *phantazein* to present to the mind] – **fantastical** *adj*, **fantastically** *adv*, **fantasticalness** *n*, **fantasticality** *n*

**²fantastic** *n, poetic* an eccentric person

**fantasticate** /fan'tastikayt/ *vt, poetic* to make fantastic – **fantastication** *n*

**¹fantasy** /'fantəsi/ *n* 1 imagination, fancy; *esp* the unrestricted free play of creative imagination 2 a creation of the unrestricted imagination, whether expressed or merely conceived: e g 2a a fantastic design or invention b a visionary or fantastic idea; an illusion c FANTASIA 1 d imaginative fiction or drama characterized esp by strange or unrealistic settings and often grotesque characters 3 a caprice, whim 4 the power or process of creating usu extravagant mental images, ideas, or daydreams in response to psychological need ⟨*an object of* ~⟩; *also* a mental image or daydream so created ⟨*sexual fantasies of adolescence*⟩ 5 *obs* a hallucination **synonyms** see IMAGINATION [ME *fantasie* – more at FANCY]

**²fantasy** *vb* to fantasize

**Fanti, Fante** /'fanti/ *n pl* **Fantis, Fantes,** *esp collectively* **Fanti, Fante** 1 a member of an African tribe of Ghana 2 the AKAN language of the Fanti

**fantoccini** /,fantə'cheeni/ *n pl* 1 puppets operated by strings or mechanical devices 2 *taking sing vb* a puppet show using fantoccini [It, pl of *fantoccino*, dim. of *fantoccio* doll, aug of *fante* child, fr L *infant-, infans* infant]

**fantom** /'fantəm/ *n* a phantom

**fan vaulting** *n* an elaborate system of vaulting, common in England in the early 14th century, in which the ribs supporting the roof diverge from a single shaft to resemble the framework of a fan

**fanwise** /'fan,wiez/ *adv or adj* in a manner or position so as to form the shape of an open fan

**fan worm** *n* any of various marine worms (family Sabellidae of the class Polychaeta) that live in long cylindrical tubes that they construct in the sea bed and from which they extend long brightly coloured feathery gills used for breathing and collecting food

**fanzine** /'fan,zeen/ *n* a magazine for fans; *esp* a magazine for fans of science fiction or of a particular pop star [³*fan* + *magazine*]

**faqir** /'faykə, fə'kiə, 'fahkiə/ *n* a fakir

**¹far** /fah/ *adv* **farther** /'fahdhə/, **further** /'fuhdhə/; **farthest** /'fahdhist/, **furthest** /'fuhdhist/ **1** to or at a considerable distance in space ⟨*wandered ∼ into the woods*⟩ **2** in total contrast – + *from* ⟨∼ *from criticizing you, I'm delighted*⟩ **3** to or at an extent or degree ⟨*as ∼ as I know*⟩ **4a** to or at a considerable distance or degree ⟨*a bright student will go ∼*⟩ ⟨*his rudeness went too ∼*⟩ **b** MUCH **1c** ⟨∼ *too hot*⟩ ⟨∼ *better methods*⟩ **5** to or at a considerable distance in time ⟨*worked ∼ into the night*⟩ ⟨*can't look ∼ beyond August*⟩ ⟨*parties are few and ∼ between*⟩ [ME *fer*, fr OE *feorr;* akin to OHG *ferro* far, OE *faran* to go – more at FARE] – **by far** by a wide margin ⟨*by far the quickest way is through London*⟩ – **far and away** by a considerable or conclusive margin ⟨*was far and away the best team*⟩ – **how far** to what extent, degree, or distance ⟨*didn't know how far to trust him*⟩ – **so far 1** to a certain extent, degree, or distance ⟨*when the water rose so far, the villagers sought higher ground*⟩ **2** up to the present ⟨*has written only one novel so far*⟩ – **thus far** *formal* SO FAR

**²far** *adj* **farther, further; farthest, furthest 1** remote in space, time, or degree ⟨*in the ∼ future*⟩ **2** of notable extent ⟨*a ∼ journey*⟩ ⟨*a man of ∼ vision*⟩ **3** being the more distant of two ⟨*the ∼ side*⟩ **4** *of a political position* extreme ⟨*the ∼ left*⟩ ⟨*a ∼ right organization*⟩ **5** in or being that subsection of the specified form of light that is farthest from the middle of the visible spectrum ⟨∼ *red*⟩ ⟨∼ *ultraviolet*⟩

**farad** /'farəd/ *n* the SI unit of CAPACITANCE (ability to store electrical charge) equal to the capacitance of a CAPACITOR (device that stores charge in an electrical circuit) between whose parallel plates there appears a POTENTIAL DIFFERENCE (difference in electric force) of 1 volt when it is charged by 1 coulomb of electricity [Michael *Faraday* †1867 E physicist]

**faraday** /'farədi, -day/ *n* the quantity of electrical charge required to remove 1 GRAM EQUIVALENT of a chemical element from solution when a solution containing the element is broken down by ELECTROLYSIS (passage of an electric current through a solution); about 96 500 coulombs [Michael *Faraday*]

**faradic** /fə'radik/ *also* **faradaic** /,farə'dayik/ *adj* of or using an asymmetrical ALTERNATING CURRENT of electricity (e g that produced by an INDUCTION COIL)

**faradism** /'farədiz(ə)m/ *n* the application of a faradic current of electricity, esp for therapeutic purposes (e g stimulating and toning muscles)

**far and near** *adv* FAR AND WIDE

**farandole** /,farən'dohl (*Fr* farãdol)/ *n* a lively Provençal dance in which men and women hold hands, form a chain, and follow a leader through a serpentine course **2** music for, or in the six-beat rhythm of, a farandole [Fr, fr Prov *farandoulo*]

**far and wide** *adv* in every direction; everywhere ⟨*advertised the event far and wide*⟩

**faraway** /,fahrə'way/ *adj* **1** lying at a great distance; remote **2** dreamy, abstracted ⟨*a ∼ look in her eyes*⟩

   *usage* Except when **faraway** is used as an adjective before a noun, one should spell it as two words ⟨*our house isn't* **far away**⟩. *antonym* nearby

**¹farce** /fahs/ *vt* to fill (poultry or meat) with stuffing [ME *farsen*, fr MF *farcir*, fr L *farcire;* akin to Gk *phrassein* to enclose]

**²farce** *n* **1** a savoury stuffing; forcemeat **2** a light comedy with an improbable plot that is concerned more with the situation than the characters ⟨*a French bedroom ∼*⟩ **3** the broad humour characteristic of farce **4a** a ridiculous or meaningless procedure or transaction **b** a mockery ⟨*this law became a ∼*⟩ [ME *farse*, fr MF *farce*, fr (assumed) VL *farsa*, fr L, fem of *farsus*, pp of *farcire*]

**farceur** /fah'suh (*Fr* farsœ:r)/ *n* **1** a joker, wag **2** a writer or actor of farce [Fr, fr MF, fr *farcer* to joke, fr OF, fr *farce*]

**farci, farcie** /fah'see (*Fr* farsi)/ *adj* filled with a (savoury) stuffing ⟨*lamb chops ∼*⟩ [Fr, fr pp of *farcir*]

**farcical** /'fahsikl/ *adj* of, or resembling a farce, esp unintentionally; ludicrous, absurd – **farcically** *adv*, **farcicality** *n*

**farcy** /'fahsi/ *n* **1** GLANDERS (disease of horses); *esp* a usu long-lasting form of glanders in which lymph vessels below the skin surface become inflamed and skin lesions form **2** a long-lasting ultimately fatal bacterial disease (ACTINOMYCOSIS) of cattle [ME *farsin, farsi,* fr MF *farcin,* fr LL *farcimen,* fr L, sausage, fr *farcire*]

**¹fard** /fahd/ *vt, archaic* **1** to paint (the face) with cosmetics **2** to gloss over [ME *farden,* fr MF *farder;* akin to OHG *faro* coloured – more at PERCH]

**²fard** *n, archaic* a cosmetic paint used on the face

**fardel** /'fahdl/ *n, archaic* **1** a bundle **2** a burden [ME, fr MF, prob fr Ar *fardah*]

**¹fare** /feə/ *vi, formal* **1** to go, travel **2** to succeed; GET ALONG ⟨*how did you ∼ in your exam?*⟩ [ME *faren,* fr OE *faran;* akin to OHG *faran* to go, L *portare* to carry, Gk *poros* passage, journey]

**²fare** *n* **1a** the price charged to transport someone **b** a paying passenger on a public conveyance **2** material provided for use, consumption, or enjoyment; *esp* the food provided for a meal ⟨*the staple ∼ of the region is a maize porridge*⟩ ⟨*good simple ∼*⟩ [ME, journey, passage, supply of food, fr OE *faru, fær;* akin to OE *faran* to go]

**fare stage** *n, chiefly Br* **1** any of the stops (e g on a bus route) between which a fare is calculated **2** a distance that can be travelled for a minimum fare or for a single increment in a fare

**fare-thee-'well** *n, chiefly NAm* a state of perfection; the ultimate degree ⟨*imitated the speaker's pompous manner to a ∼*⟩

**¹farewell** /feə'wel/ *interj* goodbye

**²farewell** *n* **1** an expression of good wishes at parting; a goodbye **2a** an act of departure or taking leave **b** a formal occasion honouring a person about to leave or retire – **farewell** *adj*

**³farewell** *vt, NAm, Austr, & NZ* to bid farewell to

**farfel, farfal** /'fahf(ə)l/ *n taking pl vb* pasta in the form of rice-like grains or small pellets [Yiddish *farfl* (pl), fr MHG *varveln*]

**farfetched** /,fah'fecht/ *adj* **1** brought from a remote time or place **2** not easily or naturally deduced or introduced; improbable, strained ⟨*a ∼ example*⟩ – **farfetchedness** *n*

**far-'flung** *adj* **1** widely spread or distributed ⟨∼ *trade connections*⟩ **2** remote ⟨*a ∼ outpost of the Empire*⟩

**far-'gone** *adj* in an advanced state, esp of something unpleasant (e g drunkenness)

**farina** /fə'reenə/ *n* **1** a flour or fine meal of vegetable matter (e g cereal grains) used chiefly as a cereal or for making puddings **2** any of various powdery or mealy substances **3** *Br* starch, esp from potato flour [L, meal, flour, fr *far* spelt – more at BARLEY]

**farinaceous** /,fari'nayshəs/ *adj* **1** containing or rich in starch; starchy ⟨*the eating of pasta ensures that the Italian diet is a highly ∼ one*⟩ **2** having a mealy texture or surface – **farinaceously** *adv*

**farinose** /'farinohs/ *adj* yielding or resembling farina

**farl, farle** /fahl/ *n, Scot* a small thin triangular cake or biscuit made with oatmeal or wheaten flour [contr of Sc *fardel*, lit., fourth part, fr ME (Sc), fr *ferde del*, fr *ferde* fourth + *del* part]

**¹farm** /fahm/ *n* **1** a leasing out of the right to collect and retain the government revenues of an area in exchange for a fixed sum **2** an area leased out for the collection of government revenues **3a** an area of land devoted to the growing of crops or the raising of animals that is worked or managed as a single unit ⟨*the estate was divided into four ∼s and leased out to tenants*⟩ ⟨*a sheep ∼*⟩ ⟨*a fruit ∼*⟩ **b** a group of buildings associated with a farm; *esp* a farmhouse ⟨*milk and eggs can be bought at the ∼*⟩ **c** an area of water used to breed or produce fish, shellfish, etc commercially ⟨*an oyster ∼*⟩ ⟨*a trout ∼*⟩ **d** something resembling a farm, esp in housing a large number of individuals under farmlike conditions ⟨*a baby ∼*⟩ [ME *ferme* rent, lease, fr OF, lease, fr *fermer* to fix, make a contract, fr L *firmare* to make firm, fr *firmus* firm]

**²farm** *vt* **1** to collect and take the proceeds of (e g taxation or a business) on payment of a fixed sum **2** to give up the proceeds of (e g an estate or a business) to another on condition of receiving in return a fixed sum **3a** to manage and cultivate (land) as farmland or as a farm ⟨*as the price of wheat rose, it became profitable to ∼ areas traditionally left uncultivated*⟩ **b** to rear (livestock) or cultivate (crops) on a farm ⟨*sheep are ∼ed on the high fells*⟩ **4** *of a batsman in cricket* to attempt to receive (all the balls bowled) so as to protect the other batsman from dismissal **5** *obs* to rent ~ *vi* to engage in the production of crops or livestock; work as a farmer

**farm out** *vt* **1** to assign (eg a job) to be carried out usu on contract **2** to put (eg children) into the care of a private individual in return for a fee

**farmer** /'fahmə/ *n* **1** a person who pays a fixed sum for some privilege or source of income **2** someone who owns, rents, or manages a farm; a producer of crops or livestock

**farmhand** /'fahm,hand/ *n* a farm worker

¹**farmhouse** /'fahm,hows/ *n* the chief dwelling house on, or formerly attached to, a farm, often incorporating facilities (eg a dairy) for the processing of farm products

²**farmhouse** *adj, esp of a food* having the qualities associated with home- rather than mass-production ⟨~ *cheese*⟩

**farming** /'fahming/ *n* the practice of agriculture – often in combination ⟨*oyster-farming*⟩

**farmland** /'fahm,land/ *n* land used or suitable for farming; *esp* cultivated arable land or pasture as opposed to rough grazing

**farmstead** /-,sted, -stid/ *n* the buildings and adjacent areas of a farm

**farmyard** /'fahm,yahd/ *n* the area round or enclosed by farm buildings

**faro** /'feəroh/ *n, pl* **faros** a gambling game in which players bet on the value of the next card to be dealt [prob alter. of earlier *pharaoh*, trans of Fr *pharaon*]

**Faroese** /,feəroh'eez/ *n or adj, pl* **Faroese** (a) Faeroese

**far-'off** *adj* remote in time or space

**farouche** /fə'roohsh, fa-/ *adj, formal* shy and lacking polish; *also* wild △ louche [Fr, wild, shy, fr LL *forasticus* belonging outside, fr L *foras* outdoors; akin to L *fores* door – more at DOOR]

,**far-'out** *adj, informal* **1** showing the qualities of outrageousness and provocation approved of by the pop and hippie cultures of the late 1960s ⟨*he had this* ~ *car painted in psychedelic colours*⟩ **2** – used as a generalized term of approval ⟨*oh,* ~ *, man!*⟩; no longer in vogue – **far-outness** *n*

**far point** *n* the point farthest from the eye at which the image of an object can be accurately focussed on the retina – compare NEAR POINT

**farraginous** /fə'rajinəs/ *adj, formal* muddled or confused; assembled (as if) at random

**farrago** /fə'rahgoh/ *n, pl* **farragoes** *formal* a confused collection; a mixture, hotchpotch [L *farragin-, farrago* mixed fodder, mixture, fr *far* spelt – more at BARLEY]

,**far-'reaching** *adj* having a wide range, influence, or effect

**farrier** /'fari·ə/ *n* **1** a blacksmith who shoes horses **2** someone who treats sick or injured horses [alter. of ME *ferrour*, fr MF, fr OF *ferreor*, fr *ferrer* to fit with iron, fr (assumed) VL *ferrare*, fr L *ferrum* iron] – **farriery** *n*

¹**farrow** /'faroh/ *vb, of a sow* to give birth (to) [ME *farwen*, fr (assumed) OE *feargian*, fr OE *fearh* young pig; akin to OHG *farah* young pig, L *porcus* pig]

²**farrow** *n* **1** a litter of piglets **2** an act of farrowing

**farseeing** /,fah'see·ing/ *adj* having foresight; farsighted

**Farsi** /'fah,see/ *n* the modern Persian language; PERSIAN 2b – compare PARSI [Per *fārsī*, fr *Fārs* Persia]

**farsighted** /,fah'sietid/ *adj* **1a** seeing or able to see to a great distance; able to see things at a distance clearly **b** having foresight or good judgment; sagacious **2** unable to see near objects clearly; affected with HYPERMETROPIA – **farsightedly** *adv,* **farsightedness** *n*

¹**fart** /faht/ *vi, vulg* to release gas from the bowels through the anus, esp loudly [ME *ferten, farten;* akin to OHG *ferzan* to break wind, ON *freta,* Gk *perdesthai,* Skt *pardate* he breaks wind]

**fart about/around** *vi, vulg chiefly Br* to spend time in pointless, aimless, or worthless activity

²**fart** *n, vulg* **1** a (loud) release of gas from the bowels through the anus **2** an unpleasant person ⟨*on first impression I thought him a bit of a* ~ *, but he's got a terrific sense of humour*⟩

¹**farther** /'fahdhə/ *adv* **1** at or to a greater distance or more advanced point ⟨~ *down the corridor*⟩ **2** ¹FURTHER **3** *usage* see ¹FURTHER [ME *ferther,* alter. of *further*]

²**farther** *adj* **1a** more distant; remoter **b** FAR 3 ⟨*the* ~ *side*⟩ **2** ²FURTHER 2

**farthermost** /-,mohst/ *adj* most distant; farthest

**farthest** /'fahdhist/ *adv or adj* **1** to or at the greatest distance in time, space, or degree ⟨*who can jump the* ~*?*⟩ ⟨*goes* ~ *towards answering the question*⟩ **2** by the greatest degree or

extent; ²MOST **1** ⟨*the essay* ~ *removed from this reviewer's comprehension – Saturday Review*⟩ *usage* see ¹FURTHER

**farthing** /'fahdhing/ *n* **1a** a former British monetary unit worth ¼ of an old penny **b** a bronze, or in former times, silver, coin representing this unit **2** something of little or no value – chiefly in *not worth a brass farthing* [ME *ferthing,* fr OE *fēorthung;* akin to MHG *vierdunc* fourth part, OE *fēortha* fourth]

**farthingale** /'fahdhing,gayl/ *n* a petticoat incorporating a hooped framework to expand a skirt at the hips and giving a characteristic line to dresses of the Elizabethan period [modif of MF *verdugale,* fr OSp *verdugado,* fr *verdugo* young shoot of a tree, fr *verde* green, fr L *viridis* – more at VERDANT]

**fasces** /'faseez/ *n taking sing or pl vb* a bundle of rods containing an axe with projecting blades carried before ancient Roman magistrates as a badge of authority and used between the two World Wars as the emblem of the Italian Fascist party [L, fr pl of *fascis* bundle; akin to L *fascia* band]

**fascia** /'fayshə; med 'fashi·ə/ *n, pl* **fasciae** /-shi·ie/, **fascias 1a** a flat horizontal band (eg of stonework) forming (part of) the load-bearing structure (ARCHITRAVE) at the top of a column in classical architecture **b** **fascia, fascia board** a board or other structure filling or masking the gap between the top of a wall and the eaves or rafters resting upon it **c** a name board over the front of a shop **2** a broad and well-defined band of colour (eg on a plant or the wing of an insect) **3** (a sheet or band of) CONNECTIVE TISSUE covering or binding together body structures or parts (eg groups of muscles) **4** *Br* the dashboard of a motor car, usu containing the speedometer and other instruments [It, fr L, band, bandage; akin to MIr *basc* necklace] – **fascial** *adj*

**fasciated** /'fashiaytid/ *adj* exhibiting fasciation

**fasciation** /-'aysh(ə)n/ *n* an abnormal enlargement and flattening of plant stems resulting from the fusion of several separate stems or side branches

**fascicle** /'fasikl/ *n* **1** FASCICULUS 1; *broadly* any small bundle or tuft **2** any of the divisions of a book published in parts [L *fasciculus,* dim. of *fascis* bundle] – **fascicled** *adj*

**fascicular** /fə'sikyoolə/ *adj* (consisting) of or arranged in small bundles of fibres ⟨~ *plant tissue*⟩ – **fascicularly** *adv*

**fasciculate** /fə'sikyoolət, -layt/ *adj* fascicular

**fasciculation** /fə,sikyoo'laysh(ə)n/ *n* muscular twitching in which linked groups of muscle fibres contract simultaneously [*fasciculus* + *-ation* (as in *fibrillation*)]

**fascicule** /'fasikyoohl/ *n* FASCICLE 2 [Fr, fr L *fasciculus*]

**fasciculus** /fə'sikyoolas/ *n, pl* **fasciculi** /-li/ **1** a slender bundle of (anatomical) fibres, esp muscle or nerve fibres **2** FASCICLE 2 [NL, fr L]

**fascinate** /'fasinayt/ *vt* **1** to hold (a person or animal) motionless (as if) by mental power or witchcraft ⟨*the rabbit lay* ~ *ed before the stoat and made no move to save itself*⟩ **2a** to capture and hold the interest of; to provide a recurrent theme or subject for (an artist, writer, etc) ⟨*the behaviour of the birds outside her window* ~*ed the old lady all winter*⟩ ⟨*Turner was* ~*ed, almost obsessed, by light*⟩ **b** to attract the curiosity of ⟨*the way that girl laughs* ~*s me*⟩ **3** *obs* to bewitch ~ *vi* to be irresistibly attractive ☐ compare CHARM [L *fascinatus,* pp of *fascinare,* fr *fascinum* witchcraft] – **fascination** *n,* **fascinator** *n*

*usage* One may be **fascinated** *by* somebody, or **fascinated** *with* or *by* something; in which case he or she or it has a **fascination** *for* one.

**fascine** /fa'seen, fə-/ *n* a long bundle of brushwood formerly used militarily (eg to reinforce gun emplacements) and now used in civil engineering as a quick means of filling holes in roads, gaps in river banks, etc [Fr, fr L *fascina,* fr *fascis* bundle]

**fascioliasis** /fə,see·ə'lie·əsis, fə,sie-/ *n, pl* **fascioliases** /-seez/ infestation with or disease caused by LIVER FLUKES [NL, fr *Fasciola,* genus of flukes + *-iasis*]

**fascism** /'fashiz(ə)m/ *n* **1** a political philosophy, movement, or regime (eg that of the Fascisti) that is aggressively nationalistic and usu hostile to socialism, exalts nation and race above the individual, and stands for a centralized autocratic government headed by a dictatorial leader, severe economic and social regimentation, and forcible suppression of opposition **2** a tendency towards or actual exercise of brutal autocratic or dictatorial control ⟨*early instances of army* ~ *and brutality* – J W Aldridge⟩ [It *fascismo,* fr *fascio* bundle, fasces, group, fr L *fascis* bundle & *fasces* fasces] – **fascist** *n or adj, often cap,* **fascistic** *adj, often cap,* **fascistically** *adv, often cap*

**Fascista** /fa'shistə/ *n, pl* **Fascisti** /-sti/ a member of the fascist political party which, under Mussolini, ruled Italy from 1922 to 1943 [It, fr *fascio*]

**fash** /fash/ *vt, chiefly Scot* to vex [MF *fascher,* fr (assumed) VL *fastidiare* to disgust, fr L *fastidium* disgust – more at FASTIDIOUS] – **fash** *n*

¹**fashion** /'fash(ə)n/ *n* **1** the make or form of something **2** a manner, way ⟨*the people assembled in an orderly* ~⟩ **3a** a prevailing and often short-lived custom, usage, or style **b** the prevailing style (e g in dress) during a particular time **c** high social standing or prominence, esp as revealed by dress or conduct; an affluent and fashionable life style ⟨*women of* ~⟩ **4** *archaic* a kind, sort [ME *facioun, fasoun* shape, manner, fr OF *façon,* fr L *faction-, factio* act of making, faction, fr *factus,* pp of *facere* to make – more at DO] – **after a fashion** in an approximate or rough way ⟨*became an artist after a fashion*⟩

²**fashion** *vt* **1a** to give shape or form to, esp using ingenuity and imagination; mould, construct **b** to mould into a particular character by influence or training; transform, adapt **2** *obs* to contrive *synonyms* see ¹MAKE – **fashioner** *n*

-**fashion** *comb form* (*n → adv*) in the manner of a ⟨*wore the scarf turban-fashion*⟩

**fashionable** /'fash(ə)nəbl/ *adj* **1** conforming to the latest custom or fashion ⟨*a novel free of* ~ *angst and introspection*⟩ **2** of high society or the group that makes or dictates fashion ⟨~ *shops*⟩ – **fashionableness** *n,* **fashionably** *adv*

**fashion plate** *n* **1** an illustration of a clothing style **2** a person who dresses exactly as the latest fashion dictates

¹**fast** /fahst/ *adj* **1a** firmly fixed or attached; not easily moved **b** tightly closed or shut ⟨*all the doors were* ~⟩ **2** firm, steadfast – chiefly in *fast friends* **3a**(1) moving or able to move rapidly; swift **a**(2) taking a comparatively short time ⟨*a* ~ *journey*⟩ **a**(3) *of a suburban train* EXPRESS **3a a**(4) accomplished quickly **a**(5) agile of mind; *esp* quick to learn **b**(1) conducive to rapidity of play or action ⟨*a* ~ *road*⟩ ⟨*cook it over a* ~ *gas*⟩ **b**(2) giving or allowing quickness of motion ⟨ *a* ~ *pitch*⟩ **c** indicating in advance of what is correct ⟨*the clock was* ~⟩ **d** having or being a high photographic speed ⟨~ *lens*⟩ ⟨~ *film*⟩ **4** *of sleep* sound, deep **5** *of a colour* permanently dyed; not liable to fade **6a** dissipated, wild ⟨*a very* ~ *set*⟩ **b** *esp of a woman* sexually free or promiscuous **7** resistant to change (e g from destructive action or fading) – often in combination ⟨*colour*fast⟩ ⟨*acid*-fast *bacteria*⟩ **8** *informal* dishonest, shady; *also* acquired by dishonest means or with unusually little effort ⟨*made a* ~ *buck*⟩ [ME, firm, strong, fr OE *fæst;* akin to OHG *festi* firm, ON *fastr,* Arm *hast*] – **play fast and loose** *informal* to behave selfishly and insincerely; toy *with* – **pull a fast one** *informal* to perpetrate a trick or fraud

*synonyms* Fast, rapid, swift, fleet, quick, speedy, hasty, expeditious: the first six are closely related and often interchangeable. Fast tends to be used of objects, while rapid is applied to actions ⟨*a fast car*⟩ ⟨*rapid progress*⟩. Swift suggests smoothness and effortlessness ⟨*more swift than swallow shears the liquid sky* – Edmund Spenser⟩. Fleet adds a suggestion of lightness and nimbleness to extreme swiftness, and is somewhat literary. Quick stresses alacrity or the short time something takes ⟨*can I have a quick word?*⟩. Speedy may also imply quickness and emphasizes haste ⟨*please send a speedy reply*⟩; it may also convey great velocity in something ⟨*a speedy motorboat*⟩. Hasty stresses hurry rather than speed, and may connote carelessness. Expeditious, on the other hand, which is rather more formal, suggests speed combined with efficiency. *antonyms* slow, halting

²**fast** *adv* **1** in a firm or fixed manner **2** sound, deeply ⟨*fell* ~ *asleep*⟩ **3a** in a rapid manner; quickly **b** in quick succession ⟨*and thick and* ~ *they came at last and more and more and more* – Lewis Carroll⟩ **4** in a reckless or dissipated manner **5** ahead of a correct time or posted schedule ⟨*the train is running 10 minutes* ~⟩ **6** *archaic* close, near ⟨*with a hill* ~ *by*⟩

³**fast** *vi* **1** to abstain from food; *esp* to do this as an act of religious devotion or commemoration **2** to eat sparingly or abstain from some foods ~ *vt* to deprive of food ⟨*the animals were* ~ed *for 24 hours before the experiment*⟩ [ME *fasten,* fr OE *fæstan*]

⁴**fast** *n* **1** the act or practice of fasting **2** a time of fasting; *also* a religious festival commemorated by fasting ⟨*the* ~ *of Ramadan*⟩

**fastback** /'fahst,bak/ *n* (a motor car with) a roof sloping backwards (nearly) to the rear bumper so that from the outside the boot does not appear to be a separate unit

**fast break** *n* a quick offensive drive (e g in basketball) in an attempt to score before the opponent's defence is organized – **fast-break** *vi*

**fast breeder reactor** *n* a NUCLEAR REACTOR in which FAST NEUTRONS are used to cause FISSION (splitting of atoms) with the release of energy, and more fissionable material is produced than is used

**fasten** /'fahs(ə)n/ *vt* **1a** to attach or secure (e g by pinning, tying, or nailing) **b** to make secure; secure against opening ⟨*make sure that the windows are* ~ed *before you go out*⟩ **2** to fix or set steadily ⟨ ~ed *his attention on the main problem*⟩ **3** to take a firm grip with – usu + a prepositional phrase ⟨ ~ *the pliers on the nut*⟩ ⟨*the dog* ~ed *its teeth into the postman's leg*⟩ **4a** to attach (oneself) persistently and usu objectionably ⟨*he* ~ed *himself to our group and insisted on leaving with us*⟩ **b** to attach, ascribe (blame, guilt, etc) ⟨*they* ~ed *responsibility for the accident on poor maintenance*⟩ ~ *vi* to become fast or fixed [ME *fastnen,* fr OE *fæstnian* to make fast; akin to OHG *festinōn* to make fast, OE *fæst* fast] – **fastener** *n*

**fasten on/upon** *vt* **1** to take a firm grip or hold on **2** to focus attention on

**fastening** /'fahs(ə)ning/ *n* something that fastens; a fastener ⟨*a gilt box with silver* ~s⟩

**fast food** *n* **1** take-away food (e g hamburgers or fried chicken) usu available on demand rather than being prepared individually for each customer **2** processed (e g frozen or packaged) food that can be prepared and served quickly – **fast-food** *adj*

**fastidious** /fa'stidi•əs, -dyəs/ *adj* **1a** excessively difficult to satisfy; hard to please **b** showing or demanding great delicacy or care **2** having complex nutritional requirements ⟨ ~ *microorganisms*⟩ **3** *archaic* scornful [ME, fr L *fastidiosus,* fr *fastidium* disgust, prob fr *fastus* arrogance (akin to L *fastigium* top) + *taedium* irksomeness] – **fastidiously** *adv,* **fastidiousness** *n*

**fastigiate** /fa'stijiət, -ayt/ *adj, biology* narrowing toward the top: **a** *of a plant* having upright usu clustered branches **b** *of body parts or organs* united in a cone-shaped bundle [deriv of L *fastigium*] – **fastigiately** *adv*

**fastigium** /fa'stijiəm/ *n* the period of greatest intensity (e g of a disease) [NL, fr L, extremity, top, gable end]

**fastness** /'fahstnis/ *n* **1** being fast: e g **1a** being fixed **b** being swift **c** colourfast quality **2a** a fortified or secure place **b** a remote and secluded place ⟨*spent the weekend in his mountain* ~⟩

**fast neutron** *n* a neutron that moves at a sufficiently high speed to cause the splitting (FISSION) of atoms with which it collides and the subsequent release of energy in a NUCLEAR REACTOR

**fast reactor** *n* a NUCLEAR REACTOR in which FAST NEUTRONS are used; *esp* FAST BREEDER REACTOR

'**fast-,talk** *vt, chiefly NAm informal* to influence or persuade by fluent, facile, and usu deceptive or tricky talk

**fastuous** /'fastyooəs/ *adj, formal* **1** haughty, arrogant **2** ostentatious, showy ⟨*a period when* ~ *living was very much the order of the day* – *TLS*⟩ [L *fastuosus,* fr *fastus* arrogance]

¹**fat** /fat/ *adj* -tt- **1** notable for having an unusually large amount of fat: **1a** plump **b** obese **c** *of a meat animal* fattened for market **2a** well filled out; thick, big ⟨*a* ~ *volume of verse*⟩ **b** full, rich ⟨*a gorgeous* ~ *bass voice* – *Irish Digest*⟩ **c** prosperous, wealthy ⟨*grew* ~ *on the war* – *Time*⟩ **3** richly rewarding or profitable; substantial ⟨*a* ~ *part in a new play*⟩ **4** productive, fertile ⟨*a* ~ *year for crops*⟩ **5a** *of soil* containing minerals that cause a greasy feel **b** *of coal* containing a high proportion of volatile matter that vaporizes when heated **c** *chiefly NAm, of wood* having a high resin content **6** *informal* practically nonexistent ⟨*a* ~ *chance*⟩ ⟨*a* ~ *lot of good it did him*⟩ **7** *informal* foolish, thick ⟨*get that idea out of your* ~ *head*⟩ [ME, fr OE *fætt,* pp of *fætan* to cram; akin to OHG *feizit* fat, L *opimus* fat, copious] – **fatly** *adv,* **fatness** *n,* **fattish** *adj*

²**fat** *n* **1** animal tissue consisting chiefly of cells full of greasy or oily matter; ADIPOSE TISSUE **2a** oily or greasy matter making up the bulk of animal fat (ADIPOSE TISSUE) and often abundant in seeds **b** any of numerous chemical compounds of carbon, hydrogen, and oxygen that form the chief constituents of plant and animal fat, are a major class of energy-rich food, are soluble in ether, chloroform, and similar organic chemical solvents but not in water, and are widely used industrially **c** a solid or semisolid fat as distinguished from an oil **3** the best or richest part ⟨*the* ~ *of the land*⟩ **4** the condition of fatness; obesity **5** excess ⟨*we must trim the* ~ *off this budget*⟩ **6** copy admitting of easy and rapid typesetting; PHAT – see also CHEW the fat

³**fat** *vt* **-tt-** to make fat; fatten

**fatal** /'faytl/ *adj* **1** fateful, decisive ⟨*a ~ hour*⟩ **2** of fate: e g **2a** like fate in proceeding according to a fixed sequence; inevitable **b** determining one's fate ⟨*that ~ day in my life*⟩ **3a** causing death **b** bringing ruin **4** *obs* fated [ME, fr MF & L; MF, fr L *fatalis*, fr *fatum* fate]

**fatalism** /-ˌiz(ə)m/ *n* (belief in) the doctrine that human beings are powerless to change events since their outcome is determined in advance (e g by God); *also* an attitude of resignation determined by this belief – **fatalist** *n*, **fatalistic** *adj*, **fatalistically** *adv*

**fatality** /fə'taləti/ *n* **1** something established by fate **2a** the quality or state of causing death or destruction **b** the quality or condition of being destined for disaster **3a** FATE **1 b** fatalism **4** the agent or agency of fate **5a** death resulting from a disaster **b** one who or that which experiences or is subject to a fatal outcome ⟨*one of the* fatalities *was a small child*⟩

**fatally** /'faytl·i/ *adv* **1** in a fatal manner; *specif* in a manner resulting in death; mortally ⟨*~ wounded*⟩ **2** as is or was fatal ⟨*~ , he refused to listen*⟩

**fata morgana** /ˌfahtə maw'gahnə/ *n* a mirage [It, lit., Morgan the fay, sorceress of Arthurian legend]

**fat body** *n* a fatty tissue distributed throughout the body of an insect, esp a nearly mature larva, that serves as a food reserve

**fat cat** *n*, *chiefly NAm informal* **1** a wealthy contributor to a political campaign fund **2** a comfortable, wealthy, and privileged person

¹**fate** /fayt/ *n* **1** the principle or determining cause or will by which events are believed to happen as they do; destiny **2a** a destiny or fortune apparently determined by fate **b** a disaster; *esp* death **3a** an outcome, end; *esp* an adverse and inevitable outcome **b** the expected result of normal development ⟨*the prospective ~ of embryonic cells*⟩ [ME, fr MF or L; MF, fr L *fatum*, lit., what has been spoken, fr neut of *fatus*, pp of *fari* to speak – more at BAN]

²**fate** *vt* to destine; *also* to doom – usu pass ⟨*the plan was ~*d *to fail*⟩

**fateful** /-f(ə)l/ *adj* **1** having a quality of ominous prophecy ⟨*a ~ remark*⟩ **2a** involving momentous and often unpleasant consequences; decisive ⟨*the ~ decision to declare war*⟩ **b** deadly, catastrophic **3** controlled by fate; foreordained – **fatefully** *adv*, **fatefulness** *n*

**Fates** /fayts/ *n pl* the three goddesses of classical mythology who determine the course of human life

**fathead** /'fatˌhed/ *n, informal* a slow-witted or stupid person; a fool – **fatheaded** *adj*, **fatheadedness** *n*

**fat hen** *n* a common plant (*Chenopodium album*) of the goosefoot family, widely distributed as a weed

¹**father** /'fahdhə/ *n* **1a(1)** the male parent of a child; *also* a father by adoption **a(2)** a male parent of an animal; a sire **b** *cap* **b(1)** GOD **1 b(2)** *the* first person of the Trinity **2** a forefather ⟨*the customs of our ~*s⟩ **3a** a man who treats or relates to another in a way suggesting the relationship of father and child, esp in receiving filial respect or reverence **b** *often cap* **b(1)** an old man – used as a respectful form of address ⟨*you are old,* Father *William, the young man cried* – Robert Southey⟩ **b(2)** something personified as an old man ⟨Father *Time*⟩ ⟨Father *Thames*⟩ **4** *often cap* an early Christian writer accepted by the church as authoritative **5a** a man who originates or institutes ⟨*the ~ of modern mathematics*⟩ **b** a source, origin **c** a very large or extreme instance of the specified thing ⟨*had the ~ of all headaches*⟩ **6** an esp Catholic priest – used esp as a title ⟨Father *Brown*⟩ **7** *usu pl* any of the leading men (e g of a city) – esp in *city fathers* [ME *fader*, fr OE *fæder*; akin to OHG *fater* father, L *pater*, Gk *patēr*] – **fatherhood** *n*, **fatherless** *adj*, **fatherlike** *adj or adv*

²**father** *vt* **1a** to be the biological cause of the conception and birth of; beget ⟨*~ed two sets of twins*⟩ **b** *of a man* to be the founder, producer, or author of; initiate ⟨*~ed a plan for improving the city's schools*⟩ **c** to be the source of **2** to fix or establish the paternity of ⟨*investigation ~*ed *the child upon the lover*⟩ **3** to foist, impose ⟨*~ a crime on a suspect*⟩ *~ vi* to care for or look after someone as a father might

**Father Christmas** *n, Br* an imaginary old man with a white beard and red suit, believed by children to deliver their presents at Christmas time

**father figure** *n* a man of particular power or influence who serves as an emotional substitute for a father

¹**father-in-ˌlaw** *n, pl* **fathers-in-law 1** the father of one's husband or wife **2** a stepfather

**fatherland** /'fahdhəˌland/ *n* **1** one's native land or country – used esp with reference to Germany; compare MOTHERLAND **2** the native land of one's father or ancestors

**fatherly** /'fahdhəli/ *adj* **1** (characteristic) of a father ⟨*~ responsibilities*⟩ **2** resembling a father (e g in care or affection) ⟨*a kind ~ old man*⟩ – **fatherly** *adv*, **fatherliness** *n*

**father of the chapel** *n, Br* the chief elected representative of a printing-office CHAPEL (trade union branch)

**Father's Day** *n* the third Sunday in June on which fathers are honoured – compare MOTHER'S DAY

¹**fathom** /'fadh(ə)m/ *n, pl* **fathoms, fathom** a unit of length equal to 6 feet (about 1.83 metres) used esp for measuring the depth of water [ME *fadme*, fr OE *fæthm* (length of the) outstretched arms; akin to ON *fathmr* fathom, L *patēre* to be open, *pandere* to spread out, Gk *petannynai*]

²**fathom** *vt* **1** to measure the depth of by using a sounding line **2** to penetrate and come to understand ⟨*couldn't ~ the problem out*⟩ *~ vi* **1** to take soundings **2** to probe – **fathomable** *adj*

**Fathometer** /fə'dhomitə/ *trademark* – used for a device that measures the depth of water by reflected sound waves

**fathomless** /-lis/ *adj* incapable of being fathomed – **fathomlessly** *adv*, **fathomlessness** *n*

**fatidic** /fay'tidik, fə-/, **fatidical** /-kl/ *adj* of prophecy – used chiefly as a technical term in theology [L *fatidicus*, fr *fatum* fate + *dicere* to say – more at DICTION]

**fatigable** /'fatigəbl/ *adj* susceptible to fatigue – **fatigability** *n*

¹**fatigue** /fə'teeg/ *n* **1a(1)** weariness from labour or exertion **a(2)** nervous exhaustion **b** the temporary loss of power to respond to a stimulus, that is induced in a nerve cell, SENSE ORGAN, muscle, etc as a result of its continued stimulation **2a** manual or menial work performed by military personnel **b** *pl* the uniform or work clothing worn on fatigue or on active duty; *also* a jumpsuit **3** the tendency of a material to break under repeated stress [Fr, fr MF, fr *fatiguer* to weary, fr L *fatigare*; akin to L af*fatim* sufficiently]

²**fatigue** *vt* **1** to weary with labour or exertion **2** to induce a condition of fatigue in (e g a muscle) *~ vi, esp of a metal* to suffer fatigue – **fatiguingly** *adv*

³**fatigue** *adj* **1** consisting of, done, or used in fatigue ⟨*a ~ detail to clean the latrines*⟩ **2** being part of fatigues ⟨*a ~ cap*⟩

**fatling** /'fatling/ *n* a young animal fattened for slaughter

**fat mouse** *n* any of several tropical and southern African short-tailed mice (genus *Steatomys*) eaten as a delicacy by the local people

**fatso** /'fatsoh/ *n, pl* **fatsoes** *informal* a fat person – often used as a disparaging form of address [prob fr *Fats*, nickname for a fat person + *-o*]

¹**fat-ˌsoluble** *adj* soluble in fats or in substances (e g ether) in which fats dissolve

**fatstock** /'fatˌstok/ *n* livestock that is fat and ready for market

**fat-tailed sheep** *n, pl* **fat-tailed sheep** (a sheep belonging to) any of several breeds of coarse-woolled meat-producing sheep that have great quantities of fat on each side of the tail bones

**fatten** /'fat(ə)n/ *vt* **1a** to make fat, fleshy, or plump – often + *up* **b** to feed up (an animal) for slaughter – often + *off* **2** to make fertile *~ vi* to become fat – **fattener** *n*

¹**fatty** /'fati/ *adj* **1** containing fat, esp in unusual amounts; *also* unduly stout; corpulent **2** greasy ⟨*avoid ~ foods*⟩ **3** (consisting) of, derived from, or chemically related to fat – **fattiness** *n*

²**fatty** *n, informal* a fat person or animal; *esp* one who is overweight

**fatty acid** *n* **1** any of a class of ORGANIC (carbon-and hydrogen-containing) chemical acids (e g ACETIC ACID) with the general formula $C_nH_{2n+1}COOH$, that are composed of usu straight chains of carbon atoms linked to each other by single chemical bonds, contain one CARBOXYL (acid) group in the molecular structure, and include many that occur naturally in fats, waxes, and ESSENTIAL OILS (class of oils occurring in plants) **2** any of numerous ORGANIC chemical acids (e g PALMITIC ACID) containing a single CARBOXYL group and usu an even number of carbon atoms, that occur naturally in combined form as GLYCERIDES in fats and oils

**fatuous** /'fatyoo-əs/ *adj* complacently or inanely foolish; silly, idiotic ⟨*a string of pointless ~ remarks*⟩ [L *fatuus* foolish – more at BATTLE] – **fatuously** *adv*, **fatuousness** *n*, **fatuity** *n*

**fat-'witted** *adj* stupid, idiotic

**faubourg** /'foh,booəg/ *n* a suburb, esp of a French city [Fr, fr MF *fauxbourg*, prob alter. of *forsbourg*, fr OF *forsborc*, fr *fors* outside + *borc* town – more at FORUM, BOURG]

**faucal** /'fawkl/ *adj* **1** of the fauces; faucial **2** *of a speech sound* deeply guttural

**fauces** /'fawseez/ *n taking sing or pl vb, pl* **fauces** the narrow passage from the back of the mouth cavity to the PHARYNX (top part of the throat) [L, pl, throat, fauces (cf SUFFOCATE)] – **faucial** *adj*

**faucet** /'fawsit/ *n, NAm* a water tap [ME, bung, tap, fr MF *fausset* bung, fr *fausser* to damage, fr LL *falsare* to falsify, fr L *falsus* false]

**faugh** /faw/ *interj* – used to express contempt, disgust, or abhorrence

**¹fault** /fawlt/ *n* **1a** a failing; *esp* a mild weakness of character less serious than a vice **b** a physical or intellectual imperfection or impairment; a defect ⟨*a ~ in my hearing*⟩ ⟨*a ~ in the gears of the bicycle*⟩ **c** a break or defect (eg a SHORT CIRCUIT) in an electrical circuit or component **2a** an action (eg an unsuccessful return) which loses a rally (eg in badminton) **b** an improper service in tennis or squash **3a** a misdemeanour ⟨*a small boy's ~s*⟩ **b** a mistake ⟨*a ~ in my adding up*⟩ **4** responsibility for wrongdoing or failure ⟨*the accident was the driver's ~*⟩ **5** a fracture in the earth's crust accompanied by a displacement (eg of the rock layers) along the fracture line **6** *obs* a lack *synonyms* see IMPERFECTION [ME *faute*, fr OF, fr (assumed) VL *fallita*, fr fem of *fallitus*, pp of L *fallere* to deceive, disappoint – more at FAIL] – **faultless** *adj*, **faultlessly** *adv*, **faultlessness** *n* – **at fault** in the wrong; liable for blame – **find fault** to criticize unfavourably – often + *with* ⟨*always finding fault with his food*⟩ – **to a fault** to an excessive degree ⟨*particular to a fault*⟩

**²fault** *vi* **1** to commit a fault; err **2** to fracture so as to produce a geological fault ~ *vt* **1** to find a fault in ⟨*can't ~ his logic*⟩ **2** to produce a geological fault in

**faultfinding** /'fawlt,fiending/ *adj* disposed to find fault; unreasonably critical ⟨*went to the film in a ~ frame of mind*⟩ – **faultfinding** *n*, **faultfinder** *n*

**faulty** /'fawlti/ *adj* having a fault, blemish, or defect; imperfect – **faultily** *adv*, **faultiness** *n*

**faun** /fawn/ *n* a figure of Roman mythology similar to the SATYR, with a human body and the horns and legs of a goat △ fawn [ME, fr L *faunus*, fr *Faunus*, Roman god of fields and cattle]

**fauna** /'fawnə/ *n, pl* **faunas** *also* **faunae** /-nie/ animals or animal life: eg **a** the animals or animal life of a region, period, or geological stratum **b** the animals or animal life developed or adapted for living in a specified environment □ compare FLORA [NL, fr LL *Fauna*, sister or wife of Faunus] – **faunal** *adj*, **faunally** *adv*

**faunistic** /faw'nistik/ *adj* of (the study of) the animals of a region or the geographical distribution of animals – **faunistically** *adv*

**Faustian** /'fowstiən/ *adj* of, belonging to, resembling, or befitting Faust or Faustus: eg **a** sacrificing spiritual values for material gains **b** striving insatiably for knowledge and mastery **c** constantly troubled and tormented by spiritual dissatisfaction or spiritual striving [*Faust, Faustus*, semi-legendary 16th-c Ger scholar & magician who allegedly sold his soul to the devil in exchange for knowledge and power]

**faute de mieux** /,foht də 'myuh (Fr foːt də mjø)/ *adv* for lack of something more suitable or desirable ⟨*sherry gave him a headache but he drank it ~*⟩ [Fr]

**fauteuil** /foh'tuh•ee (Fr fotœj)/ *n* an armchair; *also,* Br a stall seat in a theatre [Fr, fr OF *faudestuel* folding chair, of Gmc origin; akin to OHG *faltistuol* – more at FALDSTOOL]

**fauvism** /'foh,viz(ə)m/ *n, often cap* a movement in painting dating from about 1905 typified by the work of Matisse and characterized by an effort to use pure and vivid colours, a free treatment of form, and a resulting vibrant and decorative effect [Fr *fauvisme*, fr *fauve* wild animal, fr *fauve* tawny, wild, of Gmc origin; akin to OHG *falo* fallow – more at FALLOW] – **fauvist** *n, often cap*

**faux ami** /,fohz a'mee (Fr fozami)/ *n, pl* **faux amis** a foreign word or other linguistic form (eg French *actuel* meaning "current, present-day") that superficially resembles one in one's own language but has a different meaning [Fr, lit., false friend]

**faux-naïf** /,foh nah'eef (Fr foː naif)/ *adj* affecting or adopting a childlike innocence or simplicity [Fr, lit., falsely naive] – **faux-naïf** *n*

**faux pas** /,foh 'pah/ *n, pl* **faux pas** an esp social blunder [Fr, lit., false step]

**¹favour**, *NAm chiefly* **favor** /'fayvə/ *n* **1a(1)** friendly regard shown towards another, esp by a superior **a(2)** approving consideration or attention; approbation ⟨*looked with ~ on our project*⟩ **b** partiality, favouritism **c** popularity ⟨*found ~ with a wide audience*⟩ **2** (an act of) kindness beyond what is expected or due ⟨*can you do me a ~?*⟩ **3** a token of allegiance or love (eg a ribbon or badge) usu worn conspicuously **4** **favours** *pl*, **favour** *euph* consent to sexual activities, esp as given by a woman ⟨*lavished her ~s on half the regiment, who promptly reported sick*⟩ **5** *archaic* a commercial letter **6** *archaic* **6a** appearance **b** a face; facial feature [ME, fr OF *favor* friendly regard, fr L, fr *favēre* to favour, help; akin to OHG *gouma* attention] – **curry favour** to seek to gain favour by flattery or attention [¹*curry* + *favour*, by folk-etymology fr ME *favel* chestnut horse (symbolizing hypocrisy), fr OF *fauvel*] – **in favour of 1** in agreement or sympathy with; on the side of **2** to the advantage of ⟨*John gave up his rights in the house* in favour of *his wife*⟩ **3** in order to choose; out of preference for ⟨*he refused a job in industry* in favour of *an academic appointment*⟩ – **in somebody's favour 1** liked or esteemed by somebody ⟨*doing extra work to get back* in *his boss's* favour⟩ **2** to somebody's advantage ⟨*the odds were* in *his* favour⟩ – **out of favour** unpopular, disliked

**²favour**, *NAm chiefly* **favor** *vt* **1a** to regard or treat with favour **b** to do a favour or kindness for; oblige – usu + *by* or *with* ⟨*Wilson ~ed them with a kindly smile – The Listener*⟩ **c** ENDOW **2a** – usu + *by* or *with* ⟨*Nature ~ed him with a cast-iron constitution*⟩ **d** to treat gently or carefully; spare ⟨*~ed its injured leg*⟩ **2** to show partiality towards; prefer **3a** to give support or confirmation to; sustain ⟨*this evidence ~s my theory*⟩ **b** to afford advantages for success to; facilitate ⟨*good weather ~ed the outing*⟩ **4** to look like (eg a relation) ⟨*he ~s his father*⟩

**favourable** /'fayv(ə)rəbl/ *adj* **1** disposed to favour; partial **2a** expressing approval; commendatory; *also* giving a result that is in one's favour ⟨*a ~ comparison*⟩ **b** granting what is asked ⟨*a ~ answer*⟩ **c** winning approval; pleasing ⟨*a ~ impression*⟩ **3a** tending to promote or facilitate; helpful, advantageous ⟨*~ wind*⟩ **b** successful ⟨*a ~ outcome*⟩ – **favourably** *adv*

**favoured** /'fayvəd/ *adj* **1** endowed with special advantages or gifts **2** having an appearance or features of a specified kind – usu in combination ⟨*an ill-*favoured, *spoilt brat*⟩ **3** receiving preferential treatment

**¹favourite** /'fayv(ə)rit/ *n* **1** one who or that which is favoured or preferred above others; *specif* one unduly favoured by a person of high rank or authority ⟨*teachers should not have ~s*⟩ **2** the competitor (eg in a horse race) judged most likely to win, esp by a bookmaker [It *favorito*, pp of *favorire* to favour, fr *favore* favour, fr L *favor*]

**²favourite** *adj* constituting a favourite; *specif* markedly popular

**favouritism** /'fayv(ə)ri,tiz(ə)m/ *n* the showing of unfair favour; partiality

**favus** /'fayvəs/ *n* an infectious skin disease of humans and some domestic animals and fowls that is caused by a parasitic fungus and is characterized by the formation of scaly yellowish indented crusts [NL, fr L, honeycomb]

**¹fawn** /fawn/ *vi* **1** *esp of a dog* to show affection **2** to court favour by a cringing or servilely flattering manner; grovel □ usu + *on* or *upon* [ME *faunen*, fr OE *fagnian* to rejoice, fr *fægen, fagan* glad – more at FAIN] – **fawner** *n*, **fawningly** *adv*

**²fawn** *n* **1** a young deer; *esp* one still unweaned or retaining a distinctive baby coat **2** a light greyish-brown colour △ faun [ME *foun*, fr MF *feon, faon* young of an animal, fr (assumed) VL *feton-, feto*, fr L *fetus* offspring – more at FOETUS] – **fawn** *adj*

**¹fay** /fay/ *vt* to fit or join (eg timbers in shipbuilding) closely or tightly [ME *feien*, fr OE *fēgan;* akin to OHG *fuogen* to fit, L *pangere* to fasten – more at PACT]

**²fay** *n, obs* faith [ME *fai, fei*, fr OF *feid, fei* – more at FAITH]

**³fay** *n, poetic* a fairy [ME *faie*, fr MF *feie, fee* – more at FAIRY]

**⁴fay** *adj* resembling an elf △ fey

**fayre** /feə/ *n* ⁵FAIR

**faze** /fayz/ *vt, chiefly NAm informal* to disturb the composure of; disconcert, daunt [alter. of obs *feeze* to drive away, frighten, fr ME *fesen*, fr OE *fēsian* to drive away]

**F clef** /ef/ *n, music* BASS CLEF

**F distribution** *n, statistics* a PROBABILITY DENSITY FUNCTION that is used esp to compare the VARIANCES (measures of the amount of spread from the average) of two RANDOM VARIABLES, (statistical functions) that are INDEPENDENT and that both have a CHI-SQUARE DISTRIBUTION [Sir Ronald *F*isher †1962 E geneticist & statistician]

**fealty** /'fee·əlti/ *n* **1a** the allegiance of a vassal or feudal tenant to his lord **b** the obligation to show such allegiance **2** allegiance, faithfulness [ME *feute*, fr OF *feelté, fealté*, fr L *fidelitat-, fidelitas* – more at FIDELITY]

¹**fear** /fiə/ *n* **1a** an unpleasant often strong emotion caused by anticipation or awareness of danger **b** an instance of this emotion, esp occurring as a result of a specified danger or unpleasant situation 〈*a ~ of spiders*〉 〈*a ~ of physical pain*〉; *also* a state marked by this emotion 〈*in ~ of their lives*〉 **2** (a reason for or cause of) anxiety or apprehension 〈*there is some ~ that he may not pass the exam*〉 **3** profound reverence and awe 〈*the ~ of God*〉 **4** likelihood, possibility 〈*not much ~ of their team winning*〉 [ME *fer*, fr OE *fǣr* sudden danger; akin to OHG *fāra* ambush, danger, L *periculum* attempt, peril, Gk *peiran* to attempt] – **fearless** *adj*, **fearlessly** *adv*, **fearlessness** *n* – **for fear of** because of anxiety about; IN CASE OF 〈*for fear of losing electoral support*〉 – **no fear** *informal* certainly not – used interjectionally in response to a question asking one to do something dangerous or unwise 〈*will you challenge him? No fear!*〉 – **put the fear of God into** to terrify

*synonyms* Fear, dread, fright, alarm, dismay, consternation, panic, terror, horror, and trepidation all express some degree of agitation in the face of danger. **Fear** is the most general term, and may be strong or weak. **Dread** is fearful apprehension and suggests a strong feeling of helplessness to avert, or reluctance to face a threat 〈*a dread of flying*〉 〈*dread of death*〉. **Fright** is usually short-lived agitation due to a shock, while **alarm** is fright aroused by the sudden realization of imminent danger. **Alarm** is consistent with courage and self-control, but **fear** often suggests cowardice. **Dismay**, in this context, suggests a sinking of spirits and loss of courage in the face of disaster 〈*with dismay they saw the gale rip the sails to shreds*〉. **Consternation**, stronger than **dismay**, suggests great confusion which inhibits action. **Panic** is unreasoning and overmastering fear which often leads to mindless flight or counterproductive activity 〈*in her panic to get away, she left the document behind*〉. **Terror** is the strongest term, and suggests extreme fear which may paralyse or lead to panic. Unlike the other terms, it usually describes fear for one's own safety. **Horror** adds the idea of abhorrence for what is feared, especially for what may be seen 〈*saw with horror a snake in the doorway*〉. **Trepidation** suggests a trembling, hesitant apprehension 〈*approached the rostrum with trepidation*〉. *antonyms* fearlessness, assurance

²**fear** *vt* **1** to have a reverential awe of 〈*~ God*〉 **2a** to be afraid of; consider or expect with alarm **b** to be sorry or afraid to say 〈*I ~ that you have left your application too late*〉 **3** *archaic* to frighten ~ *vi* to be afraid or apprehensive – **fear-er** *n*

**fear for** *vt* to be anxious or apprehensive about 〈*I fear for his safety*〉

**fearful** /'fiəf(ə)l/ *adj* **1** causing or likely to cause fear 〈*~ storms*〉 **2a** full of fear 〈*~ of reprisals*〉 **b** showing or arising from fear 〈*a ~ glance*〉 **c** TIMID, TIMOROUS 〈*a ~ child*〉 **3** *informal* extremely bad, large, or intense 〈*a ~ waste*〉 〈*~ slum conditions*〉 – **fearfully** *adv*, **fearfulness** *n*

**fearsome** /'fiəs(ə)m/ *adj* FEARFUL 1, 2c – **fearsomely** *adv*, **fearsomeness** *n*

**feasible** /'feezəbl/ *adj* **1** capable of being done or carried out 〈*a ~ plan*〉 **2** capable of being used or dealt with successfully; suitable 〈*our ~ sources of energy are limited*〉 **3** reasonable, likely [ME *faisible*, fr MF, fr *fais-*, stem of *faire* to make, do, fr L *facere*] – **feasibly** *adv*, **feasibleness**, **feasibility** *n*

*usage* Correctly, **feasible** means "able to be done", and should not be used in the meanings "likely to happen" or "credible". A protest march or a surgical operation may be **feasible**, but a snowstorm or an epidemic are not. *antonyms* unfeasible, infeasible, chimerical, impracticable (of a scheme or project)

¹**feast** /feest/ *n* **1a** an elaborate often public meal sometimes accompanied by a ceremony or entertainment; a banquet **b** something that gives abundant pleasure 〈*a ~ of wit*〉 〈*a ~ for the eyes*〉 **2** *often cap* a periodic religious observance commemorating an event or honouring a deity, person, or thing 〈*the ~ of the Assumption*〉 [ME *feste* festival, feast, fr OF, festival, fr L *festa*, pl of *festum* festival, fr neut of *festus* solemn, festive; akin to L *feriae* holidays, *fanum* temple]

²**feast** *vi* to have or take part in a feast ~ *vt* **1** to give a feast for **2** to delight, gratify 〈*~ your eyes on her beauty*〉 – **feaster** *n*

**Feast of Tabernacles** *n* SUKKOTH (Jewish festival)
**Feast of Weeks** *n* SHABUOTH (Jewish festival)

¹**feat** /feet/ *adj, archaic* **1** neat, becoming **2** skilful, dexterous [ME *fete, fayt*, fr MF *fait*, pp of *faire*] – **featly** *adv*

²**feat** *n* **1** a notable, esp courageous, act or deed **2** an act or product of skill, endurance, or ingenuity 〈*this ship is a great ~ of engineering*〉 *synonyms* see ¹ACT [ME *fait* act, deed, fr MF, fr L *factum*, fr neut of *factus*, pp of *facere* to make, do – more at DO]

¹**feather** /'fedhə/ *n* **1a** any of the light outgrowths that form the external covering of the body of a bird and consist of a shaft bearing a set of barbs on each side that interlock to form a continuous vane – compare CONTOUR FEATHER **b** any of the feathers or pieces of feather fitted to the end of an arrow – compare FLETCHINGS **2** plumage **3** *usu pl* a long fringe or tuft of hair on the leg of a dog, carthorse, etc **4** a projecting strip, rib, etc of wood **5** the act of feathering an oar **6** *archaic* **6a** feather, feathers *pl* attire, dress 〈*I saw him in full clerical ~* – W M Thackeray〉 〈*fine ~s*〉 **b** condition, spirits 〈*in high ~*〉 [ME *fether*, fr OE; akin to OHG *federa* wing, L *petere* to go to, seek, Gk *petesthai* to fly, *piptein* to fall, *pteron* wing] – **feathered** *adj*, **feathery** *adj*, **featherless** *adj* – **a feather in one's cap** an honour or mark of distinction in which one can justly take pride

²**feather** *vt* **1a** to fit (eg an arrow) with feathers **b** to cover, clothe, or adorn with feathers **2a** to turn (an oar blade) almost horizontal after lifting from the water at the end of a stroke, in order to reduce air resistance **b(1)** to change the angle at which (an aeroplane propeller blade) meets the air so as to have minimum wind resistance; *also* to feather the propeller blades attached to (a propeller or engine) **b(2)** to allow (propeller blades) to rotate freely so as to have minimum wind resistance **3** to reduce the edge of (eg a plank) to a featheredge **4** to cut (eg air) (as if) with a wing **5** to join (eg two pieces of wood) by a TONGUE AND GROOVE (type of joint) **6** to form layers in (the hair) by skilful cutting ~ *vi* **1** to grow or form feathers **2** to have or take on the appearance of a feather or something feathered **3** *of ink or a printed impression* to soak in and spread; blur **4** to feather an oar or an aircraft propeller blade – see also **feather one's** NEST, TAR and **feather**

**featherbed** /ˌfedhə'bed, 'fedhəˌbed/ *vt* **-dd-** **1** to cushion or protect from hardship, worry, etc; pamper **2** to assist (eg an industry) financially

**feather bed** *n* (a bed with) a feather mattress

**featherbedding** /ˌfedhə'beding/ *n* rules or practices leading to overmanning in the face of technological change

**featherbrain** /'fedhəˌbrayn/ *n* a foolish scatterbrained person – **featherbrained** *adj*

**featheredge** /'fedhəˌej/ *n* (a board or plank having) a very thin sharp edge – **featheredge** *vt*

**featherhead** /'fedhəˌhed/ *n* a featherbrain – **featherheaded** *adj*

**feathering** /'fedhəring/ *n* **1a** a covering of feathers; plumage **b** a style in which feathers are attached to arrows; *also* the feathers of an arrow **2** FEATHER 3; *also* all the feathers of a dog, horse, etc

**feather star** *n* any of an order (Comatulida) of free-swimming CRINOIDS (marine animals related to starfish) having usu five feathery arms extending from a cup-shaped body

**featherstitch** /'fedhəˌstich/ *n* an embroidery stitch consisting of a line of LOOP STITCHES worked in a zigzag pattern – **featherstitch** *vb*

**featherweight** /'fedhəˌwayt/ *n* **1** one who or that which is very light in weight; *specif* a boxer who weighs not more than 9 stone (57.2 kilograms) if professional, or between 54 and 57 kilograms (between about 8 stone 7 pounds and 8 stone 13 pounds) if amateur **2** one who or that which is of limited intelligence, importance, or effectiveness

¹**feature** /'feechə/ *n* **1a** the appearance of the face or its parts 〈*gentle of ~*〉 **b** a part of the face 〈*her nose was not her best ~*〉; *also, pl* the face 〈*an embarrassed look on his ~s*〉 **2** a prominent or distinctive part or characteristic 〈*an essential ~ of the design was the flat roof*〉 **3a** a full-length film; *esp* the main film on a cinema programme **b** an important or detailed article, story, or special section in a newspaper or magazine **c** *Br* a specialized radio or television documentary –. compare DOCUMENTARY **4** an article offered for sale at cut price (eg by a chain of supermarkets) **5** *obs* physical beauty [ME *feture*, fr MF, shape, form, fr L *factura* act of making, fr *factus*, pp of *facere* to make – more at DO]

²**feature** *vt* **1** to give special prominence to (eg in a performance or newspaper) **2** to have as a characteristic or feature ~ *vi* to play an important part; be a feature – usu + in

**featured** /'feechəd/ *adj* having facial features of a specified kind – usu in combination ⟨*a heavy*-featured *man*⟩

**featureless** /'feechəlis/ *adj* having no distinctive features

**feaze** /feez, fayz/ *vt* FAZE (disconcert, perplex)

**febri-** /febri-/ *comb form* fever ⟨febri*fuge*⟩ [LL, fr L *febris*]

**febrific** /fi'brifik/ *adj, archaic* feverish

**febrifuge** /'febrifyoohj/ *n* ANTIPYRETIC (drug that alleviates fever) [Fr *fébrifuge*, deriv of LL *febri-* + *-fuga* -fuge] – **febrifuge** *adj*

**febrile** /'feebriel/ *adj* of or marked by fever; feverish [ML *febrilis*, fr L *febris* fever]

**February** /'febroo(ə)ri; *also* -rooeri/ *n* the 2nd month of the year according to the GREGORIAN CALENDAR (standard Western calendar) – see MONTH table [ME *Februarie*, fr L *Februarius*, fr *Februa*, pl, an annual feast of purification held on 15 February]

   ***usage*** The pronunciation /'febrooeri/ rather than /'febyooeri/ is recommended for BBC broadcasters.

**feces** /'feeseez/ *n pl, NAm* faeces

**feckless** /'feklis/ *adj* 1 ineffectual, weak 2 worthless, irresponsible △ reckless [Sc, fr *feck* effect, majority, fr ME (Sc) *fek*, alter. of ME *effect*] – **fecklessly** *adv*, **fecklessness** *n*

**feculent** /'fekyoolənt/ *adj, formal* filthy or foul, esp with impurities or excrement [ME, fr L *faeculentus*, fr *faec-*, *faex* dregs, sediment] – **feculence** *n*

**fecund** /'feekənd, 'fekənd/ *adj* 1 fruitful in offspring or vegetation; fertile 2 intellectually productive or inventive; prolific [ME, fr MF *fecond*, fr L *fecundus* – more at FEMININE]

**fecundate** /'fekəndayt, 'fee-/ *vt* 1 to make fecund 2 to make fertile; impregnate [L *fecundatus*, pp of *fecundare*, fr *fecundus*] – **fecundation** *n*

**fecundity** /fi'kundəti/ *n* 1 the quality or state of being fecund 2 the number of eggs or offspring produced during the lifetime of a female

¹**fed** /fed/ *past of* FEED

²**fed** *n, often cap, NAm informal* a federal agent or officer

**fedayee** /fi,dah'yee, -,da'yee/ *n, pl* **fedayeen** /-'yeen/ a member of an Arab commando group operating esp against Israel [Ar *fidā'ī*, lit., one who sacrifices himself]

**federal** /'fed(ə)rəl/ *adj* 1a formed by an agreement between political units that surrender their individual sovereignty to a central authority but retain limited powers of government ⟨*a ~ union of states*⟩ b of or being a form of government in which power is distributed between a central authority and a number of regional units c of the central government of a federation as distinguished from the governments of the constituent units ⟨*a ~ agent*⟩ 2 *cap* of the Federalist party of the USA 3 *often cap* of or loyal to the federal government or the Union armies of the USA in the American Civil War 4 *archaic* of an agreement or treaty [L *foeder-*, *foedus* compact, league; akin to L *fidere* to trust – more at BIDE] – **federally** *adv*

**Federal** *n* a supporter of the federal government or a soldier in the Union armies of the USA in the American Civil War

**federalism** /'fedrəliz(ə)m/ *n, often cap* (advocacy of) the federal principle of organization

**federalist** /-list/ *n* 1a an advocate of federalism b *often cap* WORLD FEDERALIST 2 *often cap* an advocate of a federal union between the American colonies after the American Revolution and of the adoption of the US constitution 3 *cap* a member of a major political party in the early years of the USA favouring a strong centralized national government – **federalist** *adj, often cap*

**federal·ize, -ise** /'fedrəliez/ *vt* to unite in or under a federal system – **federalization** *n*

¹**federate** /'fed(ə)rət/ *adj* united in an alliance or federation; federated [L *foederatus*, fr *foeder-*, *foedus*]

²**federate** /'fed(ə)rayt/ *vt* to join in an alliance or federation – **federative** *adj*, **federatively** *adv*

**federation** /,fedə'raysh(ə)n/ *n* 1 the act of federating; *esp* the formation of a federal union 2a a country formed by the uniting of separate states which retain control of their internal affairs but give up control of national or international affairs to the federal government b a group of organizations, societies, etc with common interests ⟨*a ~ of walking clubs*⟩

**fedora** /fi'dawrə/ *n* a low soft felt hat with a medium width brim and with the crown creased lengthways [*Fédora*, drama by V Sardou †1908 Fr playwright]

**fed up** *adj, informal* discontented, bored ⟨*~ with the nine-to-five day*⟩

¹**fee** /fee/ *n* 1a(1) an estate in land held in feudal law from a lord on condition of homage and service a(2) a piece of land so held b an inherited or heritable estate in land 2a **fees** *pl*, **fee** a sum of money paid esp for education or for a professional service ⟨*solicitor's ~* s⟩ ⟨*school ~* s⟩ b a gratuity [ME, fr OF *fé*, *fief*, of Gmc origin; akin to OE *feoh* cattle, property, OHG *fihu* cattle; akin to L *pecus* cattle, *pecunia* money, *pectere* to comb] – **in fee** in absolute and legal possession

²**fee** *vt* **feed; feeing** 1 to give a fee to 2 *chiefly Scot* to hire

**feeble** /'feebl/ *adj* 1 lacking in strength or endurance; weak ⟨*a ~ old man*⟩ ⟨*a ~ light*⟩ 2 deficient or inadequate in vigour, authority, force, efficiency, or effect ⟨*a ~ joke*⟩ ⟨*a ~ excuse*⟩ **synonyms** see WEAK **antonym** robust [ME *feble*, fr OF, fr L *flebilis* lamentable, wretched, fr *flēre* to weep – more at BLEAT] – **feebleness** *n*, **feeblish** *adj*, **feebly** *adv*

**feebleminded** /-'miendid/ *adj* 1 mentally deficient 2 foolish, stupid 3 *obs* irresolute, vacillating – **feeblemindedly** *adv*, **feeblemindedness** *n*

¹**feed** /feed/ *vb* **fed** /fed/ *vt* 1a to give food to b to give as food 2 to provide something essential to the growth, sustenance, maintenance, or operation of 3 to produce or provide food for 4a to satisfy, gratify ⟨*the acclaim* fed *his desire for recognition*⟩ b to support, encourage 5a(1) to supply for use, consumption, or processing, esp in a continuous manner, ⟨*~ the tape into the machine*⟩ ⟨*information is* fed *back to head office*⟩ a(2) to supply material to (e g a machine, esp in a continuous manner) ⟨*~ the machine with paper*⟩ b(1) to supply (a signal or power) to an electronic circuit b(2) to send (e g a radio programme) by wire to a transmitting station for broadcast 6 to act as a feed for (another performer) 7 to pass or throw a ball or puck to (a teammate), esp for a shot at the goal *~ vi* 1a to consume food; eat b to prey – + *on*, *upon*, or *off* 2 to become nourished or satisfied as if by food 3 to be moved into a machine or opening for use, processing, or storage ⟨*the grain* fed *into the silo*⟩ – see also bite the HAND that feeds one [ME *feden*, fr OE *fēdan*; akin to OE *fōda* food – more at FOOD]

   **feed up** *vt* to fatten by plentiful feeding

²**feed** *n* 1 an act of eating 2a food for livestock; *specif* a mixture or preparation for feeding livestock b the amount given at each feeding 3a material supplied (e g to a furnace or machine) b a mechanism by which the action of feeding is effected c the motion or process of carrying forward the material to be operated on (e g in a machine) 4 one who supplies cues or situations that form the basis for another esp comic performer's role 5 *informal* an esp large meal

**feedback** /'feed,bak/ *n* 1 the return to the input of a part of the output of a machine, system, or process leading to an alteration in its functioning (e g producing changes in an electronic circuit that improve performance or in an automatic control device that provide self-corrective action) 2a the modifying influence of the results or effects of an esp biological process on the start or a preceding stage of the same process b comment on or response to an action, process, etc passed back to its originator to aid evaluation and correction ⟨*got a lot of ~ on their advertising campaign*⟩

**feedback inhibition** *n* inhibition of an ENZYME controlling an early stage of a series of biochemical reactions by the END PRODUCT when it reaches a particular and critical concentration

**feeder** /'feedə/ *n* 1 a device or apparatus for supplying food (e g to a caged animal) 2 a tributary 3 a source of supply 4 a device feeding material into or through a machine 5 a road, railway, airline, etc that links remote areas with the main transport system 6 a conductor made of heavy wire that supplies electricity to some point of an electrical distribution grid 7 a transmission line running from a radio transmitter to an aerial 8 *chiefly NAm* an animal being fattened or suitable for fattening

**feeding bottle** *n* a bottle with a teat, designed to hold milk and used for feeding babies

'**feeding-,stuff** *n* feedstuff; FEED 2a

'**feed-,line** *n* a sentence or phrase that is the buildup to a punch line delivered by another person, esp a comedian

**feedlot** /'feed,lot/ *n* a plot of land on which livestock are fattened for market

**feedstock** /'feed,stok/ *n* RAW MATERIAL supplied to a machine or processing plant

**feedstuff** /'feed,stuf/ *n* FEED 2a

¹**feel** /feel, fiəl/ *vb* **felt** /felt/ *vt* 1a to handle or touch in order to examine, test, or explore some quality ⟨felt *the coat to see if it was wet*⟩ b to perceive by a physical sensation coming from

# fee

particular END ORGANS (structures at the end of a nerve) (eg of the skin or muscles) ⟨~ a draught⟩ **2a** to undergo passive experience of **b** to have one's sensibilities markedly affected by **3** to ascertain by cautious trial ⟨~ing their way⟩ – often + out ⟨felt out the opposition⟩ **4a** to be aware of by instinct or inference ⟨felt the presence of a stranger in the room⟩ **b** to believe, think ⟨I ~ that your behaviour was unwise⟩ **c** to believe oneself to be ⟨I did ~ a fool⟩ – vi **1a** to receive or be able to receive a tactile sensation **b** to search for something by using the sense of touch; grope **2** to be conscious of an inward impression, state of mind, or physical condition ⟨~s much better now⟩ **3** to seem, esp to the sense of touch ⟨~s warm⟩ **4** to have sympathy or pity ⟨really ~s for the underprivileged⟩ [ME felen, fr OE fēlan; akin to OHG fuolen to feel, L palpare to caress] – **feel like 1** to resemble or seem to be on the evidence of touch ⟨it feels like velvet⟩ **2** to wish for; be in the mood for ⟨do you feel like a drink?⟩

*usage* Feel is followed by an adjective when it means "be conscious of an inward state" ⟨**feel** happy⟩ ⟨**feel** cold⟩ ⟨**feel** sure I posted it⟩. An adverb used with **feel** describes the degree or way of feeling rather than the sensation felt ⟨**feel** very differently about it⟩ ⟨**feel** strongly that we should oppose him⟩. One **feels** bad, or **feels** well, as regards health, but as regards state of mind it is common in speech to say that one **feels** good or **feels** badly ⟨felt very badly about how we treated him⟩.

**feel up** *vt, informal* to caress intimately; *esp* to fondle the genitals of

²**feel** *n* **1** the sense of touch **2** sensation, feeling **3a** the quality of a thing as imparted through touch ⟨the material had a velvety ~⟩ **b** typical or peculiar quality or atmosphere ⟨the ~ of an old country pub⟩ **4** intuitive skill, knowledge, or ability in using or dealing with something – usu + for ⟨a ~ for words⟩

**feeler** /'feelə, 'fiələ/ *n* **1** an organ or structure (eg a tentacle or an antenna) of certain animals that is sensitive to touch **2** something (eg a proposal) ventured to ascertain the views of others – chiefly in put out feelers

**feeler gauge** *n* a set of thin steel strips of various known thicknesses that may be used singly or in combination to measure small distances between surfaces (eg the gap in a spark plug)

¹**feeling** /'feeling, 'fiəling/ *n* **1a(1)** the one of the five basic physical senses by which stimuli, esp to the skin, are interpreted by the brain as touch, pressure, and temperature **a(2)** a sensation experienced through this sense **b** generalized bodily consciousness, sensation, or awareness ⟨a ~ of nausea⟩ ⟨experienced a ~ of safety⟩ **2a** an emotional state or reaction ⟨a ~ of loneliness⟩ **b** *pl* susceptibility to impression; sensibility ⟨the remark hurt her ~s⟩ **3** a conscious recognition; a sense ⟨the harsh sentence left him with a ~ of injustice⟩ **4a** an opinion or belief, esp unreasoned; a sentiment ⟨what are your ~s on the matter?⟩ **b** an intuitive opinion ⟨I've a ~ you're right⟩; *specif* a presentiment ⟨I've a ~ she won't come⟩ **5** capacity to respond emotionally, esp with the higher emotions ⟨a man of noble ~⟩ **6** FEEL 3,4 **7** the quality of a work of art that embodies and conveys the emotion of the artist

²**feeling** *adj* **1a** sentient, sensitive **b** easily moved emotionally; sympathetic **2** expressing emotion or sensitivity ⟨gave him a ~ look⟩ **3** *obs* deeply felt – **feelingly** *adv*, **feelingness** *n*

**fee simple** *n, pl* **fees simple** *law* a FEE (land to be inherited) not limited to any particular class of heirs and without restrictions on transfer of ownership

**feet** /feet/ *pl of* FOOT

**fee tail** *n, pl* **fees tail** *law* a FEE (land to be inherited) limited to a particular class of heirs

**feet of clay** *n pl* a generally concealed or unobserved but marked weakness ⟨a towering figure, posthumously judged to have ~ – TLS⟩ [fr the feet, 'part of iron and part of clay', of the huge metal image in Dan 2:33]

**Fehling's solution** /'faylingz/ *n* a blue solution of two chemical compounds, ROCHELLE SALT and COPPER SULPHATE, used as an agent in testing substances for the presence of sugars [Hermann Fehling †1885 Ger chemist]

**feign** /fayn/ *vt* **1** to give a false appearance or impression of, on purpose ⟨~ death⟩; *also* to pretend **2** *archaic* to invent, imagine **3** *obs* to disguise, conceal ~ *vi* to pretend, dissemble **synonyms** see ¹PRETEND [ME feignen, fr OF feign-, stem of feindre, fr L fingere to shape, feign – more at DOUGH] – **feigner** *n*

¹**feint** /faynt/ *n* something feigned; *specif* a mock blow or attack directed away from the point one really intends to attack

(eg in combat sports) ⚠ faint [Fr feinte, fr OF, fr feint, pp of feindre]

²**feint** *vi* to make a feint ~ *vt* to make a pretence of as a feint ⟨he ~ed an attack and continued on his way⟩

³**feint** *adj*, of horizontal rulings on paper faint, pale [alter. of faint]

**feisty** /'fiesti/ *adj, NAm informal* **1** excited, agitated **2** fidgety, frisky **3** touchy, quarrelsome [E dial. feist mongrel dog, cur, deriv of obs fist to break wind, fr ME fisten]

**feldspar** /'fel(d)spah/ *n* any of a group of crystalline minerals that consist of silica and aluminium with either potassium, sodium, calcium, or barium and that are an essential constituent of nearly all crystalline rocks [modif of obs Ger feldspath (now feldspat), fr Ger feld field + obs Ger spath (now spat) spar]

**feldspathic** /fel(d)'spathik/ *adj, esp of a porcelain glaze* of or containing feldspar [feldspath (var of feldspar), fr obs Ger]

**feldspathoid** /'fel(d)spa,thoyd/ *n* any of a group of rock-forming minerals related to feldspar but containing less silica

**felicific** /,feli'sifik/ *adj, formal* causing or intended to cause happiness [L felic-, felix]

¹**felicitate** /fə'lisitayt/ *adj, obs* made happy [LL felicitatus, pp of felicitare to make happy, fr L felicitas]

²**felicitate** *vt* **1** *formal* to offer congratulations or compliments to – usu + on or upon **2** *archaic* to make happy – **felicitator** *n*, **felicitation** *n*

**felicitous** /fə'lisitəs/ *adj, formal* **1** very well suited or expressed; apt ⟨a ~ remark⟩; *also* marked by or given to such expression ⟨a ~ speaker⟩ **2** pleasant, delightful **synonyms** see ³FIT **antonym** infelicitous – **felicitously** *adv*, **felicitousness** *n*

**felicity** /fə'lisiti/ *n, formal* **1** (an instance of) happiness, esp when great **2** something that causes happiness **3** a felicitous faculty or quality, esp in art or language; aptness ⟨a style, which adapts itself with singular ~ to every class of subjects – J H Newman⟩ **4** a felicitous expression [ME felicite, fr MF félicité, fr L felicitat-, felicitas, fr felic-, felix fruitful, happy – more at FEMININE]

**felid** /'feelid/ *n* CAT 1b [NL Felidae, family name, fr Felis, genus of cats, fr L, cat] – **felid** *adj*

**feline** /'feelien/ *adj* **1** of cats or the cat family **2** resembling a cat; having the characteristics generally attributed to cats: **2a** sleekly graceful **b** sly, treacherous **c** stealthy [L felinus, fr felis] – **feline** *n*, **felinely** *adv*, **felinity** *n*

**feline distemper** *n* **1** PANLEUCOPAENIA (acute viral disease of cats) **2** a disease of the stomach and intestines of cats closely related to panleucopaenia

¹**fell** /fel/ *n* an animal skin or hide; a pelt [ME, fr OE; akin to OHG fel skin, L pellis]

²**fell** *vt* **1a** to cut, beat, or knock down ⟨~ a tree⟩ **b** to kill **2** to finish (a seam) by folding one raw edge under the other and sewing it flat on the wrong side [ME fellen, fr OE fellan; akin to OE feallan to fall – more at FALL] – **fellable** *adj*, **feller** *n*

³**fell** *past of* FALL

⁴**fell** *adj, archaic or poetic* **1** fierce, cruel **2** very destructive; deadly ⟨a ~ poison⟩ – see also at one fell swoop [ME fel, fr OF – more at FELON] – **fellness** *n*, **felly** *adv*

⁵**fell** *n* **1** *chiefly N Eng & Scot* a mountain **2** **fells** *pl*, **fell** a steep rugged stretch of high moorland, esp in northern England and Scotland [ME, hill, mountain, fr ON fell, fjall; akin to OHG felis rock]

**fella** /'felə/ *n, informal* FELLOW 4,7 [by alter.]

**fellah** /'felə/ *n, pl* **fellahin, fellaheen** /,felə'heen/ a peasant or agricultural labourer in an Arab country (eg Egypt) [Ar fallāh]

**fellatio** /fə'layshioh/ *also* **fellation** /fə'laysh(ə)n/ *n* oral stimulation of the penis [NL fellation-, fellatio, fr L fellatus, pp of felare, fellare to suck – more at FEMININE] – **fellate** *vt*, **fellator** *n*

**feller** /'felə/ *n, informal* FELLOW 4,7 [by alter.]

**fellmonger** /'fel,mung·gə/ *n, Br* somebody who removes hair or wool from hides in preparation for leather making – **fellmongered** *adj*, **fellmongering, fellmongery** *n*

**felloe** /'feloh/ *n* (a segment of) the exterior rim of a spoked wheel [ME fely, felive, fr OE felg; akin to OHG felga felloe]

¹**fellow** /'feloh/ *n* **1** *usu pl* a comrade, associate **2a** an equal in rank, power, or character; a peer **b** either of a pair; a mate **3** a member of a group having common characteristics; *specif, often cap* a member of an incorporated literary or scientific society ⟨Fellow of the Royal Academy⟩ **4** a man; *also* a boy **5** *often cap* an incorporated member of a college or collegiate foundation, esp in a British university **6** a person appointed to a position granting a salary and allowing for advanced study

539                    **fen**

or research **7** *informal* a boyfriend **8** *obs* a person of any of the lower social classes [ME *felawe,* fr OE *fēolaga,* fr ON *fēlagi,* fr *fēlag* partnership, fr *fē* cattle, money + *lag* act of laying]

**²fellow** *adj* being a companion, associate, or member of a group with the same characteristics – used before a noun ⟨*a ~ worker*⟩

**fellow feeling** *n* a feeling of community of interest or of mutual understanding; *specif* sympathy

**fellowship** /'felohship/ *n* **1** the condition of friendly relations between people; company, companionship **2a** community of interest, activity, feeling, or experience **b** the state of being a fellow or associate **3** *taking sing or pl vb* a group or association of people with similar interests; *specif* a group of Christians who meet together regularly for worship **4a** the position of a fellow (eg of a university) **b** (a foundation for the providing of) the salary of a fellow **5** *obs* membership, partnership

**fellow traveller** *n, chiefly derog* somebody who sympathizes with and often furthers the ideals and programme of an organized group, esp the Communist party, without membership of the group or regular participation in its activities [trans of Russ *poputchik*]

**felly** /'feli/ *n* a felloe

**felo-de-se** /ˌfeeloh də 'say, ˌfeloh, see/ *n, pl* **felones-de-se** /fə'lohneez/, **felos-de-se** /'felohz/ somebody who commits) suicide [ML *felo de se, fello de se,* lit., evildoer upon himself]

**¹felon** /'felən/ *adj, archaic* cruel, evil [ME, fr OF *felon, fel,* fr ML *fellon-, fello* evildoer, villain]

**²felon** *n* **1** somebody who has committed a felony **2** WHITLOW (inflammation of a finger or toe) **3** *archaic* a villain

**felonious** /fə'lohnyəs/ *adj* **1** (having the quality) of a felony **2** *archaic* very evil; villainous – **feloniously** *adv,* **feloniousness** *n*

**felonry** /'felənri/ *n taking sing or pl vb* felons; *specif* the convict population of a penal colony

**felony** /'feləni/ *n* a grave crime (eg murder or arson) that, until 1967, was regarded at COMMON LAW as more serious than a misdemeanour and, until 1870, involved forfeiture of property in addition to any other punishment

**felsite** /'felsiet/ *n* a dense IGNEOUS rock (rock formed by the cooling and solidification of molten lava) that consists almost entirely of FELDSPAR and QUARTZ [*felspar* + *-ite*] – **felsitic** *adj*

**felspar** /'felˌspah/ *n* FELDSPAR (type of mineral)

**¹felt** /felt/ *n* **1** a nonwoven cloth consisting of wool or fur often mixed with natural or synthetic fibres and made by applying pressure, heat, moisture, and chemicals **2** an article (eg a felt-tip pen) made of felt **3** a material resembling felt: eg **3a** a heavy paper of organic or asbestos fibres impregnated with asphalt and used in building construction **b** semirigid pressed fibre insulation used in building [ME, fr OE; akin to OHG *filz* felt, L *pellere* to drive, beat, Gk *pelas* near]

**²felt** *vt* **1** to make into felt **2** to cause to adhere and mat together **3** to cover with felt

**³felt** *past of* FEEL

**felting** /'felting/ *n* **1** the process by which felt is made **2** felt

**felt-tip pen** *n* a pen with a soft felt tip through which ink flows

**felucca** /fe'lukə/ *n* a narrow sailing ship with a LATEEN (triangular) sail used chiefly in the Mediterranean area [It *feluca,* perh deriv of Gk *epholkion* small boat]

**fem** /fem/, **femme** /fem, fam/ *n* a lesbian who adopts a passive role and extreme feminine characteristics [*fem* short for *female* or *feminine; femme* fr Fr, woman, wife]

**¹female** /'feemayl/ *n* **1** an individual that bears young or produces eggs; *esp* a woman or girl as distinguished from a man or boy **2** a plant or flower with an OVARY (structure producing seeds) but no male reproductive parts *synonyms* see LADY *antonym* male [ME, alter. (influenced by *male*) of *femel, femelle,* fr MF & ML; MF *femelle,* fr ML *femella,* fr L, girl, dim. of *femina*]

**²female** *adj* **1a** of or being a female **b** *of a plant or flower* having an OVARY (structure producing seeds) but no male reproductive parts **2** FEMININE 2 **3** designed with a hole or hollow into which a corresponding male part fits ⟨*a ~ plug*⟩ – **femaleness** *n*

*synonyms* **Female, feminine, womanly, womanlike, womanish, effeminate,** and **ladylike: Female** is opposed to *male,* and denotes sex in living things. **Feminine,** applied only to human beings, not to plants or animals, describes attributes and behaviour popularly ascribed to women rather than men. **Womanly** suggests the good qualities associated with mature women ⟨*womanly sympathy*⟩. **Womanlike** simply suggests behaviour or appearance

characteristic of women. **Womanish** is derogatory, suggesting unbecoming weakness in either men or women. **Effeminate** implies excessively feminine behaviour in men. **Ladylike** suggests the decorous behaviour expected of a lady. *antonym* male

**¹feminine** /'femənin/ *adj* **1** FEMALE 1a **2** characteristic of, appropriate to, or peculiar to women; womanly **3** of or being the gender that ordinarily includes most words or grammatical forms referring to females **4a** having an extra unstressed final syllable ⟨*~ ending*⟩ ⟨*~ rhyme*⟩ **b** having the final chord occurring on a weak beat ⟨*music in ~ cadences*⟩ *synonyms* see ²FEMALE *antonym* masculine [ME, fr MF *feminin,* fr L *femininus,* fr *femina* woman; akin to OE *delu* nipple, L *filius* son, *felix, fetus,* & *fecundus* fruitful, *felare* to suck, Gk *thēlē* nipple] – **femininely** *adv,* **feminineness** *n,* **femininity** *n*

**²feminine** *n* **1** the feminine principle in human nature – esp in *eternal feminine* **2a** a word or MORPHEME (smallest meaningful linguistic element) of the feminine gender **b** the feminine gender

**feminism** /'feminiz(ə)m/ *n* the doctrine or movement supporting women's rights, interests, and equality with men esp in political, economic, and social spheres – **feminist** *n or adj*

**femin-ize, -ise** /'feminiez/ *vt* **1** to give a feminine quality to **2** to cause (a male) to take on feminine characteristics (eg by administration of hormones) – **feminization** *n*

**femme fatale** /ˌfam fa'tahl, 'femi (*Fr* fam fatal)/ *n, pl* **femmes fatales** /fa'tahl(z) (*Fr ~*)/ a seductive and usu mysterious woman; *esp* one who lures men into dangerous or compromising situations [Fr, lit., disastrous woman]

**femoral** /'femərəl/ *adj* of the femur or thigh

**femoral artery** *n* the chief artery of the thigh lying in its anterior inner part

**femto-** /'femtoh-/ *comb form* one thousand million millionth (10⁻¹⁵) part of (a specified unit) ⟨*femtoampere*⟩ [ISV, fr Dan or Norw *femten* fifteen, fr ON *fimmtān;* akin to OE *fiftēne* fifteen]

**femur** /'feemə/ *n, pl* **femurs, femora** /'femərə/ **1** the bone of the hind or lower limb nearest the body; the thigh bone **2** the third segment of an insect's leg counting from the base [NL *femor-, femur,* fr L, thigh]

**¹fen** /fen/ *n* an area of low marshy or flooded land; *also* such an area when artificially drained [ME, fr OE *fenn;* akin to OHG *fenna* fen, Skt *paṅka* mud] – **fenny** *adj*

**²fen** *n, pl* **fen** – see *yuan* at MONEY table [Chin (Pek) *fēn* (*fĕn¹*)]

**¹fence** /fens/ *n* **1** a barrier (eg of wire or boards) intended to prevent escape or intrusion or to mark a boundary ⟨*a garden ~*⟩ **2** *informal* **2a** a receiver of stolen goods **b** a place where stolen goods are bought **3** an upright obstacle (eg one resembling a section of a fence or a wall) to be jumped by a horse (eg in showjumping or steeplechasing) **4** *archaic* a means of protection; a defence [ME *fens,* short for *defens* defence] – **fenceless** *adj,* **fencelessness** *n* – **sit on the fence** to refuse or be unable to commit oneself; remain undecided

**²fence** *vt* **1a** to enclose with a fence **b** to separate *off* or keep *out* (as if) with a fence **2** to receive or sell (stolen goods) **3** *archaic* to provide a defence for; shield, protect ~ *vi* **1a** to practise fencing **b(1)** to use tactics of attack and defence (eg thrusting and parrying) resembling those of fencing **b(2)** to engage in skilful or witty conversation, esp in order to avoid making a decisive statement **2** *of a batsman* to play at and miss the ball in cricket, esp in a tentative manner and outside the off stump – usu + *at* **3** to deal in stolen goods **4** *archaic* to provide protection – **fencer** *n*

**fencing** /'fensing/ *n* **1** the art, practice, or sport of attack and defence with the foil, épée, or sabre **2** (material used for building) fences

**fender** /'fendə/ *n* **1** a cushion (eg of foam rubber, rope, or wood) hung over the side of a ship to absorb impact and prevent chafing **2** a low metal frame or screen placed in front of a fire to confine coals, sparks, etc **3** *chiefly NAm* a device in front of a locomotive or tram to lessen injury to animals or pedestrians in case of collision – compare COWCATCHER **4** *NAm* a wing or mudguard [*fend* + ²-*er*]

**fend for** /fend/ *vt* to provide a livelihood for; support [*fend* (to defend, repel) fr ME *fenden,* short for *defenden* to defend, protect]

**fend off** *vt* to keep or ward off; repel

**fenestra** /fi'nestrə/ *n, pl* **fenestrae** /fi'nestrie/ **1** an opening in a bone or between two bones **2** a transparent spot (eg in the wings of a termite) [NL, fr L, window] – **fenestral** *adj*

**fenestra ovalis** /oh'vahlis/ *n* an oval opening between the MIDDLE EAR and the VESTIBULE (cavity) of the INNER EAR [NL, oval fenestra]

**fenestra rotunda** /roh'tundə, -'toondə/ *n* a round opening between the MIDDLE EAR and the COCHLEA (spirally coiled structure through which sound is transmitted) in the INNER EAR [NL, round fenestra]

**fenestrated** /'fenistraytid/ *adj* 1 having windows ⟨*a* ∼ *building*⟩ 2 *also* **fenestrate** having one or more openings or pores ⟨∼ *blood capillaries*⟩ [L *fenestratus,* fr *fenestra*]

**fenestration** /,feni'straysh(ə)n/ *n* 1 the arrangement of windows in a building 2 an opening in a surface (e g a wall or membrane) 3 the surgical operation of cutting an opening into the INNER EAR as a treatment for deafness

**Fenian** /'feenyən/ *n* 1 any of a legendary band of Irish warriors of the 2nd and 3rd centuries AD 2 a member of a secret 19th-century Irish and Irish-American organization dedicated to the overthrow of British rule in Ireland [IrGael *Fēinne,* pl of *Fiann,* legendary band of ancient Irish warriors] – **Fenian** *adj,* **Fenianism** *n*

**fennec** /'fenek/ *n* a small pale-fawn African fox (*Fennecus zerda*) with large ears [Ar *fanak*]

**fennel** /'fenl/ *n* a yellow-flowered European plant (*Foeniculum vulgare*) of the carrot family cultivated for its edible bulbous roots, leaves, and aromatic seeds [ME *fenel,* fr OE *finugl,* fr (assumed) VL *fenuculum,* fr L *feniculum* fennel, dim. of *fenum* hay]

**fenugreek** /'fenyoo,greek/ *n* an Asiatic plant (*Trigonella foenumgraecum*) of the pea family whose aromatic seeds are used as a flavouring [ME *fenugrek,* fr MF *fenugrec,* fr L *fenum Graecum,* lit., Greek hay]

**feoffment** /'feefmənt, 'fef-/ *n* the granting of a FIEF (feudal estate) [ME *feoffement,* fr AF, fr *feoffer* to invest with a fee, fr OF *fief* fee]

**-fer** /-fə/ *comb form* (→ *n*) somebody or something that bears ⟨*aqui*fer⟩ ⟨*coni*fer⟩ [Fr & L; Fr -*fère,* fr L -*fer* bearing, one who or that which bears, fr *ferre* to carry – more at BEAR]

**ferae naturae** /,ferie 'nachoorie/ *adj, formal* wild by nature and not usu tamed ⟨*foxes are* ∼⟩ [L, of a wild nature]

**feral** /'fiərəl, 'ferəl/ *adj* 1 *esp of animals* wild, esp after having once been domesticated or cultivated ⟨∼ *pigeons*⟩ 2 *formal* (suggestive) of a wild beast; savage △ ferial [ML *feralis,* fr L *fera* wild animal, fr fem of *ferus* wild – more at FIERCE]

**fer-de-lance** /,feə də 'lahns/ *n, pl* **fer-de-lance** a large extremely venomous PIT VIPER (*Bothrops atrox*) of Central and S America [Fr, lit., lance iron, spearhead]

**fere** /fiə/ *n, archaic* 1 a companion, comrade 2 a spouse [ME, fr OE *gefēra;* akin to OE *faran* to go, travel – more at FARE]

**feretory** /'ferit(ə)ri/ *n* (a chapel containing) an often portable shrine for the relics of a saint [ME, fr AF *fertre* & MF *fiertre,* fr ML *feretrum,* fr L, litter, bier, fr Gk *pheretron,* fr *pherein* to carry – more at BEAR]

**feria** /'fiəriə, 'feriə/ *n, pl* **ferias, feriae** a weekday of the Roman Catholic church calendar on which no feast is celebrated [ML – more at FAIR] – **ferial** *adj*

**ferine** /'fiərien/ *adj* feral [L *ferinus,* fr *fera*]

**ferity** /'ferəti/ *n, formal* the quality or state of being feral [L *feritas,* fr *ferus*]

**fermata** /fuh'mahtə/ *n* a prolongation at the discretion of the performer of a musical note, chord, or rest beyond its given time value; *also* [1]PAUSE 4 [It, lit., stop, fr *fermare* to stop, fr L *firmare* to make firm]

[1]**ferment** /fə'ment/ *vb* 1 to (cause to) undergo fermentation 2 to (cause to) work up into a state of agitation or intense activity △ foment – **fermentable** *adj,* **fermenter, fermentor** *n*

[2]**ferment** /'fuhment/ *n* 1 an agent (e g yeast) capable of bringing about fermentation 2a FERMENTATION 1 b a state of unrest or upheaval; agitation; tumult [ME, fr L *fermentum* yeast – more at BARM]

**fermentation** /,fuhmen'taysh(ə)n/ *n* 1a a chemical change with the release of many bubbles of gas b a chemical reaction in which an organic compound is broken down by the action of an ENZYME; *specif* the ANAEROBIC breakdown (breakdown occurring without the presence of oxygen) of sugar to alcohol by the action of yeast 2 FERMENT 2b – **fermentative** *adj*

**fermi** /'fuhmi/ *n, physics* a unit of length equal to $10^{-15}$ metres [Enrico *Fermi* †1954 It physicist]

**fermion** /'fuhmyən, 'feə-, -mi·ən/ *n* an ELEMENTARY PARTICLE (e g a lepton) or other system (e g the nucleus of an atom) that obeys relations (esp the EXCLUSION PRINCIPLE) stated by Fermi and Dirac [Enrico *Fermi* + E [2]-*on*] – **fermionic** *adj*

**fermium** /'fuhmyəm, -mi·əm/ *n* a radioactive metallic chemical element which is artificially produced from plutonium [NL, fr Enrico *Fermi*]

**fern** /fuhn/ *n* any of a class (*Filicineae*) of flowerless seedless lower plants; *esp* any of an order (Filicales) resembling flowering plants in having a root, stem, leaflike fronds, and a circulatory and transport system but differing in reproducing by spores [ME, fr OE *fearn;* akin to OHG *farn* fern, Skt *parṇa* wing, leaf] – **fernlike** *adj,* **ferny** *adj*

**fernery** /'fuhnəri/ *n* 1 a place or stand where ferns grow 2 a collection of growing ferns

**ferocious** /fə'rohshəs/ *adj* 1 extremely fierce, violent, or brutal 2 unbearably intense; extreme ⟨∼ *heat*⟩ [L *feroc-, ferox,* lit., fierce looking, fr *ferus* + -*oc-, -ox* looking – more at ATROCIOUS] – **ferociously** *adv,* **ferociousness** *n*

**ferocity** /fə'rosəti/ *n* the quality or state of being ferocious

**-ferous** /-fərəs/, **-iferous** /-'ifərəs/ *comb form* (→ *adj*) bearing; yielding; producing; containing ⟨*carboni*ferous⟩ ⟨*pesti*ferous⟩ [ME, fr L -*fer* & MF -*fere* (fr L -*fer*)]

**ferrate** /'ferayt/ *n* a chemical compound composed of a group containing iron and oxygen; *esp* a red SALT derived from the hypothetical ferric acid and a metal [ISV, fr L *ferrum* iron]

**ferredoxin** /,feri'doksin/ *n* an iron-containing protein that takes part in energy-producing chemical reactions in plants and some bacteria [L *ferrum* iron + E *redox* + -*in*]

[1]**ferret** /'ferit/ *n* 1 a partially domesticated usu albino European polecat that is sometimes classed as a separate species (*Mustela furo*) and is used esp for hunting small rodents (e g rats) 2 an active and persistent searcher [ME *furet, ferret,* fr MF *furet,* fr (assumed) VL *furittus,* lit., little thief, dim. of L *fur* thief] – **ferrety** *adj*

[2]**ferret** *vi* 1 to hunt with ferrets 2 *informal* to search *about* or *around* ∼ *vt* 1 to hunt (e g rats) with ferrets 2 to drive (game) esp from covert or burrows – **ferreter** *n*

**ferret out** *vt, informal* to find and bring to light by searching ⟨ferret out *the answers*⟩

**ferri-** /feri-/ *comb form* 1 iron ⟨ferri*ferrous*⟩ 2 ferric iron ⟨ferri*cyanide*⟩ [L, fr *ferrum*]

**ferriage** /'feri·ij/ *n* (the fare paid for) transport by ferry

**ferric** /'ferik/ *adj* of, being, or containing iron, esp iron having a VALENCY of three

**ferric chloride** *n* a brown chemical compound, $FeCl_3$, that readily absorbs water from the air (DELIQUESCES) to become yellow-orange and that is used in the treatment of sewage and as a disinfectant

**ferric oxide** *n* the red or black chemical compound, $Fe_2O_3$, composed of iron and oxygen that is found in nature as HAEMATITE and as rust and is also obtained synthetically and used as a pigment and a metal polish

**ferricyanide** /,feri'sie·ənied/ *n* a complex chemical compound that contains the group $Fe(CN)_6$ in a form having a VALENCY of three and that is used in making blue pigments [ISV]

**ferriferous** /fe'rifərəs/ *adj* containing or yielding iron

**ferrimagnetic** /,ferimag'netik/ *adj* of or being a substance (e g ferrite) characterized by a spontaneous magnetization in which one group of magnetic atoms is arranged in a direction opposite to the other – compare FERROMAGNETIC – **ferrimagnet** *n,* **ferrimagnetically** *adv,* **ferrimagnetism** *n*

**Ferris wheel** /'feris/ *n, chiefly NAm* BIG WHEEL [G W G *Ferris* †1896 US engineer]

**ferrite** /'feriet/ *n* any of several substances that consist essentially of a ferric oxide combined with one or more metals (e g manganese, nickel, or zinc), are strongly ferromagnetic, and are used esp in computer memories – **ferritic** *adj*

**ferritin** /'feritin/ *n* an iron-containing protein that functions in the storage of iron in the body and is found esp in the liver and spleen [*ferrite* + -*in*]

**ferro-** /feroh-/ *comb form* 1 (containing) iron ⟨ferro*concrete*⟩; iron and ⟨ferro*nickel*⟩ – chiefly in names of alloys 2 ferrous iron ⟨ferro*cyanide*⟩ [ML, fr L *ferrum*]

**ferrocyanide** /,feroh'sie·ənied/ *n* a complex chemical compound that contains the group $Fe(CN)_6$ in a form having a VALENCY of four and that is used in making blue pigments, esp PRUSSIAN BLUE

**ferroelectric** /,ferroh·i'lektrik/ *adj* of or being a crystalline substance (e g a ceramic) that can develop a positive or negative electric charge in an ELECTRIC FIELD, but does not conduct electricity and is therefore used as an insulator – **ferroelectric** *n,* **ferroelectricity** *n*

**ferromagnetic** /,ferrohmag'netik/ *adj* of or being a substance, esp iron, that can be made strongly and permanently magnetic with a magnetization in which all the magnetic atoms are arranged in the same direction – compare DIAMAGNETIC, FERRIMAGNETIC, PARAMAGNETIC – **ferromagnetic** n, **ferromagnetism** n

¹**ferrotype** /'ferə,tiep/ n a positive photograph made, esp formerly, on a thin sensitized iron plate having a darkened surface (e g of black enamel); *also* the process of producing such photographs

²**ferrotype** vt to give a gloss to (a photographic print) by pressing face down while wet on a ferrotype plate and allowing to dry

**ferrous** /'ferəs/ adj of, containing, or being iron, esp iron which has a VALENCY of two [NL *ferrosus*, fr L *ferrum*]

**ferrous oxide** n a chemical compound, FeO, that is a black powder and contains iron and oxygen

**ferrous sulphate** n a chemical compound, FeSO₄, containing iron, sulphur, and oxygen; *esp* the mineral COPPERAS

**ferrugineous** /,ferə'jeenyəs/ adj ferruginous

**ferruginous** /fə'rujinəs, fe-/ adj 1 of or containing iron ⟨a ~ soil⟩ 2 resembling iron rust in colour [L *ferrugineus, ferruginus*, fr *ferrugin-, ferrugo* iron rust, fr *ferrum*]

¹**ferrule** /'feroohl, -rəl/ n 1 a ring or cap, usu of metal, put round a slender shaft (e g a cane or a tool handle) to strengthen it or prevent it from splitting 2 a short tube or cylindrical lining (BUSH) for making a tight joint (e g between pipes) □ compare FERULE [alter. (influenced by L *ferrum* iron) of ME *virole*, fr MF, fr L *viriola*, dim. of *viriu* bracelet, of Celtic origin; akin to OIr *fiar* oblique – more at VEER]

²**ferrule** vt to supply with a ferrule

¹**ferry** /'feri/ vt 1 to carry by boat over a body of water 2 to convey (e g by car) from one place to another; transport ⟨expected to ~ my daughter's friends back and forth⟩ ~ vi to cross water in a boat [ME *ferien*, fr OE *ferian* to carry, convey; akin to OE *faran* to go – more at FARE]

²**ferry** n 1 a place where people or things are carried across a body of water (e g a river) in a boat 2 a ferryboat 3 the right to operate a ferry service across a body of water

**ferryboat** /'feri,boht/ n a boat used to ferry passengers, vehicles, or goods

**ferryman** /'ferimən, -,man/ n somebody who operates a ferry

**fertile** /'fuhtiel/ adj 1a producing or bearing fruit in great quantities; productive **b** characterized by great resourcefulness and activity; inventive ⟨a ~ imagination⟩ 2a(1) capable of sustaining abundant plant growth ⟨~ soil⟩ a(2) affording abundant possibilities for development ⟨a ~ area for research⟩ **b** capable of growing or developing ⟨a ~ egg⟩ c(1) capable of producing fruit c(2) of an anther in a flower containing pollen c(3) developing spores or spore-bearing organs **d** capable of breeding or reproducing 3 capable of being converted into material that will break down into lighter forms during radioactive reactions ⟨~ uranium 238⟩ 4 obs plentiful [ME, fr MF & L; MF, fr L *fertilis*, fr *ferre* to carry, bear – more at BEAR] – **fertilely** adv, **fertileness** n

**fertility** /fuh'tiləti/ n 1 the quality or state of being fertile 2 the birthrate of a population

**fertil·ization, -isation** /,fuhtilie'zaysh(ə)n/ n 1 an act or process of making fertile: e g 1a the application of fertilizer **b** an act or process of insemination, impregnation, or pollination 2 the process whereby two reproductive cells (e g a sperm and an egg) unite to restore the normal amount of genetic material (CHROMOSOME NUMBER) and initiate the development of a new individual – **fertilizational** adj

**fertilization membrane** n a thickened membrane surrounding a fertilized egg that prevents further penetration of the egg by sperm and is formed from the VITELLINE MEMBRANE (membrane enclosing egg cell) immediately after fertilization

**fertil·ize, -ise** /'fuhtiliez/ vt to make fertile: e g a to cause the fertilization of **b** to apply a fertilizer to ⟨~ land⟩ – **fertilizable** adj

**fertil·izer, -iser** /'fuhti,liezə/ n one who or that which fertilizes; *specif* a substance (e g manure or a chemical mixture) used to make soil more fertile

**ferula** /'feroolə/ n 1 a ferule 2 any of a genus (*Ferula*) of plants of the carrot family that yield various GUM RESINS (e g GALBANUM and ASAFOETIDA) [(2) NL, genus name, fr L, giant fennel]

**ferule** /'feroohl/ n a flat piece of wood, esp a ruler, used to punish children □ compare FERRULE [L *ferula* giant fennel, ferule]

**fervency** /'fuhv(ə)nsi/ n fervour

**fervent** /'fuhv(ə)nt/ adj 1 exhibiting deep sincere emotion; ardent ⟨a ~ believer in free speech⟩ 2 archaic or poetic very hot; glowing [ME, fr MF & L; MF, fr L *fervent-, fervens*, prp of *fervēre* to boil, glow – more at BURN] – **fervently** adv

**fervid** /'fuhvid/ adj 1 very hot; burning 2 marked by impassioned intensity or feverish urgency; too fervent ⟨his ~ manner of lovemaking offended her* – Arnold Bennett⟩ [L *fervidus*, fr *fervēre*] – **fervidly** adv, **fervidness** n

**fervour**, NAm chiefly **fervor** /'fuhvə/ n the quality or state of being fervent or fervid **synonyms** see PASSION [ME *fervour*, fr MF & L; MF *ferveur*, fr L *fervor*, fr *fervēre*]

**fescennine** /'fesinien/ adj, formal scurrilous, obscene [L *fescennini* (*versus*), ribald songs sung at rustic weddings, fr *fescenninus* of Fescennium, fr *Fescennium*, ancient town in Etruria]

**fescue** /'feskyooh/ n any of a genus (*Festuca*) of tufted grasses [ME *festu* stalk, straw, fr MF, fr LL *festucum*, fr L *festuca*]

**fess** also **fesse** /fes/ n a broad horizontal bar across the middle of a heraldic field [ME *fesse*, fr MF *faisse*, fr L *fascia* band]

**fess point** n the centre point of a heraldic shield

**fest** /fest/ n, chiefly NAm a meeting or occasion marked by a specified activity – often in combination ⟨filmfest⟩ [Ger, festival, celebration, fr MHG *vest*, fr L *festum*]

**festal** /'festl/ adj festive [L *festum* festival – more at FEAST] – **festally** adv

¹**fester** /'festə/ n a pus-producing sore; a pustule [ME, fr MF *festre*, fr L *fistula* pipe, fistulous ulcer]

²**fester** vi 1 to generate pus 2 to putrefy, rot 3 to cause increasing bitterness or irritation; rankle ⟨the injustice ~ed in their minds⟩ ~ vt 1 to cause to fester 2 to make inflamed or corrupt

¹**festinate** /'festinayt, -nət/ adj, formal hasty [L *festinatus*, pp of *festinare* to hasten] – **festinately** adv

²**festinate** /'festinayt/ vb, formal to hasten

¹**festival** /'festivl/ adj of, appropriate to, or set apart as a festival [ME, fr MF, fr L *festivus* festive]

²**festival** n 1a a time marked by special (e g customary) celebration **b** FEAST 2 2 a usu periodic programme or season of cultural events or entertainment ⟨a folk ~⟩ ⟨the Edinburgh Festival⟩

**festive** /'festiv/ adj 1 of or suitable for a feast or festival 2 joyous, merry [L *festivus*, fr *festum*] – **festively** adv, **festiveness** n

**synonyms** Festive and festal are close in meaning, but festive is the commoner word for the sense "joyous" ⟨a festive occasion⟩.

**festivity** /fe'stivəti/ n 1 FESTIVAL 1 2 **festivities** pl, festivity festive activity

¹**festoon** /fe'stoohn/ n 1 a decorative chain or strip hanging between two points 2 a carved, moulded, or painted ornament representing a decorative chain [Fr *feston*, fr It *festone*, fr *festa* festival, fr L – more at FEAST]

²**festoon** vt 1 to hang or form festoons on 2 to cover profusely and usu gaily

**festschrift** /'fest,shrift/ n, pl **festschriften** /-,shrift(ə)n/, **festschrifts** often cap a volume of writings by various authors presented as a tribute or memorial, esp to a scholar [Ger, fr *fest* festival, celebration + *schrift* writing]

**feta** /'fetə, 'fetah/ n, NAm FETTA (type of cheese)

**fetal** /'feetl/ adj foetal

¹**fetch** /fech/ vt 1 to go or come after and bring or take back ⟨go and ~ the ball⟩ 2a to cause to come; bring ⟨~ him to the police station⟩ **b** to produce as profit or return; realize ⟨will ~ £100 on the open market⟩ 3 to utter; esp to heave (a sigh) 4 to reach by sailing, esp against the wind or tide and without having to tack 5 informal to give (a blow, slap, etc) to by striking; deal ⟨~ed him one in the face⟩ ~ vi to go after something and bring it back; specif to retrieve killed game 2 to hold a course on a body of water [ME *fecchen*, fr OE *fetian, feccan*; akin to OE *fōt* foot – more at FOOT] – **fetcher** n

**fetch up** vb, informal vt 1 to bring up or out; produce 2 to bring to a stop 3 to vomit ~ vi to come to a specified standstill, stopping place, or result – usu + at or in

²**fetch** n 1 an act or instance of fetching 2 a trick, stratagem 3a the distance along open water or land over which the wind blows **b** the distance traversed by waves without obstruction

³**fetch** n DOPPELGÄNGER (ghostly double of person still alive); broadly a ghost [origin unknown]

**fetching** /'feching/ adj attractive, becoming – **fetchingly** adv

¹**fete, fête** /fayt, fet/ n 1 a festival 2 Br an event organized to raise money for charitable purposes by sideshows and the sale of various articles [Fr *fête*, fr OF *feste* – more at FEAST]

**²fete, fête** *vt* to honour or commemorate with ceremony; pay high honour to

**fête champêtre** /shom'pet(rə)/ (*Fr* fɛt ʃɑ̃pɛːtr)/ *n, pl* **fêtes champêtres** /~/ an outdoor entertainment [Fr, lit., rural festival]

**fetid** /'fetid, 'feetid/, **foetid** /'feetid/ *adj* having a heavy offensive smell; stinking [ME, fr L *foetidus*, fr *foetēre* to stink; akin to L *fumus* smoke – more at FUME] – **fetidly** *adv*, **fetidness** *n*

*usage* The pronunciation /'fetid/ is recommended for BBC broadcasters except when the word is spelt **foetid**.

**fetish** *also* **fetich** /'fetiʃ/ *n* **1** an object believed among a primitive people to have magical power, esp to protect or aid its owner; *broadly* a material object regarded with superstitious or extravagant trust or reverence **2** an object of irrational reverence or obsessive devotion ⟨*make a* ~ *of early rising*⟩ **3** an object or bodily part whose presence in reality or fantasy is psychologically necessary for sexual gratification [Fr & Pg; Fr *fétiche*, fr Pg *feitiço*, fr *feitiço* artificial, false, fr L *facticius* factitious]

**fetishism** *also* **fetichism** /'fetishiz(ə)m/ *n* **1** belief in magical fetishes **2** excessive or irrational devotion to something **3** the displacement of erotic interest and satisfaction to a fetish – **fetishist** *n*, **fetishistic** *adj*

**fetlock** /'fet,lok/ *n* **1** a projection bearing a tuft of hair on the back of the leg above the hoof of an animal of the horse family **2** the joint of the limb or tuft of hair at the fetlock [ME *fitlok, fetlak;* akin to OE *fōt* foot]

**feto-** *also* **feti-** *comb form* foeto-, foeti-

**fetor, foetor** /'feetə, -'taw/ *n, formal* a strong offensive smell; a stink [ME *fetoure*, fr L *foetor*, fr *foetēre*]

**fetta, NAm feta** /'fetə, 'fetah/ *n* a white semisoft Greek cheese made from sheep's or goat's milk and cured in brine [NGk (*tyri*) *pheta*, fr *tyri* cheese + *pheta* slice, fr It *fetta*]

**¹fetter** /'fetə/ *n* **1** a chain or shackle for the feet **2 fetters** *pl*, **fetter** something that confines; a restraint [ME *feter*, fr OE; akin to OE *fōt* foot]

**²fetter** *vt* **1** to put fetters on; shackle **2** to confine, restrain

**¹fettle** /'fetl/ *vt* **1** to cover or line the hearth of (e g a reverberatory furnace) with fettling **2** to trim or clean up the rough joints or edges of (e g pottery or a metal casting) after casting or moulding and before firing [E dial. *fettle* to clean, repair, make ready, fr ME *fetlen* to shape, prepare; prob akin to OE *fæt* vessel – more at VAT]

**²fettle** *n* **1** a state of physical or mental fitness or order; a condition ⟨*in fine* ~⟩ **2** fettling

**fettling** /'fetling/ *n* loose material (e g ore or sand) thrown on the hearth of a furnace to protect it

**fettuccine, fettucini** /,fetə'cheeni/ *n taking sing or pl vb* TAGLIATELLE (type of pasta) [It, pl of *fettuccina*, dim. of *fettuccia* small slice, ribbon, dim. of *fetta* slice]

**fetus** /'feetəs/ *n* a foetus

**feu** /fyooh/ *n, Scot* (land held under) a perpetual lease for a fixed rent [ME (Sc), fr MF *fé, fief* – more at FEE]

**¹feud** /fyoohd/ *n* a mutual enmity or quarrel that is often prolonged or long established; *esp* a lasting state of hostilities between families or clans marked by violent attacks for the purpose of revenge [alter. of ME *feide*, fr MF, of Gmc origin; akin to OHG *fēhida* hostility, feud, OE *fāh* hostile – more at FOE] – **feud** *vi*

**²feud** *n* FEE 1a (land held under feudal law) [ML *feodum, feudum*, of Gmc origin; akin to OE *feoh* cattle, property – more at FEE]

**feudal** /'fyoohdl/ *adj* **1** of a medieval FEE (estate held under feudalism) or of feudalism ⟨~ *law*⟩ **2** suggestive of feudalism (e g in servility) – **feudally** *adv*

**feudalism** /-,iz(ə)m/ *n* **1** a medieval system of political organization having as its basis the relationship of lord to vassal with all land held in FEE and as its chief characteristics homage, the service of tenants for their lords in war and court, WARDSHIP, and FORFEITURE **2** any of various political or social systems similar to medieval feudalism – **feudalist** *n*, **feudalistic** *adj*

**feudality** /fyooh'daləti/ *n* **1** the quality or state of being feudal **2** a feudal holding or domain

**feudal·ize, -ise** /'fyoohdl,iez/ *vt* to make feudal – **feudalization** *n*

**¹feudatory** /'fyoohdət(ə)ri/ *adj* **1** owing feudal allegiance **2** under the overlordship of a foreign state or sovereign [ML *feudatorius*, fr *feudatus*, pp of *feudare* to enfeoff, fr *feudum*]

**²feudatory** *n* one holding lands by feudal tenure; a vassal

**feuilleton** /'fuh·iton (*Fr* fœjtɔ̃)/ *n* **1** a part of esp a French

newspaper or magazine devoted to material designed to entertain the general reader **2** something (e g an instalment of a novel) printed in a feuilleton **3** a short literary essay, esp of a familiar anecdotal kind [Fr, fr *feuillet* sheet of paper, fr OF *foillet*, dim. of *foille* leaf – more at FOIL]

**Feulgen** /'foylgən (*Ger* fɔlgən)/ *adj* of, utilizing, or staining by the Feulgen reaction

**Feulgen reaction** *n* the chemical reaction of DNA (material in a cell carrying genetic information) with a modified SCHIFF'S REAGENT (solution used for chemical tests) to produce a brilliant purple colour used esp in staining tissue preparations for microscopy [Robert *Feulgen* †1955 Ger biochemist]

**fever** /'feevə/ *n* **1a** a rise of body temperature above the normal **b** any of various diseases of which high temperature is a prominent symptom **2a** a state of intense emotion or activity ⟨*in a* ~ *of impatience*⟩ **b** a contagious, usu transient, enthusiasm; craze ⟨*football* ~ *raged throughout the world*⟩ [ME, fr OE *fēfer*, fr L *febris;* akin to L *fovēre* to warm]

**fevered** /'feevəd/ *adj* **1** hot or flushed owing to fever or agitation ⟨*his* ~ *brow*⟩ **2** extremely fast or active ⟨*a* ~ *imagination*⟩

**feverfew** /'feevə,fyooh/ *n* a European plant (*Chrysanthemum parthenium*) of the dandelion family, with white yellow-centred flowers and small ragged leaves [ME, fr (assumed) AF *fevrefue*, fr LL *febrifugia, febrifuga* centaury, fr *febri-* + *-fuga* -fuge; fr its former use to allay fevers]

**feverish** /'feevərish/ *also* **feverous** /-rəs/ *adj* **1a** having the symptoms of a fever **b** indicating, relating to, or caused by fever **c** tending to cause or infect with fever **2** marked by intense emotion, activity, or instability – **feverishly** *adv*, **feverishness** *n*, **feverously** *adv*

**fever pitch** *n* a state of intense excitement and agitation ⟨*raised the crowd to* ~⟩

**¹few** /fyooh/ *adj* **1** amounting to only a small number ⟨*one of his* ~ *pleasures*⟩ **2** at least some though not many – + *a* ⟨*a good* ~ *drinks*⟩ ⟨*caught a* ~ *more fish*⟩ *usage* see LESS [ME *fewe*, pron & adj, fr OE *fēawa;* akin to OHG *fō* little, L *paucus* little, *pauper* poor, Gk *paid-, pais* child, Skt *putra* son] – **fewness** *n*

**²few** *n taking pl vb* **1** not many ⟨~ *were present*⟩ ⟨*ate the* ~ *that remained*⟩ ⟨~ *of his stories were true*⟩ **2** at least some though not many – + *a* ⟨*a* ~ *of them*⟩ **3** *the* elite, elect

**¹fewer** /'fyooh·ə/ *n taking pl vb* a smaller number of people or things

**²fewer** *adj, comparative of* FEW

**fey** /fay/ *adj* **1a** able to see into the future; visionary **b** marked by an otherworldly and irresponsible air **2** *chiefly Scot* **2a** fated to die; doomed **b** marked by an excited or elated state, formerly held to precede death △ **fay** [ME *feye*, fr OE *fǣge;* akin to OHG *feigi* fey] – **feyness** *n*

**fez** /fez/ *n, pl* **-zz-** *also* **-z-** a brimless hat shaped like a truncated cone that is usu red with a tassel and is traditionally worn by men in southern and eastern Mediterranean countries [Fr, fr *Fez*, city in Morocco]

**fiacre** /fi'ahkrə (*Fr* fjakr)/ *n* a small four-wheeled horse-drawn carriage for hire [Fr, fr the Hôtel de St *Fiacre* in Paris, where such vehicles were first hired out]

**fiancé, fem fiancée** /fi'onsay/ *n* somebody engaged to be married [Fr, fr MF, fr pp of *fiancer* to promise, betroth, fr OF *fiancier*, fr *fiance* promise, trust, fr *fier* to trust, fr (assumed) VL *fidare*, alter. of L *fidere* – more at BIDE]

**fianchetto** /,fee·an'chetoh/ *vb* **fianchettoing, fianchettoed** to develop (a bishop) in a chess game to the second square on the adjacent knight's file [*fianchetto*, n, fr It, dim. of *fianco* side, flank, fr OF *flanc*]

**fiasco** /fi'askoh/ *n, pl* **fiascoes** a complete and humiliating failure [Fr, fr It, lit., bottle, flask, of Gmc origin; akin to OHG *flaska* bottle]

**fiat** /'fie·ət, -at/ *n* an authoritative and often arbitrary order; a decree ⟨*government by* ~⟩ [L, let it be done, fr *fieri* to become, be done – more at BE]

**fib** /fib/ *vi* or *n* **-bb-** *informal* (to tell) a trivial or childish lie [perh by shortening & alter. fr *fable*] – **fibber, fibster** *n*

**Fibonacci number** /,feebə'nahchi, ,fib-/ *n* a number in the FIBONACCI SEQUENCE [Leonardo *Fibonacci* †*ab* 1250 It mathematician]

**Fibonacci sequence** *n* the infinite sequence of integers, 0, 1, 1, 2, 3, 5, 8, 13,... in which every number after the first two is the sum of the two numbers immediately preceding it. The Fibonacci sequence can be found in the form and development of many natural phenomena and is closely linked with the GOLDEN SECTION.

**fibr-** /'fiebr-/, **fibro-** *comb form* fibre; fibrous tissue ⟨fibr*oid*⟩; fibrous and ⟨fibro*vascular*⟩ [L *fibra*]

**fibre**, *NAm chiefly* **fiber** /'fiebə/ *n* **1** a thread or a structure or object resembling a thread: e g **1a**(1) a slender root (e g of a grass) **a**(2) an elongated tapering thick-walled plant cell **b**(1) NERVE FIBRE **b**(2) any of the filaments composing most of the packing and supporting tissue between cells **b**(3) any of the elongated elastic cells of muscle tissue **c** a slender natural or man-made thread or filament (e g of wool, cotton, asbestos, gold, glass, or rayon) typically capable of being spun into yarn **2** material made of fibres **3** essential structure or character ⟨*the very* ∼ *of his being*⟩; *also* strength, fortitude ⟨*a man of great moral* ∼⟩ [Fr, fr L *fibra*]

**fibreboard** /'fiebə,bawd/ *n* a material made by compressing fibres (e g of wood) into stiff sheets

**fibreglass** /'fiebə,glahs/ *n* **1** glass in fibrous form used in making various products (e g textiles and insulation materials) **2** any of several combinations of synthetic resins and fibreglass, used esp for making car bodies and boat frames

**fibre optics** *n taking sing vb* the technique of using very thin (bundles of) glass or plastic fibres that transmit light throughout their length by internal reflections for bending light or seeing round corners

**fibrescope** /'fiebə,skohp/ *n* a flexible instrument using fibre optics and used esp in medicine for the examination of inaccessible areas (e g the lining of the stomach)

**fibril** /'fiebril, 'fibril/ *n* a small filament or fibre: e g **a** ROOT HAIR **b**(1) any of the fine threads that make up muscle tissue **b**(2) a fine thread-like nerve [NL *fibrilla*, dim. of L *fibra*] – **fibrillar** *adj*, **fibrillose** *adj*, **fibrilliform** *adj*

**fibrillation** /,fibri'laysh(ə)n/ *n* **1** the forming of fibres or fibrils **2a** a muscular twitching involving individual muscle fibres acting without coordination **b** very rapid irregular contractions of the muscle fibres of the heart resulting in a lack of synchronization between heartbeat and pulse – **fibrillate** *vb*

**fibrin** /'fiebrin/ *n* a white insoluble fibrous protein formed from fibrinogen, esp during the clotting of blood – **fibrinous** *adj*

**fibrin, fibrino-** *comb form* fibrin ⟨fibrin*ogen*⟩

**fibrinogen** /fie'brinəj(ə)n/ *n* a GLOBULIN (type of protein) that is produced in the liver, is present esp in the liquid portion of the blood, and is converted into fibrin during clotting of blood [ISV]

**fibrinoid** /'fiebrinoyd/ *n* a material that resembles fibrin and that is formed in the walls of blood vessels and in the fibrous supporting and packing tissue (CONNECTIVE TISSUE) in some diseases and that occurs normally in the placenta

**fibrinolysin** /,fiebrinoh'liesin, ,fiebrinl'iesin/ *n* an ENZYME that takes part in fibrinolysis: e g **a** PLASMIN **b** STREPTOKINASE [ISV]

**fibrinolysis** /,fiebri'noləsis/ *n* the dissolving of blood clots as a result of the breakdown, usu by ENZYMES, of fibrin [NL] – **fibrinolytic** *adj*

**fibro** /'fiebroh/ *n, pl* **fibros** *Austr* **1** a building and insulating material made from a mixture of asbestos and cement **2** a building made from fibro [short for *fibro-cement*]

**fibroblast** /'fiebrə,blast, 'fi-/ *n* a flattened cell that produces the fibres for the supporting and packing tissue (CONNECTIVE TISSUE) in a body [ISV] – **fibroblastic** *adj*

**'fibro-ce,ment** /'fiebroh/ *n* fibro

**fibrocyte** /'fiebrə,siet/ *n* a spindle-shaped cell of fibrous tissue formed from a fibroblast [ISV] – **fibrocytic** *adj*

**¹fibroid** /'fiebroyd/ *adj* resembling, forming, or consisting of fibrous tissue

**²fibroid** *n* a mild nonlethal tumour made up of fibrous and muscular tissue that occurs esp in the wall of the womb

**fibroin** /'fiebroh·in/ *n* an insoluble protein which is the main constituent of raw silk fibres [Fr *fibroïne*, fr *fibr-* + *-ine* -in]

**fibroma** /fie'brohmə/ *n, pl* **fibromas** *also* **fibromata** /fie'brohmətə/ a mild nonlethal tumour consisting mainly of fibrous tissue [NL] – **fibromatous** *adj*

**fibrosarcoma** /,fiebrohsah'kohmə/ *n* a cancerous tumour made up chiefly of fibrous spindle-shaped cells [NL]

**fibrosis** /fie'brohsis/ *n* a condition marked by the abnormal increase of fibrous tissue in an organ or part of the body [NL] – **fibrotic** *adj*

**fibrositis** /,fiebrə'sietəs/ *n* a painful muscular condition resulting from inflammation of fibrous tissue (e g muscle sheaths) [NL, fr *fibrosus* fibrous, fr ISV *fibrous*]

**fibrous** /'fiebrəs/ *adj* **1a** containing, consisting of, or resem-

bling fibres **b** characterized by fibrosis **c** capable of being separated into fibres ⟨*a* ∼ *mineral*⟩ **2** tough, stringy [Fr *fibreux*, fr *fibre* fibre] – **fibrously** *adv*, **fibrousness** *n*

**fibrous root** *n* a root (e g in most grasses) that has no prominent central portion and that branches in all directions

**fibrovascular** /,fiebroh'vaskyoolə/ *adj, botany* having or consisting of fibres and conducting cells ⟨∼ *tissues in leaves*⟩

**fibrovascular bundle** *n* a VASCULAR BUNDLE (group of tubes transporting fluids through plants) surrounded by cells with thick fibrous walls

**fibula** /'fibyoolə/ *n, pl* **fibulae** /-lie/, **fibulas 1** an ornamented clasp fastening like a safety pin and used esp by the ancient Greeks and Romans **2a** the outer and usu the smaller of the two bones of the hind limb of VERTEBRATE animals between the knee and ankle – compare TIBIA **b** a small structure at the base of the front wing in certain moths that unites the wings by interlocking with a group of spines on the hind wing [L, prob fr *figere* to fasten, pierce] – **fibular** *adj*

**-fic** /-fik/ *suffix* (→ *adj*) making; causing ⟨*horrific*⟩ ⟨*pacific*⟩ [MF & L; MF *-fique*, fr L *-ficus*, fr *facere* to make – more at DO]

**-fication** /-fi'kaysh(ə)n/ *comb form* (→ *n*) action; production ⟨*reification*⟩ ⟨*jollification*⟩ [ME *-ficacioun*, fr MF & L; MF *-fication*, fr L *-fication-*, *-ficatio*, fr *-ficatus*, pp ending of verbs ending in *-ficare* to make, fr *-ficus*]

**fiche** /feesh/ *n, pl* **fiche** *also* **fiches** /∼/ MICROFICHE (piece of film on which information is stored)

**fichu** /'feeshooh (*Fr* fiʃy)/ *n* a woman's light triangular scarf draped over the shoulders and fastened at the bosom that was fashionable esp in the 18th and early 19th centuries [Fr, fr pp of *ficher* to stick in, throw on, fr (assumed) VL *figicare*, fr L *figere* to fasten, pierce – more at DYKE]

**ficin** /'fies(ə)n/ *n* a PROTEINASE (enzyme necessary for the digestion of protein) that is obtained from a white liquid (LATEX) found in fig trees and is used as a drug against parasitic worms [L *ficus* fig]

**fickle** /'fikl/ *adj* lacking steadfastness, constancy, or stability; capricious [ME *fikel* deceitful, inconstant, fr OE *ficol* deceitful; akin to OE *befician* to deceive, L *pigēre* to irk] – **fickleness** *n*

**fictile** /'fiktiel/ *adj* **1** moulded into shape by a potter **2** capable of being moulded ⟨∼ *clay*⟩ **3** of pottery [L *fictilis* moulded of clay, fr *fictus*]

**fiction** /'fiksh(ə)n/ *n* **1a** something invented by the imagination; *specif* an invented story ⟨*distinguish fact from* ∼⟩ **b** literature (e g novels or short stories) describing imaginary persons and events ⟨*a writer of* ∼⟩ **2** *law* an assumption of a possibility as a fact, irrespective of the question of its truth ⟨*a legal* ∼⟩ **3** the action of feigning or creating with the imagination [ME *ficcioun*, fr MF *fiction*, fr L *fiction-*, *fictio* act of fashioning, fiction, fr *fictus*, pp of *fingere* to shape, fashion, feign – more at DOUGH] – **fictional** *adj*, **fictionally** *adv*, **fictionality** *n*, **fictionist** *n*

**fictional·ize, -ise** /'fiksh(ə)nl·iez/ *vt* to make into or treat in the manner of fiction ⟨∼ *the diary he kept in prison*⟩ – **fictionalization** *n*

**fictioneer** /,fikshə'niə/ *n* one who writes fiction, esp in quantity and without high standards – **fictioneering** *n*

**fictitious** /fik'tishəs/ *adj* **1** (characteristic) of fiction; imaginary **2** not real or genuine; false △ factitious [L *ficticius* artificial, feigned, fr *fictus*] – **fictitiously** *adv*, **fictitiousness** *n*

**fictive** /'fiktiv/ *adj* **1** not genuine; feigned **2** (capable) of imaginative creation – **fictively** *adv*

**fid** /fid/ *n* **1** a bar of wood or iron used to support a topmast **2** a tapering wooden pin used in opening the strands of a rope for splicing [origin unknown]

**-fid** /-fid/ *comb form* (→ *adj*) divided into (such or so many) parts ⟨*bifid*⟩ ⟨*pinnatifid*⟩ [L *-fidus*, fr *findere* to split – more at BITE]

**¹fiddle** /'fidl/ *n* **1** a violin **2** a device (e g a frame) to keep objects from sliding off a table on board ship **3** *informal* fiddlesticks – used as an interjection **4** *informal* a dishonest practice; a swindle **5** *Br informal* an activity involving intricate manipulation ⟨*a bit of a* ∼ *to get all these wires back in place*⟩ [ME *fidel*, fr OE *fithele*, prob fr ML *vitula*] – **play second fiddle** to take a subordinate position

**²fiddle** *vi* **1** to play on a fiddle **2** *informal* **2a** to move the hands or fingers restlessly **b** to spend time in aimless or fruitless activity – often + *about* or *around* **c** to meddle, tamper *with* ∼ *vt, informal* **1** *Br* to falsify (e g accounts), esp so as to gain monetary advantage **2** *Br* to get or contrive by cheating or deception ⟨∼ d *an extra ten pounds on his expenses*⟩ – **fiddler** *n*

**fiddle away** *vt* to waste (time) on trifles

**fiddle-faddle** /ˌfadl/ *n, informal* nonsense – often used as an interjection [redupl of ¹*fiddle* 3]

**fiddlehead** /ˈfidlˌhed/ *n* ornamentation on a ship's bow curved like the scroll at the head of a violin

**fiddler crab** /ˈfidlə/ *n* a burrowing crab (genus *Uca*) the male of which has one claw much enlarged [fr the enlarged claw being held in a position like that of a violinist's arm]

**fiddlesticks** /ˈfidlˌstiks/ *n pl, informal* nonsense – used as an interjection [*fiddlestick* (violin bow, something of small value)]

**fiddling** /ˈfidling/ *adj* trifling, petty ⟨*made some ~ excuse*⟩

**fiddly** /ˈfidli/ *adj, Br informal* 1 fiddling 2 finicky

**fideism** /ˈfeedayˌiz(ə)m/ *n, philosophy* reliance on faith rather than reason, esp in METAPHYSICS [L *fides* faith + E *-ism*] – **fideist** *n*, **fideistic** *adj*

**fidelity** /fiˈdeləti/ *n* 1a the quality or state of being faithful; loyalty b accuracy in details; exactness 2 the degree to which an electronic device (eg a record player, radio, or television) accurately reproduces its original source (eg a sound or picture) [ME *fidelite*, fr MF *fidelité*, fr L *fidelitat-*, *fidelitas*, fr *fidelis* faithful, fr *fides* faith – more at BIDE]

¹**fidget** /ˈfijit/ *n, informal* 1 **fidgets** *pl*, **fidget** uneasiness or restlessness shown by nervous movements – usu + *the* 2 somebody who fidgets [irreg fr E dial. *fidge* to move restlessly, prob alter. of E dial. *fitch*, fr ME *fichen*]

²**fidget** *vb* to (cause to) move or act restlessly or nervously – **fidgety** *adj*

**fiducial** /fiˈdyoohsh(y)əl/ *adj* 1 *physics* taken as a standard of reference ⟨*a ~ mark*⟩ 2 founded on faith or trust 3 having the nature of a trust; fiduciary – **fiducially** *adv*

¹**fiduciary** /fiˈdyoohshəri/ *n* one who is entrusted to hold or manage property for another

²**fiduciary** *adj* 1 held or founded in trust or confidence 2 of or involving a confidence or trust 3 depending on public confidence for value or currency ⟨*~ money*⟩ [L *fiduciarius*, fr *fiducia* confidence, trust, fr *fidere*]

**fie** /fie/ *interj, archaic* – used to express disgust or shock [ME *fi*, fr OF]

**fief** /feef/ *n* 1 a feudal estate; a fee 2 something over which one has rights or exercises control ⟨*a politician's ~*⟩ [Fr – more at FEE]

**fiefdom** /ˈfiefdəm/ *n* a fief

¹**field** /feeld/ *n* 1a an open area of land free of woods and buildings b(1) an area of cleared enclosed land used for cultivation or pasture ⟨*a ~ of wheat*⟩ b(2) an area of land containing a natural resource ⟨*coal ~*⟩ c the place where a battle is fought; *also* a battle d a large unbroken expanse (eg of ice) e an airfield 2a an area or division of an activity ⟨*a lawyer eminent in his ~*⟩ b the sphere of practical operation outside a place of work (eg a laboratory, office, or factory) ⟨*geologists working in the ~*⟩ ⟨*~ research*⟩ c an area in which troops are operating (eg in an exercise or theatre of war) d(1) an area constructed, equipped, or marked for sports ⟨*a football ~*⟩ d(2) the part of an indoor or outdoor sports area enclosed by the running track and used for athletic field events 3 a space on which something is drawn or projected: eg 3a the ground of each division in a flag b the whole surface, esp a shield, on which a coat of arms is displayed 4 *taking sing or pl vb* 4a the participants in a sports activity, esp with the exception of the favourite or winner b all the mounted followers of a hunt except the master and hunt servants 5 *maths* a set of mathematical elements (eg all the rational numbers) that when subject to the two BINARY operations of addition and subtraction is COMMUTATIVE (independent of the order of the elements) under addition and, excluding zero (0), is commutative under multiplication. Within this set every nonzero element has an INVERSE such that if $x \neq 0$, there is an element $x^{-1}$ with $xx^{-1} = 1$ and the DISTRIBUTIVE law applies so that $x(y + z) = xy + xz$. 6 *maths* a region in which a mathematical quantity (eg a scalar or vector) is associated with every point 7 a region or space in which a given effect (eg magnetism) exists; *also* the effect itself 8 *also* field of view the area visible through the lens of an optical instrument 9 an area (eg a region of a computer disk store) in which a particular type of information is recorded [ME, fr OE *feld*; akin to OHG *feld* field, OE *flōr* floor] – **play the field** to have a number of boyfriends or girlfriends, rather than committing oneself exclusively to one person – **take the field** 1 to go onto the playing field 2 to enter upon a military campaign

²**field** *vt* 1a to stop or pick up and usu throw back (a ball), esp in cricket b to deal with by giving an impromptu answer, esp

on behalf of somebody else ⟨*~ a phone call*⟩ 2 to put into the field of play or battle ⟨*~ an army*⟩ ⟨*~ a team*⟩ ⟨*~ a candidate*⟩ ~ *vi* to play as a fielder in cricket, baseball, etc

³**field** *adj* 1 growing in or inhabiting the fields or open country 2 made, conducted, or used in the field ⟨*~ operations*⟩ 3 operating or active in the field ⟨*a ~ agent*⟩

**field allowance** *n* additional pay for an officer on campaign

**field artillery** *n* artillery, other than antiaircraft or antitank guns, used with armies in the field

**field crop** *n* an agricultural crop (eg hay, grain, or cotton) grown on large areas

**field day** *n* 1a a day for military exercises or manoeuvres b an outdoor meeting or social gathering 2 a time of great pleasure in unrestrained action ⟨*the newspaper had a ~ with the scandal*⟩ 3 *chiefly NAm* a day of sports and athletic competition, esp organized by a school

**fielder** /ˈfeeldə/ *n* any of the players whose role is to field the ball (eg in cricket)

**field event** *n* an athletic event (eg discus, javelin, or high jump) other than a race – compare TRACK EVENT

**fieldfare** /ˈfeeldˌfeə/ *n* a medium-sized Eurasian thrush (*Turdus pilaris*) with a pale grey head and chestnut-coloured wings [ME *feldefare*, fr OE *feldeware*, fr *feld* + *-ware* dweller]

**field glasses** *n pl* a hand-held optical instrument for use out of doors usu consisting of two telescopes on a single frame with a focussing device

**field goal** *n* 1 a score in American football made usu by kicking the ball over the crossbar from ordinary play 2 a goal in basketball made while the ball is in play, not from a FREE THROW

**field hockey** *n, chiefly NAm* HOCKEY 1

**field magnet** *n* a magnet for producing and maintaining a MAGNETIC FIELD, esp in a generator or electric motor

**field marshal** *n* – see MILITARY RANKS table

**field mouse** *n* any of various mice or voles that inhabit fields

**field mushroom** *n* the common edible mushroom (*Agaricus campestris*)

**field officer** *n* a commissioned officer in the army of the rank of colonel, lieutenant colonel, or major

**field of view** *n* FIELD 8

**fieldsman** /ˈfeeldzmən/ *n, pl* **fieldsmen** /-mən/ a fielder, esp in cricket

**field spaniel** *n* any of a breed of large, usu black, hunting and retrieving spaniels that have a dense flat or slightly waved coat

**field sport** *n* an open-air sport (eg hunting or shooting) involving the pursuit of animals

**field theory** *n* a detailed mathematical description of the assumed physical properties of a region under some influence (eg gravitation)

**field trial** *n* 1 a trial of gun dogs or sheep dogs in actual performance 2 *usu pl* a test for a new design, invention, variety of plant, etc under authentic working or growing conditions, rather than in the laboratory, workshop, or greenhouse

**field trip** *n* a visit made by students and usu a teacher for purposes of firsthand observation (eg to a factory or farm)

**field winding** *n* the coiled wire (WINDING) through which electric current passes in the FIELD MAGNET of a generator or motor

**fieldwork** /ˈfeeldˌwuhk/ *n* 1 a temporary fortification put up by an army in the field 2 work done in the field (eg by students) to gain practical experience through firsthand observation 3 the gathering of data (eg in anthropology, sociology, or linguistics) through the observation or interviewing of subjects in the field – **field-worker** *n*

**fiend** /feend/ *n* 1a *often cap* DEVIL 1 – + *the* b a demon c a person of great wickedness or cruelty 2 *informal* somebody excessively devoted to a specified activity or thing; a fanatic, devotee ⟨*a golf ~*⟩ ⟨*a fresh-air ~*⟩ 3 *informal* a person who uses excessive quantities of something usu specified; an addict ⟨*a dope ~*⟩ 4 *informal* somebody remarkably clever at something; WIZARD 2 ⟨*a ~ at arithmetic*⟩ [ME, fr OE *fiend*; akin to OHG *fiant* enemy, Skt *pīyant* hostile (fr *pīyati* he abuses)]

**fiendish** /ˈfeendish/ *adj* 1 extremely cruel or wicked; diabolical 2 excessively great, bad, unpleasant, or difficult ⟨*~ weather*⟩ 3 ingeniously clever or complex ⟨*a ~ scheme for evading tax*⟩ – **fiendishly** *adv*, **fiendishness** *n*

**fierce** /fiəs/ *adj* 1 violently hostile or aggressive; combative, pugnacious 2a lacking restraint or control; violent, heated ⟨*a ~ argument*⟩ ⟨*a ~ temper*⟩ b extremely intense or severe ⟨*~*

*pain*⟩ **3** furiously active or determined ⟨*make a ~ effort*⟩ **4** wild or menacing in appearance [ME *fiers,* fr OF, fr L *ferus* wild, savage; akin to Gk *thēr* wild animal] – **fiercely** *adv,* **fierceness** *n*

**fiery** /'fie·əri/ *adj* **1a** consisting of fire **b** burning, blazing ⟨*~ cross*⟩ **c** liable to catch fire or explode; inflammable ⟨*a ~ vapour*⟩ **2a** very hot ⟨*a ~ chilli sauce*⟩ **b** inflamed ⟨*a ~ boil*⟩ **3** of the colour of fire; red ⟨*a ~ sunset*⟩ **4a** full of or exuding strong emotion or spirit; passionate ⟨*a ~ speech*⟩ **b** easily provoked and very intense ⟨*a ~ temper*⟩ **5** *of a cricket pitch* allowing the bowled ball to bounce high and fast to the danger of the batsman [ME, fr *fire, fier* fire] – **fierily** *adv,* **fieriness** *n,* **fiery** *adv*

**fiery cross** *n* **1** a charred and sometimes blood-stained wooden cross formerly used by the Scottish Highlanders as a rallying signal to the clans **2** a burning cross used esp as a means of intimidation by the Ku Klux Klan

**fiesta** /fi'estə/ *n* a festival; *specif* a saint's day celebrated in Spain and Latin America with processions and dances [Sp, fr L *festa* – more at FEAST]

**fife** /fief/ *n* a small flute with six to eight finger holes and no keys that is used chiefly to accompany the drum [Ger *pfeife* pipe, fife, fr OHG *pfifa* – more at PIPE] – **fife** *vi*

**fife rail** *n, nautical* a rail round the bottom of the mast of a sailing vessel to which RUNNING RIGGING is made fast

**fifteen** /fif'teen/ *n* **1** – see NUMBER table **2** the fifteenth in a set or series **3** *taking sing or pl vb* something having 15 parts or members or a denomination of 15; *esp* a Rugby Union football team **4** the first point scored by a player or side in a game of tennis [ME *fiftene,* adj, fr OE *fiftēne, fiftīene,* fr *fif* five + *tīen* ten] – **fifteen** *adj or pron,* **fifteenth** *adj or n*

**15** *n or adj* (a film) certified in Britain as suitable for people of 15 or over – compare U, PG, 18

**fifth** /fith; *also* fifth/ *n* **1** – see NUMBER table **2a** a musical interval between one note and another five notes away from it counting inclusively in a DIATONIC scale (ordinary 8-note scale) **b** a note five notes away from another counting inclusively; *specif* the note five notes away from the first note (TONIC) of a scale; DOMINANT **2 c** the harmonic combination of two notes a fifth apart [ME *fifte, fifthe,* fr OE *fifta,* fr *fif* + *-ta* -th] – **fifth** *adj or adv,* **fifthly** *adv*

**fifth column** *n* a group within a nation or faction that sympathizes with and works secretly for an enemy or rival [name applied to rebel sympathizers in Madrid in 1936, during the Spanish Civil War, when four rebel columns were advancing on the city] – **fifth columnism** *n,* **fifth columnist** *n*

**fifth wheel** *n* **1a** a horizontal wheel or segment of a wheel that consists of two parts rotating on each other above the fore axle of a carriage, enabling it to be steered without tipping **b** a similar coupling between the tractor and trailer of an articulated lorry **2** somebody or something superfluous, unnecessary, or burdensome

**fifty** /'fifti/ *n* **1** – see NUMBER table **2** *pl* the numbers 50 to 59; *specif* a range of temperatures, ages, or dates within a century characterized by those numbers **3** something (e g a coin or note) having a denomination of 50 units; *specif, Br* a coin worth 50 pence **4** a batsman's score of between 50 and 99 runs in cricket – compare HUNDRED 2b [ME, fr *fifty,* adj, fr OE *fiftig,* fr *fiftig,* n, group of 50, fr *fif* five + *-tig* group of ten – more at EIGHTY] – **fiftieth** *adj or n,* **fifty** *adj or pron,* **fiftyfold** *adj or adv*

[1] **,fifty-'fifty** *adv* so as to share or bear evenly or equally ⟨*let's go ~*⟩ ⟨*shared the money ~*⟩

[2]**fifty-fifty** *adj* half favourable and half unfavourable; even ⟨*a ~ chance*⟩

[1]**fig** /fig/ *n* **1a** any of a genus (*Ficus* of the family Moraceae, the fig family) of trees that bear many-seeded fleshy fruits; *esp* a widely cultivated tree (*Ficus carica*) that produces pear-shaped or oblong edible fruits that are eaten fresh or dried **b** the fruit of a figtree **2** something of little value; a worthless trifle ⟨*not worth a ~*⟩ [ME *fige,* fr OF, fr OProv *figa,* fr (assumed) VL *fica,* fr L *ficus* fig tree, fig]

[2]**fig** *n* dress, array ⟨*in full Regency ~ – The Listener*⟩ [fig (to adorn), var of obs *feague* to whip, prob fr Ger *fegen* to sweep, burnish]

[1]**fight** /fiet/ *vb* **fought** /fawt/ *vi* **1a** to contend in battle or physical combat; *esp* to strive to overcome a person by blows or weapons **b** to engage in boxing **2** to put forth a determined effort; struggle ⟨*~ing for his life*⟩ *~ vt* **1a(1)** to contend against (as if) in battle or physical combat **a(2)** to engage in a boxing match with **b** to attempt to prevent the success, effectiveness,

or development of ⟨*the company fought the strike for months*⟩ ⟨*~ a bad habit*⟩ **2a** to wage ⟨*~ a war*⟩ **b** to take part in (a boxing match) **3** to struggle to endure or surmount ⟨*~ out a storm at sea*⟩ **4a** to make (one's way) by fighting ⟨*fought his way through*⟩ **b** to control by fighting – often + *down* ⟨*fought down her fear*⟩ **5** to stand as a candidate for (e g a constituency) in an election – see also **fight** SHY **of** [ME *fighten,* fr OE *feohtan;* akin to OHG *fehtan* to fight, L *pectere* to comb – more at FEE]

**fight back** *vi* to struggle to recover from a losing or disadvantageous position; resist

**fight off** *vt* to ward off by fighting; repel

**fight out** *vt* to settle (e g an argument) by fighting

[2]**fight** *n* **1a** an act of fighting; a battle, combat **b** a boxing match **c** a verbal disagreement; an argument **2** a usu protracted struggle for a goal or objective ⟨*a ~ for justice*⟩ **3** strength or disposition for fighting; pugnacity ⟨*still full of ~*⟩ □ compare [1]BATTLE

**fighter** /'fietə/ *n* **1a** a warrior, soldier **b** a pugnacious or boldly determined individual **c** [1]BOXER **2** an aeroplane of high speed and manoeuvrability with armament designed to destroy enemy aircraft

**fighting chair** /'fieting/ *n* a chair from which a salt-water angler plays a large hooked fish

**fighting chance** *n* a chance that may be realized by a struggle ⟨*a ~ of getting to the final*⟩

**fighting fit** *adj* at the peak of physical fitness

**fig leaf** *n* **1** a leaf of a fig tree **2** something that conceals or camouflages, usu inadequately or dishonestly [(2) fr the fig leaves with which Adam and Eve tried to conceal their nakedness (Gen 3:7)]

**figment** /'figmənt/ *n* something fabricated or imagined ⟨*a ~ of the author's imagination*⟩ [ME, fr L *figmentum,* fr *fingere* to shape – more at DOUGH]

**figural** /'fig(y)ərəl/ *adj* of, concerning, or consisting of human or animal figures ⟨*a ~ composition*⟩

**figurant** /'fig(y)ərənt/, *fem* **figurante** /ˌfig(y)ə'ront/ *n* a ballet dancer who dances only in a group [Fr, fr pp of *figurer* to figure, represent, appear]

**figuration** /ˌfigyoo'raysh(ə)n/ *n* **1** the creation or representation of an esp allegorical or symbolic figure ⟨*Dante's unique ~ of the underworld*⟩ **2** a form, outline **3** ornamentation of a musical passage by using esp repeated patterns of notes

**figurative** /'figyoorətiv/ *adj* **1a** representing by a figure or likeness; emblematic **b** of the representation of objects, figures, scenes, etc in art; representational ⟨*~ sculpture*⟩ **2a** not literal; metaphorical ⟨*a ~ use of the word*⟩ **b** using or characterized by FIGURES OF SPEECH ⟨*~ language*⟩ – **figuratively** *adv,* **figurativeness** *n*

[1]**figure** /'figə/ *n* **1a** an esp Arabic number symbol; a numeral, digit ⟨*a salary running into six ~s*⟩ **b** *pl* arithmetical calculations ⟨*good at ~s*⟩ **c** a written or printed character **d** value, esp as expressed in numbers; a price ⟨*the house sold at a low ~*⟩ **2a(1)** the human form, esp with regard to shape or size ⟨*a tubby ~*⟩ **a(2)** a slim or attractive bodily shape – esp in *keep/ lose one's figure* **b** an object, esp a person, noticed or recognized only as a shape or form ⟨*~s moving in the dusk*⟩ **3a** a representation of an esp human form in drawing, painting, or sculpture **b** a diagram or pictorial illustration in a text **c** a geometrical diagram or shape **4** a person, thing, or action representative of another; a symbol, emblem **5** an intentional deviation from the ordinary form or grammatical relation of words **6** the form of a SYLLOGISM (formal deductive argument) with respect to the position of the MIDDLE TERM (term common to both premises) **7** an often repeated pattern or design in a manufactured article (e g cloth) or natural product (e g wood) **8** an appearance made; a usu favourable impression produced ⟨*the couple cut quite a ~*⟩ **9a** a series of movements in a dance **b** an outline representation of a form traced by a series of evolutions (e g by a skater on an ice surface or by an aircraft in the air) **10** a personage, personality ⟨*great political ~s*⟩ **11** a short coherent group of musical notes or chords that may grow into a phrase, theme, or composition [ME, fr OF, fr L *figura,* fr *fingere*]

[2]**figure** *vt* **1** to represent (as if) by a figure or outline; portray **2** to decorate with a pattern **3** to write figures over or under (the bass line in a piece of music) in order to indicate the accompanying chords **4** to indicate or represent by numerals **5a** to calculate **b** *chiefly NAm* to conclude, decide ⟨*he ~d there was no use in further effort*⟩ **c** *chiefly NAm* to regard, consider ~

**fig** 546

*vi* **1** to take an esp important or conspicuous part – often + *in* **2** to do arithmetic; calculate **3** *informal* to seem reasonable or expected – esp in *that figures* – **figurer** *n*

**figure on** *vt, NAm* **1** to take into consideration (e g in planning) ⟨*figure on $50 a month extra income*⟩ **2** to plan ⟨*I figure on going into town*⟩

**figure out** *vt* **1** to discover, determine ⟨*try to figure out a solution*⟩ **2** to solve, fathom ⟨*figure out a problem*⟩ ⟨*I just can't figure him out*⟩

**figured** /'figəd/ *adj* **1** represented, portrayed **2** adorned with, formed into, or marked with a pattern or design ⟨∼ *muslin*⟩ ⟨∼ *wood*⟩ **3** indicated by figures **4** *of music* **4a** ornamented with a series of rapid notes **b** having the bass line marked to indicate the accompanying chords

**figured bass** *n* a musical part consisting of a set of low notes together with figures indicating the accompanying chords; CONTINUO

**figure eight** *n, chiefly NAm* FIGURE OF EIGHT

**figurehead** /'figə,hed/ *n* **1** an ornamental carved figure on a ship's bow **2** a head or chief in name only

**figure of eight** *n* something resembling the ARABIC NUMERAL eight in form or shape: e g **a** a small knot used as a stopper at the end of a rope **b** an embroidery stitch **c** a dance pattern **d** a figure performed by a skater or by an aircraft

**figure of speech** *n* a form of expression (e g a HYPERBOLE or METAPHOR) used to convey meaning or heighten effect, often by comparing or identifying one thing with another that has a meaning or connotation familiar to the reader or listener

**figure skating** *n* skating in which the skater outlines distinctive circular patterns based on the figure eight

**figurine** /figyoo'reen, '---/ *n* a small carved or moulded figure; a statuette [Fr, fr It *figurina*, dim. of *figura* figure, fr L]

**figwort** /'fig,wuht/ *n* any of a genus (*Scrophularia*) of plants of the foxglove family that have toothed leaves and clusters of greenish-yellow flowers composed of an irregular two-lipped COROLLA (ring of petals) [¹*fig* (in obs sense "piles") + *wort;* fr its supposed ability to cure piles]

**Fijian** /fee'jee·ən/ *n* **1** a member of the Melanesian people of the Fiji islands **2** the AUSTRONESIAN language of the Fijians [*Fiji* islands in the SW Pacific] – **Fijian** *adj*

**fil** /fil/ *n* (a note or coin representing) a money unit used by various Arab countries and usu worth ¹/₁₀₀₀ DINAR – see MONEY table

**filament** /'filəmənt/ *n* a single thread or a thin flexible threadlike object or part: e g **a** a slender conductor (e g in an electric light bulb) caused to glow by the passage of an electric current; *specif* such a conductor that heats the CATHODE (structure with a negative electric charge through which electricity is conducted) of an electronic device (e g a THERMIONIC VALVE) **b(1)** a thin and fine elongated constituent part of a gill (e g of a fish or a mussel) **b(2)** an elongated thin series of attached cells or a very long thin cylindrical cell (e g of some algae, fungi, or bacteria) **c** the stalk of a STAMEN (male reproductive organ of a flower) bearing the ANTHERS (pollen-containing sacs) [MF, fr ML *filamentum*, fr LL *filare* to spin – more at FILE] – **filamentary** *adj*, **filamentous** *adj*

**filar** /'filə/ *adj* **1** of a thread or line **2** *of an optical instrument* having fine threads across the eyepiece that are used for measuring objects in the FIELD OF VIEW [L *filum* thread]

**filaria** /fi'leəri·ə/ *n, pl* **filariae** /-ri,ie/ any of numerous threadlike NEMATODES (unsegmented round-bodied worms) (of *Filaria* and related genera, superfamily Filarioidea) that usu develop in biting insects, and, when adult, are parasites in the blood or tissues of mammals [NL, fr L *filum*] – **filarial** *adj*, **filariid** *adj or n*

**filariasis** /,filə'rie·əsis, fi,leəri'aysis/ *n, pl* **filariases** /-seez/ infestation with or disease (e g ELEPHANTIASIS) caused by filarial worms [NL]

**filature** /'filəchə/ *n* **1** the reeling of silk from cocoons; *also* a factory where this takes place **2** a reel for drawing off silk from cocoons [Fr, fr LL *filatus*, pp of *filare*]

**filbert** /'filbət/ *n* (the sweet thick-shelled nut of) either of two European hazels (*Corylus avellana pontica* and *Corylus maxima*); *also* the hazelnut [ME, fr AF *philber*, fr St *Philibert* †684 Frankish abbot whose feast day falls in the nutting season]

**filch** /filch/ *vt* to steal (something of small value) furtively; pilfer *synonyms* see ROB [origin unknown]

¹**file** /fiel/ *n* a tool, usu of hardened steel, with many cutting

ridges for shaping or smoothing objects or surfaces [ME, fr OE *fēol;* akin to OHG *fila* file]

²**file** *vt* to rub, smooth, or cut away (as if) with a file

³**file** *vt* **1** to arrange in order (e g alphabetically) for preservation and reference ⟨∼ *letters*⟩ **2a** to send (copy) to a newspaper ⟨∼ d *a good story*⟩ **b** to submit or record officially or as prescribed by law ⟨∼ *a lawsuit*⟩ ∼ *vi* to place items, esp papers, in a file [ME *filen*, fr MF *filer* to string documents on a string or wire, fr *fil* thread, fr L *filum*]

⁴**file** *n* **1** a folder, cabinet, etc in which papers are kept in order **2** a collection of papers or publications, usu arranged in order ⟨*a* ∼ *of back issues of a newspaper*⟩ ⟨*checked the criminal's record in the police* ∼ s⟩ **3** a collection of related data records (e g for a computer) – **on file** (as if) in a file for ready reference

⁵**file** *n* **1** a row of people, animals, or things arranged one behind the other **2** any of the rows of squares that extend across a chessboard from white's side to black's side [MF, fr *filer* to spin, fr LL *filare*, fr L *filum*]

⁶**file** *vi* to march or proceed in file

**file card** *n* a block set with many wire teeth for cleaning a metalworking file

**filefish** /'fiel,fish/ *n* any of various BONY FISHES (esp genera *Aluterus, Cantherhines*, and *Monacanthus* of the family Balistidae) with rough granular leathery skins

¹**filet** /'filit, 'filay/ *n, NAm* a fillet

²**filet** *n* a lace with a square mesh and geometrical designs [Fr, lit., net]

**filet mignon** /,filay mi'nyon (*Fr* filɛ minɔh)/ *n, pl* **filets mignons** /∼/ a small steak cut from the centre of a beef fillet [Fr, lit., dainty fillet]

**fili-** /fili-/, **filo-** *comb form* thread ⟨filiform⟩ [L *filum*]

**filial** /'fili·əl, -yəl/ *adj* **1** of or befitting a son or daughter, esp in his/her relationship to a parent ⟨∼ *obedience*⟩ **2** having or assuming the relation of a child or offspring [ME, fr LL *filialis*, fr L *filius* son – more at FEMININE] – **filially** *adv*

**filial generation** *n, genetics* a generation in a breeding experiment that is successive to a parental generation

**filiation** /,fili'aysh(ə)n/ *n* **1a** the relationship of child to parent, esp of a son to his father **b** *law* AFFILIATION (judicial establishing of the paternity of a child) **2** an offshoot or branch (e g of a culture or language) **3** (the act or process of determining) descent or derivation, esp from a culture or language ⟨*the scholar's careful* ∼ *of manuscripts*⟩ – **filiate** *vt*

**filibeg, fillibeg, philibeg** /'filibeg/ *n* a kilt [ScGael *fèile-beag*, fr *fèileadh* kilt + *beag* little]

¹**filibuster** /'fili,bustə/ *n* **1** a military adventurer engaging in unauthorized warfare against a foreign country **2** *chiefly NAm* (an instance of) the use of extreme delaying tactics, esp in a legislative assembly [Sp *filibustero*, lit., freebooter; (2) ²*filibuster*]

²**filibuster** *vi* **1** to carry out insurrectionist or revolutionary activities in a foreign country **2** *chiefly NAm* to engage in a filibuster ∼ *vt, chiefly NAm* to subject to a filibuster – **filibusterer** *n*

**filiform** /'filifawm, 'fie-/ *adj, biology* shaped like a filament; threadlike

**filigree** /'filigree/ *vt or n* (to decorate with) **a** a lacy ornamental work of fine wire of gold, silver, or copper welded or soldered to form the desired shapes and sometimes affixed to an underlying metallic surface **b** a delicate, esp intricate pattern or design ⟨*a* ∼ *of frost on a window*⟩ [Fr *filigrane*, fr It *filigrana*, fr L *filum* + *granum* grain]

**filing** /'fieling/ *n usu pl* a usu metal fragment rubbed off in filing ⟨*iron* ∼ s⟩

**filiopietistic** /,filioh,pie·ə'tistik/ *adj, formal* of an often excessive veneration of ancestors or tradition [*filial* + *-o-* + *piety* + *-istic*]

**filioque** /'fili,ok/ *n* the affirmation added to the NICENE CREED in the liturgy of Western Christian churches, and rejected by the Eastern churches, that the HOLY SPIRIT proceeds from the Son as well as from the Father [LL, and from the son]

**Filipino** /,fili'peenoh/ *n, pl* **Filipinos** a native or inhabitant of the Philippine islands [Sp, fr (*Islas*) *Filipinas* Philippine Islands] – **Filipino** *adj*

¹**fill** /fil/ *vt* **1a** to put as much as can be held or conveniently contained into ⟨∼ *a cup with water*⟩ **b** to supply with a full complement ⟨*the class is already* ∼ ed⟩ **c(1)** to cause to swell or billow ⟨*wind* ∼ ed *the sails*⟩ **c(2)** to adjust (a sail) to catch the wind **d** to raise the level of (a piece of land) with fill **e** to repair the cavities of (esp a tooth) **f** to stop up; block, plug ⟨∼ ed *the cracks in the wall before painting it*⟩ **2a** to feed, satiate **b** to

satisfy, fulfil ⟨~s *all requirements*⟩ **3a** to occupy the whole of ⟨*smoke* ~ed *the room*⟩ **b** to spread through; make full **4a** to possess and perform the duties of; hold ⟨~ *an office*⟩ **b** to appoint a person to ⟨~ *a vacancy*⟩ **5** to supply as directed; *specif, NAm* to put together the ingredients for (a prescription) ~ *vi* to become full ⟨*the stadium* ~ed *and overflowed*⟩ □ (*vt 1a, 1b, 1f; vi*) often + *up* – see also BACK **and fill, fill the** BILL/ **somebody's** SHOES [ME *fillen,* fr OE *fyllan;* akin to OE *full*]

**fill in** *vt* **1** to enrich (e g a design) with detail **2** to add what is necessary to complete; [2]MAKE OUT ⟨fill in *this form, please*⟩ **3** *informal* to give necessary or recently acquired information to ⟨*friends* filled *him in on the latest gossip*⟩ – see also FILL-IN 2 ~ *vi, informal* to take somebody's place, usu temporarily; substitute ⟨*he often* filled in *for me in emergencies*⟩ – see also FILL-IN 1

**fill out** *vi* to put on flesh ~ *vt, chiefly NAm* FILL IN 2

[2]**fill** *n* **1a** the quantity needed to fill something ⟨*a* ~ *of pipe tobacco*⟩; *esp* as much as one can eat or drink ⟨*eat your* ~⟩ **b** as much as one can bear ⟨*I've had my* ~ *of them for today*⟩ **2** material (e g gravel or earth) used to fill in a hole or hollow

[1]**filler** /'filə/ *n* one who or that which fills: e g **a** a substance added to a product (e g to increase bulk or strength) **b** a substance used to fill cracks and holes in a surface before painting or varnishing **c** a piece (e g a plate or sheet) used to cover or fill in a space between two parts of a structure **d** material (e g a brief report) used to fill extra space in a column or page of a newspaper or magazine **e** the tobacco used to form the core of a cigar **f** an utterance (e g *er* or *you know*) inserted into speech to occupy time

[2]**filler** *n, pl* **fillers, filler** – see *forint* at MONEY table [Hung *fillér*]

**filler cap** *n* a removable cover sealing the end of the filling pipe which leads to the fuel tank of a motor vehicle

[1]**fillet,** *NAm also* **filet** /'filit/ *n* **1** a ribbon or narrow strip of material used esp as a headband **2** a thin narrow strip of material: e g **2a** a band of anatomical fibres; *specif* LEMNISCUS (band of NERVE FIBRES in the brain) **b(1)** **fillet, filet** a fleshy boneless piece of meat cut from the hind loin (e g of beef or pork) or upper hind leg (e g of veal or lamb) **b(2)** a long slice of boneless fish **3a** a junction where two surfaces meet and at which the interior angle is rounded off or partly filled in **b** a usu triangular piece that partly fills such an interior angle (e g to strengthen it) **4** a narrow flat architectural moulding; *esp* the raised band between two grooves (FLUTES) on a column **5** a plain line or narrow line of repeated ornaments impressed on a book cover **6** a structure fitted to an aircraft, vehicle, etc to improve airflow, usu at a joint between two surfaces [ME *filet,* fr MF, dim. of *fil* thread – more at FILE; (2b) Fr *filet,* fr MF]

[2]**fillet** *vt* **1** to bind, provide, or adorn (as if) with a fillet **2a** to cut (meat or fish) into fillets **b** to remove the bones from (esp fish) **3** to remove inessential parts from ⟨~ *a long document*⟩

**fillibeg** /'fili,beg/ *n* FILIBEG (kilt)

**'fill-,in** *n* **1** a substitute **2** *NAm informal* a briefing

[1]**filling** /'filing/ *n* **1** something used to fill a cavity, container, or depression ⟨*a* ~ *for a tooth*⟩ **2** a food mixture used to fill pastries, cakes, or sandwiches **3** *chiefly NAm* WEFT (yarn woven across the width of the fabric)

[2]**filling** *adj, of food* satisfyingly solid and heavy

**filling station** *n* a retail establishment for selling oil and fuel to motorists

[1]**fillip** /'filip/ *n* **1** a light blow or gesture made by the sudden forcible straightening of a finger curled up against the thumb **2** something that arouses, excites, or boosts; a stimulus ⟨*this should give a* ~ *to sales*⟩ [prob imit]

[2]**fillip** *vt* **1** to strike with a fillip **2** to project quickly (as if) by a fillip **3** to stimulate

**filly** /'fili/ *n* **1** a young female horse, usu of less than four years **2** *informal* a young woman; a girl ⟨*damned good-looking* ~, *what!*⟩ [ME *fyly,* fr ON *fylja;* akin to OE *fola* foal]

[1]**film** /film/ *n* **1a** a thin skin or membranous covering; a pellicle **b** (dimness of sight resulting from) an abnormal growth on or in the eye **2a** a thin layer, covering, or coating ⟨*a* ~ *of ice on the pond*⟩ **b** a thin flexible transparent sheet (e g of plastic) used as a wrapping **3** a roll or strip of CELLULOSE ACETATE or formerly CELLULOSE NITRATE coated with a light-sensitive emulsion and used in a camera for recording optical images **4a** a series of pictures recorded on film for the cinema and projected rapidly onto a screen so as to create the illusion of movement **b** a representation (e g of an incident or story) on film **c** **films** *pl,* **film** CINEMA 1a ⟨*a* ~ *buff*⟩ ⟨*has worked in* ~s

*all his life*⟩ *synonyms* see CINEMA [ME *filme,* fr OE *filmen;* akin to Gk *pelma* sole of the foot, OE *fell* skin – more at FELL] – **filmic** *adj,* **filmically** *adv*

[2]**film** *vt* to make a film of or from ⟨~ *a scene*⟩ ⟨~ *a novel*⟩ ~ *vi* **1** to be suitable for photographing ⟨*a scene that would* ~ *well*⟩ **2** to make a film ⟨~ing *on location*⟩

**film badge** *n* a small container of sensitive photographic film worn as a badge for indicating exposure to radiation

**filmgoer** /'film,gohə/ *n* a cinemagoer

**filmography** /fil'mogrəfi/ *n* a list of films featuring the work of a prominent film figure or relating to a particular topic [*film* + *-ography* (as in *bibliography*)]

**filmsetting** /'film,seting/ *n* PHOTOCOMPOSITION (typesetting process) – **filmset** *adj,* **filmset** *vt,* **filmsetter** *n*

**filmstrip** /'film,strip/ *n* a strip of photographic film bearing photographs, drawings, diagrams, etc, for still projection

**filmy** /'filmi/ *adj* **1** of, resembling, or composed of film; gauzy **2** covered with a mist or film; hazy – **filmily** *adv,* **filminess** *n*

**filo-** – see FILI-

**fils** /fils/ *n, pl* **fils** – see *dinar* at MONEY table [Ar]

[1]**filter** /'filtə/ *n* **1** a porous article or mass (e g of paper or sand) through which a gas or liquid is passed to separate out undissolved particles in suspension **2** an apparatus containing a filter medium ⟨*a car's oil* ~⟩ **3a** a device or material for suppressing or minimizing waves (e g of light or sound) or oscillations of certain frequencies while allowing passage to other selected vibrations **b** **filter, colour filter** a transparent material (e g coloured glass) that absorbs light of certain wavelengths or colours selectively and is used for modifying emitted or received light **4** *Br* a traffic signal at a road junction consisting of a green arrow which, when illuminated, allows traffic to turn left or right when the main signals are red [ME *filtre,* fr ML *filtrum* felt, piece of felt used as a filter, of Gmc origin; akin to OHG *filz* felt – more at FELT]

[2]**filter** *vt* **1** to subject to the action of a filter **2** to remove by means of a filter ~ *vi* **1** to pass or move (as if) through a filter **2** *of a group* to move gradually ⟨*the children* ~ed *out of assembly*⟩ **3** to become known over a period of time ⟨*the news soon* ~ed *through to the public*⟩ **4** *Br, of traffic* to turn left or right in the direction of the green arrow while the main lights are still red

**filterable** *also* **filtrable** /'filt(ə)rəbl/ *adj* **1** capable of being separated by filtering **2** capable of passing through a filter – **filterability** *n*

**filterable virus** *n* an infective organism so small that a liquid containing it remains invariant after passing through a porcelain filter; a virus – no longer used technically

**filter bed** *n* a bed of sand or gravel for purifying water or sewage

**filter feeder** *n* an animal (e g a mussel or a BLUE WHALE) adapted to obtain its food by filtering small particles of matter or minute organisms from a current of water that passes through some part of its system

**filter paper** *n* porous paper used for filtering

**filter tip** *n* (a cigar or cigarette with) a tip made from a porous material that is designed to filter the smoke before it enters the smoker's mouth – **filter-tipped** *adj*

**filth** /filth/ *n* **1** foul or putrid matter; *esp* loathsome dirt or refuse **2** something loathsome or vile; *esp* obscene or pornographic material [ME, fr OE *fylth,* fr *ful* foul]

**filthy** /'filthi/ *adj* **1** covered with or containing filth; offensively dirty **2** vile, obscene *synonyms* see [1]DIRTY – **filthily** *adv,* **filthiness** *n*

[1]**filtrate** /'filtrayt/ *vb* to filter [ML *filtratus,* pp of *filtrare,* fr *filtrum*]

[2]**filtrate** *n* material that has passed through a filter

**filtration** /fil'traysh(ə)n/ *n* the process of passing (as if) through a filter; *also* diffusion ⟨*the kidney produces urine by* ~⟩

**fimbria** /'fimbriə/ *n, pl* **fimbriae** /'fimbri,ie/ a bordering fringe, esp at the entrance of the FALLOPIAN TUBES (tubes of the uterus along which eggs pass after leaving the ovaries) [NL, fr L, fringe] – **fimbrial** *adj*

**fimbriate** /'fimbri-ət, -ayt/, **fimbriated** /-,aytid/ *adj* having the edge or extremity bordered by long slender extensions; fringed ⟨~ *petals*⟩ – **fimbriation** *n*

[1]**fin** /fin/ *n* **1** an external membranous part of an aquatic animal (e g a fish or whale) used in propelling or guiding the body **2** something resembling a fin, esp in appearance or function: **2a(1)** an appendage on a submarine or boat that is shaped like a fin **a(2)** an esp vertical AEROFOIL (surface designed to control an air-

craft in flight) attached to an aircraft usu at the rear for directional stability **b** a rubber flipper worn by an underwater swimmer **c** any of the projecting ribs that dissipate heat from the surface of a radiator or engine cylinder, thus assisting cooling [ME *finn,* fr OE; akin to L *spina* thorn, spine] – **finlike** *adj,* **finned** *adj*

²**fin** *vb* **-nn-** *vi* to lash or move through the water (as if) using fins ~ *vt* to equip with fins

**finagle** /fi'naygl/ *vb, informal* to use, or obtain by, devious and often dishonest methods [alter. of E dial. *fainaigue* to renege, cheat] – **finagler** *n*

¹**final** /'fienl/ *adj* **1** not to be altered or undone; conclusive **2** being the last; occurring at the end ⟨the ~ *chapter of a book*⟩ **3** of the ultimate purpose or result of a process ⟨the ~ *goal of life*⟩ [ME, fr MF, fr L *finalis,* fr *finis* boundary, end] – **finally** *adv*

²**final** *n* something final: eg **a** a deciding match, game, trial, etc in a sport or competition; *also, pl* a round made up of these **b** *pl* the last and usu most important series of examinations in an academic or professional course

**final cause** *n, philosophy* the ultimate purpose of a thing or process

**finale** /fi'nahli/ *n* **1** the last section of an instrumental musical composition **2** a final scene or number, esp in an act of an opera **3** the last and often climactic event or item in a sequence [It, fr *finale,* adj, final, fr L *finalis*]

**finalist** /'fienl·ist/ *n* **1** a contestant in the finals of a competition **2** a student taking final examinations

**finality** /fi'naləti, fie-/ *n* **1a** the character or condition of being final, settled, irrevocable, or complete **b** the condition of being at an ultimate point, esp of development or authority **2** *philosophy* the doctrine of FINAL CAUSE **3** a fundamental fact, action, or belief

**final·ize, -ise** /'fienl·iez/ *vt* **1** to put in final or finished form; complete **2** to give final approval to – **finalization** *n*

*usage* Many people who have no objection to other words, such as **formalize** and **modernize**, formed by adding **-ize** to an adjective feel a strong dislike for **finalize**. It is a genuinely useful word in bureaucratic contexts, meaning "put into conclusive unalterable form", but should perhaps be confined to abstract contexts ⟨**finalize** *the new guidelines*⟩ and not extended to concrete objects ⟨**finalize** *the new science wing*⟩.

**final solution** *n, often cap F&S* the deportation and extermination of the Jews by the Nazis during World War II [trans of Ger *endlösung*]

¹**finance** /'fienans, fi'nans/ *n* **1** *pl* the money or other exchangeable resources of a government, business, group, or individual **2** the system that includes the circulation of money and involves banking, credit, and investment **3** the science of the management of funds **4** the obtaining of funds or capital [ME, payment, ransom, fr MF, fr *finer* to end, pay, fr *fin* end – more at FINE]

²**finance** *vt* **1** to raise or provide money for ⟨~ *a new factory*⟩ **2** to sell something to on credit; provide with credit ⟨*car manufacturers unable to* ~ *their dealers*⟩

**finance bill** *n* a parliamentary bill relating to government revenue

**finance company** *n* a company that specializes in arranging or financing HIRE PURCHASE

**finance house** *n* FINANCE COMPANY

**financial** /fie'nanshəl, fi-/ *adj* **1** of finance or financiers **2** *Austr informal* having money; well-off ⟨*motherhood is a blessing, whether you're* ~ *or not* – *Australasian Post*⟩ – **financially** *adv*

**Financial Times Index, Financial Times Industrial Ordinary Index** *n* an index of prices on the London STOCK EXCHANGE based on the daily average price of selected lists of ordinary shares – compare DOW-JONES AVERAGE [*The Financial Times,* London newspaper]

**financier** /fi'nansi·ə, fie-/ *n* one skilled in dealing with finance or investment

**finback, finback whale** /'fin,bak/ *n* RORQUAL (type of large whale); *esp* FIN WHALE

**finch** /finch/ *n* any of numerous songbirds (family Fringillidae) having a short stout conical beak adapted for crushing seeds [ME, fr OE *finc;* akin to OHG *fincho* finch, Gk *spiza* chaffinch]

¹**find** /fiend/ *vb* **found** /fownd/ *vt* **1a** to come upon, esp accidentally; encounter ⟨*found a purse lying in the street*⟩ **b** to meet with (a specific reception) ⟨*hoped to* ~ *favour*⟩ **2a** to come upon by searching or effort; obtain ⟨~ *a replacement*⟩ **b** to discover by study or experiment ⟨~ *an answer to a problem*⟩ **c**

to obtain by effort or management ⟨~ *the time to study*⟩ **d** to attain, reach ⟨*water* ~s *its own level*⟩ **e** to discover by taking soundings ⟨~ *bottom in a lake*⟩ **3a** to experience, detect ⟨*found much pleasure in their company*⟩ **b** to perceive (oneself) to be in a specified place or condition ⟨*found himself in a dilemma*⟩ **c** to regard as being; consider, think ⟨*I* ~ *her difficult to get on with*⟩ **d** to gain or regain the use or power of ⟨*trying to* ~ *his tongue*⟩ **e** to bring (oneself) to a realization of one's powers or of one's true vocation ⟨*must help her to* ~ *herself as an individual*⟩ **4a** to provide, supply ⟨*the parents must* ~ *all the school fees themselves*⟩ – sometimes + *in* ⟨*the employer's duty to* ~ *them in protective clothing*⟩ **b** to furnish (room and board), esp as a condition of employment **5a** to determine and announce (eg a conclusion) ⟨~ *a verdict of not guilty*⟩ **b** to pronounce a verdict upon ⟨*found him not guilty of fraud*⟩ ~ *vi* to determine a case judicially by a verdict ⟨~ *for the defendant*⟩ – see also find FAULT [ME *finden,* fr OE *findan;* akin to OHG *findan* to find, L *pont-, pons* bridge, Gk *pontos* sea, Skt *patha* way, course]

**find out** *vt* **1** to learn by study, observation, or search; discover **2a** to detect in an offence ⟨*the culprits were soon found out*⟩ **b** to ascertain the true character or identity of; unmask ⟨*if you pretend, you may be* found out⟩ ~ *vi* to discover, learn, or verify something ⟨*I don't know, but I'll* find out *for you*⟩

²**find** *n* **1** an act or instance of finding something, esp something valuable **2** someone or something found; *esp* a valuable object or talented person discovered ⟨*an archaeological* ~⟩ ⟨*the new player was a real* ~⟩

**finder** /'fiendə/ *n* **1** one who or that which finds **2** a small astronomical telescope attached to a larger telescope for finding an object **3** the viewfinder of a camera

**fin de siècle** /'fan də see'eklə (*Fr* fɛ̃ də sjɛkl)/ *adj* (characteristic) of the close of the 19th century and esp its literary and artistic climate of sophisticated decadence, world-weariness, and fashionable despair; decadent [Fr, end of the century]

**finding** /'fiending/ *n* **1** FIND 2 **2a** the result of a judicial inquiry **b** **findings** *pl,* **finding** the result of an investigation ⟨*the* ~s *of the welfare committee*⟩ **3** *pl, NAm* small tools and materials used by a craftsman

¹**fine** /fien/ *n* **1** a sum payable as punishment for an offence **2** a forfeiture or penalty paid to an injured party in a civil action **3** a sum payable as a premium at the beginning of a tenancy [ME, end, settlement of a suit, sum paid as compensation, fr OF *fin,* fr L *finis* boundary, end]

²**fine** *vt* to punish by a fine

³**fine** *adj* **1a** free from impurity **b** *of a metal* having a stated proportion of pure metal in the composition ⟨*gold 23 carats* ~⟩ **2a** very thin in gauge or texture ⟨~ *thread*⟩ ⟨~ *nib*⟩ **b** consisting of relatively small particles ⟨~ *sand*⟩ **c** very small ⟨~ *print*⟩ **d** sharp, keen ⟨*a knife with a* ~ *edge*⟩ **e** *nautical* almost directly in front or behind **3a(1)** having a delicate or subtle quality ⟨*a wine of* ~ *bouquet*⟩ **a(2)** keen or sensitive in perception or discrimination ⟨*a* ~ *eye for valuable old books*⟩ **b** marked by subtlety or intricacy of thought or expression ⟨*a* ~ *distinction*⟩ ⟨*very* ~ *legal points were involved*⟩ **c** on a small scale; delicate ⟨~ *workmanship*⟩ ⟨~ *stitching*⟩ ⟨fine-*boned*⟩ **4** very good of its kind; excellent: eg **4a** superior in character, nature, or ability ⟨*a* ~ *musician*⟩ ⟨*a* ~ *soldier*⟩ **b** superior in construction, execution, design, or expression ⟨*a* ~ *work of art*⟩ **c** noble, elevated ⟨~ *feelings*⟩ **d** of attractive appearance ⟨*a* ~ *young woman*⟩ ⟨*a very* ~ *garden*⟩ **e** sunny and dry ⟨~ *weather*⟩ ⟨*a* ~ *spring morning*⟩ **5** marked by or affecting often excessive elegance or refinement ⟨~ *manners*⟩ ⟨*a ball attended by* ~ *ladies and gentlemen*⟩ **6a** very well ⟨*feel* ~⟩ **b** adequate, satisfactory ⟨*that's* ~ *by me*⟩ **7** awful ⟨*that's a* ~ *thing to say!*⟩ ⟨*a* ~ *mess we're in!*⟩ **8** of, occupying, or passing through a fielding position in cricket behind the batsman and near an extension of the line between the wickets ⟨~ *leg*⟩ [ME *fin,* fr OF, fr L *finis,* n, end, limit] – **fine** *adv,* **finely** *adv,* **fineness** *n* – **cut it fine** to make the minimum allowance of time, resources, etc to accomplish something

*usage* The adverb **fine** means either "by an irreducible margin" ⟨*run it* fine⟩ or, informally, "very well" ⟨*we're doing* fine⟩ and cannot replace **finely** in its other meanings.

⁴**fine** *vt* **1** to purify, clarify ⟨~ *and filter wine*⟩ – often + *down* **2** to make finer in quality or size – often + *down* ~ *vi* **1** to become pure or clear ⟨*the ale will* ~⟩ – often + *off* **2** to become finer or smaller in lines or proportions; diminish – often + *away* or *down*

⁵**fine** /'feenay/ *n* the end – used as a direction in music to mark the closing point after a repeat [It, fr L *finis*]

⁶**fine** /feen/ *n* brandy of ordinary quality [Fr, fr *fine* fine]

**fine art** *n usu pl* (an) art (e g painting, sculpture, or music) for which aesthetic purposes are of prime importance – compare BEAUX ARTS

**fineness ratio** /'fien·nis/ *n* the ratio of the length to the maximum width of a streamlined body (e g an aeroplane)

**fine print** *n* SMALL PRINT (something deliberately obscure)

**finery** /'fienəri/ *n* dressy or showy clothing and jewels

**fines** *n pl* finely crushed or powdered material (e g ore or coal); *also* very small particles in a mixture of various sizes [³*fine*]

**fines herbes** /ˌfeenz 'eəb (*Fr* fin zɛrb)/ *n pl* a mixture of usu finely chopped herbs (e g parsley, chives, and tarragon) used as a seasoning or garnish [Fr, lit., fine herbs]

**finespun** /'fienspun/ *adj* made or developed with extreme care or delicacy; *also* developed in excessively fine or subtle detail

¹**finesse** /fi'nes/ *n* 1 refinement or delicacy of workmanship, structure, or texture 2 skilful handling of a situation; subtlety, adroitness ⟨*accomplished by* ~ *what could not have been accomplished by force*⟩ 3 the withholding of one's highest card or trump in the hope that a lower card will take the trick because the only opposing higher card is in the hand of an opponent who has already played [ME, fr MF, fr *fin*]

²**finesse** *vi* to make a finesse in playing cards – sometimes + *for* or *against* ⟨~ *for the jack*⟩ ⟨~ *against the queen*⟩ ~ *vt* 1 to play (a card) in a finesse ⟨*held back his ace and risked* finessing *the queen*⟩ 2a to bring about or manage by adroit manoeuvring **b** to evade, trick ⟨*managed to* ~ *an eagle-eyed employer*⟩

**fine structure** *n* 1 the microscopic structure of an organism or its cells, esp as revealed by an ELECTRON MICROSCOPE; ULTRASTRUCTURE 2 closely spaced spectral lines in a spectrum of an atom due to electron interaction – **fine structural** *adj*

**fine-tooth comb** *n* a comb with close-set teeth – **with a fine-tooth comb** extremely thoroughly ⟨*search through every file with a fine-tooth comb* – *Private Eye*⟩

**finfish** /'fin,fish/ *n* FISH 1b

¹**finger** /'fing·gə/ *n* 1 any of the jointed movable parts at the end of the hand; a digit of the forelimb; *esp* one other than the thumb 2a something that resembles a finger, esp in being long, relatively narrow, and often tapering in shape ⟨*a narrow* ~ *of land extending into the sea*⟩ ⟨*a* ~ *of toast*⟩ **b** a part of a glove into which a finger is inserted 3 the breadth of a finger used as a unit of measurement, esp for spirits ⟨*two* ~s *of gin*⟩ [ME, fr OE; akin to OHG *fingar* finger] – **fingerlike** *adj* – **be/feel all fingers and thumbs** to be clumsy – **burn one's fingers/get one's fingers burnt** to suffer as a result of a foolish action or mistake – **get/pull/take one's finger out** *Br slang* to start working hard; GET CRACKING – **have a finger in the/every pie** to be involved or have an interest in something/everything – **keep one's fingers crossed** to hope for the best possible outcome – **lay a finger on** to harm in the least – **lift/raise a finger** to make any effort to help ⟨*never* lifted a finger *to help with the housework*⟩ – **point the finger (at)** to accuse – **put/lay one's finger on** to identify as a reason, cause, etc; find – **put the finger on** *slang* to identify as a suspect – **slip through one's fingers** to get lost; escape ⟨*let the opportunity* slip through her fingers⟩ – **twist/wind/wrap somebody round one's (little) finger** to be able to manipulate somebody effortlessly

²**finger** *vt* 1a to play (a musical instrument) with the fingers **b** to play (e g notes or chords) with a specific fingering **c** to mark fingerings on (a music score) as a guide in playing 2 to touch or feel with the fingers; handle 3 *chiefly NAm slang* to identify; POINT OUT ⟨~ed *his associates to the police*⟩ ~ *vi* 1 to touch or handle something ⟨~s *through the cards*⟩ 2 *of a musical instrument* to have a certain fingering ⟨~s *like a clarinet*⟩

**fingerboard** /'fing·gə,bawd/ *n* the part of a stringed instrument against which the fingers press the strings to vary the pitch

**finger bowl** *n* a small water bowl for rinsing the fingers at table

**fingered** /'fing·gəd/ *adj* 1 having fingers of a specified kind or number – in combination ⟨*stubby-fingered*⟩ ⟨*five-fingered*⟩ 2 having projections or outgrowths like fingers

**finger hole** *n* 1 any of the holes in the side of a WIND INSTRUMENT (e g a recorder) which may be covered or left open by the fingers to play different notes 2 a hole (e g in a telephone dial) into which the finger is placed to provide a grip

¹**fingering** /'fing·gəring/ *n* 1 handling or touching with the fingers 2a the use or position of the fingers in sounding notes on an instrument **b** the marking (e g by figures on a musical score) of the method of fingering

²**fingering** *n* a fine wool yarn for hand-knitting [alter. of earlier *fingram*, prob fr Fr *fin grain* fine grain]

**fingerling** /'fing·gəling/ *n* a small fish, esp up to one year of age

**fingernail** /'fing·gə,nayl/ *n* the nail of a finger

**finger painting** *n* 1 a technique of spreading pigment on wet paper chiefly with the fingers 2 a picture produced by finger painting

**fingerplate** /'fing·gə,playt/ *n* a protective plate fastened to a door, usu near the handle, to prevent soiling of the door surface by finger marks

**fingerpost** /'fing·gə,pohst/ *n* a signpost whose signs are or end in the shape of a pointing finger or hand

**fingerprint** /'fing·gə,print/ *n* 1 the impression of a fingertip on any surface; *esp* an ink impression of the lines upon the fingertip taken for purposes of identification 2 unique distinguishing characteristics (e g of a recording machine or infrared spectrum) 3 the characteristic pattern of the components of a partially broken down protein or other large molecule, that is obtained when a mixture of the components is separated out by CHROMATOGRAPHY or ELECTROPHORESIS – **fingerprint** *vt*, **fingerprinting** *n*

**fingerstall** /'fing·gə,stawl/ *n* a protective covering for an injured finger

¹**fingertip** /'fing·gə,tip/ *n* 1 the tip of a finger 2 a fingerstall – **at one's fingertips** instantly or readily available to one, esp because of a full knowledge of a subject

²**fingertip** *adj* readily accessible; in close proximity ⟨~ *information*⟩ ⟨~ *controls*⟩

¹**finger-,wave** *n* a wave or curl produced by winding dampened hair round the fingers

**finial** /'fieni·əl, 'fin-/ *n* 1 an ornament forming an upper extremity of a spire, gable, pinnacle, etc, esp in Gothic architecture 2 a crowning or finishing ornament or detail (e g a decorative knob) [ME, fr *final, finial* final]

**finical** /'finikl/ *adj* finicky [prob fr ³*fine* + -*ical*] – **finically** *adv*, **finicalness** *n*

**finicking** /'finiking/ *adj* finicky [alter. of *finical*]

**finicky** /'finiki/ *adj* 1 excessively exacting or meticulous in taste or standards; fussy 2 requiring delicate attention to detail ⟨*a* ~ *job*⟩ [alter. of *finicking*] – **finickiness** *n*

**finis** /'finis/ *n* the end, conclusion – used esp to mark the end of a book or film [ME, fr L]

¹**finish** /'finish/ *vt* 1a to come to the end of; end, terminate ⟨~ed *his speech and sat down*⟩ **b** to eat, drink, use, or dispose of entirely – often + *off* or *up* ⟨~ *the meat off*⟩ 2a to bring to completion or issue; complete, perfect ⟨~ed *her new novel*⟩ – often + *off* **b** to provide with a finish; *esp* to put a final coat or surface on ⟨~ *a table with varnish*⟩ **c** to neaten (the raw edge of a piece of sewing) (e g by oversewing or facing) to prevent fraying **d** to send (a girl) to finishing school 3a to bring to an end the significance or effectiveness of ⟨*the scandal* ~ed *his career*⟩ **b** to bring about the death of **c** *informal* to exhaust ⟨*competing in the London marathon really* ~ed *me*⟩ ~ *vi* 1 to end, terminate ⟨*skirts that* ~ *just above the knee*⟩ 2a to come to the end of a course, task, or undertaking in a specified manner ⟨~ed *with a song*⟩ **b** to come to the end of a relationship ⟨*David and I have* ~ed⟩ 3 to arrive, end, or come to rest in a specified position or manner – often + *up* ⟨*we* ~ed *up in Paris*⟩ ⟨*the car* ~ed *upside down in a field*⟩; *specif* to end a competition in a specified manner or position ⟨~ed *third in the race*⟩ 4 to score a goal in soccer 5 *of a farm animal* to become suitably fat for marketing **synonyms** see ¹CLOSE [ME *finisshen*, fr MF *finiss*-, stem of *finir*, fr L *finire*, fr *finis*] – **finisher** *n*

**finish with** *vt* 1 to have no more use for ⟨*have you* finished with *the scissors yet?*⟩ ⟨*Don't go yet, I haven't* finished with *you*⟩ 2 to end a relationship or affair with ⟨finished with *her boyfriend*⟩

²**finish** *n* 1a the final stage; the end ⟨*the* ~ *of a race*⟩ **b** the cause of one's ruin; downfall 2 something that completes or perfects: e g 2a decorative features and esp woodwork used in building, but not structurally essential **b** the texture or appearance of a surface, esp after a coating has been applied ⟨*a rough* ~⟩ ⟨*eggshell* ~⟩; *also* the final treatment or coating of a surface ⟨*a veneer* ~⟩ **c** a finishing material (e g varnish) used in painting 3 the result or product of a finishing process ⟨*the*

*~ on this dress is very bad⟩* **4** the quality or state of being perfected, esp in the social graces ⟨*a pleasant young man, but he lacks ~*⟩

**finished** /'finisht/ *adj* **1** marked by the highest quality ⟨*a ~ performance*⟩ **2** at the end of an activity, undertaking, relationship, etc ⟨*we were ~ by lunchtime*⟩

**finishing school** /'finishing/ *n* a private school for girls that emphasizes cultural studies and prepares its students esp for social activities

**finite** /'fieniet/ *adj* **1a** having definite or definable limits ⟨*a ~ number of possibilities*⟩ **b** subject to limitations, esp those imposed by the laws of nature ⟨*~ beings*⟩ **2** completely determinable in theory or in fact by counting, measurement, or thought; neither infinite nor infinitesimal ⟨*a ~ distance*⟩ ⟨*the ~ velocity of light*⟩ **3a** less than some positive integer and greater than some negative integer ⟨*a ~ number*⟩ **b** having a finite number of elements ⟨*a ~ set*⟩ **4** *of a verb form* changing according to tense and subject [ME *finit*, fr L *finitus*, pp of *finire*] – **finite** *n*, **finitely** *adv*, **finiteness** *n*, **finitude** *n*

**fink** /fingk/ *n, chiefly NAm informal* **1** INFORMER 2 **2** a blackleg, strikebreaker **3** a contemptible or disliked person [origin unknown]

**fink out** *vi, chiefly NAm informal* **1** to fail miserably **2** COP OUT

**Finn** /fin/ *n* **1** a member of any people speaking Finnish or a Finnic language **2a** a native or inhabitant of Finland **b** a person of Finnish descent [Sw *Finne*]

**finnan haddie** /ˌfinən 'hadi/ *n, chiefly Scot* FINNAN HADDOCK

**finnan haddock** *n* a haddock that is split and smoked until pale yellow [*finnan* alter. of *findon*, fr *Findon*, village near Aberdeen in Scotland]

**finner** /'finə/ *n* RORQUAL (type of large whale) [¹*fin* + ²-*er*]

**Finnic** /'finik/ *adj* **1** of the Finns **2** of or constituting the branch of the Finno-Ugric subfamily of languages that includes Finnish, Estonian, and Lapp

¹**Finnish** /'finish/ *adj* (characteristic) of Finland, the Finns, or Finnish

²**Finnish** *n* a Finno-Ugric language of Finland, Karelia, and parts of Sweden and Norway

**Finno-Ugrian** /ˌfinoh 'yoohgri-ən/ *adj or n* Finno-Ugric

**Finno-Ugric** /'yoohgrik/ *adj* **1** of any of various peoples of N and E Europe and NW Siberia speaking related languages and including Finns, Hungarians, Lapps, and Estonians **2** of or constituting a subfamily of the URALIC family of languages comprising various languages spoken in Hungary, Lapland, Finland, Estonia, and the NW USSR – **Finno-Ugric** *n*

**finny** /'fini/ *adj* **1** having fins **2** *chiefly poetic* relating to or being fish

**fino** /'feenoh/ *n, pl* **finos** a light-coloured dry sherry [Sp, fr *fino* fine, fr L *finis*, n, end, limit]

**fin whale** *n* a large common widely distributed RORQUAL (*Balaenoptera physolus*)

**fiord, fjord** /fjawd, 'fee,awd/ *n* a narrow inlet of the sea between cliffs or steep slopes; *esp* one in a Scandinavian country [Norw *fjord*, fr ON *fjörthr* – more at FORD]

**fioritura** /fiˌori'tooərə/ *n, pl* **fioriture** /-'tooəray/ ORNAMENT 3 (embellishing musical note) [It, lit., flowering, fr *fiorito*, pp of *fiorire* to flower, fr (assumed) VL *florire* – more at FLOURISH]

**fipple flute** /'fipl/ *n* a tubular WIND INSTRUMENT (e g a flageolet, pipe, or recorder) characterized mainly by a whistle mouthpiece and finger holes [*fipple* (a plug at the mouth of a wind instrument) perh akin to ON *flipi* horse's lip]

**fir** /fuh/ *n* **1** any of a genus (*Abies*) of evergreen trees of the pine family that have flattish needlelike leaves and erect cones and are valued for their wood; *also* any of various similar conifers (e g the DOUGLAS FIR) **2** the wood of a fir [ME, fr OE *fyrh;* akin to OHG *forha* fir, L *quercus* oak]

¹**fire** /'fie-ə/ *n* **1a** the phenomenon of combustion manifested in light, flame, and heat **b** one of the four elements of the alchemists **2a** burning passion or emotion; ardour **b** liveliness of imagination; inspiration **3** a mass of burning fuel (e g in a fireplace or furnace) **4a** (a) destructive burning (e g of a building or forest) ⟨*insurance against ~*⟩ ⟨*acres of woodland destroyed by a forest ~*⟩ **b** a severe trial or ordeal ⟨*courage hardened in the ~s of battle*⟩ **5** brilliancy, luminosity ⟨*the ~ of a diamond*⟩ **6** the discharge of firearms **7** *Br* a small usu gas or electric domestic heater [ME, fr OE *fȳr;* akin to OHG *fiur* fire, Gk *pyr*] – **fireless** *adj* – **between two fires** under attack from both sides – **catch fire** to begin to burn – **go through fire and**

water to endure great hardship – **hang fire 1** *of a gun* to be slow in exploding **2** to delay ⟨*they're hanging fire until they know whether she's got the job*⟩ – **on fire 1** burning ⟨*the chimney's on fire*⟩ **2** eager, enthusiastic – **open/cease fire** to start/stop firing – **play with fire** to take great risks – **set fire to** to kindle accidentally or maliciously – **set the world/**(*Br*) **the Thames on fire** to cause a sensation [*Thames*, river in S England] – **under fire 1** being shot at **2** being harshly criticized ⟨*his speech had come* under fire *in the papers*⟩ – see also **out of the** FRYING PAN **into the fire, get on like a** HOUSE **on fire,** IRON **in the fire**

²**fire** *vt* **1a** to set on fire; kindle; *also* to ignite ⟨*~ a rocket engine*⟩ **b(1)** to give life or spirit to; inspire ⟨*~d the poet's imagination*⟩ **b(2)** to fill with passion; inflame ⟨*~d with enthusiasm*⟩ **2** to drive out or away (as if) by fire – usu + *out* **3a** to cause to explode; detonate ⟨*~d a charge of dynamite*⟩ **b(1)** to propel (as if) from a gun; launch ⟨*~ a rocket*⟩ ⟨*~d poisoned arrows at the invaders*⟩ **b(2)** to throw with speed; hurl **b(3)** to utter with force and rapidity ⟨*~d questions at the prisoner*⟩ **c** to discharge (a gun) ⟨*~d a pistol into the air*⟩ **d** to produce by the discharge of guns ⟨*~ a salute*⟩ **4** to apply fire or fuel to: e g **4a** to treat or process by applying heat; *specif* to bake (clay ware) in a kiln **b** to provide fuel for ⟨*an oil-fired boiler*⟩ **5** *informal* to dismiss from employment; sack ~ *vi* **1a** to catch fire; ignite **b** *of an internal-combustion engine* to undergo ignition of the air-fuel mixture **2** to become excited or angry – often + *up* **3a** to discharge a firearm ⟨*took aim and ~d at the intruder*⟩ **b** to emit or let fly an object **4** to tend a fire – **firer** *n*

**fire away** *vi, informal* to go ahead; begin – usu imper

**fire alarm** *n* (a device for producing) a signal (e g a ringing sound) to warn people of fire

**fire and brimstone** *n* eternal damnation [fr the references in Ps 11:7 & Rev 20:10]

**firearm** /'fie-ər,ahm/ *n* a weapon from which a shot is discharged by an explosive charge or compressed air – usu used only with reference to small arms

**fireback** /'fie-ə,bak/ *n* the back lining of a furnace or fireplace

**fireball** /'fie-ə,bawl/ *n* **1** a large brilliant meteor **2** lightning in the form of a ball of fire **3** the bright cloud of vapour and dust created by a nuclear explosion **4** a highly energetic person

**fire blight** *n* a destructive highly infectious disease of apples, pears, and related fruits caused by a bacterium (*Erwinia amylovora*) [fr its causing leaves to appear scorched or blackened]

**fireboat** /'fie-ə,boht/ *n* a vessel equipped for fighting fires

**firebomb** /'fie-ə,bom/ *n* an incendiary bomb – **firebomb** *vt*

**firebox** /'fie-ə,boks/ *n* a chamber (e g of a furnace or steam boiler) that contains a fire

**firebrand** /'fie-ə,brand/ *n* **1** a piece of burning material, esp wood **2** one who creates unrest or strife; an agitator, troublemaker

**firebrat** /'fie-ə,brat/ *n* a wingless BRISTLETAIL (primitive insect) (*Thermobia domestica*) that frequents warm places (e g bakeries)

**firebreak** /'fie-ə,brayk/ *n* a strip of cleared or unplanted land intended to check a forest or grass fire

**firebrick** /'fie-ə,brik/ *n* a brick that is resistant to high temperatures and is used to line fireplaces, furnaces, etc

**fire brigade** *n* **1** an organization for preventing or extinguishing fires; *esp* one maintained in Britain by local government **2** *taking sing or pl vb* the members of a fire brigade

**firebug** /'fie-ə,bug/ *n, informal* a person who deliberately sets fire to property; a fire-raiser

**fireclay** /'fie-ə,klay/ *n* clay that is resistant to high temperatures and is used esp for firebricks and crucibles

**fire control** *n* the planning, preparation, and delivery of gunfire on targets

**firecracker** /'fie-ə,krakə/ *n* a small firework that explodes loudly several times and jumps each time it explodes

**firecrest** /'fie-ə,krest/ *n* a small European bird (*Regulus ignicapillus*) that has a bright red cap and conspicuous black and white stripes about the eyes

'**fire-,cured** *adj, of tobacco* cured over open wood fires in direct contact with the smoke – compare FLUE-CURED

**firedamp** /'fie-ə,damp/ *n* (the explosive mixture of air with) a combustible mine gas that consists chiefly of METHANE

**fire department** *n, NAm* a fire fighting organization

**firedog** /'fie-ə,dog/ *n* either of two metal supports for burning logs in a grate; an andiron

**firedrake** /'fie-ə,drayk/ *n* a fire-breathing dragon, esp in Germanic mythology [ME *firdrake*, fr OE *fyrdraca*, fr *fȳr* + *draca* dragon – more at DRAKE]

**fire drill** *n* a practice drill in extinguishing or escaping from fires

'**fire-,eater** *n* **1** a performer who pretends to eat fire **2** one who is quarrelsome or violent – **fire-eating** *adj*

**fire engine** *n* a vehicle equipped with fire-fighting equipment

**fire escape** *n* a device, esp an external staircase, for escape from a burning building

**fire extinguisher** *n* an apparatus for putting out fires with chemicals

**firefight** /'fie·ə,fiet/ *n* an often spontaneous exchange of fire between opposing military units

**fire fighter** *n* a person who fights fires – **fire fighting** *n*

**firefly** /'fie·ə,flie/ *n* any of various winged night-flying beetles (esp family Lampyridae) that produce a bright intermittent light, esp for courtship purposes

**fireguard** /'fie·ə,gahd/ *n* **1** a protective metal framework placed in front of an open fire **2** *chiefly NAm* a firebreak **3** *chiefly NAm* a fire-watcher

**fire hall** *n, Can* FIRE STATION

**firehouse** /'fie·ə,hows/ *n, NAm* FIRE STATION

**fire irons** *n pl* implements (eg tongs, poker, and shovel) for tending a domestic wood or coal fire, esp in a fireplace

**firelight** /'fie·ə,liet/ *n* the light of a fire, esp of one in a fireplace

**fire lighter** *n* a piece of inflammable material used to help light a fire (eg in a grate)

**firelock** /'fie·ə,lok/ *n* (a gun with) **a** a GUNLOCK in which a slow match ignites the powder charge **b** a GUNLOCK in which a spark from a flint ignites the powder; a flintlock **c** an obsolete GUNLOCK in which the powder is ignited by sparks produced by friction between a small steel wheel and a flint; WHEEL LOCK

**fireman** /'fie·əmən/ *n* **1** somebody employed to extinguish fires **2** somebody who tends or feeds fires or furnaces; a stoker **3** *Br* SECOND MAN (driver's assistant on a diesel or electric engine)

**fire master** *n, Scot* an official in charge of a FIRE BRIGADE

**fire office** *n, chiefly Br* an insurance company specializing in fire insurance

**fire opal** *n* GIRASOL (opal that gives out fiery reflections)

**fireplace** /'fie·ə,plays/ *n* **1** a usu framed opening made in a chimney to hold a fire; a hearth; *also* a freestanding metal structure with a smoke pipe, used for the same purpose **2** an outdoor structure of brick, stone, or metal for an open fire

**fireplug** /'fie·ə,plug/ *n, chiefly NAm* a hydrant

**firepower** /'fie·ə,powə/ *n* **1** the capacity (eg of a military unit) to deliver effective fire on a target **2** the total number of effective missiles that can be placed on a target

**fireproof** /'fie·ə,proohf, -proof/ *adj* proof against or resistant to fire; *also* heatproof ⟨∼ *dishes*⟩ – **fireproof** *vt*, **fireproofing** *n*

'**fire-,raising** *n, Br* arson – **fire-raiser** *n*

**fire screen** *n* **1** a light often ornamental screen placed in front of a fireplace as a heat shield **2** *chiefly NAm* a fireguard

**fireship** /'fie·ə,ship/ *n* a ship carrying combustible materials or explosives sent into an enemy fleet or harbour to set fire to it

'**fireside** /'fie·ə,sied/ *n* **1** a place near the fire or hearth **2** the home

²**fireside** *adj* having an informal or homely quality ⟨*a ∼ chat*⟩

**fire station** *n* a building housing fire-fighting apparatus and usu firemen

**firestone** /'fie·ə,stohn/ *n* a stone that will endure high temperatures; a firebrick

'**fire-,stop** *n* a barrier designed to prevent or hinder the spread of fire (eg in a building) – **fire-stop** *vt*

**fire storm** *n* a huge uncontrollable fire that is started typically by bombs and that causes and is kept in being by an inrush of high winds

**fire tender** *n* a vehicle that is attached to a fire engine and carries fire-fighting apparatus

**fire tower** *n* a tower (eg in a forest) from which a watch for fires is maintained

**firetrap** /'fie·ə,trap/ *n* a place (eg a building) liable to catch fire or difficult to escape from in case of fire

**fire truck** *n, NAm* FIRE ENGINE

'**fire-,watcher** *n* a person who watches for the outbreak of fire (eg during an air raid) – **fire-watching** *n*

**firewater** /'fie·ə,wawtə/ *n, informal* strong alcoholic drink

**fireweed** /'fie·ə,weed/ *n* any of several plants that grow esp in clearings or areas which have been burned; *esp* ROSEBAY WILLOWHERB

**firewood** /'fie·ə,wood/ *n* wood cut for fuel; *specif, Br* kindling

**firework** /'fie·ə,wuhk/ *n* **1** a device for producing a striking display (eg of light, noise, or smoke) by the combustion of explosive or inflammable mixtures **2** *pl* a display of fireworks **3** *pl* **3a** a display of temper or intense conflict **b** a spectacular display (eg of virtuosity, oratory, or wit)

**firing** /'fie·əring/ *n* **1** the act or process of one who or that which fires **2** the process of baking and fusing ceramic products by the application of heat in a kiln **3** firewood, fuel **4** the scorching of plants, esp by unfavourable soil conditions

**firing line** *n* **1** a line from which fire is delivered against a target; *also, taking sing or pl vb* the troops stationed in a firing line **2** the forefront of an activity, esp one involving risk or difficulty – esp in *in the firing line*

**firing pin** *n* the pin in the firing mechanism of a firearm that strikes the cartridge primer to ignite the charge

**firing squad** *n taking sing or pl vb* a detachment detailed to fire a salute at a military funeral, or to carry out an execution by shooting

**firkin** /'fuhkin/ *n* **1** a small wooden vessel or cask of usu 9-gallon capacity **2** any of various British units of capacity usu equal to a quarter of a barrel (about 41 litres) [ME, deriv of MD *veerdel* fourth]

¹**firm** /fuhm/ *adj* **1a** securely or solidly fixed in place **b** not weak or uncertain; vigorous ⟨a ∼ *handshake*⟩ **c** having a solid or compact structure that resists stress or pressure **2a** not subject to change, revision, unsteadiness, or disturbance; definite, steadfast ⟨*a ∼ price*⟩ ⟨∼ *principles*⟩ ⟨∼ *arrangements*⟩ **b** not subject to price weakness; steady, stable **c** well-founded **3a** resolute, unyielding ⟨*necessary to be kind but ∼*⟩ **b** indicating firmness or resolution ⟨*a ∼ mouth*⟩ [ME *ferm*, fr MF, fr L *firmus*; akin to Gk *thronos* chair, throne] – **firm** *adv*, **firmish** *adj*, **firmly** *adv*, **firmness** *n*

   *usage* Firm as an adverb is chiefly used in certain fixed phrases ⟨*stand* firm⟩ ⟨*hold* firm⟩ and cannot replace firmly, the usual adverb ⟨*speak* firmly *to her*⟩.

²**firm** *vt* **1** to make solid, compact, firm, or secure ⟨∼ *the soil*⟩ ⟨∼ing *his grip on the racket*⟩ **2** to put into final form; settle ⟨∼ *a contract*⟩ ⟨∼ *up one's ideas*⟩ to give additional support to; strengthen ⟨*help ∼ up the franc*⟩ ∼ *vi* **1** to become firm; harden ⟨*his face ∼ed and he spoke with restrained anger*⟩ **2** to recover from a decline; improve ⟨*the market ∼ed slightly*⟩ ☐ (*vt 2&3; vi*) often + *up*

³**firm** *n taking sing or pl vb* a business partnership of two or more people, not usu recognized as a legal entity distinct from the members composing it; *broadly* any business unit or enterprise [Ger *firma* name or title of a business company, fr It, signature, deriv of L *firmare* to make firm, confirm, fr *firmus*]

**firmament** /'fuhməmənt/ *n, archaic* the vault or arch of the sky; the heavens [ME, fr LL & L; LL *firmamentum*, fr L, support, fr *firmare*] – **firmamental** *adj*

**firmer chisel** /'fuhmə/ *n* a woodworking chisel with a thin flat blade [Fr *fermoir* chisel, alter. of MF *formoir*, fr *former* to form]

**firn** /fiən/ *n* NÉVÉ (partially compacted snow at the upper end of a glacier) [Ger, fr Ger dial., of the previous year, fr OHG *firni* old]

**firring** /'fuhring/ *n, building* **1** FURRING 2a **2** a wedge-shaped strip attached to the top of joists in order to give a suitable fall to a flat roof [alter. of *furring*]

¹**first** /fuhst/ *adj* **1** preceding all the rest: eg **1a** earliest **b** being the lowest forward gear or speed of a motor vehicle **c** relating to or having the most prominent and usu highest part among a group of instruments or voices ⟨*the ∼ violins of the orchestra*⟩ ⟨*sing ∼ alto in a choir*⟩ **2** least, slightest ⟨*hasn't the ∼ idea what to do*⟩ – see also at first BLUSH, in the first INSTANCE [ME, fr OE *fyrst*; akin to OHG *furist* first, OE *faran* to go – more at FARE]

   *usage* In enumerating items, first *two*, next *three*, and last *four* should probably now be preferred to the more old-fashioned two first, three next, four last. In any case, a large number must come at the end ⟨*the* first *17 chapters*⟩.

²**first** *adv* **1** before anything else; at the beginning ⟨*came ∼ and left last*⟩ ⟨∼ *of all we had cocktails*⟩ – sometimes + *off* ⟨∼ *off he thanked us for the invitation*⟩ **2** for the first time **3** in preference to something else ⟨*won't tell you, I'll die ∼*⟩ *usage* see FIRSTLY – **first and last** always and most importantly

³**first** *n, pl (2a)* **first,** *(2b,c,d,&e)* **firsts 1** – see NUMBER table **2** something or somebody that is first: e g **2a** the first occurrence or item of a kind ⟨*was one of the* ~ *to collect Picasso*⟩ **b** the first and lowest forward gear or speed of a motor vehicle **c** the highest or chief voice or instrument of a group **d** an article of merchandise of the finest grade **e(1)** the winning or highest place in a competition, examination, or contest; *also* one who has gained such a place **e(2) first, first class** *often cap* the highest level of British honours degree **3** FIRST BASE 1 – **at first** at the beginning; initially – **from the first** from the beginning

**first aid** *n* **1** emergency care or treatment given to an ill or injured person before proper medical aid can be obtained **2** temporary emergency measures taken to alleviate a problem before a permanent solution can be found – **first-aider** *n*

**first base** *n* **1** the base that must be touched first by a batter in baseball when he/she is attempting a run; *also* the position of the player defending the area round this base **2** *chiefly NAm* the first step or stage in a course of action ⟨*the plan never got to* ~⟩ – **first baseman** *n*

**firstborn** /ˈfuhstˌbawn/ *adj* born before all others; eldest – **firstborn** *n*

**first cause** *n* a cause which does not depend on any other; *esp* God regarded as the uncaused creator of the universe – compare PRIME MOVER

¹**first class** *n* the first or highest group in a classification: e g **a** the highest of usu three classes of travel accommodation **b** a postal class that enables internal mail of the United Kingdom to be sent prepaid at the highest rate to ensure prompt delivery – compare SECOND CLASS **c** FIRST 2e(2) (academic degree) – **first-class** *adj*

²**first class** *adv* **1** in the highest quality of accommodation ⟨*travel* ~⟩ **2** as first-class mail ⟨*send a letter* ~⟩

**first cousin** *n* a child of one's uncle or aunt; COUSIN 1a

**first day cover** *n* a special envelope with a newly issued postage stamp postmarked on the first day of issue

**first-degree burn** *n* a mild burn characterized by heat, pain, and reddening of the burned surface but without blistering or charring of tissues – compare SECOND-DEGREE BURN, THIRD-DEGREE BURN

**first estate** *n, often cap F&E* the 1st of the traditional political estates; *specif* the clergy

**first floor** *n* **1** *Br* the floor immediately above the GROUND FLOOR **2** *NAm* the ground floor

ˌfirst-ˈfooter, ˌfirst-ˈfoot *n, chiefly Scot* the first person to enter a household in the New Year – **first-foot** *vi*, **first-footing** *n*

**firstfruits** /ˌfuhstˈfroohts/ *n pl* **1** the earliest agricultural produce of the season, esp when offered to God in thanksgiving **2** the earliest products or results of an endeavour

**firsthand** /ˌfuhstˈhand/ *adj* of or coming directly from the original source – **firsthand** *adv*

**first lady** *n, often cap F&L* **1** the wife or hostess of a US president or state governor **2** the leading woman in a specified activity (e g an art or profession)

**first lieutenant** *n* – see MILITARY RANKS table

**firstling** /ˈfuhstling/ *n usu pl, formal* **1** the first of a class or kind **2** the first offspring, produce, or result of something

**firstly** /-li/ *adv* in the first place; first

    *usage* Older writers on usage advised that lists of items should be formed with the adverbs **first, second,** etc rather than with **firstly, secondly,** etc but there seems no longer to be any basis for this prejudice. Perhaps **first/second/third** should be preferred where the words seem more adjectival ⟨*this organ has three important functions:* **first** ... ⟩ and **firstly/secondly/thirdly** where they seem more adverbial ⟨*we must act now:* **firstly,** *because* ... ⟩

**first mate** *n* an officer second in command to the captain of a merchant ship

**first mortgage** *n* a mortgage that has priority over all other mortgages on a property except those imposed by law

**first movement form** *n* SONATA FORM

**first name** *n* the name that stands first in a person's full name; *broadly* a forename **synonyms** see CHRISTIAN NAME

**first night** *n* **1** the night on which a theatrical production is first performed at a given place **2** the performance given on a first night

ˌfirst-ˈnighter *n* a spectator at a first-night performance

**first offender** *n* a person legally convicted of an offence for the first time

**first officer** *n* **1** FIRST MATE **2** the member of an aircraft crew second in command to the captain

**first person** *n* **1** a set of linguistic forms (e g verb forms and pronouns) referring to the speaker or writer of the utterance in which they occur **2** a linguistic form (e g *am, we*) belonging to such a set

**first post** *n, Br* the first of two bugle calls sounded in a military camp at the hour of retiring for the night

**first principles** *n pl* principles that are fundamental or self-evident

¹ˌfirst-ˈrate *adj* excellent – **first-rateness** *n*, **first-rater** *n*

²**first-rate** *adv, informal* very well

**first reading** *n* the first submitting of a bill before a legislative assembly

**first refusal** *n* the right of accepting or rejecting something before it is offered to others

**first school** *n* a PRIMARY SCHOOL for children between the ages of five and eight

**first sergeant** *n* – see MILITARY RANKS table

ˌfirst-ˈstring *adj* **1** being a regular member (e g of a sports team or orchestra) as distinguished from a substitute **2** being the top player of a team in an individual sport **3** *informal* FIRST-RATE

**first string** *n* the top player of a team (e g in tennis or squash) who usu plays first against the opposition's top player

ˌfirst-ˈup *adj, Austr informal* of the first time or attempt ⟨*finishing a creditable* ~ *fourth* – *The Age (Melbourne)*⟩ – **first-up** *n*

**first water** *n* **1** the purest lustre – used with reference to gems ⟨*a diamond of the* ~⟩ **2** the highest grade, degree, or quality ⟨*a fool of the* ~ – Thomas Wolfe⟩

**firth** /fuhth/ *n* a sea inlet or estuary, esp in Scotland [ME, fr ON *fjörthr* – more at FORD]

**fisc** /fisk/ *n* a state or royal treasury [L *fiscus*]

¹**fiscal** /ˈfiskl/ *adj* **1** of taxation, public revenues, or public debt ⟨~ *policy*⟩ **2** of financial matters ⟨~ *agent*⟩ [L *fiscalis,* fr *fiscus* basket, treasury; akin to Gk *pithos* wine jar] – **fiscally** *adv*

²**fiscal** *n* **1** PROCURATOR-FISCAL (legal officer in Scotland) **2** REVENUE STAMP (indicating payment of a tax)

**fiscal year** *n* an accounting period of 12 months

¹**fish** /fish/ *n, pl* **fish, fishes 1a** an aquatic animal – usu in combination ⟨*starfish*⟩ ⟨*cuttlefish*⟩ **b** (the edible flesh of) any of numerous cold-blooded strictly aquatic VERTEBRATE animals that have typically an elongated somewhat spindle-shaped body that is usu covered in scales and terminates in a broad tail fin, limbs that when present are in the form of fins, and gills through which the blood is circulated to be oxygenated **c** *cap* PISCES (sign of the zodiac) **2** *chiefly derog* a person – usu with a disparaging adjective ⟨*a rum* ~⟩ [ME, fr OE *fisc*; akin to OHG *fisc* fish, L *piscis*] – **fishless** *adj*, **fishlike** *adj* – **fish out of water** a person who is out of his/her proper sphere or element – **have other fish to fry** to have other, esp more important, business to attend to – **neither fish nor fowl** neither one thing nor another

    *usage* **Fish** in the edible sense is a mass noun with no plural ⟨*a wine that goes well with* **fish**⟩. The plural **fish** ⟨*caught several* **fish**⟩ is commoner today than **fishes,** which is now used chiefly for different types ⟨*valuable food* **fishes** *such as the haddock and turbot*⟩.

²**fish** *vi* **1** to try to catch fish **2** to search for something underwater (e g with a dredge) ⟨~ *for pearls*⟩ **3** *informal* **3a** to seek something by roundabout means ⟨~ing *for compliments*⟩ ⟨~ing *for tasty bits of gossip*⟩ **b** to search (as if) by groping or feeling ⟨~ing *around under the bed for his shoes*⟩ ~ *vt* **1a** to try to catch fish in ⟨~ *the stream*⟩ **b** to use (e g a net, type of rod, or bait) in fishing **2a** to catch or try to catch ⟨~ *salmon*⟩ **b** *informal* to draw forth as if fishing ⟨~ed *the ball from under the car*⟩ – often + *out* ⟨~ed *a handkerchief out*⟩ □ *(vi 2&3)* usu + *for* – see also **fish in troubled** WATERS – **fishable** *adj*, **fishability** *n*

**fish out** *vt* **1** to exhaust the supply of fish in by overfishing ⟨*this lake has been* fished *out*⟩ **2** to exhaust the supply of (fish) by fishing ⟨*herring are in danger of being* fished *out*⟩

³**fish** *n* a piece of wood or iron fastened alongside another part to strengthen it [*fish* (to mend), prob fr Fr *ficher* to fix, fr (assumed) VL *figicare,* fr L *figere*]

ˌfish-and-ˈchips *n pl* one or more pieces of fried fish, esp coated with batter, and potato chips traditionally bought ready cooked and wrapped in paper

**fishbowl** /ˈfishˌbohl/ *n* a bowl for keeping live fish in

**fishcake** /ˈfishkayk/ *n* a small round flat cake made of cooked fish mixed with mashed potato

**fisher** /ˈfishə/ *n* **1** one who or that which fishes **2** (the fur of) a large dark brown N American tree-dwelling flesh-eating mammal (*Martes pennanti*) related to the weasels

**fisherfolk** /'fishə,fohk/ *n taking pl vb* people who live in a community that is dependent on fishing

**fisherman** /'fishəmən/ *n 1 fem* 'fisher,woman one who engages in fishing as an occupation or for pleasure **2** a ship used in commercial fishing **3** the oldest type of anchor, with the stock fixed at right angles to the shank

**fisherman's bend** *n* a knot used esp to secure an anchor to its cable

**fishery** /'fishəri/ *n* **1** the activity or business of catching fish and other sea animals (e g sponges or seals); *also* a place where this is carried out **2** a place where fish are reared; FISH FARM **3** the legal right to catch fish at a particular place or in particular waters **4 fisheries** *pl*, **fishery** the technology of fishing ⟨*Ministry of Agriculture and* Fisheries⟩

'**fish-,eye** *adj* being, having, or produced by a wide-angle photographic lens that has a highly curved protruding front, covers an angle of about 180°, and gives a circular image ⟨*a* ~ *lens*⟩

**fish farm** *n* a tract of water used for the artificial cultivation of an aquatic life form (e g fishes) – **fish farming** *n*

**fish finger** *n* a small oblong piece of fish coated with breadcrumbs

**fish hawk** *n* an osprey

**fishhook** /'fish,hook/ *n* a barbed hook used on the end of a line for catching fish

**fishing** /'fishing/ *n* **1** the sport or business of catching fish **2** a place for catching fish

**fish joint** *n* a BUTT JOINT of timbers or rails in which the two pieces placed end to end are held in alignment by one or more fishplates

**fish kettle** *n* a usu deep long oval vessel used for cooking fish

**fish knife** *n* a broad-bladed table knife without a sharp edge, used for eating fish

**fish ladder** *n* a series of pools arranged like steps by which fish can pass over a dam while going upstream

**fish louse** *n* any of various small flat rounded INVERTEBRATE animals (subclass Branchiura of the class Crustacea) that have suckers and a shieldlike covering (CARAPACE) and are parasitic on fish

**fish meal** *n* ground dried fish used as fertilizer and animal food

**fishmonger** /'fish,mung-gə/ *n, chiefly Br* a retail dealer in fish

**fishnet** /'fish,net/ *n* **1** netting fitted with floats and weights or a supporting frame for catching fish **2** a coarse open-mesh fabric – **fishnet** *adj*

**fishplate** /'fish,playt/ *n* a usu metal plate used to strengthen a BUTT JOINT (joint in which pieces are placed end to end); *esp* one used between lengths of railway line [³*fish* + *plate*]

**fishpond** /'fish,pond/ *n* a pond stocked with fish for eating or ornament

**fish slice** *n* **1** a broad-bladed knife for cutting and serving fish at table **2** a kitchen implement consisting of a squarish flat perforated blade, usu of metal, that is attached to a long handle and is used esp for turning or lifting food (e g in or from a frying pan)

**fishtail** /'fish,tayl/ *vi* **1** to swing the tail of an aeroplane from side to side to reduce speed, esp when landing **2** to have the rear end slide from side to side out of control while moving forward ⟨*the car* ~ed *on the icy curve*⟩ – **fishtail** *n*

**fishway** /'fish,way/ *n* FISH LADDER

**fishwife** /'fish,wief/ *n* **1** a woman who sells or guts fish **2** a vulgar abusive woman

**fishy** /'fishi/ *adj* **1** of or like fish, esp in taste or smell **2** *informal* creating doubt or suspicion; questionable

**fissile** /'fisiel/ *adj* **1** capable of being split or divided in the direction of the grain or along natural planes of cleavage ⟨~ *wood*⟩ ⟨~ *crystals*⟩ **2** capable of undergoing (nuclear) fission [L *fissilis*, fr *fissus*] – **fissility** *n*

**fission** /'fish(ə)n/ *n* **1** a splitting or breaking up into parts **2** reproduction (e g of an amoeba) by spontaneous division into two or more parts, each of which grows into a complete organism **3a** the splitting of a molecule into simpler molecules **b** the splitting of an atomic nucleus resulting in the release of large amounts of energy [L *fission-, fissio*, fr *fissus*, pp of *findere* to split – more at BITE] – **fission** *vb*, **fissionable** *n or adj*, **fissionability** *n*, **fissional** *adj*

**fission bomb** *n* ATOM BOMB

**fissiparous** /fi'sipərəs/ *adj* **1** producing new biological units or

individuals by fission **2** *formal* tending to break up into parts; divisive ⟨~ *elements in a political party*⟩ [L *fissus* + E *-parous*] – **fissiparously** *adv*, **fissiparousness** *n*

**fissiped** /'fisiped/ *adj* of a suborder (Fissipeda) of carnivores, including the cats, dogs, and bears, that are characterized by having the digits of the feet separated [LL *fissiped-, fissipes*, fr L *fissus* + *ped-, pes* foot – more at FOOT] – **fissiped** *n*

¹**fissure** /'fishə/ *n* **1** a narrow opening or crack of considerable length and depth, usu caused by breaking or parting **2** a separation or disagreement in thought or viewpoint; a rift ⟨~s *in a political party*⟩ **3a** a natural cleft between body parts or in the substance of an organ (e g the brain or liver) **b** a break or slit in tissue, usu at the junction of skin and MUCOUS MEMBRANE **c** a crack in the surface of a tooth caused by imperfect joining of the enamel during development [ME, fr MF, fr L *fissura*, fr *fissus*]

²**fissure** *vb* to crack, divide

¹**fist** /fist/ *n* **1** the hand clenched with the fingers doubled into the palm and the thumb across the fingers **2** INDEX 5 (symbol to direct the reader's attention to another part of the text) **3** *informal* **3a** HAND 1a(1) ⟨*get your* ~s *off my book*⟩ **b** handwriting [ME, fr OE *fȳst*; akin to OHG *fūst* fist, OSlav *pęsti*]

²**fist** *vt* **1** to grip with the fist; handle ⟨~ing *acres of wet canvas*⟩ **2** to hit with the fist ⟨*the goalkeeper* ~ed *the ball clear*⟩ **-fisted** /-fistid/ *comb form (adj, n → adj)* having (such or so many) fists ⟨*two-*fisted⟩ ⟨*tight*fisted⟩

**fistfight** /'fist,fiet/ *n* a punch-up

**fistful** /'fist,f(ə)l/ *n* a handful ⟨*a* ~ *of coins*⟩

**fistic** /'fistik/ *adj, humorous* of boxing or fighting with the fists

**fisticuffs** /'fisti,kufs/ *n pl, humorous* the act or practice of fighting with the fists – no longer in vogue [alter. of *fisty cuff*, fr obs *fisty* fist + *cuff*]

**fistula** /'fistyoolə/ *n, pl* **fistulas, fistulae** /-lie/ an abnormal or surgically made passage leading from an abscess or hollow organ to the body surface or from one hollow organ to another [ME, fr L, pipe, fistula]

**fistulous** /'fistyoolas/ *adj* **1** (having the form or nature) of a fistula **2** hollow like a pipe or reed

¹**fit** /fit/ *n, archaic* a division of a poem or song [ME, fr OE *fitt*; akin to OS *fittea* division of a poem, OHG *fizza* skein]

²**fit** *n* **1a** a sudden violent attack of a disease (e g epilepsy), esp when marked by convulsions or unconsciousness; a paroxysm **b** a sudden but transient attack of a specified physical disturbance ⟨*a* ~ *of shivering*⟩ **2** a sudden outburst or flurry, esp of a specified activity or emotion ⟨*a* ~ *of letter-writing*⟩ ⟨*a* ~ *of temper*⟩ [ME, fr OE *fitt* strife] – **by/in fits and starts** in an impulsive or irregular manner – **have/throw a fit** to be shocked and angry

³**fit** *adj* **-tt-** **1a(1)** adapted or suited to an end or purpose **a(2)** adapted to the environment so as to be capable of surviving **b** acceptable from a particular viewpoint (e g of competence, morality, or qualifications); worthy ⟨*not* ~ *to be a father*⟩ **2a** in a suitable state ⟨*the house isn't* ~ *to be seen*⟩ **b** in such a state as to be ready to do or suffer something specified ⟨*so tired I was* ~ *to drop*⟩ **3** HEALTHY 1 **4** *slang, of a person* attractive [ME; akin to ME *fitten*] – **fitly** *adv*, **fitness** *n* – see fit to consider proper or advisable ⟨*saw* fit *to warn him of his impending dismissal*⟩

**synonyms** Appropriate, suitable, proper, fit, meet, becoming, fitting, apt, happy, and felicitous all describe what is right or correct in given circumstances, and are often interchangeable. **Suitable** is the mildest and most neutral term. **Fit** implies something adapted to or capable of meeting certain requirements ⟨*a feast* fit *for a king*⟩. What is **appropriate** is particularly **fit** for the occasion or action in question ⟨*red roses are an* appropriate *gift for a lover*⟩. **Proper** suggests what is expected because of its nature, or considered socially **suitable** ⟨*show a* proper *respect for the dead*⟩, while **meet**, more formal, suggests suitability for reasons of justice and morality ⟨*it is* meet *to remember, however, that he was also a loving father*⟩. **Becoming** may also mean **suitable** in a social context ⟨*becoming* modesty⟩ or attractively **suitable** with regard to personal appearance ⟨*a* becoming *hairstyle*⟩. Something **fitting** is satisfyingly appropriate ⟨*the glorious sunset made a* fitting *end to a perfect day*⟩. **Apt** describes something suited to its purpose as a result of skill or discrimination ⟨*an* apt *remark to show he had been listening*⟩. **Happy**, in this sense, describes something pleasingly **apt** ⟨*her latest novel displays a* happy *combination of wit and sensitivity*⟩. **Felicitous** is a stronger and more formal synonym for **happy**.

⁴**fit** *vb* **fitted** *also* fit; **-tt-** *vt* **1** to be suitable for or to; harmonize with ⟨*sombre music that* ~ted *her mood*⟩ **2a** to be of

the correct size or shape for ⟨*this lid doesn't* ~ *the tin*⟩ **b** to insert or adjust until correctly in place ⟨~ted *the light bulb into the socket*⟩ **c(1)** to cause to try on (clothes) in order to make adjustments in size ⟨*went to the tailor's to be* ~ted *for a new suit*⟩ **c(2)** to make or find clothes of the right size for ⟨*it's difficult to* ~ *him because he's so short*⟩ **3** to be in agreement or accord with ⟨*the theory* ~s *all the facts*⟩ **4a** to put into a condition of readiness ⟨~ted *for the position by temperament and training*⟩ **b** to bring to a required form and size; adjust **c** to cause to conform to or suit something ⟨~ted *their expenditure to their means*⟩ **5** to supply, equip ⟨~ted *the ship with new engines*⟩ – often + *out* ⟨*ships* ~ted *out for war*⟩ **6** to adjust (a curve of a specified type) to a given set of points (e g to demonstrate a mathematical or esp statistical relationship) **7** *archaic* to be seemly or proper for ⟨*it* ~s *us then to be as provident as fear may teach us* – Shak⟩ ~ *vi* **1** to conform to a particular shape or size ⟨*this dress* ~s *very nicely*⟩ **2** to be in accordance with the facts or circumstances [ME *fitten,* fr or akin to MD *vitten* to be suitable; akin to OHG *fizza* skein]

**fit in** *vt* to make room, place, or time for ⟨*fitted in an hour's jogging before supper*⟩ ~ *vi* to be in harmony or accord; conform ⟨*fitted in well with her new classmates*⟩

**fit up** *vt* **1** FIX UP **2** *Br slang* FRAME 5b ⟨*was fitted up for the murder of the policeman*⟩

**⁵fit** *n* **1** the quality, state, or manner of being fitted or adapted **2** the manner in which clothing fits the wearer **3** the degree of closeness with which surfaces are brought together in an assembly of parts **4** the conformity between an experimental result and theoretical expectation or between data and an approximating curve – esp in *goodness of fit*

**⁶fit** *dial past of* FIGHT ⟨*Joshua* ~ *the battle of Jericho*⟩

**fitch** /fich/, **fitchew** /'fichooh/ *n* **1** (the fur or pelt of) the polecat **2** a paintbrush of a type originally made from polecat hair [ME *fiche, ficheux,* fr MF or MD; MF *fichau,* fr MD *vitsau*]

**fitful** /'fitf(ə)l/ *adj* having a spasmodic or intermittent character; irregular ⟨~ *sleep*⟩ *synonyms* see PERIODIC *antonyms* continuous, steady – **fitfully** *adv,* **fitfulness** *n*

**fitment** /'fitmənt/ *n* **1** a piece of equipment; *esp* an item of built-in furniture **2** FITTING 2 [⁴*fit*]

**fitter** /'fitə/ *n* somebody who assembles or repairs machinery or appliances ⟨*a gas* ~⟩ ⟨*an air frame* ~⟩

**¹fitting** /'fiting/ *adj* appropriate to the situation ⟨*made a* ~ *answer*⟩ *synonyms* see ³FIT *antonym* unfitting – **fittingly** *adv,* **fittingness** *n*

**²fitting** *n* **1** a trying on of clothes that are being made or altered **2** a small often standardized part ⟨*a plumbing* ~⟩ ⟨*an electrical* ~⟩

**five** /fiev/ *n* **1** – see NUMBER table **2** the fifth in a set or series ⟨*the* ~ *of clubs*⟩ **3** something having five parts or members or a denomination of five **4** *pl but taking sing vb* any of several singles or doubles games in which players hit a ball with their hands against the front wall of a 3- or 4-walled court **5** *chiefly Br* **5a** a note or bill for five units of currency **b** a coin worth five new pence [ME, fr *five,* adj, fr OE *fīf;* akin to OHG *finf* five, L *quinque,* Gk *pente;* (4) perh orig played by teams of five players each] – **five** *adj or pron,* **fivefold** *adj or adv*

**five o'clock shadow** *n* a just visible beard-growth on the face of a man who has not shaved for several hours (e g between morning and late afternoon)

**fiver** /'fievə/ *n, informal* **1** *chiefly Br* a £5 note; *also* the sum of £5 **2** *chiefly NAm* a $5 bill

**five-'star** *adj* of the highest rank in a system for grading excellence applied to esp hotels ⟨*a* ~ *hotel*⟩; *broadly* of the highest standard or quality

**¹fix** /fiks/ *vt* **1a** to make firm, stable, or stationary **b** to give a permanent or final form to: e g **b(1)** to change into a stable chemical compound or available form ⟨*bacteria that* ~ *nitrogen*⟩ **b(2)** to kill, harden, and preserve for microscopic study **b(3)** to make the image of (a photographic film) permanent by removing unused sensitive chemicals **b(4)** to decide upon; establish, settle ⟨~ed *a date for the wedding*⟩ ⟨~ *a price*⟩ **2a(1)** to fasten, attach ⟨~ed *the dog's lead to his collar*⟩ **a(2)** to fasten (a bayonet) to the muzzle of a rifle **a(3)** to gaze fixedly at (somebody) with ⟨~ed *him with an accusing stare*⟩ **b** to hold or direct steadily ⟨~es *his eyes on the horizon*⟩ **c** to set or place definitely **d** to assign ⟨~ *the blame*⟩ **3a** to set in order; adjust **b** to arrange ⟨*if you want to meet them, I can* ~ *it*⟩ **4** to repair, mend ⟨~ *the clock*⟩ **5** to spay, castrate **6** *chiefly NAm* to get ready or prepare (esp food or drink) ⟨*can I* ~ *you a drink?*⟩ **7** *informal* **7a** to get even with **b** to influence the actions, outcome, or effect of by illicit means ⟨*the jury had been* ~ed⟩ **8** *slang* to inject oneself with (a narcotic drug) ⟨~ing *heroin by the time she was 15*⟩ ~ *vi* **1** to become firm, stable, or fixed **2a** to decide, arrange ⟨*I've* ~ed *to go into town tomorrow*⟩ **b** to agree *on* ⟨~ed *on George as leader*⟩ ⟨~ed *on somewhere to spend their holiday*⟩ **3** *chiefly NAm* to get ready; be about to ⟨*we're* ~ing *to leave soon*⟩ **4** *slang* to inject oneself with a narcotic drug – see also **fix one's** SIGHTS **on** [ME *fixen,* fr L *fixus,* pp of *figere* to fasten – more at DYKE] – **fixable** *adj*

**fix up** *vt, informal* **1** to provide with ⟨*fixed her up with a good job*⟩ **2** to make arrangements for ⟨*fix something up for next week*⟩ ⟨*I'm already fixed up for this weekend*⟩ **3** to adapt or repair; DO UP ⟨*fixing up the nursery for the new baby*⟩ ~ *vi, NAm* to dress carefully or formally ⟨*do I have to fix up to go to the Websters?*⟩

**²fix** *n* **1** a position of difficulty or embarrassment; a trying predicament **2** (a reckoning of) the position (e g of a ship) found by bearings, observations, or radio **3** *slang* an injection of a narcotic drug

**fixate** /'fiksayt/ *vt* **1** to make fixed, stationary, or unchanging; FIX 1a **2** to direct one's gaze on **3** to arrest the psychological development of at an immature stage ⟨*he is* ~d *at the anal stage*⟩ **4** to attach (sexual energy) to an infantile form of gratification – used technically in psychoanalysis

**fixation** /fik'saysh(ə)n/ *n* the act, process, or result of fixing or fixating: e g a stereotyped behaviour (e g in response to frustration) **b** an (obsessive or unhealthy) attachment or preoccupation **c** a concentration of the LIBIDO (sexual energy) on immature forms of gratification **d** the conversion of atmospheric nitrogen into a chemical compound

**fixative** /'fiksətiv/ *n* something that fixes or sets: e g **a** a substance added to a perfume, esp to prevent too rapid evaporation **b** a substance used to fix living tissue for study under a microscope **c** a varnish used esp for the protection of crayon drawings – **fixative** *adj*

**fixed** /fikst/ *adj* **1** securely placed or fastened; stationary **2a** not tending to vaporize; nonvolatile **b** formed into a chemical compound ⟨~ *nitrogen*⟩ **3a** not subject to or capable of change or fluctuation; settled ⟨*a* ~ *income*⟩ ⟨*a camera with a* ~ *focus*⟩ **b** intent; IMMOBILE 2 ⟨*a* ~ *stare*⟩ – **fixedly** *adv,* **fixedness** *n* – **how are you fixed** what are your circumstances (with regard to) ⟨*how are you fixed for money?*⟩

**fixed capital** *n* durable CAPITAL GOODS (e g buildings or machines) used over a period of time in the production of other goods

**fixed charge** *n* **1** a regularly recurring expense (e g rent, taxes, or interest) that must be met when due **2** FIXED COST

**fixed cost** *n* a cost (e g maintenance) that does not vary with output in the short run – compare OVERHEAD

**fixed idea** *n* an often delusional obsessive idea that dominates the mind [trans of Fr *idée fixe*]

**fixed oil** *n* an esp fatty oil which does not evaporate – compare ESSENTIAL OIL

**,fixed-'point** *adj* involving or being a mathematical notation (e g in a decimal system) in which the point separating whole numbers and fractions is fixed – compare FLOATING-POINT

**fixed point** *n* **1** a temperature (e g the boiling- or freezing-point of water) which has a constant value, and is used to calibrate a thermometer or define a temperature scale **2** a point which is left unchanged by a given mathematical transformation

**fixed star** *n* any of the stars so distant that they appear to remain in one position relative to one another

**fixer** /'fiksə/ *n* a person who is adept at bringing about a desired result (e g by enabling somebody to get round the law or officialdom)

**fixing** /'fiksing/ *n* **1** the act or process of somebody who fixes **2** *pl, NAm* trimmings ⟨*a turkey dinner with all the* ~s⟩

**fixity** /'fiksəti/ *n* **1** the quality or state of being fixed or stable **2** something that is fixed; a fixture

**fixture** /'fikschə/ *n* **1** fixing or being fixed **2a** something that is fixed or attached (e g to a building) as a permanent appendage or as a structural part ⟨*a plumbing* ~⟩ ⟨*a fluorescent light* ~⟩ **b** *law* something so annexed to land or a building that it is regarded as legally a part of it **3** somebody or something invariably present in a specified setting or long associated with a place or activity ⟨*now a* ~ *as the England wicket keeper*⟩ **4** (an esp sporting event held on) a settled date or time [modif of LL *fixura,* fr L *fixus*]

**fizgig** /'fiz,gig/ *n, archaic* **1** a flirtatious young woman **2** a firework or spinning top that makes a fizzing sound [alter. of earlier *fisgig*, prob fr *fise* intestinal wind + *gig* wanton girl, spinning top]

**¹fizz** /fiz/ *vi* **1** to make a hissing or sputtering sound **2** *of a liquid* to produce bubbles of CARBON DIOXIDE [prob imit]

**²fizz** *n* **1a** a fizzing sound **b** spirit, liveliness **2a** effervescence ⟨*all the ~ has gone out of this lemonade*⟩ **b** *informal* an effervescent drink (e g champagne) – **fizzy** *adj*

**fizzer** /'fizə/ *n* **1** something that fizzes **2** *Austr* DAMP SQUIB

**¹fizzle** /'fizl/ *vi* to make a weak fizzing sound [prob alter. of obs *fist* to break wind, fr ME *fisten*]

**fizzle out** *vi, informal* to fail or end feebly, esp after a promising start

**²fizzle** *n* **1** a feeble fizzing sound **2** an abortive effort; a failure, fiasco

**fjeld** /fyeld/ *n* a barren plateau of the Scandinavian upland [Dan]

**fjord** /fyawd, 'fee,awd/ *n* a fiord [Norw *fjord*, fr ON *fjörthr* – more at FORD]

**flab** /flab/ *n, informal* soft flabby body tissue [back-formation fr *flabby*]

**flabbergast** /'flabə,gahst/ *vt, informal* to overwhelm with shock, astonishment, or wonder; dumbfound **synonyms** see ²SURPRISE [perh fr *flabby* + *aghast*]

**flabby** /'flabi/ *adj* **1a** lacking resilience or firmness ⟨*a ~ paunch*⟩ ⟨*~ muscles*⟩ **b** having flabby flesh ⟨*fat and ~ after months of inactivity*⟩ **2** weak and ineffective; feeble ⟨*a ~ and violent movie – Time Out*⟩ [alter. of *flappy*] – **flabbily** *adv*, **flabbiness** *n*

**flabellate** /flə'belayt, -lət/ *adj, of a plant or animal part* shaped like a fan

**flabelli-** /flə'beli-/ *comb form* fan ⟨*flabelliform*⟩ [L, fr *flabellum*]

**flabellum** /flə'beləm/ *n, pl* **flabella** /-lə/ a body organ or part resembling a fan [NL, fr L, fan]

**flaccid** /'flaksid/ *adj* **1a** lacking normal or youthful firmness; flabby ⟨*~ muscles*⟩ **b** *botany* LIMP – compare TURGID 1 **2** lacking vigour or force ⟨*~ leadership*⟩ [L *flaccidus*, fr *flaccus* flabby] –**flaccidly** *adv*, **flaccidity** *n*

**¹flack** /flak/ *n, NAm informal* a person who provides publicity; *esp* PRESS AGENT [origin unknown]

**²flack** *n* FLAK

**¹flag** /flag/ *n* (the leaf of) an esp wild iris or similar plant having long bladelike leaves and growing esp in damp ground [ME *flagge* reed, rush]

**²flag, flagstone** /'flag,stohn/ *n* **1** a hard smooth-textured stone that can be split into flat pieces suitable for paving; *also* a piece of such stone **2** *pl* a floor or pavement made of flags [ME *flagge*, fr ON *flaga* slab; akin to OE *flēan* to flay – more at FLAY]

**³flag** *vt* **-gg-** to lay (e g a pavement) with flags

**⁴flag** *n* **1** a usu rectangular piece of fabric of distinctive design that is used as a symbol (e g of a nation) or as a signalling device; *esp* one flown from a single vertical staff **2** something used like a flag to signal, mark, or attract attention **3a** FLAGSHIP (ship with commanding admiral on board) **b** an admiral functioning in his office of command **c** NATIONALITY 2; *esp* the nationality of registration of a ship, aircraft, etc **4** *NAm* MASTHEAD 2b (title of a newspaper, periodical, etc printed on the first page) [perh fr ¹*flag*] – **keep the flag flying** to continue to represent opinions and ideas that one believes in, esp in the face of opposition

**⁵flag** *vt* **-gg-** **1** to decorate or mark with a flag or flags ⟨*~ged the streets in honour of the royal wedding*⟩ ⟨*~ged the important pages by clipping red tabs to the margin*⟩ **2** to signal to (as if) with a flag **3** to signal to stop – usu + *down* ⟨*~ged the train down*⟩

**⁶flag** *vi* **-gg-** **1a** to hang loose without stiffness **b** *of a plant* to droop, esp from lack of water **2** to become feeble, weary, less interesting, or less active; decline ⟨*his interest ~ged*⟩ ⟨*when everyone had had a say the topic ~ged*⟩ [origin unknown]

**flag day** *n, Br* a day on which charitable contributions are solicited in exchange for small paper flags on pins or, more recently, stickers

**flagellant** /'flajilənt/ *n* **1** a person who scourges him-/herself as a public penance **2** a person who responds sexually to being beaten by or to beating another person – **flagellant** *adj*, **flagellantism** *n*

**flagellar** /flə'jelə, 'flajələ/ *adj* of a flagellum

**¹flagellate** /'flajilayt/ *vt* to whip or flog, esp as a religious punishment or for sexual gratification [L *flagellatus*, pp of

*flagellare*, fr *flagellum*, dim. of *flagrum* whip; akin to ON *blaka* to wave]

**²flagellate** /'flajilət/, **flagellated** /-laytid/ *adj* **1a** having flagella **b** shaped like a flagellum **2** of or caused by flagellated PROTOZOANS (single-celled microorganisms) [NL *flagellatus*, fr *flagellum*]

**³flagellate** /'flajilət/ *n* a single-celled organism (PROTOZOAN) or an algal cell that has a flagellum [NL *Flagellata*, class of single-celled organisms, fr neut pl of *flagellatus*]

**¹flagellation** /,flaji'laysh(ə)n/ *n* the act or practice of flagellating; *esp* the practice of a flagellant

**²flagellation** *n* the formation or arrangement of flagella

**flagellum** /flə'jeləm/ *n, pl* **flagella** /-lə/ *also* **flagellums** any of various elongated filament-shaped appendages of plants or animals: e g **a** the slender part of an antenna furthest from an animal's body **b** a long whiplike extension that projects singly or in groups from a cell and is the primary organ of motion of many microorganisms **c** a long slender shoot [NL, fr L, whip, shoot of a plant]

**¹flageolet** /,flajə'let/ *n* a high-pitched musical instrument of the recorder family with six or eight finger holes [Fr, fr OF *flajolet*, fr *flajol* flute, fr (assumed) VL *flabeolum*, fr L *flare* to blow – more at BLOW]

**²flageolet** *n* FRENCH BEAN [Fr, modif of Prov *faioulet*, deriv of L *phaseolus* kidney bean]

**flagging** /'flaging/ *n* (a pavement or walk of) flagstones

**flagitious** /flə'jishəs/ *adj, formal* marked by outrageous or scandalous crime or vice; villainous [ME *flagicious*, fr L *flagitiosus*, fr *flagitium* shameful thing; akin to L *flagrum* whip] – **flagitiously** *adv*, **flagitiousness** *n*

**flagman** /'flagmən/ *n* a person who signals (as if) with a flag

**flag of convenience** *n* the flag of a country in which a ship is registered in order to avoid the taxes and regulations of the owner's home country

**flag officer** *n* any of the officers in the navy or coastguard above captain – compare GENERAL OFFICER [fr his being entitled to display a flag with one or more stars indicating his rank]

**flag of truce** *n* a white flag carried or displayed to an enemy as an invitation to conference or parley

**flagon** /'flagən/ *n* **1a** a large usu metal or pottery vessel with a handle and spout and often a lid, used esp for pouring alcoholic liquids at table **b** a large squat short-necked usu glass bottle that often has one or two ear-shaped handles and in which alcoholic drinks, esp cider or wine, may be sold **2** the contents of or quantity contained in a flagon [ME, fr MF *flascon*, *flacon* bottle, fr LL *flascon-*, *flasco* – more at FLASK]

**flagpole** /'flag,pohl/ *n* a usu long pole on which to raise a flag

**flag rank** *n* the rank of a flag officer

**flagrant** /'flaygrənt/ *adj* **1** conspicuously scandalous; outrageous ⟨*~ neglect of duty*⟩ **2** *archaic* flaming, glowing [L *flagrant-*, *flagrans*, prp of *flagrare* to burn – more at BLACK] – **flagrance, flagrancy** *n*, **flagrantly** *adv*

**flagrante delicto** /flə,granti di'liktoh/ *adv* IN FLAGRANTE DELICTO (in the act of committing an offence) [ML, lit., while the crime is blazing]

**flagship** /'flag,ship/ *n* **1** the ship that carries the commander of a fleet or subdivision of a fleet and flies his flag **2** the finest, largest, or most important member of a group (e g of a fleet of ships or a chain of newspapers)

**flagstaff** /'flag,stahf/ *n* a flagpole; *also* a usu short pole or stick to which a flag is attached, esp for carrying (e g by hand)

**flagstick** /'flag,stik/ *n* a removable upright stick centred in a golf hole to show its position

**flagstone** /'flag,stohn/ *n* ²FLAG (stone used for floors, pavements, etc)

**flag stop** *n, NAm* REQUEST STOP

**'flag-,waving** *n* passionate appeal to patriotic or partisan sentiment; jingoism – **flag-waver** *n*

**¹flail** /flayl/ *n* a hand threshing implement consisting of a short stout free-swinging stick attached to a wooden handle [ME *fleil, flail*, partly fr (assumed) OE *flegel* (akin to OHG *flegil* flail; both fr a prehistoric WGmc word borrowed fr LL *flagellum* flail, fr L, whip) & partly fr MF *flaiel*, fr LL *flagellum* – more at FLAGELLATE]

**²flail** *vt* **1a** to strike (as if) with a flail ⟨*~ing his opponent about the head*⟩ **b** to swing or beat as though wielding a flail ⟨*~ing his arms to ward off the insects*⟩ **2** to thresh (grain) with a flail ~ *vi* to wave, thrash ⟨*her legs ~ing in the water*⟩ – often + *about*

**flair** /fleə/ *n* **1** discriminating sense; intuitive discernment, esp in a specified field ⟨*a* ~ *for style*⟩ **2** natural aptitude; talent ⟨*shows little* ~ *for the subject*⟩ **3** a uniquely attractive quality; *esp* sophistication or smartness ⟨*cars with real* ~⟩ □ (*1&2*) usu + *for* △

**flare** [Fr, lit., sense of smell, fr OF, odour, fr *flairier* to give off an odour, fr LL *flagrare*, fr L *fragrare* – more at FRAGRANT]

**flak, flack** /flak/ *n* **1** the fire from antiaircraft guns **2** *informal* heavy criticism or opposition ⟨*this modest proposal ran into a lot of* ~⟩ [Ger *flak,* fr *fliegerabwehrkanonen,* fr *flieger* flyer + *abwehr* defence + *kanonen* guns]

¹**flake** /flayk/ *n* a platform, tray, etc for drying fish or other produce [ME, hurdle, fr ON *flaki;* akin to OHG *flah* smooth, Gk *pelagos* sea, L *placēre* to please – more at PLEASE]

²**flake** *n* **1** a small loose mass or particle ⟨*soap* ~s⟩ ⟨*a snow-flake*⟩ **2** a thin flattened piece or layer that has become detached or chipped from a surface or object **3** a pipe tobacco consisting of small irregularly cut pieces [ME, of Scand origin; akin to Norw *flak* disc]

³**flake** *vi* to come away in flakes – usu + *off* ~ *vt* **1** to form or separate into flakes ⟨~d *fish*⟩ **2** to cover (as if) with flakes – **flaker** *n*

⁴**flake** *n* the flesh of certain small sharks eaten in Australia [perh fr ²*flake*]

**flake out** *vi, informal* to collapse or fall asleep from exhaustion [perh fr obs *flake* to become languid, var of ⁶*flag,* or perh fr E dial. *flake* to lie down, bask]

**flake white** *n* pigment made from the chemical compound WHITE LEAD [²*flake*]

**flak jacket** *n* a jacket of heavy fabric containing shields (e g of metal or plastic) for protection, esp against enemy fire

**flaky** /'flayki/ *adj* **1** consisting of flakes ⟨~ *snow*⟩ **2** tending to flake ⟨~ *paint*⟩ – **flakiness** *n*

**flaky pastry** *n* rich pastry composed of numerous very thin layers and used for pies, tarts, etc

¹**flam** /flam/ *n* **1** *dial* humbug, nonsense **2** *informal* a falsehood, trick [prob short for *flimflam*]

²**flam** *n* a drumbeat of two strokes of which the first is very quick [prob imit]

¹**flambé** /'flombay (*Fr* flãbe)/ *adj, of food* sprinkled with brandy, rum, etc and ignited – used postpositively ⟨*pineapple* ~⟩ [Fr, pp of *flamber* to flame, singe, fr OF, fr *flambe* flame]

²**flambé** *vt* **flambéed; flambéing** to sprinkle (food) with brandy, rum, etc and ignite ⟨*pineapple* ~ed *with kirsch*⟩ [Fr, pp *flamber* to flame, singe, fr OF, fr *flambe* flame]

**flambeau** /'flamboh/ *n, pl* **flambeaux, flambeaus** /'flomboh(z)/ a flaming torch; *broadly* TORCH 1 [Fr, fr MF, fr *flambe* flame]

¹**flamboyant** /flam'boyənt/ *adj* **1** *often cap, of architecture* characterized by waving curves suggesting flames ⟨*windows ornamented with* ~ *tracery*⟩ **2** ornate, florid; *also* resplendent **3** given to dashing display; showy, ostentatious [Fr, fr prp of *flamboyer* to flame, fr OF, fr *flambe*] – **flamboyance, flamboyancy** *n,* **flamboyantly** *adv*

²**flamboyant** *n* a showy tropical tree (*Delonix regia*) of the pea family that is widely planted for its large stems of scarlet and orange flowers

¹**flame** /flaym/ *n* **1a** the glowing gaseous part of a fire **b** a tongue of flame **2a** **flames** *pl,* **flame** a state of blazing usu destructive combustion ⟨*the car burst into* ~⟩ ⟨*the whole city was in* ~s⟩ **b** a condition or appearance (e g a light ray) suggesting a flame, esp in having red, orange, or yellow colour **c** brilliance, brightness **d** a bright reddish-orange colour **3** ardour or passion ⟨*the* ~ *of his desire*⟩ **4** a sweetheart – usu in *old flame* [ME *flaume, flaumbe,* fr MF *flamme* (fr L *flamma*) & *flambe,* fr OF, fr *flamble,* fr L *flammula,* dim. of *flamma* flame; akin to L *flagrare* to burn – more at BLACK] – **flame** *adj*

²**flame** *vi* **1** to burn with a flame; blaze **2** to break out violently or passionately ⟨*flaming with indignation*⟩ **3** to shine brightly like flame; glow ⟨*colour flaming in her cheeks*⟩ ~ *vt* to treat or affect with flame: e g **a** to cleanse, sterilize, or destroy by fire **b** to flambé – **flamer** *n*

**flame cell** *n* a hollow cell having a tuft of small hairlike structures (CILIA) whose motion encourages the passage of material through the cell, that forms part of the excretory system of various lower INVERTEBRATE animals (e g flatworms)

**flamen** /'flaymen/ *n, pl* **flamens, flamines** /'flamineez/ a priest of ancient Rome dedicated to the service of a particular deity [ME *flamin,* fr L *flamin-, flamen*]

**flamenco** /flə'mengkoh/ *n, pl* **flamencos** **1** a vigorous rhythmic dance style of the Andalusian gypsies; *also* a dance in flamenco style **2** music or song suitable to accompany a flamenco dance [Sp, Flemish, like a gypsy, fr MD *Vlaminc* Fleming]

**flameout** /'flaym,owt/ *n* an unintentional halt in the working of an aeroplane's jet engine

**flame photometer** *n* a SPECTROPHOTOMETER (instrument that measures the intensity of light of a particular wavelength in a spectrum) in which a spray of metallic chemical compounds in solution is vaporized in a very hot flame and subjected to quantitative analysis by measuring the intensities of the spectrum lines of the metals present – **flame photometric** *adj,* **flame photometry** *n*

**flameproof** /'flaym,proohf, -proof/ *adj* resistant to the destructive action of flame; *esp* not burning on contact with flame – **flameproof** *vt,* **flameproofer** *n*

**flamethrower** /'flaym,throh·ə/ *n* a device or weapon that expels a burning stream of liquid under pressure

**flametree** /'flaym,tree/ *n* any of several ornamental Australian trees (e g the species *Brachychiton acerifolium*) with vivid scarlet bell-shaped flowers

¹**flaming** /'flayming/ *adj* **1** in flames or on fire; blazing **2** resembling or suggesting a flame in colour or brilliance ⟨*the* ~ *sunset sky*⟩ ⟨~ *red hair*⟩ **3** passionate, violent ⟨*had a* ~ *row with the boss*⟩ **4** *slang* – used as a meaningless intensive ⟨*you* ~ *idiot!*⟩ – **flamingly** *adv*

²**flaming** *adv* – used as a meaningless intensive ⟨*not* ~ *likely*⟩

**flamingo** /flə'ming·goh/ *n, pl* **flamingos** *also* **flamingoes** any of several aquatic birds (family Phoenicopteridae) with long legs and neck, webbed feet, a broad downward-bent bill, and usu rosy-white plumage with scarlet and black markings [Pg, fr Sp *flamenco,* prob fr OProv *flamenc,* fr *flama* flame, fr L *flamma*]

**flammable** /'flaməbl/ *adj* INFLAMMABLE 1 *usage* see IN-FLAMMABLE **antonym** nonflammable [L *flammare* to flame, set on fire, fr *flamma*] – **flammable** *n,* **flammability** *n*

**flan** /flan/ *n* **1** an open case of pastry or sponge cake containing a sweet or savoury filling – compare QUICHE **2** the metal disc from which a coin, token, or medal is made, as distinguished from the design and lettering stamped on it [Fr, fr OF *flaon,* fr LL *fladon-, flado* flat cake]

**flaneur** /fla'nuh (*Fr* flanœːr)/ *n* an aimless person; *esp* an idler, dilettante [Fr *flâneur* idler]

¹**flange** /flanj/ *n* a projecting collar, rib, or rim on an object for strength, for guiding, or for attachment to another object ⟨*a* ~ *on a pipe*⟩ ⟨*a* ~ *on a wheel*⟩ [perh alter. of *flanch* (a curving charge on a heraldic shield), fr ME *flaunche,* prob fr MF *flanche* flank, fr *flanc*]

²**flange** *vt* to provide with a flange – **flanger** *n*

¹**flank** /flangk/ *n* **1a** the fleshy part of the side, esp of a 4-legged animal, between the ribs and the hip; *broadly* the side of a 4-legged animal **b** a cut of meat from the flank of an animal **2a** a side ⟨*sheltering on the* ~ *of the hill*⟩ **b** the right or left of a formation ⟨*attacked the enemy on both* ~s⟩ [ME, fr OF *flanc,* of Gmc origin; akin to OHG *hlanca* loin, flank – more at LANK]

²**flank** *vt* **1** to protect a flank of **2a** to attack or threaten the flank of (e g a body of troops) **b** to pass along or round (a flank) **3a** to be situated at the side of; border ⟨*a road* ~ed *with lime trees*⟩ **b** to place something on each side of – usu + *with* ⟨~ed *the fireplace with china dogs*⟩

**flanker** /'flangkə/ *n* a player in some games (e g RUGBY UNION or AMERICAN FOOTBALL) positioned on the outside of the forward line; *esp* WING FORWARD (rugby union forward)

¹**flannel** /'flanl/ *n* **1a** a soft twilled wool or worsted fabric with a loose texture and a slightly downy surface **b** a stout cotton fabric usu downy on one side **2** *pl* garments of flannel; *esp* men's trousers **3** *Br* a cloth used for washing the skin, esp of the face **4** *Br informal* **4a** nonsense, rubbish ⟨*everything he said was a load of* ~⟩ **b** flattering or evasive talk [ME *flaunneol* woollen cloth or garment] – **flannel** *adj,* **flannelly** *adj*

²**flannel** *vb* -ll- (*NAm* -l-, -ll-) *chiefly Br informal vi* to speak or write flannel, esp with intent to deceive ~ *vt* to make (one's way) or persuade (someone) to one's advantage by flannelling

**flannelette** /,flanl'et/ *n* a downy cotton flannel

**flannel flower** *n* any of various Australian plants (genus *Actinotus*) with a white flannel-like frill beneath the flower

¹**flap** /flap/ *n* **1** a stroke with something broad; a slap **2** something broad or flat, flexible or hinged, and usu thin, that hangs loose or projects freely: e g **2a** an extended part forming a closure (e g of an envelope or carton) **b** a movable control surface on an aircraft wing for increasing lift or lift and drag **c** a piece of tissue partly severed from its place of origin, for use in surgical grafting **3** the sound or motion of something broad and flexible (e g a sail) moving to and fro or up and down; *also*

an instance of the up-and-down motion of a wing (eg of a bird) **4** a consonant sound (eg /r/ in *carrot*) made by flapping the tongue **5** *informal* a state of excitement or panicky confusion *synonyms* see ¹FUSS [ME *flappe*, prob of imit origin]

²**flap** *vb* **-pp-** *vt* **1** to cause to move esp noisily to and fro or up and down ⟨*the wind kept* ~ping *his scarf in his face*⟩ **2** to strike with a broad flexible object ⟨~ped *him in the face with the newspaper*⟩ **3** to move (wings, arms, etc) up and down (as if) in flying ~ *vi* **1** to move esp noisily to and fro or up and down ⟨*sails* ~ping *in the wind*⟩ **2a** to move wings, arms, etc up and down (as if) in flying **b** to progress by flapping ⟨*birds* ~ping *lazily across the sky*⟩ **c** to flutter ineffectively ⟨*a sparrow* ~ping *desperately against the window*⟩ **3** *informal* to be in a flap or panic

**flapdoodle** /'flap,doohdl/ *n*, *informal* nonsense [origin unknown]

**flapjack** /'flap,jak/ *n* **1** a thick pancake cooked on a griddle **2** a biscuit made with rolled oats and syrup [²*flap* + *Jack* (the name)]

**flapper** /'flapə/ *n* **1a** one who or that which flaps **b** an implement that can be flapped (eg to scare birds or swat flies) **c** FLIPPER 1 **2** *informal* a young woman; *specif* a young woman of the period of World War I and the twenties who exhibited freedom from conventions in conduct and dress

**flappy** /'flapi/ *adj* flapping or tending to flap

¹**flare** /fleə/ *vi* **1** to burn with an unsteady flame **2a** to shine or blaze with a sudden flame ⟨*a match* ~d *in the darkness*⟩ **b** to become suddenly and often violently excited, angry, or active – usu + *up* ⟨~s *up at the slightest aggravation*⟩ ⟨*fighting* ~d *up again*⟩ **c** ¹LASH 3 – usu + *out* **3** to open or spread outwards; *esp* to widen gradually towards the lower edge ⟨*the trousers* ~ *slightly*⟩ ⟨*her nostrils* ~d *angrily*⟩ ~ *vt* **1** to cause to flare **2** to signal with a flare or by flaring **3** to provide with a flare ⟨*a* ~d *skirt*⟩ [origin unknown]

²**flare** *n* **1** a (sudden) unsteady glaring light or flame **2a** (a device or substance used to produce) a fire or blaze of light used to signal, illuminate, or attract attention ⟨*the aircraft dropped* ~s *to illuminate the target*⟩ **b** a temporary outburst of energy **(1)** from a small area of the sun's surface; SOLAR FLARE (2) from a star, often amounting to an increase of several magnitudes in its brightness **3** a sudden outburst (eg of sound, excitement, or anger) **4** a spreading outward; *also* a place or part that spreads ⟨*the* ~ *of a fireplace*⟩ ⟨*jeans with wide* ~s⟩ **5** an area of flushed skin surrounding an inflamed or raised area **6** light resulting from reflection (eg between lens surfaces) or an (unwanted) effect of this light (eg a fogged or dense area in a photographic negative) △ flair

**flarepath** *n* /'fleə,pahth/ an illuminated area enabling aircraft to land or take off in low visibility

**flarestack** /-,stak/ *n* a device (eg at an oil well) for burning unwanted material (eg gas)

¹**flare-,up** *n* **1** a sudden burst of fire or light **2** an outburst of emotion, activity, or violence ⟨*a new* ~ *of border disputes*⟩

¹**flash** /flash/ *vi* **1** *of flowing water* to rush, dash **2a** to burst violently into flames ⟨*the hydrogen* ~ed⟩ **b** to break forth in or like a sudden flame or flare ⟨*lightning* ~ing *in the sky*⟩ **3a** to appear suddenly ⟨*an idea* ~es *into her mind*⟩ **b** to move with great speed ⟨*the days* ~ *by*⟩ **4a** to break forth or out so as to make a sudden display ⟨*the sun* ~ed *from behind a cloud*⟩ **b** to act or speak vehemently and suddenly, esp in anger – often + *out* **5a** to give off light suddenly or in transient bursts **b** to glow or gleam, esp with animation or passion ⟨*his eyes* ~ed *in a sinister fashion*⟩ **6** *of a liquid* to change suddenly or violently into vapour ⟨*hot water* ~ing *to steam under reduced pressure*⟩ **7** *slang* to expose the genitals in public; commit the offence of indecent exposure ~ *vt* **1a** to cause the sudden appearance or reflection of (esp light) **b(1)** to cause (eg a mirror) to reflect light **b(2)** to cause (a light) to flash **c** to convey by means of flashes of light **d** to cause to burst violently into flame; *also* to burn (a chemical compound) to determine its chemical composition by examining the resulting substances **2a** to make known or cause to appear suddenly and with great speed ⟨~ *a message on the screen*⟩ **b** to display ostentatiously ⟨*always* ~es *his fat wallet in public*⟩ **c** to expose to view suddenly and briefly ⟨~ing *a shy smile*⟩ **3** to cover with or form into a thin layer: eg **3a** to protect against rain by covering with sheet metal or a substitute **b** to coat (eg glass) with a thin layer (eg of metal or a differently coloured glass) **4** to subject (something) to a short pulse of radiation; *esp* to give (a photographic film) a

supplementary uniform exposure to light before development in order to modify detail or tone **5a** to fill (eg a river) by a sudden inflow of water **b** to carry (a vessel) along a river by flashing **6** *archaic* to splash [ME *flaschen*, of imit origin]

*synonyms* **Flash, flicker, glimmer, glance, glint, glitter, sparkle, scintillate, twinkle,** and **shimmer** all describe the emission or reflection of unsteady or discontinuous light. **Flash** implies a sudden, transient brilliance ⟨*a torch* **flashed** *in the darkness*⟩. **Flicker,** producing less light, suggests the fluctuating intensity of flames. **Glimmer,** linked to "gleam", implies subdued and unsteady light. **Glance** and **glint** both describe reflected light, darting off a surface at an oblique angle: the former stresses movement and the latter brightness. **Glitter** and **sparkle** are closely related: both suggest many points of bright light flashing continually. Figuratively, **sparkle** suggests vivacity and animation, while **glitter** has a harsh, and sometimes sinister ring to it. These connotations affect the literal meaning: a **sparkling** *sea* is inviting; a **glittering** *sea* may be cruel, and is certainly more brilliant. **Scintillate** suggests continuous sparkling, while **twinkle** implies intermittent sparkling, like a star. **Shimmer** suggests a gentler light than **scintillate,** as of light reflected off water or material ⟨*the lake* **shimmered** *in the moonlight*⟩. Compare BRIGHT, ¹GLOW

²**flash** *n* **1a** a sudden burst of light ⟨*a* ~ *of lightning*⟩ **b** a movement of a flag in signalling **2** a sudden burst of perception, emotion, etc ⟨*a* ~ *of wit*⟩ ⟨*had a* ~ *of intuition*⟩ **3** a short time ⟨*I'll be back in a* ~⟩ **4** a rush of water released down a river, canal, etc to permit passage of a boat **5a** a brief look; a glimpse **b** a brief news report, esp on radio or television **c** FLASHLIGHT 2; *also* flashlight photography **d** a quick-spreading flame or momentary intense outburst of radiant heat **6** a thin ridge on a cast or forged article, resulting from the hot metal, plastic, etc penetrating between the two parts of the mould **7** a mixture of chemical compounds (SALTS) used to give a glaze to tiles or bricks **8** a patch of bright colour against a dark background (eg on an animal's coat) **9** *Br* a patch of coloured cloth or other emblem on a uniform, vehicle, etc identifying its military unit **10** *slang* an immediate brief intensely pleasurable feeling resulting from an intravenous injection (eg of heroin or amphetamines) **11** *slang* an act of indecent exposure of the genitals **12** *archaic* a showy ostentatious person **13** *archaic* an esp vulgar or ostentatious display – **flash in the pan** (something or somebody enjoying) an apparently promising success that proves to be of no lasting worth or significance [fr the firing of the gunpowder in the pan of a flintlock musket without discharging the gun]

³**flash** *adj* **1** of sudden origin or onset and usu short duration ⟨*a* ~ *fire*⟩; *also* carried out very quickly ⟨~ *freezing of food*⟩ **2** *informal* flashy, showy **3** *archaic slang* (characteristic) of people considered social outcasts (eg criminals or tramps) ⟨~ *language*⟩

**flashback** /-,bak/ *n* **1** (an) interruption of chronological sequence in a literary, theatrical, or cinematic work by interpolation of events which occurred earlier **2** a burst of flame back or out to an unwanted position (eg in a furnace)

**flashboard** /'flash,bawd/ *n* one or more boards projecting above the top of a dam to increase its height and therefore capacity

**flashbulb** /-,bulb/ *n* an electric FLASH LAMP in which metal foil or wire is burned

**flash card** *n* a card bearing words, numbers, or pictures for brief display as a learning aid

**flashcube** /-,kyoohb/ *n* a cubical camera attachment incorporating four flashbulbs for taking four photographs in quick succession

**flasher** /'flashə/ *n* **1a** a light (eg a traffic signal or car indicator light) that catches the attention by flashing **b** a device for automatically flashing a light **2** *slang* one who commits the offence of indecent exposure

**flash flood** *n* a brief but heavy local flood, usu resulting from torrential rainfall in the immediate vicinity and occurring esp in desert or semiarid regions – **flash flood** *vi*

,**flash-'forward** *n* (an) interruption of chronological sequence of events in a literary, theatrical, or cinematic work by interpolation of events or scenes which will occur in the future

**flashgun** /-,gun/ *n* a device, attached to or incorporated in a camera, for holding and operating a photographic flashlight or flashtube

**flashing** /'flashing/ *n* sheet metal used in waterproofing a roof or the angle between a vertical surface and a roof [fr gerund of ¹*flash* vt 3a]

**flash lamp** *n* **1** a portable flashing light **2** a usu electric lamp for producing flashlight for taking photographs

**flashlight** /-,liet/ *n* **1** (the source of) a usu regularly flashing light used for signalling (eg in a lighthouse) **2 flashlight, flash** (a photograph taken with) a sudden bright artificial light used in taking photographic pictures **3** *chiefly NAm* an electric torch

**flashover** /-,ohvə/ *n* **1** an abnormal electrical discharge (eg through the air to the ground from a thundercloud or over the surface of an insulator) **2** the sudden spread of flame when the vapour above a liquid becomes heated to the FLASH POINT

**flash point** /'flash,poynt/ *n* **1** the lowest temperature at which the vapour above an easily vaporized combustible substance can be ignited in air **2** a point at which someone or something bursts suddenly into violence, action, or being

**flashtube** /-,tyoohb/ *n* a gas-filled DISCHARGE TUBE (tube in which a discharge of electricity occurs) that produces very brief intense flashes of light and is used esp in photography

**flashy** /'flashi/ *adj* **1** transitorily dazzling or attractive **2** ostentatious or showy, esp beyond the bounds of good taste – **flashily** *adv*, **flashiness** *n*

**flask** /flahsk/ *n* **1** a container or bottle typically having a relatively narrow neck and usu fitted or provided with a top: eg **1a flask, hip flask** a broad flattened bottle typically of metal or leather-covered glass that is used to carry drinks, esp alcoholic spirits, on the person (eg in a pocket or fastened to a belt) **b** any of several conical, spherical, etc narrow-necked usu glass containers used in a laboratory, esp for liquids **c** VACUUM FLASK **2** the contents of or quantity contained in a flask [MF *flasque* powder flask, deriv of LL *flascon-, flasco* bottle, prob of Gmc origin; akin to OHG *flaska* bottle]

**¹flat** /flat/ *adj* **-tt-** **1** having a continuous horizontal surface **2a** lying at full length or spread out on a surface; prostrate **b** resting with a surface against something **3** having a smooth or even surface **4** having little thickness or depth; shallow ⟨a ~ *piece of wood*⟩ ⟨a ~ *dish*⟩ **5** *of a shoe* having an unraised or only partially raised heel **6a** clearly unmistakable; downright ⟨*gave a ~ denial*⟩ **b** fixed, absolute ⟨*charged a ~ rate*⟩ **c** exact ⟨*got to work in 10 minutes ~*⟩ **7a** lacking animation, zest, or variation; dull, monotonous ⟨*how weary, stale, ~ and unprofitable, seem to me all the uses of this world* – Shak⟩ ⟨*she spoke in a ~ voice*⟩; *also* inactive ⟨*trade is a bit ~ just now*⟩ **b** having lost effervescence or sparkle ⟨~ *beer*⟩ **8a** *of a tyre* lacking air; deflated **b** *of a battery* having lost some or all of its stored electrical energy; completely or partially discharged **9a** *of a musical note* **9a(1)** lowered a semitone in pitch **a(2)** lower than the proper or intended pitch – compare ¹SHARP **7a, b** *of the vowel "a"* pronounced as in *fat* rather than as in *father* **10a** having a low trajectory ⟨*threw a fast ~ ball*⟩ **b** *of a tennis ball or shot* hit squarely without spin **11a** uniform in colour or shade **b** *of a painting* lacking illusion of depth **c(1)** *of a photograph or negative* lacking contrast **c(2)** *of lighting for photography* not emphasizing shadows or contours **d** *esp of paint* having a matt finish **12** *chiefly Br* **12a** *of races or racecourses* having no obstacles to be jumped **b** of flat racing as opposed to steeplechasing or hurdling ⟨*he's a ~ jockey*⟩ *synonyms* see ³LEVEL *usage* see ³FLAT *antonyms* concave, convex [ME, fr ON *flatr*; akin to OHG *flaz* flat, Gk *platys* – more at PLACE] – **flatly** *adv*, **flatness** *n*, **flattish** *adj* – **fall flat** to prove unsuccessful, esp by failing to amuse

**²flat** *n* **flats** *pl, also* **flat** an area of level usu low-lying ground; a plain ⟨*mud ~*⟩ **2** a flat part or surface ⟨*the ~ of one's hand*⟩ **3** (a character indicating) a musical note one semitone lower than a specified note **4a** a shallow box in which seedlings are started **b** a flat piece of theatrical scenery ( see PANE 1b **5** a flat tyre **6** *often cap* (the season of) flat racing ⟨*the end of the ~*⟩

**³flat** *adv* **1a** on or against a flat surface **b** so as to be spread out at full length **2** positively, uncompromisingly ⟨*turned the offer down ~*⟩ **3** below the proper musical pitch ⟨*she sings ~*⟩ – compare ²SHARP **3** **4** *informal* wholly, completely ⟨~ *broke*⟩ ⟨*she went ~ against his advice*⟩

*usage* The adverbs **flat** and **flatly** can each mean "completely" or "positively", but are each used in certain fixed phrases. One can **flatly** *refuse, deny,* or *oppose* something, or be **flat** *broke.*

**⁴flat** *vb* **-tt-** to flatten

**⁵flat** *n* a self-contained set of rooms used as a dwelling [alter. (influenced by ¹*flat*) of Sc *flet* floor, dwelling, fr ME, fr OE; akin to ON *flatr* flat, level]

**⁶flat** *vi* **-tt-** *NZ* to live in a flat ⟨*roughs who ~ ted over the road* – The Listener *(New Zealand)*⟩

**flatbed** /'flat,bed/ *adj, of a printing press* having a horizontal bed on which a revolving paper-bearing cylinder rests

**flatboat** /'flat,boht/ *n* a boat with a flat bottom and square ends used for bulky freight, esp in shallow waters

**flatbug** /'flat,bug/ *n* any of various broad flat TRUE BUGS (family Aradidae) that live under loose bark where they feed on fungi

**flat cap** *n* CLOTH CAP 1

**flatcar** /'flat,kah/ *n, NAm* a goods wagon without raised sides, ends, or covering

**flat-'chested** *adj, of a woman* having very small breasts

**flat-coated retriever** *n* (any of) an English breed of active medium-sized gundogs that have a close dense smooth black or liver-coloured coat and a rather long head

**flat-'earther** *n* one who believes the earth to be a flat body; *broadly* one who denies modern scientific theories

**flat feet** *n pl taking sing or pl vb* a condition in which the arches of the insteps of the feet are flattened so that the entire sole rests upon the ground

**flat fell seam** *n* a seam with two lines of stitching showing, that is produced by FELLING (method of sewing)

**flatfish** /-,fish/ *n* any of an order (Heterosomata) of chiefly marine fishes (eg the halibuts, flounders, turbots, and soles) that as adults swim along the seafloor on one side of their flattened body which has both eyes on the upper side and typically is coloured only on this side, the side facing the seafloor normally being white

**flatfoot** /-,foot/ *n, pl* (2) **flatfeet** /-,feet/, **flatfoots 1** FLAT FEET **2** *slang* a policeman

**flat-footed** /-'footid/ *adj* **1** affected with FLAT FEET; *broadly* walking with a dragging or shambling gait **2** *informal* free from reservation; forthright ⟨*had an honest ~ way of saying a thing*⟩ **3** *informal* found unprepared; unready – chiefly in *catch someone flat-footed* **4** *Br informal* clumsy, awkward – **flat-footedly** *adv*, **flat-footedness** *n*

**flat four** *n* (a vehicle having) an INTERNAL-COMBUSTION ENGINE having two sets of two cylinders horizontally opposite each other

**flat hat** *n* CLOTH CAP 1

**Flathead** /'flat,hed/ *n, pl* **Flatheads,** *esp collectively* **Flathead 1** a member of any of several N American Indian peoples that were believed to practise head-flattening by placing weights on the heads of infants **2** *not cap* any of various chiefly Indo-Pacific marine food fishes (family Platycephalidae) that have an elongated body and a flattened head covered with bony plates and spines

**flatiron** /-,ie·ən/ *n* IRON 2c; *esp* one heated on a fire, stove, etc

**flatland** /'flat,land/ *n* **1** land that lacks significant variation in height **2 flatlands** *pl,* **flatland** a region in which the land is predominantly flat – **flatlander** *n*

**flatlet** /'flatlit/ *n, Br* **1** a small flat **2** a bed-sitter provided with separate cooking and washing facilities

**flatmate** /-,mayt/ *n, Br* one who shares a flat with another

**flat out** *adv* at maximum speed, capacity, or performance ⟨*the car does 200 miles per hour ~*⟩ – **flat-out** *adj, chiefly Br*

**flat spin** *n* **1** a manoeuvre in the air or a flight condition consisting of a spin in which the aircraft is roughly horizontal **2** *informal* a state of extreme agitation ⟨*when her pet goldfish died she went into a ~*⟩

**flatten** /'flat(ə)n/ *vt* **1** to make flat **2** to lower (a musical note) in pitch, esp by a semitone – compare SHARPEN **3** *informal* to beat or overcome utterly ⟨*got ~ ed in the annual cricket match*⟩ ~ *vi* to become flat or flatter: eg **3a** to extend in or into a flat position or form ⟨*hills ~ ing into coastal plains*⟩ – often + *out* **b** to become uniform or stabilized often at a new lower level – usu + *out* ⟨*performance tended to ~ out after an initial period of improvement*⟩ – **flattener** *n*

**flatten out** *vi* **1** to manoeuvre an aircraft so that its length becomes parallel to the ground **2** *of an aircraft* to assume such a position

**¹flatter** /'flatə/ *vt* **1** to praise excessively, esp from motives of self-interest or in order to gratify another's vanity ⟨~ *ed him on his cooking*⟩ **2** to raise the hopes of or gratify, often groundlessly or with intent to deceive ⟨*I was ~ ed by the invitation*⟩ **3a(1)** to portray or represent (too) favourably ⟨*always paints pictures that ~ his subjects*⟩ **a(2)** to display to advantage ⟨*candlelight often ~ s the face*⟩ **b** to judge (oneself) (too) favourably ⟨*I ~ myself I am not a fool*⟩ **4** *archaic* to soothe, beguile ~ *vi* to use flattery [ME *flateren*, fr OF *flater* to lick, flatter, of Gmc origin; akin to OHG *flaz* flat] – **flatterer** *n*, **flatteringly** *adv*

**²flatter** *n* something used to flatten: eg **a** a block with a narrow rectangular hole through which metal is drawn in flat strips **b** a blacksmith's tool, with a flat face, that is placed on forged work and hit with a hammer to smooth the surface of the forging

**flattery** /'flatəri/ *n* **1a** the act or practice of flattering; *also* something that flatters **b** insincere or excessive praise **2** *obs* a pleasing self-deception

**flattie** /'flati/ *n, informal* **1** a flat-soled shoe or sandal **2** a policeman [(1) ¹*flat* + *-ie;* (2) *flatfoot* + *-ie*]

**flattop** /-,top/ *n, chiefly NAm informal* AIRCRAFT CARRIER

**flatulent** /'flatyoolənt/ *adj* **1** causing, marked by, or affected with accumulation of gas in the stomach or intestines **2** pretentious without real worth or substance; turgid, windy [MF, fr L *flatus*] – **flatulence, flatulency** *n,* **flatulently** *adv*

**flatus** /'flaytəs/ *n* gas generated in the stomach or intestines [L, act of blowing, act of breaking wind, fr *flatus,* pp of *flare* to blow – more at BLOW]

**flatware** /'flatweə/ *n* tableware (e g plates and saucers) that is more or less flat and usu formed or cast in a single piece; *also, chiefly NAm* cutlery for serving and eating food – compare HOLLOWWARE

**flatways** /-,wayz/ *adv* with the flat surface presented in a particular or implied position

**flatwise** /-,wiez/ *adv, chiefly NAm* flatways

**flatworm** /-,wuhm/ *n* PLATYHELMINTH (soft-bodied flattened worm); *esp* TURBELLARIAN (nonparasitic flatworm)

**flaunching** /'flawnching/, **flaunch** /'flawnch/ *n* a slope (e g of concrete) on the top of a chimney to allow rain to run off [*flanch, flaunch* (to slant, flare), perh fr Fr *flanc* flank] – **flaunch** *vb*

**flaunt** /flawnt/ *vi* **1** to wave or flutter proudly ⟨*the flag* ~s *in the breeze*⟩ **2** to parade or display oneself to public notice ~ *vt* **1** to display ostentatiously or impudently; parade ⟨~*ing his superiority*⟩ **2** *nonstandard* to flout [prob fr Scand origin; akin to ON *flana* to rush round – more at PLANET] – **flaunt** *n,* **flauntingly** *adv,* **flaunty** *adj*

> *usage* The use of **flaunt** for flout ⟨⚠ *openly* **flaunting** *the rules*⟩ is a common confusion. **synonyms** see ¹SHOW

**flautist** /'flawtist/ *n* one who plays a flute [It *flautista,* fr *flauto* flute, fr OProv *flaut*]

**flavanone** /'flavənohn, 'flay-/ *n* a KETONE, $C_{15}H_{12}O_2$; *also* any of the chemical compounds formed from it, many of which occur in plants, often in the form of GLYCOSIDES (sugar-containing compounds) [L *flavus* + ISV *-ane* + *-one*]

**flavescent** /flə'ves(ə)nt/ *adj* (turning) slightly yellow [L *flavescent, flavescens,* prp of *flavescere* to turn yellow, fr *flavus*]

**flavin** /'flayvin/ *n* any of various nitrogen-containing chemical compounds derived from ISOALLOXAZINE or containing an isoalloxazine molecule in the structure: e g **a** RIBOFLAVIN (vitamin occurring in green vegetables, milk, etc) **b** either of two compounds, FAD and FMN, that are NUCLEOTIDES containing riboflavin in their molecular structures and are important in biochemical reactions in living cells as the active nonprotein parts (COENZYMES) of flavoproteins [ISV, fr L *flavus* yellow – more at BLUE]

**flavin adenine dinucleotide** *n* FAD (compound essential for the functioning of some flavoproteins)

**flavine** /'flayvin/ *n* **1** ACRIFLAVINE or a similar yellow dye used as an antiseptic **2** a flavin [ISV, fr L *flavus*]

**flavin mononucleotide** *n* FMN (compound essential for the functioning of some flavoproteins)

**flavone** /'flayvohn/ *n* a KETONE, $C_{15}H_{10}O_2$, found in the leaves, stems, and seed capsules of many primroses; *also* any of the chemical compounds formed from it, many of which occur as yellow plant pigments in the form of GLYCOSIDES (sugar-containing compounds) and are used as dyestuffs [ISV, fr L *flavus*]

**flavoprotein** /,flayvoh'prohteen/ *n* any of a group of ENZYMES composed of a protein tightly bound to a flavin COENZYME (active nonprotein part essential for the functioning of an enzyme) and often a metal, that are important in OXIDATION reactions (e g in the breakdown of fats and carbohydrates) in living cells and act as transporters of electrons in the series of reactions by which substances derived from the breakdown of foods are oxidized to produce energy [ISV *flavin* + *-o-* + *protein*]

**¹flavour,** *NAm chiefly* **flavor** /'flayvə/ *n* **1** the blend of taste and smell sensations evoked by a substance in the mouth; *also* a distinctive flavour ⟨*condiments add* ~ *to food*⟩ **2** characteristic or predominant quality ⟨*the newspaper retains a sporting*

~⟩ **3 flavouring, flavour** a substance that flavours **4** *archaic* odour, fragrance [ME *flavour,* fr MF *flaor, flavor,* fr (assumed) VL *flator,* fr L *flare* to blow] – **flavourful** *adj,* **flavourless** *adj,* **flavoursome** *adj*

**²flavour,** *NAm chiefly* **flavor** *vt* to give or add flavour to

**¹flaw** /flaw/ *n* **1** a blemish, imperfection: e g **1a** a defect that spoils the appearance or value of an object ⟨*a* ~ *in a gem*⟩ **b** a usu hidden defect (e g a crack) that may cause failure under stress ⟨*a* ~ *in a bar of steel*⟩ **c** a weakness in something abstract ⟨*vanity was the great* ~ *in his character*⟩ ⟨*a* ~ *in his argument*⟩ **d** a fault in a legal document that may nullify it **2** *obs* a fragment **synonyms** see IMPERFECTION [ME, prob fr Scand origin; akin to Sw *flaga* flake, flaw; akin to OE *flēan* to flay] – **flawless** *adj,* **flawlessly** *adv,* **flawlessness** *n*

**²flaw** *vt* to make flaws in ⟨*your argument is seriously* ~ed⟩ ~ *vi* to become flawed

**³flaw** *n* **1** a sudden gust of wind; squall; *also* a spell of stormy weather **2** *obs* an outburst, esp of passion [of Scand origin; akin to Norw *flaga* gust; akin to L *plangere* to beat – more at PLAINT]

**flax** /flaks/ *n* **1** any of a genus (*Linum* of the family Linaceae, the flax family) of nonwoody plants; *esp* a slender erect blue-flowered plant (*Linum usitatissimum*) cultivated for its strong woody fibre and seed **2** the pale cream to greyish-yellow fibre of the flax plant, esp when cleaned and prepared for spinning into linen thread or yarn **3** any of several plants resembling flax [ME, fr OE *fleax;* akin to OHG *flahs* flax, L *plectere* to braid – more at PLY] – **flaxy** *adj*

**flaxen** /'flaks(ə)n/ *adj* **1** made of flax **2** resembling flax, esp in being a pale soft straw colour ⟨~ *hair*⟩

**flaxseed** /'flaks,seed/ *n* LINSEED (seed of flax plant)

**flay** /flay/ *vt* **1** to strip off the skin or surface of; *also* to whip savagely **2a** to strip of possessions, esp by extortion or cheating **b** to criticize or censure harshly [ME *flen,* fr OE *flēan;* akin to ON *flā* to flay, Lith *plēšti* to tear] – **flayer** *n*

**F layer** /'ef/ *n* **1** the highest layer of the IONOSPHERE (upper part of the earth's atmosphere), that consists of electrically charged atoms and free electrons and is capable of reflecting radio waves of frequencies up to $5 \times 10^7$ hertz back to earth. The F layer occurs at night at a height of about 300 kilometres (about 185 miles) above the earth's surface and during the daytime comprises the F1 LAYER and the F2 LAYER. **2** the forest soil zone marked by abundant plant remains undergoing decay

**F1 layer** *n* the lower of the two layers into which the F REGION of the IONOSPHERE (upper part of the earth's atmosphere) splits in the daytime, that occurs between about 145 to 240 kilometres (about 90 to 150 miles) above the earth's surface

**F2 layer** *n* the upper of the two layers into which the F REGION of the earth's upper atmosphere (IONOSPHERE) splits in the daytime, occurring at varying heights from about 240 to 400 kilometres (about 150 to 250 miles) above the earth's surface

**flea** /flee/ *n* **1** any of an order (Siphonaptera) of wingless blood-sucking insects that have a hard flattened body and legs adapted to leaping and that feed on warm-blooded animals **2** **flea beetle, flea** any of various small jumping beetles (family Chrysomelidae) that feed on foliage and sometimes carry virus diseases of plants [ME *fle,* fr OE *flēa;* akin to OHG *flōh* flea, OE *flēon* to flee] – **with a flea in one's ear** with a usu embarrassing reprimand ⟨*sent off* with a flea in his ear⟩

**fleabag** /-,bag/ *n, informal* **1** a dirty or neglected person or animal **2** *chiefly NAm* an inferior hotel or lodging

**fleabane** /-,bayn/ *n* any of various plants (e g of the genera *Erigeron* and *Pulicaria*) of the daisy family that were once supposed to drive away fleas; *esp* a European fleabane (*Pulicaria dysenterica*) that has golden-yellow daisylike flower heads

**fleabite** /-,biet/ *n* **1** (the red spot caused by) the bite of a flea **2** *informal* a trifling problem or expense

**'flea-,bitten** *adj* **1** bitten by or infested with fleas **2** *of a (light-coloured) horse's coat* flecked with chestnut or brown **3** *informal* shabby, run-down

**flea market** *n* a usu open-air market for secondhand articles and antiques [trans of Fr *Marché aux Puces,* a market in Paris]

**fleapit** /-,pit/ *n, chiefly Br* a shabby cinema or theatre

**flèche** /flesh (Fr flɛʃ)/ *n* a slender usu wooden spire rising from the ridge of a roof [Fr, lit., arrow]

**fléchette** /fle'shet/ *n* a small dart-shaped projectile that can be clustered in an explosive warhead, dropped as a missile from an aircraft, or fired from a hand-held gun [Fr, fr dim. of *flèche* arrow]

¹**fleck** /flek/ *vt* **1** to mark or cover with flecks; streak 〈*shoes ~ed with mud*〉 **2** to mark with touches of an abstract quality 〈*his voice is ~ed with poignancy*〉 [back-formation fr *flecked* spotted, fr ME, prob fr ON *flekkōttr*, fr *flekkr* spot]

²**fleck** *n* **1** a small spot or mark, esp of colour 〈*a brown tweed with ~s of yellow*〉 **2** a grain, particle 〈*~s of dust*〉

**flection** /'fleksh(ə)n/ *n* FLEXION (bending of a bone joint)

**fledge** /flej/ *vi, of a young bird* to acquire the feathers necessary for flight ~ *vt* **1** to rear (a young bird) until ready for flight or independent activity **2** to cover (as if) with feathers or down **3** to fit (esp an arrow) with a feather or feathers [*fledge* (capable of flying), fr ME *flegge*, fr OE *-flycge*; akin to OHG *flucki* capable of flying, OE *flēogan* to fly – more at FLY]

**fledgling, fledgeling** /'flejling/ *n* **1** a young bird just fledged **2** an inexperienced person

**flee** /flee/ *vb* **fled** /fled/ *vi* **1** to run away from danger, evil, etc **2** to pass away swiftly; vanish 〈*mists ~ing before the rising sun*〉 to run away from; shun *usage* see ¹FLY [ME *flen*, fr OE *flēon;* akin to OHG *fliohan* to flee]

¹**fleece** /flees/ *n* **1a** the coat of wool covering a sheep or similar animal **b** the wool obtained from a sheep at one shearing **2a** a soft or woolly covering like a sheep's fleece 〈*a ~ of snow lay on the ground*〉 **b** a soft bulky deep-piled synthetic fabric used chiefly for lining coats [ME *flees*, fr OE *flēos;* akin to MHG *vlius* fleece, L *pluma* feather, down]

²**fleece** *vt* **1** to remove the fleece from; shear **2** to cover with something fleecy **3** *informal* to strip of money or property, usu by fraud or extortion; *esp* to overcharge

**fleeced** /fleest/ *adj* **1** covered (as if) with a fleece **2** *of a textile* having a soft nap

**fleece-o, fleece-oh** /'fleesoh/ *n, NZ* a person who collects the fleeces of shorn sheep in a woolshed

**fleecy** /'fleesi/ *adj* covered with, made of, or resembling fleece 〈*a ~ winter coat*〉

¹**fleet** /fleet/ *vi* **1** to fly swiftly; pass rapidly 〈*clouds ~ing across the sky*〉 **2** *archaic* to flow **3** *archaic* to fade away; vanish **4** *obs* to drift [ME *fleten*, fr OE *flēotan* to float, drift; akin to OHG *fliozzan* to float, OE *flōwan* to flow]

²**fleet** *n* **1** a number of warships under a single command **2** *often cap* a country's navy – usu + *the* **3** a group of ships, aircraft, lorries, etc owned or operated under one management [ME *flete*, fr OE *flēot* ship, fr *flēotan*]

³**fleet** *adj* swift in motion; nimble *synonyms* see ¹FAST [prob fr ¹*fleet*] – **fleetly** *adv*, **fleetness** *n*

**fleet admiral** *n* – see MILITARY RANKS table

**Fleet Air Arm** *n* the branch of the Royal Navy that formerly maintained and operated naval aircraft

**fleet chief petty officer** *n* – see MILITARY RANKS table

**fleeting** /'fleeting/ *adj* passing swiftly; transitory *synonyms* see ¹TRANSIENT *antonym* lasting – **fleetingly** *adv*, **fleetingness** *n*

**Fleet Street** *n* the London press [*Fleet Street*, London, centre of the London newspaper district]

**fleishig** /'flayshik, 'flie-/ *adj* made of, prepared with, or used for meat or meat products – used in Jewish cookery; compare MILCHIG [Yiddish, fr MHG *vleischic* meaty, fr *vleisch* flesh, meat, fr OHG *fleisk*]

**Fleming** /'fleming/ *n* a member of the Germanic people inhabiting Flanders or a Flemish-speaking Belgian [ME, fr MD *Vlaminc*, fr *Vlam-* (as in *Vlamland* Flanders)]

¹**Flemish** /'flemish/ *adj* (characteristic) of Flanders, the Flemings, or Flemish

²**Flemish** *n* **1** the Germanic language of the Flemings **2** *taking pl vb* Flemings

**Flemish bond** *n* a method of laying bricks in which each row consists of alternating HEADERS (bricks laid with their ends towards the face of the wall) and STRETCHERS (bricks laid lengthways), the headers of one row being placed centrally over the stretchers of the previous row

**Flemish garden wall bond** *n* a method of laying bricks in which each row consists of one HEADER (brick laid with its end to the face of the wall) next to three or four STRETCHERS (bricks laid lengthways)

**Flemish giant** *n* (any of) a breed of rabbit, probably of Belgian origin, that is characterized by large size, vigour, and black, white, or grey coat

**flense** /flens/ *vt* to strip (e g a whale) of blubber or skin [D *flensen* or Dan & Norw *flense*]

¹**flesh** /flesh/ *n* **1a** the soft parts of the body of an animal, esp a VERTEBRATE animal; *esp* the muscular parts of the body as distinguished from the internal organs, bone, and skin **b** excess

weight; fat **2** the edible parts of an animal; *esp* the muscular tissue of any animal except usu fish and sometimes fowl **3a** the physical being of humans 〈*the spirit indeed is willing, but the ~ is weak* – Mt 26:41 (AV)〉 **b** the physical or sensual aspect of human nature, as opposed to the spiritual 〈*pleasures of the ~*〉 **4a** human beings; humankind – esp in *all flesh* **b** living beings generally **c** kindred, stock 〈*one's own ~*〉 **5** the fleshy (edible) part of a plant or fruit **6** flesh-colour [ME, fr OE *flǣsc;* akin to OHG *fleisk* flesh] – **in the flesh** in bodily form; IN PERSON – **make somebody's flesh creep** to terrify or horrify somebody – see also **go the WAY of all flesh**

²**flesh** *vt* **1** to feed (e g a hawk or hound) with flesh from the kill to encourage interest in the chase; *broadly* to initiate or habituate, esp by giving a foretaste **2** to clothe or cover (as if) with flesh; *broadly* to give substance to – usu + *out* 〈*~ed his argument out with solid fact*〉 **3** to wound the flesh of with a weapon **4** to free from flesh; *esp* to scrape (a skin) free of adhering tissue **5** *archaic* to gratify ~ *vi* to become (more) fleshy or substantial – usu + *out*

**flesh and blood** *n* **1** human nature 〈*such neglect was more than ~ could stand*〉 **2** near kindred – chiefly in *one's own flesh and blood* **3** substance, body 〈*attempting to give ~ to nebulous ideas*〉

'**flesh-,colour, flesh** *adj or n* (of) a pinkish-white colour with a slight yellow tint – **flesh-coloured** *adj*

-**fleshed** /flesht/ *comb form* (→ *adj*) having (such) flesh 〈*pink-fleshed*〉 〈*thick-fleshed*〉

**flesh fly** *n* a fly (esp family Sarcophagidae) whose maggots feed on flesh; *esp* the common flesh fly (*Sarcophaga carnaria*) whose immature larvae are deposited on animal flesh after hatching from the eggs

**fleshing** /'fleshing/ *n* **1** *pl* flesh-coloured tights worn by dancers and actors **2** *pl* material removed in fleshing a hide or skin **3a** the distribution of the lean and fat on an animal **b** the capacity of an animal to put on fat

**fleshly** /'fleshli/ *adj* **1** carnal **2** fleshy, plump *usage* The similarity of sound has led to the use of both **fleshy** and **fleshly** to mean "plump", but some writers on usage advise that **fleshly** should mean only "carnal".

**fleshpot** /-,pot/ *n* **1** *pl* bodily comfort or good living; luxury – usu + *the* **2** *usu pl* a place of luxurious or titillating entertainment 〈*a tour of the city's ~s*〉 [fr the reference in Exodus 16:3]

**flesh wound** *n* an injury involving penetration of body muscle without damage to bones or internal organs

**fleshy** /'fleshi/ *adj* **1a** consisting of or resembling flesh **b** marked by (abundant) flesh; *esp* corpulent **2** succulent, pulpy 〈*the rich ~ texture of a perfectly ripe melon*〉 *usage* see FLESHLY – **fleshiness** *n*

**fletch** /flech/ *vt* FLEDGE 3 [back-formation fr *fletcher*]

**fletcher** /'flechə/ *n* one who makes arrows [ME *fleccher*, fr OF *flechier*, fr *fleche* arrow]

**fletching** /'fleching/ *n* an arrow feather

**fletton** /'flet(ə)n/ *n* a yellowish-red brick made by compressing moist clay in a steel mould [*Fletton*, town in Cambridgeshire in England]

**fleur de coin** /,fluh də 'kwunh (*Fr* flœr də kwɛh)/ *adj, of a coin* preserved in mint condition [Fr *à fleur de coin*, lit., with the bloom of the die]

**fleur-de-lis, fleur-de-lys** /,fluh də 'lee/ *n, pl* **fleurs-de-lis, fleur-de-lis, fleurs-de-lys, fleur-de-lys** /lee(z)/ **1** IRIS 2 **2** a conventionalized iris flower with three petals, used in art and heraldry [ME *flourdelis*, fr MF *flor de lis*, lit., lily flower]

**fleuron** /'flooəron, -rən, 'fluh-/ *n* a flower-shaped ornament used for decorative effect (e g in architecture, printing, or garnishing pastry goods) [Fr, fr MF *floron*, fr *flor, flour, flur* flower]

**flew** /flooh/ *past of* FLY

**flews** /floohz/ *n pl* the drooping side parts of the upper lip of a bloodhound or similar dog [origin unknown]

¹**flex** /fleks/ *vt* **1** BEND 1 **2a** to bend or cause flexion of (a limb or joint) 〈*stretching and ~ing his knees*〉 **b** to move (a muscle or muscles) so as to flex a limb or joint 〈*~ed their biceps and went to work*〉 ~ *vi* to be bent 〈*his leg ~ed*〉 [L *flexus*, pp of *flectere*]

²**flex** *n* **1** an act or instance of flexing **2** *chiefly Br* (a length of) flexible insulated electrical cable used in connecting a portable electrical appliance to a socket [(2) short for *flexible* (cord)]

**flexible** /'fleksəbl/ *adj* **1** capable of being bent; pliant **2** yielding to influence; tractable **3** capable of changing in response to new conditions or demands; versatile ⟨*a highly ~ curriculum*⟩ **synonyms** see ¹PLASTIC **antonym** rigid – **flexibly** *adv*, **flexibility** *n*

**flexile** /'fleksiel/ *adj*, *archaic* flexible

**flexion** *also* **flection** /'fleksh(ə)n/ *n* 1 flexing or being flexed 2 a bent part; a bend 3 INFLECTION 3 4 a bending of (a limb at) a joint in such a way that the angle between the bones connected by the joint is diminished – compare EXTENSION 3b

**flexitime** /'fleksi,tiem/ *n* a system in Britain whereby employees work a set total of hours per week or month but can choose from a usu limited range of daily starting and finishing times [*flexible* + *time*]

**flexography** /flek'sogrəfi/ *n* a process of rotary LETTERPRESS printing using flexible rubber plates and rapid-drying inks [*flexible* + *-o-* + *-graphy*] – **flexographic** *adj*, **flexographically** *adv*

**flexor** /'fleksə/ *n* a muscle (eg the biceps at the front of the upper arm) that flexes or bends a body part (eg a limb) – compare EXTENSOR [NL, fr L *flexus*, pp]

**flextime** /'fleks,tiem/ *n* flexitime

**flexuous** /'fleksyoo·əs/ *adj*, *formal* 1 having turns or windings 2 lacking rigidity in structure or action ⟨*its ~ and elastic body*⟩ [L *flexuosus*, fr *flexus* bend, fr *flexus*, pp] – **flexuously** *adv*

**flexure** /'flekshə/ *n* 1 FLEXION 1 2 *formal* a turn or fold

**flibbertigibbet** /,flibəti'jibit/ *n*, *informal* a silly flighty gossipy person [ME *flepergebet*, perh of imit origin] – **flibbertigibbety** *adj*

**flic** /flik (*Fr* flik)/ *n* a Parisian policeman [Fr]

¹**flick** /flik/ *n* 1 a light sharp quick movement or blow 2 something thrown off or applied with a flick ⟨*gave the table a ~ of polish*⟩ [imit]

²**flick** *vt* **1a** to strike lightly with a quick sharp motion ⟨*~ed the old horse with a whip*⟩ **b** to remove with flicks ⟨*~ed the dust off his boots with a handkerchief*⟩ – usu + *away* or *off* 2 to cause to move with a flick ⟨*the cow ~ed its tail from side to side*⟩ ~ *vi* 1 to move lightly or quickly; dart 2 to direct flicks at something ⟨*~ed at the flies*⟩

**flick through** *vt* to leaf through (a book, magazine, etc) very quickly or perfunctorily

³**flick** *n*, *informal* 1 FILM 4a 2 *pl* (a showing of a film at) a cinema – + *the* **synonyms** see CINEMA [short for ²*flicker*]

¹**flicker** /'flikə/ *vi* 1 to move irregularly or unsteadily; quiver 2 to burn fitfully or with a fluctuating light 3 to appear or be present irregularly or indistinctly 4 *of a light* to fluctuate in intensity ~ *vt* 1 to cause to flicker 2 to produce by flickering ⟨*~ a signal with a mirror*⟩ **synonyms** see ¹FLASH [ME *flikeren*, fr OE *flicorian*] – **flickeringly** *adv*

²**flicker** *n* 1 a flickering (movement or light) 2 a momentary quickening or stirring ⟨*a ~ of interest*⟩ – **flickery** *adj*

'**flick-,knife** *n* a pocket knife with a spring-operated blade that flicks open when a button on the handle is pressed

**flier** /'flie·ə/ *n* 1 somebody or something that moves very fast 2 an airman 3 a rectangular step in a straight flight of steps – compare WINDER c 4 *informal* FLYING START 2 5 *NAm* a reckless or speculative venture ⟨*took a ~ in politics soon after getting his degree*⟩

¹**flight** /fliet/ *n* **1a** a passage through the air using wings ⟨*the ~ of a bee*⟩ **b** the ability to fly ⟨*~ is natural to birds*⟩ **2a(1)** a passage or journey through air or space ⟨*~ of a rocket to the moon*⟩; *specif* any such flight scheduled by an airline ⟨*a ~ delayed because of poor weather conditions*⟩ **a(2)** the distance covered in such a flight **b** the path of a struck or bowled ball; *esp* a relatively high curve imparted to a bowled ball in cricket **c** swift movement 3 a group of similar creatures or objects flying through the air together 4 a brilliant, imaginative, or unrestrained exercise or display ⟨*a ~ of fancy*⟩ 5 (a series of locks, hurdles, etc resembling) a continuous series of stairs from one landing or floor to another 6 any of the real or artificial feathers at the tail of a projectile (eg a dart or arrow) that provide stability 7 a small unit of (military) aircraft or personnel in the Royal Air Force [ME, fr OE *flyht*; akin to MD *vlucht* flight, OE *flēogan* to fly] – **flightless** *adj*

²**flight** *vi* to rise, settle, or fly in a flock ⟨*geese ~ing on the marsh*⟩ ~ *vt* 1 ¹FLUSH 2 2 to make (a ball, dart, etc) float slowly or deceptively esp towards a target 3 to fit (an arrow or dart) with feathers

³**flight** *n* an act or instance of fleeing [ME *fluht*, *fliht;* akin to OHG *fluht* flight, OE *flēon* to flee] – **put to flight** to force to flee; rout – **take (to) flight** to flee

**flight control** *n* 1 the control of an aircraft or spacecraft from

a ground station, esp by radio 2 the system of control devices on an aeroplane

**flight deck** *n* 1 the deck of a ship (eg an aircraft carrier) used for the takeoff and landing of aircraft 2 the compartment housing the controls and those crew who operate them in an aircraft

**flight engineer** *n* a flight crewman responsible for the operation of an aircraft's systems, including the engines, during a flight

**flight feather** *n* any of the large stiff feathers of a bird's wing or tail that are important in providing lift and control for flight – compare CONTOUR FEATHER

**flight lieutenant** *n* – see MILITARY RANKS table

**flight line** *n* 1 a parking and servicing area for aircraft 2 the line in air or space along which something (eg an aeroplane or missile) travels or is intended to travel

**flight path** *n* the (planned) course taken by an aircraft, spacecraft, etc

**flight plan** *n* a usu written statement (eg by a pilot) of the details of an intended flight, usu filed with an authority

**flight recorder** *n* a robust device fitted to an aircraft that records details of its flight, esp for use in investigating accidents

**flight sergeant** *n* – see MILITARY RANKS table

**flight sergeant aircrew** *n* – see MILITARY RANKS table

'**flight-,test** *vt* to test (eg an aircraft or spacecraft) in flight

**flighty** /'flieti/ *adj* 1 swift **2a** lacking stability or steadiness **b** easily excited or upset; skittish ⟨*a ~ horse*⟩ 3 irresponsible, silly; *also* flirtatious – **flightily** *adv*, **flightiness** *n*

¹**flimflam** /'flim,flam/ *n*, *informal* 1 deception, trickery 2 nonsense, humbug [prob of Scand origin; akin to ON *flim* mockery]

²**flimflam** *vt* **-mm-** *informal* to deceive or cheat – **flimflammer** *n*

¹**flimsy** /'flimzi/ *adj* **1a** lacking in physical strength or substance ⟨*~ silks*⟩ **b** of inferior materials or workmanship; easily destroyed or broken 2 having little worth or plausibility ⟨*a ~ excuse*⟩ **synonyms** see WEAK [perh alter. of ¹*film* + *-sy* (as in *tricksy*)] – **flimsily** *adv*, **flimsiness** *n*

²**flimsy** *n* (a document printed on) a lightweight paper used esp for multiple copies

**flinch** /flinch/ *vi* to shrink (as if) from physical pain; wince; *esp* to tense the muscles involuntarily in fear **synonyms** see ¹RECOIL [MF *flenchir* to bend, turn aside] – **flinch** *n*, **flincher** *n*

**flinders** /'flindəz/ *n pl* splinters, fragments [ME *flendris*, prob of Scand origin]

¹**fling** /fling/ *vb* **flung** /flung/ *vi* 1 to move in a hasty or violent manner ⟨*~ing out of the room in a rage*⟩ 2 *of an animal* to kick or plunge vigorously – usu + *out* ~ *vt* 1 to throw or cast (aside), esp with force or recklessness ⟨*flung the books on the table*⟩ ⟨*~ing her arms wide*⟩ ⟨*flung off all restraint*⟩ 2 to place or send suddenly and unceremoniously ⟨*the attack flung the enemy force into confusion*⟩ 3 to ejaculate or utter vigorously or offensively 4 to cast or direct (oneself or one's efforts) vigorously or unrestrainedly ⟨*flung herself into organizing the party*⟩ **synonyms** see ¹THROW [ME *flingen*, of Scand origin; akin to ON *flengja* to whip, *flā* to flay – more at FLAY] – **flinger** *n*

²**fling** *n* 1 an act or instance of flinging 2 a period devoted to self-indulgence ⟨*determined to have one last ~ before settling down*⟩ 3 *informal* a casual attempt ⟨*willing to take a ~ at almost anything*⟩

**flint** /flint/ *n* 1 flint, flintstone a dense hard rock that is a form of quartz with a very fine crystalline structure and is found esp in chalk and limestone 2 a flint implement used by primitive humans **3a** a piece of flint used, esp formerly, for producing a spark when struck or rubbed against steel **b** a piece of an alloy (eg of the metals iron and cerium) used for producing a spark (eg in a cigarette lighter) 4 something resembling flint in hard unyielding quality [ME, fr OE; akin to OHG *flins* pebble, hard stone] – **flintlike** *adj*, **flinty** *adj*

**flint corn** *n* a maize (*Zea mays indurata*) having hard horny usu rounded kernels with the soft ENDOSPERM (food reserve for the developing seedling) enclosed by a hard outer layer

**flint glass** *n* heavy brilliant glass of relatively high REFRACTIVE INDEX (measure of amount by which light entering is bent) that contains LEAD DIOXIDE and is used for cut glassware and optical devices (eg lenses and prisms); *broadly* a clear colourless glass other than PLATE GLASS

**flintlock** /-,lok/ *n* (a usu 17th- or 18th-century gun having) a mechanism for igniting the charge by means of sparks struck from a piece of flint

**¹flip** /flip/ *vb* **-pp-** *vt* **1** to toss or cause to move with a sharp movement, esp so as to be turned over in the air ⟨~ *a coin*⟩ **2** FLICK 1 **3** to turn *over* ⟨~ *ped the pages over*⟩ ~ *vi* **1** *of a small object* to make a twitching, flicking, or jerking movement **2** *slang* **2a** to lose one's sanity or self-control **b** to become extremely enthusiastic ⟨*I just ~ped over that new record*⟩ – see also **flip one's** LID [prob imit]

**flip through** *vt* to read (a newspaper, book, etc) quickly or idly

**²flip** *n* **1 a** (motion used in) flipping or a flick **2** a somersault, esp when performed in the air **3** a mixed drink consisting usu of a sweetened spiced alcoholic drink to which beaten eggs have been added

**³flip** *adj* **-pp-** *informal* flippant, impertinent

**'flip-,flap** *n* a flip-flop

**flip-flop** /'flip ,flop/ *n* **1** the sound of something flapping loosely **2** a usu electronic device or circuit (e g in a computer) capable of assuming either of two stable states **3** a rubber sandal consisting of a sole and a strap fixed between the toes **4** a backward handspring – **flip-flop** *vi*

**flippant** /'flip(ə)nt/ *adj* **1** lacking proper respect or seriousness, esp in the consideration of grave matters **2** *archaic* glib, talkative [prob fr ¹*flip*] – **flippancy** *n*, **flippantly** *adv*

**flipper** /'flipə/ *n* **1a** a broad flat limb (e g of a seal) adapted for swimming **b** a flat rubber shoe that has the front expanded into a paddle and is used in (underwater) swimming, esp SKIN DIVING **2** one who or that which flips

**flipping** /'fliping/ *adj or adv, Br slang* – used as a meaningless intensive [euphemism for *fucking*]

**flip side** *n* the side of a gramophone record, esp a single, which is not the principal marketing attraction [¹*flip*]

**¹flirt** /fluht/ *vt, archaic* to move (something) quickly and suddenly; flick ~ *vi* **1** to behave amorously without serious intent **2** *archaic* to move jerkily or erratically; flit [origin unknown] – **flirter** *n*, **flirty** *adj*, **flirtation** *n*

**flirt with** *vt* **1** to show superficial or casual interest in or liking for ⟨flirted with *the idea of getting a job*⟩ **2** to risk casually ⟨*racing drivers* flirt with *death*⟩

**²flirt** *n* **1** an act or instance of flirting **2** someone, esp a woman, who flirts

**flirtatious** /fluh'tayshəs/ *adj* **1** inclined to flirt; coquettish **2** indicative of playful sexual invitation – **flirtatiously** *adv*, **flirtatiousness** *n*

**flit** /flit/ *vi* **-tt-** **1** to pass lightly and quickly, abruptly, or irregularly from one place or condition to another; *esp* to fly in this manner ⟨*butterflies* ~ting *from flower to flower*⟩ **2** *chiefly Scot & NEng* to move house, esp rapidly and secretly; *also* to flit from rented accommodation to avoid payment of owed rent **3** *archaic* to alter, shift [ME *flitten*, of Scand origin; akin to ON *flytjask* to move, OE *flēotan* to float] – **flit** *n*, **flitter** *n*

**flitch** /flich/ *n* **1** a salted and often smoked side of pork **2** a longitudinal section of a log **3** any of the parts secured together to make a girder or beam [ME *flicche*, fr OE *flicce*]

**flitter** /'flitə/ *vi* to flutter, flicker [freq of *flit*]

**flivver** /'flivə/ *n, chiefly NAm informal* a small cheap usu old car [origin unknown]

**¹float** /floht/ *n* **1** an act or instance of floating **2** something that floats in or on the surface of a liquid: e g **2a** a cork or other device used to keep the baited end of a fishing line afloat **b** a floating platform or raft anchored close to the shore for swimmers or boats **c** something (e g a hollow ball) that floats at the end of a lever in a cistern, tank, or boiler and regulates the liquid level **d** an internal air- or gas-filled sac or bladderlike structure that buoys up the body of a plant or animal **e** a watertight structure enabling an aircraft to float on water **f** *Br* a buoyant garment or apparatus for keeping people afloat **3 a** a tool or apparatus for smoothing a surface of plaster, concrete, etc **4a** (a vehicle with) a supporting an exhibit in a parade **b** *Br* a small usu battery-powered vehicle used for making deliveries; *specif* MILK FLOAT **5a** a sum of money available for day-to-day use (e g for expenses or for giving change) **b** *chiefly NAm* the amount of money represented by cheques outstanding and in process of collection in a bank [ME *flote* boat, float, fr OE *flota* ship; akin to OHG *flōz* raft, stream, OE *flēotan* to float – more at FLEET] – **floaty** *adj*

**²float** *vi* **1** to rest on the surface of or be suspended in a liquid or gas **2a** to move buoyantly, lightly, or without definite direction; drift through a liquid or gas ⟨*yellow leaves* ~ed *down*⟩ **b**

to wander aimlessly **3** to lack firmness of purpose; vacillate **4** *of a currency* to find a value with respect to other currencies in response to the law of supply and demand and without artificial support or control ⟨*proposed that the pound be allowed to* ~⟩ ~ *vt* **1** to cause to float in or on the surface of a liquid or gas **2** to support (a structure) on a mat or raft foundation when the ground gives poor support **3** to flood or irrigate (land) naturally or artificially **4** to smooth (e g plaster or cement) with a float **5a** to present (e g an idea) for acceptance or rejection **b** to offer (stocks, bonds, etc) for sale on the STOCK MARKET **c** to establish or develop (an enterprise) by issuing and selling SECURITIES (certificates of part-ownership and rights to interest) **d** to negotiate ⟨~ *a loan*⟩ **e** to cause (currency) to float

**floatage** /'flohtij/ *n* FLOATAGE

**floatation** /floh'taysh(ə)n/ *n* FLOTATION

**floater** /'flohtə/ *n* **1a** one who or that which floats **b** a person who floats something **2** an employee without a specific job **3** a slow delivery of a cricket ball that rises after it leaves the bowler's hand before dropping towards the batsman **4** a spot appearing before the eyes due to dead cells and cell fragments in the lens and VITREOUS HUMOUR (jelly-like substance behind the lens)

**float glass** *n* a flat polished glass made by floating a continuous ribbon of molten glass over a liquid metal bath

**floating** /'flohting/ *adj* **1** suspended on or in a liquid or gas **2** located out of the normal position ⟨*a* ~ *kidney*⟩ **3a** continually drifting or changing position or abode ⟨*a large* ~ *population*⟩ **b** not presently committed or invested ⟨~ *capital*⟩ **c** *of a debt* short-term and usu not FUNDED **4** connected or constructed so as to operate and adjust smoothly ⟨*a* ~ *axle*⟩

**floating dock** *n* a large floating box-like structure that can be partly submerged to permit a ship to enter it and then raised to lift the ship out of the water

**,floating-'point** *adj* involving or being a mathematical notation in which a quantity is denoted by one number multiplied by a power of the BASE (reference number) used ⟨*the fixed-point value 99.9 could be expressed in a* ~ *system as* .999 × 10²⟩ – compare FIXED-POINT, SCIENTIFIC NOTATION

**floating policy** *n* a marine insurance policy in which only the general nature of the insured material is stated and such particulars as amount and value are fixed subsequently

**floating rib** *n* a rib (e g either of the last two pairs in humans) that has no attachment to the breastbone – compare FALSE RIB

**floating vote** *n* the aggregate of FLOATING VOTERS

**floating voter** *n* a person who does not always vote for the same political party and who may change his/her voting intentions in the period before an election

**floatplane** /'floht,playn/ *n* an aeroplane equipped with floats

**¹floc** /flok/ *n* **1** a loose fluffy or foamy mass formed by the uniting or clumping together of fine suspended particles **2** ³FLOCK 1,2,3 [short for *floccule*]

**²floc** *vb* **-cc-** *vi* to (cause to) unite into flocs

**flocculate** /'flokyoolayt/ *vb* to (cause to) form into a flocculent mass ⟨~ *clay*⟩ – **flocculant** *n*, **flocculate** *n*, **flocculator** *n*, **flocculation** *n*

**floccule** /'flokyoohl/ *n* a small loosely united bit of material (e g a collection of ore particles) suspended in or precipitated from a liquid; FLOC 1 [LL *flocculus*]

**flocculent** /'flokyoolənt/ *adj* **1** resembling wool, esp in loose fluffy structure or texture **2** made up of flocs or floccules [L *floccus* + E *-ulent*] – **flocculence** *n*

**flocculus** /'flokyooləs/ *n, pl* **flocculi** /-li/ **1** a floccule **2** a bright or dark patch on the sun [LL, dim. of L *floccus* flock of wool; akin to OHG *blaha* coarse linen]

**¹flock** /flok/ *n taking sing or pl vb* **1** a group of birds or mammals assembled or herded together **2** a church congregation in relation to its pastor **3** a large group ⟨*a whole* ~ *of tourists*⟩ [ME, fr OE *flocc* crowd, band; akin to ON *flokkr* crowd, band]

**²flock** *vi* to gather or move in a crowd ⟨*they* ~ed *to the beach*⟩

**³flock** *n* **1** a tuft of wool or cotton fibre **2** woollen or cotton refuse used for stuffing furniture, mattresses, etc **3** very short or pulverized fibre used esp to form a velvety pattern on cloth or paper or a protective covering on metal **4** FLOC 1 [ME; prob akin to MHG *vlocke* snowflake, down, tuft of wool]

**⁴flock** *vt* to fill or decorate with flock

**flocking** /'floking/ *n* a design in flock

**floe** /floh/ *n* (a sheet of) floating ice, esp on the sea; ICE FLOE [prob fr Norw *flo* flat layer]

**flog** /flog/ *vb* **-gg-** *vt* **1** to beat severely with a rod, whip, etc **2** to criticize harshly **3** to force into action; drive ⟨~ging *his keen retentive memory* – Nevil Shute⟩ **4** *informal* to repeat (something) so frequently so as to make uninteresting – esp in *flog something to death* **5** *chiefly Br slang* to sell ~ *vi, informal* to make progress painfully; slog – see also **flog a dead** HORSE (perh modif of L *flagellare* to whip – more at FLAGELLATE] – **flogger** *n*

**flong** /flong/ *n* material made of paper and used for making moulds for STEREOTYPING (form of printing) [Fr *flan* flan, flong]

¹**flood** /flud/ *n* **1** a rising and overflowing of a body of water, esp onto normally dry land **2** ²FLOW **2 3** an overwhelming quantity or volume ⟨*a* ~ *of letters*⟩ **4** a floodlight **5** *archaic* a large body of water (e g a sea) [ME, fr OE *flōd;* akin to OHG *fluot* flood, OE *flōwan* to flow]

²**flood** *vt* **1** to cover with a flood; inundate **2a** to fill abundantly or excessively ⟨*strawberries* ~ed *the market and prices dropped*⟩ **b(1)** to supply (the carburettor of an INTERNAL-COMBUSTION ENGINE) with an excess of fuel so that engine operation is hampered **b(2)** to hamper the operation of (an engine) by flooding the carburettor **3** to drive *out* of a house, village, etc by flooding ~ *vi* **1** to pour forth in a flood **2** to become filled with a flood **3** *of a carburettor or engine* to become flooded – **flooder** *n*

**floodbank** /'flud,bangk/ *n* a wall built to prevent inundation by high water

**floodgate** /-,gayt/ *n* **1** a gate for shutting out, admitting, or releasing a body of water; a sluice **2** something serving to restrain an outburst

¹**floodlight** /-,liet/ *n* (a source of) a broad beam of light for artificial illumination (e g of a sports arena or theatre stage)

²**floodlight** *vt* **floodlit** /-,lit/ to illuminate by means of floodlights

**floodmark** /'flud,mahk/ *n* a mark (e g on a wall) recording the highest level reached by a flood

**floodplain** /-,playn/ *n* an area of level land near the mouth of a river that is subject to periodic flooding and is built up by sediment deposited during flooding

**flood tide** *n* **1** the tide while flowing in or at its highest point **2** an overwhelming quantity

**floodwater** /'flud,wawtə/ *n*, **floodwaters** *n pl* the water of a flood

**floodway** /'fludway/ *n* a channel for diverting floodwaters

¹**floor** /flaw/ *n* **1** the level base of a room **2a** the lower inside surface of a hollow structure (e g a cave or body part) **b** a ground surface ⟨*the ocean* ~⟩ **3a** a structure between two storeys of a building; *also* a storey **b** *taking sing or pl vb* the occupants of a storey ⟨*the whole third* ~ *is furious*⟩ **4** the surface of a structure on which one travels ⟨*the* ~ *of a bridge*⟩ **5a** the part of an assembly in which members sit and speak **b** the members of an assembly ⟨*concluded by calling for questions from the* ~⟩ **c** the right to address an assembly ⟨*the member for Blackpool North has the* ~⟩ **6** a lower limit; a base ⟨*a* ~ *under prices or wages*⟩ [ME *flor*, fr OE *flōr*; akin to OHG *fluor* meadow, L *planus* level, Gk *planasthai* to wander] – **floor** *adj* – **cross the floor** *of a member of parliament* to transfer allegiance from a government to an opposition party or vice versa – **take the floor 1** to rise (e g at a meeting or legislative assembly) to make a formal address **2** to stand up and begin to dance – **wipe the floor with** to defeat decisively and humiliatingly

*usage* In Britain the floor of a building at ground level is the **ground floor**, and those above it the **first, second**, etc. In America the one at ground level is the **first floor** and those above it the **second, third**, etc.

²**floor** *vt* **1** to cover or provide with a floor **2a** to knock to the floor or ground **b** *informal* to reduce to silence or defeat; nonplus **3** *informal* to press (the accelerator of a vehicle) to the floor – **floorer** *n*

**floorage** /'flawrij/ *n* floor space

**floorboard** /'flaw,bawd/ *n* a board forming part of a floor

**floor exercise** *n* a gymnastics event consisting of various ballet and tumbling movements (e g jumps, somersaults, and handstands) performed without apparatus

**flooring** /'flawring/ *n* **1** a floor, base **2** material for floors ⟨*the disadvantages of softwood* ~⟩

**floor lamp** *n* STANDARD LAMP

**floor leader** *n, NAm* a member of a legislative body who directs his/her party's strategy

¹**floor-,length** *adj* reaching to the floor ⟨*a* ~ *gown*⟩

**floor manager** *n* **1** a shopwalker **2** the STAGE MANAGER of a television programme

**floor show** *n* a series of acts presented in a nightclub

**floorwalker** /-,wawkə/ *n, chiefly NAm* a shopwalker

**floozy, floozie, floosie** /'floohzi/ *n, derog* **1** a (tawdry or disreputable) woman or girl; *also* a prostitute **2** a female companion ⟨*Alf's latest* ~⟩ [perh alter. of *flossy* (showy, flashy)]

¹**flop** /flop/ *vb* **-pp-** *vi* **1** to swing or hang loosely but heavily **2** to fall, move, or drop in a heavy, clumsy, or relaxed manner ⟨~ped *into the chair with a sigh of relief*⟩ **3** *informal* to relax completely; slump **4** *informal* to fail completely ⟨*in spite of good reviews the play* ~ped⟩ ~ *vt* to move or drop heavily or with a dull noise ⟨~ped *the bundles down with a thud*⟩ [alter. of ²*flap*]

²**flop** *n* **1** (the dull sound of) a flopping motion ⟨*fell with a* ~⟩ **2** *informal* a complete failure

³**flop** *adv* with a flop

**flophouse** /'flop,hows/ *n, NAm slang* a dosshouse

**floppy** /'flopi/ *adj* tending to flop; *esp* being both soft and flexible – **floppily** *adv*, **floppiness** *n*

**floppy disk** *also* **floppy** *n* a flexible disk that is coated with a magnetic substance and is used to store data for a computer

**flor** /flaw/ *n* a crust of yeast that forms on the surface of sherry as it matures in barrel [Sp, mould, flower, fr,L *flor-, flos* flower]

**flora** /'flawrə/ *n, pl* **floras** *also* **florae** /'flawrie/ **1** a treatise on, or a work used to identify, the plants of a region or period **2** plant life; *esp* the plant life characteristic of a region, period, or special environment – compare FAUNA [NL, fr L *Flora*, Roman goddess of flowers, fr *flor-, flos* flower]

**floral** /'flawrəl, 'florəl/ *adj* of flowers or a flora [L *flor-, flos* flower – more at BLOW] – **florally** *adv*

**floral envelope** *n* the outer part of a flower consisting of the petals and SEPALS; PERIANTH

**floral leaf** *n* a modified leaf (e g a BRACT) occurring as part of or associated with the flower head (INFLORESCENCE) of a plant; *esp* a petal or SEPAL

¹**florentine** /'florəntien; *sense 2* -teen, -tien/ *adj* **1** *cap* of Florence **2** cooked or served with spinach ⟨*fish* ~⟩ [L *Florentinus*, fr *Florentia* Florence, city in Italy]

²**florentine** /'florəntien; *sense 2* -teen, -tien/ *n* **1** *cap* a native of Florence **2** a (chocolate-coated) biscuit containing nuts and dried fruit

**florescence** /flaw'res(ə)ns, flo-/ *n, formal* a state or period of flourishing or flowering [NL *florescentia*, fr L *florescent-, florescens*, prp of *florescere*, incho of *florēre* to blossom, flourish – more at FLOURISH] – **florescent** *adj*

**floret** /'flawrit, 'flo-/ *n* a small flower; *esp* any of the small flowers that together form a densely clustered flower head (e g of a daisy, dandelion, teasel, or cauliflower) – compare DISC FLORET, RAY FLORET [ME *flourette*, fr MF *flouret*, dim. of *flour* flower]

**flori-** /flawri-, flori-/ *comb form* flower; flowers ⟨*floriculture*⟩ [L, fr *flor-, flos*]

**floriated** /'flawri,aytid, 'flori-/ *adj* decorated with or shaped like a flower (motif) ⟨*a* ~ *border on a book cover*⟩ – **floriation** *n*

**floribunda** /,flori'bundə/ *n* any of various cultivated hybrid roses with open clusters of flowers [NL, fem of *floribundus* flowering freely]

**floriculture** /'flawri,kulchə, 'flori-/ *n* the cultivation and management of ornamental and flowering plants – **floricultural** *adj*, **floriculturally** *adv*, **floriculturist** *n*

**florid** /'florid/ *adj* **1** excessively flowery or ornate in style **2** tinged with red; ruddy ⟨*a* ~ *complexion*⟩ **3** fully developed; showing a complete and typical set of clinical symptoms ⟨*the* ~ *stage of a disease*⟩ **4** *archaic* healthy **5** *obs* covered with flowers [L *floridus* blooming, flowery, fr *florēre*] – **floridly** *adv*, **floridness** *n*, **floridity** *n*

**floriferous** /flaw'rifərəs/ *adj* bearing flowers; *esp* blooming freely [L *florifer*, fr *flori-*] – **floriferously** *adv*, **floriferousness** *n*

**florigen** /'florijən/ *n* a hormone or hormonal agent that promotes flowering [ISV] – **florigenic** *adj*

**florilegium** /,flawri'leeji·əm, ,flori-/ *n, pl* **florilegia** /-j(y)ə/ anthology of writings [NL, fr L *florilegus* culling flowers, fr *flori- + legere* to gather – more at LEGEND]

**florin** /'florin/ *n* **1** any of various gold coins of European countries patterned after the Florentine florin that was first struck at Florence in 1252 **2** a former British or Commonwealth silver coin worth two shillings **3** – see MONEY table **4** FORINT (Hungarian coin) [ME, fr MF, fr OIt *fiorino*, fr *fiore* flower, fr L *flor-, flos;* fr the lily (the badge of Florence) on the coins]

**florist** /'florist/ *n* one who deals in flowers and ornamental plants, or grows them for sale – **floristry** *n*

**floristic** /flo'ristik/ *adj* of flowers or a flora – **floristically** *adv*

**-florous** /-flawrəs, -flərəs/ *comb form* (→ *adj*) having or bearing (such or so many) flowers ⟨*uni*florous⟩ [LL *-florus*, fr L *flor-, flos*]

**floruit** /'floorooh·it/ *n* the date or period of flourishing (e g of a person, movement, or school) [L, he flourished, fr *florēre* to flourish]

**floss** /flos/ *n* **1** waste or short silk or silky fibres that cannot be wound on a reel; *esp* those from the outer part of a silkworm's cocoon **2a** soft thread of silk or MERCERIZED cotton (made to look silky) for embroidery **b** a lightweight wool knitting yarn **c** DENTAL FLOSS **3** fluffy fibrous material; *esp* SILK COTTON [fr or akin to D *vlos;* akin to MHG *vlus, vlius* fleece – more at FLEECE]

**flossy** /'flosi/ *adj* **1** (having the characteristics) of floss; downy **2** *NAm slang, esp of dress* showy

**flotage, floatage** /'flohtij/ *n* **1** FLOTATION 1; *also* the ability to float **2** material that floats; flotsam [²*float* + *-age*]

**flotation, floatation** /floh'taysh(ə)n/ *n* **1** the act, process, or state of floating **2** the launching, esp by financing, of a company, enterprise, etc **3** the separation of the particles of a material (e g a mass of powdered or crushed ore) according to their relative capacity for floating on a given liquid **4** the ability (e g of a tyre) to stay on the surface of soft ground or snow [²*float* + *-ation*]

**flotilla** /flə'tilə/ *n* a small fleet of ships, esp warships [Sp, dim. of *flota* fleet, fr OF *flote*, fr ON *floti;* akin to OE *flota* ship, fleet – more at FLOAT]

**flotsam** /'flots(ə)m/ *n* **1** floating wreckage, esp of a ship or its cargo – compare JETSAM **2** FLOTSAM AND JETSAM [AF *floteson*, fr OF *floter* to float, of Gmc origin; akin to OE *flotian* to float, *flota* ship]

**flotsam and jetsam** /'jets(ə)m/ *n* **1** *taking sing or pl vb* vagrants **2** unimportant miscellaneous material; ODDS AND ENDS

**¹flounce** /flowns/ *vi* **1** to move in a violent or exaggerated fashion ⟨*little girls flouncing about in their mothers' clothes*⟩ **2** to go in such a way as to attract attention, esp when extremely angry or petulant ⟨*slapped her interviewer on the left cheek and* ~d *out of the studio – The Listener*⟩ [perh of Scand origin; akin to Norw *flunsa* to hurry] – **flounce** *n*, **flouncy** *adj*

**²flounce** *n* a wide strip of fabric gathered and attached by the gathered edge (e g to the hem of a shirt or dress) [alter. of earlier *frounce*, fr ME *frouncen* to curl] – **flouncy** *adj*

**³flounce** *vt* to trim with a flounce or flounces

**flouncing** /'flownsing/ *n* material used for flounces

**¹flounder** /'flowndə/ *n, pl* **flounder**, *esp for different types* **flounders** **1** a European flatfish (*Platichthys flesus*) that is important as a food fish and has a greenish or brownish often spotted upper side and a white under side **2** any of two families (Pleuronectidae and Bothidae) of flatfishes that include some important marine food fishes; *broadly* a flatfish [ME, of Scand origin; akin to ON *flythra* flounder, *flatr* flat]

**²flounder** *vi* **1** to struggle to move or obtain footing **2** to proceed or act clumsily or ineffectually ⟨~ing *through a poor lecture*⟩ [prob alter. of *founder*] – **flounder** *n*

**¹flour** /flowə/ *n* **1** finely ground meal of wheat, often largely freed from bran; *also* a similar product obtained from cereals other than wheat, edible seeds, or other foods (e g potatoes) **2** a fine soft powder [ME – more at FLOWER]

**²flour** *vt* **1a** to coat (e g food) with flour **b** to coat as if with flour **2** to make (e g grain) into flour; mill ~ *vi, of mercury* to break up into particles on the surface of a metal instead of amalgamating with it

**flour bomb** *n* a bag of flour thrown at someone, usu as a sign of contempt

**¹flourish** /'flurish/ *vi* **1** to grow luxuriantly; thrive **2a** to achieve success; prosper **b** to be in good health **c** to reach a height of activity, development, or influence ⟨~ed *around 1850*⟩ **3a** to make bold and sweeping gestures **b** to embellish silk writing with decorative strokes ~ *vt* to wield with dramatic gestures; brandish [ME *florisshen*, fr MF *floriss-*, stem of *florir*, fr (assumed) VL *florire*, alter. of L *florēre*, fr *flor-, flos* flower] – **flourisher** *n*, **flourishingly** *adv*

**²flourish** *n* **1** a showy or flowery embellishment (e g in literature

or handwriting) or passage (e g in music) **2a** an act or instance of brandishing **b** a studied, ostentatious, or dramatic action **3** *obs* a period or state of thriving

**floury** /'flowri/ *adj* **1** coated with flour **2** resembling flour, esp in texture ⟨~ *potatoes*⟩

**flout** /flowt/ *vt* to treat with contemptuous disregard ⟨*openly* ~ing *the rules*⟩ *usage* see FLAUNT [prob fr ME *flouten* to play the flute, fr *floute* flute] – **flouter** *n*

**¹flow** /floh/ *vi* **1a** to issue or move (as if) in a stream ⟨*rivers* ~ing *to the sea*⟩ ⟨*electric current* ~ing *in the wires*⟩ ⟨*the wealth that* ~s *from our labour*⟩ **b** to circulate ⟨*blood* ~ing *round the body*⟩ **2** *of the tide* to rise – compare EBB **3** to abound ⟨~ing *with milk and honey*⟩ **4a** to proceed smoothly and readily ⟨*conversation began to* ~⟩ **b** to have a smooth graceful continuity ⟨*the* ~ing *lines of the car*⟩ **5** to hang loose or freely **6** *esp of a rock* to deform under stress without cracking or rupturing **7** *euph* to menstruate ~ *vt* **1** to cause to flow **2** to cover with water; flood [ME *flowen*, fr OE *flōwan;* akin to OHG *flouwen* to rinse, wash, L *pluere* to rain, Gk *plein* to sail, float] – **flowingly** *adv*

**²flow** *n* **1** a flowing **2** the flowing in of the tide towards the land **3a** a smooth uninterrupted movement or supply ⟨*a steady* ~ *of ideas*⟩ **b** a stream or gush of liquid or gas **c** the direction of (apparent) movement ⟨*the* ~ *of play in football*⟩ **4** the quantity that flows in a certain time **5a** the motion characteristic of liquids and gases **b** a continuous transfer of energy **6** *euph* menstruation

**³flow** *n* **1** a low-lying piece of moist land **2** an inlet of the sea – used chiefly in place-names ⟨*Scapa* Flow⟩ [of Scand origin; akin to ON *flōi* wide mouth of a river, swampy land]

**flowage** /'floh·ij/ *n* **1** a flowing or overflowing (e g onto adjacent land); *also* the liquid that flows or overflows **2** a body of water formed by overflowing or damming

**flowchart** /-ˌchaht/ *n* a diagram consisting of a set of symbols (e g rectangles or diamonds) and connecting lines, that shows step-by-step progression through a usu complicated procedure or system – **flowcharting** *n*

**flow diagram** *n* a flowchart

**¹flower** /'flowə/ *n* **1a** a blossom **b** a shoot of a FLOWERING PLANT that is specialized for reproduction and consists of a shortened axis bearing leaves modified to form petals, SEPALS, CARPELS (female reproductive structures) and/or STAMENS (male reproductive structures) **c** a plant cultivated for its blossoms **2a** the finest or most perfect part or example ⟨*the* ~ *of a nation's youth destroyed in war*⟩ **b** the finest most vigorous period; the prime **c** a state of blooming or flourishing – esp in *in flower* **3** *pl* a finely divided powder produced esp by condensation or SUBLIMATION (conversion of a gas directly to a solid) ⟨~s *of sulphur*⟩ [ME *flour* flower, best of anything, flour, fr OF *flor, flour*, fr L *flor-, flos* – more at BLOW] – **flowered** *adj*, **flowerless** *adj*, **flowerlike** *adj*

**²flower** *vi* **1** to produce flowers; blossom **2a** to reach full development or maturity ⟨~ed *into young womanhood*⟩ **b** to reach a peak condition; flourish ~ *vt* **1** to cause to bear flowers **2** to decorate with a floral design – **flowerer** *n*, **flowering** *adj*

**flowerage** /'flowərij/ *n* **1** a flowering state **2** (a mass of) flowers

**flowerbed** /'flowəˌbed/ *n* BED 2a

**flower bud** *n* a plant bud that produces only a flower

**flower child** *n* a hippie, esp of the 1960s, who advocated love, beauty, and peace and carried flowers as symbols of these beliefs

**flower girl** *n* **1** a woman who sells flowers, esp in the street **2** a young girl who carries flowers on a special occasion, esp a wedding

**flower head** *n* INFLORESCENCE; *specif* an inflorescence composed of a rounded or flattened cluster of densely packed stalkless flowers arranged so as to look like a single flower

**flowering currant** /'flow(ə)ring/ *n* a N American shrub (*Ribes sanguineum*) of the gooseberry family widely cultivated for its rosy-red fragrant flowers

**flowering plant** *n* **1** a plant that produces flowers, fruit, and seed; ANGIOSPERM **2** a plant notable for or cultivated for its ornamental flowers

**flower people** *n pl* FLOWER CHILDREN

**flowerpot** /-ˌpot/ *n* a pot, typically the shape of a small bucket and with holes in the base, in which to grow plants

**flower power** *n* the cult of the FLOWER CHILDREN

**flowery** /'flowəri/ *adj* **1** of or resembling flowers **2** marked by or using highly ornate language – **floweriness** *n*

**flowline** /'floh,lien/ *n* an ASSEMBLY LINE designed to ensure a continuous sequence of processes or operations

¹**flown** /flohn/ *past part of* FLY

²**flown** *adj, archaic* filled to excess [archaic pp of ¹*flow*]

'**flow-,on** *n, Austr* an adjustment in pay that is made to restore differentials or parity of pay following an increase in similar or related occupations ⟨*this could regenerate the wages' spiral and begin* ∼*s throughout the work force – The Age (Melbourne)*⟩

**flow sheet** *n* a flowchart

**flowstone** /'floh,stohn/ *n* a deposit of a calcium, esp CALCIUM CARBONATE, mineral formed by water flowing in a very thin sheet over limestone rocks

**flu** /flooh/ *n, informal* 1 influenza 2 any of several virus diseases marked esp by respiratory symptoms

**flub** /flub/ *vb* -**bb**- *NAm vt* to make a mess of; botch ∼ *vi* to blunder [origin unknown] – **flub** *n*

**fluctuant** /'fluktyooənt, -choo-/ *adj* 1 unstable, fluctuating 2 movable and compressible ⟨*a* ∼ *abscess*⟩

**fluctuate** /'fluktyoo,ayt, -choo,ayt/ *vi* 1 to rise and fall; swing back and forth ⟨*the price* ∼*s according to the weather*⟩ 2 to change continually and irregularly; waver ∼ *vt* to cause to fluctuate **synonyms** see ¹SWING [L *fluctuatus,* pp of *fluctuare,* fr *fluctus* flow, wave, fr *fluctus,* pp of *fluere*] – **fluctuation** *n*

**flue** /flooh/ *n* 1 a channel in a chimney for conducting gas and smoke to the outer air 2 a pipe for conveying heat (e g to water in a steam boiler) 3 an air channel leading to the lip of a wind instrument [origin unknown]

'**flue-,cured** *adj* cured by heat usu transmitted through metal flues without exposure to smoke or fumes ⟨∼ *tobacco*⟩ – compare FIRE-CURED

**fluent** /'flooh-ənt/ *adj* 1 capable of flowing; fluid 2a able to speak, write, or perform with facility ⟨∼ *in Welsh*⟩ **b** effortlessly smooth and rapid; polished ⟨*a* ∼ *performance*⟩ [L *fluent-, fluens,* prp of *fluere*] – **fluency** *n,* **fluently** *adv*

**flue pipe** *n* an organ pipe whose tone is produced by an air current striking the lip and causing the air within to vibrate – compare REED PIPE

**fluerics** /flooh'eriks/ *n taking sing vb* FLUIDICS [L *fluere* + E -*ics*] – **flueric** *adj*

**flue stop** *n* a set of flue pipes in a musical organ

¹**fluff** /fluf/ *n* **1a** small loose bits of waste material (e g hairs and threads) that stick to clothes, carpets, etc **b** soft light fur, down, etc 2 *informal* a blunder; *esp* an actor's loss of memory 3 *informal* young women considered as sexual objects or possessions – esp in *bit of fluff* ⟨*who's his latest bit of* ∼⟩ [prob alter. of *flue,* fr Flem *vluwe,* fr Fr *velu* shaggy – more at VELVET]

²**fluff** *vi* 1 to become fluffy – often + *out* or *up* 2 *informal* to make a mistake, esp in performance ∼ *vt* 1 to make fluffy – often + *out* or *up* ⟨*the bird* ∼*ed out its feathers*⟩ 2 *informal* 2a to fail to perform, achieve, or complete adequately; bungle ⟨∼ *a catch*⟩ **b** to deliver badly or forget (one's lines) in a play

**fluffy** /'flufi/ *adj* **1a** like or covered with fluff **b** light and soft or airy ⟨*a* ∼ *sponge cake*⟩ 2 *informal* lacking in intelligence, intellectual content, or decisive quality – **fluffiness** *n*

**flugelhorn** /'floohgl,hawn/ *n* a BRASS INSTRUMENT resembling a cornet but having a larger bore [Ger *flügelhorn,* fr *flügel* wing, flank + *horn* horn; fr its use to signal the flanking beaters in a shoot]

¹**fluid** /'flooh-id/ *adj* **1a** having particles that easily change their relative position without separation of the mass and that yield to pressure; capable of flowing **b** likely or tending to change or move; not fixed **c** of fluids 2 characterized by or employing a smooth easy style ⟨*the ballerina's* ∼ *movements*⟩ **3a** available for a different use **b** easily converted into cash ⟨∼ *assets*⟩ [Fr or L; Fr *fluide,* fr L *fluidus,* fr *fluere* to flow; akin to Gk *phlyzein* to boil over, L *flare* to blow – more at BLOW] – **fluidly** *adv,* **fluidity** *also* **fluidness** *n*

²**fluid** *n* 1 something capable of flowing to conform to the outline of its container; *specif* a liquid or gas 2 a liquid in the body of an animal or plant ⟨*cerebrospinal* ∼⟩ – **fluidal** *adj,* **fluidally** *adv*

**fluid drachm** /dram/, *chiefly NAm* **fluidram** /,flooh-i'dram/ a unit of capacity equal to ¹/₈ fluid ounce (about 3.55 millilitres)

**fluid drive** *n* a device (e g an automatic car gearbox) containing fluid that transmits power from an engine to a driven unit (e g the wheels of a car)

**fluidics** /flooh'idiks/ *n taking sing vb* the use of fluid flow in shaped channels to produce devices (e g an amplifier or switch) that function analogously to electronic components – **fluidic** *adj*

**fluidity** /flooh'idəti/ *n* 1 the quality or state of being fluid 2 the physical property of a substance that enables it to flow

**fluid·ize, -ise** /'flooh-i,diez/ *vt* 1 to cause to flow like a fluid 2 to suspend (e g solid particles) in a rapidly moving stream of gas or vapour to induce flowing motion of the whole; *esp* to fluidize the particles of (a loose bed of material) in an upward flow (e g of a gas) to increase the rate of a chemical or physical reaction – **fluidizer** *n,* **fluidization** *n*

**fluid ounce,** *NAm* **fluidounce** /,flooh-i'downs/ *n* 1 a British unit of liquid capacity equal to ¹/₂₀ imperial pint (about 28.41 millilitres) 2 a US unit of liquid capacity equal to ¹/₁₆ US pint (about 29.54 millilitres)

¹**fluke** /floohk/ *n* 1 a flatfish 2 a LIVER FLUKE or related TREMATODE worm [ME, fr OE *flōc;* akin to OHG *flah* smooth – more at FLAKE]

²**fluke** *n* 1 the part of an anchor that digs into the sea, river, etc bottom 2 a barbed head (e g of a harpoon) 3 either of the lobes of a whale's tail [perh fr ¹*fluke;* fr its flat shape]

³**fluke** *n* 1 an accidentally successful stroke or action 2 a stroke of luck ⟨*the discovery was a* ∼⟩ [origin unknown] – **fluke** *vt*

**fluky** *also* **flukey** /'floohki/ *adj, informal* 1 happening by or depending on chance rather than skill 2 *esp of wind* unsteady, changeable

**flume** /floohm/ *n* 1 a ravine or gorge with a stream running through it 2 an inclined channel for conveying water (e g for power generation) [prob fr ME *flum* river, fr OF, fr L *flumen,* fr *fluere*]

**flummery** /'fluməri/ *n* 1 a sweet dish typically made with flour or oatmeal, eggs, honey, cream, and an alcoholic drink (e g whisky or Madeira) 2 pretentious humbug [W *llymru*]

**flummox** /'fluməks/ *vt* to bewilder or confuse completely [origin unknown]

**flump** /flump/ *vb or n, informal* (to move or drop with) a dull heavy sound ⟨∼*ed down into his chair with a sigh*⟩ [imit]

**flung** /flung/ *past of* FLING

**flunk** /flungk/ *vb, chiefly NAm informal vi* 1 to fail, esp in an examination or course 2 to be turned *out* of a school or college for failure ∼ *vt* 1 to give a failing mark to 2 to get a failing mark in [perh blend of *flinch* and *funk*] – **flunk** *n,* **flunker** *n*

**flunky, flunkey** /'flungki/ *n* 1 a liveried servant 2 a yes-man 3 *chiefly NAm* a person performing menial duties ⟨*worked as a* ∼ *in a cookhouse*⟩ [Sc, perh fr *flanker* one who stands at somebody's side]

**fluor** /'flooh-aw/ *n* FLUORSPAR [NL, fr L, flow, fr *fluere* – more at FLUID]

**fluor-** /flooə-, flaw-/, **fluoro-** *comb form* 1 fluorine ⟨fluor*ide*⟩ ⟨fluoro*carbon*⟩ 2 *also* **fluori-** fluorescence ⟨fluoro*scope*⟩ ⟨fluori*meter*⟩ [Fr, fr *fluorine*]

**fluoresce** /flooə'res, flaw-/ *vi* to produce, undergo, or exhibit fluorescence [back-formation fr *fluorescence*] – **fluorescer** *n*

**fluorescein, fluoresceine** /flooə'resi-in, flaw-/ *n* a yellow to red dye, $C_{20}H_{12}O_5$, with a bright yellow-green fluorescence in alkaline solution

**fluorescence** /flooə'res(ə)ns, flaw-/ *n* the emission of or property of a substance of emitting ELECTROMAGNETIC RADIATION, usu as visible light, as a result of the simultaneous absorption of radiation or bombardment by particles, esp electrons, from a separate source; *also* the radiation emitted [*fluor*spar + -*escence*]

**fluorescent** /flooə'res(ə)nt, flaw-/ *adj* 1 of, having, or exhibiting fluorescence 2 bright and glowing as a result of fluorescence ⟨*a* ∼ *pink*⟩

**fluorescent lamp** *n* a tubular electric lamp having a coating of a PHOSPHOR (fluorescent material) on its inner surface and containing mercury vapour that, when an electric current flows through it, emits ultraviolet radiation which is absorbed by the phosphor causing it to emit visible light

**fluoridate** /'flooəri,dayt, flaw-/ *vt* to add a fluoride to (e g drinking water) – **fluoridation** *n*

**fluoride** /'flooəried, flaw-/ *n* a chemical compound of fluorine, esp with another chemical element or group

**fluorimeter** /flooə'rimitə, flaw-/, **fluorometer** /flooə'romitə, flaw-/ *n* an instrument for measuring the intensity, wavelength, etc of radiation produced by fluorescence and related phenomena, or the concentration of a fluorescent substance – **fluorimetry, fluorometry** *n,* **fluorimetric, fluorometric** *adj*

**fluorinate** /'flooəri,nayt, flaw-/ *vt* to treat or cause to combine with fluorine or a compound of fluorine – **fluorination** *n*

**fluorine** /'flooəreen, flaw-/ *n* a nonmetallic chemical element that belongs to the same group of elements as chlorine, bromine, and iodine (the HALOGENS), has a VALENCY of one, and occurs normally as a pale yellowish inflammable irritating toxic gas [Fr, fr NL *fluor*]

**fluorite** /'flooəriet, flaw-/ *n* fluorspar [It, fr NL *fluor*]

**fluoro-** /flooəroh-, flawroh-/ – see FLUOR-

**fluorocarbon** /,flooəroh'kahb(ə)n, flaw-/ *n* any of various chemically nonreactive (INERT) compounds containing carbon and fluorine that are used chiefly as lubricants and refrigerants and in making resins and plastics

**fluorography** /flooə'rografi, flaw-/ *n* the photography of images produced using a fluoroscope; PHOTOFLUOROGRAPHY – **fluorographic** *adj*

**fluoroscope** /'flooərə,skohp, flaw-/ *n* an instrument used for observing the internal structure of an opaque object (eg the living body) that consists of a fluorescent screen on which X-ray or gamma-ray images of the object are seen as visible light and can be viewed directly without the need for photography [ISV] – **fluoroscopy** *n*, **fluoroscopist** *n*, **fluoroscopic** *adj*, **fluoroscopically** *adv*

**fluorosis** /flooə'rohsis, flaw-/ *n* an abnormal condition (eg mottling of the teeth) caused by excessive intake of fluorine compounds [NL] – **fluorotic** *adj*

**fluorouracil** /,flooəroh'yooərəsil, ,flaw-/ *n* a fluorine-containing chemical compound, $C_4H_3FN_2O_2$, used to treat some kinds of cancer [*fluor-* + *uracil*]

**fluorspar** /'flooə,spah/ *n* a mineral consisting of calcium fluoride, $CaF_2$, that occurs in a colourless and various coloured forms, is the chief source of fluorine, and is used in the making of various glasses and as a FLUX in the manufacture and refining of metals

**fluphenazine** /flooh'fenəzeen/ *n* a chemical compound, $C_{22}H_{26}F_3N_3OS$, derived from PHENOTHIAZINE that is a tranquillizer used similarly to CHLORPROMAZINE (eg in the treatment of schizophrenia and other disturbed conditions) [*fluor-* + *phenazine*]

**¹flurry** /'fluri/ *n* **1a** a gust of wind **b** a brief light fall of snow **2** a state of nervous excitement or bustle **3** a brief rise or fall in prices; a short-lived outburst of trading activity *synonyms* see ¹FUSS [prob fr obs *flurr* to scatter, ruffle]

**²flurry** *vb* to (cause to) become agitated and confused

**¹flush** /flush/ *vi* to take wing suddenly ∼ *vt* **1** to cause (a bird) to flush **2** to expose or chase from a place of concealment 〈∼ed *the boys from their hiding place*〉 – often + *out* 〈∼ *out the criminals*〉 [ME *flusshen*, perh fr imit origin]

**²flush** *n* **1** (a cleansing with) a sudden flow, esp of water **2a** a sudden increase or expansion esp of new plant growth **b** a surge of emotion 〈*felt a ∼ of anger at the insult*〉 **3a** a tinge of red esp in the cheeks; a blush **b** a fresh and vigorous state 〈*in the first ∼ of womanhood*〉 **4** a transitory sensation of extreme heat; *specif* HOT FLUSH **5** *Br* a device for flushing toilets or drains [perh modif of L *fluxus* – more at FLUX]

**³flush** *vi* **1** to flow and spread suddenly and freely **2a** to glow brightly with a ruddy colour 〈*dawn was already* ∼ing *beyond the line of hills*〉 **b** to blush **3** to produce new growth 〈*the plants* ∼ed *twice during the year*〉 ∼ *vt* **1a** to cause to flow or be carried along on a stream of liquid; *specif* to dispose of thus **b** to pour liquid over or through; *esp* to cleanse or wash out (as if) with a rush of liquid 〈∼ *the toilet*〉 〈∼ *the lungs with air*〉 **2** to inflame, excite – usu pass 〈*was* ∼ed *with victory*〉 **3** to cause to blush **4** to prepare (a sheep) for breeding by special feeding

**⁴flush** *adj* **1** filled to overflowing **2** of a ruddy healthy colour **3a** having or forming a continuous edge or unbroken surface; not indented, recessed, or projecting 〈∼ *panelling*〉 **b** directly abutting or immediately adjacent: eg **b(1)** set even with an edge of a type page or column; having no indention **b(2)** arranged edge to edge so as to fit snugly **4** *informal* readily available; abundant **5** *informal* having a plentiful supply of money *synonyms* see ³LEVEL – **flushness** *n*

**⁵flush** *adv* **1** so as to form a level or even surface or edge **2** squarely 〈*hit him* ∼ *on the chin*〉

**⁶flush** *vt* to make flush 〈∼ *the headings on a page*〉

**⁷flush** *n* **1** a hand of playing cards, esp in a gambling game, all of the same suit **2** a 5-card hand in poker in which all the cards are of the same suit but not in sequence – compare STRAIGHT FLUSH [MF *flus, fluz*, fr L *fluxus* flow]

**¹fluster** /'flustə/ *vt* **1** to make rather drunk **2** to put into a state of agitated or nervous confusion; upset ∼ *vi* to move or behave in an agitated or confused manner [prob of Scand origin; akin to Icel *flaustur* hurry]

**²fluster** *n* a state of agitated confusion

**¹flute** /flooht/ *n* **1** a woodwind instrument of high range that consists of a cylindrical tube stopped at one end and is played by blowing air across a side hole and varying the pitch with finger-operated keys **2a** a grooved pleat (eg on a ruffle) **b** a rounded groove; *specif* any of the vertical parallel grooves on the shafts of columns in the ancient Greek or Roman styles [ME *floute*, fr MF *flahute*, fr OProv *flaut*] – **flutelike** *adj*

**²flute** *vi* to produce a flutelike sound ∼ *vt* **1** to utter with a flutelike sound **2** to form flutes in (eg the edge of a piecrust) – **fluter** *n*

**fluting** /'floohting/ *n* a series of flutes 〈*the* ∼ *of a column*〉

**flutist** /'floohtist/ *n*, *chiefly NAm* a flautist

**¹flutter** /'flutə/ *vi* **1** to flap the wings rapidly **2a** to move with quick wavering or flapping motions 〈*flags* ∼ing *in the wind*〉 **b** to beat or vibrate in irregular spasms 〈*his pulse* ∼ed〉 **3** to move about or behave in an agitated aimless manner ∼ *vt* to cause to flutter [ME *floteren* to float, flutter, fr OE *floterian*, freq of *flotian* to float; akin to OE *flēotan* to float – more at FLEET] – **flutterer** *n*, **fluttery** *adj*

**²flutter** *n* **1** a fluttering **2a** a state of (nervous) confusion or excitement **b** a flurry, commotion **c** abnormal spasmodic fluttering of a body part (eg the walls of a chamber of the heart) **3** a distortion in reproduced sound similar to but at a faster rate than wow **4** an unwanted oscillation (eg of an aircraft part or bridge) set up by natural forces **5** *chiefly Br* a small gamble or bet 〈*had a* ∼ *on the pools*〉

**flutter kick** *n* an alternating kicking motion of the legs used in various swimming styles (eg the crawl)

**fluty** /'floohti/ *adj* like the sound of a flute; light and clear

**fluvial** /'floohvi·əl, -vyəl/ *adj* of, produced by, or living in a stream or river [L *fluvialis*, fr *fluvius* river, fr *fluere*]

**fluviatile** /'floohvi·ə,til, -,tiel/ *adj* fluvial [MF, fr L *fluviatilis*, irreg fr *fluvius*]

**¹flux** /fluks/ *n* **1** a continuous flow or flowing (eg of a stream) **2a** an influx **b** continual change or fluctuation 〈*the programme was in a state of* ∼〉 **3a** a substance used to promote the melting or fluidity of a solid; *esp* a substance used in smelting ores or refining metals to promote the melting of the ore or metal and to remove impurities by combining with them to form SLAG **b** a substance (eg rosin) applied to metal surfaces to be joined by soldering, welding, etc that combines with and removes oxides formed on the metal surfaces, thus cleaning them and promoting their union **4a** the rate of flow or transfer of a liquid, gas, particles, or energy across a given surface **b** the strength or effect of the forces acting in an area of a magnetic or electric field **5** *archaic* an (abnormal) flowing of a liquid, esp watery excrement, from the body [ME, fr MF & ML; MF, fr ML *fluxus*, fr L, flow, fr *fluxus*, pp of *fluere* to flow – more at FLUID]

**²flux** *vt* **1** to cause to become fluid **2** to treat with a flux ∼ *vi* to become fluid

**flux gate** *n* a device used to indicate the direction of the earth's magnetic field

**fluxion** /'fluksh(ə)n/ *n* **1** constant change **2** *pl, archaic* CALCULUS **2b** **3** *obs* the action of flowing – **fluxional** *adj*

**flux valve** *n* FLUX GATE

**¹fly** /flie/ *vb* **flew** /flooh/; **flown** /flohn/ *vi* **1a** to move in or pass through the air by means of wings **b** to move through the air or space 〈*clouds* ∼ing *across the sky*〉 **c** to float, wave, or soar in the air 〈*flags* ∼ing *at half-mast*〉 **2a** to take flight; flee **b** to fade and disappear; vanish 〈*the shadows have* flown〉 **3a** to move, act, or pass swiftly 〈*he* flew *past me*〉 **b** to move or pass suddenly and violently into a specified state 〈flew *into a rage*〉 〈*the door* flew *open*〉 **c** to seem to pass quickly 〈*our holiday simply* flew〉 **4** to become expended or dissipated rapidly **5** to pursue or attack in flight 〈*hoped to* ∼ *at higher game*〉 **6** to operate or travel in an aircraft or spacecraft **7** *chiefly informal* to depart in haste; dash 〈*I must* ∼, *I've a meeting*〉 ∼ *vt* **1a** to cause to fly or float in the air 〈*was* ∼ing *his kite*〉 **b** to operate (eg a balloon, aircraft, or spacecraft) in flight **c** to journey over by flying 〈∼ *the Atlantic*〉 **2** to flee or escape from **3** to transport by aircraft **4** to use (a specified airline) for travelling 〈*I always* ∼ *British Airways*〉 **5** to hang (eg scenery) in the flies of a theatre [ME *flien*, fr OE *flēogan*; akin to OHG *fliogan* to fly, OE *flōwan* to flow] – **fly in the face/teeth of** to act forthrightly or brazenly in defiance of – **let fly** to aim a blow – see also **fly BLIND, with flying COLOURS, fly CONTACT, as the CROW flies, fly off the HANDLE, fly HIGH, go fly a KITE**

*usage* Both **fly** and the somewhat literary **flee** can mean "run away" or "run away from", but **fly** is not used in this sense in the past tenses. Compare ⟨we must **fly/flee** the country⟩ ⟨we **fled** (not △ **flew**) the country⟩.

**fly (out) at** *vt* to assail suddenly and violently

²**fly** *n* 1 an act or process of flying 2a a device consisting of two or more radial vanes rotating about a spindle, and used esp to govern the speed of clockwork or very light machinery b FLYWHEEL 3 *pl* the space over a stage where scenery and equipment can be hung 4 something attached by one edge: e g 4a a garment opening concealed by a fold of cloth extending over the fastener; *esp, pl* such an opening in the front of a pair of trousers ⟨*his* flies *were undone*⟩ b FLY SHEET 3 c(1) the length of an extended flag from its staff or support c(2) the outer or loose end of a flag 5 a flyleaf 6 *chiefly Br* a light covered horse-drawn carriage

³**fly** *adj, chiefly Br informal* keen, artful ⟨*the ~ boys, the real wheeler-dealers of property*⟩ [prob fr ¹*fly*]

⁴**fly** *n* 1 a winged insect – often in combination ⟨*mayfly*⟩ 2 TWO-WINGED FLY; *esp* one that is large and stout-bodied 3 a natural or artificial fly attached to a fishhook for use as bait [ME *flie*, fr OE *flēoge*; akin to OHG *flioga* fly, OE *flēogan* to fly] – **fly in the ointment** a detracting factor or element [fr the reference in Ecclesiastes 10:1] – **fly on the wall** somebody who watches others while not being noticed him-/herself – **there are no flies on** there is little or no possibility of deceiving or cheating

**fly agaric** /'agərik, ə'garik/ *n* a poisonous toadstool (*Amanita muscaria*) that has a usu bright red cap with small white scaly patches [fr its being a source of poison for flies]

**fly ash** *n* fine solid particles of noncombustible ash carried out of a bed of solid fuel during combustion, esp in power stations

**flyaway** /'flie·ə,way/ *adj* 1 lacking practical sense; flighty 2 *esp of the hair* tending not to stay in place

**flyback** /-,bak/ *n* the return of the spot of light on a CATHODE-RAY TUBE after it has traced one image and before it begins the next

**flybelt** /'flie,belt/ *n* an area infested with tsetse flies

¹**flyblow** /'flie,bloh/ *n* (infestation, esp of meat, with) an egg or young larva deposited by a FLESH FLY or blowfly [⁴*fly* + ²*blow* (deposit of insect eggs)]

²**flyblow** *vt* **flyblew** /-,blooh/; **flyblown** /-,blohn/ 1 to deposit flyblows in 2 to taint, contaminate

**flyblown** /-,blohn/ *adj* 1 infested with flyblows 2 impure, tainted ⟨*a world ~ with the vices of irresponsible power* – V L Parrington⟩ 3a not bright and new; seedy, moth-eaten b trite, hackneyed ⟨*a long list of ~ metaphors* – Horizon⟩

**fly book** *n* a case, usu in the form of a book, for storing fishing flies

**flyby** /'flie,bie/ *n, pl* **flybys** /-,biez/ 1 a flypast 2a a flight of a spacecraft close to a planet, moon, etc, esp to obtain scientific data b a spacecraft that makes a flyby

¹**fly-by-,night, fly-by-nighter** *n, informal* 1 one who seeks to evade responsibilities or debts by flight 2 someone or something lacking established reputation or standing; *esp* a shaky business enterprise

²**fly-by-night** *adj, chiefly informal* 1 given to making a quick profit, usu by disreputable or irresponsible acts ⟨*~ promoters trying to cash in* – Tom McSloy⟩ 2 transitory, passing ⟨*~ fashions*⟩ 3 not reliable

¹**fly-by-,wire** *n* a system of controlling an aircraft by having only electrical and no mechanical connections between the controls and the aircraft parts

**fly casting** *n* the casting of artificial flies in fly-fishing or as a competitive sport

**flycatcher** /-,kachə/ *n* any of several small birds (family Muscicapidae) that feed on insects caught while flying

**flyer** /'flie·ə/ *n* a flier

¹**fly-,fishing** *n* a method of fishing (e g for salmon or trout) in which an artificial fly is cast by use of a long flexible rod, a reel, and a relatively heavy line

**fly front** *n* a concealed fastening on the front of a garment – compare ²FLY 4a

**fly gallery** *n* a narrow raised platform at the side of a stage from which lines to hang scenery are operated

¹**fly-,half** *n* STAND-OFF (rugby player)

¹**fly-,in** *adj, chiefly Can* of or being a place where the only access is by aeroplane ⟨*~ communities*⟩

¹**flying** /'flie·ing/ *adj* 1a (capable of) moving in the air b rapidly moving ⟨*~ feet*⟩ c very brief hasty ⟨*a ~ visit*⟩ 2 intended for ready movement or action ⟨*~ pickets*⟩ 3 of (the operation of) or using an aircraft ⟨*belongs to a ~ club*⟩ 4 (to be) traversed (e g in speed-record trials) after a FLYING START ⟨*~ mile*⟩

²**flying** *n* 1 travel by air 2 the operation of an aircraft or spacecraft

**flying boat** *n* a seaplane with a frame adapted for floating

**flying bomb** *n* a pilotless aircraft carrying explosives

**flying bridge** *n* the highest navigational bridge on a ship

**flying buttress** *n* a projecting arched structure that supports a wall or building

**flying column** *n* a strong military detachment that operates independently of the main force

**flying disk** *n, NAm* FLYING SAUCER

**flying field** *n* a small airfield

**flying fish** *n* any of numerous fishes (family Exocoetidae), chiefly of tropical and warm seas, that have one or two pairs of long winglike fins and are able to glide some distance through the air

**flying fox** *n* FRUIT BAT (fruit-eating bat)

**flying gurnard** *n* any of several marine fishes (family Dactylopteridae) that resemble gurnards and have large PECTORAL FINS (pair of fins just behind the head) that allow them to glide above the water for short distances

**flying jib** *n* a triangular sail set furthest forward on a ship with two or more such sails

**flying lemur** *n* a tree-dwelling nocturnal mammal (genus *Cynocephalus*) of the E Indies and the Philippines, that is about the size of a cat and makes long sailing leaps using a parachute-like broad fold of skin extending from the neck to the tail and between the limbs on each side of the body

**flying mare** *n* a wrestling throw in which an opponent is seized by the wrist and thrown over the aggressor's back

**flying officer** *n* – see MILITARY RANKS table

**flying phalanger** *n* any of a group of marsupial mammals (e g genus *Petaurus*) that resemble FLYING SQUIRRELS and that have thick fur and a long bushy tail

**flying saucer** *n* any of various unidentified objects reported as seen in the air and usually described as being saucer-shaped or disc-shaped

**flying shore** *n* horizontal props between two parallel walls that provide clear working space underneath

**flying squad** *n, often cap F&S* a usu small standby group of people; esp police, ready to move or act swiftly in an emergency

**flying squirrel** *n* any of various squirrels having folds of skin connecting the forelegs and hind legs that are used in making long gliding leaps

**flying start** *n* 1 a start in racing in which the participants approach the starting line at speed but are penalized if they cross it before receiving the starting signal 2 a start to a race in which one contestant has an advantage through starting unfairly before the others 3 a privileged or successful beginning ⟨*his family's wealth gave him a ~ in life*⟩

**flying university** *n* a privately organized means of providing higher education set up in opposition to repression by the (communist) state

**flying wedge** *n* a moving formation (e g of guards or police) resembling a wedge

**flyleaf** /-,leef/, **fly** *n* a blank leaf at the beginning or end of a book; *specif* one that forms a continuous sheet with the leaf stuck to the inside of the cover [²*fly*]

**flyman** /'fliemən/ *n* a stagehand in a theatre who manipulates the curtains and scenery

¹**fly-,off** *n* a test under simulated operational conditions of aircraft competing for acceptance (e g for purchase by an air force)

**flyover** /-,ohvə/ *n, Br* (the upper level of) a crossing of two roads, railways, etc at different levels

**flypaper** /-,paypə/ *n* paper coated with a sticky, often poisonous, substance for killing flies

**flypast** /-,pahst/ *n, Br* a ceremonial usu low-altitude flight by (an) aircraft over a person or public gathering

**flyposting** /-,pohsting/ *n* the unauthorized placing of advertising material (e g posters and stickers) in public places [²*fly*] – **flypost** *vb*

**fly rail** *n* a support for the hinged leaf of a table [²*fly*]

**fly rod** *n* a light springy fishing rod used in fly-fishing

**flysch** /flish/ *n* a thick and extensive deposit, largely of sandstone, that is formed in a trough adjacent to a rising mountain belt and is common esp in the Alpine region of Europe [Ger dial.]

**fly sheet** n 1 a small pamphlet or circular 2 a sheet of a folder, booklet, or catalogue giving directions for the use of or information about the material that follows 3 also **fly** an outer protective sheet covering a tent (eg from rain or sun) [$^2$fly]

**flyspeck** /'fliespek/ n 1 a speck made by fly excrement; broadly a small spot or speck 2 something small and insignificant – **flyspeck** vt

**flyswatter** /'flieswotə/ n an implement for killing insects that consists of a flat piece of rubber, plastic, or wire netting attached to a handle

**flyting** /'flieting/ n a dispute or exchange of personal abuse in verse form (eg in an epic or drama) [gerund of E dial. flyte to quarrel, strive, scold, fr ME fliten, fr OE flītan, akin to OHG flīzan to contend, strive]

**flyway** /'flieway/ n an established route used by birds when migrating

**flyweight** /'fliewayt/ n a boxer who weighs not more than 8 stone (50.8 kilograms) if professional, or between 48 and 51 kilograms (between about 7 stone 7 pounds and 8 stone) if amateur

**flywheel** /'flieweel/ n a heavy wheel that revolves on a shaft (eg an engine crankshaft) and can either reduce fluctuations in the speed of rotation of the shaft or store energy for future use [$^2$fly]

**fly whisk** n a whisk (eg of horsehair) for brushing away flies

**flywire** /'flie,wieə/ n, chiefly Austr wire mesh, used esp for door and window screens, of such fineness that flies cannot pass through

**FM** /,ef 'em/ adj of or being a broadcasting or receiving system, usu noted for lack of interference, that transmits a signal by varying the frequency rather than the AMPLITUDE of the CARRIER wave (wave that carries the signal) [frequency modulation]

**FMN** /,ef em 'en/ n a chemical compound, $C_{17}H_{21}N_4O_9P$, formed from the vitamin riboflavin, that is the essential active nonprotein part (COENZYME) of several FLAVOPROTEIN enzymes and acts esp as a carrier of hydrogen in the breakdown and synthesis of fats and other biochemical substances in living cells [flavin mononucleotide]

**'f-,number** n the ratio of the FOCAL LENGTH to the size of the opening (APERTURE) through which light must pass in a telescope, camera, or other optical system; specif a number that expresses the size of the aperture of a camera lens and is used in conjunction with the exposure time to regulate the amount of light reaching the film. The smaller the f-number the larger the aperture and the greater the amount of light reaching the film. [focal length]

**$^1$foal** /fohl/ n 1 the young of an animal of the horse family; esp one under one year 2 a horse up to the first January after its birth [ME fole, fr OE fola; akin to L pullus young of an animal, Gk pais child – more at FEW]

**$^2$foal** vb to give birth to (a foal)

**$^1$foam** /fohm/ n 1a (a substance in the form of) a light frothy mass of fine bubbles formed in or on the surface of a liquid (eg by agitation or fermentation) b(1) a frothy mass formed in salivating or sweating b(2) froth formed in the mouth due to disease c a stabilized chemical froth discharged from fire extinguishers 2 a material (eg a plastic) in a lightweight cellular form resulting from the introduction of gas bubbles during manufacture 3 poetic the sea [ME fome, fr OE fām; akin to OHG feim foam, L spuma foam, pumex pumice] – **foamless** adj

**$^2$foam** vi 1a to produce or form foam b to froth at the mouth 2 to gush out in foam 3 to become covered (as if) with foam ⟨streets... ~ing with life – Thomas Wolfe⟩ 4 informal to be angry – chiefly in foam at the mouth ~ vt 1 to cause to foam; specif to cause air bubbles to form in 2 to convert (eg a plastic) into a foam – **foamer** n

**foam rubber** n spongy rubber of fine texture made by introducing bubbles of air into the rubber before it solidifies

**foamy** /'fohmi/ adj 1 covered with foam; frothy 2 full of, consisting of, or resembling foam – **foamily** adv, **foaminess** n

**fob** /fob/ n 1 a small pocket on or near the waistband of a man's trousers, that was originally designed to hold a watch 2 a short strap, chain, or ribbon attached to a watch carried in a fob or a waistcoat pocket 3 a seal or ornament attached to a fob chain or ribbon [perh akin to Ger dial. fuppe pocket]

**fob off** vt -bb- 1 to put off or attempt to satisfy with a trick or excuse – usu + with 2 to pass off or offer (something spurious or inferior) as genuine – usu + on 3 to put or wave aside; dismiss, ignore usage see FOIST [arch. fob to deceive, cheat, fr ME fobben – more at FOP]

**fob watch** n a large circular watch, often with a cover for the face, that is usu carried in a fob or waistcoat pocket

**focal** /'fohk(ə)l/ adj of, having, or located at a focus – **focally** adv

**focal infection** n a bacterial infection localized in an organ or region (eg the socket of a tooth); esp one causing symptoms elsewhere in the body

**focal-ize, -ise** /'fohk(ə)liez/ vb to focus – **focalization** n

**focal length** n the distance between the centre of a lens or surface of a mirror and the FOCAL POINT; also an equivalent distance when a number of lenses are used together (eg in a microscope)

**focal plane** n a plane that is perpendicular to the axis of a lens or passes through the focus

**focal point** n 1 the point at which rays of radiation, esp light, that are parallel to the axis of a lens or mirror converge or from which they (appear to) diverge 2 FOCUS 5 ⟨the fireplace was the ~ of the room⟩

**fo'c's'le** /'fohks(ə)l/ n FORECASTLE

**$^1$focus** /'fohkəs/ n, pl **focuses** /'fohkəsiz/, **foci** /'fohkie, 'fohsie/ 1a the point at which an object must be placed for an image formed by a lens or mirror to be sharp b a point at which rays (eg of light, heat, or sound) converge or from which they (appear to) diverge after reflection or REFRACTION 2a FOCAL LENGTH b adjustment (eg of the eye) for distinct vision c a state in which something must be placed in order to be clearly perceived ⟨tried to bring the issues into ~⟩ 3 a fixed point that together with a straight line (DIRECTRIX) forms a reference system for generating a curve (eg a parabola) that is a CONIC SECTION 4 a localized area of disease, or the chief site of a disease or infection that affects all or most of the body 5 a centre of activity, attraction, or attention ⟨the ~ of the meeting was on drug abuse⟩ 6 the place below the surface of the earth at which an earthquake has its origin [NL, fr L, hearth] – **focusless** adj – **out of/in focus** (not) having or giving the proper sharpness of outline due to focussing

**$^2$focus** vb -ss-, -s- vt 1 to bring (eg light rays) to a focus 2 to cause to be concentrated ⟨~sed their attention on the most urgent problems⟩ 3a to adjust the focus of b to bring into focus ~ vi 1 to come to a focus; converge 2 to bring or adjust one's eyes or a camera to a specific focus or a particular range – **focussable** adj, **focusser** n

**fodder** /'fodə/ n 1 coarse or bulk food (eg hay) for cattle, horses, sheep, or similar domestic animals 2 something that is used to supply a constant impersonal demand ⟨collected data which became computer ~⟩ – compare CANNON FODDER [ME, fr OE fōdor; akin to OHG fuotar food – more at FOOD] – **fodder** vt

**foe** /foh/ n, chiefly poetic 1 an enemy, adversary, or opponent 2 **foeman, foe** an enemy in war [ME fo, fr OE fāh, fr fāh hostile; akin to OHG gifēh hostile]

**foehn** /fuhn (Ger fœ:n)/ n FÖHN (warm dry wind)

**foetal, fetal** /'feet(ə)l/ adj of or being a foetus

**foeticide** /'feeti,sied/ n the act of killing a foetus

**foetid** /'feetid, 'fetid/ adj fetid – **foetidly** adv, **foetidness** n

**foeto-, foeti-, feto-, feti-** /'feetoh-, 'feeti-/ comb form foetus ⟨foeticide⟩; foetal and ⟨foetoplacental⟩ [NL fetus]

**foetus, fetus** /'feetəs/ n an unborn or unhatched VERTEBRATE animal, esp after attaining the basic and recognizable shape of its kind; specif a developing human embryo from usu three months after conception to birth – compare EMBRYO [NL fetus, fr L, act of bearing young, offspring; akin to L fetus fruitful – more at FEMININE]

**$^1$fog** /fog/ n 1 dead or decaying long grass on land in the winter 2 a second growth of grass after the first growth has been cut for hay; AFTERMATH 1 [ME]

**$^2$fog** n 1 a mass of fine particles of water suspended in the lower atmosphere and differing from cloud only in being near the ground 2 (a substance consisting of fine particles that are diffused through the atmosphere causing) a murky or thick condition of the atmosphere 3a a state of confusion or bewilderment b something that confuses or obscures ⟨hid behind a ~ of rhetoric⟩ 4 (an area of) cloudiness or partial opacity on on a developed photograph (eg a print, negative, or transparency), usu caused by exposure to X rays or extraneous light or chemical action resulting from incorrect developing [prob of Scand origin; akin to Dan fog spray, shower; akin to L pustula blister, pimple, Gk physan to blow]

**$^3$fog** vb -gg- vt 1 to cover, envelop, or suffuse (as if) with fog 2 to make obscure or confusing ⟨accusations which ~ged the real issues⟩ 3 to make confused ⟨arguments that ~ the mind⟩

**4** to produce fog on (eg a photographic print or negative) ~ *vi* **1** to become covered or thick with fog **2** to become blurred (as if) by a covering of fog or mist **3** *of a photographic print, negative, etc* to become cloudy or indistinct as a result of exposure to extraneous radiation or incorrect developing

**fogbound** /'fog,bownd/ *adj* **1** covered with or surrounded by fog ⟨*a ~ coast*⟩ **2** unable to move or operate because of fog ⟨*a ~ ship*⟩

**fogbow** /'fog,boh/ *n* a hazy or faint arc of white or yellowish light sometimes seen in fog

**fogey, fogy** /'fohgi/ *n, chiefly informal* a person with old-fashioned ideas – chiefly in *old fogey* [origin unknown] – **fogeyish** *adj*, **fogeyism** *n*

**foggage** /'fogij/ *n, chiefly Scot* ¹FOG 1

**foggy** /'fogi/ *adj* **1a** filled or abounding with fog **b** covered or made opaque by moisture or grime **2** blurred, obscured ⟨*hadn't the* foggiest *notion what they were voting for*⟩ **3** *of a photographic print, negative, etc* affected by fog; cloudy, indistinct – **foggily** *adv*, **fogginess** *n*

**foghorn** /'fog,hawn/ *n* **1** a horn (eg on a ship or lighthouse) sounded in a fog to give warning to ships at sea **2** *informal* a loud hoarse voice

**fog lamp** *n* an additional headlight for a vehicle, that is positioned lower on the vehicle than a normal headlight and has a powerful beam used to aid visibility in fog

**föhn** /fuhn/ (*Ger* fø:n)/ *n* a warm dry wind that blows down the sheltered side of a mountain range (eg the Alps) [Ger, deriv of L *favonius* warm west wind]

**foible** /'foybl/ *n* **1** the part of a sword blade between the middle and point – compare FORTE 2 **2** a minor weakness or short-coming in a person's character or behaviour; *also* a quirk, idiosyncrasy [obs Fr (now *faible*), fr obs *foible* weak, fr OF *feble* feeble]

**foie gras** /,fwah 'grah (*Fr* fwa gra)/ *n* the rich fatty liver of a goose, usu in the form of a pâté [Fr]

¹**foil** /foyl/ *vt* **1** to spoil or wipe out (the trail or scent of a hunted animal) by crossing or retracing **2a** to prevent (a person) from attaining an end or goal; frustrate, defeat **b** to prevent (a plan, attempt, etc) from succeeding [ME *foilen* to trample, full cloth, fr MF *fouler* – more at FULL]

²**foil** *n* **1** a light fencing sword with a circular guard to protect the hand and a flexible blade tapering to a blunted point – compare ÉPÉE, SABRE **2** foils *pl*, foil the art or sport of fencing with the foil **3** *archaic* the track or trail of a hunted animal [ME *foyle* defeat, fr *foilen;* (2,3) perh of different origin]

³**foil** *n* **1a** a curved recess or indentation between cusps or points (eg in Gothic tracery) **b** any of several arcs or curves that enclose a complex design – usu in combination; compare TREFOIL, QUATREFOIL **2a** metal in the form of a very thin sheet ⟨*silver ~*⟩ **b** a thin coat of tin or silver laid on the back of a mirror to provide a reflecting surface **3** a thin piece of metal put under a gem or an inferior stone to add colour or brilliance **4** one who or that which serves as a contrast to another ⟨*acted as a ~ for a comedian*⟩ **5** HYDROFOIL 1 [ME, leaf, fr MF *foille* (fr L *folia*, pl of *folium*) & *foil*, fr L *folium* – more at BLADE]

⁴**foil** *vt* **1** to back or cover with foil **2** to enhance by contrast; act as a foil to

**foiled** /'foyld/ *adj* ornamented with foils ⟨*a ~ arch*⟩

**foilist** /'foylist/ *n* one who fences with a foil

¹**foin** /foyn/ *vi, archaic* to thrust with a pointed weapon; lunge [ME *foinen*, fr *foin* fork for spearing fish, fr MF *foisne*, fr L *fuscina*]

²**foin** *n, archaic* a pass or thrust in fencing; a lunge

**foison** /'foyz(ə)n/ *n* **1** *chiefly Scot* **1a** physical energy or strength **b** nourishment, sustenance **2** *archaic* a rich harvest or supply; plenty, abundance **3** *pl, obs* resources [ME *foisoun* abundance, fr MF *foison*, fr L *fusion-, fusio* act of pouring – more at FUSION]

**foist** /foyst/ *vt* **1** to introduce or insert surreptitiously or without warrant *in* or *into* **2** to force another to accept (something or somebody unwanted) ⟨*foisted his company on them*⟩ **3** to pass off as genuine or worthy □ (2&3) usu + *off on, on,* or *upon* [prob fr obs D *vuisten* to take into one's hand, fr MD *vuysten*, fr *vuyst* fist; akin to OE *fyst* fist]

*usage* Correctly, one *foists* things *on* people, or *fobs* people *off with* things ⟨*I won't be* fobbed (not △ foisted) off *with that excuse*⟩.

**folacin** /'fohləsin/ *n* FOLIC ACID (type of vitamin B) [*folic acid* + *-in*]

¹**fold** /fohld/ *n* **1** an enclosure for sheep **2a** a flock of sheep **b** a

group of people adhering to a common belief, enthusiasm, or religious faith ⟨*brought him back to the ~*⟩ [ME, fr OE *falod;* akin to MLG *vält* enclosure]

²**fold** *vt* to pen (eg sheep) in a fold

³**fold** *vt* **1** to lay one part of (something) over another part ⟨*~ a letter*⟩ **2** to reduce the length or bulk of by doubling over ⟨*he ~ed up the map*⟩ **3a** to clasp together; entwine ⟨*he ~ed his hands*⟩ **b** to bring (limbs) to rest close to the body ⟨*the bird ~ed its wings*⟩ **4a** to clasp or enwrap closely; embrace ⟨*~ing her son to her breast*⟩ ⟨*~ed her in his arms*⟩ **b** to enclose; cover ⟨*~ed it carefully in a small piece of paper*⟩ **c** to wrap or wind round ⟨*~ the paper round the flowers*⟩ **5** to bend (eg a layer of rock) into folds **6** to blend (a food ingredient) into a mixture without stirring or beating ~ *vi* **1** to become or be capable of being folded **2** *informal* to fail completely; collapse; *esp* to stop production or operation because of lack of business ⟨*the new restaurant ~ed in less than a year*⟩ □ (2) often + *up;* (4b&6) usu + *in* [ME *folden*, fr OE *fealdan;* akin to OHG *faldan* to fold, Gk di*plasios* twofold] – **foldable** *adj*

⁴**fold** *n* **1a** a doubling or folding over **b** a crease or line made by folding **2** a part doubled or laid over another part; a pleat ⟨*a skirt hanging in loose ~s*⟩ **3** (a hollow inside) something that is folded together or that enfolds ⟨*held it in the ~s of her dress*⟩ **4a** a bend produced in layers of rock, usu by compression of the rock **b** *chiefly Br* an undulation in the landscape

**-fold** /-fohld/ *suffix* (→ *adj* or *adv*) **1** multiplied by (a specified number); times ⟨*a twelvefold increase*⟩ ⟨*repay you ten*fold⟩ **2** having (so many) parts ⟨*threefold aspect of the problem*⟩ [ME, fr OE *-feald;* akin to OHG *-falt* -fold, OE *fealdan*]

**foldaway** /'fohldə,way/ *adj* designed to fold out of the way or be made more compact by folding ⟨*~ doors*⟩ ⟨*~ bed*⟩

**folder** /'fohldə/ *n* **1** one who or that which folds **2** a printed circular folded usu so that the printed matter does not cross the fold **3** a folded cover or large envelope for holding or filing loose papers

**folderol, falderol** /'foldə,rol/ *n* **1** a showy useless ornament; a trifle **2** nonsense [*fol-de-rol*, a meaningless refrain in some old songs]

**folding door** *n* a door with jointed sections that can be folded together like an accordion

**folding money** *n, informal* PAPER MONEY

**folding stuff** *n, informal* PAPER MONEY

**foldout** /'fohld,owt/ *n* a folded insert (eg a map) in a book, magazine, etc, larger in size than the page

**foliaceous** /,fohli'ayshəs/ *adj* **1** of or resembling a foliage leaf **2** bearing leaves or leaflike parts **3** *esp of a rock or mineral* consisting of thin layers or plates

**foliage** /'fohli·ij/ *n* **1** the leaves of a plant or of a clump of plants **2** a cluster of leaves, flowers, and branches **3** an ornamental, usu curved, representation of leaves, flowers, and branches [MF *fuellage*, fr *foille* leaf – more at FOIL] – **foliaged** *adj*

**foliage leaf** *n* an ordinary green leaf as distinguished from a petal, scale, or similar modified or specialized leaf

**foliage plant** *n* a plant grown primarily for its decorative foliage

**foliar** /'fohli·ə/ *adj* of or applied to leaves ⟨*~ sprays*⟩

¹**foliate** /'fohli·ət/ *adj* **1** having leaves or leaflets – often in combination ⟨*tri*foliate⟩ **2** *also* **foliated** /'fohli,aytid/ shaped like a leaf ⟨*a ~ sponge*⟩ **3** foliated *also* foliate *esp of a rock or mineral* **3a** composed of thin layers **b** easily separable into layers [L *foliatus* leafy, fr *folium* leaf – more at BLADE]

²**foliate** /'fohli,ayt/ *vt* **1** to beat (metal) into a leaf or thin foil **2** to cover (glass or a mirror) with a thin coat of metal, esp tin amalgam **3** to number the leaves of (eg a manuscript or book) – compare ⁴PAGE **4a** to decorate (eg an arch) with foils **b** to decorate (eg a pedestal) with carved or painted foliage ~ *vi* **1** to divide or split into thin layers or leaves **2** *of a plant* to produce leaves

**foliation** /,fohlee'aysh(ə)n/ *n* **1** the act, process, or result of foliating **2a** the process of forming leaves or into a leaf **b** the state of being in leaf **c** the arrangement of leaves within a bud; vernation **3** the act of beating a metal into a thin plate or foil **4a** decoration with foliage **b** decoration or ornamentation (eg of an arch) with foils **5** the action of numbering the leaves of a book; *also* the total count of leaves so numbered **6** the foliated texture of a rock or mineral

**folic acid** /'fohlik/ *n* a water-soluble vitamin, $C_{19}H_{19}N_7O_6$, of the VITAMIN B COMPLEX that is found esp in green leafy vegetables and liver, is required for the normal production of

RED BLOOD CELLS, and whose lack in the diet results in anaemia – called also FOLACIN, VITAMIN BC [L *folium* leaf]

**folie à deux** /ˌfolee ah 'duh (*Fr* fɔli a dø)/ *n* the presence of the same or similar delusional ideas in two people closely associated with each other [Fr, lit., double madness]

**foliicolous** /ˌfolee'ikələs/ *adj* growing or parasitic on leaves ⟨*a ~ fungus*⟩ [L *folium* + ISV *-colous*]

¹**folio** /'fohlioh/ *n, pl* **folios** **1a** a leaf, consisting of both sides of a page, of a manuscript or book **b** a leaf number **c** a page number **2a** a sheet of paper folded once to form two leaves **b** the size of each of the two leaves formed from a folio **c** a book format in which a folded sheet forms two leaves; *also* a book in this format **d** a book of the largest size **3** a case or folder for loose papers **4** a certain number of words taken as a unit or division in a document for purposes of measurement or reference [ME, fr L, abl of *folium*]

²**folio** *vt* **folios**; **folioing**; **folioed** ²FOLIATE 3

**foliose** /'fohliohs/ *adj, of a lichen or related plant* having a flat, thin, and usu lobed THALLUS (undifferentiated plant body) attached to the substratum of rock, bark, or soil – compare CRUSTOSE, FRUTICOSE [L *foliosus* leafy, fr *folium*]

**folium** /'fohliəm/ *n, pl* **folia** /'fohli·ə/ a thin layer, occurring esp in METAMORPHIC rocks [NL, fr L, leaf

¹**folk** /fohk/ *n* **1** *taking pl vb* the great proportion of the members of a people that determines the group character and that tends to preserve its characteristic form of civilization, its customs, arts and crafts, legends, traditions, and superstitions from generation to generation **2** **folk** *taking pl vb*, **folks** *pl* a specified kind or class of people ⟨*old ~*⟩ ⟨*just plain ~*s⟩ **3** **folk music**, **folk** simple music, usu song, of traditional origin or style **4** *chiefly informal* **4a** **folk** *taking pl vb*, **folks** *pl* people generally **b** **folks** *pl*, *also* **folk** *taking pl vb* the members of one's own family; relatives **5** *taking pl vb*, *archaic* a group of kindred tribes; PEOPLE 5 [ME, fr OE *folc*; akin to OHG *folc* people] – **folkish** *adj*, **folkishness** *n*, **folky** *adj*

*usage* The use of **folk** for "people" adds a somewhat archaic and sentimental colouring. A group of **folk** waiting in the rain for a bus sound human and unpretentious and therefore more pitiable.

²**folk** *adj* **1** originating from or traditional with the common people of a country or region and typically reflecting their lifestyle **2** of (the study of) the common people

**folk etymology** *n* the transformation of words so as to bring them into an apparent relationship with other better-known or better-understood words (e g in the change of Spanish *cucaracha* to English *cockroach*)

**folklore** /'fohkˌlaw/ *n* **1** the traditional customs, knowledge, and beliefs of a people, preserved orally in legends, tales, and sayings **2** the study of the life and spirit of a people as revealed through their folklore – **folkloric** *adj*, **folklorish** *adj*, **folklorist** *n*, **folkloristic** *adj*

**folk medicine** *n* traditional medicine as practised non-professionally by people isolated from modern medical services, that involves use of remedies made from herbs, vegetables, etc

**folkmoot** /'fohkˌmooht/ *n* a general assembly of the people (e g of a shire) in early England [OE *folcmōt*, fr *folc* people + *mōt* meeting – more at MOOT]

**folkmote** /'fohkˌmoht/ *n* a folkmoot

**folksinger** /'fohksingə/ *n* one who sings FOLK SONGS – **folksinging** *n*

**folk song** *n* (a contemporary song in the style of) a simple song of traditional origin that usu has a repeating melody

**folksy** /'fohksi/ *adj, informal* **1** sociable, friendly **2a** informal, casual, or familiar in manner or style; unpretentious ⟨*play is packed with ~ dialogue full of homespun wisdom* – *Nation Review* (*Melbourne*)⟩ **b** *derog* affecting a lack of sophistication [*folks* + *-y*] – **folksily** *adv*, **folksiness** *n*

**folktale** /'fohktayl/ *n* an anonymous traditional story that is transmitted orally and in which time and place are rarely specified

**folkway** /'fohkway/ *n* a way of thinking, feeling, or acting common to a people or to a social group; *esp* a traditional social custom

**folkweave** /'fohkweev/ *n* a rough loosely woven fabric

**follicle** /'folikl/ *n* **1a** a small cavity or deep narrow-mouthed depression in the body – compare HAIR FOLLICLE **b**(1) a small sac containing an egg in the ovary of a mammal **b**(2) GRAAFIAN FOLLICLE (liquid-filled follicle containing a developing egg) **2** a dry fruit consisting of one compartment containing many seeds, that splits open along one line when ripe [NL *folliculus*,

fr L, dim. of *follis* bag – more at FOOL] – **follicular** *adj*, **folliculate** *also* **folliculated** *adj*

**follicle mite** *n* any of several minute mites (genus *Demodex*) that live as parasites in the HAIR FOLLICLES of humans and other animals

**follicle-stimulating hormone** *n* a hormone produced by the front lobe of the PITUITARY GLAND that stimulates the growth of the egg-containing GRAAFIAN FOLLICLES in the ovary of a female mammal, and activates sperm-forming cells in the testes of the male

**folliculin** /fə'likyəlin/ *n* OESTROGEN; *esp* OESTRONE – not now used technically

¹**follow** /'foloh/ *vt* **1** to go, proceed, or come after ⟨*~ed the guide*⟩ **2a** to pursue, esp in an effort to overtake **b** to seek to attain; strive after ⟨*~ knowledge*⟩ **3a** to accept as a guide or leader **b** to obey or act in accordance with ⟨*he ~ed the advice*⟩ ⟨*~ed his conscience*⟩ **4** to copy, imitate **5a** to walk or proceed along ⟨*~ a path*⟩ **b** to engage in as a calling or way of life; pursue (e g a course of action) ⟨*wheat-growing is generally ~ed here*⟩ **6a** to come or take place after in time, sequence, or order ⟨*Sunday ~s Saturday*⟩ **b** to cause to be followed – usu + *with* ⟨*~ed dinner with a liqueur*⟩ **7** to come into existence or take place as a result or consequence of ⟨*disaster ~ed the blunder*⟩ **8a** to watch steadily ⟨*~ed the ball over the fence*⟩ **b** to keep the mind on ⟨*~ a speech*⟩ **c** to attend closely to; keep abreast of ⟨*she ~ed his career with interest*⟩ **d** to understand the logic of (e g an argument) ⟨*I don't quite ~ you*⟩ *~ vi* **1** to go or come after a person or thing in place, time, sequence, or order **2** to result or occur as a consequence, effect, or inference **3** *chiefly Br* to understand the logic of a line of thought – see also **follow one's** NOSE, **follow** SUIT [ME *folwen*, fr OE *folgian*; akin to OHG *folgēn* to follow]

*usage* Even when *as* **follows** has a plural subject and introduces a list of several items ⟨*the afternoon's events will be as* **follows**⟩ it should not be pluralized to *as* **follow**.

**follow on** *vi, of a side in cricket* to bat a second time immediately after making a score that is less, by more than a predetermined amount, than that of the opposing team in its first innings – see also FOLLOW-ON

**follow through** *vi* to complete a stroke (e g in cricket or golf) by continuing the movement of the arm after the cricket ball, golf ball, etc has been struck *~ vt* **1** to continue (a stroke in cricket, golf, etc) to the end of its arc **2** *also* **follow out** to pursue or carry out (an activity or process) to a conclusion – see also FOLLOW-THROUGH

**follow up** *vt* **1** to follow with something similar, related, or supplementary ⟨*following up his promises with action*⟩ **2a** to take appropriate action about ⟨*follow up an enquiry*⟩ **b** to strengthen the effect of by further action; pursue ⟨*follow up an early advantage*⟩ **3** to maintain contact with or reexamine (a person) at usu prescribed intervals in order to evaluate a diagnosis or treatment received ⟨*patients who are* followed up *after their discharge*⟩ – see also FOLLOW-UP

²**follow** *n* **1** the act or process of following **2a** **follow shot**, **follow** a shot in billiards or snooker made by striking the CUE BALL above its centre to cause it to continue moving forwards after striking the OBJECT BALL **b** forward spin given to a ball by striking it above its centre – compare SCREW 6

**follower** /'folohə/ *n* **1** one who or that which follows: e g **1a** a person who follows the opinions or teachings of another; an adherent **b** one who or that which imitates another **2** a person in the service of another; a retainer **3** a man engaged in courtship, esp of a maidservant **4** ³FAN ⟨*a Spurs ~*⟩ **5** a machine part that receives motion from another part **6** *Br* a young domestic animal; *esp* a young cow **7** *archaic* one who or that which chases; a pursuer

¹**following** /'folohing/ *adj* **1** next after; succeeding ⟨*the ~ day*⟩ **2** that immediately follows; about to be mentioned ⟨*trains will leave at the ~ times*⟩ **3** *of a wind* blowing in the direction in which something is travelling

²**following** *n, pl* (*1*) **following**, (*2*) **followings** **1** the one about to be mentioned below or next **2** *taking sing or pl vb* a group of followers, adherents, or supporters

³**following** *prep* subsequent to ⟨*~ the lecture tea was served*⟩

*usage* The now common use of **following** to mean simply "after" is quite widely disliked; but it may be found more acceptable when it means "after and because of" ⟨**following** *a multiple pileup on the northbound carriageway, the M1 was closed for three hours*⟩.

**follow-on** /ˌfoloh 'on/ *n* the second innings of a cricket team required by the rules to follow on

**follow-'through** *n* **1** the act or an instance of following through **2** the part of the stroke in cricket, golf, etc following the striking of the ball

**follow-up** *n* **1** the act or an instance of following up **2** something that follows up or that continues or reinforces a previous action or activity – **follow-up** *adj*

**folly** /'foli/ *n* **1** lack of good sense or normal prudence and foresight; foolishness **2** a foolish act or idea **3** (criminally or tragically) foolish actions or conduct **4a** an excessively costly or unprofitable undertaking **b** a usu fanciful structure (eg a summerhouse) built esp for scenic effect or to satisfy a whim **5** *pl, often cap* a theatrical revue featuring glamorous female performers dressed in extravagant costumes **6** *obs* **6a** evil, wickedness **b** lewd behaviour [ME *folie*, fr OF, fr *fol* fool – more at FOOL]

**Folsom** /'fols(a)m/ *adj* of a prehistoric culture of N America on the E side of the Rocky mountains that is characterized by leaf-shaped flint projectile points [*Folsom*, site in New Mexico]

**foment** /foh'ment/ *vt* **1** to apply a hot moist substance to (a part of the body), esp so as to ease pain, swelling, or inflammation **2** to foster the growth or development of (eg trouble or disorder); rouse, incite ⟨~ *a rebellion*⟩ △ ferment [ME *fomenten*, fr LL *fomentare*, fr L *fomentum* fomentation, fr *fovēre* to warm, fondle, foment] – **fomentation** *n*, **fomenter** *n*

¹**fond** /fond/ *adj* **1a** having an inclination, predisposition, or appetite for something specified ⟨~ *of arguing*⟩ **b** having an affection or liking for something specified ⟨~ *of music*⟩ **2a** foolishly tender; indulgent ⟨*spoiled by a* ~ *mother*⟩ **b** affectionate, loving ⟨*a* ~ *wife*⟩ ⟨*absence makes the heart grow* ~er⟩ **3** cherished with great affection; doted on ⟨*his* ~est *hopes*⟩ **4** *archaic* foolish, silly ⟨~ *pride*⟩ □ (2) + *of* synonyms see LOVING [ME, fr *fonne* fool] – **fondness** *n*

²**fond** *n* **1** a background or basis, esp for a design – used esp with reference to lace **2** *obs* a fund [Fr, fr L *fundus* – more at FUND]

**fondant** /'fondant (*Fr* fɔ̃dɔ̃)/ *n* a soft creamy preparation of flavoured sugar and water that is used as a basis for sweets or icings; *also* a sweet consisting chiefly of fondant [Fr, fr prp of *fondre* to melt – more at FOUND]

**fondle** /'fondl/ *vt* **1** to handle tenderly, lovingly, or lingeringly **2** *obs* to pamper ~ *vi* to show affection or desire by caressing [freq of obs *fond* to fool, fr ¹*fond*]

**fondly** /'fondli/ *adv* **1** in a fond manner; affectionately **2** in a willingly credulous manner ⟨*government* ~ *imagine that cutting taxes will reduce wage demands*⟩ **3** *archaic* in a foolish manner; foolishly

**fondue** /'fond(y)ooh (*Fr* fɔ̃dy)/ *n* **1** a dish that consists of hot oil or a thick sweet or savoury sauce into which small pieces of food are dipped for cooking or coating; *esp* a traditional Swiss preparation of melted cheese, white wine, and often kirsch **2** a baked dish similar to a soufflé or savoury custard and usu containing cheese [Fr *fondue*, fr fem of *fondu*, pp of *fondre*]

¹**font** /font/ *n* **1a** a large receptacle for baptismal water **b** a receptacle for holy water **c** a receptacle for oil in a lamp **2** *chiefly NAm* a fountain, source ⟨*a* ~ *of information*⟩ [ME, fr OE, fr LL *font-, fons*, fr L, fountain] – **fontal** *adj*

²**font** *n, chiefly NAm* ²FOUNT (set of printing type)

**fontanelle**, *NAm chiefly* **fontanel** /ˌfonta'nel/ *n* a membrane-covered opening in bone or between bones; *specif* any of the membrane-covered spaces between the PARIETAL BONES of the skull of a foetus or infant [ME *fontinelle*, a bodily hollow or pit, fr MF *fontenele*, dim of *fontaine* fountain]

**fontina** /fon'teena/ *n, often cap* a usu pale yellow Italian cheese with a texture ranging from semisoft to hard and a mild to fairly sharp flavour [It]

**food** /foohd/ *n* **1a** material consisting essentially of protein, carbohydrate, and fat that is taken into the body of a living organism and used to provide energy and sustain processes (eg growth and repair of tissues) essential for life; *also* this material together with supplementary substances (eg minerals, vitamins, and condiments) **b** inorganic substances (eg carbon dioxide or phosphates) absorbed in the form of gases or solutions by plants **2** food in solid form **3** something that nourishes, sustains, or supplies ⟨*skin* ~⟩ ⟨~ *for thought*⟩ [ME *fode*, fr OE *fōda*; akin to OHG *fuotar* food, fodder, L *panis* bread, *pascere* to feed] – **foodless** *adj*

**food chain** *n* a hierarchical arrangement of the organisms of an ecological community ordered according to each organism's use of the next as a food source

**food poisoning** *n* a disorder of the stomach and intestines, typically characterized by vomiting and diarrhoea, that is caused by eating food that is naturally poisonous or that has been contaminated by bacteria, toxic substances produced by bacteria, or chemicals

**foodstuff** /'foohd,stuf/ *n* a substance with food value; *esp* the raw material of food before or after processing

**food vacuole** /'vakyoo·ohl/ *n* a small cavity (VACUOLE 2) in a cell (eg an amoeba) in which food taken into the cell is digested

**food web** *n* all the interacting food chains in an ecological community

¹**fool** /foohl/ *n* **1** a person lacking in judgment, prudence, or common sense **2a** a jester (eg in a royal household) **b** a person who is made to appear foolish as the result of trickery, practical joking, etc; a dupe **3** a harmlessly deranged person or one lacking in common powers of understanding **4** a cold dessert of fruit puree mixed with whipped cream or custard [ME, fr OF *fol*, fr LL *follis*, fr L, bellows, bag; akin to L *flare* to blow – more at BLOW; (4) perh of different origin]

²**fool** *vi* **1a** to spend time idly or aimlessly; waste time – usu + *around* or *about* ⟨*just* ~ing *around all day*⟩ **b** to act or behave in a silly or irresponsible way – often + *around* or *about* **2a** to play or improvise a comic role **b** to speak in jest; joke ⟨*I was only* ~ing⟩ to make a fool of; deceive

**fool away** *vt* to use senselessly; waste, squander

**fool (about/around) with** *vt* **1** to meddle or tamper thoughtlessly or ignorantly with ⟨*don't* fool with *that gun*⟩ **2** to philander with ⟨*stop* fooling about with *my wife*⟩ **3** to deal or contend with without serious thought, purpose, or effort ⟨*a dangerous man to* fool with⟩

³**fool** *adj, informal* foolish, silly ⟨*barking his* ~ *head off*⟩

**foolery** /'foohlari/ *n* **1** foolish behaviour **2** a foolish act, utterance, or belief

**foolhardy** /'foohl,hahdi/ *adj* foolishly adventurous and bold; rash *synonyms* see ¹ADVENTURE [ME, fr OF *fol hardi*, fr *fol* foolish + *hardi* bold – more at HARDY] – **foolhardily** *adv*, **foolhardiness** *n*

**foolish** /'foohlish/ *adj* **1a** marked by or proceeding from folly or ignorance **b** lacking, judgment or good sense **2a** absurd, ridiculous **b** nonplussed, abashed ⟨*felt extremely* ~⟩ **3** insignificant, trifling – **foolishly** *adv*, **foolishness** *n*

**foolproof** /'foohl,proohf/ *adj* so simple, plain, or reliable as to leave no opportunity for error, misuse, or failure ⟨*a* ~ *plan*⟩

**foolscap** /'foohlzkap/ *n* **1** fool's cap *also* **foolscap 1a** the cap or hood, usu with bells, worn by a jester (eg in a royal or noble household) **b** DUNCE's CAP **2** a size of paper usu 17 × 13½ inches (432 × 343 millimetres) [(2) fr the watermark of a fool's cap formerly applied to such paper]

**fool's errand** *n* a needless or fruitless task or errand

**fool's gold** *n* any of various yellow or gold-coloured minerals: eg **a** IRON PYRITES **b** CHALCOPYRITE

**fool's paradise** *n* a state of illusory happiness

**fool's parsley** *n* a poisonous European plant (*Aethusa cynapium*) of the carrot family that resembles parsley and is a weed of cultivated land

¹**foot** /foot/ *n, pl* **feet**, (3) **feet** /feet/ *also* **foot**, (9) **foot 1** the end part of the leg of a VERTEBRATE animal on which the animal stands **2** an organ of movement or attachment of an INVERTEBRATE animal; *esp* a broad muscular surface at the base or sides opposite the shell of a snail, limpet, or other MOLLUSC **3** any of various units of length originally based on the length of the human foot; *esp* a unit equal to ¹⁄₃ yard (0.3048 metre) and comprising 12 inches ⟨*6 feet tall*⟩ ⟨*a 10-foot pole*⟩ **4** the basic unit of verse metre consisting of any of various fixed combinations or groups of stressed and unstressed or long and short syllables **5** manner or motion of walking or running; step – chiefly in *fleet of foot* **6** something resembling a foot in position or use: eg **6a** the lower end of the leg of a chair, table, etc **b** either of the flat areas beside the groove, that form the base of a piece of metal printing type **c(1)** the bottom part of the spore-bearing capsule (SPOROGONIUM) in mosses **c(2)** a specialized outgrowth by which the developing spore-bearing form (SPOROPHYTE) of many ferns absorbs nourishment **d** a piece on a sewing machine that presses the cloth against the feed **7a** the lower edge (eg of a sail) **b** the lowest part; the bottom ⟨*the* ~ *of the hill*⟩ ⟨*the* ~ *of the stairs*⟩ **c** the end that is opposite the head or top ⟨*the* ~ *of the table*⟩ ⟨*the* ~ *of the bed*⟩ **8** the part (eg of a stocking) that covers the human foot **9** *taking sing or pl vb, chiefly Br* the infantry [ME *fot*, fr OE *fot*; akin to L *ped-, pes* foot, Gk *pod-, pous*] – **footlike** *adj* – **fall/land on one's feet** to be successful or happy,

esp after overcoming difficulties – **get a foot in (the door)** to obtain or reach an advantageous position from which progress may be made – **keep one's feet** to avoid overbalancing – **my foot** *informal* MY EYE – **on foot** by walking or running ⟨*tour the city* on foot⟩ – **on one's feet 1** in a standing position; not sitting down ⟨*it's nice to be sitting after being* on my feet *all day*⟩ ⟨*the speaker was* on his feet *as soon as the questioner finished*⟩ **2a** in a recovered condition (e g after illness) **b** established and usu financially sound ⟨*the business is well* on its feet⟩ – **put a foot wrong** to make a mistake – usu neg – **put one's best foot forward** to do the best one can – **put one's feet up** to take a rest – **put one's foot down 1** to take firm action; *esp* to forbid something **2** to increase speed in a car by pushing down the accelerator with one's foot – **put one's foot in it** to make an embarrassing blunder – **set foot** to go *in, on* or *inside* – **stand on one's own (two) feet** to think or act independently – **sweep somebody off his/her feet** to gain immediate and unquestioning support, approval or acceptance by somebody; *esp* to cause somebody to fall in love with one – **think on one's feet** to think and usu speak quickly and without preparation ⟨*a good politician can* think on her feet⟩
*usage* When **foot** means a unit of length, the singular is usually preferred in hyphenated constructions ⟨*a 10-*foot *pole*⟩ and the plural elsewhere ⟨*he's six* feet *tall*⟩.

**²foot** *vt* **1a** to perform the movements of (a dance) **b** to walk, run, or dance on, over, or through **2** to pay or stand credit for ⟨*agreed to ~ the bill*⟩ **3** to make or renew the foot of (e g a stocking) **4** *chiefly dial* to add *up* – **foot it 1** to dance **2** to travel on foot; walk

**footage** /'footij/ *n* **1** length or quantity expressed in feet **2** exposed film on which a scene, subject, etc has been shot; *also* the length in feet of such film

**foot-and-mouth disease, foot and mouth** *n* a contagious virus disease, esp of animals with cloven feet (e g cows, pigs, and goats), that is marked by small ulcerating blisters in the mouth, about the hoofs, and on the udder and teats

**football** /'foot,bawl/ *n* **1** any of several games that are played between two teams on a usu rectangular field having goalposts at each end, and whose object is to get the ball over a goal line or between goalposts by running, passing, or kicking: e g **1a** *Br* soccer **b** *chiefly Welsh* rugby **c** *chiefly Irish* GAELIC FOOTBALL **d** *NAm* AMERICAN FOOTBALL **e** *Austr* AUSTRALIAN RULES FOOTBALL **f** *Can* CANADIAN FOOTBALL **2** an inflated round or oval ball used in football games **3** something treated as a basis for contention rather than on its intrinsic merits ⟨*the bill became a political ~ in Parliament*⟩ – **footballer** *n*

**football pools** *n pl* a form of organized gambling based on forecasting the results of football matches

**footbath** /'foot,bahth/ *n* a bath (e g at the entrance to an indoor swimming pool) for cleaning, warming, or disinfecting the feet

**footboard** /'foot,bawd/ *n* **1** a narrow platform (e g on a vehicle) on which to stand or brace the feet **2** a board forming the foot of a bed

**footboy** /'foot,boy/ *n* a serving boy; a page, attendant

**foot brake** *n* a brake operated by foot pressure on a pedal

**footbridge** /'foot,brij/ *n* a bridge for pedestrians

**footcandle** /'foot,kandl/ *n* a former unit of illumination equal to one lumen per square foot

**'foot-,dragging** *n* failure to act with the necessary promptness or vigour

**footed** /'footid/ *adj* having a foot or feet, esp of a specified kind or number – usu in combination ⟨*a 4-*footed *animal*⟩

**footer** /'footə/ *n, chiefly Br informal* soccer [by shortening & alter. fr *football*]

**-footer** /-footə/ *comb form* (→ *n*) one who or that which is (a specified number of feet in height, length, or breadth)

**footfall** /'foot,fawl/ *n* the sound of a footstep

**foot fault** *n* a fault in tennis, badminton, etc that occurs when a server fails to keep both feet in a position required by the rules while making the serve; *esp* a fault in tennis made when the server's feet are not behind the baseline – **foot fault** *vi*

**foothill** /'foot,hil/ *n* a hill at the foot of a mountain

**foothold** /'foot,hohld/ *n* **1** a hold for the feet; FOOTING 1 **2** a usu established position or basis from which to progress ⟨*secured a ~ in the plastics market*⟩

**footie** /'footi/ *n* ²,³FOOTY

**footing** /'footing/ *n* **1** a stable position or placing of or for the feet **2** a surface or its condition, esp with respect to its suitability for walking or running on **3a** a basis or position; FOOTHOLD 2; *esp* an established position **b** a position,

status, or rank in relation to others ⟨*they all started off on an equal ~*⟩ **4** the base of a wall, column, etc that stands on the foundation and is often enlarged to distribute the load over a wider area

**foot iron** *n* a shaped iron bar embedded in a manhole wall to provide a foothold

**footle** /'foohtl/ *vi, informal* **1** to act or spend time aimlessly; potter *around* or *about* **2** to talk or act foolishly – often + *around* or *about* [alter. of *footer* (to bungle), fr Fr *foutre*, lit., to copulate] – **footle** *n*, **footler** *n*

**footless** /'footlis/ *adj* **1** having no feet **2** *NAm* stupid, inept – **footlessly** *adv*, **footlessness** *n*

**footlights** /'foot,liets/ *n pl* **1** a row of lights set across the front of a stage floor **2** the stage as a profession

**footling** /'foohtling/ *adj, informal* **1** bungling, inept ⟨*~ amateurs*⟩ **2** lacking use or value; trivial, unimportant [fr prp of *footle*]

**footloose** /'foot,loohs/ *adj* having no ties; free to go or do as one pleases

**footman** /'footmən/ *n* **1** *archaic* an infantryman **2a** a servant in livery formerly attending a rider or required to run in front of his master's carriage **b** a servant in livery hired chiefly to wait at table and guard and open doors

**footmark** /'foot,mahk/ *n* a dirty mark left by the foot; *broadly* a footprint

**¹footnote** /'foot,noht/ *n* **1** a note of reference, explanation, or comment typically placed at the bottom of a printed page below the text **2** something that is subordinately related to a larger event or work ⟨*that biography is an illuminating ~ to the history of our times*⟩

**²footnote** *vt* to supply with a footnote; annotate

**footpace** /'foot,pays/ *n* **1** a walking pace **2** a platform; dais

**¹footpad** /'foot,pad/ *n* **1** a highwayman who robbed on foot **2** *NAm* one who robs a pedestrian [*foot* + arch. *pad* highwayman]

**²footpad** *n* a broad foot on the leg of a spacecraft for distributing the weight of the craft in order to minimize sinking into a surface [*foot* + ¹*pad*]

**footpath** /'foot,pahth/ *n* a narrow path for pedestrians; *also* a pavement

**footplate** /'foot,playt/ *n, Br* the platform in the cab of a locomotive on which the crew stand

**footplateman** /'foot,playtm(ə)n/ *n, Br* a person (e g the driver) who works on the footplate of a locomotive

**'foot-,pound** *n, pl* **foot-pounds** a unit of work (equivalent to about 1.36 joules) that is equal to the work done by a force of 1 pound in moving a body through a distance of 1 foot

**foot-poundal** /,foot'powndl/ *n* an absolute unit of work (equivalent to about 0.04 joules) that is equal to the work done by a force of 1 poundal in moving a body through a distance of 1 foot

**,foot-pound-'second** *adj* being or relating to a system of units based upon the foot as the unit of length, the pound as the unit of weight or mass, and the second as the unit of time

**footprint** /'footprint/ *n* **1** an impression made by the foot of a person or animal **2** an area within which a spacecraft is intended to land

**footrace** /'foot,rays/ *n* a race run on foot

**footrest** /'foot,rest/ *n* a support (e g a low stool) for the feet

**foot rot** *n* **1** a plant disease marked by rot of the stem near the ground **2** a progressive inflammation of the feet of sheep or cattle

**footrule** /'foot,roohl/ *n* a ruler 1 foot long

**¹foots** /foots/ *n taking sing or pl vb* material deposited, esp in ageing or refining; dregs [pl of ¹*foot* (in the senses "lowest part, material at the bottom")]

**²foots** *n pl, informal* FOOTLIGHTS 1

**footsie** /'footsi/ *n, informal* **1** surreptitious amorous caresses with the feet **2** clandestine dealings □ chiefly in *play footsie with* [baby-talk dim. of *foot*]

**footslog** /'footslog/ *vi -gg- informal* to march or tramp laboriously – **footslog** *n*, **footslogger** *n*

**foot soldier** *n* an infantryman

**footsore** /'foot,saw/ *adj* having sore or tender feet, esp from much walking – **footsoreness** *n*

**footstep** /'footstep/ *n* **1a** (the sound of) a step or tread **b** distance covered by a step; a pace **2** FOOTPRINT 1 **3 footsteps** *pl*, **footstep** a way of life, conduct, or action ⟨*followed in his father's ~s*⟩

**footstone** /'foot,stohn/ *n* a stone placed at the foot of a grave

**footstool** /'foot,stoohl/ *n* a low stool used to support the feet

'**foot-,up** *n* an offence in a scrum in rugby that occurs when a front-row player lifts his foot before the ball touches the ground

**footwall** /'foot,wawl/ *n* the lower underlying wall of a mineral vein, ore deposit, or coal seam in a mine

'**foot-,warmer** *n* a device or covering for keeping the feet warm; *esp* a lined pouch into which the feet are placed

**footway** /'foot,way/ *n* a footpath

**footwear** /'footwea/ *n* shoes, boots, etc worn on the feet

**footwork** /'foot,wuhk/ *n* 1 the control and placing of the feet, esp in sport (e g in boxing or in batting in cricket) ⟨*good* ~⟩ 2 the activity of moving from place to place on foot ⟨*the investigation entailed a lot of* ~⟩

¹**footy** /'footi/ *adj, chiefly dial* insignificant, paltry [prob fr Fr *foutu*, pp of *foutre* to copulate, fr L *futuere*]

²**footy, footie** *n, Br informal* football [by shortening & alter.]

³**footy, footie** *n, informal* FOOTSIE

¹**foozle** /'foohzl/ *vt, chiefly informal* to manage or play awkwardly; bungle – used esp in golf [perh fr Ger dial. *fuseln* to work carelessly]

²**foozle** *n, chiefly informal* an act of foozling; *esp* a bungled golf stroke

**fop** /fop/ *n* a man who is devoted to or vain about his appearance or dress; a dandy [ME, fool; akin to ME *fobben* to deceive, MHG *voppen*] – **foppish** *adj*, **foppishly** *adv*, **foppishness** *n*

**foppery** /'fopəri/ *n* 1 an absurd or vain trait or action 2 the behaviour, dress, or affectations (characteristic) of a fop

¹**for** /fə; *strong* faw/ *prep* 1a – used to indicate purpose ⟨*a grant* ~ *studying medicine*⟩ ⟨*an operation* ~ *cancer*⟩ ⟨*nowhere* ~ *me to sleep*⟩ ⟨*what's this knob* ~*?*⟩, goal or direction ⟨*left* ~ *home*⟩ ⟨*acted* ~ *the best*⟩ ⟨*getting on* ~ *five*⟩, or that which is to be had or gained ⟨*now* ~ *a good rest*⟩ ⟨*run* ~ *your life*⟩ ⟨*waiting* ~ *the bus*⟩ ⟨*an eye* ~ *a bargain*⟩ ⟨*too early* ~ *dinner*⟩ **b** to belong to ⟨*the flowers are* ~ *you*⟩ 2 as being or constituting ⟨*take him* ~ *a fool*⟩ ⟨*ate it* ~ *breakfast*⟩ ⟨*I* ~ *one don't care*⟩ – compare FOR EXAMPLE 3a BECAUSE OF 1 ⟨*cried* ~ *joy*⟩ ⟨*feel better* ~ *a holiday*⟩ **b** because of the hindrance of ⟨*couldn't speak* ~ *laughing*⟩ ⟨*if it weren't* ~ *you I'd leave*⟩ 4a in place of ⟨*change* ~ *a pound*⟩ **b** on behalf of; representing ⟨*acting* ~ *my client*⟩ ⟨*red* ~ *danger*⟩ **c** in support of; in favour of ⟨*voted* ~ *Smith*⟩ 5 considered as; considering ⟨*tall* ~ *her age*⟩ ⟨*cold* ~ *April*⟩ 6 with respect to; concerning ⟨*famous* ~ *its scenery*⟩ ⟨*a stickler* ~ *detail*⟩ ⟨*full marks* ~ *English*⟩ ⟨*eggs are good* ~ *you*⟩ ⟨*it's not* ~ *me to say*⟩ 7 – used to indicate cost, payment, equivalence, or correlation ⟨£7 ~ *a hat*⟩ ⟨*all out* ~ *342 runs*⟩ ⟨*punished* ~ *talking*⟩ ⟨*wouldn't hurt her* ~ *the world*⟩ ⟨*five duds* ~ *every good one*⟩ 8 – used to indicate duration of time or extent of space ⟨~ *10 miles*⟩ ⟨*the worst accident* ~ *months*⟩ 9 on the occasion or at the time of ⟨*came home* ~ *Christmas*⟩ ⟨*invited them* ~ *nine o'clock*⟩ 10 – used to introduce a clause with a nonfinite verb ⟨*no need* ~ *you to worry*⟩ ⟨*it's dangerous* ~ *George to hurry*⟩ 11 *chiefly NAm* AFTER 5c [ME, fr OE; akin to L *per* through, *prae* before, *pro* before, for, ahead, Gk *pro*, OE *faran* to go – more at FARE] – **for all** 1 IN SPITE OF ⟨*couldn't open it* for all *their efforts*⟩ 2 to the extent that ⟨*dead* for all *I know*⟩ 3 considering how little ⟨*might as well stop talking* for all *the good it does*⟩ – **for all one is worth** with all one's might – **for it** *chiefly Br informal* likely to get into trouble ⟨*you'll be* for it *when teacher catches you*⟩ – **for nothing** 1 FREE 2 2 to no purpose; without result ⟨*didn't spend three years at college* for nothing⟩ – **for what it is worth** without guarantee of quality or accuracy ⟨*here's my advice* for what it is worth⟩ – **for you** – used after *there* or *that* in exclamations of enthusiasm or exasperation ⟨*that's country hotels* for you!⟩

²**for** *conj* 1 and the reason is that 2 BECAUSE 2

³**for** *adj* being in favour of a motion or measure

**for-** /fə-/ *prefix* 1a so as to involve prohibition or exclusion ⟨*forbid*⟩ ⟨*forfend*⟩ **b** so as to involve omission, abstention, or neglect ⟨*forgo*⟩ ⟨*forsake*⟩ ⟨*forget*⟩ 2 destructively; detrimentally ⟨*fordo*⟩ 3 completely; excessively ⟨*forspent*⟩ ⟨*forlorn*⟩ △ fore- [ME, fr OE; akin to OHG *fur-* for-, OE *for*]

**fora** /'fawrə/ *pl of* FORUM

¹**forage** /'forij/ *n* 1 food for animals; *esp* food (e g grass) taken by browsing or grazing 2 an act of foraging for provisions; *broadly* a search [ME, fr MF, fr OF, fr *forre* fodder, of Gmc origin; akin to OHG *fuotar* food, fodder – more at FOOD; (2) fr ²*forage*]

²**forage** *vt* 1 to collect or take provisions or forage from 2 to secure by foraging ⟨~d *a chicken for the feast*⟩ ~ *vi* 1 to wander in search of forage or food 2 to ravage, raid 3 to make a search; rummage – **forager** *n*

**foramen** /faw'raym(ə)n, 'forəmin/ *n, pl* **foramina** /faw'raminə/, **foramens** a small anatomical opening, perforation, or hole; FENESTRA [L *foramin-, foramen*, fr *forare* to bore – more at BORE] – **foraminal, foraminous** *adj*

**foramen magnum** /'magnəm/ *n* the large opening in the base of the skull through which the SPINAL CORD passes to become the MEDULLA OBLONGATA (stemlike part of the brain) [NL, lit., great opening]

**foramen ovale** /oh'vahli/ *n* an opening in the membrane dividing the two top chambers (ATRIA) of the heart, that is normally present only in the foetus [NL, lit., oval opening]

**foraminifer** /,forə'minifə/, **foraminiferan** /-fərən, ,forəmi-'nifərən/ *n, pl* **foraminifers, foraminifera** /,fawrəmi'nifərə/, **foraminiferans** any of an order (Foraminifera) of chiefly marine single-celled animals (PROTOZOANS) that are similar to but larger than the related amoebas and that usu have chalky shells often perforated with minute holes through which slender PSEUDOPODIA (jellylike extensions of the cell used for movement) protrude [deriv of L *foramin-, foramen* + *-fer* -fer] – **foraminiferal, foraminiferous** *adj*

**forasmuch as** /,fawrəz'much/ *conj* in view of the fact that; SINCE 2

¹**foray** /'foray/ *vt, archaic* to ravage or raid in search of spoils; pillage ~ *vi* to make a raid or brief invasion ⟨~ed *into enemy territory*⟩ [ME *forrayen*, fr MF *forrer*, fr *forre* fodder] – **forayer** *n*

²**foray** *n* 1 a sudden invasion, attack, or raid 2 a brief excursion or attempt, esp outside one's accustomed sphere ⟨*the teacher's* ~ *into politics*⟩

¹**forbear** /faw'bea/ *vb* **forbore** /-baw/; **forborne** /-bawn/ *vt* 1 to refrain or hold oneself back from, esp with an effort of self-restraint ⟨*he forbore to answer the slander*⟩ 2 *obs* to leave alone; shun ⟨~ *his presence* – Shak⟩ 3 *obs* to do without ~ *vi* 1 to abstain; HOLD BACK – usu + *from* ⟨*he forbore from expressing his disagreement*⟩ 2 *chiefly formal* to control oneself when provoked; be patient [ME *forberen*, fr OE *forberan* to endure, do without, fr *for-* + *beran* to bear]

²**forbear** /'faw,bea/ *n* a forebear

**forbearance** /faw'beərəns/ *n* 1 a refraining from the enforcement of something (e g a debt, right, or obligation) that is due 2 the act of forbearing 3 the quality of one who forbears; patience, self-restraint

**forbid** /fə'bid/ *vt* **forbidding; forbade** /fə'bad, -'bayd, -'bed/, **forbad; forbidden** 1a to refuse (as if) by authority to allow; command against ⟨*the law* ~s *shops to sell alcohol to minors*⟩ ⟨*her mother* ~s *her to go*⟩ **b** to refuse access to or use of ⟨*her father* forbade *him the house*⟩ 2 to make impracticable; hinder, prevent ⟨*space* ~s *further treatment of the subject here*⟩ [ME *forbidden*, fr OE *forbēodan*, fr *for-* + *bēodan* to bid – more at BID] – **forbiddance** *n*, **forbidder** *n*

*usage* The construction **forbid** *from* ⟨*circumstances* **forbid** *me from revealing the truth*⟩ should be replaced by ⟨*circumstances* **forbid** *my revealing the truth*⟩ or ⟨*circumstances* **forbid** *me to reveal the truth*⟩.

**forbidden** /fə'bid(ə)n/ *adj* not conforming to or occurring in accordance with simple applications of the rules of QUANTUM MECHANICS – used of phenomena relating to the energy, position, etc of atomic particles

**forbidding** /fə'biding/ *adj* 1 having a menacing or dangerous appearance ⟨~ *mountains*⟩ 2 unfriendly, hostile ⟨*his father was a stern* ~ *figure*⟩ – **forbiddingly** *adv*, **forbiddingness** *n*

**forbode** /faw'bohd/ *vb* to forebode

¹**force** /faws/ *n* 1a strength or energy exerted or brought to bear; active power ⟨*the* ~s *of nature*⟩ ⟨*the love of justice has been a powerful motivating* ~ *in his life*⟩ **b** moral or mental strength **c** capacity to persuade or convince ⟨*couldn't resist the* ~ *of his argument*⟩ **d** validity, esp in law; operative effect ⟨*an agreement having the* ~ *of law*⟩ 2a military strength **b(1)** a body (e g of troops or ships) assigned to a military purpose **b(2)** *pl* the armed services of a nation or commander **c** a body of people or things fulfilling an often specified function ⟨*a labour* ~⟩ ⟨*the combined* ~s *of the BBC Symphony Orchestra and the BBC Singers*⟩ **d** *often cap* POLICE FORCE – often + *the* **e** an individual or group having the power of effective action ⟨*police and citizens must join* ~s *to prevent violence*⟩ ⟨*he was a* ~

*behind the passing of that bill*⟩ **3** violence, compulsion, or constraint exerted on or against a person or thing **4a** (the intensity of) an agency or influence that if applied to a free body results chiefly in motion or a change in the direction or speed of motion of the body, and sometimes in deformation (e g stretching or compression) **b** an agency or influence analogous to a physical force; something capable of bringing about a change or exerting an effect ⟨*economic* ~s⟩ ⟨*the* ~ *of public opinion*⟩ **5** the quality of conveying impressions intensely in writing or speech **6** *cap* a measure of wind strength as expressed by a number on the BEAUFORT SCALE ⟨*a* Force *9 gale*⟩ [ME, fr MF, fr (assumed) VL *fortia*, fr L *fortis* strong] – **forceless** *adj* – **in force 1** in great numbers ⟨*police were summoned* in force⟩ **2** valid, operative ⟨*the new law is now* in force⟩

²**force** *vt* **1** to compel by physical, moral, or intellectual means ⟨~d *labour*⟩ **2** to make or cause through natural or logical necessity ⟨*his arguments* ~d *them to admit he was right*⟩ **3a** to press, drive, or effect against resistance or inertia ⟨~ *a bill through Parliament*⟩ ⟨~d *his way through the crowd*⟩ **b** to impose or thrust urgently, importunately, or inexorably ⟨~ *unwanted attentions on a woman*⟩ **4** to achieve or win by strength in struggle or violence: **4a** to capture or penetrate by force ⟨~ *a castle*⟩ ⟨~d *the enemy lines*⟩ **b** to break open or through ⟨~ *a lock*⟩ **5a** to raise, accelerate, or exert to the utmost ⟨forcing *the pace*⟩ **b** to produce only with unnatural or unwilling effort ⟨*she* ~d *a smile in spite of her distress*⟩ ⟨*a* ~d *laugh*⟩ **c** to wrench, strain, or use (language) unnaturally ⟨*a* ~d *metaphor*⟩ **6** to hasten the growth, onset of maturity, or rate of progress of ⟨forcing *rhubarb*⟩ **7** to induce (e g a particular bid or play by another player) in a card game by some conventional act, play, bid, or response **8** *of a batsman in cricket* to play an aggressive shot at (a delivery); *specif* to hit firmly off the back foot and with a perpendicular bat – **forcedly** *adv*, **forcer** *n*

'**force-,feed** *vt* **1** to feed (e g a person or an animal) by forcible administration of food **2** to force to take in ⟨~ *students a literary education*⟩

**forceful** /ˈfawsf(ə)l/ *adj* possessing or filled with force; effective *usage* see FORCIBLE – **forcefully** *adv*, **forcefulness** *n*

,**force-'land** *vb* to land (an aircraft) involuntarily or in an emergency [back-formation fr *forced landing*] – **forced landing**

**force majeure** /,faws ma,zhuh (*Fr* fɔrs maʒœr)/ *n* a disruptive event (e g war or civil disturbance) that cannot be reasonably anticipated or controlled; *specif* such an event operating in law to excuse a party from fulfilling a contract – compare ACT OF GOD [Fr, superior force]

**forcemeat** /ˈfawsmeet/ *n* a savoury highly seasoned mixture, usu containing breadcrumbs and often finely chopped meat, that is either used as a stuffing or served separately [*force* (alter. of ¹*farce*) + *meat*]

**force of habit** *n* the effect of repetition in making behaviour involuntary or automatic; *also* behaviour made automatic by repetition

**forceps** /ˈfawseps/ *n taking sing or pl vb, pl* **forceps** an instrument for grasping, holding firmly, or pulling something, that is used esp for operations needing delicate precise control (e g in surgery or watchmaking) [L, prob fr *formus* warm + *capere* to take – more at WARM, HEAVE] – **forcepslike** *adj*

**force pump** *n* a pump that is capable of drawing up liquids and forcing them out at a considerable height above the original level of the liquid

**forcible** /ˈfawsəbl/ *adj* **1** effected by force used against opposition or resistance ⟨*a* ~ *entry*⟩ **2** characterized by force, efficiency, or energy; powerful – **forcibleness** *n*, **forcibly** *adv* *usage* Forcible and forceful can both mean "possessing force" ⟨*a* forceful/forcible *argument*⟩ but some careful writers prefer to combine forcible to the sense "by force" ⟨forcible *expulsion*⟩.

**forcing ground** *n* HOTBED **2** (environment favouring rapid development)

¹**ford** /fawd/ *n* a shallow part of a river or similar body of water, that can be crossed by wading, in a vehicle, etc [ME, fr OE; akin to ON *fjörthr* fiord, L *portus* port, OE *faran* to go – more at FARE]

²**ford** *vt* to cross (a river, stream, etc) at a ford – **fordable** *adj*

**fordo, foredo** /faw'dooh/ *vt* **fordoes** /-'dəz, -'duz/; **fordoing; fordid** /-'did/; **fordone** /-'dun/ *archaic* to destroy; DO AWAY WITH [ME *fordon*, fr OE *fordōn*, fr *for-* + *dōn* to do]

**fordone, foredone** /faw'dun/ *adj, archaic* overcome with fatigue; exhausted ⟨*quite* ~ *with the heat*⟩

¹**fore** /faw/ *adv* **1** in, at, towards, or adjacent to the front; for-

wards; *esp* in, at, or towards the bow of a ship **2** *obs* at an earlier time or period; before [ME, fr OE; akin to OE *for*]

²**fore** *also* '**fore** *prep* **1** in the presence of **2** *chiefly dial* before

³**fore** *adj* **1** prior in order of occurrence; former **2** situated in front of something else [*fore-*]

⁴**fore** *n* something that occupies a front or forward position – **to the fore** in or into a position of prominence; forward ⟨*a younger generation of idealists is coming* to the fore⟩

⁵**fore** *interj* – used by a golfer to warn anyone within range of the probable line of flight of his/her ball [prob short for *before*]

**fore-** /faw-/ *comb form* **1a** earlier; beforehand ⟨foresee⟩ **b** occurring earlier or beforehand ⟨forepayment⟩ **2a** situated at the front; in front ⟨foreleg⟩ **b** front part of ⟨forearm⟩ △ for- [ME *for-*, *fore-*, fr OE *fore-*, fr *fore*, adv]

,**fore-and-'aft** /ahft/ *adj* **1** lying, running, or acting in the general line of the length of a construction, esp a ship; longitudinal **2** being a sail that is set lengthways in the direction of the bow and stern rather than on a yard set across the ship; *also* having fore-and-aft sails as the principal sails

**fore and aft** *adv* **1** from bow to stern; lengthways **2** in, at, or towards both the bow and stern of a ship

¹**forearm** /faw'rahm, faw'ahm/ *vt* to arm in advance; prepare

²**forearm** /ˈfawrahm/ *n* the part of the human arm between the elbow and the wrist; *also* the corresponding part in other VERTEBRATE animals

**forebear, forbear** /ˈfaw,beə/ *n* an ancestor; forefather [ME (Sc) *forebear*, fr *fore-* + *-bear* one who is (fr *been* to be)]

**forebode** *also* **forbode** /faw'bohd/ *vt* **1** to indicate or warn of in advance; portend ⟨*such heavy air* ~s *a storm*⟩ **2** to have an inward conviction or premonition of (e g impending evil or misfortune) ~ *vi* to indicate or predict the future; augur ⟨*it* ~s *ill*⟩ *synonyms* see FORETELL – **foreboder** *n*

¹**foreboding** /faw'bohding/ *n* an omen, prediction, or presentiment, esp of coming evil

²**foreboding** *adj* indicative of or marked by foreboding – **forebodingly** *adv*, **forebodingness** *n*

**forebrain** /ˈfaw,brayn/ *n* **1** the front one of the three primary divisions into which the brain of the embryo of a VERTEBRATE animal is divided **2a** the part of the adult brain that develops from the embryonic forebrain and includes the TELENCEPHALON and DIENCEPHALON **b** TELENCEPHALON

**forecaddie** /ˈfaw,kadi/ *n* a golf caddie who is stationed in the fairway and who indicates the position of balls on the course

¹**forecast** /ˈfaw,kahst/ *vb* **forecast, forecasted** *vt* **1a** to calculate or predict (some future event or condition), usu as a result of rational study and analysis of available relevant data; *esp* to predict (weather conditions) on the basis of meteorological observations **b** to indicate or anticipate as likely to occur **2** to serve as a forecast of; presage ⟨*such events may* ~ *peace*⟩ ~ *vi* to calculate or predict the future *synonyms* see FORETELL [ME *forecasten*, fr *fore-* + *casten* to cast, contrive] – **forecaster** *n*

²**forecast** /ˈfaw,kahst/ *n* **1** a prophecy, estimate, or prediction of a future happening or condition; *esp* a weather forecast **2** *archaic* the foreseeing of consequences and provision against them

**forecastle, fo'c'sle** /ˈfohksl/ *n* **1** a short raised deck at the bow of a ship **2** a part at the front of a merchant ship where the crew have their living quarters

**foreclose** /faw'klohz/ *vt* **1** to deprive (a mortgagor) of the right to redeem property, usu because of nonpayment **2** to take away the right to redeem (a mortgage or other debt) ~ *vi* to foreclose a mortgage or other debt [ME *forclosen*, fr OF *forclos*, pp of *forclore*, fr *fors* outside (fr L *foris*) + *clore* to close – more at FORUM, CLOSE]

**foreclosure** /faw'klohzhə/ *n* an act or instance of foreclosing; *specif* a legal proceeding that bars or extinguishes a mortgagor's right of redeeming a mortgaged estate

**forecourt** /ˈfaw,kawt/ *n* an open court or paved area in front of a building; *esp* the part of a petrol station where the petrol pumps are situated

**foredeck** /ˈfawdek/ *n* the front part of a ship's main deck; *also* a decked area in the bow of an otherwise open boat

**foredo** /faw'dooh/ *vt* **foredoes** /-'dəz, -'duz/; **foredoing; foredid** /-'did/; **foredone** /-'dun/ *archaic* FORDO (destroy)

**foredone** /faw'dun/ *adj, archaic* FORDONE (exhausted)

**foredoom** /faw'doohm/ *vt* to doom beforehand

'**fore-,edge** *n* the edge of a book or book page opposite the spine

**foreface** /'faw‚fays/ n the part of the head of a 4-legged animal that is in front of or below the eyes

**forefather** /'faw‚fadhə/, *fem* **foremother** /-‚mudhə/ n 1 an ancestor 2 a person of an earlier period and common heritage

**forefeel** /faw'feel/ vt **forefelt** /-'felt/ to have a presentiment or premonition of

**forefend** /faw'fend/ vt, *archaic or NAm* to forfend

**forefinger** /'faw‚fingə/ n the finger next to the thumb – called also INDEX FINGER

**forefoot** /'fawfoot/ n 1 a front foot (eg of a 4-legged animal) 2 the front part of a ship where the stem and front part of the keel meet

**forefront** /'fawfrunt/ n the foremost part, place, or position; the vanguard ⟨was in the ~ of the progressive movement⟩

**foregather** /faw'gadhə/ vi to forgather

¹**forego** /faw'goh/ vt **foregoes; foregoing; forewent** /-'went/ – **foregone** /-'gon/ *archaic* to go before; precede in time or place – **foregoer** n

²**forego** vt **foregoes; foregoing; forewent; foregone** to forgo

**foregoing** /faw'gohing, '-‚-/ adj going before; immediately preceding ⟨the ~ statement is open to challenge⟩

**foregone** /'fawgon/ adj, *archaic* previous, past

**foregone conclusion** n 1 a conclusion or decision that has preceded argument or examination 2 an inevitable result; a certainty ⟨the victory was a ~⟩

**foreground** /'faw‚grownd/ n 1 the part of a picture or view nearest to and in front of the spectator 2 a position of prominence; the forefront

**foregut** /'fawgut/ n 1 the front part of the digestive tract in an embryo of a VERTEBRATE animal, that develops into the PHARYNX, gullet, stomach, and extreme top part of the intestine 2 the front part of the gut of an insect, spider, or other ARTHROPOD

¹**forehand** /'fawhand/ n 1 the part of a horse (eg the head, neck, shoulders, and forelegs) that is in front of the rider 2 a forehand stroke in tennis, squash, etc; *also* the side of the court on which such strokes are typically made 3 *archaic* superior position or advantage; UPPER HAND

²**forehand** adv with a forehand stroke

³**forehand** adj 1 of a stroke in tennis, squash, etc made with the palm of the hand facing in the direction of movement 2a being the side of a tennis, squash, etc player on which he/she makes forehand strokes; being the right side of a right-handed player or the left side of a left-handed player **b** of or being the side of a tennis, squash, etc court corresponding to a player's forehand side 3 *obs* done or given in advance; prior

**forehanded** /‚faw'handid/ adj 1 FOREHAND 1 2 NAm 2a mindful of the future; prudent **b** well-to-do, wealthy – **forehandedly** adv, **forehandedness** n

**forehead** /'fored, -id, 'fawhed/ n the part of the face above the eyes

**forehock** /'fawhok/ n a cut of bacon or pork consisting of the front leg of a pig

**foreign** /'forən/ adj 1 (situated) outside a place or country; *esp* (situated) outside one's own country 2 born in, belonging to, or characteristic of some place or country other than the one under consideration 3 of or proceeding from some other person or material thing than the one under consideration 4 alien in character; not connected or pertinent *to* 5 of, concerned with, or dealing with other nations 6 occurring in an abnormal situation in the living body and commonly introduced from outside ⟨a ~ body in the eye⟩ 7 not being within the jurisdiction of a political unit (eg a state) [ME *forein*, fr OF, fr LL *foranus* on the outside, fr L *foris* outside – more at FORUM] – **foreignness** n

**foreign affairs** n pl matters concerned with international relations and with the interests of the home country in foreign countries

**foreign aid** n assistance (eg economic aid) provided by one nation to another usu less developed one

**foreign bill** n a BILL OF EXCHANGE (written order to pay money) that is not both drawn and payable within the same country – compare INLAND BILL

**foreign correspondent** n a correspondent, esp for a newspaper, who is based in a foreign country and who reports on that country's news and affairs

**foreigner** /'forənə/ n 1 a person belonging to or owing allegiance to a foreign country 2 something (eg a ship or animal) from or originating in a foreign country 3 *chiefly dial* STRANGER 1c; *esp* a person not native to a community

**foreign exchange** n 1 the buying and selling of foreign currencies 2 foreign currency

**foreignism** /'forənizm/ n something peculiar to a foreign language or people; *specif* a foreign idiom or custom

**foreign legion** n a body of foreign volunteers serving in a national army, esp that of France [trans of Fr *légion étrangère*]

**foreign minister** n, *often cap F&M* a government minister responsible for foreign affairs

**foreign office** n, *often cap F&O* the government department concerned with foreign affairs

**foreign policy** n the policy of a sovereign state in its interaction with other sovereign states

**foreign secretary** n, *often cap F&S, chiefly Br* FOREIGN MINISTER

¹**forejudge** /faw'juj/ vt to forjudge

²**forejudge** n to prejudge

**foreknow** /faw'noh/ vt **foreknew** /-'nyooh/; **foreknown** /-'nohn/ to have previous knowledge of; know beforehand, esp by paranormal means or by revelation – **foreknowledge** n

**foreland** /'fawlənd/ n a promontory, headland

**foreleg** /'fawleg/ n a front leg, esp of a 4-legged animal

**forelimb** /'fawlim/ n an arm, flipper, wing, or leg that is or has evolved from foreleg ⟨the ~ of a bat⟩

**forelock** /'fawlok/ n 1 a lock of hair growing just above the forehead 2 the part of a horse's mane that grows between the ears and hangs forward over the face

**foreman** /'fawmən/, *fem* **forewoman** /-woomən/ n 1 a member of a jury who acts as chairperson and spokesperson 2 a person, often an experienced or specially trained worker, who supervises a group of workers, a particular operation, or a section of a plant – **foremanship** n

**foremast** /'fawmahst/ n the mast nearest the bow or front of a ship; *specif* the lower part of such a mast having more than one part

¹**foremost** /'faw‚mohst/ adj 1 first in a series or progression 2 of first rank or position; preeminent [alter. (influenced by *fore-* and *most*) of ME *formest*, fr OE, superl of *forma* first; akin to OHG *fruma* advantage, OE *fore* fore]

²**foremost** adv 1 in the first place 2 most importantly ⟨first and ~⟩

**foremother** /'faw‚mudhə/ n a female ancestor

**forename** /'faw‚naym/ n a name that precedes a person's surname *synonyms* see CHRISTIAN NAME

**forenamed** /'faw‚naymd/ adj named or mentioned previously; aforesaid

**forenoon** /'faw‚noohn/ n, *formal* the part of the day before noon; the morning

¹**forensic** /fə'rensik/ adj 1 belonging to, used in, or suitable to courts of law; *also* of or suitable to public debate and discussion 2 of or being the investigation of crime by scientific means [L *forensis* of a forum, public, forensic, fr *forum*] – **forensically** adv

²**forensic** n 1 NAm an exercise, usu in the form of a speech or thesis, in formal argument or debate 2 pl taking sing or pl vb the art or study of argumentative discourse or debate

**forensic medicine** n a science that deals with the application of medical facts and scientific methods to criminal investigations and legal problems

**foreordain** /fawraw'dayn/ vt to settle, arrange, or appoint in advance; predestine – **foreordination** n

**forepart** /'faw‚paht/ n 1 the first or front part of something 2 the earlier part of a period of time

**forepassed, forepast** /'faw‚pahst/ adj, *archaic* bygone

**forepaw** /'faw‚paw/ n a front paw

**forepeak** /'faw‚peek/ n the compartment in the angle of a ship's bows

**foreperson** /'faw‚puhs(ə)n/ n a foreman or forewoman

**foreplay** /'faw‚play/ n erotic stimulation preceding sexual intercourse

**forequarter** /'faw‚kwawtə/ n the front half, including the leg, of a side of a 4-legged animal or of the carcass of a 4-legged animal

**forerun** /faw'run/ vt **forerunning; foreran** /faw'ran/ to come before as a token of something to follow

**forerunner** /'fawrunə/ n 1a one going or sent before to give notice of the approach of others **b** a premonitory sign or symptom 2 a predecessor, forebear 3 an original model from which later developments are derived; a prototype

**foresaddle** /'fawsadl/ n a cut of mutton, lamb, or veal that consists of the undivided forequarters of a carcass foresaid /'fawsed/ adj, archaic aforesaid

foresail /'fawsl, -sayl/ n 1 the lowest sail on the FOREMAST (mast nearest the front) of a ship having SQUARE SAILS (4-sided sails set across a ship) 2 the principal FORE-AND-AFT sail (sail set lengthways) on a schooner's foremast 3 FORESTAYSAIL (triangular sail near the front of a ship)

foresee /faw'see/ vt foresees; foreseeing; foresaw /-'saw/; foreseen /-'seen/ to be aware of (eg a development) beforehand ⟨~ difficulties⟩ – foreseeable adj, foreseer n

foreshadow /faw'shadoh/ vt to represent, indicate, or typify beforehand; suggest in advance ⟨present trends ~ future events⟩ – foreshadower n

foreshank /'fawshangk/ n a cut of beef from the lower part of a foreleg; a beef shin

foresheets /'fawsheets/ n pl the front part of an open boat in the bows

foreshore /'fawshaw/ n 1 a strip of land bordering a body of water 2 the part of a seashore between high-water and low-water marks

foreshorten /faw'shawt(ə)n/ vt 1 to shorten (a detail in a drawing or painting) according to the laws of LINEAR PERSPECTIVE so that the composition appears to have depth 2 to make more compact

foreshow /faw'shoh/ vt foreshown /-'shohn/ to tell or show beforehand; foretell, foreshadow

foreside /'faw,sied/ n, archaic the front side or part; the front

foresight /'faw,siet/ n 1 an act or the power of foreseeing 2 an act of looking forward; also a view forward 3 care or provision for the future; prudence ⟨had the ~ to invest his money wisely⟩ 4 the sight nearest the muzzle on a gun – foresighted adj, foresightedly adv, foresightedness n, foresightful adj

foreskin /'fawskin/ n a fold of skin that covers the glans of the penis

¹forest /'forist/ n 1 a tract of wooded land in Britain, formerly owned by the sovereign and used for hunting game 2 a dense growth of trees and shrubby undergrowth covering a large tract of land; also the trees of a forest 3 something resembling a profusion of trees ⟨a ~ of TV aerials⟩ [ME, fr OF, fr ML forestis, fr L foris outside – more at FORUM] – forestal, forestial adj, forested adj

²forest vt to cover with trees or forest – forestation n

forestage /'faw,stayj/ n APRON 2e (front part of a theatre stage)

forestall /faw'stawl/ vt 1 to exclude, hinder, or prevent by prior measures 2 to get ahead of; anticipate and act in advance of 3a to prevent the normal trading in (eg a market) by buying or diverting goods or by persuading people to raise prices b to buy up (goods) in order to create a short supply and thus enhance the price; CORNER 2 – not used technically 4 archaic to intercept synonyms see PREVENT [ME forstallen, fr forstall act of waylaying, fr OE foresteall, fr fore- + steall position, stall] – forestaller n, forestallment n

forestay /'faw,stay/ n a stay (eg a cable or chain) that supports the FOREMAST (mast nearest the bow or front) and runs from the head of the foremast to the bow of a ship

forestaysail /'faw,staysl/ n a triangular sail that is set on a forestay and is the first of the sails in front of the foremast

forester /'foristə/ n 1 a person trained in forestry 2 a person or animal that inhabits a forest 3 any of various moths (family Zygaenidae) that fly in daylight and have metallic-green wings

forestland /'foristland/ n land covered with forest or reserved for the growth of forests

forest ranger n an officer who patrols and guards a forest; esp one in charge of the management and protection of a portion of a public forest

forestry /'foristri/ n 1 forestland 2a the science of developing, caring for, or cultivating forests b the management of forests

foreswear /faw'sweə/ vb foreswore /faw'swaw/; foresworn /-'swawn/ to forswear

¹foretaste /'faw,tayst/ n 1 an advance indication or warning 2 a small anticipatory sample

²foretaste vt to have a foretaste of; anticipate

foretell /faw'tel/ vt foretold /-tohld/ to tell or indicate beforehand; predict – foreteller n

synonyms Foretell, now general and neutral, formerly connoted mysterious or occult power. Predict, forecast, and prophesy are chiefly restricted to people. Predict usually suggests a conclusion drawn from observations or calculations, and this always applies to forecast. Prophesy implies divine inspiration, mystic knowledge, or wisdom and assurance. Prognosticate, augur, presage, bode, and forebode, like foretell, but unlike portend, may apply either

to people foretelling the future or things betokening it. Prognosticate (formal) suggests the interpretation of signs and symptoms, as a doctor would in order to forecast the future course of an illness. Augur deals with the interpretation of omens, though it has lost its connection with the occult. Presage and portend usually mean "betoken" rather than "foretell". The former may point to favourable, unfavourable, or neutral events. Portend, however, always implies unfavourable ones, as does forebode (more common as a noun, foreboding) which suggests impending misfortune sensed in premonitions or dreams. Bode may be good or bad in implication and is qualified accordingly ⟨bode ill for⟩ ⟨bode well for⟩.

forethought /'faw,thawt/ n 1 thinking or planning out in advance; premeditation 2 consideration or thought for the future – forethought adj

foretime /'faw,tiem/ n former or past time; the time before the present

¹foretoken /'faw'tohk(ə)n/ n a sign or warning of what is to come

²foretoken vt to indicate or warn of in advance

foretop /'fawtop/ n a platform at the top of a ship's FOREMAST (lower part of frontmost mast)

fore-topgallant /,fawtop'galənt/ adj of or being the part of the frontmost mast of a ship that is next above the fore-top-mast ⟨a ~ mast⟩ ⟨a ~ sail⟩

fore-'topmast n the mast next above the FOREMAST (lower part of frontmost mast)

fore-topsail /'faw'topsl/ n a sail set on a fore-topmast; the sail next above the FORESAIL

¹forever /fə'revə/ adv 1 forever, forevermore for all future time; indefinitely ⟨wants to live ~⟩ 2 with persistence; incessantly ⟨is ~ jingling the change in his pocket⟩

usage Some British writers prefer to spell forever as two words ⟨to live for ever⟩ unless it means "persistently".

²forever n an endless length of time ⟨it took her ~ to find the answer⟩

forewarn /faw'wawn/ vt to warn in advance synonyms see WARN

forewent /faw'went/ past of FOREGO

fore wing n either of the front wings of a 4-winged insect

forewoman /'faw-woomən/ n a woman who acts as a foreman

foreword /'faw-wəd/ n a preface; esp one written by somebody other than the author of the text △ forward

¹forfeit /'fawfit/ n 1 something lost or confiscated or to which one's right is taken away as a penalty: eg 1a a small fine for breach of the rules of a club or game b a penalty imposed for an offence, breach of contract, neglect of duty, etc 2 the loss or forfeiting of something, esp civil rights 3a an article given up in the game of forfeits b pl taking sing or pl vb a game in which articles are given up (eg for making a mistake) and later redeemed usu by performing a silly task [ME forfait, fr MF, fr pp of forfaire to commit a crime, forfeit, prob fr fors outside (fr L foris) + faire to do, fr L facere – more at FORUM, DO]

²forfeit vt 1 to lose or lose the right to by some error, offence, etc 2 to subject to confiscation as a forfeit – forfeitable adj, forfeiter n

³forfeit adj forfeited or subject to forfeiture

forfeiture /'fawfichə/ n 1 the act of forfeiting something; the loss of property, money, etc as a result of a breach of a rule, legal obligation, etc 2 something (eg money, a right, or property) that is forfeited

forfend also forefend /faw'fend/ vt 1 NAm 1a to prevent; WARD OFF b to protect, preserve 2 archaic to forbid – chiefly in heaven forfend [ME forfenden, fr for- + fenden to fend]

forgather, foregather /faw'gadhə/ vi 1 to come together; assemble 2 chiefly Scot to meet somebody usu by chance – usu + with

¹forge /fawj/ n 1 an open furnace where metal, esp iron, is heated and wrought 2 a workshop with a forge; a smithy [ME, fr OF, fr L fabrica, fr fabr-, faber smith – more at DAFT]

²forge vt 1a to shape (metal or a metal object) by heating and hammering b to shape (metal or a metal object) using a press with or without heat 2 to form or bring into being, esp by an expenditure of effort ⟨made every effort to ~ party unity⟩ 3 to make (eg a document or bank note) or imitate (eg a signature) falsely, esp with intent to defraud; counterfeit ~ vi to commit forgery synonyms see ¹MAKE – forgeable adj, forgeability n, forger n

³forge vi 1 to move forwards slowly and steadily ⟨the great ship ~d through the waves⟩ 2 to move with a sudden increase

of speed and power ⟨*the horse* ~d *ahead to win the race*⟩ ⟨~d *into the lead*⟩ [prob alter. of ²*force*

**forgery** /'fawjəri/ *n* **1** an act of forging; *esp* the crime of falsely and fraudulently reproducing, making, signing, or altering a bank note, document (e g a cheque), etc **2** something forged; *esp* a forged signature, bank note, or document **3** *archaic* an invention, esp of the mind or imagination

**forget** /fə'get/ *vb* **forgetting; forgot** /-'got/; **forgotten** /-'got(ə)n/ *archaic or NAm* **forgot** *vt* **1a** to fail to remember or recall; lose the remembrance of ⟨*I ~ his name*⟩ **b** to fail to remember to do, bring, or attend to ⟨forgot *to go*⟩ ⟨forgot *my jacket*⟩ **2** to fail to give attention to; disregard, neglect ⟨forgot *his old friends*⟩ **3a** to disregard or put out of one's mind intentionally; overlook ⟨*we will ~ our differences*⟩ **b** to reject the idea or possibility of; discount ⟨*as for going out tonight, ~ it!*⟩ ~ *vi* **1** to cease remembering or noticing ⟨*forgive and ~*⟩ **2** to fail to remember at the proper time – often + *about* ⟨forgot *about the bill*⟩ [ME *forgeten*, fr OE *forgietan*, fr *for-* + *-gietan* (akin to ON *geta* to get)] – **forgetter** *n* – **forget oneself** to lose one's dignity, temper, or self-control; act unsuitably or unworthily

**forgetful** /fə'getf(ə)l/ *adj* **1** likely or apt to forget ⟨*a ~ person*⟩ **2** characterized by negligent failure to remember; neglectful – usu + *of* ⟨*~ of his manners*⟩ **3** *poetic* inducing oblivion ⟨*~ sleep*⟩ – **forgetfully** *adv*, **forgetfulness** *n*

**for'get-me-,not** *n* any of a genus (*Myosotis* of the family Boraginaceae, the forget-me-not family) with white or bright blue flowers usu arranged in a spike

**forgettable** /fə'getəbl/ *adj* apt or likely to be forgotten; *esp* unworthy of remembrance ⟨*a most ~ play*⟩

**forgive** /fə'giv/ *vb* **forgave** /-'gayv/; **forgiven** /-'giv(ə)n/ *vt* **1a** to cease to feel resentment towards ⟨*~ one's enemies*⟩ **b** to give up feeling resentment over or desire to avenge oneself for ⟨*~ the insult*⟩ **2** to pardon ⟨*~ us our trespasses*⟩ **3** to grant relief from payment of (e g a debt) ~ *vi* to grant forgiveness [ME *forgiven*, fr OE *forgifan*, fr *for-* + *gifan* to give] – **forgivable** *adj*, **forgivably** *adv*, **forgiver** *n*

**forgiveness** /fə'givnəs/ *n* the act of forgiving or state of being forgiven; pardon

**forgiving** /fə'giving/ *adj* willing or able to forgive – **forgivingly** *adv*, **forgivingness** *n*

**forgo, forego** /faw'goh/ *vt* **forgoes; forgoing; forwent** /-'went/; **forgone** /-'gon/ **1** to abstain or refrain from; renounce, relinquish ⟨*~ immediate gratification for the sake of future gains*⟩ **2** *archaic* to forsake [ME *forgon*, fr OE *forgān* to pass by, forgo, fr *for-* + *gān* to go] – **forgoer** *n*

**forint** /'fawrint/ *n* – see MONEY table [Hung, fr It *fiorino* florin]

**forjudge, forejudge** /faw'juj/ *vt* to expel, oust, or put out by judgment of a court

¹**fork** /fawk/ *n* **1** a tool or implement with two or more prongs set on the end of a handle: e g **1a** an agricultural or gardening tool for lifting, carrying, throwing, or digging **b** a small implement (e g of metal) usu having two, three, or four prongs and used for eating or serving food **2a** a forked part or piece of equipment **b fork, forks** *pl* a forked support into which a cycle wheel fits **3a** a division into branches or the place (e g in a road) where something divides into branches **b** any of the branches into which something forks ⟨*take the left ~ at the T junction*⟩ **c** a place where two or more streams meet; a confluence; *also chiefly NAm* the main tributary of a river or similar waterway **4** an attack by a chess piece (e g a knight) on two pieces simultaneously [ME *forke*, fr OE & ONF; OE *forca* & ONF *forque*, fr L *furca*] – **forkful** *n*

²**fork** *vi* **1** to divide into two or more branches ⟨*where the road ~s*⟩ **2** to make a turn into one of the branches of a fork ⟨*we ~ed left at the inn*⟩ ~ *vt* **1** to give the form of a fork to **2** to raise, pitch, dig, or work with a fork ⟨*~ hay*⟩ **3** to attack (two chess pieces) simultaneously – **forker** *n*

**fork out/over/up** *vb informal* to make a payment or contribution (of) ⟨forked out *half of his annual salary for a new car*⟩

**forked** /fawkt/ *adj* **1** having an end divided into two or more branches or points ⟨*~ lightning*⟩ **2** having a fork or forked part ⟨*a ~ road*⟩

**forklift** /'fawklift/, **forklift truck** *n* a vehicle for hoisting and transporting heavy objects by means of steel prongs inserted under the load

**forlorn** /fə'lawn/ *adj* **1a** bereft, forsaken *of* ⟨*left quite ~ of hope*⟩ **b** sad and lonely because of isolation or desertion; desolate **2** in poor condition; miserable, wretched ⟨*~ tumble-down buildings*⟩ **3** nearly hopeless ⟨*a ~ attempt*⟩ [ME *forloren*,

fr OE, pp of *forlēosan* to lose, fr *for-* + *lēosan* to lose] – **forlornly** *adv*, **forlornness** *n*

**forlorn hope** *n* **1** a desperate or extremely difficult enterprise unlikely to succeed **2** *archaic* a body of men selected to carry out a dangerous undertaking [by folk etymology fr D *verloren hoop*, lit., lost band]

¹**form** /fawm/ *n* **1a** the shape and structure of something as distinguished from its material, colour, texture, etc **b** a body (e g of a person), esp in its external appearance or as distinguished from the face **2** *philosophy* the essential nature of a thing as distinguished from the matter in which it is embodied: e g **2a** *often cap* IDEA 1 **b** that aspect of a thing that determines to which kind or species it belongs **3a** established or correct method of proceeding or behaving; procedure according to rule or convention ⟨*what is the ~?*⟩ ⟨*asked for her name as a matter of ~*⟩ **b** a prescribed and set order of words; a formula ⟨*the ~ of the marriage service*⟩ **4** a printed or typed document; *esp* one with blank spaces for insertion of required or requested information ⟨*income-tax ~s*⟩ **5a** conduct regulated by extraneous controls (e g custom or etiquette); ceremony ⟨*the rigid ~ of the imperial court*⟩ **b** manner or conduct of a specified sort as tested by a prescribed or accepted standard ⟨*rudeness is simply bad ~*⟩ **c** manner or style of doing, performing, or accomplishing according to recognized standards of technique ⟨*a strong swimmer but weak on ~*⟩ **6a** the bed or nest of a hare **b** a long usu backless seat; a bench **7** something (e g a model, frame, or mould) that holds, supports, and determines shape **8a** any of the different modes of existence, action, or manifestation of a specified thing or substance; a kind, variety ⟨*one ~ of respiratory disorder*⟩ ⟨*a ~ of art*⟩ **b** the particular way in which something is arranged, exists, or shows itself ⟨*written in the ~ of a letter*⟩ **9** a distinguishable group of organisms **10a(1)** orderly method of arrangement (e g in the presentation of ideas); manner of coordinating elements (e g of an artistic production or line of reasoning) ⟨*his work lacks ~*⟩ **a(2)** a particular kind or instance of such arrangement ⟨*the sonnet is a poetical ~*⟩ **b** a pattern, schema ⟨*arguments of the same logical ~*⟩ **c** the structural element, plan, or design of a work of art – compare CONTENT 2c **d** a visible and measurable unit defined by a contour; a bounded surface or volume (e g a sphere, cube, or triangle) **11** *taking sing or pl vb* a class organized for the work of a particular year, esp in a British school ⟨*sixth ~*⟩ **12a** the past performances of a competitor (e g a football team, horse, or runner) considered as a guide to its future performance **b** known ability to perform ⟨*a singer at the top of his ~*⟩ **c** condition suitable for performing, esp in sports – often + *in, on, out of,* or *off* ⟨*was out of ~ all season*⟩ **d** spirits; frame of mind ⟨*she's in good ~ today*⟩; *esp* good spirits **13a** LINGUISTIC FORM (meaningful unit of speech, such as a word or sentence) **b** any of the different ways in which a word may be written or spoken as a result of inflection or change of spelling or pronunciation ⟨*verbal ~s*⟩ **14** *chiefly NAm* DUMMY 3b (model of the human figure) **15** *NAm* FORME (frame enclosing printing type) **16** *Br slang* a criminal record **17** *archaic* beauty [ME *forme*, fr OF, fr L *forma*, perh modif of Gk *morphē* form, shape]

²**form** *vt* **1** to give form, shape, or existence to; fashion, construct ⟨*~ed from clay*⟩ ⟨*~ a judgment*⟩ **2a** to give a particular shape to; shape or mould into a certain state or after a particular model ⟨*~ed the dough into various shapes*⟩ ⟨*a state ~ed along the lines of the Roman Republic*⟩ **b** to arrange or organize themselves in ⟨*the women ~ed a line*⟩ **c** to model or train by instruction and discipline ⟨*a mind ~ed by a classical education*⟩ **3** to develop, acquire ⟨*~ a habit*⟩ **4** to serve to make up or constitute; be a usu essential or basic element of **5** *linguistics* **5a** to produce (e g a tense) by inflection ⟨*~s the past in -ed*⟩ **b** to combine to make (a compound word) **6** to arrange in order; DRAW UP ⟨*the battalion advanced as soon as its lines were ~ed*⟩ ~ *vi* **1** to become formed or shaped ⟨*a scab ~ed over the wound*⟩ **2** to take form; come into existence ⟨*thunderclouds were ~ing over the hills*⟩ **3** to take on a definite form, shape, or arrangement ⟨*~ into a line*⟩ *synonyms* see ¹MAKE – **formable** *adj*

**form-** /fawm-/, **formo-** /'fawmoh-/ *comb form* formic acid ⟨*formate*⟩ ⟨*formaldehyde*⟩ [*formic*]

**-form** /-fawm/ *comb form* (→ *adj*) having the form or shape of; resembling ⟨*cruciform*⟩ [MF & L; MF *-forme*, fr L *-formis*, fr *forma*]

¹**formal** /'fawml/ *adj* **1a** determining or being the essential constitution or structure ⟨*~ cause*⟩ **b** of, concerned with, or

being the outward form or appearance of something as distinguished from its content **c** having a symmetrical or orderly arrangement of elements ⟨*a* ∼ *garden*⟩ ⟨*a* ∼ *composition*⟩ **2** following or according with established form, custom, rule, or convention; not deviating from what is usual or generally accepted ⟨*lacked* ∼ *qualifications for the job*⟩ ⟨*a* ∼ *education*⟩ **3a** based on or observing conventional or prescribed forms and rules ⟨*a* ∼ *reception*⟩ ⟨∼ *landscaping*⟩ **b** characterized by punctilious respect for form or correct procedure ⟨*very* ∼ *in all his dealings*⟩ **c** rigidly ceremonious; prim **4** having the appearance without the substance; nominal ⟨∼ *Christians who go to church only at Easter*⟩ – **formally** *adv*, **formalness** *n*

²**formal** *n, NAm* something (eg a dance or dress) formal in character

**formaldehyde** /faw'maldihied/ *n* a pungent irritating gas, HCHO, used, esp in formalin, as a disinfectant and preservative and in the synthesis of other chemical compounds [ISV *form-* + *aldehyde*]

**formalin** /'fawməlin/ *n* a clear solution of formaldehyde in water used chiefly as a disinfectant and for preserving biological specimens (eg tissues, anatomical parts, and small animals) [fr *Formalin*, a trademark]

**formalism** /'fawməlizm/ *n* the practice or doctrine of strict adherence to prescribed or external forms, structures, or techniques (eg in religion, mathematics or art) often without regard to their content or inner significance – **formalist** *n or adj*, **formalistic** *adj*, **formalistically** *adv*

**formality** /faw'maliti/ *n* **1** the quality or state of being formal **2** compliance with or observance of formal or conventional rules; ceremony **3a** an established form or procedure that is required or conventional **b** something required by rule or custom that has little real significance ⟨*let's get the* formalities *over with first*⟩

**formal·ize, -ise** /'fawməliez/ *vt* **1** to give a particular or definite form to; shape **2a** to make formal **b** to give formal or official status or approval to – **formalization** *n*, **formalizer** *n*

**formal logic** *n* a system of logic (eg Aristotelian logic or SYMBOLIC LOGIC) that abstracts the forms of thought from its content as a method of investigating the structure of propositions and deductive reasoning

**formant** /'fawmənt/ *n* a characteristic component of the quality of a sound, esp a speech sound; *specif* any of several bands in which the frequencies subsidiary to the main frequency of a vowel sound are at their strongest and that differentiate the sound of one vowel from that of another [Ger, fr L *formant-, formans*, prp of *formare* to form]

¹**format** /'fawmat/ *n* **1a** the size and shape of a publication as determined by the number of times each sheet of paper has been folded ⟨*a novel in octavo* ∼⟩ **b(1)** the shape, size, and general makeup of something; *esp* the general appearance, including shape, size, layout, and binding, of a book or other publication **b(2)** the way in which information is stored in an electronic device, esp a computer **2** a general plan of organization, arrangement, or layout (eg of a television show or of data to be handled by a computer) [Fr or Ger; Fr, fr Ger, fr L *formatus*, pp of *formare* to form, fr *forma*]

²**format** *vt* to arrange (eg a book or data) in a particular format or style

**formate** /faw'mayt/ *n* any of various chemical compounds (SALTS or ESTERS) formed by combination between FORMIC ACID and a metal atom, an alcohol, or another chemical group

**formation** /faw'maysh(ə)n/ *n* **1** an act of giving form, shape, or existence to something or of taking form; development **2** something that is formed ⟨*new word* ∼s⟩ **3** the manner in which a thing is formed; structure **4** the largest unit in an ecological community comprising all the established or stable plant life of a widespread natural habitat (eg coniferous forest or prairie) **5** a body or series of rocks that share distinct well-defined properties and are considered together as a geological unit **6** an arrangement of a body or group of people (eg soldiers) or things (eg aircraft) in some prescribed manner or for a particular purpose; *also, taking sing or pl vb* such a body or group – **formational** *adj*

¹**formative** /'fawmətiv/ *adj* **1a** giving or capable of giving form; constructive ⟨*a* ∼ *influence*⟩ **b** used in word formation or inflection **2** *of a cell, tissue, etc* capable of alteration by growth and development; *also* producing new cells and tissues **3** of or characterized by formation or development or by formative effects ⟨∼ *years*⟩ – **formatively** *adv*, **formativeness** *n*

²**formative** *n, linguistics* **1** a formative AFFIX (eg *un-* in unhappy or *-s* in moves) **2** any of the basic units in TRANSFORMATIONAL GRAMMAR which play a role in determining whether a sentence is grammatically well-formed

**form class** *n* a class of LINGUISTIC FORMS (words, word parts, phrases, etc) that can be used in the same position in a construction and that have one or more grammatical features in common ⟨book *and* hat *belong to the* ∼ *of nouns*⟩ ⟨opened *and* walked *belong to the* form classes *of verbs and past tenses*⟩ – compare MAJOR FORM CLASS

**form critical** *adj* based on or applying FORM CRITICISM

**form criticism** *n* a method for determining the sources and historical authenticity of esp biblical writings by analysis of the writings in terms of traditional literary forms (eg love poems, parables, and myth) – **form critic** *n*

**forme,** *NAm* **form** /fawm/ *n* a frame enclosing metal type or blocks ready for printing [Fr *forme*, lit., form]

**formée** /'fawmay/ *adj* FORMY

¹**former** /'fawmə/ *adj* **1** of or occurring in the past ⟨*in* ∼ *times*⟩ **2** preceding in time or order ⟨*the* ∼ *Prime Minister*⟩ **3** first of two things mentioned or understood [ME, fr *forme* first, fr OE *forma* – more at FOREMOST]

²**former** *n, pl* **former** the first mentioned; the first ⟨*of puppies and kittens the* ∼ *are harder to train*⟩ – compare LATTER

*usage The* **former** should be the first of two things, if the word is used at all. Otherwise one should prefer *first* or *first-named*, or simply repeat the necessary words ⟨*Anne, Bill, and Sarah met at Anne's* (not at the **former's**) *house*⟩; but even where there are only two things it is tedious to have to look back and see what *the* **former** refers to, instead of reading straight on.

³**former** *n* **1** one who or that which forms or shapes: eg **1a** a tool or frame for giving a certain shape to a coil of electrically conducting wire **b** a structural part in an aircraft that helps to maintain the shape of the fuselage, engine case, etc **2** *chiefly Br* a member of a school form – usu in combination ⟨*a sixth* ∼⟩

**formerly** /'fawməli/ *adv* **1** at an earlier time; previously **2** *obs* just before △ **formally**

**form genus** *n* an artificial category in plant or animal classification established for organisms of obscure true relationships

**formic** /'fawmik/ *adj* of or derived from formic acid [L *formica* ant – more at PISMIRE]

**Formica** /faw'miekə/ *trademark* – used for any of various plastics made from thin sheets bonded together and used esp for hard-wearing surfaces (eg on wood)

**formic acid** /'fawmik/ *n* a colourless pungent corrosive liquid acid, HCOOH, found in plants and produced naturally by ants and used chiefly in dyeing and finishing textiles

**formicary** /'fawmikəri/ *n* an ant nest [ML *formicarium*, fr L *formica*]

**formication** /ˌfawmi'kaysh(ə)n/ *n* a sensation resembling that produced by insects creeping over the skin △ **fornication** [L *formication-, formicatio*, fr *formicatus*, pp of *formicare* to crawl like an ant, fr *formica* ant]

**formidable** /'fawmidəbl, fə'midəbl USE *the last pron is disliked by some speakers*/ *adj* **1** causing fear, dread, or apprehension ⟨*a* ∼ *prospect*⟩ **2** difficult to overcome, defeat, etc; discouraging approach or attempts to succeed or deal with **3** tending to inspire awe or respect [ME, fr L *formidabilis*, fr *formidare* to fear, fr *formido* fear; akin to Gk *mormō* she-monster] – **formidableness** *n*, **formidably** *adv*, **formidability** *n*

**formless** /'fawmlis/ *adj* **1** having no regular or definite form or shape **2** lacking order or arrangement **3** having no physical existence – **formlessly** *adv*, **formlessness** *n*

**form letter** *n* a standard letter to which pertinent details (eg name and address) are added and which is sent to a usu large number of people

**formo-** /'fawmoh-/ – see FORM-

**form of address** *n* a correct title or correct expression of politeness to be used to somebody

**form teacher** *n, Br* a teacher responsible for and often teaching one school form

**formula** /'fawmyoolə/ *n, pl* **formulas, formulae** /-li/ **1a** a set form of words for use in a ceremony, ritual, etc **b** (a conventionalized statement intended to express) a fundamental truth, principle, or procedure used esp as a basis for negotiation or action ⟨*the two sides worked out a peace* ∼⟩ ⟨*the* ∼ *for a good marriage*⟩ **2** a set of ingredients together with instructions for preparing something (eg a drug or explosive); *also* a list of ingredients required **3** a general fact, rule, or principle ex-

pressed in symbols: e g **3a** a symbolic expression of the chemical composition of a substance **b** a collection of symbols linked by mathematical operations (e g addition, multiplication, or integration) that precisely expresses a mathematical relationship and is used to solve equations, calculate the value of a physical constant, etc ⟨*the ~ for the area of a circle*⟩ ⟨*Stirling's ~*⟩ **4** a prescribed, set, or conventional form or method (e g of writing); an established rule or custom ⟨*unimaginative television programmes that were written to a ~*⟩ **5** a category of racing cars conforming to a particular size, weight, engine capacity, etc **6** *NAm* a milk mixture or substitute for feeding a baby [L, dim. of *forma* form] – **formulaic** *adj*, **formulaically** *adv*
**usage** The tendency is to prefer the Latin plural in scientific contexts ⟨*mathematical formulae*⟩ and the other plural elsewhere ⟨*political formulas*⟩.

**formular·ize, -ise** /'fawmyooləriez/ *vt* FORMULATE 1 – **formularizer** *n*, **formularization** *n*

**formulary** /'fawmyoolərɪ/ *n* **1** a book or other collection of stated and prescribed forms (e g prayers) **2** a prescribed form or model; a formula **3** a book containing a list of medicinal substances and formulas ⟨*British National* Formulary⟩

**formulate** /'fawmyoolayt/ *vt* **1** to state in or reduce to a formula; put into a standardized statement or expression **2** to devise or develop ⟨*~ policy*⟩ – **formulation** *n*, **formulator** *n*

**formul·ize, -ise** /'fawmyooliez/ *vt* FORMULATE 1 – **formulization** *n*

**formwork** /'fawmwuhk/ *n* SHUTTERING (mould to support concrete while setting)

**formy** /'fawmɪ/ *adj, of a heraldic cross* having the arms narrow at the centre and expanding towards the ends [ME *forme*, fr MF *formé*, pp of *former* to form, fr L *formare*]

**formyl** /'fawmiel, -il/ *n* the chemical group HCO that is characteristic of FORMIC ACID and ALDEHYDES [ISV]

**fornicate** /'fawnikayt/ *vi* to commit fornication [LL *fornicatus*, pp of *fornicare*, fr L *fornic-, fornix* arch, vault, brothel] – **fornicator** *n*

**fornication** /,fawni'kaysh(ə)n/ *n* **1** voluntary sexual intercourse outside marriage; adultery **2** sexual intercourse between consenting unmarried people

**fornix** /'fawniks/ *n, pl* **fornices** /'fawniseez/ an anatomical arch or fold; *esp* an arched sheet of fibres in the brain [NL, fr L, arch]

**forrader** *also* **forrarder** /'forədə/ *adv, chiefly Br informal* further ahead [E dial., compar of E *forward*]

**forsake** /fə'sayk/ *vt* **forsook** /fə'sook/; **forsaken** /fə'saykən/ **1** to renounce (e g something once cherished) without intent to recover or resume ⟨forsook *her family ties*⟩ **2** to desert, abandon ⟨*false friends ~ us in adversity*⟩ [ME *forsaken*, fr OE *forsacan*, fr *for-* + *sacan* to dispute; akin to OE *sacu* action at law – more at SAKE]
**synonyms** Abandon, desert, and forsake all mean leaving or giving up completely something or someone to whom one was formerly attached by ties of love, interest, or duty. **Abandon** strikes a note of despair, emphasizing the finality of the action ⟨abandon hope, all ye who enter here – Dante⟩. It may suggest the vulnerability of what is left behind ⟨a child abandoned on a doorstep⟩. **Desert** implies failing to fulfil a moral duty, or breaking a tie of affection or habit: someone may desert a spouse, a friend, a post, or a favourite pub. **Deserted** suggests an air of desolation. **Forsake** tends to stress the pain involved when former close attachments are renounced or repudiated ⟨forsook their families to live in the big city⟩.

**forsooth** /fə'soohth/ *adv* actually, indeed – now often used to imply contempt or doubt [ME *for soth*, fr OE *forsōth*, fr *for* + *sōth* truth – more at SOOTH]

**forspent** /faw'spent/ *adj, archaic* exhausted; WORN OUT

**forsterite** /'fawstəriet/ *n* a rock-forming mineral, $Mg_2SiO_4$, of the OLIVINE group consisting of magnesium silicate [Johann *Forster* †1798 Ger traveller]

**forswear, foreswear** /faw'sweə/ *vb* **forswore, foreswore; forsworn, foresworn** /faw'swawn/ *vt* **1** to reject or renounce solemnly, esp under oath **2a** to deny under oath **b** to perjure (oneself) (as if) under oath ~ *vi* to swear falsely [ME *forsweren*, fr OE *forswerian*, fr *for-* + *swerian* to swear]

**forsworn, foresworn** /faw'swawn/ *adj* guilty of perjury

**forsythia** /faw'siethi·ə, -thyə/ *n* any of a genus (*Forsythia*) of ornamental shrubs of the ash family with bright yellow bell-shaped flowers appearing before the leaves in early spring [NL, genus name, fr William *Forsyth* †1804 Brit botanist]

**fort** /fawt/ *n* **1a** a strong or fortified place, usu occupied only

by troops and maintained for defence **b** a fortified building (e g with rampart and parapet) built in former times for defence **2** a permanent army post – often in place names ⟨Fort *William*⟩ [ME *forte*, fr MF *fort*, fr *fort* strong, fr L *fortis*] – **hold the fort** to cope with problems for or look after the work of somebody who is absent

**fortalice** /'fawtəlis/ *n, archaic* a fortress; *specif* a small fort or outwork of a fortification [ME, fr ML *fortalitia* – more at FORTRESS]

**¹forte** /fawt; *esp sense 1* 'fawtay/ *n* **1** the area or skill in which a person excels; STRONG POINT **2** the strongest part of the blade of a fencing sword, between the middle and the hilt – compare FOIBLE [MF *fort*, fr *fort* strong]

**²forte** /'fawti, -tay/ *n, adv, or adj* (a musical note or passage performed) in a loud and forceful way – used as a direction in music [It, fr *forte* strong, fr L *fortis*]

**fortepiano** /,fawtipi'anoh/ *n* **1** a piano of the late 18th century **2** *archaic* a piano [Fr or It; Fr, fr It, fr *forte* loud + *piano* soft]

**forte-piano** /,fawti'pyahnoh/ *adv or adj* in a manner that is loud then immediately soft – used as a direction in music [It, lit., loud-soft]

**¹forth** /fawth/ *adv* **1** onwards into future time, place, or order; forwards ⟨*from that day ~*⟩ – compare AND SO FORTH, BACK AND FORTH **2** out into notice or view ⟨*put ~ leaves*⟩ **3** *archaic* away from a central location (e g a home town); abroad ⟨*went ~ to preach*⟩ [ME, fr OE; akin to OE *for*] – **forth of** *archaic* out from; OUT OF

**²forth** *prep, archaic* forth from; OUT OF

**forthcoming** /-'kuming/ *adj* **1** about to occur or appear; approaching ⟨*the ~ holidays*⟩ **2a** readily available in the near future ⟨*new funds will be ~ next year*⟩ **b** outgoing, affable ⟨*a ~, accessible, and sociable personality*⟩ [fr prp of obs *forthcome* to come forth]

**¹forthright** /'fawth,riet/ *adv, archaic* **1** directly forwards or ahead **2** immediately

**²forthright** *adj* **1** stating facts or opinions without ambiguity or hesitation; straightforward, frank ⟨*a ~ critic*⟩ ⟨*a ~ appraisal of a problem*⟩ **2** *archaic* proceeding straight on – **forthrightly** *adv*, **forthrightness** *n*

**³forthright** *n, archaic* a straight path

**forthwith** /-'widh/ *adv* immediately, straightaway

**fortification** /,fawtifi'kaysh(ə)n/ *n* **1** an act of fortifying, defending, or strengthening **2** something that fortifies ⟨*a little sherry as ~ against the cold weather*⟩ **3a** the science or art of providing defensive works **b** **fortifications** *pl*, **fortification** something (e g a rampart or ditch) constructed to defend a place or position

**fortified wine** /'fawti,fied/ *n* a wine, esp a DESSERT WINE, to which alcohol, usu in the form of grape brandy, has been added during or after fermentation

**fortify** /'fawtifie/ *vt* **1** to strengthen and secure (a strategic military position) by erecting defences or increasing the number of military personnel **2a** to give additional physical strength, courage, or endurance to; invigorate ⟨fortified *himself with a glass of wine*⟩ **b** to add mental or moral strength to; encourage ⟨fortified *by prayer*⟩ **3** to add material to for strengthening or enriching ⟨*eat a healthy diet to ~ the body against disease*⟩ ~ *vi* to erect fortifications [ME *fortifien*, fr MF *fortifier*, fr LL *fortificare*, fr L *fortis* strong] – **fortifier** *n*

**fortis** /'fawtis/ *adj* produced with relatively tense articulation and strong expiration ⟨/t/ in toe is ~, /d/ in doe is lenis⟩ [NL, fr L, strong]

**¹fortissimo** /faw'tisimoh/ *adv or adj* (in a manner that is) very loud – used as a direction in music [It, superl of *forte*]

**²fortissimo** *n, pl* **fortissimos, fortissimi** a very loud sound, note, or passage of music

**fortitude** /'fawtityoohd, -choohd/ *n* **1a** patient endurance in pain or adversity; BACKBONE **3 b** resolute courage which helps a person face danger calmly; GRIT **4 2** *obs* strength [ME, fr L *fortitudin-, fortitudo*, fr *fortis*]

**fortnight** /'fawt,niet/ *n* a period of two weeks [ME *fourtenight*, alter. of *fourtene night*, fr OE *fēowertȳne niht* fourteen nights]

**¹fortnightly** /'fawt,nietli/ *adj or adv* (occurring or appearing) once a fortnight

**²fortnightly** *n* a publication issued fortnightly

**Fortran, FORTRAN** /'fawtran/ *n* a HIGH-LEVEL (having a form that is easily understandable by humans) computer language designed primarily for mathematical and scientific applications [*formula translation*]

**fortress** /'fawtris/ *n* **1** a fortified position or place; a strong-

# for

580

hold: **1a** a permanent fortification, sometimes including a town **b** a region held under considerable military strength and considered impregnable **2** something offering protection or support [ME *forteresse*, fr MF *forteresce*, fr ML *fortalitia*, fr L *fortis* strong]

**fortuitous** /faw'tyooh·itəs, -'chooh-/ *adj* **1** occurring by chance **2** fortunate, lucky [L *fortuitus*; akin to L *fort-, fors* chance, luck] – **fortuitously** *adv*, **fortuitousness** *n*

synonyms **Accidental, chance, casual,** and **fortuitous** all describe things which happen without apparent design or cause. **Chance** is the least formal and most general ⟨*a* **chance** *meeting*⟩. **Casual** adds a sense of carelessness, indifference, or lack of importance ⟨*do not be upset by a* **casual** *remark*⟩. **Accidental** stresses absence of intention or premeditation ⟨*an* **accidental** *discovery*⟩. It often suggests unfortunate results ⟨**accidental** *damage*⟩. **Fortuitous**, on the other hand, while stressing the absence of apparent or known cause or design, usually implies fortunate results ⟨*her* **fortuitous** *arrival saved the drowning child*⟩. **Fortuitous** is often applied to physical phenomena, while **accidental** is reserved for human activities ⟨*a* **fortuitous** *concourse of atoms*⟩, but ⟨**accidental** *death*⟩. See [1]INCIDENTAL *usage* Some people dislike the use of **fortuitous** to mean "fortunate", and feel that its meaning should be confined to "occurring by chance"; so that a **fortuitous** event may well be an "unfortunate" one.

**fortuity** /faw'tyooh·əti/ *n, formal* **1** the quality or state of being fortuitous **2** a chance event or occurrence [irreg fr *fortuitous*]

**fortunate** /'fawch(ə)nət/ *adj* **1** bringing some lucky advantage not foreseen as certain; auspicious, favourable **2** receiving some unexpected good fortune – **fortunateness** *n*

**fortunately** /'fawchənətli/ *adv* **1** in a fortunate manner **2** as is or was fortunate ⟨~ *I got back in time*⟩

[1]**fortune** /'fawchən, -choohn/ *n* **1** *often cap* a supposed force or personified power that determines, favourably or unfavourably, the outcome of events affecting human beings and their endeavours **2** prosperity attained in favourable conditions; success **3a** a predetermined course of events; destiny, fate ⟨*tell his* ~ *with cards*⟩ **b** a prediction of the future ⟨*get your weight and* ~ *for ten pence*⟩ **4a** *pl* the favourable or unfavourable events in the life or progress of an individual or enterprise ⟨*tracing the* ~*s of a rags-to-riches hero*⟩ ⟨*the declining* ~*s of the film industry*⟩ **b** that which happens (as if) by chance; LUCK **1 5a** (the possession of) a stock of material possessions or resources; wealth ⟨*the family* ~⟩ ⟨*a man of* ~⟩ **b** *informal* a very large sum of money ⟨*won a* ~ *on the pools*⟩ [ME, fr MF, fr L *fortuna*; akin to L *fort-, fors* chance, luck, *ferre* to carry – more at BEAR]

[2]**fortune** *vb, archaic vt* to endow with fortune ~ *vi* to happen, chance – *usu impersonal* ⟨*so it* ~ *d*⟩

**fortune cookie** *n, NAm* a biscuit containing a slip of paper on which is printed a prediction of future events, a proverb, or a humorous statement

**fortune hunter** *n* a person who seeks wealth or prestige through personal connections, esp marriage

**fortune-teller** *n* one who claims to foretell future events – **fortune-telling** *n or adj*

**forty** /'fawti/ *n* **1** – see NUMBER table **2** *pl* the numbers 40 to 49; *specif* a range of temperatures, ages, or dates in a century characterized by those numbers [ME *fourty*, adj, fr OE *fēowertig*, fr *fēowertig* group of 40, fr *fēower* four + *-tig* -ty] – **fortieth** *adj or n*, **forty** *adj or pron*, **fortyfold** *adj or adv*

**forty-'five** *n* **1** – see NUMBER table **2** a 0.45 inch calibre pistol – *usu written* .45 **3** a disc that is designed to be played on a record player at 45 revolutions per minute – *usu written* 45 – **forty-five** *adj or pron*

**Forty Hours** *n taking sing or pl vb* a Roman Catholic devotion in which the churches of a diocese take turns every two days to have the consecrated bread of the Host exposed on the altar for continuous daytime veneration

**forty-'niner** /'niena/ *n* a person who took part in the rush to California for gold in 1849

**forty winks** *n taking sing or pl vb, chiefly informal* a short sleep; a nap

**forum** /'fawrəm/ *n, pl* **forums** *also* **fora** /-ra/ **1** the marketplace or public place of an ancient Roman city which formed the centre for judicial and public business **2a** a public meeting place for open discussion **b** a medium (e g a newspaper) through which opposing views on public matters may be aired and debated **3** the exercising of judgment concerning some issue of importance; a court, tribunal ⟨*tested in the* ~ *of public opinion*⟩ **4a** a

public meeting or lecture involving audience participation **b** a radio or television programme broadcasting discussions of public concern [L; akin to L *foris* outside, *fores* door – more at DOOR]

[1]**forward** /'faw·wood, 'faw·wəd; *sense 1 also* 'forəd *when referring to ships and aeroplanes*/ *adj* **1a** near to, located at, or directed towards the front **b** situated in advance **2** occupying a fielding position in cricket in front of the batsman's wicket ⟨~ *short leg*⟩ **3** from the original point of departure; outward ⟨*the* ~ *journey*⟩ **4a** keen to be actively involved; eager, ready **b** lacking modesty or reserve; brash, assertive **5a** advanced in development; precocious **b** *of wine* having matured early **6** moving, tending, or leading towards a position in front ⟨*England need some more* ~ *players to worry the opposition's defence*⟩ **7** of or getting ready for the future ⟨~ *planning*⟩ ⟨~ *bookings are accepted*⟩ [ME, fr OE *foreweard*, fr *fore-* + *-weard* -ward] – **forwardly** *adv*, **forwardness** *n*

[2]**forward** *adv* **1** to or towards what is ahead or in front ⟨*from that day* ~⟩ ⟨*moved slowly* ~ *through the jungle*⟩ **2** to or towards an earlier time ⟨*bring the date of the meeting* ~⟩ **3** into prominence – compare BRING FORWARD, PUT FORWARD

[3]**forward** /'faw·wood, 'faw·wəd/ *n* a mainly attacking player in any of several sports stationed at or near the front of the team or side (e g in hockey or soccer) or in the corner (e g in basketball); *also* the position of an attacking player

[4]**forward** *vt* **1** to help onwards; promote, advance ⟨~ *ed his friend's career*⟩ **2a** to send forwards; transmit ⟨*will* ~ *the goods on receipt of your cheque*⟩ **b** to send or ship onwards from an intermediate point in transit ⟨~ *all letters to the new address*⟩

**forward dive** *n* a dive made from a standing position facing the water with forward propulsion of the body – compare BACK DIVE, INWARD DIVE, REVERSE DIVE

**forwarder** /'faw·wədə/ *n* a person or business that forwards; *esp* an agent who performs services (e g receiving, transshipping, or delivering) for his client to assure and facilitate the passage of freight to its destination

**forwarding** /'faw·wəding/ *n* the act of a forwarding agent; *esp* the business of a forwarder of goods

'**forward-,looking** *adj* concerned with or planning for the future; progressive

**forward market** *n* a market in which contracts are made for the buying and selling of commodities or securities at a fixed date in the future at an agreed price

**forward pass** *n* a pass in football thrown in the direction of the opponents' GOAL LINE **a** that is illegal in rugby **b** that is legal in American or Canadian football

**forward price** *n* the price of a commodity or security on a FORWARD MARKET

**forwards** /'faw·wədz/ *adv* in a forward direction; straight ahead ⟨*this wheel rotates only* ~⟩; *broadly* forward

**forwent** *past of* FORGO

**forzando** /fawt'sandoh/ *adj or adv* SFORZANDO (musical term for emphasis) [It, verbal of *forzare* to force]

**Fosbury flop** /'fozb(ə)ri *n* a technique of high jumping in which the jumper clears the bar headfirst with his/her back to it and lands on his/her back or neck [Richard *Fosbury* b 1947 US athlete]

[1]**fossa** /'fosə/ *n, pl* **fossae** /'fosie/ a shallow anatomical cavity or depression ⟨*the temporal* ~ *of the skull*⟩ [NL, fr L, ditch] – **fossate** *adj*

[2]**fossa** *n* a slender flesh-eating catlike mammal (*Cryptoprocta ferox*) of Madagascar that resembles the related CIVET cat [Malagasy]

**fosse, foss** /fos/ *n* **1** a ditch, moat **2** a natural channel between a glacier and deposited debris [ME *fosse*, fr OF, fr L *fossa*, fr fem of *fossus*, pp]

**fossick** /'fosək/ *vt, Austr* to search for (as if) by rummaging; ferret *out* ~ *vi* **1** *Austr* to search for gold, esp by picking over abandoned workings **2** *chiefly Austr* to hunt about; rummage – *usu* + *around* [E dial. *fussick, fussock* to potter, irreg fr E *fuss*] – **fossicker** *n, chiefly Austr*

[1]**fossil** /'fosl/ *n* **1** the remains of an animal or plant of some past geological age that has been preserved in the earth's crust; *also* an impression or trace of an animal or plant preserved in this way **2** something (e g a theory) that is incapable of further development **3** an obsolete word or word element preserved only by idiom (e g *fro* in *to and fro*) **4** *informal* a person whose views are inflexible or outmoded; a fogey [L *fossilis* dug up, fr *fossus*, pp of *fodere* to dig – more at BED]

[2]**fossil** *adj* **1** having the characteristics of a fossil: e g **1a** derived

ultimately from living organisms ⟨*coal, oil, and natural gas are ~ fuels*⟩ ⟨*amber is a ~ resin*⟩ **b** preserved in a mineralized or petrified form from a past geological age ⟨*~ imprint of a raindrop*⟩ ⟨*a ~ beach*⟩ ⟨*a ~ nuclear track in mica*⟩ **c** of or being water that accumulated in an underground reservoir in a past geological age **2** like or being a fossil

**fossiliferous** /ˌfosˈlifərəs/ *adj* containing fossils ⟨*~ lime-stone*⟩

**fossil-ize, -ise** /ˈfosəliez/ *vb* **1** to (cause to) become a fossil **2** to make or become outmoded or rigid – **fossilization** *n*

**fossorial** /foˈsawri-əl/ *adj* adapted to or suitable for digging ⟨*a ~ foot*⟩ [ML *fossorius*, fr L *fossus*, pp]

**¹foster** /ˈfostə/ *adj* providing, receiving, or sharing nurture or parental care though not related by blood or legal ties ⟨*a ~ home*⟩ ⟨*a ~ child*⟩ [ME, fr OE *fōstor-*, fr *fōstor* food, feeding; akin to OE *fōda* food]

**²foster** *vt* **1** to rear or give parental care to (another's child) **2** to promote the growth or development of; encourage, cultivate ⟨*~ friendship between nations*⟩ – **fosterage** *n*, **fosterer** *n*

**fosterling** /ˈfostəling/ *n* a foster child

**fou** /fooh/ *adj, Scot* drunk [ME (Sc) *fow* full, fr ME *full*]

**fouetté** /fooh'etay/ (*Fr* fwete) *n* a quick whipping movement of the raised leg in ballet dancing, often accompanied by continuous turning on the supporting leg [Fr, fr pp of *fouetter* to whip, fr MF, fr *fouet* whip, deriv of L *fagus* beech]

**fought** /fawt/ *past of* FIGHT

**¹foul** /fowl/ *adj* **1a** offensive to the senses; loathsome, repugnant **b** filled or covered with dirty or offensive matter ⟨*~ linen*⟩ **2a** full of dirt or mud **b** encrusted, clogged, or choked with a foreign substance ⟨*the chimney was ~ and smoked badly*⟩ **3a** morally or spiritually corrupt; detestable ⟨*a ~ crime*⟩ **b** particularly unpleasant or distressing; wretched, horrid ⟨*the boss was in a ~ temper*⟩ **4** obscene, abusive ⟨*~ language*⟩ **5a** being wet and stormy ⟨*~ weather*⟩ **b** obstructive to navigation ⟨*a ~ tide*⟩ **6a** treacherous, dishonourable ⟨*fair means or ~*⟩ **b** constituting an infringement of rules, esp in a game or sport ⟨*a ~ blow in boxing*⟩ **7** marked up or defaced by changes ⟨*~ copy*⟩ **8** being odorous and impure; polluted ⟨*~ air*⟩ **9** placed in a situation that blocks or obstructs movement; entangled ⟨*a ~ anchor*⟩ *synonyms* see ¹DIRTY [ME, fr OE *fūl*; akin to OHG *fūl* rotten, L *pus* pus, *putēre* to stink, Gk *pyon* pus] – **foulness** *n* – **run foul of 1** to collide with ⟨*ran foul of a hidden reef*⟩ **2** to come into conflict with ⟨*run foul of the law*⟩

**²foul** *n* **1** an entanglement or collision in sports, esp angling, sailing, rowing, and running **2** any of several infringements of the rules in a game or sport, esp involving illegal physical contact ⟨*booked for a vicious ~ on the opposing winger*⟩

**³foul** *vi* **1** to become or be foul: eg **1a** to decompose, rot **b** to become filled, obstructed, or covered with a foreign substance **c** to become entangled or come into collision ⟨*the ropes have ~ed*⟩ **2** to commit a foul in a sport or game ~ *vt* **1** to make foul: eg **1a** to make dirty; pollute ⟨*dogs ~ the footpath*⟩ **b** to entangle or collide with **c** to cover with a foreign substance ⟨*a ship's bottom ~ed with barnacles*⟩ **d** to obstruct, block **2** to discredit, disgrace **3** to commit a foul against ⟨*~ed their centre forward*⟩

**foul up** *vt* **1** *chiefly NAm* to make dirty; contaminate **2** *informal* to entangle, block ⟨*bad weather has fouled up communications*⟩ **3** *chiefly NAm informal* to spoil or confuse by making mistakes or using poor judgment – see also FOUL-UP

**foulard** /ˈfoohlah(d)/ *n* **1** a lightweight fabric (eg silk or rayon), usu decorated with a printed pattern **2** an article of clothing (eg a scarf) made of foulard [Fr]

**foulbrood** /-ˌbroohd/ *n* a bacterial disease of honeybee larvae

**fouling** /ˈfowling/ *n* accumulated deposit; incrustation ⟨*~ on a ship's bottom*⟩

**foul line** *n* **1** either of two straight lines on a baseball or softball field, extending from the batter's position, through first and third base respectively, to the boundary. A run may not be taken for a ball hit outside the lines. **2** a line across a tenpin-bowling alley that a player delivering the ball must not cross

**foully** /ˈfowl-li/ *also* **foul** *adv* in a foul manner

**foulmouthed** /-ˈmowdhd/ *adj* given to the use of obscene, profane, or abusive language

**foul play** *n* unfair or treacherous treatment; *specif* violence leading to murder ⟨*a victim of ~*⟩

**'foul-ˌup** *n, informal* **1** a state of confusion caused by ineptitude, carelessness, or mismanagement ⟨*~s in public transport*⟩ **2** a mechanical difficulty ⟨*a ~ in the steering mechanism*⟩

**foumart** /ˈfoohmət, -maht/ *n* a polecat [ME *fulmard, folmert*, prob deriv of OE *fūl* foul + *mearth* marten]

**¹found** /fownd/ *past of* FIND

**²found** *adj* **1** having all usual or standard equipment ⟨*the boat comes fully ~, ready to go*⟩ **2** presented as an (object of) artistic value, though essentially unworked and in its natural state ⟨*sculpture made of fabric, wood, and other ~ materials*⟩ ⟨*poor quality photographs of ~ still lives – Time Out*⟩ – **all found** *chiefly Br* with free food and lodging provided in addition to wages ⟨*£30 a week and all found*⟩

**³found** *vt* **1** to take the first steps in building ⟨*~ed many places*⟩ **2** to set or ground on something solid; base – often + *on* or *upon* **3** to originate or establish (eg an institution), often with provision for continued financial support [ME *founden*, fr OF *fonder*, fr L *fundare*, fr *fundus* bottom – more at BOTTOM] – **founder** *n*, **founding** *adj*

**⁴found** *vt* **1** to melt (metal) and pour into a mould **2** to fuse or melt (substances) so as to make glass [MF *fondre* to pour, melt, fr L *fundere*; akin to OE *gēotan* to pour, Gk *chein*] – **founder** *n*

**foundation** /fownˈdaysh(ə)n/ *n* **1** founding or being founded **2** the basis or principle on which something stands or is supported ⟨*that rumour has no ~*⟩ **3a** funds donated for the permanent support of an institution or cause; an endowment **b** an organization or institution established by endowment with provision for future maintenance **4a** an underlying natural or prepared support or basic structure on which something is built up or overlaid ⟨*the city has a sandstone ~*⟩ **b** foundation, **foundations** *pl* the supporting base of a building or structure, usu below ground **5** a preparation (eg a cream or lotion) used as a base for the application of facial make-up *synonyms* see ¹BASE *antonym* superstructure – **foundational** *adj*, **foundationally** *adv*, **foundationless** *adj*

**foundation course** *n* an introductory educational course (eg the first year in a subject at certain universities)

**Foundation Day** *n* AUSTRALIA DAY – used esp in Victoria

**foundationer** /fownˈdayshənə/ *n, Br* a student who has won an award from an endowed school or college

**foundation garment** *n* a girdle, corset, or other type of supporting underwear

**foundation stone** *n* **1** a stone in the foundations of a building or other structure, often laid with public ceremony **2** *the* basis, groundwork

**founder** /ˈfowndə/ *vi* **1** *of an animal* to become disabled; *esp* to go lame **2** to collapse; GIVE WAY **3** *of a boat or ship* to sink below the surface of the water **4** to come to grief; fail ⟨*the plan has ~ed*⟩ ~ *vt* **1** to disable (eg a horse), esp by overwork **2** to cause (a ship) to sink [ME *foundren* to send to the bottom, collapse, fr MF *fondrer*, deriv of L *fundus* bottom]

**founder member** *n* one who has been a member of an institution, club, etc since its foundation

**founding father** /ˈfownding/ *n* **1** one who originates an institution or movement; a founder **2** *cap both Fs* a member of the American Constitutional Convention of 1787 which formulated the principles for the Constitution of the federal republic of the USA

**foundling** /ˈfowndling/ *n* an infant of unknown parents found abandoned

**found object** *n* OBJET TROUVÉ (natural object with aesthetic value, displayed as art)

**found poem** *n* a poem consisting of words found in a nonpoetic context (eg a newspaper) and usu rearranged by the poet

**foundry** /ˈfowndri/ *n* **1** the act, process, or art of casting metals **2** a place where founding is carried on

**foundry proof** *n* a proof taken from a FORME (body of type assembled for printing) that has been made ready for moulding

**¹fount** /fownt/ *n* a fountain, source ⟨*a ~ of information*⟩ [MF *font*, fr L *font-, fons*]

**²fount, chiefly NAm font** /font/ *n, Br* a complete set of printing type of the same size and style; *also* a complete set of characters (eg for printing by photographic processes) in one style [Fr *fonte*, fr MF, act of founding, fr (assumed) VL *fundita*, fem of *funditus*, pp of L *fundere* to pour – more at ⁴FOUND]

**¹fountain** /ˈfowntən/ *n* **1** a spring of water welling up from the earth **2** a source from which something originates ⟨*he is the ~ of honour*⟩ **3** (a structure providing) an artificially produced jet of water **4** a reservoir (eg a DRINKING FOUNTAIN) containing a supply of liquid [ME, fr MF *fontaine*, fr LL *fontana*, fr L, fem of *fontanus* of a spring, fr *font-, fons*]

**²fountain** *vi* to flow or spout like a fountain

**fountainhead** /'fowntən,hed/ *n* **1** a spring that is the source of a stream **2** a principal source; the origin

**fountain pen** *n* a pen containing a reservoir that automatically feeds the nib with ink

**four** /faw/ *n* **1** – see NUMBER table **2** the fourth in a set or series ⟨*the ~ of hearts*⟩ **3** something having four parts or members or a denomination of four: eg **3a** (the crew of) a 4-person racing rowing boat; *also, pl* races for such boats **b** a 4-cylinder engine or vehicle **c** a shot in cricket that crosses the boundary after having hit the ground, and scores four runs – compare BOUNDARY, SIX [ME, fr *four*, adj, fr OE *fēower;* akin to OHG *fior* four, L *quattuor*, Gk *tessares, tettares*] – **four** *adj or pron*, **fourfold** *adj or adv*

**four-ale bar** *n, Br* a public bar, esp considered as being a place of convivial or even disreputable merrymaking [*four ale* (a cheap mild ale orig sold at 4d a quart)]

'**four-,ball** *adj* a golf match between two partnerships in which at each hole the better individual score of one partnership is matched against the better individual score of the other – compare FOURSOME 2

,**four-by-'two** *n, Br* **1** a small piece of cloth that is attached to a cord and pulled through a gun barrel to clean it **2** *derog slang* a Jew [(1) fr its size in inches; (2) rhyming slang]

'**four-,colour** *adj* of or being a printing or photographic process using the colours CYAN (blue), MAGENTA (red), yellow, and black

,**four-di'mensional** *adj* involving four dimensions ⟨*~ spacetime continuum*⟩; *esp* consisting of elements requiring four coordinates to determine them

**fourdrinier** /fooə'drinɪə, faw-/ *n, often cap* a machine for making paper in continuous sheets by draining the web of paper on an endless wire screen [Henry *Fourdrinier* †1854 & Sealy *Fourdrinier* †1847 E papermakers & inventors]

,**four-'flush** *vi, NAm* to bluff in poker while holding a four flush; *broadly* to make a false claim; bluff – **four-flusher** *n*

**four flush** *n* a worthless hand of four cards of the same suit in a 5-card poker hand

,**four-'footed** *adj* having four feet; quadrupedal

**fourgon** /'fooəgon, 'fawgən (*Fr* furgɔ̃)/ *n* a wagon for carrying luggage [Fr]

,**four-'handed** *also* '**four-,hand** *adj* **1** designed for four hands ⟨*a ~ musical composition*⟩ **2** engaged in by four people ⟨*a ~ card game*⟩

**four horsemen** *n pl, often cap F&H* war, famine, pestilence, and death personified as the four major afflictions of humanity [fr the apocalyptic vision in Rev 6:2–8]

**four hundred, 400** *n, often cap F&H, NAm the* exclusive social set of a community; *the* elite [arbitrary smallish number]

**Fourier** /'foorɪə, 'fooriay/ *adj* of a FOURIER SERIES or FOURIER TRANSFORM

**Fourierism** /'foorɪərɪz(ə)m, 'fooriayiz(ə)m/ *n* a system for reorganizing society into small cooperative communities [Fr *fouriérisme*, fr F M C *Fourier* †1837 Fr sociologist & reformer] – **Fourierist** *n*

**Fourier series** /'foorɪ·ə, 'fooriay/ *n, maths* an infinite series in which the terms are constants multiplied by SINE or COSINE functions of integer multiples of the variable and which is used in the analysis of PERIODIC FUNCTIONS (functions whose values repeat at intervals) [Baron J B J *Fourier* †1830 Fr geometrician & physicist]

**Fourier's theorem** *n* a theorem in mathematics: any PERIODIC FUNCTION (function whose value repeats at intervals) can be resolved under suitable conditions into SINE and COSINE terms involving known constants [J B J *Fourier*]

**Fourier transform** *n, maths* a function that under suitable conditions can be obtained from a given function of $x$ by multiplying the given function by $e^{-iux}$ and integrating over all values of $x$

,**four-in-'hand** *n* **1** (a vehicle drawn by) a team of four horses driven by one person **2** *chiefly NAm* a tie worn with a slipknot at the front and the two ends hanging down

**four-leaf clover, four-leaved clover** *n* a leaf of clover with four leaflets instead of three, that is thought to bring good luck

**four-letter word** *n* any of a group of vulgar or obscene words, typically monosyllabic and referring to sex or excretion

**four of a kind** *n* four cards of the same rank in a 5-card poker hand

**fourpence** /'fawp(ə)ns/ *n, pl* (2) **fourpence, fourpences 1** the sum of four pence or pennies **2** a British silver coin worth four

old pence now specially minted for distribution by the Queen as MAUNDY MONEY

**fourpenny** /'fawp(ə)ni/ *adj* costing or worth fourpence

**fourpenny one** /'fawp(ə)ni/ *n, Br informal* a sharp blow [prob fr rhyming slang *fourpenny* (*bit*) hit]

**fourplex** /'fawpleks/ *n, Can* a small apartment block consisting of four self-contained flats [*four* + *-plex* (as in *duplex*)]

,**four-'poster** /'pohstə/ *n* a bed with tall corner posts, originally designed to support curtains or a canopy but now often ornamental

**fourragère** /,fooərah'zheə (*Fr* furaʒɛr)/ *n* a braided cord worn usu round the left shoulder of a French or US military uniform; *esp* such a cord awarded to a military unit for distinguished service [Fr]

**fourscore** /-,skaw/ *n or adj* eighty

**foursome** /'faws(ə)m/ *n* **1a** a group of four people or things; a quartet **b** two couples in company together **2a** a golf match between two pairs of partners in which each pair plays one ball – compare FOUR-BALL **b** a golf match between four players **3** a dance with four people

¹**foursquare** /-'skweə/ *adj* **1** square-shaped **2a** (giving an impression of being) soundly based or solid ⟨*the wine had ... a ~ style, good but uncompromising* – *Decanter*⟩ **b** marked by boldness and conviction; resolute ⟨*a ~ approach to a problem*⟩

²**foursquare** *adv* in a sound and unyielding manner; resolutely

,**four-'star** *adj* of the fourth rank in a system for grading excellence applied to esp hotels in which the highest standard is usu represented by the fifth rank ⟨*a ~ French restaurant*⟩

'**four-,stroke** *adj or n* (of, powered by, or being) an INTERNAL-COMBUSTION ENGINE with a cycle of four strokes for intake, compression, combustion, and exhaust

**fourteen** /faw'teen/ *n* – see NUMBER table [ME *fourtene*, fr OE *fēowertiene*, fr *fēowertiene*, adj, fr *fēower* four + *tien* ten] – **fourteen** *adj or pron*, **fourteenth** *adj or n*

**fourteener** /faw'teenə/ *n* a verse line consisting of 14 syllables

**fourth** /fawth/ *n* **1** – see NUMBER table **2a** a musical interval between one note and another four notes away from it counting inclusively in a DIATONIC scale (ordinary 8-note scale) **b** a note four notes away from another counting inclusively; *specif* the note four notes away from the first note (TONIC) of a scale; SUBDOMINANT **c** the harmonic combination of two notes a fourth apart **3** the fourth and usu highest forward gear or speed of a motor vehicle **4** the fourth and lowest class of university honours degree **5** *cap, NAm* INDEPENDENCE DAY ⟨*celebrations are planned for the Fourth*⟩ – **fourth** *adj or adv*, **fourthly** *adv*

**fourth dimension** *n* **1** a dimension in addition to length, breadth, and depth; *specif* a coordinate in addition to three RECTANGULAR COORDINATES (length, breadth, and depth), esp when interpreted as the coordinate representing time **2** something outside the range of ordinary experience ⟨*a ~ of meaning that transcends ... the issue of clarity versus obscurity* – Peter Viereck⟩ – **fourth-dimensional** *adj*

**fourth estate** *n, often cap F&E* the newspapers and journals that, as a group, are considered to wield political power; *also* the press, radio, and television collectively; the news media – compare ESTATE 1

**Fourth of July** *n* INDEPENDENCE DAY in the USA

**fourto** /'fawtoh/ *n* a quarto [*four* + *-to* (as in *quarto*)]

,**four-'way** *adj* **1** allowing passage in any of four directions **2** including four participants ⟨*a ~ dialogue*⟩

,**four-'wheel, ,four-'wheeled** *adj* **1** having four wheels **2** acting on or by means of all four wheels of a motor vehicle ⟨*~ drive*⟩

,**four-'wheeler** *n* a vehicle with four wheels

**foussa** /'foohsə/ *n* ²FOSSA (catlike mammal)

**fovea** /'fohvi·ə, -vyə/ *n, pl* **foveae** /-vi,ie/ **1** a small anatomical hollow **2** a rodless area of the retina of the eye, giving acute vision [NL, fr L, pit] – **foveal** *adj*, **foveally** *adv*, **foveate** *adj*, **foveiform** *adj*

**fovea centralis** /sen'trahlis/ *n, pl* **foveae centrales** /,fohvi·ie sen'trahleez/ FOVEA 2 [NL, central fovea]

¹**fowl** /fowl/ *n, pl* **fowls,** *esp collectively* **fowl 1** a bird that is raised or hunted for its flesh: **1a** DOMESTIC FOWL; *esp* an adult hen **b** a wild bird (eg a pheasant or duck) hunted as game **2** the flesh of birds used as food **3** *archaic* a bird [ME *foul*, fr OE *fugel*; akin to OHG *fogal* bird]

²**fowl** *vi* to hunt, snare, or shoot wildfowl – **fowler** *n*

**fowling piece** /'fowling/ *n* a light shotgun or rifle for shooting birds or small animals

**fowl pest** *n* an infectious and often fatal virus disease of domestic poultry

**fowl plague** *n* FOWL PEST

[1]**fox** /foks/, *fem* **vixen** /'viksən/ *n*, *pl* **foxes**, *esp collectively* **fox 1a** any of various alert flesh-eating mammals (esp genus *Vulpes*) of the dog family related to but smaller than wolves, with shorter legs, more pointed muzzle, large erect ears, and a long bushy tail; *esp* the RED FOX that is hunted for sport in England **b** the fur of a fox **2** a clever crafty person **3** *cap* (the language of) a member of an American Indian people formerly living in the Wisconsin area **4** rope yarns twisted and tarred to make cords used for lashings or for weaving mats **5** *archaic* a sword [ME, fr OE; akin to OHG *fuhs* fox, Skt *puccha* tail]

[2]**fox** *vt* **1a** to trick by ingenuity or cunning; outwit **b** to baffle **2a** to repair (a shoe) by renewing the upper **b** to add a strip to; *esp* to trim (a shoe) with a strip of material (e g leather) ~ *vi* **1** to act with cunning **2** to dissemble

**foxed** /fokst/ *adj* discoloured with yellowish-brown stains ⟨~ *leaves of old books*⟩ [fr the colour of a fox's fur]

**foxglove** /-,gluv/ *n* any of a genus (*Digitalis* of the family Scrophulariaceae, the foxglove family) of erect plants; *esp* a common tall European plant (*Digitalis purpurea*) cultivated for its showy RACEMES of spotted white or purple tubular flowers and as a source of the drug DIGITALIS

**foxhole** /-,hohl/ *n* a pit usu dug hastily for cover for one or several soldiers under enemy fire; *broadly* a place for concealment

**foxhound** /-,hownd/ *n* any of various breeds of large swift powerful hounds with glossy hard coats, usu black, tan, and white in colour, used in hunting foxes

**foxhunting** /-,hunting/ *n* the sport or act of hunting foxes, esp on horseback with a pack of hounds – **foxhunter** *n*

**foxie** *also* **foxy** /'foksi/ *n*, *Austr & NZ informal* FOX TERRIER [by shortening & alter.]

**foxing** /'foksing/ *n* the brownish discoloration, usu caused by dampness, of paper in old books

**foxtail** /-,tayl/ *n* **1** (something resembling) the tail of a fox **2** **foxtail**, **foxtail grass** any of several grasses (esp genera *Alopecurus*, *Hordeum*, and *Setaria*) with spikes resembling the tail of a fox

**foxtail millet** *n* a spiky coarse drought-resistant but frost-sensitive annual grass (*Setaria italica*) grown for grain, hay, and forage

**fox terrier** *n* a small lively terrier occurring in smooth-haired and wirehaired varieties, formerly used to dig out foxes

**Foxtrot** /-,trot/ – a communications code word for the letter *f*

[1]**fox-,trot** *n* **1** a short broken slow trotting gait in which the horse's hind foot hits the ground a moment before the diagonally opposite forefoot, while its head nods in time to this movement **2** a ballroom dance in a time of two beats per bar, that includes slow walking steps, quick running steps, and TWO-STEPS

[2]**fox-trot** *vi* **-tt-** to dance the fox-trot

**foxy** /'foksi/ *adj* **1** having the character or appearance of a fox: e g **1a** cunningly shrewd and crafty; wily ⟨*a narrow* ~ *face*⟩ **b** of a warm reddish-brown colour ⟨~ *eyebrows*⟩ **2** discoloured or spotted through age or decay; FOXED **3** having a sharp or musky flavour ⟨~ *wine*⟩ **4** *NAm* physically attractive ⟨*now there's a* ~ *girl*⟩ *synonyms* see SLY – **foxily** *adv*, **foxiness** *n*

**foy** /foy/ *n*, *chiefly Scot* a farewell feast or gift [D dial. *fooi* feast at end of the harvest]

**foyer** /'foy,ay, -ə (*Fr* fwaje)/ *n* an anteroom or lobby, esp of a theatre; *also* an entrance hallway or vestibule [Fr, lit., fireplace, fr ML *focarius*, fr L *focus* hearth]

**Fra** /frah/ *n* brother – used as a title preceding the name of an Italian monk or friar ⟨~ *Angelico*⟩ [It, short for *frate*, fr L *frater* – more at BROTHER]

**fracas** /'frakah/ *n*, *pl* **fracas** /'frakahz/, *NAm* **fracases** /'frakəsis/ a noisy quarrel; a brawl, uproar [Fr, din, row, fr It *fracasso*, fr *fracassare* to shatter]

**fraction** /'fraksh(ə)n/ *n* **1a** a number (e g $^3/_4$, $^5/_8$, 0.234) that is the result of dividing two numbers **b(1)** a piece broken off; a fragment **b(2)** a (small) portion or section ⟨*sold at a* ~ *of its value*⟩ **2** an act of breaking up; *specif* the breaking of the bread by a priest at Communion **3** a tiny bit; a little ⟨*a* ~ *closer*⟩ **4** *chemistry* any of several portions (e g a product of distillation separable by fractionation [ME *fraccioun*, fr LL *fraction-*, *fractio* act of breaking, fr L *fractus*, pp of *frangere* to break – more at BREAK]

*usage* Since a **fraction** may be either a "portion" or a "little bit", a **fraction** of the cost of something may be almost the whole cost, though sounding considerably less.

**fractional** /'fraksh(ə)nl/ *adj* **1** of or being a fraction **2** relatively small; inconsiderable **3** of or involving a process for separating components of a mixture through differences in physical or chemical properties ⟨~ *distillation*⟩

**fractionally** /'fraksh(ə)nli/ *adv* to a very small extent

**fractionate** /'frakshənayt/ *vt* **1** to separate (e g a mixture) into different portions **2** to divide; BREAK UP – **fractionator** *n*, **fractionation** *n*

**fractious** /'frakshəs/ *adj* **1** hard to handle or control; unruly **2** quarrelsome, irritable [*fraction* (in obs sense "discard") + *-ous*] – **fractiously** *adv*, **fractiousness** *n*

**fracto-** /fraktoh-/ *comb form* ragged in appearance; broken up – used with reference to clouds ⟨fracto*stratus*⟩ [L *fractus*, pp]

[1]**fracture** /'frakchə/ *n* **1a** breaking or being broken; *specif* the breaking of hard tissue (e g bone) **b** the rupture of soft tissue ⟨*kidney* ~⟩ **2** the result of fracturing; a break **3** the general appearance (e g texture) of a freshly broken surface of a mineral **4** *linguistics* **4a** the substitution of a diphthong for an originally simple vowel, esp under the influence of a following consonant **b** a diphthong thus substituted [ME, fr L *fractura*, fr *fractus*, pp]

[2]**fracture** *vt* **1a** to cause a fracture in; break ⟨~ *a rib*⟩ **b** to rupture, tear **2a** to damage or destroy as if by rupturing ⟨*a* ~ *d family torn apart by alcohol and insanity* – R A Sokolov⟩ **b** to cause great disorder in **c** to fractionate; BREAK UP ~ *vi* to undergo fracture

**frae** /fray/ *prep*, *Scot* from [ME (northern) *fra*, *frae*, fr ON *frā*; akin to OE *from*]

**fraenulum, frenulum** /'frenyooləm/ *n*, *pl* **fraenula, frenula** /-lə/ a fraenum [NL, dim. of L *fraenum*]

**fraenum, frenum** /'freenəm/ *n*, *pl* **fraena, frena** /-nə/ a connecting fold of membrane that supports or restrains a body part (e g the tongue) [L, lit., bridle; akin to L *firmus* firm]

**frag** /frag/ *vt* **-gg-** to injure or kill (one's military leader) deliberately by means of a grenade [*frag*, n, short for *fragmentation* (*grenade*)]

**fragile** /'frajiel/ *adj* **1a** easily shattered **b(1)** constitutionally delicate; lacking in physical or psychological strength **b(2)** somewhat weak and unwell ⟨*felt* ~ *after the previous night's party*⟩ **2** tenuous, slight *synonyms* see WEAK *antonym* durable [MF, fr L *fragilis* – more at FRAIL] – **fragility** *n*

[1]**fragment** /'fragmənt/ *n* an incomplete, broken off, or detached part [ME, fr L *fragmentum*, fr *frangere* to break – more at BREAK]

[2]**fragment** /frag'ment/ *vt* to break up or apart into fragments ~ *vi* to fall to pieces – **fragmentation** *n*

**fragmental** /frag'mentl/ *adj* fragmentary – **fragmentally** *adv*

**fragmentary** /'fragmənt(ə)ri/ *adj* consisting of fragments; incomplete – **fragmentarily** *adv*, **fragmentariness** *n*

**fragmentation bomb** /,fragmən'taysh(ə)n/ *n* a bomb or shell whose relatively thick casing is splintered on explosion and thrown in fragments in all directions

**fragrance** /'fraygrəns/ *n* **1** the quality or state of having a sweet or pleasant smell **2a** a sweet or delicate smell (e g of fresh flowers) **b** the smell of perfume, cologne, or toilet water *synonyms* see [2]SMELL

**fragrant** /'fraygrənt/ *adj* marked by fragrance [ME, fr L *fragrant-*, *fragrans*, prp of *fragrare* to smell sweetly; akin to MHG *bræhen* to smell] – **fragrantly** *adv*

**frail** /frayl/ *adj* **1** easily led into evil; morally weak ⟨~ *humanity*⟩ **2** easily broken or destroyed; fragile **3a** physically weak **b** slight, unsubstantial *synonyms* see WEAK *antonym* robust [ME, fr MF *fraile*, fr L *fragilis* fragile, fr *frangere* to break] – **frailly** *adv*, **frailness** *n*

**frailty** /'fraylti/ *n* **1** being frail **2** a fault due to weakness, esp of moral character

**fraise** /frayz/ *n* an obstacle of inclined or horizontal pointed stakes driven into the ramparts of a fortification [Fr]

**Fraktur** /frak'tooə (*Ger* fraktur)/ *n* a German style of BLACK-LETTER (Gothic or medieval-style) type [Ger, fr L *fractura* fracture]

**framboesia**, *NAm* **frambesia** /fram'beezyə, -zh(y)ə/ *n* YAWS (tropical disease) [NL, fr Fr *framboise* raspberry; fr the appearance of the sores]

**framboise** /from'bwahz (*Fr* frâbwaz)/ *n* a brandy distilled from raspberries [Fr, lit., raspberry]

[1]**frame** /fraym/ *vt* **1a** to plan; WORK OUT ⟨~d *a new method of*

*achieving their purpose*⟩ **b** to give expression to; formulate **c** to shape, construct **d** DRAW UP ⟨framing *a bill to legalize marijuana*⟩ **2** to fit or adjust for a purpose; arrange **3** to construct by fitting and uniting the parts of the skeleton of (a structure) **4** to enclose (as if) in a frame **5a** to concoct or devise (e g a criminal charge) falsely **b** to contrive the evidence against (an innocent person) so that a verdict of guilty is assured **c** to prearrange (e g a contest) so that a particular outcome is assured [ME *framen* to benefit, construct, fr OE *framian* to benefit, make progress; akin to ON *fram* forward, OE *from* from] – **framer** *n*

²**frame** *n* **1a** something composed of parts fitted together and joined **b** the physical make-up of an esp human body; physique, figure **2a** a structure composed of constructional members (e g girders or beams) that gives shape or strength (e g to a building) **b** such a structure not filled in or covered **c** a framework covered with transparent material, used for protecting plants growing out-of-doors **3a** an open case or structure made for admitting, enclosing, or supporting something ⟨a window ~⟩ **b** a machine built on or within a framework ⟨a spinning ~⟩ **c(1)** a structural unit in a vehicle chassis supported on the axles and supporting the rest of the chassis and the body **c(2)** the rigid part of a bicycle **d(1)** a part of a pair of glasses that holds one of the lenses **d(2)** *pl* that part of a pair of glasses other than the lenses **4a** an enclosing border ⟨a picture ~⟩ **b** the matter or area enclosed in such a border: e g **b(1)** any of the squares in which scores for each round are recorded (e g in bowling) **b(2)** boxed matter in a newspaper; *esp* a box of a strip cartoon **b(3)** a single picture on a length of cinefilm **b(4)** a single complete television picture made up of lines **c** a limiting, typical, or esp appropriate set of circumstances ⟨studies made within the ~ of our society and culture⟩ **d** an event that forms the background for the action of a novel or play **5** a minimal unit of programmed instruction or stimulus calling for a response by the student **6** one round of play in any of several games (e g snooker or bowling) **7** *informal* a frame-up

³**frame** *adj* having a wooden frame ⟨~ houses⟩

**frame of mind** *n* a particular mental state or disposition; a mood

**frame of reference** *n* **1** an arbitrary set of AXES (fixed lines) with reference to which the position or motion of something is described or physical laws are formulated **2** a set or system (e g of facts or ideas) serving to orient or give particular meaning (e g to a statement or a point of view)

**frameshift** /'fraym,shift/, **frameshift mutation** *n, genetics* a mutation that occurs in the genetic material of a cell, during the synthesis of proteins, caused by the addition or deletion of a complementary pair of PURINE or PYRIMIDINE bases (chemical compounds forming subunits of genetic material) from the DNA of a gene causing the CODON sequence (sequence in the genetic code) to be read incorrectly

'**frame-,up** *n, informal* a conspiracy to frame someone

¹**framework** /'fraym,wuhk/ *n* **1** a skeletal, openwork, or structural frame **2** a basic structure (e g of ideas)

²**framework** *vt* to graft parts of another variety of tree onto (a tree)

**framing** /'frayming/ *n* a frame or framework

**franc** /frangk, (Fr frâ)/ *n* – see MONEY table [Fr]

¹**franchise** /'frahnchiez, 'fran-/ *n* **1** freedom or immunity from some burden or restriction **2a** a special privilege granted to an individual or group; *esp* the right to be and exercise the powers of a corporation **b** a constitutional or statutory right or privilege; *specif* the right to vote **c** the right or licence granted to an individual or group to market a company's goods or services in a particular territory; *also* the territory involved in such a right **3** the amount of liability (e g a sum or percentage) specified in an insurance policy below which the insurer disclaims all liability [ME, fr OF, fr *franchir* to free, fr *franc* free]

²**franchise** *vt* to grant a franchise to

**franchisee** /,franchie'zee/ *n* one who is granted a franchise

**franchisor** /'franchiezə/ *n* one who grants a franchise

**Franciscan** /fran'siskən/ *n* a member of the Order of Friars Minor founded by St Francis of Assisi in 1209 and dedicated esp to preaching, missions, and charities; *also* a member of an Anglican order founded in 1921 with a similar way of life [ML *Franciscus* Francis] – **Franciscan** *adj*

**francium** /'fransi·əm/ *n* an artificially produced radioactive chemical element of the ALKALI METAL group [NL, fr *France*]

**Franco-** /frangkoh-/ *comb form* **1** French nation, people, or culture ⟨Franco*phile*⟩ **2** French and ⟨Franco-*German*⟩ [ML, fr *Francus* Frenchman, fr LL, Frank]

,**Franco-A'merican** *n* an inhabitant of the USA of French or esp French-Canadian descent – **Franco-American** *adj*

**francolin** /'frangkohlin/ *n* any of numerous partridges (*Francolinus* and related genera) of S Asia and Africa [Fr, fr It *francolino*]

**Franconian** /frang'kohniən/ *adj* of Franconia, the Franks, or Frankish [*Franconia*, former duchy of Germany] – **Franconian** *n*

**Francophile** /'frangkə,fiel/, **Francophil** /-,fil/ *adj* markedly friendly to France or French culture – **Francophile** *n*

**Francophobe** /'frangkə,fohb/ *adj* marked by a fear or strong dislike of France or French culture, customs, or people – **Francophobe** *n*

**francophone** /'frangkə,fohn/ *adj, often cap* consisting of or belonging to a French-speaking population – **Francophone** *n*

**franc-tireur** /,frong tee'ruh (Fr frâ tirœr)/ *n* a civilian fighter or sniper; *also* a guerrilla [Fr, fr *franc* free + *tireur* shooter]

**frangible** /'franjəbl/ *adj, formal* readily or easily broken [ME, fr MF & ML; MF, fr ML *frangibilis*, fr L *frangere* to break – more at BREAK] – **frangibility** *n*

**frangipane** /'franji,payn/ *n* a confection that resembles custard and is usu flavoured with almonds [Fr, frangipani (perfume), frangipane, fr It, fr Marquis Muzio *Frangipane*, 16th-c It nobleman]

**frangipani** /,franji'pahni/ *n* **1** a perfume derived from or imitating the odour of the flower of the RED JASMINE **2** any of several tropical American shrubs or small trees (genus *Plumeria*) of the periwinkle family (e g RED JASMINE) **3** an Australian tree (*Hymenosporum flavum*) with large creamy-yellow fragrant flowers [modif of It *frangipane*]

**Franglais** /'frong·glay/ *n* French with a considerable number of words borrowed from English [Fr, blend of *français* French and *anglais* English]

¹**frank** /frangk/ *adj* **1** marked by free, forthright, and sincere expression ⟨a ~ reply⟩; *also* undisguised ⟨~ admiration⟩ **2** *medicine* clinically evident; unmistakable ⟨~ pus⟩ *synonyms* see TRUTH [ME, free, generous, fr OF *franc*, fr ML *francus*, fr LL *Francus* Frank] – **frankness** *n*

²**frank** *vt* **1a** to mark (a piece of mail) with an official signature or sign indicating that the postal charges need not be paid **b** to send (a piece of mail) without charge **c** to put a stamp or mark on (a piece of mail) to indicate payment of postage **2** to enable to pass or go freely or easily ⟨the delegates will ~ the policy⟩

³**frank** *n* **1** an official signature or sign on a piece of mail indicating that postal charges need not be paid **2** a mark or stamp on a piece of mail indicating postage paid **3** a franked envelope

⁴**frank** *n, NAm informal* a frankfurter

**Frank** *n* a member of a WEST GERMANIC people that occupied the Netherlands and most of Gaul and established themselves along the Rhine in the 3rd and 4th centuries AD [ME; partly fr OE *Franca*; partly fr OF *Franc*, fr LL *Francus*, of Gmc origin (akin to OHG *Franko*, OE *Franca*)]

**Frankenstein** /'frangkən,stien/, **Frankenstein's monster**, *NAm chiefly* **Frankenstein monster** *n* **1** a work or agency that ruins its originator **2** a monster in the shape of a man [Baron *Frankenstein*, hero (who constructs a human monster) of the novel *Frankenstein* by Mary Shelley †1851 E novelist]

*usage* In the original novel, **Frankenstein** was the name of the creator, not of his monster, but the meaning has effectively changed.

**frankfurter** /'frangk,fuhtə/ *n* a smoked cooked sausage (e g of beef or beef and pork) that may be skinless or stuffed in a casing [Ger *frankfurter* of Frankfurt, fr *Frankfurt am Main*, city in W Germany]

**frankincense** /'frangkin,sens/ *n* a fragrant GUM RESIN chiefly from E African or Arabian trees (genus *Boswellia* of the family Burseraceae) that is an important resin in incense [ME *fraunk encens*, fr *fraunk*, *frank* pure, free + *encens* incense]

**franking machine** /'frangking/ *n, Br* a machine that automatically franks and postmarks letters and postcards and records the cost of postage

**Frankish** /'frangkish/ *n or adj* (the Germanic language) of the Franks

**franklin** /'frangklin/ *n* a medieval English landowner of free but not noble birth [ME *frankeleyn*, fr AF *fraunclein*, fr OF *franc* free]

**franklinite** /'frangkliniet/ *n* a black slightly magnetic mineral consisting of an oxide of iron and zinc, $ZnFe_2O_4$ [*Franklin*, town in New Jersey, USA]

**Franklin stove** /'frangklin/ *n, NAm* a freestanding metal stove resembling an open fireplace and used for heating a room [Benjamin *Franklin* †1790 US statesman & scientist, its inventor]

**frankly** /'frangkli/ *adv* 1 in a frank manner 2 to tell the truth; actually ⟨~, *I couldn't care less*⟩

**frankpledge** /'frangk,plej/ *n* an Anglo-Saxon system under which each adult male member of a TITHING (group of 10 householders) was responsible for the good conduct of the others; *also* the member himself or the TITHING

**frantic** /'frantik/ *adj* 1 emotionally out of control ⟨~ *with anger and frustration*⟩ 2 marked by fast and nervous, disordered, or anxiety-driven activity ⟨*made a ~ search for the lost child*⟩ [ME *frenetik, frantik* – more at FRENETIC] – **frantically, franticly** *adv*, **franticness** *n*

**frap** /frap/ *vt* **-pp-** to draw tight (eg with ropes or cables) ⟨~ *a sail*⟩ [ME *frapen* to strike, beat, fr MF *fraper*]

**¹frappé, frappe** /'frapay/ *adj, of a drink* chilled or partly frozen [Fr *frappé*, fr pp of *frapper* to strike, chill, fr MF *fraper* to strike]

**²frappé, frappe** *n* 1 a partly frozen drink (eg of fruit juice) 2 a liqueur served over crushed ice

**frass** /fras/ *n* excrement or other debris left by larvae or adult insects, esp after boring into wood [Ger, lit., food, feed, fr OHG *frāz* food, fr *frezzan* to devour – more at FRET]

**fraternal** /frə'tuhnl/ *adj* 1a of or involving brothers b of or being a fraternity or society 2 of twins derived from two eggs 3 friendly, brotherly [ME, fr ML *fraternalis*, fr L *fraternus*, fr *frater* brother – more at BROTHER] – **fraternalism** *n*, **fraternally** *adv*

**fraternity** /frə'tuhnəti/ *n* 1 *taking sing or pl vb* a group of people associated or formally organized for a common purpose, interest, or pleasure: eg 1a a fraternal order b a guild c a men's student organization at some American universities that is formed chiefly for social purposes and has secret rites and a name consisting of Greek letters – compare SORORITY d *NAm* a student organization for scholastic, professional, or extracurricular activities ⟨*a debating ~*⟩ 2 the quality or state of being brothers; brotherliness 3 *taking sing or pl vb* men of the same usu specified class, profession, character, or tastes ⟨*the racetrack ~*⟩ 4 the offspring of a single mating

**fratern·ize, -ise** /'fratə,niez/ *vi* 1 to associate or mingle as brothers or on fraternal terms 2a to associate on close terms with citizens or troops of a hostile country, esp during an occupation ⟨*fraternizing with the enemy*⟩ b to be friendly or amiable – **fraternizer** *n*, **fraternization** *n*

**fratricide** /'fratri,sied, 'fray-/ *n* 1 a person who kills his/her own brother or sister 2 the act of killing one's own brother or sister [ME, fr MF or L; MF, fr L *fratricida & fratricidium*, fr *fratr-, frater* brother + *-cida & -cidium* – more at -CIDE] – **fratricidal** *adj*

**Frau** /frow (*Ger* frau)/ *n, pl* **Frauen** /'frowən (*Ger* frauən)/ 1 a German-speaking married woman 2 – used of or to a German-speaking married woman (or, occasionally, an unmarried older woman) as a title equivalent to *Mrs* [Ger, woman, wife, fr OHG *frouwa* mistress, lady; akin to OE *frēa* lord]

**fraud** /frawd/ *n* 1a deceit, trickery; *specif* the use of deception for unlawful gain or unjust advantage b an act of deceiving or misrepresenting; a trick 2a a person who is not what he/she pretends to be; an impostor; *also* a cheat b something that is not what it seems or is represented to be [ME *fraude*, fr MF, fr L *fraud-, fraus*; akin to Skt *dhvarati* he bends, injures]

**fraudulent** /'frawdyoolənt/ *adj* characterized by, involving, or done by fraud; deceitful – **fraudulence** *n*, **fraudulently** *adv*, **fraudulentness** *n*

**¹fraught** /frawt/ *n, chiefly Scot* a load, cargo [ME, freight, load, fr MD or MLG *vracht, vrecht*]

**²fraught** *vt* **fraughted, fraught** *chiefly Scot* to load, fill [ME *fraughten*, fr ¹*fraught*]

**³fraught** *adj* 1 filled or charged *with* something specified ⟨*the situation is ~ with danger*⟩ 2 *Br* characterized by anxieties and tensions ⟨~ *and complex relationships*⟩ 3 *archaic* 3a laden b well supplied or provided [ME, fr pp of *fraughten*]

**fräulein** /'frawlien (*Ger* frɔilain)/ *n* 1 *cap* an unmarried German-speaking woman – used as a title equivalent to *Miss* 2 a German governess [Ger, dim. of *frau*]

**Fraunhofer lines** /'frown,hohfə (*Ger* fraunhofə)/ *n pl* the dark lines seen in spectra of the sun or stars [Joseph von *Fraunhofer* †1826 Bavarian optician & physicist]

**fraxinella** /,fraksi'nelə/ *n* a Eurasian plant (*Dictamnus albus*) of the orange family whose flowers give off an inflammable

vapour in hot weather [NL, dim. of L *fraxinus* ash tree – more at BIRCH]

**¹fray** /fray/ *vt, archaic* to scare; *also* to frighten away [ME *fraien*, short for *affraien* to affray]

**²fray** *n* a brawl, fight; *also* a dispute, debate

**³fray** *vt* 1a to wear (eg an edge of cloth) by rubbing b to separate the threads at the edge of 2 to strain, irritate ⟨*his temper became a bit ~ed*⟩ ~ *vi* to wear out or into shreds [MF *froyer, frayer* to rub, fr L *fricare* – more at FRICTION]

**⁴fray** *n* an unravelled place or worn spot (eg on fabric)

**¹frazzle** /'frazl/ *vt, informal* to put in a state of extreme physical or nervous fatigue [alter. (prob influenced by ³*fray*) of E dial. *fazle* to tangle, fray]

**²frazzle** *n, informal* a condition of fatigue or nervous exhaustion ⟨*worn to a ~*⟩

**¹freak** /freek/ *n* 1a a sudden and odd or seemingly pointless idea or turn of the mind b a seemingly capricious action or event 2 one who or that which is markedly unusual or abnormal ⟨*by some ~ of the storm one car in the queue was completely buried*⟩: eg 2a freak, freak of nature a person or animal with a physical oddity that appears in a circus, fun fair, etc b a person viewed as being highly unconventional, esp in dress or ideas c an atypical postage stamp usu caused by a unique defect in paper (eg a crease) or a unique event in the manufacturing process (eg a speck of dirt on the plate) that does not produce a constant or systematic effect d *informal* an ardent enthusiast ⟨*a film ~*⟩ ⟨*a sci-fi ~*⟩ e *slang* e(1) a sexual pervert e(2) a person who uses an illegal drug; *esp* one who has a preference for a specified drug – usu in combination ⟨*an acid*freak⟩ 3 *archaic* a whimsical quality or disposition *synonyms* see CAPRICE [origin unknown]

**²freak** *adj* having the character of a freak ⟨*a ~ accident*⟩

**³freak** *vt* 1 to streak, esp with colour ⟨*silver and mother-of-pearl ~ing the intense azure* – Robert Bridges⟩ 2 *slang* FREAK OUT ~ *vi, slang* FREAK OUT

**freak out** *vb, slang vi* 1 to withdraw from reality, esp by taking drugs 2 to experience nightmarish hallucinations as a result of taking drugs; have a bad trip 3 to behave irrationally or unconventionally (as if) under the influence of drugs ~ *vt* 1 to put under the influence of a (hallucinogenic) drug 2 to put into a state of intense excitement – see also FREAK-OUT

**freakish** /'freekish/ *adj* 1 whimsical, capricious 2 being or suitable to a freak – **freakishly** *adv*, **freakishness** *n*

**'freak-,out** *n, slang* 1 a withdrawal from reality, esp by means of drugs 2a a drug-induced state of mind characterized by nightmarish hallucinations; a bad trip b an irrational act 3 one who freaks out

**freaky** /'freeki/ *adj* being or characteristic of a freak

**¹freckle** /'frekl/ *n* any of the small brownish spots in the skin, esp of white people, that increase in number and intensity on exposure to sunlight [ME *freken, frekel*, of Scand origin; akin to ON *freknōttr* freckled; akin to OE *spearca* spark] – **freckly** *adv*

**²freckle** *vt* to sprinkle or mark with freckles or small spots ~ *vi* to become marked with freckles

**¹free** /free/ *adj* 1a having the legal and political rights of a citizen b enjoying civil and political liberty ⟨~ *citizens*⟩ c enjoying political independence or freedom from outside domination d not subject to the control or domination of another 2a not determined by external influence; able to choose ⟨*a ~ agent*⟩ b determined by the choice or wishes of a free agent ⟨~ *actions*⟩ c made, done, or given voluntarily or spontaneously; spontaneous 3a exempt, relieved, or released, esp from an unpleasant or unwanted condition or obligation – usu + *from* or *of* ⟨~ *from pain*⟩; often in combination ⟨*trouble*-free⟩ ⟨*duty*-free⟩ ⟨*a relaxed worry*-free *existence* – *Australian Women's Weekly*⟩ b not bound, confined, or detained by force ⟨*the prisoner was now ~*⟩ 4a having no trade restrictions b not subject to government regulation or official control (eg by tariffs or import quotas) 5a having no obligations (eg to work) or commitments (eg to duty or custom) ⟨*I'll be ~ this evening*⟩ b not taken up with commitments or obligations ⟨*a ~ evening*⟩ 6 having an unrestricted scope ⟨*a ~ variable*⟩ 7a(1) not obstructed or impeded; clear ⟨*a ~ and open road*⟩ a(2) not being used or occupied ⟨*waved with his ~ hand*⟩ b not hampered or restricted in its normal operation; loose 8a not fastened ⟨*the ~ end of the rope*⟩ b capable of moving or turning in any direction ⟨*a ~ particle*⟩ 9a lavish ⟨~ *spending*⟩ b outspoken c making use of something without restraint – usu + *with* ⟨*she's very ~ with her praises*⟩ d too familiar or forward in action or attitude **10** not costing or charging anything **11a(1)** not united with, attached to, or combined with something else; separate ⟨~ *ores*⟩ ⟨*a* ~ *surface of a body part*⟩ **a(2)** freestanding ⟨*a* ~ *column*⟩ **b** chemically uncombined ⟨~ *oxygen*⟩ ⟨~ *acids*⟩ **c** not permanently attached but able to move about ⟨*a* ~ *electron in a metal*⟩ **d** capable of being used alone as a meaningful linguistic form ⟨*hats is a* ~ *form*⟩ – compare ⁴BOUND 5 **12a** not literal or exact ⟨~ *translation*⟩ **b** not restricted by or conforming to conventional forms ⟨~ *skating*⟩ **13** *of a wind* not requiring a sailing vessel to be sailed as nearly against the wind as possible **14** open to all comers [ME, fr OE *frēo;* akin to OHG *frī* free, Gk *prays* gentle, Skt *priya* dear – more at FRIEND] – **freely** *adv* – **for free** without payment ⟨*now there's a charge for what she used to give* for free – Tom Lehrer⟩ – see also **give free** REIN to

²**free** *adv* **1** in a free manner **2** without charge ⟨*admitted* ~⟩ **3** not against the wind ⟨*sailing* ~⟩

*usage* Free as an adverb is used in certain phrases to mean "without restriction" ⟨*let the rope run* free⟩ but it cannot replace freely, the usual adverb ⟨freely *admitted her mistake*⟩. Only free, not freely, can mean "without payment" ⟨*to educate them* free⟩.

³**free** *vt* **1** to cause to be free – sometimes + *up* **2** to relieve or rid of that which restrains, confines, restricts, or embarrasses ⟨~ *a man from debt*⟩ **3** to disentangle, clear **4** to make available – usu + *up* ⟨~ *up more resources for welfare*⟩ – **freer** *n*

**free alongside ship** *adv or adj* without charge for delivery at the side of a carrier

**free and easy** *adj* **1** marked by informality and lack of constraint ⟨*a pleasantly* ~ *atmosphere in our office*⟩ **2** failing to observe strict standards; careless ⟨*his* ~ *literary judgments*⟩ – **free and easy** *adv*

**free association** *n* **1a** the verbal or written expression of the content of consciousness without censorship or control, used, esp in psychoanalysis, as an aid in revealing unconscious processes **b** the reporting of the first thought that comes to mind in response to a given stimulus (e g a word) **2** an idea or image brought out by free association – **free-associate** *vi*

**freebie, freebee** /'freebi/ *n, chiefly NAm informal* something (e g a theatre ticket) given or received without charge [alter. of earlier *freeby* gratis, irreg fr *free*]

**freeboard** /-,bawd/ *n* **1** the vertical distance between the waterline and the deck of a ship or boat **2** the distance between the recorded high-water mark and the top of a structure (e g a dam) associated with water

**freebooter** /-,boohtə/ *n* a pirate, plunderer [D *vrijbuiter,* fr *vrijbuit* plunder, fr *vrij* free + *buit* booty] – **freeboot** *vi*

**freeborn** /-,bawn/ *adj* **1** not born in slavery **2** of or befitting a freeborn person

**Free Church** *n, chiefly Br* a British NONCONFORMIST (e g Baptist or UNITED REFORMED) church – **Free Churchman** *n*

**free collective bargaining** *n* bargaining between trade unions and employers unhampered by government guidelines or by legal restrictions

**free diving** *n* SKIN DIVING – **free diver** *n*

**freedman** /-man/, *fem* 'freed,woman *n* someone freed from slavery

**freedom** /'freedəm/ *n* **1** being free: e g **1a** the absence of necessity or constraint in choice or action **b** liberation from slavery or restraint or from the power of another **c** the quality or state of being exempt or released, usu *from* something onerous ⟨~ *from care*⟩ **d** ease, facility ⟨*spoke the language with* ~⟩ **e** the quality of being frank, open, or outspoken ⟨*answered the questions with* ~⟩ **f** improper familiarity **g** boldness of conception or execution **h** unrestricted use *of* ⟨*gave him the* ~ *of their home*⟩ **2** an esp political right or privilege

*synonyms* Freedom, liberty, and licence all mean "the power of acting without compulsion". Freedom is the most general, suggesting absence of restraint ⟨freedom *of speech*⟩ and sometimes lack of inhibition ⟨*spoke with unembarrassed* freedom *of his past unhappiness*⟩. Liberty is often contrasted with "captivity" ⟨*restore a prisoner's* liberty⟩, and may imply a freedom granted by authority ⟨*civil* liberties⟩. Licence suggests exemption from the usual rules in special cases ⟨*poetic* licence⟩, or an abuse of freedom offensive to other people. *antonyms* constraint, servitude, slavery, captivity

**freedom of the seas** *n* the right of a merchant ship that does not belong to a country engaged in war to sail anywhere on the high seas unhindered

**freedom ride** *n, often cap F&R* a ride made by civil rights workers through states of the southern USA to check that public facilities (e g bus stations) are no longer illegally segregated on grounds of race – **freedom rider** *n*

**free enterprise** *n* an economic system that relies on private business operating competitively for profit to satisfy consumer demands, and in which government action is restricted to protecting public interest and to keeping the national economy in balance; *broadly* CAPITALISM

**free-fall** /,-'-, '-,-/ *n* **1** (the condition of) unrestrained motion in a gravitational field **2** the part of a parachute jump before the parachute opens – **free-fall** *vi*

,**free-'floating** *adj* relatively uncommitted to a particular course of action, party, etc ⟨*was not sure how the* ~ *intellectuals would vote*⟩

'**free-for-,all** *n* **1** a fight or competition open to all comers and usu with no rules **2** an often vociferous quarrel or argument involving several participants – **free-for-all** *adj*

**freehand** /-,hand/ *adj* done without the aid of drawing or measuring instruments ⟨~ *drawing*⟩ – **freehand** *adv*

**free hand** *n* freedom of action or decision ⟨*gave her a completely* ~⟩

**freehanded** /-'handid/ *adj* openhanded, generous – **freehandedly** *adv*

**freehearted** /,free'hahtid/ *adj* **1** frank, unreserved **2** generous – **freeheartedly** *adv*

**free hit** *n* an unhindered hit of the ball (e g in hockey) awarded because of a breach of the rules by an opponent

¹**freehold** /'free,hohld/ *n* **1** a tenure of property (e g land or a building) in absolute and unqualified possession ⟨*bought the* ~ *of his house*⟩; *also* a property held by such tenure **2** a tenure of an office or dignity similar to a freehold ⟨*mistaken if she thinks she has a* ~ *on the premiership*⟩ – **freeholder** *n*

²**freehold** *adj or adv* (held) in a state of freehold ⟨~ *shop and dwelling – The Age (Melbourne)*⟩ ⟨*will be sold* ~ *– The Bulletin (Sydney)*⟩

**free house** *n* a pub in Britain that is entitled to sell drinks supplied by more than one brewery – compare TIED HOUSE

**free jazz** *n* jazz that is totally improvised, lacks any regular beat, and has no predetermined harmonic or melodic structure

**free kick** *n* a kick (e g in soccer, rugby, or AMERICAN FOOTBALL) with which an opponent may not interfere; *esp* an unhindered kick (e g in soccer) in any direction awarded because of a breach of the rules by an opponent

¹**freelance** /-,lahns/, **freelancer** /-,lahnsə/ *n* a person who pursues a profession without long-term contractual commitments to any one employer – **freelance** *adj or adv*

²**freelance** *vi* to work as a freelance

**free lance** *n* a medieval knight or roving soldier available for hire by a state or commander

,**free-'living** *adj* **1** living for pleasure **2** *of a living organism* living neither on nor in association with another organism – **free-liver** *n*

**freeload** /-,lohd/ *vi, informal* to take advantage of another's generosity or hospitality without sharing in the cost or responsibility involved; sponge – **freeloader** *n*

**free love** *n* the principle or practice of having sexual relations or living together outside marriage

**freeman** /-man/ *n* **1** a person who enjoys civil or political liberty **2** a person who has the full rights of a citizen

**free market** *n* an economic market operating by free competition

**freemartin** /-,mahtin/ *n* a sexually imperfect usu sterile female calf born as a twin with a male [origin unknown]

**Freemason** /-,mays(ə)n/ *n* a member of an ancient and widespread secret fraternity called Free and Accepted Masons, that has as its aims mutual assistance and the development of friendly relations among its members

**freemasonry** /-,mays(ə)nri/ *n* **1** *cap* the principles, institutions, or practices of Freemasons **2** natural or instinctive fellowship or sympathy

**free on board** *adj, of goods* delivered on board a carrier (e g a ship) without additional charge to the buyer – **free on board** *adv*

**free place system** *n* a system whereby a certain proportion of the pupils at a maintained British secondary school were financed by the local education authority

**free port** *n* an enclosed port or section of a port where goods are received and shipped free of customs duty

**freepost** /'free,pohst/ *n, Br* a system whereby the charge for a posted item is paid by the recipient

**free radical** *n* an atom or a group of atoms having at least one unpaired electron and participating in various reactions

**free-'range** *adj* of, being, or produced by animals, esp poultry, reared in the open air and in natural conditions rather than in a battery ⟨~ *eggs*⟩

**free reed** *n* a reed in a musical instrument (e g a harmonium) that vibrates in an air opening just large enough to allow the reed to move freely – compare BEATING REED

**free rein** *n* unrestricted liberty or scope ⟨*give ~ to one's feelings*⟩

**free school** *n* a relatively informal child-centred school operated partly or wholly outside the state educational system and catering esp for problem pupils

**freesia** /'freezh(y)ə, -zyə/ *n* any of a genus (*Freesia*) of sweet-scented African plants of the iris family that have red, white, or yellow flowers [NL, genus name, fr F H T *Freese* †1876 Ger physician]

**free-'spoken** *adj* speaking freely; outspoken

**freestanding** /-'standing/ *adj* standing alone or on its own foundation, free of lateral support or attachment ⟨*a ~ column*⟩

**freestone** /-,stohn/ *n* **1** a stone that may be cut freely without splitting **2** (a fruit with) a stone to which the flesh does not cling

**freestyle** /-,stiel/ *n* (a style used in) a competition in which a contestant uses a style of his/her choice instead of a prescribed style: e g **a** CATCH-AS-CATCH-CAN (style of wrestling) **b** CRAWL 2 (style of swimming) – **freestyler, freestylist** *n*

**free-'swimming** *adj, of an animal that lives in water* able to swim about; not attached to a rock or other object ⟨*the ~ larva of the barnacle*⟩

**freethinker** /-'thingkə/ *n* a person who forms opinions on the basis of reason, independently of authority; *esp* one who questions or rejects religious dogma – **freethinking** *n or adj*

**free thought** *n* freethinking or unorthodox thought; *specif* 18th-century DEISM (belief in God based on reason)

**free throw** *n* an unhindered shot at the basket in basketball awarded because of a foul by an opponent

**free trade** *n* trade based on the unrestricted international exchange of goods, with tariffs used only as a source of revenue

**free verse** *n* verse without fixed metrical form

**free vote** *n* a vote in Parliament in which members may vote as they wish and not according to party instructions

**free walk** *n* a walking gait in which a horse is allowed complete freedom of the head and neck

**freeway** /-,way/ *n, chiefly NAm* a motorway

**¹freewheel** /-'wiəl/ *n* a device fitted to a vehicle wheel that permits forward motion when the motive power is removed

**²freewheel** *vi* **1** *of a bicycle, cyclist, or motor vehicle* to coast freely, without power from the pedals or engine **2** to move, live, or drift along freely or irresponsibly – **freewheeler** *n*

**freewill** /'free,wil/ *adj* voluntary, spontaneous

**free will** *n* the power of choosing without the constraint of divine necessity or causal law

**free world** *n* the part of the world where totalitarian or Communist political and economic systems do not prevail

**¹freeze** /freez/ *vb* **froze** /frohz/; **frozen** /'frohz(ə)n/ *vi* **1a** to become congealed into ice by cold **b** to solidify as a result of the removal of heat **2a** to become chilled with cold ⟨*almost froze to death*⟩ **b** to become coldly formal in manner **3** to stick together solidly (as if) by freezing ⟨*pressure caused the metals to ~*⟩ **4** to become clogged with ice ⟨*the water pipes froze*⟩ **5** to become fixed or motionless; *esp* to abruptly cease acting or speaking **6** to be capable of undergoing freezing for preservation ⟨*do strawberries ~ well?*⟩ – *vt* **1a** to harden into ice **b** to convert from a liquid to a solid by cold **2** to make extremely cold; chill **3a** to act on, usu destructively, by frost **b** to anaesthetize (as if) by cold ⟨*the injection froze her gum*⟩ **4** to cause to grip tightly or remain in immovable contact **5** to cause to become fixed, immovable, or unalterable, as if paralysed **6** to immobilize the expenditure, withdrawal, or exchange of (foreign-owned bank balances) by governmental regulation **7** to preserve (e g perishable food) by freezing the water content and maintaining at a temperature below 0°C [ME *fresen*, fr OE *frēosan*; akin to OHG *friosan* to freeze, L *pruina* hoarfrost] – **freezingly** *adv*

  **freeze out** *vt, informal* **1** to exclude or eliminate from competition or a position of authority or influence ⟨*the depression froze out most of his competitors*⟩ **2** to deliberately ignore or fail to respond to (someone)

**²freeze** *n* **1** a state of weather marked by low temperature, esp when below the freezing point **2a** an act or instance of freezing; *esp* a period of the holding of wages or prices at a certain level **b** the state of being frozen

**'freeze-,dry** *vt* to dehydrate (e g food) while in a frozen state under high vacuum, esp for preservation – **freeze-dried** *adj*

**freeze etching** *n* the preparation of a specimen (e g of tissue) for examination under an ELECTRON MICROSCOPE by freezing and then fracturing along natural structural lines

**freeze frame** *n* a frame of a film that is repeated so as to give the illusion of a static picture; *also* a static picture produced from a videodisc or videotape recording

**freezer** /'freezə/ *n* an apparatus that freezes or keeps cool; *esp* an insulated cabinet, compartment, or room for keeping food at a subfreezing temperature or for freezing perishable food rapidly

**freezer burn** *n* a white discoloration that appears on frozen food which is insufficiently sealed from contact with the atmosphere

**'freeze-,up** *n, informal* a spell of very cold weather

**freezing point** /'freezing/ *n* the temperature at which a liquid solidifies ⟨*the ~ of water is 0°C*⟩

**freezing works** *n, Austr & NZ* an abattoir where the carcasses are frozen ready for export

**free zone** *n* an area within which goods may be received and stored without payment of duty

**F region** *n* the highest region of the IONOSPHERE (upper part of the earth's atmosphere), occurring from 145 kilometres (about 90 miles) to more than 400 kilometres (250 miles) above the earth

**¹freight** /frayt/ *n* **1** *also* **freightage** the charge made for transporting goods **2** something that is loaded for transport; cargo **3** GOODS TRAIN **4** *chiefly formal or poetic* a load, burden [ME, fr MD or MLG *vracht, vrecht*]

**²freight** *vt* **1** to load (esp a ship) with goods for transport **2** *chiefly formal or poetic* to burden, charge

**freighter** /'fraytə/ *n* **1** a person or company that loads or charters and loads a ship **2** a shipper **3** a ship or aircraft used chiefly to carry freight

**freightliner** /-,lienə/ *n, Br* a train that transports goods prepacked in containers to make loading and unloading more efficient

**freight ton** *n* a unit of volume for cargo, usu reckoned at about 1.133 cubic metres (40 cubic feet)

**freight train** *n, NAm* GOODS TRAIN

**¹French** /french/ *adj* (characteristic) of France, its people, or their language [ME, fr OE *frencisc*, fr *Franca* Frank] – **Frenchness** *n*

**²French** *n* **1** the ROMANCE language of the people of France and of parts of Belgium, Switzerland, and Canada **2** *taking pl vb* the French people of France **3** *informal* language full of swear words and mild profanities ⟨*I wish we'd never heard of the bugger, pardon my ~* – Alan Coren⟩

**French bean** *n, chiefly Br* **1** a common bean (*Phaseolus vulgaris*) often cultivated for its slender green pods that are eaten when young **2** the pods or seeds of the French bean used as food

**French bread** *n* crusty white bread made in long thin loaves

**French Canadian** *n* a French-speaking Canadian; *esp* one of French descent

**French chalk** *n* a finely ground variety of talc used esp for drawing lines on cloth and for removing grease in dry cleaning

**French cuff** *n* a wide band turned back to make a cuff of double thickness

**French curve** *n* a curved piece of flat material (e g plastic) used as an aid in drawing noncircular curves

**French door** *n* a light door with rectangular glass panels extending the full length; *also* one of a pair of such doors in a single frame

**French dressing** *n* a dressing for salad made with oil, vinegar, and seasonings

**french fry** *n usu pl, chiefly NAm* CHIP 7a [short for *French fried (potato)*]

**French horn** *n* a spiral-shaped BRASS INSTRUMENT with finger-operated valves to vary the pitch, a funnel-shaped mouthpiece, and a much convoluted tube that flares outwards at the end

**Frenchie** /'frenchi/ *n, derog* a French person

**frenchify** /'frenchifie/ *vt, often cap, chiefly derog* to make French in qualities, traits, or typical practices – **frenchification** *n, often cap*

**French kiss** *n* a kiss made with open mouths and usu tongue-to-tongue contact – **French-kiss** *vb*

**French knickers** *n pl* wide-legged knickers

**French knot** *n* an embroidery stitch that forms a decorative knot (eg for the centre of an embroidered flower)
**French leave** *n* informal, hasty, or secret departure [fr an 18th-c French custom of leaving a reception without taking leave of the host or hostess]
**French letter** *n, Br informal* a condom
**Frenchman** /'frenchmən/, *fem* 'French,woman *n* a native or inhabitant of France
**French mustard** *n, Br* mustard mixed with vinegar
**French pastry** *n* a rich pastry filled esp with custard or fruit preparations
,**French-'polish** *vt* to apply a French polish to (wood or furniture) in order to obtain a high-gloss finish
**French polish** *n* a liquid preparation of SHELLAC and alcohol used as a finish or polish for wood
**French provincial** *n, often cap P* a style of furniture, architecture, or fabric originating in or characteristic of the 17th- and 18th-century French provinces
**French seam** *n* a double seam made by sewing the two edges with the wrong sides facing, turning the fabric, and making a second seam with the right sides facing so as to enclose the raw edges
**French toast** *n* **1** sliced bread dipped in a mixture of egg and milk and fried **2** sliced bread buttered on one side and toasted on the other
**French windows** *n pl* a pair of doors with full-length glazing that usu open onto a balcony, veranda, or garden
**frenetic** /frə'netik/ *adj* frenzied, frantic [ME *frenetik* insane, fr MF *frenetique*, fr L *phreneticus*, modif of Gk *phrenitikos*, fr *phrenitis* inflammation of the brain, fr *phren-*, *phrēn* diaphragm, mind] – **frenetically** *adv*
**frenulum** /'frenyooləm/ *n, pl* **frenula** /-lə/ **1** FRAENUM (connecting membrane) **2** a bristle or group of bristles on the front edge of the hind wings of some moths that unites the wings by interlocking with a projecting part on the front wings
**frenum** /'freenəm/ *n, pl* **frenums, frena** /-nə/ FRAENUM (connecting membrane)
**frenzied** /'frenzid/ *adj* marked by frenzy ⟨*the dog's ~ barking*⟩ – **frenziedly** *adv*
**frenzy** /'frenzi/ *n* **1a** a temporary madness **b** a state of uncontrolled mental or emotional agitation **2** intense, usu wild, and often disorderly, compulsive, or agitated activity [ME *frenesie*, fr MF, fr ML *phrenesia*, alter. of L *phrenesis*, fr *phreneticus*]
**Freon** /'free,on/ *trademark* – used for any of various nonflammable gaseous and liquid fluorine-containing chemical compounds used as refrigerants and as propellants for aerosols
**frequency** /'freekwənsi/ *n* **1** frequency, frequence the fact or condition of occurring frequently **2** *maths & statistics* **2a** the number of times that a PERIODIC FUNCTION repeats the same sequence of values as the INDEPENDENT VARIABLE varies by a specified amount **b** the number of things in a given section of an esp statistical distribution, esp as considered as a proportion of the whole ⟨*the ~ of the population between five and six feet tall*⟩ **3** the number of repetitions of a periodic process in a unit of time: eg **3a** the number of complete alternations per second of an ALTERNATING CURRENT of electricity **b** the number of sound waves per second produced by a sounding body **c** the number of complete OSCILLATIONS (periodic vibrations) per second of an ELECTROMAGNETIC WAVE (eg an X ray or ultraviolet light wave)
**frequency distribution** *n, statistics* an arrangement of statistical data that shows the frequency of the occurrence of the values of a variable
**frequency modulation** *n* a MODULATION (controlled alteration in size or state) of the frequency of a wave, esp a radio carrier wave, by the characteristics of the signal carried; *also* a method of transmitting using this – compare AMPLITUDE MODULATION
**frequency response** *n* the ability of a device (eg an audio amplifier) to deal with the various frequencies applied to it; *also* a graph representing this ability
¹**frequent** /'freekwənt/ *adj* **1** often repeated or occurring **2** habitual, persistent **3** *archaic* intimate, familiar [ME, fr MF or L; MF, fr L *frequent-*, *frequens* crowded, full] – **frequentness** *n*
²**frequent** /fri'kwent/ *vt* **1** to associate with, be in, or visit often or habitually **2** *archaic* to read systematically or habitually – **frequenter** *n*, **frequentation** *n*

**frequentative** /fri'kwentətiv/ *adj, of a verb form* denoting repeated or recurrent action or state – **frequentative** *n*
**frequently** /'freekwəntli/ *adv* at frequent or short intervals; *broadly* often
**fresco** /'freskoh/ *n, pl* **frescoes, frescos 1** the art of painting with water colours on freshly spread moist lime plaster **2** a painting done in fresco [It, fr *fresco* fresh, of Gmc origin; akin to OHG *frisc* fresh] – **fresco** *vt*
**fresco secco** /'sekoh/ *n* the art of painting in water colours on dry plaster [It, dry fresco]
¹**fresh** /fresh/ *adj* **1a** not salt ⟨*~ water*⟩ **b** free from taint; pure ⟨*~ air*⟩ **2a** *of food* not preserved (eg by tinning or freezing) ⟨*~ vegetables*⟩ **b** having its original qualities unimpaired: eg **b(1)** full of or renewed in vigour or readiness for action; refreshed ⟨*rose ~ from a good night's sleep*⟩ **b(2)** not stale, sour, or decayed ⟨*~ bread*⟩ **b(3)** not faded **b(4)** not worn or rumpled; spruce ⟨*a ~ white shirt*⟩ **3a** *of wind* rather strong **b** *of weather* cool and windy **4a** (different or alternative and) new ⟨*form ~ friendships*⟩ ⟨*make a ~ start*⟩ **b** original, vivid ⟨*a ~ approach to a familiar question*⟩ **c** newly or just come or arrived ⟨*came to undertaking ~ from teaching at a nursery school – Fair Lady (S Africa)*⟩ **d** having the milk flow recently established ⟨*a ~ cow*⟩ **5** too forward with a person of the opposite sex ⟨*he got ~ with me so I slapped his face*⟩ **synonyms** see ¹NEW **antonym** stale [ME, fr OF *freis*, of Gmc origin; akin to OHG *frisc* fresh; akin to OE *fersc* fresh; (5) prob by folk etymology fr Ger *frech* cheeky, fr OHG *freh* untamed, greedy] – **freshly** *adv*, **freshness** *n*
²**fresh** *adv* **1** just recently; newly ⟨*a ~ laid egg*⟩ **2** *chiefly NAm* as of a short time ago – esp in **fresh out of** ⟨*we're ~ out of tomatoes*⟩
³**fresh** *n* **1** an increased flow or rush (eg of water) **2** a stream of fresh water running into salt water
**fresh breeze** *n* wind having a speed of 29 to 38 kilometres per hour (about 19 to 24 miles per hour) **synonyms** see ¹WIND
**freshen** /'fresh(ə)n/ *vi* to grow or become fresh: eg **a** *of wind* to increase in strength **b** *of water* to lose saltiness ~ *vt* to make fresh; *also* to refresh, revive – often + *up*
**freshen up** *vb* to make (oneself) fresher or more comfortable, esp by washing, changing one's clothes, etc
**fresher** /'freshə/ *n, chiefly Br informal* a student in the first term at college or university [by shortening & alter. fr *freshman*]
**freshet** /'freshit/ *n* **1** a stream **2** a great rise or overflowing of a stream caused by heavy rains or melted snow **b** something resembling or suggesting a freshet, esp in being in sudden large supply [³*fresh* + *-et*]
**fresh gale** *n* wind having a speed of 62 to 74 kilometres per hour (about 39 to 46 miles per hour) **synonyms** see ¹WIND
**freshman** /-mən/ *n* **1** a novice, newcomer **2** a fresher
**freshwater** /-'wawtə/ *adj* **1** of or living in fresh water **2** accustomed to navigating only in fresh waters ⟨*a ~ sailor*⟩; *also* unskilled
**Fresnel lens** /fre'nel (*Fr* frɛnɛl)/ *n* a lens that is used esp for spotlights and has a surface consisting of a series of simple lens sections together constituting a single thin lens [Augustin *Fresnel* †1827 Fr physicist]
¹**fret** /fret/ *vb* **-tt-** *vt* **1** to torment with anxiety or worry; vex **2a** to eat or gnaw into; corrode; *also* to fray **b** to rub, chafe **c** to make by wearing away a substance ⟨*the stream ~ted a channel*⟩ **3** to pass (time) in fretting **4** to agitate, ripple ~ *vi* **1a** to eat into something **b** to affect something as if by gnawing or biting; grate **2a** to wear, corrode **b** to chafe **c** to fray **3a** to become vexed or worried **b** *of running water* to become agitated [ME *freten* to devour, fret, fr OE *fretan* to devour; akin to OHG *frezzan* to devour, *ezzan* to eat – more at EAT]
²**fret** *n* **1a** the action of wearing away; erosion **b** a worn or eroded spot **2** a state of mental agitation often accompanied by querulous speech and nervous mannerisms; irritation **3** *Br* sea mist
³**fret** *vt* **-tt-** **1a** to decorate with interlaced designs **b** to form a pattern on **2** to decorate (eg a ceiling or wooden screen) with embossed or pierced carved patterns [ME *fretten*, fr MF *freter* to bind with a ferrule, fret, fr OF, fr *frete* ferrule]
⁴**fret** *n* **1** a piece of ornamental openwork; *esp* a medieval metallic or jewelled net for a woman's headdress **2** an ornament or ornamental work consisting of small straight bars intersecting one another at right or oblique angles
⁵**fret** *n* any of a series of ridges fixed across the fingerboard of a stringed musical instrument (eg a guitar) [prob fr MF *frete* ferrule]

**⁶fret** *vt* **-tt-** to provide (a stringed instrument) with frets

**fretful** /-f(ə)l/ *adj* **1** disposed to fret; irritable **2a** *of water* rather choppy **b** *of wind* gusty – **fretfully** *adv*, **fretfulness** *n*

**fretsaw** /'fret,saw/ *n* a narrow-bladed fine-toothed saw held under tension in a deep frame and used for cutting intricate patterns in thin wood

**fretwork** /-,wuhk/ *n* **1** decoration consisting of intersecting bars **2** ornamental openwork, esp in thin wood; *also* ornamental work that stands out from a surface – **fretwork** *vt*

**Freudian** /'froydi-ən, -dyən/ *adj* of or conforming to the psychoanalytic theories or practices of S Freud [Sigmund *Freud* †1939 Austrian neurologist] – **Freudian** *n*, **Freudianism** *n*

**Freudian slip** *n* a slip of the tongue that is held to reveal some unconscious aspect of the speaker's mind

**Freund's adjuvant** /'froyndz, froynts/ *n* any of various substances (e g dead tuberculosis-causing bacteria) added to an ANTIGEN (foreign substance that activates the body's disease-fighting mechanisms) to enhance its action and thereby increase the production of ANTIBODIES [Jules *Freund* †1960 US immunologist]

**friable** /'frie-əbl/ *adj* easily crumbled or pulverized; crumbly ⟨~ *soil*⟩ [MF or L; MF, fr L *friabilis*, fr *friare* to crumble] – **friableness, friability** *n*

**friar** /'frie-ə/ *n* a member of a religious order (e g the Franciscans) combining monastic life and outside religious activity and originally owning neither personal nor community property [ME *frere, fryer,* fr OF *frere,* lit., brother, fr L *fratr-, frater* – more at BROTHER] – **friarly** *adj*

**friar's balsam** *n* a solution of BENZOIN (camphorlike chemical compound) in alcohol used mixed with hot water as an inhalant for the relief of the symptoms of a cold

**friary** /'frie-əri/ *n* a monastery of friars

**fricandeau** /'frikəndoh/ *n, pl* **fricandeaus, fricandeaux** /-doh(z)/ (a slice of) veal with strips of pork fat inserted into it, that is braised or roasted and finished off with a shiny coating made from its own juices [Fr, fr MF, irreg fr *fricasser*]

**fricassee** /'frikə,see, ,--'-/ *n* a dish of cut-up pieces of meat (e g chicken, veal, or rabbit) stewed in stock and served in a white sauce [MF, fr fem of *fricassé,* pp of *fricasser* to fricassee, perh fr *frire* to fry + *casse* ladle, dripping pan] – **fricassee** *vt*

**fricative** /'frikətiv/ *n* a consonant (e g /f, th, sh/) made by forcing air through a narrow opening formed by placing the tongue or lip close to another part of the mouth, or in languages other than English, esp Arabic, also by constricting the throat (PHARYNX) [L *fricatus,* pp of *fricare*] – **fricative** *adj*

**friction** /'friksh(ə)n/ *n* **1a** the rubbing of one body against another **b** resistance to relative motion between two bodies in contact **2** the clashing of two people or parties of opposed views; disagreement [MF or L; MF, fr L *friction-, frictio,* fr *frictus,* pp of *fricare* to rub; akin to L *friare* to crumble, Skt *bhriṇanti* they injure] – **frictionless** *adj*, **frictionlessly** *adv*

**frictional** /'frikshənl/ *adj* **1** of friction **2** moved or produced by friction – **frictionally** *adv*

**friction clutch** *n* a clutch in which connection is made through sliding friction

**friction drive** *n* a car power-transmission system that transmits motion by surface friction instead of teeth and provides a full range of variation in desired speed ratios

**Friday** /'frieday, -di/ *n* the 6th day of the week; the day falling between Thursday and Saturday [ME, fr OE *frīgedæg;* akin to OHG *frīatag;* both fr a prehistoric WGmc compound whose components are akin to OHG *Frīa,* goddess of love, & to OE *dæg* day] – **Fridays** *adv*

**fridge** /frij/ *n, chiefly Br* a refrigerator [by shortening & alter.]

**Friedmanite** /'freedmən iet/ *adj* of or advocating the economic theories of Milton Friedman; *esp* favouring strict control by the government of the supply of money in an economy [Milton *Friedman* b1912 US economist] – **Friedmanite** *n*

**friend** /frend/ *n* **1a** a person whose company, interests, and attitudes one finds sympathetic and to whom one is not closely related **b** an acquaintance **2a** someone or something that is not hostile **b** someone or something that is of the same nation, party, or group **c** someone or something that favours or promotes something (e g a charity) ⟨*a* ~ *of the poor*⟩ **3** *cap* a Quaker **4** *obs* a lover, paramour [ME *frend,* fr OE *frēond;* akin to OHG *friunt* friend; both fr the prp of a prehistoric Gmc verb represented by OE *frēon* to love; akin to OE *frēo* free] – **friendless** *adj*, **friendlessness** *n*

**¹friendly** /-li/ *adj* **1a** having the relationship of friends ⟨*Billy and Dave are quite* ~ *now*⟩ ⟨*Billy is* ~ *with Dave*⟩ **b** showing kindly interest and goodwill ⟨~ *neighbours*⟩ **c** not hostile ⟨*dealings with* ~ *nations*⟩ **d** inclined to be favourable – usu + *to* **2** cheerful, comforting **3** engaged in only for pleasure or entertainment and therefore typically not hotly contested ⟨*a* ~ *game of poker*⟩ – **friendliness** *n*

**²friendly** *adv* in a friendly manner; amicably

**³friendly** *n, chiefly Br* a match (e g in soccer) that is played for practice or pleasure and is not part of a formal sports competition

**friendly society** *n, often cap F&S, Br* a society whose members pay into a fund which is used to provide relief for the members in sickness, unemployment, and old age

**friendship** /-ship/ *n* **1** the state of being friends **2** the quality or state of being friendly; friendliness

**frier** /'frie-ə/ *n* a fryer

**Friesian** /'freezh(ə)n, -zyən/ *n, chiefly Br* **1** (any of) a breed of large black-and-white dairy cattle from N Holland and Friesland that produce large quantities of comparatively low-fat milk **2** (any of) a breed of black Dutch carriage horses [var of *Frisian*]

**¹frieze** /freez/ *n* **1** a heavy durable coarse fabric that is made of wool and SHODDY and has a rough surface **2** a carpet surface of uncut loops or of patterned cut and uncut loops [ME *frise,* fr MF, fr MD *vriese*]

**²frieze** *n* **1** the middle part of the upper section of a wall (ENTABLATURE) between the ARCHITRAVE and the CORNICE **2** a sculptured or richly ornamented decorative band (e g on a building) **3** a band, line, or series suggesting a frieze ⟨*a constant* ~ *of visitors wound its way around the ... ruins* – Molly Panter-Downes⟩ [MF, perh fr ML *phrygium, frisium* embroidered cloth, fr L *phrygium,* fr neut of *Phrygius* Phrygian, fr *Phrygia,* ancient country in Asia Minor]

**frig** /frig/ *vi* **-gg-** *vulg* **1** to masturbate **2** to have sexual intercourse [prob fr E dial. *frig* to rub, wriggle, fr ME *friggen*]

**frigate** /'frigət/ *n* **1** a square-rigged 3-masted warship next in size below a SHIP OF THE LINE **2** a general-purpose naval escort vessel between a CORVETTE and a CRUISER in size [MF, light boat, fr OIt *fregata*]

**frigate bird** *n* any of several strong-winged seabirds (family Fregatidae), chiefly of tropical regions, noted for their habit of snatching food from other birds

**frigging** /'friging/ *adj or adv, slang* – used as a meaningless intensive

**¹fright** /friet/ *n* **1** (an instance of) fear excited by sudden danger or shock; alarm **2** *informal* something or somebody unsightly, strange, ridiculous, or shocking ⟨*your hair's a* ~*; it needs cutting*⟩ *synonyms* see ¹FEAR [ME, fr OE *fyrhto, fryhto;* akin to OHG *forhta* fear]

**²fright** *vt, chiefly poetic* to alarm suddenly; frighten

**frighten** /'friet(ə)n/ *vt* **1** to make afraid; scare **2** to drive or force by frightening ⟨~*ed the boy into confessing*⟩ ~ *vi* to become frightened – **frighteningly** *adv*

**frightener** /'friet(ə)nə/ *n* one who or that which frightens – **put the frighteners on** *Br slang* to intimidate

**frightful** /-f(ə)l/ *adj* **1** causing intense fear or alarm; terrifying **2** extreme ⟨~ *thirst*⟩ **3** *informal* **3a** causing shock or horror; startling **b** very unpleasant or demanding ⟨*had a* ~ *time getting his car to start*⟩ – **frightfully** *adv*, **frightfulness** *n*

**frigid** /'frijid/ *adj* **1a** intensely cold **b** lacking warmth or intensity of feeling; indifferent **2** lacking imaginative qualities; insipid, dull **3** *esp of a woman* averse to sexual contact, esp sexual intercourse [L *frigidus,* fr *frigēre* to be cold; akin to L *frigus* frost, cold, Gk *rhigos*] – **frigidly** *adv*, **frigidness, frigidity** *n*

**frigidarium** /,friji'deəriəm/ *n, pl* **frigidaria** the chamber of a Roman bathhouse containing the cold bath – compare CALIDARIUM, LACONICUM, TEPIDARIUM [L, fr *frigidus*]

**frigid zone** *n, often cap F&Z* either of the two areas or regions between a pole of the earth and a POLAR CIRCLE – compare TEMPERATE ZONE, TORRID ZONE

**¹frill** /fril/ *vt* to provide or decorate with a frill

**²frill** *n* **1a** a gathered, pleated, or bias-cut ornamental fabric edging used on clothing **b** a small paper roll curled or fluted at one end to be slipped over the protruding end of a meat bone (e g on a chop) for decoration **2** a ruff of hair or feathers round the neck of an animal **3** *usu pl* **3a** an affectation, air ⟨*a straightforward man with no* ~*s about him*⟩ **b** something decorative but not essential; a luxury [perh fr Flem *frul*] – **frilly** *adj*, **frilliness** *n*

**frill lizard, frilled lizard** *n* a large Australian lizard (genus *Chlamydosaurus*) having a broad fold of skin on each side of the neck

¹**fringe** /frinj/ n **1** an ornamental border (eg on a garment or curtain) consisting of straight or twisted threads, strips, or tassels hanging loose from an edge (eg of a cloth or garment) or from a separate band **2** something resembling a fringe: eg **2a** a border, periphery **b** *chiefly Br* the hair that hangs over the forehead **c** any of the alternating light or dark bands produced by the INTERFERENCE or DIFFRACTION of light **3a** something that is marginal, additional, or secondary to some activity, process, or subject matter **b** *taking sing or pl vb* a group with marginal or extremist views **c** FRINGE BENEFIT **d** *often cap, taking sing or pl vb the* part of the British professional theatre featuring small-scale experimental productions, often in pubs or halls – compare OFF-OFF-BROADWAY [ME *frenge*, fr MF, fr (assumed) VL *frimbia*, fr L *fimbria*]

²**fringe** vt **1** to provide or decorate with a fringe **2** to serve as a fringe for; border ⟨*a clearing ~d with trees*⟩

**fringe benefit** n **1** a benefit (eg a pension, a paid holiday, or a car) granted by an employer to an employee in addition to basic wages **2** a gratuitous incidental gain ⟨*~s such as films and free drinks on charter flights*⟩

¹**frippery** /'fripəri/ n **1** showy, tawdry, or nonessential ornamentation, esp in clothing **2** affected elegance; ostentation [MF *friperie* rags, old clothes, deriv of ML *faluppa* piece of straw]

²**frippery** adj trifling, tawdry

**Frisbee** /'frizbi/ *trademark* – used for a small light plastic disc thrown between players by a flip of the wrist as a game

**Frise aileron** /freez/ n an AILERON (hinged flap on an aeroplane wing) having a nose portion projecting ahead of the hinge axis and a lower surface in line with the lower surface of the wing [Leslie George *Frise b* 1897 E engineer]

**friseur** /fri'zuh/ n a hairdresser [Fr, fr *friser* to curl]

¹**Frisian** /'freezh(ə)n/; *also* -zyən/ adj (characteristic) of Friesland, the Frisians, or the Frisian language [L *Frisii* Frisians]

²**Frisian** n **1** a member of a Germanic people inhabiting the Netherlands province of Friesland and the Frisian islands in the North sea **2** the Germanic language of the Frisian people, that is closely related to English

¹**frisk** /frisk/ vi to leap, skip, or dance in a lively or playful way; gambol ~ vt, *informal* to search (a person) for something (eg a concealed weapon) by running the hand rapidly over the clothing and through the pockets [obs *frisk* lively, fr ME, fr MF *frisque*, of Gmc origin; akin to OHG *frisc* fresh, lively] – **frisker** n

²**frisk** n **1** a gambol, romp **2** an act of frisking

**frisket** /'friskit/ n a device on a printing press for holding the sheet of paper in position or masking areas of the paper that are to be left blank [Fr *frisquette*, deriv of MF *frisque* lively]

**frisky** /'friski/ adj inclined to frisk; frolicsome – **friskily** adv, **friskiness** n

**frisson** /'freesonh (Fr fris5)/ n, *pl* **frissons** /'freesonh(z) (Fr ~)/ a shudder, thrill [Fr, fr LL *friction-, frictio*, irreg fr L *frigēre* to be cold]

¹**frit** /frit/ n **1** the wholly or partly fused materials of which glass is made **2** ground-up glass used as a basis for glaze or enamel [It *fritta*, fr fem of *fritto*, pp of *friggere* to fry, fr L *frigere*]

²**frit** vt **-tt-** **1** to prepare (materials for glass) by heat; fuse **2** to convert into frit

**frit fly** n a minute fly (*Oscinella frit*) whose larva is a serious pest of cereals [origin unknown]

**frith** /frith/ n FIRTH (inlet of the sea) [by alter.]

**fritillary** /fri'tiləri/ n **1** any of a genus (*Fritillaria*) of plants of the lily family that grow from bulbs and have mottled or chequered bell-shaped flowers – compare CROWN IMPERIAL, SNAKE'S-HEAD **2** any of numerous butterflies (esp genus *Argynnis*) that are usu orange with black spots on the upper side of both wings and silver markings on the underside of the hind wing [NL *fritillaria*, fr L *fritillus* dice-cup; fr the markings on the petals]

¹**fritter** /'fritə/ n a piece of fried batter often containing fruit, meat, etc ⟨apple ~⟩ [ME *fritour*, fr MF *friture*, fr (assumed) VL *frictura*, fr *frictus*, pp of *frigere* to fry – more at FRY]

²**fritter** vt to waste bit by bit; squander – usu + *away* ⟨~ing *away our natural resources*⟩ [*fritters*, n pl (fragments), alter. of E dial. *fitters* rags, fragments, fr ME *fiteres*] – **fritterer** n

**fritto misto** /ˌfreetoh 'meestoh/ n a dish of mixed fried foods; *broadly* MIXED GRILL [It, mixed fried food]

**Fritz** /frits/ n, *chiefly derog* **1** a German; *esp* a German soldier **2** German soldiers collectively □ no longer in vogue [Ger, nickname for *Friedrich*, a common forename]

**frivolous** /'frivələs/ adj **1** of little weight or importance **2a** lacking in seriousness; irresponsibly self-indulgent **b** lacking practicality or serious purpose ⟨*~ lapel pins . . . in the form of heads of young girls – New Yorker*⟩ [ME, fr L *frivolus*] – **frivolity** n, **frivolously** adv, **frivolousness** n

¹**frizz** /friz/ vt to form (eg hair) into small tight curls ~ vi, *of hair* to form a mass of tight curls [Fr *friser* to shrivel up, curl, prob fr *fris-*, stem of *frire* to fry]

²**frizz** n **1** a tight curl **2** hair that is tightly curled **3** the state of being tightly curled – **frizzy** adj, **frizzily** adv, **frizziness** n

¹**frizzle** /'frizl/ vb to frizz, curl [prob akin to OE *frīs* curly, OFris *frīsle* curl]

²**frizzle** n a crisp curl – **frizzly** adj

³**frizzle** vt **1** to fry (eg bacon) until crisp and curled **2** to burn, scorch ~ vi to cook with a sizzling noise [¹*fry* + *sizzle*]

**fro** /froh/ prep, *dial* from [ME, fr ON *frā*; akin to OE *from*]

**frock** /frok/ n **1** an outer garment worn by male members of some religious orders (eg monks and friars) **2a** an outer garment usu resembling a tunic or mantle, worn chiefly by men **b** a workman's outer shirt; *esp* SMOCK FROCK **c** a woollen jersey worn esp by sailors **3** a woman's or girl's dress [ME *frok*, fr MF *froc*, of Gmc origin; akin to OHG *hroch* mantle, coat]

**frock coat** n a usu double-breasted man's coat with knee-length skirts, worn esp by gentlemen in the 19th century

**froe, frow** /froh/ n a tool having a wedge-shaped blade set at right angles to a short handle, that is used with a mallet to split wood [perh alter. of obs *froward* turned away, fr ME; fr the position of the handle]

**froebelian** /fruh'beelyən/ adj, *often cap* relating to or derived from Friedrich Froebel or his kindergarten system of education [Friedrich *Froebel* †1852 Ger educator]

**frog** /frog/ n **1** any of various smooth-skinned web-footed largely aquatic tailless leaping amphibians (esp family Ranidae); *esp* a common European frog (*Rana temporaria*) – compare TOAD **2** the triangular elastic horny pad in the middle of the sole of a horse's foot **3a** a loop attached to a belt to hold a weapon or tool **b** a usu ornamental braiding, consisting of a button and a loop, for fastening the front of a garment **4** a shallow hollow in the face of a brick to take the mortar **5** a device permitting the wheels on one rail of a track to cross an intersecting rail **6** the nut of a violin bow **7** *informal* a condition in the throat that produces hoarseness ⟨had a *~ in his throat*⟩ **8** *often cap, informal chiefly derog* a French person [ME *frogge*, fr OE *frogga*; akin to OHG *frosk* frog, Skt *pravate* he jumps up; (8) fr the reputation of the French for eating frogs; (2,3) perh of different origin] – **froggy** adj, **froglike** adj

**frogfish** /-ˌfish/ n ANGLER FISH

**frogged** /frogd/ adj ornamented with frogs ⟨*~ jacket*⟩

**frogging** /'froging/ n FROG 3b

**froghopper** /-ˌhopə/ n any of numerous leaping insects (family Cercopidae, order Homoptera) whose larvae secrete froth

**frogman** /-mən/ n a person equipped (eg with face mask, flippers, rubber suit, and air supply) for being underwater for long periods, originally for military purposes

**frogmarch** /-ˌmahch/ vt **1** to carry (a person) face downwards by the arms and legs **2** to force (a person) to move forwards with the arms held together firmly from behind

**frogmouth** /'frogˌmowth/ n any of various SE Asian and Australian nocturnal birds (family Podargidae) resembling NIGHTJARS

**frogspawn** /-ˌspawn/ n the eggs of a frog that typically occur in a jellylike mass

**frog spit** n an alga that forms green slimy masses on quiet water

¹**frolic** /'frolik/ vi **-ck-** **1** to make merry **2** to play and run about happily; romp [*frolic*, adj (merry, frisky), fr D *vroolijk*, fr MD *vrolijc*, fr *vro* happy; akin to OHG *frō* happy, OE *frogga* frog]

²**frolic** n **1** a playful mischievous expression of high spirits **2a** fun, merriment **b** a lighthearted entertainment or game – **frolicsome** adj

**from** /frəm; *strong* from/ prep **1** – used to indicate a starting point: eg **1a** a place where a physical movement, or an action or condition suggestive of movement, begins ⟨came here *~ the city*⟩ ⟨*shot ~ above*⟩ ⟨*translated ~ French*⟩ **b** a starting point in measuring or reckoning or in a statement of extent or limits ⟨cost *~ £5 to £10*⟩ ⟨boys *~ the third form up*⟩ ⟨lives *five miles ~ the coast*⟩ ⟨*~ 60 to 80 people*⟩ **c** a point in time after which a period is reckoned ⟨a week *~ today*⟩ **d** a viewpoint ⟨seen *~ my window*⟩ ⟨*~ a practical standpoint*⟩

**2** – used to indicate separation: e g **2a** physical separation ⟨*absent* ~ *school*⟩ ⟨*took the toy away* ~ *the baby*⟩ **b** removal, abstention, exclusion, release, or differentiation ⟨*protection* ~ *the sun*⟩ ⟨*relief* ~ *anxiety*⟩ ⟨*kept the news* ~ *her*⟩ ⟨*subtract 12* ~ *15*⟩ ⟨*saved* ~ *drowning*⟩ ⟨*refrain* ~ *giggling*⟩ ⟨*different* ~ *his brother*⟩ ⟨*didn't know one* ~ *the other*⟩ **3** – used to indicate the source, cause, agent, or basis ⟨*a call* ~ *my lawyer*⟩ ⟨*a friend* ~ *Oxford*⟩ ⟨*inherited a love of music* ~ *his father*⟩ ⟨*drawn* ~ *nature*⟩ ⟨*made* ~ *flour*⟩ ⟨~ *a frail child he became a famous athlete*⟩ ⟨*read* ~ *his new book of poems*⟩ ⟨*worked hard* ~ *necessity*⟩ ⟨*suffering* ~ *mumps*⟩ ⟨~ *what I hear, they're quite rich*⟩ [ME, fr OE; akin to OHG *fram*, adv, forth, away, OE *faran* to go – more at FARE]

**frond** /frond/ *n* **1** a leaf, esp of a palm or fern **2** a leaflike plant body of a fungus, lichen, or similar plant [L *frond-, frons* foliage] – **fronded** *adj*

**frondeur** /fron'duh (*Fr* frɔdœːr)/ *n* a rebel, dissident [Fr, slinger, participant in a 17th-c revolt in which the rebels were compared to schoolboys using slings only when the teacher was not looking]

**frons** /fronz/ *n*, *pl* **frontes** the upper front part of the horny capsule enclosing the head of an insect [NL, fr L, forehead]

**¹front** /frunt/ *n* **1a** demeanour or bearing, esp in the face of a testing situation (e g danger) ⟨*put up a brave* ~⟩ **b** external and often feigned appearance **c** an artificial or self-important manner **2a(1)** the vanguard **a(2)** a line of battle **a(3)** *often cap* a zone of conflict between armies ⟨*all quiet on the Western Front*⟩ **a(4)** lateral space occupied by a military unit ⟨*fighting on a broad* ~⟩ **b(1)** a stand in reference to some issue; policy – usu + *change* ⟨*changed* ~ *and joined the enemy*⟩ **b(2)** a sphere of activity ⟨*progress on the educational* ~⟩ **b(3)** a movement linking divergent elements to achieve certain common objectives; *esp* a political coalition ⟨*a popular democratic* ~⟩ **3** a face of a building; *esp* the side that contains the principal entrance **4** the forward part or surface: e g **4a(1)** the part of the human body opposite to the back **a(2)** the part of a garment covering this part, esp the chest **b** a frontage **c** *the* beach promenade at a seaside resort **d** the boundary between two dissimilar air masses **5a** a position ahead of a person or of the foremost part of a thing **b** a position of importance, leadership, or advantage **6a** a person, group, or thing used to mask the identity or true character or activity of the actual controlling agent **b** a person who serves as the nominal head or spokesman of an enterprise or group to lend it prestige **7** *poetic* the forehead; *also* the whole face **8** *archaic* the beginning of a period of time ⟨*the* ~ *of August*⟩ [ME, fr OF, fr L *front-, frons* – more at BRINK] – **in front of 1** directly ahead of ⟨*watching the road* in front of *him*⟩ **2** in the presence of ⟨*don't swear* in front of *the children*⟩ – **out front** in the audience – **up front** as payment in advance ⟨*actors demanding* – 1 *million* up front⟩

**²front** *vi* **1** to face ⟨*the house* ~s *towards the east*⟩ – often + *on* or *onto* ⟨*a ten-acre garden* ~ing *on a lake*⟩ **2** to serve as a front – often + *for* ⟨~ing *for special interests*⟩ **3** *Austr & NZ* to appear; TURN UP ⟨*they* ~ed *at Deadleg's place at ten past* – Terry Lawsen⟩ – often + *up* – *vt* **1** to confront ⟨*went to the woods because I wished . . . to* ~ *only the essential facts of life* – H D Thoreau⟩ **2a** to be in front of ⟨*a lawn* ~ing *the house*⟩ **b** to be the leader of (a musical group) **c** to present (a television programme, film, etc) ⟨~ing *a late-night chat show*⟩ **3** to supply a front to ⟨~ed *the building with bricks*⟩ **4** to face towards ⟨*the house* ~s *the street*⟩ **5** to articulate (a speech sound) with the tongue farther forward

**³front** *adj* **1** of or situated at the front **2** *of a speech sound* articulated at or towards the front of the mouth ⟨~ *vowels*⟩ **3** being the first nine holes of an 18-hole golf course – **front** *adv*

**frontage** /'fruntij/ *n* **1a** a piece of land that fronts **b** the land between the front of a building and the street **2** the front face of a building; *also* the front width of a building

**frontage road** *n*, *NAm* SERVICE ROAD

**¹frontal** /'fruntl/ *n* **1** a cloth hanging over the front of an altar **2** a facade [(1) ME *frontel*, fr ML *frontellum*, dim. of L *front-, frons*; (2) ²*frontal*]

**²frontal** *adj* **1** of or adjacent to the forehead or the FRONTAL BONE **2a** of, situated at, or showing the front ⟨*full* ~ *nudity*⟩ **b** directed against the front or at the main point or issue; direct ⟨~ *assault*⟩ **3** parallel to the main axis of the body and at right angles to a plane dividing the body vertically into right and left sides **4** of a meteorological front [NL *frontalis*, fr L *front-, frons*] – **frontally** *adv*

**frontal bone** *n* either of a pair of MEMBRANE BONES forming the forehead

**frontality** /frun'taləti, fron-/ *n* **1** the representation of a sculptured figure in full front view without sideways movement **2** the depiction of a painted object, figure, or scene in a plane parallel to the plane of the picture surface

**frontal lobe** *n* the front lobe of either side of the brain

**front bench** *n* either of two rows of benches in Parliament on which leaders of the government and opposition parties sit; *also, taking sing or pl vb* the occupants of these benches – compare BACK BENCH – **front bencher** *n*

**,front-'end** *n* the SOFTWARE or HARDWARE (programs or machinery) of a computer that takes in and processes the raw data

**frontier** /frun'tiə/ *n* **1** a border between two countries **2a** *frontiers pl*, **frontier** the boundary between the known and the unknown with respect to a usu specified subject ⟨*the* ~s *of medicine*⟩ **b** a previously unknown or unexplored field of activity **3** *NAm* a region that forms the margin of settled or developed territory [ME *fronter*, fr MF *frontiere*, fr *front*] – **frontier** *adj*

**frontiersman** /-mən/ *n* a man living on the frontier, esp of settled territory

**frontispiece** /'fruntis,pees/ *n* an illustration preceding and usu facing the title page of a book or magazine [alter., (influenced by *piece*) of earlier *frontispice*, fr MF, front of a building, fr LL *frontispicium*, lit., view of the front, fr L *front-, frons* + *-i-* + *specere* to look at – more at SPY]

**frontless** /'fruntlis/ *adj*, *archaic* shameless

**frontlet** /'fruntlit/ *n* **1** a band worn on the forehead **2** the forehead; *esp* the forehead of a bird when distinctively marked [ME *frontlette*, fr MF *frontelet*, dim. of *frontel*, fr L *frontale*, fr *front-, frons*]

**,front-'line** *adj* **1** situated or suitable for use at a military front ⟨~ *ambulances*⟩ **2a** of the most advanced or significant activity or procedure in a field or enterprise **b** actively concerned and usu proficient in a particular field ⟨~ *teachers*⟩; *also* first-string ⟨~ *bowlers*⟩

**front line** *n* **1** a military line formed by the most advanced combat units **2** the most advanced, responsible, or significant position in a field of activity

**front man** *n* **1** a person serving as a front or figurehead **2** the leader of a musical group **3** the presenter of a television programme

**fronto-** *comb form* **1** frontal and ⟨*fronto*parietal⟩ **2** boundary of an air mass ⟨*fronto*genesis⟩ [ISV, fr L *front-, frons*; (2) ¹*front*]

**front of house** *n* the parts of a theatre (e g the auditorium and foyer) accessible to the public – **front-of-house** *adj*

**frontogenesis** /,fruntoh'jenəsis/ *n* the coming together to form a distinct FRONT of two dissimilar air masses that commonly react on each other to produce cloud and rain or snow [NL]

**frontolysis** /frun'toləsis/ *n* a process tending to destroy a meteorological FRONT [NL]

**fronton** /'fronton, -'-/ *n* a court for the game of JAI ALAI [Sp *frontón* gable, wall of a pelota court, fronton, fr dim. of *frente* forehead, fr L *front-, frons*]

**,front-'page** *adj* very newsworthy

**front room** *n* a room in a residence, used for relaxation and the entertainment of guests

**'front-,runner** *n* **1** a contestant who runs best when in the lead **2** a leading contestant in a competition

**¹frost** /frost/ *n* **1a** the process of freezing **b** the temperature that causes freezing **c** a covering of minute ice crystals on a cold surface **2a** coldness of attitude or manner **b** *informal* a failure, fiasco ⟨*the party was a terrible* ~⟩ [ME, fr OE; akin to OHG *frost*, OE *frēosan* to freeze]

**²frost** *vt* **1a** to cover (as if) with frost **b** to produce a fine-grained slightly roughened surface on (e g metal or glass) **c** to cover (e g a cake or grapes) with sugar; *also, chiefly NAm* to ice (a cake) **2** to injure or kill (e g plants) by frost **to become frosted; freeze** – often + *over*

**frostbite** /-,biet/ *n* the freezing or the local effect (e g gangrene) of a partial freezing of some part of the body

**frostbitten** /-,bit(ə)n/ *adj* afflicted with frostbite

**frosted** /'frostid/ *adj* having a frosty or sparkling sheen ⟨~ *lipstick*⟩

**frosting** /'frosting/ *n* **1** a dull or roughened finish on metal or glass; *also* a white finish produced on glass (e g by etching) **2a** *Br* thick fluffy cooked icing **b** *chiefly NAm* icing

**frostwork** /-,wuhk/ *n* **1** delicate figures that moisture sometimes forms in freezing (e g on a windowpane) **2** ornamentation (e g on silver, glass, or paper) imitative of the figures of frostwork

**frosty** /'frosti/ *adj* **1** marked by or producing frost; freezing **2** (appearing as if) covered with frost; hoary **3** marked by coolness or extreme reserve in manner ⟨*his smile was distinctly ~* – Erle Stanley Gardner⟩ – **frostily** *adv*, **frostiness** *n*

¹**froth** /froth/ *n* **1a** a mass of bubbles formed on or in a liquid; foam **b** a foamy saliva sometimes accompanying disease (e g rabies) or exhaustion **2** something insubstantial or of little value ⟨*their idle talk was a lot of ~*⟩ [ME, fr ON *frotha;* akin to OE *āfrēothan* to froth, Gk *prēthein* to blow up]

²**froth** *vt* **1** to cause (a liquid) to foam – often + *up* **2** to cover with froth ~ *vi* **1** to foam at the mouth **2** to throw froth out or up – often + *up*

**frothy** /'frothi/ *adj* **1** full of or covered with froth ⟨*~ surf*⟩ **2a** gaily frivolous or light in content or treatment ⟨*~ poetry*⟩ **b** made of light thin material ⟨*~ garments*⟩ – **frothily** *adv*, **frothiness** *n*

**frottage** /'frotahzh/ *n* the technique or process of creating a design by rubbing (e g with a pencil) over an object placed underneath the paper; *also* a composition so made [Fr, fr *frotter* to rub]

**froufrou** /'frooh,frooh/ *n* **1** a rustling sound, esp of a woman's skirts **2** frilly ornamentation, esp in women's clothing [Fr, of imit origin]

**frow** /froh/ *n* FROE (tool for splitting wood)

**froward** /'froh·əd/ *adj, archaic* **1** habitually disobedient and contrary; perverse **2** adverse, unfavourable △ forward [ME, turned away, froward, fr *fro* + *-ward*] – **frowardly** *adv*, **frowardness** *n*

¹**frown** /frown/ *vi* **1** to contract the brow in a frown **2** to show displeasure or disapproval (as if) by facial expression – often + *on* or *upon* ~ *vt* to express by frowning [ME *frounen*, fr MF *froigner* to snort, frown, of Celt origin; akin to W *ffroen* nostril] – **frowner** *n*, **frowningly** *adv*

²**frown** *n* **1** a wrinkling of the brow in displeasure, concentration, or puzzlement **2** an expression of displeasure

**frowst** /frowst/ *vi, chiefly Br* to remain indoors in a hot airless room [back-formation fr *frowsty*]

**frowsty** /'frowsti/ *adj, chiefly Br* lacking fresh air; STUFFY 2a [alter. of *frowsy*]

**frowsy, frowzy** /'frowzi/ *adj* **1** having a slovenly or uncared-for appearance; shabby **2** musty, stale [origin unknown]

**froze** /frohz/ *past of* FREEZE

**frozen** /'frohz(ə)n/ *adj* **1a** treated, affected, solidified, or crusted over by freezing **b** subject to long and severe cold ⟨*the ~ north*⟩ **2a(1)** drained or incapable of emotion; numb **a(2)** expressing or characterized by cold unfriendliness **b** incapable of being changed, moved, or undone; *specif* debarred by official action from movement or from change in status ⟨*wages were ~*⟩ **c** not available for present use ⟨*~ capital*⟩ – **frozenly** *adv*, **frozenness** *n*

**Fructidor** /,froohkti'daw (*Fr* fryktidɔr)/ *n* the 12th month of the French Revolutionary calendar, corresponding to 18 August–16 September

**fructification** /,fruktifi'kaysh(ə)n/ *n* **1** the forming or producing of fruit **2a** FRUIT 1d **b** SPOROPHORE (spore-producing plant organ)

**fructify** /'fruktifie/ *vb, formal vi* to bear fruit ~ *vt* to make fruitful or productive ⟨*social philosophy* fructified *the political thinking of liberals at the end of the century* – *TLS*⟩ [ME *fructifien*, fr MF *fructifier*, fr L *fructificare*, fr *fructus* fruit]

**fructivorous** /fruk'tivərəs/ *adj* feeding on fruit

**fructose** /'fruktohz, -tohs/ *n* any of three forms of a sugar, HOCH₂(CHOH)₃COCH₂OH; *esp* the very sweet soluble LAEVO-ROTATORY D-form that occurs esp in fruit juices and honey – called also FRUIT SUGAR, LAEVULOSE; compare GLUCOSE

**fructuous** /'fruktyooəs/ *adj, formal* fruitful ⟨*a ~ land*⟩

**frugal** /'froohg(ə)l/ *adj* characterized by or showing economy in the expenditure of resources; sparing, scanty **synonyms** see SPARING *antonym* wasteful [MF or L; MF, fr L *frugalis* virtuous, frugal, alter. of *frugi*, fr dat of *frug-*, *frux* fruit, value; akin to L *frui* to enjoy] – **frugally** *adv*, **frugality** *n*

**frugivorous** /frooh'jivərəs/ *adj* feeding on fruit [L *frug-*, *frux* + E *-vorous*] – **frugivore** *n*

¹**fruit** /frooht/ *n* **1a** a product of plant growth (e g grain, vegetables, or cotton) ⟨*the ~s of the field*⟩ **b(1)** the usu edible reproductive body of a SEED PLANT; *esp* one having a sweet pulp

associated with the seed ⟨*the ~ of the tree*⟩ **b(2)** a succulent edible plant part used chiefly in a dessert or sweet course **c** a dish, quantity, or diet of fruits ⟨*please pass the ~*⟩ **d** a product of fertilization in a plant with its modified skins or attached structures; *specif* the ripened ovary, together with its contents, of a FLOWERING PLANT **2** offspring, progeny ⟨*the ~ of her womb*⟩ **3a** the state of bearing fruit ⟨*a tree in ~*⟩ **b fruits** *pl*, **fruit** the effect or consequence of an action or operation; a product, result ⟨*the ~s of his labour*⟩; *esp* a favourable effect or consequence ⟨*his work bore ~*⟩ **4** *Br informal* a fellow – in *old fruit*; no longer in vogue **5** *chiefly NAm slang* a male homosexual [ME, fr OF, fr L *fructus* fruit, use, fr *fructus*, pp of *frui* to enjoy, have the use of – more at BROOK] – **fruited** *adj* – **bear fruit** to have a satisfying result or conclusion

²**fruit** *vb* to (cause to) bear fruit ⟨*a tree that ~s annually*⟩

**fruitarian** /frooh'teəri·ən/ *n* one whose diet consists of (uncooked) fruit [¹*fruit* + *-arian* (as in *vegetarian*)]

**fruit bat** *n* any of a suborder (Megachiroptera) of large African and Eurasian fruit-eating bats of warm regions

**fruit cake** *n* **1** a rich usu dark cake typically containing nuts, dried and candied fruits (e g currants and glacé cherries), and spices **2** *Br informal* a crazy person; a lunatic

**fruiter** /'froohtə/ *n* a plant (e g a tree) producing fruit, esp to a specified degree ⟨*that apple is a poor ~*⟩

**fruiterer** /'froohtərə/ *n* one who deals in fruit [ME, modif of MF *fruitier*, fr *fruit*]

**fruit fly** *n* any of various small flies whose larvae feed on fruit or decaying vegetable matter

**fruitful** /'froohtf(ə)l/ *adj* **1a** yielding or producing fruit **b** conducive to an abundant yield ⟨*a ~ rain*⟩ **2** abundantly productive ⟨*made several ~ suggestions*⟩ – **fruitfully** *adv*, **fruitfulness** *n*

**fruiting body** /'froohting/ *n* a plant organ (e g in lichens and mosses) specialized for producing spores

**fruition** /frooh'ish(ə)n/ *n* **1** the state of bearing fruit **2** realization, fulfilment [ME *fruicioun*, enjoyment, fr MF or LL; MF *fruition*, fr LL *fruition-*, *fruitio*, fr L *fruitus*, alter. of *fructus*, pp; current senses influenced in meaning by ¹*fruit*]

'**fruit-,knife** *n* a knife suitable for peeling and cutting up fruit, with a blade resistant to corrosion by acids in the fruit

**fruitless** /'froohtlis/ *adj* **1** lacking or not bearing fruit **2** producing no good effect; unsuccessful – **fruitlessly** *adv*, **fruitlessness** *n*

**fruitlet** /'froohtlit/ *n* a single unit of a fruit (e g a raspberry) composed of many parts – called also DRUPEL

**fruit machine** *n*, *Br* a coin-operated gambling machine that pays out according to different combinations of symbols (e g different types of fruit) visible on wheels spun by a handle or button

**fruit sugar** *n* the very sweet soluble D-form of FRUCTOSE

**fruity** /'froohti/ *adj* **1a** of or resembling a fruit **b** *of wine* having the flavour of the unfermented fruit **2** *of a voice* rich and deep **3** *informal* amusing in a sexually suggestive way ⟨*a ~ story*⟩ – **fruitily** *adv*, **fruitiness** *n*

**frumenty** /'froohmənti/ *n* a dish of wheat boiled in milk and usu flavoured with sugar and spice [ME, fr MF *frumentee*, fr *frument* grain, fr L *frumentum*, fr *frui* – more at FRUIT]

**frump** /frump/ *n, informal* **1** a dowdy unattractive girl or woman **2** a staid drab old-fashioned person [prob fr E dial. *frumple* to wrinkle, fr ME *fromplen*, fr MD *verrompelen*] – **frumpish** *adj*, **frumpy** *adj*

**frusemide** /'froohzəmied/ *n* a powerful synthetic drug, C₁₂H₁₁ClN₂O₅S, that increases the flow of urine and is used in the treatment of OEDEMA (excessive accumulation of liquid in the body tissues) and high blood pressure [alter. of *fursemide*, fr *furfural* + *sulphur* + *-emide*, prob alter. of *amide*]

**frustrate** /fru'strayt/ *vt* **1a** to balk or defeat in an endeavour; foil, thwart **b** to induce feelings of discouragement and vexation in **2** to make ineffectual; nullify ⟨*nagging daily cares that ~ a man's aspirations*⟩ [ME *frustraten*, fr L *frustratus*, pp of *frustrare* to deceive, frustrate, fr *frustra* in error, in vain; akin to L *fraus* fraud – more at FRAUD] – **frustratingly** *adv*

**frustrated** /fru'straytid/ *adj* **1** balked or discouraged in some endeavour or purpose; disappointed ⟨*looked on the critics as merely ~ writers*⟩ **2** filled with a sense of frustration

**frustration** /fru'straysh(ə)n/ *n* **1** frustrating or being frustrated **2** a deep habitual sense or state of insecurity and dissatisfaction arising from unresolved problems or unfulfilled needs; *specif* a sense of tension and dissatisfaction arising from unfulfilled sexual needs **3** something that frustrates

**frustule** /'frustyoohl/ *n* the 2-part silica-containing shell of a DIATOM (minute primitive plant) [Fr, fr L *frustulum*, dim. of *frustum*]

**frustum** /'frustəm/ *n, pl* **frustums, frusta** /'frustə/ the part of a cone or pyramid formed by cutting off the top at a plane parallel to the base; *also* the part of a solid cut off by two usu parallel planes [NL, fr L, piece, bit – more at BRUISE]

**frutescent** /frooh'tes(ə)nt/ *adj* resembling a shrub; shrubby – used in botany [L *frutex* shrub + E *-escent*]

**fruticose** /'froohtikohs/ *adj, of a lichen or related plant* having a shrubby bushy THALLUS (undifferentiated plant body) with flattened or cylindrical branches – compare CRUSTOSE, FOLIOSE [L *fruticosus*, shrubby, fr *frutic-, frutex* shrub; akin to OHG *broz* bud, OIr *broth* whisker]

**¹fry** /frie/ *vb* to cook in hot fat over a source of heat – see also **have other FISH to fry** [ME *frien*, fr OF *frire*, fr L *frigere*; akin to Gk *phrygein* to roast, fry, Skt *bhrjjati* he roasts]

**²fry** *n* **1** a dish of fried food, esp offal ⟨*lamb's* ~⟩ **2** *NAm* a social gathering (e g a picnic) at which food is fried and eaten ⟨*a fish* ~⟩

**³fry** *n, pl* **fry 1a** recently hatched fishes **b** the young of other animals, esp when occurring in large numbers **2** very small adult fishes **3** *usu pl* a small, young, or insignificant person or thing ⟨*a great part of the earth is peopled with these* ~ – Katherine Mansfield⟩ ⟨*such ideas are only small* ~⟩ [ME, prob fr ONF *fri*, fr OF *frier, froyer* to rub, spawn – more at FRAY]

**fryer** /'frie·ə/ *n* something intended for or used in frying: e g **a** a chiefly *NAm* a young chicken suitable for frying **b** a deep vessel for frying foods

**frying pan** /'frie·ing/, *chiefly NAm* **fry pan** *n* a long-handled, shallow, and usu circular metal pan that is used for frying foods – **out of the frying pan into the fire** clear of one difficulty only to fall into a greater one

**'fry-,up** *n, Br informal* an act of frying food for a simple impromptu meal; *also* a dish prepared in this way

**'f-,stop** *n* a camera lens aperture setting indicated by an F-NUMBER

**F test** *n* a statistical test using the F DISTRIBUTION

**fubsy** /'fubzi/ *adj, chiefly Br informal* chubby and somewhat squat [obs *fubs* chubby person, of imit origin]

**fuchsia** /'fyoohshə/ *n* **1** any of a genus (*Fuchsia* of the family Onagraceae, the fuchsia family) of decorative shrubs having showy nodding flowers usu in deep pinks, reds, and purples **2** a vivid reddish purple [NL, genus name, fr Leonhard *Fuchs* † 1566 Ger botanist]

**fuchsine** /'foohk,seen/, **fuchsin** /-sin/ *n* a dye, $C_{20}H_{19}N_3$, that yields a brilliant bluish red and is used in manufacturing other dyes – called also MAGENTA [Fr *fuchsine*, prob fr NL *Fuchsia*; fr its colour]

**¹fuck** /fuk/ *vb, vulg vi* to have sexual intercourse ~ *vt* **1** to have sexual intercourse with **2** – used interjectionally to express contempt or annoyance ⟨~ *you, Jack, I'm all right*⟩ ⟨~ *it! I've cut my hand*⟩ [perh of Scand origin; akin to Norw dial. *fukka* to copulate, Sw dial. *focka* to copulate, strike, push, *fock* penis; perh akin to L *pugnus* fist, *pungere* to prick, sting, Gk *pygmē* fist]

**fuck about/around** *vb, vulg vi* to act in a foolish annoying way ~ *vt* to treat (a person) harshly, interferingly, or without due consideration

**fuck off** *vi, vulg* **1** to go away; depart – often in imperative **2** *NAm* FUCK ABOUT

**fuck up** *vt, vulg* to spoil, ruin – see also FUCK-UP

**²fuck** *n, vulg* **1** an act of sexual intercourse **2** a partner in sexual intercourse ⟨*rumoured to be the best* ~ *in town*⟩ **3** the slightest bit ⟨*I don't care a* ~ *about him*⟩; *also* a least amount or degree of care or consideration ⟨*why should she give two* ~s *about it?*⟩ **4** – used as a meaningless intensive ⟨*what the* ~ *are you playing at?*⟩

**³fuck** *interj, vulg* – used to express annoyance

**,fuck-'all** *n, vulg* nothing at all

**fucker** /'fukə/ *n, vulg* **1** one who fucks **2** a stupid worthless fellow; a fool

**fucking** /'fuking/ *adj or adv, vulg* – used as a meaningless intensive ⟨*not* ~ *likely*⟩

**'fuck-,up** *n, vulg* a state of muddled confusion usu caused by a mistake

**¹fucoid** /'fyoohkoyd/ *adj* relating to or resembling seaweed (esp genus *Fucus*)

**²fucoid** *n* a fucoid seaweed or fossil

**fucose** /'fyoohkohz, -kohs/ *n* a sugar, $CH_3(CHOH)_4CHO$, that

occurs in carbohydrates in some BROWN ALGAE (type of seaweed) and in various GLYCOPROTEINS (complex substances containing protein and carbohydrate) typical of some mammalian blood groups [ISV *fuc-* (fr L *fucus*) + *-ose*]

**fucoxanthin** /,fyoohkoh'zantheen, -thin/ *n* a brown CAROTENOID pigment, $C_{42}H_{58}O_6$, occurring esp in BROWN ALGAE (type of seaweed)

**fucus** /'fyoohkəs/ *n* any of a genus (*Fucus*) of BROWN ALGAE (type of seaweed) whose ash is used as a source of iodine; *broadly* any of various seaweeds [NL, genus name, fr L, orchil, rouge, fr Gk *phykos* seaweed, orchil, rouge, of Sem origin; akin to Heb *pūkh* antimony used as a cosmetic]

**fuddle** /'fudl/ *vt* **1** to make drunk; intoxicate **2** to make confused; muddle [origin unknown] – **fuddle** *n*

**fuddy-duddy** /'fudi ,dudi/ *n, informal* a person who is old-fashioned, pompous, unimaginative, or concerned about trifles [perh alter. of *fussy* + *dud*] – **fuddy-duddy** *adj*

**¹fudge** /fuj/ *vi* **1** to exceed the proper bounds or limits of something; *also* to cheat ⟨*fudging on an exam*⟩ **2** to fail to live up to something; fail to perform as expected ⟨*fudging on her promise*⟩ **3** to avoid commitment; hedge ⟨*the company's tendency to* ~ *on matters of policy*⟩ ~ *vt* **1a** to devise or put together roughly or without adequate basis – usu + *up* ⟨*he could* ~ *up an excuse out of nothing*⟩ **b** to exaggerate, falsify ⟨~d *the figures*⟩ **2** to fail to come to grips with ⟨*a report that* ~s *the main issue*⟩ □ (*vi*) usu + *on* [prob alter. of earlier *fadge* to fit, adjust, fr ME *fage, fadge* deceit]

**²fudge** *n* **1** a soft creamy sweet made typically of sugar, milk, butter, and flavouring **2** the stop-press box or column of a newspaper **3** *informal* foolish nonsense – sometimes used, esp formerly, as an interjection to express annoyance, disappointment, or disbelief

**Fuegian** /fyoo'eej(y)ən, 'fway-/ *n* a member of an American Indian people of Tierra del Fuego [Tierra del *Fuego*, archipelago at the southern tip of the American continent]

**fuehrer** /'fyooərə (Ger fyrə)/ *n* FÜHRER (leader)

**¹fuel** /'fyooh·əl/ *n* **1a** a material used to produce heat energy or power by burning **b** material providing nutrition; food **c** a material from which ATOMIC ENERGY can be liberated, esp in a NUCLEAR REACTOR **2** a source of sustenance, strength, or encouragement ⟨*it was* ~ *for their raging passions*⟩ [ME *fewel*, fr OF *fouaille*, fr *feu* fire, fr LL *focus*, fr L, hearth – more at FOCUS]

**²fuel** *vb* **-ll-** (*NAm* **-l-, -ll-**) *vt* **1** to provide with fuel **2** to support, stimulate ⟨*inflation* ~led *by massive wage awards*⟩ ~ *vi* to take in fuel – often + *up*

**fuel cell** *n* a cell that continuously changes the chemical energy of a fuel (e g METHANOL) to electrical energy

**fuel injection** *n* the introduction of liquid fuel under pressure directly into the cylinders of an INTERNAL-COMBUSTION ENGINE, without using a carburettor – **fuel-injected** *adj*, **fuel injector** *n*

**fuel oil** *n* an oil that is used for fuel, esp in furnaces and engines

**fug** /fug/ *n, informal* the stuffy atmosphere of a poorly ventilated space [prob alter. of *²fog*] – **fuggy** *adj*

**fugacious** /fyooh'gayshəs/ *adj* **1** disappearing soon after appearing – used chiefly of plant parts (e g STIPULES) other than petals and sepals **2** *formal* lasting a short time; fleeting [L *fugac-, fugax*, fr *fugere*] – **fugacity** *n*

**fugal** /'fyoohgl/ *adj* of or in the style of a musical fugue – **fugally** *adv*

**fugato** /fooh'gahtoh/ *n, adv, or adj, pl* **fugatos** (a musical passage) in the style but not in the strict form of a fugue [It, fr pp of *fugare* to compose as a fugue, fr *fuga* fugue]

**-fuge** /-,fyoohj, -fyoohzh/ *comb form* (→ *n*) something that drives away ⟨*insectifuge*⟩ ⟨*febrifuge*⟩ [Fr, fr LL *-fuga*, fr L *fugare* to put to flight, fr *fuga*]

**¹fugitive** /'fyoohjətiv/ *adj* **1** running away or trying to escape ⟨~ *slave*⟩ ⟨~ *debtor*⟩ **2** moving from place to place; wandering **3a** of short duration; fleeting **b** difficult to grasp or retain; elusive **c** likely to evaporate, deteriorate, change, fade, or disappear **4** of transient interest; ephemeral *synonyms* see ¹TRANSIENT [ME, fr MF & L; MF *fugitif*, fr L *fugitivus*, fr *fugitus*, pp of *fugere* to flee; akin to Gk *pheugein* to flee] – **fugitively** *adv*, **fugitiveness** *n*

**²fugitive** *n* **1** a person who flees or tries to escape, esp from danger, justice, or oppression; a refugee, exile **2** something elusive or hard to find

**fugle** /'fyoohgl/ *vi, archaic* to act as fugleman [back-formation fr *fugleman*]

**fugleman** /'fyoohglmən/ *n* **1** a trained soldier formerly posted in front of a line of men at drill to serve as a model in their exercises **2** a leader [modif of Ger *flügelmann*, fr *flügel* wing + *mann* man]

**fugue** /fyoohg/ *n* **1** a musical composition for two or more voices or instrumental parts in which one or two themes are repeated or imitated by successively entering parts and developed in a continuous interweaving of those parts **2** a state of mental disturbance characterized by loss of memory and by the patient's disappearance from home [It *fuga* flight, fugue, fr L, flight, fr *fugere*] – **fugue** *vb*, **fuguist** *n*

**führer, fuehrer** /'fyooərə (*Ger* fyrə)/ *n* **1** LEADER 2c(3) – used chiefly with reference to the leader of the German Nazis **2** a leader exercising tyrannical authority [Ger, leader, guide, fr MHG *vüerer* bearer, fr *vüeren* to lead, bear, fr OHG *fuoren* to lead; akin to OE *faran* to go – more at FARE]

**¹-ful** /-f(ə)l/ *suffix* **1** (*n* → *adj*) full of ⟨*eventful*⟩ ⟨*colourful*⟩ **2** (*n* → *adj*) characterized by ⟨*peaceful*⟩ ⟨*boastful*⟩ **3** (*n* → *adj*) having the qualities of ⟨*masterful*⟩ **4** (*vb* → *adj*) tending to or able to ⟨*mournful*⟩ [ME, fr OE, fr *full*, adj]

**²-ful** *suffix* (*n* → *n*) number or amount that (a specified thing) holds or can hold ⟨*roomful*⟩ ⟨*handful*⟩
  *usage* Although such plurals as ⟨*basketsful*⟩ ⟨*packetsful*⟩ are still correct, modern writers prefer the regular plural of -ful ⟨*basketfuls*⟩ ⟨*packetfuls*⟩.

**Fula, Fulah** /'foohlah/ *n, pl* **Fulas, Fulahs,** *esp collectively* **Fula, Fulah** a member of a W African people of black African stock but showing some white features (e g straight noses and hair)

**Fulani** /'fooh'lahni, 'foohləni/ *n, pl* **Fulanis,** *esp collectively* **Fulani** **1** a Fula; *esp* the Fula of N Nigeria and adjacent areas **2** the NIGER-CONGO language of the Fula people

**fulcrum** /'fulkrəm, 'fool-/ *n, pl* **fulcrums, fulcra** **1a** the support about which a lever turns **b** something or someone providing support or assistance in an activity **2** a part of an animal (e g scales on the fins of some fishes) that serves as a hinge or support [LL, fr L, bedpost, fr *fulcire* to prop – more at BALK; (2) NL, fr LL]

**fulfil,** *NAm chiefly* **fulfill** /fool'fil/ *vt* **-ll- 1a** to put into effect; CARRY OUT ⟨~ling *the orders of the day*⟩ ⟨*the prophecy was* ~led⟩ **b** to bring to an end; complete **c** to measure up to; satisfy ⟨*this book* ~s *a long-felt need*⟩ **2** to develop the full potential of ⟨*she never* ~led *her early promise*⟩ **3** *archaic* to make full; fill ⟨*her subtle, warm, and golden breath* . . . ~s *him with beatitude* – Alfred Tennyson⟩ **synonyms** see PERFORM [ME *fulfillen*, fr OE *fullfyllan*, fr *full* + *fyllan* to fill] – **fulfiller** *n*, **fulfilment** *n*

**fulgent** /'fulj(ə)nt/ *adj, formal* dazzlingly bright [ME, fr L *fulgent-, fulgens*, prp of *fulgēre* to shine; akin to L *flagrare* to burn – more at BLACK] – **fulgently** *adv*

**fulgurant** /'fulgyoorənt/, **fulgurous** /'fulgyoorəs/ *adj, formal* flashing like lightning; dazzling

**fulgurate** /'fulgyoorayt/ *vt, formal* to emit flashes of ⟨*blue eyes that* ~d. . . *terror, love, or hate* – New Yorker⟩ [L *fulguratus*, pp of *fulgurare* to flash with lightning, fr *fulgur* lightning, fr *fulgēre*] – **fulguration** *n*

**fulgurite** /'fulgyooriet/ *n* an often tubular glassy crust produced by the fusion of sand or rock by lightning [ISV, fr L *fulgur*]

**fuliginous** /fyooh'lijinəs/ *adj, formal* **1a** sooty **b** obscure, murky **2** having a dark or dusky colour [LL *fuliginosus*, fr L *fuligin-, fuligo* soot; akin to L *fumus* smoke – more at FUME] – **fuliginously** *adv*

**¹full** /fool/ *adj* **1** containing as much or as many as is possible or normal ⟨*a bin* ~ *of corn*⟩ **2a** complete, esp in detail, number, or duration ⟨*a* ~ *report*⟩ ⟨*his* ~ *share*⟩ ⟨*gone a* ~ *hour*⟩ **b** lacking restraint, check, or qualification ⟨~ *retreat*⟩ ⟨~ *support*⟩ **c** having all distinguishing characteristics; enjoying all authorized rights and privileges ⟨~ *member*⟩ ⟨~ *colonel*⟩ **d** not lacking in any essential; perfect ⟨*in* ~ *control of his senses*⟩ **3a** at the highest or greatest degree; maximum ⟨~ *strength*⟩ ⟨~ *speed*⟩ **b** at the height of development ⟨~ *bloom*⟩ ⟨~ *moon*⟩ **4** rounded in outline; *also, chiefly euph* well filled out or plump **5a** possessing or containing a great number or amount of ⟨*a room* ~ *of pictures*⟩ **b** having an abundance of material, esp in the form of gathered, pleated, or flared parts ⟨*a* ~ *skirt*⟩ **c** rich in experience ⟨*a* ~ *life*⟩ **6** satisfied, esp with food or drink, often to the point of discomfort; replete – often + *up* **7** having both parents in common ⟨~ *sisters*⟩ **8** having volume or depth of sound ⟨~ *tones*⟩ **9a** with the at-

tention completely occupied by or centred on something ⟨~ *of gloomy thoughts about the future*⟩ ⟨*very* ~ *of himself after passing the exam*⟩ **b** filled with and expressing excited anticipation or pleasure ⟨*came in this morning* ~ *of her plans for a holiday in Fiji*⟩ **10** possessing a rich or pronounced quality ⟨*a food of* ~ *flavour*⟩ **11** – used as an intensive ⟨*won by a* ~ *four strokes*⟩ [ME, fr OE; akin to OHG *fol* full, L *plenus* full, *plēre* to fill, Gk *plērēs* full, *plēthein* to be full] – **fullness** *also* **fulness** *n*

**²full** *adv* **1a** very, extremely ⟨*knew* ~ *well he had lied to me*⟩ **b** entirely, quite ⟨~ *fathom five thy father lies* – Shak⟩ **2a** exactly ⟨~ *in the centre*⟩ **b** straight, squarely ⟨*hit him* ~ *in the face*⟩

**³full** *n* **1a** the utmost extent ⟨*enjoy life to the* ~⟩ **b** the highest or fullest state or degree ⟨*the* ~ *of the moon*⟩ **2** the requisite or complete amount – chiefly in *in full*

**⁴full** *vi, of the moon* to become full ~ *vt* to make (e g a dress) full in sewing (e g by gathers or tucks)

**⁵full** *vt* to shrink and thicken (woollen cloth) by moistening, heating, and pressing [ME *fullen*, fr MF *fouler*, fr (assumed) VL *fullare*, fr L *fullo* fuller] – **fuller** *n*

**fulla** /'foolə/ *n, NZ* a man, fellow [prob alter. of *fellow*]

**fullback** /-ˌbak/ *n* a primarily defensive player in soccer, hockey, rugby, etc, usu positioned near the defended goal; *also* the position itself

**full blood** *n* **1** descent from parents both of one pure breed **2** an individual of full blood

**full-'blooded** *adj* **1** of unmixed ancestry; purebred **2** florid, ruddy ⟨*of* ~ *face*⟩ **3a** forceful, vigorous ⟨*a* ~ *argument*⟩ **b** virile **4a** being the specified thing to a great extent ⟨*a* ~ *socialist*⟩ **b** full of rich detail ⟨*a* ~ *narrative*⟩ – **full-bloodedness** *n*

**full-'blown** *adj* **1** at the height of bloom **2** fully mature or developed; complete ⟨*the riots escalated into* ~ *civil war*⟩ **synonyms** see ²BLOSSOM

**full-'bodied** *adj* marked by richness and fullness, esp of flavour ⟨*a* ~ *wine*⟩ ⟨*a* ~ *novel*⟩

**full-bore** /-baw/ *adj* being or involving a firearm of a relatively large calibre, esp 7.62 millimetres (0.300 inch) – compare SMALL-BORE

**full circle** *adv* through a series of developments that lead back to the original source, position, or situation – chiefly in *come full circle*

**full-'dress** *adj* **1** complete down to the last point of formal procedure and therefore suitable to matters of major significance ⟨*a* ~ *debate in Parliament*⟩ ⟨*a* ~ *investigation*⟩ **2** of or being FULL DRESS ⟨~ *uniform*⟩

**full dress** *n* the style of dress prescribed for ceremonial or formal social occasions – compare MORNING DRESS, EVENING DRESS

**fuller** /'foolə/ *n* a blacksmith's hammer for grooving and spreading iron [*fuller* (to form a groove in), perh fr the name *Fuller*]

**fuller's earth** /'foolaz/ *n* a clayey substance used in fulling cloth and as a catalyst in some chemical reactions

**fuller's teasel** /'foolaz/ *n* TEASEL 1a (prickly plant)

**full-'fashioned** *adj, NAm* fully-fashioned

**full-'fledged** *adj, NAm* fully-fledged

**full house** *n* a poker hand containing three cards of one value and a pair of another value

**full-'length** *adj* **1** showing or adapted to the entire length, esp of the human figure ⟨*a* ~ *mirror*⟩ ⟨*a* ~ *dress*⟩ **2** having a full or standard length; unabridged ⟨*a* ~ *film*⟩

**full marks** *n pl, Br* due credit or commendation ⟨*give her* ~ *for trying*⟩

**full moon** *n* the moon when its whole visible disc is illuminated

**fullmouthed** /-'mowdhd/ *adj, of sheep and cattle* having a full set of teeth

**full nelson** /'nels(ə)n/ *n* a wrestling hold in which both arms are thrust under an opponent's arms from behind and the hands are clasped to press on the back of the opponent's neck – compare HALF NELSON

**full pitch** *n* FULL TOSS

**full point** *n, Br* FULL STOP

**full-ˌscale** *adj* **1** identical to an original in proportion and size ⟨*a* ~ *drawing*⟩ **2a** involving full use of available resources ⟨*a* ~ *biography*⟩ **b** total, complete

**full stop** *n* a punctuation mark . used at the end of a sentence or after an abbreviation – often used to express completion

⟨*they were just brave, clean, British success stories*. Full stop. – *Punch*⟩

,full-'term *adj* born after a pregnancy of normal length – compare PREMATURE

,full-'time *adj* employed for or involving full time ⟨~ *employees*⟩ – **full time** *adv*, **full-timer** *n*

**full time** *n* **1** the amount of time considered the normal or standard amount for working during a given period, esp a week **2** the end of a game or contest (eg in soccer)

**full toss** *n* a throw, esp a bowled ball in cricket, that has not hit the ground by the time it arrives at the point at which it was aimed

**fully** /'fooli/ *adv* **1** in a full manner or degree; completely **2** at least; not less or fewer than ⟨~ *half of us*⟩

,fully-'fashioned, *NAm* ,full-'fashioned *adj* employing or produced by a knitting process for shaping to fit the body closely ⟨~ *tights*⟩

,fully-'fledged, *NAm* ,full-'fledged *adj* **1** *of a bird* having fully developed feathers and able to fly **2** having attained complete status ⟨~ *lawyer*⟩

**fulmar** /'foolmə/ *n* a northern seabird (*Fulmarus glacialis*) of colder regions, closely related to the petrels; *also* any of several related birds of southern seas [of Scand origin; akin to ON *fülmār* fulmar, fr *füll* foul + *mār* gull (cf MEW)]

**fulminant** /'foolminənt, 'ful-/ *adj* FULMINATING 3

¹**fulminate** /'foolminayt/ *vt* **1** to utter or thunder out with denunciation **2** to cause to explode ~ *vi* **1** to thunder forth censure or invective – usu + *against* or *at* **2** to be furiously indignant; feel enraged ⟨~d *in silence*⟩ **3** to make a sudden loud noise; explode [ME *fulminaten*, fr ML *fulminatus*, pp of *fulminare*, fr L, to flash with lightning, strike with lightning, fr *fulmin-*, *fulmen* lightning; akin to L *flagrare* to burn – more at BLACK] – **fulminator** *n*, **fulmination** *n*

²**fulminate** *n* an often explosive chemical compound (eg mercury fulminate) containing the chemical group CNO [ISV *fulmin-* (fr L *fulmin-*, *fulmen* lightning) + *-ate*]

**fulminating** /'foolminayting, 'ful-/ *adj* **1** exploding with a vivid flash **2** thundering forth denunciations or threats **3** *of a disease* coming on suddenly with great severity ⟨~ *infection*⟩

**fulsome** /'fools(ə)m/ *adj* **1** abundant , copious ⟨*described in* ~ *detail*⟩ **2** offensive to the senses or to moral or aesthetic sensibility; disgusting **3a** excessively complimentary or flattering; unnecessarily effusive ⟨~ *praises*⟩ **b** obsequious **4** exceeding the bounds of good taste; overdone [ME *fulsom* copious, cloying, fr *full* + *-som* -some] – **fulsomely** *adv*, **fulsomeness** *n*

    *usage* As this is now chiefly a derogatory word, it may be misleading to use it when one means merely "generous" or "lavish".

**fulvous** /'fulvəs/ *adj* of a dull brownish-yellow colour; tawny [L *fulvus*; perh akin to L *flavus* yellow – more at BLUE]

**Fu Manchu moustache** /,fooh man'chooh/ *n* a heavy moustache with ends that turn down to the chin [*Fu Manchu*, Oriental villain in stories by Sax Rohmer (real name A S Ward) †1959 E writer]

**fumarase** /'fyoohmərayz/ *n* an ENZYME that accelerates the interconversion (eg in energy-producing biochemical reactions) of FUMARIC ACID and MALIC ACID or their derivatives

**fumarate** /'fyoohmərayt/ *n* any of various chemical compounds (SALTS or ESTERS) formed by combination between FUMARIC ACID and a metal atom, an alcohol, or another chemical group

**fumaric acid** /fyooh'marik/ *n* an acid, HOOCCH=CH COOH, found in various plants and used esp in making plastics [ISV, fr NL *Fumaria*, genus of herbs, fr LL, fumitory, fr L *fumus*]

**fumarole** /'fyoomə,rohl/ *n* a hole in or near a volcano from which hot gases and vapours issue [It *fumarola*, modif of LL *fumariolum*, fr L *fumarium* smoke chamber for aging wine, fr *fumus* fume] – **fumarolic** *adj*

**fumble** /'fumbl/ *vi* **1a** to grope for or handle something clumsily or awkwardly **b** to make awkward attempts to do or find something ⟨~d *in his pocket for a coin*⟩ **2** to feel one's way or move awkwardly ⟨*he* ~d *along the dark path*⟩ ~ *vt* **1** to bring about by clumsy handling ⟨*he* ~d *the door open*⟩ **2a** to feel or handle clumsily **b** to deal with awkwardly or clumsily; bungle **3** to make (one's way) in a clumsy manner **4** to fail to catch or stop (a ball) cleanly [prob of Scand origin; akin to Sw *fumla* to fumble] – **fumble** *n*, **fumbler** *n*, **fumblingly** *adv*

¹**fume** /fyoohm/ *n* **1 fumes** *pl*, **fume** a smoke, vapour, or gas, esp when irritating or offensive ⟨*engine exhaust* ~s⟩ **2 fumes** *pl*, **fume** something (eg an emotion) that impairs one's reason-

ing ⟨*sometimes his head gets a little hot with the* ~s *of patriotism* – Matthew Arnold⟩ **3** a state of unreasonable excited irritation or anger – chiefly in *in a fume* [ME, fr MF *fum*, fr L *fumus*; akin to OHG *toumen* to be fragrant, Gk *thymos* mind, spirit] – **fumy** *adj*

²**fume** *vt* **1** to expose to or treat with fumes ⟨~d *oak*⟩ **2** to give off in fumes ⟨*an old ship* fuming *thick black smoke*⟩ ~ *vi* **1a** to emit fumes **b** to be in a state of excited irritation or anger ⟨*she fretted and* ~d *over the delay*⟩ **2** to rise (as if) in fumes

**fumet** /'foohmay (*Fr* fymɛ)/ *n* a strong stock made from fish or game and concentrated by boiling down [Fr, odour, fume of wine or meat, fr MF, deriv of L *fumus*]

**fumigant** /'fyoohmigənt/ *n* a substance used in fumigating

**fumigate** /'fyoohmigayt/ *vt* to apply smoke, vapour, or gas to, esp for the purpose of disinfecting or of destroying pests [L *fumigatus*, pp of *fumigare*, fr *fumus* + *-igare* (akin to L *agere* to drive) – more at AGENT] – **fumigator** *n*, **fumigation** *n*

**fumitory** /'fyoohmit(ə)ri/ *n* any of several erect or climbing plants (genus *Fumaria*, esp *Fumaria officinalis*, of the family Fumariaceae, the fumitory family); *also* any of several plants of other genera of the fumitory family [ME *fumeterre*, fr MF, fr ML *fumus terrae*, lit., smoke of the earth, fr L *fumus* + *terrae*, gen of *terra* earth – more at TERRACE]

¹**fun** /fun/ *n* **1** a cause of amusement or enjoyment ⟨*swimming is good* ~⟩ **2** a mood for finding or causing amusement ⟨*the teasing was all in* ~⟩ **3a** amusement, enjoyment ⟨*sickness takes all the* ~ *out of life*⟩ **b** derisive jest; sport, ridicule ⟨*made him a figure of* ~⟩ **4** violent or excited activity or argument ⟨*let a snake loose in the classroom; then the* ~ *began*⟩ [E dial. *fun* to hoax, perh alter. of ME *fonnen*, fr *fonne* dupe] – **poke fun at** to ridicule, mock

²**fun** *adj*, *chiefly NAm informal* providing entertainment, amusement, or enjoyment ⟨*a* ~ *party*⟩ ⟨*a* ~ *person to be with*⟩

**funambulism** /fyoo'nambyooliz(ə)m/ *n*, *formal* **1** tightrope walking **2** a show of (mental) agility [L *funambulus* ropewalker, fr *funis* rope + *ambulare* to walk] – **funambulist** *n*

**fun and games** *n* *taking sing or pl vb* high-spirited amusement

¹**function** /'fungksh(ə)n/ *n* **1** an occupational duty ⟨*combines the* ~s *of chauffeur and gardener*⟩ **2** the action characteristic of a person or thing or for which a thing exists ⟨*examining the* ~ *of poetry in modern society*⟩ **3** any of a group of related actions contributing to a larger action; *esp* the normal and specific contribution of a body part to the economy of a living organism **4** an impressive, elaborate, or formal ceremony or social gathering **5a** a mathematical correspondence that assigns to each element of a set exactly one element of the same or another set; *also* the element of the RANGE (set which is mapped to by the function) defined by a particular instance of the function **b** a quality, trait, or fact dependent on and varying with another ⟨*the time they arrive is a* ~ *of how far they have to travel*⟩ **c** a facility on a keyboard-controlled device (eg a calculator) that corresponds to a mathematical function (eg taking the square root) or operation (eg addition) or that provides a nonmathematical function (eg deletion of last entry) [L *function-*, *functio* performance, fr *functus*, pp of *fungi* to perform; prob akin to Skt *bhuṅkte* he enjoys] – **functionless** *adj*

²**function** *vi* **1** to have a function; serve ⟨*an attributive noun* ~s *as an adjective*⟩ **2** to be in action; operate ⟨*a government* ~s *through numerous divisions*⟩

**functional** /'fungksh(ə)nl/ *adj* **1a** of, connected with, or being a function **b** affecting physiological or psychological functions but not the structure of the organism ⟨~ *heart disease*⟩ – compare ORGANIC 1b **2** designed or developed for practical use without ornamentation ⟨~ *furniture*⟩ **3** performing or able to perform a regular function *synonyms* see USEFUL – **functionally** *adv*

**functional group** *n* the atom or group of atoms in a chemical compound that determines its characteristic behaviour

**functional illiterate** *n* a person having had some schooling but not meeting a minimum standard of literacy – **functional illiteracy** *n*

**functionalism** /-,iz(ə)m/ *n* **1** a doctrine or practice of design (eg in architecture) that considers that form should be adapted to use, material, and structure **2** a theory that stresses the interdependence of the patterns and institutions of a society and their interaction in maintaining cultural and social unity **3** a theory or practice that evaluates everything in terms of practical usefulness – **functionalist** *n*, **functionalist, functionalistic** *adj*

**functionary** /'fungksh(ə)nəri/ *n* 1 a person who serves in a certain function 2 one holding office in a government or political party; an official, bureaucrat

**function key** *n* a keyboard key (eg on a calculator) that commands a function

**function word** *n* a word (eg a PREPOSITION, AUXILIARY, or CONJUNCTION) that primarily expresses the relationship between other words – compare CONTENT WORD

**functor** /'fungktə/ *n* FUNCTION WORD

¹**fund** /fund/ *n* 1 an available quantity of material or intangible resources; a supply ⟨~ *of knowledge*⟩ 2a a resource, esp a sum of money, whose provision or interest is set apart for a specific objective b *pl* British government bonds that yield a fixed rate of interest but give no entitlement to repayment of their face value – usu + *the;* compare CONSOL 3 *pl* an available supply of money 4 an organization administering a special fund [L *fundus* bottom, piece of landed property – more at BOTTOM]

²**fund** *vt* 1a to make provision of resources for discharging the interest or principal of b to provide funds for ⟨*research* ~ed *by the government*⟩ 2 to place in a fund; accumulate 3 to convert (a short-term debt) into a debt that is payable either at a distant date or at no definite date and that bears a fixed interest ⟨~ *a floating debt*⟩

**fundament** /'fundəmənt/ *n* 1 an underlying ground, theory, or principle 2 the part of a land surface that has not been altered by human activities 3 *chiefly euph or humorous* 3a the buttocks b the anus [ME, fr OF *fondement*, fr L *fundamentum*, fr *fundare* to found, fr *fundus*]

¹**fundamental** /ˌfundəˈmentl/ *adj* 1 serving as a basis to support existence or to determine essential structure or function; basic – often + *to* 2a of essential structure, function, or facts; radical ⟨~ *change*⟩; *specif* of or dealing with general principles rather than practical application ⟨~ *science*⟩ b adhering to fundamentalism 3a *of a musical chord or its position* having the lowest note (ROOT 7) in the bass b *physics* of or produced by a fundamental 4 of central importance; principal ⟨~ *purpose*⟩ 5 belonging to one's innate or ingrained characteristics; deep-rooted ⟨*hard to disturb his* ~ *good humour*⟩ – **fundamentally** *adv*

²**fundamental** *n* 1 something fundamental; *esp* a minimum constituent without which a thing or a system would not be what it is 2a the strongest and most audible frequency that sounds together with the HARMONICS (usu higher frequencies) in a musical note and gives the note its characteristic pitch b the lowest note of a chord in normal position 3 *physics* the lowest frequency of several component frequencies possessed by a series of sound waves, ELECTROMAGNETIC WAVES, etc

**fundamentalism** /-iz(ə)m/ *n* 1a a belief in the literal truth of the Bible b *often cap* a movement in 20th-century Protestantism emphasizing such belief c adherence to such belief 2 a movement or attitude stressing strict and literal adherence to a set of basic principles – **fundamentalist** *n*, **fundamentalist, fundamentalistic** *adj*

**fundamental law** *n* the basic law concerning the government of a state, as distinguished from legislative acts; *specif* a constitution

**fundamental particle** *n* ELEMENTARY PARTICLE

**fundamental tissue** *n* plant tissue other than the EPIDERMIS (outermost protective layer) and VASCULAR (circulatory and transporting) tissues that consists typically of relatively undifferentiated thin-walled soft cells and supportive cells

**fundamental unit** *n* BASIC UNIT (basis for a system of units of measurement)

**fundus** /'fundəs/ *n, pl* **fundi** /'fundi, -die/ the bottom, or part opposite the opening, of the internal surface of a hollow organ: eg a the upper part of the stomach below the heart and left lung b the lower back part of the bladder c the large upper end of the womb d the part of the eye opposite the pupil [NL, fr L, bottom] – **fundic** *adj*

¹**funeral** /'fyoohn(ə)rəl/ *adj* 1 of or constituting a funeral 2 FUNEREAL 2 [ME, fr LL *funeralis*, fr L *funer-*, *funus* funeral (n); perh akin to ON *deyja* to die – more at DIE]

²**funeral** *n* 1 a formal and ceremonial disposing of a dead body, esp by burial or cremation; *also, NAm* a funeral service 2 a procession connected with a funeral ⟨*the* ~ *wound its way through the grey streets*⟩ 3 an end of something's existence 4 *chiefly dial NAm* a funeral sermon 5 *informal* a matter, esp a difficulty, that is of concern only to the specified person ⟨*if you get lost in the desert, that's your* ~⟩

**funeral director** *n* UNDERTAKER 2

**funeral home** *n, NAm* FUNERAL PARLOUR

**funeral parlour** *n* an undertaker's establishment

**funerary** /'fyoohnərəri/ *adj* of, used for, or associated with burial ⟨*a pharaoh's* ~ *chamber*⟩

**funereal** /fyoohˈniəri·əl/ *adj* 1 of a funeral 2 suitable to a funeral; gloomy, solemn [L *funereus*, fr *funer-*, *funus*] – **funereally** *adv*

**fun fair** *n, chiefly Br* a usu outdoor show offering amusements (eg side-shows, rides, or games of skill)

**fungal** /'fung-gl/ *adj* fungous

**fungi-** /funji-/ *comb form* fungus ⟨fungi*form*⟩ ⟨fungi*cide*⟩ [L *fungus*]

**fungible** /'funjəbl/ *adj* 1 *law* of or being movable consumable goods (eg food and fuel) such that one specimen or part may be replaced by another of equal quantity and quality in the fulfilment of a contract 2 interchangeable [NL *fungibilis*, fr L *fungi* to perform – more at FUNCTION] – **fungibility** *n*

**fungibles** /'funjəblz/ *n pl* fungible goods

**fungicide** /'funjisied/ *n* something that kills fungi; *also* something that inhibits their growth [ISV] – **fungicidal** *adj*, **fungicidally** *adv*

**fungiform** /'funji,fawm/ *adj* shaped like a mushroom

**fungoid** /'fung-goyd/ *adj* resembling, characteristic of, or being a fungus – **fungoid** *n*

**fungous** /'fung-gəs/ *adj* 1 of or having the characteristics of fungi 2 caused by a fungus

**fungus** /'fung-gəs/ *n, pl* **fungi** /'fung-gie, -gi, -jie, -ji/ *also* **funguses** 1 any of a major group (Fungi) of organisms that lack the green pigment chlorophyll, are parasitic or feed on dead or decaying animals and plants, include moulds, rusts, mildews, smuts, mushrooms, and toadstools, and are considered to be members of either a kingdom in their own right or a subkingdom of the plant kingdom 2 something resembling a fungus, esp in rapid growth ⟨*a* ~ *of jargon obscuring the subject*⟩ [L, perh modif of Gk *spongos* sponge]

**fungus gnat** *n* any of numerous small flies (esp families Mycetophilidae and Sciaridae) whose larvae feed on fungi

**fun house** *n, NAm* AMUSEMENT ARCADE

**funicle** /'fyoohnikl/ *n* a funiculus

¹**funicular** /fyoohˈnikyoolə/ *adj* 1 dependent on the tension of a cord or cable 2 having the form of or associated with a cord 3 of or being a funiculus [L *funiculus* small rope]

²**funicular** *n* a CABLE RAILWAY ascending a mountain; *esp* one in which an ascending car counterbalances a descending car

**funiculus** /fyoohˈnikyoolǝs/ *n, pl* **funiculi** /-li, -lie/ 1 a body structure resembling a cord: eg 1a UMBILICAL CORD b a bundle of nerve fibres c SPERMATIC CORD (cord suspending testis in the scrotum) 2 the stalk connecting a plant's rudimentary seed (OVULE) to the inner wall of the seed-producing organ (OVARY) [NL, fr L, dim. of *funis* rope]

¹**funk** /fungk/ *n, informal* 1a a state of paralysing fear b a fit of inability to face difficulty 2 a person who funks; a coward [prob fr obs Flem *fonck;* (2) ²*funk*]

²**funk** *vb, informal vi* to become frightened ~ *vt* 1 to be afraid of; dread 2 to avoid doing or facing (something) because of lack of determination

³**funk** *n, slang* funky music [back-formation fr ²*funky*]

**funk hole** *n, informal* 1 a military dugout 2 a place of safe retreat

¹**funky** /'fungki/ *adj, informal* in a state of funk; panicky

²**funky** *adj* 1 *chiefly informal* having an offensive smell; foul 2 *slang* having an earthy unsophisticated style and feeling; *esp* having the style and feeling of blues ⟨~ *piano playing*⟩ 3 *slang* having an earthily sexual quality 4 *slang* – used to approve something or somebody, esp in pop culture [*funk* (offensive smell), perh fr Fr dial. *funquer* to emit smoke] – **funkiness** *n*

¹**funnel** /'funl/ *n* 1a a utensil that typically has the shape of a hollow cone with a tube extending from the smaller end and is designed to catch and direct a downward flow (eg of liquid) into a small opening b something (eg a conical hole) shaped like a funnel 2 a shaft, stack, or flue for ventilation or the escape of smoke or steam, esp from a steam engine or ship [ME *fonel*, fr OProv *fonilh*, fr ML *fundibulum*, short for L *infundibulum*, fr *infundere* to pour in, fr *in-* + *fundere* to pour – more at FOUND]

²**funnel** *vb* **-ll-** (*NAm* **-l-, -ll-**) *vi* 1 to have or take the shape of a funnel 2 to pass (as if) through a funnel ⟨*the crowd* ~led *out of the football ground*⟩ ~ *vt* 1 to form in the shape of a funnel ⟨~led *his hands and shouted through them*⟩ 2 to move to a

focal point or into a central channel ⟨*contributions were* ~ led *into one account*⟩

**funnel web, funnel web spider** *n* any of various spiders (families Agelenidae and Dipluridae) that build tube-shaped webs; *esp* an extremely poisonous large black Australian spider (*Atrax robustus*)

**funnily** /'funili/ *adv* 1 in a funny manner 2 as is curious or unexpected – often + *enough*

¹**funny** /'funi/ *adj* 1a causing mirth and laughter; amusing **b** seeking or intended to amuse; facetious 2 differing from the ordinary in a peculiar or curious way; queer 3 *informal* involving trickery, deception, or dishonesty ⟨*told his prisoner not to try anything* ~⟩ ⟨~ *business*⟩ 4 *informal* unwilling to be helpful; tending to be uncooperative ⟨*at first he was a bit* ~ *about it but in the end he agreed*⟩ 5 *informal* 5a slightly unwell **b** slightly mad – **funniness** *n*, **funny** *adv*

²**funny** *n* 1 a funny person or thing; *esp* a joke 2 *usu pl* a comic strip or comic section of a periodical

**funny bone** *n* 1 the place at the back of the elbow where the nerve supplying the hand and forearm rests against a prominence of the HUMERUS (bone of the upper arm) – not used technically 2 *informal* a sense of humour ⟨*tickled his* ~⟩ [fr the tingling felt when it is struck]

**funny farm** *n*, *humorous* a mental hospital

**funny ha-ha** *adj*, *informal* FUNNY 1 – usu contrasted with *funny peculiar*

**funnyman** /'funi,man/ *n* COMEDIAN 2

**funny peculiar** *adj*, *informal* FUNNY 2 – usu contrasted with *funny ha-ha*

¹**fur** /fuh/ *vb* -**rr**- *vt* 1 to coat or clog as if with fur – often + *up* 2 to apply FURRING (strips of wood, brick, etc) to ~ *vi* to become coated or clogged as if with fur – often + *up* [ME *furren* to line or adorn with fur, fr MF *fourrer*, fr OF *forrer*, fr *fuerre* sheath, of Gmc origin; akin to OHG *fuotar* sheath; akin to Gk *pōy* herd, Skt *pāti* he protects]

²**fur** *n* 1 a piece of the dressed pelt of an animal used to make, trim, or line garments 2 an article of clothing made of or with fur 3 the hairy coat of a mammal, esp when fine, soft, and thick; *also* such a coat with the skin 4 a coating resembling fur: eg 4a a coating of dead cells on the tongue of someone who is unwell **b** the thick pile of a fabric (eg chenille) **c** a coating formed in vessels (eg kettles or pipes) by the deposit of scale from hard water 5 any of the stylized patterns (eg ermine or vair) used in heraldry that represent animal pelts or their colours – **furless** *adj*

**furan** /'fyooəran, fyoo'ran/ *also* **furane** /-rayn/ *n* an inflammable liquid, $C_4H_4O$, that is obtained from wood oils of pines or made synthetically, and is used esp in the manufacture of nylon [ISV, fr *furfural*]

**furanose** /'fyooərənohz, -nohs/ *n* a sugar having an oxygen-containing ring of five atoms [*furan* + *-ose*]

**furanoside** /fyoo'ranəsied/ *n* a GLYCOSIDE (chemical compound derived from a sugar) containing the ring characteristic of furanose

**furbearer** /'fuh,beərə/ *n* an animal that bears fur, esp of a commercially desired quality

**furbelow** /'fuhbi,loh/ *n* 1 a pleated or gathered piece of material; *specif* a flounce on women's clothing 2 something that suggests a furbelow, esp in being showy or superfluous – often in *frills and furbelows* [by folk etymology fr Fr dial. *far-bella*] – **furbelow** *vt*

**furbish** /'fuhbish/ *vt* 1 to make lustrous; burnish, polish 2 to give a new look to; renovate – often + *up* [ME *furbisshen*, fr MF *fourbiss-*, stem of *fourbir*, of Gmc origin; akin to OHG *furben* to polish] – **furbisher** *n*

**furcate** /'fuhkayt, -kət/ *adj*, *of a plant or animal part* forked [LL *furcatus*, fr L *furca* fork] – **furcately** *adv*

**furcation** /fuh'kaysh(ə)n/ *n* 1 something that is branched; a fork 2 the act or process of branching [ML *furcation-, furcatio*, fr *furcatus*, pp of *furcare* to branch, fr L *furca*]

**furcula** /'fuhkyoolə/ *n*, *pl* **furculae** /-lie, -li/ a forked part of the body: eg **a** a wishbone **b** the forked organ on the abdomen of a SPRINGTAIL (primitive wingless insect) which enables it to leap [NL, fr L, forked prop, dim. of *furca*] – **furcular** *adj*

**furfural** /'fuhf(y)oo,ral/ *n* a liquid chemical compound (ALDEHYDE), $C_4H_3OCHO$, of penetrating smell that is usu made from plant materials and used esp in making furan or synthetic plastics and as a solvent [L *furfur* bran + ISV *-al*]

**furfuraldehyde** /,fuhf(y)oo'raldihied/ *n* furfural [L *furfur* + ISV *aldehyde*]

**furfuran** /'fuhf(y)ooran/ *n* FURAN (inflammable liquid)

**Furies** /'fyooəriz/ *n pl* EUMENIDES (avenging Greek goddesses)

**furioso** /,fyooəri'ohsoh/ *adj or adv* with great force or vigour – used as a direction in music [It, lit., furious]

**furious** /'fyooəri·əs/ *adj* 1a exhibiting or goaded by uncontrollable anger **b** giving a stormy or turbulent appearance ⟨~ *bursts of flame from the windswept fire*⟩ **c** marked by noise, excitement, or activity **d** violent ⟨*a* ~ *blow*⟩ 2 existing in an extreme degree; intense ⟨*the* ~ *growth of tropical vegetation*⟩ *synonyms* see ¹ANGER [ME, fr MF *furieus*, fr L *furiosus*, fr *furia* fury] – **furiously** *adv*

**furl** /fuhl/ *vt* to fold or roll (eg a sail, flag, or umbrella) close to or round something ~ *vi* to curl or fold as in being furled [MF *ferler*, fr ONF *ferlier* to tie tightly, fr OF *fer, ferm* tight (fr L *firmus* firm) + *lier* to tie, fr L *ligare* – more at LIGATURE] – **furl** *n*

**furlong** /'fuhlong/ *n* a unit of length equal to 220 yards (0.201168 kilometre) [ME, fr OE *furlang*, fr *furh* furrow + *lang* long]

¹**furlough** /'fuhloh/ *n* a leave of absence from duty, granted esp to a soldier; *also* a document authorizing such a leave of absence *synonyms* see ¹HOLIDAY [D *verlof*, lit., permission, fr MD, fr *ver-* for- + *lof* permission; akin to OE *for-* and to MHG *loube* permission – more at FOR-, LEAVE]

²**furlough** *vt*, *chiefly NAm* to grant a furlough to

**furmety** /'fuhməti/ *n* FRUMENTY (wheat boiled in milk) [by alter.]

**furnace** /'fuhnis/ *n* an enclosed apparatus in which heat is produced (eg for heating a building or for melting metal) [ME *furnas*, fr OF *fornaise*, fr L *fornac-, fornax;* akin to L *formus* warm – more at WARM]

**furnish** /'fuhnish/ *vt* 1 to provide with what is needed; *esp* to equip with furniture 2 to supply, give ⟨~ed *food and shelter for the refugees*⟩ [ME *furnisshen*, fr MF *fourniss-*, stem of *fournir* to complete, equip, of Gmc origin; akin to OHG *frum-men* to further, *fruma* advantage – more at FOREMOST] – **furnisher** *n*

**furnishing** /'fuhnishing/ *n usu pl* 1 an object that tends to increase comfort or utility; *specif* an article of furniture for the interior of a building – compare SOFT FURNISHINGS 2 *NAm* an article or accessory of dress

**furniture** /'fuhnichə/ *n* 1 equipment that is necessary, useful, or desirable: eg 1a the movable articles (eg tables, chairs, and beds) that make an area (eg a room in a house or office) suitable for living in or use **b** accessories ⟨*handsome brass door* ~⟩ **c** the whole movable equipment of a ship (eg rigging, sails, anchors, and boats) 2 pieces of wood, metal, or plastic placed in an arrangement of printing type to make blank spaces and secure the type in its frame 3 *archaic* the trappings of a horse [MF *fourniture*, fr *fournir*]

**furniture beetle** *n* a small wood-boring beetle (*Anobium punctatum*) whose larva is a woodworm; *broadly* any of several beetles (family Anobiidae)

**furor** /'fyooəraw/ *n, chiefly NAm* a furore

**furore** /fyoo'rawri/ *n* 1 a fashionable craze; a vogue 2a furious or hectic activity **b** an outburst of general excitement or indignation; an uproar [It *furore* & MF *furor*, fr L *furor*, fr *furere* to rage – more at DUST]

**furphy** /'fuhfi/ *n, chiefly Austr informal* an unlikely or absurd rumour [*Furphy*, name of supplier of sanitation carts in Australia during World War I]

**furred** /fuhd/ *adj* 1 lined, trimmed, or faced with fur 2 coated as if with fur; *specif, of a tongue* having a coating consisting chiefly of mucus and dead cells 3 bearing or wearing fur 4 provided with furring ⟨~ *wall*⟩

**furrier** /'furi·ə/ *n* one who prepares or deals in furs – **furriery** *n*

**furriner** /'furinə/ *n, dial or humorous* a stranger, foreigner [alter. of *foreigner*]

**furring** /'fuhring/ *n* the application of thin wood, brick, or metal to walls, floors, or ceilings to form a level surface (eg for plastering) or an air space; *also* the material used in this process

¹**furrow** /'furoh/ *n* 1a a trench in the earth made by a plough **b** rural land; a field 2 something that resembles the track of a plough: eg 2a a marked narrow depression; a groove **b** a deep wrinkle ⟨~s *in his brow*⟩ [ME *furgh, forow*, fr OE *furh;* akin to OHG *furuh* furrow, L *porca*]

²**furrow** *vb* to make or form furrows, grooves, wrinkles, or lines (in)

**furry** /'fuhri/ *adj* **1** consisting of or resembling fur ⟨*animals with* ~ *coats*⟩ **2** covered with fur **3** thick in quality ⟨*spoke with a* ~ *voice*⟩

**fur seal** *n* any of various EARED SEALS that have a double coat with a dense soft underfur used esp for clothing and trimmings

**¹further** /'fuhdhə/ *adv* **1** FARTHER **1 2** moreover **3** to a greater degree or extent ⟨~ *annoyed by a second intrusion*⟩ [ME, fr OE *furthor;* akin to OHG *furthar* further; both compars fr the root of OE *forth*] – **further to** continuing the subject of; following ⟨further to *your communication of the 4th July*⟩ – used esp in business letters

*usage* Although some writers attempt to distinguish between **farther, farthest**, used with reference to literal distance, and **further, furthest**, used for the more abstract senses of the word, **further** and **furthest** have become the commoner pair; they can be used in all the senses, while **farther** and **farthest** cannot. Only **further** can be a verb.

**²further** *adj* **1** FARTHER **1 2** extending beyond what exists or has happened; additional ⟨~ *volumes*⟩ ⟨~ *education*⟩ ⟨*closed until* ~ *notice*⟩

**³further** *vt* to help forward; promote, advance ⟨*this will* ~ *your chances of success*⟩ – **furtherance** *n*, **furtherer** *n*

**further education** *n, Br* vocational, cultural, or recreational education for people who have left school – usu taken to include formal adult education but not university education

**furthermore** /-'maw/ *adv* in addition to what precedes; moreover – used esp when introducing fresh matter for consideration

**furthermost** /-,mohst/ *adj* most distant; farthest

**furthest** /'fuhdhist/ *adv or adj* farthest *usage* see ¹FURTHER

**furtive** /'fuhtiv/ *adj* **1a** done by stealth; surreptitious **b** expressive of stealth; sly ⟨*had the* ~ *look of one with something to hide*⟩ **2** obtained in an underhand manner; stolen *synonyms* see ¹SECRET *antonym* forthright [Fr or L; Fr *furtif*, fr L *furtivus*, fr *furtum* theft, fr *fur* thief; akin to Gk *phōr* thief, L *ferre* to carry – more at BEAR] – **furtively** *adv*, **furtiveness** *n*

**furuncle** /'fyooə,rungkl/ *n* ¹BOIL – used technically [L *furunculus* petty thief, sucker, boil, dim. of *furon-*, *furo* ferret, thief, fr *fur*] – **furuncular** *adj*, **furunculous** *adj*

**furunculosis** /fyoo,rungkyoo'lohsis/ *n, pl* **furunculoses** /-seez/ **1** the condition of having or tending to develop multiple boils **2** a highly infectious disease of various fishes of the salmon family (e g trout) that is caused by a bacterium (*Bacterium salmonicida*) and is virulent esp in dense fish populations (e g in hatcheries) [NL]

**fury** /'fyooəri/ *n* **1** intense, disordered, and often destructive rage **2a** *cap* any of the avenging goddesses in Greek mythology who torment criminals and inflict plagues **b** an avenging spirit **c** one who resembles an avenging spirit; *esp* a spiteful woman **3** wild disordered force or activity **4** a state of inspired exaltation; a frenzy *synonyms* see ¹ANGER [ME *furie*, fr MF & L; MF, fr L *furia*, fr *furere* to rage – more at DUST]

**furze** /fuhz/ *n* a spiny yellow-flowered evergreen European shrub (*Ulex europaeus*) of the pea family; *broadly* any of several related plants (genera *Ulex* and *Genista*) – called also GORSE, WHIN [ME *firse*, fr OE *fyrs;* akin to Gk *pyros* wheat] – **furzy** *adj*

**fusain** /fyooh'zayn/ *n* a soft powdery constituent of coal, closely resembling charcoal [Fr]

**fuscous** /'fuskəs/ *adj* of a dark brownish-grey colour [L *fuscus* – more at DUSK]

**¹fuse** /fyoohz/ *n* **1** a continuous train of a combustible substance enclosed in a cord or cable for setting off an explosive charge by transmitting fire to it **2** *NAm chiefly* **fuze** a mechanical or electrical detonating device for setting off the explosive charge of a projectile, bomb, or torpedo [It *fuso* spindle, fr L *fusus*, of unknown origin]

**²fuse,** *NAm also* **fuze** *vt* to equip with a detonating fuse

**³fuse** *vt* **1** to reduce to a liquid or plastic state by heat; melt **2** to blend thoroughly (as if) by melting together **3** to stitch by applying heat and pressure with or without the use of an adhesive **4** to cause (e g a light bulb) to fail as a result of the melting of an electrical fuse **5** to equip (e g an electric plug) with an electrical fuse ~ *vi* **1** to become fluid with heat **2** to become blended (as if) by melting together **3** to fail because of the melting of an electrical fuse *synonyms* see ¹MIX [L *fusus*, pp of *fundere* to pour, melt – more at FOUND] – **fusible** *adj*, **fusibility** *n*

**⁴fuse** *n* an electrical safety device consisting of or including a

wire or strip of metal that melts and interrupts the circuit when the current exceeds a particular value

**fuse box** *n* a usu fireproof box containing electrical fuses

**fused quartz** /fyoohzd/ *n* QUARTZ GLASS

**fused silica** *n* QUARTZ GLASS

**fusee,** *NAm also* **fuzee** /fyooh'zee/ *n* **1** a conical spirally grooved pulley or wheel, esp in a watch or clock **2** ¹FUSE 1 **3** a match with a large head not easily blown out once lit **4** *NAm* a red flare used esp as a warning signal on railways [Fr *fusée*, lit., spindleful of yarn, fr OF, fr *fus* spindle, fr L *fusus*]

**fuselage** /'fyoohzi,lahzh/ *n* the main body of an aeroplane, designed to accommodate the crew and the passengers or cargo [Fr, fr *fuselé* spindle-shaped, fr MF, fr *fusel*, dim. of *fus*]

**fusel oil** /'fyoohzl/ *n* an acrid oily liquid occurring as a by-product during the distillation of alcoholic liquors (e g beer and whisky), consisting chiefly of AMYL ALCOHOL, and used esp as a source of chemical alcohols and as a solvent [Ger *fusel* bad liquor]

**fusi-** /fyoohzi-/ *comb form* spindle ⟨fusi*form*⟩ [L *fusus*]

**fusiform** /'fyoohzi,fawm/ *adj* tapering towards each end ⟨~ *bacteria*⟩

**fusil** /'fyoohzil/ *n* a light flintlock or firelock musket [Fr, lit., steel for striking fire, fr OF *foisil*, fr (assumed) VL *focilis*, fr LL *focus* fire – more at FUEL]

**fusilier,** *NAm also* **fusileer** /,fyoohzə'liə/ *n* **1** a soldier armed with a fusil **2** a member of any of several British regiments formerly armed with fusils [Fr *fusilier*, fr *fusil*]

**¹fusillade** /,fyoohzə'layd/ *n* **1** a number of shots fired simultaneously or in rapid succession **2** a spirited outburst, esp of criticism [Fr, fr *fusiller* to shoot, fr *fusil*]

**²fusillade** *vt* to attack or shoot down by a fusillade

**fusion** /'fyoohzh(ə)n/ *n* **1a** the act or process of liquefying or rendering plastic by heat **b** the liquid or plastic state induced by heat **2** a union (as if) by melting: e g **2a** a merging of diverse elements into a unified whole **b** a political partnership; a coalition ⟨*a* ~ *of the major parties*⟩ **c** the union of light atomic nuclei to form heavier nuclei, resulting in the release of enormous quantities of energy [L *fusion-*, *fusio*, fr *fusus*, pp]

**fusion bomb** *n* a bomb in which nuclei of a light chemical element (e g hydrogen) unite to form nuclei of heavier elements (e g helium) with a release of energy; *esp* HYDROGEN BOMB

**fusionist** /'fyoohzhənist/ *n* one who promotes or takes part in a coalition, esp of political parties

**¹fuss** /fus/ *n* **1a** needless or useless bustle or excitement; commotion **b** a show of flattering attention – often in *make a fuss of* **2a** a state of agitation, esp over a trivial matter **b** an objection, protest ⟨*kicked up a* ~ *about the new regulations*⟩ **c** an often petty controversy or quarrel [perh imit]

*synonyms* Fuss, to-do, kerfuffle, ado, commotion, flurry, flap, and bustle all mean "excited confusion". **Fuss** and the informal **to-do** and **kerfuffle** imply that the excitement is unnecessary and exaggerated ⟨*much* **fuss** *is made of the right of the parent to order the life of his child – TLS*⟩ ⟨*papers made a great* **to-do** *about her appointment*⟩. **Ado** extends this idea to include that of wasted energy, and is often used negatively ⟨*took over the job without further* **ado**⟩. **Commotion** is often noisy ⟨*there was* **commotion** *all over the house at the return of the young heir – George Meredith*⟩. **Flurry** suggests sudden troubled hurry ⟨*was in quite a* **flurry** *at the thought of such a long journey*⟩. The informal **flap** also implies some panic ⟨*get in a* **flap** *about the new regulations*⟩. **Bustle** is energetic and often self-important ⟨*the* **bustle** *of the city streets*⟩.

**²fuss** *vi* **1a** to create or be in a state of restless activity; *specif* to shower flattering attentions ⟨*doting grandparents* ~ing *over the grandchildren*⟩ **b** to pay close or undue attention to small details ⟨~ed *with her hair*⟩ **2a** to become upset; worry **b** to express annoyance or resentment ⟨*a mother who has to cope with* ~ing *children*⟩ to agitate, upset – **fusser** *n*

**fussbudget** /-,bujit/ *n, informal* a fusspot – **fussbudgety** *adj*

**fusspot** /-,pot/ *n, informal* a person who fusses about trifles

**fussy** /'fusi/ *adj* **1** easily upset; irritable **2a** showing too much concern over details **b** hard to please; fastidious ⟨*not* ~ *about food*⟩ **3** having too much or too detailed ornamentation – **fussily** *adv*, **fussiness** *n*

**fustian** /'fusti-ən, 'fuschən/ *n* **1a** a strong cotton and linen fabric, formerly used for clothing and bedding **b** a class of heavy cotton fabrics (e g corduroy, moleskin, and velveteen) usu having a pile face and twill weave **2** pretentious and banal writing or speech; bombast [ME, fr OF *fustaine*, fr ML *fustaneum*, prob fr *fustis* tree trunk, fr L, club] – **fustian** *adj*

**fustic** /'fustik/ *n* **1** (a yellow dye yielded by) the wood of a tropical American tree (*Chlorophora tinctoria*) of the fig family; *also* any of several similar woods yielding dye **2** a tree yielding fustic [ME *fustik*, fr MF *fustoc*, fr Ar *fustuq*, fr Gk *pistakē* pistachio tree – more at PISTACHIO]

**fusty** /'fusti/ *adj* **1** stale as a result of being left undisturbed for a long time; musty, mouldy **2** out-of-date **3** rigidly old-fashioned or reactionary [ME, fr *fust* wine cask, fr MF, club, cask, fr L *fustis*] – **fustily** *adv*, **fustiness** *n*

**fut** /fut/ *adv* phut

**futhark** /'foohthahk/ *n* the alphabet of RUNES used by early Germanic peoples [fr the first six letters, *f*, *u*, þ (*th*), *o* (or *a*), *r*, *c* (=k)]

**futhorc, futhork** /'foohthawk/ *n* the futhark

**futile** /'fyoohtiel/ *adj* **1** serving no useful purpose; completely ineffective ⟨*efforts to convince him were* ~⟩ **2** *of a person* lacking ability; ineffectual [MF or L; MF, fr L *futilis* that pours out easily, useless, fr *fut-* (akin to *fundere* to pour) – more at FOUND] – **futilely** *adv*, **futileness** *n*

**futility** /fyooh'tiləti/ *n* **1** the quality or state of being futile; uselessness **2** a useless act or gesture

**futtock** /'futək/ *n* any of the curved timbers joined together to form the lower part of the compound rib of a ship [prob alter. of *foothook* (futtock)]

**¹future** /'fyoohchə/ *adj* **1a** that is to be **b** existing after death ⟨~ *life*⟩ **2** of or being the verb tense that expresses action or state in the future [ME, fr OF & L; OF *futur*, fr L *futurus* about to be – more at BE]

**²future** *n* **1a** time that is to come **b** that which is going to occur **2** likelihood of success ⟨*not much* ~ *in trying to sell furs in a hot country*⟩ **3** *usu pl* something (eg a bulk commodity) bought or sold at a fixed price for future delivery ⟨*sugar* ~s⟩ **4** the future tense of a language; *also* a verb form (eg French *arrivera*) in this tense

**futureless** /'fyoohchəlis/ *adj* having no prospect of future success

**future perfect** *adj* of or being a verb tense or verb form (eg *will have finished*) that expresses completion of an action at or before a time that is yet to come – **future perfect** *n*

**futures market** *n* FORWARD MARKET

**futurism** /'fyoohchə,riz(ə)m/ *n* **1** *often cap* a movement in art, music, and literature begun in Italy about 1910 and seeking to replace traditional forms and to express esp the dynamic energy

and movement of mechanical processes **2** a point of view that finds meaning or fulfilment in the future rather than in the past or present – **futurist** *n or adj*

**futuristic** /,fyoohchə'ristik/ *adj* of the future or futurism; *esp* bearing no relation to known or traditional forms; ultramodern – **futuristically** *adv*

**futurity** /fyooh'tyooərəti, -'chooə-/ *n* **1** time to come; FUTURE 1a **2** the quality or state of being future **3** *usu pl* future events or prospects **4** *NAm* a race, esp a horse race, or competition for which entries are made well in advance of the event

**futurology** /,fyoohchə'roləji/ *n* the forecasting of the future, esp systematically on the basis of current economic or political trends in society [Ger *futurologie*, fr *futur* future + *-o-* + *-logie* -logy] – **futurologist** *n*

**fu-yung** /,fooh 'yung/ *n* (a dish containing) a mixture of egg white, cornflour, and sometimes minced chicken [Chin (Pek) *fú róng* (*fu²* *jung²*), lit., hibiscus]

**¹fuze** /fyoohz/ *n, NAm* ¹FUSE 2

**²fuze** *vt, NAm* ²FUSE

**fuzee** /fooh'zee/ *n, NAm* a fusee

**¹fuzz** /fuz/ *n* fine light particles or fibres (eg of down or fluff) [prob back-formation fr *fuzzy*]

**²fuzz** *vi* to fly off in or become covered with fluffy particles – often + *out* ~ *vt* **1** to make fuzzy **2** to envelop in a haze; blur – usu + *up*

**³fuzz** *n, slang* **1** *taking sing or pl vb* the police **2** a police officer [origin unknown]

**fuzzy** /'fuzi/ *adj* **1** of or resembling fuzz ⟨*a* ~ *covering of felt*⟩ **2** not clear; indistinct ⟨*moving the camera causes* ~ *photos*⟩ **3** *of hair* tightly curled [perh fr LG *fussig* loose, spongy; akin to OHG *fūl* rotten – more at FOUL] – **fuzzily** *adv*, **fuzziness** *n*

**fuzzy-wuzzy** /-,wuzi/ *n, Br chiefly derog* a Sudanese soldier; *broadly* any black African [redupl of *fuzzy*; fr the appearance of the hair]

**-fy** /-fie/, **-ify** *suffix* (→ *vb*) **1** become or cause to be ⟨*purify*⟩ ⟨*mollify*⟩ ⟨*solidify*⟩ **2** fill with ⟨*stupefy*⟩ ⟨*horrify*⟩ **3** give the characteristics of; make similar to ⟨*countrify*⟩ ⟨*dandify*⟩ **4** *chiefly humorous or derog* engage in (a specified activity) ⟨*argufy*⟩ ⟨*speechify*⟩ [ME *-fien*, fr OF *-fier*, fr L *-ficare*, fr *-ficus* -fic]

**fylfot** /'fil,fot/ *n* SWASTIKA (cross-shaped symbol) [ME, device used to fill the lower part of a painted glass window, fr *fillen* to fill + *fot* foot

# G

**g, G** /jee/ *n, pl* **g's, gs, G's, Gs 1a** the 7th letter of the English alphabet **b** a graphic representation of or device for reproducing the letter *g* **c** a speech counterpart of printed or written *g* **2** the 5th note of a C-major musical scale **3** one designated *g*, esp as the 7th in order or class **4** a unit of force equal to the force exerted by gravity on a body at rest and used to indicate the force to which a body is subjected when accelerated ⟨*the pilot was subjected to a force of 3g in the tight turn*⟩ **5** something shaped like the letter G **6** *chiefly NAm slang* a thousand dollars [(5) gravity; (6) grand]

¹**gab** /gab/ *vi* **-bb-** *informal* to talk in a rapid or thoughtless manner; chatter [prob short for *gabble*] – **gabber** *n*

²**gab** *n, informal* talk; *esp* idle talk – see also GIFT **of the gab**

**gabardine** /ˌgabə'deen, '--,-/ *n* **1** GABERDINE 1 **2a** a firm durable fabric (e g of wool or rayon) woven (TWILLED) with diagonal ribs on the right side **b** *chiefly Br* a waterproof coat made of gabardine

**gabble** /'gabl/ *vi* **1** to talk incoherently or foolishly; jabber **2** to utter inarticulate or animal sounds ⟨*a skein of duck... gabbling softly to themselves* – Naomi Mitchison⟩ ∼ *vt* to utter rapidly or unintelligibly [prob imit] – **gabble** *n*, **gabbler** *n*

**gabbro** /'gabroh/ *n, pl* **gabbros** a granular IGNEOUS rock formed by the slow cooling and solidification of molten rock deep below the earth's surface and composed essentially of a calcium-containing FELDSPAR, a mineral containing iron and magnesium, and accessory minerals [It, prob modif of L *glaber* smooth, bare] – **gabbroic** *adj*, **gabbroid** *adj*

**gabby** /'gabi/ *adj, informal* talkative, garrulous [²*gab* + -*y*]

**gabelle** /ga'bel/ *n* a tax on salt levied in France before 1790 [ME, fr MF, fr OIt *gabella* tax, fr Ar *qabālah*]

**gaberdine** /'gabə,deen, ,--'-/ *n* **1** a coarse long coat or smock worn chiefly by Jews in medieval times **2** GABARDINE 2 [MF *gaverdine*]

**gabfest** /'gabfest/ *n, NAm informal* **1** an informal gathering for general talk ⟨*political* ∼s ⟩ **2** a prolonged conversation [²*gab* + *fest*]

**gabion** /'gaybi·ən, -byən/ *n* a hollow cylinder of wickerwork, iron, etc filled with earth and used esp as a support in mining or by an army in building temporary works to defend a position in the field [MF, fr OIt *gabbione*, lit., large cage, aug of *gabbia* cage, fr L *cavea* – more at CAGE]

**gable** /'gaybl/ *n* **1** the vertical triangular section of wall between two slopes of a roof **2** a triangular part used in making furniture or as decoration over a window or door [ME, fr MF, of Gmc origin; akin to ON *gafl* gable – more at CEPHALIC]

**gabled** /'gaybəld/ *adj* built with a gable

**gaby** /'gaybi/ *n, dial chiefly Eng* a person lacking common sense; a simpleton [perh of Scand origin; akin to ON *gapa* to gape – more at GAPE]

¹**gad** /gad/ *n* **1** a chisel or pointed iron or steel bar for loosening ore or rock **2** *chiefly dial* a rod, stick [ME, spike, fr ON *gaddr* spike, sting; akin to OE *geard* rod – more at YARD]

²**gad** *vi* **-dd-** to go or travel in an aimless or restless manner or in search of pleasure – usu + *about* ⟨*too busy* ∼ding *about to get any work done*⟩ [ME *gadden*, prob back-formation fr *gadling* companion, fr OE *gædeling*] – **gadder** *n*

³**gad** *interj, archaic* – used as a mild oath [euphemism for *God*]

**gadabout** /'gadə,bowt/ *n* a person who goes from place to place in search of pleasure – **gadabout** *adj*

**gadarene** /'gadə,reen/ *adj, often cap* headlong, sudden ⟨*a* ∼ *rush to the cities*⟩ [fr the demon-possessed *Gadarene* swine (Mt 8:28) that rushed into the sea and drowned]

**gadfly** /-,flie/ *n* **1** any of various flies (e g a horsefly, botfly, or warble fly) that bite or annoy livestock **2** a usu intentionally annoying person who stimulates or provokes others, esp by persistent irritating criticism [¹*gad*]

**gadget** /'gajit/ *n* a usu small and often novel mechanical or electronic device, esp on a piece of machinery; a contrivance *synonyms* see ¹TOOL [perh fr Fr *gâchette* catch of a lock, trigger, dim. of *gâche* staple, hook] – **gadgeteer** *n*, **gadgetry** *n*, **gadgety** *adj*

**gadoid** /'gaydoyd/ *adj* of, resembling, or related to the cods [NL *Gadus*, genus of fishes, fr Gk *gados*, a fish] – **gadoid** *n*

**gadolinite** /'gadəli,niet/ *n* a black or brown mineral, $Be_2FeY_2Si_2O_{10}$, that is a SILICATE of the metallic chemical elements iron, BERYLLIUM, and YTTRIUM [Ger *gadolinit*, fr Johann *Gadolin* †1852 Finn chemist]

**gadolinium** /ˌgadə'linyəm, -ni·əm/ *n* a magnetic metallic chemical element belonging to the group of RARE-EARTH ELEMENTS that occurs in combination with other rare earth metals in several minerals (e g gadolinite) [NL, fr J *Gadolin*]

**gadroon** /gə'droohn/ *n* **1** an elaborately notched or indented convex moulding in architecture **2** a short often oval convex or concave series of rounded grooves (FLUTES) used in decorating silverware, glassware, etc [Fr *godron* round plait, gadroon, fr MF *goderon*, perh dim. of OF *godet* drinking cup] – **gadrooning** *n*

**gadwall** /'gadwawl/ *n, pl* **gadwalls** *esp collectively* **gadwall** a greyish-brown duck (*Anas strepera*) of similar size to the mallard [origin unknown]

**gadzooks** /gad'zooks/ *interj, often cap, archaic* – used as a mild oath [perh alter. of *God's hooks* (ie the nails by which Christ was fixed to the cross)]

**gae** /gay/ *vb* **gane** /gayn/ *Scot* to go [ME (northern) *gan*, fr OE *gān*]

**Gael** /gayl, gahl/ *n* **1** a Scottish Highlander **2** a Celtic, esp Gaelic-speaking, inhabitant of Scotland or Ireland [ScGael *Gàidheal* & IrGael *Gaedheal*]

**Gaelic** /'gaylik; *Scots* 'gahlik; *Irish* 'galik/ *adj* **1** of the Gaels, esp the Celtic Highlanders of Scotland **2** of or being the Goidelic language of the Celts in Ireland, the Isle of Man, and the Scottish Highlands ⚠ Gallic – **Gaelic** *n*

**Gaelic coffee** *n* IRISH COFFEE (coffee containing Irish whiskey)

**Gaelic football** *n* a football game that is played in Ireland and parts of the USA between teams of 15 players using a round football and a low net slung between rugby posts and in which the players score by kicking, punching, or bouncing the ball over the bar or into the net

**Gaeltacht** /'gayl,tahkh/ *n* the part of Ireland where native speakers of Irish Gaelic live [IrGael *Gaedhealtacht*, fr *Gaedheal* Gael]

¹**gaff** /gaf/ *n* **1a** a barbed spear or spearhead for killing fish or turtles **b** a pole with a hook for holding or landing heavy fish **c** a metal spur fitted to the leg of a cock in the sport of cockfighting **d** a butcher's hook **2** a round wooden or metal bar (SPAR) to which the upper edge of a 4-sided FORE-AND-AFT mainsail is attached [Fr *gaffe*, fr Prov *gaf*, fr *gafar* to seize]

²**gaff** *vt* **1** to strike or secure (e g a fish) with a gaff **2** to fit (a fighting cock) with a gaff

³**gaff** *n, archaic Br slang* a cheap theatre or music hall [origin unknown]

⁴**gaff** – **blow the gaff** to let out a usu discreditable secret [*gaff* (talk, mouth), prob alter. of *gab*]

**gaffe** /gaf/ *n* an esp social blunder; FAUX PAS [Fr, lit., gaffe]

**gaffer** /'gafə/ *n* **1** the chief lighting electrician in a film or television studio **2** *Br informal* a foreman or overseer, esp in industry; the boss **3** *dial* an old man – compare GAMMER [prob alter. of *godfather*]

¹**gag** /gag/ *vb* **-gg-** *vt* **1a** to put a gag in the mouth of (to prevent speech) **b** to hold open with a gag **2** to cause to retch **3** to obstruct, choke ⟨∼ *a valve*⟩ **4** *chiefly journalistic* to prevent from free speech or expression ∼ *vi* **1** to heave, retch **2** to be unable to endure something; balk – usu + *at* **3** to tell jokes [ME *gaggen* to strangle, of imit origin]

**²gag** *n* **1** something thrust into the mouth to keep it open or prevent speech or outcry **2** *politics* the closing of a debate in an assembly having the power to make laws, esp by calling for a vote **3** JOKE 1a **4** a hoax, trick **5** *chiefly journalistic* a check to free speech

**gaga** /'gah,gah/ *adj, informal* **1a** senile **b** slightly mad **2** marked by demonstrative or foolish enthusiasm; infatuated – often + *about* [Fr, fr *gaga* fool, of imit origin]

**¹gage** /gayj/ *n* **1** a token of defiance; *specif* a glove, cap, etc thrown on the ground in former times as a challenge to a fight **2** something deposited as a pledge of performance [ME, fr MF, of Gmc origin; akin to OHG *wetti* pledge, Goth *wadi* (cf WAGE)]

**²gage** *n* **1** *also* **gauge** relative position of a ship with reference to another ship and the wind **2** *NAm* a gauge [alter. of *gauge*]

**³gage** *vt, NAm* to gauge

**⁴gage** *n* a greengage

**gaggle** /'gagl/ *n* **1** a flock; *esp* a flock of geese when not in flight – compare SKEIN **2** *taking sing or pl vb, informal* a typically noisy or talkative group or cluster [ME *gagyll*, fr *gagelen* to cackle, prob of imit origin]

**gahnite** /'gahniet/ *n* a usu dark green mineral, $ZnAl_2O_4$, consisting of an OXIDE of zinc and aluminium [Ger *gahnit*, fr J G *Gahn* †1818 Sw chemist]

**gaiety** /'gayəti/ *n* **1** merrymaking; *also* festive activity **2** merry and lively quality, spirits, manner, or appearance [Fr *gaieté*, fr OF, fr *gai* gay]

**gaillardia** /gay'lahdiə/ *n* any of a genus (*Gaillardia*) of chiefly American plants of the daisy family often cultivated for their showy daisylike flower heads having a purple centre surrounded by yellow, reddish-orange, or white strap-shaped RAY FLOWERS [NL, genus name, fr *Gaillard* de Marentonneau, 18th-c Fr botanist]

**gaily** /'gayli/ *adv* merrily, brightly

**¹gain** /gayn/ *n* **1** resources or advantage acquired or increased; a profit ⟨*made substantial* ∼s *last year*⟩ **2** the obtaining of profit or possessions **3a** an increase in amount, magnitude, or degree ⟨*a* ∼ *in efficiency*⟩ **b** the ratio of some output parameter (e g voltage, current, or power) of an electronic device (e g an aerial or amplifier) to the corresponding input parameter; *esp* the ratio of the power of an output signal from an audio amplifier to the power of the input signal [ME *gayne*, fr MF *gaigne, gain,* fr OF *gaaigne, gaaing,* fr *gaaignier* to till, earn, gain, of Gmc origin; akin to OHG *weidanōn* to hunt for food; akin to L *vis* power – more at VIM]

**²gain** *vt* **1a(1)** to get possession of, usu by constant and steady application, merit, or craft ⟨*he stood to* ∼ *a fortune*⟩ **a(2)** to increase a lead over or catch up a rival by (esp time or distance) ⟨∼ed *35 yards on the third lap*⟩ **b** to win in competition or conflict ⟨*the attackers* ∼ed *the day*⟩ **c** to get by a natural development or process ⟨∼ *strength*⟩ **d** to make, acquire ⟨∼ *a friend*⟩ **e** to arrive at ⟨∼ed *the river that night*⟩ **2** to win to one's side; persuade ⟨∼ *adherents to a cause*⟩ **3** to cause to be obtained or given; attract ⟨∼ *attention*⟩ **4** to increase in ⟨∼ *momentum*⟩ **5** *of a timepiece* to run fast by the amount of ⟨*the clock* ∼s *a minute a day*⟩ ∼ *vi* **1** to get advantage; profit ⟨*hoped to* ∼ *from his crime*⟩ **2** to increase, specif in weight **3** *of a timepiece* to run fast – see also **gain** GROUND *synonyms* see ¹REACH, ¹WIN

**³gain** *n, building* **1** a flat shoulderlike surface that meets another at an angle above a projecting part (TENON) that is inserted into a slot (MORTISE) in making a joint in a piece of wood **2** a notch or mortise for insertion of a girder or joist [origin unknown]

**gainer** /'gaynə/ *n* one who or that which gains ⟨*you will be the* ∼ *by it*⟩

**gainful** /-f(ə)l/ *adj* profitable ⟨∼ *employment*⟩ – **gainfully** *adv*, **gainfulness** *n*

**gainly** /'gaynli/ *adj* graceful and generally pleasing [E dial. *gain* kindly, handy, fr ME *gayn*, fr OE *gēn*, fr ON *gegn* direct, favourable]

**gainsay** /gayn'say/ *vt* **gainsays** /-'sez/; **gainsaid** /-'sed/ **1** to deny, dispute ⟨*couldn't* ∼ *the statistics*⟩ **2** to stand in opposition to, esp by disputing the truth of something put forward; oppose, resist [ME *gainsayen*, fr *gain-* against (fr OE *gēan-*) + *sayen* to say – more at AGAIN] – **gainsayer** *n*

**¹gait** /gayt/ *n* **1** a manner of walking or moving on foot **2** a sequence of foot movements (e g a walk, trot, or canter) by which a horse moves forwards [ME *gait, gate* way – more at ³GATE]

**²gait** *vt* to train (a horse) to use a particular gait or set of gaits

**³gait** *n* **1** the distance between two adjoining carriages of a

lace-making frame **2** *Br* a full repeat of a pattern in weaving a repetitive design [prob alter. of ¹*gate*]

**-gaited** /'gaytid/ *comb form* (→ *adj*) having (such) a gait ⟨*slow-gaited*⟩

**gaiter** /'gaytə/ *n* **1a** a cloth or leather leg covering that reaches from the instep of the foot to ankle, mid-calf, or knee **b** a military ankle covering of stout cloth into which the bottom of the trouser leg is tucked **2** an overshoe with fabric upper [Fr *guêtre*, fr MF *guestre, guiestre*, prob of Gmc origin]

**¹gal** /gal/ *n, informal* a girl – used in writing to represent esp a US, Cockney, or upper-class pronunciation [by alter.]

**²gal** *n* a unit of acceleration equivalent to 1 centimetre per second per second [*Galileo* Galilei †1642 It astronomer & physicist]

**¹gala** /'gahlə, 'gaylə/ *n* **1** a festive gathering (that constitutes or marks a special occasion) **2** *Br* a gala sports meeting ⟨*a swimming* ∼⟩ [It, fr MF *gale* merrymaking, festivity, pleasure – more at GALLANT]

**²gala** *adj* marking or being a special occasion ⟨*a* ∼ *performance at the ballet*⟩

**galact-** /gəlakt-/, **galacto-** *comb form* **1** milk ⟨*galactopoiesis*⟩ **2** containing galactose in the molecular structure ⟨*galacturonic acid*⟩ [L *galact-*, fr Gk *galakt-, galakto-,* fr *galakt-, gala*]

**galactic** /gə'laktik/ *adj* of or within a galaxy, esp the MILKY WAY galaxy to which the sun and SOLAR SYSTEM belong

**galactic noise** *n* COSMIC NOISE (radio interference caused by radiation from the MILKY WAY galaxy)

**galactopoiesis** /gə,laktohpoy'eesis/ *n, physiology* formation and secretion of milk [NL] – **galactopoietic** *adj or n*

**galactosaemia** /gə,laktoh'seemiə/ *n, medicine* an inherited metabolic disorder in which galactose accumulates in the blood owing to the absence of an ENZYME that promotes its conversion to glucose and which, if untreated, may result in death or in liver damage, stunted growth, and often mental retardation [NL]

**galactosamine** /gə,lak'tohsə,meen/ *n* a chemical compound, $HOCH_2(CHOH)_3CH(NH_2)CHO$, derived from galactose by the addition of an AMINO group, that occurs as a constituent of cartilage

**galactose** /gə'laktohz, -tohs/ *n* a sugar, $HOCH_2(CHOH)_4CHO$, occurring in LACTOSE (sugar present in milk), that is less soluble and less sweet than glucose [Fr, fr *galact-*]

**galactosidase** /gə,lak'tohsidayz, -days/ *n* an ENZYME (e g lactase) that promotes the breakdown of a galactoside

**galactoside** /gə'laktəsied/ *n* a GLYCOSIDE (chemical compound derived from a sugar) that yields galactose on breakdown

**galacturonic acid** /gə,laktyoo'ronik/ *n* a chemical compound, $C_6H_{10}O_7$, derived from galactose by the addition of an acid group, that occurs esp as a component of substances (PECTIC SUBSTANCES) present in plant cell walls [ISV *galact-* + *-uronic*]

**galago** /gə'laygoh/ *n, pl* **galagos** BUSH BABY [NL, genus name, perh fr Wolof *golokh* monkey]

**galah** /gə'lah/ *n* **1** an Australian cockatoo (*Kakatoë roseicapilla*) with a rose-coloured breast and a grey back, that is a destructive pest in wheat growing areas and is often kept as a cage bird **2** *Austr* a fool, simpleton [native name in Australia]

**galantine** /'galənteen/ *n* a cold dish of boned and usu stuffed cooked meat or poultry glazed with aspic [Fr, fr OF *galentine, galatine* fish sauce, fr ML *galatina*, prob fr L *gelatus*, pp of *gelare* to freeze, congeal]

**Galatians** /gə'laysh(i)ənz/ *n taking sing vb* – see BIBLE table [*Galatia*, ancient country in Asia Minor]

**galavant** /'galivant/ *vi* to gallivant

**galaxy** /'galəksi/ *n* **1a** *often cap* MILKY WAY **b** any of many independent systems composed chiefly of stars, dust, and gases separated from each other by vast distances **2** an assembly of brilliant or notable people or things [ME *galaxie, galaxias*, fr LL *galaxias*, fr Gk, fr *galakt-, gala* milk; akin to L *lac* milk]

**galbanum** /'galbənəm/ *n* a yellowish to green or brown aromatic GUM RESIN obtained from any of several Asian plants (e g *Ferula galbaniflua*) and formerly used for medicinal purposes and in incense [ME, fr L, fr Gk *chalbanē*, fr Heb *ḥelbēnāh*]

**gale** /gayl/ *n* **1** a strong wind having a speed from 32 to 63 miles per hour (about 50 to 102 kilometres per hour); *esp* FRESH GALE (wind speed from 39 to 46 miles per hour) **2** a noisy outburst ⟨*his remark provoked* ∼s *of laughter*⟩ *synonyms* see ¹WIND [origin unknown]

**galea** /'gayli·ə/ *n* an anatomical part suggesting a helmet: e g **a** a helmet-shaped petal or group of petals; *esp* the upper lip of

# gal

the flower of some LABIATE plants (e g a snapdragon) **b** the outer or side lobe of the MAXILLA (mouthpart) in certain insects (e g the cockroach and honeybee) [NL, fr L, helmet] – **galeate** also **galeated** adj, **galeiform** adj

**galena** /gə'leenə/ n a bluish-grey mineral with a metallic lustre, that consists of lead sulphide, PbS, and is the commonest ore of lead [L, lead ore]

**Galenic** /gə'lenik/, **Galenical** /-kl/ adj of or being the medical methods or principles of Galen [Galen †ab 200 Gk physician] – **Galenism** n

**galenical** /gə'lenikl/ n a medicine prepared by extracting one or more active constituents of a plant

**galère** /ga'leə/ n COTERIE (exclusive group of people) [Fr, lit., galley, fr MF, fr Catal galera, fr MGk galea]

**galette** /gə'let/ n 1 a flat pastry cake traditionally baked for Twelfth Night 2 a thin fried cake of sliced or mashed potatoes [Fr, fr OF galete, fr galet pebble]

**Galibi** /gə'leebi/ n, pl **Galibis**, esp collectively **Galibi** a member, or the language, of a Carib people of French Guiana

**Galilean** /,galə'layən, -'lee·ən/ adj of or developed by Galileo Galilei, the founder of experimental physics and astronomy

**galilee** /'galə,lee/ n a chapel or porch at the entrance of some medieval churches in England [AF, fr ML galilaea, prob fr L Galilaea Galilee, region in Palestine]

**galimatias** /,gali'mayshiəs, -'matiəs/ n taking sing vb a confused and often pretentious mixture, esp of words; nonsense, gobbledygook [Fr]

**galingale** /'galing,gayl/ n a European sedge (Cyperus longus) with small spikes of pale reddish-brown flowers and aromatic roots that are used in cooking; broadly any of various related plants [ME, a kind of ginger, fr MF galingal, fr Ar khalanjān]

**galipot** /'gali,pot/ n a crude turpentine resin exuded from a S European pine tree (Pinus pinaster) [Fr]

**¹gall** /gawl/ n **1a** BILE 1a (liquid aiding fat digestion) **b** something bitter to endure **c** bitterness, rancour **2** informal brazen and insolent audacity ⟨what ~ that boy has; to say such a thing about his parents!⟩ [ME, fr OE gealla; akin to Gk cholē, cholos gall, wrath, OE geolu yellow – more at YELLOW]

**²gall** n **1** a skin sore caused by rubbing **2** a cause or state of exasperation [ME galle, fr OE gealla, fr L galla ⁴gall]

**³gall** vt **1a** to wear away by rubbing; chafe **b** to cause feelings of mortification and irritation in; vex acutely ⟨sarcasm ~ s her⟩ **2** to harass ⟨~ed by enemy fire⟩ ~ vi to become sore or worn by rubbing – **gallingly** adv

**⁴gall** n a diseased swelling of plant tissue produced by infection with fungi, insect parasites, etc [ME galle, fr MF, fr L galla]

**Galla** /'galə/ n, pl **Gallas**, esp collectively **Galla** a member or the language of any of several groups of Cushitic-speaking peoples of Kenya and S Ethiopia

**gallamine** /'galəmeen/, **gallamine triethiodide** /,trie,eth'ie·ədied/ n a synthetic drug, C₆H₃[OCH₂N(C₂H₅)₃]₃I₃, used to produce muscle relaxation, esp during anaesthesia [pyrogallol + amine + triethyl + iodide]

**¹gallant** /'galənt, gə'lahnt, gə'lant/ n **1** a fashionable young man; esp one who is particularly attentive to women **2** a woman's suitor or illicit lover

**²gallant** /sense 1 'galənt; sense 2 'galənt, gə'lahnt, gə'lant/ adj **1a** splendid, stately ⟨a ~ ship⟩ **b** spirited, courageous ⟨~ efforts against the enemy⟩ **c** nobly chivalrous and brave **2** courteously and elaborately attentive, esp to ladies **3** archaic showy in dress **synonyms** see ¹BRAVE [ME galaunt, fr MF galant, fr prp of galer to have a good time, fr gale pleasure, of Gmc origin; akin to OE wela weal – more at WEAL] – **gallantly** adv

**gallantry** /'galəntri/ n **1a** an act of marked courtesy **b** courteous attention to a lady **2** spirited and conspicuous bravery

**gallate** /'galayt, 'gawlayt/ n any of various chemical compounds (SALTS or ESTERS) formed by combination between GALLIC ACID and a metal atom, an alcohol, or another chemical group

**gall bladder** n a muscular membranous sac attached to the liver in which bile secreted by the liver is stored

**galleass** /'gali,as/ n a large fast warship equipped with both oars and sails and used esp in the 16th and 17th centuries [MF galeasse, fr OIt galeazza, deriv of MGk galea galley]

**galleon** /'gali·ən/ n a heavy 2- or 3-masted square-rigged sailing ship of the 15th to the early 18th centuries which was used, esp by the Spanish, in sea battles and for carrying cargo [OSp galeón, fr MF galion, fr OF galie galley]

**gallery** /'galəri/ n **1a** a covered passage for walking; a colonnade **b** a main corridor with windows running along one side in an old English country house **2a** an outdoor balcony **b** a railed platform around the upper part of an engine to facilitate oiling or inspection **3a** a long and narrow passage, room, or corridor ⟨a shooting ~⟩ **b** a horizontal subterranean passage in a cave or military mining system; also a horizontal passageway in a mine **c(1)** an underground passage made by a mole or ant **c(2)** a passage bored into the wood or under the bark of a tree by an insect (e g a beetle) **4a** a room or building devoted to the exhibition of works of art ⟨spent the afternoon in a ~ of Dutch seascapes⟩ **b** an institution or business exhibiting or dealing in works of art ⟨the National Gallery⟩ **c** a collection worthy of being put on display as if in an art gallery ⟨the novel contained a rich ~ of characters⟩ **5a** a structure, esp the gods in a theatre, projecting from one or more interior walls of an auditorium to accommodate additional people **b** taking sing or pl vb the members of the audience seated in a theatre gallery **6** taking sing or pl vb **6a** the undiscriminating general public ⟨a politician who always plays to the ~⟩ **b** the spectators at a sports match, esp of tennis or golf **7** a photographer's studio **8** S & Mid US a porch, veranda [ME galerie, fr ML galeria, prob alter. of galilea, galilaea galilee] – **galleried** adj – **play to the gallery** to act in a way calculated to win popular support, esp without regard to justice, honesty, etc

**gallery forest** n a forest growing along a river, stream, etc in a region otherwise devoid of trees

**galley** /'gali/ n **1** a large low ship propelled by sails and oars and used esp in the Mediterranean in ancient and medieval times in sea battles and for carrying cargo **2** a kitchen on a ship or aircraft **3a** an oblong tray with upright sides to hold type that has been set **b galley, galley proof** a proof in the form of a long sheet (taken from type on a galley) [ME galeie, fr OF galie, deriv of MGk galea]

**galley slave** n **1** a slave or criminal acting as an oarsman on a galley ship **2** one who has to do menial work; a drudge

**galley-'west** adv, chiefly NAm informal into destruction or confusion ⟨was knocked ~⟩ [prob alter. of E dial. collywest, collyweston badly askew, prob fr Collyweston, village in Northamptonshire]

**galliard** /'galyəd/ n a lively 16th-century dance often following and contrasting with a PAVANE (stately court dance); also music for this dance, that has three beats to the bar [MF gaillarde, fem of gaillard lively, valiant, fr OF, prob of Celt origin; akin to OIr gal bravery]

**Gallic** /'galik/ adj of (the people of) Gaul or France △ Gaelic [L Gallicus, fr Gallia Gaul, ancient country in W Europe]

**gallic acid** /'galik/ n an acid, C₆H₂(OH)₃COOH, widely found in plants and used esp in dyes and writing ink and as a photographic developer [Fr gallique, fr galle ⁴gall]

**Gallican** /'galikən/ adj **1** Gallic **2** often not cap of Gallicanism – **Gallican** n

**Gallicanism** /'galikə,niz(ə)m/ n a movement originating in France and advocating administrative independence from control by the Pope for the Roman Catholic church in each nation

**gallicism** /'galisiz(ə)m/ n, often cap **1** a characteristic feature (e g a word or phrase) of French occurring in another language **2** a philosophy, custom, action, etc that is characteristic of the French people

**gallic·ize, -ise** /'galisiez/ vb (to cause) to conform to French custom, philosophy, language, etc – **gallicization** n

**galligaskins** /,gali'gaskinz/ n pl loose wide hose or breeches worn in the 16th and 17th centuries [prob modif of MF garguesques, fr OSp gregüescos, fr griego Greek, fr L Graecus]

**gallimaufry** /,gali'mawfri/ n, chiefly humorous a mixture, jumble [MF galimafree hash]

**gallinaceous** /,gali'nayshəs/ adj of or belonging to an order (Galliformes) of birds, including the pheasants, turkeys, grouse, and the common DOMESTIC FOWL, that have heavy bodies and live mainly on the ground [L gallinaceus of domestic fowl, fr gallina hen, fr gallus cock]

**galling** /'gawling/ adj markedly irritating or vexing; deeply mortifying – **gallingly** adv

**gallinule** /'gali,nyoohl/ n any of several aquatic birds of the rail family with long thin toes and a shieldlike prominence at the top of the beak on the forehead [NL Gallinula, genus of birds, fr L, pullet, dim. of gallina]

**galliot** /'galiət/ n **1** a small swift galley ship formerly used in the Mediterranean **2** a long narrow Dutch merchant sailing ship that can be floated in shallow water [ME *galiote,* fr MF, fr ML *galeota,* dim. of *galea* galley, fr MGk]

**gallipot** /'gali,pot/ *n* 1 a small usu ceramic vessel formerly used to hold medicines (e g ointments) 2 *archaic* a pharmacist [ME *galy pott,* prob fr *galy, galeie* galley + *pott* pot; fr its being imported from the Mediterranean in galleys]

**gallium** /'gali-əm/ *n* a bluish-white metallic chemical element that is hard and brittle at low temperatures but melts just above room temperature and expands on freezing [NL, fr L *gallus* cock (intended as trans of Paul *Lecoq* de Boisbaudran † 1912 Fr chemist)]

**gallivant** /'galivant/ *vi* to travel or roam about for pleasure; gad about [perh alter. of ³*gallant* (to act like a gallant, flirt)]

**gall midge** *n* any of numerous minute flies (family Cecidomyiidae) most of which produce larvae that cause the formation of GALLS (abnormal tissue swellings) in plants. Members of this family of midges can be serious pests of many plants including chrysanthemums, roses, wheat, and rice.

**gall mite** *n* any of various minute 4-legged mites (family Eriophyidae) that form GALLS (abnormal tissue swellings) on plants

**gallon** /'galən/ *n* either of two units of liquid capacity equal to 8 pints: **a** IMPERIAL GALLON (standard British unit) **b** WINE GALLON (old English unit used for wine) [ME *galon,* a liquid measure, fr ONF, fr ML *galeta* pail, a liquid measure]

**gallonage** /'galənij/ *n* amount in gallons

**galloon** /gə'loohn/ *n* a narrow lace, embroidery, braid, etc trimming for dresses [Fr *galon,* fr MF, fr OF *galonner* to adorn with braid] – **gallooned** *adj*

¹**gallop** /'galəp/ *n* 1 a fast bounding gait of a 4-legged animal; *specif* the fastest natural 4-beat gait of the horse – compare ²CANTER, RUN, TROT, WALK 2 a ride or run at a gallop 3 a rapid or hasty progression ⟨*rushed through the reports at a ~* ⟩ 4 **gallops** *pl,* **gallop** *chiefly Br* a stretch of grass over which racehorses are exercised [MF *galop*]

²**gallop** *vi* 1 to progress or ride at a gallop 2 to run fast ~ *vt* 1 to cause to gallop 2 to transport at a gallop – **galloper** *n*

**Gallophile** /'galə,fiel/ *adj* FRANCOPHILE (markedly friendly to France) [L *Gallus* Gaul + E *-phile*] – **Gallophile** *n*

**galloping** /'galəping/ *adj* progressing or increasing rapidly; accelerating ⟨*~ inflation*⟩

**Galloway** /'galəway/ *n* (any of) a breed of hardy medium-sized hornless chiefly black BEEF CATTLE that are native to SW Scotland and that produce top quality meat [*Galloway,* district in SW Scotland]

**gallowglass, galloglass** /'galoh,glahs/ *n* 1 any of a group of soldiers (e g mercenaries) engaged by an Irish chieftain for military service 2 an armed Irish FOOT SOLDIER maintained by a chieftain [IrGael *gallōglach,* fr *gall* foreigner + *ōglach* soldier]

**gallows** /'galohz/ *n, pl* **gallows** *also* **gallowses** **1a** gallows *taking sing or pl vb,* **gallows tree** a frame usu of two upright posts and a crossbeam, for hanging criminals **b** *taking sing vb the* punishment of hanging ⟨*bring back the ~*⟩ 2 *taking sing or pl vb* a structure consisting of an upright frame with a crosspiece (e g a frame on a sailing ship used as a prop for spare poles, that support the rigging) [ME *galwes,* pl of *galwe,* fr OE *gealga;* akin to OHG *galgo* gallows, Arm *jatk* twig]

**gallows bird** *n, archaic informal* a person who deserves hanging

**gallows humour** *n* grim humour that makes fun of a very serious or terrifying situation

**gallstone** /'gawl,stohn/ *n* a rounded solid mass of cholesterol, calcium salts, etc formed in the GALL BLADDER or in a duct carrying bile from the liver or gall bladder to the intestine

**Gallup poll** /'galəp/ *n* a survey of public opinion on a specific issue conducted by questioning a representative sample of the population and frequently used as a means of forecasting something (e g election results) [George H *Gallup* b1901 US public opinion statistician]

**gall wasp** *n* any of several small typically dark-coloured insects (family Cynipidae) that deposit their eggs in plants (e g oak trees and roses), the resulting larvae inducing the formation of GALLS (abnormal swellings of plant tissue) in which the larvae develop and on which they feed

**galoot** /gə'looht/ *n, NAm slang* a fellow; *esp* one who is strange or foolish [origin unknown]

**galop** /'galəp/ *n* a lively dance that was popular in the 19th century; *also* music for this dance, that has two beats to the bar [Fr, lit., gallop]

**galore** /gə'law/ *adj* abundant, plentiful – used after a noun ⟨*bargains ~*⟩ [IrGael *go leor* enough]

**galosh** /gə'losh/ *n* a rubber overshoe [ME *galoche* clog, patten, fr MF] – **galoshed** *adj*

**galumph** /gə'lum(p)f/ *vi, informal* to move with a clumsy heavy tread [prob fr *gallop* + tri*umph*ant; orig formed by Lewis Carroll (C L Dodgson) †1898 E writer]

**galvanic** /gal'vanik/ *adj* 1 of or causing the production of a DIRECT CURRENT of electricity by chemical action; VOLTAIC ⟨*a ~ cell*⟩ **2a** having an electric effect; stimulating vigorous activity or vitality ⟨*a ~ personality*⟩ **b** produced as if by an electric shock; jerky, nervous ⟨*a ~ response*⟩ – **galvanically** *adv*

**galvanic couple, couple** *n* a pair of dissimilar substances (e g metals) capable of acting together as an electric source when brought in contact with an ELECTROLYTE (electrically conducting solution)

**galvanic skin response** *n* a change in the electrical potential of the skin that can be detected by a sensitive galvanometer and is brought about by arousal, emotion, etc

**galvanism** /'galvən,iz(ə)m/ *n* 1 a DIRECT CURRENT of electricity produced by chemical action 2 the therapeutic use of a direct electric current (e g in the removal of birthmarks) 3 vital or forceful activity [Fr or It; Fr *galvanisme,* fr It *galvanismo,* fr Luigi *Galvani* †1798 It physician & physicist who first described it]

**galvan·ize, -ise** /'galvaniez/ *vt* **1a** *physiology* to subject to the action of an electric current, esp for the purpose of stimulating physiological activity ⟨*~ a muscle*⟩ **b** to stimulate, excite, or rouse as if by an electric shock ⟨*the candidate ~d his supporters into action*⟩ 2 to coat (iron or steel) with zinc as a protection from rust – **galvanizer** *n,* **galvanization** *n*

**galvano-** *comb form* galvanic current ⟨*galvanometer*⟩ [*galvanic*]

**galvanometer** /,galvə'nomitə/ *n* an instrument for detecting or measuring an electric current by movements of a MAGNETIC NEEDLE in a MAGNETIC FIELD set up by the current or of a coil carrying the current in a magnetic field – **galvanometric** *adj*

**galvanoscope** /'galvənə,skohp/ *n* an instrument for detecting the presence and direction of an electric current by the deflection of a MAGNETIC NEEDLE that moves to align itself with the forces acting in the MAGNETIC FIELD set up by the current

**galyak** /'galyak, -'-/ *n* a short-haired flat or slightly wavy fur derived from the pelt of a stillborn lamb or kid [native name in the republic of Uzbekistan in the USSR]

¹**gam** /gam/ *n, slang* a leg [prob fr Fr dial. *gambe,* fr ONF, fr LL *gamba*]

²**gam** *n* a school of whales [orig sense, a social meeting of whaling ships at sea; perh short for obs *gammon* talk]

**gam-** /gam-/, **gamo-** *comb form* 1 united; joined ⟨*gamosepalous*⟩ 2 sexual ⟨*gamic*⟩ ⟨*gamogenesis*⟩ [NL, fr Gk, marriage, fr *gamos* – more at BIGAMY]

**gamba** /'gambə/ *n* VIOLA DA GAMBA (bass member of the viol family of musical instruments)

**gambier** *also* **gambir** /'gambiə/ *n* a yellowish substance obtained from a Malayan woody climbing plant (*Uncaria gambier*) of the madder family and used as an astringent and in tanning and dyeing [Malay *gambir*]

**gambit** /'gambit/ *n* 1 a planned series of moves at the beginning of a game of chess in which a player risks one or more minor pieces to gain an advantage in position **2a(1)** a remark or comment intended to start a conversation or make a revealing point in support of a point of view **a(2)** a topic of conversation ⟨*a useful conversational ~ is that of: to smoke or not to smoke*⟩ **b** a calculated move; a stratagem [It *gambetto,* lit., act of tripping someone, fr *gamba* leg, fr LL *gamba, camba,* modif of Gk *kampē* bend – more at CAMP]

¹**gamble** /'gambl/ *vi* **1a** to play a game (of chance) for money or property **b** to bet on or risk something on an uncertain outcome 2 to take on a business risk with the expectation of gain; speculate ~ *vt* 1 to risk by gambling; wager 2 to venture, hazard △ gambol [prob back-formation fr *gambler,* prob alter. of obs *gamner,* fr obs *gamen* to play] – **gambler** *n*

²**gamble** *n* 1 the playing of a game (of chance) for stakes 2 (something involving) an element of risk

**gamboge** /gam'bohj, -'boozh/ *n* 1 an orange to brown GUM RESIN obtained from some SE Asian trees (genus *Garcinia* of the family Guttiferae) and used esp as a yellow pigment for paints 2 a strong yellow [NL *gambogium,* alter. of *cambugium,* irreg fr *Cambodia,* country in SE Asia]

¹**gambol** /'gambl/ *n* a skipping or leaping about in play [modif

of MF *gambade* spring of a horse, gambol, prob fr OProv *camba* leg, fr LL]

²**gambol** *vi* -ll- (*NAm* -l-, -ll-) to skip about in play; frisk ⟨*lambs* ~*ling in the fields*⟩ △ gamble

**gambrel** /'gambrəl/ *n* **1** the hock of an animal **2** gambrel, gambrel roof a roof in which the ends and sides slope but in which the two ends each terminate at the ridge in a small vertical triangular gable **3** *NAm* gambrel, gambrel roof a roof in which the two sides have a double slope with the lower slope steeper than the upper one [ONF *gamberel* crooked stick used to hang animal carcasses, fr *gambe* leg, fr LL *gamba*]

**gambusia** /gam'byoohzhə/ *n* any of a genus (*Gambusia*) of small fish (e g killifish) introduced in warm fresh waters as valuable predators of mosquito larvae [NL, genus name, modif of AmerSp *gambusino* gambusia]

¹**game** /gaym/ *n* **1a**(1) activity engaged in for diversion or amusement; play ⟨*children happy at their* ~*s*⟩ **a**(2) the equipment for a particular esp indoor game ⟨*what* ~*s will you buy the children?*⟩ **b** often derisive or mocking jesting; fun, sport ⟨*make* ~ *of a nervous player*⟩ **2a** a procedure or strategy of manoeuvres devised for attaining some end; a tactic ⟨*playing a waiting* ~⟩ **b**(1) an illegal or fraudulent scheme; a racket ⟨*he's in the blackmail* ~⟩ **b**(2) a specified type of activity or mode of behaviour ⟨*the dating* ~⟩ **3a**(1) (the quality of play in) a physical or mental competition conducted according to rules with the participants or parties in direct opposition to each other; *also* MATCH 3a **a**(2) a division of a larger contest **a**(3) the number of points necessary to win a game **a**(4) the set of rules governing a game **b** *pl* organized sports, esp athletics ⟨*highland* ~*s*⟩ ⟨*Olympic* ~*s*⟩ **c** a situation that involves contest, rivalry, or struggle ⟨*moved into the microelectronics field early in the* ~⟩ **4a**(1) animals under pursuit or taken in hunting; *esp* wild animals, birds, and fish hunted for sport or food **a**(2) the edible flesh of game animals (e g deer and pheasant) **b** an object of ridicule or attack – often in *fair game* **5** *chiefly Br slang* prostitution – often in *on the game* **6** *informal* an occupation, profession, or other field of financial gain – **play the game** to be fair; act according to a code or set of standards – **the game is up** *informal* the crime, plot, trick, etc has been discovered or exposed – see also GIVE **the game away** [ME, fr OE *gamen*; akin to OHG *gaman* amusement]

²**game** *vi* GAMBLE 1 ~ *vt, archaic* to lose or squander by gambling

³**game** *adj* **1a** having a resolute unyielding spirit ⟨~ *to the end*⟩ **b** ready to take risks or try something new ⟨*I'm* ~ *for anything*⟩ **2** of game animals ⟨~ *laws*⟩ – **gamely** *adv*, **gameness** *n*

⁴**game** *adj* injured, crippled, or lame ⟨*a* ~ *leg*⟩ [perh fr ³*game*]

**gamebag** /'gaym,bag/ *n* a bag for holding game animals that have been killed

**gamebook** /-,book/ *n* a book for recording details of game animals that have been killed

**gamecock** /'gaym,kok/ *n* a male game fowl

**game fish** *n* a fish of a family (Salmonidae) that includes salmons, trouts, and whitefishes; *broadly* any fish sought by anglers for sport – compare COARSE FISH

**game fishing** *n* the sport of angling for game fish

**game fowl** *n* a domestic fowl of a strain developed for cock-fighting

**gamekeeper** /-,keepə/ *n* one who has charge of the breeding and protection of game animals or birds on a private preserve

**gamelan** /'gami,lan/ *n* **1** a Javanese instrument like the xylophone **2** a flute, string, and percussion orchestra of SE Asia [Jav]

**game of chance** *n* a game (e g of dice) in which chance rather than skill determines the outcome

**game of skill** *n* a game (e g chess) in which skill rather than chance determines the outcome

**game point** *n* a situation in tennis, badminton, etc in which one player will win the game by winning the next point; *also* the point won

**gamesmanship** /'gaymzmən,ship/ *n* the art or practice of winning games by means other than superior skill without actually violating the rules

**gamesome** /'gayms(ə)m/ *adj* merry, frolicsome – **gamesomely** *adv*, **gamesomeness** *n*

**gamester** /'gaymstə/ *n* a person who plays games; *esp* a gambler

**gamet-, gameto-** *comb form* gamete ⟨gameto*phore*⟩ [NL, fr *gameta*]

**gametangium** /,gami'tanji·əm/ *n, pl* **gametangia** /-jiə/ a (plant) cell or organ in which gametes are produced [NL, fr *gamet-* + Gk *angeion* vessel – more at ANGI-]

**gamete** /'gameet, gə'meet/ *n, genetics* a mature male or female reproductive cell (e g an egg or sperm cell) that possesses a single (HAPLOID) set of CHROMOSOMES (strands of gene-carrying material) and is capable of joining with a gamete of the other sex to form a fertilized cell (ZYGOTE) that contains a double (DIPLOID) set of chromosomes and from which a new organism develops [NL *gameta*, fr Gk *gametēs* husband, fr *gamein* to marry, fr *gamos* marriage – more at BIGAMY] – **gametic** *adj*, **gametically** *adv*

**game theory, games theory** *n* THEORY OF GAMES (strategic analysis of business, military, etc conflict)

**gametocyte** /gə'meetoh,siet/ *n* a cell that divides to produce gametes [ISV]

**gametogenesis** /,gamitoh'jenəsis/ *n* the production of gametes [NL] – **gametogenic, gametogenous** *adj*, **gametogeny** *n*

**gametophore** /gə'meetoh,faw/ *n* a modified branch in a plant (e g some liverworts) bearing gametangia – **gametophoric** *adj*

**gametophyte** /gə'meetoh,fiet/ *n* (a member of) the generation of a plant (e g a moss, fern, conifer, or flowering plant) exhibiting ALTERNATION OF GENERATIONS, that develops from asexual spores, bears sex organs that produce the gametes from which the SPOROPHYTE generation (generation that produces asexual spores) will develop, and that in many plants is reduced to microscopic proportions [ISV] – **gametophytic** *adj*

**gamey** /'gaymi/ *adj* gamy

**gamic** /'gamik/ *adj* requiring fertilization or the fusion of male and female gametes; sexual ⟨~ *reproduction*⟩

**gamin** /'gamin (*Fr* gamɛ̃)/ *n* a boy who hangs about in the streets; an urchin [Fr]

**gamine** /'gameen (*Fr* gamɛ̃n)/ *n* **1** a female gamin **2** a girl of elfin impish appeal [Fr, fem of *gamin*] – **gamine** *adj*

**gaming** /'gayming/ *n* **1** the practice of gambling **2** the playing of games that simulate actual conditions (e g of business or war) esp for training or testing purposes

¹**gamma** /'gamə/ *n* **1** the 3rd letter of the Greek alphabet **2** the tangent of the angle formed at a point on the straight line portion of the characteristic s-shaped curve of a photographic emulsion, with the base line of the graph – often used as an approximate indication of the degree of contrast of a developed photographic image or of a television image **3** one millionth of a gram; a microgram **4** ¹c **5** [ME, fr LL, fr Gk, of Sem origin; akin to Heb *gīmel* gimel]

²**gamma, γ-** *adj* **1** of or being an atom or chemical group third in position from a particular major or conspicuous atom or group in the molecular structure of an organic chemical compound **2** of or being the third of three or more chemical compounds closely related in structure and having the same number of each type of atom as a specified chemical compound ⟨*γ -iron*⟩

**gamma globulin** *n* any of several proteins (IMMUNO-GLOBULINS) of blood that include most antibodies and are important in the body's defence mechanisms against and development of immunity to disease-causing organisms (e g bacteria)

**gamma radiation** *n* radiation composed of GAMMA RAYS

**gamma ray** *n* a stream of high-energy ELECTROMAGNETIC RADIATION that has a shorter wavelength than X RAYS, can penetrate up to about 3 centimetres (about 1⅕ inches) of lead, and is emitted in the radioactive decay of some unstable atomic nuclei

**gammer** /'gamə/ *n, dial* an old woman – compare GAFFER [prob alter. of *godmother*]

¹**gammon** /'gamən/ *n* (the meat of) the rear end, including the hind leg, of a side of bacon removed from the carcass after curing with salt – compare HAM [ONF *gambon* ham, aug of *gambe* leg, fr LL *gamba*]

²**gammon** *n* the winning of a backgammon game before the loser removes any men from the board [perh alter. of ME *gamen* game]

³**gammon** *vt* to beat by scoring a gammon

⁴**gammon** *n* talk intended to deceive; nonsense, humbug – no longer in vogue [obs *gammon* talk]

⁵**gammon** *vi* **1** to talk gammon **2** to pretend, feign to deceive, fool □ no longer in vogue

**gammy** /'gami/ *adj, Br informal* injured or crippled ⟨*a* ~ *leg*⟩ [prob irreg fr ⁴*game* + *-y*]

**gap**

**gamodeme** /'gamə,deem/ *n, biology* a more or less isolated breeding community of organisms [*gam-* + *deme*]

**gamogenesis** /,gamoh'jenəsis/ *n* sexual reproduction [NL] – **gamogenetic** *adj,* **gamogenetically** *adv*

**gamopetalous** /,gamoh'petələs/ *adj, of a flower* (*eg a primrose or petunia*) having petals that are united to form a tube

**gamophyllous** /,gamoh'filəs/ *adj* having united leaves or leaf-like parts – used esp of a flower not differentiated into petals and SEPALS (leaflike parts surrounding the petals)

**gamosepalous** /-'sepələs/ *adj, of a flower* having SEPALS (leaf-like parts surrounding the petals) that are united

**gamp** /gamp/ *n, Br informal* a large, esp loosely tied umbrella [Sarah *Gamp,* nurse with a large umbrella in the novel *Martin Chuzzlewit* by Charles Dickens †1870 E writer]

**gamut** /'gamət/ *n* **1** the whole series of recognized musical notes **2** an entire range or series 〈*the letters she received ran the ~ from praise to contempt*〉 [ML *gamma ut,* lowest note in medieval scale of music, fr *gamma,* applied to the lowest note G on the bass clef + *ut,* applied to the first note of a hexachord (the notes of which were named after the first syllables of 6 lines of a Latin hymn: *ut, re, mi, fa, sol, la*)]

**gamy, gamey** /'gaymi/ *adj* **1** *esp of animals* brave, plucky **2** having the strong flavour or smell of game (that has been hung until high) **3** scandalous, spicy 〈*gave her all the ~ details*〉 – **gamily** *adv,* **gaminess** *n*

**-gamy** /-gəmi/ *comb form* (→ *n*) **1** marriage 〈*poly*gamy〉 **2** possession of (such) reproductive organs or (such) a mode of fertilization 〈*cleisto*gamy〉 〈*apo*gamy〉 [ME *-gamie,* fr LL *-gamia,* fr Gk – more at BIGAMY] – **gamic, -gamous** *comb form* (→ *adj*)

**gan** /gan/ *past of* GIN

**¹ganch** /gansh, ganch, gawnsh, gawnch/ *vt* to execute by impaling on stakes or hooks [modif of Turk *kancalamak* to put on a hook, fr *kanca* large hook, modif of Gk *gampsos* curved]

**²ganch** *n* the apparatus used in ganching criminals

**Ganda** /'gandə/ *n, pl* **Gandas,** *esp collectively* **Ganda 1** a member of a Bantu-speaking people of Uganda **2** the Bantu language of the Ganda people

**¹gander** /'gandə/ *n* **1** an adult male goose **2** *archaic* a simpleton [ME, fr OE *gandra;* akin to OE *gōs* goose]

**²gander** *n, informal* a look, glance 〈*talking and taking ~s at the girls – Life*〉 [prob fr **¹gander;** fr the outstretched neck of a person craning to look at something]

**Gandhian** /'gandi-ən/ *adj* of the Indian political and spiritual leader Mahatma Gandhi (†1948) or his principle of nonviolent protest

**gane** /gayn/ *past of* GAE

**¹gang** /gang/ *n taking sing or pl vb* **1** a set of articles; an outfit 〈*a ~ of cars*〉 **2** a group of people **a** working together **b** associating for criminal, disreputable, etc ends; *esp* a group of adolescents who (disreputably) spend leisure time together **c** having informal and usu close social relations 〈*have the ~ over for a party*〉 [ME, fr OE, way, passage, journey; akin to OHG *gang* act of going, Skt *jaṅghā* shank]

**²gang** *vt* **1** to assemble or operate (*eg* mechanical parts) simultaneously as a group **2** to arrange in or produce (*eg* type pages) as a gang ~ *vi* to move or act as a gang 〈*the children ~ed together*〉

**gang up** *vi* **1** to combine as a group for a specific, esp disreputable, purpose 〈*the petrol companies* ganged up *to raise prices*〉 **2** to make a joint assault *on* or *against* 〈ganged up *on him and beat him up*〉

**³gang** *vi, Scot* to go [ME *gangen,* fr OE *gangan;* akin to OE *gang* act of going]

**'gang-,bang** *n, slang* sexual intercourse usu between one woman and a succession of men on one occasion; *esp* collective rape [**¹gang** + **²bang** 4]

**ganger** /'gang-ə/ *n, Br* the foreman of a gang of workmen

**gangland** /'gang,land, -lənd/ *n, informal* the world of organized crime; the underworld

**gangli-** /gang·gli-/, **ganglio-** *comb form* ganglion 〈*gangli*ectomy〉 〈*ganglio*plexus〉 [NL, fr Gk *ganglion*]

**gangling** /'gang·gling/, **gangly** /-gli/ *adj* tall, thin, and awkward in movement 〈*a ~ gawky child*〉 [perh irreg fr Sc *gangrel* vagrant, lanky person]

**ganglion** /'gang·glion, -ən/ *n, pl* **ganglia** /-gliə/ *also* **ganglions 1a** *medicine* a small cyst on a membrane surrounding a joint or on a tendon sheath (*eg* on the back of the wrist) **b** a dense mass of NERVE CELLS; *esp* one occurring outside the brain or SPINAL CORD **2** a focus of strength, energy, or activity [LL, fr Gk] – **ganglionated** *adj,* **ganglionic** *adj*

**ganglioside** /'gang·gliə,sied/ *n* any of a group of sugar-containing fatty chemical compounds found esp in nerve tissue [ISV *ganglion* + **²**-*ose* + -*ide*]

**gangplank** /'gang,plangk/ *n* a movable bridge used in boarding or leaving a ship at a quay

**gangrel** /'gang-grəl, 'gangrəl/ *n, Scot* a vagrant [ME, irreg fr *gangen* to go – more at **³**GANG]

**¹gangrene** /'gang,green/ *n* **1** death of soft tissues in a localized area of the body, due to loss of blood supply **2** a moral evil that spreads throughout a community, civilization, etc [L *gangraena,* fr Gk *gangraina;* akin to Gk *gran* to gnaw] – **gangrenous** *adj*

**²gangrene** *vb* to make or become gangrenous

**gangster** /'gangstə/ *n* a member of a gang of criminals; a racketeer – **gangsterism** *n*

**gangue** /gang/ *n* the worthless or unwanted rock and mineral material of an ore in which valuable metals or minerals occur [Fr, fr Ger *gang* vein of metal, fr OHG, act of going]

**gangway** /-,way/ *n* **1** a passageway; *esp* a temporary way constructed from planks **2a** the opening in a ship's side or rail through which the ship is boarded **b** a gangplank; *also* a ladder or stairway slung over a ship's side by which it can be boarded by a boat **3** a main passage or level in a mine **4** an aisle dividing the front benches from the back benches in the House of Commons **5** a clear passage through a crowd – often used as an interjection **6** *Br* a narrow passage between storage bays in a warehouse, sections of seats in a theatre, etc [**¹**gang (in arch. sense "passage, road") + *way*]

**ganister, gannister** /'ganistə/ *n* **1** a fine-grained quartz rock (QUARTZITE) that can withstand high temperatures and is used in the manufacture of heat-resistant bricks for lining furnaces **2** a mixture of ground quartz and fireclay used for lining furnaces [origin unknown]

**ganja** /'ganjə/ *n* a potent preparation of cannabis used esp for smoking [Hindi *gājā,* fr Skt *gañjā*]

**gannet** /'ganit/ *n, pl* **gannets** *also esp collectively* **gannet 1** any of several large fish-eating seabirds (family Sulidae, esp *Sula bassana*) that breed in large colonies mainly on offshore islands **2** *informal* a greedy person; a scavenger [ME *ganet,* fr OE *ganot;* akin to OE *gōs* goose]

**gannetry** /'ganitri/ *n* a breeding colony of gannets

**ganoid** /'ganoyd/ *adj* of or belonging to a subclass (Ganoidei) of living and extinct BONY FISHES (*eg* the sturgeons) with usu hard enamelled scales [deriv of Gk *ganos* brightness; akin to Gk *gēthein* to rejoice – more at JOY] – **ganoid** *n*

**gantlet** /'gantlit, 'gawn-/ *n, chiefly NAm* a gauntlet

**gantry** /'gantri/ *n* **1** a frame for supporting barrels **2** a frame structure raised on side supports that spans over or round something: *eg* **2a** a platform made to carry a travelling crane and supported by towers or side frames running on parallel tracks; *also* a movable structure with platforms at different levels used for erecting and servicing rockets before launching **b** a structure spanning several railway tracks and displaying signals for each [perh modif of ONF *gantier,* fr L *cantherius* trellis]

**Ganymede** /'gani,meed/ *n* **1** a youth who serves drinks; a cupbearer **2** the 4th satellite orbiting the planet Jupiter [*Ganymede* (Gk *Ganymēdēs*), cupbearer of the gods in Gk mythology]

**gaol** /jay(ə)l/ *vt or n, chiefly Br* (to) jail

**gaoler** /'jaylə/ *n, chiefly Br* a jailer

**gap** /gap/ *n* **1** a break in a barrier (*eg* a wall, hedge, or line of military defence) **2a** a mountain pass **b** a ravine **3** SPARK GAP **4** an empty space between two objects or two parts of an object **5** a break in continuity 〈*there were unexplained ~s in his story*〉 **6** lack of balance; disparity 〈*the ~ between imports and exports*〉 **7** a wide difference in character or attitude 〈*the generation ~*〉 [ME, fr ON, chasm, hole; akin to ON *gapa* to gape] – **gappy, gapped** *adj*

**¹gape** /gayp/ *vi* **1a** to open the mouth wide **b** to open or part widely 〈*holes ~d in the pavement*〉 **2** to gaze stupidly or in openmouthed surprise or wonder **3** to yawn *synonyms* see **¹**GAZE [ME *gapen,* fr ON *gapa;* akin to L *hiare* to gape, yawn – more at YAWN] – **gapingly** *adv*

**²gape** *n* **1** an act of gaping; *esp* an openmouthed stare or yawn **2** a wide opening; a gap **3a** the average width of the open mouth or beak **b** the line along which a bird's beak closes **4** *pl but taking sing or pl vb* **4a** a disease of young birds characterized by constant gaping and caused by gapeworms infesting the windpipe **b** *informal* a fit of yawning

**gaper** /'gaypə/ *n* **1** one who or that which gapes **2** any of several large sluggish burrowing clams (family Myacidae) including several that are used as food

**gapeworm** /-ˌwuhm/ n a NEMATODE (unsegmented round-bodied parasitic worm) (*Syngamus trachea*) that causes gapes in birds

**gar** /gah/ n any of various fishes (e g the garfish) that have an elongated body resembling that of a pike and long narrow jaws [short for *garfish*]

**¹garage** /'garahzh, 'garij/ n **1** a building for sheltering (motor) vehicles **2** an establishment for providing essential services (e g supply of petrol or repair work) to motor vehicles [Fr, act of docking, garage, fr *garer* to dock, of Gmc origin; akin to OHG biwarōn to protect – more at WARE]

> *usage* There seems no reason to object to the anglicized pronunciation of **garage** as /'garij/, on the analogy of similar words borrowed from French such as *courage* /'kurij/, but many speakers prefer /'garahzh/. The American form /gə'rahzh/ is disliked in Britain.

**²garage** vt to keep or put in a garage

**garam masala** /ˌgarəm mah'sahlə/ n an aromatic mixture of ground spices (e g coriander, cumin, and cinnamon) used esp in curries [Hindi *garam masālā*, fr *garam* hot, pungent + *masālā* spice]

**garb** /gahb/ n **1** a style of clothing; dress ⟨*arrayed themselves in priestly ~*⟩ **2** an outward form; appearance ⟨*give their madness the outward ~ of sanity* – Lewis Mumford⟩ [MF or OIt; MF *garbe* graceful contour, grace, fr OIt *garbo* grace] – **garb** vt

**garbage** /'gahbij/ n **1** worthless writing or speech **2** chiefly NAm waste material; rubbish [ME, animal entrails]

**¹garble** /'gahbl/ vt **1** to sift impurities from (e g spices) **2** to distort or confuse, giving a false impression of the facts ⟨*a ~d message*⟩ [ME *garbelen*, fr OIt *garbellare* to sift, fr Ar *gharbala*, fr *ghirbāl* sieve, fr LL *cribellum*; akin to L *cernere* to sift – more at CERTAIN] – **garbler** n

**²garble** n **1** the impurities sifted from spices **2** an act or an instance of garbling

**garbo** /'gahboh/ n, *Austr informal* a dustman [by shortening & alter. fr *garbage man*]

**garboard** /'gah ˌbawd/ n the plank next to a ship's keel [obs D *gaarboord*]

**garboil** /'gahboyl/ n, *archaic* a confused disordered state; turmoil [MF *garbouil*]

**garçon** /gah'sonh (*Fr* garsɔ̃)/ n, *pl* **garçons** a waiter in a French restaurant [Fr, boy, servant]

**garda** /'gahdə/ n, *pl* **gardai** /'gahdi, -die/ (a member of) the Irish police [IrGael]

**¹garden** /'gahd(ə)n/ n **1a** a plot of ground where herbs, fruit, vegetables, or typically flowers are cultivated ⟨*rose ~*⟩ **b** a rich well-cultivated region ⟨*Kent is known as the ~ of England*⟩ **c** a container (e g a window box) planted with usu a variety of small plants ⟨*herb ~s*⟩ **2a** a public recreation area or park ⟨*a botanical ~*⟩ **b** an open-air eating or drinking place ⟨*beer ~*⟩ – see also COMMON **or garden** [ME *gardin*, fr ONF, of Gmc origin; akin to OHG *gart* enclosure – more at YARD] – **gardenful** n

**²garden** vi to work in, cultivate, or lay out a garden – **gardener** n

**garden centre** n an establishment where equipment for gardens or gardening (e g tools, furniture, plants, and seeds) is sold

**garden city** n a planned town with spacious residential areas including public parks and considerable garden space

**'garden-ˌflat** n a basement or ground-floor flat adjoining a garden

**garden heliotrope** n a Peruvian shrub (*Heliotropium arborescens*) with fragrant usu lilac or violet flowers

**gardenia** /gah'deenyə, -ni·ə/ n any of a large genus (*Gardenia*) of tropical trees and shrubs of the madder family with showy fragrant white or yellow flowers [NL, genus name, fr Alexander *Garden* †1791 Sc naturalist]

**garden party** n a usu formal party held on the lawns of a garden

**'garden-vaˌriety** adj ordinary, commonplace

**garden wall bond** n an arrangement of bricks to strengthen a wall in which a layer is laid with ends towards the wall face for every three layers laid parallel to the wall face

**garden warbler** n a brownish European warbler (*Sylvia borin*) with a beautiful song

**garderobe** /'gahdˌrohb/ n, *archaic* **1** a private room; a bedroom **2** (a part of a medieval building used as) a privy [ME, fr MF; akin to ONF *warderobe* wardrobe]

**gardyloo** /ˌgahdi'looh/ interj, *archaic* – used in Edinburgh as a

warning cry when it was customary to throw slops from the windows into the streets [perh fr Fr *garde à l'eau!* look out for the water!]

**garefowl** /'geəˌfowl/ n GREAT AUK (large flightless extinct seabird) [of Scand origin; akin to ON *geirfugl* great auk, fr *geirr* spear + *fugl* bird]

**garfish** /'gahˌfish/ n a fish (*Belone belone*) of European and N Atlantic waters with a long body and elongated jaws [ME *garfysshe*, prob fr *gar*, *gare* spear + *fysshe* fish]

**garganey** /'gahgəni/ n a small European duck (*Anas querquedula*) of which the male has a broad white curving stripe over the eye [It dial. *garganei*, of imit origin]

**gargantuan** /gah'gantyoo·ən/ adj, *often cap* of tremendous size or volume; gigantic, colossal ⟨*a ~ meal*⟩ **synonyms** see HUGE **antonym** pygmy [*Gargantua*, gigantic king in the novel *Gargantua* by François Rabelais †1553 Fr satirist]

**garget** /'gahgit/ n inflammation (MASTITIS) of the udder in domestic animals; *esp* persistent mastitis in cows, resulting in significant changes in the form and texture of the udder [prob fr ME, throat, fr MF *gargate;* akin to MF *gargouiller* to gargle] – **gargety** adj

**¹gargle** /'gahgl/ vt **1a** to blow air from the lungs through (a liquid) held in the mouth or throat **b** to cleanse or disinfect (the mouth or throat) in this manner **2** to utter with a gargling sound ~ vi **1** to use a gargle **2** to speak or sing as if gargling [MF *gargouiller*, of imit origin]

**²gargle** n **1** a liquid used in gargling **2** a bubbling liquid sound produced by gargling

**gargoyle** /'gahˌgoyl/ n a spout in the form of a grotesque human or animal figure projecting from a roof gutter to throw rainwater clear of a building [ME *gargoyl*, fr MF *gargouille;* akin to MF *gargouiller*] – **gargoyled** adj

**garibaldi** /ˌgari'bawldi/ n **1** a woman's loose long-sleeved originally bright red blouse **2** Br a biscuit with a layer of currants in it [Giuseppe *Garibaldi* †1882 It patriot; (1) fr the red shirt worn by Garibaldi and his followers]

**garish** /'geərish/ adj **1** excessively and gaudily bright or vivid **2** tastelessly showy [origin unknown] – **garishly** adv, **garishness** n

**¹garland** /'gahlənd/ n **1** a wreath of flowers or leaves worn as an ornament or sign of distinction (e g in honour of a victory) **2** an anthology or collection of verse, prose, etc [ME, fr MF *garlande*]

**²garland** vt to form into or deck with a garland

**garlic** /'gahlik/ n a European bulbous plant (*Allium sativum*) of the lily family widely cultivated for its pungent compound bulbs that are much used as a flavouring in cookery; *also* the bulb of garlic [ME *garlek*, fr OE *gārlēac*, fr *gār* spear + *lēac* leek – more at GORE] – **garlicky** adj

**garlic mustard** n a common European plant (*Alliaria petiolata*) of the cabbage family that has small white flowers and leaves that smell like garlic when crushed

**garment** /'gahmənt/ n an article of clothing [ME, fr MF *garnement*, fr OF, fr *garnir* to equip – more at GARNISH]

**¹garner** /'gahnə/ n, *formal or poetic* **1** a granary **2** a grain bin [ME, fr OF *grenier*, fr L *granarium*, fr *granum* grain]

**²garner** vt, *formal or poetic* **1** to gather, store **2** to accumulate, collect

**garnet** /'gahnit/ n **1** any of a group of hard brittle SILICATE minerals used as abrasives and, esp when a transparent deep red colour, as gemstones **2** a dark red [ME *grenat*, fr MF, fr *grenat*, adj, red like a pomegranate, fr (*pomme*) *grenate* pomegranate]

**garnetiferous** /ˌgahnət'if(ə)rəs/ adj containing garnet

**garnierite** /'gahniəˌriet/ n a soft bright green mineral that consists essentially of a SILICATE of nickel and magnesium and is an important source of nickel [Jules *Garnier* †1904 Fr geologist]

**¹garnish** /'gahnish/ vt **1a** to decorate, embellish **b** to add decorative or savoury touches to (food) **2** to garnishee **synonyms** see DECORATE [ME *garnishen*, fr MF *garniss-*, stem of *garnir* to warn, equip, garnish, of Gmc origin; akin to OHG *warnōn* to take heed – more at WARN]

**²garnish** n **1** an embellishment, ornament **2** an edible savoury or decorative addition (e g watercress) to a dish **3** an unauthorized fee formerly extorted from a new inmate of a jail or required of a new workman

**¹garnishee** /ˌgahni'shee/ n, *law* a person who is served with a garnishment

**²garnishee** vt **garnisheeing** *law* **1** to serve (someone) with a garnishment **2** to take (money or property) as garnishment

**garnishment** /-mənt/ *n* **1** a garnish **2** *law* **2a** a judicial warning to a debtor not to pay his/her debt to anyone other than the third party who seeks or has obtained judgment against the person, company, etc to whom the debtor owes money **b** a stoppage of a specified sum from wages to satisfy the person, company, etc to whom a debt is owed

**garniture** /'gahnichə/ *n* an embellishment, trimming [MF, equipment, alter. of OF *garnesture*, fr *garnir*]

**garpike** /'gah,piek/ *n* GARFISH (long-bodied fish)

**garret** /'garit/ *n* a small room just under the roof of a house [ME *garette* watchtower, fr MF *garite*, perh fr OProv *garida*, fr *garir* to protect, of Gmc origin; akin to OHG *werien* to defend]

**¹garrison** /'garis(ə)n/ *n* **1** a (fortified) town or place in which troops are stationed **2** *taking sing or pl vb* the troops stationed at a garrison [ME *garisoun* protection, fr OF *garison*, fr *garir* to protect, of Gmc origin; akin to OHG *werien* to defend – more at WEIR]

**²garrison** *vt* **1** to station troops in **2** to assign (troops) as a garrison

**garrison cap** *n* a visorless folding cap worn as part of a military uniform – compare SERVICE CAP

**garrison town** *n* a town having troops permanently garrisoned in it

**garron** /'garən/ *n, Scot & Irish* a small sturdy workhorse [IrGael *gearrān* & ScGael *gearran* gelding]

**¹garrotte, garotte,** *chiefly NAm* **garrote** /gə'rot/ *n* **1a** a Spanish method of execution by strangling or dislocating the spinal column at the base of the brain with an iron collar that is tightened by turning a screw **b** the iron collar used in garrotting **2** strangulation, esp with robbery as the motive [Sp *garrote* cudgel, garrotte, prob fr MF *garrot* heavy wooden projectile]

**²garrotte, garotte,** *chiefly NAm* **garrote** *vt* **-tt-** (*NAm* **-t-**) **1** to execute with a garrotte **2** to strangle and rob – **garrotter** *n*

**garrulous** /'gar(y)ooləs/ *adj* excessively talkative, esp about trivial things *synonyms* see TALKATIVE *antonym* taciturn [L *garrulus*, fr *garrire* to chatter – more at CARE] – **garrulously** *adv*, **garrulousness** *n*, **garrulity** *n*

**¹garter** /'gahtə/ *n* **1a** a band, usu of elastic, worn to hold up a stocking or sock **b** *NAm* suspender **2b 2** *cap* (the blue velvet garter that is the badge of) the Order of the Garter; *also* membership of the Order [ME, fr ONF *gartier*, fr *garet* bend of the knee, of Celt origin; akin to OIr *gairri* calves of the legs]

**²garter** *vt* to support (as if) with a garter

**garter snake** *n* any of numerous harmless American snakes (genus *Thamnophis*) that have longitudinal stripes on the back and give birth to live young instead of producing eggs

**garter stitch** *n* **1** KNIT STITCH **2** the pattern of alternate rows of ridges and depressions formed by a plain KNIT STITCH

**garth** /gahth/ *n* **1** the open space bounded by a cloister **2** *archaic* a small yard or enclosure [ME, fr ON *garthr* yard; akin to OHG *gart* enclosure – more at YARD]

**¹gas** /gas/ *n, pl* **-s-** *also* **-ss- 1** a substance (e g air) that has neither independent shape nor volume but tends to expand indefinitely **2a** a gas or mixture of gases with the exception of atmospheric air: e g **2a(1)** a gas or gaseous mixture used as a general anaesthetic **a(2)** a combustible gaseous mixture used as a fuel (e g for heating) **b** a substance (e g TEAR GAS or MUSTARD GAS) that can be used to produce a poisonous, suffocating, or irritant atmosphere ⟨*the troops were attacked with ~*⟩ **3** *NAm* petrol **4** *informal* empty talk **5** *slang* someone or something that has unusual appeal ⟨*the party was a real ~*⟩ – no longer in vogue; see also STEP **on the gas** [NL (orig formed by J B van Helmont †1644 D chemist, alter. of L *chaos* space, chaos, (3) short for *gasoline*]

**²gas** *vb* **-ss-** *vt* **1a** to treat chemically with gas **b** to poison or otherwise affect adversely with gas **2** *chiefly NAm* to supply with gas, esp petrol ⟨*~ up the automobile*⟩ *~ vi* **1** to give off gas **2** *NAm* to fill a tank with petrol – often + *up* **3** *informal* to talk idly

**gasbag** /-,bag/ *n, informal* an idle talker

**gas chamber** *n* a chamber in which prisoners are executed or animals killed by poison gas

**gascon** /'gaskən/ *n* **1** *cap* a native of Gascony **2** a braggart [ME *Gascoun*, fr MF *Gascon*, fr *Gascogne* Gascony, region in SW France] – **Gascon** *adj*

**gasconade** /,gaskə'nayd/ *n* bravado, boasting [Fr *gasconnade*, fr *gasconner* to boast, fr *gascon* Gascon, boaster] – **gasconade**

*vi*, **gasconader** *n*

**gaseous** /'gasiəs, 'gay-/ *adj* **1a** having the form of or being gas; *also* of gases **b** *of a vapour not in contact with its own liquid* heated so as to remain free from suspended liquid droplets **2** having the nature of a gas (e g lacking substance or solidity); tenuous – **gaseousness** *n*

**gas gangrene** *n* often rapidly progressive gangrene marked by the formation of gas in dying tissue and caused by infection of a breakage in the skin, esp an unclean wound, with a bacterium (e g some species of *Clostridium*)

**¹gash** /gash/ *vt* to make a gash in *~ vi* to make a gash; cut [ME *garsen*, fr ONF *garser*, fr (assumed) VL *charissare*, fr Gk *charassein* to scratch, engrave – more at CHARACTER]

**²gash** *n* **1** a deep long cut, esp in flesh **2** a deep narrow depression in land, whether natural (e g a gorge or cleft in rock) or man-made (e g a railway cutting)

**³gash** *n, informal* something superfluous or extra; *specif* rubbish on board ship [origin unknown]

**gasholder** /'gas,hohldə/ *n* a container for gas; *esp* a large cylindrical tank commonly having two parts, one of which telescopes into the other, and used for storing fuel gas under pressure before its distribution to consumers – called also GASOMETER

**gasify** /'gasifie, 'gay-/ *vt* to convert into gas ⟨*~ coal*⟩ *~ vi* to become gaseous – **gasifier** *n*, **gasification** *n*

**gasket** /'gaskit/ *n* **1** a line or band used to tie a furled sail to a horizontal or diagonal beam crossing the mast of a ship **2** (a specially shaped piece of) sealing material (e g of rubber or asbestos) for ensuring that a joint, esp between metal surfaces, does not leak liquid or gas [prob alter. of Fr *garcette*, fr OF, girl, dim. of *garce* girl, fem of *gars* boy]

**gaskin** /'gaskin/ *n* the upper front part of the hind leg of a 4-legged animal, esp a horse [obs *gaskin* hose, breeches, prob short for *galligaskins*]

**gaslight** /'gas,liet/ *n* **1** light given by burning gas **2** a gas flame or gas lighting fixture

**gas-liquid chromatography, gas chromatography** *n* a technique for analysing a mixture of volatile chemical substances in which the mixture is carried by an inert gas (e g argon) through a column of a stationary liquid or solid. The components are separated according to their relative velocities through the column and are identified by a detector as each leaves the column.

**gaslit** /'gas,lit/ *adj* illuminated by gaslight

**gas mantle** *n* a small cap or tube of chemically treated fibres fitted to the flame of a gas lamp to give out a brilliant glowing white light

**gas mask** *n* a mask connected to a chemical air filter and used (e g in industry or warfare) to protect the face and lungs from poisonous fumes or gases; *broadly* RESPIRATOR 1

**gasolier** /,gasə'liə/ *n* a gaslight chandelier [alter. of *gaselier*, fr *gas* + *-elier* (as in *chandelier*)]

**gasoline, gasolene** /,gasə'leen, '--,-/ *n, NAm* petrol [¹*gas* + *-ol* + *-ine* or *-ene*] – **gasolinic** *adj*

**gasometer** /ga'somitə/ *n* GASHOLDER (tank for storing gas) – not used technically [Fr *gazomètre*, fr *gaz* gas + *-o-* + *-mètre* -meter]

**'gas-,operated** *adj, of an automatic firearm* using gases produced by the burning of the propellant to operate the mechanism of reloading and firing

**gasp** /gahsp/ *vi* **1** to catch the breath suddenly and audibly (e g with shock) **2** to breathe laboriously *~ vt* to utter with gasps – usu + *out* ⟨*he ~ed out his message*⟩ [ME *gaspen*; akin to ON *geispa* to yawn] – **gasp** *n*

**gasper** /'gahspə/ *n, Br slang* a cigarette – no longer in vogue

**gas ring** *n* a hollow metal perforated ring through which jets of gas issue and over which food may be cooked

**gasser** /'gasə/ *n* **1** an oil well that yields gas **2** *informal* a talkative person

**gassy** /'gasi/ *adj* **1** full of, containing, or like gas ⟨*~ beer*⟩ **2** *informal* full of boastful or insincere talk – **gassiness** *n*

**gastarbeiter** /'gast,ahbietə/ *n* a foreign worker, esp in a German-speaking country [Ger, fr *gast* guest + *arbeiter* worker]

**gaster-** /gastə-/, **gastero-** *comb form* abdominal area ⟨*Gasteropoda*⟩ [NL, fr Gk *gastero-* belly, fr *gastr-*, *gaster-*, *gastēr*]

**gasteropod** /'gast(ə)rə,pod/ *n* GASTROPOD (snail, slug, etc)

**gastight** /'gas,tiet/ *adj* impervious to gas – **gastightness** *n*

**gastr-** /gastr-/, **gastro-** *also* **gastri-** *comb form* **1** belly ⟨*gastropod*⟩; stomach ⟨*gastritis*⟩ ⟨*gastrectomy*⟩ **2** gastric and

⟨*gastrointestinal*⟩ [Gk, fr *gastr-, gastēr*, alter. of (assumed) Gk *grastēr*, fr Gk *gran* to gnaw, eat]

**gastraea**, *NAm also* **gastrea** /ga'stree·ə/ *n, zoology* a hypothetical ancestral form of a METAZOAN (animal having cells organized into tissues and organs) corresponding in organization to the GASTRULA (2-layered cup-shaped stage) in the embryonic development of living metazoans [NL, fr Gk *gastr-, gastēr*] – **gastraeal** *adj*

**gastral** /'gastrəl/ *adj* of the stomach or digestive tract

**gastrectomy** /ga'strektəmi/ *n* surgical removal of all or part of the stomach [ISV]

**gastric** /'gastrik/ *adj* of, involving, or in the region of the stomach

**gastric juice** *n* a thin acid digestive liquid secreted by glands in the membrane lining the stomach

**gastrin** /'gastrin/ *n* a hormone secreted by the membrane lining the stomach that induces secretion of GASTRIC JUICE

**gastritis** /ga'stritəs/ *n* inflammation of esp the membrane lining the stomach [NL]

**gastrocnemius** /ˌgastrok'neemiəs/ *n, pl* **gastrocnemii** /-mi͟ˌie/ the largest and outermost muscle of the calf of the leg [NL, fr Gk *gastroknēmē* calf of the leg, fr *gastr-* + *knēmē* shin, leg]

**gastrocoel** *also* **gastrocoele** /'gastrəˌseel/ *n* ARCHENTERON (central cavity of an embryo in an early stage of development) [Fr *gastrocèle*, fr *gastr-* + *-cèle* -coele]

**gastroduodenal** /ˌgastroh‚dyooh·oh'deenl/ *adj* of or involving both the stomach and the DUODENUM (part of the intestine leading from the stomach)

**gastroenteritis** /ˌgastroh‚entə'rietəs/ *n* inflammation of the membrane lining the stomach and the intestines, usu causing painful diarrhoea [NL]

**gastroenterology** /ˌgastroh‚entə'rolǝji/ *n* the study of the diseases and abnormalities of the stomach and intestines [ISV] – **gastroenterologist** *n*, **gastroenterological** *adj*

**gastrogenic** /ˌgastrə'jenik/, **gastrogenous** /ga'strojənəs/ *adj* of gastric origin

**gastrointestinal** /ˌgastroh·in'testinl/ *adj* of or involving both the stomach and intestine

**gastronome** /'gastrəˌnohm/, **gastronomist** /ga'stronəmist/ *n* an epicure, gourmet [Fr *gastronome*, back-formation fr *gastronomie*]

**gastronomy** /ga'stronəmi/ *n* the art or science of good eating [Fr *gastronomie*, fr Gk *Gastronomia*, title of a 4th-c BC poem, fr *gastro-* belly + *-nomia* -nomy] – **gastronomic** *also* **gastronomical** *adj*, **gastronomically** *adv*

**gastro-oesophageal** /ˌgastroh-ee‚sofə'jee·əl/ *adj* of or involving both the stomach and OESOPHAGUS (gullet)

**gastropod** /'gastrəˌpod/ *n* any of a large class (Gastropoda of the phylum Mollusca) of INVERTEBRATE animals (e g snails and slugs) with a shell in one piece or no shell at all and usu with a distinct head bearing sensory organs [NL *Gastropoda*, class name, deriv of Gk *gastr-* + *pod-, pous* foot] – **gastropod** *also* **gastropodan, gastropodous** *adj*

**gastroscope** /'gastrəˌskohp/ *n* an instrument for looking at the interior of the stomach [ISV] – **gastroscopic** *adj*, **gastroscopist** *n*, **gastroscopy** *n*

**gastrotrich** /'gastrətrik/ *n* any of a small group (Gastrotricha) of minute freshwater and marine wormlike animals that have elongated bodies bearing CILIA (hairlike projections) used for movement and specialized tubular structures for attachment [deriv of Gk *gastr-* + *trich-, thrix* hair – more at TRICH-] – **gastrotrichan** *adj or n*

**gastrovascular** /ˌgastroh'vaskyoolə/ *adj* functioning in both digestion and circulation ⟨*the ~ cavity of a sea anemone*⟩ [ISV]

**gastrula** /'gastroolə/ *n, pl* **gastrulas, gastrulae** /-li/ the embryo of a METAZOAN animal (multicellular animal) at the stage in its development following the BLASTULA (hollow ball of cells stage), consisting of a hollow cup-shaped structure made up of two layers of cells that enclose the ARCHENTERON (cavity forming embryonic gut) – compare BLASTULA, MORULA [NL, fr *gastr-*] – **gastrular** *adj*

**gastrulate** /'gastroo‚layt/ *vi* to become or form a gastrula – **gastrulation** *n*

**gas turbine** *n* an INTERNAL-COMBUSTION ENGINE in which turbine blades are driven by hot gases whose pressure and velocity are intensified by compressed air introduced into the combustion chamber

**gasworks** /-ˌwuhks/ *n taking sing or pl vb, pl* **gasworks** a plant for manufacturing gas

¹**gat** /gat/ *archaic past of* GET

²**gat** *n* a natural or artificial channel or passage [prob fr D, lit., hole; akin to OE *geat* gate]

³**gat** *n, slang* a firearm [short for *Gatling (gun)*]

¹**gate** /gayt/ *n* **1** an opening in a wall or fence **2** a city or castle entrance, often with defensive structures (e g towers) **3** the usu hinged frame or door that closes an opening in a wall or fence **4a** either of a pair of barriers that **a(1)** control the level of water in a lock **a(2)** close a road at a level crossing **b** a valve for controlling the passage of a liquid or gas through a pipe or other channel **5a** a means of entrance or exit; *specif* any of the numbered exits from an airport building to the airfield ⟨*flight now boarding at ~ number 17*⟩ **b** a mountain pass **c** a space between two markers through which a skier, canoeist, etc must pass in a slalom race **d** a mechanically operated barrier used as a starting device for a race **6a** a signal that makes an electronic circuit operative for a short period **b** an electronic circuit or component with one or more inputs and one output that switches between two or more voltage levels, corresponding usu to an "on" or "off" state, according to the condition of the input signals; *specif* one comprising or used in a LOGIC CIRCUIT **7** a channel in a foundry mould through which the molten metal flows into the cavity of the mould; *also* a similar channel through which molten plastic enters a mould **8** the set of notches in a manually worked gearbox into which the gear lever is pushed to select the gears **9** the total admission receipts or the number of spectators at a sporting event **10** *NAm slang* a dismissal ⟨*gave him the ~*⟩ [ME, fr OE *geat*; akin to ON *gat* opening, Gk *chezein* to defecate] – **gated** *adj*

²**gate** *vt, Br* to punish by confinement to the premises of a school or college

³**gate** *n, archaic* a way, path [ME, fr ON *gata* road; akin to OHG *gazza* road]

**gateau** /'gatoh/ *n, pl* **gateaux** /'gatohz/ any of various rich elaborate cakes often filled and decorated with fruit, chopped nuts, and cream [Fr *gâteau* cake, fr OF *gastel*, prob of Gmc origin]

'**gate-,crasher** *n* one who enters, attends, or participates without a ticket or invitation ⟨*the party was spoilt by a number of ~s*⟩ – **gate-crash** *vb*

**gatefold** /-ˌfohld/ *n, chiefly NAm* a large folded page (e g a map) inserted in a book, journal, etc; *esp* one with a single fold that opens out like a gate

**gatehouse** /'gayt‚hows/ *n* a building (e g a lodge on an estate) beside or over a gateway

**gatekeeper** /-ˌkeepə/ *n* one who tends or guards a gate

**gateleg table** /'gaytleg/ *n* a table with hinged sections (DROP LEAVES) supported by movable paired legs

**gatepost** /-ˌpohst/ *n* the post on which a gate is hung or against which it closes

**gateway** /-ˌway/ *n* **1** an opening for a gate **2** GATE 5a

¹**gather** /'gadhə/ *vt* **1** to bring together; collect ⟨*~ firewood*⟩ ⟨*~ taxes*⟩ **2a** to pick, harvest **b** to accumulate and place in readiness ⟨*~ed up his tools*⟩ **c** to assemble (sections of a book) in order for binding **3a** to summon up ⟨*~ed her courage*⟩ **b** to gain by gradual increase; accumulate ⟨*~ speed*⟩ **c** to prepare (e g oneself) for an effort ⟨*~ed herself for her first entrance in the play*⟩ **4a** to draw about or close to something ⟨*~ing his cloak about him*⟩ **b** to clasp (e g to oneself) in an embrace ⟨*~ed her into his arms*⟩ **c** to pull (fabric) together, esp along a line of stitching, so as to create small folds or puckers **5** to reach a conclusion often intuitively from hints or through inferences ⟨*I ~ that you are ready to leave*⟩ ⟨*she soon ~ed what all the fuss was about*⟩ ~ *vi* **1** to come together in a body ⟨*a crowd had ~ed*⟩ **2a** *of a boil or similar sore* to swell and fill with pus **b** to grow, increase [ME *gaderen*, fr OE *gaderian*; akin to MHG *gatern* to unite, Skt *gadh* to hold fast – more at GOOD] – **gatherer** *n*

**synonyms Gather, collect, assemble, congregate: gather** has the widest and most general meaning, and may apply to people, objects, or abstract things. **Collect** is often used for **gather**, but may convey in addition the idea of selection, arrangement, or purpose ⟨**gather** *flowers*⟩ ⟨**collect** *flowers to press in her book*⟩. Used without an object, **collect** may suggest the gradual coming together of a group ⟨*clouds* **collected** *overhead*⟩. **Assemble**, used of people, stresses their coming together or being brought together for a particular purpose or event ⟨**assembled** *a crew to sail that morning*⟩. Used transitively with things, it suggests putting several units together to make one whole ⟨**assemble** *a model ship from a kit*⟩. **Congregate** suggests flocking together into a crowd or mass ⟨*well-*

*wishers* **congregating** *at the stage door*⟩. **antonyms** scatter, disperse, dismiss

**²gather** *n* something gathered; *esp* a small fold or pucker in cloth made by gathering

**gathering** /-ring/ *n* **1** *taking sing or pl vb* an assembly, meeting **2** a swelling (e g a boil) that discharges pus; an abscess **3** a collection, compilation **4** a gather or series of gathers in cloth **5** SECTION 13 (sheet of printed pages forming a unit in a book)

**Gatling gun** /'gatling/ *n* an early machine gun with a revolving cluster of barrels fired once each per revolution [Richard J *Gatling* †1903 US inventor]

**gauche** /gohsh/ *adj* lacking social experience or grace **synonyms** see CLUMSY [Fr, lit., left, fr MF, fr *gauchir* to turn aside] – **gauchely** *adv*, **gaucheness** *n*

**gaucherie** /'gohsh(ə)ri/ *n* (an instance of) tactless or awkward manner or behaviour [Fr, fr *gauche*]

**gaucho** /'gowchoh/ *n, pl* **gauchos** **1** a cowboy of the pampas regions in S America **2** *pl* calf-length trousers with wide legs [AmerSp, prob fr Quechua *wáhcha* poor person, orphan]

**gaud** /gawd/ *n, archaic* a gaudy ornament or trinket [ME *gaude* trick, toy, prob fr OF *gaudir* to enjoy, rejoice, fr L *gaudēre* to rejoice]

**¹gaudy** /'gawdi/ *adj* ostentatiously or tastelessly (and brightly) ornamented – **gaudily** *adv*, **gaudiness** *n*

**²gaudy** *n* a feast, esp a dinner for ex-students, in some British universities [prob fr L *gaudium* joy – more at JOY]

**gauffer** /'gohfə/ *vt* GOFFER (press frills with a heated iron)

**¹gauge, *NAm also* gage** /gayj/ *n* **1a** measurement according to some standard or system **b** dimensions, size **2** an instrument for or a means of measuring or testing: e g **2a** an instrument for measuring a dimension or for testing mechanical accuracy **b** an instrument with a graduated scale or dial for measuring or indicating quantity **3** ²GAGE 1 (position of a ship) **4a** the distance between the rails of a railway ⟨*a narrow* ~ *railway*⟩ – compare STANDARD GAUGE **b** the distance between a pair of wheels on an axle **5** *building* the quantity of plaster of paris that is mixed with mortar to make it set faster **6** the size of a shotgun expressed as the number of lead balls, each just fitting the interior diameter of the barrel, that are required to make a pound ⟨*a 12-gauge shotgun*⟩ **7a** the thickness of a thin layer of material (e g sheet metal or plastic film) **b** the diameter of wire, a hypodermic needle, a screw, etc **c** the fineness of a knitted fabric traditionally expressed by the number of loops per 1¹/₂ inches (43.75 millimetres) so that the higher the number the finer the texture [ME *gauge*, fr ONF]

**²gauge, *NAM also* gage** *vt* **1a** to measure exactly the size or dimensions of **b** to determine the capacity or contents of **c** to estimate, judge ⟨*can you* ~ *his reaction?*⟩ **2** to check for conformity to specifications or limits **3** *building* to mix (plaster) in definite proportions **4** to trim (e g bricks) to size by rubbing or chipping – **gaugeable** *adj*, **gaugeably** *adv*

**gauger** /'gayjə/ *n* **1** one who or that which gauges **2** *chiefly Scot* an exciseman who inspects bulk goods (e g whisky) on which (import) tax is to be paid

**Gaul** /gawl/ *n* **1** a Celt of ancient Gaul **2** a Frenchman [*Gaul*, ancient region in W Europe including most of what is now France, fr Fr *Gaule*, fr L *Gallia*]

**gauleiter** /'gow‚lietə/ *n* **1** *often cap* an official in charge of a district in Nazi Germany **2** an arrogant subordinate or henchman [Ger, fr *gau* district, region + *leiter* leader]

**¹Gaulish** /'gawlish/ *adj* of or being Gaul, the Gauls, or Gaulish

**²Gaulish** *n* the Celtic language of the ancient Gauls

**Gaullism** /'gaw‚liz(ə)m/ *n* **1** a French political movement during World War II led by Charles de Gaulle (†1970) in opposition to the Vichy regime **2** the political principles and policies of Charles de Gaulle in postwar France – **Gaullist** *adj or n*

**gault** /gawlt/ *n* a heavy thick clay soil [prob of Scand origin; akin to ON *gald* hard-packed snow]

**gaunt** /gawnt/ *adj* **1** excessively thin and angular as if from suffering **2** barren, desolate [ME, perh of Scand origin] – **gauntly** *adv*, **gauntness** *n*

**¹gauntlet, *NAm also* gantlet** /'gawntlit/ *n* **1** a glove to protect the hand, worn with medieval armour **2** a strong protective glove with a wide extension above the wrist, used esp for sports and in industry **3** a challenge to combat – esp in *take up/throw down the gauntlet* [ME, fr MF *gantelet*, dim. of *gant* glove, of Gmc origin; akin to MD *want* mitten, ON *vöttr* gloves] – **gauntleted** *adj*

**²gauntlet, *NAm also* gantlet** *n* **1** a double file of men facing each other and armed with clubs or other weapons with which

to strike at an individual who is made to run between them – usu in *run the gauntlet* **2** a cross fire of any kind; *broadly* an ordeal, test ⟨*ran the* ~ *of criticism and censure*⟩ **3** a stretch of railway or tram track where two lines of track overlap so that one rail of each track is within the rails of the other [by folk etymology fr arch. *gantelope*, modif of Sw *gatlopp*, fr OSw *gatulop*, fr *gata* road, lane + *lop* course, run]

**gaur** /'gowə/ *n* a large E Indian wild ox (*Bibos gaurus*) with a broad forehead and short thick conical horns [Hindi, fr Skt *gaura*; akin to Skt *go* bull, cow – more at COW]

**Gause's hypothesis** /'gowzəs/ *n* GAUSE'S PRINCIPLE

**Gause's principle** *n* a principle in ecology: two species with closely related habits or ecological requirements cannot occupy the same position in a community [G F *Gause* b1910 US ecologist]

**gauss** /gows/ *n, pl* **gauss** *also* **gausses** the CENTIMETRE-GRAM-SECOND unit of MAGNETIC FLUX DENSITY (strength of a MAGNETIC FIELD at a particular point); the magnetic flux density that will induce a voltage difference of one one-hundred millionth of a volt ($10^{-8}$ volt) across each centimetre of a wire moving with a speed of 1 centimetre per second at right angles to the LINES OF FORCE in a magnetic field [K F *Gauss* †1855 Ger mathematician & astronomer]

**Gaussian distribution** /'gowsi‚ən/ *n, statistics* NORMAL DISTRIBUTION (statistical function) [K F *Gauss*]

**gauze** /gawz/ *n* **1a** a thin often transparent fabric used chiefly for clothing or draperies **b** a loosely woven cotton surgical dressing **c** a fine mesh of metal or plastic filaments **2** a thin haze or mist [MF *gaze*, prob fr *Gaza*, town in Palestine] – **gauzy** *adj*, **gauzily** *adv*, **gauziness** *n*

**gavage** /'gavahzh, 'gavij/ *n, medicine* introduction of material, esp food, into the stomach by a tube [Fr, fr *gaver* to stuff, feed forcibly]

**gave** /gayv/ *past of* GIVE

**¹gavel** /'gav(ə)l/ *n* rent or tariff in medieval England [ME, fr OE *gafol*; akin to OE *giefan* to give]

**²gavel** *n* a small mallet with which a chairman, judge, or auctioneer commands attention or confirms a vote, sale, etc [origin unknown]

**³gavel** *vt* **-ll-** (*NAm* **-l-, -ll-**) to hammer (as if) with a gavel

**gavelkind** /-‚kiend/ *n, law* a former system of land tenure, confined chiefly to Kent, whereby tenants had certain rights (e g the right to dispose of land by will) and provision was made for the equal division of land among heirs if no will were made [ME *gavelkynde*, fr ¹*gavel* + *kinde* kind]

**gavial** /'gayvi‚əl, -vyəl/ *n* a large Indian crocodile (*Gavialis gangeticus*) [Fr, modif of Hindi *ghariyāl*]

**gavotte** /gə'vot/ *n* **1** an 18th-century dance of French peasant origin in which the feet are raised rather than slid **2** a composition or movement of music (e g in a 17th- or 18th-century series of dances) in moderately quick time having four beats in a bar [Fr, fr MF, fr OProv *gavoto*, fr *gavot* inhabitant of the Alps] – **gavotte** *vi*

**Gawd** /gawd/ *n* God – used in writing to represent a substandard pronunciation

**¹gawk** /gawk/ *vi, informal* to gawp [perh alter. of obs *gaw* to stare, fr ME *gawen*, fr ON *gā* to heed, mark] – **gawker** *n*

**²gawk** *n* a clumsy awkward person [prob fr E dial. *gawk* left-handed] – **gawkish** *adj*, **gawkishly** *adv*, **gawkishness** *n*

**gawky** /'gawki/ *adj* awkward, and usu lanky ⟨*a* ~ *child with long arms and legs*⟩ – **gawkily** *adv*, **gawky** *n*

**gawp** /gawp/ *vi, informal* to gape or stare stupidly [alter. of ME *galpen* to yawn, gape; akin to OE *gielpan* to boast, praise – more at YELP]

**gawsie, gawsy** /'gawsi/ *adj, chiefly Scot* prosperous and jolly looking [origin unknown]

**gay** /gay/ *adj* **1** happily excited; merry, cheerful **2** bright, attractive ⟨~ *sunny meadows*⟩ **3** given to social pleasures ⟨*the* ~ *life*⟩ **4** homosexual [ME, fr MF *gai*] – **gay** *adv*, **gayness** *n*

*usage* **Gay** is the preferred word used by homosexuals of themselves, and this has become such an important sense of the word that one may be misunderstood if one uses it simply to mean "cheerful"; ⟨*a* **gay** *party*⟩ has two meanings. **Synonyms** see JOYFUL **antonyms** grave, sober; straight, hetero (for 4)

**²gay** *n* a homosexual

**gayety** /'gayəti/ *n, archaic or NAm* gaiety

**gayly** /'gayli/ *adv, archaic* gaily

**¹gaze** /gayz/ *vi* to fix the eyes in a steady and intent look for a long or short time [ME *gazen*, prob fr Scand origin; akin to Sw dial. *gasa* to stare] – **gazer** *n*

**synonyms Gaze, gape, glare, stare, eye,** and **peer** all mean "look at something long or attentively", but vary widely in their motives and attitudes. **Gaze** may imply wonder, admiration, fascination, curiosity, and awe ⟨**gazed** *at the spectacle laid out before them*⟩. **Gape** suggests open-mouthed gazing as a result of stupidity or amazement ⟨**gaped** *in disbelief at the hole where his house had been*⟩. **Stare** stresses the fixity of a gaze which may be due to astonishment or curiosity, or, if directed at a person, to sometimes unintentional insolence. **Glare** adds to **stare** suggestions of fierceness and hostility. **Peer** differs from the others in suggesting a narrow, straining look, often at something quite close ⟨**peered** *at the paper without her spectacles*⟩. **Eye**, like **stare**, has a suggestion of rudeness, and implies looking at something or someone as if one were taking their measure ⟨**eyed** *her with suspicion*⟩. Compare ¹SEE

²**gaze** *n* a fixed intent look

**gazebo** /gə'zeeboh/ *n, pl* **gazebos** a freestanding roofed structure usu open at the sides and situated so as to command a view; *broadly* BELVEDERE (structure designed to command a view) [perh fr ¹*gaze* + L -*ebo* (as in *videbo* I shall see)]

**gazehound** /'gayz,hownd/ *n, archaic* a dog that hunts by sight rather than by scent; *esp* a greyhound

**gazelle** /gə'zel/ *n, pl* **gazelles**, *esp collectively* **gazelle** any of numerous small graceful African and Asian antelopes (*Gazella* and related genera) noted for their swiftness and soft lustrous eyes [Fr, fr MF, fr Ar *ghazāl*]

¹**gazette** /gə'zet/ *n* 1 a newspaper – usu in newspaper titles 2 an official journal containing announcements of honours and government appointments [Fr, fr It *gazzetta*, fr It dial. *gazeta*, fr *gazeta* small copper coin (the price of the newspaper)]

²**gazette** *vt, chiefly Br* 1 to announce or publish in a gazette 2 to announce the appointment or status of in an official gazette ⟨*he was* ~d *major*⟩

**gazetteer** /,gazə'tiə/ *n* a geographical dictionary or a dictionary of place names [*The Gazetteer's: or, Newsman's Interpreter*, a geographical index edited by Laurence Echard †1730 E historian]

**gazpacho** /gəz'pachoh, gəs-/ *n, pl* **gazpachos** a Spanish cold soup containing tomatoes, olive oil, garlic, peppers, and usu breadcrumbs [Sp]

**gazump** /gə'zump/ *vb, Br* to thwart (a would-be house purchaser) by raising the price between agreement to sell and signature of the contract [earlier *gezumph, gazoomph, gazumph* to swindle, perh fr Yiddish] – **gazumper** *n*

**G clef** /jee/ *n* TREBLE CLEF

**'G-,cramp** *n* a clamp (e g for woodworking) that is shaped somewhat like a letter G

**Ge** /zhay/ *n, pl* **Ge** *esp collectively* **Ges** 1 a member of a group of American Indian peoples of E Brazil 2 the language of the Ge peoples

**ge-** /ji-/, **geo-** *comb form* 1a ground; soil ⟨*geophyte*⟩ ⟨*geophagy*⟩ b earth; earth's surface ⟨*geophysics*⟩ ⟨*geodesic*⟩ 2 geographical; geography and ⟨*geopolitics*⟩ [ME *geo-*, fr MF & L; MF, fr L, fr Gk *gē-, geō-*, fr *gē*]

**gean** /jeen/ *n, chiefly Br* a wild SWEET CHERRY tree (*Prunus avium*); *also* its fruit [MF *guisne, guine*]

**geanticline** /ji'antiklien/ *n* an upward fold formed by the compression and arching of the earth's crust and extending over a large area of the earth's surface – compare GEOSYNCLINE – **geanticlinal** *adj*

¹**gear** /giə/ *n* 1a clothing or an article of clothing worn on a specified part of the body – often in combination ⟨*headgear*⟩ ⟨*motorcycle* ~⟩ b movable property; goods 2 a set of equipment, usu for a particular purpose ⟨*fishing* ~⟩ 3a the rigging or tackle of a ship or boat b the harness of esp horses 4a(1) a mechanism that performs a specified function in a complete machine ⟨*steering* ~⟩ a(2) a toothed wheel a(3) working relation, position, or adjustment ⟨*in* ~⟩ b any of two or more adjustments of a power-transmitting apparatus (e g of a bicycle or motor vehicle) that determine direction of travel or ratio of engine rotational speed to vehicle speed [ME *gere*, fr OE *gearwe*; akin to OHG *garuwi* equipment, clothing, OE *gearu* ready] – **change/shift gear** 1 to engage a different gear in a motor vehicle 2 to alter mood or setting

²**gear** *vt* 1a to provide (e g machinery) with gearing b to connect by gearing c to put into gear 2a to make ready for effective operation b to adjust so as to match, blend with, or satisfy something – usu + *to* ⟨*an institution* ~ed *to the needs of the blind*⟩ ~ *vi* 1 *of machinery* to be in or come into gear 2 to become adjusted so as to match, blend, or harmonize

**gearbox** /-,boks/ *n* a protective casing enclosing gears; *also* the gears so enclosed

**gear change** *n* 1 an act or the action of changing gear 2 a device (e g a gear lever) or mechanism for changing gear

**gearing** /'giəring/ *n* 1 the act or process of providing or fitting with gears 2 the parts by which motion is transmitted from one portion of machinery to another; *esp* a series of gear wheels 3 *Br* the use of supplementary capital (e g borrowed money) not in the form of shares to increase the returns, and hence the dividends that can be paid on shares; *also* the resultant economic advantage

**gear lever** *n* a lever (e g in a motor vehicle) that is connected to the gearbox and engages different gears

**gearshift** /'giə,shift/ *n, NAm* GEAR CHANGE 2

**gear wheel** *n* a toothed wheel that engages another piece of a mechanism; a cogwheel

**gecko** /'gekoh/ *n, pl* **geckos, geckoes** any of numerous small chiefly tropical and nocturnal insect-eating lizards (family Gekkonidae) noted for their ability to walk on vertical or overhanging surfaces [Malay *ge'kok*, of imit origin]

¹**gee** /jee/ *n, NAm slang* 1000 dollars [grand]

²**gee** *interj, chiefly NAm* – used as an introductory expletive or to express surprise or enthusiasm [euphemism for *Jesus*]

**geebung** /'jeebung/ *n* any of several chiefly Australian trees or shrubs (genus *Persoonia* of the family Proteaceae) with hard narrow leaves, long-lasting yellow or white flowers, and a small edible fruit; *also* this fruit [native name in Australia]

**geegaw** /'jeegaw, 'gee-/ *n* GEWGAW (trinket)

**gee-gee** /'jee-,jee/ *n, informal* a horse – used esp by or to children or in betting on horse races [redupl of *gee* (as in *gee-up*)]

**geese** /gees/ *pl of* GOOSE

**geest** /geest/ *n* old ALLUVIAL material (material deposited by flowing water) on the surface of land [Ger]

**,gee-'up** *interj* – used as a command (e g to a draught animal, esp a horse) to move ahead, or to turn to the right [origin unknown]

**gee up** *vt, informal* to stir to greater activity; give an impetus to

**,gee-'whiz** *adj, NAm informal* 1 marked by or arousing naive enthusiasm, excitement, and wonder 2 marked by spectacular or astonishing qualities or achievement

**gee whiz** /wiz/ *interj, chiefly NAm* ² GEE [euphemism for *Jesus Christ*]

**geezer** /'geezə/ *n, informal* a man, fellow; *esp* one who is thought a little odd or peculiar – chiefly in *old geezer* △ geyser [prob alter. of Sc *guiser* one in disguise, fr ME (northern) *gysar*, fr *gysen, gyzen* to dress – more at GUISARD]

**gefilte fish** /gə'filtə/ *n* a Jewish dish consisting of fish, breadcrumbs, eggs, and seasoning shaped into balls or ovals and boiled in a fish stock [Yiddish, lit., filled fish]

**gegenschein** /'gaygən,shien/ *n, often cap* a very faint round patch of light in the ECLIPTIC (apparent path of the sun among the stars) opposite the sun, probably associated in origin with the ZODIACAL LIGHT (glow in the sky seen immediately before dawn and after twilight) [Ger, fr *gegen* against, counter- + *schein* shine]

**Gehenna** /gə'henə/ *n* 1 HELL 1b 2 a place or state of misery [LL, fr Gk *Geenna*, fr Heb *Gê' Hinnōm*, lit., valley of Hinnom]

**Geiger counter** /'geigə/ *n* an electronic instrument for detecting the presence and intensity of radiation (e g COSMIC RAYS or particles from a radioactive substance) by means of its IONIZING effect on an enclosed gas, which reduces the resistance of the gas to the passage of an electric current resulting in an electrical pulse which can be registered by visible or audible means [Hans Geiger †1945 Ger physicist & W *Müller*, 20th-c Ger physicist]

**Geiger-Müller counter** /'moolə/ *n* GEIGER COUNTER

**geisha** /'gayshə/, **geisha girl** *n, pl* **geisha, geishas** a Japanese girl who is trained to provide entertaining and lighthearted company, esp for a man or a group of men [Jap, fr *gei* art + -*sha* person]

¹**gel** /jel/ *n* 1 a semi-solid jellylike COLLOID composed of a liquid evenly dispersed in a solid – compare SOL 2 JELLY 3 3 a thin coloured transparent sheet used esp to colour stage lighting [*gelatin*]

²**gel**, *chiefly NAm* **jell** *vb* -**ll**- 1 to change into a gel 2 to (cause to) take shape or become definite – **gelable** *adj*, **gelation** *n*

³**gel** /gel/ *n* a girl – used in writing to represent an upper-class pronunciation

**gelada** /'jelədə, 'gel-, ji'lahdə, gil-/ *n* a long-haired ape (*Theropithecus gelada*) of Ethiopia [prob fr Ar *qilādah* collar, mane]

**gelate** /'jelayt/ *vi* GEL 1

**gelatine, gelatin** /'jelətin, -teen/ *n* **1** a glutinous material obtained from animal tissues by boiling; *esp* a protein used as or in food (eg to set jellies), and in photography and medicine **2a** any of various substances (eg AGAR) resembling gelatine **b** an edible jelly made with gelatine **3** GEL 3 [Fr *gélatine* edible jelly, gelatin, fr It *gelatina*, fr *gelato*, pp of *gelare* to freeze, fr L – more at COLD]

**gelatin-ize, -ise** /ji'latiniez/ *vt* **1** to convert into a jelly or jellylike form **2** to coat or treat with gelatine ~ *vi* to become jellylike in consistency or change into a jelly – **gelatinization** *n*

**gelatinous** /ji'latinəs/ *adj* **1** like gelatine or jelly in consistency; viscous **2** of or containing gelatine – **gelatinously** *adv*, **gelatinousness** *n*

**gelation** /ji'laysh(ə)n/ *n* the action or process of freezing [L *gelation-*, *gelatio*, fr *gelatus*, pp of *gelare*]

¹**geld** /geld/ *vt* **1** to castrate (esp a male animal) **2** to deprive of a natural or essential part [ME *gelden*, fr ON *gelda*; akin to OE *gelte* young sow, Gk *gallos* eunuch, priest of the goddess Cybele]

²**geld** *n* a tax on land paid to the crown under Anglo-Saxon and Norman kings [OE *gield*, *geld* service, tribute; akin to OE *gieldan* to pay, yield – more at YIELD]

**gelding** /'gelding/ *n* a castrated animal; *specif* a castrated male horse [ME, fr ON *geldingr*, fr *gelda*]

**gelid** /'jelid/ *adj*, *chiefly poetic* extremely cold; icy [L *gelidus*, fr *gelu* frost, cold – more at COLD] – **gelidly** *adv*, **gelidity** *n*

**gelignite** /'jeligniet/ *n* a dynamite in which the explosive material is absorbed in a base consisting chiefly of POTASSIUM NITRATE or SODIUM NITRATE, usu with some wood pulp [*gelatin* + L *ignis* fire + *-ite* – more at IGNEOUS]

**gellant** *also* **gelant** /'jelənt/ *n* a substance used to produce gelling

**gelt** /gelt/ *n*, *chiefly NAm slang* money [D & Ger *geld* & Yiddish *gelt*]

¹**gem** /jem/ *n* **1a** a jewel **b** a precious or sometimes semiprecious stone, esp cut and polished for ornament **2a** something (eg a joke or saying) prized, esp for great beauty or perfection **b** a highly prized or well-beloved person [ME *gemme*, fr MF, fr L *gemma* bud, gem] – **gemmy** *adj*

²**gem** *vt* **-mm-** to adorn (as if) with gems

**Gemara** /ge'mahrə/ *n* a commentary on the MISHNAH (collection of Jewish traditions), forming most of the TALMUD (Jewish scriptures); *broadly* TALMUD [Aram *gĕmārā* completion] – **Gemaric** *adj*, **Gemarist** *n*

**gemeinschaft** /gə'mien,shaft/ *n*, *pl* **gemeinschaften** /-shaftən/ *often cap* a social relationship or community used as a reference norm in sociology and characterized by the common interests of individuals based on strong bonds of loyalty and kinship within a common tradition – compare GESELLSCHAFT [Ger, community, fr *gemein* common, general + *-schaft* -ship]

¹**geminate** /'jeminət/ *adj* arranged in pairs – used technically [L *geminatus*, pp of *geminare* to double, fr *geminus* twin] – **geminately** *adv*

²**geminate** /'jemi,nayt/ *vt* to double ~ *vi* to become double or paired □ used technically – **gemination** *n*

**Gemini** /'jemini, -nie/ *n* **1** a constellation of the ZODIAC (imaginary belt in the heavens) lying between Taurus and Cancer and containing the stars Castor and Pollux. It is represented as a pair of twins. **2a** the 3rd sign of the zodiac in astrology, held to govern the period May 23 - June 21 approx **b** somebody born under this sign [L, lit., the twins (Castor and Pollux, sons of the god Zeus)] – **Geminian** *adj or n*

**gemma** /'jemə/ *n*, *pl* **gemmae** /'jemie, -mee/ **1a** a plant bud; *esp* one that develops into a leaf **b** an asexual reproductive body occurring in mosses, liverworts, etc that becomes detached from the parent plant and develops into a new individual **2** an outgrowth of an animal that is produced by asexual reproduction and is capable of development into a new animal [L] – **gemmaceous** *adj*, **gemmation** *n*

**gemmate** /'jemayt/ *adj* having gemmae; reproducing by gemmae

**gemmiferous** /je'mifərəs/ *adj* **1** producing or containing gems **2** bearing or reproducing by a gemmae; gemmate

**gemmiparous** /je'mipərəs/ *adj* gemmate – **gemmiparously** *adv*

**gemmologist, gemologist** /je'molɒjist/ *n* a specialist in gems; *specif* one who values gems and assesses their quality – **gemmology** *n*, **gemmological** *adj*

**gemmulation** /,jemyoo'laysh(ə)n/ *n* formation of or reproduction by gemmules

**gemmule** /'jemyoohl/ *n* a small bud or gemma: eg **a** a hypothetical hereditary particle conceived by Darwin as the agency responsible for the production of a part in a new individual like the part in which the particle originated **b** a mass of cells inside certain animals (eg sponges) that gives rise to a new individual [Fr, fr L *gemmula*, dim. of *gemma* bud] – **gemmuliferous** *adj*

**gemsbok** /'gemzbok/ *n*, *pl* **gemsboks**, *esp collectively* **gemsbok** a large and strikingly marked ORYX (type of antelope) (*Oryx gazella*) formerly abundant in southern Africa [Afrik, lit., male chamois, fr Ger *gemsbock*, fr *gems*, *gemse* chamois + *bock* male goat]

**gemstone** /'jem,stohn/ *n* a mineral or stone that when cut and polished can be used as a gem

**gemütlich** /gə'moohtlikh (Ger gəmy:tlıç)/ *adj* snug and cheerful, often to a smothering degree or in a way suggestive of middle-class comforts; cosy; *also* congenial [Ger, fr *gemüt* spirit, heart]

**gemütlichkeit** /gə'moohtlikh,kiet (Ger gəmy:tlıçkaıt)/ *n* the quality of being gemütlich [Ger, fr *gemütlich*]

**gen** /jen/ *n*, *Br informal* the correct or complete information [short for *general (information)*]

¹**gen-** /jen-/, **geno-** *comb form* **1** race ⟨geno*cide*⟩ **2** genus; kind ⟨geno*type*⟩ [Gk *genos* birth, race, kind – more at KIN]

²**gen-** /jeen-/, **geno-** *comb form* gene ⟨geno*cline*⟩

**-gen** /-jən/ *also* **-gene** /-jeen/ *comb form* (*n* → *n*) **1** one that produces ⟨*andro*gen⟩ ⟨*carcino*gen⟩ **2** one that is (so) produced ⟨*culti*gen⟩ ⟨*phos*gene⟩ [Fr *-gène*, fr Gk *-genēs* born; akin to Gk *genos* birth]

**gendarme** /'zhon,dahm (Fr ʒɑ̃darm)/ *n* **1** a member of a body of armed police, esp in France **2** *humorous* a policeman [Fr, fr MF, back-formation fr *gensdarmes*, pl of *gent d'armes*, lit., armed people]

**gendarmerie** *also* **gendarmery** /'zhon,dahməri (Fr ʒɑ̃darməri)/ *n taking sing or pl vb* a body of gendarmes [MF *gendarmerie*, fr *gendarme*]

**gender** /'jendə/ *n* **1** sex ⟨*black divinities of the feminine* ~ – Charles Dickens⟩ **2a** a system of subdivision within a grammatical class (eg noun, pronoun, adjective, or verb) of a language that is partly arbitrary but also partly based on distinguishable characteristics (eg sex) and that determines agreement with and selection of other words or grammatical forms ⟨*the choice of* elle *to replace* la plage *in French is determined by* ~ ⟩; *also* a single subclass within such a system ⟨*masculine* ~ ⟩ **b** membership of a word or a grammatical form in such a subclass, esp as demonstrated by the form of its variable ending or of some other element of its make-up [ME *gendre*, fr MF *genre*, *gendre*, fr L *gener-*, *genus* birth, race, kind, gender – more at KIN]

**gene** /jeen/ *n* a unit of inheritance, carried on a chromosome, that consists of a molecule of DNA or sometimes RNA, is transmitted from parent to offspring, and that controls the passing on of hereditary characteristics either by specifying the structure of a particular protein or by controlling the function of other genetic material [Ger *gen*, short for *pangen*, fr *pan-* + *-gen*]

**genealogy** /,jeeni'aləji/ *n* **1** an account of the descent of a person, family, or group from an ancestor or from older forms **2** the descent of a person, family, or group from an ancestor or from older forms; pedigree; lineage **3** the study of family pedigrees [ME *genealogie*, fr MF, fr LL *genealogia*, fr Gk, fr *genea* race, family + *-logia* -logy; akin to Gk *genos* race] – **genealogist** *n*, **genealogical** *adj*, **genealogically** *adv*

**gene flow** *n* the passage and establishment of genes typical of one breeding population into the GENE POOL of another (eg by hybridization)

**gene frequency** *n* (a ratio that expresses) the frequency of occurrence of a particular version of a gene in a population, compared with the frequency of occurrence of all the alternative versions (ALLELES) of that gene

**gene pool** *n* the whole body of genes in an interbreeding population

**genera** /'jenərə/ *pl of* GENUS

**generable** /'jen(ə)rəbl/ *adj* capable of being generated

¹**general** /'jen(ə)rəl/ *adj* **1** involving or applicable to the whole **2** of, involving, or applicable to every member of a class, kind, or group **3a** applicable to or characteristic of the majority of individuals involved; prevalent **b** concerned or dealing with universal rather than particular aspects **4** of, determined by, or

concerned with main elements rather than limited details; approximate rather than strictly accurate ⟨*bearing a ~ resemblance to the original*⟩ **5** not confined by specialization or careful limitation ⟨*a ~ amnesty*⟩ **6** belonging to the common nature of a group of like individuals; generic **7** holding superior rank or taking precedence over others similarly titled ⟨*the ~ manager*⟩ [ME, fr MF, fr L *generalis*, fr *gener-, genus* kind, class – more at KIN] – **in general** usually, FOR THE MOST PART

**²general** *n* **1** something (eg a concept, principle, or statement) that involves or is applicable to the whole **2** the chief of a religious order or congregation **3** – see MILITARY RANKS table **4** *archaic* the general public; the people

**general assembly** *n* **1** *often cap G&A* the highest governing body in a religious denomination (eg the Presbyterian church) **2** *cap G&A* the supreme deliberative body of the United Nations

**general average** *n* voluntary partial loss in marine insurance that is shared proportionally by all parties concerned – compare PARTICULAR AVERAGE

**General Certificate of Education** *n* a British national examination in any of many subjects taken at three levels, the first, ORDINARY LEVEL, at about the age of 16 and the second and third, ADVANCED and SCHOLARSHIP LEVELS, which serve as university entrance qualifications, at about 18

**general degree** *n, Br* a university degree that is less specialized in content and usu lower in status than an HONOURS Degree

**general delivery** *n, NAm* POSTE RESTANTE

**general election** *n* an election in which candidates are elected in all constituencies of a nation or state

**generalissimo** /ˌjen(ə)rəˈlisimoh/ *n, pl* **generalissimos** the supreme commander of several armies acting together; *also* the supreme commander of a nation's armed forces [It, fr *generale* general + *-issimo*, superl suffix]

**generalist** /ˈjen(ə)rəlist/ *n* one whose skills, capabilities, or interests extend to several different fields or activities – compare SPECIALIST

**generality** /ˌjenəˈraləti/ *n* **1** the quality or state of being general; total applicability **2a** GENERALIZATION 2 **b** a vague or inadequate statement **3** *taking pl or sing vb* the greatest part; *the* majority

**general-ization, -isation** /ˌjen(ə)rəlieˈzaysh(ə)n/ *n* **1** the act or process of generalizing **2** a general statement, law, principle, or proposition (that does not take adequate account of the facts) ⟨*all ~s are untrue, including this one*⟩ **3** the act or process whereby a response is made to a stimulus similar to, but not identical with, a reference stimulus

**general-ize, -ise** /ˈjen(ə)rə,liez/ *vt* **1** to make general; give a general form to **2a** to derive or infer (a general conception or principle) from particulars **b** to draw a general conclusion from **3** to give general applicability to ⟨*~ a law*⟩; *also* to make indefinite ~ *vi* **1** to make generalizations; *also* to make vague or indefinite statements **2** *of a disease* to extend throughout the body – **generalizable** *adj,* **generalizer** *n*

**generalized** /ˈjen(ə)rəliezd/ *adj* made general; *esp* neither highly differentiated biologically nor strictly adapted to a particular environment

**generally** /ˈjen(ə)rəli/ *adv* **1** without regard to specific instances ⟨*~ speaking*⟩ **2** usually; AS A RULE ⟨*he ~ drinks tea*⟩ **3** collectively; AS A WHOLE ⟨*of interest to children ~*⟩

**general management committee** *n* a committee made up of ward and trade-union delegates that controls the policy of a constituency Labour Party

**general meeting** *n* a meeting that is open to all members (eg of a company, union, or society) ⟨*annual ~*⟩

**general officer** *n* a commissioned officer in the army, air force, or marines above the rank of colonel – compare COMPANY OFFICER, FIELD OFFICER

**general of the air force** *n* – see MILITARY RANKS table

**general of the army** *n* – see MILITARY RANKS table

**general paper** *n, Br* an examination paper testing general knowledge and powers of expression

**general paralysis of the insane** *n* GENERAL PARESIS

**general paresis** *n* the insanity and paralysis caused by the final stage of syphilis

**general post** *n, chiefly Br* a general exchange of positions or locations

**General Post Office** *n* – formerly used as the title of the Post Office in the United Kingdom

**general practitioner** *n* a medical doctor who treats all types of disease and is usu the first doctor consulted by a patient

**general-'purpose** *adj* suitable to be used for two or more basic purposes

**general semantics** *n taking sing or pl vb* a doctrine and educational discipline involving training in the more critical use of words and other symbols – compare SEMANTICS

**generalship** /ˈjen(ə)rəlship/ *n* **1** the (time spent in) office of a general **2** military skill in a high commander; *broadly* organizational skill in a person

**general staff** *n taking sing or pl vb* a group of officers who aid a commander in administration, training, supply, etc

**general store, general stores** *n taking sing or pl vb* a small retail shop located usu in a small or rural community that sells a wide variety of goods, including groceries, but is not divided into departments

**general strike** *n* a strike in all or many of the industries of a region or country

**general studies** *n pl* a school course (eg attended by the whole of a sixth form) designed to give subject specialists some further education outside their subject

**general theory of relativity** *n* RELATIVITY 3b

**general union** *n* a trade union which organizes workers regardless of the particular skill they possess or the industry they work in – compare CRAFT UNION, INDUSTRIAL UNION

**generate** /ˈjenə,rayt/ *vt* **1** to bring into existence: eg **1a** to beget, create **b** to originate by a physical or chemical process; produce ⟨*~ electricity*⟩ **2** to define (a mathematical or linguistic set or structure) by the application of one or more rules or operations to given quantities or items; *esp* to trace out (eg a curve) by a moving point or trace out (eg a surface) by a moving curve **3** to be the cause of (a situation, action, or state of mind) ⟨*these stories . . . ~ a good deal of psychological suspense – Atlantic*⟩ [L *generatus*, pp of *generare*, fr *gener-, genus* birth – more at KIN]

**generation** /ˌjenəˈraysh(ə)n/ *n* **1a** a group of living organisms constituting a single step in the line of descent from an ancestor **b** *taking sing or pl vb* a group of individuals born and living during the same period of time **c** *taking sing or pl vb* a group of individuals sharing a usu specified status for a limited period ⟨*the next ~ of students*⟩ **d** a type or class of objects, usu developed from an earlier type ⟨*a new ~ of computers*⟩ **2** the average span of time between the birth of parents and that of their offspring **3a** the action or process of producing offspring; procreation **b** origination by a usu mathematical or chemical process; production; *specif* the process of tracing out a geometric figure **c** the process of coming or bringing into being ⟨*~ of income*⟩ – **generational** *adj*

**generative** /ˈjen(ə)rətiv/ *adj* having the power or function of generating, originating, producing, or reproducing

**generative cell** *n* a cell that functions in sexual reproduction; GAMETE; *specif* the small cell within a POLLEN GRAIN that contains the GENERATIVE NUCLEUS

**generative grammar** *n* **1** an ordered set of rules for producing the sentences permitted by the grammar of a language **2** TRANSFORMATIONAL GRAMMAR

**generative nucleus** *n* the one of the two nuclei in a mature POLLEN GRAIN of a plant that produces seeds, that divides to form two sperm or male nuclei – compare TUBE NUCLEUS

**generative semantics** *n taking sing or pl vb* the theory that the structure of grammar and of meaning are of the same formal nature, that there is a single system of rules relating them to each other, and that grammatical well-formedness must be understood in terms of meaning, context, and the rules relating these to grammatical structure

**generator** /ˈjenə,raytə/ *n* **1** one who or that which generates **2** an apparatus in which vapour or gas is formed **3** a machine by which mechanical energy is changed into electrical energy

**generatrix** /ˌjenəˈraytriks/ *n, pl* **generatrices** /-ˈraytrəseez, -rəˈtriseez/ a point, line, or surface whose motion generates a line, surface, or solid [NL, fr L, fem of *generator*]

**¹generic** /jəˈnerik/ *adj* **1a** relating to or characteristic of a whole group or class; general **b** not having a trademark **2** relating to or having the rank of a biological genus [Fr *générique*, fr L *gener-, genus* birth, kind, class] – **generically** *adv*

**²generic** *n* a generic drug

**generosity** /ˌjenəˈrosəti/ *n* **1** the quality of being generous in spirit or act; *esp* liberality in giving **2** a generous act

**generous** /ˈjen(ə)rəs/ *adj* **1** magnanimous, kindly **2** free in giving (eg of money or help) **3** marked by abundance or ample proportions; plentiful [MF or L; MF *genereus*, fr L *generosus*, fr *gener-, genus* birth, family] – **generously** *adv,* **generousness** *n*

**genesis** /'jenəsis/ *n, pl* **geneses** /-seez/ the origin or coming into being of something [L, fr Gk, fr *gignesthai* to be born – more at KIN]

**Genesis** *n* – see BIBLE table [Gk]

**genet** /'jenit/ *n* any of several small African and European cat-like flesh-eating mammals (genus *Genetta*) related to the CIVET CATS but with scent glands less developed and claws fully retractable; *esp* one (*Genetta genetta*) found chiefly in the Iberian peninsula and parts of France [ME *genete*, fr MF, fr Ar *jar-nayț*]

**genetic** /jə'netik/ *also* **genetical** /-ikl/ *adj* **1** of or determined by the origin or development of something **2a** of or involving genetics **b** GENIC [fr *genesis*, by analogy to *antithesis: antithetic*] – **genetically** *adv*

**-genetic** /-jə'netik/ *comb form* (→ *adj*) -GENIC 1,2 ⟨*psych*ogenetic⟩ ⟨*spermato*genetic⟩

**genetic code** *n* the sequence of BASES in a strand of DNA or RNA that determines the specific AMINO ACID sequence of a protein and constitutes the biochemical basis of heredity – called also TRIPLET CODE

**genetic drift** *n* changes of GENE FREQUENCY in small populations due to chance preservation or extinction of particular genes

**genetic engineering** *n* artificial manipulation or change of the genetic constitution of living things for experimental or industrial purposes – **genetic engineer** *n*

**genetic map** *n* the arrangement of genes on a CHROMOSOME (strand of gene-carrying material)

**genetic marker** *n* a gene or genetic characteristic that serves esp to identify genes or characteristics linked with it

**genetics** /jə'netiks/ *n taking sing vb* **1** a branch of biology that deals with (the mechanisms and structures involved in) the heredity and variation of the genetic material and characteristics of organisms **2** *taking sing or pl vb* the genetic make-up of an organism, type, group, or condition – **geneticist** *n*

**geneva** /jə'neevə/ *n* a strongly alcoholic ginlike drink flavoured with juniper berries and made in the Netherlands – called also HOLLANDS [modif of obs D *genever* (now *jenever*), lit., juniper, deriv of L *juniperus*]

**Geneva bands** /je'neevə/ *n pl* two strips of white cloth hanging from the front of a clerical collar, sometimes worn by Protestant clergymen [*Geneva*, city in Switzerland; fr their use by the Calvinist clergy of Geneva]

**Geneva convention** /jə'neevə/ *n* any of a series of agreements concerning the treatment of prisoners of war and of the sick, wounded, and dead in battle, first made at Geneva in 1864, and subsequently accepted in later revisions by most nations

**Geneva gown** *n* a loose large-sleeved black gown worn by academics and some Protestant clergymen [fr its use by the Calvinist clergy of Geneva]

**Genevan** /jə'neev(ə)n/ *adj* **1** of Geneva **2** of Geneva about the time of the beginning of the Reformation; *specif* of Calvinism – **Genevan** *n*

¹**genial** /'jeenyəl, -ni·əl/ *adj* **1a** favourable to growth or comfort; mild ⟨~ *sunshine*⟩ **b** cheerfully good-tempered; kindly ⟨*our ~ host*⟩ **2** *obs* relating to marriage ⟨*the ~ bed* – John Milton⟩ △ congenial [L *genialis*, fr *genius*] – **genially** *adv*, **geniality** *also* **genialness** *n*

²**genial** /jə'nee·əl/ *adj* of the chin [Gk *geneion* chin, fr *genys* jaw – more at CHIN]

**genic** /'jeenik, 'jenik/ *adj* of or being a gene – **genically** *adv*

**-genic** /-jenik/ *comb form* **1** producing; forming ⟨*erotogenic*⟩ **2** produced by; formed from ⟨*phyto*genic⟩ **3** suitable for production or reproduction by (a specified medium) ⟨*tele*genic⟩ [ISV -*gen* & -*geny* + -*ic*; (3) *photo*genic]

**geniculate** /jə'nikyoolət/, **geniculated** /-laytid/ *adj, biology* bent abruptly at an angle like a bent knee [L *geniculatus*, fr *geniculum*, dim. of *genu* knee – more at KNEE] – **geniculately** *adv*, **geniculation** *n*

**genie** /'jeeni/ *n, pl* **genies** *also* **genii** /'jeeni,ee, -,ie/ JINN (spirit in Arab folklore) *usage* see JINN [Fr *génie*, fr Ar *jinnīy*]

**genipi** /'jenipi/ *n* a small highly aromatic silvery-haired alpine plant (*Artemisia genipi*) of the daisy family; *also* a liqueur made from this plant [Fr *génépi*, *genépi*]

**genital** /'jenitl/ *adj* **1** generative **2** of or being a sexual organ **3** of or characterized by the final stage of sexual development in psychoanalytic theory, in which oral and anal impulses are largely replaced by the satisfaction obtained from relationships with other people, esp sex partners – compare ANAL, ORAL [ME,

fr L *genitalis*, fr *genitus*, pp of *gignere* to beget – more at KIN] – **genitally** *adv*

**genitalia** /,jeni'tayli·ə, -lyə/ *n taking pl vb* the genitals [L, fr neut pl of *genitalis*] – **genitalic** *adj*

**genitals** /'jenitlz/ *n pl* the organs of the reproductive system; *esp* the external male or female sex organs

¹**genitive** /'jenətiv/ *also* **genitival** /,jeni'tievl/ *adj* of or being the grammatical genitive – often used also of English phrases introduced by the preposition *of* [ME, fr L *genetivus, genitivus*, lit., of birth, fr *genitus*] – **genitivally** *adv*

²**genitive** *n* a grammatical case expressing typically a relationship of possessor or source; *also* a form in this case – compare POSSESSIVE

**genito-** /jenitoh-/ *comb form* genital and ⟨genito*urinary*⟩ [*genital*]

**genitourinary** /-'yooərin(ə)ri/ *adj* of the genital and urinary organs or their functions

**genius** /'jeenyəs, -ni·əs/ *n, pl* (*1a*) **genii** /'jeeni,ee, -ni,ie/, (*1b&4*) **genii** *also* **geniuses**, (*2&3*) **geniuses, genii**, (*5*) **geniuses** *also* **genii 1a** an attendant spirit of a person or place **b** a person who influences another for good or bad **2** a strong leaning or inclination; a penchant ⟨*fate did not allow him to indulge his ~ till those last few years* – Norman Douglas⟩ **3a** a special, distinctive, or identifying character or spirit ⟨*optimism was the ~ of the Victorian era*⟩ **b** the associations and traditions of a place **c** a personification or embodiment, esp of a quality or condition **4** a spirit, esp in Arab folklore **5a** a single strongly marked capacity or aptitude ⟨*had a ~ for teaching maths*⟩ **b** extraordinary intellectual power, esp as displayed in creative activity ⟨*it is perhaps in* Faust *that Goethe's ~ is most evident*⟩ **c** a person endowed with extraordinary intellectual power; *specif* a a person of a very high intelligence *usage* see JINN [L, tutelary spirit, fondness for social enjoyment, fr *gignere* to beget]

**genius loci** /'lohsie, 'lohki/ *n, pl* **genii loci** /'jeeni,ee/ **1** a guardian deity of a place ⟨*Britten, then, remains the ~ of Aldeburgh – The Listener*⟩ **2** the pervading atmosphere of a place [L]

**genizah** /ge'neezə/ *n* a storeroom in a synagogue for discarded books, papers, and sacred objects [Heb *gĕnīzāh*]

**geno-** – see GEN-

**genoa** /'jenoh-ə/ *n* a large headsail, used in racing and cruising yachts, which partly overlaps the mainsail [*Genoa*, city in NW Italy]

**genocide** /'jenə,sied/ *n* the deliberate and systematic destruction of a racial or cultural group [¹*gen-* + -*cide*] – **genocidal** *adj*

**genome** *also* **genom** /'jee,nohm/ *n* the complete single or basic (HAPLOID) set of CHROMOSOMES (strands of gene-carrying material) characteristic of a particular organism; the set of chromosomes present in an egg or sperm cell; *also* the set of chromosomes present in any cell [Ger *genom*, fr *gen-* ²*gen-* + *chromosom* chromosome] – **genomic** *adj*

**genotype** /'jenoh,tiep/ *n* **1** the genetic constitution of an individual – compare PHENOTYPE **2** a group of individuals sharing a particular genotype – **genotypic** *also* **genotypical** *adj*, **genotypically** *adv*, **genotypicity** *n*

**-genous** /-jənəs/ *comb form* (→ *adj*) **1** producing; yielding ⟨*alka*ligenous⟩ **2** produced by; originating in ⟨*endo*genous⟩ [-*gen* + -*ous*]

**genre** /'zhonh-rə (*Fr* ʒãːr)/ *n* **1** a sort, type **2** a category of artistic, musical, or literary composition characterized by a particular style, form, or content ⟨*an acknowledged masterpiece of the suspense ~*⟩ [Fr, fr MF *genre* kind, gender – more at GENDER]

**genre painting** *n* painting that depicts scenes or events from everyday life usu realistically

**genro** /gen'roh/ *n taking pl vb, often cap* the elder statesmen of Japan who formerly advised the emperor [Jap *genrō*]

**gens** /jenz/ *n, pl* **gentes** /'jenteez/ **1** an ancient Roman clan embracing the families of the same stock in the male line, with the members having a common name and being united in worship of their common ancestor **2** a clan; *esp* one formed through the male line of descent [L *gent-, gens* – more at GENTLE]

**gent** /jent/ *n, nonstandard or humorous* a gentleman

**gentamicin** /,jentə'miesin/ *n* an antibiotic drug effective against many different bacteria that is obtained from a bacterium (*Micromonospora purpurea* or *Micromonospora echinospora*) and used esp in the treatment of serious infections affecting the whole body (eg septicaemia) [alter. of earlier *gentamycin*, fr *genta-* (prob irreg fr *gentian violet;* fr the colour of the bacterium from which it is produced) + *-mycin*]

**genteel** /jen'teel/ *adj* **1a** having an aristocratic quality or flavour; stylish **b** of the gentry or upper class **c** elegant or graceful in manner, appearance, or shape **d** free from vulgarity or rudeness; polite **2a** maintaining or striving to maintain the appearance of superior social status or respectability **b** marked by false delicacy, prudery, or affectation [MF *gentil* gentle] – **genteelly** *adv*, **genteelness** *n*

**genteelism** /jen'tee,liz(ə)m/ *n* a word believed by its user to be more genteel than another (eg *stomach* for *belly*)

**gentian** /'jensh(ə)n/ *n* **1** any of various plants (esp genera *Gentiana* and *Gentianella* of the family Gentianaceae, the gentian family) with smooth leaves and showy usu blue flowers **2** the underground stem (RHIZOME) and roots of a yellow-flowered gentian (*Gentiana lutea*) of S Europe that is used in bitter-tasting alcoholic drinks [ME *gencian*, fr MF *gentiane*, fr L *gentiana*, perh fr *Gentius*, 2nd-c BC Illyrian king reputed to have discovered its medicinal properties]

**gentian violet** *n, often cap G&V* a violet dye used to stain biological specimens for examination under a microscope and as a skin disinfectant and antiseptic, esp in the treatment of boils, ulcers, etc

**¹gentile** /'jentiel/ *n* **1a** *often cap* a person of a non-Jewish nation or of non-Jewish faith **b** a person who is not a Mormon **2** a heathen, pagan [ME, fr LL *gentilis*, fr L *gent-, gens* nation]

**²gentile** *adj* **1** *often cap* of the nations at large as distinguished from the Jews **2** heathen, pagan **3** of a nation, tribe, or clan [(3) L *gentilis*]

**gentilesse** /'jentiles/ *n, archaic* propriety of conduct befitting a member of the gentry [ME, fr MF, fr *gentil*]

**gentility** /jen'tiləti/ *n* **1a** the condition of belonging to the upper class **b** *taking sing or pl vb* the members of the upper class **2a(1)** proper conduct; courtesy **a(2)** attitudes or activity marked by false delicacy, prudery, or affectation **b** superior social status or prestige shown by manners, possessions, or lifestyle

**gentisic acid** /jen'tisik, -'tiz-/ *n* an acid, $C_7H_6O_4$, used medicinally as a painkiller and to stimulate sweating [ISV, fr *gentisin* (a pigment obtained from gentian root)]

**¹gentle** /'jentl/ *adj* **1a** belonging to a family of high social status **b** honourable, distinguished; *specif* of or belonging to a gentleman **c** kind, amiable – used esp in address as a complimentary epithet with archaic or humorous effect ⟨*bear with me, ~ reader*⟩ **d** suited to a person of high social station ⟨*~ pursuits*⟩ **2** free from harshness, sternness, or violence ⟨*O sleep, O ~ sleep, Nature's soft nurse* – Shak⟩ **3** soft, delicate ⟨*heard a ~ knock on the door*⟩ **4** MODERATE 1 [ME *gentil*, fr OF, fr L *gentilis* of a clan, of the same clan, fr *gent-, gens* clan, nation; akin to L *gignere* to beget – more at KIN] – **gentleness** *n*, **gently** *adv*

**²gentle** *n* **1** a maggot used as a bait in fishing **2** *archaic* a person of noble birth or status ⟨*~s, perchance you wonder at their show* – Shak⟩

**³gentle** *vt* **1a** to make mild, docile, soft, or moderate ⟨*~ a horse*⟩ **b** to mollify, placate **c** to stroke soothingly; pet **2** *obs* to raise from the ranks of the common people; ennoble

**gentle breeze** *n* wind having a speed of 12 to 19 kilometres per hour (about 8 to 12 miles per hour) *synonyms* see ¹WIND

**gentlefolk** /-,fohk/ *also* **gentlefolks** *n pl* people of good family and breeding

**gentleman** /'jentlmən/ *n* **1a** a man belonging to the landed gentry or nobility **b** a man who is chivalrous, well-mannered, and honourable (and of good birth or rank) **c** a man of independent wealth who does not work for a living **2** a man of any social class or condition – often in a courteous reference ⟨*show this ~ to a seat*⟩ or usu in the pl, in address ⟨*ladies and gentlemen*⟩ – **gentlemanly** *adj*, **gentlemanliness** *n*

*synonyms* Gentleman, man, lad, male, boy, youth: Man is the usual term, contrasting with *woman* or *child*. Except to stress a man's courtesy or chivalrousness ⟨*a perfect* gentleman⟩, gentleman is little used nowadays except as a polite form in someone's presence, or as a form of public address ⟨*Ladies and* gentlemen!⟩. A boy becomes a youth at or just after puberty; *girl* is therefore the female equivalent for either. But boy, unlike *girl*, is not used for adults, except to describe a man's circle of friends ⟨*he's out with the* boys⟩. Youth and lad both suggest immaturity, particularly the former. Lad is a more approving term than youth, but may be considered patronizing. It is more common than the equivalent female term, *lass*.

Male, like *female*, stresses biological differences and so is limited in use. See ¹MALE, compare LADY

**gentleman-at-'arms** *n, pl* **gentlemen-at-arms** any of a bodyguard of 40 gentlemen who attend the British sovereign on state occasions

**gentleman-'commoner** *n, pl* **gentlemen-commoners** any of a privileged class of COMMONERS (students without any form of grant from a college) formerly required to pay higher fees than ordinary commoners at the universities of Oxford and Cambridge

**gentleman farmer** *n, pl* **gentlemen farmers** a man of superior social position and wealth who farms mainly for pleasure rather than for profit

**gentleman's agreement, gentlemen's agreement** *n* an unwritten agreement secured only by the honour of the participants and not legally enforceable

**gentleman's gentleman** *n* a valet

**gentle sex** *n* the female sex; women in general

**gentlewoman** /'jentl,woomən/ *n* **1a** a woman of noble birth **b** a woman attendant on a lady of high rank **2** a woman of refined manners or good breeding; a lady

**gentoo** /'jentooh/ *n, pl* **gentoos 1** a penguin (*Pygoscelis papua*) common in the Falkland islands **2** *cap, archaic* a Hindu [(2) Pg *gentio*, lit., gentile, fr LL *gentilis;* (1) perh fr different origin]

**gentrify** /jentrifie/ *vt* to make into or suitable to a member of the gentry – **gentrification** *n*

**gentry** /'jentri/ *n* **1** *taking sing or pl vb* **1a** the upper or ruling class; the aristocracy **b** a class of society whose members are entitled to bear a coat of arms though not of noble rank; *esp* members of the land-owning class having such status **2** *taking pl vb* people of a specified class or kind – often used disparagingly ⟨*can't trust these academic ~*⟩ [ME *gentrie*, alter. of *gentrise* gentle birth, fr OF *genterise, gentelise*, fr *gentil* gentle]

**gents** /jents/ *n, pl* **gents** *often cap, chiefly informal* a public toilet for men [short for *gentlemen's*]

**genuflect** /'jenyoo,flekt/ *vi* **1** to bend the knee, esp in worship or as a gesture of respect (to sacred objects) **2** to be slavishly obedient or respectful; kowtow [LL *genuflectere*, fr L *genu* knee + *flectere* to bend – more at KNEE] – **genuflector** *n*, **genuflection, genuflexion** *n*

**genuine** /'jenyooin/ *adj* **1a** actually having the reputed or apparent qualities or character ⟨*~ vintage wines*⟩ **b** actually produced by or proceeding from the alleged source or author ⟨*the signature is ~*⟩ **c** sincerely and honestly felt or experienced ⟨*a deep and ~ love*⟩ **2** free from hypocrisy or pretence; sincere ⟨*a very ~ person*⟩ [L *genuinus* native, genuine; prob akin to L *gignere* to beget – more at KIN] – **genuinely** *adv*, **genuineness** *n*

*synonyms* Genuine, authentic, real, bona fide, and veritable may all describe things which are exactly what they are said to be. Authentic stresses fidelity to fact and actuality, and may suggest formal proof or authority for this ⟨*an* authentic *account of the Great Plague*⟩. Genuine emphasizes accordance with an original, without admixture or adulteration ⟨genuine *barley water*⟩; it may also be used in contrast to fraudulent or deceptive ⟨*a* genuine *smile*⟩. A ⟨genuine *Van Dyck portrait of King Charles*⟩ means that the painter was Van Dyck; an ⟨authentic *portrait of King Charles by Van Dyck*⟩ means that the portrait was painted from life. Real, less forceful than the others, simply means that something is what it appears to be ⟨real *silver*⟩. If real is affected by "reality", veritable is linked to "verity", and means truthfully being what it claims ⟨*the* veritable *words of the prophet*⟩. It is also used as an affirmative to stress the justice of a metaphor ⟨*she is a* veritable *saint*⟩. Bona fide stresses the lack of intent to deceive, and is often found in legal or commercial contexts. *antonyms* false, spurious, fraudulent, counterfeit *usage* The pronunciation of genuine to rhyme with swine is not recommended for BBC broadcasters except in humorous contexts.

**genus** /'jeenəs/ *n, pl* **genera** /'jenərə/ *also* **genuses 1** a category in the biological classification of living things ranking between a family and a species and comprising one or more related species **2** a class of objects, individuals, etc divided into several subordinate species [L *gener-, genus* birth, race, kind – more at KIN]

**-geny** /-jəni/ *comb form* (→ *n*) origin, development; method of production of ⟨*biogeny*⟩ ⟨*ontogeny*⟩ [Gk *-geneia* act of being born, fr *-genēs* born – more at -GEN]

**geo-** – see GE-

**geobotany** /jeeoh'botəni/ *n* the study of the geographical distribution of plants; PHYTOGEOGRAPHY – **geobotanist** *n*, **geobotanical** *also* **geobotanic** *adj*, **geobotanically** *adv*

**geocentric** /,jeeoh'sentrik/ *adj* **1a** relating to, measured from, or as if observed from the earth's centre – compare TOPO-CENTRIC **b** having or relating to the earth as centre – compare HELIOCENTRIC **2** taking or based on the earth as the centre of perspective and valuation – **geocentrically** *adv*

**geochemistry** /,jeeoh'kemistri/ *n* **1** a science that deals with the chemical composition of and chemical changes in the crust of the earth **2** the related chemical and geological properties of a substance – **geochemical** *adj*, **geochemically** *adv*, **geochemist** *n*

**geochronology** /-krə'noləji/ *n* the sequence of events in the distant past as indicated by geological data – **geochronologist** *n*, **geochronological** *also* **geochronologic** *adj*, **geochronologically** *adv*

**geochronometry** /,jeeoh·krə'nomətri/ *n* the measurement of past time by geochronological methods – **geochronometric** *adj*

**geode** /'jee,ohd/ *n* **1** a rounded lump of stone having a cavity lined with crystals or mineral matter **2** the cavity in a geode [L *geodes*, a gem, fr Gk *geōdēs* earthlike, fr *gē* earth] – **geodic** *adj*

¹**geodesic** /-'desik, -'deesik/ *adj* **1** geodetic **2** made of light straight structural elements mostly under tension ⟨a ~ *dome*⟩

²**geodesic, geodesic line** *n* the shortest line between two points on a given surface

**geodesy** /ji'odəsi/ *n* a branch of applied mathematics that deals with the determination of the exact positions of points, the shape and areas of large portions of the earth's surface, and the shape and size of the earth [Gk *geōdaisia*, fr *geō-* ge- + *daiesthai* to divide – more at TIDE] – **geodesist** *n*

¹**geodetic** /,jeeoh'detik/ *also* **geodetical** /-tikl/ *adj* **1** of or determined by geodesy **2** relating to the geometry of GEODETIC LINES [fr *geodesy*, by analogy to *heresy:heretic*] – **geodetically** *adv*

²**geodetic, geodetic line** *n* a geodesic on the earth's surface

**geodetic survey** *n* a survey of a large land area in which corrections are made for the curvature of the earth's surface

**Geodimeter** /,jee·ə'dimitə/ *trademark* – used for an electronic-optical device that measures distance on the basis of the speed of light

**geographer** /ji'ogrəfə/ *n* a specialist in geography

**geographical** /,jee·ə'grafikl/, **geographic** *adj* **1** of geography **2** belonging to or characteristic of a particular region – **geographically** *adv*

**geographical mile** *n* NAUTICAL MILE a (1853.2 metres)

**geography** /ji'ogrəfi/ *n* **1** a science that deals with the earth and its life; *esp* the description of land, sea, air, and the distribution of plant and animal life including human beings and their industries **2** the geographical features of an area **3** a systematic arrangement of constituent elements; a configuration ⟨*the philosophers have tried to construct geographies of human reason* – TLS⟩ **4** *informal* a layout, plan ⟨*still not used to the* ~ *of the house*⟩ [L *geographia*, fr Gk *geōgraphia*, fr *geographein* to describe the earth's surface, fr *geō-* + *graphein* to write – more at CARVE]

**geoid** /'jeeoyd/ *n* (the shape of) the surface that the earth would have if all parts of the earth had the same height as the average sea level of the oceans [Ger, fr Gk *geoeidēs* earthlike, fr *gē*] – **geoidal** *adj*

**geological time** /,jee·ə'lojikl/ *n* the long period of time occupied by the earth's geological history

**geolog·ize, -ise** /ji'oləjiez/ *vi* to study geology or make geological investigations

**geology** /ji'oləji/ *n* **1a** a science that deals with the history, composition, structure, and changes of the earth, esp as recorded in rocks **b** a study of the solid matter of a celestial body (eg the moon) **2** the geological features of an area [NL *geologia*, fr *ge-* + *-logia* -logy] – **geologist** *n*, **geological** *also* **geologic** *adj*, **geologically** *adv*

**geomagnetic** /,jeeohmag'netik/ *adj* of the earth's magnetism – **geomagnetically** *adv*, **geomagnetism** *n*, **geomagnetist** *n*

**geomagnetic storm** *n* MAGNETIC STORM

**geomancy** /'jee·ə,mansi/ *n* **1** divination by means of configurations of earth or by dots jotted down hastily at random **2** the supposed discovery and mystical interpretation of the disposition and alignment of prominent landscape features and sacred sites – compare ¹LEY [ME *geomancie*, fr MF, fr ML *geomantia*, fr LGk *geōmanteia*, fr Gk *geō-* + *-manteia* -mancy] – **geomancer**, **geomantic** *adj*

**geometer** /ji'omitə/ *n* **1** a specialist in geometry **2** a geometrid moth

**geometric** /,ji·ə'metrik/, **geometrical** /-trikl/ *adj* **1a** of or according to geometry or its laws **b** increasing in a GEOMETRIC PROGRESSION ⟨~ *population growth*⟩ **2** *cap* of or being (a style of) ancient Greek pottery characterized by geometric decorative designs **3a** (relating to art) using simple geometric designs (eg straight lines, circles, or squares) ⟨~ *abstractions*⟩ **b** *of architectural tracery* in an English Gothic style of the second half of the 13th century characterized chiefly by circles or simple circle-based openings – **geometrically** *adv*

**geometrician** /,ji,omə'trish(ə)n, jee·əmə-/ *n* GEOMETER 1

**geometric mean** *n* the *n*th ROOT of the product of *n* numbers (eg the SQUARE ROOT of two numbers) ⟨*the* ~ *of 9 and 4 is 6*⟩

**geometric progression** *n* a sequence (eg 1, ½, ¼) in which the ratio of any term to its predecessor is constant

**geometric series** *n* a series (eg 1 + x + x² + x³ + . . .) whose terms form a GEOMETRIC PROGRESSION

**geometrid** /ji'omətrid/ *n* any of a family (Geometridae) of medium-sized moths with large wings and larvae that are LOOPERS [deriv of Gk *geōmetrēs* geometer, fr *geōmetrein*; fr its looping movement, as if it were measuring the ground] – **geometrid** *adj*

**geometr·ize, -ise** /ji'omətriez/ *vt* **1** to represent geometrically **2** to cause to conform to geometric principles and laws

**geometry** /ji'omətri/ *n* **1a** a branch of mathematics that deals with the measurement, properties, and relationships of points, lines, angles, surfaces, and solids; *broadly* the study of properties of given elements that remain constant under specified transformations **b** a particular type or system of geometry ⟨*Euclidean* ~⟩ **2a** configuration **b** surface shape (eg of a mechanical part or a crystal) **3** an arrangement of objects or parts that suggests geometrical figures [ME *geometrie*, fr MF, fr L *geometria*, fr Gk *geōmetria*, fr *geōmetrein* to measure the earth, fr *geō-* ge- + *metron* measure – more at MEASURE]

**geomorphic** /,jeeoh'mawfik/ *adj* of or concerned with the form or solid surface features of the earth or of the moon, other planets, etc

**geomorphology** /-maw'foləji/ *n* **1** a science that deals with the origin, formation, and structure of the landforms of the earth's surface, or with similar features of the moon, other planets, etc **2** the features dealt with in geomorphology [ISV] – **geomorphologist** *n*, **geomorphologic, geomorphological** *adj*, **geomorphologically** *adv*

**geophagy** /ji'ofəji/ *n* the practice of eating earthy substances (eg clay or chalk), widespread among primitive peoples or those on a scanty or unbalanced diet [ISV]

**geophone** /,jee·ə,fohn/ *n* an instrument for detecting vibrations passing through rocks, soil, or ice

**geophysics** /-'fiziks/ *n taking pl vb* the physics of the earth, including the fields of meteorology, hydrology, oceanography, seismology, volcanology, magnetism, radioactivity, and geodesy [ISV] – **geophysical** *adj*, **geophysically** *adv*, **geophysicist** *n*

**geophyte** /'jee·ə,fiet/ *n* a plant that bears buds below the surface of the soil which survive the winter – compare CHAMAE-PHYTE, PHANEROPHYTE

**geopolitics** /-'politiks/ *n taking sing vb* a study of the influence of such factors as geography, economics, and DEMOGRAPHY (population statistics) on politics, esp international relations – **geopolitical** *adj*, **geopolitcally** *adv*

**Geordie** /'jawdi/ *n, Br informal* **1** a native or inhabitant of Tyneside in the NE of England **2** the dialect of Tyneside [Sc *Geordie*, nickname for *George*] – **Geordie** *adj*

**George** /jawj/ *n, Br slang* the AUTOMATIC PILOT in an aircraft [fr the forename *George*]

**georgette** /jaw'jet/, **georgette crepe** *n* a thin strong crepe fabric used for clothing, that is made of fibres woven from hard twisted yarns to produce a dull pebbly surface [fr *Georgette*, a trademark]

¹**Georgian** /'jawj(ə)n/ *n* **1** a native or inhabitant of Georgia in the Caucasus **2** the language of the people of Georgia in the Caucasus – **Georgian** *adj*

²**Georgian** *n* a native or resident of Georgia in the USA – **Georgian** *adj*

³**Georgian** *adj* **1** (characteristic) of the reigns or time of the first four King Georges of Britain (1714 to 1830) **2** (characteristic) of the reign or time of King George V of Britain (1910 to 1936) ⟨*the* ~ *poets*⟩

⁴**Georgian** *n* **1** a person living in either of the Georgian periods **2** Georgian taste or style

¹**georgic** /'jawjik/ *n* a poem dealing with agriculture [the

*Georgics*, poem by Vergil †19 BC Roman poet, fr L *Georgica*, fr neut pl of *georgicus*]

²**georgic** *adj, formal* relating to agriculture [L *georgicus*, fr Gk *geōrgikos*, fr *geōrgos* farmer, fr *geō-* ge- + *ergon* work – more at WORK]

**geoscience** / ˌjeeoh'sie•əns/ *n* (any of) the sciences (e g geology, geophysics, and geochemistry) that deal with the earth – **geoscientist** *n*

**geosphere** /'jee•ə,sfiə/ *n* LITHOSPHERE (earth's crust)

**geostationary** / ˌjeeoh'stayshən(ə)ri/ *adj* of or being an artificial satellite that travels above the equator and at the same speed as the earth rotates, so that the satellite remains above the same place on the earth

**geostrophic** /-'strofik/ *adj* of or caused by the rotation of the earth ⟨~ *wind*⟩ [ge- + Gk *strophikos* turned, fr *strophē* turning – more at STROPHE] – **geostrophically** *adv*

**geosynchronous** /-'singkrənəs/ *adj* geostationary

**geosyncline** / ˌjeeoh'singklien/ *n* a great downward fold of the earth's crust consisting of an elongated basin that becomes filled with sediment – compare GEANTICLINE – **geosynclinal** *adj*

**geotaxis** /-'taksis/ *n* the movement of an organism in response to the force of gravity [NL, fr ge- + -*taxis* ] – **geotactic** *adj*, **geotactically** *adv*

**geotectonic** / ˌjeeoh•tek'tonik/ *adj* of the form, arrangement, and structure of rock masses of the earth's crust resulting from folding or faulting – **geotectonically** *adv*

**geothermal** /-'thuhml/, **geothermic** /-'thuhmik/ *adj* of the heat of the earth's interior; *also* produced by such heat ⟨~ steam⟩ [ISV] – **geothermally** *adv*

**geotropism** / ˌjee•ə'troh,piz(ə)m/ *n* the turning or curving of a plant or plant part in the direction of or opposite to that of the force of the earth's gravity [ISV] – **geotropic** *adj*, **geotropically** *adv*

**gerah** /'girə/ *n* an ancient Hebrew unit of weight equal to ¹⁄₂₀ shekel (about 0.8 gram) [Heb *gērāh*, lit., grain]

**geraniol** /ji'rayniol, ji'rah-/ *n* a fragrant liquid chemical alcohol, $C_{10}H_{18}O$, used chiefly in perfumes and soap [ISV, fr NL *Geranium*]

**geranium** /jə'raynyəm, -nyi•əm/ *n* **1** any of a widely distributed genus (*Geranium* of the family Geraniaceae, the geranium family) of plants having usu pinkish to blue flowers and leaves that are rounded in outline and finely divided into narrow segments **2** PELARGONIUM; *specif* one cultivated as a garden plant **3** a vivid orange-red colour [NL, genus name, fr L, geranium, fr Gk *geranos* crane – more at CRANE; fr its fruit's resemblance to a crane's bill]

**gerbera** /'juhbərə, 'guh-/ *n* any of a genus (*Gerbera*) of African and Asian plants of the daisy family having tufted leaves and showy heads of yellow, pink, or orange flowers [NL, genus name, fr Traugott *Gerber* †1743 Ger naturalist]

**gerbil** *also* **gerbille** /'juh,bil/ *n* any of numerous African and Asian burrowing mouselike desert rodents (*Gerbillus* and related genera) with long hind legs adapted for jumping [Fr *gerbille*, fr NL *Gerbillus*, genus name, dim. of *jerboa*]

**gerfalcon** /juh'fawkən, -'falkən/ *n* GYRFALCON (bird of prey)

**geriatric** / ˌjeri'atrik/ *adj* **1** of or for geriatrics, the aged, or the process of aging **2** *derog* aged, decrepit [Gk *gēras* old age + E -*iatric*] – **geriatric** *n*

**geriatrician** / ˌjeriə'trish(ə)n/ *n* a specialist in geriatrics

**geriatrics** / ˌjeri'atriks/ *n taking sing vb* a branch of medicine that deals with the problems and diseases of old age and the care of aging people – compare GERONTOLOGY

**germ** /juhm/ *n* **1a** a small mass of cells (e g a bud or fertilized egg) capable of developing into an organism or into one of its parts **b** the embryo at the heart of a cereal grain that is usu separated from the starchy ENDOSPERM (surrounding nourishing layer) during milling ⟨*wheat* ~⟩ **2** something that serves as an origin; a rudiment ⟨*the* ~ *of an idea*⟩ **3** a microorganism; *esp* one that causes disease – not used technically [Fr *germe*, fr L *germin-*, *germen*, fr *gignere* to beget – more at KIN] – **germfree** *adj*, **germy** *adj*

**german** /'juhmən/ *adj* having the same parents or the same grandparents on either the mother's or father's side – usu following the noun which it modifies and joined to it by a hyphen ⟨*brothers*-german⟩ ⟨*cousin*-german⟩ [ME *germain*, fr MF, fr L *germanus* having the same parents, irreg fr *germen*]

¹**German** *n* **1a** a native or inhabitant of Germany **b** one (e g a Swiss German) who speaks German as his/her native language outside Germany **2** the Germanic language of the people of Germany, Austria, and parts of Switzerland **3** *often not cap, NAm* a dance consisting of complex routines that are improvised and intermingled with waltzes [ML *Germanus*, fr L, any member of the Germanic peoples]

²**German** *adj* (characteristic) of Germany, the Germans, or German

**German cockroach** *n* a small active winged cockroach (*Blatella germanica*), probably of African origin but now common in many parts of the world

**germander** /juh'mandə/ *n* **1** any of a genus (*Teucrium*) of plants of the mint family with small usu white, pinkish, or pale purple flowers that have a prominent liplike part **2 germander speedwell**, **germander** a common Eurasian plant (*Veronica chamaedrus*) of the foxglove family with bright blue flowers [ME *germaunder*, fr MF *germandree*, deriv of Gk *chamaidrys*, fr *chamai* on the ground + *drys* oak, tree – more at HUMBLE, TREE]

**germane** /juh'mayn/ *adj* both relevant and appropriate *to*; fitting *synonyms* see RELEVANT *antonyms* foreign [var of *german*] – **germanely** *adv*

¹**Germanic** /juh'manik/ *adj* **1** German **2** (characteristic) of the Germanic-speaking peoples **3** of Germanic

²**Germanic** *n* a branch of the INDO-EUROPEAN language family containing English, German, Dutch, Afrikaans, Flemish, Frisian, the Scandinavian languages, and Gothic

**Germanism** /'juhməniz(ə)m/ *n* **1** a characteristic feature of German occurring in another language **2** a characteristic feature (e g a custom or belief) of Germans or German culture **3a** adherence or attachment to Germany or to German customs, tastes, or ideas **b** promotion of German policies

**Germanist** /'juhmənist/ *n* a specialist in German or Germanic language, literature, or culture

**germanium** /juh'maynyəm, -ni•əm/ *n* a greyish-white hard brittle chemical element that resembles silicon in having some metallic properties although being nonmetallic, and that is used as a SEMICONDUCTOR (e g in transistors) [NL, fr ML *Germania* Germany]

**german•ize, -ise** /'juhməniez/ *vb, often cap* *vt* **1** to make German in tastes or characteristics **2** *archaic* to translate into German ~ *vi* to have or acquire German customs, tastes, or characteristics – **germanization** *n*

**German measles** *n taking sing or pl vb* a short-lasting infectious virus disease that is characterized by a slight temperature, rash, and sore throat and that is milder than typical measles but can be damaging to the foetus when occurring early in pregnancy – called also RUBELLA

**Germano-** /jə'manoh-, juhmanoh-/ *comb form* **1** German nation, people, or culture ⟨Germano*phile*⟩ **2** German and ⟨Germano-*Russian*⟩

**Germanophile** /jə'manoh,fiel/ *adj* approving of or favouring the German people and their institutions and customs – **Germanophile** *n*

**German shepherd** *n, chiefly NAm* an alsatian

**German silver** *n* NICKEL SILVER

**germ cell** *n* an egg or sperm cell, or any of the cells from which they develop

**germen** /'juhmən/ *n, pl* **germens** *also* **germina** /-minə/ **1** a mass of undifferentiated cells from which the GERM CELLS develop **2** *archaic* GERM 1a, 2 ⟨*all* ~ s *spill at once That makes ingrateful man!* – Shak⟩ [(2) L – more at GERM; (1) NL, fr L]

**germicide** /'juhmi,sied/ *n* something that kills germs – **germicidal** *adj*, **germicidally** *adv*

**germinal** /'juhminl/ *adj* **1** of or concerned with reproduction or the first stage of development; *esp* of, having the characteristics of, or giving rise to a GERM CELL or the cells and tissues of an early embryo **2a** *formal* in the earliest stage of development **b** creative, seminal [Fr, fr L *germin-*, *germen*] – **germinally** *adv*

**Germinal** /'juhminl (Fr ʒɛrminal)/ *n* the 7th month of the French Revolutionary calendar, corresponding to 21 March–19 April

**germinal disc** *n* BLASTODISC (disclike area on the yolk of an egg from which the embryo develops)

**germinal vesicle** *n* the enlarged nucleus of an egg cell before completion of its CELL DIVISION and development into the final form of the egg

**germinate** /'juhminayt/ *vt* to cause to sprout or develop ~ *vi* **1** to begin to grow; sprout **2** to come into being; evolve [L *germinatus*, pp of *germinare* to sprout, fr *germin-*, *germen* bud, germ] – **germinative** *adj*, **germination** *n*

**germ layer** *n* any of the primary layers of cells, ENDODERM,

ECTODERM, or MESODERM, in a developing embryo, that become differentiated in most embryos during and immediately following the formation of the GASTRULA and that ultimately give rise to specific adult tissues and structures

**germ plasm** *n* the hereditary material of the GERM CELLS

**germproof** /'juhm,proohf, -proof/ *adj* not allowing the penetration or action of germs

**germ warfare** *n* the use of germs to spread disease as a form of warfare

**geront-** /jeront-, jə'ront-/, **geronto-** *comb form* old person; old age ⟨geronto*logy*⟩ ⟨geronto*cracy*⟩ [Fr géront-, géronto-, fr Gk geront-, geronto-, fr geront-, gerōn old man; akin to Gk gēras old age]

**gerontic** /jə'rontik/ *adj* of or occurring in old age; *also* of senility

**gerontocracy** /,jeron'tokrəsi/ *n* rule by old men; *specif* a form of social organization in which a group of old men or a council of elders dominates or exercises control ⟨the Soviet ~ staggers on⟩ [Fr gérontocratie, fr géront- geront- + -cratie -cracy] – **gerontocrat** *n*, **gerontocratic** *adj*

**gerontology** /,jeron'toləji/ *n* a branch of biology and medicine dealing with the process of and changes associated with aging and the problems of the aged – compare GERIATRICS [ISV] – **gerontologist** *n*, **gerontological, gerontologic** *adj*

**-gerous** /-jərəs/ *comb form* (→ *adj*) bearing; producing ⟨dentigerous⟩ [L -ger, fr gerere to bear]

¹**gerrymander** /'jeri,mandə/ *n* 1 the act or method of gerrymandering 2 a district or pattern of districts varying greatly in size or population as a result of gerrymandering [Elbridge Gerry †1814 US politician + sala*mander*; fr the shape of an election district formed during Gerry's governorship of Massachusetts]

²**gerrymander** *vt* to divide (an area) into election districts in order to give one political party an electoral majority in a large number of districts, while concentrating the voting strength of the opposition in as few districts as possible – **gerrymandering** *n*

**gerund** /'jerənd/ *n* 1 a VERBAL NOUN in Latin that expresses generalized or uncompleted action and is used in all cases but the nominative 2 any of several linguistic forms similar in function to the Latin gerund in languages other than Latin; *esp* the English VERBAL NOUN ending in -ing that has the function of a noun and at the same time shows certain verbal features (e g singing in "He likes singing" and in "Singing chorales is fun") [LL gerundium, fr L gerundus, gerundive of gerere to bear, carry on] – **gerundial** *also* **gerundive** *adj*

**gerundive** /ji'rundiv/ *n* the Latin future passive participle that functions as a verbal adjective, expresses the desirability or necessity of the action to be performed, and has the same SUFFIX (ending element) as the gerund; *also* a linguistic form similar in function in another language – **gerundively** *adv*, **gerundival** *adj*

**gesellschaft** /gə'zel,shahft (Ger gəzelʃaft)/ *n* a social relationship or a society used as a reference norm in sociology and characterized by mechanistic associations between individuals based on rational division of labour, practical convenience, and self-interest – compare GEMEINSCHAFT [Ger, companionship, society, fr gesell companion + -schaft -ship]

**gesso** /'jesoh/ *n, pl* **gessoes** 1 PLASTER OF PARIS or GYPSUM (chalklike mineral) mixed with glue for use in painting or making BAS-RELIEFS (flat sculpture with projecting forms) 2 a paste made with powdered chalk that is spread on wood or occasionally canvas as a basis for painting or gilding [It, lit., gypsum, fr L gypsum]

**gest, geste** /jest/ *n* a tale of adventures; *esp* a medieval romance in verse [ME geste – more at JEST]

**gestalt** /gə'shtalt, (Ger gə'ʃtalt)/ *n, pl* **gestalten** /-tən (Ger -tn)/, **gestalts** a structure, configuration, or pattern (e g a melody) made up of psychological phenomena (e g perceptions) so integrated as to constitute a functional whole whose properties are not derivable from the sum of its parts [Ger, lit., shape, form]

**Gestalt psychology** *n* the study of perception and behaviour based on the theory that an organism responds to psychological phenomena arranged in the form of gestalts rather than as a collection of isolated elements, and that analysis of the separate elements cannot provide an understanding of the whole

**gestapo** /gə's(h)tahpoh/ *n, pl* **gestapos** a secret-police organization operating esp against people suspected of treason or plotting against the state, and often employing underhand and

terrorist methods; *specif, cap* the secret police of Nazi Germany [Ger, fr geheime staatspolizei secret state police]

**gestate** /'jestayt/ *vt* 1 to carry in the womb during pregnancy 2 to conceive and gradually develop in the mind ~ *vi* to be in the process of gestation [back-formation fr *gestation*]

**gestation** /je'staysh(ə)n/ *n* 1 the carrying of young in the womb from conception to birth; pregnancy; *also* the period during which an animal is carried in the womb 2 conception and development, esp in the mind [L gestation-, gestatio, fr gestatus, pp of gestare to bear, fr gestus, pp of gerere to bear]

**gesticulate** /je'stikyoo,layt/ *vi* to make expressive gestures, esp when speaking ⟨~d to the waiter for the bill – Rebecca West⟩ [L gesticulatus, pp of gesticulari, fr (assumed) L gesticulus, dim. of L gestus bearing, gesture, fr gestus, pp] – **gesticulant** *adj*, **gesticulative** *n*, **gesticulator** *n*, **gesticulatory** *adj*

**gesticulation** /je,stikyoo'laysh(ə)n/ *n* 1 the act of making gestures 2 a gesture; *esp* an expressive gesture made in showing strong feeling or in emphasizing points in an argument

¹**gesture** /'jeschə/ *n* 1a the use of motions of the limbs or body as a means of expression **b** a movement, usu of the body or limbs, that expresses or emphasizes an idea, feeling, or attitude 2 something said, done, or given for its effect on the attitudes of others or to convey a feeling (e g friendliness) [ML gestura mode of action, fr L gestus, pp] – **gestural** *adj*

²**gesture** *vi* to make a gesture ⟨he ~d at me urgently⟩ ~ *vt* to express or direct by a gesture

**gesture language** *n* communication by gestures; *esp* SIGN LANGUAGE

¹**get** /get/ *vb, nonstandard pres pl & 1 & 2 sing* **got** /got/; **-tt-; got; got,** *NAm also* **gotten** /'got(ə)n/ *vt* 1 to gain possession of: e g **1a** to obtain by way of benefit or advantage ⟨~ the better of an enemy⟩ ⟨got little for his trouble⟩ **b** to achieve as a result of military activity **c** to obtain by concession or entreaty ⟨~ your mother's permission to go⟩ **d** to seek out and fetch or provide ⟨~ blackberries in the wood⟩ ⟨~ a pencil from the desk⟩ ⟨~ you a present⟩ **e** to acquire by memorizing or calculation ⟨~ the verse by heart⟩ ⟨~ the answer to a problem⟩ **f** to seize 2 to receive: e g **2a** to receive as a return; earn ⟨he got a bad reputation for carelessness⟩ **b** to become affected by; catch ⟨~ the giggles⟩ ⟨got measles from his sister⟩ **c** to be subjected to; undergo ⟨got a blow on the head⟩ ⟨~ the sack⟩ **d** to suffer a specified injury to ⟨~ your fingers pinched⟩ ⟨~ his feet wet⟩ 3 to beget 4 to cause: e g **4a** to cause to come, go, or move ⟨quickly got his luggage through customs⟩ ⟨~ him out of the house⟩ ⟨grumbling won't ~ you anywhere⟩ **b** to bring into a specified condition by one's own direct action or by that of another ⟨~ my shoes mended⟩ ⟨~ the car started⟩ ⟨~ these dishes washed⟩ ⟨let me ~ this clear⟩ **c** to prevail on; induce ⟨~ the Russians to give an English broadcast – SEU W⟩ 5 to make ready; prepare ⟨~ dinner⟩ 6a to overcome ⟨I'll ~ him on that point⟩ **b** to take vengeance on; *specif* to kill ⟨out to ~ his man⟩ 7a to have – used in the present perfect tense form with present meaning ⟨I've got no money⟩ **b** to have as an obligation or necessity – used in the present perfect tense form with present meaning; used with to and an understood or expressed infinitive ⟨he has got to come⟩ ⟨I won't if I haven't got to⟩ 8a to hear ⟨didn't quite ~ that⟩ ⟨~ Peking on the radio⟩ **b** to establish communication with ⟨~ her on the telephone⟩ 9 to put out in baseball 10 *informal* to have an effect on: e g **10a** to effect emotionally ⟨the sight of her tears got him⟩ **b** to puzzle ⟨you've got me there⟩ **c** to irritate ⟨it really ~s me when you leave the washing-up⟩ 11 *informal* to hit ⟨~ him on the ear with a potato⟩ 12 *informal* to understand ⟨don't ~ me wrong⟩ 13 *informal* to look at (someone) – used as an exclamation of scorn ⟨~ you in your mother's high heels⟩ ~ *vi* 1 to reach or enter into the specified condition or activity; become ⟨~ lost⟩ ⟨~ drunk⟩ ⟨food's ~ting cold⟩ ⟨~ moving⟩ ⟨they ~ talking⟩ ⟨~ rich⟩ ⟨I'm ~ting better⟩ ⟨he's ~ting ready⟩ ⟨you're ~ting a big girl now⟩ ⟨they got married last week⟩ – used as a verbal auxiliary instead of be to form the passive ⟨wouldn't take the slightest risk of ~ting trapped inside – SEU W⟩ 2a to reach arrive ⟨where's my pen got to?⟩ ⟨~ into trouble with the law⟩ **b** to succeed in coming or going ⟨~ to the city⟩ ⟨~ into my jeans⟩ ⟨at last we're ~ting somewhere⟩ ⟨~ to sleep after midnight⟩ ⟨how to ~ clear of all the debts I owe – Shak⟩ **c** to contrive by effort, good fortune, or permission – + to and an infinitive ⟨when you ~ to know him⟩ ⟨she never ~s to drive the car⟩ 3 *slang* to leave immediately ⟨told them to ~⟩ – compare YOU GET [ME geten, fr ON geta to get, beget; akin to OE bigietan to beget, L prehendere to seize, grasp, Gk chan-

*danein* to hold, contain] – **get it** to receive a scolding or punishment – **get it together** *informal* 1 to become organized 2 to succeed in a particular field; *also* to achieve peace of mind – **get it up** *vulg* to have an erection – **get one's** *informal* to be killed ⟨*he* got his *in Korea*⟩ – **get one's own back** to revenge oneself – **getting on for** nearly (a specified age) ⟨*she's* getting on for *forty*⟩ – **get out from under** to emerge from or leave a difficult or oppressive situation – **get there** 1 to be successful 2 to understand what is meant – used ironically ⟨*you'll* get there *in the end*⟩

**usage** 1 In formal writing, it is better to avoid the overuse of **get**, and to replace it by **become, receive, obtain, buy,** etc according to the sense. 2 **Gotten** is a standard past participle in American English, but is used for the sense of "obtain" ⟨*he's just* **gotten** *a new car*⟩ rather than for merely "possess" ⟨*he has/he's* **got** (not *he's* **gotten**) *big ears*⟩. See ¹HAVE

**get about** *vi* 1 to be up and about; begin to walk ⟨*has recovered from his injuries and is able to* get about *again*⟩ 2 to become circulated, esp by word of mouth; spread ⟨*the news soon* got about⟩ 3 *informal* to travel ⟨*she* gets about *quite a lot, working for an international company*⟩

**get across** *vi* to become clear or convincing ⟨*finally the message* got across⟩ ~ *vt* 1 to make clear or convincing ⟨*she can't* get *her point* across⟩ 2 *chiefly Br informal* to annoy (someone)

**get after** *vt* to pursue with exhortation, reprimand, or attack

**get ahead** *vi* to achieve success ⟨*determined to* get ahead *in life*⟩

**get along** *vi* 1 to proceed towards a destination; progress ⟨*how is the work* getting along?⟩ 2 to meet one's needs; manage ⟨*I think I can* get along *just with that thanks*⟩ 3 to be or remain on friendly terms ⟨*I* get along *very well with her*⟩ 4 to move away; leave ⟨*I must be* getting along *now*⟩

**get around/round** *vt* 1 to get the better of; circumvent 2 to evade ⟨*if you're clever, you can sometimes* get around *the tax laws*⟩ ~ *vi* GET ABOUT

**get around/round to** *vt* to find the time for; give esp overdue attention or consideration to

**get at** *vt* 1 to reach effectively ⟨get at *the truth*⟩ ⟨*I can't* get at *the carburettor*⟩ – see also GETATABLE 2 to influence corruptly; bribe 3 to nag, tease ⟨*stop* getting at *me!*⟩ 4 to mean, imply

**get away** *vi* to escape, esp from the scene of a crime or from getting caught – see also GETAWAY

**get away from** *vt* to refuse to admit; deny – chiefly in *can't get away from* ⟨*you can't* get away from *the fact that he's dead*⟩

**get away with** *vt* to do (a reprehensible act) without criticism or penalty ⟨*you'll never* get away with *it!*⟩

**get back** *vi* 1 to come or go again to a person, place, or condition; return, revert ⟨getting back *to the main topic of the lecture*⟩ 2 to call someone back on the telephone ⟨*I'll* get back *to you as soon as I can*⟩ ~ *vt* to obtain again after loss or separation ⟨*he* got *his former job* back *after a long struggle*⟩

**get back at** *vt* to gain revenge on

**get behind/behindhand** *vi* FALL BEHIND

**get by** *vi* 1 to survive; MAKE ENDS MEET ⟨*we'll* get by *without your help*⟩ 2 to succeed with the least possible effort or accomplishment ⟨*your work will* get by, *but try to improve it*⟩ 3 to proceed without being discovered, criticized, or punished

**get down** *vi* 1 to alight, esp from a vehicle; descend 2 *of a child* to leave the table after a meal ⟨*please may I* get down?⟩ ~ *vt* 1 to cause to be physically, mentally, or emotionally exhausted; depress ⟨*the weather was* getting *her* down⟩ 2 to bring oneself to eat; swallow ⟨get *this medicine* down⟩ 3 to commit to writing; describe

**get down to** *vt* to (begin to) give one's attention or consideration to ⟨*let's* get down to *business*⟩

**get in** *vi* 1 to arrive (inside a place) ⟨*the plane* got in *late*⟩ 2a to be elected; come to power ⟨*What will you do if Labour* get in?⟩ b to be admitted (to a school, class, etc) after an examination, test, etc ⟨*did your son* get in?⟩ 3 to take part in something ⟨get in *at the start*⟩ ~ *vt* 1 to collect or buy a supply of 2 to call (someone) to one's help, esp in the house ⟨get *the doctor* in⟩ 3 to be able to deliver ⟨*did you* get *your essay* in *on time?*⟩ 4 to say (something), esp by interrupting a conversation ⟨*may I* get *a word* in *here?*⟩ 5 to cause to be admitted (eg to a

school, class etc) after an examination, test etc ⟨*didn't even get his best pupil* in⟩

**get into** *vt* 1 to possess, dominate ⟨*what's* got into *you*⟩ 2 to put (oneself or someone) into (a bad condition) ⟨*he* got (*himself*) into *trouble*⟩ 3 to start (eg a violent emotion) ⟨get into *a temper*⟩ ⟨get into *bad habits*⟩ 4 GET IN 5 5 to learn or become accustomed to ⟨*I'll soon* get into *the way of things*⟩

**get off** *vi* 1 to start, leave ⟨*intended to* get off *on his trip early in the morning*⟩ 2 to escape from a dangerous situation or punishment ⟨*expected to* get off *with a short prison sentence*⟩ 3 to leave work with permission ⟨got off *early today and went shopping*⟩ 4 to go to sleep; fall asleep ⟨*I had just* got off *when the doorbell rang*⟩ 5 *Br informal* to start a romantic or sexual relationship – often + *with* or *together* ~ *vt* 1 to secure the release of or procure a modified penalty for ⟨*his lawyers* got *him* off *with little difficulty*⟩ 2 to write and send; dispatch ⟨*I'll* get *that letter* off *tonight*⟩ 3 to leave (work) ⟨*when do you* get off *work today?*⟩ 4 to cause to go to sleep or fall asleep ⟨*I'll come as soon as I've* got *the baby* off⟩

**get off to** *vt* to make (a specified start) ⟨got off to *a good start*⟩

**get on** *vi* 1 GET ALONG 3 2 to become later or older ⟨*time's* getting on⟩ ⟨*of course, he is* getting on *a bit*⟩ 3 to continue, often after an interruption – usu + *with* ⟨get on *with your work!*⟩ 4 to hurry – usu + *with* ⟨get on *with it, we've a train to catch!*⟩ 5 to succeed – often + *in* ⟨*a young man has to think of* getting on *in his job*⟩

**get onto** *vt* 1 to be elected or appointed to ⟨get onto *the City Council*⟩ 2 to begin to talk about ⟨*how did we* get onto *that subject*⟩; *also* to begin to work at 3 *informal* to get in touch with (someone) ⟨*I'll* get onto *the director and see if he can help*⟩ 4 *informal* to learn of deceit by (someone) ⟨*he tricked people for years until the police* got onto *him*⟩

**get out** *vi* 1 to emerge, escape ⟨*doubted that he would* get out *alive*⟩ ⟨*the meeting went on late so I* got out *as soon as I could*⟩ 2 to become known; LEAK 2 ~ *vt* 1 to cause to emerge or escape ⟨got *him* out *of that trouble*⟩ 2 to bring before the public; *esp* to publish ⟨*they're* getting *a new book* out *on that*⟩ 3 to speak with difficulty ⟨*only* got *a few words* out *before he collapsed*⟩

**get out of** *vt* 1 to cause to escape responsibility for (something or doing something) ⟨*he tried to* get out of *helping his mother*⟩ ⟨*he can't* get *her* out *of that*⟩ 2 to be able to stop or leave ⟨*he couldn't* get out of *the habit*⟩ 3 to force (something) from (someone) ⟨*the police* got *the truth* out of *him*⟩ 4 to gain from ⟨*Mildred enjoys George's visits, but I don't see what he gets out of it*⟩ 5 to withdraw money, facilities, etc from ⟨*I'd advise you to* get out of *"softs"*⟩

**get outside** *vt, informal* to eat (something)

**get over** *vt* 1a to overcome, surmount ⟨*how shall we* get over *this difficulty*⟩ b to recover from ⟨got over *her illness*⟩ c to accept calmly ⟨*I can't* get over *your new hair-do!*⟩ 2 to move or travel across 3 GET ACROSS 1 4 to reach the end of (usu something unpleasant) – often + *with* ⟨*you'll be glad to* get *your operation* over *with*⟩

**get round** *vt* 1 GET AROUND 2 to cajole, persuade ⟨*he's very stubborn, but she'll* get round *him*⟩

**get round to** *vt* GET AROUND TO

**get through** *vt* 1 to reach the end of; complete; *also* to pass ⟨got through *his exams*⟩ 2a USE UP 1 ⟨got through *a lot of money*⟩ b to while away ⟨*hardly knew how to* get through *his days*⟩ 3 to pass through; be accepted by (eg a parliament) ⟨*the new bill has still to* get through *the Upper House*⟩ 4 to understand (something); cause something to be understood by (someone) ⟨*when will you* get *it* through *that thick skull of yours*⟩ ~ *vi* 1 to reach someone, esp by telephone ⟨*tried phoning him but couldn't* get through⟩ ⟨*can't* get through *to Paris*⟩ 2 to make oneself understood to (someone); convey one's feelings (to someone) ⟨*after he got back from India, I just couldn't seem to* get through *to him*⟩ 3 to be passed by a parliament, union, etc ⟨*the new law only just* got through *in time*⟩ 4 *chiefly NAm* to finish ⟨*call me when you* get through *with your work*⟩ – often + *with*

**get to** *vt* 1 to begin ⟨*she* gets to *worrying over nothing at all*⟩ 2a to have an effect on; influence b to annoy, anger ⟨*you're really beginning to* get to *me*⟩

**get together** *vt* to bring together; accumulate ~ *vi* 1 to come together; assemble 2 to unite in discussion or promotion of a project ⟨get together *over the oil deal*⟩ – see also GET-TOGETHER

**get up** *vi* **1a** to arise from bed (e g in the morning or after an illness) **b** to rise to one's feet **c** to climb, ascend **2** to go ahead or faster – used in the imperative as a command, esp to driven animals **3** *of wind, fire, etc* to increase ~ *vt* **1** to make preparations for; organize ⟨got up *a party for the newcomers*⟩ **2** to arrange as to external appearance; dress; DRESS UP – see also GETUP **3** to acquire a knowledge of; *also* to reacquaint oneself with (a subject) ⟨*I must* get up *my notes on Shakespeare*⟩ **4** to create in oneself ⟨*cannot* get up *an atom of sympathy for them*⟩ **5** to cause (someone) to rise from bed ⟨get *the children* up, *will you?*⟩ **6** to increase ⟨get up *steam*⟩ ⟨get up *speed*⟩

**get up to** *vt* **1** to reach ⟨*what page have you* got up to?⟩ **2** *informal* to be involved in ⟨*don't* get up *to mischief while I'm away*⟩

**²get** *n* **1** the entire offspring of a male animal ⟨*a stallion's* ~⟩ **2** a successful return of a difficult shot in a game (e g tennis) **3** *Br slang* a git

**getatable** /get'atəbl/ *adj, informal* accessible, approachable

**getaway** /'getə,way/ *n* an act or instance of getting away; *esp* an escape ⟨*they made a quick* ~⟩

**getter** /'getə/ *n* **1** one who gets **2** a substance included in a THERMIONIC VALVE, light bulb, etc to remove traces of gas

**'get-to,gether** *n* a meeting, esp an informal social gathering

**getup** /'get,up/ *n, informal* **1** general composition or structure; outer appearance **2** an outfit, costume

**,get-up-and-'go** *n, informal* enthusiastic energy; drive

**geum** /'jee-əm/ *n* AVENS (plant of the rose family) [NL, fr L, herb bennet]

**gewgaw** /'gyooh,gaw/ *n* something showy but worthless; a bauble, trinket [origin unknown]

**Gewürztraminer** /gə'vooəts'traminə (*Ger* gəvyrtstraminər)/ *n* a typically medium-dry white wine with a spicy bouquet; *also* the variety of grape from which this is made [Ger, fr *gewürz* spice + *traminer*, a variety of wine, fr *Tramin*, place in S Tyrol]

**gey** /gay/ *adv, chiefly Scot* very, quite [alter. of *gay*, adv]

**geyser** /'geezə; *sense 1 also* 'giezə/ *n* **1** a spring that intermittently throws out jets of heated water and steam **2** *Br* an apparatus with a boiler in which water (e g for a bath) is rapidly heated by a gas flame and may be stored △ geezer [Icel *Geysir*, name of a hot spring in Iceland, fr *geysir* gusher, fr *geysa* to rush forth, fr ON; akin to OE *gēotan* to pour – more at FOUND]

**geyserite** /'geezəriet/ *n* a SILICA mineral that is a variety of opal and is deposited in white or greyish masses round some hot springs and geysers [Fr *geysérite*, fr *geyser*, fr Icel *geysir*]

**gharial** /'geəri-əl/ *n* GAVIAL (Indian crocodile) [Hindi *ghariyāl*]

**gharry** *also* **gharri** /gari/ *n* a horse-drawn taxi used esp in India [Hindi *gāṛī*]

**ghastly** /'gahstli/ *adj* **1a** terrifyingly horrible to the senses; frightening ⟨*a* ~ *crime*⟩ **b** intensely unpleasant, disagreeable, or objectionable ⟨*such a life seems* ~ *in its emptiness and sterility* – Aldous Huxley⟩ **2** pale, wan **3** *informal* very bad ⟨*a* ~ *mistake*⟩ [ME *gastly*, fr *gasten* to terrify, fr *gast, gost* ghost] – **ghastliness** *n*

**ghat** /gawt, gaht/ *n* **1** a broad flight of steps situated on an Indian riverbank and providing access to the water (e g for bathing); *also* a landing-place **2** a mountain pass esp in India [Hindi *ghāṭ*]

**ghazi** /'gahzi/ *n, often cap* **1** a Muslim soldier fighting against non-Muslims in former times **2** a victorious Turkish sultan in former times; *broadly* any high-ranking Muslim soldier [Ar *ghāzī*]

**ghee** *also* **ghi** /gee/ *n* a semifluid clarified butter made, esp in India, from cow's or buffalo's milk [Hindi *ghī*, fr Skt *ghṛta;* akin to MIr *gert* milk]

**gherkin** /'guhkin/ *n* **1** a small prickly fruit used for pickling; *also* the slender climbing plant (*Cucumis anguria*) of the marrow family that bears it **2** the small immature fruit of the cucumber used for pickling [D *gurken*, pl of *gurk* cucumber, deriv of Pol *ogurek*, fr MGk *agouros* watermelon; cucumber]

**ghetto** /'getoh/ *n, pl* **ghettos, ghettoes** **1** an area of a city in which Jews were formerly required to live **2** an often segregated and slum area of a city in which members of a minority group live, esp because of social, legal, or economic pressures; *broadly* an area characterized by the predominance of a single type of resident or activity ⟨*official* ~s *for foreigners* – Philip Knightley⟩ [It, perh fr *getto* foundry; fr a ghetto established on the site of a foundry in Venice in 1516]

**Ghibelline** /'gibi,lien/ *n* a member of an aristocratic political party in medieval Italy supporting the authority of the German emperors in Italy – compare GUELF [It *Ghibellino*, fr OIt, fr MHG *Wibeling*, name of Salic emperors, fr *Wibeling*, castle in W Germany]

**ghibli, gibli** /'gibli/ *n* a hot desert wind of N Africa [Ar *qiblīy* south wind]

**ghillie** /'gili/ *n* **1** GILLIE **2** a low-cut shoe with decorative lacing, originally worn in Scotland

**¹ghost** /gohst/ *n* **1** a disembodied soul; *esp* the soul of a dead person believed to appear to or haunt the living **2a** a faint shadowy trace ⟨*a* ~ *of a smile*⟩ **b** the least bit ⟨*didn't have a* ~ *of a chance*⟩ **3** a false image in a photographic negative or on a television screen **4** a ghostwriter **5** a RED BLOOD CELL that has lost its haemoglobin [ME *gost, gast*, fr OE *gāst*; akin to OHG *geist* spirit, Skt *heḍa* anger] – **ghostlike** *adj*, **ghosty** *adj* – **give/yield up the ghost** to die

**²ghost** *vt* to ghostwrite ~ *vi* **1** to move silently like a ghost **2** to ghostwrite

**³ghost** *adj* **1** phantom, illusory ⟨*a* ~ *image*⟩ **2** no longer in use ⟨*a* ~ *airport*⟩

**ghost dance** *n* a group dance for communication with the spirits of the dead, characteristic of a N American Indian MESSIANIC cult (one promising future deliverance or peace and prosperity) of the late 19th century

**ghostly** /'gohstli/ *adj* **1** of, like, or being a ghost; spectral **2** *archaic* of the soul; spiritual; *also* ecclesiastical – **ghostliness** *n*, **ghostly** *adv*

**ghost town** *n* a once-flourishing town wholly or nearly deserted, usu as a result of the exhaustion of some natural resource (e g gold)

**ghostwrite** /-,riet/ *vb* **ghostwrote** /-,roht/; **ghostwritten** /-,rit(ə)n/ *vt* to write (e g a book or speech) for another who is the presumed author [back-formation fr *ghost-writer*] – **ghostwriter** *n*

**ghoul** /goohl/ *n* **1** an evil being of Arabic legend that robs graves and feeds on corpses **2** a person who enjoys the macabre [Ar *ghūl*, fr *ghāla* to seize] – **ghoulish** *adj*, **ghoulishly** *adv*, **ghoulishness** *n*

**ghyll** /gil/ *n* ³GILL

**¹GI** /jee 'ie/ *adj* **1** provided by an official US military supply department ⟨~ *shoes*⟩ **2** (characteristic) of US military personnel **3** *NAm* conforming to military regulations or customs ⟨*a* ~ *haircut*⟩ [galvanized iron; fr abbr used in listing such articles as dustbins, but taken as abbr for *government issue* or *general issue*]

**²GI** *n, pl* **GI's, GIs** a (former) member of the US armed forces; *esp* a private

**¹giant** /'jie-ənt/ *n* **1** *fem* **giantess** /-tis/ a legendary humanoid being of great size and strength **2a** a living being of great size **b** a person of extraordinary powers ⟨*a literary* ~⟩ **3** something unusually large or powerful [ME *giaunt*, fr MF *geant*, fr L *gigant-, gigas*, fr Gk] – **giantlike** *adj*

**²giant** *adj* extremely large **synonyms** see HUGE **antonyms** dwarflike, pigmy

**giant anteater** *n* a large anteater (*Myrmecophaga tridactyla*) of S America with shaggy grey fur, a black band across the chest, and a white stripe on the shoulder

**giant hogweed** *n* a very large plant (*Heracleum mantegazzianum*) of the carrot family that resembles the closely related COW PARSNIP but grows to more than 3 metres (10 feet) tall

**giantism** /'jie-əntiz(ə)m/ *n* **1** the quality or state of being a giant ⟨~ *in industry*⟩ **2** GIGANTISM 1

**'giant-,killer** *n* one who or that (e g a football team) which defeats an apparently far superior opponent – **giant-killing** *adj or n*

**giant panda** *n* PANDA 2

**giant powder** *n* a dynamite consisting of nitroglycerine absorbed usu in KIESELGUHR

**giant reed** *n* a tall European grass (*Arundo donax*) with woody stems used in making organ reeds

**giant schnauzer** *n* (any of) a breed of robust agile heavyset SCHNAUZER dogs that reach a height of about 55 to 65 centimeters (21¹/₂ to 25¹/₂ inches)

**giant sequoia** *n* BIG TREE (huge N American evergreen tree)

**giant star** *n* a star of great brightness and large mass

**giaour** /'jow·ə/ *n, derog* a non-Muslim [Turk *gâvur*]

**¹gib** /gib/ *n* a male cat; *specif* a castrated one [ME, fr *Gib*, nickname for *Gilbert*]

**²gib** *n* a plate (e g of metal or wood) machined to hold other parts in place, to afford a bearing surface, or to provide means for taking up wear [origin unknown] – **gib** *vt*

**¹gibber** /'jibə/ *vi* to make rapid, inarticulate, and usu incomprehensible utterances ⟨*a ~ing idiot*⟩ [imit] – **gibber** *n*

**²gibber** *n, Austr* a small stone; a pebble; *also* a boulder, rock [native name in Australia]

**gibberellic acid** /ˌjibə'relik/ *n* an acid, $C_{19}H_{22}O_6$, that is a gibberellin

**gibberellin** /ˌjibə'relin/ *n* any of several plant hormones that regulate growth and that in low concentrations promote the growth of shoots to many times their normal size [NL *Gibberella fujikuroi*, fungus from which it was first isolated]

**gibberish** /'jibərish/ *n* incomprehensible or meaningless language [prob fr ¹*gibber*]

**¹gibbet** /'jibit/ *n* an upright post with a projecting arm from which the bodies of executed criminals were formerly hung as a warning; *broadly* a gallows [ME *gibet*, fr OF]

**²gibbet** *vt* **1** to hang on a gibbet; *specif* to execute by so hanging **2** to expose to humiliation or public scorn

**gibbon** /'gib(ə)n/ *n* any of several tailless apes (genera *Hylobates* and *Symphalangus*) of SE Asia and the E Indies, that are the smallest of the ANTHROPOID APES and the most highly adapted to living in trees [Fr]

**gibbous** /'gibəs/ *adj* **1** *of the moon or a planet* seen with more than half but not all of the apparent disc illuminated **2** *formal* **2a** convex, protuberant **b** swollen on one side **3** *formal* having a hump; humpbacked [ME, fr MF *gibbeux*, fr LL *gibbosus* humpbacked, fr L *gibbus* hump] – **gibbously** *adv*, **gibbousness** *n*, **gibbosity** *n*

**gibbsite** /'gibziet/ *n* a mineral, $Al(OH)_3$, that consists of an oxide of aluminium chemically combined with water molecules and is an important constituent of BAUXITE (principal source of aluminium) [George *Gibbs* †1833 US mineralogist]

**gibe, jibe** /jieb/ *vi* to utter taunting or mocking words ~ *vt* to scorn or tease with taunting or mocking words **synonyms** see ²RIDICULE *usage* see ³JIBE [perh fr MF *giber* to shake, handle roughly] – **gibe** *n*, **giber** *n*

**giblets** /'jiblits/ *n pl* a fowl's heart, liver, and other edible internal organs – compare HASLET [ME *gibelet* entrails, garbage, fr MF, stew of wildfowl]

**gid** /gid/ *n* a disease, esp of sheep, caused by the presence and development in the brain of a larval form of a tapeworm (*Taenia multiceps*) and characterized by a staggering gait, loss of limb control, and finally death [back-formation fr *giddy*]

**giddy** /'gidi/ *adj* **1** lightheartedly silly; frivolous **2a** dizzy ⟨*~ from the unaccustomed exercise*⟩ **b** causing dizziness ⟨*a ~ height*⟩ **c** whirling rapidly **3** *informal* – used as an intensive, esp in *the giddy limit* [ME *gidy* mad, foolish, fr OE *gydig* possessed, mad; akin to OE *god*] – **giddily** *adv*, **giddiness** *n*

**Gideon** /'gidiən/ *n* **1** an early Hebrew hero noted for his defeat of the Midianites **2** a member of an interdenominational Christian organization whose activities include the placing of Bibles in hotel rooms [Heb *Gidh'ōn*]

**gie** /gee/ *vb, chiefly Scot* to give [by alter.]

**Giemsa stain, Giemsa** /gi'emzə/ *n* a dye consisting of a mixture of EOSIN and METHYLENE BLUE, used chiefly in staining of specimens of blood for examination under a microscope [Gustav *Giemsa* †1948 Ger specialist in chemotherapy]

**¹gift** /gift/ *n* **1** a natural capacity or talent **2** something freely given by one person to another; a present, donation **3** the act, right, or power of giving ⟨*the regional fund ... is not in M. Pompidou's ~ – The Times*⟩ **4** *Br informal* something obtained easily or cheap at the price ⟨*at £2 it's a ~*⟩ ⟨*that pass in front of the goal was a ~*⟩ [ME, fr ON, something given, talent; akin to OE *giefan* to give] – **gift of the gab** *informal* the ability to talk glibly and persuasively

**²gift** *vt* **1** to endow with some power, quality, or attribute **2** to present ⟨*he ~ed us with a book*⟩ – disliked by some speakers

**gifted** /'giftid/ *adj* **1** having or revealing great natural ability; talented **2** highly intelligent ⟨*~ children*⟩ – **giftedly** *adv*, **giftedness** *n*

**Gift of Tongues** *n* inspired ecstatic speaking; *specif* that occurring among the followers of Jesus at Pentecost

**gift token** *n* a certified statement redeemable for merchandise to the amount stated on it – compare TOKEN 5

**gift voucher** *n* GIFT TOKEN

**gift wrap** *vt* to wrap (something bought as a gift) decoratively

**¹gig** /gig/ *n* **1** a long light ship's boat propelled by oars, sails, etc **2** a light 2-wheeled one-horse carriage [ME *gigg* top, perh

of Scand origin; akin to ON *geiga* to turn aside; akin to OE *geonian* to yawn – more at YAWN]

**²gig** *n* a pronged spear for catching fish [short for earlier *fizgig*, *fishgig*, of unknown origin]

**³gig** *n* a musician's engagement for a specified time; *esp* such an engagement for one performance [origin unknown]

**⁴gig** *vi* **-gg-** *informal* to perform a gig

**giga-** /jigə-, gigə-/ *comb form* one thousand million ($10^9$) ⟨*gigavolt*⟩ [ISV, fr Gk *gigas* giant]

**gigacycle** /'gigə,siekl, 'jigə-/ *n* a gigahertz

**gigahertz** /-,huhts/ *n* a unit of frequency (e g of a radio wave) equal to $10^9$ hertz [ISV *giga-* + *hertz*]

**gigant-** /jiegant-/, **giganto-** *comb form* giant ⟨*gigantism*⟩ [Gk, fr *gigant-*, *gigas*]

**gigantesque** /ˌjiegan'tesk/ *adj* of enormous or grotesquely large proportions

**gigantic** /jie'gantik/ *adj* vastly exceeding the usual or expected; unusually enormous (e g in size, force, or prominence) ⟨*a man of ~ stature*⟩ ⟨*made a last ~ effort*⟩ **synonyms** see HUGE **antonyms** dwarflike, lilliputian – **gigantically** *adv*

**gigantism** /'jiegan,tiz(ə)m, -'-,--/ *n* **1** GIANTISM 1 **2** development to an abnormally large size **3** excessive growth in plants, often accompanied by the inhibiting of reproduction

**gigas** /'jiegəs/ *adj* of or being a POLYPLOID plant (one with more than twice the basic set of chromosomes) having a thicker stem, taller growth, darker thicker leaves, and larger flowers and seeds than the normal corresponding DIPLOID plant (plant having twice the basic set of chromosomes) [NL, fr L, giant, fr Gk]

**¹giggle** /'gigl/ *vi* to laugh in repeated short bursts; laugh in a silly manner ~ *vt* to utter with a giggle [imit] – **giggler** *n*, **gigglingly** *adv*

**²giggle** *n* **1** an act or instance of giggling **2** *chiefly Br informal* something that amuses or diverts ⟨*we only did it for a ~*⟩ – **giggly** *adj*

**gigolo** /'zhigəloh/ *n, pl* **gigolos 1** a man paid by a usu older woman for companionship or sex **2** a professional dancing partner or male escort [Fr, back-formation fr *gigolette* girl who frequents public dances, prostitute, fr *giguer* to dance, fr *gigue*]

**gigot** /'zhigoh, 'jigət/ *n* a leg of meat (e g lamb), esp when cooked [MF, dim. of *gigue* fiddle – more at JIG; fr its shape]

**gigot sleeve** *also* **gigot** /'jigət/ *n* a leg-of-mutton sleeve

**gigue** /zheeg/ *n* a lively dance movement (e g in a Baroque suite) with six quaver beats in a bar and consisting of two sections, each of which is repeated [Fr – more at JIG]

**Gila monster** /'heelə/ *n* a large orange and black venomous lizard (*Heloderma suspectum*) of the southwestern USA; *also* a related lizard (*Heloderma horridum*) of Mexico [*Gila*, river in Arizona, USA]

**gilbert** /'gilbət/ *n* the cgs unit of MAGNETOMOTIVE FORCE equivalent to $^{10}/_4\pi$ ampere-turn [William *Gilbert* †1603 E physicist]

**¹gild** /gild/ *vt* **gilded**, **gilt** /gilt/ **1** to overlay (as if) with a thin covering of gold **2** to give an attractive but often deceptive appearance to – see also **gild the** LILY [ME *gilden*, fr OE *gyldan;* akin to OE *gold*] – **gilder** *n*, **gilding** *n*
*usage* The past tense and past participle must be **gilded** in the abstract sense ⟨*gilded corruption*⟩.

**²gild** *n* a guild

**gilet** /'zheelay/ *n* **1** a bodice or part of a bodice styled like a waistcoat **2** a loose waistcoat [Fr, fr Sp *gileco*, *jaleco*, fr Ar *jalīkah*, a garment worn by slaves in Algeria, fr Turk *yelek* waistcoat]

**¹gill** /jil/ *n* a unit of liquid capacity equal to $^1/_4$ pint [ME *gille*, perh fr MF *gille*, *gelle* vat, tub, fr L *gerulus* bearer, carrier, fr *gerere* to bear]

**²gill** /gil/ *n* **1** an organ of respiration in an aquatic animal (e g a fish) for oxygenating blood using the oxygen dissolved in water **2a gills** *pl*, **gill** the flesh under or about the chin or jaws **b** any of the radiating plates forming the undersurface of the cap of some fungi (e g mushrooms) [ME *gile*, *gille*, prob of Scand origin; akin to OSw *gel*, *geel* gill, jaw] – **gilled** *adj*

**³gill, ghyll** /gil/ *n, Br* **1** a ravine **2** a narrow mountain stream or rivulet [ME *gille*, fr ON *gil*]

**gill arch** /gil/ *n* any of the bone or cartilage arches that are placed one behind the other to form part of the skeleton on each side of the PHARYNX (gullet), and that support the bases of the gills of fishes and amphibians; *also* any of the rudimentary ridges that appear at an early stage in the development of the embryos of higher VERTEBRATE animals and correspond to the gill arches

**gill cleft** /gil/ n GILL SLIT 1
**gill cover** /gil/ n OPERCULUM 2b
**gill fungus** /gil/ n a BASIDIOMYCETE fungus (eg a mushroom) having gills
**gillie, gilly** also **ghillie** /'gili/ n 1 a male attendant on a Scottish Highland chief in former times 2 an attendant to a sportsman who is hunting or fishing in Scotland [ScGael *gille* & IrGael *giolla* boy, servant] – **gillie** vi
**gillion** /'gilyən/ n, Br a thousand millions – see NUMBER table; compare BILLION [*giga-* + *million*] – **gillion** adj, **gillionth** adj or n
**gill net** /gil/ n a net suspended in water that has meshes which allow the head of a fish to pass through but entangle it as it seeks to withdraw – **gillnet** vt
**gill raker** /gil/ n any of the small bony projections on a GILL ARCH that prevent solid substances (eg food particles) from entering the gills
**gill slit** /gil/ n 1 any of the openings or clefts between the GILL ARCHES (eg of a fish) that extend from the PHARYNX (gullet) to the exterior and through which water taken in at the mouth passes to the exterior and so bathes the gills; also any of the rudimentary grooves between the GILL ARCHES of the embryos of higher VERTEBRATE animals that correspond to the gill slits 2 the external opening to the cavity containing the gills when a protective covering of the gills is present
**gillyflower, gilliflower** /'jili,flowə/ n 1 CLOVE PINK; also any of several related pinks 2 any of several plants (eg a wallflower or stock) with fragrant-smelling flowers [by folk etymology fr ME *gilofre* clove, fr MF *girofle, gilofre,* fr L *caryophyllum,* fr Gk *karyophyllon,* fr *karyon* nut + *phyllon* leaf – more at CAREEN, BLADE]
**Gilsonite** /'gilsə,niet/ trademark – used for a black lustrous asphalt occurring esp in Utah
¹**gilt** /gilt/ adj covered with gold or gilt; of the colour of gold [ME, fr pp of *gilden* to gild]
²**gilt** n 1 gold, or something that resembles gold, laid on a surface 2 superficial brilliance 3 pl gilt-edged securities △ guilt – **take the gilt off the gingerbread** to take away the part that makes the whole attractive
³**gilt** n a young female pig, esp before she has a litter [ME *gylte,* fr ON *gyltr;* akin to OE *gelte* young sow – more at GELD]
**gilt-'edged, gilt-edge** adj 1 having a gilt edge 2 of the highest quality or reliability 3 of government securities having a guaranteed fixed interest rate and redeemable at face value
**gilthead** /'gilt·hed/ n a spiny-finned food fish (*Sparus auratus*) of the Mediterranean and eastern Atlantic
**gimbal ring** n gimbals
**gimbals** /'jimblz, 'gim-/ n pl a device that permits an object (eg a ship's compass or galley stove) to incline freely in any direction, suspending it so that it will remain level when its support is tipped [alter. of obs *gemel* double ring, deriv of L *geminus* twin]
**gimcrack** /'jim,krak/ n a showy unsubstantial object of little use or value; a gewgaw [perh alter. of ME *gibecrake,* of uncertain meaning] – **gimcrack** adj, **gimcrackery** n
**gimel** /'giml/ n the 3rd letter of the Hebrew alphabet [Heb *gīmel*]
¹**gimlet** /'gimlit/ n a tool for boring small holes in wood, usu consisting of a crosswise handle fitted at right angles to a tapered screw – compare AUGER [ME, fr MF *guimbelet,* prob modif of MD *wimmelkijn,* fr *wimmel* auger + *-kijn* -kin] – **gimlet** vt
²**gimlet** adj, of eyes piercing, penetrating ⟨give him a gimlet-eyed stare⟩
**gimmal** /'giml, 'jiml/ n a pair or series of interlocked rings (eg in a machine or worn on a finger) [alter. of obs *gemel* double ring]
**gimme** /'gimi/ informal give me [by alter.]
**gimmer** /'gimə/ n, chiefly Scot & N Eng a (female) sheep until its second shearing [ME *gymbre, gymmer,* fr ON *gymbr* yearling lamb]
**gimmick** /'gimik/ n 1 a novel or attention-getting device or object 2 a scheme or angle for gaining attention or publicity [origin unknown] – **gimmickry** n, **gimmicky** adj
¹**gimp, guimpe** /gimp/ n 1 an ornamental flat braid or round cord used esp as a trimming 2 the thread used to fill in ornamental details (eg flowers) in lace [perh fr D]
²**gimp** n, informal spirit, courage [origin unknown]

¹**gin** /gin/ vb -nn-; **gan** archaic or dial to begin [ME *ginnen,* short for *beginnen*]
²**gin** /jin/ n any of various tools or mechanical devices: eg **a** a snare or trap for game **b** a machine for raising or moving heavy weights **c** COTTON GIN [ME *gin,* modif of OF *engin* – more at ENGINE]
³**gin** vt -nn- 1 to snare using a gin 2 to separate (cotton fibre) from seeds and waste material – **ginner** n, **ginning** n
⁴**gin** /gin/ conj, dial if [perh alter. of Sc & E dial. *gif,* fr ME *yif, if*]
⁵**gin** /jin/ n 1a an alcoholic spirit made by distilling a mash of grain with juniper berries **b** an alcoholic spirit similar to gin made from plain spirit flavoured with an aromatic substance 2a GIN RUMMY **b** the act of laying down a full hand of matched cards in gin rummy ⟨the bonus for going ∼ is 25 points⟩ [by shortening & alter. fr *geneva*] – **ginny** adj
⁶**gin** /jin/ n, Austr derog a female Aborigine – compare LUBRA [native name in Australia]
**gin and it** n, Br an alcoholic drink that consists of gin and Italian vermouth [*it,* short for *Italian* (*vermouth*)]
**ginger** /'jinjə/ n 1a(1) a thickened RHIZOME (underground stem) with a strong hot spicy taste, that is used in cooking and esp formerly in medicine, is dried and ground as a spice, candied as a sweet, or preserved in syrup **a(2)** the spice prepared from ginger by drying and grinding **b** any of a genus (*Zingiber* of the family Zingiberaceae, the ginger family) of plants with pungent aromatic RHIZOMES; esp a widely cultivated tropical plant (*Zingiber officinale*) that supplies most of the ginger used commercially 2 high spirit; pep 3 a strong brown colour [ME, fr OF *gimgibre,* fr ML *gingiber,* alter. of L *zingiber,* fr Gk *zingiberis,* prob modif of Skt *śrṅgavera*]
**ginger ale** n a sweetened yellowish fizzy nonalcoholic drink flavoured mainly with ginger extract
**ginger beer** n a weak alcoholic fizzy drink of milky appearance, made by the fermentation of ginger and syrup; also a similar nonalcoholic commercial preparation
**gingerbread** /-,bred/ n 1 a cake made with treacle or syrup and flavoured with ginger; also a thick biscuit made from similar ingredients 2 tawdry or excessive ornament – see also **take the** GILT **off the gingerbread** [ME *gingerbreed,* by folk etymology fr *gingebras* ginger paste, fr OF *gingembraz,* fr *gimgibre;* (2) fr the fancy shapes and gilding formerly often applied to gingerbread] – **gingerbready** adj
**ginger group** n taking sing or pl vb, Br a pressure group (eg within a political party) urging stronger action
**gingerly** /'jinjəli/ adj very cautious or careful [perh fr MF *gensor, genzor,* compar of *gent* well-born, dainty, delicate] – **gingerliness** n, **gingerly** adv
**ginger nut** n a hard biscuit flavoured with ginger and usu sweetened with golden syrup
**ginger snap** n GINGER NUT
**ginger up** vt to stir to activity; vitalize ⟨ginger up boardroom attitudes – Punch⟩ [fr the practice of stimulating a horse with ginger]
**ginger wine** n an alcoholic drink made by fermentation of ginger, water, and sugar
**gingham** /'ging·əm/ n a plain-weave often checked clothing fabric usu of yarn-dyed cotton [modif of Malay *genggang* checkered cloth]
**gingiv-** /'jinjiv-/, **gingivo-** /-oh-/ comb form gum; gums ⟨*gingivitis*⟩ [L *gingiva*]
**gingiva** /jin'jievə/ n, pl **gingivae** [-vi/ anatomy the gum [L – more at CONGER] – **gingival** adj
**gingivitis** /,jinji'vietəs/ n inflammation of the gums [NL]
**gink** /gingk/ n, derog slang a person, fellow [origin unknown]
**ginkgo** /'gingk,goh, 'ging,koh/ also **gingko** /'ging,koh/ n, pl **ginkgoes, gingkoes** a showy GYMNOSPERMOUS tree (*Ginkgo biloba*) of E China that has fan-shaped leaves and yellow fruit, and is often grown for ornament [NL *Ginkgo,* genus name, fr Jap *ginkyo*]
**gin mill** n, chiefly NAm informal a bar, saloon
**gin palace** n, Br derog a gaudy public house
**gin rummy** n a form of rummy for two players in which each player is dealt 10 cards, and in which a player may win a hand by matching all his/her cards or may end play when the value of his/her unmatched cards is less than 10 [⁵*gin*]
**ginseng** /'jin,seng/ n 1 a Chinese plant (*Panax schinseng*) of the ivy family that has leaves divided into five leaflets, scarlet berries, and an aromatic root widely valued as a tonic; also a related N American plant (*Panax quinquefolius*) 2 (a preparation of) the root of ginseng [Chin (Pek) *rénshēn* (*jen²-shen¹*)]

**gippy tummy** /'jipi/ *n, chiefly Br informal* indigestion and diarrhoea; *esp* that affecting visitors to hot countries [*gippy* by shortening & alter. fr *Egyptian*]

**gipsy** /'jipsi/ *vi* to live or roam like a Gipsy

**Gipsy,** *NAm* **Gypsy** *n* **1** a member of a dark Caucasian people coming originally from India to Europe in the 14th or 15th century and maintaining a migratory way of life chiefly in Europe and the Americas **2** ROMANY **2 3** *not cap* one who resembles a Gipsy (e g in appearance or way of life); *esp* a wanderer [by shortening & alter. fr *Egyptian*] – **gipsyhood** *n, often cap,* **gipsyish** *adj, often cap*

**gipsy moth** *n* a European TUSSOCK MOTH (*Lymantria dispar*) that has a greyish-brown mottled hairy caterpillar which feeds destructively on the leaves of many trees

**giraffe** /ji'raf, ji'rahf/ *n, pl* **giraffes**, *esp collectively* **giraffe** a large African RUMINANT (cud-chewing) mammal (*Giraffa camelopardalis*) that is the tallest living 4-legged animal and has a very long neck and a black-blotched fawn or cream coat [It *giraffa,* fr Ar *zirāfah*] – **giraffish** *adj*

**girandole** /'jirən,dohl/ *n* **1** a radiating and showy composition (e g a cluster of skyrockets fired together) **2** an ornamental branched candleholder [Fr & It; Fr, fr It *girandola,* fr *girare* to turn, fr LL *gyrare,* fr L *gyrus* circle, spiral]

**girasol, girasole** /'jirə,sol, -,sohl/ *n* an opal of varying colour, that gives out fiery reflections in bright light [It *girasole* sunflower, girasol, fr *girare* + *sole* sun, fr L *sol* – more at SOLAR]

**¹gird** /guhd/ *vb* **girded, girt** /guht/ *vt* **1a** to encircle or bind with a flexible band (e g a belt) **b** to hold secure (e g a sword by a belt, or clothing with a cord) **c** to surround **2** to provide or equip with a sword **3** to prepare (oneself) for action ~ *vi* to prepare for action – see also **gird (up) one's** LOINS [ME *girden,* fr OE *gyrdan;* akin to OE *geard* yard – more at YARD]

**²gird** *vt* to sneer at ~ *vi* to gibe, rail [ME *girden* to strike, thrust]

**³gird** *n* a sarcastic remark

**girder** /'guhdə/ *n* a horizontal main structural member (e g in a building or bridge) that supports vertical loads and that consists of a single piece or of more than one piece bound together [¹*gird* + ²*-er*]

**¹girdle** /'guhdl/ *n* **1** something that encircles or confines: e g **1a** a belt or cord encircling the body, usu at the waist **b** a woman's tightly fitting undergarment that extends from the waist to below the hips **c** either of two bony rings or arches at the front or upper and back or lower ends of the trunk of a VERTEBRATE animal, that support the forelimbs and hindlimbs respectively – compare PECTORAL GIRDLE, PELVIC GIRDLE **d** a ring made by the removal of the bark round a plant stem or tree trunk **2** the edge of a cut gem that is grasped by the setting [ME *girdel,* fr OE *gyrdel;* akin to OHG *gurtil* girdle, OE *gyrdan* to gird]

**²girdle** *vt* **1** to encircle with a girdle **2** to move round; circle (~d *the world*) **3** to cut a girdle round (a tree or plant) usu to kill by interrupting the circulation of water and nutrients

**³girdle** *n* a griddle *synonyms* see GRIDDLE [ME (Sc) *girdil,* alter. of ME *gredil*]

**girdler** /'guhdlə/ *n* a maker of girdles

**girl** /guhl/ *n* **1a** a female child **b** a young unmarried woman **2a** a female servant or employee **b** a sweetheart, girlfriend **c** a daughter **3** *informal* a woman *synonyms* see LADY *antonyms* boy, youth [ME *gurle, girle* young person of either sex] – **girlhood** *n*

**girl Friday** *n* a female general assistant, esp in an office [see MAN FRIDAY]

**girlfriend** /-,frend/ *n* **1** a frequent or regular female companion of a boy or man; *broadly* a female friend **2** a female lover

**girl guide** *n, chiefly Br* GUIDE **4** – not now used technically

**girlie, girly** /'guhli/ *adj* featuring nude or scantily clothed young women (~ *magazines*)

**girlish** /'guhlish/ *adj* of or having the characteristics of a girl or girlhood (~ *laughter*) *synonyms* see BOY – **girlishly** *adv,* **girlishness** *n*

**girl scout** *n, NAm* GUIDE **4**

**girn** /giən, guhn/ *vi, Scot & NW Eng* **1** to grimace, snarl; *also* to pull a grotesque face (*the one who* ~ed *to the judge's greatest satisfaction being declared the winner* – M F Wakelin) **2** to be peevish or fretful [ME *girnen,* alter. of *grinnen* to grin, snarl] – **girn** *n*

**giro** /'jie(ə)roh/ *n* a highly computerized low-cost system of money transfer comparable to a bank current account that is one of the national post office services in many European countries [Ger, fr It, turn, transfer, fr L *gyrus* circle, spiral]

**giron** /jie•əron/ *n, heraldry* a gyron

**Girondist** /ji'rondist/ *n* a member of the moderate republican party in the French legislative assembly in 1791; *broadly* a moderate revolutionary [Fr *girondiste,* fr *Gironde,* a political party, fr *Gironde,* department of France represented by its leaders]

**¹girt** /guht/ *past of* ¹GIRD

**²girt** *vt* to gird, encircle ~ *vi* to measure in girth [ME *girten,* alter. of *girden*]

**¹girth** /guhth/ *n* **1** a band or strap that passes under the body of a horse or other animal to fasten something (e g a saddle) on its back **2a** a measurement round a body (*he was a man of more than average* ~) **b** size, dimensions (*the river was twice its usual* ~) [ME, fr ON *gjörth;* akin to OE *gyrdan* to gird]

**²girth** *vt* **1** to encircle **2** to bind or fasten with a girth **3** to measure the girth of

**gisarme** /gi'zahm/ *n* a medieval weapon consisting of a sharpened blade mounted on a long staff and carried by a foot soldier [ME, fr OF, of Gmc origin]

**gismo** /'gizmoh/ *n* a gizmo

**gist** /jist/ *n the* main point of a matter; *the* essence (*the* ~ *of an argument*) [AF, it lies, fr MF, fr *gesir* to lie, fr L *jacēre* – more at ADJACENT]

**git** /git/ *also* **get** /get/ *n, Br slang* an unpleasant or worthless person [*git* alter. of ²*get* (in sense "offspring, bastard")]

**gittern** /'gituhn/ *n* a type of medieval guitar [ME *giterne,* fr MF *guiterne,* modif of OSp *guitarra* guitar]

**¹give** /giv/ *vb* **gave** /gayv/; **given** /'giv(ə)n/ *vt* **1** to make a present of (~ *a doll to a child*) **2a** to grant or bestow by formal action (*the law* ~s *citizens the right to vote*) **b** to accord or yield to another (~ *blood*) (~ *permission*) ( ~ *him her confidence*) **3a** to administer as a sacrament or medicine **b** to commit to another as a trust or responsibility (*gave her his coat to hold*) **c** to transfer from one's authority or custody (*the policeman gave the prisoner to the warder*) **d** to execute and deliver (~ *a legal undertaking*) **e** to convey or express to another (~ *a signal*) (~ *an order*) (~ *my regards to your family*) **4a** to proffer (a bodily part) for the action of another (*gave his hand to the visitor*) **b** to yield (oneself) to a man in sexual intercourse **5a** to present in public performance (~ *a concert*) **b** to present to view or observation (*gave evidence of real promise*) **6** to provide by way of entertainment ( ~ *a party*) **7** to propose as a toast (*I* ~ *you the Queen*) **8a** to make assignment of; allot (~ *him the best room available*) (*gave her the name Susan*) **b** to attribute, ascribe (*gave all the glory to God*) **9a** to yield as a product or effect; produce (*cows* ~ *milk*) (*84 divided by 12* ~s *7*) (*she gave him two sons*) **b** to make known; record (*the thermometer* ~s *the temperature*) **10a** to yield possession of by way of exchange; pay **b** to dispose of for a price; sell **11a** to deliver by some bodily action (*gave him a push*) **b** to make, execute (*gave a yell*) (*the ship gave a lurch*) **c** to inflict as punishment (*gave the boy a whipping*) (*the judge gave him 10 years*) **d** to cause to undergo; impose (~ *them a spelling test*) (~ *it a try*) **e** to award by formal verdict (*judgment was* ~n *against the plaintiff*) **f** to make a specified ruling on the status of (a player) (*Bowles was* ~n *offside*) **12** to offer for consideration, acceptance, or use (*gave no reason for his absence*) (*don't* ~ *me that old line*) **13a** to suffer the loss of; sacrifice (~ *his life for his principles*) **b** to apply freely or fully; devote (~ *one's time to the service of others*) (*children giving themselves to their play*) **c** to offer as a pledge (*I* ~ *you my word*) **14a** to cause to have or receive; occasion (*mountains always gave him pleasure*) **b** to cause to catch or contract (*digging* ~s *me backache*) **c** to cause (someone) (to think or wonder) (*I was given to understand that he was ill*) **15** to allow, concede (*gave him a pawn and still won*) (*it's late, I* ~ *you that*) **16** to care even to the extent of (*didn't* ~ *a hang*) ~ *vi* **1** to make a gift or gifts (*volunteers who* ~ *of their time to run Scouts* – *TES*) **2** to yield or collapse in response to pressure (*the fence gave under his weight*) **3** to afford a view or passage; open (*the door* ~s *directly upon the garden*) **4** *informal* to impart information; talk **5** *slang* to happen, GO ON (*he demanded to know what gave*) [ME *given,* of Scand origin; akin to OSw *giva* to give; akin to OE *giefan, gifan* to give, L *habēre* to have, hold] – **giver** *n* – **give me** I prefer (*give me London any day!*) – **give or take** allowing for a usu specified imprecision (*three hours, give or take a few minutes either way*) – **give somebody best** *Br* to acknowledge somebody's superiority – **give the game/show away** to reveal one's plans or a secret, usu by mistake

*synonyms* Compare **give, present, donate, bestow, confer,** and **grant: give** is the general term for handing something over to someone else. **Present** implies formality or ceremony ⟨**present** *the prizes*⟩. **Donate** suggests a public gift ⟨**donate** *a book to the school library*⟩. **Bestow** and **confer** are similar in that both suggest the giving of something prized or sought after. **Bestow** implies condescension in the giver, while **confer** stresses the giving of an honour or privilege ⟨**bestowed** *a smile on her admirers*⟩ ⟨**conferred** *an honorary degree on the poet*⟩. **Grant** stresses giving from a position of privilege or authority, and may imply justice or generosity ⟨**granted** *the town a charter in 1255*⟩. *antonym* take

**give away** *vt* **1** to make a present of **2** to hand over (a bride) to the bridegroom at a wedding **3a** to betray ⟨*you wouldn't give us away, would you?*⟩ **b** to disclose, reveal ⟨*his clothes gave him away*⟩ **4** to be at a disadvantage in a sporting contest by (e g a weight or age) compared with an opponent ⟨*giving away four years to the junior champion*⟩ **5** to lose carelessly ⟨*he gave away his last chance of winning the election when he said the wrong thing*⟩ – see also GIVEAWAY

**give back** *vt* **1** to restore to the owner or original possessor **2** to throw back (sound or light) ⟨*the cave gives back the sound of your voice*⟩

**give in** *vt* **1** to deliver, submit ⟨gave in *the money he'd found*⟩ ~ *vi* to yield under insistence or entreaty; surrender

**give off** *vt* to emit ⟨gave off *an unpleasant smell*⟩

**give out** *vt* **1** to declare, publish ⟨giving out *that the doctor ... required a few days of complete rest* – Charles Dickens⟩ **2** to emit ⟨gave out *a constant hum*⟩ **3** to issue, distribute ⟨gave out *new uniforms*⟩ ~ *vi* **1** to come to an end; RUN SHORT ⟨*our supply of sugar has* given out⟩ ⟨*his strength* gave out⟩ **2** to fail; BREAK DOWN ⟨*the engine finally* gave out⟩

**give over** *vt* **1** to cease, stop ⟨give over *crying*⟩ **2a** to yield without restraint or control; abandon ⟨gave *herself* over *completely to her work*⟩ **b** to set apart for a particular purpose or use; devote ⟨*an area* given over *to a children's playground*⟩ – + *to* **3** to deliver to somebody's care; entrust ~ *vi, informal* to bring an activity to an end; stop ⟨*told him to* give over *and let me alone* – Brendan Behan⟩

**give up** *vt* **1a** to surrender; *esp* to offer (oneself) as a prisoner ⟨*he* gave *himself* up⟩ **b** to deliver or allow to pass ⟨gave up *his seat to an old lady*⟩ **2** to desist from ⟨*refused to* give up *trying*⟩ **3a** to abandon (oneself) to a particular feeling, influence, or activity ⟨gave *himself* up *to despair*⟩ **b** to stop having or doing; renounce ⟨*I must* give up *sugar*⟩ **4** to declare incurable or insoluble ⟨*the doctors* gave him up *for dead*⟩ **5** to stop having a relationship with ⟨*she's* given me up⟩ ~ *vi* to abandon an activity or course of action; *esp* to stop trying to guess

²**give** *n* **1** capacity or tendency to yield to force or strain **2** the quality or state of being springy

,**give-and-'take** *n* **1** the practice of making mutual concessions; compromise **2** the good-natured exchange of ideas or words

**giveaway** /-ə,way/ *n* **1** an unintentional revelation or betrayal **2** something given free or at a reduced price; *esp* a free gift offered with a product or service as an incentive to purchase

**given** /'giv(ə)n/ *adj* **1** presented as a gift; bestowed without payment **2** prone, disposed ⟨~ *to swearing*⟩ **3** *of an official document* having been executed on the date specified ⟨~ *in London this ninth day of September*⟩ **4a** fixed, specified ⟨*at a ~ time*⟩ **b** assumed as actual or hypothetical ⟨~ *that all men are equal before the law*⟩ **5** immediately present in experience – **given** *n*

**given name** *n, chiefly NAm* any of one's names other than the surname

**gizmo, gismo** /'gizmoh/ *n, pl* **gizmos, gismos** *chiefly NAm* a gadget [origin unknown]

**gizzard** /'gizəd/ *n* **1** an enlargement of the digestive tract of birds, immediately following the CROP (pouch-like part of the gullet), that has thick muscular walls and usu contains small stones or grit for breaking up and grinding food **2** a thickened or enlarged muscular-walled part of the digestive tract in some INVERTEBRATE animals (e g an insect or an earthworm) that is similar in function to the gizzard of a bird [alter. of ME *giser*, fr ONF *guisier*, fr L *gigeria* (pl) giblets]

**glabella** /glə'belə/ *n, pl* **glabellae** /-li/ the smooth part of the forehead between the eyebrows [NL, fr L, fem of *glabellus* hairless, dim. of *glaber*] – **glabellar** *adj*

**glabrous** /'glabrəs/ *adj* smooth; *esp* having a surface without hairs or projections ⟨~ *skin*⟩ ⟨~ *leaves*⟩ [L *glabr-, glaber* smooth, bald – more at GLAD] – **glabrousness** *n*

**glacé** /'glasay/ *adj* **1** made or finished so as to have a smooth glossy surface ⟨~ *silk*⟩ **2** coated with a glaze; candied ⟨~

*cherries*⟩ [Fr, fr pp of *glacer* to freeze, ice, glaze, fr L *glaciare*, fr *glacies* ice]

**glacial** /'glays(h)yəl/ *adj* **1a** extremely cold ⟨*a ~ wind*⟩ **b** devoid of warmth and cordiality ⟨*a ~ smile*⟩ **2a** of or produced by glaciers **b** suggestive of the very slow movement of glaciers ⟨*progress on the bill has been ~*⟩ **c(1)** of or being any of those periods of geological time when much of the earth was covered by glaciers **c(2)** *cap* Pleistocene **3** *of a chemical compound* resembling ice in appearance, esp when frozen ⟨~ *acetic acid*⟩ [L *glacialis*, fr *glacies*] – **glacially** *adv*

**glaciate** /'glays(h)i,ayt/ *vt* **1** to freeze **2a** to cover with ice or a glacier **b** to subject to glacial action – **glaciation** *n*

**glacier** /'glasi-ə, 'glay-/ *n* a large body of ice moving very slowly down a slope or valley or spreading outwards on a land surface [Fr dial., fr MF dial., fr MF *glace* ice, fr L *glacies*; akin to L *gelu* frost – more at COLD]

**glacio-** /'glasioh-, 'glay-/ *comb form* **1** glacier ⟨glacio*logy*⟩ **2** glacial and ⟨glacio*fluvial*⟩

**glaciology** /glasi'oləji, glay-/ *n* the study of glaciers or ice accumulations and their effects [ISV *glacier* + *-o-* + *-logy*] – **glaciologist** *n*, **glaciologic, glaciological** *adj*

**glacis** /'glasi, 'glasis, 'glay-/ *n, pl* **glacis** /-sis, seez/ **1** a gentle slope; an incline **2** a slope with no cover for attackers that runs downwards from a fortification [Fr, fr *glacer* to freeze, slide]

**glacis plate** /'glasis, 'glasi/ *n* the upper frontal hull armour of an armoured fighting vehicle

¹**glad** /glad/ *adj* **-dd-** **1a** experiencing pleasure, joy, or delight; made happy **b** marked by or expressing a feeling of pleased or satisfied gratification ⟨*a ~ shout*⟩ **c** very willing ⟨~ *to do it*⟩ **2** causing happiness and joy; pleasant ⟨~ *tidings*⟩ **3** full of brightness and cheerfulness ⟨*a ~ spring morning*⟩ **4** *archaic* having a cheerful or happy temperament by nature *synonyms* see JOYFUL *antonyms* disappointed, dejected [ME, shining, glad, fr OE *glæd*; akin to OHG *glat* shining, smooth, L *glaber* smooth, bald] – **gladly** *adv*, **gladness** *n*

²**glad** *vt* **-dd-** *archaic* to gladden

³**glad** *n, informal* a gladiolus

**gladden** /'glad(ə)n/ *vt* to make glad ⟨~ *the heart*⟩

**glade** /glayd/ *n* an open space within a wood or forest [perh fr ¹*glad*] – **glady** *adj*

**glad eye** *n, informal* an amorous or sexually inviting look ⟨*he gave her the ~*⟩

¹**glad-,hand** *vt* to extend a glad hand to ⟨*candidates ~*ing *everyone they meet*⟩ ~ *vi* to extend a glad hand ⟨~ing *as if he were standing for Parliament*⟩ – **glad-hander** *n*

**glad hand** *n* a warm welcome or greeting often prompted by ulterior motives

**gladiator** /'gladi,aytə/ *n* **1** one (e g a professional combatant or slave) trained to fight in the public arena for the entertainment of ancient Romans **2** a person engaging in a public fight or controversy **3** a trained fighter; *specif* a prizefighter [L, fr *gladius* sword, of Celt origin; akin to W *cleddyf* sword; akin to L *clades* destruction, Gk *klados* sprout, branch – more at HALT] – **gladiatorial** *adj*

**gladiolus** /gladi'ohləs/ *n, pl* **gladioli** /-lie/ *also* **gladioluses** any of a genus (*Gladiolus*) of chiefly African plants of the iris family, with erect sword-shaped leaves and spikes of brilliantly coloured irregular flowers [NL, genus name, fr L, gladiolus, fr dim. of *gladius*]

**glad rags** *n pl, informal* dressy clothes

**gladsome** /'glads(ə)m/ *adj, poetic* giving or showing joy; cheerful – **gladsomely** *adv*, **gladsomeness** *n*

**Gladstone bag** /'gladstən/ *also* **Gladstone** *n, sometimes not cap* a large bag usu used when travelling, with flexible sides on a rigid frame that opens flat into two equal compartments [William Ewart *Gladstone* †1898 E statesman]

**Gladstonian** /glad'stohni-ən/ *adj* (characteristic) of William Ewart Gladstone or his political views ⟨~ *Liberalism*⟩

**glaikit, glaiket** /'glaykit/ *adj, chiefly Scot* foolish, giddy [ME (Sc) *glaikit*]

**glair, glaire** /gleə/ *n* **1** a liquid filler or adhesive made from egg white **2** a thick sticky substance resembling egg white [ME *gleyre* egg white, fr MF *glaire*, modif of (assumed) VL *claria*, fr L *clarus* clear – more at CLEAR]

**glaive** /glayv/ *n, archaic* a sword; *esp* a broadsword [ME, fr MF, javelin, sword, modif of L *gladius* sword]

¹**glam** /glam/ *vt* **-mm-** *informal* to glamorize ⟨~med *ourselves up and went down to a film premiere* – Women's Own⟩

²**glam** *adj* **-mm-** *informal* glamorous

³**glam** *n, informal* glamour

**glamor·ize, -ise** *also* **glamour·ize, -ise** /'glamǝriez/ *vt* **1** to make glamorous ⟨∼ *the living room*⟩ **2** to look upon or present as glamorous; romanticize ⟨*the novel* ∼s *war*⟩ – **glamoriza-tion** *n,* **glamorizer** *n*

**glamorous,** *also* **glamourous** /'glamǝrǝs/ *adj* having or causing glamour ⟨*a* ∼ *job*⟩ – **glamorously** *adv,* **glamorousness** *n*

**glamour,** *NAm also* **glamor** /'glamǝ/ *n* **1** a magic spell ⟨*the girls appeared to be under a* ∼ – Llewelyn Powys⟩ **2** a romantic, exciting, and often illusory attractiveness; *esp* alluring or fascinating personal attraction [Sc *glamour,* alter. of E *grammar;* fr the popular association of learning with magic] – **glamour** *vt,* **glamourless** *adj*

¹**glance** /glahns/ *vi* **1** to strike a surface obliquely so as to go off at an angle – often + *off* ⟨*the bullet* ∼d *off the wall*⟩ **2a** to flash or gleam from time to time with rays of reflected light ⟨*brooks* glancing *in the sun*⟩ **b** to make sudden quick move-ments ⟨*dragonflies* glancing *over the pond*⟩ **3** to touch on a subject or refer to it briefly or indirectly and often slightingly ⟨*the work* ∼s *at the customs of ancient cultures*⟩ **4a** *of the eyes* to move swiftly from one thing to another **b** to take a quick look at something ⟨∼d *at his watch*⟩ ∼ *vt* **1a** to cause to glance off a surface by throwing or shooting **b** to play a glance in cricket at (a ball) or at the bowling of (a bowler) **2** *archaic* to catch a glimpse of *synonyms* see ¹FLASH [ME *glencen, glenchen,* perh alter. of *glenten* to move quickly – more at GLINT]

²**glance** *n* **1** a quick flash or gleam occurring at intervals **2** a deflected impact or blow **3a** a swift movement of the eyes **b** a quick or cursory look **4** an allusion **5** a stroke in cricket that barely deflects the ball from its line of flight and sends it behind the batsman on the LEG SIDE – **at first glance** on first con-sideration ⟨at first glance *the subject seems harmless enough*⟩

³**glance** *n* any of several usu dark-coloured minerals, esp SULPHIDE minerals, that have a metallic lustre ⟨*lead* ∼⟩ [Ger *glanz* lustre, glance; akin to OHG *glanz* bright – more at GLINT]

**glancing** /'glahnsing/ *adj* **1** having a slanting direction ⟨*a* ∼ *blow*⟩ **2** incidental, indirect ⟨*made* ∼ *allusions to her past*⟩ – **glancingly** *adv*

¹**gland** /gland/ *n* **1a** a cell or group of cells that selectively removes materials from the blood, concentrates or chemically alters them, and secretes them for further use in the body or for elimination from the body **b** any of various animal struc-tures resembling glands though not secretory in function ⟨*lymph* ∼⟩ **2** any of various plant organs (e g a NECTARY) that secrete oil, nectar, resin, etc [Fr *glande,* fr OF, glandular swelling on the neck, gland, modif of L *gland-, glans* acorn; akin to Gk *balanos* acorn] – **glandless** *adj*

²**gland** *n* **1** a device for preventing leakage of fluid past a joint in machinery **2** the movable part of a STUFFING BOX (e g round a PISTON ROD) by which the packing is compressed to prevent leakage of steam or gas [origin unknown]

**glanders** /'glandǝz/ *n taking sing or pl vb* an infectious disease, esp of horses, caused by a bacterium (*Actinobacillus mallei*) and characterized by swelling of the glands beneath the jaw and a profuse discharge of mucus from the nostrils [MF *glandre* glandular swelling on the neck, fr L *glandulae,* fr pl of *glandula,* dim. of *gland-, glans*] – **glandered** *adj*

**gland of Bartholin** /'bahtǝlin/ *n* BARTHOLIN'S GLAND

**glandular** /'glandyoolǝ/ *adj* **1a** of, being, or involving glands, gland cells, or their products **b** having the characteristics or function of a gland **2** innate, inherent ⟨*the almost* ∼ . . . *instinct for adventure and romance* – *Newsweek*⟩ – **glandularly** *adv*

**glandular fever** *n* INFECTIOUS MONONUCLEOSIS

**glans** /glanz/ *n, pl* **glandes** **1** glans, **glans penis** the conical body of erectile tissue forming the head of the penis **2 glans, glans clitoridis** the small mass of erectile tissue forming the free tip of the clitoris [L *gland-, glans,* lit., acorn]

¹**glare** /gleǝ/ *vi* **1** to shine with a harsh uncomfortably bright light ⟨*light* glaring *from the unshaded bulb*⟩ **2** to stare angrily or fiercely **3** *archaic* to stand out offensively; obtrude ∼ *vt* to express (e g hostility) by staring fiercely ⟨∼d *his hatred of me*⟩ *synonyms* see ¹GAZE, ¹GLOW [ME *glaren;* akin to OE *glæs* glass]

²**glare** *n* **1a** a harsh uncomfortably bright light; *specif* painfully bright sunlight **b** cheap showy brilliance; garishness ⟨*the* ∼ *of publicity*⟩ **2** an angry or fierce stare

³**glare** *n, chiefly NAm* a surface or sheet of ice with a smooth slippery surface [prob fr ²*glare*]

**glaring** /'gleǝring/ *adj* **1** having a fixed look of hostility, fierce-ness, or anger **2a** shining with or reflecting an uncomfortably bright light **b** garish **3** painfully and obtrusively evident ⟨*a* ∼ *error*⟩ – **glaringly** *adv,* **glaringness** *n*

**glary** /'gleǝri/ *adj* having a dazzling brightness; glaring

¹**glass** /glahs/ *n* **1a** a hard brittle inorganic usu transparent or translucent substance formed by melting sand or some other form of SILICA, or sometimes oxides of phosphorus or boron, together with other oxides (e g lime or soda) and cooling the mixture rapidly to prevent the formation of crystals **b** a sub-stance resembling glass, esp in hardness and transparency ⟨*organic* ∼es *made from plastics*⟩ **c** a substance (e g pumice) produced by the quick cooling and solidification of molten rock; *esp* VOLCANIC GLASS **2a** something made of glass: e g **2a(1)** any of various glass drinking vessels (e g a tumbler or wineglass) **a(2)** a mirror, LOOKING GLASS **a(3)** a barometer **a(4)** an hourglass, sandglass **b(1)** an optical instrument (e g a magnifying glass) for viewing objects not easily seen **b(2)** *pl* a pair of glass lenses to-gether with a frame to hold them in place, for correcting defects of vision or protecting the eyes **3** the contents of or quantity contained in a drinking glass ⟨*a* ∼ *of milk*⟩ **4** glassware [ME *glas,* fr OE *glæs;* akin to OE *geolu* yellow – more at YELLOW] – **glassful** *n,* **glassless** *adj*

²**glass** *vt* **1a** to enclose, case, or wall with glass ⟨*the sun porch was* ∼ed *in*⟩ **b** to put in a glass container **2** to make glassy **3** to reflect as if in a mirror **4** to scan (e g for game or forest fires) with an optical instrument

**glassblower** /'glahs,blohǝ/ *n* a person or machine that shapes glass by blowing

**glassblowing** /'glahs,bloh·ing/ *n* the art of shaping a mass of semimolten glass by blowing air into it through a tube

**glass cloth** *n* **1** a fabric made from spun fibreglass **2** a usu linen cloth for drying glasses; *broadly* TEA TOWEL

**glass cutter** *n* a person or tool that cuts or fashions glass

**glass eye** *n* **1** an artificial eye made of glass **2** an eye having a pale, whitish, or colourless iris – **glass-eyed** *adj*

**glass fibre** *n* fibreglass

**glass harmonica** *n* a musical instrument consisting of a set of bowl-shaped glasses played by touching the edges with a wet finger

**glasshouse** /'glahs,hows/ *n* **1** a glassworks **2** *chiefly Br* a greenhouse **3** *chiefly Br slang* a military prison

**glassine** /'glaseen/ *n* a thin dense transparent or semi-transparent paper highly resistant to the passage of air and grease

**glass jaw** *n, informal* susceptibility (e g of a boxer) to knockout punches

**glassmaking** /'glahs,mayking/ *n* the art or process of manu-facturing glass – **glassmaker** *n*

**glasspaper** /'glahs,paypǝ/ *n* paper to which a thin layer of powdered glass has been glued for use as an abrasive – **glass-paper** *vt*

**glass snake** *n* a limbless snakelike lizard (*Ophisaurus ventralis*) of the southern USA with a fragile tail that readily breaks into pieces; *also* any of several similar Eurasian and N American lizards

**glass sponge** *n* a sponge (class Hexactinellida) with a SILICA skeleton that is made up of 6-rayed SPICULES and often resem-bles glass when dried

**glassware** /'glahs,weǝ/ *n* articles made of glass

**glass wool** *n* glass fibres in a mass resembling wool used esp for heat insulation and air-filters

**glasswork** /'glahs,wuhk/ *n* **1a** the manufacture of glass or glassware; *also* glaziers' work **b** glassworks *taking sing or pl vb, pl* **glassworks** a place where glass is made **2** glassware – **glassworker** *n*

**glasswort** /'glahs,wuht/ *n* any of a genus (*Salicornia*) of salt-marsh plants of the goosefoot family that have thick jointed fleshy stems and leaves reduced to fleshy sheaths [fr its former use in the manufacture of glass]

**glassy** /'glahsi/ *adj* **1** resembling glass **2** having little animation; dull, lifeless ⟨∼ *eyes*⟩ – **glassily** *adv,* **glassiness** *n*

**Glaswegian** /glaz'weejǝn, glahz-/ *n* **1** a native or inhabitant of Glasgow **2** the dialect of Glasgow [irreg fr *Glasgow,* city in Scotland] – **Glaswegian** *adj*

**glauberite** /'glowbǝ'riet/ *n* a white mineral consisting of sodium and calcium sulphate, $Na_2Ca(SO_4)_2$ [Johann *Glauber* †1668 Ger chemist]

**Glauber's salt** /'glowbǝz/ *also* **Glauber salt** *n,* **Glauber's salts** *n pl* SODIUM SULPHATE chemically combined with water molecules, Na₂SO₄.10H₂O, esp when used as a laxative [Johann *Glauber* ]

**glaucoma** /glaw'kohmə/ *n* a disease of the eye marked by increased pressure within the eyeball causing damage to the retina and gradual impairment and sometimes loss of vision [L, cataract, fr Gk *glaukōma*, fr *glaukos*]

**glauconite** /'glawkəniet/ *n* a dull green mineral consisting of a SILICATE of iron and potassium chemically combined with water molecules and occurring as a constituent of some sandstone rocks (e g greensand) [Ger *glaukonit*, irreg fr Gk *glaukos*] – **glauconitic** *adj*

**glaucous** /'glawkəs/ *adj* **1a** of a pale yellowy green colour **b** of a light bluish-grey or bluish-white colour **2a** *esp of plants or plant parts* of a dull blue or bluish-green colour **b** *of a leaf, fruit, etc* having a powdery or waxy coating that gives a frosted appearance and tends to rub off [L *glaucus* gleaming, grey, fr Gk *glaukos*] – **glaucousness** *n*

**glaucous gull** *n* a large white and pale grey gull (*Larus hyperboreus*) of Arctic regions

**glaur** /glaw/ *n, chiefly Scot* mud, mire [origin unknown]

¹**glaze** /glayz/ *vt* **1** to provide or fit with glass **2a** to coat (as if) with a glaze ⟨*the storm* ~d *trees with ice*⟩ **b** to apply a glaze to ⟨~ *apple tarts*⟩ **3** to give a smooth glossy surface to **4** to bemuse, fuddle ⟨*so* ~d *are the most of us by the purity of French culture* – Jan Morris⟩ ~ *vi* **1** to become glazed or glassy ⟨*his eyes* ~d *over*⟩ **2** to form a glaze [ME *glasen*, fr *glas* glass] – **glazer** *n*

²**glaze** *n* **1a**(1) a liquid preparation (e g a sugar syrup) applied to food to produce a glossy coating when set **a(2)** a vitreous coating made chiefly from a mixture of OXIDES and used to seal or decorate pottery **b** a transparent or translucent colour applied to modify the effect of an underlying painted or printed surface **c** a smooth glossy or lustrous surface or finish **2** a glassy film **3** *chiefly NAm* a smooth slippery coating of thin ice

**glazed** /glayzd/ *adj* **1** covered (as if) with a glassy film ⟨~ *chintz*⟩ ⟨~ *eyes*⟩ **2** marked by rigidity of expression; grimly set ⟨*the* ~ *faces of the survivors*⟩

**glazier** /'glayzi·ə, -zyə/ *n* one who fits glass, esp into windows, as an occupation – **glaziery** *n*

**glazing** /'glayzing/ *n* **1** the action, process, or trade of using or applying glaze **2a** glasswork **b** a glaze

¹**gleam** /gleem/ *n* **1a** a short-lived appearance of subdued or partly obscured light ⟨*the* ~ *of dawn in the east*⟩ **b**(1) a small bright light ⟨*the* ~ *of a match*⟩ **b(2)** a glint ⟨*a* ~ *of anticipation in his eyes*⟩ **2** a brief or faint appearance or occurrence; a trace ⟨*a* ~ *of hope*⟩ [ME *gleem*, fr OE *glǣm*; akin to OE *geolu* yellow – more at YELLOW] – **gleamy** *adj*

²**gleam** *vi* **1** to shine with subdued steady light or moderate brightness **2** to appear briefly or faintly ⟨*a light* ~ed *in the darkness*⟩ *synonyms see* ¹GLOW

**glean** /gleen/ *vi* **1** to gather produce, esp grain, left by reapers **2** to gather material (e g information) bit by bit ~ *vt* **1a** to pick up (e g grain) after a reaper to strip (e g a field) of the leavings of reapers **2a** to gather (e g information) bit by bit **b** to pick over in search of relevant material ⟨~ing *old letters for information on the history of the town*⟩ [ME *glenen*, fr MF *glener*, fr LL *glennare*; akin to MIr *digliunn* I glean, OHG *glanz* bright – more at GLINT] – **gleanable** *adj*, **gleaner** *n*

**gleanings** /'gleeningz/ *n pl* things acquired by gleaning

**glebe** /gleeb/ *n* **1** land belonging or yielding revenue to a parish church or other church estate **2** *archaic* land; *specif* a plot of cultivated land [L *gleba* clod, land – more at CLIP]

**glede** /gleed/ *n, archaic or dial* any of several birds of prey; *esp* RED KITE ⟨*the* ~, *and the kite, and the vulture after his kind* – Deut 14:13⟩ [ME, fr OE *glida*; akin to OE *glīdan* to glide]

**glee** /glee/ *n* **1** a feeling of merry high-spirited joy or delight **2** an unaccompanied song for three or more usu male solo voices [ME, fr OE *glēo* entertainment, music; akin to ON *glȳ* joy, Gk *chleuē* joke]

**glee club** *n* a choir, esp in the USA, organized for singing usu short secular pieces

**gleeful** /'gleef(ə)l/ *adj* full of glee; merry – **gleefully** *adv*, **gleefulness** *n*

**gleek** /gleek/ *vi, archaic* to make a gibe or jest [origin unknown]

**gleeman** /'gleemən/ *n, archaic* a minstrel

**gleet** /gleet/ *n* a long-lasting inflammation of a body opening (e g that of the URETHRA) usu accompanied by an abnormal discharge; *also* the discharge itself (e g that from the urethra in gonorrhoea) [ME *glet* slimy or mucous matter, fr MF *glete*, fr L

*glittus* viscous; akin to LL *glut-, glus* glue – more at CLAY] – **gleety** *adj*

**gleg** /gleg/ *adj, Scot* quick, sharp [ME, fr ON *glöggr* clear-sighted]

**glen** /glen/ *n* a secluded narrow valley; *esp* one in Scotland [ME (Sc), valley, fr (assumed) ScGael *glenn*; akin to MIr *glend* valley]

**glengarry** /glen'gari/, **glengarry bonnet** *n, often cap G* a straight-sided woollen cap with a crease in the crown from front to back and a pair of short ribbons hanging down behind, worn esp as part of Highland military uniform [*Glengarry*, valley in Scotland]

**gley** /glay/ *n* a sticky clay layer formed under the surface of some waterlogged soils [Russ *glei* clay; akin to OE *clǣg* clay – more at CLAY]

**gliadin** /'glie·ədin/ *n* PROLAMIN (simple protein in seeds); *esp* one occurring in wheat and rye as a constituent of GLUTEN [It *gliadina*, fr MGk *glia* glue – more at CLAY]

**glial** /'glie·əl, 'glee·əl/ *adj* of or being (a cell of) NEUROGLIA (cells supporting nerve cells and fibres) [NL *glia* neuroglia, fr MGk, glue]

**glib** /glib/ *adj* **-bb-** **1a** marked by ease and informality; nonchalant **b** showing little forethought or preparation; lacking depth and substance ⟨*uttering* ~ *solutions to knotty problems*⟩ **2** marked by ease and fluency in speaking or writing, often to the point of being superficial or dishonest ⟨*a* ~ *politician*⟩ **3** *archaic* smooth, slippery *synonyms see* TALKATIVE [prob modif of LG *glibberig* slippery] – **glibly** *adv*, **glibness** *n*

¹**glide** /glied/ *vi* **1a** to move noiselessly in a smooth, continuous, and effortless manner ⟨*swans gliding over the lake*⟩ **b** to move stealthily; creep ⟨*gliding along the wall until they were out of sight*⟩ **2** to pass gradually and imperceptibly **3a** *of an aircraft* to fly without the use of engines **b** to fly in a glider **4** to change the tongue position in the articulation of a glide ~ *vt* to cause to glide [ME *gliden*, fr OE *glīdan*; akin to OHG *glītan* to glide]

²**glide** *n* **1** the act or action of gliding **2a** *music* PORTAMENTO **b** a transitional sound produced by the passing of the vocal organs from one articulatory position to another

**glide path** *n* the path of descent of an aircraft in landing, esp as marked by ground radar or radio

**glider** /'gliedə/ *n* one who or that which glides; *esp* an aircraft similar to an aeroplane but without an engine

**glide slope** *n* GLIDE PATH

**glim** /glim/ *n* **1** a glimmer **2** *archaic slang* something (e g a lamp, candle, or torch) that furnishes light; *also* illumination, esp from a particular source of light – now chiefly in *douse one's glim* [perh short for ²*glimmer*]

¹**glimmer** /'glimə/ *vi* **1** to shine faintly or unsteadily **2** to appear indistinctly with a faintly luminous quality *synonyms see* ¹FLASH [ME *glimeren*; akin to OE *glǣm* gleam]

²**glimmer** *n* **1** a feeble or unsteady light **2a** a dim perception or faint idea; an inkling ⟨*I had only the vaguest* ~ *of why I was there*⟩ **b** a small sign or amount ⟨*a* ~ *of intelligence*⟩

**glimmering** /'gliməring/ *n* a glimmer

¹**glimpse** /glimps/ *vi* **1** to take a brief look **2** *archaic* to glimmer ~ *vt* to get a brief look at [ME *glimsen*; akin to MHG *glimsen* to glimmer, OE *glǣm* gleam] – **glimpser** *n*

²**glimpse** *n* **1** a brief fleeting view or look **2** *archaic* a glimmer

¹**glint** /glint/ *vi* **1** of rays of light to strike a reflecting surface obliquely and dart out at an angle **2** to shine by reflection; *specif* to shine with tiny bright flashes; sparkle, glitter **3** to appear briefly or faintly; GLEAM 2 ~ *vt* to cause to glint *synonyms see* ¹FLASH [ME *glinten* to dart obliquely, glint, alter. of *glenten*, of Scand origin; akin to Sw dial. *glänta* to clear up; akin to OHG *glanz* bright, OE *geolu* yellow – more at YELLOW]

²**glint** *n* **1** a tiny bright flash of light; a sparkle **2** a brief or faint show ⟨*detected a* ~ *of recognition in her expression*⟩

**glioma** /glee'ohmə/ *n, pl* **gliomas, gliomata** a tumour arising from NEUROGLIA (cells supporting nerve cells and fibres) [NL, fr *glia* neuroglia]

**glissade** /gli'sahd, -'sayd/ *vi* **1** to slide usu in a standing or squatting position down a slope, esp one that is snow-covered **2** to perform a sliding step in ballet [Fr, n, slide, glissade, fr *glisser* to slide, fr OF *glicier*, alter. of *glier*, of Gmc origin; akin to OHG *glītan* to glide] – **glissade** *n*, **glissader** *n*

**glissando** /gli'sandoh/ *n, pl* **glissandi** /-i/, **glissandos** a rapid sliding up or down the musical scale [prob modif of Fr *glissade*]

**¹glisten** /'glis(ə)n/ *vi* to shine, usu by reflection, with a sparkling radiance or with the lustre of a wet or oiled surface 〈*wet streets ~ing in the lamplight*〉 **synonyms** see ¹GLOW [ME *glistnen*, fr OE *glisnian*; akin to OE *glisian* to glitter, *geolu* yellow – more at YELLOW]

**²glisten** *n* a glitter, sparkle

**glister** /'glistə/ *vi, chiefly poetic* to glitter 〈*all that ~s is not gold* – Shak〉 [ME *glistren*; akin to OE *glisian*] – **glister** *n*

**glitch** /glich/ *n* **1a** an unwanted brief surge of electric power **b** a false or spurious electronic signal **2** *informal* a technical problem or mishap; hitch, malfunction 〈*a ~ in a spacecraft's fuel cell*〉 [prob fr Ger *glitschen* to slide, slip; akin to OHG *glītan* to glide – more at GLIDE]

**¹glitter** /'glitə/ *vi* **1a** to shine by reflection with a brilliant or metallic lustre 〈*~ing sequins*〉 **b** to sparkle, twinkle 〈*~ing stars*〉; *also* to look resplendently showy 〈*she ~ed with diamonds*〉 **c** to shine with a hard cold glassy brilliance 〈*his little eyes ~ed cruelly*〉 **2** to be brilliantly attractive in a superficial or deceptive way 〈*the chance of success ~ed before them*〉 **synonyms** see ¹FLASH [ME *gliteren*, fr ON *glitra*; akin to OE *geolu* yellow] – **glitteringly** *adv*

**²glitter** *n* **1** sparkling brilliance, showiness, or attractiveness **2** small glittering objects used for ornamentation – **glittery** *adj*

**gloaming** /'glohming/ *n the* twilight, dusk 〈*roaming in the ~*〉 [ME (Sc) *gloming*, fr OE *glōmung*, fr *glōm* twilight; akin to OE *glōwan* to glow]

**¹gloat** /gloht/ *vi* to observe or think about something with great and often malicious satisfaction, gratification, or relish 〈*~ over an enemy's misfortune*〉 [prob fr Scand origin; akin to ON *glotta* to grin scornfully; akin to OE *geolu* yellow] – **gloater** *n*, **gloatingly** *adv*

**²gloat** *n* a gloating feeling

**glob** /glob/ *n, informal* a blob, dollop 〈*little ~s of ink*〉 〈*great ~s of whipped cream*〉 [perh blend of *globe* and *blob*]

**global** /'glohbl/ *adj* **1** spherical 2 relating to or involving the entire world; worldwide 〈*~ warfare*〉 〈*~ communication*〉 **3** relating to or embracing all or virtually all considerations; general, comprehensive – **globally** *adv*

**globalism** /'glohbəlizm/ *n* globalization – **globalist** *n*

**global·ize, -ise** /'glohbl,iez/ *vt* to make global; *esp* to make worldwide in scope or application – **globalization** *n*

**global village** *n* the world viewed as a totally integrated ecological, socioeconomic, and political system of which all the parts are dependent on one another

**¹globe** /glohb/ *n* something spherical or rounded: eg **a** a spherical representation of the earth, a heavenly body, or the heavens **b** the earth **c** ORB 2 (symbol of royalty) [MF, fr L *globus* – more at CLIP]

**²globe** *vb* to become or form into a globe

**globe artichoke** *n* ARTICHOKE 1b

**globefish** /'glohb,fish/ *n* any of a family (Tetraodontidae) of chiefly tropical marine spiny-finned fishes which can swell themselves out to a globular form and most of which are highly poisonous

**globeflower** /'glohb,flowə/ *n* any of a genus (*Trollius*) of plants of the buttercup family with spherical yellow flowers

**¹globe·,trotter** *n* one who travels widely – **globe-trotting** *n or adj*

**globigerina** /,globijə'rienə/ *n, pl* **globigerinas, globigerinae** /-nee, -nie/ any of a genus (*Globigerina* of the phylum Protozoa) of minute single-celled marine animals that have a chalky shell and live in the surface waters of the sea [NL, genus name, deriv of L *globus* + *gerere* to carry, bear]

**globin** /'glohbin/ *n* any of a class of colourless proteins that form the protein part of haemoglobin and similar compounds (CONJUGATED PROTEINS) composed of a protein and a non-protein molecule [ISV, back-formation fr *haemoglobin*]

**globoid** /'glohboyd/ *n* SPHEROID – **globoid** *adj*

**globose** /gloh'bohs/ *adj* GLOBULAR 1 – **globosely** *adv*, **globosity** *n*

**globular** /'globyoolə/ *adj* **1** having the shape of a globe or globule 〈*~ proteins*〉 **2** having or consisting of globules [partly fr L *globus* + E *-ular;* partly fr L *globulus* + E *-ar*] – **globularly** *adv*, **globularness** *n*

**globule** /'globyoohl/ *n* a tiny globe or ball (eg of liquid or melted solid) 〈*~s of mercury*〉 [Fr, fr L *globulus*, dim. of *globus*]

**globulin** /'globyoolin/ *n* any of a class of simple proteins (eg MYOSIN) that are insoluble in pure water but are soluble in dilute solutions of SALTS and that occur widely in plant and animal tissues

**glochidiate** /gloh'kidi·ət/ *adj* **1** having glochidia 2 having barbed tips 〈*~ leaves*〉

**glochidium** /gloh'kidi·əm/ *n, pl* **glochidia** /-i·ə/ **1** a barbed hair or spine (eg on a cactus) 2 the larva of any of various freshwater mussels (family Unionidae), that develops as an external parasite on fish [NL, fr Gk *glōchis* projecting point + NL *-idium*]

**glockenspiel** /'glokən,speel, -,shpeel/ *n* a percussion instrument consisting of a series of metal bars graduated in length, tuned to the CHROMATIC SCALE, and played with two hammers to give a sound like small bells [Ger, fr *glocke* bell + *spiel* play]

**glom** /glom/ *vt* **-mm-** *NAm slang* **1** to take, steal 2 to seize, catch [prob alter. of E dial. *glaum* to grab]

**glomerule** /'glomə,roohl/ *n* a compacted CYME in the form of a head of small clustered flowers like that of a daisy or thistle [NL *glomerulus*]

**glomerulonephritis** /,glomə,r(y)oohlohnef'rietəs/ *n, pl* **glomerulonephritides** /-'rietideez/ inflammation of the tiny blood vessels (CAPILLARIES) of the glomeruli of the kidneys [NL]

**glomerulus** /glo'meryooləs/ *n, pl* **glomeruli** /-ie/ a small coiled or intertwined mass of blood vessels, nerve fibres, etc; *esp* a knot of tiny blood vessels (CAPILLARIES) at the point of origin of each NEPHRON (urine-secreting unit in a kidney) [NL, glomerulus, glomerule, dim. of L *glomer-, glomus* ball] – **glomerular** *adj*

**¹gloom** /gloohm/ *vi* **1** to look or feel sullen or despondent; mope 2 to be or become overcast **3** to loom up dimly or sombrely 〈*the castle ~ed before them*〉 *~ vi* to make dark, murky, or sombre [ME *gloumen*; akin to OE *geolu* yellow – more at YELLOW]

**²gloom** *n* **1a** partial or total darkness **b** a dark or shadowy place 〈*in the green ~s of the forest*〉 **2a** lowness of spirits; dejection **b** an atmosphere of despondency 〈*a ~ fell over the household*〉

**gloomy** /'gloohmi/ *adj* **1a** partially or totally dark; *esp* dismally and depressingly dark 〈*~ weather*〉 **b** having a frowning or scowling appearance; forbidding 〈*a ~ countenance*〉 **c** low in spirits; melancholy 〈*felt ~ after the play*〉 **2a** causing gloom; depressing 〈*a ~ story*〉 **b** marked by little or no hopefulness; pessimistic 〈*~ prophecies*〉 – **gloomily** *adv*, **gloominess** *n*

**glop** /glop/ *n, NAm slang* a jumbled or messy mass or mixture [prob imit]

**Gloria** /'glawri·ə, -riah/ *n* **1** GLORIA IN EXCELSIS **2** GLORIA PATRI

**Gloria in Excelsis** /,glawri·ə in ek'selsis, -'chel-/ *n* a Christian hymn modelled on the Psalms and usu sung as part of the Mass [LL, glory (be to God) on high; fr its opening words]

**Gloria Patri** /'pahtri/ *n* a 2-verse usu sung DOXOLOGY (formula of worship) to the Trinity [LL, glory (be) to the Father; fr its opening words]

**glorify** /'glawri,fie/ *vt* **1a** to make glorious by bestowing honour, praise, or admiration **b** to elevate to heavenly glory **2** to shed radiance or splendour on 〈*a large chandelier glorifies the whole room*〉 **3a** to give great beauty, charm, or appeal to 〈*romantic love is glorified in song and literature*〉 **b** to cause to appear better or more important than in reality 〈*his new position is just a glorified version of his old stockroom job*〉 **4** to give glory to (eg in worship) – **glorifier** *n*, **glorification** *n*

**gloriole** /'glawri·ohl/ *n* a halo, nimbus [prob blend of *glory* and *aureole*]

**glorious** /'glawri·əs/ *adj* **1a** possessing or deserving glory; illustrious **b** conferring glory 〈*a ~ victory*〉 **2** marked by great beauty or splendour; magnificent **3** delightful, wonderful 〈*had a ~ weekend*〉 – **gloriously** *adv*, **gloriousness** *n*

**¹glory** /'glawri/ *n* **1a** praise, honour, or distinction granted by common consent; renown **b** worshipful praise, honour, and thanksgiving 〈*giving ~ to God*〉 **2a** something that secures praise or renown 〈*the ~ of a brilliant career*〉 **b** a highly commendable asset 〈*her hair was her crowning ~*〉 **3a(1)** resplendence, magnificence 〈*the ~ that was Greece and the grandeur that was Rome* – E A Poe〉 **a(2)** something marked by beauty or resplendence 〈*a perfect ~ of a day*〉 **b** the splendour and beatific happiness of heaven; *broadly* eternity **4a** a state of great gratification or exaltation 〈*when she's acting she's in her ~*〉 **b** a height of prosperity or achievement **5** a ring or spot of light: eg **5a** a halo, nimbus **b** CORONA 2a, b [ME *glorie*, fr MF & L; MF, fr L *gloria*]

**²glory** *vi* to rejoice proudly; exult 〈*glories in his great physical strength*〉

**glory box** *n, Austr & NZ* BOTTOM DRAWER

**¹gloss** /glos/ *n* **1** a surface lustre or brightness; a polish **2** a deceptively attractive outer appearance; a semblance ⟨*selfishness that had a ~ of humanitarianism about it*⟩ **3** paint to which varnish has been added to give a gloss finish [prob of Scand origin; akin to Icel *glossa* to glow; akin to OE *geolu* yellow]

**²gloss** *n* **1a** a brief explanation (eg in the margin or between the lines of a text) of a difficult or obscure word or expression **b** a false and often wilfully misleading interpretation (eg of a text) **2a** a glossary **b** an interlinear translation **c** a continuous commentary accompanying a text [ME *glose*, fr OF, fr L *glossa* unusual word requiring explanation, fr Gk *glōssa, glōtta* tongue, language, unusual word; akin to Gk *glōchis* projecting point]

**³gloss** *vt* **1** to furnish glosses for **2** to interpret falsely or perversely

**gloss-** /glos-/, **glosso-** *comb form* **1** tongue ⟨gloss*algia*⟩ ⟨gloss*itis*⟩; tongue and ⟨glosso*pharyngeal*⟩ **2** language ⟨gloss*ology*⟩ [L, fr Gk *glōss-, glōsso-*, fr *glōssa*]

**glossa** /'glosǝ/ *n, pl* **glossae** /-ee, -ie/ *also* **glossas** a tongue or tonguelike structure; *esp* a tonguelike lobe in the middle of the LABIUM (lower liplike mouthpart) of an insect [NL, fr Gk *glōssa*]

**glossal** /'glos(ǝ)l/ *adj* of the tongue

**glossarist** /'glosǝrist/ *n* a glossator

**glossary** /'glosǝri/ *n* a list of terms (eg those used in a particular text or in a specialized field), usu with their meanings [ME, fr ML *glossarium*, fr L *glossa*] – **glossarial** *adj*

**glossator** /glo'saytǝ/ *n* **1** one who makes textual glosses **2** the compiler of a glossary

**glossematics** /,glosǝ'matiks/ *n taking sing vb* a system of linguistic analysis according to glossemes [ISV *glossemat-* (fr *glosseme*) + *-ics*]

**glosseme** /'gloseem/ *n* the smallest meaningful unit (eg a MORPHEME or INTONATION CONTOUR) in a language [ISV *gloss-* + *-eme*]

**glossina** /glo'sienǝ/ *n* TSETSE [NL, genus name, fr Gk *glōssa* tongue; fr its long proboscis]

**glossitis** /glo'sietǝs/ *n* inflammation of the tongue [NL]

**glosso-** – see GLOSS-

**glossolalia** /,glosoh'layli·ǝ, -lyǝ/ *n* the practice of ecstatic usu incomprehensible speaking, esp in Christian worship – compare TONGUE 4c [NL, fr Gk *gloss-* + *lalia* chatter, fr *lalein* to chatter, talk]

**glossopharyngeal** /,glosoh,farin'jee·ǝl, -fǝ'rinjǝl/ *adj* of both the tongue and PHARYNX (throat)

**glossopharyngeal nerve** *n* either of the 9th pair of CRANIAL NERVES that supply chiefly the PHARYNX (throat), the back of the tongue, and the PAROTID GLANDS (salivary glands near the ears)

**gloss over** *vt* **1** to make appear right and acceptable **2** to veil or hide by treating rapidly and superficially ⟨glossing over *humiliations, gilding small moments of glory* – TLS⟩ [¹*gloss*]

**¹glossy** /'glosi/ *adj* **1** having a surface lustre or brightness ⟨*rich ~ leather*⟩ ⟨*~ paper*⟩ **2** attractive in an artificially rich, sophisticated, or smoothly captivating manner; showy ⟨*a ~ musical*⟩ ⟨*lots of ~ and phoney chatter*⟩ – **glossily** *adv*, **glossiness** *n*

**²glossy, Br** *also* **glossy magazine** *n* a magazine expensively produced on glossy paper and often having a fashionable or sophisticated content

**-glot** /-,glot/ *comb form* (→ *n*) person who speaks a (specified) number of languages ⟨*a monoglot*⟩ [Gk *-glōttos, -glōssos*, fr *glōtta, glōssa* language, tongue]

**glott-** /glot-/, **glotto-** *comb form* language ⟨glotto*chronology*⟩ [Gk *glōtt-, glōtto-* tongue, fr *glōssa, glōtta*]

**glottal** /'glot(ǝ)l/ *adj* of or produced in or by the glottis ⟨*~ constriction*⟩

**glottal stop** *n* a speech sound (eg that between the two syllables in a Cockney pronunciation of *butter*) produced by closure of the glottis

**glottis** /'glotis/ *n, pl* **glottises, glottides** /'glotideez/ the elongated space between the vocal cords; *also* this space together with the structures that surround it – compare EPIGLOTTIS [Gk *glōttid-, glōttis*, fr *glōtta* tongue – more at GLOSS]

**glottology** /glǝ'tolǝji/ *n* linguistics – no longer used technically

**¹glove** /gluv/ *n* **1a** a covering for the hand having separate sections for each of the fingers and the thumb and often extending part way up the arm **b** ¹GAUNTLET 1,3 **2** BOXING GLOVE [ME, fr OE *glōf;* akin to ON *glōfi* glove] – **glover** *n* – **with kid gloves** with special care or consideration

**²glove** *vt* to cover (as if) with a glove

**glove box** *n* **1** a sealed protectively lined compartment having holes to which are attached gloves for use in handling dangerous materials inside the compartment **2** *chiefly Br* GLOVE COMPARTMENT

**glove compartment** *n* a small storage compartment in the dashboard of a motor car

**glove puppet** *n* PUPPET 1a

**¹glow** /gloh/ *vi* **1a** to shine (as if) with an intense heat ⟨*the fire ~ing in the darkness*⟩ **b(1)** to have a rich warm typically ruddy colour ⟨*cheeks ~ing with health*⟩ **b(2)** *euph* to sweat ⟨*horses sweat, gentlemen perspire, but ladies only ~*⟩ **2a** to experience a sensation (as if) of heat ⟨*~ing with rage*⟩ **b** to show excitement or joy ⟨*~ with pride*⟩ [ME *glowen*, fr OE *glōwan;* akin to OE *geolu* yellow – more at YELLOW] – **glowingly** *adv*

synonyms **Glow, glare, gleam, glisten,** and **shine** may all describe steady rather than flickering or intermittent light. **Glow** suggests the light given out by red-hot coals, and often has a connotation of warmth. **Glare** implies a much harsher, even dazzling light ⟨*the spotlight glared down on her*⟩. **Gleam,** by contrast, describes subdued light, often against a background of relative darkness ⟨*the gleam of a cottage window through the trees*⟩. **Glisten** may sometimes come close to "glitter", but often suggests a steadier reflection of light as if from a wet lustrous surface ⟨*the seal's coat glistened in the sun*⟩. **Shine** is the most general word of the group, and may be used in place of any of the others. Compare ¹FLASH, BRIGHT

**²glow** *n* **1** brightness or warmth of colour; *esp* redness ⟨*the ~ of his cheeks*⟩ **2a** warmth of feeling or emotion **b** a sensation of warmth ⟨*the drug produces a sustained ~*⟩ **3a** the state of glowing with heat and light **b** light from something burning without flames or smoke; incandescence

**glower** /'glowǝ/ *vi* to look or stare with sullen annoyance or anger; scowl [ME (Sc) *glowren*, perh of Scand origin; akin to Norw dial. *glȳra* to look askance, Icel *glossa* to glow] – **glower** *n*

**glowworm** /'gloh,wuhm/ *n* a luminous wingless insect; *esp* a larva or wingless female of a firefly (*Lampyris noctiluca*) that emits light from the abdomen

**gloxinia** /glok'sinyǝ, -ni·ǝ/ *n* any of a genus (*Sinningia* of the family Gesneriaceae, the gloxinia family) of Brazilian plants; *esp* a plant (*Sinningia speciosa*) widely cultivated for its showy typically white, violet, or purple bell-shaped flowers [NL, genus name, fr B P *Gloxin* 18th-c Ger botanist]

**¹gloze** /glohz/ *vt, archaic* ³GLOSS 1 [ME *glosen* to gloss, flatter, fr *glose* gloss]

**²gloze** *vt, archaic* GLOSS OVER

**gluc-** /gloohk-/, **gluco-** *comb form* **1** glucose ⟨gluc*oneogenesis*⟩ **2** chemically related to or containing a glucose molecule in the molecular structure ⟨gluc*uronic acid*⟩ [ISV]

**glucagon** /'gloohkǝ,gon, -gǝn/ *n* a protein hormone that is produced esp by the ISLETS OF LANGERHANS (cells in the pancreas) in response to low blood sugar levels and that promotes an increase in the sugar content of the blood by increasing the rate at which GLYCOGEN (type of carbohydrate) stored in the liver is broken down to glucose [*gluc-* + *-agon* (perh fr Gk *agōn*, prp of *agein* to lead, drive) – more at AGENT]

**glucocorticoid** /,gloohkoh'kawti,koyd/ *n* any of several CORTICOSTEROID hormones or drugs (eg cortisol and dexamethasone) that have important effects on carbohydrate, fat, and protein metabolism and are used widely in medicine (eg in the alleviation of the symptoms of RHEUMATOID ARTHRITIS) because of their effect in suppressing inflammation and inhibiting the activity of the immune system

**glucokinase** /,gloohkoh'kienayz/ *n* an ENZYME found esp in the liver that speeds up the rate at which glucose reacts to form GLUCOSE PHOSPHATE in various biochemical processes within the body

**gluconeogenesis** /,gloohkǝ,nee·ǝ'jenǝsis/ *n* the formation of glucose within the animal body, esp by the liver, from substances (eg proteins) other than carbohydrates [NL] – **gluconeogenic** *adj*

**gluconic acid** /glooh'konik/ *n* an acid, $C_6H_{12}O_7$, obtained by OXIDATION (chemical reaction with oxygen) of glucose and used chiefly in cleaning metals [ISV, irreg fr *glucose* + *-ic*]

**glucosamine** /glooh'kohzǝmin/ *n* a chemical compound, $C_6H_{13}NO_5$, derived from glucose by the addition of an AMINO group, that occurs esp as a constituent of MUCOPOLY-SACCHARIDES (complex sugar-containing compounds) such as CHITIN in animal supporting structures (e g the hard outer cover of an insect) and some plant cell walls

**glucose** /'gloohkohz, -kohs/ n 1 a sugar, $C_6H_{12}O_6$, that occurs in two forms, DEXTROROTATORY and LAEVOROTATORY, or as a mixture of both forms; esp the sweet colourless soluble dextrorotatory form (DEXTROSE) that occurs widely in nature and is the usual form in which carbohydrate is absorbed and used in the body by animals – compare FRUCTOSE 2 a light-coloured syrup obtained by partial breakdown of starch [Fr, modif of Gk *gleukos* must, sweet wine; akin to Gk *glykys* sweet] – **glucosic** adj

**glucose-,1-'phosphate** n a chemical compound, $C_6H_{13}O_9P$, consisting of a glucose molecule with a phosphate group attached, that is important as an intermediate in the breakdown of carbohydrates in the body and in the production of GLYCOGEN (form in which the body stores carbohydrate) [fr the position at which the phosphate radical is attached]

**glucose-,6-'phosphate** n a chemical compound, $C_6H_{13}O_9P$, consisting of a glucose molecule with a phosphate group attached that is an essential early stage in the breakdown of glucose in the body [fr the position at which the phosphate radical is attached]

**glucose phosphate** n a phosphate of glucose: e g **a** GLUCOSE-1-PHOSPHATE **b** GLUCOSE-6-PHOSPHATE

**glucosidase** /glooh'kohzidayz/ n an ENZYME that breaks down a glucoside

**glucoside** /'gloohkə,sied, -koh-/ n GLYCOSIDE (chemical compound derived from a sugar); esp a glycoside that yields glucose on breakdown – **glucosidic** adj, **glucosidically** adv

**glucuronic acid** /,gloohkyoo'ronik/ n a chemical compound, $C_6H_{10}O_7$, derived from glucose by the addition of an acid group, that occurs esp as a constituent of MUCOPOLY-SACCHARIDES (complex sugar-containing compounds) such as HYALURONIC ACID and in combination with other compounds as a glucuronide [*gluc-* + *-uronic*]

**glucuronidase** /,gloohkyoo'ronidayz/ n an ENZYME that breaks down a glucuronide

**glucuronide** /glooh'kyoorənied/ n any of various chemical compounds derived from GLUCURONIC ACID; esp one formed in the body by the combination of glucuronic acid with an unwanted or poisonous compound (e g morphine), that has greater solubility in water than the unwanted compound and can be excreted in the urine

**¹glue** /glooh/ n 1 any of various strong adhesive substances; esp a hard protein chiefly gelatinous substance that absorbs water to form a thick sticky solution with strong adhesive properties and that is obtained by boiling down animal materials (e g hides or bones) 2 a solution of glue used for sticking things together [ME *glu,* fr MF, fr LL *glut-, glus* – more at CLAY] – **gluey** adj, **gluily** adv

**²glue** vt **gluing** also **glueing** 1 to cause to stick tightly (as if) with glue ⟨~ *the wings onto the model aeroplane*⟩ 2 to fix (e g the eyes) on an object steadily or with deep concentration ⟨*don't want to stay in* ~d *to the box* – (*Bristol*) *Evening Post*⟩

**'glue-,sniffing** n the practice of breathing in the fumes from various kinds of glue as an intoxicant – **glue-sniffer** n

**gluhwein, glühwein** /'glooh,vien (*Ger* 'gly:vaɪn)/ n warmed red wine to which sugar and spices have been added; mulled red wine [Ger *glühwein,* fr *glühen* to glow, heat + *wein* wine]

**glum** /glum/ adj **-mm-** 1 sullen and brooding ⟨*became* ~ *when they heard the bad news*⟩ 2 dreary, gloomy ⟨*a* ~ *countenance*⟩ [prob akin to ME *gloumen* to gloom] – **glumly** adv, **glumness** n

**glume** /gloohm/ n a dry scale-like chaffy or membranous BRACT (specialized leaf); specif either of the two bracts at the base of the SPIKELET (flower cluster) in grasses [NL *gluma,* fr L, hull, husk; akin to L *glubere* to peel – more at CLEAVE] – **glumaceous** adj

**gluon** n an ELEMENTARY PARTICLE held to be responsible for the force that binds QUARKS together [*glue* + *²-on*]

**¹glut** /glut/ vb **-tt-** vt 1 to feed or otherwise supply to the full; satiate 2 to flood (the market) with goods so that supply exceeds demand ~ vi to eat gluttonously **synonyms** see ²SATIATE [ME *glouten, glotten,* prob fr MF *glotir, gloutir* to swallow, fr L *gluttire* – more at GLUTTON]

**²glut** n a supply (e g of a harvested crop) which exceeds market demand

**glutamate** /'gloohtəmayt/ n any of various chemical compounds (SALTS or ESTERS) formed by combination between GLUTAMIC ACID and a metal atom, an alcohol, or another chemical group; esp MONOSODIUM GLUTAMATE

**glutamic acid** /glooh'tamik/ n an AMINO ACID, $HOOCCH(NH_2)(CH_2)_2COOH$, that occurs as a constituent of most plant and animal proteins, is important in nitrogen metabolism, and is used in the form of a sodium salt, MONOSODIUM GLUTAMATE, as a seasoning [ISV *gluten* + *amino* + *-ic*]

**glutaminase** /'gloohtəminayz/ n an ENZYME that breaks down glutamine to GLUTAMIC ACID and ammonia

**glutamine** /'gloohtəmeen, -min/ n an AMINO ACID, $HOOCCH(NH_2)(CH_2)_2CONH_2$, occurring in many proteins that breaks down to yield GLUTAMIC ACID and ammonia [ISV *gluten* + *amine*]

**glutaraldehyde** /,gloohtə'raldihied/ n a chemical compound, $C_5H_8O_2$, containing two ALDEHYDE groups, that is used esp as a disinfectant, in leather tanning, and to FIX (prevent change of) biological tissues for examination under a microscope [*glutaric* acid + *aldehyde*]

**glutaric acid** /glooh'tarik/ n an acid, $COOH(CH_2)_3COOH$, used esp in the synthesis of other organic chemical compounds [prob fr *gluten* + *-aric* (as in *tartaric acid*)]

**glutathione** /,gloohtə'thie·ohn/ n a PEPTIDE (combination of a few AMINO ACIDS, smaller than a protein), $C_{10}H_{16}N_3O_6SH$, that is derived from one molecule each of the amino acids glutamic acid, cysteine, and glycine, occurs widely in plant and animal tissues, and plays an important role in biological OXIDATION-REDUCTION processes and in the activation of some ENZYMES [ISV *gluta-* (fr *glutamic acid*) + *thi-* + *-one*]

**gluten** /'gloohtən/ n a tough sticky protein substance occurring esp in wheat flour that gives dough its cohesive and elastic properties [L *glutin-, gluten* glue; akin to LL *glut-, glus* glue – more at CLAY] – **glutenous** adj

**gluteus** /'gloohti·əs, glooh'tee·əs/ n, pl **glutei** any of the large muscles of the buttocks [NL *glutaeus, gluteus,* fr Gk *gloutos* buttock – more at CLOUD] – **gluteal** adj

**glutinous** /'gloohtinəs/ adj having the quality of glue; gummy, sticky [MF or L; MF *glutineux,* fr L *glutinosus,* fr *glutin-, gluten*] – **glutinously** adv, **glutinousness** n

**glutton** /'glut(ə)n/ n **1a** one given habitually to greedy and voracious eating and drinking **b** one who has a great capacity for accepting or enduring something ⟨*he's a* ~ *for punishment*⟩ 2 WOLVERINE (flesh-eating mammal) [ME *glotoun,* fr OF *gloton,* fr L *glutton-, glutto;* akin to L *gluttire* to swallow, *gula* throat, OE *ceole*] – **gluttonous** adj, **gluttonously** adv, **gluttony** also **gluttonousness** n

**glyc-** /gliek-/, **glyco-** comb form sugar; specif glucose ⟨*glycaemia*⟩ [ISV, fr Gk *glyk-* sweet, fr *glykys*]

**glycan** /'gliekan/ n POLYSACCHARIDE (carbohydrate composed of many sugar units)

**glycer-** /glisər-/, **glycero-** comb form related to glycerol or GLYCERIC ACID ⟨*glyceraldehyde*⟩ [ISV, fr *glycerin*]

**glyceraldehyde** /,glisə'raldihied/ n a sweet chemical compound, $CH_2(OH)CH(OH)CHO$, that is formed as an intermediate in the breakdown of sugars in the body

**glyceric acid** /gli'serik/ n a syrupy acid, $CH_2OHCH(OH)COOH$, obtainable by OXIDATION of glycerol or glyceraldehyde [ISV, fr *glycerin*]

**glyceride** /'glisəried/ n a chemical compound (ESTER) formed by the combination of glycerol with an acid, esp a FATTY ACID – **glyceridic** adj

**glycerin** /'glisərin/, **glycerine** /'glisəreen, --'-/ n glycerol [Fr *glycérine,* fr Gk *glykeros* sweet; akin to Gk *glykys*]

**glycerol** /'glisərol/ n a sweet syrupy chemical ALCOHOL, $CH_2OHCH(OH)CH_2OH$, that is usu obtained from fats and is used esp as a solvent, stabilizer (e g in foods), and PLASTICIZER [*glycerin* + *-ol*] – **glycerolate** vt

**glyceryl** /'glisəril/ n a chemical group derived from glycerol by removal of one or more HYDROXYL groups; esp a chemical group, $CH_2CHCH_2$, with a VALENCY of three

**glycine** /'glieseen, --'-/ n an AMINO ACID, $NH_2CH_2COOH$, that forms part of many proteins

**glyco-** – see GLYC-

**glycogen** /'gliekohjen/ n a white tasteless POLYSACCHARIDE (carbohydrate composed of many sugar units), $(C_6H_{10}O_5)n$, that consists of linked glucose molecules and is the chief form in which carbohydrate is stored in the animal body

**glycogenesis** /,gliekoh'jenəsis/ n 1 the formation of sugar from glycogen **2** the formation of glycogen [NL] – **glyco-genetic** *adj*

**glycol** /'gliekol/ *n* ETHYLENE GLYCOL; *broadly* a related chemical ALCOHOL containing two HYDROXYL (alcohol) groups [ISV *glyc- + -ol*]

**glycolate** *also* **glycollate** /'gliekəlayt/ *n* any of various chemical compounds (SALTS or ESTERS) formed by combination between GLYCOLIC ACID and a metal atom, an alcohol, or another chemical group [ISV *glycol + -ate*]

**glycolic acid** *also* **glycollic acid** /glie'kolik/ *n* a chemical compound, $CH_2(OH)COOH$, found esp in unripe grapes and sugar beets and used esp in textile and leather processing [ISV *glycol + -ic*]

**glycolipid** /,gliekoh'lipid/ *n* a LIPID (fat) containing a carbohydrate group that occurs esp in brain tissue

**glycolysis** /glie'koləsis/ *n* the enzyme-catalysed breakdown of a carbohydrate (e g glucose) in a cell by way of phosphate derivatives, to produce PYRUVIC ACID or LACTIC ACID and energy stored in the form of high-energy phosphate bonds of ATP [NL] – **glycolytic** *adj*, **glycolytically** *adv*

**glycopeptide** /,gliekoh'peptied/ *n* a glycoprotein

**glycoprotein** /,gliekoh'prohteen/ *n* any of a class of proteins that contain one or more carbohydrate groups

**glycosaminoglycan** /glie,kohzə,mienə'agliekan/ *n* MUCOPOLYSACCHARIDE (complex sugar-containing compound) [*glycose* (fr Fr, alter. of *glucose*) + *amin-* + *glycan*]

**glycosidase** /glie'kohzidayz/ *n* an ENZYME that promotes the breakdown of a glycoside at a bond joining a sugar to a nonsugar group or another sugar unit

**glycoside** /'gliekə,sied, -koh-/ *n* any of numerous chemical compounds that contain a sugar bonded to a nonsugar group by an oxygen or nitrogen atom and that break down to yield a sugar (e g glucose) – **glycosidic** *adj*, **glycosidically** *adv*

**glycosuria** /,gliekoh'syooəri·ə/ *n* the presence of abnormal amounts of sugar in the urine [NL] – **glycosuric** *adj*

**glycosyl** /'gliekəsil/ *n* a chemical group having a VALENCY of one, that is derived from a sugar (e g glucose) by removal of the most reactive HYDROXYL group

**glycyl** /'gliesil/ *n* the chemical group, $C_2H_4NO$, having a VALENCY of one that is derived from glycine

**glyph** /glif/ *n* **1** an ornamental vertical groove, esp in a horizontal usu decorated band characteristic of DORIC (one of the five classical Greek styles of) architecture **2** a symbolic figure or character usu incised or carved in relief **3** a symbol (e g a curved arrow on a road sign) that conveys information without using words [Gk *glyphē* carved work, fr *glyphein* to carve – more at CLEAVE] – **glyphic** *adj*

**glyptal** /'glipt(ə)l/ *n* ALKYD (type of plastic)

**glyptic** /'gliptik/ *adj* relating to carving or engraving, esp on gems [Fr *glyptique*, fr Gk *glyptikos*, fr *glyphein*]

**glyptodont** /'gliptohdont, -ədont/ *n* any of various extinct mammals (genus *Glyptodont*) related to the armadillos and having the body covered with a horny armour [deriv of Gk *glyptos* carved (fr *glyphein*) + *odont-, odous* tooth]

**G-man** /'jee,man/ *n* a special agent of the US Federal Bureau of Investigation [prob fr *government man*]

**¹gnarl** /nahl/ *vi* to snarl, growl [prob freq of *gnar*, of imit origin]

**²gnarl** *n* a hard lump with twisted grain on a tree; a knot [back-formation fr *gnarled*]

**gnarled** /nahld/ *adj* **1** full of or covered with knots or lumps; knotty ⟨~ *cypresses*⟩ **2** crabbed in disposition, aspect, or character [prob alter. of *knurled*]

**gnarly** /'nahli/ *adj* gnarled

**gnash** /nash/ *vb* to strike or grind (esp the teeth) together [alter. of ME *gnasten*, prob of imit origin] – **gnash** *n*

**gnat** /nat/ *n* any of various small primitive usu biting TWO-WINGED FLIES [ME, fr OE *gnætt;* akin to OE *gnagan* to gnaw] – **gnatty** *adj*

**gnath-** /nath-/, **gnatho-** *comb form* jaw ⟨gnath*plasty*⟩ [NL, fr Gk *gnath-*, fr *gnathos;* akin to Gk *genys* jaw – more at CHIN]

**gnathic** /'nathik/, **gnathal** /-əl/ *adj* relating to the jaw

**-gnathous** *comb form* (→ *adj*) having (such) a jaw ⟨*opistho*gnathous⟩ [NL *-gnathus*, fr Gk *gnathos*]

**gnaw** /naw/ *vt* **1a** to bite or chew on with the teeth; *esp* to wear away by persistent biting or nibbling ⟨*a dog* ~ing *a bone*⟩ **b** to make by gnawing ⟨*rats* ~ed *a hole*⟩ **2a** to be a source of vexation to; plague ⟨*anxiety always* ~ing *him*⟩ **b** to affect like gnawing ⟨*hunger* ~ing *his vitals*⟩ **3** to erode, corrode ~ *vi* **1** to bite or nibble persistently ⟨~ing *at her under lip*⟩ **2** to des-

troy or reduce something (as if) by gnawing ⟨*waves* ~ing *away at the cliffs*⟩ [ME *gnawen*, fr OE *gnagan;* akin to OHG *gnagan* to gnaw] – **gnawer** *n*

**gneiss** /nies/ *n* a coarse-grained METAMORPHIC rock (one altered by heat, pressure, etc) with a layered appearance, that is typically composed of light bands of FELDSPAR and quartz alternating with dark bands of MICA [Ger *gneis*, prob alter. of MHG *gneiste, ganeiste* spark, fr OHG *gneisto*] – **gneissic, gneissoid, gneissose** *adj*

**gnocchi** /'noki, gə'noki/ *n pl* small dumplings made from flour, semolina, potatoes, or choux pastry [It, pl of *gnocco*, alter. of *nocchio* knot in wood]

**¹gnome** /nohm/ *n* a maxim, aphorism [Gk *gnōmē*, fr *gignōskein* to know – more at KNOW]

**²gnome** *n* **1** an ageless and often deformed dwarf of folklore who lives under the earth and guards precious ores or treasure **2** a wizened little man **3** *often cap* GNOME OF ZURICH [Fr, fr NL *gnomus*, prob coined by Theophrastus Paracelsus †1541 Swiss alchemist & physician] – **gnomish** *adj*

**Gnome of Zurich** /'zyooərikh/ *n, pl* **Gnomes of Zurich,** *usu pl, informal* an international banker usu considered to have great power over the financial sector of national economics [*Zurich*, city in Switzerland famous for banking]

**gnomic** /'nohmik, 'nomik/ *adj* **1** characterized by APHORISM (short wise sayings) ⟨~ *poetry*⟩ **2** *of a verb tense* expressing a general truth ⟨*"Penguins live in the Antarctic" is in the* ~ *present*⟩ **3** *of an utterance, style of writing, etc* short and mysterious; apparently wise; *also* pompous

**gnomon** /'nohmon/ *n* **1** an object that by the position or length of its shadow serves as an indicator esp of the hour of the day: e g **1a** the shadow-producing part of an ordinary sundial **b** a column or shaft erected at right angles to the horizon **2** the remainder of a PARALLELOGRAM after the removal of a similar parallelogram containing one of its corners [L, fr Gk *gnōmōn* interpreter, pointer on a sundial, fr *gignōskein*] – **gnomonic** *adj*

**gnosis** /'nohsis/ *n* secret knowledge of spiritual truth available only to the initiated, esp as held by the ancient Gnostics to be essential to salvation [Gk *gnōsis*, lit., knowledge, fr *gignōskein*]

**-gnosis** /-g'nohsis/ *comb form* (→ *n*), *pl* **-gnoses** knowledge; recognition ⟨*prognosis*⟩ [L, fr Gk *gnōsis*]

**Gnostic** /'nostik/ *n* a follower of or believer in gnosticism [LL *gnosticus*, fr Gk *gnōstikos* of knowledge, fr *gignōskein*] – **Gnostic** *adj*

**gnosticism** /'nosti,siz(ə)m/ *n, often cap* a religious outlook or system, esp of various cults of late pre-Christian and early Christian centuries, distinguished by the conviction that matter is evil and that emancipation comes through gnosis

**gnotobiotic** /,nohtohbie'otik/ *adj* of, living in, or being a controlled environment (e g a germ-free culture) containing one or only a few kinds of organisms [Gk *gnōtos* known (fr *gignōskein* to know) + *biotē* life, way of life – more at KNOW, BIOTA] – **gnotobiotically** *adv*

**gnu** /nooh/ *n, pl* **gnus,** *esp collectively* **gnu** any of several large African antelopes (genera *Connochaetes* and *Gorgon*) with a head like that of an ox, a short mane, a long tail, and horns in both sexes that curve downwards and outwards [modif of Bushman *nqu*]

**¹go** /goh/ *vb* **went** /went/; **gone** /gon/ *vi* **1** to move on a course; proceed ⟨~ *slow*⟩ ⟨*went by train*⟩ ⟨*went to France*⟩ – compare STOP **2a** to move out of or away from a place; leave, depart ⟨*I must* ~⟩ ⟨*he went early*⟩ ⟨*the ferry* ~es *every hour*⟩ – sometimes used with a further verb to express purpose ⟨*I went to see them*⟩ ⟨*I'll* ~ *and look*⟩ to make an expedition for a specified activity ⟨~ *shopping*⟩ ⟨~ *skydiving*⟩ **3a** to pass by means of a specified process or according to a specified procedure ⟨*the message went by wire*⟩ ⟨*your suggestion will* ~ *before the committee*⟩ **b(1)** to proceed without delay and in a thoughtless or reckless manner – used to intensify another verb ⟨*don't* ~ *saying that*⟩ ⟨*why did he have to* ~ *and spoil everything?*⟩ ⟨*he's been and gone and told her*⟩ **b(2)** to proceed to do something surprising – used with *and* to intensify another verb ⟨*she went and won first prize*⟩ **c(1)** to reach, run ⟨*his land* ~es *almost to the river*⟩ **c(2)** to give access; lead ⟨*that door* ~es *to the cellar*⟩ **c(3)** EXTEND 2 ⟨*his knowledge fails to* ~ *very deep*⟩ ⟨*it's true as far as it* ~es⟩ **c(4)** to speak, proceed, or develop in a specified direction or up to a specified limit ⟨*you've gone too far*⟩ ⟨*don't let's* ~ *into details*⟩ **4** to travel on foot or by moving the feet **5** to be habitually in a certain state or condition ⟨~ *bareheaded*⟩ ⟨~ *armed after dark*⟩ **6a** to become lost, consumed, or spent ⟨*my pen's* gone⟩ ⟨*the money was all* gone *by Friday*⟩ **b** to come to be applied or used ⟨*half his income* ~es *in rent*⟩ **c** to die **d** to slip away; elapse ⟨*only three weeks to* ~⟩ ⟨*the evening* went *pleasantly enough*⟩ **e** to be got rid of ⟨*these slums must* ~⟩ **f** to pass by sale ⟨~*ing cheap*⟩ **g** to become impaired or weakened; fail ⟨*his hearing started to* ~⟩ **h** to give way, succumb, crack ⟨*at last the dam* went⟩ **7a** to progress, fare ⟨*how are things* ~ing?⟩ ⟨*everything* went *well*⟩ **b** to be in general or on an average ⟨*cheap, as yachts* ~⟩ **c** to pass or be adjudged by award, assignment, or lot ⟨*the prize* went *to a French girl*⟩ **d** to turn out well; succeed ⟨*worked hard to make the party* ~⟩ **8** to put or subject oneself ⟨~ *to a lot of trouble*⟩ ⟨went *to unnecessary expense*⟩ **9** to have recourse; resort ⟨~ *to law*⟩ ⟨~ *to war*⟩ ⟨~ *to court to recover damages*⟩ **10a** to begin an action or motion ⟨*here* ~es⟩ ⟨*ready, steady,* ~!⟩ **b** to maintain or perform an action or motion ⟨*the drums had been* ~ing *strong*⟩ ⟨*her tongue* went *nineteen to the dozen*⟩ ⟨went *like this with his eyebrows*⟩ **c** to function in a proper or specified way ⟨*trying to get the motor to* ~⟩ ⟨*he felt ill, but tried to keep* ~ing⟩ **d** to make a characteristic noise; sound ⟨*the telephone* went⟩ **11a** to be known or identified as specified ⟨*now* ~es *by another name*⟩ **b(1)** to be in phrasing or content ⟨*as the saying* ~es⟩ ⟨*the story* ~es *that the expedition was a failure*⟩ **b(2)** to be sung or played in a specified manner ⟨*the song* ~es *to the tune of "Greensleeves"*⟩ **12a** to act in accordance or harmony ⟨*a good rule to* ~ *by*⟩ ⟨*not many facts to* ~ *on*⟩ **b** to occur in accordance or harmony ⟨*dreams* ~ *by contraries*⟩ **c** to contribute to a total or result ⟨*it* ~es *to show he can be trusted*⟩ ⟨*qualities that* ~ *to make a hero*⟩ ⟨*taxes that* ~ *for education*⟩ **13** to be about, intending, or destined – + *to* and an infinitive ⟨*is* ~ing *to leave town*⟩ ⟨*is it* ~ing *to rain?*⟩ ⟨*is* ~ing *to have kittens*⟩ **14a** to come or arrive at a specified state or condition ⟨~ *to sleep*⟩ ⟨~ *to waste*⟩ **b** to join a specified institution professionally or attend it habitually ⟨*to* ~ *on the stage*⟩ ⟨*does she* ~ *to school?*⟩ **c** to come to be; turn ⟨*the tyre* went *flat*⟩ ⟨*her hair* went *grey*⟩ ⟨~ *wrong*⟩ ⟨*he* went *broke*⟩ ⟨*it's just gone half six*⟩ – compare COME 4 **d(1)** to become voluntarily ⟨~ *bail for his friend*⟩ **d(2)** to change to a specified system or tendency ⟨~ *supersonic*⟩ ⟨*the company* went *public*⟩ ⟨~ *comprehensive*⟩ ⟨went *decimal*⟩ ⟨~ *metric*⟩ ⟨went *Liberal at the election*⟩ **e** to continue to be; remain ⟨~ *hungry*⟩ ⟨~ *without sugar*⟩ ⟨*jobs* went *unfilled*⟩ **15** to be compatible, suitable, or becoming; harmonize ⟨*claret* ~es *with beef*⟩ **16a** to be capable of passing, extending, or being contained or inserted ⟨*it won't* ~ *round my waist*⟩ ⟨*will these clothes* ~ *in your suitcase?*⟩ ⟨*3 into 2 won't* ~⟩ **b** to have a usual or proper place or position; belong ⟨*these books* ~ *on the top shelf*⟩ **17a** to carry authority ⟨*what she said* went⟩ **b** to be acceptable, satisfactory, or adequate ⟨*anything* ~es *here*⟩ ⟨*travellers' cheques will* ~ *anywhere*⟩ **c** to hold true; be valid ⟨*it* ~es *without saying*⟩ ⟨*and that* ~es *for you too*⟩ **18** to empty the bladder or bowels ⟨*always* ~ *after breakfast*⟩ **19** *obs* to walk ~ *vt* **1** to proceed along or according to; follow ⟨~ *one's own way*⟩ **2** to pass through (a distance); traverse ⟨~ *ten miles*⟩ **3** to undertake by travelling ⟨~ *errands*⟩ **4** to emit (a sound) ⟨*the bell* ~es *ding dong*⟩ **5** to participate to the extent of ⟨~ *shares*⟩ ⟨~ *halves*⟩ **6** to perform, effect ⟨~ *the limit*⟩ **7** to change to; adopt ⟨*you* ~ *wheels or you go bust* – R A Keith⟩ **8** *Br nonstandard* to say – used in direct speech ⟨*so she* ~es, *"Don't you ever do that again!"*⟩ [ME *gon*, fr OE *gān;* akin to OHG *gān* to go, Gk *kichanein* to reach, attain] – **go begging** to be available but in little demand – **go hang** to cease to be of interest or concern – **go it** to behave in a reckless, excited, or impromptu manner **2** to proceed rapidly or furiously – **go it alone** to act alone, esp courageously – **go missing** *chiefly Br* to disappear – **go one better** to outdo or surpass another – **go to bat for** to defend actively; champion – **leave/let go** to stop holding ⟨*let* go *of the handle*⟩ – **let oneself go 1** to behave with relaxed ease or abandonment **2** to allow one's appearance to deteriorate – **to go** *NAm, of cooked food* sold for consumption off the premises

*synonyms* Go, leave, depart, quit: go is the general word, lacking any special suggestion. Leave and depart both imply separation from people and places, but leave stresses leaving behind, and depart, contrasted with "arrive" and rather more formal, stresses the act of going away. Quit strongly implies getting free of, or away from, someone or something that binds, constricts, or otherwise holds or burdens one ⟨quit *London for the country in summer*⟩. *usage* Some people dislike going to go ⟨*he's* going to go *abroad*⟩, and prefer to form the future of the verb **go** in some other way. *antonyms* come, stay

**go about** *vi, of a sailing boat* to change from one course to another; tack ~ *vt* to undertake, SET ABOUT

**go after** *vt* to seek, pursue

**go against** *vt* **1** to act in opposition to; offend **2** to turn out unfavourably to

**go ahead** *vi* **1** to begin **2** to continue, advance – see also GO-AHEAD

**go along** *vi* **1** to move along; proceed **2** to go or travel as a companion **3** to act in cooperation

**go along with** *vt* **1** to occur as a natural accompaniment of **2** to agree with; support

**go around** *vi* **1** to pass from place to place; go here and there, esp in company ⟨*the friends she* goes around *with*⟩ **2** GO ROUND

**go at** *vt* **1** to attack, assail **2** to undertake energetically

**go back on** *vt* **1** to fail to keep (e g a promise) **2** to be disloyal to; betray

**go by** *vi* to pass ⟨*as time* goes by⟩

**go down** *vi* **1a** to fall (as if) to the ground ⟨*the plane* went down *in flames*⟩ **b** to go below the horizon; set ⟨*the sun* went down⟩ **c** to become submerged; sink ⟨*the ship* went down *with all hands*⟩ **2** to be capable of being swallowed ⟨*the medicine* went down *easily*⟩ **3** to undergo defeat; GO UNDER **4a** to find acceptance ⟨*will the plan* go down *well with the farmers?*⟩ **b** to come to be remembered, esp by posterity ⟨*he will* go down *in history as a great general*⟩ **5** to undergo a decline or decrease ⟨*his fever* went down⟩ ⟨*the market is* going down⟩ **6** to become ill – usu + *with* ⟨*he* went down *with flu*⟩ **7** *Br* to leave a university – compare COME DOWN, GO UP **8** *slang* to be sent to prison

**go down on** *vt, vulg* to perform oral sex on

**go for** *vt* **1** to serve or be accounted as ⟨*it all* went for *nothing*⟩ **2** to try to secure ⟨*he* went for *the biggest mango*⟩ **3a** to favour, accept ⟨*cannot* go for *your idea*⟩ **b** to have an interest in or liking for ⟨*I can't say I* go for *modern art*⟩ **4** to attack, assail ⟨went for *him when his back was turned*⟩

**go in** *vi* **1** to enter **2** *of the sun, moon, etc* to become obscured by a cloud **3** to form a union or alliance; join – often + *with* ⟨*asked the rest of us to* go in *with them*⟩

**go in for** *vt* **1** to engage in, esp as a hobby or for enjoyment **2** to enter and compete in (e g a test or race) ⟨*decided not to* go in for *her A-levels till next year*⟩

**go into** *vt* **1** to be contained in ⟨*5* goes into *60 12 times*⟩ **2** to investigate **3** to explain in depth; state ⟨*the book doesn't* go into *the moral aspects*⟩

**go off** *vi* **1** to explode **2** to depart, leave **3** to undergo decline or deterioration ⟨*that milk has* gone *off*⟩ **4** to follow the expected or desired course; proceed ⟨*the party* went off *well*⟩ **5** to make a characteristic noise; sound ⟨*the alarm* went off⟩

**go on** *vi* **1a** to continue (as if) with a journey **b** to continue (as if) in a course of action **2a** to proceed (as if) by a logical step ⟨*he* went on *to explain why*⟩ **b** *of time* to pass **3** to take place; happen ⟨*what's* going on?⟩ – see also GOINGS-ON **4** to be capable of being put on ⟨*her gloves wouldn't* go on⟩ **5** to talk in a lengthy and effusive or nagging manner ⟨*the way people* go on *about pollution*⟩ **6a** to come into operation, action, or production ⟨*the lights* went on *at sunset*⟩ **b** to appear on the stage ⟨*an actor waiting to* go on⟩ **7** *informal* to get along, manage ⟨*how did you* go on *for money?*⟩ ~ *vt* to have a liking for ⟨*we don't* go much *on cars* – Len Deighton⟩

**go out** *vi* **1a** to go forth or out of doors; *specif* to leave one's house **b** to participate as a principal in a duel **c** to travel to a distant place ⟨*they* went out *to Africa*⟩ **d** to work away from home ⟨*she* went out *charring*⟩ **2a** to come to an end **b** to become extinguished ⟨*the hall light* went out⟩ **c** *esp of a government* to give up office; resign **d** to become obsolete or unfashionable **e(1)** to play the last card of one's hand **e(2)** to reach or exceed the total number of points required for game in cards

**go over** *vt* **1** EXAMINE 1 **2a** REPEAT 1 **b** to study, revise ~ *vi* **1** to become converted (e g to a religion or political party) **2** to receive approval; succeed ⟨*my play should* go over *well in Scotland*⟩ – see also GOING-OVER

**go round** *vi* **1** to have currency; circulate ⟨*an amusing story is* going round⟩ **2** to be long enough to encircle something **3** to satisfy demand; meet the need ⟨*not enough jobs to* go round⟩ **4** GO AROUND

**go through** *vt* **1** to subject to thorough examination, study, or discussion **2** to experience, undergo **3** to perform, CARRY OUT ⟨went through *his work in a daze*⟩ ~ *vi* **1** to continue firmly or obstinately to the end – often + *with* ⟨*can't go through with the wedding*⟩ **2a** to receive approval or sanction **b** to come to a desired or satisfactory conclusion

**go under** *vi* to be overwhelmed, destroyed, or defeated; fail ⟨*the company was forced to* go under⟩

**go up** *vi, Br* to enter or return to a university – compare COME DOWN, GO DOWN

**go with** *vt* **1** GO ALONG WITH **1** ⟨*the responsibility that* goes with *parenthood*⟩ **2** to be the social or esp sexual companion of

²**go** *n, pl* **goes 1** the act or manner of going **2** energy, vigour ⟨*full of get up and* ∼⟩ **3a** a turn in an activity (e g a game) ⟨*told his opponent that it was his* ∼⟩ **b** an attempt, try ⟨*have a* ∼ *at painting*⟩ **c** a chance, opportunity ⟨*a fair* ∼ *at work for everyone – The Listener*⟩ **4a** a spell of activity ⟨*finished the job at one* ∼⟩ **b** *informal* an attack of illness; bout ⟨*a nasty* ∼ *of mumps*⟩ **5** a success ⟨*made a* ∼ *of the business*⟩ **6** *informal* the height of fashion; rage ⟨*shawls are all the* ∼ *at the moment*⟩ **7** *informal* an often unexpected or awkward turn of affairs ⟨*it's a rum* ∼⟩ **8** *informal* the quantity used or provided at one time ⟨*you can obtain a* ∼ *of whisky very cheaply here*⟩ ⟨*wants a third* ∼ *of treacle pudding*⟩ – **no go** *informal* to no avail; useless – **on the go** *informal* constantly or restlessly active

³**go** *adj* functioning properly; in good and ready condition ⟨*declared all systems* ∼ *for the rocket launch*⟩

⁴**go** *n* an oriental board game of ancient origin for two players, played on a board crossed by 19 vertical and 19 horizontal lines, giving 361 intersections on which the players station stones in order to dominate territory and capture the opponent's stones [Jap]

**goa** /'goh-ə/ *n* a common gazelle (*Gazella picticaudata*) of Tibet [Tibetan *dgoba*]

¹**goad** /gohd/ *n* **1** a pointed rod used to urge on an animal **2a** something that pricks like a goad; a thorn **b** something that urges or stimulates into action; a spur [ME *gode*, fr OE *gād* spear, goad; akin to Skt *hinoti* he urges on]

²**goad** *vt* **1** to drive (e g cattle) with a goad **2** to incite or rouse by nagging or persistent annoyance

¹**go-a'head** *adj* marked by energy and enterprise; progressive ⟨*a vigorous* ∼ *company*⟩ – see also GO AHEAD

²**go-a,head** *n* a sign, signal, or authority to proceed ⟨*we've just been given the* ∼ *on the project*⟩

**goal** /gohl/ *n* **1** the finishing point of a race **2** the end towards which effort is directed; the aim **3a** an area or object through or into which players in various games attempt to advance a ball or puck against the defence of the opposing side in order to score **b** the act or action of scoring a goal; *also* the resulting score [ME *gol* boundary, limit] – **goalless** *adj*

**goal area** *n* a rectangular area 20 yards (about 18 metres) wide and 6 yards (about 5.5 metres) deep in front of each goal on a soccer pitch

**goalie** /'gohli/ *n, informal* a goalkeeper

**goalkeeper** /'gohl,keepə/ *n* a player who defends the goal in hockey, lacrosse, soccer, etc – **goalkeeping** *n*

**goal kick** *n* a free kick in soccer awarded to the defending side when the ball is sent over the goal line by an opposing player

**goal line** *n* a line at either end and usu running the width of a playing area on which a goal or goal post is situated

**goalminder** /'gohl,miendə/ *n* a goalkeeper

**goalmouth** /'gohl,mowth/ *n* the area of a playing-field directly in front of the goal (e g in soccer or hockey)

**goalpost** /'gohl,pohst/ *n* either of usu two vertical posts that with or without a crossbar constitute the goal in various games (e g soccer, rugby, and hockey)

**goanna** /goh'anə/ *n, pl* **goannas**, *esp collectively* **goanna** a large Australian lizard (genus *Varanus*) [alter. of *iguana*]

¹**go-a,round** *n* **1** runaround ⟨*he's been giving me the* ∼⟩ **2** an act or instance of going round (e g in an air traffic pattern)

**goat** /goht/ *n, pl* **goats**, (*1a*) **goats**, *esp collectively* **goat 1a** any of various long-legged agile RUMINANT (cud-chewing) mammals (esp genus *Capra*) related to the sheep but of lighter build and with backwardly arching hollow horns, a short tail, and usu straight hair **b** *cap* Capricorn **2** *NAm* a scapegoat **3** *informal* a lecher **4** *informal* a foolish person [ME *gote*, fr OE *gāt;* akin to OHG *geiz* goat, L *haedus* kid] – **goatish, goatlike** *adj*, **goatling** *n* – **get somebody's goat** *informal* to annoy or irritate somebody

**goat antelope** *n* any of several mammals (e g the chamois) related to the goats but in some respects resembling the antelopes

**goatee** /'goh,tee/ *n* a small pointed or tufted beard on a man's chin [fr its resemblance to the beard of a he-goat]

**goatfish** /'gohtfish/ *n* MULLET 2

**goatherd** /'goht,huhd/ *n* one who tends goats

**goat's beard** *n* **1** a Eurasian plant (*Tragopogon pratensis*) of the daisy family with grasslike leaves and yellow flower heads that close at about midday **2** any of several plants (genus *Aruncus*) of the rose family with dense clusters of tiny yellowish-white flowers

**goatskin** /'gohtskin/ *n* the skin of a goat; *also* leather made from goatskin

**goatsucker** /'goht,sukə/ *n* a nightjar [fr the belief that it sucks milk from goats]

**goat willow** *n* a hardy shrubby willow (*Salix caprea*)

¹**gob** /gob/ *n* **1** a shapeless or sticky lump **2 gobs** *pl*, **gob**, *NAm* a large amount ⟨∼s *of money*⟩ [ME *gobbe*, fr MF *gobe* large piece of food, back-formation fr *gobet*]

²**gob** *vb* **-bb-** *slang* to spit

³**gob** *n, chiefly Br slang* a mouth [IrGael & ScGael, beak, protruding mouth]

**gobbet** /'gobit/ *n* **1** a piece or portion (e g of meat) **2** a small quantity of esp thick liquid; a drop **3** *chiefly Br* a text extract set for comment or translation by students [ME *gobet*, fr MF, mouthful, piece]

¹**gobble** /'gobl/ *vt* **1** to swallow or eat greedily or noisily **2** to take eagerly; grab **3** to read rapidly or greedily □ (*2&3*) often + *up* [prob irreg fr ¹*gob*]

²**gobble** *vi* to make the guttural sound characteristic of a male turkey or a similar sound [imit] – **gobble** *n*

**gobbledygook, gobbledegook** /'gobldi,goohk/ *n* wordy and generally incomprehensible jargon *synonyms* see DIALECT [irreg fr *gobble*, n]

**gobbler** /'goblə/ *n, informal* a male turkey

**Gobelin** /'gohbəlanh (*Fr* gɔbəlɛ̃)/ *adj* relating to or characteristic of tapestry produced at the Gobelin works in Paris – **Gobelin** *n*

'**go-be,tween** *n* an intermediate agent

**gobioid** /'gohbioyd/ *n or adj* (any) of a suborder (Gobioidea) of spiny-finned BONY FISHES, including the goby [deriv of L *gobius* gudgeon]

**goblet** /'goblit/ *n* **1** a drinking vessel (e g of glass, metal, or pottery) that has a concave and usu rounded bowl, a foot, and a stem, and is used esp for wine **2** the usu transparent vessel (e g of glass or thick plastic) that is the part of a liquidizer in which food is liquidized or ground by means of rotating blades **3** *archaic* a bowl-shaped drinking vessel (e g of metal or glass) without handles [ME *gobelet*, fr MF]

**goblet cell** *n* a specialized mucus-secreting cell shaped like a goblet that is found in MUCOUS MEMBRANES (e g those lining the intestines)

**goblin** /'goblin/ *n* a grotesque mischievous elf that is sometimes evil and malicious [ME *gobelin*, fr MF, fr ML *gobelinus*, perh deriv of Gk *kobalos* rogue]

**gobo** /'goh,boh/ *n, pl* **gobos** *also* **goboes** any of various shielding or masking pieces used in theatre, television, or film productions: e g **a** a perforated sheet used to shape a beam of light **b** a piece that shields a microphone from unwanted sounds [origin unknown]

**gobstopper** /'gob,stopə/ *n, chiefly Br* a large round hard sweet [³*gob*]

**goby** /'gohbi/ *n, pl* **gobies,** *esp collectively* **goby** any of numerous typically small spiny-finned fishes (family Gobiidae) with the PELVIC FINS (frontmost pair of fins on the underside of the body) often united to form a sucking disc for attachment to surfaces (e g rocks) [L *gobius* gudgeon, fr Gk *kōbios*]

'**go-,cart** *n, chiefly NAm* **1** a pushchair **2** a handcart

**god** /god/ *n* **1** *cap* the supreme or ultimate reality; the Being perfect in power, wisdom, and goodness whom people worship as creator and ruler of the universe **2** a being or object believed to have more than natural attributes and powers and to require man's worship; *specif* one controlling a particular aspect or part of reality **3** a person or thing of supreme value **4** a very influential person **5** *pl* the highest gallery in a theatre usu with the cheapest seats – see also put the FEAR of God into; in the LAP of the gods, for God's SAKE, take God's name in VAIN [ME, fr OE; akin to OHG *got* god]

'**god-,awful** *adj, informal* extremely unpleasant or disagreeable; abominable ⟨∼ *explosions of violence – Playboy*⟩ [*god-damned* + *awful*]

**godchild** /'god,cheild/ *n* a person for whom another person becomes godparent at baptism

[1]**goddamn, goddam** /go(d)'dam/ *n, often cap* a damn ⟨*he doesn't give a ∼ about anything*⟩

[2]**goddamn, goddam** *vb, often cap* to damn ⟨*I'll be ∼ed*⟩ ⟨*you feel like swearing and ∼ing worse and worse* – Ernest Hemingway⟩

**goddamned** /go(d)'damd, '-,-/, **goddamn, goddam** *adj or adv* damned

**goddaughter** /'god,dawtə/ *n* a female godchild

**goddess** /'godes, -dis/ *n* 1 a female deity 2 a woman whose great charm or beauty arouses adoration

**godet** /goh'det, 'goh,day/ *n* an inset, esp a triangular inset, inserted into a garment to give fullness or flare (e g in a glove or at the bottom of a skirt) [Fr, lit., drinking cup, mug, prob of Gmc origin]

**godetia** /gə'deeshə/ *n* any of several American plants (genus *Godetia*) of the fuchsia family, widely grown for their showy white, pink, or red flowers [NL, genus name, fr C H *Godet* † 1879 Swiss botanist]

'**go-,devil** *n, NAm* any of various devices for clearing pipes; *specif* a cleaning scraper rotated and propelled through a pipeline by the force of the flowing fluid

**godfather** /'god,fahdhə/ *n* 1 a male godparent 2 one having a relation to someone or something like that of a godfather to his godchild ⟨*made him the ∼ of a whole generation of rebels – TLS*⟩

'**God-,fearing** *adj* having a reverent feeling towards God; devout

**godforsaken** /'godfə,saykən/ *adj* 1 situated in a remote or desolate place ⟨*a ∼ deserted road*⟩ 2 neglected in appearance; dismal 3 in pitiable circumstances; miserable ⟨*poor ∼ orphans*⟩

**godhead** /'god,hed/ *n* 1 divine nature or essence; divinity 2 *cap* 2a God – usu + *the* b *the* nature of God, esp as existing in three persons [ME *godhed*, fr *god* + *-hed* -hood; akin to ME *-hod* -hood]

**godhood** /'god,hood/ *n* divinity

**godless** /'godlis/ *adj* not acknowledging a deity; impious – **godlessness** *n*

**godlike** /'god,liek/ *adj* resembling or having the qualities of God or a god; divine

**godly** /'godli/ *adj* 1 divine 2 pious, devout – **godliness** *n*

**godmother** /'god,mudhə/ *n* a female godparent

**godown** /'goh,down/ *n* a warehouse in an Asian country, esp in India [Malay *gudang*]

**godparent** /'god,peərənt/ *n* SPONSOR (person who accepts responsibility for the Christian upbringing of another)

**God's acre** *n, euph* a churchyard

**godsend** /'god,send/ *n* a desirable or needed thing or event that comes unexpectedly [back-formation fr *god-sent*]

**godson** /'god,sun/ *n* a male godchild

**Godspeed** /,god'speed/ *n* a prosperous journey; success ⟨*bade him ∼*⟩ [ME *god speid*, fr the phrase *God spede you* God prosper you]

**godwit** /'god,wit/ *n* any of a genus (*Limosa*) of wading birds with long upwardly curved bills, that are related to the sandpipers, snipes, and curlews [origin unknown]

**goer** /'goh-ə/ *n* 1 a regular attender – usu in combination ⟨*a theatregoer*⟩ 2a one who or that which moves or does things at high speed; *specif, chiefly Austr* a racehorse trying to win b *slang* a lively esp sexually active person; *specif* such a woman ⟨*a right little ∼*⟩ ⟨*a bit of a ∼*⟩ 3 *Austr* a proposal or idea that is acceptable or feasible

**goethite** /'gohthiet, 'guhtiet/ *n* a mineral that consists of an iron hydrogen oxide, $HFeO_2$, and is the commonest constituent of many forms of natural rust [Ger *göthit*, fr J W von *Goethe* †1832 Ger poet]

**goffer** /'gohfə/ *vt* to crimp, wave, or flute (e g linen or a lace edging), esp with a heated iron [Fr *gaufrer*, fr *gaufre* honeycomb, waffle, of Gmc origin] – **goffer** *n*

,**go-'getter** *n* an aggressively enterprising person – **go-getting** *adj or n*

[1]**goggle** /'gogl/ *vi* to stare with wide or bulging eyes [ME *gogelen* to squint] – **goggler** *n*

[2]**goggle** *adj* protuberant, staring ⟨*∼ eyes*⟩ – **goggly** *adj*

'**goggle-,box** *n, Br informal* television; *specif* a television set

,**goggle-'eyed** *adj* having bulging or rolling eyes

**goggles** /'goglz/ *n pl* protective glasses set in a flexible frame (e g of rubber or plastic) that fits snugly against the face

**go-go dancer** *n* a female dancer employed to entertain by dancing in a modern usu erotic style (e g in a disco or public house) [*a-go-go* (disco), fr *Whisky à Gogo,* café & disco in Paris, fr Fr *à gogo* galore, fr MF] – **go-go dance** *n,* **go-go dancing** *n*

[1]**Goidelic** /goy'delik/ *adj* 1 relating to or characteristic of the Gaels 2 relating to or constituting Goidelic [MIr *Gōidel* Gael]

[2]**Goidelic** *n* the group of the Celtic languages comprising Irish Gaelic, Scots Gaelic, and Manx

[1]**going** /'goh·ing/ *n* 1 an act or instance of going ⟨*comings and ∼s*⟩ – often in combination ⟨*theatregoing*⟩ 2 the usu specified condition of the ground (e g for horse racing) 3 advance towards an objective; progress ⟨*found the ∼ too slow and gave up the job*⟩ 4 the horizontal distance between consecutive risers in a stair 5 *pl, archaic* behaviour, actions ⟨*for his eyes are upon the ways of man, and he seeth all his ∼s* – Job 34:21 (AV)⟩

[2]**going** *adj* 1 working, moving ⟨*everything was in ∼ order*⟩ 2a living, existing ⟨*the best novelist ∼*⟩ b available (for use or enjoyment) ⟨*asked if there were any jobs ∼*⟩ 3 current, prevailing ⟨*∼ price*⟩ 4 conducting business with the expectation of indefinite continuance ⟨*∼ concern*⟩ – **going for** favourable to ⟨*had everything going for me*⟩ – **going on** drawing near to; approaching ⟨*sixteen, going on seventeen*⟩

,**going-'over** *n, pl* **goings-over** 1 a thorough examination or investigation 2a a severe scolding b a beating

,**goings-'on** *n pl* 1 actions, events ⟨*coming-out parties and sundry ∼*⟩ 2 irregular or reprehensible happenings or conduct ⟨*tales of scandalous ∼ in high circles*⟩

**goitre,** *NAm chiefly* **goiter** /'goytə/ *n* an abnormal enlargement of the THYROID gland, visible as a swelling of the front of the neck – compare HYPERTHYROIDISM, HYPOTHYROIDISM [Fr *goitre,* fr MF, back-formation fr *goitron* throat, fr (assumed) VL *guttrion-, guttrio,* fr L *guttur*] – **goitrous** *adj*

**goitrogen** /'goytrəjən/ *n* a substance (e g THIOUREA or THIOURACIL) that induces goitre formation – **goitrogenic** *adj,* **goitrogenicity** *n*

**go-kart** *also* **go-cart, kart** /'goh ,kaht/ *n* a tiny low-set racing car with small wheels [*go* + *kart,* alter. of *cart*]

**Golconda** /gol'kondə/ *n* a source of great wealth [*Golconda,* former city in India, capital of a kingdom containing rich diamond mines]

**gold** /gohld/ *n* 1 a yellow precious metallic chemical element that is soft and easily worked, occurs chiefly uncombined or in a few minerals, and is used esp in jewellery and electrical contacts for electronic equipment, and as a currency reserve 2a(1) gold coins a(2) a gold medal ⟨*won a ∼ in the 100 metres*⟩ b money c GOLD STANDARD d gold as a commodity in the economy 3 a deep metallic yellow colour 4 something resembling gold; *esp* something valued as the finest of its kind ⟨*a heart of ∼*⟩ 5 the golden or yellow centre spot of an archery target; *also* a shot that hits it [ME, fr OE; akin to OE *geolu* yellow – more at YELLOW]

**goldbeater** /-,beetə/ *n* one who beats gold into gold leaf – **goldbeating** *n*

**gold-beater's skin** *n* a thin sheet used esp to separate gold leaves during beating and also as a moisture-sensitive element in a HYGROMETER (instrument for measuring humidity)

[1]**goldbrick** /'gohld,brik/ *n, informal* 1 something that appears to be valuable but is actually worthless 2 *chiefly NAm* a person who shirks assigned work [fr a confidence trick in which an ordinary brick is passed off as solid gold]

[2]**goldbrick** *vt, informal* to swindle

**goldcrest** /-,krest/ *n* a very small olive-green European bird (*Regulus regulus*) that has a bright yellow crown with a black border

**gold digger** *n, informal* a woman who uses her sexual charms to extract money or gifts from men

**golden** /'gohld(ə)n/ *adj* 1 consisting of, relating to, or containing gold 2a of the colour of gold b BLOND 1a 3 lustrous, shining 4 of a high degree of excellence; superb 5 prosperous, flourishing ⟨*∼ days*⟩ 6a possessing talents that promise worldly success – often in *golden boy/girl* b highly favoured; popular 7 favourable, advantageous ⟨*a ∼ opportunity*⟩ 8 of, marking, or near a 50th anniversary ⟨*∼ wedding*⟩ 9 mellow, resonant ⟨*a smooth ∼ tenor*⟩ – **goldenly** *adv,* **goldenness** *n*

*usage* In modern use, things actually made of gold are **gold** rather than **golden** ⟨*a gold watch*⟩ ⟨*golden curls*⟩

**golden age** *n* a period of great happiness, prosperity, and achievement

**golden duck** *n* a failure of a batsman to score any runs in a cricket innings by being dismissed on the first ball received – compare KING PAIR

**golden eagle** *n* a large eagle (*Aquila chrysaëtos*) of the northern hemisphere with brownish yellow tips on the head and neck feathers

**goldeneye** /-,ie/ *n* **1** a large-headed swift-flying diving duck (*Bucephala clangula*) of northern regions, of which the male is strikingly marked in black and white **2** a lacewing fly (family Chrysopidae) with a pale green body and yellow eyes

**golden hamster** *n* a small tawny hamster (*Mesocricetus auratus*) native to Asia but kept as a pet in many parts of the world

**golden handshake** *n* a large sum of money given to an employee when he/she leaves a company, esp at retirement

**Golden Horde** /hawd/ *n taking sing or pl vb* a body of Mongol Tartars who overran eastern Europe in the 13th century and dominated Russia until 1486 [fr the golden tent of the Mongol ruler]

**golden mean** *n* **1** the medium between extremes; moderation **2** GOLDEN SECTION

**golden number** *n* a number marking a year in the Metonic cycle of 19 years that is used in calculating the date of Easter

**golden oldie** *n, informal or humorous* a well-known person or thing (esp a record) surviving from the past

**golden oriole** *n* a European oriole (*Oriolus oriolus*) of which the male is brilliant yellow with black tail and wings and the female largely greenish-yellow

**golden pheasant** *n* a brilliantly coloured pheasant (*Chrysolophus pictus*) of China and Tibet

**golden plover** *n* either of two plovers (*Pluvialis apricaria* or *Pluvialis dominica*) with brownish upper parts speckled with golden yellow and white in summer

**golden retriever** *n* a medium-sized retriever with a silky golden coat

**goldenrod** /-'rod/ *n* any of numerous plants (esp genus *Solidago*) of the daisy family with heads of small usu yellow flowers often clustered in branching spikes (PANICLES)

**golden rule** *n* **1** a moral principle deriving from Mt 7:12 and Lk 6:31: "treat others as you would like them to treat you" **2** a guiding principle

**golden section** *n* the proportion of a geometric figure or of a divided line such that the smaller dimension is to the greater as the greater is to the whole. The golden section is found in many natural phenomena and is closely related to other mathematical forms (e g the logarithmic spiral).

**golden syrup** *n* the pale yellow very sweet treacly syrup derived from cane sugar refining and used as a sauce for puddings and in cooking

**goldfield** /'gohld,feeld, -fiəld/ *n* a district in which usu workable gold-bearing minerals occur

**'gold-,filled** *adj* covered with a layer of gold ⟨~ *bracelet*⟩

**goldfinch** /-,finch/ *n* **1** a small largely red, black, yellow, and white European finch (*Carduelis carduelis*) **2** any of several small N American finches (genus *Spinus*) of which the male is yellow with black wings, tail, and crown in summer

**goldfish** /-,fish/ *n* a small usu golden-yellow or orange fish (*Carassius auratus*) related to the carps and extensively kept as an aquarium and pond fish

**gold leaf** *n* gold beaten into very thin sheets and used esp for gilding

**gold medal** *n* a medal of gold awarded to one who comes first in any of several competitions, esp in athletics – compare BRONZE 2b, SILVER MEDAL

**gold mine** *n* **1** a rich source of something desired (e g information) **2** an extremely profitable enterprise, business, etc.

**,gold-of-'pleasure** *n* a yellow-flowered plant (*Camelina sativa*) of the cabbage family found growing together with flax throughout most of Europe and formerly grown for its seeds which yield a clear oil used for lighting and skin preparations

**gold rush** *n* **1** a rush to newly discovered goldfields in pursuit of riches **2** the headlong pursuit of sudden wealth in a new or lucrative field

**goldsmith** /-,smith/ *n* one who works in gold or deals in articles of gold

**gold standard** *n* a standard of money under which the basic unit of currency is defined by a stated quantity of gold of a fixed purity and which is usu characterized by the coinage and circulation of gold, unrestricted convertibility of other money into gold, and the free export and import of gold for the settlement of international obligations

**gold tail** *n* a common European TUSSOCK MOTH (*Euproctis similis*) that is often a pest of fruit trees

**golem** /'gohlem/ *n* **1** a clay or sometimes wooden human figure of Hebrew folklore, supernaturally endowed with life **2** something (e g a robot) resembling a golem [Yiddish *goylem*, fr Heb *gōlem* shapeless mass]

**golf** /golf/ *n* a game in which a player using special clubs attempts to hit a ball into each of the 9 or 18 successive holes on a course with as few strokes as possible [ME (Sc), perh modif of MD *colf, colve* club, bat] – **golf** *vi*

**Golf** – a communications code word for the letter *g*

**golf bag** *n* a usu tubular bag with outside pockets that is designed to carry golf equipment (e g clubs, balls, and clothing)

**golf ball** *n* a sphere in an electric typewriter that is cast with characters in relief and is moved mechanically to impress them in turn on the paper

**golf car** *n* GOLF CART 2

**golf cart** *n* **1** a small cart for wheeling a golf bag round a golf course **2** a motorized cart for carrying a golfer and his/her equipment over a golf course

**golf course** *n* an area of land laid out for the game of golf with a series of 9 or 18 holes each including tee, fairway, and putting green and often natural or artificial hazards

**golfer** /'golfə/ *n* a person who plays golf

**golfing** /'golfing/ *n* the sport or practice of playing golf

**golf links** *n taking sing vb, pl* **golf links** a golf course, esp near the sea

**golf widow** *n* a woman whose husband spends a lot of time on the golf course

**Golgi** /'golji, 'golgi/ *adj* of or being the GOLGI APPARATUS or GOLGI BODIES ⟨~ *vesicles*⟩

**Golgi apparatus** *n* a specialized structure in the CYTOPLASM (jellylike material outside the nucleus) of a cell that is concerned with the secretion of cell products and appears under the ELECTRON MICROSCOPE as a series of parallel sometimes saclike membranes [Camillo *Golgi* †1926 It physician]

**Golgi body** *n* a separate particle of the Golgi apparatus as observed under the ELECTRON MICROSCOPE; *also* GOLGI APPARATUS

**Golgi complex** *n* GOLGI APPARATUS

**goliard** /'gohlyəd/ *n* any of the wandering students of the 12th or 13th centuries who wrote and performed satirical or bawdy entertainments in Latin [Fr, fr OF *goliart, goliard* glutton, drunkard, trickster, prob fr *gole* throat, gluttony, fr L *gula*] – **goliardic** *adj*

**Goliath** /gə'lie·əth/ *n* a giant [*Goliath* (Heb *Golyath*), a biblical giant of the Philistines slain by David (I Sam 17)]

**Goliath beetle** *n* a very large African beetle (*Goliathus giganteus*) that has a black body marked with white stripes and reddish-brown wing-cases

**goliath frog** *n* an African frog (*Rana goliath*) that is the largest known frog and can attain a length of 30 centimetres (about 1 foot)

**golliwog, golliwogg, gollywog** /'goli,wog/ *n* a child's doll made from soft material that is dressed as a man and has a black face and black hair standing out around its head [*Golliwogg*, an animated doll in children's fiction by Bertha Upton † 1912 US writer]

**gollop** /'goləp/ *vt or n, informal* (to) gulp [by alter.]

**'golly** /'goli/ *interj* – used to express surprise [euphemism for *God*]

**²golly** *n* a golliwog [by shortening & alter.]

**golosh** /gə'losh/ *n, chiefly Br* a galosh

**gomeril** /'goməril/, **gomeral** /-rəl/ *n, dial* a simpleton, fool [origin unknown]

**Gomorrah** /gə'morə/ *n* a place notorious for vice and depravity – compare SODOM [*Gomorrah*, biblical city destroyed by God for its wickedness (Gen 18, 19)]

**gon-** /gon-, gohn-/, **gono-** *comb form* sexual; reproductive; gonad ⟨*gonoduct*⟩ ⟨*gonidium*⟩ [Gk, fr *gonos* procreation, seed, fr *gignesthai* to be born – more at KIN]

**-gon** /-gon, -gən/ *comb form* (→ *n*) geometric figure having (so many) angles ⟨*decagon*⟩ [NL -*gonum*, fr Gk -*gōnon*, fr *gōnia* angle; akin to Gk *gony* knee – more at KNEE]

**gonad** /'gohnad; *also* 'go-/ *n* any of the primary sex glands (e g the ovaries or testes) in which the egg or sperm cells are produced [NL *gonad-, gonas*, fr Gk *gonos*] – **gonadal** *adj*

**gonadectomy** /,gohnə'dektəmi, gon-/ *n* surgical removal of an ovary or testis – **gonadectomized** *adj*

**gonadotrophic** /,gonədə'trohfik, gə,nadə-/, **gonadotropic** /-'tropik/ *adj* acting on or stimulating the gonads [ISV]

**gonadotrophin** /,gonə'dohtrəfin, go,nadoh'trohfin/, **gonado-**

**tropin** /ˌgonə'dotrəpin, goˌnadoh'trohpin/ *n* a gonadotrophic hormone (e g FOLLICLE-STIMULATING HORMONE)

**Gondi** /'gondi/ *n* a Dravidian language of central India

**gondola** /'gondələ/ *n* 1 a long narrow flat-bottomed boat with a high prow and stern used on the canals of Venice and usu propelled from the stern by a single long oar 2a an elongated cabin attached to the underside of an airship; *also* an elongated structure (e g for carrying armament or a bomb aimer) underneath an aircraft **b** an often spherical airtight enclosure suspended from a balloon for carrying passengers or instruments **c** a cabin suspended from a cable and used for transporting passengers; *esp* one used as a ski lift 3 a fixture approachable from all sides used in self-service retail shops to display goods 4 *NAm* OPEN WAGON [It, prob fr Rhaeto-Romanic *gondolà* rock, roll]

**gondolier** /ˌgondə'liə/ *n* a boatman who propels a gondola [Fr, fr It *gondoliere*, fr *gondola*]

**Gondwanian** /gond'wahnyən/ *adj* relating to the hypothetical prehistoric landmass Gondwana

**¹gone** /gon/ *adj* 1 past, bygone 2a involved, absorbed ⟨*far ~ in hysteria*⟩ **b** pregnant by a specified length of time ⟨*she's six months ~*⟩ 3 lost, ruined 4 *informal* 4a possessed with a strong attachment or a foolish or unreasoning love or desire; infatuated – often + *on* ⟨*was real ~ on that man*⟩ **b** intoxicated with alcohol, drugs, etc; *also* faint ⟨*but he was too far ~ to notice*⟩ 5 *euph* dead [fr pp of go]

**²gone** *adv, Br* later or older than; turned ⟨*didn't get home till ~ four*⟩ ⟨*I am ~ eighty-six* – Muriel Spark⟩

**goner** /'gonə/ *n, informal* one whose case or state is hopeless ⟨*if you fall behind you're a ~*⟩

**gonfalon** /'gonfələn/ *n* 1 the emblem of certain princes or states (e g the medieval republics of Italy) 2 a gonfanon [It *gonfalone*,fr OF *gonfanon, gonfalon*]

**gonfanon** /'gonfənon, -nən/ *n* a flag that hangs from a crosspiece or frame [ME *gonfanoun*, fr MF *gonfanon*, of Gmc origin; akin to OHG *gundfano* war flag, fr *gund-* battle, war + *fano* cloth]

**gong** /gong/ *n* 1 a disc-shaped percussion instrument that produces a resounding tone when struck with a usu padded hammer 2 a flat saucer-shaped bell 3 *Br slang* a medal, decoration [Malay & Jav, of imit origin] – **gong** *vi*

**Gongorism** /'gong-gəriz(ə)m/ *n* a literary style characterized by artificial elegance and the use of farfetched comparisons [Sp *gongorismo*, fr Luis de *Góngora* y Argote †1627 Sp poet] – **gongoristic** *adj*

**goni-, gonio-** *comb form* corner; angle ⟨*gonio*meter⟩ [Gk *gōnia*]

**gonidium** /go'nidi-əm/ *n, pl* **gonidia** /-diə/ 1 an asexual reproductive cell or group of cells in or on a GAMETOPHYTE (sexually reproducing form of some plants) 2 a green chlorophyll-bearing algal cell of a lichen [NL, fr *gon-* + *-idium*] – **gonidial** *adj*

**goniometer** /ˌgohni'omitə/ *n* 1 an instrument for measuring angles (e g between the faces of crystals) 2 DIRECTION FINDER – **goniometry** *n*, **goniometric** *adj*

**gonk** /gongk/ *n* an egg-shaped doll made from soft material [coined word]

**gonna** /'gonə, gənə/ *verbal auxiliary pres* going to – often used in writing to represent careless or American speech ⟨*I'm ~ wash that man right out of my hair* – Oscar Hammerstein⟩ [by alter.]

**gono-** – see GON-

**gonococcus** /ˌgonoh'kokəs/ *n, pl* **gonococci** /-'kok(s)ie, 'kok(s)i/ a pus-producing bacterium (*Neisseria gonorrhoeae*) that causes gonorrhoea [NL] – **gonococcal, gonococcic** *adj*

**gonocyte** /'gonəsiet/ *n* a cell that produces egg or sperm cells; *esp* GAMETOCYTE [ISV]

**gonogenesis** /ˌgonoh'jenəsis/ *n* the formation and maturation of egg or sperm cells [NL]

**gonophore** /'gonəfaw/ *n* 1 an elongation of the flower stalk in some plants that bears the STAMENS (male reproductive organs) and CARPELS (female reproductive organs) at its end 2 a reproductive ZOOID (individual member) of a HYDROZOAN colony (e g a Portuguese man-of-war) that remains attached to the colony [ISV] – **gonophoric** *adj*, **gonophorous** *adj*

**gonorrhoea,** *chiefly NAm* **gonorrhea** /ˌgonə'riə/ *n* a venereal disease caused by gonococcal bacteria and marked by inflammation of the MUCOUS MEMBRANES lining the genital tracts [NL, fr LL, morbid loss of semen, fr Gk *gonorrhoia*, fr *gon-* + *-rrhoia* -rrhoea] – **gonorrhoeal** *adj*

**-gony** /-g(ə)ni/ *comb form* (→ *n*) origin; reproduction; manner of coming into being ⟨*sporo*gony⟩ ⟨*cosmo*gony⟩ [L *-gonia*, fr Gk, fr *gonos*]

**goo** /gooh/ *n, informal* 1 a sticky substance; sticky matter 2 cloying sentimentality [perh alter. of *glue*] – **gooey** *adj*

**goober** /'goohbə/ *n, S & Mid US* a peanut [of African origin; akin to Kongo *nguba* peanut]

**¹good** /good/ *adj* **better** /'betə/; **best** /best/ 1a(1) of a favourable character or tendency ⟨*~ news*⟩ a(2) bountiful, fertile ⟨*~ land*⟩ a(3) handsome, attractive ⟨*~ looks*⟩ b(1) suitable, fit ⟨*~ to eat*⟩ ⟨*it's a ~ day for planting roses*⟩ b(2) free from injury or disease; whole ⟨*one ~ arm*⟩ b(3) not lessened in value ⟨*bad money drives out ~*⟩ b(4) commercially sound ⟨*a ~ risk*⟩ b(5) certain to last or live ⟨*~ for another year*⟩ b(6) certain to pay or contribute ⟨*~ for a few quid*⟩ b(7) certain to elicit a specified result ⟨*always ~ for a laugh*⟩ b(8) profitable, advantageous ⟨*made a very ~ deal*⟩ c(1) agreeable, pleasant c(2) beneficial to the health or character ⟨*whisky's ~ for a cold*⟩ ⟨*spinach is ~ for you*⟩ c(3) amusing, enjoyable ⟨*a ~ joke*⟩ c(4) not rotten; fresh ⟨*the beef is still ~*⟩ d(1) considerable, ample ⟨*a ~ margin*⟩ d(2) full ⟨*two ~ hours of slow cooking* – Elizabeth David⟩ e(1) well-founded, cogent ⟨*~ reasons*⟩ e(2) true ⟨*holds ~ for society at large*⟩ e(3) real, actualized ⟨*made ~ his promises*⟩ e(4) deserving of respect; honourable ⟨*in ~ standing*⟩ e(5) legally valid ⟨*~ title*⟩ f(1) adequate, satisfactory ⟨*~ care*⟩ f(2) conforming to a standard ⟨*~ English*⟩ f(3) choice, discriminating ⟨*~ taste*⟩ 2a(1) morally commendable; virtuous ⟨*a ~ man*⟩ a(2) right, correct ⟨*~ conduct*⟩ a(3) kind, benevolent ⟨*~ intentions*⟩ **b** reputable; *specif* upper-class ⟨*a ~ family*⟩ **c** competent, skilful ⟨*a ~ doctor*⟩ **d** loyal ⟨*a ~ party man*⟩ ⟨*a ~ Catholic*⟩ [ME, fr OE *gōd*; akin to OHG *guot* good, Skt *gadh* to hold fast] – **goodish** *adj* – **all well and good** (that is) acceptable if not ideal – **as good as** virtually; IN EFFECT ⟨*as good as dead*⟩ – **give as good as one gets** to counterattack with equal vigour – **good and** *informal* very, entirely ⟨*should be good and ready by Tuesday*⟩ – **hold good** to be true or valid – see also **in somebody's good** BOOKS, **put a good** FACE **on, in good** HANDS, **for good** MEASURE, **a (good)** RUN **for one's money, take something in good** PART, **good** SHOW, **stand one in good** STEAD, **all in good** TIME, **VERY good**

*usage* It is nonstandard to use **good** as an adverb ⟨*... he sings good*⟩. **Good** and **well** are both adjectives, but with different meanings, in ⟨*I feel* **good** (= cheerful)⟩ and ⟨*I feel* **well** (= healthy)⟩.

**²good** *n* 1a something that is good; use ⟨*it's no ~ complaining*⟩ **b** the quality of goodness ⟨*to know ~ from evil*⟩ **c** a good element or portion ⟨*recognized the ~ in him*⟩ 2 prosperity, benefit ⟨*for the ~ of the community*⟩ 3a *usu pl* something that has economic utility or satisfies an economic want *pl* personal property of value but usu excluding money, securities, transferable bills of exchange, etc **c** *pl* cloth **d** *pl* wares, merchandise ⟨*tinned ~s*⟩ 4 *pl* taking sing or pl vb, *informal* the desired or necessary article ⟨*came up with the ~s*⟩ 5 *pl, slang* proof of wrongdoing ⟨*got the ~ on him at last*⟩ – **deliver the goods** to produce the promised, desired, or expected results ⟨*the manifesto was brilliant, but once in power they couldn't deliver the goods*⟩ – **for good** forever, permanently – **good for you** *Br* – used as an expression of congratulation – **to the good** 1 for the best; beneficial ⟨*this rain is all* to the good⟩ 2 in a position of overall gain or profit ⟨*he ended the game £10* to the good⟩

**³good** *adv, nonstandard* well ⟨*he sings ~*⟩ *usage* see ¹GOOD

**good book** *n, often cap G&B* the Bible

**¹goodbye** /good'bie/ *interj* – used to express farewell to or by one departing or to end a telephone conversation [alter. of *God be with you*]

**²goodbye,** *NAm also* **goodby** *n* a concluding remark or gesture at parting ⟨*I'm afraid it's time to say our ~s*⟩

**¹'good-for-ˌnothing** *adj* of no value; useless, worthless

**²good-for-nothing** *n* an idle worthless person

**Good Friday** *n* the Friday before Easter observed in churches as the anniversary of the crucifixion of Christ [fr its special sanctity]

**ˌgood-'hearted** *adj* having a kindly generous disposition – **good-heartedly** *adv*, **good-heartedness** *n*

**ˌgood-'humoured** *adj* good-natured, cheerful – **good-humouredly** *adv*, **good-humouredness** *n*

**goodie** /'goodi/ *n* ²GOODY

**good life** *n* 1 a virtuous life 2 a life marked by a high standard of living

**good-looker** *n* a good-looking person

**,good-'looking** *adj* having a pleasing or attractive appearance
*synonyms* see BEAUTIFUL

**goodly** /'goodli/ *adj* **1** significantly large in amount; considerable ⟨*a* ~ *number*⟩ **2** *archaic* pleasantly attractive; handsome

**goodman** /'goodmən/ *n, archaic* **1** the master of a household **2** Mr

**,good-'natured** *adj* of a pleasant, cheerful, and cooperative disposition – **good-naturedly** *adv*, **good-naturedness** *n*

**goodness** /'goodnis/ *n* **1** the quality or state of being good **2** the nutritious, flavourful, or beneficial part of something ⟨*boil all the* ~ *out of the meat*⟩ – see also **goodness** KNOWS, **for goodness** SAKE

**good offices** *n pl* power or action that helps someone out of a difficulty – often in *through the good offices of*

**Good Samaritan** /sə'marit(ə)n/ *n* SAMARITAN 2a

**goods train** *n, chiefly Br* a train of wagons carrying heavy or bulk goods

**goods yard** *n, Br* a railway marshalling yard where goods are loaded and unloaded and goods trains made up

**,good-'tempered** *adj* having an even temper; not easily annoyed – **good-temperedly** *adv*, **good-temperedness** *n*

**good-time girl** *n, euph* a female prostitute

**goodwife** /'goodweif/ *n, archaic* **1** the mistress of a household **2** Mrs

**goodwill** /-'wil/ *n* **1a** a kindly feeling of approval and support; benevolent interest or concern **b** the favour or prestige that a business has acquired beyond the mere value of what it sells **2a** cheerful consent **b** willing effort – **goodwilled** *adj*
    *usage* Some British writers prefer to spell **goodwill** as two words ⟨*a gesture of good will*⟩ except in the commercial sense.

**good word** *n* **1** a favourable statement ⟨*put in a* ~ *for me*⟩ **2** *chiefly NAm* good news ⟨*what's the* ~?⟩

**¹goody** /'goodi/ *n, archaic* a usu married woman of lowly station – used as a title preceding a surname [alter. of *goodwife*]

**²goody** also **goodie** *n, informal* **1** something that is particularly attractive, pleasurable, good, or desirable ⟨*such* goodies *as model trains, cameras, microscopes, and college educations* – *Time*⟩ **2** a good person or hero – compare BADDIE

**'goody-,goody** *n or adj, informal* (one who is) affectedly or ingratiatingly prim or virtuous

**¹goof** /goohf/ *n* **1** a ridiculous stupid person **2** *chiefly NAm* a stupid blunder [prob alter. of E dial. *goff* simpleton, fr MF *goffe* clumsy]

**²goof** *vb, NAm vi* **1** *informal* to make a usu foolish or careless mistake; blunder **2** *slang* to spend time idly or foolishly – often + *off* ⟨*somebody is* ~ing *off on the job* – *Springfield (Mass) Daily News*⟩ ~ *vt, informal* to make a mess of; bungle – often + *up*

**goofball** /-,bawl/ *n, slang* **1** *chiefly NAm* a barbiturate sleeping pill **2** *NAm* a mentally abnormal person

**goofy** /'goohfi/ *adj, informal* **1** silly, daft; *esp* stupid-looking **2** *Br, of teeth* protruding – **goofily** *adv*, **goofiness** *n*

**googly** /'goohgli/ *n* a slow ball bowled in cricket by a right-handed bowler that turns towards the LEG SIDE of a right-handed batsman on bouncing although apparently delivered with an action that would make it turn the other way; *also* a similar delivery bowled by a left-handed bowler that turns unexpectedly towards the OFF SIDE [origin unknown]

**googol** /'goohgol/ *n* the figure 1 followed by 100 zeroes; $10^{100}$ [coined by a child]

**googolplex** /-,pleks/ *n* the figure 1 followed by a googol of zeroes; ten raised to the power of a googol; $10^{10^{100}}$ [*googol* + *-plex* (as in *duplex*)]

**goo-goo** /'gooh gooh/ *adj, informal* loving, enticing – chiefly in *goo-goo eyes* ⟨*make* ~ *eyes at each other* – *New Republic*⟩ [prob alter. of *²goggle*]

**gook** /goohk/ *n, NAm derog* a person of a brown or yellow race [origin unknown]

**goon** /goohn/ *n,* **1** *NAm* a man hired to terrorize or eliminate opponents **2** *slang* an idiot, dope [partly short for E dial. *gooney* simpleton; partly fr Alice the *Goon*, subhuman comic-strip creature by E C Segar †1938 US cartoonist] – **goony** *adj*

**goory** /'kooəri/ *n, NZ* a mongrel dog [modif of Maori *kuri*]

**goosander** /'gooh'sandə/ *n* a sawbill duck (*Mergus merganser*) of the northern hemisphere of which the male has a black back, pinkish-white underparts, and a greenish-black head and the female has blue-grey upper parts, whitish underparts, and a chestnut head [alter. of earlier *gossander*, prob fr *gos-* (as in *gosling*) + *berg*ander (sheldrake)]

**¹goose** /goohs/ *n, pl (1&2)* **geese** /gees/, *(3)* **gooses 1a** any of numerous large long-necked web-footed water birds (family Anatidae) that are intermediate in size and appearance between the swans and ducks **b** a female goose as distinguished from the male gander **2** a simpleton, dolt **3** a tailor's smoothing iron with a gooseneck handle [ME *gos*, fr OE *gōs*; akin to OHG *gans* goose, L *anser*] – **goosey** *adj*

**²goose** *vt, chiefly NAm vulg* to poke (a person) between the buttocks

**goose barnacle** *n* a barnacle (genus *Lepas*) with a flattened shell, that attaches itself to rocks, driftwood, the bottom of ships, etc by means of a leathery stalk

**gooseberry** /'goozb(ə)ri/ *n* **1** the edible acid usu prickly green or yellow fruit of any of several shrubs (genus *Ribes* of the family Grossulariaceae, the gooseberry family); *also* a shrub that bears gooseberries **2** an unwanted companion to two lovers – chiefly in *to play gooseberry* [perh fr *¹goose* + *berry*]

**goose bumps** *n pl, chiefly NAm* gooseflesh

**goose egg** *n, NAm informal* zero, nothing; *esp* a score of zero in a contest

**gooseflesh** /-,flesh/ *n* a bristling rough or bumpy condition of the skin produced by erection of its PAPILLAE (small projections of tissue round hair roots) usu from cold or fear

**goosefoot** /-,foot/ *n, pl* **goosefoots** any of several plants (genus *Chenopodium* of the family Chenopodiaceae, the goosefoot family) with small green flowers, that grow esp on disturbed or cultivated land [fr the shape of its leaves]

**goosegog** /'gooz,gog/ *n, Br informal or dial* a gooseberry [*goose*berry + *gog*, of unknown origin]

**goose grass** *n* CLEAVERS

**gooseneck** /-,nek/ *n* **1** something (e g a flexible jointed metal pipe) curved like the neck of a goose or U-shaped **2** a joint between a BOOM (swinging beam at bottom of sail) and a mast on a sailing vessel – **goosenecked** *adj*

**goose pimples** *n pl* gooseflesh

**goose step** *n* a straight-legged marching step used by troops of some armies when passing in review – **goose-stepper** *n*

**gopak** /'gohpak/ *n* a Ukrainian male folk dance featuring high leaps [Russ, fr Ukrainian *hopak*, fr *hop*, interj used in lively dances, fr Ger *hopp*; akin to MHG *hopfen* to hop]

**gopher** /'gohfə/ *n* **1** a burrowing edible tortoise (*Gopherus polyphemus*) of the southern USA **2a** any of several burrowing rodents (family Geomyidae) of N and Central America that are the size of a large rat and have large cheek pouches **b** any of numerous small GROUND SQUIRRELS (genus *Citellus*) of the prairie region of N America, closely related to the chipmunks [origin unknown]

**gopher snake** *n* INDIGO SNAKE

**gopher wood** *n* an unidentified type of wood used by Noah according to Gen 6:14 in building the Ark [Heb *gōpher*]

**goral** /'gawrəl/ *n* either of two mammals (*Naemorhedus goral* or *Naemorhedus cranbrooki*) of the mountains of eastern Asia that resemble small antelopes [perh deriv of Skt *gaura* gaur]

**gorblimey** /gaw'bliemi/ *interj, Br slang* – used to express surprise and indignation; also used adjectivally to suggest proletarian coarseness ⟨~ *accent*⟩ [euphemism for *God blind me*]

**Gordian knot** /'gawdi-ən, -dyən/ *n* an intricate problem; *esp* a problem insoluble in its own terms [*Gordius*, King of Phrygia, who tied an intricate knot which supposedly could be undone only by the future ruler of Asia, and which Alexander the Great cut with his sword]

**¹gore** /gaw/ *n* blood; *esp* clotted blood [ME, filth, fr OE *gor*; akin to OE *wearm* warm]

**²gore** *n* **1** a small usu triangular piece of land **2** a tapering or triangular piece of material (e g cloth) used to give shape to something (e g a garment or sail) [ME, fr OE *gāra*; akin to OE *gār* spear, Gk *chaios* shepherd's staff] – **gored** *adj*

**³gore** *vt* to pierce or wound with a horn or tusk [ME *goren*]

**¹gorge** /gawj/ *n* **1a** the throat **b** (the contents of) the stomach or belly **2** the entrance into an outwork (e g a bastion) of a fort **3** a narrow passage through land; *esp* a narrow steep-walled valley, often with a stream flowing through it ⟨*Cheddar* Gorge⟩ **4** a primitive device used instead of a fishhook that consists of an object (e g a piece of bone attached in the middle of a line) easy to swallow but difficult to eject **5** *NAm* a mass choking a passage ⟨*a river dammed by an ice* ~⟩ [ME, fr MF, fr LL *gurga*, alter. of L *gurges* throat, whirlpool – more at VORACIOUS] – **one's gorge rises** one is disgusted or sickened

**²gorge** *vi* to eat greedily or until completely full ~ *vt* **1a** to stuff to capacity; glut **b** to fill completely or to the point of swelling ⟨*veins* ~d *with blood*⟩ **2** to swallow greedily *synonyms* see ²SATIATE – **gorger** *n*

**gorgeous** /'gawjəs/ *adj* **1** splendidly brilliant or magnificent **2** very fine; pleasant ⟨*it was a ~ day for a picnic*⟩ [ME *gorgayse*, fr MF *gorgias* elegant, perh fr *gorgias* neckerchief, fr *gorge*] – **gorgeously** *adv*, **gorgeousness** *n*

**gorget** /'gawjit/ *n* **1** a piece of armour protecting the throat **2a** an ornamental collar – used in archaeology **b** a part of a WIMPLE (head-covering worn by nuns and medieval women) covering the throat and shoulders [ME, fr MF, fr *gorge*]

**gorgon** /'gawgən/ *n* **1** *cap* any of three snake-haired sisters in Greek mythology whose glance turned the beholder to stone **2** an ugly or repulsive woman [L *Gorgon-, Gorgo,* fr Gk *Gorgōn,* fr *gorgos* terrible] – **Gorgonian** *adj*

**gorgonian** /gaw'gohnyən, -ni-ən/ *n* any of an order (Gorgonacea of the class Anthozoa) of corals, including the SEA FANS and RED CORALS, that live in colonies and typically have a horny branching or treelike skeleton [deriv of L *gorgonia* coral, fr *Gorgon-, Gorgo*] – **gorgonian** *adj*

**gorgon·ize, -ise** /'gawgəniez/ *vt* to have a paralysing or mesmerizing effect on; stupefy, petrify

**Gorgonzola** /ˌgawgən'zohlə/ *n* a blue-veined strongly flavoured cheese of Italian origin [It, fr *Gorgonzola,* town in N Italy]

**gorilla** /gə'rilə/ *n* **1** an ANTHROPOID APE (*Gorilla gorilla*) of western equatorial Africa that is related to the chimpanzee but less upright and much larger **2a** an ugly or brutal man **b** a thug, hoodlum △ guerrilla [deriv of Gk *Gorillai,* a mythical African tribe of hairy women]

**gormand·ize, -ise** /'gawmənˌdiez/ *vi* to eat a lot for pleasure ~ *vt* to eat greedily; devour [*gormand,* alter. of *gourmand*] – **gormandizer** *n*

**gormless** /'gawmlis/ *adj, Br informal* lacking understanding and intelligence; stupid [alter. of E dial. *gaumless,* fr *gaum* heed, understanding (fr ME *gome,* fr ON *gaum, gaumr*) + *-less*]

**gorse** /gaws/ *n* furze [ME *gorst,* fr OE – more at HORROR] – **gorsy** *adj*

**Gorsedd** /'gawsədh/ *n, pl* **Gorseddau** /'gaw'sedhie/, **Gorsedds** the institution of bards and druids governing a Welsh EISTEDDFOD (competitive festival of music, poetry, etc) and assembling twice a year to confer bardic degrees and titles; *also* the daily assembly of bards and druids during the course of an eisteddfod [W, lit., mound, court, throne]

**gory** /'gawri/ *adj* **1** covered with gore; bloodstained **2** full of violence; bloodcurdling ⟨*a ~ film*⟩

**gosh** /gosh/ *interj* – used as a mild oath or exclamation of surprise [euphemism for *God*]

**goshawk** /'gosˌhawk/ *n* any of several long-tailed hawks (genus *Accipiter*) with short rounded wings; *esp* a hawk (*Accipiter gentilis*) of Europe, N Asia, and N America that has a conspicuous white stripe above and behind the eye [ME *goshawke,* fr OE *gōshafoc,* fr *gōs* goose + *hafoc* hawk]

**gosling** /'gozling/ *n* **1** a young goose **2** a foolish or callow person [ME, fr *gos* goose]

**go-'slow** *n, Br* a deliberate slowing down in production by workers as a means of forcing management's compliance with their demands

**¹gospel** /'gospl/ *n* **1** *often cap* **1a** the message concerning Christ, the kingdom of God, and salvation **b** any of the first four New Testament books telling of the life, death, and resurrection of Jesus Christ; *also* a similar APOCRYPHAL (not accepted as the word of God by the Christian Church) book **c** an interpretation of the Christian message ⟨*the social ~*⟩ **2** *cap* a reading from one of the New Testament Gospels as part of a church service **3** the message or teachings of a religious teacher **4a** something accepted as a guiding principle ⟨*the ~ of hard work*⟩ **b** something (eg an assertion) of such authoritative or infallible character or source as not to be questioned ⟨*they took all he said as ~*⟩ [ME, fr OE *gōdspel,* fr *gōd* good + *spell* tale, news – more at SPELL]

**²gospel** *adj* **1a** relating to the Christian gospel; evangelical **b** marked by fervent emphasis on the gospel ⟨*a ~ meeting*⟩ **2** relating to or being religious songs of American origin associated with evangelism and popular devotion and marked by simple melody and harmony and elements of folk songs, spirituals, and occasionally jazz ⟨*a ~ singer*⟩

**gospeller,** *chiefly NAm* **gospeler** /'gospələ/ *n* **1** a person who preaches or gives out a particular gospel **2** a person who reads or sings the Gospel as part of a church service

**gospel side** *n, often cap G* the left side of an altar or CHANCEL (altar, choir, and sanctuary of a church) as one faces it [fr the custom of reading the Gospel from this side]

**Gosplan** /'gosˌplan/ *n* a government department of the USSR that makes long-term economic and social plans and generally supervises their execution [Russ *Gos*udarstvennaya *Plan*ovaya (Komissiya) State Planning Commission]

**gossamer** /'gosəmə/ *n* **1** a film of cobwebs floating in the air in calm clear weather or spread over grass **2** something light, delicate, insubstantial, or tenuous; *specif* very fine gauze or silk [ME *gossomer,* fr *gos* goose + *somer* summer; prob fr its commonly appearing at the time of year when geese were ready for eating] – **gossamer** *adj,* **gossamery** *adj*

**gossan** /'gosən/ *n* a porous rusty-coloured mass of usu iron-containing oxide minerals over an ore deposit that results from the OXIDATION and dissolving away of mineral sulphides formerly present [Cornish *gossen*] – **gossanous** *adj*

**¹gossip** /'gosip/ *n* **1** a person who habitually reveals usu sensational facts concerning other people's actions or lives **2a** rumour or report of such facts **b** a chatty talk **c** the subject matter of gossip ⟨*his infidelities were common ~*⟩ **3** *archaic* a companion, crony [ME *gossib* godparent, crony, fr OE *godsibb,* fr *god* + *sibb* kinsman, fr *sibb* related – more at SIB]

**²gossip** *vi* to relate gossip *synonyms* see SPEAK – **gossiper** *n*

**gossip column** *n* a column in a newspaper relating gossip about well-known people

**gossipy** /'gosipi/ *adj* full of or given to gossip ⟨*a ~ letter*⟩ ⟨*~ neighbours*⟩

**gossoon** /go'soohn/ *n, chiefly Irish* a boy, youth; *esp* a serving boy [modif of Fr *garçon*]

**gossypol** /'gosəpol, -pohl/ *n* a poisonous plant pigment, $C_{30}H_{30}O_8$, present in cottonseed [ISV, deriv of L *gossypion* cotton]

**got** /got/ **1** *past of* GET **2** *nonstandard, pres pl & 1st & 2nd sing of* GET ⟨*I ~ news for you*⟩ ⟨*we ~ to go*⟩ – compare GOTCHA, GOTTA

**gotcha** /'gochə/ *interj, informal* **1** – used to indicate that one has understood **2** – used as a shout of triumph when seizing something or succeeding in an attempt [alter. of *got you*]

**Goth** /goth/ *n* a member of a Germanic people that invaded and settled in parts of the Roman Empire between the 3rd and 5th centuries AD [LL *Gothi,* pl, of Gmc origin]

**¹Gothic** /'gothik/ *adj* **1a** relating to or resembling the Goths, their civilization, or their language **b** Teutonic, Germanic **c** uncouth, barbarous **2a** (characteristic) of a style of architecture developed in northern France and spreading through western Europe from the middle of the 12th century to the early 16th century, that is characterized by the converging of weights and strains upon slender vertical pillars and counterbalancing buttresses and by pointed arches and vaulting **b** of an architectural style reflecting the influence of medieval Gothic **3** *often not cap* of or resembling a class of novels of the late 18th and early 19th centuries dealing with macabre or mysterious events in remote and desolate settings – **gothically** *adv,* **Gothicness** *n*

**²Gothic** *n* **1** the East Germanic language of the Goths **2** Gothic style in art or decoration; *specif* Gothic architectural style **3** a form of type or lettering with a heavy thick face and angular outlines used esp by the earliest European printers – called also BLACK LETTER; compare FRAKTUR **b** SANS SERIF

**Gothicism** /'gothiˌsiz(ə)m/ *n* **1** barbarous lack of taste or elegance **2** conformity to or practice of Gothic style – **Gothicist** *n*

**gothic·ize, -ise** /'gothisiez/ *vt, often cap* to make Gothic

**Gothic Revival** *n* an artistic style of the 18th and 19th centuries inspired by and largely imitative of Gothic style, esp in architecture

**göthite** /'gohthiet, 'guhtiet/ *n* GOETHITE (iron mineral)

**¹gotta** /'gotə/ *vt pres, nonstandard* to have a ⟨*I ~ horse*⟩ [alter. of *got a*]

**²gotta** *verbal auxiliary pres, nonstandard* to have to; must ⟨*we ~ go*⟩ [alter. of *got to*]

**gotten** /'gotn/ *NAm past part of* GET

**gouache** /goo'ahsh (Fr gwaʃ)/ *n* **1** a method of painting with opaque watercolours that have been ground in water and mixed with a gum preparation **2** a picture painted in gouache [Fr, fr It *guazzo,* lit., puddle, deriv of L *aquatio* act of fetching water, fr *aquatus,* pp of *aquari* to fetch water, fr *aqua* water – more at ISLAND]

**Gouda** /'gowdə/ *n* a mild golden-yellow cheese of Dutch origin that is similar to Edam but contains more fat [*Gouda,* town in the Netherlands]

**¹gouge** /gowj/ *n* **1** a chisel with a curved cross section and sharpened edge on the concave side of the blade **2a** the act of gouging **b** a groove or cavity scooped out **3** *chiefly NAm* an excessive or improper demand; an extortion [ME *gowge*, fr MF *gouge*, fr LL *gulbia*, of Celt origin; akin to OIr *gulban* sting]

**²gouge** *vt* **1** to scoop out (as if) with a gouge **2** to force out (an eye), esp with the thumb **3** *chiefly NAm* to subject to extortion or excessive demand; overcharge – **gouger** *n*

**gougère** /gooh'zheə (*Fr* guʒɛr)/ *n* a savoury choux pastry containing cheese [Fr]

**goulash** /'goohlash/ *n* **1** a meat stew made usu with veal or beef and highly seasoned with paprika **2** a round in bridge played with hands dealt in lots of five, five, and three cards consecutively from a pack formed by the unshuffled arranged hands from a previous deal **3** a jumble of mixed elements [Hung *gulyás* herdsman's soup]

**gourami** *also* **gouramie** /'gooərəmi/ *n, pl* **gouramis, gouramies,** *esp collectively* **gourami, gouramie 1** a large freshwater food fish (*Osphronemus goramy*) of SE Asia **2** any of various small brightly coloured fishes (family Anabantidae) often kept in aquariums [Malay *gurami*]

**gourd** /gooəd/ *n* **1** any of a family (Cucurbitaceae, the marrow family) of chiefly fleshy tendril-bearing climbing plants including the melon, squash, and pumpkin **2** the fruit of a plant of the marrow family; *esp* any of various hard-rinded inedible fruits of plants of two genera (*Lagenaria* and *Cucurbita*) often used for ornament or for vessels and utensils [ME *gourde*, fr MF, fr L *cucurbita*]

**gourde** /gooəd/ *n* – see MONEY table [AmerF, fr Fr, fem of *gourd* numb, dull, heavy, fr L *gurdus* dull, stupid]

**gourmand** /gooə'monh, gaw-/ (*Fr* gurmã)/ *n* one who is excessively fond of or heartily interested in food and drink *usage* see GOURMET [MF *gourmant*] – **gourmandism** *n*

**gourmet** /'gawmay, 'gooə- (*Fr* gurmɛ)/ *n* a connoisseur of food and drink [Fr, fr MF, alter. (prob influenced by *gourmand*) of *gromet* boy servant, vintner's assistant, fr ME *grom* groom]

*synonyms* Gourmet is polite, gourmand is usually rather rude. A hotel will advertise a complicated expensive meal as a gourmet dinner, not a gourmand one.

**gout** /gowt/ *n* **1** a disorder of the body's metabolism that results in the deposition of crystals of URIC ACID compounds in the joints, esp that of the big toe, causing painful inflammation **2** a blob, splash ⟨~s of lava⟩ [ME *goute*, fr OF, gout, drop, fr L *gutta* drop; fr the former belief that it was caused by drops of diseased matter in the blood] – **gouty** *adj*

**goutweed** /'gowt,weed/ *n* GROUND ELDER [fr the former use of its roots as a remedy for gout]

**govern** /'guv(ə)n/ *vt* **1** to exercise continuous sovereign authority over; *esp* to control and direct the making and administration of policy in **2** to control the speed of (e g a machine), esp by automatic means **3a** to control, direct, or strongly influence the actions and conduct of **b** to exert a determining or guiding influence in or over ⟨*income must* ~ *expenditure*⟩ ⟨*availability often* ~s *choice*⟩ **c** to hold in check; restrain ⟨~ *your temper*⟩ **4** to require (a word) to be in a usu specified grammatical case ⟨*in English a transitive verb* ~s *a personal pronoun in the accusative*⟩ **5** to serve as a precedent or deciding principle for ⟨*habits and customs that* ~ *human decisions*⟩ ~ *vi* **1** to prevail or have decisive influence; control **2** to exercise authority [ME *governen*, fr OF *governer*, fr L *gubernare* to steer, govern, fr Gk *kybernan*] – **governable** *adj*

**governance** /'guv(ə)nəns/ *n, formal* the act of governing; the state of being governed

**governess** /'guv(ə)nis/ *n* a woman entrusted with the teaching and often supervision of a child, esp in a private household

**governessy** /'guv(ə)nisi/ *adj* having the characteristics of or suggesting a governess; bossy, domineering

**government** /'guv(ə)nmənt, 'guvəmənt/ *n* **1** the act or process of governing; *specif* authoritative direction or control **2** the office, authority, or function of governing **3a** the continuous exercise of authority over and the performance of functions for a political unit; rule **b** the political function of policy making as distinguished from the administration of policy decisions **4** the form or system of rule by which a political unit is governed: e g **4a** the organization, machinery, or agency through which political authority is exercised and functions are performed **b** *taking sing or pl vb* the body of people that constitutes the governing authority of a political unit; *esp, often cap* a small group of people (e g a cabinet) holding the principal political executive offices of a political unit and being respon-sible for the direction and supervision of public affairs **5** POLITICAL SCIENCE – **governmental** *adj,* **governmentally** *adv*
*usage* The pronunciation /'guv(ə)nmənt/ is recommended for BBC broadcasters.

**governmentalism** /,guvə'mentl·iz(ə)m, ,guvən-/ *n* **1** a theory advocating extension of the sphere and degree of government activity **2** the tendency towards extension of the role of government – **governmentalist** *n*

**governmental·ize, -ise** /,guvə'mentl·iez, ,guvən-/ *vt* to subject to regulation or control by a government

**governor** /'guv(ə)nə/ *n* **1** one who governs: e g **1a** one who exercises authority, esp over an area or group **b** an official elected or appointed to act as ruler, chief executive, or head of a political unit **c** a commandant in the armed forces **d** the managing director and usu the principal officer of an institution or organization **e** a member of a group (e g the governing body of a school) that directs or controls an institution or society **2** a tutor **3a** *slang* one (e g a father, guardian, or employer) looked upon as governing **b** Mister, Sir – usu used as an informal term of address **4a** an attachment to a machine for automatic control (e g of fuel) or limitation of speed **b** a device giving automatic control (e g of pressure or temperature) – **governorate** *n,* **governorship** *n*

**,governor-'general** *n, pl* **governors-general, governor-generals** a governor of high rank; *esp* one representing the Crown in a Commonwealth country – **governor-generalship** *n*

**gowan** /'gowən/ *n, chiefly Scot* OXEYE DAISY; *broadly* any white or yellow meadow flower [prob alter. of ME *gollan*] – **gowany** *adj*

**gowk** /gowk/ *n, dial Scot & NEng* a fool [ME *goke, gowke* cuckoo, fr ON *gaukr*]

**gown** /gown/ *n* **1a** a loose flowing robe worn esp by a professional or academic person when acting in an official capacity **b** a woman's dress, esp one that is elegant or for formal wear **c** an outer garment worn in an operating theatre **2a** an office or profession symbolized by a distinctive robe; *esp the* legal profession **b** the body of students and staff of a college or university, esp of Oxbridge ⟨*riots between town and* ~⟩ [ME, fr MF *goune,* fr LL *gunna,* a fur or leather garment] – **gowned** *adj*

**gownsman** /'gownzmən/ *n* a professional or academic person

**gox** /goks/ *n* gaseous oxygen [gaseous oxygen]

**goy** /goy/ *n, pl* **goyim** /'goyəm, -eem/, **goys,** *chiefly derog* a Gentile – used by Jews [Yiddish, fr Heb *gōy* people, nation] – **goyish** *adj*

**Graafian follicle** /'grahfi·ən/ *n* a small liquid-filled sac or capsule in the ovary of a mammal containing a developing egg [Regnier de *Graaf* †1673 D anatomist]

**¹grab** /grab/ *vb* **-bb-** *vt* **1** to take or seize by a sudden motion or grasp **2** to obtain unscrupulously **3** to take hastily **4** *informal* to forcefully engage the attention of ⟨*he* ~s *an audience*⟩ ~ *vi* to make a grab; snatch [obs D or LG *grabben*; akin to ME *graspen* to grasp, Skt *grbhati* he seizes] – **grabber** *n*

**²grab** *n* **1a** a sudden snatch **b** an unlawful or unscrupulous seizure ⟨*a payroll* ~⟩ **c** something intended to be grabbed – often in combination ⟨*a* grab-rail⟩ **2** a mechanical device for clutching an object; *specif* the jaws of a mechanical excavator – **up for grabs** *informal* available for anyone to take or win

**grab bag** *n, chiefly NAm* **1** LUCKY DIP **2** something resembling a grab bag (e g in providing an assortment of items)

**grabble** /'grabl/ *vi* **1** to search with the hand; grope **2** to sprawl, grovel [D *grabbelen,* fr MD, freq of *grabben*] – **grabbler** *n*

**grabby** /'grabi/ *adj, informal* tending to grab; grasping, greedy

**graben** /'grahb(ə)n/ *n* RIFT VALLEY [Ger, ditch]

**¹grace** /grays/ *n* **1a** unmerited divine assistance given to human beings for their regeneration or sanctification **b** a state of being pleasing to God **c** a virtue coming from God **2** a short prayer at a meal asking a blessing or giving thanks **3a** disposition to or an act or instance of kindness or mercy **b** a special favour; a privilege ⟨*each in his place, by right, not* ~, *shall rule his heritage* – Rudyard Kipling⟩ **c** a temporary exemption; a reprieve ⟨*you have three days'* ~⟩ **d** approval, favour ⟨*stayed in his good* ~s⟩ **4a** a charming trait or accomplishment **b** a pleasingly graceful appearance or effect; a charm **c** ease and suppleness of movement or bearing **5** a musical trill, turn, or APPOGGIATURA (ornamental note) **6** – used as a title of address or reference for a duke, a duchess, or an archbishop **7** consideration, decency ⟨*had the* ~ *to blush*⟩ **8** *archaic* mercy, pardon [ME, fr OF, fr L *gratia* favour, charm, thanks, fr *gratus* pleasing, grateful; akin to OHG *queran* to sigh, Skt *grṇāti* he praises]

²**grace** *vt* 1 to confer dignity or honour on 2 to adorn, embellish

**graceful** /ˈgraysf(ə)l/ *adj* displaying grace in form, action, or movement – **gracefully** *adv*, **gracefulness** *n*

**graceless** /ˈgrayslis/ *adj* 1 lacking in divine grace; immoral, unregenerate 2a lacking a sense of propriety b devoid of elegance; awkward 3 artistically inept or unbeautiful – **gracelessly** *adv*, **gracelessness** *n*

**grace note** *n* a musical note added as an ornament

**Graces** /ˈgraysiz/ *n pl* the three beautiful sister goddesses in Greek mythology who are the givers of charm and beauty

**gracile** /ˈgrasiel/ *adj* 1 slender, slight 2 graceful [L *gracilis*] – **gracileness** *n*, **gracility** *n*

**gracioso** /ˌgrasiˈohsoh/ *n* a buffoon in Spanish comedy [Sp, fr *gracioso*, adj, agreeable, amusing, fr L *gratiosus*]

**gracious** /ˈgrayshəs/ *adj* 1a marked by kindness and courtesy b marked by tact and delicacy c characterized by charm, good taste, and generosity of spirit d having those qualities (e g comfort, elegance, and freedom from hard work) that are made possible by wealth ⟨~ *living*⟩ 2 merciful, compassionate – used conventionally of royalty and high nobility *synonyms* see ²KIND *antonym* ungracious [ME, fr MF *gracieus*, fr L *gratiosus* enjoying favour, agreeable, fr *gratia*] – **graciously** *adv*, **graciousness** *n*

¹**grackle** /ˈgrakl/ *n* any of various Asian starlings [deriv of L *graculus* jackdaw]

²**grackle, grakle** *n* a horse's noseband consisting of a strap running down the centre of the face and forking above the muzzle to form a loop [*Grakle*, Br racehorse (winner of the Grand National in 1931)]

**gradable** *also* **gradeable** /ˈgraydəbl/ *adj* that can be graded; *specif* capable of grammatical comparison or intensification ⟨*beautiful is a ~ adjective, but* atomic *is not*⟩ – **gradability** *n*

**gradate** /grəˈdayt/ *vi* to shade into the next colour, note, or stage ~ *vt* to arrange in a progression, scale, or series [back-formation fr *gradation*]

**gradation** /grəˈdaysh(ə)n/ *n* 1a a series forming successive stages b a step or place in an ordered scale 2 the act or process of grading 3 a gradual passing from one tint or shade to another (e g in a painting) 4 *linguistics* ablaut – **gradational** *adj*, **gradationally** *adv*

¹**grade** /grayd/ *n* 1a(1) a stage in a process a(2) a position in a scale of ranks or qualities b a degree of severity in illness 2a a class of things of the same stage or degree b a mark indicating a degree of accomplishment in school 3 a gradient 4 a domestic animal with one parent purebred and the other of inferior breeding 5 *NAm* 5a a form, class b *pl* the elementary school system ⟨*taught in the ~s for 19 years*⟩ [Fr, fr L *gradus* step, degree; akin to L *gradi* to step, go, Lith *gridyti* to go, wander]

²**grade** *vt* 1a to arrange in grades; sort b to arrange in a scale or series 2 to level off to a smooth horizontal or sloping surface 3 to improve (e g cattle) by breeding females to purebred males – often + *up* 4 *NAm* to assign a mark to ~ *vi* to pass from one grade to another, often by scarcely perceptible degrees

**-grade** /-grayd/ *comb form* (→ *adj*) walking ⟨*planti*grade⟩; moving ⟨*retro*grade⟩ [Fr, fr L *-gradus*, fr *gradi*]

**grade crossing** *n, chiefly NAm* LEVEL CROSSING; *also* any crossing (e g of roads or pavements) on the same level

**gradely** /ˈgraydli/ *adj, dial Eng* proper, fitting; *broadly* excellent [ME *greithly*, *graithly* ready, prompt, excellent, fr ON *greithligr* ready, prompt, fr *greithr* ready, free]

**grader** /ˈgraydə/ *n* 1 one who or that which grades 2 *chiefly NAm* a member of a school grade – usu in combination ⟨*a fifth ~*⟩

**grade school** *n, NAm* PRIMARY 6

**grade separation** *n, NAm* a road or railway crossing using an underpass or flyover

**gradgrind** /ˈgrad,griend/ *n, often cap* an uninspired and relentless seeker of facts who lacks any warm feelings [Thomas *Gradgrind*, a materialistic hardware merchant in the novel *Hard Times* by Charles Dickens †1870 E novelist] – **gradgrind** *adj*

**gradient** /ˈgraydi·ənt, -dyənt/ *n* 1a the degree of slope (e g of a road or railway); inclination b a part (e g of a road or railway) sloping upwards or downwards; an incline 2 change in the value of a quantity with change in a given variable, esp distance ⟨*vertical temperature ~*⟩ 3 a vector function that is equal to the sums of the PARTIAL DERIVATIVES of a function multiplied by their respective UNIT VECTORS and can be used to find the direction at any point in a vector field – compare CURL 6,

DIVERGENCE 4 4 a graded difference in physiological or biochemical activity along a line (e g of the body or an embryo) [L *gradient-, gradiens*, prp of *gradi*]

**gradient post** *n* a post beside a railway that indicates a change of gradient

**gradin** /ˈgraydin/, **gradine** /grəˈdeen/ *n* any of a series of steps or seats arranged in rows on a slope [Fr *gradin*, deriv of L *gradus* step]

**grading** /ˈgrayding/ *n* the relative proportion of particle sizes in concrete mixing

**gradiometer** /ˌgraydiˈomitə/ *n* an instrument for measuring the gradient of a physical quantity (e g the earth's magnetic field) [*gradient* + -o- + -*meter*]

¹**gradual** /ˈgradyoo·əl, ˈgrajoo·əl, ˈgrajəl/ *n* 1 a pair of verses usu from the Psalms that is sung or said after the Epistle in the Mass 2 a book containing the choral parts of the Mass [ML *graduale*, alter. of LL *gradale*, fr L *gradus* step; fr its being sung on the steps of the altar]

²**gradual** *adj* 1 proceeding by steps or degrees 2 moving, changing, or developing by fine, slight, or often imperceptible degrees [ML *gradualis*, fr L *gradus*] – **gradually** *adv*, **gradualness** *n*

**gradualism** /ˈgradyoo·əliz(ə)m, -jooəl-, -jəl-/ *n* the policy of approaching a desired end by gradual stages – **gradualist** *n or adj*

**graduand** /ˈgradyoo,and, -joo-/ *n, Br* one about to graduate; a candidate for a university degree [ML *graduandus*, gerundive of *graduare*]

¹**graduate** /ˈgradyoo·ət, -joo-/ *n* 1 the holder of an academic degree 2 a graduated cup, cylinder, or flask for measuring 3 *chiefly NAm* the holder of a diploma; one who has completed a course of study [ME *graduat*, fr ML *graduatus*, pp of *graduare* to graduate, fr L *gradus*]

²**graduate** *adj* 1 holding an academic degree or diploma ⟨*a ~ secretary*⟩ 2 postgraduate

³**graduate** /ˈgradyoo,ayt, -joo-/ *vt* 1a to mark with degrees of measurement b to divide into grades or intervals 2 *NAm* to grant an academic degree or diploma to 3 *NAm* to admit to a particular standing or grade ~ *vi* 1 to receive an academic degree 2 to pass from one stage of experience, proficiency, or prestige to a usu higher one 3 *NAm* to receive a diploma; complete a course of study – **graduator** *n*

**graduation** /ˌgradyooˈaysh(ə)n, -joo-/ *n* 1 a mark (e g on an instrument or vessel) indicating degrees or quantity 2 the award or acceptance of an academic degree 3 arrangement in degrees or ranks 4 *chiefly NAm* DEGREE DAY

**gradus** /ˈgraydəs/ *n* a simple dictionary of Latin synonyms and exercises in verse composition [*Gradus ad Parnassum* (L, lit., a step to Parnassus), a 17th-c dictionary of prosody formerly used in Br schools]

**Graecism** /ˈgreesiz(ə)m/ *n* 1 a Greek idiom, esp occurring in another language 2 the spirit or style of Greek culture or art; *also* a quality or feature imitative or suggestive of Greek culture or art

**graec·ize, -ise** /ˈgree,siez/ *vt, often cap* to make Greek or Hellenistic in character

**Graeco-, Greco-** *chiefly NAm* /ˈgreekoh-/ *comb form* 1 Greek nation, people, or culture ⟨Graecomania⟩ 2 Greek and ⟨Graeco-Roman⟩ [L *Graeco-*, fr *Graecus* Greek]

**Graeco-Roman** /ˌgreekoh/ *n* a style of wrestling resembling catch-as-catch-can but in which active use of the legs and holds on the legs are disallowed

**Graf** /grahf/, *fem* **Gräfin** /ˈgrayfin/ *n, pl* **Grafen** /ˈgrahfn/ a German, Austrian, or Swedish count – usu used as a title [Ger]

**graffito** /grəˈfeetoh, gra-/ *also* **graffiti** /-ti/ *n, pl* **graffiti** an inscription or drawing, now usu of an obscene or political nature, made on a rock or wall [It, dim. of *graffio* scratch, fr *graffiare* to scratch]

*usage* The plural **graffiti** is now often treated as a singular noun ⟨*this* **graffiti**⟩ but this usage is widely disliked.

¹**graft** /grahft/ *vt* 1a to cause (a plant cutting) to unite with a rooted and established growing plant (STOCK); *also* to unite (plants, or cutting and stock) to form a graft b to propagate (a plant) by grafting 2a to unite closely b to attach (a chemical unit) to a main chain of molecules 3 to implant (living tissue) surgically 4 to get (illicit gain) by graft ~ *vi* 1 to become grafted ⟨*many pears ~ well on quince rootstocks*⟩ 2 to perform grafting 3 to practise graft [ME *graften*, alter. of *graffen*, fr *graffe* graft, fr MF *grafe*, fr ML *graphium*, fr L, stylus, fr Gk *grapheion*, fr *graphein* to write – more at CARVE] – **grafter** *n*

**²graft** *n* **1a** a grafted plant **b** a plant cutting for grafting; SCION 1 **c** the point of insertion of a SCION on a rooted and established plant (STOCK) **2a** the act of grafting **b** something grafted; *specif* living tissue used in grafting **3a** the improper use of one's position (eg public office) to one's private, esp financial, advantage **b** something (eg money or position) acquired by graft

**³graft** *vi, chiefly Br slang* to work hard [E dial. *graft* to dig, alter. of ¹*grave*]

**⁴graft** *n, chiefly Br slang* hard work; *also* a trade, occupation

**graham flour** /'grayəm/ *n, NAm* wholemeal flour [Sylvester *Graham* †1851 US dietary reformer]

**grail** *n* the object of an extended or difficult quest ⟨*money and success, the twin ~s of modern life*⟩ [ME *graal* the cup or platter used (according to medieval legend) by Christ at the Last Supper and later sought for by Knights of the Round Table, fr MF, bowl, grail, fr ML *gradalis*]

**¹grain** /grayn/ *n* **1a** a seed or fruit of a cereal grass; *also* the seeds or fruits collectively of any of various food plants (eg the cereal grasses) **b** plants producing grain **2a(1)** a small hard particle or crystal (eg of sand or salt) **a(2)** a discrete particle in a rock or mineral **b** the least amount possible ⟨*not a ~ of truth in what he said*⟩ **c** fine crystallization (eg of sugar) **3a** (a scarlet dye made from) cochineal or kermes – no longer used technically **b** a fast dye **4a** a granulated surface or appearance in a photograph **b** the outer or hair side of a skin or hide **5** a unit of weight based on the weight of a grain of wheat taken as an average of the weight of grains from the middle of the wheat ear **6a** the arrangement of the fibres in wood **b** the direction or alignment of the constituent particles, fibres, or threads ⟨*the ~ of a rock*⟩ ⟨*the ~ of a fabric*⟩ **7** tactile quality **8a** natural disposition; temper **b** a basic or characteristic quality *synonyms* see ²GRAM [ME; partly fr MF *grain* cereal grain, fr L *granum;* partly fr MF *graine* seed, kermes, fr L *grana,* pl of *granum* – more at CORN] – **grained** *adj* – **against the grain** counter to one's inclination, disposition, or feeling – see also **with a grain of** SALT

**²grain** *vt* **1** to form into grains; granulate **2** to paint in imitation of the grain of wood or stone ~ *vi* to become granular; granulate – **grainer** *n*

**grain alcohol** *n* ALCOHOL 1

**grain elevator** *n* ELEVATOR 1c

**grain rust** *n* a RUST (fungus disease) that attacks a cereal grass

**grains of paradise** *n pl* the pungent seeds of a W African plant (*Aframomum melegueta*) of the ginger family that are used as a spice

**grain whisky** *n* whisky distilled from barley and maize in continuous stills and used chiefly in producing blended whiskies

**grainy** /'grayni/ *adj* **1** consisting of or resembling grains; granular **2** having or resembling the grain of wood **3** *of a photograph* having poor definition because the granules of silver forming the image have clumped together; not sharp – **graininess** *n*

**grakle** /'grakl/ *n* GRACKLE (horse's noseband)

**grallatorial** /,gralə'tawriəl/ *adj* of or belonging to the long-legged wading birds (eg the cranes) [deriv of L *grallator* one who walks on stilts, fr *grallae* stilts, fr *gradi* to go, step]

**¹gralloch** /'graləkh/ *n, Br* **1** the entrails of an animal, esp one (eg a deer) that has been hunted and killed **2** the act of gralloching [ScGael *greallach*]

**²gralloch** *vt, Br* to remove the entrails from (eg a deer), esp after killing in a hunt

**¹gram** /gram/ *n* any of several plants (eg the chick-pea) of the pea family grown esp for their edible seeds; *also* the seed of any of these plants [obs Pg (now *grão*), grain, fr L *granum*]

**²gram, gramme** *n* a metric unit of mass and weight equal to one thousandth of a kilogram (about 0.04 ounce) [Fr *gramme*, fr LL *gramma*, a small weight, fr Gk *grammat-, gramma* letter, writing, a small weight, fr *graphein* to write – more at CARVE] *synonyms* **Gram** or **gramme, grain, drachm,** and **dram** are all small units of weight: a **gram/gramme** is a unit in the metric system, while a **grain** is a smaller unit than a **dram** in the avoirdupois, troy, and apothecaries' systems. An apothecaries' **dram** is more often called a **drachm**.

**-gram** /-gram/ *comb form* (→ *n*) drawing; writing; record ⟨*ideo*gram⟩ ⟨*tele*gram⟩ ⟨*chrono*gram⟩ [L *-gramma*, fr Gk, fr *gramma*]

**gramarye** /'graməri/ *n, archaic* magic [ME, grammar, learning, occult knowledge, fr MF *gramaire* grammar, grammar book, book of sorcery]

**gram atom** *n* the quantity of a chemical element having a weight in grams numerically equal to its ATOMIC WEIGHT

**gram-atomic weight** *n* GRAM ATOM

**gram equivalent** *n* the quantity of a chemical element, chemical group, or compound having a weight in grams numerically equal to its EQUIVALENT WEIGHT

**gramercy** /grə'muhsi/ *interj, archaic* – used to express gratitude [ME *grand mercy,* fr MF *grand merci* great thanks]

**gramicidin** /,grami'siedin/ *n* an antibiotic produced by a soil bacterium (*Bacillus brevis*) and used against GRAM-POSITIVE bacteria in localized infections [*gram*-positive + *-i-* + *-cide* + *-in*]

**gramineous** /grə'mini·əs/ *adj* relating to a grass [L *gramineus,* fr *gramin-, gramen* grass]

**graminivorous** /,grami'nivərəs/ *adj* feeding on grass [L *gramin-, gramen*]

**grammage** /'gramij/ *n* the weight of paper expressed in grams per square metre

**grammalogue** /'gramə,log/ *n* a logogram [Gk *gramma* letter + E *-logue*]

**¹grammar** /'gramə/ *n* **1a** the study of the classes of words, their INFLECTIONS (variable parts), and their functions and relations in the sentence; *broadly* this study when taken to include that of PHONOLOGY (the sound system of a language) and sometimes of usage **b** the study of what is to be preferred and what avoided in inflection and SYNTAX (the construction of sentences and interrelations of their parts) **2** the characteristic system of grammar of a language **3a** a grammar textbook **b** speech or writing evaluated according to its conformity to grammatical rules **4** the principles or rules of an art, science, or technique ⟨*a ~ of the theatre*⟩ [ME *gramere,* fr MF *gramaire,* modif of L *grammatica,* fr Gk *grammatikē,* fr fem of *grammatikos* of letters, fr *grammat-, gramma*] – **grammarian** *n* *synonyms* **Grammar** is the ancient and imprecise name for the study of language, and is today usually taken to include **morphology** and **syntax** but not phonetics or semantics. **Linguistics** is the modern name for language study in the widest sense. **Morphology** deals with the ways in which words are formed, and **syntax** with the ways of putting them together into sentences.

**²grammar** *adj* relating to the type of education provided at a grammar school ⟨*the ~ stream*⟩

**grammar school** *n* **1a** a secondary school that emphasized the study of the classics **b** a British secondary school providing an academic type of education from age 11 to 18 for children selected usu by examination **2** an American school intermediate between primary school and high school **3** *NAm* PRIMARY 6

**grammatical** /grə'matikl/ *adj* **1** relating to grammar **2** conforming to the rules of grammar – **grammatically** *adv,* **grammaticalness** *n,* **grammaticality** *n*

**grammatical meaning** *n* that part of meaning which varies from one inflectional form to another (eg from *plays* to *played* to *playing*) – compare LEXICAL MEANING

**gramme** /gram/ *n* ²GRAM

**gram-molecular weight** *n* the weight in grams of a GRAM MOLECULE of a substance

**gram molecule** *n* the quantity of a chemical compound having a weight in grams numerically equal to its MOLECULAR WEIGHT

**Grammy** /'grami/ *n, pl* **Grammys** a statuette presented annually by a professional organization for notable achievement in the recording industry [*Gramophone* + *-my* (as in *Emmy*)]

**gram-'negative** *adj, of bacteria* not holding the purple dye when stained by GRAM'S METHOD – compare GRAM-POSITIVE

**gramophone** /'graməfohn/ *n* a device for reproducing sounds from the vibrations of a STYLUS (needle) resting in a spiral groove on a rotating disc; *specif, chiefly Br* RECORD PLAYER – no longer in vogue [alter. of *phonogram*]

**gramp** /gramp/, **gramps** /gramps/ *n, pl* **gramps** *informal* a grandfather – used chiefly by or when speaking to children [by shortening & alter. fr *grandpa*]

**gram-'positive** *adj, of bacteria* holding the purple dye when stained by GRAM'S METHOD – compare GRAM-NEGATIVE

**grampus** /'grampəs/ *n* **1** a marine mammal (*Grampus griseus*) of the whale family that is related to the blackfish; *broadly* any of various small whales (eg the killer whale) **2** *informal* one who breathes heavily or noisily [alter. of ME *graspey, grapay,* fr MF *graspeis,* fr *gras* fat (fr L *crassus*) + *peis* fish, fr L *piscis* – more at FISH]

**Gram's method** /gramz/ *n* a staining technique for distinguishing between different types of bacteria, in which the bacteria are stained purple with GENTIAN VIOLET followed by GRAM'S SOLUTION and then treated with a decolorizing agent (e g alcohol), some species retaining the purple dye and others losing it – compare GRAM-POSITIVE, GRAM-NEGATIVE [Hans Gram †1938 Dan physician]

**Gram's solution** n a solution of iodine and potassium iodide in water, used in staining bacteria by Gram's method

**,gram-'variable** adj staining irregularly or inconsistently by GRAM'S METHOD

**gran** /gran/ n, chiefly Br informal a grandmother – used chiefly by or when speaking to children [by shortening]

**grana** /'graynə/ pl of GRANUM

**granadilla** /,granə'dilə/ n the oblong fruit of any of various passionflowers (esp Passiflora quadrangularis of tropical America) used as a dessert [Sp, dim. of granada pomegranate]

**granary** /'granəri/ n **1a** a storehouse for threshed grain **b** a region producing grain in abundance **2** a chief source or storehouse [L granarium, fr granum grain]

**¹grand** /grand/ adj **1a** having more importance than others; foremost **b** having higher rank than others bearing the same general designation ⟨the ~ champion⟩ **c** removed in relationship by two direct stages – in combination ⟨grandfather⟩ **2** complete, comprehensive ⟨the ~ total of all money paid out⟩ **3** main, principal **4** large and striking in size, scope, extent, or conception ⟨a ~ design⟩ **5a** lavish, sumptuous ⟨a ~ celebration⟩ **b** marked by a regal form and dignity; imposing **c** fine or imposing in appearance or impression **d** lofty, sublime ⟨writing in the ~ style⟩ **6a** pretending to social superiority; supercilious ⟨my, aren't we ~!⟩ **b** intended to impress ⟨a man of ~ gestures and pretentious statements⟩ **7** informal very good; wonderful ⟨a ~ time⟩ ⟨a ~ old man⟩ [MF, large, great, grand, fr L grandis] – **grandly** adv, **grandness** n

**synonyms** Grand, magnificent, imposing, stately, majestic, and grandiose all mean "impressive in size, appearance, or theme". Grand and magnificent suggest something large-scale in a physical or aesthetic sense. Grand implies dignity, handsomeness or eminence, and excellence ⟨a grand mansion⟩. Magnificent suggests sumptuousness or superior quality ⟨magnificent state apartments⟩ ⟨magnificent acting⟩. What is imposing impresses by its size, power, bearing, or general magnificence ⟨an imposing town hall⟩ ⟨looked imposing in full regalia⟩. Stately stresses dignity, and usually suggests in addition handsome appearance, or imposing size ⟨stately progress⟩ ⟨a stately galleon⟩. Majestic adds to stately a suggestion of grandeur and solemnity, and is often used for intangible things ⟨majestic music for the procession⟩. Grandiose implies a larger-than-life grandeur which impresses ⟨things painted by a Rubens ... more grandiose than the life – Robert Browning⟩. But it frequently suggests delusions of grandeur, resulting in pretentiousness and pomposity.

**²grand** n **1** informal GRAND PIANO **2** slang **2a** Br a thousand pounds **b** NAm a thousand dollars

**grandam** /'grandam, -dəm/, **grandame** /-daym, -dəm/ n, archaic **1** a grandmother **2** an old woman [ME graundam, fr AF graund dame, lit., great lady]

**grandaunt** /-'ahnt/ n a great-aunt

**grandchild** /'gran,chield/ n the child of one's son or daughter

**granddad, grandad** /'gran,dad/ n, informal a grandfather

**granddaddy** also **grandaddy** /'gran,dadi/ n, informal **1** a grandfather **2** something that is the first, earliest, most ancient, or most venerable of its kind

**granddaughter** /'gran,dawtə/ n the daughter of one's son or daughter

**grand duchess** n **1** the wife or widow of a grand duke **2** a woman having in her own right the rank of a grand duke

**grand duchy** n the territory of a grand duke or grand duchess

**grand duke** n **1** the sovereign ruler of any of various European states **2** a son or male descendant of a Russian tsar in the male line

**grande dame** /,grond 'dahm (Fr grād dam)/ n a usu elderly woman of high rank or extremely dignified or imposing manner [Fr, lit., great lady]

**grandee** /gran'dee/ n a Spanish or Portuguese nobleman of the highest rank [Sp grande, fr grande, adj, large, great, fr L grandis]

**grandeur** /'granjə, -dyə/ n **1** the quality of being large or impressive; magnificence ⟨the glory that was Greece and the ~ that was Rome – E A Poe⟩ **2** personal greatness marked by nobility, dignity, or power [ME, fr MF, fr grand]

**grandfather** /'gran(d),fahdhə/ n the father of one's father or mother; broadly a male ancestor – **grandfatherly** adj

**grandfather clause** n a provision that existed in the constitutions of several southern states of the USA until held void in 1915, and that was designed to give to poor whites but deny to blacks the right to vote by dispensing with high qualifying requirements for the descendants of men voting before 1867

**grandfather clock** n LONG-CASE CLOCK – not used technically [fr the song My Grandfather's Clock by Henry C Work †1884 US songwriter]

**Grand Guignol** /,grong gee'nyol (Fr grā giɲɔl)/ n a dramatic entertainment featuring the gruesome or horrible [Le Grand Guignol, small theatre in Paris specializing in such plays] – **Grand Guignol** adj

**grandiloquence** /gran'diləkwəns/ n high-sounding or pompously eloquent speech or writing; bombast [prob fr MF, fr L grandiloquus using lofty language, fr grandis + loqui to speak] – **grandiloquent** adj, **grandiloquently** adv

**grandiose** /'grandiohs, -ohz/ adj **1** impressive because of uncommon largeness, scope, effect, or grandeur **2** characterized by a pretended grandeur or splendour or by absurd exaggeration synonyms see ¹GRAND [Fr, fr It grandioso, fr grande great, fr L grandis] – **grandiosely** adv, **grandioseness** n, **grandiosity** n

**grandioso** /,grandi'ohsoh/ adv or adj in a broad and noble style – used as a direction in music [It]

**grand jury** n a jury in the USA that examines accusations against people charged with crime and if the evidence warrants makes formal charges on which the accused are later tried

**Grand Lama** n DALAI LAMA

**grand larceny** n LARCENY (theft) of property of a value greater than a sum specified by US law – compare PETTY LARCENY

**grandma** /'gran,mah, 'gram,mah/ n, informal a grandmother

**grand mal** /,gronh'mal (Fr grā mal)/ n severe epilepsy characterized by convulsions affecting the whole body; also a severe epileptic fit – compare PETIT MAL [Fr, lit., great illness]

**Grand Marnier** /,grom 'mahnyay (Fr grā marnje)/ trademark – used for a liqueur made from a brandy base flavoured with orange

**grand master** n **1** a chess player who has consistently scored higher than a standardized score in international competition **2** cap G&M the head of a religious order of knighthood (e g the Templars), a friendly society, or the Freemasons

**grandmother** /'gran,mudhə, 'grand-, 'gram-/ n the mother of one's father or mother; broadly a female ancestor – **grandmotherly** adj

**grandmother clock** n a LONG-CASE CLOCK that is about two thirds the size of a grandfather clock – not used technically

**Grand National** n the major British STEEPLECHASE (an obstacle race) for horses that is run annually over a course of 4 miles 856 yards (about 7.2 kilometres) at Aintree

**grandnephew** /'grand,nefyooh/ n a great-nephew

**grandniece** /-,nees/ n a great-niece

**grand opera** n opera with usu a serious dramatic plot and no spoken dialogue

**grandpa** /'gran,pah, 'gram-/ n, informal a grandfather

**grandparent** /'gran(d),peərənt/ n the parent of one's father or mother – **grandparental** adj, **grandparenthood** n

**Grand Penitentiary** n PENITENTIARY 1b

**grand piano** n a piano with horizontal frame and strings – compare ³UPRIGHT 3

**grand prix** /,gronh 'pree (Fr grā pri)/ n, pl grand prix often cap G&P a long-distance motor vehicle race usu over a road course; specif any of a series of international FORMULA (conforming to specifications laid down by rules) car races [Fr Grand Prix de Paris, an international horse race established in 1863, lit., grand prize of Paris]

**grandsire** /'gran(d),sie-ə/ also **grandsir** /-,suh/ n, archaic **1** a grandfather **2** a forefather **3** an old man

**grand slam** n **1** (the fulfilling of) a contract to win all the tricks in one hand of a card game, specif bridge **2** a clean sweep or total success; specif the winning of all the major tournaments in a year in a usu specified sport ⟨he twice did the tennis ~⟩

**grandson** /'gran(d),sun/ n the son of one's son or daughter

**¹grandstand** /-,stand/ n **1** a usu roofed stand for spectators at a racecourse, stadium, etc in an advantageous position for viewing the play or race **2** taking sing or pl vb an audience

**²grandstand** vi, NAm informal to play or act so as to impress onlookers – **grandstander** n

**grandstanding** /'grand,standing/ n, Austr ostentatious behaviour calculated to win political support

**grand tour** n **1** an extended tour of the Continent that was formerly a usual part of the education of young British gentlemen 2 an extensive and usu educational tour

**granduncle** /-,ungkl/ *n* a great-uncle

**grange** /graynj/ *n* 1 a farm; *esp* a farmhouse with outbuildings 2 an outlying farm where a religious order or feudal lord stored crops in the late Middle Ages 3 *archaic* a granary, barn [ME, fr MF, fr ML *granica*, fr L *granum* grain]

**granger·ize, -ise** /'graynjəriez/ *vt* to illustrate by inserting engravings or photographs collected from other books; *also* to mutilate (books) to obtain material for such illustrations [James *Granger* †1776 E biographer whose *Biographical History of England* contained blank leaves on which illustrations could be added] – **grangerism** *n*, **grangerizer** *n*

**grani-** *comb form* grain; seeds ⟨gran*ivorous*⟩ [L, fr *granum*]

**granita** /grə'neetə/ *n* a coarse-grained water ice [It, fr fem of *granito*, pp]

**granite** /'granit/ *n* 1 a very hard coarse-grained typically pink, white, or grey IGNEOUS rock formed by the solidification of molten material below the earth's surface, that is composed essentially of quartz and feldspar and is used esp for building 2 unyielding firmness or endurance [It *granito*, fr pp of *granire* to granulate, fr *grano* grain, fr L *granum*] – **granitelike** *adj*, **granitoid** *adj*, **granitic** *adj*

**graniteware** /-,weə/ *n* ironware with mottled enamel usu in two tones of grey; *also* pottery with a speckled granitelike appearance

**granivorous** /gra'nivərəs/ *adj* feeding on seeds or grain

[1]**granny, grannie** /'grani/ *n, informal* a grandmother [by shortening & alter.]

[2]**granny** *adj, informal* designed for use by an older person ⟨~ *flat*⟩ ⟨~ *cottage*⟩

**granny bond** *n* a savings bond, available originally only to those over a certain age, which is guaranteed to maintain its value in line with the rate of inflation

**granny knot** *n* a REEF KNOT crossed the wrong way and therefore insecure

**Granny Smith** /smith/ *n* a large green variety of apple which can be cooked or eaten raw [Maria Ann ("Granny") *Smith* †1870 Austr gardener]

**granny specs** *n pl* glasses with small circular lenses and metal frames

**grano-** *comb form* granite; resembling granite ⟨grano*phyre*⟩ [Ger, fr *granit*, fr It *granito*]

**granodiorite** /,granoh'die·ə,riet/ *n* a coarse-grained grey IGNEOUS rock (one formed by cooling and solidification of molten material) intermediate in composition between granite and DIORITE – **granodioritic** *adj*

**granolith** /'granəlith/ *n* an artificial stone of crushed granite and cement – **granolithic** *adj*

**granophyre** /'granoh,fie·ə/ *n* an IGNEOUS rock (one formed by cooling and solidification of molten material) composed chiefly of feldspar and quartz crystals embedded in a granular matrix of the same minerals [ISV] – **granophyric** *adj*

[1]**grant** /grahnt/ *vt* **1a** to consent to carry out or fulfil (e g a wish or request) ⟨~ *a child his wish*⟩ **b** to permit as a right, privilege, or favour ⟨*luggage allowances* ~ed *to passengers*⟩ **2** to bestow or transfer formally ⟨~ *a scholarship to a student*⟩; *specif* to give the possession or title of by a deed **3a** to be willing to concede **b** to assume to be true ⟨~ ing *that you are correct, you may find it hard to prove your point*⟩ – see also TAKE **for granted** *synonyms* see [1]GIVE *antonym* withhold [ME *granten*, fr OF *creanter, graanter*, fr (assumed) VL *credentare*, fr L *credent-, credens*, prp of *credere* to believe – more at CREED] – **grantable** *adj*, **granter** *n*, **grantor** *n, law*

[2]**grant** *n* **1** the act of granting **2** something granted; *esp* a gift for a particular purpose (e g for a student's university fees and maintenance) **3a** a transfer of property by deed or writing **b** the document by which such a transfer is made; *also* the property so transferred

**grant-aided school** *n* AIDED SCHOOL

**grant-in-'aid** *n, pl* **grants-in-aid** **1** a grant or subsidy paid by a central to a local government in aid of a public undertaking **2** a grant to a school or individual for an educational or artistic project

**granul-** /granyool-/, **granuli-, granulo-** *comb form* granule ⟨granu*lose*⟩ [LL *granulum*]

**granular** /'granyoolə/ *adj* consisting of or appearing to consist of granules; having a grainy texture – **granularly** *adv*, **granularity** *n*

**granulate** /'granyoo,layt/ *vt* to form or crystallize into grains

or granules ⟨~d *sugar*⟩ ~ *vi* **1** to collect into grains or granules **2** *esp of a wound* to form GRANULATION TISSUE while beginning to heal ⟨*an open* granulating *wound*⟩ – **granulator** *n*, **granulative** *adj*

**granulation** /,granyoo'laysh(ə)n/ *n* **1** the act or process of granulating; the condition of being granulated **2a** the formation of GRANULATION TISSUE on the surface of a wound **b** an area or mass of GRANULATION TISSUE **3** GRANULE 2

**granulation tissue** *n* tissue made up largely of new CAPILLARIES (thin-walled blood vessels) that forms on the surface of and temporarily replaces lost tissue in a wound undergoing healing

**granule** /'granyoohl/ *n* **1** a small grain; *esp* any of numerous particles forming a larger unit **2** any of the small short-lived spots that give a mottled appearance to the sun's surface (PHOTOSPHERE) [LL *granulum*, dim. of L *granum* grain]

**granulite** /'granyoo,liet/ *n* a banded or layered whitish granular rock consisting of feldspar, quartz, and small red garnets – **granulitic** *adj*

**granulocyte** /'granyoolə,siet/ *n* any of various WHITE BLOOD CELLS that engulf and destroy foreign matter in the body and have CYTOPLASM (jellylike material outside the nucleus) containing large numbers of conspicuous stainable granules and a nucleus with many lobes – compare AGRANULOCYTE, BASOPHIL, EOSINOPHIL, NEUTROPHIL [ISV] – **granulocytic** *adj*

**granuloma** /,granyoo'lohmə/ *n, pl* **granulomas, granulomata** /-mətə/ a mass or lump of inflamed GRANULATION TISSUE [NL] – **granulomatous** *adj*

**granuloma inguinale** /,ing·gwi'nahli, -'nayli/ *n* a venereal disease characterized by the formation of ulcers beginning in the groin and spreading to the buttocks and genitals and caused by a bacterium (*Donovania granulomatis*) [NL, lit., inguinal granuloma]

**granuloma venereum** /və'niəriəm/ *n* GRANULOMA INGUINALE [NL, lit., venereal granuloma]

**granulose** /'granyoolohs, -lohz/ *adj* granular – **granulosity** *n*

**granulosis** /,granyoo'lohsis/ *n, pl* **granuloses** /-seez/ a virus disease of insect larvae distinguished by the presence of minute granular particles in infected cells [NL]

**granum** /'graynəm/ *n, pl* **grana** /-nə/ any of the stacks of disc-like layers of chlorophyll-containing material in plant CHLOROPLASTS (cell structures in which photosynthesis occurs) [NL, fr L, grain]

**grape** /grayp/ *n* **1** a smooth-skinned juicy greenish-white to deep red or purple berry eaten dried or fresh as a fruit or fermented to produce wine; *also* any of numerous woody vines (genus *Vitis* of the family Vitaceae, the grape family) that usu climb by tendrils, bear grapes in clusters, and are widely cultivated **2** grapeshot [ME, fr OF *crape, grape* hook, grape stalk, bunch of grapes, grape, of Gmc origin; akin to OHG *krāpfo* hook – more at CRAVE]

**grapefruit** /-,frooht/ *n* a large round citrus fruit with a bitter yellow rind and a juicy highly flavoured somewhat bitter and acidic pulp; *also* the small tree (*Citrus paradisi*) that bears grapefruits [fr its growing in clusters]

**grape hyacinth** *n* any of several small spring-flowering plants (genus *Muscari*) of the lily family that grow from bulbs and have clusters of usu blue flowers

**grapeshot** /-,shot/ *n* a cluster of small iron balls used as a cannon charge

**grape sugar** *n* DEXTROSE (kind of glucose)

**grapevine** /-,vien/ *n* **1** a vine that bears grapes **2** a secret or unofficial means of circulating information or gossip ⟨*heard about the meeting through the* ~⟩

[1]**graph** /grahf, graf/ *n* **1** a diagram (e g a series of points, a line, a curve, or an area) expressing a relation between quantities or variables, usu having two (or more) straight lines (AXES) with reference to which points or lines are located on the diagram **2** the collection of all points whose COORDINATES (numbers which specify the location of a point) satisfy a given relation (e g the equation of a mathematical function) [short for *graphic formula*]

[2]**graph** *vt* **1** to represent by a graph **2** to plot on a graph

[3]**graph** *n* **1** a symbol or spelling of a linguistic form **2** a single occurrence of a grapheme; a member of a grapheme ⟨f *and* ph *are* ~ s *of the same grapheme*⟩ [prob fr *-graph*]

**-graph** /-,grahf, -,graf/ *comb form* (→ *n*) **1** something written or represented ⟨*mono*graph⟩ ⟨*picto*graph⟩ **2** instrument for recording or transmitting (something specified or by a specified means) ⟨*seismo*graph⟩ ⟨*tele*graph⟩ [(1) MF *-graphe*, fr L

-graphum, fr Gk -graphon, fr neut of -graphos written, fr graphein to write; (2) Fr -graphe, fr LL graphus]

**grapheme** /'grafeem/ n the set of units of a writing system that represent the same sound (PHONEME) ⟨the f of fin, the ph of phantom, and the gh of laugh are members of one ∼⟩ – **graphemic** adj, **graphemically** adv

**graphemics** /gra'feemiks/ n taking sing or pl vb the study and analysis of a writing system in terms of graphemes

¹**graphic** /'grafik/ also **graphical** adj 1 formed by writing, drawing, or engraving 2 marked by clear and vivid description; sharply outlined or depicted 3a relating to the pictorial arts b relating to or involving such reproductive methods as engraving, etching, LITHOGRAPHY (method of printing), photography, silk screen printing, and woodcut c relating to the art of printing d relating to or according to graphics 4 of a rock having crystals arranged so as to resemble written or printed characters ⟨∼ granite⟩ 5 relating to or represented by a graph 6 relating to writing or to symbols that convey meaning [L graphicus, fr Gk graphikos, fr graphein] – **graphically** adv, **graphicness** n

²**graphic** n 1 a product of graphic art 2 a picture, map, or graph used for illustration or demonstration 3 a graphic representation displayed by a computer (eg on a VDU screen)

-**graphic** /-'grafik/, -**graphical** comb form (→ adj) 1 written, represented, or transmitted in (such) a way ⟨stylographic⟩ ⟨ideographic⟩ 2 relating to writing on a (specified) subject ⟨autobiographic⟩ [LL -graphicus, fr Gk -graphikos, fr graphikos]

**graphic arts** n pl the fine and applied arts of representation, decoration, and writing or printing on flat surfaces and the techniques and crafts associated with them

**graphics** /'grafiks/ n taking sing or pl vb 1a the art or science of drawing an object on a two-dimensional surface according to mathematical rules of projection b GRAPHIC ARTS c the art or technique of making designs (eg advertising posters and book jackets) containing pictorial or decorative elements as well as letters or numbers 2 the study, research, practice, etc of displaying graphics on VDU screens or computer printouts

**graphite** /'grafiet/ n a soft black lustrous form of carbon that conducts electricity and is used esp in lead pencils, in crucibles, as a lubricant, and to slow down neutrons in atomic-energy plants [Ger graphit, fr Gk graphein to write; fr its use in pencils] – **graphitic** adj

**graphit·ize, -ise** /'grafitiez/ vt 1 to convert into graphite 2 to impregnate or coat with graphite – **graphitization** n

**grapho-** comb form writing ⟨graphologist⟩ [Fr, fr MF, fr Gk, fr graphē, fr graphein to write]

**graphology** /gra'foləji/ n the study of handwriting, esp for the purpose of character analysis [Fr graphologie, fr grapho- + -logie -logy] – **graphologist** n, **graphological** adj

**graph paper** n paper ruled for drawing graphs

-**graphy** /-grəfi/ comb form (→ n) 1 writing or representation in (such) a manner or on (a specified subject) or by (a specified means) ⟨photography⟩ ⟨calligraphy⟩ ⟨biography⟩ 2 art or science of ⟨organography⟩ ⟨choreography⟩ [L -graphia, fr Gk, fr graphein] – **graphic** comb form (→ n)

**grapnel** /'grapnəl/ n 1 an instrument with several iron claws that is hurled with a line attached in order to hook on to something (eg an enemy ship before boarding, or the top of a wall) 2 a small anchor with several hooks or claws set round the shank, used for anchoring small boats; also any similar device used for grappling or dragging [ME grapenel, fr (assumed) MF grapinel, dim. of grapin, dim. of grape hook – more at GRAPE]

**grappa** /'grapə/ n an Italian spirit distilled from the fermented remains of grapes after the juice has been extracted for making wine [It]

¹**grapple** /'grapl/ n 1 a grapnel 2a the act or an instance of grappling b a hand-to-hand struggle c a contest for superiority or mastery [MF grappelle, dim. of grape hook]

²**grapple** vt 1 to seize (as if) with a grapnel 2 to come to grips with; wrestle 3 to bind closely ∼ vi 1 to make a ship fast with a grapnel 2a to come to grips with; wrestle b to attempt to deal with; cope 3 to use a grapnel – **grappler** n

**grappling iron** /'grapling/ n a grapnel

**graptolite** /'graptə,liet/ n any of numerous extinct animals (group Graptolitoidea) of the Palaeozoic era that lived as floating colonies encased in a horny skeleton and are commonly found as fossils [Gk graptos written, painted (fr graphein to write, paint) + E -lite; fr some forms resembling quill pens or written markings]

**grapy** /'graypi/ adj 1 relating to grapes or the vine that bears them 2 of wine having a grape taste as well as a wine taste

¹**grasp** /grahsp/ vi to make the motion of seizing; clutch ∼ vt 1 to take or seize eagerly 2 to clasp or embrace (as if) with the fingers or arms 3 to succeed in understanding; comprehend – see also grasp the NETTLE [ME graspen – more at GRAB] – **graspable** adj, **grasper** n

²**grasp** n 1a something (eg a handle) intended for grasping b the act or an instance of grasping; a firm hold 2 control, power ⟨he is in her ∼⟩ 3a the reach of the arms b the power of seizing and holding or attaining ⟨success was just beyond his ∼⟩ 4 comprehension ⟨showed a firm ∼ of her subject⟩

**grasping** /'grahsping/ adj eager for material possessions, often to the point of ruthlessness; rapacious, avaricious – **graspingly** adv, **graspingness** n

¹**grass** /grahs/ n 1a herbage suitable or used for grazing animals b pasture, grazing ⟨horses turned out to ∼⟩ 2 any of a large family (Gramineae, the grass family) of MONOCOTYLE-DONOUS mostly nonwoody plants with jointed stems sheathed by slender leaves and inconspicuous flowers in small spikes 3 land on which grass is grown; esp a lawn ⟨keep off the ∼⟩ 4 pl grass leaves or plants 5 slang cannabis; specif marijuana 6 Br slang a police informer [ME gras, fr OE græs; akin to OHG gras grass, OE grōwan to grow; (6) rhyming slang grass(hopper) copper (policeman)] – **grassless** adj, **grasslike** adj – **put/send out to grass** to cause (somebody) to enter usu enforced retirement ⟨an old politician put out to grass⟩

²**grass** vt 1 to feed (livestock) on grass, sometimes without grain or other concentrates 2 to cover with grass; esp to seed with grass – often + down ⟨∼ed down the newly cleared land⟩ ∼ vi 1 to produce grass 2 Br slang to inform, esp to the police – usu + on ⟨after ∼ing on his fellow criminals in order to get off himself – Private Eye⟩

**grass box** n a container attached to a lawn mower to receive the cut grass

**grass carp** n a plant-eating fish (Ctenopharyngodon idella) of Russia and China that has been introduced elsewhere to control waterweeds

**grass court** n a tennis court whose surface is grass

**grasshopper** /-,hopə/ n any of numerous plant-eating insects (order Saltoria or Orthoptera) that have the hind legs adapted for leaping – compare LOCUST

**grassie** /'grahsi/ n, Austr informal a grasshopper

**grassland** /-lənd, -,land/ n 1 farmland used for grazing 2 land on which the natural dominant plant forms are grasses

**grass of Parnassus** /pah'nasəs/ n any of a genus (Parnassia of the family Parnassiaceae) of low-growing flowering plants; esp a Eurasian plant (Parnassia palustris) with single small whitish flowers that grows in marshy areas [Parnassus, mountain in Greece]

**grass roots** n taking sing or pl vb 1 society at the local level as distinguished from the centres of political leadership ⟨widespread opposition to the plan at the ∼⟩ 2 the fundamental level or source – **grass-roots** adj

**grass skirt** n a skirt made of long grass and leaves attached to a waistband, worn by some Polynesian islanders

**grass snake** n a harmless nonpoisonous snake (Natrix natrix) that is widely distributed in Europe and has two yellow or orange patches forming a collar behind the head

**grass tip** n a thin half-length shoe for a horse at grass

**grass tree** n any of a genus (Xanthorrhoea) of Australian plants of the lily family with a thick woody trunk bearing a cluster of stiff leaves resembling grass-blades and a spike of small flowers; also any of several Australasian trees (eg a ti) having grasslike leaves – called also BLACK BOY

**grass widow**, masc **grass widower** n, often humorous a person whose spouse is temporarily away [orig sense, unmarried mother; perh referring to a bed of grass used for extramarital sex]

**grassy** /'grahsi/ adj 1a covered with or abounding with grass ⟨∼ lawns⟩ b consisting of or having a smell of grass 2 resembling grass, esp in colour

**grat** /grat/ past of ²GREET

¹**grate** /grayt/ n 1 a frame or bed of metal, esp iron, bars to hold the fuel in a fireplace, stove, or furnace 2 a fireplace [ME, fr ML crata, grata hurdle, modif of L cratis – more at HURDLE]

²**grate** vt 1 to reduce to small particles by rubbing on something rough ⟨∼ cheese⟩ 2a to gnash or grind noisily b to cause to make a rasping sound c to utter in a harsh voice 3 archaic

to abrade ~ *vi* **1** to rub or rasp noisily **2** to cause irritation; jar ⟨*his manner of talking* ~s *on my nerves*⟩ [ME *graten*, fr MF *grater* to scratch, of Gmc origin; akin to OHG *krazzōn* to scratch] – **grater** *n*

**grateful** /'graytf(ə)l/ *adj* **1a** appreciative of benefits received **b** expressing gratitude **2** affording pleasure or comfort; pleasing ⟨~ *warmth*⟩ [obs *grate* pleasing, thankful, fr L *gratus* – more at GRACE] – **gratefully** *adv,* **gratefulness** *n*

**graticule** /'gratikyoohl/ *n* **1** a usu rectangular network or scale visible when using a telescope, microscope, etc and used in locating or measuring objects **2** the network of imaginary lines of latitude and longitude on a map [Fr, fr L *craticula* fine latticework, dim. of *cratis*]

**gratification** /,gratifi'kaysh(ə)n/ *n* **1** the act of gratifying; the state of being gratified **2** a source of satisfaction or pleasure **3** *archaic* a reward, recompense; *esp* a gratuity

**gratify** /'grati,fie/ *vt* **1** to give pleasure or satisfaction to **2** to give in to; indulge, satisfy ⟨~ *a whim*⟩ **3** *archaic* to remunerate [MF *gratifier*, fr L *gratificari*, lit., to make oneself pleasing, fr *gratus* + *-ificari*, passive of *-ificare* -ify]

**gratifying** /'grati,fie·ing/ *adj* giving pleasure, esp through satisfying a craving – **gratifyingly** *adv*

**gratin** /'gratanh (*Fr* gratẽ)/ *n* a brown crust formed on food that has been cooked with a topping of breadcrumbs or grated cheese [Fr, fr MF, fr *grater* to scratch, grate]

**grating** /'grayting/ *n* **1** a partition, covering, or frame of parallel bars or crossbars **2** a wooden or metal lattice used to close any of various openings **3** a set of close equally spaced parallel lines or bars ruled on a polished surface that is used to separate a beam of light or other radiation into its constituent frequencies by DIFFRACTION

**gratis** /'gratis, 'grah-, 'gray-/ *adv or adj* without any kind of charge; free [ME, fr L *gratiis, gratis,* fr abl pl of *gratia* favour – more at GRACE]

**gratitude** /'grati,tyoohd/ *n* the state or feeling of being grateful; thankfulness [ME, fr MF or ML; MF, fr ML *gratitudo,* fr L *gratus* grateful]

**gratuitous** /grə'tyooh·itəs/ *adj* **1a** costing nothing; free **b** not involving a return benefit or compensation **2** not called for by the circumstances; unwarranted, superfluous ⟨~ *insolence*⟩ ⟨*the film contained scenes of* ~ *violence*⟩ [L *gratuitus,* fr *gratus*] – **gratuitously** *adv,* **gratuitousness** *n*

**gratuity** /grə'tyooh·əti/ *n* something given voluntarily, usu in return for or in anticipation of some service; *esp* a tip

**gratulate** /'gratyoolayt/ *vt, archaic* to congratulate [L *gratulatus,* pp of *gratulari,* fr *gratus*] – **gratulatory** *adj,* **gratulation** *n*

**graupel** /'growpl/ *n* granular snow pellets – called also SOFT HAIL [Ger, dim. of *graupe* peeled grain]

**gravamen** /grə'vaymen, -mən/ *n, pl* **gravamens, gravamina** the material or significant part of a grievance or complaint [LL, burden, fr L *gravare* to burden, fr *gravis*]

¹**grave** /grayv/ *vt* **graven** /'grayv(ə)n/, **graved 1** to impress or fix (eg a thought) deeply **2** *archaic* to carve, engrave [ME *graven* to dig, bury, engrave, fr OE *grafan*; akin to OHG *graban* to dig, OSlav po*greti* to bury]

²**grave** /grayv/ *n* a pit dug in the ground for burial of a body; *broadly* a burial place, tomb [ME, fr OE *græf*; akin to OHG *grab* grave, OE *grafan* to dig] – **graveless** *adj* – **make somebody turn in his/her grave** to cause (a person now dead) severe annoyance or worry were he/she still alive

³**grave** /grayv/ *vt* to clean by burning and then coat with tar (the bottom of a wooden ship) [ME *graven*]

⁴**grave** /grayv/ *adj* **1a** requiring serious consideration; important ⟨~ *problems*⟩ **b** likely to produce great harm or danger ⟨*a* ~ *mistake*⟩ **2** having a serious and dignified quality or demeanour ⟨*a* ~ *man little given to laughter*⟩ **3** drab in colour; sombre **4** *of a sound* low in pitch *synonyms* see SERIOUS *antonym* merry [MF, fr L *gravis* heavy, grave – more at GRIEVE] – **gravely** *adv,* **graveness** *n*

⁵**grave** /grahv/ *adj or n* (being or marked with) an accent used to show that a vowel is pronounced with a fall of pitch (eg in ancient Greek), that a vowel has a certain quality (eg *e* in French), or that the *e* of the English ending *-ed* is to be pronounced (eg in "this cursèd day")

⁶**grave** /'grahvi/ *adv or adj* slowly and solemnly – used as a direction in music [It, lit., grave, fr L *gravis*]

**graveclothes** /'grayv,klohdhz/ *n* the clothes in which a dead person is buried

**gravedigger** /'grayv,digə/ *n* **1** one who digs graves **2** one responsible for the end of something

¹**gravel** /'gravl/ *n* **1a** loose rounded fragments of rock usu mixed with sand **b** a layer or deposit of gravel; *also* a surface covered with gravel ⟨*a* ~ *road*⟩ **2** a sandy deposit of tiny stones formed in the kidneys or bladder **3** *obs* sand [ME, fr MF *gravele,* fr OF, dim. of *grave, greve* pebbly ground, beach]

²**gravel** *adj* GRAVELLY 2

³**gravel** *vt* **-ll-** (*NAm* **-l-, -ll-**) **1** to cover or spread with gravel **2a** to puzzle, confound **b** *chiefly NAm* to irritate, nettle [(2) orig referring to a ship run aground on a beach]

¹**gravel-,blind** *adj* having very weak eyesight [suggested by *sand-blind*]

**gravelly** /'gravl·i/ *adj* **1** of, containing, or covered with gravel **2** having a deep harsh grating sound ⟨*a* ~ *voice*⟩

**graven image** /'grayv(ə)n/ *n* an object of worship carved usu from wood or stone; an idol

**graver** /'grayvə/ *n* **1** a sculptor, engraver **2** any of various tools (eg a BURIN) used in engraving or in hand metal-turning

**Graves** /grahv/ *n, pl* **Graves** a dry white or occasionally red table wine produced in the Graves district of Bordeaux in France

**Graves' disease** /grayvz/ *n* HYPERTHYROIDISM (overactivity of the thyroid gland); *specif* hyperthyroidism accompanied by bulging eyes (EXOPHTHALMOS) and enlargement of the thyroid [Robert *Graves* †1853 Ir physician]

**gravestone** /-,stohn/ *n* a stone over a grave, usu inscribed with the name and details of the dead person

**Gravettian** /grə'vetiən/ *adj* (characteristic) of a late PALAEOLITHIC culture of Europe characterized by stone knives with one sharp and one blunt edge [La *Gravette,* site in SW France where remains were found]

**graveyard** /-,yahd/ *n* **1** a cemetery **2** a place characterized by disused, obsolete, or worn-out things ⟨*we dumped our car on the common which had become the local* ~⟩

**gravi-** /gravi-/ *comb form* weight; gravity ⟨gravi*meter*⟩ [MF, fr L, fr *gravis*]

**gravid** /'gravid/ *adj* **1** pregnant **2** full of eggs ⟨*a* ~ *tapeworm proglottid*⟩ □ used technically [L *gravidus,* fr *gravis* heavy] – **gravidly** *adv,* **gravidness** *n,* **gravidity** *n*

**gravida** /'gravidə/ *n, pl* **gravidas, gravidae** /-die/ a pregnant woman – often in combination with a number or figure to indicate the number of pregnancies a woman has had ⟨*a* 4-gravida⟩ [L, fr fem of *gravidus*]

**gravimeter** /grə'vimitə, 'gravi,meetə/ *n* **1** a device similar to a HYDROMETER for determining RELATIVE DENSITY (measure of the density of a substance compared with that of a standard) **2** a sensitive weighing instrument for measuring variations in the GRAVITATIONAL FIELD of the earth or moon [Fr *gravimètre,* fr *gravi-* + *-mètre* -meter]

**gravimetric** /,gravi'metrik/ *also* **gravimetrical** /-kl/ *adj* **1** of or using measurement by weight – compare VOLUMETRIC **2** of variations in the GRAVITATIONAL FIELD as measured by a gravimeter – **gravimetrically** *adv*

**gravimetry** /grə'vimətri/ *n* the measurement of weight, a GRAVITATIONAL FIELD, or density

**graving dock** /'grayving/ *n* DRY DOCK

**gravitas** /'gravitas/ *n, formal* a solemn and serious quality or manner [L, lit., heaviness, fr *gravis*]

**gravitate** /'gravitayt/ *vi* **1** to move under the influence of gravitation **2a** to move towards something **b** to become attracted *to* or *towards*; be drawn ~ *vt, physics* to move by gravitation [NL *gravitatus,* pp of *gravitare,* fr *gravitas* gravity]

**gravitation** /,gravi'taysh(ə)n/ *n* **1** a natural force of mutual attraction between bodies or particles determined by their respective masses and the distance between them **2** the action or process of gravitating – **gravitational** *adj,* **gravitationally** *adv,* **gravitative** *adj*

**gravitational field** /,gravi'taysh(ə)nl/ *n* a property of the region of space surrounding a body (eg a planet) that exerts a force of attraction on nearby bodies ⟨*the rocket entered the* ~ *of Saturn*⟩

**gravitational wave** /,gravi'taysh(ə)nl/ *n* a hypothetical pulsation (²WAVE 7a) which travels at the speed of light and by means of which gravitational attraction is effected

**graviton** /'graviton/ *n* a hypothetical ELEMENTARY PARTICLE (minute particle of matter) with zero electric charge and no mass, that is held to be responsible for gravitational interactions [ISV *gravity* + ²*-on*]

**gravity** /'gravəti/ *n* **1a** dignity or sobriety of bearing or manner **b** importance, significance; *esp* seriousness ⟨*he couldn't comprehend the* ~ *of the situation*⟩ **2** the quality of having weight

3 WEIGHT 1a **4a** the gravitational attraction of the mass of a celestial body (e g the earth) for bodies at or near its surface – compare GRAVITATIONAL FIELD **b** gravitation [MF or L; MF *gravité,* fr L *gravitat-, gravitas,* fr *gravis;* (4) NL *gravitas,* fr L] – **gravity** *adj*

**gravity feed** *n* (a system or device for) the supplying of material (e g liquid) by the action of gravity alone ⟨*the carburettor was supplied with petrol by means of a ~*⟩

**gravure** /grəˈvyooə/ *n* **1** the process of printing from an IN-TAGLIO (engraved) plate of copper or wood **2** PHOTOGRAVURE (gravure using a photographically prepared plate) [Fr, fr *graver* to grave, of Gmc origin; akin to OHG *graban* to dig, engrave – more at GRAVE]

**gravy** /ˈgrayvi/ *n* **1** the (thickened and seasoned) fat and juices from cooked meat used as a sauce **2** *slang* something pleasing or valuable that occurs or is acquired easily and unexpectedly [ME *gravey,* fr MF *gravé*]

**gravy boat** *n* a small boat-shaped vessel used for pouring gravy or other sauces

**gravy train** *n, chiefly NAm informal* a much exploited source of easy money

**gray** /gray/ *vb, n, or adj, chiefly NAm* (to) grey

**grayling** /ˈgrayling/ *n, pl* **graylings,** *esp collectively* **grayling** any of several freshwater fishes of the salmon family (genus *Thymallus*) of green-blue to silver colouring valued as food and sport fishes [ME, fr *gray* + *-ling*]

**¹graze** /grayz/ *vi* to feed on growing vegetation, attached algae, or minute water plant life ~ *vt* **1a** to crop and eat (vegetation) in the field **b** to feed on the vegetation of (e g a pasture) **2** to put to graze ⟨*~d his cows on the meadow*⟩ **3** to supply vegetation for the grazing of [ME *grasen,* fr OE *grasian,* fr *græs* grass] – **grazeable, grazable** *adj,* **grazer** *n*

**²graze** *n* **1** the act of grazing **2** vegetation for grazing

**³graze** *vt* **1** to touch lightly in passing ⟨*her bare leg ~d a nettle*⟩ **2** to abrade, scratch ⟨*~d her knee when she fell*⟩ ~ *vi* to touch or rub against something in passing ⟨*our bumpers just ~d*⟩ [perh fr ¹*graze*]

**⁴graze** *n* (a superficial abrasion, esp of the skin, made by) a scraping along a surface

**grazier** /ˈgrayzyə, -zi-ə/ *n* **1** one who grazes cattle, usu for beef production **2** *Austr* a sheep farmer

**grazing** /ˈgrayzing/ *n* **1** the (method of) feeding of animals that graze ⟨*heavy ~ will kill out some plant species*⟩ **2** vegetation or land for grazing

**¹grease** /grees/ *n* **1a** melted down animal fat **b** oily matter ⟨*he puts ~ on his hair*⟩ **c** a thick lubricant, esp used for machinery **2** wool as it comes from the sheep, retaining its natural oils and fats [ME *grese,* fr OF *craisse, graisse,* fr (assumed) VL *crassia,* fr L *crassus* thick, fat] – **greaseless** *adj,* **greaseproof** *adj* – **in the grease** *of wool or fur* in the natural uncleaned condition

**²grease** *vt* **1** to smear, lubricate, or soil with grease **2** *informal* to hasten the process or progress of; accelerate ⟨*this ~s the decline in department store sales – Wall Street Jour*⟩

**grease monkey** *n, informal* a mechanic; *esp* one working on cars and aircraft

**greasepaint** /-ˌpaynt/ *n* theatrical make-up originally made with melted grease

**greaseproof** /ˈgreesˌproohf/, **greaseproof paper** *n* paper resistant to penetration by grease, oil, or wax and used esp for wrapping food

**greaser** /ˈgreesə/ *n* **1** *Br slang* a long-haired youth usu belonging to a gang clad in black leather studded jackets and riding motorbikes **2** *chiefly NAm* a native or inhabitant of Latin America; *esp* a Mexican [¹*grease* + ²*-er*]

**greasy** /ˈgreesi, ˈgreezi/ *adj* **1a** smeared or soiled with grease ⟨*~ clothes*⟩ **b** oily in appearance, texture, or manner ⟨*his ~ smile* – Jack London⟩ **c** slippery **2** containing an excessive amount of grease ⟨*~ food*⟩ – **greasily** *adv,* **greasiness** *n*

**greasy spoon** *n, slang* a small cheap usu unsanitary restaurant

**¹great** /grayt/ *adj* **1a** notably large in size or number ⟨*a ~ tree*⟩ ⟨*~ multitudes*⟩ **b** of a relatively large kind – used in plant and animal names **c** elaborate, ample ⟨*~ detail*⟩ **2a** extreme in amount, degree, or effectiveness ⟨*~ bloodshed*⟩ **b** of importance; significant ⟨*a ~ day in European history*⟩ **3a** eminent, distinguished ⟨*a ~ poet*⟩ **b** aristocratic, grand ⟨*~ ladies*⟩ **4** main, principal ⟨*a reception in the ~ hall*⟩ **5** removed in a family relationship by at least three stages directly or two stages indirectly – chiefly in combination ⟨*~ grandfather*⟩ **6**

markedly superior in character or quality; *esp* noble ⟨*~ of soul*⟩ **7a** remarkably skilled ⟨*~ at tennis*⟩ **b** enthusiastic, keen ⟨*he was a ~ filmgoer*⟩ **8** *informal* – used as a generalized term of approval ⟨*had a ~ time*⟩ ⟨*it was just ~*⟩ **9** full of emotion ⟨*~ with anger*⟩ **10** *archaic* pregnant ⟨*~ with child*⟩ – see also **go great** GUNS, **no great** SHAKES *synonyms* see ¹LARGE *antonym* small [ME *grete,* fr OE *grēat;* akin to OHG *grōz* large] – **great** *adv,* **greatly** *adv,* **greatness** *n*

**²great** *n, pl* **great, greats** one who or that which is great ⟨*the ~s of the stage*⟩

**great ape** *n* any of the more advanced ANTHROPOID APES (e g the gorilla)

**great auk** *n* an extinct large flightless auk (*Pinguinus impennis*) formerly abundant along N Atlantic coasts

**great-ˈaunt** *n* an aunt of one's father or mother

**Great Bear** *n* URSA MAJOR (constellation close to the North Star)

**great black-backed gull** *n* a large predatory gull (*Larus marinus*) that frequents coastal regions of N Europe and the adult of which has a black back and wings

**great bustard** *n* a large Eurasian bustard (*Otis tarda*)

**great circle** *n* a circle formed on the surface of a sphere by the intersection of a plane that passes through the centre of the sphere; *esp* such a circle on the surface of the earth on the arc of which any two points are connected by the shortest distance

**greatcoat** /-ˌkoht/ *n* a heavy overcoat

**great crested grebe** *n* a large African and Eurasian GREBE (water bird) (*Podiceps cristatus*) that has black projecting ear tufts in the breeding season

**Great Dane** /dayn/ *n* (any of) a breed of massive powerful smooth-coated dogs

**great divide** *n* **1** a significant point of division **2** *euph* death – + the ⟨*he crossed the ~ bravely*⟩ [the *Great Divide,* N American watershed]

**greater** /ˈgraytə/ *adj, often cap* consisting of a central city together with adjacent areas that are geographically or administratively connected with it ⟨*Greater London*⟩ [compar of *great*]

**greater celandine** *n* CELANDINE 1 (yellow-flowered plant)

**greatest common divisor** /ˈgraytist/ *n* HIGHEST COMMON FACTOR

**greatest lower bound** *n, maths* INFIMUM

**great-ˈgrandchild** *n* a grandchild of one's son or daughter

**great-ˈgrandparent** *n* a grandparent of one's father or mother

**great grey shrike** *n* a large European SHRIKE (meat-eating bird) (*Lanius excubitor*) that is chiefly grey above with black-and-white wings and tail

**greathearted** /-ˈhahtid/ *adj* generous, magnanimous – **greatheartedly** *adv,* **greatheartedness** *n*

**great-ˈnephew** *n* a grandson of one's brother or sister

**great-ˈniece** *n* a granddaughter of one's brother or sister

**great organ** *n* the principal division of a large pipe organ that has a separate keyboard and includes the largest scale and loudest tone

**great power** *n, often cap G&P* any of the nations that exercise the most influence in international affairs

**Great Russian** *n or adj* (a member) of the Russian-speaking people of the central and NE USSR

**Greats** *n pl* the (final examination and) course in classics and philosophy for undergraduates at Oxford University [arch. *Great Go,* the final exam for the BA degree at Oxford]

**great seal** *n, often cap G&S* the official seal of a nation or monarch that is used esp for the authentication of state documents

**great skua** *n* a large stocky SKUA (large seabird) (*Stercorarius skua*) that has dusky plumage and broad rounded wings, breeds chiefly along arctic and antarctic shores, and forages over most cold and temperate seas

**great spotted woodpecker** *n* a Eurasian and N African woodpecker (*Dendrocopos major*) that has a black back with white on the shoulders

**great tit** *n* a large common Eurasian and N African tit (*Parus major*) that has a glossy black-and-white head and yellow underparts with a black band down the breast

**great-ˈuncle** *n* an uncle of one's father or mother

**Great War** *n the* first World War of 1914 to 1918

**great white shark** *n* a large man-eating shark (*Corcharodon corcharias*) that is widespread in warm and tropical seas

**great year** *n* one complete cycle (about 25 800 years) of the PRECESSION OF THE EQUINOXES

**greave** /greev/ *n* a piece of armour fitting the leg below the knee [ME *greve*, fr MF]

**grebe** /greeb/ *n* any of a family (Podicipedidae) of swimming and diving birds closely related to the LOONS but having separate toes with fleshy lobes rather than webbed feet [Fr *grèbe*]

**Grecian** /'greesh(ə)n/ *adj* **1** (characteristic) of the cultural and aesthetic ideals, esp elegance and simplicity, of classical Greece ⟨~ *profile*⟩ ⟨~ *column*⟩ **2** Greek [L *Graecia* Greece] – **Grecian** *n*, **grecianize** *vt*, *often cap*
*usage* Grecian is used today only of the art of classical Greece and of human features that remind one of this art. It cannot otherwise replace **Greek**, the general adjective.

**Grecism** /'gree,siz(ə)m/ *n*, *chiefly NAm* GRAECISM (characteristic of Greek language or culture)

**grec·ize, -ise** /'greesiez/ *vt*, *often cap*, *chiefly NAm* GRAECIZE (make Greek)

**Greco-** /greekoh-, grekoh-/ *comb form*, *chiefly NAm* Graeco-

**greed** /greed/ *n* **1** excessive desire for acquisitions, power, fame, wealth, etc; *avarice* **2** excessive desire for or consumption of food [back-formation fr *greedy*]

**greedy** /'greedi/ *adj* **1** having a strong desire for something, esp food or money **2** characterized by greed **3** eager, keen ⟨~ *for praise*⟩ [ME *gredy*, fr OE *grǣdig*; akin to OHG *grātag* greedy] – **greedily** *adv*, **greediness** *n*

'**greedy-,guts** *n taking sing vb*, *pl* **greedy-guts** *informal* one who eats too much; a glutton

¹**Greek** /greek/ *n* **1** (a descendant of) a native or inhabitant of Greece **2** the Indo-European language used by the Greeks from prehistoric times to the present; *specif* either the classical or the modern language of the Greeks **3** *not cap* something unintelligible ⟨*it's all* ~ *to me*⟩ [ME *Greke*, fr OE *Grēca*, fr L *Graecus*, fr Gk *Graikos;* (3) trans of L *Graecum* (in the medieval phrase *Graecum est; non potest legi* It is Greek; it cannot be read)]

²**Greek** *adj* **1** (characteristic) of Greece, the Greeks, or Greek **2a** (characteristic) of the Orthodox church of Greece **b** of an Eastern church using the traditional Byzantine rite in Greek

**Greek cross** *n* a cross having four equal arms forming right angles

**Greek fire** *n* an incendiary weapon used in ancient sea warfare, esp by the Byzantine Greeks, and said to have burst into flame on contact with water

**Greek key** *n* a decorative device consisting of repeated interlocking usu right-angled figures

**Greek Orthodox** *adj* ORTHODOX 2a; *specif* GREEK 2a

¹**green** /green/ *adj* **1** of the colour green **2a** covered by green growth or foliage ⟨~ *fields*⟩ **b** consisting of green (edible) plants ⟨*a* ~ *salad*⟩ **3a** youthful, vigorous ⟨*a* ~ *old age*⟩ **b** not ripened or matured; immature ⟨~ *apples*⟩ **c** fresh, new **4** appearing pale, sickly, or nauseated ⟨*during the boat trip his face went quite* ~⟩ **5** affected by intense envy or jealousy ⟨*the adulation he received made his brother* ~ *with envy*⟩ **6a** not aged ⟨*a* ~ *ham*⟩ **b** not dressed or tanned ⟨~ *hides*⟩ **c** *of wood* freshly sawn; unseasoned **7a** lacking in training, knowledge, or experience ⟨*the new recruits seemed very* ~⟩ **b** lacking sophistication; naive **8** displaying the colour green as an indication that one may proceed unhindered ⟨*the traffic lights are* ~⟩ ⟨*went through the* ~ *channel at customs*⟩; *broadly*, *chiefly NAm* in order and ready to proceed according to plan ⟨*all systems are* ~⟩ – compare GREEN LIGHT **9** being an exchange unit whose rate of exchange changes in relation to the specified currency and that is used to pay agricultural producers in the European economic community ⟨~ *pound*⟩ [ME *grene*, fr OE *grēne;* akin to OE *grōwan* to grow] – **greenly** *adv*, **greenness** *n*

²**green** *vb* to make or become green – often + *up*

³**green** *n* **1** a colour whose range of hue resembles that of new grass or the emerald and lies between blue and yellow in the spectrum **2** something of a green colour **3** *pl* green leafy vegetables (e g spinach and cabbage) whose leaves and stems are often cooked **4a** a common or park in the centre of a town or village **b** an area of closely cut grass used for a particular (sporting) purpose (e g bowling or putting) – see also RUB **of the green** – **greeny** *adj*

**green alga** *n* any of a division (Chlorophyta) of algae in which the chlorophyll is not obscured by other pigments

**greenback** /-,bak/ *n*, *NAm informal* a legal-tender note issued by the US government and supported by the credit of the country rather than by bullion

**green bacon** *n* unsmoked bacon

**green ban** *n*, *Austr* a boycott imposed by trade unions in support of an environmental issue

**green bean** *n* the narrow green edible pod of any of various beans (e g the FRENCH BEAN or the RUNNER BEAN); *also* a plant that bears green beans

**green belt** *n* a belt of parks, farmland, etc encircling an urban area and usu protected from too much new building and development

**greenbottle** /'green,botl/ *n* any of various flies (genus *Lucilia*) that have brilliant metallic green bodies

**green card** *n* a document of motor insurance protecting vehicles driven abroad

**green corn** *n* the young tender ears of sweet corn suitable for cooking

**green cross code** *n* a British code of conduct instructing people, esp children, how to cross roads more safely

**greenery** /'greenəri/ *n* green foliage or plants

'**green-,eyed** *adj* jealous

**green-eyed monster** *n* jealousy – + *the*

**greenfinch** /-,finch/ *n* a common African and Eurasian finch (*Chloris chloris*) that has olive-green and yellow plumage

**green fingers** *n pl* an exceptional ability to make plants grow – **green-fingered** *adj*

**greenfly** /-,flie/ *n*, *pl* **greenflies**, *esp collectively* **greenfly** *Br* any of various green coloured aphids that are frequently carriers of plant virus diseases and are destructive to plants; *also* an infestation of these ⟨*there is a lot of* ~ *on the roses*⟩

**greengage** /-,gayj/ *n* any of several small rounded greenish or greenish-yellow cultivated plums; *also* a tree bearing such fruit [*green* + Sir William *Gage* †1820 E botanist, who introduced it into England from France]

**green gland** *n* either of a pair of large green glands in some INVERTEBRATE animals (e g crayfishes and crabs) that have an excretory function and open at the bases of the larger antennae

**green gram** *n* MUNG BEAN (bean grown for forage)

**greengrocer** /-,grohsə/ *n*, *chiefly Br* a retailer of fresh vegetables and fruit – **greengrocery** *n*

**greenheart** /-,haht/ *n* a tropical S American evergreen tree (*Nectandra rodioei*); *also* the hard somewhat greenish wood of this tree

**greenhorn** /-,hawn/ *n* **1** an inexperienced or unsophisticated (easily cheated) person **2** *chiefly NAm* a newcomer (e g to a country) unacquainted with local manners and customs [obs *greenhorn* animal with young horns]

**greenhouse** /-,hows/ *n* an enclosure with a transparent (glass) roof and walls used for the cultivation or protection of tender plants

**greenhouse effect** *n* the warming of the lower layers of the atmosphere by absorption and reradiation of solar radiation that is thought to increase with increasing atmospheric CARBON DIOXIDE

**greening** /'greening/ *n* any of several apples having a green skin when ripe

**greenish** /'greenish/ *adj* having a tinge of green; somewhat green – **greenishness** *n*

**Greenland right whale** /'greenlənd/ *n* a large WHALEBONE WHALE (*Balaena mysticetus*) of the Arctic that is black with a light-coloured throat – called also BOWHEAD [*Greenland*, island in N Atlantic]

**green light** *n* authority or permission to undertake a project [fr the green traffic light which signals permission to proceed]

,**green-ma'nure** *vt* to fertilize with GREEN MANURE

**green manure** *n* a plant crop (e g clover) ploughed under while green to enrich the soil

**green monkey** *n* a long-tailed monkey (*Cercopithecus sabaeus*) of W Africa that has greenish-brown hair and is often tamed and trained

**green monkey disease** *n* an often fatal virus disease that causes high fever and internal bleeding and is transmitted to humans by GREEN MONKEYS

**green mould** *n* a green or green-spored mould (e g of the genera *Penicillium* or *Aspergillus*) – compare BLUE MOULD

**greenockite** /'greenə,kiet/ *n* a mineral consisting of the chemical compound cadmium sulphide, CdS, occurring in yellow crystals or as an earthy incrustation [Charles Cathcart, Lord *Greenock* †1859 E soldier, who discovered it in 1841]

**green onion** *n*, *NAm* SPRING ONION

**green paper** *n*, *chiefly Br* a set of proposals issued by a government for public comment before using them as a basis for legislation [fr the colour of its covers]

**green pepper** *n* SWEET PEPPER

**green plover** *n* LAPWING (type of crested bird)

**greenroom** /-room, -,roohm/ *n* a room in a theatre or concert hall where performers can relax when not on stage [prob fr its orig being painted green]

**greensand** /-,sand/ *n* a sedimentary deposit that consists largely of dark greenish grains of the mineral GLAUCONITE often mingled with clay or sand

**greenshank** /-,shangk/ *n* an African and Eurasian wading bird (*Tringa nebularia*) that has olive-green legs and feet

**greensick** /-,sik/ *adj* suffering from CHLOROSIS (disease caused by an iron deficiency) [back-formation fr *greensickness*] – **greensickness** *n*

**greenstick fracture** /-,stik/ *n* a bone fracture in a child or young animal in which the bone is partly broken and partly bent

**greenstone** /-,stohn/ *n* **1** any of numerous dark green compact rocks (e g DIORITE) **2** NEPHRITE (type of jade)

**greenstuff** /-,stuf/ *n* edible green vegetation; greens

**greensward** /-,swawd/ *n* turf that is green with growing grass

**green tea** *n* tea that is light in colour because the leaves have not been completely fermented

**green thumb** *n, NAm* GREEN FINGERS – **green-thumbed** *adj*

**green turtle** *n* a large edible sea turtle (*Chelonia mydas*) that is widely distributed in warm seas

**Greenwich Mean Time** /'grenich, 'grinij, -nich/ *n* the MEAN SOLAR TIME of the meridian of Greenwich, used as the primary point of reference for STANDARD TIME throughout the world – called also UNIVERSAL TIME [*Greenwich*, borough of London]

**greenwood** /-,wood/ *n* a forest green with foliage

**green woodpecker** *n* a common large African and Eurasian woodpecker (*Picus viridis*) that is chiefly green with a yellow rump and a red crown

**¹greet** /greet/ *vt* **1** to welcome with gestures and words; hail ⟨*she* ~ed *him with open arms*⟩ **2** to meet or react to in a specified manner ⟨*the candidate was* ~ed *with catcalls*⟩ **3** to be perceived by ⟨*a surprising sight* ~ed *her eyes*⟩ [ME *greten*, fr OE *grētan*; akin to OE *grātan* to weep] – **greeter** *n*

**²greet** *vi* grat /grat/; **grutten** /'grutn/ *Scot* to weep, lament [ME *greten*, fr OE *grātan*; akin to ON *grāta* to weep]

**greeting** /'greeting/ *n* **1** a salutation at meeting **2** **greetings** *pl*, **greeting** an expression of good wishes; regards ⟨*birthday* ~s⟩

**greetings card** *n* a (decorative) card with a message of goodwill that is usu sent or given on special occasions (e g an anniversary)

**gregarine** /'gregərien, -rin/ *n* any of a large order (Gregarinida) of parasitic PROTOZOANS (single-celled microorganisms) that usu occur in insects and other INVERTEBRATE animals [deriv of L *gregarius*] – **gregarine, gregarinian** *adj*

**gregarious** /gri'geəri‐əs/ *adj* **1a** tending to associate or live with others of the same kind; social ⟨*man is a* ~ *beast*⟩ **b** characterized by or indicating a liking for companionship; sociable ⟨*though now an introvert he was once very* ~⟩ **c** (characteristic) of a group, flock, crowd, etc **2a** *of a plant* growing in a cluster or a colony **b** *esp of wasps and bees* living in neighbouring nests or herding together but not forming an independent colony [L *gregarius* of a flock or herd, fr *greg-, grex* flock, herd; akin to Gk *ageirein* to collect, *agora* assembly] – **gregariously** *adv*, **gregariousness** *n*

**¹Gregorian** /gri'gawriən/ *adj* of Pope Gregory XIII or the GREGORIAN CALENDAR [Pope *Gregory* XIII †1585]

**²Gregorian** *adj* of Pope Gregory I or the chant named after him [Pope *Gregory* I †604]

**³Gregorian** *adj* of the Armenian national church [St *Gregory* the Illuminator †332, apostle of Armenia]

**Gregorian calendar** *n* a revision of the JULIAN CALENDAR now in general use that was introduced in 1582 by Pope Gregory XIII and adopted in Britain and the American colonies in 1752 and that restricts LEAP YEARS to every 4th year except for those centenary years not divisible by 400

**Gregorian chant** *n* a rhythmically free ritual chant in unison, practised in the Roman Catholic Church – called also PLAINSONG

**Gregorian telescope** *n* a REFLECTING TELESCOPE in which light that has been reflected from a secondary concave mirror passes through a perforation in the primary mirror to the eyepiece [James *Gregory* †1675 Sc mathematician & astronomer]

**greige** /grayzh/ *adj, of a textile, chiefly NAm* GREY **4** [Fr *grège* raw (of silk), fr It *greggio*]

**greisen** /'griez(ə)n/ *n* a granite rock consisting chiefly of the minerals QUARTZ and MICA that is common in Cornwall and Saxony [Ger, fr *greiszen* to split]

**gremlin** /'gremlin/ *n* **1** a mischievous creature said to be responsible for malfunctioning of machinery or equipment, esp in an aircraft **2** an invisible mischievous author of errors and inaccuracies ⟨*pestered by typographical* ~s *throughout his career – The Listener*⟩ [perh modif (influenced by *goblin*) of IrGael *gruaimīn* ill-humoured little fellow]

**grenade** /grə'nayd/ *n* **1** a small missile that contains explosive material (e g incendiary chemicals) and is thrown by hand or launched from a gun **2** a glass container filled with chemicals that is designed to burst when thrown (e g for extinguishing a fire) [MF, pomegranate, fr LL *granata*, fr L, fem of *granatus* seedy, fr *granum* grain – more at CORN]

**grenadier** /,grenə'diə/ *n* **1a** a soldier who carries and throws grenades **b** a member of a regiment or corps formerly trained specially to use grenades **c** *Br* a member of the regiment of the Grenadier Guards **2** any of various deep-sea fishes (family Macruridae) that are related to the cods and have long tapering bodies and pointed tails [Fr, fr *grenade*]

**grenadine** /,grenə'deen, '‐‐‐/ *n* **1** a plain or figured fabric (e g of silk or wool) in an open weave like that of gauze **2** a syrup made or tasting of pomegranates and used esp in cocktails or with soda water [Fr, fr *grenade*]

**Gresham's law** /'gresh(ə)mz/ *n* an observation in economics: a coin which has the same debt-paying value as another coin, but which is intrinsically worth more, tends to be hoarded or exported as bullion while the other remains in circulation [Sir Thomas *Gresham* †1579 E financier]

**grew** /grooh/ *past of* GROW

**¹grey, NAm chiefly gray** /gray/ *adj* **1** of the colour grey **2a** dull in colour or brightness ⟨~ *room*⟩ ⟨~ *day*⟩ **b** having grey hair **c** *of a horse* having both white and black hairs throughout the coat **3a** dismal, gloomy ⟨*the* ~ *office routine*⟩ **b** of an unclear or doubtful position, condition, or character ⟨*a* ~ *area*⟩ **4** *of a textile* in an unbleached undyed state as taken from the loom or knitting machine ⟨~ *goods*⟩ [ME, fr OE *grǣg*; akin to OHG *grāo* grey, ON *grār*]

**²grey, NAm chiefly gray** *n* **1** any of a series of neutral colours (e g the colour of ashes or lead) ranging between black and white **2** one who or that which is of a grey or greyish colour; *esp* a grey horse

**³grey, NAm chiefly gray** *vb* to make or become grey

**greybeard** /-,biəd/ *n* **1** an old man **2** a large (earthen) container for spirits

**grey eminence** *n* ÉMINENCE GRISE (person who exercises power behind the scenes)

**grey friar** *n, often cap G&F* a FRANCISCAN friar [fr the colour of his habit]

**greyhen** /'gray,hen/ *n* a female black grouse – compare BLACKCOCK

**grey heron** *n* a large European heron (*Ardea cinerea*) that has a long snaky neck and grey slow-beating wings and stands motionless for long periods in or near water

**greyhound** /-,hownd/ *n* (any of) a tall slender smooth-coated breed of dogs characterized by swiftness and keen sight and used for hunting down game (e g hares) and racing [ME *grehound*, fr OE *grīghund*, fr *grīg-* (akin to ON *grey* bitch) + *hund* hound]

**greyish** /-ish/ *adj, of a colour* low in SATURATION

**greylag** /-,lag/, **greylag goose** *n* a common grey Eurasian wild goose (*Anser anser*) with pink legs and an orange beak [*grey* + ²*lag* (one who lags or is last); prob fr its late migration]

**grey matter** *n* **1** nerve tissue, esp in the brain and SPINAL CORD, that contains nerve-cell bodies as well as NERVE FIBRES and has a brownish-grey colour **2** *informal* brains, intellect

**grey mullet** *n* MULLET 1

**grey plover** *n* a large Eurasian and N American PLOVER (wading bird) (*Pluvialis squatarola*) with a silver and grey mottled hood and black underparts

**grey seal** *n* a large greyish seal (*Halichoerus grypus*) found chiefly on rocky coasts of the N Atlantic

**grey squirrel** *n* a common greyish to black squirrel (*Neosciurus carolinensis*) originally native to America that has become a serious pest, esp in Britain, causing extensive damage to deciduous trees

**greywacke** /-,wakə/ *n* a coarse usu dark grey sandstone or fine grained CONGLOMERATE rock composed of cemented rock fragments (e g of the minerals quartz and feldspar) [part trans of Ger *grauwacke*]

**grey wagtail** *n* a common Eurasian WAGTAIL (water bird) (*Motacilla cinerea*) that has a slate-blue back, a long black tail, and a brilliant sulphur-yellow breast

**grey whale** *n* a large fierce WHALEBONE WHALE (*Rhachianectes glaucus*) of the N Pacific

**grey wolf** *n* a N American TIMBER WOLF

**gribble** /'gribl/ *n* any of various small marine INVERTEBRATE animals (genus *Limnoria* of the class Crustacea) related to the wood lice that bore into and destroy submerged timber [prob dim. of ²*grub*]

**grid** /grid/ *n* **1** a grating **2a(1)** an ELECTRODE (structure that conducts an electric current) of a THERMIONIC VALVE or other electronic device that usu has the form of a wire mesh and that controls the flow of electrons between the other two electrodes (the CATHODE and ANODE) when a voltage is applied to it **a(2)** a network of conductors used to distribute electric power; *also* a network of radio or television stations – compare NATIONAL GRID **b** (something resembling) a network of uniformly spaced horizontal and perpendicular lines (for locating points on a map) **3 starting grid, grid** (the lines that delineate) the starting positions of vehicles on a racetrack **4** a device (e g of glass) in a FILMSETTER on which are located the characters to be exposed on the film [back-formation fr *gridiron*] – **gridded** *adj*

**griddle** /'gridl/ *n* a flat metal surface on which scones, pancakes, etc are cooked by dry heat [ME *gredil* gridiron, fr ONF, fr LL *craticulum*, alter. of L *craticula*, dim. of *cratis* wickerwork – more at HURDLE]

> *synonyms* **Griddle, girdle, gridiron, grill.** A flat cooking surface is a **griddle** or **girdle**. A metal frame for cooking over a fire is a **gridiron** or **grill**, but the chief meaning of **grill** today is the gas or electric device that throws heat downwards.

**gridiron** /-,ie·ən/ *n* **1** a frame of metal bars on which food (e g meat or fish) is grilled (e g over a charcoal fire) **2** a framework above the stage in a theatre that supports the apparatus for changing scenery, lighting, etc **3** *NAm* the playing area of a football field *synonyms* see GRIDDLE [ME *gredire*, prob alter. (influenced by *ire, iren* iron) of *gredil*]

**grief** /greef/ *n* **1** (a cause of) deep and poignant distress (e g owing to bereavement) **2** an unfortunate outcome; disaster – chiefly in *come to grief* [ME *gref*, fr OF, heavy, grave, fr (assumed) VL *grevis*, alter. of L *gravis*] – **griefless** *adj* – **come to grief** to end badly; fail

> *synonyms* **Grief, sorrow, anguish,** and **woe** all mean "great mental suffering". **Grief** is usually felt for some definite cause, such as the death of a loved one. **Sorrow** suggests deep sadness and a sense of loss or regret. **Anguish** is stronger, suggesting almost unbearable pain. **Woe** is a now somewhat formal word for long-lasting distress (*condemned to waste eternal days in* **woe** – John Milton). Compare ²REGRET *antonyms* joy, happiness

**grievance** /'greev(ə)ns/ *n* **1** a cause of distress (e g unsatisfactory working conditions) felt to afford reason for complaint or resistance **2** a feeling of having been wronged; resentment (*they harboured many* ~s) **3** the formal expression of a grievance; a complaint (*they voiced their* ~s)

**¹grieve** /greev/ *n, Scot* a farm or estate manager; an overseer [ME *greif*, fr OE *græfa* governor, sheriff; akin to OE *geréfa* reeve]

**²grieve** *vt* to cause pain or distress to ~ *vi* to suffer grief; sorrow, esp over a bereavement – often + *for* [ME *greven*, fr OF *grever*, fr L *gravare* to burden, fr *gravis* heavy, grave; akin to Goth *kaurjos*, pl, heavy, Gk *barys*, Skt *guru*] – **griever** *n*

**grievous** /'greevəs/ *adj* **1** causing severe pain, suffering, or sorrow (*a* ~ *wound*) (*a* ~ *loss*) **2** serious, grave (~ *fault*) – **grievously** *adv*, **grievousness** *n*

**griff** /grif/ *n, Br slang* an accurate account; *esp* inside information [short for *griffin*, of unknown origin]

**griffin** /'grifin/, **griffon, gryphon** /'grifən/ *n* a mythical animal with the head, breast, and wings of an eagle and the body and tail of a lion [ME *griffon*, fr MF *grifon*, fr *grif*, fr L *gryphus*, fr Gk *gryp-, gryps*, fr *grypos* curved; akin to OE *cradol* cradle]

**griffon** /'grifən/ *n* (any of) a breed of **a** short-faced TOY DOGS of Belgian origin **b** sporting dogs with wiry greyish coats that originated in Holland [Fr, lit., griffin]

> *synonyms* A **griffon** is a kind of dog; but **griffon** and **gryphon** are also variant spellings of **griffin**. This mythical animal combining the eagle and the lion should not be confused with the **wyvern**, a mythical winged dragon.

**griffon vulture** *n* any of a genus (*Gyps*) of large African and Eurasian vultures; *esp* a large light-coloured vulture (*Gyps fulvus*)

**grift** /grift/ *vi, NAm slang* to live by slyness or ingenuity; GRAFT 3 [*grift*, n, perh alter. of *graft*] – **grift** *n*, **grifter** *n*

**grig** /grig/ *n* **1** a cricket or grasshopper **2** a young eel **3** a lively young person (*a* ~ *of a girl*) [ME *grege* dwarf]

**grigri** /'gree,gree/ *n, pl* **grigris** GRIS-GRIS (African amulet)

**grike, gryke** /griek/ *n* a cleft developed in a horizontal limestone surface and widened by the solvent action of rainwater or other natural forces [alter. of ME *crike*, fr ON *criki* crock, bend]

**¹grill** /gril/ *vt* **1** to cook under or on a grill by radiant heat (~ *the tomatoes, don't fry them*) **2a** to torture or torment with great heat (*the intense sun slowly* ~ed *them*) **b** *informal* to interrogate intensely (*the police* ~ed *the suspect*) ~ *vi* to become grilled – **griller** *n*

**²grill** *n* **1** a utensil of parallel metal bars on which food is cooked by exposure to heat (e g from a charcoal fire or electricity) **2** food cooked under or on a grill (*a mixed* ~) **3 grill, grillroom** a usu informal restaurant or dining room, esp in a hotel **4** *Br* an apparatus on a cooker under which food is cooked or browned by radiant heat *synonyms* see GRIDDLE [Fr *gril*, fr LL *craticulum* – more at GRIDDLE]

**grillage** /'grilij/ *n* **1** a framework of timber or steel used for support when building on soft soil **2** a framework for supporting a load (e g a column) [Fr, fr *grille* ]

**grille, grill** /gril/ *n* **1** a framework of upright or latticed bars forming a barrier or screen, esp between two people (e g a bank cashier and a customer) **2** an (ornamental) metal or plastic grating on the front of a car, protecting the radiator **3** a square recess at one end of a REAL TENNIS court [Fr *grille*, alter. of OF *greille*, fr L *craticula*, dim. of *cratis* wickerwork – more at HURDLE]

> *usage* A **grill** may be either a grating or a cooking utensil, but a **grille** can only be a grating.

**grilse** /grils/ *n, pl* **grilse** /~/ a young mature Atlantic salmon returning from the sea to spawn for the first time; *broadly* any of various salmon at such a stage of development [ME *grills*, perh fr MF *grisel, grisle*, grey]

**grim** /grim/ *adj* **-mm-** **1** stern or forbidding in disposition, action, or appearance (*a* ~ *overcast day*) (*a* ~ *ascetic puritan*) **2** unflinching, unyielding (~ *determination*) **3** ghastly, gloomy, or sinister in character (*a* ~ *tale*) **4** *informal* unpleasant, joyless (*that exam was pretty* ~) **5** *archaic* fierce in disposition or action; savage (~ *wolves descended on the flock*) [ME, fr OE *grimm*; akin to OHG *grimm* fierce, Gk *chromados* act of gnashing] – **grimly** *adv*, **grimness** *n*

**grimace** /'griməs, gri'mays/ *vi or n* (to make) a distorted, often self-conscious, facial expression usu of disgust, anger, or pain [n Fr, fr MF, alter. of *grimache*, of Gmc origin; akin to OE *grīma* mask; vb fr n] – **grimacer** *n*

**grimalkin** /gri'malkin/ *n* **1** – used chiefly in stories as a name for the cat, esp an old female cat **2** a spiteful or cantankerous old woman [alter. of *grey malkin*, fr *grey* + E dial. *malkin* female cat, fr ME *malkyn*, fr *Malkyn*, female forename]

**grime** /griem/ *n* soot or dirt, esp when ingrained in or sticking to a surface [Flem *grijm*, fr MD *grime* soot, mask; akin to OE *grīma* mask, Gk *chrien* to anoint – more at CHRISM] – **grime** *vt*

**Grimm's law** /grimz/ *n* a statement in historical linguistics: the consonants of the Germanic languages are related to those of Proto-Indo-European according to a recognizable system of changes (e g Latin *duo*, Sanskrit *nābhi* compared with English *two, navel*) [Jacob *Grimm* †1863 Ger philologist]

**grimy** /'griemi/ *adj* ingrained or covered with grime; dirty – **griminess** *n*

**grin** /grin/ *vb* **-nn-** *vi* to smile broadly so as to express amusement, pleasure, or pain ~ *vt* to express (something) by grinning (~ *his approval*) [ME *grennen*, fr OE *grennian*; akin to OHG *grennen* to snarl] – **grin** *n*, **grinner** *n*, **grinningly** *adv*

**¹grind** /griend/ *vb* **ground** /grownd/ *vt* **1** to reduce to small or powdered fragments by crushing between hard surfaces, often with a rotating motion (~s *corn*) (~s *food with his teeth*) **2** to wear down, polish, or sharpen by friction; whet (~ *an axe*) **3a** to stamp on or press with force (*ground the cigarette out with his heel*) (*ground his fist into his opponent's stomach*) **b** to press together with a rotating motion (~ *the teeth*) **4** to oppress, harass (*the nobility ground·down the peasants with a variety of exactions*) **5a** to operate or produce by turning a crank ⟨~ *a hand organ*⟩ **b** to produce in a mechanical way ⟨~ *out best-sellers*⟩ ~ *vi* **1** to perform the operation of grinding **2** to become pulverized, polished, or sharpened by friction **3** to move with difficulty or friction, esp so as to make a grating noise ⟨~ing *gears*⟩ **4** to work laboriously; *esp* to study hard ⟨~ *for an exam*⟩ **5** to rotate the hips in an erotic manner – see also AXE **to grind** [ME *grinden*, fr OE *grindan;* akin to L *frendere* to crush, grind, Gk *chondros* grain, OE *grēot* grit] – **grindingly** *adv*

²**grind** *n* **1** an act of grinding **2** dreary monotonous labour or routine ⟨*"oh, well, back to the ~"*⟩ **3** the result of grinding; *esp* material obtained by grinding to a particular degree of fineness **4** an act of rotating the hips in an erotic manner – compare ²BUMP **4 5** *vulg* an act of sexual intercourse; *also* a sexual partner ⟨*she's a good ~*⟩ **6** chiefly NAm a student who studies excessively; a swot

**grinder** /'grində/ *n* **1** a molar tooth **2** one who grinds **3** a machine or device for grinding

**grindstone** /-,stohn/ *n* **1** a millstone **2** (a machine consisting of) a flat circular stone (e g of natural sandstone) that revolves on an axle and is used for grinding, smoothing, or sharpening metal tools and objects – see also **keep somebody's/one's** NOSE **to the grindstone**

**gringo** /'gring-goh/ *n, pl* **gringos** chiefly derog an (English-speaking) foreigner in Spain or Latin America [Sp, prob alter. of *griego* Greek, stranger, fr L *Graecus* Greek]

¹**grip** /grip/ *vb* **-pp-** *vt* **1** to seize or hold firmly **2** to attract and hold the interest of ⟨*a story that ~s the reader*⟩ ~ *vi* to take firm hold [ME *grippen*, fr OE *grippan;* akin to OE *grīpan*] – **gripper** *n*, **grippingly** *adv*

²**grip** *n* **1a** a strong or tenacious grasp **b** manner or style of gripping ⟨*he holds his cricket bat with an unusual ~*⟩ **2a** a tenacious hold giving control, or mastery ⟨*could not free himself from the ~ of sin and guilt*⟩ **b** power of understanding ⟨*she has a good ~ of irregular German verbs*⟩ **3** a usu small device that grips ⟨*a hair ~*⟩ **4** a part by which something is grasped; *esp* a handle ⟨*what's the ~ on your tennis racket like?*⟩ **5a** one who handles and manoeuvres the cameras in a film or television studio **b** a stagehand **5** chiefly NAm a travelling bag – **get to grips with** to deal adequately with

¹**gripe** /griep/ *vt* **1** to cause intestinal gripes in **2** *archaic* to grasp, grip **3** *archaic* to afflict, distress ~ *vi* **1** to experience intestinal gripes **2** *informal* to complain continually [ME *gripen* to grasp, seize, fr OE *grīpan;* akin to OHG *grīfan* to grasp, Lith *griebti*] – **griper** *n*

²**gripe** *n* **1** *usu pl* a pinching spasmodic intestinal pain **2** *mechanics* a device (e g a brake) for grasping or holding **3** *usu pl, nautical* a fastening for securing a boat **4** *informal* a grievance, complaint **5** *archaic* **5a** a clutch, grasp **b** a handle, grip

**grippe** /grip/ *n* influenza [Fr, lit., seizure, fr *gripper* to seize] – **grippy** *adj*

**Griqua** /'greekwə, 'grikwə/ *n* a person of mixed European and HOTTENTOT descent in South Africa and esp in Griqualand [prob fr a Hottentot name]

**grisaille** /gri'zayl/ (*Fr* grizɑj)/ *n* a method of decorative painting in tones of grey, designed to produce a three-dimensional effect; *also* a painting executed by this method [Fr, fr *gris* grey]

**griseofulvin** /,grizioh'foolvin, -'ful-/ *n* an antibiotic, $C_{17}H_{17}ClO_6$, obtained from moulds (esp *Penicillium griseofulvum*) and taken orally for the treatment of fungal infections [NL *griseofulvum*, specific epithet of *Penicillium griseofulvum*, fr ML *griseus* grey + L *fulvus* yellow]

**grisette** /gri'zet/ *n* a young (vivacious) French working-class woman [Fr, fr *grisette* (dress made of) cheap grey cloth, fr *gris* grey]

**gris-gris** /'gree ,gree/ *n, pl* **gris-gris** /'gree ,greez/ an African amulet or spell [Fr, of African origin; akin to Balante *grigri* amulet]

**griskin** /'griskin/ *n, Br* the lean part from a loin of bacon [*grice* (young pig; fr ME *grys, grise*, fr ON *grīss*) + *-kin*]

**grisly** /'grizli/ *adj* **1** inspiring horror or intense fear; forbidding ⟨*houses that were dark and ~ under the blank, cold sky* – D H Lawrence⟩ **2** inspiring disgust or distaste ⟨*a ~ account of the murder*⟩ △ gristly, grizzly [ME, fr OE *grislic*, fr *gris-* (akin to OE *āgrīsan* to fear); akin to OHG *grīsenlīh* terrible] – **grisliness** *n*

**grison** /'gries(ə)n, 'griz(ə)n/ *n* any of various S American carnivorous mammals (genus *Grison*) that resemble large weasels [Fr, fr *grison* grey, fr MF, fr *gris* – more at GRIZZLED]

**grist** /grist/ *n* **1** (a batch of) grain for grinding **2** the product (e g flour) obtained from grinding grain [ME, fr OE *grīst;* akin to OE *grindan* to grind] – **grist to the/one's mill** something that can be turned to profit or advantage

**gristle** /'grisl/ *n* cartilage; *broadly* tough cartilaginous, tendinous, or fibrous matter, esp in cooked meat △ grisly, grizzly [ME *gristil*, fr OE *gristle;* akin to MLG *gristel* gristle] – **gristly** *adj*, **gristliness** *n*

**gristmill** /'grist,mil/ *n* a mill for grinding grain

¹**grit** /grit/ *n* **1** a hard sharp granule (e g of sand or stone); *also* material composed of such granules ⟨*put ~ on the garden path*⟩ ⟨*insoluble flint or granite ~ should be fed ... to all turkeys* – *Fream's Elements of Agriculture*⟩ **2 grit, gritstone** any of several rough textured sandstones **3** the grain or texture of a stone **4** determination, courage ⟨*it was stubbornness and sheer ~ that helped him to survive*⟩ [ME *grete*, fr OE *grēot;* akin to OHG *grioz* sand, L *furfur* bran, Gk *chrōs* skin]

²**grit** *vb* **-tt-** *vi* to produce a grating sound ~ *vt* **1** to cover or spread with grit ⟨*the icy roads were ~ted*⟩ **2** to clench or grind (esp one's teeth)

**grits** /grits/ *n taking sing or pl vb* grain, esp oats, husked and usu coarsely ground [ME *gryt*, fr OE *grytt;* akin to OE *grēot*]

**gritty** /'griti/ *adj* **1** containing or resembling grit ⟨*a ~ farmtrack*⟩ **2** courageously persistent or determined ⟨*a ~ character*⟩ **3** caustic, incisive ⟨*~ realism*⟩ – **grittily** *adv*, **grittiness** *n*

**grivet** /'grivit/ *n* a monkey (*Cercopithecus aethiops*) of the upper Nile and Ethiopia with a dullish-green back and white lower parts [Fr]

¹**grizzle** /'grizl/ *vi, Br informal* **1** *of a child* to cry quietly and fretfully **2** to complain in a self-pitying way – often with *about* [origin unknown]

²**grizzle** *n, Br informal* an act or instance of grizzling

**grizzled** /'grizld/ *adj* being or having grey or greyish hair ⟨*a ~ beard*⟩ [ME *griseled*, fr MF *grisel* grey, fr *gris*, of Gmc origin; akin to OHG *grīs* grey]

**grizzly** /'grizli/ *adj* somewhat grey; grizzled △ grisly, gristly [ME *grisel* grey, fr MF]

**grizzly bear, grizzly** *n* a very large powerful typically brownish-yellow bear (*Ursus horribilis*) that inhabits the highlands of western N America [*grizzly* prob var of *grisly*]

**groan** /grohn/ *vi* **1** to utter a deep moan indicative of pain, grief, or annoyance **2** to make a low creaking sound under weight or strain ⟨*the boards ~ed with the arrival of the rugby team*⟩ ~ *vt* to utter with groaning [ME *gronen*, fr OE *grānian;* akin to OHG *grīnan* to growl] – **groan** *n*, **groaner** *n*

**groat** /groht/ *n* **1** a former British coin worth four old pence **2** *archaic* a small amount of little value ⟨*not worth a ~*⟩ [ME *groot*, fr MD]

**groats** /grohts/ *n taking sing or pl vb*, **groat** *n* husked grain broken into fragments larger than grits [ME *grotes*, pl, fr OE *grotan;* akin to OE *grēot*]

**grocer** /'grohsə/ *n* a dealer in various staple foodstuffs, household supplies, and usu some fruit, vegetables, and dairy products [ME, fr MF *grossier* wholesaler, fr *gros* coarse, wholesale – more at GROSS]

**grocery** /'grohs(ə)ri/ *n* **1** *pl* consumer goods sold by a grocer **2** a grocer's shop

**grockle** /'grokl/ *n, SW Eng* a holidaymaker, tourist [origin unknown]

**grog** /grog/ *n* **1** an alcoholic spirit, esp rum, that has been watered down; *broadly* any alcoholic drink **2** heat-resistant materials (e g crushed pottery and fireclay) used as an ingredient in the manufacture of ceramic products to reduce shrinkage in drying and firing [*Old Grog*, nickname (fr the grogram cloak he sometimes wore) of Edward Vernon †1757 E admiral responsible for diluting the sailors' rum]

**groggy** /'grogi/ *adj* dazed, weak, or unsteady on the feet (e g from illness or drunkenness) [*grog* + ¹-*y*] – **groggily** *adv*, **grogginess** *n*

**grogram** /'grogrəm/ *n* a coarse loosely woven fabric of silk, silk and mohair, or silk and wool – compare GROSGRAIN [MF *gros grain* coarse texture]

**groin** /groyn/ *n* **1a** the fold or depression marking the join of the lower abdomen and the inner part of the thigh; *also* the region of this line **b** *euph* the male genitals **2** *building* the line along which two intersecting vaults meet **3** chiefly NAm GROYNE [alter. (prob influenced by E dial. *groin* snout) of ME *grynde*, fr OE, abyss; akin to OE *grund* ground]

**groined** /groynd/ *adj* furnished with groins ⟨*~ vaults*⟩

**grommet** /'gromit/ *also* **grummet** /'grumit/ *n* **1** a ring usu of twisted rope that serves as a fastening, support, or reinforcement on board ship **2** an eyelet of firm material to strengthen or protect an opening [perh fr obs Fr *gormette* curb of a bridle]

**gromwell** /'gromwəl/ *n* any of a genus (*Lithospermum*) of plants of the forget-me-not family having hard seeds [ME *gromil*, fr MF]

**¹groom** /groohm/ *n* **1a** any of several officers of the Royal Household **b** one who is in charge of the feeding, care, and stabling of horses **2** a bridegroom **3** *archaic* a manservant [ME *grom* boy, man, manservant]

**²groom** *vt* **1** to clean and care for (e g a horse) **2** to make neat or tidy ⟨*an impeccably ~ed woman*⟩ ⟨*well ~ed hair*⟩ **3** to get into readiness for a specific role or function; prepare ⟨*was being ~ed as a Tory candidate*⟩ ~ *vi* to groom oneself – **groomer** *n*

**groomsman** /'groohmzmən, 'groomz-/ *n* a male friend who attends a bridegroom at his wedding

**¹groove** /groohv/ *n* **1a** a long narrow channel or depression ⟨*he cut out a ~ in the wood with a knife*⟩ **b** the continuous spiral track on a gramophone record whose irregularities correspond to the recorded sounds **2** a fixed routine; a rut ⟨*caught in the ~ of commuting every day*⟩ **3** *informal* top form ⟨*a great saxophonist when he gets into the ~*⟩ **4** *informal* an enjoyable or exciting experience – no longer in vogue [ME *groof;* akin to OE *grafan* to dig – more at GRAVE]

**²groove** *vt* **1** to make a groove in **2** *informal* to excite pleasurably ⟨*she really ~s me*⟩ ~ *vi* **1** to form a groove ⟨*his face ~d into a smile*⟩ **2a** *esp of a jazz group* to interact harmoniously **b** to enjoy oneself intensely □ (*vt 2; vi 2*) no longer in vogue – **groover** *n*

**groovy** /'groohvi/ *adj, informal* fashionably attractive or exciting; trendy – no longer in vogue

**grope** /grohp/ *vi* **1** to feel about blindly or uncertainly in search ⟨*~d for the light switch*⟩ **2** to search blindly or uncertainly for or after ⟨*groping for the right words*⟩ ~ *vt* **1** to touch or fondle the body of (a person) for sexual pleasure **2** to find (e g one's way) by groping [ME *gropen*, fr OE *grāpian;* akin to OE *grīpan* to seize] – **grope** *n*, **groper** *n*

**grosbeak** /'grohs,beek/ *n* any of several finches (e g the hawfinch) of Europe or America having large thick conical beaks [part trans of Fr *grosbec*, fr *gros* thick + *bec* beak]

**groschen** /'grohsh(ə)n/ *n, pl* **groschen** /~/ *often cap* **1** – see *schilling* at MONEY table **2** a German coin worth 10 pfennigs [Ger]

**grosgrain** /'groh,grayn/ *n* a strong closely woven corded fabric usu of silk or rayon and with crosswise ribs – compare GROGRAM [Fr *gros grain* coarse texture]

**gros point** /'groh ,poynt/ *n* a large cross-stitch or TENT STITCH used in NEEDLEPOINT embroidery and worked across the double threads of the canvas; *also* work done in gros point – compare PETIT POINT [Fr, lit., large point]

**¹gross** /grohs/ *adj* **1** outlandish, glaring, or flagrant ⟨*~ mistake*⟩ ⟨*~ injustice*⟩ **2** excessively large, fat, or luxuriant ⟨*couldn't do up his trousers he was so ~*⟩ ⟨*~ spreading jungle*⟩ **3** consisting of an overall total before deductions (e g for taxes) are made ⟨*~ income*⟩ – compare NET **4** made up of material or perceptible elements; corporal ⟨*the ~er part of human nature*⟩ **5** coarse in behaviour; unrefined ⟨*offended by a ~ lout*⟩ **synonyms** SEE COARSE **antonyms** refined, delicate [ME, fr MF *gros* thick, coarse, fr L *grossus*] – **grossly** *adv*, **grossness** *n*

**²gross** *vt or n* (to earn or bring in) an overall total without deductions – **grosser** *n*

**³gross** *n, pl* **gross** a group of 12 dozen things ⟨*a ~ of pencils*⟩ [ME *groce*, fr MF *grosse*, fr fem of *gros*]

**gross anatomy** *n* a branch of anatomy that deals with the macroscopic rather than the microscopic structure of tissues and organs

**gross domestic product** *n* the total value of the goods and services produced in a country during a specified, usu annual, period, excluding income from possessions and investments abroad

**gross national product** *n* the total value of the goods and services produced in a country including income from possessions and investments abroad, but excluding foreign-owned income generated in the domestic economy during a specified, usu annual, period

**grosso modo** /,grosoh 'modoh/ *adv, formal* approximately, roughly [It]

**grossularite** /'grosyoolərieet/, **grossular** /'grosyoolə/ *n* a

colourless, green, pinkish, or brown garnet, $Ca_3Al_2(SiO_4)_3$ [Ger *grossularit,* fr NL *Grossularia*, genus name of the gooseberry, fr Fr *groseille* gooseberry; fr the colour of some varieties]

**grosz** /grosh/ *n, pl* **groszy** /'groshi/ – see *zloty* at MONEY table [Pol]

**¹grot** /grot/ *n, poetic* a grotto [MF *grotte*, fr It *grotta*]

**²grot** *n, Br informal* (unpleasant) dirt, soot, etc [back-formation fr *grotty*]

**¹grotesque** /groh'tesk/ *n* **1** a style of decorative art characterized by fanciful, incongruous, or fantastic human and animal forms often in combination and usu interwoven with figures of fruit, foliage, etc; *also* a piece of work in the grotesque style **2** somebody who is grotesque **3** SANS SERIF (style of typeface) [MF & OIt; MF, fr OIt (*pittura*) *grottesca,* lit., cave painting, fem of *grottesco* of a cave, fr *grotta*]

**²grotesque** *adj* (characteristic) of the grotesque: e g **a** fanciful, bizarre ⟨*a ~ horror mask*⟩ **b** absurdly incongruous ⟨*a ~ mixture of the sublime and the ridiculous*⟩ **c** departing markedly from the natural, the expected, or the typical ⟨*a ~ parody of the nature of love*⟩ – **grotesquely** *adv,* **grotesqueness** *n*

**grotesquerie** *also* **grotesquery** /-kəri/ *n* **1** something that is grotesque **2** the state of being grotesque; grotesqueness [*grotesque* + Fr *-erie* -ery or E *-ery*]

**grotto** /'grotoh/ *n, pl* **grottoes** *also* **grottos 1** an esp picturesque cave **2** an artificial and prettily decorated recess or cavelike structure [It *grotta, grotto,* fr L *crypta* cavern, crypt]

**grotty** /'groti/ *adj, Br slang* nasty and in a bad condition; unpleasant ⟨*six million homes which, by the most elementary criteria, are ~ slums – Punch*⟩ [by shortening & alter. fr *grotesque*] – **grottily** *adv*

**grouch** /growch/ *n* **1** a bad-tempered mood or complaint **2** a habitually irritable or complaining person; a grumbler [prob alter. of E dial. *grutch* grudge, fr ME *gruch, grucche,* fr *grucchen* to complain – more at GRUDGE] – **grouch** *vi,* **grouchy** *adj*

**¹ground** /grownd/ *n* **1a** the bottom of a body of water (e g the sea) **b** *pl* **b(1)** SEDIMENT 1 **b(2)** ground coffee beans after brewing **2 grounds** *pl,* **ground** a basis for belief, action, or argument ⟨*~s for complaint*⟩ **3a** a surrounding area or background; *esp* one on which a design or picture may be drawn, embroidered, etc **b** underlying material; a substratum **4a** the basic undeveloped surface of the earth ⟨*earthquakes make the ~ tremble*⟩ **b** an area used for a particular purpose ⟨*parade ~*⟩ ⟨*football ~*⟩ **c** *pl* the area round and belonging to a house or other building ⟨*the hotel was set in magnificent ~s*⟩ **d** an area to be won or defended (e g in battle) ⟨*gained much ~*⟩ **e** an area of knowledge or special interest ⟨*covered a lot of ~ in his lecture*⟩ **5** soil, earth ⟨*ploughing the ~*⟩ **6** *chiefly NAm* EARTH 8 **synonyms** see ¹BASE [ME, fr OE *grund;* akin to OHG *grunt* ground, Gk *chrainein* to touch slightly] – **break (new) ground** to do or achieve something new or original – **cover the ground 1** to cover a distance with speed **2** to deal with an assignment or examine a subject thoroughly – **(down) to the ground** *Br informal* absolutely, completely ⟨*it suits me* down to the ground⟩ – **gain ground** to make progress – **give ground** to withdraw, retreat – **lose ground** to lose or fail to improve on something already achieved or won – **into the ground** beyond what is necessary or tolerable; towards utter exhaustion ⟨*driving himself* into the ground⟩ – **off the ground** started and in progress ⟨*the programme never got* off the ground⟩ – **stand one's ground** to remain firm and unyielding in the face of opposition – **to ground** into hiding ⟨*the fox went* to ground⟩ – see also **have/keep an/one's EAR to the ground, RUN to ground**

**²ground** *vt* **1** to bring to or place on, or force down on the ground ⟨*he was ~ed by a big dog*⟩ **2a** to provide a reason or justification for ⟨*our fears were well ~ed*⟩ **b** to instruct in fundamentals (e g of a subject at school) ⟨*they were ~ed in maths and Latin*⟩ **3** to restrict (e g a pilot or aircraft) to the ground **4** *chiefly NAm* to earth (an electrical device) ~ *vi* to run aground ⟨*the boat ~ed on the soft mud bank*⟩

**³ground** *past of* GRIND

**groundbait** /-,bayt/ *n* bait scattered on the water so as to attract fish – **groundbait** *vt*

**ground bass** /bays/ *n* a short repeated sequence of bass notes on top of which (improvised) melody and harmony can be played

**ground beetle** *n* any of numerous chiefly ground-living beetles (family Carabidae)

**'ground-,cherry** *n* any of several plants (genus *Physalis*) of the potato family that have pulpy fruits surrounded by large papery husks; *also* the fruit of these plants – compare CAPE GOOSEBERRY

**ground control** *n* **1** *taking sing or pl vb* the machinery (e g computers) and operators that control or communicate with aircraft from the ground **2** *also* **ground control approach** a system for directing from the ground the landing of an aircraft whose vision is obscured

**ground cover** *n* **1** all the low-growing plants (e g mosses and ferns) in woods and forests except young trees **2** low plants (e g ivy or clover) covering the ground usu instead of turf; *also* a plant adopted for use as ground cover

**ground crew** *n taking sing or pl vb* the mechanics and technicians who maintain and service an aircraft

**ground effect** *n* a phenomenon whereby an aircraft gains extra buoyancy when close to the ground because of a dense mass of air beneath it; *also* a similar but intentionally produced effect (e g from a hovercraft's cushion of air) – **ground-effect** *adj*

**ground elder** *n* a coarse European plant (*Aegopodium podagraria*) of the carrot family that has creeping white underground stems and is a common weed of cultivated ground – called also GOUTWEED

**ground floor** *n* the floor of a building on a level with the ground – compare FIRST FLOOR

**ground frost** *n* a temperature below freezing on the ground, harmful to low-growing vegetation

**ground glass** *n* **1** glass that is translucent but not transparent owing to a light-diffusing surface produced by etching or grinding **2** glass ground into a powder

**grounding** /'grownding/ *n* fundamental training or instruction in a field of knowledge

**ground ivy** *n* a trailing plant (*Glechona hederacea*) of the mint family with rounded leaves and bluish-purple flowers

**groundless** /-lis/ *adj* having no basis or justification ⟨ ~ *fears*⟩ – **groundlessly** *adv*, **groundlessness** *n*

**groundling** /-ling/ *n* **1a** a spectator who paid the lowest price and stood in the pit of an Elizabethan theatre **b** a person of unsophisticated taste **c** somebody of low status **2a** a person who works on or near the ground rather than on water or in the air ⟨*resigned from the air force and became a* ~⟩ **b** an animal (e g a fish) or a plant that stays or grows close to the ground or at the bottom of water

**ground loop** *n* a sharp uncontrollable turn made by an aircraft on the ground in landing, taking off, or taxiing

**groundmass** /'grownd,mas/ *n* the fine-grained material of some rocks (PORPHYRIES) in which larger distinct crystals (PHENOCRYSTS) are embedded

**groundnut** /-,nut/ *n* **1** (the edible tuber of) a N American climbing plant (*Apios tuberosa*) of the pea family; *also* any of several plants having edible tuberous roots **2** *chiefly Br* the peanut

**ground pine** *n* **1** a European yellow-flowered bugle plant (*Ajuga chamaepitys*) of the mint family with a resinous smell **2** any of several CLUB MOSSES (esp *Lycopodium clavatum*) with long creeping stems and erect branches

**ground plan** *n* **1** a plan of the ground floor of a building **2** a general, first, or basic plan

**ground rent** *n* the rent paid by one who is leasing land, esp for the right to build on it

**ground rule** *n* **1** a sports rule adopted to modify play on a particular field, court, or course **2** a basic principle or rule of procedure

**groundsel** /'growns(ə)l, 'growndzl/ *n* a European plant (*Senecio vulgaris*) of the daisy family that has yellow flowers, is a common weed, and is used to feed cage birds; *also* any of several related plants (genus *Senecio*) [ME *groundeswele*, fr OE *grundeswelge*, fr *grund* ground + *swelgan* to swallow – more at SWALLOW]

**groundsheet** /-,sheet/ *n* a waterproof sheet placed on the ground, usu inside a tent, for protection against damp from the soil

**groundsman** /-mən/ *n* one who looks after the condition of a sports field (e g a cricket pitch)

**ground speed** *n* the speed (e g of an aircraft) relative to the ground – compare AIRSPEED

**ground squirrel** *n* **1** any of various burrowing rodents (genus *Citellus*) of N America that are destructive pests of agricultural land **2** a chipmunk

**groundstaff** /-,stahf/ *n taking sing or pl vb* **1** people who are employed to maintain a sports ground (e g of a cricket or soccer club) **2** GROUND CREW

**ground state** *n* the ENERGY LEVEL of a system of interacting ELEMENTARY PARTICLES (minute particles of matter) having the least energy of all its possible states

**ground stroke** *n* a stroke made (e g in tennis) by hitting the ball after it has landed on the court – compare VOLLEY 1d(1)

**ground substance** *n* a more or less uniform substance that forms the background in which differentiated elements (e g of a cell or tissue) are suspended; *esp* the typically liquid or jellylike substance in which the cells, fibres, etc of a CONNECTIVE TISSUE (e g cartilage) are embedded

**ground swell** *n* **1** a sea swell brought about by distant stormy weather or an earthquake **2** a rapid spontaneous growth (e g of political opinion) ⟨*a* ~ *of opinion in favour of front-wheel-drive cars* – Robin Davies⟩

**groundwater** /'grownd,wawtə/ *n* underground water that supplies wells and springs; *specif* water that has saturated surface soil and rocks

**ground wave** *n* a RADIO WAVE that travels along the surface of the earth rather than being reflected from the IONOSPHERE (upper part of the earth's atmosphere)

**groundwork** /-,wuhk/ *n* (preliminary work done to provide) a foundation or basis ⟨*a plan that provides the* ~ *for a bold new project*⟩ **2** a background that has not been worked upon (e g by painting or needlework) *synonyms* see [1]BASE

[1]**group** /groohp/ *n* **1** two or more figures or objects forming a complete unit in a composition (e g a painting or photograph) **2** *taking sing or pl vb* **2a** a number of individuals or objects assembled together or having some unifying relationship **b** an operational and administrative unit belonging to a command of an air force; *specif* a unit of the Royal Air Force higher than a wing and lower than a command **c** a usu small number of players of popular music, sometimes including a singer **3a** an assemblage of related organisms – often used when the kind or degree of relationship is not clearly defined **b(1)** an assemblage of atoms forming part of a molecule; RADICAL 4b ⟨*a methyl* ~⟩ **b(2)** all the (similar) chemical elements forming one of the vertical columns of the PERIODIC TABLE **c** a unit or division used in STRATIGRAPHY (study of rock layers having related characteristics) and comprising two or more related FORMATIONS that are next to each other in a SUCCESSION (ordered layers of rock deposits) **d** an assemblage of related languages ranking below a BRANCH **4** a mathematical set which has an operation defined on pairs of elements of the set such that the operation is ASSOCIATIVE (independent of the effects of bracketing), and which also has an IDENTITY ELEMENT and an INVERSE for every element [Fr *groupe*, fr It *gruppo*, of Gmc origin; akin to OHG *kropf* craw – more at CROP]

[2]**group** *vt* **1** to combine in a group **2** to assign to a group; classify ~ *vi* to form or belong to a group – **groupable** *adj*

**group captain** *n* – see MILITARY RANKS table

**grouper** /'groohpə/ *n, pl* **groupers**, *esp collectively* **grouper** any of numerous fishes (family Serranidae, esp genera *Epinephelus* and *Mycteroperca*) that are typically large solitary bottom-dwelling fishes of warm seas [Pg *garoupa*]

**groupie** /'groohpi/ *n* a fan, esp female, of a famous person, esp a rock star, who follows the object of admiration on tour [[1]*group* 2c + -*ie*]

**grouping** /'groohping/ *n* **1** the act or process of combining in groups **2** a set of individuals or objects combined in a group ⟨*a furniture* ~⟩ ⟨*an anti-fascist* ~⟩

**group practice** *n* a practice run by a group of associated medical GENERAL PRACTITIONERS

**group therapy** *n* the treatment of several individuals, often with similar psychological problems, simultaneously through group discussion and mutual aid – **group therapist** *n*

[1]**grouse** /grows/ *n, pl* **grouse** any of several birds (family Tetraonidae) that have a plump body, strong feathered legs, and reddish-brown plumage and that include many important game birds [origin unknown]

[2]**grouse** *vi, informal* to complain, grumble [origin unknown] – **grouser** *n*

[3]**grouse** *n, informal* a complaint ⟨*his main* ~ . . . *is over the inadequacy of the pay* – TLS⟩

[1]**grout** /growt/ *n* **1** **grouts** *pl*, **grout** sediment, dregs ⟨*coffee* ~*s*⟩ **2 grout, grouting 2a** thin mortar used for filling spaces (e g the joints in masonry); *also* any of various other materials (e g a mixture of cement and water or chemicals that solidify) used for a similar purpose **b** plaster that can be applied to the out-

side of buildings or as a thin finishing coat on ceilings **3** *archaic* (porridge made from) coarse meal; groats [OE *grūt* coarse meal, infusion of malt; akin to OE *grytt* grit; (2) perh of different origin]

²**grout** *vt* to fill up (joints) or finish (walls or ceilings) with grout – **grouter** *n*

**grove** /grohv/ *n* **1** a small wood or group of trees **2** a planting of esp citrus trees ⟨*orange* ~⟩ [ME, fr OE *grāf*]

**grovel** /'grovl/ *vi* **-ll-** (*NAm* **-l-**, **-ll-**) **1** to bow, lie, or creep with the body flattened on the floor so as to express complete servility or humility **2** to abase or humble oneself; cringe [back-formation fr *groveling* prone, fr *groveling*, adv, fr ME, fr *gruf*, adv, on the face (fr ON *ā grūfu*) + *-ling;* akin to OE *crēopan* to creep] – **groveller** *n*, **grovellingly** *adv*

**grow** /groh/ *vb* **grew** /grooh/; **grown** /grohn/ *vi* **1a** to spring up and develop to maturity **b** to be able to grow in some place or situation ⟨*trees that* ~ *only in the tropics*⟩ **c** to assume some relation (as if) through a process of natural growth ⟨*a tree with limbs* grown *together*⟩ ⟨*ferns* ~ing *from the rocks*⟩ **2a** to increase in size by addition of material either by assimilation into the living organism or by accumulation in a nonbiological process (e g crystallization) **b** to increase, expand ⟨*the population is* ~ing *rapidly*⟩ **3** to develop from an original source ⟨*the book* grew *out of a series of lectures*⟩ **4** to become gradually ⟨grew *pale*⟩ ~ *vt* **1** to cause to grow; cultivate ⟨~ *tomatoes*⟩ **2** DEVELOP **5** ⟨~ *wings*⟩ [ME *growen*, fr OE *grōwan;* akin to OHG *gruowan* to grow] – **grower** *n*, **growingly** *adv*

  *usage* Some people dislike the combination **grow** *smaller* as illogical.

**grow on** *vt* to have an increasing influence on; *esp* to become more pleasing to ⟨*her singing* grows on *you*⟩

**grow up** *vi* **1** *of a person* to develop towards or arrive at a mature state **2** to arise, develop, or evolve ⟨*the movement* grew up *in the 60s*⟩ **3** to begin to act sensibly – usu imper

**growing pains** /'groh-ing/ *n pl* **1** pains in the legs of growing children that have no known cause **2** the early stresses and strains attending a new project or development

**growing point** *n* the undifferentiated end of a plant shoot from which additional shoot tissues differentiate

¹**growl** /growl/ *vi* **1a** *esp of a dog* to utter a usu threatening growl ⟨*the dog* ~ed *at the stranger*⟩ **b** to make a noise like a growl; rumble ⟨*his stomach* ~ed⟩ ⟨~ing *thunder*⟩ **2** to complain gruffly or angrily ~ *vt* to utter with a growl ⟨~ed *his response*⟩ [prob imit]

²**growl** *n* a deep guttural inarticulate sound, esp expressing restrained anger – **growlingly** *adv*

**growler** /'growlə/ *n* **1** one who growls **2** a small iceberg, hazardous to ships

**growly** /'growli/ *adj* resembling a growl ⟨*a* ~ *voice*⟩ – **growliness** *n*

**grown** /grohn/ *adj* **1** fully grown; mature ⟨~ *men*⟩ **2** covered, surrounded, or overgrown with vegetation ⟨*land well* ~ *with trees*⟩ **3** cultivated or produced in a specified way or locality – used in combination ⟨*shade-*grown *tobacco*⟩

,**grown-'up** *adj* not childish or immature; adult ⟨*men and women incapable of* ~ *behaviour*⟩ – **grown-up** *n*

**growth** /grohth/ *n* **1a** (a stage in the process of) growing; size ⟨*the tree hasn't reached its full* ~⟩ **b** progressive development; evolution ⟨*art fosters the spiritual* ~ *of mankind*⟩ **c** an increase, expansion ⟨*the* ~ *of the oil industry*⟩ ⟨*mountaineering has a large and growing following ... but as a* ~ *sport it cannot compare with skiing* – *Scottish Field*⟩ **2a** something that grows or has grown ⟨*a* ~ *of bushes*⟩ **b** an abnormal proliferation of tissue (e g a tumour) **c** an outgrowth **d** the result of growth; a product ⟨*anarchy is a disturbing* ~ *from boredom*⟩ **3** cultivation ⟨*fruits of his own* ~⟩ **4** CRU – used in the classification of wine ⟨*a first-*growth *claret*⟩

**growth factor** *n* a substance (e g a vitamin) necessary for the growth of an organism

**growth hormone** *n* **1** a hormone of VERTEBRATE animals that is secreted by the front lobe of the PITUITARY GLAND and promotes and regulates growth **2** any of various plant substances (e g an AUXIN or GIBBERELLIN) that promote and regulate growth

**growth industry** *n* an industry that grows at a significantly higher rate than the average of other industries in a particular economy

**growth ring** *n* a layer of wood, shell, etc produced by a plant or animal during a particular period of growth – compare ANNUAL RING, ANNULUS

**groyne,** *chiefly NAm* **groin** /groyn/ *n* a rigid structure (e g of wood or concrete) built out from a shore to protect the shore from erosion, to trap sand (e g so as to make a beach) or to direct a current for scouring a channel – **groyned** *adj*

¹**grub** /grub/ *vb* **-bb-** *vt* **1** to clear by digging up roots and stumps **2** to dig *up* or *out* (as if) by the roots ⟨~*bed up obscure facts from a book*⟩ ~ *vi* **1** to dig in the ground, esp for something that is difficult to find or extract ⟨~*bing in the earth for potatoes*⟩ **2** to search about; rummage ⟨*always* ~*bed through junk shops*⟩ [ME *grubben;* akin to OE *grafan* to dig – more at GRAVE] – **grubber** *n*

²**grub** *n* **1** a soft thick wormlike larva of an insect (e g a beetle) **2** *informal* a slovenly person, esp a child **3** *informal* food **4** *archaic* one who does boring routine work; a drudge [ME *grubbe*, fr *grubben*]

**grubby** /'grubi/ *adj* **1** infested with grubs **2** dirty, grimy ⟨~ *hands*⟩ – **grubbily** *adv*, **grubbiness** *n*

'**grub-,kick** *vb* to kick (a rugby football) forwards along the ground – compare PUNT – **grub-kick** *n*

**grub screw** *n* a headless screw-bolt with a slotted end for turning with a screwdriver

¹**grubstake** /'grub,stayk/ *n, NAm* **1** supplies or funds given to a mining prospector on condition of a share of any profits **2** material assistance (e g money) provided for launching an enterprise or for helping a person in difficult circumstances [²*grub* **3** + *stake*]

²**grubstake** *vt, NAm* to provide with a grubstake – **grubstaker** *n*

**Grub Street** *n* the world or life-style of needy literary hacks [*Grub Street* in London, formerly inhabited by literary hacks]

¹**grudge** /gruj/ *vt* **1** to be unwilling or reluctant to give or admit; begrudge ⟨~d *the money to pay taxes*⟩ **2** to be envious of; resent ⟨~ *his success*⟩ [ME *grucchen, grudgen* to grumble, complain, fr OF *groucier*, of Gmc origin; akin to MHG *grogezen* to howl] – **grudger** *n*

²**grudge** *n* a feeling of deep-seated resentment or ill will

**grudging** /'grujing/ *adj* unwilling, reluctant – **grudgingly** *adv*

**gruel** /'grooh-əl/ *n* a thin porridge [ME *grewel*, fr MF *gruel*, of Gmc origin; akin to OE *grūt* grout]

**gruelling,** *NAm chiefly* **grueling** /'grooh-əling/ *adj* trying or exacting to the point of exhaustion; punishing ⟨*a* ~ *race*⟩ [fr prp of obs *gruel* to exhaust, punish, fr *gruel*, n] – **gruellingly** *adv*

**gruesome** /'groohs(ə)m/ *adj* horrific, repulsive, grisly ⟨~ *scenes of torture*⟩ [alter. of earlier *growsome*, fr E dial. *grow, grue* to shiver, fr ME *gruen*, prob fr MD *grüwen;* akin to OHG ingrūen to shiver] – **gruesomely** *adv*, **gruesomeness** *n*

**gruff** /gruf/ *adj* **1** rough, brusque, or stern in manner, speech, or aspect ⟨*a* ~ *reply*⟩ ⟨*a* ~ *man*⟩ **2** sounding deep and harsh; hoarse ⟨*a* ~ *voice*⟩ [D *grof;* akin to OHG *grob* coarse, *hruf* scurf – more at DANDRUFF] – **gruffly** *adv*, **gruffness** *n*

**grumble** /'grumbl/ *vi* **1** to mutter or murmur complainingly ⟨~d *about the rain*⟩ **2** to make a dull low inarticulate sound; rumble ⟨*thunder* ~d *over the horizon*⟩ ~ *vt* to express complainingly [prob fr MF *grommeler*, deriv of MD *grommen;* akin to OHG *grimm* grim] – **grumble** *n*, **grumbler** *n*, **grumblingly** *adv*, **grumbly** *adj*

**grumbling** /'grumbling/ *adj* causing intermittent pain or discomfort ⟨*a* ~ *appendix*⟩

**grummet** /'grumit/ *n* GROMMET

**grump** /grump/ *n* **1** *pl* a fit of ill humour or sulkiness ⟨*she's got the* ~s⟩ **2** a grumpy person [obs *grumps* snubs, slights, prob of imit origin]

**grumpy** /'grumpi/ *adj* moodily cross; surly – **grumpily** *adv*, **grumpiness** *n*

**Grundyism** /'grundi,iz(ə)m/ *n* excessive attachment to conventional standards, esp in sexual matters; prudishness [*Mrs Grundy*]

¹**grunt** /grunt/ *vi* to utter a grunt ~ *vt* to express with a grunt [ME *grunten*, fr OE *grunnettan*, freq of *grunian*, of imit origin] – **grunter** *n*

²**grunt** *n* **1** (a sound resembling) the deep short guttural sound characteristic of a pig **2** any of numerous chiefly tropical marine spiny-finned fishes (family Pomadasidae) capable of making a piglike grunting sound

**gruntled** /'gruntld/ *adj, informal* (made) contented or satisfied; placated [back-formation fr *disgruntled*]

**Gruyère** /'grooh-yeə (*Fr* gryjɛːr)/ *n* a pale yellow Swiss cheese with smaller holes and a slightly fuller flavour than Emmenthal [*Gruyère*, district in Switzerland]

**gryke** /griek/ n GRIKE (natural crevice)

**gryphon** /'grifən/ n a griffin *synonyms* see GRIFFON

**'G-,string** n a small piece of cloth, leather, etc covering the genitals and held in place by thongs, elastic, etc passed round the hips and between the buttocks

**G suit** n a suit designed to counteract the physiological effects of high acceleration in an aircraft or spacecraft [*gravity suit*]

**guacamole, guachamole** /,gwukə'mohli/ n a dip or hors d'oeuvre of seasoned sieved or mashed avocado [AmerSp *guacamole*, fr Nahuatl *ahuacamolli*, fr *ahuacatl* avocado + *molli* sauce, stew]

**guacharo** /'gwahchəroh/ n OILBIRD (nocturnal bird) [Sp *guácharo*]

**guaiac** /'g(w)ie,ak/ n the wood or resin of the guaiacum [NL *Guaiacum*]

**guaiacum** /'g(w)ie·əkəm/ n 1 any of a genus (*Guaiacum* of the family Zygophyllaceae) of tropical American trees and shrubs having featherlike leaves and mostly blue flowers – compare LIGNUM VITAE 2a the hard greenish-brown wood of a guaiacum (esp *Guaiacum officinale*) b a resin with a faint balsamic odour obtained from the trunk of two guaiacums (*Guaiacum officinale* and *Guaiacum sanctum*) that is used in medicine and in making varnishes [NL, genus name, fr Sp *guayaco*, fr Taino *guayacan*]

**guanaco** /gwah'nahkoh/ n, pl **guanacos**, esp collectively **guanaco** a S American mammal (*Lama guanicoe*) that has a soft thick fawn-coloured coat and is related to the camel but lacks a hump [Sp, fr Quechua *huanacu*]

**guanethidine** /gwah'nethədeen, -din/ n a synthetic drug, $C_{10}H_{22}N_4$, used esp in treating severe high blood pressure [blend of *guanidine* and *eth-*]

**guanidine** /'gwahnədeen, -din/ n a soluble chemical compound, $(NH_2)_2C:NH$, found esp in young plant and animal tissues and used esp in the synthesis of other organic chemical compounds and in medicine [ISV, fr *guanine*]

**guanine** /'gwahneen/ n a chemical compound, $C_5H_3N_4ONH_2$, that is a PURINE and is one of the four BASES whose order in the molecular chain of DNA or RNA codes genetic information – compare ADENINE, CYTOSINE, THYMINE, URACIL [*guano* + *-ine*; fr its being found esp in guano]

**guano** /'gwahnoh/ n a substance consisting chiefly of the excrement of seabirds that is rich in PHOSPHATES and is used as a fertilizer; *also* a similar product (e g of fish-cannery waste) [Sp, fr Quechua *huanu* dung]

**guanosine** /'gwahnəseen/ n a chemical compound (NUCLEOSIDE), $C_{10}H_{13}N_5O_5$, that forms part of RNA and contains guanine attached to the sugar RIBOSE [blend of *guanine* and *ribose*]

**guar** /gwah/ n a plant (*Cyanopsis psoralioides*) of the pea family that can withstand drought and is grown for animal fodder and for its seeds which produce GUAR GUM [Hindi *guār*]

**guarani** /,gwahrə'nee/ n, pl (*I*) **guarani, guaranis** (*2*) **guaranis, guaranies** 1 cap a member or the language of a people inhabiting Bolivia, Paraguay, and S Brazil 2 – see MONEY table [Sp *guaraní*]

**¹guarantee** /,garən'tee/ n 1 a guarantor 2 a written undertaking to answer for the payment of a debt or the performance of a duty of another in case of the other's default 3 an assurance for the fulfilment of a condition: e g 3a an agreement by which one person undertakes to answer for another's obligations (e g debts) in case of default b an assurance by the manufacturers of the quality or of the minimum length of use to be expected from a product offered for sale, usu accompanied by a promise to replace the product or refund the customer 4 something given as security; a pledge [prob alter. of ¹*guaranty*]

**²guarantee** vt **guaranteed; guaranteeing** 1 to undertake to answer for the debt, default, or miscarriage of ⟨~ a loan⟩ ⟨~ a cheque⟩ 2a to undertake to do or secure (something) ⟨she ~d delivery of the goods⟩ b to engage for the existence, permanence, or nature of ⟨I ~ he will come⟩ 3 to give security to

**guarantor** /,garən'taw/ n 1 a person, bank, etc that guarantees 2 one who makes or gives a guarantee [*guaranty* + ¹*-or*]

**guaranty** /'garənti/ n GUARANTEE 2,3,4 [MF *garantie*, fr OF, fr *garantir* to guarantee, fr *garant* warrant, of Gmc origin; akin to OHG *werēnto* guarantor – more at WARRANT]

**¹guard** /gahd/ n 1 a defensive position in boxing, fencing, etc 2 the act or duty of protecting or defending 3 a person or a body of men (esp soldiers) on sentinel duty 4a a person or group whose duty is to protect a place, people, etc b pl troops attached to the person of the sovereign; *specif* HOUSEHOLD TROOPS 5 something that affords protection or safety: e g 5a a device on a machine b an article of clothing that protects a part of the body ⟨shin ~⟩ 6 a basketball player who initiates offensive plays and usu marks an opposing guard 7 a strip of paper bound with book leaves onto which a loose sheet may be fastened 8 *Br* the person in charge of a railway train [ME *garde*, fr MF, fr OF, fr *garder* to guard, defend, of Gmc origin; akin to OHG *wartēn* to watch, take care – more at WARD]

**²guard** vt 1a to protect from danger, esp by watchful attention; make secure ⟨policemen ~ing our cities⟩ ⟨a room ~ed by locked doors⟩ b to stand at an entrance (as if) on guard c to protect (e g a card, chess man, etc) in a game ⟨the separated pawns could not both be ~ed⟩ 2 to watch over so as to prevent escape, disclosure, theft, or indiscretion ⟨~ing the secrets with their lives⟩; *also* to keep in check ⟨~ your tongue⟩ ~ vi to watch by way of caution or defence; stand guard *synonyms* see DEFEND – **guarder** n

**guard against** vt to attempt to prevent (something) by taking precautions

**guardant** /'gahd(ə)nt/ adj, of a heraldic animal shown from the side with the head turned towards the observer ⟨a lion passant ~⟩ [MF *gardant*, prp of *garder* to guard, look at]

**guard cell** n either of the two crescent-shaped cells that border and open and close a plant STOMA (small hole in the surface of a leaf)

**guarded** /'gahdid/ adj cautious, circumspect ⟨a ~ reply⟩ ⟨a ~ look⟩ – **guardedly** adv, **guardedness** n

**guard hair** n any of the long coarse hairs forming a protective coating over the underfur of a mammal

**guardhouse** /-,hows/ n a building used as headquarters by soldiers on guard duty or as a prison for military offenders

**guardian** /'gahdi·ən, -dyən/ n 1 one who or that which guards; a custodian ⟨~ angel⟩ 2 a person who looks after the person or property of another; *specif* a person entrusted by law with the care of a person (e g an orphan or lunatic) legally incapable of managing his/her own affairs – **guardianship** n

**guardrail** /-,rayl/ n 1 a railing (e g on a ship) for guarding against danger or trespass 2 a rail fitted on the inside of a main rail to prevent derailment of a train (e g round a corner)

**guardroom** /-,room, -,roohm/ n a room serving as a guardhouse

**guardsman** /-mən/ n a member of any military body called *guard* or *guards*

**guard's van** n, *Br* a railway wagon attached usu at the rear of a train for the use of the guard – compare CABOOSE

**guar gum** /gwah/ n a gum that consists of the ground ENDOSPERM (nutritive tissue) of GUAR seeds and is used esp as a thickening agent and as a sizing material in the manufacture of textiles

**guava** /'gwahvə/ n 1 any of several tropical American bushes or small trees (genus *Psidium*) of the eucalyptus family; *esp* a bushy tree (*Psidium guajava*) widely cultivated for its sweet acid yellow fruit 2 the edible fruit of a guava [modif of Sp *guayaba*, of Arawakan origin; akin to Tupi *guayava* guava]

**guayule** /gwə'yoohli/ n a much-branched silvery-leaved shrub (*Parthenium argentatum*) of the daisy family that occurs in Mexico and SW USA and that has been cultivated as a source of rubber [AmerSp, fr Nahuatl *cuauhuli*, lit., tree gum]

**gubbins** /'gubinz/ n, pl **gubbins** *Br informal* 1 the inner workings of a machine; gadgetry 2 a thingamajig 3 a disorganized collection of oddments 4 a group or collection of objects associated with something specified ⟨he received the catalogue and all the ~ that goes with it⟩ [pl of *gubbin* (fragment, paring), alter. of obs *gobone* gobbet, portion, fr ME *gobyn, goboun*]

**gubernatorial** /,gyoohbənə'tawri·əl/ adj of a governor [L *gubernator* governor, fr *gubernatus*, pp of *gubernare* to govern – more at GOVERN]

**guck** /guk/ n, *chiefly NAm* oozy sloppy dirt or muck [perh fr *goo* + *muck*]

**guddle** /'gudl/ vb, *chiefly Scot* vt to catch (fish) by groping with the hands (e g under stones or banks of streams) ~ vi to catch fish by guddling [prob imit]

**¹gudgeon** /'guj(ə)n/ n 1 a metal pivot fixed in the end of a wooden shaft 2 a socket fixed at the stern of a vessel, into which the rudder fits 3 an iron pin for fastening together blocks of stone [ME *gudyon*, fr MF *goujon*]

**²gudgeon** n, pl **gudgeons**, esp collectively **gudgeon** 1 a small European freshwater fish (*Gobio gobio*) related to the carps and often used for food or bait 2 any of several Australian fishes (family Electridae) [ME *gojune*, fr MF *gouvion, gougon*, fr L *gobion-, gobio*, alter. of *gobius* – more at GOBY]

**gudgeon pin** n a metal pin linking the piston and CONNECTING

ROD in an INTERNAL-COMBUSTION ENGINE – called also PISTON PIN

**guelder rose** /'geldə/ *n* an often cultivated shrub (*Viburnum opulus*) of the honeysuckle family that has clusters of white flowers [*Guelderland, Gelderland*, province of the Netherlands]

**Guelf, Guelph** /gwelf/ *n* a member of a papal and popular political party in medieval Italy that opposed the authority of the German emperors in Italy – compare GHIBELLINE [It *Guelfo*]

**guenon** /gə'non (*Fr* gənɔ̃)/ *n, pl* **guenons**, *esp collectively* **guenon** any of various long-tailed chiefly tree-dwelling African monkeys (*Cercopithecus* and related genera) [Fr]

**guerdon** /'guhd(ə)n/ *n, poetic* a reward, recompense [ME, fr MF, modif of OHG *widarlōn*, fr *widar* back, against + *lōn* reward – more at WITH, LUCRE] – **guerdon** *vt*

**guereza** /'gerizə/ *n* COLOBUS MONKEY [native name in Ethiopia]

**guernsey** /'guhnzi/ *n, often cap* **1** (any of) a breed of fawn and white dairy cattle that are larger than the JERSEY and produce rich yellowish milk **2** a thick knitted jersey traditionally worn by sailors [*Guernsey*, one of the Channel Islands]

**guerrilla, guerilla** /gə'rilə USE guerrilla *is sometimes pronounced* ge'rilə *in order to distinguish it from* gorilla/ *n* one who engages in irregular warfare, esp as a member of a small independent unit carrying out harassment and sabotage [Sp *guerrilla*, fr dim. of *guerra* war, of Gmc origin; akin to OHG *werra* strife – more at WAR]

**1guess** /ges/ *vt* **1** to form an opinion of from insufficient evidence or on dubious grounds (~ed *that rain would fall*) **2** to arrive at a correct conclusion about by conjecture, chance, or intuition (~ *the answer*) **3** *chiefly NAm informal* to believe, suppose (*I* ~ *you're right*) ~ *vi* to make a guess *synonyms* see [2]CONJECTURE *antonym* know [ME *gessen*, prob of Scand origin; akin to ON *geta* to get, guess – more at GET] – **guesser** *n*

**2guess** *n* a conjecture, estimate

**guesstimate** /'gestimət/ *n, informal* an estimate made without adequate information [blend of *guess* and *estimate*] – **guesstimate** *vt*

**guesswork** /-,wuhk/ *n* (judgment based on) the act of guessing

**1guest** /gest/ *n* **1a** a person entertained in one's home (~s *left when the drink ran out*) **b** a person taken out, entertained, and paid for by another **c** a person who pays for the services of an establishment (eg a hotel) **2** an organism (eg an insect) sharing the dwelling of another; INQUILINE **3** a person invited to participate in a public occasion or entertainment (eg a television programme) [ME *gest*, fr ON *gestr*; akin to OE *gæst* guest, stranger, L *hostis* stranger, enemy]

**2guest** *vi* to appear as a guest

**guesthouse** /-,hows/ *n* a private house offering rooms to paying guests

**guest night** *n* a social occasion to which members of a group (eg a social club) may invite nonmembers as guests

**guest worker** *n* an immigrant worker who is a temporary resident of a country, esp in the COMMON MARKET, and is usu employed in an unskilled job [trans of Ger *gastarbeiter*]

**guff** /guf/ *n, informal* nonsense, rubbish [prob imit]

**guffaw** /'gufaw, gə'faw/ *vi or n* (to utter) a burst of loud or boisterous laughter [imit]

**guggle** /'gugl/ *vi* to gurgle [imit] – **guggle** *n*

**guidance** /'gied(ə)ns/ *n* **1** the act or process of guiding **2** advice or direction given to help someone with a particular problem (eg a vocational or psychological one) (*he received much* ~ *from his father and then later from his teacher*) **3** the process of controlling the course of a projectile (eg a missile) by a built-in mechanism

**1guide** /gied/ *n* **1a** one who leads or directs another (*Beatrice was the* ~ *of Dante*) **b** one who shows and points out interesting (historical) information about a tourist attraction (eg a castle or cathedral) to a group of people **c** something (eg a guidebook) that provides a person with information about a place, activity, etc (*needed a detailed* ~ *for the gallery's endless corridors*) **d** something or somebody that directs a person in his/her conduct or course of life (*Merlin proved a powerful* ~ *to King Arthur*) **2a** a device (eg a bar or rod) for steadying or directing the motion of something (eg a part of a machine) **b** a tab projecting from a card as a label that facilitates reference **3a** a ship that is used as a marker from which other ships can regulate their movements (eg to maintain a particular formation) **b** a soldier who acts as a pivotal point (eg at the side of a line) to regulate an orderly movement or alignment **4** *often cap, chiefly Br* a

member of a worldwide movement of girls and young women that was founded with the aim of forming character and teaching good citizenship through outdoor activities and domestic skills; *specif* a member of the intermediate section of the British Guide movement for girls aged from 10 to 15 [ME, fr MF, fr OProv *guida*, of Gmc origin; akin to OE *wītan* to look after, *witan* to know – more at WIT]

**2guide** *vt* **1a** to act as a guide to; direct (~d *him through the labyrinth*) **b** to control or steer (a vehicle) (*skilfully* ~d *the glider down to the ground*) **2a** to direct or supervise, usu to a particular end (~d *the country to victory*) **b** to take charge of the training or instruction of ~ *vi* to act or work as a guide; give guidance – **guider** *n*, **guidable** *adj*

**guidebook** /-,book/ *n* a handbook; *esp* a book of information for travellers

**guided missile** *n* a missile whose course in flight is controlled electronically from the ground or by an inbuilt device (eg one that causes it to seek heat)

**guide dog** *n* a dog trained to lead a blind person

**guideline** /-,lien/ *n* **1** an indication or outline (eg by a government) of policy or conduct **2** a principle or model on which a course of action may be based (*used Buddhism as a* ~ *in sentencing the convicted*)

**guidepost** /-,pohst/ *n* a signpost

**guide rope** *n* a rope that is attached to something (eg a crane or a balloon) for guiding or steadying

**guideway** /-,way/ *n* a channel, groove, or track for controlling the line or motion of something

**guide word** *n* either of the words to the left and right at the top of a page of an alphabetical reference work (eg a dictionary) indicating the alphabetically first and last words on the page

**guiding** /'gieding/ *n* **1** the activity of one who guides **2** *chiefly Br* the activities of the Guide movement

**guidon** /'gied(ə)n/ *n* **1** a triangular or forked pennant; *esp* one carried by a military unit (eg of dragoons) as a standard **2** one who carries a guidon [MF, fr OProv *guidoo*, fr *guida* guide]

**guidwillie** /gid'wili (Scots gǒdwili)/ *adj, Scot* cordial, cheering [Sc *guidwill* goodwill]

**guild** /gild/ *n taking sing or pl vb* an association of men with similar interests or pursuits; *esp* a medieval association of merchants or craftsmen formed to further their trade interests or for mutual aid [ME *gilde*, fr ON *gildi* payment, guild; akin to OE *gield* tribute, guild – more at DANEGELD] – **guildship** *n*, **guildsman** *n*

**guilder** /'gildə/ *n* GULDEN (monetary unit of the Netherlands) [modif of D *gulden*]

**guildhall** /-'hawl/ *n* a hall where a guild or corporation usu assembles; *esp* a town hall

**guild socialism** *n* an early 20th-century British socialist theory advocating state ownership of industry with control and management of individual plants, factories, etc by guilds of workers

**guile** /giel/ *n* deceitful cunning; duplicity *synonyms* see SLY [ME, fr OF, prob of Gmc origin] – **guileful** *adj*, **guilefully** *adv*, **guilefulness** *n*

**guileless** /'giel·lis/ *adj* lacking in deceit or cunning; innocent – **guilelessly** *adv*, **guilelessness** *n*

**guillemot** /'gili,mot/ *n, pl* **guillemots**, *esp collectively* **guillemot** any of several narrow-billed AUKS (seabirds) of northern seas (genera *Uria* and *Cepphus*) [Fr, fr MF, dim. of *Guillaume* William]

**guilloche** /gi'losh/ *n* an ornament used chiefly in architecture formed of interlaced bands [Fr *guillochis*]

**guillotine** /'giləteen/ *n* **1** a machine for beheading consisting of a heavy blade that slides down between vertical grooved posts **2** an instrument (eg a paper cutter) that works like a guillotine **3** limitation of the discussion of specific sections of a bill or portions of other legislative business by the imposition of a predetermined time limit – compare CLOSURE [Fr, fr Joseph *Guillotin* †1814 Fr physician who proposed its use] – **guillotine** *vt*

**guilt** /gilt/ *n* **1** the fact of having committed an offence, esp by breaking a law **2a** responsibility for a wrong or an offence; blame (*when a spoilt child misbehaves, the* ~ *often lies with the parents*) **b** feelings of being to blame, esp for imagined offences or from a sense of inadequacy △ gilt [ME, delinquency, guilt, fr OE *gylt* delinquency]

**guiltless** /'giltlis/ *adj* innocent – **guiltlessly** *adv*, **guiltlessness** *n*

**guilty** /'gilti/ *adj* **1** justly answerable for an offence **2a** suggesting or involving guilt ⟨~ *looks*⟩ ⟨*a* ~ *deed*⟩ **b** feeling guilt ⟨*their* ~ *consciences*⟩ – **guiltily** *adv*, **guiltiness** *n*

**guimpe** /gimp/ *n* **1** a blouse worn under a pinafore **2** GIMP (braid or cord trimming) [Fr, fr OF *guimple*, of Gmc origin; akin to OE *wimpel* wimple; (2) by alter.]

**guinea** /'gini/ *n* **1** a former British gold coin worth 21 shillings **2** a monetary unit worth one pound and five pence [*Guinea*, region in W Africa, supposed source of the gold from which it was made]

**guinea fowl** /'gini/ *n* a W African bird (*Numida meleagris*) related to the pheasants, that has white-speckled slaty plumage and a bare neck and head and is widely kept for food; *broadly* any of several related birds of continental Africa and Madagascar

**guinea hen** *n* a female guinea fowl; *broadly* GUINEA FOWL

**guinea pig** *n* **1** a small stout-bodied short-eared nearly tailless rodent (*Cavia cobaya*) often kept as a pet or for use in scientific experiments **2** *chiefly informal* somebody or something used as a subject of scientific research, experimentation, or testing

**guinea worm** *n* a very long slender NEMATODE (unsegmented round-bodied worm) (*Dracunculus medinensis*) that lives as a parasite under the skin of various mammals, including human beings, in warm countries

**Guinness** /'ginis/ *trademark* – used for a type of bitter stout

**guipure** /gi'pyooa/ *n* a heavy large-patterned decorative lace on a fabric foundation [Fr, fr MF, a kind of lace, fr *guiper* to cover with silk or wool, of Gmc origin]

**guiro** /'gwiea,roh/ *n*, *pl* **guiro** a percussion instrument of Latin-American origin made of a serrated gourd and played by scraping a stick along its surface [AmerSp *güiro*, lit., gourd]

**guisard** /'giezad/ *n*, *Scot & N Eng* a mummer; *esp* one who performs at Hallowe'en [obs Sc *gyze* to disguise, fr ME *gyzen* to dress, fr *guise*, *gyze* guise]

**guise** /giez/ *n* **1** external appearance; semblance, aspect ⟨*under the* ~ *of friendship*⟩ **2** *archaic* a form or style of dress; costume ⟨*the king lived simply, and went about in the* ~ *of a peasant*⟩ △ disguise [ME, fr OF, of Gmc origin; akin to OHG *wisa* manner – more at WISE]

**guitar** /gi'tah/ *n* a flat-bodied stringed instrument whose sound may or may not be electronically modified, with a long FRETTED neck (neck with ridges against which the strings are pressed) and usu six strings plucked with a plectrum or with the fingers [Fr *guitare*, fr Sp *guitarra*, fr Ar *qītār*, fr Gk *kithara* cithara] – **guitarist** *n*

**Gujarati** /,gooja'rahti/ *n*, *pl* **Gujarati 1** Gujarati, Gujerati the INDIC language of Gujarat and neighbouring regions **2** a member of a people chiefly of Gujarat speaking the Gujarati language [Hindi *gujarātī*, fr *Gujarāt* Gujarat, region in W India]

**Gujrati** *n*, *pl* **Gujrati** GUJARATI 2

**gular** /'gyoohla/ *adj* of or situated on the throat [L *gula* throat – more at GLUTTON]

**gulch** /gulch/ *n*, *chiefly NAm* a ravine, esp with a rushing stream flowing through it [perh fr E dial. *gulch* to gulp, fr ME *gulchen*]

**gulden** /'goold(ə)n/ *n*, *pl* **guldens**, **gulden** FLORIN [ME (Sc), fr MD *gulden florijn* golden florin]

**gules** /gyoohlz/ *n*, *pl* **gules** the heraldic colour red [ME *goules*, fr MF, fr OF, fr *goles*, *goules* neck ornament made of fur usu dyed red, pl of *gole*, lit., throat]

**¹gulf** /gulf/ *n* **1** a part of the sea that is partly or almost completely enclosed by land and is usu larger than a bay ⟨*the Gulf of Mexico*⟩ **2** a deep chasm; an abyss **3** a whirlpool **4** a great area of division or difference; an unbridgeable gap ⟨*the* ~ *between theory and practice*⟩ [ME *goulf*, fr MF *golfe*, fr It *golfo*, fr LL *colpus*, fr Gk *kolpos* bosom, gulf; akin to OE *hwealf* vault, OHG *walbo*]

**²gulf** *vt* to engulf

**gulfweed** /-,weed/ *n* SARGASSUM (type of seaweed); *esp* a branching floating olive-brown seaweed (*Sargassum bacciferum*) with numerous berrylike air sacs that grows thickly in tropical American seas [*Gulf* of Mexico]

**¹gull** /gul/ *n* any of numerous long-winged web-footed usu aquatic birds (family Laridae); *esp* a largely white, grey, or black gull (e g of the genus *Larus*) [ME, of Celt origin; akin to W *gwylan* gull]

**²gull** *vt* to trick, cheat, or deceive (somebody foolish or unwary); dupe [obs *gull* gullet, fr ME *golle*, fr MF *goule*]

**³gull** *n*, *archaic* a person who is easily deceived or cheated; a dupe

**Gullah** /'gula; *also* 'goola/ *n* **1** a member of a group of Negroes inhabiting the sea islands and coastal districts of S Carolina, Georgia, and northeastern Florida **2** the English dialect of the Gullahs marked by various Africanisms

**gullet** /'gulit/ *n* **1** OESOPHAGUS (food-carrying passage between throat and stomach); *broadly* the throat **2** a groove in the living substance (PROTOPLASM) of various single-celled organisms (e g a PARAMECIUM) that sometimes functions in the intake of food [ME *golet*, fr MF *goulet*, dim. of *goule* throat, fr L *gula* – more at GLUTTON]

**gullible**, **gullable** /'guləbl/ *adj* easily deceived, cheated, or duped [²*gull* + -*ible*, -*able*] – **gullibility** *n*, **gullibly** *adv*

**gull-wing** /'gulwing/ *adj* **1** *of a car door* opening upwards **2** *of an aircraft wing* slanting upwards from the fuselage for a short distance with a long horizontal outer section

**¹gully** /'guli/ *n* **1** a trench worn in the earth by running water after rains **2** a deep gutter; a drain **3** a close fielding position in cricket just behind the stumps on the OFF SIDE; *also* the fieldsman occupying this position **4** *Austr & NZ* a valley [obs *gully* gullet, prob alter. of ME *golet*]

**²gully** *vb* to wear away into gullies; erode

**gully erosion** *n* soil erosion produced by running water

**gulosity** /gyoo'losəti/ *n*, *formal* excessive appetite; greediness [ME *gulosite*, fr LL *gulositas*, fr L *gulosus* gluttonous, fr *gula* gullet]

**gulp** /gulp/ *vt* **1** to swallow hurriedly or greedily or in one swallow **2** to keep back as if by swallowing ⟨~ *down a sob*⟩ ~ *vi* to make a sudden swallowing movement as if surprised or nervous [ME *gulpen*, fr a MD or MLG word akin to D & Fris *gulpen* to bubble forth, drink deep; akin to OE *gielpan* to boast – more at YELP] – **gulp** *n*, **gulper** *n*

**¹gum** /gum/ *n* the tissue that surrounds the teeth and covers the tooth-bearing parts of the jaws [ME *gome*, fr OE *gōma* palate; akin to OHG *guomo* palate, Gk *chaos* abyss]

**²gum** *n* **1a** any of numerous substances that are exuded by plants, consist of many repeating sugar units, and are gelatinous when moist but harden on drying – compare MUCILAGE **b** any of various substances (e g a mucilage, OLEORESIN, or GUM RESIN) that exude from plants **2** a substance prepared from or resembling a plant gum (e g in being sticky or adhesive) **3** **gum**, **gum tree 3a** a tree (e g a SAPODILLA) that yields gum **b** *chiefly Austr* a eucalyptus tree **4 gum**, **gumwood** the wood of a gum tree **5** CHEWING GUM ⟨*a packet of* ~ *containing five pieces*⟩ **6** a hard jellylike sweet; a gum-drop ⟨*a packet of fruit* ~s⟩ [ME *gomme*, fr OF, fr L *cummi*, *gummi*, fr Gk *kommi*, fr Egypt *qmy.t*]

**³gum** *vb* -**mm**- *vt* to smear, seal, or clog (as if) with gum ⟨~ *up the works*⟩ ~ *vi* to exude or form gum – **gummer** *n*

**⁴gum** *n* God – used euphemistically in the phrase *by gum* as a mild oath [euphemism]

**gum acacia** *n* GUM ARABIC

**gum ammoniac** *n* AMMONIAC (strong-smelling resin)

**gum arabic** *n* a water-soluble gum obtained from several acacias (esp *Acacia senegal* and *Acacia arabica*) and used esp in the manufacture of adhesives, in confectionery, and in pharmacy ⟨*the back of the stamp is coated with* ~⟩

**gumbo** /'gumboh/ *n* **1** a vegetable soup thickened with okra pods and usu containing meat or seafoods **2** *often cap* a PATOIS (mixture of African languages and French) used by Negroes and Creoles, esp in Louisiana **3** *NAm* OKRA **1** [AmerF *gombo*, of Bantu origin; akin to Umbundu *ochinggômbo* okra; (2) AmerF *gombo*, perh fr Kongo *nkômbô* runaway slave]

**gumboil** /'gum,boyl/ *n* an abscess in the gum

**gumboot** /-,booht/ *n* a strong waterproof rubber boot reaching usu to the knee

**gumdigger** /'gum,digə/ *n* one who digs (e g in New Zealand) for KAURI gum (commercially valuable resin of a coniferous tree)

**gum-drop** /'gum,drop/ *n* a hard jellylike sweet made of flavoured GUM ARABIC ⟨*wine* ~s⟩

**gumfield** /'gum,feeld, -,fiəld/ *n* an area (e g in New Zealand) where KAURI trees (coniferous trees) have grown that is rich in deposits of the resin that comes from them

**gumma** /'gumə/ *n*, *pl* **gummas** *also* **gummata** /'gumətə/ a rubbery tumour characteristic of the final stage of syphilis [NL *gummat-*, *gumma*, fr LL, gum, alter. of L *gummi*] – **gummatous** *adj*

**gummite** /'gumiet/ *n* a yellow to reddish-brown mixture of natural oxides of uranium chemically combined with water molecules and typically containing thorium and lead [Ger

-*gummit*, fr *gummi* gum, fr MHG, fr L; fr the gumlike appearance of some forms]

**gummosis** /gə'mohsis/ *n* the abnormal production of gum by a plant as a result of disease, injury, etc; *also* a plant disease marked by gummosis [NL, fr L *gummi* gum]

**gummy** /'gumi/ *adj* **1a** consisting of or containing gum **b** covered with gum **2** viscous, sticky – **gumminess** *n*

**gumption** /'gumpsh(ə)n/ *n* **1** shrewd practical common sense ⟨*when the pipe burst he had the* ~ *to turn off the water at the main*⟩ **2** enterprise, initiative ⟨*she had the* ~ *to start her own business*⟩ [origin unknown]

**gum resin** *n* a mixture of gum and resin, usu obtained by making an incision in a plant and allowing the juice which exudes to solidify

**gumshoe** /'gum,shooh/ *n, chiefly NAm informal* a detective [*gumshoe* (rubber shoe, one who walks stealthily)]

**gum tragacanth** /'tragəkanth/ *n* TRAGACANTH

**gum tree** *n* GUM 3; *esp* a eucalyptus – **up a gum tree** *Br informal* in serious difficulties

**gum turpentine** *n* TURPENTINE 2a (oil distilled from plant turpentines)

**gumwood** /'gum,wood/ *n* GUM 4

**¹gun** /gun/ *n* **1a** a cannon or piece of artillery; *esp* one with a high muzzle velocity that fires projectiles with a comparatively flat path through the air **b** a portable firearm (eg a rifle or pistol) **c** a device that throws a projectile **2** a discharge of a gun in a salute or as a signal ⟨*a salute of six* ~ *s was fired*⟩ **3** a person with a gun in a shooting party **4** something suggesting a gun in shape or function ⟨*a spray* ~⟩ ⟨*a cream* ~⟩ **5** *NAm* one who is skilled with a gun; *esp* a gunman [ME *gonne, gunne*, prob irreg fr *Gonnilda, Gunnilda*, fem forename, fr ON *Gunnhildr*] – **gunned** *adj* – **go great guns** *informal* to act or progress rapidly and successfully – **jump the gun 1** to start in a race before the starting signal **2** to act, move, or begin something before the proper time

**²gun** *vt* **-nn- 1a** to fire on **b** to shoot ⟨~*ned him down*⟩ **2** to open up the throttle of so as to increase speed ⟨~ *the engine*⟩ – **gun for** *vt, informal* to aim at; pursue with determination ⟨*he was gunning for that top job*⟩ ⟨*they'll gun for him until they ruin him*⟩

**¹gunboat** /'gun,boht/ *n* a relatively heavily armed ship that rides fairly shallowly on the water

**²gunboat** *adj* of or employing the high-handed use of naval or military power ⟨~ *diplomacy*⟩

**guncotton** /'gun,kot(ə)n/ *n* CELLULOSE NITRATE; *specif* cellulose nitrate with a high nitrogen content, used as an explosive

**gundog** /'gun,dog/ *n* a dog (eg a setter) trained to accompany sportsmen hunting with guns and locate, drive out of cover, or retrieve game

**gunfight** /'gun,fiet/ *n* a duel with guns – **gunfighter** *n*

**gunfire** /'gun,fieə/ *n* (the noise made by) the firing of guns

**gunflint** /'gun,flint/ *n* a piece of flint from which sparks are struck by the hammer to ignite the charge in a flintlock gun

**gunge** /gunj/ *n, Br slang* an unpleasant, dirty, or sticky substance [origin unknown] – **gungy** *adj*

**gung ho** /,gung 'hoh/ *adj, chiefly NAm informal* extremely or excessively zealous or enthusiastic [*Gung ho!*, motto (interpreted as meaning "work together") of certain US marine raiders in World War II, fr Chin (Pek) *gōnghé* (*kung¹-ho²*), short for *jōngguo gōngyè hózò shè* (*chung¹-kuo²kung¹-yeh⁴ ho²-tso⁴she⁴*) Chinese Industrial Cooperatives Society]

**gunk** /gungk/ *n, chiefly NAm slang* gunge [prob imit]

**gunlayer** /'gun,layə/ *n* somebody who adjusts a gun to the correct angle of height and direction for firing

**gunlock** /-,lok/ *n* the mechanism for igniting the charge of a firearm

**gunman** /-mən/ *n* a man armed with a gun; *esp* a professional killer

**gunmetal** /-,metl/ *n* **1** (a metal treated to imitate) a bronze formerly used for cannon **2** the colour of nearly black tarnished copper-alloy gunmetal ⟨*stockings of* ~ *silk*⟩

**gun moll** *n, slang* the girlfriend of a gangster or gunman

**gun money** *n* debased coins issued by James II in Ireland in 1689 and made partly of metal from old cannon

**¹gunnel** /'gunl/ *n* a small slimy elongated N Atlantic blenny (*Pholis gunnellus*); *also* any of several related fishes (family Pholidae) [origin unknown]

**²gunnel** *n* GUNWALE

**gunner** /'gunə/ *n* **1** a soldier or airman who operates a gun; *specif* a private in the Royal Artillery **2** one who hunts with a

gun **3** a WARRANT OFFICER who supervises naval guns and their shells and other equipment

**gunnery** /'gunəri/ *n* **1** the use of guns; *specif* the science of the flight of projectiles and of the effective use of guns **2** the firing of guns

**gunnery sergeant** *n* – see MILITARY RANKS table

**gunny** /'guni/ *n* a coarse heavy material, usu of jute, used esp for sacking [Hindi *gani*]

**gunnysack** /'guni,sak/ *n* a sack made of gunny

**gunplay** /'gun,play/ *n* the shooting of pistols, revolvers, etc with intent to scare or kill

**gunpoint** /'gun,poynt/ *n* – **at gunpoint** under threat of death by being shot

**gunpowder** /-,powdə/ *n* an explosive mixture of POTASSIUM NITRATE, charcoal, and sulphur used in gunnery and blasting; *broadly* any of various powders used in guns as propelling charges

**gun room** *n* quarters on a British warship used by junior officers

**gunrunner** /-,runə/ *n* one who carries or deals in contraband arms and ammunition – **gunrunning** *n*

**gunship** /-,ship/ *n* a heavily armed relatively slow aircraft (eg a helicopter or converted transport aeroplane) used to suppress ground fire; *also* an antitank helicopter

**gunshot** /-,shot/ *n* **1** shot or a projectile fired from a gun **2** the range of a gun ⟨*out of* ~⟩ **3** the firing of a gun

**'gun-,shy** *adj, esp of a dog* afraid of the sound of a gun

**gunslinger** /'gun,sling-ə/ *n, slang* a gunman

**gunsmith** /-,smith/ *n* somebody who designs, makes, or repairs firearms

**gunter rig** /'guntə/ *n* a FORE-AND-AFT ship's rig (with the sails attached to the mast along their leading edge) similar in shape to the BERMUDA RIG (with a triangular sail) but setting the upper part of the sail from a topmast which slides up and down the mast [Edmund *Gunter* †1626 E mathematician; fr its resemblance to a calculating instrument employing a system devised by Gunter]

**Gunter's chain** /'guntə/ *n* a surveying chain 66 feet (about 20.1 metres) long [Edmund *Gunter*]

**gunwale, gunnel** /'gunl/ *n* the upper edge of a ship's or boat's side [ME *gonnewale*, fr *gonne* gun + *wale*; fr its former use as a support for guns]

**gunyah** /'gunyə/ *n, Austr* a hut built by Australian aborigines [native name in Australia]

**gup** /'gup/ *n, slang* foolish talk; nonsense [Hindi *gap*]

**guppy** /'gupi/ *n, pl* **guppies**, *esp collectively* **guppy** a small TOPMINNOW (*Lebistes reticulatus* or *Poecilia reticulata*) of Barbados, Trinidad, and Venezuela that is frequently kept as an aquarium fish [R J L *Guppy* †1916 Trinidadian naturalist]

**gurgle** /'guhgl/ *vi* to make the sound (as if) of unevenly flowing water; *also* to flow or move with such a sound ⟨*the baby's gurgling cries of pleasure*⟩ ⟨*the brook* ~d *over the stones*⟩ ~ *vt* to utter with a gurgling sound [prob imit] – **gurgle** *n*

**Gurkha** /'guhkə/ *n* **1** a member of a group of warlike Hindu Rajputs of Nepal **2** a soldier from Nepal in the British or Indian army

**gurn** /guhn/ *vi* GIRN 2

**gurnard** /'guhnəd/ *n, pl* **gurnards**, *esp collectively* **gurnard** any of various spiny-finned fishes (family Triglidae) that have large heads covered with bony plates and three pairs of fingerlike PECTORAL FINS situated just behind the head [ME, fr MF *gornart*, irreg fr *grognier* to grunt, fr L *grunnire*, of imit origin; fr the grunting noise it makes when caught]

**guru** /'goohrooh, 'goo-/ *n, pl* **gurus 1** a personal religious teacher and spiritual guide (eg in Hinduism) **2a** a spiritual and intellectual guide; a mentor **b** *informal* the acknowledged leader or chief proponent (eg of a cult or idea) ⟨*the* ~ *of modern philosophical thought*⟩ [Hindi *gurū*, fr Skt *guru*, fr *guru*, adj, heavy, venerable – more at GRIEVE]

**¹gush** /gush/ *vi* **1** to issue copiously or violently **2** to emit a sudden copious flow **3** to make an effusive often affected display of sentiment or enthusiasm ⟨*the interviewer* ~ing *over the film star*⟩ ~ *vt* to emit in a copious free flow ⟨*the wound* ~ed *blood*⟩ [ME *guschen*, prob of imit origin]

**²gush** *n* **1** (something emitted in) a sudden outpouring **2** an effusive often affected display of sentiment or enthusiasm

**gusher** /'gushə/ *n* one who or that which gushes; *specif* an oil well with a copious natural flow

**gushy** /'gushi/ *adj* marked by effusive often affected sentiment or enthusiasm – **gushily** *adv*, **gushiness** *n*

**gusset** /'gusit/ *n* **1** a usu diamond-shaped or triangular piece of material inserted in a seam (eg of a sleeve, crotch of an undergarment, or wallet) to provide expansion or reinforcement **2** a plate or bracket for strengthening an angle in framework (eg in a building or bridge) [ME, piece of armour covering the joints in a suit of armour, fr MF *gouchet*] – **gusset** *vt*

**[1]gust** /gust/ *n* **1** a sudden brief rush of (rain carried by the) wind **2** a sudden outburst; a surge ⟨*a ~ of emotion*⟩ [prob fr ON *gustr;* akin to OHG *gussa* flood, OE *gēotan* to pour – more at FOUND] – **gusty** *adj,* **gustily** *adv,* **gustiness** *n*

**[2]gust** *vi* to blow in gusts ⟨*winds ~*ing *up to 40 mph*⟩

**gustation** /gu'staysh(ə)n/ *n, formal* the act or sensation of tasting [L *gustation-, gustatio,* fr *gustatus,* pp of *gustare* to taste – more at CHOOSE]

**gustatory** /'gustət(ə)ri/, **gustative** /-tiv/ *also* **gustatorial** /gustə'tawri·əl/ *adj, formal* relating to, associated with, or being the sense of taste – **gustatorily** *adv,* **gustativeness** *n*

**gusto** /'gustoh/ *n* enthusiastic and vigorous enjoyment or vitality ⟨*he sang with great ~*⟩ [It & Sp, fr L *gustus* taste, liking; akin to L *gustare* to taste]

**[1]gut** /gut/ *n* **1a** **guts** *pl,* **gut** the bowels, entrails **b** (a part, esp the lower part between the stomach and anus, of) the ALIMENTARY CANAL **c** **guts** *pl,* **gut** the belly, abdomen **d** catgut **2** the basic emotional or instinctively responding part of a person ⟨*wishes to appeal to the ~ rather than the mind*⟩ – Clive Barnes⟩ **3** a narrow passage; *also* a narrow waterway **4** the sac of silk taken from a silkworm ready to spin its cocoon, and drawn out into a thread for use in attaching a fishhook to a fishing line **5** *pl, informal* the inner essential parts ⟨*the ~*s *of a car*⟩ **6** *pl, informal* courage, determination **7** *pl but taking sing vb, slang* a glutton ⟨*a greedy ~*s⟩ [ME, fr OE *guttas,* pl; akin to OE *gēotan* to pour] – **hate somebody's guts** to hate somebody with great intensity

**[2]gut** *vt* **-tt-** **1** to remove the bowels from **2a** to destroy the inside of ⟨*fire ~*ted *the building*⟩ **b** to destroy the essential power or effectiveness of ⟨*inflation ~*ting *the economy of a country*⟩ **3** to extract the essentials of ⟨*~ a novel*⟩

**[3]gut** *adj* **1** arising from or concerning one's strongest emotions or instincts ⟨*~ reaction to the misery he has seen* – J A Lukas⟩ **2** having strong impact or immediate relevance ⟨*~ issues*⟩

**gutless** /-lis/ *adj* lacking courage; cowardly – **gutlessness** *n*

**gutsy** /-si/ *adj, informal* **1** courageous ⟨*a ~ little fighter*⟩ **2** expressing or appealing strongly to the physical passions; lusty ⟨*belting out ~ rock*⟩ **3** greedy – **gutsiness** *n*

**gutta-percha** /,gutə 'puhchə/ *n* a tough plastic substance derived from the milky whitish liquid (LATEX) exuded by several Malaysian trees (genera *Payena* and *Palaquium*) of the sapodilla family. It resembles rubber but contains more resin and is used esp for electrical insulation and in dentistry. [Malay *gĕtah-pĕrcha,* fr *gĕtah* sap, latex + *pĕrcha,* tree producing gutta-percha]

**guttate** /'gutayt/ *adj, biology* having or covered with small (coloured) spots or droplike markings; *also* containing small drops of matter [L *guttatus,* fr *gutta*]

**guttation** /gu'taysh(ə)n/ *n* the exudation of water or watery liquid from an uninjured surface of a plant (eg through specialized pores in the outer layer of leaves, stems, etc) [L *gutta* drop]

**[1]gutter** /'gutə/ *n* **1a** a trough along the eaves to catch and carry off rainwater **b** a low channel (eg at the edge of a street) to carry off surface water **c** a trough or groove to catch and direct something ⟨*the ~*s *of a bowling alley*⟩ **2** a white space between two pages of a book, two postage stamps on a sheet, etc **3** *the* lowest or most vulgar level or condition of human life [ME *goter,* fr OF *goutiere,* fr *goute* drop, fr L *gutta*]

**[2]gutter** *vt* **1** to cut or wear gutters in **2** to provide with a gutter ~ *vi* **1** to flow in rivulets **2a** *of a candle* to burn unevenly so that melted wax runs down one side **b** *of a flame* to burn fitfully or feebly; be on the point of going out ⟨*the candle flame ~*ing *in the breeze*⟩

**gutter out** *vi* to gradually diminish and come to an end ⟨*the candle* guttered out⟩ ⟨*his screen career had* guttered out⟩

**[3]gutter** *adj* characteristic of the gutter; *esp* marked by extreme vulgarity or cheapness ⟨*the ~ press*⟩

**guttering** /'gutəring/ *n* a length or section of a gutter; a drain ⟨*plastic ~*⟩

**guttersnipe** /-,sniep/ *n, derog* **1** a poor, badly behaved, and usu ragged town child who roams the streets and receives little social or moral training **2** a person of the lowest moral or economic station – **guttersnipish** *adj*

**guttural** /'gut(ə)rəl/ *adj* **1** of the throat **2a** formed or pro-

nounced in the throat ⟨*~ sounds*⟩ **b** of or produced with the SOFT PALATE ⟨*a ~* l *in* milk⟩ [MF, prob fr ML *gutturalis,* fr L *guttur* throat – more at COT] – **guttural** *n,* **gutturalism** *n,* **gutturality** *n,* **gutturally** *adv,* **gutturalness** *n*

**guttural·ize, -ise** /'gutərə,liez/ *vt* **1** to pronounce in a guttural manner **2** to use the SOFT PALATE in pronouncing (certain sounds, such as the *l* in *milk*) – **gutturalization** *n*

**guv** /guv/ *n, Br informal* GUVNOR 2

**guvnor** /'guvnə/ *n, Br informal* **1** a boss **2** – used as a term of address to a man, esp one in authority [alter. of *governor*]

**[1]guy** /gie/ *vt or n* (to steady or reinforce with) a rope, chain, or rod attached to something as a brace or guide [prob fr D *gei* brail]

**[2]guy** *n* **1** *often cap* a humorous effigy of a man burnt in Britain on Guy Fawkes Night **2** *informal* a man, fellow **3** *chiefly Br informal* a person of grotesque or laughable appearance [*Guy* Fawkes †1606 E conspirator]

**[3]guy** *vt* to make fun of; ridicule

**Guy Fawkes Day** /'gie ,fawks, ,- '-/ *n* GUY FAWKES NIGHT

**Guy Fawkes Night** /,gie 'fawks/ *n* November 5 observed in Britain with fireworks and bonfires in commemoration of the arrest of Guy Fawkes in 1605 for attempting to blow up the Houses of Parliament

**guzzle** /'guzl/ *vb* to consume (something) greedily, continually, or habitually [origin unknown] – **guzzler** *n*

**gwyniad** /'gwiniad/ *n* a whitefish (*Coregonus pennantii*) found in Bala lake in N Wales [W, fr *gwyn* white]

**gybe, NAm chiefly jibe** /jieb/ *vi* **1** *of a sail attached to the mast along its leading edge* to swing from one side to another when the vessel is moving in the same direction as the wind; *specif* to do so suddenly and forcibly **2** to change the course of a sailing vessel from one TACK (direction in terms of which side of the sail receives the wind) to the other, esp when going in the same direction as the wind, by allowing the sail to gybe ~ *vt* to cause (a sailing vessel) to gybe *usage* see [3]JIBE [perh modif of D *gijben*]

**gym** /jim/ *n* **1** a gymnasium **2** PHYSICAL EDUCATION by gymnastic exercises, esp in school ⟨*teaching ~*⟩ ⟨*~ shoes*⟩

**gymkhana** /jim'kahnə/ *n* a sporting event featuring competitions and displays; *specif* a meeting involving competition in horse riding, esp by children, and in carriage driving [prob modif of Hindi *gend-khāna* racket court]

**gymn-** /jimn-/, **gymno-** *comb form* naked; bare ⟨*gymno*sperm⟩ [NL, fr Gk, fr *gymnos* – more at NAKED]

**gymnasium** /jim'nayzi·əm, -zyəm/ *n, pl* **gymnasiums, gymnasia** /-zi·ə/ **1** a large room or separate building used for indoor sports and gymnastic activities **2** a German or Scandinavian secondary school that prepares students for university [L, exercise ground, school, fr Gk *gymnasion,* fr *gymnazein* to exercise naked, fr *gymnos;* (2) Ger, fr L, school]

**gymnast** /'jimnast/ *n* somebody trained in gymnastics [MF *gymnaste,* fr Gk *gymnastēs* trainer, fr *gymnazein*] – **gymnastic** *adj,* **gymnastically** *adv*

**gymnastics** /jim'nastiks/ *n pl* **1a** physical exercises designed to develop strength and coordination **b** *taking sing vb* a competitive sport in which individuals perform optional and prescribed acrobatic feats mostly on special apparatus in order to demonstrate strength, balance, and body control **2** an exercise in intellectual or artistic dexterity ⟨*verbal ~*⟩ **3** physical feats or contortions ⟨*the ~ necessary for the killer to have swung from the fire escape* – E D Radin⟩

**gymnosperm** /'jimnoh,spuhm/ *n* any of a class or subdivision (Gymnospermae) of woody seed-bearing plants (eg conifers and yews) that produce naked seeds not enclosed in an ovary – compare ANGIOSPERM [deriv of NL *gymn-* + Gk *sperma* seed – more at SPERM] – **gymnospermy** *n,* **gymnospermous** *adj*

**gym shoe** *n* a plimsoll

**[1]gymslip** /'jim,slip/ *n* a girl's tunic or pinafore dress that is worn usu with a belt as part of a school uniform

**[2]gymslip** *adj, informal* of a schoolgirl or a girl of school age ⟨*a ~ pregnancy*⟩

**gym tunic** *n, chiefly Br* a gymslip

**gyn-** /jien-/, **gyno-** *comb form* **1** woman ⟨*gyno*cracy⟩ **2** female reproductive organ; ovary ⟨*gyno*phore⟩; pistil, carpel ⟨*gynoec*ium⟩ [Gk *gyn-,* fr *gynē* – more at QUEEN]

**gynaec-** /'gienək-/, **gynaeco-, NAm chiefly gynec-, gyneco-** *comb form* woman; reproductive organs of women ⟨*gynaec*oid⟩ ⟨*gynaec*ology⟩ [Gk *gynaik-, gynaiko-,* fr *gynaik-, gynē* woman]

**gynaecology** /,gienə'koləji, jie-/ *n* a branch of medicine that deals with diseases and disorders (of the reproductive system) of women [ISV] – **gynaecologist** *n*, **gynaecologic, gynaecological** *adj*

**gynandromorph** /jie'nandrə‚mawf, ji-, gie-, -droh-/ *n* an (abnormal) individual having characteristics of both sexes in different parts of the body [ISV] – **gynandromorphic** *adj*, **gynandromorphism** *n*, **gynandromorphous** *adj*, **gynandromorphy** *n*

**gynandrous** /ji'nandrəs, jie-, gie-/ *adj, of a flower* having the male and female parts united in a column (eg in some orchids) [Gk *gynandros* of doubtful sex, fr *gynē* woman + *andr-, anēr* man – more at ANDR-]

**-gyne** /-jien/ *comb form* (→ *n*) **1** woman; female ⟨*pseudogyne*⟩ **2** female reproductive organ ⟨*trichogyne*⟩ [Gk *gynē*]

**gynoecium, gynaecium, gynaeceum,** *NAm chiefly* **gynecium** /jie'neesi‚om, gie-/ *n, pl* **gynoecia, gynaecia, gynaecea,** *NAm chiefly* **gynecia** /-si‚ə/ all the female parts of a flower [NL, alter. of L *gynaeceum* women's apartments, fr Gk *gynaikeion*, fr *gynaik-, gynē*]

**gynophore** /'jienə‚faw/ *n* an elongation of a flower stalk in some plants (eg a caper) that bears the gynoecium at its tip – **gynophoric** *adj*

**-gynous** /-jənəs/ *comb form* (→ *adj*) having (such or so many) females or female parts or organs ⟨*heterogynous*⟩ ⟨*tetrogynous*⟩ [NL *-gynus*, fr Gk *-gynos*, fr *gynē*] – **-gyny** *comb form* (→ *n*)

**¹gyp** /jip/ *n* **1** *Br* a college servant at Cambridge or Durham University – compare BEDDER, SCOUT **2** *NAm informal* **2a** a cheat, swindler **b** a fraud, swindle [prob short for *gypsy*]

**²gyp** *vb* **-pp-** *chiefly NAm informal* to cheat

**³gyp** *n, Br informal* sharp pain or punishment – chiefly in *give one gyp* [origin unknown]

**gyppo** /'jipoh/ *n or adj, pl* **gyppos** /-ohz/ *chiefly Br derog* **1** (an) Egyptian **2** (a) Gypsy [by shortening & alter.]

**gyppy tummy** /'jipi/ *n* GIPPY TUMMY

**gypsophila** /jip'sofilə; *often* jipsə'fili‚ə/ *n* any of a large genus (*Gypsophila*) of plants of the pink family having small delicate flowers in branching clusters [NL, genus name, fr L *gypsum* + *-phila* -phil]

**gypsum** /'jipsəm/ *n* **1** a widely distributed mineral, $CaSO_4.2H_2O$, that consists of calcium sulphate chemically combined with water molecules and is used esp as a soil conditioner and in making PLASTER OF PARIS **2** plasterboard [L, fr Gk *gypsos*, of Sem origin; akin to Ar *jibs* plaster] – **gypseous** *adj*, **gypsiferous** *adj*

**gypsy** /'jipsi/ *n, chiefly NAm* a gipsy

**gyr-** /jieər/, **gyro-** /'jieroh-/ *comb form* **1** ring; circle; spiral; rotation ⟨*gyromagnetic*⟩ **2** gyroscope ⟨*gyrocompass*⟩ [prob fr MF, fr L, fr Gk, fr *gyros*]

**¹gyrate** /'jie‚ərət/ *adj, biology* winding or coiled around; convoluted ⟨ ~ *branches of a tree*⟩

**²gyrate** /jie'rayt/ *vi* **1** to revolve round a point or axis **2** to move (as if) with a circular or spiral motion – **gyrator** *n*, **gyratory** *adj*

**gyration** /jie'raysh(ə)n/ *n* **1** an act or instance of gyrating **2** something (eg a coil of a shell) that is gyrate – **gyrational** *adj*

**¹gyre** /jieə/ *vi, chiefly poetic* GYRATE 2 [ME *giren*, fr LL *gyrare*, fr *gyrus*]

**²gyre** *n, chiefly poetic* GYRATION 1 [L *gyrus*, fr Gk *gyros* – more at COWER] – **gyral** *adj*

**gyrfalcon** /'juh‚faw(l)kən/ *n* an arctic falcon (*Falco rusticolus*) that occurs in several forms, is the largest of all falcons, and is more powerful though less active than the PEREGRINE falcon [ME *gerfaucun*, fr MF *girfaucon*]

**gyro** /'jie‚(ə)roh/ *n, pl* **gyros** *informal* **1** a gyroscope **2** a gyrocompass

**gyrocompass** /'jie‚əroh‚kumpəs/ *n* a compass in which the horizontal axis of a constantly spinning gyroscope always points to true north

**gyro horizon** *n* ARTIFICIAL HORIZON 2

**gyromagnetic** /‚jie‚ərohmag'netik/ *adj* of or resulting from the magnetic properties of a rotating electrically charged particle (eg an electron)

**gyromagnetic ratio** *n, physics* the ratio of the MAGNETIC MOMENT of a spinning electrically charged particle (eg an electron) to its ANGULAR MOMENTUM

**gyron** /'jie‚ərən/ *n* a heraldic figure of triangular form that usu appears in the top left-hand corner of the shield [MF *giron* ²*gore*, of Gmc origin; akin to OHG *gēra* wedge-shaped object, OE *gāra* ²*gore*]

**gyroplane** /'jie‚ərə‚playn/ *n* an aircraft supported in flight chiefly by freely rotating unpowered overhead horizontal rotors [ISV]

**gyroscope** /-‚skohp/ *n* a wheel that is mounted to spin rapidly about an axis and is free to turn in various directions but that maintains constant orientation while spinning in the absence of applied forces [Fr, fr *gyr-* + *-scope;* fr its original use to illustrate the rotation of the earth] – **gyroscopic** *adj*, **gyroscopically** *adv*

**gyrostabilizer** /‚jie‚əroh'staybəliezə/ *n* a stabilizing device (eg for a ship or aeroplane) in which a constantly spinning gyroscope opposes sideways motion

**gyrostat** /'jie‚əroh‚stat/ *n* a gyrostabilizer

**gyrus** /'jie‚ərəs/ *n, pl* **gyri** /'jie‚əree/ a convoluted ridge between anatomical grooves; *esp* any of the irregular ridges (CONVOLUTIONS) on the surface of the brain [NL, fr L, circle – more at GYRE] – **gyral** *adj*

**gyve** /jiev/ *n usu pl* a fetter, shackle [ME] – **gyve** *vt*

# H

**h, H** /aych/ *n, pl* **h's, hs, H's, Hs** **1a** the 8th letter of the English alphabet **b** a graphic representation of or device for reproducing the letter *h* **c** a speech counterpart of written *h* **2** one designated *h*, esp as the 8th in order or class **3** something shaped like the letter H

**ha** /hah/ *interj* – used esp to express surprise or joy [ME]

**haangi, hangi** /'hahng·i/ *n, pl* **haangis** an oven of a type traditional in New Zealand, that is built in a pit dug in the ground and in which the food is covered by wet sacks and earth and cooked by steam obtained from pouring water onto hot stones below the food [Maori]

**haar** /hah/ *n* a cold wet sea fog on the east coast of England or Scotland [prob fr a LG or D dial. word; akin to ON *hārr* grey, hoary]

**Habakkuk, Habacuc** /'habəkook/ *n* – see BIBLE table [*Habakkuk* (Heb *Ḥăbhaqqūq*, LL *Habacuc*), 7th-c BC Heb prophet]

**habanera** /ˌhabə'nyeərə/ *n* (slow music, with two beats to the bar, for) a Cuban dance [Sp (*danza*) *habanera*, lit., Havanan dance, fr *La Habana* Havana, capital city of Cuba]

**habdalah** /ˌhahvdə'lah, hahv'dawlə/ *n, often cap* a Jewish domestic ceremony marking the close of a Sabbath or holy day [Heb *habhdālāh* separation]

**habeas corpus** /ˌhaybi·əs 'kawpəs, -byəs/ *n* a judicial writ requiring a detained person to be brought before a court or judge so that the legality of his/her detention may be examined [ME, fr ML, lit., you should have the body (the opening words of the writ)]

**haberdasher** /'habəˌdashə/ *n* **1** a dealer in minor articles of men's clothing (e g ties and shirts) **2** *Br* a dealer in small articles (e g zips, buttons, lace, and needles) used in making or mending clothes and for sewing [ME *haberdassher*, prob modif of AF *hapertas* petty merchandise]

**haberdashery** /-ri/ *n* **1** goods sold by a haberdasher **2** a haberdasher's shop or section of a department store

**habergeon** /'habəjən/ *n* (a sleeveless mail jacket shorter than) a HAUBERK (long military tunic of mail) [ME *haubergeoun*, fr MF *haubergeon*, dim. of *hauberc* hauberk]

**habile** /'hayˌbiel/ *adj, formal* having general skill; able, skilful [Fr, fr L *habilis* – more at ABLE]

**habiliment** /hə'bilimənt/ *n* **1** *pl* characteristic apparatus; fittings ⟨*the* ∼*s of civilization* – W P Webb⟩ **2** **habiliments** *pl*, **habiliment** *archaic* clothing; *esp* the dress characteristic of an occupation or occasion ⟨*the* ∼*s of a monk*⟩ [MF *habillement*, fr *habiller* to dress a log, dress, fr *bille* log – more at BILLET]

**habilitate** /hə'bilitayt/ *vi* to qualify oneself (e g as a teacher in a German university) ⟨∼*d as a privatdocent in the theological faculty* – Jack Finegan⟩ [LL *habilitatus*, pp of *habilitare*, fr L *habilitas* ability – more at ABILITY] – **habilitation** *n*

**¹habit** /'habit/ *n* **1** a costume characteristic of a calling, rank, or function ⟨*riding* ∼⟩ ⟨*monk's* ∼⟩ **2** bodily appearance or mental make-up ⟨*a man of fleshy* ∼⟩ ⟨*a cheerful* ∼ *of mind*⟩ **3** a settled tendency or usual manner of behaviour ⟨*it was not her* ∼ *to argue*⟩ **4a** a behaviour pattern acquired by frequent repetition or physiological exposure that shows itself in regularity or increased ease of performance ⟨*acquired the* ∼ *abroad of overtaking on the left*⟩ **b** an acquired mode of behaviour that has become nearly or completely involuntary ⟨∼ *of nail-biting*⟩ **c** an addiction ⟨*the drug* ∼⟩ **5** characteristic mode of growth or occurrence (e g of a plant or animal) ⟨*a plant with a woody* ∼⟩ ⟨*the marshy* ∼ *of the coot*⟩ **6** the characteristic outward appearance or shape of a crystal [ME, fr OF, fr L *habitus* condition, character, fr *habitus*, pp of *habēre* to have, hold – more at GIVE]

*synonyms* **Habit, practice, custom,** and **wont** all mean "a pattern of behaviour fixed by constant repetition". A **habit** is usually an individual's personal mannerism or way of behaving, done unconsciously and often compulsively ⟨*trying to break a bad* **habit** *of nail-*

*biting*⟩. A **practice** is carried out regularly by an individual or group, usually from choice ⟨*made a* **practice** *of bringing in the milk every morning*⟩ ⟨*threw away the innards, as was their* **practice**⟩. A **custom** is so fixed, usually among a group and over a long period, as to have the force of unwritten law ⟨*the icy chains of* **custom** – P B Shelley⟩. The formal **wont** implies a social norm ⟨*it is ever the* **wont** *of the rich to envy the poor*⟩.

**²habit** *vt, formal* to clothe, dress

**habitable** /'habitəbl/ *adj* capable of being lived in – **habitability, habitableness** *n*, **habitably** *adv*

*synonyms* **Habitable** and **inhabitable** are not opposites. They have the same meaning, but **habitable** is usually used of buildings ⟨*make the flat* **habitable**⟩ and **inhabitable** of larger areas ⟨*the tundra was barely* **inhabitable**⟩. *antonym* uninhabitable

**habitant** /'habitənt/ *n* **1** an inhabitant, resident **2** (a descendant of) a settler of French origin, esp belonging to the farming class in Canada and Louisiana

**habitat** /'habitat/ *n* **1** the (type of) place where a plant or animal naturally grows or lives **2** the typical place of residence of a person or group **3** *formal* HABITATION 2 [L, it inhabits, fr *habitare*]

**habitation** /ˌhabi'taysh(ə)n/ *n* **1** the act of inhabiting; occupancy **2** *formal* **2a** a dwelling place a residence, home **b** a settlement, colony [ME *habitacioun*, fr MF *habitation*, fr L *habitation-, habitatio*, fr *habitatus*, pp of *habitare* to inhabit, fr *habitus*, pp]

**habit-forming** /'habitˌfawming/ *adj* tending to form an addiction

**habitual** /hə'bityooəl, -chooəl/ *adj* **1** having the nature of a habit ⟨∼ *smoking*⟩ **2** by force of habit ⟨*a* ∼ *drunkard*⟩ **3** in accordance with habit; customary ⟨*with his* ∼ *good manners he offered her his seat*⟩ **4** inherent in an individual ⟨∼ *grace*⟩ *synonyms* see USUAL *antonym* occasional – **habitually** *adv*, **habitualness** *n*

**habituate** /hə'bityooayt, -choo-/ *vt* to make used *to*; accustom *to* ⟨*night-nursing* ∼d *her to sleeping in daylight*⟩ ∼ *vi* to cause habituation ⟨*marijuana may be* habituating⟩

**habituation** /hə,bityoo'aysh(ə)n, -choo-/ *n* **1** the act or process of habituating **2a**(1) tolerance to the effects of a drug through continued use **a**(2) *psychology* reduction in sensitivity to a stimulus as a result of repeated exposure to it **b** psychological dependence on a drug after a period of use – compare ADDICTION

**habitude** /'habiˌtyoohd/ *n, formal* **1** habitual disposition or tendency **2** a custom

**habitué** /hə'bityooˌay, -chooˌay/ *n* one who frequents a specified place ⟨∼*s of Paris*⟩ ⟨∼*s of the theatre*⟩ [Fr, fr pp of *habituer* to frequent, fr LL *habituare* to habituate, fr L *habitus*]

**habitus** /'habitəs/ *n* **1** physical type or appearance; *esp* physical build and constitution, esp as related to predisposition or susceptibility to disease ⟨*a correlation between tuberculosis and the asthenic* ∼ *of the patient*⟩ **2** characteristic appearance, occurrence, or mode of growth; habit [NL, fr L, condition, character]

**haboob** /hə'boohb/ *n* a sandstorm or dust storm in N Africa [Ar *habūb* violent wind]

**Habsburg** /'hapsbuhg/ *n or adj* HAPSBURG

**haček** /'hahchek/ *n* an inverted circumflex accent (e g in *č*) [Czech *háček*, lit., little hook]

**¹hachure** /ha'shyooə/ *n* any of a series of short lines used to shade and denote hills, valleys, etc on a map and drawn in the direction of maximum slope [Fr, fr *hacher* to chop up, hatch (a map) – more at HASH]

**²hachure** *vt* to shade with or show by hachures

**hacienda** /ˌhasi'endə/ *n* (the main house of) a large estate or plantation, esp in a Spanish-speaking country [Sp, fr L *facienda*, neut pl of *faciendus*, gerundive of *facere* to make, do]

**¹hack** /hak/ *vt* **1a** to cut (as if) with repeated irregular or unskilful blows ⟨*cut the loaf in slices; don't ~ it!*⟩ **b** to sever with repeated blows ⟨~ed *off a thick branch*⟩ **2** to clear by cutting away vegetation ⟨~ed *his way through the undergrowth*⟩ **3** to kick (an opposing player or the ball) in football **4** *chiefly NAm slang* to manage successfully ⟨*he tried office work, but he just couldn't ~ it*⟩ ~ *vi* **1** to make cutting blows or rough cuts; chop **2** to cough in a short dry manner [ME *hakken*, fr OE *haccian;* akin to OHG *hacchōn* to hack, OE *hōc* hook] – **hacker** *n*

**²hack** *n* **1** any of various tools (e g a MATTOCK) used for surface digging, grubbing, or hacking **2** a nick, notch; *esp* a wound cut in a tree as a guide or marker **3** a short dry cough **4** a (wound from a) kick in football **5** a hacking blow

**³hack** *n* **1** the board on which a falcon's meat is served **2** the state of partial liberty in which a young falcon (EYAS) is kept before training – usu + *at* [blend of ¹*hatch* and E dial. *heck* hatch, rack]

**⁴hack** *n* **1a** a horse let out for common hire or used in all kinds of work **b** a horse worn out in service; **c** a light easy riding horse; *esp* one trained to walk, trot, and canter **2** an act of hacking; a ride ⟨*rode out of Aleppo as though on a morning ~ – History Today*⟩ **3** one who produces poor quality work for financial gain; *esp* a commercial writer **4** *NAm* (a driver of) a taxi [short for *hackney*]

**⁵hack** *adj* **1** performed by, suited to, or characteristic of a hack ⟨*~ writing*⟩ **2** hackneyed, trite

**⁶hack** *vt* to make trite and commonplace by indiscriminate use; to hackney ~ *vi* **1** to ride a horse at an ordinary pace, esp over roads **2** *NAm informal* to operate or ride in a taxi – **hacker** *n*

**hackamore** /'hakə,maw/ *n* a bridle with a loop capable of being tightened about the nose and used in place of a bit so that when pressure is applied above the nostrils and under the chin the horse has difficulty in breathing and is restrained [by folk etymology fr Sp *jaquima,* fr Ar *shakīmah*]

**hackbut** /'hakbut/ *n* ARQUEBUS (heavy but portable 15th-century gun) [MF *haguebute,* modif of MLG *hackebusse* ] – **hackbuteer, hackbutter** *n*

**hacking cough** /,-- '-/ *n* a repeated, harsh, dry, usu painful, chest cough [¹*hack*]

**hacking jacket** /'haking/ *n* (a fitted jacket made like) a waisted riding coat with slits in the skirt and slanting flapped pockets [⁶*hack*]

**¹hackle** /'hakl/ *n* **1** a steel comb with long teeth for splitting and combing out the fibres of flax or hemp **2a** any of the long narrow feathers on the neck of a domestic cock or other bird **b** *pl* the hairs along the neck and back of esp a dog, that can be raised to an erect position **3** *pl* temper, anger ⟨*at the insult she felt her ~s rise*⟩ **4** an artificial fishing fly made chiefly from a cock's neck feathers [ME *hakell;* akin to OHG *hāko* hook – more at HOOK]

**²hackle** *vt* **1** to comb out (e g flax) with a hackle **2** to provide (an artificial fishing fly) with a hackle – **hackler** *n*

**³hackle** *vt* to cut up or chop off roughly; hack [freq of ¹*hack*]

**⁴hackle** *n* a fracture resulting in hackly edges

**hackly** /'hakli/ *adj* having the appearance of something hacked; jagged

**hackman** /'hakmən/ *n, NAm* a taxi driver

**¹hackney** /'hakni/ *n* **1** a horse suitable for ordinary riding or driving **2** (any of) a breed of compact English horses with a conspicuous high-stepping action [ME *hakeney,* prob fr *Hakeneye* Hackney, borough of London]

**²hackney** *adj* kept for public hire ⟨*~ cab*⟩

**³hackney** *vt* to make trite, vulgar, or commonplace by frequent use

**hackneyed** /'haknid/ *adj* lacking in freshness or originality; meaningless because used or done too often

**hacksaw** /'hak,saw/ *n* a fine-toothed saw that has a blade under tension in a frame for cutting hard materials – **hacksaw** *vt*

**hackwork** /'hak,wuhk/ *n* literary, artistic, or professional work done on order usu according to formula and in conformity with commercial rather than aesthetic standards

**had** /d, əd, həd; *strong* had/ *past of* HAVE *usage* see ²BETTER, RATHER

**hadal** /'haydl/ *adj* of or being the parts of the ocean below 6000 metres (about 6562 yards) [Fr, fr *Hadès* Hades]

**haddock** /'hadək/ *n, pl* **haddocks, *also collectively* haddock** an important Atlantic food fish (*Melanogrammus aeglefinus*), usu smaller than the related common cod [ME *haddok*]

**hade** /hayd/ *n* the angle that the plane of a rock fault or a vein

makes with the vertical [*hade* (to incline from the vertical), of unknown origin]

**Hades** /'haydeez/ *n* **1** SHEOL (abode of the dead according to early Jewish thought) **2** *often not cap, euph* Hell [Gk *Haidēs,* underground abode of the dead in Gk mythology]

**hadith** /hə'deeth/ *n, often cap* the body of traditions relating to Muhammad and his companions [Ar *ḥadīth*]

**hadj** /haj/ *n* HAJJ (pilgrimage to Mecca)

**hadji** /'haji/ *n* HAJJI (Muslim pilgrim)

**hadn't** /'hadnt/ had not

**hadron** /'hadron/ *n* any of a class of ELEMENTARY PARTICLES (minute particles of matter) including the PION and all heavier particles (e g the proton and neutron) that take part in the STRONG INTERACTION (basic interaction between particles) [ISV *hadr-* thick, heavy (fr Gk *hadros*) + ²*-on*] – **hadronic** *adj*

**hadst** /hadst/ *archaic past 2 sing of* HAVE

**hae** /hay/ *vt, chiefly Scot* to have

**haem,** *chiefly NAm* **heme** /heem/ *n* a deep red iron-containing chemical compound, $C_{34}H_{32}N_4O_4Fe$, that is the nonprotein oxygen-carrying part of the HAEMOGLOBIN of blood [ISV, fr *haematin*]

**haem-** /heem-/, **haema-, haemo-,** *NAm* **hem-, hema-, hemo-** *comb form* blood ⟨*haemal*⟩ ⟨*haemoflagellate*⟩ ⟨*haemocytometer*⟩ [*haem-, haemo-* fr MF *hemo-,* fr L *haem-, haemo-,* fr Gk *haim-, haimo-,* fr *haima; haema-* fr NL, fr Gk *haima*]

**haemacytometer** *n* HAEMOCYTOMETER (instrument for counting cells)

**haemagglutinate** /,heemə'gloohtinayt, ,hemə-/ *vt* **1** to cause the clumping together of (RED BLOOD CELLS) **2** to cause the clumping together of the red blood cells in (e g a blood sample) – **haemagglutination** *n*

**haemagglutinin** /,heemə'gloohtinin/ *n* a substance that causes the clumping together of RED BLOOD CELLS [ISV]

**haemal** /'heeml/ *adj* **1** of the blood or blood vessels **2** of or situated on the side of the body containing the heart

**haemangioma** /,heemanji'ohmə/ *n* a usu noncancerous tumour made up of blood vessels that typically occurs as a purplish or reddish slightly elevated area of skin [NL, fr *haem-* + *angioma*]

**haemat-, haemato-,** *NAm* **hemat-, hemato-** *comb form* haem- ⟨*haematoid*⟩ ⟨*haematogenous*⟩ [L *haemat-, haemato-,* fr Gk *haimat-, haimato-,* fr *haimat-, haima*]

**haematein** /'heemə,teen/ *n* a reddish-brown chemical compound, $C_{16}H_{12}O_6$, that constitutes the essential dye in logwood extracts (e g HAEMATOXYLINQ and that is used chiefly to stain animal tissue for examination under the microscope

**haematic** /hi'matik/ *adj* **1** of or containing blood **2** affecting the blood

**haematin** /'hemətin, 'hee-/ *n* **1** (any of several compounds similar to) a brownish-black or bluish-black iron-containing chemical compound, $C_{34}H_{33}N_4O_5Fe$, derived from haem by OXIDATION **2** haem

**haematinic** /,heemə'tinik/ *n or adj* (something, esp a drug) tending to stimulate blood cell formation or to increase the haemoglobin content of the blood

**haematite** /'heemə,tiet, 'hemə-/ *n* a reddish-brown to black mineral that consists of an iron oxide, $Fe_2O_3$, is an important source of iron, and occurs in crystals and earthy masses – **haematitic** *adj*

**haematoblast** /'heemətə,blahst, hi'matə,blahst/, **haemoblast** /'heemə,blahst/ *n* an immature blood cell; *specif* HAEMOCYTOBLAST [ISV]

**haematocrit** /'heemətoh,krit, 'hemə-, hi'matə-/ *n* **1** an instrument for separating, usu by centrifugation, and determining the relative amounts of plasma and blood cells in a sample of blood **2** the ratio of the volume of RED BLOOD CELLS to the volume of whole blood [ISV *haemat-* + Gk *kritēs* judge, fr *krinein* to judge – more at CERTAIN]

**haematogenous** /,heemə'tojənəs/ *adj* **1** producing blood **2a** formed in or derived from the blood **b** arising in or spread by the blood ⟨*~ tuberculosis*⟩

**haematology** /,heemə'toləji/ *n* the biology and medicine of (diseases of) the blood and blood-forming organs – **haematologic, haematological** *adj*

**haematoma** /,heeemə'tohmə, ,hemə-/ *n, pl* **haemotomas, haemotomata** /-mətə/ a tumour or swelling containing blood; BRUISE 1a [NL]

**haematophagous** /,heemə'tofəgəs/ *adj* HAEMOPHAGOUS (feeding on blood)

HIJ

**haematopoiesis** /ˌheemətohpoy'eesis, ˌhemə-/ *n* HAEMOPOIESIS (formation of blood) – **haematopoietic** *adj,* **haematopoietically** *adv*

**haematoxylin** /ˌheemə'toksəlin/ *n* a colourless to yellowish chemical compound, $C_{16}H_{14}O_6$, obtained from the heartwood of the logwood tree, that turns a reddish colour on exposure to light and is used chiefly to stain specimens for examination under the microscope [ISV, fr NL *Haematoxylon,* genus of plants]

**haematoxylon** /ˌheemə'toksilon/ *n* the heartwood of the logwood tree, from which haematoxylin is extracted; LOGWOOD 1b; *also* a dye obtained from this wood [NL, fr *hemat-* + Gk *xylon* wood]

**haematuria** /ˌheemə'tyoori·ə/ *n* the abnormal presence of blood or blood cells in the urine [NL]

**haemerythrin** /hee'merəthrin/ *n* an iron-containing protein that transports oxygen in the blood of some ANNELID worms and various other INVERTEBRATE animals [*haem-* + *erythr-* + *-in*]

**haemic** /'heemik/ *adj* of blood

**haemin** /'heemin/ *n* a red-brown to blue-black chlorine-containing chemical compound, $C_{34}H_{32}N_4O_4FeCl$, derived from HAEM but usu obtained in a characteristic crystalline form from haemoglobin [ISV]

**haemo-** – see HAEM-

**haemoblast** /'heemə,blahst/ *n* HAEMATOBLAST

**haemochromatosis** /ˌheemə,krohmə'tohsis/ *n* a disorder of iron metabolism that occurs usu in males and is characterized by bronzing of the skin due to deposition of iron-containing pigments in the tissues, and frequently also by diabetic symptoms [NL, fr *haem-* + *chromat-* + *-osis*]

**haemocoele, haemocoel** /'heemə,seel/ *n* a body cavity in various INVERTEBRATE animals (e g insects) that normally contains blood and functions as part of the circulatory system

**haemocyanin** /ˌheemoh'sie·ənin/ *n* a copper-containing protein in the blood of various INVERTEBRATE animals (e g shellfish) that has the same oxygen-transporting function as haemoglobin in higher animals [ISV]

**haemocyte** /'heemoh,siet, 'hemoh-/ *n* a blood cell, esp of an insect or other INVERTEBRATE animal [ISV]

**haemocytoblast** /ˌheemoh'sietohblahst/ *n* an undifferentiated cell (STEM CELL) that gives rise to the cells and PLATELETS (disclike particles that assist in clotting) of the blood

**haemocytometer, haemacytometer** /-sie'tomitə/ *n* an instrument for counting cells (e g blood cells) suspended in a liquid, when viewed under a microscope [ISV]

**haemodialysis** /-die'aləsis/ *n* purification of the circulating blood (e g of somebody whose kidneys have failed) by DIALYSIS

**haemodynamics** /-die'namiks/ *n taking sing vb* **1** a branch of physiology that deals with the circulation of the blood **2** the forces or mechanisms involved in the circulation of the blood (e g in a particular body part) – **haemodynamic** *adj*

**haemoflagellate** /-'flajələt/ *n* a TRYPANOSOME or similar PROTOZOAN (single-celled microorganism) that moves by means of FLAGELLA (whiplike structures) and is a parasite in the blood

**haemoglobin** /-'glohbin/ *n* a red to purplish iron-containing protein that consists of a nonprotein part (HAEM) combined with a protein (GLOBIN) and that transports oxygen in the blood of VERTEBRATE and some INVERTEBRATE animals (e g earthworms). In vertebrates it occurs in the RED BLOOD CELLS and is the means of oxygen transport from the lungs to the body tissues. [ISV, short for earlier *haematoglobulin*] – **haemoglobinic, haemoglobinous** *adj*

**haemoglobinopathy** /ˌheeməglohbi'nopəthi/ *n* a blood disorder (e g SICKLE-CELL ANAEMIA) caused by a genetically determined change in the molecular structure of haemoglobin

**haemoglobinuria** /ˌheemə,glohbi'nyooəri·ə/ *n* the abnormal presence of haemoglobin in the urine [NL]

**haemolymph** /-,limf/ *n* a liquid in the tissues or body cavity of various INVERTEBRATE animals (e g insects) that is functionally comparable to the blood and LYMPH of VERTEBRATE animals

**haemolysin** /ˌheemoh'liesin/ *n* a substance that causes the disintegration of RED BLOOD CELLS [ISV]

**haemolysis** /hi'molisis/ *n* the disintegration of RED BLOOD CELLS with release of haemoglobin [NL] – **haemolyse** *vb,* **haemolytic** *adj*

**haemolytic anaemia** /ˌheemə'litik/ *n* anaemia caused by excessive destruction (e g in chemical poisoning, infection, or SICKLE-CELL ANAEMIA) of RED BLOOD CELLS

**haemolytic disease of the newborn** *n* ERYTHROBLASTOSIS FOETALIS

**haemophagous** /hee'mofəgəs/, **haematophagous** /ˌheemə'-tofəgəs/ *adj* feeding on blood

**haemophilia** /ˌheemoh'fili·ə, -mə-/ *n* a hereditary blood defect transmitted by females but occurring almost exclusively in males, in which clotting of the blood is severely delayed with consequent difficulty in controlling bleeding even after minor injuries [NL]

**haemophiliac** /ˌheemə'filik/ *n or adj* (somebody) suffering from haemophilia

**haemophilic** /ˌheemə'filik/ *adj* **1** of, resembling, or suffering from haemophilia **2** tending to thrive in blood ⟨~ *bacteria*⟩

**haemopoiesis** /ˌheemohpoy'eesis, ˌhemoh-/, **haematopoiesis** /ˌheemətohpoy'eesis, ˌhemə-/ *n* the formation of blood or blood cells in the living body; *esp* the formation of blood cells in the bone marrow and LYMPHOID tissue [NL] – **haemopoietic** *adj,* **haemopoietically** *adv*

**haemoprotein** /ˌheemə'prohteen/ *n* a protein (e g haemoglobin) containing a nonprotein group that is an iron-containing PORPHYRIN

**haemoptysis** /ˌheeməp'tiesis/ *n* the coughing up of blood from some part of the respiratory tract [NL, fr *haem-* + Gk *ptysis* act of spitting, fr *ptyein* to spit – more at SPEW]

**haemorrhage** /'hemərij/ *n* a (copious) loss of blood from the blood vessels [Fr & L; Fr *hémorrhagie,* fr L *haemorrhagia,* fr Gk *haimorrhagia,* fr *haimo-* haem- + *-rrhagia*] – **haemorrhage** *vi,* **haemorrhagic** *adj*

**haemorrhoid** /'heməroyd/ *n,* **haemorrhoids** *n pl* a mass of dilated veins in swollen tissue round or near the anus [MF *hemorrhoides,* pl, fr L *haemorrhoidae,* fr Gk *haimorrhoides,* fr *haimorthoos* flowing with blood, fr *haimo-* + *rhein* to flow]

[1]**haemorrhoidal** /ˌhemə'roydl/ *adj* **1** of or involving haemorrhoids **2** of or involving the RECTUM (lowest part of the intestines)

[2]**haemorrhoidal** *n* **1** a haemorrhoidal part (e g an artery or vein) **2** a substance used to treat haemorrhoids ⟨*various* ~s *were prescribed*⟩

**haemosiderin** /ˌheemoh'sidərin/ *n* a yellowish-brown granular pigment formed by breakdown of HAEMOGLOBIN and composed essentially of protein combined with FERRIC OXIDE [ISV]

**haemostasis** /ˌheemoh'staysis, ˌhemoh-/ *n* arrest of bleeding [NL, fr Gk *haimostasis* styptic, fr *haimo-* + *-stasis*]

**haemostat** /'heeməstat/ *n* a haemostatic; *esp* an instrument for compressing a bleeding vessel

**haemostatic** /ˌheemə'statik/ *n* something that stops or reduces bleeding; *esp* a substance that is applied to a bleeding surface to reduce bleeding – **haemostatic** *adj*

**haeremai** /'hah·ere,mie, 'hiere,mie/ *interj, NZ* welcome [Maori, lit., come here]

**haffet, haffit** /'hafit/ *n, Scot* the cheek or temple [ME (Sc) *half-heid,* fr ME *half* + *hed* head]

**hafnium** /'hafnyəm, -ni·əm/ *n* a metallic chemical element occurring in ZIRCONIUM minerals that is resistant to corrosion and is used in control rods in nuclear reactors [NL, fr *Hafnia* Copenhagen, city in Denmark]

[1]**haft** /hahft/ *n* the handle of a weapon or tool [ME, fr OE *hæft;* akin to OE *hebban* to lift – more at HEAVE]

*synonyms* A **haft** is typically a shorter handle than a **shaft.** Compare ⟨*the* **haft** *of a dagger/of a sickle*⟩ ⟨*the* **shaft** *of a spear/of a golf club*⟩.

[2]**haft** *vt* to fit with a haft

**haftarah** /ˌhəftə'rah, ˌhəf'tawrə/ *n, pl* **haftaroth** /ˌhaftə'rot/, **haftarahs** a selection from the Books of the Prophets read at the end of the Jewish synagogue service [Heb *haphṭārāh* conclusion]

[1]**hag** /hag/ *n* **1** a witch **2** an ugly and usu ill-natured old woman [ME *hagge*] – **haggish** *adj*

[2]**hag** *n, Scot & NEng* (a firm spot in) a bog [E dial., felled timber, of Scand origin; akin to ON *högg* stroke, blow; akin to OE *hēawan* to hew]

**hagbut** /'hag,but/ *n* ARQUEBUS (heavy but portable 15th-century gun)

**hagfish** /-,fish/ *n, pl* **hagfishes,** *esp collectively* **hagfish** any of several primitive eel-like marine VERTEBRATE animals (order Myxinoidae, class Cyclostomata) that are related to the LAMPREYS and have a round sucking mouth surrounded by eight tentacles enabling them to feed on fishes by boring into their bodies [[1]*hag*]

**haggadah** /hə'gahdə/ *n,* **1** *often cap* ancient Jewish lore forming the nonlegal part of the TALMUD (body of Jewish law and tradition) – compare HALAKAH **2** *cap* the narrative read at the

Passover SEDER (service) [Heb *haggādhāh*] – **haggadic** *adj, often cap*

**haggadist** /hə'gahdist/ *n, often cap* 1 a haggadic writer 2 a student of the haggadah – **haggadistic** *adj, often cap*

**Haggai** /'hagay,ie/ *n* – see BIBLE table [*Haggai*, 6th-c BC Heb prophet]

¹**haggard** /'hagəd/ *adj* 1 *of a hawk* not tamed 2 having a worn or emaciated appearance, esp through anxiety or lack of sleep [MF *hagard*] – **haggardly** *adv*, **haggardness** *n*

²**haggard** *n* an adult hawk caught wild

**Haggeus** *n* – see BIBLE table [LL, Haggai]

**haggis** /'hagis/ *n* a traditionally Scottish dish that consists of the heart, liver, and lungs of a sheep or a calf minced with suet, oatmeal, and seasonings and boiled in the stomach of the animal [ME *hagese*, perh fr *haggen* to hack, chop]

¹**haggle** /'hagl/ *vi* to bargain, wrangle ⟨*we ~d with the taxi driver over the fare*⟩ [freq of E dial. *hag* to hew] – **haggler** *n*

²**haggle** *n* an act or instance of haggling

**hagi-** /hagi-/, **hagio-** *comb form* 1 holy ⟨hagio*scope*⟩ 2 saints ⟨hagio*graphy*⟩ [LL, fr Gk, fr *hagios*]

**Hagiographa** /,hagi'ogrəfə/ *n taking sing or pl vb* the third part of the Jewish scriptures [LL, fr LGk, fr *hagio-* + *graphein* to write – more at CARVE]

**hagiography** /,hagi'ogrəfi/ *n* 1 biography of saints or venerated people 2 idealizing or idolizing biography – **hagiographer** *n*, **hagiographic**, **hagiographical** *adj*, **hagiographically** *adv*

**hagiology** /,hagi'oləji/ *n* 1 literature dealing with venerated people or writings 2 a list of venerated figures – **hagiologic**, **hagiological** *adj*, **hagiologically** *adv*

**hagioscope** /'hagi-ə,skohp/ *n* a narrow opening in an inside wall or pillar of a church, giving a view of the main altar to those in a side aisle or transept

**hagridden** /'hag,ridn/ *adj* harassed, tormented ⟨*a ~ expression on his face*⟩

**hah** /hah/ *interj* ha

¹**ha-ha** /hah 'hah/ *interj* – used to express or represent laughter, derision, or surprise at a discovery [ME, fr OE *ha ha*]

²**ha-ha** /'hah,hah/ *n* a fence hidden in a ditch or on lower ground at the boundary of a usu 18th-century garden or park, to allow uninterrupted views of the countryside beyond the grounds [Fr *haha*, prob fr *haha*, interj expressing surprise]

**hahnium** /'hahnyəm, -ni·əm/ *n* an artificially produced radioactive chemical element of ATOMIC NUMBER 105 [Otto *Hahn* † 1968 Ger chemist]

**haiku** /'hie,kooh/ *n, pl* **haiku** (a poem in) an unrhymed Japanese verse form of three lines containing 5, 7, and 5 syllables respectively – compare TANKA [Jap]

¹**hail** /hayl/ *n* 1 (a fall of) small particles of clear ice or compact snow 2 a group of things directed at somebody or something and intended to cause pain, damage, or distress ⟨*a ~ of bullets*⟩ [ME, fr OE *hægl*; akin to OHG *hagal* hail, Gk *kachlēx* pebble]

²**hail** *vi* 1 to send down hail ⟨*it's ~ing*⟩ 2 to pour down or strike like hail

³**hail** *interj* 1 – used to express acclamation ⟨*~ to the chief* – Sir Walter Scott⟩ 2 *archaic* – used as a salutation [ME, fr ON *heill*, fr *heill* healthy – more at WHOLE]

⁴**hail** *vt* **1a** to salute, greet **b** to greet with enthusiastic approval; acclaim ⟨*~ed the suggestion of a holiday with delight*⟩ 2 to greet or summon by calling ⟨*~ a taxi*⟩ *~ vi* to call out; *esp* to call a greeting to a passing ship △ hale – **hailer** *n*

**hail from** *vt* to be or have been a native or resident of

⁵**hail** *n* 1 a call to attract attention 2 hearing distance ⟨*stayed within ~*⟩ 3 *archaic* an exclamation of greeting or acclamation

'**hail-,fellow-well-'met** *adj* heartily and often excessively informal from the first moment of meeting ⟨*too ~ at his interview*⟩ [fr the archaic greeting "Hail, fellow! Well met!"]

**Hail Mary** /'meəri/ *n* a Roman Catholic prayer to the Virgin Mary that consists of salutations and a plea for her intercession [trans of ML *Ave, Maria*]

**hailstone** /-,stohn/ *n* a pellet of hail

**hailstorm** /'hayl,stawm/ *n* a storm accompanied by hail

**hair** /heə/ *n* **1a(1)** a slender threadlike outgrowth from the EPIDERMIS (surface layer) of an animal; *esp* any of the many usu coloured flexible filaments composed of dead cells impregnated with KERATIN (strong fibrous protein) that form the characteristic coat of a mammal ⟨*a cat's ~ in the milk*⟩ **a(2)** a short threadlike structure (eg on a plant) that resembles an animal hair ⟨*the ~s on a nettle leaf*⟩ **b** the hairy covering of a body

(part) ⟨*body ~*⟩; *esp* the coating of hairs on a human head ⟨*a fine head of ~*⟩ 2 haircloth ⟨*a ~ shirt*⟩ **3a** a minute distance or amount; a trifle ⟨*won by a ~*⟩ **b** a precise degree ⟨*knew to a ~ just where to place the microphone* – The Listener⟩ [ME, fr OE *hǣr*; akin to OHG *hār* hair] – **hairless** *adj*, **hairlessness** *n*, **hairlike** *adj* – **split hairs** to make oversubtle or trivial distinctions – **tear one's hair (out)** to experience or express grief, rage, or anxiety – **turn a hair** to show any reaction (eg of surprise or alarm) – usu neg ⟨*did not turn a hair when told of the savage murder* – TLS⟩; see also HIDE **or**/**nor hair**, KEEP one's **hair on**

**hair ball** *n* a compact mass of hair formed in the stomach of esp a shedding animal (eg a cat) that cleans its coat by licking

**hairbreadth** /-,bret·th, -,bredth/ *n* HAIR'S BREADTH

**hairbrush** /-,brush/ *n* a brush for the hair

**hair cell** *n* a cell with hairlike outgrowths; *esp* any of the sensory cells in the ORGAN OF CORTI (part of the ear responsible for sound perception)

**hairclip** /'heə,klip/ *n, Br* a hairgrip

**haircloth** /-,kloth/ *n* any of various stiff wiry fabrics, esp of horsehair or camel hair, used for upholstery or for stiffening in clothes

**haircut** /-,kut/ *n* (the result of) cutting and shaping of the hair – **haircutter** *n*, **haircutting** *n*

**hairdo** /-,dooh/ *n, pl* **hairdos** *informal* a hairstyle

**hairdresser** /-,dresə/ *n* somebody whose occupation is cutting, dressing, and styling the hair, esp of women – **hairdressing** *n*

**haired** /heəd/ *adj* having hair (of a specified kind) – usu in combination ⟨*fair-haired*⟩

**hair follicle** *n* a tubular sheath that surrounds the lower part of an animal hair and contains a small projection (PAPILLA) that supplies the growing root of the hair with nourishment

**hairgrip** /-,grip/ *n, Br* a flat hairpin with prongs that close together to hold the hair

**hairline** /-,lien/ *n* 1 a very slender line; *esp* a tiny line or crack on a surface 2 (a fabric with) a design consisting of lengthways or widthways lines, usu one thread wide 3 the line above the forehead beyond which hair grows – **hairline** *adj*

**hairnet** /'heə,net/ *n* a loosely woven net, usu of hair, nylon, or silk, that is worn over the hair to keep it in place

**hairpiece** /-,pees/ *n* 1 TOUPEE 2 2 a section of false hair worn to enhance a hairstyle or make a person's natural hair seem thicker or more plentiful – compare TOUPEE

¹**hairpin** /-,pin/ *n* 1 a two-pronged U-shaped pin of thin wire for holding the hair in place 2 a sharp U-shaped bend in a road

²**hairpin** *adj* having the shape of a hairpin ⟨*a ~ bend*⟩; *also* having hairpin bends ⟨*a steep ~ road*⟩

'**hair-,raiser** *n* a thriller

'**hair-,raising** *adj* causing terror, excitement, or astonishment – **hair-raisingly** *adv*

**hair's breadth** *n* a very small distance or margin

**hair seal** *n* EARLESS SEAL

**hair shirt** *n* a shirt made of rough animal hair worn next to the skin as a penance

'**hair-,slide** *n, Br* a (decorative) hinged clip for holding the hair in place

**hair space** *n* a very thin space between (the letters of) printed words

**hairsplitter** /'heə,splitə/ *n* one who emphasizes unimportant differences and points of detail in reasoning; a quibbler – **hairsplitting** *adj or n*

**hairspring** /-,spring/ *n* a slender spiral spring that regulates the motion of the BALANCE WHEEL of a timepiece

**hairstreak** /'heə,streek/ *n* any of various small butterflies (subfamily Theclinae), usu having striped markings on the underside of the wings and thin threadlike projections from the hind wings

**hairstyle** /-,stiel/ *n* a way of wearing or arranging the hair – **hairstyling** *n*, **hairstylist** *n*

'**hair-,trigger** *adj* immediately responsive to or disrupted by the slightest stimulus ⟨*a ~ temper*⟩

**hair trigger** *n* a trigger so adjusted that a very slight pressure will fire the gun

**hairworm** /'heəwuhm/ *n* 1 any of a genus (*Capillaria*)of hairlike NEMATODE worms that include serious parasites of birds and mammals 2 any of a group (Nematomorpha or Gordiacea) of very slender elongated worms that are parasitic in ARTHROPODS (eg insects) as larvae and are free-living in water as adults

¹**hairy** /'heəri/ *adj* **1a** covered with (material like) hair ⟨*a ~ woollen coat*⟩ ⟨*~ caterpillars*⟩ **b** *of a plant (part)* covered with a downy fuzz 2 *informal* presenting high risk or challenge ⟨*a ~*

scramble up a steep mountain road⟩ ⟨*a ~ adventure*⟩ – **hairiness** *n*

²**hairy** *n, informal* somebody or something hairy; *esp* a person with long hair

**Haitian** /'haysh(ə)n/ *n* **1** a native or inhabitant of Haiti **2** **Haitian Creole, Haitian** the language of Haiti based on French and various W African languages – **Haitian** *adj*

**hajj, hadj** /haj/ *n* the pilgrimage to Mecca prescribed as a religious duty for Muslims [Ar *hajj*]

**hajji** /'haji/, **hadji** *n* one who has made a pilgrimage to Mecca – often used as a title [Ar *hajjī*, fr *hajj*]

**haka** /'hahkah/ *n* a ceremonial Maori war dance [Maori]

**hake** /hayk/ *n, pl* **hake**, *esp for different types* **hakes** any of several marine food fishes (e g of the genera *Merluccius* and *Urophycis*) that are related to the common Atlantic cod [ME]

**hakenkreuz** /'hahkən,kroyts/ *n, often cap* the swastika used as a symbol of German anti-Semitism or of Nazi Germany [Ger, fr *haken* hook + *kreuz* cross]

¹**hakim** /'hakeem/ *n* a Muslim doctor in India or a Muslim country [Ar *hakīm*, lit., wise one]

²**hakim** *n* a Muslim ruler, governor, or judge in India or a Muslim country [Ar *hākim*]

**hal-, halo-** *comb form* **1** salt ⟨*halophyte*⟩ **2** halogen ⟨*halide*⟩ [Fr, fr Gk, fr *hals* – more at SALT; (2) ISV, fr *halogen*]

**halakah** /,hahlə'khah, hə'lahkə/ *n, often cap* the body of Jewish law supplementing the scriptural law and forming esp the legal part of the TALMUD (body of Jewish law and tradition) – compare HAGGADAH **1** [Heb *halākhāh*, lit., way] – **halakic** *adj, often cap*

¹**halal, hallal** /hə'lahl/ *vt* to slaughter (meat) according to Islamic law [Ar *halāl* that which is lawful]

²**halal, hallal** *n* meat from an animal slaughtered according to Islamic law

**halala** *also* **halalah** /hə'lahlə/ *n, pl* **halala, halalas** – see *riyal* at MONEY table [Ar]

**halation** /hə'laysh(ə)n/ *n* **1** the spreading of light beyond its proper boundaries (e g in a faulty photographic image) **2** a bright ring that sometimes surrounds a bright object on a television screen [*halo* + *-ation*]

**halberd** /'halbəd/ *n* a long-handled weapon combining a spear and battle-axe, used esp in the 15th and 16th centuries [ME *halberd*, fr MF *hallebarde*, fr MHG *helmbarte*, fr *heim* handle + *barte* axe] – **halberdier** *n*

**halbert** /'halbət/ *n* a halberd

¹**halcyon** /'halsi-ən/ *n, poetic* a kingfisher [ME *alceon* bird believed to breed at sea and calm the waves, fr L *halcyon*, fr Gk *alkyōn, halkyōn*]

²**halcyon** *adj* **1** calm, peaceful ⟨*~ days*⟩ **2** happy, golden ⟨*a ~ period in her life*⟩ **synonyms** see ²CALM

¹**hale** /hayl/ *adj* free from defect, disease, or infirmity; sound ⟨*a ~ and hearty old man*⟩ [partly fr ME (northern) *hale*, fr OE *hāl*; partly fr ME *hail*, fr ON *heill* – more at WHOLE

²**hale** *vt* **1** to haul, pull **2** to compel forcibly to go ⟨*~ a vagrant into court*⟩ △ **hail** [ME *halen*, fr MF *haler* – more at HAUL]

**haler** /'hahlə/ *n, pl* **halers, haleru** /'hahlə,rooh/ – see *koruna* at MONEY table [Czech]

¹**half** /hahf/ *n, pl* **halves** /hahvz/ **1a** either of two equal parts into which something is divisible; *also* a part of a thing approximately equal to a half **b** half an hour – used in designation of time ⟨*~ past three*⟩ **2a** a partner ⟨*my other ~*⟩ **b** a school term – used esp at some British public schools **3** something of (approximately) half the value or quantity: e g **3a** a child's ticket **b** *Br* the sum of or a coin representing one half of a new penny; a halfpenny **c** *Br* half a pint, esp of beer, ale, or cider **d** *NAm* a half-dollar **4** a halfback **5a** the period of play before or after the interval ⟨*neither side scored in the first ~*⟩ **b** that half of the playing area defended by a (specified) team ⟨*Liverpool were determined to keep the play in the Arsenal ~*⟩ [ME, fr OE *healf*; akin to L *scalpere* to cut, OE *sciell* shell] – **and a half** *informal* of remarkable quality ⟨*that was a party and a half*⟩ – **by half** by a great deal ⟨*too clever by half*⟩ – **by halves** less than completely; halfheartedly ⟨*he took the wrong train and lost his luggage – he never does things by halves!*⟩ – **half the battle** the most arduous part of the task ⟨*persuading him to discuss the plan was half the battle*⟩ – **in half** into two (nearly) equal parts

**usage 1 Half**, as a noun or adjective, is followed by a singular verb after a singular noun or pronoun ⟨**half** (*of*) *the lake was frozen*⟩ and by a plural verb after a plural ⟨**half** (*of*) *the children were absent*⟩. **2** Some writers on usage prefer the traditional **a half** ⟨*a half century*⟩ ⟨*a yard and a half*⟩ ⟨*a million and a half*⟩ to the newer forms ⟨*half a century*⟩ ⟨*one and a half yards*⟩ ⟨*one and a half million*⟩;

but it depends on context: in cricket, for instance, one says ⟨**a half** *century*⟩. **3** The pronunciation of **half** *past* as /'hahf,pahst/ rather than /'hah,pahst/ is recommended for BBC broadcasters.

²**half** *adj* **1a** being one of two equal parts ⟨*a ~ share*⟩ ⟨*~ a dozen*⟩ **b(1)** amounting to approximately half ⟨*~ the class*⟩ ⟨*a ~ mile*⟩ ⟨*~ my life*⟩ **b(2)** falling short of the full or complete thing; partial ⟨*~ measures*⟩ ⟨*a ~ smile*⟩ **2** extending over or covering only half ⟨*a ~ door*⟩ ⟨*~ sleeves*⟩ **3** *Br* half past ⟨*~ seven*⟩ – **halfness** *n*

³**half** *adv* **1a** in an equal part or degree ⟨*she was ~ annoyed, ~ amused at his arrogance*⟩ **b** nearly but not completely ⟨*~ persuaded*⟩ ⟨*~ cooked*⟩ ⟨*half-remembered legends from her childhood*⟩ – compare NOT HALF **2** – used with a negative to imply the opposite of what is expressed ⟨*her singing isn't ~ bad*⟩ – **half as much again** one-and-a-half times as much

**half-a-'crown** *n* HALF CROWN

**half a dozen** *n or adj* (a set of) six; *also* several

**half-and-'half** *n* something that is approximately half one thing and half another; *specif* a mixture of two beers (e g mild and bitter) – **half-and-half** *adj or adv*

**halfback** /-,bak/ *n* a player in soccer, rugby, hockey, etc positioned immediately behind the forward line – **halfback** *adj*

**half-'baked** *adj* **1** insufficiently baked; underdone **2** *informal* marked by or showing a lack of forethought or judgment; foolish ⟨*a ~ scheme for getting rich quick*⟩ ⟨*he must be ~ to believe such a tale*⟩

**halfbeak** /-,beek/ *n* any of a family (Hemiramphidae) of small slender marine and freshwater fishes with a long protruding lower jaw

**half blood** *n* **1a** the relation between people having only one parent in common **b** a person so related to another **2** a half-breed **3** GRADE 4 (crossbred domestic animal) – **half-blooded** *adj*

**half blue** *n* (the colours awarded to) one who represents either Oxford or Cambridge in a minor sport or substitutes for a full blue against the other university ⟨*got my ~ for table tennis*⟩

**half-'board** *n* provision of bed, breakfast, and midday or evening meal (e g by a hotel)

**'half-,bound** *adj, of a book* bound in two materials with the better quality or stronger material (e g leather) on the spine and corners – **half binding** *n*

**'half-,bred** *adj* having one purebred parent – **half-bred** *n*

**'half-,breed** *n* the offspring of parents of different races – **half-breed** *adj*

**half brother** *n* a brother related through one parent only

**'half-,butt** *n* a billiard cue that is longer than an ordinary cue

**'half-,caste** *n* a person of mixed racial descent; a half-breed – **half-caste** *adj*

**half cock** *n* **1** the position of the hammer or FIRING PIN of a firearm when about half retracted and held by the safety catch, so that it cannot be operated by a pull on the trigger **2** a state of inadequate preparation or information – esp in *go off at half cock*

**half-'cocked** *adj* **1** at half cock **2** lacking adequate preparation or forethought

**half crown, half-a-'crown** *n* (a former British silver coin worth) two shillings and sixpence

**half dime** *n* a silver 5-cent coin struck by the US mint in 1792 and from 1794 to 1873

**half-'dollar** *n* **1** a coin representing one half of a dollar **2** the sum of 50 cents

**half halt** *n* the checking of a horse's stride by means of the hands and leg pressure, so that it can adjust its balance for a change of gait

**half-'hardy** *adj, of a plant* able to withstand a moderately low temperature but injured by severe freezing and surviving the winter out of doors only if protected against frost

**halfhearted** /-'hahtid/ *adj* lacking enthusiasm or effort ⟨*~ attempts to start a conversation*⟩ – **halfheartedly** *adv*, **half-heartedness** *n*

**half hitch** *n* a type of simple knot made so as to be easily unfastened

**half-'holiday** *n* half a day's holiday; *esp* an afternoon's holiday

**half hour** *n* **1** a period of thirty minutes **2** the middle point of an hour – **half-hourly** *adv or adj*

**'half-,knot** *n* a knot joining the ends of two cords and used in tying other knots

**'half-,landing** *n* a landing halfway up a flight of stairs

**'half-,length** *n* a portrait showing only the upper half of the body – **half-length** *adj*

**'half-,life** *n* the time required for half of something to undergo a process: eg **a** the time required for half of the atoms of a radioactive substance to disintegrate **b** the time required for half the amount of a drug or other substance to be eliminated from an organism by natural processes

'half-,light *n* dim greyish light (eg at dusk or dawn)

,half-'mast *n* the position of a flag lowered halfway down the staff as a mark of mourning

half measures *n pl* a partial, half-hearted, or weak line of action ⟨~ *are worse than useless here*⟩

,half-'moon *n* **1** (something shaped like) the figure of the moon when half its disc is illuminated **2** LUNULE (white semicircle at the base of a fingernail)

half nelson /'nels(ə)n/ *n* a wrestling hold in which one arm is thrust from behind under the corresponding arm of an opponent and the hand placed on the back of the opponent's neck – compare FULL NELSON

half note *n, NAm* MINIM 1

half pass *n* a sideways movement in dressage in which the horse's legs cross over each other

halfpenny /'haypni; *also* ,hahf'pee *for decimal currency*/ *n* **1** (a British bronze coin representing) one half of a penny **2** a small amount – **halfpenny** *adj*

halfpennyworth /'haypəth, 'haypni,wuhth/ *n* as much as can be bought for the sum of one halfpenny; *broadly* a small amount

'half-,pint *n* **1** half a pint **2** *informal* a short, small, or inconsequential person

²half-pint *adj* **1** holding half a pint ⟨*milk in* ~ *bottles*⟩ **2** *informal* of less than average size; diminutive

'half-,plate *n or adj* **1** (a photographic plate) measuring 16.5 by 10.8 centimetres (6¹/₂ by 4¹/₄ inches) **2** (a photographic print) reproduced from a half-plate ⟨*a* ~ *illustration*⟩

half rest *n, NAm* a musical rest of the same time value as a minim

,half-'round *adj* having a cross section that is a semicircle ⟨*a* ~ *file*⟩

half sister *n* a sister related through one parent only

'half-,slip *n* a topless slip with an elasticated waistband

¹'half-,sole *n* a shoe sole extending from the instep forwards

²'half-,sole *vt* to mend or make (eg a shoe) with a half-sole ⟨~d *it with rubber*⟩

half sovereign *n* a former British gold coin worth 10 shillings

half step *n, NAm* SEMITONE (distance between adjacent notes on a piano)

half term *n, chiefly Br* a period about halfway through a school term; *also* a short school holiday taken at this time

,half-'timbered *adj* constructed of timber framework with spaces filled in by brickwork or plaster – **half-timbering** *n*

halftime /-'tiem/ *n* (an intermission marking) the completion of half of a game or contest (eg in soccer)

'half-,title *n* **1** the title of a book standing alone on a right-hand page immediately preceding the title-page **2** the page containing a half-title

halftone /-,tohn/ *n* **1** SEMITONE (distance between adjacent notes on a piano) **2a** any of the shades of grey between the darkest and the lightest parts of a photographic image **b** a photoengraving made from an image photographed through a screen and then etched so that the details of the image are reproduced in dots – **halftone** *adj*

'half-,track *n* **1** a drive system of a vehicle consisting of an endless chain or track at the back and wheels at the front **2** a motor vehicle propelled by half-tracks; *specif* one lightly armoured for military use – **half-track, half-tracked** *adj*

'half-,truth *n* a statement that is only partially true; *esp* one deliberately intended to deceive

¹'half-,volley *n* **1** a shot (eg in tennis) made at a ball just after it has bounced **2** an easily-hit delivery of the ball in cricket that bounces closer than intended to the batsman

²half-volley *vt* to strike or kick (the ball) just after it has bounced

halfway /-'way/ *adj* **1** midway between two points **2** partial – **halfway** *adv* – **meet somebody halfway** to make concessions to somebody; compromise with somebody

halfway house *n* **1a** a place (eg an inn) to stop midway on a journey **b** a halfway point or place; *esp* a compromise **2** a hostel or day-care centre for newly released prisoners, mental patients, and others who need a period in which to readjust before returning to normal living conditions

'half-,wit *n* a foolish or mentally deficient person – **half-witted** *adj*, **half-wittedness** *n*

halibut /'halibət/ *n, pl* **halibuts,** *esp collectively* **halibut 1a** a large dark green to blackish Atlantic fish (*Hippoglossus hippoglossus*) that is the largest flatfish and is much valued for food **b** an edible greenish-brown Pacific flatfish (*Hippoglossus stenolepsis*) closely related to but smaller and slimmer than the Atlantic halibut **2** any of various edible marine flatfishes of the same order (Pleuronectiformes) as the Atlantic and Pacific halibuts [ME *halybutte,* fr *haly, holy* + *butte* flatfish, fr MD or MLG *but;* fr its being eaten on holy days]

halide /'haylied/ *n* a chemical compound of a HALOGEN (eg chlorine, fluorine, or iodine) with one other chemical element or group

halieutics /,hali'oohtiks/ *n taking sing vb* the art or practice of fishing [LL *halieuticus* of fishing, fr Gk *halieutikos,* fr *halieuein* to fish, fr *hals* salt, sea] – **halieutic** *adj*

Haligonian /,hali'gohnyən/ *n* a native or inhabitant of Halifax in Canada [ML *Haligonia* Halifax]

haliotis /,hali'ohtis/ *n, pl* **haliotis** ABALONE [NL, genus name, deriv of Gk *hals* + *ōt-, ous* ear]

halite /'haliet/ *n* ROCK SALT

halitosis /,hali'tohsis/ *n* (the condition of having) offensively smelling breath [NL, fr L *halitus* breath, fr *halare* to breathe – more at EXHALE] – **halitotic** *adj*

hall /hawl/ *n* **1a** the house of a medieval king or noble **b** the chief living room in a medieval house or castle **2** the manor house of a landed proprietor **3** a large usu imposing building for public or semipublic purposes ⟨*the market* ~⟩ **4a** a building used by a college or university for some special purpose ⟨*a* ~ *of residence*⟩ **b** a (division of a) college at some universities **c** (a meal served in) the common dining room of an English college ⟨*I'll see you after* ~⟩ **5** the entrance room or passage of a building **6** a large room for public assembly or entertainment ⟨*the Quaker Meeting* Hall⟩ ⟨*a bingo* ~⟩ [ME *halle,* fr OE *heall;* akin to L *cella* small room, *celare* to conceal – more at HELL]

hallal /hə'lahl/ *vt or n* HALAL

Hallel /hə'lahl/ *n* a selection comprising Psalms 113–118 chanted during Jewish feasts (eg the Passover) [Heb *hallēl* praise]

hallelujah, halleluja /,hali'loohyə/ *n or interj* (a shout, song, etc) used to express praise, joy, or thanks [Heb *halălūyāh* praise (ye) the Lord]

halliard /'halyəd/ *n* HALYARD (hoisting rope or tackle)

¹hallmark /'hawl,mahk/ *n* **1a** an official mark stamped on gold and silver articles in Britain after their purity has been tested **b** a mark or device placed or stamped on an article of trade to indicate origin, purity, or genuineness **2** a distinguishing characteristic, feature, or object ⟨*the dramatic speeches which are the* ~ *of a barrister*⟩ [Goldsmiths' *Hall* in London, where gold and silver articles were assayed and stamped]

²hallmark *vt* to stamp (as if) with a hallmark ⟨*his confident air* ~ed *him as a leader*⟩

¹hallo /hə'loh, hu-/, **halloa** /hə'loh-ə/ *vb, interj, or n* **halloing; halloed; halloaing; halloaed;** *pl* **hallos; halloas** (to) hollo

²hallo *n or interj, pl* **hallos** *chiefly Br* (a) hello

Hall of Fame *n, chiefly NAm* (a structure housing memorials to) a group of famous or illustrious individuals

hall of residence *n* a usu large building providing accommodation for students at college

halloo /hə'looh/ *vb, interj, or n* **hallooing; hallooed;** *pl* **halloos** (to) hollo

hallow /'haloh/ *vt* **1** to make holy or set apart for holy use **2** to respect and honour greatly; venerate [ME *halowen,* fr OE *hālgian,* fr *hālig* holy – more at HOLY]

hallowed /'halohd/ *adj* sacred, revered ⟨*the* ~ *traditions from the past*⟩

Halloween, Hallowe'en /,haloh'een/ *n* October 31, the eve of ALL SAINTS' DAY, observed by dressing up in disguise, playing tricks, having jack-o'-lanterns lit, etc [short for *All Hallow Even* (All Saints' Eve)]

Hallowmas /'halohməs, -mas/ *n* ALL SAINTS' DAY (November 1) [short for ME *Alholowmesse,* fr OE *ealra halgena mæsse,* lit., all saints' mass]

hallstand /'hawl,stand/ *n* a piece of furniture with pegs for holding coats and hats, and often a rack below for umbrellas

Hallstatt, Hallstadt /'halshtat/ *adj* of the earlier period of the IRON AGE in Europe [*Hallstatt,* village in Austria where remains of the period were found]

hallucinate /hə'loohsinayt/ *vt* **1** to affect with hallucinations **2** to perceive or experience as a hallucination ~ *vi* to have hallucinations [L *hallucinatus,* pp of *hallucinari* to prate, dream, var of *alucinari,* prob fr Gk *alyein* to be distraught]

hallucination /hə,loohsi'naysh(ə)n/ *n* **1a** subjectively realistic

# hal

perception of objects that have no reality, usu arising from disorder of the brain (eg in response to certain drugs) **b** the object of a hallucinatory perception **2** a completely unfounded or mistaken impression or belief; a delusion – **hallucinational** *adj,* **hallucinative** *adj*

**hallucinatory** /həˈloohsinət(ə)ri/ *adj* **1** tending to produce hallucination ⟨~ *drugs*⟩ **2** resembling or being a hallucination ⟨~ *dreams*⟩ ⟨*a* ~ *figure*⟩ ⟨*a* ~ *painting*⟩

**hallucinogen** /həˈloohsinəjən/ *n* a substance (eg LSD) that induces hallucinations [*hallucin*ation + *-o-* + *-gen*] – **hallucinogenic** *adj*

**hallucinosis** /hə.loohsiˈnohsis/ *n* an abnormal mental state characterized by hallucinations [NL]

**hallux** /ˈhaləks/ *n, pl* **halluces** /ˈhaləseez/ the innermost digit (eg the big toe) of the hind or lower limb [NL, fr L *hallus, hallux*]

**hallway** /ˈhawl.way/ *n* an entrance hall or corridor

**halma** /ˈhalmə/ *n* a game played on a chequered board by two or four players with 19 or 13 pieces respectively which remain on the board in play, to be transferred to the corner diagonally opposite to their base corner by either of two kinds of move [Gk, leap, fr *hallesthai* to leap]

**¹halo** /ˈhayloh/ *n, pl* **halos, haloes 1** a circle of light appearing to surround the sun or moon and resulting from refraction or reflection of light by particles in the earth's atmosphere **2** something resembling a halo: eg **2a** NIMBUS 1,2 **b** a differentiated zone surrounding a central object **3** the aura of glory, veneration, or sentiment surrounding an idealized person or thing [L *halos,* fr Gk *halōs* threshing floor, disc, halo

**²halo** *vt* **haloing; haloed** to form into or surround with a halo ⟨*rainbows* ~ed *the waterfalls* – Michael Crawford⟩

**halo-** – see HAL-

**halobiont** /.haloh'bie-ənt/ *n* HALOPHILE (organism living in a salty environment) [*hal-* + Gk *biount-, biōn,* prp of *bioun* to live, fr *bios* life – more at QUICK]

**halocarbon** /ˈhalə.kahbən/ *n* any of various chemical compounds (eg a FLUOROCARBON) composed of carbon and one or more halogens

**halocline** /ˈhalə.klien/ *n* a gradient in saltness (eg in layers of a sea)

**halo effect** *n* generalization from the perception of one outstanding personality trait to an excessively favourable evaluation of the whole personality

**halogen** /ˈhaləjən/ *n* any of the five chemical elements fluorine, chlorine, bromine, iodine, and astatine that make up group VII B of the PERIODIC TABLE, are highly reactive, and occur naturally only in the form of their compounds [Sw, fr *halo-* + *-gen*] – **halogenous** *adj*

**halogenate** /ˈhaləjənayt/ *vt* to treat or cause to combine with a halogen – **halogenation** *n*

**haloperidol** /.hahloh'peridol/ *n* a synthetic drug, $C_{21}H_{23}Cl$ $FNO_2$, that depresses the activity of the CENTRAL NERVOUS SYSTEM and is used esp as a tranquillizer and sedative [*hal-* + *piperidine* + *-ol*]

**halophile** /ˈhalə.fiel/ *n* an organism that lives or grows in a salty environment (eg the sea) [ISV] – **halophilic, halophilous** *adj*

**halophyte** /ˈhaləfiet/ *n* a plant (eg SEA LAVENDER) that grows in salty soil [ISV] – **halophytic** *adj*

**halothane** /ˈhaləthayn/ *n* a nonflammable liquid general anaesthetic, $CF_3CHClBr$, given by inhalation [*halo-* + *e*thane]

**¹halt** /hawlt, holt/ *adj, archaic* lame [ME, fr OE *healt;* akin to OHG *halz* lame, L *clades* destruction, Gk *klan* to break]

**²halt** *vi* **1** to hesitate between alternative courses; waver **2** to display weakness or imperfection (eg in speech or reasoning); falter **3** *archaic* to walk or proceed lamely; limp

**³halt** *n* **1** a (temporary) stop or interruption ⟨*time to call a* ~ *to these arguments*⟩ **2** *Br* a railway stopping place for local trains, without normal station facilities [Ger, fr MHG, fr *halt,* imper of *halten* to hold, fr OHG *haltan* – more at HOLD]

**⁴halt** *vi* to come to a halt ~ *vt* **1** to bring to a stop ⟨*the strike has* ~ed *tubes and buses*⟩ **2** to cause to stop; end ⟨~ *the slaughter of seals*⟩

**¹halter** /ˈhawltə, ˈholtə/ *n* **1a** a rope or strap for leading or tying an animal **b** a band round an animal's head to which a lead may be attached **2** a noose for hanging criminals; *also* death by hanging [ME, fr OE *hælftre;* akin to OHG *halftra* halter, OE *hielfe* helve]

**²halter** *vt* **1a** to catch (as if) with a halter; *also* to put a halter on **b** to hang (a person) **2** to put restraint on; hamper

**³halter** *n* a haltere

**halterbreak** /-.brayk/ *vt* **halterbroke** /-.brohk/; **halter-**

broken /-.brohkən/ to accustom (eg a colt) to wearing a halter

**haltere** /ˈhaltiə/ *n, pl* **halteres** either of a pair of club-shaped organs in a TWO-WINGED FLY that are the modified hind pair of wings and function as sensory organs that maintain equilibrium in flight [NL *halter,* fr L, jumping weight, fr Gk *haltēr,* fr *hallesthai* to leap – more at SALLY]

**halter neck** *n* (a garment having) a neckline formed by a strap passing from the front of a garment round the neck and leaving the shoulders and upper back bare

**halting** /ˈhawlting, ˈholting/ *adj* marked by stopping and starting as if uncertain ⟨*the witness spoke in a* ~ *manner*⟩ – **haltingly** *adv*

**halvah, halva** /ˈhalvah, ˈhalvə/ *n* a sweet confection of crushed sesame seeds mixed with a syrup (eg honey) [Yiddish *halva,* fr Romanian, fr Turk *helva,* fr Ar *ḥalwā* sweetmeat]

**halve** /hahv/ *vt* **1a** to divide into two equal parts **b** to reduce to one half ⟨*halving the present cost*⟩ **2** to play (eg a hole or a match in golf) in the same number of strokes as one's opponent **3** to cut out a piece half the width of (the end of a piece of timber) to correspond with another piece of timber similarly cut [ME *halven,* fr *half*]

**¹halves** /hahvz/ *pl of* HALF

**²halves** *adv* with equal half shares ⟨*let's go* ~⟩

**halyard, halliard** /ˈhalyəd/ *n* a rope or tackle for hoisting or lowering something (eg a sail or flag) [alter. of ME *halier,* fr *halen* to pull – more at HALE]

**¹ham** /ham/ *n* **1a** the hollow of the knee **b** *usu pl* a buttock with its associated thigh **2** (the meat of) the rear end of a side of a bacon pig, esp the thigh, when removed from the carcass before curing with salt – compare GAMMON **3a** a licensed operator of an amateur radio station **b** *informal* an inexpert but showy performer; *also* an actor performing in exaggerated theatrical style [ME *hamme,* fr OE *hamm;* akin to OHG *hamma* ham, Gk *knēmē* shinbone; (3) short for *hamfatter* (bad actor), fr "The *Ham-fat* Man" Negro minstrel song] – **ham** *adj*

**²ham** *vb* **-mm-** *informal vt* to execute with exaggerated speech or gestures; overact – also in **ham it up** ~ *vi* to overact a part

**hamadryad** /.hamə'drie-ad, -əd/ *n* **1** DRYAD (wood nymph) **2a** KING COBRA **b** a baboon (*Papio hamadryas*) worshipped by the ancient Egyptians – called also SACRED BABOON [L *hamadryad-, hamadryas,* fr Gk, fr *hama* together with + *dryad-, dryas* dryad – more at SAME]

**¹hamate** /ˈhay.mayt/ *adj* shaped like a hook ⟨*a* ~ *leaf*⟩ [L *hamatus,* fr *hamus* hook]

**²hamate** *n* a bone on the inner or little finger side of the second row of bones making up the CARPUS (wrist or its equivalent) in mammals

**Hamburg** /ˈham.buhg (Ger hamburk)/ *n* (any of) a European breed of small domestic fowls with ROSE COMBS (broad flattened combs) and lead-blue legs [*Hamburg,* city in NW Germany]

**hamburger** /ˈhambuhgə/ *n* a round flat cake of minced beef; *also* a sandwich of a fried hamburger in a bread roll [Ger *Hamburger* of Hamburg, fr *Hamburg,* city in NW Germany]

**¹hame** /haym/ *n* either of two curved projections that are attached to the collar of a draught horse and to which the side straps of the harness are fastened [ME, fr MD]

**²hame** *n, Scot* home [ME (Sc & northern), var of *home*]

**hamel** /ˈhaməl/ *n, SAfr* a castrated male sheep [Afrik, fr MD; akin to OHG *hamal* castrated]

**ham-'fisted** *adj, chiefly Br informal* lacking dexterity or grace; clumsy

**ham-'handed** *adj, informal* ham-fisted

**Hamiltonian** /hamil'tohnyən/ *n* a follower or advocate of the political principles and ideas associated with Alexander Hamilton that centre on a belief in the need for a strong central government with centralization of power in the USA, encouragement of an industrial and commercial economy, and a general distrust of the political capacity or wisdom of the common man [Alexander *Hamilton* †1804 US statesman] – **Hamiltonian** *adj,* **Hamiltonianism** *n*

**Hamite** /ˈhamiet/ *n* a member of a group of chiefly N African people that are mostly Muslims and typically have a fair skin [*Ham,* son of Noah & supposed ancestor of the Egyptians & other African people (Gen 10:6–20)]

**¹Hamitic** /ha'mitik, hə-/ *adj* of or belonging to the Hamites or to one or more of the Hamitic languages

**²Hamitic** *n,* **Hamitic languages** *n pl* the BERBER, CUSHITIC, and sometimes Egyptian branches of the AFRO-ASIATIC languages

**Hamito-Semitic** /.hamitoh sə'mitik/ *adj* of or constituting the AFRO-ASIATIC languages – **Hamito-Semitic** *n*

**hamlet** /'hamlit/ *n* a small village [ME, fr MF *hamelet*, dim. of *ham* village, of Gmc origin; akin to OE *hām* village, home]

**hamman** /'hahmahm/ *n* TURKISH BATH [Ar *ḥammām* bath]

**hammer** /'hamə/ *n* **1a** a hand tool that consists of a solid head set crosswise on a handle and is used to strike a blow (eg to drive a nail) **b** a power-driven tool that substitutes a metal block or a drill for the hammerhead **2** something that resembles a hammer in the form or action: eg **2a** a lever with a stricking head for ringing a bell or striking a gong **b(1)** an arm that strikes the container holding an explosive charge in a firearm when the trigger is pulled **b(2)** a part of the mechanism of a modern gun that strikes the device that ignites the propellant **c** MALLEUS (bone of the ear) – not used technically **d** a mallet used by an auctioneer, presiding officer, etc; GAVEL **e(1)** a padded mallet in a piano for striking a string to sound a note **e(2)** a hand mallet for playing on various percussion instruments (eg a xylophone) **3** (the athletic field event using) a metal sphere weighing 7.26 kilograms (16 pounds) attached by a wire to a handle and thrown for distance [ME *hamer*, fr OE *hamor*; akin to OHG *hamar* hammer, Gk *akmē* point, edge – more at EDGE] – **under the hammer** for sale at auction

**²hammer** *vi* **1** to strike blows, esp repeatedly, (as if) with a hammer; pound **2** to make repeated efforts *at; esp* to reiterate an opinion or attitude ⟨*the lectures all* ∼ed *away at the same points*⟩ ∼ *vt* **1** to beat, drive, or shape (as if) with repeated blows of a hammer ⟨∼ed *the nail into the wall*⟩ ⟨∼ed *20 runs in one over*⟩ ⟨∼ed *home his advantage*⟩ **2** to force as if by hitting repeatedly ⟨*wanted to* ∼ *him into submission*⟩ **3** to declare formally that (a member of the Stock Exchange) is insolvent and is therefore forbidden to trade **4** *informal* to beat decisively – **hammerer** *n*

**hammer into** *vt* to cause (someone) to learn or remember (something) by continual repetition

**hammer out** *vt* to produce or bring about through lengthy discussion ⟨hammered out *a new policy*⟩

**hammer and sickle** *n* an emblem consisting of a crossed hammer and sickle used chiefly as a symbol of Communism

**hammer and tongs** *adv* with great force, vigour, or violence ⟨*went at each other* ∼⟩

**hammer beam** *n* either of the short horizontal beams, or beams supported at only one end, projecting from a pair of opposite walls to support either end of an arch or principal rafter in the rigid framework of a roof

**hammerhead** /'hamə,hed/ *n* **1** the striking part of a hammer **2** any of various medium-sized sharks (family Sphyrnidae) with eyes at the ends of bulging projections on each side of the flattened head **3** *chiefly NAm* a blockhead

**hammering** /'haməring/ *n, informal* a decisive defeat

**hammerless** /'haməlis/ *adj* having the hammer concealed ⟨*a* ∼ *gun*⟩

**hammerlock** /'hamə,lok/ *n* a wrestling hold in which an opponent's arm is held bent behind his/her back

**hammertoe** /,hamə'toh, '--,-/ *n* a toe that is bent permanently downwards

**¹hammock** /'hamək/ *n* a hanging bed usu made of netting or canvas and suspended by cords at each end [Sp *hamaca*, fr Taino]

**²hammock** *n* a fertile wooded area in the S USA, esp Florida, that is usu higher than its surroundings [var of *hummock*]

**hammy** /'hami/ *adj, chiefly informal* (characteristic) of ham actors – **hammily** *adv*, **hamminess** *n*

**¹hamper** /'hampə/ *vt* **1** to restrict the movement or operation of by bonds or obstacles; hinder **2a** to curb, restrain **b** to interfere with; encumber *synonyms* see ¹HINDER *antonyms* assist, expedite [ME *hamperen*]

**²hamper** *n, archaic* something that impedes or restricts freedom of movement; an obstruction

**³hamper** *n* a large basket, usu with a cover, for packing, storing, or transporting crockery, food, etc ⟨*picnic* ∼⟩ [ME *hampere*, alter. of *hanaper*, lit., case to hold goblets, fr MF *hanapier*, fr *hanap* goblet, of Gmc origin; akin to OE *hnæpp* bowl]

**Hampshire** /'hampshiə, -shə/ *n* **1** (any of) an American breed of black pigs with a white belt round the middle and white forelegs **2 Hampshire, Hampshire Down** (any of) a British breed of large hornless sheep that are reared for meat and produce wool of medium quality [*Hampshire*, county in S England]

**hamster** /'hamstə/ *n* any of numerous small Eurasian rodents (*Cricetus* or a related genus) having very short tails and large cheek pouches [Ger, fr OHG *hamustro*, of Slav origin; akin to OSlav *chomĕstorŭ* hamster]

**¹hamstring** /'ham,string/ *n* **1a** either of two groups of tendons at the back of the human knee **b** hamstring, hamstring muscle any of three muscles at the back of the thigh that function to extend the thigh when the leg is flexed **2** a large tendon above and behind the hock of a 4-legged animal

**²hamstring** *vt* hamstrung **1** to cripple by cutting the tendons in the leg **2** to make ineffective or powerless; cripple ⟨*teachers* . . . hamstrung *by excessive teaching schedules* – N M Pusey⟩

**hamulus** /'hamyooləs/ *n, pl* hamuli /-li/ *biology* a hook or hooked part [NL, fr L, dim. of *hamus* hook]

**Han** /han/ *n* **1** a Chinese dynasty dated 206 BC to AD 220 marked by centralized control with division of the country into a series of administrative areas ruled by centrally appointed officials, a revival of learning, and the spread of Buddhism **2** the Chinese people, esp as distinguished from Mongol, Manchu, or other non-Chinese elements in the population; ethnic Chinese

**¹hand** /hand/ *n* **1a(1)** the end of the forelimb of human beings, monkeys, etc when modified as a grasping organ **a(2)** the segment of the forelimb of a VERTEBRATE animal that corresponds anatomically to the hand (eg the end section of a bird's wing), irrespective of its form or functional specialization **b** a part (eg the pincer or claw of a crab, lobster, etc) serving the function of or resembling a hand **c** something resembling a hand: eg **c(1)** an indicator or pointer on a dial **c(2)** a stylized figure of a hand with forefinger extended to point a direction or call attention to something; *specif* INDEX 5 (printed character) **c(3)** a group of usu large leaves (eg of tobacco) reaped or tied together or of bananas growing together **d** a forehock of pork **2** *pl* **2a** personal possession ⟨*the documents fell into the* ∼s *of the enemy*⟩ **b** control, supervision ⟨*the reception was in the* ∼s *of the caterer*⟩ **3a** side, direction ⟨*men fighting on either* ∼⟩ **b** either of two sides or aspects of an issue or argument ⟨*on the one* ∼ *we can appeal for peace, or on the other declare war*⟩ **4** a pledge, esp of betrothal or marriage **5a** (style of) handwriting **b** a signature **6a** skill, ability ⟨*tried her* ∼ *at sailing*⟩ **b** an instrumental part ⟨*had a* ∼ *in the crime*⟩ **7** a unit of measure equal to 4 inches (about 102 millimetres) used esp for the height of a horse **8a** assistance or aid, esp when involving physical effort ⟨*lend a* ∼⟩ **b** participation, interest ⟨*a project in which several people had a* ∼⟩ **c** a round of applause **9a** (the cards or pieces held by) a player in a card or board game **b** a single round in a game **c** the force or solidity of one's position (eg in negotiations) **d** a turn to serve in a game (eg squash) in which only the server may score points and which lasts until the receiver wins a rally **10a** one who performs or executes a particular work ⟨*two portraits by the same* ∼⟩ **b** a worker, employee ⟨*employed over a hundred* ∼s⟩; *esp* one employed at manual labour or general tasks ⟨*a farm* ∼⟩ **c** a member of a ship's crew ⟨*all* ∼s *on deck*⟩ **d** one skilled in a particular action or pursuit – usu + *at* ⟨*she's an old* ∼ *at this job*⟩ **e** one who has long-standing experience in a specified activity or region ⟨*old British Council* ∼s⟩ ⟨*an old China* ∼⟩ **11a** handiwork **b** style of execution; workmanship ⟨*the* ∼ *of a master*⟩ [ME, fr OE; akin to OHG *hant* hand] – **handless** *adj* – **at hand** near in time or place – **at second hand** from or through an intermediary ⟨*heard the news* at second hand⟩ – **at the hands/hand of** by the act or instrumentality of – **bite the hand that feeds one** to injure a benefactor maliciously – **by hand** with the hands, usu as opposed to mechanically ⟨*sewed the dress* by hand⟩ ⟨*delivered* by hand⟩ – **change hands** to pass from the possession of one person to that of another – **eat out of somebody's hand** to accept somebody's domination – **force somebody's hand** to cause somebody to act hurriedly or against his/her will – **get/have the upper hand** to get/have a position of superiority, control, advantage, etc – **hands off** do not touch or meddle – **hands up** raise the hands in the air above the head – **have one's hands full** to be fully occupied – **have one's hands tied** to be in a position whereby one is unable to act or bound to take a certain course of action – **hold hands** to engage one's hand with another's esp as an expression of affection – **in good hands** in the care of those well-qualified and capable – **in hand 1** not used up or lost and at one's disposal ⟨*they have a game* in hand⟩ **2** *of a horse* being led rather than being ridden **3** UNDER WAY ⟨*put the work* in hand⟩ – **keep one's hand in** to remain in practice – **off one's hands** out of one's care or charge – **on hand 1** ready to use **2** in attendance; present – **on one's hands** in one's possession, care, or management – **out of hand 1** without delay; forthwith ⟨*refused it* out of hand⟩ **2** out of control ⟨*that child has got quite* out of hand⟩ – **overplay**

one's hand to overestimate one's capacities – **play into the hands of** to act so as to give an advantage to (an opponent) – **set one's hand to** to become engaged in – **sit on one's hands** to fail to take action – **take in hand** to embark on the control, discipline, or reform of – **to hand** available and ready for use; *esp* within reach – **try one's hand (at)** to make a first attempt (at) – **turn one's hand to** to apply oneself to – **wait on somebody hand and foot** to serve somebody totally and assiduously ⟨*expects me to* wait on him hand and foot⟩ – **wash one's hands of** to disclaim interest in, responsibility for, or further connection with ⟨*he* washed his hands of *the whole despicable affair*⟩ [fr Pontius Pilate's action of disclaiming responsibility for Christ's death Mt 27:24] – **with one's bare hands** without the aid of weapons or tools – see also **take the** LAW **into one's own hands,** OIL **somebody's hand**

²**hand** *vt* **1** to furl (a sail) **2** to lead, guide, or assist with the hand ⟨*he* ∼ed *her out of the car*⟩ **3a** to give or pass with the hand ⟨∼ *a letter to her*⟩ **b** to present, provide ⟨∼ed *him a surprise*⟩ – **hand it to** to give credit to; concede the excellence of

**hand down** *vt* **1** to transmit in succession (eg from father to son) **2** to give (an outgrown article of clothing) to a younger member of one's family **3** to deliver in court ⟨hand down *a judgment*⟩

**hand off** *vt* to push off (an opposing player) with the palm of the hand so as to avoid a tackle in rugby – see also HANDOFF

**hand on** *vt* HAND DOWN ⟨*the father* handed on *his good reputation to his son*⟩

**hand out** *vt* **1** to give freely or without charge ⟨handed out *sweets to the children*⟩ **2** to administer ⟨hand out *a severe punishment*⟩

**hand over** *vb* to yield control or possession (of)

**hand and spring** *n* a cut of pork consisting of the cheek, forehock, knuckle, trotter, and three or four ribs from the front end of the belly [¹*hand* 1d + *spring* (the belly or lower part of a forequarter of pork)]

**hand axe** *n* a prehistoric tool shaped from a single stone and having one end pointed for cutting and the other end rounded for holding in the hand

**handbag** /'hand,bag/ *n* a bag designed for carrying small personal articles and money, carried usu by women

**handball** /'hand,bawl/ *n* **1** (a small rubber ball used in) a game resembling fives and played in a walled court or against a single wall **2** an amateur indoor game played between two teams of seven players whose object is to direct a soccer ball into the opponent's goal by throwing and catching without physical contact between opposing players; *also* a similar game played outdoors between teams of 11 players **3** the offence of handling the ball in soccer

**handbarrow** /'hand,baroh/ *n* a workman's stretcher with handles at both ends for carrying loads

**handbasin** /'hand,bays(ə)n( *n* a wash basin

**handbell** /'hand,bel/ *n* a small bell with a handle; *esp* any of a set of small bells tuned in a scale

**handbill** /'hand,bil/ *n* a small printed sheet to be distributed (eg for advertising) by hand

**handbook** /'hand,book/ *n* a short reference book, esp on a particular subject; a manual

**hand brake** *n* a hand-operated brake in a motor vehicle

**handbreadth** /'hand,bredth, -,bret·th/ *n* any of various units of length varying from about 2¹/₂ to 4 inches (63.5 to 102 millimetres) based on the breadth of a hand

**handcar** /'hand,kah/ *n, NAm* a trolley

**handcart** /'hand,kaht/ *n* a cart drawn or pushed by hand

**handclap** /'hand,klap/ *n* a clapping action of the hands

**handclasp** /'hand,klahsp/ *n* a handshake

¹**handcraft** /'hand,krahft/ *n* (a) handicraft

²**handcraft** *vt* to fashion by handicraft

**handcuff** /'hand,kuf, 'hankuf/ *vt* **1** to apply handcuffs to; manacle **2** to hold in check; make ineffective or powerless

**handcuffs** *n pl* a pair of metal rings, usu connected by a chain or bar, that can be locked round a prisoner's wrists

**-handed** /handid/ *comb form (adj → adj)* having or using (such) a hand or (so many) hands ⟨*a large-*handed *man*⟩ ⟨*right-*handed⟩ ⟨*a one-*handed *catch*⟩ – **hander** *comb form (adj → n)*

**handedness** /'handidnis/ *n* **1** a tendency to use one hand rather than the other **2** the quality of existing in one or both of a pair of MIRROR IMAGES that cannot be superimposed on each other

**hander** /'handə/ *n* a play, film, etc having a specified number of leading roles – usu in combination ⟨*the new musical was a spectacular two-*hander⟩

,**hand-'feed** *vt* handfed /-fed/ **1** to feed (eg a baby) by hand **2** to distribute rations to (animals) at regular intervals in quantities sufficient for a single feeding – compare SELF-FEED

**handful** /'handf(ə)l/ *n, pl* **handfuls** *also* **handsful** /'handzf(ə)l/ **1** as much or as many as the hand will grasp **2** a small quantity or number ⟨*a mere* ∼ *of troops*⟩ **3** *informal* somebody or something (eg a child or animal) that is difficult to control ⟨*that boy is a real* ∼⟩

**hand gallop** *n* a moderate gallop

**hand glass** *n* **1** a small mirror with a handle **2** a hand-held magnifying glass

**handgrip** /'hand,grip/ *n* **1** a grasping with the hand **2** a sheath (eg of plastic or towelling) covering a handle on a wheelbarrow, tennis racquet, etc to make the handle easier to grip

**handgun** /'hand,gun/ *n* a firearm held and fired with one hand

,**hand-'held** *adj* held or supported only by the hand ⟨*a* ∼ *camera*⟩

**handhold** /'hand,hohld/ *n* something to hold onto for support (eg in mountain climbing)

¹**handicap** /'handi,kap/ *n* **1a** a race or contest in which an artificial advantage or disadvantage is given to a contestant so that all have an equal or more nearly equal chance of winning **b** the advantage or disadvantage so imposed, usu in the form of points, strokes (eg in golf), or weight to be carried (eg by a horse) **2** a (physical) disability or disadvantage that makes achievement unusually difficult [obs *handicap* a game in which forfeits were held in a cap, fr *hand in cap*]

²**handicap** *vt* **-pp-** **1** to assign handicaps to; impose handicaps on **2** to put at a disadvantage

**handicapper** /'handi,kapə/ *n* **1** one who assigns handicaps **2** one who competes, esp in golf, with a (specified) handicap – usu in combination ⟨*a 5-*handicapper⟩

**handicraft** /'handi,krahft/ *n* **1** (an operation requiring) manual skill **2** the articles fashioned by handicraft [ME *handi-crafte,* alter. of *handcraft*] – **handicrafter** *n*

**handicraftsman** /'handi,krahftsmən/ *n* one who engages in a handicraft; an artisan

'**hand-,in** *n* the server in a game (eg squash or badminton) in which only the server may score points

**hand in glove** *adv* in extremely close relationship or agreement ⟨*were found to be working* ∼ *with the racketeers*⟩

**hand in hand** *adv* **1** with hands clasped (eg in intimacy or affection) **2** in close association

**handiwork** /'handi,wuhk/ *n* **1** (the product of) work done by the hands rather than by machine **2** work done personally ⟨*it's all my own* ∼⟩ [ME *handiwerk,* fr OE *handgeweorc,* fr *hand* + *geweorc,* fr *ge-* (collective prefix) + *weorc* work]

**handkerchief** /'hangkə,cheef, -chif/ *n, pl* **handkerchiefs** *also* **handkerchieves** /-cheevz/ a small piece of cloth used for various usu personal purposes (eg blowing the nose or wiping the eyes) or as a clothing accessory

¹**handle** /'handl/ *n* **1** a part that is designed to be grasped by the hand **2** something that resembles a handle **3** the feel of a textile **4** *chiefly NZ* a measure of beer approximating one pint **5** *informal* a title; *also* an esp aristocratic or double-barrelled name [ME *handel,* fr OE *handle*; akin to OE *hand*] – **handled** *adj,* **handleless** *adj* – **fly off the handle** to become suddenly and violently angry

²**handle** *vt* **1a** to try or examine (eg by touching, feeling, or moving) with the hand ⟨∼ *silk to judge its weight*⟩ **b** to manage with the hands ⟨∼ *a horse*⟩ **2a** to deal with (eg a subject or idea) in speech or writing, or as a work of art **b** to manage, direct ⟨*a solicitor* ∼s *all my affairs*⟩ **3** to deal with, act on, or dispose of ⟨∼ *the day's mail*⟩ **4** to engage in the buying, selling, or distributing of (a commodity) ∼ *vi* to respond to controlling movements in a specified way ⟨*car that* ∼s *well*⟩ – **handleable** *adj*

**handlebar** /'handl,bah/ *n,* **handlebars** *n pl* a straight or bent bar with a handle at each end, esp on a cycle or scooter, for steering

**handlebar moustache** *n* a long heavy moustache that curves upwards at each end

**handler** /'handlə/ *n* **1** one who is in immediate physical charge of an animal ⟨*a police dog* ∼⟩ **2** one who helps to train a boxer or acts as his second during a match

'**hand-,line** *n* a fishing line used without a rod or reel

**handling** /'handling/ *n* **1** a process by which something is handled in a commercial transaction; *esp* the packaging and shipping of an object or material (eg to a consumer) **2** the manner in which something is treated (eg in a stage production)

**3** *Br* the offence of dealing with, receiving, or assisting in the disposal of stolen goods

**handmade** /ˌhand'mayd/ *adj* made by hand rather than by machine

**handmaid** /'hand‚mayd/ *n* a handmaiden

**handmaiden** /'hand‚mayd(ə)n/ *n* **1** a personal maid or female servant **2** something whose essential function is to serve or assist ⟨*good sense which ... is the indispensable ~ of the critical art* – Carlos Baker⟩

**'hand-me-‚down** *n, informal* **1** an article of clothing that is discarded, esp when outgrown, and passed down from person to person **2** something passed on from another □ called also REACH-ME-DOWN – **hand-me-down** *adj*

**hand mower** *n* a motorless lawn mower designed to be pushed by hand

**handoff** /'handof/ *n* the act or an instance of pushing away an opponent in rugby with the palm of the hand

**hand organ** *n* a BARREL ORGAN operated by a hand crank

**handout** /'hand‚owt/ *n* **1** something (e g food, clothing, or money) distributed free, esp to people in need **2** a folder or circular of information for free distribution **3** PRESS RELEASE

**'hand-‚out** *n* a player (e g in squash or badminton) who is not HAND-IN (server) and therefore not able to score points

**hand over fist** *adv* quickly and in large amounts ⟨*we began to make money ~*⟩

**handpick** /ˌhand'pik/ *vt* **1** to pick by hand rather than by machine **2** to select personally and carefully; choose (the best) from a group

**handpress** /'hand‚pres/ *n* a hand-operated PRINTING PRESS

**hand puppet** *n* PUPPET 1a

**handrail** /'hand‚rayl/ *n* a narrow rail for grasping with the hand as a support, esp near stairs

**handsaw** /'hand‚saw/ *n* a saw operated usu with one hand

**handsbreadth** /ˌhandz'bredth, -'bret·th/ *n* HANDBREADTH (unit of length based on the breadth of a hand)

**handscrew** /'hand‚skrooh/ *n* a metal device with two parallel jaws, that are adjusted by two threaded bolts, for holding together timbers and blocks of stone

**hands down** *adv* without much effort; easily ⟨*they won ~*⟩ [fr a jockey dropping his hands, thus loosening his grip on the reins, when winning a race easily]

**¹handsel, hansel** /'hansl/ *n* **1** a gift made as a token of good wishes or luck, esp at the beginning of a new year **2a** a first instalment, esp of money to secure a bargain or a contract **b** a first use of something; a foretaste [ME *hansell*, prob fr ON *handsal* promise or bargain confirmed by a handshake, fr *hand-, hond* hand + *sal* payment]

**²handsel, hansel** *vt* **-ll-** (*NAm* **-l-, -ll-**) **1** to give a handsel to **2** to inaugurate with a token or gesture of luck or pleasure **3** to use or do for the first time

**handset** /'hand‚set/ *n* a combined telephone transmitter and receiver that can be held in the hand

**handshake** /'hand‚shayk/ *n* a clasping and shaking of each other's usu right hand by two people (e g in greeting or farewell) – compare GOLDEN HANDSHAKE

**handsome** /'hansəm/ *adj* **1** considerable, sizable ⟨*a painting that commanded a ~ price*⟩ **2** marked by graciousness or generosity; liberal ⟨*~ contributions to charity*⟩ **3a** *of a man* having a pleasing appearance; good-looking **b** *of a woman* attractive in a dignified statuesque way **4** *NAm* marked by skill or cleverness; adroit **5** *chiefly dial* appropriate, suitable *synonyms* see BEAUTIFUL [ME *handsom* easy to handle, fr ¹*hand* + -*som* ¹-some] – **handsomely** *adv*, **handsomeness** *n*

**handspike** /'hand‚spiek/ *n* a bar used as a lever, chiefly by sailors and gunners [by folk etymology (influenced by *spike*) fr D *handspaak*, fr *hand* + *spaak* pole]

**handspring** /'hand‚spring/ *n* an acrobatic movement in which the body turns forwards or backwards in a full circle from a standing position and lands first on the hands and then on the feet

**handstand** /'hand‚stand/ *n* an act of supporting and balancing the body on only the hands with the legs in the air

**‚hand-to-'hand** *adj* involving physical contact; very close ⟨*~ fighting*⟩ – **hand to hand** *adv*

**‚hand-to-'mouth** *adj* having or providing only just enough to live on; precarious ⟨*a ~ existence*⟩

**handwork** /'hand‚wuhk/ *n* handiwork – **handworker** *n*

**handwoven** /ˌhand'wohv(ə)n/ *adj* **1** produced on a hand-operated loom **2** woven by hand

**handwrite** /'hand‚riet/ *vt* **handwrote** /-‚roht/; **handwritten** /-‚ritn/ to write by hand [back-formation fr *handwriting*]

**handwriting** /'hand‚rieting/ *n* writing done by hand; *esp* the style of writing peculiar to a particular person

**handwrought** /ˌhand'rawt/ *adj* fashioned by hand or without complex machinery

**handy** /'handi/ *adj* **1a** convenient for use; useful **b** *of a vessel or vehicle* easily handled **2** clever in using the hands, esp in a variety of practical ways; *broadly* dexterous, nimble ⟨*a ~ horse*⟩ **3** *informal* conveniently near [¹*hand* + ¹-*y*] – **handiness** *n*

**handyman** /-mon, -‚man/ *n* **1** one who does odd jobs **2** one who is competent in a variety of skills or inventive or ingenious in repair work

**¹hang** /hang/ *vb* **hung** /hung/, (*1b*) **hanged** *vt* **1a** to fasten to some elevated point by the top so that the lower part is free; suspend ⟨*~ your coat on the hook behind the door*⟩ **b** to suspend by the neck until dead – often used as a mild oath ⟨*I'll be ~ed*⟩ **c** to fasten on a point of suspension so as to allow free motion within given limits ⟨*~ a door on hinges*⟩ ⟨*~ a pendulum*⟩ **d** to suspend (meat, esp game) before cooking to make the flesh tender and develop the flavour **2** to decorate, furnish, or cover by hanging something up (e g flags or bunting) ⟨*a room hung with tapestries*⟩ **3** to hold or bear in a suspended or inclined position ⟨*hung his head in shame*⟩ **4** to fasten (something, esp wallpaper) to a wall (e g with paste) **5** to display (pictures) in a gallery ~ *vi* **1a** to remain fastened at the top so that the lower part is free; dangle **b** to die by hanging ⟨*he ~ed for his crimes*⟩ **2** to remain poised or stationary in the air ⟨*clouds ~ing low overhead*⟩ **3** to stay on; persist ⟨*the smell of the explosion hung in the afternoon air*⟩ **4** to be imminent; impend ⟨*doom hung over the nation*⟩ **5** to fall or droop from a usu tense or taut position ⟨*his mouth hung open*⟩ **6** to depend ⟨*election ~s on one vote*⟩ **7** to be uncertain or in suspense ⟨*the decision is still ~ing*⟩ **8** to lean, incline, or jut over or downwards ⟨*above the crevice ~s the rock on which the eagle has nested*⟩ **9** to fall in flowing lines ⟨*the skirt ~s well*⟩ – see also **hang in the** BALANCE, **hang** FIRE, GO **hang, hang by a** THREAD [partly fr ME *hon*, fr OE *hōn*, vt; partly fr ME *hangen*, fr OE *hangian*, vi & vt; both akin to OHG *hāhan*, vt, to hang, *hangēn*, vi] – **hangable** *adj*

*usage* **Hanged**, rather than **hung**, is the correct past tense and past participle for the sense "hang by the neck until dead", but **hung** is often used informally for this sense also ⟨*wasn't D'Alton's Father hung?* – Hilaire Belloc⟩

**hang about** *vi, informal* **1** to wait on purpose ⟨*hang about, don't go yet*⟩ **2** *Br* to wait or stay without purpose or activity ⟨*we hung about for two hours before the plane arrived*⟩ **3** *Br* to delay or move slowly; dawdle ⟨*don't hang about, we have a train to catch!*⟩

**hang around** *vi* HANG ABOUT 2

**hang back** *vi* **1** to drag behind others **2** to be reluctant to move or act; hesitate, falter

**hang in** *vi, chiefly NAm informal* to refuse to be discouraged or intimidated; persist

**hang off** *vi* HANG BACK

**hang on** *vt* **1** to take hold of for support; cling to ⟨*she hung on his arm*⟩ **2** to listen to with rapt attention ⟨*hangs on her every word*⟩ **3** to be burdensome or oppressive to ⟨*time hangs on his hands*⟩ **4** to depend on ⟨*the success of the whole project hangs on your cooperation*⟩ ~ *vi* **1** to persist tenaciously ⟨*a cold that hung on all spring*⟩ **2** to wait for a short time ⟨*hang on a second while I look it up*⟩

**hang onto** *vt* to hold or keep tenaciously ⟨*learned to hang onto his money*⟩

**hang out** *vi* **1** to protrude, esp downwards **2** *slang* to live or spend much time ⟨*the kids hang out on street corners*⟩

**hang up** *vt* **1** to place on a hook or hanger ⟨*told the child to hang up his coat*⟩ **2** to delay, suspend ⟨*the negotiations were hung up for a week*⟩ ~ *vi* to terminate a telephone conversation, often abruptly ⟨*she hung up on me*⟩

**²hang** *n* **1** the manner in which a thing hangs **2** a downward slope; *also* a droop **3** *Austr & NZ* an impressive amount – + *of a* ⟨*they got down in a ~ of a hurry* – Frank Sargeson⟩ – **get the hang of** to learn how to use, or deal with; acquire the knack of

**hangar** /'hangə/ *n* a shed; *esp* a large shed for housing aircraft △ **hanger** [Fr] – **hangar** *vt*

**hangdog** /'hang‚dog/ *adj* **1** ashamed, guilty **2** abject, cowed – **hangdog** *n*

**hanger** /'hangə/ *n* **1** a device (e g a loop or strap) by which or to which something is hung or hangs **2** something that hangs, overhangs, or is suspended: e g **2a** a small sword formerly used

by seamen **b** *chiefly Br* a small wood on steeply sloping land **3**
COAT HANGER △ hangar [(2b) OE *hangra*, fr *hangian* to hang]
,**hanger-'on** *n, pl* **hangers-on** one who attempts to associate
with a person, place, etc, esp for personal gain; a dependant
[*hang on* + *-er*]
'**hang-,glider** *n* a glider that resembles a kite and is controlled
by the body movements of one or two people harnessed to the
glider and suspended beneath it; *also* a person who flies in a
hang-glider – **hang-gliding** *n*
**hangi** /'hahng·i/ *n, pl* **hangis** HAANGI (Maori oven)
¹**hanging** /'hang·ing/ *n* **1** an execution by strangling or breaking the neck when suspended from a noose **2** something hung:
e g **2a** a curtain **b** a covering (e g a tapestry) for a wall
²**hanging** *adj* **1** situated or lying on steeply sloping ground
⟨~ *gardens*⟩ **2a** jutting out; overhanging ⟨*a* ~ *rock*⟩ **b** supported only by the wall on one side ⟨*a* ~ *staircase*⟩ **3** adapted
for sustaining a hanging object ⟨*a* ~ *rail*⟩ **4** deserving or liable
to inflict death by hanging ⟨*a* ~ *matter*⟩ ⟨*a* ~ *judge*⟩
**hanging valley** *n* a valley that ends in a steeply descending
cliff face leading to a larger valley or a shore
**hangman** /-mən/ *n* one who hangs a condemned person; *also*
a public executioner
**hangnail** /'hang,nayl/ *n* a bit of skin hanging loose at the side
or root of a fingernail [by folk etymology fr *agnail*]
**hangout** /'hang,owt/ *n, slang* a place where someone is often
to be seen
**hangover** /'hang·ohvə/ *n* **1** something (e g a surviving custom)
that remains from the past **2** the disagreeable physical effects
following heavy consumption of alcohol or from the use of drugs
'**hang-,up** *n, informal* a source of mental or emotional difficulty
**hank** /hangk/ *n* **1** a coil, loop; *specif* a coiled or looped bundle
(e g of yarn, rope, or wire) usu containing a definite length **2** a
ring or clip used to hold the LUFF (front edge) of a triangular
headsail to a STAY (wire supporting mast) [ME, of Scand origin;
akin to ON *hönk* hank; akin to OE *hangian* to hang]
**hanker** /'hangkə/ *vi* to desire strongly or persistently – usu +
*after* or *for* [prob fr Flem *hankeren*, freq of *hangen* to hang;
akin to OE *hangian*]
**hankering** /'hangkəring/ *n* a strong or persistent wish; a desire
**hankie, hanky** /'hangki/ *n, informal* a handkerchief [by
shortening & alter.]
**hanky-panky** /'pangki/ *n, informal* mildly improper or deceitful behaviour [prob alter. of *hocus-pocus*]
¹**Hanoverian** /,hanə'viəriən/ *adj* **1** of or supporting the princely
German house of Hanover **2** of or supporting the British royal
house that originated from the German house of Hanover and
reigned from 1714 to 1901 [*Hanover*, former province of
Germany]
²**Hanoverian** *n* **1** a member or supporter of the house of
Hanover **2** (any of) a breed of horses developed by crossing
heavy German horses with Thoroughbreds
**Hansa** /'hansə, 'hahnzah/ *n* (the) Hanse
**Hansard** /'hansahd/ *n* the official word-for-word report of
Parliamentary proceedings [Luke *Hansard* †1828 E printer]
**Hanse** /hans/ *n* **1** *taking sing or pl vb* **1a** a medieval merchant
guild or trading association **b** a league originally made up of
merchants from various politically independent German cities
trading abroad in the medieval period, and later of the cities
themselves, that was organized to secure greater safety and
privileges in trading **2** the entrance fee to a Hanse [*Hanse* fr
ME, fr MF, fr MLG; *Hansa* fr ML, fr MLG *hanse*] – **Han-
seatic** *n or adj*
**hansel** /'hansl/ *vt or n* -ll- (*NAm* -l-, -ll-) HANDSEL
**hansom** /'hansəm/, **hansom cab** *n* a light 2-wheeled covered
carriage with the driver's seat high up at the back △ handsome [Joseph *Hansom* †1882 E architect]
**Hanukkah, Chanukah** /'hahnook(h)ah/ *n* an 8-day Jewish holiday falling in December and commemorating the rededication
of the Temple of Jerusalem after its defilement by Antiochus
of Syria [Heb *ḥănukkāh* dedication]
**hanuman** /,hunoo'mahn/ *n* a long-tailed monkey (*Presbytis
entellus*) of S Asia considered to be sacred by Hindus [Hindi
*Hanumān*, a monkey god, hanuman, fr Skt *hanumant*, lit.,
having (large) jaws, fr *hanu* jaw]
**hào** *n* – see *dong* at MONEY table [Vietnamese]
¹**hap** /hap/ *n, archaic* **1** a happening, occurrence **2** chance, fortune [ME, fr ON *happ* good luck; akin to OE *gehæp* suitable,
OSlav *kobĭ* augury]
²**hap** *vi* -pp- *archaic* to happen
³**hap** *n, dial* something (e g a quilt or cloak) that serves as a

covering or wrap [E dial. *hap* to clothe, cover, fr ME *happen*]
**hapax legomenon** /,hapaks li'gomənon, -nən/ *n, pl* **hapax
legomena** /-nə/ a word or form of whose use there is only one
example in a language [Gk, something said only once]
**ha'penny** /'haypni/ *n* a halfpenny
¹**haphazard** /hap'hazəd/ *n, archaic* chance [¹*hap* + *hazard*]
²**haphazard** *adj* marked by lack of plan, order, or direction;
aimless – **haphazard** *adv*, **haphazardly** *adv*, **haphazardness** *n*
**haphazardry** /hap'hazədri/ *n* haphazard character or order
**hapl-, haplo-** *comb form* **1** single; simple ⟨*haplotype*⟩ **2** of the
haploid generation or condition ⟨*haplosis*⟩ [NL, fr Gk, fr
*haploos*, fr *ha-* one (akin to Gk *homos* same) + *-ploos* multiplied
by – more at SAME, DOUBLE; (2) *haploid*]
**hapless** /'haplis/ *adj* having no luck; unfortunate – **haplessly**
*adv*, **haplessness** *n*
**haplobiont** /,haploh'bie·ont, ha'plohbi,ont/ *n* a plant producing only sexual haploid individuals – **haplobiontic** *adj*
**haplography** /hap'lografi/ *n* a written haplography
¹**haploid** /'haployd/ *adj* having or being a single set of
CHROMOSOMES (strands of gene-carrying material); having
or being the basic number of chromosomes that is characteristic of the egg and sperm cells of mammals and is half that of
all other mammalian cells – compare DIPLOID, POLYPLOID [ISV,
fr Gk *haploeidēs* single, fr *haploos*] – **haploidy** *n*
²**haploid** *n* a haploid cell, individual, or generation
**haplology** /hap'loləji/ *n* contraction of a word by the omission
of one or more similar sounds or syllables in pronunciation (e g
/'liebri/ for *library*) [ISV *hapl-* + *-logy*]
**haplont** /'haplont/ *n* an organism whose SOMATIC CELLS (all cells
other than the reproductive cells) have the haploid number of
CHROMOSOMES (strands of gene-carrying material) – compare DIPLONT [ISV] – **haplontic** *adj*
**haply** /'hapli/ *adv, archaic or poetic* by chance, luck, or accident
**hap'orth, ha'porth, ha'p'orth** /'haypəth/ *n* a halfpennyworth
⟨*doesn't make a* ~ *of difference*⟩ [by contr]
**happen** /'hapn/ *vi* **1** to occur by chance – often + *it* ⟨*it so* ~s
*that I'm going your way*⟩ **2** to come into being as an event;
occur **3** to have the luck or fortune *to* ⟨*he* ~ed *to overhear the
plotters*⟩ [ME *happenen*, fr *hap*]
**synonyms** Happen, occur, befall, betide, transpire, and
materialize all mean "come about" or "take place". Happen is the
general term. Occur is often interchangeable with happen in the
sense discussed, but should be avoided when there is a possibility of
confusion with its other senses ⟨*that would never* happen *to me*⟩
rather than ⟨*that would never* occur *to me*⟩, meaning "I would never
think of it". Befall and betide suggest events outside human control, but are limited in use to formal or poetic contexts. Transpire
and materialize are now used loosely to mean "happen", but transpire essentially means "become known" ⟨*it* transpired *that she
was a secret agent*⟩. Materialize should be used only to mean
"become fact", and its use limited to what can become concrete
reality ⟨*the promised bicycle did not* materialize⟩.
**happen on/upon** *vt* to come upon by chance ⟨*happened on
an old acquaintance last week*⟩ ⟨*happened upon rich deposits
of rare minerals*⟩
**happenchance** /'hapn,chahns/ *n* happenstance
**happening** /'hap(ə)ning/ *n* **1** something that happens; an occurrence **2** an essentially unrepeatable event or series of events
designed to evoke a spontaneous audience reaction to sensory,
emotional, or spiritual stimuli: e g **2a** the creation or presentation of a nonobjective work of art (e g an ACTION PAINTING) **b** a
usu unscripted or improvised often multimedia public performance in which the audience participates *synonyms* see
OCCURRENCE
**happenstance** /'hapn,stahns, -stəns/ *n, chiefly NAm* a circumstance regarded as due to chance ⟨*balloon races have a
fixed beginning, all right, but their finishing line is a matter of*
~ – *The Observer*⟩ [*happen* + circum*stance*]
**happily** /'hapəli/ *adv* **1** by good fortune; luckily ⟨~, *he never
knew*⟩ **2** in a happy manner or state ⟨*lived* ~ *ever after*⟩ **3** in
an adequate or fitting manner; successfully ⟨*white wine goes*
~ *with fish*⟩ **4** *archaic* by chance
**happiness** /'hapinis/ *n* **1** the state of being happy **2** *obs* good
fortune; prosperity
**happy** /'hapi/ *adj* **1** favoured by luck or fortune; fortunate
⟨*their daughter's birth was a* ~ *occasion*⟩ **2** well adapted or
fitting; felicitous ⟨*a* ~ *choice*⟩ **3a** enjoying or expressing
pleasure and contentment **b** glad, pleased **4a** characterized by
a dazed irresponsible state – usu in combination ⟨*a punch*-
happy *boxer*⟩ **b** impulsively or obsessively quick to use some-

thing – usu in combination ⟨*trigger*-happy⟩ **c** enthusiastic to the point of obsession; obsessed – often in combination ⟨*that guy is stripe*-happy – Norman Mailer⟩ **d** having or marked by an atmosphere of comradeship; friendly **5** satisfied as to the fact; confident, sure ⟨*we're now quite ~ that the murder occurred at about 5:30pm*⟩ **6** euph tipsy *usage* see SATISFY *synonyms* see ³FIT, JOYFUL *antonyms* unhappy, disconsolate, sad [ME, fr *hap*]

**,happy-go-'lucky** *adj* blithely unconcerned; carefree

**happy hour** *n* a limited period of the day during which drinks are sold in a bar, pub, etc at reduced prices

**happy hunting ground** *n, informal* a choice or profitable area of activity

**¹Hapsburg** /'hapsbuhg/ *adj* of or supporting a princely German house that reigned in Austria from 1278 to 1918 and in Spain from 1516 to 1700 [*Habsburg*, castle in Aargau, Switzerland]

**²Hapsburg** *n* a member of the Hapsburg family; *esp* a Hapsburg monarch

**hapten** /'hapt(ə)n/ *also* **haptene** /-teen/ *n* a small separable part of an ANTIGEN (foreign substance that activates the body defence mechanisms) that reacts specifically with an antibody formed in response to the presence of the antigen in the body, but that does not itself stimulate the production of antibodies unless it is combined with a particular protein or other large molecule [Ger *hapten*, deriv of Gk *haptein* to fasten, bind]

**haptic** /'haptik/, **haptical** /-kl/ *adj* **1** relating to or based on the sense of touch **2** characterized by an individual preference for the sense of touch ⟨*a ~ person*⟩ [ISV, fr Gk *haptesthai* to touch]

**haptoglobin** /'haptə,glohbin/ *n* a carbohydrate-containing protein occurring in BLOOD SERUM (liquid component of blood) that can combine with haemoglobin and that functions in the removal from the serum of free haemoglobin released by the destruction of RED BLOOD CELLS [Gk *haptein* + E *-o-* + haemo*globin*]

**hara-kiri** /,harə 'kiri/ *n* suicide by ritual disembowelment practised by the Japanese samurai, esp when disgraced or found guilty of a crime carrying the death penalty for commoners [Jap *harakiri*, fr *hara* belly + *kiri* cutting]

**¹harangue** /hə'rang/ *n* **1** a speech addressed to a public assembly **2** a lengthy, ranting, and usu censorious speech or piece of writing [ME *arang*, fr MF *arenge*, fr OIt *aringa*]

**²harangue** *vi* to make a harangue; declaim ~ *vt* to address in a harangue – **haranguer** *n*

**harass** /'harəs; *also* hə'ras* USE *the last pron is disliked by some speakers*/ *vt* **1** to worry and impede by repeated raids ⟨*~ed the enemy*⟩ **2** to annoy or worry persistently **3** *archaic* to exhaust, fatigue [Fr *harasser*, fr MF, fr *harer* to set a dog on, fr OF *hare*, interj used to incite dogs, of Gmc origin; akin to OHG *hier* here – more at HERE] – **harasser** *n*, **harassment** *n*

**harbinger** /'hahbinjə/ *n* **1a** one who pioneers or initiates a major change; a precursor **b** something that gives warning of or foreshadows what is to come **2** *archaic* a person sent ahead to find lodgings [ME *herbergere*, fr OF, host, fr *herberge* hostelry, of Gmc origin; akin to OHG *heriberga*] – **harbinger** *vt*

**¹harbour**, *NAm chiefly* **harbor** /'hahbə/ *n* **1** a place of security and comfort; a refuge **2** a part of a body of water providing protection and anchorage for ships; *esp* one having facilities for loading and unloading ships [ME *herberge*; akin to OHG *heriberga* army camp, hostelry; both fr a prehistoric WGmc-NGmc compound whose constituents are akin to OHG *heri* army & to OHG *bergan* to shelter – more at HARRY, BURY]

**²harbour**, *NAm chiefly* **harbor** *vt* **1** to give shelter or refuge to ⟨*~ a fugitive*⟩ **2** to be the home or habitat of; contain ⟨*these cracks can ~ dangerous bacteria*⟩ **3** to secretly and resolutely hold on to (e g thoughts or feelings of resentment, suspicions, etc) ⟨*~ed a grudge*⟩ ~ *vi* to take shelter (as if) in a harbour

**harbourage** /'hahbərij/ *n* shelter, harbour

**harbourmaster** /'hahbə,mahstə/ *n* the officer who regulates the use of a harbour

**harbour seal** *n* a small seal (*Phoca vitulina*) that is found along N Atlantic coasts and often makes its way up rivers

**¹hard** /hahd/ *adj* **1** not easily penetrated or yielding to pressure; firm **2a** *of alcoholic drink* having a high percentage of alcohol **b** *of water* containing SALTS (e g bicarbonates or sulphates) of calcium, magnesium, etc that inhibit lathering with soap **3a** of or being radiation of relatively high penetrating power ⟨*~ X rays*⟩ **b** having or producing relatively great photographic contrast ⟨*a ~ negative*⟩ **4a** being metal as distinct from

paper ⟨*~ money*⟩ **b** *of currency* stable in value; *also* soundly backed and readily convertible into foreign currencies without large discounts **c** high and firm ⟨*~ prices*⟩ **d** available to borrowers in limited supply and at high interest rates ⟨*a ~ money policy*⟩ **5** firmly and closely twisted ⟨*~ yarns*⟩ **6a** physically fit or resistant to stress ⟨*the ~ men ran a hundred miles a week*⟩ **b** free of weakness or defects ⟨*a woman of ~ unbending will*⟩ **7a(1)** firm, definite ⟨*reached a ~ agreement*⟩ **a(2)** not speculative or conjectural; factual ⟨*~ evidence*⟩ **b** close, searching ⟨*gave a ~ look*⟩ **8a(1)** difficult to bear or endure ⟨*~ luck*⟩ ⟨*~ times*⟩ **a(2)** oppressive, inequitable ⟨*indirect taxes are ~ on the poor*⟩ **b(1)** lacking consideration, compassion, or gentleness; callous ⟨*a ~ greedy landlord*⟩ ⟨*a ~ heart*⟩ **b(2)** tough ⟨*he's a ~ man*⟩ **c(1)** harsh, severe ⟨*said some ~ things*⟩ **c(2)** resentful ⟨*~ feelings*⟩ **d** inclement ⟨*~ winter*⟩ **e(1)** forceful, violent ⟨*~ blows*⟩ **e(2)** demanding energy or stamina ⟨*~ work*⟩ **e(3)** using or performing with great energy or effort ⟨*a ~ worker*⟩ **9a** sharply defined; stark ⟨*a ~ outline*⟩ **b** lacking in delicacy or resonance ⟨*~ singing tones*⟩ **c(1)** *of* /c/ *and* /g/ pronounced /k/ and /g/ respectively **c(2)** being a consonant sound, esp in Russian, that lacks PALATALIZATION **10a(1)** difficult to accomplish or resolve; troublesome ⟨*~ problems*⟩ **a(2)** difficult to understand or explain ⟨*a ~ word*⟩ **b** having difficulty in doing something ⟨*~ of hearing*⟩ **c** difficult to magnetize or demagnetize **11a** *of pornography* graphic; HARD-CORE **2 b** *of a drug* addictive and gravely detrimental to health ⟨*such ~ drugs as heroin*⟩ **12** *of a chemical* (*e g a pesticide or a detergent*) PERSISTENT **2b** [ME, fr OE *heard*; akin to OHG *hart* hard, Gk *kratos* strength] – **hard put** barely able; faced with difficulty ⟨*was hard put to find an explanation*⟩ – **hard up** *informal* **1** short of money **2** poorly provided – + *for* ⟨*I'm hard up for summer clothes*⟩ – see also **hard** LUCK

*synonyms* Hard, difficult, and arduous describe tasks requiring effort by the mind or body. **Hard** is a general term, contrasted with "easy". **Difficult** implies obstacles or problems which it requires intelligence, skill, patience, or courage to overcome. **Arduous** stresses the need for exertion or perseverance ⟨*it had been an arduous climb, but not a difficult one. The other peaks were hard to see, because of the clouds*⟩. See POOR *antonym* easy

**²hard** *adv* **1a** with great or maximum effort or energy; strenuously ⟨*were ~ at work*⟩ **b** in a violent manner; fiercely **c** to the full extent – used in nautical directions ⟨*steer ~ aport*⟩ **d** in a searching or concentrated manner ⟨*stared ~ at him*⟩ **2a** in such a manner as to cause hardship, difficulty, or pain; severely **b** with rancour, bitterness, or grief ⟨*took his defeat ~*⟩ **3** in a firm manner; tightly **4** to the point of hardness ⟨*the water froze ~*⟩ **5** close in time or space ⟨*the house stood ~ by the river*⟩ – **die hard** to disappear or cease to exist only after a long time or a prolonged struggle ⟨*old beliefs die hard*⟩ – **hard hit** severely affected

*usage* Hard and hardly can both mean "with difficulty", but it is safer to confine hardly to the meaning "scarcely", since ⟨*they were hardly hit by the recession*⟩ has two meanings.

**³hard** *n, chiefly Br nautical* a firm usu artificial foreshore or landing place

**,hard-and-'fast** *adj* not to be modified or evaded; firm, strict ⟨*a ~ rule*⟩

**hardback** /'hahd,bak/ *n* a book bound in stiff hard durable covers – compare PAPERBACK – **hardback** *adj*

**,hard-'baked** *adj, chiefly Br* hard-boiled

**,hard-'bitten** *adj* seasoned or steeled by difficult experience; tough

**hardboard** /'hahd,bawd/ *n* (a) composition board made by compressing shredded wood chips, often with a cement at high temperatures

**,hard-'boil** *vt* to boil (an egg) in the shell until both white and yolk have solidified [back-formation fr *hard-boiled*]

**,hard-'boiled** *adj* **1** devoid of sentimentality; tough ⟨*a ~ sergeant major*⟩ **2** hardheaded, practical, shrewd ⟨*a fundamentally ~ permanently businesslike people – TLS*⟩

**hardboot** /'hahd,booht/ *n, NAm derog slang* a Kentucky horseman

**hard case** *n, informal* a tough or hardened person

**hard cash** *n* money in the form of coins or bank notes as opposed to cheques or credit

**hard cheese** *n, chiefly Br informal* HARD LUCK – often used as an interjection expressing mild sympathy

**hard coal** *n* ANTHRACITE

**hard copy** *n* computer output in a readable form (e g printed on paper)

**hardcore** /'hahd,kaw/ *n, Br* compacted rubble or clinker used esp as a foundation for roads, paving, or floors for buildings

**'hard-,core** *adj* **1** of or constituting a hard core ⟨~ *Conservative supporters*⟩ **2** *of pornography* extremely explicit; *specif* showing real rather than simulated sexual acts

**hard core** *n taking sing or pl vb* the unyielding or uncompromising members that form the nucleus of a group

**hard done by** *adj* unfairly treated

**,hard-'edge** *adj* of or being a tendency in abstract painting to use sharply defined geometric forms and pure colours – **hard-edger** *n*

**harden** /'hahdn/ *vt* **1** to make hard or harder **2** to confirm in disposition, feelings, or action; *esp* to make callous ⟨~ed *his heart*⟩ **3a** to toughen, inure ⟨~ *troops*⟩ **b** to make (eg plants) accustomed to cold or other unfavourable environmental conditions – often + *off* **4** to protect (airfields, missile launching pads, etc) from possible danger of an atomic explosion with concrete or earth or by situating underground ~ *vi* **1** to become hard or harder **2a** to become confirmed or strengthened ⟨*opposition began to* ~⟩ **b** to assume an appearance of harshness or severity ⟨*her face* ~ed *at the word*⟩ **3** to become higher or less subject to fluctuations downwards ⟨*prices* ~ed *quickly*⟩

**hardener** /'hahdn-ə/ *n* one who or that which hardens; *esp* a substance added (eg to a paint or varnish) to promote hardening

**hardening** /'hahdn·ing, 'hahdning/ *n* **1** something that hardens **2** SCLEROSIS ⟨~ *of the arteries*⟩

**hardfisted** /,hahd'fistid/ *adj* stingy, closefisted

**hardhanded** /,hahd'handid/ *adj* **1** having hands that have become hardened by hard physical work **2** strict, oppressive – **hardhandedness** *n*

**hard hat** *n* **1** a protective hat made of rigid material (eg metal or fibreglass) and worn esp by construction workers **2** *chiefly NAm* a construction worker **3** *chiefly NAm* a reactionary

**hardhead** /'hahd,hed/ *n* **1** a hardheaded person **2** a stupid person; a blockhead

**hardheaded** /,hahd'hedid/ *adj* **1** stubborn **2** sober, realistic ⟨~ *common sense*⟩ – **hardheadedly** *adv*, **hardheadedness** *n*

**hardheads** /'hahd,hedz/ *n taking sing vb, pl* **hardheads** any of several KNAPWEEDS (thistlelike plants)

**hardhearted** /,hahd'hahtid/ *adj* lacking in sympathetic understanding; unfeeling, pitiless – **hardheartedly** *adv*, **hardheartedness** *n*

**'hard-,hitting** *adj* vigorous, effective ⟨*a* ~ *series of articles*⟩

**hardihood** /'hahdihood/ *n* **1** resolute courage and fortitude **2** boldness marked by firm determination and often disdainful insolence ⟨*no historian will have the* ~ *to maintain that he commands this . . . view* – A J Toynbee⟩

**hardiment** /'hahdimənt/ *n* **1** *archaic* hardihood **2** *obs* a bold deed [ME, fr MF, fr OF, fr *hardi* bold, hardy]

**hard labour** *n* compulsory labour for imprisoned criminals as a part of prison discipline

**,hard-'line** *adj* advocating or involving a persistently firm course of action; unyielding ⟨*a* ~ *policy on inflation*⟩ – **hard-liner** *n*

**hard lines** *n pl, chiefly Br informal* hard luck – often used as an interjection expressing mild sympathy

**hard luck** *n, chiefly Br* bad luck – often used as an interjection expressing mild sympathy

**hardly** /'hahdli/ *adv* **1** in a severe manner; harshly **2** with difficulty; painfully ⟨*I could* ~ *speak for tears*⟩ **3** only just; barely ⟨*I* ~ *knew her*⟩ **4** certainly not ⟨*that news is* ~ *surprising*⟩ *usage* **1** Writers on usage advise that **hardly**, **barely**, and **scarcely** should be used with **when** or **before**, not with **than** or **till** ⟨*we had* **hardly** *arrived* **when** (not **than**) *she started scolding us*⟩ ⟨**scarcely** *was I in bed* **when** *the telephone rang*⟩. **2** Since they mean "almost not", **hardly**, **barely**, and **scarcely** should not be used with another negative ⟨⚠ *I can't* **hardly** *tell*⟩ ⟨⚠ *Nobody* **hardly** *goes there any more*⟩. See ²HARD

**hardly ever** *adv* almost never; very seldom ⟨*we* ~ *see them now*⟩

**hardmouthed** /,hahd'mowdhd/ *adj* **1** *of a horse, pony, etc* not responding satisfactorily to pressure applied to the mouth by a bit attached to a bridle **2** obstinate, stubborn ⟨~ *women who laid down the law* – John Galsworthy⟩

**hardness** /'hahdnis/ *n* **1** the quality or state of being hard **2** the resistance of a substance to being scratched, cut, or indented: eg **2a** BRINELL HARDNESS (resistance of a metal to indentation) **b** the resistance of a mineral to abrasion as determined by whether a particular mineral will scratch or be itself scratched by another – compare MOHS' SCALE

**'hard-,nosed** *adj* **1** hard-bitten, stubborn ⟨~ *student militancy* – ISIS⟩ **2** shrewd; HARDHEADED 2 ⟨~ *budgeting*⟩

**,hard-of-'hearing** *adj* partially deaf

**'hard-,on** *n, pl* **hard-ons** *vulgar* an erection of the penis

**hard pad** *n* a serious and frequently fatal virus disease of dogs that is related to distemper [fr the hardening of skin on paws & nose which the disease causes]

**hard palate** *n* the bony front part of the palate forming the roof of the mouth

**hardpan** /'hahd,pan/ *n* a hard compacted often clayey soil layer that is impervious to drainage and resistant to penetration by roots

**hard paste, hard-paste porcelain** *n* true porcelain made from a mixture of KAOLIN (a clay), quartz, and FELDSPAR fired at a high temperature – compare SOFT PASTE

**hardpoint** /'hahd,poynt/ *n* a specially strengthened point, usu on an aircraft wing, to which stores (eg armaments or fuel tanks) may be attached

**hard rock** *n* basic rock music played in its original style

**hard roe** *n* ROE 1a (eggs of a fish)

**hard rubber** *n* EBONITE (hard black rubber)

**hard sauce** *n* a creamed mixture of butter and sugar usu flavoured with brandy or rum and served esp with hot rich puddings (eg Christmas pudding)

**hardscrabble** /'hahd,skrabl/ *adj, NAm* yielding or gaining a meagre living by strenuous labour ⟨~ *farms*⟩

**hard sell** *n* aggressive high-pressure salesmanship – compare SOFT SELL

**,hard-'set** *adj* rigid, fixed

**,hard-'shell** *adj* uncompromising, confirmed ⟨*a* ~ *conservative*⟩

**hard-shell crab, hard-shelled crab** *n* a crab that has not recently shed its shell which therefore is extra hard

**hardship** /'hahdship/ *n* **1** (an instance of) suffering or privation **2** something that causes or entails suffering or privation

**hard shoulder** *n* either of two paved strips of land along a road, esp a motorway, on which stopping is allowed only in an emergency

**hard sign** *n* a symbol ъ in the Russian alphabet written after a consonant to indicate that the consonant sound lacks PALATALIZATION

**hardstanding** /'hahd,standing/, **hardstand** /'hahd,stand/ *n* a hard-surfaced area on which vehicles (eg cars or aeroplanes) may park

**hardtack** /'hahd,tak/ *n* SHIP'S BISCUIT (saltless hard biscuit)

**hardtop** /'hahd,top/ *n* a car with a rigid top of plastic or metal but styled to look like a convertible

**hardware** /'hahdweə/ *n* **1** items (eg fittings, cutlery, tools, utensils, or parts of machines) made of metal and sold by an ironmonger **2** major items of military or police equipment **3** the physical elements of an apparatus or system (eg a weapons system); *esp* the physical components (eg the electronic and electrical devices) of a computer as contrasted with the programs (SOFTWARE) that control its operation **4** devices (eg tape recorders, record players, or closed-circuit television) used as instructional equipment ⟨*educational* ~⟩

**hardwearing** /,hahd'weəring/ *adj* durable

**hard wheat** *n* a wheat producing hard grains that contain a high proportion of GLUTEN (protein substance) and that yield a flour suitable for making bread and pasta

**hard-wired** *adj, computers* being or controlled by an electronic circuit whose functions and operations are determined by its physical construction rather than by programming – **hard-wiring** *n*

**¹hardwood** /'hahd,wood/ *n* the wood of a broad-leaved tree (eg oak, ash, and beech) as distinguished from that of a coniferous tree (eg pine); *also* a tree that yields hardwood

**²hardwood** *adj* **1** having or made of hardwood ⟨~ *floors*⟩ **2** consisting of mature woody tissue ⟨~ *cuttings*⟩

**hardworking** /,hahd'wuhking/ *adj* industrious

**¹hardy** /'hahdi/ *adj* **1** bold, audacious **2a** made accustomed to fatigue or hardships; robust **b** capable of withstanding adverse conditions; *esp* capable of living outdoors over winter without artificial protection ⟨~ *plants*⟩ ⟨~ *cattle*⟩ [ME *hardi*, fr OF, fr (assumed) OF *hardir* to make hard, of Gmc origin; akin to OE *heard* hard] – **hardiness** *n*

**²hardy** *n* a wedge-tipped bar of hard iron that can be mounted on an anvil and is used in cutting and shaping metal [prob fr ¹hard + ⁴-y]

**Hardy-Weinberg law, Hardy-Weinberg principle** /ˌhahdi
'wienbuhg/ *n* a fundamental law in genetics: GENE FREQUENCIES
in a population remain constant from generation to generation
if mating is random and if mutation, selection, immigration,
and emigration do not occur [G H *Hardy* †1947 E mathematician & W *Weinberg*, 20th-c Ger scientist]
**¹hare** /heə/ *n, pl* **hares**, *esp collectively* **hare** **1** any of various
swift timid long-eared mammals (order Lagomorpha, esp genus
*Lepus*) having a divided upper lip, long hind legs, and young
that are open-eyed and furred at birth **2** a figure of a hare moved
mechanically along a dog track for the dogs to chase (e g in
greyhound racing) [ME, fr OE *hara;* akin to OHG *haso* hare, L
*canus* hoary, grey]
**²hare** *vi, informal* to run fast ⟨~d *down to the shops before
they closed*⟩
**hare and hounds** *n* PAPER CHASE
**harebell** /'heə‚bel/ *n* a slender plant (*Campanula rotundifolia* of
the family Campanulaceae, the harebell family) with blue bell-
shaped flowers that grows esp on heaths and in open woodlands
**harebrained** /'heə‚braynd/ *adj, informal* flighty, foolish
**Hare Krishna** /ˌhuri 'krishnə/ *n* a missionary Hindu cult
marked esp by the public chanting of a psalm taken from the
sacred writings of Hinduism and beginning "Hare Krishna"
[Skt *Hare Kṛṣṇa* (voc) Lord Krishna, fr *Hari* Vishnu, Lord +
*Kṛṣṇa* Krishna]
**harelip** /ˌheə'lip/ *n* a split in the upper lip, like that of a hare,
existing from birth and occurring as a nonhereditary defect –
**harelipped** *adj*
**harem** /'heərəm, hah'reem/ *n* **1a** a usu secluded (part of a) house
allotted to women in a Muslim household **b** *taking sing or pl
vb* the wives, concubines, female relatives, and female servants
occupying a harem **2** a group of females associated with one
male – used with reference to animals that have more than one
mate at a time [Ar *ḥarīm*, lit., something forbidden and *ḥaram*,
lit., sanctuary]
**haricot** /'harikoh/, **haricot bean** *n* FRENCH BEAN; *also* the ripe
seed or the unripe pod of any of several related beans (genus
*Phaseolus*) eaten as a vegetable [Fr, prob fr *haricot* stew]
**harijan** /ˌhahri'jahn, 'harijən/ *n, often cap* a Hindu belonging
to the group of outcaste people in India that were formerly
called UNTOUCHABLES [Skt *harijana* one belonging to the god
Vishnu, fr *Hari* Vishnu + *jana* person]
**hari-kari** /ˌhari 'kahri/ *n* HARA-KIRI (suicide by disembowelment
practised by the Japanese samurai)
**hark** /hahk/ *vi* to listen closely [ME *herken;* akin to OHG
*hōrechen* to listen]
**hark back** *vi* to return *to* an earlier topic or circumstance
**harken** /'hahkən/ *vb* to hearken
**harlequin** /'hahlikwin/ *n* **1a** *cap* a standard character in
comedy and pantomime with a shaved head, masked face,
coloured patterned tights, and a wooden sword **b** a clown,
buffoon **2a** a variegated pattern (e g of a textile) **b** a combination of colours in patches on a solid ground (e g in the coats of
some dogs) [It *arlecchino*, fr MF *Helquin*, a demon]
**harlequinade** /ˌhahlikwi'nayd/ *n* a part of a play or pantomime in which Harlequin has a leading role
**harlequin duck** *n* a small N American and Icelandic diving
sea duck (*Histrionicus histrionicus*), the male of which is bluish
with black, white, and chestnut markings
**Harley Street** /'hahli/ *adj* of or being an eminent medical
doctor [*Harley Street* in London, address of many eminent
physicians & surgeons]
**harlot** /'hahlət/ *n, archaic* a female prostitute [ME, fr OF *herlot*
rogue]
**harlotry** /'hahlətri/ *n, archaic* **1** prostitution **2** an unprincipled
or immoral woman ⟨*he sups tonight with a ~* – Shak⟩
**¹harm** /hahm/ *n* **1** physical or mental damage; injury **2**
mischief, wrong [ME, fr OE *hearm;* akin to OHG *harm*
injury, OSlav *sramŭ* shame] – **out of harm's way** safe from
danger
**²harm** *vt* to cause harm to *synonyms* see INJURE
**harmattan** /hah'mat(ə)n/ *n* a dry dust-laden wind that blows
off the desert onto the Atlantic coast of Africa from December
to February *synonyms* see ¹WIND [Twi *haramata*]
**harmful** /'hahmf(ə)l/ *adj* of a kind likely to be damaging; injurious – **harmfully** *adv*, **harmfulness** *n*
**harmless** /'hahmlis/ *adj* **1** free from harm, liability, or loss **2**
lacking capacity or intent to injure – **harmlessly** *adv*, **harm-
lessness** *n*

**¹harmonic** /hah'monik/ *also* **harmonical** /-kl/ *adj* **1** of musical
harmony, a harmonic, or harmonics **2** pleasing to the ear;
harmonious **3** *maths* of or being a FUNCTION that satisfies
LAPLACE'S EQUATION **4** of an integrated nature; congruous –
**harmonically** *adv*, **harmonicalness** *n*
**²harmonic** *n* **1a** any of several usu higher frequencies that
sound together with the FUNDAMENTAL (strongest and most
audible frequency) to give a musical note its characteristic tone
and determine its quality; an overtone **b** a flutelike sound
produced on a stringed instrument by lightly touching a
vibrating string at a specific point **2** *physics* any of several
component frequencies possessed by a series of sound waves,
ELECTROMAGNETIC WAVES, etc that is an integral multiple of the
FUNDAMENTAL, the lowest frequency (e g if the frequency
of the fundamental is 200 hertz, the frequencies of the harmonics are 400, 600, 800 hertz, etc)
**harmonica** /hah'monikə/ *n* a small rectangular wind instrument with reeds of graduated lengths that are recessed in air
slots where they are free to move and are made to vibrate by
breathing out and in [It *armonica*, fem of *armonico* harmoni-
ous]
**harmonic analysis** *n, maths* the expression of a PERIODIC
FUNCTION (function whose value repeats itself at regular
intervals) as a sum of SINES and COSINES and specif by means of
a FOURIER SERIES
**harmonic mean** *n* the reciprocal of the ARITHMETIC MEAN of
the reciprocals of a finite set of numbers ⟨*the ~ of 2, 4, 6, and
8 is*

$$\frac{4}{\frac{1}{2} + \frac{1}{4} + \frac{1}{6} + \frac{1}{8}} = \frac{9}{25}⟩$$

**harmonic progression** *n* a sequence whose terms are the
reciprocals of an ARITHMETIC PROGRESSION ⟨*the sequence 1,*
$\frac{1}{3}, \frac{1}{5}, \frac{1}{7} \ldots$ *is a ~*⟩
**harmonics** /hah'moniks/ *n taking sing vb* the study of the
physical characteristics of musical sounds
**harmonic series** *n* **1** *maths* a series constructed by adding
together terms in a HARMONIC PROGRESSION; *esp the* harmonic
series $1 + \frac{1}{2} + \frac{1}{3} + \frac{1}{4} + \ldots$ **2** *music* a set of frequencies
consisting of a FUNDAMENTAL (strongest and most audible fre-
quency) and all the harmonics whose frequency ratio to the
fundamental can be expressed in whole numbers
**harmonious** /hah'mohnyəs, -ni·əs/ *adj* **1** musically concordant
**2** having the parts agreeably related; congruous ⟨*the flowers
blended into a ~ whole*⟩ **3** marked by agreement in sentiment
or action – **harmoniously** *adv*, **harmoniousness** *n*
**harmonist** /'hahmənist/ *n* one who harmonizes or is skilled in
musical harmony; *esp* one who composes or performs music –
**harmonistic** *adj*, **harmonistically** *adv*
**harmonium** /hah'mohni·əm, -nyəm/ *n* a REED ORGAN in which
pedals operate a bellows that forces air through free reeds [Fr,
fr MF *harmonie, armonie*]
**harmon-ize, -ise** /'hahməniez/ *vi* **1** to play or sing in harmony
⟨*their voices ~ well*⟩ **2** to be in harmony ~ *vt* **1** to bring into
agreement or accord **2** to provide or accompany (a tune,
melody, etc) with harmony *synonyms* see AGREE *antonyms*
clash, conflict – **harmonizer** *n*, **harmonization** *n*
**harmony** /'hahməni/ *n* **1a** the combination of three or more
musical notes sounded simultaneously; a chord **b** the structure
of music with respect to the composition and progression of
chords **c** the study of the structure, relation, and progression
of chords **2a** pleasing or congruent arrangement of parts ⟨*a
painting exhibiting ~ of colour and line*⟩ **b** agreement, accord
⟨*lives in ~ with her neighbours*⟩ **3** a systematic arrangement of
parallel literary passages (e g of the Gospels) so as to show
agreement or harmony **4** *archaic* tuneful sound; melody [ME
*armony*, fr MF *armonie*, fr L *harmonia*, fr Gk, joint, harmony,
fr *harmos* joint – more at ARM]
**harmotome** /'hahmə‚tohm/ *n* a mineral of the ZEOLITE group
of minerals that consists of a SILICATE of aluminium, barium,
and potassium chemically combined with molecules of water
[Fr, fr Gk *harmos* + *tomē* section, fr *temnein* to cut – more at
TOME]
**¹harness** /'hahnis/ *n* **1a** the gear of a draught animal other
than a yoke **b** equipment; *esp* military equipment (e g armour)
for a horse or man **2** something that resembles a harness (e g in
holding or fastening something) ⟨*a safety ~*⟩ **3** a part of a
weaving loom which holds and controls one of the sets of
parallel wires that guide the warp threads [ME *herneis* baggage,
gear, fr OF, of Gmc origin; akin to OHG *hari, heri* army & to

ON *nest* provisions] – **in harness 1** in one's usual work, surroundings, or routine ⟨*back* in harness *after a long holiday*⟩ **2** in close association ⟨*working* in harness *with his colleagues*⟩

²**harness** *vt* **1a** to put a harness on (eg a horse) **b** to attach (eg a wagon) by means of a harness **2** to tie together; yoke **3** to utilize; *esp* to convert (a natural force) into energy

**harness racing** *n* the sport of racing horses, at a trotting pace, harnessed to 2-wheeled vehicles (SULKIES) carrying the driver

**harp** /hahp/ *n* **1** a musical instrument that has many parallel strings of graded length extending down a triangular frame from a long curved top piece and is played by plucking with the fingers **2** something that resembles a harp, esp in shape [ME, fr OE *hearpe;* akin to OHG *harpha* harp, Gk *karphos* dry stalk] – **harpist** *n*

**harp on** *vt, informal* to dwell on or return to (a subject) tediously or monotonously [*harp* (to play on a harp)]

**harpoon** /hah'poohn/ *n* a barbed spear or javelin used esp in hunting large fish or whales [prob fr D *harpoen,* fr OF *harpon* brooch, fr *harper* to grapple] – **harpoon** *vt,* **harpooner** *n*

**harp seal** *n* an arctic seal (*Pagophilus groenlandicus*) that has a black saddle-shaped mark on the back and lives in very large herds

**harpsichord** /'hahpsi,kawd/ *n* a keyboard instrument having a horizontal frame and strings and producing notes by the action of QUILLS (formerly crows' feathers) or leather points plucking the strings [modif of It *arpicordo,* fr *arpa* harp + *corda* string] – **harpsichordist** *n*

**harpy** /'hahpi/ *n* **1** *often cap* a rapacious creature of Greek mythology with the head of a woman and the body of a bird **2** *derog* a predatory person; *esp* a rapacious woman [L *Harpyia,* fr Gk]

**harquebus** /'hahkwibəs/ *n* ARQUEBUS (15th-century gun) – **harquebusier** *n*

**harridan** /'harid(ə)n/ *n* an ill-tempered unpleasant woman; HAG **2** [perh modif of Fr *haridelle* old horse, gaunt woman]

**harried** /'harid/ *adj* beset by worrying problems; harassed

¹**harrier** /'hari-ə/ *n* **1** a hunting dog that resembles a small foxhound and is used esp for hunting hares **2** a runner in a cross-country team [irreg fr ¹*hare*]

²**harrier** *n* any of various slender hawks (genus *Circus*) with long angled wings and long legs, that feed chiefly on small mammals, reptiles, and insects [alter. of earlier *harrower,* fr arch. *harrow* to pillage, plunder, var of *harry*]

**Harris tweed** /'haris/ *trademark* – used for a loosely woven tweed made in the Outer Hebrides

**Harrovian** /hə'rohvi-ən, -vyən/ *n or adj* (a pupil) of Harrow School [NL *Harrovia* Harrow]

¹**harrow** /'haroh/ *n* a cultivating implement set with spikes, flat curved steel teeth that can be adjusted to various angles and depths, or discs and drawn over the ground (eg by a tractor), esp to pulverize and smooth the soil [ME *harwe*]

²**harrow** *vt* **1** to cultivate (ground or land) with a harrow **2** to cause distress to; agonize – **harrower** *n*

**Harrow drive** *n* CHINESE CUT (shot off the inside edge of the bat in cricket) [*Harrow,* public school in NW London]

**harrumph** /hə'rum(p)f/ *vi or n, chiefly NAm* (to make) a guttural sound as if clearing the throat, esp as a sign of disapproval [imit]

**harry** /'hari/ *vt* **1** to make a pillaging or destructive raid on; ravage **2** to torment (as if) by constant attack; harass [ME *harien,* fr OE *hergian;* akin to OHG *heriōn* to lay waste, *heri* army, Gk *koiranos* commander]

**harsh** /hahsh/ *adj* **1** having a coarse uneven surface; rough **2** disagreeable or painful to the senses ⟨*a* ~ *light*⟩ **3** unduly exacting; severe **4** lacking in aesthetic appeal or refinement; crude *synonyms* see ¹ROUGH [ME *harsk,* prob fr Scand origin; akin to Norw *harsk* harsh] – **harshen** *vb,* **harshly** *adv,* **harshness** *n*

**hart** /haht/ *n, chiefly Br* the male of the (red) deer, esp when over five years old; a stag – compare HIND [ME *hert,* fr OE *heort;* akin to L *cervus* hart, Gk *keras* horn – more at HORN]

**hartebeest** /'hahti,beest/ *n,* **hartebeests,** *esp collectively* **hartebeest** any of several large African antelope (genus *Alcelaphus*) with ridged horns that project upwards and outwards [obs Afrik (now *hartbees*), fr D, fr *hart* deer + *beest* beast]

**hartshorn** /'hahts,hawn/ *n* a preparation of AMMONIUM CARBONATE used as smelling salts – not now used technically [fr the earlier use of hart's horns as the chief source of ammonia]

'**hart's-,tongue** *n* a Eurasian fern (*Phyllitis scolopendrium*) with undivided fronds

**harum-scarum** /,heərəm 'skeərəm/ *adj, informal* reckless, irresponsible [perh alter. of *helter-skelter*] – **harum-scarum** *adv*

**haruspex** /hə'ruspeks/ *n, pl* **haruspices** /hə'ruspi,seez/ a diviner in ancient Rome whose predictions of future events were based on an examination of the entrails of sacrificial animals [L, fr *haru-* (akin to Gk *chordē* gut, chord) + *specere* to look at] – **haruspication** *n*

¹**harvest** /'hahvist/ *n* **1** the season for gathering in agricultural crops **2** the act or process of gathering in a crop **3a** a mature crop (eg of grain or fruit); a yield **b** the quantity of grain, fruit, etc gathered in a single season **4** the product or reward of exertion [ME *hervest,* fr OE *hærfest;* akin to L *carpere* to pluck, gather, Gk *karpos* fruit, *keirein* to cut – more at SHEAR]

²**harvest** *vt* **1** to gather in (a crop); reap **2** to gather (a natural product) as if by harvesting ⟨~ *bacteria*⟩ ~ *vi* to gather in a food crop – **harvestable** *adj*

**harvester** /'hahvistə/ *n* **1** one who harvests **2** COMBINE HARVESTER

**Harvest Festival** *n* a festival of thanksgiving for the harvest, celebrated on a Sunday in September or October in British churches

**harvest home** *n* **1** the gathering or the time of harvest **2** a festival at the close of harvest **3** a song formerly sung by the reapers at the close of the harvest

**harvestman** /-mən/ *n* any of an order (Phalangida of the class Arachnida) of INVERTEBRATE animals that superficially resemble the true spiders but have small rounded bodies and very long slender legs [fr its abundance in fields at harvest time]

**harvest mite** *n* a 6-legged mite larva (family Trombiculidae) that sucks the blood of VERTEBRATE animals and causes intense irritation

**harvest moon** *n* the full moon nearest the time (EQUINOX), about September 23, when day and night are of equal length

**harvest mouse** *n* a small European FIELD MOUSE (*Micromys minutus*) that nests esp in cornfields

**Harvest Thanksgiving** *n* Harvest Festival

**has** /s, z, əz, həz; *strong* haz/ *pres 3 sing of* HAVE

'**has-,been** *n, informal* one who or that which has passed the peak of effectiveness, success, or popularity

¹**hash** /hash/ *vt* **1** to chop (eg meat and potatoes) into small pieces **2** *informal* to mix up; muddle [Fr *hacher,* fr OF *hachier,* fr *hache* battle-axe, of Gmc origin; akin to OHG *hāppa* sickle; akin to Gk *koptein* to cut – more at CAPON]

²**hash** *n* **1** chopped food; *specif* a dish consisting chiefly of reheated cooked chopped meat **2** *informal* a restatement of old material, ideas, etc in a new form – **make a hash of** *informal* to make a muddle or mess of

³**hash** *n, informal* hashish

**Hashimite, Hashemite** /'hashimiet/ *n* a member of an Arab family having common ancestry with the Muslim prophet Muhammad and founding dynasties in countries of the E Mediterranean [*Hashim,* great-grandfather of Muhammad]

**hashish** /'hashish, -sheesh/ *n* the resin from the flowering tops of the female hemp plant (*Cannabis sativa*) that is smoked, chewed, etc for its intoxicating effect – compare BHANG, CANNABIS, MARIJUANA [Ar *ḥashīsh* (cf ASSASSIN)]

**hash oil** *n, informal* LIQUID CANNABIS

**Hasid** /'hasid, 'khahsid/ *n, pl* **Hasidim** /'hasidim, khə'seedim/ **1** a member of a Jewish sect of the 2nd century BC opposed to the influence of ancient Greek culture and devoted to the strict observance of Jewish ritual forms **2** a member of a Jewish mystical sect founded in Poland about 1750 in opposition to formalistic ritualism [Heb *ḥāsīdh* pious] – **Hasidic** *adj*

**Hasidism** /'hasidiz(ə)m, 'khah-/ *n* **1** the practices and beliefs of the Hasidim **2** the Hasidic movement

**haslet** /'hazlit/ *n* the edible entrails (eg the liver and lungs) of an animal, esp a pig; *also* these cooked and compressed into a meat loaf – compare GIBLETS [ME *hastelet,* fr MF, piece of meat roasted on a spit]

**hasn't** /'haznt/ has not

**hasp** /hahsp/ *n* any of several devices for fastening; *esp* a hinged metal strap that fits over a staple and is secured by a pin or padlock to fasten a door or lid [ME, fr OE *hæsp;* akin to MHG *haspe* hasp] – **hasp** *vt*

¹**hassle** /'hasl/ *n, informal* **1** a heated often protracted argument; a wrangle **2** a violent skirmish; a fight **3** a difficult or trying situation; a struggle ⟨*it's such a* ~ *getting across London*⟩ [perh fr ²*haggle* + ²*tussle*]

²**hassle** *vb, informal vi* to argue, fight ⟨~*d with the referee*⟩ ~ *vt* to subject to usu persistent harassment

**hassock** /'hasək/ *n* **1** a tussock **2a** a cushion for kneeling on, esp in church **b** a padded cushion that serves as a seat or leg rest [ME, sedge, fr OE *hassuc*]

**hast** /hast/ *archaic pres 2 sing of* HAVE

**hastate** /'hastayt/ *adj* **1** *of a leaf* triangular with two lobes spreading outwards at the base of the stalk **2** shaped like (the head of) a spear ⟨*a ~ spot of a bird*⟩ [NL *hastatus*, fr L *hasta* spear – more at YARD] – **hastately** *adv*

¹**haste** /hayst/ *n* **1** rapidity of motion; swiftness **2** rash or headlong action; precipitateness ⟨*marry in ~, repent at leisure*⟩ **3** undue eagerness to act; urgency [ME, fr OF, of Gmc origin; akin to OE *hǣst* violence] – **make haste** to act quickly; hasten

²**haste** *vt, archaic* to urge on; hasten ⟨*with our fair entreaties ~ them on* – Shak⟩ ~ *vi, formal* to move or act swiftly

**hasten** /'hays(ə)n/ *vt* **1** to cause to hurry ⟨*~ed her to the door* – A J Cronin⟩ **2** to accelerate ⟨*~ the completion of a project*⟩ ~ *vi* to move or act quickly; hurry – **hastener** *n*

**hastily** /'haystili/ *adv* in haste; hurriedly

**hasty** /'haysti/ *adj* **1a** done or made in a hurry **b** fast and often superficial ⟨*made a ~ examination of the wound*⟩ **2** eager or impatient to do something quickly **3** precipitate, rash **4** prone to or showing anger; irritable **5** *archaic* rapid in action or movement; speedy *synonyms* see ¹FAST *antonyms* leisurely, unhurried – **hastiness** *n*

**hat** /hat/ *n* **1** a covering for the head, usu having a shaped crown and brim **2a** a distinctive head covering worn as a symbol of office **b** an office, position, role ⟨*wearing his ministerial ~*⟩ [ME, fr OE *hæt;* akin to OHG *huot* head covering – more at HOOD] – **hatless** *adj,* **hatter** *n* – **eat one's hat** – used to express one's disbelief that a usu specified event will occur ⟨*I'll eat my hat if he ever passes his driving test*⟩ – **talk through one's hat** to voice irrational or erroneous ideas, esp in an attempt to appear knowledgeable –see also **at the** DROP **of a hat**

**hatband** /'hat,band/ *n* a band of ribbon, leather, etc attached round the crown of a hat just above the brim

¹**hatch** /hach/ *n* **1** a small door or opening (eg in a wall or aircraft) **2a** (the covering for) an opening in the deck of a ship or in the floor or roof of a building **b** a hatchway **3** a floodgate in a dam, dyke, etc [ME *hache,* fr OE *hæc;* akin to MD *hecke* trapdoor]

²**hatch** *vi* **1** to incubate eggs; brood; *also* to produce young from an egg by incubation **2** to emerge from an egg or pupa ⟨*watched the chickens ~*⟩ **3** to give forth young ⟨*the egg ~ed*⟩ ~ *vt* **1a** to produce (young) from an egg by applying natural or artificial heat **b** to cause young to emerge from (an egg) by applying heat; INCUBATE 1 **2** to devise, esp secretly; originate [ME *hacchen;* akin to MHG *hecken* to mate] – **hatchable** *adj,* **hatcher** *n*

³**hatch** *n* **1** an act or instance of hatching **2** a brood of hatched young

⁴**hatch** *vt* **1** to inlay with narrow bands of distinguishable material ⟨*a silver handle ~ed with gold*⟩ **2** to mark (eg a drawing, map, or engraving) with fine closely spaced parallel lines [ME *hachen,* fr MF *hacher* to inlay, chop up – more at HASH]

**hatchback** /'hach,bak/ *n* **1** an upward-opening hatch at the back of a car, giving entry to the luggage and passenger compartment **2** a usu small car with a hatchback

**hatchery** /'hachəri/ *n* a place for hatching esp fish eggs

**hatchet** /'hachit/ *n* a light short-handled axe; *esp* one with a head suitable for alternative use as a hammer [ME *hachet,* fr MF *hachette,* dim. of *hache* battle-axe – more at HASH] – **bury the hatchet** to settle a disagreement; become reconciled [fr the N American Indian custom of burying tomahawks to signify the end of hostilities]]

**hatchet face** *n* a thin sharp face – **hatchet-faced** *adj*

**hatchet job** *n, informal* a vicious or damaging attack delivered verbally or in writing

**hatchet man** *n, slang* one hired for murder, coercion, or malicious attack

**hatching** /'haching/ *n* the engraving or drawing of fine closely spaced parallel lines, chiefly to give an effect of shading; *also* the pattern so created

**hatchling** /'hachling/ *n* a recently hatched animal

**hatchment** /'hachmənt/ *n* a square panel set cornerwise bearing the COAT OF ARMS of a deceased person for display outside a house or in a church [perh alter. of *achievement*]

**hatchway** /'hachway/ *n* a passage giving access, usu by a ladder or stairs, to an enclosed space (eg a lower deck in a ship); *also* HATCH 2a

¹**hate** /hayt/ *n* **1a** intense hostility and aversion **b** extreme dislike or antipathy; loathing ⟨*had a great ~ of hard work*⟩ **2** *informal* an object of hatred ⟨*one of my pet ~s*⟩ [ME, fr OE *hete;* akin to OHG *haz* hate, Gk *kēdos* grief]

*synonyms* Hate and hatred are not always interchangeable. Hate is preferred for the abstract emotion (as opposed to "love"), and for its use without particular reference to a person or thing ⟨hate *is a painful emotion*⟩. Hatred is preferred for personally experienced emotion. It usually implies an admixture of other feelings, according to context: resentment, jealousy, aversion, vindictiveness, etc ⟨*a long-standing* hatred *of the wealthy*⟩. It is also often used to show the effect on one who is hated ⟨*battered by* hatred*, seared by ridicule* – Flecker⟩. Compare ENMITY *antonym* love

²**hate** *vt* **1** to feel extreme enmity towards ⟨*~s his country's enemies*⟩ **2** to have a strong aversion to; find very distasteful ⟨*~ hypocrisy*⟩ ⟨*~s cabbage*⟩ ~ *vi* to express or feel hate – see also **hate somebody's** GUTS – **hater** *n*

*synonyms* Hate, detest, abominate, abhor, loathe: hate is the general term, and suggests extreme personal dislike, coupled with enmity or malice. It does not preclude grudging respect or awe ⟨*whom we fear more than love, we are not far from* hating – Richardson⟩. Detest, less strong in that it does not suggest active hostility, implies a violent antipathy ⟨detests *the idea of eating meat*⟩ ⟨*I* detest *that boy*⟩. Abhor, abominate, and loathe all suggest repugnance and disgust. Abominate suggests moral grounds for this ⟨*she* abominates *the system of apartheid*⟩. Abhor implies a shrinking or flinching from ⟨abhors *cruelty to animals*⟩. Loathe suggests utter disgust and untempered revulsion. *antonym* love

**hateful** /-f(ə)l/ *adj* **1** full of hate; malicious **2** deserving or arousing hate – **hatefully** *adv,* **hatefulness** *n*

**hath** /hath/ *archaic pres 3 sing of* HAVE

**hatha yoga** /'hatə, 'hathə, 'hahthə/ *n* a yoga consisting of physical and breathing exercises for the body in order to keep it healthy and thus leave the mind free from its demands [Skt *haṭha* force, persistence + *yoga* – more at YOGA]

**hat in hand** *adv* CAP IN HAND

**hatpin** /'hat,pin/ *n* a long usu ornamented pin used to keep a hat in place

**hatred** /'haytrid/ *n* hate ⟨*a ~ of authority*⟩ *synonyms* see ¹HATE [ME, fr *hate* + OE *rǣden* condition – more at KINDRED]

**hat trick** *n* three successes by one person or side in a usu sporting activity; *specif* the dismissing of three batsmen with three consecutive balls by a bowler in cricket [prob fr a former practice of rewarding the feat with the gift of a hat]

**hauberk** /'haw,buhk/ *n* a tunic of chain mail worn as defensive armour, esp from the 12th to the 14th century [ME, fr OF *hauberc,* of Gmc origin; akin to OE *healsbeorg* neck armour]

**haugh** /haw, hawkh, hah, hahkh/ *n* a low-lying meadow by the side of a river [ME (Sc) *holch,* fr OE *heolh* corner of land; akin to OE *holh* hole]

**haughty** /'hawti/ *adj* disdainfully proud; arrogant *synonyms* see PROUD [obs *haught,* fr ME *haute,* fr MF *haut,* lit., high, fr L *altus* – more at OLD] – **haughtily** *adv,* **haughtiness** *n*

**Hauhau** /'how,how/ *n* a religion practised by some Maoris in the mid 19th century that included some elements of Christianity [Maori]

¹**haul** /hawl/ *vt* **1** to change the course of (a ship), esp so as to sail more nearly against the main force of the wind **2a** to pull with effort; drag ⟨*~ed the wagon up the hill*⟩ **b** to transport in a vehicle, esp in a lorry **c** *informal* to take or force to go unwillingly ⟨*was continually ~ed off to parties by his friend*⟩ ~ *vi* **1** to pull, drag ⟨*~ed on the rope*⟩ **2** *of the wind* to change direction; shift – see also **haul oneself up by one's** BOOTSTRAPS, **haul over the** COALS *synonyms* see ¹PULL [ME *halen* to pull, fr OF *haler,* of Gmc origin; akin to MD *halen* to pull; akin to OE *geholian* to obtain]

**haul up** *vt, informal* to bring before an authority for judgment ⟨*hauled up before the magistrate for a traffic offence*⟩

²**haul** *n* **1** the act or process of hauling **2a** an amount gathered or acquired; a take ⟨*the burglar's ~*⟩ **b** the fish taken in a single drawing in of a net **3a** transportation by hauling **b** the distance or route over which a load is transported ⟨*a short ~*⟩ **c** a load that is transported – compare LONG HAUL

**haulage** /'hawlij/ *n* **1** the act or process of hauling **2** a charge made for hauling

**haulageway** /'hawlijway/ *n* a passage in a mine along which materials (eg broken rock or supplies) are transported

**haulier** /'hawli-ə/, *NAm* **hauler** /'hawlə/ *n* a person or commercial establishment whose business is transportation of goods, supplies, etc by lorry

**haulm** /hawm/ *n* **1** the stems or tops of cultivated plants (e g peas, beans, or potatoes), esp after the crop has been gathered **2** *Br* an individual plant stem [ME *halm*, fr OE *healm;* akin to OHG *halm* stem, L *culmus* stalk, Gk *kalamos* reed]

**haunch** /hawnch/ *n* **1a** the human hip **b** *pl* the back legs of a 4-legged animal; HINDQUARTER 2 **2** the back half of the side of a slaughtered animal; HINDQUARTER 1 〈*a* ~ *of venison*〉 **3** the lower half of either of the sides of an arch [ME *haunche*, fr OF *hanche*, of Gmc origin; akin to MD *hanke* haunch] – **on one's haunches** in a squatting position

**¹haunt** /hawnt/ *vt* **1a** to visit often; frequent **b** to continually seek the company of (a person) **2a** to recur constantly and spontaneously to 〈*the tune* ~ed *her all day*〉 **b** to reappear continually in; pervade 〈*a sense of tension that* ~s *his writing*〉 **3** to visit or inhabit as a ghost ~ *vi* **1** to stay around or persist; linger **2** to appear habitually as a ghost [ME *haunten*, fr OF *hanter*] – **haunter** *n*, **hauntingly** *adv*

**²haunt** *n* a place habitually frequented 〈*the bar was a favourite* ~ *of criminals*〉

**Hausa** /'howsə/ *n, pl* **Hausas**, *esp collectively* **Hausa 1** a member of a Negroid people of the N Nigeria and S Niger in W Africa **2** the CHAD language of the Hausa people, widely used in W Africa

**hausfrau** /'hows‚frow/ *n* a (German) housewife [Ger, fr *haus* house + *frau* woman, wife]

**hausmannite** /'howsmə‚niet/ *n* a dark brownish-black mineral consisting of a form of manganese oxide, $Mn_3O_4$ [J F L *Hausmann* †1859 Ger mineralogist]

**haustellum** /haw'steləm/ *n, pl* **haustella** /-lə/ a PROBOSCIS (elongated mouthpart) (e g of an insect) adapted to suck blood, plant juices, etc [NL, fr L *haustus*, pp of *haurire* to drink, draw – more at EXHAUST] – **haustellate** *adj*

**haustorium** /haw'stawriəm/ *n, pl* **haustoria** a projection or outgrowth from the stem or root of a parasitic plant or from a HYPHA (filament making up the body of a fungus), that serves to penetrate the host's cells and absorb food and water for the maintenance of the parasite [NL, fr L *haustus*]

**hautboy** /'ohboy/, **hautbois** *n, archaic* an oboe [MF *hautbois*, fr *haut* high + *bois* wood]

**haute couture** /‚oht kooh'tyooə (*Fr* ot kųty:r)/ *n* (the houses or designers that create) exclusive and often trend-setting fashions for women [Fr, lit., high sewing – more at COUTURE]

**haute cuisine** /kwi'zeen (*Fr* kɥizin)/ *n* elaborate cookery that reaches a high standard [Fr, lit., high cooking]

**haute école** /ay'kol (*Fr* ekɔl)/ *n* a highly stylized form of classical riding [Fr, lit., high school]

**hauteur** /oh'tuh (*Fr* otœ:r)/ *n* arrogance, haughtiness [Fr, fr *haut* high – more at HAUGHTY]

**haut monde** /‚oh 'mon(h)d (*Fr* o mɔ̃d)/ *n* high society [Fr]

**Havana** /hə'vanə/ *n* a cigar made in Cuba or from Cuban tobacco; *also* tobacco (of the type) raised in Cuba [*Havana*, city in Cuba]

**havdalah** /‚hahvdə'lah, hahv'dawlə/ *n* HABDALAH (Jewish ceremony)

**¹have** /v, əv, həv; *strong* hav/ *vb* **has** /s, z, əz, həz; *strong* haz/; **had** /d, əd, həd; *strong* had/ *vt* **1a** to hold in one's possession or at one's disposal 〈~ *a dog*〉 〈~ *no time*〉 〈~ *your cake and eat it too*〉 **b** to contain as a constituent or be characterized by 〈~ *red hair*〉 〈*coat has no pockets*〉 〈*has it in him to win*〉 **2** to own as an obligation or necessity – 〈~ *to go*〉 〈*don't* ~ *to if you don't want to*〉 **3** to stand in relationship to 〈~ *enemies*〉 〈~ *two sisters*〉 **4a** to get, obtain 〈*these shoes are the best to be had*〉 **b** to receive 〈*had news*〉 **c** to accept; *specif* to accept in marriage **d** to have sexual intercourse with (a woman or passive partner) **5a** to exhibit, show 〈*had the impudence to refuse*〉 **b** to use, exercise 〈~ *mercy on us*〉 **6a** to experience, esp by submitting, undergoing, or suffering 〈~ *a cold*〉 〈~ *my watch stolen*〉 〈~ *a good time*〉 **b** to perform, take; CARRY ON 〈~ *a bath*〉 〈~ *a fight*〉 〈~ *sex*〉 〈~ *a look at that*〉 **c** to entertain in the mind 〈~ *an opinion*〉 〈~ *a down on him*〉 〈~ *nothing against unions*〉 〈~ *it in mind to refuse*〉 **d** to engage in; hold 〈~ *a meeting*〉 **7a** to cause to by persuasive or forceful means – + infin without *to* 〈~ *the children stay*〉 〈*so he would* ~ *us believe*〉 **b** to cause to be 〈*soon* ~ *it finished*〉 〈~ *the cat down out of the tree in no time*〉 **c** to invite as a guest 〈~ *them over for drinks*〉 **8** to allow, permit 〈*I'm not having any more of that*〉 〈*can't* ~ *them crawling all over the place*〉 **9** to be competent in (a language) 〈*has only a little French*〉 **10a** to hold in a position of disadvantage or certain defeat 〈*we* ~ *him now*〉 **b** to perplex, floor 〈*you* ~ *me there*〉 **11** to be able to exercise; be entitled to 〈*I* ~ *my rights*〉 **12a** to be pregnant with or be the prospective parents of – used in the *-ing* form 〈*they're having a baby in August*〉 **b** to give birth to 〈*the cat's just had kittens*〉 **13** to partake of; consume 〈~ *dinner*〉 〈~ *a cigar*〉 **14** to bribe, suborn 〈*can be had for a price*〉 **15** *chiefly Br* to bring into a specified condition by the action of another – + the past participle 〈~ *my shoes mended*〉 **16** *chiefly NAm* to be logically inferred or supposed – + *to* and an infinitive 〈*you* ~ *to be joking!*〉 **17** *informal* to take advantage of; trick, fool 〈*been had by his partner*〉 ~ *va* **1** – used with the past participle to form the present perfect 〈*has gone home*〉 〈*why* hasn't *he?*〉, the past perfect 〈*had already eaten*〉, the future perfect 〈*will* ~ *finished dinner by then*〉, or nonfinite perfective forms 〈*having gone*〉 〈*silly not to* ~ *gone*〉; used with *got* to express obligation or necessity 〈~ *got to go*〉; used in the past tense with the past participle as a somewhat literary expression of the conditional 〈*had I known*〉 **2** WOULD 1b 〈*I had as soon not*〉 [ME *haven*, fr OE *habban;* akin to OHG *habēn* to have, *hevan* to lift – more at HEAVE] – **have been around** to be sophisticated or well-informed – **have done with** to bring to an end; have no further concern with 〈*let us* have done with *name-calling*〉 – **have had it** *informal* **1** to have had and missed one's chance **2** to have passed one's prime; be obsolete, ruined, or dead 〈*I'm afraid the car's* had it〉 – **have it 1** to maintain, affirm 〈*rumour* has it *he's been asked to resign*〉 **2** to live in the specified conditions 〈*never had it so good*〉 – **have it in for** to intend to do harm to – **have it off/away** *slang* to copulate *with* – **have it out** to settle a matter of contention by discussion or a fight – **have to do with 1** to deal with **2** to have in the way of connection or relation with or effect on 〈*the lawyer would* have *nothing* to do with *the case*〉 – compare TO DO WITH – **I have it** – used to express triumph at a discovery – **what have you** any of various other things that might also be mentioned 〈*paper clips, pins, and* what have you〉

*usage* **1** The use of **got** with **have** is commoner in British English than in American. **Have** *to* and **have got** *to* have the same meaning, but a British speaker may prefer 〈**have** *you* **got** *to go?*〉 and an American 〈*do you* **have** *to go?*〉 Some British speakers express the idea of momentary possession with **have got** 〈**have** *you* **got** *a cold?*〉 as opposed to habitual possession 〈*do you* **have** *many colds?*〉 but this distinction is disappearing under American influence 〈(*NAm*) "*do you* **have** *a cold?*" "*Yes, I do*"〉. For formal writing, it is better to avoid **got**, preferring 〈**have** *you any money?*〉 to 〈**have** *you* **got** *any money?*〉 **2** Have as an auxiliary verb is used with the past participle. It is a common confusion to introduce an extra infinitive **have** 〈⚠ *if I had* **have** *known*〉. See ¹GET

**have on** *vt* **1** to be wearing at any moment 〈*have a new suit* on〉 **2** to have plans for 〈*what do you* have on *for tomorrow?*〉 **3** *Br informal* to deceive; tease

**have up** *vt, informal* to bring before the authorities 〈*he was* had up *in court for dangerous driving*〉

**²have** *n usu pl* a wealthy person – esp in *the haves and have-nots*

**haven** /'hayv(ə)n/ *n* **1** a harbour, port **2** a place of safety or refuge [ME, fr OE *hæfen;* akin to MHG *habene* harbour, OE *hebban* to lift – more at HEAVE] – **haven** *vt*

**'have-‚not** *n usu pl* a poor person – compare ²HAVE

**haven't** /'havnt/ have not

**haver** /'hayvə/ *vi, chiefly Br* to be indecisive; hesitate [origin unknown; orig sense, to chatter idly or foolishly]

**havers** /'hayvəz/ *n taking sing vb, chiefly Scot* nonsense, poppycock [*haver*]

**haversack** /'havə‚sak/ *n* a knapsack [Fr *havresac*, fr Ger *habersack* bag for oats, fr *haber* oats + *sack* bag]

**haversian canal** /ha'vuhsh(ə)n/ *n, often cap H* any of the small canals in bone in which the blood vessels lie [Clopton *Havers* † 1702 E physician & anatomist]

**haversian system** *n, often cap H* any of the roughly cylindrical units of which dense bone is chiefly composed, that consist of a central HAVERSIAN CANAL surrounded by concentrically arranged circles of thin plates of bony tissue

**havoc** /'havək/ *n* **1** widespread destruction; devastation **2** great confusion and disorder 〈*several small children can create* ~ *in a house*〉 **synonyms** see ¹RUIN [ME *havok*, fr AF, modif of OF *havot* plunder]

**¹haw** /haw/ *n* **1** a hawthorn berry **2** the hawthorn shrub [ME *hawe*, fr OE *haga* – more at HEDGE]

**²haw** *n* NICTITATING MEMBRANE; *esp* an inflamed one of a dog, horse, or other domestic animal [origin unknown]

³**haw** vi to utter a sound resembling *haw*, esp in hesitation ⟨*hummed and ~ed before answering*⟩ – compare HUM [imit]

⁴**haw** interj – often used to indicate a hesitation in speech

**Hawaiian** /həˈwieˑən/ n 1 a native or inhabitant of Hawaii; esp one of Polynesian ancestry 2 the Polynesian language of the Hawaiians [*Hawaii*, group of islands in the Pacific Ocean] – **Hawaiian** adj

**Hawaiian guitar** n a usu electric stringed instrument consisting of a long soundboard and six to eight steel strings that are plucked while being pressed with a movable steel bar

**hawfinch** /ˈhawˌfinch/ n a large Eurasian finch (*Coccothraustes coccothraustes*) that has a large heavy beak and short thick neck and the male of which is marked with black, white, and brown [¹*haw*]

**haw-ˈhaw** interj ha-ha

¹**hawk** /hawk/ n 1 any of numerous medium-sized birds of prey (family Accipitridae) that have shortish rounded wings and long tails and that hunt during the day 2 a small board or metal sheet with a handle on the underside for holding mortar or plaster 3 one who takes a militant attitude and advocates immediate vigorous action; esp a supporter of a war or warlike policy – usu contrasted with *dove* [ME *hauk*, fr OE *hafoc*; akin to OHG *habuh* hawk, Russ *kobets*, a falcon; (2) perh of different origin] – **hawkish** adj, **hawkishly** adv, **hawkishness** n

²**hawk** vi 1 to hunt game with a trained hawk 2 to soar and strike like a hawk ⟨*birds ~ing after insects*⟩ ~ vt to hunt on the wing like a hawk

³**hawk** vt to offer for sale, esp in the street or by moving from place to place; peddle ⟨*~ing newspapers*⟩ [back-formation fr ²*hawker*]

⁴**hawk** vi to utter a harsh guttural sound (as if) in clearing the throat ~ vt to force up (e g phlegm) from the throat by hawking [imit]

⁵**hawk** n an audible effort to force up phlegm from the throat

**hawkbit** /ˈhawkˌbit/ n any of various plants (genus *Leontodon*) of the daisy family with usu golden-yellow flower heads similar to those of the dandelion

¹**hawker** /ˈhawkə/ n a falconer

²**hawker** n one who hawks goods [by folk etymology fr LG *höker*, fr MLG *hōker*, fr *hōken* to peddle; akin to OE *hēah* high]

**hawkmoth** /ˈhawkˌmoth/ n any of numerous rather large stout-bodied moths (family Sphingidae) with long strong narrow fore wings more or less pointed at the ends and small hind wings

**hawksbill** /ˈhawksˌbil/ n a flesh-eating sea turtle (*Eretmochelys imbricata*) whose shell yields a valuable tortoiseshell [fr the resemblance of its mouth to a hawk's beak]

**hawkweed** /ˈhawkˌweed/ n any of several plants (esp genus *Hieracium*) of the daisy family with usu red, orange, or yellow dandelion-like flower heads often borne in clusters

**hawse** /hawz/ n 1a **hawse, hawsehole** a hole in the front of a ship through which a cable passes b the part of the front of a ship which contains the hawses 2 the distance between the front of a ship and its anchor [ME *halse*, fr ON *hals* neck, hawse – more at COLLAR]

**hawser** /ˈhawzə/ n a large rope or small cable for towing, mooring, or securing a ship [ME, fr AF *hauceour*, fr MF *haucier* to hoist, fr (assumed) VL *altiare*, fr L *altus* high – more at OLD]

**ˈhawser-ˌlaid** adj, *of a rope* composed of three ropes twisted together from left to right with each containing three strands – compare CABLE-LAID

**hawthorn** /ˈhawˌthawn/ n any of a genus (*Crataegus*) of spring-flowering spiny shrubs of the rose family with glossy leaves, white or pink fragrant flowers, and small red berries [ME *hawethorn*, fr OE *hagathorn*, fr *haga* hedge, hawthorn + *thorn* – more at HEDGE]

¹**hay** /hay/ n 1 grass mowed and dried for use as fodder 2 reward, profit – chiefly in *make hay* 3 chiefly NAm informal bed – + *the* [ME *hey*, fr OE *hīeg*; akin to OHG *hewi* hay, OE *hēawan* to hew] – **hit the hay** informal to go to bed – **make hay of 1** to overthrow, refute ⟨*new evidence makes hay of his theories*⟩ **2** to make a muddle of ⟨*I made hay of my last exam*⟩

²**hay** vi to cut, dry and store grass for hay ~ vt to feed with hay

³**hay, hey** n 1 a country-dance featuring winding and interweaving dance figures 2 a dance figure consisting of a right

and left movement performed in a circle, straight line, or figure of eight [perh fr MF *haye* ]

**haybox** /ˈhayboks/ n an airtight box well insulated (e g with hay) that is used to keep a heated cooking vessel and its contents hot, thus enabling slow cooking to continue

**haycock** /ˈhaykok/ n a small conical pile of hay in a field

**hay fever** n acute nasal catarrh and inflammation of the lining of the eyes and eyelids occurring usu in the spring and summer through allergy to pollen

**hayfork** /ˈhayfawk/ n a fork that is mechanically operated or held in the hand and that is used for loading or unloading hay

**haylage** /ˈhaylij/ n a stored food for animals that is essentially a grass SILAGE dried to 35 to 50 per cent moisture [*hay* + si*lage*]

**hayloft** /ˈhayloft/ n a loft (e g over a stable or under a barn roof) for storing esp hay

**haymaker** /ˈhaymaykə/ n 1 one who or that which makes hay; esp one who tosses and spreads hay to dry after cutting 2 chiefly NAm a powerful swinging blow

**haynet** /ˈhaynet/ n a strong bag from which horses are fed hay (e g when travelling)

**hayrack** /ˈhayrak/ n 1 a feeding rack that holds hay for livestock 2 NAm a frame mounted on the chassis of a wagon and used esp in hauling hay or straw; *also* a wagon equipped with a hayrack

**hayrick** /ˈhayˌrik/ n a haystack

**hayseed** /ˈhayseed/ n 1 grass seed from hay 2 chiefly NAm informal a bumpkin, yokel

**haystack** /ˈhaystak/ n a large sometimes thatched outdoor pile of hay

**haywire** /ˈhaywieˑə/ adj, informal 1 out of order ⟨*the radio went ~*⟩ 2 emotionally or mentally upset; crazy ⟨*went completely ~ after the accident*⟩ [fr the use of *haywire* (wire for tying bundles of hay) for makeshift repairs]

**hazan** /khəˈzahn, ˈkhahz(ə)n/ n, pl **hazanim** /khəˈzahnim/ 1 an official of a Jewish synagogue or community in former times 2 CANTOR 2 (official in a synagogue who sings and leads prayers) [LHeb *ḥazzān*]

¹**hazard** /ˈhazəd/ n 1 a game of chance (e g CRAPS) played with two dice 2a risk, peril b a source of danger 3 chance, accident ⟨*two plants taken by ~* – Charles Darwin⟩ 4 a stroke in which a billiard ball is potted after contact with another ball – compare LOSING HAZARD, WINNING HAZARD 5 an obstacle (e g a bunker) on a golf-course *synonyms* see DANGER [ME, fr MF *hasard*, fr Ar *az-zahr* the die]

²**hazard** vt 1 to venture, risk ⟨*~ a guess*⟩ 2 to expose to danger ⟨*a captain guilty of ~ing his ship*⟩

**hazardous** /ˈhazədəs/ adj 1 depending on chance 2 involving or exposing one to risk (e g of loss or harm) ⟨*a ~ occupation*⟩ ⟨*handling ~ materials*⟩ – **hazardously** adv, **hazardousness** n

¹**haze** /hayz/ vb to make or become hazy, dull, or cloudy [prob back-formation fr *hazy*]

²**haze** n 1 fine dust, smoke, or light vapour causing a slight decrease in the air's transparency 2 vagueness or confusion of mental perception [prob back-formation fr *hazy*]

³**haze** vt 1 to harass by forcing to do unnecessary or disagreeable work 2 chiefly NAm to harass (a new student) by banter, ridicule, or criticism [origin unknown] – **hazer** n, **hazing** n

**hazel** /ˈhayzl/ n 1 (the wood or nut of) any of a genus (*Corylus*) of shrubs or small trees of the birch family bearing nuts enclosed in green leafy cups 2 a light brown to strong yellowish-brown colour [ME *hasel*, fr OE *hæsel*; akin to OHG *hasal* hazel, L *corulus*] – **hazel** adj

**hazel hen** n a European woodland grouse (*Tetrastes bonasia*)

**hazelnut** /ˈhayzlˌnut/ n the nut of a hazel – compare COBNUT, FILBERT

**hazy** /ˈhayzi/ adj 1 obscured or made dim or cloudy (as if) by haze ⟨*a ~ view of the mountains*⟩ 2 vague, indefinite ⟨*had only a ~ recollection of what happened*⟩ [origin unknown] – **hazily** adv, **haziness** n

**ˈH-ˌbomb** n HYDROGEN BOMB

¹**he** /(h)i, ee; *strong* hee/ pron 1 that male person or creature who is neither speaker nor hearer ⟨*~ is my father*⟩ – often cap when referring to God; compare SHE, HIM, HIS, IT, THEY 2 – used of either male or female when the sex of the person is unspecified ⟨*~ that hath ears to hear, let him hear* – Mt 11:15 (AV)⟩ [ME, fr OE *hē*; akin to OE *hēo* she, *hit* it, OHG *hē* he, L *cis, citra* on this side, Gk *ekeinos* that person]

*usage* **He, him, his,** and **himself** have traditionally been used to refer to either sex, since there is no English pronoun of common gender; but the use of **he** to mean "he or she" is often absurd and today may be found offensive ⟨*everyone will be able to decide for* **himself** *whether or not to have an abortion* – Albert Bleumenthal, New York State Assembly⟩. See ²ONE

²**he** /hee/ *n* 1 a male person or creature ⟨*is the baby a* ∼ *or a she?*⟩ ⟨*a he-goat*⟩ 2 ²IT 1

³**he** /hay/ *n* the 5th letter of the Hebrew alphabet [Heb *hē'*]

¹**head** /hed/ *n, pl* **heads,** *(4b)* **head** 1 the upper or foremost division of the body of an animal that contains the brain, the chief sense organs, and the mouth 2a the seat of the intellect; the mind ⟨*two* ∼ s *are better than one*⟩ **b** natural aptitude or talent ⟨*a good* ∼ *for figures*⟩ **c** mental or emotional control; composure ⟨*a level* ∼⟩ ⟨*don't lose your* ∼⟩ **d** a headache 3 **heads** *pl,* **head,** the chief side of a coin ⟨∼s, *I win*⟩ – compare TAIL 4a a person, individual ⟨*a* ∼ *count*⟩ **b** *usu pl* a single individual out of a number (eg of domestic animals) ⟨*500* ∼ *of cattle*⟩ 5a the end that is upper, higher, or opposite the foot ⟨*the* ∼ *of the table*⟩ **b** the source of a stream, river, etc **c** either end of something (eg a cask or drum) whose two ends need not be distinguished **d** DRIFT 6 (passage in a mine) 6 a director, leader: eg 6a a school principal **b** one in charge of a division or department in an office or institution ⟨*the* ∼ *of the English department*⟩ 7a CAPITULUM 2 (rounded or flattened cluster of flowers) **b** the leafy part of a plant, esp when consisting of a compact mass of leaves or fruits 8a the leading part of a military column or a procession **b** freedom to proceed on one's course or to have one's way ⟨*lengthen the reins and give the horse his* ∼⟩ ⟨*let him have his* ∼⟩ **c** headway 9a the uppermost point or projecting part of an object; the top **b** the striking part of a weapon, tool, or implement **c** the end of a muscle nearest to its main attachment to the skeleton **d** the oval part of a printed musical note 10a a body of water kept in reserve at a height **b** a mass of water in motion 11a (the pressure resulting from) the difference in height between two points in a body of liquid **b** the pressure of a liquid or gas ⟨*good* ∼ *of steam*⟩ 12a the bow and adjacent parts of a ship **b** heads *pl,* **head** a ship's toilet; *broadly, chiefly NAm* a toilet 13 a measure of length equivalent to a head ⟨*the horse won by a* ∼⟩ ⟨*he was a* ∼ *taller than his brother*⟩ 14 the place of leadership, honour, or command ⟨*at the* ∼ *of his class*⟩ 15a(1) HEADLINE 2, HEADING a(2) a separate part or topic **b** the top edge or margin of a printed page 16a the topmost edge of a book **b** the upper edge of a 4-sided sail; *also* the top corner of a triangular sail 17 the foam or froth that rises on a fermenting or effervescing liquid (eg beer) 18a the part of a boil, pimple, or abscess at which it is likely to break **b** a culminating point; a crisis – chiefly in *bring/come to a head* 19a a part or attachment of a machine or machine tool containing a device (eg a cutter or drill); *also* the part of an apparatus that performs the chief function or an often specified function **b** any of at least two electromagnetic parts which press against the MAGNETIC TAPE in a TAPE RECORDER, such that one of them can erase recorded material if desired and another may either record or play back 20a that member of an ENDOCENTRIC grammatical construction which has the same grammatical function as the whole (eg *man* in "a very old man" or "the man in the street") **b** that member of an EXOCENTRIC grammatical construction which is linked to the rest of the utterance by the supporting elements ⟨*bath in "in the bath" is the* ∼ *of a prepositional phrase*⟩ 21 *slang* one who uses a drug (eg LSD or cannabis) habitually or excessively – often in combination ⟨*acid*head⟩ [ME *hed,* fr OE *hēafod;* akin to OHG *houbit* head, L *caput*] – **bite somebody's head off** to rebuke somebody angrily – **get it into one's head** to become convinced ⟨*she* got it into her head *that I was to blame*⟩ – **go to somebody's head** 1 to make somebody confused, excited, or dizzy 2 to make somebody conceited or over-confident – **have one's head screwed on** to be sensible, practical, or provident – **heads will roll** certain people will be severely reprimanded or lose their jobs (eg because of an error or failure) – **keep one's head above water** 1 to keep out of debt 2 to survive a difficult situation – **not make head or tail of** not to understand in the least ⟨*couldn't* make head or tail of *his speech*⟩ – **off one's head** crazy, mad – **over somebody's head** 1 beyond somebody's understanding ⟨*I understand the gist but the technical language is* over my head⟩ 2 so as to pass over somebody's higher standing or authority ⟨*went* over his *supervisor's* head *to complain*⟩ – **turn somebody's head** to make somebody infatuated, vain, or deluded by notions of self-importance – see also **hit the** NAIL **on the head, off the** TOP **of one's head**

²**head** *adj* 1 of or intended for the head 2 principal, chief ⟨∼ *cook*⟩ ⟨∼ *office*⟩ 3 situated at the head

³**head** *vt* 1a to cut back the upper or end growth of (a plant or plant part) **b** to harvest (a cereal grass) by cutting off the heads 2a to provide with a head ⟨∼ *an arrow*⟩ **b** to form the head or top of ⟨*tower* ∼ed *by a spire*⟩ 3 to be at the head of; lead ⟨∼ *a revolt*⟩ – sometimes + *up* ⟨*looking for a manager to* ∼ *up the sales department* 4a to take a lead over (eg in a race); surpass **b** to go round the head of (a stream) 5a to put something at the head of (eg a list); *also* to provide with a heading **b** to stand as the first or leading member of ⟨∼s *the list of heroes*⟩ 6 to cause to take a specified course or direction ⟨∼ *a ship northwards*⟩ 7 to strike (eg a soccer ball) with the head; *also* to score (a goal) by doing this ∼ *vi* 1 to form a head ⟨*this cabbage* ∼s *early*⟩ 2 to point or proceed in a specified direction ⟨∼ing *for disaster*⟩ 3 *of a river or stream* to have a source; originate – usu + *in*

**head off** *vt* to stop the progress of or turn aside by taking preventive action; block ⟨head *them* off *at the pass*⟩ ⟨*attempts to* head off *the imminent crisis*⟩

**headache** /'hedayk/ *n* 1 a pain in the head 2 an annoying or baffling situation or problem – **headachy** *adj*

**head and shoulders** *adv* to a great degree; considerably ⟨*stood* ∼ *above the rest in character and ability*⟩

**headband** /'hed,band/ *n* 1 a band worn round the head, esp to keep hair out of the eyes 2 a plain or decorative band printed or engraved at the head of a page or chapter 3 a piece of cloth attached to the head or head and foot of the spine of a book for decoration or protection

**headboard** /'hed,bawd/ *n* a board forming the head (eg of a bed)

**head case** *n, informal* a crazy person; a lunatic

**headcheese** /'hed,cheez/ *n, NAm* BRAWN 2 (pork trimmings)

**head cold** *n* a COMMON COLD centred in the passages of the nose and adjacent mucus-producing tissues

**headdress** /'hedres/ *n* an often elaborate covering for the head

**headed** /'hedid/ *adj* 1 having a head or heading ⟨∼ *notepaper*⟩ 2 having a head or heads of a specified kind or number – in combination ⟨*a cool*headed *businessman*⟩ ⟨*a round*headed *screw*⟩

**header** /'hedə/ *n* 1 one who or that which removes heads; *esp* a grain-harvesting machine that cuts off the grain heads and lifts them up to a wagon 2a a brick or stone laid in a wall with its end towards the face of the wall – compare STRETCHER **b** TRIMMER (supporting beam or rafter) **c** a pipe or channel (eg the fitting on an INTERNAL-COMBUSTION ENGINE that receives used gases from several cylinders) into which smaller pipes or channels open **d** a mounting plate through which electrical terminals pass from a sealed device (eg a transistor) 3 a headfirst fall or dive 4 a shot or pass in soccer made by heading the ball

**headfirst** /,hed'fuhst/ *adv* with the head foremost; headlong ⟨*dived* ∼ *into the waves*⟩ – **headfirst** *adj*

**headforemost** /hed'fawmohst/ *adv* headfirst

**headgate** /'hed,gayt/ *n* a gate for controlling the water flowing into a channel (eg an irrigation ditch)

¹**head-hunting** *n* 1 cutting off and preserving the heads of enemies as trophies 2 searching for and recruitment of personnel, esp at the executive level and often from other firms – **headhunter** *n*

**heading** /'heding/ *n* 1 the compass direction in which a ship or aircraft points; *broadly* a direction 2a something that forms or serves as a head; *esp* an inscription, headline, or title standing at the top or beginning (eg of a letter or chapter) **b** a piece used in making either of the flat ends of a barrel 3 DRIFT 6 (passage in a mine)

**headlamp** /'hed,lamp/ *n* 1 a headlight 2 a light worn on the forehead (eg of a miner)

**headland** /'hedlənd/ *n* 1 unploughed land at the ends of furrows or near an edge of a field 2 a point of usu high land jutting out into a body of water; a promontory

**headless** /'hedlis/ *adj* 1 having no head 2 having no leader 3 foolish – **headlessness** *n*

**headlight** /'hed,liet/ *n* 1 (the beam cast by) the main light, with a reflector and special lens, mounted on the front of a motor vehicle 2 HEADLAMP 2

¹**headline** /'hedlien/ *n* 1 a head of a newspaper story or article, usu printed in large type and devised to summarize the story or article that follows 2 words set at the head of a passage or page to introduce or categorize 3 *pl, Br* a summary given at the beginning or end of a news broadcast

²**headline** *vt* 1 to provide with a headline 2 to publicize highly 3 *chiefly NAm* to be a star performer in (a show) ~ *vi, chiefly NAm* to be a star performer

**headliner** /'hedlienə/ *n, chiefly NAm* a star performer

**headlock** /'hed,lok/ *n* a wrestling hold in which one arm is locked round the opponent's head

¹**headlong** /'hedlong/ *adv* 1 headfirst 2 without deliberation; recklessly 3 without pause or delay [ME *hedlong*, alter. of *hedling*, fr *hed* head + *-ling* ²-ling]

²**headlong** *adj* 1 impetuous, precipitate ⟨*releasing the ~ torrent of her emotion in tears*⟩ 2 plunging headfirst 3 *archaic* steep ⟨*a ~ cliff*⟩

**head louse** *n* a louse (*Pediculus humanus capitis*) that lives on the human scalp

**headman** /-mən/ *n* 1a an overseer, foreman b a chief of a primitive community (eg a tribal village) 2 HEADSMAN (executioner)

**headmaster** /hed'mahstə/, *fem* **headmistress** /-'mistris/ *n* a person heading the staff of a school; a principal – **headmastership** *n*

**headmost** /'hedmohst/ *adj* most advanced; leading

**headnote** /'hed,noht/ *n* a note of comment or explanation at the head of a page or document

**head of state** *n, often cap H&S* the formal or titular head of a state (eg a monarch) as distinguished from the head of government (eg a PRIME MINISTER)

**head-on** *adv or adj* 1 with the head or front making the initial contact ⟨*the cars collided ~*⟩ ⟨*a ~ collision*⟩ 2 in direct opposition ⟨*what happens when primitive and civilized societies meet ~?*⟩ ⟨*a ~ confrontation*⟩

**head over heels** *adv* 1 turning over (as if) in a somersault 2 very much; completely, deeply ⟨*~ in love*⟩

**headphones** /'hedfohnz/ *n pl* a pair of earphones held over the ears by a band worn on the head; *also, sing* either of these earphones

**headpiece** /'hed,pees/ *n* 1a a protective covering (eg a helmet) for the head b HEADSTALL 2 an ornamental printed device at the head of a page or chapter

**headpin** /'hed,pin/ *n* the pin that stands nearest the bowler when the pins are arranged in TENPIN BOWLING

**headquartered** *adj* having headquarters in the specified place
*usage* Some people dislike this adjective, and prefer to say ⟨*the firm has its headquarters in Soho*⟩ rather than ⟨*the firm is headquartered in Soho*⟩.

**headquarters** /hed'kwawtəz/ *n taking sing or pl vb, pl* **headquarters** 1 a place from which a commander exercises command 2 the administrative centre of a business or operation

**headrace** /'hed,rays/ *n* a channel taking water to a mill wheel or turbine

**headrest** /'hedrest/ *n* 1 a support for the head 2 a cushioned pad at the top of the back of a motor vehicle seat, esp for preventing WHIPLASH INJURY

**head restraint** *n* HEADREST 2

**headroom** /'hed,room, -roohm/ *n* vertical space (eg beneath a bridge) in which to stand or move

**headsail** /'hed,sayl; *nautical* 'heds(ə)l/ *n* a sail (eg a JIB) set in front of the foremast

**headscarf** /'hed,skahf/ *n, pl* **headscarves, headscarfs** a scarf worn on the head by women

**head sea** *n* waves coming from a direction opposite to a ship's course

**headset** /'hed,set/ *n* 1 an attachment for holding earphones and a microphone to one's head 2 *chiefly NAm* a pair of headphones

**headship** /'hedship/ *n* the position or office of a head (eg a headmaster); leadership

**headshrinker** /'hed,shringkə/ *n* 1 a headhunter who shrinks the heads of victims 2 *humorous* a psychoanalyst or psychiatrist

**headsman** /'hedzmən/ *n* a person who beheads; an executioner

**headspace** /'hed,spays/ *n* a space left between the contents and the closure of a container (eg a tin or bottle) to allow for expansion of the contents

**headspring** /'hed,spring/ *n* a fountainhead, source

**headsquare** /'hed,skweə/ *n* a square headscarf

**headstall** /'hed,stawl/ *n* the part of a bridle or halter that fits round the head

**head start** *n* 1 an advantage granted or obtained at the start

of a race, contest, etc ⟨*a 10-minute ~*⟩ 2 an advantageous or favourable beginning

**headstock** /'hed,stok/ *n* a bearing or pedestal for a revolving or moving part in a machine; *specif* a part of a lathe that holds the revolving spindle and its attachments

**headstone** /'hed,stohn/ *n* a memorial stone placed at the head of a grave

**headstream** /'hed,streem/ *n* a stream that is the source of a river

**headstrong** /'hedstrong/ *adj* wilful, unruly ⟨*violent ~ actions*⟩ *synonyms* see UNRULY

**head teacher** *n* a headmaster or headmistress

**headtree** /'hed,tree/ *n* a wooden block attached to the top of a post to increase the load-bearing surface

**head-'up** *adj, of an instrument display* visible without the pilot's or driver's eyes having to look down from the view ahead

**headwaiter** /,hed'waytə/ *n* the head of the dining-room staff of a restaurant or hotel; MAÎTRE D'HÔTEL

**headwater** /'hed,wawtə/ *n,* **headwaters** *n pl* the upper part or source of a river

**headway** /'hedway/ *n* 1a (rate of) motion in a forward direction b advance, progress 2 headroom 3 the time interval between two vehicles (eg buses) travelling in the same direction on the same route

**headwind** /'hed,wind/ *n* a wind blowing in a direction opposite to a course, esp of a ship or aircraft

**headword** /'hed,wuhd/ *n* 1 a word or term placed at the beginning (eg of a chapter or an entry in a dictionary) 2 *linguistics* HEAD 20

**headwork** /'hed,wuhk/ *n* mental effort; thinking

**heady** /'hedi/ *adj* 1 violent, impetuous 2a tending to make giddy or exhilarated; intoxicating ⟨*~ wine*⟩ ⟨*a ~ triumph*⟩ b giddy, exhilarated ⟨*~ with his success*⟩ – **headily** *adv*, **headiness** *n*

**heal** /heel/ *vt* 1a to make sound or whole ⟨*~ a wound*⟩ b to restore to health 2 to restore to a sound, normal, or desirable state; mend ⟨*~ a breach between friends*⟩ ~ *vi* to return to a sound or healthy state [ME *helen*, fr OE *hǣlan*; akin to OHG *heilen* to heal, OE *hāl* whole – more at WHOLE] – **healer** *n*

**heald** /heeld, hiəld/ *n, chiefly Br* HEDDLE (set of cords or wires in a loom) [ME *helde*]

**health** /helth/ *n* 1a the condition of being sound in body, mind, or spirit; *esp* freedom from physical disease or pain b the general condition of the body ⟨*in poor ~*⟩ ⟨*enjoys good ~*⟩ 2 condition ⟨*the economic ~ of the country is not good*⟩; *esp* a sound or flourishing condition; well-being ⟨*indicates the continued ~ of traditional handicrafts*⟩ 3 a toast to somebody's health or prosperity ⟨*we drank his ~ on his birthday*⟩ – see also **clean** BILL **of health** [ME *helthe*, fr OE *hælth*, fr *hal*]

**health farm** *n* a residential establishment, typically in rural surroundings, that caters for people wishing to lose weight

**health food** *n* food (eg live yoghourt and untreated milk) that is usu grown without the use of artificial substances to fertilize the soil or kill pests, or produced without using chemical processes, that contains few or no artificial ingredients or additives, and that is eaten for the health-giving properties credited to it – compare WHOLEFOOD, JUNK FOOD

**healthful** /'helthf(ə)l/ *adj* 1 HEALTHY 3 2 HEALTHY 1

**health insurance** *n* insurance against financial loss through illness

**health salts** *n pl* any of various medicinal preparations (eg EPSOM SALTS or GLAUBER'S SALT) used as a laxative

**health visitor** *n* a trained person, esp a qualified nurse, who is employed by a British local authority to visit people (eg nursing mothers) in their homes and advise them on matters concerning their health

**healthy** /'helthi/ *adj* 1 having health and vigour of body, mind, or spirit 2 showing health ⟨*a ~ complexion*⟩ 3 helping to produce health ⟨*~ exercise*⟩ 4a prosperous, flourishing b not small; considerable ⟨*~ profits*⟩ – **healthily** *adv*, **healthiness** *n*

¹**heap** /heep/ *n* 1 a collection of things lying one on top of another; a pile 2 **heaps** *pl*, **heap** *informal* a great number or large quantity; a lot ⟨*we've got ~s of time before the train leaves*⟩ [ME *heep*, fr OE *hēap;* akin to OE *hēah* high]

²**heap** *vt* 1a to throw or lay in a heap; pile, amass ⟨*his sole object was to ~ up riches*⟩ b to form or round into a heap ⟨*~ed the soil into a mound*⟩ 2 to supply or bestow lavishly or in large quantities ⟨*~ed her with praise*⟩ ⟨*~ed honours upon him*⟩

**heaps** /heeps/ *adv, informal* very much 〈~ *quicker to go by car*〉 [pl of ¹*heap*]

**hear** /hiə/ *vb* **heard** /huhd/ *vt* **1** to perceive or apprehend (sound) by the ear **2** to learn by hearing 〈*I* ~d *you were leaving*〉 **3a** to listen to with attention; heed 〈~ *me out*〉 **b** to attend 〈~ *Mass*〉 **4** to give a legal hearing to 〈~ *evidence*〉 ~ *vi* **1** to have the capacity of apprehending sound **2** to gain information; learn 〈*I've* ~d *about what you did*〉 **3** – often in the expression *Hear! Hear!* indicating approval of something said [ME *heren,* fr OE *hīeran;* akin to OHG *hōren* to hear, L *cavēre* to be on guard, Gk *akouein* to hear] – **hearer** *n*

  **hear from** *vt* to receive a communication from 〈*heard from them last week*〉

  **hear of** *vt* to accept the idea of – usu neg 〈*wouldn't hear of it*〉

**hearing** /'hiəring/ *n* **1a** the process, function, or power of perceiving sound; *specif* the one of the five basic physical senses by which waves received by the ear are interpreted by the brain as sounds varying in pitch, intensity, and tone **b** earshot **2a** an opportunity to be heard or to present one's side of a case **b** a trial of a legal case in court **c** a session (e g of an official committee) in which witnesses are heard and testimony is taken

**hearing aid** *n* an electronic device worn by a deaf person for making sound louder before it reaches the ears

**hearken** *also* **harken** /'hahkən/ *vb, archaic or poetic* to listen (to); *also* to take heed (of) [ME *herknen,* fr OE *heorcnian;* akin to OHG *hōrechen* to listen – more at HARK]

**hearsay** /'hiə,say/ *n* something heard from another person; rumour

**hearsay evidence** *n* evidence which is based not on a witness's personal knowledge but on matters told to him/her by another, and which is usu inadmissible as testimony in a court of law

**hearse** /huhs/ *n* **1a** a triangular candlestick for 15 candles, used esp at certain church services (TENEBRAE) **b** an elaborate framework erected over a coffin or tomb to which decorations (e g candles) are attached **2** a vehicle for transporting a dead body in its coffin [ME *herse,* fr MF *herce* harrow, frame for holding candles, fr L *hirpic-, hirpex* harrow]

¹**heart** /haht/ *n* **1a** a hollow muscular organ of VERTEBRATE animals that by its rhythmic contraction acts as a FORCE PUMP maintaining the circulation of the blood **b** a structure in an INVERTEBRATE animal similar in function to the vertebrate heart **c** the breast, bosom 〈*clasped his wife to his* ~〉 **d** something resembling a heart in shape; *specif* a conventionalized representation of a heart **2a** a red heart-shaped figure marked on a playing card; *also* a card marked with one or more of these figures **b** *pl but taking sing or pl vb* the suit comprising cards identified by this figure **c** *pl but taking sing vb* a card game in which the object is to avoid taking tricks containing a heart or the queen of spades **3** the emotional or moral as distinguished from the intellectual nature: e g **3a** humane disposition; compassion 〈*have you no* ~?〉 **b** love, affections 〈*lost his* ~ *to her*〉 **c** courage, spirit 〈*had no* ~ *for the task*〉 **4** one's innermost character, feelings, or inclinations 〈*a man after my own* ~〉 〈*in your* ~ *you know it's true*〉 **5a** the central or innermost part; the centre 〈*the* ~ *of the sun*〉 **b** the essential or most vital part of something 〈*the* ~ *of the matter*〉 **c** the firm central part of certain leafy vegetables (e g a lettuce or cabbage) **6** *chiefly Br* fertility – chiefly in *in good heart;* used with reference to land [ME *hert,* fr OE *heorte;* akin to OHG *herza* heart, L *cord-, cor,* Gk *kardia*] – **break somebody's heart** to make somebody extremely sad or depressed, esp as a result of a failed romance, love affair, etc – **by heart** by rote or from memory – **eat one's heart out** to grieve bitterly – **lose one's heart (to)** to fall in love (with) – **set one's heart on/upon** to resolve to gain or accomplish 〈*she set her heart on a gold medal*〉 – **take heart** to gain courage or confidence – **take to heart** to be deeply affected by

  **synonyms** Something learnt *by* **heart** or *by* **rote** can be recited from memory, but *by* **rote** stresses the idea of mechanical memorizing without understanding.

²**heart** *vi, of a cabbage, lettuce, etc* to form a heart

**heartache** /'haht,ayk/ *n* mental anguish; sorrow

**heart attack** *n* an acute instance of abnormal functioning of the heart; *esp* CORONARY THROMBOSIS

**heartbeat** /'haht,beet/ *n* **1** a single complete pulsation of the heart **2** the vital centre or driving impulse

**heart block** *n* lack of coordination of the heartbeat in which the upper and lower chambers (ATRIA and VENTRICLES) of the

heart beat independently and which is marked by decreased output of blood from the heart

**heartbreak** /'haht,brayk/ *n* crushing grief; *also* something that causes heartbreak 〈*she has been a real* ~ *to her parents*〉

**heartbreaking** /'haht,brayking/ *adj* **1** causing intense sorrow or distress 〈*a* ~ *waste of talent*〉 **2** extremely trying or difficult 〈*a* ~ *task*〉 – **heartbreakingly** *adv*

**heartbroken** /'haht,brohkən/ *adj* overcome by sorrow

**heartburn** /'haht,buhn/ *n* a burning sensation behind the lower part of the breastbone, usu caused by regurgitation of acid from the stomach into the gullet

**heartburning** /'haht,buhning/ *n* intense or bitter jealousy or resentment

**heart disease** *n* an abnormal condition of the heart or of the heart and circulation

**-hearted** /-'hahtid/ *comb form (adj → adj)* having a heart of a specified kind 〈*a faint-*hearted *leader*〉 〈*warm*hearted *praise*〉

**hearten** /'hahtn/ *vt* to encourage, cheer – **hearteningly** *adv*

**heart failure** *n* **1** a condition in which the heart is unable to pump blood at an adequate rate or in adequate volume **2** stopping of the heartbeat, causing death

**heartfelt** /'haht,felt/ *adj* deeply felt; earnest **synonyms** see SINCERE

'**heart-,free** *adj* not in love

**hearth** /hahth/ *n* **1a** a brick, stone, or cement floor in front of a fireplace **b** the floor of a fireplace **c** the base of a furnace for processing metal **2** home, fireside 〈*the comforts of* ~ *and home*〉 [ME *herth,* fr OE *heorth;* akin to OHG *herd* hearth, Skt *kuḍayāti* he sings]

**hearthstone** /'hahth,stohn/ *n* **1** the stone forming a hearth **2** a soft stone or composition of powdered stone and PIPE CLAY used to whiten or scour hearths and doorsteps

**heartily** /'hahtəli/ *adv* **1** in a hearty manner **2a** with all sincerity; wholeheartedly 〈*I* ~ *recommend it*〉 **b** with zest or gusto 〈*ate* ~〉 **3** quite, thoroughly 〈~ *sick of all this talk*〉

**heartland** /'haht,land/ *n* a central or vital area

**heartless** /'hahtlis/ *adj* unfeeling, cruel – **heartlessly** *adv,* **heartlessness** *n*

**heart-lung machine** *n* a mechanical pump that shunts the body's blood away from the heart and maintains the circulation and respiration during heart surgery

**heartrending** /'haht,rending/ *adj* HEARTBREAKING 1 – **heartrendingly** *adv*

'**heart-,searching** *n* (a) close examination of one's motives or feelings 〈*reached the decision after much* ~〉

**heartsease** /'hahts,eez/ *n* **1** peace of mind; tranquillity **2** any of various violas; *esp* WILD PANSY

**heartsick** /'haht,sik/ *adj* very despondent; depressed – **heartsickness** *n*

**heartsore** /'haht,saw/ *adj* heartsick

**heartstrings** /'haht,stringz/ *n pl* the deepest emotions or affections 〈*pulled at his* ~〉 [fr the former notion of tendons or nerves supporting the heart]

**heartthrob** /'haht,throb/ *n* **1** the throb of a heart **2a** sentimental emotion; passion **b** one who arouses or who is the object of an infatuation 〈*he's a teenage* ~〉

¹**,heart-to-'heart** *adj* sincere and intimate 〈~ *confidences*〉

²**'heart-to-heart** *n, informal* a frank or intimate talk

**heart urchin** *n* any of various heart-shaped INVERTEBRATE animals (order Spatangoida of the class Echinoidea) related to the SEA URCHINS

**heartwarming** /'haht,wawming/ *adj* inspiring warm sympathetic feeling; cheering

'**heart-,whole** *adj* **1** heart-free **2** sincere, genuine

**heartwood** /'haht,wood/ *n* the older harder nonliving wood in the centre of a tree trunk, that is usu darker and denser than the surrounding SAPWOOD

¹**hearty** /'hahti/ *adj* **1a** wholehearted 〈~ *dislike of hypocrisy*〉 **b** enthusiastically or exuberantly cordial; jovial **c** expressed unrestrainedly; vigorous 〈*a* ~ *laugh*〉 **2a** robustly healthy 〈*hale and* ~〉 **b** abundant 〈*a* ~ *meal*〉 **c** nourishing 〈*a* ~ *beef stew*〉 **synonyms** see SINCERE **antonym** hollow – **heartiness** *n*

²**hearty** *n* **1** a bold brave fellow; a comrade – used esp by and to sailors **2** *chiefly Br* a sporty outgoing person 〈*rugger hearties*〉

¹**heat** /heet/ *vi* to become warm or hot – usu + *up* ~ *vt* **1** to make warm or hot – often + *up* **2** to excite, inflame [ME *heten,* fr OE *hǣtan;* akin to OE *hāt* hot] – **heatable** *adj,* **heatedly** *adv*

²**heat** *n* **1a(1)** the condition of being hot; warmth **a(2)** a marked

or notable degree of hotness **b** abnormally high bodily temperature **c** a single complete operation of heating (eg in a furnace); *also* the quantity of material so heated **d** the form of energy that is produced by the random motions of the molecules, atoms, or smaller structural units of which matter is composed and that can be transmitted by CONDUCTION, CONVECTION, or RADIATION from a body or region of higher temperature **e** the appearance, condition, or colour of a body as an indication of its temperature ⟨*at melting* ∼⟩ **f** any of a series of degrees of heating ⟨*this iron has four* ∼s⟩ **2a** intensity of feeling or reaction ⟨*the* ∼ *of passion*⟩ **b** the height or stress of an action or condition ⟨*in the* ∼ *of battle*⟩ **c** readiness for sexual intercourse in a female mammal; *specif* OESTRUS – usu in *on heat* ⟨*like a bitch on* ∼⟩ or (*chiefly NAm*) *in heat* **3** pungency of flavour **4a** a single round of a contest (eg a race) that has two or more rounds for each contestant **b** any of several preliminary contests whose winners go to the final **5** *chiefly NAm slang* **5a(1)** the intensification of police activity or investigation **a(2)** the police **b** pressure, coercion ⟨*his enemies turned the* ∼ *on him*⟩ – **heatless** *adj*

**heated** /'heetid/ *adj* marked by anger or excitement ⟨*a* ∼ *argument*⟩

**heat engine** *n* a mechanism (eg an INTERNAL-COMBUSTION ENGINE) for converting heat energy into mechanical energy

**heater** /'heetə/ *n* a device that gives off heat or holds something to be heated

**heat exchange** *n* the transference of heat from one medium to another

**heat exchanger** *n* a device (eg in a car heater or power station) that transfers heat from one liquid or gas to another without their mixing

**heat exhaustion** *n* a condition marked by weakness, sickness, dizziness, and profuse sweating that results from physical exertion in a hot environment – compare HEATSTROKE

**heath** /heeth/ *n* **1** (a) heather (esp genus *Erica*) **2a** a tract of wasteland **b** an extensive area of rather level open uncultivated land, usu with poor coarse soil, inferior drainage, and a surface rich in peat or peaty humus – compare MOOR [ME *heth*, fr OE *hǣth;* akin to OHG *heida* heather, OW *coit* forest] – **heathless** *adj*, **heathlike** *adj*, **heathy** *adj*

**heathen** /'heedh(ə)n/ *n, pl* **heathens,** *esp collectively* **heathen 1** an unconverted member of a people or nation that does not acknowledge the God of the Bible – often pl + *the* ⟨*the* ∼ *say there is no God*⟩ **2** an uncivilized or irreligious person [ME *hethen,* fr OE *hǣthen;* akin to OHG *heidan* heathen, perh orig meaning "one who lives on a heath"] – **heathen** *adj*, **heathenish** *adj*, **heathendom** *n*, **heathenism** *n*, **heathenize** *vt*

**heather** /'hedhə/ *n* **1** any of various evergreen shrubs (genera *Erica* and *Calluna* of the family Ericaceae, the heather family) that thrive on barren usu acid and ill-drained soil, and that have needlelike leaves and clusters of small flowers; *esp* a common heather (*Calluna vulgaris*) of northern and alpine regions that has small crowded stalkless leaves and tiny usu purplish-pink flowers **2** any of various plants (eg of the genera *Daboecia* and *Phyllodoce*) resembling and related to the heathers [ME (northern) *hather*]

**heather** *adj* heathery

**heathery** /'hedhəri/ *adj* **1** of or resembling heather **2** having flecks of various colours ⟨*a soft* ∼ *tweed*⟩

**heathland** /'heeth-lənd/ *n* an area of heathy land

**Heath Robinson** /,heeth 'robins(ə)n/ *adj, Br informal* impractically complex and ingenious ⟨∼ *machines constructed from old cotton bobbins* – John Lehmann⟩ [W *Heath Robinson* †1944 E artist, famous for his drawings of absurdly ingenious machines performing trivial tasks]

**heatproof** /'heet,proohf, -proof/ *adj* resistant to damage by heat

**heat pump** *n* an apparatus for transferring heat by mechanical means to a place of higher temperature (eg for heating or cooling a building)

**heat rash** *n* PRICKLY HEAT

**heat shield** *n* a part of the hull of a spacecraft designed to prevent excessive heating during reentry into the earth's atmosphere

**heat sink** *n* a means of absorbing or dissipating unwanted heat (eg from a process or an electronic device)

**heatstroke** /'heet,strohk/ *n* a condition marked esp by cessation of sweating, extremely high body temperature, and collapse, that results from prolonged exposure to high temperature – compare HEAT EXHAUSTION

**heat-,treat** *vt* to subject to heat; *esp* to treat (eg metals) by heating and cooling in a way that will produce desired properties (eg hardness) – **heat treater** *n*, **heat treatment** *n*

**heat wave** *n* a period of unusually hot weather

**heave** /heev/ *vb* **heaved, hove** /hohv/ *vt* **1** to lift upwards or onwards, esp with effort ⟨*heaving coal*⟩ **2** to throw, cast ⟨∼ *the lead*⟩ **3** to utter with obvious effort ⟨∼d *a sigh*⟩ **4** to cause to swell or rise **5** to haul, draw ∼ *vi* **1** to rise or become thrown or raised up **2** to strain to do something; labour **3a** to rise and fall rhythmically ⟨*his chest* heaving *with sobs*⟩ **b** to pant **4** to vomit **5** to pull, push – see also **heave in/into** SIGHT [ME *heven,* fr OE *hebban;* akin to OHG *hevan* to lift, L *capere* to take] – **heaver** *n*

*usage* The past tense and past participle **heaved** is commoner than **hove** except in the expressions **heave in sight** and **heave to**. *synonyms* see ¹LIFT, ¹THROW

**heave to** *vb* to bring (a ship) to a standstill with head to wind

**heave** *n* **1a** an effort to heave or raise **b** a throw, cast **2** an upward motion; a rising; *esp* a rhythmical rising ⟨*the* ∼ *of the sea*⟩ **3** the horizontal displacement (eg of rock layers) caused by a fracture in the earth's crust **4** *pl but taking sing or pl vb* BROKEN WIND (breathing disorder of horses)

**heaven** /'hev(ə)n/ *n* **1 heavens** *pl,* **heaven** the expanse of space that appears to surround the earth like a dome or vault; the sky **2a** *often cap* the dwelling place of God, his angels, and the spirits of those who have received salvation **b** a spiritual state of everlasting communion with God **3** *usu cap* GOD 1 ⟨∼ *help us all*⟩ **4** a place or condition of extreme happiness – see also **heaven** KNOWS, **for heaven's** SAKE [ME *heven,* fr OE *heofon;* akin to OHG *himil* heaven]

**heavenly** /'hev(ə)nli/ *adj* **1** of heaven or the heavens; celestial ⟨*the* ∼ *choirs*⟩ ⟨*the moon is a* ∼ *body*⟩ **2a** suggesting the blessed state of heaven; beatific ⟨∼ *peace*⟩ **b** *informal* delightful ⟨*what a* ∼ *idea*⟩ – **heavenliness** *n*

**heaven-'sent** *adj* providential

**heavenward** /'hev(ə)nwood/ *adj* directed towards heaven or the heavens

**heavenwards** /'hev(ə)nwoodz/, *NAm, chiefly* **heavenward** *adv* towards heaven or the heavens

**heavier-than-air** /'hevi·ə/ *adj, of an aircraft* weighing more than the air displaced

**heavily** /'hevəli/ *adv* **1** in a heavy manner **2** slowly and laboriously; dully **3** to a great degree; severely ⟨*crops* ∼ *damaged by frost*⟩ **4** *archaic* with sorrow; grievously ⟨*why looks your grace so* ∼ *today?* – Shak⟩

**Heaviside layer** /'hevisied/ *n* E LAYER (region of the earth's atmosphere) [Oliver *Heaviside* †1925 E physicist]

**heavy** /'hevi/ *adj* **1a** having great weight **b** having a high SPECIFIC GRAVITY; having great weight in proportion to size **c(1)** of or being an ISOTOPE (form of an atom characterized by the make-up of its nucleus) having greater than normal mass **c(2)** *of a chemical compound* containing heavy isotopes **2** hard to bear; *specif* grievous ⟨*a* ∼ *sorrow*⟩ **3** of weighty import; serious; *also* serious-minded ⟨*a* ∼ *book*⟩ **4** emotionally intense; deep, profound ⟨*a* ∼ *silence*⟩ **5a** oppressed; burdened ⟨*returned with* ∼ *spirit from the meeting*⟩ ⟨*branches* ∼ *with fruit*⟩ **b** pregnant; *esp* approaching the act of giving birth – often + *with* **6a** slow or dull from loss of vitality or resiliency sluggish ⟨∼ *movements*⟩ **b** lacking sparkle or vivacity; drab, dull ⟨*the book made* ∼ *reading*⟩ **c** lacking mirth or gaiety; sad ⟨*his heart was* ∼⟩ **d** characterized by declining prices ⟨*the stock market was* ∼⟩ **7** dulled with weariness; drowsy ⟨*his eyelids felt* ∼ *with sleep*⟩ **8** greater in quantity or quality than the average of its kind or class: eg **8a** of an unusually large amount ⟨∼ *traffic*⟩ ⟨*a* ∼ *crop*⟩ **b** of great force ⟨∼ *seas*⟩ ⟨*a* ∼ *blow*⟩ **c** overcast ⟨*a* ∼ *sky*⟩ **d(1)** impeding motion; *esp, of a racecourse* soft or muddy underfoot ⟨*the going was* ∼ *for this year's Grand National*⟩ **d(2)** *of soil* containing a high proportion of clay, inclined to hold water, and difficult to break down **e** loud and deep ⟨*the* ∼ *roll of thunder*⟩ **f** thick, coarse ⟨*a* ∼ *growth of timber*⟩ **g** oppressive ⟨∼ *odour*⟩ **h** laborious, difficult ⟨*made* ∼ *going of it*⟩ **i** of large capacity or output **j** consuming in large quantities – usu + *on* ⟨*this car is* ∼ *on petrol*⟩ **9a** digested with difficulty usu because of excessive richness ⟨∼ *fruit cake*⟩ **b** not sufficiently raised or leavened ⟨∼ *bread*⟩ **10** producing heavy usu large goods (eg coal, steel, or machinery) often used in the production of other goods ⟨∼ *industry*⟩ **11a** of the larger variety ⟨*a* ∼ *howitzer*⟩ **b** heavily armoured, armed, or equipped ⟨*the* ∼ *cavalry*⟩ **12** having stress ⟨∼ *rhythm*⟩ – used esp of syllables in accentual verse **13** relating to theatrical parts of a grave or sombre nature **14** *slang* of or being a style of loud rhythmic rock music **15** *chiefly NAm slang* frighteningly serious; *specif* threatening – often used as an interjection – see also **make heavy** WEATHER **of** [ME *hevy*, fr OE *hefig;* akin to OHG *hebīc* heavy, OE *hebban* to lift – more at HEAVE] – **heaviness** *n*

²**heavy** *adv* in a heavy manner; heavily ⟨*time hangs ∼ on us*⟩

³**heavy** *n* **1** *pl* units (eg of bombers, artillery, or cavalry) of the heavy sort **2** HEAVYWEIGHT **2 3** (an actor playing) **a** a dignified or sombre character in a dramatic production **b** a villain in a dramatic production **4** *Scot* BITTER **2** (dry beer) **5** *informal* a person of importance or significance **6** *usu pl, informal* a serious newspaper **7** *slang* one hired to compel or deter by means of threats or physical violence ⟨*set a gang of heavies on him*⟩

**heavy chain** *n* either of the two larger of the four chains of AMINO ACIDS comprising ANTIBODIES (substances produced by the body to fight disease) – compare LIGHT CHAIN

‚**heavy-'duty** *adj* able or designed to withstand unusual strain or wear

‚**heavy-'footed** *adj* heavy and slow in movement; dull ⟨*∼ literary style*⟩

‚**heavy-'handed** *adj* **1** clumsy, awkward **2** oppressive, harsh ⟨*∼ action by the government*⟩ – **heavy-handedly** *adv*, **heavy-handedness** *n*

**heavyhearted** /‚hevi'hahtid/ *adj* despondent, saddened – **heavyheartedly** *adv*, **heavyheartedness** *n*

**heavy hydrogen** *n* an ISOTOPE (form of an atom characterized by the make-up of its nucleus) of hydrogen having a MASS NUMBER greater than 1; *esp* DEUTERIUM

**heavy metal** *n* loud rhythmic rock music

**heavy spar** *n* BARYTES (type of mineral)

**heavy water** *n* water containing more than the usual proportion of heavy ISOTOPES (forms of an atom characterized by the make-up of their nuclei); *esp* water enriched with DEUTERIUM, used to slow down nuclear reactions

**heavyweight** /'hevi‚wayt/ *n* **1** somebody or something above average in weight **2** one in the usu heaviest class of contestants: eg **2a** a boxer whose weight is not limited if he is professional or is more than 81 kilograms (about 12 stone 10 pounds) if he is amateur **b** a wrestler weighing over 100 kilograms (about 15 stone 10½ pounds) **c** a weight-lifter weighing over 110 kilograms (about 17 stone 4½ pounds) **3** an important or influential person ⟨*an intellectual ∼*⟩

**hebdomad** /'hebdəmad/ *n, formal* a period of seven days; a week [L *hebdomad-, hebdomas,* fr Gk, fr *hebdomos* seventh, fr *hepta* seven – more at SEVEN] – **hebdomadal** *adj*, **hebdomadally** *adv*

**Hebdomadal Council** /heb'domədl/ *n* a representative board administering the affairs of Oxford University

**hebe** /'heebi/ *n* any of a genus (*Hebe*) of evergreen shrubs of the foxglove family, mostly native to New Zealand, that are often cultivated for their decorative leaves and usu white or purplish flowers [NL, genus name, fr *Hebe*, Greek goddess of youth, fr Gk *Hēbē*]

**hebephrenia** /‚heebi'freenyə, -ni‑ə/ *n* a mental illness (SCHIZOPHRENIA) characterized by silliness, delusions, hallucinations, and childish behaviour [NL, fr Gk *hēbē* youth] – **hebephrenic** *adj*

**hebetate** /'hebitayt/ *vt, formal* to make dull or insensitive [L *hebetatus*, pp of *hebetare*, fr *hebet-, hebes* dull] – **hebetation** *n*

**hebetude** /'hebityoohd/ *n, formal* lethargy, dullness – **hebetudinous** *adj*

**Hebraic** /hi'brayik/ *adj* (characteristic) of the Hebrews or their language or culture [ME *Ebrayke*, fr LL *Hebraicus*, fr Gk *Hebraikos*, fr *Hebraios*] – **Hebraically** *adv*

**Hebraism** /'heebray‚iz(ə)m/ *n* **1** a characteristic feature of the Hebrew language occurring in another language, esp in the Greek of the New Testament **2** the thought, spirit, or practice characteristic of the Hebrews **3** a moral theory or emphasis (eg strictness of conscience) attributed to the Hebrews

**Hebraist** /'heebray‚ist/ *n* a specialist in Hebrew and Hebraic studies

**Hebraistic** /‚heebray'istik/ *adj* **1** Hebraic **2** marked by Hebraisms

**hebra-ize, -ise** /'heebray‚iez/ *vb, often cap vi* to use Hebraisms *∼ vt* to make Hebraic in character or form – **hebraization** *n, often cap*

**Hebrew** /'heebrooh/ *n* **1** a member or descendant of any of a group of N Semitic peoples including the Israelites; *esp* an

Israelite **2** the Semitic language of the ancient Hebrews; *also* any of various later forms (eg the language used in present-day Israel) of this language [ME *Ebreu*, fr OF, fr LL *Hebraeus*, fr L, adj, fr Gk *Hebraios*, fr Aram *'Ebrai*] – **Hebrew** *adj*

**Hebrews** /'heebroohz/ *n taking sing vb* – see BIBLE table

**hecatomb** /'hekətoohm, -tohm/ *n* **1** an ancient Greek and Roman sacrifice of 100 oxen or cattle **2** the sacrifice or slaughter of many victims [L *hecatombe*, fr Gk *hekatombē*, fr *hekaton* hundred + *bous* cow – more at HUNDRED, COW]
   **usage** This word has nothing to do with "tombs". △ catacomb

**heck** /hek/ *n* HELL **2b** – used as an interjection or intensive ⟨*what the ∼!*⟩ ⟨*a ∼ of a lot of money*⟩ [euphemism]

**heckle** /'hekl/ *vt* **1** to harass and try to disconcert (eg a public speaker) with questions, challenges, or gibes **2** to molest [ME *hekelen* to hackle, fr *heckele* hackle; akin to OHG *hāko* hook – more at HOOK] – **heckler** *n*

**hect-** /hekt-/, **hecto-** *comb form* hundred (10²) ⟨*hectograph*⟩ [Fr, irreg fr Gk *hekaton*]

**hectare** /'hekteə, -tah/ *n* a metric unit of area equal to 10000 square metres [Fr, fr *hect-* + *are* ²are]

**hectic** /'hektik/ *adj* **1** of, having, or being a fluctuating but persistent fever (eg in tuberculosis) **2** red, flushed ⟨*the ∼ colour of his angry face*⟩ **3** filled with excitement or feverish activity ⟨*the ∼ days before Christmas*⟩ [ME *etyk*, fr MF *etique*, fr LL *hecticus*, fr Gk *hektikos* habitual, consumptive, fr *echein* to have – more at SCHEME] – **hectically** *adv*

**hectograph** /'hektoh‚grahf, -‚graf/ *n* a machine for making copies of a writing or drawing by use of a gelatin plate [Ger *hektograph*, fr *hekto-* hect- + *-graph*] – **hectograph** *vt*, **hectographic** *adj*

¹**hector** /'hektə/ *n* a bully, braggart [*Hector* (Gk *Hektōr*), a Trojan warrior in Greek mythology]

²**hector** *vi* to play the bully; swagger *∼ vt* to intimidate by blustering or scolding – **hectoringly** *adv*

**he'd** /eed, id, hid; *strong* heed/ he had; he would

**heddle** /'hedl/ *n* any of the sets of parallel cords or wires in a loom that with their mounting make up the harness used to guide lengthwise threads [prob alter. of ME *helde*, fr OE *hefeld;* akin to ON *hafald* heddle, OE *hebban* to lift – more at HEAVE]

**heder, cheder, chedar** /'khaydə, 'khedə/ *n, pl* **hadarim, heders, chedarim** /-‚reem/ an elementary Jewish school in which children are taught to read prayers, parts of the Bible, and other material in Hebrew [Yiddish *kheyder*, fr Heb *hedher* room]

¹**hedge** /hej/ *n* **1a** a fence or boundary formed by a dense row of shrubs or low trees; *also* a similar fence made of stones, turf, etc **b** a barrier, limit **2** a means of protection or defence (eg against financial loss) **3** a deliberately noncommittal or evasive statement [ME *hegge*, fr OE *hecg;* akin to OE *haga* hedge, hawthorn, L *colum* sieve]

²**hedge** *vt* **1** to enclose or protect (as if) with a hedge **2** to hem in or obstruct (as if) with a barrier; hinder ⟨*∼d about by qualifications*⟩ **3** to protect oneself against losing (eg a bet) by supporting more than one side ⟨*∼ a bet*⟩ *∼ vi* **1** to plant, form, or trim a hedge **2** to avoid committing oneself to a definite course of action, esp by making evasive statements **3** to protect oneself financially: eg **3a** to buy or sell FUTURES (goods bought or sold at an agreed price for later delivery) as a protection against loss due to price fluctuation – often + *against* **b** to reduce the risk of a bet – **hedger** *n*, **hedgingly** *adv*

**hedge garlic** *n* GARLIC MUSTARD

**hedgehog** /'hej‚hog/ *n* **1** any of a genus (*Erinaceus*) of African and Eurasian small spiny mammals that eat insects, are active at night, and roll themselves up into a ball for defence; *esp* a common European one (*Erinaceus europaeus*) **2** a military stronghold bristling with defences **3** *NAm* any of several spiny mammals (eg a porcupine) similar to a hedgehog

**hedgehop** /'hej‚hop/ *vi* **-pp-** to fly an aircraft close to the ground and rise over obstacles as they appear [back-formation fr *hedgehopper*] – **hedgehopper** *n*

**hedgerow** /-‚roh/ *n* a row of shrubs or small trees surrounding or separating fields

**hedge sparrow** *n* DUNNOCK (small brownish bird)

**hedonic** /hee'donik, hi-/ *adj* **1** of or characterized by pleasure **2** of hedonism; hedonistic – **hedonically** *adv*

**hedonism** /'hedə‚niz(ə)m, 'hee-/ *n* the doctrine that personal pleasure is the sole or chief good; *also* conduct or a way of life guided by or suggesting this doctrine [Gk *hēdonē* pleasure; akin to Gk *hēdys* sweet – more at SWEET] – **hedonist** *n*, **hedonistic** *adj*, **hedonistically** *adv*

**-hedral** /-heedrəl/ *comb form* (→ *adj*) having (such) a surface or (such or so many) surfaces ⟨*di*hedral⟩ [NL *-hedron*]

**-hedron** /-heedr(ə)n/ *comb form* (→ *n*), *pl* **-hedrons, -hedra** /-'heedrə/ crystal or geometric figure having (such or so many) surfaces ⟨*penta*hedron⟩ ⟨*trapezo*hedron⟩ [NL, fr Gk *-edron*, fr *hedra* seat, base – more at SIT]

**heebie-jeebies** /ˌheebi 'jeebiz/ *n pl, informal the* jitters, willies [coined by Billy DeBeck †1942 US cartoonist]

**¹heed** /heed/ *vb* to take notice (of); pay attention (to) [ME *heeden*, fr OE *hēdan;* akin to OHG *huota* guard]

**²heed** *n* attention, notice ⟨*take* ~⟩

**heedful** /'heedf(ə)l/ *adj* attentive, mindful ⟨~ *of what they were doing*⟩ – **heedfully** *adv*, **heedfulness** *n*

**heedless** /'heedlis/ *adj* inconsiderate, thoughtless – **heedlessly** *adv*, **heedlessness** *n*

**hee-haw** /'hee ˌhaw/ *n* **1** the bray of a donkey **2** a loud rude laugh; a guffaw [imit] – **hee-haw** *vi*

**¹heel** /heel/ *n* **1a** the back of the human foot below the ankle and behind the arch **b** the back of the hind limb of other VERTEBRATE animals, corresponding to the human heel **2** an anatomical structure (e g the part of the palm of the hand nearest the wrist) resembling the human heel **3** either of the crusty ends of a loaf of bread **4a** the part of a garment or an article of footwear that covers the human heel **b** a part of a shoe or boot that is attached to and often raises the sole under the heel of the foot **5** a rear, low, or bottom part: e g **5a** the rear end of a ship's keel **b** the lower end of a mast **c** the base of a tuber or cutting of a plant bearing its point of attachment to the main plant that is used for propagation **6** a backward kick with the heel in rugby, esp from a set scum **7** *slang* a contemptible person [ME, fr OE *hēla;* akin to ON *hæll* heel, OE *hōh* – more at HOCK; (7) perh of different origin] – **heeled** *adj,* **heelless** *adj* – **cool/kick one's heels** to be kept waiting or idle – **dig one's heels in** to refuse to move or change one's mind; be stubborn – **down at (the) heel** in or into a run-down or shabby condition – **kick up one's heels 1** to show sudden delight **2** to have a lively time – **on the heels of** immediately following; close behind – **show a clean pair of heels** to run quickly away (from) ⟨*when the police arrived he soon* showed a clean pair of heels⟩ – **take to one's heels** to run away; flee – **to heel 1** close behind – used in training a dog **2** into agreement or line; under control – **turn on one's heel** to turn suddenly round see also DRAG **one's heels**

**²heel** *vt* **1** to supply with a heel; *esp* to renew the heel of (e g a sock) **2** to exert pressure on, propel, or strike (as if) with the heel; *esp* to kick (a rugby ball) with the heel, esp out of a scrum ~ *vi* to move along at the heels of someone or close behind something ⟨*a dog that* ~*s well*⟩ – **heeler** *n*

**³heel** *vi* to tilt to one side; tip, list ~ *vt* to cause (a boat) to heel [alter. of ME *heelden*, fr OE *hieldan;* akin to OHG *hald* inclined, Lith *šalis* side, region]

**⁴heel** *n* a tilt (e g of a boat) to one side; *also* the extent of such a heel

**ˌheel-and-'toe** *adj* with a stride in which the heel of one foot touches the ground before the toe of the other foot leaves it ⟨~ *walking is prescribed for race walking*⟩

**heel and toe, toe and heel** *n* a technique used as an aid to gear-changing, in which the driver has one foot on the brake and accelerator at the same time so as to operate them in quick succession

**heelball** /'heel ˌbawl, 'hiəl-/ *n* a mixture of wax and lampblack used for giving a smooth polished surface to the heels of footwear and for taking brass or stone rubbings

**heel in** *vt* to plant (cuttings or plants) temporarily before setting in the final growing position [*heel*, alter. (influenced by ²*heel*) of E dial. *hele, heal* to cover over, fr ME *helen* to hide, conceal, fr OE *helian* – more at HELL]

**heeltap** /'heel ˌtap, 'hiəl-/ *n* a small quantity of alcoholic drink remaining in a glass after drinking [orig slang, one of the layers forming the heel of a shoe]

**¹heft** /heft/ *n, dial Br & NAm* weight, heaviness [irreg fr *heave*]

**²heft** *vt* **1** to test the weight of by lifting **2** *dial Br & NAm* to heave up; hoist

**hefty** /'hefti/ *adj* **1** quite heavy ⟨*a* ~ *book*⟩ **2a** large or bulky and usu strong ⟨*a* ~ *rugby forward*⟩ **b** powerful, mighty ⟨*a* ~ *blow*⟩ **c** impressively large ⟨*a* ~ *price to pay*⟩ – **heftily** *adv,* **heftiness** *n*

**Hegelian** /hay'geeli·ən, -lyən/ *adj* (characteristic) of Hegel or Hegelianism [Georg *Hegel* †1831 Ger philosopher]

**Hegelianism** /hay'geeliəˌniz(ə)m/ *n* the philosophy of Hegel that equates mind and nature so that, through DIALECTIC (pro-cess of reasoning by resolving contradictions), reason can comprehend an all-embracing ultimate reality of which finite objects are partial representations

**hegemony** /hi'gemoni; *also* hi'je-/ *n* dominating influence or authority, esp of one nation or group over others; leadership, dominance [Gk *hēgemonia*, fr *hēgemōn* leader, fr *hēgeisthai* to lead – more at SEEK] – **hegemonic** *adj*

*usage* The pronunciation /hi'gemoni/ is recommended for BBC broadcasters.

**hegira** *also* **hejira** /'hejirə/ *n* **1** a journey, esp when undertaken to escape from a dangerous or undesirable situation **2** a (mass) departure or emigration; an exodus [the *Hegira, Hejira,* flight of Muhammad from Mecca in 622, fr ML *hegira*, fr Ar *hijrah*, lit., flight]

**Heidelberg man** /'hiedl ˌbuhg/ *n* a prehistoric human being of the early PLEISTOCENE period known from a fossilized apelike lower jaw with distinctly human teeth [*Heidelberg*, city in W Germany]

**heifer** /'hefə/ *n* a young cow; *esp* one that has not had more than one calf [ME *hayfare*, fr OE *hēahfore*]

**heigh-ho** /'hay ˌhoh/ *interj* – used to express boredom, weariness, or sadness [*heigh* (var of *hey*) + *ho*]

**height** /hiet/ *n* **1** the highest or most extreme point; the zenith ⟨*at the* ~ *of his powers*⟩ **2a** the distance from the bottom to the top of something standing upright **b** the extent of elevation above a level; altitude **3** the condition of being tall or high **4a** **heights** *pl*, **height** a piece of land (e g a hill or plateau) rising to a considerable degree above the surrounding country **b** a high point or position [ME *heighthe,* fr OE *hiehthu;* akin to OHG *hōhida* height, OE *hēah* high]

**heighten** /'hiet(ə)n/ *vt* **1a** to increase the amount or degree of; augment ⟨~ed *his awareness of the problem*⟩ **b** to deepen, intensify ⟨*her colour* ~ed *by emotion*⟩ **c** to bring out more strongly; POINT UP **2a** to raise high or higher; elevate ⟨*the building was* ~ed *by another storey*⟩ **b** to raise above the ordinary or trite ~ *vi* **1** to become great or greater in amount, degree, or extent **2** to intensify

*synonyms* see INTENSIFY *antonyms* allay (for something bad), temper (for something good)

**ˌheight-to-'paper** *n* the height of printing type measured from FOOT (base) to FACE (surface that prints) and standardized at 23.317 millimetres (0.918 inch) in English-speaking countries

**Heimlich manoeuvre** /'hiemlikh (*Ger* haimlıç)/ *n* an emergency technique for saving a person from choking by pressing hard on his/her diaphragm to compress the air in the lungs so that the obstruction in the windpipe is forced out [Henry J *Heimlich* *fl*1975 US physician]

**heinous** /'haynos, 'heenəs/ *adj* hatefully or shockingly evil; abominable ⟨*a* ~ *crime*⟩ [ME, fr MF *haineus*, fr *haine* hate, fr *hair* to hate, of Gmc origin; akin to OHG *haz* hate – more at HATE] – **heinously** *adv*, **heinousness** *n*

**heinz** /hienz/ *n* a combination of bets (e g on horse races) covering six selections in different events in their 57 possible permutations of DOUBLES, TREBLES, and ACCUMULATORS [*Heinz 57 Varieties*, slogan of H J Heinz Co Ltd, manufacturers of convenience foods]

**¹heir** /eə/ *n* **1** a person who inherits or is entitled to inherit the estate of a deceased person after all debts and bequests have been paid **2** a person who inherits or is entitled to succeed to a hereditary rank, title, or office **3** a person who receives or is entitled to receive some possession, role, or quality passed on from a parent or predecessor [ME, fr OF, fr L *hered-, heres;* akin to Gk *chēros* bereaved, OE *gān* to go] – **heirless** *adj*, **heirship** *n*

**²heir** *vt, chiefly dial* to inherit ⟨*the loveliest maid . . . that ever* ~ed *a crown* – Sir Walter Scott⟩

**heir apparent** *n, pl* **heirs apparent 1** an heir whose claims are incontestable and who cannot be displaced so long as he/she outlives the person from whom he/she is to inherit **2** one whose succession, esp to a position or role, appears certain under existing circumstances

**heiress** /'eəris/ *n* a female heir; *esp* a female heir to great wealth

**heirloom** /'eəloohm/ *n* **1** a piece of (valuable) personal property that has been handed down within a family for several generations **2** something of special value handed on from one generation to another [ME *heirlome*, fr *heir* + *lome* implement – more at LOOM]

**heir presumptive** *n, pl* **heirs presumptive** an heir who can be displaced only by the birth of a child with a superior claim

**heist** /hiest/ *vt, NAm slang* **1** to commit armed robbery on **2** to take unlawfully and usu with violence; steal [alter. of ¹*hoist*] – **heist** *n*

**hejira** /'hejirə/ *n* HEGIRA (journey)

**HeLa** /'heelə/ *adj* of, derived from, or being a particular strain of human cells kept continuously growing in a culture medium for the purposes of medical research [*Henrietta La*cks *fl*1951, from whose cervical cancer the original cells were obtained]

**held** /held/ *past of* HOLD

**heldentenor** /'heldn,tenə/ *n, often cap* a tenor with a dramatic voice well suited to heroic, esp Wagnerian, roles [Ger, fr *held* hero + *tenor*]

¹**heli-** /heeli/, **helio-** *comb form* sun ⟨helio*centric*⟩ [L, fr Gk *hēli-, hēlio-*, fr *hēlios* – more at SOLAR]

²**heli-** *comb form* helicopter ⟨heli*port*⟩

**heliacal** /hi'lie·əkl/ *adj* relating to or near the sun – used esp of the last setting of a star before and its first rising after invisibility due to alignment with the sun [LL *heliacus*, fr Gk *hēliakos*, fr *hēlios*] – **heliacally** *adv*

**helic-, helico-** *comb form* helix; spiral ⟨helic*al*⟩ [Gk *helik-, heliko-*, fr *helik-, helix* spiral – more at HELIX]

**helical** /'helikl/ *adj* of or having the form of a helix; *broadly* spiral – **helically** *adv*

**helicoid** /'helikoyd/, **helicoidal** /,heli'koydl/ *adj* **1** forming or arranged in a spiral **2** having the form of a flat coil or flattened spiral ⟨~ *snail shell*⟩

**helicon** /'helikən/ *n* a large low-pitched brass instrument with a circular tube that forms a spiral round the player's body [prob fr Gk *helik-, helix* + E *-on* (as in *bombardon*)]

¹**helicopter** /'helikoptə/ *n* an aircraft which derives both lift and propulsive power from a set of horizontally rotating rotors or vanes and is capable of vertical takeoff and landing [Fr *hélicoptère*, fr Gk *heliko-* + *pteron* wing – more at FEATHER]

²**helicopter** *vb* to travel or transport by helicopter

**heliocentric** /,heelioh'sentrik/ *adj* **1** referred to, measured from, or appearing as if seen from the sun's centre **2** having or relating to the sun as a centre – compare GEOCENTRIC

¹**heliograph** /'heeliə,grahf, -,graf/ *n* **1a** PHOTOENGRAVING **2b** (type of print) **b** PHOTOHELIOGRAPH (apparatus for photographing the sun) **2** an apparatus for signalling using the sun's rays reflected from a mirror [ISV]

²**heliograph** *vt* to signal by means of a heliograph – **heliographer** *n*

**heliographic** /,heeliə'grafik/ *adj* **1** of heliography or a heliograph **2** of the sun; SOLAR **1** ⟨~ *latitude*⟩

**heliography** /,heeli'ogrəfi/ *n* **1** an early photographic process producing a PHOTOENGRAVING on a metal plate **2** the system or practice of signalling with a heliograph

**heliolatry** /,heeli'olətri/ *n* sun worship – **heliolatrous** *adj*

**heliolithic** /,heeliə'lithik/ *adj* marked by, observing, or associated with practices of sun worship and the erection of stone monuments ⟨*the* ~ *peoples of ancient Egypt*⟩

**heliometer** /,heeli'omitə/ *n* a visual telescope designed for measuring the apparent diameter of the sun but later used for measuring angles between or on planets, stars, etc [Fr *héliomètre*, fr *hélio-* heli- + *-mètre* -meter] – **heliometric** *adj*, **heliometrically** *adv*

**heliophyte** /'heeliə,fiet/ *n* a plant thriving in or tolerating full sunlight

**heliostat** /'heelioh,stat/ *n* a specialized type of COELOSTAT (astronomical instrument) for observing the sun that has a mirror mounted on an axis moved by clockwork by which a sunbeam is steadily reflected in one direction (eg into a telescope) [NL *heliostata*, fr *heli-* + Gk *-statēs* -stat]

**heliotaxis** /,heelioh'taksis/ *n* the response of a cell or organism to the stimulus of sunlight – compare PHOTOTAXIS [NL]

**heliotrope** /'heeliə,trohp/ *n* **1** any of a genus (*Heliotropium*) of plants of the forget-me-not family; *esp* a S American plant (*Heliotropium arborescens*) widely cultivated for its fragrant purplish flowers **2** BLOODSTONE (green mineral) **3** a light purple colour [L *heliotropium*, fr Gk *hēliotropion*, fr *hēlio-* heli- + *tropos* turn – more at TROPE; (1) fr its flowers' turning towards the sun; (2) fr the former belief that, if thrown into water, it would turn the sun's rays to the colour of blood]

**heliotropism** /,heeli'otrəpiz(ə)m/ *n* the turning or curving of a cell or organism towards or away from sunlight – compare PHOTOTROPISM – **heliotropic** *adj*, **heliotropically** *adv*

**heliozoan** /,heelioh'zoh·ən/ *n* any of an order (Heliozoa) of minute single-celled organisms (PROTOZOA) that live usu in fresh water, feed on algae and other small organisms, and reproduce usu by dividing into two parts or budding [NL *Heliozoa*, order name, fr *heli-* + *-zoa*; fr the resemblance to the sun and its rays] – **heliozoan** *adj*, **heliozoic** *adj*

**helipad** /'heli,pad/ *n* a heliport

**heliport** /'heli,pawt/ *n* a place for helicopters to take off and land [*helicopter* + *port*]

**helistop** /'heli,stop/ *n* a heliport

**helium** /'heeli·əm, -lyəm/ *n* a light colourless nonflammable gaseous chemical element found esp in NATURAL GASES and used chiefly for inflating airships and balloons, for filling light bulbs, and in scientific research involving low temperatures [NL, fr Gk *hēlios*; fr its discovery in the solar spectrum]

**helix** /'heeliks/ *n, pl* **helices** /'heliseez/ *also* **helixes 1** something spiral in form: eg **1a** a spiral scroll-shaped ornament in architecture **b** a coil formed by winding wire round a cylinder **2** the incurved rim of the external ear **3** a curve traced on a cylinder by the rotation of a point moving up the cylinder at a constant rate; *broadly* SPIRAL **1b 4** any of various land snails (genus *Helix*) [L, fr Gk; akin to Gk *eilyein* to roll, wrap – more at VOLUBLE; (4) NL, genus name, fr L, something spiral in form]

**hell** /hel/ *n* **1a** a nether world (eg Hades or Sheol) inhabited by the spirits of the dead **b** the home of the devil and demons in which the souls of those excluded from Paradise suffer punishment **2a** a place or state of torment, misery, or wickedness ⟨*war is* ~ – W T Sherman⟩ **b** – used as an interjection, an intensive, or a generalized term of abuse ⟨*one* ~ *of a mess*⟩ ⟨*go to* ~⟩ **c** a place or state of chaos or destruction ⟨*all* ~ *broke loose*⟩ **d** a severe scolding ⟨*got* ~ *for coming in late*⟩ **3** a hellbox [ME, fr OE; akin to OE *helian* to conceal, OHG *helan*, L *celare*, Gk *kalyptein*] – **come hell or high water** in spite of or regardless of opposition or difficulties – **for the hell of it** for the intrinsic amusement or often perverse satisfaction of an activity ⟨*threw his wicket away just for the hell of it*⟩ – **like hell 1** very hard or much ⟨*worked like hell to get the job done on time*⟩ **2** – used to intensify denial of a statement ⟨*pay you £5?* Like hell *I will!*⟩ – **raise hell 1** to act wildly; create a disturbance **2** to scold or upbraid somebody, esp loudly – **what the hell** it doesn't matter – see also **hell to** PAY

**he'll** /hil, eel, il; *strong* heel/ he will; he shall

**hell-'bent** *adj* **1** stubbornly and often recklessly determined ⟨*civilization is* ~ *on self-destruction* – R F Delderfield⟩ **2** moving at full speed; reckless

**hellbox** /'hel,boks/ *n* a receptacle into which a printer throws damaged or discarded type

**hellcat** /'hel,kat/ *n* **1** an ugly old woman; a crone **2** a spiteful ill-tempered person, esp a woman

**hellebore** /'helibaw/ *n* **1** any of a genus (*Helleborus*) of plants of the buttercup family having showy flowers; *also* the dried underground stem or an extract or powder of this formerly used in medicine **2** any of a genus (*Veratrum*) of poisonous plants of the lily family; *also* the dried underground stem of a hellebore (*Veratrum album* or *Veratrum viride*) or an extract or powder of this containing drugs and used esp as an insecticide [L *helleborus*, fr Gk *helleboros*]

**helleborine** /'helibərin, -brien/ *n* any of various plants (genera *Epipactis* and *Cephalanthera*) of the orchid family [L, a kind of hellebore, fr Gk *helleborinē*, fr *helleboros*]

**Hellene** /'heleen/ *n* a Greek [Gk *Hellēn*]

¹**Hellenic** /he'lenik, -'leenik, hə-/ *adj* (characteristic) of Greece, its people, or the (ancient) Greek language

²**Hellenic** *n* the Greek language

**Hellenism** /'heli,niz(ə)m/ *n* **1** GRAECISM **1** (Greek idiom) **2** devotion to or imitation of ancient Greek thought, customs, or styles **3** Greek civilization, esp as modified in the Hellenistic period by oriental influences **4** a body of humanistic and classical ideals (eg reason, moderation, and the pursuit of knowledge) associated with ancient Greece

**Hellenist** /'helinist/ *n* **1** a person living in ancient times who was Greek in language, outlook, and way of life but not in ancestry; *esp* a hellenized Jew **2** a specialist in the language or culture of ancient Greece

**Hellenistic** /,heli'nistik/ *adj* **1** of Greek history, culture, or art, esp in the period after the death of Alexander the Great in 323 BC **2** of the Hellenists – **Hellenistically** *adv*

**hellen·ize, -ise** /'heliniez/ *vb, often cap* to make or become Greek or Hellenistic in form or culture – **hellenization** *n, often cap*

**hell-for-'leather** *adv or adj, informal* at full speed and usu with determined recklessness ⟨*pelted* ~ *down the street*⟩ ⟨*a* ~ *gallop*⟩ [perh alter. of *all of a lather*]

**hellgrammite** /'helgrə,miet/ *n* an aquatic N American insect larva that is used for fish bait [origin unknown]

**hellhole** /'hel,hohl/ *n* **1** the pit of hell **2** *informal* a place of extreme discomfort, squalor, or evil

**hellhound** /'hel,hownd/ *n* a fiendish person

**hellion** /'heli·ən, 'helyən/ *n*, *NAm informal* a troublesome or mischievous person [prob alter. of *hallion* (scamp)]

**¹hellish** /'helish/ *adj* of, resembling, or befitting hell; diabolical ⟨*nothing more ~ than warfare within the soul* – Frank Yerby⟩ – **hellishly** *adv*, **hellishness** *n*

**²hellish** *adv* extremely, damnably ⟨*a ~ cold day*⟩

**hello** /he'loh, 'heloh, hə-/ *n*, *pl* **hellos** an expression or gesture of greeting – used interjectionally in greeting, in answering the telephone, to express surprise, or to attract attention [alter. of *hollo*]

**hell's angel** *n*, *often cap* H a member of a gang of reckless, unruly, and often violent young people who wear leather clothing and ride motorcycles – compare ROCKER

**hell's bells** *interj*, *chiefly humorous* – used esp to express irritation or impatience

**helluva** /'heləvə/ *adj*, *slang* great, terrific – often used as an intensive ⟨*a ~ din*⟩ [alter. of *hell of a*]

**¹helm** /helm/ *n*, *archaic* HELMET 1 [ME, fr OE]

**²helm** *vt*, *poetic* to cover or provide with a helmet

**³helm** *n* **1a** a tiller or wheel controlling a ship's rudder; *broadly* the entire apparatus for steering a ship **b** movement of the helm from the middle position ⟨*no amount of ~ will straighten the boat*⟩ **2** a position of control; *the head* ⟨*a new chairman is at the ~ of the company*⟩ [ME *helme*, fr OE *helma*; akin to OHG *helmo* tiller]

**⁴helm** *vt* to direct (as if) with a helm; steer

**helmet** /'helmit/ *n* **1** a protective or defensive covering for the head in ancient or medieval armour **2** any of various protective head coverings, usu made of a hard material to resist impact ⟨*a policeman's ~*⟩ **3** something resembling a helmet; *specif* a hood-shaped upper SEPAL (leaflike structure protecting developing flower bud) or petal of some flowers [MF, dim. of *helme* helmet, of Gmc origin; akin to OE *helm* helmet, OHG *helan* to conceal – more at HELL] – **helmeted** *adj*, **helmetlike** *adj*

**helminth** /'helminth/ *n* a (parasitic) worm, esp one living in the intestines of an animal – used technically [Gk *helminth-, helmis*; akin to Gk *eilyein* to roll – more at VOLUBLE] – **helminthic** *adj*

**helminth-** /'helminth-/, **helmintho-** *comb form* helminth ⟨helminth*iasis*⟩ ⟨helmintho*logy*⟩ [NL, fr Gk *helminth-, helmis*]

**helminthiasis** /,helmin'thie·əsis/ *n* infestation with or disease caused by parasitic worms [NL]

**helminthology** /,helmin'tholəji/ *n* a branch of zoology concerned with helminths; *esp* the study of parasitic worms – **helminthologist** *n*

**helmsman** /'helmzmən/ *n* the person at the helm who steers a ship – **helmsmanship** *n*

**helot** /'helət/ *n* **1** *cap* a member of a class of serfs in ancient Sparta **2** a serf, slave [L *Helotes*, pl, fr Gk *Heilōtes*, perh fr *Helos*, ancient town in S Greece] – **helotism** *n*, **helotry** *n*

**¹help** /help/ *vt* **1** to give assistance or support to ⟨*~ a child to understand his lesson*⟩ **2** to remedy, relieve ⟨*took an aspirin to ~ her headache*⟩ **3a** to be of use to; benefit **b** to further the advancement of; promote ⟨*~ing industry with loans*⟩ **4a** to refrain from ⟨*couldn't ~ laughing*⟩ **b** to keep from occurring; prevent ⟨*they couldn't ~ the accident*⟩ **c** to restrain (oneself) from taking action ⟨*tried not to say anything, but couldn't ~ myself*⟩ **5** to serve with food or drink, esp at a meal ⟨*let me ~ you to some salad*⟩ **6** to take something for the use of (oneself), esp dishonestly ⟨*~ed himself to my pen*⟩ *~ vi* to be of use or benefit ⟨*every little ~s*⟩ [ME *helpen*, fr OE *helpan*; akin to OHG *helfan* to help, Lith *šelpti*] – **helper** *n* – **help somebody on/off with** to help somebody to put on/take off (an article of clothing) – see also CANNOT **help but**

*synonyms* Help, aid, assist, and succour: the first three are often interchangeable and suggest a combined effort to achieve something or to meet a need. Help stresses, more than the other terms, advance towards the end in view ⟨*every little* helps⟩. Aid often implies the need of help or relief, and so may suggest weakness in the one aided ⟨*saints will* aid *if men will call* – S T Coleridge⟩. Assist definitely suggests helping in a subsidiary role ⟨*several nurses* assisted *the surgeon at the operation*⟩. Succour, unlike the others, suggests helping someone without their active cooperation ⟨*tended the sick and* succoured *the needy*⟩. *usage* The use of *than/as one can* help

after a negative or in a sentence with negative implication ⟨*won't cough more than I can* help⟩ has been censured as illogical, but is well established in English ⟨*your name shall occur again as little as I can* help – J H Newman⟩. It can be avoided by recasting the sentence ⟨*won't cough more than I have to*⟩. See CANNOT **antonyms** hinder, frustrate

**help out** *vb* to give assistance or aid (to), esp when in great difficulty ⟨*she helped me* out *when I was in hospital*⟩

**²help** *n* **1** aid, assistance **2** remedy, relief ⟨*there was no ~ for it*⟩ **3a** somebody, esp a woman, hired to do work, esp housework ⟨*a mother's ~*⟩ **b** the services of a paid worker; *also, chiefly NAm* the workers providing such services ⟨*~ wanted*⟩

**helpful** /'helpf(ə)l/ *adj* of service or assistance; useful – **helpfully** *adv*, **helpfulness** *n*

**helping** /'helping/ *n* a serving of food

**helpless** /'helplis/ *adj* **1** lacking protection or support; defenceless **2** lacking strength or effectiveness; powerless ⟨*was ~ to prevent his leaving*⟩ – **helplessly** *adv*, **helplessness** *n*

**helpmate** /'help,mayt/ *n* a companion and helper; *esp* a wife or husband – sometimes used ironically or patronizingly ⟨*this is Mary, my little ~*⟩ [by folk etymology (influenced by *mate*) fr *helpmeet*]

**helpmeet** /'help,meet/ *n*, *archaic* a helpmate [²*help* + ³*meet*]

**¹helter-skelter** /,heltə 'skeltə/ *adv or adj* **1** in confused haste; pell-mell ⟨*ran ~ down the stairs*⟩ **2** in haphazard order [imit]

**²helter-skelter** *n* **1** a disorderly confusion **2** a spiral slide at a fairground

**helve** /helv/ *n* a haft [ME, fr OE *hielfe*; akin to OE *healf* half]

**Helvetian** /hel'veesh(y)ən/ *adj* Swiss [NL *Helvetia* land of the Helvetii, Switzerland, fr L *Helvetii*, an ancient people of Switzerland] – **Helvetian** *n*

**¹hem** /hem/ *n* **1** the border of a cloth article when turned back and stitched down; *esp* the bottom edge of a garment (eg a skirt) finished in this manner **2** a border like a hem on an article of sheet metal, plastic, rubber, or leather [ME, fr OE; akin to MHG *hemmen* to hem in, Armenian *kamel* to press]

**²hem** *vb* -mm- *vt* **1a** to finish (eg a skirt) with a hem **b** to border, edge **2** to enclose, confine – usu + *in* or *about* ⟨*~med in by enemy troops*⟩ *~ vi* to make a hem in sewing – **hemmer** *n*

**³hem** /həm/ *interj* – often used to indicate a voiced pause in speaking [imit]

**⁴hem** *vi* -mm- to utter the sound represented by *hem*, esp in hesitation – **hem and haw** HUM AND HA

**hem-, hema-, hemo-** *comb form*, *NAm* haem-

**he-man** /'hee/ *n*, *informal* a strong virile man

**hemat-, hemato-** *comb form*, *NAm* haemat-

**heme** /heem/ *n*, *chiefly NAm* HAEM (substance in RED BLOOD CELLS)

**hemelytron** /he'melətron/ *n*, *pl* **hemelytra** /-trə/ either of the front wings, thickened at the base, of various insects (eg TRUE BUGS) [NL, fr *hemi-* + *elytron*]

**hemeralopia** /,hemərə'lohpiə/ *n* **1** a defect of eyesight characterized by reduced vision in bright light **2** NIGHT BLINDNESS – not used technically [NL, fr Gk *hēmeralōps*, fr *hēmera* day + *alaos* blind + *ōps* eye] – **hemeralopic** *adj*

**hemerocallis** /,heməroh'kalis/ *n* DAY LILY [NL, fr Gk *hēmerokalles*, fr *hēmera* + *kallos* beauty – more at CALLIGRAPHY]

**hemi-** /hemi-/ *prefix* half ⟨hemi*sphere*⟩ [ME, fr L, fr Gk *hēmi-* – more at SEMI-]

**hemiacetal** /,hemi'asitl/ *n* any of a class of chemical compounds characterized by the grouping $C(OH)(OR)$ where R is an ALKYL group

**hemicellulose** /,hemi'selyoolohs, -lohz/ *n* any of various POLYSACCHARIDES (complex sugars) forming plant cell walls that are simpler than CELLULOSE (fibrous polysaccharide) and can be easily broken down to simple sugars and other products

**hemichordate** /,hemi'kawdət, -dayt/ *n* any of a division (Hemichordata) of wormlike marine animals (eg an ACORN WORM) that have at their head end a small structure resembling a rudimentary NOTOCHORD (flexible rod of cells supporting the body) and other structures (eg gill slits) that suggest a relationship with higher CHORDATE (possessing a notochord) animals (eg lampreys, SEA SQUIRTS, and all VERTEBRATE animals) [NL *Hemichordata*, group name, fr *hemi-* + *Chordata* chordates]

**hemicycle** /'hemi,siekl/ *n* a curved or semicircular structure or arrangement [Fr *hémicycle*, fr L *hemicyclium*, fr Gk *hēmikyklion*, fr *hēmi-* + *kyklos* circle – more at WHEEL]

**hemidemisemiquaver** /ˌhemiˌdemiˌsemiˈkwayvə/ n a musical note with the time value of half a DEMISEMIQUAVER

**hemihedral** /-ˈheedrəl/ adj, of a crystal having half the surfaces required by complete symmetry – compare HOLOHEDRAL, TETARTOHEDRAL – **hemihedrally** adv

**hemihydrate** /ˌhemiˈhiedrayt/ n a chemical compound (e g PLASTER OF PARIS) formed from water and some other substance in the proportion of half a molecule of water to one molecule of the other substance – **hemihydrated** adj

**hemimetabolous** /ˌhemiməˈtabələs/ adj, of an insect having INCOMPLETE METAMORPHOSIS (gradual change from the larval stage into the mature but structurally similar adult) – compare HOLOMETABOLOUS – **hemimetabolism** n

**hemimorphic** /ˌhemiˈmawfik/ adj, of a crystal having unsymmetrical forms at its two ends [ISV] – **hemimorphism** n

**hemimorphite** /ˌhemiˈmawfiet/ n a mineral, $Zn_4Si_2O_7(OH)_2.H_2O$, that occurs in usu colourless transparent crystals and that is an important ore of zinc

**hemiola** /ˌhemiˈohlə/ n a musical rhythmic alteration consisting of three beats in place of two, or two beats in place of three [LL *hemiolia*, fr Gk *hēmiolia* ratio of one and a half to one, fr *hēmi-* + *holos* whole – more at SAFE]

**hemiparasite** /ˌhemiˈparəsiet/ n **1** a parasite that can live independently in some conditions or in some stages of its LIFE CYCLE **2** a parasitic plant (e g the mistletoe) that contains some green pigment (CHLOROPHYLL) and can therefore produce some of its own food by the process of photosynthesis [ISV] – **hemiparasitic** adj

**hemiplegia** /-ˈpleej(y)ə/ n paralysis of all or part of one side half of the body, resulting from injury to the areas of the brain that control movement and locomotion – compare PARAPLEGIA, QUADRIPLEGIA [NL, fr MGk *hēmiplēgia* paralysis, fr Gk *hēmi-* + *-plēgia* -plegia] – **hemiplegic** adj or n

**hemipteran** /hiˈmiptərən/ n TRUE BUG [deriv of Gk *hēmi-* + *pteron* wing – more at FEATHER] – **hemipteroid** adj, **hemipteron** n, **hemipterous** adj

**hemisphere** /ˈhemiˌsfiə/ n **1a** a half of the CELESTIAL SPHERE (imaginary sphere surrounding the earth on whose surface the stars, planets, etc appear to be placed) when divided into two halves by the horizon, the CELESTIAL EQUATOR, or the ECLIPTIC (apparent path travelled by the sun) **b** the northern or southern half of the earth divided by the equator, or the eastern or western half divided by a MERIDIAN (imaginary circle passing through both poles) **2** half a sphere; either of the two half spheres formed by a plane that passes through the sphere's centre **3** a map or projection of a hemisphere of the sky or earth **4** CEREBRAL HEMISPHERE (left or right half of the front portion of the brain) [ME *hemispere*, fr L *hemisphaerium*, fr Gk *hēmisphairion*, fr *hēmi-* + *sphairion*, dim. of *sphaira* sphere] – **hemispheric**, **hemispherical** adj

**hemistich** /ˈhemiˌstik/ n half of a line of verse, usu divided from the other half by a pause (CAESURA) [L *hemistichium*, fr Gk *hēmistichion*, fr *hēmi-* + *stichos* line, verse; akin to Gk *steichein* to go – more at STAIR]

**hemiterpene** /ˌhemiˈtuhpeen/ n any of various chemical compounds whose formula, $C_5H_8$, represents half that of a TERPENE; esp ISOPRENE [ISV]

**hemizygous** /ˌhemiˈziegəs, heeˈmizigəs/ adj having or characterized by a gene or a section of a CHROMOSOME (strand of gene-carrying material) that is unpaired or has no corresponding counterpart in the cell

**hemline** /ˈhemˌlien/ n the line formed by the lower hemmed edge of a garment, esp a dress

**hemlock** /ˈhemlok/ n **1a** any of several very poisonous plants of the carrot family having finely cut leaves and small white flowers; esp a common hemlock (*Conium maculatum*) **b** a poisonous drink made from the fruit of the hemlock **2** (the soft light splintery wood of) any of a genus (*Tsuga*) of evergreen cone-bearing trees of the pine family [ME *hemlok*, fr OE *hemlic*]

**hemo-** – see HEM-

**hemp** /hemp/ n **1a** a tall widely cultivated Asiatic plant (*Cannabis sativa* of the family Cannabaceae, the hemp family) that yields marijuana and a tough fibre **b** the fibre of hemp, used esp for rope and fabrics **c** an intoxicating drug (e g marijuana or hashish) obtained from hemp **2** a fibre (e g jute) from a plant other than the true hemp; also any of various plants (e g MANILA HEMP) yielding this [ME, fr OE *hænep;* akin to OHG *hanaf* hemp; both prob fr the source (prob Finno-Ugric) of Gk *kannabis* hemp] – **hempen** adj

**hemp nettle** n any of a genus (*Galeopsis*) of coarse African and Eurasian plants of the mint family; esp a bristly Eurasian plant (*Galeopsis tetrahit*)

**¹hemstitch** /ˈhemˌstich/ vt to decorate (e g a border) with hemstitch – **hemstitcher** n

**²hemstitch** n decorative needlework (DRAWN WORK) that consists of open spaces and embroidered groups of cross threads and is used esp on or next to the stitching line of hems; also a stitch used to embroider the cross threads in such needlework

**¹hen** /hen/ n **1a(1)** a female domestic fowl, esp over a year old **a(2)** the female of birds other than the domestic fowl ⟨a ~ sparrow⟩ **b** a female lobster, crab, fish, or other aquatic animal **2** chiefly Scot **³DEAR** 1b – used to girls and women **3** informal a woman; specif a fussy middle-aged woman [ME, fr OE *henn;* akin to OE *hana* cock – more at CHANT]

**²hen** adj relating to or intended for women only ⟨a ~ night⟩ ⟨a ~ party⟩

**hen and chickens** n, pl hens and chickens any of several plants (e g the houseleek) that multiply by producing shoots from the base or flowers

**henbane** /ˈhenˌbayn/ n a poisonous foul-smelling African and Eurasian plant (*Hyoscyamus niger*) of the potato family having sticky hairy toothed leaves and yellowish-brown flowers, and yielding the drugs HYOSCYAMINE and HYOSCINE [fr its containing a poison fatal to fowls]

**hence** /hens/ adv **1** from this time; later than now ⟨three days ~⟩ **2** because of this preceding fact or premise; therefore ⟨born at Christmas; ~ the name Noel⟩ **3** from this source or origin **4** formal from here; away ⟨go ~⟩ – sometimes + from ⟨depart from ~⟩; sometimes used as a literary interjection ⟨~! Depart!⟩ **5** archaic henceforth [ME *hennes, henne*, fr OE *heonan;* akin to OHG *hinnan* away, OE *hēr* here]

*usage* The construction *from* **hence** has been long established in English ⟨we sailed from hence directly to Genoa – Joseph Addison⟩, but is today disliked by some people, who prefer to use **hence** alone.

**henceforth** /ˌhensˈfawth/ adv from this time or point on ⟨promise never to get drunk ~⟩

**henceforward** /ˌhensˈfaw·wəd/ adv henceforth

**henchman** /ˈhenchmən/ n **1a** a trusted follower; a right-hand man **b** a follower, esp political, whose support is chiefly for personal advantage **c** an unscrupulous often violent member of a gang **2** obs a squire or page to a person of high rank [ME *hengestman* groom, fr *hengest* stallion (fr OE; akin to OHG *hengist* gelding) + *man*]

**hendecasyllabic** /ˌhendekəsiˈlabik/ adj consisting of 11 syllables or composed of metrical lines of verse of 11 syllables each [L *hendecasyllabus*, fr Gk *hendeka* eleven (fr *hen-, heis* one + *deka* ten) + *syllabē* syllable – more at SAME, TEN] – **hendecasyllable** n, **hendecasyllabic** n

**hendiadys** /henˈdie·ədis/ n taking sing vb the expression of an idea by the use of two independent words connected by and (e g nice and warm) instead of by combining an independent word and a modifier (e g nicely warm) [LL *hendiadys, hendiadyoin*, modif of Gk *hen dia dyoin* one through two]

**henequen** /ˈhenikin/ n a strong yellowish or reddish hard fibre obtained from the leaves of a tropical American AGAVE plant and used esp for making ropes and twine; also a plant (*Agave fourcroydes*) that yields henequen [Sp *henequén*, prob fr Taino]

**henfish** /ˈhenˌfish/ n LUMP-SUCKER (type of marine fish)

**henge** /henj/ n a ritual monument of late Neolithic or BRONZE AGE date found only in the British Isles, consisting of a circular area defined by a ditch and exterior bank and frequently including a ring of upright stones [back-formation fr *Stonehenge*, a prehistoric stone monument near Salisbury in England]

**hen harrier** n a common Eurasian hawk (*Circus cyaneus*)

**¹henna** /ˈhenə/ n **1** an African and Eurasian tropical shrub or small tree (*Lawsonia inermis* of the family Lythraceae, the henna family) that bears large branched clusters of fragrant white flowers **2** a reddish-brown dye obtained from the leaves of the henna plant and used esp on hair [Ar *ḥinnā*]

**²henna** vt hennas; hennaing; hennaed to dye or tint (e g hair) with henna

**hennery** /ˈhenəri/ n a poultry farm; also an enclosure for poultry

**henotheism** /ˈhenoh·thiˌiz(ə)m/ n the worship of one god without denying the existence of other gods [Ger *henotheismus*, fr Gk *hen-, heis* one + *theos* god] – **henotheist** n, **henotheistic** adj

**henpecked** /ˈhenˌpekt/ adj cowed or persistently nagged by a wife or female companion – **henpeck** vt

**henry** /'henri/ *n, pl* **henrys, henries** the SI unit of electrical INDUCTANCE equal to the SELF-INDUCTANCE of a closed circuit in which the variation in current of one amp per second results in an induced ELECTROMOTIVE FORCE (force driving an electric current round a circuit) of one volt [Joseph *Henry* † 1878 US physicist]

**hent** /hent/ *vt, archaic* to seize [ME *henten*, fr OE *hentan;* akin to OE *huntian* to hunt, ON *henda* to grasp]

**hen-'toed** *adj* pigeon-toed

**hep** /hep/ *adj* **-pp-** *informal* hip – no longer in vogue

**heparin** /'hepərin/ *n* a POLYSACCHARIDE (complex sugar) acid that is found esp in liver, that prolongs the clotting time of blood when injected, and that is used medically, esp in the prevention and treatment of THROMBOSIS (blocking of blood vessels by blood clots) [ISV, fr Gk *hēpar* liver] – **heparinize** *vt*

**hepat-, hepato-** *comb form* **1** liver ⟨hepat*oma*⟩ ⟨hepat*otoxic*⟩ ⟨hepat*ectomy*⟩ **2** hepatic and ⟨hepat*obiliary*⟩ [L, fr Gk *hēpat-, hēpato-*, fr *hēpat-, hēpar*]

**hepatectomy** /ˌhepə'tektəmi/ *n* surgical removal of (part of) the liver – **hepatectomize** *vt*

¹**hepatic** /hi'patik/ *adj* of or resembling the liver [L *hepaticus*, fr Gk *hēpatikos*, fr *hēpat-, hēpar;* akin to L *jecur* liver]

²**hepatic** *n* LIVERWORT (type of simple plant)

**hepatica** /hi'patikə/ *n* any of a genus (*Hepatica*) of plants of the buttercup family that have lobed leaves and delicate flowers [NL, genus name, fr ML, liverwort, fr L, fem of *hepaticus* (cf LIVERWORT)]

**hepatitis** /ˌhepə'tietəs/ *n, pl* **hepatitides** /ˌhepə'titideez/ (a condition marked by) inflammation of the liver: e g a INFECTIOUS HEPATITIS **b** SERUM HEPATITIS [NL]

**hepatocellular** /ˌhepətoh'selyoolə, hiˌpatoh-/ *adj* of or involving liver cells ⟨~ *jaundice*⟩

**hepatocyte** /hi'patəsiet, 'hepətəˌsiet/ *n* a cell of the liver; *specif* one forming part of the distinctive functional tissue of the liver and specialized to carry out various chemical activities

**hepatoma** /ˌhepə'tohmə/ *n* a usu cancerous tumour of the liver [NL]

**hepatopancreas** /ˌhepətoh'pangkriəs, hiˌpatə-/ *n* a glandular structure in many INVERTEBRATE animals (e g crabs, lobsters, and shrimps) that combines the digestive functions of the liver and pancreas of VERTEBRATE animals

**hepatopathy** /ˌhepə'topəthi/ *n* an abnormal or diseased state of the liver

**hepatotoxic** /ˌhepətoh'toksik, hiˌpatoh-/ *adj* capable of causing injury to the liver ⟨~ *drugs*⟩ – **hepatotoxicity** *n*

**hepatotoxin** /ˌhepətoh'toksin, hiˌpatoh-/ *n* a TOXIN (poisonous substance) that is capable of causing injury to the liver

**hepcat** /'hepˌkat/ *n, informal* a hipster – no longer in vogue

¹**Hepplewhite** /'hep(ə)lˌwiet/ *adj* of or being a late 18th-century English furniture style characterized by lightness, elegance, and graceful curves [George *Hepplewhite* †1786 E cabinetmaker]

²**Hepplewhite** *n* a piece of furniture made by or in the style of Hepplewhite

**hepta-, hept-** *comb form* **1** seven ⟨hepta*meter*⟩ **2** containing seven atoms, groups, or chemical equivalents in the molecular structure ⟨hept*ane*⟩ [Gk, fr *hepta* – more at SEVEN]

**heptachlor** /'heptəˌklaw/ *n* a chlorine-containing pesticide, $C_{10}H_5Cl_7$, which remains effective over a considerable period of time [*hepta-* + *chlor*ine]

**heptad** /'heptad/ *n* a group or series of seven [Gk *heptad-, heptas*, fr *hepta*]

**heptagon** /'heptəgən/ *n* a two-dimensional geometric figure having seven sides; *esp* one that is REGULAR, having seven equal sides and angles [Gk *heptagōnos* heptagonal, fr *hepta* + *gōnia* angle – more at -GON] – **heptagonal** *adj*

**heptameter** /hep'tamitə/ *n* a line of verse consisting of seven metrical FEET (units of rhythm)

**heptane** /'heptayn/ *n* an inflammable liquid, $CH_3(CH_2)_5CH_3$, that is a member of the ALKANE series of organic chemical compounds, is obtained from petroleum, and is used esp as a solvent and in determining OCTANE NUMBERS (measure of quality of fuels)

**heptarchy** /'hepˌtahki/ *n* **1** government by seven rulers; *specif* a supposed confederacy of seven Anglo-Saxon kingdoms of the 7th and 8th centuries **2** a country or state divided into seven regions

**Heptateuch** /'heptəˌtyoohk/ *n* the first seven books of the OLD TESTAMENT [LL *heptateuchos*, fr Gk, fr *hepta* + *teuchos* book]

**heptathlon** /hep'tathlən/ *n* a women's athletic contest in which all contestants compete in the 100 metres hurdles, shot put, javelin, high jump, long jump, 200 metres sprint, and 800 metres race [Gk *hepta* + *athlon* contest]

**heptose** /'heptohz, -ohs/ *n* a MONOSACCHARIDE (simple sugar), $C_7H_{14}O_7$, containing seven carbon atoms in the molecule

¹**her** /hə, ə; *strong* huh/ *adj* of her or herself, esp as possessor ⟨~ *house*⟩ ⟨~ *fuselage*⟩, agent ⟨~ *research*⟩, or object of an action ⟨~ *rescue*⟩ – used in titles of females ⟨~ *Majesty*⟩ [ME *hire*, fr OE *hiere*, gen of *hēo* she – more at HE]

²**her** *pron, objective case of* SHE – compare phrases at ME 1 [ME *hire*, fr OE *hiere*, dat of *hēo*]

   **usage 1** The spelling of **hers** meaning "the one belonging to her" as △ **her's** is a common confusion ⟨*the house became* **hers** (not △ **her's**)⟩. **2** *As she, than she* are preferable in formal writing to *as her, than her*. See ⁴AS, ²THAN, ME

¹**herald** /'herəld/ *n* **1a** an officer who officiated at tournaments in medieval times **b** an officer acting as official messenger between leaders, esp in war **c** an OFFICER OF ARMS (officer responsible for devising coats of arms) of intermediate rank; *specif* one ranking above a PURSUIVANT and below a KING OF ARMS **2** an official crier or messenger **3a** a harbinger, forerunner **b** somebody who or something that conveys news or proclaims; an announcer ⟨*it was the lark, the* ~ *of the morn* – Shak⟩ [ME, fr MF *hiraut*, fr an (assumed) Gmc compound whose components are akin to OHG *heri* army and OHG *waltan* to rule – more at HARRY, WIELD]

²**herald** *vt* **1** to give notice of; announce **2** to greet, esp with enthusiasm; hail

**heraldic** /hi'raldik/ *adj* of heralds or heraldry – **heraldically** *adv*

**heraldry** /'herəldri/ *n* **1** the system, originating in medieval times, of identifying individuals by hereditary insignia; *also* the practice of granting, classifying, and creating these **2** the study of the history, display, and description of heraldry and heraldic insignia **3** pageantry

**herb** /huhb/ *n* **1** a seed-producing plant that does not develop persistent woody tissue but dies down at the end of a growing season **2** a plant (e g parsley, thyme, or mint) or plant part valued for its medicinal, savoury, or aromatic qualities ⟨*cultivated her* ~ *garden*⟩ [ME *herbe*, fr OF, fr L *herba* grass, herb] – **herblike** *adj*, **herby** *adj*

**herbaceous** /huh'bayshəs/ *adj* **1a** of, being, or having the characteristics of a herb **b** *of a stem* having little or no woody tissue and persisting usu only for a single growing season **2** *esp of a petal or a sepal* having the texture, colour, or appearance of a leaf

**herbaceous border** *n* a permanent flower border of hardy herbaceous plants

**herbage** /'huhbij/ *n* **1** herbaceous vegetation (e g grass), esp when used for grazing **2** the succulent parts of herbaceous plants

¹**herbal** /'huhbl/ *n* a book about plants, esp with reference to their medicinal properties

²**herbal** *adj* (made) of herbs ⟨~ *tea*⟩

**herbalist** /'huhblˌist/ *n* **1** one who collects or grows herbs **2** HERB DOCTOR

**herbarium** /huh'beəri·əm/ *n, pl* **herbaria** /-riə/ a collection of dried plant specimens, usu mounted and systematically arranged for reference; *also* the place where such a collection is housed [LL, fr L *herba* + *-arium* -ary]

**herb Christopher** /'kristəfə/ *n* BANEBERRY 1 (plant of the buttercup family) [trans of ML *herba Christophori*, fr St *Christopher*, 3rd-c Christian martyr]

**herb doctor** *n* one who practises healing by the use of herbal remedies

**herbicide** /'huhbiˌsied/ *n* a chemical used to destroy or inhibit plant growth [L *herba* + ISV *-cide*] – **herbicidal** *adj*, **herbicidally** *adv*

**herbivore** /'huhbivaw/ *n* a plant-eating animal [NL *Herbivora*, group of mammals, fr neut pl of *herbivorus* feeding on plants, fr L *herba* + *-vorus* -vorous] – **herbivorous** *adj*, **herbivorously** *adv*

**herb Robert** /'robət/ *n* a very common geranium (*Geranium robertianum*) with small reddish-purple flowers [trans of ML *herba Roberti*, prob fr *Robertus* (St Robert) †1067 Fr ecclesiastic]

**herculean** /ˌhuhkyoo'lee·ən/ *adj, often cap* of extraordinary strength, size, or difficulty ⟨*a* ~ *task*⟩ [*Hercules* (Gk *Hēraklēs*), mythical Gk hero famed for his strength & his performance of twelve great tasks]

**Hercules** /'huhkyooleez/ n a very strong and usu muscular man

**Hercules beetle** /'huhkyooleez/ n a very large S American beetle (*Dynastes hercules*)

¹**herd** /huhd/ n taking sing or pl vb 1 a number of animals of one kind kept together or living as a group 2a chiefly derog a group of people usu having a common bond (the ~ instinct) b derog the masses (the common ~) [ME, fr OE heord; akin to OHG herta herd, Gk korthys heap] – **herdlike** adj

²**herd** vi to assemble or move in a herd or group ~ vt 1 to keep or move (animals) together 2 to gather, lead, or drive as if in a herd (~ed his pupils into the hall) – **herder** n

**herdsman** /-mən/ n a manager, breeder, or tender of livestock

¹**here** /hiə/ adv 1 in or at this place (turn ~) – often used interjectionally, esp in answering a roll call 2 at or in this point or particular (~ we agree) 3 to this place or position (come ~) 4 – used when introducing, offering, or drawing attention (~ he comes) (~ is the news) (~, take it) 5 – used interjectionally to attract attention (~, what's all this?) [ME, fr OE hēr; akin to OHG hier here, OE hē he] – **here and there** 1 in one place and another 2 FROM TIME TO TIME – **here goes** – used to express resolution when beginning a difficult task or action – **here's to** – used when drinking a toast (here's to your future happiness) – **here, there, and everywhere** scattered about randomly – **here we go again** the same events, actions, words, etc are being repeated – **here you are** 1 here is what you wanted (give me the paper. Here you are) 2 you have arrived (here you are at last) – **neither here nor there** of no consequence; irrelevant

*usage* Before a plural it should correctly be here *are*, although here *is* is common in spoken English today (here's *some more black-berries*).

²**here** adj 1 – used for emphasis, esp after a word such as this, that, or a possessive (this book ~) (ask my son ~) 2 substandard – used for emphasis between this or these and the following noun (this ~ book)

³**here** n this place or point (full up to ~)

**hereabouts** /'hiərə,bowts/, chiefly NAm **hereabout** /,hiərə'bowt/ adv in this vicinity

¹**hereafter** /-'ahftə/ adv 1 after this 2 in some future time or state

²**hereafter** n, often cap 1 the future 2 an existence beyond earthly life

³**hereafter** adj, archaic future

**here and now** n the immediate present time (lived in the ~ without regard for the future)

**hereaway** /'hiərəway/, **hereaways** /-wayz/ adv, dial hereabouts

**hereby** /hiə'bie, 'hiə-/ adv by this means or pronouncement (I ~ declare her elected)

**hereditable** /hə'reditəbl/ adj heritable [MF, fr LL hereditare]

**hereditament** /,heri'ditəmənt/ n, law property that can be inherited [ML hereditamentum, fr LL hereditare to inherit, fr L hered-, heres]

**hereditary** /hi'redit(ə)ri/ adj 1a genetically transmitted or transmissible from parent to offspring b characteristic of or fostered by one's predecessors; ancestral (~ pride) 2 law 2a received or passing by inheritance or required to pass by in-heritance or by reason of birth b having title or possession through inheritance or by reason of birth (~ peer) 3 tradi-tional (~ enemy) 4 of inheritance or heredity – **hereditarily** adv

**heredity** /hi'rediti/ n 1 the sum of the qualities and poten-tialities genetically derived from one's ancestors 2 the trans-mission of qualities from ancestor to descendant through a mechanism lying primarily in the CHROMOSOMES (strands of gene-carrying material) of the GERM CELLS (reproductive cells) [MF heredité, fr L hereditat-, hereditas, fr hered-, heres heir – more at HEIR]

**Hereford** /'herifəd/ n (any of) an English breed of hardy red beef cattle with white faces and markings [Hereford, Hereford-shire, former county (now incorporated in Hereford and Worcester) of England]

**herein** /hiə'rin/ adv, formal in this

**hereinabove** /,hiərinə'buv/ adv, formal in the preceding part of this writing or document

**hereinafter** /,hiərin'ahftə/ adv, formal in the following part of this writing or document

**hereinbefore** /,hiərinbi'faw/ adv, formal in the preceding part of this writing or document

**hereinbelow** /,hiərinbi'loh/ adv, formal at a subsequent point in this writing or document

**hereof** /hiə'rov/ adv, formal of this

**hereon** /hiə'ron/ adv, formal on this

**Herero** /'hiərəroh, hə'riəroh/ n, pl **Hereros,** esp collectively **Herero** a member of a BANTU people of the central part of Namibia

**heresiarch** /hi'reezi,ahk/ n an originator or chief advocate of a heresy [LL haeresiarcha, fr LGk hairesiarchēs, fr hairesis + Gk -archēs -arch]

**heresy** /'herəsi/ n 1a adherence to a religious opinion contrary to church dogma; esp denial of a revealed truth by a baptized member of the Roman Catholic church b an opinion or doc-trine contrary to church dogma 2 (adherence to) an opinion or doctrine contrary to generally accepted belief [ME heresie, fr OF, fr LL haeresis, fr LGk hairesis, fr Gk, act of taking, choice, sect, fr hairein to take]

**heretic** /'herətik/ n 1 à dissenter from established church dogma; esp a baptized member of the Roman Catholic church who disavows a revealed truth 2 one who dissents from an accepted belief or doctrine [ME (h)eretik, fr MF (h)eretique, fr LL haereticus, fr LGk hairetikos, fr Gk, able to choose, fr hairein]

**heretical** /hə'retikl/ also **heretic** adj 1 of or characterized by heresy 2 of or characterized by departure from accepted beliefs or standards; unorthodox – **heretically** adv, **hereticalness** n

**hereto** /hiə'tooh/ adv, formal to this matter or document

**heretofore** /,hiətooh'faw/ adv, formal up to this time; hitherto

**hereunder** /hiə'rundə/ adv, formal under or in accordance with this writing or document

**hereunto** /,hiərun'tooh/ adv, formal to this

**hereupon** /,hiərə'pon/ adv, formal 1 on this matter (if all are agreed ~) 2 immediately after this (let us ~ adjourn)

**herewith** /hiə'widh/ adv, formal 1 with this; enclosed in this 2 hereby

**heriot** /'heriət/ n a duty or tribute due under English law in medieval times to a lord on the death of a tenant [ME, fr OE heregeatwe, pl, military equipment, fr here army (akin to OHG heri army) + geatwe equipment – more at HARRY]

**heritable** /'heritəbl/ adj 1 capable of being inherited or of passing by inheritance 2 HEREDITARY 1a, 2a – **heritability** n

**heritage** /'heritij/ n 1 law property that descends to an heir 2 something transmitted by or acquired from a predecessor or predecessors; a legacy (a rich ~ of folklore) 3 a birthright (the ~ of natural freedom) [ME, fr MF, fr heriter to inherit, fr LL hereditare, fr L hered-, heres heir – more at HEIR]

**heritor** /'heritə/ n an inheritor

**herl** /huhl/ n 1 a BARB (side branch) of a feather used in tying an artificial fishing FLY (fishhook arranged to look like an insect) 2 an artificial FLY tied with a herl [ME herle]

**herm** /huhm/ n a square stone pillar surmounted by a bust or head, esp of Hermes, that is used as an ornament in classical architecture – compare TERM [L herma, hermes, fr Gk hermēs statue of Hermes, herm, fr Hermēs Hermes, god who served as herald and messenger of the gods]

**herma** /'huhmə/ n, pl **hermae** a herm

**hermaphrodite** /huh'mafrədiet/ n 1 an animal or plant having both male and female reproductive organs 2 something that is a combination of diverse elements [ME hermofrodite, fr L hermaphroditus, fr Gk hermaphroditos, fr Hermaphroditos, mythical son of Hermes and Aphrodite who became joined in body with the nymph Salmacis] – **hermaphrodite** adj, **herma-phroditism** n, **hermaphroditic** adj, **hermaphroditically** adv

**hermaphrodite brig** n a 2-masted vessel with, on its front mast, sails suspended from their midpoint and, on its rear mast, sails suspended along their front edge

**hermeneutical** /,huhmə'nyoohtikl/, **hermeneutic** adj of her-meneutics; interpretative [Gk hermēneutikos, fr hermēneuein to interpret, fr hermēneus interpreter] – **hermeneutically** adv

**hermeneutics** /,huhmə'nyoohtiks/ n taking sing or pl vb (the study of) the principles and methodology of esp Biblical inter-pretation

**hermetic** /huh'metik/ also **hermetical** adj 1 often cap of the GNOSTIC (of a cult believing that all matter is evil) and mys-tical ALCHEMICAL writings or teachings arising in the first three centuries AD and attributed to Hermes Trismegistus 2a airtight (a ~ seal) b impervious to external influences 3 often cap, formal difficult to understand; abstruse [NL her-meticus, fr Hermet-, Hermes Trismegistus (fr Gk Hermēs tri-smegistos, lit., Hermes thrice-greatest), legendary author of mystical & alchemical works; (2a) fr the belief that Hermes Trismegistus invented a magic seal to keep vessels airtight] – **hermetically** *adv*

**hermeticism** /huh'metə,siz(ə)m/ *n, often cap* (adherence to) a system of ideas based on hermetic teachings – **hermeticist** *n*

**hermetism** /'huhmə,tiz(ə)m/ *n, often cap* hermeticism – **hermetist** *n*

**hermit** /'huhmit/ *n* **1a** a person who withdraws from society and lives in solitude, often for religious reasons **b** a recluse **2** *obs* BEADSMAN (person who prays for the soul of another) [ME *eremite,* fr OF, fr LL *eremita,* fr LGk *erēmitēs,* fr Gk, adj, living in the desert, fr *erēmia* desert, fr *erēmos* lonely – more at RETINA] – **hermitic** *adj,* **hermitism** *n*

**hermitage** /'huhmitij/ *n* **1a** the dwelling of a hermit or hermits **b** a secluded residence or private retreat; a hideaway **2** a monastery
**Hermitage** *n* a full-bodied red or white Rhone valley wine [Tain-l'*Ermitage,* commune in SE France]

**hermit crab** *n* any of numerous chiefly marine crabs (families Paguridae and Parapaguridae) that have soft asymmetrical abdomens and occupy the empty shells of snails, whelks, etc

**hern** /huhn/ *n, dial* a heron

**hernia** /'huhni·ə, -nyə/ *n, pl* **hernias, herniae** /'huhni·ie/ a protrusion of an organ or part through CONNECTIVE TISSUE (supporting and packing tissue) or through a wall of the cavity (e g the abdomen) in which it is normally enclosed [L – more at YARN] – **hernial** *adj*

**herniate** /'huhniayt/ *vi* to protrude through an abnormal body opening – **herniation** *n*

**hero** /'hiəroh/ *n, pl* **heroes 1a** a mythological or legendary figure often held to be of divine descent and to have great strength or ability **b** an illustrious warrior **c** a person, esp a man, admired for noble achievements and qualities (e g courage) **2a** the principal male character in a literary or dramatic work **b** the central figure in an event or period [L *heros,* fr Gk *hērōs*] – **heroize** *vt*

**heroic** /hi'roh·ik/ *also* **heroical** /-kl/ *adj* **1** of or suitable to heroes **2a** showing or marked by courage and daring **b** grand, noble **3** of impressive size, power, or effect; large, powerful ⟨*an undertaking of* ~ *proportions*⟩ **4** OF HEROIC VERSE *synonyms* see ¹BRAVE – **heroically** *adv*

**heroic couplet** *n* two rhyming lines of verse, each of which consists of five IAMBS

**heroic metre** *n* HEROIC VERSE

**heroicomic** /hi,roh·i'komik, he-/, **heroicomical** /-kl/ *adj* comic by being ludicrously noble, bold, or elevated [Fr *héroïcomique,* fr *héroïque* heroic + *comique* comic]

**heroic poem** *n* an epic or a poem in epic style

**heroic quatrain** *n* HEROIC STANZA

**heroics** /hi'roh·iks/ *n pl* **1** HEROIC VERSE **2** extravagantly grand or heroic behaviour or language

**heroic stanza** *n* a rhymed group of four lines (QUATRAIN) in HEROIC VERSE with a rhyme scheme of *abab*

**heroic verse** *n* the verse form employed in epic poetry (e g the HEROIC COUPLET in English)

**heroin** /'heroh·in/ *n* a strongly addictive narcotic drug, $C_{21}H_{23}NO_5$, made from, but more potent than, morphine and used medically to relieve very severe pain △ heroine [fr *Heroin,* a trademark] – **heroinism** *n*

**heroine** /'heroh·in/ *n* **1a** a mythological or legendary woman having the qualities of a hero **b** a woman admired for her noble achievements and qualities, esp courage **2a** the principal female character in a literary or dramatic work **b** the central female figure in an event or period [L *heroina,* fr Gk *hērōīnē,* fem of *hērōs*]

**heroism** /'heroh,iz(ə)m/ *n* heroic conduct or qualities; *esp* extreme courage

**heron** /'herən/ *n, pl* **herons,** *esp collectively* **heron** any of various long-necked wading birds (family Ardeidae) with a long tapering bill, long thin legs, large wings, and soft plumage; *specif* a large grey Eurasian and N African heron (*Ardea cinerea*) that has a white head and neck [ME *heiroun,* fr MF *hairon,* of Gmc origin; akin to OHG *heigaro* heron, Gk *krizein* to creak, OHG *scrīan* to scream]

**heronry** /'herənri/ *n* a place where herons breed

**hero worship** *n* **1** veneration of a hero **2** foolish or excessive admiration for somebody – **hero-worship** *vt,* **hero-worshipper** *n*

**herpes** /'huhpeez/ *n* any of several inflammatory virus diseases of the skin characterized by clusters of blisters; *esp* HERPES SIMPLEX [L, fr Gk *herpēs,* fr *herpein* to creep – more at SERPENT] – **herpetic** *adj*

**herpes labialis** /,labi'ahlis, ,laybi-, -'aylis/ *n* COLD SORE [NL, lit., herpes of the lips]

**herpes simplex** /'simpleks/ *n* a virus disease marked by groups of watery blisters on the skin or MUCOUS MEMBRANES (e g of the mouth, lips, or genitals) [NL, lit., simple herpes]

**herpesvirus** /,huhpeez'vie·ərəs/ *n* any of a group of viruses that reproduce in cell nuclei and that cause herpes

**herpes zoster** /'zostə/ *n* SHINGLES (disease affecting nerves) [NL, lit., girdle herpes]

**herpet-, herpeto-** *comb form* **1** reptile; reptiles ⟨herpeto*fauna*⟩ ⟨herpeto*logy*⟩ **2** herpes ⟨herpeti*form*⟩ [Gk *herpeton,* fr neut of *herpetos* creeping, fr *herpein;* (2) L *herpet-, herpes*]

**herpetology** /,huhpi'toləji/ *n* a branch of zoology dealing with reptiles and amphibians – **herpetologist** *n,* **herpetologic, herpetological** *adj,* **herpetologically** *adv*

**Herr** /heə/ *n, pl* **Herren** /'heərən, 'herən/ – used of or to a German-speaking man as a title equivalent to *Mr* [Ger]

**herrenvolk** /'herən,folk/ *n, often cap* MASTER RACE; *specif* the German people held by Nazis to be the master race [Ger, fr *herr* lord, master + *volk* race, nation]

**herring** /'hering/ *n, pl* **herrings,** *esp collectively* **herring** a valuable food fish (*Clupea harengus*) that is abundant in the temperate and colder parts of the N Atlantic and is preserved in the adult state by smoking or salting; *broadly* any of several related fishes (family Clupeidae) [ME *hering,* fr OE *hæring;* akin to OHG *hārinc* herring]

¹**herringbone** /'hering,bohn/ *n* **1a** a pattern made up of rows of parallel lines with any two adjacent rows slanting in opposite directions **b** something, esp a twilled fabric, with a herringbone pattern **2** the ascent of a ski slope by herringboning

²**herringbone** *vt* to make a herringbone pattern on ~ *vi* to ascend a slope on skis by pointing the toes of the skis outwards and placing the weight on the inner side

**herringbone stitch** *n* a needlework stitch that forms a zigzag pattern

**herring gull** *n* a common large gull (*Larus argentatus*) of the northern hemisphere that as an adult is largely white with blue-grey back and wings, dark wing tips, and pink feet [fr its preying on shoals of herring]

**hers** /huhz/ *pron, pl* **hers** that which or the one who belongs to her – used without a following noun as a pronoun equivalent in meaning to the adjective *her;* compare phrases at MINE 2 *usage* see ²HER

**herself** /hə'self; *medially often* ə-/ *pron* **1** that identical female person or creature – compare SHE 1, ONESELF; used reflexively ⟨*she considers* ~ *lucky*⟩, for emphasis ⟨*she* ~ *did it*⟩ ⟨*Britain* ~⟩, or in absolute constructions ⟨~ *an orphan, she understood the situation*⟩ **2** her normal self ⟨*isn't quite* ~⟩ **3** *chiefly Irish & Scot* a woman of consequence; *esp* the mistress of the house

**hertz** /huhts/ *n, pl* **hertz** the SI unit of frequency equal to one CYCLE per second [Heinrich *Hertz* †1894 Ger physicist]

**hertzian wave** /'huhtsiən, -syən/ *n, often cap* an ELECTROMAGNETIC WAVE that is typically produced by the OSCILLATION (change in direction of flow) of electricity in a conductor (e g a radio antenna) and is of a length ranging from less than a millimetre to many kilometres [Heinrich *Hertz*]

**he's** /hiz, eez, iz; *strong* heez/ he is; he has

**Heshvan** /'kheshvən/ *n* – see MONTH table [Heb *Ḥeshwān*]

**hesitant** /'hezit(ə)nt/ *adj* tending to hesitate; irresolute – **hesitance, hesitancy** *n,* **hesitantly** *adv*

**hesitate** /'hezitayt/ *vi* **1** to hold back, esp in doubt or indecision **2** to be reluctant or unwilling *to* **3** to stammer, pause [L *haesitatus,* pp of *haesitare* to stick fast, hesitate, fr *haesus,* pp of *haerēre* to stick; akin to Lith *gaišti* to loiter] – **hesitater** *n,* **hesitatingly** *adv,* **hesitative** *adj,* **hesitation** *n*

**Hesperian** /hes'piəri·ən/ *adj, poetic* western [L *Hesperia,* the west, fr Gk, fr fem of *hesperios* of the evening, western, fr *hesperos* evening – more at WEST]

**hesperidin** /hes'peridin/ *n* a GLYCOSIDE (chemical compound derived from sugar), $C_{28}H_{34}O_{15}$, found in most citrus fruits and particularly in orange peel [NL *hesperidium* orange, fr L *Hesperides,* mythical nymphs guarding a garden in which golden apples grew]

**hesperidium** /,hespə'ridi·əm/ *n, pl* **hesperidia** /-diə/ *botany* a berry (e g an orange or lime) having a leathery rind and a pulp divided into segments [NL, orange]

**Hesperus** /'hespərəs/ *n* EVENING STAR [L, fr Gk *Hesperos*]

**hessian** /'hesi·ən/ *n* **1** a coarse heavy plain-weave fabric usu of jute or hemp, used esp for sacking and in furniture manufacture **2** a lightweight material resembling hessian and used chiefly in interior decoration [*Hesse*, region in SW Germany]

**Hessian boot** *n* a high boot extending to just below the knee, usu ornamented with a tassel and worn by men in the 19th century

**Hessian fly** *n* a small fly (*Mayetiola destructor*) that destroys wheat and other crops in America [fr the belief that it was brought to America by Hessian soldiers during the War of American Independence]

**hessonite** /'hesəniet/ *n* a reddish-brown garnet [Fr *essonit*, fr Gk *hēsson* inferior; fr its being less hard than the similar mineral jacinth]

**hest** /hest/ *n*, *archaic* behest [ME *hest*, *hes*, fr OE *hǣs*; akin to OE *hātan* to command – more at HIGHT]

**het** /het/ *adj*, *informal* heterosexual – used esp by homosexuals

**hetaera** /hi'tee·ərə/ *n*, *pl* **hetaerae** /hi'tee·ə,ree/, **hetaeras** any of a class of highly cultivated courtesans in ancient Greece; *broadly* : a prostitute [Gk *hetaira*, lit., companion, fem of *hetairos*]

**hetaira** /hi'tierə/ *n*, *pl* **hetairas**, **hetairai** /hi'tierie/ a hetaera

**heter-**, **hetero-** *comb form* **1** other; different; abnormal ⟨*heterophyllous*⟩ ⟨*heterotopic*⟩ **2** containing atoms of different kinds ⟨*heterocyclic*⟩ [MF or LL; MF, fr LL, fr Gk, fr *heteros*; akin to Gk *heis* one – more at SAME]

**hetero** /'hetəroh/ *n*, *pl* **heteros** *informal* a heterosexual

**heteroatom** /'hetəroh,atəm/ *n* an atom other than carbon in the ring of a heterocyclic chemical compound

**heteroautotrophic** /,hetəroh,awtoh'trohfik/ *adj*, *esp of a plant* requiring a simple ORGANIC (derived from plants or animals) source of carbon but utilizing an INORGANIC source of nitrogen for METABOLISM (life-supporting chemical processes)

**heterocaryon** /,hetəroh'karion, -ən/ *n* HETEROKARYON (cell containing genetically unlike nuclei)

**heterocaryosis** /,hetəroh,kari'ohsis/ *n* HETEROKARYOSIS (condition of having cells containing genetically unlike nuclei)

**heterocercal** /,hetəroh'suhkl/ *adj* **1** *of the tail fin of a fish* having the upper lobe larger than the lower with the end of the SPINAL COLUMN prolonged and somewhat upturned in the upper lobe – compare HOMOCERCAL **2** of or having a heterocercal tail fin

**heterochromatic** /-kroh'matik/ *adj* **1** of or having different colours **2** *physics* (consisting) of various wavelengths or frequencies **3** of heterochromatin – **heterochromatism** *n*

**heterochromatin** /-'krohmətin/ *n* CHROMATIN (substance in the nucleus of a cell) that stains densely with biological dyes, appears as nodules in or along CHROMOSOMES (strands of gene-carrying material), and contains relatively few genes – compare EUCHROMATIN

**heteroclite** /-,kliet/ *adj* **1** *of a word* irregular in inflection; *esp*, *of a noun* irregular in DECLENSION (addition of word parts for different grammatical cases) **2** *formal* deviating from common forms or rules [MF or LL; MF, fr LL *heteroclitus*, fr Gk *heteroklitos*, fr *heter-* + *klinein* to lean, inflect – more at LEAN] – **heteroclite** *n*

**heterocyclic** /-'siklik, -'sie-/ *adj* of, characterized by, or being a ring composed of atoms of more than one kind [ISV] – **heterocyclic** *n*, **heterocycle** *n*

**heterocyst** /'het(ə)roh,sist/ *n* a large transparent thick-walled cell that resembles a spore and occurs at intervals along the FILAMENT (strandlike chain of cells) in some BLUE-GREEN ALGAE – **heterocystous** *adj*

**heterodont** /'het(ə)roh,dont/ *adj* having or being teeth (e g those of most mammals) that are differentiated into several forms (e g incisors, canines, and molars) – compare HOMODONT [ISV]

**heterodox** /-,doks/ *adj* **1** contrary to or different from established doctrines or opinions, esp in matters of religion ⟨*a ~ sermon*⟩ **2** holding unorthodox opinions or doctrines [LL *heterodoxus*, fr Gk *heterodoxos*, fr *heter-* + *doxa* opinion – more at DOXOLOGY] – **heterodoxy** *n*

¹**heterodyne** /'het(ə)rohdien, 'het(ə)rə-/ *adj* of the combination, in a radio receiver, of an incoming radio signal and an internally generated signal of a similar frequency to produce a lower audible frequency or BEAT

²**heterodyne** *vt* to combine (a wave) with a wave of a different frequency so that a BEAT is produced

³**heterodyne** *n* a radio receiver based upon the heterodyne principle

**heteroecious**, **heterecious** /,hetə'reeshəs/ *adj*, *of a parasite* passing through the different stages in the LIFE CYCLE on or in

different and often unrelated hosts ⟨*~ insects*⟩ – compare AUTOECIOUS [*heter-* + Gk *oikia* house – more at VICINITY] – **heteroecism** *n*

**heterogamete** /,het(ə)roh'gameet/ *n* either of a pair of GAMETES (reproductive cells) that differ in form, size, or behaviour and occur typically as large nonmoving female gametes (e g eggs) and small moving male gametes (e g sperm cells) – compare ISOGAMETE [ISV]

**heterogametic** /-gə'metik/ *adj* forming two kinds of reproductive cells of which one produces male offspring and the other female offspring ⟨*the human male is ~*⟩

**heterogamy** /,hetə'rogəmi/ *n* **1** sexual reproduction involving fusion of unlike GAMETES (reproductive cells) often differing in size, structure, and physiology **2** the condition of reproducing by heterogamy – compare ANISOGAMY, ISOGAMY – **heterogamous** *adj*

**heterogeneous** /,hetərə'jeeniəs, -nyəs/ *adj* consisting of dissimilar ingredients or constituents; mixed, disparate [ML *heterogeneus*, *heterogenus*, fr Gk *heterogenēs*, fr *heter-* + *genos* kind – more at KIN] – **heterogeneously** *adv*, **heterogeneousness**, **heterogeneity** *n*

**heterogenesis** /-'jenəsis/ *n* **1** ABIOGENESIS (supposed creation of living things from lifeless matter) **2** ALTERNATION OF GENERATIONS (cycle of reproduction alternating between sexual and asexual methods) [NL] – **heterogenetic** *adj*

**heterogenous** /,hetə'rojinəs/ *adj* originating in an outside source; *esp* derived from another species ⟨*a ~ skin graft*⟩

**heterogony** /,hetə'rogəni/ *n* ALTERNATION OF GENERATIONS (cycle of reproduction alternating between sexual and asexual methods)

**heterograft** /'hetəroh,grahft/ *n* a graft of tissue taken from a donor of one species and grafted into a recipient of another species – compare HOMOGRAFT

**heterokaryon** *also* **heterocaryon** /,hetəroh'karion, -ən/ *n* a cell (e g one occurring naturally in the rootlike part of a fungus or artificially produced in culture) that contains two or more genetically unlike nuclei [NL, fr *heter-* + *karyon*, *caryon* nucleus, fr Gk *karyon* nut, kernel – more at CAREEN] – **heterokaryotic** *adj*

**heterokaryosis** *also* **heterocaryosis** /,hetəroh,kari'ohsis/ *n* the condition of having cells that are heterokaryons [NL]

**heterologous** /,hetə'roləgəs/ *adj* derived from a different species ⟨*~ transplants*⟩ [*heter-* + *-logous* (as in *homologous*)] – **heterologously** *adv*

**heterolysis** /,hetə'roləsis/ *n* the decomposition of a compound into two particles or IONS with opposite electrical charges [NL] – **heterolytic** *adj*

**heteromorphic** /,hetəroh'mawfik/, **heteromorphous** /-fəs/ *adj* **1** deviating from the usual form **2** exhibiting diversity of form or forms ⟨*~ pairs of chromosomes*⟩ ⟨*~ alternation of generations*⟩ [ISV] – **heteromorphism** *n*

**heteronomy** /,hetə'ronəmi/ *n* subjection to the law or domination of another; *esp* a lack of moral freedom or self-determination – compare AUTONOMY [*heter-* + *-nomy* (as in *autonomy*)] – **heteronomous** *adj*

**heteronym** /'hetəroh,nim/ *n* any of two or more words spelt alike but different in meaning and pronunciation (e g *sow* the noun and *sow* the verb) [back-formation fr *heteronymous*, fr LGk *heterōnymos* having different names, fr Gk *hetero-* + *onyma, onoma* name] – **heteronymous** *adj*

**heterophyllous** /,hetəroh'filəs/ *adj* having leaves of more than one form on the same plant or stem – **heterophylly** *n*

**heterophyte** /'het(ə)rə,fiet/ *n* a plant (e g a parasite or SAPROPHYTE) that is HETEROTROPHIC (requiring complex chemical compounds as an energy source) – **heterophytic** *adj*

**heteroploid** /'het(ə)rə,ployd/ *adj* ANEUPLOID (having either more or less gene-carrying material than normal) [ISV] – **heteroploid** *n*, **heteroploidy** *n*

**heteropolar** /,hetəroh'pohlə/ *adj*, *of a molecule, chemical compound or crystal* POLAR 5 (having opposite electrical charges) [ISV] – **heteropolarity** *n*

**heteropolymer** /,hetəroh'polimə/ *n* a POLYMER (complex chemical compound) (e g synthetic rubber) that is composed of a series of units of two or more substances usu of high MOLECULAR WEIGHT

**heteropteran** /,hetə'roptərən/ *n* a heteropterous insect

**heteropterous** /,hetə'roptərəs/ *adj* of or being a TRUE BUG (suborder Heteroptera) [deriv of Gk *heter-* + *pteron* wing – more at FEATHER]

¹**heterosexual** /,het(ə)rə'seksyooəl, -sh(ə)l/ *adj* **1** of, marked by,

or exhibiting heterosexuality **2** of or relating to different sexes [ISV] – **heterosexually** *adv*

²**heterosexual** *n* a heterosexual individual

**heterosexuality** /ˌhet(ə)rəˌseksyooˈaləti, -ˌsekshoo-/ *n* sexual preference for or sexual activity with people of the opposite sex – compare HOMOSEXUALITY

**heterosis** /ˌhetəˈrohsis/ *n* a marked vigour or capacity for growth often shown by crossbred animals or plants [NL] – **heterotic** *adj*

**heterospory** /ˈhetərohˌspawri, ˌhetəˈrospəri/ *n* **1** the production of asexual spores of more than one kind **2** the production (eg in ferns and seed plants) of two different forms of sexual spores (eg MICROSPORES and MEGASPORES) – **heterosporous** *adj*

**heterothallic** /ˌhetərohˈthalik/ *adj* **1** *esp of* (*a spore that produces*) *an alga or fungus* having two or more genetically incompatible but structurally similar phases that function as separate sexes or strains **2** DIOECIOUS (having separate male and female forms) [*heter-* + Gk *thallein* to sprout, grow – more at THALLUS] – **heterothallism** *n*

**heterotopic** /ˌhetərohˈtopik/ *adj* occurring in an abnormal place ⟨~ *bone formation*⟩ [*heter-* + Gk *topos* place – more at TOPIC]

**heterotrophic** /ˌhetərohˈtrofik, -ˈtrohfik/ *adj* requiring complex ORGANIC (derived from plant or animal material) nitrogen-containing chemical compounds as a source of energy and food for METABOLISM (life-supporting chemical processes) – compare AUTOTROPHIC – **heterotroph** *n*, **heterotrophically** *adv*

**heterozygote** /-ˈziegoht, -ˈzigoht/ *n* an animal, plant, or cell in which the members of at least one pair of genes that code for a particular inheritable characteristic are different versions of each other – compare HOMOZYGOTE – **heterozygosis** *n*, **heterozygosity** *n*, **heterozygous** *adj*

**heth** /het, khet/ *n* the 8th letter of the Hebrew alphabet [Heb *ḥēth*]

**hetman** /ˈhetmən/ *n*, *pl* **hetmans** a cossack leader [Pol, commander in chief, fr Ger *hauptmann* headman]

**het up** /het/ *adj*, *informal* highly excited, upset [*het*, dial. past of *heat*]

**heulandite** /ˈhyoohlənˌdiet/ *n* a ZEOLITE (type of mineral) consisting essentially of a SILICATE of sodium, aluminium, and calcium and occurring as white, red, grey, or brown crystals [Henry *Heuland*, 19th-c E mineral collector]

¹**heuristic** /ˌhyoohˈristik, hoy-/ *adj* **1** furthering investigation but otherwise unproved or unjustified ⟨*a* ~ *assumption*⟩ **2** of problem-solving techniques that proceed by trial and error ⟨*a* ~ *computer program*⟩ [Ger *heuristisch*, fr NL *heuristicus*, fr Gk *heuriskein* to discover; akin to OIr *fūar* I have found] – **heuristically** *adv*

²**heuristic** *n* **1** the study or practice of heuristic method **2** a heuristic method or procedure

**hew** /hyooh/ *vb* **hewed; hewed, hewn** /hyoohn/ *vt* **1** to strike, chop, or esp fell with blows of a heavy cutting instrument ⟨~ *off a branch*⟩ ⟨~ed *down the tree*⟩ **2** to give form or shape to (as if) with heavy cutting blows – often + *out* ⟨*she* ~ed *out a career for herself*⟩ ~ *vi* to make cutting blows [ME *hewen*, fr OE *hēawan;* akin to OHG *houwan* to hew, L *cudere* to beat] – **hewer** *n*

¹**hex** /heks/ *vb*, *chiefly NAm vi* to practise witchcraft ~ *vt* to affect as if by an evil spell; jinx [PaG *hexe*, fr Ger *hexen*, fr *hexe* witch] – **hexer** *n*

²**hex** *n*, *chiefly NAm* **1** a spell, jinx **2** a witch

**hexa-, hex-** *comb form* **1** six ⟨*hexamerous*⟩ **2** containing six atoms, groups, or chemical equivalents in the molecular structure ⟨*hexane*⟩ ⟨*hexavalent*⟩ [Gk, fr *hex* six – more at SIX]

**hexachloroethane** /ˌheksəˌklawrohˈethayn/, **hexachloroethane** /ˌheksəklawˈrethayn/ *n* a poisonous chemical compound, $C_2CL_6$, used esp in smoke bombs and in the control of parasitic LIVER FLUKES in ruminant animals (eg sheep) [ISV]

**hexachord** /ˈheksəˌkawd/ *n*, *music* six consecutive notes used, from the 11th to the 17th century, as a unit for the purposes of singing at sight [*hexa-* + Gk *chordē* string – more at YARN]

**hexad** /ˈheksad/ *n* a group or series of six [LL *hexad-, hexas*, fr Gk, fr *hex*] – **hexadic** *adj*

**hexade** /ˈheksayd/ *n* a hexad

**hexadecimal** /ˌheksəˈdesiml/ *adj* of or being a number system with a base of 16

**hexagon** /ˈheksəgən/ *n* a two-dimensional geometric figure having six sides; *esp* one that is REGULAR, having six equal

sides and angles [Gk *hexagōnon*, neut of *hexagōnos* hexagonal, fr *hexa-* + *gōnia* angle – more at -GON]

**hexagonal** /hekˈsagənl/ *adj* **1** having six angles and six sides **2** having a hexagon as section or base ⟨~ *prism*⟩ **3** relating to or being a crystal system characterized by three equal axes intersecting at angles of 60 degrees and a vertical axis of variable length at right angles – **hexagonally** *adv*

**hexagram** /ˈheksəgram/ *n* a star-shaped figure formed by drawing an equal-sided triangle on each side of a regular hexagon [ISV]

**hexahedron** /-ˈheedrən/ *n, pl* **hexahedrons** *also* **hexahedra** /-drə/ a three-dimensional geometric figure having six faces; *esp* one that is REGULAR (having six equal square faces); a cube [LL, fr Gk *hexaedron*, fr neut of *hexaedros* of six surfaces, fr *hexa-* + *hedra* seat, base – more at SIT]

**hexahydrate** /ˌheksəˈhiedrayt/ *n* a chemical compound containing six molecules of water – **hexahydrated** *adj*

**hexameter** /hekˈsamitə/ *n* a line of verse consisting of six metrical FEET (units of rhythm) [L, fr Gk *hexametron*, fr neut of *hexametros* having six measures, fr *hexa-* + *metron* measure – more at MEASURE]

**hexamethylenetetramine** /ˌheksəˌmethəleenˈtetrəmeen/ *n* a chemical compound, $C_6H_{12}N_4$, used esp as an accelerator in the process (VULCANIZATION) in which rubber is treated to give it strength, elasticity, etc, as an absorbent for PHOSGENE gas, and as a DIURETIC to control the production of urine [ISV]

**hexane** /ˈheksayn/ *n* a readily vaporizing liquid, $C_6H_{14}$, that is a member of the ALKANE series of organic chemical compounds and is found in petroleum [ISV]

**hexanoic acid** /ˌheksəˈnoh·ik/ *n* CAPROIC ACID [ISV *hexane* + *-oic*]

**hexaploid** /ˈheksəˌployd/ *adj* having or being six times the basic (HAPLOID) number of CHROMOSOMES (strands of gene-carrying material) [ISV] – **hexaploid** *n*, **hexaploidy** *n*

¹**hexapod** /ˈheksəˌpod/ *n* an insect [Gk *hexapod-, hexapous* having six feet, fr *hexa-* + *pod-, pous* foot – more at FOOT]

²**hexapod** *adj* **1** six-footed **2** of or relating to insects

**hexapody** /hekˈsapədi/ *n* a line of verse consisting of six FEET (units of rhythm) [*hex-* + *-pody* (as in *dipody*)]

**hexastich** /ˈheksəˌstik/ *n* a group, stanza, or poem of six lines [ML *hexastichon*, deriv of Gk *hexa-* + *stichos* row, line] – **hexastichic** *adj*

**hexastichon** /hekˈsastikon/ *n* a hexastich

**Hexateuch** /ˈheksəˌtyoohk/ *n* the first six books of the OLD TESTAMENT [*hexa-* + Gk *teuchos* book]

**hexavalent** /hekˈsavələnt, ˌheksəˈvaylənt/ *n, chemistry* having a VALENCY of six [ISV]

**hexobarbital** /ˌheksəˈbahbitl/ *n* a BARBITURATE drug, $C_{12}H_{16}N_2O_3$, used as a sedative and hypnotic and in the form of its soluble sodium SALT as a general anaesthetic [*hexo-* (fr *hexa-*) + *barbital*]

**hexokinase** /ˌheksohˈkienayz, -ays/ *n* any of a group of ENZYMES that accelerate the chemical reactions occurring in cells whereby phosphorus is added by PHOSPHORYLATION to hexoses (eg in the formation of glucose-6-phosphate from glucose and ATP) during the chemical processing of carbohydrates [*hexose* + *kinase*]

**hexosan** /ˈheksohˌsan/ *n* a POLYSACCHARIDE (complex sugar) yielding only hexoses when broken down

**hexose** /ˈheksohs, -sohz/ *n* a MONOSACCHARIDE (simple sugar) (eg glucose) containing six carbon atoms in the molecule [ISV]

**hexyl** /ˈheks(ə)l/ *n* a chemical group, $C_6H_{13}$, derived from a HEXANE (chemical compound occurring in petroleum) [ISV]

¹**hey** /hay/ *interj* – used esp to call attention or to express inquiry, surprise, or exultation [ME]

²**hey** *n* ³HAY (dance)

**heyday** /ˈhayˌday/ *n* the period of one's greatest strength, vigour, or prosperity [arch. *heyday*, interj expressing joy or exultation, fr earlier *heyda*, alter. of ¹*hey*]

**hey presto** /ˌhay ˈprestoh/ *interj* – used as an expression of triumph or satisfaction on completing or demonstrating something; *esp* used by conjurers on revealing the outcome of a trick

**hi** /hie/ *interj* – used esp to attract attention or as a greeting [ME *hy*]

**hiatal** /hieˈaytl/ *adj* hiatus

¹**hiatus** /hieˈaytəs/ *n* **1a** a break, gap **b** a gap or passage in an anatomical part or organ **2a** a lapse in continuity **b** the occurrence of two vowel sounds together without a pause or inter-

vening consonantal sound [L, fr *hiatus,* pp of *hiare* to yawn – more at YAWN]

²**hiatus** *adj* **1** involving a hiatus **2** *of a hernia* having a part that protrudes through the hiatus for the OESOPHAGUS (tube carrying food from mouth to stomach) in the diaphragm

**hibachi** /hi'bahchi, hi'bachi/ *n, NAm* a charcoal brazier [Jap, fr *hi* fire + *hachi* bowl]

**hibernaculum** /ˌhiebə'nakyooləm/ *n, pl* **hibernacula** /-lə/ a shelter occupied during the winter by a dormant animal (e g an insect) [NL, fr L, winter residence, fr *hibernare*]

**hibernal** /hie'buhnl/ *adj, formal* of or occurring in winter; wintry

**hibernate** /'hiebənayt/ *vi* **1** *of an animal* to pass the winter in a torpid or resting state – compare AESTIVATE **2** to be or become inactive or dormant [L *hibernatus,* pp of *hibernare* to pass the winter, fr *hibernus* of winter; akin to L *hiems* winter, Gk *cheimōn*] – **hibernator** *n,* **hibernation** *n*

¹**Hibernian** /hie'buhniən, -nyən/ *adj, chiefly poetic* (characteristic) of Ireland or the Irish [L *Hibernia* Ireland]

²**Hibernian** *n, chiefly poetic* a native or inhabitant of Ireland

**Hibernicism** /hie'buhnisiz(ə)m/ *n* a characteristic expression, idiom, etc of Irish English [ML *Hibernicus* Irish, fr L *Hibernia*]

**hibiscus** /hie'biskəs, hi-/ *n* any of a genus (*Hibiscus*) of non-woody plants, shrubs, or small trees of the hollyhock family with toothed leaves and large showy flowers [NL, genus name, fr L, marshmallow]

¹**hiccup** *also* **hiccough** /'hikup/ *n* **1** a spasmodic involuntary inhalation of air followed by closure of the GLOTTIS (opening between the throat and windpipe) and a sudden sharp sound **2 hiccups** *pl but taking sing or pl vb, also* **hiccup** an attack of hiccuping **3** *chiefly Br informal* a brief interruption or breakdown; a hitch ⟨*mistake due to a ~ in the computer*⟩ [*hiccup* of imit origin; *hiccough* by folk etymology (influenced by *cough*) fr *hiccup*]

²**hiccup** *also* **hiccough** *vb* **-p-, -pp-** *vi* to make a hiccup; *also* to be affected with hiccups ~ *vt* to say (as if) with hiccups

**hic jacet** /ˌhik 'yaket/ *n, archaic* an epitaph [L, here lies]

**hick** /hik/ *n, chiefly NAm* an unsophisticated provincial person [*Hick,* nickname for *Richard*] – **hick** *adj*

¹**hickey** /'hiki/ *n, NAm informal* a device, gadget [origin unknown]

²**hickey** *n, chiefly NAm* a lovebite [origin unknown]

**hickory** /'hikəri/ *n* (the usu tough pale wood of) any of a genus (*Carya*) of N American hardwood trees of the walnut family that often have sweet edible nuts [short for obs *pokahickory,* fr *pawcohiccora* food prepared from pounded nuts (in some Algonquian language of Virginia)] – **hickory** *adj*

**hidalgo** /hi'dalgoh/ *n, pl* **hidalgos** *often cap* a member of the lower nobility of Spain [Sp, fr OSp *fijo dalgo,* lit., son of something]

**hidden** /'hid(ə)n/ *adj* **1** out of sight; concealed **2** obscure, unexplained

**hiddenite** /'hidəniet/ *n* a transparent yellow to green variety of the mineral SPODUMENE used as a gem [William E *Hidden* † 1918 US mineralogist]

**hidden tax** *n* INDIRECT TAX

¹**hide** /hied/ *n* any of various former English units of land area based on the amount of land that would support one free family and dependants; *esp* a unit of 120 acres (about 0.5 square kilometre) [ME, fr OE *hīgid;* akin to OE *hīwan* members of a household – more at ²HIND]

²**hide** *vb* **hid** /hid/; **hidden** /'hid(ə)n/, **hid** *vt* **1** to put out of sight; secrete, conceal ⟨ *~ the key under the doormat*⟩ **2** to keep secret ⟨hid *the news from his parents*⟩ **3** to screen from view ⟨*house hidden by trees*⟩ ~ *vi* **1a** to conceal oneself **b** to remain out of sight – often + *out* **2** to seek protection or evade responsibility ⟨*unscrupulous politicians who ~ behind their elevated status*⟩ [ME *hiden,* fr OE *hȳdan;* akin to Gk *keuthein* to conceal, OE *hȳd* hide, skin] – **hider** *n*

³**hide** *n, chiefly Br* a camouflaged hut or other shelter used for observation, esp of wildlife or game

⁴**hide** *n* the raw or dressed skin of an esp large animal [ME, fr OE *hȳd;* akin to OHG *hūt* hide, L *cutis* skin, Gk *kytos* hollow vessel] – **hide or/nor hair** *informal* the least vestige or trace (of somebody or something) ⟨*hadn't seen* hide or hair *of his wife for 20 years*⟩ – **tan somebody's hide** to beat or thrash somebody severely

⁵**hide** *vt* **hided** to give a beating to; flog

'**hide-and-ˌseek** *n* a children's game in which one player covers his/her eyes while counting up to a specified number,

usu 100, after which he/she hunts for the other players who have meanwhile hidden themselves

**hideaway** /-əˌway/ *n* a retreat, hideout

**hidebound** /-ˌbownd/ *adj* **1a** *of a domestic animal* having a dry skin adhering closely to the underlying flesh **b** *of a tree* having the bark so close and constricting that it impedes growth **2** narrow or inflexible in character

**hideous** /'hidi·əs/ *adj* **1** offensive to the senses, esp the sight; exceedingly ugly **2** morally offensive; shocking [alter. of ME *hidous,* fr OF, fr *hisde, hide* terror] – **hideously** *adv,* **hideousness** *n*

**hideout** /'hiedˌowt/ *n* a place of refuge or concealment

'**hidey-ˌhole, hidy-hole** /'hiedi/ *n, informal* a hideout [alter. of earlier *hiding-hole*]

¹**hiding** /'hieding/ *n* a state or place of concealment ⟨*go into ~*⟩

²**hiding** *n, informal* a beating, thrashing ⟨*gave him a good ~*⟩; *also* a severe defeat – **(be on) a hiding to nothing** (to be engaged in) an enterprise whose only possible outcome is failure

**hidrosis** /hi'drohsis/ *n* (excretion of) sweat; perspiration [NL, fr Gk *hidrōsis,* fr *hidroun* to sweat, fr *hidrōs* sweat – more at SWEAT] – **hidrotic** *adj*

**hie** /hie/ *vb* **hying, hieing** *archaic or poetic* to hurry [ME *hien,* fr OE *hīgian* to strive, hasten; akin to OSw *hikka* to pant, Skt *śīghra* quick]

**hielaman, hieleman** /'heeləmən/ *n, pl* **hielamans, hielemans** a narrow shield of bark or wood used by Australian aborigines [native name in Australia]

**hiemal** /'hie·əməl/ *adj, formal* HIBERNAL (of or occurring in winter) [L *hiemalis,* fr *hiems* winter – more at HIBERNATE]

**hier-, hiero-** *comb form* sacred; holy ⟨*hierology*⟩ [LL, fr Gk, fr *hieros* – more at IRE]

**hierarch** /'hie·ərahk, 'hiə-/ *n* **1** a religious leader in a position of authority **2** a person with a high position in a hierarchy [MF or ML; MF *hierarche,* fr ML *hierarcha,* fr Gk *hierarchēs,* fr *hier-* + *-archēs* -arch] – **hierarchal** *adj*

**hierarchical** /ˌhie·ə'rahkikl, ˌhiə-/, **hierarchic** *adj* of or arranged in a hierarchy – **hierarchically** *adv*

**hierarchy** /'hie·ərahki, 'hiə-/ *n* **1a** a ruling body of clergy organized into orders or ranks each subordinate to the one above it; *specif* the bishops of a province or nation **b** church government by a hierarchy **2** *taking sing or pl vb* a body of people in authority **3** a graded or ranked series ⟨*the company ~ went from secretary to managing director*⟩

**hieratic** /-'ratik/ *adj* **1** of or written in a simplified form of ancient Egyptian hieroglyphics **2** (characteristic) of a priest; *esp* like a priest in dignity or stateliness of manner [L *hieraticus* priestly, fr Gk *hieratikos,* deriv of *hieros*] – **hieratically** *adv*

**hierodule** /'hie·ərəˌdyoohl/ *n* a slave in the service of a temple in ancient Greece [LL *hierodulus,* fr Gk *hierodoulos,* fr *hier-* + *doulos* slave] – **hierodulic** *adj*

**hieroglyph** /'hie·ərəˌglif, 'hiərə-/ *n* a pictorial character used in hieroglyphic writing – compare IDEOGRAM [Fr *hiéroglyphe,* fr MF, back-formation fr *hieroglyphique*]

**hieroglyphic** /ˌhie·ərə'glifik, ˌhiərə-/, **hieroglyphical** /-kl/ *adj* **1** written in, being, or belonging to a system of writing mainly in hieroglyphics **2** inscribed with hieroglyphics **3** resembling hieroglyphics in difficulty of decipherment; obscure [MF *hieroglyphique,* fr LL *hieroglyphicus,* fr Gk *hieroglyphikos,* fr *hier-* + *glyphein* to carve – more at ²CLEAVE] – **hieroglyphically** *adv*

**hieroglyphics** /ˌhie·ərə'glifiks, ˌhiərə-/ *n taking sing or pl vb* **1** a system of writing using mainly pictorial characters; *specif* the picture script of various ancient peoples, esp the Egyptians **2** something that resembles hieroglyphics, esp in difficulty of decipherment

**hierogram** /'hie·ərəˌgram, 'hiərə-/ *n* a sacred and esp hieroglyphic symbol

**hierophant** /'hie·ərəˌfant/ *n* **1** a priest in ancient Greece; *specif* the chief priest of the ELEUSINIAN MYSTERIES (religious ceremonies) **2** *formal* an expositor, interpreter [LL *hierophanta,* fr Gk *hierophantēs,* fr *hier-* + *phainein* to show] – **hierophantic** *adj*

**hi-fi** /'hie ˌfie, ˌhie 'fie/ *n, informal* **1** HIGH FIDELITY **2** equipment for the high-fidelity reproduction of sound

**higgle** /'higl/ *vi* to haggle [prob alter. of *haggle*] – **higgler** *n*

**higgledy-piggledy** /ˌhigldi 'pigldi/ *adv, informal* in confusion; topsy-turvy [perh based on *pig* (fr pigs' habit of huddling together)] – **higgledy-piggledy** *adj*

¹**high** /hie/ *adj* **1a** extending upwards for a considerable or

above average distance ⟨*rooms with* ~ *walls*⟩ **b** situated at a considerable height above a base (e g the ground) ⟨*a* ~ *plateau*⟩ **c** *of physical activity* extending to or from, or taking place at a considerable height above a base (e g the ground or water) ⟨~ *diving*⟩ **d** having a specified elevation; tall ⟨*six feet* ~⟩ – often in combination ⟨*sky*-high⟩ ⟨*waist*-high⟩ **2a** at the period of culmination or fullest development ⟨~ *summer*⟩ ⟨~ *Gothic*⟩ **b** long past; remote ⟨~ *antiquity*⟩ **3** elevated in pitch; shrill ⟨*a* ~ *note*⟩ **4** relatively far from the equator ⟨~ *latitudes*⟩ **5** slightly decomposed or tainted ⟨~ *game*⟩; *also* having a foul smell **6a** exalted in character; noble ⟨~ *principles*⟩ **b** good, favourable ⟨*has a* ~ *opinion of her*⟩ **7** of greater degree, amount, cost, value, or content than average ⟨~ *prices*⟩ ⟨*food* ~ *in iron*⟩ ⟨*submitted a* ~ *bid*⟩ **8a(1)** foremost in rank, dignity, or standing ⟨~ *officials*⟩ ⟨~ *society*⟩ **a(2)** luxurious, expensive ⟨*the* ~ *life*⟩ **b** critical, climactic ⟨*the* ~ *point of the novel is the escape*⟩ **c** marked by sublime, heroic, or stirring events or subject matter ⟨~ *tragedy*⟩ ⟨~ *adventure*⟩ **9** forcible, strong ⟨~ *winds*⟩ **10** showing elation or excitement ⟨~ *spirits*⟩ ⟨*feelings ran* ~⟩ **11** advanced in complexity, development, or elaboration ⟨~er *nerve centres*⟩ ⟨~er *mathematics*⟩ ⟨~ *technology*⟩ **12** *of a vowel* CLOSE 1b(1) (articulated with the tongue close to the palate) **13** *of a gear* designed for fast speed **14** *of words* expressive of anger **15** traditionalist ⟨*a* ~ *Tory*⟩; *specif* HIGH CHURCH ⟨~ *Anglicans*⟩ **16** *of a card* having a high value; *specif* able to win a TRICK (winning combination of cards) **17** *informal* intoxicated by alcohol or a drug; *broadly* excited, exuberant ⟨*got* ~ *on good company and happy memories*⟩ – see also **for the high** JUMP, **be high** TIME [ME, fr OE *hēah*; akin to OHG *hōh* high, L *cacumen* point, top]

    *synonyms* Compare **high** and **tall**. High is used particularly for things that extend or stand a long way above a base ⟨*a* high *mountain/shelf*⟩. Tall applies particularly to the vertical length of living things ⟨*a* tall *woman/tree*⟩ and to anything that is narrow in proportion to its height ⟨tall *buildings*⟩.

²**high** *adv* at or to a high place, altitude, or degree ⟨*climbed* ~er *on the ladder*⟩ ⟨*the bids went too* ~⟩ *usage* see HIGHLY – **fly high** to be elated

³**high** *n* **1** an elevated place or region (e g a hill or knoll) **2** a region of high atmospheric pressure **3a** a high point or level; height ⟨*sales have reached a new* ~⟩ **b** *NAm* top gear in a motor vehicle **4** *informal* an excited or stupefied state; *esp* one produced by a drug – **on high** in or to a high place, esp heaven

    *usage* Some people dislike the use of **high** to mean "a highest point".

**high altar** *n* the principal altar in a church

**high and dry** *adv* **1** *of a ship* out of reach of the current or tide; out of water **2** in a helpless or abandoned situation; without recourse

**high and low** *adv* everywhere ⟨*searched* ~ *but could not find his cuff links*⟩

‚**high-and-'mighty** *adj* arrogant, imperious

**highball** /'hie‚bawl/ *n* a drink of spirits (e g whisky) and water or a carbonated beverage served with ice in a tall glass

**highbinder** /'hie‚biendə/ *n* **1** a professional killer operating in the Chinese area of an American city **2** *NAm informal* a corrupt or scheming politician [the *Highbinders*, gang of vagabonds in New York City *ab* 1806]

**highboard** /'hie‚bawd/ *n* (diving using) a firm diving board at usu 10 metres (about 11 yards) above the water

**highborn** /-'bawn/ *adj* of noble birth

**highboy** /-‚boy/ *n, NAm* TALLBOY 1 (tall chest of drawers)

**highbred** /‚hie'bred/ *adj* coming from superior stock

**highbrow** /-‚brow/, **highbrowed** /-browd/ *adj* dealing with, possessing, or having pretensions to superior intellectual and cultural interests ⟨*a* ~ *radio programme*⟩ – **highbrow** *n*, **highbrowism** *n*

**high camp** *adj or n* (marked by) a sophisticated form of camp style or behaviour

**high chair** *n* a child's chair with long legs, a footrest, and usu a feeding tray

**High Church, high** *adj* tending, in the Anglican church, to emphasize the importance of priesthood, liturgy, ceremonial, and Catholic tradition – **High Churchman** *n*

‚**high-'class** *adj* superior, first-class

‚**high-'coloured** *adj* FLORID 2

**high comedy** *n* comedy employing subtle characterizations and witty dialogue – compare LOW COMEDY

**high command** *n* **1** the supreme headquarters of a military

force **2** *taking sing or pl vb* the commander-in-chief and high-ranking officers of a country's army, navy, and air force

**high commissioner** *n* a principal or a high-ranking commissioner; *esp* an ambassadorial representative of the government of one Commonwealth country stationed in another

‚**high-'count** *adj* having a large number of vertical and horizontal threads to the square inch ⟨~ *sheeting*⟩

**High Court, High Court of Justice** *n* the lower branch of the SUPREME COURT of England and Wales, consisting of the QUEEN'S BENCH Division, the CHANCERY Division, and the FAMILY DIVISION – compare COURT OF APPEAL

**High Court of Justiciary** *n* the superior criminal court of Scotland, dealing with treason, murder, rape, and all cases involving heavy penalties, and with appeal to the COURT OF APPEAL

**High Dutch** *n* **1** HIGH GERMAN **2** Dutch of the Netherlands rather than Afrikaans

‚**high-'energy** *adj* yielding a relatively large amount of energy when undergoing chemical breakdown (HYDROLYSIS) ⟨~ *phosphate bonds in ATP*⟩

**higher criticism** /'hie-ə/ *n* the critical study of biblical writings to determine their setting, literary sources, and the purpose and meaning of the authors – compare LOWER CRITICISM – **higher critic** *n*

**higher degree** *n* a (university) degree higher than the BA or BSc

**higher education** *n* education beyond the secondary level, esp at a college, polytechnic, or university

**higher fungus** *n* a fungus with well-developed HYPHAE (filaments making up the rootlike mass of a fungus)

‚**higher-'up** *n, informal* a person occupying a superior rank or position – compare HIGH-UP

**highest common factor** *n, maths* the largest integer or the POLYNOMIAL (series of algebraic terms) of highest degree that can be divided exactly into each of two or more integers or polynomials – called also GREATEST COMMON DIVISOR

**high explosive** *n* an explosive (e g TNT) that generates gas with extreme rapidity and has a shattering effect

**highfalutin** /-fə'loohtin/ *adj, informal* pretentious, pompous ⟨*written in a* ~ *style*⟩ [perh fr ²*high* + alter. of *fluting*, prp of *flute*]

**high fashion** *n* the style of clothing, esp HAUTE COUTURE, worn by the leaders of fashion

**high fidelity** *n* the faithful reproduction of sound – **high-fidelity** *adj*

**high finance** *n* (the major financial institutions engaged in) large and complex financial operations

‚**high-'flier, high-flyer** *n* a person who shows extreme ambition or outstanding promise (e g in business or politics)

‚**high-'flown** *adj* **1** excessively ambitious or extravagant ⟨~ *plans have given way to hardheaded financial considerations*⟩ **2** excessively elaborate or inflated; pretentious ⟨~ *rhetoric*⟩

‚**high-'flying** *adj* **1** rising to considerable height **2** marked by extravagance, pretension, or excessive ambition

**high frequency** *n* a radio frequency between 3 and 30 megahertz

**high gear** *n* TOP GEAR 2

**High German** *n* German as originally spoken in S Germany and now in standard use throughout the country

‚**high-'grade** *adj* **1** of superior grade or quality ⟨~ *bonds*⟩ **2** near the upper or most favourable extreme of a specified range ⟨*a* ~ *moron approaches normality*⟩

**high grade** *n* a grade animal that in conformation and economic qualities approximates to the breed to which its known purebred ancestors belonged

‚**high-'handed** *adj* overbearingly arbitrary – **high-handedly** *adv*, **high-handedness** *n*

‚**high-'hat** *adj* supercilious, snobbish

**High Holiday** *n* either of two important Jewish holidays: **a** ROSH HASHANAH **b** YOM KIPPUR

**high jinks** /jingks/ *n pl, informal* high-spirited fun and games

**high jump** *n* (an athletic field event consisting of) a jump for height over a bar suspended between uprights – **high jumper** *n*, **high jumping** *n*

‚**high-'key** *adj, of a photograph, print, etc* having or composed of mainly light tones with little contrast – compare LOW-KEY

¹**highland** /'hielənd/ *n*, **highlands** *n pl* high or mountainous land

²**highland** *adj* **1** of a highland or highlands **2** *cap* of the High-

lands of Scotland **3** *cap* of or being (a member of) a shaggy long-haired breed of hardy beef cattle

**Highland dancing** *n* Scottish folk dancing that involves nimble footwork and is often accompanied by bagpipe playing

**highlander** /'hieləndə/ *n* **1** an inhabitant of a highland or highlands **2** *cap* an inhabitant of the Highlands of Scotland

**Highland fling** *n* a lively solo Scottish folk dance

**Highland pony** *n* (any of) a breed of strong pony from the Highlands of Scotland that is usu brownish grey with a stripe along its back

**Highlands** /'hieləndz/ *n pl* the northwest mountainous part of Scotland

,**high-'level** *adj* **1** occurring, done, or placed at a high level **2** of high importance or rank ⟨~ *diplomats*⟩ **3** *of a computer language* having each word or symbol equal to several MACHINE CODE instructions and being easily understandable to humans

**high life** *n* the luxurious mode of living associated with the rich and fashionable

¹**highlight** /-,liet/ *n* **1** the lightest spot or area (eg in a painting or photograph) **2** an event or detail of special significance or interest ⟨~s *from the week's news*⟩ **3** a contrasting brighter part in the hair or on the face or eyes produced artificially by tinting strands of hair or applying white or sparkling make-up

²**highlight** *vt* **1a** to throw a strong light on **b** to focus attention on; emphasize **c** to emphasize (eg a figure) with light tones in painting, photography, etc **2** to give highlights to (eg the hair or eyes)

**highlighter** /'hie,lietə/ *n* white or sparkling cosmetic cream or powder used to highlight cheeks, eyes, etc

**highly** /'hieli/ *adv* **1** to a high degree; extremely ⟨~ *delighted*⟩ **2** with approval; favourably ⟨*speak ~ of someone*⟩

   **usage** Both **high** and **highly** can mean "to a high degree" ⟨*pay them* high/highly⟩ but only **highly** is used like *very* before adjectives and participles ⟨highly *intelligent*⟩ ⟨highly *paid*⟩ while **high** is closer than **highly** to the sense of figurative height ⟨*rose* high *in their profession*⟩.

,**highly-'strung, high-strung** *adj* extremely nervous or sensitive

**high mass** *n, often cap H&M* an elaborate sung mass – compare LOW MASS

,**high-'minded** *adj* having or marked by elevated principles and feelings – **high-mindedly** *adv*, **high-mindedness** *n*

**high-muck-a-muck** /,hie ,muk ee 'muk, ə 'muk/ *n, NAm informal* an important and arrogant person [by folk etymology fr Chinook Jargon *hiu muckamuck* plenty to eat]

**highness** /'hienis/ *n* **1** the quality or state of being high ⟨*the ~ of his voice*⟩ – compare HEIGHT **2** *cap* – used as a title for a person of exalted rank (eg a king or prince)

,**high-'octane** *adj* having a high OCTANE NUMBER (measure of quality of fuels) and hence not prone to producing the sharp metallic noises (PINKING) caused by faulty ignition ⟨~ *petrol*⟩

,**high-'pitched** *adj* **1** having a high pitch ⟨*a ~ voice*⟩ **2** marked by or exhibiting strong feeling; agitated ⟨*a ~ election campaign*⟩

**high place** *n* **1** a temple or altar used by the ancient SEMITES (people of SW Asia) and built usu on a hill or elevation **2** *pl* high-ranking and important positions ⟨*people in high places*⟩

**high polymer** *n* a POLYMER (complex chemical compound composed of a number of linked subunits) (eg polystyrene) of high MOLECULAR WEIGHT

,**high-'powered** *also* **high-power** *adj* having great drive, energy, or capacity; dynamic ⟨~ *executives*⟩

¹,**high-'pressure** *adj* **1** having or involving a (comparatively) high pressure, esp greatly exceeding that of the atmosphere **2a** using, involving, or being aggressive and insistent sales techniques ⟨~ *selling*⟩ **b** imposing or involving severe strain or tension ⟨~ *occupations*⟩

²**high-pressure** *vt, informal* to sell or influence by high-pressure tactics

**high priest** *n* **1** a chief priest, esp of the ancient Jewish LEVITICAL priesthood traditionally traced from Aaron **2** a priest of the higher order of priesthood in the Mormon church **3** the head or chief exponent of a movement ⟨*the ~ of rock and roll*⟩ – **high priesthood** *n*

**high priestess** *n* **1** a chief priestess **2** the female head or chief exponent of a movement ⟨*the ~ of feminism*⟩

**high relief** *n* sculptural relief in which at least half of the circumference of the design stands out from the surrounding surface – compare BAS-RELIEF

'**high-,rise** *adj* **1** (situated in a building) constructed with a large

number of storeys ⟨~ *flats*⟩ ⟨~ *blocks*⟩ **2** of or characterized by high-rise buildings ⟨*a ~ cityscape*⟩ – **high rise** *n*

**highroad** /-,rohd/ *n* **1** the easiest course *to* ⟨*the ~ to success*⟩ **2** *chiefly Br* a main road

**high roller** *n, NAm informal* **1** a person who spends extravagantly on luxurious living **2** a person who gambles recklessly or for high stakes

**high school** *n* **1** *chiefly Br* SECONDARY SCHOOL; *esp* a GRAMMAR SCHOOL, esp for girls – now used chiefly in names **2** *NAm* a school usu for pupils aged about 15-18

**high sea** *n*, **high seas** *n pl* the open part of a sea or ocean, esp outside TERRITORIAL WATERS

**high season** *n* a usu periodic time of high profitability or business opportunity; *esp* a period (eg during the summer) when the number of visitors to a holiday resort is at a peak

'**high-,sounding** *adj* pompous, but meaningless

,**high-'speed** *adj* **1** (adapted to be) operated at high speed **2** relating to the production of photographs by very short exposures

,**high-'spirited** *adj* characterized by a bold, lively, or energetic spirit; *also* highly-strung ⟨*a ~ horse*⟩ – **high-spiritedly** *adv*, **high-spiritedness** *n*

**highspot** /-,spot/ *n* **1** the most important or enjoyable feature ⟨*the ~ of his political career*⟩ **2** an exciting or interesting locality or venue ⟨*hit the ~s on their visit to the West End*⟩

'**high-,stepping** *adj, of a horse* lifting the feet high – **high-stepper** *n*

'**high ,street** *n, often cap H&S, Br* a main or principal street, esp containing shops

,**high-'strung** *adj* highly-strung

**hight** /hiet/ *adj, archaic* called, named ⟨*Childe Harold was he ~* – Lord Byron⟩ [ME, irreg pp of *hoten* to command, call, be called, fr OE *hātan*; akin to OHG *heizzan* to command, call, & prob to L *ciēre* to move, Gk *kinein*]

**high table** *n, often cap H&T* a dining-room table, usu on a platform, used by the masters and fellows of a British college, or at a formal dinner or reception (eg by distinguished guests)

**hightail** /-,tayl/ *vi, chiefly NAm* to move away at full speed – often + *it* [fr the erect tail of some animals when fleeing]

**high tea** *n, Br* a fairly substantial early evening meal at which tea is served – compare TEA 4b

,**high 'tech** /tek/ *n* **1** a style of interior decoration involving the use of (simulated) industrial building materials, fittings, etc **2** high technology – **high-tech** *adj*

,**high-'tension** *adj* having a high voltage; *also* relating to apparatus to be used at high voltage

'**high-,test** *adj* passing a difficult test; *specif* having a strong tendency to vaporize ⟨~ *gasoline*⟩

**high tide** *n* **1** (the time of) the tide when the water reaches its highest level **2** a culminating point; a climax

,**high-'toned** *adj* **1** high in social, moral, or intellectual quality; dignified **2** pretentious, pompous

**high treason** *n* TREASON 2

,**high-'up** *n, informal* a person of high rank or status – compare HIGHER-UP – **high-up** *adj*

**high water** *n* **1** water (eg in a river or lake) at its highest level or flow; *specif* HIGH TIDE **2** the time at which high water occurs – see also come HELL or **high water**

**high-water mark** *n* **1** a mark showing the highest level reached by the surface of a body of water **2** the highest point or stage; the acme

**highway** /-,way/ *n* **1** a public way; *esp* a main direct road **2** ¹BUS 2 (device for distributing electrical currents or signals)

**highway code** *n, often cap H&C* the British official code of rules and advice for the safe use of roads

**highwayman** /-mən/ *n* a person, esp on horseback, who in former times robbed travellers on the road

**highway robbery** *n, informal* overcharging, profiteering

**high yaller** /'yalə/ *n, chiefly NAm* a MULATTO (child of a Negro and a white person) or Negro of light-brown colour [*yaller*, alter. of *yellow*]

**high yellow** *n* HIGH YALLER

**hijack, high-jack** /'hiejak/ *vt* **1a** to steal (eg arms or merchandise) by stopping a vehicle in transit **b** to seize control of, and often divert, (a means of transport) by force ⟨*gunmen ~ed a plane bound for Frankfurt*⟩ **2** to steal, rob, or kidnap as if by hijacking [origin unknown] – **hijack** *n*, **hijacker** *n*

¹**hike** /hiek/ *vi* to go on a hike [perh akin to ¹*hitch*] – **hiker** *n*

**hike up** *vt, chiefly NAm* **1** to move, pull, or raise with a sudden movement ⟨*hiked himself up on the wall*⟩ **2** to increase or raise suddenly ⟨*hike up rents*⟩

**²hike** *n* **1** a long walk in the country, esp for pleasure or exercise **2** *chiefly NAm* an increase or rise ⟨*a new wage ~*⟩

**hilar** /'hielə/ *adj* of or located near a HILUM (scar on a seed)

**hilarious** /hi'leəri-əs/ *adj* marked by or causing hilarity [irreg fr L *hilarus, hilaris* cheerful, fr Gk *hilaros*] – **hilariously** *adv*, **hilariousness** *n*

**hilarity** /hi'larəti/ *n* mirth, merriment

**Hilary term** /'hiləri/ *n* the term beginning in January at Oxford and certain other universities [St *Hilary* †*ab*367 Bishop of Poitiers, whose feastday falls on 13 January]

**¹hill** /hil/ *n* **1** a usu rounded natural elevation of land lower than a mountain **2** an artificial heap or mound (e g of earth) **3** an esp steep slope [ME, fr OE *hyll;* akin to L *collis* hill, *culmen* top] – **hilly** *adj* – **over the hill** *informal* past one's prime; *specif* advanced in age

**²hill** *vt* **1** to form into a heap **2** to draw earth round the roots or base of – **hiller** *n*

**hillbilly** /'hil,bili/ *n, chiefly NAm* a person from a remote or culturally unsophisticated area (e g the mountains of the S USA) [¹*hill* + *Billy*, nickname for *William*]

**hill climb** *n* a race up a hillside for cars, motorcycles, etc

**hillfort** /-,fawt/ *n* a hilltop fortified by ramparts and ditches and characteristic of IRON AGE settlements in W Europe

**hillock** /'hilək/ *n* a small hill – **hillocky** *adj*

**Hill reaction** *n* a stage during the light-dependent phase (LIGHT REACTION) of photosynthesis that occurs in the plant CHLOROPLASTS and results in the splitting of water molecules and the release of oxygen [Robert *Hill b*1899 E biochemist]

**hillside** /'hilsied/ *n* the side or slope of a hill

**hilltop** /'hiltop/ *n* the highest part of a hill

**hilt** /hilt/ *n* a handle, esp of a sword or dagger [ME, fr OE; akin to OE *healt* lame – more at HALT] – **to the hilt** to the very limit; completely

**hilum** /'hieləm/ *n, pl* **hila** /'hielə/ **1a** a scar on a seed (e g a bean) marking its point of attachment to the stalk during development **b** the nucleus of a starch grain **2** a notch, opening, etc in a body part, usu where a vessel, nerve, etc enters [NL, fr L, trifle]

**him** /him, im/ *pron, objective case of* HE – compare phrases at ME **1** [ME, fr OE, dat of *hē* he & *hit* it – more at HE]

*usage* As *he*, *than he* are preferable in formal writing to *as him*, *than him*. See ⁴AS, ²THAN, ¹HE, HE

**Himalayan balsam** /'himə,layən/ *n* a robust thick-stemmed plant (*Impatiens glandulifera*) of the balsam family that is native to the Himalayas and bears long-stemmed clusters of large usu pinkish-purple flowers

**himation** /hi'mati,on/ *n* a rectangular cloth draped about the body and over the left shoulder, worn as a garment in ancient Greece [Gk, fr *hennynai* to clothe – more at WEAR]

**himself** /him'self; *medially often* im-/ *pron* **1a** that identical male person or creature – compare HE 1, ONESELF; used reflexively ⟨*he considers ~ lucky*⟩, for emphasis ⟨*he ~ did it*⟩ ⟨*God* Himself⟩, or in absolute constructions ⟨*~ unhappy, he understood the situation*⟩ **b** – used reflexively when the sex of the previously mentioned person or people is unspecified ⟨*everyone must fend for ~*⟩ **2** his normal self ⟨*isn't quite ~ today*⟩ **3** *chiefly NAm* oneself – used with *one* ⟨*one should wash ~*⟩ **4** *Irish & Scot* a man of consequence; *esp* the master of the house *usage* see ¹HE

**¹Himyarite** /'himyə,riet/ *n* a member or descendant of an ancient people of S Arabia [*Himyar*, legendary king in Yemen]

**²Himyarite, Himyaritic** /,himyə'ritik/ *adj* of the ancient Himyarites or their language

**hin** /hin/ *n* an ancient Hebrew unit of liquid measure equal to about 4 litres (7 pints) [Heb *hīn*, fr Egypt *hnw*]

**Hinayana** /,heenə'yahnə/ *n* THERAVADA (branch of Buddhism) [Skt *hīnayāna*, lit., lesser vehicle] – **Hinayanist** *n*, **Hinayanistic** *adj*

**¹hind** /hiend/ *n, pl* **hinds**, *esp collectively* **hind 1** a female deer; *esp* a female RED DEER – compare HART **2** any of various spotted GROUPERS (marine fish) (esp genus *Epinephelus*) [ME, fr OE; akin to OHG *hinta* hind, Gk *kemas* young deer]

**²hind** *n, archaic* **1** a farm worker, esp in N Britain **2** a rustic [ME *hine* servant, farmhand, fr OE *hīna*, gen of *hīwan*, pl, members of a household; akin to OE *hām* home – more at HOME]

**³hind** *adj* situated at the back or behind; rear ⟨*~ leg*⟩ – see also **talk the hind** LEG **off a donkey** [ME, prob back-forma-

tion fr OE *hinder*, adv, behind; akin to OHG *hintar*, prep, behind]

**hindbrain** /-,brayn/ *n* **1a(1)** the rear of the three primary divisions of the embryonic brain of a VERTEBRATE animal **a(2)** the parts (e g the cerebellum, pons, and MEDULLA OBLONGATA) of the adult brain that develop from the embryonic hindbrain **b** METENCEPHALON **c** MYELENCEPHALON **2** the rear part of the brain of an INVERTEBRATE animal

**¹hinder** /'hində/ *vt* **1** to retard or obstruct the progress of; hamper **2** to restrain, prevent – often + *from* ~ *vi* to be an obstacle or hindrance [ME *hindren*, fr OE *hindrian;* akin to OE *hinder* behind] – **hinderer** *n*

*synonyms* Hinder, hamper, impede, retard, obstruct, block, bar, dam, and balk all imply, literally or figuratively, slowing or preventing movement or progress. Hinder may suggest accidental or intentional interference with one's wishes ⟨*the crowd* hindered *him from getting to the station*⟩ ⟨*cold winds may* hinder *growth*⟩. Hamper implies encumbrances which slow down progress ⟨hampered *by the mud which clung to our boots*⟩ ⟨hampered *in her ambitions by a strong Northern accent*⟩. Impede is very similar, but stresses rather the slowing down or the difficulty of progress than its cause ⟨*do not pull the belt so tightly as to* impede *circulation*⟩. Retard stresses delay, especially figuratively. The remaining words imply the placing of obstacles in the path. Obstruct implies that this makes progress difficult, but not necessarily impossible, while block suggests effectively preventing any passage. Bar implies a ban on movement in or out, (as if) by a physical barrier. Dam suggests the blocking of an outlet for water, or may be used figuratively ⟨dammed-*up emotion must have release*⟩. Balk stresses the effective frustration of progress ⟨balked *in his ambitions by the rise of a younger man*⟩. antonyms further, promote, help

**²hinder** /'hiendə/ *adj* situated behind or at the rear; posterior [ME, fr OE *hinder*, adv]

**hindgut** /'hiend,gut/ *n* the rear section of the digestive tract of some INVERTEBRATE animals (e g insects) that in humans develops into the COLON and RECTUM

**Hindi** /'hindi/ *n* **1** a literary and official INDIC language of N India **2** a complex of INDIC dialects of N India [Hindi *hindī*, fr *Hind* India, fr Per] – **Hindi** *adj*

**hindmost** /'hiend,mohst/ *adj* furthest to the rear; last

**Hindoo** /'hindooh, -'-/ *n or adj, archaic* (a) Hindu

**Hindostani** /,hində'stahni/ *n or adj* Hindustani

**hindquarter** /,hiend'kwawtə, 'hiend,kwawtə/ *n* **1** the back half of a side (of the carcass) of a 4-legged animal including a leg and usu one or more ribs **2** *pl* the hind pair of legs of a 4-legged animal; *broadly* all the structures that lie behind the attachment of the hind legs to the body of a 4-legged animal

**hindrance** /'hindrəns/ *n* **1** the action of hindering **2** an impediment, obstacle

**hindsight** /'hiend,siet/ *n* **1** a rear sight of a firearm **2** realization of the nature and demands of a situation after it has occurred – compare FORESIGHT

**¹Hindu** /'hindooh; *also* -'-/ *n* an adherent of Hinduism; *broadly* a native or inhabitant of India [Per *Hindū* inhabitant of India, fr *Hind* India]

*synonyms* Hindi, Hindustani, and Urdu are all languages of the Indian subcontinent. Hindi is an official language of India; Hindustani is an older word for Hindi, Urdu, or any mixture of the two before they were distinguished; Urdu is an official language of Pakistan and is used also by Muslims in India. A Hindu is an adherent of Hinduism, and is in most cases a person of Indian nationality or descent.

**²Hindu** *adj* (characteristic) of the Hindus or Hinduism

**Hindu calendar** *n* a calendar using the phases of the moon, usu dating from 3101 BC and used esp in India

**Hinduism** /-,iz(ə)m/ *n* the dominant religion of India that involves belief in destiny (KARMA) and cycles of reincarnation (SAMSARA) and follows a particular moral law (DHARMA) with ritual ceremonies, mystical contemplation, and self-denying practices, and that is associated with a class system of social organization

**¹Hindustani** /,hindooh'stahni, -'stani/ *n* **1** a group of INDIC dialects of N India of which HINDI and URDU are considered diverse written forms **2** a form of speech similar to URDU, but also containing some features of HINDI, that was formerly used in the British army in India [Hindi *Hindūstānī*, fr Per *Hindūstān* India, fr *Hindū* + -*stān* country]

**²Hindustani** *adj* of Hindustan, its people, or Hindustani

**hind wing** *n* either of the rear wings of a 4-winged insect

**¹hinge** /'hinj/ *n* **1a** a jointed or flexible device on which a swinging part (eg a door or lid) turns **b** a flexible joint held together by ligaments **c** a small piece of thin gummed paper used in fastening a stamp in an album **2** a point or principle on which something turns or depends [ME *heng;* akin to MD *henge* hook, OE *hangian* to hang]

²**hinge** *vt* to attach by or provide with hinges ~ *vi* **1** to hang or turn (as if) on a hinge ⟨*the door* ~s *outwards*⟩ **2** to depend or turn on a single consideration or point – usu + *on* or *upon*

**hinge joint** *n* a joint between bones (eg at the elbow) that permits motion in only one plane

¹**hinny** /'hini/ *n* an offspring of a stallion and a female ass – compare MULE [L *hinnus*]

²**hinny, hinnie** *n, Scot & NEng* ³DEAR 1b [E dial., var of *honey*]

¹**hint** /hint/ *n* **1** a brief practical suggestion or piece of advice ⟨~s *for home decorators*⟩ **2** an indirect or veiled statement; an insinuation **3** a slight indication or trace; a suggestion – usu + *of* ⟨*a* ~ *of summer in the air*⟩ **4** *archaic* an opportunity, turn [prob alter. of obs *hent* act of seizing, fr *hent,* vb]

²**hint** *vt* to indicate indirectly and by allusion ⟨~ed *that something was up*⟩ ~ *vi* to give a hint **synonyms** see SUGGEST – **hinter** *n*

**hint at** *vt* to imply or allude to (something)

**hinterland** /'hintəland/ *n* **1** a region of land lying beyond a coast or river **2** a region remote from urban or cultural centres [Ger, fr *hinter* hinder + *land*]

¹**hip** /hip/ *n* the ripened fruit of a rose that consists of a swollen fleshy portion formed from the RECEPTACLE (tip of flower stalk bearing flower parts) containing numerous 1-seeded dry fruits (ACHENES) [ME *hipe,* fr OE *hēope;* akin to OHG *hiafo* hip]

²**hip** *n* **1a** the projecting region of each side of the lower or rear part of the mammalian body formed by parts of the pelvis and the upper part of the thighbone together with the fleshy parts covering them **b** HIP JOINT **2** the external angle formed at the junction of two sloping sides of a roof – compare VALLEY 2b [ME, fr OE *hype;* akin to OHG *huf* hip, L *cubitum* elbow, *cubare* to lie, Gk *kybos* cube, die, OE *hēah* high – more at HIGH]

³**hip** *vt* **-pp-** to make (a roof) with a hip

⁴**hip** *interj* – usu used to begin a cheer ⟨~ *hooray*⟩ [origin unknown]

⁵**hip** *adj* **-pp-** *informal* **1** characterized by a keen informed awareness of or interest in the newest developments – often + *to* **2** stylish, trendy □ no longer in vogue [alter. of *hep,* of unknown origin] – **hipness** *n*

**hipbone** /-,bohn/ *n* INNOMINATE BONE

**hip flask** *n* FLASK 1a

**hip joint** *n* the joint between the thighbone and the hipbone

**hipp-** /hip-/, **hippo-** *comb form* horse ⟨hippo*phagous*⟩ [L, fr Gk, fr *hippos* – more at EQUINE]

**hippeastrum** /,hipi'astrəm/ *n* any of a genus (*Hippeastrum*) of S American plants of the daffodil family that grow from bulbs and are cultivated esp for their large showy usu red funnel-shaped flowers [NL, genus name, fr Gk *hippeus* horseman + *astron* star]

**hipped** /hipt/ *adj* having hips, esp of a specified kind – often in combination ⟨*broad*-hipped⟩

**hippie, hippy** /'hipi/ *n* a usu young person, esp during the 1960s, who rejected the customs and morals of established society (eg by dressing unconventionally or favouring communal living), advocated nonviolence, and, in many cases, used hallucinogenic or intoxicating drugs (eg LSD) in the search for new levels of awareness; *broadly* a long-haired unconventionally dressed young person – compare HIPSTER [⁵*hip* + *-ie*] – **hippie** *adj,* **hippiedom, hippiehood** *n*

**hippo** /'hipoh/ *n, pl* **hippos** *informal* a hippopotamus

**hippocampus** /,hipoh'kampəs/ *n, pl* **hippocampi** /-pi/ a curved elongated ridge of nervous tissue that extends over part of the lower inside surface of each lateral VENTRICLE (fluid-filled cavity) in the CEREBRAL HEMISPHERES of the brain [NL, fr Gk *hippokampos* sea horse, fr *hipp-* + *kampos* sea monster] – **hippocampal** *adj*

**Hippocratic** /,hipə'kratik/ *adj* of Hippocrates or the school of medicine that took his name [*Hippocrates* (Gk *Hippokratēs*) †*ab* 377 BC Gk physician]

**Hippocratic oath** /,hipə'kratik/ *n* an oath embodying a code of medical ethics that is traditionally held to be taken by doctors before beginning medical practice and was probably taken by members of the school of Hippocrates

**hippodrome** /'hipədrohm/ *n* **1** an arena for equestrian performances or circuses **2** a MUSIC HALL, theatre, etc – esp in

names ⟨*Bristol* Hippodrome⟩ [MF, fr L *hippodromos,* fr Gk, fr *hipp-* + *dromos* racecourse – more at DROMEDARY]

**hippopotamus** /,hipə'potəməs/ *n, pl* **hippopotamuses, hippopotami** /-mie/ any of several large plant-eating 4-toed chiefly aquatic mammals (family Hippopotamidae, esp genus *Hippopotamus*) with an extremely large head and mouth, very thick almost hairless skin, and short legs [L, fr Gk *hippopotamos,* fr *hipp-* + *potamos* river, fr *petesthai* to fly, rush – more at FEATHER]

**-hippus** /-hipəs/ *comb form* (→ *n*) horse – in generic names, esp of extinct ancestors of the horse ⟨*Eohippus*⟩ [NL, fr Gk *hippos* – more at EQUINE]

**hipster** /'hipstə/ *n* **1** a person who is unusually aware of and interested in new and unconventional patterns, esp in jazz, in the use of stimulants (eg drugs), and in exotic religion – compare HIPPIE **2** a garment that hangs from the hips rather than the waist; *esp pl* trousers in this style [(1) ⁵*hip* + *-ster;* (2) based on ²*hip,* but suggested by (1)]

**hipsterism** /'hipstə,riz(ə)m/ *n* the way of life characteristic of hipsters

**hircine** /'huhsien/ *adj* of or resembling a goat, esp in smell [L *hircinus,* fr *hircus* he-goat]

¹**hire** /hie·ə/ *n* **1a** payment for the temporary use of something **b** wages ⟨*the labourer is worthy of his* ~ – Lk 10:7 (AV)⟩ **2** hiring or being hired [ME, fr OE *hӯr;* akin to MD *hūre* hire]

²**hire** *vt* **1a** to engage the services of for a set sum ⟨~ *a new crew*⟩ **b** to engage the temporary use of for an agreed sum ⟨~ *a hall*⟩ **2** to grant the services of or temporary use of for a fixed sum ⟨~ *themselves out*⟩ – **hirer** *n*

**synonyms** In British English one **hires** clothes or a bicycle or a building for a short time, and their owner **hires** them *out.* One **hires** or **rents** a car. One **rents** a room, building, or land, or a television set, for a regular **rent** or **rental,** and the owner **lets** or **rents** them to the user. (In American English, however, the user may **hire** a house for a long period or **rent** an evening suit for one night.) A landlord, or a tenant, **leases** a building or land on a **lease.** One **charters** a bus, ship, or aircraft.

**hire car** *n* a car (eg a self-drive car) available for hire

**hireling** /-ling/ *n, derog* a person who works for payment, esp purely for financial gain

**hire purchase** *n, chiefly Br* a system whereby a customer may take possession of goods after paying an initial deposit and then pay the remainder of the price in regular instalments over a specific period ⟨*bought their car on* ~⟩ – **hire-purchase** *adj*

**hirple** /'hiəpl, 'huhpl/ *vi, Scot* to limp, hobble [ME (Sc) *hirplen*]

**hirsute** /huh'syooht/ *adj* **1** *biology* covered with (coarse stiff) long hairs **2** *humorous* very hairy ⟨*her* ~ *friend*⟩ [L *hirsutus;* akin to L *horrēre* to bristle, tremble – more at HORROR] – **hirsuteness** *n*

**hirsutism** /-,tiz(ə)m/ *n, medicine* excessive growth of hair, esp of abnormal distribution

**hirudin** /hi'roohdin/ *n* a substance extracted from glands in the mouth of a leech that is used to prevent blood from clotting [Ger, fr L *hirudin-, hirudo* leech]

**hirundine** /hi'rundien/ *adj* of a bird of the swallow family [L *hirundin-, hirundo* swallow]

¹**his** /iz; *strong* hiz/ *adj* **1** of him or himself, esp as possessor ⟨~ *house*⟩ ⟨~ *tail*⟩, agent ⟨~ *writings*⟩, or object of an action ⟨~ *confirmation*⟩ – used in titles of males ⟨His *Majesty*⟩ **2** *chiefly NAm* one's – + *one* ⟨*one's duty to* ~ *public*⟩ **usage** see ¹HE [ME, fr OE, gen of *hē* he & *hit* it]

²**his** /hiz/ *pron, pl* **his** that which or the one who belongs to him – used without a following noun as a pronoun equivalent in meaning to the adjective *his;* compare phrases at MINE 2

**Hispanic** /hi'spanik/ *adj* of the people, speech, or culture of Spain, Spain and Portugal, or Latin America [L *hispanicus,* fr *Hispania* Iberian peninsula, Spain] – **Hispanicism** *n,* **Hispanicist** *n,* **Hispanicize** *vt*

**hispanism** /'hispə,niz(ə)m/ *n, often cap* **1** a movement to reassert the cultural unity of Spain and Latin America **2** a characteristic feature of Spanish occurring in another language

**hispid** /'hispid/ *adj* rough or covered with bristles, stiff hairs, or minute spines ⟨*a* ~ *plant*⟩ [L *hispidus;* prob akin to L *horrēre*] – **hispidity** *n*

**hiss** /his/ *vi* to make a sharp sound like a continuous *s,* esp as an expression of disapproval ~ *vt* **1** to show disapproval and dislike of by hissing **2** to utter with a hiss [ME *hissen,* of imit origin] – **hiss** *n,* **hisser** *n*

**hiss off** *vt* to cause (eg a performer) to leave usu the stage by hissing

**hist** /hist/ *interj* – used to attract attention [origin unknown]

**hist-** /hist-/, **histo-** *comb form* tissue ⟨histo*logy*⟩ [Fr, fr Gk *histos* mast, loom beam, web, fr *histanai* to cause to stand]

**histaminase** /hi'staminayz, -ays/ *n* a widely occurring ENZYME that takes part in biological reactions to inactivate histamine [ISV]

**histamine** /'histəmin/ *n* a chemical compound, $C_3H_3N_2CH_2$ $CH_2NH_2$, that transmits nerve impulses between nerves of the AUTONOMIC NERVOUS SYSTEM, causes contraction of some SMOOTH MUSCLE (e g in the intestines), and is released usu after injury or in the presence of an allergen (e g particles of dust or pollen, or insect stings) from the tissues and causes an allergic reaction (e g itching and local reddening and swelling) [ISV] – **histaminic** *adj*

**histaminergic** /ˌhistəmi'nuhjik/ *adj, of nerve fibres in the* AUTONOMIC NERVOUS SYSTEM liberating or activated by histamine [ISV *histamine* + Gk *ergon* work – more at WORK]

**histidine** /'histədeen, -din/ *n* an AMINO ACID, $C_3H_3N_2CH_2CH(NH_2)COOH$, that forms part of most proteins [ISV]

**histiocyte** /'histi-əsiet/ *n* a large cell (MACROPHAGE) that can take in particles of food, waste matter, etc; *specif* one fixed in loose fibrous supporting tissue [Gk *histion* web (dim. of *histos*) + ISV *-cyte*] – **histiocytic** *adj*

**histochemical** /ˌhistə'kemikl/ *adj* of histochemistry – **histochemically** *adv*

**histochemistry** /ˌhistə'kemistri/ *n* a branch of histology dealing with the use of chemical techniques in making the structure of tissues and cells visible for examination under a microscope [ISV]

**histocompatibility** /ˌhistohkəmˌpatə'bilэti/ *n* a state of mutual tolerance that allows some tissues to be grafted effectively to others (e g in blood transfusions and heart transplants)

**histogen** /'histəjən, -jen/ *n* a zone or clearly delimited region of tissue in or from which the specific parts of a plant organ are believed to grow and develop [ISV]

**histogenesis** /ˌhistoh'jenəsis/ *n* the formation and differentiation of tissues [NL] – **histogenetic** *adj*, **histogenetically** *adv*

**histogram** /'histəgram/ *n* a graph consisting of rectangles whose bases represent equal divisions of some continuous variable and whose heights represent the number of occurrences of the variable within the division [*history* + *-gram*]

**histology** /hi'toləji/ *n* 1 a branch of anatomy that deals with the minute structure of animal and plant tissues as seen with the microscope 2 a written account of histology 3 tissue structure or organization [Fr *histologie*, fr *hist-* + *-logie* -logy] – **histologist** *n*, **histological, histologic** *adj*, **histologically** *adv*

**histolysis** /hi'stoləsis/ *n* the breakdown of body tissues [NL, fr *hist-* + *-lysis*] – **histolytic** *adj*

**histone** /'histohn/ *n* any of various proteins that are found associated with DNA in the CHROMOSOMES (strands of gene-carrying material) of cells (e g blood cells, sperm cells, and cells of the thymus gland) and that may inhibit gene activity at certain points along a chromosome [ISV]

**histopathology** /ˌhistohpə'tholəji/ *n* (a branch of pathology concerned with) the tissue changes accompanying or characteristic of disease [ISV] – **histopathologist** *n*, **histopathologic**, **histopathological** *adj*, **histopathologically** *adv*

**histophysiology** /ˌhistohˌfizi'olэji/ *n* 1 a branch of biology concerned with the function and activities of tissues 2 structural and functional tissue organization – **histophysiologic**, **histophysiological** *adj*

**historian** /hi'stawri-ən/ *n* a student or writer of history; *esp* one who produces a scholarly historical work *usage* see HISTORICAL

**historic** /hi'storik/ *adj* 1 HISTORICAL 1 ⟨~ *battlefields*⟩ 2 (likely to be) famous or important in history ⟨*a* ~ *occasion*⟩ 3 *of a tense in grammar* SECONDARY 1c (past) – compare HISTORIC PRESENT *synonyms* see HISTORICAL

**historical** /hi'storikl/ *adj* 1a (having the character) of history b based on history c used in the past and reproduced in historical presentations 2 HISTORIC 3 4 DIACHRONIC (relating to changes, esp in a language, over a period of time) ⟨~ *linguistics*⟩ – **historically** *adv*, **historicalness** *n*

synonyms **Historic** means "memorable" or "likely to be famous in history", and the use of **historical** in this sense creates confusion. **Historical** is the ordinary adjective meaning "to do with history", but its chief senses today are "having really existed or happened" ⟨*was King Arthur a* **historical** *character?*⟩ or "because of past events" ⟨*for* **historical** *reasons the boundary runs down the middle of the stream*⟩ or "belonging merely to the past" ⟨*Yes, sir, "an extinct case*

of *purely* **historic** *concern," sir?'* Strickland went on...'**Historical**,' Lacon corrected him irritably. *'Not* **historic** *concern. That's the last thing we want!'* – John Le Carré⟩. *usage* Modern writers and speakers on the whole prefer *a* rather than *an* before **historian, historic, historical** ⟨*a* **historian**⟩ ⟨*a* **historic/historical** *event*⟩.

**historical materialism** *n* the Marxist theory of history and society that holds that ideas, social institutions, etc (SUPERSTRUCTURE 2) are a direct reflection of underlying economic facts – compare DIALECTICAL MATERIALISM

**historical novel** *n* a novel set in a definite period in history and dealing with historical characters and events

**historical school** *n* a school of thought, esp in economics, legal philosophy, or ETHNOLOGY (study of mankind), emphasizing evolutionary developments and historical methods of research, analysis, and interpretation

**historicism** /hi'storisiz(ə)m/ *n* a theory that emphasizes the importance of history as a standard of value or as a determiner of events – **historicist** *adj or n*

**historicity** /ˌhistə'risəti/ *n* historical reality or authenticity

**historic·ize, -ise** /hi'storisiez/ *vt* to make historical ~ *vi* to use historical material

**historico-** /hi'storikoh-/ *comb form* historical; historical and ⟨historico*philosophical*⟩ ⟨historico*social*⟩

**historic present** *n* the present tense used to relate past events

**historiographer** /ˌhistori'ogrəfə/ *n* a usu official writer of history; a historian [MF *historiographeur*, fr LL *historiographus*, fr Gk *historiographos*, fr *historia* + *graphein* to write – more at CARVE]

**historiography** /ˌhistori'ogrəfi, -awri-/ *n* 1a the writing of history; *esp* the writing of history based on the critical examination of sources and the selection of details from authentic material b the principles, theory, and history of historical writing ⟨*a course in* ~⟩ 2 the product of historical writing; a body of historical literature – **historiographic, historiographical** *adj*, **historiographically** *adv*

**history** /'histəri/ *n* 1 a tale, story 2a a record in order of time of significant events that happened in the past, usu including an explanation of their causes ⟨*a* ~ *of the university*⟩ b a written account presenting related natural phenomena systematically ⟨*a* ~ *of British birds*⟩ c an account of somebody's medical, sociological, etc background 3 a branch of knowledge that records and explains past events ⟨*medieval* ~⟩ 4a events that form the subject matter of a history b past events ⟨*that's all* ~ *now*⟩ c previous treatment, handling, or experience d an unusual or interesting past ⟨*this goblet has a* ~⟩ [L *historia*, fr Gk, inquiry, history, fr *histōr, istōr* knowing, learned; akin to Gk *eidenai* to know – more at WIT]

**histrionic** /ˌhistri'onik/ *adj* 1 of actors, acting, or the theatre 2 deliberately affected; theatrical [LL *histrionicus*, fr L *histrion-, histrio* actor, alter. of *hister*, fr Etruscan] – **histrionically** *adv*

**histrionics** /ˌhistri'oniks/ *n pl* 1 *taking sing or pl vb* theatrical performances 2 deliberate display of emotion for effect △ hysterics

**¹hit** /hit/ *vb* **-tt-; hit** *vt* **1a** to reach (as if) with a blow; strike ⟨~ *the ball*⟩ ⟨~ *by an attack of flu*⟩ b to make sudden forceful contact with ⟨*the car* ~ *the tree*⟩ **2a** to bring into contact ⟨~ *the stick against the railings*⟩ b to deliver, inflict ⟨~ *his opponent a severe blow*⟩ **3** to have a usu detrimental effect or impact on ⟨~ *hard by the drought*⟩ **4** to discover or meet, esp by chance ⟨*I seem to have* ~ *a snag*⟩ **5a** to reach, attain ⟨*prices* ~ *a new high*⟩ ⟨~ting *twenty*⟩ b *of fish* to bite at or on c to reflect accurately ⟨~ *the right note*⟩ d to cause a propelled object to reach or strike (e g a target), esp for a score in a game or contest **e** *of a batsman* to score (runs) in cricket ⟨~ *a quick fifty*⟩; *also* to score runs off a ball bowled by (a bowler) **6** *informal* to indulge in excessively ⟨~ *the bottle*⟩ **7** *informal* to arrive at or in ⟨~ *town*⟩ **8** *slang* to rob **9** *chiefly NAm slang* to kill ~ *vi* **1** to strike a blow **2a** to come into forceful contact with something b to attack ⟨*wondered where the enemy would* ~ *next*⟩ c *of a fish* to take the bait d to happen or arrive, esp with sudden or destructive force ⟨*the epidemic* ~ *that summer*⟩ **3** to come, esp by chance; arrive at or find something – + *on* or *upon* ⟨~ *on a solution*⟩ [ME *hitten*, fr ON *hitta* to meet with, hit] – **hitter** *n* – **hit it off** *chiefly informal* to get along well – often + *with* or *together* – see also **hit below the** BELT, **hit the** DECK, HARD **hit, hit the** HAY/**the** JACKPOT, **hit the** NAIL **on the head, hit the** ROAD/**the** ROOF/**the** SACK

**hit off** *vt* to represent or imitate accurately

**hit out** *vi* **1** to aim violent blows *at* ⟨*the boxer* hit out *at his opponent*⟩ **2** to aim angry verbal attacks *at*; speak violently against ⟨hitting out *at injustice and prejudice*⟩

**²hit** *n* **1a** a blow; *esp* one that strikes its target **b** a collision **2a** a stroke of luck **b** something (e g a popular tune) that enjoys great success ⟨*the show was a big ~*⟩ **3** a telling remark **4** *chiefly NAm slang* an act of murdering someone **5** *slang* a robbery – **hitless** *adj*

**hit-and-'miss** *adj* HIT-OR-MISS

**hit-and-'run** *adj* **1** being or involving a motor-vehicle driver who does not stop after involvement in an accident **2** involving rapid action and an immediate withdrawal ⟨*~ raids on coastal towns*⟩

**¹hitch** /hich/ *vt* **1** to move by jerks **2a** to catch or fasten (as if) by a hook or knot ⟨*~ed his horse to the top rail of the fence*⟩ – often + *up* **b(1)** to connect (a vehicle or implement) with a source of motive power ⟨*~ a plough to a tractor*⟩ **b(2)** to attach (a source of motive power) to a vehicle or instrument ⟨*~ the horses to the wagon*⟩ **3** to obtain (a free ride) in a passing vehicle ~ *vi* **1** to move with halts and jerks; hobble **2** to become entangled, made fast, or linked **3** *chiefly informal* to hitchhike [ME *hytchen*] – **hitcher** *n*

**hitch up** *vi* to harness and secure a draught animal or team to a vehicle (e g a wagon) ⟨*we* hitched up *and were on our way before sunrise*⟩

**²hitch** *n* **1** a sudden movement or pull; a jerk ⟨*gave his trousers a ~*⟩ **2** a sudden halt or obstruction; a stoppage ⟨*a ~ in the proceedings*⟩ **3** any of various knots used to form a temporary noose in a line or to secure a line temporarily to an object **4** *chiefly NAm* LIFT **4 5** *NAm slang* a period usu of military service

**hitchhike** /-,hiek/ *vi* to travel by obtaining free lifts in passing vehicles – **hitchhiker** *n*

**¹hither** /'hidhə/, **hitherwards** /-wədz/ *adv, chiefly formal* to or towards this place [ME *hider, hither*, fr OE *hider*; akin to Goth *hidre* hither, L *citra* on this side – more at HE] – **hither and thither** in all directions

**²hither** *adj, chiefly formal* NEAR **3a** ⟨*the ~ side of the hill*⟩

**hithermost** /'hidhə,mohst/ *adj, chiefly formal* nearest on this side

**hitherto** /-'tooh/ *adv, chiefly formal* up to this time; until now

**Hitlerian** /hit'liəri·ən/ *adj* (characteristic) of Adolf Hitler or his regime in Germany [Adolf *Hitler* †1945 Ger political leader]

**Hitlerism** /'hitləriz(ə)m/ *n* the nationalistic and totalitarian principles and policies associated with Adolf Hitler – **Hitlerite** *n or adj*

**hitman** /'hit,man/ *n, chiefly NAm slang* a hired murderer

**hit-or-'miss** *adj* marked by a lack of care or systematic thought; haphazard – **hit or miss** *adv*

**hit parade** *n* a group or listing of the most popular items of a particular kind; *esp* a list of popular songs ranked in order of the number of records of each sold

**Hittite** /'hitiet/ *n* **1** a member of a people that established an empire in Asia Minor and Syria in the 2nd millennium BC **2** the INDO-EUROPEAN language of the Hittites [Heb *Ḥittī*, fr Hitt *ḥattī*] – **Hittite** *adj*

**¹hive** /hiev/ *n* **1** a structure for housing honeybees **2** a colony of bees **3** a place swarming with busy occupants ⟨*a ~ of industry*⟩ [ME, fr OE *hȳf*; akin to Gk *kypellon* cup, OE *hēah* high – more at HIGH]

**²hive** *vt* **1** to collect into a hive **2** to store up (as if) in a hive ~ *vi* **1** *of bees* to enter and take possession of a hive **2** to reside in close association

**hive off** *vt* to separate from a group or larger unit ⟨hived off *the youngest campers into another room*⟩; *specif* to assign (e g assets or responsibilities) to a subsidiary company or agency ~ *vi* **1** to become separated from a group; form a separate or subsidiary unit **2** *informal* to leave without warning ⟨hived off *at 4.30*⟩

**³hive** *n* **1** *pl but taking sing or pl vb* URTICARIA (irritating allergic skin disorder) **2** any of the raised, usu red, irritating patches that appear on the skin during an attack of hives [origin unknown]

**ho** /hoh/ *interj* **1** – used esp to attract attention to something specified ⟨*land ~*⟩ **2** – used to express surprise or triumph; often repeated; compare HO-HO [ME]

**¹hoar** /haw/ *adj, formal* hoary [ME *hor*, fr OE *hār*; akin to OHG *hēr* hoary]

**²hoar, hoarfrost** *n* FROST **1c** [ME, hoariness, fr *hor*, adj]

**¹hoard** /hawd/ *n* **1** an often secret supply or stock (e g of money or food) stored up for preservation or future use **2** a cache of valuable archaeological remains (e g coins or treasure)

△ **horde** [ME *hord*, fr OE; akin to Gk *kysthos* vulva, OE *hȳdan* to hide]

**²hoard** *vt* **1** to lay up a hoard of ⟨*accused of ~ing food in times of scarcity*⟩ **2** to keep (e g one's thoughts) to oneself ⟨*~ed his innermost feelings*⟩ ~ *vi* to lay up a hoard

**hoarding** /'hawding/ *n* **1** a temporary board fence put round a building being erected or repaired **2** *Br* a large board designed to carry outdoor advertising [earlier *hourd, hoard*, prob deriv of OF *hourt* scaffold, platform]

**hoarse** /haws/ *adj* **1** rough or harsh in sound; grating ⟨*a ~ voice*⟩ **2** having a hoarse voice ⟨*shouted himself ~*⟩ [ME *hos, hors*, fr OE *hās*; akin to OE *hāt* hot – more at HOT] – **hoarsely** *adv*, **hoarsen** *vb*, **hoarseness** *n*

**hoary** /'hawri/ *adj* **1a** grey or white with age; *also* grey-haired **b** having a greyish appearance due to a covering of fine hairs ⟨*~ leaves*⟩ **2** impressively or venerably old; ancient **3** hackneyed ⟨*a ~ old joke*⟩ – **hoariness** *n*

**hoatzin** /hoh'atsin/ *n* a crested olive-coloured S American bird (*Opisthocomus hoazin* of the order Galliformes) with claws on the first and second fingers of the wing [AmerSp, fr Nahuatl *uatzin*]

**¹hoax** /hohks/ *vt* to trick into believing or accepting as genuine something false; deceive [prob contr of *hocus*] – **hoaxer** *n*

**²hoax** *n* **1** an attempt to trick or dupe ⟨*the warning about the bomb was a ~*⟩ **2** something false that has been passed off as genuine

**¹hob** /hob/ *n* **1** *dial Br* a goblin, elf **2** *chiefly NAm* mischief, trouble ⟨*raise ~*⟩ [ME *hobbe*, fr *Hobbe*, nickname for *Robert*]

**²hob** *n* **1** a ledge at the back or side of a fireplace on which something may be kept warm **2** a cutting tool used for cutting the teeth of GEAR WHEELS **3** *Br* a horizontal surface, either on a cooker or installed as a separate unit, that contains heating areas (e g HOT PLATES or rings) on which cooking utensils are placed [origin unknown]

**³hob** *vt* **-bb-** to cut with a hob

**Hobbesian** /'hobziən/ *adj* of Hobbes or Hobbism [Thomas *Hobbes* †1679 E philosopher]

**Hobbism** /'hobiz(ə)m/ *n* the philosophy of Hobbes; *esp* the Hobbesian theory that absolute government is necessary to prevent the war of each against all to which natural selfishness inevitably leads mankind – **Hobbist** *n or adj*

**hobbit** /'hobit/ *n* a member of an imaginary race of genial hole-dwellers that are human in appearance but half the size of man [figure in novels by J R R Tolkien †1973 E writer]

**¹hobble** /'hobl/ *vi* to move along unsteadily or with difficulty; *esp* to limp along ~ *vt* **1** to cause to limp; make lame; cripple **2** to fasten together the legs of (e g a horse) to prevent straying; fetter **3** to place under handicap; hamper, impede [ME *hoblen*; akin to MD *hobbelen* to turn, roll; (2) prob alter. of earlier *hopple*, prob fr ¹*hop*] – **hobbler** *n*

**²hobble** *n* **1** a hobbling movement **2** something (e g a rope) used to hobble an animal **3** *archaic* an awkward situation

**hobbledehoy** /,hobldi'hoy/ *n* an awkward gawky youth [origin unknown]

**hobble skirt** *n* a long skirt that is very narrow at the lower edge and restricts walking

**¹hobby** /'hobi/ *n* a leisure activity or pastime engaged in for interest or recreation [short for *hobbyhorse*] – **hobbyist** *n*

**²hobby** *n* a small falcon (*Falco subbuteo*) of Africa, Asia, and Europe that feeds esp on other small birds (e g swifts) caught on the wing and was formerly trained to catch small birds (e g larks) [ME *hoby*, fr MF *hobé*]

**hobbyhorse** /-,haws/ *n* **1** a figure of a horse fastened round the waist of a performer in a MORRIS DANCE **2a** a toy consisting of an imitation horse's head attached to one end of a stick on which a child can pretend to ride **b** ROCKING HORSE **c** a toy horse on a merry-go-round **3** a topic to which one constantly returns [arch. *hobby* small light horse, fr ME *hoby, hobyn*, prob fr *Hobbin*, nickname for *Robin*]

**hobgoblin** /,hob'goblin/ *n* **1** a goblin **2** a bugbear; BOGEY **2** [¹*hob*]

**hobnail** /'hob,nayl/ *n* a short large-headed nail for studding shoe soles [²*hob* (in arch. sense, peg or stake used as a target in games)] – **hobnailed** *adj*

**hobnob** /'hob,nob/ *vi* **-bb-** *informal* **1** to associate familiarly **2** to talk informally □ usu + *with* [fr the obs phrase *drink hobnob* to drink alternately to one another, fr earlier *habnab* in one way or another, hit or miss, prob deriv of OE *habban* to have + *nabban* to have not] – **hobnobber** *n*

**hobo** /'hohboh/ *n, pl* **hoboes** *also* **hobos** **1** *chiefly NAm* a migratory worker **2** *NAm* a tramp *usage* see ²TRAMP [perh fr *ho, bo* (assumed to be a form of greeting between tramps)]

**hobson-jobson** /,hobs(ə)n 'jobs(ə)n/ *n* FOLK ETYMOLOGY (transformation of words to produce more familiar forms) [*Hobson-Jobson,* Anglo-Indian form of a Muslim cry of mourning for Hasan & Husain, murdered grandsons of Muhammad, by folk etymology (influenced by the names *Hobson & Jobson*) fr Ar *yā Ḥasan! yā Ḥusayn!* O Hasan! O Husain!]

**Hobson's choice** /'hobs(ə)nz/ *n* an apparently free choice which offers no real alternative [prob fr Thomas *Hobson* †1631 E liveryman, who required every customer to take the horse nearest the door]

¹**hock** /hok/ *n* **1** the joint or region in the hind limb of a horse or related animal corresponding to the ankle of man but raised and bending backwards **2** a joint of a fowl's leg that corresponds to the hock of a 4-legged animal [ME *hoch, hough,* fr OE *hōh* heel; akin to ON *hāsin* hock, Skt *kaṅkāla* skeleton]

²**hock** *n, often cap, chiefly Br* a dry to medium-dry or occasionally sweet white table wine produced in the Rhine valley; *also* a similar wine produced elsewhere [modif of Ger *hochheimer,* fr *Hochheim,* town in SW Germany]

³**hock** *n, informal* **1** pawn ⟨*got his watch out of* ∼⟩ **2** debt ⟨*in* ∼ *to the bank*⟩ [D *hok* pen, prison]

⁴**hock** *vt, informal* to pawn – **hocker** *n*

**hockey** /'hoki/ *n* **1** a game played on grass between two teams of usu 11 players whose object is to direct a ball into the opponent's goal with a stick that has a flat-faced blade **2** *NAm* ICE HOCKEY [perh fr MF *hoquet* shepherd's crook, dim. of *hoc* hook, of Gmc origin; akin to OE *hōc* hook]

**hocus** /'hohkəs/ *vt* **-ss-** (*NAm* **-ss-, -s-**) **1** to trick, hoax **2** to befuddle, often with drugged drink; *also* to dope, drug ⟨∼ *sed the favourite just before the race*⟩ [obs *hocus,* n, short for *hocus-pocus*]

¹**hocus-pocus** /,hohkəs 'pohkəs/ *n* **1** SLEIGHT OF HAND **2** pointless activity or words, esp when intended to obscure or deceive [prob fr *hocus pocus,* imitation Latin phrase used by jugglers]

²**hocus-pocus** *vt* **-ss-** (*NAm* **-ss-, -s-**) to play tricks on

**hod** /hod/ *n* **1** a tray or trough mounted on a pole handle that is borne on the shoulder for carrying loads (e g of mortar or brick) **2** a coal scuttle; *also* a tall receptacle with two side handles from which coke or coal can be put onto a fire [prob fr MD *hodde;* akin to MHG *hotte* cradle, ME *schuderen* to shudder]

**hod carrier** *n* a labourer employed in carrying supplies to bricklayers, stonemasons, cement finishers, or plasterers on the job

**hodgepodge** /'hoj,poj/ *n, chiefly NAm* HOTCHPOTCH 1b (mixture) [by alter.]

**Hodgkin's disease** /'hojkinz/ *n* a cancerous disease that is characterized by progressive enlargement of the organs associated with the prevention of infection (e g LYMPH GLANDS, spleen, and liver) and by progressive anaemia [Thomas *Hodgkin* †1866 E physician]

**hodoscope** /'hodə,skohp/ *n* an instrument for tracing the paths of electrically charged particles (e g electrons and protons) occurring esp in the COSMIC RAYS falling on the earth from outer space [Gk *hodos* road, path + E *-scope* – more at CEDE]

¹**hoe** /hoh/ *n* any of various implements for tilling, mixing, or raking; *esp* an implement with a thin flat blade on a long handle, used esp for cultivating, weeding, or loosening the earth round plants [ME *howe,* fr MF *houe,* of Gmc origin; akin to OHG *houwa* mattock, *houwan* to hew – more at HEW]

²**hoe** *vi* to use a hoe; work with a hoe ∼ *vt* **1** to weed, cultivate, or thin (a crop) with a hoe **2** to remove (weeds) by hoeing **3** to prepare or cultivate (land) by hoeing – **hoer** *n*

**hoecake** /'hoh,kayk/ *n* a small cake made with maize meal [fr its formerly being baked on the blade of a hoe]

**hoedown** /-,down/ *n, chiefly NAm* **1** SQUARE DANCE **2** a gathering featuring hoedowns

¹**hog** /hog/ *n pl* **hogs,** *esp collectively* **hog** **1** a hogg **2** any of various wild pigs (family Suidae) – usu in combination ⟨*warthog*⟩ ⟨*red river* ∼⟩ **3** a stiff brush for cleaning the underwater parts of a ship **4** *Br* a castrated male pig raised for slaughter **5** *chiefly NAm* a domestic pig, esp when fully grown and weighing more than 50 kilograms (about 120 pounds); *broadly* a pig **6** *slang* a selfish, greedy, or filthy person – compare ROAD HOG [ME *hogge,* fr OE *hogg*]

²**hog** *vb* **-gg-** ∼ *vt* **1** to cut (a horse's mane) off or short **2** to cause

to arch **3** *informal* to take a selfish or excessive share of; monopolize ⟨∼ *ged the discussion*⟩ ∼ *vi, of a ship* to droop at the bow and stern owing to a structural defect

**hogan** /'hohgən/ *n* a building usu made of posts and branches covered with mud and used as a dwelling by the Navaho Indians of N New Mexico and Arizona [Navaho]

**HO gauge** *n* a gauge of track in model railways in which the rails are approximately 16.5 millimetres apart [*half* + *O gauge*]

**hogback** /-,bak/ *n, chiefly NAm* a hogsback

**hogg** /hog/ *n, Br* a young unshorn usu yearling sheep; *also* wool from the first shearing of such a sheep [var of *hog*]

**hogget** /'hogit/ *n, Br* a hogg

**hoggish** /'hogish/ *adj* grossly selfish, greedy, or filthy – **hoggishly** *adv,* **hoggishness** *n*

**Hogmanay** /'hogmənay, ,hogmə'nay/ *n, Scot* **1** the eve of New Year's Day **2** a gift requested or given at Hogmanay [origin unknown]

**hogsback** /-,bak/, **hog's back** *n* a ridge of land formed by the outcropping edges of tilted layers of rock; *broadly* a ridge or obstacle (e g for jumping) with a sharp summit and steeply sloping sides

**hog score** *n* a line which is marked across a CURLING (game played on ice in which stones are slid towards a target) rink 7 yards (about 6.5 metres) in front of the point from which the stone is propelled and beyond which the stone must slide or be removed from the ice [*hog* (curling stone that fails to reach the score)]

**hogshead** /-,hed/ *n* **1** a large cask or barrel **2** any of several measures of capacity varying according to locality and liquids contained; *esp* a measure of 52¹/₂ imperial gallons (about 238 litres)

¹**hog-,tie** *vt, chiefly NAm* to make helpless [fr the practice of making a hog or other animal helpless by tying its four feet together]

**hogwash** /-,wosh/ *n* **1** SWILL 1a, SLOP 4a **2** *slang* something worthless or nonsensical

**hogweed** /-,weed/ *n, Br* COW PARSNIP (plant of the carrot family)

¹**Hohenstaufen** /'hoh-ən,shtowfən (*Ger* hoːənʃtaʊfən)/ *adj* of a princely German family that reigned over the Holy Roman Empire from 1138 to 1254 and over Sicily from 1194 to 1266

²**Hohenstaufen** *n* a member of the Hohenstaufen family; *esp* a Hohenstaufen monarch

¹**Hohenzollern** /'hoh-ən,zolən (*Ger* hoːəntsɔlərn)/ *adj* of a princely German family that reigned in Prussia from 1701 to 1918 and in Germany from 1871 to 1918

²**Hohenzollern** *n* a member of the Hohenzollern family; *esp* a Hohenzollern monarch

**ho-ho** /hoh 'hoh/ *interj* – used to express hearty amusement

**ho hum** /'hoh ,hum/ *interj* – used to express weariness, boredom, or disdain [imit]

**hoick** /hoyk/ *vt, informal* to lift or pull abruptly; yank ⟨∼ *ed my case out of the rack*⟩ [prob alter. of ¹*hike*]

**hoi polloi** /,hoy pə'loy/ *n taking pl vb the* common people; *the* masses [Gk, the many]

**hoise** /hoyz/ *vt* **hoised** /hoyzd, hoyst/, **hoist** /hoyst/ *dial* to hoist [perh fr MD *hischen*]

**hoisin sauce** /hoy'sin/ *n* a thick reddish brown sweet spicy sauce used, esp in Chinese cookery, as a flavouring in savoury dishes (e g of fish, vegetables or pork) [prob fr Chin (Cant) *hoishin,* fr *hoi* sea + *shin* food, delicacy]

¹**hoist** /hoyst/ *vt* to raise into position (as if) by means of tackle ⟨∼ *the flag*⟩; *broadly* to raise ⟨*will not be easy to* ∼ *the price of better whiskies – The Economist*⟩ ∼ *vi* to become hoisted; rise – see also **hoist with one's own** PETARD *synonyms* see ¹LIFT [alter. of *hoise*] – **hoister** *n*

²**hoist** *n* **1** an act of hoisting; a lift **2** an apparatus for hoisting **3** (the width of) the inner end of a flag next to the staff

**hoity-toity** /,hoyti 'toyti/ *adj, informal* **1** thoughtlessly silly or frivolous; flighty **2** having an air of assumed importance; haughty [irreg redupl of E dial. *hoit* to play the fool]

**hokey** /'hohki/ *adj, chiefly NAm* **1** corny, mawkish **2** obviously contrived; phoney [irreg fr *hokum* + ¹*-y*] – **hokeyness** *n*

**hokeypokey** /,hohki'pohki/ *n, informal* HOCUS-POCUS 2 (something pointless)

**hokum** /'hohkəm/ *n, chiefly NAm* **1** a crude device, esp sentimental or comic, designed to appeal to an audience (e g of a play) **2** pretentious nonsense; bunkum [prob fr *hocus-pocus* + bun*kum*]

**hol-** /hol-/, **holo-** *comb form* **1** complete; total ⟨*holometabolism*⟩ **2** completely; totally ⟨*holographic*⟩ [ME, fr OF, fr L, fr Gk, fr *holos* whole – more at SAFE]

**holandric** /ho'landrik, hoh-/ *adj* **1** *of a hereditary characteristic* inherited solely in the male line; *specif* transmitted from male to male by a gene on a part of the male Y CHROMOSOME that has no corresponding part on the female X CHROMOSOME **2** being a gene that gives rise to a holandric characteristic □ compare HOLOGYNIC [ISV] – **holandry** *n*

**Holarctic** /ho'lahktik/ *adj* of or being the biogeographic area that includes most of the N hemisphere above the TROPIC OF CANCER

¹**hold** /hohld/ *vb* **held** /held/ *vt* **1a** to have in one's keeping; possess ⟨~s *the title to the property*⟩ **b** to retain by force ⟨*troops* ~ing *the ridge*⟩ **c** to keep control of or authority over ⟨*city is held by the enemy*⟩ **d** to keep by way of threat or force ⟨~ing *the child for ransom*⟩ **2** to impose restraint on: eg **2a** to refrain from producing ⟨~ *your noise*⟩ **b(1)** to keep under control; check ⟨*held his temper*⟩ **b(2)** to stop the action of temporarily; delay ⟨*held the presses to insert a late story*⟩ **c** to keep from advancing or from attacking successfully ⟨*held their opponents to a draw*⟩ **d** to restrict, limit ⟨~ *price increases to a minimum*⟩ **e** to bind legally or morally ⟨~ *a man to his word*⟩ **3a** to have, keep, or support in the hands or arms; grasp ⟨*held her to him*⟩ ⟨~ing *hands*⟩ **b** to keep in a specified situation, position, or state ⟨~ *a ladder steady*⟩ ⟨*held himself in readiness*⟩ **c** to support, sustain ⟨*the roof won't* ~ *much weight*⟩ **d** to retain ⟨*houses should* ~ *their value*⟩ **e** to keep in custody **f** to set aside; reserve ⟨~ *a room*⟩ **4** to bear, carry, comport ⟨*the soldierly way he* ~s *himself*⟩ **5a** to keep up without interruption; continue ⟨*ship held its course*⟩ **b** to keep the uninterrupted interest or attention of ⟨*held the audience in suspense*⟩ **6a** to contain or be capable of containing ⟨*the can* ~s *five gallons*⟩ **b** to have in store ⟨*what the future* ~s⟩ **7a** to maintain by way of opinion or feeling; harbour ⟨~ *a theory*⟩ **b** to have in regard ⟨~ing *money lightly, he spent it freely*⟩ **c** to maintain in an expressed judgment or affirmation ⟨~ing *that it is nobody's business but his* – Jack Olsen⟩ **8a** to engage in with someone else or with others; do by concerted action ⟨~ *a conference*⟩ **b** to cause to be conducted; convene ⟨~ *a meeting of the council*⟩ **9a** to occupy as a result of an appointment or election ⟨~s *a captaincy in the navy*⟩ **b** to have earned or been awarded ⟨~s *a PhD*⟩ ~ *vi* **1a** to maintain position; refuse to give ground ⟨*the defensive line is* ~ing⟩ **b** to continue unchanged; last ⟨*hopes the weather will* ~⟩ **2** to withstand strain without breaking or giving way ⟨*the anchor held in the rough sea*⟩ **3** to bear or carry oneself ⟨*asked him to* ~ *still*⟩ **4** to be or remain valid; apply ⟨*the rule* ~s *in most cases*⟩ **5** to maintain a course; continue ⟨*held south for several miles*⟩ **6** to refrain from an intended action; halt, pause – often imperative; often + *hard* **7** to stop counting during a countdown (eg in launching a spacecraft) **8** to have illegal drug material in one's possession *synonyms* see ¹KEEP *antonym* yield [ME *holden,* fr OE *healdan;* akin to OHG *haltan* to hold, L *celer* rapid] – **hold one's own** to maintain one's ground, position, or strength in the face of competition or adversity – see also **hold to** ACCOUNT/**at** BAY, **hold a** BRIEF **for/a** CANDLE **to, hold the** FORT, **hold** GOOD, **hold** HANDS, **hold one's** HORSES/**the** LINE, **hold** WATER

**hold back** *vt* **1** to hinder the progress of; restrain **2** to retain in one's keeping ~ *vi* to keep oneself in check – see also HOLDBACK

**hold down** *vt* **1** to keep within limits; *specif* to keep at a low level ⟨*try to hold prices* down⟩ **2** to hold and keep (a position of responsibility) ⟨*holding* down *two jobs*⟩

**hold forth** *vi* to speak at great length; expatiate

**hold off** *vt* **1** to keep at a distance ⟨*he tends to hold people* off⟩ **2** to resist successfully; withstand ⟨*held off the enemy attack*⟩ **3** to defer action on; postpone, delay ~ *vi* to keep off or at a distance ⟨*hope the rain holds off*⟩

**hold on** *vi* **1** to persevere in difficult circumstances **2** to wait; HANG ON ⟨*hold on a minute!*⟩

**hold on to** *vt* to keep possession of

**hold out** *vt* to present as likely or realizable; proffer ⟨*the doctors hold out every hope for his recovery*⟩ ~ *vi* **1** ¹LAST **2** ⟨*hope the car holds out till we get home*⟩ **2** to refuse to yield or give way ⟨*the garrison held out against the enemy attack*⟩

**hold out for** *vt* to insist on as the price for an agreement ⟨*held out for a shorter working week*⟩

**hold out on** *vt, informal* to withhold something (eg information) from

**hold over** *vt, NAm* to continue (eg in office) for a prolonged period ~ *vi* **1** to postpone **2** to prolong the engagement or tenure of ⟨*the show was held over for another week by popular demand*⟩ – see also HOLDOVER

**hold to** *vt* **1** to remain steadfast or faithful to; ABIDE BY **2** to cause to hold to ⟨*held him to his promise*⟩

**hold up** *vt* **1** to delay, impede ⟨*got held up in the traffic*⟩ **2** to rob at gunpoint **3** to present as an example ⟨*his work was held up to ridicule*⟩ ~ *vi* to endure a test; HOLD OUT – see also HOLDUP

**hold with** *vt* to agree with or approve of

²**hold** *n* **1** STRONGHOLD 1 **2a(1)** the act or manner of holding or grasping ⟨*released his* ~ *on the handle*⟩ **a(2)** a manner of grasping an opponent in wrestling **b** a nonphysical bond, grip, or grasp; influence, control ⟨*his father had a strong* ~ *over him*⟩ **c** possession ⟨*wants to get* ~ *of a road map*⟩ **3** something that may be grasped as a support **4** a sudden motionless posture at the end of a dance **5a** an order or indication that something is to be reserved or delayed **b** a delay in a countdown (eg in launching a spacecraft) – **take hold 1** to grasp, seize **2** to become attached or established; TAKE EFFECT

³**hold** *n* **1** a space below a ship's deck in which cargo is stored **2** the cargo compartment of an aeroplane [alter. of *hole*]

**holdall** /-,awl/ *n* a container for miscellaneous articles; *esp* a usu cloth travelling case or bag

**holdback** /'hohld,bak/ *n* **1** something that retains or restrains **2** the act of holding back

**holden** /'hohld(ə)n/ *archaic past part of* HOLD

**holder** /'hohldə/ *n* **1** a person who holds: **1a(1)** an owner **a(2)** a tenant **b** a person in possession of and legally entitled to receive payment of a bill, note, or cheque **2** a device that holds an often specified object ⟨*cigarette* ~⟩

**holdfast** /'hohld,fahst/ *n* **1a** a part by which a plant (eg a seaweed) clings to a flat surface **b** an organ by which a parasitic animal attaches itself to the organism on or in which it lives **2** something to which something else may be firmly secured

**holding** /'hohlding/ *n* **1** land held, esp as a tenant **2 holdings** *pl*, **holding** property (eg land or securities) owned

**holding company** *n* a company whose primary business is holding a controlling interest in the shares of other companies – compare INVESTMENT COMPANY, SUBSIDIARY

**holding pattern** *n* the usu oval course flown (eg over an airport) by aircraft awaiting clearance to land

**holdover** /'hohld,ohvə/ *n, NAm* somebody or something held or left over

**holdup** /-,up/ *n* **1** an armed robbery ⟨*a bank* ~⟩ **2** a delay

¹**hole** /hohl/ *n* **1** an opening into or through a thing **2a** a hollow place; *esp* a pit, cavity **b** a deep place in a body of water **c** a vacant position in a substance, esp a SEMICONDUCTOR (eg silicon), that was formerly occupied by an electron and can be regarded as equivalent to a positively charged particle **3** an animal's underground home; a burrow **4** a serious discrepancy or flaw ⟨*picked* ~s *in his story*⟩ **5a** the unit of play from the tee to the hole in golf **b** a usu lined cavity in a PUTTING GREEN into which the ball is to be played in golf **6** *informal* a mean or dingy place ⟨*lives in a dreadful* ~⟩ **7** *informal* an awkward situation; a fix ⟨*helped him out of rather a nasty* ~⟩ – see also ACE **in the hole** [ME, fr OE *hol* (fr neut of *hol,* adj, hollow) & *holh;* akin to OHG *hol,* adj, hollow, L *caulis* stalk, stem, Gk *kaulos*]

²**hole** *vt* **1** to make a hole in; *specif* to pierce the side of ⟨*the yacht was* ~d *below the waterline*⟩ **2** to drive into a hole ~ *vi* **1** to make a hole in something **2** to play one's ball into the hole in golf – usu + *out*

**hole up** *vb, informal* *vi* to take refuge or shelter ⟨*after the robbery the criminals* holed up *in a disused warehouse*⟩ ~ *vt* to place (as if) in a refuge or hiding place

,**hole-and-'corner** *adj* secret, underhand

**hole in one** *n* a golf score of one stroke on a hole; *also* a hole made in one stroke

,**hole-in-the-'corner** *adj* hole-and-corner

**holey** /'hohli/ *adj* having holes △ holy, wholly

¹**holiday** /'holiday, -di/ *n* **1** HOLY DAY **2** a day on which one does not have to do any work; *specif* a day marked by a general suspension of work in commemoration of an event ⟨*Christmas Day is a public* ~⟩ **3 holiday, holidays** *pl* a period of relaxation or recreation spent away from home or work; a vacation ⟨*went on* ~ *for a fortnight*⟩ ⟨*spent his* ~s *abroad*⟩ [ME, fr OE *hāligdæg,* fr *hālig* holy + *dæg* day]

*synonyms* **Holiday** is the general word for a day away from work.

**Holiday** or **holidays** is the usual British word for a whole period away from work ⟨*went to Ibiza for our* **holidays**⟩. **Vacation** is the usual American word for such a period, and is also the word for the interval between terms in British universities and law courts. Soldiers and certain officials go on **leave**, and this word is used also in such expressions as *sick* **leave** (for illness) and *compassionate* **leave** (for domestic problems). **Furlough** is another word for **leave**, commoner in the USA than in Britain. A **sabbatical** is a long holiday granted about every seventh year, especially to a university teacher. **Recess** is the word for the British Parliamentary vacation, and also the American word for the pause between lessons at school which British children call **break**.

²**holiday** *vi* to take or spend a holiday, esp in travel or at a resort – **holidayer** *n*

**holiday camp** *n* a place that provides accommodation and organized recreational activities for holidaymakers

**holidaymaker** /-ˌmaykə/ *n* a person who is on holiday

**holier-than-thou** /ˈhohli-ə/ *adj* marked by an air of superior holiness or morality

**holiness** /ˈhohlinis/ *n* 1 *cap* – used as a title for various high religious dignitaries ⟨*His* Holiness *Pope John Paul II*⟩ 2 the quality or state of being holy; SANCTIFICATION 2

**holism** /ˈhohˌliz(ə)m/ *n* a view of the universe, esp living nature, as composed of interacting wholes (e g of living organisms) that are more than the mere sum of their parts; *broadly* any view that emphasizes the organic or functional relation between members of a larger whole [*hol-* + *-ism*] – **holistic** *adj*

**holla** /ˈholə/ *n, vi, or interj* **hollas; hollaing; hollaed** (to) hollo

**holland** /ˈholənd/ *n, often cap* a cotton or linen fabric in PLAIN WEAVE, usu heavily stiffened or glazed and used for window blinds, bookbinding, and clothing [ME *holand*, fr *Holand* Holland, province of the Netherlands, fr MD *Holland*]

**hollandaise sauce** /holənˈdayz/ *n* a rich sauce made with butter, egg yolks, and lemon juice or vinegar [Fr *sauce hollandaise*, lit., Dutch sauce]

**Hollands** /ˈholəndz/ *n taking sing vb* gin originally made in Holland [D *hollandsch*, fr *hollandsch genever* Dutch gin]

¹**holler** /ˈholə/ *vi* 1 to gripe, complain 2 *chiefly NAm* to cry out (e g to attract attention); shout ∼ *vt, chiefly NAm* to call out (a word or phrase) [alter. of *hollo*]

²**holler** *n* 1 a complaint 2 *chiefly NAm* a shout, cry

**Hollerith** /ˈholərith/, **Hollerith code** *n* a system for converting and transferring information, (e g letters and figures) onto punched cards for use in computers [Herman *Hollerith* †1929 US engineer]

**Hollerith card** /ˈholərith/ *n* PUNCHED CARD

¹**hollo** *also* **holloa** /hoˈloh, ˈho-/ *interj* 1 – used to attract attention 2 – used as a call of encouragement or jubilation [origin unknown]

²**hollo** *also* **holloa** *vi* **hollos** *also* **holloas; holloing** *also* **holloaing; holloed** *also* **holloaed** to cry "Hollo!"; shout

³**hollo** *also* **holloa** *n, pl* **hollos** an exclamation or call of *hollo* ⟨*every day for food or play, came to the mariner's* ∼ – S T Coleridge⟩

¹**hollow** /ˈholoh/ *adj* 1 having a recessed surface; curved inwards; concave, sunken 2 having a cavity within ⟨∼ *tree*⟩ 3 echoing like a sound made in or by beating on an empty container; muffled 4a deceptively lacking in real value or significance ⟨*a* ∼ *victory*⟩ b lacking in truth or substance; false, deceitful ⟨∼ *promises*⟩ [ME *holw, holh*, fr *holh* hole, den, fr OE *holh* hole, hollow – more at HOLE] – **hollowly** *adv*, **hollowness** *n*

²**hollow** *vt* 1 to make hollow 2 to form by a hollowing action – usu + *out* ∼ *vi* to become hollow

³**hollow** *n* 1 a depressed or hollow part of a surface; *esp* a small valley or basin 2 an unfilled space; a cavity, hole

⁴**hollow** *adv* 1 in a hollow manner ⟨*his laughter rang* ∼⟩ 2 *informal* completely, comprehensively ⟨*he beat me* ∼⟩ [(2) perh of different origin]

**hollowware, holloware** /-ˌweə/ *n* vessels (e g bowls, cups, or pots), usu of pottery, glass, or metal, that have a significant depth and volume; *esp* metal cooking vessels (e g pans and kettles)

**holly** /ˈholi/ *n* 1 (the foliage or branches of) any of a genus (*Ilex* of the family Aquifoliaceae, the holly family) of trees and shrubs having thick glossy spiny-edged leaves and usu bright red berries 2 any of various trees with foliage resembling that of a holly [ME *holin, holly*, fr OE *holegn*; akin to OHG *hulis* holly, MIr *cuilenn*]

**hollyhock** /ˈholiˌhok/ *n* a tall widely cultivated Chinese plant (*Althaea rosea* of the family Malvaceae, the hollyhock family) with large coarse rounded leaves and long stems bearing several showy flowers [ME *holihoc* marshmallow, fr *holi* holy + *hoc* mallow, fr OE]

**Hollywood** /-ˌwood/ *n* the American film industry [*Hollywood*, district of Los Angeles in California, USA] – **Hollywoodish** *adj*

**holm** /hohlm, hohm/ *n, Br* a small inland or inshore island; *also* flat low-lying land near a river [ME, fr OE, fr ON *hōlmr*; akin to OE *hyll* hill]

¹**holmesian** /ˈhohmziən, ˈholmziən/ *adj, often cap* (in the manner) of the fictional detective Sherlock Holmes [Sherlock *Holmes*, detective in stories by Sir Arthur Conan Doyle †1930 Br writer]

²**holmesian** *n, often cap* a devotee of the detective series about Sherlock Holmes

**holmium** /ˈholmi-əm/ *n* a metallic chemical element of the RARE EARTH group that occurs with the related chemical element YTTRIUM and forms highly magnetic compounds [NL, fr *Holmia* Stockholm, city in Sweden]

**holm oak** *n* a S European evergreen oak (*Quercus ilex*) – called also ILEX [ME *holm* holly, alter. of *holin*; fr its foliage resembling that of the holly]

**holo-** – see HOL-

**holoblastic** /ˌholəˈblastik/ *adj, of an egg* having a pattern of division in which the whole egg divides into separate cells that together form the embryo – compare MEROBLASTIC [ISV] – **holoblastically** *adv*

**holocaust** /ˈholəˌkawst/ *n* 1 a sacrificial offering consumed by fire 2 an instance of wholesale destruction or loss of life, esp by fire 3 *often cap the* persecution and killing of European Jews by Hitler and the Nazi party during World War II [ME, fr OF *holocauste*, fr LL *holocaustum*, fr Gk *holokauston*, fr neut of *holokaustos* burnt whole, fr *hol-* + *kaustos* burnt, fr *kaiein* to burn – more at CAUSTIC]

**Holocene** /ˈholəseen/ *adj* RECENT 2 (of the present geological epoch) [ISV] – **Holocene** *n*

**holocrine** /ˈholəkrin, ˈhoh-/ *adj, of a gland* (e g a SEBACEOUS *gland in the skin*) producing a substance that contains disintegrated cells of the gland itself; *also* produced by a holocrine gland – compare APOCRINE, MEROCRINE [ISV *hol-* + Gk *krinein* to separate – more at CERTAIN]

**holoenzyme** /ˈholohˌenziem, ˈhoh-/ *n* a complete active ENZYME consisting of a protein component (APOENZYME) combined with a nonprotein activating component (COENZYME) [ISV]

**hologamous** /həˈlogəməs/ *adj* having reproductive cells of essentially the same size and appearance as nonreproductive cells – **hologamy** *n*

**hologram** /ˈholəgram/ *n* a pattern produced by interference between light scattered from an object illuminated by one part of a split laser beam and light from the other part of the beam; *also* a photographic reproduction of this pattern that when suitably illuminated produces a 3-dimensional picture

**holograph** /-grahf, -graf/ *n* a document wholly in the handwriting of its author; *also* the handwriting itself ⟨*a letter in the king's* ∼⟩ [LL *holographus*, fr LGk *holographos*, fr Gk *hol-* + *graphein* to write – more at CARVE] – **holograph, holographic** *adj*

**holography** /hoˈlogrəfi/ *n* the technique of making or using a hologram – **holograph** *vt*, **holographic** *adj*, **holographically** *adv*

**hologynic** /ˌholohˈjienik, ˌhoh-/ *adj* 1 *of a hereditary characteristic* inherited solely in the female line; transmitted from female to female (e g through receiving a gene on a part of the female X CHROMOSOME that has no corresponding part on the male Y CHROMOSOME) 2 being a gene that gives rise to a hologynic characteristic □ compare HOLANDRIC [ISV *hol-* + *-gynic* (fr Gk *gynē* woman) – more at QUEEN] – **hologyny** *n*

**holohedral** /ˌholəˈheedrəl/ *adj, of a crystal* having all the surfaces required for complete symmetry – compare HEMIHEDRAL, TETARTOHEDRAL

**holometabolous** /ˌhohlohməˈtabələs, ˌholoh-/ *adj, of an insect* undergoing a rapid and marked transformation (COMPLETE METAMORPHOSIS) from a young to a more adult stage (e g from larva to pupa and from pupa to butterfly) – compare HEMIMETABOLOUS – **holometabolism** *n*

**holomyarian** /ˌholohmieˈariən/ *adj, of a* NEMATODE *worm* having the muscle layer continuous or divided into two longitudinal zones without true muscle cells [deriv of Gk *holos* whole + *mys* muscle – more at SAFE, MOUSE]

**holophrastic** /,holə'frastik/ *adj* expressing a complex of ideas in a single word or in a fixed phrase [ISV *hol-* + *-phrastic* (fr Gk *phrazein* to point out, declare)]

**holophytic** /,holoh'fitik/ *adj* obtaining food in the manner of a green plant by photosynthesis

**holothurian** /,holə'thyooəri-ən/ *n* any of a class (Holothuroidea of the phylum Echinodermata) of marine INVERTEBRATE animals related to starfishes and SEA URCHINS that have a soft elongated muscular body with tentacles around the mouth to assist in feeding and that includes the SEA CUCUMBERS [deriv of Gk *holothourion* water polyp] – **holothurian** *adj*

**holotype** /'holə,tiep, 'hoh-/ *n* the single specimen of an organism designated as the type of a species, subspecies, or variety either by an author at the time the species is established or at a later date by another person – **holotypic** *adj*

**holozoic** /,holoh'zoh·ik/ *adj* obtaining food in the manner of most animals by eating complex matter obtained from dead or living organisms

**holp** /hohlp/ *chiefly dial past of* HELP

**holpen** /'hohlpən/ *chiefly dial past part of* HELP

**hols** /holz/ *n pl, chiefly Br informal* holidays

**holstein** /'holstien/ *n* 1 *often cap* (any of) a breed of carriage or riding horse developed by crossing the native N German breed with Thoroughbreds 2 *chiefly NAm* FRIESIAN (breed of cattle) [short for *holstein-friesian*]

**holstein-'friesian** *n* FRIESIAN 1 [*Holstein*, region in Germany, its later locality + *Friesian*]

**holster** /'hohlstə, 'hol-/ *n* a usu leather holder for a pistol [D; akin to OE *heolstor* cover, *helan* to conceal – more at HELL]

**¹holt** /hohlt/ *n, archaic* a small wood; a copse [ME, fr OE; akin to OHG *holz* wood, Gk *klados* twig – more at GLADIATOR]

**²holt** *n* a den or lair, esp of an otter [ME, alter. of ²*hold*]

**holus-bolus** /,hohləs 'bohləs/ *adv* all at once [prob redupl of *bolus*]

**holy** /'hohli/ *adj* 1 set apart to the service of God or a god; sacred ⟨*the ~ priesthood*⟩ 2a characterized by perfection and excellence; commanding absolute adoration and reverence ⟨*the ~ Trinity*⟩ b spiritually pure; godly ⟨*a ~ man given to prayer and charitable works*⟩ 3 evoking or worthy of religious respect or awe ⟨*the ~ cross*⟩ 4 terrible, awful – used as an intensive ⟨*a ~ terror*⟩ △ holey, wholly [ME, fr OE *hālig;* akin to OE *hāl* whole – more at WHOLE] – **holily** *adv*

**holy city** *n* a city that is a centre of religious worship and traditions

**Holy Communion** *n* COMMUNION 2a

**holy day** *n* a day set aside for special religious observance

**Holy Father** *n* the pope

**Holy Ghost** *n* the third person of the Trinity; HOLY SPIRIT

**Holy Hour** *n* an hour of prayer and meditation before the BLESSED SACRAMENT (bread and wine used in Communion), esp in memory of Christ's death on the cross

**Holy Innocents' Day** *n* December 28, kept by churches in memory of the children killed by Herod according to Mt 2:16

**Holy Joe** /joh/ *n, slang* a parson, chaplain; *also* a pious person [*Joe*, nickname for *Joseph*]

**Holy Land** *n the* territory of Palestine [fr its being the place of Christ's birth, ministry, and death]

**Holy Office** *n* a section of the body (CURIA) charged with protecting faith and morals in the Roman Catholic church

**holy of holies** *n* the innermost and most sacred chamber of the ancient Jewish Temple in Jerusalem; *broadly* any sacred place or thing [trans of LL *sanctum sanctorum*, trans of Heb *qōdhesh haq-qōdhāshīm*]

**holy oil** *n* olive oil blessed by a bishop for use in Christian ceremonies

**holy order** *n, often cap H&O* 1 MAJOR ORDER (grade of Christian ministry) 2 *pl* ORDINATION (ceremonial appointment to the Christian ministry) 3 *pl* the office of a Christian minister

**Holy Roller** /'rohlə/ *n, chiefly derog* a member of any of the Protestant sects whose worship meetings are characterized by frenzied excitement

**Holy Roman Empire** *n* an empire, consisting primarily of a loose confederation of mainly German and Italian territories under the control of an emperor, that existed from the 9th or 10th century to 1806

**Holy Saturday** *n* the Saturday before Easter

**Holy See** *n the* (area under the) jurisdiction of the pope

**Holy Spirit** *n the* active presence of God in human life constituting the third person of the Trinity

**¹holystone** /'hohli,stohn/ *n* a soft sandstone used to scrub a ship's decks

**²holystone** *vt* to scrub with a holystone

**Holy Synod** *n* the governing body of a national EASTERN ORTHODOX church

**Holy Thursday** *n* 1 ASCENSION DAY 2 MAUNDY THURSDAY

**holy war** *n* a war waged to promote or defend a religious cause

**holy water** *n* water blessed by a priest and used as a symbol of purification

**Holy Week** *n* the week before Easter, during which the last days of Christ's life are commemorated

**holy writ** *n, often cap H&W* 1 BIBLE 1 2 a writing or utterance having unquestionable authority

**Holy Year** *n* a Roman Catholic JUBILEE year (year of special solemnity)

**hom-** /hom-, hohm-/, **homo-** *comb form* 1 one and the same; similar; alike ⟨*homograph*⟩ ⟨*homosporous*⟩ 2 containing one more chemical group, $CH_2$, than (the specified compound) ⟨*homocysteine*⟩ [L, fr Gk, fr *homos* – more at SAME]

**homage** /'homij/ *n* 1a a ceremony by which in former times a man pledged himself as a VASSAL to serve loyally and fight for a lord in return for land b the relationship between a land-owning lord and his VASSAL c an act done or payment made in meeting the obligations of a VASSAL 2a reverential regard; deference b flattering attention [ME, fr OF *hommage*, fr *homme* man, vassal, fr L *homin-*, *homo* man; akin to OE *guma* man, L *humus* earth – more at HUMBLE]

**homalographic** /,homələ'grafik, hoh,malə-/ *adj* HOMOLOGRAPHIC (preserving the same relative positions)

**hombre** /'ombray/ *n, NAm* a man, fellow ⟨*a cabin occupied by a group of nasty-looking ~s* – Philip Hamburger⟩ [Sp, man, fr L *homin-*, *homo*]

**homburg** /'hombuhg/ *n* a felt hat with a stiff curled brim and a high crown creased lengthwise [*Homburg*, town in W Germany]

**¹home** /hohm/ *n* 1a a family's place of residence; a domicile b a house 2 the social unit formed by a family living together ⟨*comes from a broken ~*⟩ 3a a congenial and pleasant environment ⟨*the theatre is my spiritual ~*⟩ b a habitat 4a a place of origin ⟨*salmon returning to their ~ to spawn*⟩; *also* one's native country b the place where something originates or is based; headquarters ⟨*Lord's, ~ of cricket*⟩ 5 an establishment providing residence and often special care (e g for children, convalescents, old people, or disabled people) [ME *hom*, fr OE *hām* village, home; akin to Gk *kōmē* village, L *civis* citizen, Gk *koiman* to put to sleep – more at CEMETERY] – **homeless** *adj*, **homelessness** *n* – at **home** 1 relaxed and comfortable; AT EASE 2 ⟨*felt completely* at home *on the stage*⟩ 2 on familiar ground; knowledgeable ⟨*teachers* at home *in their subject fields*⟩ – **close to home** within one's personal interests so that one is strongly affected ⟨*remarks concerning tax evasion were a bit too* close to home⟩

**²home** *adv* 1 to or at home ⟨*wrote ~*⟩ 2 to a final, closed, or standard position ⟨*drive a nail ~*⟩ 3a to an ultimate objective (e g a finishing line) b to a successful or rewarding conclusion; HOME AND DRY 4 to a vital sensitive core ⟨*the truth struck ~*⟩ – **bring home** to cause to grasp or understand fully ⟨*his reply finally* brought the gravity of the situation home *to me*⟩ – **come home to roost** to rebound on the perpetrator, esp after a period of time – **nothing to write home about** nothing exceptional or worthy of pride – see also **till the cows come home** *usage* The adverb home is used without *to* when one speaks of or implies movement towards one's home, even with the verb *be* ⟨*we're nearly* home⟩. Where no movement is involved, *at* home is better than home alone in formal British writing ⟨*to stay [at]* home⟩ ⟨*is Henry [at]* home?⟩.

**³home** *adj* 1 of or being a home, place of origin, or base of operations ⟨*~ office*⟩ 2 prepared, carried out, or designed for use in the home ⟨*~ remedies*⟩ ⟨*~ cooking*⟩ ⟨*a ~ aquarium*⟩ 3 operating or occurring in a home area ⟨*the ~ team*⟩ ⟨*~ games*⟩

**⁴home** *vi* 1a to go or return home b *of an animal* to return accurately to its home or place of birth from a distance c to proceed to or towards a target using radiated energy as a guide – usu + *in on* ⟨*missiles* homing *in on their target*⟩ d to proceed or direct attention towards an objective – usu + *in on* ⟨*we're* homing *in on the right answer*⟩ 2 to have a home ~ *vt* to direct to or provide with a home

home- /ˌhomi-, ˌhohmi-/, **homeo-** *comb form* homoe-, homoeo-

**home and dry** *adv* having safely or successfully achieved one's purpose

**homebird** /-ˌbuhd/ *n, informal* a homebody

**homebody** /-ˌbodi/ *n, informal* one whose life centres on the home

¹**homebound** /ˈhohmˌbownd/ *adj* going homewards ⟨~ travellers⟩ [home + ¹bound]

²**homebound** *adj* confined to the home ⟨~ invalids⟩ [home + ⁴bound]

**homebred** /-ˈbred/ *adj* produced at home; indigenous

**home brew** *n* an alcoholic drink (eg beer) made at home

**homecoming** /-ˌkuming/ *n* 1 a return home 2 an annual celebration for former students at a college or university

**Home Counties** *n pl* the counties (Surrey, Essex, etc) surrounding London

**home economics** *n taking sing or pl vb* DOMESTIC SCIENCE – **home economist** *n*

**home from home** *n, chiefly Br* a place as comfortable or pleasant as one's own home

**home front** *n* the sphere of civilian activity in war

**homegrown** /-ˈgrohn/ *adj* 1 grown or produced at home ⟨~ vegetables⟩ 2 produced in, coming from, or characteristic of the home country ⟨~ politicians⟩

**home help** *n, Br* one who is employed (eg by a local authority) to carry out household chores, esp for those (eg the elderly or sick) incapable of doing them themselves

**homeland** /-ˌland/ *n* 1 one's native land 2 BANTUSTAN (black territory in S Africa)

**homelike** /-ˌliek/ *adj* characteristic of a home: **a** cheerful, cosy **b** simple, wholesome

**homely** /-li/ *adj* 1 suggestive or characteristic of a home 2 commonplace, familiar ⟨explained the problem in ~ terms⟩ 3 of a sympathetic character; kindly 4 simple, unpretentious ⟨she had a ~ natural manner⟩ ⟨a ~ meal of bacon and eggs⟩ 5 chiefly NAm not good-looking; plain, unattractive ⟨a ~ face redeemed by its smile⟩ □ compare HOMY – **homeliness** *n*

**homemade** /-ˈmayd/ *adj* made in the home, on the premises, or by one's own efforts ⟨~ cakes⟩

**homeo-** – see HOME-

**home office** *n, often cap H&O the* government office concerned with the internal affairs of a state (eg law and order and immigration)

**home plate** *n* a rubber slab at one corner of a baseball field at which a batter stands when batting and which constitutes the fourth base which must be touched by a base runner in order to score

**home port** *n* the port from which a ship comes or from which it is documented

¹**homer** /ˈhohmə/ *n* an ancient Hebrew unit of capacity equal to about 400 litres [Heb *hōmer*]

²**homer** *n* HOMING PIGEON

**home range** *n* the area to which the activities of an animal are confined

**Homeric** /hohˈmerik/ *adj* 1 (characteristic) of Homer, his age, or his writings 2 of epic proportions; heroic ⟨a ~ feat of endurance⟩ [Homer (Gk *Homēros*) *fl* ab 850 BC Gk epic poet] – **Homerically** *adv*

**home rule** *n* limited self-government in internal affairs by the people of a dependent political unit – compare SELF-GOVERNMENT

**home run** *n* a hit in baseball that enables the batter to make a complete circuit of the bases and score a run

**home secretary** *n, often cap H&S* a government minister for internal affairs

**homesick** /-ˌsik/ *adj* longing for home and family while absent from them [back-formation fr *homesickness*] – **homesickness** *n*

**home signal** *n* a railway signal that governs the movement of trains into a section of track – compare DISTANT SIGNAL

¹**homespun** /-ˌspun/ *adj* **1a** spun or made at home **b** made of homespun 2 lacking sophistication; simple, homely ⟨local ~ virtues – TLS⟩ ⟨~ prose⟩

²**homespun** *n* a loosely woven usu woollen or linen fabric originally made from yarn spun at home

¹**homestead** /ˈhohmstid, -sted/ *n* 1 the house and adjoining land occupied by a family 2 *Austr & NZ* the owner's living quarters on a sheep or cattle station

²**homestead** *vt* to acquire or occupy as a homestead ~ *vi* to

acquire or settle on land under a HOMESTEAD LAW – **homesteader** *n*

**homestead law** *n* any of several US legislative acts authorizing the sale of public lands in homesteads to settlers

**home straight** *n the* straight part of a racecourse between the last curve and the finish, that is usu opposite the grandstand

**homestretch** /-ˌstrech/ *n the* final stage (eg of a project)

**home student** *n* a student ordinarily resident in Britain as contrasted with an overseas student

**hometown** /ˈhohmˌtown, ˌ-ˈ-/ *n* the city or town of one's birth, upbringing, or current residence

**home truth** *n usu pl* an unpleasant but true fact about a person's character or situation

**homeward** /-wood/ *adj* being or going towards home

**homewards** /ˈhohmwədz/, chiefly NAm **homeward** *adv* towards home

**homework** /-ˌwuhk/ *n* 1 work done in one's own home for pay 2 an assignment given to a pupil to be completed outside the regular class period and esp away from school 3 preparatory reading or research (eg for a discussion) ⟨he has done his ~ on the subject⟩ – **homeworker** *n*

**homey** /ˈhohmi/ *adj, chiefly NAm* homy – **homeyness** *n*

**homicide** /ˈhomisied/ *n* (the act of) a person who kills another [ME, fr MF, fr L *homicida* & *homicidium*, fr *homo* man + *-cida* & *-cidium* – more at -CIDE ] – **homicidal** *adj*

**homiletic** /ˌhomiˈletik/, **homiletical** /-kl/ *adj* 1 of or like a homily 2 of homiletics [LL *homileticus*, fr Gk *homilētikos* of conversation, fr *homilein*] – **homiletically** *adv*

**homiletics** /ˌhomiˈletiks/ *n taking sing vb* the art of preaching

**homily** /ˈhomili/ *n* 1 a religious speech usu delivered to a congregation; a sermon 2 a lecture on moral conduct [ME *omelie*, fr MF, fr LL *homilia*, fr LGk, fr Gk, conversation, discourse, fr *homilein* to consort with, address, fr *homilos* crowd, assembly]

**homing pigeon** /ˈhohming/ *n* a domesticated pigeon trained to return home

**hominid** /ˈhominid/ *n* any of a family (Hominidae) of 2-legged mammals including recent man, his immediate ancestors, and related forms [deriv of L *homin-, homo* man] – **hominid** *adj*

**homin-ization, -isation** /ˌhominie'zaysh(ə)n/ *n* the evolutionary characteristics that differentiate man from his ancestors

**homin-ized, -ised** /ˈhominiezd/ *adj* characterized by hominization

**hominoid** /ˈhominoyd/ *adj* resembling or related to man – **hominoid** *n*

**hominy** /ˈhomini/ *n* crushed or coarsely ground maize with the husks removed, esp when prepared as food by boiling with water or milk [prob fr Algonquian origin; akin to Natick *-minne* grain]

¹**homo** /ˈhohmoh/ *n, pl* homos any of a genus (*Homo*) of mammals that includes modern man (*Homo sapiens*) and various extinct ancestors [NL *Homin-, Homo,* genus name, fr L, man]

²**homo** *n, pl* homos *derog* a homosexual [by shortening]

**homo-** – see HOM-

**homocercal** /ˌhomoh'suhkl, ˌhoh-/ *adj* 1 of the tail fin of a fish having the upper and lower lobes approximately symmetrical and the spinal column ending at or near the middle of the base – compare HETEROCERCAL 2 of or having a homocercal tail fin

**homochromatic** /ˌhoməkrə'matik, ˌhoh-/ *adj* of one colour

**homocyclic** /ˌhomə'sieklik, ˌhoh-/ *adj* relating to, characterized by, or being a ring composed of atoms of the same chemical element (eg carbon)

**homodont** /ˈhomə,dont/ *adj* having or being teeth all of one kind as in most VERTEBRATE animals other than mammals – compare HETERODONT [ISV]

**homoe-, homoeo-, home-, homeo-** *comb form* like ; similar ⟨homoeostasis⟩ [L & Gk; L *homoeo-,* fr Gk *homoi-, homoio-,* fr *homoios,* fr *homos* same – more at SAME]

**homoeomorphic** /ˌhomiə'mawfik, ˌhoh-/ *adj* characterized by homoeomorphism

**homoeomorphism** /ˌhomiə'mawfiz(ə)m, ˌhoh-/ *n* a near similarity of crystalline forms between different chemical compounds [ISV]

**homoeopath** /ˈhomi-ə,path/ *n* one who practises or supports homoeopathy

**homoeopathy** /ˌhomi'opəthi, ˌhoh-/ *n* a system of medical practice that treats disease esp by the giving of minute doses of a remedy that would in healthy people produce symptoms like those of the disease – compare ALLOPATHY [Ger *homö-opathie*, fr *homöo-* homoe- + *-pathie* -pathy]

**homoeostasis** /ˌhomiəˈstaysis, ˌhoh-, -ˈstasis, ˌhomiˈostəsis, ˌhoh-/ *n* a balance that is maintained among the constantly changing interdependent factors within an organism or group of organisms; *specif* the physiological maintenance of relatively constant conditions (e g constant internal temperature) within the body of an organism in the face of changing external conditions [NL] – **homoeostatic** *adj*, **homoeostatically** *adv*

**homogametic** /ˌhomohgaˈmetik, ˌhoh-/ *adj* forming one kind of reproductive cell; *esp* forming all reproductive cells with one type of SEX CHROMOSOME

**homogamy** /həˈmogəmi/ *n* **1a** the state of having all the flowers on a plant alike **b** the maturing of STAMENS and OVARIES (male and female reproductive parts in a flower) at the same time so that self-pollination can take place **2** reproduction within an isolated group that results in the preservation of qualities which distinguish that group from a larger one of which it is a part; *broadly* the mating of like with like; inbreeding [Ger *homogamie*, fr *hom-* + *-gamie* -gamy] – **homogamous, homogamic** *adj*

**homogenate** /hohˈmojinayt, ho-/ *n* a product of homogenizing

**homogeneity** /ˌhoməjəˈnayəti, -ˈnee-, ˌhohmoh-/ *n* **1** the quality or state of being homogeneous **2** *statistics* the state of having identical distribution functions or values ⟨*a test for ~ of variances*⟩ ⟨*~ of two statistical populations*⟩

  *usage* The pronunciation /-ˈneeəti/ rather than /-ˈnayəti/ is recommended for BBC broadcasters. *synonyms* see UNITY

**homogeneous** /ˌhoməˈjeenyəs, ˌhohmoh-, -niəs/ *adj* **1** of the same or a similar kind or nature **2** of uniform structure or composition throughout ⟨*a culturally ~ neighbourhood*⟩ **3** *of an equation, fraction, etc* having each term of the same degree if all variables are considered ⟨$x^2 + xy + y^2 = 0$ *is a ~ equation*⟩ **4** HOMOGENOUS 1 [ML *homogeneus, homogenus*, fr Gk *homogenēs*, fr *hom-* + *genos* kind – more at KIN] – **homogeneously** *adv*, **homogeneousness** *n*

  *usage* Homogeneous and homogenous have different pronunciations as well as different spellings.

**homogen·ize, -ise** /hoˈmojəniez, hə-/ *vt* **1a** to blend (diverse elements) into a smooth mixture **b** to make homogeneous **2** to reduce the particles of so that they are uniformly small and evenly distributed; *specif* to break up the fat globules of (milk) into very fine particles, esp by forcing through minute openings ~ *vi* to become homogenized – **homogenizer** *n*, **homogenization** *n*

**homogenous** /hoˈmojənəs, hə-/ *adj* **1** of or exhibiting homogeny **2** HOMOPLASTIC 2 (derived from another individual of the same species) **3** HOMOGENEOUS 1, 2, 3

**homogeny** /hoˈmojəni, hə-/ *n* correspondence between parts or organs due to descent from the same ancestral type

**homograft** /ˈhoməˌgrahft, ˈhohmə-/ *n* a graft of tissue taken from a donor of the same species as the recipient – compare HETEROGRAFT

**homograph** /ˈhoməˌgrahf, ˈhohmə-, -ˌgraf/ *n* any of two or more words spelt alike but different in meaning, derivation, or pronunciation (e g the noun *conduct* and the verb *conduct*) – compare HOMONYM, HOMOPHONE – **homographic** *adj*

**homoi-, homoio-** *comb form* homoe-, homoeo-

**homoiotherm** /həˈmoyoh,thuhm/ *n* a warm-blooded organism – **homoiothermy** *n*, **homoiothermal, homoiothermic** *adj*

**homolecithal** /ˌhomohˈlesithəl, ˌhoh-/ *adj, of an egg* having a small amount of yolk that is nearly uniformly distributed [*hom-* + Gk *lekithos* yolk]

**homologate** /hoˈmoləgayt/ *vt, formal* to sanction, allow; *esp* to approve or confirm officially [ML *homologatus*, pp of *homologare* to agree, fr Gk *homologein*, fr *homologos*] – **homologation** *n*

**homolog·ize, -ise** /hoˈmoləjiez/ *vt* to make homologous – **homologizer** *n*

**homologous** /hoˈmoləgəs/ *adj* **1a** having the same relative position, value, or structure **b(1)** exhibiting biological homology **b(2)** *of* CHROMOSOMES (*strands of gene-carrying material*) pairing with each other during MEIOSIS (division of cells to form sperm or eggs); having the same or corresponding genes usu arranged in the same order **c** belonging to or consisting of a chemical series whose members exhibit homology **2** being, derived from, or developed in response to organisms of the same species ⟨*a ~ tissue graft*⟩ [Gk *homologos* agreeing, fr *hom-* + *legein* to say – more at LEGEND]

**homolographic** /ˌhomələˈgrafik, hohˌmolə-/ *adj* preserving the mutual relations of parts, esp as to size or form ⟨*a ~ map projection*⟩ [Fr *homalographique*, fr Gk *homalos* even, level (akin to Gk *homos* same) + *graphein* to write – more at SAME, CARVE]

**homologue,** *NAm also* **homolog** /ˈhoməlog/ *n* a chemical compound, CHROMOSOME (strand of gene-carrying material), etc that exhibits homology

**homology** /hoˈmoləji/ *n* **1a** likeness in structure between parts of different organisms due to evolutionary differentiation from the same or a corresponding part of a remote ancestor – compare ANALOGY, HOMOMORPHY **b** correspondence in structure but not necessarily in function between different parts of the same individual **2a** the relation existing between chemical compounds in a series whose successive members have in composition a regular difference, esp of one carbon and two hydrogen atoms, $CH_2$ **b** the relation existing among chemical elements in the same group of the PERIODIC TABLE **3** *maths* a classification of configurations in TOPOLOGY into distinct types **4** *formal* a similarity often attributable to common origin [Gk *homologia* agreement, fr *homologos*]

**homolysis** /hoˈmoləsis, hoh-/ *n* breakdown of a chemical compound into two parts (e g atoms or chemical groups) that do not have an electric charge [NL] – **homolytic** *adj*

**homomorphism** /ˌhoməˈmawfiz(ə)m, ˌhohmoh-/ *n* **1** likeness in form (e g the condition of having flowers of only one type); homomorphy **2** a mathematical function that maps elements of one mathematical set onto elements of another and that has the property that applying the function to the sum or product of two elements is equivalent to applying the function to each element separately and adding or multiplying the result [ISV] – **homomorphic** *adj*

**homomorphy** /ˈhoməˌmawfi, ˈhohmoh-/ *n* similarity of form with different fundamental structure; *specif* superficial resemblance between organisms of different groups due to similar evolutionary adaptations – compare HOMOLOGY, HOMOPHYLY [ISV]

**homonuclear** /ˌhoməˈnyoohkliə, ˌhohmoh-/ *adj* of a molecule (e g hydrogen gas) composed of atoms having identical nuclei

**homonym** /ˈhomənim, ˈhohmə-/ *n* **1a** a homophone **b** HOMOGRAPH (word with same spelling as another) **c** any of two or more words spelt and pronounced alike but different in meaning (e g the noun *quail* and the verb *quail*) – compare SYNONYM **2** *formal* a namesake [L *homonymum*, fr Gk *homōnymon*, fr neut of *homōnymos*] – **homonymic** *adj*

**homonymous** /hoˈmoniməs, hoh-/ *adj* **1** *of words* having the relationship of homonyms **2** *formal* having the same name [L *homonymus* having the same name, fr Gk *homōnymos*, fr *hom-* + *onyma, onoma* name – more at NAME] – **homonymously** *adv*, **homonymy** *n*

**homoousion** /ˌhomohˈoohsiən, -ˈowsiən, ˌhohmoh-/ *n* the teaching of the NICENE CREED that Christ is of one substance with God the Father [LGk, fr *homoousios* of the same substance, fr Gk *hom-* + *ousia* substance]

**homophile** /ˈhoməˌfiel, ˈhoh-/ *adj* homosexual [*hom-* + ²-*phil*]

**homophone** /ˈhoməfohn/ *n* **1** any of two or more words pronounced alike but different in meaning, derivation, or spelling (e g *to, too,* and *two*) – compare HOMOGRAPH **2** a character or group of characters pronounced the same as another [ISV] – **homophonous** *adj*

**homophonic** /ˌhoməˈfonik, ˌhohmə-/ *adj* of or being music in which the parts move rhythmically in step with one another – compare CONTRAPUNTAL [Gk *homophōnos* being in unison, fr *hom-* + *phōnē* sound – more at BAN] – **homophony** *n*

**homophyly** /hoˈmofəli/ *n* resemblance due to common ancestry – compare HOMOMORPHY [ISV *hom-* + *phyl-* + *-y*]

**homoplastic** /ˌhoməˈplastik, ˌhohmoh-; *also* -ˈplahstik/ *adj* **1** relating to homoplasy **2** of or derived from another individual of the same species ⟨*~ grafts*⟩ – **homoplastically** *adv*

**homoplasy** /ˈhoməˌplaysi, ˈhohmoh-, hoˈmopləsi, hoh-/ *n* correspondence between parts or organs acquired as the result of similar evolutionary adaptations

**homopolar** /ˌhomohˈpohlə, ˌhoh-/ *adj* of a chemical bond in which there is an equal distribution of electric charge between atoms; COVALENT (of a chemical bond formed by shared electrons)

**homopolymer** /ˌhomohˈpolimə, ˌhoh-/ *n* a POLYMER (large chemical molecule composed of a series of repeating units) in which all the constituent units are identical (e g polythene)

**homopteran** /hoˈmoptərən, hoh-/ *n* a homopterous insect – **homopteran** *adj*

**homopterous** /hoh'moptərəs/ *adj* of a large suborder (Homoptera) of TRUE BUGS (e g aphids and SCALE INSECTS) that have sucking mouthparts [deriv of Gk *hom-* + *pteron* wing – more at FEATHER]

**homo sapiens** /ˌhomoh 'sapi·enz, ˌhohmoh, 'saypi·enz/ *n, often cap H* MANKIND 1 [NL, species name, fr *Homo,* genus name + *sapiens,* specific epithet, fr L, wise, intelligent – more at HOMO, SAPIENT]

**¹homosexual** /ˌhomə'seksyooə)l, -'seksh(ə)l, ˌhohmə-/ *adj* of, marked by, or exhibiting homosexuality – **homosexually** *adv*
 *usage* The pronunciation /ˌhomə-/ is recommended for BBC broadcasters, though some older speakers may prefer /ˌhohmoh-/ because of the word's derivation, from the Greek *homos* = "same" and not from the Latin *homo* = "man".

**²homosexual** *n* one who is inclined towards or practises homosexuality; a homosexual individual

**homosexuality** /ˌhoməseksyoo'aləti, -sekshoo-, ˌhohmə-/ *n* sexual preference for or sexual activity with people of one's own sex – compare HETEROSEXUALITY

**homosporous** /ho'mospərəs, ˌhomə'spawrəs, ˌhohmoh-/ *adj* producing asexual spores of one kind only

**homospory** /ho'mospəri, hoh-/ *n* the production by various plants (e g the CLUB MOSSES and HORSETAILS) of asexual spores of only one kind

**homothallic** /ˌhomoh'thalik, hoh-/ *adj* 1 *of algae and fungi* capable of undergoing sexual reproduction by interaction with a similar strain or between two of its own branches or filaments 2 MONOECIOUS (having male and female sex organs on the same individual) [*hom-* + Gk *thallein* to sprout, grow – more at THALLUS] – **homothallism** *n*

**homotransplant** /ˌhomə'trahnsplahnt, ˌhoh-, -'trans-/ *n* HOMOGRAFT (tissue transplant between individuals of the same species) – **homotransplantation** *n*

**homozygosity** /ˌhomohzie'gosəti, hoh-/ *n* the state of being a homozygote – **homozygosis** *n*

**homozygote** /ˌhohmoh'ziegoht, ˌhomoh-, -'zigoht/ *n* an animal, plant, or cell in which the genes at one or more usu specific corresponding positions on a pair of CHROMOSOMES (strands of gene-carrying material) are identical and so breed true for the characteristic(s) (e g eye colour, hairiness, the ability to produce a certain protein, etc) governed by these genes [ISV]

**homunculus** /ho'mungkyooləs/ *n, pl* **homunculi** /-li, -lie/ 1 a small man; a manikin 2 a figure of a man drawn so that the size of the parts (e g limbs, organs, etc) is proportional to the size of the area of the brain devoted to their control [L, dim. of *homin-, homo* man – more at HOMAGE]

**homy,** *chiefly NAm* **homey** /'hohmi/ *adj, informal* homelike ⟨a ~ atmosphere⟩ □ compare HOMELY

**¹hone** /hohn/ *n* a fine-grit stone for sharpening a cutting tool [ME, fr OE *hān* stone; akin to ON *hein* whetstone, L *cot-, cos,* Gk *kōnos* cone]

**²hone** *vt* 1 to sharpen, enlarge, or smooth with a hone 2 to make more acute, keen, or effective; whet, fine ⟨*finely* ~d *sarcasm*⟩ – **honer** *n*

**³hone** *vi, dial* 1 to grumble, moan 2 to yearn [MF *hoigner* to grumble]

**honest** /'onist/ *adj* 1 free from fraud or deception; legitimate, truthful ⟨*an* ~ *plea*⟩ 2 reputable, respectable ⟨*poor but* ~⟩ 3 creditable, praiseworthy ⟨*an* ~ *day's work*⟩ 4a marked by integrity; upright **b** frank, sincere ⟨*an* ~ *answer*⟩ 5 *chiefly Br* good, worthy ⟨*an* ~ *fellow*⟩ [ME, fr OF *honeste,* fr L *honestus* honourable, fr *honos, honor* honour] – **honest, honestly** *adv*

**honest broker** *n* a neutral mediator ⟨*an* ~ *between the warring parties*⟩

**honesty** /'onisti/ *n* 1a upright and straightforward conduct; integrity **b** sincerity, truthfulness 2 any of a genus (*Lunaria*) of European plants of the cabbage family that have purple flowers and broad smooth semitransparent seed capsules 3 *obs* chastity

**honewort** /'hohnˌwuht/ *n* a European plant (*Trinia glauca*) of the carrot family that has greyish leaves and stems and clusters of small white flowers; *also* any of several related plants [perh fr E dial. *hones* lumps in a cow's udder]

**¹honey** /'huni/ *n* 1a (a pale golden colour like that typical of) a sweet thick sticky liquid formed from the nectar of flowers in the HONEY SACS of various bees **b** a sweet fluid resembling honey that is collected or produced by various insects 2 something sweet or agreeable; sweetness ⟨*the* ~ *of admiration*⟩ 3 *chiefly NAm* sweetheart, dear 4 *informal* a superlative example

⟨a ~ *of a girl* – Philip Roth⟩ [ME *hony,* fr OE *hunig;* akin to OHG *honag* honey, L *canicae* bran]

**²honey** *vi* **honeyed** *also* **honied** *chiefly NAm* to use blandishments or cajolery

**³honey** *adj* 1 of or like honey 2 much loved; dear

**honey badger** *n* RATEL (badgerlike mammal) [fr its fondness for honey]

**honey bear** *n* 1 SLOTH BEAR (Asian black bear) 2 KINKAJOU (small tree-living raccoon)

**honeybee** /-ˌbee/ *n* a honey-producing bee (*Apis* or related genera) that lives in more or less organized communities; *esp* a native European bee (*Apis mellifera*) kept for its honey and wax

**honey buzzard** *n* a Eurasian and African hawk (*Pernis apivorus*) that often feeds on the larvae of wasps and bees

**¹honeycomb** /-ˌkohm/ *n* 1 a mass of 6-sided wax cells built by honeybees in their nest to contain their brood and stores of honey 2 something that resembles a honeycomb in structure or appearance; *esp* a strong lightweight cellular structural material 3 RETICULUM (second chamber of the stomach of a cow or other cud-chewing mammal)

**²honeycomb** *vt* **1a** to cause to be full of cavities like a honeycomb **b** to make into a honeycomb pattern; chequer **2a** to penetrate into every part; riddle ⟨*the ... government is* ~ed *with spies* – T H White⟩ **b** to subvert, weaken ⟨*tribes* ~ed *with rivalries*⟩ □ often pass

**honeydew** /-ˌdyooh/ *n* a sugary substance deposited on the leaves of plants usu by aphids, SCALE INSECTS, or sometimes by a fungus

**honeydew melon** *n* a pale smooth-skinned muskmelon with greenish sweet flesh

**honey eater** *n* any of several songbirds (family Meliphagidae) mostly of the S Pacific with a long tongue adapted for extracting nectar and small insects from flowers

**honeyed** *also* **honied** /'hunid/ *adj* sweetened (as if) with honey ⟨~ *words*⟩

**honey fungus** *n* a honey-coloured mushroom (*Armillaria mellea*) that grows round the base of esp decaying trees and is lethal to most plant life, particularly trees – called also BOOTLACE FUNGUS

**honey guide** *n* any of several small plainly coloured birds (family Indicatoridae, esp genera *Indicator* and *Prodotiscus*) that inhabit Africa, the Himalayas, and the E Indies and are supposed to lead humans or animals to the nests of bees

**honey locust** *n* a tall usu spiny N American tree (*Gleditsia triacanthos*) with very hard durable wood and long flattened sometimes twisted pods containing a sweet edible pulp and seeds that resemble beans

**honeymoon** /-ˌmoohn/ *n* 1 a journey or holiday taken by a newly married couple 2 the period immediately following marriage 3 a period of unusual harmony following the establishment of a new relationship ⟨*forecast that the Secretary of State would have a short* ~ *with the educational world* – TES⟩ [*honey* + ¹*moon* 2] – **honeymoon** *vi,* **honeymooner** *n*

**honey mouse** *n* a small insect-eating marsupial mammal (*Tarsipes rostratus*) of W Australia

**honey sac** *n* a swelling of the tube between the mouth and stomach of a bee, in which honey is produced

**honeysuckle** /-ˌsukl/ *n* 1 any of a genus (*Lonicera* of the family Caprifoliaceae, the honeysuckle family) of (climbing) shrubs usu with showy sweet-smelling flowers rich in nectar; *esp* a European twining shrub (*Lonicera perichymenum*) 2 any of various plants (e g a columbine or azalea) with tubular flowers rich in nectar [ME *honysoukel,* alter. of *honysouke,* fr OE *hunisūce,* fr *hunig* honey + *sūcan* to suck]

**hongi** /'hong·i/ *n, NZ* a pressing together of noses by two people that is used as a form of greeting by the Maoris [Maori] – **hongi** *vi*

**¹honk** /hongk/ *n* 1 the characteristic cry of a goose 2 a short loud unmusical tone (e g the sound made by a car's electric horn) that is like the cry of a goose [imit]

**²honk** *vi* to make the characteristic cry of a goose or a similar sound ~ *vt* to cause to honk ⟨*the driver* ~ed *his horn*⟩ – **honker** *n*

**honkie, honky** /'hongki/ *n, chiefly NAm derog* a white man – used by Blacks [origin unknown]

**honky-tonk** /'hongki ˌtongk/ *n* 1 a form of ragtime piano playing that is typically performed on an upright piano 2 *informal* a cheap nightclub or dance hall [origin unknown] – **honky-tonk** *adj*

**honorand** /'onərand/ *n* a person who is to receive an honour (e g an honorary degree) [L *honorandus*, gerundive of *honorare* to honour, fr *honos, honor* honour]

**honorarium** /ˌonəˈreəri·əm/ *n, pl* **honorariums, honoraria** /-riə/ a payment in recognition of professional services on which no price is set [L, fr neut of *honorarius*]

¹**honorary** /'on(ə)rəri/ *adj* **1a** having or conferring distinction **b** commemorative **2a** conferred or elected in recognition of achievement or service without the usual prerequisites or obligations ⟨*an ~ degree*⟩ ⟨*an ~ member*⟩ **b** unpaid, voluntary ⟨*an ~ chairman*⟩ **3** depending on honour for fulfilment ⟨*an ~ obligation*⟩ [L *honorarius*, fr *honor*] – **honorarily** *adv*

> *usage* The abbreviation **hon** stands for either **honorary** (= unpaid) or **honourable**, depending on the context.

²**honorary** *n* an honorary degree or its recipient

¹**honorific** /ˌonəˈrifik/ *adj* **1** conferring or conveying honour ⟨*~ titles*⟩ **2** belonging to or constituting a class of grammatical forms (e g in Chinese and Japanese) used in speaking to or about a social superior – **honorifically** *adv*

²**honorific** *n* an honorific word, phrase, expression, title, etc

**honor roll** *n, NAm* ROLL OF HONOUR

¹**honour, NAm chiefly honor** /'onə/ *n* **1a** good name or public esteem; reputation ⟨*his ~ was at stake*⟩ **b** outward respect; recognition ⟨*a dinner held in his ~*⟩ **2** a privilege ⟨*I have the ~ of welcoming you*⟩ **3** *cap* a person of superior social standing – now used esp as a title of address or reference for a holder of high office (e g a judge in court) ⟨*if Your* Honour *pleases*⟩ **4** one who brings respect or fame; credit ⟨*was an ~ to his profession*⟩ **5** a mark or symbol of distinction: e g **5a** an exalted title or rank **b(1)** a badge, decoration **b(2)** *pl* a ceremonial rite or observance ⟨*buried with full military ~s*⟩ **c** *pl* an academic distinction conferred on a superior student **6** *pl* a course of study for a university degree that is more exacting and specialized than that leading to a PASS DEGREE and that is now usu the standard course in Britain **7** (a woman's) chastity or purity **8a** a high standard of ethical conduct; integrity **b** one's word given as a pledge ⟨*~ bound*⟩ **9a(1)** an ace, king, queen, or jack of the trump suit in whist; *also* these cards and the ten in bridge or the four aces when there are no trumps **a(2)** *pl* the scoring value of honours held in bridge or whist **b** the privilege of playing first from the tee in golf awarded to the player who won the previous hole [ME, fr OF *honor*, fr L *honos, honor*] – **do the honours** to carry out social courtesies or civilities in the manner of a host ⟨*did the honours at the table*⟩ – **on/upon one's honour** with one's good name acting as a guarantee of the truth of a specified statement

²**honour, NAm chiefly honor** *vt* **1a** to regard or treat with honour or respect **b** to confer honour on **2a** to accept as right or appropriate; recognize, respect ⟨*the lorry-drivers were* honouring *the picket line*⟩ **b** to live up to or fulfil the terms of ⟨*~ a commitment*⟩ **c** to accept and pay when due ⟨*~ a cheque*⟩ **3** to salute (e g one's partner) with a bow in a country dance

¹**honourable, NAm chiefly honorable** /'on(ə)rəbl/ *adj* **1** worthy of honour **2** performed or accompanied with marks of honour or respect **3a** of great renown; illustrious **b** *cap* entitled to honour – used as a title for the children of certain British noblemen and for various government officials **4a** bringing credit to the possessor or doer ⟨*an ~ performance*⟩ **b** consistent with an untarnished reputation ⟨*an ~ discharge from the army*⟩ **5** characterized by (moral) integrity; ethical, upright ⟨*his intentions were ~*⟩ *usage* see HONORARY

**honourable mention** *n, often cap H&M* a distinction awarded (e g in a contest or exhibition) for work of exceptional merit that has not obtained a prize

**honour point** *n* the centre point of the upper half of a heraldic shield

**honours list** *n* a twice-yearly produced list of people who are to be honoured by the British sovereign (e g with membership of an order of chivalry or a peerage) in recognition of their public service

**hooch, hootch** /hoohch/ *n, NAm slang* spirits, esp when inferior or illicitly made or obtained [short for *hoochinoo* (a distilled liquor made by the Hoochinoo Indians of Alaska)]

¹**hood** /hood/ *n* **1a(1)** a flexible often protective covering for the top and back of the head and neck that is usu attached to the neckline of a garment **a(2)** a protective covering for the head and face **b** a usu leather covering for a hawk's head and eyes **c** a covering for a horse's, esp a racehorse's, head **2a** an orna-

mental scarf, worn over an academic gown, that indicates by its colour the wearer's university and degree **b** a hoodlike marking, crest, or expansion on the head of an animal (e g a cobra) **3a** something resembling a hood in form or use **b** a cover for (parts of) mechanical devices or machinery; *specif, NAm* a motor-vehicle bonnet **c** a folding waterproof top cover for an open car, pram, etc **d** a cover or canopy for carrying off fumes, smoke, etc [ME, fr OE *hōd;* akin to OHG *huot* head covering (cf HAT)] – **hood** *vt*, **hoodlike** *adj*

²**hood** *n, informal* a hoodlum, gangster

**-hood** /-hood/ *suffix (adj or n → n)* **1** state or condition of ⟨*priest*hood⟩ ⟨*man*hood⟩ **2** quality or character of ⟨*likeli*hood⟩ **3** time or period of ⟨*child*hood⟩ **4** instance of (a specified quality or condition) ⟨*a false*hood⟩ **5** body or class of people sharing (a specified character or state) ⟨*brother*hood⟩ [ME *-hod*, fr OE *-hād;* akin to OHG *-heit* state, condition, *heitar* bright, clear (some forms may have arisen by alter. of ME *-hed* state or OE *rǣden* condition; cf GODHEAD, MAIDENHEAD, BROTHERHOOD)]

**hooded** /'hoodid/ *adj* **1** covered (as if) by a hood ⟨*~ eyes*⟩ **2** of a plant part shaped like a hood **3a** *of an animal* **3a(1)** having the head conspicuously different in colour from the rest of the body ⟨*a ~ rat*⟩ **a(2)** having a crest on the head that suggests a hood **b** *of a cobra* having the skin at each side of the neck capable of expansion by movements of the ribs – **hoodedness** *n*

**hooded crow** *n* a Eurasian crow (*Corvus corone cornix*) with a black head, tail, and wings and a grey body, that is closely related to the CARRION CROW

**hooded seal** *n* a large seal (*Cystophora cristata*) of the N Atlantic, the male of which has a large inflatable sac on its head

**hoodie** /'hoodi/, **hoodie crow** *n, chiefly Scot* HOODED CROW

**hoodlum** /'hoohdləm/ *n* **1** a (violent) thug **2** a young ruffian [origin unknown] – **hoodlumish** *adj*, **hoodlumism** *n*

**hood moulding** *n* a stone projection to throw off rainwater over a door or window

¹**hoodoo** /'hooh,dooh/ *n, pl* **hoodoos** **1** one who or that which brings bad luck **2** a natural column of rock common in parts of W USA, that is formed by weathering and often has a strange or fantastic shape **3** *chiefly NAm* voodoo [of African origin; akin to Hausa *hu³'du³'ba¹* to arouse resentment] – **hoodooism** *n*

²**hoodoo** *vt, chiefly NAm* to cast an evil spell on; *broadly* to bring bad luck to

**hoodwink** /'hood,wingk/ *vt* **1** *informal* to deceive, delude **2** *archaic* to blindfold [¹*hood* + *wink*] – **hoodwinker** *n*

**hooey** /'hooh·i/ *n, slang* nonsense [origin unknown]

¹**hoof** /hoohf, hoof/ *n, pl* **hooves** /hoohvz/, **hoofs** **1** a curved horny casing that protects the ends of the foot of a horse, cow, or similar mammal and that corresponds to a nail or claw **2** a hoofed foot esp of a horse [ME, fr OE *hōf;* akin to OHG *huof* hoof, Skt *śapha*] – **on the hoof** *of a meat animal* before being butchered; while still alive ⟨*50p a pound* on the hoof⟩

²**hoof** *vb, informal* *vt* to kick ~ *vi* to dance – **hoof it** to go on foot; *esp* to run

**hoofbeat** /'hoohf,beet, 'hoof-/ *n* the sound of a hoof striking a hard surface

**hoofed** /hoohft, hooft/ *adj* having hoofs; UNGULATE – often in combination ⟨*cloven*-hoofed⟩

**hoofer** /'hoohfə, 'hoofə/ *n, NAm slang* a professional dancer

**hoof pick** *n* a tool for removing stones and dirt from horses' hooves

**hoofprint** /'hoohf,print, 'hoof-/ *n* an impression or hollow made by a hoof

**hoo-ha** /'hooh ,hah/ *n, informal* a fuss, to-do [perh alter. of *brouhaha*]

¹**hook** /hook/ *n* **1** a curved or bent device for catching, holding, or pulling ⟨*a fish ~*⟩ **2** something (e g a crochet hook) curved or bent like a hook **3a** a flight of a golf ball that swerves from a straight course in a direction opposite to the hand that is predominant in striking the ball, typically because of a faulty stroke; *also* a golf ball following such a course – compare SLICE **b** an attacking stroke in cricket played with a horizontal bat aimed at a ball of higher than waist height that is designed to send the ball esp behind or square with the batsman's wicket on the LEG SIDE **4** a short blow delivered in boxing with a circular motion while the elbow remains bent and rigid [ME, fr OE *hōc;* akin to MD *hoec* fishhook, corner, OHG *hāko* hook, Lith *kengè*] – **by hook or by crook** by any possible

means – **hook, line, and sinker** completely ⟨*swallowed all the lies* hook, line, and sinker⟩ – **off the hook 1** *of a telephone receiver* not resting on the main body of the telephone **2** *informal* out of trouble

²**hook** *vt* **1** to form into a hook (shape) **2** to seize, make fast, or connect (as if) by a hook **3** to make (e g a rug) by drawing loops of yarn, thread, or cloth through a coarse fabric (e g canvas) with a hook **4** to hit (a golf ball) so that a hook results **5** to gain possession of (the ball) in rugby and pass to one's team mates at the back of a scrum **6** to play a hook in cricket at (a ball) or at the bowling of (a bowler) **7** *informal* to steal, pilfer ~ *vi* **1** to form a hook; curve **2** to become hooked **3** to play a hook in cricket or golf

**hook off** *vi, NZ* to leave, disappear

**hookah** /'hookə, -kah/ *n* WATER PIPE **2** (smoking apparatus); *specif* one fitted with a long flexible tube by which the smoke is drawn through water and up into the mouth – compare NARGHILE [Ar *ḥuqqah* bottle of a water pipe]

**hook and eye** *n* a fastening device used chiefly on garments that consists of a small metal hook that links with an eye in the form of a bar or loop

**hooked** /hookt/ *adj* **1** (shaped) like a hook **2** provided with a hook **3** made by hooking ⟨*a* ~ *rug*⟩ **4** *informal* **4a** addicted to drugs **b** very enthusiastic or compulsively attached – often + *on* ⟨~ *on skiing*⟩ – **hookedness** *n*

**hooker** /'hookə/ *n* **1** (the position of) a player in rugby stationed in the middle of the front row of a scrum **2** *chiefly NAm informal* a female prostitute

**hook shot** *n* a shot in basketball made usu while standing sideways to the basket by swinging the ball up through an arc with the far hand

**hookup** /-ˌup/ *n* **1** a linking together or combination of electronic or electrical equipment (e g a radio transmitter, a satellite, and a radio receiver) for a particular often temporary purpose (e g radio transmission); *also* the plan made of such a combination **2** *chiefly NAm* an arrangement of mechanical parts

**hookworm** /-ˌwuhm/ *n* **1** any of several parasitic roundworms (family Ancylostomatidae of the phylum Nematoda) including some bloodsucking varieties harmful to humans and domestic animals, that have strong mouth hooks or plates by which they attach themselves to the lining of the host's intestine **2** infestation with or disease caused by hookworms; ANCYLOSTOMIASIS

**hooky, hookey** /'hooki/ *n* [prob fr slang *hook, hook it* to make off] – **play hooky** *chiefly NAm, Austr, & NZ informal* to play truant

**hooley** /'hoohli/ *n, chiefly NZ informal* a celebration, party; *esp* a noisy one [origin unknown]

**hooligan** /'hoohligən/ *n* a young ruffian or hoodlum [perh fr Patrick *Hooligan* fl1898 Irish criminal in London] – **hooliganism** *n*

¹**hoop** /hoohp/ *n* **1a** a large rigid circular strip (e g of iron) used for holding together the staves of a container (e g a barrel or cask) **b** a child's toy consisting of a metal, plastic, etc ring that is rolled along the ground or spun round the body **2a** a typically rigid circular figure, band, or object; a ring, circle **b** the rim of a basketball goal **c** an arch through which balls must be hit in croquet **3** a circle of flexible material (e g whalebone) or a framework of circles and curved pieces used formerly to spread out a woman's skirt [ME, fr OE *hōp*; akin to MD *hoep* ring, hoop, Lith *kabė* hook]

²**hoop** *vt* to bind or fasten (as if) with a hoop – **hooper** *n*

**hooper** /'hoohpə/ *n* a cooper

**hoopla** /'hoohp,lah/ *n* **1** a (fairground) game in which prizes are won by tossing rings over them **2** *NAm informal* **2a** excited commotion; to-do **b** nonsense [Fr *houp-là*, interj indicating sudden movement; (1) influenced by ¹ *hoop*]

**hoopoe** /'hoohpooh, -poh/ *n* any of several birds (family Upupidae) that have a slender downward-curving bill; *esp* a Eurasian and N African hoopoe (*Upupa epops*) that has pale pinkish-brown plumage and a long crest that can be erected [alter. of obs *hoop*, fr MF *huppe*, fr L *upupa*, of imit origin]

**hooray** /hoo'ray/ *interj* hurray

**hooray Henry** *n, Br chiefly humorous* a male upper-class twit [fr the forename *Henry*]

**hooroo** /'hooh,rooh, -'-/ *interj, Austr & NZ* goodbye [alter. of *hooray*]

**hoose** /hoohz/ *n* HUSK (bronchitis in cattle and sheep caused by parasitic worms) [prob akin to E *wheeze*]

**hoosegow** /'hoohs,gow/ *n, NAm slang* jail [Sp *juzgado* panel of judges, courtroom, fr pp of *juzgar* to judge, fr L *judicare*]

¹**hoot** /hooht/ *vi* **1** to utter a loud shout, usu in contempt **2a** to make the long-drawn-out throat noise of an owl or a similar cry **b** to sound the horn, whistle, etc of a motor car or other vehicle ⟨*the driver* ~ed *at me as he passed*⟩ **3** *informal* to laugh loudly ~ *vt* **1** to assail or drive out by hooting ⟨~ed *down the speaker*⟩ **2** to express in or by hoots ⟨~ed *their disapproval*⟩ [ME *houten*, of imit origin]

²**hoot** *n* **1** a sound of hooting; *esp* the characteristic cry of an owl **2** *informal* **2a** the slightest bit; DAMN **2** ⟨*I couldn't care two* ~ s⟩; *also* a least amount or degree of care or consideration ⟨*don't give a* ~ *what happens*⟩ **b** a source of laughter or amusement ⟨*the play was an absolute* ~⟩

**hootenanny** /'hoohtə,nani/ *n, NAm* a gathering at which folk singers entertain, often with the audience joining in [origin unknown]

**hooter** /'hoohtə/ *n, chiefly Br* **1** a device (e g the horn of a car) for producing a loud hooting noise **2** *slang* the nose ⟨*gave him a punch up the* ~⟩

**hoots** /hoohts, hoots/ *interj, chiefly Scot* – used to express impatience, dissatisfaction, or objection [origin unknown]

**hoover** /'hoohvə/ *vb* to clean using a vacuum cleaner

**Hoover** /'hoohvə/ *trademark* – used for a vacuum cleaner

¹**hop** /hop/ *vb* **-pp-** *vi* **1** to move by a quick springy leap or in a series of leaps; *esp* to jump on one foot **2** *informal* **2a** to make a quick trip, esp by air – usu + *off, over* or *across* ⟨~ped *across to America on important business and then back to London*⟩ **b** to board or leave a vehicle ⟨~ *onto a bus*⟩ ~ *vt* **1** to jump over ⟨~ped *the fence*⟩ **2** *NAm* to ride on, esp without authorization ⟨~ *a train*⟩ [ME *hoppen*, fr OE *hoppian*; akin to OE *hype* hip] – **hop it** *Br informal* go away

²**hop** *n* **1a** a short leap, esp on one leg **b** a bounce, rebound **2** a flight in an aircraft between two landings ⟨*flew to Bangkok in three* ~ s⟩ **3** *informal* DANCE **3** ⟨*went to the local* ~⟩ – **on the hop** *informal* **1** active, busy ⟨*been on the hop all day*⟩ **2** in a state of unreadiness; unawares ⟨*caught* on the hop⟩

³**hop** *n* **1** a climbing plant (*Humulus lupulus*) of the hemp family with inconspicuous green flowers of which the female ones are in cone-shaped catkins **2** *pl* the ripe dried female catkins of a hop plant used esp to give a bitter flavour to beer and to preserve it **3** *chiefly NAm slang* opium or a similar narcotic drug that produces numbness and dulls the consciousness [ME *hoppe*, fr MD; akin to OHG *hopfo* hop, OE *scēaf* sheaf – more at SHEAF]

⁴**hop** *vt* **-pp-** to impregnate (esp beer) with hops

**hop up** *vt, informal* **1** to excite, rouse **2** HOT UP

¹**hope** /hohp/ *vi* **1** to wish with expectation of fulfilment ⟨~s *for great things from his son*⟩ **2** *archaic* to trust ~ *vt* **1** to long for with expectation of obtainment **2** to expect with desire; trust [ME *hopen*, fr OE *hopian*; akin to MHG *hoffen* to hope] – **hoper** *n*

²**hope** *n* **1** trust, reliance ⟨*all my* ~ *is in the Lord*⟩ **2a** desire accompanied by expectation of or belief in fulfilment ⟨*has high* ~s *of an early recovery*⟩ **b** someone or something on which hopes are centred ⟨*he was our last* ~⟩ **c** something hoped for – **hope against hope** to hope without any basis for expecting fulfilment ⟨*she hoped against hope that he would be well by Christmas*⟩

**hope chest** *n, NAm* BOTTOM DRAWER

¹**hopeful** /-f(ə)l/ *adj* **1** full of hope; expectant ⟨*I'm* ~ *he'll come*⟩ **2** inspiring hope ⟨*the situation looks* ~⟩ – **hopefulness** *n*

²**hopeful** *n* a person who aspires to or is likely to succeed ⟨*political* ~s⟩

**hopefully** /-f(ə)l·i/ *adv* **1** in a hopeful manner **2** it is hoped ⟨~ *he will arrive in time*⟩

  **usage** The increasingly common use of **hopefully** to mean "it is hoped", as in sense **2**, is widely disliked both in Britain and in the USA, and in Britain is felt to be an Americanism. If one uses it, it is important to ensure that there is no ambiguity, since ⟨*they will depart* **hopefully** *in the morning*⟩ has two meanings; but it is sometimes a usefully impersonal word, since its user is not obliged to state who is doing the "hoping".

**hopeless** /-lis/ *adj* **1** having no expectation of success **2a** giving no grounds for hope ⟨*a* ~ *case*⟩ **b** incapable of solution, management, or accomplishment; impossible ⟨*a* ~ *task*⟩ **3** *chiefly informal* incompetent, useless ⟨*I'm* ~ *at sums*⟩ – **hopelessly** *adv*, **hopelessness** *n*

**hophead** /'hop,hed/ *n, chiefly NAm slang* one who uses narcotic drugs; *esp* a heroin or opium addict

**Hopi** /'hohpi/ *n, pl* (1) **Hopis**, *esp collectively* **Hopi 1** (a member of) an American Indian people of NE Arizona **2** the Shoshonean language of the Hopi people [Hopi *Hópi,* lit., good, peaceful]

**hoplite** /'hoplit/ *n* a heavily armed infantry soldier of ancient Greece [Gk *hoplitēs,* fr *hoplon* tool, weapon, fr *hepein* to care for, work at – more at SEPULCHRE]

**'hop-o'-my-,thumb** *n* a very small person

**hopper** /'hopə/ *n* **1a** one who or that which hops **b** a leaping insect; *specif* an immature hopping form of an insect **2a** a usu funnel-shaped receptacle for discharging grain, coal, etc; *also* any of various other receptacles for the temporary storage of material (e g grain) **b** *also* **hopper car** a goods wagon with a floor through which bulk materials may be discharged **c** a barge that can discharge dredged material through an opening bottom **d** a tank holding liquid and having a device for releasing its contents through a pipe [(2) fr the shaking motion of hoppers used to feed grain into a mill]

**hopping** /'hoping/ *adj* journeying or flitting about from place to place – used in combination ⟨*thus began a frenetic show-hopping existence – N Y Times*⟩

**hopping mad** *adj, informal* extremely annoyed

**hopple** /'hopl/ *n or vb* (to) hobble [prob fr ¹*hop*]

**hopsack** /'hop,sak/ *n* **1** a coarse sacking material **2** a firm rough-surfaced clothing fabric woven in BASKET WEAVE [ME *hopsak* sack for hops, fr *hoppe* hop + *sak* sack]

**hopscotch** /-,skoch/ *n* a children's game in which a player tosses an object (e g a stone) into areas of a figure outlined on the ground and hops through the figure and back to regain the object [¹*hop* + ²*scotch* (in the sense "scratched line")]

**horary** /'hawrəri/ *adj, formal* of an hour; *also* hourly [ML *horarius,* fr L *hora* hour – more at HOUR]

**Horatian** /hə'raysh(y)ən, ho-/ *adj* (characteristic) of Horace or his poetry; *esp* elegant and apt in style [L *Horatianus,* fr *Horatius* Horace (Quintus Horatius Flaccus) †8 BC Roman poet]

**Horatio Alger** /'aljə/ *adj* of or resembling the fiction of Horatio Alger in which success is achieved through self-reliance and hard work [*Horatio Alger* †1899 US clergyman and author]

**horde** /hawd/ *n* **1a** a tribe of Mongolian nomads **b** a people or tribe adopting a nomadic way of life **2 horde, hordes** *pl* a crowd, swarm ⟨*a ~ of flies buzzing about the table*⟩ ⟨*~s of children running everywhere*⟩ △ hoard [MF, Ger & Pol; MF & Ger, fr Pol *horda,* of Mongolic origin; akin to Mongolian *orda* camp, horde]

**horehound** /'haw,hownd/ *n* (any of several plants related to) a plant (*Marrubium vulgare*) of the mint family that is covered in long fine hairs and has inconspicuous whitish flowers and bitter juice that is used as a herbal remedy for coughs and colds [ME *horhoune,* fr OE *hārhūne,* fr *hār* hoary + *hūne* horehound – more at HOAR]

**hori** /'hawri, 'hori/ *n, NZ derog* MAORI **1** (Polynesian New Zealander) [Maori personal name]

**horizon** /hə'riez(ə)n/ *n* **1a horizon, visible horizon** the apparent junction of earth and sky **b(1)** the plane that is parallel to and passes through the earth's surface at an observer's position; *also* the circle formed by the intersection of this plane with the CELESTIAL SPHERE (imaginary sphere surrounding earth on which the stars, planets, etc appear to be placed) **b(2)** the plane that is parallel to such a plane but passes through the earth's centre; *also* the GREAT CIRCLE (circle with the same radius as the CELESTIAL SPHERE) formed by the intersection of this plane with the celestial sphere **c** a level mirror used esp in observing altitudes **d horizon, horizons** *pl* range of perception, experience, or knowledge ⟨*the course was intended to broaden our ~s*⟩ **2a** the geological deposit of a particular time, usu identified by distinctive fossils **b** any of the reasonably distinct layers of soil or subsoil in a vertical section of land **c** a cultural area or level of development indicated by separated groups of artefacts, esp as marked by the archaeological strata in which they are found [ME *orizon,* fr LL *horizont-, horizon,* fr Gk *horizont-, horizōn,* fr prp of *horizein* to bound, define, fr *horos* boundary; akin to L *urvus* circumference of a city] – **horizonal** *adj*

**horizontal** /,hori'zontl/ *adj* **1a** of or situated near the horizon **b** parallel to, in the plane of, or operating in a plane parallel to the horizon or to a base line; level ⟨*~ distance*⟩ ⟨*~ engine*⟩ **2** of or concerning relationships between people of the same rank in different hierarchies – compare VERTICAL 3b(2) – **horizontal** *n,* **horizontally** *adv*

**horizontal bar** *n* a steel bar supported in a horizontal position 2.5 metres (about 8 feet) above the floor and used for swinging exercises in gymnastics; *also* a usu men's gymnastics event in which the horizontal bar is used

**hormogonium** /,hawmə'gohniəm/ *n, pl* **hormogonia** /-i-ə/ a portion of a filament in many BLUE-GREEN ALGAE that becomes detached and will divide to produce another generation of the alga [NL, fr Gk *hormos* chain, necklace + *gonos* procreation, seed – more at SERIES, GON-]

**hormonal** /haw'mohnl/ *adj* of or caused by hormones – **hormonally** *adv*

**hormone** /'hawmohn/ *n* a product of living cells that usu circulates in the body liquids (e g the blood of mammals or sap of plants) and produces a specific stimulating or inhibiting effect on the activity of cells remote from its point of origin; *also* a synthetic substance that acts like a hormone [Gk *hormōn,* prp of *horman* to stir up, fr *hormē* impulse, assault – more at SERUM] – **hormonelike** *adj*

**horn** /hawn/ *n* **1a** any of the usu paired bony projecting parts on the heads of many hoofed mammals and some extinct mammals and reptiles: e g **1a(1)** either of the paired hollow sheaths of KERATIN (strong fibrous protein) that are usu present in cattle, sheep, and related mammals, are chiefly for defence, and arise from a bony core anchored to the skull **a(2)** an antler of a deer **a(3)** a permanent solid pointed projection consisting of KERATIN, that is attached to the nasal bone of a rhinoceros **a(4)** either of a pair of permanent bone projections on the skull of a giraffe or okapi, that are covered with hairy skin **b** a natural projection from an animal (e g a snail or owl) resembling or suggestive of a horn **c** the tough fibrous material, consisting chiefly of the protein KERATIN, that covers or forms hooves, the horns of cattle, sheep, etc, and other hard horny parts (e g claws or nails) **d** a hollow horn used as a container ⟨*drinking ~*⟩ **2** something resembling or suggestive of a horn: e g **2a** either of the curved ends of a crescent **b(1)** a horn-shaped body of land or water **b(2)** a pyramid-shaped peak left standing as a central mass by the development of CIRQUES (steep-walled basins) on three or more of its sides **c** a high projection (POMMEL) at the front and on top of a saddle **3a** an instrument used as a wind instrument **b(1)** HUNTING HORN **b(2)** FRENCH HORN **c** a wind instrument used in a jazz band; *esp* a trumpet **d** a device (e g on a motor car) for making loud warning noises ⟨*a fog ~*⟩ **e** *Br* a tenor SAXHORN (brass instrument) used in a military band **4** *vulg* an erect penis [ME, fr OE; akin to OHG *horn,* L *cornu,* Gk *keras*] – **horn** *adj,* **hornless** *adj,* **hornlessness** *n,* **hornlike** *adj* – **draw in one's horns** to reduce or limit one's activities or expenditure – **on the horns of a dilemma** faced with a choice between two equally undesirable alternatives

**hornbeam** /'hawn,beem/ *n* any of a genus (*Carpinus*) of trees of the birch family having smooth grey bark and hard white wood [*horn* + ¹*beam;* fr its hard smooth wood]

**hornbill** /-,bil/ *n* any of a family (Bucerotidae) of large tropical African and Asian birds with enormous beaks

**hornblende** /'hawn,blend/ *n* a dark-green to black mineral, approx $Ca_2Na(Mg,Fe)_4(Al,Fe,Ti)_3Si_6O_{22}(O,OH)_2$, that consists chiefly of silicates of calcium, magnesium, and iron, is a major constituent of many rocks, and is the commonest variety of AMPHIBOLE (large group of rock-forming minerals) [Ger, fr *horn* horn + *blende* blende] – **hornblendic** *adj*

**hornbook** /-,book/ *n* **1** a small book for teaching children to read that consisted of a sheet of parchment or paper protected by a sheet of transparent horn **2** a rudimentary treatise

**horned** /hawnd/ *adj* **1** having a horn – often in combination ⟨*one*-horned⟩ ⟨*short*-horned⟩ **2** having a part shaped like a horn

**horned owl** *n* any of various owls having conspicuous tufts of feathers on the head

**horned toad** *n* any of several small insect-eating lizards (genus *Phrynosoma*) of the W USA and Mexico with hornlike spines

**horned viper** *n* CERASTES (poisonous viper)

**hornet** /'hawnit/ *n* any of the larger wasps (family Vespidae); *esp* the European hornet (*Vespa crabro*) that has a black and yellow banded abdomen and a powerful sting [ME *hernet,* fr OE *hyrnet;* akin to OHG *hornaz* hornet, L *crabro*]

**hornet's nest** *n* an angry or hostile reaction – esp in *stir up a hornet's nest*

**hornfels** /'hawnfelz/ *n* a hard fine-grained rock formed by the alteration of slate, shale, or a similar clay rock subjected to high temperature, and commonly containing small crystals of garnet and MICA [Ger, fr *horn* horn + *fels* cliff, rock]

**horn in** *vi, informal* to participate without invitation or consent; intrude – often + *on*

**horn of plenty** *n* CORNUCOPIA

**hornpipe** /-,piep/ *n* **1** a wind instrument consisting of a wooden or bone pipe with finger holes, a bell, and a usu horn mouth-piece with a SINGLE REED 2 (a piece of music for) a lively British folk dance usu performed by one person, originally accompanied by hornpipe playing, and typically associated with sailors

'**horn-,rims** *n pl* glasses with rims made of (a material resembling) horn – **horn-rimmed** *adj*

**hornstone** /'hawn,stohn/ *n* 1 a mineral that is a variety of quartz and similar to flint but more brittle 2 hornfels or a similar compact fine-grained rock – not used technically

**hornswoggle** /'hawn,swogl/ *vt, slang* to bamboozle, hoax [origin unknown]

**horntail** /'hawn,tayl/ *n* WOOD WASP (large wasplike insect)

**hornwort** /'hawn,wuht/ *n* any of a genus (*Ceratophyllum* of the family Ceratophyllaceae) of rootless thin-stemmed submerged water plants

**horny** /'hawni/ *adj* 1a (made) of or resembling horn b hard, callous ⟨horny-*handed*⟩ 2 having a horn or horns 3 *slang* randy

**horologe** /'horəloj/ *n* a timekeeping device [ME, fr MF, fr L *horologium*, fr Gk *hōrologion*, fr *hōra* hour + *legein* to gather – more at YEAR, LEGEND]

**horologic** /,horə'lojik/ *also* **horological** /-kl/ *adj* of a horologe or horology

**horologist** /ho'roləjist/, **horologer** /-jə/ *n* 1 a person skilled in the practice or theory of horology 2 a maker of clocks or watches

**horology** /ho'roləji/ *n* 1 the science of measuring time 2 the art of constructing instruments for indicating time [Gk *hōra* + E -*logy*]

**horoscope** /'horə,skohp/ *n* a diagram of the relative positions of planets and signs of the zodiac at a specific time, esp somebody's birth, used by astrologers to infer individual character and personality traits and to foretell events in a person's life; *also* an astrological forecast based on this [MF, fr L *horoscopus*, fr Gk *hōroskopos*, fr *hōra* + *skopein* to look at – more at SPY]

**horrendous** /hə'rendəs/ *adj* dreadful, horrible [L *horrendus*, fr gerundive of *horrēre* to bristle, tremble] – **horrendously** *adv*

**horrent** /'horənt/ *adj, archaic* covered with bristling points; bristly [L *horrent-, horrens, prp of horrēre*]

**horrible** /'horəbl/ *adj* 1 marked by or arousing horror ⟨a ~ accident⟩ 2 *chiefly informal* extremely unpleasant or disagreeable ⟨~ weather⟩ [ME, fr MF, fr L *horribilis*, fr *horrēre*] – **horribleness** *n*, **horribly** *adv*

**horrid** /'horid/ *adj* 1a horrible, shocking b repulsive, nasty ⟨a ~ little boy⟩ 2 *archaic* rough, bristling [L *horridus* rough, shaggy, bristling, fr *horrēre*] – **horridly** *adv*, **horridness** *n*

**horrific** /hə'rifik/ *adj* arousing horror; horrifying ⟨a ~ account of the tragedy⟩ – **horrifically** *adv*

**horrify** /'horifie/ *vt* 1 to cause to feel horror 2 to fill with distaste or dismay; shock ⟨his uncouth table manners horrified us⟩ – **horrifyingly** *adv*

**horripilation** /ho,ripi'laysh(ə)n/ *n* gooseflesh – used technically [LL *horripilation-, horripilatio*, fr L *horripilatus*, pp of *horripilare* to bristle, be shaggy, fr *horrēre* + *pilus* hair]

**horror** /'horə/ *n* 1a intense fear, dread, or dismay; consternation ⟨astonishment giving place to ~ on the faces of the people about me – H G Wells⟩ b intense aversion or repugnance 2a the quality of inspiring horror ⟨contemplating the ~ of their lives – Liam O'Flaherty⟩ b *chiefly informal* one who or that which inspires horror or aversion ⟨that child is a perfect ~⟩ 3 *pl, chiefly informal* a state of extreme depression or apprehension *synonyms* see ¹FEAR [ME *horrour*, fr MF *horror*, fr L, action of trembling, fr *horrēre* to tremble; akin to OE *gorst* gorse, Gk *chersos* dry land]

'**horror-,struck**, '**horror-,stricken** *adj* filled with horror; shocked ⟨stood ~ before the blazing ruin⟩

**hors de combat** /,aw də 'kombah (*Fr* ɔːr də kɔ̃ba)/ *adv or adj* out of the fight; disabled [Fr]

**hors d'oeuvre** /,aw 'duhv (*Fr* ɔːr dœvr)/ *n, pl* **hors d'oeuvres** *also* **hors d'oeuvre** /aw 'duhv(z) (*Fr* ~)/ any of various savoury foods usu served as appetizers [Fr *hors-d'œuvre*, lit., outside of work]

'**horse** /haws/ *n, pl* **horses**, (3) **horse** 1a(1) a large solid-hoofed plant-eating 4-legged mammal (*Equus caballus*, family Equidae, the horse family) domesticated by humans since prehistoric times and used as a beast of burden, a draught animal, or for riding; *esp* one over 14.2 hands in height a(2) a racehorse ⟨play the ~s⟩ b a male horse; a stallion; *also* a GELDING (castrated

male) as distinguished from an uncastrated male c any living or extinct animal of the horse family 2a a usu 4-legged frame for supporting something (e g planks); a trestle b(1) POMMEL HORSE (type of gymnastics apparatus) b(2) VAULTING HORSE (type of gymnastics apparatus) 3 *taking sing or pl vb* the cavalry 4 a mass of rock occurring within a vein of ore 5 *informal* horsepower 6 *slang* heroin 7 *Br slang* a lump of sediment in the bottom of a glass of beer [ME *hors*, fr OE; akin to OHG *hros* horse] – **flog a dead horse** to waste time or energy in trying to revive worn-out or previously settled subjects – **from the horse's mouth** *informal* from the original source – **hold one's horses** to curb one's desires, enthusiasm, etc; HOLD BACK

²**horse** *vt* to provide (e g a person or vehicle) with a horse ~ *vi* 1 *of a mare* to be in heat 2 to engage in horseplay ⟨horsing around⟩

,**horse-and-'buggy** *adj, chiefly NAm* 1 of the era before the advent of certain modern inventions (e g the motor car) 2 outdated, old-fashioned

¹**horseback** /'haws,bak/ *n* – **on horseback** mounted on a horse

²**horseback** *adv, chiefly NAm* on horseback

**horsebean** /'haws,been/ *n* BROAD BEAN [*horse* (large, coarse; in names of plants & animals), fr ¹*horse*]

**horsebox** /'haws,boks/ *n* a lorry or closed trailer for transporting horses

**horse brass** *n* a brass ornament worn originally on a horse's harness

**horsebreaker** /'haws,braykə/ *n* one who breaks in or trains horses

**horse chestnut** *n* 1 a large Asiatic tree (*Aesculus hippocastanum* of the family Hippocastanaceae, the horse-chestnut family) that has 5-lobed leaves and erect cone-shaped clusters of white, pink, or red flowers, produces round prickly green fruit containing the seeds, and is widely cultivated as an ornamental and shade tree 2 the large glossy brown seed of a horse chestnut – called also CONKER

**horse coper** *n, Br* a horse dealer; COPER

**horseflesh** /'haws,flesh/ *n* horses considered collectively, esp with reference to riding, driving, or racing

**horsefly** /'haws,flie/ *n* any of a family (Tabanidae) of swift usu large flies with bloodsucking females – compare CLEG

**horsehair** /'haws,heə/ *n* 1 the hair of a horse, esp from the mane or tail 2 cloth made from horsehair

**horsehair worm** *n* a nonparasitic adult HAIRWORM (thin threadlike worm)

**horsehide** /'haws,hied/ *n* the raw or treated hide of a horse; *also* leather made from this

**horse latitudes** *n pl* either of two belts in the region of latitudes 30° N and 30° S with weather characterized by high pressure, calms, and light changeable winds

**horselaugh** /'haws,lahf/ *n* a loud boisterous laugh; a guffaw

**horseless carriage** /'hawslis/ *n, archaic* a motor car

**horse mackerel** *n* 1 any of several large tunas or related fishes of the mackerel family 2 any of various large fishes (family Carangidae); *esp* a large mackerel-like food fish (*Trachurus trachurus*) of the Atlantic

**horseman** /-mən/, *fem* **horsewoman** *n* 1a a rider on horseback b one skilled in managing horses 2 a breeder or tender of horses 3 *Can slang* a Mountie – **horsemanship** *n*

**horsemaster** /'haws,mahstə/ *n* an expert in the management and welfare of horses – **horsemastership** *n*

**horsemint** /'haws,mint/ *n* any of various coarse plants of the mint family; *esp* a European mint (*Mentha longifolia*) with spikes of pink or lilac flowers, that was formerly used for flavourings and in medicine

**horse mussel** *n* a large marine mussel (*Modiolus modiolus*) widely distributed on the shores of N Europe and America

**horse nuts** *n pl* a compound food for horses made up of many ingredients (e g oats, molasses, and vitamins)

**horse opera** *n, chiefly NAm humorous* WESTERN (film, book, etc about life in the W USA)

**horse pick** *n* HOOF PICK (tool for removing stones from a horse's hoof)

**horseplay** /'haws,play/ *n* rough or boisterous play

**horsepower** /'haws,powə/ *n* 1 the power that a horse exerts in pulling 2 an imperial unit of power equal to 745.7 watts

**horseradish** /'haws,radish/ *n* 1 a tall coarse white-flowered plant (*Armoracia rusticana*) of the cabbage family cultivated for its white pungent root; *also* the root of this plant 2 a pungent condiment prepared from the grated root of horseradish

**horse sense** *n, informal* COMMON SENSE

**horseshit** /'haws,shit/ *n, chiefly NAm vulg* nonsense, bullshit

**horseshoe** /'haws,shooh/ *n* **1** a shoe for horses usu consisting of a narrow U-shaped plate of iron made to fit the rim of the hoof **2** something (eg a valley or archway) shaped like a horseshoe **3** *pl but taking sing vb* a game like quoits played with horseshoes or with horseshoe-shaped pieces of metal – **horseshoe** *vt*, **horseshoer** *n*

**horseshoe bat** *n* any of several large-eared insect-eating bats (family Rhinolophidae or Hipposideridae) of tropical and temperate regions, that have a horseshoe-shaped pad round the nostrils

**horseshoe crab** *n* KING CRAB

**horse show** *n* an equestrian contest that usu includes competitions in riding, driving, and jumping and classes in which horses are judged for breeding

**horsetail** /'haws,tayl/ *n* any of a genus (*Equisetum*) of flowerless plants with jointed stems that are related to the ferns

**'horse-,trading** *n* negotiation accompanied by hard bargaining and reciprocal concessions

**horse trials** *n* EVENT 3b (programme of dressage, cross-country, and show-jumping events)

**horsewhip** /'haws,wip/ *vt* to flog (as if) with a whip made for horses – **horsewhipper** *n*

**horsewoman** /-,woomən/ *n* a female horseman

**horsey, horsy** /'hawsi/ *adj* **1** of or resembling a horse **2** very interested in horses, horse riding, or horse racing ⟨*boon companions of the Prince of Wales, who were ... ~ and card-playing – New York Times Book Review*⟩ **3** characteristic of horsemen – **horsily** *adv*, **horsiness** *n*

**horsie** /'hawsi/ *n* – used as a pet name for a horse

**horst** /hawst/ *n* a block of the earth's crust between two parallel faults that have caused it to be separated from and raised above the adjacent land [Ger]

**hortative** /'hawtətiv/, **hortatory** /'hawtət(ə)ri/ *adj, formal* giving exhortation [LL *hortativus*, fr L *hortatus*, pp of *hortari* to urge – more at YEARN] – **hortatively** *adv*

**horticulture** /'hawti,kulchə/ *n* the science and art of growing fruits, vegetables, flowers, and ornamental plants [L *hortus* garden + E *-i-* + *culture* – more at YARD] – **horticultural** *adj*, **horticulturally** *adv*, **horticulturist** *n*

**hosanna** /hoh'zanə/ *interj or n* (used as) a cry of acclamation and adoration [ME *osanna*, fr LL, fr Gk *hōsanna*, fr Heb *hōshī'āh-nnā* pray, save (us)!]

**HO scale** *n* a scale of approximately 3 millimetres to 30 centimetres used esp for models (eg of cars or trains) [fr its fitness for rails of HO gauge]

**'hose** /hohz/ *n, pl (1)* **hose**, *(2)* **hoses** **1** a leg covering that sometimes covers the foot: eg **1a** short breeches reaching to the knee ⟨*doublet and ~*⟩ **b** *pl, chiefly NAm* stockings; *also* tights **2** a flexible tube for conveying fluids (eg from a tap or in a car engine) [ME, fr OE *hosa* stocking, husk, akin to OHG *hosa* leg covering, Gk *kystis* bladder, OE *hȳd* hide]

**²hose** *vt* to spray, water, or wash with a hose – often + *down* ⟨*~ down a stable floor*⟩

**Hosea** /hoh'zee-ə/ *n* – see BIBLE table [*Hosea* (Heb *Hōshēa'*), 8th-c BC Heb prophet]

**hosepipe** /'hohz,piep/ *n* a length of hose for conveying water (eg for watering plants or putting out fires)

**hosiery** /'hohzəri/ *n* socks, stockings, and tights in general

**hospice** /'hospis/ *n* **1** a place of shelter for travellers or the destitute, esp when kept by a religious order **2** *Br* a nursing home, esp for terminally ill patients [Fr, fr L *hospitium*, fr *hospit-, hospes* host – more at HOST]

**hospitable** /ho'spitəbl, 'hos-/ *adj* **1a** offering a generous and cordial welcome to guests or strangers **b** offering a pleasant or sustaining environment ⟨*a ~ climate*⟩ **2** readily receptive; open ⟨*~ to new ideas*⟩ – **hospitably** *adv*

usage The pronunciation /'hospitbl/ is recommended for BBC broadcasters.

**hospital** /'hospitl/ *n* **1** a charitable institution (eg for the needy, aged, infirm, or young); HOME **5** – now used only in names ⟨*Christ's Hospital*⟩ **2** an institution where the sick or injured are given medical or surgical care – often used in British English without an article ⟨*she's in ~*⟩ ⟨*was rushed to the ~*⟩ **3** a repair shop for specified small objects ⟨*a doll's ~*⟩ [ME, fr OF, fr ML *hospitale*, fr LL, hospice, fr L, guest room, fr neut of *hospitalis* of a guest, fr *hospit-, hospes*]

**hospitality** /,hospi'taləti/ *n* hospitable treatment or reception

**hospital·ize, -ise** /'hospitl·iez/ *vt* to place in hospital as a

patient – **hospitalization** *n*

**Hospitaller,** *NAm* **Hospitaler** /'hospitələ/ *n* a member of a charitable though originally military religious order established in Jerusalem in the 12th century [ME *hospitalier*, fr MF, fr ML *hospitalarius*, fr LL *hospitale*]

**hospital ship** *n* a ship equipped as a hospital; *esp* one built or specifically assigned to assist the wounded, sick, and shipwrecked in time of war

**'host** /hohst/ *n taking sing or pl vb* **1** host, hosts *pl* a very large number; multitude **2** *chiefly poetic or archaic* an army [ME, fr OF, fr LL *hostis*, fr L, stranger, enemy – more at GUEST]

**²host** *n* **1a** an innkeeper ⟨*mine ~*⟩ **b** one who receives or entertains guests socially or officially **c** one who or that which provides facilities for an event or function ⟨*our college served as ~ for the chess tournament*⟩ **2a** *biology* **2a(1)** a living animal or plant on or in which a parasite lives **a(2)** the larger, stronger, or dominant member of a pair of organisms that live in an association (COMMENSALISM or SYMBIOSIS) in which neither organism is harmed and one or both may benefit **b** an individual into which a tissue or part is transplanted from another **3** a compere on a radio or television programme [ME *hoste* host, guest, fr OF, fr L *hospit-, hospes*, fr *hostis*]

**³host** *vt* to act as host at or of ⟨*~ed a dinner party*⟩ ⟨*~ed a series of TV programmes*⟩

usage Some people dislike the use of host as a verb.

**⁴host** *n, often cap* the bread consecrated in Communion [ME *hoste*, fr MF *hoiste*, fr LL & L; LL *hostia* Eucharist, fr L, sacrifice]

**hostage** /'hostij/ *n* a person held by one party as a pledge that promises will be kept or terms met by the other party ⟨*a man was taken ~ by the hijackers*⟩ [ME, fr OF, fr *hoste*]

**hostel** /'hostl/ *n* **1** YOUTH HOSTEL **2** *chiefly Br* a supervised residential home: eg **2a** an establishment providing accommodation for nurses, students, etc **b** an institution for junior offenders, ex-offenders, etc, providing care and encouraging social adaptation **3** *chiefly poetic or archaic* an inn [ME, lodging, inn, fr OF, fr LL *hospitale* hospice] – **hosteller** *n*

**hostelry** /-ri/ *n* an inn, hotel

**'hostess** /'hohstis/ *n* **1** a woman who entertains socially or acts as host **2a** a female employee on a ship, aeroplane, coach, or train who manages the provisioning of food and attends to the needs of passengers; *esp* AIR HOSTESS **b** a woman who acts as a companion to male patrons, esp in a nightclub; *also* a prostitute

**²hostess** *vi* to act as hostess ~ *vt* to act as hostess at or to

**hostess gown** *n* a long usu loose dress worn esp at home

**hostie** /'hohsti/ *n, Austr informal* AIR HOSTESS

**hostile** /'hostiel/ *adj* **1** of or constituting an enemy **2** antagonistic, unfriendly **3** not hospitable ⟨*a ~ environment*⟩ [MF or L; MF, fr L *hostilis*, fr *hostis*] – **hostile** *n*, **hostilely** *adv*

**hostility** /ho'stiləti/ *n* **1a** an antagonistic or unfriendly state **b** *pl* open acts of warfare; war **2** antagonism, opposition, or resistance in thought or principle ⟨*his proposal encountered much ~*⟩ synonyms see ENMITY antonym friendliness

**hostler** /'oslə/ *n* **1** *chiefly NAm* OSTLER (stableman, esp at an inn) **2** *NAm* one who services a vehicle (eg a locomotive or lorry) or machine (eg a crane)

**'hot** /hot/ *adj* **-tt-** **1a** having a relatively high temperature **b** capable of giving a sensation of heat or of burning, searing, or scalding ⟨*a ~ stove*⟩ **c** having a temperature higher than normal body heat **2a** vehement, fiery ⟨*a ~ temper*⟩ **b** violent, raging ⟨*a ~ battle*⟩ **c** of or being an exciting style of jazz with strong rhythms that became popular in the 1930s – compare COOL **2c 3** having or causing the sensation of an uncomfortable degree of body heat ⟨*~ clothes*⟩ **4** very recent; fresh ⟨*~ off the press*⟩ **5a** suggestive of heat or of burning objects ⟨*~ colours*⟩ **b** pungent, peppery ⟨*a ~ curry*⟩ **6** of a process performed on a heated material ⟨*steel ingots can be formed into tubing by ~ rolling*⟩ **7** of an atom having a higher than normal energy level due usu to nuclear processes **8** *informal* **8a** sexually excited; *also* sexually arousing **b** eager, enthusiastic ⟨*~ on the idea*⟩ **c** severe, stringent – usu + *on* ⟨*police are ~ on drunken drivers*⟩ **d** close to something sought ⟨*guess again, you're getting ~*⟩ **9** *informal* **9a** of intense and immediate interest; sensational ⟨*a ~ news story*⟩ **b** unusually lucky or favourable ⟨*~ dice*⟩ **c** performing well or strongly fancied to win (eg in a sport) ⟨*a ~ favourite*⟩ **d** currently popular; selling very well **e** very good – used as a generalized term of approval ⟨*his English is not so ~*⟩ **10** *informal* radioactive;

*also* dealing with dangerously radioactive material **11** *chiefly NAm informal* electrically live ⟨*a ~ terminal*⟩ **12** *slang* **12a** recently and illegally obtained; stolen ⟨*~ jewels*⟩ **b** wanted by the police; *also* unsafe for a fugitive [ME, fr OE *hāt;* akin to OHG *heiz* hot, Lith *kaĩsti* to get hot] – **hottish** *adj*, **hotness** *n* – **blow hot and cold** to act changeably by alternately favouring and rebuffing; vacillate [fr Aesop's fable of a man who puzzled a savage by blowing on his fingers to warm them and on his soup to cool it]]

²**hot** *adv* hotly

**hot air** *n, informal* empty talk

**hotbed** /'hot,bed/ *n* **1** a bed of soil enclosed in glass, heated esp by fermenting manure, and used for forcing or for raising seedlings **2** an environment that favours rapid growth or development, esp of something specified ⟨*a ~ of crime*⟩

,**hot-'blooded** *adj* **1** excitable, ardent **2** *of livestock* of pure or superior breeding – **hot-bloodedness** *n*

**hotbox** /'hot,boks/ *n* a rotating part (e g of an axle in a railway locomotive) that turns in a bearing and has become overheated by friction

**hotcake** /'hot,kayk/ *n* a pancake

**hotch** /hoch/ *vi, Scot* to wiggle, fidget [prob fr MF *hocher* to shake, fr OF *hochier,* of Gmc origin]

**hotchpot** /'hoch,pot/ *n, law* the combining of properties into a common lot to ensure equality of division among heirs [AF *hochepot,* fr OF, hotchpotch]

**hotchpotch** /'hoch,poch/ *n* **1a** a thick soup or stew of mixed vegetables and meat, esp mutton **b** a mixture of many usu unrelated parts; a jumble **2** *law* a hotchpot [ME *hochepot,* fr MF, fr OF, fr *hochier* to shake + *pot*]

**hot cross bun** *n* a yeast-leavened spicy bun marked with a cross and eaten esp on Good Friday

**hotdog** /'hot,dog/ *vi, NAm informal* to perform in a conspicuous or ostentatious manner; *esp* to perform stunts while riding a surfboard or skateboard [²*hot dog*] – **hotdogger** *n*

¹**hot dog** *n* **1** a frankfurter or other sausage, usu served hot in a long bread roll **2** *NAm informal* one who hotdogs; *also* a show-off

²**hot dog** *interj, NAm* – used to express approval or gratification

**hotel** /(h)oh'tel/ *n* a usu large establishment that provides meals and (temporary) accommodation for the public, esp for people travelling away from home [Fr *hôtel,* fr OF *hostel*]

*usage* Modern writers and speakers on the whole prefer *a* rather *than an* before **hotel**; the pronunciation /hoh'tel/ is recommended for BBC broadcasters.

**Hotel** – a communications code word for the letter *h*

**hotelier** /(h)oh·telyə, -yay/ *n* a proprietor or manager of a hotel [Fr *hôtelier,* fr OF *hostelier,* fr *hostel*]

**hot flash** *n, NAm* HOT FLUSH

**hot flush** *n* a sudden brief flushing and sensation of heat, usu associated with an imbalance of hormones occurring esp at the menopause

**hotfoot** /'hot,foot/ *vi or adv* (to go) in haste – **hotfoot it** to hotfoot

**hothead** /'hot,hed/ *n* a hotheaded person

**hotheaded** /,hot'hedid/ *adj* fiery, impetuous – **hotheadedly** *adv,* **hotheadedness** *n*

¹**hothouse** /'hot,hows/ *n* **1** a heated greenhouse, esp for tropical plants **2** HOTBED 2 (favourable environment for growth)

²**hothouse** *adj* **1** grown in a hothouse **2** delicate, overprotected ⟨*led a sheltered and ~ existence*⟩

**hot line** *n* a direct telephone line in constant readiness for immediate communication (e g between heads of state)

**hotly** /'hotli/ *adv* in a hot or fiery manner ⟨*a ~ debated issue*⟩

**hot metal** *n* a method of printing using type cast directly from molten metal

**hot money** *n* currency which flows rapidly between countries in response to differences in the rates of interest available in them

**hot pants** *n* women's brief shorts, typically having bibs, that were fashionable esp in the early 1970s

**hot pepper** *n* (a plant bearing) any of various small and usu thin-walled pungent capsicum fruits

**hot plate** *n* **1** a solid metal, ceramic, etc plate on the top of a cooker, esp an electric cooker, or forming part of a separate hob unit, that can be heated and on which food can be cooked; *broadly* any of the surfaces or rings on an electric cooker hob **2** *chiefly NAm* a small portable appliance used for cooking

**hot pot** *n* a stew; *specif* a mutton, lamb, or beef and potato stew cooked in a covered pot

**hot potato** *n, chiefly informal* a controversial or sensitive question or issue ⟨*a political ~*⟩

**hot rod** *n* a motor vehicle rebuilt or modified for high speed and fast acceleration – **hot-rodder** *n*

**hot seat** *n* **1** *informal* a position involving risk, embarrassment, or responsibility for decision-making ⟨*in the ~ at the interview*⟩ **2** *slang* ELECTRIC CHAIR

**hotshot** /'hot,shot/ *n, informal* a showily successful or important person ⟨*a literary ~*⟩ – **hotshot** *adj*

**hot spring** *n* a spring of naturally hot water – called also THERMAL SPRING

**hot stuff** *n, informal* **1** something or someone of outstanding ability or quality **2** something or someone that is sexually exciting ⟨*she's really ~*⟩

**Hottentot** /'hot(ə)n,tot/ *n* **1** a member of a people of southern Africa apparently of mixed Bushman and Bantu origin **2** the Khoisan language of the Hottentot people [Afrik]

**hot tub** *n* an outdoor hot bath for two or more people, equipped with underwater jets for massage – compare JACUZZI

**hot up** *vi* **1** to grow hot, lively, or exciting ⟨*the film began to* hot up *halfway through*⟩ **2** to increase in activity or intensity ⟨*air raids began to* hot up *about the beginning of February* – George Orwell⟩ *~ vt* to make hotter, livelier, or faster

**hot war** *n* a conflict involving actual fighting – compare COLD WAR

**hot water** *n, informal* a distressing predicament; *esp* one likely to lead to punishment; trouble

**hot-water bottle** *n* a usu flat rubber container that is filled with hot water and used esp to warm a bed or a person in bed

¹**hound** /hownd/ *n* **1** a dog; *esp* one of any of various hunting breeds typically with large drooping ears and a deep bark, that track their prey by scent **2** a mean or despicable person **3** one who is devoted to the pursuit of something specified ⟨*autograph ~s*⟩ [ME, fr OE *hund;* akin to OHG *hunt* dog, L *canis,* Gk *kȳon*]

²**hound** *vt* **1** to pursue (as if) with hounds **2** to drive or affect by persistent harassing ⟨*~ed from office by rumours*⟩ – **hounder** *n*

'**hound's-,tongue** *n* any of various coarse plants (genus *Cynoglossum*) of the forget-me-not family with tongue-shaped leaves; *esp* one (*Cynoglossum officinale*) with dull reddish-purple flowers

**houndstooth check, hound's-tooth check** /-,toothth/ *n* a small broken-check textile pattern

**hour** /owə/ *n* **1** a time or prescribed form of worship for daily prayer; *esp* any of the CANONICAL HOURS in the Roman Catholic church **2** the 24th part of a day; a period of 60 minutes **3a** *the* time of day reckoned in hours and minutes by the clock; *esp* the beginning of each full hour measured by the clock ⟨*the train leaves on the ~*⟩ **b** *pl* the time reckoned in one 24-hour period from midnight to midnight ⟨*attack at 0900 ~s*⟩ **4a** a fixed or customary period of time set aside for a usu specified purpose ⟨*the lunch ~*⟩ ⟨*during office ~s*⟩ **b** a particular, usu momentous, period or point of time ⟨*in his ~ of need*⟩ **c** *the* present ⟨*the story of the ~*⟩ **5** *pl* one's regular time of getting up or going to bed ⟨*kept late ~s*⟩ **6** *astronomy* a unit used to measure the position of a celestial body (e g a star or planet), that is equal to an angle of 15° in an east-west direction from a reference point (the VERNAL EQUINOX) and that represents the distance that the celestial body has travelled in 1 hour **7** the work done or distance travelled at normal rate in an hour ⟨*the city was two ~s away*⟩ ⟨*took eight machine ~s*⟩ **8** *NAm* a unit of educational credit [ME, fr OF *heure,* fr LL & L; LL *hora* canonical hour, fr L, hour of the day, fr Gk *hōra*] – **till/until all hours** until very late at night ⟨*was out drinking until all hours*⟩

**hour angle** *n, astronomy* the angle between the HOUR CIRCLE passing through a celestial body (e g a star or planet) and the hour circle passing directly above an observer (MERIDIAN), measured westward from the meridian; a measure corresponding to the time that has elapsed since a particular celestial body last passed the observer's meridian

**hour circle** *n, astronomy* any circle on the CELESTIAL SPHERE (imaginary sphere surrounding earth on whose surface the stars, planets, etc appear to be placed) that passes through both CELESTIAL POLES (two points marking the ends of the axis of the celestial sphere)

¹**hourglass** /'owə,glahs/ *n* a glass or perspex instrument for measuring time consisting of two bulbs joined by a narrow

neck, from the uppermost of which a quantity of sand, water, etc runs into the lower in the space of an hour

**²hourglass** *adj* shapely with a narrow waist ⟨*an ~ figure*⟩

**hour hand** *n* the short hand that marks the hours on the face of a watch or clock

**houri** /'hooəri/ *n* 1 any of the female virgin attendants of the blessed in the Muslim paradise 2 a voluptuously beautiful young woman [Fr, fr Per *hūri*, fr Ar *hūrīyah*]

**'hour-,long** *adj* lasting an hour

**¹hourly** /'owəli/ *adv* 1 at or during every hour; *also* continually ⟨*we're expecting him ~*⟩ 2 by the hour ⟨*~ paid workers*⟩

**²hourly** *adj* 1a done or occurring every hour ⟨*~ bus service*⟩ b continual ⟨*in ~ expectation of the rain's stopping*⟩ 2 reckoned by the hour ⟨*an ~ wage*⟩

**¹house** /hows/ *n, pl* **houses** /'howziz/ 1 a building designed for people to live in 2a an animal's shelter or refuge (e g a nest or den) b a building in which something is housed or stored ⟨*a boat ~*⟩ c a building used for a particular purpose, esp eating, drinking, or entertainment ⟨*a public ~*⟩ 3a any of the 12 equal sectors into which the CELESTIAL SPHERE (imaginary sphere surrounding earth on whose surface the stars, planets, etc appear to be placed) is divided in astrology b a sign of the zodiac in which a planet exerts its greatest influence 4a *taking sing or pl vb* the occupants of a house; the household ⟨*quiet, or you'll wake up the whole ~*⟩ b a family including ancestors, descendants, and kindred ⟨*the ~ of Tudor*⟩ 5a a residence for a religious community, students, etc b *taking sing or pl vb* the community or students in residence c *taking sing or pl vb* any of several groups into which the pupils of a British school may be divided for social purposes or for games 6a a legislative, deliberative, or consultative assembly; *esp* a division of a body consisting of two chambers b the building or chamber where such an assembly meets c a minimum number of members of such an assembly required to be present before business can be transacted 7a(1) a business organization or establishment ⟨*a publishing ~*⟩ a(2) a large building used by a business or institution – used in names ⟨*Transport* House⟩ b a gambling establishment c (the audience in) a theatre or concert hall ⟨*a full ~*⟩ d *Br* a specified performance at a theatre or cinema ⟨*shall we go to the first ~*⟩ 8 the circular area 3 yards (about 2.7 metres) in diameter surrounding the mark at which a stone is aimed in the game of curling and within which the stone must rest in order to count [ME *hous*, fr OE *hūs*; akin to OHG & ON *hūs* house] – **houseful** *n*, **houseless** *adj* – **bring the house down** to win rapturous applause – **get on like a house on fire** *informal* to get on very well ⟨got on like a house on fire *as soon as they met*⟩ – **keep house** to manage a house – **on the house** at the expense of an establishment or its management ⟨*have a drink* on the house⟩ – **put/set one's house in order** to put one's affairs straight

**²house** /howz/ *vt* 1 to provide with accommodation or storage space 2 to serve as shelter for; contain ⟨*a library ~s thousands of books*⟩

**³house** *interj* – used as an exclamation to show that one has won a game of bingo [*house*, earlier name for bingo]

**house arrest** *n* confinement often under guard to one's place of residence instead of prison

**houseboat** /-,boht/ *n* an often permanently moored boat that is fitted out as a dwelling; *also, NAm* a barge for leisure cruising

**housebound** /-,bownd/ *adj* confined to the house (e g because of illness)

**houseboy** /'hows,boy/ *n* one employed to carry out general duties in a house or hotel

**housebreak** /'hows,brayk/ *vt, NAm* to housetrain

**housebreaking** /-,brayking/ *n* an act of breaking into and entering the house of another with a criminal purpose – **housebreaker** *n*

**housebroken** /-,brohkən/ *adj, NAm* housetrained

**housecarl** /-,kahl/ *n* a member of the bodyguard of a Danish or early English king or noble [OE *hūscarl*, fr ON *hūskarl*, fr *hūs* house + *karl* man]

**housecoat** /-,koht/ *n* a woman's lightweight dressing gown for wear round the house; *also* a short overall

**housecraft** /-,krahft/ *n* 1 DOMESTIC SCIENCE 2 skill in running a household

**house cricket** *n* any of various crickets (family Gryllidae) living in or near dwellings; *esp* a widely distributed cricket (*Acheta domesticus*)

**house detective** *n, chiefly NAm* one who is employed (e g by a hotel) to prevent disorderly or improper conduct

**housefather** /-,fahdhə/ *n* a male houseparent

**housefly** /-,flie/ *n* (any of various flies similar to) a common fly (*Musca domestica*) found in most parts of the world that frequents houses and carries some diseases (e g typhoid fever)

**houseguest** /-,gest/ *n* GUEST 1a

**¹household** /-,hohld/ *n taking sing or pl vb* all the people who live together in a dwelling and benefit from the common housekeeping

**²household** *adj* 1 of a household; domestic ⟨*~ chores*⟩ 2 familiar, common ⟨*a ~ name*⟩ ⟨*a ~ word*⟩

**householder** /-,hohldə/ *n* a person who occupies a house, flat, etc as owner or tenant

**household troops** *n pl* troops appointed to attend and guard a sovereign or his/her residence

**house journal** *n* a periodical distributed by a business concern among its employees and dealing with the company's activities and internal news

**housekeeper** /-,keepə/ *n* somebody, esp a woman, employed to take charge of the running of a house – **housekeep** *vi*

**housekeeping** /-,keeping/ *n* 1 (money used for) the day-to-day running of a house and household affairs 2 the general management of an organization which ensures its smooth running (e g by the provision of equipment and keeping of records) 3 the routine tasks that have to be done in order for something (e g a computer system) to function properly

**houseleek** /-,leek/ *n* any of a genus (*Sempervivum*) of plants of the stonecrop family; *esp* a pink-flowered Eurasian plant (*Sempervivum tectorum*) that grows esp on old walls and roofs

**houselights** /-,liets/ *n pl* the lights that illuminate the auditorium of a theatre

**house longhorn** *n* a beetle (*Hylotrupes bajalus*) whose larvae feed on dead wood and are sometimes found in house timbers

**house magazine** *n* a house journal

**housemaid** /-,mayd/ *n* a female servant employed to do housework

**housemaid's knee** *n* a swelling over the knee due to the enlargement of the liquid-filled pouch (BURSA) in the front of the kneecap [fr its occurrence among servants frequently working on their knees]

**houseman** /-mən/ *n* 1 a houseboy 2 the most junior grade of British hospital doctor that is held by a usu newly qualified doctor who is still in training; *also* a doctor holding this post

**house manager** *n* one who manages all front-of-house activities in a theatre

**house martin** *n* a European martin (*Delichon urbica*) with blue-black plumage and white rump that nests on cliffs and under the eaves of houses

**housemaster** /-,mahstə/, *fem* **housemistress** *n* a teacher in charge of one school house, esp of a residential house at a boarding school

**housemother** /-,mudhə/ *n* a female houseparent

**house mouse** *n* a common usu grey mouse (*Mus musculus*) that lives and breeds in and around buildings, is found in most parts of the world, and is a serious pest causing damage to fabrics and food and carrying disease

**house of assembly** *n, often cap H&A* a legislative body or the lower house of such a body in various British colonies, protectorates, countries of the Commonwealth, etc

**house of cards** *n* a structure or situation that is insubstantial or precarious [fr the flimsy structures built by children out of playing cards]

**House of Commons** *n* the lower house of the British and Canadian parliaments

**house of correction** *n* an institution where people who had committed a minor offence were formerly confined – not used technically in Britain

**house of delegates** *n* the lower house of the legislative body in the US states of Maryland, Virginia, and West Virginia

**house of ill fame** *n, euph* a brothel

**house of ill repute** *n, euph* a brothel

**House of Keys** *n* the lower house of the Manx Parliament

**House of Lords** *n* 1 the upper house of the British Parliament composed of hereditary and invested peers 2 the body of LAW LORDS of the House of Lords which constitutes the highest COURT OF APPEAL in the United Kingdom

**House of Representatives** *n* the lower house of the US Congress or Australian Parliament

**house of studies** *n* an educational institution serving scholars of a religious order

**houseparent** /-ˌpeərənt/ *n* a person in charge of a group of young people living in care (eg in a children's home)

**house party** *n* a party lasting for one or more days and nights at a residence (eg a country house)

**houseplant** /-ˌplahnt/ *n* a plant grown or kept indoors

**'house-ˌproud** *adj* (excessively) careful about the management and appearance of one's house

**houseroom** /'howsˌroohm/ *n* – **give houseroom to** to allow or keep in one's house – usu neg ⟨*wouldn't* give *that old ornament* houseroom⟩

**house rule** *n* a rule that applies to a game only among a certain group of people or in a certain place

**house sparrow** *n* a brown sparrow (*Passer domesticus*) that is native to most of Europe, parts of Asia, and northern Africa, has been introduced into many other parts of the world (eg N America and Australia), and lives esp in or near human settlements

**house style** *n* a body of rules (eg as to punctuation and spelling) followed by a journal, publishing house, or printer

**ˌhouse-to-'house** *adj* DOOR-TO-DOOR 1

**housetop** /-ˌtop/ *n* a roof; *esp* the level surface of a flat roof – **from the housetops** for all to hear; IN PUBLIC ⟨*shouting their grievances* from the housetops⟩

**house trailer** *n*, *NAm* CARAVAN 2b

**housetrain** /-ˌtrayn/ *vt*, *chiefly Br* **1** to train (eg a pet) to defecate and urinate outdoors **2** *humorous* to teach (eg a person) to behave acceptably

**housewarming** /-ˌwawming/ *n* a party held in a house or premises to celebrate moving into it from a previous one

**housewife** /'howsˌwief; *sense 2* 'huzif/ *n* **1** a usu married woman who runs a house **2** a small container for needlework articles (eg thread) – **housewifely** *adj*, **housewifery** *n*

**housework** /-ˌwuhk/ *n* the work (eg cleaning) involved in maintaining a house

**housey-housey** /ˌhowzi 'howzi/ *n* bingo [redupl of *house*, earlier name for *bingo*]

**¹housing** /'howzing/ *n* **1** (the provision of) houses or dwelling-places collectively **2** a protective cover for machinery, sensitive instruments, etc **3** *building* a slot or groove in a structural member (eg a timber) for the insertion of part of another

**²housing** *n* an ornamental cover for a horse's saddle [ME *house, housing*, fr MF *houce*, of Gmc origin; akin to MHG *hulft* covering, OE *helan* to conceal – more at HELL]

**housing association** *n* a nonprofitmaking society that constructs, renovates, and helps tenants to rent or buy housing

**housing list** *n* a list of people waiting to be provided with council accommodation

**housing project** *n* a publicly supported and administered housing development, planned usu for low-income families

**houting** /'howting/ *n* a European sea fish (*Coregonus oxyrhynchus*) related to the salmon that ascends rivers to spawn in the autumn and is an important food fish [D, fr MD *houtic*]

**hove** /hohv/ *past of* HEAVE

**hovel** /'hovl/ *n* **1** a tabernacle **2** a small, wretched, and often dirty house or abode [ME]

**hover** /'hovə/ *vi* **1** to hang in the air or on the wing **2a** to linger or wait restlessly around a place **b** to be in a state of uncertainty, irresolution, or suspense [ME *hoveren*, freq of *hoven* to hover] – **hover** *n*, **hoverer** *n*

**hovercraft** /-ˌkrahft/ *n*, *pl* **hovercraft** a vehicle that is supported on a cushion of air produced by fans, and designed to travel over both land and sea **synonyms** see HYDROFOIL

**hoverfly** /-ˌflie/ *n* any of various brightly coloured flies (family Syrphidae) that hover in the air and frequent flowers, and many of which have yellow markings resembling those of wasps and bees

**hoverport** /-ˌpawt/ *n* a place, usu with passenger and customs facilities, where passengers embark on and disembark from hovercraft [*hovercraft* + *port*]

**hovertrain** /-ˌtrayn/ *n* a train that travels on a cushion of air along a special usu concrete track

**¹how** /how/ *adv* **1a** in what manner or way ⟨~ *do you spell it?*⟩ ⟨*know* ~ *it works*⟩ **b** with what meaning; to what effect ⟨~ *can you explain it?*⟩ **c** for what reason; why ⟨~ *could you do it?*⟩ **2** by what measure or quantity ⟨~ *much does it cost?*⟩ – often used in an exclamation as an intensive ⟨~ *nice of you to come!*⟩ **3** in what state or condition (eg of health) ⟨~ *are you?*⟩ ⟨~ *is the market today?*⟩ **4** *archaic* by what name or title ⟨~ *art thou called* – Shak⟩ [ME, fr OE *hū*; akin to OHG *hwuo* how, OE *hwā* who – more at WHO] – **how about** what do you say to or think of ⟨how about *going to London*

*for the day?*⟩ – **how do you do** – used as a formal greeting – **how's that 1** please comment ⟨how's that *for enterprise?*⟩ **2** please repeat **3** – used in cricket as an appeal to the umpire to give the batsman out

**²how** *conj* **1a** the way, manner, or state in which ⟨*remember* ~ *they fought*⟩ **b** that ⟨*told them* ~ *he had a situation* – Charles Dickens⟩ **2** however, as ⟨*a reader can shift his attention* ~ *he likes* – William Empson⟩
    **usage 1** In a sentence such as ⟨*I remember* **how** *they fought*⟩, **how** may mean either "the way in which" or "the fact that"; so it may be wise to use a different construction here. **2** The use of *as* **how** for "that" ⟨⚠ *he says as* **how** *he'll be late*⟩ is substandard.

**³how** *n* **1** a question about manner or method **2** manner, method ⟨*the* ~ *and the why of it*⟩

**⁴how** *interj* – used as a greeting by American Indians, or in usu humorous imitation of them [of Siouan origin; akin to Dakota *háo*, Omaha *hau*]

**¹howbeit** /how'bee·it/ *adv*, *formal* nevertheless

**²howbeit** *conj*, *formal* although ⟨*the room is comfortable,* ~ *small*⟩

**howdah** /'howdə/ *n* a usu canopied seat on the back of an elephant or camel [Hindi *hauda*, fr Ar *haudaj*]

**ˌhow-do-you-'do, how d'ye do** /ˌhow dyə 'dooh/ *n*, *informal* a confused or embarrassing situation [fr the phrase *how do you do?*]

**howdy** /'howdi/ *n*, *chiefly NAm informal* hello [by shortening & alter. fr *how do you do?*]

**howe** /how, hoh/ *n*, *Scot* a hollow, valley [ME (northern) *how, holl*, fr OE *hol*, fr *hol*, adj, hollow – more at HOLE]

**¹however** /how'evə/ *conj* **1** in whatever manner or way ⟨*can go* ~ *he likes*⟩ **2** *archaic* although

**²however** *adv* **1** to whatever degree or extent; no matter how ⟨~ *fast I eat*⟩ **2** in spite of that; nevertheless ⟨*still seems possible,* ~, *that conditions will improve*⟩ ⟨*would like to go;* ~, *I think I'd better not*⟩ **3** *informal* how in the world ⟨~ *did you manage it?*⟩
    **usage 1** Some writers on usage advise that **however** and *but* should not be used together ⟨⚠ *were afraid we should be late; but when we arrived,* **however,** *we found the doors still closed*⟩; but this combination is widely and respectably used. **2 However** is separated from the rest of the sentence by a comma or commas when it means "nevertheless", as in sense **2**, but not when it means "no matter how", as in sense **1**. See EVER

**howff, howf** /howf, hohf/ *n*, *Scot* a haunt, resort; *esp* a pub [D *hof* enclosure; akin to OE *hof* enclosure, *hȳf* hive]

**howitzer** /'how·itzə/ *n* a short cannon usu of medium range that projects shells at a steep angle, thus reaching targets behind cover [D *houwitser*, deriv of Czech *houfnice* ballista]

**howl** /howl/ *vi* **1a** *esp of dogs, wolves, etc* to make a loud sustained doleful cry **b** *of wind* to make a sustained wailing sound **2** to cry loudly and without restraint (eg with pain or laughter) ~ *vt* to utter with a loud sustained cry [ME *houlen*; akin to MHG *hiulen* to howl, Gk *kōkyein* to shriek] – **howl** *n* – **howl down** *vt* to express one's disapproval of (eg a speaker) by shouting

**howler** /'howlə/ *n*, *informal* a stupid and comic blunder

**howler monkey** *n* any of a genus (*Alouatta*) of monkeys of S and Central America that have a long tail adapted for seizing or grasping objects and enlarged VOCAL CORDS and surrounding structures enabling them to make loud howling noises

**howling** /'howling/ *adj*, *informal* very great, extreme, or severe ⟨*a* ~ *success*⟩

**howsoever** /ˌhowsoh'evə/ *adv* **1** in whatever manner **2** to whatever degree or extent

**how's your Father** *n*, *Br humorous* sexual play or intercourse, esp furtively indulged in [fr the catchphrase *how's your father?*, used with a wide range of meanings, orig fr a music-hall song]

**howzat** /how'zat/ *interj* HOW'S THAT 3 [by alter.]

**¹hoy** /hoy/ *interj* – used in attracting attention or in driving animals [ME]

**²hoy** *n* a small coasting vessel with sails usu set lengthways (FORE-AND-AFT) [ME, fr MD *hoei*]

**hoyden** /'hoydn/ *n* a saucy or boisterous girl or woman [perh fr obs D *heiden* country lout, fr MD, heathen; akin to OE *hǣthen* heathen] – **hoydenish** *adj*

**Hramsa** /'khramsə/ *n* a rich soft cream cheese flavoured with wild garlic [OE *hramsa* wild garlic (cf RAMSONS)]

**Hsia** /shi'ah/ *n* the legendary first dynasty of Chinese history, traditionally dated from about 2200 to 1766 BC [Chin (Pek) *Xia* (*hsia⁴*)]

# hub

**hub** /hub/ *n* **1** the central part of a wheel, propeller, fan, or similar rotating structure through which the axle passes **2** *the* centre of activity; FOCAL POINT **3** a steel punch from which a working die for a coin or medal is made [prob alter. of ²*hob*]

**hubble-bubble** /'hubl ˌbubl/ *n* **1** WATER PIPE **2** (smoking apparatus) **2** a flurry of noise or activity; a commotion [redupl of *bubble*]

**hubbub** /'hubub/ *n* a noisy confusion; uproar [prob of Celt origin; akin to ScGael *ub ub*, interj of contempt]

**hubby** /'hubi/ *n, informal* a husband [by alter.]

**hubcap** /'hubˌkap/ *n* a removable metal or plastic cap placed over the hub of a wheel, esp that of a motor vehicle

**hubris** /'hyoohbris/ *n* overweening pride, usu leading to retribution [Gk *hybris* – more at OUT] – **hubristic** *adj*

**huckaback** /'hukəˌbak/ *n* an absorbent durable fabric of cotton, linen, or both, used chiefly for towels [origin unknown]

**huckleberry** /'huklb(ə)ri, -ˌberi/ *n* **1** any of a genus (*Gaylussacia*) of N American shrubs of the heather family; *also* the edible dark blue or black berry of the huckleberry **2** a blueberry [perh alter. of arch. *hurtleberry*, fr ME *hurtilberye*]

**¹huckster** /'hukstə/ *n* **1** a hawker, pedlar **2** *chiefly NAm* one who writes advertising and publicity material for commercial clients, esp for radio or television [ME *hukster*, fr MD *hokester*, fr *hoeken* to peddle; akin to MLG *hōken* to peddle – more at HAWKER]

**²huckster** *vi* to haggle ~ *vt* **1** to deal in or bargain over **2** to promote or advertise, esp in an aggressive or underhand manner

**¹huddle** /'hudl/ *vb* **huddling** *vt* **1a** to crowd together ⟨~d *masses of people*⟩ **b** to draw or curl (oneself) up **2** to wrap tightly (e g in clothes) **3** *Br* to throw together carelessly or hurriedly ~ *vi* **1** to gather in a closely-packed group **2** to curl up; crouch [prob fr or akin to ME *hoderen* to huddle]

**²huddle** *n* **1** a closely-packed group; a bunch ⟨a ~ *of cottages*⟩ **2** a secretive or conspiratorial meeting ⟨*went into a* ~ *with his colleagues*⟩

**Hudson seal** /'huds(ə)n/ *n* the fur of the muskrat prepared to simulate seal [*Hudson* bay, inland sea in Canada]

**hue** /hyooh/ *n* **1** a complexion, aspect ⟨*political functions of every* ~⟩ **2a** a shade of a colour **b** the attribute of colours that permits them to be classed as red, yellow, green, blue, or an intermediate (e g orange) between any adjacent pair of these colours; *also* a colour having this attribute as contrasted with white, black, or grey – compare LIGHTNESS, SATURATION [ME *hewe*, fr OE *hīw*; akin to OE *hār* hoary – more at HOAR]

**hue and cry** *n* **1a** a loud cry formerly used when in pursuit of a criminal **b** a written proclamation for the capture of a suspect **2** a public outcry of alarm or protest [*hue* (outcry), fr ME *hew*, *hu*, fr OF *hue*, fr *huer* to shout, fr *hu*, interj warning of danger]

**hued** /hyoohd/ *adj* coloured – usu in combination ⟨*greenhued*⟩

**¹huff** /huf/ *vi* **1** to emit loud puffs (e g of breath or steam) **2a** to make empty threats ⟨*management* ~ed *and puffed about the chances of a lockout*⟩ **b** to take offence ~ *vt* **1** to make angry **2** to take (an opponent's piece) in a game of draughts as a penalty for failing to make a compulsory capture **3** *archaic* to treat with contempt; bully [imit; (vt 2) fr the former practice of blowing on the taken piece]

**²huff** *n* – **in a huff** in a piqued and resentful mood

**huffy** /'hufi/ *also* **huffish** /'hufish/ *adj* **1** haughty, arrogant **2a** sulky, petulant **b** easily offended; touchy – **huffily** *adv*, **huffiness** *n*

**¹hug** /hug/ *vt* **-gg- 1** to hold or press tightly, esp in the arms **2a** to feel very pleased with (oneself) **b** to cling to; cherish ⟨~ged *his miseries like a sulky child* – John Buchan⟩ **3** to stay close to ⟨*thick smoke* ~ged *the ground*⟩ [perh fr Scand origin; akin to ON *hugga* to soothe] – **huggable** *adj*

**²hug** *n* a tight clasp or embrace

**huge** /hyoohj/ *adj* great in size, scale, degree, or scope; enormous ⟨~ *mountains*⟩ ⟨a ~ *success*⟩ [ME, fr OF *ahuge*] – **hugeness** *n*

  *synonyms* Huge, vast, immense, enormous, mammoth, elephantine, giant, gigantic, colossal, gargantuan, titanic: huge is a general term, expressing great size, bulk, or capacity ⟨a **huge** man⟩ ⟨**huge** piles of wheat⟩. Vast stresses extent or range ⟨**vast** distances⟩. Immense and enormous suggest size or degree far in excess of what is usual, with **immense** sometimes implying almost infinite ⟨**immense** vistas of blue sky⟩ ⟨**enormous** strength⟩. Mammoth and elephantine suggest the large size and unwieldy

nature of the animals they recall. Used figuratively, **mammoth** can mean "excessive" or "extravagant" ⟨a **mammoth** darts tournament⟩. Giant and gigantic suggest something abnormally large; **gigantic** is preferred for figurative use ⟨a **giant** doll⟩ ⟨a **gigantic** bill for repairs⟩. Colossal suggests something of awesomely large proportions, while **titanic** implies the colossal size and primitive strength of the Titans. The hugeness of **gargantuan** is like that of Rabelais' hero: larger than life, especially with regard to food and appetites. *antonyms* tiny, minute, minuscule

**hugely** /'hyoohjli/ *adv* very much; enormously ⟨*was* ~ *excited*⟩

**hugeous** /'hyoohjəs/ *adj, archaic* huge – **hugeously** *adv*

**¹hugger-mugger** /'hugə ˌmugə/ *n* **1** secrecy **2** confusion, muddle [origin unknown] – **hugger-mugger** *adj or adv*

**²hugger-mugger** *vt* to keep secret; hush up ~ *vi, informal* to act in a confused or stealthy manner

**Huguenot** /'hyoohgənoh, -not/ *n* a member of the French Protestant church, esp of the 16th and 17th centuries [MF, fr MF dial. *huguenot*, adherent of a Swiss political movement, alter. (influenced by Besançon *Hugues* †1532 Swiss political leader) of *eidgnot*, fr Ger dial. *eidgnoss* confederate] – **Huguenotism** *n*, **Huguenotic** *adj*

**huh** /huh, hah/ *interj* – used to express surprise, disapproval, or inquiry

**hui** /'hooh-ee/ *n* **1** a tribal gathering of a widely-scattered group of Maoris **2** *NZ informal* a party [Maori & Hawaiian]

**hula** /'hoolə/ *also* **hula-hula** *n* a Polynesian dance performed by women, involving swaying of the hips and expressive movements of the hands and often accompanied by chants and rhythmic drumming; *also* music to which a hula is performed [Hawaiian]

**Hula-Hoop** /'hoohlə ˌhoohp/ *trademark* – used for a light usu cane or plastic hoop that can be made to spin round the waist by gyrating the body

**¹hulk** /hulk/ *n* **1a** a heavy unwieldy ship **b** the hull of a partially dismantled ship that is no longer seaworthy and is used as a storehouse **c** an abandoned wreck or shell, esp of a vessel **d** a ship used as a prison **2** a person, creature, or thing that is bulky or unwieldy ⟨a *big* ~ *of a man*⟩ [ME *hulke*, fr OE *hulc*, fr ML *holcas*, fr Gk *holkas*, fr *helkein* to pull – more at SULCUS]

**²hulk** *vi* **1** *dial Eng* to move ponderously **2** *NAm* to appear impressively large or massive; loom

**hulking** /'hulking/ *adj* bulky, massive

**¹hull** /hul/ *n* **1a** the outer covering of a fruit or seed **b** the usu green or leafy parts at the base of a strawberry, raspberry, or similar fruit that protected the flower in the bud stage of development **2** the main frame or body of a ship, airship, FLYING BOAT, etc; *also* the fuselage of an aeroplane **3** a covering, casing [ME, fr OE *hulu*; akin to OHG *hala* hull, OE *helan* to conceal – more at HELL] – **hull-less** *adj*

**²hull** *vt* **1** to remove the hulls of **2** to hit or pierce the hull of (e g a ship) – **huller** *n*

**hullabaloo** /ˌhuləbə'looh/ *n, pl* **hullabaloos** *informal* a confused noise; an uproar [perh irreg fr *hallo* + Sc *balloo*, interj used to hush children]

**hull down** *adv or adj, of a ship* at such a distance that only the superstructure is visible above the horizon

**hullo** /hu'loh/ *interj or n, chiefly Br* hello

**¹hum** /hum/ *vb* **-mm-** *vi* **1a** to utter a prolonged /m/ sound **b** to make the characteristic droning noise of an insect in motion or a similar sound **c** to make a low continuous vibrating sound **2** *informal* to be lively or active **3** *slang* to have an offensive smell ~ *vt* **1** to sing with the lips closed and without articulation **2** to affect or express by humming ⟨~med *me to sleep*⟩ [ME *hummen*; akin to MHG *hummen* to hum, MD *hommel* bumblebee] – **hum** *n*, **hummer** *n* – **hum and ha** *also* **hum and haw** to equivocate

**²hum** *interj* – used to express hesitation, uncertainty, disagreement, etc

**¹human** /'hyoohmən/ *adj* **1a** (characteristic) of humans ⟨~ *voice*⟩ **b** being a human **2** consisting of humans ⟨~ *race*⟩ ⟨a ~ *barrier*⟩ **3a** having the esp good attributes (e g kindness and compassion) thought to be characteristic of humans ⟨*seems austere but is really very* ~⟩ **b** having, showing, or concerned with qualities or feelings characteristic of humans ⟨*to err is* ~⟩ – see also the MILK of human kindness [ME *humain*, fr MF, fr L *humanus*; akin to L *homo* human being – more at HOMAGE] – **humanness** *n*

**²human, human being** *n* a man, woman, or child; a person *usage* Earlier writers on usage objected to the use of **human** as a noun, but today it is perfectly acceptable. It means not only "not an animal" but also "not a supernatural being".

**humane** /hyooh'mayn/ *adj* **1a** marked by compassion or consideration for other human beings or animals **b** causing the minimum pain possible ⟨~ *killing of animals*⟩ **2** characterized by broad humanistic culture; liberal ⟨~ *studies*⟩ [ME *humain*] – **humanely** *adv*, **humaneness** *n*

**human ecology** *n* the ecology of people and of human communities and populations, esp as concerned with preservation of environmental quality

**human engineering** *n* **1** management of human beings and affairs, esp in industry **2** *chiefly NAm* ERGONOMICS (science dealing with working environments and machines for human use)

**human interest** *n* a personal element (eg in a news story)

**humanism** /'hyoohmə,niz(ə)m/ *n* **1a** devotion to the humanities; literary culture **b** a cultural movement dominant during the Renaissance that was characterized by a revival of classical learning, an individualistic and critical spirit, and a shift of emphasis from religious to secular concerns **2** humanitarianism **3** a doctrine, attitude, or way of life based on human interests or values; *esp* a philosophy that asserts the intrinsic worth of humans and their capacity for fulfilment through a life governed by reason and that usu rejects religious belief – **humanist** *n or adj*, **humanistic** *adj*, **humanistically** *adv*

**humanitarian** /hyooh,mani'teəri-ən/ *n* somebody who promotes human welfare and social reform; a philanthropist – **humanitarian** *adj*, **humanitarianism** *n*

**humanity** /hyooh'manəti/ *n* **1** the quality of being humane **2a** the quality or state of being human **b** *pl* human attributes or qualities **3** *pl* the cultural branches of learning **4** humankind

**human-ize, -ise** /'hyoomə,niez/ *vt* **1a** to cause to be or seem human **b** to adapt to human nature or use **2** to make humane – **humanization** *n*, **humanizer** *n*

**humankind** /-'kiend/ *n* taking sing or pl vb human beings collectively *usage* see MANKIND

**humanly** /-li/ *adv* **1a** from a human viewpoint **b** within the range of human capacity ⟨*as perfectly as is* ~ *possible*⟩ **2a** in a manner characteristic of humans, esp in showing emotion or weakness **b** with regard to human needs, emotions, or weaknesses; with humaneness

**human nature** *n* the nature of human beings; the innate and acquired behavioural patterns, motives, attitudes, ideas, etc characteristic of human beings

**humanoid** /'hyoohmə,noyd/ *adj* having human form or characteristics ⟨~ *dentition*⟩ ⟨~ *robots*⟩ – **humanoid** *n*

**humate** /'hyoohmayt/ *n* any of various chemical compounds (SALTS or ESTERS) formed by combination between HUMIC ACID and a metal atom, an alcohol, or another chemical group

**¹humble** /'humbl/ *adj* **1** having a low opinion of oneself; unassertive **2** marked by deference or submission ⟨*a* ~ *apology*⟩ **3a** ranking low in a hierarchy or scale ⟨*man of* ~ *origins*⟩ **b** modest, unpretentious ⟨*a* ~ *dwelling*⟩ [ME, fr OF, fr L *humilis* low, humble, fr *humus* earth; akin to Gk *chthōn* earth, *chamai* on the ground] – **humbleness** *n*, **humbly** *adv*

**²humble** *vt* **1** to make humble in spirit or manner **2** to destroy the power, independence, or prestige of

*synonyms* Abase, debase, demean, degrade, humble, and humiliate can all mean "lower in one's own estimation or that of others". Abase suggests loss of rank or prestige, while debase stresses loss of inner quality or value. Demean, often reflexive, implies a loss of social standing or dignity ⟨demeaned herself by marrying out of her class⟩. Degrade suggests a much more serious loss of respect or rank, with implications of disgrace, shame, and even moral corruption. Humble stresses bringing low from a height of rank or power, and suggests a lessening of self-esteem or conceit which is salutary or deserved. Humble oneself implies no lack of self-respect, but a proper, lowly spirit. Humiliate suggests a public humbling which causes the victim extreme chagrin and mortification, and involves a loss of self-respect. *antonyms* extol, exalt (oneself)

**¹humble-,bee** *n* a bumblebee [ME *humbylbee*, fr *humbyl-* (akin to MD *hommel* bumblebee) + *bee* – more at HUM]

**humble pie** *n* [alter. (influenced by *humble*) of *umble pie* pie made of offal, fr *umbles*] – **eat humble pie** to be forced to accept humiliation or defeat; EAT CROW

**¹humbug** /'hum,bug/ *n* **1a** something designed to deceive and mislead; a fraud **b** an impostor, sham ⟨*he's no doctor, he's a* ~⟩ **2** pretence, deception **3** drivel, nonsense **4** a hard usu pepper-

mint-flavoured striped sweet made from boiled sugar [origin unknown] – **humbuggery** *n*

**²humbug** *vb* **-gg-** to deceive with a hoax

**humdinger** /'hum,dingə/ *n, informal* an excellent or remarkable person or thing [origin unknown]

**humdrum** /'hum,drum/ *adj* monotonous, dull [irreg redupl of *hum*] – **humdrum** *n*

**humectant** /hyooh'mekt(ə)nt/ *n* a substance (eg glycerin) that promotes retention of moisture [L *humectant-*, *humectans*, prp of *humectare* to moisten, fr *humectus* moist, fr *humēre* to be moist – more at HUMOUR] – **humectant** *adj*

**humeral** /'hyoohmərəl/ *adj* **1** (situated in the region) of the humerus or shoulder **2** of or being a part of the body analogous to the humerus or shoulder – **humeral** *n*

**humeral veil** *n* an oblong shawl worn round the shoulders and over the hands by a priest or subdeacon holding a sacred vessel

**humerus** /'hyoohmərəs/ *n, pl* **humeri** /-ri, -rie/ the long bone of the upper arm or forelimb extending from the shoulder to the elbow [NL, fr L, upper arm, shoulder; akin to Goth *ams* shoulder, Gk *ōmos*]

**humic** /'hyoohmik/ *adj* of or derived at least in part from humus

**humic acid** /'hyoohmik/ *n* any of various organic acids obtained from humus

**humid** /'hyoohmid/ *adj, esp of weather* (uncomfortably) moist and warm ⟨*a* ~ *climate*⟩ *synonyms* see ¹WET [Fr or L; Fr *humide*, fr L *humidus*, fr *humēre* to be moist]

**humidifier** /hyooh'midi,fie-ə/ *n* a device for supplying or maintaining humidity

**humidify** /hyooh'midifie/ *vt* to make humid – **humidification** *n*

**humidity** /hyooh'midəti/ *n* (the degree of) moisture, esp in the atmosphere; dampness – compare RELATIVE HUMIDITY

**humidor** /'hyoohmidaw/ *n* a case or room for storing cigars, tobacco, etc at the correct humidity [*humid* + *-or* (as in *cuspidor*)]

**humify** /'hyoohmifie/ *vb* to convert into or form humus – **humification** *n*

**humiliate** /hyooh'miliayt/ *vt* to lower the dignity or self-respect of; humble *synonyms* see ²HUMBLE *antonym* exalt [LL *humiliatus*, pp of *humiliare*, fr L *humilis* low – more at HUMBLE] – **humiliatingly** *adv*, **humiliation** *n*

**humility** /hyooh'miləti/ *n* the quality or state of being humble △ humiliation

**hummingbird** /'huming,buhd/ *n* any of numerous tiny brightly coloured usu tropical American birds (family Trochilidae) related to the swifts, that have a slender bill and narrow wings that beat rapidly making a humming sound

**hummingbird moth** *n* a hawkmoth [fr its hovering flight resembling that of a hummingbird]

**humming top** *n* a top that hums as it spins

**hummock** /'humək/ *n* **1** a hillock **2** a ridge of ice **3** ²HAMMOCK (fertile area in the S USA) [origin unknown] – **hummocky** *adj*

**hummus, houmous, houmus** /'hoohməs, 'hoomas, 'hooh,-moohs/ *n* a thick paste or spread made from chick-peas, and TAHINI (sesame-seed paste), flavoured with lemon juice and garlic, and served esp as an appetizer [Turk *humus* mashed chick-peas, fr *hummus* chick-pea, fr Ar *ḥummuṣ, ḥimmiṣ*]

**humoral** /'hyoohmərəl/ *adj* **1** of, proceeding from, or involving a body secretion (eg a hormone) **2** of any of the four humours of medieval physiology

**humoresque** /,hyoomə'resk/ *n* a musical composition that is whimsical or fanciful in character; a capriccio [Ger *humoreske*, fr *humor* humour, fr E]

**humorist** /'hyoohmərist/ *n* a person (eg a writer) specializing in or noted for humour – **humoristic** *adj*

**humorous** /'hyoohmərəs/ *adj* full of humour; funny – **humorously** *adv*, **humorousness** *n*

**¹humour**, *chiefly NAm* **humor** /'hyoohmə/ *n* **1a** a liquid (eg the blood) involved in the functioning of the body **b** a secretion (eg a hormone) that stimulates activity of a nerve, gland, etc – not now used technically **2** a liquid or juice of an animal or plant; *specif* any of the four fluids regarded formerly as entering into the constitution of the body and determining by their relative proportions a person's health and temperament – used in medieval physiology **3** temperament ⟨*a man of cheerful* ~⟩ **4** a state of mind; temper ⟨*he was in no* ~ *to listen to further argument*⟩ **5** a sudden inclination; a whim ⟨*when the* ~ *takes him*⟩ **6a** comic or amusing quality ⟨*saw the* ~ *of his predica-*

# hum

*ment*⟩ **b** the faculty of expressing or appreciating the comic or amusing **c** something designed to be comic or amusing *synonyms* see WIT [ME *humour,* fr MF *humeur,* fr ML & L; ML *humor,* fr L, moisture; akin to L *humēre* to be moist, Gk *hygros* wet] – **humourless** *adj,* **humourlessness** *n*

²**humour** *vt* to comply with the mood or wishes of; indulge

¹**hump** /hump/ *n* **1 a** a rounded part projecting from its surroundings: eg **1a** HUNCHBACK **1 b** a fleshy lump on the back of an animal (eg a camel, bison, or whale) **c** a mound, hummock **2** *Br* a fit of sulking, vexation, or depression – + *the* [akin to MLG *hump* bump, L in*cumbere* to lie down, Gk *kymbē* bowl, OE *hype* hip] – **humplike** *adj* – **over the hump** having completed the worst or most difficult part

²**hump** *vt* **1** to hunch **2** *chiefly Br informal* to put or carry on the back; *broadly* to carry (eg something heavy) with difficulty ⟨~ing *suitcases around*⟩ **3** *vulg* to have sexual intercourse with ~ *vi* **1** to rise in a hump **2** *NAm slang* to exert oneself **3** *vulg* to have sexual intercourse

**humpback** /'hump,bak/ *n* **1** a hunchback **2** *also* **humpback whale** a large WHALEBONE WHALE (genus *Megaptera*) related to the RORQUALS but having very long flippers – **humpbacked** *adj*

**humpback bridge, humpbacked bridge** *n* a road bridge with a short steep incline and decline

**humped** /humpt/ *adj* having a hump; *esp* hunchbacked

**humped cattle** *n* domestic cattle developed from an Indian species (*Bos indicus*) and characterized by a hump of fat and muscle above the shoulders; Brahman cattle

¹**humph** /hǝmf/ *interj* – used to express doubt or contempt [imit of a grunt]

²**humph** *vi* to utter a humph ~ *vt* to utter (eg a remark) in a tone suggestive of a humph

**humpty** /'humpti/ *n, Br* a low cushioned seat; a tuffet [perh fr *Humpty-Dumpty*]

**humpty-'dumpty** /'dumpti/ *n, often cap H&D* something that once damaged can never be repaired or made operative again [*Humpty-Dumpty,* egg-shaped nursery-rhyme character who fell from a wall and broke into bits]

¹**humpy** /'humpi/ *adj* **1** full of or covered in humps **2** having the form of a hump **3** having the hump; irritable

²**humpy** *n, Austr* a small or primitive hut [native name in Australia]

**humus** /'hyoohmǝs/ *n* a brown or black material that results from partial decomposition of plant or animal matter and forms the fertile organic portion of the soil [NL, fr L, earth – more at HUMBLE]

**Hun** /hun/ *n, pl* **Huns, (2b) Huns,** *esp collectively* **Hun 1** a member of a nomadic Mongolian people gaining control of a large part of central and eastern Europe under Attila about AD 450 **2a** *often not cap* a person who is wantonly destructive; a vandal **b** *derog* a German; *esp* a German soldier or aircraft in World Wars I & II [LL *Hunni,* pl] – **Hunnish** *adj*

¹**hunch** /hunch/ *vi* to assume a bent or crooked posture ~ *vt* to bend into a hump or arch ⟨~ed *his shoulders*⟩ [origin unknown]

²**hunch** *n* **1** a hump **2** a thick piece; a lump **3** a strong intuitive feeling

**hunchback** /'hunch,bak/ *n* **1** a humped or crooked back; *also* KYPHOSIS (abnormal curvature of the spine) **2** a person with a hunchback – **hunchbacked** *adj*

**hundred** /'hundrǝd/ *n, pl* **hundreds, (1) hundred 1** – see NUMBER table **2a** 100 units or digits; *specif* 100 pounds ⟨*must have cost* ~s⟩ **b** a score of 100 or more runs made by a batsman in cricket – compare FIFTY 4 **3** the number occupying the position three to the left of the decimal point in the Arabic notation; *also, pl* this position **4** *pl* the numbers 100 to 999 **5** something (eg a bank note) having a denomination of 100 **6** a historical subdivision of some English and American counties **7** *pl the* hundred years of a specified century ⟨*the 17* ~s⟩ **8** *pl, informal* an indefinitely large number [ME, fr OE; akin to ON *hundrath* hundred; both fr a prehistoric WGmc-NGmc compound whose constituents are akin to OE *hund* hundred & to Goth gar*athjan* to count; akin to L *centum* hundred, Gk he*katon,* Avestan *satam,* OE *tien* ten – more at TEN, REASON; (6) prob fr its orig consisting of 100 hides of land] – **hundred** *adj,* **hundredfold** *adj or adv,* **hundredth** *adj or n*

,**hundred-per'center** *n, NAm informal* a thoroughgoing nationalist [*hundred-percent (American)*] – **hundred-percentism** *n*

**hundreds and thousands** *n pl* very small balls or thin strands of brightly coloured sugar used as a decoration (eg on cakes and trifles)

**hundredweight** /'hundrǝd,wayt/ *n, pl* **hundredweight, hundredweights 1** METRIC HUNDREDWEIGHT **2a** *Br* a unit of weight equal to 112 pounds (about 50.80 kilograms) **b** *chiefly NAm* a unit of weight equal to 100 pounds (about 45.36 kilograms)

**hung** /hung/ *past of* HANG

**Hungarian** /hung'geǝri-ǝn/ *n* **1** a native or inhabitant of Hungary; *specif* MAGYAR **2** the language of the Magyars [*Hungary,* country in central Europe] – **Hungarian** *adj*

¹**hunger** /'hung-gǝ/ *n* **1a** a craving or urgent need for food **b** an uneasy sensation caused by the lack of food **c** a weakened condition brought about by prolonged lack of food **2** a strong desire; a craving [ME, fr OE *hungor;* akin to OHG *hungar* hunger, Skt *kānksati* he desires]

²**hunger** *vi* **1** to feel or suffer hunger **2** to have an eager desire ~ *vt, archaic* to make hungry

**hunger march** *n* a march undertaken by a group of people, esp unemployed workers, as a protest against their neediness – **hunger marcher** *n*

**hunger strike** *n* refusal to eat enough to sustain life as an act of protest (eg against imprisonment) – **hunger striker** *n*

**hung jury** *n taking sing or pl vb* a jury that fails to reach a verdict

**hung over** *adj* suffering from a hangover

**hungry** /'hung-gri/ *adj* **1a** feeling hunger **b** characterized by or characteristic of hunger or appetite **2** eager, avid ⟨*cash*-hungry *development programmes – Sunday Times*⟩ **3** not rich or fertile; barren – **hungrily** *adv,* **hungriness** *n*

**hunk** /hungk/ *n* **1** a large lump or piece **2** a large muscularly built person, usu a man [Flem *hunke*]

**hunkers** /'hungkǝz/ *n pl, informal* the haunches ⟨*sitting crouched on his* ~⟩ [*hunker* (to crouch, squat), perh of Scand origin; akin to ON *hūka* to squat]

**hunks** /hungks/ *n taking sing vb, informal* a surly ill-natured person; *esp* a miser [origin unknown]

¹**hunky** /'hungki/ *n, NAm* BOHUNK [prob by shortening & alter. fr *Hungarian*]

²**hunky** *adj, informal, of a person, esp a man* attractively well built [*hunk* + ¹-*y*]

**hunky-dory** /,hungki 'dawri/ *adj, chiefly NAm informal* quite satisfactory; fine [obs E (NAm) dial. *hunk* (home base, goal; fr D *honk*) + -*dory* (origin unknown)]

¹**hunt** /hunt/ *vt* **1a** to pursue for food or sport ⟨~ *foxes*⟩ **b** to manage in the search for game ⟨~s *a pack of hounds*⟩ **2a** to pursue with intent to capture ⟨~ed *the escaped prisoner*⟩ **b** to search out; seek **3** to drive or chase, esp by harrying ⟨*innocent people* ~ed *from their homes*⟩ **4** to scour in search of prey ⟨~s *the woods*⟩ ~ *vi* **1** to take part in a hunt **2** to attempt to find something – often + *for* ⟨~ing *for their slippers*⟩ **3** *esp of a device or machine* to run alternately faster and slower instead of steadily; *also* to oscillate [ME *hunten,* fr OE *huntian;* akin to OE *hentan* to seize, attack, OHG heri*hunda* battle spoils]
**synonyms** In Britain, to go **hunting** is to pursue a fox, deer, or hare with a pack of hounds, and usually on horseback, and to go **shooting** is to pursue animals (or, more often, birds) with a gun; in the USA **hunting** is the word for both activities.

²**hunt** *n* **1** the act, the practice, or an instance of hunting **2** *taking sing or pl vb* **2a** a group of mounted hunters and their hounds **b** an association of people who hunt a particular district ⟨*secretary of the local* ~⟩

**huntaway** /'huntǝ,way/ *n, Austr & NZ* a sheepdog that drives sheep away from the shepherd

**hunter** /'huntǝ/, *fem (1a,2a,& b)* **huntress** /'huntrǝs/ *n* **1a** a person who hunts game, esp with hounds **b** a dog used or trained for shooting **c** a horse with the stamina, weight-bearing ability, and boldness required for cross-country work and hunting, esp fox hunting **2a** a person who searches for something **b** a fortune hunter **3** a watch with a hinged lid that protects the face **4** *cap* the constellation of Orion [(3) fr its being orig designed to protect the glass from damage in hunting]

**hunter clip** *n* a manner of clipping a horse's coat so as to leave long hair on the lower legs and in a saddle-shaped patch on the back

**hunter's moon** *n* the FULL MOON after HARVEST MOON (the full moon nearest the Autumn equinox)

**hunting** /'hunting/ *n* **1** the act of one who hunts; *specif* the pursuit of game on horseback with hounds **2** the process of hunting **3a** a periodic variation in speed of an electrical machine; *also* oscillation **b** a self-induced and undesirable oscillation of a variable (e g engine speed) above and below the desired value in an automatically controlled system

**hunting box** *n* a small house used only during the hunting season

**hunting cat** *n* a cheetah

**hunting ground** *n* **1** a region where game is hunted **2** an area of operation or exploitation ⟨*the British Empire is a favourite* ~ *these days for historians*⟩

**hunting horn** *n* a horn used for signalling in hunting

**Huntington's chorea** /'huntingtənz/ *n* a hereditary disorder of the brain in which CHOREA (involuntary spasmodic movement) develops usu in middle age followed by gradual deterioration of mental health and death from degeneration of the nervous system [George *Huntington* †1916 US neurologist]

**huntsman** /-mən/ *n* **1** HUNTER 1a **2** a person employed to train the hounds and manage them during a hunt

**hup** /həp, hup/ *interj* **1** – used to urge a horse to start, go faster, etc **2** – used to mark a marching beat [origin unknown]

**¹hurdle** /'huhdl/ *n* **1a** a portable panel usu of interlaced branches and stakes used esp for enclosing land or livestock **b** a frame or sledge formerly used in Britain for dragging traitors to execution **2a** an artificial barrier which must be jumped over in certain races **b** *pl* any of various athletics races in which a series of hurdles are placed at regular intervals along the track **c** *pl* a horse race over a course longer than 2 miles (about 3.2 kilometres) containing hurdles that are a minimum of 3 feet 6 inches high (about 1.06 metres) but are lower and flimsier than the fences used in steeplechases – compare STEEPLECHASE 1, ¹FLAT 12 **3** a barrier, obstacle [ME *hurdel*, fr OE *hyrdel;* akin to OHG *hurd* hurdle, L *cratis* wickerwork, hurdle]

**²hurdle** *vt* **1** to jump over, esp while running **2** to overcome, surmount ~ *vi* to run in a hurdles race △ **hurtle** – **hurdler** *n*

**hurdy-gurdy** /,huhdi 'guhdi/ *n* a musical instrument in which the sound is produced by turning a crank; *esp* BARREL ORGAN [prob imit]

**hurl** /huhl/ *vt* **1** to drive or thrust violently ⟨~ed *his forces against the Turks*⟩ **2** to throw forcefully; fling ⟨~ed *the manuscript into the fire*⟩ ⟨~ed *himself over the fence*⟩ **3** to utter or shout violently ~ *vi* to play the game of hurling **synonyms** see ¹THROW [ME *hurlen*, prob fr imit origin] – **hurl** *n*, **hurler** *n*

**hurley, hurly** /'huhli/ *n* **1** hurling **2** a stick used for playing hurling [*hurl* + *-y*]

**hurling** /'huhling/ *n* a game resembling hockey played, esp in Ireland, between two teams of 15 players each [fr gerund of *hurl* ]

**hurly-burly** /,huhli 'buhli/, **hurly** *n* uproar, tumult [prob alter. & redupl of *hurling*, gerund of *hurl*]

**Huron** /'hyooərən, -ron/ *n*, *pl* **Hurons**, *esp collectively* **Huron 1** *pl* a confederation of American Indian peoples originally living along the St Lawrence valley **2** a member of any of the Huron peoples [Fr, lit., boor]

**hurrah, hoorah** /hoo'rah/ *interj, vi, or n* (to) hurray

**¹hurray, hooray** /hə'ray/ *interj* – used to express joy, approval, or encouragement [perh fr Ger *hurra*]

**²hurray, hooray** /hoo'ray/ *vi or n* (to shout) a cheer of joy, approval, or encouragement

**hurricane** /'hurikən/ *n* **1** a tropical cyclone with winds of 117 kilometres per hour (about 73 miles per hour) or greater that is usu accompanied by rain, thunder, and lightning and that sometimes moves into temperate latitudes; *broadly* a violent storm **2** something resembling a hurricane, esp in violence **synonyms** see WHIRLWIND [Sp *huracán*, fr Taino *hurakán*]

**hurricane lamp** *n* a candlestick or oil lamp equipped with a glass chimney to protect the flame

**hurried** /'hurid/ *adj* done or working under pressure; hasty ⟨~ *instructions*⟩ – **hurriedly** *adv*, **hurriedness** *n*

**¹hurry** /'huri/ *vt* **1a** to transport or cause to go with haste; rush ⟨~ *him to hospital*⟩ **b** to impel to rash or precipitate action ⟨*was hurried into making a decision*⟩ **2a** to impel to greater speed ⟨*hates to be* hurried *at mealtimes*⟩ **b** to hasten the progress or completion of ⟨*don't* ~ *this passage of the music*⟩ ~ *vi* to move or act with haste ⟨*please* ~ *up*⟩ [perh fr ME *horyen*, prob of imit origin] – **hurrier** *n*

**²hurry** *n* **1** flurried and often bustling haste; rush **2** a state of eagerness or urgency; a need for haste ⟨*there's no* ~ *for it*⟩ – **in a hurry** without delay; as rapidly as possible ⟨*the police got there in a hurry*⟩

**hurry-'scurry, hurry-skurry** *n, informal* a confused rush [redupl of ²*hurry*] – **hurry-scurry** *adj or adv*

**¹hurt** /huht/ *vb* **hurt** *vt* **1a** to afflict with physical pain; wound **b** to do substantial or material harm to; damage ⟨*the dry summer has* ~ *the land*⟩ **2a** to cause mental pain or anguish to; offend ⟨*his feelings were* ~ *by the snub*⟩ **b** to be detrimental to; harm ⟨*charges of dishonesty* ~ *his chances of being elected*⟩ ~ *vi* **1** to feel pain; suffer **2** to cause damage or distress ⟨*hit where it* ~s⟩ **synonyms** see INJURE [ME *hurten, hirten* to strike, injure, prob fr OF *hurter* to collide with, prob of Gmc origin] – **hurter** *n*

**²hurt** *n* **1** a cause of injury or damage; a blow **2a** a body injury or wound **b** mental distress or anguish; suffering **3** a wrong, harm – **hurtless** *adj*

**hurtful** /'huhtf(ə)l/ *adj* causing injury or anguish; damaging ⟨*a* ~ *remark*⟩ – **hurtfully** *adv*, **hurtfulness** *n*

**hurtle** /huhtl/ *vi* **1** to move with a crashing sound; clatter ⟨*rocks* hurtling *down the cliff*⟩ **2** to move very rapidly ⟨*police car* ~d *along the road*⟩ ~ *vt* to hurl, fling [ME *hurtlen* to collide, freq of *hurten*] – **hurtle** *n*

**¹husband** /'huzbənd/ *n* a married man, esp in relation to his wife [ME *husbonde*, fr OE *husbonda* master of a house, fr ON *húsbōndi*, fr *hūs* house + *bōndi* householder (cf ¹BOND)] – **husbandly** *adj*

**²husband** *vt* **1** to use sparingly and economically; conserve ⟨~ *one's strength and resources*⟩ **2** *archaic* to find a husband for – **husbander** *n*

**husbandman** /'huzbəndmən/ *n* **1** one who ploughs and cultivates land; a farmer **2** a specialist in a branch of farm husbandry

**husbandry** /'huzbəndri/ *n* **1** the management of resources; *esp* thrift **2a** the cultivation or production of plants and animals; farming **b** the scientific control and management of a branch of farming, esp that concerned with domestic animals

**¹hush** /hush/ *vt* **1** to silence, quiet ⟨~ed *the children as they entered the library*⟩ **2** to put at rest; appease ⟨~ed *his conscience by bringing her flowers*⟩ **3** to keep from public knowledge; suppress – often + *up* ⟨~ed *up the affair*⟩ ~ *vi* to become quiet **synonyms** see ²QUIET [back-formation fr *husht* (hushed), fr ME *hussht*, fr *huissht*, interj used to demand silence]

**²hush** *adj, archaic* silent, still

**³hush** *n* a silence or calm, esp following noise

**⁴hush** *vt, N Eng* to wash away (soil) to expose minerals, ores, etc for mining [imit]

**hush-'hush** *adj, informal* secret, confidential

**hush money** *n* money paid to prevent the disclosure of information

**¹husk** /husk/ *n* **1** a typically dry or membranous outer covering of a seed or fruit **2** the esp worthless outer layer of something; a shell [ME, prob modif of MD *huuskijn*, dim. of *huus* house, cover] – **husky** *adj*

**²husk** *vt* to strip the husk from – **husker** *n*

**¹husky** /'huski/ *adj, of a voice* slightly rasping; hoarse [prob fr *husk* (huskiness), fr obs *husk* to have a dry cough, of imit origin] – **huskily** *adv*, **huskiness** *n*

**²husky** *n or adj, informal* (one who is) hefty or burly [prob fr ¹*husk*]

**³husky** *n* ESKIMO DOG [prob by shortening & alter. fr *Eskimo*]

**huss** /hus/ *n* (the flesh, when prepared for sale, of) a dogfish [alter. of ME *husk, huske*, of unknown origin]

**hussar** /hoo'zah/ *n* **1** a Hungarian horseman of the 15th century **2** *often cap* a member of any of various European cavalry regiments originally modelled on the Hussars, noted esp for their stylish dress [Hung *huszár* hussar, (obs) highway robber, fr Serb *husar* pirate, fr ML *cursarius* – more at CORSAIR]

**Hussite** /'husiet/ *n* a member of the Bohemian religious and nationalist movement led by John Huss [NL *Hussita*, fr John *Huss* †1415 Bohemian religious reformer] – **Hussite** *adj*, **Hussitism** *n*

**hussy** /'husi/ *n* **1** a disreputable and immoral woman **2** a pert or mischievous girl [alter. of *housewife*]

**hustings** /'hustingz/ *n taking sing or pl vb* **1** a raised platform used until 1872 for the nomination of candidates for Parliament and for election speeches **2** a place or occasion for election speeches **3** the proceedings of an election campaign [ME, local court, fr OE *hūsting* deliberative assembly or council, fr ON *hūsthing*, fr *hūs* house + *thing* assembly]

**hustle** /'husl/ *vt* **1a** to jostle, shove **b** to convey forcibly or hurriedly ⟨~d *him into a taxi*⟩ **c** to force hurriedly ⟨~d *her into accepting*⟩ **2** *informal* **2a** to obtain by energetic, esp underhanded, activity ⟨~ *drugs on the black market*⟩ **b** to swindle, cheat ⟨*there are usually people to be* ~d *out of their money*⟩; *also, chiefly NAm* to sell something to, or obtain something from, by swindling ~ *vi* **1** to shove, press **2** to hasten, hurry **3** *chiefly NAm* **3a** to make strenuous, often dishonest, efforts to secure money or business **b** to obtain money by fraud or deception **c** *informal* to engage in prostitution **4** *chiefly NAm* to play a game or sport aggressively [D *husselen* to shake, fr MD *hutselen*, freq of *hutsen*; akin to MD *hodde* hod] – **hustle** *n*, **hustler** *n*

**hustle up** *vt* to obtain or prepare quickly ⟨hustled up *some breakfast*⟩

¹**hut** /hut/ *n* an often small and temporary dwelling of simple construction [MF *hutte*, of Gmc origin; akin to OHG *hutta* hut; akin to OE *hȳd* skin, hide]

²**hut** *vb* **-tt-** *vt* to furnish with a hut ~ *vi* to live in a hut

³**hut** *interj* – used to mark a marching cadence [prob alter. of *hup*]

¹**hutch** /huch/ *n* **1** a chest or compartment for storage **2** a pen or coop for a small animal (eg a rabbit) **3** a trough **3a** for kneading dough **b** for washing ore **4** *derog* a shack, shanty [ME *huche*, fr OF]

²**hutch** *vt* to keep (as if) in a hutch

**hutment** /'hutmənt/ *n* a collection of huts; an encampment

¹**huzzah, huzza** /həˈzah/ *vt* **huzzahing, huzzaing; huzzahed, huzzaed** to cheer, applaud [origin unknown]

²**huzzah, huzza** *vi, n, or interj* (to) hurrah

**hwan** /hwahn, wahn/ *n, pl* **hwan 1** a Korean monetary unit worth $\frac{1}{10}$ WON **2** a coin representing one hwan [Korean]

**hyacinth** /'hie-ə,sinth/ *n* **1** JACINTH (reddish-orange gem) **2a** any of a genus (*Hyacinthus*) of plants of the lily family that grow from bulbs and bear clusters of flowers at the top of leafless stems; *esp* a common garden plant (*Hyacinthus orientalis*) widely grown for the beauty and fragrance of its typically blue, pink, or white flowers **b** any of several other plants of the lily family **3** a colour varying from a light violet to a medium purplish blue [L *hyacinthus*, a precious stone, a flowering plant, fr Gk *hyakinthos*] – **hyacinthine** *adj*

**hyaena** /hie'eenə/ *n* a hyena

**hyal-, hyalo-** *comb form* glass; hyaline ⟨hyal*escent*⟩ ⟨hyalo*gen*⟩ [LL, glass, fr Gk, fr *hyalos*]

¹**hyaline** /'hie-əlin/ *adj* **1** of glass **2a** *of biological materials or structures* transparent or semitransparent and free from obvious fibres, granules, etc ⟨*a* ~ *membrane*⟩ **b** of a mineral glass, vitreous [LL *hyalinus*, fr Gk *hyalinos*, fr *hyalos*]

²**hyaline** *n* **1** *also* **hyalin** any of several translucent nitrogen- and sugar-containing substances related to CHITIN (substance forming the hard outer cover of insects) **2** *chiefly poetic* something transparent, esp a clear sky or a smooth sea ⟨*the morning is as clear as diamond or as* ~ – Sacheverell Sitwell⟩

**hyaline cartilage** *n* a common translucent bluish-white cartilage without obvious fibres that is present in joints and respiratory passages and forms most of the foetal skeleton

**hyalite** /'hie-əliet/ *n* a colourless clear or translucent opal [Ger *hyalit*, fr Gk *hyalos*]

**hyaloid** /'hie-əloyd/ *adj, of biological materials or structures* glassy, transparent [Gk *hyaloeidēs*, fr *hyalos*]

**hyaloid membrane** *n* a thin membrane enclosing the VITREOUS HUMOUR of the eye

**hyaloplasm** /'hie-əloh,plaz(ə)m/ *n* the clear nongranular apparently homogeneous substance of CYTOPLASM (jellylike material inside a cell) in which the nucleus and other ORGANELLES are suspended

**hyaluronic acid** /,hie-əlyooə'ronik/ *n* a viscous MUCOPOLYSACCHARIDE (complex sugar-containing compound) with lubricating properties that occurs esp in the VITREOUS HUMOUR of the eye, the umbilical cord, and the SYNOVIAL fluid (lubricating fluid secreted at joints) and as a cementing substance in the tissue lying below the skin [ISV]

**hyaluronidase** /,hie-əlyooə'ronidayz/ *n* an ENZYME that breaks down and lowers the viscosity of HYALURONIC ACID and is used to enable liquids to spread more easily through tissues containing the acid [ISV, irreg fr *hyaluronic* (*acid*) + *-ase*]

**hybrid** /'hiebrid/ *n* **1** an offspring of two animals or plants of different races, breeds, varieties, species, etc **2** a person produced by the blending of two diverse cultures or traditions **3a** something consisting of parts differing in origin or composition; a composite ⟨*artificial* ~s *of DNA and RNA*⟩ **b** a word (eg *television*) composed of elements from different languages [L *hybrida*] – **hybrid** *adj*, **hybridism** *n*, **hybridity** *n*

**hybrid bill** *n* a legislative bill some of whose provisions are general in effect while others only affect a particular class, individual, or locality – compare PRIVATE BILL, PUBLIC BILL

**hybridist** /'hiebridist/ *n* one who produces hybrid organisms by selective breeding

**hybrid·ize, -ise** /'hiebridiez/ *vb* to (cause to) produce hybrids; interbreed – **hybridizer** *n*, **hybridization** *n*

**hybrid vigour** *n* HETEROSIS (marked capacity for growth shown by some hybrids)

**hybris** /'hiebris/ *n* HUBRIS (excessive pride)

**hydatid** /'hiedətid/ *n* a sac or cyst filled with clear watery liquid; *esp* a larval stage in the development of some tapeworms that typically consists of a liquid-filled bladder or cyst from the inner walls of which grow smaller daughter cysts containing heads that will ultimately form the future tapeworms [Gk *hydatid-, hydatis* watery cyst, fr *hydat-, hydōr*]

**hydr-, hydro-** *comb form* **1a** water ⟨hydr*ous*⟩ ⟨hydro*electricity*⟩ **b** liquid ⟨hydro*kinetics*⟩ ⟨hydro*meter*⟩ **2** hydrogen; containing or combined with hydrogen ⟨hydro*carbon*⟩ ⟨hydro*chloric*⟩ **3** hydroid ⟨hydro*medusa*⟩ [ME *ydr-, ydro-*, fr OF, fr L *hydr-, hydro-*, fr Gk, fr *hydōr* – more at WATER]

**hydra** /'hiedrə/ *n, pl* **hydras, hydrae** /-ree/ **1** a persistent evil that is not easily overcome **2** any of numerous small freshwater INVERTEBRATE animals (class Hydrozoa, esp genus *Hydra*) that are single POLYPS having a hollow tubular body attached at one end to a rock, plant, etc and with a mouth at the other end surrounded by tentacles [*Hydra*, a serpent in Gk mythology with many heads that regrew when cut off, fr ME *Ydra*, fr L *Hydra*, fr Gk; (2) NL, genus name, fr L, Hydra]

'**hydra-,headed** *adj* having many centres or branches ⟨*a* ~ *organization*⟩

**hydrallazine** /hie'draləzeen/ *n* a synthetic drug, $C_8H_8N_4$, used to treat high blood pressure [irreg fr *hydr-* + phth*alazine* ($C_8H_6N_2$), fr *phthal-* + *-azine*]

**hydrangea** /hie'draynjə/ *n* any of a genus (*Hydrangea* of the family Hydrangeaceae) of woody shrubs that are widely cultivated for their large showy clusters of usu white, pink, or pale blue flowers [NL, genus name, fr *hydr-* + Gk *angeion* vessel – more at ANGI-; fr its cup-shaped seed vessel]

**hydrant** /'hiedrənt/ *n* a discharge pipe with a valve and nozzle from which water may be drawn from a water main, esp for fighting fires

**hydranth** /'hiedranth/ *n* any of the individual members (POLYPS) making up a HYDROZOAN colony that are specialized for feeding [ISV *hydr-* + Gk *anthos* flower – more at ANTHOLOGY]

**hydrastine** /hie'drasteen/ *n* a chemical compound, $C_{21}H_{21}NO_6$, that is an active constituent of hydrastis and whose hydrochloride has been used as an antiseptic and in the treatment of uterine haemorrhage [ISV]

**hydrastinine** /hie'drastineen *n* a chemical compound derived from hydrastine and having the same uses [ISV]

**hydrastis** /hie'drastis/ *n* the dried underground stem (RHIZOME) and root of a N American plant (*Hydrastis canadensis*) of the buttercup family, that causes contraction of the womb and has been used to check bleeding from the womb and in the relief of painful menstruation [NL, genus name]

¹**hydrate** /'hiedrayt/ *n* a chemical compound or complex ION (group of atoms having electrical charge) formed by the chemical combination of water with another substance

²**hydrate** /'hiedrayt, hie'drayt/ *vb, chemistry vt* to cause to take up or combine with water or the elements of water ~ *vi* to become a hydrate – **hydrator** *n*, **hydration** *n*

**hydraulic** /hie'drolik/ *adj* **1** operated, moved, or effected by means of liquid, esp water **2a** of hydraulics ⟨~ *engineer*⟩ **b** of liquid, esp water, in motion ⟨~ *erosion*⟩ **3** operated by the transmission of pressure in a liquid being forced through pipes, tubes, etc ⟨~ *brakes*⟩ **4** hardening or setting under water ⟨~ *cement*⟩ [L *hydraulicus*, fr Gk *hydraulikos*, fr *hydraulis* hydraulic organ, fr *hydr-* + *aulos* reed instrument – more at ALVEOLUS] – **hydraulically** *adv*

**hydraulic ram** *n* a pump that forces running water to a higher level by using the KINETIC ENERGY (energy of motion) of the flow of water

**hydraulics** /hie'droliks/ *n taking sing vb* a branch of physics that deals with the practical applications (eg the transmission of energy or the effects of flow) of liquid (eg water) in motion

**hydrazide** /'hiedrəzied/ *n* any of a class of chemical compounds derived from hydrazine or one of its derivatives by replacement of hydrogen by another atom or a chemical group [ISV]

**hydrazine** /'hiedrəzeen, -zin/ *n* (any of various organic chemical compounds derived from) a colourless fuming corrosive liquid, $N_2H_4$, that is a strong REDUCING AGENT and is used esp in fuels for rocket and jet engines [ISV]

**hydrazoic acid** /,hiedrə'zoh·ik/ *n* a colourless poisonous explosive liquid, $HN_3$, that has a foul smell and that reacts with heavy metals (e g lead) to yield explosive compounds that are AZIDES [*hydr-* + *azo-* + *-ic*]

**hydric** /'hiedrik/ *adj* characterized by, relating to, or requiring an abundance of moisture ⟨*a ~ habitat*⟩ ⟨*a ~ plant*⟩ – compare MESIC, XERIC – **hydrically** *adv*

**-hydric** /-hiedrik/ *suffix* (→ *adj*) 1 containing (so many) hydrogen atoms that will dissociate in water to yield HYDROGEN IONS ⟨*monohydric acids*⟩ 2 containing (so many) hydroxyl groups ⟨*hexahydric alcohols*⟩

**hydride** /'hiedried/ *n* a chemical compound of hydrogen with one other chemical element or group that is usu more ELECTROPOSITIVE (has a greater tendency to release electrons) than hydrogen

**hydriodic acid** /,hiedri'odik/ *n* a solution of HYDROGEN IODIDE in water that is a strong acid and a strong REDUCING AGENT [ISV]

¹**hydro** /'hiedroh/ *n, pl* **hydros** *Br* a hotel or establishment offering facilities for HYDROPATHIC treatment (the use of water in treating disease) [short for *hydropathic establishment*]

²**hydro** *adj, informal* HYDROELECTRIC ⟨*~ energy*⟩

**hydro-** – see HYDR-

**hydrobiology** /,hiedroh-bie'oləji/ *n* the biology of bodies of water; the study of the plant and animal life of lakes, rivers, etc – **hydrobiologist** *n*, **hydrobiological** *adj*

**hydrobromic acid** /,hiedroh'brohmik/ *n* a solution of HYDROGEN BROMIDE in water that is a strong acid but a weak REDUCING AGENT [ISV]

**hydrocarbon** /,hiedroh'kahb(ə)n, ,--'--, 'hiedrə-/ *n* an organic chemical compound (e g benzene) containing only carbon and hydrogen – **hydrocarbonaceous, hydrocarbonic, hydrocarbonous** *adj*

**hydrocele** /'hiedroh,seel/ *n* an abnormal accumulation of watery liquid in a body cavity (e g the scrotum) [L, fr Gk *hydrokēlē*, fr *hydr-* + *kēlē* tumour – more at -CELE]

**hydrocephalus** /,hiedroh'sefələs/ *also* **hydrocephaly** /-'sefəli/ *n* an abnormal increase in the amount of CEREBROSPINAL FLUID (nourishing and shock-absorbing liquid) within the system of interconnecting cavities of the brain, that is accompanied by expansion of these cavities, enlargement of the skull, and wasting of the brain [NL *hydrocephalus*, fr LL, hydrocephalic, fr Gk *hydrokephalos*, fr *hydr-* + *kephalē* head – more at CEPHALIC] – **hydrocephalic** *adj*

**hydrochloric acid** /,hiedrə'klorik/ *n* a solution of HYDROGEN CHLORIDE in water that is a strong corrosive acid, is normally present in dilute form in the digestive juice secreted by the stomach, and is widely used in industry and in laboratories [ISV]

**hydrochloride** /,hiedrə'klawried/ *n* a chemical compound of HYDROCHLORIC ACID, esp with an organic BASE (compound that reacts with an acid to form a SALT)

**hydrochlorothiazide** /,hiedroh,klawrə'thie·əzied, -,klorə-/ *n* a drug, $C_7H_8O_4N_3ClS_2$, with diuretic properties that has actions and uses similar to those of CHLOROTHIAZIDE (drug used to treat high blood pressure and excess water retention) [*hydr-* + *chlor-* + *thiazine* + *-ide*]

**hydrocortisone** /,hiedroh'kawtizohn, -sohn/ *n* a STEROID hormone, $C_{21}H_{30}O_5$, that is produced by the CORTEX (outer region) of the ADRENAL GLAND and is used in the treatment of RHEUMATOID ARTHRITIS, allergies, and various skin disorders

**hydrocyanic acid** /,hiedrohsie'anik/ *n* a solution of HYDROGEN CYANIDE in water that is an extremely poisonous weak acid – called also PRUSSIC ACID [ISV]

**hydrodynamic** /,hiedrohdie'namik, ,hiedrə-, -di-/ *also* **hydrodynamical** /-kl/ *adj* of or involving principles of hydrodynamics [NL *hydrodynamicus*, fr *hydr-* + *dynamicus* dynamic] – **hydrodynamically** *adv*

**hydrodynamics** /,hiedrohdie'namiks, ,hiedrə-, -di-/ *n taking sing vb* a branch of science that deals with the motion of liquids and the forces acting on solid bodies immersed in liquids – compare HYDROKINETIC, HYDROSTATICS – **hydrodynamicist** *n*

**hydroelectric** /,hiedrohi'lektrik/ *adj* of the production of electricity by using the power generated by water in motion [ISV] – **hydroelectrically** *adv*, **hydroelectricity** *n*

**hydrofluoric acid** /,hiedrohflooh'orik/ *n* a solution of HYDROGEN FLUORIDE in water that is a poisonous weak acid and is used esp in finishing and etching glass and in cleaning metals (e g copper or cast iron) [ISV]

**hydrofoil** /'hiedrə,foyl/ *n* 1 hydrofoil, foil a structure fixed to the underside of a boat that is designed to lift the hull of the boat clear of the water when moving at speed – compare AEROFOIL 2 a boat fitted with hydrofoils

  *synonyms* A **hovercraft** can travel over either land or water; a **hydrofoil** can travel over water only, and rises out of the water only when it is going fast.

**hydrogen** /'hiedrəj(ə)n/ *n* a nonmetallic chemical element that is the simplest, lightest, and most abundant of the elements, is normally a colourless odourless highly inflammable gas, and occurs chiefly in combined form as a constituent esp of water and organic chemical compounds (e g natural gas, petroleum, fats, proteins, and carbohydrates) – compare DEUTERIUM, TRITIUM [Fr *hydrogène*, fr *hydr-* + *-gène* -gen; fr the production of water by its combustion] – **hydrogenous** *adj*

**hydrogenase** /hie'drojənayz/ *n* an ENZYME of various microorganisms (e g some bacteria and algae) that promotes the formation and use of gaseous hydrogen

**hydrogenate** /hie'drojinayt/ *vt* to combine or treat with or expose to hydrogen; *esp* to add hydrogen to the molecule of (an organic chemical compound) – **hydrogenation** *n*

**hydrogen bomb** *n* a bomb whose violent explosive power is due to the sudden release of atomic energy resulting from the union of hydrogen nuclei to form helium nuclei at very high temperature and pressure produced usu by the explosion of an atom bomb

**hydrogen bond** *n* a weak chemical bond (e g between molecules of water) consisting of a hydrogen atom bonded between two ELECTRONEGATIVE atoms (atoms having the power to attract electrons) (e g fluorine, oxygen, or nitrogen) with one side of the linkage being a COVALENT BOND and the other being electrostatic in nature

**hydrogen bromide** *n* a colourless pungent irritating gas, HBr, that dissolves in water to form HYDROBROMIC ACID and is used esp in the synthesis of organic chemical compounds that are bromides

**hydrogen chloride** *n* a colourless pungent poisonous gas, HCl, that dissolves in water to form HYDROCHLORIC ACID and is used esp in the synthesis of organic chemical compounds that are chlorides

**hydrogen cyanide** *n* 1 an extremely poisonous gaseous or liquid chemical compound, HCN, that has the smell of bitter almonds, dissolves in water to form HYDROCYANIC ACID, and is used chiefly to exterminate rodents and insects by fumigation 2 HYDROCYANIC ACID

**hydrogen fluoride** *n* a colourless corrosive poisonous usu gaseous chemical compound, HF, that dissolves in water to form HYDROFLUORIC ACID and is used esp as a catalyst in the petroleum industry and in the synthesis of organic chemical compounds that are fluorides

**hydrogen iodide** *n* an acrid colourless gas, HI, that dissolves in water to form HYDRIODIC ACID and is used esp in the synthesis of organic chemical compounds that are iodides

**hydrogen ion** *n* 1 the positively charged ION, $H^+$, characteristic of acids, that consists of a hydrogen atom that has lost an electron; a proton 2 a hydrogen ion combined with water that is present in solutions of acids; HYDRONIUM

**hydrogen peroxide** *n* an unstable chemical compound, $H_2O_2$, used esp as an OXIDIZING AGENT and bleaching agent, an antiseptic, and a rocket fuel

**hydrogen sulphide** *n* an inflammable poisonous gas, $H_2S$, that has a smell of rotten eggs and is found esp in many MINERAL WATERS and in decaying matter

**hydrography** /hie'drogrəfi/ *n* 1 the detailed description, measurement, and mapping of bodies of water (e g oceans, seas, lakes, and rivers) 2 (the representation on a map of) bodies of water [MF *hydrographie*, fr *hydr-* + *-graphie* -graphy] – **hydrographer** *n*, **hydrographic** *adj*, **hydrographically** *adv*

**hydroid** /'hiedroyd/ *n* a HYDROZOAN; *esp* one that is a POLYP (hollow tubular usu stationary animal) or colony of joined polyps or in which the polyp stage in the animal's life cycle is dominant, as distinguished from a MEDUSA (jellyfish or umbrella-shaped form of a hydrozoan) [NL *Hydroida*, order name, fr *Hydra*] – **hydroid** *adj*

**hydrokinetic** /,hiedroh-ki'netik, -kie-/, **hydrokinetical** /-kl/ *adj* of the motions of liquids or the forces that produce or affect such motions – compare HYDROSTATIC, HYDRODYNAMICS – **hydrokinetics** *n taking sing vb*

**hydrolase** /'hiedrəlayz/ *n* an ENZYME that promotes hydrolysis

**hydrology** /hie'droləji/ *n* a science dealing with the properties, distribution, and circulation of water on the surface of the earth, in the soil and underlying rocks, and in the atmosphere [NL *hydrologia*, fr L *hydr-* + *-logia* -logy] – **hydrologic, hydrological** *adj*, **hydrologically** *adv*, **hydrologist** *n*

**hydrolysate** /hie'drolisayt, -zayt/ *also* **hydrolyzate** /-zayt/ *n* a product of hydrolysis

**hydrolyse,** *chiefly NAm* **hydrolyze** /'hiedrəliez/ *vb* to undergo or subject to hydrolysis [ISV, fr NL *hydrolysis*] – **hydrolysable** *adj*

**hydrolysis** /hie'droləsis/ *n, pl* **hydrolyses** the chemical breakdown of a compound into two or more other compounds by reaction with water involving the splitting of a bond and addition of the elements of water [NL] – **hydrolytic** *adj*, **hydrolytically** *adv*

**hydromagnetic** /,hiedroh·mag'netik/ *adj* MAGNETOHYDRODYNAMIC [*hydr-* + *magnetic*] – **hydromagnetics** *n taking sing or pl vb*

**hydromancy** /'hiedrəmansi/ *n* divination by the appearance or motion of liquids, esp water [ME *ydromancie*, fr MF, fr L *hydromantia*, fr *hydr-* + *-mantia* -mancy]

**hydromedusa** /,hiedrohmi'dyoohzə/ *n, pl* **hydromedusae** /-zi/ the MEDUSA (umbrella-shaped sexually reproducing form) of a HYDROZOAN animal, that is produced as a bud from a hydroid [NL] – **hydromedusan** *adj or n*, **hydromedusoid** *adj*

**hydromel** /'hiedrəmel/ *n* a mixture of honey and water; *esp* mead [ME *ydromel*, fr MF & L; MF, fr L *hydromeli*, fr Gk, fr *hydr-* + *meli* honey – more at MELLIFLUOUS]

**hydrometallurgy** /,hiedroh·mə'taləji, -'metə,luhji/ *n* the extraction of metals from ores by using water to dissolve the worthless material or concentrate the metal ions [ISV] – **hydrometallurgical** *adj*

**hydrometeor** /,hiedroh'meetiə, -'meeti,aw/ *n* a product of water in the atmosphere (e g rain, fog, hail, snow, or clouds) [ISV]

**hydrometeorology** /,hiedroh,meetiə'roləji/ *n* a branch of meteorology that deals with water in the atmosphere, esp rain, hail, or snow – **hydrometeorologist** *n*, **hydrometeorological** *adj*

**hydrometer** /hie'dromitə/ *n* an instrument for measuring the RELATIVE DENSITY (density compared with that of water or another standard) of a liquid, that consists usu of a bulb with a graduated stem from which a reading is taken when the instrument is floated in the liquid – compare HYGROMETER – **hydrometric, hydrometrical** *adj*, **hydrometry** *n*

**hydromorphic** /,hiedrə'mawfik/ *adj, of a soil (e g that in a bog)* developed in the presence of or containing an excess of moisture

**hydronium** /hie'drohni·əm, -nyəm/, **hydronium ion** *n* the positively charged ion $H_3O^+$, that consists of a HYDROGEN ION combined with a water molecule and is present in solutions of acids – called also HYDROXONIUM [ISV *hydr-* + *-onium*]

**hydropathy** /hie'dropəthi/ *n* HYDROTHERAPY [ISV] – **hydropathic** *adj*, **hydropathically** *adv*

**hydroperoxide** /,hiedrəpə'roksied/ *n* a chemical compound containing an $O_2H$ group

**hydrophane** /'hiedrə,fayn/ *n* a semitranslucent opal that becomes translucent or transparent in water – **hydrophanous** *adj*

**hydrophilic** /,hiedrə'filik/, **hydrophile** *adj, chemistry* of or having a strong attraction for water; easily soluble in water – compare HYDROPHOBIC 2 [NL *hydrophilus*, fr Gk *hydr-* + *-philos* -philous] – **hydrophilicity** *adv*

**hydrophilous** /,hie'drofiləs/ *adj, of a plant* 1 pollinated by the agency of water 2 living or growing in water; hydrophytic

**hydrophobia** /,hiedrə'fohbi·ə/ *n* 1 the abnormal fear of water 2 rabies [LL, fr Gk, fr *hydr-* + *-phobia* fear of something – more at PHOBIA]

**hydrophobic** /-'fohbik/ *adj* 1 of or suffering from hydrophobia 2 *chemistry* lacking an attraction for or repelling water; soluble in fats or oils rather than water – compare HYDROPHILIC – **hydrophobicity** *n*

**hydrophone** /'hiedrə,fohn/ *n* an instrument for listening to sound transmitted through water

**hydrophyte** /'hiedroh,fiet/ *n* a plant that grows on or in waterlogged soil [ISV] – **hydrophytic** *adj*

¹**hydroplane** /'hiedrə,playn/ *n* 1a HYDROFOIL 1 b a broad float fixed to the underside of an aeroplane, enabling it to land or glide on water 2a a speedboat fitted with hydrofoils or a stepped bottom so that the hull is raised wholly or partly out of the water when moving at speed b a rudder on a horizontal axis on a submarine for steering it upwards or downwards 3 a seaplane

²**hydroplane** *vi* 1 to skim over the water with the hull largely clear of the surface 2 to ride in a hydroplane – **hydroplaner** *n*

**hydroponics** /,hiedroh'poniks, -drə-/ *n taking sing vb* the growing of plants without soil in a solution containing nutrients or in a supporting medium (e g gravel or sand) through which nutrient solutions are pumped [*hydr-* + Gk *-ponikos* cultural (in *geōponikos* agricultural, fr *geōponein* to plough, fr *gē* earth + *ponein* to toil)] – **hydroponic** *adj*, **hydroponically** *adv*

**hydroquinone** /,hiedrohkwi'nohn/, **hydroquinol** /-ol/ *n* a chemical compound, $C_6H_4(OH)_2$, that is a strong REDUCING AGENT and is used esp as a photographic developer and as an antioxidant [ISV]

**hydroscope** /'hiedrə,skohp/ *n* a device for observing underwater objects – compare PERISCOPE [ISV]

**hydrosere** /'hiedrə,siə/ *n* a SERE (progressive sequence of changes in the make-up of an ecological community) originating in a wet or aquatic environment – **hydroseral** *adj*

**hydrosol** /'hiedrə,sol/ *n* a SOL in which the liquid medium in which the solid particles are suspended is water [*hydr-* + *-sol* (fr *solution*)] – **hydrosolic** *adj*

**hydrosphere** /'hiedrə,sfiə/ *n* the whole of the watery parts of the earth including all bodies of water (e g lakes and oceans) and the WATER VAPOUR in the atmosphere [ISV] – **hydrospheric** *adj*

**hydrostatic** /,hiedrə'statik/ *also* **hydrostatical** /-kl/ *adj* of or concerned with liquids at rest or the pressure they exert or transmit – **hydrostatically** *adv*

**hydrostatics** /,hiedrə'statiks/ *n taking sing vb* a branch of physics that deals with the characteristics of liquids at rest, esp the pressure in a liquid or exerted by a liquid on an immersed body – compare HYDROKINETIC, HYDRODYNAMICS

**hydrosulphide** /,hiedrə'sulfied/ *n* a chemical compound that contains the chemical group SH, and is derived from HYDROGEN SULPHIDE by the replacement of one of its hydrogen atoms by a chemical element or group [ISV]

**hydrosulphite** /,hiedrə'sulfiet/ *n* a chemical compound (SALT) containing the chemical group $S_2O_4$; *esp* a sodium salt used as a reducing and bleaching agent [ISV]

**hydrotaxis** /,hiedrə'taksis/ *n* the movement of a cell or organism towards or away from water or moisture [NL] – **hydrotactic** *adj*

**hydrotherapy** /,hiedro'therəpi/ *n* the use of water in the treatment of disease [ISV]

**hydrothermal** /,hiedrə'thuhml/ *adj* of or caused by the action of hot water, esp in forming rocks and minerals [ISV] – **hydrothermally** *adv*

**hydrothorax** /,hiedroh'thawraks/ *n* an excess of watery liquid in the PLEURAL cavity (gap between membranes surrounding the lungs) usu resulting from failing circulation (e g in heart disease) or from lung infection [NL]

**hydrotropism** /hie'drotrəpiz(ə)m/ *n* the turning or curving of an organism, esp a plant, or of one of its parts towards or away from water or WATER VAPOUR [ISV] – **hydrotropic** *adj*, **hydrotropically** *adv*

**hydrous** /'hiedrəs/ *adj* containing water; *esp* chemically combined with water molecules

**hydroxide** /hie'droksied/ *n* a chemical compound containing a HYDROXIDE ION or hydroxyl group [ISV]

**hydroxide ion** *n* the negatively charged ion, $OH^-$, characteristic of hydroxides – called also HYDROXYL ION

**hydroxonium** /hiedrok'sohni·əm, -nyəm/, **hydroxonium ion** *n* HYDRONIUM

**hydroxy** /hie'droksi/ *adj* containing one or more hydroxyl groups; *esp* containing hydroxyl in place of hydrogen – often in combination ⟨hydroxy*acetic acid*⟩ [ISV, fr *hydroxyl*]

**hydroxyapatite** /hie,droksi'apətiet/ *n* a complex phosphate of calcium, $Ca_5(PO_4)_3OH$, that occurs as a mineral and is the chief structural element of the bone of VERTEBRATE animals

**hydroxybutyric acid** /hie,droksibyoo'tirik/ *n* a chemical compound, $CH_3CHOHCH_2COOH$, derived from BUTYRIC ACID by the replacement of one hydrogen atom by a hydroxyl group

**hydroxyl** /hie'droksil, -siel/ *adj or n* (being or containing) the chemical group OH$_1$, that has a VALENCY of one, consists of one atom of hydrogen and one of oxygen, and is the characteristic group esp of hydroxides, alcohols, GLYCOLS, and PHENOLS; *also* (being or containing) a HYDROXIDE ION [*hydr-* + *ox-* + *-yl*] – **hydroxylic** *adj*

**hydroxylamine** /ˌhiedrok'siləmeen, hieˌdroksilə'meen/ *n* a colourless odourless nitrogen-containing chemical compound, NH$_2$OH, that resembles ammonia in its reactions and that is used esp as a REDUCING AGENT [ISV]

**hydroxylase** /hie'droksilayz/ *n* an ENZYME that promotes the hydroxylation of a compound

**hydroxylate** /hie'droksilayt/ *vt* to introduce one or more hydroxyl groups into – **hydroxylation** *n*

**hydroxyl ion** *n* HYDROXIDE ION

**hydroxyproline** /hieˌdroksi'prohleen/ *n* an AMINO ACID, C$_5$H$_9$NO$_3$, that occurs naturally as a constituent of COLLAGEN (protein in tendons, the membrane round bones, etc) [*hydroxy-* + *proline*]

**hydroxytryptamine** /hieˌdroksi'triptəmeen/ *n* SEROTONIN

**hydroxyurea** /hieˌdroksiyoo'ree·ə, -'yoooriə/ *n* a chemical compound, H$_2$NCONHOH, used esp as an anticancer drug

**hydrozoan** /ˌhiedrə'zoh·ən/ *n* any of a class (Hydrozoa of the phylum Coelenterata) of INVERTEBRATE animals that includes simple POLYPS (hollow tubular usu stationary forms) (e g the hydras), branching seaweedlike colonies of polyps, some brightly coloured corals, and compound forms that resemble jellyfish (e g the PORTUGUESE MAN-OF-WAR). The majority of the class exhibits ALTERNATION OF GENERATIONS with the usu dominant HYDROID form (polyp or colony of polyps) giving rise to the MEDUSOID form (jellyfish or umbrella-shaped individual) that bears eggs and sperm for SEXUAL REPRODUCTION. [deriv of Gk *hydr-* + *zōion* animal – more at ZO-] – **hydrozoan** *adj*

**hyena, hyaena** /hie'eenə/ *n* any of several large strong doglike flesh-eating mammals (family Hyaenidae), of Africa and Asia, that usu feed as scavengers [L *Hyaena*, fr Gk *hyaina*, fr *hys* hog – more at SOW] – **hyenic** *adj*, **hyenoid** *adj*

**hyet-, hyeto-** *comb form* rain ⟨*hyeto*logy⟩ [Gk, fr *hyetos*, fr *hyein* to rain – more at SUCK]

**hygiene** /'hie·jeen/ *n* **1** the science of the establishment and maintenance of health **2** conditions or practices (e g of cleanliness) conducive to health [Fr *hygiène* & NL *hygieina*, fr Gk, neut pl of *hygieinos* healthful, fr *hygiēs* healthy; akin to Skt *su* well & to L *vivus* living – more at QUICK] – **hygienic** *adj*, **hygienically** *adv*, **hygienist** *n*

**hygienics** /hie'jeeniks/ *n taking sing vb* HYGIENE 1

**hygr-, hygro-** *comb form* humidity; moisture ⟨*hygro*scope⟩ [Gk, fr *hygros* wet – more at HUMOUR]

**hygrograph** /'hiegrəˌgrahf, -ˌgraf/ *n* an instrument for recording variations in atmospheric humidity [ISV]

**hygrometer** /hie'gromitə/ *n* any of several instruments for measuring the humidity of the atmosphere – compare HYDROMETER [prob fr Fr *hygromètre*, fr *hygr-* + *-mètre* -meter] – **hygrometric** *adj*, **hygrometrically** *adv*, **hygrometry** *n*

**hygrophilous** /hie'grofiləs/ *adj* living or growing in moist places (e g marshes)

**hygroscope** /'hiegrəˌskohp/ *n* an instrument that indicates changes in the humidity of the air, without actually measuring it

**hygroscopic** /ˌhiegrə'skopik/ *adj* **1** readily taking up and retaining moisture from the air **2** *botany* **2a** sensitive to moisture ⟨~ *tissues*⟩ **b** induced by the uptake or loss of moisture ⟨*turgid movements are* ~⟩ [fr the use of such materials in the hygroscope] – **hygroscopically** *adv*, **hygroscopicity** *n*

**hying** /'hie·ing/ *pres part of* HIE

**Hyksos** /'hiksos/ *adj or n pl* (of) a Semite dynasty that ruled Egypt from about the 18th to the 16th century BC [Gk *Hyksōs*, dynasty ruling Egypt, fr Egypt *ḥq'š' sw ruler* of the countries of the nomads]

**hyl-** /hiel-/, **hylo-** *comb form* **1** matter; material ⟨*hylo*zoism⟩ **2** wood ⟨*hylo*phagous⟩ [Gk, fr *hylē*, lit., wood]

**hyla** /'hielə/ *n* any of a genus (*Hyla*) of TREE FROGS [NL, fr Gk *hylē* wood]

**hylotheism** /ˌhielə'thee·iz(ə)m/ *n* a doctrine that equates God and matter

**hylozoism** /ˌhielə'zoh·iz(ə)m/ *n* a doctrine held esp by early Greek philosophers that all matter has life [Gk *hylē* + *zōos* alive, living; akin to Gk *zōē* life – more at QUICK] – **hylozoist** *n*, **hylozoistic** *adj*

**hymen** /'hiemen/ *n* a fold of MUCOUS MEMBRANE that partly covers the opening of the vagina and is usu ruptured by the first instance of sexual intercourse – called also MAIDENHEAD [LL, fr Gk *hymēn* membrane] – **hymenal** *adj*

¹**hymeneal** /ˌhieme'nee·əl/ *adj*, *poetic* of marriage [L *hymenaeus* wedding song, wedding, fr Gk *hymenaios*, fr *Hymēn* Hymen, god of marriage] – **hymeneally** *adv*

²**hymeneal** *n*, *archaic* a wedding song or hymn – compare PROTHALAMION

**hymenium** /hie'meeni·əm/ *n, pl* **hymenia, hymeniums** a spore-bearing layer in fungi consisting of a group of spore-bearing cells often interspersed with sterile structures [NL, fr Gk *hymēn* membrane] – **hymenial** *adj*

**hymenopteran** /ˌhiemi'noptərən/ *n* any of an order (Hymenoptera) of highly specialized usu stinging insects (e g bees, wasps, or ants) that often associate in large colonies and have usu four membranous wings and the abdomen generally attached to the rest of the body by a slender stalk [NL *hymenopteron*, fr Gk, neut of *hymenopteros* membrane-winged, fr *hymēn* + *pteron* wing – more at FEATHER] – **hymenopteran, hymenopterous** *adj*

**hymenopteron** /ˌhiemi'noptərən/ *n, pl* **hymenoptera** /-tərə/ *also* **hymenopterons** a hymenopteran

¹**hymn** /him/ *n* **1a** a song of praise to God **b** a rhythmic composition adapted for singing in a religious service **2** a song in praise of a god, saint, nation, etc [ME *ymne*, fr OF, fr L *hymnus* song of praise, fr Gk *hymnos*]

²**hymn** *vt* to praise or worship in hymns ~ *vi* to sing a hymn

**hymnal** /'himnəl/ *n* (a book containing) a collection of church hymns [ME *hymnale*, fr ML, fr L *hymnus*]

**hymnary** /'himnəri/ *n* a hymnal

**hymnbook** /'himˌbook/ *n* a hymnal

**hymnody** /'himnədi/ *n* **1** the singing or writing of hymns **2** the hymns of a time, place, or church [LL *hymnodia*, fr Gk *hymnōidia*, fr *hymnos* + *aeidein* to sing – more at ODE]

**hymnography** /him'nogrəfi/ *n* the writing of hymns

**hymnology** /him'noləji/ *n* **1** the writing of hymns **2** the study of hymns [Gk *hymnologia* singing of hymns, fr *hymnos* + *-logia* -logy]

**hyoid** /'hie·oyd/ *adj* of the HYOID BONE [NL *hyoides* hyoid bone]

**hyoid bone** *n* a complex of joined bones situated at the base of the tongue and supporting the tongue and its muscles [NL *hyoides*, fr Gk *hyoeidēs* shaped like the letter upsilon (Y, ν), being the hyoid bone, fr *y*, *hy* upsilon]

**hyoscine** /'hie·əˌseen/ *n* a drug, C$_{17}$H$_{21}$NO$_4$, found in various plants of the potato family, including DEADLY NIGHTSHADE and henbane, that has effects (e g the reduction of salivation and sweating and the dilation of the pupil of the eye) on the PARASYMPATHETIC NERVOUS SYSTEM similar to those of the drug ATROPINE but depresses the CENTRAL NERVOUS SYSTEM and tends to slow heart rate and induce drowsiness. Hyoscine is used esp to reduce muscular rigidity and tremor and, together with morphine, as a light sedative to induce a state of TWILIGHT SLEEP during childbirth and in the preparation of patients for surgery under a general anaesthetic. – called also SCOPOLAMINE [ISV *hyos*cyamine + *-ine*]

**hyoscyamine** /ˌhie·ə'sie·əmeen, -min/ *n* a chemical compound, C$_{17}$H$_{23}$NO$_3$, found esp in DEADLY NIGHTSHADE and henbane that is the LAEVOROTATORY form of the drug ATROPINE and has actions on the nervous system and uses similar to those of atropine [Ger *hyoscyamin*, fr NL *Hyoscyamus*, genus of herbs, fr L, henbane, fr Gk *hyoskyamos*, lit., swine's bean, fr *hyos* (gen of *hys* swine) + *kyamos* bean – more at SOW]

**hyp-** – see HYPO-

**hypabyssal** /ˌhipə'bisl/ *adj* of or being an IGNEOUS rock formed by the cooling and solidification of molten material at a moderate depth below the earth's surface [ISV] – **hypabyssally** *adv*

**hypaethral**, *chiefly NAm* **hypethral** /hie'peethrəl, hi-/ *adj* **1** having a roofless central space open to the sky ⟨~ *temple*⟩ **2** *formal* outdoor, open-air [L *hypaethrus* exposed to the open air, fr Gk *hypaithros*, fr *hypo-* + *aithēr* ether, air – more at ETHER]

**hypallage** /hie'paləji/ *n* the reversal of two words for rhetorical effect [LL, fr Gk *hypallagē*, lit., interchange, fr *hypallassein* to interchange, fr *hypo-* + *allassein* to exchange, fr *allos* other – more at ELSE]

**hypanthium** /hie'panthiəm/ *n, pl* **hypanthia** /-iə/ an enlargement of the RECEPTACLE (tip of the flower-bearing stalk) of some plants, that encircles the OVARY (seed-bearing structure), bears the STAMENS (male reproductive structures), petals, and sepals on its rim, and may enlarge further to surround the fruit (eg in the rose) [NL, fr *hypo-* + *anth-* + *-ium*] – **hypanthial** *adj*

**¹hype** /hiep/ *n, slang* **1** HYPODERMIC **2** a drug addict **3** a cheat, put-on **4** extravagant and usu false publicity ⟨*media* ~⟩ [by shortening & alter. fr *hypodermic*]

**²hype** *vt, slang* **1** to cheat, trick **2** to publicize extravagantly and often falsely

**,hyped-'up** *adj, slang* stimulated; KEYED UP

**hyper-** /hiepə-/ *prefix* **1** above; beyond; super- ⟨hyper*physical*⟩ **2a** excessively ⟨hyper*sensitive*⟩ ⟨hyper*critical*⟩ **b** excessive ⟨hyper*aemia*⟩ ⟨hyper*tension*⟩ **3** that exists in, or is a space of, more than three dimensions ⟨hyper*cube*⟩ ⟨hyper*space*⟩ □ compare HYPO- [ME *iper-*, fr L *hyper-*, fr Gk, fr *hyper* – more at OVER]

**hyperacid** /,hiepər'asid/ *adj* containing more than the normal amount of acid; *esp of the stomach* secreting more acid than is normal – **hyperacidity** *n*

**hyperactive** /,hiepər'aktiv/ *adj* excessively or abnormally active – **hyperactivity** *n*

**hyperaemia**, *chiefly NAm* **hyperemia** /,hiepə'reemi·ə, -myə/ *n* an excess of blood in a body part; congestion [NL] – **hyperaemic** *adj*

**hyperaesthesia**, *NAm* **hyperesthesia** /-ees'theezyə, -zh(y)ə/ *n* an abnormally increased sensitivity to sensory stimuli (eg touch) [NL, fr *hyper-* + *-aesthesia* (as in *anaesthesia*)] – **hyperaesthetic** *adj*

**hyperbaric** /,hiepə'barik/ *adj* of or using greater than normal pressure, esp of oxygen ⟨~ *oxygen chambers*⟩ ⟨~ *medical treatment*⟩ [*hyper-* + *bar-* + *-ic*] – **hyperbarically** *adv*

**hyperbaton** /hie'puhbəton/ *n* a reversal of the usual order of words (eg in "beer I love") [L, fr Gk, neut of *hyperbatos* transposed, fr *hyperbainein* to step over, fr *hyper-* + *bainein* to step, walk – more at COME]

**hyperbola** /hie'puhbələ/ *n, pl* **hyperbolas, hyperbolae** /-bəli/ a two-dimensional curve generated by a point so moving that the difference of its distances from two fixed points (FOCUSES) is a constant; the intersection of two RIGHT CIRCULAR CONES joined at the apexes with a plane that cuts both of the cones – compare ELLIPSE, PARABOLA [NL, fr Gk *hyperbolē*]

**hyperbole** /hie'puhbəli/ *n* a figure of speech based on extravagant exaggeration (eg in "mile-high ice-cream cones") [L, fr Gk *hyperbolē* excess, hyperbole, hyperbola, fr *hyperballein* to exceed, fr *hyper-* + *ballein* to throw – more at DEVIL] – **hyperbolist** *n*

**¹hyperbolic** /,hiepə'bolik/ *also* **hyperbolical** /-kl/ *adj* of, characterized by, or given to hyperbole – **hyperbolically** *adv*

**²hyperbolic** *also* **hyperbolical** *adj* **1** of or like a hyperbola **2** of or being a space in which more than one line parallel to a given line passes through a point ⟨~ *geometry*⟩

**hyperbolic function** *n* any of a set of six mathematical functions that are related to the hyperbola and analogous to the TRIGONOMETRIC FUNCTIONS (sine, cosine, and tangent)

**hyperbol·ize, -ise** /hie'puhbəliez/ *vi* to indulge in hyperbole ~ *vt* to exaggerate (something) to a hyperbolic degree

**hyperboloid** /hie'puhbə,loyd/ *n* a curved surface generated by an ellipse of variable size moving in such a way that it touches the curves of two equal hyperbolas whose planes are perpendicular to each other and which have one axis in common. The hyperboloid may have either of two different forms, one of a single somewhat hourglass-shaped surface, the other of two surfaces stretching to infinity; the cross sections of the hyperboloids are either hyperbolas or ellipses. – compare ELLIPSOID, PARABOLOID [NL] – **hyperboloidal** *adj*

**¹hyperborean** /,hiepə'bawri·ən/ *adj* **1** of an extreme northern region **2** of any of the Arctic peoples

**²hyperborean** *n* **1** *often cap* a member of a people held by the ancient Greeks to live beyond the north wind in a region of perpetual sunshine **2** an inhabitant of the far north [L *Hyperborei* (pl), fr Gk *Hyperboreoi*, fr *hyper-* + *Boreas* (god of the north wind]

**hypercalcaemia,** *chiefly NAm* **hypercalcemia** /,hiepəkal'seemyə, -miə/ *n* an excess of calcium in the blood – compare HYPOCALCAEMIA [NL, fr *hyper-* + *calc-* + *-aemia*] – **hypercalcaemic** *adj*

**hypercapnia** /,hiepə'kapniə/ *n* the presence of an excessive

amount of CARBON DIOXIDE in the blood [NL, fr *hyper-* + Gk *kapnos* smoke] – **hypercapnic** *adj*

**hypercharge** /'hiepə,chahj/ *n* a QUANTUM property of an ELEMENTARY PARTICLE (minute particle of matter) occurring in different forms that undergo the STRONG INTERACTION, that is related to STRANGENESS and is represented by a number equal to twice the average value of the electric charges of the different forms in which the particle can occur

**hypercholesteraemia** /,hiepəkə,lestə'reemyə, -miə/ *n* hypercholesterolaemia [NL]

**hypercholesterolaemia** /,hiepəkə,lest(ə)ro'leemyə, -miə/ *adj* the presence of excess cholesterol in the blood [NL]

**hyperconscious** /,hiepə'konshəs/ *adj* acutely aware or sensitive

**hypercritical** /,hiepə'kritikl/ *adj* excessively critical or faultfinding; captious △ hypocritical – **hypercritically** *adv*

**hyperemia** /,hiepə'reemyə, -miə/ *n, chiefly NAm* HYPERAEMIA [NL] – **hyperemic** *adj*

**hypereutectic** /,hiepəyooh'tektik/, **hypereutectoid** /-oyd/ *adj, of an alloy or other mixture* containing more of the minor component than is contained in the EUTECTIC mixture (that with the lowest melting point) – compare HYPOEUTECTIC

**hyperexcitability** /,hiepərik,sietə'biləti/ *n* the state or condition of being unusually or excessively excitable

**hyperfine** /'hiepə,fien/ *adj* of or being very closely spaced ENERGY LEVELS in an atom; *also* of or being very closely spaced SPECTRAL lines (lines corresponding to electromagnetic radiation of different frequencies) that occur as a result of the interaction either between the SPIN of the electrons in an atom and the spin of the atom's nucleus, or between the electrons' spin and an external electric or magnetic field

**hyperfocal distance** /'hiepə,fohkl, ,-'-/ *n* the nearest distance upon which a photographic lens may be focussed to produce satisfactory definition at infinity [ISV]

**hypergamy** /hie'puhgəmi/ *n* marriage into an equal or higher caste or social group

**hyperglycaemia** /,hiepəglie'seemyə, -mi·ə/ *n* an excess of sugar in the blood (eg in DIABETES MELLITUS) – compare HYPOGLYCAEMIA [NL] – **hyperglycaemic** *adj*

**hypergol** /'hiepəgol, -gohl/ *n* a hypergolic rocket fuel [Ger, fr *hyper-* + *erg-* + *-ol*]

**hypergolic** /,hiepə'golik/ *adj* **1** *esp of a rocket fuel* igniting spontaneously on contact with an OXIDIZING AGENT without external means of ignition (eg a spark) **2** of or using hypergolic fuel ⟨*a* ~ *engine*⟩ – **hypergolically** *adv*

**hypericum** /hie'perikəm/ *n* SAINT-JOHN'S-WORT [NL, genus name, fr L *hypericum, hypericon* Saint-John's-wort, fr Gk *hyperikon, hypereikos*, prob fr *hypo-* + *ereikē* heath, heather]

**hyperinflation** /,hiepərin'flaysh(ə)n/ *n* very rapid economic inflation – **hyperinflationary** *adj*

**hyperinsulinism** /,hiepər'insyooliniz(ə)m/ *n* the presence of excess insulin in the body, usu resulting in HYPOGLYCAEMIA (low blood sugar) – compare HYPOINSULINISM [ISV]

**hyperirritability** *n* abnormally great or uninhibited response to stimuli – **hyperirritable** *adj*

**hyperkinesia** /,hiepəki'neezh(y)ə, -kie-/ *n* abnormally increased and usu purposeless and uncontrollable muscular movement; spasm [NL, fr *hyper-* + *-kinesia* movement, fr Gk *kinēsis* – more at KINESIS] – **hyperkinetic**

**hyperkinesis** /,hiepəki'neesis, -kie-/ *n* hyperkinesia [NL, fr *hyper-* + Gk *kinēsis*]

**hyperlipaemia** /,hiepəli'peemiə/ *n* the presence of excess fat or LIPIDS in the blood [NL, fr *hyper-* + *lip-* + *-aemia*]

**hyperlipidaemia** /,hiepə,lipi'deemiə/ *n* hyperlipaemia [NL, fr ISV *hyper-* + *lipid* + *-aemia*]

**hypermarket** /'hiepə,mahkit/ *n* **1** a large indoor market composed of a number of stalls trading usu in a similar type of merchandise ⟨*an antique* ~⟩ **2** a very large self-service retail store selling a wide range of household and consumer goods (eg food, clothes, toys, and electrical appliances) and usu situated on the outskirts of a major town or city

**hypermetamorphosis** /,hiepə,metə'mawfəsis, -,metəmaw'fohsis/ *n* a method of development (METAMORPHOSIS) in some insects (eg the BLISTER BEETLE) in which the larva passes through two or more INSTARS (forms assumed between moulting) each markedly different in structure from the others [NL]

**hypermetropia** /-me'trohpi·ə, -pyə/ *n* a condition in which visual images come to a focus behind the retina of the eye and vision is better for distant than for near objects; longsightedness – compare MYOPIA [NL, fr Gk *hypermetros* beyond measure (fr *hyper-* + *metron* measure) + NL *-opia*] – **hypermetropic, hypermetropical** *adj*, **hypermetropy** *n*

**hypermorph** /'hiepə,mawf/ *n* a mutant gene having an effect resembling but greater than that of the corresponding naturally occurring (WILD-TYPE) gene – compare HYPOMORPH – **hypermorphic** *adj*, **hypermorphism** *n*

**hyperon** /'hiepərɔn/ *n* any of a group of unstable ELEMENTARY PARTICLES (minute particles of matter) (e g SIGMA and LAMBDA particles) that are greater in mass than the proton or neutron and belong to the BARYON group [prob fr *hyper-* + *-on*]

**hyperopia** /,hiepə'rohpi-ə, -pyə/ *n* hypermetropia [NL] – **hyperopic** *adj*

**hyperostosis** /,hiepəro'stohsis/ *n, pl* **hyperostoses** excessive growth or thickening of bone tissue [NL] – **hyperostotic** *adj*

**hyperparasite** /,hiepə'parəsiet/ *n* a parasite that lives on or in another parasite – **hyperparasitic** *adj*, **hyperparasitism** *n*

**hyperparathyroidism** /,hiepə,parə'thieroydiz(ə)m/ *n* an excess of PARATHYROID hormone in the body; *also* the resulting abnormal state marked esp by an excess of calcium in the blood and urine and the withdrawal of calcium from bones – compare HYPOPARATHYROIDISM

**hyperphysical** /,hiepə'fizikl/ *adj* beyond or independent of the physical world; supernatural – **hyperphysically** *adv*

**hyperpituitarism** /,hiepəpi'tyooh·itəriz(ə)m/ *n* excessive production of hormones (e g GROWTH HORMONE) by the PITUITARY GLAND – compare HYPOPITUITARISM [ISV] – **hyperpituitary** *adj*

**hyperplasia** /,hiepəplayzyə, -zh(y)ə/ *n* an (excessive) increase in the number of cells of a body part; *esp* an abnormal or unusual growth or increase in the size of a tissue, organ, or other body part caused by an increase in the number of cells – compare HYPERTROPHY [NL] – **hyperplastic** *adj*

**hyperploid** /'hiepə,ployd/ *n or adj* (an organism or cell) having a slightly greater number of CHROMOSOMES (strands of gene-carrying material) than an exact multiple of the HAPLOID number (single or basic set as found in an egg or sperm cell) of chromosomes – compare HYPOPLOID [ISV] – **hyperploidy** *n*

**hyperpnoea,** *NAm* **hyperpnea** /,hiepə'nee-ə, ,hiepə'nee-ə/ *n* abnormally rapid or deep breathing; HYPERVENTILATION – compare HYPOPNOEA [NL] – **hyperpnoeic** *adj*

**hyperpolar·ize, -ise** /,hiepə'pohləriez/ *vt* to produce an increase in POTENTIAL DIFFERENCE across (a biological membrane) ⟨*a ~d nerve cell*⟩ – compare DEPOLARIZE – **hyperpolarization** *n*

**hyperpyretic** /,hiepəpie'retik/ *adj* of or affected with hyperpyrexia [ISV]

**hyperpyrexia** /,hiepəpie'reksiə/ *n* the condition of having a dangerously high body temperature (e g in heatstroke) – **hyperpyrexial** *adj*

**hypersensitive** /,hiepə'sensətiv/ *adj* **1** excessively or abnormally sensitive **2** abnormally susceptible (e g to a drug) – **hypersensitiveness** *n*, **hypersensitivity** *n*

**hypersonic** /,hiepə'sonik/ *adj* **1** of or being a speed five or more times that of sound in air – compare SONIC **2** moving, capable of moving, or using air currents that move at hypersonic speed ⟨*~ wind tunnel*⟩ [ISV] – **hypersonically** *adv*

**hyperspace** /'hiepə,spays/ *n* space of more than three dimensions

**hypersthene** /'hiepəs,theen/ *n* a greyish, greenish-black, or dark brown rock-forming PYROXENE mineral consisting of a SILICATE of magnesium and iron, (MgFe)SiO₃ [Fr *hypersthène*, fr Gk *hyper-* + *sthenos* strength] – **hypersthenic** *adj*

**hypertension** /,hiepə'tensh(ə)n/ *n* abnormally high blood pressure – compare HYPOTENSION [ISV]

**hypertensive** /,hiepə'tensiv/ *adj* causing or marked by high blood pressure or a rise in blood pressure

**hyperthermia** /,hiepə'thuhmi-ə/ *n* very high body temperature, esp when intentionally induced for therapeutic purposes (e g in some treatments for cancer) – compare HYPOTHERMIA, HYPERPYREXIA [NL, fr *hyper-* + *therm-* + *-ia*] – **hyperthermic** *adj*

**hyperthyroidism** /,hiepə'thieroy,diz(ə)m/ *n* an excess of THYROID hormones in the body; *also* the resulting condition marked esp by increased metabolic rate, enlargement of the thyroid gland, rapid heart rate, high blood pressure, protrusion of the eyeball, thinness, and nervousness – compare HYPOTHYROIDISM [ISV] – **hyperthyroid** *adj*

**hypertonic** /,hiepə'tonik/ *adj* **1** *esp of a muscle or muscular tissue* exhibiting excessive tone or tension **2** having a higher

OSMOTIC PRESSURE than a surrounding medium or a liquid under comparison ⟨*animals that produce a ~ urine*⟩ □ compare HYPOTONIC, ISOTONIC [ISV] – **hypertonicity** *n*

¹**hypertrophy** /hie'puhtrəfi/ *n* **1** excessive development or increase in size of a tissue, organ, or other body part; *specif* the enlargement or growth of a body part caused by an increase in the size of the cells or fibres without an increase in their number – compare HYPERPLASIA **2** exaggerated growth or complexity [NL *hypertrophia*, fr *hyper-* + *-trophia* -trophy] – **hypertrophic** *adj*

²**hypertrophy** *vb* to (cause to) undergo hypertrophy

**hyperuricaemia** /,hiepə,yooəri'seemyə, -miə/ *n* the presence of excess URIC ACID in the blood [NL]

**hyperventilation** /,hiepə,venti'laysh(ə)n/ *n* excessively fast and deep breathing leading to abnormal loss of CARBON DIOXIDE from the blood and often dizziness – **hyperventilate** *vi*

**hypha** /'hiefə/ *n, pl* **hyphae** /-,fee/ any of the threadlike filaments that make up the MYCELIUM (major part of the body) of a fungus [NL, fr Gk *hyphē* web; akin to Gk *hyphos* web – more at WEAVE] – **hyphal** *adj*

**hyphen** /'hief(ə)n/ *n* a punctuation mark - used to divide or to compound words, word elements, or numbers [LL & Gk; LL, fr Gk, fr *hyph' hen* under one, fr *hypo* under + *hen*, neut of *heis* one – more at UP, SAME] – **hyphenless** *adj*

**hyphenate** /'hiefənayt/, **hyphen** *vt* to connect or separate (e g words, word elements, or numerals) with a hyphen – **hyphenation** *n*

**hypn-, hypno-** *comb form* **1** sleep ⟨hypno*phobia*⟩ **2** hypnotism ⟨hypno*genesis*⟩ [Fr, fr LL, fr Gk, fr *hypnos* – more at SOMNOLENT]

**hypnagogic, hypnogogic** /,hipnə'gojik/ *adj* of or associated with the drowsiness preceding sleep – compare HYPNOPOMPIC [Fr *hypnagogique*, fr Gk *hypn-* + *-agōgos* leading, inducing, fr *agein* to lead – more at AGENT]

**hypnoanalysis** /,hipnoh-ə'naləsis/ *n* the treatment of mental illness using psychoanalytical techniques on a hypnotized patient

**hypnogenesis** /,hipnoh'jenəsis/ *n* the induction of a hypnotic state [NL] – **hypnogenetic** *adj*, **hypnogenetically** *adv*

**hypnoid** /'hipnoyd/, **hypnoidal** /-dl/ *adj* of mild hypnotic or suggestible states resembling sleep or hypnosis

**hypnopaedia** /,hipnoh'peediə/ *n* learning or conditioning during sleep [*hypn-* + Gk *paideia* education, fr *paid-*, *pais* child]

**hypnopompic** /,hipnoh'pompik/ *adj* of or associated with the semiconsciousness preceding waking ⟨*~ illusions*⟩ – compare HYPNAGOGIC [*hypn-* + Gk *pompē* act of sending – more at POMP]

**hypnosis** /hip'nohsis/ *n, pl* **hypnoses** /-seez/ **1** any of various trancelike conditions that (superficially) resemble sleep; *specif* such a condition induced by a person to whose suggestions the subject is then markedly susceptible **2** HYPNOTISM **1** [NL]

**hypnotherapy** /,hipnoh'therəpi/ *n* the treatment of mental illness, physical disease, compulsive behaviour, etc using hypnotism

¹**hypnotic** /hip'notik/ *adj* **1** tending to produce sleep; soporific **2a** of, tending to induce, resembling, or being a state of hypnosis **b** of or susceptible to hypnotism [Fr or LL; Fr *hypnotique*, fr LL *hypnoticus*, fr Gk *hypnōtikos*, fr *hypnoun* to put to sleep, fr *hypnos*] – **hypnotically** *adv*

²**hypnotic** *n* **1** something (e g a drug) that induces sleep **2** one who is or can be hypnotized

**hypnotism** /'hipnə,tiz(ə)m/ *n* **1** the study or process of inducing hypnosis **2** HYPNOSIS **1** – **hypnotist** *n*

**hypnot·ize, -ise** /'hipnətiez/ *vt* **1** to induce hypnosis in **2** to dazzle or overcome (as if) by hypnotic suggestion ⟨*a voice that ~s its hearers*⟩ ⟨*drivers ~d by speed*⟩ – **hypnotizable** *adj*, **hypnotizer** *n*, **hypnotization** *n*

¹**hypo** /'hiepoh/ *n, pl* **hypos** SODIUM THIOSULPHATE used as a fixing agent in photography [short for *hyposulphite*]

²**hypo** *n, pl* **hypos**, *informal* HYPODERMIC

**hypo-, hyp-** *prefix* **1** under; beneath ⟨hypo*blast*⟩ ⟨hypo*dermic*⟩ **2** less than normal or normally ⟨hyp*aesthesia*⟩ ⟨hypo*tension*⟩ **3** in a lower state of oxidation ⟨hypo*chlorous acid*⟩ □ compare HYPER- [ME *ypo-*, fr OF, fr LL *hypo-*, *hyp-*, fr Gk, fr *hypo* – more at UP]

**hypoblast** /'hiepə,blast/ *n* the innermost layer of cells of an embryo at a very early stage in its development; the cells that give rise to the ENDODERM; *broadly* ENDODERM – **hypoblastic** *adj*

**hypocalcaemia,** *chiefly NAm* **hypocalcemia** /ˌhiepoh-·kal'seemyə, -miə/ *n* a deficiency of calcium in the blood – compare HYPERCALCAEMIA [NL, fr *hypo-* + *calc-* + *-aemia*] – **hypocalcaemic** *adj*

**hypocaust** /'hiepəˌkawst/ *n* an ancient Roman central heating system with an underground furnace and tiled flues to distribute the heat [L *hypocaustum,* fr Gk *hypokauston,* fr *hypokaiein* to light a fire under, fr *hypo-* + *kaiein* to burn – more at CAUSTIC]

**hypocentre** /'hiepoh,sentə/ *n* **1** the point on the earth's surface directly below the centre of a nuclear bomb explosion **2** the point of origin (FOCUS) of an earthquake

**hypochlorite** /ˌhiepə'klawriet/ *n* any of various chemical compounds (SALTS or ESTERS) formed by combination between HYPOCHLOROUS ACID and a metal atom, an alcohol, or another chemical group

**hypochlorous acid** /ˌhiepə'klawrəs/ *n* an unstable weak acid, HClO, obtained in solution along with HYDROCHLORIC ACID by reaction of chlorine with water and used esp in the form of its SALTS as a strong OXIDIZING AGENT, bleach, disinfectant, and chlorinating agent [ISV]

**hypochondria** /ˌhiepə'kondri·ə/ *also* **hypochondriasis** /ˌhiepəkon'drie·əsis/ *n* morbid concern about one's health; *specif* such a concern when accompanied by the persistent but unfounded belief that one is suffering from physical disease [NL, fr LL, pl, upper abdomen (formerly regarded as the seat of hypochondria), fr Gk, lit., the parts under the cartilage (of the breastbone), fr *hypo-* + *chondros* cartilage, granule, grain – more at GRIND]

[1]**hypochondriac** /ˌhiepə'kondriak/ *also* **hypochondriacal** /ˌhiepəkon'drie·əkl/ *adj* **1** of the hypochondrium **2** of or affected or produced by hypochondria [Fr *hypochondriaque,* fr Gk *hypochondriakos,* fr *hypochondria*]

[2]**hypochondriac** *n* one who is affected by hypochondria

**hypochondrium** /ˌhiepə'kondriəm/ *n, pl* **hypochondria** /-ri·ə/ either of two regions lying, one on each side, in the upper part of the abdomen and below the ribs [NL, fr Gk *hypochondrion* abdomen, sing. of *hypochondria*]

**hypocorism** /hie'pokəriz(ə)m/ *n* (the use of) a pet name or euphemism [LL *hypocorisma,* fr Gk *hypokorisma,* fr *hypokorizesthai* to call by pet names, fr *hypo-* + *korizesthai* to caress, fr *koros* boy, *korē* girl] – **hypocoristic, hypocoristical** *adj,* **hypocoristically** *adv*

**hypocotyl** /ˌhiepə'kotil/ *n* the part of the stem of a plant embryo or seedling below the COTYLEDON (first leaf produced by a germinating seed) and above the root (RADICLE) [ISV *hypo-* + *cotyl*edon]

**hypocrisy** /hi'pokrəsi/ *n* **1** the pretence of possessing virtues, beliefs, or qualities that one does not really have, esp in matters of religion or morality 〈~ *is saying one thing and thinking another*〉 **2** an act or instance of hypocrisy [ME *ypocrisie,* fr OF, fr LL *hypocrisis,* fr Gk *hypokrisis* act of playing a part on the stage, hypocrisy, fr *hypokrinesthai* to answer, act on the stage, fr *hypo-* + *krinein* to decide – more at CERTAIN]

**hypocrite** /'hipəkrit/ *n* one given to hypocrisy [ME *ypocrite,* fr OF, fr LL *hypocrita,* fr Gk *hypokritēs* actor, hypocrite, fr *hypokrinesthai*] – **hypocrite** *adj*

**hypocritical** /ˌhipə'kritikl/ *adj* characterized by hypocrisy 〈*affected a* ~ *regret*〉; *also* being a hypocrite 〈*a most* ~ *liar*〉 ⚠ hypercritical – **hypocritically** *adv*

**hypocycloid** /ˌhiepə'siekloyd/ *n* a curve traced by a point on the circumference of a circle that rolls round the inside of a fixed circle

**hypoderm** /'hiepəˌduhm/ *n* the hypodermis [NL *hypoderma,* fr *hypo-* + *-derma*]

[1]**hypodermic** /ˌhiepə'duhmik/ *adj* **1** of the parts or region just beneath the skin **2** adapted for use in or administered by injection beneath the skin [ISV] – **hypodermically** *adv*

[2]**hypodermic** *n* **1** HYPODERMIC INJECTION **2** HYPODERMIC SYRINGE; *also* HYPODERMIC NEEDLE

**hypodermic injection** *n* an injection made into the tissues beneath the skin

**hypodermic needle** *n* **1** a hollow needle used, esp as part of a HYPODERMIC SYRINGE, for introducing or removing material from the body; NEEDLE 1c(2) **2** a HYPODERMIC SYRINGE complete with needle

**hypodermic syringe** *n* a small syringe used with a hollow needle for the injection or withdrawal of material beneath the skin

**hypodermis** /ˌhiepə'duhmis/ *n* **1** the layer of tissue immedi-

ately beneath the EPIDERMIS (outer layer of cells) of a plant, esp when modified to serve as a supporting and protecting or water-storing layer **2** the layer of cells that underlies and secretes the material of the outer protective cover (CUTICLE) of an insect, crab, etc [NL] – **hypodermal** *adj*

**hypoeutectic** /ˌhiepohyooh'tektik/, **hypoeutectoid** /-oyd/ *adj,* of an alloy or other mixture containing less of the minor component than is contained in the EUTECTIC mixture (that with the lowest melting point) – compare HYPEREUTECTIC

**hypogastrium** /ˌhiepə'gastriəm/ *n, pl* **hypogastria** /-i·ə/ the middle region of the lower part of the abdomen beneath the navel – compare EPIGASTRIUM [NL, fr Gk *hypogastrion,* fr *hypo-* + *gastr-, gastēr* belly – more at GASTRIC] – **hypogastric** *adj*

**hypogeal** /ˌhiepə'jee·əl/, **hypogean** /-'jee·ən/, **hypogeous** /-'gee·əs/ *adj* **1** growing, living, or occurring below the surface of the ground 〈~ *insects*〉 〈*an* ~ *stem*〉 **2a** of a COTYLEDON (*first leaf produced by a germinating seed*) remaining below the ground when the seed germinates **b** of or being plant germination in which the COTYLEDON remains underground while the EPICOTYL (part of seedling stem above the cotyledon) elongates ☐ compare EPIGEAL [LL *hypogeus* underground, fr Gk *hypogaios,* fr *hypo-* + *gē* earth] – **hypogeally** *adv*

**hypogene** /'hiepəˌjeen/ *adj,* of rock formed or occurring at depths below the earth's surface – compare EPIGENE [*hypo-* + Gk *-genēs* born, produced – more at -GEN]

**hypoglossal** /ˌhiepə'glos(ə)l/ *adj* lying beneath the tongue

**hypoglossal nerve** /ˌhiepə'glosl/ *also* **hypoglossal** *n* either of the 12th and final pair of CRANIAL NERVES that supply the muscles of the tongue in higher VERTEBRATE animals

**hypoglycaemia** /ˌhiepohglie'seemyə, -mi·ə/ *n* an abnormally low amount of sugar in the blood – compare HYPERGLYCAEMIA [NL] – **hypoglycaemic** *adj*

**hypognathous** /hie'pognəthəs/ *adj* **1** having the lower jaw longer than and protruding beyond the upper jaw; UNDERSHOT **2** of an insect having the mouthparts turned downwards

**hypogynous** /hie'pojinəs/ *adj* **1** of a floral organ (e g a petal or sepal) attached to the RECEPTACLE (end of the flower-bearing stalk) or stem below the OVARY (seed-bearing structure) and free from it **2** of a flower having hypogynous floral organs ☐ compare EPIGYNOUS, PERIGYNOUS – **hypogyny** *n*

**hypoid gear** /'hiepoyd/ *also* **hypoid** *n* a system of two gears with the PINION (smaller gear) not intersecting the axis of the main gear [short for *hyperboloidal*]

**hypoinsulinism** /ˌhiepoh'insyooliniz(ə)m/ *n* a deficiency of insulin in the body, usu resulting in HYPERGLYCAEMIA (high blood sugar) – compare HYPERINSULINISM

**hypolimnion** /ˌhiepoh'limni·ən/ *n, pl* **hypolimnia** /-ni·ə/ the cold lower layer of water in a lake, that is rich in nutrients, and usu very low in oxygen – compare EPILIMNION [NL, fr *hypo-* + Gk *limnion,* dim. of *limnē* lake – more at LIMNETIC]

**hypomania** /ˌhiepə'maynyə/ *n* a mild form of mania [NL] – **hypomanic** *adj*

**hypomorph** /'hiepəˌmawf, 'hiepoh-/ *n* a mutant gene having an effect resembling but weaker than that of the corresponding naturally occurring (WILD-TYPE) gene – called also LEAKY GENE; compare HYPERMORPH – **hypomorphic** *adj,* **hypomorphism** *n*

**hyponasty** /'hiepəˌnasti/ *n* the occurrence of stronger or more rapid growth of the under surface of a plant part (e g a flower petal) than of the upper surface, causing the part to bend inwards and often upwards – compare EPINASTY [ISV *hypo-* + *-nasty*] – **hyponastic** *adj*

**hyponymy** /hie'ponimi/ *n* the relationship between two words such that the meaning of one (e g *scarlet*) always includes that of the other (e g *red*) but not the reverse [*hypo-* + *-onymy* (as in *synonymy*)] – **hyponymous** *adj*

**hypoparathyroidism** /ˌhiepoh,parə'thieroydiz(ə)m, ˌhiepə-/ *n* a deficiency of PARATHYROID hormone in the body; *also* the resulting abnormal state marked esp by abnormally low amounts of calcium in the blood, often resulting in TETANY (condition of involuntary prolonged muscular contraction) – compare HYPERPARATHYROIDISM

**hypopharynx** /ˌhiepə'faringks, ˌhiepoh-/ *n, pl* **hypopharynges** /-injeez/, **hypopharynxes** /-inksiz/ **1** an appendage or thickened fold of tissue on the floor of the mouth of many insects, that resembles a tongue **2** the end of the OESOPHAGUS nearest the mouth [NL]

**hypophysectomy** /ˌhie,pofi'sektəmi/ *n* surgical removal of the PITUITARY GLAND – **hypophysectomize** *vt*

**hypophysis** /hie'pofəsis/ *n, pl* **hypophyses** /-seez/ PITUITARY GLAND (hormone-secreting gland at the base of the brain) [NL, fr Gk, attachment underneath, fr *hypophyein* to grow beneath, fr *hypo-* + *phyein* to grow, produce – more at BE] – **hypophyseal, hypophysial** *adj*

**hypopituitarism** /ˌhiepoh·pityooh·itəriz(ə)m/ *n* deficient production of hormones (e g GROWTH HORMONE) by the PITUITARY GLAND – compare HYPERPITUITARISM [ISV] – **hypopituitary** *adj*

**hypoplasia** /ˌhiepə'playzyə, -zh(y)ə/ *n* a condition of arrested or defective development in which an organ or other body part remains below the normal size or in an immature state [NL] – **hypoplastic** *adj*

**hypoploid** /'hiepoh,ployd/ *n or adj* (an organism or cell) having slightly fewer CHROMOSOMES (strands of gene-carrying material) than an exact multiple of the HAPLOID number (single or basic set as found in an egg or sperm cell) of chromosomes – compare HYPERPLOID – **hypoploidy** *n*

**hypopnoea,** *NAm* **hypopnea** /ˌhiepoh'neeə/ *n* abnormally shallow breathing – compare HYPERPNOEA [NL] – **hypopnoeic** *adj*

**hyposensit·ize** /ˌhiepoh'sensitiez/, **-ise** *vt* to reduce the sensitivity of, esp to something that causes an allergic reaction; desensitize – **hyposensitization** *n*

**hypostasis** /hie'postəsis/ *n, pl* **hypostases** /-seez/ **1a** something that settles at the bottom of a liquid; sediment **b** the settling of blood in the lower parts of an organ or body, esp owing to impaired circulation **2** PERSON 2 **3** *philosophy* **3a** the substance or essential nature of something **b** a concept that is hypostatized **4** the failure of a gene to produce its usual effect when coupled with another gene that is not its ALLELE – compare EPISTASIS [LL, substance, sediment, fr Gk, support, foundation, substance, sediment, fr *hyphistasthai* to stand under, support, fr *hypo-* + *histasthai* to be standing – more at STAND] – **hypostatic, hypostatical** *adj*, **hypostatically** *adv*

**hypostat·ize, -ise** /hie'postə,tiez/ *vt* to think of (a concept) as having concrete reality; REIFY [Gk *hypostatos* substantially existing, fr *hyphistasthai*] – **hypostatization** *n*

**hypostoma** /hie'postəmə/ *n, pl* **hypostomas, hypostomata** /ˌhiepəstə'mahtə/ a hypostome [NL]

**hypostome** /'hiepə,stohm/ *n* any of several structures associated with the mouth: e g **a** the liplike part that forms the posterior edge of the mouth of a crab, lobster, etc **b** the rounded or slightly raised area at the unattached end of a HYDRA or related POLYP (marine animal with a hollow tubular body) that bears the mouth **c** a rodlike organ that arises at the base of the beak in various mites and ticks [ISV *hypo-* + *-stome* (fr Gk *stoma* mouth) – more at STOMACH]

**hypostyle** /'hiepə,stiel/ *n or adj* (a building) having the roof resting on a grid of columns [Gk *hypostylos*, fr *hypo-* + *stylos* pillar – more at STEER]

**hyposulphite** /ˌhiepoh'sulfiet/ *n* **1** THIOSULPHATE – used esp in photography **2** HYDROSULPHITE

**hypotaxis** /ˌhiepə'taksis/ *n* the subordination of one clause to another (e g by a conjunction) [NL, fr Gk, subjection, fr *hypotassein* to arrange under, fr *hypo-* + *tassein* to arrange – more at TACTICS] – **hypotactic** *adj*

**hypotension** /ˌhiepoh'tensh(ə)n/ *n* abnormally low blood pressure – compare HYPERTENSION [ISV]

**hypotensive** /ˌhiepoh'tensiv/ *adj* causing or marked by low blood pressure or a lowering of blood pressure ⟨~ *drugs*⟩

**hypotenuse** /hie'pot(ə)n,yoohz/ *also* **hypothenuse** *n* the side of a right-angled triangle that is opposite the right angle [L *hypotenusa*, fr Gk *hypoteinousa*, fr fem of *hypoteinōn*, prp of *hypoteinein* to subtend, fr *hypo-* + *teinein* to stretch – more at THIN]

**hypothalamic** /ˌhiepoh·thə'lamik/ *adj* **1** located below the THALAMUS of the brain **2** of the hypothalamus

**hypothalamus** /ˌhiepə'thaləməs/ *n* a part of the brain that lies beneath the THALAMUS and includes centres that regulate body temperature, appetite, secretion of hormones by the PITUITARY GLAND, and other AUTONOMIC functions [NL]

**hypothec** /hie'pothik/ *n* a legal right in favour of a creditor over the property of his/her debtor – used in Roman and Scots law [Fr & LL; Fr *hypothèque*, fr MF, fr LL *hypotheca*, fr Gk *hypothēkē* deposit, pledge, fr *hypotithenai*]

**hypothermal** /ˌhiepə'thuhml/ *adj* of or being deposits of metal-bearing ores formed at high temperatures by the action of hot mineral-bearing water solutions

**hypothermia** /ˌhiepoh'thuhmi·ə/ *n* the condition of having a dangerously or abnormally low body temperature; *also* low body temperature when intentionally induced in order to

reduce the oxygen requirements of the tissue in surgery esp of the heart and brain – compare HYPERTHERMIA [NL, fr *hypo-* + *therm-* + *-ia*] – **hypothermic** *adj*

**hypothesis** /hie'pothəsis/ *n, pl* **hypotheses** /-seez/ **1** a proposed possible explanation for a phenomenon, set of circumstances, etc **2** a proposition assumed for the sake of argument [Gk, fr *hypotithenai* to put under, suppose, fr *hypo-* + *tithenai* to put – more at DO]

**hypothes·ize, -ise** /hie'pothə,siez/ *vi* to form a hypothesis ~ *vt* to adopt as a hypothesis; assume

**hypothetical** /ˌhiepə'thetikl/ *adj* **1** involving logical hypothesis; conditional **2** of or depending on supposition; conjectural – **hypothetically** *adv*

**hypothyroidism** /ˌhiepoh'thieroy,diz(ə)m/ *n* a deficiency of THYROID hormones in the body; *also* a condition (e g cretinism or MYXOEDEMA) resulting from this – compare HYPERTHYROIDISM [ISV] – **hypothyroid** *adj*

**hypotonic** /ˌhiepə'tonik/ *adj* **1** *esp of a muscle or muscular tissue* having deficient tone or tension **2** having a lower OSMOTIC PRESSURE than a surrounding medium or a liquid under comparison □ compare HYPERTONIC, ISOTONIC [ISV] – **hypotonicity** *n*

**hypoxaemia** /ˌhiepok'seemyə, ˌhipok-, -miə/ *n* deficient oxygenation of the blood; an abnormally low amount of oxygen in the blood [NL, fr *hypo-* + *ox-* + *-aemia*] – **hypoxaemic** *adj*

**hypoxanthine** /ˌhiepə'zantheen, -thin/ *n* a nitrogen-containing chemical compound, $C_5H_4N_4O$, that is a breakdown product of DNA and RNA and is found in plant and animal tissues [ISV]

**hypoxia** /hie'poksi·ə, hi-/ *n* a deficiency of oxygen reaching the tissues of the body [NL, fr *hypo-* + *ox-* + *-ia*] – **hypoxic** *adj*

**hyps-, hypsi-, hypso-** *comb form* height; altitude ⟨*hypsography*⟩ [Gk, fr *hypsos* height; akin to OE *ūp* up]

**hypsography** /hip'sografi/ *n* **1** the measurement and mapping of the earth's surface with reference to elevation **2** the elevations or inequalities of a land surface, or the means (e g colour shadings) by which they are shown on maps [ISV] – **hypsographic, hypsographical** *adj*, **hypsographically** *adv*

**hypsometer** /hip'somitə/ *n* **1** an apparatus for estimating altitudes in mountainous regions from the boiling points of liquids **2** any of various instruments for determining the height of trees by TRIANGULATION (calculation of distances by the measurement of angles) [ISV]

**hypsometry** /hip'somətri/ *n* the measurement of heights, esp with reference to sea level – **hypsometric** *adj*

**hyrax** /'hieraks/ *n, pl* **hyraxes** *also* **hyraces** /'hierəseez/ any of several small thickset plant-eating mammals (order Hyracoidea) with short legs and ears, a rudimentary tail, and feet with soft pads and broad nails resembling hooves [Gk *hyrak-, hyrax* shrewmouse]

**hyssop** /'hisəp/ *n* **1** a plant used in purificatory sprinkling rites by the ancient Hebrews **2** a Eurasian plant (*Hyssopus officinalis*) of the mint family with spikes of small blue flowers and aromatic and pungent leaves that are sometimes used as a herb [ME *ysop*, fr OE *ysope*, fr L *hyssopus*, fr Gk *hyssōpos*, of Sem origin; akin to Heb *ēzōbh* hyssop]

**hyster-, hystero-** *comb form* **1** womb ⟨*hysterotomy*⟩ **2** hysteria ⟨*hysterogenic*⟩; hysteria and ⟨*hysteroneurasthenia*⟩ [(1) Fr or L; Fr *hystér-*, fr L *hyster-*, fr Gk, fr *hystera;* (2) NL, fr *hysteria*]

**hysterectom·ize, -ise** /ˌhistə'rektəmiez/ *vt* to remove the womb of by surgery

**hysterectomy** /ˌhistə'rektəmi/ *n* surgical removal of the womb

**hysteresis** /ˌhistə'reesis/ *n, physics* a delay between the production of an effect and the event producing it; *esp* an apparent lag in the degree of magnetization produced in a magnetic material (e g iron) by a changing magnetizing force with respect to that force [NL, fr Gk *hysterēsis* shortcoming, fr *hysterein* to be late, fall short, fr *hysteros* later – more at OUT] – **hysteretic** *adj*

**hysteria** /hi'stiəri·ə/ *n* **1** a mental disorder marked by emotional excitability and disturbances (e g paralysis) of the normal body processes **2** unmanageable emotional excess; *esp* fits of laughing or weeping [NL, fr E *hysteric*, adj, fr L *hystericus*, fr Gk *hysterikos*, fr *hystera* womb; fr the former belief that hysteric women were suffering from disturbances of the womb]

**hysteric** /hi'sterik/ *n* someone suffering from hysteria

**hysterical** /hi'sterikl/ *adj* **1** **hysterical, hysteric** of or marked by hysteria **2** *informal* extremely funny – **hysterically** *adv*

**hysterics** /hi'steriks/ *n taking sing or pl vb* a fit of uncontrollable laughter or crying; hysteria

**hysteroid** /'histəroyd/ *adj* resembling hysteria

**hysteron proteron** /ˌhistəron 'protəron/ *n* **1** a figure of speech consisting of the reversal of a natural or rational order (e g in "thunder and lightning") **2** *philosophy* a logical fallacy in which the proposition to be proved is assumed as a premise in its own proof [LL, fr Gk, lit., (the) later earlier, (the) latter

first]

**hysterotely** /'histərohˌteli/ *n* the retention or manifestation of one or more structures or characteristics associated with an earlier stage of development (e g the retention of larval characteristics in a pupa) – compare PROTHETELY [Gk *hysteros* later + *telein* to complete, perfect, fr *telos* end – more at WHEEL]

**hysterotomy** /ˌhistə'rotəmi/ *n* surgical incision of the womb; *esp* a caesarean [NL *hysterotomia*, fr *hyster-* + *-tomia* -tomy]

# I

**i, I** /ie/ *n, pl* **i's, is, I's, Is 1a** the 9th letter of the English alphabet **b** a graphic representation of or device for reproducing the letter *i* **c** a speech counterpart of printed or written *i* **2** one designated *i*, esp as the 9th in order or class **3** one **4** something shaped like the letter I **5** *maths* a UNIT VECTOR parallel to the x-axis **6** the symbol used to represent the square root of minus one ⟨*i* = √−1⟩

**I** /ie/ *pron* **1** the one who is speaking or writing ⟨∼ *feel fine*⟩ ⟨*my wife and* ∼⟩ – compare ME, MINE, MY, WE **2** *nonstandard or dial* me ⟨*between you and* ∼⟩ ⟨*"will they chase* ∼?" *asks one* – *TES*⟩ [ME, fr OE *ic;* akin to OHG *ih* I, L *ego*, Gk *egō*] *usage* The use of I for *me* as the second of two objects after a preposition or verb ⟨△ *he interviewed my wife and* I⟩ ⟨△ *for people like you and* I⟩ is a common confusion. Those who are unsure of the difference between I and me sometimes avoid the difficulty by using **myself** ⟨*best wishes from George and* **myself**⟩ even as the second of two subjects ⟨*you and* **myself** *are the best drivers*⟩, but the second construction in particular is disapproved of by writers on usage. See ¹BETWEEN, ²LET, ME

**-i-** – used as a connective vowel to join word elements, esp of Latin origin ⟨*matri*linear⟩ ⟨*rati*cide⟩ [ME, fr OF, fr L, stem vowel of most nouns and adjectives in combination]

**¹-ia** /-iə, yə/ *suffix* (→ *n*) **1** pathological condition of ⟨*hyster*ia⟩ ⟨*anaem*ia⟩ **2** genus of (specified plant or animal) ⟨*Fuchs*ia⟩ **3** territory, world, or society of ⟨*suburb*ia⟩ ⟨*Austral*ia⟩ [NL, fr L & Gk, suffix forming feminine nouns]

**²-ia** *suffix* (→ *n taking pl vb*) **1** higher taxonomic category (e g class or order) consisting of (specified plants or animals) ⟨*Saur*ia⟩ **2** things derived from or relating to ⟨*rega*lia⟩ ⟨*juveni*lia⟩ [NL, fr L (neut pl of *-ius*, adj ending) & Gk, neut pl of *-ios*, adj ending]

**³-ia** *pl of* -IUM

**-ial** /-iəl/ – see ¹-AL ⟨*manor*ial⟩ [ME, fr MF, fr L *-ialis*, fr *-i-* + *-alis* -al]

**iamb** /'ie·am(b)/ *n* **1** a unit (FOOT) of verse consisting of one short or unstressed syllable followed by one long or stressed syllable (e g in *above*) **2** a line of verse written in iambs – compare TROCHEE [L *iambus*, fr Gk *iambos*] – **iambic** *adj or n*

**iambus** /ie'ambəs/ *n* an iamb

**-ian** /-iən/ – see -AN

**-iana** /-i'ahnə/ – see -ANA

**-iasis** /-ie·əsis/ *suffix* (→ *n*), *pl* **-iases** /-seez/ disease resembling or produced by ⟨*hypochondr*iasis⟩ ⟨*psor*iasis⟩ [NL, fr L, fr Gk, suffix of action, fr denominative verbs in *-ian, -iazein*]

**-iatric** /-i'atrik/ *also* **-iatrical** /-kl/ *comb form* (→ *adj*) of (a specified medical treatment) ⟨*paed*iatric⟩ [NL *-iatria*]

**-iatrics** /-i'atriks/ *comb form* (→ *n taking sing or pl vb*) medical treatment ⟨*paed*iatrics⟩

**iatro-** *comb form* medical; healing ⟨*iatro*genic⟩ ⟨*iatro*chemistry⟩ [NL, fr Gk, fr *iatros* physician]

**iatrogenic** /ie,atroh'jenik/ *adj* induced inadvertently by a medical doctor or his/her treatment ⟨*an* ∼ *rash*⟩ [Gk *iatros* + E *-genic*] – **iatrogenically** *adv*

**-iatry** /-'ie·ətri/ *comb form* (→ *n*) medical treatment ⟨*psych*iatry⟩ [Fr *-iatrie*, fr NL *-iatria*, fr Gk *iatreia* art of healing, fr *iatros*]

**I beam** *n* an iron or steel beam or girder that is I-shaped in cross section

**¹Iberian** /ie'biəri·ən/ *n* a member of any of the peoples inhabiting the Caucasus between the Black and Caspian seas in ancient times [*Iberia*, ancient region of the Caucasus] – **Iberian** *adj*

**²Iberian** *n* **1a** a member of any of the white peoples that in ancient times inhabited Spain and Portugal and that were probably related in origin to the peoples of northern Africa **b** a native or inhabitant of Spain or Portugal **2** any of the languages of the ancient Iberians [*Iberia*, peninsula in SW Europe containing Spain & Portugal] – **Iberian** *adj*

**ibex** /'iebeks/ *n, pl* **ibexes**, *esp collectively* **ibex** any of several wild goats living chiefly in high mountain areas of Europe, Asia, and N Africa and having large ridged backward-curving horns; *esp* a wild goat (*Capra hircus*) of Asia Minor believed to be the ancestor of the domestic goat [L]

**ibidem** /'ibidem, i'biedem/ *adv* in the same place; *specif* in the same book, chapter, or passage as previously mentioned [L]

**-ibility** /-ə'biləti/ – see -ABILITY

**ibis** /'iebis/ *n, pl* **ibises**, *esp collectively* **ibis** any of several wading birds (family Threskiornithidae) of warm regions that are related to the herons but are distinguished from them by a long slender downward-curving bill [L, fr Gk, fr Egypt *hby*]

**-ible** /-ibl, -əbl/ – see -ABLE

**Ibo** /'eeboh/ *n, pl* **Ibos**, *esp collectively* **Ibo 1** a member of a Negro people of the area round the lower Niger in W Africa **2** a Kwa language widely used in S Nigeria

**IC** *n* INTEGRATED CIRCUIT

**¹-ic** /-ik/ *suffix* (*n* → *adj*) **1** having the character or form of; being ⟨*panoram*ic⟩ ⟨*run*ic⟩ **2a** (characteristic) of or associated with ⟨*Byron*ic⟩ ⟨*Homer*ic⟩ ⟨*quixot*ic⟩ **b** related to, derived from, or containing ⟨*alcohol*ic⟩ ⟨*ole*ic⟩ **3** utilizing ⟨*electron*ic⟩ ⟨*atom*ic⟩ **4** exhibiting ⟨*nostalg*ic⟩; affected with ⟨*allerg*ic⟩ **5** characterized by; producing ⟨*analges*ic⟩ **6** *chemistry* having a VALENCY relatively higher than in (specified compounds or ions named with an adjective ending in *-ous*) ⟨*ferric iron*⟩ ⟨*mercur*ic⟩ [ME, fr OF & L; OF *-ique*, fr L *-icus* – more at -Y]

**²-ic** *suffix* (→ *n*) **1** one having the nature or character of ⟨*fanat*ic⟩ **2** one belonging to or associated with ⟨*ep*ic⟩ **3** one affected by ⟨*alcohol*ic⟩ **4** one who or that which produces ⟨*emet*ic⟩

**-ical** /-ikl/ *suffix* (*n* → *adj*) -ic ⟨*symmetr*ical⟩ ⟨*geolog*ical⟩ – sometimes differing from *-ic* in that adjectives formed with *-ical* have a wider or more transferred range of meaning than corresponding adjectives in *-ic* ⟨*econom*ic⟩ ⟨*econom*ical⟩ [ME, fr LL *-icalis* (as in *clericalis* clerical, *radicalis* radical)]

**ICBM** *n, pl* **ICBM's, ICBMs** an intercontinental BALLISTIC MISSILE

**¹ice** /ies/ *n* **1a** frozen water **b** a sheet or stretch of ice **2** a substance resembling ice; *esp* a substance reduced to the solid state by cold ⟨*ammonia* ∼ *in the rings of Saturn*⟩ **3** (a serving of) a frozen dessert containing a flavouring (e g fruit juice): e g **3a** *Br* ICE CREAM **b** WATER ICE **4** *NAm slang* diamonds; *broadly* jewellery [ME *is*, fr OE *īs;* akin to OHG *īs* ice, Avestan *isu-* icy] – **iceless** *adj* – **break the ice** to relieve the formality or tension of a situation (e g by starting a conversation) – **cut no ice** *informal* to fail to impress; have no importance or influence ⟨*her confident manner cuts no ice with me*⟩ – **on ice** in abeyance; in reserve for later use ⟨*kept their plans* on ice *for the time being*⟩ – **skate on thin ice** to be in a dangerous or delicate situation

**²ice** *vt* **1a** to coat with or convert into ice **b** to chill with ice **c** to supply with ice **2** to cover (as if) with icing **3** to shoot (an ice hockey puck) the length of the rink and beyond the opponents' GOAL LINE ∼ *vi* **1** to become ice-cold **2** to become covered or clogged with ice – often + *up* or *over* ⟨*the carburettor* ∼d *up*⟩

**ice age** *n* **1** a time of widespread glaciation **2** *cap I&A* the Pleistocene glacial epoch

**ice axe** *n* a combination pick and adze with a spiked handle that is used in climbing on snow or ice (e g to cut ice steps)

**ice bag** *n* a waterproof bag of ice for local application to the body (e g in the relief of the pain of a bruise)

**iceberg** /-,buhg/ *n* **1** a large floating mass of ice detached from a glacier **2** an emotionally cold person – see also **the** TIP **of the iceberg** [prob part trans of Dan or Norw *isberg*, fr *is* ice + *berg* mountain]

**iceblink** /-,blingk/ *n* a glare in the sky over an ICE FIELD, caused by the reflection of light

**iceblock** /'ies,blok/ *n, Austr & NZ* ICE LOLLY

**ice blue** *adj & n* (of) a very pale blue colour

**iceboat** /-,boht/ *n* a skeleton boat or frame on runners propelled on ice, usu by sails

**icebound** /'ies,bownd/ *adj* surrounded or obstructed by ice

**icebox** /-,boks/ *n* **1** *Br* the freezing compartment of a refrigerator **2** *NAm* a refrigerator

**icebreaker** /-,brayka/ *n* **1** a structure that protects a bridge pier from floating ice **2** a ship equipped to make and maintain a channel through ice

**ice cap** /-,kap/ *n* a cover of perennial ice and snow; *specif* a glacier permanently covering an extensive area of relatively level land (eg in the polar regions) – called also ICE SHEET

**ice cream** /,ies 'kreem, 'ies ,kreem/ *n* a sweet flavoured frozen food containing cream or a cream substitute and often eggs

**icefall** /'ies,fawl/ *n* a steeply descending part of a glacier in the form of a mass of usu jagged blocks

**ice field** *n* **1** an extensive sheet of sea ice; a large ICE FLOE **2** ICE CAP

**ice floe** *n* a sheet of floating ice, esp on the sea

**ice fog** *n* a fog composed of ice particles

**'ice-,foot** *n, chiefly Can* ice that is anchored to the shore and extends into the sea as a shelf

**ice hockey** *n* a game played on an ice rink by two teams of six players on skates whose object is to drive a PUCK (rubber disc) into the opponent's goal with a hockey stick

**icehouse** /'ies,hows/ *n* a building in which ice is made or stored; *esp* a structure, often vaulted and usu adjacent to a pond or moat, used formerly to store ice between layers of straw in winter for use in summer

**Icelander** /'ies,landa, -landa/ *n* a native or inhabitant of Iceland [Dan *Islænder*, fr *Island* Iceland, island between the Arctic & Atlantic oceans]

**'Icelandic** /ies'landik/ *adj* (characteristic) of Iceland, the Icelanders, or their language

**'Icelandic** *n* the NORTH GERMANIC language of the Icelandic people

**Iceland moss** *n* an edible lichen (*Cetraria islandica*) of mountainous and arctic regions used as food and in the manufacture of some cosmetics

**Iceland poppy** *n* **1** a poppy (*Papaver nudicaule*) of subarctic regions with large fragrant usu yellow or white flowers **2** any of various cultivated poppies that have rather small single or double flowers of usu pastel colours

**Iceland spar** *n* a transparent form of CALCITE (calcium carbonate mineral), with crystals having the property of BIREFRINGENCE

**ice lolly** /,ies 'loli, 'ies ,loli/ *n* a sweet frozen confection, esp a flavoured piece of ice, on a stick

**iceman** /'ies,man/ *n* one who sells or delivers ice, esp in the USA

**Iceni** /ie'seenie/ *n pl* an ancient British people of eastern England who revolted against the Romans in AD 61 under their queen Boadicea (Boudicca) [L] – **Icenian**, **Icenic** *adj*

**ice pack** *n* **1** an expanse of PACK ICE **2** ICE BAG

**ice pick** *n* a hand tool ending in a spike for chipping ice (eg for drinks)

**ice plant** *n* a southern African mesembryanthemum (*Mesembryanthemum crystallinum*) that has fleshy leaves covered with glistening blisterlike swellings and pink or white flowers

**ice point** *n* the temperature of 0° Celsius at which ice is in equilibrium with liquid water under air saturated with water at standard atmospheric pressure

**ice sheet** *n* ICE CAP

**ice show** *n* an entertainment consisting of various acrobatic, dance, etc routines by ice skaters, usu with musical accompaniment

**ice skate** *n* a shoe with a metal runner attached for skating on ice – **ice-skate** *vi*, **ice skate** *n*

**ice yacht** *n* an iceboat

**I Ching** /ee ching/ *n* an ancient Chinese book that is a source of Confucian and Taoist philosophy and presents 64 symbolic 6-line figures each containing information relevant to daily life and future events [Chin (Pek) *yi jīn* (*i⁴ ching¹*) classic (book) of changes]

**ichn-** /ikn-/, **ichno-** *comb form* footprint; track ⟨ichno*logy*⟩ [Gk, fr *ichnos*]

**ichneumon** /ik'nyoohman/ *n* **1** a mongoose **2 ichneumon fly, ichneumon** any of a large superfamily (Ichneumonoidea) of 4-winged insects with long antennae, whose larvae are usu internal parasites of other insect larvae, esp caterpillars [L, fr Gk *ichneumōn*, lit., tracker, fr *ichneuein* to track, fr *ichnos*]

**ichnology** /ik'nolaji/ *n* the study of fossilized footprints

**ichor** /'iekaw/ *n* **1** an ethereal liquid that took the place of blood in the veins of the ancient Greek gods **2** a thin watery or blood-tinged discharge [Gk *ichōr*] – **ichorous** *adj*

**ichthy-** /ikthi-/, **ichthyo-** *comb form* fish ⟨ichthyo*saur*⟩ [L, fr Gk, fr *ichthys;* akin to Arm *jukn* fish]

**ichthyology** /,ikthi'olaji/ *n* a branch of zoology that deals with fishes – **ichthyologist** *n*, **ichthyological** *adj*, **ichthyologically** *adv*

**ichthyophagous** /,ikthi'ofagas/ *adj* eating or subsisting on fish; PISCIVOROUS [Gk *ichthyophagos*, fr *ichthy-* + *-phagos* -phagous]

**ichthyornis** /,ikthi'awnis/ *n* any of a genus (*Ichthyornis*) of extinct toothed seabirds [NL, genus name, fr *ichthy-* + Gk *ornis* bird – more at ERNE]

**ichthyosaur** /'ikthi-a,saw/ *n* any of an order (Ichthyosauria) of extinct marine reptiles with fish-shaped bodies and elongated snouts [deriv of Gk *ichthy-* + *sauros* lizard – more at SAURIAN] – **ichthyosaurian** *adj or n*

**ichthys** /'ikthis/ *n* a representation of a fish symbolizing Christ in Christian iconography [Gk, fish]

**-ician** /-ish(a)n/ *suffix* (→ *n*) specialist in or practitioner of ⟨beauti*cian*⟩ ⟨techni*cian*⟩ [ME, fr OF *-icien*, fr L *-ica* (as in *rhetorica* rhetoric) + OF *-ien* -ian]

**icicle** /'iesikl/ *n* a hanging tapering mass of ice formed by the freezing of dripping water [ME *isikel*, fr *is* ice + *ikel* icicle, fr OE *gicel*; akin to OHG *ihilla* icicle, MIr *aig* ice]

**icing** /'iesing/ *n, chiefly Br* a sweet and either creamy or hard coating for cakes, biscuits, etc, that is often made with icing sugar, a liquid (eg water or egg white), and flavouring, and that is often coloured and decorated with rosettes, piping, etc

**icing sugar** *n* finely powdered sugar used in making cake icings and sweets

**icky** /'iki/ *adj, informal* cloying, sentimental [perh baby-talk alter. of *sticky*]

**icon, ikon** /'iekon/ *n* **1** a usu pictorial representation; an image **2** a conventional religious image (eg of Christ, the Virgin Mary, or a saint) typically painted on a small wooden panel and used as an aid to devotion in the Eastern Orthodox church **3** an object of uncritical devotion; an idol [L, fr Gk *eikōn*, fr *eikenai* to resemble; (2) LGk *eikōn*, fr Gk] – **iconic** *adj*, **iconically** *adv*, **iconicity** *n*

**icon-** /iekon-/, **icono-** *comb form* image; likeness ⟨icono*later*⟩ ⟨icono*grapher*⟩ [Gk *eikon-*, *eikono-*, fr *eikon-*, *eikōn*]

**iconoclasm** /ie'kona,klaz(a)m/ *n* the doctrine, practice, or attitude of an iconoclast [fr *iconoclast*, by analogy to *enthusiast : enthusiasm*]

**iconoclast** /-,klast/ *n* **1** a person who destroys religious images or opposes their veneration **2** one who attacks established beliefs or institutions [ML *iconoclastes*, fr MGk *eikonoklastēs*, fr Gk *eikono-* + *klan* to break – more at HALT] – **iconoclastic** *adj*, **iconoclastically** *adv*

**iconographic** /ie,kona'grafik/, **iconographical** *adj* **1** of iconography **2** representing something by pictures or diagrams – **iconographically** *adv*

**iconography** /,ieka'nografi/ *n* **1** pictorial material illustrating a subject; a pictorial record of a subject **2** the traditional or conventional images or symbols associated with a subject, esp a religious or legendary subject **3** the imagery or symbolism of a work of art, an artist, or a body of art **4** iconology **5** a published work dealing with or featuring iconography [Gk *eikonographia* sketch, description, fr *eikonographein* to describe, fr *eikon-* + *graphein* to write – more at CARVE] – **iconographer** *n*

**iconolatry** /,ieka'nolatri/ *n* the worship of images or icons

**iconology** /,ieka'nolaji/ *n* the study of icons or of artistic symbolism [Fr *iconologie*, fr *icono-* icon- + *-logie* -logy] – **iconological** *adj*

**iconoscope** /ie'konaskohp/ *n* an early type of television CAMERA TUBE (part of camera where optical images are converted into electrical impulses) that uses a beam of relatively high velocity electrons to scan the pattern of electrical charge produced on a screen by the emission of electrons in proportion to the intensity of light falling on various parts of the screen [fr *Iconoscope*, a trademark]

**iconostasis** /,ieka'nostasis/ *n, pl* **iconostases** /-seez/ a screen or partition with doors and tiers of icons that separates the sanctuary from the nave in Eastern Orthodox churches [MGk *eikonostasi*, fr LGk *eikonostasion* shrine, fr *eikon-* + Gk *histanai* to stand]

**icosahedron** /,iekasa'heedran/ *n, pl* **icosahedrons, icosahedra** a three-dimensional geometric figure having 20 faces; *esp* one that is REGULAR, having 20 equal equilateral triangular faces [Gk *eikosaedron*, fr *eikosi* twenty + *-edron* -hedron – more at VIGESIMAL] – **icosahedral** *adj*

**-ics** /-iks/ *suffix* (→ *n taking sing or pl vb*) **1** study, knowledge, skill, or practice of ⟨*linguis*tics⟩ ⟨*electron*ics⟩ **2** actions, activities, or mode of behaviour characteristic of (a specified person or thing) ⟨*histrion*ics⟩ ⟨*acroba*tics⟩ **3** qualities, operations, or phenomena relating to ⟨*mecha*nics⟩ ⟨*acous*tics⟩ [*-ic* + *-s;* trans of Gk *-ika,* fr neut pl of *-ikos* -ic]
*usage* Names of studies and activities ending with **-ics** take a singular verb when a singular noun follows ⟨*linguistics is his hobby*⟩ or when strictly used ⟨*acoustics deals with sound*⟩, but a plural verb in a looser sense ⟨*the acoustics of the hall are poor*⟩ ⟨*his politics are unusual*⟩. Kinds of behaviour ending with **-ics** are plural ⟨*these histrionics are ridiculous!*⟩.

**icterus** /'iktərəs/ *n* jaundice [NL, fr Gk *ikteros;* akin to Gk *iktis,* a yellow bird] – **icteric** *adj*

**ictus** /'iktəs/ *n* rhythmic or metrical stress in verse as distinct from prose [L, fr *ictus,* pp of *icere* to strike; akin to Gk *aichmē* lance]

**icy** /'iesi/ *adj* **1a** covered with, full of, or consisting of ice **b** intensely cold **2** characterized by personal coldness; frigid ⟨*an ~ stare*⟩ – **icily** *adv,* **iciness** *n*

**id** /id/ *n* the one of the three divisions of the mind in psychoanalytic theory that is completely unconscious and is the source of psychic energy derived from instinctual needs and drives – compare EGO, SUPEREGO [NL, fr L, it]

¹**-id** /-id, -əd/ *suffix* (→ *n*) **1** member of (a specified zoological family) ⟨*arach*nid⟩ **2** meteor associated with or radiating from (a specified constellation or comet) ⟨*Perse*id⟩ [(1) L *-ides,* masc patronymic suffix, fr Gk *-idēs;* (2) It *-ide,* fr L *-id-, is,* fem patronymic suffix, fr Gk]

²**-id** *suffix* (→ *n*) (such) a body, particle, or structure ⟨*energ*id⟩ [prob fr L *-id-, -is,* fem patronymic suffix, fr Gk]

**I'd** /ied, ahd/ I had; I should; I would

**-idae** /-idie/ *suffix* (→ *n taking pl vb*) members of (a specified zoological family) ⟨*Feli*dae⟩ [NL, fr L, fr Gk *-idai,* pl of *-idēs*]

**ID card** /,ie 'dee/ *n* IDENTITY CARD

**ide** /ied/ *n* a European freshwater food fish (*Idus idus*) of the carp family [Sw *id*]

**-ide** /-ied/ *also* **-id** /-id, -əd/ *suffix* (→ *n*) **1** chemical compound composed of two chemical elements or groups – added to the shortened name of the nonmetallic or more electronegative element ⟨*hydrogen sulph*ide⟩ or chemical group ⟨*cyan*ide⟩ **2** chemical compound derived from or related to (a specified compound) ⟨*glucos*ide⟩ ⟨*lanthan*ide⟩ [Ger & Fr; Ger *-id,* fr Fr *-ide* (as in *ox*ide)]

**idea** /ie'diə/ *n* **1** *often cap, philosophy* a transcendent archetype of which an existing thing is an imperfect representation (eg in the philosophy of Plato) ⟨*the Platonic Idea*⟩ **2** a plan of action; an intention **3** an indefinite or vague impression; a fancy ⟨*I'd an ~ you were coming*⟩ **4** something (eg a thought, concept, sensation, or image) actually or potentially present in the mind ⟨*the ~ of death never occurred to him*⟩ **5** a formulated thought or opinion ⟨*tell me your ~s on the subject*⟩ **6** whatever is known or supposed about something; a notion ⟨*the foreigner's ~ of England*⟩ **7** an individual's conception of the perfect or typical example of something specified ⟨*she's my ~ of an attractive woman*⟩ ⟨*not my ~ of a good time*⟩ **8** the central meaning or aim of a particular action or situation ⟨*the ~ of the game is to score goals*⟩ [L, fr Gk, fr *idein* to see – more at WIT] – **idealess** *adj*
*synonyms* Idea, concept, conception, thought, and notion all describe something existing in the mind as a result of thinking, feeling, or willing. Idea is the most general word, and has the widest range. Concept, in precise use, means a certain idea of a category formed by generalizing from particulars ⟨*had only seen donkeys, so had no concept of "horse"*⟩; but it is often used more loosely to express any widely accepted idea of what a thing should be ⟨*the concept of conservation is now well-established*⟩. Conception is the word used to describe the process of formulating ideas, but it may also be used for concept in its wider sense. It then tends to stress the ideas of an individual or group ⟨*everyone has his/her own conception of conservation, which may be different from those of others*⟩. Thought, in this sense, means an idea which results from reasoning rather than imagination. It contrasts with notion, an often vague or fanciful and unreasoned idea. Notion may also, like concept, suggest a general idea ⟨*no notion of punctuality*⟩. Notion may, too, resemble conception in suggesting the meaning understood by a term ⟨*no notion of what we mean by good manners*⟩.

¹**ideal** /ie'deel, ie'diəl/ *adj* **1a** existing only in the mind ⟨*to confuse ~ and concrete things*⟩; *broadly* lacking practicality **b** of or constituting mental images, ideas, or conceptions; conceptual **2** of or embodying an ideal; perfect ⟨*~ beauty*⟩ ⟨*an ~ spot for a picnic*⟩ **3a** *philosophy* existing as an archetypal idea **b** of philosophical idealism [Fr or LL; Fr *idéal,* fr LL *idealis,* fr L *idea*]
*usage* Since there can be no degrees in the ideal, some people dislike expressions such as ⟨*one of the most ideal spots for a holiday*⟩.

²**ideal** *n* **1** a standard of morality, perfection, beauty, or excellence ⟨*a man of high ~s*⟩ **2** one looked up to as embodying an ideal or as a model for imitation **3** an ultimate object or aim; a goal **4** *maths* a subset of a RING that is closed under addition (the addition of any two elements in the ring yields a further element of the ring) and is such that the product of any element of the ring with any element of the subset is a member of the subset ⟨*the integers ending in 0 are an ~ in the ring of all integers*⟩ – **idealless** *adj*

**idealism** /ie'dee,liz(ə)m, -'diə-/ *n* **1** *philosophy* **1a(1)** a theory that ultimate reality lies in a realm transcending the perceptible world and that objects in the perceptible world are imperfect copies of the ideal – compare MATERIALISM **a(2)** a theory that the essential nature of reality lies in consciousness or reason **b** a theory that only what is immediately perceived (eg sensations or ideas) is real and knowable **2** the practice of living according to one's ideals **3** a literary or artistic theory or practice that affirms the preeminent value of imagination and representation of ideal types as compared with faithful copying of nature – compare REALISM

**idealist** /ie'deelist, -'diə-/ *n* **1a** an adherent of a philosophical theory of idealism **b** an artist or author who advocates or practises idealism in art or writing **2** somebody guided by ideals; *esp* one who places ideals before practical considerations

**idealistic** /,iedee'listik, -diə-/, **idealist** *adj* of or characterized by idealists or idealism – **idealistically** *adv*

**ideality** /,iedi'aləti/ *n* **1a** the quality or state of being ideal **b** existence only in idea **2** something imaginary or idealized

**ideal·ize, -ise** /ie'deeliez, -'diə-/ *vt* **1** to attribute qualities of excellence or perfection to; glorify **2** to represent in an ideal form ~ *vi* to form ideals – **idealizer** *n,* **idealization** *n*

**ideally** /-li/ *adv* **1** in idea or imagination; mentally **2a** in accordance with an ideal; perfectly ⟨*~ suited for the job*⟩ **b** for best results ⟨*~, we should allot twice as much time to the project*⟩

**ideal point** *n, maths* an imaginary point at infinity where two parallel lines meet

**ideal type** *n* a hypothetically constructed entity (eg a type of society, institution, or activity) used in making comparisons with and developing theoretical explanations of the real world

**ideate** /'iedi,ayt/ *vb* to form an idea or conception (of) – **ideation** *n,* **ideational** *adj*

**idée fixe** /,eeday 'feeks (*Fr* ide fiks)/ *n, pl* **idées fixes** /~/ a fixed or obsessive idea; FIXED IDEA [Fr]

**idem** /'idem, 'iedem/ *pron* the same as previously mentioned (eg in a book or newspaper article) [L, same – more at IDENTITY]

**idempotent** /ie'dempətənt/ *adj* of or being a mathematical quantity which is not zero and which remains the same if multiplied by itself – compare NILPOTENT [ISV *idem-* (fr L *idem* same) + L *potent-, potens* having power – more at POTENT] – **idempotent** *n*

**identic** /ie'dentik/ *adj* constituting a diplomatic action or expression in which two or more governments follow precisely the same course or use the same wording in dispatches, or in which one government follows precisely the same course or uses the same wording with reference to two or more other governments ⟨*~ notes*⟩ [short for *identical*]

**identical** /ie'dentikl/ *adj* **1** being the same; selfsame ⟨*the ~ place where we stopped before*⟩ **2** very similar or exactly alike ⟨*~ hats*⟩ ⟨*the copy was ~ with the original*⟩ **3a** having the same cause or origin ⟨*the infections appeared to be ~*⟩ **b** of twins, triplets, *etc* derived from a single egg [ML *identicus,* fr LL *identitas*] – **identically** *adv,* **identicalness** *n*
*usage* The combination identical with is always correct, but identical to is now also becoming common. *synonyms* see ¹SAME *antonym* diverse

**identification** /ie,dentifi'kaysh(ə)n/ *n* **1a** identifying or being identified **b** evidence of identity ⟨*employees must carry ~ at all times*⟩ **2a** the putting of oneself mentally in the position of another that results in a feeling of close emotional association ⟨*she feels an ~ with Scarlett O'Hara*⟩ **b** the usu unconscious attribution of the characteristics of another to oneself in order to attain gratification, emotional support, or relief from mental conflict

**identification card** *n* IDENTITY CARD

**identification parade** *n, chiefly Br* a line-up of people, including one suspected of having committed a crime, arranged by the police for the purpose of inspection by a witness, who may thus be able to identify the suspect

**identify** /ie'dentifie/ *vt* **1a** to cause to be or become identical **b** to associate or link closely ⟨*groups that are* identified *with conservation*⟩ **2a** to establish the identity of ⟨*they* identified *him by his fingerprints*⟩ **b** to determine the TAXONOMIC category (e g the species) to which (a plant or animal) belongs ~ *vi* to experience psychological identification ⟨~ *with the hero of a novel*⟩ – **identifiable** *adj*, **identifiably** *adv*, **identifier** *n*

¹**identikit** /ie'dentikit/ *n, often cap* a set of drawings or photographs of alternative facial characteristics used by the police to build up a likeness, esp of a suspect or wanted criminal; *also* a likeness constructed in this manner or from witnesses' descriptions [fr *Identi-kit*, a trademark]

²**identikit** *adj* **1** *often cap* of or composed of identikit ⟨*police issued an* ~ *picture of the wanted man*⟩ **2** combining the representative features of something; stereotyped ⟨*the type of bland, middlebrow,* ~ *novel . . . with which the market is flooded* – Paul Bailey⟩

**identity** /ie'dentəti/ *n* **1** the condition of being exactly alike; sameness **2** the distinguishing character or personality of an individual; individuality ⟨*she has a distinct* ~ *, even though she is only four years old*⟩ **3** the condition of being the same as something or somebody known or supposed to exist ⟨*establish the* ~ *of stolen goods*⟩ ⟨*a case of mistaken* ~⟩ **4** an algebraic equation that remains true whatever values are substituted for the symbols ⟨$(x + y)^2 = x^2 + 2xy + y^2$ *is an* ~⟩ **5 identity element, identity** *maths* an element that leaves any element of the set to which it belongs unchanged when combined with it by a specific mathematical operation ⟨*zero is the* ~ *for addition*⟩ **6** *Austr & NZ* a personality, character ⟨*he was a well-known television* ~⟩ [MF *identité*, fr LL *identitat-, identitas*, irreg fr L *idem* same, fr *is* that – more at ITERATE]

**identity bracelet** *n* a bracelet that has its owner's name engraved on it

**identity card** *n* a card bearing information (e g a photograph or signature) that establishes the identity of the holder

**identity crisis** *n* a psychological maladjustment that arises in people when they are unable to establish their identity in relation to society

**identity matrix** *n, maths* UNIT MATRIX

**identity parade** *n* IDENTIFICATION PARADE

**ideo-** *comb form* idea ⟨ideogram⟩ [Fr *idéo-*, fr Gk *idea*]

**ideogram** /'idi·ə,gram/ *n* **1** a picture or symbol used in a system of writing to represent a thing or an idea but not the word or sound for it; *esp* one that represents not the object pictured but some thing or idea evoked by it **2** LOGOGRAM (letter or symbol representing a word) ☐ compare PICTOGRAPH, HIEROGLYPH – **ideogramic, ideogrammic** *adj*, **ideogrammatic** *adj*

**ideograph** /'idi·ə,grahf, -,graf/ *n* an ideogram – **ideographic** *adj*, **ideographically** *adv*

**ideography** /,idi'ografi/ *n* the use of ideograms

**ideological** /,iediə'lojikl, -,-'---/ *also* **ideologic** *adj* of or based on ideology – **ideologically** *adv*

**ideologue** /'iedee·ə,log/ *n* **1** a theorist, visionary **2** an advocate or adherent of a particular ideology [Fr *idéologue*, back-formation fr *idéologie*]

**ideology** /,iedi'olaji/ *n* **1** visionary speculation **2a** a systematic body of concepts **b** a manner of thinking characteristic of an individual, group, or culture ⟨*medical* ~⟩ **c** the integrated assertions, theories, and aims that constitute a social, political, or cultural programme [Fr *idéologie*, fr *idéo-* ideo- + *-logie* -logy] – **ideologist** *n*

**ides** /iedz/ *n taking sing or pl vb* the 15th day of March, May, July, or October or the 13th day of any other month in the ancient Roman calendar; *broadly* this day and the seven days preceding it [MF, fr L *idus*]

**-idine** *NAm also* **-idin** /-ədeen/ *suffix* (→ *n*) nitrogen-containing chemical compound related in origin or structure to (a specified compound) ⟨tolu*idine*⟩ ⟨pyrrol*idine*⟩ [ISV *-ide* + *-ine, -in*]

**idio-** *comb form* one's own; personal; distinct ⟨idio*blast*⟩ ⟨idio*lect*⟩ [Gk, fr *idios* – more at IDIOT]

**idioblast** /'idioh,blast/ *n* a plant cell that differs markedly from neighbouring cells [ISV] – **idioblastic** *adj*

**idiocy** /'idi·əsi/ *n* **1** extreme mental deficiency **2** something notably stupid or foolish ⟨*bureaucratic* idiocies⟩

**idiographic** /'idiə'grafik/ *adj* of or dealing with the concrete, individual, or unique [ISV]

**idiolect** /'idi·ə,lekt/ *n* the language or speech pattern of an individual [*idio-* + *-lect* (as in *dialect*)] – **idiolectal** *adj*

**idiom** /'idi·əm/ *n* **1a** the language peculiar to a people or to a district, community, or class; a dialect **b** the syntactic, grammatical, or structural form peculiar to a language **2** an expression in the usage of a language that is peculiar to itself either grammatically (e g *no, it wasn't me*) or esp in having a meaning that cannot be derived from the sum of the meanings of its elements (e g *Monday week* for "the Monday a week after next Monday") **3** a characteristic style or form of artistic expression ⟨*a poet writing in the Eliot* ~⟩ ⟨*the modern jazz* ~⟩ *synonyms* see LANGUAGE [MF & LL; MF *idiome*, fr LL *idioma* individual peculiarity of language, fr Gk *idiōmat-, idiōma*, fr *idiousthai* to make one's own, fr *idios*]

**idiomatic** /,idi·ə'matik/ *adj* **1** of or conforming to idiom **2** peculiar to a particular group, individual, or style – **idiomatically** *adv*, **idiomaticity** *n*

**idiomorphic** /,idiə'mawfik/ *adj, of minerals* having the proper crystalline structure [Gk *idiomorphos*, fr *idio-* + *-morphos* -morphous] – **idiomorphically** *adv*

**idiopathic** /,idi·ə'pathik/ *adj, medicine* **1** peculiar to the individual **2** arising spontaneously or from an obscure or unknown cause ⟨~ *disease*⟩ – **idiopathically** *adv*

**idioplasm** /'idiə,plaz(ə)m, -dioh-/ *n* a part of PROTOPLASM (living material of a cell) once held to function in the transmission of hereditary characteristics [ISV] – **idioplasmatic, idioplasmic** *adj*

**idiosyncrasy** /,idioh'singkrəsi/ *n* **1** a characteristic peculiarity of habit or structure **2a** a characteristic of thought or behaviour peculiar to an individual or group; *esp* an eccentricity **b** allergic sensitivity of an individual to a drug, food, etc [Gk *idiosynkrasia*, fr *idio-* + *synkerannynai* to blend, fr *syn-* + *kerannynai* to mingle, mix – more at CRATER] – **idiosyncratic** *adj*, **idiosyncratically** *adv*

**idiot** /'idi·ət/ *n* **1** an (ineducable) person afflicted with idiocy, esp from birth **2** a silly or foolish person [ME, fr L *idiota* ignorant person, fr Gk *idiōtēs* one in a private station, layman, ignorant person, fr *idios* one's own, private; akin to L *sed, se* without, *sui* of oneself] – **idiot** *adj*, **idiotic, idiotical** *adj*, **idiotically** *adv*

**idiot board** *n, informal* a device (e g a movable roll of paper with the text printed on it) that is used to prompt a performer on television; an autocue

**idiotism** /'idiətiz(ə)m/ *n* **1** IDIOM **2** *2 obs* IDIOM 1 [MF *idiotisme*, fr L *idiotismus* common speech, fr Gk *idiōtēs*, fr *idiōtēs*]

**idiot savant** /,eedyoh sa'vonh (Fr idjo savah)/ *n, pl* **idiots savants, idiot savants** /~/ a mentally defective person who exhibits exceptional skill or brilliance in some limited field [Fr, lit., learned idiot]

**idiotype** /'idioh,tiep/ *n* any of several closely related variant structures of an ANTIBODY considered without reference to the ANTIGEN (substance that stimulates production of an antibody) with which that antibody specifically combines – **idiotypic** *adj*

**-idium** /-idi·əm/ *suffix* (→ *n*), *pl* **-idiums, -idia** /-'idiə/ small or lesser kind of ⟨anth*eridium*⟩ [NL, fr Gk *-idion*, dim. suffix]

¹**idle** /'iedl/ *adj* **1** having no particular purpose or value; vain, useless ⟨~ *curiosity*⟩ **2** lacking foundation; groundless ⟨~ *rumour*⟩ **3** not occupied or employed: e g **3a** not in use or operation ⟨*machines lying* ~⟩ **b** not turned to appropriate use ⟨~ *funds*⟩ **4** shiftless, lazy ⟨~ *fellows*⟩ *synonyms* see INACTIVE *antonyms* working, active, busy △ idol, idyll [ME *idel*, fr OE *īdel*; akin to OHG *ītal* worthless] – **idleness** *n*, **idly** *adv*

²**idle** *vi* **1a** to spend time in idleness **b** to move idly **2** *esp of an engine* to run without being connected to the part (e g the wheels of a car) that is driven, so that no useful work is done ~ *vt* to pass in idleness – usu + *away* ⟨*they* ~d *the hours away*⟩ – **idler** *n*

**idler wheel** /'iedlə/ *n* **1** a wheel, gear, or roller used to transfer motion or to guide or support something **2** a guide or tightening pulley for a belt or chain

**Ido** /'eedoh/ *n* an artificial international language based on Esperanto [Esperanto, offspring, fr Gk *-idēs*, patronymic suffix]

**idocrase** /'iedə,krayz, 'idə-/ *n* a mineral, $Ca_{10}(MgFe)_2Al_4Si_9O_{34}(OH)_4$, that is a complex SILICATE of calcium, magnesium, iron, and aluminium, occurs in limestones, and is used as a gemstone – called also VESUVIANITE [Fr, fr Gk *eidos* + *krasis* mixture, fr *kerannynai* to mix – more at CRATER]

**idol** /'iedl/ *n* **1** a symbol, esp a carved figure, of a god or other object of worship; *broadly* a false god **2** something visible but without substance ⟨*an enchanted phantom, a lifeless* ~ – P B Shelley⟩ **3** an object of passionate or excessive devotion ⟨*a* pop ∼〉 **4** a false conception; fallacy △ idle, idyll [ME, fr OF *idole*, fr LL *idolum*, fr Gk *eidōlon* phantom, idol; akin to Gk *eidos* form – more at IDYLL]

**idolater** /ie'dolətə/ *n* **1** a worshipper of idols **2** a passionate and often uncritical admirer [ME *idolatrer*, fr MF *idolatre*, fr LL *idololatres*, fr Gk *eidōlolatrēs*, fr *eidōlon* + *-latrēs* -later]

**idolatrous** /ie'dolətrəs/ *adj* **1** of or marked by idolatry **2** having the character of idolatry 〈*the religion of ∼ nationalism* – Aldous Huxley〉 **3** practising or given to idolatry – **idolatrously** *adv*, **idolatrousness** *n*

**idolatry** /ie'dolətri/ *n* **1** the worship of a physical object as a god **2** excessive attachment or devotion to something

**idol·ize, -ise** /'ied(ə)l,iez/ *vt* to worship idolatrously; *broadly* to love or admire to excess 〈*the common people whom he so* ∼d – *TLS*〉 ∼ *vi* to practise idolatry **synonyms** see ¹REVERE – **idolizer** *n*, **idolization** *n*

**idyll** *also* **idyl** /'idil/ *n* **1** a simple descriptive work either in poetry or prose that deals with rustic life or pastoral scenes or suggests a mood of peace and contentment **2** an episode suitable for an idyll **3** a pastoral or romantic musical composition △ idle, idol [L *idyllium*, fr Gk *eidyllion*, fr dim. of *eidos* form; akin to Gk *idein* to see – more at WIT] – **idyllic** *adj*, **idyllically** *adv*

**i e** /ie 'ee/ *adv* that is to say 〈*minors, ∼ those under 18 years of age, will not be admitted*〉 [L *id est*]

**-ie** /-ee/ *suffix* (*n → n*) ⁴-Y

**-ier** /-iə/ – see ²-ER

**¹if** /if/ *conj* **1a** in the event that 〈*∼ she should telephone, let me know*〉 **b** supposing 〈*∼ you'd listened, you'd know*〉 **c** on condition that 〈*you can go out ∼ you put on your scarf*〉 **2** whether – used in indirect questions 〈*asked ∼ the post had come*〉 **3** – used to introduce an exclamation expressing a wish 〈*∼ it would only rain*〉 **4** even if, although 〈*∼ she's stupid, at least she's honest*〉 〈*an interesting ∼ untenable argument*〉 **5a** that – used after expressions of emotion 〈*I don't care ∼ she's busy*〉 〈*it's not surprising ∼ you're annoyed*〉 **b** – used with a negative when certain expletives introduce startling news 〈*blow me ∼ he didn't hit her!*〉 [ME, fr OE *gif*; akin to OHG *ibu* if] – **if anything** on the contrary even; perhaps even 〈*if anything, you ought to apologize*〉

**usage** In formal writing, **whether** is to be preferred to **if** in indirect questions and clauses expressing doubt 〈*I wonder* **whether**/**if** *he heard*〉. Where both words are possible, **whether** is often clearer than **if**, as 〈*let me know* **if** *you intend to come*〉 has two meanings. See WERE

**²if** *n* **1** a condition, stipulation 〈*the question ... depends on too many* ∼s *to allow an answer* – *Encounter*〉 **2** a supposition 〈*a theory full of* ∼s〉

**-iferous** /-if(ə)rəs/ – see -FEROUS [ME, fr L *-ifer*, fr *-i-* + *-fer* -ferous]

**iffy** /'ifi/ *adj, informal* full of contingencies and uncertainties 〈*the situation is far too ∼ for any predictions* – *N Y Times*〉 [¹*if* + ¹*-y*] – **iffiness** *n*

**-iform** /-ifawm/ – see -FORM 〈*rami*form〉 [MF & L; MF *-iforme*, fr L *-iformis*, fr *-i-* + *-formis* -form]

**-ify** /-ifie, -ofie/ – see -FY [ME *-ifien*, fr OF *-ifier*, fr L *-ificare*, fr *-i-* + *-ficare* -fy]

**Igbo** /'igboh/ *n, pl* **Igbos**, *esp collectively* **Igbo** (an) Ibo

**igloo** /'iglooh/ *n, pl* **igloos** **1** a dome-shaped Eskimo dwelling made of blocks of hard snow **2** a structure shaped like a dome [Eskimo *iglu, igdlu* house]

**igneous** /'igni·əs/ *adj* **1** of or resembling fire; fiery **2** *of a rock* formed by the cooling and solidification of MAGMA (molten rock material below the earth's surface) or lava on or below the earth's surface – compare PLUTONIC, VOLCANIC [L *igneus*, fr *ignis* fire; akin to Skt *agni* fire]

**ignescent** /ig'nes(ə)nt/ *adj* capable of emitting sparks [L *ignescent-, ignescens*, prp of *ignescere* to catch fire, fr *ignis*]

**igni-** /igni-/ *comb form* fire; burning 〈*igni*tron〉 [L, fr *ignis*]

**ignis fatuus** /,ignis 'fatyoo·əs/ *n, pl* **ignes fatui** /,igneez 'fatyoo,ee/ WILL-O'-THE-WISP [ML, lit., foolish fire]

**ignite** /ig'niet/ *vt* **1** to subject to fire or intense heat; *esp* to make incandescent by heat **2a** to set fire to; *also* to kindle **b** to cause (an air-fuel mixture) to burn **3** to inflame, excite 〈*oppression that ∼d the hatred of the people*〉 ∼ *vi* **1** to catch fire **2** to begin to glow **3** to burst forth suddenly into violence or conflict 〈*situation could ∼ if not properly handled*〉 [L *ignitus*, pp of *ignire*, fr *ignis*] – **ignitable, ignitible** *adj*, **igniter, ignitor** *n*

**ignition** /ig'nish(ə)n/ *n* **1** the act or action of igniting **2** the process or means (e g an electric spark) of igniting an air-fuel mixture

**ignoble** /ig'nohbl/ *adj* **1** of low birth or humble origin; plebeian

**2** base, dishonourable **synonyms** see ¹MEAN **antonym** noble [L *ignobilis*, fr *in-* ¹in- + *gnobilis, nobilis* noble] – **ignobleness** *n*, **ignobly** *adv*, **ignobility** *n*

**ignominious** /,ignə'mini·əs/ *adj* **1** marked by or causing disgrace or discredit; shameful **2** despicable, contemptible **3** humiliating, degrading 〈*suffered an ∼ defeat*〉 – **ignominiously** *adv*, **ignominiousness** *n*

**ignominy** /'ignəmini/ *n* **1** deep personal humiliation and disgrace **2** disgraceful or dishonourable conduct or quality [MF or L; MF *ignominie*, fr L *ignominia*, fr *ig-* (as in *ignorare* to be ignorant of, ignore) + *nomin-, nomen* name, repute – more at NAME]

**ignoramus** /,ignə'rayməs, -'rahməs/ *n* an ignorant person; a dunce [*Ignoramus*, ignorant lawyer in *Ignoramus*, play by George Ruggle †1622 E dramatist, fr NL *ignoramus* endorsement by a Grand Jury on a bill of indictment giving insufficient evidence for prosecution, fr L, we do not know, fr *ignorare*]

**ignorance** /'ignərəns/ *n* the state of being ignorant

**ignorant** /'ignərənt/ *adj* **1a** lacking knowledge or education 〈*an ∼ society*〉; *also* lacking knowledge or comprehension of something specified 〈*parents ∼ of modern mathematics*〉 **b** caused by or showing lack of knowledge 〈*∼ errors*〉 **2** unaware, uninformed **3** *informal* lacking social training; impolite – **ignorantly** *adv*

**ignoratio elenchi** /ignaw,ratioh e'lengki/ *n, philosophy* the logical fallacy of proving a conclusion which is irrelevant to the point at issue [L, lit., ignorance of proof]

**ignore** /ig'naw/ *vt* to refuse to take notice of; disregard **synonyms** see ¹NEGLECT **antonyms** notice, pay heed (to) [obs *ignore* to be ignorant of, fr Fr *ignorer*, fr L *ignorare*, fr *ignarus* ignorant, unknown, fr *in-* ¹in- + *gnoscere, noscere* to know – more at KNOW] – **ignorable** *adj*, **ignorer** *n*

**Igorot** /'igəroht, 'eegə-/ *n, pl* **Igorots**, *esp collectively* **Igorot** a member of any of several related peoples of NW Luzon in the Philippines; *also* their Austronesian languages

**iguana** /,igyoo'ahnə, i'gwahnə/ *n* any of various large plant-eating typically dark-coloured tropical American lizards (family Iguanidae) that have a serrated or spiny crest on the back and are important as human food in heir native habitat; *broadly* any of various large lizards [Sp, fr Arawak *iwana*]

**iguanid** /i'gwahnid/ *n* any of a family (Iguanidae) of tropical American lizards that includes the iguana

**iguanodon** /,igyoo'ahnədon, i'gwah-/ *n* any of a genus (*Iguanodon*) of gigantic erect long-tailed plant-eating dinosaurs from the early Cretaceous period of Belgium and Britain [NL *Iguanodont-, Iguanodon*, genus name, fr Sp *iguana* + NL *-odon* (as in *mastodon*)]

**IHS** – used as a Christian symbol and monogram for *Jesus* [LL, part transliteration of Gk ΙΗΣ, abbreviation for ΙΗΣΟΥΣ *Iēsous* Jesus]

**ikebana** /,ikay'bahnə, ,iki-, ,eek-/ *n* the Japanese art of flower arranging that emphasizes form and balance [Jap, fr *ikeru* to keep alive, arrange + *hana* flower]

**ikey** /'ieki/ *n, derog* a Jew [*Ike*, nickname for *Isaac*] – **ikey** *adj*

**ikon** /'iekon/ *n* an icon

**il-** /il-/ – see IN-

**ilang-ilang** /,eelang 'eelang/ *n* (an) ylang-ylang

**ile-** /ili-/ *also* **ileo-** *comb form, medicine* **1** ILEUM (small intestine) 〈*ile*itis〉 **2** ileal and 〈*ileocaecal*〉 [NL *ileum*]

**¹-ile** /-iel/ *suffix* (→ *adj*) (capable) of or liable to (so act or be acted upon) 〈*prehens*ile〉 〈*volat*ile〉 〈*frag*ile〉 [ME, fr MF, fr L *-ilis*]

**²-ile** *suffix* (→ *n*), *statistics* segment of (a specified size) in a FREQUENCY DISTRIBUTION 〈*dec*ile〉 [prob fr *-ile* (as in *quart*ile, n)]

**ileitis** /,ili'ietəs/ *n* inflammation of the ileum [NL]

**ileostomy** /,ili'ostəmi/ *n* the surgical formation of an opening through the abdominal wall into the ileum, that acts as an artificial anus [ISV]

**ileum** /'ili·əm, 'ieliəm/ *n, pl* **ilea** /-liə/ the last part of the SMALL INTESTINE extending between the JEJUNUM and the LARGE INTESTINE [NL, fr L, groin, entrails] – **ileal** *adj*

**ileus** /'ili·əs, 'ieliəs/ *n* mechanical or functional obstruction of the bowel [L, fr Gk *eileos*, fr *eilyein* to roll – more at VOLUBLE]

**ilex** /'ieleks/ *n* **1** HOLM OAK **2** a holly tree or shrub [L]

**iliac** /'iliak/ *also* **ilial** /'iliəl/ *adj* of or located near the ilium [LL *iliacus*, fr L *ilium*]

**Iliad** /'iliad/ *n* **1** a long narrative; *esp* an epic in the Homeric tradition **2a** a series of exploits suitable for an epic **b** a series of woes or disasters [the *Iliad*, ancient Gk epic poem (describing the siege of Troy by the Greeks) by Homer, fr L *Iliad-, Ilias*, fr Gk, fr *Ilion* Troy] – **Iliadic** *adj*

**ilio-** *comb form* iliac and 〈*ilio*lumbar〉 [NL *ilium*]

**ilium** /'ili-əm/ *n, pl* **ilia** /'ili-ə/ the upper and largest of the three principal bones composing either side of the pelvis [NL, fr L *ilium, ileum*]

¹**ilk** /ilk/ *pron, chiefly Scot that* same – esp in the names of landed Scottish families ⟨*Stuart of that* ~⟩ [ME, fr OE *ilca*, fr a prehistoric compound whose constituents are akin to Goth *is* he (akin to L *is* he, that) and OE *gelīc* like – more at ITERATE, LIKE]

²**ilk** *n* sort, kind ⟨*politicians and others of that* ~⟩
  **usage** Some people dislike the originally humorous extension of the Scottish ilk to mean simply "sort".

³**ilk** *adj, chiefly Scot* each, every [ME, adj & pron, fr OE *ylc, ælc* – more at EACH]

**ilka** /'ilkə/ *adj, chiefly Scot* each, every [ME, fr *ilk* + *a* (indef article)]

¹**ill** /il/ *adj* **worse** /wuhs/; **worst** /wuhst/ **1** bad: eg **1a** morally evil ⟨~ *deeds*⟩ **b** malevolent, hostile ⟨~ *feeling*⟩ ⟨*held an* ~ *opinion of his neighbours*⟩ **c** harsh ⟨~ *weather*⟩ ⟨~ *treatment*⟩ **d** not normal or sound ⟨~ *health*⟩ **e** unlucky, disadvantageous ⟨*an* ~ *omen*⟩ ⟨~ *fortune*⟩ **f** difficult ⟨*an* ~ *man to please*⟩ **g** socially improper ⟨~ *manners*⟩ **2** not in good health; *also* nauseated, sick **3** *chiefly Br* hurt, wounded ⟨*still very* ~ *after the accident*⟩ **4** *chiefly Scot* immoral, vicious **5** *archaic* notably unskilful or inefficient [ME, fr ON *illr*]
  **usage** Ill and sick both mean "in bad health"; but since in British English the primary meaning of be sick is to vomit, and of feel sick to feel like vomiting, British speakers prefer to refer to general bad health by saying (*I was ill last week*). Ill cannot be used before a noun in British English, however, so it is usual to speak of ⟨a sick (not △ an ill) *child*⟩ and of ⟨sick pay⟩ and ⟨sick leave⟩. People who are ill are the sick. In American English the two words are interchangeable, ill being somewhat more formal and used of more serious complaints. In American English one can speak of ⟨an ill child⟩.

²**ill** *adv* **worse**; **worst 1** with displeasure or hostility; unfavourably ⟨*spoke* ~ *of his neighbours*⟩ **2** hardly, scarcely ⟨~ *at ease*⟩ ⟨*can* ~ *afford such extravagances*⟩ **3** in a reprehensible, harsh, faulty, or deficient manner; badly – often in combination ⟨*fared* ~⟩ ⟨*ill-adapted to city life*⟩

³**ill** *n* something bad: eg **a** the reverse of good; evil ⟨*spoke no* ~ *of him*⟩ **b** an ailment, sickness **c** a misfortune, trouble ⟨*economic and social* ~s⟩

**I'll** /iel, ahl/ I will; I shall

,**ill-ad'vised** *adj* showing lack of proper consideration or sound advice ⟨*an* ~ *decision*⟩ – **ill-advisedly** *adv*

**ill at ease** *adj* feeling uneasy; uncomfortable

**illative** /i'laytiv/ *n* a word ⟨eg *therefore*⟩ or phrase ⟨eg *as a consequence*⟩ introducing an inference [LL *illativum* conclusion, fr neut of *illativus* inferential, fr L *illatus*, suppletive pp of *inferre* – more at INFER] – **illation** *n*, **illative** *adj*, **illatively** *adv*

,**ill-'bred** *adj* **1** having or showing bad upbringing; impolite **2** genetically inferior by reason of being the offspring of badly matched parents

,**ill-di'sposed** *adj* unfriendly, unsympathetic

**illegal** /i'leegl/ *adj* not according to or authorized by law; unlawful; *also* not sanctioned by official rules ⟨eg of a game⟩ [Fr or ML; Fr *illégal*, fr ML *illegalis*, fr L *in-* ¹in-+ *legalis* legal] – **illegally** *adv*, **illegality** /,ili'galəti/ *n*

**illegible** /i'lejəbl/ *adj* not legible; undecipherable ⟨~ *handwriting*⟩ △ eligible – **illegibly** *adv*, **illegibility** *n*

**illegitimacy** /,ili'jitiməsi/ *n* the quality or state of being illegitimate

**illegitimate** /,ili'jitimət/ *adj* **1** not recognized as lawful offspring; *specif* born of parents not married to each other **2** incorrectly deduced or inferred; illogical **3** departing from the regular; erratic **4a** not sanctioned by law; illegal **b** not authorized by good usage; *specif* substandard or incorrect in grammar – **illegitimately** *adv*

,**ill-'fated** *adj* suffering, leading to, or destined for misfortune; unlucky ⟨*an* ~ *expedition*⟩

,**ill-'favoured** *adj* **1** unattractive in physical appearance; *esp* having an ugly face **2** offensive, objectionable

,**ill-'gotten** *adj* acquired by illicit or improper means – chiefly in *ill-gotten gains*

,**ill-'humoured** *adj* surly, irritable

**illiberal** /,i'librəl/ *adj* not liberal: eg **a** lacking culture and refinement **b(1)** not broad-minded; bigoted **b(2)** opposed to liberalism **c** *archaic* lacking a liberal education **d** *archaic* not generous; stingy [MF or L; MF, fr L *illiberalis* ignoble, stingy, fr L *in-* ¹in-+ *liberalis* liberal] – **illiberally** *adv*, **illiberalness** *n*, **illiberality** *n*

**illiberalism** /i'librəliz(ə)m/ *n* opposition to or lack of liberalism

**illicit** /i'lisit/ *adj* not permitted; unlawful ⟨~ *love affairs*⟩ △ elicit [L *illicitus*, fr *in-* ¹in- + *licitus* lawful – more at LICIT] – **illicitly** *adv*

**illimitable** /i'limitəbl/ *adj, formal* without limits; measureless ⟨*the* ~ *reaches of space and time*⟩ – **illimitableness** *n*, **illimitably** *adv*, **illimitability** *n*

**Illinois** /'ilinoy, --'-/ *n, pl* **Illinois** /-noy, -noyz/ **1** *pl* a confederation of American Indian peoples of Illinois, Iowa, and Wisconsin **2** a member of any of the Illinois peoples [Fr, of Algonquian origin; akin to Shawnee *hilenawe* man]

**illiquid** /i'likwid/ *adj* **1** *of a financial asset* not being cash or readily convertible into cash ⟨~ *holdings*⟩ **2** *of an organization, company, etc* deficient in liquid assets – **illiquidity** *n*

**illite** /'iliet/ *n* (any of) a group of clay minerals formed by the decomposition of various SILICATE minerals [*Ill*inois, state of the USA + *-ite*] – **illitic** *adj*

**illiteracy** /i'lit(ə)rəsi/ *n* **1** the quality or state of being illiterate; *esp* inability to read or write **2** a mistake or crudity (eg in speaking) made by or typical of one who is illiterate

**illiterate** /i'lit(ə)rət/ *adj* **1** unable to read or write; *broadly* having little or no education – compare INNUMERATE **2a** showing or marked by a lack of familiarity with language and literature **b** violating approved patterns of speaking or writing ⟨*an* ~ *letter*⟩ **3** showing or marked by a lack of acquaintance with the fundamentals of a particular field of knowledge [L *illiteratus*, fr *in-* ¹in- + *litteratus* literate] – **illiterate** *n*, **illiterately** *adv*, **illiterateness** *n*

,**ill-'mannered** *adj* having bad manners; rude

,**ill-'natured** *adj* having a disagreeable disposition; cross, surly – **ill-naturedly** *adv*

**illness** /'ilnis/ *n* (an) unhealthy condition of body or mind

**illocutionary force** /,ilə'kyoohshənri/ *n* the linguistic act (eg assertion, promise, request) performed by a speaker – compare PERLOCUTIONARY FORCE [*il-* + *locution* + *-ary*]

**illogical** /i'lojikl/ *adj* **1** contrary to the principles of logic **2** devoid of logic; senseless – **illogically** *adv*, **illogicalness** *n*, **illogicality** *n*

,**ill-'sorted** *adj* not well matched ⟨*he and his wife were an* ~ *pair* – Lord Byron⟩

,**ill-'starred** *adj* ill-fated, unlucky ⟨*an* ~ *venture*⟩

,**ill-'tempered** *adj* ill-natured, quarrelsome – **ill-temperedly** *adv*

,**ill-'timed** *adj* badly timed; *esp* inopportune ⟨~ *remark*⟩

,**ill-'treat** *vt* to treat cruelly or improperly; maltreat **synonyms** see ¹MISUSE – **ill-treatment** *n*

**illume** /i'lyoohm/ *vt, poetic* to illuminate [short for *illumine*]

**illuminant** /i'l(y)oohminənt/ *n* an illuminating device or substance

¹**illuminate** /i'l(y)oohminayt/ *vt* **1a(1)** to cast light on; fill with light ⟨*a picture* ~d *by a spotlight*⟩ **a(2)** to brighten, light ⟨*her face* ~d *by a smile*⟩ **b** to enlighten spiritually or intellectually **2** to make clear; elucidate ⟨*facts which* ~ *a historical period*⟩ **3** to decorate, esp in the Middle Ages, (a manuscript) with elaborate embellishments of initial letters or with independent designs in the margins that are usu in gold, silver, and brilliant colours [L *illuminatus*, pp of *illuminare*, fr *in-* ²in- + *luminare* to light up, fr *lumin-*, *lumen* light – more at LUMINARY] – **illuminatingly** *adv*, **illuminative** *adj*, **illuminator** *n*

²**illuminate** /i'l(y)oohminət, -nayt/ *n, archaic* one having or claiming unusual enlightenment

**illuminati** /i,l(y)oohmi'nahti/ *n taking pl vb* **1** *cap* any of various groups claiming special religious enlightenment **2** people who are or who claim to be unusually enlightened [It & NL; It, fr NL, fr L, pl of *illuminatus*]

**illumination** /i,loohmi'naysh(ə)n, i,lyooh-/ *n* **1** illuminating or being illuminated: eg **1a** spiritual or intellectual enlightenment **b(1)** an act of lighting up **b(2) illuminations** *pl*, **illumination** decorative lighting or lighting effects ⟨*the Blackpool* ~s⟩ **c** decoration of a manuscript by the art of illuminating **2** the amount of light per unit area of a surface on which it falls **3** any of the decorative features used in the art of illuminating or in decorative lighting

**illumine** /i'l(y)oohmin/ *vt, poetic* to illuminate [ME *illuminen*, fr MF or L; MF *illuminer*, fr L *illuminare*] – **illuminable** *adj*

**Illuminism** /i'loohminiz(ə)m, i'lyooh-/ *n* beliefs or claims forming the doctrine or principles of Illuminati – **illuminist** *n*

**ill-use** /yoohz/ *vt* to treat harshly or unkindly; maltreat, abuse – **ill-usage** *n*

**illusion** /i'l(y)oohzh(ə)n/ *n* **1** a false impression or notion; misapprehension ⟨*I have no* ~s *about my ability*⟩ **2a(1)** a misleading image presented to the vision **a(2)** something that deceives or misleads intellectually **b(1)** perception of an object in such a way that it presents a misleading image to the eye ⟨*an optical* ~⟩ **b(2)** a hallucination **3** a fine plain transparent gauze or tulle usu made of silk and used for veils, trimmings, and dresses *synonyms* see DELUSION △ allusion [ME, fr MF, fr LL *illusion-, illusio*, fr L, act of mocking, fr *illusus*, pp of *illudere* to mock at, fr *in-* ²*in-* + *ludere* to play, mock – more at LUDICROUS] – **illusional** *adj*

**illusionary** /i'loohzhən(ə)ri, i'lyooh-/ *adj* illusory

**illusionism** /i'loohzhəniz(ə)m, i'lyooh-/ *n* the use of the artistic techniques of perspective or shading to create the illusion of reality, esp in a work of art; TROMPE L'OEIL – **illusionist** *n or adj*, **illusionistic** *adj*

**illusive** /i'l(y)oohsiv/ *adj* illusory – compare ELUSIVE – **illusively** *adv*, **illusiveness** *n*

**illusory** /i'l(y)oohsəri, -zəri/ *adj* based on or producing illusion; deceptive, unreal ⟨~ *hopes*⟩ *synonyms* see APPARENT *antonyms* real, actual, factual – **illusorily** *adv*, **illusoriness** *n*

**illustrate** /'iləstrayt/ *vt* **1a** to make clear by giving or serving as an example or instance; clarify ⟨*used many anecdotes to* ~ *his lecture on humour*⟩ **b** to provide with visual features intended to explain or decorate ⟨~ *a book*⟩ **2** to show clearly; demonstrate **3** *archaic* to make illustrious **4** *obs* to light up **5** *obs* to adorn ~ *vi* to give an example or instance [L *illustratus*, pp of *illustrare*, fr *in-* ²*in-* + *lustrare* to purify, make bright – more at LUSTRE] – **illustrator** *n*

**illustration** /,ilə'straysh(ə)n/ *n* **1** illustrating or being illustrated **2** something that serves to illustrate: eg **2a** an example that explains or clarifies something **b** a picture or diagram that helps to make something clear or attractive *synonyms* see ¹INSTANCE – **illustrational** *adj*

**illustrative** /'iləstrətiv, -stray-/ *adj* serving or intended to illustrate ⟨~ *examples*⟩ – **illustratively** *adv*

**illustrious** /i'lustri·əs/ *adj* marked by distinction or renown; eminent [L *illustris*, prob back-formation fr *illustrare*] – **illustriously** *adv*, **illustriousness** *n*

**illuviation** /i,loohvi'aysh(ə)n/ *n* the deposition and accumulation in a soil layer (HORIZON) of dissolved or suspended materials removed and transported from an upper soil layer by rainwater – compare ELUVIATION [²*in-* + *-luviation* (as in *eluviation*)] – **illuviate** *vi*

**illuvium** /i'loohviəm/ *n, pl* **-viums, -via** /-viə/ material removed by the action of liquid from one soil layer (HORIZON) and deposited in a lower layer [NL, fr *in-* + *-luvium* (as in *alluvium*)] – **illuvial** *adj*

**ill will** *n* unfriendly feeling

**Illyrian** /i'liriən/ *n* **1** a native or inhabitant of ancient Illyria **2** the extinct and almost unknown Indo-European languages of the Illyrians [*Illyria*, ancient country in S Europe] – **Illyrian** *adj*

**ilmenite** /'ilməniet/ *n* a common iron-black mineral, FeTiO₃, composed of iron, titanium, and oxygen [Ger *ilmenit*, fr *Ilmen*, range of the Ural mountains in USSR]

**Ilocano, Ilokano** /,eeloh'kahnoh/ *n, pl* **Ilocanos, Ilokanos,** *esp collectively* **Ilocano, Ilokano** **1** a major people of northern Luzon in the Philippines; *also* their language **2** a member of the Ilocano

**im-** /im-/ – see IN-

**I'm** /iem/ I am

¹**image** /'imij/ *n* **1** a representation (eg a statue) of a person or thing **2a** the optical counterpart of an object produced by a lens, mirror, etc or an electronic device **b** a likeness of an object produced on a photographic material **3a** exact likeness; semblance ⟨*God created man in his own* ~ – Gen 1:27 (RSV)⟩ **b** a person who strikingly resembles another specified person ⟨*he is the* ~ *of his father*⟩ **4** a typical example or embodiment (eg of a quality); incarnation ⟨*he is the* ~ *of goodness*⟩ **5a** a mental picture of something not actually present; an impression **b** an idea, concept **6** a vivid or graphic representation or description **7** FIGURE OF SPEECH; *esp* one (eg a metaphor or simile) involving a likeness **8** a conception (eg of a person, institution, or nation) created in the minds of people, esp the general public, often by manipulation of newspapers, television, etc by public relations experts ⟨*a politician worried about his public* ~⟩ ⟨*a corporate* ~ *of warmth and humanity*⟩ **9** *maths* an element in a set (the RANGE) onto which an element of another set (the DOMAIN) is mapped by a mathematical function [ME, fr OF, short for *imagene*, fr L *imagin-, imago*; akin to L *imitari* to imitate]

²**image** *vt* **1** to describe or portray in language, esp vividly **2** to reflect, mirror **3a** to create a representation of; *also* to form an image of **b** to represent symbolically

**image converter** *n* IMAGE TUBE

**image orthicon** *n* a highly sensitive television CAMERA TUBE (part of camera where optical images are converted into electrical impulses) in which electrons emitted from a surface in proportion to the intensity of light are focussed onto a target from which greater numbers of electrons are emitted, leaving the target with an intensified pattern of electrostatic charge which is then scanned by an electron beam – compare VIDICON

**imagery** /'imij(ə)ri/ *n* **1** (the art of making) images **2** language rich in metaphor and simile; *esp* such language used in verse **3** mental images; *esp* the products of imagination

**image tube** *n* an electronic device in which an intensified or visible image of electromagnetic radiation (eg visible or infrared light or X-rays) is produced on a fluorescent screen

**imaginable** /i'majinəbl/ *adj* capable of being imagined; conceivable – **imaginableness** *n*, **imaginably** *adv*

¹**imaginal** /i'majinl/ *adj* of imagination, images, or imagery [*imagine* + *-al*]

²**imaginal** *adj* of the insect imago [NL *imagin-, imago*]

**imaginary** /i'majin(ə)ri/ *adj* **1** existing only in imagination; lacking factual reality **2** *maths* of or containing an IMAGINARY NUMBER – **imaginarily** *adv*, **imaginariness** *n*

**imaginary number** *n* (the product of a REAL NUMBER and) the positive square root of minus one $(+\sqrt{-1})$

**imaginary part** *n, maths* the part of a COMPLEX NUMBER (eg *3i* in *2 + 3i*) that contains the IMAGINARY NUMBER

**imagination** /i,maji'naysh(ə)n/ *n* **1** the act or power of forming a mental image of something not present to the senses or never before known or wholly perceived in reality **2** creative ability **3a** a creation of the mind; *esp* an idealized or poetic creation **b** a fanciful or empty notion

*synonyms* **Imagination, fancy,** and **fantasy** are usually contrasted when they apply to aesthetic, especially literary, contexts. Here, **imagination** stresses the power to convey or imagine what is real or could be real, depicting not only outward appearance, but also feelings and thoughts, even where situations and characters are invented. **Fancy,** on the other hand, delights in inventing unreal situations or beings. The **imagination** of Shakespeare can convey the suffering of King Lear, but the enchanted forest of *A Midsummer Night's Dream* is a product of his **fancy.** Fantasy goes even further from reality, and may be bizarre, extravagant, and wildly fanciful ⟨**fantasy** *worlds of science fiction*⟩.

**imaginative** /i'maj(i)nətiv/ *adj* **1** of or characterized by imagination **2** given to imagining; having a lively imagination **3** of images; *esp* showing a command of imagery – **imaginatively** *adv*, **imaginativeness** *n*

**imagine** /i'maj(ə)n/ *vt* **1** to form a mental image of (something not present) **2** to suppose, think ⟨*I* ~ *it will rain*⟩ **3** to believe without sufficient basis; fancy ⟨~s *himself to be indispensable*⟩ ~ *vi* to use the imagination □ often with a clause as object ⟨*can't* ~ *where they went*⟩ [ME *imaginen*, fr MF *imaginer*, fr L *imaginari*, fr *imagin-, imago* image]

**imagism** /'imi,jiz(ə)m/ *n, often cap* an early 20th-century movement in poetry, in England and America, advocating free verse and the expression of ideas and emotions through clear precise images – **imagist** *n*, **imagist, imagistic** *adj*, **imagistically** *adv*

**imago** /i'maygoh/ *n, pl* **imagoes, imagines** /i'mayjineez, -'mah-, -nayz/ **1** an insect in its final adult sexually mature and typically winged state **2** *psychology* a subconscious idealized mental image of a person, esp a parent, formed usu in childhood [NL, fr L, image]

**imam** /i'mahm, '--/ *n* **1** the leader of prayer in a mosque **2** *cap* a Shiite leader held to be a divinely appointed sinless infallible successor of Muhammad **3** CALIPH (Muslim ruler); *also* any of various Islamic doctors of law or theology [Ar *imām*]

**imamate** /i'mahmayt, -mət/ *n, often cap* **1** the office of an imam **2** the region or country ruled over by an imam

**imaret** /i'mahret/ *n* an inn or hospice in Turkey [Turk, fr Ar *'imārah* building]

**imbalance** /im'baləns/ *n* lack of balance: eg **a** a lack of functional balance in a physiological system ⟨*hormonal* ~⟩ **b** lack of balance between segments of a country's economy **c** a numerical disproportion (eg between males and females in a population or racial elements in a school)

**imbecile** /'imbəseel, -siel/ *n* **1** MENTAL DEFECTIVE **2** a fool, idiot [Fr *imbécile*, fr *imbécile* weak, weak-minded, fr L *imbecillus*, prob fr *in-* ¹*in-* + *baculum* stick, staff] – **imbecile, imbecilic** *adj*, **imbecilely** *adv*

**imbecility** /ˌimbə'siləti/ *n* 1 being imbecilic or an imbecile 2 utter foolishness or nonsense; *also* an instance of such foolishness

**imbed** /im'bed/ *vb*, **-dd-** to embed

**imbibe** /im'bieb/ *vt* 1 to receive into the mind and retain; assimilate ⟨~ *moral principles*⟩ 2 to drink 3 to take in or up; absorb, assimilate ⟨*a sponge* ~s *moisture*⟩ ~ *vi* 1 DRINK 2 2a to take in liquid **b** to absorb or assimilate moisture, gas, light, or heat [L *imbibere* to drink in, conceive, fr *in-* + *bibere* to drink – more at POTABLE] – **imbiber** *n*

**imbibition** /ˌimbi'bish(ə)n/ *n* the act or action of imbibing; *esp* the taking up of a liquid (e g water) by a COLLOIDAL system (mixture having particles of one substance suspended in another) resulting in swelling – **imbibitional** *adj*

**imbosom** /im'booz(ə)m/ *vt* to embosom

**¹imbricate** /'imbrikət, -kayt/ *adj* having or being tiles, scales, etc that overlap each other in regular order (LL *imbricatus*, pp of *imbricare* to cover with pantiles, fr L *imbric-, imbrex* pantile, fr *imbr-, imber* rain; akin to Gk *ombros* rain] – **imbricately** *adv*

**²imbricate** /'imbrikayt/ *vb* to overlap, esp in regular order

**imbrication** /ˌimbri'kaysh(ə)n/ *n* 1 the state of being imbricated 2 a decoration or pattern resembling overlapping tiles, scales, etc

**imbroglio** /im'brohlioh/ *n, pl* **imbroglios** 1 a confused mass ⟨*an* ~ *of papers and books*⟩ 2a an intricate or complicated situation (e g in a play, film, or novel) **b** a confused or complicated misunderstanding or disagreement [It, fr *imbrogliare* to entangle, fr MF *embrouiller* – more at EMBROIL]

**imbrown** /im'brown/ *vt* to embrown

**imbrue** /im'brooh/ *vt, formal* to stain, drench ⟨*the soldiers* ~d *their hands in the blood* – Edward Gibbon) [ME *enbrewen*, prob fr MF *abrevrer, embevrer* to soak, drench, deriv of L *bibere* to drink]

**imbrute** /im'brooht/ *vb, formal* to sink or degrade to the level of a brute

**imbue** /im'byooh/ *vt* 1 to tinge or dye deeply 2 to cause to become permeated; infuse ⟨*a man* ~d *with a strong sense of duty*⟩ [L *imbuere*]

**imidazole** /ˌimi'dazohl, -'day-, ˌimidə'zohl/ *n* (any of various compounds derived from) a chemical BASE, $C_3H_4N_2$, with a characteristic HETEROCYCLIC (containing a ring of atoms not all of which are carbon) structure, that is used esp in the synthesis of other organic chemical compounds [ISV, fr *imide* + *azole*]

**imide** /'imied/ *n* any of a class of chemical compounds containing the chemical group NH, that are derived from ammonia by replacement of two hydrogen atoms by one or two metal atoms or acid groups – compare AMIDE [ISV, alter. of *amide*] – **imidic** *adj*

**imido** /'imidoh/ *adj* of or containing the chemical group NH or a substituted group NR united to one or two chemical groups of acid character

**imine** /i'meen, '--/ *n* any of a class of chemical compounds containing the chemical group NH, that are derived from ammonia by replacement of two hydrogen atoms by a nonacid organic chemical group (e g an ETHYL group) [ISV, alter. of *amine*]

**imino** /'iminoh/ *adj* of or containing the chemical group NH or a substituted group NR united to a nonacid chemical group

**imipramine** /i'miprəmeen/ *n* an antidepressant drug, $C_{19}H_{24}N_2$ [*imide* + *propyl* + *amine*]

**imitate** /'imitayt/ *vt* 1 to follow as a pattern, model, or example 2 to produce a copy of; reproduce 3 to be or appear like; resemble 4 to mimic, take off ⟨*can* ~ *his father's booming voice*⟩ [L *imitatus*, pp of *imitari* – more at IMAGE] – **imitator** *n*, **imitable** *adj*

**¹imitation** /ˌimi'taysh(ə)n/ *n* 1 an act or instance of imitating 2 something produced as a copy; a counterfeit 3 the repetition in one musical part of the melodic theme, phrase, or motive previously found in another musical part – compare OSTINATO, SEQUENCE 2c 4 *psychology* the assumption of the modes of behaviour observed in other individuals – **imitational** *adj*

**²imitation** *adj* made in imitation of something else that is usu genuine and of better quality; not real ⟨~ *leather*⟩

**imitative** /'imitətiv/ *adj* 1a marked by or given to imitation ⟨*acting is an* ~ *art*⟩ **b** reproducing a natural sound; ONOMATOPOEIC ⟨"*hiss*" *is an* ~ *word*⟩ **c** exhibiting mimicry 2 imitating something superior; counterfeit – **imitatively** *adv*, **imitativeness** *n*

**immaculate** /i'makyoolət/ *adj* 1 having no stain or blemish; pure 2 free from flaw or error 3a spotlessly clean ⟨*his nails were* ~⟩ **b** *biology* having no coloured spots or marks ⟨*petals* ~⟩ [ME *immaculat*, fr L *immaculatus*, fr *in-* ¹*in-* + *maculatus*,

pp of *maculare* to stain, fr *macula* spot, stain] – **immaculacy** *n*, **immaculately** *adv*, **immaculateness** *n*

**Immaculate Conception** *n* (December 8 observed as a Roman Catholic festival in commemoration of) the conception of the Virgin Mary, held in Roman Catholic dogma to have preserved her soul free from original sin

**immanent** /'imənənt/ *adj* 1 existing as an inner force or principle; indwelling 2 *philosophy* having existence only in the mind 3 *esp of God* pervading nature or the souls of men – compare TRANSCENDENT [LL *immanent-, immanens*, prp of *immanēre* to remain in place, fr L *in-* ²*in-* + *manēre* to remain – more at MANSION] – **immanence, immanency** *n*, **immanently** *adv*

**immaterial** /ˌimə'tiəri·əl/ *adj* 1 not consisting of matter; incorporeal 2 of no great consequence; unimportant ⟨*that is a minor point,* ~ *to the argument*⟩ [ME *immateriel*, fr MF, fr LL *immaterialis*, fr L *in-* ¹*in-* + LL *materialis* material] – **immaterially** *adv*, **immaterialness** *n*, **immateriality** *n*

**immaterialism** /ˌimə'tiəriəliz(ə)m/ *n, philosophy* a theory that the reality of matter consists in its being conceived by the mind – **immaterialist** *n*

**immature** /ˌimə'tyooə/ *adj* 1a lacking complete growth, differentiation, or development ⟨*a thin* ~ *soil*⟩ ⟨~ *fruit*⟩ **b(1)** not having arrived at a definitive form or state; crude, unfinished ⟨*a vigorous but* ~ *school of art*⟩ **b(2)** *of a land surface or topographic feature (e g a valley)* in an early stage of erosion; YOUTHFUL 3 **c** exhibiting less than an expected degree of maturity; lacking judgment; unstable ⟨*emotionally* ~ *adults*⟩ 2 *archaic* premature □ compare PREMATURE **synonyms** see ¹YOUNG [L *immaturus*, fr *in-* ¹*in-* + *maturus* mature] – **immature** *n*, **immaturely** *adv*, **immatureness** *n*, **immaturity** *n*

**immeasurable** /i'mezh(ə)rəbl/ *adj* incapable of being measured; *broadly* indefinitely extensive – **immeasurableness** *n*, **immeasurably** *adv*

**immediacy** /i'meedi·əsi/ *n* 1 the quality or state of being immediate; *esp* freedom from an intervening agent 2 *usu pl* something requiring immediate attention ⟨*the immediacies of life*⟩

**immediate** /i'meedi·ət, -dyət/ *adj* 1a acting or being without any intervening agency or factor; direct ⟨*the* ~ *cause of death*⟩ **b** *philosophy* involving or derived from a single premise ⟨*an* ~ *inference*⟩ 2 next in line or relationship ⟨*only the* ~ *family was present*⟩ 3a occurring at once; instant ⟨*an* ~ *reply*⟩ **b** of or near to the present time ⟨*too busy with* ~ *concerns to worry about the future*⟩ 4 in close or direct physical proximity ⟨*the* ~ *neighbourhood*⟩ 5 directly touching or concerning a person or thing ⟨*the child's* ~ *world is the classroom*⟩ [LL *immediatus*, fr L *in-* ¹*in-* + LL *mediatus* intermediate – more at MEDIATE] – **immediateness** *n*

**immediate constituent** *n* any of the meaningful constituents directly forming a larger linguistic construction ⟨*subject and predicate are the* immediate constituents *of a sentence*⟩

**¹immediately** /-li/ *adv* 1 in direct relation or proximity; directly ⟨*the parties* ~ *involved in the case*⟩ ⟨*the house* ~ *beyond this one*⟩ 2 without delay

**²immediately** *conj* as soon as

**immedicable** /i'medikəbl/ *adj, formal* incurable [L *immedicabilis*, fr *in-* ¹*in-* + *medicabilis* medicable] – **immedicably** *adv*

**immemorial** /ˌimi'mawri·əl/ *adj* extending beyond the reach of memory, record, or tradition ⟨*existing from time* ~⟩ [prob fr Fr *immémorial*, fr MF, fr *in-* + *memorial*] – **immemorially** *adv*

**immense** /i'mens/ *adj* very great, esp in size, degree, or extent; vast, huge ⟨*the* ~ *and boundless universe*⟩ **synonyms** see HUGE **antonym** minute [MF, fr L *immensus* immeasurable, fr *in-* ¹*in-* + *mensus*, pp of *metiri* to measure – more at MEASURE ] – **immensely** *adv*, **immenseness** *n*, **immensity** *n*

**immensurable** /i'mensh(ə)rəbl/ *adj, formal* immeasurable [LL *immensurabilis*, fr L *in-* ¹*in-*+ LL *mensurabilis* measurable]

**immerge** /i'muhj/ *vi* to plunge into or immerse oneself in something [L *immergere*] – **immergence** *n*

**immerse** /i'muhs/ *vt* 1 to plunge into something that surrounds or covers; *esp* to plunge or dip into a liquid 2 to baptize by complete submersion 3 to engross, absorb ⟨*completely* ~d *in his work*⟩ [L *immersus*, pp of *immergere*, fr *in-* ²*in-* + *mergere* to merge] – **immersible** *adj*

**immersed** /i'muhst/ *adj, of a plant* growing wholly under water

**immersion** /i'muhsh(ə)n, -zh(ə)n/ *n* 1 immersing or being immersed; *specif* baptism by complete submersion of the person

**2** *astronomy* disappearance of a celestial body behind or into the shadow of another

**immersion heater** *n* an electric apparatus for heating a liquid in which it is immersed; *esp* an electric water-heater fixed inside a domestic hot-water storage tank

**immesh** /i'mesh/ *vt* to enmesh

**immigrant** /'imigrənt/ *n* one who or that which immigrates: **a** a person who comes to a country to take up permanent residence **b** a plant or animal that becomes established in an area where it was previously unknown *synonyms* see EMIGRANT – **immigrant** *adj*

**immigrate** /'imigrayt/ *vi* to enter and usu become established; *esp* to come into a country of which one is not a native for permanent residence ~ *vt* to bring in or send as immigrants *synonyms* see EMIGRANT [L *immigratus*, pp of *immigrare* to remove, go in, fr *in-* ²*in-* + *migrare* to migrate] – **immigration** *n*, **immigrational** *adj*

**imminence** /'iminəns/ *n* **1** **imminence, imminency** the quality or state of being imminent **2** something imminent; *esp* impending evil or danger

**imminent** /'iminənt/ *adj* about to take place; *esp* impending, threatening ⟨*was in* ~ *danger of being run over*⟩ △ eminent [L *imminent-, imminens*, prp of *imminēre* to project, threaten, fr *in-* ²*in-* + *-minēre* (akin to L *mont-, mons* mountain) – more at MOUNT] – **imminently** *adv*, **imminentness** *n*

**immiscible** /i'misəbl/ *adj* incapable of being mixed – used technically – **immiscibly** *adv*, **immiscibility** *n*

**immitigable** /i'mitigəbl/ *adj*, *formal* incapable of being mitigated [LL *immitigabilis*, fr L *in-* ¹*in-* + *mitigare* to mitigate] – **immitigableness** *n*, **immitigably** *adv*

**immittance** /i'mit(ə)ns/ *n* electrical ADMITTANCE (property of a circuit of allowing current flow) or IMPEDANCE (opposition of a circuit to current flow) [*impedance* + ad*mittance*]

**immobile** /i'mohbiel/ *adj* **1** incapable of being moved; fixed **2** not moving; motionless ⟨*keep the patient* ~⟩ [ME *in-mobill*, fr L *immobilis*, fr *in-* ¹*in-* + *mobilis* mobile] – **immobility** *n*

**immobil·ize, -ise** /i'mohbiliez/ *vt* to make immobile: e g **a** to prevent freedom of movement or effective use of ⟨*the planes were* ~d *by bad weather*⟩ **b** to reduce or eliminate motion of (the body or a part) by mechanical means or by strict bed rest **c** to withhold (money or capital) from circulation – **immobilizer** *n*, **immobilization** *n*

**immoderate** /i'mod(ə)rət/ *adj* lacking in moderation; excessive ⟨~ *pride*⟩ ⟨*an* ~ *appetite*⟩ [ME *immoderat*, fr L *immoderatus*, fr *in-* ¹*in-* + *moderatus*, pp of *moderare* to moderate] – **immoderacy** *n*, **immoderately** *adv*, **immoderateness** *n*, **immoderation** *n*

**immodest** /i'modist/ *adj* not modest; *specif* not conforming to standards of sexual propriety [L *immodestus*, fr *in-* ¹*in-* + *modestus* modest] – **immodestly** *adv*, **immodesty** *n*

**immolate** /'imohlayt/ *vt* **1** to offer in sacrifice; *esp* to kill as a sacrificial victim **2** to kill, destroy [L *immolatus*, pp of *immolare*, fr *in-* ²*in-* + *mola* mill, meal; fr the custom of sprinkling victims with sacrificial meal] – **immolator** *n*, **immolation** *n*

**immoral** /i'morəl/ *adj* not moral; *esp* not conforming to conventional moral standards (e g in sexual matters) – compare AMORAL – **immorally** *adv*

**immoralist** /i'morəlist/ *n* an advocate of immorality

**immorality** /,imə'raləti/ *n* **1** the quality or state of being immoral; *esp* unchastity **2** an immoral act or practice

**¹immortal** /i'mawtl/ *adj* **1** exempt from death ⟨*the* ~ *gods*⟩ **2** of or connected with immortality ⟨~ *longings*⟩ **3** enduring forever; imperishable ⟨~ *fame*⟩ [ME, fr L *immortalis*, fr *in-* ¹*in-* + *mortalis* mortal] – **immortalize** *vt*, **immortally** *adv*

**²immortal** *n* **1a** one exempt from death **b** *pl, often cap* the gods of the ancient Greeks and Romans **2** a person of lasting fame

**immortality** /,imaw'taləti/ *n* the quality or state of being immortal: **a** eternal existence **b** lasting fame

**immortelle** /,imaw'tel/ *n* EVERLASTING **3** (flower that keeps its colour and form when dried) [Fr, fr fem of *immortel* immortal, fr L *immortalis*]

**immotile** /i'mohtiel/ *adj* lacking motility – used esp of an organism or of one of its parts – **immotility** *n*

**¹immovable** /i'moohvəbl/ *adj* **1** incapable of being moved; *broadly* not moving or not intended to be moved **2a** steadfast, unyielding **b** incapable of being moved emotionally △ irremovable – **immovableness, immovability** *n*, **immovably** *adv*

**²immovable** *n* **1** one who or that which cannot be moved **2** *pl* REAL ESTATE

**immune** /i'myoohn/ *adj* **1a** free, exempt ⟨~ *from further taxation*⟩ **b** marked by protection ⟨*some criminal leaders are* ~ *from arrest*⟩ **2** not susceptible or responsive ⟨~ *to all pleas*⟩; *esp* having a high degree of resistance to a disease ⟨~ *to diphtheria*⟩ **3a** having or producing ANTIBODIES in response to a corresponding ANTIGEN (foreign substance entering a body) ⟨*an* ~ *serum*⟩ **b** produced in response to the presence of a corresponding ANTIGEN ⟨~ *agglutinins*⟩ **c** concerned with, involving, or bringing about immunity ⟨~ *globulins*⟩ [L *immunis*, fr *in-* ¹*in-* + *munia* services, obligations; akin to L *munus* service] – **immune** *n*

*usage* One is immune *from* taxation or arrest, immune *to* disease.

**immune response** *n* the reaction of a body to the introduction of a foreign substance (ANTIGEN) whereby ANTIBODIES are produced which bind onto and destroy the antigen

**immunity** /i'myoohnəti/ *n* the quality or state of being immune; *specif* a condition of being able to resist the development of a disease-causing parasite, esp a microorganism, or counteract the effects of its products

*synonyms* The chief sense of **immunity** is now "lack of susceptibility to disease", but it also means "freedom from obligation"; **impunity** chiefly means "freedom from punishment".

**immun·ize, -ise** /'imyooniez/ *vt* to make immune – **immunization** *n*

**immuno-** *comb form* immunity; immunology and ⟨*immunobiology*⟩ ⟨*immunogenetics*⟩ [ISV, fr *immune*]

**immunoadsorbent** /,imyoonoh·əd'zawb(ə)nt/ *n* an insoluble chemical compound consisting of an antibody and another substance (e g cellulose) that can selectively remove a specific ANTIGEN (foreign substance activating antibody production) from solution and is used esp in biochemistry (e g in the separation of CELL MEMBRANE fragments from a mixture of broken cell fragments)

**immunoassay** /,imyoonoh·ə'say, ,imyoonoh'asay/ *n* the identification and measurement of the concentration of a substance (e g a protein) through its capacity to act as an ANTIGEN (foreign substance activating antibody production) in the presence of specific antibodies that react with it – **immunoassayable** *adj*

**immunochemistry** /,imyoonoh'keməstri/ *n* a branch of chemistry that deals with the chemical aspects of immunology and immunological products (e g antibodies) [ISV] – **immunochemical** *adj*, **immunochemically** *adv*

**immunocytochemistry** /,imyoonoh,sietoh'kemistri/ *n* a branch of chemistry that deals with the chemical aspects of cells (e g lymphocytes) concerned with immunity, esp antibody formation – **immunocytochemical** *adj*, **immunocytochemically** *adv*

**immunodepression** /,imyoonoh·di'presh(ə)n/ *n* reduction in the responses of the immune system – **immunodepressant** *n*, **immunodepressive** *adj*

**immunodiffusion** /,imyoonoh·di'fyoohzh(ə)n/ *n* the separation of ANTIGENS (foreign substances activating antibody production) into discrete parts through differences in their ability to pass through a filter or diffuse through a gelatinous or similar medium

**immunoelectrophoresis** /,imyoonoh·i,lektrəfə'reesis/ *n, pl* **immunoelectrophoreses** /-seez/ separation of proteins by ELECTROPHORESIS (movement of particles in a gas or liquid under the influence of an electric current) followed by their identification through specific immunological reactions – **immunoelectrophoretic** *adj*, **immunoelectrophoretically** *adv*

**immunofluorescence** /,imyoonoh·flə'res(ə)ns, -flooə-/ *n* **1** ANTIBODY (substance produced by the body to counteract an antigen) detection by use of a fluorescent dye to stain the antibody **2** the fluorescence emitted by a stained antibody – **immunofluorescent** *adj*

**immunogen** /i'myoohnəjən, -jen/ *n* an ANTIGEN (foreign substance that enters a body) that produces an IMMUNE RESPONSE (e g antibody formation) [fr *Immunogen*, a trademark]

**immunogenesis** /,imyoonoh'jenəsis/ *n* the production of immunity – **immunogenic** *adj*, **immunogenically** *adv*, **immunogenicity** *n*

**immunogenetics** /,imyoonoh·jə'netiks/ *n taking sing vb* a branch of immunology concerned with the interrelations of heredity, disease, and the immune system and its components (e g antibodies) – **immunogenetic** *adj*, **immunogenetically** *adv*

**immunoglobulin** /,imyoonoh'globyoolin/ *n* a protein (e g an antibody) that is made up of linked units (LIGHT and HEAVY CHAINS) of AMINO ACIDS and usu binds specifically to a particular ANTIGEN (foreign substance activating antibody production)

**immunohaematology** /ˌimyoonohˌheemə'toləji/ *n* a branch of immunology that deals with the immunological properties of blood

**immunology** /ˌimyoo'noləji/ *n* a branch of biology that deals with the phenomena and causes of immunity [ISV] – **immunologist** *n*, **immunologic, immunological** *adj*, **immunologically** *adv*

**immunopathology** /ˌimyoonohpə'tho:ləji/ *n* a branch of medicine that deals with immunological abnormalities and disease – **immunopathologist** *n*, **immunopathologic, immunopathological** *adj*

**immunoreactive** /'imyoonoh·riˌaktiv/ *adj* reacting to particular substances (ANTIGENS or HAPTENS) that either stimulate the production of antibodies or react with them (*serum ~ insulin*) – **immunoreactivity** *n*

**immunosuppression** /ˌimyoonoh·sə'presh(ə)n/ *n* suppression (e g by drugs) of natural IMMUNE RESPONSES (e g production of antibodies) – **immunosuppress** *vt*, **immunosuppressant** *n or adj*, **immunosuppressive** *adj*

**immunotherapy** /-'therəpi/ *n* treatment of or preventative measures against disease by means of administration of ANTIGENS (foreign substances activating antibody production) or antigenic preparations [ISV]

**immure** /i'myooə/ *vt* **1a** to enclose (as if) within walls **b** to imprison **2** to build into a wall; *esp* to entomb in a wall [ML *immurare*, fr L *in-* ²in- + *murus* wall – more at MUNITION] – **immurement** *n*

**immutable** /i'myoohtəbl/ *adj* not capable of or susceptible to change [ME, fr L *immutabilis*, fr *in-* ¹in- + *mutabilis* changeable, fr *mutare* to change] – **immutableness** *n*, **immutably** *adv*, **immutability** *n*

¹**imp** /imp/ *n* **1a** a small devil or demon **b** a mischievous child; a scamp **2** *obs* a shoot, bud; *also* a graft [ME *impe*, fr OE *impa*, fr *impian* to imp]

²**imp** *vt*, *archaic* to graft or repair (e g a falcon's wing or tail) with a feather to improve flight [ME *impen*, fr OE *impian*; akin to OHG *impfōn* to graft; both from a prehistoric WGmc word derived fr L *in-* ²in- + *putare* to prune – more at PAVE]

¹**impact** /im'pakt/ *vt* **1** to fix or press firmly (as if) by packing or wedging **2a** to have an impact on; impinge on **b** to (cause to) strike forcefully ~ *vi* **1** to have an impact **2** to impinge or make contact, esp forcefully [L *impactus*, pp of *impingere* to push against – more at IMPINGE] – **impactive** *adj*

²**impact** /'impakt/ *n* **1a** an impinging or striking, esp of one body against another **b** a violent contact or collision; *also* the impetus produced (as if) by a collision (*caught the full ~ of the blow*) **2** a strong or powerful effect or impression (*the ~ of modern science on our society*)

**impacted** /im'paktid/ *adj* **1** *of a tooth* obstructed by a bone, other teeth, or lack of space in the jaw and so unable to grow into the proper position **2** *of a fracture* having the broken ends wedged together

**impaction** /im'paksh(ə)n/ *n* the act of becoming or the state of being impacted; *esp* lodgment of something (e g faeces) in a passage or cavity of the body

**impair** /im'peə/ *vt* to diminish in quality, strength, or amount; injure, weaken (*his health was ~ed by overwork*) (*the strike seriously ~ed community services*) **synonyms** see INJURE [ME *empeiren*, fr MF *empeirer*, fr (assumed) VL *impejorare*, fr L *in-* ²in- + LL *pejorare* to make worse – more at PEJORATIVE] – **impairer** *n*, **impairment** *n*

**impaired** /im'peəd/ *adj*, *Can*, *of a driver or driving* under the influence of alcohol or narcotics (*being convicted for the fourth time in four years of ~ driving resulted in a four-month jail term* – *Sudbury Star (Ontario)*)

**impala** /im'pahlə/ *n* a large brownish African antelope (*Aepyceros melampus*) of which the male has slender horns with a configuration resembling the shape of a lyre [Zulu]

**impale** /im'payl/ *vt* **1** to pierce (as if) with something pointed; *esp* to torture or kill by fixing on a sharp stake **2** to join together (two COATS OF ARMS) so that they appear side by side on a heraldic shield divided in half vertically [MF & ML; MF *empaler*, fr ML *impalare*, fr L *in-* ²in- + *palus* stake – more at POLE] – **impalement** *n*

**impalpable** /im'palpəbl/ *adj* **1a** incapable of being sensed by touch; intangible (*the ~ aura of power that emanated from*

*him* – Osbert Sitwell) **b** containing no grains or grit; very fine (*rock worn to an ~ powder*) **2** not easily discerned or grasped by the mind [¹*in-* + *palpable*] – **impalpably** *adv*, **impalpability** *n*

**impanel** /im'panl/ *vt* to empanel

**imparadise** /im'parədies/ *vt*, *chiefly poetic* **1** to make blissfully happy; enrapture **2** to make (a place) like a paradise [²*in-* + *paradise*]

**imparisyllabic** /im,parisi'labik/ *adj*, *of a noun or verb* having differing numbers of syllables in different grammatical forms (INFLECTIONS) [L *impar* unequal + E *syllabic*]

**imparity** /im'parəti/ *n*, *formal* inequality, disparity [LL *imparitas*, fr L *impar* unequal, fr *in-* ¹in- + *par* equal]

**impart** /im'paht/ *vt* **1** to convey, transmit (*his assurance ~ed authority to his words*) (*the flavour ~ed by herbs*) **2** to make known; disclose **synonyms** see ¹REVEAL [MF & L; MF *impartir*, fr L *impartire*, fr *in-* ²in- + *partire* to divide, part] – **impartable** *adj*, **impartation, impartment** *n*, **imparter** *n*

**impartial** /im'pahsh(ə)l/ *adj* favouring neither one side nor another; not biased **synonyms** see ¹FAIR **antonyms** partial, biased **impartially** *adv*, **impartiality** *n*

**impartible** /im'pahtəbl/ *adj*, *law* not partible; not subject to partition or division (*an ~ inheritance*) [LL *impartibilis*, fr L *in-* ¹in- + LL *partibilis* divisible, fr L *partire*] – **impartibly** *adv*

**impassable** /im'pahsəbl/ *adj* incapable of being passed, traversed, or surmounted – **impassableness** *n*, **impassably** *adv*, **impassability** *n*

**impasse** /'ampas; *also* 'impas *(Fr* ɛ̃pas*)* USE the pron 'impas *is disliked by some speakers*/ *n* **1** a predicament from which there is no obvious escape **2** a deadlock [Fr, fr *in-* ¹in-+ *passer* to pass]

**impassible** /im'pasəbl/ *adj* **1** *Christianity* incapable of suffering or of experiencing pain or injury **2** *formal* incapable of feeling or emotion; impassive △ impassable [ME, fr MF or LL; MF, fr LL *impassibilis*, fr L *in-* ¹in- + LL *passibilis* passible] – **impassibly** *adv*, **impassibility** *n*

**impassion** /im'pash(ə)n/ *vt* to arouse the feelings or passions of [It *impassionare*, fr *in-* ²in- + *passione* passion, fr LL *passion-*, *passio*]

**impassioned** /im'pash(ə)nd/ *adj* filled with passion or zeal; showing great warmth or intensity of feeling

**impassive** /im'pasiv/ *adj* **1a** not susceptible to physical feeling; inanimate **b** incapable of or not susceptible to emotion; apathetic **2** showing no feeling or emotion; expressionless [¹*in-* + *passive*] – **impassively** *adv*, **impassiveness** *n*, **impassivity** *n*

**impasto** /im'pastoh/ *n* the technique or practice of applying pigment thickly in painting; *also* the body of pigment so applied [It, fr *impastare* to make into a paste or crust, fr *in-* ²in-+ *pasta* paste, fr LL] – **impastoed** *adj*

**impatiens** /im'payshi,enz/ *n* BALSAM 2b (type of plant) [NL, genus name, fr L, impatient; fr the bursting of its ripe seed pods at a touch]

**impatient** /im'paysh(ə)nt/ *adj* **1a** not patient; restless or quickly roused to anger or exasperation **b** intolerant (*~ of delay*) **2** showing or caused by a lack of patience (*an ~ reply*) **3** eagerly desirous; anxious (*~ to see her boyfriend*) [ME *impacient*, fr MF, fr L *impatient-*, *impatiens*, fr *in-* ¹in- + *patient-*, *patiens* patient] – **impatience** *n*, **impatiently** *adv*

**impawn** /im'pawn/ *vt*, *archaic* to put in pawn; pledge

**impeach** /im'peech/ *vt* **1a** to bring an accusation against **b** to charge with a usu serious crime or misdemeanour; *specif*, *chiefly NAm* to charge (a public official) before a competent tribunal with misconduct in office **2** to cast doubt on; *esp* to challenge the credibility or validity of (*~ the testimony of a witness*) **synonyms** see ACCUSE [ME *empechen* to impede, accuse, fr MF *empeechier* to hinder, fr LL *impedicare* to fetter, fr L *in-* ²in- + *pedica* fetter, fr *ped-*, *pes* foot – more at FOOT] – **impeachable** *adj*, **impeachment** *n*, **impeachability** *n*

**impeccable** /im'pekəbl/ *adj* **1** not capable of sinning or liable to sin **2** free from fault or blame; flawless (*spoke ~ French*) [L *impeccabilis*, fr *in-* ¹in- + *peccare* to sin] – **impeccably** *adv*, **impeccability** *n*

**impecunious** /ˌimpi'kyoohnyəs, -ni·əs/ *adj*, *chiefly formal* having very little or no money; penniless **synonyms** see POOR [¹*in-* + *obs pecunious* rich, fr ME, fr L *pecuniosus*, fr *pecunia* money – more at FEE] – **impecuniously** *adv*, **impecuniousness** *n*, **impecuniosity** *n*

**impedance** /im'peed(ə)ns/ *n* something that impedes; a hindrance: e g **a** the opposition in an electrical circuit to the flow of an ALTERNATING CURRENT that is analogous to the electrical resistance to a direct current; the ratio of the greatest value of the ELECTROMOTIVE FORCE (energy which causes current to flow) to the greatest value of the current produced **b** the ratio of the sound pressure to the rate of volume displacement at a given surface in a sound-transmitting medium that is vibrating to produce the sound *synonyms* see IMPEDIMENT

**impede** /im'peed/ *vt* to interfere with or retard the progress of; hinder *synonyms* see [1]HINDER *antonyms* assist, promote [L *impedire*, fr *in-* [2]*in-* + *ped-*, *pes* foot – more at FOOT] – **impeder** *n*

**impediment** /im'pedimənt/ *n* **1** something that impedes; *esp* a physiological speech defect (e g a cleft palate) **2** something (e g an existing marriage) that prevents a marriage from taking place legally

*synonyms* Impedance and impediment are both formed from impede; but **impedance** is confined virtually to physics and electronics while **impediment**, the more general word, is also the physiological and legal one.

**impedimenta** /im,pedi'mentə/ *n taking pl vb* **1** unwieldy baggage or equipment; *esp* the travelling equipment of an army **2** things that impede; encumbrances [L, pl of *impedimentum* impediment, fr *impedire*]

**impel** /im'pel/ *vt* **-ll-** **1** to urge forward or force into action; drive ⟨*felt* ~*led to speak his mind*⟩ **2** to impart motion to; propel *synonyms* see [1]PUSH [L *impellere*, fr *in-* [2]*in-*+ *pellere* to drive – more at FELT] – **impellent** *adj or n*

**impeller** *also* **impellor** /im'pelə/ *n* **1** one who or that which impels **2** (a blade of) a rotor; *also* a disc of angled blades which impart motion to a gas or liquid by rotating

**impend** /im'pend/ *vi* **1** to hover threateningly; menace **b** to be about to happen **2** *archaic* to be suspended; hang [L *impendēre*, fr *in-* [2]*in-* + *pendēre* to hang – more at PENDANT]

**impendent** /im'pend(ə)nt/ *adj, formal* impending [L *impendent-*, *impendens*, prp of *impendēre*] – **impendence**, **impendency** *n*

**impending** /im'pending/ *adj* about to happen; approaching, threatening ⟨~ *doom*⟩ ⟨*the* ~ *storm*⟩

**impenetrability** /im,penitrə'biləti/ *n* **1** the quality or state of being impenetrable **2** *physics* the inability of two portions of matter to occupy the same space at the same time

**impenetrable** /im'penitrəbl/ *adj* **1a** incapable of being penetrated or pierced **b** inaccessible to intellectual influences or ideas **2** incapable of being comprehended; inscrutable **3** *physics* having the property of impenetrability [ME *impenetrabel*, fr MF *impenetrable*, fr L *impenetrabilis*, fr *in-* [1]*in-* + *penetrabilis* penetrable] – **impenetrableness** *n*, **impenetrably** *adv*

**impenitent** /im'penit(ə)nt/ *adj* not penitent [LL *impaenitent-*, *impaenitens*, fr L *in-* [1]*in-* + *paenitent-*, *paenitens* penitent] – **impenitence**, **impenitency** *n*, **impenitently** *adv*

[1]**imperative** /im'perətiv/ *adj* **1a** of or being the grammatical form (MOOD) that expresses the will to influence the behaviour of another **b** expressive of a command, plea, or exhortation **c** having power to restrain, control, and direct; authoritative **2** not to be put off or evaded; urgent ⟨*an* ~ *duty*⟩ □ compare IMPERATIVE, IMPERIOUS [LL *imperativus*, fr L *imperatus*, pp of *imperare* to command – more at EMPEROR] – **imperatively** *adv*, **imperativeness** *n*

[2]**imperative** *n* **1** the imperative MOOD or a verb form or verbal phrase expressing it **2** something that is imperative: e g **2a** a command, order **b** an obligatory act or duty **c** an imperative judgment or proposition

**imperator** /,impə'rahtaw/ *n* a COMMANDER-IN-CHIEF or emperor of the ancient Romans [L – more at EMPEROR] – **imperatorial** *adj*

**imperceptible** /impə'septəbl/ *adj* **1** not perceptible by the mind or the senses **2** extremely slight, gradual, or subtle ⟨*an* ~ *change in his attitude towards her*⟩ [MF, fr ML *imperceptibilis*, fr L *in-* [1]*in-* + LL *perceptibilis* perceptible] – **imperceptibly** *adv*, **imperceptibility** *n*

**imperceptive** /,impə'septiv/ *adj* not perceptive – **imperceptiveness** *n*

**impercipient** /,impə'sipi-ənt/ *adj* not percipient; unperceptive – **impercipience** *n*

[1]**imperfect** /im'puhfikt/ *adj* **1** not perfect: e g **1a** defective **b** deficient **c** DICLINOUS (having the male and female reproductive organs in separate flowers) ⟨*an* ~ *flower*⟩ **d** lacking or not involving sexual reproduction ⟨*the* ~ *stage of a fungus*⟩ **2** of or constituting a verb tense that expresses a continuing state or an incomplete action, esp in the past **3** not legally enforceable **4** *of a musical cadence* passing from a TONIC chord to a DOMINANT chord, giving a feeling of incompletion [ME

*imperfit*, fr MF *imparfait*, fr L *imperfectus*, fr *in-* [1]*in-* + *per-fectus* perfect] – **imperfectly** *adv*, **imperfectness** *n*

[2]**imperfect** *n* an imperfect tense; *also* the verb form expressing it

**imperfect fungus** *n* a fungus (order Fungi Imperfecti) of which only the CONIDIAL stage (form in which asexual reproduction occurs) is known and which can cause serious diseases in animals and people

**imperfection** /,impə'feksh(ə)n/ *n* the quality or state of being imperfect; *also* a fault, blemish ⟨*many* ~s *in his character*⟩

*synonyms* Blemish, flaw, fault, and defect are all forms of imperfection. A **blemish** is a minor or superficial imperfection which spoils the appearance of something, either literally or figuratively ⟨*no blemishes spoilt her complexion/reputation*⟩. A **flaw** suggests a small but fundamental weakness in what would otherwise approach perfection. **Fault** suggests an inherent deficiency or shortcoming, while a **defect** is a structural imperfection which may prevent or impair the functioning of a machine or something similar.

**imperfective** /,impə'fektiv/ *adj, of a verb form* (e g *in Russian*) showing that an action or event is still in progress at a particular time and not yet completed – compare PERFECTIVE – **imperfective** *n*

**imperforate** /im'puhf(ə)rət/ *also* **imperforated** *adj* **1** having no opening or aperture; *specif* lacking the usual or normal opening **2** *of a stamp or a sheet of stamps* lacking perforations or ROULETTES (small slits between rows of stamps in a sheet) [[1]*in-* + *perforate*]

[1]**imperial** /im'piəri-əl/ *adj* **1a** of or befitting an empire, emperor, or empress **b** of the British Empire **2a** sovereign, royal **b** regal, imperious **3** of superior or unusual size or excellence **4** belonging to an official nonmetric British series of weights and measures [ME, fr MF, fr LL *imperialis*, fr L *imperium* command, empire] – **imperially** *adv*

[2]**imperial** *n* **1** *cap* a follower or soldier of the Holy Roman emperor **2** a size of paper usu 30 x 22 inches (762 × 559 millimetres) or in the USA 31 × 23 inches (787 × 584 millimetres) **3** a small pointed beard growing below the lower lip **4** something of unusual size or excellence [(3) Fr *impériale*, fr fem of *impérial* imperial; fr the beard worn as a young man by Napoleon III † 1873 Emperor of France]

**imperial gallon** *n* a unit of liquid capacity used as a standard in Britain and equal to about 4.546 litres

**imperialism** /im'piəri-ə,liz(ə)m/ *n* **1** government by an emperor **2** the policy, practice, or advocacy of extending the power and dominion of a nation, esp by territorial acquisitions or by gaining indirect control over the political or economic life of other areas – **imperialist** *n or adj*, **imperialistic** *adj*, **imperialistically** *adv*

**imperil** /im'perəl/ *vt* **-ll-** (*NAm* **-l-**, **-ll-**) to bring into peril; endanger – **imperilment** *n*

**imperious** /im'piəri-əs/ *adj* **1** marked by arrogant assurance; domineering, overbearing ⟨*his* ~ *arbitrariness*⟩ **2** urgent, imperative ⟨*the* ~ *problems of the new age* – J F Kennedy⟩ □ compare IMPERATIVE, IMPERIAL [L *imperiosus*, fr *imperium*] – **imperiousness** *n*, **imperiously** *adv*

**imperishable** /im'perishəbl/ *adj* **1** not perishable or subject to decay **2** enduring permanently ⟨~ *fame*⟩ – **imperishable** *n*, **imperishableness** *n*, **imperishably** *adv*, **imperishability** *n*

**imperium** /im'piəri-əm/ *n* supreme power or absolute dominion; control, sovereignty [L – more at EMPIRE]

**impermanent** /im'puhmənənt/ *adj* not permanent; transient – **impermanence**, **impermanency** *n*, **impermanently** *adv*

**impermeable** /im'puhmi-əbl/ *adj* not permitting passage, esp of liquids or gases, through its substance; impervious [LL *impermeabilis*, fr L *in-* [1]*in-* + LL *permeabilis* permeable] – **impermeableness** *n*, **impermeably** *adv*, **impermeability** *n*

**impermissible** /,impə'misəbl/ *adj* not permissible – **impermissibly** *adv*, **impermissibility** *n*

**impersonal** /-'puhs(ə)nl/ *adj* **1a** *of a verb* denoting the verbal action of an unspecified agent and hence used with no expressed subject (e g *methinks*) or with a merely formal subject (e g *rained* in *it rained*) **b** *of a pronoun* INDEFINITE (not referring to a specific person or thing) **2a** having no personal reference or connection; objective ⟨~ *criticism*⟩ **b** not involving or reflecting the human personality or emotions ⟨*spoke in a flat* ~ *tone*⟩ **c** not existing as a person; not having personality ⟨*an* ~ *deity*⟩ [LL *impersonalis*, fr L *in-* [1]*in-* + LL *personalis* personal] – **impersonally** *adv*, **impersonality** *n*, **impersonalize** *vt*, **impersonalization** *n*

**impersonate** /im'puhsənayt/ *vt* to assume or act the character of; pretend to be (another person) ⟨*the comedian could ~ most leading politicians*⟩ ⟨*caught trying to ~ an officer*⟩ – **impersonator** *n*, **impersonation** *n*

**impertinence** /im'puhtinəns/, **impertinency** /im'puhtinənsi/ *n* 1 the quality or state of being impertinent: e g 1a incivility, insolence b *formal* irrelevance, inappropriateness 2 an instance of impertinence ⟨*I thought his comment an ~*⟩

**impertinent** /im'puhtinənt/ *adj* 1 not restrained within due or proper bounds ⟨*~ curiosity*⟩ ; *also* rude, insolent ⟨*an ~ answer*⟩ 2 *formal* not pertinent; irrelevant [ME, fr MF, fr LL *impertinent-, impertinens*, fr L *in-* [^1]*in-* + *pertinent-, pertinens*, prp of *pertinēre* to pertain] – **impertinently** *adv*

**imperturbable** /,impə'tuhbəbl, -puh-/ *adj* marked by extreme calm and composure; serene [ME, fr LL *imperturbabilis*, fr L *in-* [^1]*in-* + *perturbare* to perturb] – **imperturbably** *adv*, **imperturbability** *n*

**impervious** /im'puhvi·əs/ *adj* 1 not allowing entry or passage; impenetrable ⟨*a coat ~ to rain*⟩ 2 not capable of being affected or disturbed ⟨*~ to criticism*⟩ □ usu + *to* [L *impervius*, fr *in-* [^1]*in-* + *pervius* pervious] – **imperviously** *adv*, **imperviousness** *n*

**impetigo** /,impə'tiegoh/ *n* an acute contagious skin disease characterized by blisters, pimples, and yellowish crusts on the sores [L, fr *impetere* to attack – more at IMPETUS] – **impetiginous** *adj*

**impetrate** /'impitrayt/ *vt* to obtain by request or entreaty, esp by prayer [L *impetratus*, pp of *impetrare*, fr *in-* [^2]*in-* + *patrare* to accomplish – more at PERPETRATE] – **impetration** *n*

**impetuosity** /im,petyoo'osəti/ *n* 1 the quality or state of being impetuous 2 an impetuous action

**impetuous** /im'petyoo·əs/ *adj* 1 marked by rash and impulsive action ⟨*an ~ temperament*⟩ 2 *poetic* marked by forceful and violent movement ⟨*an ~ wind*⟩ [ME, fr MF *impetueux*, fr LL *impetuosus*, fr L *impetus*] – **impetuously** *adv*, **impetuousness** *n*

**impetus** /'impitəs/ *n* 1a a driving force; an impulse b an incentive, stimulus ⟨*gave a new ~ to the ailing economy*⟩ 2 the property possessed by a moving body by virtue of its mass and its motion – used of bodies moving suddenly or violently to indicate the origin and intensity of the motion [L, assault, impetus, fr *impetere* to attack, fr *in-* [^2]*in-* + *petere* to go to, seek – more at FEATHER]

**impi** /'impi/ *n, taking sing or pl vb, pl* **impis**, *SAfr* an armed usu organized band of Africans [Zulu]

**impiety** /im'pie·əti/ *n* 1 the quality or state of being impious; irreverence 2 an impious act

**impinge** /im'pinj/ *vi* 1 to strike, dash ⟨*I heard the rain ~ upon the earth* – James Joyce⟩ 2 to make an impression ⟨*waiting for the germ of a new idea to ~ upon my mind* – Phyllis Bentley⟩ 3 to encroach, infringe ⟨*~ on other people's rights*⟩ □ usu + *on* or *upon* [L *impingere*, fr *in-* [^2]*in-* + *pangere* to fasten, drive in – more at PACT] – **impingement** *n*

   **synonyms** Impinge and infringe can now both mean "encroach" ⟨*impinge/infringe on my rights*⟩, although in older use infringe was only a transitive verb. △ impugn

**impious** /'impi·əs/ *adj* not pious; lacking in reverence or proper respect (e g for God or one's parents); irreverent [L *impius*, fr *in-* [^1]*in-* + *pius* pious] – **impiously** *adv*

**impish** /'impish/ *adj* of or characteristic of an imp; *esp* mischievous – **impishly** *adv*, **impishness** *n*

**implacable** /im'plakəbl/ *adj* not capable of being appeased or pacified; inexorable ⟨*an ~ enemy*⟩ [MF or L; MF, fr L *implacabilis*, fr *in-* [^1]*in-* + *placabilis* placable] – **implacableness** *n*, **implacably** *adv*, **implacability** *n*

[^1]**implant** /im'plahnt/ *vt* 1a to fix or set securely or deeply ⟨*a ruby ~ed in the idol's forehead*⟩ b to set permanently in the consciousness or habit patterns; inculcate 2 to insert in the tissue of a living organism (e g for growth, slow release, or formation of an organic union) ⟨*subcutaneously ~ed hormone pellets*⟩ – **implantable** *adj*, **implanter** *n*

[^2]**implant** /'im,plahnt/ *n* something (e g a graft or pellet) implanted in tissue

**implantation** /,implahn'taysh(ə)n/ *n* implanting or being implanted; *specif* the attachment of the early embryo (BLASTOCYST) of a mammal to the wall of the uterus before the formation of the placenta

**implausible** /im'plawzəbl/ *adj* not plausible; provoking disbelief – **implausibly** *adv*, **implausibility** *n*

**implead** /im'pleed/ *vt* to take legal action against [ME *empleden*, fr MF *emplaider*, fr OF *emplaidier*, fr *en-* + *plaidier* to plead]

[^1]**implement** /'implimənt/ *n* 1 an article serving to equip ⟨*the ~s of religious worship*⟩ 2 an object that enables some purpose to be achieved or furthered and that is caused to act by some applied force (e g via the human hand); a tool, utensil 3 one who or that which serves as an instrument or tool ⟨*propaganda as an ~ of peace*⟩ 4 the fulfilment or performance of an obligation – used in Scots Law *synonyms* see [^1]TOOL [ME, fr LL *implementum* act of filling up, fr L *implēre* to fill up, fr *in-* [^2]*in-* + *plēre* to fill – more at FULL]

[^2]**implement** /'impliment, -mənt/ *vt* to carry out; accomplish; *esp* to give practical effect to ⟨*plans not yet ~ed owing to lack of funds*⟩ – **implemental** *adj*, **implementation** *n*

**implicate** /'implikayt/ *vt* 1 to involve as a consequence, corollary, or inference; imply 2a to bring into intimate or esp incriminating connection ⟨*~d in the murder*⟩ b to involve in the nature or operation of something; affect ⟨*the brain is pathologically ~d in insanity*⟩ 3 *archaic* to fold or twist together; entwine [L *implicatus*, pp of *implicare* – more at EMPLOY]

**implication** /,impli'kaysh(ə)n/ *n* 1a the act of implicating; the state of being implicated b close connection; *esp* incriminating involvement 2a the act of implying; the state of being implied b(1) a logical relation between two propositions that fails to hold only if the first is true and the second is false b(2) a logical relation between two propositions such that if the first is true the second must be true 3 something implied – **implicative** *adj*, **implicatively** *adv*, **implicativeness** *n*

**implicit** /im'plisit/ *adj* 1a understood though not directly expressed; implied ⟨*an ~ assumption*⟩ b potentially present though not realized or visible ⟨*a sculptor may see different figures ~ in a block of stone* – John Dewey⟩ 2 without doubt or reservation; unquestioning, absolute ⟨*~ obedience*⟩ □ compare EXPLICIT [L *implicitus*, pp of *implicare*] – **implicitly** *adv*, **implicitness** *n*

**implicit function** *n* a mathematical function that is not expressed or is not expressible with the DEPENDENT VARIABLE on one side of an equation and the one or more INDEPENDENT VARIABLES on the other – compare EXPLICIT FUNCTION

**implode** /im'plohd/ *vi* 1a to collapse inwards suddenly ⟨*a blow causing a vacuum tube to ~*⟩ b to undergo violent compression ⟨*massive stars which ~*⟩ 2 to come (as if) to a centre ⟨*the imploding or contracting energies of our world* – Marshall McLuhan⟩ ~ *vt* 1 to cause to implode 2 to pronounce (a consonant sound) with IMPLOSION [[^2]*in-* + *-plode* (as in *explode*)]

**implore** /im'plaw/ *vt* 1 to call on in humility or prayer; beseech 2 to call or beg for earnestly; entreat *synonyms* see BEG [MF or L; MF *implorer*, fr L *implorare*, fr *in-* [^2]*in-* + *plorare* to cry out (cf DEPLORE, EXPLORE)]

**implosion** /im'plohzh(ə)n/ *n* 1 the action of imploding 2 the inrush of air in forming a SUCTION STOP (consonant pronounced by sucking air inwards) 3 the act or action of coming (as if) to a centre ⟨*the rush of students into our universities is not explosion but ~* – Marshall McLuhan⟩ [[^2]*in-* + *-plosion* (as in *explosion*)] – **implosive** *adj or n*

**imply** /im'plie/ *vt* 1 to involve or indicate as a necessary though not expressly stated consequence ⟨*the rights of citizenship ~ certain obligations*⟩ 2 to involve by very nature ⟨*war implies fighting*⟩ 3 to express indirectly; hint at ⟨*his silence implied consent*⟩ *synonyms* see SUGGEST *usage* see INFER [ME *emplien* to enwrap, entangle, fr MF *emplier*, fr L *implicare*]

**impolite** /,impə'liet/ *adj* not polite; rude [L *impolitus*, fr *in-* [^1]*in-*+ *politus* polite] – **impolitely** *adv*, **impoliteness** *n*

**impolitic** /im'polətik/ *adj, formal* not politic; unwise, illadvised – **impolitical** *adj*, **impoliticly, impolitically** *adv*

**imponderable** /im'pond(ə)rəbl/ *adj* not ponderable; incapable of being precisely weighed or evaluated [ML *imponderabilis*, fr L *in-* [^1]*in-* + LL *ponderabilis* ponderable] – **imponderable** *n*, **imponderableness** *n*, **imponderably** *adv*, **imponderability** *n*

[^1]**import** /im'pawt/ *vt* 1 to bring from a foreign or external source; *esp* to bring (e g merchandise) into a place or country from another country 2 *formal* to convey as meaning or portent; signify, imply b *archaic* to express, state 3 *archaic* to be of importance to; concern ~ *vi, formal* to be of consequence; matter [ME *importen*, fr L *importare* to bring into, fr *in-* [^2]*in-* + *portare* to carry – more at FARE] – **importable** *adj*, **importer** *n*

[^2]**import** /'impawt/ *n* 1 something that is imported 2 importing, esp of merchandise 3 *formal* purport, meaning 4 *formal* importance; *esp* relative importance ⟨*it is hard to determine the ~ of this decision*⟩

**importance** /im'pawt(ə)ns/ *n* the quality or state of being important; consequence, significance

**important** /im'pawt(ə)nt/ *adj* 1 of considerable significance or consequence; weighty ⟨*an* ~ *matter*⟩ 2 marked by a pompous or self-important manner 3 having considerable authority, influence, or social distinction ⟨*a very* ~ *person*⟩ [MF, fr OIt *importante*, fr L *important-*, *importans*, prp of *importare*]

**importantly** /im'pawt(ə)ntli/ *adv* 1 in an important way 2 as is important

   *usage* Some people dislike the use of **importantly** to mean "as is important" ⟨*he's experienced with poultry, and perhaps more* **importantly** *he's a good worker*⟩, and prefer to use *more* **important** in such sentences.

**importation** /,impaw'taysh(ə)n/ *n* 1 the act or practice of importing 2 something imported

**importunate** /im'pawtyoonət, -chənət/ *adj, chiefly formal* troublesomely urgent; extremely persistent in request or demand – **importunately** *adv*, **importunateness** *n*, **importunity** *n*

¹**importune** /im'pawtyoohn, -choohn/ *adj, formal* importunate [ME, fr MF & L; MF *importun*, fr L *importunus*, fr *in-* ¹in- + *-portunus* (as in *opportunus* fit) – more at OPPORTUNE] – **importunely** *adv*

²**importune** *vb, chiefly formal* *vt* 1 to press or urge with repeated requests; solicit with troublesome persistence 2a to annoy, trouble b to solicit for purposes of prostitution ~ *vi* to beg, urge, or solicit importunately *synonyms* see BEG – **importuner** *n*

**impose** /im'pohz/ *vt* 1a to enforce or apply as compulsory; levy ⟨~ *a tax*⟩ b to establish or make prevail by force ⟨~d *himself as their leader*⟩ 2 to arrange (e g typeset pages) in order for printing as a SIGNATURE (sheet of pages) 3 PALM OFF ⟨~ *fake antiques on the public*⟩ 4 to force into the company or on the attention of another ⟨~ *oneself on others*⟩ 5 *archaic* to place, set ~ *vi* 1 to take unwarranted advantage ⟨~d *on his good nature*⟩; *also* to be an excessive requirement or burden ⟨*mother always says she doesn't want to* ~ *on us*⟩ 2 to practise deception □ (*vt 3&4; vi 1&2*) + *on* or *upon* [MF *imposer*, fr L *imponere*, lit., to put upon (perf indic *imposui*), fr *in-* ²in- + *ponere* to put – more at POSITION] – **imposer** *n*

**imposing** /im'pohzing/ *adj* impressive because of size, bearing, dignity, or grandeur; commanding *synonyms* see ¹GRAND *antonyms* unimposing, insignificant – **imposingly** *adv*

**imposition** /,impə'zish(ə)n/ *n* 1 the act of imposing 2 something imposed: e g 2a a levy, tax b an excessive or unwarranted requirement or burden c the copying or memorizing of something as a punishment (e g at an English school) 3 a deception, imposture 4 the ordering of pages to be printed so that they will appear in the correct order in the finished product

**impossibility** /im,posə'biləti, ,---'---/ *n* 1 the quality or state of being impossible 2 something impossible

**impossible** /im'posəbl/ *adj* 1a incapable of being or occurring; not possible b seemingly incapable of being done, attained, or fulfilled; insuperably difficult; hopeless ⟨*an* ~ *task*⟩ c difficult to believe ⟨*an* ~ *story*⟩ 2 extremely undesirable or difficult to put up with; unacceptable, unbearable ⟨*life became* ~ *because of lack of money*⟩ ⟨*an* ~ *child*⟩ [ME, fr MF & L; MF, fr L *impossibilis*, fr *in-* ¹in- + *possibilis* possible] – **impossibleness** *n*, **impossibly** *adv*

   *usage* Since there can be no degrees in impossibility, some people dislike expressions such as ⟨*even more* **impossible**⟩.

¹**impost** /'impohst/ *n* 1 something imposed or levied; a tax 2 the extra weight carried by a racehorse in a handicap race [MF, fr ML *impositum*, fr L, neut of *impositus*, pp of *imponere*]

²**impost** *n* a bracket, top part of a pillar, or moulding that supports an arch [Fr *imposte*, deriv of L *impositus*]

**impostor, imposter** /im'postə/ *n* a person who assumes a false identity or title for fraudulent purposes [LL *impostor*, fr *impostus*, pp]

**imposthume, imposthume** /im'postyoohm/ *n, archaic* an abscess [ME *emposteme*, deriv of Gk *apostēma*, fr *aphistanai* to remove, fr *apo-* + *histanai* to cause to stand – more at STAND]

**imposture** /im'poschə/ *n* (an instance of) fraud, deception; *esp* deception practised by an impostor [LL *impostura*, fr L *impositus*, *impostus*, pp of *imponere*]

**impotent** /'impət(ə)nt/ *adj* 1 not potent; lacking in effectiveness, strength, or vigour; powerless ⟨~ *rage*⟩ ⟨*the* ~ *ruling classes*⟩ 2a unable to copulate through an inability to maintain an erection of the penis b *of a male* sterile – not used technically *synonyms* see STERILE *antonyms* virile, potent △ **impudent**

[ME, fr MF & L; MF, fr L *impotent-*, *impotens*, fr *in-* ¹in- + *potent-*, *potens* potent] – **impotence, impotency** *n*, **impotent** *n*, **impotently** *adv*

**impound** /im'pownd/ *vt* 1a to shut up (as if) in a pound; confine b to take and hold in (temporary) legal custody ⟨~ *stolen goods*⟩ 2 to collect and confine (water) (as if) in a reservoir – **impoundable** *adj*, **impoundage, impoundment** *n*

**impoverish** /im'pov(ə)rish/ *vt* 1 to make poor ⟨~ed *by misfortune*⟩ 2 to deprive of strength, richness, or fertility ⟨~ *the soil*⟩ *synonyms* see POOR *antonym* enrich [ME *enpoverisen*, fr MF *empovriss-*, stem of *empovrir*, fr *en-* + *povre* poor – more at POOR] – **impoverisher** *n*, **impoverishment** *n*

**impracticable** /im'praktikəbl/ *adj* 1a not practicable; incapable of being put into effect or carried out ⟨*an* ~ *plan*⟩ b impassable ⟨*an* ~ *road*⟩ 2 *archaic* intractable, unmanageable – **impracticableness** *n*, **impracticably** *adv*, **impracticability** *n*

   *synonyms* A plan, method, or suggestion that cannot be carried out is both **impracticable** and **impractical**, but **impracticable** emphasizes sheer impossibility while **impractical** implies uselessness and ineffectiveness.

**impractical** /im'praktikl/ *adj* not practical: e g a incapable of dealing sensibly with practical matters b impracticable ⟨*a totally* ~ *scheme*⟩ ⟨*economically* ~⟩ c idealistic ⟨*an* ~ *pipe dream* – James Laughlin⟩ – **impractically** *adv*, **impracticalness, impracticality** *n*

**imprecate** /'imprikayt/ *vb, formal* *vt* to invoke evil on; curse ~ *vi* to swear, curse [L *imprecatus*, pp of *imprecari* to invoke by prayer, fr *in-* ²in- + *precari* to pray – more at PRAY]

**imprecation** /,impri'kaysh(ə)n/ *n, formal* 1 the act of imprecating 2 a curse – **imprecatory** *adj*

**imprecise** /,impri'sies/ *adj* not precise; inexact, vague – **imprecisely** *adv*, **impreciseness** *n*, **imprecision** *n*

¹**impregnable** /im'pregnəbl/ *adj* 1 incapable of being taken by assault; unconquerable ⟨*an* ~ *fortress*⟩ 2 beyond criticism or question; unassailable ⟨*an* ~ *social position*⟩ [ME *imprenable*, fr MF, fr *in-* ¹in- + *prenable* vulnerable to capture, fr *prendre* to take – more at PRIZE] – **impregnableness** *n*, **impregnably** *adv*, **impregnability** *n*

²**impregnable** *adj* capable of being impregnated

**impregnant** /im'pregnənt/ *n* a substance used for impregnating another substance

¹**impregnate** /im'pregnayt, -nət/ *adj* filled, saturated

²**impregnate** /im'pregnayt/ *vt* 1a(1) to make pregnant a(2) to introduce SPERM CELLS into b to fertilize 2a to cause to be imbued, permeated, or saturated *with* b to permeate thoroughly; interpenetrate [LL *impraegnatus*, pp of *impraegnare*, fr L *in-* ²in- + *praegnas* pregnant] – **impregnation** *n*, **impregnator** *n*

**impresario** /,impri'sahrioh/ *n, pl* **impresarios** one who organizes, puts on, or sponsors a public entertainment (e g a sports event); *esp* the manager or conductor of an opera or concert company [It, fr *impresa* undertaking, fr *imprendere* to undertake, fr (assumed) VL *imprehendere*, fr L *in-* ²in- + *prehendere* to seize – more at PREHENSILE]

**imprescriptible** /,impri'skriptəbl/ *adj* that cannot be legally taken away or revoked; inalienable ⟨*the* ~ *rights of man*⟩ [MF, fr *in-* ¹in- + *prescriptible* subject to prescription, fr ML *prescriptibilis*, fr *prescriptus*, pp of *prescribere* – more at PRESCRIBE]

¹**impress** /im'pres/ *vt* 1a to apply with pressure so as to imprint ⟨~ *a signet ring on wax*⟩ b to produce (e g a mark) by pressure ⟨~ *one's name on a metal strip*⟩ c to mark (as if) by pressure or stamping ⟨~ed *his children with the right ideas*⟩ 2a to fix strongly or deeply (e g in the mind or memory) ⟨*the value of hard work was* ~ed *upon me*⟩ b to produce a deep and usu favourable impression on ⟨*his boss was* ~ed *by his efficiency*⟩ 3 to transmit (force or motion) by pressure; *esp* to apply (e g voltage) to a circuit from an outside source ~ *vi* to produce an impression, esp a favourable one ⟨*performances that failed to* ~⟩ *synonyms* see ¹MOVE [ME *impressen*, fr L *impressus*, pp of *imprimere*, fr *in-* ²in- + *premere* to press – more at PRESS]

²**impress** /'impres/ *n* 1 the act of impressing 2a a mark made by pressure; an imprint b an image of something formed (as if) by pressure; *esp* a seal 3 a characteristic or distinctive mark; a stamp ⟨*the* ~ *of a fresh and vital intelligence is stamped . . . in his work* – Lytton Strachey⟩ 4 an impression, effect

³**impress** /im'pres/ *vt* 1 to levy or take by force for public service; *esp* to force into naval service; press-gang 2 to procure or enlist by forcible persuasion ⟨*they had* ~ed *a small school*

... *to assist in the performances* – Charles Dickens⟩ [²*in-* + ³*press*]

**impressible** /im'presəbl/ *adj* capable of being impressed; sensitive – **impressibly** *adv*, **impressibility** *n*

**impression** /im'presh(ə)n/ *n* **1** the act or process of impressing **2** the effect produced by impressing: eg **2a** a stamp, form, or figure produced by physical contact **b** an imprint of the teeth and adjacent portions of the jaw for use in dentistry **c** an influence or effect, esp a marked one, on the mind or senses ⟨*make a good* ~⟩; *esp* a favourable impression ⟨*the new singer made quite an* ~⟩ **3a** a characteristic, trait, or feature resulting from some influence ⟨*the* ~ *on behaviour produced by the social milieu*⟩ **b** an effect of alteration or improvement ⟨*the settlement left little* ~ *on the wilderness*⟩ **c** impression, impressions *pl* a telling image impressed on the mind or senses ⟨*first* ~s *of Greece*⟩ **4a** the amount of pressure with which an inked printing surface deposits its ink on the paper **b** a single instance of the meeting of a printing surface and the material being printed; *also* a print or copy so made **c** all the copies of a publication (eg a book) printed in one continuous operation **5** a usu indistinct or imprecise notion or recollection **6** a coat of paint for ornament or preservation **7** an imitation of a person by another; *esp* an imitation in caricature of a noted personality as a form of theatrical entertainment – **impressional** *adj*

**impressionable** /im'presh(ə)nəbl/ *adj* capable of being easily impressed: **a** easily influenced **b** easily moulded; plastic – **impressionableness** *n*, **impressionably** *adv*, **impressionability** *n*

**impressionism** /im'preshə,niz(ə)m/ *n* **1** *often cap* a theory or practice in painting, esp among French painters of about the 1870s, of depicting the natural appearances of usu informal and outdoor scenes by means of dabs or strokes of primary unmixed colours in order to simulate actual reflected light **2a** the literary depiction of scene, emotion, or character by details intended to achieve a vividness or effectiveness more by evoking subjective and sensory impressions than by recreating an objective reality **b** a style of musical composition designed to create impressions and moods through rich and varied harmonies and tones **3** a theory or practice of describing and examining one's subjective reactions to a work of art [Fr *impressionisme*, fr *impression* + *-isme* -ism; orig fr the painting "Impression, soleil levant" ("Impression, sunrise") by Claude Monet †1926 Fr artist]

**impressionist** /im'preshənist/ *n* **1** *often cap* a person (eg a painter) who practises or adheres to the theories of impressionism **2** an entertainer who does impressions

**impressionistic** /im,preshə'nistik/ *adj* **1** impressionistic, **impressionist** of or constituting impressionism **2** based on or involving subjective impression as distinct from knowledge, fact, or systematic thought – **impressionistically** *adv*

**impressive** /im'presiv/ *adj* making a marked impression; stirring deep feelings, esp of awe or admiration – **impressively** *adv*, **impressiveness** *n*

**impressment** /im'presmənt/, **impress** *n* the act of seizing for public use or of impressing into public service [³*impress* + *-ment*]

**imprest** /'imprest/ *n* a loan or advance of money; *esp* a loan from a government for public business [obs *imprest* to lend, prob fr It *imprestare*]

**imprimatur** /,impri'mahtə, -'maytə/ *n* **1** a licence to print or publish, esp by the authority of the ROMAN CATHOLIC church **2** sanction, approval [NL, let it be printed, fr *imprimere* to print, fr L, to imprint, impress – more at IMPRESS]

**imprimis** /im'priemis/ *adv* in the first place – used to introduce a list of items [ME *inprimis*, fr L *in primis* among the first (things)]

¹**imprint** /im'print/ *vt* **1** to mark (as if) by pressure; impress **2a** to fix indelibly or permanently (eg on the memory) **b** to affect by imprinting ⟨*a chance to become* ~ed *with a loving female figure* – Woman's Own⟩

²**imprint** /'imprint/ *n* something imprinted or printed: eg **a** a mark or depression made by pressure ⟨*the fossil* ~ *of a dinosaur's foot*⟩ **b**(1) a publisher's name, often with address and date of publication, printed at the foot of a TITLE PAGE **c**(2) a printer's name or device printed on the back of the TITLE PAGE **c** an indelible distinguishing effect or influence ⟨*their work bears a sort of regional* ~ – Malcolm Cowley⟩ [MF *empreinte*, fr fem of *empreint*, pp of *empreindre* to imprint, fr L *imprimere*]

**imprinting** /im'printing/ *n* a rapid learning process that takes place early in the life of a member of a social species of animals, esp birds, that establishes a behaviour pattern involving

attachment to an object or creature, esp the animal's mother, seen just after hatching or birth

**imprison** /im'priz(ə)n/ *vt* to put (as if) in prison; confine [ME *imprisonen*, fr OF *emprisoner*, fr *en-* + *prison*] – **imprisonable** *adj*, **imprisonment** *n*

**improbability** /im,probə'biləti, ,---'---/ *n* **1** the quality or state of being improbable **2** something improbable

**improbable** /im'probəbl/ *adj* unlikely to be true or to occur [MF or L; MF, fr L *improbabilis*, fr *in-* ¹*in-* + *probabilis* probable] – **improbableness** *n*, **improbably** *adv*

**improbity** /im'prohbəti/ *n, formal* lack of probity or integrity; dishonesty [MF or L; MF *improbité*, fr L *improbitat-*, *improbitas*, fr *improbus* bad, dishonest, fr *in-* ¹*in-* + *probus* good, honest – more at PROVE]

¹**impromptu** /im'promptyooh/ *adj* **1** made or done on the spur of the moment; improvised ⟨*an* ~ *change of plan*⟩ **2** composed or uttered without previous preparation ⟨*a short* ~ *speech*⟩ [Fr, fr *impromptu* extemporaneously, fr L *in promptu* in readiness] – **impromptu** *adv*

²**impromptu** *n, pl* **impromptus 1** something that is impromptu **2** a musical composition suggesting improvisation

**improper** /im'propə/ *adj* not proper: eg **a** not in accordance with fact, truth, or correct procedure; incorrect ⟨~ *inference*⟩ **b** not suitable or appropriate to the occasion or purpose in hand ⟨~ *medicine*⟩ **c** not in accordance with propriety or modesty; indecent ⟨~ *language*⟩ [MF *impropre*, fr L *improprius*, fr *in-* ¹*in-* + *proprius* proper] – **improperly** *adv*, **improperness** *n*

**improper fraction** *n* a fraction whose numerator is equal to, larger than, or of equal or higher degree than the denominator ⟨$^4/_3$ *and* $(x^3 + 1) / (x + 4)$ *are improper fractions*⟩

**improper integral** *n, maths* a DEFINITE INTEGRAL whose region of INTEGRATION includes a point at which the INTEGRAND (quantity to be integrated) is undefined or tends to infinity or whose limits of integration are not all finite

**impropriate** /im'prohpriət, -ayt/ *adj* having been transferred from ecclesiastical to lay ownership or control [ML or NL *impropriatus*, pp of *impropriare* to appropriate, fr L *in-* ²*in-* + *propriare* to appropriate] – **impropriate** *vt*

**impropriety** /,imprə'prie-əti/ *n* **1** the quality or state of being improper **2** an improper act or remark; *esp* an unacceptable use of a word [Fr or LL; Fr *impropriété*, fr LL *improprietat-*, *improprietas*, fr L *improprius*]

**improvable** /im'proohvəbl/ *adj* capable of improving or being improved ⟨~ *land*⟩ – **improvably** *adv*, **improvability** *n*

**improve** /im'proohv/ *vt* **1a** to enhance in value or quality; make better **b** to increase the value of (land or property) by making better (eg by cultivation or the erection of buildings) **2** to use to good purpose ⟨~ *one's time by studying*⟩ **3** *archaic* to employ, use ~ *vi* to advance or make progress in what is desirable [alter. (prob influenced by *approve*) of earlier *emprowe*, *improwe*, *improue*, fr AF *emprouer* to invest profitably, fr OF *en-* + *prou* advantage, fr LL *prode* – more at PROUD]

**improve on** *vt* to make useful additions or amendments to ⟨*the new version* improves on *the original*⟩

**improvement** /-mənt/ *n* **1** the act or process of improving **2a** the state of being improved; *esp* increased value or excellence ⟨~ *in the standard of living*⟩ **b** an instance of such improvement; something that increases value or excellence ⟨~s *to an old house*⟩

*usage* When something has improved, there is an **improvement** *in* it; when two things are compared, one can be an **improvement** *on* the other ⟨*today's weather is an* **improvement** *on yesterday's*⟩.

**improver** /im'proohvə/ *n* **1** one who or that which improves **2** *chiefly Br* one who works for low wages in order to gain instruction and experience in a trade or occupation, esp while serving an apprenticeship

**improvident** /im'provid(ə)nt/ *adj* lacking foresight; not providing for the future [LL *improvident-*, *improvidens*, fr L *in-* ¹*in-* + *provident-*, *providens* provident] – **improvidence** *n*, **improvidently** *adv*

**improvisation** /,imprəvie'zaysh(ə)n/ *n* **1** the act or art of improvising **2** something (eg a musical or dramatic composition) improvised – **improvisational** *adj*

**improvisator** /im'provizaytə, 'imprəviezaytə/ *n* one who improvises – **improvisatorial** *adj*, **improvisatory** *adj*

**improvise** /'imprəviez/ *vt* **1** to compose, recite, or perform impromptu or without a set script, musical score, etc ⟨~d *music*⟩ **2** to make, devise, or provide without preparation ⟨*had to* ~ *a policy*⟩ **3** to concoct out of what is conveniently to hand ⟨*a hastily* ~d *shelter*⟩ ~ *vi* to improvise something [Fr *improviser*, fr It *improvvisare*, fr *improvviso* sudden, fr L *improvisus*, lit., unforeseen, fr *in-* ¹*in-* + *provisus*, pp of *providēre* to see ahead – more at PROVIDE] – **improviser, improvisor** *n*

**imprudence** /im'proohd(ə)ns/ *n* **1** the quality or state of being imprudent **2** an imprudent act

**imprudent** /im'proohd(ə)nt/ *adj* not prudent; lacking discretion or caution [ME, fr L *imprudent-, imprudens*, fr *in-* ¹*in-* + *prudent-, prudens* prudent] – **imprudently** *adv*

**impudent** /'impyood(ə)nt/ *adj* marked by contemptuous or cocky boldness or disregard of others; insolent, forward △ impotent [ME, shameless, fr L *impudent-, impudens*, fr *in-* ¹*in-*+ *pudent-, pudens*, prp of *pudēre* to feel shame] – **impudence** *n*, **impudently** *adv*

**impudicity** /,impyoo'disəti/ *n, formal* lack of modesty; shamelessness [MF *impudicité*, fr L *impudicus* immodest, shameful, fr *in-* ¹*in-* + *pudicus* modest, fr *pudēre*]

**impugn** /im'pyoohn/ *vt* to attack by words or arguments; call into question the validity or integrity of ⟨ ~ *a rival's motives*⟩ △ infringe, impinge, impute [ME *impugnen*, fr MF *impugner*, fr L *impugnare* to attack, assail, fr *in-* ²*in-* + *pugnare* to fight – more at PUNGENT] – **impugnable** *adj*, **impugner** *n*, **impugnment** *n*

¹**impulse** /'impuls/ *n* **1a** the act of driving onwards with sudden force; an impulsion, thrust **b** motion produced by such an impulse **c** a wave of electrical energy transmitted through tissues, esp NERVE FIBRES and muscles, that results in physiological activity or inhibition **2a** a force so communicated as to produce motion suddenly **b** an inspiration, stimulus ⟨*the creative* ~⟩ **3a** a sudden spontaneous inclination or incitement to some unpremeditated action **b** a propensity or natural tendency, usu other than rational ⟨*sexual* ~⟩ **4** *physics* **4a** the product of the average value of a force and the time during which it acts, being a quantity equal to the change in momentum produced by the force **b** PULSE 4a (temporary fluctuation in the value of an electric current or voltage) [L *impulsus*, fr *impulsus*, pp of *impellere* to impel] – **on (an) impulse** without prior thought or planning; spontaneously ⟨*went to the seaside* on impulse⟩

²**impulse** *vt* to give an impulse to ⟨*economic developments as* ~d *by scientific discovery* – *Nature*⟩

**impulse buying** *n* the buying of merchandise on impulse

**impulsion** /im'pulsh(ə)n/ *n* **1a** the action of impelling; the state of being impelled **b** an impelling force **c** an onward tendency derived from an impulsion; impetus **2** IMPULSE 3a **3** COMPULSION 2 (irresistible desire)

**impulsive** /im'pulsiv/ *adj* **1** having the power of driving or impelling **2** actuated by or likely to act on impulse **3** *esp of electrical forces* acting in very short bursts; momentary ⟨*an electric motor giving* ~ *thrusts*⟩ **synonyms** see SPONTANEOUS **antonym** deliberate – **impulsively** *adv*, **impulsiveness** *n*

**impunity** /im'pyoohnəti/ *n* exemption or freedom from punishment, harm, loss, or retribution – often in *with impunity* ⟨*trespassing with* ~⟩ **synonyms** see IMMUNITY [MF or L; MF *impunité*, fr L *impunitat-, impunitas*, fr *impune* without punishment, fr *in-* ¹*in-* + *poena* pain]

**impure** /im'pyooə/ *adj* not pure: e g **a** lewd, unchaste **b** containing something unclean; foul ⟨ ~ *water*⟩ **c** ritually unclean **d** mixed with an extraneous and usu inferior substance; adulterated ⟨*an* ~ *chemical*⟩ **e** mixed, bastard ⟨*an* ~ *style of ornamentation*⟩ [Fr & L; Fr, fr L *impurus*, fr *in-* ¹*in-* + *purus* pure] – **impurely** *adv*, **impureness** *n*

**impurity** /im'pyooərəti/ *n* **1** the quality or state of being impure **2** something that is impure or makes something else impure

**impute** /im'pyooht/ *vt* **1** to lay the responsibility or blame for, often unjustly; charge **2** to credit to a person or a cause; *esp* to attribute unjustly ⟨*imputing to me better qualities than I possess*⟩ **synonyms** see ASCRIBE △ impugn [ME *inputen*, fr L *imputare*, fr *in-* ²*in-* + *putare* to consider – more at PAVE] – **imputable** *adj*, **imputative** *adj*, **imputation** *n*, **imputability** *n*

¹**in** /in/ *prep* **1a(1)** – used to indicate location within or inside something three-dimensional ⟨*swimming* ~ *the lake*⟩ **a(2)** – used to indicate location within or not beyond limits ⟨ ~ *reach*⟩ ⟨ ~ *sight*⟩ ⟨*wounded* ~ *the leg*⟩ ⟨*playing* ~ *the street*⟩ **a(3)** at – used with the names of cities, countries, and seas ⟨ ~ *London*⟩ **a(4)** attending or undergoing treatment at ⟨ ~ *hospital*⟩ ⟨ ~ *church*⟩ **a(5)** occurring as the subject matter of ⟨*a character* ~ *a play*⟩ **a(6)** during ⟨ ~ *the summer*⟩ ⟨ ~ *future*⟩ ⟨ ~ *1959*⟩ ⟨*lost* ~ *transit*⟩ **a(7)** by or before the end of ⟨*wrote it* ~ *a week*⟩ ⟨*will come* ~ *an hour*⟩ **b(1)** into ⟨*went* ~ *the house*⟩ **b(2)** through in an inward

direction ⟨*came* ~ *the door*⟩ **b(3)** towards ⟨ ~ *the wrong direction*⟩ ⟨*the sun* ~ *my eyes*⟩ **2a** – used to indicate means, or instrumentality, or medium of expression ⟨*drawn* ~ *pencil*⟩ ⟨*bound* ~ *leather*⟩ ⟨*written* ~ *French*⟩ ⟨*covered* ~ *jam*⟩ ⟨*drink your health* ~ *cider*⟩ ⟨*a symphony* ~ *G*⟩ **b** – used to describe costume ⟨*a child* ~ *gumboots*⟩ ⟨*a girl* ~ *red*⟩ **3a** – used to indicate qualification, manner, or circumstance ⟨ ~ *fun*⟩ ⟨ ~ *exile*⟩ ⟨ ~ *public*⟩ ⟨ ~ *step*⟩ ⟨ ~ *anger*⟩ ⟨ ~ *his sleep*⟩ ⟨ ~ *a hurry*⟩ **b** so as to be ⟨*broke* ~ *pieces*⟩ – compare INTO **c** – used to indicate occupation or membership ⟨*a job* ~ *insurance*⟩ ⟨*everyone* ~ *the team*⟩ **4a** AS REGARDS ⟨*equal* ~ *distance*⟩ ⟨*weak* ~ *arithmetic*⟩ **b** BY WAY OF ⟨*said* ~ *reply*⟩ ⟨*the latest thing* ~ *shoes*⟩ **5a** – used to indicate division, arrangement, or quantity ⟨*packed* ~ *dozens*⟩ ⟨*standing* ~ *a circle*⟩ ⟨*arrived* ~ *their thousands*⟩ **b** – used to indicate the larger member of a ratio ⟨*one* ~ *six is eligible*⟩ ⟨*a tax of 40p* ~ *the £*⟩ **6** *of an animal* pregnant with ⟨ ~ *lamb*⟩ **7** – used to introduce indirect objects ⟨*rejoice* ~⟩ or to form adverbial phrases; compare IN FACT, IN RETURN [ME, fr OE; akin to OHG *in* in, L *in*, Gk *en*] – **in all** as a total; altogether – **in it** of advantage (e g between competitors or alternatives) ⟨*there's not much* in it *between them*⟩ ⟨*what's* in it *for me?*⟩ – **in that** BECAUSE 1

**synonyms** In American English one gets **on/onto** or **off** a train, bus, or boat, in British English it is also possible to get **in/into** or **out** of them. Americans live **on** a street, the British live in one ⟨*a house* in/(*NAm*) on *Park Lane*⟩. **usage 1** The central meaning of **in** is to convey the idea of position or state. It is very commonly used also to convey that of motion, but may be less vivid than into ⟨*dive* in/into *the lake*⟩. **2** Within or **inside** are clearer words than **in** to express the idea of "not beyond". Does ⟨*it'll arrive* in *a week*⟩ mean before the end of the week or on the seventh day?

²**in** *adv* **1a** to or towards the inside or centre ⟨*come* ~ *out of the rain*⟩ **b** so as to incorporate ⟨*mix* ~ *the flour*⟩ **c** to or towards home, the shore, or one's destination ⟨*three ships came sailing* ~⟩ **d** at a particular place, esp at one's home or business ⟨*be* ~ *for lunch*⟩ **e** into concealment ⟨*the sun went* ~⟩ **2a** so as to be added or included ⟨*fit a piece* ~⟩ ⟨*write a paragraph* ~⟩ **b** in or into political power ⟨*voted them* ~⟩ **c(1)** on good terms ⟨ ~ *with the boss*⟩ **c(2)** in a position of assured or definitive success **c(3)** into a state of efficiency or proficiency ⟨*work a horse* ~⟩ **d** in or into vogue or fashion **e** *of an oil well* in production **f** in or into a centre, esp a central point of control ⟨*letters pouring* ~⟩ ⟨*after harvests are* ~⟩ ⟨*went* ~ *to bat*⟩ **3** chiefly NAm in a specified relation ⟨ ~ *bad with the boss*⟩ – **in between** between ⟨*neither green nor blue but something* in between⟩ ⟨*likes wine before, after, and* in between *meals*⟩ – **in for** certain to experience – compare LET IN FOR – **in on** having a share in ⟨*she's* in on *the deal*⟩

³**in** *adj* **1a** located inside; internal **b** being in operation or power ⟨*the fire's still* ~⟩ **c** shared by a select group; INSIDE 3 ⟨*an* ~ *joke*⟩ **2** directed or serving to direct inwards ⟨*the* ~ *tray*⟩ **3a** keenly aware of and responsive to fashion ⟨*the* ~ *crowd*⟩ **b** extremely fashionable ⟨*the* ~ *place to go*⟩

⁴**in** *n* **1** one who is in office or power or on the inside ⟨*a matter of* ~s *versus outs*⟩ **2** influence, pull ⟨*enjoys a good deal of* ~ *with the manager*⟩

¹**in-** /in-/, **il-** /il-/, **im-** /im-/, **ir-** /ir-/ *prefix* not; non-; un- – usu *il-* before *l* ⟨*illogical*⟩, *im-* before *b, m*, or *p* ⟨*imbalance*⟩ ⟨*immoral*⟩ ⟨*impractical*⟩, *ir-* before *r* ⟨*irreducible*⟩, and *in-* before other sounds ⟨*inconclusive*⟩ **synonyms** see NON- [ME, fr MF, fr L; akin to OE *un-*]

²**in-, il-, im-, ir-** *prefix* **1** in; within; into; towards; on ⟨*influx*⟩ ⟨*immerse*⟩ ⟨*irradiance*⟩ – usu *il-* before *l, im-* before *b, m*, or *p, ir-* before *r*, and *in-* before other sounds **2** ¹EN- ⟨*imperil*⟩ ⟨*inspirit*⟩ [ME, fr MF, fr L, fr *in* in, into]

¹**-in** /-in/ *suffix* (→ *n*) chemical compound: e g **a** hydrolytic enzyme ⟨*pepsin*⟩ **b** antibiotic ⟨*streptomycin*⟩ **c** ²-INE 1 ⟨*glycerin*⟩ [Fr *-ine*, fr L *-īna*, fem of *-īnus* of or belonging to – more at -EN]

²**-in** *comb form* (→ *n*) **1** organized public protest by means of or in favour of; demonstration ⟨*teach*-in⟩ ⟨*love*-in⟩ **2** public group activity ⟨*sing*-in⟩ [²*in* (as in *sit*-in)]

**inability** /,inə'biləti/ *n* lack of sufficient power, resources, or capacity ⟨*his* ~ *to do maths*⟩ △ disability [ME *inabilite*, fr MF *inhabilité*, fr *in-* ¹*in-* + *habilité* ability]

**in absentia** /,in ab'sentiah, -shiah/ *adv* in absence ⟨*gave him the award* ~⟩ [L]

**inaccessible** /,inak'sesəbl/ *adj* not accessible [MF or LL; MF, fr LL *inaccessibilis*, fr L *in-* ¹*in-* + LL *accessibilis* accessible] – **inaccessibly** *adv*, **inaccessibility** *n*

**inaccuracy** /in'akyoorəsi/ *n* **1** the quality or state of being inaccurate **2** a mistake, error

**inaccurate** /in'akyoorət/ *adj* not accurate; faulty – **inaccurately** *adv*

**inaction** /in'aksh(ə)n/ *n* lack of action or activity

**inactivate** /in'aktivayt/ *vt* to make inactive – **inactivation** *n*

**inactive** /in'aktiv/ *adj* **1** not given to action or effort **2** out of use; not functioning **3** relating to members of the armed forces who are not performing or available for military duties **4** *of a disease* not progressing; dormant **5** chemically inert **6** optically neutral in POLARIZED light (light that vibrates only in a restricted number of directions) **7** biologically inert, esp because of the loss of some quality (e g infectivity or antigenicity) – **inactively** *adv*, **inactivity** *n*

synonyms **Inactive, idle, inert, passive, supine,** and **dormant** all mean "not engaged in work or activity". **Inactive** is a neutral term simply meaning "not currently in action" ⟨*an* **inactive** *machine*⟩ ⟨**inactive** *because of a bad leg*⟩. **Idle,** usually applied to people, but sometimes also to tools, also describes an absence of activity, but implies a cause for this such as unemployment, leisure, or laziness. **Inert** things have no power to move themselves or to activate processes, while **inert** people are habitually lethargic and difficult to arouse to (especially mental) activity. **Passive** is similar, but stresses lack of reaction to stimuli or provocation. **Supine** people are abjectly inert, through apathy or lethargy. **Dormant** means "temporarily inactive", with the possibility or likelihood of some return to activity in the future. *antonym* active

**inadequacy** /in'adikwəsi/ *n* the quality or state or an instance of being inadequate

**inadequate** /in'adikwət/ *adj* not adequate: e g **a** insufficient **b** characteristically unable to cope, esp in demanding situations ⟨*he has an ~ personality*⟩ – **inadequately** *adv*, **inadequateness** *n*

**inadmissible** /,inəd'misəbl/ *adj* not admissible – **inadmissibly** *adv*, **inadmissibility** *n*

**inadvertence** /,inəd'vuht(ə)ns/, **inadvertency** /,inəd'vuht(ə)nsi/ *n* **1** the fact or action of being inadvertent; inattention **2** a result of inattention; an oversight [ML *inadvertentia*, fr L *in-* ¹in- + *advertent-, advertens,* prp of *advertere* to advert]

**inadvertent** /,inəd'vuht(ə)nt/ *adj* **1** heedless, inattentive **2** unintentional [back-formation fr *inadvertence*] – **inadvertently** *adv*

**inadvisable** /,inəd'viezəbl/ *adj* not advisable – **inadvisability** *n*

**-inae** /-inie/ *suffix* (→ *n pl*) members of the subfamily of – used in all names of zoological subfamilies in recent classification ⟨*Felinae*⟩ [NL *-īnae,* fr L, fem pl of *-īnus*]

**inalienable** /in'aylyənəbl/ *adj* incapable of being alienated, surrendered, or transferred ⟨*~ rights*⟩ – **inalienably** *adv*, **inalienability** *n*

**inamorata** /,inamə'rahtə, in,amə-/, *masc* **inamorato** /-rahtoh/, *n, pl* **inamoratas,** *masc* **inamoratos** a person with whom one is in love or is having a sexual relationship [It *innamorato* (masc), *innamorata* (fem), fr pp of *innamorare* to inspire with love, fr *in-* ²in- + *amore* love, fr L *amor* – more at AMOROUS]

**in-and-'in** *adv or adj* in repeated generations of the same or closely related stock ⟨*a freak colour in horses caused by breeding ~*⟩

**in-and-'out** *n* an obstacle consisting of two fences in close proximity for a horse to jump successively

**inane** /in'ayn/ *adj* **1** empty, insubstantial **2** lacking significance, meaning, or point; silly [L *inanis*] – **inanely** *adv*, **inaneness** *n*

**inanimate** /in'animət/ *adj* **1** not animate: e g **1a** not having life or spirit **b** lacking consciousness or power of motion **2** not animated or lively [LL *inanimatus,* fr L *in-* ¹in- + *animatus,* pp of *animare* to animate] – **inanimately** *adv*, **inanimateness** *n*

**inanition** /,inə'nish(ə)n/ *n, formal* the quality or state of being empty: **a** the loss of energy that results from lack of food or water **b** the absence or loss of social, moral, or intellectual vitality or vigour; lethargy

**inanity** /i'nanəti/ *n* **1** the quality or state of being inane **2** something that is inane ⟨*the suggestion was an ~*⟩

**inappetence** /in'apit(ə)ns/, **inappetency** /-ənsi/ *n* loss or lack of appetite [¹*in-* + *appetence, appetency*] – **inappetent** *adj*

**inapplicable** /in'aplikəbl/, /,inə'plikəbl/ *adj* not applicable; unsuitable – **inapplicably** *adv*, **inapplicability** *n*

**inapposite** /in'apəzit/ *adj* not apposite; irrelevant – **inappositely** *adv*, **inappositeness** *n*

**inappreciable** /,inə'preesh(y)əbl/ *adj* too small or slight to be perceived ⟨*an ~ difference in the temperature*⟩ [Fr *inappré-*

*ciable,* fr MF *inappreciable,* fr *in-* ¹in- + *appreciable*] – **inappreciably** *adv*

**inapprehensible** *adj* /,inapri'hensəbl/ incapable of being apprehended by the mind or the senses

**inappropriate** /,inə'prohpri-ət/ *adj* not appropriate – **inappropriately** *adv*, **inappropriateness** *n*

**inapt** /in'apt/ *adj* **1** not suitable or appropriate **2** inept – **inaptly** *adv*, **inaptness** *n*

synonyms **Inapt, inept,** and **unapt** all mean "not apt", but in careful modern use **inapt** is confined to the sense "not appropriate" ⟨*an* **inapt** *quotation*⟩, **inept** largely means "foolish" or "incompetent", and **unapt** means chiefly "not likely" ⟨**unapt** *to agree*⟩.

**inaptitude** /in'aptityoohd/ *n* lack of aptitude

**inarguable** /in'ahgyooəbl/ *adj* not arguable – **inarguably** *adv*

**inarticulate** /,inah'tikyoolət/ *adj* **1a** not understandable as spoken words ⟨*~ cries*⟩ **b(1)** incapable of speech, esp under stress of emotion; mute **b(2)** incapable of being expressed by speech ⟨*~ longings*⟩ **2a** not giving or not able to give coherent, clear, or effective expression to one's ideas or feelings ⟨*an ~ person*⟩ **b** not coherently, clearly, or effectively expressed ⟨*an ~ speech*⟩ **3** of or being a BRACHIOPOD (marine shelled INVERTEBRATE animal) lacking a shell hinge [LL *inarticulatus,* fr L *in-* ¹in- + *articulatus,* pp of *articulare* to utter distinctly – more at ARTICULATE; (3) NL *inarticulatus,* fr L *in-* + NL *articulatus* articulate] – **inarticulately** *adv*, **inarticulateness** *n*

**inartistic** /,inah'tistik/ *adj* **1** not conforming to the principles of art **2** not appreciative of art **3** lacking in artistic skill

**inasmuch** *adv* – **inasmuch as** to the extent or degree that; INSOFAR AS

**inattention** /,inə'tensh(ə)n/ *n* failure to pay attention; disregard

**inattentive** /,inə'tentiv/ *adj* not attentive synonyms see ABSTRACTED – **inattentively** *adv*, **inattentiveness** *n*

**inaudible** /in'awdəbl/ *adj* not audible [LL *inaudibilis,* fr L *in-* ¹in-+ LL *audibilis* audible] – **inaudibly** *adv*, **inaudibility** *n*

¹**inaugural** /in'awgyoorəl/ *adj* **1** of an inauguration **2** marking a beginning; first in a projected series ⟨*an ~ meeting*⟩ [Fr, fr *inaugurer* to inaugurate, fr L *inaugurare*]

²**inaugural** *n* an inaugural address

**inaugurate** /in'awgyoorayt/ *vt* **1** to induct into office with suitable ceremonies **2a** to dedicate ceremoniously; observe formally the beginning of **b** to bring about the beginning of [L *inauguratus,* pp of *inaugurare,* lit., to practise augury, fr *in-* ²in- + *augurare* to augur; fr the rites connected with augury] – **inaugurator** *n*

**inauguration** /i,nawgyoo'raysh(ə)n/ *n* an act of inaugurating; *esp* a ceremonial induction into office

**Inauguration Day** *n* January 20 following a presidential election, on which the president of the USA is inaugurated

**inauspicious** /,inaw'spishəs/ *adj* not auspicious – **inauspiciously** *adv*, **inauspiciousness** *n*

**inauthentic** /,inaw'thentik/ *adj* ɪ.ot authentic – **inauthenticity** *n*

¹**inboard** /in'bawd/ *adv* **1** within the body (HULL) of a vessel; towards the centre line of a ship **2** in a position closer or closest to the long axis of an aircraft

²**inboard** /'inbawd/ *adj* located, moving, or being inboard ⟨*an ~ engine*⟩; *also* having an inboard engine ⟨*~ boats*⟩

**inborn** /-'bawn/ *adj* **1** born in or with a person; forming part of one's natural make-up **2** hereditary, inherited ⟨*phenylketonuria is an ~ error of metabolism*⟩ synonyms see CONGENITAL

**inbreathe** /in'breedh/ *vt* to breathe (something) in; inhale

**inbred** /-'bred/ *adj* **1** rooted and ingrained in one's nature as deeply as if implanted by heredity ⟨*an ~ love of freedom*⟩ **2** subjected to or produced by inbreeding

**inbreed** /in'breed/ *vb* **in-bred** /-'bred/ to subject to or engage in inbreeding – **inbreeder** *n*

**inbreeding** /-,breeding/ *n* **1** the interbreeding of closely related individuals, esp to preserve and fix desirable characteristics of and to eliminate unfavourable characteristics from a stock (e g of domestic animals) **2** confinement to a narrow range or a local or limited field of choice

**inbuilt** /-'bilt/ *adj* built-in; *esp* inherent

**inbye, inby** /'inbie, -'-/ *adj, dial Br* situated close by, esp near to the house ⟨*the ~ land*⟩ [²*in* + *bye,* var of *by,* adv]

**Inca** /'ingkə/ *n* **1** a member of the QUECHUAN peoples of Peru who maintained an extensive empire until the Spanish conquest **2** a king or noble of the Inca empire [Sp, fr Quechua *inka* king, prince] – **Incan** *adj*, **Incaic** *adj*

**incalculable** /in'kalkyoolǝbl/ *adj* **1** not capable of being calculated; *esp* too large or numerous to be calculated **2** unpredictable, uncertain – **incalculably** *adv*, **incalculability** *n*

**in camera** *adv* in private; secretly [NL, lit., in a chamber]

**incandesce** /,inkan'des/ *vb* to make, be, or become incandescent [L *incandescere*]

**incandescence** /,inkan'des(ǝ)ns/ *n* the quality or state of being incandescent; *esp* the emission of radiation by a hot body so as to make that body visible

**incandescent** /,inkan'des(ǝ)nt/ *adj* **1a** white, glowing, or luminous with intense heat **b** strikingly bright, radiant, or clear; brilliant **c** glowing, ardent ⟨∼ *affection*⟩ **2a** of or being light produced by incandescence **b** producing light by incandescence ⟨*an* ∼ *bulb*⟩ [Fr or L; Fr, fr L *incandescent-, incandescens*, prp of *incandescere* to become hot, fr *in-* ²*in-* + *candescere* to become hot, incho of *candēre* to glow – more at CANDID] – **incandescently** *adv*

**incandescent lamp** *n* an electric lamp in which a filament gives off light when heated to incandescence by an electric current

**incantation** /,inkan'taysh(ǝ)n/ *n* the use of spoken or sung spells as a part of a ritual of magic; *also* a written or recited magical formula of words designed to produce a particular effect [ME *incantacioun*, fr MF *incantation*, fr LL *incantation-, incantatio*, fr L *incantatus*, pp of *incantare* to enchant – more at ENCHANT] – **incantational, incantatory** *adj*

**incapable** /in'kaypǝbl/ *adj* lacking capacity, ability, or qualification for the purpose or end in view: e g **a** not in a state or of a kind to admit of ⟨∼ *of precise measurement*⟩ **b** not able or fit for the doing or performance of ⟨*he's* ∼ *of spelling correctly*⟩ [MF, fr *in-* ¹*in-* + *capable*] – **incapableness** *n*, **incapably** *adv*, **incapability** *n*

*synonyms* Incapable suggests a more permanent lack of ability than does unable. Compare ⟨*he's incapable of lying*⟩ ⟨*he's unable to attend the meeting*⟩.

**incapacitate** /,inkǝ'pasitayt/ *vt* **1** to deprive of capacity or natural power; disable **2** to make legally incapable (e g by unsoundness of mind) or ineligible (e g by bankruptcy) – **incapacitator** *n*, **incapacitation** *n*

**incapacity** /,inkǝ'pasǝti/ *n* **1** lack of ability or natural power ⟨*his apparent* ∼ *for telling the truth*⟩ **2** lack of legal ability, entitlement, or qualification [Fr *incapacité*, fr MF, fr *in-* ¹*in-* + *capacité* capacity]

**incarcerate** /in'kahsǝrayt/ *vt* to confine (as if) in a prison [L *incarceratus*, pp of *incarcerare*, fr *in-* ²*in-* + *carcer* prison] – **incarceration** *n*

**incardination** /in,kahdi'naysh(ǝ)n/ *n* the formal acceptance by a diocese of a clergyman from another diocese [LL *incardination-, incardinatio*, fr *incardinatus*, pp of *incardinare* to ordain as chief priest, fr *in-* ²*in-* + *cardinalis* principal – more at CARDINAL]

¹**incarnadine** /in'kahnǝdien/ *adj, poetic* **1** flesh-coloured **2** red; *esp* bloodred [MF *incarnadin*, fr OIt *incarnadino*, fr *incarnato* flesh-coloured, fr L incarnare to in-

²**incarnadine** *vt, poetic* to make incarnadine; redden

¹**incarnate** /in'kahnǝt, -nayt/ *adj* **1** invested with bodily and esp human nature and form **2** that is the essence of; typified ⟨*evil* ∼⟩ **3** made manifest or comprehensible; embodied ⟨*a fiend* ∼⟩ [ME *incarnat*, fr LL *incarnatus*, pp of *incarnare* to incarnate, fr L *in-* ²*in-* + *carn-, caro* flesh – more at CARNAL]

²**incarnate** /'inkah,nayt/ *vt* to make incarnate

**incarnation** /,inkah'naysh(ǝ)n/ *n* **1** the act of making incarnate; the state of being incarnate **2a(1)** the embodiment of a deity or spirit in an earthly form **a(2)** *cap, Christianity* the union of divinity with humanity in Jesus Christ **b** a quality or concept typified or made concrete, esp in a person ⟨*she is the* ∼ *of goodness*⟩ **3** any of several successive bodily manifestations or lives ⟨*in another* ∼ *he might be a brilliant cricketer*⟩

**incase** /in'kays/ *vt* to encase

**incautious** /in'kawshǝs/ *adj* lacking in caution; rash – **incautiously** *adv*, **incautiousness** *n*

**incendiarism** /in'sendyǝriz(ǝ)m/ *n* incendiary action or behaviour: **a** arson **b** the promotion of civil unrest; sedition – **incendiarist** *n*

¹**incendiary** /in'sendyǝri/ *n* **1a** a person who deliberately sets fire to property (e g a building) **b** an incendiary device (e g a bomb) **2** a person who inflames or stirs up factions, quarrels, or sedition; an agitator [L *incendiarius*, fr *incendium* fire, fr *incendere*]

²**incendiary** *adj* **1** of or involving the deliberate burning of property **2** tending to inflame or stir up trouble; inflammatory

⟨∼ *speeches*⟩ **3a** able to (spontaneously) catch alight; combustible **b** relating to, being, or involving the use of a missile containing chemical compounds that ignite on bursting or on contact

¹**incense** /'insens/ *n* **1** material used to produce a fragrant smell when burned **2** the perfume given off by some spices and gums when burned; *broadly* a pleasing scent **3** pleasing attention; flattery [ME *encens*, fr OF, fr LL *incensum*, fr L, neut of *incensus*, pp of *incendere* to set on fire, fr *in-* ²*in-* + *-cendere* to burn; akin to L *candēre* to glow – more at CANDID]

²**incense** /in'sens/ *vt* **1** to apply or offer incense to **2** to perfume with incense

³**incense** /in'sens/ *vt* to arouse the extreme anger or indignation of; enrage [ME *encensen* to set on fire, inflame, fr MF *incenser*, fr L *incensus*]

**incentive** /in'sentiv/ *n* something that motivates or spurs one on (e g to action or effort) ⟨*it gave me the* ∼ *to carry on*⟩ ⟨*workers who lack* ∼⟩ [ME, fr LL *incentivum*, fr neut of *incentivus* stimulating, fr L, setting the tune, fr *incentus*, pp of *incinere* to set the tune, fr *in-* ²*in-* + *canere* to sing – more at CHANT] – **incentive** *adj*

**incept** /in'sept/ *vt* to take in; *esp* to ingest [L *in-* ²*in-* + *-ceptus*, fr *captus*, pp of *capere* to take] – **inceptor** *n*

**inception** /in'sepsh(ǝ)n/ *n* an act, process, or instance of beginning; a start *synonyms* see ORIGIN [L *inception-, inceptio*, fr *inceptus*, pp of *incipere* to begin, fr *in-* ²*in-* + *capere* to take – more at HEAVE]

¹**inceptive** /in'septiv/ *n* an INCHOATIVE (denoting the beginning of an action) verb

²**inceptive** *adj* **1** of a beginning **2** *of a verb* denoting the beginning of an action; INCHOATIVE **2** – **inceptively** *adv*

**incertitude** /in'suhtityoohd/ *n* uncertainty, doubt [MF, fr LL *incertitudo*, fr L *in-* ¹*in-* + LL *certitudo* certitude]

**incessant** /in'ses(ǝ)nt/ *adj* continuing without interruption; unceasing *synonyms* see CONTINUAL *antonym* intermittent [ME *incessaunt*, fr LL *incessant-, incessans*, fr L *in-* ¹*in-* + *cessant-, cessans*, prp of *cessare* to delay – more at CEASE] – **incessancy** *n*, **incessantly** *adv*

**incest** /'insest/ *n* SEXUAL INTERCOURSE between people (e g brother and sister) so closely related that they are forbidden by law to marry [ME, fr L *incestum*, fr neut of *incestus* impure, fr *in-* ¹*in-* + *castus* pure – more at CASTE]

**incestuous** /in'sestyoo-ǝs/ *adj* **1** constituting or involving incest **2** guilty of incest **3** unhealthily closed to outside influences ⟨∼ *quoting of one another's works*⟩ – **incestuously** *adv*, **incestuousness** *n*

¹**inch** /inch/ *n* **1** a unit of length equal to $\frac{1}{36}$ yard (about 25.4 millimetres) **2** a small amount, distance, or degree ⟨*escaped death by an* ∼⟩ **3** *pl* stature, height ⟨*a man of his* ∼*es would be easily seen in a crowd*⟩ **4** a fall (e g of rain or snow) sufficient to cover a surface to the depth of one inch [ME, fr OE *ynce*, fr L *uncia* – more at OUNCE] – **every inch** in every respect; completely ⟨*looks every inch a winner*⟩ – **within an inch of** very close to ⟨*was within an inch of being run down*⟩ – **within an inch of somebody's life** almost to the point of death ⟨*flogged him within an inch of his life*⟩

²**inch** *vi* to move by small degrees ⟨*the long line of people* ∼*ing up the stairs*⟩ ∼ *vt* to cause to move slowly ⟨*to* ∼ *the prices back up*⟩

³**inch** *n, chiefly Scot* an island – usu in place-names [ME, fr ScGael *innis*]

**-in-'chief** *comb form* (*n* → *n*) having superiority over all others

**inchoate** /'inkoh·ayt, in'koh·ayt/ *adj, formal* only partly in existence or operation; *esp* imperfectly formed or formulated ⟨*an* ∼ *longing*⟩ [L *inchoatus*, pp of *inchoare*, lit., to hitch up, fr *in-* ²*in-* + *cohum* strap fastening a plough beam to the yoke] – **inchoately** *adv*, **inchoateness** *n*

**inchoative** /in'koh·ǝtiv/ *adj* **1** initial, formative ⟨*the* ∼ *stages*⟩ **2** *of a verb* denoting the beginning of an action, state, or occurrence – **inchoative** *n*, **inchoatively** *adv*

**inchworm** /'inch,wuhm/ *n* LOOPER **1** (type of caterpillar)

**incidence** /'insid(ǝ)ns/ *n* **1a** an occurrence **b** the rate of occurrence or influence ⟨*a high* ∼ *of crime*⟩ **2a** the arrival of something (e g a projectile or a ray of light) at a surface **b** ANGLE OF INCIDENCE (angle which an incident projectile, ray of light, etc makes with a surface)

¹**incident** /'insid(ǝ)nt/ *n* **1** an occurrence of an action or situation that is a separate unit of experience; a happening ⟨*it was a remarkable* ∼⟩ **2** an action likely to lead to grave consequences, esp in diplomatic matters ⟨*a serious border* ∼⟩ **3** an

event occurring as part of a series or as dependent on or subordinate to something else ⟨*there are various ~s of this kind throughout the play*⟩ *synonyms* see OCCURRENCE [ME, fr MF, fr ML *incident-, incidens*, fr L, prp of *incidere* to fall into, fr *in-* ²*in-* + *cadere* to fall – more at CHANCE]

²**incident** *adj* **1** occurring or likely to occur esp as a minor consequence or accompaniment ⟨*the confusion ~ to moving house*⟩ **2** *esp of property rights* dependent on or relating to another thing in law **3** falling or striking on something ⟨*~ light rays*⟩

¹**incidental** /ˌinsi'dentl/ *adj* **1** occurring merely by chance or without intention or calculation **2** likely to ensue as a chance or minor consequence ⟨*social obligations ~ to his job*⟩

**synonyms** Incidental, accidental, adventitious, and contingent all mean "nonessential", "arising from external circumstances". The first two stress comparative lack of importance, while **adventitious** insists on the lack of innateness and is more likely to be the result of chance. **Contingent** is applied to what may happen but is subject to events. *usage* Some careful writers like to confine **incidental** to the sense "ensuing as a minor consequence" ⟨*incidental expenses*⟩ and to use **accidental** for "happening by chance".

²**incidental** *n* **1** something that is incidental **2** *pl* minor items (e g of expenses)

**incidentally** /ˌinsi'dentl·i/ *adv* **1** by chance; casually **2** as a digression; BY THE WAY

**incidental music** *n* background music that enhances the dramatic action of a play, film, television programme, etc

**incinerate** /in'sinərayt/ *vt* to burn to ashes [ML *incineratus*, pp of *incinerare*, fr L *in-* ²*in-* + *ciner-, cinis* ashes; akin to Gk *konis* dust, ashes] – **incineration** *n*

**incinerator** /in'sinəraytə/ *n* a machine that incinerates; *esp* a furnace or a container for incinerating waste materials

**incipiency** /in'sipiənsi/, **incipience** /-əns/ *n* the state or fact of being incipient; beginning

**incipient** /in'sipi·ənt/ *adj* beginning to come into being or to become apparent; commencing ⟨*evidence of ~ racial tension*⟩ [L *incipient-, incipiens*, prp of *incipere* to begin – more at INCEPTION] – **incipiently** *adv*

**incipit** /'insipit, 'inkipit/ *n* the first part; beginning; *specif* the opening words of a text of a medieval manuscript or early printed book [L, it begins, fr *incipere*]

**incise** /in'siez/ *vt* **1** to cut into **2a** to carve designs or letters into (e g a block of stone); engrave **b** to carve (e g an inscription) into a surface [MF or L; MF *inciser*, fr L *incisus*, pp of *incidere*, fr *in-* ²*in-* + *caedere* to cut – more at CONCISE]

**incised** /in'siezd/ *adj* **1a** cut in; engraved; *esp* decorated with incised figures **b** *of a wound* made (as if) with a sharp knife **2** having an edge that is naturally formed with deep and sharp notches ⟨*an ~ leaf*⟩

**incision** /in'sizh(ə)n/ *n* **1a** a sharp notch or indentation (e g in the natural shape of a leaf's edge) **b** a cut, gash; *specif* an incised wound made esp in medical surgery into the body **2** an act of incising

**incisive** /in'siesiv/ *adj* impressively direct and decisive (e g in manner or presentation) – **incisively** *adv*, **incisiveness** *n*

**incisor** /in'siezə/ *n* a tooth adapted for cutting; *specif* any of the cutting teeth in mammals in front of the CANINES

**incite** /in'siet/ *vt* to move to action; stir up; spur on [MF *inciter*, fr L *incitare*, fr *in-* ²*in-* + *citare* to put in motion – more at CITE] – **incitant** *n*, **incitation** *n*, **inciter** *n*

**incitement** /in'sietmənt/ *n* **1** an act of inciting; the state of being incited ⟨*~ to riot*⟩ **2** something that incites

**incivility** /ˌinsi'viləti/ *n* **1** the quality or state of being uncivil; rudeness **2** a rude or discourteous act [MF *incivilité*, fr LL *incivilitat-, incivilitas*, fr *incivilis*, fr L *in-* ¹*in-* + *civilis* civil]

**inclement** /in'klemənt/ *adj* **1** physically severe; stormy ⟨*~ weather*⟩ **2** *archaic* not clement; unmerciful [L *inclement-, inclemens*, fr *in-* ¹*in-* + *clement-, clemens* clement] – **inclemency** *n*, **inclemently** *adv*

**inclinable** /in'klienəbl/ *adj* having a tendency or inclination *to*; *also* disposed to favour or think well of

**inclination** /ˌinkli'naysh(ə)n/ *n* **1** an act or the action of bending or inclining: e g **1a** a bow, nod **b** a tilting of something **2** a particular tendency or propensity; *esp* a liking ⟨*had little ~ for housekeeping*⟩ **3a** a deviation from the true vertical or horizontal; a slant; *also* the degree of such deviation **b** an inclined surface; a slope **c(1)** the angle between two lines or planes ⟨*the ~ of two rays of light*⟩ **c(2)** *maths* the angle made by a line with the x-axis measured anticlockwise from the

positive direction of that axis *synonyms* see TENDENCY – **inclinational** *adj*

¹**incline** /in'klien/ *vi* **1** to bend the head or body forwards; bow **2** to lean, tend, or become drawn towards an opinion or course of conduct **3** to deviate from a line, direction, or course; *specif* to deviate from the vertical or horizontal ~ *vt* **1** to cause to stoop or bow; bend **2** to have influence on; persuade ⟨*his love of books ~d him towards a literary career*⟩ **3** to give a bend or slant to [ME *inclinen*, fr MF *incliner*, fr L *inclinare*, fr *in-* ²*in-* + *clinare* to lean – more at LEAN] – **incliner** *n*

²**incline** /'inklien/ *n* an inclined plane; a slope

**inclined** /in'kliend/ *adj* **1** having inclination, disposition, or tendency **2a** having a leaning or slope **b** making an angle with a line or plane

**inclined plane** *n* a plane surface that makes an oblique angle with the horizontal

**inclining** /in'kliening/ *n* **1** an inclination, tendency **2** *archaic* a party, following

**inclinometer** /ˌinkli'nomitə/ *n* **1** an apparatus for determining the direction of the earth's MAGNETIC FIELD with reference to the plane of the horizon **2** an instrument for indicating the inclination to the horizontal of an axis of a ship or aircraft

**inclose** /in'klohz/ *vt* to enclose

**inclosure** /in'klohzhə/ *n* an enclosure

**include** /in'kloohd/ *vt* **1** to contain, comprise **2** to take in or comprise as a part of a larger group, set, or principle *synonyms* see COMPRISE [ME *includen*, fr L *includere*, fr *in-* ²*in-* + *claudere* to close – more at CLOSE] – **includable, includible** *adj*

**included** /in'kloohdid/ *adj* that is enclosed or embraced; *esp*, *of a male or female plant reproductive structure* not projecting beyond the mouth of the COROLLA (circle of petals) ⟨*~ stamens*⟩

**inclusion** /in'kloohzh(ə)n/ *n* **1** the act of including; the state of being included **2** something that is included: e g **2a** a gaseous, liquid, or solid foreign body enclosed in a mass (e g of a mineral) **b** something (e g a starch grain) taken up by, or stored within, a living cell **3** the relation between two mathematical sets when all members of the first are also members of the second – compare MEMBERSHIP 3 [L *inclusion-, inclusio*, fr *inclusus*, pp of *includere*]

**inclusion body** *n* a rounded or oval body within a cell that is characteristic of some virus diseases, and is believed to represent a stage in the multiplication of the virus

**inclusive** /in'kloohsiv, -ziv/ *adj* **1a** broad in orientation or scope **b** covering or intended to cover all items, costs, or services **2** including the stated limits or extremes ⟨*from Monday to Friday ~*⟩ – **inclusively** *adv*, **inclusiveness** *n* – **inclusive of** taking into account; including ⟨*the cost of building inclusive of materials*⟩

**inclusive disjunction** *n* a complex sentence in logic that is true when either one or both of its constituent sentences are true

**incoercible** /ˌinkoh'uhsəbl/ *adj* incapable of being controlled, checked, or confined [¹*in-* + *coercible*]

**incogitant** /in'kojitənt/ *adj, formal* thoughtless, inconsiderate [L *incogitant-, incogitans*, fr *in-* ¹*in-* + *cogitant-, cogitans*, prp of *cogitare* to think]

¹**incognito** /ˌinkog'neetoh, in'kognitoh/ *adv or adj* with one's identity concealed [It, fr L *incognitus* unknown, fr *in-* ¹*in-* + *cognitus*, pp of *cognoscere* to know – more at COGNITION]

²**incognito** *n, pl* **incognitos** (the state or disguise of) one who is incognito

**incognizant** /in'kogniz(ə)nt/ *adj* lacking awareness or consciousness *of* [¹*in-* + *cognizant*] – **incognizance** *n*

**incoherent** /ˌinkoh'hiərənt/ *adj* lacking coherence: e g **a** not sticking closely or compactly together; loose **b** not logically connected; uncoordinated ⟨*the victim told an ~ story*⟩ **c** not clearly intelligible; inarticulate ⟨*a voice ~ with rage*⟩ – **incoherence, incoherency** *n*, **incoherently** *adv*

**in coitu** /in 'koh·itooh/ *adv, euph* while copulating [L]

**incombustible** /ˌinkəm'bustəbl/ *adj* not combustible; incapable of being burned [ME, prob fr MF, fr *in-* ¹*in-* + *combustible*] – **incombustible** *n*, **incombustibility** *n*

**income** /'inkum, 'inkəm/ *n* **1** a coming in; an input, influx ⟨*fluctuations in the nutrient ~ of a body of water*⟩ **2** a gain or recurrent benefit usu measured in money that derives from one's work, property, or investment; *also* the amount of such gain received in a period of time ⟨*a small yearly ~*⟩

**incomer** /'inˌkumə/ *n, chiefly Br* one who comes in: e g **a** an immigrant **b** an intruder **c** a successor

**incomes policy** *n* a political strategy for managing the rate of growth and distribution of incomes in an economy; *specif* an attempt to control wage inflation by direct government intervention (e g setting limits on wage increases) in the process of wage bargaining – compare FREE COLLECTIVE BARGAINING
**income tax** *n* a tax on income
¹**incoming** /'in,kuming/ *n* **1** the act of coming in; an arrival **2** *pl* INCOME 2
²**incoming** *adj* **1** coming in; arriving ⟨*an* ~ *ship*⟩ ⟨*the* ~ *tide*⟩ **2** just starting, beginning, or succeeding ⟨*the* ~ *president*⟩
**incommensurable** /,inkə'mensh(ə)rəbl/ *adj* **1** not having a common measure; *broadly* lacking a common basis of comparison in respect to a quality normally subject to comparison **2** having no common factor ⟨√2 *and* 3 *are* ~⟩ [¹*in-* + *commensurable*] – **incommensurable** *n*, **incommensurably** *adv*, **incommensurability** *n*
**incommensurate** /,inkə'menshərət/ *adj* not commensurate; *esp* not adequate in proportion
**incommode** /,inkə'mohd/ *vt, formal* to give inconvenience or distress to; disturb [MF *incommoder*, fr L *incommodare*, fr *incommodus* inconvenient, fr *in-* ¹*in-* + *commodus* convenient – more at COMMODE]
**incommodious** /,inkə'mohdi·əs/ *adj, formal* inconvenient or uncomfortable, esp because of being too small – **incommodiously** *adv*, **incommodiousness** *n*
**incommunicable** /,inkə'myoohnikəbl/ *adj* **1** incapable of being communicated or imparted **2** *archaic* uncommunicative [MF or LL; MF, fr LL *incommunicabilis*, fr L *in-* ¹*in-* + LL *communicabilis* communicable] – **incommunicably** *adv*, **incommunicability** *n*
**incommunicado** /,inkə,myoohni'kahdoh/ *adv or adj* without or deprived of means of communication; *also* in solitary confinement [Sp *incomunicado*, fr pp of *incomunicar* to deprive of communication, fr *in-* ¹*in-* + *comunicar* to communicate, fr L *communicare*]
**incommunicative** /,inkə'myoohnikətiv/ *adj* uncommunicative
**incommutable** /,inkə'myoohtəbl/ *adj* **1** not interchangeable **2** unchangeable [ME, fr L *incommutabilis*, fr *in-* ¹*in-* + *commutabilis* commutable] – **incommutably** *adv*
**incomparable** /in'komp(ə)rəbl/ *adj* **1** of such quality as to be beyond comparison; matchless **2** not suitable for comparison [ME, fr MF, fr L *incomparabilis*, fr *in-* ¹*in-* + *comparabilis* comparable] – **incomparably** *adv*, **incomparability** *n*
**incompatibility** /,inkəm,patə'bilati/ *n* **1a** the quality or state of being incompatible **b** the condition in which two plants are unable to fertilize each other **2** *pl* mutually incompatible things or qualities
**incompatible** /,inkəm'patəbl/ *adj* **1a** incapable of association because incongruous, discordant, or disagreeing ⟨~ *colours*⟩ ⟨*conduct* ~ *with sense of honour*⟩ **b** unsuitable for use in association because of undesirable chemical or physiological effects ⟨~ *drugs*⟩ **2** mutually exclusive ⟨~ *propositions*⟩ [MF & ML; MF, fr ML *incompatibilis*, fr L *in-* ¹*in-* + ML *compatibilis* compatible] – **incompatible** *n*, **incompatibly** *adv*
**incompetent** /in'kompit(ə)nt/ *adj* **1** lacking the qualities needed for effective action ⟨~ *to teach*⟩ **2** not legally qualified or competent ⟨*an* ~ *witness*⟩ **3** inadequate to or unsuitable for a particular purpose ⟨*an* ~ *heart valve*⟩ ⟨*an* ~ *system of government*⟩ **4** of or being rock structures or layers that are not strong enough to withstand or transmit pressure and hence crush or flow under stress [MF *incompétent*, fr *in-* ¹*in-* + *compétent* competent] – **incompetence, incompetency** *n*, **incompetent** *n*, **incompetently** *adv*
**incomplete** /,inkəm'pleet/ *adj* **1** not complete; unfinished **2** lacking a part; *esp, of a flower* lacking one or more sets of the floral organs (e g petals) present in a perfect flower [ME *incompleet*, fr LL *incompletus*, fr L *in-* ¹*in-* + *completus* complete] – **incompletely** *adv*, **incompleteness** *n*, **incompletion** *n*
**incomplete metamorphosis** *n* a method of development (METAMORPHOSIS) in an insect (e g a cockroach or grasshopper) in which the immature stages differ from the adult insect only in size and in the absence of reproductive organs and fully developed wings – compare COMPLETE METAMORPHOSIS
**incompliant** /,inkəm'plie·ənt/ *adj* not compliant or pliable; unyielding
**incomprehensible** /,inkompri'hensəbl, -,--'---/ *adj* impossible to understand; unintelligible [ME, fr L *incomprehensibilis*, fr *in-* ¹*in-* + *comprehensibilis* comprehensible] – **incomprehensibleness** *n*, **incomprehensibly** *adv*, **incomprehensibility** *n*

**incomprehension** /,inkompri'hensh(ə)n/ *n* lack of comprehension or understanding
**incompressible** /,inkəm'presəbl/ *adj* incapable of or resistant to compression – **incompressibly** *adv*, **incompressibility** *n*
**inconceivable** /,inkən'seevəbl/ *adj* **1** impossible to conceive; unimaginable **2** unbelievable – **inconceivableness** *n*, **inconceivably** *adv*, **inconceivability** *n*
**inconclusive** /,inkən'kloohsiv/ *adj* leading to no conclusion or definite result – **inconclusively** *adv*, **inconclusiveness** *n*
**incondite** /in'kondit, -diet/ *adj* badly put together; crude ⟨*turgid* ~ *prose*⟩ [L *inconditus*, fr *in-* ¹*in-* + *conditus*, pp of *condere* to put together, store up, hide – more at CONDIMENT]
**incongruent** /in'kong·grooənt/ *adj* not mathematically CONGRUENT (equal in all respects) ⟨~ *triangles*⟩ [L *incongruent-*, *incongruens*, fr *in-* ¹*in-* + *congruent-*, *congruens* congruent] – **incongruently** *adv*
**incongruous** /in'kong·groo·əs/ *adj* out of place; incompatible, discordant ⟨~ *colours*⟩ ⟨*conduct* ~ *with his principles*⟩ [LL *incongruus*, fr L *in-* ¹*in-* + *congruus* congruous] – **incongruously** *adv*, **incongruousness** *n*, **incongruity** *n*
**inconsequent** /in'konsikwənt/ *adj* **1** lacking reasonable sequence; illogical **2** irrelevant **3** INCONSEQUENTIAL 2 [LL *inconsequent-*, *inconsequens*, fr L *in-* ¹*in-* + *consequent-*, *consequens* consequent] – **inconsequence** *n*, **inconsequently** *adv*
**inconsequential** /,inkonsi'kwensh(ə)l/ *adj* **1a** illogical **b** irrelevant **2** of no significance; unimportant – **inconsequentially** *adv*, **inconsequentiality** *n*
**inconsiderable** /,inkən'sid(ə)rəbl/ *adj* not worth considering; trivial ⟨*exercised no* ~ *influence*⟩ [MF, fr *in-* ¹*in-* + *considerable*, fr ML *considerabilis* considerable] – **inconsiderableness** *n*, **inconsiderably** *adv*
**inconsiderate** /,inkən'sid(ə)rət/ *adj* **1** heedless, thoughtless **2** careless of the rights or feelings of others [L *inconsideratus*, fr *in-* ¹*in-* + *consideratus* considerate] – **inconsiderately** *adv*, **inconsiderateness**, **inconsideration** *n*
**inconsistent** /,inkən'sist(ə)nt/ *adj* lacking consistency: e g **a** not compatible with another fact or assertion ⟨~ *statements*⟩ **b** containing incompatible elements ⟨*an* ~ *argument*⟩ **c** incoherent or illogical in thought or actions; changeable **d** *maths* not satisfiable by any set of values for the unknowns ⟨~ *equations*⟩ ⟨~ *inequalities*⟩ – **inconsistence, inconsistency** *n*, **inconsistently** *adv*
**inconsolable** /,inkən'sohləbl/ *adj* incapable of being consoled; broken-hearted ⟨*the widower's* ~ *grief*⟩ ⟨*she was* ~ *after the loss of her child*⟩ [L *inconsolabilis*, fr *in-* ¹*in-* + *consolabilis* consolable] – **inconsolableness** *n*, **inconsolably** *adv*
**inconsonant** /in'kons(ə)nənt/ *adj* not harmonious; discordant [¹*in-* + ²*consonant*] – **inconsonance** *n*
**inconspicuous** /,inkən'spikyoo·əs/ *adj* not readily noticeable [L *inconspicuus*, fr *in-* ¹*in-* + *conspicuus* conspicuous] – **inconspicuously** *adv*, **inconspicuousness** *n*
**inconstant** /in'konst(ə)nt/ *adj* not constant: e g **a** likely to change frequently without apparent reason **b** unfaithful ⟨*an* ~ *wife*⟩ [ME, fr MF, fr L *inconstant-*, *inconstans*, fr *in-* ¹*in-* + *constant-*, *constans* constant] – **inconstancy** *n*, **inconstantly** *adv*
**incontestable** /,inkən'testəbl/ *adj* not contestable; indisputable ⟨~ *proof*⟩ [Fr, fr *in-* ¹*in-* + *contestable*, fr *contester* to contest] – **incontestably** *adv*, **incontestability** *n*
**incontinence** /in'kontinəns/ *n* the quality or state of being incontinent: e g **a** failure to restrain sexual appetite; unchastity **b** lack of control of urination or defecation
**incontinent** /in'kontinənt/ *adj* not continent: e g **a** lacking self-restraint **b** suffering from urinary or faecal incontinence **c** not under control ⟨*that play . . . is singularly* ~ *and full of loose ends – TLS*⟩ [ME, fr MF or L; MF, fr L *incontinent-*, *incontinens*, fr *in-* ¹*in-* + *continent-*, *continens* continent]
¹**incontinently** /in'kontinəntli/ *adv* without delay; immediately [MF *incontinent*, fr LL *in continenti (tempore)* in continuous time]
²**incontinently** *adv* in an incontinent or unrestrained manner; *esp* without moral restraint
**incontrovertible** /,inkontrə'vuhtəbl, in,kon-/ *adj* not open to question; indisputable ⟨~ *evidence*⟩ [¹*in-* + *controvertible*] – **incontrovertibly** *adv*
¹**inconvenience** /,inkən'veeniəns/ *n* **1** the quality or state of being inconvenient; difficulty, discomfort **2** something that is inconvenient
²**inconvenience** *vt* to subject to inconvenience
**inconvenient** /,inkən'veenyənt, -ni·ənt/ *adj* not convenient,

esp in causing difficulty, discomfort, or annoyance; inopportune [ME, fr MF, fr L *inconvenient-, inconveniens*, fr *in-* ¹*in-* + *convenient-, conveniens* convenient] – **inconveniently** *adv*

**inconvertible** /ˌinkən'vuhtəbl/ *adj* not convertible: eg **a** *of paper money* not exchangeable on demand for money in coin **b** *of a currency* not exchangeable for a foreign currency – **inconvertibly** *adv*, **inconvertibility** *n*

**incoordination** /ˌinkoh,awdi'naysh(ə)n/ *n* lack of coordination, esp of muscular movements that results from loss of voluntary control – **incoordinated, incoordinate** *adj*

**incorporate** /in'kawpərayt/ *vt* **1a** to unite thoroughly with or work indistinguishably into something already existent **b** to admit to membership in a corporate body **2a** to blend or combine thoroughly to form a consistent whole **b** to form into a legal corporation **3** to give material form to; embody ~ *vi* **1** to unite in or as one body **2** to form or become a legal corporation [ME *incorporaten*, fr LL *incorporatus*, pp of *incorporare*, fr L *in-* ²*in-* + *corpor-, corpus* body] – **incorporator** *n*, **incorporable** *adj*, **incorporative** *adj*, **incorporation** *n*

**incorporated** /in'kawpəraytid/, **incorporate** /-ərət/ *adj* **1a** united in one body **b** admitted to membership in a corporate body **2** *NAm* formed into a legal corporation – compare LIMITED COMPANY

**incorporeal** /ˌinkaw'pawri-əl/ *adj* **1** not corporeal; having no material body or form **2** of or constituting a legal right that is attached to property (eg copyrights or patents) which has no physical existence [L *incorporeus*, fr *in-* ¹*in-* + *corporeus* corporeal] – **incorporeally** *adv*, **incorporeity** *n*

**incorrect** /ˌinkə'rekt/ *adj* **1** not true; factually wrong ⟨*all your answers are* ~⟩ **2** improper; *esp* not in accordance with an established social standard or set of rules ⟨*he scolded his son for* ~ *behaviour*⟩ [ME, fr MF or L; MF, fr L *incorrectus*, fr *in-* ¹*in-* + *correctus* correct] – **incorrectly** *adv*, **incorrectness** *n*

**incorrigible** /in'korijəbl/ *adj* **1** incapable of being corrected or amended; *esp* incurably bad **2** not manageable; uncontrollable **3** unwilling or unlikely to change ⟨~ *habits*⟩ [ME, fr LL *incorrigibilis*, fr L *in-* ¹*in-* + *corrigere* to correct – more at CORRECT] – **incorrigible** *n*, **incorrigibleness** *n*, **incorrigibly** *adv*, **incorrigibility** *n*

**incorrupt** /ˌinkə'rupt/ *also* **incorrupted** *adj* free from corruption: eg **a** not defiled or depraved; upright **b** free from error **c** *obs* not affected with decay [ME, fr L *incorruptus*, fr *in-* ¹*in-* + *corruptus* corrupt] – **incorruptly** *adv*, **incorruptness** *n*

**incorruptible** /ˌinkə'ruptəbl/ *adj* incapable of corruption: eg **a** not subject to decay or dissolution **b** incapable of being bribed or morally corrupted – **incorruptible** *n*, **incorruptibly** *adv*, **incorruptibility** *n*

**incorruption** /ˌinkə'rupsh(ə)n/ *n*, *archaic* the quality or state of being free from physical decay

**incrassate** /in'krasət, -sayt/ *adj*, *biology* swollen, inflated [LL *incrassatus*, pp of *incrassare* to thicken, fr L *in-* ²*in-* + *crassare* to thicken, fr *crassus* thick]

¹**increase** /in'krees/ *vi* **1** to become progressively greater (eg in size, amount, number, or intensity); *specif*, *of a mathematical sequence, series, or function* to have each term greater than the one preceding it **2** to multiply by the production of young ~ *vt* **1** to make greater; augment **2** *obs* to enrich [ME *encresen*, fr MF *encreistre*, fr L *increscere*, fr *in-* ²*in-* + *crescere* to grow – more at CRESCENT] – **increasable** *adj*, **increaser** *n*

**synonyms** Increase, enlarge, augment, and multiply all mean "make greater or more numerous"; increase has the most general application. Used intransitively, it often stresses progressive or proportionate growth ⟨*the child's wisdom increased with age*⟩. Enlarge carries its literal meaning of "make larger" over into figurative use ⟨*enlarge one's circle of friends*⟩. Augment implies that what is being increased, whether literally or figuratively, was already large or great ⟨*this concert augmented the pianist's reputation*⟩. Multiply suggests increasing something by repetition ⟨*multiplied his protestations of gratitude to the point of embarrassment*⟩. Compare INTENSIFY **antonym** decrease

²**increase** /'inkrees/ *n* **1** the act or process of increasing; addition or enlargement in size, extent, quantity, etc **2** something (eg offspring, produce, or profit) added to an original stock by addition or growth

**increasingly** /in'kreesingli/ *adv* to an increasing degree

**incredible** /in'kredəbl/ *adj* **1** too extraordinary and improbable to be believed; *also* hard to believe **2** *informal* wonderful, amazing – often used as a generalized term of approval ⟨*he has the most* ~ *way with women*⟩ △ incredulous [ME, fr L

*incredibilis*, fr *in-* ¹*in-* + *credibilis* credible] – **incredibleness** *n*, **incredibly** *adv*, **incredibility** *n*

**incredulity** /ˌinkri'dyoohləti/ *n* the quality or state of being incredulous; disbelief

**incredulous** /in'kredyooləs/ *adj* **1** unwilling to admit or accept what is offered as true; not credulous **2** expressing disbelief ⟨*an* ~ *stare*⟩ △ incredible [L *incredulus*, fr *in-* ¹*in-* + *credulus* credulous] – **incredulously** *adv*

**increment** /'ingkrimənt, in-/ *n* **1** an increase, esp in quantity or value; an enlargement; *also* a quantity **2a** something gained or added **b(1)** any of a series of regular consecutive additions **b(2)** a regular increase in pay resulting from an additional year's service ⟨*gets his* ~ *plus a cost-of-living increase*⟩ **c** a minute increase in a mathematical quantity **3** a positive or negative change in the value of one or more of a set of variable mathematical quantities [ME, fr L *incrementum*, fr *increscere*] – **incremental** *adj*, **incrementally** *adv*

**incriminate** /in'kriminayt/ *vt* to involve in or to demonstrate involvement in a crime or fault [LL *incriminatus*, pp of *incriminare*, fr L *in-* ²*in-* + *crimin-, crimen* crime] – **incriminatory** *adj*, **incrimination** *n*

**incross** /'in,kros/ *n* an individual produced by crossing inbred lines of the same breed or strain

**incrossbred** /in'kros,bred/ *n* an individual produced by crossing inbred lines of separate breeds or strains

**incrust** /in'krust/ *vb* to encrust

**incrustation** /ˌinkru'staysh(ə)n/ *n* **1** the act of encrusting; the state of being encrusted **2a** a crust or hard coating **b** a growth or accumulation (eg of habits, opinions, or customs) resembling a crust [L *incrustation-, incrustatio*, fr *incrustatus*, pp of *incrustare* to encrust]

**incubate** /'ingkyoobayt, 'in-/ *vt* **1** to sit upon (eggs) so as to hatch by the warmth of the body; *also* to maintain (eg an embryo or a chemically active system) under conditions favourable for hatching, development, or reaction **2** to cause (eg an idea) to develop ~ *vi* **1** to sit on eggs **2** to undergo incubation [L *incubatus*, pp of *incubare*, fr *in-* ²*in-* + *cubare* to lie – more at HIP] – **incubative** *adj*, **incubatory** *adj*

**incubation** /ˌingkyoo'baysh(ə)n, ˌin-/ *n* **1** the act or process of incubating **2** the period between the infection of an individual by a disease-causing agent and the manifestation of the disease it causes – **incubational** *adj*

**incubator** /'ingkyoo,baytə, 'in-/ *n* one who or that which incubates: eg **a** an apparatus in which eggs are hatched artificially **b** an apparatus that maintains controlled conditions, esp for the housing of premature or sick babies or the cultivation of microorganisms

**incubus** /'ingkyoobəs, 'in-/ *n, pl* **incubuses, incubi** /-bi, -bie/ **1** a demon assuming male form to have sexual intercourse with women in their sleep – compare SUCCUBUS **2** a nightmare **3** one who or that which oppresses or burdens like a nightmare [ME, fr LL, fr L *incubare*]

**inculcate** /'inkulkayt/ *vt* to teach or instil (eg into a person) by frequent repetitions or admonitions ⟨~ *d a sense of social responsibility in her children*⟩ ⟨*student* ~ *d with a desire for knowledge*⟩ [L *inculcatus*, pp of *inculcare*, lit., to tread on, fr *in-* ²*in-* + *calcare* to trample, fr *calc-, calx* heel – more at CALKIN] – **inculcator** *n*, **inculcation** *n*

**inculpable** /in'kulpəpl/ *adj* free from guilt; blameless [LL *inculpabilis*, fr L *in-* ¹*in-* + *culpabilis* culpable]

**inculpate** /'inkulpayt/ *vt* to incriminate [LL *inculpatus*, fr L *in-* ²*in-* + *culpatus*, pp of *culpare* to blame – more at CULPABLE] – **inculpation** *n*, **inculpatory** *adj*

**incult** /in'kult/ *adj* coarse, uncultured [L *incultus*, fr *in-* ¹*in-* + *cultus*, pp of *colere* to cultivate – more at WHEEL]

**incumbency** /in'kumb(ə)nsi/ *n* **1** the quality or state of being incumbent **2** something that is incumbent; a duty **3** the sphere of action or period of office of an incumbent

¹**incumbent** /in'kumb(ə)nt/ *n* the holder of an office or post, or of an Anglican BENEFICE [ME, fr L *incumbent-, incumbens*, prp of *incumbere* to lie down on, fr *in-* ²*in-* + *-cumbere* to lie down; akin to L *cubare* to lie – more at HIP]

²**incumbent** *adj* **1a** lying or resting on something else **b** *of a geologic stratum* lying over other material; superimposed **2** imposed as a duty or obligation – usu + *on* or *upon* ⟨~ *on us to help*⟩ **3** occupying a specified office ⟨*the* ~ *caretaker*⟩ **4** bent over so as to rest on or touch an underlying surface □ compare RECUMBENT

**incumbrance** /in'kumbrəns/ *n* an encumbrance

**incunable** /in'kyoohnəbl/ *n* an incunabulum [Fr, fr NL *incunabulum*]

**incunabulum** /,inkyoo'nabyooləm/ *n, pl* **incunabula** /-lə/ **1** a book printed before 1501 **2** a work of art or of industry of an early period [NL, fr L *incunabula*, pl, swaddling clothes, cradle, fr *in-* [2]*in-* + *cunae* cradle – more at CEMETERY]

**incur** /in'kuh/ *vt* **-rr-** to become liable or subject to; bring upon oneself ⟨*she* ∼red *several debts*⟩ [L *incurrere*, lit., to run into, fr *in* [2]*in-* + *currere* to run – more at CAR] – **incurrence** *n*

**incurable** /in'kyoorərəbl/ *adj* not curable [ME, fr MF or LL; MF, fr LL *incurabilis*, fr L *in-* [1]*in-* + *curabilis* curable] – **incurable** *n*, **incurableness** *n*, **incurably** *adv*, **incurability** *n*

**incurious** /in'kyoorəri·əs/ *adj* lacking a normal or usual curiosity; uninterested ⟨*a blank* ∼ *stare*⟩ **synonyms** see INDIFFERENT **antonyms** curious, inquisitive [L *incuriosus*, fr *in-* [1]*in-* + *curiosus* curious] – **incuriously** *adv*, **incuriousness** *n*, **incuriosity** *n*

**incurrent** /in'kurənt/ *adj, of an anatomical duct, channel, etc* carrying an inwardly flowing current of liquid (eg water or blood) – compare EXCURRENT [L *incurrent-, incurrens*, prp of *incurrere*]

**incursion** /in'kuhsh(ə)n/ *n* **1** a sudden usu temporary invasion; an unexpected usu brief entrance, esp into another's territory **2** an intrusive demand ⟨∼s *into my leisure time*⟩ [ME, fr MF or L; MF, fr L *incursion-, incursio*, fr *incursus*, pp of *incurrere*] – **incursive** *adj*

**incurve** /in'kuhv/ *vt* to bend so as to curve inwards [L *incurvare*, fr *in-* [2]*in-* + *curvare* to curve, fr *curvus* curved – more at CROWN] – **incurvation** *n*

**incus** /'ingkəs/ *n, pl* **incudes** /in'kyoohdeez/ the middle of a chain of three small bones that transmit sound in the ear of a mammal – called also ANVIL; compare MALLEUS, STAPES [NL, fr L, anvil, fr *incudere*]

**incuse** /in'kyoohz/ *n or adj* (an impression) formed by stamping or punching in – used chiefly of old coins or features of their design [L *incusus*, pp of *incudere* to stamp, strike, fr *in-* [2]*in-* + *cudere* to beat – more at HEW]

**ind-** /ind-/, **indi-, indo-** *comb form* **1** indigo ⟨ind*oxyl*⟩ **2** resembling indigo (eg in colour) ⟨indo*phenol*⟩ [ISV, fr L *indicum* – more at INDIGO]

**Ind-** /ind-/, **Indo-** *comb form* **1a** India or the East Indies **b** Indian ⟨Indo-*British*⟩; Indian and ⟨Indo-*African*⟩ **2** Indo-European ⟨Indo-*Hittite*⟩ [Gk, fr *India* India]

**indaba** /in'dahbə/ *n, chiefly SAfr* a conference, parley [Zulu *indaba* affair]

**indamine** /'ində,meen, -min/ *n* any of a series of organic chemical BASES that form SALTS that are unstable blue and green dyes [ISV *ind-* + *amine*]

**indebted** /in'detid/ *adj* **1** owing money ⟨*heavily* ∼ *to a finance company for loans*⟩ **2** owing gratitude or recognition to another; beholden [ME *indetted*, fr OF *endeté*, pp of *endeter* to involve in debt, fr *en-* + *dete* debt]

**indebtedness** /in'detidnis/ *n* **1** the condition of being indebted **2** something (eg an amount of money) that is owed

**indecency** /in'dees(ə)nsi/ *n* **1** the quality or state of being indecent; indecorum **2** something (eg a word or action) that is indecent

**indecent** /in'dees(ə)nt/ *adj* **1** not decent; indecorous **2** hardly suitable; unseemly ⟨*he remarried with* ∼ *haste*⟩ **3** morally offensive [MF or L; MF *indécent*, fr L *indecent-, indecens*, fr *in-* [1]*in-* + *decent-, decens* decent] – **indecently** *adv*

**indecent assault** *n* an assault involving some sexual element but not amounting to rape

**indecent exposure** *n* intentional exposure of part of one's body (eg the genitals) in circumstances in which such exposure is likely to be an offence against generally accepted standards of decency

**indecipherable** /,indi'sief(ə)rəbl/ *adj* incapable of being deciphered ⟨∼ *handwriting*⟩

**indecision** /,indi'sizh(ə)n/ *n* a wavering between two or more possible courses of action; irresolution [Fr *indécision*, fr *indécis* undecided, fr LL *indecisus*, fr L *in-* [1]*in-* + *decisus*, pp of *decidere* to decide]

**indecisive** /,indi'siesiv/ *adj* **1** not decisive; *esp* giving an uncertain result ⟨*an* ∼ *battle*⟩ **2** marked by or prone to indecision; irresolute – **indecisively** *adv*, **indecisiveness** *n*

**indeclinable** /,indi'klienəbl/ *adj* having no grammatical inflections [MF, fr LL *indeclinabilis*, fr L *in-* [1]*in-* + LL *declinabilis* capable of being inflected, fr L *declinare* to inflect – more at DECLINE]

**indecorous** /in'dek(ə)rəs/ *adj* not decorous; in bad taste [L *indecorus*, fr *in-* [1]*in-* + *decorus* decorous] – **indecorously** *adv*, **indecorousness** *n*

**indecorum** /,indi'kawrəm/ *n* lack of decorum; impropriety [L, neut of *indecorus*]

**indeed** /in'deed/ *adv* **1** without any question; truly, undeniably ⟨*it is* ∼ *remarkable*⟩ – often used in agreement ⟨∼ *I will*⟩ **2** – used for emphasis after *very* and an adjective or adverb ⟨*very cold* ∼⟩ **3** in point of fact; actually ⟨*I don't mind*; ∼, *I'm pleased*⟩ ⟨*if* ∼ *they want to marry him.*" "Indeed?" "Does she ∼!"⟩ ⟨"*What's this?*" "*What* ∼! *You may well ask*"⟩ [ME *in dede* in reality, fr [1]*in* + *dede* deed]

**indefatigable** /,indi'fatigəbl/ *adj* incapable of being fatigued; tireless [MF, fr L *indefatigabilis*, fr *in-* [1]*in-* + *defatigare* to fatigue, fr *de* down + *fatigare* to fatigue] – **indefatigableness** *n*, **indefatigably** *adv*, **indefatigability** *n*

**indefeasible** /,indi'feezəbl/ *adj* not capable of being annulled, forfeited, or made void ⟨*an* ∼ *right*⟩ [[1]*in-* + *defeasible*] – **indefeasibly** *adv*, **indefeasibility** *n*

**indefectible** /,indi'fektəbl/ *adj* **1** not subject to failure or decay; lasting **2** free of faults; flawless [[1]*in-* + obs *defectible* liable to fail, fr *defect* + *-ible*] – **indefectibly** *adv*, **indefectibility** *n*

**indefensible** /,indi'fensəbl/ *adj* **1** incapable of being defended or justified ⟨∼ *conduct*⟩ **2** incapable of being protected against physical attack – **indefensibly** *adv*, **indefensibility** *n*

**indefinable** /,indi'fienəbl/ *adj* incapable of being precisely described or analysed – **indefinable** *n*, **indefinableness** *n*, **indefinably** *adv*, **indefinability** *n*

**indefinite** /in'definət/ *adj* not definite: eg **a** typically designating an unidentified or not immediately identifiable person or thing ⟨*the* ∼ *articles* a *and* an⟩ **b** not precise; vague ⟨*an* ∼ *answer*⟩ **c** having no exact limits ⟨*an* ∼ *period*⟩ [L *indefinitus*, fr *in-* [1]*in-* + *definitus* definite] – **indefinite** *n*, **indefinitely** *adv*, **indefiniteness** *n*

**indefinite integral** *n* a function whose DERIVATIVE is a given function

**indehiscent** /,indi'his(ə)nt/ *adj* not opening (eg to release seeds) at maturity ⟨∼ *fruits*⟩ [[1]*in-* + *dehiscent*] – **indehiscence** *n*

**indelible** /in'deləbl/ *adj* **1** incapable of being removed or erased **2** making marks not easily erased ⟨*an* ∼ *pencil*⟩ [ML *indelibilis*, alter. of L *indelebilis*, fr *in-* [1]*in-* + *delēre* to delete] – **indelibly** *adv*, **indelibility** *n*

**indelicacy** /in'delikəsi/ *n* **1a** the quality or state of being indelicate **2** something (eg an act or utterance) that is indelicate

**indelicate** /in'delikət/ *adj* offensive to good manners or refined taste; improper – **indelicately** *adv*, **indelicateness** *n*

**indemnification** /in,demnifi'kaysh(ə)n/ *n* **1a** the action of indemnifying **b** the condition of being indemnified **2** INDEMNITY 2b

**indemnify** /in'demnifie/ *vt* **1** to secure against harm, loss, or damage **2** to make compensation to for incurred harm, loss, or damage [L *indemnis* unharmed, fr *in-* [1]*in-* + *damnum* damage] – **indemnifier** *n*

**indemnity** /in'demnəti/ *n* **1a** security against harm, loss, or damage **b** exemption from incurred penalties or liabilities **2a** INDEMNIFICATION 1 **b** something that indemnifies

**indemonstrable** /,indi'monstrəbl/ *adj* incapable of being demonstrated; not subject to proof – **indemonstrably** *adv*

**indene** /'indeen/ *n* a liquid chemical compound, $C_9H_8$, obtained from COAL TAR and used esp in making resins [ISV, fr *indole*]

[1]**indent** /in'dent/ *vt* **1a** to cut or otherwise divide (a document carrying two or more copies) to produce sections with irregular edges that can be matched for authentication **b** to draw up (eg a deed) in two or more exactly corresponding copies **2a** NOTCH **1 b** to cut into for the purpose of mortising or dovetailing **3** to indenture **4** to set (eg a line of a paragraph) a few spaces in from the margin **5** to join together (as if) by mortises or dovetails **6** *chiefly Br* to order (goods) by an indent ∼ *vi* **1** to form an indentation **2** *chiefly Br* to make out an official requisition – often + *on* and *for* ⟨∼ *on HQ for supplies*⟩ [ME *indenten*, fr MF *endenter*, fr OF, fr *en-* + *dent* tooth, fr L *dent-, dens* – more at TOOTH] – **indenter** *n*

[2]**indent** /'indent/ *n* **1** INDENTURE 1 **2** an indentation; indention **3** *chiefly Br* **3a** an official requisition **b** a purchase order for goods, esp when sent from a foreign country

[3]**indent** /-'-/ *vt* **1** to force inwards so as to form a depression **2**

to form a dent or depression in [ME *endenten,* fr *en-* + *denten* to dent] – **indenter** *n*

⁴**indent** /'--/ *n* an indentation

**indentation** /,inden'taysh(ə)n/ *n* **1a** an angular cut in an edge; a notch **b** a usu deep recess (eg in a coastline) **2** indenting or being indented **3** a dent **4** an indention in printing

**indention** /in'densh(ə)n/ *n* **1** indenting or being indented **2** the blank space produced by indenting

¹**indenture** /in'denchə/ *n* **1a** a document or a section of a document that is indented **b** a formal or official document, usu executed in two or more copies **c indentures** *pl,* **indenture** a contract binding one person to work for another for a given period of time **2a** a formal certificate (eg an inventory or voucher) prepared for purposes of control **b** a document stating the terms under which a security (eg a bond) is issued

²**indenture** *vt* to bind (eg an apprentice) by indentures

**independence** /,indi'pend(ə)ns/ *n* the quality or state of being independent

**Independence Day** *n* (July 4 observed as a legal holiday in the USA in commemoration of) the adoption of the Declaration of Independence in 1776

**independency** /,indi'pend(ə)nsi/ *n* **1** independence **2** *cap* the Independent movement or form of organization

¹**independent** /,indi'pend(ə)nt/ *adj* **1** not dependent: eg **1a(1)** not subject to control by others; self-governing **a(2)** not affiliated with a larger controlling unit **b(1)** not requiring or relying on something else; not contingent ⟨an ~ *conclusion*⟩ **b(2)** not looking to others for one's opinions or for guidance in conduct **b(3)** not bound by or committed to a political party **c(1)** not requiring or relying on others (eg for care or livelihood) ⟨~ *of his parents*⟩ **c(2)** enough to free one from the necessity of working for a living ⟨a man of ~ *means*⟩ **d(1)** refusing to accept help from or to be under obligation to others **d(2)** showing a desire for freedom ⟨an ~ *manner*⟩ **e(1)** having LINEAR INDEPENDENCE ⟨an ~ *set of vectors*⟩ **e(2)** having the property that the joint probability (eg of events or samples) or the joint PROBABILITY DENSITY FUNCTION equals the product of the separate probabilities or probability density functions **2** *cap* relating to the Independents **3a** MAIN **5** ⟨the ~ *clause*⟩ **b** neither deducible from nor incompatible with another statement ⟨~ *postulates*⟩ – **independently** *adv*

²**independent** *n* **1** *cap* a sectarian of an English religious movement for congregational autonomy originating in the late 16th century and giving rise to Congregationalists, Baptists, and Quakers **2** somebody who is independent; *specif, often cap* a person who is not bound by or definitively committed to a political party

**independent assortment** *n* the process by which ALLELES (genes producing alternative forms of a particular hereditary characteristic) coding for different hereditary characteristics and carried on different CHROMOSOMES (strands of gene-carrying material) become separated and are distributed to reproductive cells (eg egg and sperm cells) independently of each other, so that each reproductive cell receives a random combination of alleles

**independent school** *n* a school providing full-time education for pupils of school age without support from public funds; a private school

**independent suspension** *n* an arrangement of the suspension in a motor vehicle by which the suspension and springing of a wheel act independently of any other wheel

**independent variable** *n* any of an arbitrary set of variables in an equation whose values may be freely chosen without unbalancing the equation ⟨in $z = x^2 + 3xy + y^2$, *x and y may be taken as* independent variables⟩ – compare DEPENDENT VARIABLE, DUMMY VARIABLE

**in-'depth** *adj* having detailed thoroughness; searching ⟨~ *questions*⟩ ⟨an ~ *study*⟩

**indescribable** /,indi'skriebəbl/ *adj* **1** that cannot be described ⟨an ~ *sensation*⟩ **2** surpassing description ⟨~ *joy*⟩ – **indescribableness** *n,* **indescribably** *adv*

**indestructible** /,indi'struktəbl/ *adj* not destructible – **indestructibleness** *n,* **indestructibly** *adv,* **indestructibility** *n*

**indetectable** *also* **indetectible** /,indi'tektəbl/ *adj* resisting detection; not easily noticed or proved ⟨this poison would be ~ *in a corpse*⟩ – **indetectably** *adv,* **indetectability** *n*

**indeterminable** /,indi'tuhminəbl/ *adj* incapable of being definitely decided or ascertained △ indeterminate – **indeterminableness** *n,* **indeterminably** *adv*

**indeterminacy principle** /,indi'tuhminəsi/ *n, physics* UNCERTAINTY PRINCIPLE

**indeterminate** /,indi'tuhminət/ *adj* **1** not definitely or precisely determined or fixed; vague **2** *of simultaneous equations* having an infinite number of solutions by reason of certain relations between the coefficients, or from insufficient data **3** being an undefined mathematical expression (eg $\%$) **4** *botany* RACEMOSE △ indeterminable [ME *indeterminat,* fr LL *indeterminatus,* fr L *in-* ¹in- + *determinatus,* pp of *determinare* to determine] – **indeterminately** *adv,* **indeterminateness** *n,* **indetermination** *n*

**indeterminate cleavage** *n* cleavage of a fertilized egg in which each of the cells formed has the potential for developing into any of the tissues, structures, etc of the adult organism – compare DETERMINATE CLEAVAGE

**indeterminate vowel** *n* SCHWA

**indeterminism** /,indi'tuhmi,niz(ə)m/ *n* **1** a theory that deliberate actions and choices are not determined by antecedent physical or mental events **2** a theory that not every event has a cause – **indeterminist** *n,* **indeterministic** *adj*

¹**index** /'indeks/ *n, pl* **indexes, indices** /'indiseez/, (4) *usu* **indices 1** a guide or list to aid reference: eg **1a** an alphabetical list of items (eg topics or names) treated in a printed work that gives for each item the page number where it appears ⟨an ~ *at the back of the book*⟩ **b** a list of items of a specified type ⟨an ~ *of personal names*⟩ **c** CARD INDEX **d** THUMB INDEX **e** a bibliographical record of groups of publications that is usu published periodically **2a** a device (eg a pointer on a scale) that indicates a value or quantity **b** something that points towards or demonstrates a particular state of affairs; an indication ⟨the *fertility of the land is an ~ of the country's wealth*⟩ **3** a list of restricted or prohibited material; *specif, cap* the list of books the reading of which is prohibited or restricted for Roman Catholics by the church authorities **4** *maths* a usu nonnegative integer, esp a subscript, that indicates the position of an element in an array, sum, or sequence ⟨the indices 2 *and* 3 *locate the element* $a_{23}$ *in the second row and third column of a determinant*⟩ **5** a character representing a pointing fist that is used to direct attention (eg to a note or paragraph) **6** a ratio or other number derived from a series of observations and used as an indicator or measure (eg of a condition, property, or phenomenon); *specif* INDEX NUMBER [L *indic-, index* forefinger, informer, guide, fr *indicare* to indicate; (3) NL *Index librorum prohibitorum* List of forbidden books, the official list issued by the Roman Catholic church] – **indexical** *adj*

²**index** *vt* **1a** to provide with an index **b** to list in an index **2** to serve as an index of **3** to cause to be index-linked ~ *vi* to prepare an index – **indexer** *n*

**indexation** /,indek'saysh(ə)n/ *n* **1** the act or process of making something (eg a pension) index-linked **2** a wage or salaries scheme by which an increase in the index of retail prices results in a corresponding increase in pay

**index card** *n* a card on which an entry in an index or catalogue is recorded

**index finger** *n* the forefinger

**index fossil** *n* a fossil, usu with a narrow time range and wide geographical distribution, that is used in the identification of related geological formations

**index-'linked** *adj* increasing or decreasing proportionally to a rise or fall in an index, esp the cost-of-living index

**index number** *n* a number used to indicate change in value (eg of cost or price) as compared with the value, usu taken to be 100, at some earlier time

**index of refraction** *n, physics* REFRACTIVE INDEX

**indi-** /indi-/ – see ind-

**India** /'indi-ə/ – a communications code word for the letter *i*

**india ink** *n, often cap 1st I, NAm* INDIAN INK

**Indiaman** /'indi-əmən/ *n, pl* **Indiamen** /-mən/ a merchant ship formerly used in trade with India or the E Indies; *esp* a large sailing ship used in this trade

**Indian** /'indi-ən/ *n* **1** a native or inhabitant of India **2a** a member of any of the indigenous peoples of N, Central, or S America excluding the Eskimos **b** any of the native languages of American Indians [*India,* subcontinent of Asia, fr L, fr Gk, fr *Indos* India, Indus (river in NW India), fr OPer *Hindu* India; (2) fr the mistaken belief of Columbus that America was part of Asia] – **Indian** *adj*

**Indian agent** *n* an official representative of the US federal government to American Indian tribes, esp on reservations

**Indian club** *n* a usu wooden club shaped like a large bottle that is swung for gymnastic exercise

**Indian corn** *n, chiefly NAm* maize

**Indian file** *n* SINGLE FILE [fr the (American) Indian practice of walking through woods in this way]

**Indian hemp** *n* HEMP 1

**indian ink** *n, often cap 1st I* 1 a solid black pigment consisting of LAMPBLACK (powdered black soot) mixed with a binder and used in drawing and lettering 2 a fluid ink consisting usu of a fine suspension of indian ink in a liquid

**Indian meal** *n* meal ground from INDIAN CORN; maize meal

**Indian meal moth** *n* a moth (*Plodia interpunctella*) whose larva is a serious pest in granaries and flour mills

**Indian red** *n* 1 a naturally occurring yellowish-red earth containing HAEMATITE (reddish iron oxide mineral) and used as a pigment 2 any of various light red to purplish-brown pigments made by heating and OXIDIZING iron SALTS

**Indian summer** *n* 1 a period of warm weather in late autumn or early winter 2 a happy or flourishing period occurring towards the end of something, esp of a person's life [fr its frequent occurrence in a region of the USA formerly occupied by Indians]

**Indian wrestling** *n, NAm* ARM WRESTLING

**India paper** *n* a thin tough opaque printing paper

**india rubber** *n, often cap I* ¹RUBBER 2a

**Indic** /'indik/ *adj* 1 of the subcontinent of India; Indian 2 of or being the Indian branch of the Indo-European languages – **Indic** *n*

**indican** /'indikən/ *n* 1 a chemical compound (GLUCOSIDE), $C_{14}H_{17}NO_6$, derived from glucose and INDOXYL that occurs esp in the indigo plant and is a source of natural indigo 2 an unstable substance, $C_8H_7NO_4S$, found, usu in the form of its potassium SALT, in the urine of mammals [L *indicum* indigo – more at INDIGO]

**indicate** /'indikayt/ *vt* 1a(1) to point to; point out a(2) to show or demonstrate as or by means of a sign or pointer **b** to be a sign, symptom, or index of ⟨*the high fever* ~s *a serious condition*⟩ **c** to demonstrate or suggest the necessity or advisability of ⟨*radical surgery is usually* ~d *in this situation*⟩ – usu pass 2 to state or express briefly; suggest ⟨ ~d *his desire to cooperate*⟩ [L *indicatus*, pp of *indicare*, fr in- ²in- + *dicare* to proclaim, dedicate – more at DICTION]

**indication** /,indi'kaysh(ə)n/ *n* 1 the action of indicating 2a something (e g a sign or suggestion) that serves to indicate ⟨*gave no* ~ *that he heard me*⟩ **b** something (e g a treatment or procedure) that is indicated as advisable or necessary 3 the degree indicated on a graduated instrument; a reading – **indicational** *adj*

¹**indicative** /in'dikətiv/ *adj* 1 of or constituting the grammatical mood that represents the denoted act or state as an objective fact ⟨*an* ~ *verb form*⟩ 2 serving to indicate ⟨*actions* ~ *of fear*⟩ – **indicatively** *adv*

²**indicative** *n* the indicative mood; *also* a verb form or verbal phrase expressing it

**indicator** /'indikaytə/ *n* 1 a person, sign, or thing that indicates or is an indication: e g **1a** a hand or needle on an instrument (e g a dial); a pointer **b** an instrument for giving visual readings (e g of measurements) that is attached to a machine or apparatus **c** a light on a vehicle that flashes to indicate an intention to turn left or right **2a** a substance (e g litmus) used to show visually, usu by a change of colour, the condition (e g the degree of acidity or alkalinity) of a solution, the presence of a particular material, or the end point of a particular chemical reaction **b** TRACER 4 (substance for tracing the course of a chemical or biological process) 3 an organism or ecological community so strictly associated with particular environmental conditions that its presence is indicative of the existence of those conditions ⟨ ~ *species*⟩ 4 a statistic (e g the level of industrial production or the balance of imports and exports) that gives an indication of the state of a national economy – compare LEADING INDICATOR – **indicatory** *adj*

**indices** /'indiseez/ *pl of* INDEX

**indicia** /in'dishi-ə/ *n pl* distinctive marks; indications [L, pl of *indicium* sign, fr *indicare*]

**indict** /in'diet/ *vt* 1a to charge with an offence; accuse **b** to condemn – not used in law 2 to charge with a crime to be tried by a judge and jury 3 *NAm, of a grand jury* to make a formal accusation against as a means of bringing to trial *synonyms* see ACCUSE △ indite [alter. of earlier *indite*, fr ME *inditen*, fr AF *enditer*, fr OF, to write down – more at INDITE] – **indicter, indictor** *n*

**indictable** /in'dietəbl/ *adj* 1 subject to being indicted; liable to indictment 2 making one liable to indictment

**indictable offence** *n* a serious crime triable by a judge and jury in the Crown Court

**indictment** /in'dietmənt/ *n* 1 the action or the legal process of indicting 2 a formal written statement drawn up by a prosecuting authority accusing one or more people of an offence to be tried by a judge and jury 3 grounds for severe censure; condemnation ⟨*such practices are a searing* ~ *of contemporary society*⟩

**Indies** /'indiz/ *n pl* India and neighbouring regions – + *the* [pl of obs *Indie, Indy* India]

**indifference** /in'dif(ə)rəns/ *n* 1 the quality, state, or fact of being indifferent 2 absence of interest or importance ⟨*it's a matter of complete* ~ *to me*⟩

**indifferent** /in'difrənt/ *adj* 1 that does not matter one way or the other; neutral 2 not interested in or concerned about something ⟨*completely* ~ *to the outcome*⟩ ⟨*remained* ~ *to her pleas*⟩ **3a** neither good nor bad; mediocre ⟨*does* ~ *work at the office*⟩ ⟨*is the food good, bad, or* ~?⟩ **b** not very good; inferior ⟨*a very* ~ *wine*⟩ 4 chemically, magnetically, etc neutral **5a** *of cells, tissues, etc* not differentiated; not modified or specialized for a particular function **b** having the potential for development into more than one type of tissue, structure, etc; *esp* not yet having undergone embryological DETERMINATION (irreversible fixing of the ultimate nature of embryonic tissue) [ME, fr MF or L; MF, regarded as neither good nor bad, fr L *indifferent-, indifferens*, fr in- ¹in- + *different-, differens*, prp of *differre* to be different – more at DIFFER] – **indifferently** *adv*

*synonyms* **Indifferent, unconcerned, incurious, disinterested, detached, uninterested,** and **apathetic: indifferent** and **unconcerned** simply mean "not feeling or showing interest", but there is often a suggestion that interest or concern should be shown ⟨**unconcerned** *that her daughter was out late*⟩ ⟨**indifferent** *to the noise the children were making*⟩. **Incurious** suggests docile acceptance of facts or a lack of proper (especially intellectual) interest ⟨**incurious** *as to the origin of the universe/the food we eat/his family fortune*⟩. To be **detached** is to take an objective, dispassionate attitude, while **disinterested** in one sense stresses lack of selfish interest and so implies impartiality. **Uninterested** simply means "not interested". **Apathetic** may suggest a state of mind or character as well as an attitude to a particular thing. It suggests a deplorable absence of interest or involvement, through inertia, unconsciousness, or absence of feeling ⟨*an* **apathetic** *attitude towards unemployment*⟩. *usage* One is **indifferent** *to* or *as to* (not △ *for*) something, or **indifferent** *whether* something happens.

**indifferentism** /in'difrəntiz(ə)m/ *n* indifference; *specif* the belief that all religions are equally valid – **indifferentist** *n*

**indigence** /'indij(ə)nt/ *n* a level of poverty in which real hardship and deprivation are suffered and the comforts of life are wholly lacking

**indigene** /'indijeen/ *also* **indigen** /'indijən/ *n* an animal, plant, etc indigenous to a particular locality; NATIVE 2b [L *indigena*]

**indigen·ize, -ise** /in'dijə,niez/ *vt* to make (something introduced from elsewhere) less alien ⟨ ~ *the Liturgy to meet local needs*⟩ – **indigenization** *n*

**indigenous** /in'dij(ə)nəs/ *adj* 1 originating, growing, or living naturally in a particular region or environment ⟨ ~ *to Australia*⟩ 2 innate, inborn *synonyms* see ¹NATIVE *antonyms* exotic, naturalized [LL *indigenus*, fr L *indigena*, n, native, fr OL *indu, endo* in, within (akin to L *in* and to L *de* down) + L *gignere* to beget – more at DE-, KIN] – **indigenously** *adv*, **indigenousness** *n*

**indigent** /'indij(ə)nt/ *adj* needy, poor *synonyms* see POOR [ME, fr MF, fr L *indigent-, indigens*, prp of *indigēre* to need, fr OL *indu* + L *egēre* to need; akin to OHG *ekrōdi* thin] – **indigent** *n*

**indigested** /,indi'jestid/ *adj* not carefully thought out or arranged; formless

**indigestible** /,indi'jestəbl/ *adj* 1 not digestible; not easily digested 2 not easy to take in or understand ⟨*an* ~ *mass of facts*⟩ [LL *indigestibilis*, fr L in- ¹in- + LL *digestibilis* digestible] – **indigestible** *n*, **indigestibility** *n*

**indigestion** /,indi'jeschən/ *n* 1 inability to digest or difficulty in digesting something 2 pain or discomfort in the digestive system often resulting from difficulty in digesting something

**indign** /in'dien/ *adj, archaic* unworthy, undeserving [ME *indigne*, fr MF, fr L *indignus*]

**indignant** /in'dignənt/ *adj* filled with or marked by indignation ⟨*became* ~ *at the accusation*⟩ *synonyms* see ¹ANGER [L *indignant-, indignans*, prp of *indignari* to be indignant, fr *indignus*

unworthy, fr *in-* ¹in- + *dignus* worthy – more at DECENT] –
**indignantly** *adv*
**indignation** /ˌindigˈnaysh(ə)n/ *n* anger aroused by something
judged unjust, unworthy, or mean *synonyms* see ¹ANGER
**indignity** /inˈdignəti/ *n* **1a** an act that offends against a
person's dignity or self-respect; an insult **b** humiliating treatment ⟨the ~ of being stripped and searched⟩ **2** *obs* lack or loss
of dignity or honour [L *indignitat-, indignitas*, fr *indignus*]
**indigo** /ˈindigoh/ *n, pl* **indigos, indigoes 1a(1)** a blue dye
formerly obtained from plants, esp indigo plants, and now
made artificially **a(2) indigo, indigo blue** a chemical compound,
$C_{16}H_{10}N_2O_2$, that is the principal colouring matter of natural
indigo and is usu prepared synthetically as a blue powder with
a coppery lustre **b** any of several blue VAT DYES derived from
or closely related to indigo **2** a dark greyish-blue colour whose
hue lies between violet and blue in the spectrum **3 indigo
plant, indigo** a plant that yields indigo; *esp* any of a genus
(*Indigofera*) of tropical plants of the pea family [It dial., fr L
*indicum*, fr Gk *indikon*, fr neut of *indikos* Indic, fr *Indos* India]
**indigo snake** *n* a large harmless blue-black snake (*Drymarchon
corais couperi*) of the S USA – called also GOPHER SNAKE
**indigotin** /inˈdigətin, ˌindiˈgohtin/ *n* the principal colouring
matter of indigo; INDIGO 1a(2) [ISV *indigo* + connective *-t-* +
*-in*]
**indirect** /ˌindiˈrekt, -die-/ *adj* not direct: e g **a(1)** deviating from
a direct line or course; roundabout **a(2)** not going straight to
the point ⟨an ~ accusation⟩ **b** not straightforward and open;
deceitful **c** not directly aimed at or achieved ⟨~ consequences⟩
**d** stating what a real or supposed original speaker said with
changes of tense, person, etc that adapt the statement grammatically to the sentence in which it is included ⟨~ speech⟩ –
compare DIRECT 5c **e** not effected directly by the action of the
people or the electorate ⟨~ government representation⟩ [ME,
fr ML *indirectus*, fr L *in-* ¹in- + *directus* direct] – **indirectly**
*adv*, **indirectness** *n*
**indirect discourse** *n, NAm* indirect speech; REPORTED SPEECH
**indirect fire** *n* gunfire by indirect aiming at a target not visible
from the gun
**indirect free kick** *n* a free kick in soccer that is awarded for
any of several minor offences and from which a direct attempt
at goal may not be made – compare DIRECT FREE KICK, PENALTY
KICK
**indirection**/ˌindiˈreksh(ə)n, -die-/*n*1lack of straightforwardness
and openness; deceitfulness **2a** indirect action or procedure **b**
aimlessness
**indirect labour** *n* labour (e g administration) that is necessary
to but not directly concerned with manufacture or the provision of a service – compare DIRECT LABOUR
**indirect lighting** *n* lighting in which the source of light is
concealed and the light emitted is diffusely reflected (e g by the
ceiling)
**indirect object** *n* a grammatical object (e g *her* in *I gave her
the book*) representing the secondary goal of the action of its
verb
**indirect proof** *n* REDUCTIO AD ABSURDUM (method of proving
something to be false)
**indirect tax** *n* a tax levied on goods, services, etc and paid
indirectly by a person or organization purchasing these goods
or services at an increased price – compare DIRECT TAX
**indiscernible** /ˌindiˈsuhnəbl/ *adj* incapable of being discerned:
**a** incapable of being perceived or recognized ⟨features ~ in
the dark⟩ **b** not recognizable as separate or distinct ⟨thought
good was ~ from evil⟩ – **indiscernibly** *adv*
**indisciplinable** /ˌindisəˈplinəbl/ *adj* not subject to or capable
of being disciplined; unruly
**indiscipline** /inˈdisiplin/ *n* lack of discipline; unruliness – **indisciplined** *adj*
**indiscreet** /ˌindiˈskreet/ *adj* not discreet; imprudent [ME *indiscrete*, fr MF & LL; MF *indiscret*, fr LL *indiscretus*, fr L,
indistinguishable, fr *in-* ¹in- + *discretus*, pp of *discernere* to
separate – more at DISCERN] – **indiscreetly** *adv*, **indiscreetness**
*n*
**indiscrete** /ˌindiˈskreet/ *adj* not separated into distinct parts
⟨an ~ mass⟩ [L *indiscretus*]
**indiscretion** /ˌindiˈskresh(ə)n/ *n* **1** lack of discretion; imprudence **2** an indiscreet act or remark
**indiscriminate** /ˌindiˈskriminət/ *adj* **1** not marked by careful
distinction; lacking in discrimination and discernment ⟨~
reading habits⟩ **2** not differentiated; confused ⟨their language
is an ~ mixture of French and English⟩ **antonym** selective –

**indiscriminately** *adv*, **indiscriminateness** *n*, **indiscriminative**
*adj*
**indiscrimination** /ˌindiˌskrimiˈnaysh(ə)n/ *n* lack of discrimination
**indispensable** /ˌindiˈspensəbl/ *adj* that cannot be done without; essential ⟨carbon dioxide is ~ for plants⟩ **synonyms** see
²NECESSARY **antonym** dispensable – **indispensable** *n*, **indis-
pensableness** *n*, **indispensably** *adv*, **indispensability** *n*
**indispose** /ˌindiˈspohz/ *vt* **1a** to make unfit **b** to make averse;
disincline **2** *archaic* to cause to be in poor physical health [prob
back-formation fr *indisposed*]
**indisposed** /ˌindiˈspohzd/ *adj* **1** slightly ill **2** averse [ME, not
prepared for, unfitted, fr ¹in- + *disposed*]
**indisposition** /ˌindispəˈzish(ə)n/ *n* the condition of being indisposed: **a** disinclination **b** a usu slight illness
**indisputable** /ˌindiˈspyoohtəbl/ *adj* not disputable; incontestable ⟨~ proof⟩ [LL *indisputabilis*, fr L *in-* ¹in- + *dis-
putabilis* disputable] – **indisputableness** *n*, **indisputably** *adv*
**indissoluble** /ˌindiˈsolyoobl/ *adj* incapable of being dissolved,
decomposed, undone, or annulled ⟨an ~ contract⟩ – **indis-
solubleness** *n*, **indissolubly** *adv*, **indissolubility** *n*
**indistinct** /ˌindiˈstingkt/ *adj* not distinct: e g **a** not sharply
outlined or separable; not clearly seen ⟨~ figures in the fog⟩ **b**
not clearly recognizable or understandable; uncertain [L *indis-
tinctus*, fr *in-* ¹in- + *distinctus* distinct] – **indistinctly** *adv*, **indistinctness** *n*
**indistinctive** /ˌindiˈstingktiv/ *adj* lacking distinctive qualities
or features
**indistinguishable** /ˌindiˈsting-gwishəbl/ *adj* incapable of being
distinguished: **a** indistinct, faint ⟨an ~ shape in the mist⟩ **b**
not capable of being discriminated ⟨~ from his brother⟩ –
**indistinguishableness** *n*, **indistinguishably** *adv*, **indistinguish-
ability** *n*
**indite** /inˈdiet/ *vt* **1** *formal* to put down in writing ⟨~ a
message⟩ **2** *archaic* to make up; compose ⟨~ a poem⟩ △
indict [ME *enditen*, fr OF *enditer* to write down, proclaim, fr
(assumed) VL *indictare* to proclaim, fr L *indictus*, pp of *indicere*
to proclaim, fr *in-* ²in- + *dicere* to say – more at DICTION] –
**inditer** *n*
**indium** /ˈindi-əm/ *n* a rare soft silvery metallic chemical element
that occurs in small amounts in zinc ores, is easily melted, and
is used as a plating for bearings, in alloys melting at a low
temperature, and in the making of transistors [NL, fr ISV *ind-*
+ NL *-ium;* fr the two indigo-blue lines in its spectrum]
**indivertible** /ˌindiˈvuhtəbl, -die-/ *adj* not to be diverted or
turned aside – **indivertibly** *adv*
¹**individual** /ˌindiˈvidyooəl, -jəl/ *adj* **1a** of or being an individual **b** intended for one person ⟨an ~ serving⟩ **2** existing
as a distinct entity; separate ⟨they each had ~ copies⟩ **3** having
marked individuality ⟨an ~ style⟩ **4** *obs* inseparable **synonyms**
see ¹CHARACTERISTIC, ¹SINGLE **antonyms** general, common [ML
*individualis*, fr L *individuus* indivisible, fr *in-* ¹in- + *dividuus*
divided, fr *dividere* to divide] – **individually** *adv*
²**individual** *n* **1a** a particular being or thing as distinguished
from a class, species, or collection: e g **1a(1)** a single human being
as contrasted with a social group or institution **a(2)** a single
organism as distinguished from a group **b** a particular person;
*esp* one viewed with disfavour ⟨a cantankerous ~⟩ **2** *philosophy* an indivisible entity
   *usage* Writers on usage advise that **individual** should be used only
   when contrast is made with a group ⟨*safeguard the rights of the
   individual in society*⟩ and not to mean simply "person".
**individualism** /ˌindiˈvidyooəˌliz(ə)m, -jəliz(ə)m/ *n* **1a** a doctrine
that the interests of the individual are or should be the foundation of morality; *also* conduct guided by such a doctrine **b** a
social theory maintaining the political and economic
independence of the individual and stressing individual
initiative, action, and interests; *also* conduct or practice guided
by such a theory **2** individuality
**individualist** /ˌindiˈvidyooəˌlist, -jəlist/ *n* **1** one who shows
marked individuality or independence in thought or behaviour
**2** one who advocates or practises individualism – **individualist,
individualistic** *adj*, **individualistically** *adv*
**individuality** /ˌindiˌvidyooˈaləti, -joo-/ *n* **1a** the total character
peculiar to and distinguishing an individual from others **b** the
distinctive character that makes a person unusual; *esp* the
tendency to pursue one's course with marked independence or
self-reliance **2** an individual, person **3** separate or distinct
existence
**individual·ize, -ise** /ˌindiˈvidyooəˌliez, -jəliez/ *vt* **1** to make

individual in character **2** to treat or notice individually; particularize **3** to adjust or adapt to suit a particular individual ⟨*efforts to ~ teaching to suit each pupil's needs*⟩ – **individualization** *n*

**individual medley** *n* a swimming race in which each contestant swims each quarter of the course with a different stroke, specif the butterfly, backstroke, breaststroke, and crawl

**individuate** /ˌindiˈvidyoo͵ayt, -joo-/ *vt* to give individuality or individual form to

**individuation** /ˌindi͵vidyooˈaysh(ə)n, -joo-/ *n* **1** the act or process of individuating: eg **1a** the development of the individual from the universal or the general **b** the process by which individuals in society become differentiated from one another **c** the formation of the separate but interdependent functional units making up a colony (e g a coral) **d** differentiation of tissue into regions with the potential for different types of development along a primary axis of an embryo **2** the state of being an individual; *specif* individuality

**indivisible** /ˌindiˈvizəbl/ *adj* not divisible [ME, fr LL *indivisibilis*, fr L *in*- ¹in- + LL *divisibilis* divisible] – **indivisible** *n*, **indivisibleness** *n*, **indivisibly** *adv*, **indivisibility** *n*

**indo** /indoh-/ – see IND-

**Indo-** /indoh-/ – see IND-

**Indo-ˈAryan** *n* **1** a member of any of the peoples of India of Indo-European language and Caucasian physique **2** any of the early Indo-European invaders of Persia, Afghanistan, and India **3** the Indo-Iranian languages of India and Pakistan – **Indo-Aryan** *adj*

**Indo-Chiˈnese** *n* **1** a native or inhabitant of Indochina **2** Sino-Tibetan [(1) *Indochina*, former region of SE Asia; (2) *Ind*- + *Chinese*] – **Indo-Chinese** *adj*

**indoctrinate** /inˈdoktrinayt/ *vt* **1** to instruct esp in fundamentals or rudiments; teach **2** to imbue with a usu partisan or sectarian opinion, point of view, or ideology [prob fr ME *endoctrinen*, fr MF *endoctriner*, fr OF, fr *en*- + *doctrine* teaching, something taught] – **indoctrinator** *n*, **indoctrination** *n*

**Indo-Euroˈpean** *adj* relating to or being the INDO-EUROPEAN LANGUAGES – **Indo-European** *n*

**Indo-European languages** *n pl* a family of languages comprising those spoken in most of Europe, Asia as far east as N India, and N and S America

**Indo-Gerˈmanic** *n* Indo-European – **Indo-Germanic** *adj*

**Indo-ˈHittite** *n* a language family including Indo-European and Anatolian; *also* the hypothetical parent language of this family – **Indo-Hittite** *adj*

**Indo-Iˈranian** *adj* of, characteristic of, or constituting a subfamily of the INDO-EUROPEAN LANGUAGES comprising the Indic and the Iranian branches – **Indo-Iranian** *n*

**indole** /ˈindohl/ *n* a chemical compound, $C_8H_7N$, that is present in some plant oils and COAL TAR, occurs in the intestines and faeces as a product of the decomposition of some proteins, and is used in minute amounts in some perfumes; *also* a chemical compound derived from indole [ISV *ind*- + *-ole*]

**indoleacetic acid** /ˌindohləˈsetik/ *n* a plant hormone, $C_8H_6NCH_2CO_2H$, that promotes growth and root formation of plants

**indolebutyric acid** /ˌindohlbyoohˈtirik/ *n* a synthetic acid, $C_8H_6N(CH_2)_3COOH$, similar to INDOLEACETIC ACID in its effects on plants

**indolent** /ˈindələnt/ *adj* **1a** causing little or no pain **b** slow to develop or heal ⟨*an ~ ulcer*⟩ **2a** averse to activity, effort, or movement; habitually lazy ⟨*an ~ pupil*⟩ **b** conducive to or exhibiting laziness ⟨*~ weather*⟩ ⟨*an ~ sigh*⟩ **synonyms** see LETHARGY **antonyms** active, industrious [LL *indolent-*, *indolens* insensitive to pain, fr L *in*- ¹in- + *dolent-*, *dolens*, prp of *dolēre* to feel pain – more at CONDOLE] – **indolence** *n*, **indolently** *adv*

**indomethacin** /ˌindohˈmethəsin/ *n* a synthetic drug, $C_{19}H_{16}ClNO_4$, used esp to relieve pain and inflammation (e g in the treatment of arthritis) [*indole* + *meth*- + *ac*etic acid + *-in*]

**indomitable** /inˈdomitəbl/ *adj* incapable of being subdued; unconquerable ⟨*~ courage*⟩ [LL *indomitabilis*, fr L *in*- ¹in- + *domitare* to tame – more at DAUNT] – **indomitableness** *n*, **indomitably** *adv*, **indomitability** *n*

**Indonesian** /ˌindəˈneezh(ə)n, -zyən/ *n* **1** a native or inhabitant of Indonesia or of the Malay archipelago **2** a branch of the Austronesian language family of the East Indies; *esp* BAHASA INDONESIA [*Indonesia*, country & archipelago in SE Asia] – **Indonesian** *adj*

**indoor** /inˈdaw/ *adj* **1** relating to the interior of a building ⟨*an ~ scene*⟩ **2** done, living, or belonging indoors ⟨*an ~ sport*⟩ ⟨*an ~ plant*⟩ [alter. (influenced by *in*) of obs *within-door*, fr the phrase *within door* in a building]

**indoors** /inˈdawz/ *adv* in or into a building ⟨*stay ~ till the rain stops*⟩

**indophenol** /ˌindohˈfeenol/ *n* any of various chemically related blue or green dyes used esp for wool and cotton [ISV]

**indorse** /inˈdaws/ *vt* to endorse

**indoxyl** /inˈdoksil/ *n* an unstable chemical compound, $C_8H_7NO$, that occurs in combined form in plants and in the urine of animals, and is produced as an intermediate step in indigo manufacture [ISV *ind*- + *hydroxyl*]

**indraught** /ˈindrahft/ *n* **1** a drawing or pulling in **2** an inward flow or current (e g of air or water)

**indrawn** /inˈdrawn/ *adj* **1** drawn in ⟨*an ~ breath*⟩ **2** aloof, reserved

**indri** /ˈindri/ *n* a large lemur of Madagascar (*Indris brevicaudatus*) that has a rudimentary tail and black and white markings [Fr, fr Malagasy *indry* look! (mistaken for the animal's name by an 18th-c Fr naturalist)]

**indris** /ˈindris/ *n* the indri [NL, genus name, fr Fr *indri*]

**indubitable** /inˈdyoohbitəbl/ *adj* too evident to be doubted; unquestionable [Fr or L; Fr, fr L *indubitabilis*, fr *in*- ¹in- + *dubitabilis* dubitable] – **indubitableness** *n*, **indubitably** *adv*, **indubitability** *n*

**induce** /inˈdyoohs/ *vt* **1** to lead on to do something; move by persuasion or influence **2a(1)** to cause to appear or to occur; bring on or bring about **a(2)** to cause (labour) to begin by the use of drugs **b** to cause the formation of **c** to produce (e g an electric current) by induction **d** *psychology* to arouse by indirect stimulation **3** to establish by logical induction; *specif* to infer (a general principle) from particular cases – compare DEDUCE [ME *inducen*, fr L *inducere*, fr *in*- ²in- + *ducere* to lead – more at TOW] – **inducible** *adj*, **inducibility** *n*

**inducement** /inˈdyoohsmənt/ *n* **1** the act or process of inducing **2** something that induces; *esp* a motive or consideration that encourages one to do something ⟨*they offered a higher salary as an ~ to stay*⟩

**inducer** /inˈdyoohsə/ *n* **1** one who or that which induces **2** a substance that induces or increases the production of an enzyme or other protein; *specif* a substance that causes genetic induction by combining with and inactivating a REPRESSOR (substance that indirectly prevents the synthesis of a protein by a gene)

**induct** /inˈdukt/ *vt* **1** to place formally in office; install ⟨*was ~ed as president*⟩ **2a** to introduce, initiate ⟨*it is essential that teachers be ~ed properly into the profession*⟩ **b** *NAm* to enrol for military training or service [ME *inducten*, fr ML *inductus*, pp of *inducere*, fr L]

**inductance** /inˈdukt(ə)ns/ *n* **1a** a property of an electrical circuit by which an ELECTROMOTIVE FORCE is induced in it by a variation of current either in the circuit itself or in a neighbouring circuit, giving rise to a variation in the strength of the MAGNETIC FIELD linked with the circuit **b** the degree to which an ELECTROMOTIVE FORCE is induced in an electrical circuit; *also* the measure of inductance equal to the ratio of the electromotive force induced to the inducing current **2** a circuit or a device possessing inductance

**inductee** /inˈduktee/ *n, NAm* a person inducted into military service

**induction** /inˈduksh(ə)n/ *n* **1a** the act or process of inducting (e g into office) **b** an initial experience; an initiation; *specif* preparatory training before embarking on a longer programme **c** a formal introduction (e g by means of a lecture) to an organization; *esp* an introduction for new employees **d** the ceremony of giving the ecclesiastical revenues of a benefice to a clergyman newly instituted to it **2a** the act or an instance of reasoning from particular premises to a general conclusion **b** a conclusion reached by logical induction **c induction, mathematical induction** a mathematical demonstration of the validity of a law concerning all the positive integers, by proving that the law holds for the first integer and that if it holds for all the integers preceding a given integer it must hold for the given integer **3a** the act of bringing forward or adducing (e g facts or particulars) **b** the act of causing or bringing on or about **c** the production of an electric charge, magnetism, or ELECTROMOTIVE FORCE in an object (e g an electrical conductor, a magnetized body, or an electrical circuit) by the proximity of, but not contact with, a similarly energized body or by the variation of a MAGNETIC

FLUX **d** the drawing of the fuel-air mixture from the carburettor into the combustion chamber of an INTERNAL-COMBUSTION ENGINE **e** the process by which a cell or tissue influences neighbouring cells or tissues; *esp* the sum of the processes by which one embryonic tissue induces and directs the development and differentiation of other embryonic cells and tissues **f** the activation of a STRUCTURAL GENE (gene responsible for the synthesis of a particular protein) by a substance that combines with and inactivates a genetic REPRESSOR (substance that indirectly represses the function of a structural gene); *also* (an increase in) the production of a protein (e g an ENZYME) by induction **4** *NAm* the formality by which a civilian is inducted into military service

**induction coil** *n* a transformer for producing intermittent pulses of high voltage electricity

**induction heating** *n* the heating of material by means of an electric current induced to flow in the material or its container

**inductive** /in'duktiv/ *adj* **1** of or employing mathematical or logical induction ⟨~ *reasoning*⟩ – compare DEDUCTIVE 1 **2a** relating to or possessing inductance ⟨*an* ~ *circuit*⟩ **b** of, produced by, or operating by electrical induction **3** introductory **4** involving the action of an embryological inductor; tending to produce induction – **inductively** *adv*, **inductiveness** *n*

**inductor** /in'duktə/ *n* **1** one who or that which inducts **2a** a part of an electrical apparatus that is acted upon or acts by induction **b** an electrical component that has inductance; *esp* a component that is included in an electrical circuit to provide inductance and that usu consists of a coiled electrical conductor which is sometimes wound on a laminated steel core to increase the inductive effect **3** a part of an embryo or a substance produced by embryonic tissue that is capable of inducing a specific type of development and differentiation in previously undifferentiated tissue – called also ORGANIZER

**indue** /in'dyooh/ *vt* to endue

**indulge** /in'dulj/ *vt* **1a** to give free rein to (e g a taste) **b** to allow (oneself) to do something pleasurable or gratifying ⟨*he thought he would* ~ *himself by opening another bottle*⟩ **2** to treat with great or excessive leniency, generosity, or consideration; pamper ~ *vi* to indulge oneself – often + *in* ⟨~ *in another cigarette*⟩ [L *indulgēre* to be complaisant] – **indulger** *n*

¹**indulgence** /in'dulj(ə)ns/ *n* **1** remission of part or all of the punishment that according to Roman Catholicism is due, esp in purgatory, for sins whose guilt has been pardoned **2** indulging or being indulgent ⟨*treated her moody child with* ~⟩ **3** an indulgent act **4** something indulged in

²**indulgence** *vt* to attach an indulgence to ⟨~ d *prayers*⟩

**indulgent** /in'dulj(ə)nt/ *adj* indulging or characterized by indulgence; lenient [L *indulgent-, indulgens*, prp of *indulgēre*] – **indulgently** *adv*

**induline** /'indyoolin, -leen/ *n* any of numerous blue or violet dyes related to the SAFRANINES [ISV *ind-* + *-ule* + *-ine*]

**indult** /in'dult/ *n* a special often temporary dispensation granted in the Roman Catholic church for a particular purpose [ME (Sc), fr ML *indultum*, fr LL, grant, fr L, neut of *indultus*, pp of *indulgēre*]

**induna** /in'doohnə/ *n, SAfr* a headman [Zulu *in-duna* captain, councillor]

¹**indurate** /'indyoorət/, **indurated** /'indyoo,raytid/ *adj* physically or morally hardened

²**indurate** /'indyoorayt/ *vt* **1** to make unfeeling, stubborn, or obdurate **2** to make hardy; inure **3a** to make hard ⟨*great heat* ~s *clay*⟩ **b** to increase the fibrous elements of ⟨~d *tissue*⟩ **4** to establish firmly; confirm ~ *vi* **1** to grow hard; harden **2** to become established [L *induratus*, pp of *indurare*, fr *in-* ²*in-* + *durare* to harden, fr *durus* hard – more at DURING] – **induration** *n*, **indurative** *adj*

**indusium** /in'dyoohzi·əm/ *n, pl* **indusia** /-ziə/ **1** an enveloping or covering layer or membrane **2** an outgrowth of the surface layer of a fern frond that covers and protects a cluster of spores [NL, fr L, tunic, prob fr *induere* to put on]

¹**industrial** /in'dustri·əl/ *adj* **1** relating to industry **2** characterized by highly developed industries ⟨*an* ~ *nation*⟩ **3** engaged in industry ⟨*the* ~ *classes*⟩ **4** derived from human industry ⟨~ *wealth*⟩ **5** used in industry ⟨~ *diamonds*⟩ △ **industrious** – **industrially** *adv*

²**industrial** *n* **1** a person or company employed or engaged in industry or industrial production **2** *usu pl* a share or bond issued by an industrial enterprise

**industrial action** *n* action (e g a strike or go-slow) taken by a body of workers to force an employer to comply with demands

**industrial archaeology** *n* the scientific study of the products and remains of past industrial activity

**industrial engineering** *n* engineering that deals with the development and application of cost and work standards for the various operations involved in manufacture

**industrial estate** *n* an area that is usu at a distance from the centre of a city or town and that is designed esp for a community of industries and businesses

**industrialism** /in'dustri·ə,liz(ə)m/ *n* social and economic organization in which industries, esp large-scale mechanized industries, are dominant

**industrialist** /in'dustri·əlist/ *n* one who owns or is engaged in the management of an industry; a manufacturer

**industrial-ize, -ise** /in'dustri·ə,liez/ *vt* to make industrial; introduce industry to ⟨~ *an agricultural region*⟩ ~ *vi* to become industrial – **industrialization** *n*

**industrial melanism** *n* genetically determined darkening, esp in insects (e g the PEPPERED MOTH), that occurs in areas blackened by industrial pollution

**industrial relations** *n pl* the dealings or relationships between the management of a usu large business or industrial enterprise and the employees, esp trade unions, operating within it

**industrial revolution** *n* a rapid major development of an economy (e g in England in the late 18th century) marked by the general introduction of mechanized techniques and large-scale production

**industrial school** *n* a school specializing in the teaching of manual skills and familiarity with tools and machines; *specif* a public institution of this kind for juvenile delinquents

**industrial tribunal** *n* a usu official tribunal set up to handle legal disputes (e g over alleged unfair dismissal) between employers and employees

**industrial union** *n* a trade union that admits to membership workers in an industry irrespective of their occupation or craft – compare CRAFT UNION, GENERAL UNION

**industrious** /in'dustri·əs/ *adj* **1** persistently diligent; hard-working **2** constantly, regularly, or habitually occupied **synonyms** see ¹BUSY *antonyms* lazy, indolent △ **industrial** – **industriously** *adv*, **industriousness** *n*

**industry** /'indəstri/ *n* **1** diligence and application in an employment or pursuit **2a** systematic work, esp for the creation of value **b** a department or branch of a craft, art, business, or manufacture; *esp* a manufacturing concern with substantial capital and a large personnel **c(1)** a usu specified group of productive or profit-making enterprises ⟨*the car* ~⟩ **c(2)** an organized field of activity regarded in its commercial aspects ⟨*the growth of the knowledge* ~⟩ ⟨*the Shakespeare* ~⟩ **d** manufacturing activity as a whole ⟨*the nation's* ~⟩ [MF *industrie* skill, employment involving skill, fr L *industria* diligence, fr *industrius* diligent, fr OL *indostruus*, fr *indu* in + *-struus* (akin to L *struere* to build) – more at INDIGENOUS, STRUCTURE]

**usage** A new pronunciation /in'dustri/ is widely disliked.

**indwell** /,in'dwel/ *vb* to exist within as an activating spirit, force, or principle – **indweller** *n*

**indwelling** /'in,dweling/ *adj, of a tube* (e g a catheter) *inserted into the body* left within a body organ or passage, esp to promote drainage

¹**-ine** /-ien, -een, -in/ *suffix* (→ *adj*) **1** relating to or resembling ⟨*equine*⟩ ⟨*feminine*⟩ **2** made of; like ⟨*opaline*⟩ ⟨*crystalline*⟩ [ME *-in, -ine*, fr MF & L; (1) MF *-in*, fr L *-inus*; (2) MF *-in*, fr L *-inus*, fr Gk *-inos* – more at -EN]

²**-ine** *suffix* (→ *n*) **1** chemical compound: e g **1a** basic or base-containing carbon compound (e g an amino acid or alkaloid) that contains nitrogen ⟨*morphine*⟩ ⟨*leucine*⟩ ⟨*glycine*⟩ **b** mixture of compounds (e g of hydrocarbons) ⟨*kerosine*⟩ **c** usu gaseous hydride ⟨*arsine*⟩ **2** *-in* [ME *-ine, -in*, fr MF & L; MF *-ine*, fr L *-ina*, fr fem of *-īnus*, adj suffix]

**inebriant** /in'eebriənt/ *n* an intoxicant – **inebriant** *adj*

¹**inebriate** /in'eebriayt/ *vt* **1** to make drunk; intoxicate **2** to exhilarate or stupefy as if by liquor ⟨*a crowd* ~d *by news of victory*⟩ [L *inebriatus*, pp of *inebriare*, fr *in-* ²*in-* + *ebriare* to intoxicate, fr *ebrius* drunk – more at SOBER] – **inebriate** *adj*, **inebriation** *n*, **inebriety** *n*

²**inebriate** /in'eebriət/ *n* a drunkard

**inebriated** /in'eebriaytid/ *adj* exhilarated or confused (as if) by alcohol; intoxicated

**inedible** /in'edəbl/ *adj* **1** not safe to be eaten ⟨*an* ~ *fungus*⟩ **2** not fit to be eaten ⟨*a badly cooked and* ~ *meal*⟩

**inedited** /in'editid/ *adj* unedited [NL *ineditus*, fr L, not made known, fr *in-* ¹*in-* + *editus*, pp of *edere* to proclaim – more at EDITION ]

**ineducable** /in'edyookəbl, -djoo-/ *adj* incapable of being educated, esp because of mental retardation – **ineducability** *n*

**ineffable** /in'efəbl/ *adj* **1** too great to be expressed in words; unutterable ⟨~ *joy*⟩ **2** not to be uttered; taboo ⟨*the ~ name of Jehovah*⟩ [ME, fr MF, fr L *ineffabilis*, fr *in-* ¹*in-* + *effabilis* capable of being expressed, fr *effari* to speak out, fr *ex-* + *fari* to speak – more at BAN] – **ineffableness** *n*, **ineffably** *adv*, **ineffability** *n*

**ineffective** /,ini'fektiv/ *adj* **1** not effective; not producing an intended effect ⟨*an ~ law*⟩ **2** *of a person* not capable of performing efficiently or achieving results ⟨*an ~ leader*⟩ – **ineffectively** *adv*, **ineffectiveness** *n*

**ineffectual** /,ini'fektyooəl, -chooəl/ *adj* **1** not producing or not able to give the proper or intended effect; futile ⟨*all his attempts were ~*⟩ **2** unable to get things done; weak in character ⟨*a very ~ person*⟩ – **ineffectuality** *n*, **ineffectually** *adv*, **ineffectualness** *n*

**inefficacious** /,inefi'kayshəs/ *adj* lacking the power to produce a desired effect; ineffective ⟨*the therapy proved to be ~*⟩ ⟨*my strictures were quite ~*⟩ – **inefficaciously** *adv*, **inefficaciousness** *n*

**inefficacy** /in'efikəsi/ *n* lack of power to produce a desired effect; ineffectiveness [LL *inefficacia*, fr L *inefficac-*, *inefficax* inefficacious, fr *in-* ¹*in-* + *efficac-*, *efficax* efficacious]

**inefficiency** /,ini'fish(ə)nsi/ *n* **1** the quality or state of being inefficient **2** something that is inefficient

**inefficient** /,ini'fish(ə)nt/ *adj* not efficient; not producing the effect intended or desired, esp in a capable or economical way ⟨*an ~ method*⟩ ⟨*an ~ worker*⟩ – **inefficient** *n*, **inefficiently** *adv*

**inegalitarian** /,ini,gali'teəriən/ *adj* not egalitarian

**inelastic** /,ini'lastik/ *adj* not elastic: **a** slow to react or respond to changing conditions; unadaptable **b** inflexible, unyielding *synonyms* see ¹STIFF – **inelasticity** *n*

**inelastic collision** *n* a collision in which part of the KINETIC ENERGY of the colliding particles or bodies changes into another form of energy (eg radiation) or in which some other property (eg electric charge) is exchanged between the colliding particles

**inelegant** /in'eligənt/ *adj* lacking in refinement, grace, or good taste [MF, fr L *inelegant-*, *inelegans*, fr *in-* ¹*in-* + *elegant-*, *elegans* elegant] – **inelegance** *n*, **inelegantly** *adv*

**ineligible** /in'elijəbl/ *adj* not eligible; not qualified or not worthy to be chosen or preferred (eg for an office) [Fr *inéligible*, fr *in-* ¹*in-* + *éligible* eligible] – **ineligible** *n*, **ineligibility** *n*

**ineluctable** /,ini'luktəbl/ *adj*, *formal* not to be avoided, changed, or resisted; inevitable [L *ineluctabilis*, fr *in-* ¹*in-* + *eluctari* to struggle out, fr *ex-* + *luctari* to struggle – more at LOCK] – **ineluctably** *adv*, **ineluctability** *n*

**inenarrable** /,ini'narəbl/ *adj* incapable of being narrated; indescribable [ME, fr MF, fr L *inenarrabilis*, fr *in-* ¹*in-* + *enarrare* to explain in detail, fr *e-* + *narrare* to narrate]

**inept** /i'nept/ *adj* **1** not suitable or apt to the time, place, or occasion **2** lacking sense or reason; foolish **3** generally incompetent; bungling *synonyms* see CLUMSY, INAPT *antonyms* apt, adept [Fr *inepte*, fr L *ineptus*, fr *in-* ¹*in-* + *aptus* apt] – **ineptly** *adv*, **ineptitude** *n*, **ineptness** *n*

**inequality** /,ini'kwoləti/ *n* **1** the quality of being unequal or uneven: eg **1a** lack of evenness **b** social disparity **c** disparity of distribution or opportunity **d** the condition of being variable; changeableness ⟨~ *of temperament*⟩ **2** an instance of being unequal **3** a formal statement of mathematical inequality between two expressions, usu with a sign of inequality (eg ⟨, ⟩, or ≠ signifying respectively *is less than*, *is greater than*, and *is not equal to*) between them [MF *inequalité*, fr L *inaequalitat-*, *inaequalitas*, fr *inaequalis* unequal, fr *in-* ¹*in-* + *aequalis* equal]

**inequitable** /in'ekwitəbl/ *adj* not equitable; unfair – **inequitably** *adv*

**inequity** /in'ekwiti/ *n* **1** injustice, unfairness **2** an instance of injustice or unfairness

**ineradicable** /,ini'radikəbl/ *adj* incapable of being rooted out – **ineradicability** *n*, **ineradicably** *adv*

**inerrant** /in'erənt/ *adj* free from error; infallible [L *inerrant-*, *inerrans*, fr *in-* ¹*in-* + *errant-*, *errans*, prp of *errare* to err] – **inerrancy** *n*

**inert** /i'nuht/ *adj* **1** lacking the power to move **2** deficient in active properties: eg **2a** chemically unreactive **b** *of a drug* not having the expected or desired biological action or effects **3** not moving; inactive, indolent *synonyms* see INACTIVE [L *inert-*, *iners* unskilled, idle, fr *in-* ¹*in-* + *art-*, *ars* skill – more at ARM] – **inert** *n*, **inertly** *adv*, **inertness** *n*

**inert gas** *n* NOBLE GAS (eg helium or neon)

**inertia** /i'nuhshə/ *n* **1a** a property of matter by which it remains at rest or in uniform motion in the same straight line unless acted upon by some external force **b** an analogous property of other physical quantities (eg electricity) **2** indisposition to motion, exertion, or change; inertness ⟨*failed to make a needed change in the system through sheer ~*⟩ [NL, fr L, lack of skill, idleness, fr *inert-*, *iners*] – **inertial** *adj*, **inertially** *adv*

**inertial guidance** *n* guidance or navigation (eg of an aircraft or spacecraft) by comparison of preprogrammed data with data collected by measurement of inertial forces within the craft

**inertial navigation** *n* INERTIAL GUIDANCE

**inertia reel** *n* a reel that permits steady unwinding but resists a sudden sharp jerk ⟨*an ~ seat belt*⟩

**inertia selling** *n*, *chiefly Br* the practice of sending unrequested goods to people with the intention of demanding payment if the goods are not returned

**inescapable** /,ini'skaypəbl/ *adj* incapable of being avoided, ignored, or denied; unavoidable – **inescapably** *adv*

¹**inessential** /,ini'sensh(ə)l/ *adj* **1** having no essence **2** not essential; unessential

²**inessential** *n* something that is not essential

**inestimable** /in'estiməbl/ *adj* **1** incapable of being estimated or computed; *specif* too great to be estimated ⟨*storms caused ~ damage along the coast*⟩ **2** too valuable or excellent to be measured ⟨*has performed an ~ service for his country*⟩ [ME, fr MF, fr L *inaestimabilis*, fr *in-* ¹*in-* + *aestimabilis* estimable] – **inestimably** *adv*

**inevitable** /in'evitəbl/ *adj* incapable of being avoided or evaded; bound to happen or to confront one [ME, fr L *inevitabilis*, fr *in-* ¹*in-* + *evitabilis* avoidable, fr *evitare* to avoid, fr *e-* + *vitare* to shun] – **inevitableness** *n*, **inevitably** *adv*, **inevitability** *n*

**inexact** /,inig'zakt/ *adj* not precisely correct or true; inaccurate ⟨*an ~ translation*⟩ [Fr, fr *in-* ¹*in-* + *exact*] – **inexactitude** *n*, **inexactly** *adv*, **inexactness** *n*

**inexcusable** /,iniks'kyoohzəbl/ *adj* without excuse or justification ⟨~ *rudeness*⟩ [L *inexcusabilis*, fr *in-* ¹*in-* + *excusabilis* excusable] – **inexcusableness** *n*, **inexcusably** *adv*

**inexhaustible** /,inig'zawstəbl/ *adj* not exhaustible; incapable of being used up or worn out ⟨~ *patience*⟩ – **inexhaustibleness** *n*, **inexhaustibly** *adv*, **inexhaustibility** *n*

**inexistent** /,inig'zistənt/ *adj* not having existence; nonexistent [LL *inexsistent-*, *inexsistens*, fr L *in-* ¹*in-* + *exsistent-*, *exsistens*, prp of *exsistere* to exist] – **inexistence** *n*

**inexorable** /in'eks(ə)rəbl/ *adj* **1** not to be persuaded or moved by entreaty **2** continuing inevitably; that cannot be averted ⟨*the ~ passage of time*⟩ [L *inexorabilis*, fr *in-* ¹*in-* + *exorabilis* pliant, fr *exorare* to prevail upon, fr *ex-* + *orare* to speak – more at ORATION] – **inexorableness** *n*, **inexorably** *adv*, **inexorability** *n*

**inexpedient** /,inik'speediənt/ *adj* not expedient; inadvisable – **inexpedience**, **inexpediency** *n*, **inexpediently** *adv*

**inexpensive** /,inik'spensiv/ *adj* reasonable in price; cheap – **inexpensively** *adv*, **inexpensiveness** *n*

**inexperience** /,inik'spiəri•əns/ *n* **1** lack of practical experience; *esp* lack of the skill gained from experience **2** lack of knowledge of the ways of the world [MF, fr LL *inexperientia*, fr L *in-* ¹*in-* + *experientia* experience] – **inexperienced** *adj*

**inexpert** /in'ekspuht/ *adj* not expert; unskilled [ME, fr MF, fr L *inexpertus*, fr *in-* ¹*in-* + *expertus* expert] – **inexpert** *n*, **inexpertly** *adv*, **inexpertness** *n*

**inexpiable** /in'ekspiəbl/ *adj* not capable of being expiated [L *inexpiabilis*, fr *in-* ¹*in-* + *expiare* to expiate] – **inexpiably** *adv*

**inexplicable** /,inik'splikəbl, in'eksplikəbl/ *adj* incapable of being explained, interpreted, or accounted for [MF, fr L *inexplicabilis*, fr *in-* ¹*in-* + *explicabilis* explicable] – **inexplicableness** *n*, **inexplicably** *adv*, **inexplicability** *n*

**inexplicit** /,inik'splisit/ *adj* not explicit

**inexpressible** /,inik'spresəbl/ *adj* beyond one's power to express; indescribable – **inexpressibleness** *n*, **inexpressibly** *adv*, **inexpressibility** *n*

**inexpressive** /,inik'spresiv/ *adj* **1** lacking expression or meaning ⟨*an ~ face*⟩ **2** *archaic* inexpressible – **inexpressively** *adv*, **inexpressiveness** *n*

**inexpugnable** /,inik'spugnəbl/ *adj* incapable of being subdued

# ine

752

or overthrown; **impregnable** ⟨*an* ~ *position*⟩ [MF, fr L *inexpugnabilis*, fr *in-* [1]*in-* + *expugnare* to take by storm, fr *ex-* + *pugnare* to fight – more at PUNGENT] – **inexpugnableness** *n*, **inexpugnably** *adv*

**inexpungible** /ˌinikˈspunjəbl/ *adj* incapable of being obliterated ⟨*an* ~ *smell of garlic*⟩ [*in-* + *expunge*]

**in extenso** /ˌin ikˈstensoh/ *adv* at full length [ML]

**inextinguishable** /ˌinikˈstingˌgwishəbl/ *adj* not extinguishable; unquenchable ⟨*an* ~ *flame* ⟩ ⟨*an* ~ *longing*⟩ – **inextinguishably** *adv*

**in extremis** /ˌin ikˈstreemis/ *adv* in extreme circumstances; *esp* at the point of death [L]

**inextricable** /inˈekstrikəbl/ *adj* 1 from which one cannot extricate oneself 2a incapable of being disentangled or untied ⟨*an* ~ *knot*⟩ b indissolubly mixed up; inseparable ⟨*the history of Hitler and the history of World War II ... are* ~ – J K Galbraith⟩ [MF or L; MF, fr L *inextricabilis*, fr *in-* [1]*in-* + *extricabilis* extricable] – **inextricably** *adv*, **inextricability** *n*

**infallible** /inˈfaləbl/ *adj* 1 incapable of error; unerring ⟨*an* ~ *memory*⟩ 2 not liable to fail; certain ⟨*an* ~ *remedy*⟩ 3 *of the Pope* incapable of error in defining doctrines relating to faith or morals [ML *infallibilis*, fr L *in-* [1]*in-* + LL *fallibilis* fallible] – **infallibly** *adv*, **infallibility** *n*

**infamous** /ˈinfəməs/ *adj* 1 having a reputation of the worst kind; notorious ⟨~ *traitor*⟩ – sometimes used humorously ⟨~ *for his practical jokes*⟩ 2 causing or bringing infamy; disgraceful 3 convicted of an offence bringing infamy [ME, fr L *infamis*, fr *in-* [1]*in-* + *fama* fame]

**infamy** /ˈinfəmi/ *n* 1 evil reputation brought about by something grossly criminal, shocking, or brutal 2a an extreme and publicly known criminal or evil act b the state of being infamous

**infancy** /ˈinf(ə)nsi/ *n* 1 early childhood 2 a beginning or early period of existence ⟨*when sociology was in its* ~⟩ 3 the legal status of an infant

[1]**infant** /ˈinf(ə)nt/ *n* 1 a child in the first period of life 2 a minor [ME *enfaunt*, fr MF *enfant*, fr L *infant-, infans*, fr *infant-, infans* incapable of speech, young, fr *in-* [1]*in-* + *fant-, fans*, prp of *fari* to speak – more at BAN]

[2]**infant** *adj* 1 of or being in infancy; in an early stage of development ⟨*the* ~ *Christian Church*⟩ 2 concerned with or intended for young children or for children in British schools aged from five to seven or eight ⟨*an* ~ *teacher*⟩

**infanta** /inˈfantə/ *n* a daughter of a Spanish or Portuguese monarch [Sp & Pg, fem of *infante*]

**infante** /inˈfanti/ *n* a younger son of a Spanish or Portuguese monarch [Sp & Pg, lit., infant, fr L *infant-, infans*]

**infanticide** /inˈfantisied/ *n* 1 the killing of an infant; *also* the practice of killing newborn infants 2 the crime, punishable as manslaughter, of a mother killing her child under the age of 12 months 3 one who kills an infant [LL *infanticidium* (sense 1 & 2) & *infanticida* (sense 3), fr L *infant-, infans* + *-i-* + *-cidium* & *-cida* -cide]

**infantile** /ˈinf(ə)ntiel/ *adj* 1 of infants or infancy 2 suitable to or characteristic of an infant; *esp* very immature ⟨~ *humour*⟩ 3 in a very early stage of development – **infantility** *n*

**infantile paralysis** *n* POLIOMYELITIS

**infantilism** /inˈfantiˌliz(ə)m/ *n* 1 retention of childish physical, mental, or emotional qualities in adult life; *esp* failure to attain sexual maturity 2 an act or expression that indicates lack of maturity – used technically

**infantry** /ˈinf(ə)ntri/ *n* 1 *taking pl vb* soldiers trained, armed, and equipped to fight on foot 2 *taking sing or pl vb* an infantry regiment or branch of an army [MF & OIt; MF *infanterie*, fr OIt *infanteria*, fr *infante* boy, foot soldier, fr L *infant-, infans*]

**infantryman** /ˈinf(ə)ntrimən/ *n* an infantry soldier

**infant school** *n, Br* a school for children aged five to seven or eight; *broadly* a kindergarten

**infarct** /inˈfahkt/ *n* an area of death in a tissue or organ (eg the heart) resulting from obstruction of the blood circulation in that area by a clot, air bubble, etc [L *infarctus*, pp of *infarcire* to stuff, fr *in-* [2]*in-* + *farcire* to stuff – more at FARCE] – **infarcted** *adj*

**infarction** /inˈfahksh(ə)n/ *n* (the development or production of) an infarct

**infatuate** /inˈfatyooayt/ *vt* 1 to affect with folly 2 to inspire with powerful but superficial or short-lived feelings of love and desire [L *infatuatus*, pp of *infatuare*, fr *in-* [2]*in-* + *fatuus* fatuous] – **infatuated** *adj*, **infatuation** *n*

**infauna** /ˈinˌfawnə/ *n* aquatic animals living on the bottom,

esp in a soft sea bed – compare EPIFAUNA [NL, fr [2]*in-* + *fauna*] – **infaunal** *adj*

**infect** /inˈfekt/ *vt* 1 to contaminate (eg air or food) with a disease-producing substance or agent (eg a bacterium) 2a to pass on a disease or a disease-causing agent to b *of a disease-causing organism* to invade (an individual or organ), usu by penetration 3a to contaminate, corrupt ⟨*manages to* ~ *her with a sense of guilt*⟩ b to work upon or seize upon so as to induce sympathy, belief, or support ⟨*the teacher* ~ed *his pupils with his enthusiasm*⟩ [ME *infecten*, fr L *infectus*, pp of *inficere* to dip in, stain, taint, fr *in-* [2]*in-* + *facere* to make, do – more at DO] – **infector** *n*

**infection** /inˈfeksh(ə)n/ *n* 1 the act or result of infecting or contaminating 2 an act or process of infecting; *also* the establishment of a disease-causing agent in its host after invasion 3 the state produced by the establishment of an infective agent in or on a suitable host; *also* a contagious or infectious disease 4 an infective agent; *also* material contaminated with an infective agent 5 the communication of emotions or qualities through example or contact

**infectious** /inˈfekshəs/ *adj* 1a infectious, infective capable of causing infection b *of a disease* caused and communicable by infection with a disease-causing microorganism (eg a bacterium) – compare CONTAGIOUS 2 readily spread or communicated to others ⟨~ *excitement*⟩ – **infectiously** *adv*, **infectiousness** *n*, **infectivity** *n*

**infectious hepatitis** *n* a serious highly infectious virus disease that is characterized by inflammation of the liver, accompanied by jaundice, fever, nausea, vomiting, and abdominal discomfort

**infectious mononucleosis** *n* an infectious disease characterized by fever, swollen and painful LYMPH GLANDS, and an increase in the number of LYMPHOCYTES in the blood – called also GLANDULAR FEVER

**infelicitous** /ˌinfəˈlisitəs/ *adj* not apt; not suitably chosen for the occasion ⟨*his* ~ *remark at the garden party*⟩ – **infelicitously** *adv*

**infelicity** /ˌinfəˈlisəti/ *n* 1 the quality or state of being infelicitous 2 something that is infelicitous [ME *infelicite*, fr L *infelicitas*, fr *infelic-, infelix* unhappy, fr *in-* [1]*in-* + *felic-, felix* fruitful – more at FEMININE]

**infelt** /ˈinfelt/ *adj* felt inwardly; heartfelt

**infer** /inˈfuh/ *vb* **-rr-** *vt* 1 to derive as a conclusion from facts or premises ⟨*to see smoke and* ~ *fire*⟩ 2 to guess, surmise ⟨*I* ~ *from your letter that all is well*⟩ 3 to point out; indicate ⟨*this doth* ~ *the zeal I had to see him* – Shak⟩ 4 to suggest, imply ⟨*this survey* ~s *that the installations are not profitable*⟩ ~ *vi* to draw inferences ⟨*men ... have observed,* ~red, *and reasoned ... to all kinds of results* – John Dewey⟩ [MF or L; MF *inferer*, fr L *inferre*, lit., to carry or bring into, fr *in-* [2]*in-* + *ferre* to carry – more at BEAR] – **inferable, inferrible** *adj*, **inferrer** *n*

*usage* Correctly, the writer or speaker **implies** (= "hints") to the reader, listener, or observer **infers** (= "guesses by reasoning"). **Infer** has been used on occasion for **imply** since the 16th century ⟨*Great or Bright* infers *not Excellence* – John Milton⟩ but today this usage is widely disliked. To avoid ambiguity it may be safer to provide either word with an adequate context ⟨*I* infer *from your silence that you disagree*⟩.

**inference** /ˈinf(ə)rəns/ *n* 1 the act or process of inferring: eg 1a the act or an instance of passing from one proposition accepted as true to another whose truth is believed to follow from that of the former b the assumption of statistical generalizations (eg of the value of population PARAMETERS) usu with calculated degrees of certainty, based on actual sample values determined by experiment 2 something that is inferred; *esp* a proposition arrived at by inference [ML *inferentia*, fr L *inferent-, inferens*, prp of *inferre*]

**inferential** /ˌinfəˈrensh(ə)l/ *adj* 1 relating to, involving, or resembling inference 2 deduced or deducible by inference – **inferentially** *adv*

**inferior** /inˈfiori-ə/ *adj* 1 situated lower down; lower 2 of low or lower degree or rank 3 of little or less importance, value, or merit ⟨*always felt* ~ *to his older brother*⟩ 4a *of an animal structure* situated below or behind another part, esp a corresponding part b *of a plant part* situated below or at or near the base of another part or organ: eg b(1) *of a calyx* lying below the OVARY (seed-bearing organ) b(2) *of an ovary* lying below the petals or sepals 5 relating to or being a symbol or letter written as a SUBSCRIPT 6 *of a planet* nearer the sun than the earth is

[ME, fr L, compar of *inferus* – more at UNDER] – **inferior** *n*, **inferiorly** *adv*, **inferiority** *n*
  **usage** Things are **inferior** *to*, not *than*, other things ⟨△ *a man of greatly* **inferior** *abilities than mine*⟩. Compare SUPERIOR
**inferior conjunction** *n* a conjunction in which a lesser or secondary celestial body passes between the observer and the primary body round which it revolves ⟨~ *of Venus*⟩
**inferiority complex** /in‚fiəri'orəti/ *n* an acute sense of personal inferiority resulting either in timidity or, through overcompensation, in exaggerated aggressiveness; *broadly* a feeling of being inferior or inadequate
**infernal** /in'fuhnl/ *adj* **1** relating to a nether world of the dead **2a** of hell **b** hellish, diabolical ⟨~ *wickedness*⟩ **3** *informal* damnable, damned – used chiefly to express anger or irritation ⟨*an* ~ *nuisance*⟩ [ME, fr OF, fr LL *infernalis*, fr *infernus* hell, fr L, lower; akin to L *inferus* inferior] – **infernally** *adv*
**infernal machine** *n* a machine or apparatus maliciously designed to explode and destroy life or property; *esp* a concealed or disguised bomb
**inferno** /in'fuhnoh/ *n, pl* **infernos** a place or a state that resembles or suggests hell, esp in intense heat or raging fire ⟨*the* ~ *of war*⟩ ⟨*the roaring* ~ *of the blast furnace*⟩ [It, hell, fr LL *infernus*]
**infero-** *comb form* below and ⟨*infero*lateral⟩ [L *inferus*]
**infertile** /in'fuhtiel/ *adj* not fertile or productive ⟨~ *eggs*⟩ ⟨~ *fields*⟩ **synonyms** see STERILE [MF, fr LL *infertilis*, fr L *in-* ¹in- + *fertilis* fertile] – **infertility** *n*
**infest** /in'fest/ *vt* **1** to spread or swarm in or over in a troublesome manner ⟨*shark*-infested *waters*⟩ **2** to live in or on as a parasite [MF *infester*, fr L *infestare*, fr *infestus* hostile] – **infestant** *n*, **infester** *n*, **infestation** *n*
**infibulation** /in‚fibyoo'laysh(ə)n/ *n* the partial closure of the female genitals, by stitching up or fastening with a clasp, to prevent sexual intercourse [L *infibulatus*, pp of *infibulare* to fasten with a clasp or buckle, fr *in-* ²in- + *fibula* clasp, pin]
**infidel** /'infidl/ *n* **1** a person who is not a Christian or who opposes Christianity **2a** an unbeliever in or opponent of a particular religion (e g Islam) **b** a person who acknowledges no religious belief **3** a disbeliever in something specified or understood [MF *infidele*, fr LL *infidelis* unbelieving, fr L, unfaithful, fr *in-* ¹in- + *fidelis* faithful – more at FIDELITY] – **infidel** *adj*
**infidelity** /‚infi'deləti/ *n* **1** lack of belief in a religion **2a** unfaithfulness to a moral obligation; disloyalty **b** marital unfaithfulness or an instance of it
¹**infield** /'infeeld/ *n* **1** a field near a farmhouse **2a** the area of a cricket field relatively near the wickets or of a baseball field enclosed by the bases **b** the fielding positions that lie in a cricket or baseball infield; *also, taking sing or pl vb* the players who field in these positions
²**infield** /-'-/ *adv* away from the edge of a playing field
**infielder** /'infeeldə/ *n* a cricket or baseball player who is fielding in the infield
**infighting** /'in‚fieting/ *n* **1** fighting or boxing at close quarters **2** rough-and-tumble fighting **3** prolonged and often bitter dissension among members of a group or organization ⟨*bureaucratic* ~⟩ – **infighter** *n*
**infill** /'infil/ *vt* to fill in (a gap or cavity); *esp* to build houses in between (houses already standing) – **infill** *n*
**infilling** /'in‚filing/ *n* material (e g hardcore) used to fill in spaces between structural members (e g walls) or to make up levels (e g floors)
**infiltrate** /'infiltrayt/ *vt* **1** to cause (e g a liquid) to permeate something (e g by penetrating its pores or interstices) **2** to pass into or through (a substance) by filtering or permeating **3** to pass (troops) singly or in small groups through gaps in the enemy line **4** to enter or become established in gradually or unobtrusively ⟨*the intelligence staff had been* ~d *by spies*⟩ ~ *vi* to enter, permeate, or pass through a substance or area by filtering or by insinuating gradually – **infiltrative** *adj*, **infiltrator** *n*, **infiltration** *n*
**infimum** /in'fieməm/ *n* the greatest number less than or equal to all members of a given set of numbers – called also GREATEST LOWER BOUND; compare SUPREMUM [L, neut of *infimus*, superl of *inferus* lower – more at UNDER]
¹**infinite** /'infinət/ *adj* **1** subject to no limitation or external determination; boundless **2** extending indefinitely; endless ⟨~ *space*⟩ **3** immeasurably or inconceivably great or extensive; inexhaustible ⟨~ *patience*⟩ **4a** extending beyond, lying beyond, or being greater than any arbitrarily chosen finite value, however large ⟨*there are an* ~ *number of positive inte-*

gers⟩ **b** extending to infinity ⟨~ *plane surface*⟩ **c** having an infinite number of elements or terms ⟨*an* ~ *set*⟩ ⟨*an* ~ *series*⟩ – **infinitely** *adv*, **infiniteness** *n* [ME *infinit*, fr MF or L; MF, fr L *infinitus*, fr *in-* ¹in- + *finitus* finite]
  **usage** An immeasurably small thing is better described as **infinitesimal** than as **infinitely** *small*.
²**infinite** *n* **1** diviness, sublimity – + *the* **2** an incalculable or very great number **3** an infinite quantity or magnitude
¹**infinitesimal** /‚infini'tesiml/ *n* an infinitesimal variable or quantity [NL *infinitesimus* infinite in rank, fr L *infinitus*]
²**infinitesimal** *adj* **1** taking on values arbitrarily close to zero **2** immeasurably or incalculably small – **infinitesimally** *adv*
**infinitesimal calculus** *n, maths* CALCULUS 2b
¹**infinitive** /in'finətiv/ *adj* formed with the infinitive [LL *infinitivus*, fr L *infinitus*] – **infinitively** *adv*
²**infinitive** *n* a verb form that performs some functions of a noun and that in English is used with *to* (e g *go* in "I asked him *to go*") except with auxiliary and various other verbs (e g *go* in "I must go") – **infinitival** *adj or n*
**infinitude** /in'finityoohd/ *n* **1** the quality or state of being infinite; infinity **2** something that is infinite, esp in extent **3** an infinite number or quantity
**infinity** /in'finəti/ *n* **1a** the quality of being infinite **b** unlimited extent of time, space, or quantity; boundlessness **2** an indefinitely great number or amount **3a** the limit of a mathematical function when its value becomes arbitrarily large **b** a part of a geometric figure that lies beyond any part whose distance from a given position is finite ⟨*do parallel lines ever meet if they extend to* ~?⟩ **c** a TRANSFINITE number (e g the number of NATURAL NUMBERS) **4** a distance so great that the rays of light from a POINT SOURCE at that distance may be regarded as parallel
**infirm** /in'fuhm/ *adj* **1** of poor or deteriorated vitality; *esp* feeble from age **2** weak in mind, will, or character; irresolute, vacillating ⟨~ *of purpose*⟩ **3** not solid or stable; insecure **synonyms** see WEAK *antonym* hale [ME, fr L *infirmus*, fr *in-* ¹in- + *firmus* firm] – **infirmly** *adv*
**infirmary** /in'fuhməri/ *n* a hospital
**infirmity** /in'fuhməti/ *n* **1** the quality or condition of being infirm, frail, or weak **2** a disease, malady
¹**infix** /in'fiks/ *vt* **1** to fasten or fix by piercing or thrusting in **2** to instil, inculcate **3** to insert (e g a sound or letter) as an infix [L *infixus*, pp of *infigere*, fr *in-* ²in- + *figere* to fasten – more at DYKE]
²**infix** /'infiks/ *n* an AFFIX appearing in the body of a word or root – compare PREFIX, SUFFIX
**in flagrante delicto** /in flə'granti di'liktoh/ *adv* **1** in the very act of committing a misdeed; red-handed ⟨*caught the thief* ~⟩ **2** in the very act of having sexual intercourse, esp illicitly [ML, lit., in blazing crime]
**inflame** /in'flaym/ *vt* **1** to set on fire; kindle **2a** to excite or arouse passion or excessive action or feeling in **b** to make more heated or violent; intensify ⟨*insults served only to* ~ *the feud*⟩ **3** to cause to redden or grow hot from anger or excitement ⟨*cheeks* ~d *by rage and resentment*⟩ **4** to cause inflammation in (body tissue) ~ *vi* **1** to burst into flame **2** to become excited or angered **3** to become affected with inflammation [ME *enflamen*, fr MF *enflamer*, fr L *inflammare*, fr *in-* ²in- + *flamma* flame] – **inflamer** *n*
**inflammable** /in'flaməbl/ *adj* **1** capable of being easily ignited and of burning with extreme rapidity **2** easily inflamed, excited, or angered [Fr, fr ML *inflammabilis*, fr L *inflammare* to inflame] – **inflammable** *n*, **inflammableness** *n*, **inflammably** *adv*, **inflammability** *n*
  **usage** Despite appearances, **inflammable** and **flammable** are not opposites but synonyms. Since **inflammable** looks as if it might mean "not flammable", on the analogy of *independent* or *insensitive*, it is safer to use **flammable** in technical contexts to do with fire prevention. Only **inflammable** can be used in the figurative meaning "easily excited". *antonyms* nonflammable, noninflammable △ inflammatory
**inflammation** /‚inflə'maysh(ə)n/ *n* **1** inflaming or being inflamed **2** a local reaction to injury or infection that is marked by dilation of the minute blood vessels (CAPILLARIES) and infiltration of WHITE BLOOD CELLS into the affected area, accompanied by redness, heat, pain, and swelling
**inflammatory** /in'flamət(ə)ri/ *adj* **1** tending to inflame or excite the senses **2** tending to excite agitation, disorder, or tumult; seditious ⟨~ *propaganda*⟩ **3** accompanied by or tending to cause inflammation – **inflammatorily** *adv*

**¹inflatable** /in'flaytəbl/ *adj* capable of being inflated ⟨*an ~ boat*⟩

**²inflatable** *n* something (eg a toy) that is capable of being inflated; *specif* an inflatable dinghy

**inflate** /in'flayt/ *vt* **1** to swell or distend with air or gas **2** to puff up; cause to swell **3** to expand or increase abnormally or imprudently **4** to increase (a price level) or cause (a volume of credit or the economy) to expand – compare DEFLATE **3** ~ *vi* to become inflated *synonyms* see EXPAND *antonym* deflate [L *inflatus*, pp of *inflare*, fr *in-* ²*in-* + *flare* to blow – more at BLOW] – **inflater, inflator** *n*

**inflated** /in'flaytid/ *adj* **1** distended with air or gas **2** bombastic, exaggerated ⟨*an ~ style of writing*⟩ **3** expanded to an abnormal or unjustifiable volume or level ⟨*~ prices*⟩ **4** *chiefly botany* hollow and swelled out or enlarged

**inflation** /in'flaysh(ə)n/ *n* **1** inflating or being inflated: eg **1a** distension **b** empty pretentiousness; pomposity **2** a substantial and continuing rise in the general level of prices

**inflationary** /in'flayshən(ə)ri/ *adj* of, characterized by, or productive of inflation ⟨*~ wage rises*⟩

**inflationary spiral** *n* a continuous rise in prices that is sustained by the tendency of wage increases and cost increases to react on each other

**inflationism** /in'flayshə,niz(ə)m/ *n* the policy of economic inflation, esp through expansion of currency or bank deposits – **inflationist** *n or adj*

**inflect** /in'flekt/ *vt* **1** to turn from a direct line or course; curve **2** to vary (a word) by inflection; decline, conjugate **3** to change or vary the pitch of (a voice or note); modulate ~ *vi* to become modified by inflection [ME *inflecten*, fr L *inflectere*, fr *in-* ²*in-* + *flectere* to bend] – **inflective** *adj*

**inflection, Br also inflexion** /in'fleksh(ə)n/ *n* **1** the act or result of curving or bending; a bend **2** change in pitch or loudness of the voice **3a** the change of form that words undergo to mark grammatical distinctions (eg those of case, gender, number, tense, person, mood, or voice) usu within the same part of speech **b** a form, suffix, or element involved in such variation **c** the relation of a word to its root by inflection ⟨*harder is related to* hard *by ~*⟩ – compare DERIVATION **d** the part of grammar dealing with inflection; accidence **4a** change of curvature with respect to a fixed line from concave to convex or conversely **b** POINT OF INFLECTION (point on a curve where the tangent changes its sign)

**inflectional** /in'flekshənl/ *adj* of or characterized by inflection ⟨*an ~ suffix*⟩ – **inflectionally** *adv*

**inflexed** /in'flekst/ *adj, biology* bent or turned abruptly inwards, downwards, or towards the axis ⟨*~ petals*⟩ [L *inflexus*, pp of *inflectere*]

**inflexible** /in'fleksəbl/ *adj* rigidly firm: eg **a** lacking or deficient in suppleness; unbendable **b** unbending; resolutely firm ⟨*~ courage*⟩ **c** incapable of change, unalterable *synonyms* see ¹STIFF [ME, fr L *inflexibilis*, fr *in-* ¹*in-* + *flexibilis* flexible] – **inflexibleness** *n*, **inflexibly** *adv*, **inflexibility** *n*

**inflict** /in'flikt/ *vt* to force or impose (something damaging or painful) on someone ⟨*~ punishment*⟩ [L *inflictus*, pp of *infligere*, fr *in-* ²*in-* + *fligere* to strike – more at PROFLIGATE] – **inflicter, inflictor** *n*, **inflictive** *adj*

*usage* Compare **inflict** and **afflict**. Damage and trouble are inflicted *on* people, and people are afflicted *with* them ⟨*she afflicted* (not △ inflicted) *me with lots of extra work*⟩.

**infliction** /in'fliksh(ə)n/ *n* **1** the act of inflicting **2** something (eg punishment or suffering) that is inflicted

**in-'flight** *adj* made, carried out, or provided for use or enjoyment while in flight ⟨*~ refuelling*⟩ ⟨*~ meals*⟩

**inflorescence** /,inflaw'res(ə)ns, -flə-/ *n* **1a(1)** the (mode of) arrangement of flowers on a stem **a(2)** a flower-bearing stem; a floral axis of a plant together with its flower-bearing branches or stalks **a(3)** a flower cluster; *also* a solitary flower **b** (the area bearing) a cluster of reproductive organs in a moss **2** the budding and unfolding of blossoms; flowering [NL *inflorescentia*, fr LL *inflorescent-, inflorescens*, prp of *inflorescere* to begin to bloom, fr L *in-* ²*in-* + *florescere* to begin to bloom – more at FLORESCENCE] – **inflorescent** *adj*

**inflow** /'infloh/ *n* a flowing in ⟨*a pipe of sufficient diameter to take the maximum rate of ~*⟩ ⟨*~ of foreign currency*⟩

**¹influence** /'infloo-əns/ *n* **1** an ethereal fluid held to flow from the stars and to affect the actions of men **2** the act or power of producing an effect without apparent exertion of force or direct exercise of command ⟨*his ~ changed me a great deal*⟩ **3** the power to achieve something desired by the often secret or unfair use of wealth or position ⟨*he got that job by using ~*⟩ **4** the power or capacity of causing an effect in indirect or intangible ways; sway ⟨*under the ~ of drugs*⟩ **5** one who or that which exerts influence; *esp* one who tends to produce a moral or immoral effect on another ⟨*thought his brother was a bad ~*⟩ [ME, fr MF, fr ML *influentia*, fr L *influent-, influens*, prp of *influere* to flow in, fr *in-* ²*in-* + *fluere* to flow – more at FLUID] – **under the influence** affected by alcohol; drunk ⟨*was arrested for driving under the influence*⟩

**²influence** *vt* **1** to affect or alter by indirect or intangible means; sway **2** to have an effect on the condition or development of; modify **3** to persuade ⟨*Mr Foot . . . ~d Mr Callaghan not to call a general election* – *The Times*⟩ *synonyms* see ¹MOVE – **influenceable** *adj*, **influencer** *n*

**¹influent** /'in,flooh·ənt, -'--/ *adj* flowing in

**²influent** *n* **1** a tributary stream **2** an organism, esp an animal, that has a modifying effect on the balance and stability of an ecological community

**¹influential** /,infloo'ensh(ə)l/ *adj* exerting or possessing influence – **influentially** *adv*

**influenza** /,infloo'enzə/ *n* **1** a highly infectious virus disease characterized by sudden onset, fever, exhaustion, severe aches and pains, and inflammation of the MUCOUS MEMBRANES lining the nose, throat, and other respiratory passages **2** any of numerous feverish usu virus diseases of domestic animals marked by respiratory symptoms [It, lit., influence, fr ML *influentia;* fr the belief that epidemics were due to the influence of the stars]

**influx** /'influks/ *n* a usu sudden increase in flowing in; the arrival of large amounts or numbers ⟨*an ~ of foreign capital*⟩ ⟨*an ~ of tourists*⟩ [LL *influxus*, fr L, pp of *influere*]

**info** /'infoh/ *n, informal* information

**infold** /in'fohld/ *vt* to enfold

**inform** /in'fawm/ *vt* **1** to impart an essential quality or character to ⟨*here alone a sense of style ~s all life's activities* – Jan Morris⟩ **2** to communicate knowledge to ⟨*~ a prisoner of his rights*⟩ **3** *obs* to make known ~ *vi* **1** to give information or knowledge **2** to act as an informer – + *against* or *on* [ME *informen*, fr MF *enformer*, fr L *informare*, to give shape to, fr *in-* ²*in-* + *forma* form]

*usage* One can **inform** somebody *of* a fact, or **inform** somebody *that* a fact is true, but one cannot correctly **inform** somebody *to* do something ⟨△ *please* inform *the customer to wait*⟩.

**informal** /in'fawml/ *adj* **1** marked by an absence of formality or ceremony ⟨*an ~ meeting*⟩ ⟨*an ~ group*⟩ **2** characteristic of or appropriate to casual or everyday use ⟨*~ English*⟩ ⟨*~ clothes*⟩ – **informally** *adv*, **informality** *n*

**informant** /in'fawmənt/ *n* one who gives information: eg **a** an informer **b** one who supplies an investigator (eg a foreign scholar) with cultural or linguistic data

**information** /,infə'maysh(ə)n/ *n* **1** the communication or reception of facts or ideas **2a** knowledge obtained from investigation, study, or instruction **b** news **c** facts, data **d** a signal or character (eg in a radio transmission or computer) representing data **e** something (eg a message, experimental data, or a picture) which justifies change in a construct (eg a plan or theory) that represents physical or mental experience or another construct **f** a measure of the content of information; *specif* a measure of the probability that any particular message may occur that represents the degree of choice available in interpreting a particular message **3** a formal accusation or complaint presented to a magistrate *synonyms* see KNOWLEDGE – **informational** *adj*

**information retrieval** *n* the location and recovery of desired information, esp from a computer

**information science** *n* the collection, classification, storage, retrieval, and distribution of recorded knowledge, treated both as a pure and as an applied science

**information theory** *n* a theory that deals statistically with information, the measurement of its content in terms of its distinguishing characteristics, and with the efficiency of processes of communication of information between humans and machines (eg in telecommunication or in computing machines)

**informative** /in'fawmətiv/, **informatory** /in'fawmət(ə)ri/ *adj* conveying facts or ideas; instructive – **informatively** *adv*, **informativeness** *n*

**informed** /in'fawmd/ *adj* **1a** possessing information ⟨*~ sources*⟩ ⟨*~ observers*⟩ **b** based on possession of information ⟨*an ~ estimate of next year's tax receipts*⟩ **2** knowledgeable about matters of contemporary interest; educated ⟨*what the ~ person should know about Marxism*⟩

**informer** /in'fawmə/ *n* **1** one who supplies information **2** a person who informs against another; *specif* one who makes a practice, esp for a financial reward, of informing against others to the police

**infra** /'infrə/ *adv* BELOW 5 ⟨*for additional examples see ~*⟩ [L]

**infra-** /infrə-/ *prefix* **1** below ⟨infra*renal*⟩ ⟨infra*structure*⟩; less than ⟨infra*human*⟩ **2** within ⟨infra*specific*⟩ ⟨infra*territorial*⟩ **3** below in a scale or series ⟨infra*red*⟩ [L *infra* – more at UNDER]

**infract** /in'frakt/ *vt* to violate, infringe [L *infractus*, pp of *infringere* to break off – more at INFRINGE] – **infractor** *n*

**infraction** /in'fraksh(ə)n/ *n* a violation, infringement ⟨*an ~ of the law*⟩

**infra dig** /,infrə 'dig/ *adj, informal* beneath one's dignity; undignified ⟨*children are encouraged ... to think of their former homes as somehow ~ – Observer Magazine*⟩ [short for L *infra dignitatem*]

**infrahuman** /,infrə'hyoohmən/ *adj* less or lower than human; *esp* ANTHROPOID – **infrahuman** *n*

**infrangible** /in'franjəbl/ *adj* **1** not capable of being broken or separated into parts **2** not to be infringed or violated [MF, fr LL *infrangibilis*, fr L *in-* ¹*in-* + *frangere* to break – more at BREAK] – **infrangibleness** *n*, **infrangibly** *adv*, **infrangibility** *n*

¹**infrared** /,infrə'red/, **infrared radiation** *n* ELECTROMAGNETIC RADIATION lying outside the visible spectrum, that has a wavelength between red light and microwaves, and is commonly perceived as heat

²**infrared** *adj* **1** being, relating to, producing, or using infrared radiation ⟨*~ therapy*⟩ ⟨*an ~ grill*⟩ **2** sensitive to infrared radiation ⟨*~ photographic film*⟩

**infrasonic** /,infrə'sonik/ *adj* **1** having or relating to a frequency below the lower threshold of human hearing **2** of, being, using, or produced by infrasonic waves or vibrations

**infraspecific** /,infrəspə'sifik/ *adj* included within or being a subdivision of a species ⟨*~ categories*⟩

**infrastructure** /'infrə,strukchə/ *n* **1** the underlying foundation or basic framework (e g of a system or organization) **2** the permanent installations (e g airfields) required for military purposes

**infrequent** /in'freekwənt/ *adj* **1** not often happening or occurring; rare ⟨*~ contributions*⟩ **2** not habitual or persistent ⟨*an ~ contributor*⟩ [L *infrequent-, infrequens*, fr *in-* ¹*in-* + *frequent-, frequens* frequent] – **infrequence, infrequency** *n*, **infrequently** *adv*

**infringe** /in'frinj/ *vt* to encroach upon in a way that violates law or the rights of another ⟨*~ a patent*⟩ ~ *vi* to encroach, trespass – usu + *on* **synonyms** see IMPINGE △ impugn [L *infringere*, lit., to break off, fr *in-* ²*in-* + *frangere* to break – more at BREAK] – **infringer** *n*

**infringement** /in'frinjmənt/ *n* (an) encroachment or trespass on a right or privilege; (a) violation

**infundibular** /,infun'dibyoolə/,**infundibulate** /-lət/ *adj* **1** funnel-shaped **2** of or having an infundibulum

**infundibulum** /,infun'dibyooləm/ *n, pl* **infundibula** /-lə/ any of various conical or dilated organs or parts; *esp* the funnel-shaped mass of GREY MATTER that connects the PITUITARY GLAND to the brain [NL, fr L, funnel – more at FUNNEL]

¹**infuriate** /in'fyooəriayt/ *vt* to make furious; enrage ⟨*the delay ~d him*⟩ [ML *infuriatus*, pp of *infuriare*, fr L *in-* ²*in-* + *furia* fury] – **infuriatingly** *adv*, **infuriation** *n*

²**infuriate** /in'fyoohzəbl/ *adj* furiously angry

**infuse** /in'fyoohz/ *vt* **1a** to cause to be permeated with something (e g a principle or quality) ⟨*~d the whole team with enthusiasm*⟩ **b** to introduce, inject **2** to inspire, animate ⟨*a sense of purpose that ~d scientific research*⟩ **3** to steep in liquid (e g water) without boiling so as to extract the soluble properties or constituents ~ *vi* to be in process of infusing ⟨*let the tea ~ for a few minutes*⟩ [ME *infusen*, fr MF & L; MF *infuser*, fr L *infusus*, pp of *infundere* to pour in, fr *in-* ²*in-* + *fundere* to pour – more at FOUND] – **infuser** *n*

**infusible** /in'fyoohzəbl/ *adj* very difficult or impossible to fuse or melt – **infusibleness** *n*, **infusibility** *n*

**infusion** /in'fyoohzh(ə)n/ *n* **1** infusing **2** the continuous slow introduction of a solution, esp into a vein **3** an extract obtained by infusing

**infusorian** /,infyooh'zawri-ən/ *n* any of a group of minute organisms found esp in decomposing organic matter; *esp* a single-celled organism (PROTOZOAN) that bears CILIA (small hair-like structures used for movement) – not now used technically [NL *Infusoria*, group name, fr L *infusus*, pp; fr their being found in infusions of organic matter] – **infusorian** *adj*, **infusorial** *adj*

¹**-ing** /-ing/ *suffix* (→ *vb or adj*) – used to form the present participle ⟨*sailing*⟩ and sometimes to form an adjective resembling a present participle but not derived from a verb ⟨*swashbuckling*⟩ [ME, alter. of *-ende*, fr OE, fr *-e-*, verb stem vowel + *-nde*, prp suffix – more at -ANT] – **-ingly** (→ *adv*)

²**-ing** *suffix* (→ *n*) **1** action or process of ⟨*running*⟩ ⟨*sleeping*⟩; *also* instance of (a specified action or process) ⟨*a meeting*⟩ – sometimes used to form a noun resembling a gerund but not derived from a verb ⟨*skydiving*⟩ **2 -ings** (→ *n pl*), **-ing** product or result of (a specified action or process) ⟨*an engraving*⟩ ⟨*earnings*⟩ **3** activity or occupation connected with ⟨*boating*⟩ ⟨*banking*⟩ **4a** collection or aggregate of ⟨*shipping*⟩ ⟨*housing*⟩ **b** something connected with, consisting of, or used in making ⟨*scaffolding*⟩ ⟨*skirting*⟩ **5** something related to (a specified concept) ⟨*offing*⟩ [ME, fr OE, suffix forming nouns from verbs; akin to OHG *-ung*, suffix forming nouns from verbs]

³**-ing** *suffix* (→ *n*) one of a (specified) kind ⟨*sweeting*⟩ ⟨*lording*⟩ ⟨*greening*⟩ [ME, fr OE; akin to OHG *-ing* belonging to, of the kind of]

**ingather** /in'gathə/ *vt* to gather in; *esp* to harvest – **ingathering** *n*

**ingeminate** /in'jeminayt/ *vt* to redouble, reiterate [L *ingeminatus*, pp of *ingeminare*, fr *in-* ²*in-* + *geminare* to double, fr *geminus* twin]

**ingenious** /in'jeeni-əs/ *adj* **1** marked by special aptitude for discovering, inventing, or contriving **2** marked by originality, resourcefulness, and cleverness in conception or execution ⟨*an ~ gadget*⟩ **3** *obs* showing or requiring intelligence, aptitude, or discernment **synonyms** see CLEVER △ ingenuous [MF *ingenieux*, fr L *ingeniosus*, fr *ingenium* natural capacity – more at ENGINE] – **ingeniously** *adv*, **ingeniousness** *n*

**ingenue, ingénue** /,anzhay'nooh (*Fr* ɛ̃ʒeny)/ *n* **1** a naive or artless young woman **2** the stage role of an ingenue; *also* an actress playing such a role [Fr *ingénue*, fem of *ingénu* ingenuous, fr L *ingenuus*]

**ingenuity** /,inji'nyooh-əti/ *n* **1a** cleverness in contriving; inventiveness **b** cleverness of invention or construction **2** *obs* candour, ingenuousness

**ingenuous** /in'jenyoo-əs/ *adj* **1** showing innocent or childlike simplicity; natural ⟨*an ~ smile*⟩ **2** lacking subtlety or guile; frank, candid **synonyms** see ¹NATURAL *antonyms* disingenuous, cunning △ ingenious [L *ingenuus* native, free born, fr *in-* ²*in-* + *gignere* to beget – more at KIN] – **ingenuously** *adv*, **ingenuousness** *n*

**ingest** /in'jest/ *vt* to take in (as if) for digestion; absorb [L *ingestus*, pp of *ingerere* to carry in, fr *in-* ²*in-*+ *gerere* to bear] – **ingestible** *adj*, **ingestion** *n*, **ingestive** *adj*

**ingesta** /in'jestə/ *n pl* material taken into the body by way of the digestive tract [NL, fr L, neut pl of *ingestus*]

**ingle** /'ing-gl/ *n* **1** a flame, blaze **2** a fireplace **3** a corner, angle [ScGael *aingeal*]

**inglenook** /'ing-gl,nook/ *n* an alcove by a large open fireplace; *also* a bench or settle occupying this alcove

**inglorious** /in'glawri-əs/ *adj* **1** not glorious; lacking fame or honours **2** shameful, ignominious [L *inglorius*, fr *in-* ¹*in-* + *gloria* glory] – **ingloriously** *adv*, **ingloriousness** *n*

'**in-,goal** *n* the area on a rugby field between the goal line and the dead-ball line

**ingoing** /'ingoh-ing/ *adj* going in; entering

**ingot** /'ing-gət/ *n* a (bar-shaped) mass of cast metal, esp gold or silver, which can be stored or transported and later processed [ME, mould for casting metal, prob fr OE *in* + *goten*, pp of *gēotan* to pour, cast in metal – more at ⁴FOUND]

**ingot iron** *n* iron containing only small proportions of impurities (e g less than 0.05 per cent carbon)

¹**ingrain** /in'grayn/ *vt* to force or impress (e g an idea, principle, substance, or pattern) indelibly into a mental or moral constitution or into a fibre or fabric

²**ingrain** /'in·grayn/ *n or adj* **1** (an article) made of fibres that are dyed to various colours before being spun into yarn **2** (an article, esp a carpet) made of yarn that is dyed before being woven or knitted

**ingrained** /'ingraynd/ *adj* **1** *esp of dirt* worked into the grain or fibre **2 ingrained, ingrain** firmly and deeply implanted; deep-rooted ⟨*~ prejudice*⟩ – **ingrainedly** *adv*

**ingrate** /'ingrayt, -'-/ *n, formal* an ungrateful person [L *ingratus* ungrateful, fr *in-* ¹*in-* + *gratus* grateful – more at GRACE]

**ingratiate** /in'grayshi,ayt/ *vt* to gain favour for (oneself) by deliberate effort – usu + *with* ⟨~ *themselves with the public*⟩ [²*in*- + L *gratia* grace] – **ingratiatory** *adj*, **ingratiation** *n*

**ingratiating** /in'grayshi,ayting/ *adj* showing a desire to gain favour ⟨*an* ~ *smile*⟩ – **ingratiatingly** *adv*

**ingratitude** /in'gratityoohd/ *n* forgetfulness or scant recognition of kindness received; ungratefulness [ME, fr MF, fr ML *ingratitudo*, fr L *in*- ¹*in*- + LL *gratitudo* gratitude]

**ingravescent** /,ingrə'ves(ə)nt/ *adj, esp of disease* growing worse [L *ingravescent-, ingravescens*, prp of *ingravescere* to become heavier or worse, fr L ²*in*- + *gravis* heavy, severe – more at GRIEVE] – **ingravescence** *n*

**ingredient** /in'greedi-ənt/ *n* something that forms a component part of a compound, combination, or mixture; a constituent [ME, fr L *ingredient-, ingrediens*, prp of *ingredi* to go into, fr *in*- ²*in*- + *gradi* to go – more at GRADE] – **ingredient** *adj*

**ingress** /'in-gres/ *n* 1 the act of entering; an entrance; *specif* the entrance of a celestial body (eg the sun, the moon, or a planet) into a position in front of another (eg eclipse, OCCULTATION, or TRANSIT) 2 the right of entrance or access [ME, fr L *ingressus*, fr *ingressus*, pp of *ingredi*] – **ingression** *n*

**ingressive** /ing'gresiv/ *adj* 1 of or involving ingress ⟨*an* ~ *current of air*⟩ 2 *of a verb* INCHOATIVE 2 – **ingressive** *n*, **ingressiveness** *n*

**ingrowing** /'in,groh-ing/ *adj* growing or tending inwards; *specif* having the free tip or edge embedded in the flesh ⟨*an* ~ *toenail*⟩

**ingrown** /'in-grohn/ *adj* 1 inward-looking in activities or interests; withdrawn 2 *chiefly NAm* ingrowing – **ingrownness** *n*

**ingrowth** /'in,grohth/ *n* 1 a growing inwards (eg to fill a space) 2 something that grows in or into a space

**inguinal** /'ing-gwinl/ *adj* of or situated in the region of the groin [L *inguinalis*, fr *inguin-, inguen* groin – more at ADEN-]

**ingurgitate** /in'guhjitayt/ *vt* to swallow greedily or in large quantities; guzzle [L *ingurgitatus*, pp of *ingurgitare*, fr *in*- ²*in*- + *gurgit-, gurges* whirlpool – more at VORACIOUS] – **ingurgitation** *n*

**INH** *trademark* – used for the drug ISONIAZID that is used in the treatment of tuberculosis [*isonicotinic acid hydrazide*]

**inhabit** /in'habit/ *vt* 1 to occupy permanently; live in ⟨*people who* ~ *the lands to the West*⟩ 2 to be present in ⟨*the hopes and fears that* ~ *the human mind*⟩ ~ *vi, archaic* to reside in a place; dwell *synonyms* see HABITABLE [ME *enhabiten*, fr MF & L; MF *enhabiter*, fr L *inhabitare*, fr *in*- ²*in*- + *habitare* to dwell, fr *habitus*, pp of *habēre* to have – more at GIVE] – **inhabitable** *adj*, **inhabitancy** *n*, **inhabitant** *n*, **inhabitation** *n*, **inhabiter** *n*

¹**inhalant** /in'haylənt/ *n* something (eg a medical preparation) that is inhaled

²**inhalant** *also* **inhalent** *adj* INCURRENT (carrying an inwardly flowing current of liquid)

**inhalation** /,inhə'laysh(ə)n/ *n* 1 the act or an instance of inhaling 2 material (eg medical preparations) to be taken in by inhaling – **inhalational** *adj*

**inhalator** /'inhə,laytə/ *n* a respirator

**inhale** /in'hayl/ *vb* to breathe in [²*in*- + -*hale* (as in *exhale*)] – **inhale** *n*

**inhaler** /in'haylə/ *n* 1 one who inhales 2 a device used for inhaling a medical preparation, esp as a treatment for asthma

**inharmonious** /,inhah'mohnyəs, -ni-əs/ *adj* 1 not harmonious; discordant 2 not congenial or compatible; conflicting ⟨~ *interests*⟩ – **inharmoniously** *adv*, **inharmoniousness** *n*

**inhere** /in'hiə/ *vi* to be inherent; belong, reside ⟨*power to make laws* ~ *in the state*⟩ [L *inhaerēre*, fr *in*- ²*in*- + *haerēre* to adhere – more at HESITATE]

**inherent** /in'herənt, -'hiə-/ *adj* intrinsic to the constitution or essence of something; innate, inseparable [L *inhaerent-, inhaerens*, prp of *inhaerēre*] – **inherence** *n*, **inherently** *adv*

  *usage* The pronunciation /in'hiərənt/ is recommended for BBC broadcasters. *synonyms* see CONGENITAL

**inherit** /in'herit/ *vt* 1 to come into possession of; receive **1a** (a title or piece of property) as a legal right from an ancestor at his/her death **b** (a characteristic) from ancestors by genetic transmission ⟨~ *a strong constitution*⟩ 2 to receive or come to possess as if from an ancestor ⟨~ed *the problem from his predecessor*⟩ ~ *vi* to take or receive property or rights by inheritance [ME *enheriten* to make heir, inherit, fr MF *enheriter* to make heir, fr LL *inhereditare*, fr L *in*- ²*in*- + *hereditas* inheritance – more at HEREDITY] – **inheritor** *n*, **inheritress, inheritrix** *n*

**inheritable** /in'heritəbl/ *adj* 1 capable of being inherited;

transmissible 2 capable of inheriting – **inheritableness** *n*, **inheritability** *n*

**inheritance** /in'herit(ə)ns/ *n* **1a** (the act of) inheriting property **b** the transmission of genetic qualities from parent to offspring **c** the acquisition of a possession, condition, or trait from past generations 2 something that is or may be inherited 3 something material or immaterial that is acquired or derived from the past

**inheritance tax** *n, NAm* DEATH DUTY

**inhesion** /in'heezh(ə)n/ *n* the quality, state, or fact of inhering; inherence [L *inhaesus*, pp of *inhaerēre* to inhere]

**inhibit** /in'hibit/ *vt* 1 to prohibit *from* doing something ⟨*creditors . . . might be* ~ed *from lending the company money* – *The Times*⟩ **2a** to hold in check; restrain **b** to discourage from free or spontaneous activity, esp through the operation of psychological or social controls ~ *vi* to cause inhibition *synonyms* see RESTRAIN *antonym* allow [ME *inhibiten*, fr L *inhibitus*, pp of *inhibēre*, fr *in*- ²*in*- + *habēre* to have – more at GIVE] – **inhibitive** *adj*, **inhibitory** *adj*

**inhibition** /,inhi'bish(ə)n/ *n* **1a** inhibiting or being inhibited **b** something that forbids, debars, or restricts 2 an inner restraint on free activity, expression, or functioning: eg **2a** an unconscious psychological restraint on a psychological or physical activity ⟨*sexual* ~s⟩ **b** a restraining of a function (eg of a bodily organ or an ENZYME) 3 an order by an Anglican bishop suspending a minister from parochial duty

**inhibitor, inhibiter** /in'hibitə/ *n* one who or that which inhibits; *esp* an agent that slows or interferes with a chemical action (eg rusting)

**inhomogeneous** /,inhomə'jeenyəs, -ni-əs, -hohmə-/ *adj* not homogeneous – **inhomogeneity** *n*

**inhospitable** /,inho'spitəbl/ *adj* 1 not showing hospitality; not friendly or welcoming ⟨*an* ~ *person*⟩ 2 providing no shelter or means of support; barren ⟨~ *mountain areas*⟩ – **inhospitableness** *n*, **inhospitably** *adv*

**inhospitality** /,inhospi'taləti/ *n* being inhospitable

**in-'house** *adj* of or carried on within a group or organization ⟨*is she an* ~ *lexicographer?*⟩ – **in-house** *adv*

**inhuman** /in'hyoohmən/ *adj* **1a** lacking in kindness or compassion; brutal ⟨*an* ~ *tyrant*⟩ **b** cold, impersonal ⟨*the* ~ *manner of an interviewer*⟩ **c** failing to conform to basic human needs ⟨~ *living conditions*⟩ 2 being other than human ⟨*an* ~ *form lurked in the shadows*⟩ [MF & L; MF *inhumain*, fr L *inhumanus*, fr *in*- ¹*in*- + *humanus* human] – **inhumanly** *adv*, **inhumanness** *n*

**inhumane** /,inhyooh'mayn/ *adj* not humane; lacking in kindness or compassion [MF *inhumain* & L *inhumanus*] – **inhumanely** *adv*

**inhumanity** /,inhyooh'manəti/ *n* **1a** the quality or state of being pitiless or cruel ⟨*man's* ~ *to man* – Robert Burns⟩ **b** a cruel or barbarous act 2 absence of warmth or feeling; impersonality

**inhume** /in'hyoohm/ *vt, formal* to bury, inter [L *inhumare*, fr *in*- ²*in*- + *humus* earth – more at HUMBLE] – **inhumation** *n*

**inimical** /i'nimik(ə)l/ *adj* **1a** having the attitude of an enemy; hostile **b** indicating hostility; unfriendly ⟨*a voice apparently cold and* ~ – Arnold Bennett⟩ 2 adverse in tendency, influence, or effects; harmful ⟨*a policy* ~ *to the interests of the company*⟩ [LL *inimicalis*, fr L *inimicus* enemy – more at ENEMY] – **inimically** *adv*

**inimitable** /i'nimitəbl/ *adj* defying imitation; matchless [MF or L; MF, fr L *inimitabilis*, fr *in*- ¹*in*- + *imitabilis* imitable] – **inimitableness** *n*, **inimitably** *adv*

**iniquity** /i'nikwəti/ *n* 1 gross injustice; wickedness 2 an iniquitous act or thing; a sin [ME *iniquite*, fr MF *iniquité*, fr L *iniquitat-, iniquitas*, fr *iniquus* uneven, fr *in*- ¹*in*- + *aequus* equal] – **iniquitous** *adj*

¹**initial** /i'nish(ə)l/ *adj* 1 of the beginning; incipient ⟨*the* ~ *symptoms of a disease*⟩ 2 placed at the beginning; first ⟨*the* ~ *number of a code*⟩ [MF & L; MF, fr L *initialis*, fr *initium* beginning, fr *initus*, pp of *inire* to go into, fr *in*- ²*in*- + *ire* to go – more at ISSUE] – **initially** *adv*, **initialness** *n*

²**initial** *n* **1a** the first letter of a name **b** *pl* the first letter of each word in a full name ⟨*found that their* ~s *were identical*⟩ 2 a large, often decorated, letter beginning (a chapter or paragraph of) a text 3 a cell, or group of cells, giving rise to new tissues or structures; a precursor; *specif* a MERISTEMATIC plant cell

³**initial** *vt* -ll- (*NAm* -l-, -ll-) to put initials on, esp to indicate authorization ⟨~ *a memorandum*⟩

**initial·ize, -ise** /i'nishəliez/ *vt, computers* to give an initial value to (a variable or storage location) in a computer program

**initial teaching alphabet** *n* a 44-character phonetic alphabet designed esp for use in the first stages of teaching children to read English

¹**initiate** /i'nishiayt/ *vt* **1** to cause or enable the beginning of; set going ⟨~ *a road-building programme*⟩ ⟨*enzymes that ~ fermentation*⟩ **2** to instil with rudiments or principles, esp of something complex or obscure ⟨~ *pupils into the mysteries of algebra*⟩ **3** to induct into membership (as if) by formal rites [LL *initiatus*, pp of *initiare*, fr L, to induct, fr *initium*] – **initiator** *n*, **initiatory** *adj*

²**initiate** /i'nishi·ət/ *adj* **1** initiated or formally admitted (eg to membership or an office) **2** instructed in secret knowledge

³**initiate** /i'nishiət/ *n* **1** somebody who is undergoing or has undergone initiation **2** somebody who is instructed or proficient in a complex or specialized field

**initiation** /i,nishi'aysh(ə)n/ *n* **1** the act or an instance of initiating or being initiated **2** the ceremony or formal procedure with which somebody is made a member of a society or club **3** the condition of being initiated

¹**initiative** /i'nish(y)ətiv/ *adj* of initiation; introductory, preliminary

²**initiative** *n* **1** a first step, esp in the attainment of an end or goal ⟨*took the ~ in dealing with the issue*⟩ ⟨*news of a fresh peace ~*⟩ **2** energy or resourcefulness displayed in initiation of action; enterprise ⟨*a man of great ~*⟩ **3a** the right to initiate legislative action **b** a procedure, esp in N America and Switzerland, enabling a specified number of voters to propose a law by petition and secure its submission to the electorate or to the legislature for approval – compare REFERENDUM – **on one's own initiative** without being prompted; independently of outside influence or control

**inject** /in'jekt/ *vt* **1a** to throw, drive, or force into something ⟨~ *fuel into an engine*⟩ **b** to force a fluid into (eg for medical purposes) **2** to introduce as an element or factor ⟨~ed *some humour into his speech*⟩ [L *injectus*, pp of *inicere*, fr *in-* ²in- + *jacere* to throw – more at JET] – **injectable** *adj*, **injector** *n*

**injectant** /in'jekt(ə)nt/ *n* a substance that is injected into something

**injection** /in'jeksh(ə)n/ *n* **1a** an act or instance of injecting **b** the placing of an artificial satellite or a spacecraft into an orbit or on a TRAJECTORY (curved path); *also* the time or place at which injection occurs **2** something (eg a medical preparation) that is injected **3** a mathematical mapping that relates each element of a set to just one element of another set such that no two elements of the first set correspond to the same element of the second – compare BIJECTION, SURJECTION

**injection moulding** *n* the manufacture of rubber or plastic articles by injecting heated material into a mould – **injection-moulded** *adj*

**injective** /in'jektiv/ *adj* being a mathematical injection – called also ONE-TO-ONE

**injudicious** /,injooh'dishəs/ *adj* not judicious; indiscreet, unwise – **injudiciously** *adv*, **injudiciousness** *n*

**Injun** /'injən/ *n, informal* a N American Indian [alter. of *Indian*]

**injunction** /in'jungksh(ə)n/ *n* **1** the act or an instance of enjoining; an order, admonition **2** an order granted by a court requiring somebody to do or refrain from doing a particular act [MF & LL; MF *injonction*, fr LL *injunction-*, *injunctio*, fr L *injunctus*, pp of *injungere* to enjoin – more at ENJOIN] – **injunctive** *adj*

**injure** /'injə/ *vt* **1a** to do injustice to; wrong **b** to offend ⟨~ *a man's pride*⟩ **2a** to inflict bodily hurt on **b** to impair the soundness of ⟨~ *your health*⟩ **c** to inflict damage or loss on ⟨~ *your authority*⟩ ⟨*this tax will ~ all business*⟩ [back-formation fr *injury*] – **injurer** *n*

synonyms **Injure, hurt, harm, wound, damage, impair, spoil, mar: injure** is the most general term and has the widest application, to physical and mental damage, and to loss of value or reputation. **Hurt, harm,** and **wound** may all describe the causing of physical or mental distress to a living being; **harm** stresses the infliction of pain or loss; **hurt** the pain itself or what is hurt; and **wound** implies actual damage to the body or, figuratively, the feelings. In addition, **injure, hurt,** and **harm** may be applied to things, and then suggest actions which diminish their value ⟨**hurt** *sales*⟩ ⟨**harm** *your public image*⟩. **Damage** suggests an injury leading to loss of soundness, worth, or effectiveness ⟨**damaged** *his car in a crash*⟩ ⟨**damaged** *by his experiences in the war*⟩. **Impair** suggests rather a deterioration than a loss ⟨*the continual noise* **impaired** *his hearing for a while*⟩.

**Mar** either physically disfigures or figuratively impairs what would otherwise be sound or perfect. **Spoil** goes further than **mar** in suggesting irremediable damage leading to ruin or destruction. Compare MISUSE

**injurious** /in'jooəri·əs/ *adj* **1** inflicting or tending to inflict injury; detrimental ⟨~ *to health*⟩ **2** abusive, insulting ⟨*speak not ~ words* – George Washington⟩ – **injuriously** *adv*, **injuriousness** *n*

**injury** /'injəri/ *n* **1a** an act that damages or hurts; a wrong **b** a violation of another's rights, for which the law allows an action to recover damages **2** hurt, damage, or loss sustained; *specif* a bodily hurt [ME *injurie*, fr L *injuria*, fr *injurus* injurious, fr *in-* ¹in- + *jur-, jus* right – more at JUST]

'**injury-,time** *n* time added on to the end of a match in certain sports (eg rugby and soccer) to compensate for time lost owing to injuries to players

**injustice** /in'justis/ *n* **1** absence of justice, esp as manifest in the violation of another's rights; unfairness **2** an unjust act or state of affairs ⟨*the report did him an ~*⟩ ⟨*the ~s of apartheid*⟩ [ME, fr MF, fr L *injustitia*, fr *injustus* unjust, fr *in-* ¹in- + *justus* just]

¹**ink** /ingk/ *n* **1** a coloured usu liquid material used for writing and printing **2** the black secretion of an octopus, squid, or related animal that serves to hide it from a predator or prey [ME *enke*, fr OF, fr LL *encaustum*, fr neut of L *encaustus* burned in, fr Gk *enkaustos*, verbal of *enkaiein* to burn in – more at ENCAUSTIC] – **inky** *adj*, **inkiness** *n*

²**ink** *vt* to apply ink to ⟨~ *a printing plate*⟩; *also* to write on, draw, or sign in ink ⟨~ *in a pencil drawing*⟩

**inkblot test** /'ingkblot/ *n* RORSCHACH TEST (psychological test based on interpretation of ink blots)

**ink cap** *also* **inky cap** *n* any of several edible mushrooms (genus *Coprinus*) whose PILEUS (cap) melts into an inky fluid after the spores have matured; *esp* one (*Coprinus atramentarius*) with a brownish-grey cap scaly in the centre

**inked** /ingkt/ *adj, Austr & NZ informal* drunk, incapacitated [¹*ink* (in the sense "cheap wine")]

**inkfish** /'ingk,fish *n* a squid

¹**inkhorn** /'ingk,hawn/ *n* a small portable bottle (eg made of horn) for holding ink

²**inkhorn** *adj* ostentatiously learned; pedantic ⟨~ *terms*⟩

**inkle** /'ingkl/ *n* a coloured linen tape or braid woven on a very narrow loom and used for trimming; *also* the thread used [origin unknown]

**inkling** /'ingkling/ *n* **1** a faint indication or suggestion; a hint ⟨*there was no path – no ~ even of a track* – New Yorker⟩ **2** a slight knowledge or vague idea ⟨*hasn't got an ~ of how to darn socks*⟩ [ME *yngkiling*, prob fr *inclen* to hint at; akin to OE *inca* suspicion, Lith *ingis* sluggard]

**inkslinger** /'ingk,sling·ə/ *n* one who writes professionally or copiously without maintaining a high standard; a hack

**inkstand** /'ingk,stand/ *n* a stand or tray kept on a desk, with fittings for holding ink and often p:ns

**inkwell** /'ingk,wel/ *n* an often porcelain container for ink (eg one slotted into a special hole in a school desk)

**inlaid** /in'layd/ *adj* **1** set into a surface in a decorative design in such a way that the surface remains level ⟨*marble tables with ~ ebony*⟩ **2** decorated with a design or material set into a surface ⟨*a table with an ~ top*⟩

¹**inland** /'inlənd/ *adj* **1** of the interior of a country **2** *chiefly Br* not foreign; domestic ⟨~ *revenue*⟩

²**inland** /in'land, 'in-/ *adv or n* (into or towards) the interior of a country

**inland bill** *n* a BILL OF EXCHANGE (order to pay money) that is both drawn and payable within the same country – compare FOREIGN BILL

**inlander** /'inləndə/ *n* one who lives inland

**Inland Revenue** *n* the government department responsible for collecting taxes in Britain

'**in-,law** *n usu pl, informal* a relative by marriage ⟨*all her ~s turned up for the christening*⟩ [back-formation fr *mother-in-law*, etc]

¹**inlay** /in'lay/ *vt* **inlaid** /in'layd/ **1a** to set into a surface or ground material for decoration or reinforcement **b** to decorate with inlaid material **2** to rub, beat, or fuse (eg wire) into a prepared space in metal, wood, or stone – **inlayer** *n*

²**inlay** /'inlay/ *n* **1** inlaid work or a decorative inlaid pattern **2** a dental filling usu of gold or porcelain that is shaped to fit a cavity and then cemented into place

**inlet** /'inlet, -lit/ *n* **1a** a bay or recess in the shore of a sea, lake, or river; *also* CREEK 1 **b** a narrow water passage between peninsulas or through a barrier island leading to a bay or lagoon 2 a means of entry; *esp* an opening for intake ⟨*a fuel* ~⟩ [fr its letting water in]

**inlier** /'in,lie-ə/ *n* an outcrop of rock surrounded by rock of younger age [³*in* + -*lier* (as in *outlier*)]

**in-line engine** *n* an INTERNAL-COMBUSTION ENGINE in which the cylinders are arranged in one or more straight lines

¹**in loco parentis** /in ‚lohkoh pə'rentis/ *adv* in the place of and esp having the responsibilities of a parent ⟨*while you are at school your headmaster is* ~⟩ [L]

²**in loco parentis** *n* regulation or supervision by an administrative body (e g at a university) acting in loco parentis ⟨*still discussing the concept of* ~⟩

**inly** /'inli/ *adv, poetic* 1 inwardly 2 in an intimate manner; thoroughly ⟨~ *know all knowledge* – John Masefield⟩

**inmate** /'inmayt/ *n* somebody who is confined in an institution (e g a prison or hospital); *broadly* any of a group occupying a single dwelling

**in medias res** /in ‚meedias 'rayz/ *adv* in or into the middle of a narrative or plot ⟨*the reader is plunged* ~ *with the discovery of a dead body*⟩ [L, lit., into the midst of things]

**in memoriam** /‚in mi'mawri-əm, -am/ *prep* in memory of – used esp in epitaphs [L]

**inmost** /'inmohst/ *adj* 1 furthest within ⟨*the* ~ *cells of a prison*⟩ 2 most intimate ⟨*knew his* ~ *thoughts*⟩ [ME, fr OE *innemest*, superl of *inne*, adv, in, within, fr *in*, adv]

**inn** /in/ *n* 1a an establishment (e g a small hotel) providing lodging and food, esp for travellers **b** PUBLIC HOUSE 1 2 *often cap* a hall of residence formerly provided for students, esp of law, in London ⟨*Gray's Inn*⟩ – compare INNS OF COURT [ME, fr OE; akin to ON *inni* dwelling, inn, OE *in*, adv]

**innards** /'inədz/ *n pl, informal* 1 the internal organs of a person or animal; *esp* the viscera 2 the internal parts of a structure or mechanism ⟨*the* ~ *of a typewriter*⟩ [alter. of *inwards*]

**innate** /i'nayt/ *adj* 1a existing in or belonging to an individual from birth; native, natural **b** belonging to the essential nature of something; inherent ⟨*the* ~ *defects of a plan*⟩ **c** originating in the intellect or the structure of the mind rather than in perception of the external world ⟨~ *ideas*⟩ 2a *of a plant or animal part* attached to the tip of the support – compare ADNATE **b** ENDOGENOUS (developing within a body) **c** immersed in or embedded in **synonyms** see CONGENITAL [ME *innat*, fr L *innatus*, pp of *innasci* to be born in, fr *in-* ²in- + *nasci* to be born – more at NATION] – **innately** *adv*, **innateness** *n*

¹**inner** /'inə/ *adj* 1a situated within; internal, interior ⟨*an* ~ *chamber*⟩ **b** situated near to a centre, esp of influence ⟨*an* ~ *circle of government ministers*⟩ 2 of the mind or soul ⟨*the* ~ *life of man*⟩ [ME, fr OE *innera*, compar of *inne* within – more at INMOST] – **inner** *n*, **innerly** *adv*, **innermost** *adj*

²**inner** *n* (a shot that hits) the ring on a shooting target next to the bull's-eye

**inner city** *n* a usu older and more densely populated central section of a city; *esp* such an area characterized by unemployment, poor housing, and a rootless population, caused esp by the decentralization of industry – **inner-city** *adj*

‚**inner-di'rected** *adj, psychology* guided in thought and action by one's own values rather than by external influences

**inner ear** *n* the essential organ of hearing and balance located in the bone covering the temple (TEMPORAL BONE) and supplied by the AUDITORY NERVE which transmits sound as nerve impulses to the brain

**Inner House** *n the* higher branch of the Court of Session in Scotland

**inner light** *n, often cap I&L* a divine presence held, esp in Quaker doctrine, to enlighten and guide the soul

**inner man** *n* 1 the soul, mind 2 *humorous* the stomach, appetite ⟨*the* ~ *will consume most of your bank balance*⟩

**inner planet** *n* any of the planets Mercury, Venus, Earth, and Mars that as a group have orbits nearer the sun than the other planets

**inner product** *n, maths* SCALAR PRODUCT (product of two vectors)

**innersole** /'inə,sohl/ *n* an insole

**inner space** *n* 1 space at or near the earth's surface, esp under the sea 2 the unconscious human mind

**innerspring** /‚inə'spring/ *adj, NAm* interior-sprung

**inner tube** *n* an inflatable airtight tube placed inside the casing of a pneumatic tyre

**innervate** /'inəvayt/ *vt* to supply with nerves – **innervation** *n*, **innervational** *adj*

**innerve** /i'nuhv/ *vt* to give nervous energy to; animate

**inning** /'ining/ *n* 1 the reclaiming of land, esp from the sea 2a a division of a baseball game consisting of a turn at batting for each team; *also* a baseball team's turn at batting **b** a player's turn (e g in croquet) [(1) fr gerund of E dial. *in* to enclose, reclaim, fr ME *innen*, fr OE *innian* to include, go in, fr ²*in*; (2) ²*in* + -*ing*]

**innings** /'iningz/ *n taking sing vb, pl* **innings** 1a any of the alternating divisions of a cricket match during which one side bats and the other bowls **b** the turn of one player to bat; *also* the manner of playing or the runs scored in such an innings ⟨*a rather slow* ~⟩ ⟨*an* ~ *of 110*⟩ **c** an unplayed innings of a side ⟨*won by an* ~ *and 32 runs*⟩ 2a a period during which a person has opportunity for action or achievements ⟨*on the verge of that momentous* ~ *which was to project him into world politics* – TLS⟩ **b** *chiefly Br informal* the duration of a person's life ⟨*he had a good* ~⟩

**innit** /'init/ *chiefly Br nonstandard* isn't it – used at the end of a statement to elicit agreement or for rhetorical emphasis ⟨*well, that's up to them* ~? – Daily Mirror⟩ [by alter.]

**innkeeper** /'in‚keepə/ *n* the landlord of an inn

**innocence** /'inəs(ə)ns/ *n* 1a freedom from guilt or sin through being unacquainted with evil; blamelessness **b** chastity **c** freedom from legal guilt of a particular crime or offence **d** freedom from guile or sophistication; artlessness, naiveté **e** lack of knowledge; ignorance ⟨*written in entire* ~ *of English grammar*⟩ 2 one who is innocent ⟨*she's* ~ *itself!*⟩

**innocent** /'inəs(ə)nt/ *adj* 1a free from guilt or sin, esp through lack of knowledge of evil; pure ⟨*an* ~ *child*⟩ **b** harmless in effect or intention ⟨*refused to believe they were having a quite* ~ *conversation*⟩ **c** free from legal guilt or fault; *also* lawful ⟨*a wholly* ~ *transaction*⟩ 2 lacking or deprived of something ⟨*a face* ~ *of make-up*⟩ 3a lacking sophistication, affectation, or guile; artless, ingenuous **b** ignorant, unaware [ME, fr MF, fr L *innocent-*, *innocens*, fr *in-* ¹in- + *nocent-*, *nocens* wicked, fr prp of *nocēre* to harm – more at NOXIOUS] – **innocency** *n*, **innocent** *n*, **innocently** *adv*

**innocuous** /i'nokyoo-əs/ *adj* 1 having no harmful effects; harmless 2 unlikely to provoke or offend; inoffensive, insipid [L *innocuus*, fr *in-* ¹in- + *nocēre*] – **innocuously** *adv*, **innocuousness** *n*

**innominate** /i'nominət/ *adj, formal* having no name; unnamed; *also* anonymous [LL *innominatus*, fr L *in-* ¹in- + *nominatus*, pp of *nominare* to nominate]

**innominate artery** *n* a short artery that arises from the arch of the AORTA (main artery from the heart) and divides into the CAROTID and SUBCLAVIAN arteries of the right side

**innominate bone** *n* the large bone that forms half of the PELVIS (bowl-shaped frame of bones at base of backbone) in mammals and is composed of the ILIUM, ISCHIUM, and PUBIS which are joined into one bone in the adult; the hipbone

**innominate vein** *n* either of a pair of veins that receive blood from the head and neck and join to form the SUPERIOR VENA CAVA (large vein returning blood to the heart)

**innovate** /'inəvayt/ *vt* 1 to introduce (as if) new 2 *archaic* ALTER 1 ~ *vi* to make changes; introduce something new [L *innovatus*, pp of *innovare*, fr *in-* ²in- + *novus* new – more at NEW] – **innovative** *adj*, **innovator** *n*, **innovatory** *adj*

**innovation** /‚inə'vaysh(ə)n/ *n* 1 the introduction of something new 2 a new idea, method, or invention – **innovational** *adj*

**innoxious** /i'nokshəs/ *adj* innocuous, harmless ⟨*an* ~ *substance*⟩ [L *innoxius*, fr *in-* ¹in- + *noxius* noxious]

**Inns of Court** *n pl* the four private societies of law students and practising barristers in London which have the exclusive right of admission to the English Bar; *also* the four sets of buildings owned and used by the Inns of Court

**innuendo** /‚inyoo'endoh/ *n, pl* **innuendos**, **innuendoes** an oblique allusion; a hint, insinuation; *esp* a veiled slight on somebody's character or reputation [L, by hinting, fr *innuere* to hint, fr *in-* ²in- + *nuere* to nod – more at NUMEN]

**innumerable** /i'nyoohmərəbl/ *adj* too many to be counted; countless [ME, fr L *innumerabilis*, fr *in-* ¹in- + *numerabilis* numerable] – **innumerableness** *n*, **innumerably** *adv*

¹**innumerate** /i'nyoohmərət/ *adj, chiefly Br* showing or marked by a lack of understanding of the mathematical approach; not numerate – **innumeracy** *n*

²**innumerate** *n, chiefly Br* somebody who is innumerate

**innumerous** /i'nyoohm(ə)rəs/ *adj* innumerable [L *innumerus*, fr *in-* ¹in- + *numerus* number – more at NIMBLE]

**innutrition** /ˌinyoo'trish(ə)n/ *n* failure of nourishment

**inobservance** /ˌinəb'zuhvəns/ *n* **1** lack of attention; disregard **2** failure to observe something (eg a custom or rule) [Fr & L; Fr, fr L *inobservantia*, fr *in-* ¹*in-* + *observantia* observance] – **inobservant** *adj*

**inoculant** /i'nokyoolənt/ *n* an inoculum

**inoculate** /i'nokyoolayt/ *vt* **1a** to introduce a microorganism (eg a virus or bacterium) into ⟨~ *mice with anthrax*⟩ **b** to introduce (eg a microorganism) into a suitable situation for growth (eg a culture or an animal) **c** VACCINATE 2 **2** to introduce something into the mind of; imbue *synonyms* see VACCINATE [ME *inoculaten* to insert a bud in a plant, fr L *inoculatus*, pp of *inoculare*, fr *in-* ²*in-* + *oculus* eye, bud – more at EYE] – **inoculator** *n*, **inoculative** *adj*, **inoculativity** *n*

**inoculation** /iˌnokyoo'laysh(ə)n/ *n* **1** an act, process, or instance of inoculating; *esp* the introduction of a disease-causing or foreign agent (eg a PATHOGEN or ANTIGEN) into a living organism to stimulate the production of ANTIBODIES (substances produced by the body to fight disease) **2** an inoculum

**inoculum** /i'nokyooləm/ *n, pl* **inocula** /-lə/ material used for inoculation [NL, fr L *inoculare*]

**inodorous** /in'ohd(ə)rəs/ *adj* emitting no smell; odourless [L *inodorus*, fr *in-* ¹*in-* + *odorus* odorous]

**in-'off** *n* LOSING HAZARD [fr the phrase *in off the red/white ball*]

**inoffensive** /ˌinə'fensiv/ *adj* **1** not causing any harm; innocuous **2** not objectionable to the senses – **inoffensively** *adv*, **inoffensiveness** *n*

**inoperable** /in'op(ə)rəbl/ *adj* **1** not suitable for surgery **2** impracticable

**inoperative** /in'op(ə)rətiv/ *adj* not functioning; having no effect – **inoperativeness** *n*

**inopportune** /ˌinopə'tyoohn/ *adj* inconvenient, unseasonable ⟨*an* ~ *time for a visit*⟩ ⟨*her* ~ *arrival*⟩ [L *inopportunus*, fr *in-* ¹*in-* + *opportunus* opportune] – **inopportunely** *adv*, **inopportuneness** *n*

**inordinate** /in'awdinət/ *adj* **1** disorderly, indisciplined ⟨~ *conduct*⟩ **2** exceeding reasonable limits; immoderate ⟨~ *wage demands*⟩ [ME *inordinat*, fr L *inordinatus*, fr *in-* ¹*in-* + *ordinatus*, pp of *ordinare* to arrange – more at ORDAIN] – **inordinately** *adv*, **inordinateness** *n*

**inorganic** /ˌinaw'ganik/ *adj* **1a(1)** being or composed of matter other than plant or animal; mineral **a(2)** forming or belonging to the inanimate world **b** of, being, or dealt with by a branch of chemistry concerned with substances that do not contain carbon **2** not arising through natural growth; artificial – **inorganically** *adv*

**inosculate** /i'noskyoolayt/ *vb* **1** *esp of blood vessels* to unite by contact; blend **2** *formal* to unite intimately ⟨~ *past and present*⟩ [²*in-* + L *osculatus*, pp of *osculare* to provide with a mouth or outlet, fr *osculum*, dim. of *os* mouth] – **inosculation** *n*

**inositol** /i'nohsitol/ *n* any of several alcohols, $C_6H_6(OH)_6$, that occur in microorganisms, plants, and animals including man, esp in the VITAMIN B COMPLEX; *esp* MYOINOSITOL [ISV, fr *inosite* inositol, fr Gk *inos*, gen of *is* sinew]

**inotropic** /ˌinə'trohpik, ˌeenə-, -'tropik/ *adj* of or influencing the force of contraction of (heart) muscles [ISV *ino-* (fr Gk *in-*, *is* sinew) + *-tropic*]

**inpatient** /'inˌpaysh(ə)nt/ *n* a hospital patient who receives board and lodging as well as treatment – compare OUTPATIENT

**in personam** /ˌin puh'sohnam/ *adv or adj, of a legal action or judgment* against a specific person for the purpose of imposing a liability or obligation – compare IN REM [LL, against a person]

**in petto** /in 'petoh/ *adv or adj* **1** in private; secretly – used of Roman Catholic cardinals before their names are officially announced **2** in miniature [It, lit., in the breast; (2) influenced in meaning by E *petty*]

**in propria persona** /in ˌpropriə puh'sohnə, ˌprohpriə/ *adv* in one's own person or character; personally; *specif* without the assistance of a lawyer [ML]

¹**input** /'inpoot/ *n* **1** something that is put in: eg **1a** an amount coming or put in ⟨*increased* ~ *of fertilizer may increase crop yield*⟩ **b** something (eg power, energy, material, or data) supplied to a machine or system **c** a component of production (eg land, labour, or raw materials) **2** the point at which an input (eg of energy, material, or data) is made

²**input** *vt* **-tt-** to enter (eg data) into a computer or data-processing system

**input/output** *n* (the operations that control) the equipment controlling the passage of information into and out of a computer – **input/output** *adj*

**inquest** /'in(g)kwest/ *n* **1a** a judicial or official inquiry, esp by a coroner's court into the cause of a death **b** *taking sing or pl vb* a body of people (eg a jury) assembled to hold such an inquiry **c** the finding or decision of such an inquiry **2** an inquiry or investigation, esp into something that has failed [ME, fr OF *enqueste*, fr (assumed) VL *inquaestus*, pp of *inquaerere* to inquire]

**inquietude** /in'kwie-ətyoohd/ *n, formal* a disturbed state; uneasiness, restlessness [ME, fr MF or LL; MF, fr LL *inquietudo*, fr L *inquietus* disturbed, fr *in-* ¹*in-* + *quietus* quiet]

**inquiline** /'inkwilien/ *n* an animal (eg the cuckoo) that lives habitually in the nest or abode of some other species [L *inquilinus* tenant, lodger, fr *in-* ²*in-* + *colere* to cultivate, dwell – more at WHEEL] – **inquiline** *adj*, **inquilinism** *n*, **inquilinity** *n*, **inquilinous** *adj*

**inquire, enquire** /in'kwie-ə/ *vt* ASK 1b ⟨~ *when the next train is due*⟩ ⟨~ *the way to the station*⟩ ~ *vi* **1** to seek information by questioning ⟨~d *about the price of dairy products*⟩ **2** to make a search or inquiry – often + *into* ⟨*a government cannot* ~ *into religious conviction* – W R Inge⟩ *usage* see ENQUIRE [ME *enquiren*, fr OF *enquerre*, fr (assumed) VL *inquaerere*, alter. of L *inquirere*, fr *in-* ²*in-* + *quaerere* to seek] – **inquirer** *n*, **inquiringly** *adv*

**inquire after** *vt* to ask about the health of

**inquiry, enquiry** /in'kwie-əri/ *n* **1** a request for information **2** a systematic investigation, esp of a matter of public concern ⟨*an official* ~ *following a train crash*⟩

**inquiry agent** *n, Br* PRIVATE DETECTIVE

**inquisition** /ˌinkwi'zish(ə)n/ *n* **1** the act of inquiring **2** a judicial or official inquiry or examination, usu before a jury **3a** *cap* a former Roman Catholic tribunal for the discovery and punishment of heresy; *esp* the Spanish Inquisition **b** a ruthless investigation or examination [ME *inquisicioun*, fr MF *inquisition*, fr L *inquisition-, inquisitio*, fr *inquisitus*, pp of *inquirere*] – **inquisitional** *adj*

**inquisitive** /in'kwizətiv/ *adj* **1** eager for knowledge or understanding; inquiring ⟨*an* ~ *mind*⟩ **2** fond of making inquiries; *esp* unduly curious about the affairs of others – **inquisitively** *adv*, **inquisitiveness** *n*

**inquisitor** /in'kwizitə/ *n* somebody who inquires or conducts an inquisition; *esp* one who is unduly harsh or hostile in making an inquiry

**inquisitorial** /inˌkwizi'tawri-əl/ *adj* of or being an inquisition; *specif* of a system of criminal procedure in which the judge is also the prosecutor – compare ACCUSATORIAL – **inquisitorially** *adv*

**in re** /in 'ray/ *prep* in the matter of; concerning, re – often used in the title or name of a law case [L]

**in rem** /in 'rem/ *adv or adj, of a legal action or judgment* against a thing (eg a right or piece of property) for the purpose of recovering or acquiring it – compare IN PERSONAM [LL]

**in-'residence** *adj* officially associated with an organization in a specified capacity – usu in combination ⟨*writer-in-residence at the university*⟩

**inroad** /'inˌrohd/ *n* **1** a sudden hostile incursion; a raid ⟨*an* ~ *into enemy country*⟩ **2 inroads** *pl*, **inroad** a serious or forcible encroachment or advance ⟨*an illness made* ~s *on his savings*⟩

**inrush** /'inˌrush/ *n* a crowding or flooding in; an influx

**insalivate** /in'salivayt/ *vt* to soak (food) with saliva to make swallowing and digestion easier

**insalubrious** /ˌinsə'l(y)oohbri-əs/ *adj, formal* unhealthy ⟨*an* ~ *climate*⟩ [L *insalubris*, fr *in-* ¹*in-* + *salubris* healthful – more at SAFE] – **insalubriously** *adv*, **insalubrity** *n*

**ins and outs** *n pl, informal* characteristic peculiarities and complexities; ramifications ⟨*explained all the* ~ *of his theory*⟩

**insane** /in'sayn/ *adj* **1** mentally disordered; mad **2** used by, typical of, or intended for insane persons ⟨*an* ~ *asylum*⟩ **3** *informal* utterly absurd ⟨*an* ~ *climate*⟩ [L *insanus*, fr *in-* ¹*in-* + *sanus* sane] – **insanely** *adv*, **insaneness** *n*

**insanitary** /in'sanit(ə)ri/ *adj* unclean enough to endanger health; filthy, contaminated – **insanitation** *n*

**insanity** /in'sanəti/ *n* **1** a severely deranged state of the mind that is not the result of mental deficiency **2** a degree of unsoundness of mind or lack of understanding that prevents somebody from being legally responsible for his/her actions or from taking legal action **3** (an act or instance of) extreme foolishness

**insatiable** /in'saysh(y)əbl/ *adj* incapable of being satisfied ⟨*an ~ desire for wealth*⟩ [ME *insaciable*, fr MF, fr L *insatiabilis*, fr *in-* ¹*in-* + *satiare* to satisfy – more at SATIATE] – **insatiableness** *n*, **insatiably** *adv*, **insatiability** *n*

**insatiate** /in'sayshi·ət/ *adj* insatiable – **insatiately** *adv*, **insatiateness** *n*

**inscape** /'inskayp/ *n* a unity perceived in natural objects or in somebody's mental life that is expressed in literature [²*in-* + *-scape* (as in *landscape*); orig formed by Gerard Manley Hopkins †1889 E poet]

**inscribe** /in'skrieb/ *vt* **1a** to write, engrave, or print, esp as a lasting record ⟨*~d his name in the visitors' book*⟩ **b** to enter on a list; enrol **2a** to write, engrave, or print characters upon ⟨*~d the visitors' book with his name*⟩ **b** to address or dedicate (e g a book or poem) to someone, esp by a handwritten note ⟨*an ~d copy of a first edition*⟩ **3** to draw within a geometrical figure so as to touch at as many points as possible ⟨*a regular polygon ~d in a circle*⟩ **4** *Br* to register the name of the holder of (a security) [L *inscribere*, fr *in-* ²*in-* + *scribere* to write – more at SCRIBE] – **inscriber** *n*

**inscription** /in'skripsh(ə)n/ *n* **1a** something that is inscribed; *also* a superscription **b** EPIGRAPH **2 c** the wording on a coin, medal, or seal; a legend **2** the (handwritten) dedication of a book or work of art **3a** the act of inscribing **b** the entering of a name (as if) on a list; an enrolment **4** *Br* **4a** the act of inscribing securities **b** *pl* inscribed securities [ME *inscripcioun*, fr L *inscription-*, *inscriptio*, fr *inscriptus*, pp of *inscribere*] – **inscriptional** *adj*, **inscriptive** *adj*

**inscroll** /in'skrohl, in'skrol/ *vt, archaic* to write on a scroll; record

**inscrutable** /in'skroohtəbl/ *adj* hard to interpret or understand; enigmatic, mysterious ⟨*an ~ smile*⟩ ⟨*the judge remained silent and ~*⟩ [ME, fr LL *inscrutabilis*, fr L *in-* ¹*in-* + *scrutari* to search – more at SCRUTINY] – **inscrutableness** *n*, **inscrutably** *adv*, **inscrutability** *n*

**inseam** /'in,seem/ *n* an inner seam of a garment or shoe

**insect** /'insekt/ *n* **1** any of a class (Insecta of the phylum Arthropoda) of INVERTEBRATE animals having a body divided into three well-defined parts including the head, the central thorax bearing only three pairs of legs and typically one or two pairs of wings, and the abdomen **2** any of various small animals (e g earthworms, spiders, or woodlice) – not used technically ⟨*whatever creeps the ground, ~ or worm* – John Milton⟩ **3** a worthless or insignificant person [L *insectum*, fr neut of *insectus*, pp of *insecare* to cut into, fr *in-* ²*in-* + *secare* to cut – more at SAW; fr the segmented body (cf ENTOMOLOGY)] – **insect** *adj*, **insectan** *adj*

**insectarium** /,insek'teəri·əm/ *n, pl* **insectariums, insectaria** /-riə/ an insectary [NL]

**insectary** /in'sektəri/ *n* a place where living insects are kept and reared

**insecticidal** /in,sekti'siedl/ *adj* **1** destroying or controlling the growth of insects – used esp of a chemical substance **2** of an insecticide – **insecticidally** *adv*

**insecticide** /in'sektisied/ *n* something, esp a commercially produced chemical preparation, that destroys insects [ISV]

**insectifuge** /in'sektifyoohj, -fyoohzh/ *n* an insect repellent

**insectile** /in'sektiel/ *adj* resembling or being an insect; *also* consisting of insects ⟨*an ~ population*⟩

**insectivore** /in'sekti,vaw/ *n* **1** any of an order (Insectivora) of mammals (e g moles, shrews, and hedgehogs) that are mostly small and nocturnal and eat insects **2** an insect-eating plant or animal [deriv of L *insectum* + *-vorus* -vorous]

**insectivorous** /,insek'tivərəs/ *adj* feeding on insects – **insectivory** *n*

**insecure** /,insi'kyooə/ *adj* **1** uncertain, apprehensive ⟨*feeling somewhat ~ of his reception*⟩ **2** lacking adequate protection or guarantee; unsafe ⟨*an ~ investment*⟩ ⟨*an ~ job*⟩ **3** not firmly fixed or supported; shaky ⟨*the hinge is loose and ~*⟩ **4a** not stable or well-adjusted ⟨*an ~ marriage*⟩ **b** deficient in (self-)confidence; beset by fear and anxiety ⟨*always felt ~ in a group of strangers*⟩ [ML *insecurus*, fr L *in-* ¹*in-* + *securus* secure] – **insecurely** *adv*, **insecureness** *n*, **insecurity** *n*

**inseminate** /in'seminayt/ *vt* **1** sow 1b,c **2** to introduce semen into the reproductive system of (a female) **3** to introduce ideas, principles, etc into the mind of [L *inseminatus*, pp of *inseminare*, fr *in-* ²*in-* + *semin-*, *semen* seed – more at SEMEN] – **insemination** *n*

**inseminator** /in'seminaytə/ *n* one who practises artificial insemination, esp on domestic animals

**insensate** /in'sensayt, -sət/ *adj* **1** insentient **2** lacking wisdom or discernment; *also* foolish **3** lacking in human feeling; inhuman [LL *insensatus*, fr L *in-* ¹*in-* + LL *sensatus* having sense, fr L *sensus* sense] – **insensately** *adv*, **insensateness** *n*

**insensible** /in'sensəbl/ *adj* **1** incapable or bereft of feeling or sensation: e g **1a** insentient, lifeless ⟨*~ earth*⟩ **b** unconscious ⟨*knocked ~ by a sudden blow*⟩ **c** lacking or deprived of sensory perception ⟨*~ to pain*⟩ ⟨*hands ~ from cold*⟩ **2** very slight; imperceptible ⟨*an ~ change*⟩ **3a** apathetic, indifferent ⟨*~ to fear*⟩ **b** unaware ⟨*~ of their danger*⟩ **4** not intelligible; meaningless [ME, fr MF & L; MF, fr L *insensibilis*, fr *in-* ¹*in-* + *sensibilis* sensible] – **insensibleness** *n*, **insensibly** *adv*, **insensibility** *n*

**insensitive** /in'sensətiv/ *adj* **1a** not responsive or susceptible ⟨*~ to the demands of the public*⟩ **b** lacking in feelings or consideration; callous ⟨*so ~ as to laugh at someone in pain*⟩ **2** not physically or chemically sensitive ⟨*~ to light*⟩ – **insensitively** *adv*, **insensitiveness** *n*, **insensitivity** *n*

**insentient** /in'senshi·ənt/ *adj, formal* not endowed with the capacity to perceive; inanimate – **insentience** *n*

**inseparable** /in'sep(ə)rəbl/ *adj* incapable of being separated ⟨*~ friends*⟩ [ME, fr L *inseparabilis*, fr *in-* ¹*in-* + *separabilis* separable] – **inseparable** *n*, **inseparableness** *n*, **inseparably** *adv*, **inseparability** *n*

¹**insert** /in'suht, -'zuht/ *vt* **1** to put or thrust in ⟨*~ the key in the lock*⟩ ⟨*~ a spacecraft into orbit*⟩ **2** to put or introduce into the body of something; interpolate ⟨*~ an advertisement in a newspaper*⟩ **3** to set in and make fast; *esp* to insert by sewing between two cut edges ~ *vi, of a muscle* to be in attachment to the part to be moved ⟨*muscles ~ on bone*⟩ [L *insertus*, pp of *inserere*, fr *in-* ²*in-* + *serere* to join – more at SERIES] – **inserter** *n*

²**insert** /'insuht, 'inzuht/ *n* something that is inserted or is designed for insertion; *esp* written or printed material inserted (e g between the leaves of a book)

**insertion** /in'suhsh(ə)n, -'zuh-/ *n* **1** inserting **2** something that is inserted: e g **2a** the part of a muscle that inserts – compare ORIGIN **b** the mode or place of attachment of an organ or part **c** embroidery or needlework inserted as ornament between two pieces of fabric **d** a single appearance of an advertisement (e g in a newspaper) – **insertional** *adj*

**insertion braid** *n* BEADING 4

**in-'service** *adj* **1** of or being one who is fully employed ⟨*~ teachers*⟩ ⟨*~ police officers*⟩ **2** *of training* undertaken in mid-career

¹**inset** /'inset/ *n* **1a** a place where something flows in; a channel **b** a setting or flowing in **2** something that is inset: e g **2a** a small illustration (e g a map or picture) set within a larger one **b** a piece of cloth set into a garment for decoration, for shaping, or to allow expansion **c** a part or section of a utensil that fits into an outer part **d** a section of a book that is placed inside another for binding

²**inset** *vt* **-tt-**; **inset, insetted** to insert as an inset

¹**inshore** /'inshaw/ *adj* **1** situated or carried on near shore ⟨*~ fishing*⟩ **2** moving towards the shore ⟨*an ~ current*⟩

²**inshore** /in'shaw/ *adv* to or towards the shore ⟨*boats driven ~ by the storm*⟩

¹**inside** /in'sied/ *n* **1** an inner side or surface **2a** an internal part; the region within a boundary ⟨*fire destroyed the ~ of the house*⟩ **b** inward nature, thoughts, or feeling **c** the middle or main part of a division of time ⟨*the ~ of a week*⟩ **d** **insides**, *pl* **inside** *informal* viscera, entrails – not used technically **3** a position of confidence or of access to confidential information ⟨*only someone on the ~ could have told*⟩ **4** the area nearest a specified or implied point of reference: e g **4a** the side of HOME PLATE nearest the batter in baseball **b** the middle portion of a playing area **c** the area near or underneath the basket in basketball **d** the side of a pavement nearer the wall **5a** the side of a double seat in a bus nearer the window **b** the downstairs part of a double-decker bus – **inside out 1** with the inner surface on the outside ⟨*turned his socks inside out*⟩ **2** *informal* in a very thorough manner ⟨*knows his subject inside out*⟩

²**inside** *adj* **1** of, on, near, or towards the inside ⟨*an ~ lavatory*⟩ **2** of or being the inner side of a curve or near the side of the road ⟨*driving on the ~ lane*⟩ **3** known or relating to a select group ⟨*an ~ joke*⟩

³**inside** *prep* **1a** in or into the interior of (something, esp something small) ⟨*~ my mouth*⟩ **b** on the inner side of **2** within ⟨*~ an hour*⟩

⁴**inside** *adv* **1** to or on the inner side **2** in or into the interior **3**

indoors 4 *chiefly Br slang* in or into prison ⟨*did a spell ~ for rape*⟩ – **inside of 1** *informal* in less time than ⟨*should be there inside of an hour*⟩ **2** *chiefly NAm* inside, within
**inside job** *n, informal* a crime, esp a robbery, committed by or with the help of someone (e g an employee) with knowledge of the victim's premises or organization
**insider** /in'siedə/ *n* somebody recognized or accepted as a member of a group, category, or organization; *esp* somebody who has access to confidential information (e g by being a director or a holder of 10 per cent or more of an equity security in a company) or who is in a position of power ⟨~ *dealings*⟩
**inside track** *n* **1** the inner side or lane of a curved racetrack **2** *chiefly NAm* an advantageous competitive position ⟨*the owner's son has the ~ for the job*⟩
**insidious** /in'sidi·əs/ *adj* **1a** ready to entrap the unwary; treacherous ⟨*an ~ stratagem*⟩ **b** harmful but enticing; seductive ⟨~ *drugs that destroy the young*⟩ **2a** acting gradually and imperceptibly but with grave consequences; subtle ⟨*the ~ pressures of modern life*⟩ **b** *of a disease* developing so gradually as to be well established before becoming apparent △ invidious [L *insidiosus*, fr *insidiae* ambush, fr *insidēre* to sit in, sit on, fr *in-* 2in- + *sedēre* to sit – more at SIT] – **insidiously** *adv*, **insidiousness** *n*
**insight** /'in,siet/ *n* **1** the power of discerning the true or underlying nature of a situation; penetration; *esp* the power of understanding one's own actions, motives, etc **2** an act or result of discerning the true or underlying nature of something ⟨~s *into rural life at the turn of the century*⟩ **synonyms** see DISCERNMENT – **insightful** *adj*
**insigne** /in'signi/ *n, pl* **insignia** a badge of authority or honour [L, mark, badge, fr neut of *insignis* marked, distinguished, fr *in-* 2in- + *signum* mark, sign]
**insignia** /in'signi·ə/ *n taking pl vb, pl* **insignia, insignias 1** badges of authority or honour; emblems **2** distinguishing marks or signs □ sometimes treated as sing. in American English
**insignificant** /,insig'nifikənt/ *adj* not significant: e g **a** lacking meaning or import; inconsequential ⟨*an ~ remark*⟩ **b** lacking influence or social standing ⟨*this ~ hanger-on*⟩ **c** very small in size, amount, or number – **insignificance, insignificancy** *n*, **insignificantly** *adv*
**insincere** /,insin'siə/ *adj* not sincere; hypocritical [L *insincerus*, fr *in-* 1in-+ *sincerus* sincere] – **insincerely** *adv*, **insincerity** *n*
**insinuate** /in'sinyoo,ayt/ *vt* **1a** to introduce (e g an idea) gradually or in a subtle or indirect way ⟨~ *doubts into a trusting mind*⟩ **b** to suggest (something unpleasant) by oblique or covert references ⟨~d *that the witness had been bribed*⟩ **2** to gain acceptance for (e g oneself) by stealthy or subtle means ⟨~d *himself into the favour of the wealthy*⟩ ~ *vi* to make insinuations **synonyms** see SUGGEST [L *insinuatus*, pp of *insinuare*, fr *in-* 2in- + *sinuare* to bend, curve, fr *sinus* curve] – **insinuative** *adj*, **insinuator** *n*
**insinuation** /in,sinyoo'aysh(ə)n/ *n* something that is insinuated; *esp* a sly, subtle, and usu derogatory reference
**insipid** /in'sipid/ *adj* **1** devoid of any definite flavour; tasteless **2** devoid of interesting or stimulating qualities; dull, vapid ⟨*an ~ character*⟩ [Fr & LL; Fr *insipide*, fr LL *insipidus*, fr L *in-* 1in- + *sapidus* savoury, fr *sapere* to taste – more at SAGE] – **insipidly** *adv*, **insipidity** *n*
**insist** /in'sist/ *vi* **1** to take a resolute stand; refuse to give way ⟨~ed *on his innocence*⟩ **2** to place great emphasis or importance ⟨*teachers who ~ on punctuality*⟩ ⟨*I'll come if you ~*⟩ ~ *vt* to maintain persistently; declare firmly ⟨~ed *that his story was true*⟩ □ (*vi 1&2*) usu + *on* or *upon* [MF or L; MF *insister*, fr L *insistere* to stand upon, persist, fr *in-* 2in- + *sistere* to stand; akin to L *stare* to stand – more at STAND]
**insistent** /in'sist(ə)nt/ *adj* **1** insisting forcefully or repeatedly; emphatic ⟨*he's very ~ that he can afford the car*⟩ **2** demanding attention; persistent [L *insistent-, insistens*, prp of *insistere*] – **insistently** *adv*, **insistence** *n*
**in situ** /in 'sityooh/ *adv or adj* in the natural or original position [L, in position]
**insobriety** /,insə'brie·əti/ *n, formal* lack of sobriety or moderation; *esp* intemperance in drinking
**insociable** /in'sohsh(y)əbl/ *adj* not sociable [L *insociabilis*, fr *in-* 1in- + *sociabilis* sociable] – **insociably** *adv*, **insociability** *n*
**insofar** /insə'fah, insoh'fah/ *conj* – **insofar as** to the extent or degree that ⟨*I'll help you insofar as I can*⟩
**insolate** /'insohlayt/ *vt* to expose to the sun's rays △ insu-

late [L *insolatus*, pp of *insolare*, fr *in-* 2in- + *sol* sun – more at SOLAR]
**insolation** /,insə'laysh(ə)n/ *n* **1** sunstroke **2** solar radiation that has been received on a given surface
**insole** /'in,sohl/ *n* **1** an inside sole of a shoe **2** a strip of rubberized or cotton padded material the shape of the sole that is placed inside a shoe for warmth, comfort, or hygiene
**insolent** /'insələnt/ *adj* showing disrespectful rudeness; impudent ⟨*an ~ child*⟩ ⟨~ *behaviour*⟩ [ME, fr L *insolent-, insolens;* akin to L *insolescere* to grow haughty] – **insolence** *n*, **insolent** *n*, **insolently** *adv*
**insolubil·ize, -ise** /in'solyoobl,iez/ *vt* to make insoluble – **insolubilization** *n*
**insoluble** /in'solyoobl/ *adj* not soluble: e g **a** having or admitting of no solution or explanation **b** incapable of being dissolved in a liquid; *also* soluble only with difficulty or to a slight degree **c** *archaic* indissoluble [ME *insolible*, fr L *insolubilis*, fr *in-* 1in- + *solvere* to free, dissolve – more at SOLVE] – **insoluble** *n*, **insolubleness** *n*, **insolubility** *n*, **insolubly** *adv*
**insolvable** /in'solvəbl/ *adj, chiefly NAm* impossible to solve ⟨*an apparently ~ problem*⟩ – **insolvably** *adv*
**insolvent** /in'solvənt/ *adj* **1a** unable to pay debts as they fall due; *specif* having liabilities in excess of the value of assets held **b** insufficient to pay all debts ⟨*an ~ estate*⟩ **2** relating to or for the relief of insolvency or insolvents – **insolvency** *n*, **insolvent** *n*
**insomnia** /in'somni·ə/ *n* prolonged (abnormal) inability to obtain adequate sleep [L, fr *insomnis* sleepless, fr *in-* 1in- + *somnus* sleep – more at SOMNOLENT] – **insomniac** *adj or n*
**insomuch** /insə'much, insoh'much/ *adv* – **insomuch as 1** to the extent or degree that; INSOFAR AS **2** in view of the fact that; because – **insomuch that** to such a degree that; THAT 2a(1)
**insouciance** /in'soohsyəns (Fr ɛ̃su:sjɑ̃:s)/ *n* lighthearted unconcern; nonchalance [Fr, fr *in-* 1in- + *soucier* to trouble, disturb, fr L *sollicitare*] – **insouciant** *adj*, **insouciantly** *adv*
**inspan** /in'span/ *vb, S Afr* to yoke, harness [Afrik, fr D *inspannen*, fr *in* in + *spannen* to stretch, yoke]
**inspect** /in'spekt/ *vt* **1** to examine closely and critically; scrutinize ⟨~ed *his fingernails for dirt*⟩ **2** to view or examine officially ⟨~s *the barracks every Friday*⟩ ~ *vi* to inspect something [L *inspectus*, pp of *inspicere*, fr *in-* 2in- + *specere* to look – more at SPY] – **inspection** *n*, **inspective** *adj*
**inspector** /in'spektə/ *n* a person employed to inspect something: e g **a** a police officer who ranks below a superintendent and above a sergeant **b** an official consultant who visits British schools to advise on and assess the teaching – **inspectorate** *n*, **inspectorship** *n*
**inspiration** /,inspi'raysh(ə)n/ *n* **1a** a divine influence or action on a person which qualifies him/her to receive and communicate sacred revelation, esp in the form of written scripture **b** the action or power of stimulating the intellect or emotions **2** the act of drawing in; *specif* the drawing of air into the lungs **3a** the quality or state of being inspired ⟨*architecture that reveals a lack of ~*⟩ **b** an inspired idea ⟨*I've had an ~, let's go to the seaside*⟩ **4** an inspiring agent or influence ⟨*she was the ~ for his greatest orchestral works*⟩ – **inspirational** *adj*, **inspirationally** *adv*
**inspirator** /'inspi,raytə/ *n* a device (e g an injector or respirator) by which something (e g gas or vapour) is drawn in
**inspiratory** /in'spie·ərətri/ *adj* relating to, used for, or associated with inspiration
**inspire** /in'spie·ə/ *vt* **1** to inhale **2a** to influence, shape, move, or guide by divine or supernatural inspiration **b** to exert an animating or exalting influence on ⟨*was particularly ~d by the Impressionists*⟩ ⟨*inspiring music*⟩ **c** to impel, encourage ⟨*threats don't necessarily ~ people to work*⟩ **d** to affect – usu + *with* ⟨*seeing the old room again ~d him with nostalgia*⟩ **3a** to communicate to an agent supernaturally ⟨*writings ~d by God*⟩ **b** to give rise to; occasion ⟨*music ~d by a holiday in the mountains*⟩ **4** to incite, instigate ⟨*riots ~d by fascists*⟩ **5** *archaic* to breathe or blow into or upon ~ *vi* to inhale [ME *inspiren*, fr MF & L; MF *inspirer*, fr L *inspirare*, fr *in-* 2in- + *spirare* to breathe – more at SPIRIT] – **inspirer** *n*
**inspired** /in'spie·əd/ *adj* outstanding or brilliant in a way that suggests divine inspiration ⟨*gave an ~ rendering of the piano sonata*⟩ ⟨*made an ~ guess*⟩
**inspirit** /in'spirit/ *vt* to fill with spirit; animate, encourage
**inspissate** /in'spisayt/ *vt, formal* to make thick or thicker, esp by condensation [LL *inspissatus*, pp of *inspissare*, fr L *in-* 2in- + *spissare* to thicken, fr *spissus* thick; akin to Gk *spidios* extended, L *spatium* space] – **inspissator** *n*, **inspissation** *n*

inst /inst/ *adj, humorous when spoken* INSTANT 2

**instability** /,instə'biləti/ *n* the quality or state of being (mentally or emotionally) unstable

**instable** /in'staybl/ *adj* unstable [MF or L; MF, fr L *instabilis*, fr *in*- ¹in- + *stabilis* stable]

**install, instal** /in'stawl/ *vt* -ll- **1** to induct into an office, dignity, rank, or order, esp with ceremonies or formalities (e g by seating in a stall or official seat) **2** to establish in a specified place, condition, or status ⟨~ing *herself in front of the fire*⟩ **3** to place in usu permanent position for use or service ⟨*had a shower* ~ed *in the bathroom*⟩ [MF *installer*, fr ML *installare*, fr L *in*- ²in- + ML *stallum* stall, fr OHG *stal*] – **installer** *n*

**installation** /,instə'laysh(ə)n/ *n* **1** a device, apparatus, or piece of machinery fixed or fitted in place to perform some specified function ⟨*a new gas central-heating* ~⟩ **2** a military camp, fort, base, or establishment ⟨*US* ~s *in Europe*⟩

¹**instalment,** *NAm chiefly* **installment** /in'stawlmənt/ *n* installing or being installed

²**instalment,** *NAm chiefly* **installment** *n* **1** any of the parts into which a debt is divided when payment is made at intervals **2a** any of several parts (e g of a publication) presented at intervals **b** a single part of a serial story [alter. of earlier *estalment* payment by instalment, deriv of OF *estaler* to place, fix, fr *estal* place, of Gmc origin; akin to OHG *stal* place, stall]

**instalment plan** *n, NAm* HIRE PURCHASE

¹**instance** /'inst(ə)ns/ *n* **1** an example cited as an illustration or proof **2** the institution of a legal action – chiefly in *court of first instance* **3** a situation viewed as one stage in a process or series of events ⟨*prefers, in this* ~, *to remain anonymous* – *TLS*⟩ **4** *formal* a solicitation, request ⟨*am writing to you at the* ~ *of my client*⟩ [ME *instaunce*, fr MF *instance* act of urging, motive, instant, fr L *instantia* presence, urgency, fr *instant*-, *instans*] – **for instance** as an example – **in the first instance** firstly, originally ⟨*the position will be located in Sydney* in the first instance – *The Sun (Melbourne)*⟩

**synonyms Instance, example,** and **illustration** can all mean a "typical case". **Instance** may mean no more than "case" ⟨*in most instances the houses have no garage*⟩. Both an **instance** and an **example** may be, and an **illustration** must be, specifically brought forward to clarify a point ⟨*he gave as an* **instance/example** *the danger of fire in old buildings*⟩. An **illustration** is often more extended and detailed ⟨*told this story as an* **illustration** *of what he meant*⟩.

²**instance** *vt* **1** to exemplify by an instance **2** to put forward as a case or example; cite

**instancy** /'inst(ə)nsi/ *n* **1** urgency, insistence **2** imminence **3** immediacy, instantaneousness

¹**instant** /'inst(ə)nt/ *n* **1** an infinitesimal space of time; *esp* a point in time separating two states ⟨*at the* ~ *of death*⟩ **2** the present or current month [ME, fr ML *instant*-, *instans*, fr *instant*-, *instans*, adj, instant, fr L]

²**instant** *adj* **1a** present, current ⟨*previous felonies not related to the* ~ *crime*⟩ **b inst, instant** of or occurring in the present month – used in commercial communications **2** immediate ⟨*the play was an* ~ *success*⟩ **3a(1)** premixed or precooked and sold frozen, tinned, or dried for easy final preparation ⟨~ *mashed potatoes*⟩ **a(2)** appearing (as if) in ready-to-use form ⟨~ *culture*⟩ ⟨*updating ... your image with* ~ *beards, mustaches, and sideburns* – *Playboy*⟩ **b** immediately soluble in water ⟨~ *coffee*⟩ **4** *formal* demanding, urgent [ME, fr MF or L; MF, fr L *instant*-, *instans*, fr prp of *instare* to stand upon, urge, fr *in*- ²in- + *stare* to stand – more at STAND] – **instantness** *n*

**instantaneous** /,inst(ə)n'tayni-əs/ *adj* **1** done, occurring, or acting in an instant or instantly; IMMEDIATE 3a ⟨*death was* ~⟩ **2** occurring or present at a particular instant ⟨~ *velocity*⟩ ⟨~ *value*⟩ [ML *instantaneus*, fr *instant*-, *instans*, n] – **instantaneously** *adv*, **instantaneity** *n*, **instantaneousness** *n*

**instanter** /in'stantə/ *adv, formal* instantly, immediately [ML, fr *instant*-, *instans*]

**instantiate** /in'stanshiayt/ *vt* to represent (an abstraction) by a concrete instance – **instantiation** *n*

**instantly** /'inst(ə)ntli/ *adv* **1** immediately; AT ONCE **2** *archaic* with importunity; urgently

**instant replay** *n* ACTION REPLAY – **instant-replay** *adj*

**instar** /'in,stah/ *n* a stage in the life of an insect, crab, spider, or related animal between two successive moults; *also* an individual in a specified instar

**instate** /in'stayt/ *vt* **1** to set or establish in a rank or office; install **2** *obs* **2a** to invest, endow **b** to bestow, confer

**in statu pupillari** /in ,statyooh ,pyoohpi'lahri/ *adv* in the status of a pupil or undergraduate [ML]

**in statu quo** /in ,statyooh 'kwoh/ *adv* in the former or same state [NL, lit., in the state in which]

**instauration** /,instaw'raysh(ə)n/ *n, formal* **1** restoration after decay or a lapse **2** *obs* an act of instituting or establishing something [L *instauration*-, *instauratio*, fr *instauratus*, pp of *instaurare* to renew, restore – more at STORE]

**instead** /in'sted/ *adv* as a substitute or alternative ⟨*was going to write but called* ~⟩ ⟨*sent his son* ~⟩ – compare STEAD – **instead of** as a substitute for or alternative to; IN PLACE OF

**instep** /'in,step/ *n* **1** the arched middle portion of the human foot in front of the ankle joint; *esp* its upper surface **2** the part of the hind leg of the horse between the HOCK and the PASTERN joint **3** the part of a shoe or stocking over the instep

**instigate** /'instigayt/ *vt* **1** to goad or urge forwards; provoke, incite **2** to initiate (a course of action or procedure, e g a legal investigation) [L *instigatus*, pp of *instigare* – more at STICK] – **instigator** *n*, **instigative** *adj*, **instigation** *n*

**instil,** *NAm chiefly* **instill** /in'stil/ *vt* -ll- **1** to cause to enter drop by drop ⟨~ *medication into the infected eye*⟩ **2** to impart gradually ⟨~ling *in children a love of learning*⟩ – *in* or *into* [MF & L; MF *instiller*, fr L *instillare*, fr *in*- ²in- + *stillare* to drip – more at DISTIL] – **instiller** *n*, **instillment** *n*, **instillation** *n*

¹**instinct** /'instingkt/ *n* **1** a natural or inherent aptitude, impulse, or capacity ⟨*had an* ~ *for the right word*⟩ **2a** a largely inheritable and unalterable tendency of an organism to make a complex and specific response to environmental stimuli without involving reason **b** behaviour that is carried on without conscious thought [ME, fr L *instinctus* impulse, fr *instinctus*, pp of *instinguere* to incite; akin to L *instigare* to instigate] – **instinctual** *adj*

²**instinct** *adj, formal* profoundly imbued; infused ⟨*a man* ~ *with justice*⟩ – usu + *with*

**instinctive** /in'stingktiv/ *adj* of, being, or prompted by instinct ⟨~ *behaviour*⟩; arising spontaneously and being independent of judgment or will ⟨*an* ~ *doubt of their honesty*⟩ **synonyms** see SPONTANEOUS **antonym** intentional – **instinctively** *adv*

¹**institute** /'instityooht/ *vt* **1** to instate, install **2** to originate and establish; initiate, inaugurate ⟨~d *many social reforms*⟩ **3** to establish in a position or office; *esp* to invest (a minister) with spiritual charge of a BENEFICE (paid office of the Church of England) [ME *instituten*, fr L *institutus*, pp of *instituere*, fr *in*- ²in-+ *statuere* to set up – more at STATUTE]

²**institute** *n* **1** something that is instituted: e g **1a(1)** an elementary principle recognized as authoritative **a(2)** *pl* a collection of authoritative principles and precepts; *esp* a summary of laws **b** an organization for the promotion of a cause or pursuit ⟨*a research* ~⟩ ⟨*an* ~ *for the blind*⟩; *also* the premises used by an institute **c** an educational institution **d** *NAm* an intensive and usu brief course of instruction on selected topics relating to a usu specified field ⟨*an urban studies* ~⟩ **2** *obs* an act of instituting

**institute of education** *n, often cap I&E* any of several institutions that oversee teacher training in England and Wales

**institution** /,insti'tyoohsh(ə)n/ *n* **1** an act of instituting; an establishment **2a** an established, significant, and sanctioned practice, relationship, or organization in a society or culture ⟨*the* ~ *of marriage*⟩; *also* an accustomed or familiar activity or object ⟨*his bow tie is an* ~⟩ **b(1)** (a building housing) an established organization or body (e g a university or hospital); *esp* one catering to public needs **b(2)** *euph* a mental hospital **3** *archaic* something that serves to instruct; *also* instruction, training

**institutional** /,insti'tyoohsh(ə)nl/ *adj* **1** (typical) of an institution; *esp* dull and repetitive ⟨~ *food*⟩ **2** of esp legal principles or institutes – **institutionally** *adv*

**institutionalism** /insti'tyoohsh(ə)nl,iz(ə)m/ *n* **1** emphasis on organization (e g in religion) at the expense of other factors **2** the system of public institutional care of defective, delinquent, or dependent people **3** an economic school of thought that emphasizes the role of social institutions in influencing economic behaviour – **institutionalist** *n*

**institutional-ize, -ise** /insti'tyoohsh(ə)nl,iez/ *vt* **1** to make into or give the character of an institution to ⟨~d *idiomatic phrases*⟩ ⟨*it was her contemporaries who codified and* ~d *modern dance* – John Percival⟩ **2a** to put or keep in the care of an institution **b** to cause or allow to acquire personality or behaviour traits typical of people in an institution ⟨*guards ... as* ~d *as the men they guard* – Jeremy James⟩ – **institutionalization** *n*

**instruct** /in'strukt/ vt 1 to impart knowledge to, esp in a systematic manner; teach 2a to direct authoritatively b COMMAND 1 3 to engage (a lawyer, specif a barrister) to conduct a case *synonyms* see TEACH [ME *instructen*, fr L *instructus*, pp of *instruere*, fr *in-* ²*in-* + *struere* to build – more at STRUCTURE]

**instruction** /in'struksh(ə)n/ n 1a **instructions** pl, **instruction ORDER** 7b, **COMMAND** 2a ⟨*had* ~s *not to admit strangers*⟩ b pl an outline or manual of technical procedure c a word, sequence of words, numerical code, etc, that tells a computer to perform a particular operation 2 teaching – **instructional** adj

**instructive** /in'struktiv/ adj carrying a lesson; enlightening – **instructively** adv, **instructiveness** n

*synonyms* The material and processes of "instruction" are **instructional** ⟨*an* **instructional** *course*⟩ but may not succeed in being **instructive**.

**instructor** /in'struktə/, *fem* **instructress** /-tris/ n one who instructs; a teacher: eg **a** a teacher of a technical or practical subject ⟨*a swimming* ~⟩ **b** NAm a college teacher below professorial rank – **instructorship** n

¹**instrument** /'instrəmənt/ n 1a a means whereby something is achieved, performed, or furthered **b** a dupe; TOOL 3 2 an implement, tool, or device designed esp for delicate work (eg surgery) or for measurement ⟨*scientific* ~s⟩ 3 a device used to produce music 4 a formal legal document (eg a deed, bond, or agreement) 5 an electrical or mechanical device used in navigating an aircraft; *esp* such a device used as the sole means of navigating *synonyms* see ¹TOOL [ME, fr L *instrumentum*, fr *instruere* to arrange, instruct]

²**instrument** /'instrəmənt, -ment/ vt 1 to score for musical performance; orchestrate 2 to equip with instruments

**instrumental** /,instrə'mentl/ adj 1a serving as an instrument, means, agent, or tool ⟨*was* ~ *in organizing the strike*⟩ **b** of or done with an instrument or tool 2 relating to, composed for, or performed on a musical instrument; *esp* for instruments but not voice 3 of or being a grammatical case or form expressing means or agency – **instrumental** n, **instrumentally** adv

**instrumentalism** /,instrə'mentl·iz(ə)m/ n a doctrine that ideas are instruments of action and that their usefulness determines their truth; pragmatism

**instrumentalist** /,instrə'mentl,ist/ n 1 a player on a musical instrument 2 a student or exponent of instrumentalism – **instrumentalist** adj

**instrumentality** /,instrəmen'taləti/ n a means, agency

**instrumentation** /,instrəmən'taysh(ə)n, -men-/ n 1 the use or provision of instruments 2 the arrangement or composition of music for instruments, esp for a band or orchestra 3a technology concerned with the development and manufacture of instruments **b** instruments for a particular purpose

**instrument flying** n the navigation of an aircraft by instruments only (eg when visibility is poor)

**instrument landing** n an aircraft landing made when visibility is very poor or nonexistent, by means of instruments and by ground radio or radar directing devices

**instrument panel** n a panel on which instruments are mounted; *esp* a dashboard

**insubordinate** /,insə'bawdinət/ adj unwilling to submit to authority; disobedient – **insubordinate** n, **insubordinately** adv, **insubordination** n

**insubstantial** /,insəb'stansh(ə)l/ adj 1 lacking substance or material nature; imaginary, unreal 2 lacking firmness or solidity; flimsy [Fr or LL; Fr *insubstantiel*, fr LL *insubstantialis*, fr L *in-* ¹*in-* + LL *substantialis* substantial] – **insubstantiality** n

**insufferable** /in'suf(ə)rəbl/ adj incapable of being endured; intolerable ⟨*an* ~ *bore*⟩ – **insufferableness** n, **insufferably** adv

**insufficiency** /,insə'fish(ə)nsi/ *also* **insufficience** /,insə'fish(ə)ns/ n 1a lack of adequate supply **b** lack of physical power or capacity; *specif* the inability of an organ or body part (eg the heart or kidneys) to function normally 2 something insufficient ⟨*he was aware of his* insufficiencies⟩

**insufficient** /,insə'fish(ə)nt/ adj not sufficient; *esp* deficient in power, capacity, or competence ⟨*we received* ~ *help*⟩ [ME, fr MF, fr LL *insufficient-, insufficiens*, fr L *in-* ¹*in-* + *sufficient-, sufficiens* sufficient] – **insufficiently** adv

**insufflate** /'insu,flayt/ vt 1 *medicine* to blow (eg a powder or gas), esp into a body cavity (eg the lungs) 2 *formal* to blow on or into ⟨~ *a room with insecticide*⟩ [LL *insufflatus*, pp of *insuf-*

*flare*, fr L *in-* ²*in-* + *sufflare* to blow up, fr *sub-* up + *flare* to blow – more at SUB-, BLOW] – **insufflator** n

**insufflation** /,insu'flaysh(ə)n/ n an act or instance of insufflating; *also* a Christian rite performed by breathing on a person to symbolize the action of the Holy Spirit

**insula** /'insyoolə/ n, pl **insulae** /-lie/ a small lobe of the forebrain in mammals [NL, fr L, island]

**insular** /'insyoolə/ adj 1a of or being an island **b** living or situated on an island ⟨~ *residents*⟩ 2 *of a plant or animal* having a restricted or isolated natural range or habitat 3a *of island people* ⟨*surviving* ~ *customs*⟩ **b** that results (as if) from lack of contact with other peoples or cultures; narrow-minded, illiberal 4 *anatomy* of an island of cells or tissue [LL *insularis*, fr L *insula* island] – **insularism** n, **insularly** adv, **insularity** n

**insulate** /'insyoolayt/ vt 1 to place in a detached situation; isolate; *esp* to separate from conducting bodies by means of nonconducting material so as to prevent transfer or loss of electricity, heat, or sound 2 to preserve or keep safe from unpleasant circumstances ⟨*civil servants are* ~d *from the effects of inflation as their salaries are index-linked*⟩ [L *insula* island]

**insulation** /,insyoo'laysh(ə)n/ n 1 insulating or being insulated 2 material used in insulating

**insulator** /'insyoo,laytə/ n something that insulates; *esp* a (device made of) material that is a poor conductor of electricity and that is used for separating or supporting conductors to prevent undesired flow of electricity

**insulin** /'insyoo,lin/ n a protein hormone secreted by the ISLETS OF LANGERHANS (groups of cells located in the pancreas) that is essential esp for controlling the amount of sugar in the blood and is used in the treatment and control of DIABETES MELLITUS [NL *insula* islet (of Langerhans), fr L, island]

¹**insult** /in'sult/ vi, *archaic* to behave with pride or arrogance; vaunt ~ vt to treat with insolence, indignity, or contempt; *also* to cause offence or damage to ⟨*arguments that* ~ *the reader's intelligence*⟩ ⟨*foods that* ~ *the body*⟩ [MF or L; MF *insulter*, fr L *insultare*, lit., to spring upon, fr *in-* ²*in-* + *saltare* to leap – more at SALTATION] – **insulter** n, **insultingly** adv

²**insult** /'insult/ n 1 an act of insulting; something that insults 2 an injury to the body or one of its parts; *also* something that causes or has a potential for causing such insult ⟨*pollution and other environmental* ~s⟩ 3 *archaic* an act of attacking

**insuperable** /in's(y)oohprəbl/ adj incapable of being surmounted, overcome, or passed over ⟨~ *difficulties*⟩ [ME, fr MF & L; MF, fr L *insuperabilis*, fr *in-* ¹*in-* + *superare* to surmount, fr *super* over – more at OVER] – **insuperably** adv

**insupportable** /,insə'pawtəbl/ adj 1 unendurable ⟨~ *pain*⟩ 2 incapable of being sustained; unjustifiable ⟨~ *charges*⟩ [MF or LL; MF, fr LL *insupportabilis*, fr L *in-* ¹*in-* + *supportare* to support] – **insupportableness** n, **insupportably** adv

**insuppressible** /,insə'presəbl/ adj not suppressible – **insuppressibly** adv

**insurable** /in'shoorəbl, in'shaw-/ adj that may be insured – **insurability** n

**insurance** /in'shoorəns, -'shaw-/ n 1 insuring or being insured 2a the business of insuring people or property **b** a contract whereby one party undertakes to guarantee another against loss by a specified contingency or risk; *also* the protection afforded by this contract **c**(1) the premium demanded under such a contract **c**(2) the sum for which something is insured

**insure** /in'shooə, in'shaw/ vt 1 to give, take, or procure insurance on or for 2 *chiefly NAm* to ensure ~ vi to contract to give or take insurance; *specif* to underwrite [ME *insuren*, prob alter. of *assuren* to assure] – **insurer** n

*usage* **Insure** and **ensure** have the same pronunciation.

**insured** /in'shooəd, in'shawd/ n, pl **insured** somebody whose life or property is insured – usu + *the*

**insurgency** /in'suhj(ə)nsi/, **insurgence** /in'suhj(ə)ns/ n the quality, state, or action of being insurgent; *specif* a condition of revolt against a government that is less than an organized revolution and that is not recognized as warfare

¹**insurgent** /in'suhj(ə)nt/ n a person who revolts against civil authority or an established government; *esp* a rebel not recognized as a soldier [L *insurgent-, insurgens*, prp of *insurgere* to rise up, fr *in-* ²*in-* + *surgere* to rise – more at SURGE]

²**insurgent** adj rising in opposition to civil authority or established leadership; rebellious – **insurgently** adv

**insurmountable** /,insə'mowntəbl/ adj insuperable ⟨~ *problems*⟩ – **insurmountably** adv

**insurrection** /,insə'reksh(ə)n/ n (an act or instance of) revolt against civil authority or an established government *synonyms* see REBELLION [ME, fr MF, fr LL *insurrection-*, *insurrectio*, fr *insurrectus*, pp of *insurgere*] – **insurrectional** *adj*, **insurrectionary** *adj or n*, **insurrectionist** *n*

**insusceptible** /ˌinsəˈseptəbl/ *adj* not susceptible ⟨~ *to flattery*⟩ – **insusceptibly** *adv*, **insusceptibility** *n*

**inswing** /ˈinˌswing/ *n* the swing of a bowled cricket ball from the off to the leg side – compare OUTSWING – **inswinger** *n*

**intact** /inˈtakt/ *adj* 1 untouched, esp by anything that harms or diminishes; whole, uninjured 2 *of a living body or its parts* having no relevant part removed or destroyed: 2a being a virgin b not castrated [ME *intacte*, fr L *intactus*, fr in- ¹in- + *tactus*, pp of *tangere* to touch – more at TANGENT] – **intactness** *n*

**intaglio** /inˈtahlioh/ *n*, *pl* **intaglios 1a** an incised or engraved sunken design made in hard material, esp precious or semiprecious stone, so that an impression (eg in sealing wax) from the design gives an image in relief **b** the art or process of making intaglios **c** printing (eg in GRAVURE) done from a plate in which the image is sunk below the surface 2 something (eg a gem) carved in intaglio [It, fr *intagliare* to engrave, cut, fr ML *intaliare*, fr L in- ²in- + LL *taliare* to cut – more at TAILOR]

**intake** /ˈinˌtayk/ *n* 1 an opening through which liquid or gas enters an enclosure or system ⟨*the air ~ of a jet engine*⟩ 2a a taking in b(1) *taking sing or pl vb* the amount or number taken in ⟨*our total annual ~ of students*⟩ b(2) something (eg energy) taken in; an input

**Intal** /ˈintal/ *trademark* – used for the asthma-controlling drug SODIUM CROMOGLYCATE

¹**intangible** /inˈtanjəbl/ *adj* not tangible; impalpable [Fr or ML; Fr, fr ML *intangibilis*, fr L in- ¹in- + LL *tangibilis* tangible] – **intangibleness** *n*, **intangibly** *adv*, **intangibility** *n*

²**intangible** *n* something intangible; *specif* a business asset (eg goodwill) that does not physically exist

**intarsia** /inˈtahsiə/ *n* 1 (the art or process of making) a mosaic usu of wood fitted into a supporting wood background 2 a geometric knitting pattern resembling an intarsia [Ger, modif of It *intarsio*, fr *intarsiare* to inlay, fr in- ²in- + *tarsia* intarsia, fr Ar *tarṣī*]

**integer** /ˈintijə/ *n* 1 the number one (1) or any number (eg 6, 0, -23) obtainable by once or repeatedly adding one to or subtracting one from the number one 2 a complete entity [L, adj, whole, entire – more at ENTIRE]

**integrable** /ˈintigrəbl/ *adj* capable of being integrated – **integrability** *n*

¹**integral** /ˈintigrəl; *esp in maths* inˈtegrəl/ *adj* **1a** essential to completeness; constituent – chiefly in *integral part* **b(1)** of or being a mathematical integer **b(2)** of or concerned with mathematical integrals or integration **c** formed as a unit with another part 2 composed of integral parts; integrated 3 lacking nothing essential; whole – **integrally** *adv*, **integrality** *n*

*usage* The pronunciation /ˈintigrəl/ is recommended for BBC broadcasters.

²**integral** *n* 1 a mathematical function whose DERIVATIVE is a given function, and which is essentially the sum of a large number of infinitely small quantities, and one form of which can be used to find the area under a given curve – compare DEFINITE INTEGRAL, INDEFINITE INTEGRAL 2 a solution of a DIFFERENTIAL EQUATION

**integral calculus** *n* a branch of mathematics dealing with methods of finding integrals and with their applications (eg to the determination of lengths, areas, and volumes and to the solution of DIFFERENTIAL EQUATIONS)

**integrand** /ˈintiˌgrand/ *n* a mathematical expression to be integrated [L *integrandus*, gerundive of *integrare*]

**integrant** /ˈintigrənt/ *adj* integral, essential – **integrant** *n*

**integrate** /ˈintigrayt/ *vt* 1 to form or blend into a whole; unite 2a to combine together or with something else b to incorporate into a larger unit – usu + *into* 3 to find the integral of (eg a mathematical function or DIFFERENTIAL EQUATION) **4a** to end the segregation of (eg a racial minority group) and bring into full membership of society or an organization b to desegregate ⟨~ *school districts*⟩ ~ *vi* to become integrated [L *integratus*, pp of *integrare*, fr *integr-*, *integer*] – **integrative** *adj*

**integrated circuit** *n* a tiny electronic circuit formed in or on a single slice of semiconductor material (eg silicon) – **integrated circuitry** *n*

**integrated day** *n* a day of esp infant-school activity planned as a whole without a formal timetable

**integration** /ˌintiˈgraysh(ə)n/ *n* 1 the act or process or an instance of integrating: eg **1a** the incorporation of individuals from different groups (eg races) as equals into a society or an organization b *psychology* the coordination of mental processes into an effective personality 2 *mathematics* **2a** the operation of calculating a mathematical integral **b** the operation of solving a DIFFERENTIAL EQUATION

**integration by parts** *n* a method of mathematical integration using the formula $\int u(dv/dx)\,dx = uv - \int v(du/dx)\,dx$

**integrationist** /ˌintiˈgraysh(ə)nist/ *n* a person who believes in, advocates, or practises social integration – **integrationist** *adj*

**integrator** /ˈintigraytə/ *n* one who or that which integrates; *esp* a device (eg in a computer) that performs the equivalent of mathematical integration or solution of DIFFERENTIAL EQUATIONS

**integrity** /inˈtegrəti/ *n* 1 an unimpaired condition; soundness 2 uncompromising adherence to a code of esp moral or artistic values; honesty, incorruptibility 3 the quality or state of being complete or undivided; wholeness, completeness ⟨*the ~ of the Empire was threatened*⟩ *synonyms* see UNITY *antonym* (sense 2) duplicity

**integument** /inˈtegyoomənt/ *n* something that covers or encloses; *esp* an enveloping layer (eg a skin, membrane, or husk) of a living organism or one of its parts [L *integumentum*, fr *integere* to cover, fr in- ²in- + *tegere* to cover – more at THATCH] – **integumental** *adj*, **integumentary** *adj*

**intellect** /ˈint(ə)lekt/ *n* 1 the capacity for intelligent thought, esp when highly developed; understanding 2 a person with great intellectual powers [ME, fr MF or L; MF, fr L *intellectus*, fr *intellectus*, pp of *intellegere* to understand – more at INTELLIGENT]

**intellection** /ˌint(ə)ˈleksh(ə)n/ *n*, *formal* the exercise of the intellect; reasoning; *also* an act of this – **intellective** *adj*

¹**intellectual** /ˌint(ə)ˈlektyooˑəl, -chəl/ *adj* **1a** of or requiring the intellect or its use **b** developed or chiefly guided by the intellect rather than by emotion or experience ⟨*a coldly ~ artist*⟩ 2 given to the use of the intellect ⟨*an ~ family*⟩; *also* having great intellect – **intellectually** *adv*, **intellectualness** *n*, **intellectuality** *n*, **intellectualize** *vb*, **intellectualization** *n*, **intellectualizer** *n*

²**intellectual** *n* 1 an intellectual person 2 *pl*, *archaic* intellectual powers

**intellectualism** /ˌint(ə)ˈlektyooˑ əl,iz(ə)m, -chəl-/ *n* (excessive) devotion to the exercise of intellect or to intellectual pursuits – **intellectualist** *n*, **intellectualistic** *adj*

**intelligence** /inˈtelijəns/ *n* 1 the ability to learn, understand, apply knowledge, or think abstractly, esp in relation to new or trying situations; *also* the skilled use of intelligence or reason 2a an intelligent entity; *esp* an angel b intelligent minds or mind ⟨*cosmic ~*⟩ 3 the act of understanding; comprehension **4a** news; INFORMATION 2a,c **b** information concerning (possible) enemies or an area; *also*, *taking sing or pl vb* an agency engaged in obtaining such information [ME, fr MF, fr L *intelligentia*, fr *intelligent-*, *intelligens* intelligent]

**intelligence quotient** *n* a number expressing the ratio of somebody's apparent intelligence as determined by a test to the average for his/her age, the average being regarded as 100 ⟨*she must be a genius, her ~ is 160*⟩ – compare MENTAL AGE

**intelligencer** /inˈtelijənsə/ *n*, *archaic* 1 a secret agent; a spy 2 a bringer of news; REPORTER b(1)

**intelligence test** *n* a test designed to determine the relative mental capacity of somebody

**intelligent** /inˈtelijənt/ *adj* 1 having or indicating intelligence, esp to a high degree 2 able to perform some of the functions of a computer ⟨*an ~ computer terminal*⟩ [L *intelligent-*, *intelligens*, prp of *intelligere*, *intellegere* to understand, fr *inter-* + *legere* to gather, select – more at LEGEND] – **intelligently** *adv*, **intelligential** *adj*

*synonyms* **Intelligent, clever, quick-witted, bright, brilliant,** and **brainy** all mean "mentally quick or keen". **Intelligent** suggests higher than average mental capacity and the ability to apply the mind effectively to whatever situation may arise. **Clever** stresses quick, apt facility or resourcefulness, sometimes suggesting that this is at the expense of profundity or soundness of reasoning. **Quick-witted** implies an alert mind which can cope swiftly with emergencies or react intelligently to a stimulus. **Bright**, often used of children, implies a lively alertness and quickness to learn and understand. **Brilliant** suggests an impressive and evident intelligence which compels respect and admiration. **Brainy** is an (envious) informal term applied, usually by schoolchildren, to those they consider unusually knowledgeable or intelligent ⟨*R is an* **intelligent** *pupil,* **quick-witted** *in debate,* **clever** *at composing essays,* **bright** *in class, labelled* brainy *by her fellow pupils – she should make a* brilliant *student at university"*⟩. Compare ¹INTELLECTUAL, SHREWD *antonyms* unintelligent, slow-witted, dull

**intelligentsia** /in‚teliˈjen(t)si·ə/ *n taking sing or pl vb* the group of intellectuals who form an artistic, social, or political vanguard or elite [Russ *intelligentsiya*, fr L *intelligentia* intelligence]

**intelligible** /inˈtelijəbl/ *adj* **1** capable of being understood or comprehended **2** able to be apprehended by the intellect only [ME, fr L *intelligibilis*, fr *intelligere*] – **intelligibleness** *n*, **intelligibly** *adv*, **intelligibility** *n*

**intemperance** /inˈtemp(ə)rəns/ *n* lack of moderation, esp in satisfying an appetite or passion; *esp* habitual or excessive drinking of alcohol

**intemperate** /inˈtemp(ə)rət/ *adj* **1** going beyond the bounds of reasonable behaviour; unbridled, immoderate **2** given to excessive use of alcohol [ME *intemperat*, fr L *intemperatus*, fr *in-* ¹*in-* + *temperatus*, pp of *temperare* to temper] – **intemperately** *adv*, **intemperateness** *n*

**intend** /inˈtend/ *vt* **1** to mean, signify **2a** to have in mind as a purpose or goal **b** to design for a specified use or future ⟨*poems* ∼ed *for reading aloud*⟩ ⟨∼ed *as a compliment*⟩ **3** *archaic* to proceed on (a course) ∼ *vi, archaic* to set out; start [ME *intenden, intenden*, fr MF *entendre* to purpose, fr L *intendere* to stretch out, to purpose, fr *in-* ²*in-* + *tendere* to stretch – more at THIN] – **intender** *n*

*usage* One **intends** something *to* happen, or **intends** *that* something should happen, but one cannot correctly **intend** *for* something to happen ⟨⚠ *I didn't* **intend** *for her to hear*⟩.

**intendance** /inˈtend(ə)ns/, **intendancy** /-si/ *n* management, superintendence

**intendant** /inˈtend(ə)nt/ *n* an administrative official (eg a governor), esp under the French, Spanish, or Portuguese monarchies [Fr, fr MF, fr L *intendent-, intendens*, prp of *intendere* to intend, attend]

¹**intended** /inˈtendid/ *adj* **1** planned for the future; proposed, designed **2** intentional – **intendedly** *adv*, **intendedness** *n*

²**intended** *n, informal* one's future spouse ⟨*she was his* ∼⟩

**intending** /inˈtending/ *adj* prospective, aspiring ⟨*an* ∼ *teacher*⟩

**intendment** /inˈtendmənt/ *n* the true meaning or intention, esp of a law

**intenerate** /inˈtenərayt/ *vt, formal* to make tender; soften [²*in-* + L *tener* soft, tender – more at TENDER] – **inteneration** *n*

**intense** /inˈtens/ *adj* **1a** existing or occurring in an extreme degree **b** having or showing a usual characteristic in extreme degree ⟨*an* ∼ *sun shone*⟩ **2** highly concentrated; intensive **3a** feeling emotion deeply, esp by nature or temperament **b** deeply felt; ardent [ME, fr MF, fr L *intensus*, fr pp of *intendere* to stretch out] – **intensely** *adv*, **intenseness** *n*

*synonyms* Both **intense** and **intensive** can mean "highly concentrated" ⟨**intense/intensive** *effort*⟩, but otherwise **intense** means chiefly "extreme" ⟨**intense** *heat*⟩ ⟨**intense** *effort*⟩ while **intensive** extends the idea of "concentration" into its grammatical, medical, and industrial senses.

**intensifier** /inˈtensi‚fie·ə/ *n* one who or that which intensifies; *esp* a linguistic element (eg *very*) that gives force or emphasis

**intensify** /inˈtensi‚fie/ *vt* **1** to make (more) intense; strengthen **2** to increase the density and contrast of (a photographic image) by chemical treatment ∼ *vi* to become (more) intense; grow stronger or more acute – **intensification** *n*

*synonyms* Intensify, aggravate, heighten, and enhance all mean "increase markedly in degree or measure". Intensify suggests a deepening and strengthening, particularly of a characteristic quality ⟨*in the lustrous air all colours were* intensified – Mary Webb⟩. Aggravate suggests making an already serious condition or situation noticeably worse ⟨*the cold air* aggravated *his cough*⟩. Heighten and enhance both imply a lifting above normal levels of effectiveness or enjoyment. Enhance stresses attractiveness and value. heighten suggests poignancy and keenness of feeling ⟨*mature trees* enhance *the beauty of any garden*⟩ ⟨*the presence of her father* heightened *his embarrassment*⟩. Compare ¹INCREASE *antonyms* mitigate, allay, abate, temper

**intension** /inˈtensh(ə)n/ *n* **1** intensity **2** *philosophy* CONNOTATION **3** – **intensional** *adj*, **intensionally** *adv*

**intensity** /inˈtensəti/ *n* **1** the quality or state of being intense; *esp* an extreme degree of strength, force, or energy **2** the magnitude of force or energy per unit (eg of surface, charge, or mass) **3** SATURATION **4** (purity of a colour)

¹**intensive** /inˈtensiv/ *adj* **of** or marked by intensity or intensi-

fication: eg **a** highly concentrated ⟨∼ *study*⟩ **b** *of a grammatical construction* tending to strengthen or increase; being an intensifier **c** of or constituting a method designed to increase productivity by the expenditure of more capital and labour rather than by increase in the land or raw materials used ⟨∼ *farming*⟩ **d** using a specified factor of production to a greater extent than others – usu in combination ⟨*labour*-intensive⟩ ⟨*capital*-intensive⟩ – **intensively** *adv*, **intensiveness** *n*

²**intensive** *n* a linguistic intensifier

**intensive care** *n* the continuous care and treatment of a gravely ill patient, usu in a special section of a hospital ⟨*an* ∼ *unit*⟩

¹**intent** /inˈtent/ *n* **1a** the act or fact of intending; a purpose, intention ⟨∼ *to kill*⟩ **b** the state of mind with which an act is done ⟨*with good* ∼⟩ ⟨*with bad* ∼⟩ **2** an intention to commit a crime ⟨*loitering with* ∼⟩ **3** meaning, significance [ME *entent*, fr OF, fr LL *intentus*, fr L, act of stretching out, fr *intentus*, pp of *intendere*] – **to all intents and purposes** in every practical or important respect; virtually

²**intent** *adj* **1** directed with strained or eager attention; concentrated **2** having the mind, attention, or will concentrated on something or some end or purpose ⟨∼ *on his work*⟩ [L *intentus*, fr pp of *intendere*] – **intently** *adv*, **intentness** *n*

**intention** /inˈtensh(ə)n/ *n* **1** a determination to act in a certain way; a resolve **2** *pl* purpose with respect to proposal of marriage ⟨*are his* ∼s *honourable?*⟩ **3a** what one intends to do or bring about; an aim **b** the object for which a prayer, mass, or pious act is offered **4** *philosophy* a concept; *esp* a concept considered as the product of attention directed to an object of knowledge **5** the purpose or resolve with which a person commits or fails to commit an act, as considered in law **6** *medicine* a natural healing process of a wound, in which the edges grow together **7** *archaic* import, significance

**intentional** /inˈtensh(ə)nl/ *adj* **1** done by intention or design ⟨∼ *damage*⟩ **2a** *philosophy* of conceptual intention **b** pointing or referring to something beyond itself ⟨∼ *consciousness*⟩ *synonyms* see ¹VOLUNTARY *antonyms* instinctive, inadvertent – **intentionally** *adv*, **intentionality** *n*

¹**inter** /inˈtuh/ *vt* **-rr-** to deposit (a dead body) in the earth or in a tomb; bury [ME *enteren*, fr OF *enterrer*, fr (assumed) VL *interrare*, fr *in-* ²*in-* + L *terra* earth – more at TERRACE]

²**inter** /ˈintə/ *n, informal* any of various intermediate university examinations ⟨*swotting for my* ∼⟩ [short for *intermediate*]

**inter-** /intə-/ *prefix* **1** between; among; in the midst ⟨inter*city*⟩ ⟨inter*penetrate*⟩ ⟨inter*stellar*⟩ **2a** reciprocal ⟨inter*relation*⟩ **b** reciprocally ⟨inter*marry*⟩ **3** located between ⟨inter*face*⟩ **4** carried on between ⟨inter*national*⟩ **5** occurring between ⟨inter*glacial*⟩ ⟨inter*lunar*⟩ ☐ compare INTRA- [ME *inter-, enter-*, fr MF & L; MF *inter-, entre-*, fr L *inter-*, fr *inter*; akin to OHG *untar* between, among, Gk *enteron* intestine, OE *in* in]

**interabang** /inˈterə‚bang/ *n* INTERROBANG (punctuation mark)

**interact** /‚intəˈrakt/ *vi* to act upon each other; act reciprocally – **interactant** *n*, **interaction** *n*

**interactive** /‚intəˈraktiv/ *adj* characterized by interaction; *specif* characterized by the exchange of information between a computer and user while a program is being run

**inter alia** /‚intə ˈrayli·ə/ *adv* among other things [L]

**inter alios** /‚intə ˈrayliohs/ *adv* among other people [L]

**interatomic** /‚intərəˈtomik/ *adj* existing or acting between atoms

**interbrain** /ˈintə‚brayn/ *n* DIENCEPHALON (part of the brain)

**interbreed** /‚intəˈbreed/ *vb* **interbred** /-ˈbred/ *vi* to breed together: eg **a** to crossbreed **b** to breed within a closed population ∼ *vt* to cause to breed together

**intercalary** /inˈtuhkəl(ə)ri/ *adj* **1a** inserted in a calendar to resynchronize it with some objective time-measure (eg the solar year) ⟨*an* ∼ *day*⟩ **b** *of a year* containing an intercalary period **2** inserted between other elements or layers; interpolated [L *intercalarius*, fr *intercalare*]

**intercalate** /inˈtuhkə‚layt/ *vt* **1** to insert (eg a day) in a calendar **2** to insert between or among existing periods, elements, or layers ⟨*modern languages students spending an* ∼d *year abroad*⟩ [L *intercalatus*, pp of *intercalare*, fr *inter-* + *calare* to call, summon – more at LOW] – **intercalation** *n*

**intercede** /‚intəˈseed/ *vi* to intervene between parties with a view to reconciling differences; beg or plead on behalf of another ⟨*she it was who* ∼d *for the old woman with her uncle* – Hilaire Belloc⟩ [L *intercedere*, fr *inter-* + *cedere* to go – more at CEDE] – **interceder** *n*

**intercellular** /‚intəˈselyoolə/ *adj* occurring between cells ⟨∼ *spaces*⟩ – **intercellularly** *adv*

**¹intercept** /ˌintəˈsept/ *vt* **1** to stop, seize, or interrupt in progress, course, or movement, esp from one place to another **2** to intersect **3** to gain possession of (an opponent's pass, e g in soccer) **4** *obs* to prevent, hinder **5** *obs* to interrupt communication or connection with [L *interceptus*, pp of *intercipere*, fr *inter-* + *capere* to take, seize – more at HEAVE]

**²intercept** /ˈintəsept/ *n* **1** *maths* the distance from the zero point (ORIGIN) on a graph to another point where the graph crosses one of the axes **2** an interception; *esp* the interception of a missile by an interceptor or of a target by a missile

**interception** /ˌintəˈsepsh(ə)n/ *n* something that is intercepted; *esp* an intercepted pass (e g in soccer)

**interceptor, intercepter** /ˌintəˌseptə/ *n* one who or that which intercepts; *specif* a high-speed fast-climbing fighter plane or missile designed for defence against raiding bombers or missiles

**intercession** /ˌintəˈsesh(ə)n/ *n* the act of interceding (e g with God) esp by prayer, petition, or entreaty [MF or L; MF, fr L *intercession-, intercessio*, fr *intercessus*, pp of *intercedere*] – **intercessional** *adj*, **intercessor** *n*, **intercessory** *adj*

**¹interchange** /ˌintəˈchaynj/ *vt* **1** to put each of (two things) in the place of the other **2** EXCHANGE **3** ~ *vi* to change places reciprocally [ME *entrechaungen*, fr MF *entrechangier*, fr OF, fr *entre-* inter- + *changier* to change] – **interchangeable** *adj*, **interchangeableness** *n*, **interchangeably** *adv*, **interchangeability** *n*, **interchanger** *n*

**²interchange** /ˈintəchaynj/ *n* **1** (an) interchanging; (an) exchange **2** a (motorway) junction of two or more roads by a system of separate levels that permit traffic to pass from one to another without the crossing of traffic streams

**intercity** /ˌintəˈsiti/ *adj* **1** existing or travelling (fast) between cities **2** of, involving, or being an express train that operates between large towns – **intercity** *n*

**interclavicle** /ˌintəˈklavikl/ *n* a bone lying in front of the STERNUM (breastbone) and between the CLAVICLES (collarbones) (e g in a reptile) – **interclavicular** *adj*

**intercollegiate** /ˌintəkəˈleeji·ət/ *adj* between colleges ⟨~ *athletics*⟩

**intercolumniation** /ˌintəkəˌlumniˈaysh(ə)n/ *n, building* **1** the clear space between the columns of a series **2** the system of spacing of the columns in a structure [L *intercolumnium* space between two columns, fr *inter-* + *columna* column]

**intercom** /ˈintəˌkom/ *n* a local communication system (e g in a ship or building) with a microphone and loudspeaker at each station [short for *intercommunication (system)*]

**intercommunicate** /ˌintəkəˈmyoohnikayt/ *vi* to communicate with each other: e g **a** to hold conversation; exchange information **b** to have free passage from one to another ⟨*the rooms* ~⟩ – **intercommunication** *n*

**intercommunion** /ˌintəkəˈmyoohnyən/ *n* the practice between denominations of the Christian faith of admitting one another's members to Communion

**interconnect** /ˌintəkəˈnekt/ *vt* to connect with each other ~ *vi* to be or become connected with one another – **interconnection** *n*

**intercontinental** /ˌintəˌkontiˈnentl/ *adj* extending among continents or carried on, travelling, or capable of travelling between continents ⟨~ *ballistic missile*⟩

**interconversion** /ˌintəkənˈvuhsh(ə)n/ *n* mutual conversion ⟨~ *of chemical compounds*⟩ – **interconvert** *vt*, **interconvertible** *adj*, **interconvertibility** *n*

**intercostal** /ˌintəˈkostl/ *adj* situated between the ribs; *also* of an intercostal part [NL *intercostalis*, fr L *inter-* + *costa* rib] – **intercostal** *n*, **intercostally** *adv*

**intercourse** /ˈintəˌkaws/ *n* **1** connection or dealings between people or groups **2** exchange, esp of thoughts or feelings; communion **3** physical sexual contact between individuals that involves the genitals of at least one person ⟨*heterosexual* ~⟩ ⟨*anal* ~⟩ ⟨*oral* ~⟩; *esp* SEXUAL INTERCOURSE 1 [ME *intercurse, entercourse*, fr MF & ML; MF *entrecours*, fr ML *intercursus*, fr L, act of running between, fr *intercursus*, pp of *intercurrere* to run between, fr *inter-* + *currere* to run – more at CURRENT]

**intercrop** /ˈintəˌkrop/ *vb* **-pp-** *vt* to grow a crop in between rows, plots, etc of (another crop) ~ *vi* to grow two or more crops simultaneously (e g in alternate rows) on the same plot – **intercrop** *n*

**¹intercross** /ˌintəˈkros/ *vb* to crossbreed

**²intercross** /ˈintəˌkros/ *n* (a product of) crossbreeding

**intercrystalline** /ˌintəˈkristlˌien/ *adj* occurring between crystals

**intercurrent** /ˌintəˈkurənt/ *adj* occurring in the midst of another process; intervening; *specif* occurring during the course of another disease ⟨*died of an* ~ *infection*⟩ [L *intercurrent-, intercurrens*, prp of *intercurrere*] – **intercurrently** *adv*

**intercut** /ˌintəˈkut/ *vb* **-tt-**; **intercut** *vt* **1** to insert a contrasting camera shot into (a film sequence) by cutting; *broadly* to insert contrasting matter into **2** to insert (a contrasting camera shot) into a film sequence by cutting; *broadly* to insert (contrasting matter) into a narrative ~ *vi* to alternate contrasting matter by cutting

**interdenominational** /ˌintədiˌnomiˈnaysh(ə)nl/ *adj* occurring between or involving different (Christian) denominations – **interdenominationalism** *n*

**interdental** /ˌintəˈdentl/ *adj* **1** situated or intended for use between the teeth **2** *of a consonant* formed with the tip of the tongue between the upper and lower front teeth ⟨~ th *in* think *and that*⟩ – **interdentally** *adv*

**interdepartmental** /ˌintəˌdeepahtˈmentl/ *adj* carried on between or involving different departments (e g of a firm or an educational institution) ⟨*strong* ~ *rivalry*⟩ – **interdepartmentally** *adv*

**interdepend** /ˌintədiˈpend/ *vi* to depend upon each other – **interdependence, interdependency** *n*, **interdependent** *adj*

**¹interdict** /ˈintəˌdikt, -ˌdiet/ *n* **1** a Roman Catholic disciplinary measure withdrawing most sacraments and Christian burial from a person or district **2** *law* a prohibitory decree; a prohibition [ME *entredit*, fr OF, fr L *interdictum* prohibition, fr neut of *interdictus*, pp of *interdicere* to interpose, forbid, fr *inter-* + *dicere* to say – more at DICTION]

**²interdict** /ˌintəˈdikt/ *vt* **1** to forbid in a usu formal or authoritative manner, esp by an interdict **2** to destroy, cut, or damage (e g an enemy line of supply) by firepower to stop or hamper an enemy – **interdictive** *adj*, **interdictor** *n*, **interdiction** *n*, **interdictory** *adj*

**interdiffuse** /ˌintədiˈfyoohz/ *vi* to diffuse and mix freely so as to become a uniform mixture – **interdiffusion** *n*

**interdigitate** /ˌintəˈdijitayt/ *vi* to be interlocked like the fingers of folded hands ⟨*retinal ganglion cells* . . . ~ *with neighbouring ones* – *Nature*⟩ [*inter-* + L *digitus* finger – more at TOE] – **interdigitation** *n*

**interdisciplinary** /ˌintəˈdisiplinəri/ *adj* involving two or more fields of study

**¹interest** /ˈint(ə)rest, -rəst/ *n* **1a(1)** a right, title, or legal share in something **a(2)** participation in advantage and responsibility **b** a business in which one has an interest **2** benefit, ADVANTAGE 2; *specif* self-interest ⟨*always acting in their own* ~⟩ ⟨*it is to your* ~ *to speak first*⟩ **3a** a charge for borrowed money that is generally a percentage of the amount borrowed **b** something added above what is due **4** a group financially interested in an industry or enterprise **5a** readiness to be concerned with, moved by, or have one's attention attracted by something; curiosity ⟨*takes a great* ~ *in politics*⟩ **b** the quality in a thing that arouses interest ⟨*sport doesn't hold much* ~ *for me*⟩; *also* something one finds interesting ⟨*has many* ~s⟩ [ME, prob alter. of earlier *interesse*, fr AF & ML; AF, fr ML, fr L, to be between, make a difference, concern, fr *inter-* + *esse* to be – more at IS] – **declare an interest** to disclose a personal connection, esp financial, with a subject under discussion (e g in Parliament)

**²interest** *vt* **1** to induce or persuade to participate or engage, esp in an enterprise **2** to concern or engage (somebody, esp oneself) in an activity or cause – usu + *in* **3** to engage the attention or arouse the interest of

**interested** /ˈint(ə)restid, ˈintrəstid/ *adj* **1** having the interest aroused or attention engaged ⟨~ *listeners*⟩ **2** affected or involved; not impartial ⟨~ *parties*⟩ – compare DISINTERESTED – **interestedly** *adv*

**interest group** *n taking sing or pl vb* a group of people having a common identifying interest; *esp* an organized social group whose defence of a particular interest provides a basis for action – compare PRESSURE GROUP

**interesting** /ˈint(ə)resting, ˈintrəsting/ *adj* holding the attention; arousing interest – **interestingly** *adv*

**¹interface** /ˈintəˌfays/ *n* **1** a surface forming a common boundary of two bodies, spaces, or phases ⟨*an oil-water* ~⟩ **2a** the place at which (diverse) independent systems meet and act on or communicate with each other ⟨*the man-machine* ~⟩; *broadly* an area in which diverse things interact **b** the means by which interaction or communication is effected at an interface (e g by an electrical circuit or electronic component connecting computers) – **interfacial** *adj*

**usage** The modern use of **interface** in an abstract sense to mean "common frontier" ⟨*the* **interface** *between literary studies and social history*⟩ is disliked by some people as jargon.

²**interface** /ˌintəˈfays/ *vt* **1** to apply interfacing to **2** to connect by means of an interface ⟨∼ *a machine with a computer*⟩ **3** to serve as an interface for ∼ *vi* **1** to become interfaced **2** to serve as an interface

**interfacing** /ˈintəˌfaysing/ *n* stiffening material attached (e g by sewing) between two layers of fabric in a garment, esp in the lapels and collar

**interfaith** /ˌintəˈfayth/ *adj* involving people of different religious faiths

**interfascicular** /ˌintəfəˈsikyoolə/ *adj* situated between FASCICLES (clusters of branches, leaves, etc)

**interfere** /ˌintəˈfiə/ *vi* **1** to get in the way of, hinder, or impede another; come into collision or be in opposition – + *with* ⟨*noise* ∼*s with my work*⟩ **2** to enter into or take a part unwelcomely in matters that do not concern one ⟨∼ *between husband and wife*⟩ **3** of waves to act reciprocally so as to augment, diminish, or otherwise affect one another **4** to claim priority for an invention in patent law **5** to hinder illegally an attempt by a player to catch or hit a ball or puck – usu + *with* **6** *euph* to assault somebody sexually – usu + *with* [MF (*s'*)*entreferir* to strike one another, fr OF, fr *entre*- inter- + *ferir* to strike, fr L *ferire* – more at BORE] – **interferer** *n*

**interference** /ˌintəˈfiərəns/ *n* **1** something that interferes; an obstruction **2** the mutual effect of the meeting of two WAVE TRAINS (succession of equal waves) (e g of light or sound) of the same type in which the resulting neutralization at some points and reinforcement at others produces in the case of light waves alternate bright and dark bands and in that of sound waves silence, increased intensity, or beats **3** the illegal hindering of an opponent in hockey, ice hockey, etc **4a** the confusion of received radio signals by unwanted signals or atmospherics **b** something that produces such a confusion – **interferential** *adj*

**interferogram** /ˌintəˈfiərəgram/ *n* a photographic record made by an apparatus for recording optical interference phenomena

**interferometer** /ˌintəfəˈromitə/ *n* an instrument that uses light interference phenomena for precise measurements (e g of wavelength, fine structure of spectra, or distance) [ISV] – **interferometry** *n*, **interferometric** *adj*, **interferometrically** *adv*

**interferon** /ˌintəˈfiəron/ *n* a small soluble protein that inhibits the action of a virus and is produced by cells in response to invasion by a virus or sometimes another intracellular parasite (e g a brucella), or experimentally to the action of certain chemicals [*interfer*ence + -*on*]

**interfertile** /ˌintəˈfuhtiel/ *adj* capable of interbreeding – **interfertility** *n*

**interfile** /ˌintəˈfiel/ *vt* ³FILE 1; *esp* to put (e g an ordered set of documents) into an existing file ∼ *vi* ³FILE; *also* to fit in with an existing file

**interfuse** /-ˈfyoohz/ *vt* **1** to combine by fusing; blend, mix **2** INFUSE 1a ∼ *vi* to blend, mix, or mingle together [L *interfusus*, pp of *interfundere* to pour between, fr *inter*- + *fundere* to pour – more at FOUND] – **interfusion** *n*

**intergalactic** /ˌintəgəˈlaktik/ *adj* situated or occurring (in the spaces) between galaxies

**intergenerational** /ˌintəˌjenəˈraysh(ə)nl/ *adj* existing or occurring between (the members of) two or more generations ⟨∼ *marriage – The Economist*⟩ – **intergenerationally** *adv*

**intergenic** /ˌintəˈjenik/ *adj* involving two genes or their activities; *esp* involving the action of one gene on another ⟨∼ *suppression*⟩

¹**interglacial** /ˌintəˈglaysiəl/ *adj* occurring or formed between two periods of glacial activity when much of the earth was covered by ice sheets

²**interglacial** *n* an interglacial period of relatively mild climate marked by a temporary retreat or shrinking of the ice

**intergovernmental** /ˌintəˌguvənˈment(ə)l/ *adj* existing or occurring between two or more governments or levels of government

¹**intergrade** /-ˈgrayd/ *vi* to merge gradually one with another through a continuous series of intermediate forms – **intergradation** *n*, **intergradational** *adj*

²**intergrade** /ˈintəˌgrayd/ *n* an intermediate or transitional form

**intergrowth** /-ˌgrohth/ *n* (the product of) a growing between or together

¹**interim** /ˈintərim/ *n* an intervening time; INTERVAL 1a ⟨*in the* ∼⟩ [L, adv, meanwhile, fr *inter* between – more at INTER-]

²**interim** *adj* designed or occurring for an interim; temporary, provisional

**interionic** /ˌintəieˈonik/ *adj* situated, existing, or acting between IONS (atoms or groups of atoms having electrical charge) ⟨∼ *distance*⟩

¹**interior** /inˈtiəri-ə/ *adj* **1** lying, occurring, or functioning within the limits or interior; INNER 1a **2** away or remote from the border or shore; inland **3** of the inner constitution or concealed nature of something ⟨∼ *meaning of a poem*⟩ **4** INNER 2 ⟨*a simple* ∼ *piety*⟩ □ compare EXTERIOR [MF & L; MF, fr L, compar of (assumed) OL *interus* inward, on the inside; akin to L *inter*] – **interiorly** *adv*, **interiority** *n*

²**interior** *n* **1** the internal or inner part of a thing; *also* the inland **2** the internal affairs of a country ⟨*the minister of the* ∼⟩ **3** a representation of the interior of a building

**interior angle** *n* **1** an angle contained within any two adjacent sides of a square, triangle, or other figure whose sides are straight lines **2** any of the angles contained within two parallel lines and an intersecting line

**interior decoration** *n* (the art or practice of planning and supervising) the decorating and furnishing of interiors of buildings or rooms – **interior decorator** *n*

**interior design** *n* interior decoration – **interior designer** *n*

**interior·ize, -ise** /inˈtiəriəˌriez/ *vt* to make interior; *esp* to make into a part of one's own inner being or personality ⟨*women interiorizing a culturally suggested inferiority*⟩ – **interiorization** *n*

**interior monologue** *n* a literary device in which a character's sequence of thought and feeling is presented in the form of a speech

**in·terior-'sprung** *adj* having (coil) springs within a padded casing ⟨∼ *mattress*⟩

**interject** /ˌintəˈjekt/ *vt* to throw in (e g a comment) abruptly among or between other things [L *interjectus*, pp of *intericere*, fr *inter*- + *jacere* to throw – more at JET] – **interjector** *n*, **interjectory** *adj*

**interjection** /-ˈjeksh(ə)n/ *n* **1a** the act of interjecting or exclaiming; ejaculation **b** something (e g a remark) interjected or interrupting **2a** an ejaculatory word (e g *Wonderful!*) or utterance (e g *ah!* or *good heavens!*); an exclamation **b** a cry or inarticulate utterance (e g *ouch!*) expressing an emotion – **interjectional** *adj*, **interjectionally** *adv*

**interlace** /-ˈlays/ *vt* **1** to unite (as if) by lacing together; interweave **2** to mingle, blend, intersperse ⟨*narrative* ∼d *with anecdotes*⟩ ∼ *vi* to cross one another intricately; intertwine [ME *entrelacen*, fr MF *entrelacer*, fr OF *entrelacier*, fr *entre*- inter- + *lacier* to lace] – **interlacement** *n*

**interlaminate** /ˌintəˈlamiˌnayt/ *vt* **1** to insert between layers or thin plates **2** to arrange in alternate layers or thin plates ⟨∼d *clay and quartz*⟩ – **interlamination** *n*

**interlard** /-ˈlahd/ *vt* to intersperse, esp *with* something foreign or irrelevant ⟨*text* ∼ed *with photographs*⟩ [MF *entrelarder*, fr OF, fr *entre* inter-+ *larder* to lard, fr *lard*, n]

**interleading** /ˌintəˈleeding/ *adj*, *SAfr* adjoining ⟨*large lounge with* ∼ *sun lounge – The Cape Times (Cape Town)*⟩

¹**interleaf** /ˌintəˈleef/ *vt* to interleave

²**interleaf** /ˈintəˌleef/ *n* **1** a usu blank leaf inserted between two leaves of a book (e g for protecting colour plates) **2** SLIP SHEET (paper inserted between two newly printed sheets)

**interleave** /-ˈleev/ *vt* **1** to provide with interleaves **2** to insert between layers or leaves **3** to arrange (as if) in alternate layers or leaves

**interlibrary** /ˌintəˈliebrəri/ *adj* taking place between libraries ⟨*an* ∼ *loan*⟩

¹**interline** /ˌintəˈlien/ *vt* to insert between written or printed lines [ME *enterlinen*, fr ML *interlineare*, fr L *inter*- + *linea* line] – **interlineation** *n*

²**interline** *vt* to provide (a garment) with an interlining [ME *interlinen*, fr *inter*- + *linen* to line]

**interlinear** /-ˈlini-ə/ *adj* **1** inserted between written or printed lines ⟨∼ *gloss*⟩ **2** written or printed in different languages or texts in alternate lines [ME *interliniare*, fr ML *interlinearis*, fr L *inter*- + *linea* line] – **interlinearly** *adv*

**interlingua** /ˌintəˈling-gwə/ *n* an artificial international language largely based on Latin elements in the chief European languages [It, fr *inter*- + *lingua* language, tongue, fr L – more at TONGUE]

**interlining** /-ˌliening/ *n* (fabric used to make) a lining (e g of a coat) sewn between the ordinary lining and the outside fabric to give additional warmth or bulk

**interlink** /,intə'lingk/ *vt* to link together – **interlink** *n*

**¹interlock** /-'lok/ *vi* to become engaged, interrelated, or interlaced with one another ⟨~ing *fingers*⟩ ~ *vt* 1 to lock together; unite 2 to connect so that motion of any part is constrained by another; *esp* to arrange the connections of (railway signals and points) to ensure movement in proper sequence – **interlocker** *n*

**²interlock** /'intə,lok/ *n* something interlocked; *specif* a fabric knitted with interlocking stitches – **interlock** *adj*

**interlocution** /,intəlo'kyoohsh(ə)n/ *n* dialogue, conversation [L *interlocution-, interlocutio*, fr *interlocutus*, pp of *interloqui* to speak between, fr *inter-* + *loqui* to speak]

**interlocutor** /-'lokyootə/, *fem* **interlocutress** /-tris/, **interlocutrice** /-tris/, **interlocutrix** /-triks/ *n* 1 one who takes part in dialogue with another 2 a judgment or order of a court – used in Scots Law [(2) ML *interlocutorium*, fr neut of *interlocutorius* provisional, fr LL *interlocutus*, pp of *interloqui* to pronounce a provisional sentence, fr L, to speak between]

**interlocutory** /-'lokyoot(ə)ri/ *adj* 1 (consisting) of dialogue ⟨~ *observations*⟩ 2 pronounced during a legal action and having only partial, provisional, or interim force ⟨~ *decree*⟩

**interlope** /,intə'lohp/ *vi* 1 to encroach on the rights (e g in trade) of others 2 to intrude, interfere [prob back-formation fr *interloper*, fr *inter-* + *-loper* (akin to MD *lopen* to run, OE *hlēapan* to leap) – more at LEAP] – **interloper** *n*

**interlude** /-,loohd/ *n* 1 a light or farcical entertainment presented between the acts of a medieval play (MYSTERY PLAY, MORALITY PLAY) at a festival 2 an intervening or interruptive period, space, or event, esp of a contrasting character; an interval ⟨*darkness with* ~s *of light*⟩ ⟨*brief* ~ *of sanity*⟩ 3 a musical composition inserted between the parts of a longer composition, a drama, or a religious service [ME *enterlude*, fr ML *interludium*, fr L *inter-* + *ludus* play – more at LUDICROUS]

**interlunar** /,intə'l(y)oohnə/ *also* **interlunary** /-n(ə)ri/ *adj* of the interval between old and new moon when the moon is invisible [deriv of L *interlunium* interlunary period, fr *inter-* + *luna* moon – more at LUNAR]

**intermarriage** /-'marij/ *n* 1 marriage between members of different groups (e g families or tribes) 2 marriage within a specific group as required by custom or law

**intermarry** /-'mari/ *vi* 1 to marry each other or somebody from the same group 2 to become connected by marriage with another group or with each other ⟨*the different races* ~ *freely*⟩

**intermeddle** /,intə'medl/ *vi* to meddle impertinently and officiously [ME *entermedlen*, fr MF *entremedler*, fr OF, fr *entre-* *inter-* + *medler* to mix – more at MEDDLE] – **intermeddler** *n*

**intermediacy** /,intə'meediəsi/ *n* 1 the act of intermediating 2 the quality of being intermediate; intermediateness

**¹intermediary** /,intə'meedyəri/ *adj* 1 intermediate 2 acting as a mediator

**²intermediary** *n* somebody or something acting as a mediator or go-between

**¹intermediate** /,intə'meedi,ayt/ *vi* to act as an intermediary; mediate, intervene [ML *intermediatus*, pp of *intermediare*, fr L *inter-* + LL *mediare* to mediate] – **intermediation** *n*

**²intermediate** /,intə'meedi-ət/ *adj* being or occurring at or near the middle place, stage, or degree or between two others or extremes [ML *intermediatus*, fr L *intermedius*, fr *inter-* + *medius* mid, middle – more at MID] – **intermediately** *adv*, **intermediateness** *n*

**³intermediate** /,intə'meedi-ət/ *n* 1 an intermediary 2 a chemical compound formed as an intermediate step between the starting material and the final product in a chemical reaction or process involving a series of reactions 3 a US motor car that is larger than a compact but smaller than full-size

**intermediate host** *n* an animal or plant (HOST) in or on which a parasite lives for part of its LIFE CYCLE but which is not the host in which the parasite becomes a sexually mature adult

**intermedin** /,intə'meedin/ *n* MELANOCYTE-STIMULATING HORMONE (hormone stimulating the darkening of skin)

**interment** /in'tuhmənt/ *n* burial △ internment [ME *enterment*, fr MF *enterrement*, fr OF, fr *enterrer* to inter]

**intermezzo** /,intə'metsoh/ *n, pl* **intermezzi** /-see/, **intermezzos** 1 a short light entertainment (e g a dance) coming between the acts of a play or an opera 2a a movement coming between the major sections of an extended musical work (e g an opera) b a short independent instrumental composition [It, deriv of L *intermedius* intermediate]

**interminable** /in'tuhminəbl/ *adj* having or seeming to have no end; *esp* wearisomely long ⟨*an* ~ *sermon*⟩ [ME, fr LL *interminabilis*, fr L *in-* ¹in- + *terminare* to terminate] – **interminableness** *n*, **interminably** *adv*, **interminability** *n*

**intermingle** /-'ming·gl/ *vb* to mix or mingle together or with something else

**intermission** /-'mish(ə)n/ *n* 1 intermitting or being intermitted 2 an intervening period of time (e g between attacks of a disease) 3 *chiefly NAm* INTERVAL 3 [L *intermission-, intermissio*, fr *intermissus*, pp of *intermittere*]

**intermit** /-'mit/ *vb* **-tt-** *formal vt* to cause to cease for a time or at intervals; discontinue ⟨*never* ~ted *his habit of smoking*⟩ ~ *vi* to be intermittent; stop for a time [L *intermittere*, fr *inter-* + *mittere* to send] – **intermitter** *n*

**intermittent** /-'mit(ə)nt/ *adj* coming and going at intervals; not continuous ⟨~ *rain*⟩ *synonyms* see PERIODIC *antonyms* continuous, incessant [L *intermittent-, intermittens*, prp of *intermittere*] – **intermittence** *n*, **intermittently** *adv*

**intermix** /,intə'miks/ *vb* to intermingle [back-formation fr obs *intermixt* intermingled, fr L *intermixtus*, pp of *intermiscēre* to intermix, fr *inter-* + *miscēre* to mix] – **intermixture** *n*

**intermolecular** /-mə'lekyoolə/ *adj* situated, existing, or acting between molecules

**intermundane** /,intə'mundayn, ,intəmun'dayn/ *adj* existing between worlds

**¹intern, interne** /in'tuhn/ *adj, archaic* internal [MF *interne*, fr L *internus*]

**²intern** /in'tuhn/ *vt* to confine or impound, esp during a war ⟨~ *enemy aliens*⟩ [Fr *interner*, fr *interne*, adj] – **internment** *n*

**³intern, interne** /'intuhn/ *n, NAm* an advanced student or graduate, usu in a professional field (e g medicine or teaching), gaining supervised practical experience (e g in a hospital or classroom) [Fr *interne*, fr *interne*, adj] – **internship** *n*

**⁴intern** /'intuhn/ *vi, NAm* to act as an intern

**¹internal** /in'tuhnl/ *adj* **1a** existing or situated within the limits or surface of something **b(1)** *anatomy* situated within the body ⟨*an* ~ *organ*⟩ **b(2)** situated on or towards the inner side or the side towards the centre of an organism or one of its parts ⟨*an* ~ *layer of muscle*⟩ ⟨~ *phloem*⟩ **2** taken inside the body (e g by being swallowed) ⟨*an* ~ *remedy*⟩ **3** of or existing within the mind ⟨~ *doubts*⟩ **4** depending only upon the properties of the thing under consideration, without reference to things outside it ⟨~ *evidence of forgery in a document*⟩ **5** present or arising within an organism or one of its parts ⟨*an* ~ *stimulus*⟩ ⟨*an* ~ *disorder*⟩ **6** existing or operating only within a state ⟨~ *strife*⟩ ⟨~ *affairs*⟩ ⟨*Linjeflyg, the Swedish* ~ *airline* – *Flight International*⟩ [L *internus*; akin to L *inter* between] – **internally** *adv*, **internality** *n*

**²internal** *n* a medical examination of the vagina, uterus, or adjacent structures – not used technically

**internal-combustion engine** *n* a HEAT ENGINE (engine that converts heat into mechanical energy) in which the combustion that generates the heat takes place inside the engine itself (e g in a cylinder) instead of in a furnace outside it

**internal degree** *n* a degree taken in the normal manner by attending the university that awards it – compare EXTERNAL DEGREE

**internal examiner** *n* an examiner who is on the staff of the institution whose candidates he/she examines

**internal-ize, -ise** /in'tuhnl·,iez/ *vt* to make internal; *specif* to incorporate (e g learnt values or patterns of behaviour) within the self as conscious or subconscious guiding principles – **internalization** *n*

**internal respiration** *n* exchange of gases between the cells of the body and the blood – compare EXTERNAL RESPIRATION

**Internal Revenue** *n* the government department responsible for collecting taxes in the USA

**internal rhyme** *n* rhyme between a word within a line and another either at the end of the same line or nearby within another line

**internal secretion** *n* a hormone; *specif* one secreted into the blood of an animal

**¹international** /-'nash(ə)nl/ *adj* **1** affecting, involving, or having members in two or more nations ⟨~ *trade*⟩ ⟨~ *movement*⟩ **2** known, recognized, or renowned in more than one country ⟨*an* ~ *celebrity*⟩ – **internationally** *n*, **internationality** *n*

**²international** *n* **1** (one who competes in) a sports, games, etc match between two national teams ⟨*was an England* ~⟩ **2** *also* **internationale** *often cap* an organized group that transcends national limits; *esp* any of several socialist or communist organizations of international scope [(2) Fr *internationale*, fr fem of *international*, adj, fr E]

**international date line** *n often cap I, D, & L* an arbitrary line approximately along the 180th MERIDIAN (line of longitude), east and west of which the date differs by one calendar day

**internationalism** /-,iz(ə)m/ *n* **1** international character, interests, or outlook **2** (an attitude favouring) a policy of cooperation among nations, esp of the development of close international political and economic relations – **internationalist** *n or adj*

**international·ize, -ise** /-,iez/ *vb* to make or become international; *esp* to place under international control – **internationalization** *n*

**international law** *n* a body of rules accepted as governing the relations between nations

**International Phonetic Alphabet** *n* an alphabet designed to represent each human speech sound with a unique symbol – called also IPA

**international relations** *n taking sing vb* a branch of POLITICAL SCIENCE concerned with relations between nations and primarily with foreign policies

**international style** *n* functional architectural design employing modern materials and avoiding regional and traditional influences

**international unit** *n* a quantity of a biological substance (e g a vitamin or hormone) that produces a standard internationally agreed biological effect

**interne** /'intuhn/ *n* INTERN (advanced student)

**internecine** /,intə'neesien, -'nesien/ *adj* **1** mutually destructive **2** of or involving conflict within a group ⟨*bitter* ∼ *feuds*⟩ [L *internecinus* murderous, deadly, fr *internecare* to destroy entirely, exterminate, fr *inter-* + *necare* to kill, fr *nec-, nex* violent death – more at NOXIOUS]

    *usage* **1** The Latin word from which internecine comes has no suggestion of conflict "within a group" ⟨*an* internecine *trades union dispute*⟩ but that is the chief meaning of the word today. **2** The pronunciation /,intə'neesien/ is recommended for BBC broadcasters.

**internee** /,intuh'nee/ *n* an interned person

**interneuron** /,intə'nyooəron/, **interneurone** /-rohn/ *n* an internuncial NERVE CELL – **interneuronal** *adj*

**internist** /in'tuhnist, '---/ *n, NAm* a doctor who specializes in the esp nonsurgical treatment of internal diseases and disorders

**internode** /-,nohd/ *n* **1** the part of a plant stem between two NODES (points from which leaves or side branches grow) **2** the part of a nerve fibre between two NODES OF RANVIER (constrictions in the sheath covering some nerve fibres) [L *internodium*, fr *inter-* + *nodus* knot] – **internodal** *adj*

**internuclear** /-'nyoohkli·ə/ *adj* situated, existing, or occurring between the nuclei of atoms or of cells

**internuncial** /-'nunshl/ *adj* **1** of an internuncio **2** serving to link NERVE CELLS that convey impulses to the brain and SPINAL CORD and those that carry them from there to a muscle, gland, etc – **internuncially** *adv*

**internuncio** /,intə'nunshi,oh/ *n* a papal ambassador (LEGATE) of lower rank than a NUNCIO [It *internunzio*, fr L *internuntius, internuncius* conveyor of messages, go-between, fr *inter-* + *nuntius, nuncius* messenger]

**interoceptive** /-roh'septiv/ *adj* of or being stimuli arising within the body, esp in the heart, lungs, intestines, or similar body organs [*inter-* (as in *interior*) + *-o-* + *-ceptive* (as in *receptive*)]

**interoceptor** /,intəroh'septə/ *n* a specialized structure or nerve ending that responds to and transmits interoceptive stimuli

**interpellate** /in'tuhpilayt/ *vt* to question (e g a government minister) formally concerning an action or policy △ interpolate [L *interpellatus*, pp of *interpellare* to interrupt, fr *inter-* + *-pellare* (fr *pellere* to drive)] – **interpellator** *n*, **interpellation** *n*

**interpenetrate** /,intə'penitrayt/ *vt* to penetrate thoroughly ∼ *vi* to penetrate mutually – **interpenetration** *n*

**interpersonal** /,intə'puhs(ə)nl/ *adj* of, being, or involving relations between people – compare INTRAPERSONAL – **interpersonally** *adv*

**interphase** /-,fayz/ *n* the interval between the end of one division of a cell and the beginning of another in the process of CELL DIVISION (splitting of a cell to form two or four new cells)

**interplanetary** /-'planit(ə)ri/ *adj* existing, carried on, or taking place between planets ⟨∼ *space*⟩

**interplant** /,intə'plahnt/ *vt* to plant a crop between (plants of another kind); *also* to set out young trees among (existing vegetation)

**interplay** /-,play/ *n* interaction – **interplay** *vi*

**interplead** /,intə'pleed/ *vi* to go to law with each other in order to determine which is the rightful claimant against a THIRD PARTY [AF *enterpleder*, fr *enter-* inter- + *pleder* to plead, fr OF *plaidier* – more at PLEAD]

**interpleader** /,intə'pleedə/ *n* a legal proceeding by which two parties making the same claim against a THIRD PARTY are compelled to determine between themselves which is the rightful claimant [AF *enterpleder*, fr *enterpleder*, vb]

**Interpol** /-,pol/ *n* an international police organization that provides liaison between national police forces [*Inter*national *pol*ice (orig the telegraphic address of the International Criminal Police Commission)]

**interpolate** /in'tuhpəlayt/ *vt* **1** to alter or corrupt (e g a text) by inserting new or foreign matter **2** to insert between other things or parts; *esp* to insert (words) into a text or conversation **3** to estimate values that lie between two known values of (a curve or other mathematical function) – compare EXTRAPOLATE **1** ∼ *vi* to make insertions or interruptions [L *interpolatus*, pp of *interpolare* to refurbish, alter, corrupt, fr *inter-* + *-polare* (fr *polire* to polish)] – **interpolator** *n*, **interpolative** *adj*, **interpolation** *n*

**interpose** /,intə'pohz/ *vt* **1** to place between two things or in an intervening position ⟨*tending to* ∼ *objects of worship between God and man* – W R Inge⟩ **2** to put forth by way of interference or intervention ⟨*prevented a decision by* interposing *a veto*⟩ **3** to introduce (words) as an interruption during a conversation or argument ∼ *vi* **1** to be or come in an intervening position **2** INTERVENE 3 **3** to interrupt [MF *interposer*, fr L *interponere* (perf indic *interposui*), fr *inter-* + *ponere* to put – more at POSITION] – **interposer** *n*

**interposition** /,intəpə'zish(ə)n/ *n* **1** the act of interposing **2** something interposed

**interpret** /in'tuhprit/ *vt* **1** to expound the meaning of; present in understandable terms ⟨∼ *a dream*⟩ **2** to conceive of in the light of one's beliefs, judgments, or circumstances; construe ⟨*the Trojan horse was* ∼ed *as a friendly gift*⟩ **3** to represent by means of art; bring (e g a score or script) to realization by performance ⟨∼s *a role*⟩ ∼ *vi* to act as an interpreter [ME *interpreten*, fr MF & L; MF *interpreter*, fr L *interpretari*, fr *interpret-, interpres* agent, negotiator, interpreter] – **interpretable** *adj*, **interpretability** *n*, **interpretive, interpretative** *adj*, **interpretively, interpretatively** *adv*

**interpretation** /in,tuhpri'taysh(ə)n/ *n* **1** the act or result of interpreting ⟨∼ *of a law*⟩ ⟨*Freudian* ∼ *of nightmares*⟩ **2** an instance of artistic interpretation in performance or adaptation ⟨*famous for her* ∼s *of several dramatic roles*⟩ – **interpretational** *adj*

**interpreter** /in'tuhpritə/ *n* **1** one who or that which interprets; *esp* one who translates orally for people speaking in different languages **2** a computer program (e g one for use with a system in which the computer gives an immediate response to a user) that translates an instruction into a form directly usable by a computer for immediate execution of that instruction

**interpretive semantics** /in'tuhpritiv/ *n taking sing vb* the theory that sentences are related to their meanings by a system of rules separate from those concerned with syntax

**interracial** /,intə'raysh(ə)l/ *adj* of, involving, or designed for members of different races

**interred** /in'tuhd/ *past of* INTER

**interregnum** /,intə'regnəm/ *n, pl* **interregnums, interregna** /-'regnə/ **1** the time during which **1a** a throne is vacant between two successive reigns **b** the normal functions of government are suspended **2** a lapse or pause in a continuous series [L, fr *inter-* + *regnum* reign – more at REIGN]

**interrelate** /-ri'layt/ *vb* to bring into or be in a relationship where each one depends upon or is acting upon the other – **interrelation** *n*, **interrelationship** *n*

**interreligious** /,intəri'lijəs/ *adj* existing between or involving (members of) different religions

**interring** /in'tuhring/ *pres part of* INTER

**interrobang** *also* **interabang** /in'terə,bang/ *n* a punctuation mark ‽ designed for use esp at the end of an exclamatory rhetorical question [*interro*gation mark + *bang* (printers' slang for exclamation mark)]

**interrogate** /in'terəgayt/ *vt* **1** to question formally and systematically, esp with intense pressure, so as to extract information ⟨∼d *the prisoners*⟩ 2 to give or send out a signal to (e g a computer) to trigger an appropriate response [L *interrogatus*, pp of *interrogare*, fr *inter-* + *rogare* to ask – more at RIGHT] – **interrogation** *n*, **interrogational** *adj*

**interrogation mark** *n* QUESTION MARK

¹**interrogative** /ˌintəˈrogətiv/ *adj* **1a** of or constituting the grammatical distinction of form (²MOOD 2) that expresses a question **b** used in a question **2** inquisitive, questioning – **interrogatively** *adv*

²**interrogative** *n* **1** an interrogative utterance; a question **2** a word or particle used in asking questions **3** the interrogative MOOD (distinction of form) of a language

**interrogator** /inˈterəˌgaytə/ *n* **1** one who interrogates **2** a radio device containing a transmitter and receiver which sends out a signal to trigger a TRANSPONDER (type of radio or radar set) and which receives and displays the reply

¹**interrogatory** /ˌintəˈrogət(ə)ri/ *n* a formal question or inquiry; *esp* a written question to be answered on oath on the order of a court

²**interrogatory** *adj* interrogative

¹**interrupt** /ˌintəˈrupt/ *vt* **1** to break the flow or action of (e g a speaker or speech) **2** to break the uniformity or continuity of ⟨*blue skies suddenly* ∼ed *by storm clouds*⟩ ∼ *vi* to interrupt an action; *esp* to interrupt another's utterance with one's own [ME *interrupten*, fr L *interruptus*, pp of *interrumpere*, fr *inter-* + *rumpere* to break – more at BEREAVE] – **interruptible** *adj*, **interruption** *n*, **interruptive** *adv*

²**interrupt** *n* (a circuit that conveys) a signal to a computer to halt a program and begin processing data from another source

**interrupter** /ˌintəˈruptə/ *n* one who or that which interrupts; *esp* an automatic device for periodically interrupting or breaking an electric current

**inter se** /ˌintə ˈsay/ *adv or adj* among or between themselves [L]

**intersect** /-ˈsekt/ *vt* to pierce or divide (e g a line or area) by passing through or across; cross ∼ *vi* **1** to meet and cross at a point **2** OVERLAP 2 [L *intersectus*, pp of *intersecare*, fr *inter-* + *secare* to cut – more at SAW]

**intersection** /ˈintəˌseksh(ə)n, ˌ--ˈ--/ *n* **1** the act or process of intersecting **2** a place where two or more things (e g streets) intersect **3** the set of elements common to two or more mathematical sets; *also* the set of points common to two geometric configurations – compare UNION 2d

**intersegmental** /ˌintəˈsegmentl/ *adj* existing or arising between the segments of an organism (e g a worm or insect)

**intersex** /-ˌseks/ *n* (the condition of being) an intersexual individual [ISV]

**intersexual** /-ˈseksyoʊəl, -sh(ə)l/ *adj* **1** existing between the sexes ⟨∼ *hostility*⟩ **2** intermediate in sexual characteristics between a typical male and a typical female [ISV] – **intersexually** *adv*, **intersexuality** *n*

¹**interspace** /ˈintəˌspays/ *n* an intervening space; an interval

²**interspace** /ˌintəˈspays/ *vt* **1** to separate (e g printed letters) by spaces **2** to occupy or fill the space between

**interspecies** /-ˈspeeshiz/ *adj* interspecific

**interspecific** /-spəˈsifik/ *adj* existing or arising between different species ⟨∼ *hybrid*⟩

**intersperse** /-ˈspuhs/ *vt* **1** to insert at intervals among other things; scatter ⟨∼d *drawings throughout the text*⟩ **2** to diversify or vary with things scattered at intervals ⟨∼d *the text with drawings*⟩ [L *interspersus* interspersed, fr *inter-* + *sparsus*, pp of *spargere* to scatter – more at SPARK] – **interspersion** *n*

**interstadial** /ˌintəˈstaydiəl/ *n* INTERGLACIAL; *esp* a subdivision within a stage of glacial activity, that is marked by a temporary retreat of the ice and is typically shorter or less marked than an interglacial [ISV *inter-* + NL *stadium* stage, phase] – **interstadial** *adj*

¹**interstate** /-ˈstayt/ *adj* of, connecting, or existing between two or more states, esp of the USA or of Australia ⟨*an* ∼ *highway*⟩

²**interstate** *adv, Austr* from the state one is in to another ⟨*wanted a car, $2000, cartridges, and a girl to go* ∼ – *The Sun* (*Melbourne*)⟩

**interstellar** /-ˈstelə/ *adj* existing, carried on, or taking place among or between the stars

**intersterile** /ˌintəˈsteriel/ *adj* incapable of producing offspring by interbreeding – **intersterility** *n*

**interstice** /inˈtuhstis/ *n* a small intervening space esp between closely placed things; a chink, crevice [Fr, fr LL *interstitium*, fr L *interstitus*, pp of *intersistere* to stand still in

the middle, fr *inter-* + *sistere* to come to a stand; akin to L *stare* to stand]

**interstitial** /ˌintəˈstishl/ *adj* **1** of, having, or situated in interstices **2a** *of a cell or tissue* situated within but not restricted to or characteristic of the cells of a particular organ or tissue – used esp of fibrous tissue **b** affecting the interstitial cells or tissues of an organ or part **3a** of or being a crystalline compound in which (small) atoms or IONS (atoms having an electrical charge) of a nonmetal occupy holes between the larger metal atoms or ions in the crystal **b** of or occupying a hole in an interstitial compound ⟨*an* ∼ *atom*⟩ – **interstitially** *adv*

**interstitial-cell-stimulating hormone** *n* LUTEINIZING HORMONE; *specif* luteinizing hormone when produced in males, causing increased production of SEX HORMONES and stimulating sperm formation

**interstratify** /ˌintəˈstratiˌfie/ *vt* to insert between other strata ⟨*lava flow* interstratified *with sedimentary rock*⟩ – **interstratification** *n*

**intersubjective** /ˌintəsubˈjektiv/ *adj* accessible to or occurring between two or more conscious minds ⟨∼ *reality*⟩ ⟨∼ *communication*⟩ – **intersubjectively** *adv*, **intersubjectivity** *n*

**intertestamental** /ˌintətestəˈment(ə)l/ *adj* of or forming the period of two centuries between the composition of the last book of the OLD TESTAMENT and the first book of the NEW TESTAMENT

**intertidal** /-ˈtiedl/ *adj* of or being the part of a seashore between the high and low watermarks – **intertidally** *adv*

**intertropical** /ˌintəˈtropik(ə)l/ *adj* (of or being regions) situated between or within the tropics

**intertwine** /ˌintəˈtwien/ *vt* to unite or join together by twining ∼ *vi* to twine about one another – **intertwinement** *n*

**intertwist** /ˌintəˈtwist/ *vb* to intertwine – **intertwist** *n*

**interurban** /ˌintəˈuhbən/ *adj* connecting or between cities or towns

**interval** /ˈintəv(ə)l/ *n* **1** an intervening space: e g **1a** a time between events or states; a pause **b** a distance or gap between objects, units, or states ⟨*lamp posts placed at regular* ∼s⟩ **c** the difference in pitch between two musical notes **2** a set of REAL NUMBERS between two numbers, that either includes or excludes one or both of them; *also* the set of real numbers greater or less than and including or excluding a real number **3** *Br* a break in the presentation of an entertainment (e g a play); an intermission [ME *intervalle*, fr MF, fr L *intervallum* space between ramparts, interval, fr *inter-* + *vallum* rampart – more at WALL]

**intervalometer** /ˌintəvəˈlomitə/ *n* a device that operates a control (e g for a camera shutter) at regular intervals

**intervene** /-ˈveen/ *vi* **1** to enter or appear as something irrelevant or extraneous ⟨*unforeseeable events always* ∼ ⟩ **2** to occur, fall, lie, or come between two things, esp points of time or events ⟨*intervening years*⟩ **3** to come in or between so as to hinder or modify ⟨∼ *to settle a quarrel*⟩ **4a** to enter a lawsuit as a THIRD PARTY in order to protect an alleged interest **b** to interfere usu by force or threat of force in another nation's internal affairs, esp to compel or prevent an action or to maintain or alter a condition **5** to interfere in the economic processes of the market, esp in order to affect the price of a commodity ⟨*the Bank of England* ∼d *to stabilize the pound*⟩ [L *intervenire* to come between, fr *inter-* + *venire* to come – more at COME] – **intervenor** *n*, **intervention** *n*

**intervention** /ˌintəˈvensh(ə)n/ *adj, of a commodity* purchased from the producer by the European economic community at the point at which the market price falls to a specified level ⟨∼ *butter*⟩

**interventionism** /-ˌiz(ə)m/ *n* the theory or practice of intervening; *specif* governmental intervention in economic affairs at home or in political affairs of another country – **interventionist** *n or adj*

**intervertebral** /ˌintəˈvuhtibrəl/ *adj* situated between vertebrae of the backbone – **intervertebrally** *adv*

**intervertebral disc** /ˌintəˈvuhtibrəl/ *n* any of the discs of tough elastic material that are situated between adjoining vertebrae in the backbone and help to cushion the vertebrae against shock

**interview** /-vyooh/ *n* **1** a formal usu face-to-face meeting or consultation usu to evaluate qualifications (e g of a prospective student or employee) **2a** a meeting at which information is obtained (e g by a reporter) from somebody **b** a report or reproduction of information so obtained [MF *entrevue*, fr (*s'*)*entrevoir* to see one another, meet, fr *entre-* inter- + *voir* to see – more at VIEW] – **interview** *vb*, **interviewer** *n*, **interviewee** *n*

**inter vivos** /,intə 'veevos/ *adv or adj* between living people; *esp* from one living person to another ⟨~ *gifts*⟩ ⟨*property transferred* ~⟩ [LL]

**intervocalic** /,intəvoh'kalik/ *adj, of a speech sound* immediately preceded and immediately followed by a vowel ⟨~ "*r*"⟩

**interwar** /,intə'waw/ *adj* occurring or falling between wars, esp World Wars I and II ⟨*the* ~ *years*⟩

**interweave** /-'weev/ *vb* **interwove** /-'wohv/ *also* **interweaved; interwoven** /-'wohv(ə)n/ *also* **interweaved** *vt* **1** to weave together **2** to intermingle, blend ⟨*we can never get divorced, because the financial arrangements between us are too* interwoven – Ian Smith⟩ ~ *vi* to intertwine, intermingle – **interwoven** *adj*, **interweave** *n*

**intestacy** /in'testəsi/ *n* the quality or state of being or dying intestate

**¹intestate** /in'testayt, -tət/ *adj* **1** having made no valid will ⟨*he died* ~⟩ **2** not disposed of by will ⟨*an* ~ *estate*⟩ [ME, fr L *intestatus*, fr in-¹in- + *testatus* testate]

**²intestate** *n* a person who dies intestate

**intestinal** /in'testinl, in,tes'tien(ə)l/ *adj* **1** of, being, or affecting the intestine **2** occurring or living in the intestine ⟨~ *flora*⟩ ⟨~ *bacteria*⟩ – **intestinally** *adv*

**¹intestine** /in'testin/ *adj* internal, domestic; *specif* of the internal affairs of a state or country ⟨~ *war*⟩ [MF or L; MF *intestin*, fr L *intestinus*, fr *intus* within – more at ENT-]

**²intestine** *n* the tubular part of the digestive tract that extends from the stomach to the anus – compare LARGE INTESTINE, SMALL INTESTINE [MF *intestin*, fr L *intestinum*, fr neut of *intestinus*]

**intima** /'intimə/ *n, pl* **intimae** /'inti,mee/, **intimas** the innermost lining coat of a blood vessel, body organ, etc [NL, fr L, fem of *intimus*]

**intimacy** /'intiməsi/ *n* **1** the state of being intimate; familiarity **2** *euph* SEXUAL INTERCOURSE

**¹intimate** /'intimayt/ *vt* to make known: e g **a** to announce **b** to hint, imply *synonyms* see SUGGEST [LL *intimatus*, pp of *intimare* to put in, announce, fr L *intimus* innermost, superl of (assumed) OL *interus* inward – more at INTERIOR] – **intimater** *n*, **intimation** *n*

**²intimate** /'intimət/ *adj* **1a** intrinsic, essential **b** belonging to or characterizing one's deepest nature ⟨*shared his* ~ *reflections*⟩ **2** marked by very close association, contact, or familiarity ⟨~ *knowledge of the law*⟩ **3a** marked by a warm friendship developing through long association ⟨*on* ~ *terms with his neighbours*⟩ **b** suggesting informal warmth or privacy ⟨*a very* ~ *atmosphere*⟩ **4** of a very personal or private nature ⟨*an* ~ *diary*⟩ **5** *euph* involved in a sexual relationship; *specif* engaging in an act of sexual intercourse ⟨*in six months they were* ~ *six times in the car and twice on a mountainside – News of the World*⟩ [alter. of obs *intime*, fr L *intimus*] – **intimately** *adv*, **intimateness** *n*

**³intimate** *n* a close friend or confidant

**intimidate** /in'timidayt/ *vt* to frighten; *esp* to compel or deter (as if) by threats *synonyms* see THREATEN [ML *intimidatus*, pp of *intimidare*, fr L in-²in- + *timidus* timid] – **intimidator** *n*, **intimidatory** *adj*, **intimidation** *n*

**intimism** /'intimizm/ *n, often cap* a style of painting of the early 20th century applying the techniques of IMPRESSIONISM to domestic interiors rather than to landscape ⟨*the* ~ *of Bonnard and Vuillard*⟩ [Fr *intimisme*, fr *intime* intimate, fr L *intimus*]

**intinction** /in'tingksh(ə)n/ *n* the administration of Communion by dipping the bread in the wine and giving both together to the communicant [LL *intinction-, intinctio* immersion, fr L *intinctus*, pp of *intingere* to dip in, fr in- + *tingere* to dip, moisten – more at TINGE]

**intine** /'intin,'intien,'inteen/ *n* the inner layer of the wall of a spore (e g a POLLEN GRAIN) [prob fr Ger, fr L *intus* within + NL in- fibrous tissue, fr Gk *in-, is* tendon]

**intitule** /in'tityoohl/ *vt, Br* to furnish (e g a legislative act) with a title or designation [MF *intituler*, fr LL *intitulare*, fr L in-²in- + *titulus* title]

**into** /'intə *before consonants; otherwise* 'intooh/ *prep* **1a** so as to be inside ⟨*come* ~ *the house*⟩ **b** so as to be ⟨*grow* ~ *a woman*⟩ ⟨*turn* ~ *a frog*⟩ ⟨*divide it* ~ *sections*⟩ ⟨*roll it* ~ *a ball*⟩ **c** so as to be in (a state) ⟨*get* ~ *trouble*⟩ ⟨*scared them* ~ *silence*⟩ **d** so as to be expressed in ⟨*translate it* ~ *French*⟩, dressed in ⟨*changed* ~ *his uniform*⟩, occupied in ⟨*go* ~ *farming*⟩, or a member of ⟨*get* ~ *the team*⟩ ⟨*enter* ~ *an alliance*⟩ – compare COME INTO **e** – used in division as

the inverse of *by* or *divided by* ⟨*divide 35* ~ *70*⟩ **2** – used to indicate a partly elapsed period of time or a partly traversed extent of space ⟨*far* ~ *the night*⟩ ⟨*deep* ~ *the jungle*⟩ **3** in the direction of; *esp* towards the centre of ⟨*look* ~ *the sun*⟩ ⟨*inquire* ~ *the matter*⟩ **4** to a position of contact with; against ⟨*ran* ~ *a wall*⟩ **5** *informal* involved with ⟨*they were* ~ *hard drugs*⟩; *esp* keen on ⟨*are you* ~ *yoga?*⟩ [ME, fr OE *intō*, fr ²in- + *tō* to]

**usage** Into should not be confused with in *to*, where in is an adverb. Compare ⟨*they came* **into** *the house*⟩ ⟨*they came* in *to see me*⟩. See ¹IN

**intolerable** /in'tol(ə)rəbl/ *adj* not tolerable ; unbearable ⟨~ *pain*⟩ [ME, fr L *intolerabilis*, fr in-¹in- + *tolerabilis* tolerable] – **intolerableness** *n*, **intolerably** *adv*, **intolerability** *n*

**intolerance** /in'tolərəns/ *n* **1** the quality or state of being intolerant **2** exceptional sensitivity (e g to a drug or food)

**intolerant** /in'tolərənt/ *adj* **1** unable or unwilling to endure ⟨*a plant* ~ *of direct sunlight*⟩ ⟨~ *of criticism*⟩ **2** unwilling to grant or share social, professional, political, or religious rights; bigoted – **intolerantly** *adv*, **intolerantness** *n*

**intonate** /'intohnayt/ *vt* to intone, utter

**intonation** /,intə'naysh(ə)n/ *n* **1** the act of intoning; esp liturgical chanting **2** something that is intoned; *specif* the opening notes of a GREGORIAN CHANT **3** performance of music with respect to correctness of pitch and harmony **4** the rise and fall in pitch of the voice in speech – **intonational** *adj*

**intonation contour** *n* INTONATION PATTERN

**intonation pattern** *n* a unit of speech melody with particular levels of pitch and at least one peak of prominence (NUCLEUS) that contributes to the total meaning of an utterance ⟨*a falling* ~ *makes "He is" into a statement, a rising one makes it a question*⟩

**intone** /in'tohn/ *vb* to utter (something) in musical or prolonged tones; recite in singing tones or in a monotone [ME *entonen*, fr MF *entoner*, fr ML *intonare*, fr L in-²in- + *tonus* tone] – **intoner** *n*

**in toto** /in 'tohtoh/ *adv* totally, entirely ⟨*accepted the plan* ~⟩

**intoxicant** /in'toksikənt/ *n* something that intoxicates; *esp* an alcoholic drink – **intoxicant** *adj*

**intoxicate** /in'toksikayt/ *vt* **1** to poison – used esp in medicine **2a** to excite or stupefy by the action of alcohol or a drug, esp to the point where physical and mental control is markedly diminished **b** to cause to lose self-control through excitement or elation ⟨~d *with joy*⟩ [ML *intoxicatus*, pp of *intoxicare*, fr L in-²in- + *toxicum* poison – more at TOXIC]

**intoxicated** /in'toksikaytid/ *adj* affected (as if) by alcohol; inebriated – **intoxicatedly** *adv*

**intoxicating** /in'toksikayting/ *adj* causing or producing intoxication ⟨~ *drinks*⟩ ⟨~ *beauty*⟩

**intoxication** /in,toksi'kaysh(ə)n/ *n* the condition of being drunk; inebriation

**intra-** /intrə-/ *prefix* **1a** within; inside ⟨intracontinental⟩ ⟨intrauterine⟩ **b** during (intranatal) **c** between layers of ⟨intradermal⟩ **2** intro- ⟨*an* intramuscular *injection*⟩ □ compare INTER- [LL, fr L *intra*, fr (assumed) OL *interus*, adj, inward – more at INTERIOR]

**intraarterial** /,intraah'tiəriel/ *adj* situated within or entering by way of an artery; *also* used in intraarterial procedures – **intraarterially** *adv*

**intracardiac** /,intrə'cahdi,ak/ *also* **intracardial** /-dial/ *adj* situated, occurring, or performed within the heart ⟨~ *surgery*⟩; *also* used in intracardiac procedures ⟨*an* ~ *catheter*⟩ – **intracardially** *adv*

**intracellular** /,intrə'selyoolə/ *adj* situated, occurring, or functioning within a living cell ⟨~ *enzymes*⟩ – **intracellularly** *adv*

**intracerebral** /,intrə'serəbrəl/ *adj* (affecting or involving structures) within the CEREBRUM of the brain ⟨~ *injections*⟩ – **intracerebrally** *adv*

**intracranial** /-'kraynəl, -ni-əl/ *adj* (affecting or involving structures) within the skull – **intracranially** *adv*

**intractable** /in'traktəbl/ *adj* **1** not easily governed, managed, or directed; OBSTINATE 1 ⟨*an* ~ *child*⟩ **2** not easily manipulated, wrought, or solved ⟨~ *metal*⟩ ⟨*an* ~ *problem*⟩ **3** not easily relieved or cured ⟨~ *pain*⟩ ⟨*an* ~ *disease*⟩ *synonyms* see UNRULY *antonym* tractable [L *intractabilis*, fr in-¹in- + *tractabilis* tractable] – **intractableness** *n*, **intractably** *adv*, **intractability** *n*

**intracutaneous** /,intrəkyooh'tayniəs/ *adj* intradermal – **intracutaneously** *adv*

**intradermal** /ˌintrəˈduhm(ə)l/ *adj* situated, occurring, or done within or between the layers of the skin – **intradermally** *adv*

**intradermal test** *n* a test for immunity or hypersensitivity made by injecting a minute amount of diluted ANTIGEN (substance stimulating the production of antibodies) into the skin

**intrados** /inˈtraydos/ *n, pl* **intrados, intradoses** the underside of an arch – compare EXTRADOS [Fr, fr L *intra* within + Fr *dos* back – more at DOSSIER]

**intragalactic** /ˌintrəgəˈlaktik/ *adj* situated or occurring within the confines of a single galaxy

**intramolecular** /ˌintrəmohˈlekyoohlə/ *adj* existing or acting within the molecule; *also* formed by reaction between different parts of the same molecule [ISV] – **intramolecularly** *adv*

**intramural** /ˌintrəˈmyooərəl/ *adj* **1a** within the limits usu of a community or institution (e g a university) **b** competitive only within the student body ⟨~ *sports*⟩ **2** *anatomy & physiology* situated or occurring within the substance of the walls of an organ – **intramurally** *adv*

**intramuscular** /-ˈmuskyoolə/ *adj* in or going into a muscle [ISV] – **intramuscularly** *adv*

¹**intransigent** /inˈtransij(ə)nt/ *adj* refusing to compromise or to abandon an extreme position or attitude, esp in politics; uncompromising, irreconcilable [Sp *intransigente*, fr *in-* ¹*in-* + *transigente*, prp of *transigir* to compromise, fr L *transigere* to transact – more at TRANSACT] – **intransigence** *n*, **intransigently** *adv*

²**intransigent** *n* an intransigent person

**intransitive** /-ˈtransitiv, -ˈtrahn-, -zitiv/ *adj* not transitive; *esp* not having a direct object ⟨*an* ~ *verb such as "rise"*⟩ [LL *intransitivus*, fr L *in-* ¹*in-* + LL *transitivus* transitive] – **intransitive** *n*, **intransitively** *adv*, **intransitiveness** *n*, **intransitivity** *n*

**intrant** /ˈintrənt/ *n, archaic* an entrant [L *intrant-, intrans*, prp of *intrare* to enter – more at ENTER]

**intranuclear** /ˌintrəˈnyoohkliə/ *adj* situated or occurring within a nucleus ⟨*the* ~ *location of DNA synthesis – Nature*⟩ [ISV]

**intraperitoneal** /ˌintrəˌperitəˈnee(ə)l/ *adj* in or going into the cavity of the abdomen; *also* introduced through the PERITONEUM (lining of the cavity of the abdomen) – **intraperitoneally** *adv*

**intrapersonal** /ˌintrəˈpuhsən(ə)l/ *adj* occurring within the individual mind or self rather than interpersonally

**intraspecies** /ˌintrəˈspeesheez/ *adj* INTRASPECIFIC

**intraspecific** /ˌintrəspəˈsifik/ *adj* occurring within a species or involving members of one species – **intraspecifically** *adv*

**intrastate** /ˌintrəˈstayt/ *adj* (occurring) within a state, esp of the USA ⟨*interstate and* ~ *commerce*⟩

**intrauterine** /-ˈyoohtərin, -rien/ *adj* situated, used, or occurring within the uterus; *also* involving the part of development that takes place in the uterus [ISV]

**intrauterine device, intrauterine contraceptive device** *n* a device (e g a coil or loop of metal or plastic) inserted and left in the uterus to prevent conception

**intravascular** /-ˈvaskyoolə/ *adj* situated or occurring within a vessel, esp a blood vessel ⟨~ *thrombosis*⟩ – **intravascularly** *adv*

**intravenous** /-ˈveenəs/ *adj* (situated or occurring within, or entering the body or blood stream) by way of a vein ⟨*an* ~ *injection*⟩ ⟨~ *feeding*⟩; *also* used in intravenous procedures ⟨*an* ~ *needle*⟩ [ISV] – **intravenously** *adv*

**intravital** /ˌintrəˈviet(ə)l/ *adj* intravitam [ISV] – **intravitally** *adv*

**intravitam** /ˌintrəˈviet(ə)m/ *adj* **1** performed upon or found in a living subject **2** *of a dye used to colour cells, tissues, etc for examination* having the property of staining living cells without killing them – compare SUPRAVITAL [NL *intra vitam* during life]

**intrazonal** /ˌintrəˈzohn(ə)l/ *adj* of or being a soil or class of soils marked by relatively well-developed characteristics that are determined primarily by local factors (e g the parent material) rather than by climate and vegetation – compare AZONAL, ZONAL

**intreat** /inˈtreet/ *vb, archaic* to entreat

**intrench** /inˈtrench/ *vb* to entrench

**intrepid** /inˈtrepid/ *adj* fearless, bold, and resolute ⟨*an* ~ *explorer*⟩ **synonyms** see ¹BRAVE [L *intrepidus*, fr *in-* ¹*in-* + *trepidus* alarmed – more at TREPIDATION] – **intrepidly** *adv*, **intrepidness** *n*, **intrepidity** *n*

**intricacy** /ˈintrikəsi/ *n* **1** the quality of being intricate **2** something intricate ⟨*the intricacies of a plot*⟩

**intricate** /ˈintrikət/ *adj* **1** having many complexly interrelating parts or elements; complicated ⟨*an* ~ *pattern*⟩ **2** difficult to resolve or analyse ⟨~ *puzzles*⟩ **synonyms** see ¹COMPLEX [ME, fr L *intricatus*, pp of *intricare* to entangle, fr *in-* ²*in-* + *tricae* trifles, impediments] – **intricately** *adv*, **intricateness** *n*

**intrigant, intriguant** /ˈintrigont/ *fem* **intrigante, intriguante** /ˌintriˈgont/ *n* one who engages in intrigue; an intriguer [Fr *intrigant*, fr It *intrigante*, prp of *intrigare*]

¹**intrigue** /inˈtreeg/ *vt* **1** to bring or accomplish by intrigue ⟨~ *oneself into office*⟩ **2** to arouse the interest or curiosity of ⟨~d *by the tale*⟩ **3** to captivate; FASCINATE 2 ⟨*her beauty* ~s *me*⟩ ~ *vi* to carry on an intrigue; *esp* to plot, scheme [Fr *intriguer*, fr It *intrigare*, fr L *intricare* to entangle, perplex] – **intriguer** *n*

²**intrigue** /ˈintreeg, -ˈ-/ *n* **1a** a secret scheme; a machination, plot **b** the practice of engaging in or using scheming or underhand plots ⟨*treachery and* ~ *brought him to power*⟩ **2** a clandestine love affair

**intriguing** /inˈtreeging/ *adj* engaging the interest to a marked degree; fascinating ⟨*a thoroughly* ~ *young woman*⟩ – **intriguingly** *adv*

**intrinsic** /inˈtrinzik/ *adj* **1a** belonging to the essential nature or constitution of a thing ⟨*an ornament of no* ~ *worth but of great sentimental value*⟩ **b** of or being a SEMICONDUCTOR (solid that conducts electricity to a limited extent) that has practically no impurities and whose ability to conduct electricity is a property of the material itself rather than the result of any impurities it contains **2** originating or situated within (a part of) the body ⟨~ *asthma*⟩ **antonym** extrinsic [MF *intrinsèque* internal, fr LL *intrinsecus*, fr L, adv, inwardly; akin to L *intra* within – more at INTRA] – **intrinsically** *adv*, **intrinsicalness** *n*

**intrinsical** /inˈtrinsikl/ *adj, archaic* intrinsic

**intrinsically ordered** *adj, of a grammatical rule* applied in an order dictated by the fact that the conditions for the application of one rule come about through the application of another

**intrinsic factor** *n* a protein produced by the lining of the intestines that is required for the absorption of VITAMIN B₁₂ – compare EXTRINSIC FACTOR

**intro** /ˈintroh/ *n, pl* **intros** *informal* INTRODUCTION 1

**intro-** *prefix* **1** in; into ⟨*intro*jection⟩ **2** inwards; within ⟨*intro*vert⟩ – compare EXTRO- [ME, fr MF, fr L, fr *intro* inside, to the inside, fr (assumed) OL *interus*, adj, inward]

**introduce** /ˌintrəˈdyoohs/ *vt* **1** to lead or bring in, esp for the first time ⟨~ *a rare plant species into the country*⟩ **2a** to bring into play ⟨~ *a new line of approach into the argument*⟩ **b** to bring into practice or use; institute ⟨~d *reforms in court practice*⟩ **3** to lead to or make known by a formal act, announcement, or recommendation: e g **3a** to cause to be acquainted; make (oneself or a person) known to another **b** to present formally (e g at court or into society) **c** to present or announce formally or officially or by an official reading ⟨~d *a private bill in Parliament*⟩ **d** to make preliminary explanatory or laudatory remarks about (e g a subject or speaker) **4** PLACE 2a, INSERT 2 ⟨*the risk of* introducing *harmful substances into the body*⟩ **5** to bring to a knowledge or discovery of something ⟨~ *her to the works of Byron*⟩ [L *introducere*, fr *intro-* + *ducere* to lead – more at TOW] – **introducer** *n*

**introduction** /ˌintrəˈduksh(ə)n/ *n* **1** something that introduces: e g **1a(1)** a part of a book, lecture, or treatise preliminary to the main portion ⟨*the long rambling* ~ *dwarfed the text*⟩ **a(2)** a preliminary treatise or course of study ⟨*a two-week* ~ *into philosophy*⟩ **b** a short introductory musical passage **2** introducing or being introduced; *esp* a formal presentation of one person to another **3** something introduced; *specif* a plant or animal new to an area [ME *introduccioun* act of introducing, fr MF *introduction*, fr L *introduction-, introductio*, fr *introductus*, pp of *introducere*]

**introductory** /ˌintrəˈdukt(ə)ri/ *adj* of or being a first step that sets something going or in proper perspective; preliminary ⟨*the speaker's* ~ *remarks established his point of view*⟩ ⟨*an* ~ *course in calculus*⟩ – **introductorily** *adv*

**introgression** /ˌintrəˈgreshən/ *n* the entry or introduction of a gene from the complex of genes of one species into that of another species in crossbreeding [*intro-* + *-gression* (as in *regression*)] – **introgressant** *adj or n*, **introgressive** *adj*

**introit** /ˈintroyt/ *n* **1** *often cap* the ANTIPHON or psalm sung as the priest approaches the altar to celebrate Communion or Mass **2** a piece of music sung or played at the beginning of a service of worship [MF *introite*, fr ML *introitus*, fr L, entrance, fr *introitus*, pp of *introire* to go in, fr *intro-* + *ire* to go – more at ISSUE]

**introject** /ˌintrə'jekt/ *vt* to incorporate (attitudes or ideas) unconsciously into one's personality [*intro-* + *-ject* (as in *project*, vb)] – **introjection** *n*

**intromission** /-'mish(ə)n/ *n* the act or process of intromitting; *esp* the insertion or period of insertion of the penis in the vagina in copulation [Fr, fr MF, fr L *intromissus*, pp of *intromittere*]

**intromit** /-'mit/ *vt* **-tt-** to send or put in; insert [L *intromittere*, fr *intro-* + *mittere* to send] – **intromittent** *adj*, **intromitter** *n*

**introrse** /in'traws/ *adj* turned inwards or towards the axis of growth; *esp* of or being an ANTHER (pollen-containing flower structure) opening towards the centre of the flower – compare EXTRORSE [L *introrsus*, adv, inwards, fr *intro-* + *versus* towards, fr pp of *vertere* to turn – more at WORTH] – **introrsely** *adv*

**introspect** /-'spekt/ *vi* to examine the contents of one's mind (eg thoughts and feelings) reflectively [L *introspectus*, pp of *introspicere* to look inside, fr *intro-* + *specere* to look – more at SPY] – **introspective** *adj*, **introspectively** *adv*, **introspectiveness** *n*, **introspection** *n*

**introspectionism** /ˌintrə'spekshəˌniz(ə)m/ *n* a theory holding that psychology must be based essentially on data derived from introspection – compare BEHAVIOURISM – **introspectionist**, **introspectionistic** *adj*, **introspectionist** *n*

**¹introvert** /-'vuht/ *vt* **1** to turn inwards or in on itself or oneself: eg **1a** to bend inwards; *also* to draw in (a tubular body part) usu by INVAGINATION (process of folding in) **b** to concentrate or direct (the mind, thoughts, or emotions) on oneself ⟨his ∼ed *despair*⟩ **2** to produce psychological introversion in ⟨∼ed *by a childhood trauma*⟩ [*intro-* + *-vert* (as in *divert*)] – **introversion** *n*

**²introvert** /'intrəˌvuht/ *n* **1** something (eg the eyestalk of a snail) that is or can be drawn in **2** one whose attention and interests are directed wholly or predominantly towards his/her own mental life – compare EXTROVERT

**intrude** /in'troohd/ *vi* **1** to thrust oneself in without invitation, permission, or welcome; to enter or come unsuitably **2** to enter as a geological intrusion ∼ *vt* **1** to thrust or force in or upon, esp without permission, welcome, or suitable reason ⟨∼d a *trite moral into his play*⟩ **2** to cause (eg rock) to intrude □ compare OBTRUDE, PROTRUDE [L *intrudere* to thrust in, fr *in-* ²in- + *trudere* to thrust – more at THREAT] – **intruder** *n*

**intrusion** /in'troohzh(ə)n/ *n* **1** intruding or being intruded; *specif* the act of wrongfully entering upon, seizing, or taking possession of the land of another **2a** the flowing or forcible entry of molten rock into cavities in or between other rock formations **b** a body or mass of rock formed by intrusion; an intrusive rock [ME, fr MF, fr ML *intrusion-*, *intrusio*, fr L *intrusus*, pp of *intrudere*]

**intrusive** /in'troohsiv, -ziv/ *adj* **1** characterized by (a tendency to) intrusion **2** *of a rock* formed below the earth's surface by the slow cooling and solidification of rock forced while in a plastic state into cavities or between layers of existing rock; *also* PLUTONIC **3** *linguistics* inserted where there is no corresponding letter in spelling or etymology ⟨∼ /r/ *after "idea" in "the idea of"*⟩ □ compare OBTRUSIVE – **intrusively** *adv*, **intrusiveness** *n*

**intrust** /in'trust/ *vt* to entrust

**intubation** /ˌintyoo'baysh(ə)n/ *n* the introduction of a tube into a hollow organ (eg the windpipe) – **intubate** *vt*

**intuit** /in'tyooh-it/ *vb* to receive knowledge or learn of (something) by intuition – **intuitable** *adj*

**intuition** /ˌintyooh'ish(ə)n/ *n* **1a** (knowledge gained from) immediate apprehension or understanding **b** the power of attaining direct knowledge or understanding without evident rational thought and the drawing of conclusions from evidence available **2** quick and ready insight *synonyms* see ¹REASON [LL *intuition-*, *intuitio* act of contemplating, fr L *intuitus*, pp of *intueri* to look at, contemplate, fr *in-* ²in- + *tueri* to look at] – **intuitional** *adj*

**intuitionism** /ˌintyooh'ishəniz(ə)m/ *n* **1** a doctrine that knowledge rests upon basic truths that can be known intuitively **2** a doctrine that moral values and principles can be discerned intuitively – **intuitionist** *adj or n*

**intuitive** /in'tyooh-itiv/ *adj* **1** of (the nature of) intuition ⟨the ∼ *faculty*⟩ **2** known or perceived by intuition; directly apprehended ⟨had an ∼ *awareness of his sister's feelings*⟩ **3** possessing or given to intuition or insight ⟨an ∼ *mind*⟩ – **intuitively** *adv*, **intuitiveness** *n*

**intumesce** /ˌintyoo'mes/ *vi, of a body organ or part* to enlarge or swell (eg with blood) [L *intumescere* to swell up, fr *in-* ²in- + *tumescere*, incho of *tumēre* to swell – more at THUMB] – **intumescence** *n*, **intumescent** *adj*

**intussusception** /ˌintəsə'sepsh(ə)n/ *n* a drawing or turning in of something from without; *esp* the slipping of a length of intestine into an adjacent portion usu producing obstruction [deriv of L *intus* within + *susceptus*, pp of *suscipere* to take up – more at SUSCEPTIBLE] – **intussuscept** *vb*, **intussusceptive** *adj*

**inulin** /'inyoolin/ *n* a tasteless white carbohydrate found esp dissolved in the sap of the roots and RHIZOMES (underground plant stems) of plants of the daisy family where it functions as an energy store for the plant [prob fr Ger *inulin*, fr L *inula* elecampane]

**inunction** /in'ungksh(ə)n/ *n* an act of applying or anointing with oil or ointment [ME, fr L *inunction-*, *inunctio*, fr *inunctus*, pp of *inunguere* to anoint – more at ANOINT]

**inundate** /'inundayt/ *vt* **1** to cover with a flood; overflow **2** OVERWHELM 1b ⟨∼d *with telephone calls*⟩ [L *inundatus*, pp *inundare*, fr *in-* ²in- + *unda* wave – more at WATER] – **inundator** *n*, **inundatory** *adj*, **inundation** *n*

**inure** /i'nyooə/ *vt* to accustom *to* something undesirable; habituate ⟨∼d *to the smell of greasepaint*⟩ ∼ *vi* to become operative or of use or advantage; *esp* to accrue [ME *enuren*, fr *en-* + *ure*, n, use, custom, fr MF *uevre* work, practice, fr L *opera* work – more at OPERA] – **inurement** *n*

**inurn** /i'nuhn/ *vt* to place (eg cremated remains) in an urn; *broadly* ENTOMB 2

**in utero** /in 'yoohtəroh/ *adv* in the uterus – used chiefly with reference to a foetus before birth [L]

**inutile** /in'yoohtiel/ *adj, formal* useless, unusable [ME, fr MF, fr L *inutilis*, fr *in-* ¹in- + *utilis* useful – more at UTILITY] – **inutility** *n*

**in vacuo** /in 'vakyoo,oh/ *adv* **1** *chemistry & physics* in a vacuum **2** without being related to practical application, relevant facts, etc [NL]

**invade** /in'vayd/ *vt* **1** to enter (eg a country) for hostile purposes **2** to encroach upon; infringe ⟨a noise ∼d *his privacy*⟩ **3a** to spread over or into as if invading; PERMEATE 1 ⟨doubts ∼ *his mind*⟩ **b** to affect injuriously and progressively ⟨gangrene ∼s *healthy tissue*⟩ [ME *invaden*, fr L *invadere*, fr *in-* ²in- + *vadere* to go – more at WADE] – **invader** *n*

**invaginate** /in'vajinayt/ *vb, biology* *vt* **1** to enclose, sheathe **2** to fold or push in so that an outer becomes an inner surface ∼ *vi* to undergo invagination [ML *invaginatus*, pp of *invaginare*, fr L *in-* ¹in- + *vagina* sheath] – **invaginate** *adj*

**invagination** /inˌvaji'naysh(ə)n/ *n* **1** an act or process of invaginating **2** the formation of a GASTRULA (hollow cupshaped form of a developing animal embryo) by an infolding of part of the wall of the BLASTULA (early form of an embryo consisting of a hollow ball of cells) – compare INVOLUTION 3b **3** an invaginated part

**¹invalid** /in'valid/ *adj* **a** without foundation or force in fact, truth, or law; *specif* legally void ⟨his will is technically ∼⟩ **b** logically inconsistent ⟨∼ *arguments were revealed by Socrates*⟩ [L *invalidus* weak, fr *in-* ¹in- + *validus* strong – more at VALID] – **invalidly** *adv*, **invalidness**, **invalidity** *n*

**²invalid** /'invəlid; *also* -ˌleed/ *adj* **1** suffering from disease or disability; ill **2** of or suited to one who is ill ⟨∼ *chair*⟩ [L & Fr; Fr *invalide*, fr L *invalidus*]

**³invalid** /'invəlid/ *n* one who is ill or disabled – **invalidism** *n*

**⁴invalid** /'invəlid, ˌinvə'leed/ *vt* **1** to make ill or disabled **2** to remove from active duty by reason of sickness or disability ⟨he was ∼ed *out of the army*⟩

**invalidate** /in'validayt/ *vt* to make invalid; *esp* to weaken or destroy the convincingness of (eg an argument or claim) *synonyms* see ABROGATE – **invalidator** *n*, **invalidation** *n*

**invaluable** /in'valyooəbl/ *adj* valuable beyond estimation; priceless ['in- + *value*, vb + *-able*] – **invaluableness** *n*, **invaluably** *adv*

> **synonyms** Things that are more **valuable** than can be estimated are **invaluable** or **priceless**; things of no **value** are **valueless** or **worthless**. A thing may be **valued** (= highly esteemed) without being **valuable**, or **valuable** without being **valued**.

**Invar** /in'vah/ *trademark* – used for an iron and nickel alloy having a low degree of expansion when heated

**invariable** /in'veəri-əbl/ *adj* not (capable of) changing; constant – **invariable** *n*, **invariableness** *n*, **invariably** *adv*, **invariability** *n*

**invariant** /-'veəri-ənt/ *adj* constant, unchanging; *specif* unaffected by a particular mathematical operation ⟨~ *under rotation of the coordinate axes*⟩ – **invariant** *n*, **invariance** *n*

**invasion** /in'vayzh(ə)n/ *n* **1** an act of invading; *esp* incursion of an army for conquest or plunder **2** the incoming or spread of something usu harmful [ME *invasioune*, fr MF *invasion*, fr LL *invasion-*, *invasio*, fr L *invasus*, pp of *invadere* to invade]

**invasive** /in'vayziv, -siv/ *adj* **1** of or characterized by military aggression or invasion **2** tending to spread; *esp* tending to invade healthy tissue ⟨~ *cancer cells*⟩ – **invasiveness** *n*

**invective** /in'vektiv/ *n* **1** an abusive attack in words ⟨~s *against sin*⟩ **2** insulting or abusive language; VITUPERATION **1** *synonyms* see ²ABUSE [ME *invectif*, adj, fr MF, fr L *invectivus*, fr *invectus*, pp of *invehere*] – **invective** *adj*, **invectively** *adv*

**inveigh** /in'vay/ *vi* to speak or protest bitterly or vehemently *against*; rail [L *invehi* to attack, inveigh, passive of *invehere* to carry in, fr *in-* ²in- + *vehere* to carry – more at WAY] – **inveigher** *n*

**inveigle** /in'vaygl/ *also* -'veegl/ *vt* to win (something or somebody) over by ingenuity, flattery, or deceit ⟨subtly ~d *him into the trap*⟩ ⟨cleverly ~d *information from her*⟩ [modif of MF *aveugler* to blind, hoodwink, fr OF *avogler*, fr *avogle* blind, fr ML *ab oculis*, lit., lacking eyes] – **inveiglement** *n*, **inveigler** *n*
*usage* The pronunciation /in'vaygl/ is recommended for BBC broadcasters. *Synonyms* see ²LURE

**invent** /in'vent/ *vt* **1** to think up; imagine ⟨~ *a name*⟩ **2** FABRICATE **2** ⟨~ *an excuse*⟩ **3** to produce (eg something useful) for the first time through the use of the imagination or of ingenious thinking and experiment ⟨~ *a new machine*⟩ [ME *inventen* to find, discover, fr L *inventus*, pp of *invenire* to come upon, find, fr *in-* ²in- + *venire* to come – more at COME] – **inventor** *n*, **inventress** *n*
*synonyms* One **invents** something new; one **discovers** something already in existence.

**invention** /in'vensh(ə)n/ *n* **1** productive imagination; inventiveness **2** something invented: eg **2a(1)** a (misleading or fanciful) product of the imagination **a(2)** a device, contrivance, or process originated after study and experiment **b** *music* a short keyboard composition, usu in DOUBLE COUNTERPOINT **3** the act or process of inventing

**inventive** /in'ventiv/ *adj* **1** good at producing inventions; creative **2** characterized by invention – **inventively** *adv*, **inventiveness** *n*

¹**inventory** /'invəntri/ *n* **1a** an itemized list of current assets (eg of the property of an individual or estate) **b** a list of traits, preferences, attitudes, interests, etc used to evaluate personal characteristics or skills **2** the items listed in an inventory **3** *NAm* the quantity of goods, components, or raw materials on hand; STOCK **5b** **4** the taking of an inventory [ML *inventorium*, alter. of LL *inventarium*, fr L *inventus*, pp] – **inventorial** *adj*, **inventorially** *adv*

²**inventory** *vt* to make an inventory of; catalogue

**inverness** /,invə'nes/ *n* a loose belted coat having a cape with a closely-fitting round collar [*Inverness*, town in Scotland]

¹**inverse** /in'vuhs, '--/ *adj* **1** opposite in order, direction, nature, or effect ⟨~ *snobbery*⟩ **2** *maths* **2a** being or relating to an INVERSE FUNCTION ⟨*an ~ sine*⟩ **b** having or being a relationship between two quantities (eg the pressure and volume of a gas) in which one quantity increases in the same proportion as the other decreases [L *inversus*, fr pp of *invertere*] – **inversely** *adv*

²**inverse** *n* **1** a direct opposite; a reverse **2** the result of an inversion; *specif, philosophy* a proposition obtained by negating the subject term of another logical proposition **3a(1) inverse function, inverse** a mathematical function (eg the operation of squaring a number) that exactly reverses the effect of another given function (eg the operation of taking the SQUARE ROOT of a number) **a(2)** a mathematical operation that exactly reverses another ⟨*division and multiplication are* ~s⟩ **b** a number, quantity, or other element of a mathematical set that is related to another element of the set in such a way that the result of applying a given operation to them is an IDENTITY ELEMENT of the set

**inversion** /in'vuhsh(ə)n/ *n* **1** the act or process of inverting **2** a reversal of position, order, form, or relationship: eg **2a(1)** *linguistics* a change in normal word order; *esp* the placing of a verb before its subject **a(2)** *music* the process or result of changing, converting, or reversing the relative positions of the elements of a musical interval, chord, or phrase (eg by repeating a phrase with its intervals in the contrary order) **b** (the abnormal condition of a body organ or part of) being turned inwards or inside out ⟨~ *of the foot*⟩ ⟨~ *of the uterus*⟩ **c** *genetics* a breaking off of a

section of a CHROMOSOME (strand of gene-carrying material) and its subsequent reattachment in inverted position resulting in a reversal of the order of the genes carried on this section; *also* a section of a chromosome that has undergone this process **3** the operation in mathematics of forming the inverse of a quantity, operation, or element **4** homosexuality **5** *chemistry* a conversion of a substance showing DEXTROROTATION into one showing LAEVOROTATION or vice versa ⟨~ *of sucrose*⟩ **6** *electronics* the conversion of DIRECT CURRENT (eg from a battery) into ALTERNATING CURRENT **7** a reversal of the normal TEMPERATURE GRADIENT of the atmosphere so that warm air overlies a layer of cooler air – **inversive** *adj*

¹**invert** /in'vuht/ *vt* **1a** to turn inside out or upside down **b** to turn (eg a body organ or part) inwards **2** to reverse in position, order, or relationship; subject to inversion: eg **2a** to subject to musical inversion **b** to subject to chemical inversion **c** to subject to mathematical inversion [L *invertere*, fr *in-* ²in- + *vertere* to turn – more at WORTH] – **invertible** *adj*

²**invert** /'invuht/ *n* something or somebody characterized by inversion; *esp* a homosexual

³**invert** /in'vuht/ *adj* subjected to chemical inversion

**invertase** /in'vuhtayz, -tays/ *n* an enzyme capable of breaking down SUCROSE (ordinary commercially available sugar) into INVERT SUGAR [ISV]

**invertebrate** /in'vuhtibrət, -brayt/ *adj* **1a** *of an animal* lacking a backbone **b** of invertebrate animals **2** lacking in strength, vitality, character; weak, spineless [NL *invertebratus*, fr L *in-* ¹in- + NL *vertebratus* vertebrate] – **invertebrate** *n*

**inverted comma** *n* **1** a comma in type printed upside down at the top of the line **2** either of a pair of punctuation marks " " or ' ' that in English are typically used to indicate the beginning and end of a quotation in which the exact phraseology of a person or text is directly quoted – sometimes used to disclaim responsibility for an expression ⟨*using the term "natural death" in* ~s – Philip Toynbee⟩

**inverted pleat** *n* a pleat made by forming two folded edges which are secured to face each other on the right side of the fabric – compare BOX PLEAT

**inverter** /in'vuhtə/ *n* **1** one who or that which inverts **2** a device for converting DIRECT CURRENT (eg from a battery) into ALTERNATING CURRENT by mechanical or electronic means

**invert sugar** *n* a mixture of the sugars glucose and fructose that occurs naturally in fruits and is produced artificially by the breakdown of SUCROSE (ordinary commercially available sugar); *also* glucose obtained from the breakdown of starch

¹**invest** /in'vest/ *vt* **1** to confer (the symbols of) authority, office, or rank on **2** to clothe, cover, or surround completely (as if) with something ⟨~ed *with an air of mystery*⟩ ⟨~ed *himself with a raincoat*⟩ **3** to surround with troops or ships so as to prevent escape or entry; besiege **4** to endow with a quality or characteristic; INFUSE **1a** ⟨*events* ~ed *with significance*⟩ [L *investire* to clothe, surround, fr *in-* ²in- + *vestis* garment – more at WEAR; (1) ML *investire*, fr L, to clothe; (3) MF *investir*, fr OIt *investire*, fr L, to surround]

²**invest** *vt* **1** to commit (money) to a particular use (eg buying shares or new capital outlay) in order to earn a financial return ⟨*the company* ~ed *one million pounds in a new factory*⟩ **2** to devote or commit (eg time or effort) to something for future benefit ⟨~ *his talents well*⟩ ~ *vi* to make an investment ⟨~ *in a new car*⟩ [It *investire* to clothe, invest money, fr L, to clothe] – **investable** *adj*, **investor** *n*

**investigate** /in'vestigayt/ *vb* **1** to make a systematic examination or study (of) **2** to conduct an official inquiry (into) [L *investigatus*, pp of *investigare* to track, investigate, fr *in-* ²in- + *vestigium* footprint, track (cf VESTIGE)] – **investigative** *adj*, **investigator** *n*, **investigatory** *adj*, **investigation** *n*, **investigational** *adj*

**investiture** /in'vestichə/ *n* the act of investing somebody (eg with authority or a quality); *esp* a formal ceremony conferring an office or honour on somebody [ME, fr ML *investitura*, fr *investitus*, pp of *investire*]

¹**investment** /in'vestmənt/ *n* **1** *biology* an outer layer or envelope covering an organism, body part, etc **2** an investiture **3** a blockade, siege **4** *archaic* VESTMENT **1** [¹ *invest*]

²**investment** *n* (a sum of) money invested for income or profit; capital outlay; *also* the asset (eg property) purchased ⟨*sell off all* ~s *in South Africa*⟩ [²*invest*]

**investment company** *n* a company whose primary business is to acquire the shares or securities of other companies purely for investment purposes – compare HOLDING COMPANY

**investment trust** *n* an INVESTMENT COMPANY that purchases securities on behalf of its investors – compare UNIT TRUST

**inveteracy** /in'vet(ə)rəsi/ *n* the quality of being obstinate or persistent; tenacity [*inveterate* + *-cy*]

**inveterate** /in'vet(ə)rət/ *adj* **1** firmly and obstinately established by long persistence ⟨*the* ~ *tendency to overlook the obvious*⟩ **2** confirmed in a habit; HABITUAL ⟨*an* ~ *smoker*⟩ [L *inveteratus*, fr pp of *inveterare* to age (vt), fr *in-* ²*in-* + *veter-, vetus* old – more at WETHER] – **inveterately** *adv*

**inviable** /in'vie-əb(ə)l/ *adj* not capable of living or surviving, esp because of abnormal genetic make-up ⟨*many mutants are* ~⟩ [ISV] – **inviability** *n*

**invidious** /in'vidi-əs/ *adj* **1** tending to cause discontent, ill will, or envy **2** of an unpleasant or objectionable nature; of a kind causing or likely to cause harm or resentment ⟨*a most* ~ *comparison*⟩ △ insidious [L *invidiosus* envious, invidious, fr *invidia* envy – more at ENVY] – **invidiously** *adv*, **invidiousness** *n*

**invigilate** /in'vijilayt/ *vb, chiefly Br vi* to supervise students at an examination ~ *vt* to supervise (an examination or those taking it) [L *invigilatus*, pp of *invigilare*, fr *in-* ²*in-* + *vigilare* to keep watch – more at VIGILANT ] – **invigilator** *n*, **invigilation** *n*

**invigorate** /in'vigərayt/ *vt* to give fresh life and energy to; ANIMATE 2 [deriv of L *in-* ²*in* + *vigor* vigour] – **invigoratingly** *adv*, **invigorator** *n*, **invigoration** *n*

**invincible** /in'vinsəbl/ *adj* incapable of being conquered, overcome, or subdued [ME, fr MF, fr LL *invincibilis*, fr L *in-* ¹*in -* + *vincere* to conquer – more at VICTOR] – **invincibleness** *n*, **invincibly** *adv*, **invincibility** *n*

**inviolable** /in'vie-ələbl/ *adj* **1** secure from violation, profanation, or assault ⟨~ *moral principles*⟩ **2** that must not be violated [MF or L; MF, fr L *inviolabilis*, fr *in-* ¹*in-* + *violare* to violate] – **inviolableness** *n*, **inviolably** *adv*, **inviolability** *n*

**inviolacy** /in'vie-ələsi/ *n* the quality of being inviolate

**inviolate** /in'vie-ələt, -,layt/ *adj* not violated or profaned – **inviolately** *adv*, **inviolateness** *n*

**invisible** /in'vizəbl/ *adj* **1a** incapable by nature of being seen **b** inaccessible to view; hidden ⟨*clouds rendered the stars* ~⟩ **2a** not appearing in published financial statements ⟨~ *assets*⟩ **b** not reflected in statistics ⟨~ *earnings*⟩ **c** of or being trade in services (e g insurance or tourism) rather than in goods – compare VISIBLE 4 **3** too small or unobtrusive to be seen or noticed; imperceptible, inconspicuous ⟨*an* ~ *hair net*⟩ ⟨~ *to the human eye*⟩ [ME, fr MF, fr L *invisibilis*, fr *in-* ¹*in-* + *visibilis* visible] – **invisible** *n*, **invisibleness** *n*, **invisibly** *adv*, **invisibility** *n*

**invisible ink** *n* a liquid used for writing communications (e g secret messages) that remains invisible on paper until developed (e g by heating the paper)

**invitation** /,invi'taysh(ə)n/ *n* **1a** the act of inviting **b** an often formal request to be present or participate **2** an incentive, inducement

**invitational** /,invi'taysh(ə)n(ə)l/ *adj* limited to invited participants ⟨*an* ~ *lecture*⟩

¹**invitatory** /in'vietətəri/ *adj* containing an invitation ⟨~ *note*⟩

²**invitatory** *n* an invitatory psalm (e g Psalm 95) or other invitation to prayer

¹**invite** /in'viet/ *vt* **1a** to offer an incentive or inducement to; entice **b** to (unintentionally) increase the likelihood of ⟨*his actions* ~ *trouble*⟩ **2a** to request the presence or participation of **b** to request formally ⟨~ *him to be a member*⟩ **c** to urge politely; WELCOME **3** ⟨*donations are* ~d⟩ [MF or L; MF *inviter*, fr L *invitare*] – **inviter** *n*, **invitee** *n*

²**invite** /'inviet/ *n, informal* an invitation

**inviting** /in'vieting/ *adj* attractive, tempting – **invitingly** *adv*

**in vitro** /in 'veetroh, 'vitroh/ *adv or adj* outside the living body of a plant or animal and in an artificial environment ⟨~ *cultivation of tissues*⟩ [NL, lit., in glass]

**in vivo** /in 'veevoh/ *adv or adj* in the living body of a plant or animal [NL, lit., in the living]

**invocate** /'invə,kayt/ *vt, archaic* to invoke

**invocation** /,invə'kaysh(ə)n/ *n* **1a** the act or process of petitioning for help or support (e g from God or the Muses); supplication; *specif, often cap* an invocatory prayer at the beginning of a religious service **b** a calling upon for authority or justification ⟨*an* ~ *of sound reasons to justify the decision*⟩ **2** a formula for conjuring; an incantation **3** an act of legal or moral implementation; an enforcement ⟨~ *of treaty provisions*⟩ [ME *invocacioun*, fr MF *invocation*, fr L *invocation-,*

*invocatio*, fr *invocatus*, pp of *invocare*] – **invocational** *adj*, **invocatory** *adj*

¹**invoice** /'invoys/ *n* **1** ⁴BILL 3a; *specif* an itemized list of goods shipped, usu specifying the price and the terms of sale **2** a consignment of merchandise [modif of MF *envois*, pl of *envoi* message – more at ¹ENVOY]

²**invoice** *vt* to submit an invoice for or to

**invoke** /in'vohk/ *vt* **1a** to petition (e g a god) for help or support **b** to appeal to or cite as an authority **2** to call forth (e g a spirit) by uttering a spell or magic formula **3** to make an earnest request for; SOLICIT 4 ⟨~d *their forgiveness*⟩ **4** to put into effect or operation; implement ⟨~ *economic sanctions*⟩ **5** to call forth; excite ⟨*adverse conditions* ~ *a new patriotism*⟩ [ME *invoken*, fr MF *invoquer*, fr L *invocare*, fr *in-* ²*in-* + *vocare* to call – more at VOICE] – **invoker** *n*

**involucre** /,invə'loohkə/ *n* a plant structure consisting of one or more WHORLS (circular arrangements) of BRACTS (usu tiny narrow leaflike or spiny parts) situated below and close to a flower, flower cluster, or fruit [Fr, fr NL *involucrum*] – **involucral** *adj*, **involucrate** *adj*, **involucred** *adj*

**involucrum** /,invə'loohkrəm/ *n, pl* **involucra** a surrounding envelope or sheath; *esp* an involucre [NL, sheath, involucre, fr L, sheath, fr *involvere* to wrap]

**involuntary** /in'volənt(ə)ri/ *adj* **1** done contrary to or without choice **2** compulsory ⟨~ *servitude*⟩ **3** not subject to conscious control; reflex ⟨~ *movement*⟩ *synonyms* see SPONTANEOUS [LL *involuntarius*, fr L *in-* ¹*in-* + *voluntarius* voluntary] – **involuntarily** *adv*, **involuntariness** *n*

**involuntary muscle** *n* muscle (e g that lining the digestive tract) not under conscious control

¹**involute** /'invəlooht/ *adj* **1** *biology* **1a(1)** curled spirally **a(2)** *of a shell* having the whorls closely coiled **b** curled or curved inwards; *esp, of a leaf* having the edges rolled over the upper surface towards the centre **2** having the form of an involute **3** involved, intricate [L *involutus* involved, fr pp of *involvere*] – **involutely** *adv*

²**involute** *n* the curve that would be traced by a point on a thread kept taut as it is unwound from another curve (the EVOLUTE)

³**involute** /,invə'looht/ *vi* **1** to become involute **2** *esp of a body organ or part* to return to a former normal condition or size ⟨*after pregnancy the uterus* ~s⟩

**involution** /,invə'loohsh(ə)n/ *n* **1a(1)** the act or an instance of enfolding or entangling; involvement ⟨*his* ~ *in political activities*⟩ **a(2)** an involved grammatical construction usu characterized by the insertion of clauses between subject and predicate **b** complexity, intricacy ⟨*a novel containing much* ~⟩ **2** the act or process of raising a mathematical quantity to a particular power; EXPONENTIATION – compare EVOLUTION 4 **3a** an inward curvature; *also* a part curving inwards **b** the formation of a GASTRULA (hollow cupshaped form of a developing animal embryo) by the ingrowth of some of the cells making up the hollow ball of cells (BLASTULA) that comprises the previous stage in the development of the embryo – compare INVAGINATION 2 **4** a shrinking or return, esp of a body organ or part, to a former normal size ⟨~ *of the uterus after pregnancy*⟩ **5** the regressive alterations or degeneration of a body or its parts characteristic of the aging process [L *involution-, involutio*, fr *involutus*, pp of *involvere*] – **involutional** *adj*, **involutionary** *adj*

**involve** /in'volv/ *vt* **1a** to engage as a participant ⟨*workmen* ~d *in building a house*⟩ **b** to cause to be associated or take part; concern, implicate ⟨*the questionable right of a government to* ~ *the nation in war*⟩ **c** to occupy (e g oneself) absorbingly; *esp* to commit (e g oneself) emotionally ⟨*she became* ~d *with a married man*⟩ **2** to surround as if with a wrapping; envelop ⟨~d *in a massive crowd*⟩ **3** to relate closely; connect ⟨*this problem is closely* ~d *with many others*⟩ **4a** to have within or as part of itself; include **b** to require as a necessary accompaniment; entail **c** to have an effect on; affect ⟨*the decision will* ~ *his future*⟩ **5** *archaic* to wind, coil, or wreathe about; entwine [ME *involven* to roll up, wrap, fr L *involvere*, fr *in-* ²*in-* + *volvere* to roll – more at VOLUBLE] – **involvement** *n*, **involver** *n*

**involved** /in'volvd/ *adj* marked by extreme and often needless complexity; intricate *synonyms* see ¹COMPLEX *antonym* straightforward – **involvedly** *adv*

**invulnerable** /in'vulnərəbl/ *adj* **1** incapable of being wounded, injured, or harmed ⟨~ *fortress*⟩ **2** immune to or proof against attack; impregnable ⟨~ *to criticism*⟩ [L *invulnerabilis*, fr *in-*

# inw

¹in- + *vulnerare* to wound – more at VULNERABLE] – **invulnerableness** *n*, **invulnerably** *adv*, **invulnerability** *n*
  *usage* Since one either is or is not **invulnerable**, some people dislike expressions such as ⟨*render us fairly* **invulnerable**⟩.

¹**inward** /'inwəd/ *adj* 1 situated within or directed towards the inside 2 of the mind or spirit ⟨*struggled to achieve* ~ *peace*⟩ [ME, fr OE *inweard;* akin to OHG *inwert* inward; both fr a prehistoric WGmc compound whose constituents are represented by OE *in* & OE *-weard* -ward]

²**inward** *n* 1 something that is inward 2 *pl* innards

**inward dive** *n* a dive made from a standing position facing away from the water with forward rotation of the body – compare FORWARD DIVE, BACK DIVE, REVERSE DIVE

**inwardly** /-li/ *adv* 1 in the innermost being; mentally, spiritually ⟨*outwardly energetic but* ~ *barren*⟩ 2a beneath the surface; internally ⟨*bled* ~⟩ b to oneself; privately; *specif* so as not to be audible ⟨*cursed* ~⟩ *antonym* outwardly

**inwardness** /'inwoodnis/ *n* 1 close acquaintance; familiarity, intimacy 2 fundamental nature; ESSENCE 1a ⟨*could not grasp the* ~ *of her being*⟩ 3 internal quality or substance 4 absorption in (esp one's own) mental or spiritual life

**inwards** /'inwoodz/, *chiefly NAm* **inward** *adv* 1 towards the inside, centre, or interior 2 towards the inner being *antonym* outwards

**inweave** /in'weev/ *vt* **inwove** *also* **inweaved; inwoven** *also* **inweaved** to interweave, interlace

**in-'wrought** *adj* 1 *of a fabric* decorated with a pattern woven or worked in; *esp* decorated with embroidery 2 *of a pattern* woven or worked in (e g to a fabric)

**inyala** /in'yahlə/ *n, pl* **inyalas**, *esp collectively* **inyala** NYALA (type of antelope) [Zulu *inxala*]

**iod-, iodo-** *comb form* iodine ⟨*iodize*⟩ ⟨*iodoform*⟩ [Fr *iode*]

¹**iodate** /'ie-ə,dayt/ *n* a chemical compound (SALT) formed by combination between IODIC ACID and a metal atom or other chemical group [Fr, fr *iode*]

²**iodate** *vt* to impregnate or treat with iodine; iodize [*iod-* + *-ate*] – **iodation** *n*

**iodic** /ie'odik/ *adj* of or containing iodine, esp with a VALENCY of five [Fr *iodique*, fr *iode*]

**iodic acid** *n* a solid, $HIO_3$, formed from iodine and able to dissolve in water to form an acidic solution

**iodide** /'ie-ə,died/ *n* a compound of iodine with one other chemical element or group; *esp* any of various chemical compounds (SALTS or ESTERS) formed by combination between HYDRIODIC ACID and a metal atom, an alcohol, or another chemical group [ISV]

**iodinate** /ie'odinayt/ *vt* to treat or cause to combine with (a compound of) iodine – **iodination** *n*

**iodine** /'ie-ə,deen/ *n* a nonmetallic chemical element belonging to the group containing chlorine, fluorine, and bromine (HALOGEN group), that is prepared usu as heavy shining blackish-grey crystals and is used, esp in the form of its compounds, in medicine, photography, and chemical analysis [modif of Fr *iode*, fr Gk *iōdēs* violet-coloured, fr *ion* violet; fr the violet vapour it forms when heated]

**iod·ize, -ise** /'ie-ə,diez/ *vt* to treat with iodine or an iodide ⟨~d *salt*⟩

**iodoform** /ie'odə,fawm/ *n* a yellow solid chemical compound, $CHI_3$, with a characteristic penetrating smell, that is a mild disinfectant and has been used as an antiseptic for dressing wounds [ISV *iod-* + *-form* (as in *chloroform*)]

**iodophor** /ie'odə,faw/ *n* a complex of iodine with an organic chemical compound, that releases iodine gradually and is used as a disinfectant [*iod-* + Gk *-phoros* carrier – more at -PHORE]

**iodopsin** /ˌie-ə'dopsin/ *n* a light-sensitive pigment in the CONES (structures that receive light) of the retina of the eye, whose presence is responsible for the perception of colour [Gk *iōdēs* violet-coloured + *opsis* sight, vision + E *-in* – more at OPTIC]

**iodous** /ie'odəs/ *adj* of or containing iodine, esp with a VALENCY of three [ISV]

**ion** /'ie-ən/ *n* 1 an atom or group of atoms that carries a positive or negative electrical charge as a result of having lost or gained one or more ELECTRONS (atomic particles having a single negative electrical charge) – compare ANION, CATION 2 an electron or other electrically charged subatomic particle that is not bound, either chemically or physically, to an atom, ion, etc [Gk, neut of *iōn*, prp of *ienai* to go – more at ISSUE]

**-ion** /-i·ən/ *suffix* (*vb → n*) 1a act or process of ⟨*validation*⟩ b result of (a specified act or process) ⟨*regulation*⟩ 2 quality or condition of ⟨*hydration*⟩ ⟨*ambition*⟩ [ME *-ioun, -ion,* fr OF *-ion,* fr L *-ion-, -io*]
  *synonyms* The suffixes **-ion** and **-ment** are attached to verbs, and the nouns so formed mean either a process or the result of one; the suffix **-ness** is attached to adjectives, and the nouns so formed mean a quality. Compare ⟨*correction*⟩ ⟨*correctness*⟩.

**ion engine** *n* a hypothetical rocket engine that obtains thrust from a stream of ionized particles

**ion exchange** *n* a reversible process in which an ion present in an insoluble solid is interchanged with another ion that has the same electrical charge and is present in a surrounding solution, and which is used esp for softening or demineralizing water, the purification of chemicals, or the separation of substances – **ion-exchanger** *n*

**ionian mode** /ie'ohniən/ *n, often cap* a MODE (fixed arrangement of eight notes) which may be represented on the white keys of the piano on a scale from C to C

**ionic** /ie'onik/ *adj* 1 of, existing as, or characterized by ions ⟨~ *gases*⟩ ⟨*the* ~ *charge*⟩ 2 based on or functioning by means of ions ⟨~ *conduction*⟩ [ISV] – **ionicity** *n*

¹**Ionic** /ie'onik/ *adj* 1 (characteristic) of Ionia or the Ionians 2 of that one of the three Greek orders of architecture that is characterized esp by the scroll-shaped ornament of its CAPITAL (upper part of a column) – compare DORIC 2, CORINTHIAN 2 [L & MF; MF *ionique*, fr L *ionicus*, fr Gk *iōnikos*, fr *Iōnia* Ionia, ancient region of Asia Minor]

²**Ionic** *n* a dialect of ancient Greek used in Ionia, in which is written much important literature

**ionic bond** *n* ELECTROVALENT BOND (chemical bond linking ions having opposite electrical charges)

**ionium** /ie'ohni-əm/ *n* a naturally occurring radioactive form of the chemical element thorium, having a MASS NUMBER (number of protons and neutrons in the nucleus of an atom) of 230 [*ion;* fr its ionizing action]

**ionization chamber** /ˌie-ənie'zaysh(ə)n/ *n* a device (e g in a GEIGER COUNTER) for detecting or measuring radioactivity, that consists of a tube containing gas at low pressure and ELECTRODES (metal wires, plates, etc that conduct an electric current) between which a high voltage is applied. The size of the current that flows between the electrodes is proportional to the degree of ionization of the gas in the tube, which in turn depends on the amount of radioactivity present.

**ion·ize, -ise** /'ie-ə,niez/ *vb* to convert or become converted wholly or partly into ions [ISV] – **ionizable** *adj*, **ionizer** *n*, **ionization** *n*

**ionophore** /ie'onə,faw/ *n* a compound that facilitates the transport of an ION (particle having electrical charge) across a CELL MEMBRANE or similar barrier by temporarily combining with the ion and increasing the permeability of the barrier to it

**ionosphere** /ie'onə,sfiə/ *n* 1 the part of the earth's atmosphere beginning at a height of about 40 kilometres (25 miles) and extending outwards to at least 400 kilometres (250 miles) above the earth, that consists of several regions each having one or more layers that vary in height and degree of ionization. The ionosphere contains electrically charged particles by means of which RADIO WAVES are transmitted to great distances around the earth. 2 a region of electrically charged particles similar to the earth's ionosphere, surrounding a celestial body (e g Venus or Mars) □ compare E LAYER – **ionospheric** *adj*, **ionospherically** *adv*

**iontophoresis** /ei,ontohfə'reesis/ *n* the introduction of a substance (e g a drug) into living tissue, esp into a single cell, by applying a voltage to a hollow ELECTRODE or similar device that contains the substance and is inserted into the tissue [NL, fr *ionto-* ion (fr Gk *iont-, iōn*, prp of *ienai* to go) + *-phoresis*] – **iontophoretic** *adj*, **iontophoretically** *adv*

**iota** /ie'ohtə/ *n* 1 the 9th letter of the Greek alphabet 2 an infinitesimal amount; a jot [L, fr Gk *iōta*, of Sem origin; akin to Heb *yōdh* yod]

**iotacism** /ei'ohtə,siz(ə)m/ *n* excessive conversion of other vowel sounds into that of iota, esp in modern Greek [LL *iotacismus* repetition of iota, fr Gk *iōtakismos*, fr *iōta*]

**IOU** /ˌie oh 'yooh/ *n* a paper that has on it the letters IOU, a stated sum, and a signature and that is given as an acknowledgment of debt; *also* a debt [prob fr the pronunciation of *I owe you*]

**-ious** /-i·əs/ *suffix* (*n → adj*) *-ous* ⟨*captious*⟩ [ME; partly fr OF *-ious, -ieux,* fr L *-iosus,* fr *-i-* (penultimate vowel of some noun stems) + *-osus* -ous; partly fr L *-ius,* adj suffix]

**IPA** *n* INTERNATIONAL PHONETIC ALPHABET

**ipecac** /'ipi,kak/ *n* ipecacuanha

**ipecacuanha** /,ipi,kakyoo'ahnə/ *n* the dried underground stem (RHIZOME) and roots of a tropical S American creeping plant used in medicine esp as an EMETIC (substance causing vomiting) and an EXPECTORANT (substance aiding removal of bronchial secretions); *also* the plant (*Cephaelis ipecacuanha*) of the madder family that yields ipecacuanha [Pg *ipecacuanha*, fr Tupi *ipekaagu'ene*]

**ipse dixit** /,ipsay 'diksit/ *n* an arbitrary dogmatic assertion; a dictum [L, he himself said it]

**ipsilateral** /,ipsi'lat(ə)rəl/ *adj* situated or appearing on or affecting the same side of the body – compare CONTRALATERAL [ISV, fr L *ipse* self, himself + *later-*, *latus* side] – **ipsilaterally** *adv*

**ipsissima verba** /ip'sisimə 'vuhbə/ *n pl* the exact words used by someone quoted [NL, lit., the selfsame words]

**ipso facto** /,ipsoh 'faktoh/ *adv* by the very fact or nature of the case [NL, lit., by the fact itself]

**IQ** *n* INTELLIGENCE QUOTIENT ⟨*an ~ of 100 is average*⟩

**ir-** – see [1]IN-

**Iranian** /i'rayni·ən, i'rahni·ən/ *n* **1** a native or inhabitant of Iran **2** a branch of the Indo-European family of languages that includes Persian [*Iran*, country in SW Asia] – **Iranian** *adj*

**Iraqi**, *Austr chiefly* **Iraki** /i'rahki, i'raki/ *n* **1** a native or inhabitant of Iraq **2** the dialect of Modern Arabic spoken in Iraq [Ar '*irāqīy*, fr '*Irāq* Iraq, country in SW Asia] – **Iraqi** *adj*

**irascible** /i'rasibl/ *adj* easily provoked into anger; quick-tempered [MF, fr LL *irascibilis*, fr L *irasci* to become angry, be angry, fr *ira*] – **irascibleness** *n*, **irascibly** *adv*, **irascibility** *n*

**irate** /ie'rayt/ *adj* roused to or arising from anger ⟨*an ~ tax-payer*⟩ ⟨*~ words*⟩ **synonyms** see [1]ANGER [L *iratus*, fr *ira*] – **irately** *adv*, **irateness** *n*

**ire** /ie·ə/ *n*, *chiefly poetic* intense and usu openly displayed anger **synonyms** see [1]ANGER [ME, fr OF, fr L *ira*; akin to OE of*ost* haste, GK *hieros* holy, *oistros* gadfly, frenzy] – **ireful** *adj*

**irenic** /ie'reenik,-'ren-/ *also* **irenical** /-ikal/ *adj* conducive to or operating towards peace or conciliation ⟨*take ~ measures*⟩ [GK *eirēnikos*, fr *eirēnē* peace] – **irenically** *adv*

**irid-** /irid-/, **irido-** *comb form* **1** rainbow ⟨*iridescent*⟩ **2** iris of the eye ⟨*iridectomy*⟩ **3** iridium ⟨*iridic*⟩; iridium and ⟨*iridosmium*⟩ [(1) L *irid-*, *iris*; (2) NL *irid-*, *iris*; (3) NL *iridium*]

**iridaceous** /iri'dayshəs/ *adj* of or belonging to the iris family (Iridaceae)

**iridescence** /iri'des(ə)ns/ *n* a play of changing colours producing rainbow effects (eg in a soap bubble or bird's plumage); *also* a glittering quality or effect suggestive or iridescence ⟨*the ~ of his prose*⟩ – **iridescent** *adj*, **iridescently** *adv*

**iridic** /ei'ridik, i'ridik/ *adj* **1** of or containing iridium, esp with a VALENCY of four **2** of the iris of the eye

**iridium** /i'ridi·əm/ *n* a silver-white chemical element that is a hard brittle very heavy metal belonging to the same group of elements as platinum [NL, fr L *irid-*, *iris* rainbow; fr the colours produced by its dissolving in hydrochloric acid]

**iridosmine** /,iri'dosmine,,ieri-/ *n* a mineral that is a naturally occurring alloy of the metals iridium and osmium, usu containing some rhodium and platinum [G, fr *irid-* + NL *osmium*]

[1]**iris** /'ieris/ *n pl* (*1*) **irises**, **irides** /'ierideez/ (*2*) **irises**, **irides**, *esp collectively* **iris 1a** the small opaque sheet of muscle around the pupil of the eye, that forms the coloured portion of the eye and expands or contracts to regulate the size of the pupil and thus the amount of light entering the eye **b(1) iris, iris diaphragm** an adjustable device of thin overlapping usu metal plates that can be moved to change the size of an opening and that is used to regulate the amount of light entering a camera or similar optical instrument **b(2)** an effect in films similar to a fade-in or a fade-out in which the size of the picture is regulated by its dissolving from a usu circular frame **2** any of a large genus (*Iris* of the family Iridaceae, the iris family) of plants with long straight basal leaves and large showy flowers [(2) NL *Irid-*, *Iris*, genus name, fr L *irid-*, *iris* rainbow, iris plant, fr Gk, rainbow, iris plant, iris of the eye – more at WIRE; (1) NL *irid-*, *iris*, fr Gk]

[2]**iris** *vt* to operate the iris of a film camera so as to fade (a picture) – + *in* or *out*

[1]**Irish** /'ierish/ *adj* **1** of Ireland or the Irish language **2** amusingly illogical *usage* see BRITISH [ME, adj, fr (assumed) OE *Irisc*, fr OE *Iras* Irishmen, of Celt origin; akin to OIr *Eriu* Ireland]

[2]**Irish** *n* **1** *taking pl vb* the people of Ireland **2 Irish, Irish Gaelic** the Celtic language of Ireland, esp as used since the end of the medieval period **3** English as spoken and written in Ire-

land **4 Irish, Irish bull** an amusingly illogical expression (eg "it was hereditary in his family to have no children")

**Irish coffee** *n* hot sugared coffee with Irish whiskey, topped with whipped cream

**Irish confetti** *n* a stone, brick, or fragment of stone or brick used as a missile

**Irish draught horse** *n* (any of) a native Irish breed of heavy working horse, the mares of which are often crossed with Thoroughbreds to produce high-class hunters

**Irishism** /'ierishiz(ə)m/ *n* a characteristic feature of Irish English; *esp* IRISH 4

**Irishman** /'ierishmən/, *fem* **Irishwoman** *n* a native or inhabitant of Ireland

**Irish martingale** *n* a device for keeping a horse's reins in place that consists of a short strap with a ring at each end through which the reins pass beneath the horse's neck

**Irish moss** *n* CARRAGEEN (edible purplish-red seaweed)

**Irishry** /'ierishri/ *n* Irish quality or character; *also* an Irish trait

**Irish setter** *n* (any of) a breed of gundogs similar to ENGLISH SETTERS but with a chestnut-brown or mahogany-red coat

**Irish stew** *n* a stew consisting chiefly of meat, esp mutton, potatoes, and onions in a thick gravy

**Irish terrier** *n* (any of) a breed of active medium-sized terriers developed in Ireland and having a short thick usu reddish wiry coat

**Irish water spaniel** *n* (any of) a breed of large retrievers developed in Ireland and having a heavy curly liver-coloured coat and an almost hairless tail

**Irish whiskey** *n* whiskey made in Ireland, chiefly of barley

**Irish wolfhound** *n* (any of) a breed of very large tall hounds that have the general form of a greyhound but are much larger and stronger and have a long rough coat

**irk** /uhk/ *vt* to make weary, irritated, or bored **synonyms** see ANNOY [ME *irken*]

**irksome** /-s(ə)m/ *adj* tedious, tiresome ⟨*an ~ task*⟩ – **irksomely** *adv*, **irksomeness** *n*

[1]**iron** /'ie·ən/ *n* **1** a heavy silver-white metallic element that is magnetic, may be worked with relative ease, readily rusts in moist air, occurs native in meteorites and combined in most IGNEOUS (formed by the cooling and solidification of molten material) rocks, is the most used of metals, and is vital to biological processes **2** something made of or originally made of iron: eg **2a** *usu pl* something (eg handcuffs or fetters) used to bind or restrain ⟨*clapped him in ~*⟩ **b** a heated metal implement used for branding or CAUTERIZING (treating a wound by burning) **c** a metal implement with a smooth flat typically triangular base that is heated (eg by electricity or by placing on a hot surface) and used to smooth or press cloth or clothing **d** a stirrup **e** a golf club with a metal head; *specif* any of a numbered series of usu nine such clubs with heads of varying angles for hitting the ball various distances **3** great strength or hardness [ME, fr OE *īsern*, *īren*; akin to OHG *īsarn* iron] – **iron in the fire** an iron or project which may come to fruition ⟨*I'm hoping to get this job but I have several other irons in the fire*⟩ [fr a blacksmith heating pieces of iron for forging]

[2]**iron** *adj* **1** (made) of iron **2** resembling iron (eg in appearance or strength) **3a** strong and healthy; robust ⟨*an ~ constitution*⟩ **b** inflexible, unrelenting ⟨*~ determination*⟩ ⟨*an ~ will*⟩ **c** holding or binding fast ⟨*the ~ ties of kinship*⟩ – **ironness** *n*

[3]**iron** *vt* **1** to furnish or cover with iron **2** to shackle with irons **3a** to smooth (as if) with a heated iron ⟨*~ed his shirt*⟩ **b** to remove (eg wrinkles) by ironing – often + *out* ~ *vi* to be capable of being ironed ⟨*this skirt ~s well*⟩

**iron out** *vt* **1** to make tolerable or harmonious by suppression or modification of extremes; *broadly* to remove ⟨*ironed out their differences*⟩ **2** to solve esp after intense practical investigation ⟨*ironed out the difficulties*⟩

**Iron Age** *n* one of the traditional archaeological divisions of human culture, characterized by the smelting and widespread use of iron, beginning somewhat before 1000 BC in western Asia and Egypt but some centuries later in western Europe – compare BRONZE AGE

**ironbound** /-'bownd/ *adj* bound (as if) with iron: eg **a** rugged, harsh ⟨*~ coast*⟩ **b** stern, rigorous ⟨*~ traditions*⟩

[1]**ironclad** /-'klad/ *adj* **1** *esp* of naval vessels sheathed in iron or steel armour **2** rigorous, rigid

[2]**ironclad** *n* an armoured naval vessel, esp in the 19th and early 20th centuries

**Iron Cross** *n* a German medal awarded for outstanding bravery in war [trans of Ger *eiserne kreuz*]

**iron curtain** n, often cap I&C **1** the heavily guarded border between W Europe and the Communist countries of E Europe **2** an esp political and ideological barrier (eg to the movement of people and ideas) between the Communist countries of E Europe and the democracies of the West and their allies

**ironfisted** /ˌie-ən'fistid/ adj being both harsh and ruthless ⟨~ methods⟩

**¹iron grey** adj, of a horse having predominantly black hairs and few white ones throughout the coat

**²iron grey** n **1** an iron grey horse **2** a dark grey colour with a greenish tinge

**iron hand** n stern or rigorous control ⟨ruled with an ~⟩ – **ironhanded** adj, **ironhandedly** adv, **ironhandedness** n

**iron horse** n **1** NAm an early locomotive engine **2** archaic a bicycle

**ironic** /ie'ronik/, **ironical** /-ikl/ adj **1** relating to, containing, or constituting irony **2** given to irony – **ironicalness** n

　usage Some people dislike the now common use of **ironic(al)** to mean simply "paradoxical" ⟨it is ironical that he should be taxed at the top rate on his unemployment benefit⟩ and of **ironically** to mean simply "strangely enough". **Synonyms** see SARCASTIC

**ironically** /ie'ronikli/ adv **1** in an ironic way **2** it is ironical that

**ironing** /'ie-əning/ n **1** the action or process of smoothing or pressing (as if) with a heated iron **2** clothes and cloth articles (eg towels and tablecloths) that have been or are to be ironed

**ironing board** n a long relatively narrow flat board that is usu mounted on collapsible legs and has a padded cloth-covered surface on which clothes are ironed

**ironist** /'ierənist/ n someone who uses irony, esp in the development of a literary work or theme

**iron lung** n a device for maintaining breathing artificially, in which rhythmic alternations in the air pressure in a chamber surrounding a patient's chest, force air into and out of the lungs

**ironmaster** /'ie-ən,mahstə/ n an owner of an iron works or foundry, esp in the 19th century

**ironmonger** /-,mung-gə/ n, Br a dealer in esp household hardware (eg pots, pans, and nails)

**ironmongery** /'ie-ən,mung-gəri/ n, Br **1** articles sold by an ironmonger; hardware **2** humorous metallic items of technical equipment (eg firearms or tools)

**iron mould** n a spot (eg on cloth) due to staining by rusty iron or by ink [mould, alter. of mole spot]

**iron oxide** n any of several chemical compounds consisting of iron and oxygen: eg **a** FERRIC OXIDE **b** FERROUS OXIDE

**iron pyrites** n a common mineral, $FeS_2$, that consists of iron and sulphur, has a pale brass-yellow colour and metallic lustre, and is burnt in making SULPHUR DIOXIDE and SULPHURIC ACID

**iron ration** n an emergency food ration, esp as supplied to a soldier [fr its orig consisting mainly of tinned food]

**ironsides** /'ie-ən,siedz/ n, pl **ironsides 1** a man of great strength or bravery **2** taking pl vb the cavalry regiment of the Parliamentary side in the English Civil War; broadly the entire Parliamentary army

**ironstone** /-,stohn/ n a hard SEDIMENTARY rock (rock formed from material deposited by natural forces) rich in iron; esp a SIDERITE occurring in a coal region

**ironstone china** n a type of hard durable white pottery developed in England early in the 19th century

**ironwood** /'ie-ən,wood/ n (the wood of) any of numerous trees and shrubs with exceptionally tough or hard wood

**ironwork** /'ie-ən,wuhk/ n **1** work in iron; articles made of iron **2** pl but taking sing or pl vb an establishment where iron or steel is smelted or heavy iron or steel products are made – **ironworker** n

**irony** /'ierəni/ n **1** SOCRATIC IRONY **2a** the use of words to express something other than and esp the opposite of the literal meaning **b** an ironic expression or utterance **3a** (an event or situation showing) incongruity between the actual circumstances or result of events and the normal, appropriate, or expected circumstances or result **b** DRAMATIC IRONY **4** an attitude of detached awareness of incongruity ⟨looked with ~ on the craze for individuality⟩ synonyms see WIT [L ironia, fr Gk eirōneia, fr eirōn dissembler]

**Iroquoian** /ˌirə'kwoyən/ n a language family of eastern N America including CHEROKEE, ERIE, and MOHAWK – **Iroquoian** adj

**Iroquois** /'irəkwoy(z)/ n, pl **Iroquois 1** pl an allied group of American Indian peoples formerly living in New York state **2** a member of any of the Iroquois peoples [Fr, fr Algonquin Irinakhoiw, lit., real adders]

**irradiance** /i'raydiəns/ n, physics **1** the quality or state of being radiant; radiance **2** the amount of RADIANT FLUX (emission or transmission of energy travelling in waveform) for a given surface area usu expressed in joules per square metre

**irradiate** /i'raydiayt/ vt **1a** to light up; brighten **b** to give intellectual or spiritual insight to **c** to affect or treat by radiant energy (eg heat); specif to treat by exposure to radiation **2** to emit like rays of light; RADIATE **1** ⟨irradiating strength and comfort⟩ ~ vi, archaic to emit rays; shine [L irradiatus, pp of irradiare, fr in- ²in- + radius ray] – **irradiator** n, **irradiative** adj

**irradiation** /i,raydi'aysh(ə)n/ n **1** an act or instance of irradiating **2** emission of radiant energy (eg heat or light) **3** exposure to radiation (eg X rays)

**irradicable** /i'radikəbl/ adj impossible to eradicate or stamp out; deep-rooted ⟨an ~ prejudice⟩ [ML irradicabilis, fr L in-¹in- + radic-, radix root – more at ROOT] – **irradicably** adv

**irrational** /i'rash(ə)nl/ adj not rational: eg **a** not governed by or according to reason ⟨~ fears⟩ **b**(1) of a syllable in Greek and Latin verse having a length other than that required by the metre **b**(2) of a foot in Greek or Latin verse containing such a syllable **c** of, involving, or being (a mathematical expression containing) an IRRATIONAL NUMBER ⟨an ~ root of an equation⟩ [ME, fr L irrationalis, fr in- ¹in- + rationalis rational] – **irrationally** adv, **irrationalness** n, **irrationality** n

**irrationalism** /i'rash(ə)nəlizm/ n (an) irrational belief or action – **irrationalist** n or adj, **irrationalistic** adj

**irrational number** also **irrational** n a number (eg $\sqrt{2}$ or π) that cannot be expressed as the ratio of two integers – compare RATIONAL NUMBER, SURD

**irrebuttable** /ˌiri'butəbl/ n, law not capable of being REBUTTED (shown to be false by legal argument) ⟨an ~ presumption in law⟩

**irreclaimable** /ˌiri'klayməbl/ adj incapable of being reclaimed – **irreclaimably** adv

**¹irreconcilable** /i'rekən,sieləbl, -,--'---, ,---'---/ adj impossible to reconcile: eg **a** resolutely opposed; implacable ⟨~ enemies⟩ **b** INCOMPATIBLE 2 ⟨~ statements⟩ – **irreconcilableness** n, **irreconcilably** adv, **irreconcilability** n

**²irreconcilable** n one who or that which is irreconcilable; esp a member of a group (eg a political party) that opposes compromise or collaboration

**irrecoverable** /ˌiri'kuv(ə)rəbl/ adj incapable of being recovered or rectified; irreparable ⟨~ debts⟩ ⟨~ injuries⟩ – **irrecoverableness** n, **irrecoverably** adv

**irrecusable** /ˌiri'kyoohzəbl/ adj not subject to exception or rejection [LL irrecusabilis, fr L in- ¹in- + recusare to reject, refuse – more at RECUSANCY] – **irrecusably** adv

**irredeemable** /ˌiri'deeməbl/ adj **1** not redeemable: eg **1a** not able to be finally settled by payment of the PRINCIPAL (sum of money originally lent or invested) ⟨~ bond⟩ **b** of paper money not able to be exchanged for precious metal by the issuing bank; inconvertible **2** being beyond remedy; hopeless ⟨~ mistakes⟩ – **irredeemably** adv

**irredentism** /ˌiri'den,tiz(ə)m/ n (advocacy of) a political principle or policy directed towards the restoration of territories to the political units to which they are related historically or by reason of the nationality of their inhabitants [It irredentismo, fr It Italia irredenta Italian-speaking territory not incorporated in Italy, lit., unredeemed Italy] – **irredentist** n or adj

**irreducible** /ˌiri'dyoohsəbl/ adj impossible to bring into a desired, normal, or simpler state ⟨an ~ matrix⟩; specif, of a mathematical expression incapable of being split up into factors whose variables have lower powers (than those in the expression) ⟨~ polynomials⟩ ⟨an ~ equation⟩ [¹in- + reducible] – **irreducibly** adv, **irreducibility** n

**irrefragable** /i'refrəgəbl/ adj, formal **1** impossible to deny or refute ⟨~ arguments⟩ **2** impossible to break or alter ⟨~ rules⟩ ⟨an ~ cement⟩ [LL irrefragabilis, fr L in- ¹in- + refragari to oppose, fr re- + -fragari (as in suffragari to vote for); akin to L suffragium suffrage] – **irrefragably** adv, **irrefragability** n

**irrefrangible** /ˌiri'franjəbl/ adj not capable of being bent or deflected: eg **a** inviolable, absolute **b** esp of waves of visible light not capable of being deflected (REFRACTED) when passing from one medium to another (eg air to glass) [¹in- + refrangible]

**irrefutable** /ˌiri'fyoohtəbl, i'refyootəbl/ adj impossible to refute; **incontrovertible** ⟨~ *proof*⟩ [LL *irrefutabilis*, fr L *in-* ¹*in-* + *refutare* to refute] – **irrefutably** *adv*, **irrefutability** *n*

**irregardless** /ˌiri'gahdlis/ *adv, nonstandard* regardless [prob blend of *irrespective* and *regardless*]

¹**irregular** /i'regyoolə/ *adj* **1a** failing to accord with or conform to what is usual, proper, accepted, or right; contrary to rule, custom, or moral principles ⟨~ *behaviour*⟩ **b** not conforming to the normal manner of INFLECTION (change in the form of a word according to its grammatical function) ⟨*sell, put, feed are* ~ *verbs*⟩; *specif* STRONG 16 **c** improper or inadequate because of failure to conform to a prescribed course ⟨*an* ~ *marriage service*⟩ **d** *of troops* not belonging to the regular army organization but raised for a special purpose **2** lacking symmetry or evenness ⟨*an* ~ *coastline*⟩; *esp* ZYGOMORPHIC (having only one plane of symmetry) **3a** lacking continuity or regularity esp of occurrence or activity ⟨~ *employment*⟩ **b** *NAm, esp of students* part-time [ME *irreguler*, fr MF, fr LL *irregularis*, fr L *in-* ¹*in-* + *regularis* regular] – **irregularly** *adv*

²**irregular** *n* one who is irregular; *esp* a soldier who is not a member of a regular military force

**irregularity** /iˌregyoo'larəti, ˌ---'---/ *n* **1** the quality or state of being irregular **2** something that is irregular (eg not conforming with accepted professional or ethical standards)

**irrelative** /i'relətiv/ *adj* not relative: **a** not related **b** irrelevant – **irrelatively** *adv*

**irrelevance** /i'reliv(ə)ns/, **irrelevancy** /-nsi/ *n* **1** the quality or state of being irrelevant **2** something irrelevant

**irrelevant** /i'reliv(ə)nt/ *adj* **1** not relevant; inapplicable ⟨*that statement is* ~ *to your argument*⟩ **2** unimportant – **irrelevantly** *adv*

**irreligion** /ˌiri'lij(ə)n/ *n* hostility or indifference to (a) religion [MF or L; MF, fr L *irreligion-*, *irreligio*, fr *in-* ¹*in-* + *religion-*, *religio* religion] – **irreligionist** *n*, **irreligious** *adj*, **irreligiously** *adv*

> **synonyms** Irreligious means "against religion"; **nonreligious** means "not religious", "secular"; **unreligious** may mean either.

**irremeable** /i'remiəbl, i'reemiəbl/ *adj, archaic* offering no possibility of return [L *irremeabilis*, fr *in-* ¹*in-* + *remeare* to go back, fr *re-* + *meare* to go – more at PERMEATE]

**irremediable** /ˌiri'meedi·əbl, -dyəbl/ *adj* not able to be put right or remedied; *specif* incurable [L *irremediabilis*, fr *in-* ¹*in-* + *remediabilis* remediable] – **irremediableness** *n*, **irremediably** *adv*

**irremissible** /ˌiri'misəbl/ *adj* **1** not remissible; unpardonable **2** not to be remitted; OBLIGATORY 3 [MF, fr LL *irremissibilis*, fr *in-* ¹*in-* + *remissibilis* remissible] – **irremissibly** *adv*

**irremovable** /ˌiri'moohvəbl/ *adj* not able to be removed esp from an official position △ immovable

**irreparable** /i'rep(ə)rəbl/ *adj* not able to be put right or repaired ⟨~ *damage to his reputation*⟩ [ME, fr MF, fr L *irreparabilis*, fr *in-* ¹*in-* + *reparabilis* reparable] – **irreparableness** *n*, **irreparably** *adv*

> **synonyms** Harm and damage are **irreparable** ⟨*an irreparable loss*⟩; material objects that cannot be mended are **unreparable**.
> **usage** The pronunciation /i'rep(ə)rəbl/ rather than /ˌiri'peərəbl/ is recommended for BBC broadcasters.

**irreplaceable** /ˌiri'playsəbl/ *adj* not replaceable; having no adequate substitute – **irreplaceableness** *n*, **irreplaceably** *adv*, **irreplaceability** *n*

**irrepressible** /ˌiri'presəbl/ *adj* impossible to repress, restrain, or control ⟨~ *curiosity*⟩ – **irrepressibly** *adv*, **irrepressibility** *n*

**irreproachable** /ˌiri'prohchəbl/ *adj* not reproachable; impeccable ⟨~ *conduct*⟩ – **irreproachableness** *n*, **irreproachably** *adv*, **irreproachability** *n*

**irresistible** /ˌiri'zistəbl/ *adj* impossible to resist successfully ⟨*an* ~ *puppy*⟩ ⟨*the* ~ *escalation of the arms race*⟩ – **irresistibleness** *n*, **irresistibly** *adv*, **irresistibility** *n*

**irresolute** /i'rezəl(y)ooht/ *adj* uncertain how to act or proceed; hesitant, vacillating [¹*in-* + *resolute*] – **irresolutely** *adv*, **irresoluteness** *n*, **irresolution** *n*

**irresolvable** /ˌiri'zolvəbl/ *adj* incapable of being resolved; *esp* not analysable into component parts

**irrespective of** /ˌiri'spektiv/ *prep* without regard or reference to; regardless of ⟨*a college open to all* ~ *race, colour or creed*⟩

**irrespirable** /i'respirəbl, ˌiri'spie·ərəbl/ *adj* unfit for breathing [Fr, fr LL *irrespirabilis*, fr L *in-* ¹*in-* + *respirare* to breathe – more at RESPIRE]

**irresponsible** /ˌiri'sponsəbl/ *adj* not responsible: eg **a** not answerable to higher authority ⟨*an* ~ *dictatorship*⟩ **b** said or done with no sense of responsibility **c** lacking a sense of responsibility **d** unable esp mentally or financially to bear responsibility – **irresponsibility** *n*, **irresponsibly** *adv*

**irresponsive** /ˌiri'sponsiv/ *adj* not responsive; *esp* not able, ready, or inclined to respond – **irresponsiveness** *n*

**irretentive** /ˌiri'tentiv/ *adj* not retentive; *esp* lacking the ability to retain knowledge ⟨*an* ~ *memory*⟩

**irretrievable** /ˌiri'treevəbl/ *adj* not retrievable; irrecoverable – **irretrievably** *adv*, **irretrievability** *n*

**irreverence** /i'rev(ə)rəns/ *n* (an act or utterance showing) lack of reverence [ME, fr L *irreverentia*, fr *irreverent-*, *irreverens* irreverent, fr *in-* ¹*in-* + *reverent-*, *reverens* reverent] – **irreverent** *adj*, **irreverently** *adv*, **irreverential** *adj*

**irreversible** /ˌiri'vuhsəbl/ *adj* **1** incapable of being reversed ⟨*an* ~ *judgment*⟩ **2** *of a chemical reaction* capable of change in one direction only so that completion is reached – **irreversibly** *adv*, **irreversibility** *n*

**irrevocable** /i'revəkəbl/ *adj* incapable of being revoked; unalterable ⟨*an* ~ *decision*⟩ [ME, fr L *irrevocabilis*, fr *in-* ¹*in-* + *revocabilis* revocable] – **irrevocableness** *n*, **irrevocably** *adv*, **irrevocability** *n*

> **usage** The pronunciation /i'revəkəbl/ rather than /ˌiri'vohkəbl/ is recommended for BBC broadcasters.

**irrigate** /'irigayt/ *vt* **1** to wet, moisten: eg **1a** to supply (eg land) with water by artificial means **b** to flush (a body part) with a stream of liquid (eg in removing a foreign body from the eye) **2** to refresh as if by watering ~ *vi* to practise irrigation [L *irrigatus*, pp of *irrigare*, fr *in-* ²*in-* + *rigare* to water] – **irrigator** *n*, **irrigation** *n*

**irritability** /ˌiritə'biləti/ *n* **1** the quality or state of being irritable: eg **1a** quick excitability to annoyance, impatience, or anger; petulance **b** abnormal or excessive excitability of an organ or part of the body **2** the property of living organisms that permits them to react to stimuli

**irritable** /'iritəbl/ *adj* capable of being irritated: eg **a** easily exasperated or excited; ill-tempered **b** responsive to stimuli – **irritableness** *n*, **irritably** *adv*

**irritant** /'irit(ə)nt/ *n* something that irritates or excites – **irritant** *adj*

**irritate** /'iritayt/ *vt* **1** to provoke impatience, anger, or displeasure in; annoy **2** to induce irritability in or of ~ *vi* to cause or induce displeasure or irritation [L *irritatus*, pp of *irritare* to excite, arouse] – **irritatingly** *adv*

> **synonyms** Irritate, exasperate, nettle, provoke, aggravate, rile, and peeve, all mean "excite a feeling of annoyance or anger". They may be distinguished by the reactions they provoke. **Irritate** implies annoying someone to the extent of making him/her impatient and possibly angry. **Exasperate** takes this further by suggesting the limits of someone's patience have been reached. **Nettle** suggests a momentary irritation, and stinging or piquing rather than rousing to anger ⟨*her taunts nettled them*⟩. **Provoke** implies an often deliberate irritation which usually evokes an angry response ⟨*provoked by his silence, she flounced off*⟩. **Aggravate** is like **provoke**, and often implies repeated or prolonged irritating action. **Rile** suggests something which disturbs one's serenity and may lead to agitation or to open anger. **Peeve**, the weakest term, suggests some minor or petty source of irritation evoking a querulous or resentful response. Compare ANNOY **antonyms** mollify, soothe, calm

**irritated** /'iritaytid/ *adj* subjected to irritation; *esp* roughened, reddened, or inflamed by an irritant ⟨~ *eyes*⟩

**irritation** /ˌiri'taysh(ə)n/ *n* **1** irritating or being irritated; something irritating **2** a condition of irritability, soreness, roughness, or inflammation of a body part

**irritative** /'iritətiv/ *adj* **1** serving to provoke; irritating **2** accompanied with or produced by irritation ⟨~ *coughing*⟩

**irrotational** /ˌiroh'taysh(ə)nl/ *adj* **1** not rotating or involving rotation ⟨*an* ~ *electric field*⟩ **2** free of VORTICES (whirling masses of liquid or gas) ⟨~ *flow*⟩

**irrupt** /i'rupt/ *vi* **1** to rush in forcibly or violently **2** *of a natural population* to undergo a sudden upsurge in numbers, esp when natural ecological balances and checks are disturbed **3** *chiefly NAm* ERUPT 1c ⟨*the crowd* ~*ed in a fervour of patriotism –* *Time*⟩ **synonyms** see ERUPT [L *irruptus*, pp of *irrumpere*, lit., to break in, fr *in-* ²*in-* + *rumpere* to break – more at BEREAVE] – **irruption** *n*

**irruptive** /i'ruptiv/ *adj* **1** irrupting or tending to irrupt **2** *of a rock* INTRUSIVE (formed from molten rock forced between layers of the earth) – **irruptively** *adv*

**is** /iz; *strong* iz, *pres 3 sing of* BE, *dial pres* 1 & 2 *sing of* BE, *substandard pres pl of* BE [ME, fr OE; akin to OHG *ist* is (fr *sīn* to be), L *est* (fr *esse* to be), Gk *esti* (fr *einai* to be)]

**is-** /ies-/, **iso-** *comb form* **1** equal; homogeneous; uniform ⟨*is-acoustic*⟩ **2** *of a specified chemical compound or group* having the same atomic composition but a different structure from (ISOMERIC with) ⟨*isopropyl*⟩ **3** for or from different individuals of the same species ⟨*isoagglutination*⟩ [LL, fr Gk, fr *isos* equal]

**Isaiah** /ie'zie-ə/ *n* – see BIBLE table [*Isaiah* (Heb *Yĕsha'āyāhū*), 8th-c BC Hebrew prophet]

**Isaias** *n* – see BIBLE table [LL, Isaiah]

**isallobar** /ie'saləbah/ *n* a line on a map or chart connecting places of equal change of atmospheric pressure within a specified time [ISV *is- + all- + -bar* (as in *isobar*)] – **isallobaric** *adj*

**ischaemia**, *chiefly NAm* **ischemia** /is'keemi-ə/ *n* localized lack of oxygen in a tissue due to obstruction of the inflow of blood from an artery [NL, fr *ischaemus* styptic, fr Gk *ischaimas*, fr *ischein* to restrain + *haima* blood] – **ischaemic** *adj*

**ischium** /'iski-əm/ *n, pl* **ischia** /'iskiə/ the lower and posterior of the three principal bones composing either half of the PELVIS (bowl-shaped frame of bones at base of backbone) [L, hip joint, fr Gk *ischion*] – **ischial** *adj*

**-ise** /-iez/ *suffix*, (→ *vb*), *chiefly Br* **-ize**

**isentropic** /,iesen'tropik/ *adj, physics* relating to equal or constant ENTROPY (amount of disorder in a system); *esp* taking place without change of entropy ⟨*an ~ expansion*⟩ – **isentropically** *adv*

**-ish** /-ish/ *suffix* **1** (*n* → *adj*) of or belonging to (a specified country or national group) ⟨*Finn*ish⟩ **2a** (*n* → *adj*) having the characteristics of ⟨*boy*ish⟩ ⟨*mul*ish⟩ – often used disparagingly ⟨*child*ish⟩ ⟨*book*ish⟩ **b**(1) (*adj, n* → *adj*) having a touch or trace of ⟨*summer*ish⟩; slightly ⟨*purpl*ish⟩ **b**(2) (*n* → *adj*) having the approximate age of ⟨*forty*ish⟩ **b**(3) (*n* → *adj*) being or occurring at the approximate time of ⟨*eight*ish⟩ [ME, fr OE *-isc*; akin to OHG *-isc* -ish, Gk *-iskos*, dim. suffix]

**Ishmael** /'ishmay(ə)l/ *n* a social outcast [*Ishmael*, the outcast son of Abraham and Hagar (Gen 16-21)]

**Ishmaelite** /'ishmay(ə)liet/ *n* an Ishmael – **Ishmaelitish** *adj*, **Ishmaelitism** *n*

**isinglass** /'iezing,glahs/ *n* **1** a semitransparent whitish very pure GELATINE (jellylike protein) prepared from the air bladders of fishes (e g sturgeons) and used esp as a clarifying agent, in jellies and glue, and for preserving eggs **2** MICA (glasslike material) [prob by folk etymology fr obs D *huizenblas*, fr MD *huusblase*, fr *huus* sturgeon + *blase* bladder]

**Islam** /'izlahm, -lam/ *n* **1** the religious faith of Muslims including belief in Allah as the sole deity and in Muhammad as his prophet **2a** the civilization or culture accompanying Islamic faith **b** the group of modern nations in which Islam is the dominant religion *synonyms* see MUSLIM [Ar *islām* submission (to the will of God)] – **Islamic** *adj*, **Islamics** *n taking sing vb*

**Islamism** /'izlamiz(ə)m, -lahm-/ *n* the faith, doctrine, or cause of Islam – **Islamist** *n*

**Islam·ize, -ise** /'izləmiez, -lahm-/ *vt* to make Islamic; *esp* to convert to Islam – **Islamization** *n*

¹**island** /'ieland/ *n* **1** a tract of land surrounded by water and smaller than a continent **2** something resembling an island esp in its isolated or surrounded position **3** **island, traffic island** an area in the middle of a road from which traffic is excluded for the safety of pedestrians **4** an isolated superstructure on the deck of a ship (e g on one side of an aircraft carrier) **5** an isolated person, group, or area [alter. (influenced by ¹*isle*) of earlier *iland*, fr ME, fr OE *īgland*; akin to ON *eyland* island; both fr a prehistoric NGmc-WGmc compound whose constituents are represented by OE *īg* island (akin to OE *ēa* river, L *aqua* water) and OE *land*]

²**island** *vt* **1a** to make (as if) into an island **b** to dot (as if) with islands **2** ISOLATE 1

**islander** /'ieləndə/ *n* a native or inhabitant of an island

**island universe** *n* a galaxy other than the MILKY WAY – no longer used technically

¹**isle** /iel/ *n* an island; *esp* a small island ⟨*Isle of Wight*⟩ [ME, fr OF, fr L *insula*]

²**isle** *vt* **1** to make into an isle **2** to place (as if) on an isle

**islet** /'ielit/ *n* **1** a little island **2** a small isolated mass of one type of tissue within a different type **3** ISLET OF LANGERHANS

**islet of Langerhans** /'lang-ə,hanz/ *n* any of the groups of small spherical or oval cells that are scattered throughout the PANCREAS (digestive gland close to stomach) and secrete the hormone INSULIN to regulate the levels of sugar in the blood [Paul *Langerhans* †1888 Ger physician]

**ism** /'iz(ə)m/ *n, chiefly derog* a distinctive doctrine, cause, theory, or practice [*-ism*]

**-ism** /-iz(ə)m/ *suffix* (→ *n*) **1a** act, practice, or process of ⟨*critic*ism⟩ ⟨*plagiar*ism⟩ **b** mode of behaviour characteristic of (a specified person or thing) ⟨*animal*ism⟩ **2a** state, condition, or property of ⟨*barbarian*ism⟩ ⟨*magnet*ism⟩ **b** diseased state or condition resulting from excessive use of (a specified drug) ⟨*alcohol*ism⟩ or marked by resemblance to (a specified person or thing) ⟨*gigant*ism⟩ **3a** doctrine, theory, or cult of ⟨*Buddh*ism⟩ **b** adherence to (a specified doctrine, system, or class of principles) ⟨*stoic*ism⟩ **4** characteristic or peculiar feature of (a specified language or variety of language) ⟨*colloquial*ism⟩ ⟨*Anglic*ism⟩ **5** discrimination on the grounds of ⟨*ugly*ism – *The Listener*⟩ [ME *-isme*, fr MF & L; MF, fr L *-isma* & *-ismus*, fr Gk *-isma* & *-ismos*, fr verbs in *-izein* -ize]

**isn't** /'iznt/ is not

**iso-** – see IS-

**isoagglutination** /,iesoh-ə,gloohti'naysh(ə)n/ *n* AGGLUTINATION (clumping together) of the blood cells of one individual by the addition of blood of another of the same species or of the same blood group – **isoagglutinative** *adj*

**isoagglutinin** /,iesoh-ə'gloohtinin/ *n* an ANTIBODY (substance made in the body to fight disease) produced by an individual that reacts with ANTIGENS (substances that stimulate the production of antibodies) on blood cells produced by other individuals of the same species

**isoalloxazine** /,iesoh-ə'loksəzeen/ *n* a yellow solid chemical compound, $C_{10}H_6N_4O_2$, containing three rings of atoms in the molecular structure, that is the parent compound from which the vitamin riboflavin and other chemically related compounds (FLAVINS) are derived [*iso- + all*antoic + *ox*alic + *azine*]

**isoantibody** /,iesoh'antibodi/ *n* an ANTIBODY (substance made in the body to fight disease) that is produced only by some individuals of a species against an ANTIGEN (substance that stimulates the production of antibodies) which they lack and other individuals of the species have, if that antigen is introduced into the system

**isoantigen** /,iesoh'antijən/ *n* an ANTIGEN (substance that stimulates the production of antibodies) that is present only in some individuals of a species (e g of a particular blood group) and is capable of causing the production of an isoantibody by individuals which lack it [ISV] – **isoantigenic** *adj*, **isoantigenicity** *n*

**isobar** /'iesohbah, 'iesə-/ *n* **1** a line on a map or chart connecting places where the atmospheric pressure reduced to sea level is the same **2** any of two or more atoms or chemical elements having the same ATOMIC WEIGHTS or MASS NUMBERS but different ATOMIC NUMBERS [ISV *is- + -bar* (fr Gk *baros* weight); akin to Gk *barys* heavy – more at GRIEVE] – **isobaric** *adj*

**isobutylene** /,iesoh'byoohtileen/ *n* a gaseous chemical compound, $CH_2{=}C(CH_3)_2$, used esp in making a synthetic rubber [ISV]

**isochromatic** /,iesoh-krə'matik, -kroh-/ *adj, of a photographic film or emulsion* ORTHOCHROMATIC (sensitive to all colours except red)

**isochron** /'iesə,kron/, **isochrone** /-krohn/ *n* a line on a chart connecting points at which events occur at the same time or which represents the same time or time difference [ISV *is- + -chron* (fr Gk *chronos* time)]

**isochronal** /ie'sokrənl/ *adj* uniform in time; lasting an equal amount of time; recurring at regular intervals [Gk *isochronos*, fr *is-* + *chronos* time] – **isochronally** *adv*, **isochronism** *n*

**isochronous** /ie'sokrənəs/ *adj* isochronal [Gk *isochronos*] – **isochronously** *adv*

¹**isoclinal** /,iesoh'klienl/ *adj* relating to, having, or indicating equality of slope or dip [ISV] – **isoclinally** *adv*

²**isoclinal** *n* isoclinic line

**isocline** /'iesoh,klien/ *n* a folding in the layers of the earth that is so closely folded that the rock beds of the two sides have the same dip

**isoclinic** /,iesoh'klinik/ *adj* isoclinal [ISV] – **isoclinically** *adv*

**isoclinic line** /,iesoh'klinik/ *n* a line on a map or chart joining points on the earth's surface at which a magnetic needle has the same inclination to the vertical

**isocyanate** /,iesoh'sie-ənayt, -nət/ *n* any of various chemical compounds (SALTS or ESTERS) formed by combination between CYANIC ACID and a metal atom, an alcohol, or another chemical group and used esp in the manufacture of plastics and adhesives [ISV]

**isodiametric** /ˌiesoh͵die·ə'metrik/ *adj* having equal diameters [ISV]

**isodynamic** /ˌiesohdie'namik/ *adj* **1** relating to equality or uniformity of force **2** connecting points at which the magnetic intensity is the same ⟨~ *line*⟩ [ISV]

**isoelectric** /-i'lektrik/ *adj* having or representing no difference of electric potential

**isoelectric point** *n* the degree (pH) of acidity or alkalinity at which a solution is electrically neutral and its particles will not migrate in an electric field [ISV]

**isoelectronic** /ˌiesoh·i͵lek'tronik, -͵elek-/ *adj* having the same number or pattern of electrons [ISV] – **isoelectronically** *adv*

**isoenzyme** /-'enziem/ *n* ISOZYME (protein with same function but different chemical properties from another) – **isoenzymatic** *adj*, **isoenzymic** *adj*

**isogamete** /ˌiesoh-gə'meet, -'gameet/ *n* a GAMETE (reproductive cell)(eg a sperm)indistinguishablein form, size, or behaviour from another gamete (eg an egg) with which it can unite to form a ZYGOTE – compare HETEROGAMETE [ISV] – **isogametic** *adj*

**isogamous** /ie'sogəməs/ *adj* having or characterized by the fusion of isogametes – compare HETEROGAMOUS – **isogamy** *n*

**isogeneic** /ˌiesoh·jə'nayik, -'nee·ik/ *adj* SYNGENEIC (having same origin) [*is-* + *-geneic* (as in *syngeneic*)]

**isogenetic** /ˌiesoh·jə'netik/ *adj* isogenic

**isogenic** /-'jenik/ *adj* characterized by essentially identical genes ⟨*identical twins are* ~⟩ [*is-* + *gene* + *-ic*]

**isogloss** /-͵glos/ *n* an imaginary line dividing places or regions that differ in a particular linguistic feature; *also* a line on a map representing this [ISV *is-* + Gk *glōssa* language – more at GLOSS] – **isoglossal** *adj*

¹**isogonic** /ˌiesə'gonik/, **isogonal** /ie'sogənl/ *adj* relating to or having equal angles [ISV *is-* + Gk *gōnia* angle – more at -GON]

²**isogonic, isogonal** /ie'sogənl/ *n* ISOGONIC LINE

³**isogonic** *adj* exhibiting equivalent relative growth of parts such that size relations remain constant [*isogony* (fr *is-* + *-gony*) + *-ic*] – **isogony** *n*

**isogonic line** *n* a line on a map or chart joining points on the earth's surface at which the DECLINATION (angle between magnetic North and true North) is the same

**isogram** /'iesoh͵gram, 'iesə-/ *n* ISOPLETH 2 (line on a map joining constant values)

**isohaemolysis** /ˌiesoh·hi'moləsis/ *n* disintegration of the red blood cells of one individual by ANTIBODIES (substances produced by the body to fight disease) in the blood of another of the same species [NL]

**isohel** /'iesoh͵hel, 'iesə-/ *n* a line on a map or chart connecting places having an equal period of sunshine [*is-* + Gk *hēlios* sun – more at SOLAR]

**isohyet** /ˌiesoh'hie·ət/ *n* a line on a map or chart connecting areas of equal rainfall [ISV *is-* + Gk *hyetos* rain – more at HYET-] – **isohyetal** *adj*

¹**isolate** /'iesəlayt/ *vt* **1** to set apart from others; *also* to quarantine **2** to select from among others; *esp* to separate from another substance so as to obtain pure or in a free state **3** to insulate [back-formation fr *isolated* set apart, fr Fr *isolé*, fr It *isolato*, fr *isola* island, fr L *insula*] – **isolator** *n*, **isolable** *also* **isolatable** *adj*

²**isolate** /'iesəlat, -layt/ *n* a product of isolating; an individual or kind obtained by selection or separation

**isolating** /'iesəlayting/ *adj, of a language* ANALYTIC (not using changes in the form of words to express grammatical relationships)

**isolation** /ˌiesə'laysh(ə)n/ *n* isolating or being isolated **synonyms** see SOLITUDE

**isolationism** /ˌiesə'layshən͵iz(ə)m/ *n* a policy of isolation; *esp* such a policy pursued by a nation deliberately abstaining from international political and economic relations (eg alliances or trade agreements) – **isolationist** *n or adj*

**isoleucine** /ˌiesoh'loohseen, -sin, ͵iesə-/ *n* an ESSENTIAL AMINO ACID, $CH_3CH_2CH(CH_3)CH(NH_2)COO$ H, that is required by the body for normal development and health and forms part of many proteins, and that is isomeric with LEUCINE [ISV]

**isoline** /'iesoh͵lien/ *n* ISOPLETH 2 (line on a map joining constant values)

**isomagnetic** /ˌiesoh·mag'netik/ *adj* **1** of points of equal magnetic intensity or of equal value of a component of such intensity **2** connecting isomagnetic points ⟨~ *line on a map*⟩ [ISV]

**isomer** /'iesəmə/ *n* a chemical compound, group, ion, or atom exhibiting isomerism [ISV, back-formation fr *isomeric*]

**isomerase** /ie'somərayz, -rays/ *n* an ENZYME that speeds up the conversion of the substance (SUBSTRATE) upon which it acts to an isomeric form

**isomeric** /ˌiesoh'merik/ *adj* relating to or exhibiting isomerism [ISV, fr Gk *isomerēs* equally divided, fr *is-* + *meros* part – more at MERIT]

**isomerism** /ie'somə͵riz(ə)m/ *n* **1** the relation of two or more chemical compounds, groups, or ions that contain the same numbers of atoms of the same elements but differ in structural arrangement and properties **2** the relation of two or more NUCLIDES (atoms characterized by the composition of their nuclei) with the same MASS NUMBERS and ATOMIC NUMBERS but different energy states and rates of radioactive decay **3** the condition of being isomerous

**isomer·ize, -ise** /ie'soməriez/ *vi* to become changed into an isomeric form ~ *vt* to cause to isomerize – **isomerization** *n*

**isomerous** /ie'somərəs/ *adj* having an equal number of parts (eg ridges or markings); *esp, of a flower* having the members of each floral WHORL (arrangement of petals around the stem) equal in number

**isometric** /ˌiesoh'metrik, ͵iesə-/ *also* **isometrical** /-kl/ *adj* **1** relating to or characterized by equality of measure: eg **1a** relating to or being an ISOMETRIC DRAWING or ISOMETRIC PROJECTION **b** relating to or being a crystal structure or crystallization system characterized by three equal axes at right angles **2** relating to or involving isometrics – **isometrically** *adv*

**isometric drawing** *n* a three-dimensional representation of an object in which the lines in all three dimensions are drawn to scale

**isometric line** *n* **1** ISOPLETH 2 (line on a map joining constant values) **2** a line representing changes of pressure or temperature under conditions of constant volume

**isometric projection** *n* a method of drawing a three-dimensional object in which the three faces shown are equally inclined to the drawing surface so that all the edges are equally foreshortened – compare AXONOMETRIC PROJECTION

**isometrics** /ˌiesoh'metriks, ͵iesə-/ *n taking sing or pl vb* exercise or a system of exercises in which opposing muscles are so contracted that there is little shortening but great increase in TONE (condition of tension and elasticity) of muscle fibres involved

**isometry** /ie'somətri/ *n, maths* a mapping of a METRIC SPACE onto another SPACE so that the distance between any two points in the original space is the same as the distance between their images in the second space ⟨*rotation and translation are* isometries *of the plane*⟩

**isomorph** /'iesoh͵mawf/ *n* something identical with or similar to something else in form or structure: eg **a** one of two or more substances related by isomorphism **b** an individual or group exhibiting isomorphism [ISV] – **isomorphous** *adj*

**isomorphic** /ˌiesoh'mawfik, iesoh-/ *adj* **1** being of identical or similar form, shape, or structure; *esp, of some lower plants* having the generations bearing nonsexual (SPOROPHYTIC) and sexual (GAMETOPHYTIC) stages alike in size and shape ⟨*some algae and fungi are* ~⟩ **2** related by an isomorphism ⟨~ *mathematical rings*⟩ – **isomorphically** *adv*

**isomorphism** /ˌiesoh'mawfiz(ə)m/ *n* **1** superficial or apparent similarity in organisms of different ancestry resulting from evolution along similar lines **2a** similarity of crystalline form between substances of closely similar composition **b** HOMOEOMORPHISM (similarity of crystalline form between unlike substances) **3** *maths* a HOMOMORPHISM (type of mapping) that is BIJECTIVE (associating each element of one set uniquely with another) [ISV]

**isoniazid** /ˌiesoh'nie·əzid/ *n* a synthetic antibacterial drug, $NC_5H_4CONHNH_2$, used in treating tuberculosis [*isoni*cotinic acid hydr*azide*]

**isooctane** /ˌiesoh'oktayn/ *n* an inflammable liquid OCTANE (constituent of petroleum), $(CH_3)_3CCH_2CH(CH_3)_2$, used to determine the OCTANE NUMBER (indication of content) of fuels [ISV]

**isophote** /'iesə͵foht, 'iesoh-/ *n* a curve on a chart joining points of equal light intensity from a given source [ISV *is-* + *-phote*, fr Gk *phōt-, phōs* light – more at FANCY] – **isophotal** *adj*

**isopiestic** /ˌiesoh·pie'estik/ *adj* relating to or marked by equal pressure [*is-* + Gk *piestos*, verbal of *piezein* to press]

**isopleth** /'iesoh͵pleth, 'iesə-/ *n* **1** a line on a meteorological graph joining constant values (eg of temperature, pressure, or rainfall) and showing the occurrence or frequency of a phenomenon as a function of two variables **2** a line (eg an ISOBAR) on a map connecting points at which a given variable (e g height above SEA LEVEL) has, or is assumed to have, a specified constant value – called also ISOGRAM, ISOLINE, ISOMETRIC LINE [ISV *is-* + Gk *plēthos* quantity; akin to Gk *plēthein* to be full – more at FULL] – **isoplethic** *adj*

**isopod** /'iesə,pod/ *n* any of a large order (Isopoda of the class Crustacea) of small freshwater, marine, or terrestrial licelike INVERTEBRATE animals (e g a wood-louse) with eyes not borne on stalks and the body composed of seven free segments each bearing a pair of similar legs [deriv of Gk *is-* + *pod-*, *pous* foot – more at FOOT] – **isopod** *adj*, **isopodan** *adj or n*

**isoprenaline** /,iesə'prenəleen/ *n* a synthetic drug, $(HO)_2C_6H_3CH(OH)CH_2NHCH(CH_3)_2$, that has the same stimulatory effect as the hormone ADRENALIN and is used esp to treat asthma and to stimulate the heart [prob fr *isopropyl* + *adrenaline*]

**isoprene** /-,preen/ *n* an inflammable liquid chemical compound, $CH_2=C(CH_3)CH=CH_2$, used esp in the manufacture of rubber [prob fr *is-* + *propyl* + *-ene*]

**isoprenoid** /,iesə'preenoyd/, **isoprenoidal** /,iesoh'preenoydl, -pree'noydl/ *adj* relating to, containing, or being a chemical grouping characteristic of isoprene

**isopropyl alcohol** /,iesoh'prohpil/ *n* an inflammable alcohol, $CH_3CH(OH)CH_3$, that vaporizes readily and is used esp as a solvent and for cleansing wounds

**isoproterenol** /,iesəproh'terənol, -nohl/ *n* isoprenaline [*isopropyl* + ar*terenol* (norepinephrine), fr *Arterenol*, a trademark]

**isopteran** /ie'soptərən/ *n* a termite [deriv of Gk *isos* equal + *pteron* wing]

**isosceles** /ie'sosəleez/ *adj*, *of a triangle* having two sides of equal length [LL, fr Gk *isoskelēs*, fr *is-* + *skelos* leg]

**isoseismal** /,iesoh'siezməl, ,iesə-/ *adj* relating to or marked by equal intensity of earthquake shock

**isosmotic** /,iesoz'motik/ *adj*, *of solutions* relating to or exhibiting equal OSMOTIC PRESSURE [ISV] – **isosmotically** *adv*

**isospin** /'iesə,spin/ *n* a QUANTUM NUMBER used to characterize a group of closely related ELEMENTARY PARTICLES (minute parts of an atom) (e g a proton and a neutron) that differ only in electric charge – called also ISOTOPIC SPIN

**isospondylous** /,iesoh'spondələs/ *adj* relating to an order (Isospondyli) of primitive soft-finned BONY FISHES that includes many important food fishes (e g the herring and salmon) [deriv of Gk *isos* equal + *spondylos* vertebra – more at SPONDYLITIS]

**isosporous** /,iesə'spawrəs, ie'sospərəs/ *adj* producing sexual or nonsexual spores of only one kind – **isospory** *n*

**isostasy** /ie'sostəsi/ *n* 1 the quality or state of being subjected to equal pressure from every side 2 general EQUILIBRIUM (balance) in the earth's crust maintained by a yielding flow of rock material beneath the surface under the stress of gravity [ISV *is-* + Gk *-stasia* condition of standing, fr *histanai* to cause to stand – more at STAND] – **isostatic** *adj*, **isostatically** *adv*

**isotach** /'iesə,tak/ *n* a line on a map or chart connecting points of equal wind speed [ISV *is-* + *-tach* (fr Gk *tachys* quick)]

**isotherm** /'iesoh,thuhm, 'iesə-/ *n* 1 a line on a map or chart connecting points having the same temperature at a given time or the same average temperature for a given period 2 a line on a chart representing changes of volume or pressure under conditions of constant temperature [Fr *isotherme*, adj]

**isothermal** /,iesoh'thuhml, iesə-/ *adj* 1 relating to or marked by equality of temperature 2 relating to or marked by changes of volume or pressure under conditions of constant temperature [Fr *isotherme*, fr *is-* + Gk *thermos* hot – more at WARM] – **isothermally** *adv*

**isotonic** /,iesə'tonik/ *adj* 1 relating to or exhibiting equal tension 2 *of solutions* isosmotic [ISV] – **isotonically** *adv*, **isotonicity** *n*

**isotope** /'iesə,tohp/ *n* 1 any of two or more species of atoms of a chemical element with the same ATOMIC NUMBER and position in the PERIODIC TABLE of elements and nearly identical chemical behaviour, but with differing ATOMIC MASS or MASS NUMBER and different physical properties 2 NUCLIDE (atom characterized by composition of its nucleus) [*is-* + Gk *topos* place – more at TOPIC] – **isotopic** *adj*, **isotopically** *adv*, **isotopy** *n*

**isotopic spin** /,iesə'topik/ *n* isospin

**isotropic** /iesoh'tropik, ,iesə-/ *adj* exhibiting properties (e g velocity of light transmission) with the same values when measured along axes in all directions ⟨*an ~ crystal*⟩ [ISV] – **isotropy** *n*

**isozyme** /-,ziem/ *n* any of two or more ENZYMES (proteins that promote biological reactions) that are chemically distinct but perform the same function – **isozymic**

**I-spy** /ie 'spie/ *n* a children's game in which an object which can be seen by the players is guessed from the initial letter of its name

**Israel** /'izrayəl, 'izrie-əl/ *n* 1 the Jewish people 2 a people chosen by God ⟨*Christian claims to be the true ~*⟩ [ME, fr OE, fr LL, fr Gk *Israēl*, fr Heb *Yiśrā'ēl*] – **Israel** *adj*

¹**Israeli** /iz'rayli/ *adj* of modern Israel [NHeb *yiśrĕ'ēlī*, fr Heb, Israelite, n & adj, fr *Yiśrā'ēl*]

²**Israeli** *n*, *pl* **Israelis** *also* **Israeli** a native or inhabitant of modern Israel

**Israelite** /'izrəliet/ *n* a descendant of the Hebrew patriarch Jacob; *specif* a native or inhabitant of the ancient northern kingdom of Israel [ME, fr LL *Israelita*, fr Gk *Israēlitēs*, fr *Israēl*] – **Israelite**, **Israelitish** *adj*

**issuable** /'ishooəbl, 'isyooəbl/ *adj* 1 open to contest, debate, or LITIGATION (legal proceedings) 2 authorized for issue ⟨*bonds ~ under the merger terms*⟩ 3 possible as a result or consequence – **issuably** *adv*

**issuance** /'ishooəns/ *n*, *formal* the act of issuing; ISSUE 2, 8a

**issuant** /'ishooənt, 'isyoo-/ *adj* 1 *of a heraldic animal* having only the upper part depicted 2 *archaic* coming forth; emerging

¹**issue** /'ish(y)ooh, 'isyooh/ *n* 1 *pl* proceeds from a source of revenue (e g an estate) 2 the action of going, coming, or flowing out; EMERGENCE 1 3 a means or place of going out; an exit, outlet 4 offspring, progeny ⟨*died without ~*⟩ 5 an outcome that usu constitutes a solution (e g of a problem), resolution (e g of a difficulty), or decision; a result 6a a matter that is in dispute between two or more parties; a point of debate or controversy b the point at which an unsettled matter is ready for a decision ⟨*brought the matter to an ~*⟩ 7 something coming forth from a specified source ⟨*~s of a disordered imagination*⟩ 8a the act of publishing or officially giving out or making available ⟨*the next ~ of commemorative stamps*⟩ ⟨*~ of supplies by the quartermaster*⟩ b the thing or the whole quantity of things given out at one time; *specif* a number of a magazine, periodical, etc ⟨*read the latest ~*⟩ 9 *archaic* a final outcome or solution; a termination 10 *archaic* a discharge (e g of blood) from the body [ME, exit, proceeds, fr MF, fr OF, fr *issir* to come out, go out, fr L *exire* to go out, fr *ex-* + *ire* to go; akin to Goth *iddja* he went, Gk *ienai* to go, Skt *eti* he goes] – **issueless** *adj* – **at issue** under discussion or consideration; in dispute – **join/take issue** to take an opposing or conflicting stand; disagree *with*

²**issue** *vi* 1a to go, come, or flow out b to come forth; emerge c to come to an issue of law or fact in pleading 2 to accrue ⟨*profits issuing from the sale of the stock*⟩ 3 to descend from a specified parent or ancestor 4 to be a consequence; emanate – *in* 5 to have a consequence; result 6 to appear or become available through being officially put forth or distributed; appear through issuance or publication ⟨*no new editions are expected to ~ from that press*⟩ ~ *vt* 1 to cause to come forth; discharge, emit 2a to give out or distribute officially ⟨*government ~d a new airmail stamp*⟩ b to provide or equip officially; supply ⟨*why are we being ~d with Privy Council stationery? – Punch*⟩ c to send out for sale or circulation; PUBLISH 2b – **issuer** *n*

**issuing house** /'ish(y)ooing, 'isyooing/ *n* a financial institution that acts as sponsor to a company seeking to raise capital by issuing shares for it. Normally an issuing house will buy the entire share issue of a company and then sell it to the public.

¹**-ist** /-ist/ *suffix* (→ *n*) 1a one who performs (a specified action) ⟨*cyclist*⟩ b one who makes or produces (a specified thing) ⟨*novelist*⟩ c one who plays (a specified musical instrument) ⟨*harpist*⟩ d one who operates (a specified mechanical instrument or device) ⟨*motorist*⟩ 2 one who specializes in or practises (a specified art, science, skill, or profession) ⟨*geologist*⟩ ⟨*ventriloquist*⟩ 3 one who adheres to or advocates (a specified doctrine, system, or code of behaviour) ⟨*socialist*⟩ ⟨*royalist*⟩ ⟨*hedonist*⟩ ⟨*Calvinist*⟩ 4 one who is prejudiced on grounds of ⟨*sexist*⟩ [ME *-iste*, fr OF & L; OF *-iste*, fr L *-ista*, *-istes*, fr Gk *-istēs*, fr verbs in *-izein* *-ize*]

*usage* Where a word can be formed with either **-ist** or **-alist** ⟨*education(al)ist*⟩ it is reasonable to prefer the shorter version.

²**-ist** *suffix* (→ *adj*) 1 relating to or characteristic of ⟨*dilettantist*⟩ ⟨*obscurantist*⟩ 2 showing prejudice on grounds of ⟨*racist*⟩

¹**isthmian** /'isthmiə/ a native or inhabitant of an isthmus

²**isthmian**, **isthmic** *adj* of or situated in or near an isthmus:

e g a *often cap* of the Isthmus of Corinth in Greece or the games held there in ancient times **b** *often cap* of the Isthmus of Panama

**isthmus** /'isməs; *also* 'isthməs/ *n* **1** a narrow strip of land connecting two larger land areas **2** a narrow part or passage of an animal's body connecting two larger structures or cavities [L, fr Gk *isthmos*]

**istle** /'istli/ *n* a strong fibre (e g for ropes or baskets) made from various tropical American plants [AmerSp *ixtle*, fr Nahuatl *ichtli*]

**¹it** /it/ *pron* **1** that thing, creature, or group – used as subject or object ⟨*took a quick look at the house and noticed that ~ was very old*⟩ ⟨*had a baby but lost ~*⟩ ⟨*the government realizes that ~ must act*⟩ ⟨*beauty is everywhere and ~ is a source of joy*⟩; – compare HE, ITS, THEY, **²THERE 2a** – used as subject of an impersonal verb ⟨*~'s raining*⟩ ⟨*~'s not far to London*⟩ ⟨*~ says so in the paper*⟩ **b** – used as the impersonal subject of a sentence which makes a promise ⟨*~'s a promise*⟩, confirms an arrangement ⟨*~'s a date*⟩, or seals a contract ⟨*~'s a deal*⟩ **3a** – used as anticipatory subject or object of a verb ⟨*~'s no fun being a secretary*⟩ ⟨*~ seems that they went*⟩ ⟨*I take ~ that you refuse*⟩ ⟨*he can't keep ~ if he's stupid*⟩ **b** – used to highlight part of a sentence ⟨*~ was the President who arrived yesterday*⟩ ⟨*~ was yesterday that he arrived*⟩ **c** – used with many verbs and prepositions as a meaningless object ⟨*run for ~*⟩ ⟨*footed ~ back to camp*⟩ **4a** this, that – used to refer to previous or following information ⟨*he failed. It's a shame*⟩ **b** – used to refer to an explicit or implicit state of affairs ⟨*how's ~ going?*⟩ **5** that which is available ⟨*one boiled egg and that's ~*⟩, important ⟨*yes, that's just ~*⟩, or appropriate ⟨*a bit tighter – that's ~*⟩ [ME, fr OE *hit* – more at HE]

**usage 1** The spelling of **its** meaning "of it" as ⚠ **it's** is a common confusion ⟨⚠ **it's** roadholding puts Viceroy in the forefront of cars – *The Times*⟩. Compare ⟨**it's** (= it is) *ready*⟩ ⟨**it's** (= it has) *gone*⟩ but ⟨**its** *climate*⟩ ⟨**its** *kennel*⟩. **2** One should avoid using **it** unless the meaning is clear. In ⟨*drank some coffee because* **it** *was cold*⟩ was the coffee cold, or the weather?

**²it** *n* **1** the player in a game who performs a function (e g trying to catch others in a game of tag) essential to the nature of the game ⟨*who's ~? He is*⟩ **2** a neuter or sexless creature ⟨*our cat's an ~*⟩ – sometimes used offensively of people **3** SEX APPEAL; *also* SEXUAL INTERCOURSE ⟨*the next most difficult thing to doing ~ standing up in a hammock* – Len Deighton⟩

**³it** *n, informal* ITALIAN VERMOUTH

**itacolumite** /ˌitə'koləmiet/ *n* a granular rock derived from QUARTZ that resembles the mineral MICA and is flexible when split into thin slabs [*Itacolumi*, mountain in Brazil]

**itaconic acid** /ˌitə'konik/ *n* a solid chemical compound, $CH_2=C(CO_2H)CH_2CO_2H$, obtained usu by fermentation of sugars with moulds (genus *Aspergillus*) and used in the manufacture of vinyls and plastics [ISV, anagram of *aconitic acid*, $C_3H_3(COOH)_3$, from the decomposition of which it can be obtained]

**Italian** /i'tali·ən/ *n* **1** a native or inhabitant of Italy **2** the ROMANCE (Latin-based) language of the Italians [*Italy*, country in S Europe] – **Italian** *adj*

**italianate** /i'talyənayt/ *vt* to italianize

**Italianate** /i'talyənət, -nayt/ *adj* **1** Italian in quality or characteristics ⟨*a dark ~ beauty*⟩ **2** resembling the art or architecture of Italy esp from the 14th to the 16th century

**Italian greyhound** *n* (any of) a breed of TOY DOGS developed by selective breeding from standard greyhounds

**Italianism** /i'talyəniz(ə)m/ *n* **1a** a characteristic feature (e g a custom, belief, or artistic style) of Italians or Italian culture **b** a characteristic feature of Italian occurring in another language **2a** adherence or attachment to Italy or to Italian customs, tastes, or styles **b** promotion of Italian policies

**italian·ize, -ise** /i'talyəniz/ *vb, often cap* **vi** to have or acquire Italian customs, tastes, or characteristics; *specif* to follow the style or technique of recognized Italian painters ~ *vt* to make Italian (e g in appearance, behaviour, or outlook) – **Italianization** *n*

**Italian ryegrass** *n* a European grass (*Lolium multiflorum*) much used for hay

**Italian sonnet** *n* PETRARCHAN SONNET (14-line verse form with characteristic rhyme pattern)

**Italian vermouth** *n* a usu dark reddish-brown sweet vermouth

**Italian warehouseman** *n* a seller or importer of Italian groceries (e g pasta, olive oil, and dried fruits)

**¹italic** /i'talik/ *adj* **1** *cap* of ancient Italy, its peoples, or their Indo-European languages **2** of a type style with characters that slant upwards to the right (e g in "*these words are italic*") **3** of a style of handwriting, usu using a broad-nibbed pen, in which vertical and horizontal strokes are thick and slanting strokes are thin ⟨*an ~ pen*⟩ [(2) fr this type style having been introduced by Aldus Manutius †1515 It printer]

**²italic** *n* **1a** an italic type or handwriting style **b** a character in italic type or script ⟨*a word in ~s for emphasis*⟩ **2** *cap* the Italic branch of the Indo-European language family

**Italicism** /i'talisiz(ə)m/ *n* ITALIANISM 1b

**italic·ize, -ise** /i'tali,siez/ *vt* to print in italics or underline with a single line to indicate italic type to the printer – **italicization** *n*

**Italo-** /italoh-/ *comb form* Italian; Italian and ⟨*Italo-Austrian*⟩

**¹itch** /ich/ *vi* **1a** to have an itch ⟨*her arm ~ed*⟩ **b** to produce an itching sensation ⟨*long underwear that ~es*⟩ **2** to have a restless desire or hankering ⟨*were ~ing to go outside*⟩ ~ *vt* to cause to itch [ME *icchen*, fr OE *giccan;* akin to OHG *jucchen* to itch]

**²itch** *n* **1a** an uneasy irritating sensation in the upper surface of the skin that makes one want to scratch **b** a skin disorder accompanied by such a sensation; *esp* SCABIES (infection of skin with parasitic mites) **2** a restless usu constant often compulsive desire ⟨*an ~ to travel*⟩ – **itchiness** *n*, **itchy** *adj*

**it'd** /'itəd/ it had; it would

**¹-ite** /-iet/ *suffix* (→ *n*) **1a** one who belongs to (a specified place, country, tribe, or group) ⟨*Israelite*⟩ ⟨*socialite*⟩ ⟨*Hittite*⟩ **b** adherent or follower of (a specified doctrine or movement) ⟨*Puseyite*⟩ ⟨*Pre-Raphaelite*⟩ **2a(1)** product of ⟨*metabolite*⟩ ⟨*catabolite*⟩ **a(2)** commercially manufactured product ⟨*ebonite*⟩ **b** -itol ⟨*inosite*⟩ **3** fossil ⟨*ammonite*⟩ **4** mineral ⟨*bauxite*⟩ ⟨*bentonite*⟩ **5** segment or constituent part of (a specified body or organ) ⟨*somite*⟩ ⟨*dendrite*⟩ [ME, fr OF & L; OF, fr L *-ita*, *-ites*, fr Gk *-itēs;* (3) NL *-ites*, fr L; (5) Fr, fr L *-ita*, *-ites*]

**²-ite** *suffix* (→ *n*) salt or ester of (a specified acid with a name ending in *-ous*) ⟨*sulphite*⟩ [Fr, alter. of *-ate* -ate, fr NL *-atum*]

**¹item** /'ietəm/ *adv* and in addition; also – used to introduce each article in a list [ME, fr L, fr *ita* thus]

**²item** *n* **1** a separate particular in a list, account, or series; an article **2** a separate piece of news or information ⟨*column of local ~s*⟩ – **item** *vt*

**item·ize, -ise** /'ietəmiez/ *vt* to state or set down in detail or by particulars; list ⟨*~d all expenses*⟩ – **itemization** *n*

**iterance** /'itərəns/ *n* REPETITION 1 ⟨*what needs this ~, Woman? I say, thy husband!* – Shak⟩ – **iterant** *adj or n*

**iterate** /'itərayt/ *vt* to say or do again or repetitively; reiterate *usage* see REITERATE [L *iteratus*, pp of *iterare*, fr *iterum* again; akin to L *is* he, that, *ita* thus, Skt *itara* the other, *iti* thus] – **iteration** *n*

**iterative** /'itərətiv/ *adj* involving repetition: e g **a** *of a verb form* FREQUENTATIVE (marking repeated state of affairs) **b** relating to or being an arithmetical procedure in which repetition of a cycle of operations produces results which are ever closer approximations to an unknown value – **iteratively** *adv*

**ithyphallic** /ˌithi'falik/ *adj* **1** relating to the PHALLUS (model of a penis) carried in procession in ancient festivals of the Greek god, Bacchus **2a** having an erect penis – usu used of figures in pictures or statues **b** *formal* obscene, lewd [LL *ithyphallicus*, fr Gk *ithyphallikos*, fr *ithyphallos* erect phallus, fr *ithys* straight + *phallos* phallus]

**itineracy** /ie'tinərəsi, i'tin-/ *n* itinerancy

**itinerancy** /ie'tinərənsi, i'ti-/ *n* **1** itinerating or being itinerant **2a** a system (e g in the Methodist Church) of itinerant ministers who are appointed to different groups of congregations by rotation **b** a group of people (e g preachers or judges) who travel from place to place in the course of their work or duty

**¹itinerant** /ie'tinərənt/ *adj* travelling from place to place; *esp* covering a circuit ⟨*~ preacher*⟩ [LL *itinerant-, itinerans*, prp of *itinerari* to journey, fr L *itiner-, iter* journey, way, fr *ire* to go – more at ISSUE] – **itinerantly** *adv*

**²itinerant** *n* one who moves from place to place; *esp, formal* a tramp, vagrant

**itinerary** /ie'tinərəri, i'ti-/ *n* **1** (the proposed outline of) the route of a journey **2** a travel diary **3** a traveller's guidebook – **itinerary** *adj*

**itinerate** /ie'tinərayt, i'ti-/ *vi* to travel from place to place, esp on a preaching or judicial circuit – **itinerate** *adj*, **itineration** *n*

**-itious** /-ishəs/ *suffix* (→ *adj*) relating to or having the characteristics of ⟨*fictitious*⟩ ⟨*expedi*tious⟩ [L *-icius, -itius*]

**-itis** /-ietəs/ *suffix* (→ *n*), *pl* **-itises** *also* **-itides** *sometimes* **-ites** 1 disease or inflammation of ⟨*bronch*itis⟩ 2a suffering caused by a surfeit or excess of ⟨*television*itis⟩ b infatuation or obsession with ⟨*jazz*itis⟩ c excess of the qualities of ⟨*big-business*itis⟩ [NL, fr L & Gk; L, fr Gk, fr fem of -*itēs* -ite]

**it'll** /'itl/ it will; it shall

**-itol** /-itol/ *suffix* (→ *n*) ALCOHOL usu related to a sugar ⟨*mann*itol⟩ [ISV -*īte* (fr [1]-*ite*) + -*ol*]

**its** /its/ *adj* of it or itself, esp as possessor ⟨~ *climate*⟩ ⟨*going to ~ kennel*⟩, agent ⟨*a child proud of ~ first drawings*⟩ ⟨*war and all ~ horrors – SEU S*⟩, or object of an action ⟨~ *final enactment into law*⟩ *usage* see [1]IT

**it's** /its/ it is; it has

**itself** /it'self/ *pron* 1 that identical thing, creature, or group – compare [1]IT 1; used reflexively ⟨*a cat washing ~*⟩ ⟨*history repeating ~*⟩, for emphasis ⟨*the letter ~ was missing*⟩, or in absolute constructions ⟨~ *a splendid specimen of classic art, it is sure to be exhibited throughout the world*⟩; compare ONESELF 2 its normal self – **(all) by itself** without help; alone – **in itself** without considering the rest; as such ⟨*not dangerous* in itself⟩

**itsy-bitsy** /,itsi 'bitsi/ *adj, informal* extremely small; tiny ⟨*perhaps I could just manage an ~ slice of that cake*⟩ [prob fr baby talk for *little bit*]

**itty-bitty** /,iti 'biti/ *adj, informal* itsy-bitsy

**-ity** /-əti/ *suffix* (→ *n*) 1 quality or state of ⟨*author*ity⟩ ⟨*theatrical*ity⟩; *also* instance of (a specified quality or state) ⟨*an obscen*ity⟩ 2 amount or degree of ⟨*humid*ity⟩ ⟨*salin*ity⟩ *usage* see -TY [ME -*ite*, fr OF or L; OF -*ité*, fr L -*itat*-, -*itas*, fr -i- (stem vowel of adjs) + -*tat*-, -*tas* -ty; akin to Gk -*tēt*-, -*tēs* -ity]

**IUD** *n* INTRAUTERINE DEVICE (contraceptive device)

**-ium** /-i-əm/ *suffix* (→ *n*), *pl* **-iums, -ia** /-iə/ 1a usu metallic chemical element ⟨*sod*ium⟩ b positive ion ⟨*imidazol*ium⟩ ⟨*ammon*ium⟩ 2 small kind of; mass of – esp in botanical terms ⟨*pollin*ium⟩ 3 biological part; part or region of body ⟨*epi*-*the*lium⟩ ⟨*hypogastr*ium⟩ [(1) NL, fr L, ending of some neut nouns; (2,3) NL, fr L, fr Gk -*ion*]

**[1]-ive** /-iv/ *suffix* (→ *adj*) 1 tending to; disposed to ⟨*correc*tive⟩ ⟨*spor*tive⟩ 2 performing (a specified function) ⟨*descrip*tive⟩ ⟨*genera*tive⟩ [ME -*if*, -*ive*, fr MF & L; MF -*if*, fr L -*ivus*]

**[2]-ive** *suffix* (→ *n*) 1 one who or that which performs or serves to accomplish (a specified action) ⟨*seda*tive⟩ ⟨*detec*tive⟩ 2 one who is in or affected by (a specified state or condition) ⟨*cap*tive⟩ ⟨*consump*tive⟩

**I've** /iev/ I have

**ivied** /'ievid/ *adj* overgrown with ivy ⟨~ *walls*⟩

**ivory** /'ievəri/ *n* 1a the hard creamy-white modified DENTINE (tooth material) that composes the tusks of a tusked mammal, esp the elephant b a tusk (e g of an elephant) that yields ivory 2 a creamy slightly yellowish white colour 3 *pl, informal* things (e g dice or piano keys) made of ivory or of a similar substance 4 *slang* a tooth [ME *ivorie*, fr OF *ivoire*, fr L *eboreus* of ivory, fr *ebor*-, *ebur* ivory, fr Egypt ;*b*, ;*bw* elephant, ivory] – **ivory** *adj*

**ivory black** *n* black pigment made from charred ivory

**ivory gull** *n* a gull (*Pagophila eburnea*) of the arctic regions

**ivory nut** *n* the nutlike seed of a S American palm (*Phytelephas macrocarpa*) containing a very hard kernel used for carving and turning – compare VEGETABLE IVORY

**ivory tower** *n* 1 an impractical often escapist aloofness from practical concerns 2 a secluded place (e g for meditation); a retreat ⟨*viewing college as an ~*⟩ [trans of Fr *tour d'ivoire*; orig used by C A Sainte-Beuve †1869 Fr poet & critic] – **ivory-tower** *also* **ivory-towered, ivory-towerish** *adj*

**ivy** /'ievi/ *n* 1 a very common and widely cultivated climbing, ground-covering, or sometimes shrubby Eurasian woody plant (*Hedera helix* of the family Araliaceae, the ivy family) with ever-green leaves, small yellowish flowers, and black berries 2 *NAm* POISON IVY [ME, fr OE *īfig*; akin to OHG *ebah* ivy]

**Ivy League** *adj, NAm* (characteristic) of a group of long-established eastern US universities (e g Harvard) widely regarded as high in scholastic and esp social prestige – **Ivy Leaguer** *n*

**iwis** /ee'wis/ *adv, archaic* certainly [ME, fr OE *gewis* certain; akin to OHG *giwisso* certainly, OE *witan* to know – more at WIT]

**ixia** /'iksiə/ *n* any of a genus (*Ixia*) of plants of the iris family of southern Africa, with large ornamental flowers [NL, genus name, fr Gk *ixos* mistletoe, birdlime]

**ixodid** /'iksədid, ik'sohdid/ *adj* relating to or being a typical tick [deriv of Gk *ixōdēs* sticky, fr *ixos* birdlime] – **ixodid** *n*

**Iyar** /'ee,yah/ *n* – see MONTH [Heb *Iyyār*]

**izard** /'izəd/ *n* a CHAMOIS (goatlike antelope) found in the Pyrenees Fr

**-ize, -ise** /-iez/ *suffix* (→ *vb*) 1a(1) cause to be, conform to, or resemble ⟨*liquid*ize⟩ ⟨*popular*ize⟩ a(2) subject to (a specified action) ⟨*plagiar*ize⟩ ⟨*critic*ize⟩ a(3) impregnate, treat, or combine with ⟨*albumin*ize⟩ ⟨*oxid*ize⟩ b treat like; make into ⟨*lion*ize⟩ ⟨*proselyt*ize⟩ c treat according to the method of ⟨*bowdler*ize⟩ 2a become; become like ⟨*crystall*ize⟩ b engage in (a specified activity) ⟨*philosoph*ize⟩ c experience (a specified feeling) ⟨*sympath*ize⟩ [ME -*isen*, fr OF -*iser*, fr LL -*izare*, fr Gk -*izein*]

*usage* 1 The sole American form of this suffix is **-ize**, and it is also a common British one, endorsed by the "house style" of many British publishing houses and newspapers. The following verbs must be spelt with **-ise** in both British and American English: *advertise, advise, apprise, chastise, circumcise, comprise, demise, despise, devise, disfranchise, disguise, enfranchise, excise, exercise, improvise, incise, merchandise, premise, revise, supervise, surmise, surprise, televise*. Sooner than learn the foregoing list, some British writers find it safer to use **-ise** all the time. The spelling of verbs ending in -*yse*, such as *analyse*, with a *z* is purely American. 2 The free creation of new verbs such as *containerize* and *privatize* is disapproved of by some people. One can sometimes replace an **-ize** verb such as *martyrize* by an already existing word such as the verb to *martyr*.

**izzard** /'izəd/ *n, archaic or dial NAm* the letter *z* [alter. of earlier *ezod, ezed*, prob fr MF *et zede* and Z]

**izzat** /'izət/ *n, chiefly Ind* personal dignity or reputation; honour [Hindi *'izzat*, fr Ar *'izzah* glory]

# J

**j, J** /jay/ *n, pl* **j's, js, J's, Js 1a** the 10th letter of the English alphabet **b** a graphic representation of or device for producing the letter *j* **c** a speech counterpart of printed or written *j* **2** *maths* a UNIT VECTOR parallel to the y-axis **3** one who or that which is designated *j*, esp as the 10th in order or class **4** something shaped like the letter J

**¹jab** /jab/ *vb*, **-bb-** *vt* **1a** to pierce (as if) with a sharp object; stab **b** to poke quickly or abruptly; thrust **2** to strike with a short straight blow ~ *vi* **1** to make quick or abrupt thrusts (as if) with a sharp or pointed object **2** to strike a person with a short straight blow [var of ³*job*]

**²jab** *n* an act of jabbing: eg **a** a short straight boxing punch delivered with the leading hand **b** *informal* an injection; esp one given (eg to someone travelling abroad) as protection against infection or disease (eg cholera) ⟨*has she had all her* ~s *for Indonesia yet?*⟩

**¹jabber** /'jabə/ *vi* to talk or chatter rapidly, indistinctly, or incomprehensibly ~ *vt* to utter rapidly or indistinctly [ME *jaberen*, of imit origin] – **jabberer** *n*

**²jabber** *n* rapid or unintelligible talk or chatter

**jabberwocky** /'jabəwoki/ *n* nonsensical speech or writing [*Jabberwocky*, nonsense poem in *Through the Looking-Glass* by Lewis Carroll (C L Dodgson) †1898 E writer]

**jabiru** /'jabirooh/ *n* any of several large tropical storks [Pg, fr Tupi & Guarani *jabirú*]

**jaborandi** /jabə'randi/ *n* the dried leaves of either of two S American shrubs (*Pilocarpus jaborandi* and *Pilocarpus microphyllus*) of the rue family that are a source of PILOCARPINE (drug formerly used to induce sweating) [Pg, fr Tupi *yaborandi*]

**jabot** /'zhaboh/ *n* a pleated frill of lace or cloth attached down the centre front of a woman's bodice; *also* a similar length of lace or cloth attached to the front of a neckband and worn, esp by men, in the 18th century [Fr]

**jacana** /ˌzhahsə'nah, jas-/ *n* any of several long-legged and long-toed wading birds (family Jacanidae) that frequent coastal freshwater marshes and ponds in warm regions [Pg *jaçanã*, fr Tupi & Guarani]

**jacaranda** /jakə'randə/ *n* (the wood of) any of a genus (*Jacaranda* of the family Bignoniaceae, the jacaranda family) of tropical American trees with showy blue flowers [NL, genus name, fr Pg, a tree of this genus, fr Tupi *yacarandá*]

**jacinth** /'jasinth/ *n* **1** a reddish-orange transparent form of the mineral ZIRCON used as a gem **2** *archaic* HYACINTH 2 (flowering plant) [ME *iacinct*, fr OF *jacinthe*, fr L *hyacinthus*, a flowering plant, a gem]

**jacinthe** /'jasinth, zhah'sant/ *n* a moderately intense orange colour [Fr, lit., hyacinth]

**¹jack** /jak/ *n* **1a** MAN 1a(1), 1e,3 – usu used as an intensive in such phrases as *every man jack* **b jack, jack tar** *often cap* a sailor **c**(1) a servant, labourer **c**(2) a lumberjack **c**(3) a steeplejack **2** any of various mechanical devices: eg **2a** a device for turning a spit **b** any of various mechanisms for exerting a force to lift a heavy body a short distance ⟨*car* ~⟩ **c** the part of the action of a keyboard instrument that drives the hammer or PLECTRUM (implement for plucking a string) **3** something that supports or holds in position **4a**(1) any of several fishes **a**(2) **jack** *also* **jackfish** a young pike **b** a male donkey **5a** a small national flag flown at the bow of a ship – compare UNION JACK **b**(1) *pl but taking sing vb* a game played with a set of small objects that are tossed, caught, and moved in successive numbers usu to the bounce of a small rubber ball **b**(2) a small 6-pointed metal object used in the game of jacks **6** a small ball rolled down the bowling green to serve as a target in bowls and boule **7** a playing card carrying the figure of a soldier or servant and ranking usu below the queen **8** JACKPOT 1 **9a** JACK PLUG (electrical plug) **b** JACK SOCKET (electrical socket) **10** *NAm slang* money [ME *jacke*, fr *Jacke*, nickname for *Johan* John]

**²jack** *vt* **1a** to move or lift (as if) by a jack **b** to raise the level or quality of ⟨~ *up the price*⟩ **2** to give up; abandon – usu + *in* or *up* ⟨*I was fed up with my job so I* ~ed *it in*⟩ **3** *NZ* to settle, fix □ (*1&3*) usu + *up* – **jacker** *n*

**jackal** /'jakl/ *n* **1** any of several wild dogs from Africa, Asia, and Europe that are smaller than the related wolves **2a** someone who performs routine or menial tasks for another **b** someone who serves or collaborates with another esp in wrong doing [Turk *çakal*, fr Per *shagāl*, fr Skt *sṛgāla*; (2) fr the former belief that the jackal flushed prey for the lion]

**jackanapes** /'jakəˌnayps/ *n* **1** an impudent or conceited fellow **2** a saucy or mischievous child **3** *archaic* a monkey, ape [perh alter. of (assumed) *Jack Ape*, name given to a pet ape]

**jackass** /'jakˌas/ *n* **1** a male ass; *also* a donkey **2** a stupid person; a fool – **jackassery** *n*

**jack bean** *n* a bushy tropical American plant (genus *Canavalia*) of the pea family; *esp* a plant (*Canavalia ensiformis*) grown esp for forage

**jackboot** /-ˌbooht/ *n* **1** a heavy military leather boot extending above the knee and worn esp during the 17th and 18th centuries **2** a laceless military boot reaching to the calf **3** a repressive fascist or military rule

**Jack-by-the-'hedge** *n* GARLIC MUSTARD

**jackdaw** /'jakˌdaw/ *n* a common black and grey Eurasian bird (*Corvus monedula*) that is related to but smaller than the common crow [¹*jack* + *daw*]

**jackeroo** *also* **jackaroo** /jakə'rooh/ *n*, *Austr informal* a young inexperienced worker on a cattle or sheep station [*jackeroo* alter. of *jackaroo*, fr ¹*jack* + *-aroo* (as in *kangaroo*)]

**¹jacket** /'jakit/ *n* **1a** an outer garment for the upper body usu having sleeves and opening the full length of the centre front **b** something that is worn or fastened round the body and serves a specific function: eg **b**(1) a lifejacket **b**(2) a straitjacket **2a** the natural covering (eg of fur or wool) of an animal **b** the skin of a potato esp when baked **3** an outer covering or casing: eg **3a**(1) an insulating cover (eg for a hot water tank) **a**(2) a covering that encloses an intermediate space through which a temperature-controlling liquid or gas circulates **a**(3) a tough metal casing that forms the outer shell of certain kinds of bullet **b** *chiefly NAm* **b**(1) a wrapper or open envelope for a document **b**(2) an envelope for enclosing registered mail during delivery from one post office to another **c**(1) DUST JACKET **c**(2) the cover of a paperback book **c**(3) the outside leaves for a booklet, pamphlet, or catalogue that is to be stitched or wired through the centre of the fold **c**(4) *chiefly NAm* a gramophone record sleeve [ME *jaket*, fr MF *jaquet*, dim. of *jaque* short jacket, prob fr *jacque* peasant, fr the name *Jacques* James]

**²jacket** *vt* to put a jacket on; enclose in or with a jacket

**jackfish** /'jakˌfish/ *n* PIKE 1

**Jack Frost** *n* frost or frosty weather personified

**jackfruit** /'jakˌfrooht/ *n* **1** (the fruit of) a large widely cultivated tropical tree (*Artocarpus heterophyllus*) of the fig family and closely related to the breadfruit, that yields a fine-grained yellow wood and immense fruits which contain an edible pulp and nutritious seeds **2** DURIAN [Pg *jaca* jackfruit (fr Malayalam *cakka*) + E *fruit*]

**jackhammer** /-ˌhamə/ *n* **1** a usu hand-held pneumatic hammer drill used for rock drilling **2** *NAm* PNEUMATIC DRILL

**'jack-in-ˌoffice** *n* a pretentious self-important petty official

**'jack-in-theˌbox** *n*, *pl* jack-in-the-boxes, jacks-in-the-box a toy consisting of a small box out of which a figure (eg of a clown's head) springs when the lid is raised

**Jack Ketch** /kech/ *n*, *Br informal* the public hangman [*Jack Ketch* †1686 E executioner]

**¹jackknife** /-ˌnief/ *n* **1** a large clasp knife for the pocket **2** a dive executed headfirst in which the diver bends from the waist, touches the ankles while keeping the knees straight, and then straightens out before hitting the water

**²jackknife** *vt* **1** to cut with a jackknife **2** to cause to double up like a jackknife ~ *vi* **1** to double up like a jackknife **2** to turn or rise and form an angle of 90° or less with each other – used esp of a pair of vehicles (eg a tractor and its trailer) that are fastened together

**jack-of-'all-,trades** *n, pl* **jacks-of-all-trades** one who can do passable work in various fields; a handy versatile person

**jack off** *vb, chiefly NAm vulgar* to masturbate [prob alter. of *jerk off*]

**'jack-o'-,lantern** *n* **1a** IGNIS FATUUS; WILL-O'-THE-WISP (appearance of fire in marshy ground) **b** SAINT ELMO'S FIRE (discharge of electricity during stormy weather) **2** a lantern made from a hollowed out pumpkin cut to look like a human face

**jack plane** *n* a medium-sized plane used in the first rough stages of planing wood

**jack plug** *n* a single-pronged electrical plug for insertion into a JACK SOCKET

**jackpot** /-,pot/ *n* **1** a large pot (eg in poker) formed by the accumulation of stakes from previous play **2a** a combination on a FRUIT MACHINE that wins a top prize or all the coins in the machine **b** the amount of jackpot won **3** a large amount of money or other prize (eg in a lottery or contest) often formed by the accumulation of unwon prizes ['jack 6 + 'pot 4; fr a form of poker in which a player needs two jacks or better to open] – **hit the jackpot 1** to win the jackpot **2** *informal* to have a big success

**jackrabbit** /'jak'rabit/ *n* any of several large hares (genus *Lepus*) of western N America that have very long ears and long hind legs [jackass + rabbit; fr its long ears]

**jack rafter** *n* a short rafter (eg one supporting an extension from the main roof)

**Jack Russell, Jack Russell terrier** /'jak 'rusl/ *n* (any of) a breed of small aggressive terrier dogs originally bred to hunt rats [*Jack* (John) *Russell* †1883 E clergyman & dog-fancier]

**jacksnipe** /-,sniep/ *n* a true SNIPE (wading bird with long beak) (*Lymnocryptes minimus*) from Africa, Asia, and Europe that is smaller and more highly coloured than the common snipe

**jack socket** *n* an electrical terminal usu consisting of a thin hollow cylindrical socket designed for speed and ease of connection

**jackstaff** /'jak,stahf/ *n* a short flagpole erected at the bow of a ship

**jackstone** /'jak,stohn/ *n* JACK 5b(2)

**jackstraw** /'jak,straw/ *n* **1** SPILLIKIN 1 **2** *pl but taking sing vb* SPILLIKIN 2

**jack tar** *n, often cap* a sailor

**jack towel** *n, dial Br* ROLLER TOWEL

**Jacobean** /,jakə'bee-ən/ *adj* of (the age of) James I [NL *Jacobaeus*, fr *Jacobus* James]

**Jacobin** /'jakəbin/ *n* **1** a Dominican friar **2** a member of a radical political group advocating a democracy in which all should be equal, and engaging in terrorist activities during the French Revolution of 1789; *broadly* a member of an extremist, radical, or terrorist political group **3** *often not cap* a type of pigeon with a cowl-like crest of feathers about the head [(1) ME, fr MF, fr ML *Jacobinus*, fr LL *Jacobus* (St James); fr the location of the first Dominican convent in the Rue St-Jacques (street of St James) in Paris; (2) Fr, fr *Jacobin* Dominican; fr the group's meeting in the former Dominican convent in Paris; (3) Fr *Jacobine*, fem of *Jacobin*] – **Jacobinism** *n*, **jacobinize** *vt, often cap*, **Jacobinic, Jacobinical** *adj*

**Jacobite** /'jakəbiet/ *n* a supporter of James II or of the Stuarts after the revolution of 1688 [*Jacobus* (James II)] – **Jacobitical** *adj*, **Jacobitism** *n*

**Jacob's ladder** /'jaykəbz/ *n* **1** any of a genus (*Polemonium*) of plants of the phlox family that have bell-shaped flowers; *esp* a plant (*Polemonium caeruleum*) of European origin that is widely grown for its bright blue or white flowers **2** a rope or wire ladder used on board ship [fr the ladder seen in a dream by Jacob in Gen 28:12]

**jaconet** /'jakənit/ *n* a lightweight cotton cloth used for clothing and bandages [modif of Urdu *jagannāthī*, fr *Jagannath* (Puri), city in E India]

**jacquard** /'jakahd/ *n, often cap* **1a jacquard, jacquard loom** a loom for weaving patterned fabrics **2** a fabric of intricate weave or pattern [Joseph *Jacquard* †1834 Fr inventor]

**jacquerie** /'zhakəri (Fr zakri)/ *n, often cap* a peasants' revolt [Fr (orig applied to the French peasant revolt in 1358), fr MF, fr *jacque* peasant – more at JACKET]

**jactation** /jak'taysh(ə)n/ *n* **1** JACTITATION 1 **2** *archaic* BOAST 1

[L *jactation-, jactatio*, fr *jactatus*, pp of *jactare* to throw, shake, speak out, boast – more at JET]

**jactitation** /,jakti'taysh(ə)n/ *n* **1** a tossing to and fro or jerking and twitching of the body **2a** *archaic* BOAST 1 **b** a false claim; *specif* one of marriage, formerly actionable at law [LL *jactitation-, jactitatio*, fr *jactitatus*, pp of *jactitare*, freq of *jactare* to throw]

**Jacuzzi** /jə'koohzi/ *trademark* – used for a system of underwater jets to be fitted into a HOT TUB

**'jade** /jayd/ *n* **1** a vicious or worn-out old horse **2** a flirtatious or disreputable woman; a hussy [ME]

**²jade** *n* either of two tough compact typically green gemstones that takes a high polish: **a** JADEITE **b** NEPHRITE [Fr, fr obs Sp (*piedra de la*) *ijada*, lit., loin stone; fr the belief that jade cures renal colic]

**jaded** /'jaydid/ *adj* **1** fatigued (as if) by overwork; exhausted **2** dulled by surfeit or excess [fr pp of *jade* to wear out (a horse) by overwork, fr 'jade] – **jade** *vb*, **jadedly** *adv*, **jadedness** *n*

**jade green** *n* a light bluish green colour

**jadeite** /'jaydiet/ *n* a mineral that when cut constitutes the more valuable variety of jade and that varies in colour from white to green, red, or blue [Fr] – **jaditic** *adj*

**jaeger** /'yaygə/ *n* **1** *also* **jäger** a German or Austrian rifleman or sniper **2** *NAm* SKUA (large seabird) [Ger *jäger, jaeger*, lit., hunter]

**Jaffa** /'jafə/ *n, often cap* a large type of orange grown esp in Israel [*Jaffa* (Joppa), former port in Israel]

**'jag** /jag/ *vt* **-gg-** **1** to cut or tear unevenly or raggedly **2** to cut indentations into; *also* to form teeth on (a saw) by cutting indentations [ME *jaggen* to stab, slash] – **jagger** *n*

**²jag** *n* a sharp projecting part

**³jag** *n* **1** *archaic dial Br or archaic dial Am* a small load (eg of hay) **2** *slang* a period of indulgence (eg in an activity or emotion); a spree ⟨*a crying ~*⟩; *esp* a drinking bout [origin unknown]

**jagged** /'jagid/ *adj* **1** having a sharply uneven edge or surface **2** having a harsh, rough, or irregular quality *synonyms* see 'ROUGH – **jaggedly** *adv*, **jaggedness** *n*

**jaggery** /'jagəri/ *n* an unrefined brown sugar made from palm sap [Hindi *jāgrī*]

**jaggy** /'jagi/ *adj* jagged, notched

**jaguar** /'jagyoo-ə/ *n* a big wildcat (*Panthera onca*) of tropical America that is larger and stockier than the leopard and is brownish yellow or buff with black spots [Sp *yaguar* & Pg *jaguar*, fr Guarani *yaguara* & Tupi *jaguara*]

**jaguarundi** /,jagwə'roondi/ *n* a slender long-tailed short-legged greyish wildcat (*Felis yagouaroundi*) of Central and S America [AmerSp & Pg, fr Tupi *jaguarundi* & Guarani *yaguarundi*]

**Jahveh, Jahweh** /'yahway/ *n* Yahweh

**jai alai** /,khay ah'lay/ *n* a mainly Spanish court game played by two or four players who use a long curved wicker basket strapped to the wrist to catch and hurl the ball against a wall [Sp, fr Basque, fr *jai* festival + *alai* merry]

**'jail, Br also gaol** /jayl/ *n* (a) prison [ME *jaiole*, fr OF, fr (assumed) VL *caveola*, dim. of L *cavea* cage – more at CAGE]

**²jail, Br also gaol** *vt* to confine (as if) in a jail

**jailbird** /-,buhd/ *n* a person confined or who has been confined in jail; *esp* a habitual criminal

**jailbreak** /-,brayk/ *n* an escape from jail

**jail delivery** *n* **1** the clearing of a jail by bringing the prisoners to trial, esp formerly **2** the freeing of prisoners by force

**jailer, jailor** *Br also* **gaoler** /'jaylə/ *n* **1** a keeper of a jail **2** one who restricts another's liberty as if by imprisonment

**Jain** /jayn, jien/, **Jaina** /-nə/ *n* an adherent of Jainism [Hindi *Jain*, fr Skt *Jaina*, fr *Jina* saint, victorious]

**Jainism** /'jayniz(ə)m, 'jie-/ *n* a religion of India originating from Hinduism in the 6th century BC emphasizing the perfectibility of man and teaching liberation of the soul, esp by the practice of self-denial and AHIMSA (non-violence)

**jake** /jayk/ *adj, chiefly NAm slang* satisfactory, OK origin unknown

**jakes** /jayks/ *n taking sing or pl vb, slang* a toilet, privy [perh fr Fr *Jacques* James]

**jalap** /'jaləp/ *n* **1** the dried root of a Mexican plant (*Exogonium purga*) of the bindweed family; *also* a powder prepared from this root that was formerly used as a strong laxative **2** a plant yielding jalap [Fr & Sp; F *jalap*, fr Sp *jalapa*, fr *Jalapa*, city in Mexico]

**jalopy** /jə'lopi/ *n, informal* a dilapidated old vehicle or aeroplane [origin unknown]

**jalousie** /'zhaləzi, 'zhaloo,zee/ *n* **1** a blind with adjustable horizontal slats for admitting light and air while excluding sun and rain **2** a window made of adjustable glass LOUVRES (horizontal parallel slats sloping outwards) that control ventilation [Fr, lit., jealousy, fr OF *jelous* jealous]

**¹jam** /jam/ *vb* **-mm-** *vt* **1a** to press, squeeze, or crush into a close or tight position; wedge **b(1)** to cause to become wedged so as to be unworkable ⟨~ *the typewriter keys*⟩ **b(2)** to make unworkable by jamming **c** to block passage of or along; obstruct ⟨*traffic was* ~*med by the procession*⟩ ⟨*crowds* ~*ming the streets*⟩ **d** to fill often to excess; pack ⟨*a book* ~*med with useful information*⟩ **2** CRUSH 1b; *also* to bruise by crushing ⟨~*med his hand in the door*⟩ **3** to send out interfering signals or cause reflections so as to make **a** (a radio signal) unintelligible **b** (a radio device) ineffective ~ *vi* **1a** to become blocked or wedged **b** to become unworkable through the jamming of a movable part **2** to force one's way into a restricted space; crowd or squash tightly together ⟨*they all* ~*med into the room*⟩ **3** to take part in a JAM SESSION (informal jazz concert) [perh imit]

**jam on** *vt* to apply (brakes) suddenly and violently

**²jam** *n* **1** an instance of jamming or result of being jammed: e g **1a** a crowded mass that impedes or blocks ⟨*traffic* ~⟩ **b** the pressure or congestion of a crowd; a crush **2** a difficult state of affairs **3** JAM SESSION (informal jazz concert)

**³jam** *n* **1** a preserve made by boiling fruit and sugar to a thick consistency **2** *chiefly Br informal* something agreeable or easy ⟨*money for* ~⟩ [prob fr ¹*jam*]

**jamb** /jam/ *n* **1** an upright piece or surface forming the side of an opening (e g for a door, window, or fireplace) **2** a projecting part or mass that resembles a column in shape △ jam [ME *jambe*, fr MF, lit., leg, fr LL *gamba* – more at GAMBIT]

**jambalaya** /ˌjambəˈlie-ə/ *n* a dish of rice typically cooked with ham, sausage, chicken, shrimp, or oysters and seasoned with herbs [LaF, fr Prov *jambalaia*]

**jambeau** /ˈjamboh/ *n, pl* **jambeaux** /-bohz/ a piece of medieval armour for the leg below the knee [ME, fr (assumed) AF, fr MF *jambe*]

**jamboree** /ˌjambəˈree/ *n* **1** a noisy or unrestrained revel or spree **2a** a large festive gathering **b** a national or international camping assembly of scouts or guides [origin unknown]

**James** /jaymz/ *n* – see BIBLE table [Saint *James* †*ab* 62 disciple (and prob brother) of Christ]

**Jamesian** /ˈjaymziən/ *adj* (characteristic) of Henry James or his writings; *esp* displaying elaborate sentence structure and qualified rather than direct statement for the description of subtle human relationships [Henry *James* †1916 E (US-born) writer]

**jammer** /ˈjamə/ *n* one who or that which jams; *esp* a usu tuned radio transmitter that emits a signal intended to jam other radio or radar signals

**jammy** /ˈjami/ *adj* **1** covered or spread with jam **2** of or resembling jam (e g in consistency) **3** *chiefly Br* **3a** lucky **b** crafty **c** easy

**jam-ˈpacked** *adj, informal* full to overflowing; extremely crowded

**jam session, jam** *n* an unrehearsed performance by a group of jazz or pop musicians characterized by group improvisation [²*jam*]

**jandal** /ˈjandl/ *n, NZ* a flip-flop [prob alter. of *sandal*]

**jane** /jayn/ *n, chiefly NAm slang* a woman fr the forename *June*

**Janeite** /ˈjayniet/ *n* an uncritical over-enthusiastic admirer of the novels of Jane Austen [*Jane* Austen †1817 E novelist]

**¹jangle** /ˈjang-gl/ *vi* **1** to make a harsh or discordant often ringing noise **2** to be in a state of tense irritation ⟨*his nerves were* jangling *as he walked into the room*⟩ ~ *vt* **1** to utter or sound in a discordant, babbling, or chattering way **2a** to cause to sound harshly or inharmoniously **b** to excite (e g nerves) to tense irritation [ME *janglen*, fr OF *jangler*, of Gmc origin; akin to MD *jangelen* to grumble] – **jangler** *n*, **jangly** *adj*

**²jangle** *n* **1** a jangling noise **2** noisy quarrelling

**janissary** /ˈjanisəri/ *n* **1** *often cap* a soldier of an elite corps of Turkish troops organized in the 14th century and abolished in 1826 **2** a member of a group of loyal or subservient troops, officials, or supporters [It *gianizzero*, fr Turk *yeniçeri*, fr *yeni* new + *çeri* soldier, corps]

**janitor** /ˈjanitə/ *n* **1** a doorkeeper; ¹PORTER **2** *chiefly NAm* a caretaker [L, fr *janua* door, fr *janus* arch, gate] – **janitorial** *adj*, **janitress** *n*

**janizary** /ˈjanizəri/ *n* a janissary

**Jansenism** /ˈjansəniz(ə)m/ *n* (the doctrine of) a 17th and 18th

century movement among esp French Roman Catholics which held, like many Protestant sects of the time, that one would be saved less because of one's good deeds than because God had chosen one for salvation [Fr *jansénisme*, fr Cornelis *Jansen* † 1638 D theologian] – **Jansenist** *n*, **Jansenistic** *adj*

**January** /ˈjanyoo(ə)ri; *also* -yooeri/ *n* the 1st month of the year according to the GREGORIAN CALENDAR (standard Western calendar) – see MONTH table [ME *Januarie*, fr L *Januarius*, 1st month of the Roman year, fr *Janus*]

*usage* The pronunciation /ˈjanyoori/ is recommended for BBC broadcasters.

**ˈJanus-ˌfaced** /ˈjaynəs/ *adj* **1** looking in opposite directions at the same time **2** two-faced, hypocritical [*Janus*, Roman god of doors, gates, and beginnings, who was usu depicted with two faces looking in opposite directions]

**Janus green** /ˈjaynəs/ *n* a dye used esp as a biological stain (e g for revealing parts of a cell) [prob fr *Janus*, a trademark]

**Jap** /jap/ *n or adj* (a) Japanese – usu used more disparagingly in the USA than in Britain

**¹japan** /jəˈpan/ *adj* of or originating in Japan; of a style characteristic of or imitating Japanese workmanship [*Japan*, country in E Asia]

**²japan** *n* **1a** a varnish giving a hard brilliant finish **b** a hard dark coating of BITUMEN (tarlike substance) that is applied like a varnish, esp to metal, and is fixed by heating **2** work (e g lacquer ware) finished and decorated in the Japanese manner

**³japan** *vt* **-nn-** **1** to cover (as if) with a coat of japan **2** to give a high gloss to – **japanner** *n*

**Japanese** /ˌjapəˈneez/ *n, pl* **Japanese 1** a native or inhabitant of Japan; *also* a person of Japanese descent **2** the language of the Japanese – **Japanese** *adj*

**Japanese cedar** *n* CRYPTOMERIA (evergreen tree)

**Japanese lantern** *n* CHINESE LANTERN (paper lantern)

**Japanese millet** *n* a coarse grass (*Echinochloa frumentacea*) cultivated esp in Asia for its edible seeds

**Japanese quince** *n* japonica

**Japanese vellum** *n* a thick tough handmade paper usually cream in colour

**japan·ize, -ise** /ˈjapəniez/ *vt, often cap* **1** to make Japanese **2** to bring (an area) under the influence of Japan – **japanization** *n, often cap*

**Japan wax** *n* a yellowish fat obtained from the berries of any of several sumach shrubs or trees (e g *Rhus vernicifllua* and *Rhus succedanea*) and used chiefly in polishes

**¹jape** /jayp/ *vi* to say or do something jokingly or mockingly; jest [ME *japen*] – **japer, japester** *n*, **japery** *n*

**²jape** *n* something designed to arouse amusement or laughter; a jest, joke

**japonica** /jəˈponikə/ *n* a Chinese ornamental shrub (*Chaenomeles speciosa*) of the rose family with clusters of scarlet or white flowers [NL (specific epithet of *Pyrus japonica*, with which this species was orig confused), fr fem of *Japonicus* Japanese, fr *Japonia* Japan]

**¹jar** /jah/ *vb* **-rr-** *vi* **1a** to make a harsh or discordant noise **b(1)** to be out of harmony; clash – usu + *with* **b(2)** to bicker **c** to have a harshly disagreeable or disconcerting effect – + *on* or *upon* **2** to undergo severe vibration (e g from a blow) ~ *vt* **1** to cause to jar: e g **1a** to affect disagreeably; shock **b** to make unstable; shake **2** to injure with a sharp blow [prob imit] – **jarringly** *adv*

**²jar** *n* **1** a jarring noise **2a** a sudden or unexpected shake **b** an unsettling shock (e g to nerves or feelings)

**³jar** *n* **1** a usu cylindrical short-necked and wide-mouthed container, made typically of earthenware or glass **2a** the contents of or quantity contained in a jar **b** *chiefly Br informal* a glass of an alcoholic drink, esp beer ⟨*fancy a* ~?⟩ [MF *jarre*, fr OProv *jarra*, fr Ar *jarrah* earthen water vessel] – **jarful** *n*

**⁴jar** *n, archaic* the position of being ajar – esp in *on the jar* [alter. of earlier *char* turn, fr ME – more at CHORE]

**jardiniere** /ˌzhahdiˈnyeə (Fr ʒardinjɛːr)/ *n* **1** an ornamental stand or large pot for plants or flowers **2** a garnish consisting of several vegetables cut into pieces, cooked, and arranged in separate groups round meat [Fr *jardinière*, lit., female gardener]

**jargon** /ˈjahg(ə)n/ *n* **1a** confused incomprehensible language **b** a strange, outlandish, or barbarous language or dialect **c** PIDGIN (simplified hybrid language used for trading) **2** the technical vocabulary or idiom of a special activity or group ⟨*scientific* ~⟩ **3** obscure and often pretentious language marked by a roundabout way of expression and use of long words *synonyms* see DIALECT [ME, fr MF, prob of imit origin] – **jargonize** *vb*, **jargonistic** *adj*

**jargoon** /jah'goohn/, **jargon** /jah'gon/ *n* a colourless, pale yellow, or smoky ZIRCON (type of gemstone) [Fr *jargon* – more at ZIRCON]

**jarl** /yahl/ *n* a medieval Scandinavian noble ranking immediately below the king [ON – more at EARL]

**jarrah** /'jarə/ *n* (the tough wood of) a W Australian eucalyptus tree (*Eucalyptus marginata*) with rough bark and ovate leaves [native name in Australia]

**jasmine** /'jasmin, 'jaz-/ *n* **1a** any of numerous often climbing shrubs (genus *Jasminum*) of the olive family that usu have extremely fragrant flowers; *esp* a high-climbing half-evergreen Asian shrub (*Jasminum officinale*) with fragrant white flowers from which a perfume is extracted **b** any of numerous plants having sweet-scented flowers; *esp* YELLOW JASMINE **2** a light yellow colour [Fr *jasmin*, fr Ar *yāsamīn*, fr Per]

**jaspé** /'jaspay/ *adj, of a fabric* variegated, mottled [Fr, fr pp of *jasper* to mottle, fr *jaspe* jasper, fr MF *jaspe, jaspre*]

**jasper** /'jaspə/ *n* an opaque quartz, usu red brown, yellow, or dark green, used as a gemstone [ME *jaspre*, fr MF, fr L *jaspis*, fr Gk *iaspis*, of Sem origin; akin to Heb *yāshĕpheh* jasper] – **jaspery** *adj*

**jasperware** /'jaspə,weə/ *n* a fine-grained unglazed stoneware developed by Josiah Wedgwood, usu decorated with raised white classical motifs on a coloured ground

**jassid** /'jasid/ *n* any of a large family (Jassidae) of small leaf-hoppers found throughout the world that includes many economically significant pests of cultivated plants; *broadly* a leaf-hopper [deriv of Gk *Iassos, Iasos*, ancient town in Asia Minor]

**Jat** /jaht/ *n* a member of an Indo-Aryan people of the Punjab and Uttar Pradesh [Hindi *Jāṭ*]

**jato** /'jaytoh/ *n, pl* **jatos** an auxiliary power unit that is used for assisting the takeoff of an aircraft and consists of one or more jet engines (e g rockets) to provide temporary extra thrust; *also* a takeoff so assisted [*jet-assisted takeoff*]

**jaundice** /'jawndis/ *n* **1** yellowish coloration of the skin, tissues, and body fluids caused by the deposition of BILE (digestive juice produced by the liver) pigments **2** a disease or abnormal condition, esp of the liver, characterized by jaundice **3** a state or attitude characterized by bitterness, envy, or distaste [ME *jaundis*, fr MF *jaunisse*, fr *jaune* yellow, fr L *galbinus* yellowish green, fr *galbus* yellow]

**jaundiced** /'jawndist/ *adj* **1** affected (as if) with jaundice **2** exhibiting or influenced by bitterness, envy, or distaste

**jaunt** /jawnt/ *vi or n* (to make) a short journey for pleasure [origin unknown]

**jaunting car** /'jawnting/ *n* a light 2-wheeled open horse-drawn vehicle, used esp formerly in Ireland, with sideways-facing seats

**jaunty** /'jawnti/ *adj* sprightly in manner or appearance; lively, rakish [alter. of obs *jentee* genteel, fr Fr *gentil*] – **jauntily** *adv*, **jauntiness** *n*

**Java man** /'jahvə/ *n* either of two small-brained prehistoric men (*Homo erectus* and *Homo robustus*) known chiefly from more or less fragmentary skulls found in Trinil in Java

**Javanese** /jahvə'neez/ *n, pl* **Javanese** **1** a member of an Indonesian people inhabiting the island of Java **2** an AUSTRONESIAN language of the Javanese [*Java* + *-nese* (as in *Japanese*)] – **Javanese** *adj*

**Java sparrow** *n* a finchlike Javanese weaverbird (*Padda oryzivora*)

**javelin** /'jav(ə)lin/ *n* **1** a light spear thrown as a weapon in hunting or war **2** a slender usu metal shaft at least 2-6 metres (about 8$\frac{1}{2}$ feet) long that is thrown for distance in an athletic field event; *also* this event [MF *javeline*, alter. of *javelot*, of Celt origin; akin to OIr *gabul* forked stick]

**Javelle water, Javel water** /zhə'vel, zha–/ *n* a solution of SODIUM HYPOCHLORITE in water used as a disinfectant and bleaching agent [*Javel*, former village in France]

**¹jaw** /jaw/ *n* **1a** either of two structures composed of bone or cartilage that in most VERTEBRATE animals form a framework above and below the mouth, support the soft parts enclosing it, and usu bear teeth at their outer edges: **1a(1)** MANDIBLE (lower jaw) **a(2)** MAXILLA (upper jaw) **b** *usu pl* a jaw with its associated parts constituting the walls of the mouth and serving to open and close it **c** any of various organs of INVERTEBRATE animals that perform the function of the vertebrate jaws **2** *pl* something resembling the jaws of an animal: e g **2a** the entrance of a narrow pass or channel **b** two or more opposable parts that

open and close for holding or crushing something between them ⟨*the* ∼s *of a clamp*⟩ **c** a position or situation in which one is faced with an imminent threat ⟨*stared into the* ∼s *of death*⟩ **3** *informal* **3a** continual talk; loquacity; *esp* impudent or offensive talk **b** a friendly chat; a chin-wag **c** a moralizing talking-to; a sermon, lecture [ME]

**²jaw** *vb, informal vt* to talk to or at in a scolding or boring manner ∼ *vi* to talk, gossip; *esp* to talk for a long time or long-windedly

**jawbone** /'jaw,bohn/ *n* the bone of esp a lower jaw

**jawbreaker** /'jaw,braykə/ *n, informal* a word difficult to pronounce

**jawed** /jawd/ *adj* having jaws, esp of a specified type or shape – usu in combination ⟨*square-jawed*⟩

**jawless fish** /'jawlis/ *n* any of a group (Agnatha) of primitive fishlike animals without jaws that includes CYCLOSTOMES (e g lampreys) and extinct related forms

**jawline** /'jaw,lien/ *n* the outline of the lower jaw

**jay** /jay/ *n* **1a** a predominantly fawn-coloured Eurasian and African bird (*Garrulus glandarius*) of the crow family with a black-and-white crest and wings marked with black, white, and blue **b** any of various usu crested and largely blue birds related to the common jay **2a** an impertinent chatterer **b** DANDY 1 **c** a gullible or unsophisticated person; a simpleton [ME, fr MF *jai*, fr LL *gaius*, prob fr the name *Gaius*]

**jaywalk** /'jay,wawk/ *vi* to cross a street carelessly or in a dangerous manner so as to be endangered by traffic [¹*jay* 2c + *walk*] – **jaywalker** *n*

**¹jazz** /jaz/ *vi* **1** to dance to or play jazz **2** *informal* to go here and there energetically; gad – often + *around* [prob fr E (NAm Negro) slang *jazz* copulation, frenzy, prob fr W African origin] – **jazz up** *vt* **1** to play (e g a piece of music) in the style of jazz **2** to enliven, accelerate **3** to make bright, esp in a vivid or garish way

**²jazz** *n* **1a** music of American Negro origin developed esp from RAGTIME and BLUES, played solo or by a group, and characterized by SYNCOPATED rhythms (displacement of the accent onto a weak beat) and usu by improvisation, often with special melodic features peculiar to the individual interpretation of the player **b** popular dance music influenced by jazz and played in a loud rhythmic manner **2** *informal* empty pretentious talk; humbug ⟨*spouted a lot of scientific* ∼⟩ **3** *informal* similar but unspecified things; stuff ⟨*planting, weeding, cropping, and all that* ∼ – *Evening Argus (Brighton)*⟩

**jazzer** /'jazə/ *n* a jazzman

**jazzman** /'jazman/ *n* a jazz musician

**jazzy** /'jazi/ *adj* **1** having the characteristics of jazz **2** *informal* garish, gaudy – **jazzily** *adv*, **jazziness** *n*

**JCB** /,jay,see'bee/ *trademark* – used for a mechanical earth-mover

**jealous** /'jeləs/ *adj* **1a** intolerant of rivalry or unfaithfulness ⟨*the Lord your God is a* ∼ *God* – Ex 20:5 (AV)⟩ **b** disposed to suspect rivalry or unfaithfulness; apprehensive of the loss of another's exclusive devotion **2** hostile towards a rival or one believed to enjoy an advantage; envious **3** vigilant in guarding a possession, right, etc ⟨∼ *of his honour*⟩ **4** distrustfully watchful; suspicious ⟨*kept a* ∼ *eye on her husband*⟩ [ME *jelous*, fr OF, fr (assumed) VL *zelosus*, fr LL *zelus* zeal – more at ZEAL] – **jealously** *adv*, **jealousness, jealousy** *n*

**jean** /jeen/ *n* **1** a durable twilled cotton cloth used esp for sportswear and work clothes **2** a brand or type of jeans ⟨*they make a very good* ∼⟩ [short for *jean fustian*, fr ME *Gene* Genoa, city in NW Italy + *fustian*]

**jeans** /jeenz/ *n pl* casual trousers that are usu closely fitting; *esp* such trousers made of blue denim – **jean** *adj*

**jeep** /jeep/ *n* a small tough general-purpose motor vehicle with 4-wheel drive, esp used in military service [alter. of *gee pee*, fr *general-purpose*]

**jeepers** /'jeepəz/, **jeepers creepers** *interj, chiefly NAm slang* – used to express surprise [euphemism for *Jesus, Jesus Christ*]

**¹jeer** /jiə/ *vi* to speak or cry out with derision or mockery to deride with jeers; taunt [origin unknown] – **jeerer** *n*, **jeeringly** *adv*

**²jeer** *n* a jeering remark or sound; a taunt

**Jeeves** /jeevz/ *n* a perfect valet and discreetly resourceful confidant [*Jeeves*, valet in novels by P G *Wodehouse* †1975 E writer]

**Jeffersonian** /jefə'sohniən/ *adj* (characteristic) of Thomas Jefferson or his political principles or policies [Thomas *Jefferson* †1826 US president] – **Jeffersonian** *n*, **Jeffersonianism** *n*

**jehad** /ji'hahd/ *n* JIHAD (Islamic holy war)

**Jehovah** /ji'hohvə/ *n* GOD 1 ⟨*in the Lord* ~ *is everlasting strength* – Isa 26:4 (AV)⟩ [NL, false reading (as *Yĕhōwāh*) of Heb *Yahweh*]

**Jehovah's Witness** *n* a member of a FUNDAMENTALIST (accepting the whole Bible as literally true) Christian sect practising personal spreading of the Christian message, rejecting the authority of the secular state, and preaching that the end of the present world is imminent

**jehu** /'jayh(y)ooh/ *n, humorous* a fast or reckless driver [*Jehu* (Heb *Yēhū*), 9th-c BC king of Israel recognized by his furious chariot-driving (2 Kings 9:20)]

**jejun-** /jijoohn-/, **jejuno-** *comb form* jejunum ⟨jejun*ectomy*⟩ [L *jejunum*]

**jejune** /ji'joohn/ *adj* 1 lacking nutritive value or substance ⟨~ *diets*⟩; *also* barren 2 lacking interest or significance; dull, unsatisfying ⟨~ *lectures*⟩ 3 lacking maturity; puerile ⟨~ *remarks on world affairs*⟩ [L *jejunus*] – **jejunely** *adv*, **jejuneness** *n*

**jejunum** /ji'joohnəm/ *n* the section of the SMALL INTESTINE in mammals that is between the DUODENUM and the ILEUM [L, fr neut of *jejunus*] – **jejunal** *adj*

**Jekyll and Hyde** /,jekəl ənd 'hied/ *n* a person having a split personality, one side of which is good and the other evil [Dr *Jekyll* & Mr *Hyde*, the two sides of the split personality of the chief character in the story *The Strange Case of Dr Jekyll and Mr Hyde* by R L Stevenson †1894 Sc writer] – **Jekyll-and-Hyde** *adj*

**jell** /jel/ *vb, chiefly NAm* to gel [back-formation fr *jelly*]

**jellaba** /jə'lahbə/ *n* DJELLABA (loose hooded garment)

¹**jelly** /'jeli/ *n* **1a** a soft fruit-flavoured transparent dessert set with gelatin **b** a savoury food product of similar consistency, made esp from meat stock and gelatin **2** a clear fruit preserve made by boiling sugar and the juice of fruit **3** a substance resembling jelly in consistency **4** a state of fear or irresolution ⟨*he was reduced to a quivering* ~⟩ [ME *gelly*, fr MF *gelee*, fr fem of *gelé*, pp of *geler* to freeze, congeal, fr L *gelare* – more at COLD] – **jellify** *vb*, **jellylike** *adj*

²**jelly** *vi* to gel ~ *vt* **1** to bring to the consistency of jelly; cause to set **2** to set in a jelly ⟨jellied *beef*⟩

**jelly baby** *n* a small soft gelatinous sweet in the shape of a person

**jelly bag** *n* a bag (eg of muslin) through which juice (eg from pulped fruit) is strained in making jelly

**jellyfish** /'jeli,fish/ *n* **1a** any of a class (Scyphozoa of the phylum Coelenterata) of free-swimming marine animals that have a nearly transparent saucer-shaped body and extendable tentacles studded with stinging cells; *also* a structurally similar organism that is the sexually reproducing form of a related class of animals **b** SIPHONOPHORE (colonial marine animals resembling jellyfish) **2** a person lacking backbone or firmness of character

**jelly roll** *n, NAm* a SWISS ROLL with a jelly filling

¹**jemmy** /'jemi/ *n, Br* a short steel crowbar used esp by burglars for forcing open doors and windows [*Jemmy*, nickname for *James*]

²**jemmy** *vt, Br* to force open (as if) with a jemmy ⟨*the burglar jemmied a window*⟩

**je ne sais quoi** /,zhə nə say 'kwah (*Fr* ʒə nə sɛ kwa)/ *n* a quality that cannot be adequately described or expressed [Fr, lit., I know not what]

**jennet** /'jenit/ *n* **1** a small Spanish riding horse **2a** a female donkey **b** HINNY (offspring of stallion and female donkey) [ME *genett*, fr MF *genet*, fr Catal *ginet*, *genet* Zenete (member of a Berber people), horse; (2) influenced in meaning by *jenny*]

**jenny** /'jeni/ *n* **1a** – used as a familiar name for a wren **b** a female donkey **2** SPINNING JENNY (early spinning machine) [*Jenny*, nickname for *Jane*]

**jeon** /jun/ *n* – see *won* at MONEY table [Korean]

**jeopard·ize, -ise** /'jepədiez/ *vt* to put in danger; imperil

**jeopardy** /'jepədi/ *n* **1** exposure to or risk of death, loss, or injury; danger **2** liability to conviction and punishment faced by a defendant in a criminal trial *synonyms* see DANGER [ME *jeopardie*, fr AF *juparti*, fr OF *jeu parti* alternative, uncertainty, lit., divided game]

**jequirity bean** /ji'kwirəti/ *n* **1** the poisonous scarlet and black seed of the ROSARY PEA that is often used as a bead **2** ROSARY PEA 1 [Pg *jequiriti*]

**jerbil** /'juhbil/ *n* GERBIL (small rodent)

**jerboa** /juh'boh·ə/ *n* any of several nocturnal African and Eurasian jumping rodents (family Dipodidae) with long hind legs and a long tail [Ar *yarbū'*]

**jeremiad** /,jerə'mie·əd/ *n* a prolonged lamentation or complaint [Fr *jérémiade*, fr *Jérémie* Jeremiah, fr LL *Jeremias*]

**Jeremiah** /,jerə'mie·ə/ *n* **1** – see BIBLE table **2** one who is pessimistic about the present and foresees a calamitous future [*Jeremiah* (LL *Jeremias*, fr Gk *Hieremias*, fr Heb *Yirmĕyāh*), 6th-c BC Heb prophet, known for his pessimism]

**Jeremias** /,jeri'mie·əs/ *n* – see BIBLE table

**jerid** /jə'reed/ *n* a blunt javelin used by horsemen in the Middle East [Ar *jarīd* rod, lance]

¹**jerk** /juhk/ *vt* **1** to give a quick suddenly arrested push, pull, twist, or jolt to ⟨*she* ~ed *the chair I was sitting on*⟩ **2** to propel with short abrupt motions **3** to utter in an abrupt, snappy, or sharply broken manner **4** to stimulate; JOG **2** ⟨~ *one's memory*⟩ ~ *vi* **1** to make a sudden spasmodic motion **2** to move in short abrupt motions or with frequent jolts **3** to throw an object with a jerk [prob alter. of E dial. *yerk* to thrash, attack, excite, fr ME *yerken* to bind tightly] – **jerker** *n*

**jerk off** *vb, chiefly NAm vulg* to masturbate

²**jerk** *n* **1** a single quick motion (eg a pull, twist, or jolt) **2a** an involuntary spasmodic muscular motion due to reflex action **b** *pl* involuntary twitchings due to nervous excitement **3** the pushing of a weight from shoulder height to a position above the head in weight-lifting – compare ⁴CLEAN **2** **4** *chiefly NAm informal* a stupid, foolish, or naive person [(4) prob fr *jerk off*]

³**jerk** *vt* to preserve (eg beef or venison) in the form of long slices or strips dried in the sun [back-formation fr *jerky* dried meat, modif of AmerSp *charqui*, fr Quechua *ch'arki*]

**jerkin** /'juhkin/ *n* **1** a close-fitting hip-length sleeveless jacket, made esp of leather and worn by men in the 16th and 17th centuries **2** a man's or woman's sleeveless jacket [origin unknown]

**jerkwater** /'juhk,wawtə/ *adj, NAm* insignificant, piddling ⟨~ *towns*⟩ [*jerkwater* (rural train), fr ¹*jerk* + *water*; fr its formerly taking on water carried in buckets from the source of supply]

**jerky** /'juhki/ *adj* **1** moving along with or marked by fits and starts **2** characterized by abrupt or awkward transitions ⟨*a* ~ *prose style*⟩ – **jerkily** *adv*, **jerkiness** *n*

**jeroboam** /,jerə'boh·am, -əm/ *n* an outsize wine bottle: e g **a** a Bordeaux bottle holding six times the usual amount **b** a Champagne bottle holding four times the usual amount – compare REHOBOAM [*Jeroboam* I †*ab* 912 BC king of the northern kingdom of Israel]

**jerry** /'jeri/ *n, Br informal* CHAMBER POT [prob by shortening & alter. fr *jeroboam*]

**Jerry** /'jeri/ *n, chiefly Br* **1** a German; *esp* a German soldier in World War II **2** a German aircraft in World War II **3 Jerries** *pl*, **Jerry** the German armed forces in World War II; *also* a unit of these forces [by shortening & alter.]

**jerry-build** /'jeri-/ *vt* **jerry-built** /-,bilt/ to build cheaply and flimsily [back-formation fr *jerry-built*] – **jerry-builder** *n*

'**jerry-,built** *adj* **1** built cheaply and unsubstantially ⟨~ *houses*⟩ **2** carelessly or hastily put together [origin unknown]

**jerry can, jerrican** /'jeri,kan/ *n* a narrow flat-sided container for carrying liquids, esp petrol or water, with a capacity of about 25 litres (about 5 gallons) [*Jerry* + *can*; fr its German design]

**jersey** /'juhzi/ *n* **1** a plain machine-knitted fabric made of wool, nylon, etc and used esp for clothing **2** a jumper **3** *often cap* (any of) a breed of small short-horned mainly yellowish-brown or fawn dairy cattle noted for their rich milk [*Jersey*, one of the Channel islands]

**Jerusalem artichoke** /jə'roohsələm/ *n* a sunflower (*Helianthus tuberosus*) grown for its sweet-fleshed TUBERS (fleshy underground stems) that are used as a vegetable, a livestock feed, and a source of the sugar, LAEVULOSE [*Jerusalem* by folk etymology fr It *girasole* girasol]

**Jerusalem Bible** *n* a translation of the Bible based on the work of the Roman Catholic Ecole Biblique in Jerusalem and published in English in 1966

**Jerusalem cherry** *n* either of two plants (*Solanum pseudocapsicum* or *Solanum capsicastrum*) of the nightshade family grown as ornamental house plants for their orange to red berries [*Jerusalem*, city in Palestine

**jess** /jes/ *n* a short strap made esp of leather which is secured to the leg of a hawk used for falconry, and usu has a ring on the other end for attaching a leash [ME *ges*, fr MF *gies*, fr pl of *jet* throw, fr *jeter* to throw – more at JET] – **jessed** *adj*

¹**jest** /jest/ *n* **1** something intended to provoke laughter: eg **1a**

a comic or taunting act; a prank; PRACTICAL JOKE **b** an utterance (e g a jeer or a witty quip) intended to be taken as mockery or humour rather than literal truth **2** a frivolous mood or manner; fun, merriment ⟨*spoken in* ~⟩ **3** a laughingstock [ME *geste* deed, exploit, fr OF, fr L *gesta* deeds, fr neut pl of *gestus*, pp of *gerere* to bear, wage]

²**jest** *vi* **1** to speak or act without seriousness **2** to make a witty remark; joke **3** *archaic* to utter taunts; gibe

**jester** /'jestə/ *n* **1** an employee formerly kept in great households to provide casual amusement and commonly dressed in a brightly coloured costume with cap, bells, and BAUBLE (mock staff of office) **2** one given to jesting

**Jesu** /'jeezyooh/ *n, poetic* Jesus

**Jesuit** /'jezyoo-it/ *n* **1** a member of the Roman Catholic Society of Jesus, founded by St Ignatius Loyola in 1534 and devoted to missionary and educational work **2** one given to intrigue or deception [NL *Jesuita*, fr LL *Jesus*] – **jesuitic, jesuitical** *adj, often cap*, **jesuitically** *adv, often cap*, **jesuitism, jesuitry** *n, often cap*, **jesuitize** *vb, often cap*

**Jesus** /'jeezəs/, **Jesus Christ** /'kriest/ *n* **1** the Jewish religious teacher whose life, death, and resurrection as reported in the New Testament are the basis of the Christian message of salvation **2** *slang* – used interjectionally as an expression of surprise, dismay, annoyance, etc [LL, fr Gk *Iēsous*, fr Heb *Yēshūa'*]

**Jesus freak** *n, informal* a usu young member of any of various EVANGELICAL (energetically preaching the faith) Christian groups characterized by a simple, usu communal way of life

¹**jet** /jet/ *n* **1** a compact velvet-black LIGNITE (form of coal) that takes a good polish and is often used for jewellery **2** an intense black colour [ME, fr MF *jaiet*, fr L *gagates*, fr Gk *gagatēs*, fr *Gagas*, town & river in Asia Minor]

²**jet** *vb* **-tt-** *vi* to spout forth in a jet or jets ~ *vt* **1** to emit in a stream; spout **2** to direct a jet of liquid or gas at [MF *jeter*, lit., to throw, fr L *jactare* to throw, fr *jactus*, pp of *jacere* to throw; akin to Gk *hienai* to send]

³**jet** *n* **1a** a usu forceful stream of fluid (e g water or gas) discharged from a narrow opening or a nozzle **b** a nozzle or other narrow opening for emitting a jet of liquid **2** something issuing as if in a jet ⟨*talk poured from her in a brilliant* ~ *– Time*⟩ **3a** JET ENGINE **b** an aircraft powered by one or more jet engines

⁴**jet** *vi* **-tt-** to travel by jet aircraft

**jet-'black** *adj* very dark black

**jeté** /zhə'tay (*Fr* ʒəte)/ *n* a high arching leap in ballet in which the dancer has one leg stretched forwards and the other backwards [Fr, fr pp of *jeter*]

**jet engine** *n* an engine that produces motion in one direction as a result of the discharge of a jet of gas in the opposite direction; *specif* an aircraft engine having one or more exhaust nozzles for discharging a jet of heated air and exhaust gases to produce propulsion or lift

**Jeth** /jet/ *n* – see MONTH table [Hindi *Jēṭh*, fr Skt *Jyaiṣṭha*]

**jet lag** *n* any of various disruptions of normal bodily rhythms (e g extreme tiredness) experienced after a long aeroplane flight to a widely different time zone

**jetliner** /'jet,lienə/ *n* a jet airliner

**'jet-pro,pelled** *adj* **1** moving by jet propulsion **2** suggestive of the speed and force of a jet aeroplane

**jet propulsion** *n* propulsion of a body produced by the forwardly directed forces of the reaction resulting from the backward discharge of a jet of fluid; *specif* propulsion of an aeroplane by jet engines

**jetsam** /'jetsəm/ *n* **1** goods thrown overboard to lighten a ship in distress; *esp* such goods when washed ashore **2** FLOTSAM AND JETSAM [alter. of *jettison*]

**jet set** *n taking sing or pl vb* an international social group of wealthy individuals who frequent fashionable resorts all over the world – compare BEAUTIFUL PEOPLE [³*jet*] – **jet-set** *adj*, **jet-setter** *n*

**jet stream** *n* a current of strong winds high in the atmosphere, usu blowing from a generally westerly direction and often exceeding a speed of 400 kilometres per hour (250 miles per hour)

¹**jettison** /'jetis(ə)n/ *n* **1** the act of jettisoning cargo **2** rejection, abandonment [ME *jetteson*, fr AF *getteson*, fr OF *getaison* act of throwing, fr L *jactation-, jactatio*, fr *jactatus*, pp of *jactare* – more at ²JET]

²**jettison** *vt* **1** to throw (e g goods or cargo) overboard to lighten the load of a ship in distress **2** to cast off as superfluous or encumbering; abandon **3** to eject (e g unwanted material) from an aircraft or spacecraft in flight – **jettisonable** *adj*

**jetton** /'jetən/ *n* COUNTER 1 [Fr *jeton*, fr MF, fr *jeter* to throw, calculate]

¹**jetty** /'jeti/ *n* **1a** a structure (e g a pier or breakwater) built out into the sea, a lake, or a river to shelter a harbour or to break the force of waves and currents **b** a protecting frame of a pier **2** a small landing wharf; a pier **3** the overhanging upper storey of a timber-framed house; the overhang [ME *jette*, fr MF *jetee*, fr fem of *jeté*, pp of *jeter* to throw – more at ²JET]

²**jetty** *vi, of an upper storey* to project; jut out

³**jetty** *adj, chiefly poetic* jet-black

**jeu de mots** /,zhuh də 'moh (*Fr* zə də mo)/ *n, pl* **jeux de mots** /~/ a play on words; a pun [Fr]

**jeu d'esprit** /,zhuh de'spree (*Fr* ʒo dɛspri)/ *n, pl* **jeux d'esprit** /~/ a witty comment or composition [Fr, lit., play of the mind]

**jeunesse dorée** /zhuh,nes daw'ray (*Fr* ʒɔnes dɔre)/ *n taking sing or pl vb* young people of wealth and fashion [Fr, gilded youth]

**jew** /jooh/ *vt, derog* **1** to get the better of financially, esp by hard bargaining ⟨~ *him out of £10*⟩ **2** to reduce (a price) by bargaining – + *down* [fr the alleged sharpness of Jews in business dealings]

**Jew**, *fem* **Jewess** /'joohes, -is/ *n* **1a** a member of the ancient tribe of Judah **b** an Israelite **2** a member of a Semitic people existing in Palestine from the 6th century BC to the 1st century AD, some of whom now live in Israel and others in various countries throughout the world **3** a person belonging to a continuation through descent or conversion of the ancient Jewish people **4** a person whose religion is Judaism **5** *often not cap, derog* **5a** one given to hard financial bargaining **b** a miser □ sometimes considered offensive in attributive use ⟨*your* ~ *friend*⟩ [ME, fr OF *gyu*, fr L *Judaeus*, fr Gk *Ioudaios*, fr Heb *Yĕhūdhī*, fr *Yĕhūdhāh* Judah, Jewish kingdom]

**'Jew-,baiting** *n* active or systematic persecution of Jews – **Jew-baiter** *n*

**jewboy** /'jooh,boy/ *n, derog* a Jewish male

**jewel** /'jooh-əl/ *n* **1** an ornament of precious metal often set with stones and worn as an accessory of dress **2** one who or that which is highly esteemed **3** a precious stone; a gem **4** a bearing for a pivot (e g in a watch or compass) made of crystal, precious stone, or glass [ME *juel*, fr OF, dim. of *jeu* game, play, fr L *jocus* game, joke – more at JOKE] – **jewelled** *adj*

**jeweller**, *NAm chiefly* **jeweler** /'jooh-ələ/ *n* one who deals in, makes, or repairs jewellery and often watches

**jewellery**, *NAm chiefly* **jewelry** /'jooh-əlri, 'jooləri/ *n* jewels, esp as worn for personal adornment
  *usage* The pronunciation /'jooh-əlri/ rather than /'jooləri/ is recommended for BBC broadcasters.

**jewfish** /'jooh,fish/ *n* any of various large GROUPERS (types of fish) esp of southern seas

**Jewish** /'joohish/ *adj* relating to or characteristic of the Jews; *also* being a Jew or Jewess – **Jewishly** *adv*, **Jewishness** *n*

**Jewish calendar** *n* a calendar in use among Jewish people that is reckoned from the year 3761 BC and dates in its present form from about AD 360

**Jewry** /'joohri, 'jooəri/ *n* **1** a Jewish quarter (e g of a town); a ghetto **2** *taking sing or pl vb* the Jewish people collectively

**Jew's harp, Jews' harp** *n* a small lyre-shaped instrument that is placed between the teeth and sounded by striking a metal tongue with the finger

**jezail** /jə'ziel, -'zayl/ *n* a long heavy Afghan rifle [Per *jazā'il*]

**Jezebel** /'jezəbel, -bl/ *n, often not cap* a shameless or immoral woman [*Jezebel* (Heb *Izebel*), wife of the king of Israel, notorious for her wickedness (I & II Kings)]

**JHVH** *n* YHWH

¹**jib** /jib/ *n* a triangular sail set on a STAY (cable or rope) extending from the foremast to the bow or the BOWSPRIT (pole projecting from the bow of a ship) [origin unknown]

²**jib** *vb* **-bb-** *chiefly NAm* to gybe

³**jib** *n* **1** the projecting arm of a mechanical crane **2** the beam that pivots from the foot of the upright mast of a DERRICK (simple crane) [prob by shortening & alter. fr *gibbet*]

⁴**jib** *vi* **-bb-** *esp of a horse* to refuse or show unwillingness to proceed further; baulk [prob fr *jib* to swing round like a sail, fr ¹*jib*] – **jibber** *n*

**jib at** *vt* to recoil or baulk at

**jibbah** /'jibə/ *n* JUBBAH (loose robe) [Egyptian Ar, var of Ar *jubbah*]

**'jib-,boom** *n* a pole (SPAR) that forms an extension of the

BOWSPRIT (pole projecting from the bow of a ship) [¹*jib* + *boom*]

¹**jibe** /jieb/ *vb, chiefly NAm* to gybe

²**jibe** *vb* to gibe

³**jibe** *vi, NAm informal* to be in accord; agree ⟨*his account of the accident* ~s *pretty well with other accounts*⟩ [origin unknown]

    *usage* Of the three verbs pronounced /jieb/, **gibe** rather than **jibe** is the chief spelling of the one meaning "taunt"; **gybe** is the chief British and **jibe** the chief American spelling of the nautical one meaning "swing across the ship"; and **jibe** is the chief spelling of the American one meaning "be in accord".

**jiff** /jif/ *n* a jiffy [by shortening]

**jiffy** /'jifi/ *n, informal* a moment, instant ⟨*ready in a* ~⟩ [origin unknown]

¹**jig** /jig/ *n* **1a** any of several lively springy dances in triple rhythm **b** music to which a jig may be danced **c** GIGUE **2a** any of several angling lures that jerk up and down in the water **b** a device used to hold a piece of work in the correct relationship to a tool or to another piece of work during assembly **c** a device in which crushed ore is concentrated or coal is cleaned by agitating in water **3** *archaic* a trick, game ⟨*the* ~ *is up*⟩ [prob fr MF *giguer* to dance, fr *gigue* fiddle, of Gmc origin; akin to OHG *gīga* fiddle; akin to ON *geiga* to turn aside – more at GIG]

²**jig** *vb* -gg- *vt* **1** to dance in the rapid lively manner of a jig **2a** to cause to make a rapid jerky movement **b** to separate (a mineral or ore from waste) with a jig **3** to catch (a fish) with a jig **4** to machine by using a jig ~ *vi* **1a** to dance a jig **b** to move with rapid jerky motions **2** to fish with a jig **3** to work with the aid of a jig

¹**jigger** /'jigə/ *n* **1** one who or that which jigs or operates a jig **2** a mould or a machine incorporating a revolving mould on which ceramic items (e g plates) are formed **3** a variable measure of spirits that is used in mixing drinks; *also* the small container holding a jigger **4** *chiefly NAm* something, esp a gadget or small piece of apparatus, which one is (temporarily) unable to designate accurately – compare THINGAMAJIG

²**jigger** *n* HARVEST MITE [of African origin; akin to Wolof *jiga* insect]

**jiggered** /'jigəd/ *adj* **1** *NEng* tired out; exhausted **2** *informal* blowed, damned ⟨*well, I'll be* ~!⟩ [origin unknown]

**jiggery-pokery** /,jigəri 'pohkəri/ *n, chiefly Br* dishonest underhand dealings or scheming [alter. of Sc *joukery-pawkery*, fr *joukery* trickery (fr *jouk* to dodge, cheat) + *pawkery* slyness, trickiness, fr *pawk* trick (cf PAWKY)]

**jiggle** /'jigl/ *vb, informal* to (cause to) move with quick little jerks up and down or from side to side [freq of ²*jig*] – **jiggle** *n*

¹**jigsaw** /'jig,saw/ *n* **1** a power-driven fret saw **2** JIGSAW PUZZLE ⟨*the architects are fitting a brand new piece of* ~ *into an old environment – Observer Magazine*⟩

²**jigsaw** *vt* to cut or form (as if) by a jigsaw

**jigsaw puzzle** *n* a puzzle consisting of small irregularly cut pieces, esp of wood or card, that are fitted together to form a picture; *broadly* something assembled from many disparate parts or elements

**jihad, jehad** /ji'hahd/ *n* **1** a holy war waged on behalf of Islam as a religious duty **2** a crusade for a principle or belief [Ar *jihād*]

¹**jilt** /jilt/ *n* a person, esp a woman, who at a whim or unfeelingly casts off a lover [prob alter. of *jillet* (flirtatious girl), fr *Jill* (nickname for *Gillian*) + *-et*]

²**jilt** *vt* to cast off (one's lover) at a whim or unfeelingly

**jim crow** /jim/ *n, often cap J&C,* *NAm* **1** racial discrimination, esp against black Americans, by legal enforcement or tradition ⟨~ *laws*⟩ **2** *derog* a Negro ⟨~ *schools*⟩ [*Jim Crow,* stereotype Negro in a 19th-c song-and-dance act] – **jim crowism** *n, often cap J&C*

'**jim-'dandy** *n or adj, NAm chiefly dial* (something) excellent [*Jim,* nickname for *James* + *dandy*]

**jimjams** /'jim,jamz/ *n pl, informal* **1** DELIRIUM TREMENS **2** the jitters □ + *the* [perh alter. of *delirium tremens*]

¹**jimmy** /'jimi/ *n, NAm* a jemmy [*Jimmy,* nickname for *James*]

²**jimmy** *vt, NAm* to jemmy

³**jimmy** *n, chiefly Scot* ²MATE 1c [fr the name *Jimmy*]

**jimsonweed** /'jims(ə)n,weed/ *n, often cap, NAm* THORN APPLE 2 [*jimson* alter. of *Jamestown,* town in Virginia, USA]

¹**jingle** /'jing-gl/ *vi* **1** to make a light clinking or tinkling sound **2** to rhyme or sound in a catchy repetitious manner ~ *vt* to cause to jingle [ME *ginglen,* of imit origin] – **jingler** *n*

²**jingle** *n* **1** a jingling sound (e g of small bells) **2a** something that jingles **b** a short catchy song or rhyme characterized by repetition of phrases and used esp in advertising – **jingly** *adj*

**jingo** /'jing-goh/ *interj* – used as a mild oath in *by jingo* [prob euphemism for *Jesus*]

**jingoism** /'jing-goh,iz(ə)m/ *n* extreme fanatical patriotism or nationalism marked esp by a warlike foreign policy [*jingo* (a chauvinist); fr the use of the phrase *by jingo* in the chorus of a popular song in 1878 supporting British belligerence towards Russia] – **jingoist** *n,* **jingoistic** *adj,* **jingoistically** *adv*

¹**jink** /jingk/ *n* **1** a quick evasive turn (e g in rugby) **2** *pl* pranks, frolics – esp in *high jinks* [origin unknown]

²**jink** *vi* to move quickly or unexpectedly with sudden turns and shifts (e g in dodging) ~ *vt* to dodge, elude

**jinn, djin, djinn** /jin/ *n, pl* **jinns, jinn 1** any of a class of spirits that according to Muslim demonology inhabit the earth, assume various forms, and exercise supernatural power **2** a supernatural spirit that often takes human form and serves whoever summons it [Ar *jinnīy* demon]

    *usage* This Arabic word is also variously represented as **jinni, djinni, djini,** and **genie.** The last form has a pural **genii,** which makes it easily confused with one sense of **genius** (plural also **genii**) meaning "an attendant spirit"; but **genius** and **jinn** are quite different in origin.

**jinni, djinni, djini** /ji'nee, 'jini/ *n* a jinn

**jinrikisha** /jin'rikshə/ *n* a rickshaw [Jap, fr *jin* man + *riki* strength, power + *sha* carriage]

**jinx** /jingks/ *n, informal* a force, curse, etc that brings bad luck ⟨*she put a* ~ *on him*⟩ [prob alter. of *jynx* (wryneck); fr the use of this bird in witchcraft] – **jinx** *vt*

**jipijapa** /,heepee'hahpə/ *n* a panama hat [Sp, a palmlike tree, fr *Jipijapa,* town in Ecuador]

**jitney** /'jitni/ *n, NAm* **1** a motor car or small bus that carries passengers over a regular route according to a flexible timetable **2** *slang* a US 5-cent piece; NICKEL 2a [(2) origin unknown; (1) fr the original 5-cent fare]

¹**jitter** /'jitə/ *vi* **1** to be nervous or act in a nervous way **2** to make continuous fast repetitive movements [origin unknown]

²**jitter** *n* **1** *pl* the sense of panic or extreme nervousness ⟨*had a bad case of the* ~s *before his performance*⟩ **2** an irregular random movement (e g of a pointer or an image on a screen) – **jittery** *adj*

**jitterbug** /-,bug/ *n* **1** a jazz variation of the two-step dance that was popular esp in the 1940s and in which couples swing, balance, and twirl often with vigorous acrobatics **2** one who dances the jitterbug – **jitterbug** *vi*

**jiu-jitsu, jiu-jutsu** /,jooh 'jitsooh/ *n* ju-jitsu

¹**jive** /jiev/ *n* **1** swing music; *also* the energetic dancing performed to it **2** *chiefly NAm* glib, deceptive, or obscure talk; JARGON 2,3; *specif* the jargon of jazz musicians [origin unknown]

²**jive** *vi* **1** to dance to or play jive **2** *NAm* to fool around ~ *vt* **1** SWING 4 **2** *NAm* to cajole; TEASE 3

³**jive** *adj, chiefly NAm slang* phony ⟨*don't give me any of that* ~ *talk*⟩

**jo** /joh/ *n, pl* **joes** *chiefly Scot* a sweetheart, dear [alter. of *joy*]

**joanna** /joh'anə/ *n, Br slang* a piano [rhyming slang]

¹**job** /job/ *n* **1a** a piece of work; *esp* a small piece of work undertaken on order at a stated rate **b** the object or material on which work is being done **c** something produced by work ⟨*do a better* ~ *next time*⟩ **2a(1)** something that has to be done; a task **a(2)** something requiring unusual exertion ⟨*it was a real* ~ *to talk over that noise*⟩ **b** a specific duty, role, or function ⟨*it's not our* ~ *to interfere*⟩ **c** a regular remunerative position ⟨*a part-time* ~ *as a waitress*⟩ **3** *chiefly Br* a state of affairs; thing – + *bad* or *good* ⟨*make the best of a bad* ~⟩ ⟨*it's a good* ~ *you came when you did*⟩ **4** *informal* **4a** an example of a usu specified type; an item ⟨*bought myself a brand new V-8 sports* ~⟩ **b** something done, esp under the guise of public or official business, for private advantage ⟨*suspected the whole incident was a put-up* ~⟩ *specif* a robbery ⟨*did a bank* ~ *over in Finchley*⟩ **d** a damaging or destructive bit of work ⟨*did a* ~ *on him*⟩ **synonyms** see ¹TASK [perh fr obs *job* lump, fr ME *jobbe,* perh alter. of *gobbe* – more at GOB] – **just the job** exactly what is needed – **on the job 1** engaged in one's occupation; AT WORK 1 ⟨*this burglar is known to wear gloves when he is* on the job⟩ **2** *vulg* engaged in sexual intercourse

²**job** *vb* -bb- *vi* **1** to do odd or occasional pieces of work, usu at a stated rate **2** to carry on public business for private gain

3a to carry on the business of a middleman or wholesaler **b** to work as a stockjobber ~ *vt* **1** to buy and sell (e g shares) for profit; speculate **2** to hire or let for a definite job or period of service **3** to get, deal with, or effect by jobbery **4** to subcontract – usu + *out* **5** *NAm informal* to swindle, trick

³**job** *vb, chiefly dial* to jab [ME *jobben*, prob of imit origin] – **job** *n*

**Job** /johb/ *n* – see BIBLE table [*Job* (fr L, fr Gk *Iōb*, fr Heb *Iyyōbh*), Old Testament patriarch who suffered many calamities, bewailed his fate, but retained his faith in God]

**jobation** /joh'baysh(ə)n/ *n, chiefly Br* a long-winded reproof; LECTURE **1** [arch. *jobe* to scold, lecture, fr *Job;* fr the reproofs Job received from his friends]

**jobber** /'jobə/ *n* one who jobs: e g a(1) a stockjobber a(2) a wholesaler; *specif* one who operates on a small scale or who sells only to retailers and institutions **b** one who works by the job or on job work

**jobbery** /'jobəri/ *n* the act or practice of making improper private gain from public office

**jobbing** /'jobing/ *adj* of or engaging in small, miscellaneous, or subcontracted jobs (e g of printing)

**Job Centre** *n* a British government employment office

**job description** *n* a precise written description of the duties belonging to a particular job

**job evaluation** *n* the determination of the relationship between jobs, used as a basis for establishing a structure of wage rates for them

**jobholder** /'job,hohldə/ *n* one having a regular or specific job

**jobless** /'jobləs/ *adj* **1** having no job **2** relating to those having no job – **joblessness** *n*

**job lot** *n* **1** a miscellaneous collection of goods for sale as one lot **2** a miscellaneous and usu inferior collection or group

**Job's comforter** /johbz/ *n* somebody whose attempts to encourage or comfort have the opposite effect [fr the tone of the speeches made to Job by his friends]

**Job's tears** *n pl* **1** hard pearly white seeds that are often used as beads **2** *taking sing vb* an Asiatic grass (*Coix lacryma-jobi*) whose seeds are Job's tears

¹**jock** /jok/ *n, informal* JOCKEY **1**

²**jock** *n, NAm informal* an athlete [*jockstrap*]

**Jock** *n, Br informal* a Scotsman; *esp* a Scottish soldier – often used informally to address a Scotsman whose name is not known [Sc nickname for *John*]

**jockette** /jo'ket/ *n, chiefly derog* a female jockey

¹**jockey** /'joki/ *n* **1** one who rides a horse, esp as a professional in a race **2** *NAm* one who operates or works with a specified vehicle, device, or object; an operator ⟨a truck ~⟩ [*Jockey*, Sc nickname for *John*]

²**jockey** *vt* **1** to deal shrewdly or fraudulently with **2** to ride (a horse) as a jockey **3** to manoeuvre or manipulate by adroit or devious means ⟨~ed *me into handing over the money*⟩ **4** *chiefly NAm* to drive, operate; *also* to manoeuvre ⟨~ *a truck into position*⟩ ~ *vi* **1** to act as a jockey **2** to manoeuvre for advantage ⟨~ *for a starting position on the team*⟩ – **jockeyship** *n*

**jockey club** *n* an association for the promotion and regulation of horse racing

**jockstrap** /'jok,strap/ *n* a support for the genitals worn by men taking part in sports or strenuous activities [E slang *jock* penis + E *strap*]

**jocose** /jə'kohs/ *adj, formal or poetic* **1** given to joking; JOCULAR **1 2** characterized by joking; playful [L *jocosus*, fr *jocus* joke] – **jocosely** *adv*, **jocoseness** *n*, **jocosity** *n*

**jocular** /'jokyoolə/ *adj* **1** given to joking; habitually jolly or jocund **2** characterized by joking; playful [L *jocularis*, fr *joculus*, dim. of *jocus*] – **jocularly** *adv*, **jocularity** *n*

**jocund** /'jokənd/ *adj, formal or poetic* marked by or suggestive of high spirits and lively merriment ⟨a *poet could not but be gay, in such a* ~ *company* – William Wordsworth⟩ [ME, fr LL *jocundus*, alter. of L *jucundus*, fr *juvare* to help, delight] – **jocundly** *adv*, **jocundity** *n*

**jodhpurs** /'jodpəz/ *n pl* riding trousers cut full at the hips and closely fitting from knee to ankle [*Jodhpur*, city in India] – **jodhpur** *adj*

**Joel** /'joh·əl/ *n* – see BIBLE table [*Joel* (fr L, fr Gk *Iōēl*, fr Heb *Yō'ēl*), Heb prophet]

**joey** /'joh·i/ *n, Austr* **1** a young kangaroo **2** a young animal [native name in Australia]

¹**jog** /jog/ *vb* **-gg-** *vt* **1** to give a slight shake or push to; nudge; *also* to give or act as an impetus to ⟨~ *things along*⟩ **2** to rouse to alertness ⟨~ged *his memory*⟩ **3** to cause (e g a horse) to go at a jog **4** to align the edges of (piled sheets of paper) by hitting or shaking against a flat surface ~ *vi* **1** to move up and down or about with a short heavy motion ⟨his *rucksack* ~ging *against his back*⟩ **2a** to run or ride at a slow trot; *specif* to run in such a way regularly in order to keep fit **b** to go at a slow, leisurely, or monotonous pace; trudge [prob alter. of *shog* (to shake, shove), fr ME *shoggen*]

²**jog** *n* **1** a slight shake; a push, nudge **2a** a jogging movement, pace, or trip **b** a slow trot

**jogger** /'jogə/ *n* one who or that which jogs: a one who regularly jogs to keep fit **b** a device for jogging piled sheets of paper

¹**joggle** /'jogl/ *vb* to (cause to) move or shake slightly [freq of ¹*jog*] – **joggle** *n*, **joggler** *n*

²**joggle** *n* **1** a notch or tooth in a joining surface (e g of a piece of building material) to prevent slipping **2** a peg or pin (DOWEL) for joining two neighbouring blocks of stone [dim. of *jog* (projecting part), prob alter. of ²*jag*] – **joggle** *vt*

**jog trot** *n* **1** a slow regular trot (e g of a horse) **2** a routine, leisurely, or monotonous course or progression

**johannes** /joh'(h)aneez/ *n, pl* **johannes** a Portuguese gold coin of the 18th and 19th centuries [*Johannes* John V †1750 King of Portugal]

**Johannine** /joh'hanien/ *adj* relating to or characteristic of the apostle John or the New Testament books ascribed to him [LL *Johannes* John]

**john** /jon/ *n, chiefly NAm* **1** *informal* a toilet **2** *slang* a prostitute's male client [fr the name *John*]

**John** /jon/ *n* – see BIBLE table [*John* (LL *Johannes*, fr Gk *Iōannēs*, fr Heb *Yōhānān*), apostle of Christ & reputed author of the fourth Gospel, three Epistles, and the Book of Revelation]

**John Barleycorn** /'bahli,kawn/ *n, chiefly humorous* alcoholic drink personified

**John Bull** /bool/ *n* **1** the English nation personified; the English people **2** a typical Englishman; esp one regarded as truculently insular [*John Bull*, character typifying the English nation in *The History of John Bull* by John Arbuthnot †1735 Sc physician & writer] – **John Bullish** *adj*, **John Bullishness** *n*, **John Bullism** *n*

**John Doe** /'doh/ *n* **1** a party to legal proceedings whose true name is unknown or withheld **2** *chiefly NAm* an average man [arbitrary name]

**John Dory** /'dawri/ *n* a common yellow to olive European food fish (*Zeus faber*) with an oval compressed body, long spines on its back, and a dark spot on each side; *also* a closely related and possibly identical fish (*Zeus capensis*) widely distributed in southern seas [earlier *dory*, fr ME *dorre*, fr MF *doree*, lit., gilded one]

**Johne's disease** /'yohnəz/ *n* a long-lasting often fatal ENTERITIS (inflammation of the intestines), esp of cattle, that is caused by a rod-shaped bacterium (*Mycobacterium paratuberculosis*) and is characterized by persistent diarrhoea and gradual wasting away [Heinrich *Johne* †1910 Ger bacteriologist]

**John Hancock** /'hangkok/ *n, NAm informal* a person's signature [*John Hancock* †1793 US statesman; fr the prominence of his signature on the US Declaration of Independence]

**John Henry** /'henri/ *n, NAm informal* a person's signature [fr the name *John Henry*]

**johnny** /'joni/ *n, informal* **1** *often cap* a man, fellow **2** a condom [*Johnny*, nickname for *John*]

**johnnycake** /'joni,kayk/ *n* an American cake or bread made with meal from maize [prob fr the name *Johnny*]

**Johnny-come-'lately** *n, pl* **Johnny-come-latelies, Johnniescome-lately** a late or recent arrival; a newcomer

**Johnsonese** /,jonsə'neez/ *n* a literary style characterized by balanced sentence structure and words of Latin derivation [Samuel *Johnson* †1784 E writer]

**Johnson grass** /'jons(ə)n/ *n* a tall grass (*Sorghum halepense*) naturalized for hay and forage in warm regions [William *Johnson* †1859 US farmer]

**Johnsonian** /jon'sohnyən, -ni·ən/ *adj* relating to or characteristic of Samuel Johnson or his writings; *esp* expressed in or making use of Johnsonese

**John Thomas** /'toməs/ *n, Br euph* a penis [fr the names *John Thomas*]

**joie de vivre** /,zhwah də 'veev/ *(Fr ʒwa də viːvr)/ *n* keen or demonstrative enjoyment of life [Fr, lit., joy of living]

¹**join** /joyn/ *vt* **1a** to put or bring together so as to form a unit; fasten ⟨~ *two blocks of wood with glue*⟩ **b** to connect (e g

points) by a line c to adjoin, meet ⟨*where the river* ~s *the sea*⟩ **2** to put or bring into close association or relationship; unite ⟨~ed *in marriage*⟩ **3a** to come into the company of ⟨~ed *us for lunch*⟩ **b** to associate oneself with ⟨~ed *him in the campaign*⟩ **c** to become a member of ⟨~ed *the church*⟩ ~ *vi* **1a** to come together so as to be connected **b** to adjoin, meet ⟨*the two estates* ~⟩ **2** to come into close association or relationship: e g **2a** to form an alliance ⟨~ed *to combat crime*⟩ **b** to become a member of a group **c** to take part in a collective activity ⟨~ *in singing*⟩ [ME *joinen*, fr OF *joindre*, fr L *jungere* – more at YOKE] – **joinable** *adj*

**synonyms Join, combine, unite, connect, link, associate**, and **relate** can all mean "bring together one or more people or things". **Join** implies the bringing together of clearly separate things into a close relationship ⟨**join** *two pieces of string*⟩ ⟨**join** *hands*⟩. **Combine** implies merging things, often with a purpose, so that they lose their separate identities ⟨**combine** *flour and water to make a paste*⟩. **Unite** stresses the one whole which results from **joining** or **combining**. **Connect** and **link** both suggest joining things in such a way that they retain their separate identities. This often involves some intervening element ⟨*a coach service* **links** *the village with the station*⟩ ⟨*a bridleway* **connects** *the station to the road*⟩. Used figuratively to imply an association between abstracts or facts, **connect** suggests a much more tenuous or vague association than **link** ⟨*her name was* **linked** *with the murder*⟩ ⟨*she claimed her visit was not* **connected** *with his death*⟩. **Associate**, of people, implies a relationship on equal terms. With abstracts, **associate** suggests they are naturally connected in one's thoughts ⟨*I always* **associate** *spring with daffodils*⟩. **Relate** suggests rather a connection based on, or claiming to be based on, logic ⟨**related** *his ambitious nature to a frustrated childhood*⟩. **antonyms** separate, disengage

**join up** *vi* to enlist in an armed service

²**join** *n* **1** JOINT 2a **2** UNION 2d (set of mathematical elements)

**joinder** /'joyndə/ *n* **1** a joining of parties or causes in a legal action **2** *formal* the act of joining; conjunction [Fr *joindre* to join]

**joiner** /'joynə/ *n* one who joins: e g **a** a person whose occupation is to construct or repair the wooden fittings (e g doors and window frames) of a building **b** a sociable or public-spirited person who joins many organizations

**joinery** /'joynəri/ *n* **1** the craft or trade of a joiner **2** woodwork constructed by a joiner

**joining** /'joyning/ *n* the act or an instance of joining one thing to another; a juncture ⟨*the* ~s *in shorthand*⟩

¹**joint** /joynt/ *n* **1a(1)** the point of contact between elements of an animal skeleton with the parts that surround and support it **a(2)** NODE 3b (point on a plant stem at which a leaf or branch emerges) **b** a part or space included between two articulations, knots, nodes, etc **c** a large piece of meat cut from a carcass and often suitable for roasting **2a** a place where two things or parts are joined **b** a space between the adjacent surfaces of two bodies joined and held together (e g by cement or mortar) **c** a fracture or crack in rock not accompanied by dislocation **d** the hinge of the case or binding of a book along the back edge of each cover **e** the junction of two or more members of a framed structure **f** a union formed by two rails that meet on a railway line, including the elements (e g fishplates and bolts) necessary to hold the abutting rails together **g** an area at which two ends, surfaces, or edges are attached **3** *informal* **3a** a shabby or disreputable place of entertainment (e g a bar or nightclub) **b** a place, establishment **c** a fairground stall or sideshow **4** *slang* a cigarette containing marijuana [ME *jointe*, fr OF, fr *joindre*] – **jointed** *adj*, **jointedly** *adv*, **jointedness** *n* – **out of joint 1** *of a bone* dislocated **2** disordered, disorganized – see also **put somebody's** NOSE **out of joint**

²**joint** *adj* **1** united, combined ⟨*the* ~ *influences of culture and climate*⟩ **2** common to two or more: e g **2a(1)** involving the united activity of two or more ⟨*a* ~ *effort*⟩ **a(2)** constituting an activity, operation, or organization in which elements of more than one armed service participate ⟨~ *manoeuvres*⟩ **a(3)** constituting an action or expression of two or more governments ⟨~ *peace talks*⟩ **b** shared by or affecting two or more ⟨*a* ~ *fine*⟩ ⟨~ *property*⟩ **3** united, joined, or sharing with another (e g in a right or status) ⟨~ *heirs*⟩ ⟨~ *tenancy*⟩ **4** *statistics* being a function of or involving two or more variables, esp RANDOM VARIABLES ⟨*a* ~ *probability density function*⟩ [ME, fr MF, fr pp of *joindre*]

³**joint** *vt* **1a** to unite by a joint; fit together **b** to provide with a joint; articulate **c** to prepare (e g a board) for joining by planing

the edge **2** to separate the joints of (e g meat); *also* to cut (e g a chicken) into joints, ~ *vi, esp of small grains* to form joints as a stage in growth [¹*joint*]

**joint account** *n* a bank account held in the names of more than one person (e g of a husband and wife)

**jointer** /'joyntə/ *n* one who or that which joints; *esp* any of various tools used in making joints

**joint honours** *n pl* a combination of subjects studied for a British university honours degree

**jointly** /-li/ *adv* in a joint manner; together

**joint resolution** *n* a resolution passed by both houses of a legislative body that has the force of law when signed by the chief executive

**jointress** /'joyntrəs/ *n* a woman holding a legal jointure

**joint-stock company** *n* a company consisting of individuals organized to conduct a business for gain and having a joint stock of capital represented by shares owned individually by the members and transferable without the consent of the group

**jointure** /'joynchə/ *n* property secured to a wife as provision for her, should she survive her husband

**joist** /joyst/ *n* any of the parallel small timbers or metal beams that support a floor or ceiling [ME *giste*, fr MF, fr (assumed) VL *jacitum*, fr L *jacēre* to lie – more at ADJACENT]

**jojoba** /hə'hohbə/ *n* a shrub or small tree (*Simmondsia californica*) of the box family of southwestern N America with edible seeds that yield a valuable liquid wax [MexSp]

¹**joke** /johk/ *n* **1a** something said or done to provoke laughter; *esp* a brief spoken narrative with a humorous twist as its climax – compare PRACTICAL JOKE **b(1)** the humorous or ridiculous element in something ⟨*where's the* ~ *in that?*⟩ **b(2)** an instance of joking or making fun ⟨*can't take a* ~⟩ ⟨*he played a* ~ *on me*⟩ **c** a laughingstock **2** something of little difficulty or seriousness; a trifling matter ⟨*that exam was a* ~⟩ – often used in neg constructions ⟨*it is no* ~ *to be lost in the desert*⟩ [L *jocus*; akin to OHG *gehan* to say, Skt *yācati* he implores] – **jokey, joky** *adj*

²**joke** *vi* to make jokes; jest ~ *vt* to make the object of a joke; kid – **jokingly** *adv*

**joker** /'johkə/ *n* **1** a person given to joking **2** a playing card, usu depicting a jester, added to a pack as a card whose value is chosen by the holder, or as the highest-ranking card **3a** something (e g an emergency measure or stratagem) held in reserve to gain an end or escape from a predicament **b** *chiefly NAm* **b(1)** an unsuspected or misunderstood clause, phrase, or word in a document that greatly alters it or makes it unworkable or uncertain in some respect **b(2)** a readily apparent fact, factor, or condition that negates a seeming advantage **4** *informal* a fellow, guy; *esp* an insignificant, obnoxious, or incompetent person ⟨*a shame to let a* ~ *like this win* – Harold Robbins⟩

**jolie laide** /,zholi 'led (Fr ʒɔli lɛd)/ *n, pl* **jolies laides** /,zholi 'led(z) (Fr* ~*)/* a woman whose conventionally unattractive looks enhance her fascination and charm [Fr, lit., pretty ugly woman]

**jollification** /,jolifi'kaysh(ə)n/ *n* the state or an instance of merrymaking; a festivity, jollity

**jollity** /'joləti/ *n* the quality or state of being jolly; merriment

¹**jolly** /'joli/ *adj* **1a(1)** full of high spirits; joyous ⟨*a* ~ *laugh*⟩ **a(2)** given to conviviality; jovial ⟨*a* ~ *fellow*⟩ **b** expressing, suggesting, or inspiring gaiety; cheerful ⟨*a* ~ *tune*⟩ **2** *informal* extremely pleasant or agreeable; delightful ⟨*the nobility ... have always found* ~ *ways of killing wild animals* – David Frost & Anthony Jay⟩ **3** *Br euph* slightly drunk [ME *joli*, fr OF] – **jollily** *adv*, **jolliness** *n*

²**jolly** *adv, informal* very ⟨*it was a* ~ *good thing I was there*⟩ △ jollily

³**jolly** *vt, informal* **1** to put or try to put in good humour, esp to gain an end; wheedle – usu + *along* ⟨~ *him along*⟩ **2** *informal* to make cheerful or bright – + *up* ⟨~ *up the room with colourful cushions and bright lighting*⟩

⁴**jolly** *n, chiefly Br* a good time; jollification ⟨*rumbustious Australians out for a* ~ – Edward Heath⟩

**jolly boat, jolly** *n* a ship's boat of medium size used for general work [origin unknown]

**Jolly Roger** /'rojə/ *n* a pirate's black flag with a white skull and crossbones [prob fr ¹*jolly* + the name *Roger*]

¹**jolt** /johlt/ *vt* **1** to cause to move with a sudden jerky motion **2** to give a knock or blow to; *specif* to jar with a quick or hard blow **3** to disturb abruptly the composure of; jar ⟨*crudely* ~ed

*out of that mood* – Virginia Woolf⟩ ~ *vi* to move with a jerky motion; bump [prob blend of obs *joll* to strike and *jot* to bump] – **jolter** *n*

²**jolt** *n* **1** an unsettling blow, movement, or shock **2** a small potent or bracing portion; a shot ⟨*a* ~ *of fresh air*⟩ – **jolty** *adj*

**Jonah** /'johnə/ *n* **1** – see BIBLE table **2** a person believed to bring bad luck [*Jonah* (Heb *Yōnāh*), Heb prophet who was held responsible for a storm striking a ship he travelled on]

**Jonas** /'johnəs/ *n* – see BIBLE table [LL, Jonah]

**Jonathan** /'jonəthən/ *n, archaic* an American; *esp* a New Englander [fr the forename *Jonathan*, common among early English settlers in America]

**Joneses** *n pl* – **keep up with the Joneses** to compete with and attempt to impress one's friends, neighbours, etc, esp by spending lavishly [fr the common surname *Jones*]

**jongleur** /ˌzhong'gluh (*Fr* ʒɔglœːr)/ *n* a wandering medieval minstrel [Fr, fr OF *jogleour* – more at JUGGLER]

**jonquil** /'jongkwil/ *n* a Mediterranean plant (*Narcissus jonquilla*) of the daffodil family that grows from a bulb and is widely cultivated for its yellow or white fragrant short-tubed clustered flowers – compare DAFFODIL [Fr *jonquille*, fr Sp *junquillo*, dim. of *junco* reed, fr L *juncus*; akin to ON *einir* juniper, L *juniperus*]

**Jordan almond** /'jawd(ə)n/ *n* a large Spanish almond that is often salted or coated with sugar of various colours [by folk etymology (influenced by *Jordan*, river in Palestine) fr ME *jardin almande*, fr MF *jardin* garden + ME *almande* almond]

**Jordan curve** *n* SIMPLE CLOSED CURVE (e g a circle or ellipse) [Camille *Jordan* †1922 Fr mathematician]

**jorum** /'jawrəm/ *n* a large drinking vessel or its contents [perh fr *Joram* in the Bible who "brought with him vessels of silver" (2 Sam 8:10–AV)]

¹**josh** /josh/ *vb, chiefly NAm vt* to make fun of; tease to engage in banter; joke [origin unknown] – **josher** *n*

²**josh** *n, chiefly NAm* a good-humoured joke

**Joshua** /'josh(y)oo·ə/ *n* – see BIBLE table [*Joshua* (Heb *Yehōshūa*'), successor of Moses & leader of the Israelites]

**joss** /jos/ *n* a Chinese idol or cult image [Pidgin E, fr Pg *deus* god, fr L – more at DEITY]

**joss house** *n* a Chinese temple or shrine

**joss stick** *n* a slender stick of incense (e g for burning in front of a joss)

**jostle** /'josl/ *vi* **1a** to come in contact or into collision **b** to make one's way by pushing and shoving **2** to vie in gaining an objective; contend ~ *vt* **1a** to come in contact or into collision with **b** to force (as if) by pushing; elbow **2** to vie with in attaining an objective [alter. of *justle*, freq of ¹*joust*] – **jostle** *n*

**Josue** *n* – see BIBLE table [LL, Joshua]

¹**jot** /jot/ *n* the least bit; an iota ⟨*nothing ... has caused the author to change his mind one* ~ – *TLS*⟩ [L *iota*, *jota* iota]

²**jot** *vt* **-tt-** to write briefly or hurriedly; set down in the form of a note ⟨~ *this down*⟩

**jotter** /'jotə/ *n* **1** one who jots down brief notes **2** a small book or pad for notes or memoranda

**jotting** /'joting/ *n* a brief note; a memorandum

**Jotun** *also* **Jotunn** /'yohtən/ *n* a member of a race of giants in Norse mythology [ON *jöttun*]

**joual** /zhooh'al/ *n* a Canadian dialect of French [CanF, fr CanF dial., horse, alter. of Fr *cheval*]

**joule** /'joohl/ *n* the SI unit of work or energy equal to the work done when a force of one newton moves its point of application through a distance of one metre [James *Joule* † 1889 E physicist]

**jounce** /jowns/ *vi* to move in an up-and-down manner; bounce ~ *vt* to cause to jounce; jolt [ME *jouncen*] – **jounce** *n*

**journal** /'juhnl/ *n* **1a** a record of current transactions: e g **1a(1)** a daily account book; DAYBOOK **2 a(2)** an account book (BOOK OF ORIGINAL ENTRY) in DOUBLE ENTRY bookkeeping **b** an account of day-to-day events **c** a private record of experiences, ideas, or reflections kept regularly **d** a record of the transactions of a public body, learned society, etc **e** *nautical & computers* LOG 3,4 **2a** a daily newspaper **b** a periodical dealing esp with matters of current interest or specialist subjects **3** the part of a rotating shaft, axle, roll, or spindle that turns in a bearing [ME, service book containing the day hours, fr MF, fr *journal* daily, fr L *diurnalis*, fr *diurnus* of the day, fr *dies* day – more at DEITY; (3) perh of different origin]

**journal box** *n* a metal housing to support and protect a journal bearing

**journalese** /ˌjuhnə'leez/ *n* a style of writing regarded as

characteristic of newspapers; *specif* loose or cliché-ridden writing

**journalism** /'juhnəlˌiz(ə)m/ *n* **1** the collection and editing of material of current interest for presentation through news media; *also* the editorial or business management of such media **2a** writing designed for publication in a newspaper or popular magazine **b** writing characterized by a direct presentation of facts or description of events without an attempt at interpretation **c** writing designed to appeal to current popular taste or public interest **3** newspapers and magazines

**journalist** /'juhnəlist/ *n* **1** a person engaged in journalism; *esp* a writer or editor for a news medium **2** one who keeps a journal

**journalistic** /ˌjuhnə'listik/ *adj* relating to or characteristic of journalism or journalists – **journalistically** *adv*

**journal·ize, -ise** /'juhnəliz/ *vt* to enter or record in a journal ~ *vi* to keep a journal (e g in accounting or for personal use) – **journalizer** *n*

¹**journey** /'juhni/ *n* **1** travel or passage from one place to another, esp by land and over a considerable distance – compare ¹VOYAGE, ²TRIP, ¹TOUR, JAUNT, EXCURSION, EXPEDITION, ²CRUISE, PILGRIMAGE **2** the distance involved in a journey, esp as defined by the time taken to cover it ⟨*a day's* ~⟩ **3** something suggesting travel or passage from one place to another ⟨*the* ~ *through life*⟩ [ME, fr OF *journee* day's journey, fr *jour* day, fr LL *diurnum*, fr L, neut of *diurnus*]

²**journey** *vi* to go on a journey; travel ~ *vt* to travel over or through; traverse – **journeyer** *n*

**journeyman** /'juhnimən/ *n* **1** a worker who has learned a trade and is employed by another person, usu by the day **2** an experienced reliable worker or performer, esp as distinguished from one who is brilliant or outstanding [ME, fr *journey* journey, a day's labour + *man*]

**journeywork** /'juhniˌwuhk/ *n* **1** work done by a journeyman **2** uninspired or mediocre work; hackwork

¹**joust** /jowst/ *vi* **1** to fight in a joust or tournament **2** *journalistic* to engage in personal combat or competition [ME *jousten*, fr OF *juster* to gather, unite, fight in a joust, fr (assumed) VL *juxtare*, fr L *juxta* near; akin to L *jungere* to join – more at YOKE] – **jouster** *n*

²**joust** *n* **1a** a combat on horseback between two knights or men-at-arms with lances, esp as part of a medieval tournament **b** *pl* a tournament **2** *journalistic* a personal combat or competition; a struggle

**Jove** /johv/ *n* the Roman god Jupiter – often used interjectionally to express surprise or agreement, esp in *by Jove* [L *Jov-, Juppiter*]

**jovial** /'johvi·əl/ *adj* markedly good-humoured; jolly, convivial [MF *jovial* born under the planet Jupiter (considered by astrologers as the source of happiness), fr LL *jovialis* of the god or planet Jupiter, fr *Jov-, Juppiter*] – **jovially** *adv*, **joviality** *n*

**Jovian** /'johvi·ən/ *adj* relating to or characteristic of the planet Jupiter [L *jovius* of the god or planet Jupiter]

¹**jowl** /jowl/ *n* **1** JAW 1a, 1b; *esp* MANDIBLE (lower jaw) **2a** CHEEK 1 **b** the cheek meat of a pig [alter. of ME *chavel*, fr OE *ceafl*; akin to MHG *kivel* jaw]

²**jowl** *n*, **jowls** *n pl* usu slack flesh (e g a DEWLAP, WATTLE, or the part of a double chin that hangs down) associated with the lower jaw or throat – see also CHEEK **by jowl** [ME *cholle*, prob fr OE *ceole* throat]

³**jowl** *n* the head of a fish and usu neighbouring parts, esp as a cut of fish [ME *choll* head]

¹**joy** /joy/ *n* **1a** the emotion or state of great happiness, pleasure, or delight (e g produced by success, good fortune, or the prospect of possessing what one desires) **b** the expression or showing of such emotion **2** a source or cause of delight **3** *Br informal* success, satisfaction ⟨*he had no* ~ *at the first shop he went into*⟩ **synonyms** see ¹PLEASURE **antonyms** grief, sorrow [ME, fr OF *joie*, fr L *gaudia*, pl of *gaudium*, fr *gaudēre* to rejoice; akin to Gk *gēthein* to rejoice] – **joyless** *adj*, **joylessly** *adv*, **joylessness** *n*

²**joy** *vi* to experience joy; rejoice ~ *vt, archaic* to gladden

**joyance** /'joyəns/ *n, poetic* delight, enjoyment

**Joycean** /'joysi·ən/ *adj* relating to or characteristic of James Joyce or his writings; *esp* making use of compound or invented words and recording the unspoken reflections of his characters [James *Joyce* †1941 Ir writer]

**joyful** /'joyf(ə)l/ *adj* filled with, causing, or expressing joy; happy – **joyfully** *adv*, **joyfulness** *n*

**synonyms Joyful, joyous, glad, happy, cheerful, lighthearted,**

and **gay** all describe a mood of keen pleasure or delight. **Joyful** and **joyous** are the strongest terms, suggesting elation and rejoicing. While **joyful** describes the people experiencing this emotion, or their behaviour, **joyous** often describes whatever itself inspires joy or is by nature full of joy ⟨*streets full of* **joyful** *people celebrating the peace*⟩ ⟨*all that ever was* **joyous***, and clear, and fresh, thy music doth surpass* – P B Shelley⟩. **Glad** suggests delight tinged with unspecified gratitude or gratification ⟨**glad** *did I live and gladly die* – R L Stevenson⟩. **Happy** stresses contentment and well-being, and suggests a more passive pleasure than the preceding terms. **Cheerful**, **lighthearted**, and **gay** all describe the expression of one's happiness in outward mood and behaviour. **Cheerful** suggests unfailing good spirits either as a characteristic or as a result of feeling happy. **Lighthearted** stresses the absence of care and implies gaiety and high spirits. It now replaces **gay**, which more strongly suggested happiness and high spirits, as this sense of **gay** has been eclipsed by its adoption as a label by the homosexual community. *antonyms* sad, depressed, melancholy

**joyous** /'joyəs/ *adj* joyful *synonyms* see JOYFUL – **joyously** *adv*, **joyousness** *n*

**joyride** /'joy,ried/ *n* **1a** a ride in a car taken for pleasure and often without the owner's consent **b** a short pleasure flight in an aircraft **2** a course of conduct or action resembling a joyride, esp in its happy disregard of cost or consequences – **joyrider** *n*, **joyriding** *n*

**joystick** /'joy,stik/ *n* **1** the control column of an aeroplane **2** a control for any of various devices (e g video games) that resembles an aeroplane's joystick, esp in being capable of motion in two or more directions [prob fr E slang *joystick* penis]

**JP** /jay'pee/ *n* a local magistrate; JUSTICE OF THE PEACE

**jubbah** /'joobə, 'jubə/ *n* a long loose outer garment traditionally worn in Muslim countries [Ar (cf ²JUMPER)]

**jubilant** /'joohbilant/ *adj* filled with or expressing great joy; exultant – **jubilance** *n*, **jubilantly** *adv*

**jubilarian** /,joohbi'leəri·ən/ *n* one celebrating a jubilee; *specif* a priest, monk, or nun celebrating the fiftieth anniversary of entering the religious life

**jubilate** /'joohbilayt/ *vi* to rejoice, exult [L *jubilatus*, pp of *jubilare*; akin to MHG *jū* (exclamation of joy), Gk *iȳgē* shout]

**Jubilate** /,joohbi'lahti/ *n* **1** the 100th Psalm in the Authorized Version of the Bible **2** the third Sunday after Easter [L, 2 pl imper of *jubilare*; (1) fr its opening word; (2) fr Psalm 66 (AV), also beginning with the word *Jubilate*, used as the introit for the third Sunday after Easter]

**jubilation** /,joohbi'laysh(ə)n/ *n* rejoicing; the state of being jubilant; *also* an expression of great joy

**jubilee** /'joohbi'lee, '--,-/ *n* **1** *often cap* a year of emancipation and restoration provided by ancient Hebrew law to be kept every 50 years, and celebrated by the freeing of Hebrew slaves, return of misappropriated lands to their former owners, and omission of all cultivation of the land **2a** a special anniversary (e g of a sovereign's accession to the throne) **b** a celebration of such an anniversary ⟨*remembered Queen Victoria's diamond* ~⟩ **3** a period of time, proclaimed by the Pope usually every 25 years, during which a special PLENARY INDULGENCE (forgiveness of sins) is granted to Roman Catholics who perform certain works of repentance and piety **4a** jubilation **b** a season or occasion of celebration [ME, fr MF & LL; MF *jubilé*, fr LL *jubilaeus*, modif (influenced by L *jubilare* to rejoice) of LGk *iōbēlaios*, fr Heb *yōbhēl* ram's horn, jubilee]

**Judaeo-Christian**, *NAm chiefly* **Judeo-Christian** /jooh,dayo'krischən/ *adj* having historical roots in both Judaism and Christianity ⟨~ *morality*⟩ [L *Judaeus* Jew – more at JEW]

**Judaeo-Spanish**, *NAm chiefly* **Judeo-Spanish** /jooh'dayoh, jooh'dee·oh/ *n* the Romance language of SEPHARDIC Jews (those of Spanish or Portuguese descent) living in the Balkans and Asia Minor; ¹LADINO 1

**Judaic** /jooh'dayik/ *also* **Judaical** /-k(ə)l/ *adj* of or characteristic of Jews or Judaism [L *judaicus*, fr Gk *ioudaikos*, fr *Ioudaios* Jew – more at JEW]

**Judaica** /jooh'dayikə/ *n pl* literary or historical materials relating to Jews or Judaism [L, neut pl of *Judaicus*]

**Judaism** /'joohday,iz(ə)m/ *n* **1** a religion developed among the ancient Hebrews and characterized by belief in one God, external to creation but operating in it, who has revealed himself to Abraham, Moses, and the Hebrew prophets, and by a religious life in accordance with Scriptures and traditions handed down and interpreted by the religious leaders **2** conformity to Jewish rites, ceremonies, and practices **3** the cultural,

social, and religious beliefs and practices of the Jews **4** the Jewish people

**Judaist** /'joohdayist/ *n* a person who believes in or practises Judaism – **Judaistic** *adj*

**Juda·ize, -ise** /'joohdayiez/ *vi* to adopt the customs, beliefs, or character of a Jew ~ *vt* to make Jewish – **Judaization** *n*, **Judaizer** *n*

**Judas** /'joohdəs/ *n* **1** a traitor; *esp* one who betrays under the guise of friendship **2** **judas, judas hole** a peephole in a door [*Judas* (fr LL, fr Gk *Ioudas*, fr Heb *Yĕhūdhāh*), apostle who betrayed Christ]

**Judas tree** *n* any of a genus (*Cercis*) of trees and shrubs of the pea family that are often grown for their showy flowers; *esp* a Eurasian tree (*Cercis siliquastrum*) with purplish-pink flowers [fr the tradition that the apostle Judas hanged himself from a tree of this kind]

**judder** /'judə/ *vi, chiefly Br* to vibrate with jerky intensity ⟨*the engine stalled and* ~ed⟩ [prob alter. of *shudder*] – **judder** *n*

**Jude** /joohd/ *n* – see BIBLE table [*Jude* (LL *Judas*), disciple of Christ]

**¹judge** /juj/ *vt* **1** to form an opinion about through careful weighing of evidence and testing of assumed truths **2a** to sit in judgment on; try **b** to decide the result of (a competition or contest); act as a judge in **3** to determine or pronounce after enquiry and deliberation **4** *of a Hebrew tribal leader* to govern, rule **5** to form an estimate or evaluation of ⟨~ *the distance*⟩ **6** to hold as an opinion; infer, think ~ *vi* **1** to form a judgment or opinion **2** to act as a judge ⟨*to* ~ *between us*⟩ [ME *juggen*, fr OF *jugier*, fr L *judicare*, fr *judic-, judex* judge, fr *jus* right, law + *dicere* to decide, say – more at JUST, DICTION] – **judger** *n*

*synonyms* The verb **judge** is either transitive or intransitive, but **adjudge** is transitive only. In the legal senses one **judges/adjudges** a case, **judges/adjudges** a prisoner guilty; one **judges** an accused person, and **adjudges** (= "awards") legal costs. In the more general senses one **judges/adjudges** something to be true; one **judges** a flower show or beauty competition, and **judges** (= "estimates") time, distance, temperature, etc.

**²judge** *n* one who judges: e g **a** a public official authorized to hear and decide questions brought before a court of law **b** *often cap* a tribal hero and leader among the Hebrews after the death of Joshua **c** a person appointed to decide in a contest or competition; *esp* any of a panel of adjudicators who award marks for style and performance in certain sporting contests (e g diving or ice skating) **d** one who gives an authoritative opinion ⟨*a good* ~ *of character*⟩ **e** CRITIC 1a [ME *juge*, fr MF, fr L *judex*] – **judgeship** *n*

**judge advocate** *n* an officer appointed to superintend the trial and advise on points of military law at a court-martial

**judge advocate general** *n* the senior nonmilitary legal officer in charge of the administration of justice in the army or air force

**judge-made law** *n* legal principles based on previous judicial decision rather than on written (STATUTE) law

**Judges** /'jujiz/ *n taking sing vb* – see BIBLE table

**Judges' Rules** *n* the rules governing police interrogation of suspects

**judgmatic** /juj'matik/, **judgmatical** /-k(ə)l/ *adj, informal* judicious, discreet [prob irreg fr *judgment*] – **judgmatically** *adv*

**judgment, judgement** /'jujmənt/ *n* **1a** a formal utterance of an authoritative opinion **b** an opinion so pronounced **2a** a formal decision given by a court **b(1)** an obligation (e g a debt) created by the decision of a court **b(2)** a certificate embodying such a decision **3a Judgment, Last Judgment** *the* final judging of mankind by God **b** a divine sentence or decision; *specif* a calamity held to be sent by God as a punishment **4a** the process of forming an opinion or evaluation by discerning and comparing **b** an opinion or estimate so formed **5a** the capacity for judging; discernment **b** the exercise of this capacity **6** a statement (PROPOSITION) in logic stating something believed or asserted *synonyms* see ¹REASON – **judgmental** *adj*

**Judgment Day** *n* the day of God's judgment of mankind at the end of the world, according to various theologies

**judicature** /'joohdikəchə/ *n* **1** the administration of justice in general **2** a court of justice **3** JUDICIARY 1 **4a** (the extent of) the power, authority, or jurisdiction of a judge **b** (the duration of) the office or function of a judge [MF, fr ML *judicatura*, fr L *judicatus*, pp of *judicare*]

**judicial** /jooh'dish(ə)l/ *adj* **1** relating to a judgment, the function of judging, the administration of justice, or the judiciary ⟨~

*processes*⟩ – compare EXECUTIVE, LEGISLATIVE **2** ordered or enforced by a court ⟨~ *decisions*⟩ **3** of, characterized by, or expressing judgment; CRITICAL 1c **4** arising from a judgment of God **5** belonging or appropriate to a judge or the judiciary [ME, fr L *judicialis*, fr *judicium* judgment, fr *judex*] – **judicially** *adv*

**judicial murder** *n* a sentence of death pronounced in due course of law but nevertheless considered to be unjust

**judicial review** *n* **1** a reexamination by judges (eg of the proceedings of a lower court) **2** a constitutional doctrine of some countries that gives to a court system the power to cancel legislative or executive acts which the judges declare to be unconstitutional ⟨~ *has ... been termed America's distinctive contribution to the science of politics* – F A Ogg and P O Ray⟩

**judicial separation** *n* a court order that a married couple should live apart

**judiciary** /jooh'dishəri/ *n* **1a** a system of courts of law **b** *taking sing or pl vb* the judges of these courts **2** a judicial branch of the US government [*judiciary*, adj, fr L *judiciarius* judicial, fr *judicium*] – **judiciary** *adj*

**judicious** /jooh'dishəs/ *adj* having, exercising, or characterized by sound judgment; discreet, discerning – **judiciously** *adv*, **judiciousness** *n*

**Judith** /'joohdith/ *n* – see BIBLE table [*Judith* (fr LL, fr Gk *Ioudith*, fr Heb *Yĕhūdhīth*), Jewish heroine (prob legendary)]

**judo** /'joohdoh/ *n* an Oriental MARTIAL ART developed from ju-jitsu that emphasizes the use of quick movement and leverage to throw an opponent [Jap *jūdō*, fr *jū* weakness, gentleness + *dō* art] – **judoist** *n*

**judoka** /'joohdoh,kah/ *n* one who practises judo [Jap *jūdōka*, fr *jūdō*]

**judy** /'joohdi/ *n*, *often cap*, *slang* a girl [*Judy*, nickname for *Judith*]

**¹jug** /jug/ *n* **1a** a vessel for holding liquids: **1a(1)** *chiefly Br* a vessel for holding and pouring liquids that usu has a handle and a lip or spout **a(2)** *chiefly NAm* a large deep earthenware or glass vessel for liquids that usu has a handle and a narrow mouth often fitted with a cork; FLAGON 1b **b** the contents of or quantity contained in a jug; a jugful **2** a large secure handhold in mountaineering or rock climbing **3** *informal* prison ⟨*three years in* ~⟩ [perh fr *Jug*, nickname for *Joan*; (2) short for *jug-handle*] – **jugful** *n*

**²jug** *vt* -gg- **1** to stew (esp a hare) in an earthenware vessel **2** *informal* to imprison

**jugate** /'jooh,gayt/ *adj* **1** *esp of a leaf* having parts arranged in pairs; paired **2** having a jugum [NL *jugum*]

**jug band** *n* a band that uses crude improvised musical instruments

**juggernaut** /'jugə,nawt/ *n* **1a** a massive irresistible force or object that crushes whatever is in its path **b** an object of devotion for which one sacrifices oneself or others **2** *Br* a very large heavy usu articulated lorry, esp when considered a threat to safety or the environment [Hindi *Jagannāth*, title of the god Vishnu, lit., lord of the world, fr Skt *Jagannātha*; fr the former belief that some devotees of Vishnu threw themselves beneath the wheels of a cart bearing his image in procession]

**juggins** /'juginz/ *n*, *pl* **juggins**, **jugginses** *informal or humorous* a naive or simpleminded person; a simpleton – no longer in vogue [prob fr the name *Juggins* (cf MUGGINS)]

**juggle** /'jugl/ *vi* **1** to perform the tricks of a juggler **2** to engage in manipulation, esp in order to achieve a desired end ~ *vt* **1** to manipulate esp in order to achieve a desired end ⟨~ *an account to hide a loss*⟩ **2a** to toss in the manner of a juggler **b** to hold or balance precariously [ME *jogelen*, fr MF *jogler* to joke, fr L *joculari*, fr *joculus*, dim. of *jocus* joke] – **juggle** *n*

**juggler** /'juglə/ *n* **1** one skilled in keeping several objects in motion in the air at the same time by alternately tossing and catching them **2** one who manipulates, esp in order to achieve a desired end [ME *jogelour*, fr OE *geogelere*, fr OF *jogleour*, fr L *joculator*, fr *joculatus*, pp of *joculari*] – **jugglery** *n*

**¹jugular** /'jugyoolə/ *adj* **1a** of the throat or neck **b** of the jugular vein **2a** *of a fish* having the VENTRAL (of the lower body surface) fins on the throat located further forward than the PECTORAL FINS **b** *of a ventral fin of a fish* located on the throat [LL *jugularis*, fr L *jugulum* collarbone, throat; akin to L *jungere* to join – more at YOKE]

**²jugular, jugular vein** *n* any of several veins of each side of the neck that return blood from the head

**jugulum** /'jugyooləm/ *n*, *pl* **jugula** /-lə/ **1** the part of the neck just above the breast of a bird **2** the jugum [NL, fr L]

**jugum** /'joohgəm/ *n*, *pl* **juga** /-gə/, **jugums 1** a pair of opposite leaflets **2** the hindmost and base region of an insect's wing, modified in some moths into a lobe that joins the fore and hind wings during flight [NL, fr L, yoke – more at YOKE]

**¹juice** /joohs/ *n* **1** the extractable liquid contents of cells or tissues **2a** *pl* the natural liquids of an animal body **b** the liquid or moisture contained in something **3** the inherent quality of a thing; spirit, essence; *esp* basic force or vigour **4** *informal* **4a** alcoholic drink **b** electricity **c** petrol [ME *jus*, fr OF, broth, juice, fr L; akin to Skt *yūṣ* broth]

**²juice** *vt* **1** to extract the juice of **2** to add juice to

**juice up** *vb*, *NAm informal* to give life, energy, or spirit to

**juicer** /'joohsə/ *n*, *NAm* an appliance for extracting juice from fruit or vegetables

**juicy** /'joohsi/ *adj* **1** containing much juice; succulent **2** *informal* financially rewarding; profitable ⟨*a* ~ *deal*⟩ **3** *informal* **3a** rich in interest ⟨*a* ~ *problem*⟩; *esp* interesting because of racy or spicy content ⟨~ *scandal*⟩ **b** sexually attractive; LUSCIOUS 2 – **juicily** *adv*, **juiciness** *n*

**ju-jitsu, jiu-jitsu** /,jooh 'jitsooh/ *n* an Oriental MARTIAL ART employing holds, throws, and paralysing blows to subdue or disable an opponent – compare JUDO [Jap *jūjutsu*, fr *jū* weakness, gentleness + *jutsu* art]

**juju** /'jooh,jooh/ *n* **1** a FETISH (object believed to have magical power), charm, or amulet of W African peoples **2** the magic attributed to or associated with jujus [of W African origin; akin to Hausa *djudju* fetish]

**jujube** /'jooh,joohb/ *n* **1** an edible berrylike fruit of any of several trees (genus *Ziziphus*) of the buckthorn family; *also* a tree that produces this fruit **2** a fruit-flavoured gum or lozenge [ME, fr ML *jujuba*, alter. of L *zizyphum*, fr Gk *zizyphon*]

**ju-jutsu, jiu-jutsu** /,jooh 'jitsooh/ *n* ju-jitsu

**jukebox** /'joohk,boks/ *n* a coin-operated record player that automatically plays records chosen from a limited selection [Gullah *juke* disorderly, of W African origin; akin to Bambara *dzugu* wicked]

**julep** /'joohlip/ *n* **1** a drink consisting of sweet syrup, flavouring, and water **2** a chiefly American drink consisting of an alcoholic spirit and sugar poured over crushed ice and garnished with mint [ME, fr MF, fr Ar *julāb*, fr Per *gulāb*, fr *gul* rose + *āb* water]

**Julian calendar** /'joohlyən, -li-ən/ *n* a calendar introduced in Rome in 46 BC establishing the 12-month year of 365 days, with an extra day every fourth year, and each month having 31 or 30 days, except for February which has 28, or 29 in leap years – compare GREGORIAN CALENDAR [L *julianus*, fr Gaius *Julius* Caesar †44 BC Roman general & statesman]

**¹julienne** /,joohli'en/ *n* **1** a clear soup containing julienne vegetables **2** a garnish of julienne vegetables [Fr, prob fr the name *Jules*, *Julien*]

**²julienne** *adj* cut into long thin strips ⟨~ *potatoes*⟩ ⟨*green beans* ~⟩

**juliet cap** /'joohli•ət, -et/ *n* a woman's small close-fitting brimless cap worn esp by brides [prob fr *Juliet*, heroine of Shakespeare's tragedy *Romeo and Juliet*]

**Juliett** /,joohli'et/ – a communications code word for the letter *j* [prob irreg fr *Juliet*]

**July** /joo'lie/ *n* the 7th month of the year according to the GREGORIAN CALENDAR (standard Western calendar) – see MONTH table [ME *Julie*, fr OE *Julius*, fr L, fr Gaius *Julius* Caesar, whose birthday fell in this month (previously named *Quintilis*, ie 'fifth month')]

**Jumada** /jooh'mahdə/ *n* – see MONTH table [Ar *Jumādā*]

**¹jumble** /'jumbl/ *vb* to move or mix in a confused or disordered manner – often + *up* [perh imit]

**²jumble** *n* **1a** a mass of things mingled together without order or plan; a hotchpotch **b** a state of confusion **2** *Br* articles for a jumble sale

**³jumble, jumbal** *n* a small thin usu ring-shap•d sweet biscuit or cake [perh alter. of obs *gimbal* ring]

**jumble sale** *n*, *Br* a sale of donated secondhand articles held by a nonprofitmaking organization (eg a church or charity) to help support its work

**jumbo** /'jumboh/ *n*, *pl* **jumbos** a very large specimen of its kind [prob fr *mumbo-jumbo*; influenced in meaning by *Jumbo*, a huge elephant exhibited in London & the USA in the late 19th c] – **jumbo** *adj*

**jumbo jet** *n* a large thin jet aeroplane capable of carrying several hundred passengers

**jumbuck** /'jum,buk/ *n, Austr* a sheep [native name in Australia]

**¹jump** /jump/ *vi* **1a** to spring into the air; leap; *esp* to spring free from the ground or other base by the muscular action of feet and legs **b** to move suddenly or involuntarily (eg from shock or surprise); start **c** to move over a position occupied by an opponent's man in a board game, often thereby capturing the man **d** to begin a forward movement – usu + *off* **e** to move quickly or energetically (as if) with a jump; *also* to act immediately ⟨*he expected everyone to ~ at his command*⟩ **f** to go from one sequence of instructions in a computer program to another ⟨*~ to a subroutine*⟩ **2** to pass or change rapidly, suddenly, or abruptly; *esp* to pass in this manner (as if) over some intervening thing: eg **2a** to skip ⟨*this record ~s*⟩ ⟨*~ed to the end of the book*⟩ **b** to rise suddenly in rank or status ⟨*~ed from captain to colonel*⟩ **c** to make a mental leap ⟨*her mind ~ed from one thing to another*⟩ **d** to come to or arrive at a position or judgment without due deliberation ⟨*~ to conclusions*⟩ **e** LEAP 2 ⟨*scandals that ~ into the headlines*⟩ **f** to undergo a sudden sharp increase ⟨*prices ~ed sky-high*⟩ **3** to move haphazardly or aimlessly ⟨*~ed from job to job*⟩ **4** to make a jump in bridge **5** to make a sudden physical or verbal attack – usu + *on* or *upon* ⟨*~ed on him for his criticism*⟩ **6** *NAm* to bustle with activity ⟨*by midnight the place was really ~ing*⟩ **7** *archaic* to coincide, agree – usu + *with* ~ *vt* **1a** to leap over ⟨*~ a hurdle*⟩ **b** to move over (a man) in a board game **c** to pass over, esp to a point beyond; skip, bypass ⟨*~ electrical connections*⟩ **d** to act, move, or begin before (eg a signal); anticipate ⟨*~ the green light*⟩ **2a** to escape or run away from ⟨*~ prison*⟩ **b** to leave hastily or in violation of an undertaking or contract ⟨*~ ship*⟩ ⟨*~ bail*⟩ **c** to depart from (a normal course) ⟨*the train ~ed the rails*⟩ **3** to seize or take possession of summarily or in violation of another's rights; occupy illegally ⟨*~ a mining claim*⟩ **4** to cause or help to jump ⟨*~ed the child down from the chair*⟩ ⟨*~ed her horse over the gate*⟩ **5** to raise (a bridge partner's bid) by more than one rank **6** *chiefly NAm* to leap aboard, esp so as to travel illegally ⟨*~ a train*⟩ **7** *informal* to make a sudden or surprise attack on [prob akin to LG *gumpen* to jump] – **jump to it** *informal* to hurry – see also **jump on the** BANDWAGON, **jump the** GUN/**the** QUEUE, **jump out of one's** SKIN

**jump at** *vt* to accept eagerly ⟨*jump at the chance*⟩

**²jump** *n* **1a(1)** an act of jumping; a leap **a(2)** any of several sports contests (eg the long jump) that include a jump, spring, or bound **a(3)** a space, height, or distance cleared or covered by a jump **a(4)** an obstacle to be jumped over ⟨*my horse fell at the last ~*⟩ **b** a sudden involuntary movement; a start **c** a move made in a board game by jumping **d** a transfer from one sequence of instructions in a computer program to a different sequence ⟨*conditional ~*⟩ **2a(1)** a sharp sudden increase (eg in amount, price, or value) **a(2)** a bid in bridge of more TRICKS than are necessary to outbid the preceding bid, made in order to discourage one's opponents from further bidding, or to convey information to one's partner about a hand with a high point value – compare SHIFT **b** a sudden change or transition; *esp* one that leaves a break in continuity **c** any of a series of moves from one place or position to another; a move ⟨*stayed two ~s ahead of his opponent*⟩ **3** *pl, informal* the fidgets **4** *chiefly NAm informal* an advantage at the start ⟨*getting the ~ on our competition*⟩ **5** *Br slang* an act of sexual intercourse – **for the high jump** about to receive a severe reprimand or punishment

**jump ball** *n* a toss of a basketball by an official into the air between two opponents who jump up and attempt to tap the ball to a teammate

**jump cut** *n* a discontinuity or acceleration in the action of a filmed scene caused by the removal of the middle part of the shot

**,jumped-'up** *adj, derog* recently risen in wealth, rank, or status; upstart

**¹jumper** /'jumpǝ/ *n* **1** a person who jumps **2a** any of various devices operating with a jumping motion **b** a short wire used to close a break or cut out part of an electrical circuit **3** an animal that jumps; *esp* a riding horse trained to jump fences

**²jumper** *n* **1** *Br* a knitted or crocheted garment usu without fastenings that is worn on the upper body **2** *NAm* PINAFORE 2 [prob fr E dial. *jump* loose jacket, prob alter. of *jupe* coat, jacket, fr ME *juype*, fr OF *jupe*, fr Ar *jubbah*]

**jumping bean** /'jumping/ *n* a seed of any of several Mexican shrubs (genera *Sebastiania* and *Sapium*) of the spurge family that tumbles about because of the movements of the larva of a small moth (*Carpocapsa saltitans*) inside it

**jumping jack** *n* **1** a toy figure of a man that is jointed and made to jump or dance by means of strings or a sliding stick **2** a firework that jumps about when lit

**jumping-off place** *n* a place or point from which an enterprise is launched

**jumping-off point** *n* a jumping-off place

**jumping plant louse** *n* any of numerous plant lice (family Psyllidae) with the FEMURS (upper leg joints) thickened and adapted for leaping

**jumping spider** *n* any of a family (Salticidae) of small spiders that stalk and leap upon their prey

**'jump-,jet** *n, chiefly Br* a jet aircraft able to take off and land vertically

**jump leads** *n pl* a pair of heavy-duty electric cables for starting the engine of a motor vehicle with a flat battery, by connecting the engine to a second battery; *also, sing* either of these cables

**'jump-,off** *n* the last round of a showjumping competition, in which those riders who have previously jumped clear perform again, usu against the clock – **jump off** *vi*

**jump pass** *n* a pass made by a player (eg in basketball) while jumping

**jump seat** *n* a folding seat between the front and rear seats of a large car; *also* a similar folding seat for temporary use in other vehicles or aircraft

**jump shot** *n* a shot in basketball made by jumping into the air and releasing the ball with one or both hands at the peak of the jump

**jump start** *n* the starting of a motor vehicle's engine using jump leads – **jump start** *vt*

**jumpsuit** /'jump,s(y)ooht/ *n* a one-piece garment combining top and trousers or shorts

**'jump-,up** *n, WI* DANCE 3 – **jump up** *vi*

**jumpy** /'jumpi/ *adj* **1** characterized by jumps or sudden variations **2** nervous, jittery – **jumpiness** *n*

**jun** /jun/ *n, pl* **jun** – see *won* at MONEY table [Korean]

**junco** /'jungkoh/ *n, pl* **juncos, juncoes** any of a genus (*Junco*) of small widely distributed American finches [NL, genus name, fr Sp, reed – more at JONQUIL]

**junction** /'jungksh(ǝ)n/ *n* **1** joining or being joined **2a** a place of meeting **b** an intersection of roads, esp where one terminates **c** a point (eg in a thermocouple) at which dissimilar metals make contact **d** an INTERFACE (area of contact) in a semiconductor device (eg a transistor) between regions with different electrical characteristics **3** something that joins □ compare JUNCTURE [L *junction-, junctio*, fr *junctus*, pp of *jungere* to join – more at YOKE] – **junctional** *adj*

**junction box** *n* a box containing connections between separate electric circuits

**junctural** /'jungkchǝrǝl/ *adj, linguistics* relating to juncture

**juncture** /'jungkchǝ/ *n* **1** an instance of joining; a union **2a** a connection; JOINT 2a **b** the manner of transition between two consecutive speech sounds **3** a point of time; *esp* one made critical by a concurrence of circumstances □ compare JUNCTION

**June** /joohn/ *n* the 6th month of the year according to the GREGORIAN CALENDAR (standard Western calendar) – see MONTH table [ME, fr MF & L; MF *Juin*, fr L *Junius*, prob fr *Junius*, name of a Roman clan]

**june bug** *n* CHAFER (type of beetle)

**Jungian** /'yoong·i·ǝn/ *adj* relating to or characteristic of the school of analytical psychology founded by C G Jung [Carl Gustav *Jung* †1961 Swiss psychologist] – **Jungian** *n*

**jungle** /'jung·gl/ *n* **1** an area of land overgrown with thickets or tangled masses of vegetation (eg in the tropics) **2a** a confused, disordered, or complex mass ⟨*the ~ of tax laws*⟩ **b** a place of ruthless struggle for survival ⟨*the blackboard ~*⟩ [Hindi *jangal* waste land, forest, fr Skt *jāngala*] – **jungly** *adj*

**jungle fever** *n* a severe malarial fever

**jungle fowl** *n* any of several Asiatic wild birds (genus *Gallus*); *esp* a bird (*Gallus gallus*) of SE Asia from which domestic fowls have probably descended

**¹junior** /'joohnyǝ/ *n* **1** a person who is younger than another ⟨*she is five years his ~*⟩ **2a** a person holding a lower or subordinate position in a hierarchy of ranks ⟨*the little office ~ straight from school* – Colin MacInnes⟩ **b** a person who is below a designated age (eg 18) **c** a member of a younger form in a school ⟨*the ~s go to bed earlier*⟩ **3** *NAm* a student in the next-to-the-last year before graduating **4** *NAm informal* a male child; a son – used esp as a term of address [L, n & adj]

**²junior** *adj* **1** younger – used chiefly in the USA to distinguish a son with the same name as his father **2** lower in standing or rank ⟨~ *partners*⟩ **3** concerned with or intended for children aged from 7 to 11 ⟨*both infant and* ~ *classes*⟩ [L, compar of *juvenis* young – more at YOUNG]

**juniorate** /'joohnyərayt, -rət/ *n* **1** a course of secondary or higher study for candidates for the priesthood, brotherhood, or sisterhood; *specif* one preparatory to the course in philosophy **2** a SEMINARY (training college) for juniorate training

**junior college** *n* a US educational institution that offers two years of studies corresponding to those in the first two years of a four-year college; *also* a similar institution elsewhere (e g in Britain) ⟨*the present grammar school will become a* Junior College *for pupils aged 16–19 – TES*⟩

**Junior Common Room** *n* **1** a sitting room in a college for the use of the students **2** *taking sing or pl vb* the student community in a college

**junior high school** *n* a US school usu for children aged 12 to 14

**junior lightweight** *n* a professional boxer who weighs not more than 9 stone 4 pounds (59.0 kilograms) – called also SUPER FEATHERWEIGHT

**junior middleweight** *n* a professional boxer who weighs not more than 11 stone (69.9 kilograms)

**junior school** *n* **1** a primary school for children aged from 7 to 11 **2** the junior department of a fee-paying secondary school preparing pupils for the senior school

**junior seaman** *n* – see MILITARY RANKS table

**junior technician** *n* – see MILITARY RANKS table

**junior welterweight** *n* a professional boxer who weighs not more than 10 stone (63.5 kilograms)

**juniper** /'joohnipə/ *n* **1** any of several evergreen shrubs or trees (genus *Juniperus*) of the cypress family; *esp* a trailing or shrubby one **2** any of several coniferous trees resembling true junipers [ME *junipere*, fr L *juniperus* – more at JONQUIL]

**juniper oil** *n* a bitter strong-tasting oil obtained from the fruit of the common juniper and used esp in gin and liqueurs

**¹junk** /jungk/ *n* **1a** secondhand, worn, or discarded articles or material; *broadly* RUBBISH 1 **b** something of little value or inferior quality **2a** *slang* narcotic drugs; *esp* heroin **b** *Austr informal* JUNKIE 1 **3** *archaic* pieces of old cable or cordage used esp to make mats, swabs, or OAKUM (rope fibre used to seal wooden boats) **4** *archaic* hard salted meat, esp beef, for consumption on board ship [ME *jonke*] – **junky** *adj*

**²junk** *vt, informal* to get rid of as worthless; discard

**³junk** *n* any of various types of boat used in the Far East having a steep and overhanging bow, a high stern, a flat bottom, squarish sails (LUGSAILS) often stiffened with horizontal battens, and a deep rudder [Pg *junco*, fr Jav *joñ*]

**junk art** *n* three-dimensional art made from pieces of discarded material (e g metal, glass, or wood) – **junk artist** *n*

**Junker** /'yoongkə/ *n* a member of the Prussian land-owning aristocracy [Ger, fr OHG *junchērro*, lit., young lord] – **Junkerdom** *n*, **Junkerism** *n*

**¹junket** /'jungkit/ *n* **1** a dessert of sweetened flavoured milk curdled with RENNET (substance prepared from the stomachs of calves) **2** *informal* **2a** a festive social affair **b** *chiefly NAm* a trip, journey; *esp* a trip made by an official at public expense [ME *ioncate*, deriv of (assumed) VL *juncata*, fr L *juncus* rush; fr its being orig made or served in a rush basket]

**²junket** *vi, informal* **1** to feast, banquet **2** *chiefly NAm* to go on a junket – **junketer**, **junketeer** *n*

**junk food** *n, informal* food (e g hot dogs, chips, and candy floss) that is usu prepared and eaten away from the home, is often processed to an extensive degree, and typically has a high carbohydrate content but overall low nutritional value – compare WHOLEFOOD

**junkie, junky** /'jungki/ *n, informal* **1** a drug addict; *also* a drug peddler **2** *NAm* a junk dealer

**junk mail** *n* material (e g advertising circulars) received through the post but not requested, often addressed to "occupant" or "resident"

**junk shop** *n* a shop selling secondhand articles or usu inferior antique goods

**Junoesque** /joohnoh'esk/ *adj, of a woman* having stately beauty [*Juno*, Roman goddess of women & marriage, wife of Jupiter]

**junta** /'juntə, 'hoontə/ *n taking sing or pl vb* **1** a council or committee for political or governmental purposes; *esp* a group of people controlling a government, esp after a revolutionary seizure of power **2** a group of people joined for a common

purpose [Sp, fr fem of *junto* joined, fr L *junctus*, pp of *jungere* to join – more at YOKE]

**junto** /'juntoh/ *n taking sing or pl vb, pl* **juntos** JUNTA 2 [prob alter. of *junta*]

**Jupiter** /'joohpitə/ *n* the planet fifth in order from the sun that is the largest planet of the solar system [L *Juppiter, Jupiter* the god Jove, the planet Jupiter, fr OL *Jovis* Jove + L *pater* father]

**Jura** /'jooərə/ *n* the Jurassic geological period or the rocks belonging to it [*Jura*, mountain range between France & Switzerland]

**jural** /'jooərəl/ *adj* of law, rights, or obligations [L *jur-, jus* law] – **jurally** *adv*

**Jurassic** /joo'rasik/ *adj* relating to or being the geological period of the MESOZOIC era between the CRETACEOUS and the TRIASSIC or the corresponding system of rocks, marked by the presence of dinosaurs and the first appearance of birds [Fr *jurassique*, fr *Jura*, mountain range] – **Jurassic** *n*

**jurat** /'jooərat/ *n* **1** a certificate added to an AFFIDAVIT (sworn declaration in writing) stating when, before whom, and where it was made **2** *Br* **2a** an officer, esp of the CINQUE PORTS of the SE coast of England, similar in function to an ALDERMAN (member of English borough or county council) **b** a magistrate in the Channel Islands [(2) ME *jurate*, fr ML *juratus*, fr L, pp of *jurare* to swear; (1) short for L *juratum* (*est*) it has been sworn, 3 sing. perf passive of *jurare*]

**juridical** /joo'ridikl/ *also* **juridic** *adj* **1** relating to the administration of justice or the office of a judge **2** relating to law in general or jurisprudence; legal ⟨~ *terms*⟩ [L *juridicus*, fr *jur-, jus* + *dicere* to say – more at DICTION] – **juridically** *adv*

**jurisconsult** /jooəris'konsult/ *n* a jurist; *esp* one learned in international and CIVIL LAW [L *jurisconsultus*, fr *juris* (gen of *jus*) + *consultus*, pp of *consulere* to consult]

**jurisdiction** /-'diksh(ə)n/ *n* **1** the power, right, or authority to interpret and apply the law ⟨*the* ~ *of the court*⟩ **2** the authority of an independent power to govern or legislate **3** the limits or territory within which authority may be exercised; control [ME *jurisdiccioun*, fr OF & L; OF *juridiction*, fr L *jurisdiction-, jurisdictio*, fr *juris* + *diction-, dictio* act of saying – more at DICTION] – **jurisdictional** *adj*, **jurisdictionally** *adv*

**jurisprudence** /-'proohd(ə)ns/ *n* **1** a legal system or body of law **2** the science or philosophy of law **3** a branch of law ⟨*medical* ~⟩ – **jurisprudential** *adj*, **jurisprudentially** *adv*

**jurist** /'jooərist/ *n* **1** a person having a thorough knowledge of law; *esp* one who writes on the subject of law – compare JUROR **2** *NAm* a lawyer; *specif* a judge [MF *juriste*, fr ML *jurista*, fr L *jur-, jus*]

**juristic** /joo'ristik/, **juristical** /-kl/ *adj* **1** of a jurist or jurisprudence **2** of or recognized in law – **juristically** *adv*

**juror** /'jooərə/ *n* **1** a member of a jury – compare JURIST **2** a person who takes an oath (e g of allegiance) – compare NON-JUROR

**¹jury** /'jooəri/ *n taking sing or pl vb* **1** a body of usu 12 people drawn from the community to hear evidence in court in serious criminal trials and in some civil cases and sworn to give an honest answer, esp a verdict of guilty or not guilty, based on this evidence to questions put before them **2** a committee for judging and awarding prizes at a contest or exhibition [ME *jure*, fr AF *juree*, fr OF *jurer* to swear, fr L *jurare*, fr *jur-, jus*]

**²jury** *adj, nautical* improvised for temporary use, esp in an emergency; makeshift ⟨*a* ~ *mast*⟩ ⟨*a* ~ *rig*⟩ [origin unknown]

**jury box** *n* that part of a courtroom where the jury sits during a trial

**juryman** /-mən/, *fem* **jurywoman** *n* JUROR 1

**jussive** /jusiv/ *n* a word, form, grammatical case, or MOOD of a verb expressing command [L *jussus*, pp of *jubēre* to order; akin to Gk *hysminē* battle] – **jussive** *adj*

**¹just** /just/ *adj* **1a** having a basis in or conforming, sometimes rigidly, to fact or reason; reasonable ⟨*a* ~ *but not a generous decision*⟩ ⟨~ *anger*⟩ **b** conforming to a standard of correctness; proper ⟨~ *proportions*⟩ **2a(1)** acting or being in conformity with what is morally upright or fair; righteous ⟨*a* ~ *ruler*⟩ ⟨*a* ~ *society*⟩ **a(2)** being what is merited; deserved ⟨*a* ~ *punishment*⟩ **b** legally correct; lawful ⟨~ *title to an estate*⟩ **synonyms** see ¹FAIR *antonym* unjust [ME, fr MF & L; MF *juste*, fr L *justus*, fr *jus* right, law; akin to Skt *yos* welfare] – **justly** *adv*, **justness** *n*

**²just** *adv* **1a** exactly, precisely – not with negatives ⟨~ *right*⟩ ⟨~ *the thing for your cold*⟩ ⟨~ *how do you plan to get there?*⟩

**b** at this moment and not sooner ⟨*he's only ~ arrived*⟩ – increasingly used with the past tense in British as well as American English ⟨*the bell ~ rang*⟩ **c** only at this moment and not later ⟨*I'm ~ coming*⟩ **2a** by a very small margin; barely ⟨*~ too late*⟩ ⟨*~ above his elbow*⟩ ⟨*only ~ possible*⟩ **b** only, simply ⟨*~ a note*⟩ **3** quite ⟨*not ~ yet*⟩ ⟨*~ as well I asked*⟩ **4** *informal* very, completely ⟨*~ wonderful*⟩ **5** *informal* indeed – expressing irony ⟨*didn't he ~!*⟩ – **just about 1** almost **2** not more than ⟨*just about room to cook*⟩ – **just now 1** at this moment **2** a moment ago – **just on** exactly – used with reference to numbers and quantities – **just the same** nevertheless; EVEN SO – **just so 1** tidily arranged **2** – used to express agreement

    **usage 1** Some writers on usage advise against *just exactly*, preferring that either *just* or *exactly* should be used alone. **2** *Just not* can mean either "by a small margin not" or "simply not", but *not just* means "not only". Compare ⟨*he's not just a friend of mine* (= he's more than a friend, or he's a friend of other people too)⟩ ⟨*he's just* (= simply) *not a friend of mine*⟩. **3** The pronunciation /jest/ is disliked by some people.

**justice** /'justis/ *n* **1a** the maintenance or administration of what is just, esp by the impartial adjustment of conflicting claims or the assignment of merited rewards or punishments **b** the administration of law ⟨*court of ~*⟩ **c(1)** a judge of a SUPERIOR COURT **c(2)** *Br* – used as a title for a HIGH COURT judge ⟨*Mr Justice Smith*⟩ **c(3)** JUSTICE OF THE PEACE **2a** the quality of being just, impartial, or fair **b(1)** the principle or ideal of just dealing or right action **b(2)** conformity to this principle or ideal; righteousness **c** the quality of conforming to law **3** conformity to truth, fact, or reason; correctness [ME, fr OF, fr L *justitia*, fr *justus*] – **do justice 1a** to treat fairly or adequately ⟨*to do him justice, you never explained it to him*⟩ **b** to show appreciation for **2** to acquit (oneself) in a way worthy of one's abilities

**justice of the peace** *n* a magistrate empowered chiefly to administer immediate (SUMMARY) justice in minor cases and to commit for trial

**justiciable** /ju'stishi·əbl/ *adj* **1** liable to trial in a court of justice ⟨*a ~ offence*⟩ **2** capable of being decided by legal principles or by a court of justice ⟨*a ~ issue*⟩ △ justifiable – **justiciability** *n*

**justiciar** /ju'stishiah/ *n* the chief political and judicial officer of the Norman and later kings of England until the 13th century [ME, fr ML *justitiarius*, fr L *justitia*]

**justifiable** /'justifie·əbl; *also* ,--'--/ *adj* capable of being justified; defensible ⟨*~ family pride – Current Biog*⟩ – **justifiability** *n*, **justifiably** *adv*

**justifiable homicide** *n* an act of killing a person (eg in the course of trying to arrest someone or in carrying out a judicial death sentence) to which no legal blame attaches

**justification** /,justifi'kaysh(ə)n/ *n* **1** the act, process, or state of being justified by God **2a** justifying or being justified **b** something (eg a defence or excuse) that justifies **3** the spacing out of a line of text

**justificatory** /'justifi,kaytəri, ,---'---/ *adj* tending or serving to justify; vindicatory

**justify** /'justifie/ *vt* **1** to prove or show to be just, right, or reasonable **2** to judge, regard, or treat as righteous and worthy of salvation **3** to adjust or arrange exactly; *specif* to space out (eg a passage of text) to make lines equally long and ensure that

there are even margins **4** *archaic* **b** to absolve **4a** to administer justice to ~ *vi* **1** to show a sufficient lawful reason for an act done **2** to fit exactly; *specif* to fill a full line **3** to justify lines of text [ME *justifien*, fr MF or LL; MF *justifier*, fr LL *justificare*, fr L *justus*] – **justifier** *n*

¹**jut** /jut/ *vb* **-tt-** *vi* to extend out, up, or forwards; project, protrude ⟨*mountains ~ting into the sky*⟩ – often + *out* ~ *vt* to cause to project [alter. (influenced by obs *jutty* to project) of ²*jet* (in sense "to project")]

²**jut** *n* something that juts (out); a projection

**jute** /jooht/ *n* the glossy fibre of either of two Indian plants (*Corchorus olitorius* and *Corchorus capsularis*) of the linden family used chiefly for sacking and twine; *also* a plant that produces jute [Hindi & Bengali *jūṭ*]

**Jute** *n* a member of a Germanic people that invaded England and esp Kent along with the Angles and Saxons in the 5th century AD and merged with them to form the Anglo-Saxon people [ME, fr ML *Jutae* Jutes, of Gmc origin] – **Jutish** *adj*

**jutty** /'juti/ *n, obs* a projecting part of a building [ME, prob alter. of *jette* jetty]

**juvenescence** /,joovə'nes(ə)ns/ *n, formal* the state of being or becoming youthful [L *juvenescent-, juvenescens*, prp of *juvenescere* to reach the age of youth, become young again, fr *juvenis*] – **juvenescent** *adj*

¹**juvenile** /'joovəniel/ *adj* **1a** physiologically immature or undeveloped body; young **b** *esp of water or gas* derived from sources within the earth and coming to the surface for the first time **2** (characteristic) of or suitable for children or young people ⟨*~ books*⟩ ⟨*stop this ~ behaviour!*⟩ **synonyms** see ¹YOUNG [Fr or L; Fr *juvénile*, fr L *juvenilis*, fr *juvenis* young person – more at YOUNG]

²**juvenile** *n* **1a** a young person **b** a book for children or young people **2** a young individual resembling an adult of its kind except in size and ability to reproduce (eg a fledged bird not yet in adult plumage) **3** an actor who plays youthful parts

**juvenile court** *n* a court that follows procedures differing from those of the ordinary criminal courts and has special authority over dependent young people below a particular age and young criminal offenders

**juvenile delinquent** *n* a child or young person below a particular age who has committed a criminal offence and may be tried before a JUVENILE COURT – **juvenile delinquency** *n*

**juvenile hormone** *n* an insect hormone that controls development and maturation to the adult and plays a role in reproduction

**juvenilia** /,joohvə'nili·ə/ *n taking pl vb* **1** artistic or literary compositions produced in the artist's or author's youth **2** artistic or literary compositions suited to or designed for the young [L, neut pl of *juvenilis*]

**juvenility** /,joohvə'niləti/ *n* **1** the quality or state of being juvenile; youthfulness **2a** immaturity of thought or conduct **b** *usu pl* an instance of being juvenile (eg in thought or action)

**juxta-** /jukstə-/ *comb form* situated near ⟨juxta*glomerular cells*⟩; beside ⟨juxta*pose*⟩ [L *juxta* near – more at JOUST]

**juxtapose** /,jukstə'pohz/ *vt* to place side by side [prob back-formation fr *juxtaposition*]

**juxtaposition** /,jukstəpə'zish(ə)n/ *n* the act or an instance of placing two or more things side by side; *also* the state of being so placed [L *juxta* near + E *position*] – **juxtapositional** *adj*

# K

**k, K** /kay/ *n, pl* **k's, ks, K's, Ks 1a** the 11th letter of the English alphabet **b** a graphic representation of or device for producing the letter *k* **c** a speech counterpart of printed or written *k* **2** one designated *k*, esp as the 11th in order or class **3** a unit of computer storage capacity equal to 1024 bytes ⟨*a computer memory of 64K*⟩ **4** *maths* a UNIT VECTOR parallel to the z-axis **5** something shaped like the letter K [(5) *kilo*-]

**K1** *n* a single-seater KAYAK (type of canoe)

**K2** *n* a 2-seater KAYAK (type of canoe)

**K4** *n* a 4-seater KAYAK (type of canoe)

**Kaaba** /'kahbə/ *n* a small stone building in the court of the Great Mosque at Mecca that contains a sacred black stone and is the goal of Islamic pilgrimage and the point towards which Muslims turn in praying [Ar *ka'bah*, lit., square building]

**kabala, kabbala, kabbalah** /kə'bahlə/ *n* CABALA (Jewish or other mystical lore) – **kabalism** *n*, **kabalist** *n*, **kabalistic** *adj*

**kabob** /kə'bob/ *n* KEBAB (grilled meat usu served on a skewer)

**Kabuki** /kə'boohki/ *n, often not cap* traditional Japanese popular drama with singing and dancing performed in a highly stylized manner by males only [Jap, lit., art of singing and dancing]

**Kabyle** /kə'biel/ *n* **1** a BERBER (Muslim people of N Africa) of the mountainous coastal area east of Algiers **2** the language of the Kabyles, belonging to the BERBER branch of the AFRO-ASIATIC language family [Ar *qabā'il*, pl of *qabīlah* tribe]

**kaddish** /'kadish/ *n, pl* **kaddishim** /-shim/ *often cap* a Jewish prayer recited in the daily ritual of the synagogue and by mourners at public services after the death of a close relative [Aram *qaddīsh* holy]

**kadi** /'kahdi, 'kaydi/ *n* QADI (Muslim judge)

**kaffeeklatsch** /'kafay,klach, 'kafee-/ *n, often cap, NAm* an informal social gathering for coffee and conversation [Ger, fr *kaffee* coffee + *klatsch* gossip]

**Kaffir, Kafir** /'kafə/ *n* **1** a member of a group of southern African Bantu-speaking peoples **2** *often not cap, chiefly SAfr derog* a S African Black [Ar *kāfir* infidel]

**Kaffir lily** *n* **1** a plant (*Schizostylus coccinea*) of the iris family with fleshy strap-shaped leaves and showy usu red funnel-shaped flowers **2** a plant (*Clivia miniata*) of the daffodil family with strap-shaped fleshy leaves and showy funnel-shaped flowers

**kaffiyeh** /kə'feeyə/ *n* a shawl worn on the head by BEDOUINS (wandering Arab tribesmen living in desert areas) [Ar *kūfiyah*, *kaffiyah*]

**kafir** /'kafə/ *n* a SORGHUM (type of grass) that is grown for its grain and has stout short-jointed somewhat juicy stalks and erect heads [short for *kafir corn*, fr *Kaffir, Kafir*]

**Kafir** *n* a member of a people of the Hindu Kush mountain range in NE Afghanistan [Ar *kāfir* infidel]

**Kafiri** /'kafəri/ *n* the language of the Kafirs in Afghanistan, belonging to the DARDIC group of the INDO-EUROPEAN language family

**Kafkaesque** /,kafkə'esk/ *adj* suggestive of the writings of Franz Kafka, esp in expressing, symbolizing, or encapsulating the anxieties of 20th-century man and his sense of isolation and unreality [Franz *Kafka* †1924 Austrian writer]

**kaftan** /'kaf,tan/ *n* a caftan

**kahawai** /'kah·həwie, 'kah·wie/ *n, pl* **kahawai**, *esp for different types* **kahawais** a marine food fish (*Arripis trutta*) of the perch family found in New Zealand and Australia [Maori]

**kai** /kie/ *n, NZ* food [Maori]

**kail** /kayl/ *n* KALE (type of cabbage)

**kailyard** /'kayl,yahd/ *n* KALEYARD (vegetable garden)

**kainite** /'kieniet, 'kay-/ *also* **kainit** /kie'neet/ *n* a naturally occurring chemical compound (SALT), $KMg(SO_4)Cl.3H_2O$, that is a sulphate and chloride of magnesium and potassium chemically combined with water and is used as a fertilizer [Ger *kainit*, fr Gk *kainos* new – more at RECENT]

**kaiser** /'kiezə/ *n* either of the two emperors of Germany during the period from 1871 to 1918; *also* the emperor of Austria or head of the Holy Roman Empire in former times [Ger, fr OHG *keisur* emperor, fr a prehistoric Gmc word borrowed fr L *Caesar*, cognomen of the Emperor Augustus] – **kaiserdom** *n*, **kaiserism** *n*

**kaiserin** /'kiezərin/ *n* the wife of a kaiser [Ger, fem of *kaiser*]

**kaka** /'kahkə/ *n* an olive brown New Zealand parrot (*Nestor meridionalis*) with grey and red markings [Maori]

**kakapo** /'kahkə,poh/ *n, pl* **kakapos** a chiefly nocturnal burrowing New Zealand parrot (*Strigops habroptilus*) with green and brown barred plumage [Maori]

**kakemono** /,kaki'mohnoh/ *n, pl* **kakemonos** a Japanese painting or ornamentally handwritten inscription on a silk or paper scroll which is mounted on a roller and designed to be hung on a wall as decoration [Jap]

**kala-azar** /,kahlə ə'zah, ,kalə/ *n* a severe infectious disease chiefly of Asia marked esp by fever, blood disorders, and enlargement of the spleen and liver and caused by a PROTOZOAN (single-celled microorganism) (*Leishmania donovani*) transmitted by the bite of SAND FLIES [Hindi *kālā-āzār* black disease, fr Hindi *kālā* black + Per *āzār* disease]

**kale, kail** /kayl/ *n* **1a** a hardy cabbage (*Brassica oleracea acephala*) with curled often finely cut leaves that do not form a dense head **b** *Scot* **b(1)** (a) cabbage **b(2)** a broth of cabbage, esp kale **2** *NAm slang* money [Sc, fr ME (northern) *cal*, fr OE *cāl* – more at COLE]

**kaleidoscope** /kə'liedə,skohp/ *n* **1** a tubular instrument containing loose chips of coloured glass between two flat plates and two plane mirrors so placed that an endless variety of symmetrical patterns is produced as the instrument is rotated and the chips of glass change position; *also* a similar instrument producing such patterns in another way (e g by mirrors alone) **2** something that is continually changing: e g **2a** a multicoloured changing pattern or scene ⟨ *. . . the ever-changing seashore, a ~ of sea, sand, jetsam, pipelines and filth – Punch*⟩ **b** a succession of changing phases or actions ⟨*a new era in the ~ of European affairs*⟩ [Gk *kalos* beautiful + *eidos* form + E *-scope* – more at CALLIGRAPHY, IDOL] – **kaleidoscopic, kaleidoscopical** *adj*, **kaleidoscopically** *adv*

**kalends** /'kaləndz/ *n taking sing or pl vb* CALENDS (first day of the month according to the ancient Roman calendar)

**kaleyard, kailyard** /'kaylyahd/ *n, Scot* **1** a cabbage patch; KITCHEN GARDEN **2** *also* **kaleyard school** a late 19th-century literary movement specializing in a parochial and sentimentalized depiction of Scottish Lowland life ⟨*It certainly wasn't dull: old Thingmyjig up from Bloomsbury trailing a ~ scribbler – Scottish Field*⟩

**kalinite** /'kayliniet, 'kaliniet/ *n* ALUM (chemical compound containing aluminium and potassium) [*kali*- (fr NL *kalium* potassium, fr *kali* alkali, potassium) + connective *-n-* + *-ite*]

**kaliph, kalif** /'kaylif, 'kalif/ *n* CALIPH (former Islamic leader) – **kaliphate** *n*

**kallidin** /'kalidin/ *n* any of several KININS (types of protein) formed from GLOBULIN in the liquid portion (PLASMA) of the blood by the action of kallikrein [Ger, fr *kalli*krein + -*d*- (prob fr *deka*-) + -*in*]

**kallikrein** /'kalikrien/ *n* an ENZYME that liberates KININS (types of protein) from the liquid portion (PLASMA) of the blood [Ger, fr *kalli*- beautiful (fr Gk) + pan*krea*s pancreas + -*in;* prob fr its use to treat pancreatic disorders]

**Kalmuck, Kalmuk** /'kalmook/ *n* **1** a member of a group of Mongolian peoples inhabiting a region stretching from W China to the Caspian Sea **2** the MONGOLIC language of the Kalmucks [Russ *Kalmyk*, fr Kazan Tatar]

**Kalmyk** /'kalmik/ *n* (a) Kalmuck
**kalpa** /'kahlpə, 'kal-/ *n* a period in which, according to Hindu belief, the universe undergoes a cycle of creation and destruction [Skt]
**kame** /kaym/ *n* a short ridge, hill, or mound of drift material deposited in layers by water from a melting glacier [Sc, kame, comb, fr ME (northern) *camb* comb, fr OE]
[1]**kamikaze** /,kami'kahzi/ *n* **1** a member of the Japanese air force in World War II who volunteered to crash an explosive-laden aircraft suicidally on a target (eg a ship) **2** an aircraft used in a kamikaze attack [Jap, lit., divine wind; orig applied to a storm which destroyed a Mongol fleet attacking Japan in 1281]
[2]**kamikaze** *adj* **1** of or being a kamikaze **2** *humorous* suicidal ⟨the city's ~ taxi drivers⟩
**kampong** /'kampong, -'-/ *n* a hamlet or village in a Malay-speaking country [Malay]
**Kampuchean** /,kampoo'chee·ən/ *n or adj* (a native or inhabitant) of Kampuchea [*Kampuchea* (formerly Khmer Republic, formerly Cambodia), country in SE Asia]
**kana** /'kahnə/ *n* any of various Japanese SYLLABARIES (lists of signs representing the syllables of a language) [Jap, fr *ka-* temporary, false + *na* name]
**kanaka** /kə'nakə, 'kanəkə/ *n, often cap* **1** a South Sea islander; *specif* a member of the native people of Hawaii **2** a South Sea islander formerly employed in forced labour on Australian sugar plantations [Hawaiian, person, human being]
**Kanarese** /,kanə'reez/ *n, pl* **Kanarese** **1** a member of a Kannada-speaking people of Mysore in S India **2** KANNADA [*Kanara*, district in SW India]
**kangaroo** /,kang·gə'rooh/ *n, pl* **kangaroos** any of various plant-eating marsupial mammals (family Macropodidae) of Australia, New Guinea, and neighbouring islands that hop on their long powerful hind legs rather than run, and have a small head, large ears, a long thick tail used as a support, and rather small forelegs not used for locomotion [prob native name in Australia]
**kangaroo court** *n* **1** a mock court in which the principles of law and justice are disregarded or perverted **2** a court characterized by irresponsible, unauthorized, or irregular status or procedures **3** judgment or punishment given outside of legal procedure
**kangaroo rat** *n* any of numerous NW American pouched nocturnal burrowing rodents (genus *Dipodomys*) that hop on well-developed hind legs rather than run
**kanji** /'kanji, 'kahnji/ *n* a Japanese SYLLABARY (list of signs representing the syllables of a language) or style of writing derived from Chinese writing [Jap, fr *kan* Chinese + *ji* character, letter]
**Kannada** /'kanədə/ *n* the major DRAVIDIAN language of Mysore in S India [Kannada *kannaḍa*]
**Kantian** /'kanti·ən, 'kahn-/ *adj* of Kant or his philosophy [Immanuel *Kant* †1804 Ger philosopher] – **Kantian** *n*, **Kantianism** *n*
**kaolin** /'kayəlin/ *also* **kaoline** /-lin, -leen/ *n* a fine usu white clay formed from decomposed FELDSPAR that is used esp in the manufacture of pottery and china and in medicine in the treatment of stomach disorders; CHINA CLAY [Fr *kaolin,* fr *Gaoling* (*Kao-ling*), hill in SE China where it was originally obtained]
**kaolinite** /'kayəliniet/ *n* a clay mineral, Al$_2$Si$_2$O$_5$(OH)$_4$, consisting of an aluminium silicate that constitutes the principal mineral in kaolin – **kaolinitic** *adj*
**kaon** /'kay,on/ *n* an unstable ELEMENTARY PARTICLE (minute particle of matter) of the MESON family that exists in forms having positive or negative electric charge with a mass about 966 times that of the electron and in neutral forms with a mass about 975 times that of the electron [ISV *ka* K (fr *K-meson,* its earlier name) + [2]*-on*]
**kapellmeister** /kə'pel,miestə (Ger kapelmaistər)/ *n, pl* **kapellmeister** *often cap* the director of a choir or orchestra [Ger, fr *kapelle* choir, orchestra + *meister* master]
**kaph** /kahf/ *n* the 11th letter of the Hebrew alphabet [Heb, lit., palm of the hand]
**kapok** /'kaypok/ *n* a mass of silky fibres that surround the seeds of the CEIBA tree and are used esp as a filling for mattresses, life jackets, and sleeping bags, and as insulation [Malay]
**kappa** /'kapə/ *n* the 10th letter of the Greek alphabet [Gk, of Sem origin; akin to Heb *kaph*]
**kaput** *also* **kaputt** /kə'poot/ *adj, informal* **1** utterly finished,

defeated, or destroyed **2** unable to function; useless, broken [Ger, fr Fr *capot* not having made a trick at piquet]
**karabiner** /,karə'beenə/ *n* CARABINER (soldier carrying short rifle, esp formerly)
**Karaism** /'karə,iz(ə)m/ *n* a Jewish doctrine originating in the 8th century that rejects scholarly commentary and later tradition and bases its beliefs on Scripture alone [LHeb *qĕrāīm* Karaites, fr Heb *qārā* to read] – **Karaite** *n*
**karakul, caracul** /'karəkl/ *n* **1** *often cap* (any of) a breed of hardy fat-tailed sheep from Bukhara, having a narrow body and a coarse wiry brown fleece **2** the tightly curled glossy black coat of the newborn lamb of a karakul, valued as fur [*Karakul,* village in Bukhara in W Asia]
**karat** /'karət/ *n, NAm* CARAT 1 (unit of fineness for gold) ⚠ caret
**karate** /kə'rahti/ *n* an Oriental MARTIAL ART in which an attacker is disabled by crippling kicks and punches [Jap, lit., empty hand] – **karateist** *n*
**Karelian** /kə'reelyən/ *n* **1** a native or inhabitant of Karelia in the far NE of Europe **2** the language of the Karelians, that belongs to the FINNO-UGRIC language family [*Karelia,* region in NE Europe] – **Karelian** *adj*
**Karen** /kə'ren/ *n, pl* **Karen, Karens** **1a** a group of peoples of E and S Burma **b** a member of any of these peoples **2a** a group of languages spoken by the Karen peoples **b** a language of this group
**karma** /'kahmə/ *n, often cap* the force generated by a person's actions, believed in Hinduism and Buddhism to determine his/her destiny in the next existence [Skt *karman* (nom *karma*), lit., work] – **karmic** *adj, often cap*
**karoo, karroo** /kə'rooh/ *n, pl* **karoos, karroos** an area of dry high flat land in southern Africa [Afrik *karo*]
**kaross** /kə'ros/ *n* a simple garment or rug of skins used esp by native tribesmen of southern Africa [Afrik *karos*]
**karri** /'kahri/ *n* an Australian eucalyptus tree (*Eucalyptus diversicolor*); *also* the hard wood of this tree [native name in W Australia]
**karst** /kahst/ *n* an irregular limestone region with underground streams, caverns, and potholes [Ger] – **karstic** *adj*
**kart** /kaht/ *n* GO-KART (miniature racing car)
**Kartik** /'kahtik/ *n* – see MONTH table [Hindi *Kārtik,* fr Skt *Kārttika*]
**karting** /'kahting/ *n* the sport of racing GO-KARTS (miniature racing cars)
**kary-** /kari-/, **karyo-** *also* **cary-, caryo-** *comb form* **1** nucleus of a cell ⟨karyo*kinesis*⟩ **2** nut; kernel ⟨karyo*psis*⟩ [NL, fr Gk *karyon* nut – more at CAREEN]
**karyokinesis** /,kariohkineesis, -kie-/ *n* **1** the movement of CHROMOSOMES (strands of gene-carrying material), division of the nucleus, and other phenomena occurring in the nucleus of a cell, that are characteristic of MITOSIS (CELL DIVISION producing two new cells) **2** the whole process of MITOSIS [NL] – **karyokinetic** *adj*
**karyology** /,kari'oləji/ *n* a branch of CYTOLOGY (biology of plant and animal cells) that deals with the minute anatomy of cell nuclei, esp the nature and structure of CHROMOSOMES (strands of gene-carrying material) [ISV] – **karyological** *also* **karyologic** *adj*
**karyolymph** /'kariə,limf/ *n* NUCLEAR SAP (clear liquid in a cell nucleus) [ISV]
**karyolysis** /,kari'oləsis/ *n, pl* **karyolyses** /-seez/ the dissolution of a cell's nucleus during MITOSIS (CELL DIVISION producing two new cells) [NL]
**karyosome** /'kariə,sohm/ *n* **1** a mass of CHROMATIN (substance composed of protein and NUCLEIC ACID) resembling a NUCLEOLUS (small spherical body) in a cell nucleus **2** a cell nucleus [ISV]
**karyotype** /'karioh,tiep/ *n* the sum of the specific characteristics of the CHROMOSOMES (strands of gene-carrying material) of a cell; *also* the chromosomes themselves [ISV] – **karyotypic, karyotypical** *adj*
**karzy, kazi, carsey** /'kahzi/ *n, Br informal* a toilet [modif of It *casa* house]
**kasbah** /'kazbah, 'kas-/ *n* CASBAH (Arab quarter or market)
**Kashmir goat** /'kashmiə/ *n* an Indian goat bred esp for its undercoat of fine soft wool that constitutes the cashmere wool sold commercially [*Kashmir,* region in the Indian subcontinent]
**Kashmiri** /kash'miəri/ *n, pl* **Kashmiris,** *esp collectively* **Kashmiri** **1** a native or inhabitant of Kashmir **2** the Indic language of Kashmir

KLM

# kas

**kashruth, kashrut** /'kash,root/ n 1 the state of being KOSHER (permissible for strict Jews to eat) 2 the Jewish laws concerning food (eg the correct method of killing animals for food) [Heb *kashrūth, kashrŭt*, lit., fitness]

**kat** also **khat** /kaht, kat/ n a shrub (*Catha edulis*) of the spindle tree family cultivated by the Arabs for its leaves and buds that are the source of an addictive drug similar to AMPHETAMINE when chewed or used as a tea [Ar *qāt*]

**kata** /'kahtah/ n a formal training exercise in an Oriental MARTIAL ART (eg karate) [Jap]

**katabatic** /,katə'batik/ adj, of a wind moving downwards; sinking [LGk *katabatikos* of descent, fr Gk *katabatos* descending, fr *katabainein* to descend, fr *kata-* cata- + *bainein* to go]

**katabolism** /kə'tabəliz(ə)m/ n CATABOLISM (process by which the body breaks down complex substances to release energy)

**Katharevusa** /,kahthə'revəsah/ n modern Greek conforming to classical Greek usage [NGk *kathareuousa*, fr Gk, fem of *kathareuōn*, prp of *kathareuein* to be pure, fr *katharos* pure]

**katharsis** /kə'thahsis/ n CATHARSIS (relief of pent-up feelings)

**kathode** /'kathohd/ n CATHODE

**katydid** /'kaytidid/ n any of several large green N American long-horned grasshoppers, the males of which usu have STRIDULATING (sound-producing) organs on the fore-wings that produce a loud shrill sound when rubbed together [imit]

**kauri** /'kow(ə)ri/ n any of various trees (genus *Agathis* of the family Araucariaceae); esp a tall timber tree (*Agathis australis*) of New Zealand having fine white straight-grained wood 2 also **kauri copal, kauri gum, kauri resin** a brown resin obtained from the kauri tree found as a fossil or collected from living trees and used esp in varnishes and linoleum [Maori *kawri*]

**kava** /'kahvə/ n 1 an Australasian shrubby pepper plant (*Piper methysticum*) from whose crushed root an intoxicating drink is made 2 the intoxicating drink made from kava [Tongan & Marquesan, lit., bitter]

**kayak** /'kie(y)ak/ n an Eskimo canoe made of a frame covered with skins except for a small opening in the centre and propelled by a double-bladed paddle; also a similar canvas-covered or fibreglass canoe [Eskimo *qajaq*] – **kayaker** n

¹**kayo** /kay'oh/ n, pl **kayos** chiefly NAm KNOCKOUT 1 [pronunciation of KO]

²**kayo** vt **kayoes, kayos; kayoing; kayoed** chiefly NAm to knock out

**Kazan Tartar** /kə'zan, kə'zahn/ n a member, or the Turkic language, of a people living in the Tartar Republic of the USSR

**kazi** /'kahzi/ n, Br informal a karzy, toilet

**kazoo** /kə'zooh/ n, pl **kazoos** a toy musical instrument consisting of a tube into which one sings or hums to vibrate a thin skin, usu of paper, covering a side hole [imit]

**kea** /'kayə/ n a large mainly green New Zealand parrot (*Nestor notabilis*) that normally eats insects but sometimes destroys sheep by slashing the back to feed on the kidney fat [Maori]

**kebab** /ki'bab/ n cubed or minced meat (eg lamb or beef) often MARINATED (soaked in a spiced liquid), served usu on a skewer and grilled with vegetables (eg onions, mushrooms, and pieces of green pepper) [Per & Hindi *kabāb*, fr Ar, fr Turk *kebap*]

**Kechumaran, Quechumaran** /kechəmə'ran, kə,chooh-/ n a S American language family comprising AYMARA and QUECHUA [*Kechu*a (var of *Quechua*) + Aymara + *-an*]

**keck** /kek/ vi, chiefly NAm 1 to retch or make the sound of retching 2 to feel or show loathing [imit]

**ked** /ked/ n SHEEP KED (parasitic sheep fly) [origin unknown]

¹**kedge** /kej/ vt to pull (a ship) along by means of a line attached to an anchor dropped in an appropriate position [ME *caggen*]

²**kedge** n a small anchor used esp in kedging

**kedgeree** /,kejə'ree, '---/ n 1 a dish originating in India that has as its chief constituents rice and lentils, beans, peas, or other PULSE 2 a European dish based on kedgeree and containing rice, flaked fish (eg haddock), and chopped hard-boiled eggs [Hindi *khicaṛī*, fr Skt *khiccā*]

**keek** /keek/ vi, chiefly Scot to peep, look [ME *kiken*, prob fr MD *kīken* to look] – **keek** n, **keeker** n

¹**keel** /kie:l/ n 1 a flat-bottomed ship; esp a barge used on the river Tyne to carry coal 2 the amount of coal carried in a keel; specif a unit of weight equal to 21.2 tons (about 1016 kilograms) [ME *kele*, fr MD *kiel*; akin to OE *cēol* ship, *cot* small house – more at COT]

²**keel** n 1a a timber or set of plates which runs lengthways along the centre of the bottom of a vessel and from which the framework of the hull is built up. It also acts as ballast and improves stability. b the main load-bearing member (eg in an airship or aeroplane) 2 biology a projection or ridge suggesting a keel; specif CARINA (pair of lower linked flower petals) 3 poetic a ship [ME *kele*, fr ON *kjǫlr*; akin to OE *ceole* throat, beak of a ship – more at GLUTTON] – **keeled** adj, **keelless** adj – **on an even keel** without any sudden changes or trouble; steady, calm

³**keel** vt to cause to turn over or collapse ~ vi 1 to tip or turn over; esp, of a ship to tip or turn so that the keel is uppermost 2 to fall (as if) in a faint; collapse ⟨~ed over with laughter – Bud Freeman⟩ □ usu + over

⁴**keel** n 1 a coloured marking crayon used esp for chalking lines or marking timber 2 chiefly dial RED OCHRE (stain used for marking sheep) [ME (Sc) *keyle*, prob fr ScGael *cīl*]

**keelhaul** /-,hawl/ vt 1 to haul under the keel of a ship as punishment or torture 2 to rebuke severely [D *kielhalen*, fr *kiel* keel + *halen* to haul]

**keelson** /'kelsən, 'keel-/, **kelson** /'kelsən/ n a structure fastened to the keel of a ship and running lengthways above it in order to stiffen and strengthen its framework and support the floor [prob of Scand origin; akin to Sw *kölsvin* keelson]

¹**keen** /keen/ adj 1a having a fine edge or point; sharp ⟨a ~ sword⟩ b affecting one as if by cutting or piercing ⟨~ sarcasm⟩ ⟨a ~ wind from the sea⟩ c making a strong impression on a particular sense; vivid ⟨a ~ scent⟩ 2a enthusiastic, eager ⟨a ~ swimmer⟩ ⟨was ~ to go⟩ b of emotion or feeling intense ⟨took a ~ interest⟩ 3a intellectually alert; having or characteristic of a quick penetrating mind ⟨a ~ wit⟩ ⟨had a ~ awareness of the problem⟩; also shrewdly astute ⟨~ bargainers⟩ b serving to challenge; competitive ⟨~ debate⟩; specif, chiefly Br, of prices low in order to be competitive c extremely sensitive in perception ⟨~ eyesight⟩ 4 NAm wonderful, excellent synonyms see ¹SHARP antonym blunt [ME *kene* brave, sharp, fr OE *cēne* brave; akin to OHG *kuoni* brave, OE *cnāwan* to know – more at KNOW] – **keenly** adv, **keenness** n – **keen on** interested in; attracted to ⟨he seems to be very keen on her⟩

²**keen** vi to utter a keen; lament loudly or in a way suggestive of a keen ~ vt to utter (as if) with a keen [IrGael *caoinim* I lament] – **keener** n

³**keen** n a lamentation for the dead uttered usu in a loud wailing voice, esp at Irish funerals

¹**keep** /keep/ vb **kept** /kept/ vt 1 to take notice of by appropriate conduct; fulfil: eg 1a to be faithful to ⟨~ a promise⟩ ⟨~ an appointment⟩ b to act fittingly in relation to (a feast or ceremony) ⟨~ the Sabbath⟩ c to conform to in habits or conduct ⟨~ late hours⟩ ⟨~ open house⟩ d to stay in accord with (a beat) ⟨~ time⟩ ⟨~ step⟩ 2 to preserve, maintain: eg 2a to watch over and defend; guard ⟨may God ~ you⟩ ⟨~ us from harm⟩ ~s goal for the local team⟩ b(1) to take care of, esp as an owner; tend ⟨~ a sheep⟩ ⟨~ goldfish⟩ b(2) to support ⟨earns enough to ~ himself⟩ b(3) to maintain in a specified condition – often in combination ⟨a well-kept garden⟩ c to continue to maintain ⟨~ order⟩ ⟨~ a lookout⟩ d(1) to cause to remain in a specified place, situation, or condition ⟨~ him waiting⟩ ⟨a net to ~ the birds out⟩ d(2) to store habitually for use ⟨where do you ~ the butter?⟩ d(3) to preserve (food) in an unspoilt condition ⟨how long can you ~ fish in a freezer?⟩ e to have or maintain in one's service or at one's disposal ⟨~ a car⟩ ⟨~ a mistress⟩ ⟨~ them on a while longer⟩ – usu disparaging in adjectival use ⟨a kept woman⟩ f to record by entries in a book ⟨~ accounts⟩ ⟨~ a diary⟩ g to have customarily in stock for sale ⟨do you ~ this brand?⟩ 3a to delay, detain ⟨what kept you so long?⟩ b to restrain; HOLD BACK ⟨~ him from going⟩ c to save, reserve ⟨~ some for later⟩ d to refrain from revealing or releasing ⟨~ a secret⟩ 4 to retain possession or control of ⟨kept the money he found⟩ ⟨~ a copy of the letter⟩ ⟨~ your temper⟩ 5 to stay or remain on or in, often against opposition; hold ⟨kept his ground⟩ ⟨kept her job⟩ ⟨~ your seat⟩ ⟨~ guard⟩ 6 to manage, run ⟨~ a shop⟩ ⟨~s house for her father⟩ 7 archaic to continue to follow ⟨~ the path⟩ 8 archaic to confine oneself to ⟨~s to her room⟩ ~ vi 1a to maintain a course ⟨~ to the right⟩ b to continue, usu without interruption ⟨~ talking⟩ – often + on ⟨~ on smiling⟩; compare KEEP ON c to persist in a practice ⟨kept bothering them⟩ – often + on ⟨kept on smoking in spite of warnings⟩; compare KEEP ON 2a to stay or remain in a specified desired place, situation, or condition ⟨~ warm⟩ ⟨~ fine⟩ ⟨~ out of the way⟩ ⟨~ off the grass⟩ b to remain in good condition ⟨meat will ~ in the freezer⟩ ⟨knowledge doesn't ~ any better than fish –

A N Whitehead⟩ **c** to remain in a specified condition of health ⟨*how are you* ∼ing?⟩ **d** to call for no immediate action ⟨*the matter will* ∼ *till morning*⟩ **3** to act as wicketkeeper or goalkeeper ⟨*he* ∼s *for Watford*⟩ [ME *kepen*, fr OE *cēpan* to observe, seek, seize; akin to OHG *chapfen* to look] – **keep one's hair/shirt on** *informal* to remain calm; keep one's temper

**synonyms** Keep, retain, hold, withhold, detain, and reserve may all mean "have in one's possession or custody and not let go". Keep is the most general and least precise of these terms. Retain stresses continued possession in the face of threatened seizure or loss. Hold suggests resisting efforts to take what is in one's custody. Withhold, detain, and reserve all convey the idea of "keeping back". Withhold implies unwillingness or refusal to let go, while detain implies a delay in letting a person or thing go free, which may or may not be due to acceptable motives. Reserve stresses keeping something back for use in future. *antonym* relinquish

**keep at** *vt* to persist in doing or concerning oneself with ⟨*the work is tiring but he'll* keep at *it until he's finished*⟩
**keep back** *vt* **1** to prevent from approaching or coming forwards ⟨*police* kept *the crowds* back⟩ **2** to prevent from advancing; retard; HOLD BACK ⟨*a strike at the plant* kept *plans for expansion* back *another year*⟩ **3a** to prevent from being revealed; conceal ⟨kept back *vital information*⟩ **b** to keep (usu some of something) in one's possession ⟨*I* kept *a few books* back *and gave him the rest*⟩ **4** DETAIN 1 ⟨kept back *after school*⟩ – compare KEEP IN
**keep down** *vt* **1** to keep in control; *esp* to prevent from increasing ⟨keep *expenses* down⟩ **2** to prevent from growing, advancing, or succeeding ⟨*can't* keep *a good man* down⟩ **3** to prevent (food) from being vomited
**keep from** *vt* **1** to prevent (someone) from (something or doing something) ⟨*don't let me* keep *you* from *your work*⟩ **2** to refrain from; help ⟨*can't* keep from *laughing*⟩
**keep in** *vt* **1** to cause to stay indoors, esp in school as a punishment **2** to take care of; not allow to cease ⟨keep *the fire* in⟩ ∼ *vi* to stay indoors (e g for health reasons)
**keep in with** *vt* to (try to) remain friendly with
**keep off** *vi* to remain at a distance; not happen ⟨*if the rain* keeps off, *we can go*⟩ ∼ *vt* to cause to keep off; prevent the effect of ⟨*draw the curtain to* keep *the sun* off⟩
**keep on** *vi* to talk continuously ⟨keeps on *about his operation*⟩; *esp* to nag ⟨*don't* keep on!⟩ – compare KEEP ON AT ∼ *vt* to retain in one's employment or possession ⟨kept *the cook* on *until he found another job*⟩ ⟨kept *the flat* on *for the summer*⟩
**keep on at** *vt* to talk to continuously or ask repeatedly; nag ⟨*his wife* kept on at *him until he bought her a new car*⟩
**keep out** *vb* to (cause to) not enter ⟨*that should* keep *them* out!⟩
**keep out of** *vb* to (cause to) stay away from (usu something bad) ⟨*I hope you'll* keep (*him*) out of *trouble while I'm away*⟩
**keep to** *vt* **1** to stay in or on ⟨keep to *the left*⟩ **2** to not deviate from; ABIDE BY ⟨keep to *the point!*⟩
**keep under** *vt* **1** to control ⟨*Jim always* kept *his feelings* under⟩ ⟨*we tried to* keep *the fire* under⟩ **2** to limit the freedom of ⟨*previous rulers had* kept *the people* under⟩
**keep up** *vt* **1** to cause to remain high ⟨*the farmers are* keeping *prices* up⟩ ⟨*she* kept up *her spirits by singing*⟩ **2** to keep in good condition ⟨*how do you manage to* keep up *such a big house?*⟩ **3** to continue ⟨keep up *the good work*⟩ ⟨keep *it* up!⟩ **4** to cause to remain out of bed ⟨*I hope I'm not* keeping *you* up⟩ ∼ *vi* **1** to remain out of bed ⟨*no, we often* keep up *late*⟩ **2** to remain the same ⟨*do you think the weather will* keep up⟩ **3** to remain level ⟨*I had to run to* keep up⟩ **4** to keep adequately informed ⟨keep up *on international affairs*⟩
**²keep** *n* **1** the fortified inner tower of a medieval castle; *broadly* a fortress, castle **2** the means or provisions, food, by which one is kept; maintenance ⟨*earned his* ∼⟩ **3** *archaic* KEEPING 1 – **for keeps** *informal* **1** with the provision that one keeps as one's own what one wins or receives ⟨*he gave it to me* for keeps⟩ **2** for an indefinitely long time; FOR GOOD ⟨*came home* for keeps⟩
**keeper** /'keepə/ *n* **1** one who keeps, manages, or guards: e g **1a** a protector, guardian **b** a gamekeeper **c** a custodian **d** a curator **e** *informal* a goalkeeper **f** *informal* a wicketkeeper **2** any of various devices (e g a stitched loop on a strap) for keeping something in position **3** ARMATURE 2a (bar placed across a magnet's poles to prevent loss of magnetization)
**keep fit** *n* instruction in activities, esp physical exercises, designed to keep one's body healthy and supple

**keeping** /'keeping/ *n* **1** the act of one who keeps; *esp* custody, care ⟨*entrusted to his* ∼⟩ **2** maintenance, support **3** conformity, accordance ⟨*in* ∼ *with good taste*⟩ ⟨*out of* ∼ *with accepted standards*⟩
**keepnet** /-ˌnet/ *n* a large usu cylindrical net suspended in the water in which an angler keeps the day's catch alive for later release
**keepsake** /-'sayk/ *n* something kept or given to be kept as a memento, esp of the giver [¹*keep* + -*sake* (as in *namesake*)]
**keeshond** /'kays,hond, 'kees-/ *n*, *pl* **keeshonden** /-d(ə)n/, **keeshonds** (any of) a breed of small grey heavy-coated dogs that have a thick coat around the neck, shoulders, and chest, a face and head suggesting those of a fox, and small pointed ears [D, prob fr *Kees* (nickname for *Cornelis* Cornelius) + *hond* dog, fr MD; akin to OE *hund* hound]
**kef** /kef/ *n* **1** a state of drowsy tranquillity **2** a smoking material (e g marijuana) that produces kef □ called also KIF [Ar *kayf* pleasure]
**keg** /keg/ *n* **1** a small cask or barrel: e g **1a** *Br* a small barrel having a capacity of 10 gallons (about 45.5 litres) or less; *specif* a metal beer barrel from which the beer is pumped by pressurized gas **b** *NAm* a barrel having a capacity of 30 gallons (about 136.5 litres) or less **2** the contents of a keg **3 keg beer, keg** *Br* beer infused with gas and served under pressure ⟨*I'll have a pint of* ∼, *please*⟩ [ME *kag*, of Scand origin; akin to ON *kaggi* cask]
**keloid** /'keeloyd/ *n* a thick scar resulting from excessive growth of fibrous tissue at the point of injury [Fr *kiloïde*, fr Gk *chēlē* claw] – **keloidal** *adj*
**kelp** /kelp/ *n* **1a** any of various large brown seaweeds (orders Laminariales and Fucales) **b** a mass of large seaweeds **2** the ashes of seaweed used esp as a source of iodine [ME *culp*]
**¹kelpie** /'kelpi/ *n* a water spirit of Scottish folklore usu in the guise of a horse, that delights in or brings about the drowning of travellers [prob of Celt origin; akin to ScGael *cailpeach* colt]
**²kelpie** *n* a dog bred in Australia from British collies and used there as a sheep dog [*Kelpie*, name of an early specimen of this breed]
**kelson** /'kelsən/ *n* KEELSON (supporting structure fastened to the keel of a ship)
**kelt** /kelt/ *n* a salmon or SEA TROUT that is weak and emaciated after producing eggs [ME (northern), prob fr ScGael *cealt*]
**Kelt** /kelt/ *n*, *archaic* a Celt – **Keltic** *adj*
**kelter** /'keltə/ *n*, *Br* KILTER (working order)
**kelvin** /'kelvin/ *n* the SI unit of temperature defined by the Kelvin scale and equal to $1/_{273.16}$ of the temperature of the TRIPLE POINT of water
**Kelvin** *adj* relating to, conforming to, or being a scale of temperature on which ABSOLUTE ZERO (hypothetically coldest temperature possible) is at 0° and water freezes at 273.16° under standard conditions [William Thomson, Lord *Kelvin* †1907 Sc physicist]
**kemp** /kemp/ *n* a coarse animal fibre that is usu white and is used in mixed wools (e g in carpets) [ME *kempe* coarse hair, of Scand origin] – **kempy** *adj*
**kempt** /kem(p)t/ *adj*, *esp of hair* neatly kept; trim, tidy [ME, fr pp of *kemben* to comb, fr OE *cemban;* akin to OE *camb* comb]
**¹ken** /ken/ *vb* **-nn-** *vt* **1** *chiefly dial* to recognize (as if) by sight **2** *chiefly Scot* to have acquaintance with or knowledge of; know ⟨*d'ye* ∼ *John Peel?*⟩ ∼ *vi*, *chiefly Scot* to have knowledge; know [ME *kennen*, fr OE *cennan* to make known & ON *kenna* to perceive; both akin to OE *can* know – more at CAN]
**²ken** *n* **1** the range of perception, understanding, or knowledge ⟨*beyond our* ∼⟩ **2** *chiefly archaic* the range of vision; sight, view ⟨*when a new planet swims into his* ∼ – John Keats⟩
**kenaf** /kə'naf/ *n* an E Indian HIBISCUS plant (*Hibiscus cannabinus*) widely cultivated for its fibre; *also* the fibre, used esp for ropes [Per]
**kendo** /'kendoh/ *n* a Japanese MARTIAL ART consisting of fencing with bamboo sticks [Jap *kendō*, fr *ken* sword + *dō* art]
**¹kennel** /'kenl/ *n* **1a** a shelter for a dog **b kennels** *pl but taking sing or pl vb*, **kennel** an establishment for the breeding or boarding of dogs ⟨*runs a* ∼s *in the country*⟩ **2** a pack of dogs, esp hounds **3** *derog* a small mean dwelling or room [ME *kenel*, deriv of (assumed) VL *canile*, fr L *canis* dog – more at HOUND]
**²kennel** *vb* **-ll-**, **-l-** (*NAm* **-l-**, **-ll-**) *vi* to take shelter (as if) in a kennel ∼ *vt* to put or keep (as if) in a kennel or kennels
**Kennelly-Heaviside layer** /'kenəli 'hevisied/ *n* E LAYER (layer of the atmosphere) [Arthur *Kennelly* †1939 US electrical engineer & Oliver *Heaviside* †1925 E physicist]

**kenning** /'kening/ *n* a metaphorical compound word or phrase used esp in Old English and Old Norse poetry (e g *swan-road* for *ocean*) [ON, fr *kenna* to perceive, know, name]

**keno** /'keenoh/ *n, pl* **kenos** *NAm* a game resembling bingo [Fr *quine* set of five winning numbers in a lottery + E *-o* (as in *lotto*)]

**kenosis** /ki'nohsis/ *n* Christ's act of emptying himself of certain divine qualities (e g inability to feel pain) when he took on human form [LGK *kenōsis*, fr Gk, act of emptying, fr *kenoun* to purge, empty, fr *kenos* empty] – **kenotic** *adj*

**kenspeckle** /'ken,spekl/ *adj, chiefly Scot* conspicuous [prob of Scand origin; akin to Norw *kjennspak* quick to recognize]

**Kentish fire** /'kentish/ *n, chiefly Br* a prolonged bout of usu slow handclapping in unison, esp to express disapproval or dissent [*Kent*, county in SE England]

**Kentishman** /'kentishmən/ *n* a native or inhabitant of the county of Kent; *specif* one from west of the river Medway – compare MAN OF KENT

**kentledge** /'kentlij/ *n* crude iron or scrap metal used as permanent ballast in a ship [prob fr Fr *quintelage* ballast]

**Kentucky coffee tree** *n* a tall N American tree (*Gymnocladus dioica*) of the pea family with clusters of greenish-white flowers and large dark brown woody pods containing lens-shaped seeds formerly used as a substitute for coffee

**kepi** /'kaypee/ (*Fr* kepi)/ *n* a round cap with a flat top and a horizontal peak worn esp by French officers, policemen, and officials [Fr *képi*, deriv of LL *cappa* head-covering, cloak]

**Keplerian** /kep'liəri-ən/ *adj* of the astronomer Kepler, or his laws concerning the motions of the planets in their orbits [Johannes *Kepler* †1630 Ger astronomer]

**kept** /kept/ *past of* KEEP

**keramic** /ki'ramik/ *n or adj* (a) ceramic

**kerat-, kerato-** *comb form* **1** cornea ⟨kerat*itis*⟩ **2** – see CERAT-

**keratin** /'kerətin/ *n* any of various sulphur-containing fibrous proteins that form the chemical basis of nails, claws, and other horny tissue and hair [ISV] – **keratinous** *adj*

**keratin·ize, -ise** /ki'ratiniez, 'kerətiniez/ *vt* to make into keratin or keratinous tissue ⟨*tissue* ~d *by friction*⟩ ~ *vi* to become keratinous – **keratinization** *n*

**keratinophilic** /ki,ratinə'filik, ,kerətinə'filik/ *adj, esp of a fungus* showing an attraction to keratin (e g in hair, skin, feathers, or horns)

**keratitis** /,kerə'tietəs/ *n, pl* **keratitides** /,kerə'titədeez/ inflammation of the CORNEA (transparent protective covering on the front outer surface of the eye) [NL]

**keratoconjunctivitis** /,kerətoh-kən,jungkti'vietəs/ *n* combined inflammation of the transparent coverings (CORNEA and CONJUNCTIVA) protecting the eye [NL]

**keratogenous** /,kerə'tojinəs/ *adj* developing or producing horny tissue

**keratose** /'kerətohs, -tohz/ *adj, esp of a sponge* having a horny skeleton

**keratosis** /,kerə'tohsis/ *n, pl* **keratoses** /-seez/ an area of skin marked by overgrowth of horny tissue [NL] – **keratotic** *adj*

**kerb,** *NAm* **curb** /kuhb/ *n, Br* **1** an edging (e g of concrete or stone) built along the side of a pavement, marking it off from the road **2** *also* **kerb market** a (street) market for trading in stocks, shares, etc after the stock exchange has closed [*kerb* alter. of *curb;* (2) fr its having orig traded on the street]

**kerb crawler** *n* one who drives slowly close to a pavement with the intention of enticing or forcing a potential sexual partner into the car – **kerb crawling** *n*

**kerb drill** *n, Br* a sequence of actions, esp looking to right and left, performed before crossing a road

**kerbstone** /'kuhb,stohn/ *n, Br* a block of stone forming a kerb

**kerchief** /'kuhchif/ *n, pl* **kerchiefs** /'kuhchivz/ *also* **kerchieves** /'kuhchivz, -cheevz/ **1** a square or triangle of cloth used as a head-covering or worn as a scarf round the neck **2** a handkerchief [ME *courchef*, fr OF *cuevrechief*, fr *covrir* to cover + *chief* head – more at CHIEF]

**kerf** /kuhf/ *n* (the width of) a slit or notch made by a saw or cutting torch [ME, fr OE *cyrf* act of cutting; akin to OE *ceorfan* to carve – more at CARVE]

**kerfuffle** /kə'fufl/ *n, chiefly Br informal* a fuss, commotion *synonyms* see ¹FUSS [Sc *curfuffle* disorder, agitation]

**kermes** /'kuhmiz/ *n* the dried bodies of the females of various SCALE INSECTS (genus *Kermes*) that are found on the KERMES OAK and are used as a red dyestuff [Fr *kermès,* fr Ar *qirmiz*]

**kermesite** /'kuhmiziet, -siet/ *n* a cherry-red mineral, $Sb_2S_2O$, consisting of an antimony sulphide [Fr *kermésite,* fr *kermès*]

**kermes oak** /kuh'mes, keə'mes (*Fr* kɛrmɛs)/ *n* a dwarf often shrubby Mediterranean oak tree (*Quercus coccinea*) that is the host of the kermes insect

**kermesse** *n* a bicycle race consisting of several laps of a very short circuit, usu in a town centre [Fr, lit., kermis, fr D *kermis*]

**kermis, kermess** /'kuhmis/ *n* **1** an annual outdoor festival in the Low Countries **2** *NAm* a fair held usu for charitable purposes [D *kermis,* fr MD *kercmisse,* fr *kerc* church + *misse* mass, church festival]

¹**kern, kerne** /kuhn/ *n* **1** a lightly-armed foot soldier of medieval Ireland or Scotland **2** *archaic* a peasant, yokel [ME *kerne,* fr MIr *cethern* band of soldiers]

²**kern** *n* a part of a letter that overhangs the piece of type on which it is cast [Fr *carne* corner, fr L *cardin-, cardo* hinge – more at CARDINAL]

³**kern** *vt* to form with a kern ⟨~ed *letters*⟩

**kernel** /'kuhnl/ *n* **1** the inner softer often edible part of a seed, fruit stone, or nut **2** a whole seed of a cereal **3** a central or essential part; CORE 2 **4** *maths* a subspace of a VECTOR SPACE that is mapped to the zero element of another vector space by a given LINEAR TRANSFORMATION [ME, fr OE *cyrnel,* dim. of *corn* seed, corn]

**kernite** /'kuhniet/ *n* a mineral, $Na_2B_4O_7.4H_2O$, that consists of a sodium borate chemically combined with water and is an important source of the chemical compound BORAX [*Kern* County in California, USA]

**kerogen** /'kerəjən/ *n* tarlike material occurring in SHALE (rock formed by compression of clay layers) and yielding oil when heated [Gk *kēros* wax + E *-gen* – more at CERUMEN]

**kerosene, kerosine** /'kerəseen, -sin/ *n, NAm, Austr, & NZ* PARAFFIN **3** [Gk *kēros* + E *-ene* (as in *camphene*)]

**kerry** /'keri/ *n, often cap* (any of) an Irish breed of small hardy long-lived black dairy cattle [County *Kerry* in SW Ireland]

**Kerry blue terrier, Kerry blue** *n* (any of) an Irish breed of medium-sized terriers with a long head, deep chest, and silky bluish coat

**Kerry Hill** *n* (any of) a breed of hardy English meat-producing sheep [*Kerry Hill* in Kerry, town in Wales]

**kersey** /'kuhzi/ *n* a heavy compact ribbed woollen cloth with a short NAP (soft raised surface) [ME, prob fr *Kersey,* village in Suffolk, England]

**kerseymere** /-miə/ *n* a fine woollen fabric with a close NAP (soft raised surface) made in fancy TWILL (having an appearance of parallel diagonal ribs) weaves [alter. (influenced by *kersey*) of *cassimere* (cashmere), fr obs *Cassimere* Kashmir]

**kerygma** /kə'rigmə/ *n, pl* **kerygmata** /-mətə/ the proclamation of salvation through Jesus Christ [Gk *kērygma,* fr *kēryssein* to proclaim, fr *kēryx* herald] – **kerygmatic** *adj*

**Kesp** /kesp/ *trademark* – used for a meat substitute woven from spun fibres of TEXTURED VEGETABLE PROTEIN

**kestrel** /'kestrəl/ *n* a small common Eurasian and N African falcon (*Falco tinnunculus*) that is noted for its habit of hovering in the air against a wind and is about 30 centimetres (1 foot) long, bluish grey above in the male, and reddish brown in the female [ME *castrel,* fr MF *crecerelle,* fr *crecelle* rattle, prob of imit origin]

**ket-** /keet-/, **keto-** *comb form* ketone ⟨ket*osis*⟩ [ISV]

**ketal** /'keetal/ *n* any of various chemical compounds similar to ACETALS but obtained by heating ketones with ETHANOL

**ketch** /kech/ *n* a FORE AND AFT rigged sailing vessel with two masts, the AFTER (rear) mast being shorter than the foremast and located forward of the sternpost [ME *cache,* prob fr *cacchen* to chase, catch]

**ketchup** /'kechəp, -up/, *NAm chiefly* **catchup** /~, 'kachəp/ *n* any of several sauces made with vinegar and seasonings and used as a relish; *esp* a sauce made from seasoned tomato puree [Malay *kēchap* spiced fish sauce]

**keto** /'keetoh/ *adj* of a ketone; *also* containing a ketone group [*ket-*]

**ketogenesis** /,keetoh'jenəsis/ *n* the production of KETONE BODIES (e g in the disease DIABETES) [NL] – **ketogenic** *adj*

**ketoglutaric acid** /,keetoh-glooh'tarik/ *n* either of two keto derivatives, $C_5H_6O_5$, of GLUTARIC ACID; *esp* the ALPHA keto derivative formed in various biochemical processes (e g the KREBS CYCLE) in the body

**ketone** /'keetohn/ *n* a carbon-containing chemical compound (e g acetone) with a CARBONYL group attached to two carbon atoms [Ger *keton,* alter. of *aketon* acetone] – **ketonic** *adj*

**ketone body** n any of the three chemical compounds ACETO-ACETIC ACID, ACETONE, and beta-HYDROXYBUTYRIC ACID found in the blood and urine in abnormal amounts in conditions where the body's METABOLISM (biochemical processes) are impaired (e g in the disease DIABETES MELLITUS)

**ketose** /'keetohz/ n a sugar (e g fructose) containing one ketone group per molecule [ISV]

**ketosis** /ki'tohsis/ n an abnormal increase of KETONE BODIES in the body [NL] – **ketotic** adj

**ketosteroid** /‚keetoh'stiəroyd/ n a STEROID (complex carbon-containing chemical compound) (e g CORTISONE or OESTRONE) containing a ketone group [ISV]

**kettle** /'ketl/ n 1 a metal vessel used esp for boiling liquids; esp one with a lid, handle, and spout that is placed on top of a stove or cooker or contains an electric heating element and is used to boil water **2a** a pothole **b** a steep-sided hollow without surface drainage, esp in a deposit of glacial drift [ME ketel, fr ON ketill; akin to OE cietel kettle; both fr a prehistoric Gmc word borrowed fr L catillus, dim. of catinus bowl!]

**kettledrum** /-‚drum/ n a drum that consists of a hollow brass or copper bowl with a covering of parchment or plastic stretched across it, the tension of which can be changed to vary the pitch

**kettle of fish** n, informal **1** a state of affairs; esp an awkward or muddled state of affairs or predicament (a pretty ~!) **2** a matter (that's a different ~)

**Kewpie** /'kyoohpi/ trademark – used for a small chubby doll with a topknot of hair

**¹key** /kee/ n **1a** a usu metal instrument by which the bolt of a lock is turned **b** any of various devices having the form or function of such a key (a ~ for a clock) **2a** a means of gaining or preventing entrance, possession, or control **b** a helpful or deciding factor (the ~ to success) **3a** something that gives an explanation or identification or provides a solution (the ~ to a riddle) **b** a list of words or phrases giving an explanation of symbols or abbreviations **c** an aid to interpretation or identification; a clue **d** an arrangement of the important characteristics of a group of plants or animals designed to facilitate identification usu by means of successive choices between the presence or absence of differentiating characteristics in a particular specimen (a ~ to the families of British flowering plants) **e** an explanatory list (e g of symbols or abbreviations) used on a map or chart **4a** a metal pin that can be inserted to keep two parts together **b** a keystone in an arch **c** a small piece of wood or metal used as a wedge or for preventing motion between parts **5a** any of the levers of a keyboard musical instrument that are pressed by a finger or foot to work the mechanism and produce the notes **b** a lever that controls an air hole in the side of a woodwind musical instrument or a valve in a brass instrument **c key**, **keybutton** a part in the keyboard of a machine (e g a typewriter) that when pushed down by a finger works, usu by lever action, to set another part in motion **6** a dry usu single-seeded fruit (e g of an ash or elm tree); SAMARA **7** a system of seven notes based on their relationship to the first and lowest note, after which the key is named. It provides the overall tonal framework for a piece of music (a symphony in the ~ of G major) **8a** characteristic style or tone (the seminar started in a rather low ~) **b** the tone or pitch of a voice **c** the predominant tone of a photograph with respect to its lightness or darkness – compare HIGH-KEY, LOW-KEY **9** a decorative motif resembling a key – compare GREEK KEY **10** the indentation or roughness of a surface to improve sticking (e g of plaster or glue) **11** a small switch for opening or closing an electric circuit **12** a set of instructions for the production and interpretation of CRYPTOGRAMS (communications in code) [ME, fr OE cæg; akin to MLG keige spear] – **keyed** adj, **keyless** adj

**²key** vt **1** to lock (as if) with a key; fasten: e g **1a** to secure (e g a pulley on a shaft) by a key **b** to finish off (an arch) by inserting a keystone **2** to roughen (a surface) preparatory to applying plaster, paint, etc **3** to bring into harmony or conformity; make appropriate; attune (remarks ~ed to a situation) **4** to identify (a biological specimen) by use of a key **5** to provide with identifying or explanatory cross-references or symbols (instructions ~ed to accompanying drawings – John Gartner) **6** to keyboard – often + in ~ vi **1** to use a key **2** to work as a keyboarder

**key up** vt to make nervous, tense, or excited – usu pass (was keyed up over her impending operation)

**³key** adj **1** of basic importance; fundamental (~ issues) **2** indispensable, irreplaceable (~ workers)

**⁴key** n a low island or reef; specif any of the small coral islands off the southern coast of Florida △ quay [Sp cayo, fr Lucayo]

**⁵key** n, slang a kilogram (about 2¼ pounds) of marijuana [by shortening & alter. fr kilogram]

**¹keyboard** /-‚bawd/ n **1a** a bank of keys on a musical instrument (e g a piano) that consists of seven usu white and five raised usu black keys to the OCTAVE (eight whole notes considered as a set) **b** also **keyboards** pl an instrument having a keyboard (Bach's works for ~) (started playing ~s in a band in college – Melody Maker) **2** an array of systematically arranged keys by which a machine is operated – called also KEYSET

**²keyboard** vi to operate a machine (e g for setting printing type) by means of a keyboard ~ vt to capture or set (e g data or text) by means of a keyboard – **keyboarder** n

**key grip** n the chief GRIP (stagehand) in a film or television studio

**keyhole** /-‚hohl/ n a hole in a lock into which the key is put

**keyhole limpet** n any of various INVERTEBRATE animals (family Fissurellidae of the class Gastropoda) related to the limpets that have a hole at the top of the shell

**keyhole saw** n a narrow pointed fine-toothed saw used for cutting tight curves

**key money** n a lump sum paid in addition to rent for the granting or renewing of a property tenancy

**Keynesian** /'kaynziən/ adj (characteristic) of J M Keynes or his economic theories [John Maynard Keynes †1946 E economist] – **Keynesian** n

**Keynesianism** /'kaynzi•əniz(ə)m/ n the economic theories of J M Keynes and his followers; specif the theory that the monetary and taxation policies of a government directly affect actual demand, inflation, and employment

**¹keynote** /'key‚noht/ n **1** the first note of a musical scale considered as the base note for purposes of harmony **2** the fundamental or central fact, principle, idea, or mood

**²keynote** adj being or delivered by a speaker who presents the issues of primary interest to an assembly, esp in a way that arouses unity and enthusiasm (a ~ speech)

**³keynote** vt **1** to set the keynote of **2** NAm to deliver the keynote address at (e g a rally or conference) – **keynoter** n

**keypunch** /-‚punch/ n a machine with a keyboard used to cut holes or notches in PUNCHED CARDS – **keypunch** vt, **keypuncher** n

**keyset** /'keeset/ n to keyboard

**key signature** n the sharp or flat signs placed at the beginning of the musical stave to indicate the set of notes (KEY 7) on which the following piece or passage of music is based

**keystone** /-‚stohn/ n **1** the wedge-shaped piece at the highest point of an arch that locks the other pieces in place – compare VOUSSOIR **2** something on which associated things depend for support (collective bargaining – the ~ of industrial democracy – Adlai Stevenson) – compare CORNERSTONE

**keystroke** /'kee‚strohk/ n the act or an instance of pressing down a key on a keyboard – **keystroke** vb

**keyway** /'keeway/ n **1** a groove or channel for a key **2** the slot for the key in a lock that has a flat metal key

**key word** n a word that is a key: e g **a** a word exemplifying the meaning or value of a letter or symbol **b** a significant word from a title or document that is used as an index to content

**KGB** n the secret police of the USSR [Russ Komitet Gosudarstvennoye Bezopastnosti State Security Committee]

**khaddar** /'kahdə/ n Indian cotton cloth woven in the home [Hindi khādar, khādī]

**khadi** /'kahdi/ n khaddar

**¹khaki** /'kahki/ n **1a** a khaki-coloured cloth, made usu of cotton or wool and used esp for military uniforms **b** a garment of this cloth; esp a military uniform **2a** Br a dull yellowish brown colour **b** NAm a light yellowish brown colour [Hindi khākī dust-coloured, fr khāk dust, fr Per]

**²khaki** adj **1** made of or having the colour of khaki **2** informal having a skin colour intermediate between those of white-skinned and dark-skinned peoples

**khalif** /'kaylif, 'kalif/ n CALIPH (former Islamic leader) – **khalifate** n

**Khalkha** /'kalkə/ n the official language of the Mongolian People's Republic

**khamsin** /'kamsin, kam'seen/ n a hot southerly Egyptian wind coming from the Sahara desert synonyms see ¹WIND [Ar rīḥ al-khamsīn the wind of the fifty (days between Easter and Pentecost)]

¹**khan** /kahn/ *n* **1** a medieval supreme ruler over the Turkish, Tartar, and Mongol tribes; *also* a medieval sovereign of China **2** a local chieftain or man of rank in some countries of central Asia [ME *caan*, fr MF, of Turkic origin; akin to Turk *han* prince] – **khanate** *n*

²**khan** *n* CARAVANSERAI (large courtyard of Eastern inn to accommodate caravans) [Ar *khān*]

**khapra beetle** /'kaprə, 'kahprə/ *n* a beetle (*Trogoderma granarium*) that is native to the Indian subcontinent and is now a serious pest of stored grain in most parts of the world [Hindi *khaprā*, lit., destroyer]

**khat** /kaht, kat/ *n* KAT (shrub whose leaves are chewed as a drug)

**khedive** /ki'deev/ *n* any of the rulers of Egypt during the period from 1867 to 1914, governing as representatives of the sultan of Turkey [Fr *khédive*, fr Turk *hidiv*] – **khedivial, khedival** *adj*

**Khmer** /kmeə/ *n*, *pl* **Khmers**, *esp collectively* **Khmer 1** a member of one of the main ethnic groups of Kampuchea **2** the official language of Kampuchea – **Khmerian** *adj*

**Khoisan** /'koysahn, -'-/ *n* a group of African languages comprising HOTTENTOT and the BUSHMAN languages

**Khotanese** /,kohtə'neez/ *n* an extinct eastern Iranian language of central Asia belonging to the INDO-EUROPEAN language family [*Khotan*, region in central Asia]

**khoum** /khoom/ *n* – see *ouguiya* at MONEY table [of Ar origin]

**Khowar** /'koh,wah/ *n* a language of NW Pakistan belonging to the DARDIC group of the INDO-EUROPEAN language family

**khyber** /'kiebə/ *n*, *Br slang* the arse, buttocks [rhyming slang *Khyber (pass)* arse, fr the *Khyber Pass* between Afghanistan & Pakistan]

**kiang** /ki'ang/ *n* an Asiatic wild ass (*Equus hemionus*) usu having a reddish back and sides and white underparts, muzzle, and legs [Tibetan *rkyaṅ*]

¹**kibble** /'kibl/ *vt* to grind (e g grain) coarsely [origin unknown] – **kibbler** *n*

²**kibble** *n* coarsely ground meal or grain

**kibbutz** /ki'boots/ *n*, *pl* **kibbutzim** /,kiboot'seem/ a farm or settlement in Israel run as a cooperative [NHeb *qibbūṣ*, fr Heb, gathering]

**kibbutznik** /ki'bootsnik/ *n* a member of a kibbutz [Yiddish, fr *kibbutz* (fr NHeb *qibbūṣ*) + *-nik*]

**kibe** /kieb/ *n* an inflamed open sore, esp on the heel ⟨*the toe of the peasant comes so near the heel of the courtier, he galls his ~* – Shak⟩ [ME, perh fr W *cibi, cibwst*]

**kibitzer** /'kibitsə/ *n* one who looks on and often offers unwanted advice or comment, esp at a card game [Yiddish *kibitser*, fr *kibitsen*, to kibitz, fr Ger *kiebitzen*, fr *kiebitz* lapwing, busybody, fr MHG *gîbitz* lapwing, of imit origin] – **kibitz** *vb*

**kibosh** /'kie,bosh/ *n* [origin unknown] – **kibosh** *vt* – **put the kibosh on** *informal* to put an end to (a hope, plan, etc); ruin

¹**kick** /kik/ *vi* **1a** to strike out with the foot or feet **b** to make a kick in football **2** to show opposition; resist, rebel ⟨*~ing against authority*⟩ **3** *of a firearm* to jerk backwards when fired ~ *vt* **1** to strike suddenly and forcefully (as if) with the foot **2** to score by kicking a ball ⟨*~ed three goals for Arsenal*⟩ **3** *slang* to free oneself of (esp a drug or drug-using habit) [ME *kiken*] – **kick oneself** to reprove oneself for stupidity or for failure to do something – see also **kick the** BUCKET/**one's** HEELS, **kick up one's** HEELS, **kick against the** PRICKS, **kick over the** TRACES, **kick** UPSTAIRS

**kick against** *vt* to oppose or dislike ⟨*he kicked against the idea from the start*⟩

**kick around/about** *vb*, *informal vt* **1** to treat in an inconsiderate or high-handed fashion **2** to consider, examine, or discuss from various angles, esp in an unsystematic or experimental way ⟨*kick the problem around for a while and see what ideas emerge*⟩ ~ *vi* **1** to wander aimlessly or idly; go from one place to another as circumstances or fancy dictates ⟨*spent the last few years kicking around in Africa*⟩ **2** to lie unnoticed or out of place; remain unused or unwanted ⟨*there's a spare blanket kicking around in one of these rooms*⟩

**kick off** *vi* **1** to start or resume play with a kickoff **2** *informal* to begin proceedings; start **3** *NAm slang* to die – see also KICKOFF

**kick out** *vt*, *informal* to dismiss or throw out forcefully or unceremoniously ⟨*kick the Americans out!*⟩

**kick up** *vt* **1** to cause to rise upwards; raise ⟨*clouds of dust kicked up by passing cars*⟩ **2** *informal* to stir up; cause ⟨*kick up a fuss*⟩ ~ *vi* to create a row or fuss

²**kick** *n* **1a** a blow or sudden forceful thrust with the foot; *specif* a sudden propelling of an object (e g a ball) with the foot **b** the power to kick **c** a repeated motion of the legs used in swimming **d** a sudden burst of speed, esp in a running race **2** a sudden forceful jolt or thrust suggesting a kick: e g **2a** the sudden backward jerk when a gun is fired **b** an abnormal and unintended movement of a ball, esp in snooker, billiards, etc, when struck by the cue or by another ball **3** power or strength to resist; *broadly* resilience ⟨*still has some ~ in him*⟩ **4a** a stimulating effect or quality ⟨*this drink has quite a ~ in it*⟩ **b** *usu pl* a stimulating or pleasurable experience or feeling; a thrill ⟨*he did it for ~s*⟩ **c** an absorbing or obsessive new interest ⟨*on a health food ~ at present*⟩

³**kick** *n* an indentation in the base of a glass vessel, esp a bottle [origin unknown]

**kickback** /-,bak/ *n* **1** a sharp violent reaction **2** a money return received, usu because of help or favours given or sometimes because of confidential agreement or as a result of force applied

**kicker** /'kikə/ *n* one who or that which kicks; *esp* a horse with a habit of kicking

'**kicking-,strap** /'kiking/ *n* **1** a strap fixed behind the hindquarters of a horse that is to be driven, to prevent it from kicking **2** a rope, wire, or block and tackle running from a point some way along the BOOM (horizontal beam to which a sail is attached) of a sailing dinghy to the bottom of the mast and designed to prevent the boom rising and letting wind escape from the sail

**kickoff** /-,of/ *n* **1** a kick that begins a football game by putting the ball into play **2** *informal* an act or instance of beginning

**kick pleat** *n* a short pleat consisting of a layer of fabric sewn under an opening at the lower edge of a narrow skirt to allow freedom of movement

**kickshaw** /'kikshaw/ *n*, *archaic* **1** a fancy dish; a delicacy **2** a bauble [modif of Fr *quelque chose* something]

**kickstand** /-,stand/ *n* a swivelling metal bar or rod for holding up a 2-wheeled vehicle when not in use [fr its being put in position by a kick]

'**kick-,start** *also* **kick-starter** *n* a lever which when kicked down starts the engine of esp a motorcycle – **kick-start** *vb*

**kick turn** *n* a standing half turn in skiing made by swinging one ski high with a jerk and planting it in the desired direction and then lifting the other ski into a parallel position

¹**kid** /kid/ *n* **1a** a young goat **b** a young individual of various animals related to the goat **2a** kidskin ⟨*shoes made of ~*⟩ **b** the flesh of a kid **3** *informal* a child; *also* a young person (e g a teenager) – see also **with kid** GLOVES [ME *kide*, of Scand origin; akin to ON *kith* kid] – **kiddish** *adj*

²**kid** *vi* **-dd-** *of a goat or antelope* to give birth to young

³**kid** *vb* **-dd-** *informal vt* **1** to deceive as a joke; hoax, fool ⟨*it's the truth; I wouldn't ~ you*⟩ **b** to convince (oneself) of something untrue or improbable ⟨*~ded themselves that they were better writers than they were* – The Listener⟩ **2** to make fun of; tease ~ *vi* to engage in good-humoured fooling or horseplay; joke – often + *around* [prob fr ¹*kid*] – **kidder** *n*, **kiddingly** *adv*

**Kidderminster** /'kidə,minstə/ *n* a type of carpet made of INGRAIN yarn (yarn dyed before weaving) [*Kidderminster*, town in England]

**kiddie, kiddy** /kidi/ *n*, *informal* a small child [¹*kid* + *-ie, -y*]

**kiddiwink** /-wingk/ *n*, *informal* a kiddie [*kiddie* + *wink* (of unknown origin)]

**kiddush** /'kidash, ki'doohsh/ *n* a ceremonial blessing pronounced over wine or bread in a Jewish home or synagogue on a sabbath or other holy day [LHeb *qiddūsh* sanctification]

**kiddush hashem** /hə'shaym/ *n*, *often cap K&H* an act of moral uprightness or religious heroism by a Jew that causes others to reverence God; *specif* martyrdom in the cause of Judaism [LHeb *qiddūsh hash-shēm* sanctification of the name (of God)]

,**kid-'glove** *adj* using or involving gentle, considerate, or tactful methods ⟨*~ diplomacy*⟩

**kidnap** /'kidnap/ *vt* **-pp-** (*NAm* **-pp-, -p-**) to seize and detain (a person) by unlawful force and often with a demand for ransom money [prob back-formation fr *kidnapper*, fr ¹*kid* + obs *napper* thief, fr *nap* to seize] – **kidnapper**, *NAm also* **kidnaper** *n*

**kidney** /'kidni/ *n* **1a** either of a pair of organs of VERTEBRATE animals, situated in the body cavity near the SPINAL COLUMN, that excrete waste products of METABOLISM (biochemical processes) present in the blood, in humans are bean-shaped organs lying behind the PERITONEUM (inner lining of the abdomen) in a mass of fatty tissue, and consist chiefly of minute tubes (NEPHRONS) by which urine is secreted, collected, and discharged into a main cavity, from where it is conveyed by the URETER to the bladder **b** any of various excretory organs of INVERTEBRATE animals having a similar function to the kidneys of VERTEBRATE animals **2** the kidney of an animal eaten as food **3** *formal* a sort, kind, or type, esp with regard to temperament ⟨*a man of a different* ∼⟩ [ME]

**kidney bean** *n* **1** FRENCH BEAN **2** any of the kidney-shaped seeds of the FRENCH BEAN, esp when mature and dark red in colour

**kidney machine** *n* a machine that artificially purifies the blood of someone whose kidneys do not function properly

**kidney vetch** *n* a Eurasian plant (*Anthyllis vulneraria*) of the pea family having heads of yellow or red flowers [fr its former use as a remedy for kidney disorders]

**kidskin** /'kid,skin/, **kid** *n* the skin of a kid; *also* a soft supple leather made from this or from goatskin or lambskin

**kids' stuff,** *NAm chiefly* **kid stuff** *n, slang* something befitting or appropriate to children; *specif* something extremely simple or easy

**kier** /kiə/ *n* a large vat used in boiling or bleaching cloth [prob of Scand origin; akin to ON *ker* tub, vessel]

**kieselguhr, kieselgur** /'keezl,gooə/ *n* loose or porous DIATOMITE (material derived from silicon-containing skeletons of minute organisms) used for polishing, in the manufacture of dynamite, and for filtering wines and beers [Ger *kieselgur,* fr *kiesel* pebble, flint + *gur, guhr* earthy deposit in rocks]

**kieserite** /'keezəriet/ *n* a white mineral, $MgSO_4.H_2O$, that consists of a magnesium sulphate chemically combined with water [Ger *kieserit,* fr Dietrich *Kieser* †1862 Ger physician]

**kif** /kif, keef/ *n* KEF (drug or drugged state)

**kike** /kiek/ *n, chiefly NAm derog* a Jew [prob alter. of *kiki,* redupl of *-ki,* common ending of names of Jews who lived in Slavonic countries]

**Kikongo** /ki'kong,goh/ *n* KONGO 2 (African language)

**Kikuyu** /ki'kooh,yooh/ *n, pl* **Kikuyus,** *esp collectively* **Kikuyu** **1** a member of a BANTU-speaking people of Kenya **2** the BANTU language of the Kikuyu people

**kilderkin** /'kildəkin/ *n* **1** a small cask having a capacity of 16 or 18 gallons (about 73 or 82 litres) **2** a British unit of capacity equal to $^1/_2$ barrel (about 82 litres) [ME, fr MD *kindekijn,* fr ML *quintale* quintal]

**¹kill** /kil/ *vt* **1a** to deprive of life **b(1)** to slaughter (eg a pig) for food **b(2)** to convert a food animal into (eg pork) by slaughtering **2a** to put an end to; destroy ⟨∼ *his hopes*⟩ **b** to defeat, veto ⟨∼ *the Bill!*⟩ **3a** to destroy the vital, active, or essential quality of ⟨∼ed *the pain with drugs*⟩ ⟨*his tactless remark* ∼ed *the conversation*⟩ **b** to spoil, subdue, or neutralize the effect of ⟨*that colour* ∼s *the room*⟩ **4** to cause (time) to pass without boredom ⟨∼ed *time by playing cards*⟩ **5** to hit (a shot) so hard in a racket game that a return is impossible **6** *informal* to cause to stop; TURN OFF ⟨∼ *the motor*⟩ ⟨∼ *the lights*⟩ **7** *informal* **7a** to cause extreme pain to ⟨*my feet are* ∼ing *me*⟩ **b** to tire almost to the point of collapse **8** *informal* to consume (eg a bottle of alcoholic drink) totally **9** *informal* to overwhelm with admiration or amusement ⟨*his jokes really* ∼ *me*⟩ **10** *journalistic* to discard or abandon further investigation of (a story) ∼ *vi* to destroy life ⟨*would you* ∼ *for your principles?*⟩ [ME *killen, cullen* to strike, beat, kill; perh akin to OE *cwellan* to kill – more at QUELL] – **to kill** so as to create a great impression; showily ⟨*dressed to kill*⟩

**synonyms** **Kill, slay, murder, assassinate, dispatch,** and **execute: kill** is the most general term, and may be applied to people, creatures, and plants, and figuratively to plans, feelings, and similar things which may be said to have life. **Slay,** now chiefly literary, suggests violent and intentional killing. **Murder,** which like **assassinate** and **execute** is applied to people rather than animals or other living matter, implies a deliberate, often premeditated killing which constitutes a criminal act. **Assassinate** implies a stealthy or treacherous murder, usually with a political motive. **Dispatch** is a euphemism for **kill,** implying speed and efficiency, and often used for the humane killing of animals. **Execute** describes the carrying out of a sentence of death, usually officially.

**kill off** *vt* to destroy totally or in very large numbers

**²kill** *n* **1** an act or instance or the moment of killing ⟨*in at the* ∼⟩ **2** something killed: eg **2a(1)** an animal shot for food or sport **a(2)** animals killed in a hunt, season, or particular period of time **b** an enemy aircraft, submarine, or ship destroyed by military action **c** a return shot in a racket game that is too hard for an opponent to handle

**killdeer** /'kil,diə/ *n, pl* **killdeers,** *esp collectively* **killdeer** a PLOVER (type of bird) (*Charadrius vociferus*) of N America characterized by a mournful penetrating cry [imit]

**killer** /'kilə/ *n* **1** one who or that which kills **2 killer whale** *also* **killer** a flesh-eating black-and-white TOOTHED WHALE (*Orcinus orca*) 6 to 9 metres (20 to 30 feet) long found in most seas of the world

**killick** /kilik/ *n* an anchor, esp of stone [origin unknown]

**killifish** /'kili,fish/ *n* **1** any of numerous small egg-laying fishes (family Cyprinodontidae) much used as bait and in the control of mosquitoes whose larvae it eats **2** TOPMINNOW 1 [*killie, killy* (killifish), fr *kill* (channel, river, stream), fr D *kil,* fr MD *kille*]

**¹killing** /'kiling/ *n* **1** the act of one who kills **2** a sudden notable gain or profit ⟨*made a* ∼ *on the stock exchange*⟩

**²killing** *adj* **1** that kills or relates to killing **2** *informal* extremely exhausting or difficult to endure **3** *informal* highly amusing – **killingly** *adv*

**killjoy** /-,joy/ *n* one who spoils the pleasure of others

**kiln** /kiln/ *n* an oven, furnace, or heated enclosure used for processing a substance (eg clay or porcelain) by burning, firing, or drying [ME *kilne,* fr OE *cyln,* fr L *culina* kitchen, fr *coquere* to cook – more at COOK] – **kiln** *vt*

**Kilner jar** /'kilnə/ *trademark* – used for a wide glass jar that has an airtight lid and is used for preserving foods, esp fruit and vegetables

**kilo** /'keeloh/ *n, pl* **kilos** a kilogram

**Kilo** – a communications code word for the letter *k*

**kilo-** *comb form* thousand ($10^3$) ⟨*kiloton*⟩ – compare MILLI- [Fr, modif of Gk *chilioi* – more at MILE]

**kilobit** /'kiləbit/ *n* either of two units of computer information: **a** one equal to 1000 bits **b** one equal to 1024 bits [ISV]

**kilobyte** /-,biet/ *n* either of two units of computer storage: **a** one equal to 1000 bytes **b** one equal to 1024 bytes

**kilocalorie** /-,kaləri/ *n* CALORIE 1b (measure of heat) [ISV]

**kilocycle** /-,siekl/ *n* a kilohertz [ISV]

**kilogram** /-,gram/ *n* **1** the SI unit of mass and weight equal to the mass of a platinum-iridium cylinder kept near Paris, and approximately equal to the weight of a litre of water **2** a unit of force equal to the weight of a kilogram mass under the earth's gravitational attraction [Fr *kilogramme,* fr *kilo-* + *gramme* gram]

**kilogram calorie** *n* CALORIE 1b (measure of heat)

**kilogram-'metre** *n* the METRE-KILOGRAM-SECOND system gravitational unit of work and energy equal to the work done by a force of 1 kilogram acting through a distance of 1 metre in the direction of the force

**kilohertz** /-,huhts/ *n* a unit of frequency equal to 1000 hertz [ISV]

**kilojoule** /-,joohl/ *n* a unit of work or energy equal to 1000 joules

**kilolitre** /-,leetə/ *n* a unit of volume equal to 1000 litres (about 220 gallons) [Fr, fr *kilo-* + *litre*]

**kilometre** /'kilə,meetə, ki'lomitə USE *the last pron is disliked by some speakers*/ *n* a unit of length equal to 1000 metres (about 0.62 mile) [Fr *kilomètre,* fr *kilo-* + *mètre* metre]

**kiloton** /-,tun/ *n* **1** a unit of mass or weight equal to 1000 tons **2** an explosive force equivalent to that of 1000 tons of TNT; about $5 \times 10^6$ joules

**kilovolt** /-,volt/ *n* a unit of POTENTIAL DIFFERENCE equal to 1000 volts [ISV]

**kilowatt** /-,wot/ *n* a unit of electrical power equal to 1000 watts [ISV]

**kilowatt-'hour** *n* a unit of work or energy equal to that expended by 1 kilowatt in 1 hour

**¹kilt** /kilt/ *vt, chiefly dial* to tuck up (eg a skirt) [ME *kilten,* of Scand origin; akin to ON *kjalta* fold of a gathered skirt]

**²kilt** *n* a skirt traditionally worn by Scotsmen that is formed usu from a length of tartan, is pleated at the back and sides, and is wrapped round the body and fastened at the front

**kilter** /'kiltə/ *n* [origin unknown] – **out of kilter** not in proper working order

**Kimbundu** /kim'boondooh/ *n* a BANTU language of N Angola

**kimono** /ki'mohnoh/ *n, pl* **kimonos** **1** a loose robe with wide sleeves and a broad sash traditionally worn by the Japanese **2** a loose dressing gown worn chiefly by women [Jap, clothes]

**¹kin** /kin/ *n* **1** a group of people of common ancestry; a clan **2a** *taking sing or pl vb* one's relatives; kindred **b** a kinsman, relation ⟨*he wasn't any* ∼ *to you* – Jean Stafford⟩ **3** *archaic* kinship ⟨*claim* ∼ *with them*⟩ [ME, fr OE *cyn;* akin to OHG *chunni* race, L *genus* birth, race, kind, Gk *genos,* L *gignere* to beget, Gk *gignesthai* to be born]

**²kin** *adj* kindred, related

**-kin** /-kin/ *also* **-kins** *suffix* (→ *n*) small kind of ⟨*cat*kin⟩ ⟨*mann*ikin⟩ [ME, fr MD *-kin;* akin to OHG *-chīn,* dim. suffix]

**kina** /'keenə/ *n* – see MONEY table [native name in Papua New Guinea]

**kinaesthesia,** *chiefly NAm* **kinesthesia** /ˌkinəs'theezi·ə, -zh(y)ə, ˌkie-/ *n* the sense of the position and movement of the joints of the body [NL, fr Gk *kinein* to move + *aisthēsis* perception] – **kinaesthetic** *adj,* **kinaesthetically** *adv*

**kinaesthesis,** *chiefly NAm* **kinesthesis** /ˌkinəs'theesis/ *n* kinaesthesia

**kinase** /'kienayz, -ays/ *n* an ENZYME that speeds up the transfer of PHOSPHATE groups from the energy-storing chemical compounds ATP or ADP to another substance (SUBSTRATE) involved in the chemical reaction [ISV, fr *kinetic*]

**¹kind** /kiend/ *n* **1** fundamental nature or quality; essence ⟨*problems differing in degree rather than in* ∼⟩ **2a** a group united by common features or interests; a category ⟨*biting insects with habits characteristic of their* ∼⟩ **b** a specific or recognized variety ⟨*what* ∼ *of car do you drive?*⟩ – often in combination ⟨*how delinquents differ from the rest of juvenile-kind – TLS*⟩ **c** a doubtful or barely admissible member of a category ⟨*a* ∼ *of grey*⟩ **3** *archaic* nature ⟨*laws of* ∼⟩ **4** *archaic* a family, lineage **5** *archaic* a manner ⟨*in this* ∼⟩ [ME *kinde,* fr OE *cynd;* akin to OE *cyn* kin] – **in kind 1** in goods, commodities, or natural produce as distinguished from money **2** in a similar way or with the equivalent of what has been offered or received ⟨*repaid his generosity* in kind⟩ – **kind of 1** to a moderate degree; somewhat **2** in a manner of speaking **3** roughly, approximately ⟨*all you can do is* kind of *nurse it* – SEU S⟩

> *usage* **1** In formal writing **kind, sort,** and **type** should be treated as singular, not plural ⟨*this* **kind**/**sort**/**type** *of* book is (not △ *these* **kind**/**sort**/**type** *of books are*) *interesting*⟩, although the plural construction has been long established in English ⟨*these* **kind** *of knaves I know* – Shak⟩ and is common in speech. The plural is perhaps more acceptable in questions after *what* or *which* ⟨*what* **sort** *of things are they?*⟩ and it is of course correct where **kind, sort,** and **type** are themselves plural ⟨*many* **types** *of error/errors*⟩. The idea of plurality can always be expressed by rephrasing ⟨*books of that* **kind**/**sort**/**type** *are interesting*⟩. **2** Some writers on usage object to **kind** *of a,* **sort** *of a* ⟨*what* **kind** *of a car is it?*⟩ and advise that *a* should be omitted here. *synonyms* see ¹TYPE

**²kind** *adj* **1a** of a generous nature; disposed to be helpful and benevolent **b** of a forbearing, considerate, or compassionate nature; gentle **c** arising from or characterized by sympathy, benevolence, or forbearance ⟨*a* ∼ *act*⟩ **2** cordial, friendly ⟨∼ *regards*⟩ **3** not harmful; mild; beneficial ⟨*a climate that is* ∼ *to the skin*⟩

> *synonyms* Kind, kindly, kindhearted, gracious, benign, benevolent, charitable, compassionate, and sympathetic all mean "showing concern and sympathy for another or others". **Kind** and **kindly** are often interchangeable to convey benevolence, gentleness, and a desire to be helpful to others, but **kind** is more usually applied to people and their natures, and **kindly** to the expression of kindness ⟨*a* **kind** *lady with a* **kindly** *smile*⟩. **Kindhearted** suggests an innate tendency to kindness. **Benign** stresses gentleness, mildness, serenity, and mercifulness, in people or their actions ⟨*found a* **benign** *old man beaming down at them*⟩. **Gracious** suggests kindly courtesy, especially from a superior or to someone in need ⟨*a* **gracious** *gift*⟩. **Benevolent** may suggest a disposition to care for another's welfare, or a more generally directed goodwill ⟨*bestowed* **benevolent** *smiles on all and sundry*⟩. **Charitable** may also suggest generosity and goodwill, but it often stresses mercifulness and leniency in judging the behaviour of others. **Sympathetic** carries this further by actually sharing the problems of others or displaying a kindly understanding of them. **Compassionate** suggests a nature easily moved to pity. *antonyms* unkind, uncaring, unfeeling

**kinda** /'kiendə/ *adv* KIND OF – used in writing to suggest casual speech

**kindergarten** /'kində,gahtn/ *n* a school or class for small children [Ger, fr *kinder* children + *garten* garden]

**kindhearted** /ˌkiend'hahtid/ *adj* marked by a sympathetic nature; KINDLY 2 *synonyms* see ²KIND – **kindheartedly** *adv,* **kindheartedness** *n*

**¹kindle** /'kindl/ *vt* **1** to set burning; light ⟨∼ *a fire*⟩ ⟨∼ *wood*⟩ **2** to stir up (e g emotion); arouse, incite **3** to cause to glow; illuminate ∼ *vi* **1** to catch fire; begin to burn **2** to become

animated or aroused; flare up ⟨*interest had* ∼d⟩ **3** to become illuminated; brighten ⟨*her eyes* ∼d⟩ [ME *kindlen,* fr ON *kynda;* akin to OHG *cunt*esal fire] – **kindler** *n*

**²kindle** *vb, esp of a rabbit* to give birth (to) [ME *kindlen,* prob fr *kinde* kind]

**kindliness** /'kiendlinis/ *n* kindness

**kindling** /'kindling/ *n* material (e g dry wood and leaves) that is easily set light to and is used for starting a fire

**¹kindly** /'kiendli/ *adj* **1** of an agreeable or beneficial nature; pleasant ⟨*a* ∼ *climate*⟩ **2** of a sympathetic or generous nature; friendly ⟨∼ *men*⟩ **3** *archaic* lawful, legitimate *synonyms* see ²KIND *antonyms* unkindly, harsh

**²kindly** *adv* **1** readily ⟨*did not take* ∼ *to the suggestion*⟩ **2a** in a kind manner; sympathetically **b** in an appreciative or sincere manner; favourably ⟨*would take it* ∼ *if you'd put in a good word for the boy*⟩ **c(1)** – used to add politeness or emphasis to a request ⟨∼ *fill in the attached questionnaire*⟩ **c(2)** – used to convey irritation or anger in a command ⟨*will you* ∼ *shut that door*⟩

**kindness** /'kiendnis/ *n* **1** a kind deed; *also* kind behaviour **2** the quality or state of being kind – see also **the** MILK **of human kindness**

**¹kindred** /'kindrid/ *n* **1** *taking sing or pl vb* **1a** a group of related individuals **b** one's relatives **2** family relationship; kinship [ME, fr *kin* + OE *ræden* condition, fr *rædan* to advise, read]

**²kindred** *adj* of a similar nature or character; like

**kine** /kien/ *archaic pl of* COW [ME *kyne,* fr OE *cÿna, cūna,* gen pl of *cū* cow]

**kinematics** /ˌkini'matiks, ˌkie-/ *n taking sing vb* a branch of DYNAMICS that deals with aspects of motion without consideration of force or interaction [Fr *cinématique,* fr Gk *kinēmat-, kinēma* motion – more at CINEMATOGRAPH] – **kinematic, kinematical** *adj,* **kinematically** *adv*

**kinescope** /'kinəskohp, 'kie-/ *n* **1** *NAm* PICTURE TUBE (television tube) **2** TELERECORDING (film recorded from television) [fr *Kinescope,* a trademark] – **kinescope** *vt*

**kinesics** /ki'neesiks, kie-/ *n taking sing vb* the systematic study of the relationship between bodily cues or movements (e g blushes, shrugs, or eye movements) and communication [Gk *kinēsis* + E *-ics*]

**kinesis** /ki'neesis, kie-/ *n, pl* **kineses** /-seez/ a movement made by an organism in response to the intensity rather than the direction of a stimulus, in which the organism moves at random until a better environment is reached [NL, fr Gk *kinēsis* motion, fr *kinein* to move]

**-kinesis** /-ki'neesis/ *comb form* (→ *n*), *pl* **-kineses** /-seez/ division ⟨*karyo*kinesis⟩ [NL, fr Gk *kinēsis*]

**kinesthesia** /ˌkinəs'theezi·ə, -zh(y)ə, ˌkie-/ *n, chiefly NAm* KINAESTHESIA (sense of position and movement of body joints) – **kinesthetic** *adj,* **kinesthetically** *adv*

**kinesthesis** /ˌkinəs'theesis/ *n, chiefly NAm* KINAESTHESIA (sense of position and movement of body joints)

**kinet-, kineto-** *comb form* movement; motion ⟨*kineto*genic⟩ ⟨*kineto*scope⟩ [Gk *kinētos* moving]

**kinetheodolite** /ˌkinithi'odəliet/ *n* an instrument (THEODOLITE) for measuring horizontal and vertical angles that has a camera for recording data (e g the deviation of a missile flight) [Gk *kinēsis* motion + E *theodolite*]

**kinetic** /ki'netik, kie-/ *adj* relating to motion [Gk *kinētikos,* fr *kinētos* moving, fr *kinein*] – **kinetically** *adv*

**kinetic art** *n* art (e g sculpture) depending for its effect on the actual or suggested movement of surfaces or volumes – **kinetic artist** *n*

**kinetic energy** *n* energy that a body or system has by virtue of its motion

**kinetics** /ki'netiks/ *n taking sing or pl vb* **1** a branch of science that deals with the effects of forces upon the motions of material bodies, or with changes in a physical or chemical system **2** the mechanism by which a physical or chemical change is effected – **kineticist** *n*

**kinetic theory** *n* any of several theories in physics based on the fact that constituent particles of a substance are in vigorous motion; *esp* KINETIC THEORY OF GASES

**kinetic theory of gases** *n* a theory in physics: the particles of a gas move in straight lines with high average velocity, continually encounter one another and thus change their individual velocities and directions, and cause pressure by their impact against the walls of a container

**kinetin** /'kienətin/ *n* a plant hormone that promotes MITOSIS

(CELL DIVISION producing two new cells) and the formation of CALLUSES (repair tissue) esp in the presence of an AUXIN (growth-promoting hormone) [kinet- + -in]

**kinetochore** /ki'netəkaw, kie-/ n, genetics CENTROMERE [kinet- + Gk chōros place]

**kinetograph** /ki'netəgrahf, kie-, -graf/ n an early form of film camera

**kineton** /'kientən/ n a horse's noseband with a secondary and lower loop attached on the nose to the main loop [Kineton, village in Warwickshire in England, where its inventor lived]

**kinetonucleus** /ki,netoh'nyoohkliəs, kie-/ n a kinetoplast [NL, fr Gk kinētos + NL nucleus]

**kinetoplast** /ki'netoh,plahst, kie-, -,plast/ n a specialized cell part (ORGANELLE), esp of TRYPANOSOMES (parasitic single-celled organisms), that contains DNA and has some characteristics of a MITOCHONDRION (energy-producing organelle) [ISV] – **kinetoplastic** adj

**kinetoscope** /ki'netə,skohp, kie-/ n an apparatus for viewing a sequence of pictures on an endless band of film moved continuously over a light source and a rapidly rotating shutter that creates an illusion of motion [fr Kinetoscope, a trademark]

**kinetosome** /ki'netəsohm, kie-/ n BASAL BODY (small structure at the base of hairlike projections from a cell)

**kinfolk** /'kinfohk/, chiefly NAm **kinfolks** n pl relatives

**king** /king/ n **1a** a male monarch of a major territorial unit; esp one who inherits his position and rules for life **b** a supreme chief (eg of a group of tribes) **2** cap God, Christ **3** the holder of a preeminent position ⟨Keegan, ~ of Wembley⟩; esp a chief among competitors ⟨a cotton ~⟩ **4** the principal piece of each colour in a set of chessmen, having the power to move ordinarily one square in any direction and to capture opposing men but being obliged never to enter or remain in check **5** a playing card that is marked with a stylized figure of a king and ranks usu below the ace **6** a draughtsman that has reached the opposite side of the board and can therefore move both forwards and backwards, its rank being shown by placing another draughtsman of the same colour on top of it – see also **turn king's** EVIDENCE [ME, fr OE cyning; akin to OHG kuning king, OE cyn kin]

**kingbird** /'king,buhd/ n any of various American TYRANT FLYCATCHERS (types of bird) (genus Tyrannus)

**kingbolt** /-,bohlt/ n a vertical bolt by which the forward axle and wheels of a vehicle, or the BOGIES (undercarriage with two or more pairs of wheels) of a railway vehicle, are connected with the other parts

**King Charles spaniel** /king chahlz/ n any of a breed of small spaniels with a well-rounded upper skull projecting forwards towards the short turned-up nose [King Charles II of England †1685]

**king cobra** n a large venomous cobra (Naja hannah) of SE Asia and the Philippines

**king crab** n any of a small group of marine INVERTEBRATE animals (order Xiphosura of the class Merostomata, phylum Arthropoda) that are related to spiders and scorpions, have a broad horseshoe- or crescent-shaped CEPHALOTHORAX (combined head and central region of the body) and an abdomen ending in a long spike, and that were most abundant several millions of years ago – called also HORSESHOE CRAB

**kingcraft** /-,krahft/ n the art of governing as a king

**kingcup** /-,kup/ n MARSH MARIGOLD

**kingdom** /-d(ə)m/ n **1** a territorial unit having a monarchical form of government headed by a king or queen **2** often cap **2a** the eternal kingship of God **b** the realm in which God's will is fulfilled **3a** a realm or region in which something is dominant ⟨in the untroubled ~ of reason – Bertrand Russell⟩ **b** an area or sphere in which someone holds a preeminent position **4** any of the three primary divisions into which natural objects are commonly classified – compare ANIMAL KINGDOM, MINERAL KINGDOM, PLANT KINGDOM

**kingfish** /-,fish/ n OPAH (very large brilliantly coloured sea fish)

**kingfisher** /-,fishə/ n any of numerous fish-eating birds (family Alcedinidae) that live near water, are usu brightly coloured, and have a short tail and long stout sharp beak; esp a kingfisher (Alcedo atthis) of Eurasia and N Africa that has cobalt blue and green upperparts and chestnut underparts

**King James Version** /king jaymz/ n AUTHORIZED VERSION (of the Bible) [King James I of England †1625 who commissioned this translation of the Bible]

**kingklip** /-,klip/ n an edible eel-like marine fish [short for kingklipfish, part trans of Afrik koningklipvis, fr koning king + klip rock, stone + vis fish]

**kinglet** /'kinglit/ n **1** a weak or petty king; esp one who rules over a small territory **2** any of several small birds (genus Regulus) that resemble warblers (eg the goldcrest or firecrest)

**kingly** /'kingli/ adj **1** of a king; monarchical, royal **2** befitting a king; majestic – **kingliness** n, **kingly** adv

**kingmaker** /-,maykə/ n somebody having great influence over the choice of candidates for (political) office

**king of arms** n, heraldry an OFFICER OF ARMS (person responsible for devising armorial bearings) of the highest rank; a chief herald

**king pair** n a failure of a batsman to score any runs in either innings of a cricket match by being dismissed on the first ball in each one – compare GOLDEN DUCK

**king penguin** n a large antarctic penguin (Aptenodytes patagonica)

**kingpin** /-,pin; also sense 1 ,-'-/ n **1** the chief or key person or thing in a group or undertaking **2a** KINGBOLT (vertical bolt linking parts of a vehicle) **b** a pin connecting the two parts of a KNUCKLE JOINT **3** the pin which stands at the front of the triangle of pins to be aimed at in TENPIN BOWLING

**king post** n a vertical supporting post connecting the apex of a triangular framework supporting a roof or other structure with the base – compare QUEEN POST

**king prawn** n any of several large prawns (genus Penaeus, esp Penaeus plebejus and Penaeus latisulcatus) found in Australian waters

**Kings** /kingz/ n taking sing vb – see BIBLE table

**King's Bench** n QUEEN'S BENCH (division of the HIGH COURT) – used when the reigning British monarch is a man

**King's Counsel** n QUEEN'S COUNSEL (senior barrister) – used when the reigning British monarch is a man

**King's English** n standard or correct S British English speech or usage – used when the reigning British monarch is a man

**king's evidence** n QUEEN'S EVIDENCE – used when the reigning British monarch is a man

**king's evil** n, often cap K&E SCROFULA (type of tuberculosis) [fr the former belief that it could be healed by a king's touch]

**kingship** /'kingship/ n the position or office of a king

**king-,size, king-sized** adj larger or longer than the regular or standard size

**king snake** n any of numerous brightly marked nonvenomous American snakes (genus Lampropeltis)

**king's shilling** n, often cap K&S a shilling whose acceptance by a recruit from a recruiting officer constituted until 1879 a binding enlistment in the British army ⟨he's taken the ~⟩

**kingwood** /'kingwood/ n a beautiful hard Brazilian wood used esp for cabinetwork; also any of various trees (genus Dalbergia, esp Dalbergia cearensis) that yield it

**kinin** /'kienin/ n **1** any of various hormones that are formed locally in the tissues and have their chief effect on SMOOTH MUSCLE **2** CYTOKININ (plant growth hormone) [Gk kinein to move, stimulate + E -in]

**kininogen** /kie'ninəjən/ n an inactive substance from which a kinin is formed – **kininogenic** adj

**kink** /kingk/ n **1** a short tight twist or curl caused by something doubling or winding upon itself **2** an eccentricity or quirk; esp such an eccentricity in sexual behaviour or preferences **3** chiefly NAm a cramp in some part of the body **4** chiefly NAm an imperfection likely to cause difficulties in the operation of something [D; akin to MLG kinke kink] – **kink** vb

**kinkajou** /'kingkə,jooh/ n a slender nocturnal tree-dwelling carnivorous mammal (Potos caudivolvulus, family Procyonidae) of Mexico and Central and S America that is about 1 metre (3 feet) long and has a long prehensile tail, large lustrous eyes, and soft woolly yellowish-brown fur [Fr, of Algonquian origin; akin to Ojibwa qwingwâage wolverine]

**kinky** /'kingki/ adj **1** closely twisted or curled; having many kinks ⟨~ hair⟩ **2** informal **2a** idiosyncratic, offbeat; broadly unusual **b** sexually perverted or deviant – **kinkiness** n

**kinnikinnick** also **kinnikinic** /'kinikinik/ n a mixture of dried leaves and bark and sometimes tobacco smoked by the American Indians and pioneers, esp in the Ohio valley; also a plant (eg a sumach or dogwood) used in it [of Algonquian origin; akin to Natick kinukkinuk mixture]

**kino** /'keenoh/, **kino gum** n a red gum obtained from various trees (esp Pterocarpus erinaceus) of the pea family and used in tanning and in medicine for its astringent properties [of African origin; akin to Mandingo keno, kano]

**kinsfolk** /'kinz,fohk/ n taking pl vb relatives

**kinship** /'kinship/ n **1** blood relationship **2** similarity, likeness

**kinsman** /'kinzmən/, *fem* **kinswoman** *n* a (male) relative

**kiosk** /'kee,osk/ *n* 1 an open summerhouse or pavilion common in Turkey or Iran 2 a small stall or stand with one or more open sides used esp for the sale of newspapers, cigarettes, sweets, or tickets 3 *Br* a public telephone box [Turk *köşk,* fr Per *kūshk* portico, palace; (2,3) Fr *kiosque,* fr Turk *köşk*]

**Kiowa** /'kie·əwə/ *n, pl* **Kiowas,** *esp collectively* **Kiowa** 1 a member of an American Indian people of Colorado, Kansas, New Mexico, Oklahoma, and Texas 2 the language of the Kiowa people

¹**kip** /kip/ *n* a bundle of untreated hides of young or small animals; *also* a hide from such a bundle [obs D; akin to MLG *kip* bundle of hides]

²**kip** *n, chiefly Br informal* 1 a place to sleep 2 (a period of) sleep [perh fr Dan *kippe* cheap tavern]

³**kip** *vi* **-pp-** *chiefly Br informal* 1 to sleep 2 to lie down to sleep – often + *down*

⁴**kip** *n* a unit of weight equal to 1000 pounds (about 453.6 kilograms) used to express deadweight load [*kilo-* + *pound*]

⁵**kip** *n, pl* **kip, kips** – see MONEY table [Thai]

¹**kipper** /'kipə/ *n* 1 a male salmon or SEA TROUT during or after the spawning season 2 a kippered fish, esp a herring – compare BUCKLING [ME *kypre,* fr OE *cypera;* akin to OE *coper* copper]

²**kipper** *vt* to cure (a split dressed fish) by salting and drying, usu in smoke

**kipper tie** *n* a very wide tie worn esp during the 1960s [partly fr its kipper-like shape; partly suggested by the name of Michael *Fish* fl1966 E clothes designer]

**kir** /kiə/ *n, often cap* a drink consisting of white wine mixed with a dash of blackcurrant liqueur or syrup [Felix *Kir* †1968 mayor of Dijon in France, its alleged inventor]

**Kirghiz** /'kuhgiz/ *n, pl* **Kirghizes,** *esp collectively* **Kirghiz** 1 a member of a Mongolian people inhabiting chiefly the Central Asian steppes 2 the TURKIC language of the Kirghiz

**kirk** /kuhk/ *n* 1 *cap* the national Church of Scotland as distinguished from the Church of England or the Episcopal Church in Scotland 2 *chiefly Scot* a church [ME (northern), fr ON *kirkja,* fr OE *cirice* – more at CHURCH]

**Kirman** /kuh'mahn, kiə-/ *n* a Persian carpet or rug characterized by elaborate fluid designs and soft colours [*Kirman,* province in Iran]

**kirmess** /'kuhmis/ *n* KERMIS (fair or festival)

**kirsch** /kiəsh/ *n* a dry colourless spirit distilled from the fermented juice of the black morello cherry [Ger, short for *kirschwasser,* fr *kirsche* cherry + *wasser* water]

**kirtle** /'kuhtl/ *n* 1 a tunic or coat worn by men, esp in the Middle Ages 2 a long gown or dress worn by women [ME *kirtel,* fr OE *cyrtel,* fr (assumed) OE *curt* short, fr L *curtus* shortened – more at SHEAR]

**Kislev** /'kislef/ *n* – see MONTH table [Heb *Kislēw*]

**kismet** /'kizmet, 'kis-/ *n, often cap* FATE 1,2a [Turk, fr Ar *qismah* portion, lot]

¹**kiss** /kis/ *vt* **1a** to touch with the lips, esp as a mark of affection or greeting **b** to touch in this way in order to express or effect ⟨*he* ~ed *her good night*⟩ 2 to touch gently or lightly ⟨*wind gently* ~ing *the trees*⟩ ~ *vi* 1 to touch or caress one another with the lips, esp as a mark of love or sexual desire 2 to come into gentle contact [ME *kissen,* fr OE *cyssan;* akin to OHG *kussen* to kiss] – **kissable** *adj*

²**kiss** *n* 1 an act or instance of kissing; *specif* a caress with the lips **2a** a CANNON in billiards which is made when the CUE BALL touches both OBJECT BALLS lightly **b** a light brief contact between two balls in billiards, snooker, etc 3 a small piece of confectionery (eg a sweet or meringue) ⟨*coconut* ~es⟩

'**kiss-,curl** *n* a small curl of hair falling on the forehead or cheek

**kisser** /'kisə/ *n* 1 somebody who kisses 2 *slang* **2a** the mouth **b** the face

**kiss of death** *n* an action or relationship bound to cause ruin or failure [fr the kiss with which Judas betrayed Jesus (Mk 14:44-46)]

**kiss of life** *n* 1 ARTIFICIAL RESPIRATION in which the rescuer blows air into the victim's lungs with mouth-to-mouth contact 2 an action or occurrence that restores or revitalizes – usu + *the* ⟨*injection of funds by private investors gave ailing industry the* ~⟩

**kiss of peace** *n* a ceremonial kiss, embrace, or handclasp used in Christian services of worship, esp Communion

**kist** /kist/ *n, chiefly dial or SAfr* a large chest or trunk; *esp, SAfr* one used for storing a bride's trousseau [ME *kiste,* fr ON

*kista* – more at CHEST; in SAfr, fr Afrik *kis,* fr D *kist,* fr MD *kiste*]

¹**kit** /kit/ *n* 1 a set of tools or implements ⟨*a carpenter's* ~⟩ **2a(1)** a set of parts ready to be assembled ⟨*a model aeroplane* ~⟩ **a(2)** an assembled collection of related printed matter or other material ⟨*instruction* ~⟩ **b** a container for any of such sets or collections 3 a set of clothes and equipment for use in a usu specified situation ⟨*riding* ~⟩ ⟨*travel* ~⟩; *esp* the equipment carried by a member of one of the armed forces 4 *dial Br* a wooden tub (eg for holding fish) [ME *kitt, kyt* tub, prob fr MD *kitte, kit* jug, vessel]

²**kit** *vt* **-tt-** *chiefly Br* to supply with kit; equip; *esp* to clothe – usu + *out* or *up* ⟨*all* ~ted *out for climbing*⟩

³**kit** *n* a small narrow violin used esp in the 18th and early 19th centuries [origin unknown]

⁴**kit** *n* a kitten

⁵**kit** *n* a Maori handbag or basket made of flax [Maori *kete*]

**kitbag** /-,bag/ *n* a large cylindrical usu canvas bag that is carried on the back, supported by a strap over one shoulder, and is used by soldiers and travellers to carry their kit

**kitchen** /'kichin/ *n* a place (eg a room in a house or hotel) with facilities for preparing and cooking food [ME *kichene,* fr OE *cycene;* akin to OHG *chuhhina* kitchen; both fr a prehistoric WGmc word borrowed fr LL *coquina,* fr L *coquere* to cook – more at COOK]

**kitchen cabinet** *n* an informal group of advisers to the head of a government

**kitchenette** /,kichi'net/ *n* (a part of a large room containing) a small kitchen

**kitchen garden** *n* a garden in which vegetables are grown

**kitchen midden** *n* a domestic refuse heap, usu including food remains; *specif* a refuse mound marking the site of a prehistoric settlement

**kitchen paper** *n* absorbent paper used chiefly in the kitchen (eg for draining food cooked in fat)

**kitchen police** *n taking pl vb, NAm* soldiers detailed to assist the cooks in a military mess

**,kitchen-'sink** *adj, Br, esp of drama* portraying modern daily life in a realistic and often sordid manner

**kitchen unit** *n* a fitment (eg a sink, cupboard, or cooker) of a modern kitchen; *also* a combination of kitchen fitments arranged compactly

**kitchenware** /'kichin,weə/ *n* utensils and equipment for use in a kitchen

¹**kite** /kiet/ *n* 1 any of various hawks (family Accipitridae) with long narrow wings, a deeply forked tail, and feet adapted for taking insects and small reptiles as prey; *esp* RED KITE 2 a light frame covered with thin material (eg paper or cloth), often provided with a balancing tail, and designed to be flown in the air at the end of a long string 3 *archaic* a person who preys on others [ME, fr OE *cȳta* owl; akin to MHG *kūze* owl, Gk *goan* to lament] – **go fly a kite** *chiefly NAm* to stop being an annoyance or disturbance ⟨*got mad and told him to go fly a kite*⟩

²**kite** *vi* 1 to move rapidly or in a carefree manner 2 *chiefly NAm* to rise rapidly; soar ⟨*the prices of necessities continue to* ~⟩ ~ *vt* to cause to move or rise rapidly

'**Kite-,mark** *n* a mark in the form of a stylized kite on goods (eg electrical appliances) approved by the British Standards Institution

**kith** /kith/ *n taking sing or pl vb* familiar friends, neighbours, or relatives ⟨~ *and kin*⟩ [ME, fr OE *cȳthth,* fr *cūth* known – more at UNCOUTH]

**kitsch** /kich/ *n* artistic or literary material that is usu designed to appeal to popular or sentimental taste and is pretentious or inferior [Ger, fr *kitschen* to slap together] – **kitschy** *adj*

¹**kitten** /'kitn/ *n* a young cat; *also* an immature individual of any of various species of small mammal [ME *kitoun,* fr (assumed) ONF *caton,* dim. of ONF *cat,* fr LL *cattus*] – **have kittens** *informal* to be extremely worried or upset

²**kitten** *vi* to give birth to kittens

**kittenish** /'kitn·ish/ *adj* resembling a kitten; *esp* coyly playful or flirtatious – **kittenishly** *adv,* **kittenishness** *n*

**kittiwake** /'kiti,wayk/ *n* any of various gulls (genus *Rissa,* esp *Rissa tridactyla*) that have mainly white plumage and a short or rudimentary hind toe [imit

¹**kittle** /'kitl/ *vt, Scot* 1 to tickle 2 to perplex [ME (northern) *kytyllen,* prob fr ON *kitla*]

²**kittle** *adj, Scot* difficult or risky to deal with; unpredictable

¹**kitty** /'kiti/ *n* a cat; *esp* a kitten – used chiefly as a pet name or calling name

**²kitty** /n/ **1** a fund in a card game (e g poker) made up of contributions from each pot and used (e g to pay expenses or buy refreshments) for the players **2** a usu jointly held fund of money or collection of goods made up of small contributions; a pool [¹*kit*]

**kiva** /'keevə/ *n* a chamber that is usu round and partly underground and is used by the Pueblo Indians of the SW USA for religious rituals [Hopi]

**kiwi** /'keewi/ *n* **1** a flightless New Zealand bird (genus *Apteryx*) with rudimentary wings, stout legs, a long bill, and greyish-brown hairlike plumage **2** *cap* a native or resident of New Zealand – used as a nickname **3a** a climbing plant (*Actinidia chinensis*) found in Asia **b** **kiwi, kiwi fruit** an edible oval fruit of this plant that has a brown hairy skin, green flesh, and black seeds □ (3) called also CHINESE GOOSEBERRY [Maori, of imit origin; (3) fr the fruit's being commercially exported from New Zealand]

**Klan** /klan/ *n* KU KLUX KLAN – **Klanism** *n*, **Klansman** *n*

**Klaxon** /'klaks(ə)n/ *trademark* – used for a powerful electrically operated horn or warning signal

**klebsiella** /‚klebzi'elə/ *n* any of a genus (*Klebsiella*) of plump nonmobile frequently encapsulated rod-shaped bacteria that can cause disease (e g pneumonia) [NL, genus name, fr Edwin *Klebs* †1913 Ger pathologist]

**Kleenex** /'kleeneks/ *trademark* – used for a paper handkerchief

**Klein bottle** /klien/ *n, maths* a one-sided surface that is formed by passing the narrow end of a tapered tube through the side of the tube and flaring this end out to join the other end – compare MÖBIUS STRIP [Felix *Klein* †1925 Ger mathematician]

**klepht** /kleft/ *n, often cap* a Greek belonging to any of several independent guerrilla communities formed after the Turkish conquest of Greece in the 15th century [NGk *klephtēs*, lit., robber, fr Gk *kleptēs*, fr *kleptein* to steal] – **klepthic** *adj, often cap*

**kleptomania** /‚kleptə'maynyə/ *n* an irresistible desire to steal, esp when not accompanied by economic motives or desire for financial gain [NL, fr *klepto*- (fr Gk *kleptein*) + *mania*] – **kleptomaniac** *n*

**klieg light, kleig light** /kleeg/ *n* a powerful ARC LAMP used in film studios [John *Kliegl* †1959 & Anton *Kliegl* †1927 US (German-born) lighting experts]

**Klinefelter's syndrome** /'klien‚feltəz/ *n* an abnormal condition in a man caused by the presence of two X CHROMOSOMES and one Y CHROMOSOME (chromosomes that determine sex) instead of only one of each, and resulting in infertility and smallness of the testicles [Harry *Klinefelter* b 1912 US physician]

**klinostat** /'klienəstat/ *n* a revolving stand used esp for experiments on plant growth (e g to test plants' response to gravitational pull) [Ger, fr *klino*- clin- + -*stat* -stat]

**klipspringer** /'klip‚spring-ə/ *n* a small African antelope (*Oreotragus oreotragus*) [Afrik, fr *klip* cliff, rock + *springer* leaper]

**kloof** /kloohf/ *n, SAfr* a deep glen; a ravine [Afrik, fr D]

**klystron** /'klistron, 'klie-/ *n* an electronic device in which the speed of a beam of electrons is regulated by electric fields and which is used for the generation and amplification of ultrahigh-frequency electric current [fr *Klystron*, a trademark]

**knack** /nak/ *n* **1** a special usu intuitive or innate ability or capacity that enables a person to do something, esp of a technical, difficult, or unusual nature, with ease ⟨*skating is easy once you've got the ~*⟩; *broadly* APTITUDE 2 ⟨*has a ~ for saying the wrong thing*⟩ **2** *archaic* an ingenious device; *broadly* a toy, knick-knack [ME *knak, knakke* trick, prob fr *knak* sharp blow or sound, of imit origin]

**¹knacker** /'nakə/ *n, Br* **1** somebody who buys and slaughters worn-out horses for use esp as animal food or fertilizer ⟨*a ~'s yard*⟩ **2** a buyer of old structures, esp ships or houses, for their constituent materials [prob fr E dial., saddlemaker] – **knackery** *n*

**²knacker** *vt, chiefly Br slang* to wear out or make unfit for work; exhaust – usu pass ⟨*after working all night I felt* ~ed⟩

**³knacker** *n usu pl, Br vulg* a testicle [prob fr E dial. *knack* to make a cracking noise, strike]

**¹knap** /nap/ *n, chiefly dial* **1** a crest of a hill; a summit **2** a small hill [ME, fr OE *cnæp*; akin to OE *cnotta* knot]

**²knap** *vt* -pp- to hit or break with a quick blow; *esp* to shape (e g flints) by breaking off pieces [ME *knappen*, of imit origin] – **knapper** *n*

**knapsack** /'nap‚sak/ *n* a (soldier's) bag, usu of canvas or leather, that is strapped on the back and used for carrying supplies or personal belongings *synonyms* see RUCKSACK [LG *knappsack* or D *knapzak*, fr LG & D *knappen* to make a snapping noise, eat + LG *sack* or D *zak* sack]

**knapweed** /-‚weed/ *n* any of various plants (genus *Centaurea*) of the daisy family; *esp* a thistle-like European plant (*Centaurea nigra*) with tough wiry stems and knobby heads of purple flowers [ME *knopwed*, fr *knop* knob + *wed* weed]

**knave** /nayv/ *n* **1** an unprincipled or deceitful man; a rogue **2** JACK 7 (playing card) **3** *archaic* **3a** a male servant **b** a man of humble birth or position [ME, fr OE *cnafa* servant, boy; akin to OHG *knabo* boy] – **knavery** *n*, **knavish** *adj*, **knavishly** *adv*

**knead** /need/ *vt* **1** to work and press into a mass (as if) with the hands ⟨*~ing dough*⟩ **2** to manipulate (as if) by kneading ⟨*~ the idea into shape*⟩ [ME *kneden*, fr OE *cnedan*; akin to OHG *knetan* to knead, OE *cnotta* knot] – **kneadable** *adj*, **kneader** *n*

**¹knee** /nee/ *n* **1a** (the part of the legs that includes) a joint in the middle part of the human leg that is the articulation between the FEMUR (thighbone), TIBIA (shinbone), and kneecap **b(1)** the joint in the hind leg of a 4-footed VERTEBRATE animal that corresponds to the human knee **b(2)** the CARPAL joint of the foreleg of a 4-footed VERTEBRATE animal **c** the TARSAL joint of a bird **d** the joint between the FEMUR and TIBIA of an insect **e** the part of an article of clothing that covers the knees ⟨*went through the ~s of his trousers*⟩ **2a** something (e g a piece of wood or iron) resembling the human knee, esp in its angular bent form **b** a rounded or conical outgrowth rising from the roots of any of several swamp-growing trees and projecting above the water [ME, fr OE *cnēow*; akin to OHG *kneo* knee, L *genu*, Gk *gony*] – **kneed** *adj* – **bring/force somebody to his/her knees** to cause somebody to submit or accept defeat or failure

**²knee** *vt* to strike or touch with the knee

**¹kneecap** /'nee‚kap/ *n* **1** PATELLA **2** a protective covering for the knee (e g of a horse)

**²kneecap** *vt* -pp- to smash or shoot the kneecap of (somebody) as a punishment or torture

**‚knee-'deep** *adj* **1** knee-high **2a** immersed up to the knees ⟨*~ in mud*⟩ **b** deeply engaged or occupied ⟨*~ in work*⟩

**‚knee-'high** *adj* high or deep enough to reach up to the knees

**kneehole** /'nee‚hohl/ *n* a space (e g under a desk) for the knees

**'knee-‚jerk** *adj* occurring as a conditioned response; automatic ⟨*~ radicalism – The Economist*⟩

**knee jerk** *n* an involuntary forward kick produced by a light blow on the tendon below the kneecap

**kneel** /neel/ *vi* **knelt** /nelt/, **kneeled** /neeld, nield, nelt/ to fall or rest on the knee or knees [ME *knelen*, fr OE *cnēowlian*; akin to OE *cnēow* knee]

**kneeler** /'neelə, 'niələ/ *n* **1** somebody who kneels **2** a hassock or low stool for kneeling

**'knees-‚up** *n, pl* **knees-ups** *chiefly Br informal* **1** a party dance in which alternate knees are raised in time with the increasing tempo of the music **2** a party or celebration with dancing and boisterous merrymaking

**¹knell** /nel/ *vi* **1** *of a bell* to ring, esp for a death, funeral, or disaster; to toll **2** to sound in an ominous manner or with an ominous effect ~ *vt* to summon, announce, or proclaim (as if) by a knell [ME *knellen*, fr OE *cnyllan*; akin to MHG er*knellen* to toll]

**²knell** *n* **1** the sound of a bell, esp when rung slowly (e g for a funeral or disaster) **2** an indication of the end or the failure of something ⟨*this decision sounded the death ~ for our hopes*⟩

**Knesset** /'knesit/ *n* the legislative assembly of Israel [NHeb *kĕneseth* gathering, assembly, fr Heb *kānas* to gather]

**knew** /nyooh/ *past of* KNOW

**Knickerbocker** /'nikə‚bokə/ *n* a descendant of the early Dutch settlers of New York [Diedrich *Knickerbocker*, fictitious author of *History of New York* by Washington Irving †1859 US writer]

**knickerbocker glory** *n* an elaborate dessert or sundae, typically consisting of layers of fruit, jelly, ice cream, and cream served in a tall glass

**knickerbockers** /'nikə‚bokəz/ *n pl* short baggy trousers gathered on a band at the knee [fr the knee-breeches worn by *Knickerbocker* in George Cruikshank's illustrations to Irving's *History of New York*]

**¹knickers** /'nikəz/ *n pl* **1** *Br* women's or girls' pants **2** *NAm* knickerbockers [short for *knickerbockers*] – **get one's knickers in a twist** *humorous* to become agitated or confused

**²knickers** *interj, Br slang* – used as an exclamation of defiance or contempt

**knick-knack, nick-nack** /'nik,nak/ *n* a small trivial ornament or trinket [redupl of *knack*]

**¹knife** /nief/ *n, pl* **knives** /nievz/ **1a** a cutting implement consisting of a blade fastened to a handle **b** such an instrument used as a weapon **2** a sharp cutting blade or tool in a machine [ME *knif*, fr OE *cnīf*; akin to MLG *knīf* knife, OE *cnotta* knot] – **knifelike** *adj*

**²knife** *vt* **1** to cut, slash, or wound with a knife **2** to mark or spread with a knife **3** *chiefly NAm informal* to try to defeat or harm by underhand means ∼ *vi* to cut a way (as if) with a knife blade ⟨*the cruiser* ∼d *through the heavy seas*⟩

**'knife-,edge** *n* **1** the edge of a knife **2** something (eg a ridge of rock) resembling the edge of a knife in sharpness and narrowness **3** a sharp wedge of hard material (eg steel) used as a fulcrum or pivot in a pair of scales, a pendulum, etc **4** an uncertain or precarious position or condition – esp in *on a knife-edge*

**knife pleat** *n* a narrow flat pleat; *esp* any of a series of such pleats that overlap and fall in the same direction

**¹knight** /niet/ *n* **1a(1)** a mounted armed soldier serving a feudal superior; *esp* a man ceremonially inducted into special military rank usu after completing service as page and squire **a(2)** a man honoured by a sovereign for merit and in Britain having a nonhereditary rank below a baronet entitling him to put the word *Sir* before his name **a(3)** a person equal to a knight in rank **b** a man devoted to the service of a lady as her attendant or champion **c** a member of any of various orders or societies **2** either of two pieces of each colour in a set of chessmen having a move from one corner to the diagonally opposite corner of a rectangle of three by two squares one of which may be occupied [ME, fr OE *cniht*; akin to OHG *kneht* youth, military follower, OE *cnotta* knot] – **knightly** *adj or adv*, **knightliness** *n*

**²knight** *vt* to confer a knighthood on

**knight bachelor** *n, pl* **knights bachelors, knights bachelor** a knight of the oldest and lowest order of knighthood

**,knight-'errant** *n, pl* **knights-errant 1** a knight travelling in search of adventures in which to exhibit military prowess and chivalrous conduct **2** an impractically idealistic or chivalrous person

**,knight-'errantry** *n* **1** the practice or conduct of a knight-errant **2** chivalrous conduct

**knighthood** /'niet-hood/ *n* **1** the rank or profession of a knight **2** the qualities befitting a knight; chivalry **3** *taking sing or pl vb* knights as a class or body

**Knight Templar** /'templə/ *n, pl* **Knights Templars, Knights Templar** TEMPLAR 1 (knight of a religious military order)

**¹knit** /nit/ *vb* **-tt-; knit, knitted** *vt* **1a** to link firmly or closely ⟨∼ted *her hands together*⟩ **b** to unite intimately **2a** to cause to grow together ⟨*time and rest will* ∼ *a fractured bone*⟩ **b** to contract into wrinkles ⟨∼ted *her brow in thought*⟩ **3a** to form (eg a fabric, garment, or design) by working one or more continuous yarns or threads into a series of interlocking loops using two needles or a knitting machine **b** to work (eg a specified number of rows) using a knitting stitch, specif KNIT STITCH ⟨∼ *1, purl 1*⟩ ∼ *vi* **1a** to practise or engage in knitting; make knitted fabrics or articles **b** to work yarn or thread in a knitting stitch, specif KNIT STITCH ⟨∼ *to the end of the row*⟩ **2a** to grow together **b** to become joined or drawn together [ME *knitten*, fr OE *cnyttan*; akin to OE *cnotta* knot] – **knitter** *n*

*usage* The inflection **knit** is commoner in the general senses ⟨*a closely* knit *group*⟩, and **knitted** is usual in the sense of making things from wool ⟨*a* knitted *jacket*⟩.

**²knit, knit stitch** *n* a basic knitting stitch that produces a raised pattern on the front of the work and is usu made by inserting the right needle through a loop on the left needle from the back to the front, bringing the yarn from the back of the work round the right needle in a clockwise direction, and pulling it through the first loop to form a new loop – compare PURL STITCH

**knitting** /'niting/ *n* **1** the act, action, or work of one who or that which knits **2** work that has been or is being knitted

**knitwear** /'nit,weə/ *n* knitted clothing

**knob** /nob/ *n* **1a** a rounded protuberance **b** a small rounded ornament (eg on the top of a bedpost), handle (eg on a drawer), or control attachment (eg on a television set) **2** a small piece or lump (eg of coal or butter) **3** *chiefly NAm* a rounded usu isolated hill or mountain **4** *Br vulg* the penis [ME *knobbe*; akin to MLG

*knubbe* knob, OE *-cnoppa* – more at KNOP] – **knobbed** *adj*, **knobby** *adj* – **with knobs on** *informal* to an even greater degree

**knobble** /'nobl/ *n* a small knob or lump [ME *knoble*, fr *knobbe* + *-le*, dim. suffix] – **knobbly** *adj*

**knobkerrie** /'nob,keri/ *n* a short wooden club with a knobbed head used esp by S African tribesmen for striking or throwing [Afrik *knopkierie*, fr *knop* knob + *kierie* club, fr Hottentot *kīrri* stick]

**¹knock** /nok/ *vi* **1** to strike something with a sharp, esp audible, blow; *esp* to strike a door so as to indicate one's desire to gain admittance ⟨∼ *before you enter*⟩ **2** to collide with something **3a** to make a sharp pounding noise **b** *of an internal-combustion engine* to make a metallic rapping noise because of a mechanical defect; *also* ⁷PINK ∼ *vt* **1a(1)** to strike sharply **a(2)** to drive, force, make, or take (as if) by so striking ⟨∼ed *a hole in the wall*⟩ ⟨*her earnings would be* ∼ed *off her mother's benefit* – *The Times*⟩ **b** to set forcibly in motion with a blow **2** to cause to collide ⟨∼ed *their heads together*⟩ **3** *informal* to find fault with ⟨*always* ∼ing *those in authority*⟩ – see also **knock into a** COCKED HAT, **knock** COLD, **knock the** STUFFING **out of somebody** [ME *knoken*, fr OE *cnocian*; akin to MHG *knochen* to press]

**knock about/around** *vb, informal vi* **1** to be present, usu without any clearly defined aim or purpose ⟨*she's been* knocking about *here for years*⟩ **2** to be involved in a relationship (*with*) ⟨*those two have been* knocking about *together for ages*⟩ ∼ *vt* to strike repeatedly, beat ⟨knocks *her* about *when he's had too much to drink*⟩

**knock back** *vt, chiefly Br informal* **1** to drink (an esp alcoholic beverage) rapidly **2** to cost; SET BACK **2** ⟨*that new car must have* knocked *her* back *a bit*⟩ **3** to surprise, disconcert ⟨*the news really* knocked *him* back⟩

**knock down** *vt* **1a** to strike to the ground (as if) with a sharp blow or a vehicle ⟨*was* knocked down *by a car in the High Street*⟩ **b** to demolish ⟨*the houses were* knocked down *to make room for a motorway*⟩ **2** to dispose of (an item for sale at an auction) *to* a bidder **3** to take apart; disassemble **4** to (cause to) reduce (a price) ⟨knock *the price* down *to £4*⟩ ⟨knocked *him* down *to £25 000*⟩

**knock off** *vi* to stop doing something, esp one's work ∼ *vt* **1** to do hurriedly or routinely ⟨knocked off *a painting in an afternoon*⟩ **2** to discontinue, stop ⟨knocked off *work at five*⟩ **3** to deduct ⟨knocked off *a pound to make the price more attractive*⟩ **4** *informal* to kill; *esp* to murder **5** *informal* to rob or steal ⟨knocked off *a couple of thousand*⟩ **6** *Br slang* to have sexual intercourse with

**knock on** *vb* to handle (the ball) in rugby so as to cause a KNOCK-ON

**knock out** *vt* **1** to empty (a tobacco pipe) by striking on or with something **2a** to defeat (a boxing opponent) by a knockout **b** to make unconscious **c** to make inoperative or useless ⟨*telephone communications were* knocked out *by the storm*⟩ **3** to tire out; exhaust **4** to eliminate (an opponent) from a knockout competition **5** *informal* to overwhelm with amazement or pleasure

**knock together** *vt* to make or assemble, esp hurriedly or in a makeshift way ⟨knocked together *a new skirt in an afternoon*⟩

**knock up** *vt* **1** *informal* to make, prepare, or arrange hastily ⟨*can you* knock up *some lunch for us?*⟩ **2** *informal* to make ill or exhausted **3** *informal* to achieve a total of ⟨knocked up *300 miles in the first day of travelling*⟩ **4** *Br informal* to awaken, rouse **5** *chiefly NAm slang* to make pregnant ∼ *vi* to practise informally before a match of tennis, squash, etc

**²knock** *n* **1a(1)** a sharp blow; a rap **a(2)** the sound of a knock; an audible blow or rap ⟨*a* ∼ *at the door*⟩ **b** a piece of bad luck or misfortune; a setback **2** a harsh and often petty criticism ⟨*likes praise but can't stand the* ∼s⟩ **3** *informal* INNINGS 1b

**knockabout** /'nokə,bowt/ *adj* **1** suitable for rough use ⟨∼ *clothes*⟩ **2** characterized by or employing boisterous antics; slapstick ⟨∼ *comedy*⟩

**¹knockdown** /-,down/ *n* **1** the action of knocking down, esp by a blow; *also* a blow that knocks down ⟨*the first* ∼ *came just after the beginning of the fight*⟩ **2** something (eg a piece of furniture) that can be easily assembled or dismantled

**²knockdown** *adj* **1** having such force as to strike down or overwhelm ⟨*a* ∼ *argument*⟩ **2** constructed so as to be easily assembled or dismantled ⟨*a* ∼ *table*⟩ **3** *of a price* very low or substantially reduced; *esp* being the lowest acceptable to the seller

**knocker** /'nokə/ *n* **1** one who or that which knocks; *specif* a metal ring, bar, or hammer hinged to a door for use in knocking **2** *usu pl, vulg* a woman's breast

**knock-for-'knock** *adj* of or being an agreement between insurance companies whereby if more than one insured person has sustained a loss (e g in a road accident) each company indemnifies its own policyholder regardless of legal liability for the loss

**knocking shop** /'noking/ *n, chiefly Br vulg* a brothel [¹*knock* (to copulate with)]

**knock-'knee** *n,* **knock-knees** *n taking sing or pl vb* a condition in which the legs curve inwards at the knees – **knock-kneed** *adj*

**¹'knock-ˌon** *n* (an instance of) hitting the ball towards the opponent's GOAL LINE with the hand or arm that is a violation of the rules in rugby

**²ˌknock-'on** *adj* characterized by a series of events, actions, etc each caused by the preceding one ⟨*a ~ effect throughout industry – The Guardian*⟩

**knockout, knock-out** /'nokˌowt/ *n* **1a** the act of knocking out; the condition of being knocked out **b(1)** (the termination of a boxing match resulting from) a blow that knocks out a boxing opponent or knocks him down for longer than a particular time, usu 10 seconds **b(2)** TECHNICAL KNOCKOUT **2** a competition or tournament with successive rounds in which losing competitors are eliminated until a winner emerges in the final ⟨*a ~ competition*⟩ **3** *informal* somebody or something sensationally striking or attractive – **knockout** *adj*

**knockout drops** *n pl* drops containing a drug (e g CHLORAL HYDRATE) which are put into a drink, esp surreptitiously, in order to produce unconsciousness or stupefaction

**¹knoll** /nol/ *n* a small round hill; a mound [ME *knol,* fr OE *cnoll;* akin to ON *knollr* mountaintop, OE *cnotta* knot]

**²knoll** *vb, archaic* to knell [ME *knollen*]

**knop** /nop/ *n* a usu ornamental knob [ME, fr OE *-cnoppa* knob; akin to OE *cnotta*] – **knopped** *adj*

**¹knot** /not/ *n* **1a** an interlacing of (parts of) one or more strings, threads, etc that forms a lump or knob **b** a particular manner of forming a knot ⟨*had to learn six different ~s to gain his badge*⟩ **c** a piece of material (e g ribbon or braid) tied as an ornament **d** a (sense of) tight constriction ⟨*his stomach was all in ~s*⟩ **2** something hard to solve; a problem **3** a bond of union; *esp* the marriage bond **4a** a protuberant lump or swelling in tissue **b(1)** the base of a woody branch enclosed in the stem from which it arises **b(2)** the cross-section of the base of a branch that appears in timber as a rounded usu cross-grained area **5** *taking sing or pl vb* a cluster of people or things; a group **6a** a speed of one NAUTICAL MILE per hour **b** one NAUTICAL MILE – not used technically [ME, fr OE *cnotta;* akin to OHG *knoto* knot, Lith *gniusti* to press; (6) fr the knots tied on a ship's logline to measure speed] – **tie somebody in knots** to confuse somebody utterly; bewilder – **tie the knot** to get married

**²knot** *vb* **-tt-** *vt* **1** to tie in or with a knot; form knots in **2** to unite closely or intricately *~ vi* to form a knot or knots; become knotted – **knotter** *n*

**³knot** *n, pl* **knots,** *esp collectively* **knot** a sandpiper (*Calidris canutus*) with grey plumage that breeds in the Arctic and winters in temperate or warm parts of the world [ME *knott*]

**knotgrass** /-ˌgrahs/ *n* any of several plants (genus *Polygonum*) of the dock family; *esp* a widely occurring weed (*Polygonum aviculare*) with jointed stems and minute green flowers

**knothole** /-ˌhohl/ *n* a hole in a board or tree trunk where a knot or branch has come out

**knotted** /'notid/ *adj* **1** tied in or with a knot or knots **2** full of knots; gnarled – **get knotted** *slang* – used to rebuke impertinence or reject a proposal

**knotting** /'noting/ *n* a preparation (e g shellac) used to cover knots in wood before painting to prevent resin seeping through the paint

**knotty** /'noti/ *adj* **1** marked by or full of knots **2** difficult to solve; complicated *synonyms* see ¹COMPLEX – **knottiness** *n*

**knotweed** /'notˌweed/ *n* knotgrass

**knout** /nowt/ *n* a whip formerly used in Russia for flogging criminals [Russ *knut,* of Scand origin; akin to ON *knūtr* knot; akin to OE *cnotta*] – **knout** *vt*

**¹know** /noh/ *vb* **knew** /nyooh/; **known** /nohn/ *vt* **1a(1)** to perceive directly; have direct cognition of **a(2)** to have understand-

ing of ⟨*~ thyself*⟩ **a(3)** to recognize the nature of; discern ⟨*knew right from wrong*⟩ **b(1)** to recognize, identify ⟨*would ~ her again*⟩ **b(2)** to be acquainted or familiar with ⟨*I've ~n her all my life*⟩ **b(3)** to have experience of ⟨*has ~n both success and failure*⟩ **b(4)** to be confined by or subject to ⟨*their grief knew no bounds*⟩ **2a** to be aware of the truth or factuality of; be convinced or certain of ⟨*I ~ that the earth is round*⟩ ⟨*"she's about 35." "Oh I don't ~, I think she's nearer 40"*⟩ **b** to have a practical understanding or knowledge of ⟨*~s how to write*⟩ ⟨*she ~s Italian*⟩ **3** *archaic* to have sexual intercourse with *~ vi* to have knowledge of something [ME *knowen,* fr OE *cnāwan;* akin to OHG *bichnāan* to recognize, L *gnoscere, noscere* to come to know, Gk *gignōskein*] – **knowable** *adj,* **knower** *n* – **be to know** to be expected to discern or have any knowledge of ⟨*how was I to know it would bite?*⟩ – **goodness/heaven/ Lord knows 1** it is not known ⟨*goodness knows where they are*⟩ **2** – used to emphasize a statement ⟨*goodness knows it wasn't me*⟩ – **you know** – used for adding emphasis to a statement ⟨*you'll have to try harder,* you know, *if you want to succeed*⟩ – see also **not know somebody from** ADAM, **know one's** ONIONS

*usage* The very common use of **you know** as a meaningless addition to speech is widely disliked.

**²know** *n* – **in the know** in possession of confidential or otherwise exclusive knowledge or information

**'know-ˌall** *n* a person who behaves as if he/she knows everything

**'know-ˌhow** *n* knowledge of how to do something smoothly and efficiently; expertise

**¹knowing** /'noh·ing/ *n* the action, fact, or condition of knowing or understanding something ⟨*there's no ~ what will happen*⟩

**²knowing** *adj* **1** shrewdly and astutely alert; *esp* implying knowledge of a secret ⟨*a ~ look*⟩ **2** deliberate, conscious ⟨*~ interference in the affairs of another*⟩ – **knowingly** *adv*

**'know-it-ˌall** *n* a know-all – **know-it-all** *adj*

**knowledge** /'nolij/ *n* **1a** the fact or condition of knowing something or somebody through experience or association ⟨*a remarkable ~ of human nature*⟩ **b** acquaintance with or understanding of something, esp a branch of learning ⟨*a ~ of foreign languages*⟩ **c** the fact or condition of being conscious of something; awareness ⟨*depressed by the ~ of what still had to be done*⟩ **2a** the range of information, perception, or understanding enjoyed by an individual or group **b** the fact or condition of having information or of being learned; erudition ⟨*a woman of unusual ~*⟩ **3** the sum of what is known; the body of truth, information, and principles acquired by mankind **4** SEXUAL INTERCOURSE – archaic except in *carnal knowledge* **5** *archaic* a branch of learning [ME *knowlege,* fr *knowlechen* to acknowledge, irreg fr *knowen*] – **to one's knowledge** as far as one knows or is able to judge ⟨*to my knowledge he's never ventured outside the British Isles*⟩

*synonyms* Knowledge, science, learning, erudition, scholarship, information, lore, and wisdom all describe what can be known. Information in the popular sense is simply the data serving as a basis for knowledge. Knowledge includes not only information, whether formally acquired or not, but also what can be deduced or inferred from experience and reasoning. Science, in this context, suggests a body of knowledge systematically acquired and scientifically tested. Learning and erudition generally apply to the humanities rather than to the sciences. Learning suggests individual knowledge acquired by long study, while erudition stresses profundity, bookishness, and often specialized knowledge. Scholarship implies possession of learning rather than the learning itself; it stresses academic attainment, scrupulous care, and detailed knowledge. Lore describes a body of knowledge acquired by the senses or tradition rather than formally or scientifically. Wisdom may describe occult lore, but in its more general meaning implies the ability to use one's knowledge sensibly and prudently. Compare KNOWLEDGEABLE, WELL-INFORMED, ERUDITE, SCHOLARLY, WISE, and LEARNED, which all reflect the meanings of their related nouns. *antonym* ignorance

**knowledgeable** /'nolijəbl/ *adj* having or exhibiting knowledge or intelligence; well informed – **knowledgeableness** *n,* **knowledgeably** *adv,* **knowledgeability** *n*

**known** /nohn/ *adj* generally recognized ⟨*a ~ authority on this topic*⟩

**¹knuckle** /'nukl/ *n* **1** the rounded prominence formed by the ends of the two adjacent bones at a joint; *specif* any of the joints between the hand and the fingers or the finger joints closest to these **2** a cut of meat consisting of the lowest leg joint of a pig, sheep, etc with the adjoining flesh **3a(1)** any of the cylindrical parts of a hinge through which a pin or rivet passes **a(2)** **knuckle joint, knuckle** a hinge joint retained by a pin or rivet **b** the meeting of two surfaces at a sharp angle (e g in a roof) [ME *knokel;* akin to MHG *knöchel* knuckle, OE *cnotta* knot] – **near the knuckle** *chiefly Br informal* approaching indecency – **rap over the knuckles** (to give) a scolding ⟨*she really rapped him over the knuckles*⟩ ⟨*gave him a rap over the knuckles for his disobedience*⟩

²**knuckle** *vi* to place the knuckles on the ground in shooting a marble ∼ *vt* to hit, press, or rub with the knuckles
  **knuckle down** *vi, informal* to apply oneself earnestly ⟨*let's knuckle down to business*⟩
  **knuckle under** *vi* to give in; submit ⟨*refused to knuckle under to any dictatorship*⟩

**knucklebone** /-₁bohn/ *n* any of the bones forming a knuckle; *esp* a METACARPAL or METATARSAL bone of a sheep formerly used in gambling or divination

'**knuckle-₁duster** *n* **1** a set of metal finger rings or guards attached to a bar and worn over the front of the doubled fist for use as a weapon **2** *informal* a large and ostentatious ring

**knucklehead** /'nukl₁hed/ *n, informal* a stupid person – **knuckleheaded** *adj*

**knur,** *Br also* **knurr** /nuh/ *n* a hard lump or knot (e g on a tree trunk); a gnarl [ME *knorre;* akin to OE *cnotta* knot]

**knurl** /nuhl/ *n* a small knob or protuberance; *esp* any of a series of small ridges, beads, etc on a surface to aid in gripping [prob alter. of *knur*] – **knurled** *adj,* **knurly** *adj*

¹**KO** /₁kay'oh/ *n, pl* **KOs** *informal* a kayo [knock out]

²**KO** *vt* **KO's; KO'ing; KO'd** *informal* to kayo

**koa** /'koh·ə/ *n* a Hawaiian tree (*Acacia koa*) of the pea family grown for its fine-grained red wood; *also* the wood of the koa used esp for furniture [Hawaiian]

**koala** /koh'ahlə/, **koala bear** *n* an Australian tree-dwelling marsupial mammal (*Phascolarctos cinereus*) about 60 centimetres (2 feet) long that feeds on eucalyptus leaves and has large hairy ears, grey fur, and sharp claws [native name in Australia]

**koan** /'koh₁ahn/ *n* a paradox to be meditated on that is used to train Zen Buddhist monks to abandon reason and develop intuition in order to gain enlightenment [Jap *kōan,* fr *kō* public + *an* proposition]

**kob** /kob/ *n* any of various medium-sized African antelopes (genus *Kobus*) the male of which has long ridged curved horns [of Niger-Congo origin; akin to Wolof *koba,* an antelope]

**kobo** /'koh₁boh/ *n* – see *naira* at MONEY table [alter. of *copper*]

**kobold** /'kobohld/ *n* **1** a gnome in German folklore that inhabits underground places **2** an often mischievous domestic spirit of German folklore [Ger – more at COBALT]

**Köchel number** /'kuhkəl (*Ger* kœçəl)/ *n* any of a group of numbers used as a cataloguing system for Mozart's works [Ludwig von *Köchel* †1877 Austrian naturalist & cataloguer of Mozart's works]

**kodiak bear** /'kohdi₁ak/ *n* a brown bear (*Ursus middendorffi*) of Alaska [*Kodiak* Island in Alaska]

**kofta** /'koftə/ *n* an Indian dish of minced meat or vegetables formed into small balls and fried [Hindi *koftā*]

**kohl** /kohl/ *n* (a cosmetic preparation made with) a black powder used, originally chiefly by Asian women, to darken the eyelids [Ar *kuhl*]

**kohlrabi** /'kohl₁rahbi/ *n, pl* **kohlrabies** (any of) a variety of cabbage (*Brassica oleracea caulorapa*) having a greatly enlarged, fleshy, turnip-shaped edible stem [Ger, fr It *cavolo rapa,* fr *cavolo* cabbage + *rapa* turnip]

**koine** /'koyni/ *n* **1** *cap* the Greek language as used in E Mediterranean countries in the Hellenistic and Roman periods **2** a language of a region that has become the LINGUA FRANCA of a larger area [Gk *koinē,* fr fem of *koinos* common]

**kola nut, cola nut** *n* the bitter caffeine-containing seed of any of several trees (genus *Cola,* esp *Cola nitida*) of the cocoa family that is chewed esp as a stimulant and is used in beverages [*kola* of African origin; akin to Temne *k'ola* kola nut, Mandingo *kolo*]

**kolinsky, kolinski** /kə'linski/ *n, pl* **kolinskies** (the fur or pelt of) any of several Asiatic minks (esp *Mustela siberica*) [Russ *kolinskii* of Kola, fr *Kola,* town & peninsula in USSR]

**kolkhoz** /kol'hawz, kol'khawz/ *n, pl* **kolkhozy** /-zi/, **kolkhozes** a COLLECTIVE FARM of the USSR [Russ, fr *kollektivnoe khozyaĭstvo* collective farm]

**kolkhoznik** /kol'hawznik, -'khawz-/ *n, pl* **kolkhozniki** /-ki/, **kolkhozniks** a member of a kolkhoz [Russ, fr *kolkhoz* + *-nik*]

**Kol Nidre** /₁kol 'nidri, -rə/ *n* a formula for the annulment of private vows chanted in the synagogue on the eve of YOM KIPPUR [Aram *kol nidhrē* all the vows; fr the opening phrase of the prayer]

**komodo dragon** /kə'mohdoh/ *n* an Indonesian MONITOR lizard (*Varanus komodoensis*) that is the largest of all known lizards, reaching 3 metres (about 10 feet) in length [*Komodo* Island in Indonesia]

**Komsomol** /₁komso'mol/ *n* the Communist youth organization of the USSR [Russ, fr *Kommunisticheskiĭ Soyuz Molodezhi* Communist Union of Youth)

**Kongo** /'kong·goh/ *n, pl* **Kongos,** *esp collectively* **Kongo 1** a member of a BANTU people of the lower Zaire river **2** the BANTU language of the Kongo people

**Konkani** /'kongkəni/ *n* an INDIC language of the W coast of India [Marathi *Koṅkaṇī*]

**koodoo** /'kooh₁dooh/ *n, pl* **koodoos,** *esp collectively* **koodoo** KUDU (type of antelope)

**kook** /koohk/ *n, chiefly NAm informal* an eccentric, unusual, or crazy person [by shortening & alter. fr *cuckoo*] – **kookie, kooky** *adj,* **kookiness** *n*

**kookaburra** /'kookə₁burə/ *n* a large Australian kingfisher (*Dacelo gigas*) that is about the size of a crow and has a call resembling loud laughter [native name in Australia]

**kopeck** *also* **kopek** /'kohpek/ *n* – see *ruble* at MONEY table [Russ *kopeĭka*]

**kopje, koppie** /'kopi/ *n* a small hill on the S African veld; *broadly, SAfr* a small hill [Afrik *koppie,* fr D *kopje,* dim. of *kop* head, peak, cup]

**Koran, Qur'an** /kaw'rahn/ *n* the book composed of writings accepted by Muslims as revelations made to Muhammad by Allah through the angel Gabriel [Ar *qur'ān,* fr *qara'a* to read, recite] – **Koranic** *adj*

**Korean** /kə'ree·ən/ *n* **1** a native or inhabitant of Korea **2** the language of the Koreans [*Korea,* peninsula in E Asia] – **Korean** *adj*

**korfball** /'kawf₁bawl/ *n* a game played by two mixed teams of 12 members each who try to shoot a ball into a high net [D *korfbal,* fr *korf* basket + *bal* ball]

**korma** /'kawmə/ *n* an Indian dish of meat or sometimes vegetables braised in water, stock, yoghourt, or cream [Hindi *kormā* braised meat]

**koruna** /ko'roohnə/ *n, pl* **koruny** /-ni/, **korunas** – see MONEY table [Czech, lit., crown, fr L *corona*]

¹**kosher** /'kohshə/ *adj* **1a** *of food* prepared according to Jewish law **b** selling or serving kosher food ⟨*a ∼ butcher*⟩ ⟨*a ∼ restaurant*⟩ **2** *informal* proper, legitimate ⟨*perfectly ∼ evidence*⟩ [Yiddish, fr Heb *kāshēr* fit, proper]

²**kosher** *n* (a shop selling) kosher food

³**kosher** *vt* to make (food) kosher

**koskas** *n, pl* **koskaste** *SAfr* a cupboard for storing food [Afrik, fr *kos* food (fr D *kost*) + *kas* cupboard (fr D *kast*)]

**koto** /'koh₁toh/ *n, pl* **kotos** a Japanese musical instrument with a long rectangular wooden body and 13 silk strings [Jap]

**koumiss, kumiss** /'koohmis/ *n* an alcoholic drink of fermented (mare's) milk made originally by the nomadic peoples of central Asia and used medicinally and as a beverage [Russ *kumys*]

**kowhai** /'koh₁wie/ *n* a golden-flowered shrub or small tree (*Sophora tetraptera*) of the pea family that occurs in Australasia and Chile [Maori]

¹**kowtow** /'kow₁tow, 'koh-/ *n* a (Chinese) gesture of deep respect which consists of kneeling down and touching the ground with one's forehead [Chin (Pek) *ke tóu* (*k'o*¹ *t'ou*²), fr *ke* (*k'o*¹) to bump + *tóu* (*t'ou*²) head]

²**kowtow** /₁-'-/ *vi* **1** to make a kowtow **2** to show obsequious deference

¹**kraal** /krahl/ *n* **1** a village of southern African tribesmen, often enclosed by a fence **2** an enclosure for domestic animals in southern Africa [Afrik, fr Pg *curral* pen for cattle, enclosure, fr (assumed) VL *currale* enclosure for vehicles – more at CORRAL]

²**kraal** *vt* to pen in a kraal

**kraft** /krahft/ *n* a strong paper or board made from wood pulp boiled in an alkaline solution containing SODIUM SULPHATE [Sw or Ger, lit., strength]

**kragdadige** /'krahkh₁dahdikh·ə/ *n, SAfr* an advocate of hard-line policies ⟨*well-known Government ∼s in all these fields* – *The Star (Johannesburg)*⟩ – compare VERLIGTE, VERKRAMPTE [Afrik *kragdadig* forceful, determined, fr D *krachtdadig*]

**kragdadigheid** /'krakh͵dahdikh͵hiet/ *n, SAfr* uncompromising toughness (e g by government in response to demands for liberalization) [Afrik, lit., forcefulness, fr *kragdadig*]

**krait** /kriet/ *n* any of several brightly banded extremely venomous nocturnal snakes (genus *Bungarus*) of E Asia and adjacent islands [Hindi *karait*]

**kraken** /'krahkən/ *n* a mythical Scandinavian sea monster [Norw dial.]

**krater** /'kraytə/ *n* CRATER 3 (large Greek jar) [Gk *kratēr* – more at CRATER]

**K ration** *n* a lightweight packaged ration of emergency foods developed for the US armed forces in World War II [A B Keys *b*1904 US physiologist]

**kraut** /krowt/ *n, often cap, derog* a German [Ger, sauerkraut, cabbage – more at SAUERKRAUT]

**Krebs cycle** /krebz/ *n* a sequence of chemical reactions in the living cell which provides energy for storage in high-energy PHOSPHATE bonds of ADP and ATP [Sir Hans (Adolf) *Krebs* †1981 Br (German-born) biochemist]

**kremlin** /'kremlin/ *n* **1** a citadel or strongly fortified area within a Russian town or city **2** *cap the* government of the USSR [Fr *kremlin* or obs Ger *kremelin*, fr Russ *kreml'*; (2) the *Kremlin*, citadel of Moscow and governing centre of the USSR]

**kremlinology** /͵kremli'noləji/ *n, often cap* the study of the policies and practices of the Soviet government – **kremlinologist** *n, often cap*

**kreuzer** /'kroytsə/ *n* any of several small coins formerly used in Austria and Germany [Ger]

**krill** /kril/ *n* small marine INVERTEBRATE animals (esp genus *Euphausia*, of the class Crustacea) that resemble shrimps and constitute the principal food of many sea animals (e g WHALEBONE WHALES) [Norw *kril* fry of fish]

**kris** /krees/ *n* a Malay or Indonesian dagger with a scalloped blade [Malay *kĕris*]

**Kriss Kringle** /͵kris 'kring·gl/ *n, NAm* FATHER CHRISTMAS [modif of Ger *Christkindl* Christ child, Christmas gift, dim. of *Christkind* Christ child]

**kromesky** /krə'meski/ *n* a breaded or batter-coated croquette usu of minced meat or poultry wrapped in bacon [modif of Russ *kromochki*, pl of *kromochka* slice of bread, dim. of *kroma* slice of bread]

**¹krona** /'krohnə/ *n, pl* **kronur** /~/ – see MONEY table [Icel *krōna*, lit., crown]

**²krona** /'kroohnə/ *n, pl* **kronor** /-naw/ – see MONEY table [Sw, lit., crown]

**¹krone** /'krohnə/ *n, pl* **kronen** /-ən/ **1** the basic monetary unit of Austria from 1892 to 1925 **2** a coin representing one krone [Ger, lit., crown]

**²krone** *n, pl* **kroner** /~/ – see MONEY table [Dan, lit., crown]

**Kronecker delta** /'krohnekə/ *n, maths* a function of two variables that is defined to be equal to one (1) when the variables are equal and zero (0) otherwise [Leopold *Kronecker* †1891 Ger mathematician]

**Kru** /krooh/ *n, pl* **Krus**, *esp collectively* **Kru 1** a member of a Negro people of the Liberian coast **2** the language of the Kru

**Krugerrand** /'kroohgə͵rahnt, -͵rand/ *n* a 1-ounce (28.35-gram) gold coin of the Republic of S Africa [S J P *Kruger* †1904 SAfr statesman + *rand*]

**krummholz** /'kroomholts/ *n taking sing or pl vb* stunted forest characteristic of the TIMBERLINE (upper limit of tree growth) [Ger, fr *krumm* crooked + *holz* wood]

**krummhorn** /'kroom͵hawn, 'krum-/ *n* CRUMHORN (medieval woodwind instrument)

**krypton** /'kript(ə)n, 'kripton/ *n* a colourless relatively inert gaseous chemical element found in very small amounts in air and used esp in fluorescent lights [Gk, neut of *kryptos* hidden – more at CRYPT]

**Kshatriya** /'kshatri·ə/ *n* a Hindu of an upper caste traditionally assigned to military occupations [Skt *kṣatriya*]

**kudos** /'k(y)oohdos/ *n* fame and renown, esp resulting from an act or achievement; prestige [Gk *kydos*; akin to Gk *akouein* to hear – more at HEAR]

**kudu, koodoo** /'kooh͵dooh/ *n, pl* **kudus, koodoos**, *esp collectively* **kudu, koodoo** either of two greyish brown African antelopes (*Tragelaphus strepsiceros* and *Tragelaphus imberbis*) with large spirally twisted horns [Afrik *koedoe*]

**Kufic, Cufic** /'koohfik, 'kyoohfik/ *adj or n* (of or being) an early form of Arabic lettering, used esp in manuscripts of the Koran and inscriptions [*Kufa, Cufa*, ancient city in SW Asia]

**Ku Klux Klan** /͵k(y)ooh ͵kluks 'klan/ *n* **1** a secret society that

was active in the USA after the Civil War and that opposed the right of blacks to vote **2** a secret political organization in the USA that confines its membership to American-born Protestant whites and that is hostile to blacks [perh fr Gk *kyklos* circle + E *clan*]

**kukri** /'kookri/ *n* a short curved knife used esp by Gurkhas [Hindi *kukṛī*]

**kulak** /'kooh͵lak/ *n* **1** a prosperous peasant farmer in pre-revolutionary Russia **2** a member of a class of Russian peasant-proprietors working for personal profit and opposing collectivization – used technically in Marxist literature △ muzhik [Russ, lit., fist]

**kultur** /kool'tooə/ *n, often cap* **1** CULTURE **5** **2** *chiefly derog* German culture conceived of as emphasizing individual subordination to the state and practical efficiency [Ger, fr L *cultura* culture]

**Kulturkampf** /-͵kampf/ *n* a conflict between civil and religious authorities, esp over control of education and ecclesiastical appointments; *specif* the conflict between the German government and the Papacy in the late 19th century [Ger, fr *kultur* + *kampf* conflict]

**kumara** /'koomərə/ *n, NZ* SWEET POTATO [Maori]

**kumiss** /'koohmis/ *n* KOUMISS (drink made from fermented milk)

**kümmel** /'kooml/ *n* a colourless aromatic liqueur flavoured principally with caraway and cumin seeds [Ger, lit., caraway seed, fr OHG *kumīn* cumin]

**kumquat, cumquat** /'kumkwot/ *n* any of several small orange citrus fruits with sweet spongy rind and somewhat acid pulp that are used chiefly for preserves; *also* any of several trees or shrubs (genus *Fortunella*) of the rose family that bear kumquats [Chin (Cant) *kam kwat*, fr *kam* gold + *kwat* orange]

**kung fu** /͵kung 'fooh/ *n* a Chinese MARTIAL ART resembling karate [Chin dial., alter. of Pek *quán fǎ* (*chüan² fa³*), lit., boxing principles]

**kunzite** /'koontsiet/ *n* a SPODUMENE (type of mineral) that occurs in pinkish lilac crystals and is used as a gem [G F *Kunz* †1932 US gem expert]

**kurchatovium** /͵kuhchə'tohvyəm, -vi·əm/ *n* RUTHERFORDIUM [Igor *Kurchatov* †1960 Russ nuclear physicist]

**Kurd** /kuhd/ *n* a member of a pastoral and agricultural people who inhabit adjoining parts of Turkey, Iran, Iraq, and Syria and the Armenian and Azerbaijan sectors of the Soviet Caucasus – **Kurdish** *adj*

**Kurdish** /'kuhdish/ *n* the Iranian language of the Kurds

**Kurdistan** /͵kuhdi'stan, -'stahn/ *n* an oriental rug woven by the Kurds and noted for fine colours and durability [*Kurdistan*, region in Asia]

**kurgan** /'kooəgən (*Russ* kuə'gan)/ *n* a prehistoric burial mound found in E Europe and esp S Russia [Russ, of Turkic origin; akin to Turk *kurgan* fortress, castle]

**kuri** /'koori/ *n, pl* **kuris 1** *NZ* a mongrel dog **2** *NZ informal* an unpopular man or woman **3** *Austr derog* a Maori [Maori]

**kurrajong** /'kurə͵jong/ *n* any of several Australian trees or shrubs yielding strong woody fibre [native name in Australia]

**kurtosis** /kuh'tohsis/ *n, statistics* the peakedness or flatness of the graph of a FREQUENCY DISTRIBUTION, esp as determining the concentration of values near the MEAN (average) as compared with the NORMAL DISTRIBUTION [Gk *kyrtōsis* convexity, fr *kyrtos* convex; akin to L *curvus* curved – more at CROWN]

**kuru** /'koorooh/ *n* a fatal progressive disease of the nervous system that occurs esp among tribesmen in eastern New Guinea [native name in New Guinea, lit., trembling]

**kurus** /koo'roohsh/ *n, pl* **kurus** – see *lira* at MONEY table [Turk *kuruş*]

**kvass, kvas** /k'vahs/ *n* a sour-sweet beverage of slight alcoholic content made in E Europe usu by fermenting mixed cereals and adding flavouring (e g fruit or peppermint) [Russ *kvas*]

**Kwa** /kwah/ *n* a branch of the NIGER-CONGO language family that is spoken along the W African coast and a short distance inland and includes IBO and YORUBA

**kwacha** /'kwahchə/ *n, pl* **kwacha** – see MONEY table [native name in Zambia, lit., dawn]

**kwanza** /'kwahnzə/ *n, pl* **kwanzas, kwanza** – see MONEY table [of Bantu origin]

**kwashiorkor** /͵kwashi'awkə/ *n* severe malnutrition in infants and children that is caused by a diet high in carbohydrate and low in protein [native name in Ghana, lit., red boy; fr the reddening of the hair it causes]

**kyanite** /'kie·əniet/ *n* a mineral, $Al_2SiO_5$, containing aluminium, silicon, and oxygen that occurs usu in blue thin-bladed crystals and crystalline rocky masses and is sometimes used as a gemstone [Ger *zyanit*, fr Gk *kyanos* dark blue enamel, lapis lazuli]

**kyat** /ki'aht/ *n* – see MONEY table [Burmese]

**kye, ky** /kie/ *n taking pl vb, dial* cattle [ME *ky*, fr OE *cȳ*, pl of *cū* cow]

**kyle** /kiel/ *n, Scot* a narrow channel between islands or between an island and the mainland [ScGael *caol*, fr *caol* narrow]

**kymogram** /'kieməgram/ *n* a record made by a kymograph [ISV]

**kymograph** /'kieməgrahf, -graf/ *n* a rotating cylindrical device that graphically records motion or pressure (eg heartbeat or

muscle contraction( [Gk *kyma* wave + ISV *-graph* – more at CYME] – **kymographic** *adj*

**Kymric** /'kimrik/ *adj or n* CYMRIC (Welsh)

**kyphosis** /kie'fohsis/ *n* abnormal backward curvature of the spine – compare LORDOSIS, SCOLIOSIS [NL, fr Gk *kyphōsis*, fr *kyphos* humpbacked; akin to OE *hēah* high] – **kyphotic** *adj*

**kyrie** /'kiri,ay, 'kiri,ee/, **kyrie eleison** *n, often cap* a short prayer, often set to music, that begins with or consists of the words "Kyrie eleison" or their English translation "Lord, have mercy" [NL, fr LL *kyrie eleison*, transliteration of Gk *kyrie eleēson* Lord, have mercy]

# L

**l, L** /el/ *n, pl* **l's, ls, L's, Ls 1a** the 12th letter of the English alphabet **b** a graphic representation of or device for reproducing the letter *l* **c** a speech counterpart of printed or written *l* **2** one designated *l*, esp as the 12th in order or class **3** fifty **4** something shaped like the letter L; *specif* ²ELL **5** *NAm* ELEVATED

**l-** /el-/ *prefix* **1** laevorotatory ⟨*l-tartaric acid*⟩ **2** having a similar CONFIGURATION (arrangement of atoms) at an optically active carbon atom to the configuration of laevorotatory GLYCERALDEHYDE – usu printed as a small capital ⟨*L-fructose*⟩ [ISV, fr *laev-*]

**¹la** /lah/ *n* LAH (musical note)

**²la** *interj, archaic* – used for expressing emphasis or surprise [ME (northern), fr OE *lā*]

**laager** /'lahgə/ *n* a camp; *esp* an encampment, esp in Africa, protected by a circle of wagons or armoured vehicles [obs Afrik *lager* (now *laer*), fr Ger] – **laager** *vb*

**lab** /lab/ *n, informal* a laboratory

**labarum** /'labərəm/ *n, pl* **labara** an imperial standard or banner of the later Roman emperors resembling the VEXILLUM; *esp* the standard adopted by Constantine after his conversion to Christianity [LL]

**labdanum** /'labdənəm/ *n* a soft dark fragrant bitter OLEORESIN (mixture of oil and plant resin) derived from various rockroses (genus *Cistus*) and used in perfumery [ML *lapdanum*, fr L *ladanum, ledanum*, fr Gk *ladanon, ledanon*, fr *ledon* rockrose, of Sem origin]

**labefaction** /,labi'faksh(ə)n/ *n, formal* an impairment or decline, esp of moral principles or civil order [LL *labefaction-, labefactio*, fr L *labefactus*, pp of *labefacere* to shake, cause to totter, fr *labare* to totter + *facere* to make]

**¹label** /'laybl/ *n* **1** a heraldic figure (CHARGE 1) that consists of a narrow horizontal band with usu three pendants **2** a slip (e g of paper, cloth, or metal) inscribed and attached to something to give information (e g identification, description, or directions) **3** a descriptive or identifying word or phrase: e g **3a** an epithet **b** a word or phrase used with a dictionary definition to provide additional information (e g about level of usage) **c** material used in radioactive labelling **4** a sticker **5** TRADE NAME 1b, 2: e g **5a** (a name used by) a company producing commercial recordings ⟨*the group has transferred to a new* ∼⟩ ⟨*the band's British* ∼ . . . *hope the new single will be recorded in the next fortnight – Melody Maker*⟩ **b** a name under which a shop, esp a chain store, sells certain goods [ME, narrow band, strip, fr MF, fr OF, ribbon, fringe, prob of Gmc origin]

**²label** *vt* **-ll-** (*NAm* **-l-, -ll-**) **1a** to attach a label to **b** to describe or categorize (as if) with a label ⟨*had him* ∼*led as a troublemaker*⟩ **2a** to make (a chemical element or atom) traceable by using a radioactive ISOTOPE (form in which an atom can occur) or an isotope of unusual mass for following through chemical reactions or biological processes **b** to distinguish (e g a chemical compound or molecule) by introducing a labelled atom – **labellable** *adj*, **labeller** *n*

**labellum** /lə'beləm/ *n, pl* **labella** /-lə/ **1** the often large and distinctive middle petal of an orchid **2** an end part of the LABIUM (lower mouthpart) or LABRUM (upper mouthpart) of various insects [NL, fr L, dim. of *labrum* lip – more at LIP] – **labellate** *adj*

**¹labial** /'laybi-əl/ *adj* **1** of the lips or labia **2** articulated using one or both lips ⟨*the* ∼ *sounds* /f/, /p/, and /ooh/⟩ [ML *labialis*, fr L *labium* lip] – **labially** *adv*, **labialize** *vt*, **labialization** *n*

**²labial** *n* a labial consonant (e g /f/ and /p/)

**labia majora** /,laybi-ə mə'jawrə/ *n pl* the outer fatty folds surrounding the opening of the vagina [NL, lit., larger lips]

**labia minora** /mi'nawrə/ *n pl* the inner folds consisting largely of CONNECTIVE TISSUE which surround the opening of the vagina [NL, lit., smaller lips]

**¹labiate** /'laybiət, -ayt/ *adj* **1** *of a plant* having the petals (COROLLA) or sepals (CALYX) arranged in two unequal portions that project one over the other like lips ⟨*the snapdragon is* ∼⟩ **2** of the mint family [NL *labiatus*, fr L *labium*]

**²labiate** *n* a plant of the mint family

**labile** /'laybil, -biel/ *adj* **1** readily or continually undergoing chemical, physical, or biological change or breakdown; unstable ⟨*a* ∼ *mineral*⟩ **2** *formal* readily open to change ⟨*an emotionally* ∼ *person*⟩ [Fr, fr MF, prone to err, fr LL *labilis*, fr L *labi* to slip – more at SLEEP] – **lability** *n*

**labio-** /laybioh-/ *comb form* labial and ⟨labio*dental*⟩ [L *labium*]

**labiodental** /,laybioh'dentl/ *adj*, of a consonant articulated using the bottom lip and the teeth ⟨*the* ∼ *sounds* /f/ *and* /v/⟩ – **labiodental** *n*

**labionasal** /,laybioh'nayzl/ *adj* both labial and nasal ⟨*the* ∼ *sound* /m/⟩ [ISV]

**labiovelar** /,laybioh'veelə/ *adj* both labial and VELAR (articulated with the tongue and SOFT PALATE) ⟨*the* ∼ *sound* /w/⟩ [ISV] – **labiovelar** *n*

**labium** /'laybi-əm/ *n, pl* **labia** /'laybiə/ **1** any of the folds at the margin of the opening of the vagina – compare LABIA MAJORA, LABIA MINORA **2** the (lower) lip of a COROLLA (all the petals of a flower) that is divided into two liplike parts **3a** a lower mouthpart of an insect that is formed by the joining of a pair of MAXILLAE (accessory mouthparts) **b** a liplike part of various INVERTEBRATE animals [NL, fr L, lip – more at LIP]

**laboratory** /lə'borətri/ *n* a place equipped for scientific experiment, testing, and analysis; *broadly* a place providing opportunity for research or practice in a field of study [ML *laboratorium*, fr L *laboratus*, pp of *laborare* to labour, fr *labor*]

**laborious** /lə'bawri-əs/ *adj* **1** industrious, diligent **2** involving or characterized by strenuous effort; laboured – **laboriously** *adv*, **laboriousness** *n*

**labor union** *n, NAm* TRADE UNION

**¹labour,** *NAm chiefly* **labor** /laybə/ *n* **1a** expenditure of effort, esp when difficult or compulsory; toil **b** human activity that provides the goods or services in an economy **c** (the period of) the physical activities involved in the birth of young **2** an act or process requiring labour; a task **3a** *taking sing or pl vb* an economic group comprising those who do manual work or work for wages ⟨*local* ∼ *isn't suitable*⟩ **4** *taking sing or pl vb, cap* the Labour party *synonyms see* ¹WORK [ME, fr OF, fr L *labor*]

**²labour,** *NAm chiefly* **labor** *vi* **1** to exert one's powers of body or mind, esp with painful or strenuous effort; work, strive **2** to move with great effort ⟨*was* ∼*ing up the stairs with the heavy shopping*⟩ **3** to be in the process of giving birth **4** to suffer from some disadvantage or distress ⟨∼ *under a delusion*⟩ **5** *of a ship* to pitch or roll heavily ∼ *vt* **1** to treat or work out in often laborious detail ⟨∼ *the obvious*⟩ ⟨∼ *the point*⟩ **2** *archaic* **2a** to spend labour on or produce by labour; *esp* to till, cultivate **b** to strive to effect or achieve

**³labour** *adj* **1** of labour **2** *cap* of or being a political party, specif one in the UK, advocating a planned socialist economy and associated with working-class interests

**Labour Day** *n* a day set aside for special recognition of working people; e g **a** the first Monday in September observed in the USA and Canada as a public holiday **b** MAY DAY

**laboured** /'laybəd/ *adj* characterized by labour and effort; *esp* lacking ease of expression ⟨*a* ∼ *speech*⟩

**labourer** /'layb(ə)rə/ *n* somebody who does unskilled manual work, esp outdoors

**labour exchange** *n, often cap L&E* a former government office that sought to find jobs for unemployed people and was responsible for paying out unemployment benefit

**labour force** *n* WORKFORCE

**'labour-in,tensive** *adj* using proportionately more labour than capital or land in the process of production – compare CAPITAL-INTENSIVE

**labourite** /'laybəriet/ *n, often cap* a member or supporter of the Labour party

**labour of love** *n* a task performed for the pleasure it yields rather than for personal gain

**labour pain** *n usu pl* one of the regularly recurrent pains that are characteristic of childbirth

**laboursaving** /-,sayving/ *adj* adapted to replace or decrease human, esp manual, labour ⟨~ *domestic appliances*⟩

**labour theory of value** *n* a theory in (Marxist) economics: the relative prices of goods are determined by the amounts of labour going into producing them

**labour ward** *n* a hospital ward or room designed to accommodate women during childbirth

**labrador** /'labrədaw/ *n, often cap* LABRADOR RETRIEVER

**labradorite** /,labrə'dawriet/ *n* a FELDSPAR (type of crystalline mineral) showing a play of several colours due to the breaking up (DIFFRACTION) of light into the colours of the spectrum [*Labrador*, region in E Canada]

**Labrador retriever** *n* a retriever largely developed in England from stock originating in Newfoundland and characterized by a short dense black or golden coat and notable breadth of head and chest [*Labrador* in Canada]

**labret** /'laybret/ *n* an ornament (e g a piece of shell) worn in a perforation of the lip [L *labrum* lip]

**labrid** /'labrid, 'laybrid/ *n* any of various important food fish (family Labridae, the wrasse family) that live in both the Mediterranean and the waters of N Europe [deriv of L *labrus, labros*, a fish]

**labroid** /'labroyd, 'lay-/ *n* a labrid

**labrum** /'labrəm, 'lay-/ *n, pl* **labra** an upper or front mouthpart of a spider, crab, shrimp, or other ARTHROPOD consisting of a single central piece in front of or above the MANDIBLES [NL, fr L, lip, edge – more at LIP]

**laburnum** /lə'buhnəm/ *n* any of a small genus (*Laburnum*) of Eurasian shrubs and trees of the pea family with pendulous bright yellow flowers and poisonous seeds; *esp* an ornamental tree (*Laburnum anagyroides*) [NL, genus name, fr L, laburnum]

**labyrinth** /'labərinth/ *n* **1** a structure of intricate passageways and blind alleys; a maze **2** something perplexingly complex or tortuous in structure, arrangement, or character **3** a tortuous anatomical structure; *esp* the INNER EAR or its bony or membranous part [ME *laborintus*, fr L *labyrinthus*, fr Gk *labyrinthos*]

**labyrinthine** /,labə'rinthien/, **labyrinthian** /,labə'rinthiən/ *adj* **1** of, like, or forming a labyrinth; intricate, involved **2** of, affecting, or originating in the INNER EAR ⟨*severe ~ irritation*⟩

**¹lac** /lak/ *n* a substance resembling RESIN (saplike plant secretion) that is secreted by a SCALE INSECT (*Laccifer lacca*) and that is purified to form SHELLAC [Per *lak* & Hindi *lākh*, fr Skt *lākṣā*]

**²lac** *n* LAKH (100 000)

**laccolith** /'lakəlith/ *n* a mass of IGNEOUS rock that is forced between beds of existing rock and produces domed bulging of the overlying layers [Gk *lakkos* cistern + E *-lith*]

**¹lace** /lays/ *n* **1** a cord or string used for drawing together two edges (e g of a garment or shoe) **2** an ornamental braid for trimming coats or uniforms **3** an openwork usu figured fabric made of thread, yarn, etc and used for trimmings, household furnishings and covers (e g curtains and tablecloths), and entire garments [ME, net, noose, cord, fr OF *laz*, fr L *laqueus* snare – more at DELIGHT] – **laced** *adj*, **laceless** *adj*, **lacelike** *adj*

**²lace** *vt* **1** to draw together the edges of (as if) by means of a lace passed through eyelets **2** to draw or pass (e g a lace) through something **3** to confine or compress by tightening laces ⟨~d *her into her corsets*⟩ **4a** to adorn (as if) with lace **b** to mark *with* streaks of colour ⟨*a red sky ~d with gold*⟩ **5a** to add a dash of an alcoholic drink, esp a spirit, to **b** to give savour, variety, or spice to ⟨*a mundane story line ~d with witty repartee*⟩ **6** *informal* to beat, lash ~ *vi* to be fastened or tied *up* with a lace [ME *lacen*, fr OF *lacier*, fr L *laqueare* to ensnare, fr *laqueus*] – **lacer** *n*

**lace into** *vt, informal* to attack vigorously

**lacebug** /'lays,bug/ *n* any of a family (Tingidae) of small TRUE BUGS that feed on plants [fr the lacy network of raised lines covering the body and wings]

**¹lacerate** /'lasərət, -rayt/, **lacerated** *adj* having the edges deeply and irregularly cut ⟨*a ~ petal*⟩

**²lacerate** /'lasərəyt/ *vt* **1** to tear or rend roughly; *esp* to wound

jaggedly **2** to cause sharp mental or emotional pain to [L *laceratus*, pp of *lacerare* to tear; akin to L *lacer* mangled, Gk *lakis* torn] – **laceration** *n*

**lacertian** /lə'suhsh(ə)n/ *adj* lacertilian

**lacertilian** /,lasə'tilyən/ *adj* of or like lizards [deriv of L *lacerta* lizard] – **lacertilian** *n*

**'lace-,up** *n, chiefly Br* a shoe or boot that is fastened with laces

**lacewing** /-,wing/ *n* any of an order (Neuroptera) of insects having delicate wings with a fine network of veins, long antennae, and brilliant eyes – called also NEUROPTERAN

**lacework** /'lays,wuhk/ *n* objects or patterns consisting of or resembling lace

**laches** /'lachiz/ *n, pl* **laches** *law* negligence in carrying out a legal duty or undue delay in asserting a legal claim [ME *lachesse*, fr MF *laschesse*, fr OF *lasche* lax, deriv of L *laxare* to loosen]

**lachrymal** /'lakriməl/, **lacrimal** *adj* **1** of or being the glands that produce tears **2** *formal* of or marked by tears [MF or ML; MF *lacrymal*, fr ML *lacrimalis, lachrymalis*, fr L *lacrima* tear – more at TEAR]

**lachrymation, lacrimation** /,lakri'maysh(ə)n/ *n* the esp abnormal or excessive secretion of tears [L *lacrimation-, lacrimatio*, fr *lacrimatus*, pp of *lacrimare* to weep, fr *lacrima*]

**lachrymator** /'lakri,maytə/ *n* a tear-producing substance (e g a TEAR GAS)

**lachrymatory** /'lakrimətri/ *adj* of or prompting tears

**lachrymose** /'lakrimohs/ *adj* **1** given to tears or weeping; tearful **2** tending to cause tears; mournful – **lachrymosely** *adv*

**lacing** /'laysing/ *n* **1** the action of one who or that which laces **2** something that laces; LACE 1 **3** a contrasting marginal band of colour (e g on a feather) **4a** a dash of spirits in a food or esp a beverage (e g coffee) that adds flavour or spice **b** a trace or sprinkling that adds savour, variety, or spice **5** a course usu of brick added to a wall of stone or rubble to increase strength **6** *informal* a beating, thrashing

**laciniate** /lə'siniayt, -ət/ *adj, of a plant or animal part* bordered with a fringe; *esp* cut into deep irregular usu pointed lobes ⟨~ *petals*⟩ [L *lacinia* flap, fringe; akin to L *lacer* mangled] – **laciniation** *n*

**¹lack** /lak/ *vi* **1** to be deficient or missing ⟨*nothing is ~ing but the will*⟩ **2** to be short or have need of something – usu + *for* ⟨*he will not ~ for advisers*⟩ ~ *vt* to stand in need of; suffer from the absence or deficiency of ⟨*he ~s skill in debate*⟩ [ME *laken*, fr MD; akin to ON *leka* to leak]

**synonyms Lack, want, need**, and **require** all mean "be without something necessary or desirable". **Lack** stresses the absence of something ⟨*she lacks confidence*⟩. **Want** may suggest a deplorable lack, or it may stress urgent necessity. As this use may be confused with **want's** other sense of "desire" ⟨*your hair wants cutting*⟩, **need** is often preferred for this meaning ⟨*your hair needs cutting*⟩, since **need** stresses necessity rather than absence. **Require** is often interchangeable with **need**, but tends to imply more compelling or significant urgency, and is rather more formal ⟨*great acts require great means of enterprise* – John Milton⟩. As a noun, **lack** suggests the total or partial failure of something expected to be found. It is often qualified, to avoid ambiguity ⟨*a total lack of proper concern*⟩. **Want** is similar, but applies only to what is desired or desirable. **Dearth** suggests scarcity rather than a complete lack of something ⟨*a dearth of good novels this season*⟩. **Absence**, unless qualified, does suggest that something is missing altogether ⟨*in the absence of brains, she got by on common sense*⟩.

**²lack** *n* **1** the fact or state of being wanting or deficient **2** something that is lacking

**lackadaisical** /,lakə'dayzikl/ *adj* lacking life, spirit, or zest; *also* (reprehensibly) casual or negligent [alter. of *lackaday* + *-ical*] – **lackadaisically** *adv*

**lackaday** /,lakə'day/ *interj, archaic* – used to express regret, dismay, or disapproval [alter. of *alack the day*]

**¹lackey** /'laki/ *n* **1** a usu liveried servant; a footman **2** a servile follower; a toady [MF *laquais*]

**²lackey** *vb* to act as a lackey (for)

**lacking** /'laking/ *adj, euph* mentally deficient; stupid

**lacklustre** /-,lustə/ *adj* lacking in sheen, radiance, or vitality; dull

**Lacombe** /lə'kohm, lə'koohm/ *n* (any of) a breed of white bacon-producing pigs developed in Canada from LANDRACE, CHESTER WHITE, and BERKSHIRE stock [*Lacombe* Experiment Station in Alberta, Canada]

**laconic** /lə'konik/ *adj* using or involving the use of a minimum

of words; concise, terse *synonyms* see CONCISE *antonyms* prolix, verbose [L *laconicus* Spartan, fr Gk *lakŏnikos;* fr the Spartan reputation for terseness of speech] – **laconically** *adv*
**laconicism** /lə'konisiz(ə)m/ *n* (a) laconism
**laconicum** /lə'konikəm/ *n, pl* **laconica** the hot dry chamber of a Roman bathhouse – compare CALIDARIUM, FRIGIDARIUM, TEPIDARIUM [L, fr neut of *laconicus*]
**laconism** /'lakə,niz(ə)m/ *n* **1** brevity or terseness of expression or style **2** a laconic expression
¹**lacquer** /'lakə/ *n* **1a** a clear or coloured varnish obtained by dissolving a substance (e g shellac) in a solvent (e g alcohol) **b** any of various durable natural varnishes; *esp* a varnish obtained from an Asiatic shrub (*Rhus verniciflua*) of the sumach family **2** a substance consisting of shellac and alcohol that is sprayed onto the hair to fix it in place [Pg *lacré* sealing wax, fr *laca* lac, fr Ar *lakk,* fr Per *lak*]
²**lacquer** *vt* to coat with lacquer – **lacquerer** *n*
**lacrimal** /'lakriml/ *adj* LACHRYMAL (of tear glands or tears)
**lacrimation** /,lakri'maysh(ə)n/ *n* LACHRYMATION (producing tears)
**lacrosse** /lə'kros/ *n* a game played on grass by two teams of 10 players whose object is to throw a ball into the opponents' goal using a long-handled stick that has a triangular head with a loose mesh pouch for catching and carrying the ball [CanF *la crosse,* lit., the crosier]
**lact-** /lakt-/, **lacti-**, **lacto-** *comb form* **1** milk ⟨lacto*flavin*⟩ **2a** LACTIC ACID ⟨lact*ate*⟩ **b** lactose ⟨lact*ase*⟩ [Fr & L; Fr, fr L, fr *lact-, lac* – more at GALAXY]
**lactase** /'laktayz, -ays/ *n* an ENZYME that breaks down certain sugars (e g LACTOSE) and occurs esp in the intestines of young mammals and in yeasts [ISV]
¹**lactate** /'laktayt/ *n* any of various chemical compounds (SALTS or ESTERS) formed by combination between LACTIC ACID and a metal atom, an alcohol, or another chemical group
²**lactate** /'laktayt, -'-/ *vi* to secrete milk [L *lactatus,* pp of *lactare,* fr *lact-, lac*]
**lactation** /lak'taysh(ə)n/ *n* (the duration of) the secretion of milk by a mammal after giving birth – **lactational** *adj*, **lactationally** *adv*
¹**lacteal** /'lakti-əl/ *adj* **1** consisting of, producing, or resembling milk **2a** conveying or containing a milky fluid **b** of the lacteals [L *lacteus,* fr *lact-, lac*]
²**lacteal** *n* any of the vessels transporting LYMPH (body fluid bathing tissues) that arise from the VILLI (fingerlike outgrowths) of the SMALL INTESTINE and convey CHYLE (type of lymph) to the THORACIC DUCT (main lymph vessel)
**lactescent** /lak'tes(ə)nt/ *adj, esp of a plant* secreting a milky juice [L *lactescent-, lactescens,* prp of *lactescere* to turn to milk, incho of *lactēre* to be milky, fr *lact-, lac* milk] – **lactescence** *n*
**lactic** /'laktik/ *adj* **1a** of milk **b** obtained from sour milk or whey **2** involving the production of LACTIC ACID
**lactic acid** *n* an acid, $C_3H_6O_3$, present normally in tissue, produced in carbohydrate matter usu by bacterial fermentation, and used esp in food and medicine and in industry
**lactiferous** /lak'tifərəs/ *adj* **1** secreting or conveying milk **2** yielding a milky juice ⟨~ *plants*⟩ [Fr or LL; Fr *lactifère,* fr LL *lactifer,* fr L *lact-, lac* + *-fer*] – **lactiferousness** *n*
**lactobacillus** /,laktohbə'siləs/ *n* any of a genus (*Lactobacillus*) of bacteria that form LACTIC ACID [NL]
**lactogenic** /,laktə'jenik/ *adj* inducing the secretion of milk
**lactoglobulin** /,laktoh'globyoolin/ *n* a protein fraction that is obtained from the whey of milk
**lactose** /'laktohz, -tohs/ *n* a sugar, $C_{12}H_{22}O_{11}$, that is a DI-SACCHARIDE consisting of the simple sugars glucose and GALACTOSE, is present in milk, and yields esp LACTIC ACID when fermented [ISV]
**lacto-vegetarianism** /laktoh-/ *n* vegetarianism that allows the consumption of certain animal products (e g milk, cheese, and sometimes eggs) – **lacto-vegetarian** *n*
**lacuna** /lə'kyoohnə/ *n, pl* **lacunae**, **lacunas 1** a blank space or missing part; a gap **2** a small cavity, pit, or discontinuity in an anatomical structure [L, pool, pit, gap – more at LAGOON] – **lacunal, lacunar, lacunary, lacunate** *adj*
**lacunar** /lə'kyoohnə/ *n, pl* **lacunaria** /,lakyoo'neəriə/ COFFER 4 (recessed panel) [L, fr *lacuna* pit]
**lacustrine** /lə'kustrien/ *adj* of, growing in, or living in lakes [Fr or It *lacustre,* fr L *lacus* lake]
**lacy** /'laysi/ *adj* like or consisting of lace
**lad** /lad/ *n* **1** a male person of any age between early boyhood and maturity; boy, youth **2** a man, fellow – used to express

male togetherness ⟨*having a few jars with the* ~s⟩ or protective affection ⟨*the* ~s *played a blinder last night*⟩ **3** *Br* STABLE LAD ⟨*the head* ~⟩ *synonyms* see GENTLEMAN *antonym* lass [ME *ladde*]
**ladanum** /'ladənəm/ *n* LABDANUM (oily substance used in perfumery)
¹**ladder** /'ladə/ *n* **1** a structure for climbing up or down that has two long sidepieces of metal, wood, rope, etc joined at intervals by crosspieces on which one may step **2** something that resembles or suggests a ladder in form or use; *specif, Br* a vertical line in hosiery or knitting caused by stitches becoming unravelled **3** a series of usu ascending steps or stages; a scale ⟨*the promotion* ~⟩ [ME, fr OE *hlæder;* akin to OHG *leitara* ladder, OE *hlinian* to lean – more at LEAN]
²**ladder** *vb, chiefly Br vi* to develop a ladder ⟨*her tights* ~ed⟩ ~ *vt* to cause a ladder to develop in ⟨*she* ~ed *her tights*⟩
¹**ladder-,back** *n or adj* (a chair) having a back consisting of two upright posts connected by horizontal slats
**ladder stitch** *n* an embroidery stitch consisting of transverse bars worked between raised often parallel lines
**laddie** /'ladi/ *n, chiefly Scot* an esp young lad
**lade** /layd/ *vb* **laded; laded, laden** /'layd(ə)n/ *vt* **1** to put a load or burden on or in; load **2** to put or place as a load, esp for shipment; ship **3** to load heavily or oppressively ⟨*trees* ~n *with fruit*⟩ ⟨~n *with sorrow*⟩ ~ *vi* to take on a load, esp cargo; load [ME *laden,* fr OE *hladan;* akin to OHG *hladan* to load, OSlav *klasti*]
*usage* This old verb has been mostly replaced by **load,** except in such phrases as ⟨*a heavily-laden bus*⟩.
**la-di-da, lah-di-dah** /,lah di 'dah/ *adj, Br informal* affectedly refined or polished; pretentiously elegant, esp in voice and pronunciation ⟨*a* ~ *accent*⟩ [perh alter. of *lardy-dardy*]
**ladies** /'laydiz/ *n taking sing vb, often cap, chiefly Br informal* a public toilet for women [short for *ladies' room, ladies' lavatory,* etc]
**ladies' man** *also* **lady's man** *n* a man who shows a marked fondness for and attentiveness to women
**ladies' room** *n* a public toilet for women
**ladies' tresses** *n taking sing or pl vb* any of a widely distributed genus (*Spiranthes*) of orchids with slender often twisted spikes of white irregular flowers
**Ladin** /la'deen/ *n* **1** ROMANSH (group of esp Swiss dialects) **2** one who speaks Romansh as a mother tongue [Rhaeto-Romanic, fr L *Latinum* Latin]
**lading** /'layding/ *n* cargo, freight [fr gerund of *lade*]
**ladino** /lə'deenoh/ *n, pl* **ladinos 1** JUDAEO-SPANISH (language) **2** *often cap* a Spanish-American of mixed descent [Sp, fr *ladino* cunning, learned, lit., Latin, fr L *latinus;* (2) AmerSp, fr Sp]
¹**ladle** /'laydl/ *n* **1** a deep-bowled long-handled spoon used esp for taking up and conveying liquids or semiliquid foods (e g soup) **2** a vessel for carrying molten metal [ME *ladel,* fr OE *hlædel,* fr *hladan*]
²**ladle** *vt* **1** to take up and convey in a ladle **2** to distribute lavishly or effusively ⟨ladling *out compliments*⟩
**lady** /'laydi/ *n* **1a** a woman having authority or rights of property, esp as a feudal superior **b** a woman receiving the homage or devotion of a knight or lover **2a** a woman of superior social position **b** a woman of refinement and gentle manners ⟨*a real* ~⟩ **c** a woman, female ⟨*the new sales director is quite a formidable* ~⟩ ⟨*Harlow's dinner ladies are still dishing up – Harlow Gazette*⟩ – often in courteous reference ⟨*show the* ~ *to a seat*⟩ or usu pl in address ⟨ladies *and gentlemen*⟩ **3** a wife ⟨*the captain and his* ~⟩ – compare OLD LADY **4** *cap* any of various titled women in Britain – used as a customary title for a marchioness, countess, viscountess, or baroness, for the wife of a knight, baronet, member of the peerage, or man having the courtesy title of *lord,* and as a courtesy title before the name and surname of the daughter of a duke, marquess, or earl **5** a female member of an order of knighthood – compare DAME [ME, fr OE *hlæfdīge,* fr *hlāf* bread + *-dīge* (akin to *dæge* kneader of bread) – more at LOAF, DAIRY]
*synonyms* **Lady, woman, girl, lass, female: woman** is the usual term for a female human being, and the term usually to be preferred ⟨*the* **woman** *next door*⟩ ⟨*a* **woman** *doctor*⟩. **Lady,** because of its earlier implications of higher social status, is retained as a term of politeness, e g in a woman's presence, and where several women are being publicly addressed ⟨**Ladies!** *please be seated*⟩. In other situations, **lady** smacks of snobbishness or gentility, though in North America, where democracy has reacted in the opposite way, there is a tendency to call all women **ladies**, and there is some tendency for

the word to be used among feminists ⟨*she's a very able* lady⟩. **Girl**, the usual term for a young human female, is increasingly applied informally, and usually without insulting intentions, to women of almost any age, married and unmarried. **Lass** is a less common alternative, applied to a more limited, younger age range. **Female** stresses biological differences and so is jocular or derogatory in other contexts. Compare GENTLEMAN, ²FEMALE

**ladybird** /-,buhd/ *n* any of numerous small nearly hemispherical often brightly coloured beetles (family Coccinellidae) of temperate and tropical regions that usu feed both as larvae and adults on other insects; *esp* any of several ladybirds that have red wing cases with black spots [Our *Lady*, the Virgin Mary]

**lady bountiful** *n, often cap L&B* a woman noted for patronizing and interfering generosity [*Lady Bountiful*, character in the play *The Beaux' Stratagem* by George Farquhar †1707 Ir dramatist]

**ladybug** /-,bug/ *n, NAm* a ladybird

**lady chapel** *n, often cap L&C* a chapel dedicated to the Virgin Mary that is usu part of a larger church

**Lady Day** *n* March 25 observed as the feast of the Annunciation

**lady-in-'waiting** *n, pl* **ladies-in-waiting** a lady of a queen's or princess's household appointed to wait on her

**'lady-,killer** *n, informal* a man who captivates women

**ladylike** /-,liek/ *adj* **1** resembling a lady, esp in manners; well-bred **2** suitable to a lady *synonyms* see ²FEMALE *antonym* gentlemanly

**ladylove** /'laydi,luv/ *n* a sweetheart, mistress

**lady's bedstraw** /'bed,straw/ *n* a common Eurasian BEDSTRAW (type of plant) (*Galium verum*) with bright yellow flowers

**lady's fingers** *n pl* OKRA (green vegetable in the form of pods)

**ladyship** /-ship/ *n* – used as a title to address or refer to a woman having the rank of lady ⟨*her* Ladyship *is not at home*⟩

**lady's slipper** *n* any of several temperate-zone orchids (genus *Cypripedium*) having flowers whose shape suggests a slipper

**'lady's-,smock** *n* CUCKOOFLOWER 1

**Laetare Sunday** /li'teəri, lay'tahri/ *n* the fourth Sunday in Lent [L *laetare*, 2 sing. imper of *laetari* to rejoice, the opening word of the introit for this day]

**Laetrile** /'laytriel/ *trademark* – used for the drug AMYGDALIN that is believed to be of use in the treatment of cancer

**laev-** /leev-/, **laevo-**, *NAm* **lev-**, **levo-** *comb form* **1** laevorotatory ⟨*laevulose*⟩ **2** to the left ⟨*laevorotatory*⟩ [L *laevus* left; akin to Gk *laios* left]

**laevo** /'leevoh/ *adj* laevorotatory

**laevodopa** /'leevoh,dohpə/ *n* L-DOPA (type of AMINO ACID)

**laevorotatory** /-'rohtət(ə)ri, -roh'tayt(ə)ri/, **laevorotary** /-'rohtəri/ *adj* turning towards the left or anticlockwise; *esp, of a chemical compound* rotating the plane of POLARIZATION of light to the left – compare DEXTROROTATORY – **laevorotation** *n*

**laevulose** /'levyoolohs, -lohz/ *n* FRUCTOSE (type of sugar) [ISV, irreg fr *laev-* + *-ose*]

**'lag** /lag/ *vi* **-gg-** **1a** to stay or fall behind; linger, loiter – often + *behind* **b** to move, advance, or develop with comparative slowness; fail to keep pace – often + *behind* **2** to slacken or weaken gradually; flag **3** to toss or roll a marble towards a line or a billiard ball towards the top cushion to determine order of play [prob of Scand origin; akin to Norw *lagga* to go slowly] – **lagger** *n*

**²lag** *n* **1** the act or an instance of lagging **2** comparative slowness or retardation **3** an interval, esp between related events or phenomena; *specif* TIME LAG

**³lag** *vt* **-gg-** *slang* **1** to send to prison **2** to arrest [origin unknown]

**⁴lag** *n, slang* **1** a convict **2** an ex-convict – esp in *old lag* **3** a term of imprisonment

**⁵lag** *n* lagging [orig sense, stave of a barrel, wooden covering or casing; prob of Scand origin; akin to ON *lögg* rim of a barrel]

**⁶lag** *vt* **-gg-** to cover or provide with lagging – **lagger** *n*

**lagan** /'lagən/ *n* goods thrown into the sea with a buoy attached so that they may be found again; *also* goods lying on the seabed [MF *lagan* or ML *laganum* debris washed up from the sea, prob of Gmc origin]

**lagend** /'lagənd/ *n* lagan

**lager** /'lahgə/ *n* a light beer brewed by slow fermentation and stored in refrigerated cellars for maturing [Ger *lagerbier* beer made for storage, fr *lager* storehouse + *bier* beer]

**laggard** /'lagəd/ *n* one who or that which lags behind or lingers – **laggardly** *adj or adv*

**lagging** /'laging/ *n* **1** material for thermal insulation (e g wrapped round a boiler or laid in a roof) **2** planking used esp for preventing cave-ins in earthwork or for supporting an arch during construction

**lagniappe** /lan'yap, '--/ *n, chiefly NAm* a small gift given to a customer by a merchant at the time of a purchase; *broadly* something given or obtained gratuitously or by way of good measure [AmerF, fr AmerSp *la nâpa* the lagniappe]

**lagomorph** /'lagə,mawf/ *n* any of an order (Lagomorpha) of gnawing mammals having two pairs of INCISORS (biting teeth) in the upper jaw one behind the other and comprising the rabbits, hares, and PIKAS [deriv of Gk *lagōs* hare + *morphē* form] – **lagomorphic, lagomorphous** *adj*

**lagoon** /lə'goohn/ *n* **1** a shallow channel or pool usu separated from a larger body of water by a sandbank, reef, etc **2** a shallow artificial pool or pond (e g for the processing of sewage or sludge or storage of a liquid) [Fr & It; Fr *lagune*, fr It *laguna*, fr L *lacuna* pit, pool, fr *lacus* lake]

**laguna** /lə'goohnə/ *n* a small lake or pond [Sp, fr L *lacuna*]

**lah, la** /lah/ *n* the 6th note of the scale in the SOL-FA method of representing the musical scale [ME *la*, fr ML – more at GAMUT]

**lah-di-dah** /,lah di 'dah/ *adj* la-di-da

**Lahnda** /'lahndə/ *n* an INDIC language of the W Punjab

**laic** /'layik/, **laical** /'layikl/ *adj* of the laity; secular [LL *laicus*, fr LGk *laikos* fr Gk, of the people, fr *laos* people] – **laically** *adv*

**laicism** /'layi,siz(ə)m/ *n* a political movement or programme having secularization as its principal aim

**laic·ize, -ise** /'layi,siez/ *vt* **1** to change to lay status **2** to put (e g a school) under the direction of laymen; *also* to open to laymen – **laicization** *n*

**¹laid** /layd/ *past of* LAY

**²laid** *n* paper watermarked with fine lines running across the grain – compare WOVE [*laid (paper)*, fr pp of ¹*lay*]

**,laid-'back** *adj, informal* relaxed, casual – compare COOL

**lain** /layn/ *past part of* LIE

**¹lair** /leə/ *n* **1** the resting or living place of a wild animal; a den **2** a refuge or place for hiding [ME, fr OE *leger* act of lying, grave, bed; akin to OHG *legar* bed, OE *licgan* to lie – more at LIE]

**²lair** *vi* to go to or rest in a lair ~ *vt* to place in a lair

**³lair** *n, Austr derog* a showily dressed young man [back-formation fr *lairy*]

**laird** /leəd/ *n, Scot* a member of the landed gentry [ME (northern) *lord*, *lard* lord] – **lairdly** *adj*

**lairy** /'leəri/ *adj, slang* **1** *Br* artful **2** *Austr* flashy [prob alter. of *leery* (in the sense "wide-awake, knowing")]

**laissez-aller** /,lesay 'alay (Fr lese ale)/ *n, formal* lack of constraint [Fr, fr *laissez aller* let (someone) go

**laissez-faire, *Br also* laisser-faire** /,lesay 'feə (Fr lese fεr)/ *n* **1** a doctrine opposing government interference in economic affairs **2** *chiefly derog* deliberate refraining from interference with esp individual freedom of choice and action [Fr *laissez faire*, imper of *laisser faire* to let (people) do (as they choose)] – **laissez-faire** *adj*

**laissez-passer** /,lesay pa'say (Fr lese pase)/ *n, formal* a permit, pass [Fr, fr *laissez passer* let (someone) pass]

**laitance** /'layt(ə)ns/ *n* an accumulation of fine particles on the surface of fresh concrete due to an upward movement of water (e g when excessive mixing water is used) [Fr, fr *lait* milk, fr L *lact-, lac* – more at GALAXY]

**laity** /'layəti/ *n taking sing or pl vb* **1** the people of a religion other than its clergy **2** the mass of the people as distinguished from those of a particular profession or those specially skilled [⁵*lay* + *-ity*]

**¹lake** /layk/ *n* **1** a large inland body of water; *also* a pool of other liquid (e g lava, oil, or pitch) **2** an accumulation of some surplus liquid (agricultural) product ⟨*a wine* ~⟩ – compare MOUNTAIN 2a [ME, fr OF *lac*, fr L *lacus*; akin to OE *lagu* sea, Gk *lakkos* pond]

**²lake** *n* **1a** a deep purplish-red pigment originally prepared from substances derived from certain insects **b** any of numerous usu bright translucent pigments composed essentially of a soluble organic dye and a chemical compound of a metal **2** a vivid red colour; CARMINE 2 [Fr *laque* lac, fr OProv *laca*, fr Ar *lakk* – more at LACQUER] – **laky** *adj*

**lake dwelling** *n* a dwelling built on posts in a lake; *esp* one built in prehistoric times – **lake dweller** *n*

**Lakeland terrier** /'layklənd/ *n* (any of) an English breed of rather small wirehaired straight-legged terriers [*Lakeland* (Lake District), region in NW England where the breed was developed]

**lakh** /lak/ *n, pl* **lakhs** *also* **lakh** *chiefly Ind* **1** one hundred thousand ⟨*50* ∼s *of rupees*⟩ **2** a great number [Hindi *lākh*, fr Skt *lakṣa*, lit., mark, sign]

**-lalia** /-'laylyə/ *comb form* (→ *n*) speech disorder (of a specified type) ⟨*echolalia*⟩ [NL, fr Gk *lalia* chatter, fr *lalein* to chat]

**Lallan** /'lalən/ *adj, Scot* of the Lowlands of Scotland [var of *lowland*]

**Lallans** /'lalənz/ *n taking sing vb* Lowland Scots dialect

**lallation** /la'laysh(ə)n/ *n* a speech fault whereby /r/ is pronounced as /l/ [L *lallare* to sing a lullaby]

**¹lam** /lam/ *vb* **-mm-** *informal vt* to beat soundly; thrash ∼ *vi* **1** to strike, thrash **2** *NAm* to flee hastily; scram [of Scand origin; akin to ON *lemja* to thrash; akin to OE *lama* lame]

**²lam** *n, NAm informal* sudden or hurried flight, esp from the law

**lama** /'lahmə/ *n* a Lamaist monk ⚠ **llama** [Tibetan *blama*]

**Lamaism** /'lahmə,iz(ə)m/ *n* a form of Buddhism of Tibet and Mongolia in which the monks practise elaborate ritual and are headed by the DALAI LAMA – **Lamaist** *n or adj*, **Lamaistic** *adj*

**Lamarckism** /lah'mah,kiz(ə)m/ *n* a theory of evolution proposing that structural changes acquired by plants and animals in response to changes in their environment can be transmitted to their offspring – compare CLADISTICS, LYSENKOISM, NEO-DARWINISM [J B de Monet *Lamarck* †1829 Fr naturalist] – **Lamarckian** *adj or n*

**lamasery** /'lahməsəri/ *n* a monastery of lamas [Fr *lamaserie*, fr *lama* + Per *sarāī* palace]

**¹lamb** /lam/ *n* **1a** a young sheep, esp one that is less than one year old or without permanent teeth **b** the young of various animals (e g the smaller antelopes) other than sheep **2a** a gentle, meek, or innocent person **b** a dear, pet **3a** the flesh of a lamb used as food **b** lambskin [ME, fr OE; akin to OHG *lamb* lamb, *elaho* elk – more at ELK]

**²lamb** *vi* to give birth to a lamb ∼ *vt* **1** to give birth to (a lamb) **2** to tend (ewes) at lambing time – **lamber** *n*

**lambaste** /lam'bayst, lam'bast/, **lambast** *vt* **1** to beat, thrash **2** to attack verbally; censure, scold [prob fr ¹*lam* + *baste*]

**lambda** /'lamdə/ *n* **1** the 11th letter of the Greek alphabet **2** a minute particle of matter that has no electric charge and has a mass 2183 times that of an electron [Gk, of Sem origin; akin to Heb *lāmedh* lamed]

**lambdacism** /'lamdə,siz(ə)m/ *n* LALLATION (a speech defect) [LL *labdacismus*, fr Gk *labdakismos*, fr *labda*, *lambda* lambda]

**lambent** /'lamb(ə)nt/ *adj, chiefly poetic* **1** playing lightly on or over a surface; flickering ⟨∼ *flames*⟩ **2** softly bright or radiant ⟨*eyes* ∼ *with love*⟩ **3** marked by lightness or brilliance, esp of expression ⟨*a* ∼ *wit*⟩ *synonyms* see BRIGHT [L *lambent-, lambens*, prp of *lambere* to lick – more at ⁴LAP] – **lambently** *adv*, **lambency** *n*

**lambert** /'lambət/ *n* a unit of surface brightness equal to one LUMEN per square centimetre [Johann *Lambert* †1777 Ger physicist & philosopher]

**Lambeth degree** /'lambəth/ *n* an honorary degree conferred by the Archbishop of Canterbury [*Lambeth* Palace in London, residence of the Archbishop of Canterbury]

**lambkin** /'lamkin/ *n* **1** a little lamb **2** – used as an affectionate name for a small child

**lambrequin** /'lamb(r)ə,kin/ *n* **1** a scarf used to cover a knight's helmet **2** *chiefly NAm* a short decorative piece of drapery for a shelf edge or for the top of a window or door; a valance [Fr]

**lambskin** /'lam,skin/ *n* **1** (the leather made from) the skin of a lamb or small sheep **2** lambskin leather with the wool on, used esp for winter clothing

**¹lame** /laym/ *adj* **1a** having a body part, esp a leg, so disabled as to prevent freedom of movement; *esp* having a limp caused by a disabled leg **b** *of a body part* disabled **2** weak, unconvincing ⟨*a* ∼ *excuse*⟩ [ME, fr OE *lama*; akin to OHG *lam* lame, Lith *limti* to break down] – **lamely** *adv*, **lameness** *n*

**²lame** *vt* **1** to make lame; cripple **2** to make weak or ineffective; disable

**³lame** *n* **1** a thin plate, esp of metal; LAMINA 1 **2** *pl* small overlapping steel plates joined to slide on one another (e g in medieval armour) [MF, fr L *lamina*]

**lamé** /'lahmay/ *n* a lustrous clothing fabric made from any of various fibres combined with transverse metallic threads, often of gold or silver [Fr, fr *lamé* worked with gold or silver thread, fr *lame* thin metal plate, gold or silver thread]

**lamebrain** /-,brayn/ *n, NAm informal* a hopelessly ineffectual or foolish person; a crackpot – **lamebrain, lamebrained** *adj*

**lamed** /'lahmid/ *n* the 12th letter of the Hebrew alphabet [Heb *lāmedh*, lit., ox goad]

**lame duck** *n* **1** somebody or something (e g a person or business) that is weak, ineffective, or incapable **2** *NAm* an elected officer or group continuing to hold political office during a usu brief interim before the election and inauguration of a successor

**lamell-** /-lə'mel-/, **lamelli-** *comb form* lamella ⟨lamelli*form*⟩ ⟨lamel*lose*⟩ [NL, fr *lamella*]

**lamella** /lə'melə/ *n, pl* **lamellae** /-li/ *also* **lamellas** a thin flat scale, membrane, or part: e g **a** any of the thin plates composing the gills of oysters, mussels, or similar shellfish **b** a gill of a mushroom [NL, fr L, dim. of *lamina* thin plate] – **lamellar** *adj*, **lamellarly** *adv*, **lamellate** *adj*

**lamellation** /,lamə'laysh(ə)n/ *n* **1** formation or division into lamellae **2** a lamella

**lamellibranch** /lə'meli,brangk/ *n, pl* **lamellibranchs** any of a class (Lamellibranchia of the phylum Mollusca) of INVERTEBRATE animals (e g clams, oysters, and mussels) that have a flattened body enclosed within a fold of skin (MANTLE 2b(1)) that produces a shell whose right and left parts are connected by a hinge over the animal's back – called also BIVALVE [NL *Lamellibranchia*, class name, fr *lamell-* + L *branchia* gill – more at BRANCHIA] – **lamellibranch** *adj*, **lamellibranchiate** *adj or n*

**lamellicorn** /lə'meli,kawn/ *adj* of or belonging to a group (superfamilies Scarabaeoidea or Lamellicornia) of large beetles (e g the STAG BEETLE) that are characterized by their club-shaped antennae [deriv of NL *lamell-* + L *cornu* horn – more at HORN] – **lamellicorn** *n*

**lamelliform** /lə'meli,fawm/ *adj* having the form of a thin plate

**¹lament** /lə'ment/ *vi* to feel or express grief, sorrow, or deep regret; mourn aloud – often + *for* or *over* ∼ *vt* to lament or mourn for, esp demonstratively [MF & L; MF *lamenter*, fr L *lamentari*, fr *lamentum*, n, lament; akin to ON *lōmr* loon, L *latrare* to bark, Gk *lēros* nonsense]

**²lament** *n* **1** an expression of grief; a wail **2** a dirge, elegy

**lamentable** /'lamәntәbl; *also* lə'mentəbl *the last pron is disliked by some speakers*/ *adj* **1** that is to be regretted or lamented; deplorable **2** expressing grief; mournful ⟨*a faint and* ∼ *cry* – Walter de la Mare⟩ – **lamentableness** *n*, **lamentably** *adv*

**lamentation** /,lamən'taysh(ə)n/ *n* an act or instance of lamenting

**Lamentations** /,lamən'taysh(ə)nz/ *n taking sing vb* – see BIBLE table

**lamia** /'laymiə/ *n* a female demon in classical mythology, esp one who preyed on human beings and sucked their blood [ME, fr L, fr Gk, devouring monster – more at LEMUR]

**lamin-** /lamin-/, **lamini-**, **lamino-** *comb form* lamina; laminae ⟨lamin*ar*⟩ ⟨lamin*itis*⟩

**lamina** /'laminə/ *n, pl* **laminae** /-ni/, **laminas 1** a thin plate, scale, layer, or flake **2** the broad flat part of a leaf, as distinct from its stem **3** any of the narrow thin parallel plates of soft sensitive tissue that cover the flesh within the wall of a hoof [L]

**lamina propria** /'prohpriə/ *n, pl* **laminae propriae** /-pri,ee/ *anatomy* BASEMENT MEMBRANE [NL, lit., lamina proper]

**laminar** /'laminə/ *adj* arranged in, consisting of, or resembling laminae

**laminar flow** *n* a smooth nonturbulent flow of gases or liquids passing over or near a solid usu streamlined surface – compare TURBULENT FLOW

**laminaria** /,lami'neəriə/ *n* any of various usu large chiefly perennial brown seaweeds (KELPS) (order Laminarides, esp genus *Laminaria*) that typically have an unbranched stalk with a broad, flattened, and smooth or convoluted blade [NL, genus name] – **laminarian** *adj or n*

**laminarin** /,lami'neərin/ *n* a starchlike chemical compound that is found in various seaweeds (e g laminaria) [ISV *laminar-* (fr NL *Laminaria*) + *-in*]

**¹laminate** /'lami,nayt/ *vt* **1** to roll or compress (e g metal) into a thin plate **2** to separate into laminae **3** to make by uniting superimposed layers of one or more materials **4** to cover with a thin sheet or sheets of material (e g metal or plastic) ∼ *vi* to separate into laminae – **laminator** *n*

**²laminate** /'laminət, -nayt/ *adj* **1** consisting of laminae **2** bearing or covered with laminae

[3]**laminate** /'laminət, -nayt/ *n* a product made by laminating

**laminated** /'laminaytid/ *adj* 1 LAMINATE 1 2a composed of layers of firmly united material b made by bonding or impregnating superimposed layers (eg of paper, wood, or fabric) with resin and compressing under heat

**lamination** /ˌlami'naysh(ə)n/ *n* 1 laminating or being laminated 2 a laminate structure 3 a lamina

**Laminboard** /'laminˌbawd/ *trademark* – used for a plywood similar to BLOCKBOARD but made of thinner strips of wood

**lamington** /'lamingtən/ *n* an esp Australian cake that is made by dipping a cube of sponge cake in chocolate and coconut [prob fr Charles Baillie, Lord *Lamington* †1940 Br Governor of Queensland]

**laminitis** /ˌlami'nietəs/ *n* inflammation of the lining of the hoof of esp a horse, accompanied by heat, pain, and lameness and caused by overeating or by excessive exertion on hard surfaces [NL]

**Lammas** /'laməs/ *n* 1 *also* **Lammas Day** August 1 formerly celebrated in England as a harvest festival 2 *also* **Lammastide** /-ˌtied/ the time of the year around Lammas [ME *Lammasse*, fr OE *hlāfmæsse*, fr *hlāf* loaf, bread + *mæsse* mass; fr the former consecration on this day of loaves made from the first ripe grain]

**lammergeier, lammergeyer** /'laməˌgie-ə/ *n* a large vulture (*Gypaetus barbatus*) that lives in mountain regions from the Pyrenees to N China and in flight resembles a huge falcon [Ger *lämmergeier*, fr *lämmer* lambs + *geier* vulture]

**lamp** /lamp/ *n* 1 any of various devices for producing visible light: eg **1a** a vessel containing an inflammable substance (eg oil, gas, or wax) that is burnt to give out artificial light – compare HURRICANE LAMP, SAFETY LAMP b a usu portable electric device containing a light bulb 2 any of various light-emitting devices (eg a sunlamp) used for the invisible radiation (eg heat) which they produce 3 a source of intellectual or spiritual illumination [ME, fr OF *lampe*, fr L *lampas*, fr Gk, fr *lampein* to shine; akin to ON *leiptr* lightning]

**lampblack** /-ˌblak/ *n* a finely powdered black soot used chiefly as a pigment (eg in paints, enamels, and printing inks) [fr the black soot deposited by the flame of a smoking oil lamp]

**lampbrush chromosome** /'lampˌbrush/ *n* a greatly enlarged CHROMOSOME (strand of gene-carrying material) that is covered with fine hairlike loops and is characteristic of some animal reproductive cells dividing to form eggs [fr its resemblance to a brush for cleaning oil lamps or bottles]

**lamper eel** /'lampə/ *n* a lamprey [by alter.]

**lampern** /'lampən/ *n* a European river lamprey (*Lampetra fluviatilis*) [ME *lamproun*, fr MF *lamprion*, dim. of *lamproie* lamprey, fr OF *lampreie*]

**lamplighter** /-ˌlietə/ *n* one whose occupation was to light and extinguish street lamps

[1]**lampoon** /lam'poohn/ *n* 1 a harsh and scathing written attack usu ridiculing an individual; a satire – compare CARICATURE, SKIT 2 a light and mocking satire against somebody or something [Fr *lampon*, prob fr *lampons* let us drink (a common refrain in drinking songs), fr *lamper* to drink, guzzle]

[2]**lampoon** *vt* to make the subject of a lampoon; ridicule – **lampooner, lampoonist** *n*, **lampoonery** *n*

**lamp post** *n* a post, usu of metal or concrete, that supports a light which illuminates a street or other public area (eg a park)

**lamprey** /'lampri/ *n* any of several eel-like aquatic vertebrates (order Petromyzonida) that are widely distributed in both fresh and salt water and have a large jawless mouth adapted for sucking by which they attach themselves to fishes on which they feed parasitically [ME, fr OF *lampreie*, fr ML *lampreda* (cf LIMPET)]

**lampshade** /-ˌshayd/ *n* a usu decorative, translucent, and removable cover placed round a source of artificial light, esp an electric light bulb, to reduce glare

**lampshell** /'lampˌshel/ *n* BRACHIOPOD (marine shellfish that has tentacles with which it feeds) [fr the resemblance of the shell and its protruding stalk to an ancient oil lamp with the wick protruding]

**lamp standard** *n* LAMP POST

**lanai** /lah'nie, lə-/ *n* a porch or verandah that serves, esp in summer, as an open-air living room [Hawaiian]

**lanate** /'laynayt/ *adj* woolly [L *lanatus*, fr *lana* wool]

**Lanby buoy** /'lanbi/ *n* a large navigational buoy fitted with a light, fog signal, and radar beacon and designed to replace lightships [*Large automatic navigational buoy*]

**Lancashire** /'langkəshiə, -shə/ *n* a whitish-yellow crumbly-textured cheese with a high fat content and a flavour that ranges from mild to tangy as the cheese matures [*Lancashire*, county in NW England]

**Lancastrian** /lang'kastri-ən/ *n or adj* 1 (a supporter) of the English royal house of Lancaster that ruled from 1399 to 1461 2 (a native or inhabitant) of Lancashire [John of Gaunt, Duke of *Lancaster* †1399; (2) *Lancaster*, county town of Lancashire]

[1]**lance** /lahns/ *n* 1 a weapon of war consisting of a long shaft with a sharp steel head carried by horsemen for use in charging 2 any of various sharp objects suggestive of a lance: eg **2a** a lancet b a spear used for killing whales 3 LANCER 1b [ME, fr OF, fr L *lancea*]

[2]**lance** *vt* **1a** to pierce (as if) with a lance b to open (as if) with a lancet ⟨~ *a boil*⟩ 2 to throw out or forward· ~ *vi* to move forward (as if) by cutting one's way ⟨*bombers would buzz overhead and* ~ *towards shore* – Norman Mailer⟩ [ME *launcen*, fr MF *lancer*, fr LL *lanceare*, fr L *lancea*]

**lance corporal** *n* – see MILITARY RANKS table [*lance* fr obs *lancepesade* lance corporal, fr MF *lancepessade*, fr OIt *lancia spezzata* seasoned soldier, lit., broken lance]

**lancelet** /'lahnslit/ *n* any of various small marine fishlike animals (subphylum Cephalochordata) that live usu buried in sand and resemble the probable ancestors of VERTEBRATE animals [[1]*lance* + *-let*]

**lanceolate** /'lahnsi-əlayt, -lət/ *adj* shaped like a lance head; *specif* tapering to a point at the tip and sometimes at the base ⟨~ *leaves*⟩ [LL *lanceolatus*, fr L *lanceola*, dim. of *lancea*] – **lanceolately** *adv*

**lancer** /'lahnsə/ *n* **1a** one who carries a lance b a member of a military unit formerly composed of lightly armed cavalry that carry lances 2 *pl but taking sing vb* (the music for) a dance consisting of five movements arranged for groups of four or more couples

**lancet** /'lahnsit/ *n* 1 a sharp-pointed and commonly two-edged surgical instrument used to make small cuts 2 a narrow opening (eg for a window) with a pointed top [ME *lancette*, fr MF, dim. of *lance*]

**lancet window** *n* a high window composed of one or more lancets, that has an acutely pointed head and no ornamental stonework

**lancewood** /'lahnsˌwood/ *n* (a tree that produces) a tough elastic wood used esp for shafts, fishing rods, and bows

**lancinating** /'lahnsiˌnayting/ *adj* piercing, stabbing ⟨~ *pain*⟩ [fr prp of *lancinate* (to pierce, lacerate), fr L *lancinatus*, pp of *lancinare*; akin to L *lacer* mangled – more at LACERATE] – **lancination** *n*

[1]**land** /land/ *n* **1a** the solid part of the surface of the earth; *also* a corresponding part of the moon, a planet, etc b ground or soil of a specified situation, nature, or quality ⟨*wet* ~⟩ ⟨*ploughed* ~⟩ c the surface of the earth and all its natural resources 2 a portion of the earth's solid surface distinguishable by boundaries or ownership: eg **2a** a country ⟨*campaigned in every corner of the* ~⟩ b **land, lands** *pl* privately or publicly owned land ⟨*had some* ~ *in the country*⟩ 3 a realm, domain ⟨*in the* ~ *of dreams*⟩ 4 *taking sing or pl vb* the people of a country ⟨*the* ~ *rose in rebellion*⟩ 5 (*the* way of life in) *the* rural and esp agricultural regions of a country ⟨*going back to the* ~⟩ 6 land left unploughed between furrows 7 an area of a surface that is left between holes, grooves, etc, (eg the space between the grooves of a rifle bore or of a musical record) [ME, fr OE; akin to OHG *lant* land, OIr *lann* open space] – **landless** *adj*

[2]**land** *vt* 1 to set or put on shore from a ship **2a** to set down (eg passengers or goods) after transporting b to cause to reach or come to rest in a particular place or position ⟨*never* ~ed *a punch*⟩ c to bring to a specified condition ⟨*his carelessness* ~ed *him in trouble*⟩ d to bring (eg an aeroplane) to a landing 3 to catch and bring in (eg a fish) 4 *Br informal* to present *with* something unwanted; burden ⟨~ed *me with the job of cleaning up the mess*⟩ 5 *informal* to hit (someone) with (a blow) ⟨~ed *him one on the nose*⟩ 6 *informal* to gain, secure ⟨~ *a job*⟩ ~ *vi* **1a** to go ashore from a ship; disembark **b(1)** *of a ship, boat, etc* to come to shore **b(2)** to arrive on shore in a boat, ship, etc 2a to come to the end of a course or to a stage in a journey; end up – often + *up* ⟨*took the wrong bus and* ~ed *up on the other side of town*⟩ b to strike or meet a surface (eg after a fall) ⟨~ed *on his head*⟩ **c(1)** *of an aircraft or spacecraft* to alight on a surface **c(2)** to arrive in an aircraft, spacecraft, etc which has alighted on a surface – see also **land on one's** FEET (at FOOT), **land in somebody's** LAP

**Land** /land (Ger lant)/ *n*, *pl* **Länder** /'landə (Ger 'lɛndər)/ a province in the Federal Republic of Germany or in Austria [Ger, land, country, province, fr OHG *lant* land]

**land agent** *n* ESTATE AGENT

**landau** /'landaw/ *n* **1** a four-wheeled carriage that has a raised seat outside for the driver and a folding top divided into two sections that can be let down, folded back, or removed **2** a closed car body with a folding top over the rear passenger compartment [*Landau*, town in S Germany where it was first made]

**landaulet** /,landə'let/ *n* a small landau

**land breeze** *n* a breeze blowing seawards from the land, generally at night

**land crab** *n* any of various crabs (family Gecarcinidae) that live mostly on land and breed in the sea

**landed** /'landid/ *adj* **1** owning land ⟨~ *gentry*⟩ **2** consisting of or derived from land or REAL ESTATE ⟨~ *property*⟩

**lander** /'landə/ *n* one who lands; also a space vehicle that is designed to land on the moon, a planet, etc

**landfall** /-,fawl/ *n* **1** an act or instance of sighting or reaching land after a voyage or flight **2** the land first sighted on a voyage or flight

**landform** /-,fawm/ *n* a feature of the earth's surface attributable to natural causes (e g a hill, lake, or beach)

**land-grabber** *n* one who seizes land by illegal or unfair means

**landholder** /-,hohldə/ *n*, *NAm* a holder or owner of land – **landholding** *adj or n*

**landing** /'landing/ *n* **1** an act or process of going or bringing to a surface from the air or to shore from the water **2** a place for discharging and taking on passengers and cargo **3** a level space at the top of a flight of stairs or between two flights of stairs

**landing craft** *n* a naval craft designed for putting troops and equipment ashore

**landing field** *n* a field where aircraft may land and take off

**landing gear** *n* the undercarriage of an aircraft

**landing net** *n* a small net with a handle, used to land hooked fish from the water

**landing stage** *n* a usu floating and moored platform for landing passengers or cargo

**landing strip** *n* a runway without normal airfield or airport facilities; an airstrip

**landlady** /-,laydi/ *n* **1** a female landlord **2** the wife of a landlord **3** the female proprietor of a guesthouse or lodging house

**land-line** *n* a telecommunications link using cables as opposed to radio transmission

**landlocked** /-,lokt/ *adj* **1** (nearly) enclosed by land ⟨*a ~ country*⟩ **2** confined to fresh water by some barrier ⟨~ *salmon*⟩

**landlord** /-,lawd/ *n* **1** a person who owns land, buildings, or accommodation for lease or rent **2** one who keeps a pub or lodging house

**landlordism** /'land,lawdiz(ə)m/ *n* an economic system or practice by which a landowner becomes a landlord by leasing esp agricultural land to tenants

**landlubber** /-,lubə/ *n*, *informal* a person unacquainted with the sea or seamanship; a landsman – **landlubberly** *adj*

**landmark** /'land,mahk/ *n* **1** an object (e g a stone or tree) that marks a boundary of land **2a** a conspicuous object on land that can be used to identify a locality **b** a structure in the body used as a point of orientation in locating other structures **3** an event or development that marks a turning point or a stage ⟨*this novel is a ~ in modern literature*⟩

**landmass** /-,mas/ *n* a large area of land ⟨*continental ~es*⟩

**land office** *n*, *NAm* a government office in which entries on and sales of public land are registered

**land-office business** *n*, *NAm informal* extensive and rapid business

**landowner** /'land,ohnə/ *n* an owner of land – **landownership** *n*, **landowning** *adj or n*

**land plaster** *n* a finely ground chalklike rock used as a fertilizer

**Landrace** /'landrays/ *n* a pig of any of several breeds locally developed in northern Europe [Dan, fr *land* + *race*]

**land rail** *n* CORNCRAKE (bird found in cornfields)

**land reform** *n* a measure designed to bring about a fair and even distribution of agricultural land, esp by government action; *also* the resulting redistribution

**¹landscape** /-,skayp/ *n* **1** natural, esp inland, scenery **2** an area of land that can be seen in a single view **3** a picture (e g a

painting or photograph) of natural inland scenery; *also* such pictures as an artistic category [D *landschap*, fr *land* + *-schap* -ship]

**²landscape** *vt* to improve (a natural landscape) by altering the plant cover ~ *vi* to engage in the occupation of landscape gardening – **landscaper** *n*

**³landscape** *adj* OBLONG b ⟨*a ~ page*⟩ – compare PORTRAIT

**landscape architect** *n* one whose profession is the arrangement of land for human use and enjoyment involving the siting of roads, buildings, and planted areas – **landscape architecture** *n*

**landscape gardener** *n* one skilled in the development and decorative planting of gardens and grounds – **landscape gardening** *n*

**'land-shark** *n* a land-grabber

**landside** /'land,sied/ *n* the flat part of a plough that guides it along a furrow and takes the side pressure when the earth is turned

**landslide** /-,slied/ *n* **1** a usu rapid movement of a mass of solid material (e g rock) down a slope; *also* the mass that moves down **2** an overwhelming victory, esp in an election

**landslip** /-,slip/ *n* a small landslide

**Landsmål, Landsmaal** /'lahntsmawl/ *n* NYNORSK (Norwegian language) [Norw, lit., language of the country]

**landsman** /'landzmən/ *n* one who lives on the land; *esp* one who knows little or nothing of the sea or seamanship

**landward** /'landwood/ *adj* lying or being towards the land or on the side towards the land

**landwards** /'landwoodz/, *NAm chiefly* **landward** *adv* to or towards the land

**¹lane** /layn/ *n* **1** a narrow passageway or road, esp between fences or hedges; *also* a narrow street **2** a relatively narrow way or track: e g **2a** an ocean route used by or prescribed for ships **b** a strip of road for a single line of vehicles **c** AIR LANE **d** any of several parallel courses in which a competitor must stay during a race **e** a narrow hardwood surface having pins at one end and a shallow channel along each side that is used in tenpin bowling; BOWLING ALLEY [ME, fr OE *lanu*; akin to MD *lane* lane]

**²lane** *adj*, *Scot* lone [ME (Sc), var of *lone*]

**laneway** /-,way/ *n*, *chiefly Can* a lane running between or behind houses and now usu used for parking cars

**langbeinite** /'langbie,niet/ *n* a chemical compound, $K_2Mg_2(SO_4)_3$, that is much used in the fertilizer industry [Ger *langbeinit*, fr A *Langbein*, 19th-c Ger chemist]

**langlauf** /'lahng,lowf, 'lang-/ *n* cross-country running or racing on skis [Ger, fr *lang* long + *lauf* race, run] – **langlaufer** *n*

**Langobard** /'lang-gə,bahd/ *n* LOMBARD **1a** (invader of Italy in the sixth century) [L *Langobardus* Lombard] – **Langobardic** *adj*

**langouste** /'long-goohst, -'-/ *n* SPINY LOBSTER [Fr]

**lang syne** /,lang 'sien; *often* 'zien/ *n or adv*, *chiefly Scot* (times) long ago ⟨*should auld acquaintance be forgot, and days o' auld ~* – Robert Burns⟩ [ME (Sc), fr *lang* long + *syne* since]

**language** /'lang-gwij/ *n* **1a** those words, their pronunciation, and the methods of combining them which are used and understood by a particular people, nation, etc ⟨*the English ~*⟩ **b(1)** (the ability to make and use) audible, articulate, meaningful sound by the action of the vocal organs **b(2)** a systematic means of communicating ideas or feelings by the use of conventionalized signs, sounds, gestures, or marks having understood meanings **b(3)** the suggestion by objects, actions, or conditions of associated ideas or feelings ⟨*body ~*⟩ **b(4)** the means by which animals communicate **b(5)** a formal system of signs and symbols (e g for use in programming a computer) together with rules for their use **b(6)** MACHINE LANGUAGE **2a** a particular form or manner of verbal expression; *specif* style **b** the specialized vocabulary and phraseology belonging to a particular group or profession ⟨*legal ~*⟩ **c** abusive, impolite or irreligious speech ⟨*mind your ~*⟩ ⟨*pardon my ~*⟩ **3** the study of language, esp as a school subject [ME, fr OF, fr *langue* tongue, language, fr L *lingua* – more at TONGUE] – **speak the same language** to have the same interests, ideas, etc; get on well together

synonyms Language, speech, tongue, idiom: language is the usual term for the body of words used by a people, or for that employed by specialists in a given field amongst themselves. Tongue may refer to a dialect of some kind, as well as to a standard language. Speech refers almost always to the spoken language. Idiom suggests a distinctive use of language by the people of a country, or sometimes a district ⟨*the British* idiom *is not always easy for Ameri-*

*cans to understand*⟩. **Idiom** may also be used for the private or distinctive language of a group or literary school ⟨*a poem in the pastoral idiom*⟩. Compare DIALECT

**language laboratory** *n* a room equipped with tape recorders in cubicles and sometimes with other audiovisual equipment where foreign languages are learnt by listening and speaking; *also* this method of language learning

**langue** /long·g (*Fr* lä:g)/ *n* language regarded as a system of elements or a set of habits common to a community of speakers – compare PAROLE, COMPETENCE 2 [Fr, lit., language]

**langue de chat** /,long də 'shah (*Fr* lä də ʃa)/ *n* a long thin finger-shaped piece of chocolate; *also* a crisp biscuit of the same shape [Fr, lit., cat's tongue]

**langue d'oc** /'long·gə ,dok (*Fr* lä:g dɔk)/ *n* PROVENÇAL 2 (language spoken in France); *esp* medieval Provençal [Fr, fr OF, lit., language of *oc*; fr the Provençal use of the word *oc* for "yes"]

**langue d'oïl** /do'eel (*Fr* dɔil)/ *n* (the medieval French dialects of N France which formed the basis of) modern French [Fr, fr OF, lit., language of *oïl*; fr the French use of the word *oïl* for "yes"]

**languet** /'lang·gwet/ *n* something resembling the tongue in form or function [ME, fr MF *languete*, dim. of *langue*]

**languid** /'lang·gwid/ *adj* **1** drooping or flagging (as if) from exhaustion; weak **2a** sluggish in character or disposition; listless, apathetic **b** *of a literary style* lacking colour, uninteresting **3** lacking force, vigour, or quickness of movement; slow, dull [MF *languide*, fr L *languidus*, fr *languēre* to languish – more at SLACK] – **languidly** *adv*, **languidness** *n*

**languish** /'lang·gwish/ *vi* **1a** to be or become feeble or weak **b** to be or live in a state of depression or decreasing vitality **2a** to become dispirited; pine – often + *for* **b** to lose intensity or urgency (e g from being neglected or disregarded) ⟨*his interest* ~ed⟩ **c** to suffer hardship or neglect ⟨~ed *in prison for two years*⟩ **3** to assume an expression of grief or emotion appealing for sympathy [ME *languishen*, fr MF *languiss-*, stem of *languir*, fr (assumed) VL *languire*, fr L *languēre*] – **languisher** *n*, **languishingly** *adv*, **languishment** *n*

**languor** /'lang·gə/ *n* **1** weakness or weariness of body or mind **2** listless indolence; dreaminess **3** heavy or sleep-inducing stillness ⟨*a certain* ~ *in the air*⟩ *synonyms* see LETHARGY [ME, fr OF, fr L, fr *languēre*] – **languorous** *adj*, **languorously** *adv*

**langur** /lung'gooə/ *n* any of various Asiatic slender long-tailed monkeys (family Colobidae) with bushy eyebrows and a chin tuft [Hindi *lāgūr*]

**laniard** /'lanyəd/ *n* LANYARD (piece of rope or cord)

**laniary** /'lani·əri/ *n or adj* (a tooth, esp a canine tooth) adapted for tearing [L *laniarius* of a butcher, fr *lanius* butcher; akin to L *laniare* to tear]

**laniferous** /lə'nif(ə)rəs/, **lanigerous** /lə'nijərəs/ *adj* bearing (something resembling) wool [*laniferous* fr L *lanifer*, fr *lana* wool + *ferre* to bear, carry; *lanigerous* fr L *laniger*, fr *lana* + *gerere* to bear]

**lank** /langk/ *adj* **1** not well filled out; meagre, gaunt ⟨~ *cattle*⟩ **2** tall and weak ⟨~ *grass*⟩ **3** straight and limp without spring or curl ⟨~ *hair*⟩ [(assumed) ME, fr OE *hlanc*; akin to OHG *hlanca* loin, L *clingere* to girdle] – **lankly** *adv*, **lankness** *n*

**lanky** /'langki/ *adj* ungracefully tall and thin – **lankiness** *n*

**lanner** /'lanə/, *masc* **lanneret** /'lanə,ret/ *n* a falcon (*Falco biarmicus*) of S Europe, SW Asia, and Africa; *specif* a female lanner [ME *laner*, fr MF *lanier*]

**lanolin, lanoline** /'lanəlin/ *n* WOOL GREASE, esp when refined for use in ointments and cosmetics – called also WOOL FAT [L *lana* wool + ISV *-ol* + *-in*]

**lantana** /lan'tahnə, -'tay-/ *n* any of a genus (*Lantana*) of shrubs having heads of brightly coloured flowers and juicy plumlike fruit [NL, genus name, deriv of It dial., viburnum]

**lantern** /'lantən/ *n* **1** a usu portable protective case with transparent openings that houses a light (e g a candle) **2a** the chamber in a lighthouse containing the light **b** a structure with glazed or open sides above an opening in a roof for light or ventilation **c** a small tower surmounting a dome **3** *archaic* MAGIC LANTERN [ME *lanterne*, fr MF, fr L *lanterna*, fr Gk *lamptēr*, fr *lampein* to shine – more at LAMP]

**lantern fish** *n* any of numerous small deep-sea fishes (family Myctophidae) that have rows of luminous spots on the body

**lantern fly** *n* any of several large brightly marked insects (family Fulgoridae) having the front of the head prolonged into a hollow structure that was once thought to emit light

**lantern jaw** *n* **1** a long narrow lower jaw that projects beyond the upper jaw **2** *pl* long narrow jaws that give a hollow look to the cheeks and face – **lantern-jawed** *adj*

**lantern pinion** *n* a gear wheel having cylindrical pins instead of teeth

**lantern slide** *n* a transparency, esp of glass, used formerly for projecting pictures with a MAGIC LANTERN

**lanthanide** /'lanthənied/ *n* any one of a series of chemical elements of increasing ATOMIC NUMBER beginning with lanthanum (57) or CERIUM (58) and ending with LUTETIUM (71) [ISV, fr NL *lanthanum*]

**lanthanum** /'lanthənəm/ *n* a white soft metallic chemical element that is one of the RARE-EARTH ELEMENTS [NL, fr Gk *lanthanein* to escape notice]

**lanthorn** /'lant·hawn, 'lantən/ *n*, *chiefly Br archaic* a lantern [by alter. (influenced by *horn*, from which lanterns were formerly made)]

**lanugo** /lə'nyoohgoh/ *n* a dense cottony or downy growth; *specif* the soft woolly hair that covers the unborn young of some mammals, including humans [L, down – more at WOOL]

**lanyard** *also* **laniard** /'lanyəd/ *n* **1** a piece of rope or line for fastening something on board ship **2a** a cord worn round the neck to hold something (e g a knife or whistle) **b** a cord worn as a symbol of a military award or honour **3** a cord used in firing certain cannon [ME *lanyer*, fr MF *laniere*, fr OF *lasniere*, fr *lasne* strap, thong]

**Lao** /low/ *n or adj, pl* **Laos**, *esp collectively* **Lao** (a member or the language) of a Tai people living in Laos and adjacent parts of NE Thailand and constituting an important branch of the Tai race – **Lao** *adj*

**Laodicean** /,layohdi'see·ən/ *n or adj* (one who is) lukewarm or indifferent with regard to religion or politics [*Laodicea* (now Latakia), ancient city in Asia Minor; fr the reproach to the church of the Laodiceans in Rev 3:15-16]

**Laotian** /lay'ohsh(ə)n, 'lowsh(ə)n/ *n or adj* (a) Lao [prob fr Fr *laotien*, adj & n, irreg fr *Lao*]

¹**lap** /lap/ *n* **1** (the clothing covering) the front part of the lower body and thighs of a seated person **2** a hollow place amongst hills **3** *archaic* a loose panel or hanging flap, esp of a garment [ME *lappe*, fr OE *læppa*; akin to OHG *lappa* flap, L *labi* to slide – more at SLEEP] – **lapful** *n* – **drop/land in somebody's lap** to (cause to) become somebody's responsibility – **in the lap of luxury** in an environment of great ease, comfort, and wealth – **in the lap of the gods** beyond human influence or control

²**lap** *vb* **-pp-** *vt* **1a** to fold over or round something; wind, wrap **b** to envelop entirely; swathe **2** to fold over, esp into layers **3** to hold protectively (as if) in the lap **4a** to place over and cover a part of; overlap ⟨~ *shingles on a roof*⟩ **b** to unite (e g beams or timbers) so as to preserve the same breadth and depth throughout **5a** to smooth or polish (e g a metal surface) to a high degree of refinement or accuracy **b** to work (two surfaces) together with or without abrasives until a very close fit is produced **6a** to overtake and thereby lead or increase the lead over (another contestant) by a full circuit of a racetrack **b** to complete a circuit of (a racetrack) ~ *vi* **1** to fold, wind **2a** to project beyond or spread over something **b** to lie partly over or alongside something or one another **3** to traverse or complete a circuit of a course – **lapper** *n*

³**lap** *n* **1a** the amount by which one object overlaps or projects beyond another **b** the part of an object that overlaps another **2** a smoothing and polishing tool (e g for metal or precious stones) usu comprising a piece of wood, leather, felt, or soft metal covering a rotating disc **3a** a layer of a flexible substance: e g **3a(1)** cotton, wool, etc wound round something, esp a roller, before spinning **a(2)** a sheet of paper cut to a particular size for handling and shipping **b** a surface defect, usu in metal, caused by the folding over on itself of a part of the molten material **4a** (the distance covered during) the act or an instance of moving once round a closed course (e g a racetrack) **b** (the distance covered during) the act or an instance of travelling the length of a straight course (e g a swimming pool) **c** one stage or segment of a larger unit (e g a journey) **d** one complete turn (e g of a rope round a drum)

⁴**lap** *vb* **-pp-** *vi* **1** to take in liquid with the tongue **2a** to make a gentle splashing sound ⟨*all silent except for the waves* ~ping *against the shore*⟩ **b** to move in little waves; wash ⟨*the sea* ~ ped *gently over the edge of the quay*⟩ ~ *vt* **1a** to take in (liquid) with the tongue **b** to take in or absorb eagerly or quickly – usu + *up* ⟨*the crowd* ~ped *up every word he said*⟩ **2** to flow or splash against in little waves [ME *lapen*, fr OE *lapian*; akin

to OHG *laffan* to lick, L *lambere*, Gk *laphyssein* to devour] –
**lapper** *n*

⁵**lap** *n* **1a** an act or instance of lapping **b** the amount that can
be carried to the mouth by one lick or scoop of the tongue **2 a**
gentle splashing sound

**laparoscope** /'lapəroh,skohp/ *n* an instrument used to examine the abdomen; *specif* a fine tube which when inserted
into the abdomen can be illuminated to allow direct observation of the contents without the need for surgery [Gk *lapara*
flank (fr *laparos* slack, soft) + E *-scope*] – **laparoscopy** *n*

**laparotomy** /,lapə'rotəmi/ *n* surgical incision through the
abdominal wall [Gk *lapara* + ISV *-tomy*]

**lap belt** *n* a seat belt that fastens across the lap

**lapdog** /'lap,dog/ *n* **1** a small docile dog **2** somebody, esp in a
dependent position, who shows an excessive or fawning admiration or devotion to another [¹*lap*] – **lapdog** *adj*

**lapel** /lə'pel/ *n* the part of a garment that is turned back; *specif*
a fold of the top front edge of a coat or jacket that is continuous with the collar [dim. of ¹*lap*]

**lapidarian** /,lapi'deəriən/ *adj* LAPIDARY 2

¹**lapidary** /'lapidəri/ *n* **1** one who cuts, polishes, or engraves
precious stones usu other than diamonds **2** the art of cutting
gems

²**lapidary** *adj* **1a** sculptured in or engraved on stone **b** of (the
art of cutting) precious stones **2** *formal, of literary style* having
the elegance and precision associated with inscriptions on
monumental stone [L *lapidarius* of stone, fr *lapid-*, *lapis* stone;
akin to Gk *lepas* crag]

**lapillus** /lə'piləs/ *n usu pl, pl* **lapilli** /-lie/ a small stony or glassy
fragment of lava thrown out in a volcanic eruption [L, dim. of
*lapis*]

**lapin** /'lapin/ *n* (the fur of) a rabbit [Fr, rabbit]

**lapis lazuli** /,lapis 'lazyoolie, -li/ *n* (the colour of) a rich blue
semiprecious stone [ME, fr ML, fr L *lapis* + ML *lazuli*, gen of
*lazulum* lapis lazuli, fr Ar *lāzaward* – more at AZURE

**lap joint** *n* a joint made by overlapping two ends or edges and
fastening them together – **lap-jointed** *adj*

**Laplace's equation** *n* an equation stating that the sum of the
PARTIAL DERIVATIVES of the second ORDER of a function is equal
to zero

**Laplander** /'lap,landə/ *n* LAPP 1

**Lapp** /lap/ *n* **1** a member of a people of N Scandinavia, Finland, and the Kola peninsula of N Russia who are mainly
nomadic herders of reindeer, fishermen, and hunters of sea
mammals **2** *also* **Lappish** any or all of the FINNO-UGRIC languages of the Lapps [Sw; perh akin to MHG *lappe* simpleton]
– **Lapp** *adj*, **Lappish** *adj*

**lappet** /'lapit/ *n* **1** a fold or flap on a garment or headdress **2** a
flat overlapping or hanging piece, esp of flesh (eg the wattle of
a bird) [¹*lap* + *-et*]

**lap robe** *n, NAm* TRAVELLING RUG

¹**lapse** /laps/ *n* **1a** a slight error or slip ⟨*a ~ of memory*⟩ **b** a
deviation or aberration, esp of a temporary nature, from what
is correct or acceptable ⟨*a ~ in table manners*⟩ **2a** a drop;
*specif* a decrease of temperature, humidity, or pressure as the
height increases – compare LAPSE RATE **b** a fall, decline ⟨*a
sudden ~ of confidence*⟩; *esp* a moral fall or decline to a lower
state ⟨*a ~ from grace*⟩ **3a(1)** the termination of a right or
privilege through failure to exercise it within some limit of time
**a(2)** termination of insurance cover for nonpayment of premiums **b** a decline into disuse ⟨*the ~ of a custom*⟩ **4** an abandonment of religious faith **5** a continuous passage or elapsed
period; an interval ⟨*the ~ of time*⟩ ⟨*returned after a ~ of
several years*⟩ [L *lapsus*, fr *lapsus*, pp of *labi* to slip – more at
SLEEP]

²**lapse** *vi* **1a** to fall *from* an attained and usu high level (eg of
morals or manners) to one much lower; depart *from* an accepted
or previous standard or state **b** to sink or slip gradually; subside ⟨*the guests ~d into silence when the speech began*⟩ **2** to
go out of existence or use; cease ⟨*our friendship ~d when we
left college*⟩ **3** to pass from one proprietor to another by omission or negligence **4** *of time* to run its course; pass ~ *vt* to let
slip; forfeit ⟨*to ~ one's membership*⟩ – **lapser** *n*

**lapse rate** *n* the rate of change of temperature, humidity, or
pressure associated with a change in height

**lapstrake** /'lap,strayk/ *adj or n* (being) a CLINKER-BUILT boat
(one made with overlapping planks) – **lapstraked** *adj* [³*lap* +
*strake*]

**lapstreak** /'lap,streek/ *adj or n* (being) a lapstrake

**lapsus linguae** /,lapsəs 'ling-gwi/ *n* a slip of the tongue [L]

**laputan** /lə'pyooht(ə)n/ *adj, often cap, of a person or idea* absurd,
improbable [*Laputa*, flying island in Jonathan Swift's *Gulliver's
Travels* whose inhabitants engage in impractical projects]

**lapwing** /'lap,wing/ *n* a crested plover (*Vanellus vanellus*) noted
for its slow irregular flapping flight and its shrill wailing cry
[ME, by folk etymology fr OE *hlēapewince*; akin to OE *hlēapan*
to leap & to OE *wincian* to wink]

**Lar** /lah/ *n, pl* **Lares** /'lahreez, 'leə-/ a god or spirit associated
with VESTA and the PENATES as a guardian of the household
by the ancient Romans [L – more at LARVA]

**larboard** /'lahbəd/ *n, archaic* ⁴PORT [ME *ladeborde*] – **larboard**
*adj*

**larceny** /'lahsəni/ *n* **1** theft **2** *law* the common-law offence
abolished in 1968 of unlawfully taking and carrying away personal property with intent to deprive the rightful owner of it
permanently [ME, fr MF *larcin* theft, fr L *latrocinium* robbery,
fr *latron-*, *latro* mercenary soldier; akin to OE *unlæd* poor, Gk
*latron* pay]

**larch** /lahch/ *n* (the wood of) any of a genus (*Larix*) of trees of
the pine family with short needle-shaped deciduous leaves
arranged in small clusters [deriv of L *laric-*, *larix*]

¹**lard** /lahd/ *vt* **1a** to dress (eg meat) for cooking by inserting or
covering with fat or fatty meat (eg bacon) to prevent drying **b**
to cover with grease; apply grease to **2** to decorate or intersperse *with* something; garnish ⟨*the book is well ~ed with
anecdotes*⟩

²**lard** *n* a soft white solid fat obtained by rendering the internal
esp abdominal fat of a pig [ME, fr OF, fr L *lardum*; akin to L
*laetus* glad, *largus* abundant, Gk *larinos* fat] – **lardy** *adj*

**larder** /'lahdə/ *n* **1** a place where food is stored; a pantry **2** a
supply of food [ME, fr MF *lardier*, fr OF, fr *lard*]

**lardon** /'lahd(ə)n/ *n* a strip (eg of pork fat or bacon) with which
meat is larded; *specif* one inserted into lean meat before cooking – compare BARD [Fr *lardon* piece of fat pork, fr OF, fr
*lard*]

**lardoon** /lah'doohn/ *n* a lardon

**lardy-dardy** /,lahdi 'dahdi/ *adj* la-di-da [imit of an affected
manner of speech]

**lares and penates** /,lahreez ənd pe'nahteez, ,leə-/ *n pl* **1** *cap*
L&P the Roman gods of the household worshipped in close
association with VESTA **2** personal or household goods

**Largactil** /lah'gaktil/ *trademark* – used for the tranquillizing
drug CHLORPROMAZINE

¹**large** /lahj/ *adj* **1** having more than usual power, capacity, or
scope; comprehensive ⟨*establishing a ~r social justice*⟩ **2** exceeding most other things of like kind, esp in quantity or size;
big **3** dealing in great numbers or quantities; operating on an
extensive scale ⟨*a ~ and highly profitable business*⟩ ⟨*a ~ exporter*⟩ **4** *of a wind* favourable **5** extravagant, boastful ⟨*~
talk*⟩ **6** *obs* extensive, broad [ME, fr OF, fr L *largus*] – **largeness** *n*, **largish** *adj*

  **synonyms** Large, big, and great are often interchangeable. Large
  is often preferred to describe physical dimensions, quantity, amount,
  or capacity ⟨*a large garden/portion/number/bucket*⟩. Big is more
  appropriate for bulk, mass, or weight ⟨*a big man/heap/book*⟩ and
  for volume of sound ⟨*a big voice*⟩. Great, when applied to material
  objects, has some additional sense, as of admiration, awe, or annoyance ⟨*this great lorry overtook me*⟩ ⟨*a great library full of books*⟩.
  Applied to abstractions, it suggests degree ⟨*showed me great kindness*⟩. Used figuratively, big, large, and great have similar connotations to their literal use. Great may mean eminent, significant,
  or in some way superior. Large implies broadness, generosity, and
  comprehensiveness ⟨*take the large view*⟩. Big suggests importance
  and impressiveness but often in contrast to genuine worth. Compare
  HUGE **antonyms** little, small **usage** Things *loom*, *bulk*, or are writ
  **large**, not **largely**. Largely means "to a large extent" ⟨*success was
  largely due to his efforts*⟩ and not "in a large way".

²**large** *adv* with the wind blowing favourably from behind
⟨*sailing ~*⟩ – **bulk large** to appear as an important or prominent factor ⟨*a consideration that bulks large in everyone's thinking*⟩ – **by and large** ON THE WHOLE; IN GENERAL – **writ large**
manifested on an expanded scale or in a clearer manner [*writ*,
pp of write]

³**large** *n* – **at large 1** without restraint or confinement; AT
LIBERTY ⟨*the escaped prisoner is still at large*⟩ **2** AS A WHOLE
⟨*society at large*⟩

**large calorie** *n* CALORIE 1b

**largehearted** /,lahj'hahtid/ *adj* bighearted, generous – **large-
heartedness** *n*

**large intestine** *n* the rear division of the intestine of a

VERTEBRATE animal that is wider and shorter than the SMALL INTESTINE, typically divided into CAECUM, COLON, and RECTUM, and concerned esp with the absorption of water and formation of solid waste matter

**largely** /'lahjli/ *adv* to a large extent *usage* see [1]LARGE

**,large-'minded** *adj* liberal in outlook, range, or capacity; broad-minded – **large-mindedly** *adv*, **large-mindedness** *n*

**,large-'scale** *adj* larger than others of its kind: e g a involving great numbers or quantities; extensive ⟨~ *preparations*⟩ **b** *of a map* having a scale that shows much detail

**largess, largesse** /lah'jes/ *n* 1 liberal giving, esp (as if) to an inferior 2 something (e g money) given generously as a gift [ME *largesse*, fr OF, fr *large*]

**large white** *n* any of a British breed of large long-bodied white pigs

**larghetto** /lah'getoh/ *n, adv, or adj, pl* **larghettos** (a movement that is) slow but not so slow as largo – used as a TEMPO (speed) direction in music [adj It, somewhat slow, fr *largo;* n & adv fr adj]

**largo** /'lahgoh/ *n, adv, or adj, pl* **largos** (a movement that is) played in a very slow and broad manner – used as a TEMPO (speed) direction in music; compare LENTO [adj It, slow, broad, fr L *largus* abundant – more at LARD; n & adv fr adj]

**lari** /'lahri/ *n* – see *rupee* at MONEY table [Per *lārī*]

**lariat** /'lari-ət/ *n, chiefly NAm* a lasso [AmerSp *la reata* the lasso, fr Sp *la* the + AmerSp *reata* lasso, fr Sp *reatar* to tie again, fr *re-* + *atar* to tie, fr L *aptare* to fit – more at ADAPT]

[1]**lark** /lahk/ *n* any of numerous singing, usu ground-nesting, birds (family Alaudidae) found mostly in Europe, Asia, and N Africa; *esp* a skylark [ME, fr OE *lāwerce;* akin to OHG *lērihha* lark]

[2]**lark** *vi* to have fun; frolic, sport – usu + *about* or *around* [prob alter. of E dial. *lake* to frolic, fr ME *laiken*, fr ON *leika* to play, dance] – **larker** *n*

[3]**lark** *n, informal* 1 a merry adventure; a frolic; *also* a prank 2 *Br* a type of activity; a way of behaving ⟨*it's a good* ~ – *two hundred quid a week, own car, and no questions asked*⟩ – **larky** *adj*

**larkspur** /'lahk,spuh/ *n* DELPHINIUM (flower of the buttercup family); *esp* a cultivated annual delphinium grown for its showy irregular flowers [[1]*lark* + *spur;* fr its spur-shaped calyx]

**larrikin** /'larikin/ *n* 1 *chiefly Austr* an unruly youth; a hooligan 2 *Austr* an urchin; *esp* one who is adolescent [E dial. *larrikin* frolicsome or mischievous youth] – **larrikin** *adj*

**larrup** /'larəp/ *vt, dial or informal* to beat soundly; thrash; *also* to defeat decisively [perh imit]

**larum** /'larəm/ *n, archaic* an alarm [short for *alarum*]

**larva** /'lahvə/ *n, pl* **larvae** /-vi/ *also* **larvas** 1 the immature, wingless, and often wormlike feeding form that hatches from the egg of many insects, alters, chiefly in size, while passing through several moults, and is finally transformed into a pupa or chrysalis from which the adult emerges 2 the early form (e g a tadpole) of an animal (e g a frog) that at birth or hatching is fundamentally unlike its parent and must METAMORPHOSE (change in structure and way of life) before assuming the adult characters [NL, fr L, spectre, mask; akin to L *lar*] – **larval** *adj*

**larvi-** /lahvi-/ *comb form* larva ⟨*larvicide*⟩ [NL, fr *larva*]

**larvicide** /'lahvi,sied/ *n* a chemical for killing larval pests

**laryng-** /larinj-, laring-g-/, **laryngo-** *comb form* 1 larynx ⟨*laryngitis*⟩ 2 laryngeal and ⟨*laryngopharyngeal*⟩ [NL, fr Gk, fr *laryng-, larynx*]

[1]**laryngeal** /,larin'jee-əl, lə'rinjiəl/ *adj* 1 of or used on the larynx 2 produced by or with constriction of the larynx ⟨~ *articulation of sounds*⟩ – **laryngeally** *adv*

[2]**laryngeal** *n* 1 an anatomical part (e g a nerve or artery) that supplies or is associated with the larynx 2a a laryngeal sound b any of a set of several hypothetical PHONEMES (speech sounds that distinguish meaning) reconstructed for Proto-Indo-European

**laryngectomee** /-'jektəmee/ *n* a person who has undergone laryngectomy

**laryngectomy** /,larin'jektəmi/ *n* surgical removal of (part of) the larynx

**laryngitis** /,larin'jietəs/ *n* inflammation of the larynx [NL] – **laryngitic** *adj*

**laryngology** /,laring'goləji/ *n* a branch of medicine dealing with diseases of the larynx, throat, and nasal passages [ISV]

**laryngoscope** /lə'ring-gə,skohp/ *n* an instrument for examining the interior of the larynx [ISV] – **laryngoscopic, laryngoscopical** *adj*, **laryngoscopically** *adv*, **laryngoscopy** *n*

**larynx** /'laringks/ *n, pl* **larynges** /lə'rinjeez/, **larynxes** the modified upper part of the windpipe of air-breathing vertebrates that contains the vocal cords in human beings, most other mammals, and a few lower forms – compare PHARYNX [NL *laryng-, larynx*, fr Gk]

**lasagne** /lə'zanyə, lə'sanyə/ *n* (a baked dish of minced meat, tomatoes, cheese sauce, and) pasta in the form of broad flat ribbons often flavoured and coloured with spinach [It, pl of *lasagna*, fr (assumed) VL *lasania*, fr L *lasanum* cooking pot, fr Gk *lasanon* chamber pot]

**lascar** /'laskə/ *n, often cap* an E Indian sailor, army servant, or soldier [modif (influenced in meaning by Hindi *lashkarī* soldier, sailor) of Hindi *lashkar* army, fr Per, fr Ar *al-'askar* the army]

**lascivious** /lə'sivi-əs/ *adj* inclined to or inciting uncontrolled sexual desire; lustful, lewd [L *lascivia* wantonness, fr *lascivus* wanton – more at LUST] – **lasciviously** *adv*, **lasciviousness** *n*

**lase** /layz/ *vi* to function as a laser [back-formation fr *laser*]

**laser** /'layzə/ *n* an apparatus that generates an intense narrow beam of light or other electromagnetic radiation of a single wavelength in the ultraviolet, visible, or infrared regions of the spectrum ⟨~ *beams*⟩ – compare MASER [*light amplification* by *stimulated emission* of *radiation*]

[1]**lash** /lash/ *vi* 1 to move violently or suddenly 2 to beat, pour ⟨*rain* ~ed *down*⟩ 3a to strike (as if) with a whip – often + *at, against*, or *out* b to make a verbal attack or retort – usu + *out* 4 *Br* to spend money recklessly – usu + *out* ~ *vt* 1a to strike with a lash; whip b to strike quickly and forcibly; beat on or against ⟨*rain* ~es *the window*⟩ 2a to attack with stinging words b to drive (as if) with a whip; rouse, goad ⟨~ed *them into a fury with his fiery speech*⟩ c to cause to lash ⟨~ed *its tail from side to side*⟩ [ME *lashen*, perh of imit origin] – **lasher** *n*

**lash out** *vt, Br informal* to spend unrestrainedly – often + *on* ⟨*lashed out £800 on a fur coat*⟩ ~ *vi* 1 to make a sudden violent or physical attack – usu + *at* or *against* 2 *of a horse* to kick 3 *Br informal* to spend money freely or recklessly – often + *on*

[2]**lash** *n* 1a(1) a stroke (as if) with a whip a(2) (the flexible part of) a whip b a sudden swinging movement or blow 2 violent onslaught ⟨*the* ~ *of a north wind*⟩ ⟨*gave him a* ~ *with her tongue*⟩ 3 an eyelash 4 *Austr & NZ* an attempt, go

[3]**lash** *vt* to bind or fasten with a rope, cord, etc [ME *lasschen* to lace, fr MF *lacier* – more at LACE] – **lasher** *n*

[1]**lashing** /'lashing/ *n* the act of one who lashes; a physical or verbal beating [[1]*lash*]

[2]**lashing** *n* something used for binding, wrapping, or fastening [[3]*lash*]

**lashings** /'lashingz/ *n pl, informal* a great plenty; an abundance – usu + *of* ⟨~ *of domestic hot water* – *Kent & Sussex Courier*⟩ [fr gerund of [1]*lash*]

**'lash-,up** *n* something improvised; a makeshift, contrivance [[3]*lash*] – **lash-up** *adj*

**L-asparaginase** /,el aspə'rajinayz, -nays/ *n* an ENZYME that breaks down the amino acid ASPARAGINE, is obtained esp from bacteria, and is used esp to treat leukaemia

**lass** /las/ *n* 1 a young woman; a girl 2 one's sweetheart *synonyms* see LADY *antonym* lad [ME *las*]

**lassa fever** /'lasə/ *n* an acute severe often fatal virus disease of tropical countries [*Lassa*, village in NE Nigeria where the disease was first reported]

**lassie** /'lasi/ *n* a lass, girl

**lassitude** /'lasityoohd/ *n* 1 fatigue, weariness 2 languor, listlessness *synonyms* see LETHARGY [MF, fr L *lassitudo*, fr *lassus* weary – more at LET]

[1]**lasso** /la'sooh, 'lasoh/ *n, pl* **lassos, lassoes** a rope or long thong of leather with a running noose that is used esp for catching horses and cattle [Sp *lazo*, fr L *laqueus* snare – more at DELIGHT]

[2]**lasso** *vt* **lassos, lassoes; lassoing; lassoed** to catch (as if) with a lasso; rope – **lassoer** *n*

[1]**last** /lahst/ *vi* 1 to continue in time; go on 2a to remain in good or adequate condition, use,.or effectiveness; endure b to manage to continue (e g in a course of action) ⟨*he* ~ed *for a week without cigarettes*⟩ c to continue to live ⟨*he won't* ~ *much longer*⟩ d to continue to be available or unexhausted; be sufficient or enough ⟨*the money* ~ed *until the end of the month*⟩ ~ *vt* 1 to continue in existence or action as long as or longer than – often + *out* ⟨*couldn't* ~ *out the training*⟩ 2 to be enough for the needs of during a length of time ⟨*the supplies will* ~ *them a week*⟩ *synonyms* see CONTINUE [ME *lasten*, fr OE *lǣstan* to last, follow; akin to OE *lǣst* footprint] – **laster** *n*

**²last** *adj* **1** following all the rest: eg **1a** final, latest **b** being the only remaining ⟨*his ~ pound*⟩ **2** administered to the seriously sick or dying ⟨*the ~ rites of the church*⟩ **3a** next before the present; most recent ⟨*~ week*⟩ ⟨*Thursday ~*⟩ ⟨*this is better than his ~ book*⟩ **b** most up-to-date; latest **4** least suitable or likely ⟨*he'd be the ~ person to fall for flattery*⟩ **5a** conclusive, definitive ⟨*the ~ word on the subject*⟩ **b** highest in degree; utmost ⟨*of the ~ importance*⟩ **c** single – used as an intensive ⟨*ate every ~ scrap*⟩ – see also FIRST and last, **on one's last LEGS** [ME, fr OE *latost,* superl of *læt* late] – **lastly** *adv*

synonyms Since **last** may mean "final" ⟨*famous* **last** *words*⟩ it is clearer to use **latest** rather than **last** to express the idea of "most recent" ⟨*her* **latest**, *but we hope not her* **last**, *book*⟩ except in certain set phrases such as **last week. usage** see ¹FIRST

**³last** *adv* **1** after all others; at the end ⟨*came ~ and left first*⟩ **2** on the most recent occasion ⟨*when we ~ met*⟩ **3** in conclusion; lastly ⟨*and ~, the economic aspect*⟩

**⁴last** *n, pl* **last** somebody or something that is last – **at (long) last** after everything; finally; *esp* after much delay – **to the last** till the end

**⁵last** *n* a form (eg of metal or plastic) which is shaped like the human foot and over which a shoe is shaped or repaired [ME, fr OE *læste,* fr *lāst* footprint; akin to OHG *leist* shoemaker's last, L *lira* furrow – more at LEARN]

**‚last-'ditch** *adj* made as a final effort, esp to avert disaster ⟨*a ~ attempt to raise the money*⟩

**last ditch** *n* a place or position of final defence

**¹lasting** /'lahsting/ *adj* existing or continuing permanently or for a long while; enduring – **lastingly** *adv,* **lastingness** *n*

**²lasting** *n* a sturdy cotton or woollen cloth used esp in shoes and luggage [¹*lasting*]

**Last Judgment** *n the* final judgment of humankind before God at the end of the world – compare DOOM

**last minute** *n* the moment just before some climactic, decisive, or disastrous event

**last name** *n* a surname

**last post** *n* the second of two bugle calls sounded at the hour for retiring in a military camp; *also* such a bugle call sounded at a military funeral or tattoo

**last straw** *n the* last of a series (eg of events or indignities) that brings one beyond the point of endurance [fr the fable of the last straw that broke the camel's back when added to his burden]

**Last Supper** *n the* supper eaten by Jesus and his disciples on the night of his betrayal

**last thing** *adv* as the final action, esp before going to bed ⟨*always has a cup of cocoa ~ at night*⟩

**Last Things** *n pl* events (eg the resurrection and divine judgment of all humankind) marking the end of the world; *specif* death, judgment, Heaven, and Hell in Catholic theology [trans of ML *Novissima*]

**last word** *n* **1** *the* final remark in a verbal exchange **2a** *the* power of final decision; *the* final judgment **b** *the* definitive statement or treatment ⟨*his study will surely be the ~ on the subject for many years*⟩ **3** – *the* most advanced, up-to-date, or fashionable example of its kind ⟨*the ~ in sports cars*⟩

**latakia** /‚lata'kia/ *n, often cap* a highly aromatic oriental smoking tobacco [*Latakia,* seaport in Syria]

**¹latch** /lach/ *vi* **1** to attach oneself; hold tightly ⟨*~ed onto a rich widow*⟩ **2** *informal* to gain understanding or comprehension □ usu + *on* or *onto* [ME *lachen,* fr OE *læccan;* akin to Gk *lambanein* to take, seize]

**²latch** *n* any of various devices in which mating mechanical parts engage to fasten but usu not to lock something: **a** a fastener (eg for a gate) with a pivoted bar that falls into a notch on the gatepost **b** a fastener (eg for a door) in which a spring slides a bolt into a hole; *also* NIGHT LATCH – **latch** *vt*

**latchkey** /-‚kee/ *n* a key to an outside door, esp a front door

**latchkey child** *n, chiefly Br* a child whose parents are regularly absent from home (eg because of working) on his/her return from school; *specif* one given a key to let him-/herself in

**latchstring** /'lach‚string/ *n* a string attached to a latch that may be left hanging outside the door to permit the raising of the latch from the outside

**¹late** /layt/ *adj* **1a(1)** occurring, coming, being, or done after the due, usual, or proper time ⟨*a ~ spring*⟩ **a(2)** continuing after the usual time or until an advanced hour ⟨*a ~ session in the House*⟩ **b** of an advanced stage in point of time or development ⟨*the ~ Middle Ages*⟩; *esp* far advanced towards the close of the day or night ⟨*~ hours*⟩ **2a** *of a specified*

person no longer alive; *esp* comparatively recently deceased ⟨*the ~ James Scott*⟩ ⟨*his ~ wife*⟩ – compare ¹EX- **c** existing, happening, or holding a position just previous to the present time, esp as the most recent of a succession; recent ⟨*the ~ government*⟩ ⟨*some ~ news has just arrived*⟩ **3** far on in the day or night ⟨*it's too ~ to go now*⟩ synonyms see ¹MODERN, TARDY antonyms present, current; early, punctual, prompt [ME, late, slow, fr OE *læt;* akin to OHG *laz* slow, OE *lætan* to let] – **lateness** *n*

**²late** *adv* **1a** after the usual or proper time ⟨*stayed up ~*⟩ **b** at or near the end of a period of time or of a process or series – often + *on* ⟨*~ on in the experiment*⟩ **2** until lately; recently ⟨*Dr Evans, ~ of Birmingham, now lectures at Durham*⟩ – **of late** in the period shortly or immediately preceding; recently ⟨*have not seen him of late*⟩

**late bottled** *adj, often cap, of port* resembling vintage port but matured in wooden barrels instead of in bottles

**latecomer** /'layt‚kuma/ *n* one who arrives late

**lateen** /la'teen/ *adj* of or being a type of ship's rigging used esp in the Mediterranean and the Indian ocean and characterized by a triangular sail hung from a long spar set at an angle on a low mast [Fr (*voile*) *latine* lateen sail, lit., Latin sail]

**Late Greek** *n* the Greek language as used in the 3rd to 6th centuries

**Late Latin** *n* the Latin language as used in the 3rd to 6th centuries

**lately** /'laytli/ *adv* recently; OF LATE ⟨*has been friendlier ~*⟩

**laten** /'layt(ə)n/ *vi* to grow late ~ *vt* to cause to grow or become late

**latency** /'layt(ə)nsi/ *n* **1** the quality or state of being latent; dormancy **2** a latency period **3** LATENT PERIOD 2

**latency period** /'layt(ə)nsi/ *n* **1** a stage of personality development, according to Freudian psychology, observed in some cultures (eg that of W Europe and N America) that extends from about the age of five to puberty and during which sexual urges appear to lie dormant **2** LATENT PERIOD 2

**La Tène** /lah 'ten (*Fr* la ten)/ *adj* of the later period of the IRON AGE in Europe dating from the 5th century BC to the Roman conquests [*La Tène,* shallows of the Lake of Neuchâtel in Switzerland, where remains of the period were first discovered]

**latensification** /lay‚tensifi'kaysh(ə)n/ *n* the developing of a photographic negative or print by intensification of the latent image, using chemicals or exposing it to light of low intensity [blend of ¹*latent* and *intensification*] – **latensify** *vt*

**¹latent** /'layt(ə)nt/ *adj* present and capable of becoming visible or active though not now so ⟨*a ~ infection*⟩ ⟨*his desire for success remained ~*⟩ [L *latent-, latens,* fr prp of *latēre* to lie hidden; akin to OHG *luog* den, Gk *lanthanein* to escape notice]

**²latent** *n, NAm* a fingerprint (eg at the scene of a crime) that is scarcely visible but can be developed for study

**latent heat** *n* heat given off or absorbed in a change of PHASE (eg from a liquid to a gas) without a change in temperature

**latent image** *n* the invisible image first produced on photographic film, paper, etc by a reaction with light which is then made visible by usu chemical developers

**latent period** *n* **1** the incubation period of a disease **2** the interval between stimulation and response

**¹lateral** /'lat(ə)rəl/ *adj* **1** of the side; situated on, directed towards, or coming from the side **2** made by allowing air to escape on either or both sides of the tongue ⟨/*l*/ is a ~ consonant⟩ [L *lateralis,* fr *later-, latus* side] – **laterally** *adv*

**²lateral** *n* **1** something having a lateral situation, growth, or extension: eg **1a** a side ditch or conduit (eg in a water system) **b** a mining drift to one side of and parallel to a main drift **c** a side branch or root **d** either of the left-hand or right-hand pairs of a 4-legged animal's (eg a horse's) legs **2** a lateral consonant

**lateral bud** *n* a bud that develops in the joint between a leaf stalk and a stem

**lateral line** *n* a duct along the side of a fish containing pores that open into tubes supplied with SENSE ORGANS sensitive to low vibrations; *also* one of these tubes or sense organs

**lateral thinking** *n* thinking that ranges over unusual aspects of a problem or topic and often furnishes unexpected conclusions

**laterite** /'latə‚riet/ *n* a red clay formed by the weathering of rocks that consists esp of compounds of iron and aluminium [L *later* brick] – **lateritic** *adj*

**later·ization, -isation** /‚latərie'zaysh(ə)n/ *n* the process of conversion of rock to laterite

¹**latest** /'laytist/ *adj* most up-to-date ⟨*what's the ~ news*⟩
*synonyms* see ²LAST

²**latest** *n* the most recent or currently fashionable style or
development ⟨*the ~ in diving techniques*⟩ – **at the latest** and
no later ⟨*be home by one at the latest*⟩

**Late Summer Holiday** *n* AUGUST BANK HOLIDAY

**latex** /'layteks/ *n, pl* **latices** /'latə‚seez/, **latexes** **1** a milky usu
white fluid that is produced by cells of various flowering plants
(e g of the spurge and poppy families) and is used to make
rubber, chewing gum, etc **2** a water emulsion of a synthetic
rubber or plastic used esp in paints and adhesives [NL *latic-*,
*latex*, fr L, fluid] – **laticiferous** *adj*

¹**lath** /lahth/ *n, pl* **laths** /lahths, lahdhz/, **lath** **1** a thin narrow
strip of wood nailed to rafters, joists, or studding as a
groundwork for slates, tiles, or plaster **2** a building material in
sheets used as a base for plaster △ **lathe** [ME, fr OE *lætt;*
akin to OHG *latta* lath, W *llath* yard]

²**lath** *vt* to cover or line with laths

¹**lathe** /laydh/ *n* an administrative district of Kent in former
times [ME, fr OE *lǣth;* akin to ON *lǣth* landed property]

²**lathe** *n* a machine in which work is rotated about a horizontal
axis and shaped by a fixed tool [prob fr ME *lath* supporting
stand, prob of Scand origin]

³**lathe** *vt* to cut or shape on a lathe

¹**lather** /'lahdhə/ *n* **1a** a foam or froth formed when a detergent
(e g soap) is agitated in water **b** foam or froth from profuse
sweating (e g on a horse) **2** an agitated or overwrought state; a
dither [(assumed) ME, fr OE *lēathor;* akin to OE *lēag* lye –
more at LYE ] – **lathery** *adj*

²**lather** *vt* **1** to spread lather over **2** *informal* to beat severely;
flog ~ *vi* to form a (froth like) lather – **lathering** *n*, **latherer** *n*

**lathi** /'lahti/ *n* a heavy stick often of bamboo bound with iron
used in India as a weapon, esp by police [Hindi *lāṭhī*]

**lathing** /'lahdhing; *also* 'lahthing/ *n* **1** the action or process of
placing laths **2** a quantity or installation of laths

**lathyrism** /'lathə‚riz(ə)m/ *n* poisoning produced by eating the
seeds of a pealike plant (genus *Lathyrus*) and characterized by
spasmodic paralysis of the legs [NL *Lathyrus*, genus name, fr
Gk *lathyros*, a type of pea]

**lathyritic** /,lathə'ritik/ *adj* of, affected with, or characteristic
of lathyrism ⟨*~ rats*⟩ ⟨*~ cartilage*⟩

**latices** /'latə‚seez/ *pl of* LATEX

**laticifer** /'lay'tisifə/ *n* a plant cell or vessel that contains latex
[ISV *latici-* (fr NL *latic-*, *latex*) + *-fer*]

**latifundium** /,lati'fundi·əm/ *n, pl* **latifundia** /-diə/ a great
landed estate (e g in ancient Italy) with primitive agriculture and
labour often in a state of partial servitude [L, fr *latus* wide +
*fundus* piece of landed property – more at BOTTOM]

**latimeria** /,lati'miəri·ə/ *n* any of a genus (*Latimeria*) of
COELACANTH fishes (large primitive fish formerly thought
to be extinct) that have fleshy fins and are found in deep seas
off southern Africa [NL, genus name, fr Marjorie Courtenay-
*Latimer b* 1907 SAfr museum director]

¹**Latin** /'latin/ *adj* **1** of Latium or the Latins **2a** of or composed
in Latin **b** Romance **3** of the part of the Christian church that
until recently used a Latin text for the order of service; ROMAN
CATHOLIC **4** of the peoples or countries using Romance
languages **5** *chiefly NAm* of the peoples or countries of Latin
America [ME, fr OE, fr L *Latinus*, fr *Latium*, ancient country
of Italy]

²**Latin** *n* **1** the Italic language of ancient Latium and of Rome
and until modern times the dominant language of school,
church, and state in W Europe **2** a member of the people of
ancient Latium **3** a Catholic using the Latin form of service **4**
a member of any of the Latin peoples **5** the Latin alphabet **6**
*chiefly NAm* a native or inhabitant of Latin America

**Latinate** /'latinət, -nayt/ *adj* of, resembling, or derived from
Latin

**Latin cross** *n* a cross having a long upright shaft and a shorter
crossbar traversing it above the middle

**Latinian** /lə'tinian/ *n* the group of Italic languages that includes
Latin

**Latinism** /'latiniz(ə)m/ *n* **1** a characteristic feature of Latin occurring in another language **2** Latin quality, character, or mode
of thought

**Latinist** /'latinist/ *n* a specialist in the Latin language or
Roman culture

**latinity** /lə'tinəti/ *n, often cap* **1** a manner of speaking or writing Latin **2** LATINISM 2

**latin·ize, -ise** /'latiniez/ *vt* **1a** to give a Latin form to **b** to

introduce Latinisms into **c** ROMANIZE 2 **2** to make Latin or
Italian in doctrine, ideas, or traits; *specif* to cause to resemble
the Roman Catholic church **3** *obs* to translate into Latin ~ *vi*
**1** to use Latinisms **2** to show the influence of the Romans or
of the Roman Catholic church – **latinization** *n*

**Latin Quarter** *n* a section of Paris on the LEFT BANK of the
Seine frequented by students and artists [trans of Fr *Quartier
Latin*]

**Latin square** *n* a square array of symbols in which each
symbol appears once and once only in each row and column
and which is used in the design of statistical experiments

**latish** /'laytish/ *adj* somewhat late

**latitude** /'latityoohd/ *n* **1a** angular distance of a point on the
surface of a celestial body, esp the earth, measured north or
south from the equator – compare LONGITUDE **b** angular distance of a celestial body from the ECLIPTIC (apparent path
travelled by the sun) **c** latitude, latitudes *pl* a region or locality
as marked by its latitude **2** (permitted) freedom of action or
choice **3** *archaic* scope, range [ME, fr L *latitudin-*, *latitudo*
breadth, width, fr *latus* wide; akin to Arm *lain* wide] – **lati-
tudinal** *adj*, **latitudinally** *adv*

**latitudinarian** /,lati,tyoohdi'neəri·ən/ *n* a person who is broad
and liberal in standards of religious belief and conduct; *specif*
a member of the Church of England who favours freedom of
doctrine and practice within it – **latitudinarian** *adj*, **lati-
tudinarianism** *n*

**latosol** /'latəsol/ *n* a red and yellow tropical soil [irreg fr L
*later* brick + E *-sol* (as in *podsol*, var of *podzol*)] – **latosolic**
*adj*

**latrine** /lə'treen/ *n* a small pit dug in the earth and used as a
toilet, esp in a military camp, barracks, etc; *broadly* a toilet
[Fr, fr L *latrina*, contr of *lavatrina*, fr *lavere* to wash – more at
LYE]

**-latry** /-lətri/ *comb form* (→ *n*) worship ⟨*heliolatry*⟩ [ME *-latrie*,
fr OF, fr LL *-latria*, fr Gk, fr *latreia*] – **-later** *comb form* (→ *n*)

**latten, lattin** /'lat(ə)n/ *n* **1** a yellow alloy identical to or resembling brass typically hammered into thin sheets, and formerly
much used for church utensils **2** metal in thin sheets ⟨*gold ~*⟩
[ME *laton* metal resembling brass, fr MF]

¹**latter** /'latə/ *adj* **1** of the end; later, final ⟨*the ~ stages of a
process*⟩ **2** recent, present ⟨*these ~ days*⟩ **3** second of two
things or last of several things mentioned or understood ⟨*of
ham and beef the ~ meat is cheaper today*⟩ [ME, fr OE *lætra*,
compar of *læt* late]

²**latter** *n, pl* **latter** the second or last mentioned

*usage The* **latter** *should be the second of two things, if the word is
used at all. It is often used for the last of three or more, but there it is
clearer to use third, last, or last-named, or simply to repeat the
necessary words* ⟨*Anne, Bill, and Sarah met at Sarah's* (not *at the*
**latter's** *house*)⟩; *even where there are only two things it is tedious to
have to look back and see what the* **latter** *refers to, instead of
reading straight on.*

'**latter-‚day** *adj* of present or recent times; modern

**Latter-Day Saint** *n* a member of a religious body tracing its
origin to Joseph Smith in 1830 and accepting the Book of
Mormon as divine revelation; a Mormon [fr the Mormons'
name for themselves, the Church of Jesus Christ of *Latter-Day
Saints*]

**latterly** /-li/ *adv* **1** towards the end or latter part of a period **2**
lately

**lattice** /'latis/ *n* **1a** a framework or structure of crossed wooden
or metal strips with open spaces between **b** something (e g a
screen, window, or door) having a lattice **c** a network or design
resembling a lattice **2** a regular geometrical arrangement of
points or objects over an area or in space: e g **2a** SPACE LATTICE
(geometrical arrangement of atoms or ions in a crystal) **b** a geometric arrangement of reactive materials in a nuclear reactor **c**
a PARTIALLY ORDERED mathematical set for any two elements
of which there exist a SUPREMUM (smallest element larger than
the two elements) and an INFIMUM (largest element smaller than
the two elements) [ME *latis*, fr MF *lattis*, fr *latte* lath] – **lattice**
*vt*, **latticed** *adj*

**lattice girder** *n* a girder with flat plates at top and bottom
connected by a latticework web

**latticework** /-,wuhk/ *n* a lattice; *also* something latticed

**latus rectum** /,lahtəs 'rektəm/ *n, pl* **latera recta** /,latərə 'rektə/
a straight line passing through a FOCUS of a CONIC SECTION
(ellipse, parabola, etc) parallel to the DIRECTRIX (line that with a
focus can be used to define a curve) [NL, lit., straight side]

**Latvian** /'latvi·ən/ *n* **1** a native or inhabitant of Latvia; *also*

LETT **2** the Baltic language of the Latvians [*Latvia*, country in N Europe (now a republic of the USSR)] – **Latvian** *adj*
**lauan** /lowˈahn, ˈlooˌahn, -ˈ-/ *n* any of various Philippine timbers (e g of trees of the genera *Shorea* and *Parashorea*) that are light yellow to reddish brown or brown, are of moderate strength and durability, and include some which are sold commercially as PHILIPPINE MAHOGANY [Tagalog *lawaan*]
¹**laud** /lawd/ *n* **1** *pl but taking sing or pl vb, often cap* a religious service usu immediately following matins and forming with it the first of the CANONICAL HOURS **2** (a hymn of) praise [ME *laudes* (pl), fr ML, fr L, pl of *laud-, laus* praise; akin to OHG *liod* song]
²**laud** *vt* **1** to praise or extol, esp with hymns **2** to praise enthusiastically or extravagantly [L *laudare*, fr *laud-, laus*] – **laudation** *n*
**laudable** /ˈlawdəbl/ *adj* worthy of praise; commendable △ laudatory – **laudableness** *n*, **laudably** *adv*, **laudability** *n*
**laudanum** /ˈlawdənəm/ *n* **1** any of various preparations of opium formerly used in medicine **2** a solution of opium in alcohol [NL, prob fr ML *lapdanum, laudanum* labdanum]
**laudatory** /ˈlawdət(ə)ri/, **laudative** /ˈlawdətiv/ *adj, chiefly formal* of or expressing praise △ laudable
¹**laugh** /lahf/ *vi* **1a** to show amusement, mirth, joy, or scorn by making explosive vocal sounds usu accompanied by smiling and movements of the facial muscles **b** to experience amusement, mirth, joy, or contempt ⟨*he* ~ed *inwardly though his face remained grave*⟩ **2** to be of a kind that inspires joy; *esp* to have a cheerful or lively appearance **3** *chiefly poetic* to produce a sound of or resembling laughing ⟨*a* ~ing *brook*⟩ ~ *vt* **1** to influence, move, or bring to a specified state by laughter ⟨~ed *him out of his fears*⟩ **2** to utter or express (as if) with a laugh ⟨~ed *her consent*⟩ **3** to minimize or dismiss by treating as amusingly trivial – + *off* or *away* ⟨*you can't* ~ *off a royal commission* – Alan Villiers⟩ [ME *laughen*, fr OE *hliehhan*; akin to OHG *lachēn* to laugh, OE *hlōwan* to moo – more at LOW] – **laugher** *n*, **laughingly** *adv*
**laugh at** *vt* to treat lightly, carelessly, or as an object of fun
²**laugh** *n* **1** the act or sound of laughing **2** an expression of mirth or scorn **3 laugh, laughs** *pl* a means of entertainment; a diversion ⟨*we had a lot of* ~s *on holiday*⟩ **4** *informal* a cause for derision or merriment; a joke ⟨*swim in that current? That's a* ~⟩
**laughable** /ˈlahfəbl/ *adj* of a kind to provoke laughter or sometimes derision; amusingly ridiculous – **laughableness** *n*, **laughably** *adv*
  **synonyms** Compare **absurd, laughable, ridiculous, ludicrous, preposterous, crazy,** and **crackpot. Laughable** is the mildest term in this group. **Absurd** emphasizes inappropriateness or unreasonableness, and is the most general term. **Ridiculous** and **ludicrous** suggest scornful or derisive laughter: a person may be **ridiculous** but not **ludicrous,** which applies to ideas or things, especially their appearance ⟨*a* **ludicrous** *hat with birds' wings on it*⟩. What is **preposterous** is so absurd as to be unworthy of serious consideration. **Crazy** and **crackpot** are informal terms suggesting absurdity to the point of insanity.
**laughing gas** /ˈlahfing/ *n* NITROUS OXIDE [fr the initial feelings of exhilaration it produces]
**laughing jackass** *n* KOOKABURRA (Australian kingfisher) [fr its call, resembling loud laughter]
**laughingstock** /-ˌstok/ *n* an object of ridicule; a butt
**laughter** /ˈlahftə/ *n* **1** a sound (as if) of laughing **2** the action of laughing **3** *archaic* a cause of merriment [ME, fr OE *hleahtor*; akin to OE *hliehhan*]
¹**launch** /lawnch/ *vt* **1a** to throw forward; hurl **b** to release or send off (e g a self-propelled object) ⟨~ *a rocket*⟩ **2a(1)** to set (a boat or ship) afloat **a(2)** to set (a newly built boat or ship) afloat **b** to start or set in motion (e g on a course or career); introduce ⟨~ed *his son in business*⟩ **c** to introduce (a new product) onto the market ⟨*a party to* ~ *a new book*⟩ ~ *vi* **1** to throw oneself energetically; plunge – + *into* or *out into* ⟨~ed *into a brilliant harangue*⟩ **2** to make a start – usu + *out* or *forth* ⟨~ed *forth on a long-winded explanation*⟩ [ME *launchen*, fr ONF *lancher*, fr LL *lanceare* to wield a lance – more at LANCE]
²**launch** *n* an act or instance of launching
³**launch** *n* **1** the largest boat carried by a warship **2** a large open or half-decked motorboat [Sp or Pg; Sp *lancha*, fr Pg, perh fr Malay *lanchar* swift]
**launcher** /ˈlawnchə/ *n* that which launches: e g **a** a device for firing a grenade from a rifle **b** a device for launching a rocket or rocket shell **c** a catapult

**launching pad** /ˈlawnching/ *n* a launchpad
**launchpad** /ˈlawnchˌpad/ *n* **1** a noninflammable platform from which a rocket, launch vehicle, or guided missile can be launched **2** a base from which something is set in motion; a starting point ⟨*the project is still on the* ~⟩
**launch vehicle** *n* the rocket power source or sources used to launch a spacecraft
**launch window** *n* WINDOW 8 (time during which a spacecraft must be launched)
¹**launder** /ˈlawndə/ *n* a trough; *esp* an inclined box used when mining to convey particles of ore suspended in water [ME, launderer, fr MF *lavandier*, fr ML *lavandarius*, fr L *lavandus,* gerundive of *lavare* to wash – more at LYE]
²**launder** *vt* **1** to wash (e g clothes) in water **2** to make ready for use by washing, sometimes starching, and ironing **3** to give (something, esp money, obtained illegally) the appearance of being respectable or legal ~ *vi* **1** to wash or wash and iron clothes or cloth articles (e g household linens) **2** to become clean by washing, ironing, etc ⟨*clothes that* ~ *well*⟩ [ME *launder*, n] – **launderer,** *fem* **laundress** *n*
**launderette, laundrette** /ˌlawnd(ə)ˈret/ *n* a commercial laundry equipped with washing machines and dryers to be operated esp by the customer [fr *Launderette,* a trademark]
**Laundromat** /ˈlawndrəˌmat/ *trademark* – used for a self-service laundry
**laundry** /ˈlawndri/ *n* **1** clothes or cloth articles that have been or are to be laundered, esp by being sent to a laundry **2** a place where laundering is done; *esp* a commercial laundering establishment
**laundryman** /ˈlawndrimən/, *fem* **laundrywoman** *n* a laundry worker
**laura** /ˈlawrə/ *n* a monastery of an Eastern Orthodox church consisting of partly reclusive monks [LGk, fr Gk, lane]
**laureate** /ˈlawri-ət, ˈlori-ət/ *n* a person specially honoured for achievement in an art or science; *specif* POET LAUREATE [L *laureatus* crowned with laurel, fr *laurea* laurel wreath, fr fem of *laureus* of laurel, fr *laurus*] – **laureate** *adj*, **laureateship** *n*
**laurel** /ˈlorəl/ *n* **1** any of a genus (*Laurus* of the family Lauraceae, the laurel family) of trees or shrubs that have smooth shiny leaves, small flowers, and oval-shaped berries; *specif* ³BAY 1a **2** a tree or shrub that resembles the true laurel **3 laurels** *pl,* **laurel** a crown of laurel leaves awarded as a token of victory or preeminence; a distinction, honour [ME *lorel,* fr OF *lorier,* fr *lor* laurel, fr L *laurus*]
**lauric acid** /ˈlawrik, ˈlorik/ *n* a FATTY ACID, $CH_3(CH_2)_{10}COOH$, that forms part of several fats and oils, is found esp in coconut oil, and is used in making soaps and lauryl alcohol [ISV, fr L *laurus*]
**lauryl alcohol** /ˈlawril, ˈloril/ *n* an alcohol, $CH_3(CH_2)_{11}OH$, used in making WETTING AGENTS and detergents
**lav** /lav/ *n, informal* a toilet [short for *lavatory*]
**lava** /ˈlahvə/ *n* (solidified) molten rock that issues from a volcano or from a crack in the earth's surface [It, fr L *labes* fall or *lavare* to wash] – **lavalike** *adj*
**lavabo** /ləˈvahboh, ləˈvayboh/ *n, pl* **lavabos** *often cap* a ceremony at Mass in which the officiating priest washes his hands after the OFFERTORY (offering of the unconsecrated bread and wine to God) and says Psalm 25:6–12 (Vulgate) [L, I shall wash, fr *lavare;* fr the opening word of Psalm 25:6 (Vulgate)]
**lavage** /ˈlavij (Fr lavaːʒ)/ *n* washing; *esp* the therapeutic washing of an organ of the body [Fr, fr MF, fr *laver* to wash, fr L *lavare*]
**lava lava** /ˈlahvə ˌlahvə/ *n* a rectangular cloth of cotton print worn like a kilt or skirt in Polynesia and esp in Samoa [Samoan, clothing]
**lavation** /laˈvaysh(ə)n/ *n, formal* the act or an instance of washing, cleansing, or lavage [L *lavation-, lavatio,* fr *lavatus*] – **lavational** *adj*
**lavatorial** /ˌlavəˈtawri-əl/ *adj* characterized by excessive reference to lavatories and (the bodily functions associated with) their use; *broadly* vulgar ⟨~ *humour*⟩
**lavatory** /ˈlavətri/ *n* **1** a vessel (e g a basin) for washing **2** a toilet **3** *NAm* a washbasin; *also* a room with facilities for washing and usu with one or more toilets [ME *lavatorie* washbasin, fr ML *lavatorium,* fr L *lavatus,* pp of *lavare* to wash – more at LYE] – **lavatory** *adj*
**lavatory paper** *n* TOILET PAPER
¹**lave** /layv/ *n, chiefly Scot* something that is left; a residue [ME (northern), fr OE *lāf;* akin to OE *belīfan* to remain – more at LEAVE]

²**lave** *vt, poetic* **1** to wash, bathe **2** to flow along the edge of [ME *laven,* fr OE *lafian;* akin to OHG *labōn* to wash; both fr a prehistoric WGmc word borrowed fr L *lavare*]

¹**lavender** /'lavində/ *n* **1** a Mediterranean plant (*Lavandula officinalis*) of the mint family widely cultivated for its narrow aromatic leaves and spikes of lilac-purple flowers which are dried and used in perfume sachets; *also* any of several related plants (genus *Lavandula*) used similarly **2** a pale purple colour [ME *lavendre,* fr AF, fr ML *lavandula,* perh deriv of L *lividus* bluish or *lavare* to wash]

²**lavender** *vt* to perfume (eg linen) by sprinkling or interlayering with lavender

**lavender water** *n* a perfume consisting essentially of lavender oils and alcohol

¹**laver** /'layvə/ *n* a large basin used for ceremonial washings in the ancient Jewish Tabernacle and Temple worship [ME *lavour,* fr MF *lavoir,* prob fr ML *lavatorium*]

²**laver** *n* any of several mostly edible seaweeds: eg **a** a SEA LET-TUCE **b** any of several common red seaweeds (genus *Porphyra,* esp *Porphyra umbilicalis*) whose fronds can be eaten as a salad but are usu boiled, made into flat cakes, and fried as a breakfast dish [NL, fr L, a water plant]

**laver bread** *n* a flattened cake made from seaweed and eaten esp in Wales for breakfast

**laverock** /'lavərək/ *n, chiefly Scot* ¹LARK (bird) [ME *laverok,* fr OE *lāwerce*]

¹**lavish** /'lavish/ *adj* **1** expending or bestowing profusely; prodigal **2** expended, bestowed, or produced in abundance *synonyms* see PROFUSE *antonym* sparing [ME *lavas* abundance, fr MF *lavasse* downpour of rain, fr *laver* to wash – more at LAVAGE] – **lavishly** *adv,* **lavishness** *n*

²**lavish** *vt* to expend or bestow with (undue) profusion

**lavolta** /lə'voltə/ *n* an early French dance characterized by constant turning and high leaps [It *la volta,* lit., the turn, fr *la* the + *volta* turn – more at VOLTE]

**lavvie, lavvy** /'lavi/ *n, Br euph* a toilet [by shortening & alter. fr *lavatory*]

**law** /law/ *n* **1a(1)** a binding custom or practice of a community; a rule of conduct or action prescribed or formally recognized as binding or enforced by a controlling authority **a(2)** the whole body of such customs, enactments, practices, and rules so recognized and enforced ⟨*the ~ of the land*⟩ **a(3)** COMMON LAW **b(1)** the control brought about by the existence or enforcement of such law – chiefly in *law and order* **b(2)** the action of laws considered as a means of redressing wrongs; *also* litigation ⟨*always ready to go to ~*⟩ **c** a rule or order that it is advisable or obligatory to observe ⟨*the ~ of self-preservation*⟩ **d** something compatible with or enforceable by established law ⟨*such decrees are not ~ and should be rescinded*⟩ **e** control, authority **2a** *often cap* the revelation of the will of God set out in the Old Testament **b** *cap* the first part of the Jewish scriptures; PENTATEUCH **3** a rule of action, construction, or procedure ⟨*the ~s of cricket*⟩ ⟨*the ~s of poetry*⟩ **4** the whole body of laws relating to one subject ⟨*company ~*⟩ **5a** *often cap* the legal profession **b** law as a branch of knowledge; JURIS-PRUDENCE **6a** a statement of an order or relation of phenomena that is made on the basis of evidence and that so far as is known is invariable under the given conditions ⟨*the first ~ of thermodynamics*⟩ ⟨*Boyle's ~*⟩ **b** a relation between mathematical or logical expressions that holds for all cases **c** the observed regularity (of nature) **7** *taking sing or pl vb, often cap, chiefly informal* a person, group, or agency that enforces the law; *esp* the police ⟨*look out, the ~ are coming*⟩ [ME, fr OE *lagu,* of Scand origin; akin to ON *lög* law; akin to OE *licgan* to lie – more at LIE] – **have the law on somebody** *informal* to enforce the law against somebody, esp by reporting him/her to the police – **in/at law** according to the law ⟨*enforceable at law*⟩ – **lay down the law** to give orders or express one's opinions with great force, often when one has no right to – **law unto him-/her-/itself** somebody or something that does not follow accepted conventions – **take the law into one's own hands** to take action (against injustice) oneself without making use of the official methods or rules of law

¹**law-a,biding** *adj* abiding by or obedient to the law – **law-abidingness** *n*

**lawbreaker** /-,braykə/ *n* one who violates the law – compare OUTLAW – **lawbreaking** *adj or n*

**lawful** /'lawf(ə)l/ *adj* **1** allowed by law **2** constituted, authorized, or established by law; rightful ⟨*your ~ Queen*⟩ – **lawfully** *adv,* **lawfulness** *n*

*synonyms* **Lawful, legal, legitimate,** and **licit** all mean "sanctioned by law". **Lawful** can imply conformity with any sort of law, such as divine, common, or canon law, and may mean "rightful" ⟨*the lawful heir*⟩. **Legal** applies to statute law or that administered by the courts: the **lawful** owner of a piece of property is one whose **legal** right to it is certain; a **lawful** marriage is one to which there is no **legal** impediment, such as close family relationship. **Legitimate** can imply a legal status, particularly that of being born in wedlock ⟨*his legitimate children*⟩, or in more general use apply to what is sanctioned not only by the law but by custom, the proper authorities, or simple logic ⟨*took a perfectly legitimate interest in her daughter's prospects*⟩. The rare and formal **licit** usually implies strict conformity to the law ⟨*licit use of property does not include creating a nuisance*⟩. *antonym* unlawful

**lawgiver** /-,givə/ *n* **1** a person who gives a code of laws to a people ⟨*Moses the ~*⟩ **2** a legislator

¹**law-,hand** *n* a special style of handwriting used in old legal documents in England

**lawks** /lawks/ *interj, dial or archaic Br* – used to express surprise [euphemism for *Lord*]

**lawless** /'lawlis/ *adj* **1** not regulated by or based on law **2a** not restrained or controlled by law; unruly **b** illegal – **lawlessly** *adv,* **lawlessness** *n*

**Law Lord** *n* a member of the House of Lords with legal experience obtained usu by holding or having held high judicial office, who takes part in its judicial proceedings as the highest COURT OF APPEAL

**lawmaker** /-,maykə/ *n* a person who makes or enacts laws; a legislator – **lawmaking** *n*

**lawman** /'law,man, -mən/ *n, NAm* an official (eg a sheriff or police officer) who enforces the law

**law merchant** *n, pl* **laws merchant** (the body of) international customary law that formerly regulated dealings between merchants [ME *lawe marchaund* (trans of ML *lex mercatoria*), fr *lawe* law + *marchaund, marchant,* adj, merchant]

¹**lawn** /lawn/ *n* a fine sheer linen or cotton fabric of plain weave that is thinner than CAMBRIC [ME, fr *Laon,* town in N France] – **lawny** *adj*

²**lawn** *n* **1** an area of ground (eg round a house or in a garden or park) that is covered with grass and is kept mowed **2** *archaic* an open space between woods; a glade [ME *launde,* fr MF *lande* heath, of Celt origin; akin to OIr *land* open space – more at LAND] – **lawn, lawny** *adj*

**lawn bowling** *n, NAm* bowls played on a green

**lawn mower** *n* a machine for cutting grass on lawns

**lawn tennis** *n* tennis played on a grass court

**law of averages** *n* the principle that one extreme will be cancelled out by its opposite, and the balance restored

**law of dominance** *n, genetics* MENDEL'S LAW 3

**law officer** *n* an official appointed to administer and interpret the law; *specif* a British ATTORNEY GENERAL or SOLICITOR GENERAL

**law of independent assortment** *n, genetics* MENDEL'S LAW 2

**law of large numbers** *n* a theorem in mathematical statistics: the probability that the MEAN (average) of a random sample differs from the mean of the population from which the sample is drawn by more than a given amount approaches zero as the size of the sample approaches infinity. In principle the law of large numbers states that the larger the sample chosen the more closely and accurately it will represent the total population.

**law of nations** *n* INTERNATIONAL LAW

**law of segregation** *n, genetics* MENDEL'S LAW 1

**law of war** *n* a rule or code that governs the rights and duties of the participants in international war

**lawrencium** /law'rensi-əm, lo-/ *n* a short-lived radioactive chemical element that is produced artificially from CALIFORNIUM [NL, fr Ernest O *Lawrence* †1958 US physicist]

**law report** *n* a published account of a legal proceeding stating the facts of the case, the reasons given by the court for its decision, and the legal principles on which the decision was based

**lawsuit** /-,s(y)ooht/ *n* a noncriminal case in a court of law

**lawyer** /'lawyə, 'loyə/ *n* a person whose profession is to conduct lawsuits for clients or to advise as to legal rights and obligations

**lax** /laks/ *adj* **1a** *of the bowels* loose, open **b** having loose bowels **2** not strict or stringent; careless, negligent ⟨*~ morals*⟩ ⟨*~ in his duties*⟩; *also* deficient in firmness or precision ⟨*his ideas are a bit ~*⟩ **3a** not tense, firm, or rigid; slack ⟨*a ~ rope*⟩ **b** not compact or closely joined; open, loose ⟨*a* ~ *flower cluster*⟩ **4** *of a speech sound* pronounced with the muscles in a relatively relaxed state (e g of the vowel /i/ in contrast with the vowel /ee/) [ME, fr L *laxus* loose – more at SLACK] – **laxity, laxness** *n*, **laxly** *adv*, **laxation** *n*

**¹laxative** /'laksətiv/ *adj* **1** having a tendency to loosen or relax; *specif* relieving constipation **2** subject to or having loose bowels [ME *laxatif*, fr ML *laxativus*, fr L *laxatus*, pp of *laxare* to loosen, fr *laxus*] – **laxatively** *adv*, **laxativeness** *n*

**²laxative** *n* something (e g a medicine) taken to relieve constipation

**¹lay** /lay/ *vb* **laid** /layd/ *vt* **1** to beat or strike down with force ⟨*a blow that* laid *him to the ground*⟩ ⟨*wheat* laid *flat by the wind and rain*⟩ **2a** to put or set down **b** to place for rest or sleep; *esp* to bury **3** to bring forth and deposit (an egg) **4** to calm, allay ⟨~ *the dust*⟩ ⟨~ *a ghost*⟩ **5** to bet, wager ⟨~ *odds on the favourite*⟩ ⟨~ *my life on it*⟩ **6** to press (cloth) down, giving a smooth and even surface **7a** to dispose or spread over or on a surface ⟨~ *a carpet*⟩ ⟨~ *a cloth on the table*⟩ **b** to set in order or position ⟨~ *a table for dinner*⟩ ⟨~ *bricks*⟩ **c** to put (strands) in place and twist to form a rope, hawser, or cable; *also* to make by so doing ⟨~ *up rope*⟩ **8a** to put or impose as a duty, burden, or punishment – esp + *on* or *upon* ⟨~ *a tax on land*⟩ **b** to put as a burden of reproach ⟨laid *the blame on him*⟩ **c** to advance as an accusation; impute ⟨*the disaster was* laid *to faulty inspection*⟩ ⟨laid *a charge of manslaughter*⟩ **9** to place (something immaterial) on something ⟨~ *stress on grammar*⟩ **10** to prepare, contrive ⟨*a well-*laid *plan*⟩ **11a** to bring into position or against or into contact with something; place, apply ⟨laid *the watch to his ear*⟩ ⟨*the horse* laid *his ears back*⟩ **b** to prepare or position for action or operation ⟨~ *a fire in the fireplace*⟩; *also* to adjust (a gun) to the proper direction and elevation **12** to bring to a specified condition ⟨~ *waste the land*⟩ **13a** to assert, allege ⟨~ *claim to an estate*⟩ **b** to submit for examination and judgment ⟨laid *his case before the tribunal*⟩ **14** to place fictitiously; locate ⟨*the scene is* laid *in wartime London*⟩ **15** *slang* to copulate with or persuade to copulation ~ *vi* **1** to produce and deposit eggs **2** to wager, bet **3a** to apply oneself vigorously ⟨laid *to his oars*⟩ **b** *nautical* to proceed to a specified place or position ⟨~ *close to the wind*⟩ **4** *dial* to plan, prepare ⟨~ *for a chance to escape*⟩ **5** *nonstandard* ¹LIE [ME *leyen*, fr OE *lecgan*; akin to OE *licgan* to lie – more at LIE] – **lay about one** to deal blows indiscriminately; lash out on all sides – **lay it on** to exaggerate, esp in order to flatter or impress ⟨*he was really* laying it on *a bit thick*⟩ – see also **lay one's** CARDS **on the table, lay** CLAIM **(to), lay a** FINGER **on, lay something on the** LINE, **lay** LOW/OPEN, **lay** SIEGE **to**

*usage* One of the commonest errors in English is to use **lay** (**laid, laid**) instead of **lie** (**lay, lain**). The two verbs have been confused by **distinguished writers** ⟨△ *there let him* lay – Lord Byron⟩ ⟨△ *Eddy went forward and* laid *down* – Ernest Hemingway⟩. This confusion is caused partly by the fact that **lay** is also the past of **lie**; but **lain** is not part of **lay** and **laid** is not part of **lie**. While **lay** is chiefly transitive ⟨*lay the table*⟩ with a few intransitive senses ⟨*hens have stopped* laying⟩, **lie** is intransitive only ⟨*lie on the floor*⟩. One can **lay** somebody **low** (= bring him/her down) or **lie low** (= stay in hiding). In the following examples, **lie** is used correctly ⟨*I always* lie (not △ lay) *down in the afternoons*⟩ ⟨*I'm* lying (not △ laying) *down now*⟩ ⟨*I* lay (not △ laid) *down yesterday afternoon*⟩ ⟨*I have never* lain (not △ laid) *down in the morning*⟩.

**lay aside** *vt* **1** to put aside for future use; store, reserve **2** to put out of use or consideration; abandon

**lay by** *vt* LAY ASIDE ~ *vi, of a ship* to come to a standstill; HEAVE TO

**lay down** *vt* **1** to surrender; GIVE UP ⟨lay down *your arms*⟩ ⟨laid down *his life for the cause*⟩ **2** to establish, prescribe ⟨lay down *a scale for a map*⟩; *esp* to dictate ⟨lay down *the law*⟩ **3** to store; *specif* to store (wine) in a cellar **4** to direct towards a target ⟨lay down *a barrage*⟩ **5** to begin to construct (e g a ship or railway) – see also **lay down the** LAW

**lay in** *vt* to collect for storage in preparation ⟨*must* lay in *some candles before the power cuts*⟩

**lay into** *vt, informal* to attack physically or verbally ⟨laid into *the government*⟩ ⟨*should have seen them* lay into *those scones*⟩

**lay off** *vt* **1** to cease to employ (a worker) temporarily **2** to add (a card) to a matched set already exposed on the table (e g in rummy, canasta, etc) **3** *informal* **3a** to let alone **b** to avoid ⟨lay off *pastry and pud* – The Times⟩ ~ *vi, informal* to stop or desist, *specif* from an activity causing annoyance

**lay on** *vt, chiefly Br* **1** to supply (e g water or gas) to a building **2** to supply facilities for; organize ⟨*cars were* laid on⟩

**lay out** *vt* **1** to prepare (a corpse) for a funeral **2** to arrange according to a plan ⟨*flower beds and lawns were* laid out *in a formal pattern*⟩ **3** *informal* to knock flat or unconscious **4** *informal* to spend **5** *informal* to exert (oneself) for a purpose ⟨*he wouldn't* lay *himself* out *to please the chairman of the board*⟩

**lay to** *vt* to check the motion of (a ship) ~ *vi* LIE TO

**lay up** *vt* **1** LAY ASIDE **1 2** LAY IN **3** to cause to remain inactive – usu pass ⟨*was* laid up *in bed for a week with a bad back*⟩

**²lay** *n* **1a** a place where something lies or is laid; a covert, lair **b** a mussel or oyster bed **2** a share of profit (e g from a whaling voyage) paid in lieu of wages **3** the direction or amount of twist in strands of rope **4** the state of one that lays eggs ⟨*hens coming into* ~⟩ **5** a guide against which a sheet is laid in a printing press **6** *chiefly NAm* the way in which a thing lies or is laid in relation to something else ⟨*the* ~ *of the land*⟩ **7** *informal* a line of work; occupation **8** *slang* an act of, or partner in, sexual intercourse

**³lay** *past of* LIE

**⁴lay** *n* **1** a simple narrative poem intended to be sung; a ballad **2** a melody, song; *specif* a 14th-century French song with usu 12 unequal stanzas sung to different tunes [ME, fr OF *lai*]

**⁵lay** *adj* **1** of or performed by the laity; not ecclesiastical or clerical **2** of members of a religious house occupied with domestic or manual work ⟨*a* ~ *brother*⟩ **3** not belonging to a particular profession; nonprofessional ⟨*the* ~ *public*⟩ *synonyms* see ³PROFANE *antonyms* clerical, ecclesiastical [ME, fr OF *lai*, fr LL *laicus*, fr Gk *laikos* of the people, fr *laos* people]

**layabout** /'layəbowt/ *n, chiefly Br* a lazy shiftless person; an idler

**'lay-,by** *n, pl* **lay-bys** *Br* a branch from or a widening of a road to permit vehicles to stop without obstructing traffic

**lay day** *n* a day allowed for loading or unloading a vessel [prob fr ¹*lay*]

**¹layer** /'layə/ *n* **1** someone or something that lays: e g **1a** a hen that produces eggs ⟨*the leghorn is a splendid* ~⟩ **b** a workman who lays bricks **2** a single thickness of some substance spread or lying over, on, or under another, often as part of a series **3a** a branch or shoot of a plant treated to induce it to take root while still attached to the parent plant **b** a plant developed by layering **4** any of a series of gradations or depths (e g of complexity or feeling) ⟨*fanning out harmonies . . . adding* ~ *upon* ~ *to the melody* – Nation Review (Melbourne)⟩ ⟨*pain that penetrates through the* ~ s *of sleep*⟩

**²layer** *vt* **1a** to arrange or form (as if) in layers ⟨*potato slices* ~ed *with cheese*⟩ **b** to form out of or with layers ⟨*you can see in the excavation how the Romans used to* ~ *their roads*⟩ **2** to propagate (a plant) by means of layers **3** to cut (hair) in layers ~ *vi, of a plant* to form roots where a stem or shoot comes in contact with the ground

**layerage** /'layərij/ *n* the practice or art of layering plants

**layette** /lay'et/ *n* a complete outfit of clothing and equipment for a newborn infant [Fr, fr MF, dim. of *laye* box, fr MD *lade*; akin to OE *hladan* to load – more at LADE]

**lay figure** *n* **1** a jointed model of the human body used by artists, esp to show the arrangement of drapery **2** a person likened to a dummy or puppet [obs *layman* lay figure, fr D *leeman*, fr *lid* limb + *man* man]

**laying on of hands** *n* the act of laying hands on a person's head to confer a spiritual blessing (e g in Christian ordination, confirmation, or faith healing)

**layman** /'laymən/, *fem* **laywoman** /-,woomən/ *n* **1** a person who is not a member of the clergy **2** a person without special (e g professional) knowledge of some field [⁵ *lay*]

**layoff** /-,of/ *n* **1** the laying off of an employee or a work force **2** a period of unemployment, inactivity, or idleness

**layout** /-,owt/ *n* **1** arranging or laying out **2** the plan, design, or arrangement of something (e g rooms in a building or matter to be printed) laid out **3a** something laid out ⟨*a model train* ~⟩ **b** a set or outfit, esp of tools

**lay reader** *n* a lay person authorized to conduct parts of church services

**lay shaft** *n* an intermediate shaft that receives and transmits power, esp in a gearbox [prob fr ¹*lay*]

**'lay-,up** *n* a shot in basketball made from near the basket usu by bouncing the ball off the backboard

**lazar** /'lazə/ *n, archaic* one afflicted with a repulsive disease;

*specif* a leper [ME, fr ML *lazarus,* fr LL *Lazarus,* a diseased beggar mentioned in Lk 16:20]

**lazaret, lazarette** /ˌlazəˈret/ *n* a lazaretto [Fr, fr It dial. *lazareto*]

**lazaretto** /ˌlazəˈretoh/ *n, pl* **lazarettos** **1** a hospital for contagious diseases **2** a building or a ship used for detention in quarantine **3** a ship's storeroom [It dial. *lazareto,* alter. (influenced by It *lazzaro* leper, fr ML *lazurus*) of *nazareto,* fr *Santa Maria di Nazaret,* church in Venice that maintained a hospital]

**laze** /layz/ *vi* to act or rest lazily; idle ⟨*he* ~d *in the garden all afternoon*⟩ ~ *vt* to pass (time) *away* in idleness or relaxation ⟨*he* ~d *away the whole afternoon*⟩ [back-formation fr *lazy*] – **laze** *n*

**lazulite** /ˈlazyooliet/ *n* an often crystalline azure-blue mineral that is a phosphate of aluminium, iron, and magnesium, $(Mg,Fe)Al_2(PO_4)_2(OH)_2$ [Ger *lazulith,* fr ML *lazulum* lapis lazuli] – **lazulitic** *adj*

**lazurite** /ˈlazyooriet/ *n* a blue mineral that consists essentially of a complex sulphur-containing silicate of aluminium and sodium and is the main constituent of the gemstone LAPIS LAZULI [Ger *lasurit,* fr ML *lazur* lapis lazuli, fr Ar *lāzaward*]

**lazy** /ˈlayzi/ *adj* **1a** disinclined or averse to activity; indolent; *also* not energetic or vigorous ⟨*a* ~ *manner*⟩ **b** encouraging inactivity or indolence ⟨*a* ~ *afternoon*⟩ **2** moving slowly; sluggish ⟨*a* ~ *river*⟩ **synonyms** see LETHARGY **antonyms** active, energetic [perh fr MLG *lasich* feeble; akin to MHG *erleswen* to become weak] – **lazily** *adv,* **laziness** *n*

**lazybones** /-ˌbohnz/ *n, pl* **lazybones** *informal* a lazy person

**lazy eye** *n* AMBLYOPIA (impaired vision unaccompanied by damage to the eye)

**lazy Susan** /ˈsoohz(ə)n/ *n* a revolving tray placed on a dining table for serving food, condiments, or relishes [fr the forename *Susan*]

**lazy tongs** *n* an arrangement of jointed and pivoted bars capable of great extension, used for picking up or handling something at a distance

**LCD** *n* a display of numbers, symbols, etc (e g in a digital watch) produced by applying an electric current to LIQUID CRYSTAL units in order to increase the amount of light they reflect [*liquid crystal display*]

**L-dopa** /ˌel ˈdohpə/ *n* a chemical compound that is the form of DOPA that occurs naturally in plant and animal cells and is used as a drug, esp in the treatment of PARKINSON'S DISEASE [*l- + dopa*]

**lea, ley** /lee/ *n, chiefly poetic* (an area of) grassland; pasture [ME *leye,* fr *leye* fallow, unploughed, fr OE *læg-;* akin to OE *liegan* to lie]

¹**leach** /leech/ *n* **1** a perforated vessel used in leaching; *esp* one used to hold wood ashes through which water is passed to extract the LYE (alkaline liquid used in making soap) **2** a solution or product obtained by leaching **3** leaching [prob alter. of E dial. *letch* muddy ditch, fr ME *lache, leche* stream flowing through boggy land, fr OE *læcc, lecc,* fr *leccan* to wet, moisten – more at LEAK; (2,3) ²*leach*]

²**leach** *vt* **1** to separate the soluble components from (a mixture) by the action of a percolating liquid (e g water) **2** to remove (soluble matter) by the action of a percolating liquid – often + *out* ⟨~ *out alkali from ashes*⟩ ~ *vi* to pass out or through (as if) by percolation – **leacher** *n*

³**lead** /leed/ *vb* **led** /led/ *vt* **1a(1)** to guide on a way, esp by going in advance ⟨*led him by the hand*⟩ **a(2)** to cause to go with one (under duress) ⟨*led the condemned man to the scaffold*⟩ **b** to direct or guide on a course, or to a state or condition; influence ⟨*reflection led him to a better understanding of the problem*⟩ ⟨*he was easily led*⟩ **c** to serve as a channel or route for ⟨*a pipe* ~s *water to the house*⟩ ⟨*the road led her to a small village*⟩ **2** to go through; live ⟨~ *a quiet life*⟩ **3a(1)** to direct the operations, activity, or performance of; have charge of ⟨*led a safari into little-known territory*⟩ **a(2)** to act as or be a leader in or of ⟨~ *fashion*⟩ ⟨~ *an orchestra*⟩ **b** to go or be at the head or ahead of ⟨*Cambridge were* ~ing *Oxford all the way in the last boat race*⟩ **4** to begin play, esp at a card game, with ⟨~ *trumps*⟩ **5** to begin a series of blows with ⟨*led a short jab to the head*⟩ ~ *vi* **1a(1)** to guide somebody or something along a way **a(2)** to act as or be a leader **b(1)** to lie or run in a specified place or direction ⟨*the path* ~s *uphill*⟩ **b(2)** to serve as an entrance or passage ⟨*this door* ~s *us to the garden*⟩ **2a** to be first or ahead **b(1)** to begin, open – usu + *off* ⟨*led off with a speech by the chairman*⟩ **b(2)** to play the first card of a trick, round, or

game **3** to tend or be directed towards a specified result ⟨*study* ~ing *to a degree*⟩ **4** to direct the first of a series of blows at an opponent in boxing (*with* the right or left hand) – see also **lead somebody a merry** DANCE, **lead by the** NOSE [ME *leden,* fr OE *lǣdan;* akin to OHG *leiten* to lead, OE *līthan* to go]

**lead back** *vt* to lead (a card) from a suit that one's partner has originally led

**lead off** *vb* to make a start (on); open – see also LEAD-OFF

**lead on** *vt* **1** to entice or induce to proceed in a (mistaken or unwise) course **2** to cause to believe something that is untrue; DECEIVE 1

**lead up to** *vt* to prepare the way for, esp by using a gradual or indirect approach

²**lead** /leed/ *n* **1a(1)** position at the front or ahead **a(2)** the act or privilege of leading in cards; *also* the card or suit led **a(3)** the first of a series or exchange of blows in boxing **a(4)** a pattern of movement of a horse in which one or other of the front feet strikes the ground first **b** guidance, direction; *also* an example, precedent **c** a margin or position of advantage or superiority **2a(1)** a deposit of ore; a lode **a(2)** a gold-bearing gravel deposit in an old river bed **b** a channel of water **(1)** leading to a mill **(2)** through an icefield **c** an indication, clue **d** (one who plays) a principal role in a dramatic production **e** a line or strap for leading or restraining an animal (e g a dog) ⟨*dogs must be kept on a* ~⟩ **f(1)** an introductory section of a news story **f(2)** a news story of chief importance **3** an insulated wire or cable that conducts an electric current **4** ⁴PITCH 2b(2) (distance between two threads of a screw)

³**lead** /leed/ *adj* acting or serving as a lead or leader ⟨*a* ~ *article*⟩ ⟨*the* ~ *singer in the group*⟩

⁴**lead** /led/ *n* **1** a heavy dense bluish-white metallic chemical element occurring chiefly in the mineral GALENA, that is soft and easily worked and is used esp in pipes, cable sheaths, batteries, and shields against radioactivity, and as a constituent of solder and the alloy (TYPE METAL) from which printing type is made **2a** the (lead) weight on a line for taking soundings at sea **b** *pl* lead framing for panes in windows **c** a thin strip of metal used to separate lines of type in printing **3a** a thin stick of GRAPHITE (blackish soft form of carbon) or crayon in or for a pencil – compare LEAD PENCIL **b** WHITE LEAD (white lead-containing pigment used, esp formerly, in paints) **4** bullets, projectiles ⟨*the* ~ *was flying*⟩ **5** TETRAETHYL LEAD (poisonous liquid added to petrol to improve its combustion properties) **6** *pl, Br* (a usu flat roof covered with) thin sheets of lead △ **led** [ME *leed,* fr OE *lēad;* akin to MHG *lōt* lead] – **leadless** *adj* – **swing the lead** to neglect one's work or responsibilities, esp by inventing excuses; malinger [*lead* 2a; fr the leadsman's job being considered easy]

⁵**lead** /led/ *vt* **1** to cover, line, or weight with lead **2** to fix (window glass) in position with leads ⟨*an old window with* ~ed *panes*⟩ **3** to separate lines of (type) with leads **4** to treat or mix with lead or a lead compound ⟨~ed *petrol*⟩

**lead acetate** *n* an ACETATE of lead; *esp* a poisonous chemical compound, $Pb(CH_3COO)_2$, that readily dissolves in water and is used in dyeing and printing cottons

**lead arsenate** *n* an ARSENATE of lead; *esp* an acidic chemical compound, $PbHAsO_4$, used in insecticides

**lead azide** *n* an explosive chemical compound, $Pb(N_3)_2$, used as a detonating agent in explosive charges

**lead carbonate** /led/ *n* a carbonate of lead; *esp* WHITE LEAD (white pigment used, esp formerly, in paints)

**lead chromate** *n* a CHROMATE of lead; *esp* CHROME YELLOW (yellow pigment used, esp formerly, in paints)

**lead colic** *n* severe abdominal pains occurring as a symptom of LEAD POISONING – called also PAINTER'S COLIC

**lead dioxide** *n* a poisonous chemical compound, $PbO_2$, that gives off oxygen when heated and is used in the manufacture of dyes and pigments, and as an ELECTRODE (plate that conducts electricity) in some batteries (e g those in cars)

**leaden** /ˈled(ə)n/ *adj* **1a** made of lead **b** dull grey ⟨*a* ~ *sky*⟩ **2a** oppressively heavy ⟨~ *limbs*⟩ ⟨*a* ~ *silence*⟩ **b** lacking spirit or animation; sluggish ⟨~ *prose*⟩ – **leadenly** *adv,* **leadenness** *n*

**leader** /ˈleedə/ *n* **1a** a main or end shoot of a plant **b** *pl* dots or hyphens used (e g in an index) to lead the eye horizontally **c** a short length of material for attaching the end of a fishing line to a lure or hook **d** an article offered at a special low price to stimulate business; LOSS LEADER **e** a blank section at the beginning or end of a reel of film or recording tape **2** a person who leads: e g **2a** a guide, conductor **b(1)** a person who directs a military force or unit **b(2)** a person who has commanding authority or influence **c(1)** the principal officer of a political party **c(2)** either of two government ministers who have charge of the disposition of government business in Parliament ⟨*the* Leader *of the Commons*⟩ **c(3)** the principal member of the party elite in a totalitarian system **d(1)** a member of a musical ensemble who leads its performance **d(2)** *Br* the principal first violinist and usu assistant conductor of an orchestra **d(3)** *NAm* CONDUCTOR **c 3** a horse or either of a pair of horses placed in advance of the other horses of a team **4** *chiefly Br* a newspaper editorial **5** *Br* LEADING COUNSEL – **leaderless** *adj*, **leadership** *n*

**leader of the opposition** *n* the principal member of the opposition party in Parliament who is given a salary and an important role in organizing the business of the house

**lead glass** /led/ *n* glass containing LEAD MONOXIDE; *esp* a tough brilliant high quality glass containing 30 per cent or more lead monoxide

**ˈlead-ˌin** /leed/ *n* **1** introductory matter **2** the cable that runs from an aerial to a transmitter or receiver **3** that part of the groove on a record before the recording – **lead-in** *adj*

**ˈleading** /ˈleeding/ *adj* coming or ranking first; foremost, principal ⟨*the* ~ *role*⟩

**²leading** /ˈleding/ *n* the process of spacing typeset lines (e g by inserting leads); *also* a space between printed lines made (as if) with a lead

**leading aircraftman** /ˈleeding/ *n* – see MILITARY RANKS table

**leading article** *n*, **1** *chiefly Br* LEADER **4 2** *chiefly NAm* the article given the most significant position or most prominent display in a periodical

**leading case** *n* a legal case which establishes a precedent and is used in deciding subsequent cases

**leading counsel** *n*, *Br* a QUEEN'S COUNSEL who is retained to conduct a case in court, usu assisted by a junior barrister

**leading diagonal** *n*, *maths* PRINCIPAL DIAGONAL (upper left to lower right)

**leading edge** *n* the foremost edge of an aerofoil (e g a propeller blade or wing)

**leading indicator** *n* an economic variable which has a pattern of movement similar to that of the general business cycle, but which generally predates it. It can thus be used to forecast economic change.

**leading lady,** *masc* **leading man** *n* an actress who plays the female lead in a film, play, etc

**leading light** *n* a prominent and influential person in a particular sphere

**leading note** *n* the seventh note of a DIATONIC scale (ordinary 8-note musical scale), represented in sol-fa by *te* – called also SEVENTH

**leading question** *n* a question so phrased as to suggest the expected answer

   *usage* **Leading question** has a precise meaning in law; it is not merely a "principal", "embarrassingly direct", "unfair", or "difficult" question. A true **leading question** is helpful rather than hostile in intention.

**leading rein** *n* **1** a rein used for leading a horse; *esp* one for controlling the horse of a pupil **2** *pl* straps by which children are supported when beginning to walk

**leading seaman** *n* – see MILITARY RANKS table

**leading strings** *n pl* **1** LEADING REINS **2 2** a state of dependence or tutelage – usu in *in leading strings*

**lead line** /led/ *n* SOUNDING LINE

**lead monoxide** *n* a poisonous chemical compound, PbO, that exists in a yellow form and a brownish-red form and is used in making rubber, LEAD GLASS, and varnishes and as a glaze for pottery – compare LITHARGE, MASSICOT

**lead-off** /leed/ *n* a beginning or leading action; a start – **lead-off** *adj*

**lead pencil** /led/ *n* a pencil containing a lead of GRAPHITE (blackish soft form of carbon)

**lead poisoning** *n* poisoning that results from the absorption of lead into the body and is characterized by severe pains in the abdomen, a dark line along the gums, and paralysis of muscles

**leadscrew** /ˈleedˌskrooh/ *n* a screw that moves the carriage of a lathe

**leadsman** /ˈledzmən/ *n* a man who uses a sounding lead to determine the depth of water

**lead time** /leed/ *n* the period between the initiation and completion of a new production process ⟨*a long* ~ *on a new aircraft*⟩

**leadwork** /ˈledˌwuhk/ *n* **1** something made of lead **2** work that is done with lead

**¹leaf** /leef/ *n, pl* **leaves** /leevz/ **1a(1)** any of the usu green, flat, and typically broad-bladed outgrowths from the stem of a plant that function primarily in the manufacture of food for the plant by photosynthesis **a(2)** a modified leaf (e g a petal or SEPAL) **b(1)** (the state of having) foliage ⟨*the trees are already in* ~⟩ **b(2)** the leaves of a plant (e g of the tea or tobacco plants) as an article of commerce **b(3)** a category of FLUE-CURED tobacco (tobacco cured by drying without direct exposure to smoke) consisting of the leaves pulled from above the centre of the plant stalk **2** something suggestive of a leaf: e g **2a** a part of a book or folded sheet of paper containing a page on each side **b(1)** a part (e g of a window shutter, folding door, or table) that slides or is hinged – compare DROP LEAF **b(2)** a section that can be inserted into a tabletop to extend it **c(1)** a thin sheet of metal, marble, etc **c(2)** metal (e g gold or silver) in sheets usu thinner than foil **c(3)** any of the metal strips of a LEAF SPRING [ME *leef*, fr OE *lēaf*; akin to OHG *loub* leaf, L *liber* bast, book] – **leafless** *adj*, **leaflike** *adj*

**²leaf** *vi* to send out or produce leaves

   **leaf through** *vt* to turn over the pages of (e g a book) quickly while only glancing at the contents – compare FLICK THROUGH

**leafage** /ˈleefij/ *n* **1** leaves, foliage **2** a representation of leaves for ornamentation

**leaf beet** *n* CHARD (vegetable with thick stalks and spinachlike leaves)

**leaf beetle** *n* any of a family (Chrysomelidae) of numerous small brightly coloured leaf-eating beetles

**leaf blotch** *n* a plant disease caused by a fungus (*Rhynchosporium secalis*) that attacks the leaves of cereals, esp barley, and adversely affects the development of the grain

**leaf bud** *n* a plant bud that develops into a leafy shoot and does not produce flowers

**leaf butterfly** *n* any of a genus (*Kallima*) of butterflies of S Asia and the E Indies that mimic leaves

**leaf curl** *n* any of various plant diseases characterized by curling of the leaves

**leaf-cutter bee** *n* any of various bees (genus *Megachile*) that live alone rather than in organized colonies and damage garden flowers (e g roses) by cutting pieces from the leaves for use in building the nests in which they lay their eggs

**-leafed** /leeft/ *comb form* (*adj* → *adj*) -leaved

**leaf fat** *n* the fat that lines the cavity of the abdomen and encloses the kidneys; *esp* that of a pig, used in the manufacture of LEAF LARD

**leafhopper** /-ˌhopə/ *n* any of numerous small often brightly coloured leaping insects (family Cicadellidae, order Homoptera) that suck the juices of plants and often cause damage to crops

**leaf insect** *n* any of various insects (family Phyllidae) common in S Asia that are related to the STICK INSECTS and whose flat green bodies and flaps on the legs closely resemble plant leaves

**leaf lard** *n* high-quality lard made from LEAF FAT

**leaflet** /ˈleeflit/ *n* **1a** any of the parts into which a COMPOUND LEAF is divided **b** a small or young leaf **2** a single sheet of paper or small loose-leaf pamphlet containing printed matter (e g advertising)

**leaf miner** *n* any of various small insects (e g some moths and flies) that as larvae burrow in and eat the internal tissues of leaves

**leaf mould** *n* **1** a mould or mildew of leaves **2** a compost or soil layer composed chiefly of decayed vegetable matter

**leaf roll** *n* a virus disease of the potato that is transmitted by aphids, is characterized by an upward and inward rolling of the leaf edges, and results in stunted growth and a much reduced yield

**leaf roller** *n* any of various moths and butterflies (esp superfamily Tortricoidea) whose caterpillars make a shelter by rolling up plant leaves

**leaf rust** *n* a plant disease (RUST), esp of cereal grasses (e g wheat), that is characterized by reddish-brown discoloration chiefly of the leaves

**leaf shutter** *n* a shutter for a camera that is usu found within or immediately behind the lens and is made of usu five thin metallic leaves that swing out of the light path when a picture is taken

**leaf spot** *n* any of various plant diseases typically caused by fungi and characterized by dark often circular spots on the leaves

**leaf spring** *n* a spring (eg between the body and the back axle of a motor vehicle) made of superimposed metal strips

**leafstalk** /-,stawk/ *n* the stalk attaching a leaf to the stem of a plant; PETIOLE

**leaf stripe** *n* any of various plant diseases characterized by striped discolorations on the leaves

**leafy** /'leefi/ *adj* **1a** having or thick with leaves ⟨~ *woodlands*⟩ **b** *of a plant* having broad-bladed leaves **c** consisting chiefly of leaves ⟨*green* ~ *vegetables*⟩ **2** resembling or having the form of a leaf or thin layer – **leafiness** *n*

¹**league** /leeg/ *n* any of various units of distance of about 3 miles (5 kilometres) [ME *leuge, lege,* fr LL *leuga,* of Gaulish origin]

²**league** *n* **1a** *taking sing or pl vb* an association of nations, groups, or people for a common purpose or to promote a common interest **b** (a competition for an overall title, in which each person or team plays all the others at least once, held by) an association of people or sports clubs ⟨*a chess* ~⟩ ⟨*the Football League*⟩ **2** a class, category ⟨*the top* ~⟩ [ME (Sc) *ligg,* fr MF *ligue,* fr OIt *liga,* fr *ligare* to bind, fr L – more at LIGATURE] – **leaguer** *n* – **in league** in alliance

³**league** *vb* to form into a league

**leaguer** /'leegə/ *n* LAAGER (military camp) [D *leger;* camp, siege, couch, lair; akin to OHG *legar* act of lying down – more at LAIR]

**league table** *n* a table showing the relative positions of competitors in a league; *broadly* a list in order of merit

¹**leak** /leek/ *vi* **1** to (let liquid, gas, or light) enter or escape through a crack or hole, usu by a fault or mistake ⟨*fumes* ~ *in*⟩ ⟨*this bucket* ~s⟩ ⟨*all the water has* ~ed *away*⟩ **2** to become known despite efforts at concealment – often + *out* ~ *vt* **1** to permit to enter or escape (as if) through a leak **2** to give out (information) surreptitiously ⟨~ed *the story to the press*⟩ [ME *leken,* fr ON *leka;* akin to OE *leccan* to moisten, OIr *legaim* I melt] – **leakage** *n*

²**leak** *n* **1a** a crack or hole through which something (eg a liquid or gas) is admitted or escapes, usu by mistake **b** a means by which something (eg secret information) is admitted or escapes, usu with prejudicial effect **c** a loss of electricity due to faulty insulation; *also* the point or the path at which such loss occurs **2** a leaking or that which is leaked; *esp* a disclosure **3** *slang* an act of urinating – often + *have* or *take* △ **leak**

**leaky** /'leeki/ *adj* **1** permitting liquid, information, etc to leak in or out; *broadly* not watertight ⟨*a* ~ *argument*⟩ **2** *of a mutant organism* having a LEAKY GENE; showing some of the characteristics typical of the normal gene and some typical of the mutant gene – **leakiness** *n*

**leaky gene** *n* HYPOMORPH (mutant gene that retains some of the normal gene's function)

**leal** /leel/ *adj, chiefly Scot* loyal, true [ME *leel,* fr OF *leial, leel* – more at LOYAL] – **leally** *adv*

¹**lean** /leen/ *vb,* **leant** /lent/, **leaned** /leend, lent/ *vi* **1a** to incline or bend from a vertical position ⟨~t *forward to look*⟩ **b** to rest supported on or against something in a sloping position **2** to incline in opinion, taste, etc ~ *vt* to place *on/against* for support ⟨*he* ~t *his bike against the wall*⟩ – see also **lean over** BACKWARDS [ME *lenen,* fr OE *hleonian;* akin to OHG *hlinēn* to lean, Gk *klinein,* L *clinare*] – **lean** *n*

*usage* **Leant** and **leaned** are equally common in British English, but **leaned** is the commoner American form.

**lean on** *vt* **1** to rely for support or inspiration on; depend on **2** *informal* to exert pressure on; use coercion on

²**lean** *adj* **1a** lacking or deficient in flesh or bulk **b** *of meat* containing little or no fat **2** lacking richness, sufficiency, or value **3** deficient in an essential or important quality or ingredient: eg **3a** *of an ore* containing little valuable mineral **b** *esp of an air-fuel mixture* low in the fuel component [ME *lene,* fr OE *hlǣne*] – **leanly** *adv,* **leanness** *n*

³**lean** *n* the part of meat that consists principally of fat-free muscular tissue

**leaning** /'leening/ *n* a definite but weak attraction, tendency, or partiality

'**lean-,to** *n, pl* **lean-tos** a small building with a roof that rests on the side of a larger building or wall

¹**leap** /leep/ *vb* **leapt** /lept/, **leaped** /leept, lept/; **leaping** *vi* **1** to jump in or through the air ⟨~ *over a fence*⟩ ⟨*a fish* ~s *out of the water*⟩ **2** to pass abruptly from one state or topic to another or from nonexistence to existence; *esp* to rise quickly ⟨*he* ~t *into prominence from obscurity*⟩ ⟨*the idea* ~t *into his mind*⟩ ~

*vt* to pass over by leaping [ME *lepen* to run, jump, fr OE *hlēapan;* akin to OHG *hlouffan* to run] – **leaper** *n*

*usage* **Leapt** is the commoner inflection in British English, but **leaped** is the commoner American form.

**leap at** *vt* to seize eagerly at an opportuntiy, offer, etc

²**leap** *n* **1a** (the distance covered by) a jump **b** a place leapt over or from **2** a sudden transition, esp a rise or increase

¹**leapfrog** /-,frog/ *n* a game in which one player bends down and another leaps over him/her

²**leapfrog** *vb* **-gg-** **1** to leap (over) (as if) in leapfrog **2** to go or send ahead of (each other) in turn; (cause to) progress by overtaking ⟨*to* ~ *two military units*⟩

**leap year** *n* a year with an extra day added to make it coincide with the solar year; *esp* a year in the GREGORIAN CALENDAR with February 29th as the 366th day [prob fr the "leap" made by any date after February in a leap year over the weekday on which it would normally fall]

**learn** /luhn/ *vb* **learnt** /luhnt/, **learned** /luhnd, luhnt/ *vt* **1a(1)** to gain knowledge or understanding of or skill in by study, instruction, or experience ⟨~ *a trade*⟩ **a(2)** to memorize ⟨~ *the lines of a play*⟩ **b** to come to be able – + *infin* ⟨~ *to dance*⟩ **c** to come to realize or know ⟨*we* ~t *that he was ill*⟩ **2** *substandard* to teach ⟨*that teacher never* ~t *me nothing*⟩ ~ *vi* to acquire knowledge or skill [ME *lernen,* fr OE *leornian;* akin to OHG *lernēn* to learn, L *lira* furrow, track] – **learnable** *adj,* **learner** *n*

*usage* **Learnt** and **learned** are equally common in British English, but **learned** is the commoner American form. It may be clearer to use **learnt,** to avoid confusion with the adjective **learned** /'luhnid/ (= "erudite").

**learned** /'luhnid; *sense 2* luhnd/ *adj* **1** characterized by or associated with learning; erudite **2** acquired by learning ⟨~ *versus innate behaviour patterns*⟩ – **learnedly** *adv,* **learnedness** *n*

**learning** /'luhning/ *n* **1** the acquiring of knowledge or skill ⟨~ *for pleasure*⟩ **2** knowledge or skill acquired by instruction or study ⟨*his* ~ *astonished them*⟩ **3** modification of a behavioural tendency by experience (eg exposure to conditioning) **synonyms** see KNOWLEDGE

¹**lease** /lees/ *n* **1** a contract putting the land or other property of one party at the disposal of another, usu for a stated period and rent **2** a piece of land or property that is leased **3** a (prospect of) continuance – esp in *lease of life* ⟨*his recovery gave him a new* ~ *of life*⟩

²**lease** *vt* **1** to grant by lease **2** to hold under a lease **synonyms** see ²HIRE [AF *lesser,* fr OF *laissier* to let go, fr L *laxare* to loosen, fr *laxus* slack – more at SLACK]

**leasehold** /-,hohld/ *n* tenure by or property held by lease – **leaseholder** *n*

**leash** /leesh/ *n* **1a** ²LEAD **2e b** a restraint, check **2** *taking sing or pl vb* **2a** a set of three animals (eg greyhounds, foxes, or hares) **b** a set of three ⟨*a* ~ *of drawers . . . as Tom, Dick, and Francis* – Shak⟩ [ME *lees, leshe,* fr OF *laisse,* fr *laissier*] – **leash** *vt*

¹**least** /leest/ *adj* **1** lowest in rank, degree, or importance **2a** smallest in quantity or extent **b** being of a kind distinguished by small size – used in names of plants and animals ⟨~ *bittern*⟩ **c** smallest possible; slightest ⟨*haven't the* ~ *idea*⟩ [ME *leest,* fr OE *lǣst,* superl of *lǣssa* less]

²**least** *n* the smallest quantity, number, or amount ⟨*it's the* ~ *I can do*⟩ ⟨*to say the* ~⟩ ⟨*nobody would worry in the* ~ – SEU S⟩ – **at least 1** as a minimum; if not more ⟨*costs at least £5*⟩ **2** if nothing else; IN ANY CASE ⟨*at least it's legal*⟩

³**least** *adv* to the smallest degree or extent ⟨*least-known*⟩ ⟨*when we* ~ *expected it*⟩ – **least of all** especially not ⟨*no one,* least of all *the children, paid attention*⟩

**least common denominator** *n, maths* LOWEST COMMON DENOMINATOR

**least squares** *n pl* a method of fitting a curve to a set of points representing statistical data, in such a way that the sum of the squares of the distances of the points from the curve is a minimum

**least upper bound** *n, maths* SUPREMUM

**leastways** /'leestwayz/, **leastwise** /'leestwiez/ *adv, chiefly dial* AT LEAST 2

¹**leather** /'ledhə/ *n* **1** animal skin dressed for use **2** the dangling flap of a dog's ear **3** something wholly or partly made of leather; *esp* a piece of chamois, used esp for polishing metal or glass **4** STIRRUP LEATHER [ME *lether,* fr OE *lether-;* akin to OHG *leder* leather] – **leatherlike** *adj*

²**leather** *vt* to beat with a strap; thrash

**leatherback** /'ledhə,bak/ *n* the largest existing sea turtle (*Dermochelys coriacea*) distinguished by its flexible CARAPACE (back covering) that is composed of a mosaic of small bones embedded in a thick leathery skin

**leathercloth** /'ledhə,kloth/ *n* fabric coated to resemble leather

**Leatherette** /,ledhə'ret/ *trademark* – used for a product coloured, finished, and embossed in imitation of leather grains

**leatherjacket** /-,jakit/ *n, chiefly Br* the larva of a CRANE FLY (e g the DADDY LONGLEGS), that lives in the soil and causes serious damage to plants (e g crops) by feeding on their roots

**leathern** /'ledhən/ *adj, archaic* made of or resembling leather

**leatherneck** /-,nek/ *n, slang* a soldier; *esp* MARINE 2a – used esp by sailors [fr the leather neckband formerly part of a marine's uniform]

**leatherwood** /'ledhə,wood/ *n* 1 a small tree (*Dirca palustris* of the family Thymeleaceae) with yellow flowers and tough pliant stems, whose bark can be used to make ropes, baskets, etc 2 a tree (*Cyrilla racerniflora* of the family Cyrillaceae) of S America and southeastern parts of the USA, that is cultivated for its attractive white flowers and shiny green leaves 3 an embossed hardboard with a leatherlike finish, used in interior decoration

**leathery** /'ledhəri/ *adj* resembling leather in appearance or consistency; *esp* tough ⟨*his ~ old face*⟩ ⟨*~ overcooked omelettes*⟩

**¹leave** /leev/ *vb* **left** /left/ *vt* **1a(1)** to bequeath ⟨left *a fortune to his son*⟩ **a(2)** to pass members of one's family) remaining after one's death ⟨*~s a widow and two children*⟩ **b** to cause to remain as an aftereffect ⟨*oil ~s a stain*⟩ ⟨*the wound* left *an ugly scar*⟩ **2a** to cause or allow to be or remain in a specified or unaltered condition ⟨*~ the door open*⟩ ⟨*his manner* left *me cold*⟩ ⟨*~ the washing-up for tomorrow*⟩ **b** to fail to include, use, or take along ⟨left *his notes at home*⟩ – sometimes + *off* or *out* ⟨left *his name off the list*⟩ **c** to have remaining or as a remainder ⟨*10 from 12 ~s 2*⟩ **d** to permit to be or remain subject to the action or control of a specified person or thing ⟨*just ~ everything to me*⟩ ⟨*nothing* left *to chance*⟩ **e** to allow to do or continue something without interference ⟨left *him to take care of himself*⟩ **3a** to go away from ⟨*told him to ~ the room*⟩ **b** to desert, abandon ⟨left *his wife*⟩ **c** to end association with; withdraw from ⟨left *school at 15*⟩ **4** to put, station, deposit, or deliver, esp before departing ⟨*the postman* left *a package for you*⟩ ⟨*don't ~ your van outside my gate*⟩ *~ vi* to depart; SET OUT [ME *leven*, fr OE *læfan*; akin to OHG ver*leiben* to leave, OE be*līfan* to be left over, Gk *lipos* fat] – **leaver** *n* – **leave alone/be/** LET ALONE/BE

*usage* Leave should not be used for let in the sense of "allow to" ⟨⚠ leave *me go*⟩. **synonyms** see ¹GO **antonym** remain

**leave off** *vb* to stop, cease ⟨*I wish the rain would* leave off⟩ ⟨leave off *teasing him*⟩

**²leave** *n* **1** permission to do something **2** authorized (extended) absence (e g from duty or employment) *synonyms* see ¹HOLIDAY – **take leave of 1** to say farewell to ⟨*courteously* took leave of *their hosts*⟩ **2** to depart from ⟨*have you* taken leave of *your senses?*⟩ – **take one's leave** to say farewell when leaving a person or place ⟨*I must now* take my leave⟩ [ME *leve*, fr OE *lēaf*; akin to MHG *loube* permission, OE a*lȳfan* to allow – more at BELIEVE]

**³leave** *vi* to produce leaves; leaf [ME *leven*, fr *leef* leaf]

**-leaved** /-leevd/ *comb form* (*adj → adj*) having (such or so many) leaves ⟨*palmate-*leaved⟩ ⟨*4-*leaved *clover*⟩

**¹leaven** /'lev(ə)n/ *n* **1a** a substance (e g yeast) used to produce fermentation in dough; *esp* a mass of fermenting dough reserved for this purpose **b** a substance (e g baking powder) used to produce a gas that lightens dough or batter; RAISING AGENT **2** something that modifies or lightens [ME *levain*, fr MF, fr (assumed) VL *levamen*, fr L *levare* to raise – more at LEVER]

**²leaven** *vt* **1** to raise or make lighter (as if) with a leaven **2** to mingle or permeate with some modifying, tempering, or enlivening element

**leaves** /leevs/ *pl of* LEAF

**'leave-,taking** *n* a departure, farewell

**leavings** /'leevingz/ *n pl* remains, residue

**Lebanese** /,lebə'neez/ *n or adj, pl* **Lebanese** (a native or inhabitant) of the Lebanon [*Lebanon*, country in SW Asia]

**lebensraum** /'layb(ə)nz,rowm (Ger 'le:bənzrəum)/ *n, often cap* **1** territory believed to be necessary for national existence or economic self-sufficiency – used chiefly with reference to the land Nazi Germany attempted to take in World War II **2** space required for life, growth, or activity [Ger, fr *leben* living, life + *raum* space]

**lecher** /'lechə/ *n* a man who engages in lechery [ME *lechour*, fr OF *lecheor*, fr *lechier* to lick, live in debauchery, of Gmc origin; akin to OHG *leckōn* to lick – more at LICK]

**lechery** /'lechəri/ *n* inordinate indulgence in sexual activity; debauchery, lasciviousness – **lecherous** *adj*, **lecherously** *adv*

**lecithin** /'lesəthin/ *n* any of several PHOSPHOLIPIDS (phosphorus-containing fatty chemical compounds) that are widely distributed in animals and plants (e g in nerve tissue and egg yolk) and are used in the manufacture of margarine, chocolate, etc because of their ability to stabilize oil and water mixtures and retard the deterioration of fats and oils; *also* a mixture of or substance rich in lecithins [ISV, fr Gk *lekithos* yolk of an egg]

**lecithinase** /'lesəthinayz, -nays/ *n* any of several ENZYMES that break down lecithins and related chemical compounds

**lectern** /'lek,tuhn/ *n* READING DESK; *esp* one from which the Bible is read in church [ME *lettorne*, fr MF *letrun*, fr ML *lectorinum*, fr L *lector* reader]

**lection** /'leksh(ə)n/ *n* **1** a passage from the Bible proper to be read on a particular day of the church year **2** a variant reading in a particular copy or edition of a text [(1) LL *lection-*, *lectio*, fr L, act of reading, fr *lectus*, pp; (2) NL *lection-*, *lectio*, fr L]

**lectionary** /'leksh(ə)nri/ *n* a book or list of scriptural texts proper to each day of the church year

**lector** /'lektaw/ *n* the reader of a lesson in a church service [LL, reader of the lessons in a church service, fr L, reader, fr *lectus*, pp of *legere* to read – more at LEGEND]

**¹lecture** /'lekchə/ *n* **1** a discourse given to an audience or class, esp for instruction **2** a reproof delivered at length; a long reprimand [ME, act of reading, fr LL *lectura*, fr L *lectus*, pp]

**²lecture** *vi* to deliver a lecture or series of lectures *~ vt* **1** to deliver a lecture to **2** to reprove at length or severely

**lecturer** /'lekchərə/ *n* **1** one who lectures **2** the holder of the lowest regular teaching rank esp in a British university or college; *broadly* a British university or college teacher below professorial rank

**lectureship** /-ship/ *n* the office, duties, or position of an academic lecturer

**led** /led/ *past of* LEAD

**LED** /,el ,ee 'dee; *also* led/ *n* a DIODE that emits light when an electric current is passed through it and that is used esp to display numbers, symbols, etc on a screen (e g in a pocket calculator) [*light-emitting diode*]

**lederhosen** /'laydə,hohz(ə)n (Ger 'le:dərho:zən)/ *n pl* traditional leather shorts that often have braces and are worn in parts of northern Europe, esp Bavaria [Ger, fr MHG *lederhose*, fr *leder* leather + *hose* trousers]

**ledge** /lej/ *n* **1** a usu narrow horizontal edge or shelflike surface that projects from a vertical or steep surface (e g a wall or rock face) ⟨*a window ~*⟩ **2** an underwater ridge or reef, esp near the shore **3** a mineral-bearing lode or vein [ME *legge* bar of a gate, prob fr *leggen* to lay] – **ledgy** *adj*

**¹ledger** /'lejə/ *n* **1** a book containing accounts, into which debits and credits are copied from BOOKS OF ORIGINAL ENTRY **2** a horizontal piece of timber secured to the uprights of scaffolding to support the underfloor timbers [ME *legger*, prob fr *leyen*, *leggen* to lay]

**²ledger** *vi* to fish with LEDGER TACKLE *~ vt* to use (e g a hook or bait) in ledgering

**ledger board** *n* **1** a horizontal board forming the top rail of a simple fence or the handrail of a balustrade **2** a board fitted into the studs of a wall to support the ceiling or floor joists

**ledger line, leger line** *n* a short line added above or below a musical stave to extend its range

**ledger tackle** *n* fishing tackle arranged so that the weight and bait rest on the bottom

**¹lee** /lee/ *n* **1** protecting shelter **2 lee, lee side** the side (e g of a ship) sheltered from the wind [ME, fr OE *hlēo*; akin to OHG *lāo* lukewarm, L *calēre* to be warm]

**²lee** *adj* of the lee ⟨*the rocky point . . . was in sight, broad on the ~ bow* – Frederick Marryat⟩ – compare WEATHER

**leeboard** /-,bawd/ *n* either of two movable flat surfaces attached to the outside of the hull of a sailing vessel that reduce leeway when lowered

**¹leech** /leech/ *n* **1** any of numerous flesh-eating or bloodsucking usu freshwater worms (class Hirudinea of the phylum Annelida) that typically have a flattened segmented body with a sucker at each end **2** one who gains or seeks to gain profit or advantage from another, esp by clinging persistently **3** *archaic* a physician, surgeon [ME *leche*, fr OE *lǣce*; akin to OHG *lāhhi* physician; (1) perh fr its former use by physicians for bleeding patients, but perh of different origin]

²**leech** vt to bleed by the use of leeches ~ vi to attach oneself to a person in the manner of a leech – usu + onto ⟨she ~ed onto him the moment he appeared⟩

³**leech** n 1 either vertical edge of a SQUARE SAIL (4-sided sail set across a boat) 2 the rear edge of a FORE-AND-AFT sail (sail set in the lengthways direction of a boat) [ME *leche*, fr MLG *līk* boltrope; akin to MHG ge*leich* joint – more at LIGATURE]

**Lee-Enfield** /ˌlee ˈenfeeld, -fiəld/ n a magazine-fed British military rifle [James P *Lee* †1904 US (Scottish-born) inventor + *Enfield*, district of London (site of the Royal Small Arms Factory)]

**leek** /leek/ n a plant (*Allium porrum*) of the lily family that is related to onions, chives, and garlic and has mildly pungent leaves and a thick white edible stalk for which it is grown △ leak [ME, fr OE *lēac*; akin to OHG *louh* leek]

**leer** /liə/ vi or n (to give) a lascivious, knowing, or sly look [prob fr obs *leer* cheek, face, fr ME *ler, lere*, fr OE *hlēor*]

**leery** /ˈliəri/ adj suspicious, wary ⟨he was ~ of strangers⟩ [*leer* + -y]

**lees** /leez/ n pl the sediment of a liquor (eg wine) during fermentation and aging; the dregs [ME *lie*, fr MF, fr ML *lia*, prob of Celt origin]

**lee shore** n a shore lying off a ship's LEE SIDE

**lee side** /ˈlee sied/ n LEE 2

¹**leeward** /ˈleewood; *naut* ˈlooh-əd/ adj or adv in or facing the direction towards which the wind is blowing – compare WINDWARD

²**leeward** n LEE 2

**leeway** /-ˌway/ n 1a off-course sideways movement of a ship caused by the force of the wind b the horizontal angle between the longitudinal axis of an aircraft and its path relative to the ground; the angle between the HEADING and the TRACK of an aircraft 2a an allowable margin of freedom or variation; tolerance b a margin of shortcoming in performance ⟨she has a lot of ~ to make up after her absence⟩

¹**left** /left/ adj 1a of, situated on, or being the side of the body in which most of the heart is located b(1) located nearer to the left hand than to the right ⟨the ~ pocket⟩; *esp* located on the left hand when facing in the same direction as an observer ⟨the ~ wing of an army⟩ b(2) located on the left when facing downstream ⟨the ~ bank of a river⟩ 2 *often cap* of the Left in politics [ME, fr OE, weak; akin to MLG *lucht* left; fr the left hand's being the weaker in most people] – **left** adv

²**left** n 1a (a blow struck with) the left hand b the location or direction of the left side c the part on the left side 2 *taking sing or pl vb, often cap* the members of a European legislative body occupying the left of a legislative chamber as a result of holding more radical political views than other members 3 *taking sing or pl vb* 3a *cap* those professing socialist or radical political views b *often cap* LEFT WING 1 ⟨the Labour Left⟩

³**left** *past of* LEAVE

**left atrioventricular valve** /ˌaytriohven'trikyoolə/ n the heart valve, consisting of two flaps, that is situated on the left-hand side of the heart between the left ATRIUM (upper chamber) and the left VENTRICLE (lower chamber) and that stops blood flowing back from the ventricle to the atrium – called also BICUSPID VALVE, MITRAL VALVE; compare RIGHT ATRIOVENTRICULAR VALVE

**Left Bank** n the bohemian district of Paris situated on the left bank of the Seine [trans of fr *Rive Gauche*]

¹**left-ˌhand** adj 1 situated on the left 2 left-handed

ˌ**left-ˈhanded** adj 1 using the left hand habitually or more easily than the right; *also* swinging from left to right ⟨a ~ batsman⟩ 2 of, designed for, or done with the left hand 3 of a marriage morganatic 4 clumsy, awkward 5 ambiguous, double-edged ⟨a ~ compliment⟩ 6 anticlockwise – used of a twist, rotary motion, or spiral curve as viewed from a given direction with respect to the axis of rotation – **left-handed, left-handedly** adv, **left-handedness** n

ˌ**left-ˈhander** n 1 a left-handed person 2 a blow struck with the left hand

**leftism** /ˈlefˌtiz(ə)m/ n, *often cap* (advocacy of) the principles and policy of the Left – **leftist** n or adj

**left-luggage office** n, Br a room (eg at a railway station) where luggage may be left, usu for a small fee

**leftover** /-ˌohvə/ n usu pl an unused or unconsumed residue; *esp* uneaten food consumed at a later meal – **leftover** adj

**leftward** /ˈleftwood/ adj towards or on the left

**leftwards** /ˈleftwədz/, *chiefly NAm* **leftward** adv towards the left

**left wing** n *taking sing or pl vb, often cap L&W* 1 the more socialist division of a group or party 2 LEFT 3a – **left-wing** adj, **left-winger** n

**lefty, leftie** /ˈlefti/ n, *informal* a left-winger

¹**leg** /leg/ n 1 a limb of an animal used esp for supporting the body and for walking: eg 1a (an artificial replacement for) either of the lower limbs of a human b a hind leg of a meat animal, esp above the hock ⟨a ~ of lamb⟩ c any of the jointed appendages that occur in pairs on the segments of the body of an insect, spider, crab, centipede, etc and are used in walking and crawling 2a a pole or bar serving as a support or prop ⟨the ~s of a tripod⟩ ⟨a table ~⟩ b a branch of a forked or jointed object ⟨the ~s of a compass⟩ 3a the part of a garment that covers (part of) the leg b the part of the upper (eg of a boot) that extends above the ankle 4 either side of a triangle as distinguished from the base or hypotenuse 5a LEG SIDE ⟨hit the ball to ~⟩ b a fielding position in cricket on the LEG SIDE of the pitch; *also* the fieldsman occupying this position – usu in combination ⟨fine ~⟩ ⟨short ~⟩ 6a the course and distance sailed on a single tack b a portion of a trip; a stage c the part of a relay race run by one competitor ⟨ran the first ~ for the English team⟩ d any of a set of events or games that must all be won to decide a competition ⟨Liverpool are at home in the first ~⟩ 7.a branch, part, or link of a system (eg an electrical circuit or a communications network) made up of several interconnecting or interdependent parts [ME, fr ON *leggr*; akin to OE *līra* muscle, calf, L *lacertus* muscle, upper arm] – **not have a leg to stand on** to have no support or basis for one's position, esp in a controversy – **on one's last legs** at or near the end of one's resources; on the verge of failure, exhaustion, or ruin – **pull somebody's leg** to deceive somebody playfully; tease – see also LEG-PULL – **shake a leg 1** to hasten – usu imper **2** to dance – **talk the hind leg off a donkey** to talk excessively

²**leg** vi -gg- – **leg it** to walk or run fast ⟨you must leg it if you want to catch the 9.30 bus⟩

³**leg** adj 1 *esp of a ball bowled in cricket* moving or tending to move in the direction of the OFF SIDE ⟨~ spin⟩ ⟨~ cutter⟩ 2 in, on, through, or towards the LEG SIDE of a cricket field ⟨~ slip⟩ ⟨his first ball knocked the ~ stump out of the ground⟩

**legacy** /ˈlegəsi/ n 1 a gift of money or property by will; a bequest 2 something passed on or remaining from an ancestor or predecessor or from the past ⟨the ~ of the ancient philosophers⟩ ⟨the bitter ~ of colonialism⟩ [ME *legacie* legateship, bequest, fr MF or ML; MF, legateship, fr ML *legatia*, fr L *legatus* legate]

**legal** /ˈleegl/ adj 1 of law 2a deriving authority from law b established by or having a formal status derived from law ⟨a corporation is a ~ but not a real person⟩ 3 permitted by law 4 recognized in COMMON LAW as distinguished from EQUITY (system based on natural justice) **synonyms** see LAWFUL **antonym** illegal [ME, fr MF, fr L *legalis*, fr *leg-, lex* law] – **legally** adv

**legal age** n the age at which a person assumes full legal rights and responsibilities

**legal aid** n (a system of) payments made from public funds to assist those who cannot afford legal advice or representation

**legal cap** n a white often ruled writing paper for legal use that is usu 330 x 203 millimetres ($13\frac{1}{2} \times 8$ inches) in size [-cap (as in foolscap)]

**legal eagle** n, *slang* a skilful and often unscrupulous lawyer

**legalese** /ˌleegl'eez/ n the specialized language or jargon of the legal profession

**legal fiction** n an assertion recognized by the law as fictitious but accepted for convenience as true, usu so as to bring a case within the operation of a rule of law

**legal holiday** n, *chiefly NAm* a public holiday established by legal authority and characterized by legal restrictions on work and the transaction of official business – compare BANK HOLIDAY

**legalism** /-ˌiz(ə)m/ n strict, literal, or excessive conformity to the law or to a religious or moral code

**legalist** /ˈleegl-ist/ n 1 an advocate or adherent of moral legalism 2 one who views things from a legal standpoint; *esp* a person who places primary emphasis on legal principles or on the formal structure of governmental institutions – **legalistic** adj, **legalistically** adv

**legality** /li'galəti/ n 1 being legal; lawfulness 2 pl the requirements and procedures of the law ⟨*the procedure for adoption is hedged about with* legalities⟩

**legal·ize, -ise** /'leegl·iez/ *vt* to make legal; *esp* to give legal validity or sanction to – **legalization** *n*

**legal reserve** *n* a (minimum amount of) readily available (LIQUID 4) assets which a bank or insurance company is required by law to maintain to meet claims by depositors

**legal tender** *n* currency which a creditor is bound by law to accept as payment of a money debt

**legate** /'legət/ *n* an official delegate or representative; an emissary [ME, fr OF & L; OF *legat*, fr L *legatus* deputy, emissary, fr pp of *legare* to depute, send as emissary, bequeath, fr *leg-, lex* law] – **legateship** *n*, **legatine** *adj*

**legatee** /,legə'tee/ *n* one to whom a legacy is bequeathed

**legation** /li'gaysh(ə)n/ *n* (the official residence of) a diplomatic mission in a foreign country headed by a minister

**legato** /li'gahtoh/ *n, adv, or adj, pl* **legatos** (a manner of performing or passage of music performed) in a smooth and connected manner [It, lit., tied, fr pp of *legare* to tie, fr L *ligare*]

**leg before wicket** *adj, of a batsman in cricket* out because of having obstructed with a part of the body, esp the legs, a ball that would otherwise have hit the wicket

**'leg-,break** *n* a slow bowled ball in cricket that turns from the LEG SIDE towards the OFF SIDE when it bounces

**leg bye** *n* a run scored in cricket after the ball has touched a part of the batsman's body (e g his legs) but not his bat or hands that is credited to his side's but not his own score – compare BYE, EXTRA

**legend** /'lej(ə)nd/ *n* **1a(1)** a story coming down from the past; *esp* one popularly regarded as historical although not verifiable **a(2)** a body of such stories ⟨*a character in Celtic* ~⟩ **a(3)** a popular myth of recent origin b a person, act, or thing that inspires legends ⟨*a ~ in her own lifetime*⟩ **2a** an inscription or title on an object (e g a coin) **b** CAPTION 2 **c** the key explaining the symbols and conventions used in a map, chart, etc [ME *legende*, fr MF & ML; MF *legende*, fr ML *legenda*, fr L, fem of *legendus*, gerundive of *legere* to gather, select, read; akin to Gk *legein* to gather, say, *logos* speech, word, reason]

   *synonyms* A **legend** and a **myth** are both stories handed down from the past; but while a **legend** may have its origin in fact ⟨*the* **legend** *of Alfred and the cakes*⟩ a **myth** has been invented, often to account for something ⟨*the* **myth** *of Pandora's box, which explains the existence of evil*⟩.

**legendary** /'lejənd(ə)ri/ *adj* **1** (characteristic) of legend or a legend; *esp* told of in legend **2** celebrated as a legend ⟨*the ~ W G Grace*⟩ – **legendarily** *adv*

**legendry** /'lej(ə)ndri/ *n* a body of legends

**legerdemain** /,lejədə'man, -'mayn/ *n* **1** SLEIGHT OF HAND **2** a display of artful skill, trickery, or adroitness ⟨*political ~*⟩ [ME, fr MF *leger de main* light of hand]

**leger line** /'lejə/ *n* LEDGER LINE

**-legged** /-'legid; *also* -'legd/ *comb form* (*adj* → *adj*) having (such or so many) legs ⟨*bow*-legged *men*⟩ ⟨*a* 4-legged *animal*⟩

**legging** /'leging/ *n usu pl* a closely fitting covering (e g of leather) that reaches from the ankle to the knee or thigh

**'leggy** /'legi/ *adj* **1** having disproportionately long legs ⟨*a ~ colt*⟩ **2** *esp of a woman* having attractively long legs **3** *of a plant* spindly

**'leggy** *n, informal* **1** a leg-break **2** a bowler of leg-breaks

**leghorn** /'leg,hawn; *sense 2* le'gawn/ *n* **1a** fine plaited straw made from an Italian wheat **b** a hat of this straw **2** (any of) a Mediterranean breed of small hardy domestic fowls noted for their large production of white eggs [*Leghorn* (Livorno), town in Italy]

**legible** /'lejəbl/ *adj* capable of being read or deciphered ⟨*~ handwriting*⟩ [ME, fr LL *legibilis*, fr L *legere* to read] – **legibly** *adv*, **legibility** *n*

**'legion** /'leej(ə)n/ *n taking sing or pl vb* **1** the principal unit of the ancient Roman army consisting of 3000 to 6000 foot soldiers together with cavalry **2** a very large number; a multitude **3** a national association of ex-servicemen ⟨*the Royal British Legion*⟩ [ME, fr OF, fr L *legion-, legio*, fr *legere* to gather – more at LEGEND]

**'legion** *adj* many, numerous ⟨*the problems are ~*⟩

**'legionary** /'leejən(ə)ri/ *adj* of or being a legion [L *legionarius*, fr *legion-, legio*]

**'legionary** *n* a legionnaire

**legionary ant** *n* ARMY ANT

**legionnaire** /,leejə'neə/ *n* a member of a legion; *esp* a member of the French foreign legion [Fr *légionnaire*, fr L *legionarius*]

*synonyms* An ancient Roman soldier was a **legionary**; a member of the French foreign legion is a **legionary** or **legionnaire**, and so is a British or American ex-serviceman, the Americans preferring the latter word.

**legionnaire's disease** *n* a serious sometimes fatal infectious disease that has symptoms like those of pneumonia, is caused by a bacterium, and usu affects groups of people associated in one place (e g a hotel or hospital) [fr its outbreak amoung a group of US ex-servicemen in 1976]

**Legion of Honour** *n* a French order conferred as a reward for civil or military merit [trans of Fr *Légion d' Honneur*]

**legislate** /'leji,slayt/ *vi* to make or enact laws ~ *vt* to cause, provide, or bring about by legislation [back-formation fr *legislator*]

**legislation** /,leji'slaysh(ə)n/ *n* **1** legislating; *specif* the making of laws that have the force of authority by virtue of their being proclaimed and put into action by an official organ of a state or other organization **2** the laws proclaimed and put into action by a legislator or a legislative body **3** a prospective law for or under consideration by a legislative body □ compare LEGISLATURE

**'legislative** /'lejislətiv/ *adj* **1** having the power or performing the function of legislating – compare EXECUTIVE, JUDICIAL **2a** of a legislature ⟨*~ committees*⟩ ⟨*~ immunity*⟩ **b** created by a legislature, esp as distinguished from an executive or judicial body **3** of, concerned with, or created by legislation – **legislatively** *adv*

**'legislative** *n* the legislature

**legislator** /'leji,slaytə/, *fem* **legislatress** /-tris/, **legislatrix** /-triks/ *n* a maker of laws; *esp* a member of a legislative body [L*legis lator*, lit., proposer of a law, fr *legis*, gen of *lex* law + *lator* proposer, fr *latus*, suppletive pp of *ferre* to carry, propose – more at TOLERATE, BEAR] – **legislatorship** *n*, **legislatorial** *adj*

**legislature** /'lejisləchə/ *n* a body of people having the power to legislate; *specif* an organized body having the authority to make laws for a political unit – compare LEGISLATION

**legist** /'leejist/ *n* a specialist in law [MF *legiste*, fr ML *legista*, fr L *leg-, lex*]

**legit** /lə'jit/ *adj, slang* legitimate ⟨*a racket boy with a lot of ~ business* – Harold Robbins⟩

**'legitimate** /lə'jitimət/ *adj* **1** lawfully begotten; *specif* born in wedlock **2** neither spurious nor false; genuine ⟨*~ grievance*⟩ **3a** in accordance with law ⟨*a ~ government*⟩ **b** ruling by or based on the strict principle of hereditary right ⟨*a ~ king*⟩ **4** conforming to recognized principles or accepted rules and standards **5** relating to plays acted by professional actors but not including revues, music hall, or some forms of musical comedy ⟨*the ~ theatre*⟩ **6** in accord with reason or logic; following logically ⟨*a ~ deduction*⟩ *synonyms* see LAWFUL *antonym* illegitimate [ML *legitimatus*, pp of *legitimare* to legitimate, fr L *legitimus* legitimate, fr *leg-, lex* law] – **legitimacy** *n*, **legitimately** *adv*

**'legitimate** /lə'jitimayt/, **legitimat·ize, -ise** /lə'jitimətiez/, **legitim·ize, -ise** /lə'jitimiez/ *vt* to make or show to be legitimate: **a(1)** to give legal status or authorization to **a(2)** to show or affirm to be justified **b** to give (an illegitimate child) the legal status of one legitimately born – **legitimation** *n*, **legitimatization, legitimization** *n*

**legitimism** /lə'jiti,miz(ə)m/ *n, often cap* adherence to the principles of political legitimacy or to a person claiming a throne by descent – **legitimist** *n, often cap*, **legitimist** *adj*

**legless** /'leglis/ *adj, chiefly Br informal* drunk

**legman** /'leg,man/ *n, chiefly NAm informal* a newspaper reporter who goes to the scene of an occurrence to gather his/her own information

**Lego** /'legoh/ *trademark* – used for a toy construction kit

**,leg-of-'mutton, leg-o'-mutton** *adj* having the approximately triangular shape or outline of a leg of mutton ⟨*~ sleeves*⟩ ⟨*a ~ sail*⟩

**'leg-,pull** *n* a playful trick or hoax intended to deceive someone [fr the phrase *pull somebody's leg*]

**legroom** /'legroohm, -,room/ *n* space in which to extend the legs while seated

**leg show** *n, informal* a theatrical performance featuring scantily-dressed girls dancing in unison

**leg side** *n the* part of a cricket field on the side of a line joining the middle stumps in which the batsman stands when playing a ball; the left-hand part of the field as viewed by a right-handed batsman looking directly at the bowler – compare OFF SIDE

**leg spin** *n* spin that causes a cricket ball bowled at a slow speed to turn from the LEG SIDE towards the OFF SIDE when it bounces

**leg spinner** *n* 1 a bowler who imparts LEG SPIN to a ball; a bowler of LEG-BREAKS 2 LEG-BREAK

**legume** /'legyoohm, li'gyoohm/ *n* 1 the edible pod or seed of a leguminous plant (e g pea or bean) used as a vegetable 2 any of a large family (Leguminosae) of plants, shrubs, and trees, including important food and forage plants (e g peas, beans, and clovers), that bear fruits that are legumes or LOMENTS (pods constricted between the seeds) and have swellings (NODULES) on the roots that contain NITROGEN-FIXING bacteria 3 the long-celled fruit of a leguminous plant, that typically contains several seeds and splits longitudinally into two halves to disperse the seeds; a pod [Fr *légume*, fr L *legumin-, legumen*, fr *legere* to gather – more at LEGEND]

**leguminous** /li'gyoohminəs/ *adj* (consisting) of, resembling, or being plants that are legumes

**'leg-,up** *n, informal* 1 assistance in mounting an object (e g a horse) 2 a helping hand; a boost

**'leg-,warmer** *n usu pl* a knitted legging ⟨*ballet dancers rehearsing in* ~s⟩

**legwork** /-,wuhk/ *n* work (e g gathering information) that involves physical activity and forms the basis of more creative or mentally exacting work

**lehr** /liə/ *n* a long oven in which glass is annealed [Ger]

**'lei** /lay/ *n* a wreath or necklace usu of flowers or leaves that is a symbol of affection in Polynesia [Hawaiian]

**²lei** /lay/ *pl of* LEU

**Leibnizian** /lieb'nitsiən, liep-/ *adj* of Leibniz or his philosophy [Gottfried Wilhelm von *Leibniz* †1716 Ger philosopher & mathematician] – **Leibnizianism** *n*

**Leicester** /'lestə/ *n* 1 (any of) a breed of white-faced meat-producing English sheep with long exceptionally fine white fleece 2 an orange-red mild-flavoured cheese with a flaky texture [*Leicester*, county in England]

**leishmania** /leesh'maynyə/ *n* any of a genus (*Leishmania* of the family Trypanosomatidae) of single-celled organisms (PROTOZOANS) that move by means of long whiplike structures (FLAGELLA) and live as parasites in the tissues of VERTEBRATE animals, including humans; *broadly* any of several similar organisms of the same families [NL, genus name, fr Sir William *Leishman* †1926 Sc bacteriologist]

**leishmaniasis** /,leeshmə'nie-əsis/ *n* infection with or a disease (e g KALA-AZAR) caused by leishmanias [NL]

**leister** /'leestə/ *vt or n* (to catch with) a spear armed with three or more barbed prongs for spearing fish, esp salmon [of Scand origin; akin to ON *ljōstr* leister, *ljōsta* to strike, stab]

**leisure** /'lezhə/ *n* 1 freedom provided by the cessation of activities; *esp* time free from work or duties 2 unhurried ease [ME *leiser*, fr OF *leisir*, fr *leisir* to be permitted, fr L *licēre* – more at LICENCE] – **leisure** *adj*, **leisureless** *adj* – **at (one's) leisure** 1 at an unhurried pace 2 at one's convenience

**leisured** /'lezhəd/ *adj* 1 having plenty of free time, esp because of not needing to work 2 leisurely ⟨*at a* ~ *pace*⟩

**'leisurely** /-li/ *adv* without haste; deliberately

**²leisurely** *adj* characterized by leisure; unhurried – **leisureliness** *n*

**leitmotiv, leitmotif** /'lietmoh,teef/ *n* 1 a musical phrase that accompanies the reappearance of and represents an idea, person, or situation, esp in a Wagnerian music drama 2 a (dominant) recurring theme, esp in a literary work [Ger *leitmotiv*, fr *leiten* to lead + *motiv* motive, fr Fr *motif*]

**'lek** /lek/ *n* – see MONEY table [Albanian]

**²lek** *n* an assembly area where BLACK GROUSE or other birds congregate to carry on display and courtship behaviour [prob fr Sw, sport, play]

**lekker** /'lekə/ *adj, SAfr informal* pleasant, nice [Afrik, fr D]

**leman** /'lemən/ *n, archaic* a sweetheart, lover; *esp* a mistress [ME *lefman, leman*, fr *lef* lief + *man*]

**'lemma** /'lemə/ *n, pl* **lemmas, lemmata** /'lemətə/ 1a a proposition accepted as true for the sake of demonstrating another proposition b(1) *maths* a minor proposition that must be proved before proceeding to the proof of the main theorem b(2) a theorem 2 the argument or theme of a composition prefixed as a title or introduction; *broadly* (a subsidiary part of) a heading or introduction 3 an annotated word or phrase [L, fr Gk *lēmma* thing taken, assumption, fr *lambanein* to take – more at LATCH]

**²lemma** *n* the lower of the two scalelike leaves that enclose

each flower in a grass – compare PALEA 2 [Gk, husk, fr *lepein* to peel – more at LEPER]

**lemming** /'leming/ *n* 1 any of several small short-tailed furry volelike rodents of northern and polar regions of N America, Europe, and Asia; *esp* one (*Lemmus Lemmus*) of northern mountains that periodically undergoes mass migration which often results in the death of many through drowning in the sea 2 a member of a group mindlessly pursuing a course of action that will lead to mass destruction [Norw; akin to ON *lōmr* guillemot, L *latrare* to bark – more at LAMENT]

**lemniscate** /lem'niskət/ *n, maths* a figure-of-eight shaped curve whose equation in POLAR COORDINATES is $\rho^2 = a^2 \cos 2\theta$ [NL *lemniscata*, fr fem of L *lemniscatus* with hanging ribbons, fr *lemniscus*]

**lemniscus** /lem'niskəs/ *n, pl* **lemnisci** /-ski/ *anatomy* a band of fibres, esp NERVE FIBRES [NL, fr L, ribbon, fr Gk *lēmniskos*]

**'lemon** /'lemən/ *n* 1 an oval yellow citrus fruit with a thick rind and acid flesh; *also* a stout thorny tree (*Citrus limon*) related to the orange and grapefruit trees that bears lemons 2 a pale yellow colour 3 *informal* one who or that which is unsatisfactory or worthless; a dud [ME *lymon*, fr MF *limon*, fr ML *limon-, limo*, fr Ar *laymūn*] – **lemony** *adj*

**²lemon** *adj* 1a consisting of, containing, or made with lemon b having the flavour or scent of lemon 2 of a pale yellow colour

**lemonade** /,lemə'nayd/ *n* 1 a soft drink consisting of sweetened lemon juice mixed with water 2 a carbonated soft drink flavoured with lemon

**lemon balm** *n* a bushy Eurasian plant (*Melissa officinalis*) of the mint family that has white or pinkish flowers and is often cultivated for its fragrant lemon-scented leaves

**lemongrass** /-,grahs/ *n* a robust grass (*Cymbopogon citratus*) of tropical regions that is the source of an oil that smells of lemon or verbena and is used as a perfume in soaps

**lemon sole** *n* a flatfish (*Microstomus kitt*) that is found in N Atlantic and European waters and is highly valued for food [*lemon* fr Fr *limande* flatfish, dab]

**lemon squash** *n, Br* a noncarbonated soft drink made from a sweetened lemon concentrate mixed with water

**lemon squeezer** *n* a device (e g of glass or plastic) for pressing the juice from citrus fruits that consists of a ridged and pointed centre part rising from a shallow dish

**lemon thyme** *n* a cultivated variety of the common European thyme with lemon-scented flowers and leaves used for flavouring food

**le mot juste** /lə ,mot 'zhoost (*Fr* lə mo ʒyst)/ *n* the most appropriate word ⟨*the house is . . . a bargain to boot, which is* ~*, since the Duke of Wellington bought it . . . – Punch*⟩ [Fr]

**lempira** /'lempirə/ *n* – see MONEY table [AmerSp, fr *Lempira*, 16th-c Indian chief]

**lemur** /'leemə/ *n* any of numerous tree-dwelling mammals, esp of Madagascar, that are related to the monkeys but are usu regarded as constituting a distinct superfamily (Lemuroidea), are active chiefly at night, and usu have a muzzle like a fox, large eyes, very soft woolly fur, and a long furry tail [NL, fr L *lemures*, pl, ghosts; akin to Gk *lamia* devouring monster]

**lemures** /'lemyooreez/ *n taking pl vb* spirits of the unburied dead, exorcised from homes in early Roman religious observances [L]

**'lend** /lend/ *vb* **lent** /lent/ *vt* 1a to give for temporary use on condition that the same or its equivalent be returned ⟨*can you* ~ *me £10?*⟩ b to let out (money) for temporary use on condition of repayment with interest 2a to give the assistance or support of; afford, contribute ⟨*a dispassionate and scholarly manner which* ~s *great force to his criticisms – TLS* ⟩ b to adapt or apply (oneself); accommodate ⟨*a topic that* ~s *itself admirably to class discussion*⟩ ~ *vi* to make a loan *usage* see ²LOAN [ME *lenen, lenden*, fr OE *lǣnan*, fr *lǣn* loan – more at LOAN] – **lender** *n*

**²lend** *n, nonstandard* LOAN 2a ⟨*let's have a* ~ *of your bike*⟩

**lending library** /'lending/ *n* 1 a library that lends its books either publicly as part of a state-run service or privately (e g to subscribers) 2 *chiefly Br* the lending department of a public library

**'lend-,lease** *n* the transfer of goods and services to an ally to aid in a common cause, with payment being made by a return of the original items or their use in the common cause or by a similar transfer of other goods and services – used esp with reference to the system by which the USA gave material aid to the Allies in World War II – **lend-lease** *vt*

**length** /leng(k)th; *also* lenth/ *n* 1a(1) the longer or longest dimension of an object a(2) the extent from end to end ⟨*walked the* ~

*of the street*⟩ ⟨*the whole ~ of a book*⟩ **b** a measured distance or dimension ⟨*a 2-metre ~ of tube*⟩ **c** the quality or state of being long rather than short ⟨*an essay is not judged only on its ~*⟩ **2a** duration or extent in or with regard to time ⟨*the ~ of a broadcast*⟩ **b** relative duration or stress of a sound **3a** distance or extent in space ⟨*an arm's ~ apart*⟩ **b** the length of something taken as a unit of measure ⟨*his horse led by a ~*⟩ **4 lengths** *pl*, **length** the degree to which something (eg a course of action or a line of thought) is carried; a limit, extreme ⟨*went to great ~s to learn the truth*⟩ **5a** a long expanse or stretch ⟨*brushed her ~s of hair*⟩ **b** a piece, esp of a certain length, being or usable as part of a whole or of a connected series; a section ⟨*a ~ of pipe*⟩ **6** the distance down a cricket pitch which the bowled ball travels before pitching; *also* the length of a delivery that is most likely to compel the batsman to play a defensive stroke and that is the bowler's ideal ⟨*one ball ... lifted off a ~* – John Arlott⟩ **7** the vertical extent of something (eg an article of clothing), esp with reference to the position it reaches on the body – usu in combination ⟨*shoulder-length hair*⟩ [ME *lengthe*, fr OE *lengthu*, fr *lang* long] – **at length 1** fully, comprehensively **2** for a long time **3** finally; AT LAST
    *usage* The pronunciation /length/ rather than /lenth/ is *recommended* for BBC broadcasters.
**lengthen** /'length(ə)n, 'lengkth(ə)n/ *vb* to make or become longer *antonyms* shorten, curtail, abbreviate – **lengthener** *n*
**lengthways** /-,wayz/, **lengthwise** /'leng(k)th,wiez/ *adv or adj* in the direction of the length ⟨*bricks are generally laid ~*⟩
**lengthy** /'leng(k)thi/ *adj* of great or unusual length; long ⟨*a ~ book*⟩; *also* excessively or tediously protracted – **lengthily** *adv*, **lengthiness** *n*
**lenient** /'leenyənt, 'leeni-ənt/ *adj* **1** of a mild or merciful nature; not severe ⟨*~ laws*⟩ **2** *archaic* exerting a soothing or easing influence; relieving pain or stress *synonyms* see MERCY *antonym* severe [L *lenient-, leniens*, prp of *lenire* to soften, soothe, fr *lenis* soft, mild – more at LET] – **lenience, leniency** *n*, **leniently** *adv*
**Leninism** /'leni,niz(ə)m/ *n* the political, economic, and social principles and policies advocated by Lenin; *esp* the theory and practice of communism developed by or associated with Lenin; Marxism-Leninism [Vladimir Ilich *Lenin* (real name Ulyanov) † 1924 Russ Communist leader] – **Leninist** *n or adj*, **Leninite** *n or adj*
**lenis** /'leenis/ *adj* produced with relatively little force and weak expulsion of breath ⟨/d/ *in* doe *is ~*, /t/ *in* toe *is fortis*⟩ [NL, fr L, mild, smooth]
**lenitive** /'lenətiv/ *adj* relieving pain or stress ⟨*a ~ drug*⟩ [MF *lenitif*, fr ML *lenitivus*, fr L *lenitus*, pp of *lenire*] – **lenitive** *n*
**lenity** /'lenəti/ *n, formal* gentleness, mercy; *also* a merciful or lenient act *synonyms* see MERCY *antonym* severity
**leno** /'leenoh/ *n* **1** an open weave in which pairs of warp yarns cross one another and lock the weft yarns in position **2** a fabric (eg gauze) made with a leno weave [perh fr Fr *linon* linen fabric]
**lens** /lenz/ *n* **1a** a piece of glass or other transparent material that has two shaped sides, at least one of which is curved either outwards or inwards, and that is used either singly or combined with one or more similar devices in an optical instrument (eg a camera or microscope) to form an image by focussing rays of light **b** a combination of two or more single lenses **2** a device for directing or focussing radiation other than light (eg sound waves or electrons) **3** something shaped like an optical lens with both sides convex **4** a transparent lens-shaped body in the eye, that has two outward-curving sides and that focusses light rays onto the retina [NL *lent-, lens*, fr L, lentil; fr its shape] – **lensed** *adj*, **lensless** *adj*
**Lent** /lent/ *n* the 40 weekdays from Ash Wednesday to Easter observed by the Roman Catholic, Eastern, and some Protestant churches as a period of penitence and fasting [ME *lente* springtime, Lent, fr OE *lengten*; akin to OHG *lenzin* spring]
**Lenten** /'lent(ə)n/ *adj* **1** of Lent **2** suitable to Lent; *esp* meagre ⟨*~ fare*⟩
**lentic** /'lentik/ *adj* of or living in still waters (eg lakes, ponds, or swamps) – compare LOTIC [L *lentus* sluggish]
**lenticel** /'lenti,sel, -s(ə)l/ *n* a pore in the stem of a woody plant through which gases are exchanged between the atmosphere and the stem tissues [NL *lenticella*, dim. of L *lent-, lens* lentil]
**lenticular** /len'tikyoolə/ *adj* **1** having the shape of a lens with both sides convex ⟨*~ clouds with a smooth, elliptical outline*⟩ **2** of a lens [L *lenticularis* lentil-shaped, fr *lenticula* lentil] – **lenticular** *n*
**lentiginous** /len'tijinəs/, **lentiginose** /-nohs/ *adj* dotted or

speckled (as if) with freckles [L *lentiginosus*, fr *lentigin-, lentigo* birthmark, mole, fr *lent-, lens* lentil]
**lentil** /'lentl/ *n* **1** a widely cultivated Eurasian plant (*Lens culinaris*) of the pea family that bears edible seeds and leafy stalks used as animal fodder **2** the small flattish circular seed of the lentil that is typically yellow, orange, or brownish-red in colour, is rich in protein, and is used as a vegetable and in soups [ME, fr OF *lentille*, fr L *lenticula*, dim. of *lent-, lens*; akin to Gk *lathyros* vetch]
**lento** /'lentoh/ *adv or adj* in a slow manner – used as a direction in music; compare LARGO [It, fr L *lentus* pliant, sluggish, slow – more at LITHE]
**Leo** /'lee-oh/ *n* **1** a constellation of the ZODIAC (imaginary belt in the heavens) lying between Cancer and Virgo and represented as a lion **2a** the 5th sign of the zodiac in astrology, held to govern the period July 23 - August 22 approx **b** somebody born under this sign [L, lit., lion – more at LION]
**leone** /li'ohni/ *n* – see MONEY table [*Sierra Leone*, country in W Africa]
¹**leonine** /'lee-ənien/ *adj* **1** of a lion **2** resembling a lion; having the characteristics (eg courage and nobility) popularly ascribed to a lion [ME, fr L *leoninus*, fr *leon-, leo*]
²**leonine** *adj* having internally rhyming lines [prob fr some medieval poet named *Leo, Leonius*, or *Leoninus*
**leopard** /'lepəd/, *fem* **leopardess** /'lepədis, ,lepə'des/ *n* **1** a BIG CAT (*Felis pardus*) of S Asia and Africa that usu has a tawny or buff coat with black spots arranged in broken rings or rosettes – called also PANTHER **2** a heraldic representation of a lion walking (PASSANT) with its head turned towards the observer (GUARDANT) [ME, fr OF *leupart*, fr LL *leopardus*, fr Gk *leopardos*, fr *leōn* lion + *pardos* leopard]
**leopard moth** *n* a black-spotted white moth (*Zeuzera pyrina*) whose caterpillar bores holes in many trees, causing damage to the wood
**leotard** /'lee-ə,tahd/ *n* a close-fitting one-piece garment worn by dancers or others performing physical exercises [Jules *Léotard* †1870 Fr trapeze artist]
**Lepcha** /'lepchə/ *n, pl* **Lepcha, Lepchas 1** a member of a Mongoloid people of Sikkim in India **2** the Tibeto-Burman language of the Lepcha people
**leper** /'lepə/ *n* **1** someone suffering from leprosy **2** a person shunned for moral or social reasons; an outcast [ME, fr *lepre* leprosy, fr OF, fr LL *lepra*, fr Gk, fr *lepein* to peel; akin to OE *læfer* reed]
**lepid-** /lepid-/, **lepido-** *comb form* flake; scale ⟨*Lepidoptera*⟩ [NL, fr Gk, fr *lepid-, lepis* scale, fr *lepein*]
**lepidolite** /le'pidəliet/ *n* a pink to violet-coloured mineral, typically $K(Li,Al)_3(Si,Al)_4 O_{10}(F,OH)_2$, that consists of a MICA (common mineral with a flaky texture) containing the chemical element lithium and is used esp in glazes and enamels [Ger *lepidolith*, fr *lepid-* + *-lith*]
**lepidopteran** /,lepi'doptərən/ *n* any of a large order (Lepidoptera) of insects comprising the butterflies, moths, and SKIPPERS that are caterpillars in the larval stage, and as adults have four wings usu covered with minute overlapping and often brightly coloured scales [NL *Lepidoptera*, order of insects, fr *lepid-* + *pteron* wing – more at FEATHER] – **lepidopteran** *adj*, **lepidopterous** *adj*
**lepidopterist** /,lepi'doptərist/ *n* a specialist in the study of lepidopterans
**lepidopteron** /,lepi'doptərən/ *n, pl* **lepidoptera** /-rə/ *also* **lepidopterons** a lepidopteran [NL, sing. of *Lepidoptera*]
**lepidosis** /,lepi'dohsis/ *n, pl* **lepidoses** /-seez/ the arrangement and character of scales or shields (eg on a snake) [NL]
**lepidote** /'lepidoht/ *adj* covered with flakes or flaky scales ⟨*~ rhododendrons*⟩ [Gk *lepidōtos* scaly, fr *lepid-, lepis*]
**leporine** /'lepərien/ *n* of or resembling the hare [L *leporinus*, fr *lepor-, lepus* hare (cf LEVERET)]
**leprechaun** /'leprik(h)awn/ *n* a mischievous elf of Irish folklore, usu believed to reveal the hiding place of a pot of gold if caught [IrGael *leipreachān*, fr MIr *lūchorpān*, fr *lū* small + *corpān*, dim. of *corp* body, fr L *corpus*]
**leprosarium** /,leprə'seəriəm/ *n, pl* **leprosariums, leprosaria** /-riə/ a hospital for lepers [ML, fr LL *leprosus* leprous]
**leprosy** /'leprəsi/ *n* **1** a long-lasting disease that is caused by a bacillus (*Mycobacterium leprae*), transmitted by prolonged contact with an infected person, and characterized by the formation of lumps or patches on the skin that enlarge and spread, loss of sensation with eventual paralysis, wasting of muscle, and production of deformities and mutilations **2** a morally or

spiritually harmful influence ⟨the ~ of poverty⟩ [leprous + -y]
– **leprotic** adj

**leprous** /'leprəs/ adj **1a** infected with leprosy **b** of or resembling leprosy or a leper **2** scaly, scurfy [ME, fr LL leprosus, fr lepra leprosy] – **leprously** adv, **leprousness** n

**-lepsy** /-,lepsi/ comb form (→ n) attack; seizure ⟨catalepsy⟩ [MF -lepsie, fr LL -lepsia, fr Gk -lēpsia, fr lēpsis, fr lambanein to take, seize – more at LATCH]

**lepto-** comb form narrow; slender ⟨leptophyllous⟩ ⟨leptocephalous⟩ [Gk, fr leptos, lit., peeled, fr lepein to peel]

**leptocephalus** /,leptoh'sefələs; also -'kef-/ n, pl **leptocephali** /-li, -lie/ the long thin small-headed transparent first larva of various eels [NL, fr Gk leptos + kephalē head – more at CEPHALIC]

**¹lepton** /'lep,ton/ n, pl **lepta** – see drachma at MONEY table [NGk, fr Gk, small bronze coin, fr neut of leptos small]

**²lepton** n any of a group of ELEMENTARY PARTICLES (minute particles of matter) (e g an electron or MUON) that take part in WEAK INTERACTIONS but not STRONG INTERACTIONS and are also FERMIONS [Gk leptos + E ²-on] – **leptonic** adj

**leptorrhine** /'leptərin/ adj having a long narrow high-bridged nose [deriv of Gk leptos + rhin-, rhis nose]

**leptospirosis** /,leptohspie-ə'rohsis/ n, pl **leptospiroses** /-seez/ any of several diseases of human beings and domestic animals that are caused by infection with any of various SPIROCHAETES (spiral-shaped bacteria) (genus Leptospira) and are typically characterized by fever, muscle pains, and in some cases jaundice [NL, fr Leptospira, genus of spirochaetes, fr Gk leptos + L spira coil, twist]

**leptotene** /'leptəteen/ n the first stage in the initial phase (PROPHASE) of MEIOSIS (division of a cell and its nucleus to form four new cells), in which the CHROMOSOMES (strands of gene-carrying material) appear as fine discrete threads [ISV] – **leptotene** adj

**lesbian** /'lezbi-ən/ n, often cap a female homosexual [Lesbos, island in the Aegean Sea, the home of Sappho fl ab 600 BC Gk poetess & reputed homosexual] – **lesbian** adj, **lesbianism** n

**lese majesty** /leez, lez/, **lèse majesté** /(Fr lez maʒeste)/ n **1a** a crime (e g treason) committed against a sovereign power **b** an offence violating the dignity of a ruler as the representative of a sovereign power **2** an affront to dignity or importance [Fr lèse majesté, fr MF lese majesté, fr L laesa majestas, lit., injured majesty]

**lesion** /'leezh(ə)n/ n **1** injury, harm **2** an abnormal change in the structure of an organ or part due to injury or disease; esp a well defined area or patch of structural change [ME, fr MF, fr L laesion-, laesio, fr laesus, pp of laedere to injure]

**lespedeza** /,lespə'deezə/ n any of a genus (Lespedeza) of plants of the pea family including some widely used for forage, soil improvement, and esp hay [NL, irreg fr V M de Zespedes or Céspedez fl 1785 Sp governor of East Florida]

**¹less** /les/ adj **1** fewer ⟨~ than three⟩ ⟨emerging from the mêlée with ~ wounds than his brothers – Alan Sillitoe⟩ – disapproved of by some speakers **2** lower in rank, degree, or importance ⟨James the Less⟩ ⟨no ~ a person than the President himself⟩ **3** smaller in quantity or extent ⟨of ~ importance⟩ ⟨in ~ time⟩ ⟨weighs three pounds ~⟩ – compare NEITHER/NOTHING MORE OR LESS THAN [ME, partly fr OE lǣs, adv & n; partly fr lǣssa, adj; akin to OFris lēs less, Gk limos hunger]

*usage* Correctly, **less** means "not so much". The noun takes a singular verb ⟨less is expected of him⟩ and the adjective is used of mass nouns with no plural ⟨less sugar⟩ and of abstractions that cannot be counted ⟨less opportunity⟩. **Few** and **fewer** mean "not many", "not so many". The nouns take plural verbs ⟨few are ready⟩ and the adjectives are used of things that can be counted ⟨to buy less (not fewer) beer and fewer (not less) cigarettes⟩; many fewer is more formally correct than much fewer. The use of **less** for **fewer** ⟨less people than usual⟩ has been established in English since the 9th century, but is widely disliked, and should be avoided in formal writing. Numbers themselves are measured with **less than**, meaning "under", rather than with **fewer** ⟨less than six weeks⟩ ⟨less than £50⟩.

**²less** adv to a lesser degree or extent ⟨sleeps ~ in summer⟩ ⟨much ~ angrily⟩ ⟨doesn't seem any the ~ healthy⟩ – compare MORE OR LESS, MUCH LESS – **less and less** to a progressively smaller size or extent – **less than** by no means; not at all ⟨he was being less than honest in his replies⟩

**³less** prep diminished by; minus ⟨£100 ~ tax⟩

**⁴less** n, pl **less 1** a smaller portion or quantity **2** something of less importance – **less of 1** not so truly ⟨she's less of a fool than I thought⟩ **2** informal stop perpetrating ⟨less of your cheek!⟩

**-less** /-lis/ suffix (→ adj) **1a** destitute of; not having ⟨brainless⟩ ⟨childless⟩ **b** free from ⟨painless⟩ ⟨careless⟩ **2** unable to (so act or be acted on) ⟨tireless⟩ ⟨stainless⟩ [ME -les, -lesse, fr OE -lēas, fr lēas devoid, false; akin to OHG lōs loose, OE losian to get lost – more at LOSE]

**lessee** /le'see/ n somebody who holds land or other property under a lease – compare LESSOR [ME, fr AF, fr lessé, pp of lesser to lease – more at LEASE]

**lessen** /'les(ə)n/ vb to reduce in size, extent, etc; diminish, decrease

**lesser** /'lesə/ adj or adv less in size, quality, or significance ⟨lesser-known⟩ ⟨the ~ of two evils⟩ – not used in comparatives

**Lesser Bear** n URSA MINOR (constellation)

**lesser black-backed gull** n a common Eurasian gull (Larus fuscus) that is about the size of a HERRING GULL and has a greyish-black back

**lesser celandine** /'seləndien/ n CELANDINE 2 (plant of the buttercup family)

**lesser spotted woodpecker** n the smallest European woodpecker (Dendrocopos minor) that is the size of a sparrow and has a back marked with closely spaced black and white bars

**¹lesson** /'les(ə)n/ n **1** a passage from sacred writings read in a service of worship **2a** a piece of instruction **b** a reading or exercise to be studied **c** a period of instruction **3a** something, esp a piece of wisdom, learnt by study or experience ⟨his years of travel had taught him valuable ~s⟩ **b** an instructive or warning example ⟨the ~s history holds for us⟩ [ME, fr OF leçon, fr LL lection-, lectio, fr L, act of reading, fr lectus, pp of legere to read – more at LEGEND]

**²lesson** vt, archaic **1** to give a lesson to; instruct **2** to lecture, rebuke

**lessor** /'lesaw, -'-/ n somebody who conveys property by lease – compare LESSEE [ME lessour, fr AF, fr lesser to lease]

**lest** /lest/ conj **1** so that ... not; IN CASE ⟨obeyed her ~ she should be angry⟩ **2** that – used after an expression of fear ⟨feared ~ she be angry⟩ [ME les the, leste, fr OE thȳ lǣs the, fr thȳ (instrumental of thæt that) + lǣs less + the, relative particle]

*usage* **Lest** is correctly used with should or with the subjunctive ⟨lest he forget⟩, but not with will or would or ordinary indicative verb forms ⟨△ lest he forgets⟩.

**¹let** /let/ n **1** a serve or rally in tennis, squash, etc that does not count and must be replayed **2** formal something that impedes; an obstruction ⟨without ~ or hindrance⟩ [ME, obstruction, fr letten to hinder, fr OE lettan to delay, hinder; akin to OHG lezzen to delay, hurt, OE læt late]

**²let** vb let; **-tt-** vt **1** to offer or grant for rent or lease ⟨~ rooms⟩ **2a** to give opportunity to, whether by positive action or by failure to prevent; allow to ⟨he ~ his beard grow⟩ ⟨please ~ me know⟩ ⟨~ the prisoner go⟩ ⟨a break in the clouds ~ him see his objective⟩ **b** to allow to escape, enter, or pass ⟨~ blood⟩ ⟨the dogs loose⟩ ⟨~ them through⟩ ⟨she ~ out a scream⟩ **3** – used in the imperative to introduce a request or proposal ⟨~ us pray⟩ ⟨~ me see⟩, a challenge ⟨just ~ him try⟩, a command ⟨~ it be known⟩, or something to be supposed for the sake of argument ⟨~ AB be equal to BC⟩; compare LET'S ~ vi to become rented or leased [ME leten, fr OE lǣtan; akin to OHG lāzzan to permit, L lassus weary, lenis soft, mild] – **let alone** to say nothing of; esp still less ⟨can't walk, let alone run⟩ – **let alone/be** to stop or refrain from molesting, disturbing, or interrupting ⟨please let the cat alone⟩ – **let fall/drop** to express casually and as if accidentally

*usage* **Let** should be followed by object pronouns ⟨let you and me (not △ I) go⟩, but subject pronouns are correct with **let's** = "let us" ⟨let us go now, you and I – T S Eliot⟩. synonyms see ²HIRE

**let down** vt **1** to make (a garment) longer **2** to fail in loyalty or support; disappoint – see also LETDOWN

**let in for** vt to involve in (something undesirable ⟨let myself in for a lot of work⟩

**let in on** vt to allow to share

**let into** vt to insert into (a surface) ⟨a tablet let into the wall⟩

**let off** vt **1** to cause to explode ⟨let the fireworks off⟩ **2** to excuse from punishment **3** chiefly Br to offer (part of a building) for rent

**let on** vi **1** to reveal, admit ⟨knows more than he lets on⟩; esp to divulge secret information ⟨nobody let on about the surprise party⟩ **2** informal to pretend ⟨let on that he was a stranger⟩

**let out** vt **1** to make (a garment) wider (e g by inserting an inset) – compare TAKE IN 2 to express publicly; *esp* to blab 3 to excuse, exculpate – see also LET-OUT

**let up** *vi* **1a** to diminish, slow down, or cease **b** to relax or cease one's efforts or activities **2** to become less severe ⟨*his own blunder taught him to let up on the faults of others*⟩

³**let** *n*, *Br* **1** an act or period of letting premises (eg a flat or bed-sitter) ⟨*most agents take more trouble over long ∼s – Cosmopolitan*⟩ **2** premises rented or for rent

**-let** /-lit/ *suffix* (→ *n*) **1** -ETTE 1 ⟨*book*let⟩ ⟨*star*let⟩ **2** article worn on (a specified part of the body) ⟨*ank*let⟩ [ME, fr MF *-elet*, fr *-el*, dim. suffix (fr L *-ellus*) + *-et*]

**letdown** /-,down/ *n*, *informal* **1** a disappointment, disillusionment **2** the descent of an aircraft or spacecraft to the point at which a landing approach is begun

**lethal** /'leeth(ə)l/ *adj* **1** relating to or (capable of) causing death ⟨∼ *chemicals*⟩ ⟨∼ *injury*⟩ ⟨*a ∼ parasite*⟩ **2** gravely damaging or destructive; devastating ⟨*a ∼ attack on his reputation*⟩ [L *lethalis*, fr *lethum*, var (prob influenced by Gk *lēthē* forgetfulness, oblivion) of *letum* death] – **lethally** *adv*, **lethality** *n*

**lethal factor** *n* LETHAL GENE

**lethal gene** *also* **lethal** *n* a gene that may prevent development or cause the death of an organism at any time in its development from the embryo to the adult

**lethal mutation** *also* **lethal** *n* (a genetic mutation that produces) a LETHAL GENE

**lethargic** /lə'thahjik/ *adj* **1** sluggish **2** indifferent, apathetic – **lethargically** *adv*

**lethargy** /'lethəji/ *n* **1** abnormal drowsiness **2** lack of energy or interest [ME *litargie*, fr ML *litargia*, fr LL *lethargia*, fr Gk *lēthargia*, fr *lēthargos* forgetful, lethargic, fr *lēthē* + *argos* lazy – more at ARGON]

synonyms Lethargy, sluggishness, lassitude, languor, listlessness, laziness, sloth, and indolence all mean "inability or a disinclination to be active". Lethargy describes a state of drowsiness or apathy brought about by illness, tiredness, exhaustion, or constant frustration. Sluggishness emphasizes slowness of movement in mind or body. Lassitude, languor, and listlessness all suggest a state of inertia. In lassitude, this is brought about by overwork, strain, poor health, or intense worry, so that one's energy seems to have drained away. Languor is more often the result of indolence, luxurious living, amorousness, or a warm climate. Listlessness stresses lack of energy or enthusiasm without suggesting a cause. Indolence and laziness are habits of mind; the former stresses a love of ease, the latter stresses a disinclination to work or exert oneself in any way. Sloth is a somewhat literary term for either. Compare STUPOR, INACTIVE

**lethe** /'leethi/ *n*, *poetic* oblivion, forgetfulness [*Lethe*, mythical river in the underworld whose waters caused drinkers to forget their past, fr L, fr Gk *Lēthē*, fr *lēthē* forgetfulness; akin to Gk *lanthanein* to escape notice, *lanthanesthai* to forget – more at LATENT] – **lethean** *adj*

'**let-,out** *n*, *informal* something (eg an exclusion clause in a contract) that provides an opportunity to escape or be released from an obligation or expected course of action

**let's** /lets/ let us – used of a group that includes the one addressed ⟨∼ *face it*⟩ ⟨∼ *dance, Mary*⟩ ⟨∼ *not have lunch yet*⟩; compare ²LET 3 *usage* see ²LET

**Lett** /let/ *n* a member of a people closely related to the Lithuanians and mainly inhabiting Latvia [Ger *Lette*, fr Latvian *Latvi*]

¹**letter** /'letə/ *n* **1** a symbol, usu written or printed, representing a speech sound and constituting a unit of an alphabet **2a** a written or printed message addressed to a person, number of people, or organization and usu sent through the post **b letters** *pl*, *letter* a formal written communication containing a grant or authorization **3** *pl but taking sing or pl vb* **3a** literature; BELLES LETTRES **b** learning; *esp* scholarly knowledge of or achievement in literature ⟨*a man of ∼s*⟩ **4** the precise wording; the strict or literal meaning ⟨*the ∼ of the law*⟩ ⟨*obeyed the instructions to the ∼*⟩ **5a** a single piece of type **b** a style of type [ME, fr OF *lettre*, fr L *littera* letter of the alphabet, *litterae*, pl, epistle, literature]

²**letter** *vt* **1** to set down in letters ⟨*he carefully ∼ed his greeting in red and blue*⟩ **2** to mark with letters ⟨∼ *the diagram and provide a key*⟩ – **letterer** *n*

³**letter** *n* a person who rents or leases his/her property [³*let* + ²*-er*]

**letter bomb** *n* an explosive device concealed in an envelope or package and sent through the post to the intended victim

**letter box** *n*, *Br* a box designed to receive mail: eg **a** a postbox

**b** a hole or box (eg in a door) to receive material delivered by post

**letter card** *n* a card that can be folded and sent as a letter

**lettered** /'letəd/ *adj* **1** learned, educated **2** inscribed (as if) with letters

**letterhead** /-,hed/ *n* a sheet printed with a letterheading; *also* the heading itself

**letterheading** /'letə,heding/ *n* a printed heading on a sheet of writing paper showing the name and address of a person or organization

**lettering** /'letəring/ *n* the letters used in an inscription, esp as regards their style or quality ⟨*a memorial tablet with gold ∼*⟩

**letter of credit** *n* **1** a letter addressed by a banker to a correspondent certifying that a person named in it is entitled to draw on that correspondent or his/her agent up to a certain sum **2** a letter addressed by a banker to a person to whom credit is given, authorizing him/her to draw on the issuing bank or on its agent in another country up to a certain sum and guaranteeing to accept the drafts if duly made

,**letter-'perfect** *adj* correct to the smallest detail; *esp* word-perfect

**letterpress** /-,pres/ *n* **1a** (work produced by) printing from an inked raised surface, esp when the paper is impressed directly on the surface **b** a press for letterpress printing **2** *chiefly Br* text (eg of a book) as distinct from pictorial illustrations

**letters of administration** *n pl* a legal document giving authority to administer the estate of an INTESTATE (person who dies without making a valid will)

**letters of credence** *n pl* a formal document authorizing a diplomatic agent to act for his/her government

**letters of marque** *n pl* a licence formerly granted by a government to a private person to fit out an armed ship to plunder enemy shipping as a privateer [obs *marque* reprisals, fr ME fr MF, fr OProv *marca*, fr *marcar* to mark, sieze as a pledge, of Gmc origin]

**letters patent** *n pl* a formal document (eg from a sovereign) conferring on somebody a right or privilege, esp the sole right to exploit his/her invention

**Lettic** /'letik/ *adj* BALTIC 2 [*Lett - ic*]

**letting** /'leting/ *n*, *chiefly Br* property, esp a house or flat, that is let

¹**Lettish** /'letish/ *adj* of the Latvians or their language

²**Lettish** *n* LATVIAN 2

**lettre de cachet** /,let(rə)də ka'shay (*Fr* lɛtr də kaʃɛ)/ *n*, *pl* **lettres de cachet** /∼/ a letter bearing an official seal (eg of a sovereign) and usu authorizing imprisonment without trial of a named person [Fr, lit., letter with a seal]

**lettuce** /'letis/ *n* any of a genus (*Lactuca*) of plants of the daisy family; *esp* a common garden vegetable (*Lactuca sativa*) whose succulent edible green or whitish-green leaves are used esp in salads [ME *letuse*, fr OF *laitues*, pl of *laitue*, fr L *lactuca*, fr *lact-*, *lac* milk – more at GALAXY; fr its milky juice]

**letup** /'letup/ *n* a cessation or lessening of effort, activity, or intensity

**leu** /'layooh/ *n*, *pl* **lei** /'lay/ – see MONEY table [Romanian, lit., lion, fr L *leo* – more at LION]

**leuc-** /l(y)oohk-/, **leuco-**, **leuk-**, **leuko-** *comb form* **1** white; colourless ⟨leuco*cyte*⟩ ⟨leucor*rhoea*⟩ **2** WHITE MATTER of the brain ⟨leuco*tomy*⟩ [NL, fr Gk *leuk-*, *leuko-*, fr *leukos* white – more at LIGHT]

**leucine** /'lyoohseen/ *n* an ESSENTIAL AMINO ACID, $(CH_3)_2CHCH_2CH(NH_2)COOH$, found in most proteins and required in the diet of human beings for normal health and growth [ISV *leuc-* + *-ine*]

**leucite** /'l(y)oohsiet/ *n* a white or grey mineral, $KAlSi_2O_6$, containing potassium, aluminum, and silicon that is sometimes used as a fertilizer [Ger *leuzit*, fr *leuz-* leuc-] – **leucitic** *adj*

**leucocidin** /,l(y)oohkə'siedin/ *n* a substance made by some bacteria that destroys WHITE BLOOD CELLS [ISV *leuc-* + *-cide* + *-in*]

**leucocyt-**, **leucocyto-**, **leukocyt-**, **leukocyto-** *comb form* leucocyte; WHITE BLOOD CELL ⟨leucocy*tosis*⟩ [ISV]

**leucocyte** /'l(y)oohkə,siet/ *n* WHITE BLOOD CELL [ISV]

**leucocytosis** /,l(y)oohkəsie'tohsis/ *n* a condition, characteristic of infection or tissue damage (eg a burn), in which the number of WHITE BLOOD CELLS in the circulating blood is abnormally high [NL]

**leucoma** /l(y)ooh'kohmə/ *n* a patch of dense white tissue in the CORNEA (outer transparent covering) of the eye [LL, fr Gk *leukōma*, fr *leukos*]

leu 842

leucopenia /ˌl(y)oohkə'peenyə/ n a condition, characteristic of some diseases, in which the number of WHITE BLOOD CELLS circulating in the blood is abnormally low [NL, fr leuc- + Gk penia poverty, lack]

leucoplakia /ˌl(y)oohkə'plakiə/ n an abnormal condition that can develop into cancer, in which white patches of thickened tissue occur on the MUCOUS MEMBRANES (e g of the lips, genitals, or lining the mouth) [NL, fr leuc- + Gk plak-, plax flat surface – more at PLEASE] – leucoplakic adj

leucoplast /'l(y)oohkə,plast/ n a colourless PLASTID (minute body in a plant cell) occurring esp in tissues deep within the plant and not exposed to sunlight, that stores starch, fat, or protein and is potentially capable of developing into a CHROMOPLAST (plastid containing red or yellow colouring matter) [ISV]

leucoplastid /ˌl(y)oohkə'plastid/ n a leucoplast

leucopoiesis /ˌl(y)oohkoh·poy'eesis/ n the formation of WHITE BLOOD CELLS [NL] – leucopoietic adj

leucorrhoea, NAm chiefly leukorrhea /ˌl(y)oohkə'riə/ n a thick whitish discharge from the vagina resulting esp from inflammation of its lining [NL] – leucorrhoeal adj

leucosis /l(y)ooh'kohsis/ n, pl leucoses /-seez/ any of various disease conditions characterized by an abnormal increase in the number of WHITE BLOOD CELLS; leukaemia [NL]

leucotomy /l(y)ooh'kotəmi/ n a lobotomy

leuk- /l(y)oohk-/, leuko- comb form leuc-, leuco-

leukaemia, NAm leukemia /l(y)ooh'keemyə, -mi·ə/ n any of several short- or long-lasting usu fatal types of cancer that are characterized by an abnormal increase in the number of WHITE BLOOD CELLS in the body tissues, esp the blood [NL] – leukaemic adj

leukocyt-, leukocyto- comb form leucocyt-, leucocyto-

lev /lef/ n, pl leva /'levə/ – see MONEY table [Bulgarian, lit., lion]

lev- /leev-/, levo- comb form, chiefly NAm laev-, laevo-

Levalloisian /ˌlevə'loyziən/ adj of any late and middle PALAEOLITHIC culture of 3 million years ago, that was characterized by a technique of manufacturing tools by striking flakes from a flat flint nodule [Levallois-Perret, suburb of Paris in France]

levant /li'vant/ vi, chiefly Br to abscond; esp to run away from a debt (eg of unpaid bets) [perh fr Sp levantar to break camp, deriv of L levare] – levanter n

levanter /lə'vantə/ n a strong easterly Mediterranean wind [Levant, name for the countries bordering on the E Mediterranean, fr Fr levant, prp of lever to rise]

levator /li'vaytə, 'levətaw/ n, pl levatores /ˌlevə'tawreez/, levators a muscle that serves to raise a part of the body – compare DEPRESSOR [NL, fr L levatus, pp of levare to raise – more at LEVER]

¹levee /'levi/ n 1 a reception of visitors formerly held by a person of distinction on rising from bed 2 an afternoon assembly at which the British sovereign receives only men 3 a formal reception, usu in honour of a particular person △ levy [Fr lever, fr MF, act of arising, fr (se) lever to rise]

²levee n, NAm 1a a man-made embankment for preventing flooding a river landing place; a pier 2 a continuous dyke or ridge (eg of earth) for confining areas of land to be irrigated 3 the natural embankment of silt deposited by a river [Fr levée, fr OF, act of raising, fr lever to raise – more at LEVER]

³levee vt leveeing; leeveed NAm to provide with a levee

levée /'levi, 'levay/ n the lifting of a dancer by her partner [Fr]

levée en masse /ˌlevi on 'mas (Fr lɔve ã mas)/ n, pl levées en masse /~/ LEVY EN MASSE (spontaneous uprising) [Fr]

¹level /'levəl/ n 1 a device for establishing a horizontal line or plane: eg 1a SPIRIT LEVEL b WATER LEVEL 2 a measurement of the difference in height of two points by means of a level 3a horizontal condition; esp equilibrium of a liquid marked by a smooth horizontal surface ⟨water seeks its own ~⟩ b an (approximately) horizontal line, plane, or surface 4a a position of height in relation to the ground; a height ⟨eye ~⟩ ⟨a garden arranged on two ~s⟩ b level, levels pl a practically horizontal or flat area, esp of land 5 a position or place in a scale or rank (eg of value, importance, or achievement) or in relation to an arbitrary reference value ⟨a high ~ of academic excellence⟩ 6 an interconnecting series of horizontal passages in a mine 7 a concentration or amount of a constituent, esp a liquid in the body (eg blood) 8 the size or amount of something specified and often measurable ⟨noise ~⟩ ⟨the ~ of production⟩ 9 physics ENERGY LEVEL (stable amount of energy) [ME, fr MF livel, fr (assumed) VL libellum, alter. of L libella, fr dim. of libra weight, balance] – on the level honest; BONA FIDE

²level vb -ll- (NAm -l-, -ll) vt 1a to make (a line or surface) horizontal; make flat or level ⟨~ a field for planting⟩ b to raise or lower to the same height – often + up ⟨~ up the picture with the one next to it⟩ 2a to bring to a horizontal aiming position ⟨~led the gun at his head⟩ b to aim, direct – + at or against ⟨~led a charge of fraud at him⟩ 3 to bring to a common level, plane, or standard; equalize ⟨love ~s all ranks – W S Gilbert⟩ 4 to lay level with the ground; raze 5 to make (colour) even or uniform by dyeing 6 to find the elevations of different points in (a piece of land), esp with a surveyor's level 7 informal to knock (a person) down ~ vi 1 to attain or come to a level – usu + out or off ⟨the plane ~led off at 10000 feet⟩ 2 to aim a gun or other weapon horizontally 3 of a surveyor to measure the heights of sections of land 4 informal to deal or speak frankly and openly – usu + with

³level adj 1a having no part higher than another; flat b of a spoon, cup, etc filled just to the edge or rim ⟨a ~ teaspoonful of sugar⟩ c parallel with the plane of the horizon; conforming to the curvature of the liquid parts of the earth's surface 2a even or unvarying in magnitude ⟨a ~ temperature⟩ b equal in advantage, progression, or standing c steady, unwavering ⟨gave him a ~ look⟩ ⟨spoke in ~ tones⟩ 3 reasonable, balanced ⟨arrive at a justly proportional and ~ judgment on this affair – Sir Winston Churchill⟩ 4 distributed evenly ⟨~ stress⟩ 5 suited to a particular rank or plane (eg of ability or achievement) – usu in combination ⟨top-level thinking⟩ – levelly adv, levelness n – level best very best ⟨he did his level best⟩

synonyms Level, flat, plane, even, smooth, and flush describe a surface like that of a calm piece of water. What is level is parallel to the horizon, while what is flat is not always horizontal. A flat surface does not have any irregularities, but these may be present in something level ⟨a level plain dotted with hillocks⟩ ⟨a flat cliff-face offering no handholds⟩. A plane surface is one which can be demonstrated mathematically to be flat. Even implies a visible uniformity ⟨your hemline is not even⟩. Smooth suggests a surface so free of irregularities that it might have been polished; unlike the other words, it may be applied to a curved surface ⟨a smooth wooden ball⟩. Flush implies matching an adjoining surface in the same plane ⟨the river is now flush with its banks and may overflow⟩.

level crossing n, Br a place where a railway crosses a road or another railway

levelheaded /-'hedid/ adj having sound judgment; sensible – levelheadedness n

leveller, NAm chiefly leveler /'levələ/ n 1 one who or that which levels 2 cap a member of a group of radicals which arose during the English Civil War and advocated legal equality for everyone and freedom of religious worship 3 one favouring the removal of political, social, or economic inequalities 4 something that tends to reduce or eliminate differences between people

levelling screw n a screw for adjusting the level of an apparatus (eg a record turntable)

levelling staff /'levəling/ n a graduated staff used in measuring the vertical distance between a point on the ground and the line of sight of a surveyor's level

level of significance n the probability that a given statistical outcome could have arisen by chance rather than as a result of some specific cause – called also SIGNIFICANCE LEVEL

¹lever /'leevə/ n 1a a bar used for prizing up or dislodging something b an inducing or compelling force; a tool ⟨attempts to use food as a political ~ – Time⟩ 2a a rigid piece that transmits and modifies force or motion when forces are applied at two points and it turns about a third; specif a rigid bar used to exert a force or sustain a weight at one point of its length by the application of a force at a second and turning at a third on a support b a projecting piece by which a mechanism is operated or adjusted [ME, fr OF levier, fr lever to raise, fr L levare; akin to L levis light in weight – more at ⁴LIGHT]

²lever vt 1 to prize, raise, or move (as if) with a lever – often + up or off ⟨~ed himself out of bed⟩ 2 to operate (a device) in the manner of a lever ⟨~ed the throttle back⟩

leverage /'leevərij/ n 1 the action of a lever or the mechanical advantage gained by it 2 power, influence 3 NAm economics GEARING

leveret /'lev(ə)rit/ n a young hare, esp one in its first year [ME, fr (assumed) MF levret, fr MF levre hare, fr L lepor-, lepus]

leviable /'leviəbl/ adj capable of being levied or LEVIED ON

leviathan /lə'vie·əthən/ n 1a a large sea animal b a large ocean-going ship 2 cap the political state; esp a totalitarian state having a vast bureaucracy **3** something large or formidable [*Leviathan,* a huge sea animal in the Bible, fr ME, fr LL, fr Heb *liwyāthān;* (2) fr the political treatise *Leviathan* by Thomas Hobbes †1679 E philosopher, in which "Leviathan" represents sovereign power] – **leviathan** *adj*

¹**levigate** /'levigayt/ *vt* **1** to grind to a fine smooth powder while in moist condition **2** to separate (fine powder) from coarser material by suspension in a liquid **3** to make into a mixture of uniform texture (e g a gel) [L *levigatus,* pp of *levigare* to polish, make smooth, fr *levis* smooth + *-igare* (akin to *agere* to drive) – more at LIME, AGENT] – **levigation** *n*

²**levigate** /'levigayt, -gət/ *adj, botany* without hairs; smooth

**levitate** /'levi,tayt/ *vb* to (cause to) rise or float in the air, esp in seeming defiance of gravity ⟨*saw several objects* ~d *during a spiritualistic seance*⟩ ⟨*a particle* ~d *by an electromagnetic device*⟩ [*levity* + *-ate*]

**levitation** /,levi'taysh(ə)n/ *n* levitating; *esp* the rising or lifting of a person or thing by apparently supernatural means – **levitational** *adj*

**Levite** /'leeviet/ *n* a member of the priestly Hebrew tribe of Levi; *specif* a Levite of non-Aaronic descent assigned to lesser ceremonial offices under the priests of the family of Aaron [ME, fr LL *Levita, Levites,* fr Gk *Leuites,* fr *Leui* Levi, son of Jacob, fr Heb *Lēwī*]

**Levitical** /lə'vitikl/ *adj* of the Levites or the Old Testament book of Leviticus [LL *Leviticus*]

**Leviticus** /lə'vitikəs/ *n* – see BIBLE table [LL, lit., of the Levites]

**levity** /'levəti/ *n* **1a** lack of seriousness; *esp* excessive or unseemly frivolity **b** lack of steadiness; changeableness **2** *archaic* the quality or state of being light in weight [L *levitat-, levitas,* fr *levis* light in weight, trivial – more at ⁴LIGHT]

**levodopa** /'leevoh,dohpə/ *n, chiefly Br* L-DOPA (substance used in treating PARKINSON'S DISEASE)

¹**levy** /'levi/ *n* **1a** the imposing or collection of a tax, fine, etc **b** an amount levied **2a** enlistment or conscription for military service **b** *taking sing or pl vb* troops raised by levy △ levee [ME, fr MF *levee,* fr OF, act of raising – more at ²LEVEE]

²**levy** *vt* **1** to impose, collect, or require by legal authority ⟨~ *a tax*⟩ **2** to enlist or conscript for military service **3** to prepare for and make (war) – usu + *on* or *upon*

**levy on/upon** *vt* to obtain (payment that is owing) by seizing the debtor's possessions officially

**levy en masse** /,levi on 'mas/ *n, pl* **levies en masse** the spontaneous act of the people of a territory of taking up arms for self-defence on the approach of an enemy without having had time to organize in accordance with recognized rules of warfare [part trans of Fr *levée en masse*]

**lewd** /l(y)oohd/ *adj* **1a** sexually coarse or suggestive; lustful ⟨*a* ~ *wink*⟩ **b** obscene ⟨~ *songs*⟩ **2** *obs* evil, wicked [ME *lewed* vulgar, fr OE *lǣwede* laical, ignorant] – **lewdly** *adv,* **lewdness** *n*

**lewis** /'looh·is/ *n* a device consisting of wedges or curved metal bars for gripping and hoisting large stones or blocks [prob fr the name *Lewis*]

**Lewis gun** *n* a light magazine-fed air-cooled gas-operated machine gun [Isaac *Lewis* †1931 US army officer & inventor]

**lewisite** /'looh·i,siet/ *n* a colourless or brown irritant and blister-inducing liquid, ClCH=CHAsCl₂, developed as a poison gas for war use [Winford *Lewis* †1943 US chemist]

**lewisson** /'looh·isən/ *n* a lewis

**lexeme** /'lekseem/ *n* a minimal unit of the vocabulary of a language that can have independent meaning without being added to another word or word part; a word – compare MORPHEME [*lexicon* + *-eme*]

**lexical** /'leksikl/ *adj* **1** of words or the vocabulary of a language, as distinguished from its grammar and construction **2** of a lexicon or lexicography – **lexically** *adv,* **lexicality** *n*

**lexical meaning** *n* the meaning of the ROOT (e g *play*) in a set of inflectional forms (e g *plays, played, playing*) – compare GRAMMATICAL MEANING

**lexicography** /,leksi'kogrəfi/ *n* **1** the editing or compiling of a dictionary **2** the principles and practices of dictionary making [LGk *lexikographos* dictionary writer, fr *lexikon* + Gk *-graphos* -grapher] – **lexicographer** *n,* **lexicographical, lexicographic** *adj,* **lexicographically** *adv*

**lexicology** /,leksi'koləji/ *n* a branch of linguistics concerned with the meaning and use of words [Fr *lexicologie,* fr *lexico-* (fr LGk *lexiko-,* fr *lexikon*) + *-logie* -logy] – **lexicologist** *n*

**lexicon** /'leksikən/ *n, pl* **lexica** /-kə/, **lexicons 1** a book containing an alphabetical arrangement of the words in a language and their definitions; a dictionary **2** the vocabulary of a language, an individual speaker, or a subject **3** the total stock of MORPHEMES (meaningful units of language) in a language [LGk *lexikon,* fr neut of *lexikos* of words, fr Gk *lexis* word, speech, fr *legein* to say – more at LEGEND]

**lexigraphy** /lek'sigrafi/ *n* a system of writing in which each character stands for a word [Gk *lexis* + E *-graphy*]

**lexis** /'leksis/ *n, pl* **lexes** /-seez/ LEXICON 2,3 [Gk, speech, word]

¹**ley** /lee, lay/, **ley line** an alignment of landmarks held to mark the course of a prehistoric trackway [*lea, ley* (tract of open ground), fr ME *lee, leye,* fr OE *lēah;* akin to OHG *lōh* thicket, L *lucus* grove]

²**ley** *n* **1** LEA (grassland) **2** agricultural land used temporarily for hay or grazing [var of *ley*]

**Leyden jar** /'liedən/ *n* an early form of electrical CAPACITOR (device for storing electrical energy) consisting of a glass jar coated inside and outside with metal foil and having the inner coating connected to a conducting rod passed through the insulating stopper [*Leiden, Leyden,* city in the Netherlands]

**ley farming** *n* a system of farming in which the CROP ROTATION includes a period under grass

'**L-,form** *n* a form of some bacteria that resembles a MYCOPLASMA (extremely small usu parasitic organism) and that may be a specialized reproductive body which appears chiefly when the environment is unfavourable [Lister Institute, London, where it was first isolated]

**Lhasa apso** /,lahsə 'apsoh/ *n, pl* **Lhasa apsos** (any of) a Tibetan breed of small dogs that have a dense coat of long hard straight hair, a tail curled over the back, and that are used as guard dogs [*Lhasa,* city in Tibet + Tibetan *apso*]

**li** /lee/ *n, pl* **li** *also* **lis** any of various Chinese units of distance; *esp* one equal to about 0·5 kilometre (about ¹/₃ mile) [Chin (Pek) *li* (*li³*)]

**liability** /,lie·ə'bilǝti/ *n* **1** the quality, state, or condition of being liable **2** something for which one is liable; *esp* debts **3** *chiefly informal* hindrance, drawback ⟨*china cups are a bit of a* ~ *when you're camping*⟩ ⟨*she's so clumsy; she's a real* ~⟩

**liable** /'lie·əbl/ *adj* **1a** legally responsible ⟨~ *for the debts incurred by his son*⟩ **b** subject to appropriation or attachment ⟨*all his property is* ~ *to pay his debts*⟩ **2** exposed *to,* subject *to,* or in a position to incur some usu adverse circumstance or action ⟨~ *to hurt yourself if you do that*⟩ **3** habitually likely *to;* apt ⟨*he's* ~ *to get annoyed*⟩ [(assumed) AF, fr OF *lier* to bind, fr L *ligare* – more at LIGATURE]

**liaise** /lee'ayz/ *vi* **1** to establish or maintain liaison **2** to act as a liaison officer [back-formation fr *liaison*]

**liaison** /lee'ayzon, -z(ə)n, -zonh/ *n* **1a** a close bond or connection **b** a secret or extramarital sexual relationship; an affair **2** the pronunciation of an otherwise silent consonant (e g *t* in the French *est-il*) at the end of the first of two consecutive words, the second of which begins with a vowel sound **3** the communication or association that establishes and maintains mutual understanding and cooperation, esp between parts of an armed force **4** a substance (e g flour, cornflour, or potato) or mixture (e g of egg yolk and cream) used in cooking to thicken or bind liquids (e g soups and sauces) [Fr fr MF, fr *lier*]

**liana** /li'ahnə/ *n* a climbing soft-stemmed or woody plant, esp of tropical rain forests, that roots in the ground [Fr *liane,* prob fr *lier*] – **lianoid** *adj*

**liane** /li'ahn/ *n* a liana

**liang** /li'ahng/ *n, pl* **liang** *also* **liangs** an old Chinese unit of weight equal to ¹/₁₆ CATTY (about 38 grams) [Chin (Pek) *liǎng* (*liang³*)]

**liar** /'lie·ə/ *n* one who tells lies, esp habitually △ lyre [ME, fr OE *lēogere,* fr *lēogan* to lie – more at ³LIE]

**Lias** /'lie·əs/ *adj or n* (of or being) a subdivision of the European JURASSIC rock system [n Fr, fr E *lias* a blue limestone rock, fr ME *lyas,* fr MF *liois;* adj fr n] – **Liassic** *adj*

**lib** /lib/ *n, often cap, informal* LIBERATION 2 ⟨*gay* ~⟩

**libation** /lie'baysh(ə)n/ *n* **1a** an act of pouring a liquid as a sacrifice, esp to a deity **b** a liquid (e g wine) used as a libation **2a** an act or instance of drinking; esp ceremoniously **b** *formal or humorous* a beverage; *esp* a drink containing alcohol [L *libation-, libatio,* fr *libatus,* pp of *libare* to pour as an offering; akin to Gk *leibein* to pour] – **libationary** *adj*

**libber** /'libə/ *n, informal* an advocate of equal rights and status in a specified field; a liberationist ⟨*a women's* ~⟩ [*lib* + ²*-er*]

¹**libel** /'liebl/ *n* **1a** the harming of a person's good name or reputation by means of published writing, print, or pictorial

representation as distinguished from mere spoken words or gestures; *also* an act of publishing such libel – compare SLANDER **b** a false and insulting statement **2** a written statement made by a PLAINTIFF (person who brings an action in a court of law against another) [ME, written declaration, fr MF, fr L *libellus*, dim. of *liber* book – more at LEAF]

²**libel** *vb* **-ll-** (*NAm* **-l-**, **-ll-**) *vi* to make libellous statements ~ *vt* to make or publish a libel against (someone) *synonyms* see ²MALIGN – **libellant, libeller, libellist** *n*

**libellee**, *NAm chiefly* **libelee** /ˌliebəˈlee/ *n* a person against whom a libel action has been brought in court

**libellous**, *NAm chiefly* **libelous** /ˈliebələs/ *adj* constituting or including a libel; defamatory ⟨*a* ~ *statement*⟩

¹**liberal** /ˈlibrəl/ *adj* **1** of or based on LIBERAL STUDIES ⟨~ *education*⟩ **2a** generous and openhanded ⟨*a* ~ *giver*⟩ **b** given or provided in a generous and openhanded way; ample ⟨*a* ~ *donation*⟩ **3** not literal; loose ⟨*a* ~ *translation*⟩ **4** broad-minded, tolerant; *esp* not bound by authoritarianism, orthodoxy, or traditional forms **5a** of, favouring, or based on the principles of liberalism **b** *cap* of or being a political party that advocates the principles of political liberalism; *specif* of or being a political party of the UK associated with ideals of individual esp economic freedom, greater individual participation in government, and constitutional, political, and administrative reforms designed to secure these objectives **6** *archaic* of or befitting a man of free birth [ME, fr MF, fr L *liberalis* suitable for a freeman, generous, fr *liber* free; akin to OE *lēodan* to grow, Gk *eleutheros* free] – **liberally** *adv*, **liberalness** *n*

²**liberal** *n* a person who is liberal: e g **a** one who is open-minded or not strict in the observance of orthodox, traditional, or established forms or ways **b** *cap* a member or supporter of a Liberal political party **c** an advocate or adherent of liberalism, esp in individual rights

**liberal arts** *n pl* **1a** the medieval studies comprising the TRIVIUM (grammar, rhetoric, and logic) and QUADRIVIUM (music, geometry, arithmetic, and astronomy) **b** the arts generally (e g humanities and languages) **2** *chiefly NAm* LIBERAL STUDIES

**liberalism** /ˈlibrəliz(ə)m/ *n* **1** breadth of mind; tolerance **2a** *often cap* a movement in modern Protestantism emphasizing intellectual freedom and the spiritual and ethical content of Christianity **b** a political philosophy based on belief in progress, the essential goodness of human beings, and the freedom and independence of the individual, and standing for the protection of political and civil liberties **c** *cap* the principles and policies of a Liberal party – **liberalist** *n or adj*, **liberalistic** *adj*

**liberality** /ˌlibəˈraləti/ *n* the quality or state of being liberal in attitude or in giving; *also, formal* a liberal gift

**liberal·ize, -ise** /ˈlibrəˌliez/ *vb* to make or become (more) liberal – **liberalization** *n*, **liberalizer** *n*

**Liberal Judaism** *n* REFORM JUDAISM

**liberal studies** *n taking sing or pl vb* the studies (e g language, philosophy, history, literature, and abstract science) in a college or university which are intended to provide chiefly general knowledge and to develop the general intellectual capacities rather than professional or vocational skills

**liberate** /ˈlibəˌrayt/ *vt* **1** to set at liberty; release; *specif* to free (a country) from domination by a foreign power **2** to release (e g a gas or atom) from combination (in a chemical compound) **3** *euph or humorous* to take, steal [L *liberatus*, pp of *liberare*, fr *liber*] – **liberator** *n*

**liberation** /ˌlibəˈraysh(ə)n/ *n* **1** liberating or being liberated **2** the action of seeking equal rights and status ⟨*women's* ~⟩ – **liberationist** *n*

**libertarian** /ˌlibəˈteəri·ən/ *n* **1** a believer in free will **2** one who upholds the principles of absolute and unrestricted liberty of thought and action △ libertine – **libertarian** *adj*, **libertarianism** *n*

**liberticide** /liˈbuhtisied/ *n* **1** the destruction of liberty **2** a destroyer of liberty – **liberticidal** *adj*

**libertine** /ˈlibəteen/ *n* **1** a person who is unrestrained by convention or morality; *specif* one leading a dissolute life **2** *chiefly derog* a freethinker, esp in religious matters △ libertarian [ME *libertyn* freedman, fr L *libertinus*, fr *libertinus*, adj, of a freedman, fr *libertus* freedman, fr *liber*] – **libertinage, libertinism** *n*, **libertine** *adj*

**liberty** /ˈlibəti/ *n* **1** the quality or state of being free: **1a** the power to do as one pleases **b** freedom from physical restraint **c** freedom from arbitrary or dictatorial control **d** the possession of various social, political, or economic rights and privileges **e** the power of choice **2a** a right or immunity awarded or granted; a privilege **b** permission; *esp* permission to go freely within specified limits **3** an action going beyond normal limits; an instance of unnecessary, unwarranted, or improper freedom: e g **3a** a breach of etiquette or socially acceptable conduct **b** a risk, chance ⟨*took foolish* liberties *with his health*⟩ **4** a short authorized absence from naval duty, usu for less than 48 hours *synonyms* see FREEDOM *antonyms* captivity, imprisonment, bondage, slavery [ME, fr MF *liberté*, fr L *libertat-*, *libertas*, fr *liber* free – more at LIBERAL] – **at liberty 1** free ⟨*you are* at liberty *to leave*⟩ **2** unoccupied; AT LEISURE

**liberty cap** *n* a close-fitting conical cap worn as a symbol of liberty, esp by by the French revolutionaries

**Liberty Hall** *n, informal* a place where one can do as one likes

**liberty horse** *n* a circus horse that performs without a rider

**libidinous** /liˈbidinəs/ *adj* **1** of the libido **2** *formal* having or marked by lustful desires; lascivious [ME, fr MF *libidineus*, fr L *libidinosus*, fr *libidin-*, *libido*] – **libidinously** *adv*, **libidinousness** *n*

**libido** /liˈbeedoh/ *n, pl* **libidos 1** emotional or mental energy that according to PSYCHOANALYTIC theory is derived from primitive biological urges **2** sexual drive [NL *libidin-*, *libido*, fr L, desire, lust, fr *libēre* to please – more at LOVE] – **libidinal** *adj*, **libidinally** *adv*

**Lib-Lab** /ˌlib ˈlab/ *adj* concerning or involving both the Labour and Liberal parties ⟨*the* ~ *pact*⟩ [*Liberal* + *Labour*]

**libra** /ˈleebrə, ˈliebrə/ *n, pl* **libras, (2a) librae** /-brie, -bree/ **1** *cap* **1a** a small constellation of the ZODIAC (imaginary belt in the heavens) lying between Virgo and Scorpius and represented as a pair of scales **b(1)** the 7th sign of the zodiac in astrology, held to govern the period September 23 - October 22 approx **b(2)** somebody born under this sign **2a** an ancient Roman unit of weight equal to 327.45 grams (about 11½ ounces) **b** any of various Spanish, Portuguese, Colombian, or Venezuelan units of weight [(1) ME, fr L, lit., scales, pound (cf LIRA, LIVRE); (2a) L; (2b) Sp & Pg, fr L] – **Libran** *adj or n*

**librarian** /lieˈbreəri·ən/ *n* a person who manages or assists in a library

**librarianship** /lieˈbreərianship/ *n, chiefly Br* the study or the principles and practices of library care and administration

**library** /ˈliebrəri/ *n* **1a** a place in which literary, musical, artistic, or reference materials (e g books, manuscripts, recordings, or films) are kept for use but not for sale ⟨*a lending* ~⟩ **b** a collection of such materials **2** a collection resembling or suggesting a library ⟨*a* ~ *of computer programs*⟩ **3** a series of related books issued by a publisher **4** *Br* a theatre ticket agency – used esp by people working in the theatre trade [ME, fr ML *librarium*, fr L, neut of *librarius* of books, fr *libr-*, *liber* book – more at LEAF]

*usage* The pronunciation /ˈliebrəri/ rather than /ˈlieb(ə)ri/ is recommended for BBC broadcasters.

**library science** *n, chiefly NAm* librarianship

**librate** /lieˈbrayt/ *vi* **1** to oscillate or vibrate like a balance; sway **2** to stay poised [L *libratus*, pp of *librare* to balance, fr *libra* scales]

**libration** /lieˈbraysh(ə)n/ *n* **1** the action or state of librating **2** a real or apparent oscillation of a planet or satellite, esp the moon, that causes parts at the edge of the disc to become alternately visible and invisible. The librations of the moon enable us to see 59 per cent of the moon's surface from earth. – **librational, libratory** *adj*

**libretto** /liˈbretoh/ *n, pl* **librettos, libretti** /-ti/ (a book containing) the text of a work (e g an opera) that is both theatrical and musical [It, dim. of *libro* book, fr L *libr-*, *liber*] – **librettist** *n*

**Librium** /ˈlibri·əm/ *trademark* – used for the tranquillizing drug CHLORDIAZEPOXIDE

**Libyan** /ˈlibi·ən/ *n* **1** a native or inhabitant of Libya **2** an ancient Berber language of N Africa [*Libya*, country in N Africa] – **Libyan** *adj*

**lice** /lies/ *pl of* LOUSE

**licence**, *NAm chiefly* **license** /ˈlies(ə)ns/ *n* **1a** permission to act **b** freedom of action **2a** permission granted by an authorized body to engage in a particular business (e g selling alcohol) or activity (e g driving a vehicle or possessing a firearm) which would otherwise be unlawful ⟨*granted export* ~ s⟩ **b** an official document, sign, or tag showing that a licence has been granted ⟨*lost her dog* ~⟩ **3** deviation from fact, form, or rule by an artist or writer, esp for the sake of the effect gained ⟨*poetic* ~⟩ **4** *formal* **4a** freedom that allows or is used with irresponsibility; excessive liberty **b** disregard for rules of personal conduct or what is socially acceptable [ME, fr MF *licence,* fr L *licentia,* fr *licent-, licens,* prp of *licēre* to be permitted; akin to Latvian *līkt* to come to terms]

  **usage** In British English, the noun is spelt **licence** and the verb **license**: in American English both noun and verb are spelt **license**; but both forms are used in such expressions as **licensed/licenced premises** ( = a place where one can drink) according to whether one feels the establishment to have received a **licence** or to have been **licensed. synonyms** see FREEDOM **antonyms** constraint, restraint

**license** *also* **licence** /'lies(ə)ns/ *vt* **1** to issue a licence to **2** to permit or authorize, esp by formal licence – **licensable** *adj,* **licenser, licensor** *n*

**licensed victualler** *n, Br* a publican holding a licence to sell food and alcoholic drink on his/her premises

**licensee** /ˌlies(ə)n'see/ *n* a person who is licensed; *esp* a person having a licence to sell alcoholic drinks

**license plate, licence plate** *n, chiefly NAm* a renewable number plate usu fixed to the bumper of a vehicle showing that it has been licensed

**licensing laws** /'liesənsing/ *n pl, Br* laws governing when, where, and to whom alcoholic drinks may be sold

**licentiate** /lie'sensh(i)·ət, -ayt/ *n* **1** one who is licensed to practise a profession **2** (the holder of) an academic degree that ranks below that of doctor and is given by some European universities [ML *licentiatus,* fr pp of *licentiare* to allow, fr L *licentia*]

**licentious** /lie'senshəs/ *adj* **1** lacking legal or moral restraints; *esp* disregarding sexual restraints **2** *formal* marked by disregard for strict rules of correctness [L *licentiosus,* fr *licentia*] – **licentiously** *adv,* **licentiousness** *n*

**lichee** /'liechee, -'-/ *n* LITCHI (Chinese tree or its fruit)

**lichen** /'liekən, 'lichin/ *n* **1** any of numerous complex plants (group Lichenes) made up of an alga and a fungus growing in mutually beneficial association (SYMBIOSIS) on a solid surface (e g a rock or tree trunk) **2** any of several skin diseases characterized by raised spots [L, fr Gk *leichēn, lichēn*] – **lichened** *adj,* **lichenous** *adj*

**lich-gate** /lich/ *n* LYCH-GATE (roofed gate)

**licit** /'lisit/ *adj, formal* not forbidden by law; *broadly* permissible **synonyms** see LAWFUL **antonym** illicit [MF *licite,* fr L *licitus,* fr pp of *licēre* to be permitted – more at LICENCE] – **licitly** *adv*

¹**lick** /lik/ *vt* **1a(1)** to draw the tongue over, esp in order to taste, moisten, or clean ⟨~ *a stamp*⟩ **a(2)** to flicker or play over like a tongue **b** to take into the mouth with the tongue; lap – usu + *up* **2** *informal* **2a** to beat, thrash **b** to get the better of; overcome ⟨*has* ~ed *every problem*⟩ to lap (as if) with the tongue; *also* to dart like a tongue ⟨*flames* ~ing *at the windows*⟩ – see also **lick into** SHAPE [ME *licken,* fr OE *liccian;* akin to OHG *leckōn* to lick, L *lingere,* Gk *leichein*]

²**lick** *n* **1a** an act or instance of licking **b** a small amount; a touch ⟨*a* ~ *of paint*⟩ **2** a blow **3 lick, salt lick** a place (e g a salt spring) to which animals regularly go to lick a salt deposit; *also* a block of selected minerals provided for animals to lick **4** an improvised piece of dance music usu added into a written composition **5** *informal* a (fast) speed or pace ⟨*going at quite a* ~⟩ – **a lick and a promise** *informal* a perfunctory performance of a task; *esp* a hasty and careless wash

**lickerish, liquorish** /'likərish/ *adj, archaic* **1a** fond of good food; eager to taste or enjoy **b** greedy, desirous **2** lecherous [alter. of obs *lickerous,* fr ME *likerous,* fr (assumed) ONF, fr ONF *leckeur* lecher; akin to OF *lecheor* lecher] – **lickerishly** *adv,* **lickerishness** *n*

**lickety-split** /ˌlikəti 'split/ *adv, NAm informal* at great speed [prob irreg fr ¹*lick + split*]

**licking** /'liking/ *n* **1** the act or action of one who licks **2** *informal* a sound thrashing; a beating **3** *informal* a severe setback; a defeat

**lickspittle** /'lik,spitl/ *n* a crawling subordinate; a toady

**licorice** /'likərish, -ris/ *n, chiefly NAm* liquorice

**lictor** /'liktə/ *n* an ancient Roman officer who bore the FASCES (bundle of rods and an axe) as the insignia of his office and whose duties included accompanying the chief magistrates in public appearances [L; perh akin to L *ligare* to bind]

**lid** /lid/ *n* **1** a movable cover that is hinged or detachable; *esp* one for the opening of a hollow container (e g a vessel or box) **2** an eyelid **3** the OPERCULUM (flap covering seeds or spores) in mosses **4** *slang* a hat **5** *slang* an ounce of marijuana [ME, fr OE *hlid;* akin to OHG *hlit* cover, OE *hlinian, hleonian* to lean – more at LEAN] – **lidded** *adj* – **flip one's lid 1** to lose one's self control; go mad **2** to become wildly excited or eager – often + *over* – **put the (tin) lid on** *chiefly Br informal* to ruin;

PUT PAID TO – **take the lid off** to make revelations about; expose

**lidar** /'liedah/ *n* a device that is similar in operation to radar but emits pulses of light from a laser instead of RADIO WAVES [*light* + ra*dar*]

**lidless** /'lidlis/ *adj* **1** having no lid **2** *of eyes* having no eyelids **3** *archaic, of eyes* watchful

**lido** /'liedoh, 'lee-/ *n, pl* **lidos 1** a fashionable beach resort **2** a public open-air swimming pool [*Lido,* resort near Venice in Italy, fr L *litus* shore]

¹**lie** /lie/ *vi* **lying; lay** /lay/; **lain** /layn/ **1a** to be or stay at rest in a horizontal position; rest, recline ⟨~ *motionless*⟩ ⟨~ *asleep*⟩ **b** to assume a horizontal position – often + *down* **c** to be or remain in a specified state or condition ⟨~ *in wait*⟩ ⟨*the town lay at the mercy of the invaders*⟩ ⟨*machinery* lying *idle*⟩ **2** *of something inanimate* to be or remain in a flat or horizontal position on a surface ⟨*books* lying *on the table*⟩ **3** *of snow* to remain on the ground without melting **4** to have direction; lead ⟨*the route* lay *to the west*⟩ **5a** to occupy a specified place or position ⟨*hills* ~ *behind us*⟩ ⟨*the real reason* ~s *deeper*⟩ **b** to have an esp adverse effect through mere presence, weight, or relative position ⟨*remorse* lay *heavily on him*⟩ **c** to be sustainable or admissible in a court of law ⟨*the case will* ~⟩ **6** ⁴to remain at anchor or becalmed **7** *of a corpse* to be buried **8** *archaic* to reside temporarily; stay for the night; lodge **9** *archaic* to have sexual intercourse – + *with* or *together* – see also **lie LOW, lie in** STATE *usage* see ¹LAY [ME *lien,* fr OE *licgan;* akin to OHG *ligen* to lie, L *lectus* bed, Gk *lechos*] – **lier** *n*

  **lie down** *vi* **1** to submit weekly or abjectly to defeat, disappointment, or insult ⟨*won't take that criticism* lying *down*⟩ **2** to fail to perform or to neglect one's part deliberately ⟨lying *down on the job*⟩

  **lie down under** *vt* to accept without protest or resistance

  **lie in** *vi* **1** to be confined to bed during childbirth **2** to stay in bed later than usual – see also LIE-IN

  **lie off** *vi, of a ship* to be a small distance from the shore or another ship

  **lie over** *vi* to await attention at a later time ⟨*several jobs* lying *over from last week*⟩

  **lie to** *vi, of a ship* to be stationary or nearly so, with the bows pointing into the wind

  **lie up** *vi* **1** to stay in bed, esp because of illness **2** *of a ship* to remain in dock or out of service **3** to remain inactive or at rest

²**lie** *n* **1** the way, position, or situation in which something lies ⟨*the* ~ *of the land*⟩ **2** the position of a golf ball to be played ⟨*an awkward* ~ *in the bunker*⟩ **3** a place frequented by animals or fish

³**lie** *vb* **lying** *vi* **1** to make an untrue statement with intent to deceive; speak falsely **2** to create a false or misleading impression ⟨*the camera cannot* ~⟩ – *vt* to bring about by telling lies ⟨*managed to* ~ *his way out of trouble*⟩ – see also **lie in/ through one's back** TEETH (at TOOTH) [ME *lien,* fr OE *lēogan;* akin to OHG *liogan* to lie, OSlav *lŭgati*]

⁴**lie** *n* **1** an untrue or false statement; *esp* a false statement made with intent to deceive **2** something that misleads or deceives – **give the lie to 1** to show (something) to be false **2** to accuse (somebody) of lying

**liebfraumilch** /'leebfrow,milkh (*Ger* liːpfraumilç)/ *n, often cap* a dry white wine made in the Rhine valley; a type of HOCK; *also* a similar wine made elsewhere [Ger, alter. of *liebfrauenmilch,* fr *Liebfrauenstift,* religious foundation in Worms, Germany + *milch* milk]

**lied** /leed (*Ger* liːt)/ *n, pl* **lieder** /'leedə (*Ger* liˑdər)/ a German song; *esp* a 19th-century setting of a poem to music [Ger, song, fr OHG *liod* – more at LAUD]

**lie detector** *n* an instrument that detects changes occurring in certain physiological activities (e g pulse or breathing rates) as evidences of the tension that accompanies lying – compare POLYGRAPH

'**lie-,down** *n, chiefly Br informal* a brief rest, esp on a bed

¹**lief** /leef/ *adj, archaic* **1** dear, beloved **2** willing, glad [ME *lief, lef,* fr OE *lēof;* akin to OE *lufu* love – more at LOVE]

²**lief** *adv, archaic* soon, gladly ⟨*I'd as* ~ *go as not*⟩

¹**liege** /leej/ *adj* **1a** having the right to feudal allegiance or service ⟨*his* ~ *lord*⟩ **b** owing feudal allegiance and service **2** faithful, loyal [ME, fr OF, fr LL *laeticus,* fr *laetus* serf, of Gmc origin; akin to OFris *let* serf]

²**liege** *n* **1 liege, liege man 1a** a person bound to feudal service and allegiance; VASSAL **b** a loyal follower **2 liege, liege lord** a feudal superior to whom allegiance and service were due

846

**'lie-,in** *n, chiefly Br informal* a longer stay than usual in bed in the morning

**lien** /'lee-ən, leen/ *n* the legal right to hold another's property until a debt is paid [MF, tie, band, fr L *ligamen*, fr *ligare* to bind – more at LIGATURE]

**lierne** /li'uhn, li'eən/ *n* a nonstructural rib in a vaulted ceiling that passes from one main rib to another [Fr, fr MF, fr *lier* to bind, tie, fr L *ligare*]

**lieu** /l(y)ooh/ *n* [MF, place, fr L *locus* – more at STALL] – **in lieu** in substitution; instead ⟨*I'm phoning in lieu of sending a letter*⟩

**lieutenant** /lef'tenənt; *Royal Navy* lə'tenənt; *NAm* looh'tenənt/ *n* 1 an official empowered to act for a higher official; deputy **2a** – see MILITARY RANKS table **b** *NAm* a fire or police officer ranking below a captain [ME, fr MF, fr *lieu* place + *tenant* holding, fr *tenir* to hold, fr L *tenēre* – more at THIN] – **lieutenancy** *n*

**lieutenant colonel** *n* – see MILITARY RANKS table

**lieutenant commander** *n* – see MILITARY RANKS table

**lieutenant general** *n* – see MILITARY RANKS table

**lieutenant governor** *n* a deputy or subordinate governor: eg **a** an elected official serving as deputy to the governor of a US state **b** the formal head of the government of a Canadian province appointed by the federal government as the representative of the crown – **lieutenant governorship** *n*

**lieutenant junior grade** *n, pl* **lieutenants junior grade** – see MILITARY RANKS table

**¹life** /lief/ *n, pl* **lives** /lievz/ **1a** the quality that distinguishes a living and functional being from a dead body or inanimate object **b** a principle or force that is considered to underlie the distinctive quality of animate beings – compare VITALISM **c** a state of matter (eg a cell or an organism) characterized by capacity for biochemical processing (METABOLISM), growth, reaction to stimuli, and reproduction **2a** the sequence of physical and mental experiences that make up the existence of an individual **b** one or more aspects of the process of living ⟨*the sex ~ of the frog*⟩ **3** a biography ⟨*Boswell's Life of Johnson*⟩ **4** spiritual existence transcending physical death ⟨*passed from death unto ~* – Jn 5.24 (AV)⟩ **5a** the period from birth to death or to the present time ⟨*had a long and happy ~*⟩ ⟨*I've lived here all my ~*⟩ **b(1)** the state or condition of earthly existence **b(2)** a specific phase of earthly existence ⟨*adult ~*⟩ **c** the period from an event or the present time until death ⟨*a member for ~*⟩ **d** a sentence of imprisonment for the remainder of a convicted person's life **6** a way or manner of living ⟨*it's a man's ~ in the army*⟩ **7** *usu pl* a living being; *specif* a person ⟨*many* lives *were lost in the disaster*⟩ **8** an animating and shaping force or principle **9** the source of pleasure, interest, or enjoyment in living; reason for living ⟨*his work was his whole ~*⟩ **10** spirit, animation ⟨*there was no ~ in her dancing*⟩ **11** the form or pattern of something existing in reality ⟨*painted from ~*⟩ **12** the period of usefulness, effectiveness, or functioning of something inanimate ⟨*the expected ~ of torch batteries*⟩ **13** a period of existence (eg of a subatomic particle) – compare HALF-LIFE **14** living beings (eg of a specified kind or environment) ⟨*forest ~*⟩ **15a** the active part of human existence, esp in a wide range of circumstances or experiences ⟨*left home to see ~*⟩ **b** animate activity and movement ⟨*stirrings of ~*⟩ **c** the activities of a specified sphere, area, or time ⟨*the political ~ of the country*⟩ **16** a person providing interest and activity ⟨*~ of the party*⟩ **17** sparkle or effervescence (eg of wine) **18** another chance given to one likely to lose – see also **within an** INCH **of one's/somebody's life** [ME *lif*, fr OE *līf*; akin to OE *libban* to live – more at LIVE] – **come to life 1** to regain consciousness or vitality **2** to take on a real or lifelike quality ⟨*a writer whose characters* come to life⟩

**²life** *adj* **1** of animate being **2** lifelong ⟨*a ~ member*⟩ **3** using a living model ⟨*a ~ drawing*⟩ **4** of or provided by life insurance ⟨*a ~ policy*⟩

**,life-and-'death** *adj* involving or culminating in life or death; having vital importance as if involving life or death

**life assurance** *n, chiefly Br* LIFE INSURANCE

**life belt** *n* a belt of buoyant material designed to keep a person afloat in the water

**lifeblood** /-,blud, ,-'-/ *n* **1** the blood necessary to life **2** a vital or life-giving force ⟨*freedom of enquiry is the ~ of a university*⟩

**lifeboat** /-,boht/ *n* **1** a robust shore-based and often self-righting boat specifically designed for use in saving lives at sea **2** a boat carried by a ship for use in an emergency

**life buoy** /boy/ *n* an often ring-shaped float to which a person may cling in the water

**life class** *n* an art class in which students draw or paint a living model

**life cycle** *n* **1** the series of stages in form and functional activity through which an organism passes between successive recurrences of a specified primary stage which is usu the fertilized egg **2** LIFE HISTORY 1 **3** a series of stages through which an individual, group (eg a family), or culture passes during its lifetime **4** the series of levels in sales and profitability through which a product passes from its launch to its withdrawal from the market

**life expectancy** *n* the expected length of somebody's or something's life based on statistical evidence

**'life-,force** *n* ÉLAN VITAL (vital force contained in all living things)

**life form** *n* the body form that characterizes a kind of organism (eg a species) at maturity

**'life-,giving** *adj* giving or having power to give life or spirit; invigorating

**lifeguard** /-,gahd/ *n* a usu expert swimmer employed (eg at a beach or a swimming pool) to safeguard other swimmers – **lifeguard** *vi*

**life history** *n* **1** a history of the changes through which an organism passes in its development from the primary stage to its natural death **2** the history of an individual's development in his/her social environment

**life insurance** *n* a type of insurance providing for the payment of a stipulated sum of money to a named beneficiary when the insured person dies or reaches a certain age

**life jacket** *n* a device that is either inflatable or made of buoyant material and is designed to keep a person afloat in the water; *specif* one with a collar for the neck

**lifeless** /-lis/ *adj* having no life: eg **a** dead **b** inanimate **c** having no living beings **d** lacking qualities expressive of life and vigour; dull ⟨*~ voice*⟩ – **lifelessly** *adv*, **lifelessness** *n*

**lifelike** /-,liek/ *adj* accurately representing or imitating real life ⟨*a ~ portrait*⟩ – **lifelikeness** *n*

**lifeline** /-,lien/ *n* **1a** a rope for saving or safeguarding life: eg **1a(1)** one stretched along the deck of a ship in rough weather **a(2)** one fired to a ship in distress by means of a rocket **b** the line by which a diver is lowered and raised **c** a rope line for lowering or raising a person to safety **2** something, esp the sole means of communication, regarded as indispensable for the maintaining or protection of life

**lifelong** /-,long/, **life** *adj* lasting or continuing throughout life – compare LIVELONG

**life office** *n, chiefly Br* an insurance company specializing in LIFE INSURANCE

**life of Riley** /'rieli/ *n, informal* a lazy, carefree, comfortable, and usu luxurious way of living – usu + *the* [fr the name *Riley* or *Reilly*]

**,life-or-'death** *adj* life-and-death

**life peer**, *fem* **life peeress** /'piəris/ *n* a British peer whose title has been conferred for the duration of his/her life only – **life peerage** *n*

**life preserver** *n* **1** *chiefly NAm* a device (eg a LIFE JACKET or LIFE BUOY) designed to save a person from drowning **2** *chiefly Br archaic* a small club that has a lump of metal enclosed in its head; a cosh

**lifer** /'liefə/ *n, informal* **1** a person sentenced to imprisonment for life **2** a person who makes a career of one of the armed forces

**life raft** *n* a raft that is either inflatable or made of buoyant material and is carried on ships and in aircraft for use in an emergency

**liferent** /'lief,rent/ *n* the Scottish legal right of possession and use of inheritable property without the right to destroy its substance

**lifesaver** /-,sayvə/ *n* **1** someone or something that saves life or prevents difficulty or distress **2** something timely and effective in the relief of distress ⟨*this gin and tonic's a real ~*⟩ – **lifesaving** *adj or n*

**life science** *n* a branch of science (eg biology, medicine, anthropology, or sociology) that deals with living organisms and life processes – **life scientist** *n*

**'life-,size, life-sized** *adj* of natural size; of the size of the original ⟨*a ~ statue*⟩

**life span** *n* **1** the duration of existence of an individual **2** the average length of life of a kind of organism or of a material object, esp in a particular environment or in specified circumstances

**'life-,style** *n* an individual's typical way of life

**life-support system** *n* a system that provides all or some of the items necessary for maintaining the life and health of a person (e g in a spacecraft)

**life table** *n* MORTALITY TABLE (chart showing statistics relating to deaths)

**lifetime** /-,tiem/ *n* **1** the duration of existence, utility, validity, or activity of a living being or a thing **2** *physics* the duration of the existence of an ion or atomic particle

**lifework** /-'wuhk/ *n* the entire or principal work of one's lifetime; *also* a work extending over a lifetime

**life zone** *n* an area of the earth having a characteristic collection of living organisms

**'lift** /lift/ *vt* **1a** to raise **(1)** from a lower to a higher position; elevate **(2)** in rank or condition **(3)** in rate, amount, or intensity **b** to hit (e g a cricket ball) or the bowling of (a bowler) into the air **2** to put an end to (a blockade or siege) by withdrawing the surrounding forces **3** to revoke, rescind ⟨∼ *an embargo*⟩ **4a** to plagiarize **b** to take out of normal setting ⟨∼ *a word out of context*⟩ **5** to take up (e g a root crop) from the ground ⟨∼ing *potatoes*⟩ **6a** to shift (artillery fire) from one area to another **b** to withhold (artillery fire) from an area **7** to move from one place to another (e g by aircraft); transport **8** to take up (a fingerprint) from a surface **9** *NAm* to pay off (a debt, esp a mortgage) **10** *informal* to steal ⟨*had her purse* ∼ed⟩ ∼ *vi* **1a** to ascend, rise **b** to appear elevated (e g above surrounding objects) **2a** to disperse upwards ⟨*until the fog* ∼s⟩ **b** *of bad weather* to cease, usu temporarily ⟨*the rain finally* ∼ed⟩ **3** *of a bowled ball in cricket* to rise at a sharper angle than expected after pitching ⟨*one ball* ∼ed *off a length* – John Arlott⟩ – see also **lift a** FINGER [ME *liften*, fr ON *lypta;* akin to OE *lyft* air – more at LOFT] – **liftable** *adj*, **lifter** *n*

**synonyms** Lift, raise, rear, elevate, hoist, boost, and heave: **lift** often stresses the effort involved in moving something upwards; this implication is absent from **raise**, which often involves bringing something up to a natural or expected upright or higher position ⟨**raise** *your hands/a tentpole/the Union Jack*⟩. **Rear** also means "make upright", but is often used intransitively ⟨*the horse* **reared**⟩. **Elevate** is rather more formal than **lift** or **raise**, and is more often used figuratively than literally, meaning "exalt". **Hoist** usually implies mechanical assistance in lifting something, while **heave** stresses the exertion involved. The somewhat informal **boost** suggests a helping push from below, and correspondingly, in a figurative sense, an increase in status, degree, or amount. See ROB *antonym* lower

**lift-off** *vi* TAKE OFF 2d – see also LIFT-OFF

**²lift** *n* **1** the amount that may be lifted at one time; a load **2a** the action or an instance of lifting **b** the lifting up of a dancer, usu by her partner **3** a device, apparatus, or machine for lifting (e g for raising a vehicle for repair) **4** a usu free ride as a passenger in a vehicle ⟨*managed to get* ∼s *all the way to London*⟩ **5** any of the layers forming the heel of a shoe **6** a rise or advance in position or condition **7** a slight rise or elevation of ground **8** the distance or extent to which something (e g water in a canal lock) rises **9** a usu temporary feeling of cheerfulness, pleasure, or encouragement ⟨*new haircut gave her a real* ∼⟩ **10** the component of the total aerodynamic force acting on an aircraft or wing that is perpendicular to the relative wind and that for an aircraft in steady flight constitutes the upward force that opposes the pull of gravity **11** an organized movement of people or cargo by some form of transport; *esp* an airlift **12** a face-lift **13** *chiefly Br* a device for conveying people or objects from one level to another, esp in a building

**liftman** /'lift,man/ *n, Br* a lift operator

**'lift-,off** *n* a vertical take-off by an aircraft, rocket, or missile

**ligament** /'ligəmənt/ *n* **1** a tough band of tissue connecting two or more movable bones or cartilages or supporting an organ in place in the body **2** a connecting or unifying bond ⟨*the law of nations, the great* ∼ *of mankind* – Edmund Burke⟩ [ME, fr ML & L; ML *ligamentum,* fr L, band, tie, fr *ligare*] – **ligamentary, ligamentous** *adj*

**ligand** /'ligənd, 'lie-/ *n* a chemical group, ion, or molecule joined by many bonds to a central atom, ion, etc in a complex chemical compound [L *ligandus,* gerundive of *ligare*]

**ligase** /'liegayz, -gays/ *n* an ENZYME that accelerates the chemical reaction in which two molecules are linked together usu using energy stored in the form of the chemical compound ATP [ISV *lig-* (fr L *ligare*) + *-ase*]

**ligate** /'lie,gayt, -'-/ *vt* to tie with a ligature [L *ligatus,* pp]

**ligation** /lie'gaysh(ə)n/ *n* **1** an act of ligating **2** something that binds; a ligature

**ligature** /'ligəchə/ *n* **1a** something that is used to bind; *specif* a thread used in surgery **b** something that unites or connects **2** the action of binding or tying **3a** a compound note indicating a group of musical notes to be sung to one syllable **b** a slur in vocal music showing that two or more notes covered by the sign are to be sung to the same syllable **4** a character consisting of two or more letters or characters joined together; *esp* one (e g ﬀ) consisting of letters that do not represent a single sound **5** an adjustable metal band securing the reed to the mouthpiece of instruments of the clarinet and saxophone family [ME, fr MF, fr LL *ligatura,* fr L *ligatus,* pp of *ligare* to bind, tie; akin to MHG ge*leich* joint, Alb *lith* I tie]

**'light** /liet/ *n* **1a** that which makes vision possible ⟨*enough* ∼ *to read*⟩ **b** the sensation aroused by stimulation of the sense of sight; brightness; *also* a manifestation of this ⟨*flashing* ∼s *that accompany severe headaches*⟩ **c** an ELECTROMAGNETIC RADIATION in the wavelength range including infrared, visible, ultraviolet, and X rays; *specif* the part of this range that is visible to the human eye **2** daylight **3** a source of light: e g **3a** something shining in the sky ⟨*saw strange* ∼s *in the west*⟩ **b** a burning candle **c** a source of light powered by gas or esp electricity ⟨*turn the* ∼ *on*⟩ **4a** spiritual illumination **b** INNER LIGHT (divine presence in the soul) **c** enlightenment **d** *the* truth – esp in *see the light* **5a** public knowledge ⟨*facts brought to* ∼⟩ **b** a particular aspect or appearance in which something is viewed ⟨*now saw the matter in a different* ∼⟩ **6** a particular illumination in a place ⟨*studio with a north* ∼⟩ **7** something that enlightens or informs ⟨*he shed some* ∼ *on the problem*⟩ **8** a medium (e g a window or windowpane) through which light is admitted **9** *pl* a set of principles, standards, or opinions ⟨*true by your* ∼s⟩ **10** a person in a particular place or field ⟨*one of the leading* ∼s *in the group*⟩ ⟨*the lesser* ∼s⟩ **11** a specified expression perceived as being in a person's eyes ⟨*had a wicked* ∼ *in her eye*⟩ **12** a lighthouse ⟨*the Eddystone* ∼⟩ **13** TRAFFIC LIGHT **14** the effect of light on objects or scenes as represented in art **15** a flame or spark for lighting something, esp a cigarette **16** *Br* **16a** an answer to a crossword-puzzle clue **b** any of the words in an acrostic which, when guessed from clues given, form with their initial or other letters the hidden word that is the answer to the puzzle – compare UPRIGHT [ME, fr OE *lēoht;* akin to OHG *lioht* light, L *luc-, lux* light, *lucēre* to shine, Gk *leukos* white] – **lightless** *adj* – **bring/come to light** (to cause) to become known – **in (the) light of** taking into consideration – **see the light 1a** to be born **b** to be published **2a** to undergo conversion **b** to grasp or understand suddenly

**²light** *adj* **1** having plenty of light; bright ⟨*a* ∼ *airy room*⟩ **2a** pale in colour or colouring **b** *of a colour* medium in SATURATION (absence of dilution) and high in LIGHTNESS ⟨*a* ∼ *blue*⟩

**³light** *vb* **lighted, lit** /lit/ *vi* to catch fire ∼ *vt* **1** to set fire to; ignite **2a** to lead with a light; guide ⟨*torches* lit *the way*⟩ **b** to illuminate ⟨*room* lit *by a bay window*⟩ – often + *up* ⟨*fireworks* lit *up the sky*⟩ **c** to animate, brighten – usu + *up* ⟨*a smile* lit *up her face*⟩

**usage** Lit is a commoner inflection than **lighted** except where the verb is used as an attributive adjective, before the noun. Compare ⟨*I* lit *a candle*⟩ ⟨*the fire's not* lit *yet*⟩ ⟨*a* **lighted** *cigarette*⟩.

**light up** *vi* **1** to become light; brighten ⟨*her face* lit up⟩ **2** to start smoking a cigarette, pipe, etc

**⁴light** *adj* **1a(1)** having little weight; not heavy **a(2)** of the smaller variety ⟨*a* ∼ *portable gun*⟩ **b** designed to carry a comparatively small load ⟨*a* ∼ *truck*⟩ **c** (made of materials) having relatively little weight in proportion to bulk ⟨*aluminium is a* ∼ *metal*⟩ **d** containing less than the legal, standard, or usual weight ⟨*a* ∼ *coin*⟩ **2a** of little importance; trivial **b** not abundant; scanty ⟨∼ *rain*⟩ **3a** *of sleep or a sleeper* easily disturbed **b** exerting a minimum of force or pressure; gentle ⟨*a* ∼ *touch*⟩ ⟨*a* ∼ *breeze*⟩ **c** resulting from a very slight pressure; faint ⟨∼ *print*⟩ **4a** easily endurable ⟨*a* ∼ *illness*⟩ ⟨∼ *taxation*⟩ **b** requiring little effort ⟨∼ *work*⟩ **5** capable of moving swiftly or nimbly ⟨∼ *on his feet*⟩ **6** lacking seriousness; frivolous ⟨∼ *conduct*⟩ **7** free from care; cheerful **8** intended chiefly to entertain ⟨∼ *verse*⟩ **9a** having a comparatively low alcoholic content ⟨*a* ∼ *white wine*⟩ **b** having a relatively mild flavour **10a** easily digested ⟨*a* ∼ *dessert*⟩ **b** well risen ⟨*a* ∼ *cake*⟩ **11** lightly armoured, armed, or equipped ⟨∼ *cavalry*⟩ **12** coarse and sandy or easily pulverized ⟨∼ *soil*⟩ **13** dizzy, giddy ⟨*felt* ∼ *in the head*⟩ **14a** carrying little or no cargo ⟨*the ship returned* ∼⟩ **b** requiring relatively small investment and usu devoted to the production of goods for direct consumption by the consumer ⟨~ *industry*⟩ **15** not bearing a stress or accent ⟨*a* ~ *syllable*⟩ **16** having a clear soft quality ⟨*a* ~ *voice*⟩ **17** in debt to the kitty in a poker game ⟨*three chips* ~⟩ **18** having failed to make the required number of tricks in a game of bridge **19** *informal* short of (a sum of) money ⟨*paying for the dinner has left me a bit* ~⟩ [ME, fr OE *lēoht*; akin to OHG *līhti* light, L *levis*, Gk *elachys* small] – **lightish** *adj*

**⁵light** *adv* **1** in a light manner; lightly **2** with the minimum of luggage ⟨*travel* ~⟩

**⁶light** *vi* **lighted, lit** /lit/ **1** to settle, alight ⟨*a bird* lit *on the lawn*⟩ **2** to fall unexpectedly **3** to arrive by chance; happen – + *on* or *upon* ⟨lit *upon a solution*⟩ [ME *lighten*, fr OE *līhtan*; akin to OE *lēoht* light in weight]

  **light out** *vi, chiefly NAm informal* to leave in a hurry

**light adaptation** *n* the processes by which the eye adapts to conditions of increased illumination (e g in bright sunlight) that include contraction of the pupil and reduction in the speed and frequency of nerve impulses reaching the brain owing to the decrease of the light-sensitive pigment (RHODOPSIN) in the RODS (cells in the retina of the eye) – compare DARK ADAPTATION – **light-adapted** *adj*

**light air** *n* wind having a speed of 1 to 5 kilometres per hour (about 1 to 3 miles per hour)

**light ale** *n, Br* a usu bottled pale beer of comparatively low alcoholic content

**light breeze** *n* wind having a speed of 6 to 11 kilometres per hour (4 to 7 miles per hour) *synonyms* see ¹WIND

**light bulb** *n* INCANDESCENT LAMP

**light chain** *n* either of the two smaller of the four chains of AMINO ACIDS comprising ANTIBODIES (substances produced by the body to fight disease) – compare HEAVY CHAIN

**¹lighten** /'liet(ə)n/ *vt* **1** to make light or clear; illuminate **2** to make (e g a colour) lighter ~ *vi* **1a** to shine brightly **b** to grow lighter; brighten **2** to discharge flashes of lightning [ME *lightenen*, fr *light* ²light] – **lightener** *n*

**²lighten** *vt* **1** to relieve of a burden in whole or in part ⟨*the news* ~ed *his mind*⟩ **2** to reduce the load or weight of **3** to make less wearisome; alleviate ⟨~ed *his gloom*⟩; *broadly* to cheer, gladden ~ *vi* **1** to become lighter or less burdensome **2** to become more cheerful ⟨*his mood* ~ed⟩ *synonyms* see RELIEVE [ME *lightenen*, fr *light* ⁴light] – **lightener** *n*

**¹lighter** /'lietə/ *vt or n* (to carry or transport in) a large usu flat-bottomed barge used esp in unloading or loading ships [ME, fr (assumed) MD *lichter*, fr MD *lichten* to unload; akin to OE *lēoht* light in weight]

**²lighter** *n* **1** one who lights or sets a fire **2** a device for lighting a fire; *esp* a mechanical or electrical device that operates typically by producing a spark which ignites a small enclosed supply of gas or liquid petroleum and is used for lighting cigarettes, cigars, or pipes

**lighterage** /'lietərij/ *n* the loading, unloading, or transport of goods by means of a lighter; *also* the charge for this

**lighter-than-'air** *adj, of an aircraft* of less weight than an equivalent volume of air

**lightface** /'liet,fays/ *n* the comparatively light thin form of a typeface that is used for setting ordinary text; *also* printing in lightface – compare BOLDFACE – **lightfaced** *adj*

**light-'fingered** *adj* **1** expert at or given to stealing, esp by picking pockets **2** having a light and dexterous touch; nimble – **light-fingeredness** *n*

**light-'flyweight** *n* an amateur boxer who weighs not more than 48 kilograms (about 7 stone 7 pounds)

**light-'footed** *also* **'light-,foot** *adj* **1** having a light and springy step **2** moving gracefully and nimbly

**light grey** *adj, of a horse* having predominantly white hairs and few black ones throughout the coat

**light-'headed** *adj* **1** dizzy, giddy; *also* euphoric **2** lacking in maturity or seriousness; frivolous – **light-headedly** *adv*, **light-headedness** *n*

**lighthearted** /-'hahtid/ *adj* free from care or worry; cheerful *synonyms* see JOYFUL *antonym* despondent – **lightheartedly** *adv*, **lightheartedness** *n*

**light-'heavyweight** *n* a boxer who weighs not more than 12 stone 7 pounds (79.4 kilograms) if professional, or between 75 and 81 kilograms (between about 11 stone 11 pounds and 12 stone 10 pounds) if amateur

**lighthouse** /-,hows/, **light** *n* a structure (e g a tower) equipped with a powerful beacon light to warn or guide shipping at sea

**lighting** /'lieting/ *n* **1** the action or an instance of making or becoming light **2** artificial light; *also* the apparatus providing it

**lightly** /'lietli/ *adv* **1** with little weight or force; gently **2** in a small degree or amount ⟨~ *salted food*⟩ **3** with little difficulty; easily ⟨*expected trouble but got off* ~⟩ **4** in an agile manner; nimbly **5** with indifference or carelessness; unconcernedly ⟨*such problems should not be passed over* ~⟩ **6** without reason or thought; readily ⟨*an offer not* ~ *made*⟩

**light meter** *n* a small and often portable device for measuring the degree of illumination; *esp* EXPOSURE METER (device measuring photographic exposure)

**light-'middleweight** *n* an amateur boxer who weighs between 67 and 71 kilograms (between about 10 stone 8 pounds and 11 stone 2 pounds)

**¹lightness** /'lietnis/ *n* **1** the quality or state of being illuminated **2** the characteristic of the colours of an object by which that object appears to reflect or transmit more or less light

**²lightness** *n* **1** the quality or state of being light in weight **2a** the quality or state of being nimble **b** an ease or gaiety of style or manner; lack of seriousness ⟨*speech had a* ~ *of tone which hardly fitted its subject*⟩ **3** a lack of weightiness or force; delicacy

**¹lightning** /'lietning/ *n* the flashing of light produced by a discharge of atmospheric electricity from one cloud to another or between a cloud and the earth △ lightening [ME, fr gerund of *lightenen* to lighten]

**²lightning** *adj* moving or done with or as if with the speed and suddenness of lightning ⟨~ *reflexes*⟩

**lightning arrester** *n* a device that protects electrical apparatus (e g telegraphs or aerials) from injury by lightning

**lightning conductor** *n* a metallic rod fixed to the highest point of a building or mast and connected to the moist earth or water below to protect the building from damage by lightning

**lightning rod** *n, NAm* LIGHTNING CONDUCTOR

**lightning strike** *n* an industrial strike called at very short notice

**light-o'-love** /,liet ə 'luv/ *n, pl* **light-o'-loves** *archaic* **1** a prostitute **2** a fickle woman

**light opera** *n* OPERETTA (romantic comic opera)

**light pen** *n* a pen-shaped PHOTOELECTRIC device that is held or moved over a VDU screen to draw lines, identify symbols, etc in order to communicate with a computer

**light pencil** *n* LIGHT PEN

**lightproof** /'liet,proohf, -proof/ *adj* impenetrable by light

**light reaction** *n* the phase of photosynthesis that is dependent on the presence of light and that involves the conversion of light energy to chemical energy for storage in the form of the chemical compound ATP and the splitting of water molecules into hydrogen and oxygen – compare DARK REACTION

**lights** /liets/ *n pl* the lungs of a slaughtered animal (e g a sheep or pig) [ME *lightes*, fr *light* light in weight]

**lightship** /-,ship/ *n* a moored vessel equipped with a powerful beacon light to warn or guide shipping at sea

**light show** *n* an entertainment of constantly changing coloured light, often in time to music ⟨*went to a laser* ~⟩

**¹lightsome** /'liets(ə)m/ *adj, archaic or poetic* **1** airy, nimble ⟨*walked with a* ~ *step*⟩ **2** free from care; lighthearted – **lightsomely** *adv*, **lightsomeness** *n*

**²lightsome** *adj, poetic* **1** giving light; luminous **2** well lighted; bright

**'lights-,out** *n* **1** a command or signal for putting out lights; *specif* the last bugle call of the day in a military establishment **2** a prescribed bedtime for people living in an institution (e g boarding school)

**lighttight** /'liet,tiet/ *adj* lightproof

**light trap** *n* **1** a device that allows a person or object to enter (e g into a darkroom) but excludes light **2** a device for collecting or destroying insects (e g moths) that consists of the lure of a bright light or ultraviolet light in association with a trapping or killing mechanism

**¹lightweight** /'liet,wayt/ *n* **1** one of less than average weight; *specif* a boxer who weighs not more than 9 stone 9 pounds (61.2 kilograms) if professional, or between 57 and 60 kilograms (between about 8 stone 13 pounds and 9 stone 6 pounds) if amateur **2** a person of little ability or importance

**²lightweight** *adj* **1** of a lightweight ⟨*the* ~ *championship*⟩ **2** having less than average weight **3** lacking in seriousness or profundity; inconsequential

**light-'welterweight** *n* an amateur boxer who weighs between 60 and 63.5 kilograms (between about 9 stone 6 pounds and 10 stone)

**'light-ˌyear** *n* a unit of length in astronomy equal to the distance that light travels in one year in a vacuum; 9460 thousand million kilometres (about 5878 thousand million miles)

**lign-** /lign-/, **ligni-, ligno-** *comb form* **1** wood ⟨lign*in*⟩ ⟨ligne*ous*⟩ **2** lignin and ⟨ligno*cellulose*⟩ [L *lign-, ligni-,* fr *lignum*]

**ligneous** /'lignios/ *adj* of or resembling wood; woody [L *ligneus,* fr *lignum* wood, fr *legere* to gather – more at LEGEND]

**lignify** /'lignifie/ *vt* to convert into wood or woody tissue ~ *vi* to become wood or woody [Fr *lignifier,* fr L *lignum*] – **lignification** *n*

**lignin** /'lignin/ *n* a substance that together with cellulose forms the woody cell walls of plants and the cementing material between them

**lignite** /'ligniet/ *n* a usu brownish black coal intermediate between peat and BITUMINOUS COAL; *esp* one in which the texture of the original wood is distinct [Fr, fr L *lignum*] – **lignitic** *adj*

**lignocaine** /'lignoˌkayn/ *n* a synthetic chemical compound, $(CH_3)_2C_6H_3NHCOCH_2N(C_2H_5)_2$, that is used as a local anaesthetic and to control fluctuations of the heartbeat

**lignocellulose** /ˌlignoh'selyoolohs/ *n* any of several closely related substances constituting the essential part of woody cell walls and consisting of cellulose intimately associated with lignin [ISV] – **lignocellulosic** *adj*

**lignum vitae** /ˌlignəm 'vieti/ *n* any of several tropical American trees (genus *Guaiacum* of the family Zygophyllaceae) with very hard heavy dark wood; *also* the wood of a lignum vitae [NL, lit., wood of life]

**ligroin** /'ligroh·in/ *n* any of several petroleum extracts that boil usu in the range 20° to 135°C and are used esp as solvents [origin unknown]

**ligula** /'ligyoolə/ *n*, **ligulae** /-lie/ *also* **ligulas 1** a ligule **2** the end lobed part of the LABIUM (lower lip) of an insect [NL]

**ligulate** /'ligyoolət, -layt/ *adj* **1** shaped like a strap ⟨*the ~ corolla of a ray plant*⟩ **2** having ligules, ligulae, or ligulate COROLLAS (circular arrangements of petals)

**ligule** /'ligyoohl/ *n* a scalelike or strap-shaped projection, esp on a plant: eg **a** a membranous outgrowth of a leaf, esp of the sheath of a blade of grass **b** the strap-shaped petals of a RAY FLOWER in a composite flower head (eg a daisy) [NL *ligula,* fr L, small tongue, strap; akin to L *lingere* to lick – more at LICK]

**likable** *also* **likeable** /'liekəbl/ *adj* having qualities that cause people to react favourably; pleasant, agreeable – **likableness** *n,* **likability** *n*

**¹like** /liek/ *vt* **1a** to find agreeable, acceptable, or pleasant; enjoy ⟨~s *games*⟩ ⟨~s *playing games*⟩ **b** to feel towards; regard ⟨*how would you ~ a change?*⟩ **2** to wish or choose to have, be, or do; want ⟨~s *to help*⟩ ⟨~s *us to come early*⟩ **3** *archaic* to be agreeable to ⟨*it ~s me not*⟩ to feel inclined; choose ⟨*you can leave any time you ~*⟩ [ME *liken,* fr OE *lician;* akin to OE *gelīc* alike] – **if you like** to put it another way

**²like** *n usu pl* a liking, preference ⟨*one's ~s and dislikes*⟩

**³like** *adj* **1a** the same or nearly the same (eg in appearance, character, or quantity) ⟨*suits of ~ design*⟩ **b** bearing a close resemblance; *esp* faithful ⟨*portrait is very ~*⟩ **2** likely to ⟨*the one discipline ~ to give accuracy of mind* – H J Laski⟩ [ME, alter. of *ilich,* fr OE *gelīc* like, alike; akin to OHG *gilīh* like, alike; both fr a prehistoric Gmc compound whose constituents are represented by OE *ge-* (associative prefix) and by OE *līc* body; akin to Lith *lygus* like]

**⁴like** *prep* **1a** having the characteristics of; similar to ⟨*his house is ~ a barn*⟩ **b** typical of ⟨*was ~ him to do that*⟩ **c** close to ⟨*cost something ~ £5*⟩ **2a** in the manner of; similarly to ⟨*act ~ a fool*⟩ ⟨*do it ~ this*⟩ **b** to the same degree as ⟨*fits ~ a glove*⟩ **3** appearing to be, threaten, or promise ⟨*you seem ~ a sensible man*⟩ **4a** of the class of ⟨*a subject ~ physics*⟩ **b** – used to introduce an example ⟨*several people interested, ~ Mrs Jones and Dr Simpson*⟩

**⁵like** *n* one who or that which is like another, esp in high value; a counterpart, equal ⟨*never saw the ~ of it*⟩ ⟨*had no use for the ~s of him*⟩ ⟨*her ~ will never be seen again*⟩ – **the like** similar things ⟨*football, tennis, and the like*⟩

**⁶like** *adv* **1** likely, probably ⟨*be thirsty as ~ as not*⟩ **2** nearly ⟨*the actual interest is more ~ 18 per cent*⟩ **3** *nonstandard* SO TO SPEAK ⟨*went up to her casually, ~*⟩ **4** *archaic* equally

**⁷like** *conj* **1** in the same way as ⟨*they raven down scenery ~ children do sweetmeats* – John Keats⟩ **2** as if ⟨*middle-aged men who looked ~ they might be out for their one night of the year*

– Norman Mailer⟩ □ disapproved of by some speakers – **like anything** – used to emphasize a verb ⟨*run* like anything⟩ – **like that 1** in that way ⟨*don't snort* like that⟩ **2** without demur or hesitation ⟨*can't change jobs just* like that⟩

*usage* **1** When **like** means "similar to" or "in the same way as", and no verb follows, it should be preferred to **as** ⟨*sing* like *a bird*⟩ ⟨*it is tyrannous to use it* like *a giant* – Shak⟩. There is a difference of meaning between ⟨*let me speak to you* like *a father* ( = in the way your own father might)⟩ and ⟨*let me speak to you* as *a father* ( = in my capacity as your father)⟩. In these sentences **like** is functioning in the role of a preposition, so any pronouns that follow must be in the form **like** *me/him/her/them,* not △ **like** *I/he/she/they.* **2** When **like** means "similarly to" or "in the same way as" and a verb does follow, **as** is to be preferred, although the construction with **like** has long been current in English ⟨*few have observed* like *you have done* – Charles Darwin⟩ ⟨*we are overrun by them,* like *the Australians were by rabbits* – Sir Winston Churchill⟩. **3** When **like** means "as if", "as though", or "such as" it should be replaced by one of these in formal writing ⟨*a subject such as* (not **like**) *physics*⟩ especially when a verb follows ⟨*lying on the floor as if* (not △ **like**) *they were dead*⟩.

**-like** /-liek/ *comb form* (→ *adj*) resembling or characteristic of ⟨*bell-like*⟩ ⟨*ladylike*⟩

**likeable** /'liekəbl/ *adj* likable

**likelihood** /'liekli,hood/ *n* probability ⟨*a strong ~ that it will happen as predicted*⟩

**likelihood function** *n, statistics* a PROBABILITY DISTRIBUTION in which the random variables are considered as constants and one or more parameters (eg variances) are considered as variables

**¹likely** /'liekli/ *adj* **1** having a high probability of being or occurring ⟨~ *to succeed*⟩ ⟨*the ~ result*⟩ **2a** reliable, credible ⟨*a ~ enough story*⟩ **b** incredible – used ironically ⟨*a ~ tale!*⟩ **3** apparently qualified; suitable ⟨*a ~ place*⟩ **4** promising ⟨~ *lads*⟩ [ME, fr ON *glīkligr,* fr *glīkr* like; akin to OE *gelīc*]

**²likely** *adv* in all probability; probably ⟨*he'll very ~ say you're wrong*⟩

*usage* In formal writing the adverb **likely** is used only with *quite, very, more,* or *most,* or in the phrases *more than* **likely,** *as* **likely** *as not.* It should not stand alone ⟨△ *they will* **likely** *betray themselves by loud breathing* – Scribner's⟩.

**ˌlike-'minded** *adj* having a similar outlook or disposition – **like-mindedly** *adv,* **like-mindedness** *n*

**liken** /'liekən/ *vt* to find or point out similarities in; compare – often + *to*

**likeness** /-nis/ *n* **1** the quality or state of being like; a resemblance **2** a portrait considered as being faithful to the original ⟨*not a good ~ of mother*⟩

**likewise** /-ˌwiez/ *adv* **1** in like manner; similarly ⟨*go and do ~*⟩ **2** moreover; IN ADDITION **3** similarly so with me ⟨*answered "~" to "Pleased to meet you"*⟩

**liking** /'lieking/ *n* favourable regard; fondness ⟨*took a ~ to the newcomer*⟩ ⟨*things were not to his ~*⟩

**likuta** /li'k(y)oohtə/ *n, pl* **makuta** /mah-/ – see *zaire* at MONEY table [of Niger-Congo origin; prob akin to obs Nupe *kuta* stone]

**lilac** /'lielək, -lak/ *n* **1** any of various trees or shrubs (genus *Syringa*) of the ash family; *esp* a European shrub (*Syringa vulgaris*) that has deep green leaves and large oval clusters of fragrant white or purple flowers **2** a pale pinkish purple colour [obs Fr (now *lilas*), fr Ar *līlak,* fr Per *nīlak* bluish, fr *nīl* blue, fr Skt *nīla* dark blue]

**lilangeni** /ˌlilən'geni/ *n, pl* **emalangeni** /ˌemələn'geni/ – see MONEY table [native name in Swaziland]

**liliaceous** /ˌlili'ayshəs/ *adj* of lilies or the lily family

**lilliputian** /ˌlili'pyoohsh(ə)n/ *n or adj, often cap* (somebody or something) remarkably small or tiny [*Lilliput,* imaginary country of tiny people in *Gulliver's Travels* by Jonathan Swift †1745 Ir satirist]

**Li-lo** /'lie loh/ *trademark* – used for an AIR BED

**¹lilt** /lilt/ *vi* to sing or speak rhythmically and with fluctuating pitch [ME *lulten*]

**²lilt** *n* **1** a spirited and usu merry song or tune **2** a rhythmic swing or flow ⟨*the ~ of the questioner's voice* – Elizabeth Hardwick⟩ **3** a light springy movement ⟨*a ~ in her step*⟩

**lilting** /'lilting/ *adj* **1** characterized by a rhythmical flow of sounds or fluctuating pitch ⟨*a ~ voice*⟩ **2** characterized by springiness or buoyancy – **liltingly** *adv,* **liltingness** *n*

**¹lily** /'lili/ *n* **1** any of a genus (*Lilium* of the family Liliaceae, the lily family) of erect leafy-stemmed plants that grow from bulbs, are native to the northern hemisphere, and are widely cultivated for their showy flowers; *broadly* any of various other plants of the lily or the related daffodil or iris families **2** any of various plants with showy flowers: eg **2a** a scarlet anemone (*Anemone coronaria*) that grows wild in Palestine **b** WATER LILY **c** CALLA (type of house plant) **3** one resembling a lily in fairness, purity, or fragility ⟨*a virgin, a . . . ~ –* Shak⟩ ⟨*my lady's ~ hand –* John Keats⟩ **4** FLEUR-DE-LIS 2 (heraldic flower) [ME *lilie*, fr OE, fr L *lilium*] – **gild the lily** to add unnecessary ornamentation to something beautiful in its own right

**'lily-,livered** /'livəd/ *adj* lacking courage; cowardly

**lily of the valley** *n, pl* **lilies of the valley** a low plant (*Convallaria majalis*) of the lily family that has two large leaves and fragrant nodding bell-shaped white flowers

**lily pad** *n* a floating leaf of a WATER LILY

**¹,lily-'white** *adj* **1** white as a lily; pure white **2** irreproachable, pure **3** *chiefly NAm* characterized by or favouring the exclusion of Negroes, esp from politics

**²'lily-,white** *n, chiefly NAm* a member of a lily-white political organization

**Lima** /'leemə/ *n* – a communications code word for the letter *l*

**lima bean** /'limə/ *n* **1** any of various widely cultivated bushy or tall-growing beans derived from a tropical American bean (*Phaseolus limensis*); *also* the flat edible usu pale green or whitish seed of a lima bean **2** SIEVA BEAN [*Lima*, city in Peru]

**limaciform** /li'masifawm, lie-, -'maysi-/ *adj* resembling a slug ⟨*~ insect larvae*⟩ [deriv of L *limac-, limax* slug + *-iformis* -iform]

**limacine** /'limsin, 'lie-, -sin/ *adj* (characteristic) of slugs [NL *limacinus*, fr L *limac-, limax*]

**limaçon** /'limsən/ *n, maths* a geometric curve which can occur in three forms, one of which is somewhat heart-shaped, and that has the equation in POLAR COORDINATES $r = b + 2a\cos\theta$ [Fr, lit., snail, fr OF, dim. of *limaz* slug, snail, fr L *limax*]

**¹limb** /lim/ *n* **1** any of the projecting paired structures of an animal body used esp for movement and grasping but sometimes modified into sensory or sexual organs; *esp* a leg or an arm of a human being **2** a large primary branch of a tree **3** an extension, branch; *specif* any of the four branches or arms of a cross **4** *chiefly humorous* an active member or agent ⟨*~s of the law*⟩ **5** *archaic* a mischievous child [ME *lim*, fr OE; akin to ON *limr* limb, L *limes* limit, *limen* threshold, Gk *leimōn* meadow] – **limbless** *adj*, **limby** *adj* – **out on a limb** in an exposed and unsupported position

**²limb** *vt* to dismember; *esp* to cut off the limbs of (a felled tree)

**³limb** *n* **1** the graduated margin of a curve or circle in an instrument for measuring angles **2** the outer edge of the apparent disc of a planet, moon, star, etc **3** the expanded portion of an organ or structure; *esp* the spreading upper portion of a SEPAL (leaflike structure protecting developing flower bud) or petal [L *limbus* border – more at LIMP]

**limbed** /limd/ *adj* having limbs, esp of a specified kind or number – usu in combination ⟨*strong-*limbed⟩

**¹limber** /'limbə/ *n* the detachable front part of a gun carriage by which the gun can be towed and which consists usu of a frame supporting two wheels and an ammunition box used as a seat [ME *lymour*]

**²limber** *adj* **1** capable of being shaped; flexible **2** having a supple quality (eg of mind or body); agile [origin unknown] – **limberly** *adv*, **limberness** *n*

**³limber** *n usu pl* a gutter or pipe on each side of a ship that provides a passage for water to be pumped out [modif of Fr *lumière*, fr OF, light, opening, fr L *luminare* window – more at LUMINARY]

**limber up** *vb* to (cause to) become agile, supple, or flexible ⟨*limber up her fingers*⟩ ⟨*limber up before taking part in the race*⟩

**limbic** /'limbik/ *adj* of or being the LIMBIC SYSTEM of the brain [NL *limbicus* of a border or margin, fr L *limbus*]

**limbic system** *n* a group of structures (eg the HYPOTHALAMUS, the HIPPOCAMPUS, and the AMYGDALA) of the brain that are concerned esp with emotion and motivation

**¹limbo** /'limboh/ *n, pl* **limbos 1** *often cap* an abode of souls that, according to Roman Catholic theology, are barred from heaven because of not having received Christian baptism **2a** a place or state of restraint or confinement **b** a place or state of neglect or oblivion ⟨*proposals kept in ~*⟩ **c** an intermediate or transitional place or state [ME, fr ML, abl of *limbus* limbo, fr L, border – more at LIMP]

**²limbo** *n, pl* **limbos** a W Indian acrobatic dance that involves bending over backwards and passing under a horizontal pole lowered slightly for each successive pass [native name in W Indies]

**Limburger** /'lim,buhgə/ *n* a creamy soft white to yellow cheese with a brown rind and a strong smell and flavour [Flem, one from Limburg, fr *Limburg*, province in NE Belgium]

**¹lime** /liem/ *n* **1** BIRDLIME (sticky substance used to catch birds) **2a** a caustic solid mixture of chemical compounds that consists of calcium oxide often together with MAGNESIUM OXIDE, is obtained by heating forms of CALCIUM CARBONATE (eg shells or limestone), and is used esp in building (eg in mortar and plaster) and in agriculture – called also CAUSTIC LIME, QUICKLIME **b** a dry white powder consisting essentially of the chemical compound calcium hydroxide that is made by treating caustic lime with water **c** CALCIUM ⟨*carbonate of ~*⟩ [ME, fr OE *līm*; akin to OHG *līm* birdlime, L *linere* to smear, *levis* smooth, Gk *leios*]

**²lime** *vt* **1** to smear with a sticky substance, esp BIRDLIME **2** to trap (as if) with BIRDLIME **3** to treat or cover with lime ⟨*~ the soil in the spring*⟩

**³lime** *adj* of or containing lime or limestone

**⁴lime** *n* (the light fine-grained white wood of) a linden tree [alter. of ME *lind*, fr OE; akin to OHG *linta* linden]

**⁵lime** *n* **1** a spiny tropical citrus tree (*Citrus aurantifolia*) cultivated for its small spherical greenish yellow fruit; *also* the fruit of the lime whose acid juicy pulp is used as a flavouring and as a source of VITAMIN C **2** a soft drink made from sweetened lime juice ⟨*lager and ~*⟩ [Fr, fr Prov *limo*, fr Ar *līm*]

**limeade** /,liem'ayd/ *n* a soft drink consisting of sweetened lime juice mixed with plain or carbonated water

**'lime-,juicer** /'joohsə/ *n, NAm slang* a British ship or sailor [fr the former drinking of lime juice on British ships to prevent scurvy]

**limekiln** /'liem,kiln/ *n* a kiln or furnace for reducing calcium-containing material (eg limestone or shells) to lime for burning

**limelight** /-,liet/ *n* **1a** a stage lighting instrument producing illumination by means of an intense flame directed on a cylinder of lime **b** the white light produced by such an instrument **2** *the* centre of public attention

**limen** /'liemən, -men/ *n* THRESHOLD 3a (beginning of a physiological or psychological effect) [L *limin-, limen* – more at LIMB]

**limerick** /'limərik/ *n* a humorous and often indecent verse form of five lines with the first, second, and fifth lines rhyming and the third and fourth lines rhyming [*Limerick*, city & county in SW Ireland]

**limestone** /-,stohn/ *n* a rock that is formed chiefly by the accumulation of animal or plant remains (eg shells or coral), consists mainly of the chemical compound CALCIUM CARBONATE, is extensively used in building, and yields lime when burned

**'lime-,twig** *n* a twig covered with BIRDLIME to catch birds

**limewash** /-,wosh/ *n* a solution of lime and water used as a coating (eg for walls)

**limewater** /-,wawtə/ *n* **1** an alkaline solution of the chemical compound calcium hydroxide in water **2** natural water containing the chemical compound CALCIUM CARBONATE or calcium sulphate in solution

**limey** /'liemi/ *n, pl* **limeys** *often cap, NAm derog slang* a British person, esp a sailor [*lime-juicer* + *-y*]

**liminal** /'liminəl/ *adj* **1** of a sensory THRESHOLD (beginning of a physiological or psychological effect) **2** barely perceptible [L *limin-, limen* threshold]

**¹limit** /'limit/ *n* **1a** a geographical or political boundary ⟨*outside the 200-mile ~*⟩ **b** *pl* the place enclosed within a boundary ⟨*must not go off ~s*⟩ **2a** something that bounds, restrains, or confines ⟨*worked within the ~s of his knowledge*⟩ ⟨*set a ~ on his spending*⟩ **b limits** *pl*, the furthest extent ⟨*the ~s of knowledge*⟩ **c** a line or point that cannot or should not be passed **3** a prescribed maximum or minimum amount, quantity, or number ⟨*the speed ~*⟩: eg **3a** the maximum quantity of game or fish that may be taken legally in a specified period **b** a maximum amount decided on for a gambling bet or raise **c** *the* maximum level of alcohol in the blood at which one may legally drive a vehicle ⟨*fined for driving while over the ~*⟩ **4a** a number whose difference from the value of a function approaches zero as the value of the INDEPENDENT VARIABLE approaches some given number **b** a number that for an infinite sequence of numbers is such that ultimately each of the remaining terms of the sequence differs from this number by less than any given amount **5** a person, situation, or thing that is exasperating or intolerable – + *the* [ME, fr MF *limite*, fr L *limit-*, *limes* boundary – more at LIMB] – **limitless** *adj*, **limitlessly** *adv*, **limitlessness** *n*

**²limit** *vt* **1** to assign certain limits to ⟨*reserved the right to ~ use of the land*⟩ **2a** to restrict to specific bounds or limits ⟨*the specialist can no longer ~ himself to his speciality*⟩ **b** to curtail or reduce in quantity or extent; curb ⟨*we must ~ the power of aggressors*⟩ – **limitable** *adj*, **limiter** *n*

  *synonyms* One limits ( = "restricts") people or activities; one de-limits ( = "fixes") boundaries or distances. *antonym* widen

**limitary** /'limitəri/ *adj*, *archaic* **1** subject to limits **2** of or serving as a boundary

**limitation** /ˌlimi'taysh(ə)n/ *n* **1** an act or instance of limiting **2** the quality or state of being limited **3** something that limits; *esp* a limit of capability **4** a period defined by law after which a claimant is barred from bringing a legal action – **limitational** *adj*

**limitative** /'limitaytiv/ *adj* serving to limit or restrict

**limited** /'limitid/ *adj* **1** confined within limits; restricted ⟨*~ success*⟩ **2** characterized by enforceable limitations prescribed (eg by a constitution) on the scope or exercise of powers ⟨*a ~ monarchy*⟩ **3** lacking the ability to grow or do better ⟨*a bit ~; a bit thick in the head* – Virginia Woolf⟩ **4** *NAm*, of a train having a limited number of carriages and making a limited number of stops – **limitedly** *adv*, **limitedness** *n*

**limited company** *n*, *Br* a company in which the responsibility of an individual shareholder for the company's debts is limited according to the NOMINAL VALUE of his/her shares

**limited edition** *n* an edition of a publication limited to a specific number of copies and usu printed in a special format

**limited liability** *n* liability (eg of a shareholder or shipowner) limited by law or contract

**limited war** *n* a war whose objective is less than the total defeat of the enemy

**limiting** /'limiting/ *adj* **1** functioning as a limit; restrictive ⟨*~ factors*⟩ **2** serving to specify the application of the modified noun ⟨this *in "this book" is a ~ word*⟩

**limit point** *n* a point that is related to a mathematical set of points in such a way that every NEIGHBOURHOOD of the point no matter how small contains another point belonging to the set

**limitrophe** /'limiˌtrohf/ *adj*, *of a country or region* situated on a border or frontier; adjacent [Fr, fr L *limitrophus* set apart to support troops on the frontier, fr L *limit-*, *limes* boundary + Gk *trophos* supporting]

**limmer** /'limə/ *n*, *chiefly Scot* **1** a scoundrel **2** a prostitute [ME (Sc)]

**limn** /lim/ *vt* **limned** /limd/; **limning** /'liming, 'limning/ *archaic or poetic* **1** to represent by drawing or painting ⟨*if he be ~ed aright* – *Cornhill Magazine*⟩ **2** to describe in words △ limb [ME *luminen*, *limnen* to illuminate (a manuscript), fr MF *en-luminer*, fr L *illuminare* to illuminate] – **limner** *n*

**limnetic** /lim'netik/, **limnic** /'limnik/ *adj* of or inhabiting the open water of a lake ⟨*~ environment*⟩ [ISV, fr Gk *limnē* pool, marshy lake; akin to L *limen* threshold – more at LIMB]

**limnology** /lim'noləji/ *n* the scientific study of physical, chemical, meteorological, and biological conditions in bodies of fresh water (eg lakes) [Gk *limnē* + ISV *-logy*] – **limnological** *adj*, **limnologically** *adv*, **limnologist** *n*

**limonene** /'liməneen/ *n* a widely distributed chemical compound, $C_{10}H_{16}$, that occurs in ESSENTIAL OILS (eg of oranges or lemons), smells of lemons, and is used in the manufacture of resins and as a solvent [ISV, fr Fr *limon* lemon]

**limonite** /'liməˌniet/ *n* a common mineral FERRIC OXIDE of variable composition that is a major source of iron [Ger *limonit*, fr Gk *leimōn* meadow – more at LIMB] – **limonitic** *adj*

**limousine** /ˌliməˈzeen, '---/ *n* a large luxurious often chauffeur-driven car that sometimes has a glass partition separating the driver's seat from the passenger compartment [Fr, lit., cloak, fr *Limousin*, region in France]

**¹limp** /limp/ *vi* **1** to walk lamely; *esp* to walk so as to avoid placing weight on one foot **2** to proceed slowly or with difficulty ⟨*commerce ~ed toward a standstill* – *Time*⟩ [prob fr ME *lympen* to fall short; akin to OE *limpan* to happen, L *limbus* border, *labi* to slide – more at SLEEP] – **limper** *n*

**²limp** *n* a limping movement or gait

**³limp** *adj* **1a** lacking or seeming to lack firmness and body and consequently drooping or shapeless ⟨*~ curtains*⟩ **b** not stiff or rigid ⟨*~ leather bookbinding*⟩ **2** lacking energy [akin to ¹*limp*] – **limply** *adv*, **limpness** *n*

**limpet** /'limpit/ *n* **1** a marine INVERTEBRATE animal (esp families Acmaeidae and Patellidae of the class Gastropoda, phylum Mollusca) that has a low conical shell open on the underside, browses over rocks or timbers along coasts, and clings very tightly when disturbed **2** one who or that which clings tenaciously to someone or something **3** **limpet mine**, **limpet bomb**, **limpet** an adhesive explosive device; *esp* one designed to cling to the hull of a ship [ME *lempet*, fr OE *lempedu*, fr ML *lampreda* (cf LAMPREY)]

**limpid** /'limpid/ *adj* **1** transparent ⟨*~ streams*⟩ **2** clear and simple in style ⟨*~ prose*⟩ **3** calm, serene □ compare CLEAR [Fr or L; F *limpide*, fr L *limpidus*, fr *lympha*, *limpa* water – more at LYMPH] – **limpidly** *adv*, **limpidness** *n*, **limpidity** *n*

**limulus** /'limyooləs/ *n*, *pl* **limuli** /-li/ any of a genus (*Limulus*) of KING CRABS [NL, genus name, fr L *limus* sidelong]

**limy** /'liemi/ *adj* **1** smeared with or consisting of lime; sticky **2** containing lime or limestone **3** resembling or having the qualities of lime

**linac** /'linak/ *n* LINEAR ACCELERATOR (device for accelerating atomic particles) [*lin*ear *ac*celerator]

**linage** *also* **lineage** /'lienij/ *n* **1** the number of lines of printed or written matter **2** payment for writing at so much a line △ lineage

**linalool** /li'naloh,ol, 'linəloohl/ *n* a liquid alcohol, $C_{10}H_{17}OH$, that has a smell similar to bergamot and is used in perfumes, soaps, and flavouring materials [ISV, fr MexSp *lináloe*, tree yielding perfume, fr ML *lignum aloes*, lit., wood of the aloe]

**linchpin** /'linch,pin/ *n* **1** a locking pin inserted crosswise (eg through the end of an axle or shaft) **2** someone or something that acts as a vital or coordinating part ⟨*the ~ of the argument*⟩ [ME *lynspin*, fr *lyns* linchpin (fr OE *lynis*) + *pin*]

**Lincoln** /'lingkən/ *n* (any of) an English breed of long-woolled meat-producing sheep similar to but heavier than the Leicester [*Lincoln*, *Lincolnshire*, county in E England where the breed was developed]

**Lincoln green** /'lingkən/ *n* **1** a bright green colour **2** cloth of Lincoln green [*Lincoln*, city in E England where the cloth was orig made]

**lincomycin** /ˌlingkə'miesin/ *n* an antibiotic, $C_{18}H_{34}N_2O_6S$, obtained from a bacterium (*Streptomyces lincolnensis* var *lincolnensis*) and used esp to treat serious infections caused by bacteria (esp STREPTOCOCCI and STAPHYLOCOCCI) [*linco-* (fr *Streptomyces lincolnensis*) + *-mycin*]

**linctus** /'lingktəs/ *n* any of various syrupy usu medicated liquids used to relieve throat irritation and coughing [NL, fr L, pp of *lingere* to lick – more at LICK]

**lindane** /'lindayn/ *n* an insecticide that consists of the chemical compound benzene hexachloride and is broken down by living organisms very slowly [T van der *Linden* b 1884 D chemist]

**linden** /'lind(ə)n/ *n* any of a genus (*Tilia* of the family Tiliaceae, the linden family) of widely planted trees native to temperate regions, that have a winglike BRACT (leaflike structure) attached to the stalk of the flower and fruit and usu have heart-shaped leaves; *esp* a European tree (*Tilia europaea*) much used for ornamental planting [ME, made of linden wood, fr OE, fr *lind* linden tree]

**¹line** /lien/ *vt* **1** to cover the inner surface of ⟨*~ a cloak with silk*⟩ **2** to put something in the inside of; fill **3** to serve as the lining of ⟨*tapestries ~d the walls*⟩ [ME *linen*, fr *line* flax, fr OE *līn* – more at LINEN]

**²line** *n* **1a** a thread, string, cord, or rope: eg **1a(1)** a comparatively strong slender cord **a(2)** a clothesline **a(3)** a rope used on a ship **b** a device for catching fish that consists of a cord with hooks and is attached to a rod or other fishing gear **c** a length of material (eg cord) used in measuring and levelling **d** piping for conveying a liquid or gas (eg steam) **e(1)** a wire or pair of wires connecting one telegraph or telephone station with another; *also* a whole system of such wires **e(2)** the principal circuits of an electric power system **2a** a horizontal row of written or printed characters **b(1)** a single row of words in a poem **b(2)** *pl* a piece of poetry ⟨*~s on the death of a favourite goldfish*⟩ **b(3)** a unit in the rhythmic structure of verse formed by the grouping of a number of the smallest units of the rhythm **c** a short letter; a note **d** a short sequence of words spoken by an actor playing a particular role; *also*, *pl* all of the sequences making up a particular role **3a** something (eg a ridge or seam) that is distinct, elongated, and narrow **b** a narrow crease (eg on the face); a wrinkle **c(1)** the course or direction of something in motion ⟨*the ~ of march*⟩ **c(2)** the trail of scent left by a hunted animal **d(1)** a real or imaginary straight line oriented in terms of stable points of reference ⟨*lies on a ~ between London and Glasgow*⟩ **d(2)** a state of agreement, conformity ⟨*bring into ~*⟩ ⟨*stray out of ~*⟩ **e** a boundary of an area ⟨*the state ~*⟩ **f** a railway track **4a** a course of conduct, action, or thought **b** *also* **line of country** a field of activity, interest, or business ⟨*he's in the clothing ~*⟩ **c** a specified way or theme of talking or writing ⟨*a hefty ~ in home psychoanalysis* – Derek Jewell⟩ **5** a limit, restraint **6a(1)** a related series of people or things coming one after the other in time; a family **a(2)** a strain produced and maintained by selective breeding **a(3)** a chronological series **b lines** *pl*, **line** a linked series of trenches and fortifications, esp facing the enemy **c** a military formation in which the different elements (e g men or companies) are abreast of each other **d** naval ships arranged in a regular order ⟨*the fleet changed from ~ ahead to ~ abreast*⟩ **e** a rank of objects of one kind; a row **f** (the company owning or operating) a group of vehicles, ships, aeroplanes, etc carrying passengers or goods regularly over a route ⟨*a shipping ~*⟩ **g** a succession of musical notes, esp in melodic phrases **h** an arrangement of operations in industry permitting various stages of manufacture to take place in sequence ⟨*assembly ~*⟩ ⟨*production ~*⟩ **7** a narrow elongated mark drawn or projected: e g **7a(1)** a circle of latitude or longitude on a sphere (e g the earth or a celestial sphere) **a(2)** *the equator* ⟨*crossing the ~*⟩ **b line symbol, line** a mark (e g on a map) indicating the position of a boundary, division, or other linear feature in two dimensions or the outline of an area **c** any of the horizontal parallel strokes on a musical STAVE on or between which notes are placed – compare SPACE 3 **d** a mark (e g in pencil) that forms part of the formal design of a picture as distinguished from the shading or colour; *also* the way in which an artist uses such lines ⟨*purity of ~*⟩ **e** a division on a bridge score dividing the points for tricks both bid and made from the other points scored – chiefly in *above/below the line* ⟨*my four honours in trumps gave me 100 points below the ~*⟩ **f** a marked or imaginary line across or at the limit of a playing area (e g a football field) with reference to which the playing of a game or sport is regulated ⟨*grounded the ball over the ~ for a try*⟩ **g** (a single passage of the scanning spot tracing) a thin horizontal section of the image on a television screen **h** a narrow part of a spectrum (e g of light from the sun) distinguished by being noticeably more or less bright than neighbouring areas ⟨*the sodium ~s occur in the yellow part of the spectrum*⟩ **8** a straight or curved path that is traced by a moving point and has length but no breadth; *esp* a straight line **9a** a defining outline; a contour ⟨*the ~ of a building*⟩ **b lines** *pl*, **line** a general plan; a model ⟨*writing something on the ~s of a guidebook*⟩ **10** the unit of fineness of HALFTONES expressed as the number of screen lines to the linear inch **11** merchandise or services of the same general class for sale or regularly available ⟨*we don't carry that ~*⟩ **12** an indication (e g of intention) based on insight or investigation ⟨*got a ~ on their plans*⟩ **13** *pl*, *Br* a row of tents or huts in a military camp **14** *chiefly Br* ¹PICA (unit of printing-type size) **15** *pl*, *Br* a specified number of lines of writing esp to be copied as a school punishment **16a** *Br* the regular and numbered infantry regiments of the army as opposed to auxiliary forces or troops guarding the sovereign ⟨*a regiment of the ~*⟩ **b** *NAm* the combatant forces of an army as distinguished from the staff corps and supply services **17** *Br* the path through the air followed by a bowled cricket ball before it bounces; *also* the direction in which such a ball travels, esp as viewed in terms of the difficulty it causes the batsman ⟨*he bowls a good ~ and length*⟩ **18** *archaic* one's position in life; one's lot – compare HARD LINES [ME; partly fr OF *ligne*, fr L *linea*, fr fem of *lineus* made of flax, fr *linum* flax; partly fr OE *līne*; akin to OE *līn* flax] – **liny** *also* **liney** *adj* – **all along the line** at every stage – **draw a/the line 1** to fix an arbitrary boundary between things that tend to merge ⟨*the difficulty of* drawing a line *between art and pornography*⟩ **2** to fix a boundary excluding what one will not tolerate or engage in – **get a line on** *informal* to obtain information about – **hold the line** to keep a telephone line open – **in line for** in the right position for; likely to get – **lay (something) on the line 1** to state (something) honestly and openly **2** to expose to risk or loss – **on line** *of a computer terminal* switched on and connected to the main computer – **read between the lines** to understand or perceive meaning that is not directly expressed or stated – **shoot a line** *informal* to boast – **step out of line** to act differently from others or from what is expected – **toe the line** to conform to expected behaviour; obey – see also HOOK, **line, and sinker**

**³line** *vt* **1** to mark or cover with a line or lines **2** to place or form a line along ⟨*pedestrians ~ the pavements*⟩

**line out** *vt* to indicate (as if) with lines; outline – see also LINE-OUT

**line up** *vi* to assume an orderly arrangement in a straight line ~ *vt* **1** to produce, organize, and assemble ⟨line up *some arguments*⟩ **2** to form into a line; align ⟨line up *troops*⟩ – see also LINE-UP

**⁴line** *adj* made up of lines and solid areas without gradations of tone

**¹lineage** /'lini·ij/ *n* a line of descent from a common ancestor or source; *also* the descendants of such a line △ **linage** [ME *linage*, fr MF *linage, lignage*, fr OF, fr *ligne*]

**²lineage** /'lienij/ *n* LINAGE

**lineal** /'lini·əl/ *adj* **1** linear **2** composed of or arranged in lines **3a** consisting of or being in a direct line of ancestry or descent – usu contrasted with *collateral* **b** of or derived from ancestors; hereditary **4** of or dealing with a lineage – **lineally** *adv*, **lineality** *n*

**lineament** /'lini·əmənt/ *n* **1** *usu pl* a distinctive outline, feature, or contour of a body or figure, esp a face **2** a linear geological feature (e g of the earth or a planet) that reveals a characteristic (e g a fault) in the underlying structure △ liniment [ME, fr L *lineamentum*, fr *linea*] – **lineamental** *adj*

**linear** /'lini·ə/ *adj* **1a(1)** of or resembling a line; straight **a(2)** involving a single dimension **b** of or based on LINEAR EQUATIONS or LINEAR TRANSFORMATIONS **c(1)** characterized by an emphasis on line; *esp* having clearly defined outlines ⟨*~ art*⟩ **c(2)** composed of simply drawn lines with little attempt at pictorial representation ⟨*~ script*⟩ **d** consisting of a straight chain of atoms **2** elongated with nearly parallel sides ⟨*~ leaf*⟩ **3** involving or expressed by a LINEAR EQUATION; *esp* having or being a response or output that is directly proportional to the input ⟨*~ amplifier*⟩ – **linearly** *adv*, **linearity** *n*

**Linear A** *n* a simple nonpictorial (LINEAR 1c(2)) form of writing used in Crete from the 18th to the 15th centuries BC

**linear accelerator** *n* a device in which charged particles (e g electrons) are accelerated in a straight line by successive impulses from a series of electric fields

**linear algebra** *n* a branch of mathematics concerned with VECTOR SPACES, MATRICES, and LINEAR TRANSFORMATIONS

**Linear B** *n* a simple nonpictorial (LINEAR 1c(2)) form of writing employing characters standing for syllables and used at Knossos on Crete and on the Greek mainland from the 15th to the 12th centuries BC for documents in the MYCENAEAN language

**linear combination** *n* a mathematical expression (e g $4x + 5y + 6z$) which is composed only of additions or subtractions of elements (e g variables or equations)

**linear dependence** *n* the property of a mathematical set (e g of MATRICES or VECTORS) of having at least one LINEAR COMBINATION equal to zero when the elements of the set are multiplied by nonzero constants (COEFFICIENTS) that are taken from a given set (e g the REAL NUMBERS) – **linearly dependent** *adj*

**linear equation** *n* an equation of the first degree in any number of variables (e g $x + y = 9$)

**linear function** *n* **1** a mathematical function in which the variables appear only in the first degree, are multiplied by constants, and are combined only by addition and subtraction **2** LINEAR TRANSFORMATION

**linear independence** *n* the property of a mathematical set (e g of MATRICES or VECTORS) of having no LINEAR COMBINATION of the elements equal to zero when the elements of the set are multiplied by constants (COEFFICIENTS) taken from a given set unless all the elements of the LINEAR COMBINATION are equal to zero – **linearly independent** *adj*

**linear-ize, -ise** /'liniəriez/ *vt* to give a linear form to; *esp* to transform an equation into a LINEAR EQUATION – **linearizable** *adj*, **linearization** *n*

**linear measure** *n* **1** a measure of length **2** a system of measures of length

**linear motor** *n* an electric motor that produces thrust directly in a straight line rather than by rotational force

**linear perspective** *n* the representation in a drawing or painting of parallel lines as converging in order to give the illusion of depth and distance

**linear programming** *n* a mathematical method of solving practical problems (e g the most profitable allocation of resources) by finding the maximum or minimum value of LINEAR FUNCTIONS subject to various constraints

**linear transformation** *n* a mathematical function that maps one VECTOR SPACE onto another one over the same FIELD in such a way that the image of the sum of two vectors equals the sum of their images, and the image of the product of a SCALAR and a vector equals the product of the scalar and the image of the vector

**lineation** /ˌliniˈaysh(ə)n/ *n* 1 the action of marking with lines; delineation 2 an arrangement of lines [ME *lineacion* outline, fr L *lineation-*, *lineatio*, fr *lineatus*, pp of *lineare* to make straight, fr *linea*]

**linebreed** /ˈlienˌbreed/ *vb* **linebred** /-ˌbred/ to interbreed (animals) within a particular line of descent, usu to perpetuate desirable characteristics

**linecaster** /ˈlienˌkahstə/ *n* a machine that casts pieces of metal type by squirting molten lead into rows of moulds one line at a time – **linecasting** *n*

**line drawing** *n* a drawing composed only of lines (e g drawn with a pen or pencil)

**line engraving** *n* 1 a method of engraving in metal in which the effects are produced by lines of differing widths and closeness 2 a plate engraved in this way; *also* a print made from such a plate – **line engraver** *n*

**line gauge** *n* a printer's ruler showing the size of printing type

**lineman** /ˈlienmən/ *n*, *chiefly NAm* LINESMAN 2

¹**linen** /ˈlinin/ *adj* 1 made of flax 2 made of or resembling linen [ME, fr OE *linen*, fr *lin* flax; akin to OHG *lin* flax; both fr a prehistoric Gmc word borrowed fr L *linum* flax] – **wash one's dirty linen in public** to make public facts and details that are generally regarded as private

²**linen** *n* 1a cloth made of flax and noted for its strength, coolness, and sheen **b** thread or yarn spun from flax 2 clothing or household articles (e g sheets, pillowcases, and tablecloths) made of a usu washable cloth, esp linen 3 paper made from linen fibres or with a linen finish

**linenfold** /ˈlininˌfohld/ *n* a carved or moulded ornament representing vertical folds of linen, characteristic of Tudor panelling

**line of country** *n* LINE 4b (specialist field)

**line of duty** *n* all that is authorized, required, or normally associated with some field of responsibility

**line of force** *n* a line in a field of force (e g a magnetic or electric field) whose TANGENT at any point gives the direction of the force at that point

**line of sight** *n* 1 a line from an observer's eye to a distant point towards which he/she is looking 2 the straight path between a radio or television transmitter and receiving aerials when unobstructed by the horizon

**lineolate** /ˈliniəlayt/, **lineolated** /-laytid/ *adj*, *botany & zoology* marked with fine lines or grooves [NL *lineolatus*, fr *lineola*, dim. of *linea* line – more at LINE]

¹**line-ˌout** *n* the method in Rugby Union by which the ball is returned to play by being thrown in between two lines of players from each team; *also* the two lines of players [*line out* (vb) to line up, form a line]

**line printer** *n* a high-speed printing device (e g for a computer) that prints each line as a unit rather than character by character – **line printing** *n*

¹**liner** /ˈlienə/ *n* 1 one who or that which makes, draws, or uses lines 2 a ship belonging to a shipping company that carries passengers on scheduled routes

²**liner** *n* one who or that which lines or is used to back something; *esp* a removable metal lining for reducing wear in machinery

**linesman** /ˈlienzmən/ *n* 1 an official who assists a referee or umpire in various games (e g soccer, rugby, or tennis), esp in determining if a ball or player is out of bounds 2 *chiefly Br* one who sets up or repairs telephone lines, electric power cables, etc

**line spectrum** *n* a SPECTRUM that is produced by atoms and consists of sharp lines – compare BAND SPECTRUM, CONTINUOUS SPECTRUM

**line squall** *n* a squall or thunderstorm occurring along a COLD FRONT (edge of mass of cold air)

¹**line-ˌup, lineup** *n* 1 a line of people arranged for inspection or for identification by police 2a a group of people or items assembled for a particular purpose ⟨*the* ∼ *for tonight's show*⟩ **b** a list of players playing for a team; *also* the players on such a list ⟨*England's* ∼ *includes Brooking and Keegan*⟩

¹**ling** /ling/ *n* any of various fishes of the cod family (Gadidae); *esp* a large fish (*Molva molva*) of shallow seas of Greenland and Europe that is an important food fish [ME; akin to D *leng* ling, OE *lang* long]

²**ling** *n* heather [ME, fr ON *lyng*; akin to Lith *lenkti* to bend – more at -LING]

¹**-ling** /-ling/ *suffix* (*n* → *n*) 1 one connected with ⟨*hireling*⟩ ⟨*sibling*⟩ 2 young, small, or lesser kind of ⟨*duckling*⟩ ⟨*princeling*⟩ 3 one having (a specified quality or attribute) ⟨*underling*⟩ [ME, fr OE; akin to OE *-ing* one of a (specified) kind]

²**-ling, -lings** *suffix* (*n or adj* → *adj or adv*) in (such) a direction or manner ⟨*darkling*⟩ ⟨*flatlings*⟩ [ME *-ling* (fr OE), *-linges* (fr *-ling* + *-es* -s); akin to OHG *-lingun* -ling, Lith *lenkti* to bend]

**linga** /ˈlingɡə/ *n* a stylized phallic symbol (of the Hindu god Siva) – compare YONI [Skt *liṅga* (nom *liṅgam*), lit., characteristic]

**Lingala** /lingˈgahlə/ *n* a BANTU language of the Congo

**lingam** /ˈlingɡəm/ *n* a linga

**Lingayat** /lingˈgah-yət/ *n* a member of a SAIVA sect of S India marked by wearing of the linga and characterized by denial of distinctions between social classes (CASTES) [Kannada *liṅgāyata*]

**linger** /ˈlingɡə/ *vi* 1a to delay going, esp because of reluctance to leave; tarry **b** to dwell on a subject – usu + *over*, *on*, or *upon* 2 to continue in a failing or morbid state unduly or unhappily – often + *on* 3 to be slow to act; procrastinate 4 to be protracted or slow in disappearing *synonyms* see ³STAY [ME (northern) *lengeren* to dwell, freq of *lengen* to prolong, fr OE *lengan*; akin to OE *lang* long] – **lingerer** *n*, **lingeringly** *adv*

**lingerie** /ˈlonh-zhəri, ˈlan(h)-/ *(Fr* lɛ̃ʒri*)/ n* women's underwear and nightclothes [Fr, fr MF, fr *linge* linen, fr L *lineus* made of flax – more at ²LINE]

*usage* The alternative pronunciation ending in /-ray/ is disliked by some people.

**lingo** /ˈling-goh/ *n*, *pl* **lingoes** *derog or humorous* strange or incomprehensible language or speech: e g **a** a foreign language **b** the special vocabulary of a particular subject; JARGON 2 **c** the language characteristic of an individual; IDIOLECT *synonyms* see DIALECT [Prov *lingo* tongue or Pg *lingoa*, both fr L *lingua* – more at TONGUE]

**lingu-** /ˈling-g-/, **lingui-**, **linguo-** *comb form* 1 language ⟨*lingui*st⟩ 2 tongue ⟨*linguiform*⟩ [L *lingu-*, fr *lingua*]

**lingua** /ˈling-gwə/ *n*, *pl* **linguae** /ˈling-gwie/ a tongue; *also* an organ or structure resembling a tongue – used technically [L]

**lingua franca** /ˌling-gwə ˈfrangkə/ *n*, *pl* **lingua francas**, **linguae francae** /ˌling-gwie ˈfrangkie/ 1 a common language that consists of Italian mixed with French, Spanish, Greek, and Arabic and is spoken in Mediterranean ports 2 any of various languages (e g Swahili) used as common or commercial tongues among people with different native languages 3 something resembling a common language ⟨*the* ∼ *of popular music – Punch*⟩ [It, lit., Frankish language]

**lingual** /ˈling-gwəl/ *adj* 1a of or resembling the tongue **b** lying near or next to the tongue **c** pronounced with the tongue 2 linguistic – **lingually** *adv*

**linguini** /lingˈgweeni/ *n* pasta in the form of flat strands [It, pl of *liguina*, dim. of *lingua* tongue, fr L]

**linguist** /ˈling-gwist/ *n* 1 a person accomplished in languages; *esp* POLYGLOT 1 2 *also* **linguistician** somebody who specializes in linguistics

**linguistic** /lingˈgwistik/ *also* **linguistical** *adj* of language or linguistics – **linguistically** *adv*

**linguistic atlas** *n* a publication containing a set of maps on which speech variations are recorded

**linguistic form** *n* a meaningful unit of speech (e g a MORPHEME, word, or sentence)

**linguistic geography** *n* local or regional variations of a language or dialect, studied as a field of knowledge

**linguistic philosophy** *n* ORDINARY-LANGUAGE PHILOSOPHY

**linguistics** /lingˈgwistiks/ *n taking sing vb* the study of human language including its units, nature, structure, and modification – compare PHILOLOGY *synonyms* see GRAMMAR

**lingulate** /ˈling-gyoolayt, -lət/ *adj* shaped like a tongue; LIGULATE ⟨*a* ∼ *leaf*⟩ [L *lingulatus*, fr *lingula*, dim. of *lingua*]

**liniment** /ˈlinimənt/ *n* a liquid or semiliquid preparation that is applied to the skin to reduce pain or soothe irritation △ **lineament** [ME, fr LL *linimentum*, fr L *linere* to smear – more at LIME]

**lining** /ˈliening/ *n* 1 (a piece of) material used to line a garment, curtains, etc; *esp* a layer of fabric when cut and constructed to the shape of a garment and attached to the inner surface 2 the act or process of providing something with a lining

**¹link** /lingk/ *n* **1** a connecting structure: e g **1a(1)** a single ring or division of a chain **a(2)** a standardized division of a surveyor's chain that is 7.92 inches (about 20.12 centimetres) long and serves as a measure of length **b** CUFF LINK **c** link, linkage *chemistry* BOND 3b (mechanism which holds atoms together) **d** an intermediate rod or piece in a mechanism for transmitting force or motion **e** the part of an electrical fuse that breaks under an excess load **2** something resembling a link of chain: e g **2a** a segment of sausage in a chain **b** a connecting element ⟨*sought a* ∼ *between smoking and cancer*⟩ **c** a unit in a communications system [ME, of Scand origin; akin to ON *hlekkr* chain; akin to OE *hlanc* lank] – **linker** *n*

**²link** *vt* **1** to join, connect ⟨*road that* ∼s *two towns*⟩ – often + *up* **2** to act as a linkman for ⟨∼s . . . *the two-hour pop marathon* – George Melly⟩ ∼ *vi* **1** to become connected by a link – often + *up* **2** *dial* to join together by intertwining arms *synonyms* see ¹JOIN *antonym* sunder

**³link** *n* a torch, esp of flaming pitch, formerly used to light somebody's way through the streets [perh modif of ML *linchinus* candle, alter. of L *lychnus*, fr Gk *lychnos;* akin to Gk *leukos* white – more at LIGHT]

**⁴link** *vi, Scot* to skip smartly along [origin unknown]

**linkage** /'lingkij/ *n* **1** the manner or style of being joined: e g **1a** the manner in which atoms or chemical groups are linked in a molecule **b** BOND 3b (mechanism which holds atoms together) **2** the quality or state of being linked; *esp* the relationship between genes on the same CHROMOSOME (strand of gene-carrying material) that causes them to be inherited together **3a** a system of links **b** the degree of electromagnetic interaction expressed as the number of turns of wire in an electric COIL multiplied by the MAGNETIC FLUX (measure of the strength of the magnetism) linked by the coil

**linkage group** *n* a set of genes at different positions on the same CHROMOSOME (strand of gene-carrying material) that tend to act as a single pair of genes in MEIOSIS (process of cell division to form sex cells) instead of undergoing INDEPENDENT ASSORTMENT, so that the characteristics coded for by these genes remain together for several generations

**linkboy** /'lingk,boy/ *n* a male attendant formerly employed to bear a light, esp a torch of burning pitch, for a person on the streets at night [³*link* + *boy*]

**linked** /lingkt/ *adj* **1** marked by linkage, esp genetic linkage ⟨∼ *genes*⟩ **2** having or provided with links

**linking verb** /'lingking/ *n* COPULA b (e g *be* or *seem*)

**¹linkman** /'lingkmən/ *n* a linkboy

**²linkman** *n* a broadcaster whose function is to link and introduce separate items, esp in a news magazine programme

**links** /lingks/ *n, pl* **links 1** GOLF COURSE; *esp* one near the seaside **2** *pl, Scot* sand hills, esp along the seashore [ME, rising ground, sand hills, fr OE *hlincas*, pl of *hlinc* ridge; akin to OE *hlanc* lank]

**linkup** /'lingk,up/ *n* **1** the establishment of contact; a meeting ⟨*the* ∼ *of two spacecraft*⟩ **2a** something that serves as a linking device or factor **b** a functional whole that is the result of a linkup

**linn** /lin/ *n, chiefly Scot* **1** a waterfall **2** a precipice [ScGael *linne* pool]

**Linnaean, Linnean** /li'nee·ən/ *adj* of or following the systematic methods of the Swedish botanist Linné, who established the system of BINOMIAL NOMENCLATURE (scheme of naming things using two terms) for all living organisms [Carolus *Linnaeus*, Latinized name of Carl von Linné †1778 Sw botanist]

**linnet** /'linit/ *n* a common small African and Eurasian finch (*Acanthis cannabina*) having variable reddish-brown feathers [MF *linette*, fr *lin* flax, fr L *linum;* fr its feeding on the seed of flax and other plants]

**lino** /'lienoh/ *n, pl* **linos** *chiefly Br* linoleum

**linocut** /-,kut/ *n* a design cut in relief on a piece of linoleum; *also* a print made from such a design

**linoleate** /li'nohli,ayt/ *n* any of various chemical compounds (SALTS or ESTERS) formed by combination between LINOLEIC ACID and a metal atom, an alcohol, or another chemical group

**linoleic acid** /,linə'layik, -'lee-/ *n* a liquid FATTY ACID, $C_{18}H_{32}O_2$, found in DRYING oils and SEMIDRYING oils (e g linseed or peanut oil), held to be essential in animal nutrition and used in making paint and synthetic resins [Gk *linon* flax + ISV *oleic* (acid)]

**linolenate** /,linə'laynayt, -'lee-/ *n* any of various chemical compounds (SALTS or ESTERS) formed by combination be-

tween LINOLENIC ACID and a metal atom, an alcohol, or another chemical group

**linolenic acid** /,linə'laynik, -'lee-/ *n* a liquid FATTY ACID, $C_{18}H_{30}O_2$, found esp in DRYING OILS (e g LINSEED OIL) and considered an essential animal nutrient [ISV, irreg fr *linoleic*]

**linoleum** /li'nohli·əm/ *n* a usu patterned hardwearing glossy floor covering made with a burlap or canvas backing and a surface of a mixture of solidified LINSEED OIL with gums, cork dust, pigments, etc [L *linum* flax + *oleum* oil – more at OIL]

**Linotype** /'lienə,tiep, -noh-/ *trademark* – used for a keyboard-operated typesetting machine that produces each line of type in the form of a solid metal slug

**linsang** /'linsang/ *n* any of various Asiatic mammals (*Prionodon* and related genera) with thick spotted or banded fur, that resemble long-tailed cats and are related to the civets and genets [Malay]

**linseed** /'linseed/ *n* the seed of flax used esp as a source of linseed oil, as a medicine, or as animal feed [ME, fr OE *līnsǣd*, fr *līn* flax + *sǣd* seed – more at LINEN]

**linseed oil** *n* a yellowish DRYING OIL obtained from flaxseed and used esp in making paint, varnish, printing ink, and linoleum and for conditioning cricket bats

**linsey-woolsey** /,linzi 'woolzi/ *n* a coarse sturdy fabric of wool and linen or cotton [ME *lynsy wolsye*, prob fr *Lindsey*, village in Suffolk + *wolle* wool + rhyming ending]

**linstock** /'lin,stok/ *n* a staff having a pointed foot adapted for sticking into the ground and a forked tip and formerly used to hold a lighted match for firing cannon [D *lontstok*, fr *lont* match + *stok* stick]

**lint** /lint/ *n* **1** a soft absorbent material with a fleecy surface that is made from linen usu by scraping and is used chiefly for surgical dressings **2** the fibrous coat of thick convoluted hairs borne by cotton seeds **3** *chiefly NAm* FLUFF 1a [ME, deriv of L *linum* flax, linen] – **linty** *adj*

**lintel** /'lintl/ *n* a horizontal architectural beam spanning and usu carrying the load above an opening (e g a door or window) [ME, fr MF, fr LL *limitaris* threshold, fr L, constituting a boundary, fr *limit-, limes* boundary – more at LIMB]

**linter** /'lintə/ *n, NAm* **1** a machine for removing linters **2** *pl* the fuzz of short fibres that adheres to cottonseed after GINNING (separating fibre from raw cotton) [*lint* + ²*-er*]

**lion** /'lie·ən/, *fem* **lioness** /'lie·ənis, ,lie·ə'nes/ *n, pl* **lions**, *(1a)* **lions**, *esp collectively* **lion 1a** a large flesh-eating chiefly nocturnal cat (*Felis leo*) that lives and hunts in groups on the plains or rocky areas of Africa and formerly southern Asia, and that has a tawny body with a tufted tail and in the male a shaggy blackish or dark brown mane **b** *cap* Leo **2a** a person resembling a lion (e g in courage or ferocity) – used in the West Indies to address a man **b** a person of interest or importance ⟨*literary* ∼s⟩ [ME, fr OF, fr L *leon-, leo*, fr Gk *leōn*] – **lionlike** *adj*

**lioncel** /'lie·ənsel/ *n* a heraldic representation of a lion, usu in a group of four or more [Fr, fr MF, dim. of *lion*]

**lionhearted** /,lie·ən'hahtid/ *adj* courageous, brave

**lion-ize, -ise** /'lie·ə,niez/ *vt* **1** to treat as an object of great interest or importance **2** *archaic Br* to show the sights of a place to [(2) fr the lions formerly kept at the Tower of London and considered one of the city's chief attractions] – **lionizer** *n*, **lionization** *n*

**lion's mouth** *n* a place of great danger

**lion's share** *n* the largest or best portion

**¹lip** /lip/ *n* **1** either of two fleshy folds that surround the mouth in many VERTEBRATE animals including man and in man are organs of speech **2a** a fleshy edge or margin (e g of a wound) **b** LABIUM (insect lower lip) **c** LABELLUM 1 (petal of orchid) **d** one part of a two-lipped COROLLA (flower head) **3a** the edge of a hollow vessel, esp a jug, or of a cavity; *esp* one shaped to make pouring easy **b** a projecting edge (e g of the mouth of an organ flue pipe or on the end of an AUGER) **4** EMBOUCHURE (use of the lips in playing a wind instrument) **5** *slang* impudent or insolent talk, esp in reply ⟨*don't give us any* ∼, *sonny*⟩ [ME, fr OE *lippa;* akin to OHG *leffur* lip, & prob to L *labium, labrum* lip] – **lipless** *adj*, **liplike** *adj* – (**keep a) stiff upper lip** (to show or maintain) stoical courage

**²lip** *adj* **1** spoken with the lips only; insincere – often in combination ⟨lip-*worship*⟩ **2** *linguistics* LABIAL 2 ⟨∼ *consonants*⟩

**³lip** *vt* **-pp-** **1** to touch with the lips; *esp* to kiss **2** *of water* to lap against **3** *of a golf ball* to reach the edge of (the hole) without dropping in

**lip-** /ˈlip-, liep-/, **lipo-** *comb form* fat; fatty tissue; fatty ⟨lipo-*protein*⟩ ⟨lipoma⟩ [NL, fr Gk, fr *lipos* – more at LEAVE]

**lipase** /ˈlipayz, -ays, 'lie-/ *n* an ENZYME present in many organs of the body, in the blood, and in plants and seeds that accelerates the breakdown or synthesis of fats or the breakdown of LIPOPROTEINS [ISV]

**lipbrush** /ˈlip,brush/ *n* a brush for applying colour to the lips

**lip gloss** *n* a cosmetic cream or jelly for giving a glossy often tinted sheen to the lips

**lipid** /ˈlipid, 'lie-/ *also* **lipide** /ˈlipid, 'liepied/ *n* any of various substances, usu insoluble in water but soluble in alcohol and ether, that with proteins and carbohydrates constitute the principal structural components of living cells, and that include fats, waxes, PHOSPHATIDES, CEREBROSIDES, and related and derived compounds [ISV] – **lipidic** *adj*

**Lipizzaner, Lipizaner** /ˌlipit'sahnə/ *n* (any of) a breed of shapely spirited usu grey horses developed at the Austrian Imperial Stud and used esp in dressage displays at the Spanish Riding School in Vienna [Ger, fr *Lipizza, Lippiza,* stud in NW Yugoslavia (formerly the Austrian Imperial Stud)]

**lipogenesis** /ˌliepə'jenəsis/ *n* the formation of FATTY ACIDS in the cells of the living body [NL]

**lipoic acid** /li'poh·ik, lie-/ *n* a chemical compound, $C_8H_{14}O_2S_2$, that is required for the growth of various microorganisms and is concerned with the processing of carbohydrates in cells [*lip-, lipo- + -ic*]

**¹lipoid** /ˈlipoyd, 'lie-/, **lipoidal** /li'poydl, lie-/ *adj* resembling fat [ISV]

**²lipoid** *n* a lipid [ISV]

**lipolysis** /li'poləsis/ *n* the breakdown of fat [NL] – **lipolytic** *adj*

**lipoma** /li'pohmə/ *n, pl* **lipomas, lipomata** /-mətə/ a tumour of fatty tissue [NL] – **lipomatous** *adj*

**lipophilic** /ˌlipə'filik, lie-/ *adj* having an attraction for lipids (eg fats) ⟨*a ~ metabolite*⟩ – **lipophilicity** *n*

**lipopolysaccharide** /ˌlipoh,poli'sakəried, ˌlie-/ *n* a large molecule consisting of lipids (eg fats) and sugars joined by chemical bonds

**lipoprotein** /ˌlipoh-, ˌliepoh-/ *n* a CONJUGATED PROTEIN that is a complex of protein and lipid (eg fat)

**lipotropic** /ˌlipoh'trohpik, -'tropik, ˌliepoh-/ *adj* promoting the physiological use of fat [ISV] – **lipotropism** *n*

**lipotropin** /ˈlipə,trohpin, 'lie-/ *n* either of two PEPTIDES that are produced in the mammalian PITUITARY (gland located below the brain) and that stimulate the breakdown of lipids (eg fats)

**lipped** /lipt/ *adj* having a lip or lips, esp of a specified kind or number – often in combination ⟨*tight-lipped*⟩

**lipping** /ˈliping/ *n* 1 outgrowth of bone in liplike form at a joint margin 2 a piece of wood set in an archer's bow where a flaw has been cut out 3 *music* EMBOUCHURE

**Lippizaner** /ˌlipit'sahnə/ *n* a Lippizaner

**'lip-,read** *vb* **lip-read** /-,red/ *vt* to understand by lipreading ~ *vi* to use lipreading – **lip-reader** *n*

**lipreading** /ˈlip,reeding/ *n* the interpreting (eg by the deaf) of a speaker's words without hearing his/her voice by watching the movements of the lips

**lip service** *n* support in words but not in deeds ⟨*paid ~ to hygiene by washing down the building once a year*⟩

**lipstick** /ˈlip,stik/ *n* a waxy solid cosmetic usu in stick form for colouring the lips; *also* a stick of such cosmetic with its case

**lip strap** *n* a strap that passes under a horse's chin to hold the bit and curb chain in position

**liquate** /ˈliekwayt/ *vt* to separate (esp a metal) out of a combination or mixture by the application of heat ⟨*~ metallic lead from its ore*⟩ – usu + *out* [L *liquatus,* pp of *liquare;* akin to L *liquēre*] – **liquation** *n*

**liquefacient** /ˌliekwi'faysh(ə)nt/ *n* something that liquefies a substance or promotes liquefaction [L *liquefacient-, liquefaciens,* prp of *liquefacere*] – **liquefacient** *adj*

**liquefaction** /-'faksh(ə)n/ *n* 1 the process of making or becoming liquid 2 the state of being liquid [ME, fr LL *liquefaction-, liquefactio,* fr L *liquefactus,* pp of *liquefacere,* fr *liquēre* to be fluid + *facere* to make – more at DO]

**liquefy** *also* **liquify** /ˈliekwifie/ *vt* to reduce to a liquid state ~ *vi* to become liquid [MF *liquefier,* fr L *liquefacere*] – **liquefiable** *adj,* **liquefier** *n,* **liquefiability** *n*

**liquescent** /li'kwes(ə)nt/ *adj* being or tending to become liquid; melting [L *liquescent-, liquescens,* prp of *liquescere* to become fluid, incho of *liquēre*] – **liquesce** *vt*

**liqueur** /li'kyooə, li'kuh/ *n* any of several usu sweetened spirits

(eg Cointreau or Bénédictine) variously flavoured (eg with fruit or aromatics) and drunk in small quantities after a meal △ liquor [Fr, fr OF *licour* liquid – more at LIQUOR]

**¹liquid** /ˈlikwid/ *adj* 1 flowing freely like water 2 neither solid nor gaseous; characterized by free movement of the constituent molecules among themselves but without the tendency to separate like those of gases ⟨*~ mercury*⟩ 3a shining and clear ⟨*large ~ eyes*⟩ b *of a sound* flowing, pure, and free of harshness c smooth and unconstrained in movement d *of a consonant* (eg /r/ *or* /l/) articulated without friction and capable of being prolonged like a vowel 4 consisting of or capable of ready conversion into cash ⟨*~ assets*⟩ [ME, fr MF *liquide,* fr L *liquidus,* fr *liquēre* to be fluid; akin to L *lixa* water, lye, OIr *fliuch* damp] – **liquidly** *adv,* **liquidness** *n,* **liquidity** *n*

**²liquid** *n* 1 a liquid substance 2 a liquid consonant (eg /r/ *or* /l/)

**liquid air** *n* air in the liquid state that can be prepared by subjecting purified air to great pressure and that is intensely cold and used chiefly as a refrigerant and in the production of pure oxygen and nitrogen

**liquidambar** /ˌlikwi'dambə/ *n* 1 any of a genus (*Liquidambar*) of trees (eg SWEET GUM) of the WITCH HAZEL family that bear a round fruit composed of many woody segments 2 a resin from the SWEET GUM (*Liquidambar styraciflua*) [NL, genus name, fr L *liquidus* + ML *ambar, ambra* amber]

**liquidate** /ˈlikwidayt/ *vt* 1a(1) to determine by agreement or by law the precise amount of (debts, damages, or accounts) a(2) to settle the accounts of (eg a business) and use the assets towards paying off the debts b to settle (a debt), esp by payment 2 to get rid of; *specif* to kill, esp as a ruthless political measure 3 to convert (assets) into cash 4 *archaic* to make clear ~ *vi* 1 to liquidate debts, damages, or accounts 2 to settle the accounts of a business or other organization and use the assets towards paying off the debts 3 to be or become liquidated △ liquidize [LL *liquidatus,* pp of *liquidare* to melt, fr L *liquidus*] – **liquidation** *n*

**liquidator** /ˈlikwi,daytə/ *n* a person appointed by law to liquidate a company

**liquid cannabis** *n* a potent psychoactive drug made by distilling cannabis – called also OIL

**liquid crystal** *n* a liquid having certain physical, esp optical, properties usu shown by crystalline solids but not by ordinary liquids

**liquidity preference** /li'kwidəti/ *n, economics* the propensity to hold money in liquid form (eg cash) rather than in the less readily convertible form of assets

**liquid·ize, -ise** /ˈlikwidiez/ *vt* to make liquid; *esp* to pulverize (eg fruit or vegetables) into a liquid △ liquidate

**liquid·izer, -iser** /ˈlikwidiezə/ *n, chiefly Br* one who or that which liquidizes; *esp* a domestic electrical appliance for grinding, pureeing, liquidizing, or blending foods

**liquid measure** *n* a unit or series of units for measuring liquid capacity

**liquid paraffin** *n* a colourless oily mixture of chemical compounds obtained from petroleum that is used esp as a laxative

**liquidus** /ˈlikwidəs/ *n* a curve, usu on a graph showing the relationship between temperature and the composition of a mixture (eg of a substance when melting or solidifying), above which only the liquid phase can exist – compare SOLIDUS [L, liquid]

**liquify** /ˈlikwifie/ *vb* to liquefy

**¹liquor** /ˈlikə/ *n* 1 a liquid substance: eg a a solution of a drug in water b BATH 2b(1) (liquid contained for a special purpose) c a liquid, esp water, in which food has been cooked d a solution bathing food in a tin and having preservative properties e *chiefly NAm* a usu distilled rather than fermented alcoholic drink; spirits f *Br informal* the liquid from mashed tinned peas sold as a gravy with steak pies in eel and pie shops △ liqueur [ME *licour,* fr OF, fr L *liquor,* fr *liquēre*]

**²liquor** *vt* 1 to dress (eg leather) with oil or grease 2 *informal* to make drunk with alcohol – usu + *up* ~ *vi, informal* to drink alcohol, esp to excess – usu + *up*

**liquorice,** *chiefly NAm* **licorice** /ˈlikərish, -ris/ *n* 1 a European plant (*Glycyrrhiza glabra*) of the pea family that has spikes of blue flowers and is cultivated for its roots 2a the pungent black dried root of liquorice; *also* an extract of this used esp in brewing, confectionery, and as a laxative b a sweet flavoured with liquorice ⟨*~ allsorts*⟩ [ME *licorice,* fr OF, fr LL *liquiritia,* alter. of L *glycyrrhiza,* fr Gk *glykyrrhiza,* fr *glykys* sweet + *rhiza* root]

**lira** /ˈliərə/ *n, pl* (*1*) **lire** *also* **liras,** (*2*) **liras** *also* **lire,** (*3*) **liroth,**

**lirot 1** – see MONEY table **2** a Turkish or Syrian pound, divided into 100 piastres **3** the former Israeli pound [(1) It, fr L *libra,* a unit of weight; (2) Turk, fr It; (3) NHeb, fr It]

**liriodendron** /ˌlirioh'dendrən/ *n, pl* **liriodendrons, liriodendra** /-drə/ TULIP TREE [NL, genus name, fr Gk *leirion, lirion* lily + *dendron* tree]

**liripipe** /'liri,piep/ *n* an elongated extension to the top of a medieval hood that usu hung down behind the head; *also* the tip of a graduate's hood [ML *liripipium*]

**lisente** /li'sente/ *n, pl* **lisente** – see *loti* at MONEY table [of Bantu origin]

**lisle** /liel/ *adj or n* (of or being) a smooth tightly twisted thread usu made of long-staple cotton 〈~ *stockings*〉 [*Lisle* (now *Lille*), city in N France]

**¹lisp** /lisp/ *vi* **1** to pronounce /s/ and /z/ imperfectly, esp by giving them the sounds of /th/ and /dh/ **2** to speak falteringly, childishly, or with a lisp ~ *vt* to utter falteringly or with a lisp [ME *lispen,* fr OE *-wlyspian;* akin to OHG *lispen* to lisp] – **lisper** *n*

**²lisp** *n* **1** a speech defect or affectation characterized by lisping **2** a sound resembling a lisp

**lissom, lissome** /'lis(ə)m/ *adj* easily flexed; lithe, nimble [alter. of *lithesome*] – **lissomely** *adv,* **lissomeness** *n*

**lissotrichous** /li'sotrikəs/ *adj* having straight smooth hair [deriv of Gk *lissos* smooth + *trich-, thrix* hair]

**¹list** /list/ *vb, archaic vt* to please, suit ~ *vi* to wish, choose [ME *lysten,* fr OE *lystan;* akin to OE *lust*]

**²list** *vb, archaic vi* to listen ~ *vt* to listen to [ME *listen,* fr OE *hlystan,* fr *hlyst* hearing, fr *hlysnan* to listen]

**³list** *n* **1a** a band or strip of material; *esp* a selvage **b** a dark line along the back of an animal (e g a horse) **2** *pl but taking sing or pl vb* **2a** (the fence surrounding) a TILTYARD **b** a scene of competition 〈*entered the political* ~*s in 1954*〉 [ME, fr OE *līste;* akin to OHG *līsta* edge, Albanian *leth*]

**⁴list** *vt* **1** to cut away a narrow strip (e g of sapwood) from the edge of (a board, plank, etc) **2** to prepare or plant (land) with ridges and furrows

**⁵list** *n* a roll or catalogue of words or numbers (e g representing people or objects belonging to a class) usu arranged in order, one beneath the other, so as to be easily found 〈*a guest* ~〉〈*a shopping* ~〉 – see also on the DANGER list [Fr *liste,* fr It *lista,* of Gmc origin; akin to OHG *līsta*]

**⁶list** *vt* **1a** to make a list of **b** to include on a list; register; *specif, Br* to include (a building) in an official list as being of architectural or historical importance and hence protected from demolition **2** to place (oneself) in a specified category 〈~s *himself as a political liberal*〉 **3** to enter in a catalogue with a selling price 〈*a car* ~ed *at £5000*〉 **4** *archaic* to recruit ~ *vi, archaic* to enlist

**⁷list** *vb* to (cause to) lean to one side; tilt 〈*the ship was* ~ing *badly*〉 [origin unknown] – **list** *n*

**¹listen** /'lis(ə)n/ *vi* **1** to pay attention to sound 〈~ *to music*〉 **2** to hear or consider with thoughtful attention; to heed 〈~ *to a plea*〉 **3** to be alert to catch an expected sound 〈~ *for his step*〉 [ME *listnen,* fr OE *hlysnan;* akin to Skt *śroṣati* he hears, OE *hlūd* loud] – **listener** *n*

**listen in** *vi* to tune in to or monitor a broadcast – **listener-in** *n*

**²listen** *n, informal* an act of listening 〈*here, have a* ~〉

**listenable** /'lis(ə)nəbl/ *adj* agreeable to hear

**lister** /'listə/ *n* somebody who lists or catalogues

**listing** /'listing/ *n* **1** an act or instance of making or including in a list **2** something listed

**listless** /'listlis/ *adj* characterized by indifference, lack of energy, and disinclination for exertion; languid *synonyms* see LETHARGY [ME *listles,* fr *list* inclination, desire (prob fr *lysten, listen* to please) + *-les* -less – more at ¹LIST] – **listlessly** *adv,* **listlessness** *n*

**list price** *n* the basic price of an item as published in a catalogue, price list, or advertisement but subject to discounts (e g trade or quantity discounts)

**lit** /lit/ *past of* LIGHT

**litany** /'lit(ə)n·i/ *n* **1** a prayer consisting of a series of petitions by the leader (e g the minister) with alternate responses by the congregation **2** *cap* a prayer consisting of set petitions and responses which is included in the Anglican Book of Common Prayer – usu + *the* △ liturgy [ME *letanie,* fr OF, fr LL *litania,* fr LGk *litaneia,* fr Gk, entreaty, fr *litanos* entreating; akin to OE *līm* lime]

**litchi, lichee, lychee** /'liechee, -'-/ *n* a small oval fruit that has

a hard scaly outer covering and a small hard seed surrounded by edible pulp and that is firm, sweetish, and black when dried, and soft, white, and fragrant when tinned; *also* a Chinese tree (*Litchi chinensis* of the family Sapindaceae) that bears litchis [Chin (Pek) *lìzhī* (*li⁴ chih¹*)]

**lit crit** /ˌlit 'krit/ *n, informal* literary criticism 〈*knows every* ~ *cliché in the book* – R A Sokolov〉

**-lite** /-liet/ *comb form* (→ *n*) mineral 〈*rhodolite*〉; rock 〈*aerolite*〉; fossil 〈*ichnolite*〉 [Fr, alter. of *-lithe,* fr Gk *lithos* stone]

**liter** /'leetə/ *n, NAm* a litre

**literacy** /'lit(ə)rəsi/ *n* the quality or state of being literate

**¹literal** /'lit(ə)rəl/ *adj* **1a** according with the exact letter of a written text; *specif* according with the letter of the scriptures **b** following the usual meaning of a specified term or expression; having no embellishment (e g metaphor or allegory) 〈*freedom in the* ~ *sense is an impossibility*〉 – often used, though with the disapproval of some speakers, to stress the aptness of a metaphor 〈*a* ~ *mountain of correspondence*〉 **c** characterized by a lack of imagination; prosaic 〈*a very* ~ *man*〉 **2** of or expressed in letters **3** reproduced word for word; exact, verbatim 〈*a* ~ *translation*〉 [ME, fr MF, fr ML *litteralis, literalis,* fr L, of a letter, fr *littera, litera* letter] – **literalness** *n,* **literality** *n*

**²literal** *n* a misprint usu involving a single letter

**literalism** /'litrəliz(ə)m/ *n* the rejection of allegorical or metaphysical interpretations of esp biblical texts – **literalist** *n,* **literalistic** *adj*

**literally** /'litrəli/ *adv* **1** in the literal sense; without metaphor or exaggeration **2** with exact equivalence; verbatim 〈*follow the instructions* ~〉 **3** – used to intensify a metaphorical or hyperbolic expression 〈*she was* ~ *tearing her hair out*〉; disapproved of by some speakers

**literary** /'lit(ə)rəri/ *adj* **1a** of, being, or about literature 〈~ *criticism*〉 **b** characteristic of or being in a formal, rather than colloquial, style **2a** well-read **b** producing, well versed in, or connected with literature 〈*Disraeli was a* ~ *as well as a political figure*〉 – **literarily** *adv,* **literariness** *n*

**literary executor** *n* a person entrusted with the management of the papers and unpublished works of a deceased author

**¹literate** /'lit(ə)rət/ *adj* **1a** educated, cultured **b** able to read and write **2** versed in literature or creative writing [ME *literat,* fr L *litteratus* marked with letters, literate, fr *litterae* letters, literature, fr pl of *littera*] – **literately** *adv,* **literateness** *n*

**²literate** *n* **1** an educated person **2** somebody who can read and write

**literati** /ˌlitə'rahti/ *n pl* **1** the educated class; the intelligentsia **2** scholars and authors [obs It *litterati,* fr L, pl of *litteratus*]

**literatim** /ˌlitə'rahtim/ *adv or adj* letter for letter 〈*copied* ~ *from the manuscript*〉 [ML, fr L *littera*]

**literation** /ˌlitə'raysh(ə)n/ *n* the representation of sounds or words by letters [L *littera* + E *-ation*]

**literature** /'lit(ə)rəchə/ *n* **1** the production of literary work esp as an occupation **2a** writings in prose or verse; *esp* writings having excellence of form or style and expressing ideas of permanent or universal interest **b** the body of writings on a particular subject or of a particular culture or language 〈*scientific* ~〉〈*French* ~〉 **c** printed matter (e g leaflets giving information) 〈*campaign* ~〉 **3** the aggregate of musical compositions 〈*the piano* ~ *of Brahms*〉 **4** *archaic* literary culture

**lith-** /lith-/, **litho-** *comb form* **1** stone 〈*lithograph*〉〈*lithotomy*〉 **2** lithium 〈*lithic*〉 [(1) L, fr Gk, fr *lithos;* (2) NL *lithium*]

**-lith** /-lith/ *comb form* (→ *n*) **1a** structure or implement of stone 〈*megalith*〉〈*eolith*〉 **b** artificial stone 〈*granolith*〉 **2** stone in (a specified body cavity) 〈*urolith*〉 **3** -lite 〈*laccolith*〉 [NL *-lithus* & Fr *-lithe,* fr Gk *lithos*]

**litharge** /'lithahj/ *n* a LEAD MONOXIDE, PbO, used in making rubber, paint, etc – compare MASSICOT [ME, fr MF, fr L *lithargyrus,* fr Gk *lithargyros,* fr *lithos* + *argyros* silver – more at ARGENT]

**lithe** /liedh/ *adj* **1** easily bent or flexed 〈*a* ~ *plant stem*〉 **2** marked by graceful suppleness 〈*a* ~ *dancer*〉〈*treading with a* ~ *silent step*〉 [ME, fr OE *līthe* gentle; akin to OHG *lindi* gentle, L *lentus* slow] – **lithely** *adv,* **litheness** *n*

**lithesome** /'liedhs(ə)m/ *adj* lissom

**lithia** /'lithi·ə/ *n* a white oxide of lithium, Li₂O, used for absorbing CARBON DIOXIDE and water vapour [NL, fr Gk *lithos*]

**lithiasis** /li'thie·əsis/ *n, pl* **lithiases** /-seez/ the formation of CALCULI (stones) in the body (e g in the gall bladder or kidney) [NL, fr Gk, fr *lithos*]

**lithia water** *n* a mineral water containing lithium salts

**lithic** /'lithik/ *adj* **1** (made) of stone **2** of lithium – **lithically** *adv*

**-lithic** /-'lithik/ *comb form* (→ *adj*) relating to or characteristic of (a specified stage) in the use by human beings of stone implements ⟨*Neolithic*⟩

**lithium** /'lithi-əm/ *n* **1** a soft silver-white chemical element of the ALKALI METAL group that is the lightest metal known and that is used esp in nuclear reactions, in batteries, and in metallurgy **2** the lithium ION when used, esp in the form of LITHIUM CARBONATE, in the treatment of manic-depressive conditions [NL, fr *lithia*]

**lithium carbonate** *n* a chemical compound, $Li_2CO_3$, used in the glass and ceramic industries and medically to treat manic-depressive conditions

**lithium fluoride** *n* a white chemical compound, LiF, used esp in making prisms and ceramics and as a FLUX (substance promoting fusion of metals or minerals)

**litho** /'liethoh/ *n, pl* **lithos 1** a lithograph **2** lithography

¹**lithograph** /'lithə,grahf, -,graf/ *vt* to produce, copy, or portray by lithography – **lithographer** *n*

²**lithograph** *n* a print made by lithography – **lithographic** *adj*, **lithographically** *adv*

**lithography** /li'thogrəfi/ *n* **1** the process of printing from a flat surface (eg a smooth stone or metal plate) on which the image to be printed is ink-receptive and the blank area ink-repellent **2** PLANOGRAPHY (printing from a flat surface) [Ger *lithographie*, fr *lith-* + *-graphie* -graphy]

**lithoid** /'lithoyd/, **lithoidal** /li'thoydl/ *adj* of or resembling stone or rock

**lithology** /li'tholəji/ *n* **1** the study of rocks **2** the character (eg the composition or shape) of a rock (formation) – **lithologic** *also* **lithological** *adj*, **lithologically** *adv*

**lithophyte** /'lithə,fiet/ *n* **1** a living organism (eg a coral) having a hard stony structure or skeleton **2** a plant that grows on rock [Fr, fr *lith-* + *-phyte*] – **lithophytic** *adj*

**lithopone** /'lithə,pohn/ *n* a white pigment consisting essentially of the chemical compounds ZINC SULPHIDE and BARIUM SULPHATE [ISV *lith-* + Gk *ponos* work]

**lithosol** /'lithəsol/ *n, chiefly NAm* a shallow soil overlying rocks [*lith-* + L *solum* soil]

**lithosphere** /'lithə,sfiə/ *n* the solid crust of the earth or another celestial body, composed of rock essentially like that exposed at the surface and usu considered to be about 80 kilometres (50 miles) in thickness [ISV]

**lithotomy** /li'thotəmi/ *n* surgical incision of the bladder for removal of a stone [LL *lithotomia*, fr Gk, fr *lithotomein* to perform a lithotomy, fr *lith-* + *temnein* to cut – more at TOME]

**lithotrity** /li'thotrəti/ *n* the surgical process of crushing a stone in the bladder so that it may be passed easily through the URETHRA (tube carrying urine to the exterior) [deriv of Gk *lithōn thyrptikos* stone-crushing]

**Lithuanian** /,lithyoo'aynyən, -ni-ən/ *n* **1** a native or inhabitant of Lithuania **2** the Baltic language of the Lithuanians [*Lithuania*, country in NE Europe (now a republic of the USSR)] – **Lithuanian** *adj*

**litigant** /'litigənt/ *n* a person engaged in a lawsuit – **litigant** *adj*

**litigate** /'litigayt/ *vi* to carry on a lawsuit ~ *vt* to contest (an issue) at law [L *litigatus*, pp of *litigare*, fr *lit-*, *lis* lawsuit + *agere* to drive – more at AGENT] – **litigable** *adj*, **litigation** *n*

**litigious** /li'tijəs/ *adj* **1** eager or prone to engage in lawsuits **2** subject to litigation **3** *formal* disputatious, contentious [ME, fr MF *litigieux*, fr L *litigiosus*, fr *litigium* dispute, fr *litigare*] – **litigiously** *adv*, **litigiousness** *n*

**litmus** /'litməs/ *n* a colouring matter from lichens that turns red in acid solutions and blue in alkaline solutions and is used as an acid-alkali indicator [of Scand origin; akin to ON *litmosi* herbs used in dyeing, fr *litr* colour (akin to OHG ant*lizzi* face) + *mosi* moss (akin to OE *mōs* moss)]

**litmus paper** *n* absorbent paper coloured with litmus and used as an indicator to determine whether a mixture is acid or alkaline

**litotes** /'lietə,teez, 'li-, lie'tohteez/ *n, pl* **litotes** /~/ understatement, esp when used for literary effect, in which an affirmative is expressed by the negative of its opposite (eg in "not a bad singer", "they were not a little drunk") [Gk *litotēs*, fr *litos* simple; akin to Gk *leios* smooth – more at LIME]

**litre**, *NAm chiefly* **liter** /'leetə/ *n* a metric unit of capacity used as a standard in Britain and equal to 1.000028 cubic decimetres (0.219975 gallon) [Fr *litre*, fr ML *litra*, a measure, fr Gk, a weight]

¹**litter** /'litə/ *n* **1a** a covered and curtained couch provided with

shafts and carried by people or animals **b** a stretcher or other device for carrying a sick or injured person **2a** material used as bedding for animals **b** the uppermost slightly decayed layer of organic matter (eg leaves or pine needles) on the forest floor **3** *taking sing or pl vb* a group of offspring of an animal, born at one birth **4a** rubbish or waste products, esp in a public place **b** an untidy accumulation of objects (eg papers) [ME, fr OF *litiere*, fr *lit* bed, fr L *lectus* – more at LIE] – **littery** *adj*

²**litter** *vt* **1a** to provide (eg a horse) with litter as a bed **b** to spread litter or straw on **2** to give birth to (young) **3a** to strew with scattered articles **b** to scatter about in disorder ~ *vi* **1** to give birth to a litter **2** to strew litter

**litterae humaniores** /,litəri hyooh,mani'awreez/ *n pl* **1** the classics as a university subject **2** *chiefly NAm* the humanities [ML, lit., more humane letters]

**litterateur** *also* **littérateur** /,litərə'tuh (*Fr* literatœ:r)/ *n* a literary man; *esp* a professional writer [Fr *littérateur*, fr L *litterator* critic, fr *litteratus* literate]

**litter bin** *n, chiefly Br* a bin or basket in a public place for litter to be placed in

**litterbug** /'litə,bug/ *n, NAm* a litterlout

**litterer** /'litərə/ *n* a litterlout

**litterlout** /'litə,lowt/ *n, informal* somebody who litters a public area

**littermate** /'litə,mayt/ *n* any of the offspring in a litter in relation to the others; a sibling

¹**little** /'litl/ *adj* **littler**, (2a) **less** /les/, (1b, 1d, 1e) **lesser** /'lesə/; **littlest**, (1b&2a) **least** /leest/ **1** not big: eg **1a** small in size or extent; tiny ⟨*his* ~ *feet*⟩ **b** *of a plant or animal* small in comparison with related forms – used in vernacular names ⟨~ *owl*⟩ **c** small in number **d** small in condition, distinction, or scope ⟨~ *men with big ambitions*⟩ **e** narrow, mean ⟨*the pettiness of* ~ *minds*⟩ **f** pleasingly small ⟨*he's a cute* ~ *thing*⟩ **2a** amounting to only a small quantity; not much ⟨*had* ~ *or no time*⟩ ⟨*unfortunately he has* ~ *money*⟩ **b** at least some though not much – + *a* ⟨*fortunately he had a* ~ *money in the bank*⟩ **3** small in importance or interest; trivial □ the comparative and superlative forms **littler** and **littlest** are used esp (as if) by or to children *synonyms* see ¹SMALL [ME *littel*, fr OE *lytel*; akin to OHG *luzzil* little, Lith *liūsti* to be sad] – **littleness** *n*

²**little** *adv* **less** /les/; **least** /leest/ **1** to no great degree or extent; not much – often in combination ⟨*little-known*⟩ **2** not at all ⟨~ *does he care*⟩ **3** rarely, infrequently – **little by little** by small degrees or amounts; gradually

³**little** *n* **1a** only a small portion or quantity; not much ⟨*understood* ~ *of his speech*⟩ ⟨*there is very* ~ *to spare*⟩ ⟨*do what* ~ *I can*⟩ **b** at least some though not much – + *a* ⟨*have a* ~ *of this cake*⟩ **2** a short time or distance ⟨*walk for a* ~⟩ – **a little** somewhat, rather ⟨*a little over 50 years*⟩ ⟨*found the play a little boring*⟩ – **in little** on a small scale; *esp* in miniature – **make little of 1** to disparage **2** to understand only partially

**little auk** *n* a small short-billed AUK (diving seabird) (*Plautus alle*) that breeds on arctic coasts and migrates south in winter

**Little Bear** *n* URSA MINOR

**Little Dipper** /'dipə/ *n, chiefly NAm* URSA MINOR

**little end** *n, Br* the smaller end of a CONNECTING ROD in an engine operated by pistons – compare BIG END

**little englander** /'ingləndə/ *n, often cap L&E* an opponent of the territorial expansion of the British Empire, esp in the 19th century

**little finger** *n* the fourth and smallest finger of the hand, counting the index finger as the first

'**little-,go** *n* a former preliminary examination for the Cambridge BA degree

**little grebe** *n* a common small red-necked African and Eurasian GREBE (diving bird) (*Tachybaptus ruficollis*) – called also DABCHICK

**Little Hours** *n pl* the offices of PRIME, TERCE, SEXT, and NONE forming part of the CANONICAL HOURS of the Roman Catholic church

**little leaf** *n* any of several plant disorders characterized by small and often discoloured and distorted leaves

**Little League** *n* a commercially sponsored N American baseball league for boys from 8 to 12 years old – **Little Leaguer** *n*

**little magazine** *n* a small usu noncommercial literary magazine publishing esp experimental writing appealing to a relatively limited number of readers

**Little Office** *n* an OFFICE (series of psalms and prayers) in honour of the Virgin Mary like but shorter than the Divine Office of the Roman Catholic church

**little owl** *n* an African and Eurasian partly DIURNAL (active in daytime) insect-eating owl (*Athene noctua*) that is distinguished by its small size, yellow eyes, speckled plumage, and squat flat-headed appearance

**little people** *n pl* the tiny imaginary beings (e g fairies, elves, and esp leprechauns) of folklore

**Little Russian** *n* a member of the Slavonic-speaking peoples of the southern and southwestern USSR – **Little Russian** *adj*

**little slam** *n* (the fulfilling of) a contract to win all but one of the tricks in one hand of a card game, specif bridge – called also SMALL SLAM; compare GRAND SLAM

**little tern** *n* a very small widely distributed tern (*Sterna albifrons*) breeding on sand banks and beaches, and now much reduced in numbers in Britain

**little toe** *n* the outermost and smallest toe of the foot

**little woman** *n, humorous & often derog* one's wife

¹**littoral** /'litərəl/ *adj* of, situated, or growing on or near a (sea) shore △ literal [L *litoralis*, fr *litor-, litus* seashore]

²**littoral** *n* a coastal region; *esp* the shore zone between high and low watermarks

**lit up** *adj, slang* drunk

**liturgical** /li'tuhjikl/ *adj* 1 (having the characteristics) of liturgy 2 using or favouring the use of liturgy ⟨~ *churches*⟩ – **liturgically** *adv*

**liturgics** /li'tuhjiks/ *n taking sing or pl vb* the practice or study of formal public worship

**liturgiology** /li,tuhji'oləji/ *n* the study of formal public worship – **liturgiologist** *n*

**liturgist** /'litəjist/ *n* 1 a person who follows, compiles, or leads a liturgy 2 a specialist in liturgiology

**liturgy** /'litəji/ *n* 1 *often cap* the form of service used in the celebration of Communion, esp in the Orthodox church 2 a prescribed form of public worship △ litany [LL *liturgia*, fr Gk *leitourgia*, fr (assumed) Gk (Attic) *leitos* public (fr Gk *laos* – Attic *leōs* – people) + *-ourgia* -urgy]

**livable** *also* **liveable** /'livəbl/ *adj* 1 suitable for living in or with 2 endurable – **livableness** *n*

¹**live** /liv/ *vi* 1 to be alive; have the life of an animal or plant 2 to continue alive ⟨*will he* ~, *doctor?*⟩ 3 to maintain oneself; subsist ⟨~ *by enthusiasm*⟩ 4 to conduct or pass one's life ⟨~d *only for his work*⟩ 5 to occupy a home; dwell ⟨living *in a shabby room*⟩ ⟨*they had always* ~d *in the country*⟩ 6 to attain eternal life ⟨*though he were dead, yet shall he* ~ – Jn 11:25 (AV)⟩ 7 to remain in human memory or record 8 to have a life rich in experience ⟨*during his time in China he really* ~d⟩ 9 to co-habit – + *together* or *with* 10 *chiefly Br informal* to be found in a specified place, esp normally or usually ⟨*a big freezer that* ~s *elsewhere – Doing Up Your Home*⟩ ~ *vt* 1 to pass, spend, or experience ⟨*she* ~d *three years as a nun*⟩ 2 to enact, practise ⟨~ *a lie*⟩ 3 to exhibit vigour, gusto, or enthusiasm in ⟨~d *life to the fullest*⟩ [ME *liven*, fr OE *libban*; akin to OHG *lebēn* to live, L *caelebs* unmarried] – **live it up** *informal* to enjoy an exciting or extravagant social life or social occasion ⟨lived it up *with wine and song – Newsweek*⟩ – see also **live in** SIN

**live down** *vt* to cause (e g a crime or mistake) to be forgotten, esp by subsequent good behaviour ⟨*made a mistake and couldn't* live it down⟩

**live in** *vi, esp of a servant* to live in one's place of employment

**live out** *vi, esp of a servant* to live outside one's place of employment ~ *vt* to live till the end of ⟨*will the sick man* live out *the month?*⟩; *also* to live longer than ⟨*will communism* live *capitalism* out?⟩

**live up to** *vt* to act or be in accordance with (esp a standard expected by somebody)

²**live** /liev/ *adj* 1 having life; living 2a abounding with life; vivid **b** containing living organisms; unsterilized ⟨~ *yoghurt*⟩ 3 exerting force or containing energy: e g **3a** afire, glowing ⟨~ *coals*⟩ **b** connected to electric power **c** charged with explosives and containing shot or a bullet ⟨~ *ammunition*⟩; *also* unexploded ⟨*a* ~ *bomb*⟩ **d** driven by or imparting motion or power **e** *of a nuclear reactor or nuclear bomb* charged with material capable of undergoing FISSION 4 of continuing or current interest ⟨~ *issues*⟩ 5 *esp of a rock* in a pure native state; *specif* not quarried or cut 6 in play in a game ⟨*a* ~ *ball*⟩ **7a** not yet printed from or plated ⟨~ *type*⟩ **b** not yet typeset ⟨~ *copy*⟩ **8a** of or involving the actual presence or participation of real people ⟨*a* ~ *audience*⟩ ⟨~ *music*⟩ **b** broadcast while happening; not prerecorded ⟨*a* ~ *television programme*⟩ [short for *alive*]

³**live** /liev/ *adv* during, from, or at a live production ⟨*the Wedding was seen* ~ *by millions throughout the world*⟩ ⟨*appearing* ~ *every Tuesday*⟩

¹**livebait** /,liev'bayt/ *n* fishing bait that is alive

²**livebait** *vi* to fish using livebait

¹**live-,bearer** *n* a fish that brings forth living young rather than eggs

,**live-'bearing** /liev/ *adj* VIVIPAROUS (producing live young)

,**live-,born** /liev/ *adj* born alive – compare STILLBORN

**-lived** /-livd/ *comb form* (→ *adj*) having a life of (a specified kind or length) ⟨*long*-lived⟩ [ME, fr *lif* life]

,**live-'in** /liv/ *adj* 1 living in one's place of employment ⟨*a* ~ *maid*⟩ 2 living with another in his/her home ⟨*her* ~ *lover*⟩

**livelihood** /'livli,hood/ *n* a means of support or sustenance [alter. of ME *livelode* course of life, fr OE *līflād*, fr *līf* + *lād* course – more at LODE]

**live load** *n* a variable load or force on a structure (e g moving traffic on a bridge) – compare DEAD LOAD

**livelong** /'liv,long/ *adj, chiefly poetic* whole, entire ⟨*the* ~ *day*⟩ – compare LIFELONG [ME *lef long*, fr *lef* dear + *long* – more at LIEF]

**lively** /'lievli/ *adj* 1 briskly alert and energetic; vigorous, animated ⟨*a* ~ *discussion*⟩ ⟨~ *children racing home from school*⟩ 2 active, keen ⟨*takes a* ~ *interest in the people around her*⟩ 3 brilliant, vivid ⟨*a* ~ *flashing wit*⟩ ⟨*a* ~ *colour*⟩ 4 imparting spirit or vivacity; stimulating ⟨*many a peer of England brews* livelier *liquor than the Muse* – A E Housman⟩ 5 quick to rebound; resilient 6 responding readily to the helm ⟨*a* ~ *boat*⟩ 7 full of life, movement, or incident ⟨*the crowded streets made a* ~ *scene*⟩ 8 *humorous* full of possibly disagreeable or dangerous action; eventful ⟨*given a* ~ *time by enemy artillery*⟩ [ME, fr OE *līflīc*, fr *līf* life] – **livelily** *adv*, **liveliness** *n*, **lively** *adv*

**synonyms** Active, lively, energetic, strenuous, vigorous, and dynamic all describe the application of strength or vitality to human activity. Active stresses movement and lack of rest ⟨*an* **active** *life*⟩ ⟨*an* **active** *mind*⟩. Lively is an approving synonym of **active** – it suggests the vitality and animation connected with being fully alive. Energetic may apply to people or their activities; it suggests intense or enthusiastic effort, not necessarily crowned with success ⟨*in spite of their* **energetic** *attempts to free the rope, it would not budge*⟩. Strenuous is also often used to describe effort, and adds to **energetic** a sense of either urgency ⟨**strenuous** *attempts to close the gates before the mob arrived*⟩, or sustained effort ⟨*the* **strenuous** *life of a pioneer*⟩. Vigorous stresses strength and capacity ⟨*her* **vigorous** *mind made her well able to hold her own in debates*⟩. Dynamic adds a suggestion of machine-like drive which evokes admiration ⟨*a* **dynamic** *go-getter who will get the company back on its feet*⟩. See BUSY **antonyms** sluggish, torpid

**liven** /'liev(ə)n/ *vb* to make or become lively – often + *up*

**live oak** /liev/ *n* any of several N American evergreen oaks; *esp* one (*Quercus virginia*) often cultivated for its very tough durable wood that is used in shipbuilding

¹**liver** /'livə/ *n* **1a** a large glandular highly VASCULAR (well supplied with blood vessels) organ of VERTEBRATE animals that secretes bile and causes important changes in many of the substances contained in the blood (e g by converting blood sugar into GLYCOGEN which it stores until required, and by forming UREA for the excretion of poisonous waste materials) **b** any of various large compound glands associated with the digestive system of INVERTEBRATE animals and probably concerned with the secretion of digestive ENZYMES 2 the liver of an animal (e g a calf or pig) eaten as food 3 a greyish reddish brown colour; maroon ⟨*a white dog with* ~ *spots*⟩ 4 *archaic* the liver considered as the seat of emotions or character traits [ME, fr OE *lifer*; akin to OHG *lebra* liver]

²**liver** *n* somebody who lives, esp in a specified way ⟨*a clean* ~⟩

**liver fluke** *n* any of various parasitic flatworms (e g *Fasciola hepatica*) that invade and damage the liver of mammals, esp sheep

**liveried** /'livərid/ *adj* wearing a livery ⟨*a* ~ *chauffeur*⟩

**liverish** /'livərish/ *adj* 1 suffering from liver disorder; bilious 2 peevish, irascible; *also* glum – **liverishness** *n*

**liver of sulphur** *n* a mixture of sulphur-containing potassium compounds used in the treatment of skin diseases [¹*liver* 3]

**Liverpudlian** /,livə'pudli‧ən/ *n* 1 a native or inhabitant of Liverpool 2 *informal* the dialect of Liverpool [*Liverpudl*- (alter. - influenced by *puddle* - of *Liverpool*, city in England) + E *-ian*] – **Liverpudlian** *adj*

**liver sausage** *n* a sausage consisting chiefly of cooked minced liver, often with pork trimmings

**liverwort** /-,wuht/ *n* 1 a BRYOPHYTE (type of simple plant) of a class (Hepaticae) related to and resembling the mosses but differing in reproduction and development 2 HEPATICA (plant of the buttercup family) [fr its liver-like lobed leaves & former reputation as a cure for liver ailments]

**liverwurst** /'livə,vooəst, -,vuhst/ *n* LIVER SAUSAGE [part trans of Ger *leberwurst*, fr *leber* liver + *wurst* sausage]

¹**livery** /'livəri/ *n* 1a the distinctive clothing worn by a member of a livery company or guild b the uniform of servants employed by an individual or a single household c distinctive colouring or marking d distinctive dress; garb e a distinctive colour scheme (eg on aircraft or trains) distinguishing the operating company 2 the feeding, stabling, and care of horses for pay – usu + *at* ⟨*three horses at* ~⟩ 3 the former act or method of delivering or transferring legal possession of property, esp freehold land 4 chiefly *NAm* LIVERY STABLE 5 archaic the provision of food and clothing to servants or retainers 6 taking *sing or pl vb, archaic* the members of a British livery company [ME, fr OF *livree*, lit., delivery, fr *livrer* to deliver, fr L *liberare* to free – more at LIBERATE]

²**livery** *adj* 1 resembling liver (eg in colour or texture) 2 liverish

**livery company** *n* any of various London craft or trade associations that are descended from medieval guilds and formerly wore distinctive livery

**liveryman** /'livərimən/ *n* a freeman of the City of London who is a member of a LIVERY COMPANY

**livery stable** *n* a stable where horses and vehicles are kept for hire; *also* an establishment where horses are stabled and fed for their owners

**lives** /lievz/ *pl of* LIFE

**live steam** /liev/ *n* steam direct from a boiler and under full pressure

**livestock** /'liev,stok/ *n* taking *sing or pl vb* 1 animals kept or raised for use or pleasure; *esp* farm animals kept for use and profit 2 *Br humorous* small verminous creatures (eg lice or fleas)

**live trap** *n* a trap for catching an animal alive and uninjured – **livetrap** *vt*

**live wire** /'liev/ *n, informal* an alert, active, or aggressive person

**liveyer** /'livyə/ *n, Can* a permanent resident, esp on the Labrador coast, as opposed to a visiting fisherman [prob alter. of *live here*]

**livid** /'livid/ *adj* 1 discoloured by bruising; black-and-blue 2 ashen, pallid ⟨*this cross, thy* ~ *face, thy pierced hands and feet* – Walt Whitman⟩ 3 reddish ⟨*a fan of gladiolas blushed* ~ *under the electric letters* – Truman Capote⟩ 4 *informal* very angry; enraged ⟨*was* ~ *at his son's disobedience*⟩ **synonyms** see ¹ANGER [Fr *livide*, fr L *lividus*, fr *livēre* to be blue; akin to OE *slāh* sloe, Russ *sliva* plum] – **lividness** *n*, **lividity** *n*

¹**living** /'living/ *adj* 1a having life; alive b existing in use ⟨~ *languages*⟩ 2a exhibiting the life or motion of nature; natural ⟨*the forest is a* ~ *museum of ecology*⟩ b ²LIVE 3a 3 of feelings, ideas, *etc* 3a full of life or vigour ⟨*made mathematics a* ~ *subject*⟩ b true to life; vivid ⟨*the programme was televised in* ~ *colour*⟩ 4 suited for living ⟨*the* ~ *area*⟩ 5 involving living people 6 *informal* – used as an intensive ⟨*scared the* ~ *daylights out of him*⟩ [fr prp of ¹*live*; (4) fr gerund of ¹*live*] – **livingness** *n*

²**living** *n* 1 the condition of being alive 2 a manner of life 3a means of subsistence; a livelihood ⟨*earning a* ~⟩ b *Br* BENEFICE 1 c archaic an estate, property

**living death** *n* a life so full of misery that it is worse than being dead

**living fossil** *n* an organism (eg a HORSESHOE CRAB or a coelacanth fish) that has remained essentially unchanged from earlier geological times and whose close relatives are usu extinct

**living room** *n* a room in a residence used for the common social activities of the occupants **synonyms** see SITTING ROOM

**living space** *n* LEBENSRAUM

**living standard** *n* STANDARD OF LIVING

**living unit** *n, formal* a flat or house for use by one family

**living wage** *n* 1 a subsistence wage 2 a wage sufficient to provide the necessities and comforts essential to an acceptable STANDARD OF LIVING

**livre** /'leevrə, (*Fr* livr)/ *n* (a coin representing) a former French monetary unit worth 20 SOLS [Fr, fr L *libra*, a unit of weight]

**lixiviate** /lik'siviayt/ *vt* to extract a soluble constituent from (a solid mixture) by washing or percolation; leach [LL *lixivium* lye, fr L *lixivius* made of lye, fr *lixa* lye – more at LIQUID] – **lixiviation** *n*

**lizard** /'lizəd/ *n* 1 any of a suborder (Lacertilia) of reptiles distinguished from the snakes by a solid inseparable lower jaw, two pairs of well differentiated functional legs which may be lacking in burrowing forms, external ears, and eyes with movable lids 2 the skin of a lizard used to make shoes, handbags, etc [ME *liserd*, fr MF *laisarde*, fr L *lacerta*; akin to L *lacertus* muscle – more at LEG] – **lizard** *adj*

'**ll** /-l/ *vb* will, shall ⟨*you'll be late*⟩ **usage** see SHALL

**llama** /'lahmə/ *n* 1 any of several wild and domesticated S American cud-chewing mammals (genus *Lama*) related to the camels but smaller and without a hump; *esp* the domesticated GUANACO used in the Andes as a beast of burden and a source of wool 2 cloth made from the hair of the llama ⚠ lama [Sp, fr Quechua]

**llano** /'l(y)ahnoh/ *n, pl* llanos an open grassy plain in Spanish America or the southwestern USA [Sp, plain, fr L *planum* – more at PLAIN]

**Lloyd's** /loydz/ *n* taking *sing or pl vb* an association of underwriters in London specializing in marine insurance and shipping news and insuring against losses of almost every kind [Edward *Lloyd* † *ab* 1730 E coffee-house keeper whose premises in London became the centre of shipbroking & marine insurance business]

**lo** /loh/ *interj, archaic* – used to call attention or to express wonder or surprise [ME, fr OE *lā*]

**loach** /lohch/ *n* any of a family (Cobitidae) of small African and Eurasian freshwater fishes related to the carps and having a long slender body and spines round the mouth [ME *loche*, fr MF]

¹**load** /lohd/ *n* 1a whatever is put on a man or pack animal to be carried; a pack b whatever is put in a ship or vehicle or aircraft for conveyance; a cargo; *esp* a quantity of material assembled or packed as a shipping unit c the quantity that can be carried at one time by a specified means; *esp* a measured quantity of a commodity fixed for each type of carrier – often in combination ⟨*a boat*load *of tourists*⟩ 2a a mass or weight supported by something ⟨*branches bent low by their* ~ *of fruit*⟩ b the forces to which a structure is subjected ⟨*the* ~ *on the vault*⟩ 3a a burden of responsibility, anxiety, etc ⟨*took a* ~ *off her mind*⟩ b a burdensome or laborious responsibility ⟨*always carried his share of the* ~⟩ 4a a charge for a firearm b the quantity of material loaded into a device at one time 5 external resistance overcome by a machine or other source of power 6a power consumed or required; *also, NAm* power output (eg of a power plant) b a device to which power is delivered 7a(1) the amount of work that a person carries or is expected to carry a(2) the amount of authorized work to be performed by a machine, group, department, or factory b the demand on the operating resources of a system (eg a telephone exchange or a refrigerating apparatus) 8 the decrease in capacity for survival of the average individual in a population due to the presence of harmful genes in the GENE POOL (whole body of genes in a population) ⟨*genetic* ~⟩ ⟨*mutational* ~⟩ 9 *informal* an intoxicating amount of alcohol 10 **loads** *pl, load informal* a large quantity or amount; a lot ⟨*there's* ~s *of room on the back seat*⟩ [ME *lod*, fr OE *lād* support, carrying – more at LODE] – **get a load of** *slang* to pay attention to – usu imper ⟨*get a load of this, everybody!*⟩

²**load** *vt* 1a to put a load in or on ⟨~ *a van with furniture*⟩ b to place in or on a means of conveyance ⟨~ *cargo*⟩ 2a to encumber or oppress with something heavy, laborious, or disheartening; burden ⟨*a company* ~ed *down with debts*⟩ b to place as a burden or obligation ⟨~ *more work on him*⟩ 3a to increase the weight of by adding something heavy b to add a conditioning substance (eg a mineral salt) to in order to give body c to add filler to (paper) d to weight or shape (dice) to fall unfairly e to cause to contain one-sided or prejudicial influences; bias f to cause to contain emotional associations or hidden implications ⟨*a* ~ed *statement*⟩ g to weight (eg a test) with factors influencing validity or outcome 4a to put a load or charge in (a device or piece of equipment) ⟨~ *a gun*⟩ b to place or insert as a load in a device or piece of equipment ⟨~ *film in a camera*⟩ 5 to alter (eg an alcoholic drink) by adding an adulterant or drug 6 to add loading to (an insurance premium) 7 *of one stage of an electrical circuit* to affect, often adversely (the output of a preceding stage) ~ *vi* 1 to receive a load 2 to put a load on or in a carrier, device, or container; *esp* to insert the charge or cartridge in the chamber of a firearm -- **loader** *n*

**load displacement** *n* the displacement of a fully loaded ship

**loaded** /'lohdid/ *adj* **1** *esp of a question, argument, etc* misleading, biassed **2** *informal* drunk **3** *informal* having a large amount of money

**loading** /'lohding/ *n* **1** a cargo, weight, or stress placed on something **2** an amount added (eg to the net premium in insurance) to represent business expenses, extra risks, or profit **3** material (eg china clay or size) used to load something; filler **4** *Austr* WEIGHTING (extra allowance)

**loading gauge** *n, Br* a railway warning device (eg a bar suspended over tracks at the regulation height) that shows how high a train may be loaded

**load line** *n* the line, esp the PLIMSOLL LINE, on the side of a ship indicating the maximum depth to which it should sink in the water when properly and safely loaded

**loads** /lohdz/ *adv, informal* very much ⟨*felt* ~ *better*⟩ [fr pl of ¹*load*]

**loadstar** /'lohd,stah/ *n* LODESTAR

**loadstone** /'lohd,stohn/ *n* LODESTONE

¹**loaf** /lohf/ *n, pl* **loaves** /lohvz/ **1** a mass of bread often having a regular shape and standard weight **2** a shaped or moulded often symmetrical mass of food (eg sugar or chopped cooked meat) ⟨*meat* ~⟩ **3** *Br slang* the head, brains – esp in *use one's loaf* [ME *lof*, fr OE *hlāf*; akin to OHG *hleib* loaf; (3) rhyming slang *loaf (of bread)* head]

²**loaf** *vi* to spend time in idleness [prob back-formation fr *loafer*]

**loafer** /'lohfə/ *n* **1** one who loafs; an idler **2** *chiefly NAm* a low leather shoe similar to a moccasin but with a broad flat heel [perh short for *landloafer*, fr Ger *landläufer* tramp, fr *land* + *läufer* runner; (2) fr *Loafer*, a trademark]

**loam** /lohm/ *n* **1** a mixture (eg for plastering) composed chiefly of moistened clay **2** ³SOIL 2a; *specif* crumbly soil consisting of a mixture of clay, silt, and sand [ME *lom*, fr OE *lām* clay; akin to OE *līm* lime] – **loamy** *adj*

¹**loan** /lohn/ *n* **1a** money lent at interest **b** something lent, usu for the borrower's temporary use **2** the grant of temporary use **3** a loanword [ME *lon*, fr ON *lān*; akin to OE *lǣn* loan, *lēon* to lend, L *linquere* to leave, Gk *leipein*]

²**loan** *vt, chiefly NAm or nonstandard* to grant a loan of, esp formally or for a long period ⟨*paintings* ~ed *to a public gallery*⟩ – **loanable** *adj*

    *usage* The verb **loan** should be avoided in formal British English, though it was once as correct as **lend** and is coming back under American influence. In American use, the participle **loaned**, with reference to material wealth or objects, is often preferred to **lent** ⟨*pictures* loaned *to the gallery*⟩.

**lo and behold** /loh/ *interj* – used to express wonder or surprise

**loaning** /'lohning/ *n, N Eng & Scot* **1** a lane **2** an open space for milking [ME *loning*, fr *lone*, alter. of *lane*]

**loan shark** *n, chiefly NAm informal* one who lends money to individuals at exorbitant rates of interest

**loan translation** *n* a word or phrase introduced into a language through translation of the constituents of a term in another language (eg *superman* from German *übermensch*) – called also CALQUE

**loanword** /-,wuhd/ *n* a word taken from another language and at least partly naturalized

**loath, loth** /lohth/ *also* **loathe** /lohdh/ *adj* unwilling *to* do something disliked; reluctant [ME *loth* loathsome, fr OE *lāth*; akin to OHG *leid* loathsome, OIr *liuss* aversion] – **loathness** *n*

    *usage* It is probably better to spell the adjective **loath** and to reserve the spelling **loathe** for the related verb.

**loathe** /lohdh/ *vt* to dislike greatly, often with disgust or intolerance; detest *synonyms* see ²HATE *antonym* dote on [ME *lothen*, fr OE *lāthian*, fr *lāth*] – **loather** *n*

**loathing** /'lohdhing/ *n* extreme disgust; detestation

¹**loathly** /'lohdhli/ *adj, poetic* loathsome

²**loathly** *adv* not willingly; reluctantly

**loathsome** /'lohdhs(ə)m, 'lohth-/ *adj* giving rise to loathing; disgusting [ME *lothsum*, fr *loth* evil, fr OE *lāth*, fr *lāth*, adj] – **loathsomely** *adv*, **loathsomeness** *n*

**loaves** /lohvz/ *pl of* LOAF

¹**lob** /lob/ *n, dial Br* a dull heavy person; a lout [prob of LG origin; akin to LG *lubbe* coarse person]

²**lob** *vb* **-bb-** *vt* **1** to throw, hit, or propel (eg a tennis ball) easily or in a high arc **2** to hit a lob against ⟨~bed *him as he came into the net*⟩ ~ *vi* **1** to move in an arc **2** to hit a ball easily in a high arc, esp in tennis or squash **3** *Austr* to

arrive ⟨*he* ~ bed *home at eight*⟩ [¹*lob* (in arch. sense, a loosely hanging object)]

³**lob** *n* a ball that is lobbed

**lob-, lobo-** *comb form* lobe ⟨*lobar*⟩ ⟨*lobotomy*⟩ [*lobe*]

**lobar** /'lohbə/ *adj* of or affecting a lobe

**lobate** /'lohbayt/ *also* **lobated** /-baytid/ *adj* **1** having or resembling a lobe or lobes **2** *of a bird* having separate fringed toes [NL *lobatus*, fr LL *lobus*] – **lobately** *adv*

**lobation** /loh'baysh(ə)n/ *n* **1a** the quality or state of being lobed **b** the formation of lobes or LOBULES (small lobes) **2a** a lobe **b** LOBULE

¹**lobby** /'lobi/ *n* **1** a porch or small entrance hall: eg **1a** an anteroom of a legislative chamber; *esp* either of two anterooms to which members of either of the Houses of Parliament go to vote during a division **b** *chiefly NAm* a large entrance hall serving as a foyer (eg in a hotel or theatre) **2** *taking sing or pl vb* a group of people who frequent a lobby; *esp* a group of people engaged in lobbying as representatives of a particular interest group [ML *lobium* gallery, of Gmc origin; akin to OHG *louba* porch (cf LODGE)]

²**lobby** *vi* to conduct activities aimed at influencing public officials, esp members of a legislative body (eg Members of Parliament), towards an action ~ *vt* **1** to promote (eg a project) or secure the passage of (eg legislation) by influencing public officials **2** to attempt to influence or sway (eg a member of a legislative body) towards an action – **lobbyer** *n*, **lobbyism** *n*, **lobbyist** *n*

**lobby correspondent** *n, Br* a parliamentary correspondent (eg of a newspaper) given information unofficially by Ministers, which may be used without naming the source

**lobe** /lohb/ *n* **1** a curved or rounded projection or division; *specif* a usu somewhat rounded projection or division of a body organ or part **2** an earlobe [MF, fr LL *lobus*, fr Gk *lobos* – more at SLEEP] – **lobed** *adj*

**lobectomy** /loh'bektəmi/ *n* the surgical removal of a lobe of an organ (eg a lung) or gland (eg the thyroid) [ISV]

**'lobe-,fin** *also* **lobe-finned fish** *n* any of a large group (Crossopterygii) of fishes (eg a LATIMERIA) that have paired fins resembling legs, that may be ancestral to the ground-living VERTEBRATE animals, and that are mostly extinct – **lobe-finned** *adj*

**lobelia** /loh'beelyə/ *n* **1** any of a genus (*Lobelia* of the family Lobeliaceae, the lobelia family) of widely distributed nonwoody plants often cultivated for their clusters of showy lipped blue flowers [NL, genus name, fr Matthias de *Lobel* †1616 Flem botanist]

**loblolly** /'lob,loli/ *n, dial* **1** a thick gruel – used esp by sailors **2** a lout **3** *NAm* a mire, mudhole [prob fr E dial. *lob* to boil + obs E dial. *lolly* broth]

**loblolly pine** *n* a pine (*Pinus taeda*) of the southern USA with flaky reddish bark, long needles in groups of three, and spiny tipped cones

**lobo** /'lohboh/ *n, pl* **lobos** *NAm* TIMBER WOLF [Sp, wolf, fr L *lupus* – more at WOLF]

**lobo-** – see LOB-

**lobotomy** /lə'botəmi, loh-/ *n* a brain operation used, esp formerly, in the treatment of some mental disorders (eg violent psychoses) in which nerve fibres in the CEREBRAL CORTEX (area of brain controlling higher thought ability), esp in the FRONTAL LOBES, are cut in order to change behaviour [ISV] – **lobotomize** *vt*

**lobscouse** /'lob,skows/ *n* a dish prepared by stewing or baking meat with vegetables and SHIP BISCUIT that was originally served to sailors [origin unknown]

**lobster** /'lobstə/ *n, pl* **lobsters**, *esp collectively* **lobster 1** any of a family (Homaridae, esp genus *Homarus* of the class Crustacea) of large edible 10-legged marine INVERTEBRATE animals that have stalked eyes, a pair of large claws, and a long abdomen and that include species from coasts on both sides of the N Atlantic **2** SPINY LOBSTER [ME, fr OE *loppestre*, modif (prob influenced by OE *loppe* spider) of L *locusta* crustacean, lobster]

**lobsterman** /'lobstəmən/ *n* one whose business is catching lobsters

**lobster pot** *n* (a round wicker basket with an inverted funnel in the top used as) a trap for catching lobsters

**lobulate** /'lobyoolayt/ *also* **lobulated** /-laytid/ *adj* made up of or having lobules ⟨*the pancreas is a* ~ *organ*⟩ – **lobulation** *n*

**lobule** /'lobyoohl/ *n* a small lobe; *also* a subdivision of a lobe – **lobulose** *adj*

**lobworm** /'lob,wuhm/ *n* a large earthworm used as bait by anglers; LUGWORM [¹*lob* + *worm*]

¹**local** /'lohk(ə)l/ *adj* **1** of or characterized by position in space **2** of, belonging to, or characteristic of a particular place; not general or widespread ⟨∼ *news*⟩ **3a** primarily serving the needs of a particular limited district ⟨∼ *government*⟩ **b** *of a public conveyance* making all the stops on a route **4** involving or affecting only a restricted part of a living organism ⟨∼ *anaesthetic*⟩ [ME *localle*, fr MF *local*, fr LL *localis*, fr L *locus* place – more at STALL] – **locally** *adv*

²**local** *n* a local person or thing ⟨*spoke to the friendly* ∼s⟩: eg **a** *Br* the neighbourhood pub **b** *chiefly NAm* a local public conveyance (eg a train or bus) **c** *NAm* a local or particular branch, lodge, or chapter of an organization; *esp* a union branch

**local authority** *n taking sing or pl vb* the body of both elected and salaried people who administer British LOCAL GOVERNMENT

**local colour** *n* vividness in writing derived from the presentation of the features and peculiarities of a particular locality and its inhabitants

**locale** /loh'kahl/ *n* a place or locality, esp when viewed in relation to a particular event or characteristic; a scene [modif of Fr *local*, fr *local*, adj]

**local education authority** *n taking sing or pl vb* the department of a British LOCAL AUTHORITY responsible for state education in the area

**local government** *n* the government of a specific local area constituting a subdivision of a major political unit (eg a nation or state)

**localism** /'lohk(ə)l,iz(ə)m/ *n* **1** affection or partiality for a particular place, esp to the exclusion of others **2** a local idiom or custom

**locality** /loh'kaləti/ *n* **1** the fact or condition of having a location in space or time **2** a particular place, situation, or location

**local-ize, -ise** /'lok(ə)l,iez/ *vt* **1** to give local characteristics to **2** to assign to or keep within a definite locality ∼ *vi* to collect in a specific or limited area – **localization** *n*

**local oscillator** *n* a device in certain radio receivers that generates a local signal (OSCILLATION) that is mixed with the incoming signal to produce an amplified and much improved output

**local time** *n* time based on the meridian through a particular place as contrasted with that of a TIME ZONE (area in which the time is standardized)

**locate** /loh'kayt/ *vi, NAm* to establish oneself or one's business; settle ∼ *vt* **1** to determine or indicate the place, site, or limits of **2** to set or establish in a particular spot **3** to find the location of ⟨*we eventually* ∼d *him in the pub*⟩ [L *locatus*, pp of *locare* to place, fr *locus*] – **locatable** *adj*, **locater** *n*

**location** /loh'kaysh(ə)n/ *n* **1** a particular place or position **2** a place outside a studio where a picture or part of it is filmed – usu in **on location 3** *Austr* a farm, station – **locational** *adj*, **locationally** *adv*

**locative** /'lokətiv/ *n* a grammatical case expressing place where or wherein; *also* a form in this case [L *locus* place + E *-ative* (as in *vocative*)] – **locative** *adj*

**loch** /lokh/ *n* **1a** a lake in Scotland **b** *Scot* a lake **2** a bay or arm of the sea off the Scottish coast, esp when nearly landlocked [ME (Sc) *louch*, fr ScGael *loch*; akin to L *lacus* lake]

**lochia** /'lokiə/ *n* a discharge of blood, mucus, etc, from the womb following childbirth and usu lasting several days or weeks [NL, fr Gk, fr neut pl of *lochios* of childbirth, fr *lochos* childbirth] – **lochial** *adj*

**lochside** /'lokh,sied/ *n* the shore of a loch

**loci** /'lohsi, -sie; *also* 'lohki, kie/ *pl of* LOCUS

¹**lock** /lok/ *n* **1a** a portion (eg a tuft, tress, or ringlet) of hair **b** *pl* the hair of the head **2** a bunch of wool, cotton, flax, etc; a tuft [ME *lok*, fr OE *locc*; akin to OHG *loc* lock, L *luctari* to struggle, *luxus* dislocated]

²**lock** *n* **1a** a fastening that can be opened and often closed only by means of a particular key or combination **b** a gunlock **c** a mechanism that can lock a part of a device in position **2a** an enclosed section of waterway (eg a canal) which has gates at each end and in which the water level can be varied to raise or lower boats from one level to another **b** AIR LOCK **3a** a locking or fastening together **b** a hold in wrestling secured on a usu specified part of the body; *broadly* any controlling hold **4** *chiefly Br* the (maximum) extent to which the front wheels of a vehicle are turned to change the direction of travel ⟨*from* ∼ *to* ∼ *is* 3⁵/₈ *turns of the steering wheel*⟩ [ME *lok*, fr OE *loc*; akin to OHG *loh* enclosure, OE *locc* lock of hair]

³**lock** *vt* **1a** to fasten the lock of **b** to make fast (as if) with a lock ⟨∼ *up the house*⟩ **2a** to shut in or out or make secure or inaccessible (as if) by means of locks ⟨∼ed *himself away from the curious world*⟩ ⟨∼ed *her husband out*⟩ **b** to hold fast or inactive; fix in a particular situation or method of operation ⟨*a team firmly* ∼ed *in last place*⟩ ⟨*afraid of being* ∼ed *into the system*⟩ **3a** to make fast by the interlacing or interlocking of parts **b** to hold in a close embrace **c** to grapple in combat; *also* to bind closely – often pass ⟨*administration and students were* ∼ed *in conflict*⟩ **d** to fasten (printing type, blocks, or plates) in a metal frame (⁵CHASE) or on the bed of a press by tightening the QUOINS; *also* to attach (a curved plate) to the plate cylinder of a rotary press – often + *up* **4** to invest (capital) without assurance of easy convertibility into money – often + *up* **5** to move or permit (a ship) to pass by raising or lowering in a lock ∼ *vi* **1** to interlace, interlock **2** to go or pass by means of a lock (eg in a canal) – **lockable** *adj*

**lock on** *vt* to sight and follow automatically by means of a radar beam or sensor – compare ACQUIRE 2

**lock out** *vt* to subject (a body of employees) to a lockout

**lockage** /'lokij/ *n* **1** an act or process of passing a ship through a lock **2** a system of locks **3** the tariff charged for passing through a lock

**locker** /'lokə/ *n* **1** a cupboard or compartment that may be closed with a lock; *esp* one for individual storage use in a cloakroom, CHANGING ROOM, etc **2** a chest or compartment on board ship in which articles are stowed **3** *NAm* a freezer; *esp* one rented in a shop or other establishment

**locker room** *n, chiefly NAm* CHANGING ROOM

**locket** /'lokit/ *n* a small case usu of precious metal that opens on a hinge, has space for a memento (eg a small picture or a lock of hair), and is usu worn on a chain round the neck [MF *loquet* latch, fr MD *loke*; akin to OE *loc*]

**lock forward** *n* either of two players positioned inside the second row of the scrum in rugby

**lockjaw** /'lok,jaw/ *n* an early symptom of a tetanus infection characterized by spasm of the jaw muscles and inability to open the jaws; *also* tetanus

**lockkeeper** /-,keepə/ *n* somebody who looks after and often lives next to a canal or river lock

**locknut** /-,nut/ *n* **1** a nut screwed hard up against another to prevent either of them from moving **2** a nut so constructed that it locks itself when screwed up tight

**lockout** /-,owt/ *n* the whole or partial closing of a business establishment by an employer in order to gain concessions from or resist demands of employees

**locksmith** /-,smith/ *n* somebody who makes or mends locks as an occupation – **locksmithing** *n*

**lockstep** /-,step/ *n* a mode of marching in step by a body of people going one after another as closely as possible

**lockstitch** /-,stich/ *n* a sewing machine stitch formed by the looping together of two threads, one on each side of the material being sewn – **lockstitch** *vb*

**lock, stock, and barrel** *adv* wholly, completely ⟨*the only thing which had not been sold* ∼ *with the ... house was this piano* – Marcia Davenport⟩ [fr the principal parts of a firearm]

**lockup** /-,up/ *n* **1** (the time of) locking; the state of being locked **2** a prison; *esp* a small local prison where people are detained before a court hearing **3** *Br* a lock-up shop or garage

¹**lock-,up** *adj, Br, of a building* able to be locked up and left when not in use; *esp* without a house or living quarters attached ⟨*a* ∼ *shop*⟩ ⟨*a* ∼ *garage*⟩

¹**loco** /'lohkoh/ *n, pl* **locos** locoweed

²**loco** *adj, chiefly NAm slang* out of one's mind; crazy, frenzied ⟨*most of the resident foreigners ... take to drink, driven* ∼ *by the Portuguese peculiarities* – Mary McCarthy⟩ [Sp]

³**loco** *adv or adj* in the register as written – used as a direction in music [It dial., there, fr L *in loco* in the place]

⁴**loco** *n* a locomotive

**loco citato** /,lohkoh si'tahtoh, ki'tahtoh/ *adv* in the place or passage already quoted [L]

**loco disease** *n* a disease of cattle caused by eating locoweed

**locomotion** /,lohkə'mohsh(ə)n/ *n* **1** an act or the power of moving from place to place **2** TRAVEL 1, 2a [L *locus* place + E *motion*]

¹**locomotive** /,lohkə'mohtiv/ *adj* **1** of or functioning in locomotion **2** of travel **3** of or being a machine that moves about by operation of its own mechanism

²**locomotive** *n* an engine that runs on rails, uses any of several

forms of energy for producing motion, and is used for moving railway carriages and wagons

**locomotor** /-'mohtə/ *adj* **1** LOCOMOTIVE 1 **2 locomotor, locomotory** affecting or involving parts of the body used for locomotion

**locomotor ataxia** /ə'taksi-ə/ *n* a disorder of the nervous system during TERTIARY SYPHILIS marked esp by disturbances of gait and difficulty in coordinating voluntary movements

**locoweed** /'lohkoh,weed/ *n* any of several western N American plants (genera *Astragalus* and *Oxytropis*) of the pea family that cause madness in livestock [MexSp *loco*, fr Sp, crazy]

**locular** /'lokyoolə/ *adj* having or composed of loculi – often in combination ⟨*multi*locular⟩

**loculate** /'lokyoolət, -layt/, **loculated** /-laytid/ *adj* having or divided into loculi – **loculation** *n*

**locule** /'lokyoohl/ *n* a loculus; *esp* any of the cells of a compound OVARY (seed-producing organ) of a plant [Fr, fr L *loculus*] – **loculed** *adj*

**loculicidal** /,lokyoolə'siedl/ *adj, of a fruit* splitting lengthways so as to bisect each loculus [NL *loculus* + L *-cidere* to cut, fr *caedere* – more at CONCISE] – **loculicidally** *adv*

**loculus** /'lokyooləs/ *n, pl* **loculi** /-li/ **1** a small chamber or cavity, esp in a plant or animal body **2** a compartment in a Roman or early Christian tomb (eg in a catacomb) [NL, fr L, dim. of *locus*]

**locum** /'lohkəm/ *n, chiefly Br* somebody filling an office for a time or temporarily taking the place of another – used esp with reference to a doctor, paramedical worker, therapist, or clergyman; *also* a period of work as a locum [ML *locum tenens*, lit., one holding a place]

**locum tenens** /'tenenz/ *n, pl* **locum tenentes** /te'nenteez, -tiz/ *formal* a locum

**locus** /'lohkəs, 'lokəs/ *n, pl* **loci** /'lohsi, -sie; *also* 'lohki, -kie/ *also* **locuses 1** a place, locality **2** *maths* the set of all points whose location is determined by stated conditions **3** the position on a CHROMOSOME (strand of gene-carrying material) of a particular gene [L – more at STALL; (2,3) NL, fr L]

**locus classicus** /'klasikəs/ *n, pl* **loci classici** /'klasiki, -kie/ **1** the best-known and most authoritative passage or work on a particular subject **2** the central or most typical example; the standard case [NL]

**locus standi** /'standi, -die/ *n* the right to appear in court or be heard on any question [L, lit., place of standing]

**locust** /'lohkəst/ *n* **1** any of numerous migratory SHORT-HORNED GRASSHOPPERS (eg of the genera *Locusta* and *Melanophus*); *esp* one (*Locusta migratoria*) that often travels in vast swarms in warm and tropical parts of Asia and Africa stripping the areas passed of all vegetation **2a** any of various hard-wooded trees of the pea family: eg **2a(1)** CAROB (Mediterranean tree) **a(2)** a tall N American tree (*Robinia pseudoacacia*) of the pea family with hanging clusters of fragrant white flowers, thorns, and hard wood **b** the wood of a locust tree [ME, fr L *locusta*; (2) fr its pods allegedly resembling locusts]

**locust bean** *n* the fruit of the CAROB tree

**locution** /loh'kyoohsh(ə)n, lə-/ *n* **1** a peculiar or typical word or expression; *esp* one characteristic of a region, group, or cultural level **2** style of discourse; phraseology [ME *locucioun*, fr L *locution-, locutio*, fr *locutus*, pp of *loqui* to speak]

**lode** /lohd/ *n* an ore deposit △ load [ME, way, waterway, fr OE *lād* course, support; akin to OE *līthan* to go – more at LEAD]

**loden** /'lohd(ə)n/ *n* **1** a thick woollen cloth used for outer clothing **2** a dull greyish-green colour [Ger, fr OHG *lodo* coarse cloth]

**lodestar, loadstar** /'lohd,stah/ *n* **1** a star that leads or guides; *esp* POLE STAR **2** something that serves as a guiding star [ME *lode sterre*, fr *lode* course, fr OE *lād*]

**lodestone, loadstone** /-,stohn/ *n* **1** (a piece of) MAGNETITE (black iron-containing mineral) that has been magnetized **2** something that strongly attracts; a magnet [obs *lode* course, fr ME]

**¹lodge** /loj/ *vt* **1a** to provide temporary, esp rented, accommodation for **b** to establish or settle in a place **2** to serve as a receptacle for; contain, house **3** *esp of wind or rain* to beat (eg a crop) flat to the ground **4** to fix in place (eg by throwing or thrusting) **5** to deposit for safeguard or preservation ⟨~ *the jewellery at the bank*⟩ **6** to place or vest (eg power), esp in a source, means, or agent **7** to lay (eg a complaint) before a proper authority ~ *vi* **1a** to occupy a place, esp temporarily **b(1)** to have a residence; dwell **b(2)** to be a lodger **2** to come to rest; settle ⟨*the bullet* ~d *in his chest*⟩ **3** *esp of hay or grain crops* to fall or lie down

**²lodge** *n* **1a** the meeting place of a branch of an organization, esp a fraternal organization ⟨*Masonic* ~⟩ **b** *taking sing or pl vb* the body of members of such a branch **2a** a house set apart for residence in a particular season (eg the hunting season) **b** *often cap* a hotel, esp at a resort **3a** a house on an estate originally for the use of a gamekeeper, caretaker, gardener, or porter **b** a shelter or room for an employee (eg a porter) at the entrance to a college, block of flats, etc **c** the house where the head of a university college lives, esp in Cambridge **4** a den or lair of an animal or a group of animals (eg beavers or otters) **5a** a wigwam **b** *taking sing or pl vb* a family of N American Indians **6** *chiefly dial* a usu temporary shelter or abode [ME *loge*, fr OF, of Gmc origin; akin to OHG *louba* porch (cf LOBBY)]

**lodger** /'lojə/ *n* somebody who lodges; *esp* somebody who occupies a rented room in another's house

**lodging** /'lojing/ *n* **1** a place to live; a dwelling **2a** a temporary place to stay ⟨*a* ~ *for the night*⟩ **b lodgings** *pl*, **lodging** a room or rooms for living in that is usu rented and is in a private house rather than a hotel

**lodging house** *n* a house where lodgings are provided and let

**lodgment, lodgement** /'lojmənt/ *n* **1a** the act, faċt, or manner of lodging **b** a placing, depositing, or coming to rest **2** an accumulation or collection deposited in a place or remaining at rest

**lodicule** /'lodikyoohl/ *n* either of usu two delicate membranous scales at the base of the OVARY (seed-producing organ) of a grass [L *lodicula*, dim. of *lodic-, lodix* cover]

**loess** /'loh·is, les/ *n* an unlayered usu yellowish brown fine-grained loamy deposit found in Europe, Asia, and N America and believed to be chiefly deposited by the wind [Ger *löss, loess*, fr Ger dial. *lösch* loose] – **loessial** *adj*

**¹loft** /loft/ *n* **1** the space immediately under a pitched roof; *also* a room occupying this space; an attic **2a** a gallery in a church or hall; *esp* one intended for an organist or other musicians **b** an upper floor of a barn or warehouse used for storage, esp when not partitioned – sometimes in combination ⟨*a hay*loft⟩ **c** a shed or coop for pigeons **3a** the backward slant of the face of a golf-club head **b** the height of flight ⟨*gave the ball too little* ~⟩ **4** *NAm* an upper room or floor [ME, fr OE, fr ON *lopt* air; akin to OE *lyft* air, OHG *luft*]

**²loft** *vt* **1** to propel through the air or into space ⟨~ed *the ball over mid-wicket*⟩ ⟨*instruments* ~ed *by a powerful rocket*⟩ **2** to lay out a full sized working drawing of the lines and contours of (eg a ship's hull) ~ *vi* **1** to propel a ball high into the air **2** to rise high

**lofted** /'loftid/ *adj, of a golf club* having a head with an appreciably backward-slanting face

**lofty** /'lofti/ *adj* **1** having a haughty overbearing manner; supercilious **2a** elevated in character and spirit; noble **b** elevated in position; superior **3a** rising to a great height; impressively high ⟨~ *mountains*⟩ **b** remote, esoteric – **loftily** *adv*, **loftiness** *n*

**¹log** /log/ *n* **1** a usu bulky piece or length of unshaped timber; *esp* a length of a tree trunk ready for sawing or for use as firewood ⟨*a* ~ *cabin*⟩ **2** an apparatus for measuring the rate of a ship's motion through the water, formerly consisting of a wooden float tied to a line **3a** the record of the rate of a ship's speed or of her daily progress; *also* the full nautical record of a ship's voyage **b** the full record of a flight by an aircraft **4** any of various records of performance ⟨*a computer* ~⟩ [ME *logge*, prob of Scand origin; akin to ON *lāg* fallen tree; akin to OE *licgan* to lie – more at LIE; (3,4) short for *logbook*]

**²log** *vb* **-gg-** *vt* **1a** to cut (trees) for timber **b** to clear (land) of trees **2** to enter details of or about in a log ⟨~ *one's petrol consumption*⟩ **3a** to move or attain (eg an indicated distance, speed, or time) as noted in a log **b(1)** to sail a ship or fly an aircraft for (an indicated distance or period of time) **b(2)** to have (an indicated record) to one's credit; achieve ⟨~ged *about 30000 miles a year in his car*⟩ ⟨*racing drivers* ~ging *record speeds*⟩ ~ *vi* to cut logs for timber

**³log** *n* a logarithm – **log** *adj*

**log-, logo-** *comb form* thought, speech ⟨*logo*gram⟩ ⟨*logo*rrhoea⟩ [Gk, fr *logos* – more at LEGEND]

**-log** /-log/ *comb form* (→ *n*), *chiefly NAm* -logue

**loganberry** /'lohgənb(ə)ri, -,beri/ *n* an upright-growing hybrid raspberry (*Rubus loganobaccus*) cultivated for its large sweet edible red berries; *also* the berry of a loganberry [James Logan †1928 US lawyer + E *berry*]

**logaoedic** /,logə'eedik/ *adj, esp of classical verse* marked by the mixture of several metres; *specif* having a rhythm that uses both DACTYLS and TROCHEES or ANAPAESTS and IAMBS [LL *logaoedicus*, fr LGk *logaoidikos*, fr Gk *log-* + *aoidē* song, poetry, fr *aeidein* to sing – more at ODE] – **logaoedic** *n*

**logarithm** /'logə,ridh(ə)m/ *n* the power to which a number (the BASE) must be raised in order to produce a given number ⟨*the ~ of 100 to base 10 is 2*⟩ [NL *logarithmus*, fr *log-* + Gk *arithmos* number – more at ARITHMETIC] – **logarithmic** *adj*, **logarithmically** *adv*

**logarithmic function** *n, maths* a function (e g $y = \log x$) that is the inverse of an EXPONENTIAL FUNCTION (e g $x = e^y$)

**logbook** /-,book/ *n* 1 LOG 3,4 2 *Br* a document containing details of registration, ownership, etc of a motor vehicle – not now used technically; compare REGISTRATION DOCUMENT

**loge** /lohzh/ *n* a box in a theatre [Fr – more at LODGE]

**logger** /'logə/ *n, NAm* somebody engaged in logging; a lumberjack

**loggerhead** /'logə,hed/ *n* 1 any of various very large marine turtles (family Cheloniidae); *esp* a flesh-eating turtle (*Caretta caretta*) of the warmer parts of the western Atlantic 2 an iron tool consisting of a long handle ending in a ball or bulb that is heated and used to melt tar or to heat liquids [prob fr E dial. *logger* block of wood + *head*; orig senses, blockhead, large head] – **at loggerheads** in a state of quarrelsome disagreement

**loggia** /'loj(i)ə/ *n, pl* **loggias** *also* **loggie** /'lojie/ a roofed open gallery behind a colonnade or arcade [It, fr Fr *loge*]

**logic** /'lojik/ *n* **1a(1)** a branch of philosophy that deals with the formal principles and structure of sound thought and reasoning **a(2)** a specified branch or system of logic ⟨*modal ~*⟩ ⟨*Boolean ~*⟩ **a(3)** the formal principles of a branch of knowledge ⟨*the ~ of ecology*⟩ **b(1)** a particular mode of reasoning viewed as valid or faulty ⟨*was quite unable to follow his ~*⟩ **b(2)** relevance, propriety **c** the interrelation or sequence of facts or events when seen as inevitable or predictable **d** the fundamental principles and the connection of circuit elements for performing BOOLEAN operations (e g those needed for arithmetical computation) in a computer; *also* the circuits themselves **2** something that forces a decision apart from or in opposition to reason ⟨*the ~ of war*⟩ [ME *logik*, fr MF *logique*, fr L *logica*, fr Gk *logikē*, fr fem of *logikos* of reason, fr *logos* reason – more at LEGEND] – **logician** *n* – **chop logic** to argue over minor points

**logical** /'lojikl/ *adj* **1** of or conforming to the rules of logic ⟨*a ~ argument*⟩ **2** capable of reasoning or of using reason in an orderly fashion; skilled in logic ⟨*a ~ thinker*⟩ **3** of, being, or forming part of a LOGIC CIRCUIT in a computer ⟨*~ elements*⟩ – **logically** *adv*, **logicalness** *n*, **logicality** *n*

**logical positivism** *n* a philosophical movement originating in Vienna in the 1920s and later popular at Oxford, stressing the linguistic analysis of statements that holds characteristically that statements can be meaningful only if based on observable phenomena and so verifiable and that metaphysical theories are therefore meaningless – **logical positivist** *n*

**logic circuit** *n* any of various electronic circuits used extensively in computers to perform simple logical operations, that consist of one or more GATES whose output signal is dependent on the condition of one or more input signals and corresponds usu to an "on" or "off" state that represents a single unit of computer information (⁴BIT)

**logico-** /lojikoh-/ *comb form* logical; logical and ⟨*logicomathematical*⟩

**logion** /'logion/ *n, pl* **logia** /'logiə/, **logions** a saying; *esp* a saying attributed to Jesus [Gk, dim. of *logos*]

**logistic** /lo'jistik, lə-/, **logistical** /-kl/ *adj* **1** *philosophy* of SYMBOLIC LOGIC **2** of logistics – **logistically** *adv*

**logistic curve** *n* an S-shaped curve having an EXPONENTIAL component and used to represent population growth mathematically

**logistician** /,loji'stish(ə)n/ *n* a specialist in logistics

**logistics** /lo'jistiks, lə-/ *n taking sing or pl vb* **1** the aspect of military science dealing with the transportation, quartering, and supplying of troops in military operations **2** the handling of the details of an operation [Fr *logistique* art of calculating, logistics, fr Gk *logistikē* art of calculating, fr fem of *logistikos* of calculation, fr *logizein* to calculate, fr *logos* reason]

**logjam** /'log,jam/ *n, chiefly NAm* a deadlock, impasse [orig referring to logs jammed together in a river]

**lognormal** /log'nawməl/ *adj, statistics* of or being a LOGARITHMIC FUNCTION (e g the logarithm of a RANDOM VARIABLE) that has a NORMAL DISTRIBUTION – **lognormally** *adv*, **lognormality** *n*

**logo** /'logoh/ *n, pl* **logos** **1** LOGOTYPE 2 **2** an identifying statement; a motto

**logo-** – see LOG-

**logogram** /'logə,gram/ *n* a letter, symbol, or sign used (e g in shorthand) to represent an entire word – **logogrammatic** *adj*

**logograph** /'logə,grahf, -,graf/ *n* a logogram – **logographic** *adj*, **logographically** *adv*

**logogriph** /-,grif/ *n* a word puzzle (e g an anagram) [*log-* + Gk *griphos* reed basket, riddle – more at CRIB]

**logomachy** /lo'gomək/ *n, pl* **logomachies** **1** a dispute over or about words **2** a controversy depending merely on the meaning of words [Gk *logomachia*, fr *log-* + *machesthai* to fight]

**logorrhoea** /,logə'riə/ *n* usu pathologically excessive and often incoherent and uncontrollable talkativeness or wordiness; *broadly* verbosity, long-windedness [NL] – **logorrhoeic** *adj*

**Logos** /'logos/ *n, pl* **Logoi** /'logoy/ **1** cosmic reason that in ancient Greek philosophy gives order and form to the world **2** WORD 4a [Gk, speech, word, reason – more at LEGEND]

**logotype** /'logə,tiep/ *n* **1** a single block or piece of type that prints a whole item (e g the name of a newspaper or a trademark) **2** an identifying symbol (e g for advertising)

**logrolling** /'log,rohling/ *n, chiefly NAm* **1** the rolling of logs in water by treading; *also* a sport in which men treading logs try to dislodge one another **2** the trading of votes by members of a legislature to secure mutual advantage [(2) fr a former American custom of neighbours helping one another to roll logs into a pile for burning] – **logroll** *vb*, **logroller** *n*

**-logue**, *NAm ehiefly* **-log** /-log/ *comb form* (→ *n*) **1** conversation; talk ⟨*duologue*⟩ **2** student; specialist ⟨*sinologue*⟩ [ME *-logue*, fr OF, fr L *-logus*, fr Gk *-logos*, fr *legein* to speak – more at LEGEND]

**logwood** /'log,wood/ *n* **1a** a Central American and W Indian tree (*Haematoxylon campechianum*) of the pea family with hard heavy wood **b** the brown or reddish-brown heartwood of the logwood tree **2** a dye extracted from logwood – compare HAEMATEIN, HAEMATOXYLIN

**logy**, *also* **loggy** /'lohgi/ *adj, NAm* sluggish, listless [perh fr D *log* heavy; akin to MLG *luggish* lazy] – **loginess** *n*

**-logy** /-ləji/ *comb form* (→ *n*) **1** oral or written expression ⟨*phraseology*⟩; *esp* body of writings of (a specified kind) or on (a specified subject) ⟨*trilogy*⟩ ⟨*hagiology*⟩ **2** doctrine; theory; science ⟨*ethnology*⟩ ⟨*semiology*⟩ [ME *-logie*, fr OF, fr L *-logia*, fr Gk, fr *logos* word]

**loin** /loyn/ *n* **1a** the part of a human being or 4-legged animal on each side of the spinal column between the hipbone and the lower ribs **b** a cut of meat comprising this part of one or both sides of a carcass with the adjoining half of the vertebrae included **2** *pl* **2a** the upper and lower abdominal regions and the region about the hips **b(1)** the pubic region; the crotch **b(2)** *euph or poetic* the genitals [ME *loyne*, fr MF *loigne*, fr (assumed) VL *lumbea*, fr L *lumbus*; akin to OE *lendenu* loins] – **gird (up) one's loins** to prepare for action; muster one's resources

**loincloth** /'loyn,kloth/ *n* a cloth worn about the hips and covering the genitals

**loiter** /'loytə/ *vi* **1** to remain in an area for no obvious reason but possibly for an illicit purpose; HANG ABOUT **2a** to make frequent pauses while travelling; dawdle **b** to lag behind [ME *loiteren*, prob fr MD *loteren* to waggle, be loose] – **loiterer** *n*

**loll** /lol/ *vi* **1** to hang down loosely ⟨*his tongue ~ed out*⟩ **2** to recline, lean, or move in a lazy or excessively relaxed manner or position; lounge ~ *vt* to let (e g one's limbs or tongue) droop or dangle [ME *lollen*, prob of imit origin] – **loll** *n*, **loller** *n*

**Lollard** /'loləd/ *n* any of the followers of Wycliffe who travelled in the 14th and 15th centuries as lay preachers throughout England and Scotland [ME, fr MD *lollaert*, lit., mumbler (orig applied to a charitable brotherhood, & later to various religious groups), fr *lollen* to mumble] – **Lollardism** *n*, **Lollardy** *n*

**lollipop, lollypop** /'loli,pop/ *n* **1** a large often round flat sweet of boiled sugar on the end of a stick **2** *chiefly Br* ICE LOLLY [prob fr E dial. *lolly* tongue + *pop*]

**lollipop man**, *fem* **lollipop lady** *n, Br* someone wearing a white coat who stops traffic with a large round sign on a pole to let children travelling to and from school cross the road safely

**lollop** /'loləp/ *vi* **1** to move or proceed with a slouching or loping motion **2** *dial Eng* to loll [*loll* + *-op* (as in *gallop*)]

**lolly** /'loli/ *n* **1a** a lollipop **b** ICE LOLLY **2** *Br slang* money

**Lombard** /'lombahd, -bəd/ *n* **1a** a member of a Teutonic people that invaded Italy and settled in the Po valley in the 6th century

AD **b** a native or inhabitant of Lombardy **2** a banker, money-lender [ME *Lumbarde*, fr MF *lombard*, fr OIt *lombardo*, fr L *Langobardus*; (2) fr the prominence of Lombards as money-lenders] – **Lombardian, Lombardic** *adj*

**Lombardy poplar** /'lombədi, 'lum-/ *n* a much planted European poplar tree (*Populus nigra italica*) that is distinguished by its tall narrow shape and upward-sloping branches [*Lombardy*, region in N Italy]

**loment** /'lohment/ *n* a long dry nonopening (INDEHISCENT) 1-celled fruit that has constrictions between the seeds and breaks transversely into several usu 1-seeded segments at maturity [NL *lomentum*, fr L, wash made of bean meal, fr *lotus*, pp of *lavare* to wash – more at LYE]

**lomentum** /loh'mentəm/ *n, pl* **lomenta** /loh'mentə/, **lomentums** a loment

**Lomotil** /'lohmə,til/ *trademark* – used for DIPHENOXYLATE HYDROCHLORIDE

**London particular** *n, archaic* a very dense fog; a pea-souper [fr its former prevalence in London]

**London plane** /'lundən/ *n* a fast-growing smoke-resistant hybrid plane tree (*Platanus x hybrida*) that is widely used for street planting in towns [*London*, capital city of England]

**London pride** *n* a plant (*Saxifraga umbrosa*) of the saxifrage family with small pinkish-white flowers growing out of a rosette of leaves

**lone** /lohn/ *adj* **1** only, sole **2** situated alone or separately; isolated **3** *formal* having no company; solitary [ME, short for *alone*] – **loneness** *n*

**lonely** /'lohnli/ *adj* **1a** being without company; lone **b** cut off from others; solitary **2** not frequented by people; desolate **3a** sad as a result of being alone or without friends **b** causing a feeling of loneliness ⟨*my ~ bed*⟩ **4** producing a feeling of bleakness or desolation ⟨*a ~ hillside*⟩ – **lonelily** *adv,* **loneliness** *n*

**lonely hearts** *adj* of or for lonely people who are seeking companions or spouses ⟨*a ~ club*⟩

**loner** /'lohnə/ *n, informal* a person or animal that prefers solitude

**¹lonesome** /'lohns(ə)m/ *adj* **1** LONELY **3 2a** remote, unfrequented ⟨*look down, look down that ~ road* – Gene Austin⟩ **b** LONE **2** ⟨*on the trail of the ~ pine* – Ballard Macdonald⟩

**²lonesome** *n, informal* self ⟨*sat all on his ~*⟩

**lone wolf** *n* a person who prefers to work, act, or live alone

**¹long** /long/ *adj* **longer** /'long·gə/; **longest** /'long·gist/ **1a** extending for a considerable distance **b** having greater length than usual **c** having greater height than usual; tall **d** having greater length than breadth; elongated **e** having an apparently greater length than that specified ⟨*ten ~ days before we meet again*⟩ **2a** having a specified length ⟨*six feet ~*⟩ **b** forming the chief linear dimension ⟨*the ~ side of the room*⟩ **3a** extending over a considerable time ⟨*a ~ friendship*⟩ **b** having a specified duration ⟨*two hours ~*⟩ **c** prolonged beyond the usual time ⟨*a ~ look*⟩ **4a** containing many items in a series ⟨*a ~ list*⟩ **b** having a specified number of units ⟨*300 pages ~*⟩ **c** consisting of a greater number or amount than usual – compare LONG DOZEN **5a** *of a speech sound or syllable* having a relatively long duration **b** being one of a pair of similarly spelt vowel sounds that is longer in duration ⟨*~ a in* fate⟩ **c** *of a syllable in poetry* **c(1)** of relatively extended duration **c(2)** bearing a stress or accent **6a** having the capacity to reach or extend a considerable distance ⟨*a ~ left jab*⟩ **b** hit for a considerable distance ⟨*a very ~ drive from the tee*⟩ **7a** extending far into the future or past ⟨*the thoughts of youth are ~, ~ thoughts* – H W Longfellow⟩ **b** payable after a considerable period ⟨*a ~ note*⟩ **8** possessing a high degree or a great deal of something specified; strong **on** ⟨*~ on common sense*⟩ **9a** of an unusual degree of difference between the amounts wagered on each side ⟨*~ odds*⟩ **b** of the larger amount wagered ⟨*take the ~ end of the bet*⟩ **10** subject to great odds ⟨*it's a ~ chance, but it just might work*⟩ **11** owning or accumulating securities or goods, esp in anticipation of a rise in prices ⟨*they are now ~ on wheat*⟩ ⟨*take a ~ position in steel*⟩ [ME *long, lang,* fr OE; akin to OHG *lang* long, L *longus,* Gk *dolichos*] – **longness** *n* – **before long** in a short time; soon – **not long for** having little time left to do or enjoy ⟨*he's not long for this world*⟩ – see also **by a long** CHALK, **at long** LAST, **in the long** RUN, **by a long** SHOT, **long in the** TOOTH

**²long** *adv* **1** for or during a long time ⟨*not ~ returned*⟩ **2** for the duration of a specified period ⟨*how ~ was he away?*⟩ **3** at a point of time far before or after a specified moment or event

⟨*was excited ~ before the big day*⟩ **4** after or beyond a specified time ⟨*said it was no ~er possible*⟩ **5** *esp of financial dealings* in or into a long position (e g in a market) ⟨*went ~ 500 shares*⟩ – **as/so long as 1** during and up to the end of the time that; while **2** providing **3** *chiefly NAm* to the extent or degree that; since ⟨*as long as you're going, I'll go too*⟩

**³long** *n* **1** a long period of time ⟨*couldn't stay for ~*⟩ **2** a long syllable **3** a size in clothing for tall men – **the long and (the) short** the final outcome or essential meaning ⟨*the long and the short of it was that he paid for the wine*⟩

**⁴long** *vi* to feel a strong desire or craving, esp *for* something not likely to be attained ⟨*they ~ for peace but are driven to war*⟩ [ME *longen*, fr OE *langian*; akin to OHG *langēn* to long, OE *lang* long] – **longer** *n*

**long ago** *n* the distant past ⟨*in the days of ~*⟩ – **long-ago** *adj*

**longan** /'long·gən/ *n* **1** a tropical Asian tree (*Euphoria longana* of the family Sapindaceae) related to the litchi, that has small yellowish-white flowers and bears an edible fruit **2** the small somewhat spherical yellowish-brown edible fruit of the longan that has a juicy white pulp [Chin (Pek) *lóng yăn* (*lung*² *yen*³), lit., dragon's eye]

**longanimity** /,long·gə'niməti/ *n, formal* patience, forbearance [LL *longanimitas*, fr *longanimis* patient, fr L *longus* long + *animus* soul – more at ANIMATE]

**longboat** /'long,boht/ *n* the largest boat carried aboard a sailing vessel

**long bone** *n* any of the long bones supporting a limb of a VERTEBRATE animal and consisting of a cylindrical shaft that contains marrow and ends in enlarged heads for articulation with other bones

**longbow** /-,boh/ *n* the medieval English yew or ash bow of about 2 metres (6 feet) in length; *also* a similar bow used in archery – **longbowman** *n*

**long-case clock** *n* GRANDFATHER CLOCK

**¹long-,chain** *adj* having a relatively long chain of atoms, esp carbon atoms, in the molecule ⟨*~ hydrocarbons*⟩

**¹long-,day** *adj, of a plant* producing flowers only on exposure to long periods of daylight – compare DAY-NEUTRAL, SHORT-DAY

**¹,long-'distance** *adj* **1a** *of a running race* covering a long distance **b** effective over a long distance ⟨*~ listening devices*⟩ **2** of or being telephone communication with a distant place ⟨*there's a ~ call for you*⟩

**²long-distance** *adv* by long-distance telephone ⟨*I called her ~*⟩

**long division** *n* arithmetical division in which all the calculations involved are written out, usu in a systematic way

**long dozen** *n* one more than a dozen; thirteen

**,long-drawn-'out** *also* **long-drawn** *adj* extended to a great length; protracted

**longe** /lunj, lonj/ *n or vb* ³,⁴LUNGE

**long-eared owl** *n* a medium-sized European owl (*Asio otus*) with long ear tufts

**longeron** /'lonjərən/ *n* a fore-and-aft framing structural part of an aircraft fuselage [Fr, fr *allonger* to make long]

**longeval** /lon'jeev(ə)l/, **longevous** /lon'jeevəs/ *adj, formal* long-lived [L *longaevus*, fr *longus* long + *aevum* age – more at AYE]

**longevity** /lon'jevəti; *also* long'gevəti/ *n* **1** unusually long length of life **2** length of life ⟨*a study of ~*⟩ [LL *longaevitas*, fr L *longaevus*]

*usage* The pronunciation /lon'jevəti/ is recommended for BBC broadcasters.

**long face** *n* a facial expression of sadness or melancholy

**longhair** /'long,heə/ *n, chiefly derog* a person with, or thought of as having, long hair: e g a a hippie **b** someone of an artistic, esp avant-garde, temperament **c** an unworldly intellectual [back-formation fr *long-haired*] – **long-hair, long-haired** *adj*

**longhand** /'long,hand/ *n* ordinary writing; handwriting

**long haul** *n* **1** a lengthy usu difficult period of time ⟨*the ~ back to health*⟩ **2** the transport of goods over long distances – **long-haul** *adj*

**longhead** /'long,hed/ *n* a person with a long skull

**longheaded** /-'hedid/ *adj* **1** having unusual foresight or wisdom **2** having a long skull – **longheadedness** *n*

**long hop** *n* a short-pitched delivery of a cricket ball that can be easily hit

**longhorn** /'long,hawn/ *n* (any of) a breed of long-horned cattle of Spanish derivation

**long-horned beetle, long horn beetle** *n* any of various

beetles (family Cerambycidae) usu distinguished by their very long antennae

**long-horned grasshopper** *n* any of various grasshoppers (family Tettigoniidae) distinguished by their very long antennae

**long horse** *n* VAULTING HORSE

**longhouse** /'long,hows/ *n* a long communal dwelling, esp as used in Borneo, Malaya, etc and by the Iroquois and other N American Indians

**long hundredweight** *n*, *Br* HUNDREDWEIGHT 2a

**longi-** /lonji-; *also* long·gi-/ *comb form* long ⟨longi*pennate*⟩ ⟨longi*tude*⟩ [ME, fr L, fr *longus*]

**longicorn** /'lonji,kawn/ *adj* 1 of or being LONG-HORNED BEETLES 2 having long antennae [deriv of *longi-* + L *cornu* horn – more at HORN] – **longicorn** *n*

**longing** /'long·ing/ *n* a strong desire, esp for something difficult to attain – **longingly** *adv*

**longish** /'long·ish/ *adj* somewhat long; moderately long

**longitude** /'lonjityoohd; *also* 'long·gi,tyoohd/ *n* the angular distance of a point on the surface of a celestial body, esp the earth, measured east or west along the equator from a PRIME MERIDIAN (e g that of Greenwich) and expressed in degrees; *also* the time difference corresponding to this – compare LATITUDE [ME, fr L *longitudin-, longitudo* length, fr *longus*]
    *usage* The pronunciation /'lonjityoohd/ is recommended for BBC broadcasters.

**longitudinal** /-'tyoohdinl/ *adj* 1 of length or the lengthways dimension 2 placed or running lengthways 3 dealing with the growth and change of an individual or group over a period of years ⟨~ *studies*⟩ – **longitudinally** *adv*

**longitudinal wave** *n* a wave (e g a sound wave) in which the particles of the medium (e g air) through which the wave is transmitted vibrate in the same direction as that of the line of advance of the wave – compare TRANSVERSE WAVE

**long johns** /jonz/ *n pl, informal* woollen underpants with legs extending usu down to the ankles [fr the forename *John*]

**long jump** *n* (an athletic field event consisting of) a jump for distance from a running start – **long jumper** *n*, **long jumping** *n*

**long leg** *n* a fielding position in cricket near the boundary behind the batsman on the LEG SIDE of the pitch; *also* the fieldsman occupying this position

**long-'life** *adj*, *of a commercial product* (processed so as to be) long-lasting

**long-'lived** /livd/ *adj* 1 having a long life; characterized by long life ⟨*a* ~ *family*⟩ 2 lasting a long time; enduring – **long-livedness** *n*

**Longobard** /'long·gə,bahd/ *n, pl* **Longobards, Longobardi** /,long·gə'bahdi, -die/ LOMBARD 1a [L *Langobardus, Longobardus*] – **Longobardic** *adj*

**long off** *n* a fielding position in cricket near the boundary behind the bowler on the OFF SIDE of the pitch; *also* the fieldsman occupying this position

**long on** *n* a fielding position in cricket near the boundary behind the bowler on the LEG SIDE of the pitch; *also* the fieldsman occupying this position

**long pig** *n* human flesh as food, esp as consumed in the South Seas and New Zealand

**long-'playing** *adj* having a relatively long playing time – used esp of a gramophone record that plays at 33¹/₃ revolutions per minute

**long-'range** *adj* 1 involving or taking into account a long period of time ⟨~ *planning*⟩ 2 relating to or fit for long distances ⟨~ *rockets*⟩

**long run** *n* a relatively long period of time – usu in *in the long run* – **long-run** *adj*

**long s** *n* a written or printed form ʃ of the letter *s* disused since the 19th century except for archaic effect

**longship** /'long,ship/ *n* a long open ship propelled by oars and a sail and used by the Vikings principally to carry warriors for the purpose of invasion and conquest

**longshoreman** /-,shawmən/ *n, NAm* a docker [*longshore*, short for *alongshore*]

**long shot** *n* 1 a competitor, esp in a horse race, given little chance of winning; *also* a bet on such a competitor made at long odds 2 a venture involving considerable risk but promising a rich reward if successful; *also* a venture with little chance of success – **by a long shot** by a great deal

**longsighted** /,long'sietid/ *adj* farsighted – **longsightedness** *n*

**long since** *adv* 1 long ago ⟨*programmes which have* ~ *ceased to be useful*⟩ 2 for a long time ⟨*has* ~ *been recognized as a great writer*⟩

**long-'standing** *adj* of long duration

**long stop** *n* 1 a now largely disused fielding position in cricket directly behind the wicketkeeper and relatively far from the batsman; *also* the fieldsman occupying this position whose object was to stop balls missed by the wicketkeeper 2 *Br* one who or that which provides a final line of defence should normal procedures fail

**long-'suffering** *n* long and patient endurance of provocation, pain, or difficulty – **long-suffering** *adj*, **long-sufferingly** *adv*

**long suit** *n* 1 a hand in a card game containing more than the average number of cards in a suit 2 *informal* the activity or quality in which a person excels ⟨*diplomacy is not exactly my* ~⟩

**long-tailed duck** *n* a small sea duck (*Clangula hyemalis*) of the northern parts of the northern hemisphere, the drake of which has a long thin tail

**long-tailed tit** *n* a very small Eurasian tit (*Aegithalos caudatus*) with a long tail and largely black, pink, and white plumage

**long-'term** *adj* 1 occurring over or involving a relatively long period of time 2a of or constituting a financial operation or obligation based on a considerable period, esp one of more than 10 years ⟨~ *bonds*⟩ b generated by financial assets held for longer than six months ⟨*a* ~ *capital gain*⟩

**long-time** /'long,tiem/ *adj* long-standing

**long ton** *n* a British unit of weight equal to 2240 pounds (about 1016.05 kilograms)

**longueur** /long'guh (Fr lɔ̃gœːr)/ *n usu pl, pl* **longueurs** /long'guh(z) (Fr ~)/ a dull and tedious passage or section (e g of a book); *also* a dull and tedious period ⟨*the* ~s *of travel*⟩ [Fr, lit., length]

**long vacation** *n* the summer holiday of British law courts and universities

**long view** *n* an approach to a problem or situation that emphasizes long-range factors rather than short-term advantages

**long-'waisted** *adj* of more than average length from the shoulder to the waist

**long wave** *n* a band of RADIO WAVES much used for sound broadcasting and having wavelengths of 1000 metres or more

**longways** /'longwayz/ *adv* lengthways

**long weekend** *n* a short holiday including a weekend

**long-'winded** /-'windid/ *adj* 1 not easily subject to loss of breath 2 tediously long in speaking or writing – **long-windedly** *adv*, **long-windedness** *n*

**longwise** /'long,wiez, -wiz/ *adv*, *chiefly NAm* lengthways

**long-'woolled** *adj*, *esp of a sheep* having long but coarse wool

**¹loo** /looh/ *n* 1 an old card game in which the winner of each trick or a majority of tricks takes a portion of the pool while losing players have to contribute to the next pool 2 money staked at loo [short for obs *lanterloo*, fr Fr *lanturelu* piffle]

**²loo** *vt* to oblige to contribute to a new pool at loo for failing to win a trick

**³loo** *n, chiefly Br informal* TOILET 1 [perh modif of Fr *l'eau* the water]

**looby** /'loohbi/ *n* an awkward clumsy fellow [ME *loby*]

**loofah** /'loohfə/ *n* the fibrous skeleton of the fruit of a tropical plant (genus *Luffa*) of the marrow family, that is dried and used as a bath sponge [NL *Luffa*, genus name, fr Ar *lūf*]

**¹look** /look/ *vt* 1 to make sure or take care (that something is so or is done) ⟨~ *that the liquor is clear* – *National Times* (Sydney)⟩ 2 to find out or learn by the use of one's eyes ⟨~ *what time it starts*⟩ ⟨~ *what you've done!*⟩ 3 to regard intensely; examine ⟨~ *him in the eye*⟩ ⟨~ *a gift horse in the mouth*⟩ 4 to express by the eyes or facial expression ⟨~ed *daggers at her*⟩ ~ *vi* 1a to use the power of sight; *esp* to make a visual search b to direct one's attention ⟨~ *upon the future with hope*⟩ c to direct the eyes ⟨~ *at him!*⟩ 2a to have a specified import when seen; seem ⟨*his hat* ~s *ridiculous*⟩ b to have an appearance that befits or accords with the specified thing ⟨*really* ~ed *the part*⟩ 3 to have a specified outlook ⟨*the house* ~ed *east*⟩ 4 to gaze in wonder or surprise; stare [ME *looken*, fr OE *lōcian*; akin to OS *lōcōn* to look] – **look here** – used to attract attention, for emphasis, etc – see also **look down one's** NOSE **at, (look) like a drowned** RAT
    *usage* **Look** is followed by an adjective when it means "appear when seen" ⟨**look** *bad*⟩. An adverb used with **look** describes the way of using one's eyes ⟨**look** *carefully*⟩.

**look after** *vt* to take care of

**look back** *vi* 1 to remember – often + *to* or *on* 2 to show signs of interrupted progress – usu in the negative ⟨*exchanged* *a knight for a queen and never* looked back〉

**look down** *vi* to have an attitude of superiority or contempt – + *on* or *upon* 〈*snobbishly* looks down *on the poor*〉

**look for** *vt* 1 to await with hope or anticipation 2 to search for

**look forward to** *vt* to expect with pleasure 〈*I* look forward to *your return*〉

**look in** *vi, Br* 1 to pay a short visit 〈*will* look in *on the party*〉 2 to watch television – no longer in vogue

**look into** *vt* to investigate

**look on** *vi* to be a spectator

**look out** *vt* 1 to direct one's sight from the inside (eg of a room) to the outside 2 to keep watching 〈look out *for your parents*〉 3 to take care – often imperative 〈look out! *This fence is barbed wire!*〉 ~ *vi, chiefly Br* to choose by inspection; select 〈look out *a suit for the interview*〉 – see also LOOKOUT

**look over** *vt* to examine (quickly) part by part 〈*just look this over and tell me what you think*〉

**look up** *vi* to improve in prospects or conditions 〈*business is* looking up〉 ~ *vt* 1 to search for (as if) in a reference work 〈look up *a phone number in the directory*〉 2 to pay a usu short visit 〈looked *my friend up while I was there*〉

**look up to** *vt* to have an attitude of respect towards 〈*always* looked up to *their parents*〉

²**look** *n* 1a the act of looking **b** ²GLANCE 3 2a the appearance of the face; an expression **b** *pl* (attractive) physical appearance 〈*he's kept his* ~s〉 3 the state or form in which something appears 〈*a new* ~ *in knitwear*〉 〈*has the* ~ *of a loser about him*〉

'**look-a,like** *n, chiefly NAm* one who or that which looks like another; a double 〈*are you entering the Ronald Reagan* ~ *competition?*〉

**looker** /'lookə/ *n, informal* an attractive person, esp a woman – compare GOOD-LOOKER

,**looker-'on** *n, pl* **lookers-on** an onlooker

'**look-,in** *n, informal* a chance to take part; *also* a chance of success

**looking glass** /'looking/ *n* a mirror

**lookout** /'look,owt/ *n* 1 one engaged in keeping watch 2 a place or structure affording a wide view for observation 3 a careful looking or watching 4 a matter of care or concern 〈*it's your* ~ *if you do such a silly thing*〉 5 *chiefly Br* a future possibility; a prospect

'**look-,see** *n, informal* a relatively quick assessment or investigation

¹**loom** /loohm/ *n* a frame or machine for weaving together yarns or threads into cloth [ME *lome* tool, loom, fr OE *gelōma* tool; akin to MD al*lame* tool]

²**loom** *vi* 1 to come into sight indistinctly, in enlarged or distorted and menacing form, often as a result of atmospheric conditions 2a to appear in an impressively great or exaggerated form **b** to take shape as an impending occurrence – often + *large* 〈*the bankruptcy proceedings* ~ed *large*〉 [origin unknown]

³**loom** *n* the indistinct and exaggerated appearance of something seen on the horizon or through fog or darkness; *also* a looming shadow or reflection

¹**loon** /loohn/ *n* 1 a crazy person 2 an eccentric or silly person [ME *loun* rogue; influenced in meaning by *loony*]

²**loon** *vi, slang* to behave in a crazy or excited manner, usu as a result of intoxication

³**loon** *n, chiefly NAm* DIVER 3 (large diving bird) [of Scand origin; akin to ON *lōmr* loon – more at LAMENT]

**loons** /loohnz/ *n pl, informal* closely fitting flared trousers that hang from the hips and have no waistband [short for *pantaloons*]

**loony, looney** /'loohni/ *adj, informal* absurdly or amusingly eccentric or irrational; crazy 〈*some* ~ *scheme to import Tasmanian turnips*〉 [by shortening & alter. fr *lunatic* ] – **looniness** *n*, **loony** *n*

**loony bin** *n, humorous* a lunatic asylum

¹**loop** /loohp/ *n, archaic* LOOPHOLE 1a [ME *loupe;* perh akin to MD *lupen* to watch, peer]

²**loop** *n* 1a a (partially) closed figure that has a curved outline surrounding a central opening **b** such a figure of folded material (eg cord or ribbon) serving as an ornament 2a something shaped like a loop **b** a manoeuvre in which an aircraft passes successively through a climb, inverted flight, a dive, and then returns to normal flight 3 a ring or curved piece used to form a fastening or handle 4 a loop- or zigzag-shaped INTRA-

UTERINE DEVICE 5 a closed electric circuit 6 a piece of film or magnetic tape whose ends are spliced together so as to project or play back the same material continuously 7 a series of instructions (eg for a computer) that is repeated until a terminating condition is reached [ME *loupe,* of unknown origin]

³**loop** *vi* 1 to make or form a loop 2 to perform a loop in an aircraft 3 to move in loops or in an arc 〈*the black mamba* ~ed *from one branch to another*〉 ~ *vt* **1a** to make a loop in, on, or about **b** to fasten with a loop 2 to join (two courses of loops) in knitting 3 to connect (electrical conductors) so as to complete a loop 4 to cause to move in an arc – **loop the loop** to perform a loop in an aircraft

**looper** /'loohpə/ *n* 1 any of the usu rather small hairless caterpillars that are mostly larvae of moths (families Geometridae and Noctuidae) and that move in a series of loops by drawing the hindmost legs up to the front legs so that the body is arched – called also MEASURING WORM, INCHWORM 2 one who or that which loops; *esp* a device on a sewing machine for making loops

¹**loophole** /'loohp,hohl/ *n* 1a a small usu vertical opening in a wall or fortification through which missiles, firearms, etc may be discharged **b** a similar opening to admit light and air or to permit observation 2 a means of escape; *esp* an ambiguity or omission in the text of a contract, statute, etc through which an obligation or penalty may be evaded [¹*loop* + *hole*]

²**loophole** *vt* to make loopholes in

**loop line** *n* a railway line that leaves and later rejoins a main line

**loop of Henle** /'henli/ *n* a U-shaped tubular part of a NEPHRON (urine-secreting unit in a kidney) that lies between the PROXIMAL CONVOLUTED TUBULE and the DISTAL CONVOLUTED TUBULE and in which reabsorption of water and dissolved substances (eg glucose) from the urine into the blood takes place [F G J *Henle* †1885 Ger pathologist]

**loop stitch** *n* a needlework stitch consisting of a series of interlocking loops

**loopy, loopey** /'loohpi/ *adj* 1 having or characterized by loops 2 *informal* slightly crazy or foolish

¹**loose** /loohs/ *adj* **1a** not rigidly fastened or securely attached **b(1)** having worked partly free from attachments 〈*the masonry is* ~ *at the base of the wall*〉 **b(2)** having relative freedom of movement **c** of a cough produced freely and accompanied by production of mucus **d** not tight-fitting 2a free from a state of confinement, restraint, or obligation 〈*a lion* ~ *in the streets*〉 〈*spend* ~ *funds wisely*〉 **b** not brought together in a bundle, container, or binding; separate 3 not dense, close, or compact in structure or arrangement 4a lacking in (power of) restraint 〈*a* ~ *tongue*〉 〈~ *bowels*〉 **b** *esp of a woman* having or seeking many sexual adventures; promiscuous 5a not tightly drawn or stretched; slack **b** having a flexible or relaxed character 6a lacking in precision, exactness, or care 〈*a* ~ *translation*〉 **b** permitting freedom of interpretation 〈*the wording of the document is very* ~〉 [ME *lous,* fr ON *lauss;* akin to OHG *lōs* loose – more at -LESS] – **loosely** *adv*, **looseness** *n* – **break loose** to escape – **have a screw/slate loose** to be slightly mad or eccentric – **let loose** to allow to escape; send forth 〈let loose *a torrent of abuse on them*〉 – **let loose on** to give freedom of access to or of action with respect to 〈*can't* let *him* loose on *the computer just yet*〉 – see also **at a loose** END

²**loose** *vt* **1a** to release; LET LOOSE **b** to free from restraint 2 to make loose; untie 〈~ *a knot*〉 3 to cast loose; detach 4 to let fly (eg a bullet); discharge △ lose

³**loose** *n* open play in rugby that is characterized by free passing of the ball – often + *the* – **on the loose** free from restraint; *specif* having escaped from prison

⁴**loose** *adv* in a loose manner; loosely 〈*the rope hung* ~〉 – see also **play** FAST **and loose**

**loose box** *n, Br* an individual 4-walled enclosure within a barn or stable in which an animal, esp a horse, may move freely without a restraining device (eg a tether)

,**loose-'cover** *n, chiefly Br* a fitted usu cloth cover for a piece of furniture (eg an upholstered armchair or sofa) that may be unzipped and removed for cleaning

,**loose-'jointed** *adj* having joints apparently not closely articulated; supple – **loose-jointedness** *n*

,**loose-'leaf** *adj* 1 bound in a cover whose spine may be opened for the removal, rearrangement, or replacement of leaves 〈*a* ~ *notebook*〉 2 of or used with a loose-leaf binding 〈~ *paper*〉

,**loose-'limbed** /limd/ *adj* having flexible or supple limbs

**loosen** /'loohs(ə)n/ *vt* 1 to release from restraint 2 to make loose or looser **3** to relieve (the bowels) of constipation **4** to cause or permit to become less strict ~ *vi* to become loose or looser

**loose scrum** *n* MAUL 2

**loose smut** *n* a disease of cereal grains caused by parasitic SMUT fungi, in which the entire head is transformed into a dusty mass of spores

**loosestrife** /'loohs,strief/ *n* **1** any of several plants (genus *Lysimachia*) of the primrose family with leafy stems and yellow or white flowers **2** any of a genus (*Lythrum*) of plants of the henna family including some with showy spikes of purple flowers; *esp* PURPLE LOOSESTRIFE [intended as trans of Gk *lysimacheios* loosestrife (as if fr *lysis* act of loosing + *machē* battle, strife, fr *Lysimachos*, name of its reputed discoverer]

¹**loot** /looht/ *n* **1** goods, usu of considerable value, taken in war; spoils **2** something resembling goods of value seized in war: eg **2a** something taken by force or violence **b** illicit gains by public officials **3** *informal* money ⟨*lots of lovely* ~⟩ [Hindi *lūṭ*, fr Skt *luṇṭati* he robs]

²**loot** *vt* **1a** to plunder or sack in war **b** to rob or steal, esp on a large scale, usu by violence or corruption **2** to seize and carry away by force, esp in war ~ *vi* to engage in robbing or plundering, esp in war or public disturbance – **looter** *n*

¹**lop** /lop/ *n* small branches and twigs cut away from a tree [ME *loppe*]

²**lop** *vt* **-pp- 1a(1)** to cut off branches or twigs from; trim **a(2)** to sever (eg branches) from a woody plant **b** to cut from a person **2** to remove or do away with as unnecessary or undesirable – usu + *off* or *away* ⟨~ped *several thousands off the annual budget*⟩ **3** *archaic* to cut off the head or limbs of – **lopper** *n*

³**lop** *vi* **-pp-** *esp of animal ears* to hang downwards; droop [perh imit]

¹**lope** /lohp/ *n* **1** an easy bounding gait capable of being sustained for a long time **2** *NAm* an easy natural gait of a horse resembling a canter [ME *loup*, *lope* leap, fr ON *hlaup*; akin to OE *hlēapan* to leap – more at LEAP]

²**lope** *vi* to go, move, or ride at a lope – **loper** *n*

'**lop-,eared** *adj* having ears that droop

**lophophore** /'lohfə,faw/ *n* a circular or horseshoe-shaped tentacle-bearing organ about the mouth of various INVERTEBRATE animals, esp BRACHIOPODS and BRYOZOANS, that functions esp in the collection of food [Gk *lophos* crest + E *-phore*]

**loppy** /'lopi/ *adj* hanging loose; limp

**lopsided** /,lop'siedid/ *adj* **1** having one side heavier or lower than the other **2** lacking in balance, symmetry, or proportion – **lopsidedly** *adv*, **lopsidedness** *n*

**loquacious** /lə'kwayshəs/ *adj*, *formal* given to excessive talking; garrulous **synonyms** see TALKATIVE [L *loquac-*, *loquax*, fr *loqui* to speak] – **loquaciously** *adv*, **loquaciousness** *n*, **loquacity** *n*

**loquat** /'lohkwət, -kwot/ *n* an often cultivated ornamental Asian evergreen tree (*Eriobotrya japonica*) of the rose family, with reddish branches and white flowers; *also* the yellow edible plumlike fruit of the loquat, used esp for preserves [Chin (Cant) *logwad* (*lō-kwat*)]

**loran** /'lawrən/ *n* a navigational system operating over long distances in which the relative time of reception of synchronized pulsed signals transmitted from two or more sets of radio stations is used to determine the geographical position of a ship or aircraft – compare DECCA [*long-range navigation*]

¹**lord** /lawd/ *n* **1** somebody having power and authority over others: eg **1a** a ruler by hereditary right to whom service and obedience are due **b** one from whom a feudal fee or estate is held **c** one who has achieved domination or who exercises leadership or great power in some area ⟨*press* ~s⟩ **2** *cap* **2a** God **b** Jesus – often + *Our* **3** a man of rank or high position: eg **3a** a feudal tenant holding land directly from the king **b** a British nobleman: eg **b(1)** a member of the lowest grade of the peerage; a baron **b(2)** a marquess, earl, or viscount **b(3)** the son of a duke or a marquess or the eldest son of an earl **b(4)** a bishop of the Church of England – often + *my* when used in address **c** *pl*, *cap* HOUSE OF LORDS – often + *the* **4** – used as part of an official title ⟨Lord *Advocate*⟩ **5** a person chosen to preside over a festival – see also Lord KNOWS, take the Lord's NAME in vain [ME *loverd*, *lord*, fr OE *hlāford*, fr *hlāf* loaf + *weard* keeper – more at LOAF, WARD]

²**lord** *vi* – **lord it** to behave in a domineering or arrogant manner – often + *over* ⟨lords it *over his friends*⟩; compare QUEEN IT

**Lord** *interj* – used to express surprise, amazement, or dismay, esp in such phrases as *Oh Lord!*, *Good Lord!*, etc

**lord advocate** *n*, *often cap L&A* the chief law officer of the Crown in Scotland

**Lord Chamberlain** *n* the chief officer of the British Royal Household

**lord chancellor** *n*, *often cap L&C* an officer of state who is the Speaker of the House of Lords, serves as the head of the British legal system, and is usu a leading member of the cabinet

**Lord Chief Justice** *n*, *pl* **Lords Chief Justice** the president of the QUEEN'S BENCH Division of the HIGH COURT who is second to the Lord Chancellor in the English legal system

**Lord High Admiral** *n* a title given in former times to the commander-in-chief of the British Navy and now given to the British Sovereign

**lording** /'lawding/ *n*, *archaic* a lord

**Lord Justice of Appeal** *n*, *pl* **Lords Justices of Appeal** a judge of the COURT OF APPEAL

**Lord Lieutenant** *n*, *pl* **Lords Lieutenant**, **Lord Lieutenants** an official appointed to represent the sovereign in a British county

**lordling** /'lawdling/ *n* a little or insignificant lord

**lordly** /'lawdli/ *adj* **1a** (having the characteristics) of a lord; dignified **b** grand, noble **2** disdainful and arrogant – **lordliness** *n*, **lordly** *adv*

**Lord of Appeal in Ordinary** *n*, *pl* **Lords of Appeal in Ordinary** a person with a minimum of 15 years experience as a barrister or advocate or 2 years in high judicial office who is appointed a life peer to hear appeals in the House of Lords

**lord of misrule** *n* a master of Christmas revels in England, esp in the 15th and 16th centuries

**lordosis** /law'dohsis/ *n* abnormal forward curvature of the spine, esp in the waist or lower (LUMBAR) region – compare KYPHOSIS, SCOLIOSIS [NL, fr Gk *lordōsis*, fr *lordos* curving forwards; akin to OE be*lyrtan* to deceive] – **lordotic** *adj*

**Lord President of the Council** *n*, *pl* **Lord Presidents of the Council** the president of the PRIVY COUNCIL

**Lord Privy Seal** /'privi/ *n*, *pl* **Lords Privy Seal** a senior member of the British Cabinet with no departmental duties

**Lord Protector of the Commonwealth** *n* PROTECTOR 2b

**lords and ladies** *n taking sing vb* cuckoopint [fr its contrasting dark and light flower-spikes]

**Lord's day** *n*, *often cap D* Sunday – usu + *the* [fr the Christian belief that Christ rose from the dead on Sunday]

**lordship** /'lawdship/ *n* **1a** the rank or dignity of a lord – used as a title to address or refer to a bishop, a HIGH COURT judge, or a peer ⟨*his* Lordship *is not at home*⟩ **b** the authority or power of a lord; dominion **2** the territory under the jurisdiction of a lord

**Lord's Prayer** *n* the prayer beginning "Our Father" that was taught by Jesus and is found in variant versions in Matthew and Luke

**Lord's Supper** *n* COMMUNION 2a [ME *Lordis sopere*, trans of LL *dominica cena*, trans of Gk *kyriakon deipnon*]

**Lord's table** *n*, *often cap T* an altar

¹**lore** /law/ *n* **1** erudition, scholarship **2** a specified body of knowledge or tradition ⟨*bird* ~⟩ ⟨*ghost* ~⟩ **3** *archaic* something that is taught; a lesson **synonyms** see KNOWLEDGE [ME, fr OE *lār* doctrine, lesson; akin to OHG *lēra* doctrine, OE *leornian* to learn]

²**lore** *n* the region between the eye and beak in a bird or the corresponding region in a reptile or fish [NL *lorum*, fr L, thong, rein; akin to Gk *eulēra* reins] – **loreal** *adj*

**lorgnette** /law'nyet/(*Fr* lɔrŋɛt)/ *n* a pair of glasses or opera glasses without earpieces, held to the face by a single handle [Fr, fr *lorgner* to take a sidelong look at, fr MF, fr *lorgne* cross-eyed]

**lorgnon** /law'nyon (*Fr* lɔrŋɔ̃)/ *n* a lorgnette [Fr, fr *lorgner*]

**lorica** /lo'riekə/ *n*, *pl* **loricae** /-kie/ **1** an ancient Roman breastplate of leather or metal **2** the hard protective case or shell of various minute aquatic INVERTEBRATE animals (eg a ROTIFER) [L, fr *lorum*; (2) NL, fr L] – **loricate**, **loricated** *adj*

**lorikeet** /'lorikeet, --'-/ *n* any of numerous small chiefly Australasian tree-dwelling parrots (subfamily Lorunae), that have bright-coloured plumage and usu have long slender protuberances on the upper surface of the tongue that form a brushlike organ used for extracting nectar from flowers [*lory* + *-keet* (as in *parakeet*)]

**lorimer** /'lorimə/ *n* a maker of the metal parts of bridles and saddles [ME *lorimer, loriner,* fr OF *lormier, lorenier,* deriv of L *lorum* strap]

**loriner** /'lorinə/ *n* a lorimer

**loris** /'lawris/ *n* any of several small nocturnal slow-moving tree-dwelling primate mammals (family Lorisidae) of S and SE Asia – compare SLENDER LORIS, SLOW LORIS [Fr, perh fr obs D *loeris* simpleton] – **lorisiform** *adj*

**lorn** /lawn/ *adj, poetic* desolate, forsaken [ME, fr *loren,* pp of *lesen* to lose, fr OE *lēosan* – more at LOSE] – **lornness** *n*

**-lorn** /-lawn/ *comb form* (→ *adj*) deprived of ⟨*lovelorn*⟩ ⟨*parent-lorn*⟩

**lorry** /'lori/ *n* 1 a large low horse-drawn wagon without sides 2 any of various trucks running on rails 3 *Br* a large motor vehicle for carrying loads (e g goods or raw materials) by road [perh fr E dial. *lurry* to pull, drag]

**lory** /'lawri/ *n* any of numerous large lorikeets [Malay *nuri, luri*]

**lose** /loohz/ *vb* **lost** /lost/ *vt* **1a** to bring to destruction – usu pass ⟨*the ship was* lost *on the reef*⟩ **b** to damn – usu pass ⟨lost *souls*⟩ **2** to miss from one's possession or from a customary or supposed place; be unable to find ⟨lost *her glasses*⟩ **3** to suffer deprivation of; part with, esp in an unforeseen or accidental manner ⟨lost *his leg in an accident*⟩ **4a** to suffer loss through the death or removal of or final separation from (a person) ⟨lost *a son in the war*⟩ **b** to fail to keep control of or allegiance of ⟨~ *votes*⟩ **5a** to fail to use; let slip by ⟨~ *the tide*⟩ **b(1)** to fail to win, gain, or obtain ⟨~ *a prize*⟩ ⟨~ *a contest*⟩ **b(2)** to undergo defeat in ⟨lost *every battle*⟩ **c** to fail to catch with the senses or the mind ⟨lost *part of what was said*⟩ **6** to cause the loss of ⟨*one careless statement* lost *him the election*⟩ **7** to fail to keep, sustain, or maintain ⟨lost *his balance*⟩ **8a** to cause to miss one's way or bearings ⟨lost *themselves in the maze of streets*⟩ **b** to withdraw (oneself) from immediate reality ⟨lost *himself in daydreaming*⟩ **9a** to wander or go astray from ⟨lost *the road*⟩ **b** to draw away from; outstrip ⟨lost *his pursuers*⟩ **10** to fail to keep in sight or in mind **11** to free oneself from; get rid of ⟨*dieting to* ~ *some weight*⟩ **12** *of a timepiece* to run down by the amount of ⟨*my watch* ~ s *a minute each day*⟩ ~ *vi* **1** to undergo deprivation of something of value **2** to undergo defeat ⟨~ *with good grace*⟩ **3** *of a timepiece* to run slow – see also LOSE GROUND, lose one's HEART (to), lose one's RAG/one's WOOL △ loose [ME *losen,* fr OE *losian* to perish, lose, fr *los* destruction; akin to OE *lēosan* to lose; akin to ON *losa* to loosen, L *luere* to release, atone for, Gk *lyein* to loosen, dissolve, destroy] – **losable** *adj,* **losableness** *n*

**lose out** *vi* to fail to win in competition; fail to receive an expected reward or gain – often + *on*

**losel** /'lohzl/ *n, archaic & dial* a worthless person [ME, fr *losen* (pp of *lesen* to lose), alter. of *loren* – more at LORN] – **losel** *adj*

**loser** /'loohzə/ *n* **1** one who loses, esp consistently **2** one or that which does poorly or is likely to do poorly; a failure

**losing hazard** /'loohzing/ *n* the pocketing of the CUE BALL after it strikes another ball in billiards

**loss** /los/ *n* **1a** the act of losing possession **b** the harm or privation resulting from loss or separation **c** an instance of losing **2** a person, thing, or amount that is lost: e g **2a** *pl* killed, wounded, or captured soldiers ⟨~ es *are estimated at several hundreds*⟩ **b(1)** power or energy lost in an electrical system or apparatus equal to the difference between the input power and output power **b(2)** the decrease in power attributable to a particular element of an electrical circuit and corresponding to the conversion of electrical power into heat **3a** failure to gain, win, obtain, or use **b** an amount by which the cost of producing an article or service exceeds the selling price **4** decrease in amount, size, or degree **5** destruction, ruin **6** the amount of a financial claim for death or damage suffered by an insured person or group that the insurer becomes liable for [ME *los,* prob back-formation fr *lost,* pp of *losen* to lose] – **at a loss** uncertain, puzzled

**loss adjuster** *n* ASSESSOR 3 (investigator of insurance claims)

**loss leader** *n* an article sold at a loss in order to draw customers

**loss ratio** *n* the ratio of insurance losses incurred by an insurance company to premiums earned during a given period

**lossy** /'losi/ *adj* causing the reduction or dissipation of electrical energy ⟨*a* ~ *transmission line*⟩ ⟨*a* ~ *dielectric*⟩ [*loss* + ¹-*y*]

**lost** /lost/ *adj* **1** not made use of, won, or claimed **2a** unable to find the way **b** no longer visible **c** lacking assurance or self-

confidence; helpless **3** ruined or destroyed physically or morally **4a** no longer possessed ⟨*he mourned his* ~ *hair*⟩ **b** no longer known ⟨*the music of the ancient Greeks is* ~ *to us*⟩ **5a** taken away or beyond reach or attainment; denied ⟨*regions* ~ *to the faith*⟩ **b** insensible, hardened ⟨~ *to shame*⟩ **6** rapt, absorbed ⟨~ *in reverie*⟩ [fr pp of *lose*] – **lostness** *n* – **get lost** *informal* to go away – usu imper

*usage* Since there can be no degrees in being **lost**, some people dislike expressions such as ⟨*very* **lost** *to grace*⟩.

**lost cause** *n* a cause that has lost all prospect of success

**lost generation** *n* **1** the generation considered socially and emotionally disadvantaged as a result of reaching adulthood during and immediately following World War I **2** the potentially talented young men killed in World War I

**lost-wax process** *n* CIRE PERDUE (method of casting bronze)

¹**lot** /lot/ *n* **1** an object used as a counter in deciding a question by chance ⟨*they drew* ~ s⟩ **2** (the use of lots as a means of making) a choice **3a** something that comes to somebody by lot; a share **b** one's way of life or worldly fate; one's fortune ⟨*it's my* ~ *to be misunderstood*⟩ **4** an article or a number of articles offered as one item (e g in an auction sale) ⟨*what am I bid for* ~ *16?*⟩ **5a** *taking sing or pl vb* a number of associated people; a set ⟨*hello you* ~ – Margaret Drabble⟩ **b** *taking sing or pl vb* a batch or quantity of a substance or of people or things ⟨*the next* ~ *of students*⟩ ⟨*another* ~ *of wine*⟩ **c** a portion, share ⟨*the money was divided into two* ~ s⟩ **d** a kind, sort – chiefly in *a bad lot* **e** *chiefly Br informal* a minor ordeal ⟨*after that* ~ *I need a drink*⟩ **6** *chiefly NAm* **6a** a portion of land; *esp* one with fixed boundaries that is designated on a plot or survey **b** a film studio and its adjoining property **7** *lot, lots pl, informal* a considerable amount or number ⟨*a* ~ *of illness*⟩ ⟨~ s *of friends*⟩ **8** *chiefly Br* the whole amount or number ⟨*ate the* ~⟩ [ME, fr OE *hlot*; akin to OHG *hlōz*, Lith *kliudyti* to hook on] – **a lot 1** lots ⟨*drove* a lot *faster*⟩ **2** *informal* often, frequently ⟨*goes there* a lot⟩

²**lot** *vt* **-tt-** **1** to form or divide (e g land) into lots **2** to allot, apportion

**loth** /lohth/ *adj* loath

**lothario** /loh'thahrioh/ *n, pl* **lotharios** *often cap* a man whose chief interest is seducing women [*Lothario,* seducer in the play *The Fair Penitent* by Nicholas Rowe †1718 E dramatist]

**loti** /'lohti/ *n, pl* **maloti** /mə'lohti/ – see MONEY table [native name in Lesotho]

**lotic** /'lohtik/ *adj* of or living in actively moving water ⟨~ *biology*⟩ – compare LENTIC [L *lotus,* pp]

**lotion** /'lohsh(ə)n/ *n* a liquid preparation for cosmetic or external medicinal use [ME *loscion, locion,* fr L *lotion-, lotio* act of washing, fr *lotus,* pp of *lavere* to wash – more at LYE]

**lots** /lots/ *adv, informal* much, considerably ⟨*is* ~ *older than me*⟩ [pl of ¹*lot*]

**lotta** /'lotə/ (a) lot of – used in writing to represent nonstandard speech

**lottery** /'lot(ə)ri/ *n* **1** a way of raising money by the sale of numbered tickets, some of which are later randomly selected entitling the holder to a prize **2** an event or affair whose outcome is (apparently) decided by chance ⟨*buying a secondhand car is a* ~⟩ [MF *loterie,* fr MD, fr *lot* lot; akin to OE *hlot* lot]

**lotto** /'lotoh/ *n* bingo [It, lottery, lotto, fr Fr *lot* lot, of Gmc origin; akin to OE *hlot* lot]

**lotus** /'lohtəs/ *n* **1** *also* **lotos** a fruit considered in Greek legend to cause lazy forgetfulness and dreamy contentment **2** any of various tropical African and Asian water lilies including several represented in ancient Egyptian and Hindu art and religious symbolism **3** any of a genus (*Lotus*) of widely distributed upright plants (e g BIRD'S-FOOT TREFOIL) or small shrubs of the pea family with yellow, pink, or white flowers [L & Gk; L *lotus,* fr Gk *lōtos,* fr Heb *lōt* myrrh; (3) NL, genus name, fr L]

¹**lotus-ˌeater** *n* one who lives in dreamy laziness [the *Lotus-eaters* (Gk *Lōtophagoi*), race of people in Greek mythology who ate the lotus and lived in idle contentment] – **lotus-eating** *n*

**lotus position** *n* a yoga position in which one sits with legs folded and the arms resting on the knees [trans of Skt *padmāsana,* fr *padma* lotus (symbolizing transcendence of external impulse & sensation) + *āsana* seat, posture]

**louche** /loohsh/ *adj* morally dubious; disreputable, seedy △ farouche [Fr, lit., cross-eyed, fr L *luscus* one-eyed]

**loud** /lowd/ *adj* **1a** marked by intensity or volume of sound **b** producing a loud sound **2** clamorous, noisy **3** obtrusive or offensive in appearance; flashy ⟨*a* ~ *checked suit*⟩ [ME, fr OE *hlūd*; akin to OHG *hlūt* loud, L *inclutus* famous, Gk *klytos,*

Skt *śṛṇoti* he hears] – **loud, loudly** *adv,* **loudness** *n* – **out loud aloud** – **for crying out loud** *informal* – used to express exasperation and annoyance

usage The adverbs **loud** and **loudly** can each mean "noisily" ⟨*don't shout so* **loud/loudly**⟩ but only **loudly** can mean "obtrusively" ⟨**loudly** *dressed in orange velvet*⟩.

**louden** /'lowd(ə)n/ *vb* to make or become loud

**loud-'hailer** *n, chiefly Br* a megaphone

**loudmouth** /-,mowth/ *n* a person given to much loud offensive talk – **loudmouthed** *adj*

**loudspeaker** /,lowd'speekə/ *n* (a cabinet that contains) an electromechanical device that converts electrical energy into sound waves and that is used to reproduce audible sounds in a room, hall, etc

**lough** /lokh/ *n* **1a** a lake in Ireland **b** *Irish* a lake **2** a bay or inlet of the sea in Ireland [ME, of Celt origin; akin to OIr *loch* lake; akin to L *lacus* lake]

**louis d'or** /,looh·i 'daw (*Fr* lwi dɔr)/ *n, pl* **louis d'or** /~/ **1** a French gold coin first struck in 1640 and issued up to the Revolution **2** the French 20-franc gold piece issued after the Revolution [Fr, fr *Louis* XIII †1643 King of France + *d'or* of gold]

**Louis Quatorze** /,looh·i ka'tawz (*Fr* ~ katɔrz)/ *adj* (characteristic) of the architecture or furniture of the reign of Louis XIV of France [Fr, Louis XIV †1715 King of France]

**Louis Quinze** /kanhz (*Fr* kẽz)/ *adj* (characteristic) of the architecture or furniture of the reign of Louis XV of France [Fr, Louis XV †1774 King of France]

**Louis Seize** /sez (*Fr* sɛz)/ *adj* (characteristic) of the architecture or furniture of the reign of Louis XVI of France [Fr, Louis XVI †1793 King of France]

**Louis Treize** /trez (*Fr* trɛz)/ *adj* (characteristic) of the furniture or architecture of the reign of Louis XIII of France [Fr, Louis XIII]

¹**lounge** /lownj/ *vi* to act or move idly or lazily; loll ~ *vt* to pass (time) idly ⟨~ *away the afternoon*⟩ [origin unknown] – **lounger** *n*

²**lounge** *n* **1** a place for lounging: eg **1a** a room in a private house for sitting in; a sitting room **b** a room in a public building or vehicle providing comfortable seating; *also* a waiting room (eg at an airport) **2** a long couch *synonyms see* SITTING ROOM

**lounge bar** *n, Br* SALOON 4a

**lounge lizard** *n* a man who passes his time idly in fashionable society, esp in the company of women – no longer in vogue

**loungeroom** /'lownj,roohm, -,room/ *n, Austr* a lounge

**lounge suit** *n* a man's suit for wear during the day and on informal occasions

**loup** /lowp, lohp/ *vb, chiefly Scot* to leap [ME *loupen,* fr ON *hlaupa;* akin to OE *hlēapan* to leap – more at LEAP] – **loup** *n*

**loupe** /loohp/ *n* a small optical magnifying instrument used esp by jewellers and watchmakers △ loop [Fr, gem of imperfect brilliancy, loupe]

**loup-garou** /,looh ga'rooh (*Fr* lu garu)/ *n, pl* **loups-garous** /~/ a werewolf [MF]

**lour** /'lowə; *also* 'loh·ə/ *vi or n, chiefly Br* (to) lower – **louring, loury** *adj*

usage The pronunciation /'lowə/ is recommended for BBC **broadcasters.**

¹**louse** /lows/ *n, pl* (*1*) **lice** /lies/; (*2*) **louses 1a** any of various small wingless insects (orders Anoplura and Mallophaga) with usu flattened bodies, that live as parasites on warm-blooded animals, including human beings **b** any of various small usu sluggish insects or related animals that live on other animals (eg fish) or on plants and suck their blood or juices – usu in combination ⟨*plant* ~⟩ **c** any of several small nonparasitic insects or related animals – usu in combination ⟨*book* ~⟩ ⟨*wood* ~⟩ **2** *informal* a contemptible person [ME *lous,* fr OE *lūs;* akin to OHG *lūs* louse, W *llau* lice]

²**louse** *vt* to pick lice from; delouse

**louse up** *vt, informal* to make a mess of; spoil ⟨*she really loused that deal up*⟩

**lousewort** /-,wuht/ *n* any of a genus (*Pedicularis*) of plants of the foxglove family with spikes of variously coloured two-lipped flowers [fr the former belief that sheep feeding on it become infested with vermin]

**lousy** /'lowzi/ *adj* **1** infested with lice **2** *of silk* fuzzy and specked because of splitting of the fibre **3** *informal* **3a** totally repulsive; disgusting **b** wretchedly poor, useless, or inferior **c** amply or excessively supplied; replete – usu + *with* ⟨~ *with money*⟩ ⟨*the place was* ~ *with police*⟩ – **lousily** *adv,* **lousiness** *n*

¹**lout** /lowt/ *vi, archaic* to bow in respect [ME *louten,* fr OE *lūtan;* akin to ON *lūta* to bow down, OE *lȳtel* little]

²**lout** *n* **1** an awkward clownish man or youth; an oaf **2** a rough ill-mannered man or youth [perh fr ON *lūtr* bent down, fr *lūta*] – **loutish** *adj,* **loutishly** *adv,* **loutishness** *n*

**louvre,** *NAm* **louver** /'loohvə/ *n* **1** a structure on a roof with horizontal slatted apertures for the escape of smoke or admission of light **2** an opening provided with one or more slanted fixed or movable horizontal strips (eg of metal, glass, or wood) to allow flow of air but to exclude rain or sun or to provide privacy; *also* a similar device for controlling the passage of air, light, etc **3** a slanted strip of a louvre [ME *lover,* fr MF *lovier*] – **louvred** *adj*

**lovable** *also* **loveable** /'luvəbl/ *adj* having qualities that deserve love; worthy of love – **lovableness** *n,* **lovably** *adv*

**lovage** /'luvij/ *n* any of several fragrant plants of the carrot family; *esp* a European plant (*Levisticum officinale*), often cultivated as a herb, the fruits of which are sometimes used to flavour food [ME *lovache,* fr AF, fr LL *levisticum,* alter. of L *ligusticum,* fr neut of *ligusticus* of Liguria (ancient country in SW Europe, now part of Italy), fr *Ligur-, Ligus* inhabitant of Liguria]

¹**love** /luv/ *n* **1a(1)** strong affection for another arising out of kinship or personal ties ⟨*maternal* ~ *for a child*⟩ **a(2)** attraction based on sexual desire; strong affection and tenderness felt by lovers **a(3)** affection based on admiration, benevolence, or common interests ⟨~ *for his old schoolmates*⟩ **b** an assurance of love ⟨*give her my* ~⟩ **2** warm attachment, enthusiasm, or devotion ⟨~ *of the sea*⟩ **3a** the object of attachment, devotion, or admiration ⟨*football was his first* ~⟩ **b** a beloved person; a darling, dear **4a** unselfish, loyal, and benevolent concern for the good of another: **4a(1)** the fatherly concern of God for human beings **a(2)** brotherly concern for others **b** a person's adoration of God **5** a god or personification of love **6** an amorous episode; LOVE AFFAIR ⟨*My Life and* Loves – Frank Harris⟩ **7** a score of zero in various games (eg tennis) **8** *euph* SEXUAL INTERCOURSE [ME, fr OE *lufu;* akin to OHG *lupa* love, OE *lēof* dear, L *lubēre, libēre* to please; (8) fr the phrase *to play for love* to play for nothing (ie without stakes)] – **fall in love (with)** to become strongly emotionally and usu sexually attracted (to) – **for love or/nor money** in any possible way – usu neg ⟨*couldn't get a ticket for love or money*⟩ – **in love (with)** strongly emotionally attached (to) – **make love to 1** to have sexual intercourse with **2** to woo, court

²**love** *vt* **1** to hold dear; cherish **2a** to feel a lover's passion, devotion, or tenderness for **b(1)** to caress **b(2)** to fondle amorously **b(3)** *euph* to have sexual intercourse with **3** to like or desire actively; take pleasure in ⟨~d *to play the violin*⟩ **4** to thrive in ⟨*the rose* ~s *sunlight*⟩ ~ *vi* to feel love

**love affair** *n* **1** an often temporary romantic attachment between lovers, esp a man and a woman **2** a lively enthusiasm ⟨*he had a* ~ *with hang-gliding*⟩

**love apple** *n, archaic* a tomato [prob fr its alleged aphrodisiac properties]

**lovebird** /'luv,buhd/ *n* **1** any of various small usu grey or green parrots (eg the budgerigar) that show great affection for their mates **2** *pl, humorous* two human lovers ⟨*a pair of* ~s⟩

**lovebite** /'luv,biet/ *n* a temporary red mark produced in lovemaking by biting and sucking the skin, esp of the neck

**love child** *n, euph* an illegitimate child

**love drug** *n, informal* cannabis

**love feast** *n* a meal eaten in common by a Christian congregation to symbolize brotherly love [trans of LL *agape* – more at AGAPE]

**love-in-a-'mist** *n* a European plant (*Nigella damascena*) of the buttercup family, that is cultivated as a garden plant and has pale blue or white flowers enveloped in numerous very finely cut leaves

**love knot** *n* a stylized knot sometimes embroidered or made of ribbon and used as an emblem of love

**loveless** /-lis/ *adj* **1** not giving love; unloving **2** without love ⟨*a* ~ *marriage*⟩ **3** not loved; unloved – **lovelessly** *adv,* **lovelessness** *n*

**love-lies-'bleeding** *n* any of various plants (genus *Amaranthus,* esp *Amaranthus caudatus*) of the amaranth family widely cultivated for their drooping spikes of small usu scarlet or purple flowers

**lovelock** /'luv,lok/ *n* a long lock of hair worn over the shoulder by men in the 17th and 18th centuries

**lovelorn** /-,lawn/ *adj* sad because of unrequited love – **lovelornness** *n*

**¹lovely** /'luvli/ *adj* **1** delicately or delightfully beautiful **2** very pleasing; fine ⟨*a ~ view*⟩ **synonyms** see BEAUTIFUL **antonym** unlovely – **lovelily** *adv*, **loveliness** *n*

**²lovely** *n, informal* a beautiful woman; *esp* a glamorous showgirl ⟨*two lovelies on the stage*⟩ ⟨*hallo, my ~*⟩

**lovemaking** /'luv,mayking/ *n* **1** courtship **2** sexual activity; *esp* SEXUAL INTERCOURSE

**love match** *n* a marriage or engagement undertaken for love rather than financial or other advantages

**love nest** *n, journalistic* a small secret flat, room, or house used for conducting a usu illicit sexual relationship

**lover** /'luvə/ *n* **1a** a person in love **b** a person with whom somebody has a (long-term) sexual relationship outside marriage **c** *pl* two people in love with each other; *esp* two people who habitually have sexual relations **2** DEVOTEE 2

**loverly** /'luvəli/ *adj, nonstandard or humorous* lovely

**love seat** *n* an S-shaped double chair or settee allowing two people to sit side by side while facing each other

**lovesick** /'luv,sik/ *adj* **1** languishing with love **2** expressing a lover's longing – **lovesickness** *n*

**lovey** /'luvi/ *n, chiefly Br informal* LOVE 3b

**lovey-dovey** /'luvi ,duvi/ *adj, Br informal* (excessively) loving [*lovey* + *dovey*, fr *dove* + ⁴*-y*]

**loving** /'luving/ *adj* feeling or showing love; affectionate ⟨*~ care*⟩ ⟨*a ~ glance*⟩ – **lovingly** *adv*, **lovingness** *n*

**synonyms** **Loving**, **affectionate**, **fond**, **tender**, **devoted**, and **doting** may all mean "feeling or showing love or liking". **Loving** suggests sincerity and depth of feeling, and stresses the inward emotion, while **affectionate** stresses its outward expression and often suggests demonstrativeness. **Devoted** suggests a love that shows itself in attentiveness and loyalty, while **tender** implies gentle and considerate care for the loved one. **Fond** may replace **loving** or **affectionate** but often suggests a blinkered or foolish tenderness ⟨*fond parents who believe their child can do no wrong*⟩. **Doting** suggests fondness taken to extremes. Compare AMOROUS **antonyms** unloving, indifferent

**loving cup** *n* a large ornamental drinking vessel with two or more handles that is passed round among a group of people (eg in a ceremony or at a banquet) for all to drink from

**loving-'kindness** *n* tender and benevolent affection

**¹low** /loh/ *vi or n* (to) moo [vb ME *loowen*, fr OE *hlōwan;* akin to OHG *hluoen* to moo, L *calare* to call, summon, Gk *kalein;* n fr vb]

**²low** *adj* **1a** measuring little from base to top ⟨*a ~ wall*⟩ **b** situated or passing only a little above a reference line, point, or plane ⟨*~ bridges*⟩ **c** low-necked **2a** situated or passing below the normal level or surface or below the base of measurement ⟨*~ ground*⟩ ⟨*the ~ countries*⟩ **b** marking a nadir or bottom ⟨*the ~ point of his career*⟩ **3a** *of sound* not loud; soft; *also* flat **b** depressed in pitch ⟨*a ~ note*⟩ **4a** near the equator ⟨*~ latitudes*⟩ **b** near the horizon ⟨*the sun ~ in the sky*⟩ **5** humble in character or status ⟨*~ birth*⟩ **6a** lacking strength, health, or vitality; weak, prostrate ⟨*very ~ with pneumonia*⟩ **b** lacking spirit or vivacity; depressed ⟨*~ spirits*⟩ **7a** of lesser degree, size, or amount than average or ordinary ⟨*~ pressure*⟩ **b** less than usual in number, amount, or value ⟨*~ prices*⟩ **8** falling short of some standard: eg **8a** lacking dignity or formality ⟨*a ~ style of writing*⟩ **b** morally reprehensible ⟨*a ~ trick*⟩ **c** coarse, vulgar ⟨*~ language*⟩ **9** often *cap* LOW CHURCH **10** unfavourable, disparaging ⟨*had a ~ opinion of him*⟩ **11** *of a gear* designed for slow speed **12** *of a vowel* open **synonyms** see ¹MEAN [ME *lah, low*, fr ON *lāgr;* akin to MHG *læge* low, flat] – **lowness** *n*

**³low** *n* **1** something that is low: eg **1a** a depth, nadir ⟨*sales have reached a new ~*⟩ **b** a region of low atmospheric pressure; a depression **2** *NAm* bottom gear in a motor vehicle

**⁴low** *adv* at or to a low place, altitude, or degree ⟨*she fired ~ and hit him in the leg*⟩ – **lay low 1** to knock or bring down; *esp* to destroy **2** to cause to be ill or physically weakened – **lie low 1** to stay in hiding; avoid being noticed **2** to bide one's time

**usage** The adverb **low** is used after many verbs ⟨*sing/curtsey/aim low*⟩. The rarer adverb **lowly** should probably be reserved for the sense "in a humble manner".

**lowborn** /,low'bawn/ *adj* born to parents of low social rank

**lowboy** /'loh,boy/ *n, NAm* a low chest or side table with drawers that is supported on short legs – compare TALLBOY

**lowbred** /,low'bred/ *adj* rude, vulgar

**lowbrow** /'loh,brow/ *adj, derog* of, dealing with, or having unsophisticated or unintellectual tastes, esp in the arts – **lowbrow** *n*

**Low Church** *adj* tending, esp in the Church of England, to minimize emphasis on the priesthood, sacraments, and ceremonial and often to emphasize evangelical principles – **Low Churchman** *n*

**low cloud** *n* cloud with an average height of less than 2000 metres (about 6500 feet)

**low comedy** *n* comedy bordering on farce and depending on physical action and situation rather than wit and characterization – compare HIGH COMEDY

**lowdown** /'loh,down/ *n, informal* inside information – usu + the

**,low-'down** *adj, informal* contemptible, base

**¹lower, lour** /'lowə/ *vi* **1** to look sullen; frown **2** *of the weather* to become dark, gloomy, and threatening [ME *louren;* akin to MHG *lūren* to lie in wait] – **lower** *n*

**²lower** *adj* **1** relatively low in position, rank, or order **2** less advanced in the scale of evolutionary development ⟨*~ organisms*⟩ **3** constituting the popular, more representative, and often (eg in Britain) more powerful branch of a legislative body consisting of two houses ⟨*the ~ chamber*⟩ **4a** (held to be) situated beneath the earth's surface **b** *cap* being an earlier division of the named geological or archaeological period or series of rocks ⟨*Lower Cretaceous*⟩ ⟨*Lower Palaeolithic*⟩ **5** being the southern part of a specified area ⟨*~ New York State*⟩

**³lower** /'loh·ə/ *vi* to move down; drop; *also* to diminish ~ *vt* **1a** to cause to descend; let down ⟨*~ the boats!*⟩ **b** to reduce the height of ⟨*~ed the ceiling*⟩ **2a** to reduce in value or amount ⟨*~ the price*⟩ **b** to bring down; degrade; *also* to humble **c** to reduce the objective of ⟨*~ed their sights and accepted less*⟩ **3** to reduce or diminish the strength, intensity, or pitch of (music, sounds, etc)

**lower bound** *n, maths* a number less than or equal to every element of a given set

**,lower-'case** *adj, of a letter* of or conforming to the series (eg a, b, c rather than A, B, C) typically used elsewhere than at the beginning of sentences or proper names ⟨*proper nouns should not be ~*⟩

**lower case** *n* **1** a type case containing lower-case letters and usu spaces and QUADS (type-metal spaces) **2** lower-case letters [fr its being orig the lower of a pair of type cases]

**lower class** *n*, **lower classes** *n pl* a social class occupying a position below the MIDDLE CLASS and having the lowest status in a society by virtue of a low material standard of living, often caused by lack of working skills, and often social instability and a low level of personal ambition and aspiration, esp towards education – compare MIDDLE CLASS, UPPER CLASS – **lower-class** *adj*

**lower criticism** *n* textual criticism, esp of scripture – compare HIGHER CRITICISM

**lower deck** *n* **1** a deck below the main deck of a ship **2** *taking sing or pl vb, chiefly Br informal* the PETTY OFFICERS and men of a ship or navy as distinguished from the officers – compare QUARTERDECK

**lower fungus** *n* a fungus with absent or rudimentary HYPHAE (filaments making up the rootlike mass)

**lowermost** /-,mohst, -məst/ *adj* lowest

**lower school** *n* a school or part of a school for younger pupils

**,lower-'second** *n, often cap L&S* a level of honours degree between an UPPER-SECOND and a third

**lower sixth** *n, often cap L&S* the 1st year of a school SIXTH FORM

**lowery** /'lowəri/ *adj, New Eng US* gloomy, lowering

**lowest common denominator** /'loh·ist/ *n* **1** *maths* the lowest common multiple of two or more DENOMINATORS – called also LEAST COMMON DENOMINATOR **2** *derog* something (eg a level of taste) that typifies or is common to the greatest possible number of people

**lowest common multiple** *n, maths* the smallest number that can be obtained by multiplying two or more other numbers

**lowest terms** *n pl, maths* the form of a fraction in which the numerator and denominator have no factor in common ⟨*reduce a fraction to ~*⟩

**low frequency** *n* a radio frequency in the range between 30 and 300 kilohertz

**Low German** *n* **1** the German dialects of N Germany; PLATTDEUTSCH **2** the WEST GERMANIC languages (eg Dutch) other than HIGH GERMAN

,**low-'grade** *adj* **1** of inferior grade or quality ⟨~ *bonds*⟩ **2** being near the lower or least favourable extreme of a range ⟨*a ~ fever*⟩ ⟨*a ~ imbecile*⟩

,**low-'key** *also* **low-keyed** *adj* **1** of low intensity; restrained **2** *of a photograph, print, etc* having or composed of mainly dark tones with few highlights – compare HIGH-KEY

[1]**lowland** /'lohlənd/ *n*, **lowlands** *n pl* low or level country

[2]**lowland** *adj* **1** of a lowland or lowlands **2** *cap* (characteristic) of the Lowlands of Scotland – **lowlander** *n*

**Low Latin** *n* the Latin language in its later stages (e g Vulgar or Medieval Latin)

,**low-'level** *adj* **1** being of low importance or rank **2** occurring, done, or placed at a low level **3** *of a computer language* having each word, symbol, etc equal to one MACHINE CODE instruction (instruction in a form directly usable by a computer) and less like a human language than a HIGH-LEVEL computer language

**low life** *n* the life of the lower classes as treated in the arts, esp in its more picturesquely sordid aspects – compare HIGH LIFE

,**low-'loader** *n* a vehicle with a low load-carrying platform

[1]**lowly** /'lohli/ *adv* **1** in a humble or meek manner **2** in a low position, manner, or degree *usage* see [4]LOW

[2]**lowly** *adj* **1** humble and modest in manner or spirit **2** low in the scale of biological or cultural evolution **3** ranking low in some hierarchy (e g a social or economic order) **4** not lofty or sublime; prosaic – **lowliness** *n*

,**low-'lying** *adj* **1** rising relatively little above the base of measurement ⟨~ *hills*⟩ **2** lying below the normal level or surface or below the base of measurement ⟨~ *clouds*⟩

**low mass** *n, often cap L&M* a Roman Catholic mass that is recited by a single celebrant, without a choir, and without the use of incense – compare HIGH MASS

'**low-,necked**, **low-neck** *adj* having a low-cut neckline

,**low-'pitched** *adj* **1** *of sound* not shrill; deep **2** *of a roof* sloping gently

,**low-'profile** *adj* **1** having little height; low **2** intended to attract little attention; unobtrusive

**low profile** *n* an inconspicuous mode of operation or behaviour ⟨*the Government has been keeping a ~ over the disturbances* – *The Guardian*⟩

**low relief** *n* BAS-RELIEF (sculpture with forms barely projecting from the background)

'**low-,rise** *adj* **1** constructed with one or two storeys ⟨*a ~ classroom building*⟩ **2** of or characterized by low-rise buildings – compare HIGH-RISE

**low season** *n* a usu periodic time of low or reduced profitability (e g from sales) or business opportunity; *esp* a seasonal decline in the number of visitors to a holiday resort

**low silhouette** *n* LOW PROFILE

,**low-'spirited** *adj* dejected, depressed – **low-spiritedly** *adv*, **low-spiritedness** *n*

**Low Sunday** /'sunday, -di/ *n* the Sunday following Easter [prob fr its relative unimportance, compared with the high feast of Easter]

,**low-'tension** *adj* having a low voltage; *also* relating to apparatus for use at low voltages

**low tide** *n* the tide when the water reaches its lowest level; *also* the time when this occurs

**low water** *n* **1** water (e g in a river or lake) at its lowest level or ebb **2** LOW TIDE

[1]**lox** /loks/ *n* liquid oxygen [*l*iquid *ox*ygen]

[2]**lox** *n, pl* **lox, loxes** smoked salmon [Yiddish *laks*, fr MHG *lahs* salmon]

**loxodrome** /'loksə,drohm/ *n* RHUMB LINE [ISV, back-formation fr *loxodromic*]

**loxodromic** /,loksə'dromik/ *adj* relating to a RHUMB LINE or to sailing on rhumb lines [deriv of Gk *loxos* oblique (akin to L *ulna* elbow) + *dromos* course] – **loxodromically** *adv*

**loyal** /'loyəl/ *adj* **1** unswerving in allegiance: e g **1a** faithful to one's lawful sovereign or government **b** faithful to a private person to whom fidelity is due **c** faithful to a cause, ideal, or custom **2** showing loyalty ⟨*her ~ determination to help the party*⟩ [MF, fr OF *leial, leel*, fr L *legalis* legal] – **loyally** *adv*

**loyalist** /'loyəlist/ *n* somebody who is or remains loyal to a government or sovereign, esp in time of revolt

**loyalty** /'loyəlti/ *n* **1** being loyal **2** the tie binding a person to something to which he/she is loyal [ME *loyaltee*, fr MF *loialté*, fr OF *leialté*, fr *leial*]

**lozenge** /'lozinj/ *n* **1** a figure with four equal sides and two acute and two obtuse angles; a diamond-shaped figure **2** something shaped like a lozenge; *esp, heraldry* a diamond-shaped design on a COAT OF ARMS **3** a small often medicated sweet ⟨*a cough ~*⟩ [ME *losenge*, fr MF *losange*]

**LP** /,el 'pee/ *n* a gramophone record designed to be played at $33\frac{1}{3}$ revolutions per minute and typically having a diameter of 30.5 centimetres (12 inches) and a playing time of 20-25 minutes [*l*ong *p*laying]

'**L-,plate** *n* a sign bearing a letter L fixed to the front and back of a motor vehicle, esp in Britain, to show that the driver is not yet qualified [*Learner*]

**LSD** /,el es 'dee/ *n* a drug, $C_{20}H_{25}N_3O$, that induces psychotic symptoms and hallucinations similar to those of schizophrenia and is taken illegally for its potent action in producing altered perceptions [*ly*sergic acid *d*iethylamide]

**luau** /'looh·ow/ *n* a Hawaiian feast [Hawaiian *lu'au*]

**lubber** /'lubə/ *n* **1** a big clumsy fellow **2** a clumsy seaman [ME *lobre, lobur*] – **lubberliness** *n*, **lubberly** *adj or adv*

**lubber line** *n* a fixed line on the compass of a ship or aircraft that is aligned with the fore-and-aft line of the craft

**lubra** /'loohbrah, -brə/ *n, Austr chiefly derog* a female aborigine – compare [6]GIN [native name in Tasmania]

**lubricant** /'loohbrikənt/ *n* **1** a substance (e g grease or oil) capable of reducing friction, heat, and wear when introduced as a film between solid surfaces **2** something that lessens or prevents friction or difficulty ⟨*alcohol is a great ~ when strangers meet*⟩ – **lubricant** *adj*

**lubricate** /'loohbrikayt/ *vt* **1** to make smooth or slippery **2** to apply a lubricant to ~ *vi* to act as a lubricant [L *lubricatus*, pp of *lubricare*, fr *lubricus* slippery - more at SLEEVE] – **lubricator** *n*, **lubricative** *adj*, **lubrication** *n*

**lubricious** /looh'brishəs/ *adj* **1** marked by wantonness; lecherous; *also* salacious **2** having a smooth or slippery quality ⟨*a ~ skin*⟩ [(1) ML *lubricus*, fr L, slippery, easily led astray; (2) L *lubricus*] – **lubriciously** *adv*, **lubricity** *n*

**lubricous** /'loohbrikəs/ *adj* lubricious

**Lucan, Lukan** /'loohkən/ *adj* of Luke or the Gospel ascribed to him [LL *lucanus*, fr *Lucas* Luke, fr Gk *Loukas*]

**Lucayo** /looh'kie·oh/ *n* (the language of) the Lucayo people of the Bahamas in former times

**lucent** /'loohs(ə)nt/ *adj* **1** glowing with light; luminous **2** marked by clarity or translucence; clear [L *lucent-, lucens*, prp of *lucēre* to shine – more at LIGHT] – **lucency** *n*, **lucently** *adv*

**lucerne** *also* **lucern** /looh'suhn/ *n, chiefly Br* a deep-rooted European plant (*Medicago sativa*) of the pea family widely grown for fodder – called also ALFALFA [Fr *luzerne*, fr Prov *luserno*]

**lucid** /'loohsid/ *adj* **1a** suffused with light; luminous **b** translucent **2** having full use of one's faculties; sane **3** clear to the understanding; plain *antonyms* obscure, vague, dark [L *lucidus*; akin to L *lucēre*] – **lucidity** *n*, **lucidly** *adv*, **lucidness** *n*

**Lucifer** /'loohsifə/ *n* **1** – used as a name of the devil **2** the planet Venus when appearing as the MORNING STAR [ME, fr OE, fr L, the morning star, fr *lucifer* light-bearing, fr *luc-, lux* light + *-fer* -ferous – more at LIGHT; (1) fr a reference in Isaiah 14:12 to the King of Babylon falling like the morning star, interpreted by later writers as an allusion to Satan] – **luciferous** *adj*

**luciferase** /looh'sifə,rayz, -,rays/ *n* an ENZYME that activates or increases the rate of OXIDATION of luciferin [ISV, fr *luciferin*]

**luciferin** /looh'sifərin/ *n* a substance occurring in light-emitting organisms (e g fireflies and glowworms) that gives out practically heatless light when undergoing OXIDATION [ISV, fr L *lucifer* light-bearing]

**Lucina** /looh'sienə/ *n, archaic* a midwife [L, Roman goddess of childbirth]

**Lucite** /'loohsiet/ *trademark* – used for an ACRYLIC RESIN or plastic consisting essentially of long chains of METHYL METH-ACRYLATE units

**luck** /luk/ *n* **1** whatever good or bad events happen to a person by chance **2** the tendency for a person to be consistently fortunate or unfortunate **3** success as a result of good fortune [ME *lucke*, fr MD *luc*; akin to MHG *gelücke* luck] – **hard/tough/worse luck!** *informal* – used to express commiseration at somebody's misfortune – **push one's luck** *informal* to push an advantage up to or over the brink of failure ⟨*take the money, don't push your luck*⟩

**luck out** *vi, NAm* to prosper or succeed, esp through chance or good fortune

**lucky** /'luki/ *adj* **1** having good luck **2** resulting from good luck; fortuitous **3** producing or resulting in good by chance;

favourable **4** seeming to bring good luck ⟨*a* ~ *rabbit's foot*⟩ – **luckily** *adv*, **luckiness** *n*

**lucky dip** *n, Br* an attraction (e g at a party or fair) in which small prizes can be drawn unseen from a sawdust-filled barrel, box, etc, on payment of a small charge; *also* the receptacle used

**lucrative** /'loohkrətiv/ *adj* producing wealth; profitable [ME *lucratif*, fr MF, fr L *lucrativus*, fr *lucratus*, pp of *lucrari* to gain, fr *lucrum*] – **lucratively** *adv*, **lucrativeness** *n*

**lucre** /'loohkə/ *n, chiefly humorous* monetary gain; profit; *also* money – esp in *filthy lucre* [ME, fr L *lucrum;* akin to OE *lēan* reward, OHG *lōn*, Gk *leia* booty]

**lucubration** /,loohkyoo'braysh(ə)n/ *n*, **lucubrations** *n pl, formal* **1** laborious study or meditation, esp when done at night **2** studied or pretentious expression in speech or writing [L *lucubration-, lucubratio* study by night, work produced at night, fr *lucubratus*, pp of *lucubrare* to work by lamplight; akin to L *luc-, lux*] – **lucubrate** *vi*

**luculent** /'loohkyoolənt/ *adj, formal* clear in thought or expression; lucid [ME, fr L *luculentus*, fr *luc-, lux* light] – **luculently** *adv*

**Lucullan** /looh'kulən/, **Lucullian** /,loohkə'lee·ən/ *adj* lavish, luxurious ⟨*a* ~ *feast*⟩ [L *lucullanus* of Lucullus, fr Lucius Licinius *Lucullus* † *ab* 57 BC Roman general & epicure]

**Luddite** /'ludiet/ *n* **1** a member of various groups of early 19th century English textile workers organized to destroy labour-saving manufacturing machinery as a protest against unemployment **2** an opponent of industrial or technological innovation; *broadly* somebody opposed to change [Ned *Ludd* *fl* 1779 half-witted Leicestershire workman who destroyed stocking frames]

**ludic** /'loohdik/ *adj, formal* playful – used in sociology and literary criticism [Fr *ludique*, fr L *ludus* play]

**ludicrous** /'loohdikrəs/ *adj* **1** amusing or laughable through obvious absurdity or incongruity **2** meriting derisive laughter or scorn as absurdly inept, false, or foolish *synonyms* see LAUGHABLE [L *ludicrus* playful, fr *ludus* play, sport; akin to L *ludere* to play, Gk *loidoros* abusive] – **ludicrously** *adv*, **ludicrousness** *n*

**ludo** /'loohdoh/ *n, chiefly Br* a simple board game played with counters and dice, in which from two to four people advance their counters in turn towards the home square [L, I play, fr *ludere*]

**lues** /'looh·eez/ *n, pl* **lues** syphilis [NL, fr L, plague; akin to Gk *lyein* to loosen, destroy – more at LOSE] – **luetic** *adj*, **luetically** *adv*

**¹luff** /luf/ *n* the forward edge of a FORE-AND-AFT sail (one attached to the mast along its edge) [ME, weather side of a ship, luff, fr MF *lof* weather side of a ship]

**²luff** *vi* to sail more nearly against the main force of the wind – often + *up*

**luffa** /'lufə/ *n* a loofah

**Luftwaffe** /'looft,vahfə, (Ger* lʊftvafə)/ *n* the German Air Force just before and during World War II [Ger, fr *luft* air + *waffe* weapon]

**¹lug** /lug/ *vb* **-gg-** *informal* *vt* **1** to drag, pull, or carry with great effort **2** to introduce in a forced and often irrelevant manner ⟨ ~ *his name into the talk*⟩ ~ *vi* to pull with great effort; tug [ME *luggen* to pull by the hair or ear, drag, prob of Scand origin; akin to Norw *lugga* to pull by the hair]

**²lug** *n* **1** a large basket used by wholesalers for vegetables or fruit **2** *informal* an act of lugging

**³lug** *n* **1** something that projects like an ear: e g **1a** a handle **b** a leather loop on the saddle of a carthorse through which a shaft passes **2** a category of FLUE-CURED tobacco comprised of the leaves pulled from the base of the plant stalk **3** *chiefly dial Br or informal* an ear [ME (Sc) *lugge* earflap of a cap, perh fr ME *luggen*]

**Luganda** /looh'gandə, -'gahndə/ *n* GANDA **2** (African language)

**luge** /loohzh/ *n* a small toboggan that is ridden by a person lying on his/her back and used esp in racing [Fr]

**luggage** /'lugij/ *n* **1** (suitcases, bags, etc containing) the belongings which accompany a traveller **2** suitcases, bags, etc, esp when matching ⟨*a set of matching pigskin* ~⟩ [¹*lug* + *-age*]

**lugger** /'lugə/ *n* a small fishing or coasting boat that carries one or more lugsails [*lugsail*]

**lughole** /'lug,hohl/ *n, chiefly dial Br or informal* the ear hole; *broadly* the ear

**lugsail** /'lug,sayl, -səl/, **lug** *n* a 4-sided FORE-AND-AFT sail (one

---

attached to the mast at its edge) attached also to a spar hanging from the mast [perh fr ³*lug*]

**lugubrious** /looh'goohbri·əs, lə-/ *adj* mournful; *esp* exaggeratedly or affectedly mournful [L *lugubris*, fr *lugēre* to mourn; akin to Gk *lygros* mournful] – **lugubriously** *adv*, **lugubriousness** *n*

**lugworm** /'lug,wuhm/, **lug** *n* any of a genus (*Arenicola* of the class Polychaeta) of marine segmented worms that burrow in sand, have a row of tufted gills along each side of the back, and that are used for bait [origin unknown]

**Lukan** /'loohkən/ *adj* Lucan

**Luke** /loohk/ *n* – see BIBLE table [*Luke* (L *Lucas*, fr Gk *Loukas*), 1st-c physician, companion of St Paul, and reputed author of the third Gospel & the Acts of the Apostles, fr Gk *Loukas*]

**lukewarm** /,loohk'wawm/ *adj* **1** moderately warm; tepid **2** lacking conviction; indifferent [ME, fr *luke* lukewarm + *warm;* akin to OHG *lāo* lukewarm – more at LEE] – **lukewarmly** *adv*, **lukewarmness** *n*

**¹lull** /lul/ *vt* **1** to cause to sleep or rest; soothe **2** to cause to relax vigilance, esp by deception or guile ~ *vi* to become less in intensity or strength ⟨*the storm gradually* ~ed⟩ [ME *lullen*, prob of imit origin]

**²lull** *n* **1** a temporary pause or decline in activity ⟨*the early morning* ~ *in urban noise*⟩: e g **1a** a temporary calm before or during a storm **b** a temporary drop in business activity **2** *archaic* something that lulls; *esp* a lullaby

**¹lullaby** /'lulləbie/ *n* a song to quieten children or lull them to sleep [obs *lulla*, interj used to lull a child (fr ME) + *bye*, interj used to lull a child, fr ME *by*]

**²lullaby** *vt* to quieten with a lullaby

**lulu** /'looh,looh/ *n, chiefly NAm slang* someone or something remarkable or wonderful [prob fr *Lulu*, nickname for *Louise*]

**lum** /lum/ *n, chiefly Scot* a chimney [origin unknown]

**lumb-** /lumb-/, **lumbo-** *comb form* **1** lumbar and ⟨*lumbosacral*⟩ **2** loin ⟨*lumbago*⟩ [L *lumbus* loin – more at LOIN]

**lumbago** /lum'baygoh/ *n* muscular pain of the lumbar region of the back [L, fr *lumbus*]

**lumbar** /'lumbə/ *adj* of or being the region of the loins, between the ribs and hips, or the vertebrae of this region between the THORACIC vertebrae and the SACRUM (lowest part of the backbone) [NL *lumbaris*, fr L *lumbus*]

**¹lumber** /'lumbə/ *vi* to move heavily or clumsily [ME *lomeren*]

**²lumber** *n* **1** surplus or disused articles (e g furniture) that are stored away **2** *NAm* timber or logs, esp when dressed for use [perh fr *Lombard* (in obs sense, pawnshop); or perh fr ¹*lumber*] – **lumber** *adj*

**³lumber** *vt* **1** to heap together in disorder **2** *NAm* to cut down and saw the timber of **3** *chiefly Br informal* to clutter (as if) with lumber; encumber, saddle – usu pass + *with* ⟨*I was* ~ed *with the bill as usual*⟩ ⟨*parents,* ~ed *with the unenviable task of guiding choice* – *The Economist*⟩ ~ *vi, NAm* to cut and prepare timber – **lumberer** *n*

**lumberjack** /-,jak/ *n, chiefly NAm* a person engaged in lumbering

**'lumber-,jacket** *n* a heavy hip-length usu brightly checked woollen jacket that is fastened up to the neck

**lumberman** /'lumbəmən/ *n, NAm* a lumberjack

**lumberyard** /'lumbə,yahd/ *n, chiefly NAm* a wood-yard

**lumbosacral** /,lumboh'sakrəl, -'saykrəl/ *adj* of the lumbar and SACRAL (at or round the base of the backbone) regions or parts of the body

**lumen** /'loohmin/ *n, pl* **lumina** /'l(y)oohminə/, **lumens** **1** the cavity of a tubular organ or structure of the body ⟨*the* ~ *of a blood vessel*⟩ **2** the bore of a tube (e g a hollow needle or catheter) **3** the SI unit of LUMINOUS FLUX equal to the amount of light emitted in a SOLID ANGLE of 1 steradian by a POINT SOURCE of light with an intensity of 1 candela [NL *lumin-, lumen*, fr L, light, air shaft, opening] – **luminal, lumenal** *adj*

**lumin-** /loohmin-/, **lumini-, lumino-** *comb form* light ⟨*luminiferous*⟩ [ME *lumin-*, fr L *lumin-, lumen*]

**luminaire** /,loohmi'neə/ *n, chiefly NAm* a light fitting [Fr, lamp, lighting]

**luminance** /'loohminəns/ *n* **1** being luminous **2** (a measure of) the intensity of light radiating or reflected from a surface in a given direction per unit of projected area; the brightness of a point on a surface

**luminary** /'loohmin(ə)ri/ *n* a source of light or illumination: e g **a** a person brilliantly outstanding in some respect **b** *formal* a natural body that gives light (e g the sun or moon) [ME *luminarye*, fr MF & LL; MF *luminaire* lamp, fr LL *luminaria*, pl of

**luminare** lamp, heavenly body, fr L, window, fr *lumin-, lumen* light; akin to L *lucēre* to shine – more at LIGHT] – **luminary** *adj*

**luminesce** /ˌloohmiˈnes/ *vi* to exhibit luminescence [back-formation fr *luminescent*]

**luminescence** /ˌloohmiˈnes(ə)ns/ *n* (the emission of) light not due to INCANDESCENCE (light emission resulting from heating of a body), that occurs at low temperatures and that is produced by physiological processes (e g in the firefly), by chemical action, by friction, or by electrical action – **luminescent** *adj*

**luminiferous** /ˌloohmiˈnifərəs/ *adj* transmitting, producing, or yielding light

**luminosity** /ˌl(y)oohmiˈnosəti/ *n* **1a** being luminous **b** something luminous **2a** the relative quantity of light **b** the relative brightness of something; *specif* BRIGHTNESS 2

**luminous** /ˈloohminəs/ *adj* **1a** emitting or full of light; bright **b** of light or LUMINOUS FLUX **2** bathed in or exposed to steady light ⟨*a public square ~ with sunlight*⟩ **3** easily understood; *also* explaining clearly **4** intelligent, enlightened ⟨*awed at being in the presence of a ~ intellect*⟩ *synonyms* see BRIGHT [ME, fr L *luminosus*, fr *lumin-, lumen*] – **luminously** *adv*, **luminousness** *n*

**luminous flux** *n* the rate of emission or flow of light energy; RADIANT FLUX in the visible-wavelength range, usu expressed in lumens

**luminous paint** *n* paint containing a phosphorescent compound causing it to glow in the dark after exposure to light

**lumme** /ˈlumi/ *interj, Br informal* – used to express surprise [contr of ⟨*Lord*⟩ *love me*]

**lummox** /ˈluməks/ *n, informal* a clumsy person [origin unknown]

**¹lump** /lump/ *n* **1** a usu compact piece or mass of indefinite size and shape ⟨*a ~ of coal or sugar*⟩ **2a** a protuberance; *esp* an abnormal swelling **b** a bruise **3** *informal* a heavy thickset person; *specif* one who is stupid or dull **4** *taking sing or pl vb, Br informal* casual nonunion building workers as a group – + *the* [ME]

**²lump** *vt* **1** to group without discrimination – usu + *together* **2** to make lumps on, in, or of ~ *vi* to become formed into lumps

**³lump** *adj* not divided into parts; entire ⟨*a ~ sum*⟩

**⁴lump** *vt, informal* [prob imit; earlier senses, to look sulky, be displeased at] – **lump it** to put up with a state of affairs – esp in *like it or lump it*

**lumpen** /ˈloompən/ *adj, derog* of or being dispossessed and uprooted individuals cut off from the economic and social class, esp the working class, with which they might normally be identified ⟨*~ proletariat*⟩ [Ger *lumpenproletariat* lowest section of the proletariat, fr *lump* contemptible person (fr *lumpen* rags) + *proletariat*]

**lumper** /ˈlumpə/ *n, NAm* a labourer employed to handle freight or cargo

**lumpish** /ˈlumpish/ *adj* **1** dull, sluggish **2** heavy, awkward **3** tediously slow or dull; boring – **lumpishly** *adv*, **lumpishness** *n*

**'lump-ˌsucker** *n* a sea fish (*Cyclopterus lumpus*) of the northern N Atlantic that has a large rounded body and its PELVIC FINS (frontmost pair of fins on the underside of the body) modified into an efficient sucker by which the fish attaches itself to rocks, stones, etc

**lumpy** /ˈlumpi/ *adj* **1a** filled or covered with lumps **b** *of the sea* characterized by choppy waves **2** having a thickset clumsy appearance – **lumpily** *adv*, **lumpiness** *n*

**lumpy jaw** *n* ACTINOMYCOSIS (disease characterized by hard swollen masses of tissue); *esp* actinomycosis of the head in cattle

**lunacy** /ˈloohnəsi/ *n* **1a** insanity (interrupted by lucid intervals) – not now used technically **b** insanity amounting to lack of capability or responsibility in law **2** wild foolishness; extravagant folly **3** a foolish act [*lunatic* + *-cy*]

**luna moth** /ˈloohnə/ *n* a large mostly pale green N American SATURNIID moth (*Actias luna*) with crescent-shaped markings and long tails on the hind wings [NL *luna* (specific epithet of *Actias luna*), fr L, moon]

**lunar** /ˈloohnə/ *adj* **1a** of the moon **b** designed for use on the moon ⟨*~ vehicles*⟩ **2** shaped like a crescent; lunate **3** measured by the moon's revolution ⟨*~ month*⟩ [L *lunaris*, fr *luna* moon; akin to L *lucēre* to shine – more at LIGHT]

**lunar caustic** *n* SILVER NITRATE esp when melted and moulded into sticks for use in cauterizing [obs *luna* silver, fr ML, fr L, moon]

**lunar eclipse** *n* an eclipse in which the moon passes partially or wholly through the earth's shadow

**lunar excursion module, lunar module** *n* a space vehicle module designed to carry astronauts from the COMMAND MODULE to the surface of the moon and back

**lunar month** *n* a period of time averaging 29 days, 12 hours, 44 minutes, and 2.8 seconds between two successive new moons

**lunate** /ˈloohnayt/ *adj* shaped like a crescent [L *lunatus*, pp of *lunare* to bend in a crescent, fr *luna*] – **lunately** *adv*

**lunatic** /ˈloohnətik/ *adj* **1a** affected with lunacy; insane **b** designed for the care of insane people ⟨*~ asylum*⟩ **2** wildly foolish [ME *lunatik*, fr OF or LL; OF *lunatique*, fr LL *lunaticus*, fr L *luna*; fr the former belief that lunacy fluctuates with the phases of the moon] – **lunatic** *n*

**lunatic fringe** *n taking sing or pl vb* a group of eccentric or fanatical members of a usu extreme political or social movement

**lunation** /loohˈnaysh(ə)n/ *n* LUNAR MONTH [ME *lunacioun*, fr ML *lunation-, lunatio*, fr L *luna*]

**¹lunch** /lunch/ *n* **1** a light midday meal; *broadly, NAm* a light meal **2** the food prepared for a lunch [prob short for *luncheon*]

**²lunch** *vi* to eat lunch ~ *vt* to provide lunch for – **luncher** *n*

**luncheon** /ˈlunch(ə)n/ *n* **1** a midday social gathering at which a formal usu relatively large meal is eaten **2** *formal* lunch [E dial. *luncheon* large lump, alter. of earlier *lunch* lump, piece (esp of food), prob alter. of *lump*]

**luncheonette** /ˌlunchəˈnet/ *n, chiefly NAm* a café

**luncheon meat** *n* a precooked mixture of meat (e g pork) and cereal shaped in a loaf and containing preservatives

**luncheon voucher** *n* a voucher for a specified amount of money given to a British employee as a benefit additional to pay and exchangeable for food in some restaurants or shops

**lune** /loohn/ *n* a crescent-shaped figure formed on a plane surface by two intersecting arcs or on a sphere by two GREAT CIRCLES (circles having the same centre as the sphere) [L *luna* moon – more at LUNAR]

**lunette** /loohˈnet/ (*Fr* lynɛt) *n* **1a** an oval or circular window opening in a vault or dome **b** a semicircular section of wall that is partly surrounded by a vault and that is often filled by windows or by mural painting **2** a temporary fortification consisting of two walls forming a projecting angle [Fr, fr OF *lunete* small object shaped like the moon, fr *lune* moon]

**lung** /lung/ *n* **1a** either of the usu paired spongy saclike respiratory organs in the chest of air-breathing VERTEBRATE animals **b** any of various respiratory organs of INVERTEBRATE animals **2 iron lung, lung** a mechanical device for regularly introducing fresh air into and withdrawing stale air from the lung; a respirator **3** an area of open ground (e g a park or field) in a town or city – compare GREEN BELT [ME *lunge*, fr OE *lungen;* akin to OHG *lungun* lung, *līhti* light in weight – more at LIGHT]

**lungan** /ˈlungˌgən/ *n* LONGAN

**lung book** *n* BOOK LUNG (respiratory organ of spiders, scorpions, etc)

**¹lunge** /lunj/ *vt* to thrust or push with a lunge ~ *vi* to make a lunge [by shortening & alter. fr obs *allonge* to make a thrust with a sword, fr Fr *allonger* to make long, extend (an arm)]

**²lunge** *n* **1** a sudden thrust or forceful forward movement (e g with a sword or foil) **2** the act of plunging forward – **lunger** *n*

**³lunge** *n* a long rein or line used to guide a horse in training [Fr *longe*, fr OF, fr fem of *lonc* long, fr L *longus*]

**⁴lunge** *vt* to guide or exercise (a horse) on a lunge in a circular course round the trainer

**lunged** /lungd/ *adj* **1** having lungs; PULMONATE **2** having a lung or lungs of a specified kind or number – in combination ⟨*one-lunged*⟩

**lungfish** /ˈlungˌfish/ *n* any of various freshwater fishes (order Dipneusti or Cladistia) that breathe by means of a modified lunglike AIR BLADDER as well as by gills

**lungi** /ˈloongˌgi/ *n* a usu cotton cloth worn variously as a loincloth, turban, sash, or skirt esp by male Indians [Hindi *luṅgī*, fr Per]

**lungworm** /ˈlungˌwuhm/ *n* any of various parasitic NEMATODE worms that infest the lungs and air passages of mammals

**lungwort** /-ˌwuht/ *n* a European plant (*Pulmonaria officinalis*) of the forget-me-not family with usu white-spotted leaves covered in rough hairs, and bluish flowers [fr the supposed resemblance of its leaves to a diseased lung, & its former use to treat lung ailments]

**lunisolar** /ˌloohni'sohlə/ *adj* relating or attributed to the moon and the sun [L *luna* moon + E *-i-* + *solar*]

**lunitidal** /ˌloohni'tiedl/ *adj* relating to or being tidal movements dependent on the moon [L *luna* + E *-i-* + *tidal*]

**lunule** /'loohnyoohl/ *n* a crescent-shaped body part or marking (eg the whitish mark at the base of a fingernail) [NL *lunula*, fr L, crescent-shaped ornament, fr dim. of *luna* moon]

**luny** /'loohni/ *n or adj* (a) loony

**Lupercalia** /ˌloohpuh'kaylyə/ *n* an ancient Roman festival celebrated on February 15th to ensure fertility for the people, fields, and flocks [L, pl, fr *Lupercus*, god of flocks] – **Lupercalian** *adj*

**lupin**, *NAm* **lupine** /'loohpin/ *n* 1 any of a genus (*Lupinus*) of plants of the pea family that have tall spikes of variously coloured flowers and some of which are cultivated as garden plants, or for fertilizer, fodder, or their edible seeds 2 an edible lupin seed [ME, fr L *lupinus*, *lupinum*, perh fr *lupinus*, adj]

**lupine** /'loohpien/ *adj* of or resembling a wolf; wolfish [L *lupinus*, fr *lupus* wolf – more at WOLF ]

**lupinosis** /ˌloohpi'nohsis/ *n* a liver disease of sheep and cattle caused by eating a fungus growing on lupins [NL]

**lupulin** /'loohpyoolin/ *n* a fine yellow resinous powder extracted from hops, that has the characteristic hop flavour and smell and mild sedative properties [NL *lupulus* (specific epithet of the hop plant *Humulus lupulus*), fr dim. of L *lupus* wolf, hop]

**lupus** /'loohpəs/ *n* any of several diseases characterized by skin disorders; *esp* LUPUS VULGARIS [ML, fr L, wolf]

**lupus erythematosus** /ˌerəˌtheemə'tohsəs/ *n* 1 a long-lasting progressively worsening disease affecting much of the body that is marked by degenerative changes of CONNECTIVE TISSUE, reddish skin lesions, inflammation of joints, lesions and scarring of internal organs (eg the kidneys), and wasting 2 a degenerative disease affecting the skin of the head and face and often the lining of the mouth and marked by the formation of slightly raised reddened scaly patches [NL, lit., erythematous lupus]

**lupus vulgaris** /vool'gahris, vul-/ *n* a long-lasting tuberculosis of the skin marked by the formation of soft yellowish transparent swellings, ulcers and abscesses, and scarring [NL, lit., common lupus]

**¹lurch** /luhch/ *n* a decisive defeat (eg in cribbage) in which an opponent wins a game by more than double the defeated player's score [MF *lourche*, adj, defeated by a lurch, deceived] – **in the lurch** *informal* in a vulnerable and unsupported position; deserted

**²lurch** *n* an act or instance of swaying or tipping; *esp* a staggering gait [origin unknown]

**³lurch** *vi* to roll or tip abruptly; pitch; *also* to stagger

**lurcher** /'luhchə/ *n* 1 a spy, lurker 2 any of several types of swift-running long-haired hunting dogs that are crosses between the greyhound or whippet and another breed (eg the collie or terrier) 3 *archaic* a petty thief; a pilferer [E dial. *lurch* to lurk, cheat, steal, fr ME *lorchen*, prob alter. of *lurken* to lurk]

**¹lure** /lyooə, looə/ *n* 1 a bunch of feathers and often meat attached to a long cord and used by a falconer to recall a hawk 2a something or someone used to entice or decoy b the power to appeal or attract ⟨the ∼ of success⟩ 3 a decoy for attracting animals to capture: eg 3a an artificial bait used for catching fish b a structure on the head of some fish that is often luminous and used to attract prey [ME, fr MF *loire*, of Gmc origin; akin to MHG *luoder* bait; akin to OE *lathian* to invite, OHG *ladōn*]

**²lure** *vt* 1 to recall (a hawk) by means of a lure 2 to tempt with a promise of pleasure or gain – **lurer** *n*

*synonyms* Lure, entice, inveigle, decoy, tempt, and seduce can all mean "attract out of one's usual or proper course into danger or harm". Lure suggests the use of ruses or promises, or simply an irresistible influence drawing one on, not necessarily to one's detriment ⟨the sun lured her out of doors⟩ ⟨universities seeking to lure the best students to their faculties⟩. Entice, often interchangeable with lure, but more personal, usually implies artfulness and coaxing. Inveigle may imply the use of flattery or deceit as well as artful adroitness to achieve one's ends. Decoy suggests misleading appearances which lead people astray or into a trap. Tempt and seduce often imply an attempt (successful in the case of seduce) to overcome moral scruples, though tempt may sometimes simply refer to action against one's better judgment, and in general use may be so weakened as to mean simply "attract". Compare CATCH, CHARM

**lurex** /'looəreks, 'lyooəreks/ *n or adj* (fabric) made with Lurex thread

**Lurex** *trademark* – used for a type of thread which is (partly) coated so as to give a metallic appearance

**lurid** /'l(y)ooərid/ *adj* 1 wan and ghastly pale in appearance 2 shining with the red glow of fire seen through smoke or cloud 3a causing horror or revulsion; gruesome b highly coloured; sensational ⟨∼ newspaper reports of the crime⟩ [L *luridus* pale yellow, sallow, fr *luror* pale yellowish colour] – **luridly** *adv*, **luridness** *n*

**lurk** /luhk/ *vi* 1a to lie hidden in wait, esp with evil intent b to move furtively or inconspicuously 2a to be concealed but capable of being discovered; *specif* to constitute a latent threat b to lie hidden [ME *lurken*; akin to MHG *lüren* to lie in wait – more at LOWER] – **lurker** *n*

**luscious** /'lushəs/ *adj* 1 having a delicious taste or smell; sweet 2 having sensual appeal; seductive 3 richly luxurious or appealing to the senses; *also* excessively ornate 4 *archaic* excessively sweet; cloying [ME *lucius*, perh alter. of *licius*, short for *delicious*] – **lusciously** *adv*, **lusciousness** *n*

**¹lush** /lush/ *adj* 1a producing or covered by luxuriant growth ⟨∼ grass⟩ ⟨∼ pastures⟩ b characterized by abundance; plentiful 2 opulent, sumptuous *synonyms* see PROFUSE [ME *lusch* soft, tender] – **lushly** *adv*, **lushness** *n*

**²lush** *n* 1 *NAm slang* intoxicating liquor; drink 2 *chiefly NAm derog* a habitual heavy drinker; a drunkard, alcoholic [perh fr ¹*lush*]

**Luso-** /'loohsoh-/ *comb form* Portuguese and ⟨Luso-*Brazilian*⟩ ⟨Luso-*African*⟩ [Pg, fr *lusitano* Portuguese, fr L *lusitanus* of Lusitania (ancient region corresponding approximately to modern Portugal)]

**¹lust** /lust/ *n* 1 strong sexual desire, esp as opposed to love 2 an intense longing; a craving [ME, pleasure, appetite, sexual desire, fr OE; akin to OHG *lust* pleasure, L *lascivus* wanton] – **lustful** *adj*, **lustfully** *adv*, **lustfulness** *n*

**²lust** *vi* to have an intense desire or need; crave; *specif* to have an intense sexual need – often + *after* or *for*

**lustral** /'lustrəl/ *adj* 1 purificatory 2 *archaic* happening at intervals of five years: quinquennial [L *lustralis*, fr *lustrum*]

**lustrate** /'lustrayt/ *vt* to purify ceremonially [L *lustratus*, pp of *lustrare* to brighten, purify] – **lustration** *n*

**¹lustre**, *NAm chiefly* **luster** /'lustə/ *n* a lustrum [ME *lustre*, fr L *lustrum*]

**²lustre**, *NAm chiefly* **luster** *n* 1 a glow of reflected light; a sheen; *specif* the property of a mineral that is determined by the amount and quality of light reflected from its surface 2a a glow of light (as if) from within b radiant beauty 3 glory, distinction ⟨he has added ∼ to his name⟩ 4a a glass pendant used esp to ornament a candlestick or chandelier b a decorative object (eg a chandelier) hung with glass pendants 5 a lustrous fabric with cotton warp and a wool, mohair, or alpaca weft 6 lustreware [MF *lustre*, fr OIt *lustro*, fr *lustrare* to brighten, fr L; akin to L *lucēre* to shine – more at LIGHT] – **lustreless** *adj*

**³lustre**, *NAm chiefly* **luster** *vt* 1 to give lustre or distinction to 2 to coat or treat with a substance that imparts lustre

**lustreware** /-ˌweə/ *n* pottery or porcelain decorated with an iridescent glaze before firing

**¹lustring** /'lustring/ *n* LUTESTRING (silk fabric) [modif of It *lustrino*]

**²lustring** /'lust(ə)ring/ *n* a finishing process (eg CALENDERING) for giving a gloss to yarns and cloth [fr gerund of ³*lustre*]

**lustrous** /'lustrəs/ *adj* 1 having lustre; shining ⟨a ∼ satin⟩ ⟨the ∼ glow of an opal⟩ 2 radiant in character or reputation; illustrious *synonyms* see BRIGHT – **lustrously** *adv*, **lustrousness** *n*

**lustrum** /'lustrəm/ *n, pl* **lustrums**, **lustra** /'lustrə/ a period of five years [L, a ceremonial purification of the Roman people made every five years after the census; akin to L *lustrare* to brighten, purify]

**lusty** /'lusti/ *adj* 1 full of vitality; healthy 2 full of strength; vigorous – **lustihood** *n*, **lustily** *adv*, **lustiness** *n*

**lusus naturae** /ˌloohsəs na'tooərie, 'natyoorie, -ree/ *n* a sport or freak of nature; a monster, mutant [NL, lit., game of nature]

**¹lute** /looht/ *n* an ancient stringed instrument with a large pear-shaped body, a neck with a fretted fingerboard, and pairs of strings tuned in unison [ME, fr MF *lut*, fr OProv *laut*, fr Ar *al-'ūd*, lit., the wood]

**²lute, luting** *n* a substance (eg cement or clay) used esp for sealing or packing joints or for coating a porous surface to make it impervious to a liquid or gas [ME *lute*, fr L *lutum* mud – more at POLLUTE]

³**lute** *vt* to seal or coat with lute

¹**lute-** /looht-/, **luteo-** *comb form* yellowish ⟨luteo*lin*⟩

²**lute-, luteo-** *comb form* CORPUS LUTEUM ⟨luteo*trophic*⟩ [NL (*corpus*) *luteum*]

**luteal** /'loohti·əl/ *adj* of or involving the CORPUS LUTEUM (hormone-producing body present in the ovary during pregnancy)

**lutecium** /looh'teesh(y)əm/ *n* LUTETIUM

**lutein** /'loohti·in, -teen/ *n* an orange XANTHOPHYLL (type of pigment), $C_{40}H_{56}O_2$, occurring in plants, animal fat, egg yolk, and the CORPUS LUTEUM (hormone-producing body present in the ovary during pregnancy)

**lutein·ize, -ise** /'loohti·i,niez, -teeniez/ *vt* to cause the production of a CORPUS LUTEUM (hormone-producing body present in the ovary during pregnancy) in ~ *vi* to undergo transformation into a CORPUS LUTEUM – **luteinization** *n*

**luteinizing hormone** /'loohti·iniezing, 'loohtee-/ *n* a hormone produced by the front lobe of the PITUITARY GLAND that stimulates ovulation and the development of the CORPUS LUTEUM (body of tissue that produces hormones needed in pregnancy) in the female, and in the male causes the development of the INTERSTITIAL tissue of the testis resulting in increased production of male SEX HORMONES

**luteinizing hormone-releasing hormone** *n* a local hormone produced by the brain that causes the release of LUTEINIZING HORMONE from the PITUITARY GLAND

**lutenist** /'loohtinist/, **lutanist** /-tən-/ *n* a lute player [ML *lutanista*, fr *lutana* lute, prob fr MF *lut*]

**luteotrophic** /,loohtioh'trofik, -'trohfik/, **luteotropic** *adj* promoting the growth of the CORPUS LUTEUM (hormone-producing body present in the ovary during pregnancy)

**luteotrophic hormone** *n* PROLACTIN (hormone inducing milk production in humans)

**luteotrophin** /-'trohfin/, **luteotropin** *n* PROLACTIN (hormone inducing milk production in humans) [*luteotroph*ic, *luteotrop*ic + *-in*]

**luteous** /'loohti·əs/ *adj* yellow tinged with green or brown [L *luteus* yellowish, fr *lutum*, a plant used for dyeing yellow]

**lutestring** /'looht,string/ *n* a plain glossy silk formerly much used for women's dresses and ribbons [by folk etymology fr It *lustrino* glossy fabric, fr *lustro* lustre]

**lutetium** *also* **lutecium** /looh'teesh(y)əm/ *n* a silvery-white chemical element that is a metal and a member of the RARE-EARTH group of elements [NL, fr L *Lutetia*, ancient name of Paris, city in France]

¹**Lutheran** /'loohthərən/ *n* a member of a Lutheran church

²**Lutheran** *adj* 1 of the religious doctrines (eg justification by faith alone) developed by Martin Luther or his followers 2 of the Protestant churches adhering to Lutheran doctrines, liturgy, and forms of organization [Martin *Luther* †1546 Ger religious reformer] – **Lutheranism** *n*

**luting** /'loohting/ *n* ²LUTE (material for sealing holes, joints, etc)

**lutz** /loots/ *n* a jump in ice-skating from the outside backward edge of one skate with a complete turn in the air and a return to the outside backward edge of the other skate [prob irreg fr Gustave *Lussi* b1898 Swiss figure-skater, its inventor]

**Luwian** /'looh·iən, -wiən/ *n* an Anatolian language of the Indo-European language family [*Luwi* (an ancient people of the southern coast of Asia Minor)] – **Luwian** *adj*

**lux** /luks/ *n, pl* **lux, luxes** the SI unit of illumination equal to one lumen per square metre [L, light – more at LIGHT]

**luxate** /'luksayt/ *vt* to throw out of place or out of joint; displace, dislocate – used in medicine and dentistry [L *luxatus*, pp of *luxare*, fr *luxus* dislocated – more at LOCK] – **luxation** *n*

**luxe** /luks, looks/ *n* luxury [Fr, fr L *luxus* – more at LUXURY] – **luxe** *adj*

**luxuriant** /lug'zhooəri·ənt/ *adj* 1 characterized by abundant growth 2a exuberantly rich and varied; prolific b richly or excessively ornamented ⟨~ *prose*⟩ **synonyms** see PROFUSE – **luxuriance** *n*, **luxuriantly** *adv*

**luxuriate** /lug'zhooəriayt/ *vi* 1 to grow extensively or profusely 2 to enjoy oneself consciously; revel – often + *in* [L *luxuriatus*, pp of *luxuriare*, fr *luxuria*]

**luxurious** /lug'zhooəri·əs/ *adj* 1 of unrestrained gratification of the senses; voluptuous 2 fond of luxury or self-indulgence 3 characterized by opulence and rich abundance – **luxuriously** *adv*, **luxuriousness** *n*

**luxury** /'lukshəri/ *n* 1 great ease or comfort based on habitual or liberal use of expensive items without regard to cost ⟨lived

*in* ~⟩ 2a something desirable but costly or difficult to obtain ⟨a ~ *few can afford*⟩ b something relatively expensive adding to pleasure or comfort but not indispensable 3 an enjoyable self-indulgence ⟨a weekly box of chocolates is her one ~⟩ – see also **in the** LAP **of luxury** [ME *luxurie* lechery, lust, fr MF, fr L *luxuria* rankness, luxury, excess; akin to L *luxus* luxury, excess] – **luxury** *adj*

**lwei** /lə'way/ *n, pl* **lwei** *also* **lweis** – see *kwanza* at MONEY table [native name in Angola]

¹**-ly** /-li/ *suffix* (→ *adj*) 1 like in appearance, manner, or nature; having the characteristics of ⟨*fatherly*⟩ ⟨*queenly*⟩ 2 recurring regularly at intervals of; every ⟨*hourly*⟩ ⟨*daily*⟩ [ME, fr OE *-līc, -lic;* akin to OHG *-līh;* both fr a prehistoric Gmc noun represented by OE *līc* body – more at LIKE]

²**-ly** *suffix* (→ *adv*) 1 in (such) a manner ⟨*slowly*⟩ 2 from (such) a point of view ⟨*musically speaking*⟩ 3 with respect to ⟨*partly*⟩ 4 as is (specified); it is (specified) that ⟨*naturally*⟩ ⟨*regrettably*⟩ 5 speaking (in a specified way) ⟨*frankly*⟩ ⟨*briefly*⟩ [ME, fr OE *-līce, -lice,* fr *-līc*, adj suffix]

**usage** Adjectives ending in *-ical* ⟨*practical*⟩ ⟨*political*⟩ form adverbs with *-ly* ⟨*practically*⟩ ⟨*politically*⟩; adjectives ending in *-ic* ⟨*scenic*⟩ ⟨*sarcastic*⟩ usually form adverbs with *-ally* ⟨*scenically*⟩ ⟨*sarcastically*⟩. The only well-known words ending in *-icly* are ⟨*publicly*⟩ and the variant spelling ⟨*frantically*⟩.

**lyart** /'lie·ət/ *adj, chiefly Scot* (streaked with) grey [ME, fr MF *liart*]

**lyase** /'lie·ayz, -ays/ *n* any of a group of enzymes (eg a DECARBOXYLASE) that catalyse reactions, or their reversal, in which a DOUBLE BOND (chemical bond in which two bonds join two atoms) is formed in a molecule by removing a chemical group from the molecule by a process other than HYDROLYSIS (reaction with water) [Gk *lyein* to loosen, release + E *-ase* – more at LOSE]

**lycaenid** /lie'seenid/ *n* any of a family (Lycaenidae) of medium-sized often brilliantly coloured butterflies (eg the blues, coppers, and hairstreaks) [deriv of NL *Lycaena*, genus of butterflies, fr Gk *lykaina*, fem of *lykos* wolf]

**lycanthrope** /'liekən,throhp, lie'kanthrohp/ *n* 1 a person displaying lycanthropy 2 a werewolf [NL *lycanthropus*, fr Gk *lykanthrōpos* werewolf, fr *lykos* wolf + *anthrōpos* man – more at WOLF]

**lycanthropy** /lie'kanthrəpi/ *n* 1 *psychology* a delusion that one has become a wolf 2 the changing of a human being into a wolf, that is held to be possible by witchcraft or magic and is often thought to be associated with the occurrence of the full moon – **lycanthropic** *adj*

**lycée** /'leesay (Fr lise)/ *n* a French public secondary school that prepares for university [Fr, fr MF, lyceum, fr L *Lyceum*]

**lyceum** /lie'see·əm/ *n* 1 a lycée 2 *often cap* a public building, cinema, theatre, etc 3 *chiefly NAm* a hall for public lectures or discussions; *also* an organization responsible for presenting such a programme [L *Lyceum*, gymnasium near Athens where Aristotle taught, fr Gk *Lykeion*, fr neut of *lykeios*, epithet of Apollo, god of poetry]

**lychee** /'liechi/ *n* a litchi

**lych-gate** /lich/ *n* a roofed gate at the entrance to a churchyard, that is traditionally used as resting place for a coffin during the first part of the burial service [ME *lycheyate*, fr *lich* body, corpse (fr OE *līc*) + *gate, yate* gate]

**lychnis** /'liknis/ *n* any of a genus (*Lychnis*) of plants of the pink family (eg RAGGED ROBIN) with heads of showy mostly red or white flowers [NL, genus name, fr L, a red flower, fr Gk; akin to Gk *lychnos* lamp, L *lux* light – more at LIGHT]

**Lycian** /'lisiən/ *n* 1 a native or inhabitant of Lycia 2 an Anatolian language of the Indo-European language family [*Lycia*, ancient region in SW Asia Minor] – **Lycian** *adj*

**lycopod** /'liekə,pod/ *n* LYCOPODIUM 1; *broadly* CLUB MOSS [NL *Lycopodium*]

**lycopodium** /,liekə'pohdi·əm/ *n* 1 any of a large genus (*Lycopodium*) of upright or creeping CLUB MOSSES (group of primitive plants) with evergreen leaves having one vein 2 a fine yellowish inflammable powder composed of lycopodium spores and used, esp formerly, in pharmacy (eg as a covering for pills) and as a component of fireworks [NL, genus name, fr Gk *lykos* wolf + *podion*, dim. of *pod-, pous* foot – more at FOOT; fr the clawlike shape of its root]

**lycosid** /lie'kohsid/ *n, pl* **lycosidae** any of a genus (*Lycosa*) of WOLF SPIDERS [NL *Lycosa*, genus name, fr L *lycos*, a spider, fr Gk *lykos*, lit., wolf] – **lycosid** *adj*

**Lycra** /'liekrə/ *trademark* – used for a synthetic yarn resembling elastic, made from polyurethane and used chiefly in corsetry and swimwear

**lyddite** /'lidiet/ *n* a powerful explosive composed chiefly of PICRIC ACID [*Lydd*, town in Kent, England, near which it was first tested in 1888]

**lydian mode** /'lidiən/ *n* a MODE (fixed arrangement of eight notes) which may be represented on the white keys of the piano from F to F [*Lydia*, ancient country in W Asia Minor]

**lye** /lie/ *n* a strong alkaline liquid rich in POTASSIUM CARBONATE, that is leached from wood ashes and used esp in making soap; *broadly* a strong alkaline solution (e g of SODIUM HYDROXIDE or POTASSIUM HYDROXIDE) △ lie [ME, fr OE *lēag;* akin to OHG *louga* lye, L *lavare, lavere* to wash, Gk *louein*]

**lygus bug** /'liegəs/ *n* any of various small TRUE BUGS (genus *Lygus*) with sucking mouthparts, including some that transmit virus diseases of plants [NL *Lygus,* genus name]

**,lying-'in** /'lie·ing/ *n, pl* **lyings-in, lying-ins** confinement for childbirth

**lying in state** *n* (the period of) the ceremonial display of (a coffin containing) the dead body of a person of high rank to which people may pay homage

**lyme grass** /liem/ *n* any of various rough creeping grasses (genus *Elymus*); *esp* one (*Elymus arenarius*) often planted on sand to hold it together and prevent erosion [prob fr obs *lyme* birdlime – more at LIME]

**lymph** /limf/ *n* 1 a pale liquid containing WHITE BLOOD CELLS but normally no RED BLOOD CELLS, that drains from spaces between the cells of body tissues into a system of channels and ducts through which it circulates and is purified before passing into the bloodstream – compare TISSUE FLUID 2 *archaic* a spring or stream of water; *also* pure water [L *lympha* water goddess, water, fr Gk *nymphē* nymph – more at NUPTIAL; (1) NL, fr L]

**lymph-** /limf-/, **lympho-** *comb form* lymph; lymphoid tissue ⟨lympho*cyte*⟩ [NL *lympha*]

**lymphadenitis** /lim,fadi'nietəs, ,---'--/ *n* inflammation of LYMPH NODES [NL, fr *lymphaden* lymph node, fr *lymph-* + Gk *adēn* gland – more at ADEN-]

**¹lymphatic** /lim'fatik/ *adj* **1a** of, involving, or produced by lymph, lymphoid tissue, or lymphocytes **b** conveying lymph ⟨~ *vessels*⟩ ⟨~ *system*⟩ **2** lacking physical or mental energy; sluggish – **lymphatically** *adv*

**²lymphatic** *n* a vessel that contains or conveys lymph

**lymph cell** *n* a cell that occurs in lymph; *specif* a lymphocyte

**lymph gland** *n* LYMPH NODE

**lymph node** *n* any of the rounded masses of tissue containing lymphocytes and lymphoblasts, that occur along the course of the lymphatic vessels and through which lymph passes and is purified (e g by removal of bacteria) before entering the bloodstream

**lymph nodule** *n* a small simple LYMPH NODE

**lymphoblast** /'limfoh,blast, -,blahst/ *n* a cell that produces lymphocytes [ISV] – **lymphoblastic** *adj*

**lymphocyte** /'limfəsiet/ *n* a WHITE BLOOD CELL that is present in large numbers in lymph and lymphoid tissue, makes up 20 to 30 per cent of the white blood cells of normal human blood, and forms part of the immune system that defends the body against invading or foreign matter (e g by producing antibodies) [ISV] – **lymphocytic** *adj*

**lymphocytosis** /,limfoh-sie'tohsis/ *n* an increase in the number of lymphocytes in the blood usu associated with long-lasting infections (e g GLANDULAR FEVER) [NL, fr ISV *lymphocyte*] – **lymphocytotic** *adj*

**lymphogranuloma** /,limfoh-granyoo'lohmə/ *n, pl* **lymphogranulomas, lymphogranulomata** /-mətə/ **1** an area of swollen inflamed tissue in a LYMPH NODE **2 lymphogranuloma, lymphogranuloma inguinale, lymphogranuloma venereum** a contagious VENEREAL DISEASE caused by a virus and marked by swelling and ulceration of lymphoid tissues in the groin and pelvic regions [NL] – **lymphogranulomatous** *adj*

**lymphogranulomatosis** /,limfoh-granyoo,lohmə'tohsis/ *n, pl* **lymphogranulomatoses** /-seez/ the development of lymphogranulomas in various parts of the body; *also* a condition characterized by lymphogranulomas [NL *lymphogranulomat-, lymphogranuloma* + *-osis*]

**lymphography** /lim'fografi/ *n* the taking of X-ray photographs showing LYMPH NODES and lymphatic vessels – **lymphographic** *adj*

**lymphoid** /'limfoyd/ *adj* **1** of, resembling, or conveying lymph **2** of or being the tissue characteristic of the LYMPH NODES

**lymphoma** /lim'fohmə/ *n, pl* **lymphomas, lymphomata** /-mətə/ a tumour of lymphoid tissue [NL] – **lymphomatoid** *adj*, **lymphomatous** *adj*

**lymphomatosis** /,limfoh-mə'tohsis/ *n, pl* **lymphomatoses** /-seez/ the presence of multiple lymphomas in the body [NL *lymphomat-, lymphoma* + *-osis*]

**lymphopoiesis** /,limfəpoy'eesis/ *n, pl* **lymphopoieses** /-seez/ the formation of lymphocytes by the body [NL] – **lymphopoietic** *adj*

**lymphosarcoma** /,limfoh-sah'kohmə/ *n, pl* **lymphosarcomas, lymphosarcomata** /-mətə/ a cancerous lymphoma that tends to spread from the original site and form new growths freely, esp along the adjacent lymphatic vessels [NL] – **lymphosarcomatous** *adj*

**lyncean** /lin'see·ən/ *adj* sharp-sighted [L *lync-, lynx* lynx; but prob sometimes taken as a reference to *Lynceus*, mythological figure famous for his sharp sight (L *Lynceus*, fr Gk *Lynkeus*)]

**lynch** /linch/ *vt* to put to death illegally by mob action [*lynch law*] – **lyncher** *n*

**lynchet** /'linchit/ *n, Br* a terrace formed on a hillside as a result of prehistoric ploughing [*lynch* (alter. of *link* ridge of land) + *-et* – more at LINKS]

**lynch law** *n* the punishment of presumed crimes or offences usu by death without due process of law [prob fr William *Lynch* †1820 US citizen who organized extralegal tribunals in Virginia]

**lynchpin** /-,pin/ *n* a linchpin

**lynx** /lingks/ *n, pl* **lynxes,** *esp collectively* **lynx** any of various Eurasian and N American wildcats with relatively long legs, a short stubby tail, mottled coat, and often tufted ears: e g **a** the common lynx (*Felis lynx*) of N Europe and Asia **b** the bobcat [L, fr Gk; akin to OE *lox* lynx, Gk *leukos* white – more at LIGHT]

**'lynx-,eyed** *adj* sharp-sighted

**lyo-** /lioh-/ *comb form* dissolved or dispersed state; dispersion ⟨*lyophilic*⟩ [prob fr NL, fr Gk *lyein* to loosen, dissolve – more at LOSE]

**lyonnaise** /,lee·ə'nez, ,lie·ə'nayz/ (*Fr* ljɔnɛz) *adj* prepared with onions ⟨~ *potatoes*⟩ [Fr (*à la*) *lyonnaise* in the manner of Lyons, fr fem of *lyonnais* of Lyons, fr *Lyon* Lyons, city in France]

**lyophile** /'lie·ə,fiel/ *adj* **1** lyophilic **2** of or obtained by freeze-drying [ISV]

**lyophilic** /,lie·ə'filik/ *adj, chemistry, esp of a* COLLOID marked by a strong attraction between a dispersed substance and the liquid in which it is dispersed – compare LYOPHOBIC

**lyophil·ize, -ise** /lie'ofiliez/ *vt* to freeze-dry – **lyophilizer** *n*, **lyophilization** *n*

**lyophobic** /,lie·ə'fohbik/ *adj, chemistry, esp of a* COLLOID marked by a lack of strong attraction between a dispersed substance and the liquid in which it is dispersed – compare LYOPHILIC

**lyrate** /'lie·ərət/ *adj* shaped like a lyre ⟨*the* ~ *horns of the impala*⟩ – **lyrately** *adv*

**lyre** /'lie·ə/ *n* a stringed instrument of the harp family used by the ancient Greeks esp to accompany song and recitation △ liar [ME *lire*, fr OF, fr L *lyra*, fr Gk]

**lyrebird** /-,buhd/ *n* either of two Australian pheasantlike songbirds (genus *Menura*), of which the male has very long tail feathers that are displayed during courtship in the shape of a lyre

**¹lyric** /'lirik/ *adj* **1** suitable for singing to the lyre **2** suitable for being set to music and sung **3** expressing direct usu intense personal emotion ⟨~ *poetry*⟩ **4** *of a singer* having a light voice and a melodic style – compare DRAMATIC [MF or L; MF *lyrique* of a lyre, fr L *lyricus*, fr Gk *lyrikos*, fr *lyra*]

**²lyric** *n* **1** a lyric composition; *specif* a lyric poem **2** *pl* the words of a popular song or musical-comedy number

**lyrical** /'lirikl/ *adj* **1** lyric **2** full of admiration or enthusiasm ⟨*he was* ~ *about Bournemouth*⟩ – **lyrically** *adv*, **lyricalness** *n*

**lyricism** /'lirisiz(ə)m/ *n* **1a** the quality or state of being lyric; songfulness **b** a directly personal and intense style or quality in an art (e g poetry or music) **2** great enthusiasm or exuberance

**lyricist** /'lirisist/ *n* a writer of lyrics

**lyrist** /'lie·ərist; sense 2 'lirist/ *n* **1** somebody who plays the lyre **2** a lyricist

**lys-** /lies-/, **lysi-, lyso-** *comb form* breakdown; lysis ⟨lys*in*⟩ [NL, fr Gk *lys-, lysi-* loosening, fr *lysis*]

**lysate** /'liesayt/ *n* a product of lysis or breakdown

**lyse** /lies, liez/ *vb* to (cause to) undergo lysis or breakdown [back-formation fr NL *lysis*]

**-lyse**, *NAm chiefly* **-lyze** /-liez/ *comb form* (→ *vb*) produce or undergo lysis or breakdown ⟨*electrolyse*⟩ [ISV, prob irreg fr NL *-lysis*]

**Lysenkoism** /li'sengkoh·iz(ə)m/ *n* a biological doctrine that, in contradiction to orthodox genetics, asserts the fundamental influence of environmental and other nongenetic factors on evolution, and the passing-on from one generation to the next of characteristics acquired during the parent's lifetime – compare LAMARCKISM, NEO-DARWINISM [Trofim *Lysenko* b1898 Russ geneticist]

**lysergic acid** /lie'suhjik/ *n* an acid, $C_{16}H_{16}N_2O_2$, that is obtained from chemical substances present in ERGOT (fungus that grows on rye) and used in the manufacture of drugs for medical use [*lys-* + *ergot*]

**lysergic acid diethylamide** /~ ˌdieˌethil'aymied, -ˌeethil-, ˌdie·ə'thieləmied/ *n* LSD

**lysimeter** /lie'simitə/ *n* a device for measuring the percolation of water through soils and for determining the (amount of) soluble constituents removed in the drainage – **lysimetric** *adj*

**lysin** /'liesin/ *n* a substance capable of causing lysis or breakdown; *esp* an antibody capable of causing disintegration of RED BLOOD CELLS or microorganisms

**lysine** /'lieseen, -sin/ *n* an ESSENTIAL AMINO ACID, $NH_2(CH_2)_4CH(NH_2)COOH$, that is required by the body for normal growth and health

**lysis** /'liesis/ *n, pl* **lyses** /-seez/ 1 the gradual decline of a disease process (e g fever) 2 a process of disintegration or breakdown (e g of cells) [NL, fr Gk, act of loosening, dissolution, remission of fever, fr *lyein* to loosen – more at LOSE]

**-lysis** /-ləsis/ *comb form* (→ *n*), *pl* **-lyses** /-ləseez/ decomposition; disintegration; breakdown ⟨*electrolysis*⟩ ⟨*autolysis*⟩ [NL, fr L & Gk; L, loosening, fr Gk, fr *lysis*]

**lyso-** /liesoh-/ – see LYS-

**lysogen** /'liesəjen/ *n* a lysogenic bacterium or strain of bacteria

**lysogenic** /ˌliesə'jenik/ *adj* 1 *of a bacterium or strain of bacteria* having a virus (PROPHAGE) incorporated into the hereditary material that destroys other bacteria whilst being harmless to the virus carrier 2 TEMPERATE 3 ⟨~ *viruses*⟩ – **lysogenicity** *n*, **lysogeny** *n*

**lysogen·ize, -ise** /lie'sojəniez/ *vt* to make lysogenic – **lysogenization** *n*

**Lysol** /'liesol, -sohl/ *trademark* – used for a disinfectant consisting of a brown solution containing CRESOLS

**lysosome** /'liesəˌsohm/ *n* any of the membrane-surrounded sacs or cavities that occur in CYTOPLASM (jellylike material inside a cell) and contain various enzymes that are capable of breaking down unwanted or ingested material or of causing the breakdown and disintegration of the cell itself (AUTOLYSIS) [ISV *lys-* + ³*-some*] – **lysosomal** *adj*, **lysosomally** *adv*

**lysozyme** /'liesəˌziem/ *n* an enzyme present in egg white and in human tears and saliva, that destroys various bacteria by dissolving their protective cell walls

**-lyte** /-liet/ *comb form* (→ *n*) substance capable of undergoing (a specified process or change) ⟨*electrolyte*⟩ [Gk *lytos* that may be untied, soluble, fr *lyein*]

**lythe** /liedh/ *n, Br* a pollack [origin unknown]

**lytic** /'litik/ *adj* of breakdown (LYSIS) or a substance (LYSIN) causing breakdown; *also* producing or effecting lysis (e g of cells) [Gk *lytikos* able to loosen, fr *lyein*] – **lytically** *adv*

**-lytic** /-'litik/ *suffix* (→ *adj*) of or effecting (such) breakdown or decomposition ⟨*hydrolytic enzymes*⟩ [Gk *lytikos*]

**-lyze** /-liez/ *comb form* (→ *vb*), *NAm* -lyse

# M

**m, M** /em/ *n, pl* **m's, ms, M's, Ms 1a** the 13th letter of the English alphabet **b** a graphic representation of or device for reproducing the letter *m* **c** a speech counterpart of printed or written *m* **d** one designated *m*, esp as the 13th in order or class **2** one thousand **3** something shaped like the letter M **4a** EM 1 (unit of width used by printers) **b** ¹PICA 2

**'m** /-m/ *vb* am ⟨*I'm going*⟩

**M60 machine gun** *n* a 0.30 inch calibre gas-operated air-cooled machine gun fed by a cartridge belt and currently used by some NATO troops

**ma** /mah/ *n, informal* a mother – used chiefly as a term of address [short for *mama*]

**ma'am** /mam, mahm; *unstressed* məm/ *n* madam – used widely in the USA and in Britain, esp by servants and when addressing the Queen or a royal princess

**mac, mack** /mak/ *n, Br informal* an often casual coat or jacket made from waterproof or water-resistant material (e g plastic or rubberized fabric); a raincoat [short for *mackintosh*]

**Mac** *n, informal* **1** – used to address a Scotsman **2** *NAm* – used to address a man whose name is not known

**macabre** /mə'kahb(r)ə/ *adj* **1** having death as a subject; including a personification of death **2** dwelling on the gruesome; morbid **3** tending to produce horror in an onlooker [Fr, fr (*danse*) *macabre* dance of death, fr MF (*danse de*) *Macabré*]

**macadam** /mə'kadəm/ *n* **1** (a) macadamized road or pavement – compare TARMACADAM **2** material used in making a macadamized road [John *McAdam* †1836 Sc engineer]

**macadamia** /ˌmakə'daymiə/ *n* any of a genus (*Macadamia*, esp *Macadamia ternifolia*, of the family Proteaceae) of Australian evergreen trees with edible nuts resembling filberts [NL, genus name, fr John *Macadam* †1865 Australian chemist]

**macadam·ize, -ise** /mə'kadəmiez/ *vt* to construct or surface (a road) by compacting successive layers of small broken stones into a solid mass and often binding them together with tar, asphalt, etc

**macaque** /mə'kahk/ *n* any of numerous monkeys (*Macaca* and related genera) chiefly of S Asia and the E Indies, that typically have short tails and cheek pouches in which food is stored; *esp* RHESUS MONKEY △ macaw [Fr, fr Pg *macaco*]

**macaroni** /makə'rohni/ *n, pl* (2) **macaronis, macaronies 1** pasta made from DURUM WHEAT and shaped in hollow tubes wider in diameter than spaghetti **2a** an English dandy of the late 18th and early 19th centuries who affected continental ways **b** an affected young man; a fop [It *maccheroni, pl of maccherone*, fr It dial. *maccarone* dumpling, macaroni]

**macaronic** /ˌmakə'ronik/ *adj* characterized by a mixture of two languages, esp by a mixture of Latin with vernacular words that sometimes have Latin endings – usu used of burlesque verses [NL *macaronicus*, fr It dial. *maccarone* macaroni] – **macaronic** *n*, **macaronically** *adv*

**macaroon** /ˌmakə'roohn/ *n* a small cake or biscuit composed chiefly of egg whites, sugar, and ground almonds or occasionally coconut △ meringue [Fr *macaron*, fr It dial. *maccarone*]

**macassar oil** /mə'kasə/ *n, often cap M* an oil formerly used for dressing the hair, reputedly made from ingredients obtained from Makassar; *also* any of several similar oils used esp as a hairdressing [*Macassar, Makassar*, city on Celebes in Indonesia]

**macaw** /mə'kaw/ *n* any of numerous long-tailed parrots (esp genus *Ara*) of S and Central America, including some of the largest and showiest △ macaque [Pg *macau*]

**Maccabees, Machabees** /'makəˌbeez/ *n taking sing vb* – see BIBLE table [*Maccabees*, a priestly family leading a Jewish revolt against Syrian rule in the 2nd c BC & ruling Palestine until 63 BC, fr Gk *Makkabaioi*, fr pl of *Makkabaios*, surname of Judas

Maccabaeus †160 BC Jewish patriot] – **Maccabean** *adj*

**maccaboy** /'makəboy/ *n* a snuff from Martinique [Fr *macouba*, fr *Macouba*, district in Martinique]

**McCarthyism** /mə'kahthi,iz(ə)m/ *n* fanatical opposition to elements held to be subversive (e g members of Communist parties), typically accompanied by the use of tactics involving personal attacks on individuals by means of widely publicized indiscriminate allegations, esp on the basis of unsubstantiated charges [Joseph R *McCarthy* †1957 US politician] – **McCarthyite** *n*

**McCoy** /mə'koy/ *n, informal* something that is neither imitation nor substitute – usu in the phrase *the real McCoy* [alter. of *Mackay* (in the phrase *the real Mackay* the true chief of the Mackay clan, a position often disputed)]

**¹mace** /mays/ *n* **1** a heavy spiked staff or club used esp in the Middle Ages as a weapon for breaking armour **2a** an ornamental staff used as a symbol of authority by a public official or a legislative body **b** a person who carries a mace [ME, fr MF, fr (assumed) VL *mattia*; akin to OHG *medela* plough, L *mateola* mallet]

**²mace** *n* an aromatic spice consisting of the dried outer fibrous covering of a nutmeg [ME, fr MF *macis*, fr L *macir*, an East Indian spice, fr Gk *makir*]

**³mace** *vt, chiefly NAm* to attack with Mace

**Mace** *trademark* – used for a temporarily disabling liquid containing TEAR GAS, that is often employed as a riot control agent and causes tears, dizziness, and sometimes nausea

**macédoine** /ˌmasə'dwahn, 'masədoyn/ (*Fr* masedwan) *n* a mixture of diced fruits or vegetables served as a salad or cocktail, in jelly, or as a garnish [Fr, fr *Macédoine* Macedonia; perh fr the mixture of races in Macedonia]

**Macedonian** /ˌmasi'dohniən/ *n* **1** a native or inhabitant of Macedonia **2** the Slavonic language of modern Macedonia **3** the language of ancient Macedonia, of uncertain affinity but probably Indo-European [*Macedonia*, region in S Europe]

**macerate** /'masərayt/ *vt* **1** to cause to waste away (as if) by excessive fasting **2** to cause to become soft or separated into constituent elements (as if) by steeping in fluid ~ *vi* to soften and wear away, esp as a result of being wetted or steeped [L *maceratus*, pp of *macerare* to soften, steep] – **macerator** *n*, **maceration** *n*

**Mach** /mak, mahk/ *n* a usu high speed expressed by a stated MACH NUMBER ⟨*an aeroplane flying at* ~ *two*⟩ △ Mark

**Machabees** /'makəbeez/ *n taking sing vb* MACCABEES [LL *Machabaei*, modif of Gk *Makkabaioi*]

**machete** /mə'sheti, -'chayti/ *n* a broad heavy knife used, esp in the W Indies, for cutting sugarcane and undergrowth and as a weapon [Sp]

**Machiavellian** /ˌmaki·ə'veli·ən/ *adj* of or suggesting the principles of conduct laid down by Machiavelli; *specif* characterized by cunning, duplicity, or opportunism [Niccolò *Machiavelli* † 1527 It statesman & political philosopher] – **Machiavellian** *n*

**Machiavellianism** /ˌmakiə'veliəniz(ə)m/ *n* the political theory of Machiavelli; *esp* the view that politics is amoral and that any means however unscrupulous can justifiably be used in securing or retaining political power

**machicolated** /mə'chikəlaytid/ *adj* furnished with machicolations [ML *machicolatus*, pp of *machicolare*, fr OF *machicoller*, fr *machicoleis* machicolation, fr *macher* to crush + *col* neck, fr L *collum* – more at COLLAR]

**machicolation** /maˌchikə'laysh(ə)n/ *n* **1** an opening between the brackets of a projecting parapet (e g on a tower or castle wall) or in the floor of a gallery or gatehouse, used for dropping missiles upon assailants below **2** a gallery or parapet containing such openings

**machinate** /'makinayt/ *vi* to plan or plot, esp to do harm; intrigue [L *machinatus*, pp of *machinari*, fr *machina* machine, contrivance] – **machinator** *n*

**machination** /,maki'naysh(ə)n/ *n* **1** an act of machinating **2** a scheme or crafty design intended to carry out some usu evil intent

¹**machine** /mə'sheen/ *n* **1a** any of various devices formerly used to produce stage effects **b** a combination of parts that transmit forces, motion, and energy one to another in a predetermined manner ⟨*a sewing* ∼⟩: eg **b(1)** a bicycle **b(2)** a motorcycle **c** an instrument (eg a lever or pulley) designed to transmit or modify the application of power, force, or motion **d** a combination of mechanically, electrically, or electronically operated parts for performing a task ⟨*a calculating* ∼⟩ ⟨*a card-sorting* ∼⟩ **e** a coin-operated device ⟨*a cigarette* ∼⟩ **f** machinery – + *the* or in pl ⟨*man must not become the servant of the* ∼⟩ **2a** a person or organization that acts like a machine ⟨*the party* ∼⟩ **b(1)** a combination of people (eg an organization) acting together for a common end along with the agencies they use ⟨*a powerful propaganda* ∼⟩ **b(2)** a highly organized political group under the leadership of a boss or small clique **3** *archaic* a constructed thing, whether material or immaterial **4** *archaic* a military engine *synonyms* see ¹TOOL [MF, structure, fabric, fr L *machina*, fr Gk *mēchanē* (Doric dial. *machana*), fr *mēchos* means, expedient – more at MAY]

²**machine** *vi* **1** to use a machine to perform a particular operation or activity (eg sewing) ⟨∼ *along the edge of the material*⟩ **2** to be acted on with a machine ⟨*this material* ∼s *easily*⟩ ∼ *vt* to shape, finish, or operate on by a machine; *esp* to sew using a sewing machine ⟨∼ *the zip in place*⟩ – **machinable** *also* **machineable** *adj*, **machinability** *n*

**machine code** *n* a system of symbols and rules for coding information in a form understandable and usable by a machine (eg a computer); *also* information so coded

**machine finish** *n* a moderately smooth finish given to paper by the CALENDER rolls of a papermaking machine; *also* a type of paper given this finish – **machine-finished** *adj*

**machine gun** *n* an automatic gun which uses belt-fed ammunition for rapid continuous firing – **machine-gun** *vb*, **machine gunner** *n*

**machine language** *n* **1** information recorded in a form usable by a machine (eg a computer) **2** numbers or instructions expressed in a form directly usable by a computer

**machinelike** /mə'sheen,liek/ *adj* resembling a machine, esp in regularity of action or stereotyped uniformity of product

**ma,chine-'readable** *adj* directly understandable and usable by a computer ⟨∼ *text*⟩

**machinery** /mə'sheen(ə)ri/ *n* **1a** machines in general or as a functioning unit: eg **1a(1)** apparatus for producing stage effects **a(2)** literary devices used esp for dramatic effect **b** the working parts of a machine **2** the system or organization by which an activity or process, esp of the state, is controlled ⟨*the cumbersome* ∼ *of the law*⟩

**machine shop** *n* a workshop in which products are machined to size and assembled

**machine tool** *n* a usu power-driven machine designed for cutting or shaping wood, metal, etc

**machinist** /mə'sheenist/ *n* **1a** a worker who makes, assembles, or repairs machinery **b** a craftsman skilled in the use of machine tools **c** one who operates a machine, esp a sewing machine **2** *archaic* a person in charge of the mechanical aspects of a theatrical production

**machismo** /mə'kizmoh, -'chiz-/ *n* an excessive sense of masculine pride; an exaggerated awareness and assertion of masculinity [MexSp, fr Sp *macho* male]

**machmeter** /'mak,meetə, 'mahk-/ *n* an instrument for indicating the Mach number of an aircraft in flight

**Mach number** *n* a number representing the ratio of the speed of a body to the speed of sound in the surrounding atmosphere ⟨*a* ∼ *of two indicates a speed that is twice that of sound*⟩ [Ernst *Mach* †1916 Austrian physicist]

¹**macho** /'machoh, 'mahchoh, -koh/ *n or adj* (one who is) aggressively virile *synonyms* see ¹MALE [Sp, male, fr L *masculus* – more at MALE]

²**macho** *n* machismo

**mack** /mak/ *n, Br* a mac

**mackerel** /'mak(ə)rəl/ *n, pl* **mackerels**, *esp collectively* **mackerel 1** a fish (*Scomber scombrus*) of the N Atlantic that is one of the most important food fishes, has a greenish back striped with dark blue bars, a silvery belly, and a forked tail, and reaches

a length of about 45 centimetres (18 inches) **2** any of various fishes of the suborder (Scombroidea) to which the common mackerel belongs; *esp* a comparatively small member of this group as distinguished from a BONITO or tuna [ME *makerel*, fr OF]

**mackerel shark** *n* any of a family (Lamnidae) of large fierce sharks of the northern open sea; *esp* PORBEAGLE

**mackerel sky** *n* a sky covered with rows of ALTOCUMULUS or CIRROCUMULUS clouds resembling the patterns on a mackerel's back

**mackinaw** /'makinaw/ *n, NAm* **1** a heavy cloth of wool (and other fibres) often with a plaid design and usu heavily napped and felted **2** a short coat of heavy fabric, esp mackinaw [*Mackinaw* City in Michigan, USA, formerly an Indian trading post]

**mackintosh** *also* **macintosh** /'makintosh/ *n, chiefly Br* **1** a mac, raincoat **2** a lightweight waterproof fabric originally of rubberized cotton [Charles *Macintosh* †1843 Sc chemist & inventor]

¹**mackle** /'makl/ *n* a blur or double impression on a printed sheet [Fr *macule* spot, mackle, fr L *macula* spot, stain]

²**mackle** *vb* to blur (eg a printed sheet) or become blurred

**Maclaurin's series** /mə'klawrinz/ *n, maths* a TAYLOR'S SERIES in which the EXPANSION is about the reference point zero [Colin *Maclaurin* †1746 Sc physician]

**macle** /'makl/ *n* **1** TWIN **3** (compound crystal of similar parts grown together) **2** a dark or discoloured spot (eg in a mineral) [Fr, wide-meshed net, lozenge, macle, fr OF, mesh, lozenge, of Gmc origin; akin to OHG *masca* mesh – more at MESH] – **macled** *adj*

**Mâcon** /'makonh (*Fr* mək5)/ *n* a heavy red or dry white table wine made in S Burgundy in France [Fr, fr *Mâcon*, city in France]

**macr-, macro-** *comb form* **1** long ⟨macro*diagonal*⟩ ⟨macro*biotic*⟩ **2a** large ⟨macro*spore*⟩ **b** exceptionally or abnormally large ⟨macro*cyte*⟩ **3** including or more comprehensive than ⟨*Macro-Ge*⟩ – used of a language group [Fr & L, fr Gk *makr-, makro-* long, fr *makros* – more at MEAGRE]

**macramé** /mə'krahmi/ *n* a piece of ornamental work, eg lace or fringe, made by knotting coarse threads or cords in a geometrical pattern; *also* the art of tying knots in patterns [Fr or It; Fr *macramé*, fr It *macramè*, fr Turk *makrama* napkin, towel, fr Ar *migramah* embroidered veil]

¹**macro** /'makroh/ *adj* **1** being large, thick, or exceptionally prominent **2** of, involving, or intended for use with relatively large quantities or on a large scale **3** GROSS **1b** [*macr-*]

²**macro, macroinstruction** *n, pl* **macros, macroinstructions** a single computer instruction that stands for a sequence of operations

**macroaggregate** /,makroh'agrigət/ *n* a relatively large particle (eg of soil) – **macroaggregated** *adj*

**macrobiotic** /,makrəbie'otik, -kroh-/ *adj* of or being a restricted diet (eg one consisting chiefly of whole grains and vegetables) that is usu undertaken with the intention of promoting health and prolonging life

**macrocarpa** /,makrə'kahpə/ *n* a New Zealand cypress (*Cupressus macrocarpa*) used esp for hedging [NL, specific epithet, fr *macr-* + *-carpa*, fem of *-carpus* -carpous]

**macrocephalous** /,makroh'sefələs/, **macrocephalic** /-si'falik/ *adj* having or being an exceptionally large head or cranium [Fr *macrocéphale*, fr Gk *makrokephalos* having a long head, fr *makr-* + *kephalē* head – more at CEPHALIC] – **macrocephaly** *n*

**macroclimate** /'makroh,kliemət/ *n* the predominant or normal climate of a large region – **macroclimatic** *adj*

**macrocosm** /'makrə,koz(ə)m/ *n* **1** the great world; universe **2** a complex structure or entity that is a large-scale reproduction of one of its constituents [Fr *macrocosme*, fr ML *macrocosmos*, fr L *macr-* + Gk *kosmos* order, universe] – **macrocosmic** *adj*, **macrocosmically** *adv*

**macrocyte** /'makroh,siet/ *n* an exceptionally large RED BLOOD CELL that may appear in the blood, esp in some anaemia conditions [ISV] – **macrocytic** *adj*

**macrocytosis** /,makroh·sie'tohsis/ *n, pl* **macrocytoses** /-seez/ the occurrence of macrocytes in the blood [NL]

**macroeconomics** /,makroh·ekə'nomiks, -eekə-/ *n taking sing or pl vb* a study of economics in terms of whole systems (eg of nations), esp with reference to general levels of output and income and to the interrelation between sectors of the economy – compare MICROECONOMICS – **macroeconomic** *adj*

**macroevolution** /,makroh·eevə'loohsh(ə)n, -'lyooh-/ *n* evolutionary change affecting broad groups of organisms (e g families and genera) and involving relatively large and complex steps or changes – **macroevolutionary** *adj*

**macrofossil** /'makroh,fosl/ *n* a fossil large enough to be observed by the naked eye

**macrogamete** /,makroh'gameet/ *n* the larger and usu female GAMETE (mature reproductive cell) of an organism that reproduces by fusion of dissimilar male and female gametes [ISV]

**macroglobulin** /,makroh'globyoolin/ *n* a large GLOBULIN (type of protein) [ISV]

**macroinstruction** /,makroh·in'struksh(ə)n/ *n, computers* MACRO

**macromere** /'makrəmiə/ *n* a large BLASTOMERE (cell produced by division of an egg into many cells)

**macromolecule** /-'molikyoohl/ *n* a large molecule (e g of a protein or rubber) built up from repeating units of smaller chemical structures [ISV] – **macromolecular** *adj*

**macron** /'makron/ *n* a mark ¯ placed over a vowel to indicate a long sound or over a syllable or alone to indicate a stressed or long syllable in a metrical foot [Gk *makron*, neut of *makros* long]

**macronucleus** /,makroh'nyoohklias/ *n* a relatively large cell nucleus; *specif* the larger of two nuclei in most PROTOZOANS (single-celled animals) provided with CILIA (hairlike structures), that is primarily concerned with feeding and growth functions – compare MICRONUCLEUS [NL]

**macronutrient** /,makroh'nyoohtri·ənt/ *n* a chemical element (e g carbon, hydrogen, or oxygen) that is essential in relatively large quantities for the normal growth and development of a plant, tissue, etc – compare TRACE ELEMENT

**Macro-Pano-Tacanan** /,makroh ,pahnoh tə'kahnən/ *n* an American Indian language group of Peru, Brazil, Southern Patagonia, and Tierra del Fuego [*macr- + Pano,* a language family including languages spoken by the Panoan peoples of the Amazon basin + *Tacana,* a language family of the Tacana peoples of S America]

**macrophage** /-,fayj, -,fahzh/ *n* any of various large cells that defend the body by ingesting foreign matter and debris, form part of the RETICULOENDOTHELIAL SYSTEM (system of cells and tissues providing body defence), and are widely distributed throughout the body's CONNECTIVE TISSUES where they may be mobile or attached to the tissue fibres; *broadly* a large PHAGOCYTE (cell that ingests harmful or unwanted material) [Fr, fr *macr- + -phage*] – **macrophagic** *adj*

**macrophage system** *n* RETICULOENDOTHELIAL SYSTEM (system of cells and tissues providing defence for the body)

**macrophyte** /'makrə,fiet/ *n* a member of the macroscopic plant life of esp a body of water – **macrophytic** *adj*

**macropterous** /ma'kroptərəs/ *adj* having long or large wings or fins [Gk *makropteros*, fr *makr- + pteron* wing – more at FEATHER]

**macroscopic** /-'skopik/ *also* **macroscopical** /-kl/ *adj* 1 large enough to be observed by the naked eye 2 considered in terms of large units or elements [ISV *macr- + -scopic* (as in *microscopic*)] – **macroscopically** *adv*

**macrosociology** /,makroh,sohs(h)i'oləji/ *n* the study of total social systems, esp entire societies – **macrosociological** *adj,* **macrosociologically** *adv*

**macrosporangium** /,makroh·spə'ranjiəm/ *n* MEGASPORANGIUM (plant structure housing immature female reproductive cells)

**macrospore** /'makroh,spaw/ *n* MEGASPORE (plant spore that develops into a female reproductive cell)

**macrostructure** /-,strukchə/ *n* the structure (e g of metal, a body part, or the soil) that can be seen without using a microscope; the macroscopic structure – **macrostructural** *adj*

**macula** /'makyoolə/ *n, pl* **maculae** /-lie/ *also* **maculas** 1 a blotch, spot; *esp* a macule 2 an anatomical structure (e g the MACULA LUTEA) having the form of a spot differentiated from the surrounding tissues [L] – **macular** *adj*

**macula lutea** /'loohti·ə/ *n, pl* **maculae luteae** /,makyoolie 'loohti·ie/ a small yellowish area lying slightly to the side of the centre of the RETINA of the eye, that constitutes the region of best vision – called also YELLOW SPOT [NL, lit., yellow spot]

**maculate** /'makyoolət/, **maculated** /-laytid/ *adj* marked with spots; blotched

**maculation** /,makyoo'laysh(ə)n/ *n* 1 a blemish in the form of a discrete spot ⟨*acne scars and* ~s⟩ 2 the arrangement of spots and markings on an animal or plant

**macule** /'makyoohl/ *n* a patch of skin altered in colour but usu not raised, that is a characteristic feature of various diseases (e g smallpox) [Fr, fr L *macula*]

**¹mad** /mad/ *adj* **-dd-** 1 mentally disordered; insane – not now used technically 2a completely unrestrained by reason and judgment; senseless ⟨*he'll do anything for a dare; he's utterly* ~⟩ **b** incapable of being explained or accounted for; illogical ⟨*I know it sounds* ~, *but it's true*⟩ 3 carried away by enthusiasm or desire 4 affected with rabies; rabid ⟨*a* ~ *dog*⟩ 5 wildly exciting or enjoyable ⟨*a* ~ *party*⟩ 6 intensely excited; frantic ⟨*the dog was* ~ *with fear*⟩ 7 marked by intense and often chaotic activity; wild ⟨*made a* ~ *dash for cover*⟩ 8 *informal* carried away by intense anger; furious ⟨*she's fighting* ~⟩ *synonyms* see ¹ANGER [ME *medd, madd,* fr OE *gemǣd,* pp of (assumed) *gemǣdan* to madden, fr *gemād* silly, mad; akin to OHG *gimeit* foolish, crazy, Skt *methati* he hurts] – **like mad** very hard, fast, loud, etc ⟨*shouted* like mad⟩

**²mad** *vt* **-dd-**, *NAm* to madden

**³mad** *n, NAm* a fit or mood of anger; fury

**Madagascar periwinkle** *n* ¹PERIWINKLE C

**madam** /'madəm/ *n, pl* **madams,** (1) **mesdames** /'may,dam/ **1a** *often cap* – used without a name as a form of respectful or polite address to a woman ⟨*will* ~ *have the fish?*⟩ **b** *cap* – used with *Dear* as a conventional form of address at the beginning of a letter 2 *cap* – used in direct address as a conventional title of respect before a woman's title of office ⟨Madam *Chairman*⟩ ⟨Madam *President*⟩ 3 the female head of a brothel ⟨*he paid the* ~⟩ 4 *Br* a conceited or petulant young lady or girl ⟨*a little* ~⟩ [ME, fr OF *ma dame,* lit., my lady]

**madame** /'madəm (*Fr* madam)/ *n, pl* **mesdames** /'may,dam/ *often cap* – used as a title equivalent to *Mrs* before the name of a married woman (or, occasionally, an unmarried older woman) not of English-speaking nationality, esp one whose native language is French, or used without a name as a generalized term of direct address [Fr, fr OF *ma dame*]

**madcap** /'mad,kap/ *adj* marked by impulsiveness or recklessness ⟨*a* ~ *scheme*⟩ – **madcap** *n*

**madden** /'madn/ *vt* 1 to drive mad; craze 2 to make intensely angry; enrage – **maddeningly** *adv*

**madder** /'madə/ *n* 1 a Eurasian plant (*Rubia tinctorum* of the family Rubiaceae, the madder family) with leaves growing in a circle round the stem, small yellowish flowers, and a red fleshy root; *broadly* any of several plants (genus *Rubia*) 2a the root of the Eurasian madder used formerly in dyeing; *also* a dye prepared from it **b** a medium to strong red colour [ME, fr OE *mædere;* akin to OHG *matara* madder]

**madding** /'mading/ *adj* 1 acting as if mad; frenzied ⟨*far from the* ~ *crowd's ignoble strife* – Thomas Gray⟩ 2 tending to infuriate; maddening

**made** /mayd/ *adj* 1 assembled or prepared, esp by putting together various ingredients ⟨~ *mustard*⟩ ⟨*a* ~ *dish*⟩ 2 assured of success ⟨*now I am a* ~ *man forever* – Christopher Marlowe⟩ [ME, fr pp of *maken* to make] – **get/have it made** to be certain of success; be in a fortunate situation ⟨*with this new job he's really* got it made⟩

**made ground** *n* rubbish or excavated soil deposited in a depression or pit; FILL 2

**Madeira** /mə'diərə/ *n* any of several rich fortified white wines from Madeira; *also* a similar wine made elsewhere [Pg, fr *Madeira* islands in the Atlantic Ocean]

**Madeira cake** *n, Br* a rich sponge cake often flavoured with lemon

**madeleine** /'madəlin, -layn/ *n* a small rich cake made from a sponge mixture and baked in a small mould (e g a DARIOLE) [Fr, prob fr *Madeleine* Paulmier, 19th-c Fr pastry-cook]

**mademoiselle** /,madmwə'zel (*Fr* madmwazɛl)/ *n, pl* **mademoiselles, mesdemoiselles** /,may- (*Fr* medmwazel)/ **1a** an unmarried French-speaking girl or woman **b** *often cap* – used of or to an unmarried French-speaking girl or woman as a title equivalent to *Miss* 2 a French governess or female language teacher [Fr, fr OF *ma damoisele,* lit., my (young) lady]

**,made-to-'measure** *adj, of a garment* made by a tailor according to an individual's measurements in order to achieve a good fit – compare OFF-THE-PEG

**,made-to-'order** *adj* produced to meet a special or an individual requirement

**,made-'up** *adj* 1 wearing make-up 2 fancifully conceived or falsely devised; fictional 3 fully manufactured or assembled 4 made, concocted 5 *of a road* covered in tarmac; metalled

**madhouse** /'mad,hows/ *n* 1 a lunatic asylum – not used technically **2** a place of bewildering uproar or confusion ⟨*it's like a ~ in there, I can't hear myself speak*⟩

**Madison Avenue** /'madis(ə)n/ *n* the American advertising industry [*Madison Avenue* in New York City, centre of the American advertising business]

**Madison race** /'madis(ə)n/ *n* a bicycle relay race held on a track between teams of two or three in which all riders remain on the track but only one is competing at any one time [*Madison* Square Garden, sports arena in New York City where such races were formerly held]

**madly** /-li/ *adv* **1** in a mad manner; *also* to a degree suggestive of madness **2** very, extremely ⟨*~ gay*⟩ ⟨*~ expensive*⟩

**madman** /-mən/, *fem* **madwoman** *n* a person who is or acts as if insane; a lunatic – not used technically

**madness** /-nis/ *n* **1** the quality or state of being mad: eg **1a** insanity – not now used technically **b** extreme folly **c** frenzy, rage **d** ecstasy, enthusiasm **2** any of several ailments of animals marked by frenzied behaviour; *specif* rabies

**Madonna** /mə'donə/ *n* **1** VIRGIN MARY **2** *obs* an Italian lady [It, fr OIt *ma donna*, lit., my lady]

**Madonna lily** *n* a white lily (*Lilium candidum*), native to Mediterranean regions, with trumpet-shaped flowers

**madras** /mə'dras, -'drahs/ *n* **1** a fine plain-woven shirt and dress fabric usu of cotton and typically in brightly coloured checked or striped designs **2** a light open usu cotton fabric with a heavy design, used for curtains [*Madras*, city in SE India]

**madrepore** /,madri'paw/ *n* any of various corals (order Madreporaria) of tropical seas that form coral reefs [Fr *madrépore*, fr It *madrepora*, fr *madre* mother (fr L *mater*) + *poro* pore (fr L *porus*) – more at MOTHER] – **madreporian** *adj or n*, **madreporic** *adj*

**madreporite** /'madri,pawriet/ *n* a perforated or porous plate on the upper surface of a starfish, SEA URCHIN, or related animal, through which water enters to pass into the system of tubes that make up the WATER-VASCULAR SYSTEM [ISV *madrepore* + ¹-*ite* (segment); fr the resemblances of the perforations to those of a madrepore]

**madrigal** /'madrig(ə)l/ *n* **1** a short medieval love poem suitable for being set to music **2a** a complex unaccompanied song for several voices on a secular text, developed esp in the 16th and 17th centuries **b** a part-song; *esp* a glee [It *madrigale*, fr ML *matricale*, fr neut of (assumed) *matricalis* simple, fr LL, of the womb, fr L *matric-*, *matrix* womb] – **madrigalian** *adj*, **madrigalist** *n*

**maduro** /mə'dyooəroh/ *n, pl* **maduros** a dark-coloured relatively strong cigar [Sp, fr *maduro* ripe, fr L *maturus* – more at MATURE]

**madwort** /'mad,wuht/ *n* **1** ALYSSUM 1 (yellow-flowered plant) **2** a low-growing Eurasian plant (*Asperugo procumbens*) of the forget-me-not family, that has leaves covered in coarse hairs, blue flowers, and a root that yields a red dye that has been used as a substitute for MADDER [prob fr the former belief that it could heal the bite of a mad dog (cf ALYSSUM)]

**Maecenas** /mie'seenəs/ *n* a generous patron, esp of literature or art [L, fr Gaius *Maecenas* †8 BC Roman statesman & patron of literature]

**maelstrom** /'maylstrohm/ *n* **1** a powerful often violent whirlpool **2** something resembling a maelstrom in turbulence and violence [obs D (now *maalstroom*), fr *malen* to grind + *strom* stream; akin to OHG *malan* to grind & to OHG *stroum* stream – more at MEAL, STREAM]

**maenad** /'meenad/ *n* **1** a woman participant in orgies in honour of Dionysus, the Greek god of wine; a bacchante **2** an unnaturally excited or distraught woman [L *maenad-*, *maenas*, fr Gk *mainad-*, *mainas*, fr *mainesthai* to be mad; akin to Gk *menos* spirit – more at MIND] – **maenadic** *adj*

**maestoso** /mie'stohsoh/ *adj or adv* in a majestic stately manner – used as a direction in music [It, fr L *majestosus*, fr *majestas* majesty]

**maestro** /'miestroh/ *n, pl* **maestros, maestri** /'miestri/ a master in an art or specific field of activity, *esp* an eminent composer, conductor, or teacher of music [It, lit., master, fr L *magister* – more at MASTER]

**Mae West** /,may 'west/ *n, informal* an inflatable life jacket in the form of a collar extending down the chest, worn by airmen in World War II [*Mae West* †1980 US actress noted for her full figure]

**maffick** /'mafik/ *vi* to celebrate with boisterous rejoicing and riotous behaviour [back-formation fr *Mafeking night*, English

celebration of the lifting of the siege of Mafeking in S Africa on 17 May 1900]

**Mafia, maffia** /'mafi·ə/ *n taking sing or pl vb* **1** a secret society of affiliated Sicilian political terrorists **2** an organized secret body of criminals originating in Sicily and now prevalent esp in the USA, that controls many international and national illicit activities (e g vice and narcotics) **3** *often not cap* an excessively influential coterie of a usu specified kind; a clique ⟨*the presumptions of the mental-health* mafia – R J Neuhaus⟩ ⟨*the literary ~ will plug it even if it is rubbish* – The Bookseller⟩ △ maquis [It, fr It dial., boldness, bragging]

**mafic** /'mafik/ *adj* of or being a group of usu dark-coloured minerals rich in magnesium and iron [NL *magnesium* + L *ferrum* iron + E -*ic*]

**mafioso** /,mafi'ohzoh, -soh (*It* mafioso)/ *n, pl* **mafiosi** a member of the Mafia [It, fr *Mafia*]

**mag** /mag/ *n, informal* a magazine

**magazine** /,magə'zeen, '---/ *n* **1a** a room in which arms, ammunition, or explosives (e g gunpowder) are kept **b** an accumulation of munitions of war **2a** a periodical bound in paper covers that consists of miscellaneous pieces (e g articles, stories, and poems) by different authors, is often illustrated, and usu contains advertisements **b** a regularly occurring television or radio programme containing a number of usu topical items often without a common theme and usu on relatively unserious subjects **3** a supply chamber: e g **3a** a holder in or on a gun for cartridges to be fed into the gun chamber mechanically **b** a lightproof chamber for films or plates on a camera or for film on a projector [MF, warehouse, fr OProv, fr Ar *makhāzin*, pl of *makhzan* storehouse]

**magdalen** /'magdələn/, **magdalene** /-een/ *n, often cap, archaic* **1** a reformed prostitute **2** a house of refuge or reform for prostitutes [Mary *Magdalen* or *Magdalene*, woman healed by Jesus of evil spirits (Lk 8:2), dubiously identified with a reformed prostitute (Lk 7:36–50)]

**Magdalenian** /,magdə'leenyən, -ni-ən/ *adj* of the latest Palaeolithic culture in Europe, between about 15000 and 10000 BC, that was characterized by ivory, flint, and bone implements, esp harpoons, decorative carving, and cave paintings [Fr *magdalénien*, fr *La Madeleine*, rock shelter in SW France]

**Magellanic Cloud** /,magi'lanik/ *n* either of the two nearest galaxies to the Milky Way system, located within 25 degrees of the south celestial pole and appearing as conspicuous patches of light [Ferdinand *Magellan* †1521 Pg navigator]

**Magen David** /,mawgən 'dayvid/ *n* STAR OF DAVID (Jewish symbol) [Heb *māghēn Dāwīdh*, lit., shield of David, fr *Dāwīdh* David † *ab*973 BC king of Judah & Israel]

**magenta** /mə'jentə/ *n* **1** FUCHSINE (bluish-red dye) **2** a deep purplish-red **3** a pinkish-red – used in photography and colour printing of one of the PRIMARY COLOURS; compare CYAN, YELLOW [*Magenta*, town in N Italy, site of a battle in 1859 just before magenta was discovered]

**maggot** /'magət/ *n* **1** a soft-bodied legless grub that is the larva of a TWO-WINGED FLY (e g the housefly), and which usu lives on decaying matter **2** a fantastic or eccentric idea; a whim ⟨*he has a ~ in his brain*⟩ [ME *mathek*, *maddok*, *magotte*, of Scand origin; akin to ON *mathkr* maggot; akin to OE *matha* maggot] – **maggoty** *adj*

**Magh** /mahj/ *n* – see MONTH table [Skt *māgha*]

**magi** /'mayjie/ *pl of* MAGUS

¹**Magian** /'mayjiən/ *n* MAGUS

²**Magian** /'mayjiən, 'mayjie-ən/ *adj* of the Magi – **Magianism** *n*

¹**magic** /'majik/ *n* **1** the use of means (e g charms, rites, incantations, or spells) believed to have supernatural power over natural forces **2a** an extraordinary power or influence producing surprising results and defying explanation **b** something that seems to cast a spell ⟨*the ~ of the voice*⟩ **3** the art of producing illusions by sleight of hand [ME *magik*, fr MF *magique*, fr L *magice*, fr Gk *magikē*, fem of *magikos* Magian, magical, fr *magos* magus, sorcerer, of Iranian origin; akin to OPer *mogush* sorcerer]

²**magic** *adj* **1** of or used in magic **2a** having seemingly supernatural qualities or powers **b** giving a feeling of enchantment **3** *informal* – used as a generalized term of approval ⟨*this new record is really ~*⟩ ⟨*the last goal was sheer ~, Brian*⟩ – **magical** *adj*, **magically** *adv*

³**magic** *vt*, **-ck-** to affect, influence, or take away (as if) by magic

**magic eye** n 1 PHOTOELECTRIC CELL 2 2 a miniature CATHODE-RAY TUBE that emits a variable light and can be used as a visual indicator for tuning a device (e g a radio worked by valves)

**magician** /mə'jish(ə)n/ n 1 one (e g a sorcerer) skilled in magic 2 a conjurer

**magic lantern** n an early form of slide projector

**magic square** n a square array of numbers in which the numbers in each row, column, and diagonal add up to the same total

**magilp** /mə'gilp/ n MEGILP (medium for oil painting)

**Maginot Line** /'mazhinoh (Fr maʒino)/ n a defensive position blindly relied on [The *Maginot Line* (Fr *Ligne Maginot*), a line of fortifications on the NE frontier of France which failed to prevent the German invasion of France in 1940, fr André *Maginot* †1932 Fr minister of war]

**magisterial** /,maji'stiəri-əl/ adj 1a of, being, or having the characteristics of a master or teacher b marked by masterly skill; authoritative ⟨*they are getting a* ~ *translation* – *TLS*⟩ 2 of (the office or duties of) a magistrate [LL *magisterialis* of authority, fr *magisterium* office of a master, fr *magister*] – **magisterially** adv

**magisterium** /,maji'stiəriəm/ n teaching authority, esp of the Roman Catholic church [L]

**magistracy** /'majistrəsi/ n 1 the state of being a magistrate 2 the office, power, or dignity of a magistrate 3 *taking sing or pl vb* a body of magistrates 4 the district under a magistrate

**magistral** /'majistrəl/ adj of or characteristic of a master; magisterial [LL *magistralis*, fr L *magistr-, magister*] – **magistrally** adv

**magistrate** /'majistrayt, -strət/ n an official entrusted with administration of the laws: e g a a principal official exercising governmental powers over a major political unit (e g a nation) ⟨*let the* ~s *be labouring men* – Shak⟩ b a paid or unpaid local judicial officer presiding in a magistrates' court – compare JUSTICE OF THE PEACE, STIPENDIARY MAGISTRATE c a local official exercising administrative and often judicial functions [ME *magistrat*, fr L *magistratus* magistracy, magistrate, fr *magistr-, magister* master, political superior – more at MASTER] – **magistratical** adj, **magistratically** adv

**magistrates' court** n a court of summary jurisdiction for minor criminal cases and preliminary hearings of INDICTABLE OFFENCES and with certain civil and administrative functions, involving two or more magistrates

**magistrature** /'majistrəchə/ n the magistracy

**Maglemosian** /,magli'mohsi-ən, -sh(ə)n/ adj of the first MESOLITHIC culture of N Europe, between about 8000 and 5000 BC, that was characterized by its forest and lakeside settlements and its woodworking tools, fishing tackle, and dugout canoes [*Maglemose*, site on the island of Sjælland (Zealand) in Denmark]

**magma** /'magmə/ n 1 a thin pasty SUSPENSION (substance mixed but undissolved in liquid) 2 molten rock material within the earth from which an IGNEOUS rock results by cooling and solidification – compare LAVA [NL, fr L *magmat-, magma* dregs, fr Gk, thick unguent, fr *massein* to knead – more at MINGLE] – **magmatic** adj

**Magna Carta** *also* **Magna Charta** /,magnə 'kahtə/ n a document constituting a fundamental guarantee of rights and privileges [*Magna Carta, Magna Charta*, a charter of liberties granted by King John in 1215, fr ML, lit., great charter]

**magnanimity** /,magnə'nimoti/ n 1 the quality of being magnanimous 2 a magnanimous act

**magnanimous** /mag'naniməs/ adj 1 showing or suggesting a lofty and courageous spirit ⟨*the irreproachable lives and* ~ *sufferings of their followers* – Joseph Addison⟩ 2 showing or suggesting nobility of feeling and generosity of mind; not subject to petty feelings (e g jealousy or resentment) [L *magnanimus*, fr *magnus* great + *animus* spirit – more at MUCH, ANIMATE] – **magnanimously** adv, **magnanimousness** n

**magnate** /'magnayt/ n a person of wealth, influence, or distinction often in a specified area of business or industry △ magnet [ME *magnates*, pl, fr LL, fr L *magnus*]

**magnesia** /mag'neezh(y)ə, -zyə/ n 1 a white oxide of magnesium, MgO, used esp in making heat-resistant materials to line furnaces, fireplaces, etc, in cements, insulators, fertilizers, and rubber, and in medicine as an antacid and mild laxative 2 magnesium [NL, fr *magnes carneus*, a white earth which adhered to a person's lips, lit., flesh magnet] – **magnesian** adj

**magnesite** /'magnəsiet/ n MAGNESIUM CARBONATE occurring

naturally as a white mineral and used esp in making heat-resistant materials (e g bricks for lining furnaces)

**magnesium** /mag'neezyəm/ n a silver-white lightweight metallic chemical element that occurs abundantly in nature, is soft and easily worked, and is used in the manufacture of fireworks because of the intense white light it produces on burning, and in construction, esp in the form of light alloys [NL, fr *magnesia*]

**magnesium carbonate** n a chemical compound, $MgCO_3$, that is a white carbonate of magnesium and occurs naturally as the minerals dolomite and magnesite

**magnesium chloride** n a chemical compound, $MgCl_2$, that is a chloride of magnesium that readily absorbs moisture from the atmosphere and is used esp as a source of magnesium metal

**magnesium hydroxide** n a slightly alkaline compound, $Mg(OH)_2$, used esp as a laxative and antacid (e g in MILK OF MAGNESIA)

**magnesium oxide** n MAGNESIA 1

**magnesium sulphate** n a chemical compound that is a sulphate of magnesium: e g a a white compound, $MgSO_4$, that is a natural constituent of MINERAL WATER and is used in medicine as a laxative b EPSOM SALTS

**magnet** /'magnit/ n 1a LODESTONE 1 (magnetized magnetite) b a body having the property of attracting iron and producing a MAGNETIC FIELD outside itself; *specif* a mass of iron, steel, etc that has this property artificially imparted 2 something that attracts ⟨*the island is a* ~ *for tax evaders*⟩ △ magnate [ME *magnete*, fr MF, fr L *magnet-, magnes*, fr Gk *magnēs* (*lithos*), lit., stone of Magnesia, ancient city in Asia Minor]

**magnet-, magneto-** *comb form* magnetic force; magnetism; magnetic; magnetic force and ⟨*magnetoelectric*⟩ ⟨*magneton*⟩ [L *magnet-, magnes*]

**¹magnetic** /mag'netik/ adj 1a of magnetism or a magnet b of, produced by, or characterized by the earth's magnetism ⟨~ *equator*⟩ c (capable of being) magnetized d working by magnetism or magnetic attraction ⟨*a* ~ *compass*⟩ 2 possessing an extraordinary power or ability to attract or charm ⟨*a* ~ *personality*⟩ – **magnetically** adv

**²magnetic** n a magnetic substance

**magnetic declination** n DECLINATION 3

**magnetic dip** n ²DIP 3

**magnetic equator** n ACLINIC LINE

**magnetic field** n the region of space near a magnetic body or a body carrying an electric current in which magnetic forces set up by the body or current can be detected; *also* the forces of magnetic attraction or repulsion acting in this region and considered esp with reference to their strength or the direction in which they act

**magnetic flux** n 1 (LINES OF FORCE used to represent) the strength or effect of the magnetic forces acting in a particular area of a MAGNETIC FIELD 2 MAGNETIC FIELD

**magnetic flux density** n the strength or effect of the magnetic forces acting at a particular point in a MAGNETIC FIELD

**magnetic head** n a device used in MAGNETIC RECORDING for converting electrical signals into magnetized areas on a tape, disk, etc, converting a magnetic recording into electrical signals, or erasing a magnetic recording

**magnetic moment** n a measure of the TORQUE (force producing rotation) exerted on a MAGNETIC NEEDLE, a particle or group of particles having electric charge, or a similar magnetic system when placed in a MAGNETIC FIELD; the quantity obtained by multiplying the distance between the poles of a magnet by the strength of either pole

**magnetic needle** n a slender bar of magnetized iron, steel, etc that, when freely suspended, turns to align itself with the direction of the forces acting in a MAGNETIC FIELD in which it is placed, and that is the essential part of a compass that works by magnetism

**magnetic north** n the northerly direction in the earth's MAGNETIC FIELD as indicated by a horizontal MAGNETIC NEEDLE

**magnetic pole** n 1 either of the regions of a magnet at which the magnetic forces set up by the magnet are strongest 2 either of two small nonstationary regions that are located respectively in the polar areas of the N and S hemispheres of the earth and towards which a MAGNETIC NEEDLE points from any direction; *also* either of two comparable regions on a celestial body (e g a star or planet) other than the earth

**magnetic recording** n the process of recording sound, television pictures, or data (e g for a computer) by producing areas magnetized to different degrees on a moving tape, disk, etc; *also* sound, pictures, or data recorded in this way – **magnetic recorder** *n*

**magnetic resonance** *n* the absorption or emission of ELECTROMAGNETIC RADIATION by atoms or atomic nuclei in a MAGNETIC FIELD and their transition between different ENERGY LEVELS, esp to a higher energy level, when subjected to RADIO WAVES at particular frequencies

**magnetic storm** *n* a marked temporary disturbance of the earth's MAGNETIC FIELD, probably related to events occurring on the sun's surface

**magnetic tape** *n* a ribbon of thin plastic impregnated with a powder that can be magnetized, for use in MAGNETIC RECORDING

**magnetism** /'magni‚tiz(ə)m/ *n* **1a** a physical phenomenon existing in various forms, that is associated with moving particles having electric charge and involves the setting up of a field of force, is shown by magnets and electric currents, and includes the attraction for iron observed in magnets **b** a branch of physics dealing with magnetic phenomena **2** an ability to attract or charm

**magnetite** /'magni‚tiet/ *n* a black mineral, Fe₃O₄, that is an oxide of and an important source of iron and has the property of being strongly attracted by a magnet – **magnetitic** *adj*

**magnetization** /‚magnitie'zaysh(ə)n, -ti-/ *n* magnetizing or being magnetized; *also* the degree to which a body is magnetized

**magnet·ize, -ise** /-tiez/ *vt* **1** to attract like a magnet; charm **2** to cause to be magnetic; make into a magnet – **magnetizable** *adj*, **magnetizer** *n*

**magneto** /mag'neetoh/ *n, pl* **magnetos** a magnetoelectric device; *esp* a generator with PERMANENT MAGNETS used to produce a high voltage for the ignition of some petrol engines (e g on motorcycles)

**magneto-** – see MAGNET-

**magnetoelectric** /mag‚neetoh·i'lektrik/ *adj* of or characterized by an electric current or a voltage produced by magnetic means ⟨∼ *induction*⟩ – **magnetoelectrically** *adv*, **magnetoelectricity** *n*

**magnetograph** /mag'neetoh‚grahf, ‚graf/ *n* an automatic instrument for recording measurements of and variations in the forces in a MAGNETIC FIELD (e g of the earth or the sun) – **magnetographic** *adj*

**magnetohydrodynamic** /mag‚neetoh·hiedrohdie'namik/ *adj* of or being phenomena arising from the movement of gases and liquids that conduct electricity, in the presence of an electric field or a MAGNETIC FIELD – **magnetohydrodynamics** *n taking sing or pl vb*

**magnetometer** /‚magni'tomitə/ *n* an instrument for measuring magnetic intensity, esp of the forces acting in the earth's MAGNETIC FIELD – **magnetometry** *n*, **magnetometric** *adj*

**magnetomotive force** /mag‚neetoh'mohtiv/ *n* a factor that is the cause of a MAGNETIC FLUX (magnetic effects operating in a particular area)

**magneton** /'magniton, mag'nieton/ *n* a unit for measuring the MAGNETIC MOMENT of a particle (e g an electron or atom) [ISV *magnet-* + ²-*on*]

**magnetopause** /mag'neetoh‚pawz/ *n* the outer boundary of a magnetosphere [*magneto*sphere + L *pausa* stop – more at PAUSE]

**magnetoresistance** /mag'neetoh·ri‚zist(ə)ns/ *n* a change in the resistance to the flow of an electric current due to the presence of a MAGNETIC FIELD

**magnetosphere** /mag'neetoh‚sfiə/ *n* a region that surrounds the earth or other celestial body (e g a planet), extends out for thousands of kilometres, and is dominated by the body's MAGNETIC FIELD so that electrically charged particles are trapped in it – **magnetospheric** *adj*

**magnetostatic** /mag‚neetoh'statik/ *adj* of or being a stationary MAGNETIC FIELD

**magnetostriction** /-'striksh(ə)n/ *n* the change in the dimensions of a FERROMAGNETIC body (body having magnetic properties like those of iron) caused by magnetization or demagnetization [ISV *magnet-* + -*striction* (as in *constriction*)] – **magnetostrictive** *adj*, **magnetostrictively** *adv*

**magnetron** /'magnitron/ *n* an electronic valve that in the presence of an externally applied MAGNETIC FIELD is used as a high-power microwave source (e g for a radar transmitter) [blend of *magnet* and -*tron*]

**magnific** /mag'nifik/, **magnifical** *adj, archaic* magnificent; *also* sublime [MF *magnifique*, fr L *magnificus*] – **magnifical** *adj*, **magnifically** *adv*

**magnificat** /mag'nifikat/ *n* **1** *cap* **1a** the song (CANTICLE) of the Virgin Mary in Luke 1:46–55 **b** a musical setting for the Magnificat **2** an utterance or song of praise [ME, fr L, (it) magnifies, fr *magnificare* to magnify; fr the first word of the canticle]

**magnification** /‚magnifi'kaysh(ə)n/ *n* **1** the act of magnifying or state of being magnified **2** the apparent enlargement of an object by an optical instrument (e g a microscope) – called also POWER

**magnificent** /mag'nifis(ə)nt/ *adj* **1** marked by stately grandeur and splendour ⟨*a* ∼ *way of life*⟩ **2** sumptuous in structure and adornment ⟨*a* ∼ *cathedral*⟩; *broadly* strikingly beautiful or impressive ⟨*a* ∼ *physique*⟩ **3** impressive to the mind or spirit; sublime ⟨∼ *prose*⟩ **4** exceptionally fine or excellent ⟨*a* ∼ *day*⟩ **synonyms** see ¹GRAND **antonym** modest [L *magnificent-* (e g in *magnificentia* magnificence), irreg fr *magnificus* noble, splendid, fr *magnus* great – more at MUCH] – **magnificence** *n*, **magnificently** *adv*

**magnifico** /mag'nifikoh/ *n, pl* **magnificoes, magnificos 1** a nobleman of Venice **2** a person of high position or distinguished appearance and manner [It, fr *magnifico*, adj, magnificent, fr L *magnificus*]

**magnify** /'magnifie/ *vt* **1a** to extol, laud **b** to cause to be held in greater esteem or respect **2a** to increase in significance; intensify **b** to exaggerate ⟨*he has* magnified *his own part in the fight*⟩ **3** to enlarge in fact or in appearance ⟨*a telescope* magnifies *distant objects*⟩ ∼ *vi* to have the power of causing objects to appear larger than they are [ME *magnifien*, fr MF *magnifier*, fr L *magnificare*, fr *magnificus*] – **magnifier** *n*

**magnifying glass** *n* a single magnifying lens

**magniloquent** /mag'niləkwənt/ *adj* speaking in or characterized by a high-flown often bombastic style or manner; grandiloquent [back-formation fr *magniloquence*, fr L *magniloquentia*, fr *magniloquus* magniloquent, fr *magnus* + *loqui* to speak] – **magniloquence** *n*, **magniloquently** *adv*

**magnitude** /'magnityoohd/ *n* **1a** (great) size or extent **b** a quantity, number **2** the importance or quality of something ⟨*he did not realize the* ∼ *of the problem*⟩ **3** the intrinsic or apparent brightness of a celestial body, esp a star, as represented by a number on a logarithmic scale in which lower numbers correspond to greater brightnesses – compare ABSOLUTE MAGNITUDE **4** a measure of quantity expressed as a number that represents a multiple of a standard unit (e g a litre or kilogram) [ME, fr L *magnitudo*, fr *magnus*]

**magnolia** /mag'nohli·ə, -lyə/ *n* **1** any of a genus (*Magnolia* of the family Magnoliaceae, the magnolia family) of N American and Asian shrubs and trees with evergreen or deciduous leaves and usu showy white, yellow, rose, or purple flowers that appear in early spring **2** a very pale pinkish-white colour [NL, genus name, fr Pierre *Magnol* †1715 Fr botanist]

**Magnox** /'magnoks/ *trademark* – used for an alloy of magnesium with small quantities of the metals aluminium and beryllium that is used to enclose rods of uranium fuel in some NUCLEAR REACTORS

**magnum** /'magnəm/ *n* an outsize wine bottle holding twice the usual amount (about 1.5 litres) [L, neut of *magnus* great]

**magnum opus** /'ohpəs/ *n* a great work; *esp* the greatest achievement of an artist or writer [L]

**magpie** /'magpie/ *n* **1a** any of numerous European and N American birds (genus *Pica*, esp *Pica pica*) of the crow family having a long tail, black-and-white plumage, and a chattering call **b** any of various birds related to or resembling the magpies; *esp* either of two Australian birds (genus *Gymnorhina*) with black-and-white plumage **2** (a shot that hits) the ring on a shooting target between the inner and the outer ring **3** *informal* a person who chatters noisily **4** *Br informal* one who collects objects in a random fashion [*Mag* (nickname for *Margaret*) + ¹*pie*]

**magpie moth** *n* a white moth (*Abraxas grossulariata*) with black and yellow markings, whose caterpillar feeds on the leaves of currant and gooseberry bushes

**maguey** /'magway/ *n* **1a** any of various fleshy-leaved AGAVES: e g **1a(1)** a Mexican agave (e g *Agave atrovirens*) used to make PULQUE (alcoholic drink) **a(2)** an agave (*Agave cantala*) whose leaves yield CANTALA (type of hard fibre) **b** any of various plants (genus *Furcraea*) related to the agaves **2** any of several hard fibres derived from magueys and used esp for twine; esp CANTALA [Sp, fr Taino]

**magus** /'maygəs/ *n, pl* **magi** /'mayjie/ **1a** a member of a ZOROASTRIAN or pre-Zoroastrian hereditary priestly class in ancient Persia **b** *often cap* any of the traditionally three wise men from the East who paid homage to the infant Jesus according to Mt 2:1–12 **2** a magician, sorcerer, or astrologer in ancient times [ME, fr L, fr Gk *magos* – more at MAGIC]

**Magyar** /'magyah/ *n* (the language of) a member of the FINNO-UGRIC people that forms the predominant part of the population of Hungary [Hung] – **Magyar** *adj*

**magyar sleeve** *n* a loosely fitting sleeve that is cut in one piece with the bodice

**maharajah, maharaja** /ˌmah·hah'rahjə/ *n* a Hindu prince, esp a ruler over the former native states, ranking above a rajah [Skt *mahārāja*, fr *mahat* great (akin to Gk *megas* great – more at MUCH) + *rājan* raja]

**maharani, maharanee** /ˌmah·hah'rahnee/ *n* **1** the wife of a maharajah **2** a Hindu princess ranking above a RANI [Hindi *mahārānī*, fr *mahā* great (fr Skt *mahat*) + *rānī* rani]

**maharishi** /ˌmah·hah'rishi/ *n* a Hindu teacher of religious and mystical knowledge [Skt *mahārṣi*, fr *mahat* + *ṛṣi* sage and poet]

**mahatma** /mah'hatmə/ *n* **1** a person revered for outstanding wisdom or moral and spiritual qualities – used as a title of honour, esp by Hindus **2** a person regarded by THEOSOPHISTS (adherents of a mystical religion) as having special wisdom or skills [Skt *mahātman*, fr *mahātman* great-souled, fr *mahat* + *ātman* soul – more at ATMAN]

**Mahayana** /ˌmah·hə'yahnə/ *n* a liberal Buddhist sect, chiefly in Tibet, China, and Japan, that is THEISTIC (believing in one God), recognizes a large body of non-Buddhist scripture, and teaches social concern and universal salvation – compare THERAVADA [Skt *mahāyāna*, lit., great vehicle] – **Mahayanist** *n*, **Mahayanistic** *adj*

**Mahdi** /'mahdi/ *n* (a leader claiming to be) the expected messiah of Muslim tradition who will forcibly convert all mankind to Islam △ mufti [Ar *mahdīy*, lit., one rightly guided] – **Mahdism** *n*, **Mahdist** *n*

**Mahican, Mohican** /mə'heekən/ *n*, *pl* **Mahicans**, *esp collectively* **Mahican** a member or the language of a N American Indian people formerly living in the environs of the Hudson river – **Mahican** *adj*

**mah-jong, mah-jongg** /ˌmah 'jong/ *n* a game of Chinese origin usu played by four people with 144 tiles that are drawn and discarded until one player secures a winning hand [Chin *máquè* (*ma²-ch'üh⁴*), lit., sparrows]

**mahlstick** /'mawlˌstik/ *n* MAULSTICK (stick to steady a painter's hand)

**mahogany** /mə'hog(ə)ni/ *n* **1a** the usu dark-coloured wood of any of various chiefly tropical trees (esp genera *Swietenia* and *Khoya* of the family Meliaceae, the mahogany family); *esp* the durable yellowish-brown to reddish-brown usu moderately hard and heavy wood of a W Indian tree (*Swietenia mahogani*), that is widely used for fine cabinetwork **b** a tree that yields mahogany **2** (any of various trees that yield) a wood (eg PHILIPPINE MAHOGANY) resembling or used in place of mahogany **3** the reddish-brown colour of mahogany [origin unknown]

**mahonia** /mə'hohnyə/ *n* any of a genus (*Mahonia*) of N American and Eurasian evergreen shrubs (eg OREGON GRAPE) of the barberry family with spiny leaves and clusters of small yellow flowers [NL, genus name, fr Bernard Mc*Mahon* †1816 US (Irish-born) botanist]

**Mahound** /mə'hownd, -'hoohnd/ *n*, *archaic* Muhammad regarded as a deity [ME *Mahun, Mahoun*, fr OF *Mahom, Mahun*, short for *Mahomet*]

**mahout** /mə'howt/ *n* a keeper and driver of an elephant [Hindi *mahāwat, mahāut*]

**mahratta** /mə'rahtə/ *n* MARATHA (member of a S Indian people)

**maid** /mayd/ *n* **1** an unmarried girl or woman; *also* a female virgin **2** a female servant [ME *maide*, short for *maiden*] – **maidish** *adj*, **maidishness** *n*

**maidan** /mie'dahn/ *n* an African or Asiatic parade ground or esplanade [Hindi *maidān*, fr Ar]

¹**maiden** /'mayd(ə)n/ *n* **1** an unmarried girl or woman **2** a former Scottish beheading device resembling a guillotine **3** a horse that has never won a race **4 maiden, maiden over** an over in cricket in which no runs are credited to the batsman [ME, fr OE *mægden, mǣden*, dim. of *mægeth;* akin to OHG *magad* maiden, OIr *mug* serf, *macc* son] – **maidenish** *adj*, **maidenlike** *adj*, **maidenly** *adj*, **maidenliness** *n*, **maidenship** *n*

²**maiden** *adj* **1a(1)** not married ⟨*a* ~ *aunt*⟩ **a(2)** VIRGIN 2, 3 **b** *of a female animal* **b(1)** never having been mated **b(2)** never having borne young **c** that has not been altered from its original state; intact, fresh **2** of or suitable to a maiden **3** being the first or

earliest of its kind ⟨*the ship's* ~ *voyage*⟩ ⟨*the MP's* ~ *speech in Parliament*⟩

**maidenhair, maidenhair fern** /-ˌheə/ *n* any of a genus (*Adiantum*) of ferns with fronds that have delicate feathery branches

**maidenhair tree** *n* GINKGO (primitive tree related to the conifers)

**maidenhead** /-ˌhed/ *n* **1** the quality or state of being a maiden; virginity **2** the hymen – not used technically [ME *maidenhed*, fr *maiden* + *-hed* -hood; akin to ME *-hod* -hood]

**maidenhood** /'mayd(ə)nhood/ *n* the quality, state, or time of being a maiden

**maiden name** *n* the surname of a woman prior to marriage

**maid-in-'waiting** *n*, *pl* **maids-in-waiting** a young woman of a queen's or princess's household appointed to attend her

**maid of all work** *n*, *pl* **maids of all work** a maid who does general housework; *broadly* one who or that which does many jobs

**maid of honour** *n*, *pl* **maids of honour 1** an unmarried lady, usu of noble birth, whose duty it is to attend a queen or princess **2** a bride's principal unmarried wedding attendant **3** a puff pastry tartlet filled with a thick rich almond-flavoured custard

**maidservant** /-ˌsuhv(ə)nt/ *n* a female servant

**maieutic** /may'yoohtik/ *adj* of or resembling the SOCRATIC method of eliciting ideas latent in the mind of another by a series of questions and answers [Gk *maieutikos* of midwifery, deriv of *maia* midwife]

**maigre** /'maygə/ *adj* **1** *of days in the calendar of the Roman Catholic church* prescribed for fasting or for not eating meat **2** suitable for eating on maigre days; *specif* not containing meat or meat juices [Fr, lit., meagre, fr MF]

¹**mail** /mayl/ *n* **1a** a bag of posted items (eg letters) conveyed from one post office to another **b** the postal matter that makes up one particular consignment ⟨*unload the* ~ *for Nottingham*⟩ ⟨*sat down to open his* ~⟩ **c** a conveyance that transports mail **2** a postal system [ME *male* pack, bag, fr OF, of Gmc origin; akin to OHG *malaha* bag]

²**mail** *vt* ⁴POST 1

³**mail** *n* **1** armour made of interlocking metal rings, chains, or sometimes plates **2** the hard enclosing covering of an animal (eg a tortoise) [ME *maille*, fr MF, fr L *macula* spot, mesh] – **mailed** *adj*, **mailless** *adj*

⁴**mail** *vt* to clothe (as if) with mail

**mailable** /'mayləbl/ *adj*, *NAm* adapted for posting; legally admissible as mail – **mailability** *n*

**mailbag** /-ˌbag/ *n* **1** a bag used for transporting mail **2** *NAm* a postbag

**mailbox** /-ˌboks/ *n*, *NAm* LETTER BOX b; *also* a box near a dwelling for the occupant's mail

**mailcoach** /'maylˌkohch/ *n* a railway coach specially adapted to carry mail

**mail drop** *n*, *NAm* **1** a receptacle or slot for deposit of mail **2** an address used in transmitting secret communications

**mailing** /'mayling/ *n*, *Scot* a rented farm [ME *mailling*, fr *maille, male* rent, tribute – more at BLACKMAIL]

**mailing list** /'mayling/ *n* a list, kept by an organization, of names and addresses to which it regularly posts information

**maillot** /mie·yoh/ (*Fr* majo) /*n* **1** tights for dancers, acrobats, or gymnasts **2** a jersey **3** a woman's one-piece usu strapless swimsuit [Fr, lit., swaddling cloth]

**mailman** /-ˌman/ *n*, *NAm* a postman

**mail order** *n* an order for goods that is received and fulfilled by post – **mail-order** *adj*

¹**maim** /maym/ *vt* to mutilate, disfigure, or wound seriously [ME *maynhen, maymen*, fr OF *maynier* (cf MAYHEM)] – **maimer** *n*

²**maim** *n*, *obs* serious physical injury or defect; *esp* loss of a limb

¹**main** /mayn/ *n* **1** physical strength; force – in *with might and main* **2a main, mains** *pl the* chief pipe, duct, or cable of a public service (eg gas, electricity, or water) ⟨*the water* ~⟩ ⟨*turned off the gas at the* ~s⟩ **b** *pl but taking sing vb, chiefly Br* a source of electricity produced centrally for use by a large number of consumers – usu + *the* **3a** MAINMAST **b** MAINSAIL **4a** *archaic* a mainland **b** *poetic* HIGH SEA [ME, fr OE *mægen;* akin to OHG *magan* strength, OE *magan* to be able – more at MAY; (2–4) fr ²*main* & by shortening] – **in/for the main** on the whole; FOR THE MOST PART

²**main** *adj* **1** chief, principal **2** fully exerted; sheer ⟨~ *force*⟩

⟨*by* ~ *strength*⟩ **3** *of an academic subject* being that which is studied in most depth and to which most time is devoted **4** connected with or located near the MAINMAST or MAINSAIL **5** *of a clause* functioning as the chief element in a complex sentence and able to stand alone as a sentence (eg *he laughed* in *he laughed when he heard*) – see also **have an** EYE **to the main chance** [ME, fr OE *maegen-*, fr *mægen* strength]

³**main** *n* a number exceeding four and not exceeding nine called by the player before throwing the dice in the game of HAZARD [prob fr ²*main*]

**main beam** *n* the brighter and more far-reaching illumination provided by a vehicle headlight

**main chance** *n the* chance that promises most advantage or profit ⟨*always has an eye to the* ~⟩

**maincrop** /'mayn,krop/ *adj* of or being a crop gathered in the main harvest as distinguished from an early or late harvest – **maincrop** *n*

**main deck** *n* **1** the highest deck that extends the full width and length of a naval vessel **2** the upper deck of a merchant vessel between the POOP (structure at rear of ship) and FORE-CASTLE (forward part of ship)

**mainframe** /-,fraym/ *n* a large computer that can run several independent programs simultaneously or is connected to other smaller computers

**mainland** /-lənd/ *n* the largest land area of a continent, country, etc, as distinguished from a smaller offshore island or sometimes from a cape or peninsula – **mainlander** *n*

**mainline** /-,lien/ *vb, slang* to inject (heroin or a similar drug) into a vein [*main line* (principal vein)] – **mainline** *adj or n,* **mainliner** *n*

**main line** *n* a principal road or railway line

**mainly** /-li/ *adv* in most cases; for the most part; chiefly

**mainmast** /-,mahst; *naut* -məst/ *also* **main** *n* (the lowest section of) a sailing vessel's principal mast

**mainplane** /'mayn,playn/ *n* any of the chief supporting structures of an aeroplane; *esp* either of the wings or both considered together

**mains** /maynz/ *adj* of or (suitable to be) powered by electricity from the mains ⟨*a* ~ *razor*⟩

**mainsail** /-,sayl; *naut* -s(ə)l/ *also* **main** *n* **1** the principal and lowest sail on the mainmast of a SQUARE-RIGGED ship **2** the principal sail set on the side of the mainmast nearest the stern of a FORE AND AFT rigged sailing vessel (eg a racing or cruising yacht)

**mainsheet** /'mayn,sheet/ *n* a rope by which the mainsail is controlled and secured

**mainspring** /-,spring/ *n* **1** the chief spring in a mechanism, esp of a watch or clock **2** the chief or most powerful motive, agent, or cause of something

**mainstay** /-,stay/ *n* **1** a rope or wire stretching forward from the head of the mainmast and providing its chief support **2** a chief support of something

**mainstream** /-,streem/ *n* a prevailing current or direction of activity or influence – **mainstream** *adj*

**Main Street** *n* a place where people hold materialistic self-satisfied ideals [*Main Street*, novel by Sinclair Lewis †1951 US novelist] – **Main Streeter** *n*

**maintain** /mayn'tayn/ *vt* **1** to keep in an existing state (eg of operation, repair, efficiency, or validity); preserve from failure or decline ⟨~ *one's health*⟩ ⟨~ *machinery*⟩ **2** to sustain against opposition or danger; uphold and defend ⟨~ *a position*⟩ **3** to continue or persevere in; KEEP UP ⟨*couldn't* ~ *his composure*⟩ **4a** to support or provide for; bear the expense of ⟨*has a family to* ~⟩ **b** to sustain ⟨*enough food to* ~ *life*⟩ **5** to affirm (as if) in argument; assert ⟨~ed *that all men are not equal*⟩ **synonyms** see ¹SUPPORT [ME *mainteinen,* fr OF *maintenir,* fr ML *manu-tenēre,* fr L *manu tenēre* to hold in the hand] – **maintainable** *adj,* **maintainer** *n,* **maintainability** *n*

**maintained school** *n* a school provided, controlled, or aided by a British local education authority

**maintenance** /'mayntinəns/ *n* **1** maintaining or being maintained **2** the upkeep of property or equipment ⟨*car* ~⟩ **3** *chiefly Br* ALIMONY 1 **4** the former offence of interference in a legal case by an uninvolved party (eg by the providing of funds for the continuation of the action) – compare CHAMPERTY [ME, fr MF, fr OF, fr *maintenir*]

**maintop** /'mayn,top/ *n* a platform at the junction of the MAINMAST (lowest part of principal mast) and the main-topmast of a ship with SQUARE SAILS (4-sided sails set across the ship in a side-to-side direction)

,**main-'topmast** *n* a mast next above the MAINMAST (lowest part of principal mast) in a sailing ship

**main yard** *n* the pole used to suspend a sail from a mainsail

**mair** /meə/ *adj, adv, or n, chiefly Scot* more

**maisonette** /,mays(ə)n'et/ *n* **1** a small house **2** a part of a house, usu on two floors, let or sold separately [Fr *maisonnette,* fr OF, dim. of *maison* house, fr L *mansion-, mansio* dwelling place – more at MANSION]

**maître d'** /,metrə 'dee/ *n, pl* **maître d's,** *NAm* MAÎTRE D'HÔTEL

¹**maître d'hôtel** /,metrə doh'tel/ *n, pl* **maîtres d'hôtel** /~/ **1** MAJORDOMO (head steward of a household) **2** a headwaiter [Fr, lit., master of house]

²**maître d'hôtel** *adj* containing or cooked with parsley and lemon juice ⟨~ *butter*⟩ ⟨~ *sauce*⟩

**maize** /mayz/ *n* (the ears or edible seeds of) a tall widely cultivated originally American cereal grass (*Zea mays*) bearing seeds on elongated ears – called also INDIAN CORN △ maze [Sp *maiz,* fr Taino *mahiz*]

**majesty** /'majəsti/ *n* **1** sovereign power or authority **2** *often cap* – used in addressing or referring to a king or queen ⟨*Your* Majesty⟩ ⟨*Her* Majesty's *Government*⟩ **3a** impressive bearing or aspect **b** greatness or splendour of quality or character **synonyms** see ¹GRAND [ME *maieste,* fr OF *majesté,* fr L *majestat-, majestas;* akin to L *major* greater] – **majestic, majestical** *adj,* **majestically** *adv*

**majolica** /mə'jolikə, -'yol-/ *also* **maiolica** /mə'yolikə/ *n* a type of early Italian earthenware covered with an opaque tin glaze and decorated with bright-coloured metallic OXIDES on the glaze before firing [It *maiolica,* fr ML *Majolica* Majorca, largest of the Balearic Islands in the Mediterranean, fr LL *Majorca*]

¹**major** /'mayjə/ *adj* **1** greater in importance, size, rank, or degree ⟨*one of our* ~ *poets*⟩ **2** having attained the age of majority **3** notable or conspicuous in effect or scope; considerable ⟨*a* ~ *improvement*⟩ **4** involving serious risk to life; serious ⟨*a* ~ *illness*⟩ **5a** *esp of a musical scale or* MODE having SEMITONES (smallest intervals between two notes) between the third and fourth and the seventh and eighth steps, giving the pattern: tone, tone, semitone, tone, tone, tone, semitone ⟨~ *scale*⟩ **b** being or based on a (specified) major scale ⟨*in a* ~ *key*⟩ ⟨*sonata in C* ~⟩ **c** being a musical interval (equivalent to the distance) between the first and the second, third, sixth, or seventh notes of a major scale ⟨~ *third*⟩ – compare AUG-MENTED, DIMINISHED, MINOR 3c, PERFECT 5a **d** *of a chord* having a musical interval of four SEMITONES (smallest intervals between two notes) between the lowest note and the next note above it. Minor chords have three semitones in this position. **6** *chiefly NAm* of a main subject or course of academic study [ME *maiour,* fr L *major,* compar of *magnus* great, large – more at MUCH]

²**major** *n* **1** a person who has attained the age of majority **2** a major musical interval, scale, key, or MODE **3** – see MILITARY RANKS table **4** *chiefly NAm* (a student specializing in) a main subject of academic study ⟨*he is a history* ~⟩

³**major** *vi, chiefly NAm* to take courses in one's major subject

**major axis** *n* the longest AXIS of an ellipse; the chord passing through the focuses of an ellipse

**majordomo** /,mayjə'dohmoh/ *n, pl* **majordomos** **1** a man (eg a head steward) having charge of a large household (eg a palace) **2** a butler or steward [Sp *mayordomo* or obs It *maiordomo,* fr ML *major domus,* lit., chief of the household]

**majorette** /,mayjə'ret/ *n* a girl who twirls a baton and accompanies a marching band [short for *drum majorette,* fem of *drum major* leader of a marching band]

**major form class** *n* any of the PARTS OF SPEECH of traditional grammar (eg noun, verb, or preposition)

**major general** *n* – see MILITARY RANKS table [Fr *major général,* fr *major,* n + *général,* adj, general]

**majoritarianism** /mə,jori'teəriəniz(ə)m/ *n* the philosophy or practice according to which decisions of an organized group should be made by a numerical majority of its members – **majoritarian** *adj or n*

**majority** /mə'jorəti/ *n* **1** the (status of one who has attained the) age at which full legal rights and responsibilities are acquired **2a** a number greater than half of a total **b** the amount by which a majority exceeds the remaining smaller number ⟨*a* ~ *of seven*⟩ **3** *taking sing or pl vb* the greatest in number of two or more groups constituting a whole; *specif* (the excess of votes over its rival obtained by) a group having sufficient votes to obtain control – compare PLURALITY 3b **4** the military office, rank, or commission of a major [MF *majorité*, fr ML *majoritat-, majoritas*, fr L *major*, adj; (4) Fr *majorité*, fr *major*, n]

*usage* A **majority** is strictly a greater number, not the greater part of a single thing. Expressions such as ⟨△ the **majority** *of the garage is filled with rubbish*⟩ are best avoided. Compare BULK

**major league** *n* a league of highest classification in US professional sport, esp baseball

**major order** *n usu pl* any of the holy orders of bishops, priests, or deacons of the Roman Catholic or Eastern Orthodox church

**major premise** *n* the statement that contains the description of the subject of the conclusion drawn in a SYLLOGISM (logical exercise of the form "All As are B, C is an A, so C must be B") ⟨*if Venus is a goddess, and we accept the* ∼ *that all goddesses are immortal, we conclude that Venus must be immortal*⟩

**major prophet** *n* any of the prophets Ezekiel, Isaiah, and Jeremiah or their books in the Old Testament

**major seminary** *n* a Roman Catholic SEMINARY (training college for priests) giving usu the entire training required for MAJOR ORDERS

**major suit** *n* either of the suits of hearts or spades that in bridge are of superior scoring value – compare MINOR SUIT

**major term** *n* the term that states what is asserted of the subject of a MAJOR PREMISE (e g "are immortal" in "all goddesses are immortal")

**majuscule** /'majəskyoohl/ *n* (a letter in) any of several styles of handwriting using only capital or UNCIAL (rounded or curved capital) letters – compare MINUSCULE [Fr, fr L *majusculus* rather large, dim. of *major*] – **majuscule** *adj*, **majuscular** *adj*

**makar** /'mahkə, 'may-/ *n, chiefly Scot* a poet [ME *maker* maker, poet]

¹**make** /mayk/ *vb* **made** /mayd/ *vt* **1a** to create or produce (for someone) by work or action ⟨∼ *a dress*⟩ ⟨∼ *a road*⟩ ⟨made *in Korea*⟩ ⟨*she* made *herself a cup of coffee*⟩ **b** to cause; BRING ABOUT ⟨∼ *a disturbance*⟩ ⟨∼ *peace*⟩ **c** to fit or destine (as if) by creating ⟨*was* made *for his profession*⟩ **2** to formulate in the mind ⟨∼ *plans*⟩ ⟨∼ *no doubt of it*⟩ **3** to put together from ingredients or components ⟨*jam is* made *from fruit*⟩ ⟨*do you think I'm* made *of money?*⟩ – often + *up* **4** to compute or estimate to be ⟨*what time do you* ∼ *it?*⟩ **5a** to assemble and set alight the materials for (a fire) **b** to renew or straighten the bedclothes on (a bed) **c** to shuffle (a pack of cards) in preparation for dealing **6a** to cause to be or become ⟨made *himself useful*⟩ ⟨made *him bishop*⟩ ⟨*couldn't* ∼ *himself heard*⟩ **b** to cause (something) to appear or seem to; represent as ⟨*in the film they* ∼ *the battle take place in winter*⟩ **c(1)** to change, transform ⟨∼ *the material into a skirt*⟩ **c(2)** to produce as an end product ⟨*the navy will* ∼ *a man of you*⟩ ⟨made *a mess of the job*⟩ **d** to carry on right through (a period of time) ⟨*take sandwiches and* ∼ *a day of it*⟩ **7a** to enact, establish ⟨∼ *laws*⟩ ⟨∼ *a distinction*⟩ ⟨∼ *a price*⟩ **b** to draft or produce a version of ⟨∼ *a will*⟩ **8** to cause (an electric circuit) to be completed – compare BREAK 13c **9a** to perform; CARRY OUT ⟨∼ *a speech*⟩ ⟨∼ *an early start*⟩ ⟨∼ *war*⟩ ⟨*a sweeping gesture*⟩ ⟨∼ *a detour*⟩ ⟨*a postman making his rounds*⟩ **b** to eat ⟨∼ *a good breakfast*⟩ **c** to put forward for acceptance ⟨∼ *an offer*⟩ ⟨∼ *a promise*⟩ **10** to cause to act in a specified way; compel ⟨*rain* ∼s *the flowers grow*⟩ ⟨*she was* made *to return*⟩ **11a** to amount to; count as ⟨*four and four* ∼ *eight*⟩ ⟨*that* ∼s *the third time he's said it*⟩ ⟨∼s *a great difference*⟩ **b** to be integral or essential to the existence or success of ⟨*the bright paint really* ∼s *the room*⟩ ⟨*it* made *my day*⟩ **c** to combine to form; constitute ⟨∼ *a quorum*⟩ ⟨*hydrogen and oxygen* ∼ *water*⟩ **12** to be capable of becoming or of serving as ⟨*rags* ∼ *the best paper*⟩ ⟨*she will* ∼ *a rotten secretary*⟩ **13** to reach, attain ⟨*never* ∼ *the airfield*⟩ ⟨*the story* made *the papers*⟩ – often + *it* ⟨*you'll never* ∼ *it that far*⟩ **14** to gain (e g money) by working, trading, dealing, etc ⟨∼ *£10*⟩ ⟨∼ *a loss*⟩ **15a** to act so as to acquire ⟨∼ *enemies*⟩ **b** to score (e g points) in a game or sport ⟨∼ *30 runs*⟩ **16a** to fulfil (a CONTRACT) in bridge or another card game **b** to win a TRICK with (a card) **17** to ensure the success or prosperity of ⟨*anyone he takes a fancy to is* made⟩ **18** *slang* to persuade to consent to sexual intercourse **19** *archaic* to translate into a specified language ⟨*making those two authors English* – John Dryden⟩ ∼ *vi* **1a** to behave so as to seem ⟨made *as though he were angry*⟩ **b** to behave as if beginning a specified action ⟨made *to go*⟩ ⟨made *as if to hand it over*⟩ **c** to act so as to be ⟨∼ *merry*⟩ ⟨∼ *ready to leave*⟩ **2** to set out or go (in a specified direction) ⟨made *towards the door*⟩ ⟨*we're* making *for the coast*⟩ **3** to undergo manufacture or processing – usu + *up*

⟨*the silk* ∼s *up beautifully*⟩ **4** to increase in height or size ⟨*the tide is* making *now*⟩ **5** *archaic* to compose poetry [ME *maken*, fr OE *macian*; akin to OHG *mahhōn* to prepare, make, OSlav *mazati* to anoint] – **makable** *adj* – **make believe** to pretend, feign – **make do** to get along or manage with the means at hand – **make it 1** *informal* to be successful ⟨*actors trying to* make *it in the big time*⟩ **2** *slang* to achieve sexual intercourse – often + *with*

*synonyms* Make, create, form, fashion, fabricate, produce, manufacture, and forge may all mean "cause something to come into being". **Make** is the most general and the most widely applicable. **Create** most strongly stresses conscious intention, power, control, and aesthetic purpose. It suggests too that the end product is very different from the raw materials used ⟨*God* **created** *the world from chaos*⟩. **Form** implies shape, design, or structure in the finished article, whether concrete or abstract ⟨**form** *a circle/a plan*⟩. **Fashion** adds to **form** a suggestion of intelligent or ingenious invention ⟨**fashioned** *a skirt from the curtains*⟩. **Fabricate** suggests making something from many parts, or according to a pattern ⟨**fabricated** *hundreds of containers a week*⟩; its more usual use, however, is figurative, when it often suggests imaginative invention of what is not true ⟨**fabricated** *some story about having to visit his mother*⟩. **Produce** is another general term which basically means "turning out work", with the emphasis on the result rather than the process. **Manufacture** adds the idea of mechanical or mechanized activity, which sometimes makes it a derogatory substitute for **create** ⟨he **manufactures** *five thrillers every year*⟩. The literal meaning of **forge** is carried over into its figurative sense, to stress the physical or mental effort involved in creating something real and enduring ⟨**forge** *a friendship*⟩. It may also mean "make a counterfeit". *antonyms* unmake, destroy

**make away with** *vt* **1** *also* **make off with** to steal or abduct **2** to destroy

**make for** *vt* **1** to go towards, esp in haste **2** to be conducive to ⟨*courtesy* makes for *safer driving*⟩

**make like** *vt, informal* to act the part of; imitate

**make of** *vt* **1** to attribute a specified degree of significance to ⟨*tends to* make *too much of her problems*⟩ **2** to understand by; conclude as to the meaning of ⟨*could* make *nothing of the play*⟩

**make off** *vi* to leave in haste

**make out** *vt* **1** to draw up in writing **2** to complete (e g a printed form or document) by writing information in appropriate spaces **3** to find or grasp the meaning of ⟨*tried to* make *out what had happened*⟩ **4** to claim or pretend to be true ⟨made *out that he had never heard of me*⟩ **5** to identify (e g by sight or hearing) with difficulty or effort ∼ *vi* **1** to fare, manage ⟨*how is he* making *out in his new job*⟩ **2** *chiefly NAm slang* to engage in sexual activity or intercourse

**make over** *vt* **1** to transfer the title of (property) ⟨made *over the estate to his eldest son*⟩ **2** *chiefly NAm* to remake, remodel ⟨made *the whole house* over⟩

**make up** *vt* **1a** to invent (e g a story), esp in order to deceive **b** to set (an account) in order **2a** to arrange typeset matter into (columns or pages) for printing **b** to produce (e g curtains or clothes) by cutting and sewing **c** PREPARE 3a ⟨make *up a prescription*⟩ **3** to wrap or fasten up ⟨make *the books up into a parcel*⟩ **4** to compensate for (a deficiency); *esp* to make (e g a required amount or number) complete ⟨make *up a foursome for tennis*⟩ **5** to settle, decide ⟨made *up his mind to leave*⟩ ⟨made *up their differences*⟩ **6a** to prepare in physical appearance for a role **b** to apply cosmetics to ∼ *vi* **1** to become reconciled ⟨*quarrelled but later* made *up*⟩ **2** to compensate for ⟨*we* made *up for lost time*⟩ **3** to put on costumes or makeup (e g for a play) **4** to assemble a finished article; *esp* to complete a garment by sewing together **5** to act ingratiatingly and flatteringly *to* ⟨made *up to the play's director, hoping for a part*⟩

**make with** *vt, chiefly NAm slang* to produce, perform usu + *the*

²**make** *n* **1a** the manner or style in which a thing is constructed **b** a place or origin of manufacture; BRAND 3b **2** the physical, mental, or moral constitution of a person ⟨*men of his* ∼ *are rare*⟩ **3** the type or process of making or manufacturing **4** the act of shuffling cards; *also* a player's turn to shuffle *synonyms* see ¹TYPE – **make or break** a (last) chance to prove oneself or achieve something – **on the make 1** rising or attempting to rise to a higher social or financial status **2** in search of a sexual partner or sexual adventure

**makebate** /'mayk,bayt/ *n, archaic* one who excites contention and quarrels [¹*make* + obs *bate* strife, fr ME, fr *baten* to contend, argue, beat the wings – more at ²BATE]

'**make-be,lieve** *n or adj* (something) imaginary or pretended

,**make-'do** *adj* makeshift – **make-do** *n*

**maker** /'maykə/ *n* 1 one who or that which makes 2 *cap* GOD 1 3 a person who borrows money on a PROMISSORY NOTE (specific promise of payment) 4a the player in a card game (e g EUCHRE) who decides on the trumps suit and alone or in partnership must make at least three tricks or pay a penalty **b** a DECLARER in bridge 5 a manufacturer 6 *archaic* a poet

**makeready** /-,redi/ *n* (material used in) final preparation for printing

**makeshift** /-,shift/ *adj or n* (being) a usu crude and temporary expedient

'**make-,up** *n* **1a** the way in which the parts or ingredients of something are put together; composition **b** physical, mental, and moral constitution **2a** cosmetics (e g lipstick and mascara) applied, esp to the face, to give colour or emphasis **b** the effect achieved by the application of make-up **c** materials (e g wigs and cosmetics) used for special costuming (e g for a play) 3 the operation of making up (e g of matter for printing); *also* the arrangement of such matter

**makeweight** /-,wayt/ *n* 1 something added to bring a weight to a desired value 2 someone or something of little importance added to compensate for a lack

**making** /'mayking/ *n* 1 the act or process of forming, causing, doing, or coming into being ⟨*can spot problems in the* ∼⟩ 2 a process or means of advancement or success ⟨*even misfortune can be the* ∼ *of a person*⟩ **3a makings** *pl*, **making** the essential qualities for becoming something specified ⟨*had the* ∼s *of a great artist*⟩ **b** *pl* the material from which something is to be made; *esp, chiefly NAm & Austr* paper and tobacco used for rolling one's own cigarettes

**mako** /'mahkoh/ *also* **mako shark** *n, pl* **makos** either of two MACKEREL SHARKS (*Isurus glaucus* and *Isurus oxyrhynchus*) found in Australian seas and elsewhere that are notable sport fishes and are considered dangerous to man [Maori]

**makuta** /mah'koohtə/ *pl of* LIKUTA (Zaïrean money)

**mal-** /mal-/ *comb form* 1a bad ⟨mal*practice*⟩; faulty ⟨mal*function*⟩ **b** badly ⟨mal*odorous*⟩; deficiently ⟨mal*nourished*⟩ **2a** abnormal ⟨mal*formation*⟩ **b** abnormally ⟨mal*formed*⟩ 3 not ⟨mal*content*⟩ ⟨mal*adroit*⟩ [ME, fr MF, fr OF, fr *mal* bad (fr L *malus*) & *mal* badly, fr L *male*, fr *malus* – more at SMALL]

**malabsorption** /malab'zawpsh(ə)n; *also* -əb'saw-/ *n* the faulty absorption of a vitamin, mineral (e g iron), protein, or other nutrient from the stomach and intestines

**malac-, malaco-** *comb form* soft ⟨mala*coid*⟩ [L, fr Gk *malak-, malako-*, fr *malakos*; akin to L *molere* to grind]

**malacca cane** /mə'lakə/ *n* an often mottled cane obtained from the stem of an Asiatic RATTAN palm (*Calamus rotang*) and used esp for walking sticks [*Malacca*, city and state in Malaya]

**Malachi** /'malə,kie/ *n* – see BIBLE table [*Malachi*, supposed to be the name of a 5th-c BC prophet, fr Heb *Mal'ākhī*, lit., my (i e God's) messenger]

**Malachias** /,malə'kie-əs/ *n* Malachi [LL, fr Gk, fr Heb *Mal'ākhī*]

**malachite** /'malə,kiet/ *n* a green mineral, $Cu_2CO_3(OH)_2$, that consists of a carbonate of copper and is used as a source of copper and for making ornaments △ marcasite [ME *melochites*, fr L *molochites*, fr Gk *molochītēs*, fr *molochē* mallow]

**malacology** /,malə'koləji/ *n* a branch of zoology dealing with MOLLUSCS (large group of animals including the snails, oysters, and squids) [Fr *malacologie*, contr of *malacozoologie*, fr NL *Malacozoa*, zoological group including soft-bodied animals (fr *malac-* + *-zoa*) + Fr *-logie* -logy] – **malacologist** *n*, **malacological** *also* **malacologic** *adj*

**malacostracan** /,malə'kostrəkən/ *n* any of a major subclass (Malacostraca of the class Crustacea) of INVERTEBRATE animals including most of the well-known marine, freshwater, and ground-living members of the group (e g the crabs, lobsters, shrimps, and woodlice) [deriv of Gk *malakostrakos* soft-shelled, fr *malak-* + *ostrakon* shell – more at OYSTER] – **malacostracan** *adj*

**maladapted** /,malə'daptid/ *adj* unsuited or poorly suited (e g to a particular use, purpose, or situation) – **maladaptation** *n*, **maladaptive** *adj*

**maladjusted** /,malə'justid/ *adj* poorly or inadequately

adjusted, specif to one's social environment and conditions of life – **maladjustive** *adj*, **maladjustment** *n*

**maladminister** /,maləd'ministə/ *vt* to administer incompetently or corruptly, esp in public office – **maladministration** *n*

**maladroit** /malə'droyt/ *adj* clumsy, inept *synonyms* see CLUMSY *antonyms* diplomatic, adroit [Fr, fr MF, fr *mal-* + *adroit*] – **maladroitly** *adv*, **maladroitness** *n*

**malady** /'malədi/ *n* a disease, illness, or disorder; *broadly* any unhealthy or morbid condition [ME *maladie*, fr OF, fr *malade* sick, fr L *male habitus* in bad condition]

**mala fide** /,malə 'fiedi/ *adv or adj* with or in bad faith [LL]

**Malaga** /'maləgə/ *n* any of several usu sweet fortified wines from the Málaga region of Spain; *also* a similar wine made elsewhere

**Malagasy** /,malə'gasi/ *n, pl* **Malagasies**, *esp collectively* **Malagasy** (the language of) a native or inhabitant of the Malagasy Republic [*Malagasy* Republic (formerly Madagascar), island in the Indian Ocean] – **Malagasy** *adj*

**malaguena** /,malə'gaynyə/ *n* a folk dance-tune that originated in Málaga and is similar to a FANDANGO [Sp *malagueña*, fr fem of *malagueño* of Málaga, fr *Málaga*, city and province in S Spain]

**malaise** /ma'lez, -'layz/ *n* 1 an indeterminate feeling of weakness or lack of health, often indicative of or accompanying the onset of an illness 2 a vague sense of mental or moral unease 3 a lack of wellbeing, esp as shown in reduced activity ⟨*Britain's economic* ∼⟩ [Fr, fr OF, fr *mal-* + *aise* comfort – more at EASE]

**malamute, malemute** /'maləmyooht/ *n* ALASKAN MALAMUTE (powerful Alaskan dog) [*Malemute*, an Alaskan Eskimo people]

**malanders, mallanders, mallenders** /'maləndəz/ *n taking sing vb* a condition characterized by the formation of an inflamed scaly area on the back of the knee of a horse's foreleg [ME *malawnder* sore on a horse's knee, fr MF *malandre*, fr L *malandria* sore on a horse's neck]

**malapert** /,malə'puht/ *adj, archaic* impudently bold; saucy [ME, fr MF, unskilful, fr *mal-* + *apert* skilful, modif of L *expertus* expert] – **malapertly** *adv*, **malapertness** *n*

**malapropism** /'maləpro,piz(ə)m/ *n* (an instance of) an incongruous misapplication of a word (e g in "always said 'polobears' . . . and 'neonstockings'" – *Time*) [Mrs *Malaprop*, character noted for her misuse of words in the comedy *The Rivals* by R B Sheridan †1816 Ir dramatist] – **malapropian** *adj*

**malapropos** /,maləprə'poh/ *adv* in an inappropriate or inopportune way [Fr *mal à propos*] – **malapropos** *adj*

¹**malar** /'maylə/ *adj* of or in the region of the cheek or the side of the head [NL *malaris*, fr L *mala* jawbone, cheek]

²**malar, malar bone** *n* ZYGOMATIC BONE (cheekbone)

**malaria** /mə'leəri•ə/ *n* **1a** a disease of humans that is caused by parasitic PROTOZOANS (single-celled animals) (genus *Plasmodium*) in the RED BLOOD CELLS, is transmitted by the bite of mosquitoes, and is characterized by periodic attacks of chills and fever **b** any of various diseases of birds and mammals caused by protozoans in the blood 2 *archaic* an unwholesome atmosphere caused by exhalations from marshes [It, fr *mala aria* bad air; fr the former belief that it was caused by gases from marshy places] – **malarial** *adj*, **malarian** *adj*, **malarious** *adj*

**malarkey** /mə'lahki/ *n, informal* foolishness, nonsense; *esp* insincere or foolish talk [origin unknown]

**malate** /'malayt, 'may-/ *n* any of various chemical compounds (SALTS or ESTERS) formed by combination between MALIC ACID and a metal atom, an alcohol, or another chemical group

**malathion** /,malə'thie,on, -ən/ *n* a brown to yellow general-purpose liquid insecticide, $C_{10}H_{19}O_6PS_2$, used against household flies and garden pests (e g greenfly) [fr *Malathion*, a trademark]

**Malay** /mə'lay/ *n* (the language of) a member of a people of the Malay peninsula, E Sumatra, parts of Borneo, and some nearby islands [obs D *Malayo* (now *Maleier*, fr Malay *Mēlayu*] – **Malay** *adj*, **Malayan** *n or adj*

**Malayalam** /mə'layələm, ,mali'ahləm/ *n* a DRAVIDIAN language of SW India

**Malayo-** /məlayoh-/ *comb form* Malayan and ⟨Malayo-*Indonesian*⟩

**Ma,layo-Poly'nesian** *adj* AUSTRONESIAN

¹**malcontent** /,malkən'tent/ *n* a discontented person; *esp* somebody violently opposed to a government

**²malcontent, malcontented** *adj* dissatisfied with the existing state of affairs ⟨*awed by the greatness of the universe and ~ with what the philosophers told me* – W S Maugham⟩ [MF, fr OF, fr *mal-* + *content*] – **malcontentedly** *adv*, **malcontentedness** *n*

**mal de mer** /ˌmal də 'meə/ *n* seasickness [Fr]

**maldevelopment** /ˌmaldi'veləpmənt/ *n* abnormal or deficient growth or development – **maldeveloped** *adj*

**¹male** /mayl/ *adj* **1a**(1) of or being the sex that produces the relatively small SEX CELLS (eg the SPERMATOZOIDS of ferns, mosses, algae, etc or the SPERMATOZOA of animals) that are usually capable of movement and that fertilize the eggs of a female **a**(2) *of a plant or flower* having STAMENS (structures that produce the male reproductive cells) but no OVARIES (seed-producing female reproductive structures) and not producing fruit or seed **b**(1) (characteristic of) the male sex ⟨*a deep ~ voice*⟩ **b**(2) made up of male individuals ⟨*a ~ choir*⟩ **2** designed for fitting into a corresponding hollow part ⟨*a ~ electric plug*⟩ [ME, fr MF *masle, male,* adj & n, fr L *masculus,* dim. of *mar-, mas* male] – **maleness** *n*

synonyms Male, masculine, manly, manlike, mannish, gentlemanly, manful, virile, and macho: male is opposed to "female", and denotes sex in living things. Masculine describes qualities and characteristics regarded as typical of men as opposed to women; it may be applied to men or women, but not to plants or animals. Manly suggests those virtues expected of a mature man. Manlike simply implies a correspondence with what is characteristic of men, especially their failings ⟨*a manlike bluntness*⟩, or, of animals etc, a similarity to human beings. Mannish describes masculine behaviour by women or the women themselves. Manful, like manly, implies the best qualities imputed to males, but stresses courage and resolution. Virile, unlike manly and manful, may be applied only to mature men, and stresses masterfulness, forcefulness, and specifically the ability to procreate. Gentlemanly stresses the gentler qualities associated with masculinity: gentleness, protectiveness, chivalry, and courtesy. Macho, in contrast, exaggerates virility to the point of boastful aggressiveness. Compare ²FEMALE, GENTLEMAN *antonym* female

**²male** *n* a male person, animal, or plant *synonyms see* GENTLEMAN *antonym* female

**male alto** *n* COUNTERTENOR (high-voiced adult male singer)

**maleate** /məˈlee-ət, -ˈlay-/ *n* any of various chemical compounds (SALTS or ESTERS) formed by combination between MALEIC ACID and a metal atom, an alcohol, or another chemical group

**male chauvinist** *n* a man who adheres excessively to a traditional view of male and female roles, esp to a belief in the inherent superiority of men over women, and is overly loyal to his own sex – **male-chauvinist** *adj*, **male chauvinism** *n*

**male chauvinist pig** *n, derog* MALE CHAUVINIST

**malediction** /ˌmalə'diksh(ə)n/ *n, formal* **1** a curse **2** a slanderous statement [ME *malediccioun,* fr LL *malediction-, maledictio,* fr *maledictus,* pp of *maledicere* to curse, fr L, fr *male* badly + *dicere* to speak, say – more at MAL-, DICTION] – **maledictive, maledictory** *adj*

**malefaction** /ˌmali'faksh(ə)n/ *n, formal* an evil deed

**malefactor** /ˈmaliˌfaktə/ *n, formal* **1** a criminal; *esp* FELON **2** one who does evil [ME, fr L, fr *malefactus,* pp of *malefacere* to do evil, fr *male* + *facere* to do – more at DO]

**male fern** *n* a fern (*Dryopteris filix-mas*) that has scaly stalks and large leaves with spore-producing bodies enclosed in kidney-shaped covers on the underside, and from which an extract is obtained that is used to treat tapeworm infestation

**malefic** /mə'lefik/ *adj, formal* **1** having a malicious influence; baleful, harmful **2** criminal [L *maleficus* wicked, mischievous, fr *male*]

**maleficence** /mə'lefis(ə)ns/ *n, formal* **1** (an instance of) evildoing **2** the quality or state of being maleficent

**maleficent** /mə'lefis(ə)nt/ *adj, formal* **1** causing harm or evil; baleful **2** of the nature of a crime; criminal [back-formation fr *maleficence*]

**maleic acid** /mə'lee-ik/ *n* an acid, HOOCCH=CHCOOH, used esp in making plastics [Fr *acide maléique,* alter. of *acide malique* malic acid; fr its formation by dehydration of malic acid]

**maleic hydrazide** /ˈhiedrəzied/ *n* a synthetic chemical compound, $C_4H_4N_2O_2$, that has the ability to inhibit or retard plant growth

**malemute** /ˈmaləˌmyooht/ *n* ALASKAN MALAMUTE (powerful Alaskan dog)

**malentendu** /ˌmalonton'dooh (*Fr* malãtãdy)/ *n, pl* **malentendus** *formal* a misunderstanding [Fr, fr *mal entendu* misunderstood]

**malevolence** /mə'levələns/ *n* **1** being malevolent **2** malevolent behaviour

**malevolent** /mə'levələnt/ *adj* having, showing, or arising from an often intense desire to do harm *antonym* benevolent [L *malevolent-, malevolens,* fr *male* badly + *volent-, volens,* prp of *velle* to wish – more at MAL-, WILL] – **malevolently** *adv*

**malfeasance** /mal'feez(ə)ns/ *n* wrongdoing or misconduct, esp by a public official [*mal-* + obs *feasance* doing, execution, fr MF *faisance,* fr OF, fr *fais-,* stem of *faire* to do, fr L *facere*]

**malformation** /ˌmalfaw'maysh(ə)n/ *n* anomalous, abnormal, or faulty formation or structure – **malformed** *adj*

**malfunction** /-'fungksh(ə)n/ *vi* to fail to operate in the normal or usual manner – **malfunction** *n*

**Malibu board** /ˈmalibooh/ *n* a highly manoeuvrable surfboard with a fin and a rounded nose [*Malibu* Beach in California, USA]

**malic acid** /ˈmalik/ *n* an acid, $C_4H_6O_5$, that occurs naturally in the juices of various plants and fruits (eg apples) and is formed as an intermediate compound in the KREBS CYCLE (final stage in the breakdown of sugars and fats to produce energy) [Fr *acide malique,* fr L *malum* apple, fr Gk *mēlon, malon*]

**malice** /ˈmalis/ *n* conscious desire to harm; *esp* a premeditated desire to commit a crime [ME, fr OF, fr L *malitia,* fr *malus* bad – more at SMALL] – **malicious** *adj*, **maliciously** *adv*, **maliciousness** *n*

**malice aforethought** *n* predetermination to commit an esp violent crime, which must be proved in order to make a killing constitute an act of murder

**¹malign** /mə'lien/ *adj* **1a** harmful in nature, influence, or effect; injurious **b** *of a disease* malignant, virulent **2** bearing or showing (vicious) ill will or hostility; malevolent *synonyms see* SINISTER [ME *maligne,* fr MF, fr L *malignus,* fr *male* badly + *gigni* to be born, passive of *gignere* to beget (cf BENIGN)] – **malignly** *adv*

**²malign** *vt* to utter injuriously misleading or false reports about; speak evil of [ME *malignen,* fr MF *maligner* to act maliciously, fr LL *malignari,* fr L *malignus*]

synonyms Malign, traduce, cast aspersions, vilify, calumniate, defame, slander, and libel may all mean "speak ill of in order to harm". Malign implies malicious falsehood and misrepresentation, though deliberate lying is not always involved ⟨*Richard III is a much-*malign*ed king*⟩. Traduce (formal) stresses the results of such action, in bringing someone into undeserved disrepute. Casting aspersions implies an indirect attack on someone's reputation, by innuendo and oblique suggestions, but vilify suggests an open and often virulently abusive direct attack. Calumniate, more formal than malign, implies malice, falsehood, and often actual damage to someone's good name. Defame stresses a definite loss of reputation. Libel and slander are often interchangeable in general use to imply false accusations and damage to one's reputation, though slander stresses the suffering of the victim. Legally, slander applies to oral defamation, and libel to written or pictorial defamation. Compare ¹ABUSE, DISPARAGE *antonym* praise

**malignancy** /mə'lignənsi/ *n* **1** being malignant **2a** the showing (eg by a tumour) of malignant qualities or the degree to which these are shown **b** a malignant tumour

**malignant** /mə'lignənt/ *adj* **1a** MALIGN **1a b** passionately and relentlessly malevolent **2a** *of a disease* very severe or deadly ⟨*~ malaria*⟩ **b** *of a tumour* tending to spread, esp rapidly and over large areas, and cause death – compare BENIGN [LL *malignant-, malignans,* prp of *malignari*] – **malignantly** *adv*

**malignity** /mə'lignəti/ *n* malignancy, malevolence

**malines** /ma'leen/ *n, pl* **malines** /~/ **1** MECHLIN (fine lace) **2** *also* **maline** a fine stiff net with a six-sided mesh that is usu made of silk or rayon and is often used for veils [Fr, fr *Malines* (Mechelen), city in N Belgium]

**malinger** /mə'ling-gə/ *vi* to pretend illness or incapacity so as to avoid duty or work [Fr *malingre* sickly, deriv of OF *mal* badly + *haingre* thin, weak] – **malingerer** *n*

**Malinke** /mə'lingki/ *n, pl* **Malinkes,** *esp collectively* **Malinke** (the language of) a member of a Negro people of W Africa who use a type of shell as currency

**malison** /ˈmaliz(ə)n, -s(ə)n/ *n, archaic* a curse [ME, fr OF *maleïçon,* fr LL *malediction-, maledictio* – more at MALEDICTION]

**malkin** /ˈmawkin, ˈmawl-, ˈmal-/ *n* **1** *dial chiefly Br* an untidy woman; a slattern **2** *archaic* a cat – compare GRIMALKIN [ME *malkyn* woman of the lower classes, mop, fr *Malkyn,* fem name, dim. of *Malde* Maud, Matilda]

**mall** /mawl, mal/ *n* **1** an alley used for PALL-MALL (17th-century ball game) **2** a public promenade, often bordered by trees **3** *NAm* a shopping precinct, usu with associated parking space [short for *pall-mall;* (2) The *Mall,* promenade in London, orig a pall-mall alley]

**mallanders** /'maləndəz/ *n taking sing vb* MALANDERS (horse disease)

**mallard** /'malahd, -ləd/ *n, pl* **mallards,** *esp collectively* **mallard** a common large wild duck (*Anas platyrhynchos*) of the northern hemisphere that is the ancestor of the domestic ducks, and the male of which has a bright green head and a reddish-brown breast [ME, fr MF *mallart,* prob fr *male, masle* male + *-art* -ard]

**malleable** /'mali·əbl/ *adj* **1** *esp of a metal* capable of being beaten or rolled into a desired shape – compare DUCTILE 2 **2** easily shaped by outside forces or influences ⟨a ~ *character*⟩ **synonyms** see [1]PLASTIC **antonym** refractory [ME *malliable,* fr MF or ML; MF *malleable,* fr ML *malleabilis,* fr *malleare* to hammer, fr L *malleus* hammer – more at MAUL] – **malleableness, malleability** *n*

**mallee** /'mali/ *n* **1** any of several low-growing shrubby Australian eucalyptus trees (e g *Eucalyptus dumosa* and *Eucalyptus oleosa*) **2** a dense thicket or growth of mallees; *also* land covered by such growth [native name in Australia]

**mallee fowl** /'mali/ *n* a large Australian bird (*Leipoa ocellata*) whose eggs are laid and hatched in mounds of sand and vegetation

**mallemuck** /'malimuk/ *n* any of several large sea birds (e g the albatross, fulmar, or petrel) [D *mallemuk,* fr *mal* silly + *mok* gull]

**mallenders** /'maləndəz/ *n* MALANDERS (horse disease)

**malleolus** /mə'lee·ələs/ *n, pl* **malleoli** either of the two bony projections, one at each side of the ankle, that form the lower ends of the leg bones [NL, fr L, dim. of *malleus* hammer]

**mallet** /'malit/ *n* **1** a hammer with a large esp barrel-shaped head of relatively soft material for driving a tool (e g a chisel) or for striking a surface without marking it; *specif* one with a large wooden head **2** an implement with a large usu cylindrical wooden head for striking the ball in polo, croquet, etc **3** a light hammer with a small rounded or spherical usu padded head used in playing certain musical instruments (e g a vibraphone) [ME *maillet,* fr MF, fr OF, dim. of *mail* hammer, fr L *malleus*]

**malleus** /'mali·əs/ *n, pl* **mallei** /'mali,ee/ the outermost of a chain of three small bones that transmit sound in the ear of a mammal – compare INCUS, STAPES [NL, fr L, hammer]

**mallow** /'maloh/ *n* any of a genus (*Malva*) of plants of the hollyhock family, with usu lobed or notched leaves and showy purplish, pink, or white flowers; *also* any of several other related plants (e g the marshmallow) [ME *malwe,* fr OE *mealwe,* fr L *malva*]

**malm** /mahm/ *n* a soft crumbly limestone or limestone soil [ME *malme,* fr OE *mealm-;* akin to OE *melu* meal – more at MEAL]

**malmsey** /'mahmzi/ *n, often cap* the sweetest variety of Madeira wine [ME *malmesey,* fr ML *Malmasia* Monemvasia, village in Greece where it was orig produced]

**malnourished** /,mal'nurisht/ *adj* undernourished

**malnutrition** /,malnyooh'trish(ə)n/ *n* faulty or inadequate nutrition

**malocclusion** /,malə'kloohzh(ə)n/ *n* a defect in the meeting and alignment of the upper and lower teeth when the jaws are brought together

**malodorous** /-'ohd(ə)rəs/ *adj, formal* **1** smelling bad **2** unsavoury ⟨~ *practices*⟩ – **malodorously** *adv,* **malodorousness** *n*

**malolactic** /,maloh'laktik/ *adj* of or involved in the conversion by bacteria of MALIC ACID (acid found in fruits) to LACTIC ACID in wine ⟨~ *fermentation*⟩

**Malpighian body** /mal'pigi·ən/ *n* MALPIGHIAN CORPUSCLE

**Malpighian corpuscle** *n* the part of a NEPHRON (any of the urine-secreting units in a kidney) that consists of a network of tiny blood vessels (GLOMERULUS) together with its enclosing membrane (BOWMAN'S CAPSULE) [Marcello *Malpighi* †1694 It anatomist]

**Malpighian layer** *n* the innermost part of the outer layer (EPIDERMIS) of the skin [Marcello *Malpighi*]

**Malpighian tube** *n* MALPIGHIAN TUBULE

**Malpighian tubule** *n* any of a group of long tubes in most insects and some related animals (e g spiders, scorpions, and centipedes), that function primarily as excretory organs and have only one open end through which waste material is discharged into the hind part of the digestive tract [Marcello *Malpighi*]

**malpractice** /mal'praktis/ *n* **1** failure to exercise due professional (e g legal or medical) skill or care which results in injury, loss, or damage ⟨*sued the dentist for* ~⟩ **2** an instance of improper conduct – **malpractitioner** *n*

[1]**malt** /mawlt, molt/ *n* **1** grain softened in water, allowed to germinate, and used esp in brewing and distilling **2** unblended MALT WHISKY produced in a particular area ⟨*the finest Highland* ~s⟩ [ME, fr OE *mealt;* akin to OHG *malz* malt, OE *meltan* to melt] – **malty** *adj*

[2]**malt** *vt* **1** to convert (grain) into malt **2** to make or treat with malt or MALT EXTRACT ~ *vi* to become malt

**Malta fever** /'mawltə/ *n* human BRUCELLOSIS (bacterial disease) [*Malta,* island in the Mediterranean]

**maltase** /'mawltayz, -ays/ *n* an enzyme that accelerates the breakdown of the sugar maltose to glucose, is found in plants, bacteria, and yeasts, and is secreted by the intestines during digestion

**malted milk** *n* **1** a soluble powder prepared from dried milk and malted cereals; *also* a beverage made by dissolving this powder usu with milk **2** *NAm* a beverage made by dissolving malted milk in milk and adding ice cream and flavouring

**Maltese** /mawl'teez/ *n, pl* **Maltese 1** (the Semitic language of) a native or inhabitant of Malta **2** (any of) a breed of TOY DOGS that have long white coats, black noses, and very dark eyes – **Maltese** *adj*

**Maltese cat** *n* a bluish-grey domestic short-haired cat

**Maltese cross** *n* a cross consisting of four equal arms that widen from the centre and have their outer ends indented by a V [orig the emblem of the Knights of Malta (Hospitallers), rulers of Malta from 1530 to 1798]

**malt extract** *n* a sweet light-brown syrup prepared from an infusion of malt and water

**Malthusian** /mal'thyoohzh(ə)n, -zi·ən/ *adj* of Malthus or his theory that population tends to increase at a faster rate than its means of subsistence and that widespread poverty and degradation inevitably result unless population growth is checked by sexual restraint or by disaster (e g disease, famine, or war) [Thomas *Malthus* †1834 E economist] – **Malthusian** *n,* **Malthusianism** *n*

**maltings** /'mawltingz/ *n, pl* **maltings** an establishment where malt is prepared and stored

**malt liquor** *n* a fermented alcoholic drink (e g beer or ale) made with malt

**maltose** /'mawltohz, -tohs/ *n* a fermentable sugar, $C_{12}H_{22}O_{11}$, that consists of two linked glucose units and is formed esp by the breakdown of starch [Fr, fr E [1]*malt*]

**maltreat** /,mal'treet/ *vt* to treat cruelly or roughly; abuse **synonyms** see [1]MISUSE [Fr *maltraiter,* fr MF, fr *mal-* + *traiter* to treat, fr OF *traitier* – more at TREAT] – **maltreatment** *n*

**maltster** /'mawltstə/ *n* a person who makes or deals in malt

**malt sugar** *n* maltose

**malt whisky** *n* whisky distilled from malted barley

**malvasia** /,malvə'siə/ *n* the variety of grape used to make MALMSEY (sweet Madeira wine) [It, fr *Monemvasia,* village in Greece]

**malversation** /,malvuh'saysh(ə)n/ *n, formal* corruption in office [MF, fr *malverser* to be corrupt, fr *mal* + *verser* to turn, handle, fr L *versare,* fr *versus,* pp of *vertere* to turn – more at WORTH]

**mam** /mam/ *n, dial Br* mother [baby talk]

[1]**mama, mamma** /mə'mah/ *n* mother – formerly used as a term of address [baby talk]

[2]**mama, mamma** /'mumə; *NAm* 'mahmə/ *n* mummy – used informally and by children

**mamba** /'mambə/ *n* any of several large venomous snakes (genus *Dendraspis*) of tropical and southern Africa, that are related to the cobras and hunt small animals in trees; *esp* an aggressive southern African snake (*Dendraspis angusticeps*) that grows to a length of 4 metres (about 12 feet) and readily inflicts its often fatal bite [Zulu *im-amba*]

**mambo** /'mamboh/ *n, pl* **mambos** (the music for) a ballroom dance of Haitian origin that resembles the RUMBA and the CHA-CHA – compare SAMBA, CONGA [AmerSp] – **mambo** *vi*

**mamelon** /'mamilən/ *n* a small rounded hillock [Fr, lit., nipple, fr MF, dim. of *mamele* breast, nipple, fr L *mamilla*]

**mameluke** /'mami,loohk/ *n* **1** *cap* a member of a politically powerful Egyptian military class, originally Turkish slaves, occupying the sultanate from 1250 to 1517 and remaining powerful until the early 19th century **2** *often cap* a white or oriental slave in Muslim countries [Ar *mamlūk*, lit., slave]

**mamilla**, *NAm chiefly* **mammilla** /ma'milə/ *n*, *pl* **mamillae**, *NAm chiefly* **mammillae** /-lie/ **1** a nipple **2** a nipple-shaped part, structure, or protuberance [L *mammilla*, *mamilla* breast, nipple, dim. of *mamma*] – **mamillary** *adj*, **mamillate**, **mamillated** *adj*

**mamluk** /'mamloohk/ *n* a mameluke

**mamma** /'mamə/ *n*, *pl* **mammae** /'mamie/ MAMMARY GLAND [L, mother, breast, of baby-talk origin] – **mammate** *adj*

**mammal** /'maməl/ *n* any of a class (Mammalia) of warm-blooded VERTEBRATE animals comprising humans and all other animals that nourish their young with milk secreted by MAMMARY GLANDS and have the skin usu more or less covered with hair [deriv of LL *mammalis* of the breast, fr L *mamma* breast] – **mammalian** *adj* or *n*

**mammalogy** /ma'maləji/ *n* a branch of zoology dealing with mammals [ISV, blend of *mammal* and *-logy*] – **mammalogist** *n*, **mammalogical** *adj*

**mammary** /'maməri/ *adj* of, like, lying near, or affecting a MAMMARY GLAND or breast

**mammary gland** *n* any of the large glands (e g a breast) that in female mammals are modified to secrete milk, are situated on the front or underside of the body in one or more pairs, and that usu end in a nipple

**mammee** /ma'mee/, **mammee apple** *n* a tropical American tree (*Mammea americana* of the family Guttiferae) that bears a large edible fruit having a thick reddish rind and sweet juicy yellow or reddish flesh; *also* the fruit of this tree [Sp *mamey*, fr Taino]

**mammer** /'mamə/ *vi*, *archaic or dial* to waver, hesitate [ME *mameren* to stammer, of imit origin]

**¹mammock** /'mamək/ *n*, *dial Br* a broken piece; a scrap [origin unknown]

**²mammock** *vt*, *dial Br* to tear into fragments; mangle

**mammogram** /'maməgram/ *n* an X-ray photograph of the breasts [*mamma* + *-o-* + *-gram*]

**mammography** /ma'mogrəfi/ *n* examination of the breasts by taking X-ray photographs (e g for early detection of cancer)

**Mammon** /'mamən/ *n* material wealth or possessions, esp considered as having an evil influence ⟨*you cannot serve God and* ~ – Mt 6:24 (RSV)⟩ [LL *mammona*, fr Gk *mamōna*, fr Aram *māmōnā* riches]

**mammonist** /'mamənist/, **mammonite** /'maməniet/ *n* one devoted to the ideal or greedy in the pursuit of wealth – **mammonish** *adj*, **mammonism** *n*, **mammonist**, **mammonistic** *adj*

**¹mammoth** /'maməth/ *n* **1** any of numerous extinct elephants distinguished from recent elephants by their large size, very long tusks that curve upwards, and long thick hair **2** something immense of its kind; a giant ⟨*a company that is a* ~ *of the industry*⟩ [Russ *mamont, mamot*]

**²mammoth** *adj* of very great size; gigantic *synonyms* see HUGE *antonym* microscopic

**mammy** /'mami/ *n* **1** mama, mummy – used esp by children in Br **2** *NAm* a Negro nanny of white children, esp formerly in the southern USA [alter. of *mamma*]

**mammy wagon** *n* a W African vehicle used for carrying both people and goods [*mammy* of unknown origin]

**¹man** /man/ *n*, *pl* **men** /men/ **1a(1)** a human being; *esp* an adult male as distinguished from a woman or child **a(2)** a man belonging to a usu specified category (e g by birth, residence, membership, or occupation) – usu in combination ⟨*townsman*⟩ ⟨*businessman*⟩ **a(3)** a husband – esp in *man and wife* **a(4)** a male sexual partner **b** the human race **c** a two-legged PRIMATE mammal (*Homo sapiens*) that is the sole representative of a distinct family (Hominidae) and is anatomically related to the GREAT APES but is distinguished from them esp by greater brain development and a capacity for articulate speech and abstract reasoning; *broadly* any extinct ancestor (family Hominidae) of modern man **d** one possessing the qualities associated with manhood (e g courage and strength) ⟨*be a* ~⟩ **e** a fellow, chap **2a** a feudal tenant; VASSAL **b** *pl* the members of (the ranks of) a military force ⟨*officers and* men⟩ **c** *pl* the working force, as distinguished from the employer and usu the management **d** *pl* the members of a team **3a** an individual, person ⟨*a* ~ *could get killed there*⟩ **b** the most suitable man ⟨*if you want a good worker, he's your* ~⟩ **4** any of the pieces moved by each player in various board games (e g chess or draughts) **5** *slang* – used

interjectionally to express intensity of feeling ⟨~, *what a game*⟩ **6** *often cap*, *NAm slang the* police **7** *often cap*, *NAm slang the* white establishment – used by blacks *synonyms* see GENTLEMAN *antonym* woman [ME, fr OE (nearly always in the sense "human being"); akin to OHG *man* man, Skt *manu*] – **manless** *adj*, **manlike** *adj* – **as one man** with the agreement and consent of all – **to a man** without exception – see also be **one's** OWN **man**

**²man** *vt* **-nn-** **1** to supply with the man or men necessary ⟨~ *a fleet*⟩ **2** *of a member of a ship's crew* to take up station by ⟨~ *the capstan*⟩ **3** to serve in the force or complement of ⟨*workers who* ~ *the production lines*⟩ ⟨~ned *the pumps*⟩

**mana** /'mahnə/ *n* **1** the power of the elemental forces of nature embodied in an object or person **2** *chiefly NZ* moral authority; prestige [of Melanesian & Polynesian origin; akin to Hawaiian & Maori *mana*]

**man-about-'town** *n*, *pl* **men-about-town** a worldly and socially active man

**¹manacle** /'manəkl/ *n*, **manacles** *n pl* **1** a shackle or handcuff **2** a restraint [ME *manicle*, fr MF, fr L *manicula*, dim. of *manus* hand – more at MANUAL]

**²manacle** *vt* **1** to confine (the hands) with manacles **2** to subject to a restraint

**¹manage** /'manij/ *vt* **1a** to make and keep submissive ⟨~ *difficult children*⟩ **b** to use (e g money) economically ⟨~d *his resources carefully*⟩ **2** to influence by unfair means; manipulate ⟨~ *an election*⟩ **3** to succeed in handling (e g something difficult) ⟨*I can't* ~ *the crate by myself*⟩ **4** to succeed in accomplishing ⟨*she could only* ~ *a smile*⟩ ⟨*always* ~s *to win*⟩ **5** to conduct the running of (a business); *also* to take or have charge of (e g a sports team or athlete) – *vi* **1** to direct or carry on business or affairs **2** to be able to cope with a difficult situation; *esp* to use one's finances to the best advantage [It *maneggiare*, fr *mano* hand, fr L *manus*] – **manageable** *adj*, **manageableness** *n*, **manageably** *adv*, **manageability** *n*

**²manage** *n* MANEGE [It *maneggio* management, training of a horse, fr *maneggiare*]

**management** /-mənt/ *n* **1** the act or art of managing **2** *taking sing or pl vb* the collective body of those who manage or direct an enterprise – **managemental** *adj*

**manager** /'manijə/, *fem* **manageress** /'manijə,res/ *n* **1** one who conducts business or household affairs; *esp* a person whose work or profession is management **2** a person who controls the activities of a sports team, entertainer, etc **3** a person able to manage with the specified degree of efficiency – **managership** *n*, **managerial** *adj*, **managerially** *adv*

**managing director** /'manijing/ *n* the chief director of a company, responsible for the overall management of the company's business

**managing editor** *n* one who has charge of all editorial activities of a publication (e g a newspaper)

**manakin** /'manəkin/ *n* any of numerous small short-billed birds (family Pipridae) of Central and S America that have elaborate courtship behaviour [var of *manikin*]

**mañana** /man'yahnə/ *adv or n* (at) an indefinite time in the future [Sp, lit., tomorrow, fr earlier *cras mañana* early tomorrow, fr *cras* tomorrow (fr L) + *mañana* early, fr L *mane* early in the morning]

**man ape** *n* an ape-man

**man-at-'arms** *n*, *pl* **men-at-arms** a (heavily armed and usu mounted) soldier

**manatee** /,manə'tee/ *n* any of several large chiefly tropical aquatic mammals (genus *Trichechus*) that feed on plants, have a stout body and a squarish head, and differ from the related DUGONG esp in having a broad and rounded tail [Sp *manatí*, of Cariban origin]

**Manchester terrier** /'manchestə/ *n* (any of) a breed of small slightly built short-haired black-and-tan terriers [*Manchester*, city in NW England]

**manchineel** /,manchi'niəl/ *n* a tropical American tree (*Hippomane mancinella*) of the spurge family, that has poisonous yellow to reddish sweet-scented applelike fruit and a milky sap that causes blisters [Fr *mancenille*, fr Sp *manzanilla*, fr dim. of *manzana* apple]

**Manchu** /man'chooh/ *n*, *pl* **Manchus**, *esp collectively* **Manchu** (the language of) a member of the original nomadic Mongolian race of Manchuria that conquered China, established a dynasty there in 1644, and has largely assimilated Chinese culture – **Manchu** *adj*

**manciple** /'mansipl/ *n* a steward or caterer, esp in a college or monastery [ME, fr ML *mancipium* office of steward, fr L, act of purchase, fr *mancip-*, *manceps* purchaser – more at EMANCIPATE]

**Mancunian** /mang'kyoohni•ən/ *n or adj* (a native or inhabitant) of Manchester [LL *Mancunium* Manchester]

**-mancy** /-mənsi/ *comb form* (→ *n*) divination ⟨*necromancy*⟩ [ME *-mancie*, fr OF, fr L *-mantia*, fr Gk *-manteia*, fr *manteia*, fr *mantis* diviner, prophet – more at MANTIS]

**Mandaean** /man'dee•ən/ *n* 1 a member of a baptizing sect of GNOSTICS (adherents of a mystical religion heretical to Christians) in Iraq 2 a form of the ARAMAIC language found in documents written by Mandaeans [Mandaean *mandayyā* having knowledge] – **Mandaean** *adj*

**mandala** /'mahndələ/ *n* a Hindu or Buddhist graphic symbol used in ritual and meditation; *specif* a circle enclosing a square with a god on each of its four sides used to represent the universe [Skt *maṇḍala* circle] – **mandalic** *adj*

**mandamus** /man'daymэs/ *n* a COURT ORDER requiring something specified to be carried out (eg by an inferior court or tribunal) [L, we command, fr *mandare*]

**mandarin** /'mandərin, ,--'-/ *n* **1a** a public official in the Chinese Empire ranked according to any of nine grades **b** a reactionary official; *also* a bureaucrat ⟨*the* ~ *s of Whitehall*⟩ **c** a person of position and influence, esp in intellectual or literary circles; *esp* an elder and often traditionalist or reactionary member of such a circle **2** *cap* **2a** the primarily northern dialect of Chinese used by the court and officials of the Empire **b** the chief dialect of Chinese that has a standard variety spoken in the Beijing (Peking) area **3 mandarin, mandarin orange 3a** a small spiny Chinese orange tree (*Citrus reticulata*) widely cultivated for its edible fruit **b** the yellow to reddish-orange loose-skinned fruit of a mandarin tree **synonyms** see TANGERINE [Pg *mandarim*, fr Malay *mĕntĕri*, fr Skt *mantra* counsellor, fr *mantra* counsel – more at MANTRA; (3) Fr *mandarine*, fr Sp *mandarina*, prob fr *mandarín* mandarin (prob referring to the yellow colour of a mandarin's robes), fr Pg *mandarim*] – **mandarinic** *adj*, **mandarinism** *n*

**mandarin collar** *n* a narrow stand-up collar

**mandarin duck** *n* an often domesticated originally Asian duck (*Aix galericulata*), the male of which has bright markings and a small crest on the head

¹**mandate** /'mandayt, -dət/ *n* 1 an authoritative command from a superior; *esp* a formal order from a SUPERIOR COURT or official to an inferior one 2 an authorization to act on behalf of another; *specif* the political authority given by electors to parliament ⟨*accepted the* ~ *of the people*⟩ **3a** an order granted by the League of Nations to a member nation for the establishment of a responsible government over a conquered territory **b** a mandated territory [MF & L; MF *mandat*, fr L *mandatum*, fr neut of *mandatus*, pp of *mandare* to entrust, command, prob irreg fr *manus* hand + *-dere* to put – more at MANUAL, DO]

²**mandate** /'mandayt/ *vt* to administer or assign (eg a territory) under a mandate – **mandator** *n*

¹**mandatory** /'mandət(ə)ri/ *adj* 1 containing or constituting a command 2 compulsory, obligatory – **mandatorily** *adv*

    *usage* The pronunciation /'mandət(ə)ri/ rather than /man'dayt(ə)ri/ is recommended for BBC broadcasters.

²**mandatory** *n* a nation or person holding a mandate

**man-day** *n* a unit of one day's work by one person

**Mande** /'mahnday, -'-/ *n* a branch of the NIGER-CONGO language family spoken in W Africa

**mandible** /'mandibl/ *n* **1a** JAW 1a; *esp* a lower jaw consisting of a single bone or a set of completely fused bones **b** the lower jaw with its surrounding soft parts **c** the upper or lower segment of a bird's bill **2** any of various mouthparts in INVERTEBRATE animals, used to hold or bite food materials; *esp* either member of the front pair of mouth parts of an insect, spider, etc, that often form strong biting jaws [MF, fr LL *mandibula*, fr L *mandere* to chew – more at MOUTH] – **mandibular** *adj*, **mandibulate** *adj or n*

**Mandingo** /man'ding•goh/ *n, pl* **Mandingoes, Mandingos,** *esp collectively* **Mandingo** (the language of) a member of any of a number of black peoples of W Africa

**mandola** /man'dohlə/ *n* a 16th-17th century lute that is the ancestor of the smaller mandolin [It, fr Fr *mandore*, modif of LL *pandura* three-stringed lute – more at BANDORE]

**mandolin** *also* **mandoline** /,mandə'lin/ *n* a musical instrument of the lute family that has a neck with FRETS (means of altering length and therefore pitch of strings) and usu four pairs of strings [It *mandolino*, dim. of *mandola*] – **mandolinist** *n*

**mandragora** /man'dragərə/ *n* MANDRAKE 1 [ME]

**mandrake** /'mandrayk/ *n* 1 a Mediterranean plant (*Mandragora officinarum*) of the potato family with whitish or purple flowers and a large forked root traditionally thought to resemble the human form – called also MANDRAGORA 2 the root of a mandrake, formerly used esp to promote conception, as a laxative, or to induce sleep or hypnosis [ME, prob alter. of *mandragora*, fr OE, fr L *mandragoras*, fr Gk]

**mandrel** *also* **mandril** /'mandrəl/ *n* 1 an axle or spindle inserted into a hole in a workpiece to support it during machining 2 a metal bar round which material (eg metal) may be shaped (eg by casting, moulding, or forging) [prob modif of Fr *mandrin*]

**mandrill** /'mandril/ *n* a large baboonlike monkey (*Mandrillus mormon*) of W Africa that has a stout body, a short tail and brown hair, and the male of which has brilliant red and blue cheeks [prob fr ¹*man* + ³*drill*]

**mane** /mayn/ *n* 1 the long thick hair growing about the neck of some mammals (eg a horse or male lion) 2 *chiefly humorous* long thick hair on a person's head [ME, fr OE *manu*; akin to OHG *mana* mane, L *monile* necklace] – **maned** *adj*

¹**man-,eater** *n* 1 a person or animal that eats human flesh: eg **1a** a cannibal **b** MACKEREL SHARK; *esp* WHITE SHARK **c** GREAT WHITE SHARK **d** a big cat (eg a lion or tiger) that has acquired the habit of feeding on human flesh 2 *informal* a woman with many lovers – **man-eating** *adj*

**manege** *also* **manège** /ma'nezh/ *n* 1 a school for teaching horsemanship and training horses; *specif* an enclosed arena for schooling in DRESSAGE (complex exact manoeuvres for horses) 2 the art of horsemanship or of training horses 3 the movements or paces of a trained horse △ ménage [Fr *manège*, fr It *maneggio* training of a horse – more at ²MANAGE]

**manes** /'mahnayz/ *n pl* 1 the deified spirits of the ancient Roman dead honoured with graveside sacrifices 2 the venerated or appeased spirit of a dead person [L]

**maneuver** /mə'noohvə/ *vb or n, NAm* (to) manoeuvre

**,man-for-'man** *adj* MAN-TO-MAN 2

**man for man** *adv* comparing each individual with his/her opposite number on the other side or sides ⟨ ~ , *England was the stronger team*⟩

**man Friday** *n* a trustworthy male employed on general duties [*Friday*, native servant in the novel *Robinson Crusoe* by Daniel Defoe †1731 E writer]

**manful** /'manf(ə)l/ *adj* having or showing courage and resolution **synonyms** see ¹MALE **antonym** feeble – **manfully** *adv*, **manfulness** *n*

**mangabey** /'mang•gəbi/ *n* any of a genus (*Cercocebus*) of long-tailed African monkeys [*Mangaby*, region in the Malagasy Republic]

**mangan-** /mang•gən/, **mangano-** *comb form* manganese ⟨*manganous*⟩ [Ger *mangan*, fr Fr *manganèse*]

**manganate** /'mang•gənayt/ *n* a chemical compound containing manganese in the form of the ION (group of atoms having electrical charge) $MnO_4^-$

**manganese** /,mang•gə'neez/ *n* a greyish-white usu hard and brittle metallic chemical element that resembles iron but is not magnetic [Fr *manganèse*, fr It *manganese* magnesia, manganese, fr ML *magnesia*] – **manganesian** *adj*

**manganese bronze** *n* brass containing up to four per cent manganese and having a high resistance to corrosion

**manganese dioxide** *n* a dark-brown to black chemical compound, $MnO_2$, that occurs naturally as various minerals and is used esp as an OXIDIZING AGENT and in making glass and ceramics

**manganese spar** *n* RHODOCHROSITE (pink to red mineral)

**manganese steel** *n* a very hard alloy of steel with up to 14 per cent manganese that is used (eg in railway points) where resistance to shock and wear is required

**manganic** /mang'ganik/ *adj* of, containing, or derived from manganese, esp with a VALENCY of three or six

**manganin** /'mang•gənin/ *n* an alloy of copper, manganese, and nickel that has a high degree of resistance to the flow of an electric current and that is much used for RESISTORS (electrical components used to retard current flow) in electrical goods since temperature changes do not greatly affect its degree of resistance

**manganite** /'mang•gəniet/ *n* 1 a grey to black mineral, $MnO(OH)$, that consists of manganese hydroxide and is a minor source of manganese 2 any of various unstable manganese compounds made by reaction of MANGANESE DIOXIDE with an alkali or chemical base

**manganous** /'mang-gənəs, mang'ganəs/ adj of, containing, or derived from manganese, esp with a VALENCY of two

**mange** /manj, maynj/ n any of various persistent contagious skin diseases that affect domestic animals or sometimes humans, are marked by inflammation and loss of hair, and are caused by a minute parasitic mite [ME manjewe, fr MF mangene itching, fr mangier to eat]

**mangel-wurzel** /'mang-gl ,wuhzl/, **mangel** n a large coarse yellow to reddish-orange type of beet extensively grown as food for livestock [Ger mangoldwurzel, mangelwurzel, fr mangold beet + wurzel root]

**manger** /'maynjə/ n a trough or open box in a stable for holding feed – see also DOG **in the manger** [ME mangeour, manger, fr MF maingeure, fr mangier to eat, fr L manducare to chew, devour, fr manducus glutton, fr mandere to chew – more at MOUTH]

**¹mangle** /'mang-gl/ vt 1 to hack or crush (as if) by repeated blows ⟨bodies ~d in the car accident⟩ 2 to spoil by bad work, mistakes, etc ⟨~d the pronunciation of the word⟩ [ME manglen, fr AF mangler, freq of OF maynier to maim] – **mangler** n

**²mangle** vt or n (to pass through) a machine with rollers for squeezing water from and pressing laundry [n MD mangel, fr Ger, fr MHG, dim. of mange mangonel, mangle, fr L manganum; vb fr n] – **mangler** n

**mango** /'mang-goh/ n, pl **mangoes, mangos** 1 an edible yellowish-red fruit with a firm skin, large hard stone, and juicy aromatic slightly acid pulp; also a tropical evergreen tree (Mangifera indica) of the sumach family that bears mangoes [Pg manga, fr Tamil mān-kāy]

**mangold** /'mang-gohld, -gəld/ n a mangel-wurzel [short for mangold-wurzel, fr Ger mangoldwurzel]

**mangonel** /'mang-gə,nel/ n a large military apparatus formerly used to throw rocks, stones, etc [ME, fr MF, prob fr ML manganellus, dim. of LL manganum philtre, mangonel, fr Gk manganon; akin to MIr meng deception]

**mangosteen** /'mang-goh,steen/ n an edible dark reddish-brown fruit with thick rind and juicy flesh having a flavour suggestive of both peach and pineapple; also an E Indian tree (Garcinia mangostana of the family Guttiferae) that bears mangosteens [Malay mangustan]

**mangrove** /'mang,grohv/ n 1 any of a genus (Rhizophora, esp Rhizophora mangle of the family Rhizophoraceae) of tropical trees or shrubs that grow in dense thickets along coasts and muddy banks and whose trunks and branches produce many roots (PROP ROOTS) that form intertwined impenetrable masses 2 any of several trees (genus Avicennia) of the teak family with growth habits like those of the true mangroves [prob fr Pg mangue mangrove (fr Sp mangle, fr Taino) + E grove]

**mangy, mangey** /'manji, 'maynji/ adj 1 suffering or resulting from mange 2 having many worn or bare spots; seedy, shabby – **mangily** adv, **manginess** n

**manhandle** /man'handl, '-,--/ vt 1 to move or manage by human force 2 to handle roughly

**manhattan** /man'hatn/ n, often cap a cocktail consisting of vermouth, whisky, and sometimes a dash of bitters [Manhattan, borough of New York City, USA]

**manhole** /'man,hohl/ n a covered opening through which a person may go, esp to gain access to an underground or enclosed structure (e g a sewer)

**manhood** /-hood/ n 1 manly qualities (e g courage) 2 the condition of being an adult male as distinguished from a child or female 3 taking sing or pl vb adult males collectively ⟨the ~ of England⟩ 4 euph a penis

**man-'hour** n a unit of one hour's work by one person, used esp as a basis for COST ACCOUNTING and wage calculation

**manhunt** /-,hunt/ n an organized and usu intensive hunt for a person, esp a criminal

**mania** /'maynyə/ n 1 abnormal excitement and euphoria marked by mental and physical hyperactivity and disorganization of behaviour; specif the manic phase of a manic-depressive disorder 2 excessive or unreasonable enthusiasm; a craze ⟨had a ~ for saving things⟩ – often in combination ⟨Beatlemania⟩ [ME, fr LL, fr Gk, fr mainesthai to be mad; akin to Gk menos spirit – more at MIND]

**maniac** /'mayniak/ n 1 one who is or acts as if (violently) insane; a lunatic – not used technically 2 a person characterized by an inordinate or uncontrollable enthusiasm for something [LL maniacus maniacal, fr Gk maniakos, fr mania]

**maniacal** /mə'nie·əkl/ also **maniac** /'mayniak/ adj 1 affected with or suggestive of madness ⟨~ laughter⟩ 2 characterized by ungovernable excitement or frenzy; frantic – **maniacally** adv

**¹manic** /'manik/ adj of, like, affected by, or exhibiting mania – **manically** adv

**²manic** n a person suffering from mania

**¹manic-de'pressive** adj of, affected by, or being a mental disorder that is characterized by alternating mania and usu extreme depression

**²manic-depressive** n a person suffering from a manic-depressive disorder

**Manichaean, Manichean** /,mani'kee·ən/, **Manichee** /'manikee/ n 1 a believer in a religious DUALISM (doctrine of the separate existence of good and evil) originating in Persia in the 3rd century AD and teaching the release of the spirit from matter through austere living 2 a believer in religious or philosophical DUALISM, regarded as heretical esp by the Roman Catholic church [LL manichaeus, fr LGk manichaios, fr Manichaios Manes †ab276 Per founder of the sect] – **Manichaean** adj, **Manichaeanism, Manichaeism** n

**manicotti** /,mani'koti/ n taking sing or pl vb tubular pasta shells that may be stuffed with ricotta cheese or a meat mixture; also a dish of stuffed manicotti baked usu with tomato sauce [It, pl of manicotto muff, fr manica sleeve, fr L, fr manus hand]

**¹manicure** /'manikyooə/ n 1 a manicurist 2 (a) treatment for the care of the hands and fingernails [Fr, fr L manus hand + Fr -icure (as in pédicure pedicure) – more at MANUAL]

**²manicure** vt 1 to give a manicure to; esp to trim and polish the fingernails of 2 to trim closely and evenly ⟨~d lawns⟩

**manicurist** /'manikyooərist/ n one who gives manicure treatments

**¹manifest** /'manifest/ adj readily perceived by the senses (e g sight) or mind; obvious *synonyms* see EVIDENT *antonyms* latent, hidden, concealed [ME, fr MF or L; MF manifeste, fr L manifestus, lit., hit by the hand, fr manus + -festus (akin to L infestus hostile) – more at DARE] – **manifestly** adv, **manifestness** n

**²manifest** vt to make evident or certain by showing or displaying ⟨his political beliefs ~ themselves in his every action⟩ ~ vi, of a spirit, ghost, etc to appear in visible form *synonyms* see ¹SHOW – **manifestable** adj, **manifester** n

**³manifest** n a list of passengers or an invoice of cargo, esp for a ship

**manifestation** /,manife'staysh(ə)n/ n 1a the act, process, or an instance of manifesting b something that manifests; evidence c a sign (e g materialization) of the presence of a spirit 2 a public demonstration of power and purpose – **manifestational, manifestative** adj

**manifesto** /,mani'festoh/ n, pl **manifestos, manifestoes** a public declaration of intentions, motives, or views; esp one issued by a political party before an election, setting out its policies [It, denunciation, manifestation, fr manifestare to manifest, fr L, fr manifestus]

**¹manifold** /'manifohld/ adj 1 including, uniting, or marked by a diversity or variety of features ⟨a ~ personality⟩ 2 consisting of or operating many of one kind combined ⟨a ~ bellpull⟩ [ME, fr OE manigfeald, fr manig many + -feald -fold] – **manifoldness** n

usage The idea of "many times" is expressed by many + fold rather than by manifold ⟨recoup our expenses manyfold⟩

**²manifold** n 1 a whole that unites or consists of many diverse elements 2 a pipe fitting with several lateral outlets for connecting one pipe with others; also a fitting on an INTERNAL-COMBUSTION ENGINE that receives the exhaust gases from several cylinders

**³manifold** vt to make (many) copies of – **manifolder** n

**manikin, mannikin** /'manikin/ n 1 a mannequin 2 a little man; a dwarf 3 an anatomical model of the body for use in medical or art instruction [D mannekijn little man, fr MD, dim. of man; akin to OE man]

**manila** also **manilla** /mə'nilə/ adj, often cap made of MANILA PAPER or the plant fibre ABACA – **manila** n

**Manila hemp** n ABACA (plant fibre) [Manila, city in the Philippine Islands]

**manila paper** n, often cap M a strong and durable paper of a brownish or buff colour with a smooth finish made originally from the plant fibre ABACA

**manilla** /mə'nilə/ n a horseshoe-shaped metal bracelet used as money by some peoples of W Africa [Pg manilha or Sp manilla]

**manille** /mə'nil/ *n* the second highest trump in various card games (e g OMBRE) [Fr, fr Sp *malilla*, fr *malo* bad]

**man in the street** *n* an average or typical person, esp for statistical purposes

**manioc** /'mani,ok/ *n* CASSAVA (starch-yielding tropical plant) [Fr *manioc* & Sp & Pg *mandioca*, of Tupian origin; akin to Tupi *manioca* cassava]

**manioca** /,mani'ohkə/ *n* CASSAVA (starch-yielding tropical plant)

**maniple** /'manipl/ *n* 1 a long narrow strip of silk worn at mass over the left arm by clerics of or above the order of SUBDEACON 2 a subdivision of the ancient Roman legion consisting of either 120 or 60 men [(1) ML *manipulus*, fr L, handful, fr *manus* hand + *-pulus* (akin to L *plēre* to fill); fr its having been originally held in the hand; (2) L *manipulus*, fr *manipulus* handful; fr the custom of using a handful of hay on the end of a pole as a military standard] – **manipular** *adj*

**manipulate** /mə'nipyoolayt/ *vt* 1 to handle or operate, esp skilfully 2a to manage or use skilfully b to control or influence by artful, unfair, or insidious means, esp to one's own advantage 3 to examine and treat (a fracture, sprain, etc) by moving bones into the proper position manually [back-formation fr *manipulation*, fr Fr, fr *manipule* handful, fr L *manipulus*] – **manipulator** *n*, **manipulatable, manipulable** *adj*, **manipulability** *n*, **manipulative** *adj*, **manipulatively** *adv*, **manipulatory** *adj*, **manipulation** *n*

**manitou, manitu** /'manitooh/ *n* a supernatural force held by the ALGONQUIAN Indians of N America to pervade the natural world – used as a name [of Algonquian origin; akin to Ojibwa *manito* spirit, god]

**man jack** *n* individual man ⟨every ∼⟩

**mankind** /man'kiend/ *n taking sing or pl vb* 1 the human race 2 men as distinguished from women

  *usage* Some people today do not like the use of **mankind** to include women, and prefer to refer to human beings as **humankind**; others find **humankind** ridiculous.

**manlike** /-,liek/ *adj* 1 resembling or characteristic of humans rather than animals ⟨*curious ∼ gestures of a monkey*⟩ 2 resembling or characteristic of a man rather than a woman or a child *synonyms* see ¹MALE

**manly** /-li/ *adj* (marked by the good qualities) befitting a man ⟨∼ *sports*⟩ *synonyms* see ¹MALE *antonym* effeminate – **manliness** *n*

**man-'made** *adj* made or produced by human beings rather than nature; *also* synthetic

**manna** /'manə/ *n* 1a food miraculously supplied to the Israelites in their journey through the wilderness b divinely supplied spiritual nourishment c a usu sudden and unexpected source of benefit 2 a sweet substance exuded from the trunk of esp the European flowering ash (*Fraxinus ornus*) that yields MANNITOL and acts as a mild laxative [ME, fr OE, fr LL, fr Gk, fr Heb *mān*]

**manned** /mand/ *adj* 1 equipped with men/women 2 *of a spacecraft* carrying a human crew

**mannequin** /'manikin/ *n* 1 an artist's, tailor's, or dressmaker's model of the human figure; *also* a form representing the human figure used esp for displaying clothes 2 a woman who models clothes, esp at a fashion show [Fr, fr D *mannekijn* little man – more at MANIKIN]

**manner** /'manə/ *n* 1 a kind, sort ⟨*what ∼ of man is he?*⟩; *also* sorts ⟨*all ∼ of information*⟩ 2a(1) the mode or method in which something is done or happens ⟨*worked in a ∼*⟩ ⟨*dressed in a contemporary ∼*⟩ a(2) method of artistic execution or mode of presentation; style b *pl* social conduct or rules of conduct as shown in the prevalent customs ⟨*Victorian ∼s*⟩ c a characteristic or distinctive bearing, air, or deportment ⟨*his poised gracious ∼*⟩ ⟨*a cool offhand ∼*⟩ d *pl* social behaviour evaluated as to politeness; *esp* conduct indicating good background ⟨*this oaf has no ∼s*⟩ *synonyms* see BEHAVIOUR [ME *manere*, fr OF *maniere* way of acting, fr (assumed) VL *manuaria*, fr L, fem of *manuarius* of the hand, fr *manus* hand – more at MANUAL] – **mannerless** *adj* – **in a manner of speaking** in one sense; IN A WAY – **to the manner born** accustomed (as if) from birth

**mannered** /'manəd/ *adj* 1 having manners of a specified kind – usu in combination ⟨*well-mannered*⟩ 2 having an artificial or stilted character ⟨*passages . . . so ∼ as to be unintelligible* – R G G Price⟩

**mannerism** /'manə,riz(ə)m/ *n* 1a exaggerated or affected following of a particular style or manner in art or literature b *often cap* a style of art in late 16th-century Europe characterized by the use of distorted proportion, esp of the human figure, to intensify the emotional impact of a work 2 a characteristic and often unconscious mode or peculiarity of action, bearing, or treatment – **mannerist** *n or adj, often cap*, **manneristic** *adj*

**mannerly** /-li/ *adj* showing or having good manners – **mannerliness** *n*, **mannerly** *adv*

**mannikin** /'manikin/ *n* MANIKIN

**mannish** /'manish/ *adj* resembling, befitting, typical of, or more usually associated with a man rather than a woman ⟨*she has a ∼ stride*⟩ *synonyms* see ¹MALE *antonyms* womanish, effeminate – **mannishly** *adv*, **mannishness** *n*

**mannite** /'maniet/ *n* mannitol [Fr, fr *manna*, fr LL] – **mannitic** *adj*

**mannitol** /'manitol/ *n* a slightly sweet-tasting ALCOHOL, $C_6H_8(OH)_6$, that is obtained from MANNA and seaweeds and used esp for testing the functioning of the kidneys [ISV, fr *mannite* + *-ol*]

**mannose** /'manohz, -nohs/ *n* a sugar, $C_6H_{12}O_6$, obtained from mannitol [ISV, fr *manna* + *-ose*]

**¹manoeuvre,** *NAm chiefly* **maneuver** /mə'noohvə/ *n* 1a a military or naval movement b **manoeuvre, manoeuvres** *pl* an armed forces training exercise; *esp* an extended and large-scale training exercise involving military and naval units separately or in combination 2 an intended and controlled variation from a straight and level flight path in the operation of an aircraft 3 a skilful or dexterous movement 4 an adroit and clever management of affairs, often using trickery and deception [Fr *manoeuvre*, fr OF *maneuvre* work done by hand, fr ML *manuopera*, fr L *manu operare* to work by hand (cf MANURE)]

**²manoeuvre,** *NAm chiefly* **maneuver** *vi* 1a to perform a manoeuvre b to perform a military or naval manoeuvre, esp in order to secure an advantage 2 to use stratagems or trickery; scheme ∼ *vt* 1 to cause (e g troops) to execute manoeuvres 2 to manage or guide into or out of a specified position or condition 3 to manipulate with adroitness and design 4 to bring about or secure as a result of contriving – **manoeuvrable** *adj*, **manoeuvrability** *n*, **manoeuvrer** *n*

**man of God** *n* 1 a godly man (e g a saint or prophet) 2 a clergyman

**Man of Kent** /kent/ *n* a native or inhabitant of Kent; *specif* one from east of the river Medway – compare KENTISHMAN

**man of letters** *n* 1 a scholar 2 an author whose works are admired in literary circles

**man of straw** *n* 1a a weak or imaginary opposition (e g an argument or opponent) set up only to be easily defeated b a person set up to serve as a cover for a usu questionable transaction 2 a weak and indecisive person

**man of the cloth** *n* a clergyman

**man of the house** *n* the chief male in a household

**man of the world,** *fem* **woman of the world** *n* someone of wide experience

**man-of-'war** *n, pl* **men-of-war** a warship of the days of sail; *broadly* a warship

**manometer** /mə'nomitə/ *n* 1 an instrument typically consisting of a U-shaped tube filled with a liquid (e g mercury) that is used for comparing pressures exerted by gases and vapours with reference to a standard pressure (e g atmospheric pressure) 2 SPHYGMOMANOMETER (instrument for measuring blood pressure) [Fr *manomètre*, fr *mano-* gas, vapour (fr Gk *manos* sparse, loose, rare) + *-mètre* -meter – more at MONK] – **manometry** *n*, **manometric, manometrical** *adj*, **manometrically** *adv*

**manor** /'manə/ *n* 1 a landed estate 2 a former unit of English rural territorial organization; *esp* such a unit in the Middle Ages consisting of an estate under a lord who held a variety of rights over land and tenants including the right to hold court 3 **manor, manor house** the (former) house of the lord of a manor 4 *slang* a district or area of police administration [ME *maner*, fr OF *manoir*, fr *manoir* to sojourn, dwell, fr L *manēre* – more at MANSION] – **manorial** *adj*

**man-o'-war bird** *n* FRIGATE BIRD; *esp* one (*Fregata magnificens*) the male of which has a red patch on the throat, and the female a white breast

**manpower** /'man,powə/ *n* 1 power available from or supplied by the physical effort of human beings 2 the total supply of people available and equipped for service (e g in the armed forces or industry)

**manqué** /'mong,kay (*Fr* māke)/ *adj* that could have been but failed to be – used after the noun ⟨*a poet ∼*⟩ [Fr, fr pp of *manquer* to lack, fail, fr It *mancare*, deriv of L *mancus* having a crippled hand, maimed, infirm]

**mansard** /'mansahd, -səd/, **mansard roof** *n* a roof with two slopes on both sides and both ends, the lower slope being steeper and longer than the upper one [Fr *mansarde*, fr François *Mansart* †1666 Fr architect] – **mansarded** *adj*

**manse** /mans/ *n* the residence of an esp Presbyterian or Baptist clergyman [ME *manss* mansion, fr ML *mansa, mansus, mansum,* fr L *mansus,* pp of *manēre*]

**manservant** /'man‚suhv(ə)nt/ *n, pl* **menservants** a male servant, esp a valet

**-manship** /-mənship/ *suffix* (→ *n*) art or skill of one who practises or is interested in ⟨*horse*manship⟩

**mansion** /'mansh(ə)n/ *n* **1a** a **mansion, mansion-house** the house of the lord of a manor **b** a large imposing residence **2** *pl* a large building divided into flats **3** HOUSE 3b (division of the zodiac) **4** *archaic* a dwelling, abode [ME, fr MF, fr L *mansion-, mansio,* fr *mansus,* pp of *manēre* to remain, dwell; akin to Gk *menein* to remain]

**'man-‚size, man-sized** *adj* **1** suitable for or requiring a man ⟨*a ~ job*⟩ **2** larger than normal ⟨*a ~ meal*⟩

**manslaughter** /'man‚slawtə/ *n* the unlawful killing of somebody without malicious intent (eg by avoidable negligence or in the course of an unlawful act)

**mansuetude** /'manswityoohd/ *n, archaic* meekness, gentleness [ME, fr L *mansuetudo,* fr *mansuetus* tame, mild, fr pp of *mansuescere* to tame, fr *manus* hand + *suescere* to accustom; akin to Gk *ēthos* custom – more at MANUAL, ETHICAL]

**manta ray, manta** /'mantə/ *n* any of several large flat ray fish (genera *Manta* and *Mobula*) that feed on plankton and are widely distributed in warm seas [AmerSp *manta,* fr Sp, blanket; fr its being caught in traps resembling large blankets]

**mantelet** /'manti‚let, 'mantlit/ *n* **1** a very short cape or cloak **2** MANTLET (movable shield) [ME, fr MF, dim. of *mantel, manteau* mantle]

**mantelletta** /‚manti'letə/ *n* a knee-length mantle formerly worn by a prelate of the Roman Catholic church [It, dim. of *mantello* mantle]

**mantelpiece** /'mantl‚pees/, **mantel** *n* an ornamental structure round a fireplace; *also* a mantelshelf △ **mantle** [MF *mantel* mantle]

**mantelshelf** /-‚shelf/, **mantel** *n* a shelf forming part of or situated above a mantelpiece

**mantic** /'mantik/ *adj* relating to the faculty of divination; prophetic [Gk *mantikos,* fr *mantis*]

**mantid** /'mantid/ *n* a mantis [NL *Mantidae,* group name, fr *Mantis,* genus name] – **mantid** *adj*

**mantilla** /man'tilə/ *n* **1** a light usu lace scarf worn over the head and shoulders, esp by Spanish and Latin-American women **2** a short light cape or cloak [Sp, dim. of *manta* blanket, cloak]

**mantis** /'mantis/ *n, pl* **mantises, mantes** /-teez/ any of several insects (order Dictyoptera and family Mantidae) that feed on other insects and clasp their prey in forelimbs that are held up as if in prayer; *esp* PRAYING MANTIS [NL, fr Gk, lit., diviner, prophet; akin to Gk *mainesthai* to be mad – more at MANIA]

**mantissa** /man'tisə/ *n* the part of a COMMON LOGARITHM (logarithm whose base is 10) following the decimal point (eg .5359 of the logarithm 3.5359) – compare CHARACTERISTIC 2 [L *mantisa, mantissa* makeweight, fr Etruscan]

**mantis shrimp** *n* any of an order (Stomatopoda) of marine INVERTEBRATE animals (eg a squilla) that are shrimplike and have two grasping appendages which resemble the front legs of a PRAYING MANTIS – called also STOMATOPOD

**'mantle** /'mantl/ *n* **1a** a loose sleeveless garment worn over other clothes; a cloak **b** a symbol of superiority or authority ⟨*invested his people with the ~ of universal champions of justice* – Denis Goulet⟩ **2a** something that covers, envelops, or conceals **b**(1) a fold or lobe in the body wall of snails, mussels, etc that lines the wall and contains shell-secreting glands **b**(2) the soft external BODY WALL that lines the hard outer covering of barnacles, SEA SQUIRTS, and related animals **3** the feathers covering the back and wings of a bird, esp when different in colour from the rest of the plumage **4** a lacy hood or sheath treated with a solution of the chemical elements cerium and thorium that when placed over the flame of a gas or oil lamp increases the amount of light given off **5a** mantlerock **b** the part of the earth that lies between the crust and the central core **6** a mantelpiece △ **mantel** [ME *mantel,* fr OF, fr L *mantellum*]

**²mantle** *vt* to cover (as if) with a mantle; cloak ~ *vi* **1** to become covered with a coating; *esp, of a liquid* to become covered in scum **2** to blush ⟨*her rich face* mantling *with emotion* – Benjamin Disraeli⟩

**mantlerock** /'mantl‚rok/ *n* a layer of loose rock, including soil and sediments, that rests on the earth's solid rock and forms the land surface

**mantlet** /'mantlit/ *n* a movable shield or shelter: eg **a** a movable shelter formerly used by besiegers when attacking **b** the movable frontal plate of the turret of an armoured fighting vehicle [var of *mantelet*]

**‚man-to-'man** *adj* **1** characterized by frankness and honesty ⟨*a ~ talk*⟩ **2** of or being a system of defence in soccer, hockey, basketball, etc in which each defensive player marks a specific opponent

**Mantoux test** /man'tooh (*Fr* mãtu)/ *n* a test to detect past or present tuberculosis infection, by studying the skin's reaction to a preparation (TUBERCULIN) of specific substances extracted from the bacterium causing tuberculosis [Charles *Mantoux* †1947 Fr physician]

**mantra** /'mantrə/ *n* a sacred word or sound used as an invocation or incantation (eg in Hinduism or Buddhism) [Skt, sacred counsel, formula, fr *manyate* he thinks; akin to L *mens* mind – more at MIND]

**mantrap** /'man‚trap/ *n* a trap for catching people

**mantua** /'mantyooə/ *n* a usu loosely fitting gown worn esp in the 17th and 18th centuries [modif (influenced by *Mantua,* town in N Italy) of Fr *manteau, mantel* cloak]

**¹manual** /'manyooəl/ *adj* **1a** of or involving the hands ⟨*~ dexterity*⟩ **b** worked or done by hand and not by machine or automatically ⟨*a ~ gear change*⟩ ⟨*~ indexing*⟩ **2** requiring or using physical skill and energy ⟨*~ labour*⟩ ⟨*~ workers*⟩ [ME *manuel,* fr MF, fr L *manualis,* fr *manus* hand; akin to OE *mund* hand, Gk *marē*] – **manually** *adv*

**²manual** *n* **1** a book of instructions and information; a handbook **2** the set movements in the handling of a military item (eg a weapon) during a drill or ceremony ⟨*the ~ of arms*⟩ **3** a keyboard for the hands; *specif* any of the several keyboards of an organ that control separate divisions of the instrument

**manual alphabet** *n* an alphabet for deaf-mutes in which the letters are represented by finger positions

**manubrium** /mə'nyoohbri‚əm/ *n, pl* **manubria** /-briə/ *also* **manubriums** a projecting anatomical part shaped like a handle: eg **a** the section of the breastbone nearest the head of human beings and many other mammals **b** the tubular projection incorporating the mouth that hangs down from the centre of the umbrella-shaped body of a jellyfish or related COELENTERATE animal [NL, fr L, handle, fr *manus*]

**¹manufacture** /‚manyoo'fakchə/ *n* **1a** the process of making articles by hand or machinery, esp when carried on systematically on a large scale with specialized machinery and an organized workforce **b** a productive industry using mechanical power and machinery **2** the act or process of producing something [MF, fr L *manu factus* made by hand]

**²manufacture** *vt* **1** to make (materials) into a product suitable for use **2** to make (articles) from raw materials by hand or machinery, esp on a large scale **3** to invent, fabricate **4** *chiefly derog* to produce as if by manufacturing; create ⟨*writers who ~ stories for television*⟩ to engage in manufacture **synonyms** see ¹MAKE – **manufacturing** *n*

**manufactured gas** *n* a combustible gaseous mixture made from coal, coke, or petroleum products

**manufacturer** /‚manyoo'fakchərə/ *n* someone who manufactures; *esp* an employer of workers in a manufacturing industry

**manuka** /'mahnookə/ *n* an evergreen New Zealand shrub (*Leptospermum scoparium*) of the eucalyptus family that has hard wood and aromatic leaves and forms large areas of scrub [Maori]

**manumission** /‚manyoo'mish(ə)n/ *n* the act or process of manumitting; *esp* formal release from slavery [ME, fr MF, fr L *manumission-, manumissio,* fr *manumissus,* pp of *manumittere*]

**manumit** /‚manyoo'mit/ *vt* **-tt-** to release from slavery [ME *manumitten,* fr MF *manumitter,* fr L *manumittere,* fr *manus* hand + *mittere* to let go, send – more at SMITE]

**¹manure** /mə'nyooə/ *vt* to spread manure on (land) [ME *manouren* to till, cultivate, fr MF *manouvrer,* lit., to do work by hand, fr L *manu operare* (cf MANOEUVRE)] – **manurer** *n*

**²manure** *n* material that fertilizes land; *esp* animal excrement from stables and farmyards that is usu mixed with straw or some other form of litter – **manurial** *adj*

**manus** /'maynəs/ *n, pl* **manus** the farthest section of the forelimb of a VERTEBRATE animal, consisting of the wrist and hand in a human being or the equivalent part in other vertebrates [NL, fr L, hand]

**¹manuscript** *adj* written by hand or typed ⟨~ *letters*⟩ [L *manu scriptus* written by hand]

**²manuscript** *n* a handwritten or typewritten composition or document as distinguished from a printed copy; *esp* an author's original ⟨*sent in her novel in* ~⟩

**¹Manx** /mangks/ *adj* (characteristic) of the Isle of Man, the Manx people, or the Manx language [alter. of earlier *Maniske*, fr (assumed) ON *manskr*, fr *Mana* Isle of Man]

**²Manx** *n* 1 *taking pl vb* the people of the Isle of Man 2 the almost extinct Celtic language of the Manx people

**Manx cat** *n* (any of) a breed of short-haired domestic cats, some of which have no external tail

**Manxman** /-mən/, *fem* **Manxwoman** *n* a native or inhabitant of the Isle of Man

**manx shearwater** *n, often cap M* a small black-and-white SHEARWATER (seabird) (*Puffinus puffinus*) common in the N Atlantic

**¹many** /'meni/ *adj* more /maw/; most /mohst/ 1 amounting to a large number; more than several ⟨*worked for* ~ *years*⟩ – sometimes in combination ⟨*many-worded*⟩ 2 being one of a large number ⟨~ *a man*⟩ ⟨~ *another student*⟩ ⟨~'s *the time I've wondered*⟩ [ME, fr OE *manig*; akin to OHG *manag* many, OSlav *mŭnogŭ* much] – **as many** the same in number ⟨*saw three plays in as many days*⟩

**²many** *n taking pl vb* 1 a large number; more than several ⟨*a good* ~ *of them*⟩ ⟨*how* ~ *are coming?*⟩ 2 the great majority of people ⟨*the* ~⟩ – compare ONE TOO MANY

**³many** *adv* BY FAR – with plurals ⟨~ *more cars than usual*⟩

**many-'sided** *adj* 1 having many sides or aspects 2 having many interests or aptitudes – **many-sidedness** *n*

**many-'valued** *adj* possessing more than the customary two TRUTH-VALUES of truth and falsehood ⟨*a* ~ *logic*⟩

**Manzanilla** /ˌmanzə'nilə/ *n* a pale very dry sherry [Sp, lit., camomile, dim. of *manzana* apple]

**Maoism** /'mow.iz(ə)m/ *n* the theory and practice of Marxist-Leninist communism developed in China chiefly by Mao Tse-tung [*Mao Zedong* (*Mao* Tse-tung) †1976 Chin political leader] – **Maoist** *n or adj*

**Maori** /'mowri, 'mahri/ *n, pl* **Maoris**, *esp collectively* **Maori** 1 a member of the indigenous Polynesian people of New Zealand 2 the language of the Maori, which is one of the AUSTRONESIAN family of languages

**Maoritanga** /ˌmowri'tahng.ə/ *n, NZ* Maori culture [Maori]

**¹map** /map/ *n* 1a(1) a representation on a reduced scale and usu a flat surface of (part of) the earth's surface, showing geographical features, political divisions, population distribution, etc a(2) a similar representation of the surface of another planet, the moon, etc b a representation of (part of) the CELESTIAL SPHERE, showing the positions of the stars and other celestial bodies 2 a representation of something in a maplike form 3 GENETIC MAP (theoretical arrangement of genes along a chromosome) 4 *maths* a mapping [ML *mappa*, fr L, napkin, towel] – **off the map** into oblivion; out of any position of importance ⟨*several bad matches put the player* off the map *in the world rankings*⟩ – **on the map** widely known or recognized ⟨*the by-election had put Biggleswade right* on the map⟩

**²map** *vb* -pp- *vt* 1a to make a map of ⟨~ *the surface of the moon*⟩ b to portray as if on a map ⟨*sorrow was* ~ped *on her face*⟩ c to survey in order to make a map 2 to apply a mapping to (a mathematical element or set) 3 to plan in detail – often + *out* ⟨~ *out a programme*⟩ ~ *vi, of a gene* to be located on a GENETIC MAP (theoretical arrangement of genes along a chromosome) – **mappable** *adj*, **mapper** *n*

**maple** /'maypl/ *n* 1 any of a genus (*Acer*) of trees of the sycamore family that have broad leaves with three to seven pointed lobes and clusters of paired broad flat winged seeds 2 the hard light-coloured close-grained wood of a maple, used esp for flooring and furniture [ME, fr OE *mapul-*; akin to ON *möpurr* maple]

**maple sugar** *n* sugar made by boiling maple syrup

**maple syrup** *n* syrup made by concentrating the sap of maple trees, esp the SUGAR MAPLE

**mapmaker** /'map.maykə/ *n* someone who makes maps; a cartographer – **mapmaking** *n*

**mapping** /'maping/ *n* a correspondence between two mathematical sets in which each element of one set corresponds exactly to one element of the other set

**maquette** /ma'ket/ *n* a sculptor's usu small preliminary model (eg in wax or clay) [Fr, fr It *macchietta*, dim. of *macchia* sketch, deriv of L *macula* spot]

**maquillage** /ˌmaki'yahzh (*Fr* makijaʒ)/ *n* MAKE-UP 2 [Fr, fr *maquiller* to make up]

**maquis** /ma'kee/ *n, pl* **maquis** /~/ 1 (an area of) scrubland vegetation of Mediterranean coastal areas, consisting mainly of broad-leaved evergreen shrubs (eg laurels and myrtles) or small trees (eg olives and figs) 2 *often cap* 2a a member of the French Resistance during World War II b *taking sing or pl vb* a band of maquis △ Mafia [Fr, fr It *macchie*, pl of *macchia* thicket, spot, fr L *macula* spot]

**mar** /mah/ *vt* -rr- 1 to detract from the perfection or wholeness of; spoil 2 *archaic* 2a to inflict serious bodily harm on b to destroy **synonyms** see INJURE [ME *marren*, fr OE *mierran* to obstruct, waste; akin to OHG *merren* to obstruct]

**mara** /mə'rah/ *n* a long-legged rodent (*Dolichotis magellanica*) that resembles a hare and lives in herds on the pampas of Argentina and Patagonia [AmerSp *mará*]

**marabou, marabout** /'marəbooh/ *n* 1a a large grey and white African stork (*Leptoptilos crumeniferus*) that has an inflatable pouch of pink skin at its throat and feeds esp on carrion b a soft fluffy material prepared from marabou or turkey feathers and used for trimming esp women's hats or clothes 2 (fabric made from) a fine silk which has been THROWN (twisted to make a stronger thread) and usu dyed before its waxy outer covering has been removed [Fr *marabout*, lit., marabout]

**marabout** /'marəbooh/ *n, often cap* (a shrine marking the grave of) a Muslim holy man of N Africa [Fr, fr Pg *marabuto*, fr Ar *murābiṭ* hermit, monk]

**maraca** /mə'rakə/ *n* a rhythm instrument made from the shell of a dried gourd, or a similar object (eg made of plastic), that contains dried seeds, pebbles, beads, etc, has a handle, and is usu played as one of a pair, esp in Latin-American dance music △ marimba [Pg *maracá*]

**marae** /mah'rie/ *n* the central meeting ground of a Maori village and the meetinghouse and dining hall that stand there [Tahitian & Maori]

**maraging steel** /'mah.rayjing/ *n* a strong corrosion-resistant steel containing a relatively low proportion of carbon and up to 25 per cent nickel [*martensite* + *aging*]

**maraschino** /ˌmarə'sheenoh, -'skeenoh/ *n, pl* **maraschinos** *often cap* 1 a sweet liqueur distilled from the fermented juice of a bitter wild cherry 2 **maraschino cherry, maraschino** a usu large cherry preserved in true or imitation maraschino, used to decorate food or drinks [It, fr *marasca* bitter wild cherry]

**marasmic** /mə'razmik/ *n* one who suffers from marasmus

**marasmus** /mə'razməs/ *n* progressive wasting, esp in infants and young children, associated usu with a poor diet or a prolonged stomach disorder that has resulted in the inability to digest and absorb food efficiently [LL, fr Gk *marasmos*, fr *marainein* to waste away – more at SMART] – **marasmic** *adj*

**Maratha** /mə'rahtə/ *n* a member of a people of the S central part of India; *specif* the native people of the state of Maharashtra [Marathi *Marāṭhā* & Hindi *Marhaṭṭā*, fr Skt *Mahārāṣṭra* Maharashtra]

**Marathi** /mə'rahti/ *n* the chief language of the state of Maharashtra in India [Marathi *marāṭhī*]

**marathon** /'marəth(ə)n/ *n* 1 a long-distance race; *specif* one of 26 miles 385 yards (about 42.2 kilometres) that is contested on an open course in major athletics championships (eg the Olympic Games) 2a an endurance contest ⟨*a dance* ~⟩ b something (eg an event or activity) characterized by great length or concentrated effort [*Marathon*, site in Greece of a victory of Greeks over Persians in 490 BC, the news of which was carried to Athens by a long-distance runner]

**maraud** /mə'rawd/ *vi* to roam about and raid in search of plunder ~ *vt* to raid, pillage [Fr *marauder*, fr *maraud* vagabond, rogue] – **marauder** *n*

**maravedi** /ˌmarə'vaydi/ *n, pl* **maravedis** a medieval Spanish copper coin unit worth 1/34 REAL [Sp *maravedi*, fr Ar *Murābiṭīn*, 11th- & 12th-c Muslim dynasty in N Africa & Spain]

**¹marble** /'mahbl/ *n* 1a(1) crystalline limestone in which the original crystals have dissolved slowly under the influence of usu heat and pressure and recrystallized to form a hard rock that can be polished to a very smooth finish and is used esp in architecture or sculpture a(2) a hard rock formed from material (eg fragments of rocks and minerals or shells or skeletons of sea urchins, corals, etc) that is deposited by wind, water, or ice, accumulates, and hardens to resemble marble ⟨*Purbeck* ~⟩ **b** a sculpture or carving made of marble **c** something suggesting marble (e g in hardness, coldness, or smoothness) ⟨*she has a heart of* ~⟩ **2a** a little ball made of a hard substance (e g glass) and used in various usu children's games **b** *pl but taking sing vb* any of several games played with marbles, the object of which is to hit a mark or hole, to hit another player's marble, or to knock as many marbles as possible out of a ring **3** marbling **4** *pl, informal* elements of common sense; *esp* sanity ⟨*he's completely lost his* ~!⟩ ⟨*persons who are born without all their* ~s – Arthur Miller⟩ [ME, fr OF *marbre*, fr L *marmor*, fr Gk *marmaros*] – **marbly** *adj*

²**marble** *vt* to give a veined or mottled appearance to ⟨~ *the edges of a book*⟩

³**marble** *adj* resembling, made of, or suggestive of marble ⟨~ *floors*⟩

**marbled** /'mahbəld/ *adj* **1a** made of or veneered with marble **b** marked by an extensive use of marble as an architectural or decorative feature ⟨*ancient* ~ *cities*⟩ **2** *of meat* marked by a mixture of fat and lean

**marble-ize, -ise** /'mahbəliez/ *vt* to marble

**marbling** /'mahbling/ *n* coloration or markings resembling or suggestive of marble

**marc** /mahk/ *n* the residue remaining after grapes or other fruit have been pressed; *also* brandy made from this residue [Fr, fr MF, fr *marchier* to trample]

**Marcan, Markan** /'mahkən/ *adj* (characteristic) of the apostle Mark or the Gospel according to Mark [LL *Marcus* Mark]

**marcasite** /,mahkə'seet, 'mahkə,siet/ *n* **1** a white or pale yellow form of the mineral IRON PYRITES used esp for jewellery **2** polished steel or a similar white metal used for making jewellery △ malachite [ME *marchasite*, fr ML *marcasita*, fr Ar *marqashīthā*] – **marcasitical** *adj*

¹**marcel** /mah'sel/ *n* a deep soft wave made in the hair by a heated curling iron [*Marcel* Grateau †1936 Fr hairdresser]

²**marcel** *vt* **-ll-** to make a marcel in

¹**march** /mahch/ *n*, **marches** *n pl, often cap* a border region; frontier; *esp* a tract of land between two countries whose ownership is disputed ⟨*the Welsh* Marches⟩ [ME *marche*, fr OF, of Gmc origin; akin to OHG *marha* boundary – more at MARK]

²**march** *vi* to have common borders or frontiers – + *with* or *together* ⟨*a region that* ~es *with Canada in the north*⟩

³**march** *vi* **1** to walk along steadily, usu with a rhythmic stride and in step with others **2a** to move in a direct purposeful manner **b** to make steady progress; advance ⟨*time* ~es *on*⟩ **3** to stand in orderly array suggestive of marching ⟨*tall plane trees* ~ed *either side of the drive*⟩ **4** to participate in an organized march ~ *vt* **1** to cause to march ⟨~ed *the children off to bed*⟩ **2** to cover by marching; traverse ⟨~ed *20 miles*⟩ [MF *marchier* to trample, march, fr OF, to trample, prob of Gmc origin; akin to OHG *marcōn* to mark]

⁴**march** *n* **1a(1)** the action or an instance of marching **a(2)** the distance covered within a specified period of time by marching ⟨*a day's* ~ *away*⟩ **a(3)** a regular measured stride or rhythmic step used in marching **b** steady forward movement; progress ⟨*the* ~ *of a film towards the climax*⟩ **2** a musical composition, usu with two or four beats to the bar, that has a strongly accentuated beat and is designed or suitable to accompany marching **3** a procession of people organized as a demonstration of support for a particular cause, to draw attention to a problem, etc – **on the march** moving steadily; advancing – **steal a march on/upon** to gain an advantage over, usu by stealthy or underhand means

**March** *n* the 3rd month of the year according to the GREGORIAN CALENDAR (standard Western calendar) – see MONTH table [ME, fr OF, fr L *martius*, fr *martius* of Mars, fr *Mart-, Mars* Mars, Roman god of war]

¹**marcher** /'mahchə/ *n* one who inhabits a border region

²**marcher** *n* one who or that which marches; *esp* one who marches for a usu specified cause ⟨*a peace* ~⟩

**marchesa** /ma'kaysə/ *n, pl* **marchese** /-se/ an Italian woman holding the rank of a marchese; a marchioness [It, fem of *marchese*]

**marchese** /mah'kayse/ *n, pl* **marchesi** /-si/ an Italian nobleman corresponding in rank to a British marquess [It, fr ML *marcensis*, fr *marca* border region, of Gmc origin; akin to OHG *marha*]

**marching orders** /'mahching/ *n pl* **1** official notice for troops to leave one place for another **2** *Br informal* notice of dismissal ⟨*the player was given his* ~ *after the brutal foul*⟩

**marchioness** /,mahshə'nes, 'mahshənis/ *n* **1** the wife or widow of a marquess **2** a woman having in her own right the rank of a marquess [ML *marchionissa*, fr *marchion-, marchio* marquess, fr *marca*]

**marchpane** /'mahch,payn/ *n, archaic* marzipan [It *marzapane*]

'**march-,past** *n* a marching by, esp of troops on parade

**marconigram** /mah'kohnigram/ *n* a radiogram [Guglielmo *Marconi* †1937 It electrical engineer, inventor of wireless telegraphy]

**Mardi Gras** /,mahdi 'grah/ *n* **1** SHROVE TUESDAY, often observed (e g in New Orleans) with parades and festivities **2** a carnival period climaxing on Shrove Tuesday [Fr, lit., fat Tuesday]

¹**mare** /meə/ *n* a female horse or other member of the horse family, esp when fully mature or of breeding age [ME, fr OE *mere;* akin to OHG *merha* mare, OE *mearh* horse, W *march*]

²**mare** /'mahray/ *n, pl* **maria** any of several large dark areas on the surface of the moon or the planet Mars [NL, fr L, sea – more at MARINE]

**mare clausum** /,mahray 'klows(ə)m/ *n* a navigable body of water (e g a sea) that is under the jurisdiction of one nation and is closed to other nations [NL, lit., closed sea]

**Marek's disease** /'marik/ *n* a cancerous disease of poultry caused by a virus and characterized by the development of tumours and often by paralysis of the legs [József *Marek* † 1952 Hung veterinarian]

**mare liberum** /,mahray 'leebərəm/ *n* a navigable body of water (e g a sea) that is open to all nations [NL, lit., free sea]

**mare nostrum** /,mahray 'nostrəm/ *n* a navigable body of water (e g a sea) that belongs to a single nation or is mutually shared by two or more nations [L, our sea]

**mare's nest** /meəz/ *n, pl* **mare's nests, mares' nests** a false discovery, illusion, or deliberate hoax

**mare's tail** *n, pl* **mare's tails, mares' tails 1** a wispy high-altitude cloud (CIRRUS) with a long slender flowing appearance **2a** a common aquatic plant (*Hippuris vulgaris* of the family Hipparidaceae) with elongated shoots covered with dense rings of short very narrow leaves **b** HORSETAIL (flowerless plant)

**margaric acid** /mah'garik/ *n* a synthetic FATTY ACID, $CH_3(CH_2)_{15}COOH$, that is intermediate between PALMITIC ACID and STEARIC ACID [Fr *margarique*, fr *margarine*]

**margarine** /,mahjə'reen; *also* ,mahgə'reen, '---/ *n* a food product made usu from vegetable oils churned with skimmed milk to a smooth emulsion, usu fortified with vitamins A and D, and used as a substitute for butter [Fr, fr Gk *margaron* pearl]

*usage* The pronunciation with /g/ rather than /j/ is now rare, but follows more correctly the spelling and etymology of the word.

**margay** /'mahgay/ *n* a small American spotted wildcat (*Felis tigrina*) resembling the ocelot and inhabiting an area extending from S USA to Brazil [Fr, fr Tupi *maracaja*]

¹**marge** /mahj/ *n, poetic* MARGIN 1, 2 [MF, fr L *margo*]

²**marge** *n, informal* margarine [by shortening & alter.]

**margent** /'mahj(ə)nt/ *n, archaic* MARGIN 1a, 2

¹**margin** /'mahjin/ *n* **1a** the part of a page or sheet outside the main body of printed or written matter **b** a vertical line, usu on the left-hand side of a page (e g of an exercise book), marking a margin **2** the outside limit and adjoining surface of something; the edge ⟨*at the* ~ *of the woods*⟩ **3a** a spare amount or measure or degree allowed or given more than that which is strictly necessary ⟨*left no* ~ *for error in his calculations*⟩ **b(1)** a bare minimum below which or an extreme limit beyond which something becomes impossible or is no longer desirable ⟨*a joke that was on the* ~ *of good taste*⟩ **b(2)** the limit below which the level of return is insufficient to warrant continued economic activity **4a** the difference between net sales and the cost of merchandise sold, from which expenses are usu met or profit derived **b** the difference provided by a stockbroker between the amount of a loan and the current value of the securities deposited as COLLATERAL for the loan **c(1)** cash or collateral that is deposited by a client with a broker (e g a stockbroker) to protect the broker from loss on a contract **c(2)** the value of a client's shares, bonds, etc bought with the aid of credit obtained specifically (e g from a broker) for that purpose **d** a range about a specified figure within which a purchase is to be made **5** measure or degree of difference ⟨*the bill was passed by a one-vote* ~⟩ [ME, fr L *margin-, margo* border – more at MARK] – **margined** *adj*

²**margin** *vt* **1** to provide with notes in the margin **2** to provide with an edging or border

¹**marginal** /'mahjinl/ *adj* **1** written or printed in the margin of

a page or sheet ⟨~ *notes*⟩ **2a** of or situated at a margin or border ⟨*regards violence as a ~ rather than a central problem*⟩ **b** characterized by the incorporation of habits and values from two different cultures and by incomplete adoption of either ⟨*the ~ cultural habits of new immigrant groups*⟩ **3** located at the fringe of consciousness ⟨~ *sensations*⟩ **4a(1)** close to the lower limit of qualification, acceptability, or function ⟨*a semi-literate man of ~ ability*⟩ **a(2)** slight, small ⟨*a ~ but important improvement*⟩ – disapproved of by some people **b(1)** likely to yield a supply of goods which when marketed will barely cover the cost of production ⟨~ *land*⟩ **b(2)** of or derived from goods produced and marketed with a marginal result ⟨~ *profits*⟩ **5** being a constituency where the Member of Parliament was elected with only a small majority – compare SAFE [ML *margi-nalis*, fr L *margin-, margo*] – **marginally** *adv*, **marginality** *n*

²**marginal** *n* a marginal constituency

**marginalia** /ˌmahjiˈnaylyə/ *n pl* notes written in the margin (e g of a book) [NL, fr ML, neut pl of *marginalis*]

**marginal utility** *n* the amount of additional worth provided by the consumption of an extra unit of economic goods or services

**marginate** /ˈmahjinayt/, **marginated** /-aytid/ *adj* having a margin that is distinct in colour, shape, etc ⟨~ *leaves*⟩

**margravate** /ˈmahgrəvət/ *n* the territory of a margrave

**margrave** /ˈmahgrayv/ *n* **1** a military governor, esp of a German border province **2** a member of the German nobility corresponding in rank to a British marquess [D *markgraaf*, fr MD *marcgrave;* akin to OHG *marcgrāvo;* both fr a prehistoric D-G compound whose constituents are akin to OHG *marha* boundary and to OHG *grāvo* count – more at MARK] – **margravial** *adj*

**margraviate** /mahˈgrayviət/ *n* a margravate

**margravine** /ˈmahgrəˌveen/ *n* the wife of a margrave

**marguerite** /ˌmahgəˈreet/ *n* **1** OXEYE DAISY **2** any of various flowers of the daisy family: e g **2a** any of various single-flowered chrysanthemums; *esp* a white or yellow variety (*Chrysanthemum frutescens*) **b** any of several cultivated camomiles (genus *Anthemis*) [Fr, fr MF *margarite* pearl, daisy, fr L *margarita* pearl, fr Gk *margaritēs*, fr *margaron*]

**Marian** /ˈmeəriən/ *adj* **1** of Mary Tudor or her reign (1553-58) **2** of the Virgin Mary

**Marianist** /ˈmeəriənist/ *n* a member of the Roman Catholic Society of Mary of Paris founded by William Joseph Chaminade in France in 1817 and devoted esp to education – compare MARIST

**Maria Theresa dollar** /məˌreeˈə təˈraysə, -zə/ *n* a silver coin with the image of Maria Theresa and the date 1780 used as a trade coin in the Middle East [*Maria Theresa* †1780 Archduchess of Austria & Queen of Hungary]

**mariculture** /ˈmariˌkulchə/ *n* the cultivation of marine plants and animals using their natural environment [L *mare* sea + E *-culture* (as in *agriculture*)]

**marigold** /ˈmarigohld/ *n* **1** POT MARIGOLD **2** any of a genus (*Tagetes*) of plants of the daisy family with showy yellow or orange flower heads [ME, fr *Mary*, mother of Jesus + ME *gold*]

**marijuana, marihuana** /ˌmarəˈwahnə; *also* -ˈhwahnə, -yooˈahnə/ *n* **1** the hemp plant **2** a usu mild form of cannabis usu smoked for its intoxicating effect – compare HASHISH, BHANG [MexSp *mariguana, marihuana*]

**marimba** /məˈrimbə/ *n* a percussion instrument of southern Africa and Central America which resembles a large xylophone, has a dried gourd shell or similar object beneath each bar to give resonance, and is played with soft-headed hammers ⚠ maraca [of African origin; akin to Kimbundu *marimba* xylophone]

**marina** /məˈreenə/ *n* a dock or basin providing secure moorings for pleasure craft, yachts, etc and often offering special facilities (e g workshops) [It & Sp, seashore, fr fem of *marino*, adj, marine, fr L *marinus*]

¹**marinade** /ˌmariˈnayd/ *n* a blended liquid of oil, wine or vinegar, herbs, and spices in which meat, fish, etc is soaked before cooking to enrich its flavour or to tenderize it [Fr, fr Sp *marinada*, fr *marinar* to pickle in brine, fr *marino* marine]

²**marinade** *vt* to soak in a marinade

**marinate** /ˈmarinayt/ *vt* to marinade [prob fr It *marinato*, pp of *marinare*, fr *marino* marine]

¹**marine** /məˈreen/ *adj* **1a** of or living in the sea ⟨~ *life*⟩ ⟨~ *biology*⟩ **b** of or used in the navigation of the sea; nautical ⟨*a ~ chart*⟩ **c** of or concerning the commerce of the sea; maritime

⟨~ *law*⟩ ⟨~ *insurance*⟩ **d** depicting the sea, seashore, or ships ⟨*a ~ painter*⟩ **2** of or used by marines ⟨~ *barracks*⟩ [ME, fr L *marinus*, fr *mare* sea; akin to OE *mere* sea, pool, OHG *meri* sea, OSlav *morje*]

²**marine** *n* **1** seagoing ships collectively, esp in relation to nationality or class ⟨*the mercantile ~*⟩ **2a** any of a class of soldiers serving on shipboard or in close association with a naval force **b** – see MILITARY RANKS table **3** an executive department (e g in France) having charge of naval affairs **4** a marine picture; a seascape

**mariner** /ˈmarinə/ *n* one who travels by sea and does or assists in doing the work required to sail the vessel; a seaman, sailor [ME, fr AF, fr OF *marinier*, fr ML *marinarius*, fr L *marinus* marine]

**Mariolatry** /ˌmeəriˈolətri/ *n* excessive veneration of the Virgin Mary – **Mariolater** *n*

**Mariology** /ˌmeəriˈoləji/ *n* study or doctrine relating to the Virgin Mary – **Mariological** *adj*

**marionette** /ˌmariˈəˈnet/ *n* a small-scale usu wooden figure (e g of a person or animal) with jointed limbs that is moved from above by attached strings or wires [Fr *marionnette*, fr MF *maryonete*, fr *Marion*, dim. of *Marie* Mary]

**marish** /ˈmarish/ *adj or n, archaic* (like) a marsh

**Marist** /ˈmeərist/ *n* a member of the Roman Catholic Society of Mary founded by Jean Claude Colin in France in 1816 and devoted to education – compare MARIANIST [Fr *mariste*, fr *Marie* Mary]

**marital** /ˈmaritl/ *adj* **1** of marriage or the married state ⟨~ *vows*⟩ **2** of a husband and his role in marriage ⟨~ *rights*⟩ ⚠ martial [L *maritalis*, fr *maritus* husband] – **maritally** *adv*

**maritime** /ˈmariˌtiem/ *adj* **1** of navigation or commerce on the sea **2** of or bordering on the sea ⟨*a ~ province*⟩ **3** having the characteristics of a mariner [L *maritimus*, fr *mare* sea]

**marjoram** /ˈmahjərəm, -rəm/ *n* any of various usu fragrant and aromatic plants (genus *Origanum*) of the mint family with small pale purple or pink flowers, whose leaves are used as a herb in cookery; *also* oregano [alter. of ME *majorane*, fr MF, fr ML *majorana*]

¹**mark** /mahk/ *n* **1a(1)** a conspicuous object serving as a guide for travellers **a(2)** something (e g a line, notch, or fixed object) designed to record position **b** any of the points on a SOUNDING LINE (rope for measuring water depth) that correspond to a depth in whole fathoms and are distinctively marked (e g by a piece of leather or coloured cloth) – compare DEEP 1 **c** an object to be aimed at: e g **c(1)** a target **c(2)** the jack in a game of bowls **c(3)** a boxer's midriff **d** the starting line or position in a track event **e(1)** a goal or desired object **e(2)** the point under discussion ⟨*that comment was rather off the ~*⟩ **f** a standard of performance, quality, or condition ⟨*his singing was hardly up to the ~*⟩ **2a(1)** a sign, token ⟨*gave her the necklace as a ~ of his esteem*⟩ **a(2)** an impression on the surface of something; *esp* a scratch, stain, etc that spoils the appearance of a surface **a(3)** a distinguishing characteristic ⟨*he bears the ~s of an educated man*⟩ **b** a symbol used for identification or indication of ownership **c** a symbol, esp a cross, made in place of a signature by a person who cannot write **d** a written or printed symbol ⟨*punctuation ~s*⟩ **e(1)** a trademark **e(2)** *cap* – used with a number to specify a particular model of a vehicle, weapon, machine, etc ⟨Mark *4 sports car*⟩ ⚠ Mach **f** a symbol used as a judgment of merit, esp one used by a teacher to express an estimate of a student's work or conduct **g** a figure that registers a point or level reached or achieved ⟨*the halfway ~ in the first period of play*⟩ **3a** attention, notice ⟨*nothing worthy of ~ occurred*⟩ **b** importance, distinction ⟨*a person of little ~*⟩ **c** a lasting or strong impression ⟨*years of warfare have left their ~ on the country*⟩ **d** an assessment of merits; rating ⟨*got high ~s for honesty*⟩ **4a** the action of a rugby player making a mark in the ground with his heel and shouting "mark" after catching a ball which has been kicked, knocked, or thrown forward by a member of the opposing team, after which he is awarded a free kick; *also* the mark so made **b** a catch, made by a player of AUSTRALIAN RULES FOOTBALL, of a ball which has been kicked at least 10 yards by an opponent, after which a free kick is awarded **5** *informal* an object of attack, ridicule, or abuse; *specif* a victim of a swindle **6** *archaic* a boundary territory; a frontier [ME, fr OE *mearc* boundary, frontier, sign; akin to OHG *marha* boundary, L *margo*] – **on your marks** – used as a command to competitors in a race to take their starting positions

²**mark** *vt* **1a(1)** to fix or trace *out* the bounds or limits of **a(2)** to

plot the course of; chart **b** to set apart (as if) by a line or boundary – usu + *off* **2a(1)** to designate (as if) by a mark ⟨~ed *for greatness*⟩ **a(2)** to make or leave a mark on **a(3)** to label (merchandise) so as to indicate price or quality **a(4)** to add appropriate symbols, characters, or other marks to or on ⟨~ *the manuscript for the printer*⟩ – usu + *up* **b(1)** to indicate by a mark or symbol ⟨~ *an accent*⟩ ⟨*X* ~s *the spot*⟩ **b(2)** to register, record ⟨~ *the date in your diary*⟩ **b(3)** to evaluate by means of marks or symbols ⟨~ *examination papers*⟩ **b(4)** to put something inside a book so as to identify (a page) **c(1)** to characterize, distinguish ⟨*the flamboyance that* ~s *her stage appearance*⟩ **c(2)** to be a sign of ⟨*this treaty will* ~ *the friendship between our countries*⟩ **c(3)** to be the occasion of (something notable); to indicate as a particular time ⟨*this year* ~s *the 50th anniversary of the organization*⟩ **3** to take notice of; observe ⟨~ *my words*⟩ **4** to pick up (one's golf ball) from a putting green and substitute a marker **5** to make a mark on catching (the ball) in rugby or AUSTRALIAN RULES FOOTBALL **6** *Br* to stay close to and hamper the movements of (an opponent in a team sport), esp to prevent him/her from getting the ball or scoring ~ *vi* **1** to take careful notice **2** to become or make something stained, scratched, etc ⟨*it won't* ~, *will it?*⟩ **3a** to evaluate something by marks **b** to keep score in a game (e g of billiards or darts) **4** to make a mark in rugby or AUSTRALIAN RULES FOOTBALL **5** *Br* to mark an opposing player or team – see also **mark** TIME [ME *marken,* fr OE *mearcian;* akin to OHG *marcōn* to determine the boundaries of, OE *mearc* boundary]

**mark down** *vt* **1** to put a lower price on ⟨marked down *all the merchandise for the sale*⟩ **2** *Br* to select as a victim – see also MARKDOWN

**mark up** *vt* to set a higher price on – see also MARKUP

³**mark** *n* **1** any of various old European units of weight used esp for gold and silver; *esp* a unit equal to about 227 grams (about 8 ounces) **2** a monetary unit: **2a** a former English unit worth 13s 4d **b** any of various former Scandinavian or German monetary units; *specif* a unit and corresponding silver coin of the 16th century worth ¹/₂ TALER **c** – see MONEY table **d** MARKKA (Finnish monetary unit) [ME, fr OE *marc,* prob of Scand origin; akin to ON *mörk* mark; akin to OE *mearc* sign]

**Mark** *n* – see BIBLE table [*Mark* (L *Marcus*), Christian apostle & evangelist]

**Markan** /'mahkən/ *adj* MARCAN

**markdown** /'mahk,down/ *n* **1** a reduction in the price of an article **2** the amount by which an original selling price is reduced

**marked** /mahkt/ *adj* **1a** having natural marks (of a specified type) ⟨*wings* ~ *with white*⟩ **b** made identifiable by marking ⟨*a* ~ *card*⟩ **2** having a distinctive or emphasized character; noticeable ⟨*a* ~ *American accent*⟩ **3** being an object of attack, suspicion, or vengeance ⟨*a* ~ *man*⟩ **4** distinguished from the basic form (e g the singular) by the presence of a particular linguistic feature (e g *s* indicating the plural) – **markedly** *adv*

**marker** /'mahkə/ *n* **1** one who or that which marks **2** something used for marking **3** GENETIC MARKER (identifiable gene used in genetic analysis to identify associated genes) – **marker** *adj*

¹**market** /'mahkit/ *n* **1a(1)** a meeting together of people for the purpose of trade by purchase and sale **a(2)** *taking sing or pl vb* the people assembled at such a meeting **b** a public place (e g an open space or building) where a market is held; *esp* a place where goods (e g provisions or livestock) are sold **2** the rate or price offered for a commodity or SECURITY (e g a share or bond) **3a** a geographical area or section of the community in which there is a demand for commodities ⟨*the foreign* ~⟩ **b** the course of commercial activity by which the exchange of commodities is effected; extent of trading ⟨*the* ~ *is dull*⟩ **c** an opportunity for selling ⟨*create new* ~s *for our product*⟩ **d** the area of economic activity in which buyers and sellers come together and the forces of supply and demand affect prices ⟨~ *value*⟩ **4** *archaic* the act or an instance of buying and selling [ME, fr ONF, fr L *mercatus* trade, marketplace, fr *mercatus,* pp of *mercari* to trade, fr *merc-, merx* merchandise; akin to Oscan *amiricadut* without remuneration (cf COMMERCE)] – **in the market** interested in buying ⟨in the market *for a good house*⟩ – **on the market** available for purchase; up for sale – see also DRUG **on the market**

²**market** *vi* to deal in a market ~ *vt* **1** to offer for sale in a market **2** to sell – **marketer** *n*

**marketable** /'mahkitəbl/ *adj* **1a** fit to be offered for sale in a market ⟨*contaminated food that is not* ~⟩ **b** wanted by purchasers; salable ⟨~ *securities*⟩ **2** relating to buying or selling – **marketability** *n*

**market cross** *n* (a structure incorporating) a cross originally erected in a market place

**market garden** *n* a large area of land on which fruit and vegetables are grown for market – **market gardener** *n,* **market gardening** *n*

**marketing** /'mahkiting/ *n* **1** the act or process of buying or selling in a market **2** the skills and functions (e g packaging, promotion, and distribution) that are involved in selling goods or services

**marketing research** *n* research conducted to establish the extent and location of the market for a particular product, or to analyse the problems and costs associated with products and processes as compared with those of alternative or competitive products or processes; research dealing with the marketing of a particular product

**marketplace** /'mahkit,plays/ *n* **1a** an open square or place in a town where markets or public sales are held **b** MARKET 3c,d ⟨*the* ~ *is the interpreter of supply and demand*⟩ **2** the world of trade or economic activity; the everyday world ⟨*a conviction that religion belongs in the* ~ – *Current Biog*⟩

**market price** *n* a price actually given in current market dealings

**market research** *n* the gathering of factual information as to consumer preferences for goods and services; research into the patterns or state of demand in a market; *also* MARKETING RESEARCH

**market town** *n* a town which has the right to hold a public market

**market value** *n* the value of an asset if sold in a free market; a price at which both buyers and sellers are willing to do business – compare BOOK VALUE

**markhor** /'mah,kaw/ *n* a large Himalayan wild goat (*Capra falconeri*) with long spiralled horns and a coat that is reddish brown in summer and grey and silky in winter [Per *mārkhōr,* lit., snake eater, fr *mār* snake + *-khōr* eating, fr *khurdan* to eat]

**marking** /'mahking/ *n* **1** the act or process, or an instance of making or giving a mark **2a** a mark made **b** an arrangement, pattern, or disposition of marks ⟨*the* ~s *of its wings*⟩ **3** the act or process of staying close to an opposing player

**marking ink** *n* indelible ink for marking fabric

**markka** /'mahkə/ *n, pl* **markkaa** /-kah/, **markkas** – see MONEY table [Finn, fr Sw *mark,* a unit of value; akin to ON *mörk* mark]

**Markov chain** *also* **Markoff chain** /'mahkof/ *n* a sequence of random events or states in which the probability of each event or state occurring is dependent on the outcome of the preceding event [A A *Markov* †1922 Russ mathematician]

**Markovian** /mah'kohviən/, **Markov** *also* **Markoff** /'mahkof/ *adj* of or resembling a MARKOV PROCESS or MARKOV CHAIN, esp by having probabilities defined in terms of progression from the possible existing states to other states ⟨~ *models*⟩

**Markov process** *also* **Markoff process** *n* a random or probabilistic process (e g BROWNIAN MOVEMENT) that resembles a MARKOV CHAIN except that the states are continuous; *also* MARKOV CHAIN

**marksman** /'mahksmən/, *fem* **markswoman** *n* a person skilled or practised at hitting a mark or target; *esp* a person who has reached a high standard of rifle shooting – **marksmanship** *n*

**markup** /'mahk,up/ *n* **1** an increase in the price of an article **2** the amount added (e g by the retailer) to the cost price to determine the selling price

¹**marl** /mahl/ *n* a fine-grained mixture of chiefly clay and silt and a high percentage of CALCIUM CARBONATE that is used esp as a fertilizer for soils that are deficient in lime [ME, fr MF *marle,* fr ML *margila,* dim. of L *marga,* fr Gaulish] – **marly** *adj*

²**marl** *vt* to dress (land) with marl

³**marl** *vt* to bind or fasten with marline [D *marlen,* back-formation fr *marling*]

**marlin** /'mahlin/ *n, pl* **marlins,** *esp collectively* **marlin** any of several large marine fishes (genera *Makaira* and *Tetrapturus*) related to the SAILFISHES and SPEARFISHES that have a spear-shaped projection extending from the snout, feed mainly on other fish, and are highly prized game fish [short for *marlinspike;* fr the appearance of its beak]

**marline, marlin** /'mahlin/ *n* a thin usu tarred rope made of two strands loosely twisted together left-handed and used, esp on board ship, for binding things together and as a covering for wire rope [D *marlijn*, alter. (influenced by *lijn* line) of *marling*, fr *meren*, *marren* to tie, moor, fr MD *meren*, *maren* – more at MOOR]

**marlinespike, marlinspike** /-ˌspiek/ *n* a pointed steel tool used to separate strands of rope or wire (e g in splicing)

**marlite** /'mahliet/ *n* a marl that does not decompose when exposed to air – **marlitic** *adj*

¹**marmalade** /'mahməˌlayd/ *n* a jam made from the pulp and usu peel of citrus fruits, esp oranges, and sugar [Pg *marmelada* quince conserve, fr *marmelo* quince, fr L *melimelum*, a sweet apple, fr Gk *melimēlon*, fr *meli* honey + *mēlon* apple – more at MELLIFLUOUS]

²**marmalade** *adj, esp of a cat* brownish orange – **marmalade** *n*

**marmite** /'mahmiet/ *n* a large usu earthenware or cast-iron cooking pot with a lid [Fr]

**Marmite** /'mahmiet/ *trademark* – used for a concentrated yeast extract that is added to soups and stews to give flavour and is used as a savoury spread; compare BOVRIL

**marmoreal** /mah'mawri·əl/ *also* **marmorean** /-ri·ən/ *adj* of or resembling marble or a marble statue [L *marmoreus*, fr *marmor* marble, fr Gk *marmaros*] – **marmoreally** *adv*

**marmoset** /'mahməzet/ *n* any of numerous long-tailed S and Central American monkeys (family Callithricidae) that have silky fur, have claws instead of nails on all the digits except the big toe, feed mainly on insects, and live in family groups [ME *marmusette*, fr MF *marmoset* grotesque figure, fr *marmouser* to mumble, of imit origin]

**marmot** /'mahmət/ *n* any of several stout-bodied short-legged burrowing rodents (genus *Marmota*) that have coarse fur, a short bushy tail, and very small ears, and that feed on a variety of green vegetation [Fr *marmotte*]

**marocain** /'marəkayn/ *n* a crepe fabric with crosswise ridges [Fr (*crêpe*) *marocain*, lit., Moroccan crepe]

**Maronite** /'marəniet/ *n* a member of a Syrian Christian church now existing chiefly in the Lebanon [ML *maronita*, fr *Maron-*, *Maro*, 5th-c Syrian monk]

¹**maroon** /mə'roohn/ *n* **1** *cap* (a descendant of) a fugitive Negro slave of the W Indies and Guiana in the 17th and 18th centuries **2** a person who is marooned [modif of AmerSp *cimarrón*, fr *cimarrón* wild, savage, lit., living on mountaintops, fr Sp *cima* peak, fr L *cyma* young sprout of cabbage]

²**maroon** *vt* **1** to put ashore and abandon on a desolate island or coast **2** to isolate in a helpless state

³**maroon** *n* **1** a dark brownish-red colour **2** an explosive rocket used esp as a distress signal [Fr *marron* Spanish chestnut] – **maroon** *adj*

**marplot** /'mahˌplot/ *n* one who frustrates or ruins a plan or undertaking by meddling

¹**marque** /mahk/ *n* **1** LETTERS OF MARQUE (licence esp to fit out an armed ship) **2** *obs* a reprisal, retaliation [ME, fr MF, fr OProv *marca*, fr *marcar* to mark, seize as pledge, of Gmc origin; akin to OHG *marcōn* to mark]

²**marque** *n* a brand or model of a product (e g a sports car) [Fr, mark, brand, fr MF, fr *marquer* to mark, of Gmc origin; akin to OHG *marcōn* to mark]

**marquee** /mah'kee/ *n* **1** a large tent (e g for an outdoor party, reception, or exhibition) **2** *NAm* a permanent canopy usu of metal and glass projecting over an entrance (e g of a hotel or theatre) [modif of Fr *marquise*, lit., marchioness]

**Marquesan** /mah'kayz(ə)n/ *n* **1** a native or inhabitant of the Marquesas islands **2** the language of the Marquesans, which belongs to the AUSTRONESIAN family of languages – **Marquesan** *adj*

**marquess, marquis** /'mahkwis/ *n, pl* **marquesses, marquises, marquis 1** a nobleman of hereditary rank in Europe and Japan **2** a member of the British peerage ranking below a duke and above an earl [ME *marquis*, *markis*, fr MF *marquis*, alter. of *marchis*, fr *marche* ¹march] – **marquessate, marquisate** *n*

**marquetry** *also* **marqueterie** /'mahkətri/ *n* decorative work in which a design is made up of pieces of wood veneer applied to a surface (e g of a piece of furniture) sometimes with additional inlays of wood, shell, ivory, brass, etc – compare PARQUETRY [MF *marqueterie*, fr *marqueter* to chequer, inlay, fr *marque* mark]

**marquise** /mah'keez/ *n* **1** MARCHIONESS (wife of a marquess) **2** a gem, ring setting, or the oblique face of a cut gem that is usu oval in shape but with pointed ends **3** *archaic* MARQUEE 1 [Fr, fem of *marquis*]

**marquisette** /ˌmahki'zet, -kwi-/ *n* a thin transparent meshed fabric used for clothing, curtains, and mosquito nets [*marquise* + *-ette*]

**marram grass** /'marəm/ *n* any of several strong wiry grasses (genus *Ammophila*, esp *Ammophila arenaria*) that grow on sandy shores and help prevent erosion [of Scand origin; akin to ON *maralmr*, a beach grass]

**Marrano** /mə'rahnoh/ *n, pl* **Marranos** a Christianized Jew or Moor of medieval Spain [Sp, lit., pig]

**marriage** /'marij/ *n* **1a** the mutual relation of husband and wife; the state of being husband and wife **b** the customary practice whereby a man and a woman are joined in a special kind of social and legal dependence **2** an act of marrying or the rite by which the married status is effected; *esp* the wedding ceremony and attendant festivities or formalities **3** an intimate or close union ⟨*the ~ of painting and poetry* – J T Shawcross⟩ *synonyms* see WEDDING [ME *mariage*, fr MF, fr *marier* to marry] – **marriageable** *adj*

**marriage lines** *n, informal* a marriage certificate

**marriage of convenience** *n* a marriage contracted for social, political, or economic advantage rather than for mutual affection

¹**married** /'marid/ *adj* **1a** joined in marriage; wedded **b** of marriage or married people; connubial **2** united, joined

²**married** *n, pl* **marrieds, married** a married person ⟨*young ~s*⟩

**marron** /'maronh (*Fr* marɔ̃)/ *n* **1** an edible chestnut; *esp* SPANISH CHESTNUT **2** *pl* MARRONS GLACÉS [Fr]

**marrons glacés** /ˌmaronh 'glasay, (*Fr* marɔ̃ glase)/ *n, pl* chestnuts candied or preserved in syrup [Fr, lit., glazed marrons]

**marrow** /'maroh/ *n* **1a** a soft tissue that fills the cavities and porous part of most bones and in which RED BLOOD CELLS and certain WHITE BLOOD CELLS are produced **b** the substance of the SPINAL CORD **2** the inmost, best, or essential part; core ⟨*is personal liberty the ~ of democracy?*⟩ **3** *chiefly Br* VEGETABLE MARROW [ME *marowe*, fr OE *mearg*; akin to OHG *marag* marrow, Skt *majjan*] – **marrowless** *adj*, **marrowy** *adj*

**marrowbone** /'marəˌbohn, -roh-/ *n* **1** a bone (e g a shinbone) rich in marrow **2** *pl, humorous* the knees

**marrowfat** /'marəˌfat, -roh-/ *n* any of several types of large pea

¹**marry** /'mari/ *vt* **1a** to join as husband and wife according to law or custom ⟨*they were* married *yesterday*⟩ **b** to give in marriage ⟨married *his daughter to the town clerk's son*⟩ **c** to take as wife or husband in marriage; wed ⟨married *the girl next door*⟩ **d** to perform the ceremony of marriage for ⟨*the couple were* married *by the Archbishop*⟩ **e** to obtain by marriage ⟨married *a fortune*⟩ **2** to bring together in close or harmonious relationship; unite ~ *vi* **1a** to take a wife or husband **b** to become husband and wife **2** to join in a close or harmonious relationship ⟨*these wines ~ well*⟩ [ME *marien*, fr *marier*, fr L *maritare*, fr *maritus* husband]

**marry into** *vt* to become a member of or obtain by marriage ⟨married into *a prominent family*⟩

**marry off** *vt, informal* to find a spouse for ⟨married off *her daughter to an oil sheikh*⟩

²**marry** *interj, archaic* – used formerly for emphasis and esp to express amused or surprised agreement [ME *marie*, fr *Marie*, the Virgin Mary]

**Mars** /mahz/ *n* the planet fourth in order from the sun that is noted for its red colouring [L *Mart-*, *Mars*, Roman god of war]

**Marsala** /mah'sahlə/ *n* a usu sweet fortified wine from Sicily [*Marsala*, town in Sicily]

**Marseilles** /mah'say/ *n* a firm cotton fabric that is similar to PIQUÉ [*Marseilles*, city in SE France]

**marsh** /mahsh/ *n* an area of soft wet land covered chiefly with sedges, rushes, and grasses [ME *mersh*, fr OE *merisc*, *mersc*; akin to MD *mersch* marsh, OE *mere* sea, pool – more at MARINE]

¹**marshal** *also* **marshall** /'mahsh(ə)l/ *n* **1a** a high official in a medieval royal household, originally having charge of the cavalry but later usu in command of the military forces **b** a person who arranges and directs a ceremony, parade, etc **c** a person who arranges the procedure at races **2a** FIELD MARSHAL **b** an officer of the highest military rank **3a** a chief officer in the USA responsible for the processes of the court in a judicial district **b** the administrative head of a US city police department or fire brigade [ME, fr OF *mareschal*, of Gmc origin; akin to OHG *marahscalc* marshal, fr *marah* horse + *scalc* servant] – **marshalcy** *n*, **marshalship** *n*

²**marshal** vb **-ll-** (NAm **-l-, -ll-**) vt **1** to place in proper rank or position ⟨~ling the troops⟩ **2** to bring together and arrange in an appropriate or effective order ⟨~ one's arguments⟩ ⟨~ two coats of arms on one shield⟩ **3** to lead ceremoniously or solicitously; usher ⟨~ling her little group of children down the street⟩ ~ vi to take form or order ⟨ideas ~ling neatly⟩

**marshalling yard** /'mahshəling/ n, chiefly Br a place where railway vehicles are shunted and made up into trains

**marshal of the Royal Air Force** n – see MILITARY RANKS table

**marsh crocodile** n MUGGER 1

**marsh gas** n methane

**marsh harrier** n a small brown bird of prey (Circus aeruginosus), the male of which has grey plumage on its wings and tail, that nests in large dense reed-beds and is seen over open fields and marshes in Europe, N Africa, and Asia

**marsh hawk** n a small N American bird of prey, closely related to the Eurasian HEN HARRIER

**marshland** /'mahsh·lənd/ n a marshy district; a marsh

**marshmallow** /,mahsh'maloh/ n **1** a pink-flowered hairy Eurasian plant (Althaea officinalis) of the hollyhock family that grows in marshes, usu near the sea, and has a root that contains a sweet gumlike substance sometimes used in confectionery and medicine **2** a confection made from the root of the marshmallow or from sugar, egg white, and gelatine beaten to a light spongy consistency

**marshmallowy** /mahsh'maloh·i/ adj resembling a marshmallow in softness or sweetness; esp sentimental

**marsh marigold** /'mari,gohld/ n a European and N American plant (Caltha palustris) of the buttercup family that is common in marshes, damp woods, and other wet places and has shiny kidney-shaped leaves and large bright yellow flowers – called also KINGCUP

**marsh samphire** n GLASSWORT (fleshy plant with jointed stems)

**marsh tit** n a Eurasian tit (Parus palustris) with a black cap and chin, that is common in deciduous woodland and scrubland

**marshy** /'mahshi/ adj **1** resembling or being a marsh; boggy ⟨~ ground⟩ **2** of or occurring in marshes ⟨~ vegetation⟩ – **marshiness** n

¹**marsupial** /mah'syoohpi·əl, -'sooh-/ adj **1** of or being a marsupial **2** of or forming a marsupium

²**marsupial** n any of an order (Marsupialia) of lower mammals comprising kangaroos, wombats, bandicoots, opossums, and related animals of Central and S America and Australasia, in which the young are born in an incomplete state of development and usu continue their development in the protection of a pouch at the mother's abdomen [deriv of NL marsupium]

**marsupium** /mah'syoohpiəm, -'sooh-/ n, pl **marsupia** /-piə/ **1** an abdominal pouch of most marsupials, formed by a fold of the skin, in which the young are carried and suckled **2** any of several structures in various esp aquatic INVERTEBRATE animals (e g sandhoppers) for enclosing or carrying eggs or young [NL, fr L, purse, pouch, fr Gk marsypion, dim. of marsypos pouch]

**mart** /maht/ n a place of trade (e g an auction room or a market) [ME, fr MD marct, mart, prob fr ONF market]

**Martello** /mah'teloh/, **Martello tower** n a circular masonry fort formerly used (e g in Britain) for coastal defence [alter. of Cape Mortella in Corsica, where such a tower was captured by a British fleet in 1794]

**marten** /'mahtin/ n, pl **martens**, esp collectively **marten** any of several slender-bodied mammals (genus Martes) related to but larger than weasels that live mainly in trees and feed on other animals, fruit, and carrion; also the fur or pelt of a marten △ martin [ME martryn, fr MF martrine marten fur, fr OF, fr martre marten, of Gmc origin; akin to OE mearth marten]

**martensite** /'mahtin,ziet/ n the chief constituent of rapidly cooled steel that is responsible for the hardness of steel formed in this way [Adolf Martens †1914 Ger metallurgist] – **martensitic** adj, **martensitically** adv

**martial** /'mahsh(ə)l/ adj **1** of or suited for war or a warrior **2** of an army or military life **3** experienced in or inclined to war; warlike △ marital [ME, fr L martialis of Mars, fr Mart-, Mars Mars, Roman god of war] – **martially** adv

**martial art** n any of the Oriental arts of combat (e g judo, karate, and kendo) widely practised as sports

**martial law** n the law administered by military forces in an occupied territory or in an emergency

¹**Martian** /'mahsh(ə)n/ adj of or coming from the planet Mars

²**Martian** n a supposed inhabitant of Mars

**martin** /'mahtin/ n any of various birds of the swallow family: eg **a** HOUSE MARTIN **b** SAND MARTIN △ marten [MF, fr St Martin; prob fr the migration of martins around Martinmas]

**martinet** /,mahti'net/ n a strict disciplinarian [Jean Martinet † 1672 Fr army officer]

**martingale** /'mahtin,gayl/ n **1** a device for steadying a horse's head or checking its upward movement, consisting of one or more straps fastened to the girth, passing between the forelegs, and attached to the reins, noseband, or bit **2** any of several systems of betting in which the stake is doubled each time a bet is lost [MF]

**martini** /mah'teeni/ n a cocktail made of gin and vermouth; esp DRY MARTINI [prob fr Martini & Rossi, It firm selling vermouth]

**Martini** trademark – used for a brand of sweet or dry vermouth

**Martinmas** /'mahtinməs, -,mas/ n November 11 celebrated as the feast of St Martin [ME martinmasse, fr St Martin †397 patron saint of France + ME masse mass]

**martlet** /'mahtlit/ n a representation, used in heraldry, of a bird that resembles the martin but has no feet [MF, prob alter. of martinet, dim. of martin]

¹**martyr** /'mahtə/ n **1** a person who is put to death for adherence to a cause, esp a religion **2** a victim esp of constant, sometimes self-inflicted, suffering ⟨made a ~ of herself in the hope of being praised⟩ ⟨he was a ~ to rheumatism⟩ [ME, OE, fr LL, fr Gk martyr-, martys, lit., witness; akin to L memor mindful] – **martyrize** vt, **martyrization** n

²**martyr** vt **1** to put to death for adhering to a belief, faith, or practice **2** to inflict agonizing pain on; torture

**martyrdom** /'mahtədəm/ n **1** the suffering of death on account of adherence to a cause, esp one's religious faith **2** affliction, torture

**martyrologist** /,mahtə'roləjist/ n a writer of or specialist in martyrology

**martyrology** /,mahtə'roləji/ n **1** a catalogue of martyrs and saints arranged by the dates of their feast days **2** ecclesiastical history concerned with the lives and sufferings of martyrs – **martyrological** adj

**martyry** /'mahtəri/ n a shrine erected in honour of a martyr [LL martyrium, fr LGk martyrion, fr Gk martyr-, martys]

¹**marvel** /'mahv(ə)l/ n **1** something that causes wonder or astonishment **2** someone who is marvellous [ME mervel, fr OF merveille, fr LL mirabilia marvels, fr L, neut pl of mirabilis wonderful, fr mirari to wonder – more at SMILE]

²**marvel** vb **-ll-** (NAm **-l-, -ll-**) to become filled with surprise, wonder, or amazed curiosity (at) ⟨~led at the magician's skill⟩ ⟨~led that they had escaped unhurt⟩

**marvellous**, NAm chiefly **marvelous** /'mahvələs/ adj **1** causing wonder; astonishing **2** miraculous, supernatural **3** of the highest kind or quality ⟨has a ~ way with children⟩ – **marvellously** adv, **marvellousness** n

**Marxism** /'mahksiz(ə)m/ n the political, economic, and social principles and policies advocated by Karl Marx; esp a theory and practice of socialism including the labour theory of value, dialectical and historical materialism, the class struggle, and dictatorship of the proletariat until the establishment of a classless society [Karl Marx †1883 Ger political philosopher]

**Marxism-'Leninism** /'leniniz(ə)m/ n a theory and practice of communism developed by Lenin from the doctrines of Marx, which states that the dictatorship of the proletariat is necessary in order to build a socialist society – **Marxist-Leninist** n or adj

**Marxist** /'mahksist/ also **Marxian** /'mahksiən/ adj of, developed by, or influenced by the doctrines of Marx – **Marxist** n

**Mary** /'meəri/ n the mother of Jesus [LL Maria, fr Gk Mariam, Maria, fr Heb Miryām]

**Maryland** /'meərilənd/ n an air-cured tobacco that is grown in N America, often blended with other tobacco types, and used esp in cigarettes – compare VIRGINIA [Maryland, state of the USA]

**Mary Poppins** /'popinz/ n an ideal nanny ⟨Mary Poppins needed . . . by . . . working mother – The Times⟩ [Mary Poppins, nanny in children's books by P L Travers b 1906 Br (Austr-born) writer]

**marzipan** /'mahzi,pan/ n a paste made from ground almonds, sugar, and egg whites that is used as a coating for cakes or shaped into various forms as small sweets [Ger, fr It marza-

*pane*, a medieval coin, marzipan, fr Ar *mawthabān*, a medieval coin]

**Masai** /'masie/ *n, pl* **Masais,** *esp collectively* **Masai 1** a member of a pastoral and hunting people of Kenya and Tanzania **2** a NILOTIC language of the Masai

**mascara** /ma'skahra/ *n* a cosmetic for colouring, esp darkening, the eyelashes [It *maschera* mask]

**mascon** /'maskon/ *n* any of the areas of dense rock that are situated just under the surface of the moon, and held to cause deviations of the paths of orbiting spacecraft by their greater gravitational pull [²*mass* + *concentration*]

**mascot** /'maskot, -kət/ *n* a person, animal, or object adopted as a symbol, esp to bring good luck [Fr *mascotte*, fr Prov *mascoto*, fr *masco* witch, fr ML *masca*]

**¹masculine** /'maskyoolin/ *adj* **1a** male **b** having qualities appropriate to a man ⟨*her deep ~ voice*⟩ **2** of, belonging to, or being the gender that normally includes most words or grammatical forms referring to males **3a** *of verse, poetry, etc* having or occurring in a stressed final syllable ⟨*~ rhyme*⟩ ⟨*~ ending*⟩ **b** *of a piece of music* having the final chord occurring on a strong beat ⟨*~ cadence*⟩ **synonyms** see ¹MALE **antonym** feminine [ME *masculin*, fr MF, fr L *masculinus*, fr *masculus*, n, male, dim. of *mas* male] – **masculinely** *adv*, **masculineness** *n*, **masculinity** *n*

**²masculine** *n* **1** a word or language form of the masculine gender **2** the masculine gender

**masculin·ize, -ise** /'maskyooliniez/ *vt* to give a predominantly masculine character to; *esp* to cause (a female) to take on male characteristics

**maser** /'mayzə/ *n* a device that uses the internal energy of vibrating atoms or molecules to produce a very powerful beam of microwaves – compare LASER [*m*icrowave *a*mplification by *s*timulated *e*mission of *r*adiation]

**¹mash** /mash/ *n* **1** crushed malt or grain meal soaked and stirred in hot water to convert starch to sugar (e g prior to the production of beer or whisky) **2** a mass of mixed ingredients (e g bran) used either dry or moistened with hot water for feeding livestock **3** a soft pulpy mass **4** *Br informal* mashed potatoes ⟨*bangers and ~*⟩ [ME, fr OE *māx-*; akin to MHG *meisch* mash]

**²mash** *vt* **1a** to reduce to a soft pulpy state by crushing, pounding, etc **b** to crush, smash ⟨*~ a finger*⟩ **2** to heat and stir (e g crushed malt) in water as part of the process of brewing beer **3** *chiefly N & Mid Eng* to infuse (tea) with hot water

**³mash** *vt* to flirt with or seek to gain the affection of [prob fr ²*mash*]

**⁴mash** *n* an infatuation; a crush

**¹masher** /'mashə/ *n* one who or that which mashes ⟨*a potato ~*⟩

**²masher** *n* a man who makes passes at women

**mashie** *also* **mashy** /'mashi/ *n* a metal golf club used for shots of medium distance and for height – no longer in vogue [perh fr Fr *massue* club, fr (assumed) VL *mattiuca*, fr *mattia* mace]

**Mashona** /mə'shohnə/ *n, pl* **Mashonas,** *esp collectively* **Mashona** a member of a Bantu-speaking people of Zimbabwe

**mash tun** *n* a vessel in which malt and other grain is MASHED

**¹mask** /mahsk/ *n* **1a** a (partial) cover for the face used for disguise or protection **b(1)** a figure of a head worn on the stage in ancient times to identify the character and project the voice **b(2)** a grotesque false face worn at carnivals or in rituals **c** an often grotesque carved head or face used as an ornament (e g on the keystone of an arch) **d** a copy of a face made by sculpting or by means of a mould – compare DEATH MASK **2a** something that disguises or conceals; *esp* a pretence, facade **b** a translucent or opaque screen to cover part of the sensitive surface in taking or printing a photograph, so that only part of the image or scene appears in the final picture **3a** a device covering the mouth and nose, used **(1)** to promote breathing (e g by connection to an oxygen supply) **(2)** to remove noxious gases from the air **(3)** to prevent the spread of infective material breathed out (e g by a surgeon) **b** GAS MASK **4** a face-pack **5** the head or face of an animal (e g a fox or dog) **6** MASQUE **7** *archaic* a person wearing a mask [MF *masque*, fr OIt *maschera*]

**²mask** *vt* **1** to provide, cover, or conceal (as if) with a mask: e g **1a** to conceal from view ⟨*~ a gun battery*⟩ **b** to make indistinct or imperceptible ⟨*~s the strong flavour*⟩ **c** to cover up ⟨*~ed his real purpose*⟩ **2** to cover for protection **3** to modify the size or shape of (e g a photograph) by means of a mask – **maskable** *adj*

**masked** /'mahskt/ *adj* **1** marked by the use of masks ⟨*a ~ ball*⟩ **2** failing to present or produce the usual symptoms;

latent ⟨*~ infection*⟩ ⟨*a ~ virus*⟩

**masker** *also* **masquer** /'mahskə/ *n* a person who wears a mask; *esp* a participant in a masquerade

**masking tape** /'mahsking/ *n* an adhesive tape used to cover a surface, esp an edge of a surface, and keep it free from paint when painting an adjacent area

**masochism** /'masə̇,kiz(ə)m/ *n* **1** a sexual perversion in which pleasure is experienced from being physically or mentally abused, esp by somebody who is a love object – compare SADISM **2** pleasure from something tiresome or painful – not used technically [ISV, fr Leopold von Sacher-*Masoch* † 1895 Austrian novelist] – **masochist** *n*, **masochistic** *adj*, **masochistically** *adv*

**¹mason** /'mays(ə)n/ *n* **1** a skilled worker with stone **2** *cap* a freemason **3** *NAm* a bricklayer [ME, fr OF *maçon*, prob of Gmc origin; akin to OE *macian* to make]

**²mason** *vt* **1** to construct of or repair with masonry **2** to build stonework or brickwork about, under, in, or over

**,Mason-'Dixon line** /'diks(ə)n/ *also* **Mason and Dixon's line** *n* the S boundary line of Pennsylvania; *also* the boundary line between the N and S states of the USA [Charles *Mason* †1787 and Jeremiah *Dixon* *fl*1767 E surveyors]

**Masonic** /mə'sonik/ *adj* (characteristic) of Freemasons or Freemasonry

**masonry** /'mays(ə)nri/ *n* **1a** something built of stone or brick **b** the art, trade, or occupation of a mason **c** work done by a mason **2** *cap* FREEMASONRY

**mason's mark** *n* a mark carved by a mason to identify his work

**mason wasp** *n* any of various wasps that do not live in social groups and that build nests of hardened mud

**Masora, Masorah** /mə'sawrə/ *n* a body of notes on the text of the Hebrew Old Testament compiled by scribes during the first thousand years of the Christian era [NHeb *mĕsōrāh*, fr LHeb *māsōreth* tradition, fr Heb, bond]

**Masorete, Massorete** /'masəreet/ *n* any of the scribes who compiled the Masora [MF *massoreth*, fr LHeb *māsōreth*] – **Masoretic** *adj*

**masque** *also* **mask** /mahsk/ *n* **1** MASQUERADE 1 **2** a short allegorical dramatic entertainment of the 16th and 17th centuries which was performed, often at court, by masked actors, and was originally mimed to music but later included poetic dialogue, songs, and dance [MF *masque*, fr OIt *maschera* mask]

**masquer** /'mahskə/ *n* a masker

**¹masquerade** /,maskə'rayd/ *n* **1** a social gathering of people wearing masks and often fantastic costumes **2** something that is merely show; a pretence [MF, fr OIt dial. *mascarada*, fr OIt *maschera*]

**²masquerade** *vi* **1a** to disguise oneself; *also* to wear a disguise **2** to assume the appearance of something that one is not – usu + *as* ⟨*was arrested for* masquerading *as a policeman*⟩ – **masquerader** *n*

**¹mass** /mas/ *n* **1** *cap* the form of service used in the celebration of the Eucharist, esp in Roman Catholic and Anglo-Catholic churches **2** *cap* a celebration of the Eucharist ⟨*Sunday* Masses *held at three different hours*⟩ **3** a musical setting for the regular parts (ORDINARY) of the Mass [ME, fr OE *mæsse*, modif of (assumed) VL *messa*, lit., dismissal at the end of a religious service, fr LL *missa*, fr L, fem of *missus*, pp of *mittere* to send – more at SMITE]

**²mass** *n* **1a** a quantity of matter or the form of matter that holds or clings together in one body **b(1)** an (unbroken) expanse; a bulk ⟨*a mountain ~*⟩ ⟨*a ~ of colour*⟩ **b(2)** massive quality or effect **b(3)** the principal part or main body **b(4)** a total, whole ⟨*men in the ~*⟩ **c** the property of a body that is a measure of its resistance to having its speed or position changed when a force is applied to it, that is commonly taken as a measure of the amount of material it contains and causes it to have weight in a gravitational field, and that together with length and time constitutes one of the fundamental quantities on which all physical measurements are based **2 masses** *pl but taking sing or pl vb*, **mass** a large quantity, amount, or number ⟨*a great ~ of material*⟩ ⟨*there was* masses *of food left over*⟩ **3a** a large body of people in a compact group **b** *pl* the body of ordinary people as contrasted with the élite [ME *masse*, fr MF, fr L *massa*, fr Gk *maza*; akin to Gk *massein* to knead – more at MINGLE] – **massless** *adj*

**³mass** *vb* to assemble in or collect into a mass ⟨*thousands of students ~ed in the street*⟩

**⁴mass** *adj* **1a** of, designed for, or consisting of the mass of the people ⟨*a* ~ *market*⟩ ⟨~ *education*⟩ **b** participated in by or affecting a large number of individuals ⟨~ *murder*⟩ ⟨~ *demonstrations*⟩ **c** large-scale, wholesale ⟨~ *production*⟩ **2** viewed as a whole; total ⟨*the* ~ *effect of a design*⟩

**Massachuset** /ˌmasə'choohsit/ *n, pl* **Massachusets** *also* **Massachusetts,** *esp collectively* **Massachuset 1** a member of an American Indian people of Massachusetts **2** the ALGONQUIAN language of the Massachuset [Massachuset *Massa-adchu-es-et,* a locality, lit., about the big hill]

**¹massacre** /'masəkə/ *vt* **1** to kill in a massacre; slaughter **2** *informal* to defeat severely ⟨*the amateur team were* ~d *by the professionals*⟩; *also* to spoil, mangle ⟨*the student* ~d *the translation*⟩ – **massacrer** *n*

**²massacre** *n* **1** the ruthless and indiscriminate killing of large numbers of people **2** a wholesale slaughter of animals **3** complete defeat or destruction [MF]

**¹massage** /'masahj, 'masahzh/ *n* (an act of) rubbing, stroking, kneading, or tapping) of (part of) the body with the hand or an instrument in order to relieve aches, tone muscles, give relaxation, etc [Fr, fr *masser* to massage, fr Ar *massa* to stroke]

**²massage** *vt* to perform massage on – **massager** *n*

**mass defect** /'deefekt/ *n* the difference between the mass of the nucleus of an atom and the sum of the individual masses of protons and neutrons in that nucleus

**massé** /'masi/ *n* a shot in billiards or snooker made with a (nearly) vertical cue so as to drive the CUE BALL round one ball in order to strike another [Fr, fr pp of *masser* to make a massé shot, fr *masse* sledgehammer, fr MF *mace* mace]

**mass-energy equation** *n* an equation for the interconversion of mass and energy: $E = mc^2$ where $E$ is energy, $m$ is mass, and $c$ is the velocity of light

**masseter** /ma'seetə/ *n* a large muscle that raises the lower jaw and is used in chewing [NL, fr Gk *masētēr,* fr *masasthai* to chew] – **masseteric** *adj*

**masseur** /ma'suh/, *fem* **masseuse** /-'suhz/ *n* someone who practises massage and physiotherapy [Fr, fr *masser* to massage]

**massicot** /'masiˌkot/ *n* a soft yellow mineral of lead monoxide, PbO, used esp as a pigment – compare LITHARGE [ME *masticot,* fr MF *massicot, masticot,* fr OIt *massicotto* pottery glaze]

**massif** /'maseef/ *n* **1** a principal mountain mass that gives rise to a number of peaks towards its summit **2** a mountainous block of the earth's crust bounded by faults or folds and displaced as a unit [Fr, fr *massif,* adj]

**massive** /'masiv/ *adj* **1** forming or consisting of a large mass: eg **1a** large, solid, or heavy ⟨~ *walls*⟩ ⟨*a* ~ *volume*⟩ **b** impressively large or ponderous **c(1)** *of a rock* fairly uniform in appearance; homogeneous ⟨~ *sandstone*⟩ **c(2)** *of a mineral* not obviously crystalline **2a** large, solid, or heavy in structure ⟨*a* ~ *jaw*⟩ **b** large in scope or degree ⟨*a* ~ *feeling of frustration*⟩ **c(1)** large in comparison to what is typical ⟨*a* ~ *dose of penicillin*⟩ **c(2)** extensive and severe ⟨~ *haemorrhage*⟩ ⟨~ *collapse of a lung*⟩ **d** imposing in excellence or grandeur; monumental ⟨~ *simplicity*⟩ [ME *massiffe,* fr MF *massif,* fr *masse* mass] – **massively** *adv,* **massiveness** *n*

**mass media** *n pl* ²MEDIA

**mass noun** *n* a noun (eg *sand* or *justice*) that characteristically denotes a substance or concept and not an individual item, that does not form a plural, and that cannot be used with the indefinite article – compare COUNT NOUN

**mass number** *n* the total number of protons and neutrons in the nucleus of an atom that is used to express the mass of an ISOTOPE

**mass observation** *n, Br* the study and reporting of human behaviour, habits, and opinions in the context of everyday life

**Massorete** /'masəreet/ *n* MASORETE

**mass-pro'duce** /prə'dyoohs/ *vt* to produce (goods) in large quantities by standardized mechanical processes [back-formation fr *mass production*] – **mass production** *n*

**mass society** *n* a form of society characteristic of highly developed industrialized consumer societies in which the same activities, habits, tastes, and opinions are offered to and shared by the great majority of the population – compare ALTERNATIVE SOCIETY

**mass spectrograph** *n* a MASS SPECTROSCOPE in which the stream of electrically charged particles is detected photographically

**mass spectrometer** *n* a MASS SPECTROSCOPE in which the stream of electrically charged particles is detected by electric means – **mass spectrometric** *adj,* **mass spectrometry** *n,* **spectrometrist** *n*

**mass spectroscope** *n* an apparatus that separates electrically charged particles according to their charge-to-mass ratios by subjecting them to magnetic and electric fields. The resulting MASS SPECTRUM is received or detected either electrically or photographically and can be used in the identification of ISOTOPES of chemical elements, the dating of geological samples, the analysis of chemical compounds, etc. – **spectroscopy** *n,* **spectroscopist** *n*

**mass spectrum** *n* the spectrum of a stream of electrically charged particles (eg electrons or IONS) dispersed according to their mass

**massy** /'masi/ *adj, formal* massive, heavy ⟨*the* ~ *gold bracelet*⟩ ⟨*a* ~ *city wall*⟩

**¹mast** /mahst/ *n* **1a** a long pole rising from the keel or deck of a ship from which a sail can be set; *broadly* a tall pole or structure on a ship **b** any of the sections of a compound mast ⟨*topgallant* ~⟩ **2a** a (nearly) vertical pole (eg an upright post in various cranes) **b** a vertical pole or lattice upright supporting a radio or television aerial **3** a disciplinary proceeding at which the commanding officer of a naval unit hears and disposes of cases against his men [ME, fr OE *mæst;* akin to OHG *mast,* L *malus*] – **masted** *adj* – **before the mast** as an ordinary sailor, not an officer

**²mast** *vt* to equip with a mast

**³mast** *n* beechnuts, acorns, etc accumulated on the forest floor and often serving as food for animals (eg pigs) [ME, fr OE *mæst;* akin to OHG *mast* food, mast, OE *mete* food – more at MEAT]

**mast-** /mast-/, **masto-** *comb form* breast; nipple; MAMMARY GLAND ⟨*mastitis*⟩ [NL, fr Gk, fr *mastos* – more at MEAT]

**mastaba** /'mastəbə/ *n* an originally mudbrick superstructure built over Egyptian tombs of the earliest dynasties, that is oblong in shape with sloping sides and a flat roof [Ar *maṣṭabah* stone bench]

**mast cell** *n* a large cell that occurs esp in CONNECTIVE TISSUE (loose fibrous supporting tissue) and contains HISTAMINE, SEROTONIN, and HEPARIN which may be released on disruption of the cell (eg as a result of an antigen-antibody reaction at the cell surface) and may cause responses such as inflammation or an allergic reaction [part trans of Ger *mast zelle,* fr *mast* food, mast (fr OHG) + *zelle* cell]

**mastectomy** /ma'stektəmi/ *n* the removal of a breast by surgery (eg to treat cancer)

**-masted** /-mahstid/ *comb form* (*adj* → *adj*) having (such or so many) masts

**¹master** /'mahstə/ *n* **1a(1)** a male teacher **a(2)** a person holding an academic degree higher than a bachelor's but lower than a doctor's **b** *often cap* a revered religious leader **c** a workman qualified to teach apprentices ⟨*a* ~ *carpenter*⟩ **d(1)** an artist, performer, player, etc who is extremely skilled or accomplished **d(2)** a painting by a master artist **e** a great figure of the past (eg in science or art) whose work serves as a model or ideal **2a** someone having control or authority over another; a ruler, governor **b** one who or that which conquers or masters; a victor, superior ⟨*in this young, obscure challenger the champion found his* ~⟩ **c** a person qualified to command a merchant ship **d(1)** an owner, esp of a slave or animal **d(2)** *often cap* one who directs a hunt and has overall control of the pack of hounds (eg foxhounds or beagles) used in it **e** an employer **f** the male head of a household **3a** – used as a title for a youth or boy too young to be called *Mr* **b** the eldest son of a Scottish viscount or baron **4a** a presiding officer in an institution or society (eg a Masonic lodge) or at a function **b** *often cap* an officer of the SUPREME COURT of England and Wales with responsibility esp for preliminary or procedural matters in HIGH COURT cases **5a** a mechanism or device that controls the operation of another **b** an original from which copies can be made: eg **b(1)** a master recording **b(2)** MATRIX **2d 6** *archaic* MR [ME, fr OE *magister* & OF *maistre,* both fr L *magister;* akin to L *magnus* great – more at MUCH]

**²master** *vt* **1** to become master of; overcome **2a** to become skilled or proficient in the use of ⟨~ *a foreign language*⟩ **b** to gain a thorough understanding of ⟨*haven't* ~ed *all the details yet*⟩

**³master** *adj* being a master: eg **a** having chief authority; dominant **b** skilled, proficient ⟨~ *builder*⟩ ⟨~ *chef*⟩ **c** principal, main **d** superlative – often in combination ⟨*a master-liar*⟩ **e** being a device or mechanism that controls the operation of another mechanism or that establishes a standard (eg a dimen-

sion or weight(⟨*a* ~ *gauge*⟩ **f** being a copy, mould, or MATRIX from which duplicates are made
**master aircrew** *n* – see MILITARY RANKS table
**master-at-'arms** *n, pl* **masters-at-arms** a PETTY OFFICER responsible for maintaining discipline aboard ship
**master bedroom** *n* a principal bedroom in a house; *esp* one that is occupied by the head of the household
**master chief petty officer** *n* – see MILITARY RANKS table
**master class** *n* a class in which an eminent musician listens to and corrects advanced pupils
**masterful** /-f(ə)l/ *adj* **1** inclined to take control and dominate **2** having or showing the technical, artistic, or intellectual power and skill of a master ⟨~ *drawings*⟩ *usage* see MASTERLY – **masterfully** *adv*, **masterfulness** *n*
**master gunnery sergeant** *n* – see MILITARY RANKS table
**master key** *n* a key designed to open several different locks
**masterly** /-li/ *adj* suitable to or resembling a master; *esp* showing superior knowledge or skill ⟨~ *performance*⟩ – **masterly** *adv*, **masterliness** *n*
*usage* Writers on usage advise that the meaning "skilful" should be expressed by **masterly**, while **masterful** should be used only in the sense of "dominating".
**master mason** *n* a Freemason who has reached the third degree and is therefore fully qualified
**¹mastermind** /'mahstə‚miend/ *n* **1** a person who masterminds a project **2** a person of outstanding intellect
**²mastermind** *vt* to be the intellectual force behind (a project)
**master of arts** *n, often cap M&A* **1** the recipient of a master's degree, usu in an arts subject **2** the degree making one a master of arts
**master of ceremonies**, *fem* **mistress of ceremonies** *n* **1** a person in charge of procedures on a state or public occasion **2** a person who acts as host, esp by introducing speakers, performers, etc, at an event
**master of science** *n, often cap M&S* **1** the recipient of a master's degree, usu in a scientific subject **2** the degree making one a master of science
**Master of the Rolls** *n* the presiding judge of the COURT OF APPEAL
**masterpiece** /'mahstə‚pees/ *n* **1** a piece of work presented to a medieval organization of craftsmen (GUILD) as evidence of qualification for the rank of master **2** a work done with extraordinary skill; *esp* the supreme creation of a type, period, or person [prob trans of D *meesterstuk* or Ger *meisterstück*]
**master race** *n taking sing or pl vb* a people who are held or who hold themselves to be racially superior and hence fitted to rule or enslave other peoples [trans of Ger *herrenvolk*]
**master sergeant** *n* – see MILITARY RANKS table
**mastership** /'mahstəship/ *n* **1** the authority or control of a master **2** the status, office, or function of a master **3** the proficiency of a master
**mastersinger** /'mahstə‚sing·ə/ *n* MEISTERSINGER
**masterstroke** /'mahstə‚strohk/ *n* a masterly performance or move
**masterwork** /'mahstə‚wuhk/ *n* a masterpiece
**mastery** /'mahstəri/ *n* **1a** the authority of a master; dominion **b** the upper hand in a contest or competition **2a** possession or display of great skill or technique **b** skill or knowledge that makes one master of a subject; command [ME *maistrie*, fr OF, fr *maistre* master]
**masthead** /'mahst‚hed/ *n* **1** the top of a mast **2a** the printed matter in a newspaper or periodical that gives the title and details of ownership, advertising rates, and subscription rates **b** the name of a newspaper displayed at the top of the first page
**mastic** /'mastik/ *n* **1** an aromatic resin that is obtained from MASTIC TREES and is used chiefly in varnishes **2** a puttylike material made esp with asphalt and used for coating, filling, sealing, or cementing wood, masonry, etc [ME *mastik*, fr L *mastiche*, fr Gk *mastichē*; akin to Gk *mastichan*]
**mastic asphalt** *n* a tarry mixture of BITUMEN with sand and gravel, used for roofing or floor finishing
**masticate** /'mastikayt/ *vt* **1** to grind or crush (food) (as if) with the teeth in preparation for swallowing; chew **2** to soften or reduce to pulp by crushing or kneading ~ *vi* to chew [LL *masticatus*, pp of *masticare*, fr Gk *mastichan* to gnash the teeth; akin to Gk *masasthai* to chew – more at MOUTH] – **masticator** *n*, **mastication** *n*
**¹masticatory** /'mastikət(ə)ri/ *adj* **1** used for or adapted to

chewing ⟨~ *limbs of an insect*⟩ **2** of or involving the organs of mastication ⟨~ *paralysis*⟩
**²masticatory** *n* a substance (e g gum) that is chewed but not swallowed; *esp* a medicinal substance chewed to increase the production of saliva
**mastic tree** *n* a small S European evergreen tree (*Pistacia lentiscus*) of the sumach family that yields mastic
**mastiff** /'mastif/ *n* (any of) a breed of very large powerful deep-chested smooth-coated dogs used chiefly as watchdogs and guard dogs [ME *mastif*, modif of MF *mastin*, fr (assumed) VL *mansuetinus*, fr L *mansuetus* tame – more at MANSUETUDE]
**mastigophoran** /‚masti'gofərən/ *n* any of a class (Mastigophora) of single-celled organisms (PROTOZOANS) (e g a euglena or trypanosome) including all those forms with FLAGELLA (whiplike structures) and including many often treated as algae [deriv of Gk *mastig-, mastix* whip + *pherein* to carry – more at BEAR] – **mastigophoran** *adj*
**mastitis** /ma'stietəs/ *n, pl* **mastitides** /ma'stitədeez/ inflammation of the breast or udder, usu caused by bacterial infection [NL, fr *mast-* + *-itis*] – **mastitic** *adj*
**masto-** – see MAST-
**mastodon** /'mastə‚don/ *n* any of numerous extinct mammals (esp genus *Mammut*) that are similar to the mammoths and existing elephants but have a different form of molar teeth [NL *mastodont-, mastodon*, fr Gk *mast-* + *odont-, odōn, odous* tooth – more at TOOTH] – **mastodont** *adj or n*, **mastodontic** *adj*
**¹mastoid** /'mastoyd/ *adj* **1** being a somewhat conical prominent or projecting part of the TEMPORAL BONE behind the ear; *also* being any of several bony parts that occupy a similar position in the skull of less evolutionarily advanced VERTEBRATE animals **2** of or near the mastoid [NL *mastoides* resembling a nipple, mastoid, fr Gk *mastoeidēs*, fr *mastos* breast – more at MEAT]
**²mastoid** *n* a mastoid bone or projection
**mastoid cell** *n* one of the small cavities in the mastoid that develop after birth and are filled with air
**mastoidectomy** /‚mastoy'dektəmi/ *n* surgical removal of the MASTOID CELLS or of the mastoid bone [ISV]
**mastoiditis** /‚mastoy'dietəs/ *n* inflammation of the mastoid, esp the MASTOID CELLS [NL]
**masturbate** /'mastəbayt/ *vi* to practise masturbation ~ *vt* to practise masturbation on [L *masturbatus*, pp of *masturbari*]
**masturbation** /‚mastə'baysh(ə)n/ *n* stimulation of the genital organs commonly resulting in orgasm and accomplished by means (e g manual manipulation) other than sexual intercourse – **masturbational** *n*
**masturbatory** /'mastə‚baytəri/ *adj* of or involving masturbation ⟨~ *fantasies*⟩
**¹mat** /mat/ *n* **1a(1)** a piece of coarse usu woven, felted, or plaited fabric (e g of rushes or rope) used esp as a covering for an area of floor; *also* RUG 1 **a(2)** DOORMAT 1 **a(3)** a relatively thin usu decorative piece of material (e g cork or plastic) used under an object, esp to protect a surface (e g from heat, moisture, or scratches) – compare TABLEMAT **c** a large thick pad or cushion used as a surface for wrestling, tumbling, and gymnastics **d** a mat, usu of rubber, used by players of darts, bowls, etc to mark the correct place to stand while throwing or bowling **2** something made up of many intertwined or tangled strands **3** a large slab usu of reinforced concrete used as the supporting base of a building [ME, fr OE *meatte*, fr LL *matta*, of Sem origin; akin to Heb *miṭṭāh* bed] – **on the mat** *informal* in trouble; due to be punished – compare ON THE CARPET
**²mat** *vb* **-tt-** *vt* **1** to provide with a mat or matting **2a** to form into a tangled mass **b** to pack down so as to form a dense mass ~ *vi* to become tangled or intertwined
**³mat** *vt, adj, or n* **-tt-** (to) matt
**⁴mat** *n* MATRIX 2a
**Matabele** /‚matə'beeli, -'beli/ *n, pl* **Matabeles**, *esp collectively* **Matabele 1** a member of a Zulu tribe of Zimbabwe **2** the Bantu language of the Matabele
**matador** /'matədaw/ *n* someone who has the principal role and who kills the bull in a bullfight [Sp, fr *matar* to kill]
**¹match** /mach/ *n* **1a** a person or thing equal or similar to another **b** one able to cope with another **c** a person or thing exactly like another **2** two people or things that go well together ⟨*carpet and curtains are a* ~⟩ **3a** a contest between two or more teams or individuals ⟨*a golf* ~⟩ ⟨*a soccer* ~⟩ **b** a tennis contest completed when one player or side wins a specified number of sets **4a** a marriage union **b** a prospective partner in marriage [ME *macche*, fr OE *mǣcca*; akin to OE *macian* to make – more at MAKE]

²**match** vt **1a** to be equal to (an opponent) **b(1)** to set in competition or opposition; pit ⟨~ing *his strength against his enemy's*⟩ **b(2)** to provide with worthy competition **c** to set in comparison **2a(1)** to put in a set possessing equal or harmonizing qualities **a(2)** to cause to correspond ⟨~ing *life-style to income*⟩ **b(1)** to be the exact counterpart or equal of ⟨*this vase ~es that*⟩ ⟨*no one can ~ her for working under pressure*⟩ **b(2)** to harmonize with **c** to find a counterpart for **d** to provide funds complementary to ⟨*the government will ~ any money the local authority raises*⟩ **3** to fit together or make suitable for fitting together **4a** to toss coins with **b** *NAm* to flip or toss (coins) and compare exposed faces **5** *archaic* to join or give in marriage ~ vi **1** to be exactly or nearly alike **2** to go well together; correspond *synonyms* see ³RIVAL – **matchable** *adj*, **matcher** *n*

**match up with** vt to correspond to; equal

³**match** n **1** a chemically prepared wick or cord formerly used in firing firearms or powder **2** a short slender piece of inflammable material (e g wood) tipped with a mixture that bursts into flame when slightly heated through friction (e g by being scratched against a rough surface); *esp* SAFETY MATCH [ME *macche* wick, fr MF *meiche*]

**matchboard** /'mach,bawd/ n a board with a groove cut along one edge and a ridge (TONGUE) along the other so as to fit snugly with the edges of similarly cut boards

**matchbox** /'mach,boks/ n a box that contains matches and that has a surface on which the matches can be struck

**matchless** /-lis/ adj having no equal; peerless – **matchlessly** adv

**matchlock** /'mach,lok/ n **1** a mechanism by which a slow-burning cord is lowered over a hole in the breech of a musket to ignite the charge **2** a musket equipped with a matchlock

**matchmaker** /'mach,mayka/ n a person who arranges marriages; *also* one who derives vicarious pleasure from contriving to arrange marriages – **matchmaking** n

**match play** n a golf competition scored by the number of holes won rather than of strokes played – compare STROKE PLAY

**match point** n a situation in tennis, badminton, etc in which one player will win the match by winning the next point; *also* the point contested ⟨*he saved two ~s when 3–5 down in the final set but went on to win*⟩

¹**matchstick** /'mach,stik/ n ³MATCH 2; *specif* a wooden one after use

²**matchstick** adj **1** made (as if) of matchsticks ⟨*a ~ house*⟩ **2** resembling a matchstick in being relatively long and thin ⟨*the child drew ~ men*⟩

**matchwood** /'mach,wood/ n wood suitable for matches; *also* wood splintered into minute pieces

¹**mate** /mayt/ vt or n (to) checkmate [vb ME *maten*, fr MF *mater*, fr OF *mat*, n, checkmate, fr Ar *māt* (in *shāh māt*); n ME *mat*, fr MF, fr OF]

²**mate** n **1a** an associate, companion – often in combination ⟨*flatmate*⟩ ⟨*playmate*⟩ **b** an assistant to a more skilled workman ⟨*plumber's ~*⟩ **c** *chiefly Br & Austr* a friend, chum – used esp as a familiar form of address between men **2** an officer on a merchant ship ranking below the captain **3** either of a pair: e g **3a** a marriage partner **b** either member of a breeding pair of animals ⟨*a sparrow and his ~*⟩ **c** either of two matched objects ⟨*a ~ to this glove*⟩ **4** *archaic* a match, peer [ME, prob fr MLG *māt;* akin to OE *gemetta* guest at one's table, *mete* food – more at MEAT]

³**mate** vt **1** to join or fit together; couple **2a** to join together as mates **b** to provide a mate for **3** *archaic* to equal, match ~ vi **1** to become mated ⟨*gears that ~ well*⟩ **2** to copulate

**maté, mate** /'matay, 'mahtay/ n **1** a tealike aromatic beverage drunk chiefly in S America **2** a S American holly (*Ilex paraguayensis*); *also* its leaves and shoots used in making maté [Fr & AmerSp; Fr *maté*, fr AmerSp *mate*, fr Quechua]

**matelassé** /'mat'lasay/ adj, of a textile having a raised or embossed design (e g of quilting) [Fr, fr pp of *matelasser* to cushion, quilt, fr *matelas* mattress, fr MF *matelas, materas* – more at MATTRESS]

**matelot** /'mat(ə)loh/ n, Br informal SAILOR 1b [Fr, fr MF, fr MD *mattenoot*, fr *matte* mat, bed + *noot* companion]

**matelote** /'matəloht/, **matelotte** /-lot/ n (a method of cooking) a stew made usu with pieces of fish in a seasoned wine and onion sauce [Fr *matelote*, fr *matelot*]

**mater** /'maytə/ n, chiefly Br humorous a mother [L – more at MOTHER]

**materfamilias** /,maytəfə'mili-əs/ n a female head of a household [L, fr *mater* + *familias*, archaic gen of *familia* household – more at FAMILY]

¹**material** /mə'tiəri-əl/ adj **1a(1)** (consisting) of or derived from matter; *esp* physical ⟨*the ~ world*⟩ **a(2)** bodily ⟨*~ needs*⟩ **b** of matter or content rather than form ⟨*~ cause*⟩ **2** important, significant – often + *to* ⟨*facts ~ to the investigation*⟩ **3** concerned with physical rather than spiritual things ⟨*~ progress*⟩ **4** relevant to the issue before a law court; *esp* offering or being very significant facts or testimony [ME *materiel*, fr MF & LL; MF, fr LL *materialis*, fr L *materia* matter – more at MATTER] – **materially** adv, **materialness** n, **materiality** n

*synonyms* **Material, physical,** and **corporeal** differ in emphasis when describing things which have actual, perceptible existence. **Material** stresses substance as opposed to the spiritual, ideal, or otherwise intangible ⟨**material** *possessions*⟩ ⟨*the* **material** *world which surrounds us*⟩. **Physical** chiefly stresses an opposition to mental, metaphysical, or imaginary, and is applied particularly to what can be perceived by the senses or measured in some way ⟨**physical** *laws*⟩. It may also apply to the body, as opposed to the mind or spirit ⟨**physical** *exhaustion*⟩. **Corporeal** adds to **physical** the quality of tangibility and of having a body, or something like one ⟨*energy has* **physical** *but not* **corporeal** *existence*⟩. Used with reference to the human body, it stresses a contrast with immaterial or spiritual ⟨*human beings are said to have spiritual as well as corporeal existence*⟩. See RELEVANT. Compare PERCEPTIBLE *antonym* immaterial

²**material** n **1a(1)** the elements, constituents, or substances of which something is composed or can be made **a(2)** matter that has usu specified qualities which give it individuality ⟨*the table was covered with a film of sticky ~*⟩ ⟨*explosive ~s*⟩ **b(1)** data that may be worked into a more finished form – compare RAW MATERIAL **b(2)** a person or people considered with a view to his/her/their potential for successful development or training in a specified sphere of activity ⟨*I don't think he's officer ~*⟩ **c** MATTER 4 **d** cloth **2a** pl apparatus necessary for doing or making something **b** MATÉRIEL (military equipment)

**materialism** /mə'tiəri̇əliz(ə)m/ n **1a** a theory that only physical matter is real and that all processes and phenomena can be explained by reference to it – compare IDEALISM **b** a doctrine that the highest values lie in material well-being and progress **c** a doctrine that political and social change is caused by change in the material and economic basis of society – compare DIALECTICAL MATERIALISM, HISTORICAL MATERIALISM **2** a preoccupation with or stress upon material rather than intellectual or spiritual things – **materialist** n or adj, **materialistic** adj, **materialistically** adv

**materialization, -isation** /mə,tiəriəlie'zaysh(ə)n/ n **1** the action of materializing or becoming materialized **2** something that has been materialized; *esp* an apparition

**material·ize, -ise** /mə'tiəri-ə,liez/ vt **1a** to make material ⟨*materializing an idea in words*⟩ **b** to cause to appear in bodily form ⟨*~ the spirits of the dead*⟩ **2** to cause to be materialistic ~ vi **1** to assume bodily form **2a** to come into existence; become tangible ⟨*promises of money which never ~d*⟩ **b** to put in an appearance; *esp* TURN UP ⟨*agreed to meet at seven but he failed to ~*⟩ *synonyms* see HAPPEN – **materializer** n

**materia medica** /mə,tiəriə 'medikə/ n taking pl vb **1** substances used in the composition of medical remedies; drugs, medicine **2a** the branch of medical science that deals with the sources, nature, properties, and preparation of drugs **b** a written account of materia medica [NL, lit., medical matter]

**matériel,** NAm chiefly **materiel** /mə,tieri'el/ n equipment, apparatus, and supplies used by an organization or institution (e g the armed forces) [Fr *matériel*, fr *matériel*, adj]

**maternal** /mə'tuhnl/ adj **1** (characteristic) of a mother; motherly **2a** related through a mother ⟨*his ~ aunt*⟩ **b** inherited or derived from the female parent ⟨*~ genes*⟩ [ME, fr MF *maternel*, fr L *maternus*, fr *mater* mother] – **maternally** adv, **maternalism** n, **maternalistic** adj

¹**maternity** /mə'tuhnəti/ n **1a** the quality or state of being a mother; motherhood **b** the qualities of a mother; motherliness **2** a hospital department designed for the care of women before and during childbirth and for the care of newborn babies

²**maternity** adj designed for wear during pregnancy ⟨*a ~ dress*⟩

**mateship** /'maytship/ n, Austr good fellowship between friends and working companions; camaraderie ⟨*men ... live in a cocoon of ~ and mother love* – Helen Jarvis⟩

¹**matey** /'mayti/ *n, chiefly Br* ²MATE 1c [²*mate* + ⁴-*y*]
²**matey** *adj, chiefly Br informal* on good terms; friendly [²*mate* + ¹*ly*] – **mateyness, matiness** *n*
**math** /math/ *n, NAm* mathematics
**mathematic-, mathematico-** *comb form* mathematical and ⟨mathematico*logical*⟩
**mathematical** /,mathə'matikl/ *also* **mathematic** *adj* 1a of, using, or consistent with mathematics **b** designed for use in connection with mathematics ⟨*slide rules and other* ~ *instruments*⟩ 2 rigorously exact; precise 3 possible but highly improbable ⟨*only a* ~ *chance*⟩ [L *mathematicus*, fr Gk *mathēmatikos*, fr *mathēmat-, mathēma* learning, mathematics, fr *manthanein* to learn; akin to Goth *mundon* to pay attention, Skt *medhā* intelligence] – **mathematically** *adv*
**mathematical induction** *n* INDUCTION 2c (type of proof)
**mathematical logic** *n* SYMBOLIC LOGIC
**mathematician** /,mathəmə'tish(ə)n/ *n* a specialist or expert in mathematics
**mathematic·ize, -ise** /,mathə'matisiez/ *vt* to express in mathematical form – **mathematicization** *n*
**mathematics** /,mathə'matiks/ *n* 1 *taking sing vb* the science of numbers and their operations, interrelations, combinations, generalizations, and abstractions and of space configurations and their structure, measurement, transformations, and generalizations 2 *taking sing or pl vb* the mathematics or mathematical operations involved in a particular problem, field of study, etc ⟨*the* ~ *of physical chemistry*⟩
**mathemat·ize, -ise** /'mathəmətiez/ *vt* to mathematicize – **mathematization** *n*
**maths** /maths/ *n taking sing or pl vb, chiefly Br informal* mathematics
**matin, mattin** /'matin/, **matinal** /'matinl/ *adj* of matins or early morning
**matinee, matinée** /'matinay/ *n* a daytime, esp afternoon, performance of a musical or dramatic production [Fr *matinée*, lit., morning, fr OF, fr *matin* morning, fr L *matutinum*, fr neut of *matutinus* of the morning, fr *Matuta*, goddess of morning; akin to L *maturus* ripe – more at MATURE]
**matinee coat** *n, Br* a short coat worn by babies
**matinee idol** *n* a handsome actor romantically appealing to women – used esp of actors of the 1930s and 1940s
**matinee jacket** *n, Br* MATINEE COAT
**matins, mattins** /'matinz/ *n taking sing or pl vb, often cap* 1 the first of the seven CANONICAL HOURS (prayer services observed daily), originally observed at night, but now often recited at dawn with LAUDS 2 MORNING PRAYER [ME *matines*, fr OF, fr LL *matutinae*, fr L, fem pl of *matutinus*]
  *usage* The spelling **mattins** is used more in the Church of England than elsewhere.
**matr-, matri-, matro-** *comb form* mother ⟨matri*arch*⟩ ⟨matro*nymic*⟩ [L *matr-, matri-*, fr *matr-, mater*]
**matriarch** /'maytri,ahk/ *n* 1 a woman who rules a family, group, or state; *specif* a mother who is the head and ruler of her family 2 an old and venerated woman – **matriarchal** *adj*
**matriarchate** /'maytri,ahkət, -kayt/ *n* 1 a matriarchal family or society 2 a theoretical stage in primitive society in which matriarchs hold the chief authority
**matriarchy** /'maytri,ahki/ *n* 1 a matriarchate 2 a system of social organization in which the female is the head of the family and descent and inheritance are traced through the female line
**matric** /mə'trik/ *n, Br informal* MATRICULATION 2
**matricide** /'maytri,sied/ *n* (the act of) one who kills his/her mother [L *matricida* & *matricidium*, fr *matr-* + *-cida* & *-cidium* – more at -CIDE] – **matricidal** *adj*
**matriclinous** /,matri'klienəs/, **matriclinic** /-klinik/ *adj, of an animal or plant* showing inherited characteristics of the female parent – compare PATRICLINOUS
**matriculate** /mə'trikyoolayt/ *vt* 1 to admit as a member of a body, esp a college or university 2 to record (heraldic arms) in an official register ~ *vi* (to become eligible) to be matriculated [ML *matriculatus*, pp of *matriculare*, fr LL *matricula* public roll, dim. of *matric-, matrix* list, fr L, womb] – **matriculant** *n*, **matriculator** *n*
**matriculation** /mə,trikyoo'laysh(ə)n/ *n* 1 matriculating or being matriculated 2 *Br* a former qualifying examination for university entrance now superseded by the General Certificate of Education
**matrilineal** /,matri'lini·əl, ,maytri-/ *adj* of or tracing descent through the maternal line ⟨~ *society*⟩ – **matrilineally** *adv*

**matrilocal** /'matri,lohkl, 'maytri-/ *adj* of or having a marriage system in which the married couple live with the wife's family
**matrimonial** /,matri'mohniəl/ *adj* of marriage, the married state, or married people – **matrimonially** *adv*
**matrimony** /'matriməni/ *n* MARRIAGE 1a,2 [ME, fr MF *matremoine*, fr L *matrimonium*, fr *matr-, mater* mother, matron – more at MOTHER]
**matrimony vine** *n* any of various shrubs (genus *Lycium*) of the potato family with often showy flowers and bright berries
**matrix** /'maytriks/ *n, pl* **matrices** /-seez/, **matrixes** 1 a substance, environment, etc within which something else originates or develops 2a a mould from which a surface in relief (e g a piece of type or a stereotype) is made by pouring or pressing **b** a photographic negative of a type character that forms the image of the character in making printing plates **c** an engraved or inscribed die or stamp **d** an impression of a gramophone record used to mass-produce duplicates of the original 3a the natural material (e g rock) in which a fossil, metal, gem, crystal, or pebble is embedded **b** material in which something is enclosed or embedded (e g for protection or study) 4a(1) the substance in which tissue cells (e g of bone or CONNECTIVE TISSUE) are embedded a(2) the substance in which specialized structures in an organ or organelle are embedded **b** the thickened tissue at the base of a fingernail or toenail from which new nail substance develops **c** an outer layer surrounding a CHROMOSOME (strand of gene-carrying material) **d** a body or substance on which a fungus or a lichen grows 5 the metal that is the major component of an alloy 6a a rectangular array of numbers or other mathematical elements that can be manipulated and transformed according to special mathematical rules and that can be used to find solutions to sets of simultaneous equations **b** something resembling a mathematical matrix, esp in rectangular arrangement of elements into rows and columns 7 *obs* the womb [L, womb, fr *matr-, mater*]
**matrix printer** *n* a printer that uses a character-sized matrix of needles for printing and forms each character from dots printed by the needles
**matrix sentence** *n, linguistics* that one of a pair of joined sentences that maintains its essential external structure (e g "the book is gone" in "the book that I want is gone")
**matro-** *comb form* – see MATR-
**matron** /'maytrən/ *n* 1a a usu mature, dignified or staid married woman; *esp* a middle-aged woman with children **b** a woman in charge of living arrangements in a school, residential home, etc **c** *NAm* a wardress in a prison 2 *Br* a woman in charge of the nursing in a hospital – not now used technically [ME *matrone*, fr MF, fr L *matrona*, fr *matr-, mater*] – **matronal** *adj*, **matronhood, matronship** *n*, **matronlike** *adj*
**matron·ize, -ise** /'maytrəniez/ *vt* 1 to make matronly 2 to superintend as a matron; chaperone
**matronly** /'maytrənli/ *adj* of or suitable for a matron; *esp* staid or portly – **matronliness** *n*
**matron of honour** *n* a bride's principal married wedding attendant
**matronymic** /,matrə'nimik/ *n* a name derived from that of the bearer's mother or maternal ancestor – called also METRONYMIC; compare PATRONYMIC [*matr-* + *-onymic* (as in *patronymic*)]
¹**matt, mat, matte** /mat/ *vt* 1 to make (e g metal or colour) matt 2 to give (a picture) a matt
²**matt, mat, matte** *adj* lacking lustre or gloss; *esp* having an even surface free from shine or highlights ⟨~ *metals*⟩ ⟨*a* ~ *white face*⟩ [Fr *mat*, fr OF, defeated, fr L *mattus* drunk; akin to L *madēre* to be wet – more at MEAT]
³**matt, mat, matte** *n* 1 a border round a picture acting as a frame or as a contrast between picture and frame 2 a roughened or dull finish (e g on gilt or paint) [Fr *mat* dull colour, unpolished surface, fr ²*mat, adj*]
**matte** /mat/ *n* an impure mixture of SULPHIDES (sulphur-containing chemical compounds) formed during the process (SMELTING) of heating ores to obtain metals (e g copper, lead, or nickel) [Fr]
¹**matter** /'matə/ *n* 1a a subject of interest or concern **b** a subject of disagreement or proceedings at law **c** something to be dealt with; an affair, concern ⟨*a few personal* ~s *to take care of*⟩ ⟨*it's no laughing* ~⟩ **d** material (for treatment) in thought, fields of knowledge, discourse, or writing ⟨*style is elegant, but the* ~ *is so dull*⟩ ⟨~s *of faith*⟩ **e(1)** that part of a legal case which deals with facts rather than principles of law **e(2)** something to be proved in a court of law **f** a condition affecting a person or

# mat

thing usu unfavourably ⟨*what's the* ~?⟩ **g** a source, esp of feeling or emotion ⟨~ *for wonder*⟩ **2** the content of or ideas contained in verbal or written material as distinguished from the form in which this content is expressed **3a** the substance of which a physical object is composed **b** physical substance occupying space and having mass **c** something of a particular kind or for a particular purpose ⟨*vegetable* ~⟩ ⟨*reading* ~⟩ **d** material (e g faeces, urine, or pus) discharged from the living body **4** the formless substance that in Aristotelian philosophy can take form to become any existing thing **5** a more or less definite amount or quantity ⟨*a* ~ *of 10 years*⟩ **6a** something written or printed **b(1)** type set up for printing **b(2)** text material, esp typed sheets as distinguished from illustrations **7** *obs* sensible or serious material as distinguished from nonsense or drollery ⟨*more* ~, *less art* – Shak⟩ [ME *matere*, fr OF, fr L *materia* matter, physical substance, fr *mater* mother] – **as a matter of fact** in truth; actually – **for that matter** so far as that is concerned – **in the matter of** concerning; IN REGARD TO – **no matter 1** that is of no importance ⟨*I've missed the bus.* No matter, *I'll come and collect you*⟩ **2** regardless or irrespective of ⟨*would be calm* no matter *what the provocation*⟩ – see also not MINCE **matters**

²**matter** *vi* **1** to be of importance **2** to form or discharge pus; SUPPURATE ⟨~ ing *wound*⟩

**matter of course** *n* something routine or to be expected as a natural or logical consequence

,**matter-of-'fact** *adj* adhering to or concerned with fact; *esp* not fanciful or imaginative – **matter-of-factly** *adv*, **matter-of-factness** *n*

**mattery** /'matəri/ *adj* producing or containing pus or material resembling pus ⟨*eyes all* ~⟩

**Matthean, Matthaean** /mə'thee-ən/ *adj* (characteristic) of the apostle Matthew or the Gospel according to Matthew [LL *Mattheus, Matthaeus* Matthew]

**Matthew** /'mathyooh/ *n* – see BIBLE table [*Matthew* (fr Fr *Mathieu*, fr LL *Matthaeus*, fr Gk *Matthaios*, fr Heb *Mattithyāh*), Christian apostle and evangelist]

**mattin** /'matin/ *adj* MATIN

¹**matting** /'mating/ *n* material (e g hemp) for mats ⟨*coconut* ~⟩ **2** mats ⟨*rush* ~ *on the floor*⟩ [fr gerund of ²*mat*]

²**matting** *n* a dull lustreless surface (e g on gilding, metalwork, or satin) [fr gerund of ¹*matt*]

**mattins** /'matinz/ *n taking sing or pl vb, often cap* matins

**mattock** /'matək/ *n* a digging tool with a head like that of a pick at one end and usu a blade like that of an axe or ADZE at the other [ME *mattok*, fr OE *mattuc*]

**mattress** /'matris/ *n* **1** a fabric case filled with resilient material (e g feathers, foam rubber, or an arrangement of coiled springs) used as, or on, a bed **2a** a mass of interwoven brush and poles to protect a bank from erosion; *also* a similar mass serving as a foundation in soft ground **b** a concrete slab or raft used as a foundation or footing [ME *materas*, fr OF, fr Ar *maṭrah* place where something is thrown]

**maturate** /'matyoorayt/ *vt* to bring to maturity ~ *vi* **1** to mature **2** SUPPURATE – **maturative** *adj*

**maturation** /,matyoo'raysh(ə)n/ *n* **1** the process of becoming mature **2** the final stages during the development of cells, tissues, or organs in which they differentiate and become specialized **3** the entire process by which GAMETES (sperm or eggs) are produced and which includes both MEIOSIS (division of a cell to form four new cells) and any physiological and structural changes that fit the gamete for its future role – **maturational** *adj*

¹**mature** /mə'tyooə/ *adj* **1** based on slow careful consideration ⟨*a* ~ *judgment*⟩ **2a** having completed natural growth and development; ripe **b** having attained a final or desired state ⟨~ *wine*⟩ **3a** (characteristic) of or being in a condition of full or adult development **b** older or relatively more advanced physically, emotionally, or mentally than others of his/her kind **4** due for payment ⟨*a* ~ *loan*⟩ **5** *of a land surface or feature* being in the middle stage of a cycle of erosion; characterized by erosion caused by running water so that slopes predominate over flat areas [ME, fr L *maturus* ripe; akin to L *mane* in the morning, *manus* good] – **maturely** *adv*, **matureness** *n*

²**mature** *vt* to bring to maturity or completion ~ *vi* **1** to become mature **2** to become due for payment ⟨*a savings bond that* ~s *in 10 years*⟩

**mature student** *n* an older-than-usual entrant to British higher education

**maturity** /mə'tyooərəti/ *n* **1** the quality or state of being

mature; *esp* full development **2** the date when a bond, note, insurance policy, etc becomes due

**matutinal** /,matyoo'tienl/ *adj, chiefly formal* of or occurring in the morning; early [LL *matutinalis*, fr L *matutinus* – more at MATINEE] – **matutinally** *adv*

**matzo** /'matsoh/ *n, pl* **matzoth** /'matsot, -soth/, **matzos** (a wafer of) unleavened bread eaten esp at the Passover [Yiddish *matse*, fr Heb *maṣṣāh*]

**maud** /mawd/ *n* a travelling-rug or Scots shepherd's shawl of grey striped wool plaid [prob fr the forename *Maud*]

**maudlin** /'mawdlin/ *adj* **1** weakly, tearfully, and gushingly sentimental **2** drunk enough to be emotional and foolish [*Maudlin* Mary Magdalen, often depicted as a weeping, penitent sinner – more at MAGDALEN]

**maugre** /'mawgə/ *prep, archaic* IN SPITE OF [ME, fr OF *maugré*, fr *maugré* displeasure, fr *mau, mal* evil + *gré* pleasure]

¹**maul** /mawl/ *n* **1** a heavy two-handed hammer often with a wooden head used esp for driving wedges or piles **2** a situation in Rugby Union football, during the run of play, in which one or more players from each team close round the player carrying the ball who tries to get the ball out to his own team – called also LOOSE SCRUM; compare RUCK, SET SCRUM **3** a confused and noisy struggle; brawl [(1) ME *malle*, fr OF *mail*, fr L *malleus*; akin to L *molere* to grind – more at MEAL; (2, 3) ²*maul*]

²**maul** *vt* **1a** to beat, bruise **b** *esp of an animal* to attack and tear the flesh of **c** to handle clumsily; paw **2** to handle roughly; criticize heavily ⟨*the critics* ~ed *the play*⟩ – **mauler** *n*

**maulstick, mahlstick** /'mawl,stik/ *n* a stick used by painters to support and steady the hand holding the brush [part trans of D *maalstok*, fr obs D *malen* to paint + D *stok* stick]

**Mau Mau** /'mow ,mow/ *n* a secret political organization founded in 1952 with the aim of driving Europeans out of Kenya by terrorist methods [origin unknown]

**maun** /mawn/ *verbal auxiliary, chiefly Scot* must [ME *man*, fr ON, will, shall]

**maund** /mawnd/ *n* any of various Asian, esp Indian, units of weight; *esp* a unit equal to 37.4 kilograms (82.28 pounds) [Hindi *man*]

**maunder** /'mawndə/ *vi* **1** to wander or act slowly and idly **2** to speak in a rambling or indistinct manner – often + *on* ⟨*must you go* ~ing *on about it?*⟩ **3** *dial Br* to grumble [prob imit] – **maunderer** *n*

**maundy** /'mawndi/ *n, often cap* **1** the washing of the feet of poor people on MAUNDY THURSDAY observed by some churches as a commemoration of Jesus washing his disciples' feet **2** (the distribution of) maundy money [ME *maunde*, fr OF *mandé*, fr L *mandatum* command – more at MANDATE; fr Jesus' words in John 13:34]

**maundy money** *n, often cap 1st or 1st & 2nd M* specially minted coins given to selected poor people by the British Sovereign in a ceremony on Maundy Thursday

**Maundy Thursday** *n* the Thursday before Easter observed in commemoration of the LAST SUPPER

**mausoleum** /,mawsə'lee-əm/ *n, pl* **mausoleums** *also* **mausolea** /-'lee-ə/ **1** a large and elaborate tomb; *esp* a usu stone building with places for entombment of the dead above ground **2** a large gloomy usu ornate building, room, or structure [L, fr Gk *mausōleion*, fr *Mausōlos* Mausolus †*ab* 353 BC, ruler of Caria in Asia Minor for whom a magnificent tomb was erected]

**mauve** /mohv/ *n* **1** any of a range of pinkish purple to bluish purple colours **2** a dyestuff that produces a mauve colour [Fr, mallow, fr L *malva*]

**maverick** /'mav(ə)rik/ *n* **1** an independent individual who refuses to conform with his/her group **2** *NAm* an unbranded range animal; *esp* a motherless calf [Samuel A *Maverick* †1870 US pioneer who did not brand his calves]

**mavis** /'mayvis/ *n, chiefly poetic* SONG THRUSH [ME, fr MF *mauvis*]

**mavourneen** *also* **mavournin** /mə'vooəneen/ *n, Irish* my darling [IrGael *mo mhuirnīn*, fr *mo* my + *muirnīn* darling]

**maw** /maw/ *n* **1a(1)** an animal's stomach or CROP (first chamber in the digestive tract of a bird) **a(2)** the last of the four stomachs of a ruminant (e g a cow) **b** the throat, gullet, or jaws, esp of a voracious flesh-eating animal **2** something resembling a maw, esp in being gaping or tending to swallow things up ⟨*huge sums of money have disappeared into the* ~ *of bureaucracy*⟩ [ME, fr OE *maga*; akin to OHG *mago* stomach, Lith *makas* purse]

**mawkin** /'mawkin/ *n, dial Br* MALKIN (slut)

**mawkish** /'mawkish/ *adj* **1** having an insipid often unpleasant taste **2** falsely or feebly sentimental, esp in a maudlin way [ME *mawke* maggot, fr ON *mathkr* – more at MAGGOT] – **mawkishly** *adv*, **mawkishness** *n*

**maxi** /'maksi/ *n, pl* **maxis** a floor-length woman's coat, skirt, etc – compare MINI, MIDI [*maxi-*]

**maxi-** /maksi-/ *comb form* **1** extra long; *esp* floor-length ⟨maxi-*skirt*⟩ **2** extra large ⟨maxi-*budget*⟩ [fr *maximum*, by analogy to *minimum*:*mini-*]

**maxilla** /mak'silə/ *n, pl* **maxillae** /-lie/, **maxillas 1a** JAW 1a **b(1)** an upper jaw, esp of mammals including humans, in which the bony elements are closely joined **b(2)** either of two MEMBRANE BONE elements of the upper jaw bearing most of the teeth in VERTEBRATE animals and humans **2** either of the first pair or any of the first two pairs of mouthparts behind the MANDIBLES in insects, centipedes, shrimps, and related animals [L, dim. of *mala* jaw] – **maxillary** *adj or n*

**maxilliped** /mak'sili,ped/ *n* any of the first three pairs of mouthparts of shrimps, crabs, lobsters, etc that are situated immediately behind the maxillae and that help transfer food to the mouth [ISV] – **maxillipedary** *adj*

**maxillipede** /mak'sili,peed/ *n* a maxilliped

**maxillo-** /maksiloh-/ *comb form* maxillary and ⟨maxillo*facial*⟩ [L *maxilla*]

**maxillofacial** /,maksiloh'faysh(ə)l/ *adj* of or treating the maxilla and the face ⟨a ~ *surgeon*⟩

**maxim** /'maksim/ *n* (a succinct expression of) a general truth, fundamental principle, or rule of conduct [ME *maxime*, fr MF, fr ML *maxima*, fr L, fem of *maximus*, superl of *magnus* great – more at MUCH]

**maximal** /'maksiml/ *adj* **1** most comprehensive; complete **2** being an upper limit; highest; *specif, of an element in a mathematical set* being greater than or equal to every other element in the set – **maximally** *adv*

**maximalist** /'maksiml,ist/ *n* one who favours immediate and direct action without compromise to secure all of his/her goals; *specif* a socialist advocating the immediate seizure of power by revolutionary means – compare MINIMALIST

**Maxim gun** *n* an obsolete single-barrelled water-cooled automatically firing machine gun [Sir Hiram Stevens *Maxim* †1916 Br (US-born) inventor]

**maximin** /'maksimin/ *n* the maximum of a mathematical set of minimum values (MINIMA); *esp* the largest of a set of minimum possible gains each of which occurs in the least advantageous outcome of a strategy followed by a participant in a situation governed by the THEORY OF GAMES – compare MINIMAX [*maximum* + *minimum*] – **maximin** *adj*

**maxim·ize, -ise** /'maksi,miez/ *vt* **1** to increase or use to a maximum or to the highest possible degree **2** to find a maximum value of (a mathematical function) *antonym* minimize – **maximizer** *n*, **maximization, maximization** *n*

**maximum** /'maksiməm/ *n, pl* **maxima** /-mə/, **maximums 1a** the greatest quantity or degree attainable or attained **b** the period of highest, greatest, or most extreme development **2** an upper limit allowed by law or other authority ⟨*driving with blood alcohol over the* ~⟩ **3** the largest element of a mathematical set; *esp* the largest value assumed by a CONTINUOUS function on a closed interval [L, neut of *maximus*] – **maximum** *adj*

**maximum likelihood** *n* a method for estimating statistical quantities (e g the MEAN and VARIANCE) by choosing an ESTIMATOR (statistical function) that maximizes the probability of obtaining the observed values of the data

**maxixe** /mə'sheesh, mak'seeks, mə'sheeshay/ *n* a Brazilian dance that was the forerunner of the tango [Pg]

**maxwell** /'makswəl, -wel/ *n* a unit of MAGNETIC FLUX (strength of a MAGNETIC FIELD) in the CENTIMETRE-GRAM-SECOND system equal to a flux of one gauss per square centimetre; $10^8$ weber [James Clerk *Maxwell* †1879 Sc physicist]

**¹may** /may/ *verbal auxiliary, pres sing & pl* **may**; *past* **might** /miet/ **1a** have permission to ⟨*you* ~ *go now*⟩; have liberty to – used almost interchangeably with *can* but now sometimes considered authoritarian except in the first person ⟨*what's this,* ~ *I ask?*⟩ **b** be in some degree likely to ⟨*you* ~ *be right*⟩ ⟨*the road* ~ *well be closed*⟩ **2** – used to express a wish or desire, esp in prayer, cursing, or blessing ⟨*long* ~ *he reign*⟩ **3** – used to express purpose or expectation ⟨*I laugh that I* ~ *not weep*⟩, contingency ⟨*he'll do his duty come what* ~⟩, or concession ⟨*he* ~ *be slow but he is thorough*⟩; used in questions to emphasize ironic uncertainty ⟨*and who* ~ *you be?*⟩ **4** shall, must – used in law where the sense, purpose, or policy requires this

interpretation **5** *archaic* have the ability to; can [ME (1 & 3 sing. pres indic), fr OE *mæg*; akin to OHG *mag* (1 & 3 sing. pres indic) have power, am able (infin *magan*), Gk *mēchos* means, expedient]

**usage** Traditionally, **may** and **might** have different meanings when used with the perfect tense. Compare ⟨*he* **may** *have* (= perhaps he has) *been drowned*⟩ ⟨*he* **might** *have been* (= but he was not) *drowned*⟩. An increasing modern tendency to use **may** for **might** in these and similar situations ⟨*if I hadn't been there he* **may** *have been drowned*⟩ ⟨*try as they* **may**, *they had no alternative but to give in*⟩ is widely disliked. See ¹CAN

**²may** *n, archaic* a maiden [ME, fr OE *mæg* kinsman, kinswoman, maiden]

**May** *n* **1** the 5th month of the year according to the GREGORIAN CALENDAR (standard Western calendar) – see MONTH table **2** *often not cap* the early vigorous blooming part of human life; prime **3** the springtime festivities of May Day ⟨*Queen of the* ~⟩ **4** *not cap* **4a** (the blossom of) hawthorn **b** flowering branches, esp of hawthorn, used as decoration on May Day [ME, fr OF & L; OF *mai*, fr L *Maius*, fr *Maia*, Roman goddess]

**maya** /'mie·ə/ *n* the material world as perceived by the senses, held in Hinduism to conceal the unity of absolute being; *broadly* deceptive appearance or illusion [Skt *māyā*]

**Maya** /'mie·ə/ *n, pl* **Mayas,** *esp collectively* **Maya 1** a member of a group of American Indian peoples chiefly of the Yucatán peninsula who before the discovery of America had established a developed civilization **2a** any of the languages of the ancient Maya peoples **b** YUCATEC; *esp* the older form of that language [Sp]

**Mayan** /mie·ən/ *adj or n* **1** (of) a Maya **2** (of) a language of any of the Mayas

**mayapple** /'may,apl/ *n* (the edible egg-shaped yellow fruit of) a N American plant (*Podophyllum peltatum*), of the barberry family [*May*]

**maybe** /'may,bee/ *adv* perhaps [ME, fr (*it*) *may be*]

**maybug** /'may,bug/ *n* a cockchafer

**Mayday** /'may,day/ – used as an international radiotelephone distress signal [Fr *m'aider* help me]

**May Day** *n* May 1 celebrated as a springtime festival and in many countries as a public holiday in honour of working people

**mayest** /'mayist/, **mayst** /mayst/ *archaic pres 2 sing of* MAY

**mayflower** /-,flowə/ *n* any of various spring-blooming plants

**mayfly** /-,flie/ *n* any of an order (Ephemeroptera) of insects with an aquatic larva and a short-lived fragile adult having membranous wings and two or three long slender bristles at the hind end of the body

**mayhap** /'mayhap/ *adv, archaic* perhaps [fr the phrase (*it*) *may hap*, fr ¹*may* + ²*hap*]

**mayhem** /'mayhem/ *n* **1** needless or wilful damage **2** a state of great confusion or disorder [ME *mayme* the crime of depriving a person of a limb, fr AF *mahaim*, fr OF, loss of a limb, fr *maynier* to maim]

**maying** /'maying/ *n, often cap* the traditional celebrating of May Day

**mayn't** /maynt/ may not

**mayonnaise** /,mayə'nayz/ *n* a thick dressing or cold sauce (e g for salad or salmon) made with egg yolks, vegetable oil, and vinegar or lemon juice [Fr, perh fr *mahonnais* of Mahón, fr *Mahón*, port in Minorca]

**mayor** /meə/ *n, fem* **mayoress** an official elected or appointed to act as chief executive or nominal head of a city or borough [ME *maire*, fr OF, fr L *major* greater – more at MAJOR] – **mayoral** *adj*, **mayorship** *n*

**mayoralty** /'meərəlti/ *n* the (term of) office of a mayor [ME *mairaltee*, fr MF *mairalté*, fr OF, fr *maire*]

**mayoress** /'meəris/ *n* the wife of a mayor; *also* someone fulfilling the role of hostess at mayoral functions

**maypole** /'may,pohl/ *n* a tall painted flower-wreathed pole around which people dance on May Day

**May queen** *n* a girl chosen to preside over a May-Day festival

**mayst** /mayst/ *verbal auxiliary* mayest

**Maytide** /'maytied/ *n* the month of May

**Maytime** /'maytiem/ *n* maytide

**mayweed** /'mayweed/ *n* STINKING MAYWEED

**May Week** *n* a Cambridge university festival period in June with boat races between the colleges, balls, etc – compare EIGHTS WEEK

**mazaedium** /mə'zeediəm, ,mazə'eediəm/ *n, pl* **mazaedia** /-diə/ a spore-producing organ (e g of some lichens) consisting of a

# maz

powdery mass of spores in an enclosing sac [NL, fr Gk *maza* lump, mass + L *aedes* temple, house – more at MASS, EDIFY]

**mazard, mazzard** /'mazəd/ *n* **1** a mazer **2** *archaic* the head, face [by alter.]

**mazarine** /ˌmazə'reen, 'mazərin/ *adj or n* (of) a deep rich blue colour [perh fr Jules *Mazarin* †1661 Fr (It-born) cardinal & statesman, or Duchesse de *Mazarin* †1699 Fr noblewoman]

**¹maze** /mayz/ *vt, archaic* to bewilder, perplex △ maize [ME *mazen*, prob fr (assumed) OE *masian* to confuse; perh akin to Sw *masa* to be sluggish] – **mazement** *n*

**²maze** *n* **1a** (a drawn representation of) a network of paths (e g separated by hedges or turf) designed to confuse and puzzle those who attempt to walk through it; *also* a similar shaped construction used in learning experiments usu with rats or mice **b** something intricately or confusingly elaborate or complicated ⟨*a ~ of regulations*⟩ **2** *archaic* a state of bewilderment – **mazy** *adj*, **mazelike** *adj*

**mazer** /'mayzə/ *n* a large drinking bowl used in former times and originally of a hard wood [ME *mazere*, of Gmc origin; akin to OHG *masar* gnarled outgrowth on a tree]

**mazuma** /mə'zoohmə/ *n, NAm slang* money [Yiddish *mezumen*, fr Heb *mēzūmān* fixed, appointed]

**mazurka** *also* **mazourka** /mə'zuhkə/ *n* (music for or in the rhythm of) a Polish folk dance in moderate time with three beats to the bar [Fr, fr Polish, fr *Mazur* inhabitant of the province Mazovia]

**mazzard, mazard** /'mazəd/ *n* SWEET CHERRY; *esp* wild or seedling sweet cherry used as a rootstock for grafting [origin unknown]

**mbira** /em'biərə/ *n* an African musical instrument that consists of a varying number of tuned metal or wooden strips, mounted on a gourd resonator or wooden box, that vibrate when plucked with the thumb or fingers [of Bantu origin]

**MC** *n* MASTER OF CEREMONIES

**'M-,day** *n* a day on which a military mobilization is to begin [*mobilization day*]

**¹me** /mee/ *pron, objective case of* I ⟨*looked at ~*⟩ ⟨*fatter than ~*⟩ ⟨*it's ~*⟩ [ME, fr OE *mē;* akin to OHG *mih* me, L *me,* Gk *me,* Skt *mā*]

*usage* **1** As I, than I are preferable in formal writing to *as* **me***, than* **me***,* but **me***,* not I, should follow prepositions ⟨△ *a girl like* I⟩. **2** *It is* (or *it's*) **me/him/her/us/them** is more natural in speech than *it is* I/he/she/we/they ⟨*regardless of grammar, they all cried "That's him!"* – R H Barham⟩ though the subject pronouns should be used in formal writing, or where a verb follows ⟨*it was* I *who wrote the letter*⟩. See ⁴AS, ²THAN

**²me** *n* something suitable for me ⟨*that dress isn't really ~*⟩

**³me** *adj, substandard* my

**⁴me, mi** *n* the 3rd note of the scale in the SOL-FA method of representing the musical scale [*Me* alter. of *mi,* fr ML – more at GAMUT]

**mea culpa** /ˌmayah 'koolpah/ *n* a formal acknowledgment of personal guilt or error – often used interjectionally [L, through my fault]

**¹mead** /meed/ *n* a fermented alcoholic drink made of water, honey, malt, yeast, and sometimes spices [ME *mede,* fr OE *medu;* akin to OHG *metu* mead, Gk *methy* wine]

**²mead** *n, archaic or poetic* a meadow [ME *mede,* fr OE *mǣd*]

**meadow** /'medoh/, **meadowland** *n* a piece of grassland: **a** moist low-lying usu level ground often near a river **b** an area used for hay or grazing animals [ME *medwe,* fr OE *mǣdwe,* oblique case form of *mǣd;* akin to OE *māwan* to mow – more at MOW]

**meadow fescue** *n* a tall vigorous Eurasian grass (*Festuca pratarsis*) with broad flat leaves, widely cultivated for permanent pasture and hay

**meadow grass** *n* any of various grasses (e g of the genus *Poa*) that thrive in the presence of abundant moisture

**meadowlark** /'medoh,lahk/ *n* any of several N American songbirds (genus *Sturnella*) that are largely brown and buff with a yellow breast marked with a black crescent

**meadow pipit** /'pipit/ *n* a common African and Eurasian PIPIT (type of songbird) (*Anthus pratensis*) that has olive-brown and white plumage

**meadow rue** *n* any of a genus (*Thalictrum*) of plants of the buttercup family with leaves resembling those of RUE and clusters of small yellowish-green, purple, or white flowers

**meadow saffron** *n* COLCHICUM **1** (genus of plants); *esp* a European colchicum (*Colchicum autumnale*) – called also AUTUMN CROCUS

**meadowsweet** /'medoh,sweet/ *n* a tall Eurasian plant (*Filipendula ulmaria*) of the rose family with creamy-white fragrant flowers

**meagre,** *NAm chiefly* **meager** /'meegə/ *adj* **1** having little flesh; thin **2** lacking desirable qualities (e g richness or strength) ⟨*leading a ~ life*⟩ **3** deficient in quality or quantity ⟨*a ~ diet*⟩ ⟨*a ~ meal*⟩ [ME *megre,* fr MF *maigre,* fr L *macr-, macer* lean; akin to OE *mæger* lean, Gk *makros* long] – **meagrely** *adv,* **meagreness** *n*

**¹meal** /meel, mial/ *n* **1** the portion of food taken or provided at one time to satisfy appetite **2** (the time of) eating a meal [ME *meel* appointed time, meal, fr OE *mǣl;* akin to OHG *māl* time, L *metiri* to measure – more at MEASURE] – **make a meal of** *informal* to carry out in an unduly laborious way

**²meal** *n* **1** (a product resembling, esp in texture) the usu coarsely ground seeds of a cereal grass or pulse – compare FLOUR **2a** *Scot* oatmeal **b** *NAm* maize flour [ME *mele,* fr OE *melu;* akin to OHG *melo* meal, L *molere* to grind, Gk *mylē* mill]

**mealie** /'meeli/ *n, SAfr* (an ear of) maize [Afrik *mielie,* fr Pg *milho* millet, fr L *milium* – more at MILLET]

**meal moth** *n* a moth (*Pyralis farinalis*) that has a larva which is a serious pest of cereal products

**meals on wheels** *n taking sing or pl vb* a service providing meals for the housebound

**mealtime** /'mial,tiem, 'meel-/ *n* the usual time for a meal

**mealworm** /'mial,wuhm, 'meel-/ *n* the larva of various beetles (family Tenebrionidae) that infests and pollutes grain products; *esp* that of a black beetle (*Tenebrio molitor*) raised as food for insect-eating animals, for laboratory use, or as bait for fishing

**mealy** /'meeli/ *adj* **1** soft, dry, and crumbly **2** containing meal **3a** covered with meal or with fine granules **b** *esp of a horse* flecked with another colour **4** pallid, blanched ⟨*a ~ complexion*⟩ **5** MEALY-MOUTHED – **mealiness** *n*

**mealybug** /-,bug/ *n* any of numerous SCALE INSECTS (family Pseudococcidae) that have a white powdery covering and are destructive pests, esp of fruit trees

**mealy-'mouthed** *adj* unwilling to speak plainly or directly, esp when this may offend – **mealy-mouthedness** *n*

**¹mean** /meen/ *adj* **1** lacking distinction or eminence; humble ⟨*the ~est flower that blows* – William Wordsworth⟩; *specif* of low social position ⟨*of ~ birth*⟩ **2** merely ordinary – usu + neg ⟨*no ~ feat* – Benny Green⟩ **3** of poor shabby inferior quality or status ⟨*~er quarters of the city*⟩ **4** not honourable or worthy; base; *esp* SMALL-MINDED **5a** not generous; stingy **b** characterized by petty malice; spiteful, nasty ⟨*what a ~ trick to play*⟩ **6** *chiefly NAm* particularly bad-tempered, unpleasant, or disagreeable ⟨*that was a ~ storm last night*⟩ ⟨*the ~est horse I ever saw*⟩ **7** *NAm* being in low spirits or health ⟨*he felt ~*⟩ **8** *informal* excellent, impressive ⟨*blows a ~ trumpet* – Globe & Mail (Toronto)⟩ [ME *mene,* fr *imene,* fr OE *gemǣne;* akin to OHG *gimeini* common, L *communis* common, *munus* service, gift] – **meanly** *adj,* **meanness** *n*

*synonyms* **Mean, ignoble, low, abject, sordid, base,** and **vile** all describe what falls below accepted standards of human worth and dignity. **Mean** suggests a petty, ungenerous nature and implies small-mindedness. **Ignoble** stresses the lack of any noble qualities, while **low** implies a failure to meet basic standards of decency, and often involves meanly taking advantage of someone. **Abject** is the least derogatory of these terms, and implies an extremely humble or degraded situation or condition, often adding a strong sense of hopelessness or servility. **Sordid** adds corruption and squalor to the degradation of **abject. Base** is strongly condemnatory and implies self-seeking, dishonourable behaviour. **Vile** is stronger still, suggesting abhorrence for what is considered foul or depraved. See STINGY *antonyms* honourable, noble

**²mean** *vb* **meant** /ment/ *vt* **1** to have in mind as a purpose; intend ⟨*I ~ to go*⟩ ⟨*she ~*t *no offence*⟩ **2** to serve or intend to convey, produce, or indicate; signify ⟨*this ~s war*⟩ ⟨*red ~s danger*⟩ **3** to intend for a particular use or purpose ⟨*it isn't ~*t *to relieve pain*⟩ **4** to have significance or importance to the extent or degree of ⟨*her family ~s a lot to her*⟩ ⟨*health ~s everything*⟩ ~ *vi* to have an intended purpose – chiefly + *well* or *ill* ⟨*he ~s well*⟩ [ME *menen,* fr OE *mǣnan;* akin to OHG *meinen* to have in mind, OSlav *měniti* to mention]

*usage* One **means** something to happen, or **means** *that* something should happen, but one cannot correctly **mean** *for* something to happen ⟨△ *I didn't* **mean** *for you to know*⟩.

**³mean** *n* **1a** a middle point between extremes **b** a value that lies within a range of values and is estimated according to a prescribed law: e g **b(1)** ARITHMETIC MEAN **b(2)** EXPECTED VALUE **c**

either of the middle two terms of a proportion (e g *b* and *c* in *a:b::c:d*) **2** *taking sing or pl vb* that which enables a desired purpose to be achieved ⟨~s *of production*⟩; *also* the method used to attain an end ⟨*use any* ~s *at their disposal*⟩ **3** *pl* resources available for disposal; *esp* wealth ⟨*a man of* ~s⟩ [ME *mene*, fr MF *meien*, fr *meien*, adj] – **by all means** without doubt or hesitation; certainly ⟨*go ahead* by all means⟩ – **by means of** with the help or use of ⟨*escaped* by means of *a ladder*⟩ – **by no means** not at all; in no way ⟨*he is* by no means *rich*⟩

⁴**mean** *adj* **1** occupying a middle position; intermediate in space, order, time, kind, or degree **2** occupying a position about midway between extremes: e g **2a** near the average **b** being the mean of a set of values; average ⟨~ *temperature*⟩ [ME *mene*, fr MF *meien*, fr L *medianus* – more at MEDIAN]

¹**meander** /mi'andə/ *n* **1** a turn or winding of a stream **2** a winding path, course, or pattern [L *maeander*, fr Gk *maiandros*, fr *Maiandros* (now *Menderes*), river in Asia Minor] – **meandrous** *adj*

²**meander** *vi* **1** to follow a winding or intricate course **2** to wander aimlessly or casually without definite direction – **meanderer** *n*, **meandering** *adj*, **meanderingly** *adv*

**mean deviation** *n*, *statistics* the mean of the values of the numerical differences between the numbers of a set (e g statistical data) and their mean or MEDIAN (value in the middle of the range)

**mean distance** *n* the ARITHMETIC MEAN (average) of the maximum and minimum distances of a planet, satellite, or secondary star from its PRIMARY (that round which it orbits)

**mean free path** *n* the average distance travelled by a molecule in a gas between collisions with other molecules

**meanie, meany** /'meeni/ *n*, *informal* a narrow-minded or ungenerous person ⟨*you old* ~⟩ [¹*mean* + *-ie*, ⁴*-y*]

**meaning** /'meening/ *n* **1a** that which one intends to convey, esp by language **b** that which is conveyed, esp by language **2** something meant or intended; an aim ⟨*a mischievous* ~ *was apparent*⟩ **3** a significant quality; *esp* implication of a hidden or special significance ⟨*a glance full of* ~⟩ **4** sense, significance ⟨*the* ~ *of a dream*⟩ ⟨*the* ~ *of life*⟩ **5** *philosophy* **5a** CONNOTATION (set of properties implied by a term) **b** DENOTATION (reference of a term) – **meaning** *adj*, **meaningly** *adv*, **meaningful** *adj*, **meaningfully** *adv*, **meaningfulness** *n*

**meaningless** /'meeninglis/ *adj* devoid of meaning; futile – **meaninglessly** *adv*, **meaninglessness** *n*

**mean life** *n* the average time during which an atom, nucleus or other, usu unstable, system exists in a particular form

**mean solar time** *n* MEAN TIME

**mean square** *n*, *statistics* the ARITHMETIC MEAN (average) of the squares of a set of values

**mean square deviation** *n*, *statistics* VARIANCE 5 (measure of spread of a set of data)

**means test** /meenz/ *n* an examination of someone's financial state to determine his/her eligibility for public assistance, for a student grant for his/her child, etc

**mean sun** *n* a fictitious sun used for timekeeping that moves uniformly along the CELESTIAL EQUATOR (circle round an imaginary sphere representing the extent of the universe) and maintains a constant rate of apparent motion

**meant** /ment/ *adj* **1** SUPPOSED 2,3,4 **2** *Br* SUPPOSED 1b,1c ⟨*to get a mature student's place . . . you are* ~ *to have a minimum of five O-levels* – *Observer Magazine*⟩

¹**meantime** /'meen,tiem/ *n* the intervening time ⟨*in the* ~⟩

²**meantime** *adv* meanwhile

**mean time** *n* time that is based on the motion of the MEAN SUN and that has the mean solar second as its unit

**mean value theorem** *n*, *maths* a theorem in calculus: if a CONTINUOUS function of one variable is represented as a smooth curve on a closed interval and DIFFERENTIABLE on the interval minus its end points there is at least one point where the DERIVATIVE (slope) of the function is equal to the slope of the line joining the end points

¹**meanwhile** /'meen,wiel/ *n* meantime

²**meanwhile** *adv* **1** during the intervening time **2** during the same period ⟨~, *down on the farm . . .*⟩

**meany** /'meeni/ *n* a meanie

**measles** /'meezlz/ *n taking sing or pl vb* **1a** an infectious virus disease marked by a rash of distinct red circular spots **b** any of various rash-producing diseases (e g German measles) **2** infestation with or disease caused by larval parasitic worms in the muscles and tissues [(1) ME *meseles*, pl of *mesel* measles, spot

characteristic of measles, alter. (influenced by *mesel* leper) of *masel;* akin to MD *masel* spot characteristic of measles; (2) ME *mesel* infested with tapeworms, lit., leprous, fr OF, fr ML *misellus* leper, fr L, wretch, fr *misellus,* dim. of *miser* miserable]

**measly** /'meezli/ *adj* **1** infected with measles **2** containing larval parasitic worms ⟨~ *pork*⟩ **3** *informal* contemptibly small; *also* worthless

**measurable** /'mezh(ə)rəbl/ *adj* **1** capable of being measured; *specif* large or small enough to be measured **2** belonging to a class of sets on which a mathematical measure is defined – **measurably** *adv*, **measurableness, measurability** *n*

¹**measure** /'mezhə/ *n* **1a(1)** an appropriate or due portion ⟨*give them their just* ~⟩ **a(2)** a moderate extent, amount, or degree ⟨*a* ~ *of respectability*⟩ **a(3)** a fixed, suitable, or conceivable limit ⟨*wisdom beyond* ~⟩ **b(1)** the dimensions, capacity, or amount of something ascertained by measuring **b(2)** the character, nature, or capacity of somebody or something ascertained by assessment – used esp in *get the measure of* **b(3)** the width of a full line or column of type or printing **c** a measured quantity ⟨*a* ~ *of whisky*⟩ ⟨*short* ~⟩ **2a** an instrument or utensil for measuring **b(1)** a standard or unit of measurement ⟨*the metre is a* ~ *of length*⟩ **b(2)** a system of standard units of measure ⟨*metric* ~⟩ ⟨*liquid* ~⟩ **3** the act or process of measuring **4a** a (slow and stately) dance **b** rhythmic structure or movement; cadence: e g **b(1)** poetic rhythm; *specif* METRE **b(2)** musical time ⟨*a piece in* ¾ ~⟩ **c(1)** a metrical unit; FOOT 4 **c(2)** *music* a bar **5a** a number that divides exactly into a quantity **b** a mathematical function that assigns nonnegative REAL NUMBERS to sets in such a way that the value of the EMPTY (containing no elements) set is zero and the sum of the values of two DISJOINT (having no elements in common) sets is that of their UNION (set containing all elements of both other sets) **6** a basis or standard of comparison; a criterion **7a** a step planned or taken as a means to an end ⟨*we must take* ~s *to improve sales*⟩ ⟨*hard* ~s⟩ **b** a proposed legislative act ⟨~s *to combat unemployment*⟩ [ME *mesure*, fr OF, fr L *mensura*, fr *mensus*, pp of *metiri* to measure; akin to OE *māth* measure, Gk *metron*] – **for good measure** as an extra precaution or beyond that required ⟨*add an extra dash of brandy* for good measure⟩ – **made to measure** of clothes made to fit a particular person – **out of measure** to an exceedingly great degree

²**measure** *vt* **1** to choose or control with cautious restraint; regulate ⟨~ *his words to suit the occasion*⟩ **2** to take or allot in measured amounts ⟨~ *out 3 cups*⟩ **3** to mark off by making measurements – often + *off* **4** to ascertain or fix the measurements of – often + *off* or *out* **5** to estimate or appraise by a criterion – usu + *against* or by ⟨~s *his skill against his rival*⟩ **6** to serve as a measure of ⟨*a thermometer* ~s *temperature*⟩ **7** *archaic* to travel over; traverse ~ *vi* **1** to take or make a measurement **2** to have a specified measurement ⟨~s *2 feet from end to end*⟩ – **measurer** *n*

**measure up** *vi* to have necessary qualifications; be adequate for – often + *to* ⟨*didn't measure up to the standard*⟩

**measured** /'mezhəd/ *adj* **1** slow and regular ⟨*a* ~ *tread*⟩ **2** rhythmical; regularly recurrent **3** carefully thought out ⟨*spoken with* ~ *contempt*⟩ – **measuredly** *adv*

**measureless** /-lis/ *adj* **1** having no observable limit; immeasurable ⟨*the* ~ *universe*⟩ **2** very great ⟨*treated them with* ~ *contempt*⟩

**measurement** /-mənt/ *n* **1** measuring **2** a figure, extent, or amount obtained by measuring; a dimension **3** MEASURE 2b

**measurement ton** *n* FREIGHT TON

**measuring worm** /'mezh(ə)ring/ *n* LOOPER 1 (type of caterpillar)

**meat** /meet/ *n* **1a** food; *esp* solid food as distinguished from drink **b** the edible part of something as distinguished from its covering (e g a husk or shell) ⟨*coconut* ~⟩ **2** animal tissue used as food: **2a** FLESH 2 **b** FLESH 1a; *specif* flesh of domesticated animals **3** the core or essence of something **4** *archaic* a meal; *esp* dinner [ME *mete*, fr OE; akin to OHG *maz* food, L *madēre* to be wet, Gk *madaros* wet, *mastos* breast]

**meatball** /'meet,bawl/ *n* **1** a small ball of chopped or minced meat often mixed with breadcrumbs and spices before cooking **2** *NAm slang* a boring or stupid person

**meatus** /mi'aytəs/ *n*, *pl* **meatuses, meatus** (the opening to the outside of) a natural body passage [LL, fr L, going, passage, fr *meatus*, pp of *meare* to go – more at PERMEATE]

**meaty** /'meeti/ *adj* **1** full of meat; fleshy **2** of or resembling meat **3** rich in matter for thought

**mecamylamine** /,mekə'miləmeen/ *n* a drug, $C_{11}H_{21}N.HCl,$

used to treat high blood pressure [fr *Mecamylamine*, a trademark]

**mecca** /'mekə/ *n, often cap* a place regarded as a goal, or with special reverence or affection, esp by a specified group of people ⟨*Lord's is the cricketer's* ~⟩ [*Mecca*, city in Saudi Arabia, birthplace of Muhammad and holy city of Islam]

**Meccano** /mi'kahnoh/ *trademark* – used for a toy construction set usu of perforated strips of metal or plastic

**mechan-, mechano-** *comb form* machine ⟨mechano*morphic*⟩; mechanical ⟨mechan*ize*⟩ [ME *mechan-*, fr MF or L, fr Gk *mēchan-*, fr *mēchanē* machine – more at MACHINE]

**mechanic** /mi'kanik/ *n* 1 a skilled worker who operates or maintains machinery ⟨*a motor* ~⟩ 2 mechanic, mechanical a manual worker; an artisan

**mechanical** /-kl/ *adj* 1a of or using machinery or tools ⟨~ *aptitude*⟩ b made, operated by, or being a machine or tool ⟨*a* ~ *saw*⟩ c being or made from pulp from wood that has been ground by machine – compare WOOD-FREE 2 of machinists or other skilled workers ⟨*the* ~ *trades*⟩ 3 done as if by machine; lacking in spontaneity and originality ⟨*her singing was cold and* ~⟩ 4a of, dealing with, or in accordance with the principles of mechanics ⟨~ *work*⟩ ⟨~ *energy*⟩ b relating to the quantitative relations of force and matter ⟨~ *pressure of wind on a tower*⟩ 5 caused by, resulting from, or relating to a process that involves a purely physical as opposed to a chemical change ⟨~ *erosion of rock*⟩ **synonyms** see SPONTANEOUS [ME *mechanicall*, fr MF or L; MF *mechanique*, fr L *mechanicus*, fr Gk *mēchanikos*, fr *mēchanē* machine – more at MACHINE] – **mechanicalism** *n*, **mechanically** *adv*, **mechanicalness** *n*

**mechanical advantage** *n* the advantage gained by the use of a mechanism in transmitting force; *specif* the ratio of the force that performs the useful work of a machine to the force that is applied to the machine

**mechanical drawing** *n* (a) drawing of a machine, architectural plan, etc done with the aid of instruments

**mechanician** /ˌmekə'nish(ə)n/ *n* a mechanic, machinist

**mechanics** /mi'kaniks/ *n* 1 *taking sing vb* a branch of physical science that deals with (the effect on moving and stationary bodies of) energy and forces 2 *taking sing vb* the practical application of mechanics to the design, construction, or operation of machines or tools 3 *taking sing or pl vb* mechanical or functional details

**mechanism** /'mekəniz(ə)m/ *n* 1a a piece of machinery; *also* something resembling this, esp in the arrangement and working of its parts ⟨~ *of the ear*⟩ b a process or technique for achieving a result 2 mechanical operation or action 3 a theory that all natural processes are mechanically determined and capable of exhaustive explanation by the laws of physics and chemistry – compare DYNAMISM, VITALISM 4 the fundamental physical or chemical processes involved in or responsible for a natural phenomenon (e g an action or reaction), a natural development (e g organic evolution), or a synthetic chemical reaction 5a the way in which psychological factors operate and interact b a psychological system influencing the behaviour of a person ⟨*defence* ~⟩

**mechanist** /'mekənist/ *n* 1 an adherent of the doctrine of mechanism 2 *archaic* a mechanician

**mechanistic** /ˌmekə'nistik/ *adj* 1 mechanically determined ⟨~ *universe*⟩ 2 relating to the doctrine of mechanism 3 MECHANICAL 4 – **mechanistically** *adv*

**mechan·ize, -ise** /'mekəniez/ *vt* 1 to make mechanical, automatic, or monotonous 2a to equip with machinery, esp in order to replace human or animal labour b to equip with armed and armoured motor vehicles – **mechanizable** *adj*, **mechanizer** *n*, **mechanization** *n*

**mechanoreceptor** /'mekənoh·riˌseptə/ *n* a sensory END ORGAN of a nerve (e g a touch receptor) that responds to a mechanical stimulus (e g a change in pressure or tension) – **mechanoreception** *n*, **mechanoreceptive** *adj*

**mechanotherapy** /ˌmekənoh'therəpi/ *n* the treatment of clinical disorders or injuries by manual or mechanical means, esp by providing specific exercises

**Mechlin** /'meklin/ *n* a delicate PILLOW LACE used for dresses and millinery that has floral designs on a heavier mesh ground made up of 6-sided shapes [*Mechlin*, town in N Belgium]

**meconium** /mi'kohni·əm/ *n* 1 a dark greenish mass that accumulates in the bowels during foetal life and is discharged shortly after birth 2 a faecal liquid expelled from the anus of certain insects on emergence of the adult form from the pupa [L, lit., poppy juice, fr Gk *mēkōnion*, fr *mēkōn* poppy; akin to OHG *mago* poppy]

**mecopterous** /mi'koptərəs/ *adj* of or being any of an order (Mecoptera) of primitive flesh-eating insects (e g SCORPION FLIES) usu with membranous wings and a long beak with biting mouthparts at the tip [NL *Mecoptera*, group name, fr *meco-* long (fr Gk *mēkos* length; akin to Gk *makros* long) + Gk *pteron* wing – more at MEAGRE, FEATHER]

**medal** /'medl/ *n* a piece of metal, often resembling a coin, having a design, emblem, inscription, etc that commemorates a person or event or is awarded for excellence or achievement; *also* a similar metal disc bearing a religious emblem or picture △ meddle [MF *medaille*, fr OIt *medaglia* coin worth half a denarius, medal, prob fr (assumed) VL *medalis* half, fr LL *medialis* middle, fr L *medius* – more at MID]

**medallic** /mi'dalik/ *adj* relating to or shown on a medal ⟨*a* ~ *sculptor*⟩

**medallion** /mi'dalyən/ *n* 1 a large medal 2 something resembling a large medal; *esp* a decorative tablet, panel, etc in a wall or window often bearing a figure or portrait in relief 3 a medal bearing a religious emblem or picture [Fr *médaillon*, fr It *medaglione*, aug of *medaglia*]

**medallist, NAm chiefly medalist** /'medəlist/ *n* 1 a designer, engraver, or maker of medals 2 a recipient or winner of a (specified) medal as an award, esp in sport ⟨*an Olympic bronze* ~⟩

**medal play** *n* STROKE PLAY (golf scored by the number of strokes played)

**meddle** /'medl/ *vi* to interest oneself in what is not one's concern; interfere unduly – usu + *in* or *with* △ medal [ME *medlen*, fr OF *mesler, medler*, fr (assumed) VL *misculare*, fr L *miscēre* to mix – more at MIX] – **meddler** *n*, **meddlingly** *adv*

**meddlesome** /'medəlsəm/ *adj* given to meddling – **meddlesomeness** *n*

**Mede** /meed/ *n* a native or inhabitant of ancient Media in Persia [ME, fr L *Medus*, fr Gk *Mēdos*]

**medi-** /meedi-/, **medio-** *comb form* middle ⟨medi*eval*⟩ [L, fr *medius*]

**¹media** /'meedi·ə/ *n, pl* **mediae** /'meedi·ie, -ee/ 1 the middle layer of the wall of a blood or LYMPH vessel consisting chiefly of circular muscle fibres 2 the longitudinal vein running through the central region of an insect's wing [NL, fr L, fem of *medius*]

**²media** *n pl* means of mass communication (e g newspapers, radio, and television) ⟨*the* ~ *have given full coverage to the story*⟩ – called also MASS MEDIA [pl of *medium*]

**usage** Although **media** is strictly plural, it is now coming to be treated as an aggregate singular noun ⟨*the* **media** *is responsible*⟩. This usage, and the plural form ⟨*these* **medias**⟩, are widely disliked.

**mediaeval** /ˌmedi'eevl/ *adj* medieval

**medial** /'meedi·əl/ *adj* 1 being, occurring in, or extending towards the middle 2 median – **medial** *n*, **medially** *adv*

**¹median** /'meedi·ən/ *n* 1 a medial part (e g a vein or nerve) 2a a statistical value in an ordered set of values below and above which there is an equal number of values or which is the ARITHMETIC MEAN of the two middle values if there is no one middle value b a vertical line that divides the HISTOGRAM (type of graph) of a FREQUENCY DISTRIBUTION into two parts of equal area c a value of a RANDOM VARIABLE (statistical quantity) for which all greater values make the DISTRIBUTION FUNCTION greater than one half and all lesser values make it less than one half 3a a line from a point of intersection of two sides of a triangle to the midpoint of the opposite side b a line joining the midpoints of the nonparallel sides of a TRAPEZIUM (4-sided geometrical figure with one pair of parallel sides)

**²median** *adj* 1 being in the middle or in an intermediate position 2 of or constituting a statistical median 3 lying in the plane dividing an organ or organism into right and left equal halves [MF or L; MF, fr L *medianus*, fr *medius* middle – more at MID]

**median strip** *n, NAm* a central reservation (e g between the two halves of a dual carriageway)

**mediant** /'meedi·ənt/ *n, music* the third note of a DIATONIC scale (ordinary 8-note musical scale) represented in sol-fa by *me* – called also THIRD [It *mediante*, fr LL *mediant-, medians*, prp of *mediare* to be in the middle]

**media pack** *n* an educational package comprising notes, slides, and an audio cassette or disc

**mediastinum** /ˌmeedi·ə'stienəm/ *n, pl* **mediastina** /-nə/ the central space in the chest between the PLEURA (membranes enclosing the lungs), that contains all the organs of the chest except the lungs; *also* the contents or walls of this space [NL, fr L, neut of *mediastinus* medial, fr *medius*] – **mediastinal** *adj*

¹**mediate** /'meedi•ət/ *adj* acting through an intervening agent or agency; indirect [ME, fr LL *mediatus* intermediate, fr pp of *mediare*] – **mediacy** *n*, **mediately** *adv*, **mediateness** *n*

²**mediate** /'meedi,ayt/ *vi* **1** to intervene between parties in order to reconcile them **2** to reconcile differences **3** to be in a middle or intermediate position ~ *vt* **1a** to effect by action as an intermediary **b** to bring about (a settlement) by mediation **2a** to act as intermediary agent in bringing, effecting, or communicating **b** to transmit as an intermediate mechanism or agency [ML *mediatus*, pp of *mediare*, fr LL, to be in the middle, fr L *medius* middle – more at MID] – **mediative, mediatory, mediatorial** *adj*, **mediatorially** *adv*

**mediation** /,meedi'aysh(ə)n/ *n* the act or process of mediating; *esp* intervention by a neutral person or body between conflicting parties (e g warring states or trades unions and employers) to bring about reconciliation, settlement, or compromise – **mediational** *adj*

**mediat·ize, -ise** /'meediətiez/ *vt* to annex (a state) to a larger state while leaving the former ruler with a title and often some governing rights [Ger *mediatisieren*, fr *mediat* mediate, fr LL *mediatus*]

**mediator** /'meediaytə/, *fem* **mediatrice** /'meediaytris/, **mediatrix** /-triks/ *n* **1** one who or that which mediates; *esp* one who mediates between parties at variance **2** something (e g an enzyme or hormone) that mediates in a chemical or biological process

¹**medic** /'medik/ *n*, *NAm* MEDICK (plant of the pea family)

²**medic** *n*, *informal* **1** one engaged in medical work; *esp* a medical doctor or student **2** a usu noncombative doctor or medical orderly attached to a military unit [L *medicus* physician]

**medicable** /'medikəbl/ *adj* curable, remediable [L *medicabilis*, fr *medicare* to heal]

¹**medical** /'medikl/ *adj* **1** of or concerned with physicians or the practice of medicine **2** requiring or devoted to medical treatment [Fr or LL; Fr *médical*, fr LL *medicalis*, fr L *medicus* physician, fr *mederi* to heal; akin to Avestan *vī-mad-* healer, L *meditari* to meditate] – **medically** *adv*

²**medical** /'medikl/, **medical examination** *n* an examination of the body functions and condition of an individual to determine their physical fitness for an insurance policy, job, etc

**medicament** /mi'dikəmənt/ *n* MEDICINE 1 – **medicamentous, medicamental, medicamentary** *adj*

**Medicare** /'medikeə/ *n* a comprehensive medical insurance, esp for the aged, sponsored by the US and Canadian governments [blend of *medical* and *care*]

**medicate** /'medikayt/ *vt* **1** to treat medicinally **2** to impregnate with a medicinal substance (~d *soap*) [L *medicatus*, pp of *medicare* to heal, fr *medicus*]

**medication** /medi'kaysh(ə)n/ *n* **1** the act or process of medicating **2** a medicinal substance; MEDICINE 1

**medicinal** /mə'dis(ə)nl/ *adj* **1** tending or used to cure disease or relieve pain **2** SALUTARY (producing a beneficial effect) – **medicinal** *n*, **medicinally** *adv*

**medicinal leech** *n* a large European freshwater leech (*Hirudo medicinalis*) formerly used by physicians for bleeding patients

**medicine** /'med(ə)sin/ *n* **1** a substance or preparation used (as if) in treating disease **2a** the science and art of the maintenance of health and the prevention, alleviation, or cure of disease **b** the branch of medicine concerned with the nonsurgical treatment of disease **3** the profession or practice of medicine (*she's going in for* ~) **4** something held by primitive people, esp of N America, to have remedial or magical properties; *also* the magical power of the object or the ritual in which it is used – not used technically in ethnology [ME, fr OF, fr L *medicina*, fr fem of *medicinus* of a physician, fr *medicus*] – **take one's medicine** to accept one's due punishment; submit to something unpleasant

*usage* The pronunciation /'medsin/ with two syllables is recommended for BBC broadcasters

**medicine ball** *n* a heavy stuffed leather-covered ball that is usu thrown between people for exercise

**medicine chest** *n* a box or cabinet containing medicines, bandages, etc

**medicine dropper** *n* DROPPER 2 (device for measuring medicines)

**medicine man** *n* a healer or sorcerer believed to have supernatural powers of healing esp among the N American Indians; a shaman – compare WITCH DOCTOR

**medick**, *NAm* **medic** /'medik/ *n* any of a genus (*Medicago*) of small plants (e g lucerne) of the pea family that have purple or yellow flowers [ME *medike*, fr L *medica*, fr Gk *mēdikē*, fr fem of *mēdikos* of Media, fr *Mēdia* Media, ancient country in SW Asia]

**medico** /'medikoh/ *n*, *pl* **medicos** *informal* ²MEDIC [It *medico* or Sp *médico*, both fr L *medicus*]

**medico-** *comb form* medical (*medicopsychology*); medical and (*medicolegal*) [NL. fr L *medicus*]

**medieval, mediaeval** /,medi'eevl/ *adj* **1** (characteristic) of the Middle Ages **2** *informal* old-fashioned, primitive [*medi-* + L *aevum* age – more at AYE] – **medievally** *adv*

**medievalism** /,medi'eevəliz(ə)m/ *n* **1** medieval qualities, character, or beliefs **2** devotion to or copying of the institutions, arts, and practices of the Middle Ages

**medievalist** /,medi'eevəlist/ *n* a specialist in or devotee of medieval history, culture, or languages – **medievalistic** *adj*

**Medieval Latin** *n* the Latin used esp for liturgical and literary purposes from the 7th to the 15th centuries

**medio-** – see MEDI-

**mediocre** /,medi'ohkə/ *adj* **1** neither good nor bad; indifferent; *esp* conspicuously lacking distinction or imagination **2** not good enough; fairly bad [MF, fr L *mediocris*, lit., halfway up a mountain, fr *medi-* + *ocris* stony mountain; akin to L *acer* sharp – more at EDGE]

*usage* Some people dislike expressions such as (*a very* **mediocre** *performance*), and feel that things either are or are not **mediocre**.

**mediocrity** /medi'okrəti/ *n* **1a** the quality or state of being mediocre **b** mediocre ability or value **2** a mediocre person

**meditate** /'meditayt/ *vt* **1** to focus one's thoughts on; consider or plan in the mind – often + *on* **2** to plan or project in the mind ~ *vi* **1** to engage in deep or serious reflection (*he* ~d *for two days before giving a reply*) **2** to empty the mind of thoughts and fix the attention on one matter, esp for religious or therapeutic reasons or to develop mental faculties [L *meditatus*, pp of *meditari* – more at METE] – **meditator** *n*, **meditative** *adj*, **meditatively** *adv*, **meditativeness** *n*, **meditation** *n*

**Mediterranean** /,meditə'raynyən, -ni-ən/ *adj* **1a** of or characteristic of the (region around the) Mediterranean sea **b** *of a climate* characterized by hot summers and mild rainy winters **2** of a group or physical type of the CAUCASIAN (white-skinned) race characterized by medium or short stature, slender build, and dark complexion **3** *not cap, obs* enclosed or nearly enclosed with land [(3) L *mediterraneus*, fr *medi-* + *terra* land; (1, 2) the *Mediterranean* sea, between Europe & Africa]

**Mediterranean fever** *n* BRUCELLOSIS (disease of humans and cattle)

**Mediterranean flour moth** *n* a small largely grey and black widely distributed moth (*Ephestia kuehniella*) whose larva destroys processed grain products

**Mediterranean fruit fly** *n* a widely distributed fly (*Ceratitis capitata*) with black and white markings whose larva lives and feeds in ripening fruit

¹**medium** /'meedi-əm/ *n*, *pl* **mediums, media** /-diə/, (2e) **mediums,** (2b&3b) **media** *also* **mediums 1** (something in) a middle position or state **2** a means of effecting or conveying something: e g **2a(1)** a substance regarded as the means of transmission of a force or effect (*air is the* ~ *that conveys sound*) **a(2)** a surrounding or enveloping substance; *esp* MATRIX **3 b** a channel or means of communication; *esp* one (e g television) designed to reach large numbers of people **c** a mode of artistic expression (*discovered his true* ~ *as a writer*) **d** an intermediary, go-between **e** someone through whom others seek to communicate with the spirits of the dead **f** a material or technical means of artistic expression (*found watercolour a satisfying* ~) **3a** a condition or environment in which something may function or flourish **b(1)** a nutrient system for the artificial cultivation of cells or organisms, esp bacteria **b(2)** a liquid or solid in which animal or plant structures are placed (e g for preservation) **c** a liquid (e g oil or water) with which dry colouring material (PIGMENT) can be mixed **4** a size of paper usu 23 x 18 inches (584 × 457 millimetres) *usage* see MEDIA [L, fr neut of *medius* middle – more at MID]

²**medium** *adj* intermediate in amount, quality, position, or degree

**medium frequency** *n* a radio frequency in the range between 300 and 3000 kilohertz

**mediumistic** /,meedi∂'mistik/ *adj* (having the qualities) of a spiritualistic medium

**medium of exchange** *n* something commonly accepted in

exchange for goods and services and recognized as representing a standard of value

**medium wave** *n* a band of radio waves, typically used for sound broadcasting, having wavelengths between about 180 metres and 600 metres

**medlar** /'medlə/ *n* a small Eurasian tree (*Mespilus germanica*) of the rose family that bears a fruit resembling a crab apple; *also* the fruit of the medlar that is not eaten until it has begun to decay and that is used in preserves [ME *medeler*, fr MF *meslier*, *medlier*, fr *mesle*, *medle* medlar fruit, fr L *mespilum*, fr Gk *mespilon*]

**¹medley** /'medli/ *n* 1 a (confused) mixture 2 a musical composition made up of a series of songs or short musical pieces 3 a swimming race composed of distances swum by each competitor in backstroke, breaststroke, butterfly and freestyle [ME *medle*, fr MF *medlee*, fr fem of *medlé*, pp of *medler* to mix – more at MEDDLE]

**²medley** *adj* mixed, motley

**medley relay** *n* a relay race in swimming usu of 400 metres (about 437 yards) and between teams of four in which the first member of each team swims backstroke, the second member breaststroke, the third butterfly, and the last freestyle

**medulla** /mi'dulə/ *n, pl* (*1*) **medullae** /-lie/, (*2*) **medullas** *also* **medullae** 1a MARROW 1 (soft material inside bones) b MEDULLA OBLONGATA 2a the inner or deep part of an animal or plant structure 〈the *adrenal* ∼〉 b MYELIN SHEATH (insulating membrane round nerves) [L]

**medulla oblongata** /oblong'gahtə/ *n, pl* **medulla oblongatas, medullae oblongatae** /-ie/ the (pyramid-shaped) last part of the brain of VERTEBRATE animals whose back part merges with the SPINAL CORD [NL, lit., oblong medulla]

**medullary** /mi'duləri/ *adj* 1 of or located in a medulla, esp the MEDULLA OBLONGATA 2 of or located in the PITH (central spongelike core of a stem) of a plant

**medullary ray** *n* 1 any of several wedges of tissue consisting of living thin-walled cells that radiate between the water- and food-conducting tissue (VASCULAR BUNDLES) in the stems of many non-woody plants and connect the PITH (central spongelike core) with the CORTEX (outer layers) 2 VASCULAR RAY (tissue radiating between VASCULAR BUNDLES)

**medullary sheath** *n* 1 MYELIN SHEATH (insulating membrane round nerves) 2 a layer of thick-walled cells surrounding the medulla of the stem in some plants

**medullated** /'med(ə)l,aytid, mi'dul-/ *adj* 1 *of a nerve fibre* MYELINATED 2 having a medulla

**medusa** /mi'dyoohzə/ *n, pl* **medusae** /-sie, -zie/, **medusas** a jellyfish; *also* the umbrella-shaped free-swimming form of a class (Hydrozoa) of related animals that produces sperm and eggs for sexual reproduction [NL, fr *Medusa*, one of the mythical Gorgons, fr L, fr Gk *Medousa*; fr the resemblance of some species to a head with snaky curls] – **medusan** *adj or n*, **medusoid** *adj or n*

**meed** /meed/ *n, archaic* a reward, fitting return, or recompense [ME, fr OE *mēd*; akin to OHG *miata* reward, Gk *misthos*]

**meek** /meek/ *adj* 1 patient and without resentment; long-suffering, mild 2 lacking spirit and courage; submissive [ME, of Scand origin; akin to ON *mjūkr* gentle; akin to L *mucus*] – **meekly** *adv*, **meekness** *n*

**meerkat** /'miə,kat/ *n* any of several small flesh-eating S African mammals (esp *Cynictis penicillata* and *Suricata swicatta*) that are related to the mongooses – called also SURICATE [Afrik, fr D, a kind of monkey, fr MD *meercatte* monkey, fr *meer* sea + *cattle* cat]

**meerschaum** /'miəshəm/ *n* 1 a fine light white clayey mineral that is a water-containing form of the chemical compound magnesium silicate found chiefly in Turkey and used esp for tobacco pipes 2 a tobacco pipe with a bowl made of meerschaum [Ger, fr *meer* sea + *schaum* foam]

**¹meet** /meet/ *vb* met /met/ *vt* 1a to come into the presence of by accident or design b to be present to greet the arrival of 〈*I'll* ∼ *you off the train*〉 c to come into contact or conjunction with; join 〈*where the river* ∼s *the sea*〉 d to appear to the perception of 〈*a terrible scene* met *her eye*〉 2 to encounter as antagonist or foe; oppose 3 to answer, esp in opposition 〈*his speech was* met *with loud catcalls*〉 4 to conform to, esp with exactitude and precision; satisfy 〈*expand a concept to* ∼ *new problems*〉 5 to pay fully; settle 〈∼ *the cost*〉 6 to cope with; match 〈*was able to* ∼ *every social situation*〉 7 to provide for 〈*had enough money to* ∼ *the needs of the moment*〉 8 to become acquainted with 〈*we* met *the professor at the conference*〉 9 to

encounter or experience during the course of something 〈*they* ∼ *many difficulties in their work*〉 10 to receive or greet in an official capacity ∼ *vi* 1 to come together **a** from different directions 〈*the cars* met *in a head-on collision*〉 **b** for a common purpose 〈*the athletes* met *last Wednesday*〉 **c** as contestants, opponents, or enemies 2 to join at a fastening 〈*the waistcoat won't* ∼〉 3 to become acquainted 〈*we* met *at the party*〉 – see also **meet somebody** HALFWAY, **make both** ENDS **meet, more than meets the** EYE *synonyms* see ¹PASS [ME *meten*, fr OE *mētan*; akin to OHG *muoz* meeting, Arm *matčim* I approach] – **meeter** *n*

**meet up with** *vt* to encounter, esp by chance 〈met up with *him at the zoo*〉 – disapproved of by some people

**meet with** *vt* to experience, undergo 〈*his efforts* met *with much criticism*〉 – disapproved of by some people

**²meet** *n* 1 the assembling of participants for a hunt or for competitive sports 2 *chiefly NAm* an athletics meeting

**³meet** *adj, formal* suitable, proper. *synonyms* see ³FIT *antonym* unmeet [ME *mete*, fr OE *gemāte*; akin to OE *metan* to mete] – **meetly** *adv*

**meeting** /'meeting/ *n* 1 a coming together 〈*a chance* ∼〉: e g 1a an assembly of people for a common purpose 〈*a committee* ∼〉 b a session of horse or greyhound racing 2 a permanent organizational unit of the Quakers 3 an intersection, junction 4 *chiefly Br* a competition between teams or individuals (e g athletes)

**meetinghouse** /'meeting,hows/ *n* a building used for worship, esp by Quakers

**mega-** /megə-/, **meg-** *comb form* 1a great; large 〈*mega*lith〉 b having a (specified) part of large size 〈*mega*cephalic〉 2 million (10⁶) 〈*mega*hertz〉 [Gk, fr *megas* large – more at MUCH]

**megabit** /'megə,bit/ *n* a unit of computer information **a** equal to 1 million bits **b** equal to $2^{20}$ bits

**megabyte** /-,biet/ *n* a unit of computer storage **a** equal to 1 million bytes **b** equal to $2^{20}$ bytes

**megacephaly** /,megə'sefəli/ *n* a condition of having an unusually large head either at birth or by abnormal overgrowth of the facial bones

**megacycle** /-,siekl/ *n* a megahertz

**megadeath** /-,deth/ *n* one million deaths – used as a unit in predicting the effects of atomic warfare

**megagamete** /,megəgə'meet/ *n* MACROGAMETE (female reproductive cell)

**megagametophyte** /,megəgə'meetəfiet/ *n* the female GAMETOPHYTE (plant reproductive cell) produced by a MEGASPORE

**megahertz** /-,huhts/ *n* a unit of frequency equal to 10⁶ hertz [ISV]

**megakaryocyte** /,megə'kariəsiet/ *n* a very large cell with a single nucleus that is found in the bone marrow and from which BLOOD PLATELETS (particles assisting blood-clotting) develop by division of the CYTOPLASM (jellylike material inside a cell) [*mega-* + *kary-* + *-cyte*] – **megakaryocytic** *adj*

**megal-** /meg(ə)l-/, **megalo-** *comb form* 1 large; of giant size 〈*megalo*polis〉 2 grandiose 〈*megalo*mania〉 [NL, fr *megal-*, *megas* – more at MUCH]

**megalecithal** /,megə'lesithəl/ *adj, of an egg* containing very large amounts of yolk – compare HOMOLECITHAL, TELOLECITHAL [*mega-* + Gk *lekithos* yolk]

**megalith** /'megəlith/ *n* a huge undecorated block of stone; esp one used in prehistoric monuments – **megalithic** *adj*

**megaloblast** /'megəloh,blahst/ *n* a large ERYTHROBLAST (cell that develops into a RED BLOOD CELL) that appears in the blood, esp in PERNICIOUS ANAEMIA (disease of the blood) – **megaloblastic** *adj*

**megalocephaly** /,megəloh'sefəli/ *n* MEGACEPHALY (abnormal enlargement of the head)

**megalomania** /,meg(ə)lə'maynγ-ə/ *n* 1 a mania for grandiose things 2 a mental disorder that is marked by delusions of personal omnipotence and grandeur [NL] – **megalomaniac** *adj or n*, **megalomaniacal** *adj*, **megalomaniacally** *adv*

**megalopolis** /,meg(ə)l'opəlis/ *n* 1 a very large city 2 a densely populated urban region centred in a city or embracing several cities – **megalopolistic** *adj*, **megalopolitan** *n or adj*, **megalopolitanism** *n*

**megalopteran** /,megə'loptərən/ *n* any of a small suborder (Megaloptera) of insects (e g alder flies and snake flies) having wings with a fine network of veins and developing from aquatic larvae [NL *Megaloptera*, group name, fr *megal-* + Gk *pteron* wing – more at FEATHER] – **megalopterous** *adj*

**megaphone** /'megə,fohn/ *n* a hand-held, often funnel-shaped device used to amplify or direct the spoken voice – **megaphonic** *adj*, **megaphonically** *adv*

**megascopic** /,megə'skopik/ *adj* **1** MACROSCOPIC **2** of or based on observations made with the unaided eye [*mega-* + *-scopic* (as in *microscopic*)] – **megascopically** *adv*

**megasporangium** /,megəspaw'ranjiəm/ *n* a SPORANGIUM (plant structure producing spores) that develops only megaspores [NL]

**megaspore** /'megəspaw/ *n* a spore in plants that gives rise to female GAMETOPHYTES (reproductive cells) and is generally larger than the male MICROSPORE [ISV] – **megasporic** *adj*

**megasporogenesis** /,megə,spawrə'jenəsis/ *n* the formation and maturation of a megaspore [NL]

**megasporophyll** /,megə'spawrəfil/ *n* a SPOROPHYLL (leaflike plant structure) that develops only megasporangia

**megathere** /'megə,thiə/ *n* any of an extinct genus (*Megatherium*) of huge mammals resembling the sloths [NL *Megatherium*, genus name, fr *mega-* + Gk *thērion* wild animal – more at TREACLE]

**megaton** /-tun/ *n* an explosive force equivalent to that of $10^6$ tons of TNT (about $5 \times 10^9$ joules)

**megawatt** /'megə,wot/ *n* one million watts [ISV]

**megilp, magilp** /mə'gilp/ *n* a gelatinous mixture of LINSEED OIL and a varnish made from the resin of mastic trees that is used as an oil-painting medium [origin unknown]

**megohm** /'meg,ohm/ *n* one million ohms [ISV]

**¹megrim** /'meegrəm/ *n* **1a** a migraine **b** *usu pl* vertigo, dizziness **2a** a fancy, whim **b** *pl* low spirits [ME *migreime*, fr MF *migraine*]

**²megrim** *n* any of several small flatfishes; *esp* a European flatfish (*Lepidorhombus whiffiagonis*) [origin unknown]

**meinie, meiny** /'mayni/ *n* **1** *chiefly Scot* a crowd of people **2** *archaic* a retinue, household [ME *meynie* – more at MENIAL]

**meiosis** /mie'ohsis/ *n, pl* **meioses** /-seez/ **1** an understatement aimed at enhancing the esteem in which something is held **2** the specialized cellular process by which the number of CHROMOSOMES (strand of gene-carrying material) in cells producing the GAMETES (sperm and eggs) is reduced by one half and that involves usu a REDUCTION DIVISION in which one of each pair of corresponding chromosomes passes to each newly formed cell followed by a subsequent division (MITOSIS) to produce four new cells – compare MITOSIS [NL, fr Gk *meiōsis* diminution, fr *meioun* to diminish, fr *meiōn* less – more at MINOR] – **meiotic** *adj*, **meiotically** *adv*

**Meissen** /'mies(ə)n/ *n* a type of European HARD-PASTE porcelain developed in the 18th century at Meissen near Dresden and used for both ornamental and table wares

**Meistersinger** /'miestə,zingə (*Ger* maistərzigər)/ *n, pl* **Meistersinger, Meistersingers** a member of any of various German guilds formed chiefly in the 15th and 16th centuries by workingmen and craftsmen for the cultivation of poetry and music △ minnesinger [Ger, fr MHG, fr *meister* master + *singer*]

**melamine** /'melə,min, -,meen/ *n* **1** a chemical compound, $C_3H_6N_6$, with a high melting point, that is used esp in MELAMINE RESINS **2** a MELAMINE RESIN or a plastic made from such a resin [Ger *melamin*]

**melamine resin** *n* a THERMOSETTING (becoming permanently rigid after heating) resin made from melamine used esp in moulded products, adhesives, and coatings

**melan-, melano-** *comb form* **1** black; dark ⟨melan*osis*⟩ ⟨melan*in*⟩ **2** melanin ⟨melan*oid*⟩ [ME, fr MF, fr LL, fr Gk, fr *melan-, melas* – more at MULLET]

**melancholia** /,melən'kohli-ə/ *n* a mental condition characterized by extreme depression and feelings of worthlessness that is often associated with a manic-depressive illness [NL, fr LL, melancholy] – **melancholiac** *n*

**melancholic** /,melən'kolik/ *adj* **1** of or subject to melancholy or melancholia; depressed **2** tending to depress the spirits; saddening – **melancholic** *n*, **melancholically** *adv*

**¹melancholy** /'melənkəli, -koli/ *n* **1a** an abnormal state characterized by irascibility or depression that in medieval physiology was attributed to an excess of BLACK BILE **b** BLACK BILE (body fluid believed in medieval physiology to cause depression) **c** melancholia **2a** depression of mind or spirits; dejection **b** a pensive mood often coupled with sadness [ME *malencolie*, fr MF *melancolie*, fr LL *melancholia*, fr Gk, fr *melan-* + *cholē* bile – more at GALL]

**²melancholy** *adj* characterized by or causing depression, sadness, or pensiveness ⟨*a* ~ *thought*⟩ ⟨*a* ~ *man*⟩

**Melanesian** /,melə'neezh(y)ən, -zyən/ *n* **1** a member of the main group of native inhabitants of the Pacific islands of Melanesia **2** a language group consisting of the Austronesian languages of Melanesia – **Melanesian** *adj*

**mélange** /'maylonhzh (*Fr* melã:ʒ)/ *n* a mixture of often incongruous elements [Fr, fr MF, fr *mesler, meler* to mix – more at MEDDLE]

**melanin** /'melənin/ *n* a dark brown or black pigment of animal or plant structures (e g skin or hair)

**melanism** /'melə,niz(ə)m/ *n* **1** an increased amount of black or nearly black pigmentation (e g of skin, feathers, or hair) **2** intense pigmentation in humans in skin, eyes, and hair – **melanist** *n*, **melanistic** *adj*, **melanic** *adj or n*

**melanite** /'meləniet/ *n* a black garnet gemstone containing the metal titanium [Ger *melanit*, fr *melan-* + *-it* -ite] – **melanitic** *adj*

**melan·ize, -ise** /'meləniez/ *vt* **1** to convert into or increase the amount of melanin in **2** to make dark or black – **melanization** *n*

**melano-** *comb form* – see MELAN-

**melanoblast** /mi'lanoh,blahst, 'melənoh-, -blast/ *n* a cell from which a melanocyte or melanophore develops [ISV] – **melanoblastic** *adj*

**melanoblastoma** /mi,lanoh-bla'stohmə, ,melənoh-/ʟ *n, pl* **melanoblastomas, melanoblastomata** /-mətə/ a cancerous tumour derived from melanoblasts [NL]

**melanochroi** /,melə'nokroh-ie/ *n pl* CAUCASIANS (white-skinned people) having dark hair and pale complexion [NL, irreg fr *melan-* + Gk *ōchroi*, nom pl masc of *ōchros* pale] – **melanochroid** *adj*

**melanocyte** /mi'lanəsiet, 'melənoh-/ *n* a cell in the EPIDERMIS (outer skin layer) that produces melanin [ISV]

**melanocyte-stimulating hormone** /mi'lanəsiet, 'melənoh-/ *n* a hormone produced in the PITUITARY GLAND of VERTEBRATE animals that causes darkening of the skin by stimulating melanin dispersion in pigment-containing cells – compare MELATONIN

**melanogenesis** /mi,lanoh'jenəsis, 'melənoh-/ *n* the formation of the pigment melanin [NL]

**melanoid** /'melənoyd/ *n* a pigment (e g one contributing esp to the yellow colour of the skin) that is a disintegration product of MELANIN [ISV]

**melanoma** /,melə'nohmə/ *n, pl* **melanomas** *also* **melanomata** /-mətə/ a usu cancerous tumour, esp of the skin, containing dark pigment [NL]

**melanophore** /mi'lanoh,faw, 'melənoh-/ *n* a melanin-containing CHROMATOPHORE (pigment-bearing cell), esp of fishes, amphibians, and reptiles

**melanophore-stimulating hormone** *n* MELANOCYTE-STIMULATING HORMONE

**melanosis** /,melə'nohsis/ *n* a condition characterized by abnormal deposition of pigments, esp melanins, in the tissues of the body [NL] – **melanic** *adj*

**melanotic** /,melə'notik/ *adj* having or characterized by black pigmentation

**melanterite** /mi'lantəriet/ *n* COPPERAS (iron-containing mineral) [Ger *melanterit*, deriv of Gk *melantēria* pigment used to black shoes, fr *melan-* + *tērein* to watch, preserve]

**melatonin** /,melə'tohnin/ *n* a hormone produced in the PINEAL GLAND of VERTEBRATE animals that produces lightening of the skin by stimulating concentration of the pigment melanin in pigment-containing cells – compare MELANOCYTE-STIMULATING HORMONE [prob fr *melanocyte* + *serotonin*]

**Melba sauce** /'melbə/ *n* a sweet sauce (e g for ice cream) made with raspberries [Nellie *Melba* †1931 Austr operatic soprano]

**Melba toast** *n* very thin crisp toast [Nellie *Melba*]

**¹meld** /meld/ *vt* to declare or disclose (a card or combination of cards) for a score in a card game, esp by placing face up on the table ~ *vi* to declare a meld [Ger *melden* to announce, fr OHG *meldōn*; akin to OE *meldian* to announce, OSlav *moliti* to ask for]

**²meld** *n* (the act of laying down) a card or combination of cards that is or can be melded in a card game

**³meld** *vb, chiefly NAm* to merge [blend of *melt* and *weld*]

**mêlée, melee** /'melay/ *n* a confused, riotous, or lively struggle; *esp* a general hand-to-hand fight [Fr *mêlée*, fr OF *meslee*, fr *mesler* to mix – more at MEDDLE]

**melic** /'melik/ *adj, of poetry* intended to be sung [L *melicus*, fr Gk *melikos*, fr *melos* song – more at MELODY]

**melilot** /'melilot/ *n* any of a genus (*Melilotus*) of plants of the pea family widely cultivated to enrich the soil and for hay; *esp* a yellow-flowered melilot (*Melilotus officinalis*) that is a common weed of cultivated land – called also SWEET CLOVER [ME *mellilot*, fr MF *melilot*, fr L *melilotos*, fr Gk *melilōtos*, fr *meli* honey + *lōtos* clover, lotus – more at MELLIFLUOUS]

**meliorate** /'meeli·ə,rayt/ *vb* to ameliorate [LL *melioratus*, pp of *meliorare*, fr L *melior* better; akin to L *multus* much, Gk *mala* very] – **meliorator** *n*, **melioration** *n*, **meliorative** *adj*

**meliorism** /'meeliəriz(ə)m/ *n*-the belief that the world can be improved by human effort – **meliorist** *adj or n*, **melioristic** *adj*

**melisma** /mə'lizmə/ *n*, *pl* **melismata** /-mətə/ 1 a group of notes sung to one syllable, esp in PLAINSONG (medieval Christian chant) 2 melodic embellishment; a cadenza [NL, fr Gk, song, melody, fr *melizein* to sing, fr *melos* song] – **melismatic** *adj*

**melliferous** /mə'lifərəs/ *adj* producing or yielding honey [L *mellifer*, fr mell-, *mel* + *-fer* -ferous]

**mellific** /mə'lifik/ *adj* melliferous

**mellifluent** /mə'liflooənt/ *adj* mellifluous [LL *mellifluent-*, *mellifluens*, fr L *mell-*, *mel* + *fluent-*, *fluens*, prp of *fluere*] – **mellifluently** *adv*, **mellifluence** *n*

**mellifluous** /mə'lifloo·əs/ *adj* smoothly or sweetly flowing ⟨*a* ~ *voice*⟩ [LL *mellifluus*, fr L *mell-*, *mel* honey + *fluere* to flow; akin to Goth *milith* honey, Gk *melit-*, *meli*] – **mellifluously** *adv*, **mellifluousness** *n*

**mellophone** /'melə,fohn/ *n* a brass musical instrument having a range of notes and tone similar to that of the French horn [¹*mellow* + *-phone*]

¹**mellow** /'meloh/ *adj* **1a** *of a fruit* tender and sweet because ripe **b** *of a wine* well aged and pleasingly mild **2a** made gentle by age or experience **b** rich and full but free from harshness ⟨*a* ~ *sound*⟩ ⟨~ *colours*⟩ **c** pleasantly intoxicated **d** pleasing, agreeable ⟨*in a* ~ *mood*⟩ **3** *of soil* having a consistency that is soft and like that of LOAM (rich soil of sand and clay) [ME *melowe*] – **mellowly** *adv*, **mellowness** *n*

²**mellow** *vb* to make or become mellow

**melodeon, melodion** /mə'lohdi·ən/ *n* a small REED ORGAN worked by suction; AMERICAN ORGAN [Ger *melodion*, fr *melodie* melody, fr OF]

**melodic** /mə'lodik/ *adj* **1** of melody; melodious **2** *of a part in a musical composition* playing the melody – **melodically** *adv*
  *usage* Writers on usage advise that **melodic** should be reserved for the technical senses connected with "melody", and **melodious** used for the sense "pleasantly tuneful".

**melodious** /mə'lohdi·əs/ *adj* of or producing (a pleasing) melody – **melodiously** *adv*, **melodiousness** *n*

**melodist** /'melədist/ *n* **1** a singer **2** a composer of melodies

**melod·ize, -ise** /'melədiez/ *vt* **1** to make melodious **2** to set to a melody ~ *vi* to sing, play or compose melodies – **melodizer** *n*

**melodrama** /'melə,drahmə/ *n* **1a** a work (e g a film or play) making a crude appeal to the emotions and in which plot and action are more important than character or motive **b** the dramatic genre comprising such works **2** sensational or sensationalized events or behaviour [modif of Fr *mélodrame* (orig a sensational play interspersed with songs), fr Gk *melos* + Fr *drame* drama, fr LL *drama*] – **melodramatic** *adj*, **melodramatically** *adv*

**melodramatics** /,melədrə'matiks/ *n taking sing or pl vb* over-emotional behaviour designed to impress or influence others

**melodramat·ize, -ise** /,melə'dramətiez/ *vt* **1** to make melodramatic ⟨~ *a situation*⟩ **2** to make a melodrama of (e g a novel) – **melodramatization** *n*

**melody** /'melədi/ *n* **1** an agreeable succession or arrangement of sounds **2a** a rhythmic succession of single notes organized as a distinct sequence; a tune **b** a musical line represented horizontally in written music **c** the chief part in harmonized music [ME *melodie*, fr OF, fr LL *melodia*, fr Gk *melōidia* chanting, music, fr *melos* limb, musical phrase, song (akin to Bret *mell* joint) + *aeidein* to sing – more at ODE]

**melon** /'melən/ *n* **1** (any of various plants of the cucumber family having) a fruit (e g a watermelon) containing sweet edible flesh and usu eaten raw **2** *NAm slang* a surplus of profits available for distribution to stockholders [ME, fr MF, fr LL *melon-*, *melo*, short for L *melopepon-*, *melopepo*, fr Gk *mēlopepōn*, fr *mēlon* apple + *pepōn*, an edible gourd – more at PUMPKIN ]

¹**melt** /melt/ *vi* **1** to become altered from a solid to a liquid state usu by heating **2a** to dissolve, disintegrate ⟨*the meringue* ~ed *in her mouth*⟩ **b** to disappear as if by dissolving ⟨*her anger* ~ed *at his kind words*⟩ **3** to become mild, tender, or gentle **4** to lose distinct outline; blend – often + *into* ⟨*the images* ~ed *into one another*⟩ ~ *vt* **1** to reduce from a solid to a liquid state usu by heating **2** to cause to disappear or disperse **3** to make tender or gentle; soften *synonyms* see MOLTEN [ME *melten*, fr OE *meltan*; akin to L *mollis* soft, *molere* to grind – more at MEAL] – **meltable** *adj*, **meltability** *n*, **melter** *n*, **meltingly** *adv*, **meltingness** *n*
  **melt down** *vt* to melt (e g scrap metal) for reuse

²**melt** *n* **1a** molten material **b** the mass melted at a single operation **2** melting or being melted; *esp* a thaw ⟨*roads softened during the spring* ~⟩

³**melt** *n* the spleen; *esp* that of slaughtered animals for use as feed or food [ME *milte*, fr OE; akin to OHG *miltzi* spleen]

**melting** /'melting/ *adj*, *of a voice* soft, gentle – **meltingly** *adv*

**melting point** /'melting/ *n* the temperature at which a solid melts

**melting pot** *n* **1** a vessel for melting something; a crucible **2** a place or situation in which there is a mixing of diverse ideas, peoples, traditions, or cultures; *also* the resulting mixture, esp of peoples – **in the melting pot** in a state of flux or indecision

**melton, melton cloth** /'melt(ə)n/ *n* a heavy smooth woollen or wool and cotton fabric with a short NAP (raised fibres) used esp for overcoats [*Melton* Mowbray, town in Leicestershire]

**meltwater** /'melt,wawtə/ *n* water derived from the melting of (glacial) ice or snow

**mem** /mem/ *n* the 13th letter of the Hebrew alphabet [Heb *mēm*, lit., water]

**member** /'membə/ *n* **1** a part or organ of the body: e g **1a** a limb **b** *euph* the penis **2** a unit of structure in a plant body **3a** an individual or unit belonging to or forming part of a group or organization (e g a church) **b** *often cap* a person entitled to sit in a legislative body; *esp* a member of Parliament **4** a constituent part of a whole: e g **4a** a division of a sentence; *esp* CLAUSE 2 **b** a proposition of a SYLLOGISM (deductive argument) **c** *maths* ELEMENT 2b(4) (part of a mathematical set) **d** any of the components of a logical class **e** either of the expressions on either side of a mathematical equation or inequality **5** a beam or similar (load-bearing) structure, esp in a building [ME *membre*, fr OF, fr L *membrum*; akin to Goth *mimz* flesh, Gk *mēros* thigh, *mēninx* membrane]

**membership** /-ship/ *n* **1** the state or status of being a member **2** *taking sing or pl vb* the body of members ⟨*an organization with a large* ~⟩ **3** the relation between an element of a mathematical class and the class – compare INCLUSION 3

**membrane** /'membrayn/ *n* **1** a thin soft pliable sheet or layer, esp in an animal or plant **2** a piece of parchment forming part of a roll [L *membrana* skin, parchment, fr *membrum*] – **membranal** *adj*, **membraned** *adj*

**membrane bone** *n* a bone (e g in the skull) that forms from CONNECTIVE TISSUE (loose fibrous supporting tissue) without previously existing as cartilage

**membranous** /'membraynəs/ *adj* **1a** of or resembling (a) membrane **b** thin, pliable, and often somewhat transparent ⟨~ *leaves*⟩ **2** characterized or accompanied by the formation of a usu abnormal membrane or membranous layer ⟨~ *croup*⟩ – **membranously** *adv*

**membranous labyrinth** *n* the sensory structures of the INNER EAR

**memento** /mə'mentoh/ *n*, *pl* **mementos, mementoes** something that serves as a reminder of a person, past event, etc; a souvenir [ME, fr L, remember, imper of *meminisse* to remember; akin to L *ment-*, *mens* mind]

**memento mori** /'mawri/ *n*, *pl* **memento mori** a reminder of mortality; *esp* a death's-head [L, remember that you must die]

**memo** /'memoh/ *n*, *pl* **memos** a memorandum

**memoir** /'memwah/ *n* **1a** a narrative composed from personal experience **b** *pl* an autobiography **c** a biography, esp of a person known to the writer **2a** a learned essay on a particular topic **b** *pl* the record of the proceedings of a learned society [Fr *mémoire*, lit., memory, fr L *memoria*] – **memoirist** *n*

**memorabilia** /,mem(ə)rə'bili·ə/ *n taking pl vb* (records of) memorable things or events [L, fr neut pl of *memorabilis*]

**memorable** /'mem(ə)rəbl/ *adj* worth remembering; notable [ME, fr L *memorabilis*, fr *memorare* to remind, mention, fr *memor* mindful] – **memorably** *adv*, **memorability** *n*

**memorandum** /,memə'randəm/ *n*, *pl* **memorandums, memoranda** /-də/ **1** an informal record, communication, or reminder **2** a short legal document recording the terms of an agreement, establishment of a company, etc **3** an informal diplomatic communication **4** a usu brief communication for internal circulation (e g within an office) [ME, fr L, neut of *memorandus* to be remembered, gerundive of *memorare*]

**usage** The plural **memoranda** is now sometimes treated as a singular noun ⟨*this* **memoranda**⟩, but this usage is widely disliked.

¹**memorial** /mə'mawri·əl/ *adj* **1** serving to preserve the memory of a person or event **2** of or involving memory – **memorially** *adv*, **memorialize** *vt*, **memorializer** *n*, **memorialization** *n*

²**memorial** *n* **1** something, esp a monument, that commemorates a person or event **2a** a historical record **b** a memorandum, note; *specif* an informal diplomatic communication **c** a statement of facts addressed to a government or parliament and often accompanied by a petition or remonstrance

**memorialist** /mə'mawriəlist/ *n* a person who writes or signs a memorial or memoir

**memor·ize, -ise** /'meməriez/ *vt* to commit to memory; learn by heart – **memorizable** *adj*, **memorizer** *n*, **memorization** *n*

**memory** /'mem(ə)ri/ *n* **1a** a person's capacity to remember **b** the store of things learned and retained from an organism's activity or experience as evidenced by recall and recognition; *also* the power or process of realizing or recalling these things **2a** commemorative remembrance ⟨erected a statue in ~ of the hero⟩ **b** the fact or condition of being remembered ⟨days of recent ~⟩ **3a** a particular act of recall or recollection ⟨had no ~ of the incident⟩ **b** an image or impression of someone or something that is remembered ⟨his ~ will stay with us⟩ **c** the time within which past events can be or are remembered ⟨within the ~ of living men⟩ **4a** memory, memory bank a device in which information, esp for a computer, can be inserted and stored, and from which it may be extracted when wanted **b** the capacity of a device for storing information ⟨a computer with 16K of ~⟩ **5** a capacity of a metal, plastic, etc for showing effects as the result of past treatment, or for returning to a former condition [ME *memorie*, fr MF *memoire*, fr L *memoria*, fr *memor* mindful; akin to OE *mimorian* to remember, L *mora* delay, Gk *mermēra* care, Skt *smarati* he remembers]

**synonyms** Memory, remembrance, recollection, retrospect, and reminiscence all involve the recall of past experience. Memory applies to the mental faculty involved, while remembrance stresses the act or process of remembering. Recollection suggests conscious recall of something, usually for a purpose. Retrospect suggests the returning of the mind to the past in order to contemplate or evaluate it. Reminiscence is pleasurable, often shared, recall of the past. A memory, or memories, are more likely to have been kept in mind, and cherished, than a recollection, or recollections, which suggest a conscious effort of recall, often for practical reasons. **antonym** oblivion

**memory trace** *n* an alteration within the CENTRAL NERVOUS SYSTEM postulated as constituting the physical basis of learning – compare ENGRAM

**memsahib** /'mem,sah·hib/ *n* – used, esp among the indigenous population in colonial India, when addressing or speaking of an esp married European woman [Hindi *memṣaḥib*, fr E *ma'am* + Hindi *ṣāḥib* sahib]

**men** /men/ *pl of* MAN

**men-** /men-/, **meno-** *comb form* menstruation ⟨menorrhagia⟩ [NL, fr Gk *mēn* month – more at MOON]

¹**menace** /'menis/ *n* **1** a show of intention to inflict harm; a threat ⟨demanded money with ~s⟩ **2a** a source of danger **b** a person who causes annoyance [ME, fr MF, fr L *minacia*, fr *minac-, minax* threatening, fr *minari* to threaten – more at MOUNT]

²**menace** *vt* **1** to threaten or show intent to harm **2** to represent or pose a threat to; endanger ~ *vi* to act in a threatening manner **synonyms** SEE THREATEN – **menacer** *n*, **menacing** *adj*, **menacingly** *adv*

**menad** /'meenad/ *n* MAENAD (female worshipper of Dionysus)

**menadione** /,menə'die·ohn/ *n* a yellow, synthetic chemical compound, $C_{11}H_8O_2$, related to, and having the same biological activity as natural VITAMIN K, and used in fungicides and animal feeds – called also VITAMIN K₃ [*methyl + naphthoquinone + di- + ketone*]

**ménage** /me'nahzh, '--/ *n* a household [Fr, fr OF *mesnage* dwelling, fr (assumed) VL *mansionaticum*, fr L *mansion-, mansio* mansion]

**ménage à trois** /ah trwah/ *n* a relationship in which three people, esp a married couple and the lover of one of the couple, live together [Fr, lit., household for three]

**menagerie** /mə'najəri/ *n* a place where animals are kept and

trained, esp for exhibition; *also* a zoo [Fr *ménagerie*, fr MF, management of a household or farm, fr *menage*]

**menaphthone** /me'nafthohn/ *n* menadione [*methyl + naphthoquinone*]

**menaquinone** /,menəkwi'nohn/ *n* VITAMIN K₂ [*methyl + naphthoquinone*]

**menarche** /'menahki/ *n* the beginning of the menstrual function; *esp* the first menstrual period of an individual [NL, fr *men-* + Gk *archē* beginning] – **menarcheal** *adj*

¹**mend** /mend/ *vt* **1a** to improve in manners or morals ⟨~ one's ways⟩ **b** to set right by correcting or removing ⟨~ a hole⟩ **2a** to restore to sound condition or working order ⟨~ a shirt⟩ ⟨~ a car⟩ **b** to restore to health; cure **3** to add fuel to (a fire) ~ *vi* **1** to improve morally **2** to become corrected or improved **3** to improve in health; *also* to heal [ME *menden*, short for *amenden* – more at AMEND] – **mendable** *adj*, **mender** *n*

²**mend** *n* **1** an act of mending **2** a mended place or part – **on the mend** improving, esp in health

**mendacious** /men'dayshəs/ *adj* given to or characterized by deception or falsehood; lying [L *mendac-, mendax* – more at AMEND] – **mendaciously** *adv*, **mendaciousness** *n*

**mendacity** /men'dasəti/ *n* **1** (a tendency to) untruthfulness **2** a lie; falsehood △ mendicity

**mendelevium** /,mendə'leevi·əm/ *n* an artificially produced radioactive metallic chemical element [NL, fr Dmitri *Mendeleev* †1907 Russ chemist]

**Mendelian** /men'deeli·ən/ *adj* of or according with MENDEL'S LAWS or MENDELISM – **Mendelian** *n*, **Mendelianist** *n*

**Mendelian factor** *n* a gene

**Mendelian inheritance** *n* inheritance of characteristics transmitted by genes in accordance with MENDEL'S LAWS

**Mendelism** /'mendəliz(ə)m/ *n* the principles or operations of MENDEL'S LAWS; *also* MENDELIAN INHERITANCE – **Mendelist** *adj* or *n*

**Mendel's law** /'mendlz/ *n* **1** a principle in genetics: hereditary units occur in pairs that separate during GAMETE (sex cell) formation so that each gamete receives only one member of a pair – called also LAW OF SEGREGATION **2** a principle in genetics limited and modified by the subsequent discovery of the phenomenon of LINKAGE (nonseparation of genes during CELL DIVISION): the different pairs of hereditary units are distributed to the gametes independently of each other, the gametes combine at random, and the various combinations of hereditary pairs occur in the ZYGOTES (structure formed by fusion of male and female sex cells) according to the laws of chance – called also LAW OF INDEPENDENT ASSORTMENT **3** a principle in genetics proved subsequently to be subject to many limitations: because one of each pair of hereditary units dominates the other in expression, characteristics are inherited as alternatives on an all-or-nothing basis – called also LAW OF DOMINANCE [Gregor *Mendel* †1884 Austrian botanist]

**mendicancy** /'mendikənsi/ *n* begging or being a beggar

**mendicant** /'mendikənt/ *n* **1** BEGGAR 1 **2** *often cap* a friar living off alms [L *mendicant-, mendicans*, prp of *mendicare* to beg, fr *mendicus* beggar – more at AMEND] – **mendicant** *adj*, **mendicancy** *n*

**mendicity** /men'disəti/ *n* mendicancy △ mendacity [ME *mendicite*, fr MF *mendicité*, fr L *mendicitat-, mendicitas*, fr *mendicus*]

**mending** /'mending/ *n* something, esp clothes, to be mended

**menfolk** /'men,fohk/ *n taking pl vb*, *NAm also* **menfolks** *n pl* **1** men in general **2** the men of a family or community

**menhaden** /men'hayd(ə)n/ *n*, *pl* **menhaden, menhadens** a sea fish (*Brevoortia tyrannus*) of the herring family abundant along the Atlantic coast of the USA where it is used for bait or converted into oil or fertilizer [of Algonquian origin; prob akin to Narraganset *munnawhatteaûg* menhaden]

**menhir** /'menhiə/ *n* a single upright roughly shaped stone, usu of prehistoric origin [Fr, fr Bret, fr *men* stone + *hir* long]

¹**menial** /'meenyəl, -ni·əl/ *adj* **1** of servants; lowly **2a** degrading; *also* servile ⟨answered in ~ tones⟩ **b** lacking in interest or status ⟨foreign workers employed in ~ tasks⟩ [ME *meynial*, fr *meynie* household, retinue, fr OF *mesnie*, fr (assumed) VL *mansionata*, fr L *mansion-, mansio* dwelling] – **menially** *adv*

²**menial** *n* a domestic servant or retainer

**Ménière's disease** /mə'nyeəz/ *n* a disorder of the MEMBRANOUS LABYRINTH (sensory structures) of the INNER EAR that is marked by recurrent attacks of dizziness, ringing in the ears, and deafness [Prosper *Ménière* †1862 Fr physician]

**mening-, meningo-** *also* **meningi-** *comb form* meninges ⟨mening*itis*⟩; meninges and ⟨meningo*encephalitis*⟩ [NL, fr *mening-, meninx*]

**meningeal** /mə'ninjiəl/ *adj* of or affecting the meninges

**meninges** /mə'ninjeez/ *pl of* MENINX

**meningioma** /mə,ninji'ohmə/ *n, pl* **meningiomas, meningiomata** /-mətə/ a slow-growing tumour arising from the meninges and often causing damage by pressure on the brain [NL]

**meningitis** /,menin'jietəs/ *n, pl* **meningitides** /-'jitədeez/ inflammation of the meninges, esp the two inner membranes (PIA MATER and ARACHNOID), usu caused by bacterial, fungal, or viral infection [NL] – **meningitic** *adj*

**meningococcus** /mə,ning·goh'kokəs/ *n, pl* **meningococci** /-'kok(s)i, 'kok(s)ie/ a bacterium (*Neisseria meningitidis*) that causes meningitis of the brain and SPINAL CORD [NL] – **meningococcal** *also* **meningococcic** *adj*

**meningoencephalitis** /mə,ning-goh·in,sefə'lietəs/ *n, pl* **meningoencephalitides** /-'litədeez/ inflammation of the brain and meninges [NL] – **meningoencephalitic** *adj*

**meninx** /'meningks, 'mee-/ *n, pl* **meninges** /mə'ninjeez/ any of the three membranes (DURA MATER, ARACHNOID, and PIA MATER) that envelop the brain and SPINAL CORD [NL, fr Gk *mēning-, mēninx* membrane; akin to L *membrana* membrane]

**meniscus** /mə'niskəs/ *n, pl* **menisci** /mə'nisee, -sie/ *also* **meniscuses 1** a crescent-shaped body or figure **2** a fibrous cartilage within a joint, esp of the knee **3** a CONCAVO-CONVEX (having one surface curving inwards and one curving outwards) lens **4** the curved upper surface of a liquid standing in a column that is CONCAVE when the containing walls are wetted by the liquid and CONVEX when not [NL, fr Gk *mēniskos,* fr dim. of *mēnē* moon, crescent – more at MOON]

**Mennonite** /'menəniet/ *n* a member of any of various Protestant groups derived from the Anabaptist movement in Holland that reject infant baptism, formal church organization, and military service [Ger *Mennonit,* fr *Menno* Simons †1561 Frisian religious reformer]

**meno-** – see MEN-

**meno mosso** /,menoh 'mosoh/ *adv* less rapid; slower – used as a direction in music [It]

**menopause** /'menə,pawz/ *n* (the time of) the natural cessation of menstruation occurring usu between the ages of 45 and 50 [Fr *ménopause,* fr *méno-* men- + *pause*] – **menopausal** *adj*

**menorah** /mi'nawrə/ *n* a many-branched candelabrum used in Jewish worship [Heb *mĕnōrāh* candlestick]

**menorrhagia** /,menaw'rayjyə/ *n* abnormally profuse menstrual bleeding [NL] – **menorrhagic** *adj*

**menorrhoea** /menə'riə/ *n* normal menstrual bleeding [NL]

**mensal** /'mensl/ *adj, formal* of or done at the table [LL *mensalis,* fr L *mensa* table]

**menses** /'menseez/ *n taking sing or pl vb* the menstrual flow [L, lit., months, pl of *mensis* month – more at MOON]

**Menshevik** /'menshəvik/ *n, pl* **Mensheviks, Mensheviki** /-'veeki/ a member of the less radical wing of the Russian Social Democratic party before and during the Russian Revolution, believing in the gradual achievement of socialism by parliamentary methods – compare BOLSHEVIK [Russ *men'shevik,* fr *men'she* less; fr their forming the minority group of the party] – **Menshevism** *n,* **Menshevist** *n or adj*

**mens rea** /,menz 'ree-ə/ *n* criminal intent [NL, lit., guilty mind]

**men's room** *n, chiefly NAm* a public toilet for men

**menstrual** /'menstrooəl/ *adj* of or being menstruation or the approximately 28-day cycle that includes an instance of menstruation

**menstruate** /'menstrooayt/ *vi* to undergo menstruation [LL *menstruatus,* pp of *menstruari,* fr L *menstrua* menses, fr neut pl of *menstruus* monthly, fr *mensis* month]

**menstruation** /,menstroo'aysh(ə)n/ *n* a discharging of blood, secretions, and tissue debris from the womb that recurs in nonpregnant women of breeding age at approximately monthly intervals and that is considered to represent a readjustment of the womb to the nonpregnant state following changes accompanying the preceding OVULATION (release of eggs from the ovary); *also* PERIOD 3c

**menstruous** /'menstrooəs/ *adj* menstrual [L *menstruus*

**menstruum** /'menstroo-əm/ *n, pl* **menstruums, menstrua** /'menstrooə/ a solvent; *esp* one used in drug preparation [ML, lit., menses, alter. of L *menstrua;* fr the comparison made by alchemists of a base metal in a solvent undergoing transmuta-

tion to gold with an ovum in the womb being (supposedly) transformed by menstrual blood]

**mensurable** /'menshərəbl/ *adj* capable of being measured; measurable [LL *mensurabilis,* fr *mensurare* to measure, fr *mensura* measure – more at MEASURE] – **mensurability, mensurableness** *n*

**mensural** /'menshərəl/ *adj* **1** of or being POLYPHONIC (several-part vocal) music originating in the 13th century with each note having a definite and exact time value **2** or or involving measurement [LL *mensuralis* measurable, fr L *mensura*]

**mensuration** /,menshə'raysh(ə)n/ *n* **1** the act of measuring; measurement **2** geometry applied to the estimation of lengths, areas, or volumes from given dimensions or angles

**menswear** /'menz,weə/ *n* clothing for men

**-ment** /-mənt/ *suffix* (*vb → n*) **1a** a concrete result, object, or agent of (a specified action) ⟨*embank*ment⟩ ⟨*entangle*ment⟩ **b** concrete means or instrument of (a specified action) ⟨*entertain*ment⟩ **2a** action; process ⟨*encircle*ment⟩ ⟨*develop*ment⟩ **b** place of (a specified action) ⟨*encamp*ment⟩ *usage* see -ION [ME, fr OF, fr L *-mentum;* akin to L *-men,* suffix denoting concrete result, Gk *-mat-, -ma*]

¹**mental** /'mentl/ *adj* **1a** of the mind or its activity; *specif* of the total emotional and intellectual response of an individual to his/her environment ⟨~ *health*⟩ **b** relating to intellectual as contrasted with emotional or physical activity ⟨~ *ability*⟩ ⟨*a* ~ *age of three*⟩ **c** performed by or existing in the mind ⟨~ *arithmetic*⟩ ⟨~ *anguish*⟩ **d** relating to spirit or idea as opposed to matter **2a** of or affected by a psychiatric disorder ⟨*a* ~ *patient*⟩ ⟨~ *illness*⟩ **b** intended for the care or treatment of people affected by psychiatric disorders ⟨~ *hospitals*⟩ **3** of or having telepathic or mind-reading powers ⟨*a* ~ *medium*⟩ **4** *chiefly Br* crazy; *also* stupid ⟨*he must be* ~ *to take that job*⟩ **5** *substandard* mad [ME, fr MF, fr LL *mentalis,* fr L *ment-, mens* mind – more at MIND] – **mentally** *adv*

²**mental** *adj* of the chin; ²GENIAL [L *mentum* chin; akin to L *mont-, mons* mountain – more at MOUNT]

**mental age** *n* a measure used in psychological testing that expresses an individual's mental attainment in terms of the number of years it takes an average child to reach the same level – compare INTELLIGENCE QUOTIENT

**mental defective** *n* someone who is mentally deficient

**mental deficiency** *n* failure in intellectual development resulting in a need for continuing parental or institutional care

**mentalism** /-,iz(ə)m/ *n* **1** a doctrine that only individual minds are real and that the external world exists or has properties only to the extent that it is represented in a conscious mind **2** a doctrine that holds that the aim of psychology should be to study minds using methods of INTROSPECTION (thinking about or observing one's own thought processes) rather than to study behaviour under experimental conditions – compare BEHAVIOURISM

**mentalist** /'mentəlist/ *n* MIND READER

**mentality** /men'taləti/ *n* **1** mental power or capacity; intelligence ⟨*a man of low* ~⟩ **2** mode or way of thought; mental disposition or outlook ⟨*a provincial* ~⟩

**mentation** /men'taysh(ə)n/ *n, formal* mental activity [L *ment-, mens* + E *-ation*]

**menthol** /'menthol/ *n* a chemical alcohol, $C_{10}H_{19}OH$, that occurs esp in mint oils and has the smell and cooling properties of peppermint [Ger, deriv of L *mentha* mint]

**mentholated** /'menthəlaytid/ *adj* containing or impregnated with menthol

¹**mention** /'mensh(ə)n/ *n* **1** a brief reference to something; a passing remark **2** a formal citation for outstanding achievement [ME *mencioun,* fr OF *mention,* fr L *mention-, mentio,* fr *ment-, mens* mind]

²**mention** *vt* to make mention of; refer to; *also* to cite for outstanding achievement – **mentionable** *adj,* **mentioner** *n*

**mentor** /'mentaw/ *n* a wise and trusted adviser [*Mentor* (Gk *Mentōr*), tutor of Odysseus' son Telemachus in Homer's *Odyssey*] – **mentorship** *n*

**mentum** /'mentəm/ *n, pl* **menta** /-tə/ **1** a chin **2** a hard plate forming part of the LABIUM (lower lip) of an insect [L – more at MENTAL]

**menu** /'menyooh/ *n, pl* **menus** (a list of) the dishes that may be ordered (e g in a restaurant) or that are to be served (e g at a banquet) [Fr *menu* small, detailed, fr L *minutus* very small – more at MINUTE]

**meow** /mee'ow/ *vi or n* (to) miaow [imit]

**meperidine** /mə'perədeen, -din/ *n, chiefly NAm* PETHIDINE (pain-killing drug) [*methyl* + pi*peridine*]

**Mephistopheles** /ˌmefis'tofəleez/ *n* a diabolical or fiendish person [Ger, name for the devil in various versions of the Faust legend] – **Mephistophelian, Mephistophelean** *adj*

**mephitis** /mi'fietəs/ *n* a poisonous or foul gas emitted from the earth; *also* a foul stench [L, fr Oscan] – **mephitic** *adj*

**meprobamate** /mə'prohbəmayt, ˌmeprə'bohmayt/ *n* a synthetic drug, $(NH_2CO_2CH_2)_2C(CH_3)(C_3H_7)$, that is used as a mild tranquillizer [*methyl* + *propyl* + dicar*bamate*]

**mer-** *comb form* sea ⟨mer*maid*⟩ [ME, fr *mere*, fr OE]

**-mer** /-mə/ *comb form* (→ *n*) 1 something that is a (specified type of) polymer or isomer ⟨*tautomer*⟩ 2 something that has (such or so many) parts ⟨*pentomer*⟩ [ISV, fr Gk *meros* part – more at MERIT] – **-merism** *comb form* (→ *n*), **-merous** *comb form* (→ *adj*)

**merbromin** /mə'brohmin/ *n* a green chemical compound, $C_{20}H_8Br_2HgNa_2O_6$, that forms a red solution in water and that is used as an antiseptic [*mercuric acetate* + di*brom-* + fluoresc*ein*]

**mercantile** /'muhkəntiel/ *adj* 1 of or concerned with merchants or trading ⟨~ *law*⟩ 2 (having the characteristics) of mercantilism ⟨~ *system*⟩ [Fr, fr It, fr *mercante* merchant, fr L *mercant-, mercans*, fr prp of *mercari* to trade – more at MERCHANT]

**mercantilism** /'muhkəntlˌiz(ə)m, -ˌtielˌiz(ə)m/ *n* 1 the theory or practice of mercantile pursuits; commercialism 2 an economic system that developed esp in the 17th century with the rise of the modern centralized nation state and that was intended to increase the power and esp the monetary wealth of a nation by strict regulation of the national economy usu through policies designed to secure an accumulation of bullion, a favourable balance of trade, the development of agriculture and manufactures, and the establishment of foreign trading monopolies – **mercantilist** *n or adj*, **mercantilistic** *adj*

**mercapt-** /muh'kapt-/, **mercapto-** *comb form* containing the chemical group –SH in the molecular structure ⟨mercapto*purine*⟩ [ISV, fr *mercaptan*]

**mercaptan** /muh'kaptan/ *n* any of various chemical compounds with the general formula RSH, that are similar to the alcohols and phenols but contain sulphur in place of oxygen and that often have disagreeable smells [Ger, fr Dan, fr ML *mercurium captans*, lit., seizing mercury]

**mercaptopurine** /məˌkaptə'pyooərin/ *n* a drug, $C_5H_4N_4S$, that interferes with the synthesis in the body of DNA and RNA and that is sometimes useful in the treatment of leukaemia

**Mercator projection** /muh'kaytə/, **Mercator's projection** *n* a CYLINDRICAL PROJECTION in which all RHUMB LINES (imaginary lines on the earth's surface cutting all meridians at the same angle) are represented by straight lines and small areas are represented in their true shape. This projection is unsuitable for general use as the shapes of large areas become greatly distorted with increasing distance from the equator. [Gerhardus *Mercator* (Gerhard Kremer) †1594 Flem geographer]

[1]**mercenary** /'muhs(ə)nri/ *n* a hired (foreign) soldier; *broadly* one for whom financial reward is the chief motive [ME, hireling, fr L *mercenarius*, fr *merced-, merces* wages – more at MERCY]

[2]**mercenary** *adj* 1 serving merely for (monetary) reward 2 hired for service in the army of a foreign country – **mercenarily** *adv*, **mercenariness** *n*

**mercer** /'muhsə/ *n, Br* a dealer in (fine quality) fabrics [ME, fr OF *mercier* merchant, fr *mers* merchandise, fr L *merc-, merx* – more at MARKET]

**mercer·ize, -ise** /'muhsəˌriez/ *vt* to give (e g cotton yarn) lustre, strength, and receptiveness to dyes by chemical treatment under tension with an alkali (e g CAUSTIC SODA) [John *Mercer* † 1866 E calico printer] – **mercerization** *n*

**mercery** /'muhsəri/ *n, Br* a mercer's wares, shop, or occupation

[1]**merchandise** /'muhchənˌdies/ *n* 1 the commodities that are bought and sold in commerce 2 goods for sale (e g in a shop) [ME *marchaundise*, fr OF *marcheandise*, fr *marcheant*]

[2]**merchandise** /'muhchənˌdiez/ *vt* 1 to buy and sell in business 2 to promote the sale or sales of – **merchandiser** *n*

**merchandising** /'muhchəndiezing/ *n* sales promotion, including market research, development of new products, coordination of manufacture and marketing, and effective advertising and selling

[1]**merchant** /'muhchənt/ *n* 1 a buyer and seller of commodities;

a wholesaler; *also, chiefly NAm* a shopkeeper 2 *chiefly derog* a person who is given to a specified activity ⟨*a speed* ~⟩ [ME *marchant*, fr OF *marcheant*, fr (assumed) VL *mercatant-, mercatans*, fr prp of *mercatare* to trade, fr L *mercatus*, pp of *mercari* – more at MARKET] – **merchant** *vt*, **merchantlike** *adj*

[2]**merchant** *adj* of or used in commerce; *esp* of a MERCHANT NAVY

**merchantable** /'muhchəntəbl/ *adj* of commercially acceptable quality; marketable – **merchantability** *n*

**merchant bank** *n* a firm of private bankers that specializes in accepting foreign BILLS OF EXCHANGE and in the purchase and sale of stocks and shares – **merchant banker** *n*

**merchantman** /-mən/ *n, pl* **merchantmen** /-mən/ a trading ship as opposed to a warship

**merchant marine** *n* MERCHANT NAVY

**merchant navy** *n* (the personnel of) the privately or publicly owned commercial ships of a nation

**Mercian** /'muhsh(y)ən/ *n* 1 a native or inhabitant of Mercia 2 the Old English dialect of Mercia [*Mercia*, ancient kingdom in central England] – **Mercian** *adj*

**merciful** /'muhsif(ə)l/ *adj* having, showing, or inclined to mercy – **mercifully** *adv*, **mercifulness** *n*

**merciless** /'muhsilis/ *adj* having no mercy; pitiless – **mercilessly** *adv*, **mercilessness** *n*

**mercur-, mercuro-** *comb form* mercury ⟨mercur*ous*⟩ [ISV, fr *mercury*]

**mercurate** /'muhkyoorayt/ *vb* to combine or treat with mercury or a mercury salt – **mercuration** *n*

[1]**mercurial** /muh'kyooəri-əl/ *adj* 1a of the planet Mercury b born under or influenced astrologically by the planet Mercury 2 having qualities of eloquence, ingenuity, or thievishness attributed to the god Mercury or to the influence of the planet Mercury 3 characterized by rapid and unpredictable changeableness of mood 4 of, containing, or caused by mercury – **mercurially** *adv*, **mercurialness** *n*

[2]**mercurial** *n* a drug or chemical containing mercury

**mercuric** /muh'kyooərik/ *adj* of or containing mercury; *esp* containing mercury having a VALENCY of two

**mercuric chloride** *n* a white poisonous chemical compound, $HgCl_2$, used as a disinfectant and fungicide and in photography – called also CORROSIVE SUBLIMATE

**mercuric oxide** *n* a poisonous chemical compound, $HgO$, existing as a red or yellow powder and used as a pigment

**mercuric sulphide** *n* a chemical compound, $HgS$, existing as a black solid or a red solid (VERMILION) used as a pigment

**Mercurochrome** /mə'kyooərəˌkrohm/ *trademark* – used for the chemical compound MERBROMIN

**mercurous** /'muhkyooərəs/ *adj* of or containing mercury; *esp* containing mercury having a VALENCY of one

**mercurous chloride** *n* an insoluble chemical compound, $Hg_2Cl_2$, used as a fungicide and formerly as a purgative – called also CALOMEL

**mercury** /'muhkyoori/ *n* 1a a heavy silver-white poisonous metallic chemical element that is liquid at ordinary temperatures and used esp in scientific instruments – called also QUICKSILVER b the mercury in a thermometer or barometer 2 *cap* the planet nearest to the sun 3 a poisonous European plant (*Mercurialis perennis*) of the spurge family [ME *mercurie*, fr ML *mercurius*, fr L *Mercurius* Mercury, god of commerce, travel, etc (fr *merc-, merx*), & the planet Mercury]

**mercury chloride** *n* a chemical compound that is a CHLORIDE of mercury: a MERCUROUS CHLORIDE b MERCURIC CHLORIDE

**mercury-vapour lamp, mercury lamp** *n* a lamp in which an electric discharge takes place through mercury vapour causing a characteristic greenish-blue light that is used for street lighting and as a source of ultraviolet radiation

**mercy** /'muhsi/ *n* 1 compassion or forbearance shown esp to an offender or to one subject to one's power 2a an act of divine favour; a blessing b a fortunate circumstance ⟨*it was a* ~ *they found her before she froze*⟩ 3 compassionate treatment of those in distress ⟨*nuns who do works of* ~ *among the poor*⟩ [ME, fr OF *merci*, fr ML *merced-, merces*, fr L, price paid, wages, fr *merc-, merx* merchandise – more at MARKET] – **at the mercy of** wholly under the power or control of

synonyms **Mercy, clemency, lenience, lenity,** and **charity**: **mercy** stresses compassion and kindliness; **clemency** is a more neutral term, suggesting a mild disposition inclined to mercy, which may however be due to expediency as much as compassion, and is applied mainly to those in authority, with power to judge or punish. **Lenience**, and its more formal synonym **lenity**, both stress the absence of severity, sometimes to the point of indulgence. **Charity** suggests general goodwill with a capacity for understanding and tolerance ⟨*with malice toward none, with* **charity** *toward all* – Abraham Lincoln⟩. Compare ²KIND **antonyms** harsh, severe

**mercy killing** *n* euthanasia

**mercy seat** *n* **1** the gold plate resting on the ancient Jewish ark according to the account in Exodus **2** the throne of God

¹**mere** /miə/ *n* a (small) lake or marsh [ME, fr OE, sea, lake – more at MARINE]

²**mere** /miə/ *n, archaic* a boundary, landmark [ME, fr OE *māre* – more at MUNITION]

³**mere** /miə/ *adj* being what is specified and nothing else; nothing more than ⟨*a ~ child*⟩ [ME, fr L *merus* pure, unmixed – more at MORN] – **merely** *adv*

⁴**mere** /'miəri, 'meri/ *n* a ceremonial Maori hand weapon made of bone or greenstone that is held by someone speaking formally in public [Maori]

**-mere** /-miə/ *comb form* (→ *n*) part; segment ⟨*blasto*mere⟩ [Fr *-mère*, fr Gk *meros* part – more at MERIT]

**meretricious** /,merə'trishəs/ *adj* **1** tawdrily and falsely attractive ⟨*~ glamour*⟩ **2** based on pretence or insincerity; specious ⟨*~ argument*⟩ **3** *archaic* of or like a prostitute [L *meretricius*, fr *meretric-, meretrix* prostitute, fr *merēre* to earn – more at MERIT] – **meretriciously** *adv*, **meretriciousness** *n*

**merganser** /muh'gansə/ *n, pl* **mergansers, merganser** any of various usu crested fish-eating and diving sawbill ducks (genus *Mergus*); *esp* RED-BREASTED MERGANSER [NL, fr L *mergus*, a waterfowl (fr *mergere*) + *anser* goose – more at GOOSE]

**merge** /muhj/ *vt* **1** to cause to combine, unite, or coalesce **2** to blend gradually by stages that blur the distinctness of ⟨*as cultures are ~d and traditions lost*⟩ ~ *vi* **1** to become combined into one **2** to blend or come together without abrupt change ⟨*merging traffic*⟩ **synonyms** see ¹MIX [L *mergere* to dip, plunge; akin to Skt *majjati* he dives] – **mergence** *n*

**merger** /'muhjə/ *n* **1** a legal process involving the absorption of one estate, a contract, or interest into another **2** a combining of two or more organizations (e g business concerns) by absorption of one by the other(s) – compare CONSOLIDATION 2 [*merge* + *-er* (as in *waiver*)]

**meridian** /mə'ridi•ən/ *n* **1a**(1) a GREAT CIRCLE (circle with the same radius as the earth) on the surface of the earth passing through the geographic poles **a**(2) the half of such a circle included between the poles **b** a representation of such a circle or half circle numbered for longitude on a map or globe **2** a GREAT CIRCLE of the CELESTIAL SPHERE (imaginary sphere surrounding earth on whose surface the stars, planets, etc appear to be placed) passing through its poles and the ZENITH (highest point) above a given place **3** a high point, esp of success or greatness **4** a line or circle (e g on a projection of a planet or a lens) comparable to a meridian of longitude **5 meridian, meridian curve** the curve formed by the intersection of the surface of a revolving body and a plane passing through the axis of revolution **6** *archaic* the hour of noon; midday [ME, fr MF *meridien*, fr *meridien* of noon, fr L *meridianus*, fr *meridies* noon, south, irreg fr *medius* mid + *dies* day – more at MID, DEITY] – **meridian** *adj*

**meridional** /mə'ridi•ənl/ *adj* **1** of or situated in the south; southern **2** of or characteristic of people living in the south, esp of France **3** of a meridian [ME, fr MF *meridionel*, fr LL *meridionalis*, irreg fr L *meridies* noon, south] – **meridional** *n*, **meridionally** *adv*

**meringue** /mə'rang/ *n* **1** a mixture of stiffly beaten egg whites and sugar baked until crisp **2** any of various confections (e g a small cake, fruit-filled shell, or pie) made with meringue or having a meringue topping △ macaroon [Fr]

**merino** /mə'reenoh/ *n, pl* **merinos 1** (any of) a breed of fine-woolled white sheep originating in Spain and producing a heavy fleece of exceptional quality **2** a soft wool or wool and cotton clothing fabric resembling cashmere **3** a fine wool and cotton yarn used for hosiery and knitwear [Sp]

**meristem** /'meristem/ *n* a plant tissue that is the major area of growth and is usu made up of small cells capable of dividing indefinitely and giving rise to similar cells or to cells that develop and become specialized to produce the definitive tissues and organs [Gk *meristos* divided (fr *merizein* to divide, fr *meros* part) + E *-em* (as in *system*)] – **meristematic** *adj*, **meristematically** *adv*

**meristic** /mə'ristik/ *adj* **1** segmental **2** involving modification in number or in geometrical relation of body parts ⟨*~ variation in flower petals*⟩ [Gk *meristos*] – **meristically** *adv*

¹**merit** /'merit/ *n* **1a** the quality of deserving well or ill ⟨*payment by ~*⟩ **b** a praiseworthy quality; virtue ⟨*an answer that had the ~ of honesty*⟩ **c** worth, excellence ⟨*an idea of great ~*⟩ **2** spiritual credit held to be earned by good works and to ensure future benefits **3** *pl* the intrinsic rights and wrongs of a (legal) case without reference to technicalities [ME, fr OF *merite*, fr L *meritum*, fr neut of *meritus*, pp of *merēre* to deserve, earn; akin to Gk *meros* part, L *memor* mindful – more at MEMORY] – **meritless** *adj*

²**merit** *vt* to be worthy of or entitled or liable to; deserve – **meritedly** *adv*

**meritocracy** /,meri'tokrəsi/ *n* **1** an educational system that favours the talented (e g by using competitive examinations) **2** (a social system based on) leadership by the talented [¹*merit* + *-o-* + *-cracy*] – **meritocratic** *adj*

**meritorious** /,meri'tawri•əs/ *adj* deserving of reward or honour – **meritoriously** *adv*, **meritoriousness** *n*

**merit system** *n, NAm* a system by which appointments and promotions in the civil service are based on competence rather than political favouritism

**merl, merle** /muhl/ *n, Scot* the European blackbird [MF *merle*, fr L *merulus;* akin to OE *ōsle* blackbird, OHG *amsla*]

**merlin** /'muhlin/ *n* a small N American and European falcon (*Falco columbarius*) with pointed wings and prominently streaked underparts [ME *meriloun*, fr AF *merilun*, fr OF *esmerillon*, aug of *esmeril*, of Gmc origin; akin to OHG *smiril* merlin]

**merlon** /'muhlən/ *n* any of the solid upright sections between indentations of a battlemented parapet [Fr, fr It *merlone*, aug of *merlo* battlement, fr ML *merulus*, fr L, merl]

**mermaid** /'muh,mayd/ *n* a mythical sea creature usu represented with a woman's body to the waist and a fish's tail instead of legs [ME *mermaide*, fr *mer-* + *maide* maid] .

**mermaid's purse** *n* the leathery egg case of the dogfish or related fishes

**merman** /'muhmən/ *n* a mythical sea creature usu represented with a man's body to the waist and a fish's tail instead of legs

**meroblastic** /,merə'blastik/ *adj, of an egg* having a pattern of division in which only part of the egg divides to form the embryo as a result of the presence of an impeding mass of yolk material – compare HOLOBLASTIC [Gk *meros* part + ISV *-blastic*] – **meroblastically** *adv*

**merocrine** /'merəkrin, -krien/ *adj* producing or being a secretion that is discharged without major damage to the secreting cells ⟨*a ~ gland*⟩ – compare HOLOCRINE, APOCRINE [ISV, fr Gk *meros* part + *krinein* to separate – more at CERTAIN]

**meromyosin** /,merə'mie•əsin/ *n* either of two structural subunits that constitute MYOSIN (muscle fibre protein) [Gk *meros* + E *myosin*]

**-merous** /-mərəs/ *comb form* (→ *adj*) having the specified number of parts ⟨*hexa*merous⟩ [NL *-merus*, fr Gk *-merēs*, fr *meros* – more at MERIT]

**Merovingian** /,meroh'vinji•ən/ *n or adj* (a member) of the first Frankish dynasty reigning from about 500 to 751 AD [Fr *mérovingien*, fr ML *Merovingi* Merovingians, fr *Merovaeus* Merowig †458 Frankish founder of the dynasty]

**merriment** /'merimənt/ *n* **1** lighthearted gaiety or fun; mirth **2** a lively celebration or party

**merry** /'meri/ *adj* **1** full of gaiety or high spirits **2** marked by festivity **3** *informal* slightly drunk; tipsy [ME *mery*, fr OE *myrge, merge* pleasant, delightful; akin to OHG *murg* short – more at BRIEF] – **merrily** *adv*, **merriness** *n*

**merry-andrew** /'androoh/ *n, often cap M&A* one who clowns publicly; a buffoon [*merry* + the forename *Andrew*]

**merry-go-round** *n* **1** a fairground machine with seats often shaped like horses that revolve about a fixed centre **2** a whirl of activity or events ⟨*the ~ of the social calendar*⟩

**merrymaking** /'meri,mayking/ *n* **1** lively or festive activity; conviviality **2** a convivial occasion; a festivity – **merrymaker** *n*

**merrythought** /'meri,thawt/ *n, chiefly Br* a wishbone

**mes-** /meez-/, **meso-** *comb form* **1** mid; in the middle ⟨*mesocarp*⟩ ⟨*Meso*lithic⟩ **2** intermediate (e g in size or type) ⟨*mesomorph*⟩ ⟨*meson*⟩ [L, fr Gk, fr *mesos* – more at MID]

**mesa** /'maysə/ *n* a usu isolated hill, esp in SW USA, having steeply sloping sides and a level top; *also* a broad terrace with an abrupt slope on one side [Sp, lit., table, fr L *mensa*]

**mésalliance** /me'zali•əns/ *n* a marriage with a person of inferior social position [Fr, fr *més-* mis- + *alliance*]

**mesarch** /'mezahk/ *adj* of or being the XYLEM (water-conducting tissue) of a plant having METAXYLEM (part of the first-formed xylem) developed both inside and outside the PROTOXYLEM (first-formed xylem)

**mescal** /me'skal/ *n* **1** a small cactus (*Lophophora williamsii*) with rounded stems covered with small jointed protuberances that contain mescaline and are used for their hallucinogenic effects, esp among the Mexican Indians **2a** a usu colourless Mexican spirit distilled esp from the central leaves of maguey plants **b** a plant from which mescal is produced; *esp* MAGUEY [Sp *mezcal, mescal,* fr Nahuatl *mexcalli* mescal liquor]

**mescal button** *n* any of the dried disc-shaped tops of the mescal

**mescaline, mescalin** /'meskəlin, -leen/ *n* a hallucinogenic drug, $(CH_3O)_3C_6H_2(CH_2)_2NH_2$, that is obtained from any of several PEYOTE cacti

**mesdames** /may'dam/ *pl of* MADAM *or of* MADAME *or of* MRS

**mesdemoiselles** /,maydəmwah'zel/ *pl of* MADEMOISELLE

**meseems** /mi'seemz/ *vb impersonal, past* **meseemed** /mi'seemd/ *archaic* it seems to me

**mesembryanthemum** /,mezimbri'anthiməm/ *n* any of a genus (*Mesembryanthemum* of the family Aizoaceae, the mesembryanthemum family) of chiefly S African fleshy-leaved nonwoody plants or undershrubs with brightly coloured flowers [NL, genus name, fr Gk *mesēmbria* midday (fr *mes-* + *hēmera* day) + *anthemon* flower, fr *anthos* – more at ANTHOLOGY]

**mesencephalon** /,mesen'sef(ə)lon/ *n* the middle division of the brain; the midbrain – compare PROSENCEPHALON, RHOMBENCEPHALON [NL] – **mesencephalic** *adj*

**mesenchyme** /'mesengkiem/ *n* a loosely organized fibrous tissue of the MESODERM (embryonic tissue layer) of an embryo giving rise to such structures as CONNECTIVE TISSUES, blood, bone, cartilage, etc [Ger *mesenchym,* fr *mes-* + NL *-enchyma*] – **mesenchymal, mesenchymatous** *adj*

**mesenteron** /mes'entəron/ *n, pl* **mesentera** /-rə/ the middle part of the digestive tract of VERTEBRATE animals that is developed from the ARCHENTERON (cavity forming embryonic gut) [NL]

**mesentery** /'mez(ə)n,teri, 'mes-/ *n* **1a** one or more membranes in VERTEBRATE animals that consist of a double fold of the PERITONEUM (skin lining the abdomen) and that envelop the intestines and their associated structures and connect them with the rear wall of the abdominal cavity **b** a fold of membrane comparable to a mesentery and supporting an internal organ (e g the heart) that is not a part of the digestive tract **2** a support or partition in an INVERTEBRATE animal similar or comparable to the vertebrate mesentery [NL *mesenterium,* fr MF & Gk; MF *mesentere,* fr Gk *mesenterion,* fr *mes-* + *enteron* intestine – more at INTER-] – **mesenteric** *adj*

¹**mesh** /mesh/ *n* **1** an open space in a net, network, etc **2a** the cords, wires, etc that make up a net; NETWORK 1 ⟨*wire* ∼⟩ **b** a woven, knitted, or knotted fabric with evenly spaced small holes **3a** an interlocking or intertwining arrangement or construction **b** *pl* a web, snare **4** working contact (e g of the teeth of gears) ⟨*in* ∼⟩ [prob fr obs D *maesche;* akin to OHG *masca* mesh, Lith *mazgos* knot]

²**mesh** *vt* **1** to catch or entangle (as if) in the openings of a net **2** to cause to engage **3** to coordinate closely ∼ *vi* **1** to become entangled (as if) in meshes **2** *of gears* to be in or come into mesh **3** to fit together properly; coordinate

**mesial** /'meezi-əl/ *adj* **1** (in or directed towards the) middle; *esp, of a plane* dividing an animal into right and left halves **2** of being the surface of a tooth that is next to the tooth in front of it or that is nearest to the middle of the front of the jaw [*mes-* + *-ial*] – **mesially** *adv*

¹**mesic** /'meezik/ *adj* characterized by, relating to, or requiring a moderate amount of moisture ⟨*a* ∼ *habitat*⟩ ⟨*a* ∼ *plant*⟩ – compare HYDRIC, XERIC [*mes-* + *-ic*] – **mesically** *adv*

²**mesic** *adj* of a meson [*meson* + *-ic*]

**mesio-** /meezioh-, meesioh-/ *comb form* mesial and ⟨*mesiodistal*⟩ ⟨*mesiobuccal*⟩

**mesitylene** /mə'sitəleen, 'mesitəleen/ *n* an oily chemical compound, $C_6H_3(CH_3)_3$, that is found in COAL TAR and petroleum or made synthetically and that is a powerful solvent [*mesityl* (the radical $C_3H_5$), fr Gk *mesitēs* mediator]

**mesityl oxide** /'mesitil/ *n* a fragrant liquid chemical compound, $(CH_3)_2C=CHCOCH_3$, used esp as a solvent [*mesityl* (the radical $C_3H_5$)]

**mesmerism** /'mezmə,riz(ə)m/ *n* **1** hypnotism **2** hypnotic appeal [F A *Mesmer* †1815 Austrian physician & hypnotist] – **mesmerist** *n,* **mesmeric** *adj*

**mesmer·ize, -ise** /'mezməriez/ *vt* **1** to hypnotize **2** to spellbind, fascinate – **mesmerizer** *n*

**meso-** – see MES-

**mesoblast** /'meezə,blast, 'mesoh-/ *n* the embryonic cells that give rise to mesoderm; *broadly* mesoderm – **mesoblastic** *adj*

**mesocarp** /'meezoh,kahp/ *n* the middle layer of the PERICARP (ripened ovary wall enclosing the seeds) of a fruit

**mesoderm** /-,duhm/ *n* the middle of the three primary layers of cells (GERM LAYERS) of an embryo that is the source of various adult structures (e g bone, muscle, CONNECTIVE TISSUE, and the inner layer of the skin) in the mature animal; *broadly* tissue derived from this germ layer – compare ENDODERM, ECTODERM [ISV] – **mesodermal, mesodermic** *adj*

**mesogloea, mesoglea** /,meesoh'glee·ə, ,mesoh-/ *n* a gelatinous substance between the outer and inner tissue layers (ENDODERM and ECTODERM) of sponges, jellyfish, SEA ANEMONES, and related animals [NL, fr *mes-* + LGk *gloia, glia* glue – more at CLAY] – **mesogloeal** *adj*

**Mesolithic** /,mesoh'lithik/ *adj* of or being a transitional period of the STONE AGE between the Palaeolithic and the Neolithic [ISV]

**mesomere** /'meesoh,miə, 'mesoh-/ *n* a primitive segment of an embryo

**mesomerism** /mi'soməriz(ə)m/ *n, chemistry* RESONANCE 4 (variations in the possible structure of a molecule) [*mes-* + *-merism*]

**mesomorph** /'mesoh,mawf/ *n* a mesomorphic person [*mesoderm* + *-morph*]

**mesomorphic** /,mesoh'mawfik/ *adj* **1** being or concerning a state intermediate between a true liquid and a true solid **2** having or being a robust muscular body build – compare ECTOMORPHIC, ENDOMORPHIC [(1) *mes-* + *-morphic;* (2) *mesoderm* + *-morphic* (fr the predominance in such types of structures developed from the mesoderm)] – **mesomorphism, mesomorphy** *n*

**meson** /'meezon/ *n* any (e g PIONS or KAONS) of the family of HADRONS (strongly interacting particles) that are also BOSONS [ISV *mes-* + ²*-on*] – **mesonic** *adj*

**mesonephros** /,mesoh'nefrəs/ *n, pl* **mesonephroi** /-'nefroy/ either member of the middle pair of the three pairs of embryonic kidneys of VERTEBRATE animals that in the mature animal remain functional only in fishes and amphibians – compare METANEPHROS, PRONEPHROS [NL, fr *mes-* + Gk *nephros* kidney] – **mesonephric** *adj*

**mesopause** /'mesoh,pawz/ *n* the transition zone between the mesosphere and the EXOSPHERE (outer atmospheric region) [*mesosphere* + *pause*]

**mesophyll** /'mesoh,fil/ *n* the PARENCHYMA (soft tissue composed of thin-walled cells) between the outer protective layers (EPIDERMIS) of a leaf [NL *mesophyllum,* fr *mes-* + Gk *phyllon* leaf – more at BLADE] – **mesophyllic, mesophyllous** *adj*

**mesophyte** /-,fiet/ *n* a plant that grows under medium conditions of moisture [ISV] – **mesophytic** *adj*

**mesorrhine** /'mesoh,rien/ *adj* having a moderately broad nose [*mes-* + *-rrhine*]

**mesoscale** /'mesoh,skayl/ *adj* of a weather phenomenon approximately extending from 1 to 100 kilometres (about ⁵/₈ to 62¹/₂ miles) horizontally ⟨∼ *cloud pattern*⟩ ⟨∼ *wind circulation*⟩

**mesosome** /'mesoh,sohm/ *n* an ORGANELLE (specialized cell part) of bacterial cells that appears in images produced by an ELECTRON MICROSCOPE as an infolding of the membrane surrounding the cell and is a site of localization of ENZYMES used in RESPIRATION (energy-producing chemical reactions) [*mes-* + ³*-some*]

**mesosphere** /-,sfiə/ *n* a layer of the upper atmosphere which extends from the top of the STRATOSPHERE to an altitude of about 80 kilometres (50 miles) and in which light-based chemical reactions take place – **mesospheric** *adj*

**mesothelioma** /-theeli'ohmə/ *n, pl* **mesotheliomas, mesotheliomata** /-mətə/ a tumour of the lining of the heart, lungs, etc, often occurring after prolonged contact with blue asbestos dust [NL]

**mesothelium** /,mesoh'theelyəm/ *n, pl* **mesothelia** /-lyə/ EPITHELIUM (surface tissue) derived from MESODERM (embryonic tissue layer) that lines the body cavity of an embryo of a VERTEBRATE animal and gives rise to epithelia (e g of the linings of the abdomen, heart, and lungs), muscle, and several minor structures [NL, fr *mes-* + epi*thelium*] – **mesothelial** *adj*

**mesothoracic** /,mesoh·thaw'rasik/ *adj* of the mesothorax

**mesothorax** /ˌmesoh'thawraks/ *n* the middle of the three segments of the THORAX (body part between head and abdomen) of an insect [NL]

**mesothorium** /ˌmesoh'thawriəm/ *n* either of two radioactive products intermediate between the chemical element thorium and its ISOTOPE (form of an atom characterized by the makeup of its nucleus) radiothorium: **a** an isotope of radium **b** an isotope of actinium [NL]

**mesotrophic** /ˌmesoh'trohfik/ *adj, of a body of water* having a moderate amount of dissolved nutrients (eg chemical compounds or food) – compare EUTROPHIC, OLIGOTROPHIC

**Mesozoic** /ˌmezoh'zoh·ik/ *adj* of or being an era of geological history, including the interval between the PERMIAN and the TERTIARY, marked esp by the dinosaurs, marine and flying reptiles, and evergreen trees; *also* relating to the system of rocks formed in this era – **Mesozoic** *n*

**mesquite** /me'skeet/ *n* a spiny deep-rooted tree or shrub (*Prosopis juliflora*) of the pea family that forms extensive thickets in the southwestern USA and Mexico, bears pods rich in sugar, and is important as a livestock feed [Sp, fr Nahuatl *mizquitl*]

**¹mess** /mes/ *n* **1** a quantity of food: eg **1a** a prepared dish of soft or liquid food; *also* a usu unappetizing mixture of ingredients cooked or eaten together **b** enough of a specified food for a dish or a meal 〈*picked a* ~ *of greens for dinner*〉 **2a(1)** *taking sing or pl vb* a group of people (eg servicemen or servicewomen) who regularly take their meals together **a(2)** a meal so taken **b** a place where meals are regularly served to a group 〈*officers'* ~〉 **3a** a confused, dirty, or offensive state or condition; a jumble 〈*the whole house is a* ~〉 **b** a disordered situation or state resulting from misunderstanding, blundering, or misconduct 〈*got himself into a real* ~〉 [ME *mes*, fr OF, fr LL *missus* course at a meal, fr *missus*, pp of *mittere* to put, fr L, to send]

**²mess** *vt, archaic* to supply with meals ~ *vi* **1** to take meals with a mess 〈~ed *together during the war*〉 **2** to make a mess **3a** to dabble, potter **b** to handle or play with something, esp carelessly 〈*told the child not to* ~ *with his father's camera*〉 **c** to interfere, meddle 〈~ing *in other people's affairs*〉 □ (3) often + *about* or *around*

**mess about/around** *vb, chiefly Br vi* **1a** to waste time; dawdle, idle 〈*spent the whole day just messing about*〉 〈*stop messing about and say what happened*〉 **b** MESS 3a 〈*mess about with paint*〉 **c** to work according to one's whim or mood 〈*nothing . . . half so much worth doing as simply messing about in boats* – Kenneth Grahame〉 **2** *informal* to conduct an affair with 〈*messing about with another man's wife*〉 ~ *vt* to treat roughly, interferingly, or without due consideration 〈*he shouldn't mess the men about too much, they know their job . . . – The Lorry Driver*〉

**mess up** *vt* to make a mess of; spoil 〈*messed our plans up*〉

**¹message** /'mesij/ *n* **1** a communication in writing, in speech, or by signals **2** a messenger's errand or function **3** an important (central) theme or idea intended to inspire, urge, warn, enlighten, advise, etc 〈*Be True To Thyself was the* ~ *that adorned the ancient Greek temples*〉 [ME, fr OF, fr ML *missaticum*, fr L *missus*, pp of *mittere*]

**²message** *vt* **1** to send as a message or by messenger **2** to order or instruct by message ~ *vi* to communicate by message

**messaline** /ˌmesə'leen, '--,-/ *n* a soft lightweight silk dress fabric with a satin weave [Fr, fr *Messaline* Messalina †48 wife of the Roman Emperor Claudius]

**Messapian** /mə'saypiən/ *n* the poorly attested language of ancient Messapia in SE Italy

**messeigneurs** /mayse'nyuh (*Fr* mesɛɲœr)/ *pl of* MONSEIGNEUR

**messenger** /'mesinjə/ *n* **1** one who bears a message or does an errand: eg **1a** a dispatch bearer in government or military service **b** an employee who carries messages or dispatches **2** a light line used in hauling a heavier line (eg between ships) **3** *archaic* a forerunner, herald [ME *messager, messangere*, fr OF *messagier*, fr *message*]

**messenger RNA** *n* an RNA that carries the code for a particular protein from the cell's DNA to the RIBOSOME (specialized structure in a cell) and there acts as a TEMPLATE (device from which a replica is made) for the formation of that protein – called also MRNA; compare TRANSFER RNA

**messiah** /mə'sie·ə/ *n* **1** *often cap* **1a** *the* expected king and deliverer of the Jews **b** Jesus **2** a professed or accepted leader of some hope or cause [Heb *māshīaḥ* & Aram *mĕshīḥā*, lit., anointed] – **messiahship** *n*

**messianic** /ˌmesi'anik/ *adj* **1** of a messiah **2** marked by idealistic enthusiasm on behalf of a cherished cause 〈*a* ~ *sense of*

*historic mission* – Edmond Taylor〉 **3** of a time of blessedness associated in the Judaeo-Christian tradition with the end of the temporal world 〈~ *age*〉 – compare ESCHATOLOGY [(assumed) NL *messianicus*, fr LL *Messias* + L *-anicus* (as in *romanicus* Romanic)]

**messianism** /mə'sie·ə,niz(ə)m, 'mesiə-/ *n* **1** belief in a messiah **2** belief in the absolute rightness of a cause

**Messias** /mə'sie·əs/ *n* MESSIAH 1 [ME, fr LL, fr Gk, fr Aram *mĕshīḥā*]

**Messidor** /'mesidaw (*Fr* mesidɔːr)/ *n* the 10th month of the French Revolutionary calendar, corresponding to 20 June–19 July [Fr, fr L *messis* harvest + Gk *dōron* gift]

**messieurs** /'mesyuh, 'mesəz (*Fr* mesjø)/ *pl of* MONSIEUR

**mess jacket** *n* a short fitted man's jacket reaching to the waist and worn as part of a uniform on formal occasions in the mess

**mess kit** *n* a compact kit of cooking and eating utensils for soldiers, campers, etc

**messmate** /-,mayt/ *n* a member of a mess (eg on a ship)

**Messrs** /'mesəz/ *pl of* MR 〈~ *Jones, Brown, and Robinson*〉 – used in commerce

**messuage** /'meswij/ *n* a dwelling house with its outbuildings and adjacent land [ME, fr AF, prob alter. of OF *mesnage* – more at MÉNAGE]

**messy** /'mesi/ *adj* **1** marked by confusion, disorder, or dirt; untidy 〈*a* ~ *room*〉 **2** lacking neatness or precision; careless, slovenly 〈~ *thinking*〉 **3** unpleasantly or tryingly difficult to conclude 〈~ *lawsuits*〉 – **messily** *adv*, **messiness** *n*

**mestizo** /me'steezoh/, *fem* **mestiza** /-zə/ *n, pl* **mestizos**, *fem* **mestizas** a person of mixed blood; *specif* a person of mixed European and American Indian ancestry [Sp, fr *mestizo* mixed, fr LL *mixticius*, fr L *mixtus*, pp of *miscēre* to mix – more at MIX]

**mestranol** /'mestrənol, -,nohl/ *n* a synthetic OESTROGEN (SEX HORMONE), $C_{21}H_{26}O_2$, used in oral contraceptives [meth- + estrogen (var of *oestrogen*) + pregnane ($C_{21}H_{36}$) + -*ol*]

**¹met** /met/ *past of* MEET

**²met** *adj* meteorological 〈*the* ~ *office forecast*〉

**meta-** /metə-/, **met-** *prefix* **1a** occurring later than; after 〈*metapneumonia*〉 〈*metoestrus*〉 **b** situated behind or beyond 〈*metacarpus*〉 〈*metagalaxy*〉 **c** later or more highly organized or specialized form of 〈*metaxylem*〉 **2** change; transformation 〈*metamorphosis*〉 〈*metabolism*〉 **3** more comprehensive; transcending; of a higher or second order 〈*metapsychology*〉 – used with the name of a discipline to designate a new but related discipline designed to deal critically with the original one 〈*metalanguage*〉 **4a** related to 〈*metaldehyde*〉 **b** involving substitution at two positions in the BENZENE RING (circular arrangement of carbon atoms) that are separated by one carbon atom – compare ORTHO-, PARA- **c** derived from (a specified compound) by loss of water 〈*metaphosphoric acid*〉 [NL & ML, fr L or Gk; L, change, fr Gk, among, with, after, change, fr *meta* among, with, after; akin to OE *mid, mith* with, OHG *mit*]

**metabolism** /mə'tabə,liz(ə)m/ *n* **1a** the sum of the processes in the building up and destruction of living tissue; *specif* the chemical changes in living cells by which energy is provided for life-supporting processes and activities and new material is assimilated **b** all the processes by which a specified substance is dealt with in the living body 〈*fat* ~〉 **c** all the metabolic activities taking place in a particular environment 〈*the* ~ *of a lake*〉 **2** METAMORPHOSIS 2 (abrupt change in structure and form of an organism) – usu in combination 〈*holo*metabolism〉 [ISV, fr Gk *metabolē* change, fr *metaballein* to change, fr *meta-* + *ballein* to throw – more at DEVIL]

**metabolite** /mə'tabə,liet/ *n* **1** a product of metabolism **2** a substance essential to the metabolism of a particular organism or to a particular metabolic process

**metabol·ize, -ise** /mə'tabə,liez/ *vt* to subject to metabolism ~ *vi* to perform metabolism

**metacarpal** /ˌmetə'kahpl/ *n* a metacarpal bone

**metacarpus** /-'kahpəs/ *n* the part of the hand in human beings or forefoot in four-legged animals between the wrist and fingers that typically contains five (elongated) bones – compare CARPUS [NL, fr *meta-* + *carpus*] – **metacarpal** *adj*

**metacentre** /-,sentə/ *n* the point of intersection of the vertical line through the centre of buoyancy of a floating body (eg a ship) with the vertical line through the new centre of buoyancy when the body is displaced (eg by being heeled over) [Fr *métacentre*, fr *méta-* meta- + *centre* centre]

**metacentric** /ˌmetə'sentrik/ *adj* **1** of a metacentre **2** of or being a CHROMOSOME (strand of gene-carrying material in a cell) having two equal arms because of the middle position of the CENTROMERE (specialized region of chromosome) [(1) *meta- centre* + *-ic;* (2) *meta-* + *-centric*] – **metacentric** *n*

**metacercaria** /ˌmetəsə'keəri·ə/ *n, pl* **metacercariae** /-ri·ee/ a tail-less late larval stage in the development of a parasitic flatworm (TREMATODE) in which the larva is enclosed in a cyst and that is usu the form which infects the DEFINITIVE HOST (animal harbouring the sexually-reproducing form of a parasite) [NL, fr *meta-* + *cercaria*] – **metacercarial** *adj*

**metachromatic** /ˌmetəkroh'matik/ *adj* **1** *of a biological structure* (characterized by) staining in a different colour or shade from what is typical ⟨~ *granules in a bacterium*⟩ **2** having the capacity to stain different elements of a cell or tissue in different colours or shades ⟨~ *stains*⟩

**metagalaxy** /ˌmetə'galəksi/ *n* the entire system of galaxies; the universe [ISV] – **metagalactic** *adj*

**metagenesis** /-'jenəsis/ *n* ALTERNATION OF GENERATIONS; *esp* regular alternation of a sexual and an asexual generation [NL] – **metagenetic** *adj,* **metagenetically** *adv*

**¹metal** /'metl/ *n* **1** any of various non-transparent and typically bright shiny substances that can be worked and shaped into wires or thin sheets, are good conductors of electricity and heat, and form atoms (CATIONS) having positive electric charge by loss of electrons; *esp* one that is a chemical element as distinguished from an ALLOY (mixture containing metals) **2** either of the heraldic tinctures gold and silver **3** glass in its molten state **4a** printing type metal **b** set type matter **5** *chiefly Br* ROAD METAL (stones used in road construction) △ **mettle** [ME, fr OF, fr L *metallum* mine, metal, fr Gk *metallon*]

**²metal** *vt* **-ll-** (*NAm* **-l-, -ll-**) **1** to cover or provide with metal **2** *chiefly Br* to surface (a road) with broken stones

**metalanguage** /'metə,lang·gwij/ *n* a language used to talk about language

**metalled,** *NAm chiefly* **metaled** /'metld/ *adj, chiefly Br, of a road* covered or made with a surface of broken stones

**metallic** /mi'talik/ *adj* **1a** of or being a metal ⟨*a* ~ *element*⟩ **b** made of or containing a metal **c** having properties of a metal **2** yielding metal **3** resembling metal: e g **3a** having iridescent and reflective properties ⟨*a* ~ *car finish*⟩ **b** having an acrid quality ⟨*the tea has a* ~ *taste*⟩ **4** having a harsh resonance; grating ⟨*a* ~ *voice*⟩ – **metallically** *adv*

**metalliferous** /ˌmetə'lifərəs/ *adj* yielding or containing metal [L *metallifer,* fr *metallum* + *-fer* -ferous]

**metalling,** *NAm chiefly* **metaling** /'metə)ling/ *n, chiefly Br* the process of metalling a road; *also* material for metalling

**metall·ize, -ise,** *NAm also* **metalize** /'metl·iez/ *vt* to treat, combine, or coat with a metal ⟨~d *polycarbonate*⟩ – **metallization** *n*

**metallography** /ˌmetl'ogrəfi/ *n* the study of the (microscopic) structure of metals [Fr *métallographie,* fr L *metallum* + Fr *-graphie* -graphy] – **metallographer** *n,* **metallographic** *adj,* **metallographically** *adv*

**¹metalloid** /'metl·oyd/ *n* **1** a nonmetal that can combine with a metal to form an ALLOY (mixture containing a metal) **2** an element (e g arsenic) having some properties of typical metals and some of typical nonmetals

**²metalloid** *also* **metalloidal** /-dl/ *adj* **1** resembling a metal **2** of or being a metalloid

**metallurgy** /mə'taləji, 'metl,uhji/ *n* the science and technology of metals [NL *metallurgia,* fr Gk *metallon* + NL *-urgia* -urgy] – **metallurgist** *n,* **metallurgical** *adj,* **metallurgically** *adv*

*usage* The pronunciation with the stress on the second syllable is recommended for BBC broadcasters.

**metalware** /'metl,weə/ *n* ware (e g household utensils) made of metal

**metalwork** /-,wuhk/ *n* the craft or product of metalworking – **metalworker** *n*

**metalworking** /'metl,wuhking/ *n* the act or process of shaping things out of metal

**metamathematics** /ˌmetə,mathə'matiks/ *n taking sing vb* the philosophy of mathematics; *esp* the logical system of mathematics – **metamathematical** *adj*

**metamere** /'metə,miə/ *n* SOMITE (body segment) [ISV] – **metameric** *adj,* **metamerically** *adv*

**metamerism** /mə'tamə,riz(ə)m/ *n* the condition of having or the stage of evolutionary development characterized by a body made up of SOMITES (similarly structured segments)

**metamorphic** /ˌmetə'mawfik/ *adj* **1** of or involving meta-

morphosis **2** *of a rock* of or produced by metamorphism – **metamorphically** *adv*

**metamorphism** /ˌmetə'mawfiz(ə)m/ *n* a change in the constitution of rock; *specif* a pronounced change effected by pressure, heat, and water resulting in a more compact and more highly crystalline condition

**metamorphose** /metə'mawfohz, ,---'-/ *vt* **1a** to change into a different physical form, esp by supernatural means ⟨*Circe* ~d *her guests into pigs*⟩ **b** to change strikingly the appearance or character of; transform ⟨*you are so* ~d *I can hardly think you my master* – Shak⟩ **2** to cause (rock) to undergo metamorphism ~ *vi* to undergo metamorphosis [MF *metamorphoser,* fr *meta- morphose* metamorphosis, fr L *metamorphosis*]

**metamorphosis** /ˌmetə'mawfəsis, -maw'fohsis/ *n, pl* **metamorphoses** /-seez/ **1a** change of physical form, structure, or substance, esp by supernatural means **b** a striking alteration in appearance, character, or circumstances ⟨~ *from rags to riches*⟩ **2** a marked (abrupt) change in the form or structure of an animal (e g a butterfly or a frog) occurring in the course of development [L, fr Gk *metamorphōsis,* fr *metamorphoun* to transform, fr *meta-* + *morphē* form]

**metanephros** /ˌmetə'nefros/ *n, pl* **metanephroi** /-froy/ either member of the rear pair of the three pairs of embryonic kidneys of VERTEBRATE animals that persists as a definitive kidney only in mature reptiles, birds, and mammals – compare MESONEPHROS, PRONEPHROS [NL, fr *meta-* + Gk *nephros* kidney] – **metanephric**

**metaphase** /-,fayz/ *n* the stage of the two processes (MITOSIS and MEIOSIS) whereby cells divide in which the CHROMOSOMES (strands of gene-carrying material) become arranged in the EQUATORIAL PLANE (central region) of the SPINDLE (spindle-shaped arrangement of fibres) [ISV]

**metaphase plate** *n* EQUATORIAL PLATE (region of genetic material in the nucleus of a dividing cell)

**metaphor** /'metəfə, -,faw/ *n* **1** a figure of speech in which a word or phrase literally denoting one kind of object or idea is used in place of another to suggest a likeness or analogy between them (e g in *the ship ploughs the sea*); *broadly* figurative language – compare SIMILE **2** an object, activity, or idea treated as a metaphor [MF or L; MF *metaphore,* fr L *metaphora,* fr Gk, fr *metapherein* to transfer, fr *meta-* + *pherein* to bear – more at BEAR] – **metaphoric, metaphorical** *adj,* **metaphorically** *adv*

**metaphosphate** /ˌmetə'fosfayt/ *n* any of various chemical compounds (SALTS or ESTERS) formed by the combination between METAPHOSPHORIC ACID and a metal atom, an alcohol, or another chemical group [ISV]

**metaphosphoric acid** /ˌmetəfos'forik/ *n* a glassy solid acid, $HPO_3$ or $(HPO_3)n$, formed by heating ORTHOPHOSPHORIC ACID

**metaphrase** /'metə,frayz/ *n* a close translation [NL *meta- phrasis,* fr Gk, fr *metaphrazein* to translate, fr *meta-* + *phrazein* to show, tell]

**metaphysic** /-'fizik/ *n* **1** a particular system of metaphysics ⟨*the Hegelian* ~⟩ **2** the principles underlying a particular discipline or branch of knowledge ⟨*undermining the* ~ *of ethical values*⟩ [ME *metaphesyk,* fr ML *Metaphysica*] – **metaphysic** *adj*

**metaphysical** /-'fizikl/ *adj* **1** of metaphysics **2** of a realm beyond the senses or reason **3** highly abstract or abstruse ⟨~ *reasoning*⟩ **4** *often cap* of or being (English) poetry, esp of the early 17th century, that is marked by ingenious witty imagery (CONCEIT 2) expressing subtleties of thought and emotion – **metaphysically** *adv*

**Metaphysical** *n* a metaphysical English poet of the 17th century

**metaphysician** /ˌmetəfi'zish(ə)n/ *n* a student of or specialist in metaphysics

**metaphysics** /ˌmetə'fiziks/ *n taking sing vb* **1a** a division of philosophy concerned with ultimate causes and the underlying nature of things; *esp* ONTOLOGY (study of being or existence) **b** pure or speculative philosophy **2** METAPHYSIC 2 [ML *Meta- physica,* title given to Aristotle's treatise on the subject, fr Gk *(ta)meta(ta)physika,* lit., the (works) after the physical (works); fr its position in his collected works]

**metaplasia** /-'playzi·ə, -zh(y)ə/ *n* **1** transformation of one tissue into another **2** (abnormal) replacement of cells of one type by cells of another [NL] – **metaplastic** *adj*

**metaplasm** /'metə,plaz(ə)m/ *n* alteration of the regular structure of words, sentences, etc by transposition of letters, syllables, or words [L *metaplasmus,* lit., transformation, fr Gk *metaplasmos,* fr *metaplassein* to remould, fr *meta-* + *plassein* to mould – more at PLASTER] – **metaplasmic** *adj*

**metaprotein** /ˌmetəˈprohteen/ *n* any of various products derived from proteins through the action of acids or alkalies by which the solubility and sometimes the composition of the proteins is changed

**metasediment** /ˌmetəˈsedimənt/ *n* a METAMORPHIC (changed by natural processes) rock of sedimentary origin – **metasedimentary** *adj*

**metasequoia** /ˌmetəsiˈkwoy·ə/ *n* any of a genus (*Metasequoia*) of extinct and living deciduous coniferous trees of the pine family [NL, genus name, fr *meta-* + *Sequoia*]

**metasomatism** /ˌmetəˈsohməˌtiz(ə)m/ *n* METAMORPHISM (change in the constitution of rock) that involves changes in the chemical composition as well as in the texture of rock [*meta-* + Gk *sōmat-, sōma* body – more at SOMAT-] – **metasomatic** *adj,* **metasomatically** *adv*

**metastable** /-ˈstaybl/ *adj* having or characterized by only a slight margin of (chemical) stability ⟨*a ~ compound*⟩ [ISV] – **metastably** *adv,* **metastability** *n*

**metastasis** /miˈtastəsis/ *n, pl* **metastases** /-seez/ change of position, state, or form: e g **a** transfer of a disease-producing agency (e g bacteria) from the site of the disease to another part of the body **b** a secondary growth of a cancerous tumour at a site distant from the primary growth [NL, fr LL, transition, fr Gk, fr *methistanai* to change, fr *meta-* + *histanai* to cause to stand, set – more at STAND] – **metastatic** *adj,* **metastatically** *adv*

**metastas·ize, -ise** /miˈtastəsiez/ *vi* to spread by metastasis

**metatarsal** /ˌmetəˈtahsl/ *n* a metatarsal bone

**metatarsus** /-ˈtahsəs/ *n* the part of the foot in human beings or of the hind foot in four-legged animals between the ankle and toes – compare TARSUS [NL, fr *meta-* + *tarsus*] – **metatarsal** *adj,* **metatarsally** *adv*

**metathesis** /məˈtathəsis/ *n, pl* **metatheses** /-seez/ a change of place or condition: e g **a** transposition of two PHONEMES (units of sound) in a word (e g in Old English *bridd,* Modern English *bird*) **b** a chemical reaction in which different kinds of molecules exchange parts to form other kinds of molecules [Gk, fr *metatithenai* to transpose, fr *meta-* + *tithenai* to place – more at DO] – **metathetical, metathetic** *adj,* **metathetically** *adv*

**metathorax** /-ˈthawraks/ *n* the rear segment of the THORAX (body part between head and abdomen) of an insect [NL] – **metathoracic** *adj*

**metaxylem** /ˌmetəˈzielem/ *n* the part of the primary XYLEM (water-conducting tissue) of a plant that develops after the PROTOXYLEM (first-formed xylem) and is distinguished typically by broader tubular elements (TRACHEIDS) and vessels with rough or pitted walls

**metazoan** /-ˈzoh·ən/ *n* any of a group (Metazoa) that comprises all animals having the body composed of cells developed and differentiated into tissues and organs and usu a digestive cavity lined with specialized cells [NL *Metazoa,* group name, fr *meta-* + *-zoa*] – **metazoan** *adj,* **metazoal** *adj*

1**mete** /meet/ *vt* **1** to assign by measure; allot – usu + *out* ⟨~ *out punishment*⟩ **2** *archaic* MEASURE 4 [ME *meten,* fr OE *metan;* akin to OHG *mezzan* to measure, L *modus* measure, *meditari* to meditate]

2**mete** *n* a boundary ⟨~s *and bounds*⟩ [AF, fr L *meta*]

**metempsychosis** /ˌmetəmsieˈkohsis/ *n* the passing of the soul at death into another body [LL, fr Gk *metempsychōsis,* fr *meta-* + *en-* + *psychē* soul – more at PSYCHE]

**metencephalon** /ˌmetenˈsefəˌlon/ *n* the front segment of the RHOMBENCEPHALON (hindbrain); *also* the two specialized regions (CEREBELLUM and PONS) that evolve from this segment [NL] – **metencephalic** *adj*

**meteor** /ˈmeeti·ˌə, -ˌaw/ *n* **1** a phenomenon or appearance in the atmosphere (e g lightning, a rainbow, or a snowfall) **2a** any of the small particles of matter in the SOLAR SYSTEM observable directly only when heated by friction so that they glow as they fall into the atmosphere **b** the streak of light produced by the passage of a meteor [ME, fr MF *meteore,* fr ML *meteorum,* fr Gk *meteōron* phenomenon in the sky, fr neut of *meteōros* high in air, fr *meta-* + *-eōros* (akin to Gk *aeirein* to lift)]

**meteoric** /ˌmeetiˈorik/ *adj* **1** of or derived from the earth's atmosphere **2** of a meteor **3** resembling a meteor in speed or in sudden and temporary brilliance ⟨~ *rise to fame*⟩ – **meteorically** *adv*

**meteorite** /ˈmeeti·əˌriet/ *n* a meteor that reaches the surface of the earth without being completely vaporized – **meteoritic, meteoritical** *adj*

**meteoritics** /ˌmeetiəˈritiks/ *n taking sing vb* a branch of science that deals with meteors

**meteorograph** /ˈmeeti·ərəˌgrahf, -ˌgraf/ *n* an apparatus for recording automatically and simultaneously several meteorologic elements – **meteorographic** *adj*

**meteoroid** /ˈmeeti·əˌroyd/ *n* **1** a meteor revolving around the sun **2** a meteor particle itself without relation to the phenomena it produces when entering the earth's atmosphere – **meteoroidal** *adj*

**meteorology** /ˌmeeti·əˈroləji/ *n* **1** a branch of science that deals with the atmosphere and its phenomena and esp with weather and weather forecasting **2** the atmospheric phenomena and weather of a region ⚠ metrology [Fr or Gk; Fr *météorologie,* fr MF, fr Gk *meteōrologia,* fr *meteōron* + *-logia* -logy] – **meteorologist** *n,* **meteorologic, meteorological** *adj,* **meteorologically** *adv*

**meteor shower** *n* the phenomenon observed when members of a group of meteors encounter the earth's atmosphere and their luminous paths appear to spray out from a single point

1**meter** /ˈmeetə/ *n, NAm* a metre

2**meter** *n* **1** an instrument for measuring (and recording) the amount of something (e g gas, electricity, or parking time) used **2** an impression of a franking machine [2*-meter*]

3**meter** *vt* **1** to measure by means of a meter **2** to supply in a measured or regulated amount **3** to print postal data on by means of a franking machine

1**-meter** /-mətə/ *comb form* (→ *n*) measure or unit of metrical verse ⟨*penta*meter⟩ – compare FOOT 4 [1*metre*]

2**-meter** *comb form* (→ *n*) instrument or means for measuring ⟨*baro*meter⟩ [Fr *-mètre,* fr Gk *metron* measure]

**meter maid** *n, chiefly NAm informal* a woman TRAFFIC WARDEN [(*parking*) *meter*]

**meth-** /meth-/, **metho-** *comb form* methyl ⟨meth*acrylic*⟩ [ISV, fr *methyl*]

**methacrylate** /methˈakriˌlayt/ *n* **1** any of various chemical compounds (SALTS or ESTERS) formed by the combination between METHACRYLIC ACID and a metal atom, an alcohol, or another chemical group **2** an ACRYLIC RESIN (glassy plasticlike substance) or plastic made from a derivative of METHACRYLIC ACID [ISV]

**methacrylic acid** /ˌmethəˈkrilik/ *n* an acid, $CH_2C(CH_3)CO_2H$, used esp in making ACRYLIC RESINS (glassy plasticlike substances) or plastics [ISV]

**methadon** /ˈmethəˌdon/ *n* methadone

**methadone** /ˈmethəˌdohn/ *n* a synthetic addictive drug, $C_{21}H_{27}NO$, used for the relief of pain and as a substitute drug in the treatment of heroin addiction [6-di-*meth*yl*a*mino-4, 4-*d*iphenyl-3-heptan*one*]

**methaemoglobin** /metˌheeməˈglohbin, meˌtheemə-/ *n* a soluble brown blood pigment that differs from the red haemoglobin in containing iron in its FERRIC form and in being unable to combine reversibly with oxygen [ISV]

**methamphetamine** /ˌmethamˈfetəmin/ *n* an AMPHETAMINE (stimulant drug), $C_6H_5CH_2CH(NHCH_3)CH_3$, used as a stimulant for the CENTRAL NERVOUS SYSTEM and in the treatment of obesity [*meth-* + *amphetamine*]

**methane** /ˈmeeˌthayn/ *n* a colourless odourless inflammable gas, $CH_4$, that is a member of the ALKANE series of organic chemical compounds, is a product of decomposition of plant or animal matter in marshes and mines or of the CARBONIZATION (decomposition by heat) of coal, and is used as a fuel and as a raw material in synthesis of chemical compounds [ISV]

**methane series** *n* ALKANES (series of related chemical compounds)

**methanol** /ˈmethənol/ *n* a light inflammable poisonous liquid alcohol, $CH_3OH$, formed in the DESTRUCTIVE DISTILLATION (decomposition by heat) of wood or made synthetically, that is used esp as a solvent, antifreeze, or a raw material in chemical synthesis and is added to ETHYL ALCOHOL to make it unfit to drink [ISV]

**Methedrine** /ˈmethədrin/ *trademark* – used for methamphetamine

**metheglin** /məˈtheglin/ *n* a drink usu made of fermented honey and water; mead [W *meddyglyn,* fr *meddyg* physician + *llyn* liquor, lake]

**methicillin** /ˌmethəˈsilin/ *n* a type of penicillin used esp to treat infections by penicillin-resistant STAPHYLOCOCCI (type of bacteria) [*meth-* + pen*icillin*]

**methinks** /mi'thingks/ *vb impersonal* **methought** /mi'thawt/ *archaic* it seems to me [ME *me thinketh*, fr OE *mē thincth*, fr *mē* (dat of *ic* I) + *thincth* (it) seems, fr *thyncan* to seem – more at I, THINK]

**methionine** /mi'thie·ə,neen, -,nien/ *n* a sulphur-containing ESSENTIAL AMINO ACID, $CH_3S(CH_2)_2CH(NH_2)COOH$, that is required by the body for normal development and health, and forms part of many proteins [ISV, fr *methyl* + *thion-* + *-ine*]

**metho** /'methoh/ *n*, *Austr* METHYLATED SPIRITS (e g drunk as a source of alcohol) [by shortening & alter.]

**method** /'methəd/ *n* **1a** a systematic plan or procedure for doing something **b** a regular way or process of doing something **2a** an orderly arrangement or system **b** the habitual practice of regularity and orderliness **3** *cap* a dramatic technique by which an actor seeks to gain complete identification with the inner personality of the character being portrayed – often + *the* [MF or L; MF *methode*, fr L *methodus*, fr Gk *methodos*, fr *meta-* + *hodos* way – more at CEDE]

**methode champenoise** *n* a method of producing sparkling wine that entails allowing the wine to ferment for a second time after it has been bottled [Fr *méthode champenoise*, lit., method of Champagne – more at CHAMPAGNE]

**methodical** /mə'thodikl/, *NAm also* **methodic** *adj* **1** arranged, characterized by, or performed with method or order ⟨*a ~ treatment of the subject*⟩ **2** habitually proceeding according to method; systematic ⟨*~ in his daily routine*⟩ – **methodically** *adv*, **methodicalness** *n*

**Methodism** /'methədiz(ə)m/ *n* **1** the doctrines and practice of Methodists **2** the Methodist churches

**Methodist** /'methədist/ *n* a member of any of the denominations deriving from the Wesleyan revival in the CHURCH OF ENGLAND, having an evangelical character, and stressing personal and social morality [*method* + *-ist;* orig sense, one devoted to a particular method] – **Methodist** *adj*, **Methodistic** *adj*

**method·ize, -ise** /'methədiez/ *vt* to reduce to method; systematize

**methodological** /,methədə'lojikl/ *adj* of method or methodology – **methodologically** *adv*

**methodology** /,methə'doləji/ *n* **1** a body of methods and rules employed by a science or discipline **2** the analysis of the principles or procedures of inquiry in a particular field [NL *methodologia*, fr L *methodus* + *-logia* -logy] – **methodologist** *n*

**methotrexate** /,methə'treksayt/ *n* a synthetic anticancer drug, $C_{20}H_{22}N_8O_5$, that is an ANTIMETABOLITE (substance that inhibits life-supporting processes) and is used esp to treat LYMPHOMAS (tumours of certain glandular tissues) and some forms of leukaemia [*meth-* + *-trexate*, of unknown origin]

**meths** /meths/ *n taking sing vb*, *Br informal* METHYLATED SPIRITS [by contr]

**'meths-,drinker** *n*, *Br* an alcoholic who habitually drinks methylated spirits

**Methuselah** /mi'thyoohzələ/ *n* an outsize champagne bottle holding eight times the usual amount [*Methuselah* (Heb *Mĕthūshā'ĕl*), biblical character said to have lived 969 years (Gen 5:27)]

**methyl** /'methil, 'meethil, -,thiel/ *n* a chemical group, $CH_3$, derived from the gas methane by removal of one hydrogen atom [ISV, back-formation fr *methylene*] – **methylic** *adj*

**methyl acetate** *n* an inflammable fragrant liquid, $CH_3CO_2CH_3$, used esp as a solvent and paint remover

**methylal** /'methi,lal/ *n* an inflammable liquid, $CH_2(OCH_3)_2$ of pleasant smell used esp as a solvent, in perfumery, and in making adhesives [ISV]

**methyl alcohol** *n* METHANOL

**methylamine** /,methilə'meen, -'amin, mə'thiləmeen/ *n* an inflammable explosive gas, $CH_3NH_2$, that has a strong smell of ammonia and is used esp in the synthesis of other chemical compounds (e g dyes and insecticides) [ISV]

**methylase** /'methi,layz, -,lays/ *n* an ENZYME that speeds up methylation (e g of RNA or DNA)

**methylate** /'methilayt/ *vt* **1** to impregnate or mix with METHANOL (type of alcohol) **2** to introduce the methyl group into – **methylator** *n*, **methylation** *n*

**methylated spirits** *n taking sing or pl vb* any of several

mixtures of alcohol treated (e g with methanol) to make them undrinkable but often abused

**methyl bromide** *n* a poisonous gaseous chemical compound, $CH_3Br$, used chiefly as a fumigant against rodents, worms, insects, etc

**methylcholanthrene** /,methilkə'lanthreen/ *n* a potent cancer-producing chemical compound, $C_{21}H_{16}$ [*methyl* + *cho*lic acid + *anthracene*]

**methyldopa** /,methil'dohpə/ *n* a synthetic drug, $HO_2C_6H_3CH_2C(NH_2)(CH_3)CO_2H$, used to treat high blood pressure

**methylene** /'methə,leen/ *n* a chemical group, $CH_2$, with a VALENCY of two that is derived from the gas methane by removal of two hydrogen atoms [Fr *méthylène*, fr Gk *methy*wine + *hylē* wood – more at MEAD]

**methylene blue** *n* a dye, $C_{16}H_{18}ClN_3S.3H_2O$, used esp to stain biological specimens, as an antidote in cyanide poisoning, and as an INDICATOR to show completion of certain chemical reactions

**methylene chloride** *n* a nonflammable liquid, $CH_2Cl_2$, used esp as a solvent, paint remover, and refrigerant

**methyl methacrylate** *n* a flammable liquid, $C_5H_8O_2$, that is able to combine chemically (POLYMERIZE) with itself to form chainlike structures and is used esp in the production of resins

**methylnaphthalene** /,methil'nafthəleen, -'napthə-/ *n* either of two chemical compounds, $C_{11}H_{10}$; *esp* an oily liquid used in determining CETANE NUMBERS (measure of quality of diesel fuels)

**methyl parathion** *n* a potent synthetic phosphorus-containing insecticide, $C_8H_{10}NO_5PS$, that is more poisonous than PARATHION

**methysergide** /,methə'suhjied/ *n* a synthetic drug, $C_{21}H_{27}N_3O_2$, used in the treatment and prevention of some types of headache (e g migraine) [*methyl* + ly*serg*ic acid + am*ide*]

**metic** /'metik/ *n* an alien resident of an ancient Greek city who had some civil privileges [Gk *metoikos*, fr *meta-* + *oikos* house – more at VICINITY]

**metical** /meti'kal/ *n* – see MONEY table [Pg, fr Ar *mithqāl*, a unit of weight]

**meticulous** /mə'tikyooləs/ *adj* marked by extreme or excessive care in the consideration or treatment of details [L *meticulosus* fearful, fr *metus* fear + *-iculosus* (as in *periculosus* dangerous)] – **meticulously** *adv*, **meticulousness** *n*, **meticulosity** *n*
**usage** The use of **meticulous(ly)** in a favourable sense ⟨*a meticulously spotless kitchen*⟩ is now well established though disapproved of by some old-fashioned writers on usage. **synonyms** see CAREFUL

**métier** /'maytyay/ *n* **1** one's vocation, trade **2** an area of activity in which one is expert or successful; one's forte [Fr, fr (assumed) VL *misterium*, alter. of L *ministerium* work, ministry]

**metif** /may'teef/ *n* OCTOROON (person with some Negro blood) [Fr *métif*, alter. of *métis*]

**métis** /me'tees/ *n*, *pl* **métis** one of mixed blood: **a** a half-breed **b** a crossbred animal [Fr, fr LL *mixticius* mixed – more at MESTIZO]

**metoestrus** /me'teestrəs/ *n* the period of regression and recuperation that follows OESTRUS (period of sexual excitement) in a mammal's sexual cycle [NL]

**Metol** /'meetol/ *trademark* – used for a photographic developer

**Metonic cycle** /mi'tonik/ *n* a period of almost exactly 19 years covering all the phases of the moon, after which the new moons occur again on the same dates in the calendar year [*Meton*, 5th-c BC Gk astronomer]

**metonym** /'metənim/ *n* a word used in metonymy [back-formation fr *metonymy*]

**metonymy** /mi'tonəmi/ *n* a figure of speech in which the name of an attribute of a thing is used instead of the thing itself (e g in "lands belonging to the *crown*") [L *metonymia*, fr Gk *metōnymia*, fr *meta-* + *-ōnymia* -onymy]

**'me-,too** *adj* imitative, unoriginal ⟨*inept advertising expenditure and ~ product development – Handbook for Managers*⟩ – **me-tooer** *n*, **me-tooism** *n*

**metope** /'metohp, 'metəpi/ *n* the space between two square projections (TRIGLYPHS) of an ornamental band (FRIEZE) in DORIC architecture, often adorned with carved work [Gk *metopē*, fr *meta-* + *opē* opening; akin to Gk *ōps* eye, face – more at EYE]

**metr-, metro-** *comb form* uterus ⟨*metritis*⟩ ⟨*metrorrhagia*⟩ [NL, fr Gk *mētr-*, fr *mētra*, fr *mētr-*, *mētēr* mother – more at MOTHER]

**¹metre**, *NAm chiefly* **meter** /'meetə/ *n* **1** systematically arranged and measured rhythm in verse: eg **1a** rhythm that continuously imposes a single basic pattern on a line of verse ⟨*iambic* ∼⟩ **b** rhythm characterized by regular recurrence of a systematic arrangement of basic patterns in larger figures ⟨*ballad* ∼⟩ **2** a basic recurrent rhythmical pattern of accents and beats per bar in music [ME, fr OE & MF; OE *mēter*, fr L *metrum*, fr Gk *metron* metre, measure; MF *metre*, fr OF, fr L *metrum* – more at MEASURE]

**²metre**, *NAm chiefly* **meter** *n*, the SI unit of length equal to 1 650 763.73 wavelengths of the radiation corresponding to the transition between two specific ENERGY LEVELS of the krypton ISOTOPE (form of an atom characterized by the makeup of its nucleus) $_{36}Kr^{86}$ (about 1.094 yards) [Fr *mètre*, fr Gk *metron* measure]

**,metre-,kilogram-'second** *adj* of or being a system of units based on the metre as the unit of length, the kilogram as the unit of mass, and the mean solar second as the unit of time – compare SI

**¹metric** /'metrik/ *n* **1** *pl* a part of prosody that deals with metrical structure **2** a mathematical function that associates with each pair of elements of a set a nonnegative REAL NUMBER representing their distance apart and satisfying the conditions that the number is zero only if the two elements are identical, the number is the same regardless of the order in which the two elements are taken, and the number associated with one pair of elements plus that associated with one member of the pair and a third element is equal to or greater than the number associated with the other member of the pair and the third element

**²metric** *adj* **1** metric, metrical **1a** based on the metre as a standard of measurement – compare SI **b** of the metric system ⟨*a* ∼ *study*⟩ **2** metrical – **metrically** *adv*

**-metric** /-'metrik/, **-metrical** /-kl/ *comb form* (→ *adj*) **1** of, employing, or obtained by (a specified meter) ⟨*galvano*metric⟩ **2** of the art, process, or science of measuring (something specified) ⟨*chrono*metric⟩ ⟨*gravi*metrical⟩

**metrical** /'metrikl/, **metric** *adj* **1** of or composed in metre **2** of measurement – **metrically** *adv*

**metricate** /'metrikayt/ *vt* to change into or express in the METRIC SYSTEM ∼ *vi* to adopt the METRIC SYSTEM – **metrication** *n*

**metric hundredweight** *n* a unit of weight equal to 50 kilograms

**metric·ize, -ise** /'metri,siez/ *vb* to metricate

**metric space** *n* a mathematical set for which a metric is defined for any pair of elements

**metric system** *n* a decimal system of weights and measures based on the metre and the kilogram

**metric ton** *n* a tonne

**metrist** /'metrist/ *n* one skilled in the handling of poetic metre

**metro** /'metroh/ *n, pl* **metros** an underground railway system in a city ⟨*the Leningrad* ∼⟩ [Fr *métro*, short for (*chemin de fer*) *métropolitain* metropolitan railway]

**Metro** /'metroh/ *adj, Can* of the inner urban area of a Canadian city, esp of Toronto ⟨*gave* ∼ *police a description* – *Globe & Mail* (*Toronto*)⟩ [short for *metropolitan*]

**metro-** – see METR-

**metrology** /mi'troləji/ *n* **1** the science of weights and measures or of measurement **2** a system of weights and measures △ meteorology [Fr *métrologie*, fr Gk *metrologia* theory of ratios, fr *metron* measure – more at MEASURE] – **metrologist** *n*, **metrological** *adj*, **metrologically** *adv*

**metronidazole** /,metrə'niedə,zohl/ *n* a synthetic drug, $C_6H_9N_3O_3$, used to treat infections by PROTOZOA (single-celled organisms), esp of the vagina [*methyl* + *-tron-* (prob fr *nitro*) + *imide* + *azole*]

**metronome** /'metrə,nohm/ *n* an instrument designed to mark exact time by a regularly repeated tick [Gk *metron* + *-nomos* controlling, fr *nomos* law – more at NIMBLE]

**metronomic** /,metrə'nomik/ *also* **metronomical** /-kl/ *adj* mechanically regular in action or tempo – **metronomically** *adv*

**metronymic** /,metrə'nimik/ *n* MATRONYMIC [MGk *mētrōnymikos* named after one's mother, fr Gk *mētr-, mētēr* mother + *onyma, onoma* name] – **metronymic** *adj*

**metropolis** /mi'tropəlis/ *n* **1** the mother city or state of a colony, esp in ancient Greece **2** the chief or capital city of a country, state, or region **3a** a centre of a usu specified activity ⟨*a great business* ∼⟩ **b** a large or important city [LL, fr Gk *mētropolis*, fr *mētr-, mētēr* mother + *polis* city – more at MOTHER, POLICE]

**¹metropolitan** /,metrə'polit(ə)n/ *n* **1** the primate (eg an archbishop) of an ecclesiastical province **2** one who lives in a metropolis or displays metropolitan conduct or customs

**²metropolitan** *adj* **1** of or constituting a metropolitan or his ecclesiastical jurisdiction (SEE) **2** (characteristic) of a metropolis **3** of or constituting a mother country [LL *metropolitanus* of the see of a metropolitan, fr *metropolita*, n, metropolitan, fr LGk *mētropolitēs*, fr *mētropolis* see of a metropolitan, fr Gk, chief city]

**metropolitan area** *n* a large urban area in Britain (eg Greater Manchester) governed by a single local authority with wide powers

**metrorrhagia** /,meetrə'rayjyə, ,met-, -raw'ray-/ *n* profuse bleeding from the womb, esp between menstrual periods [NL, fr *metr-* + *-rrhagia*] – **metrorrhagic** *adj*

**-metry** /-mətri/ *comb form* (→ *n*) art, process, or science of measuring (something specified) ⟨*chrono*metry⟩ ⟨*photo*metry⟩ [ME *-metrie*, fr MF, fr L *-metria*, fr Gk, fr *metrein* to measure, fr *metron* – more at MEASURE]

**metteur en scène** /me,tuh on 'sen (*Fr* metœr ã sɛn)/ *n* **1** a theatre producer **2** a film director [Fr, lit., one who puts on stage]

**mettle** /'metl/ *n* **1** quality of temperament or disposition ⟨*gentlemen of brave* ∼ – Shak⟩ **2a** vigour and strength of spirit or temperament; ardour ⟨*suspected to have more tongue in his head than* ∼ *in his bosom* – Sir Walter Scott⟩ **b** staying quality; stamina ⟨*trucks had proved their* ∼ *in army transport* – Pioneer & Pacemaker⟩ △ metal [alter. of *metal*] – **mettled** *adj* – **on one's mettle** ready to do one's best

**mettlesome** /-s(ə)m/ *adj* full of mettle; spirited

**meuniere** /muh'nyeə (*Fr* mønjɛːr)/ *adj* served with a sauce of melted butter, parsley, and lemon juice ⟨*sole* ∼⟩ [Fr (*à la*) *meunière*, lit., in the manner of a miller's wife, fr *meunière* miller's wife, fem of *meunier* miller, fr L *molinarius*, fr *molina* mill]

**¹mew** /myooh/ *n* a gull; *esp* a Eurasian gull (*Larus canus*) [ME, fr OE *mǣw*; akin to ON *mār* gull (cf FULMAR)]

**²mew** *vi* to utter a miaow or similar sound ⟨*gulls* ∼ed *over the bay*⟩ ∼ *vt* to utter by mewing; miaow [ME *mewen*, of imit origin]

**³mew** *n* a miaow

**⁴mew** *n* **1** *pl but taking sing or pl vb, chiefly Br* **1a** stables, usu with living quarters, built round an open courtyard **b** living quarters adapted from such stables **2** *archaic* a cage for hawks, esp while moulting [ME *mewe* cage for hawks, fr MF *mue*, fr *muer* to moult, fr L *mutare* to change – more at MISS; (1) the *Mews*, the royal stables in London, built on the site of the former royal hawks' mews]

**⁵mew** *vt* to shut in; confine – often + *up*

**mewl** /myoohl/ *vi* **1** to cry weakly; whimper **2** to mew, miaow [imit]

**Mexican** /'meksikən/ *n* **1** a native or inhabitant of Mexico **2** NAHUATL **2** (American Indian language) [*Mexico*, country in N America] – **Mexican** *adj*

**mezereon** /mə'ziəri-ən/ *n* a small European shrub (*Daphne mezereum* of the family Thymelaeaceae) with fragrant lilac purple flowers [ME *mizerion*, fr ML *mezereon*, fr Ar *māzariyūn*, fr Per]

**mezuzah, mezuza** /mə'zoohzə/ *n* a small oblong case containing a parchment inscribed with Deut 6:4–9 and 11:13–21 and the name Shaddai and fixed to the doorpost by some Jewish families as a sign and reminder of their faith [Heb *mězūzāh* doorpost]

**mezzanine** /'mezəneen/ *n* **1** a low-ceilinged storey between two main storeys (eg the ground and first floors) of a building; *esp* an intermediate storey that projects in the form of a balcony **2** *Br* the area beneath the stage in a theatre [Fr, fr It *mezzanino*, fr *mezzano* middle, fr L *medianus* middle, median]

**mezza voce** /,metsə 'vohchi/ *adv or adj* with medium or half volume of tone – used as a direction in music [It, half voice]

**mezzo** /'metsoh/, **mezzo-soprano** *n, pl* **mezzos, mezzo-sopranos** a woman's voice of a compass between that of the SOPRANO and CONTRALTO; *also* a singer having this voice [It *mezzosoprano*, fr *mezzo* + *soprano*]

**mezzo forte** /,metsoh 'fawti/ *adj or adv* moderately loud – used as a direction in music [It]

**mezzo piano** /,metsoh pi'annoh, 'pyahnoh/ *adj or adv* moderately soft – used as a direction in music [It]

**mezzo-rilievo, mezzo-relievo** /,metsoh ri'leevoh, ri'lyayvoh/ *n, pl* **mezzo-rilievos, mezzo-relievos** sculptural technique (RELIEF 6a) which is halfway between BAS-RELIEF and HIGH RELIEF and in which about half of the circumference of the modelled form stands out from the flat background [It *mezzorilievo*, fr *mezzo* middle, moderate, half + *rilievo* relief]

**mezzotint** /'metsoh͵tint/ *n* a method of engraving on copper or steel in which the whole plate is uniformly roughened and parts then scraped smooth or left rough to produce light and shade; *also* a print produced by this method [modif of It *mezzatinta*, fr *mezza* (fem of *mezzo*) + *tinta* tint]

**mho** /moh/ *n, pl* **mhos** SIEMENS (unit of electrical conductance) [backward spelling of *ohm*]

**mi** /mee/ *n, music* [4]ME

**mi-** /'mie-/, **mio-** *comb form* less ⟨Mio*cene*⟩ [prob fr NL *meio-*, fr Gk, fr *meiōn* – more at MINOR]

**MI5** /͵em ie 'fiev/ *n* the security service of British Military Intelligence – not now in official use [*military* intelligence]

**MI6** /͵em ie siks/ *n* the espionage service of British Military Intelligence – not now in official use

**Miami** /mie'ami/ *n, pl* **Miamis**, *esp collectively* **Miami** a member of an American Indian people originally of Wisconsin and Indiana

**miaow** /mi'ow, myow/ *n* **1** the characteristic cry of a cat **2** a spiteful or malicious remark [imit] – **miaow** *vi*

**miasma** /mi'azmə/ *n, pl* **miasmas** *also* **miasmata** /-mətə/ **1** a heavy vapour (eg from a swamp) formerly believed to cause disease; *broadly* any heavy or foul-smelling vapour or atmosphere ⟨a ~ *of tobacco smoke*⟩ **2** a pervasive influence or atmosphere that tends to weaken or corrupt ⟨*freed from the* ~ *of poverty* – Sir Arthur Bryant⟩ [NL, fr Gk, defilement, fr *miainein* to pollute] – **miasmal** *adj*, **miasmatic** *adj*, **miasmic** *adj*

**mica** /'miekə/ *n* any of various coloured or transparent silicon-containing minerals occurring as crystals that readily separate into very thin flexible leaves [NL, fr L, grain, crumb; akin to Gk *mikros* small] – **micaceous** *adj*

**Micah** /'miekə/ *n* – see BIBLE table [*Micah* (Heb *Mīkhāh*, short for *Mīkhāyāh*), 8th-c BC Heb prophet]

**mice** /mies/ *pl of* MOUSE

**micelle** /mi'sel/ *n* a unit of structure built up from chains of molecules or ions: eg **a** an ordered region in a fibre (eg of cellulose or rayon) **b** a molecular aggregate that forms a particle in a COLLOID (solution containing suspended particles) [NL *micella*, fr L *mica*] – **micellar** *adj*

**Michaelmas** /'mik(ə)lməs/ *n* (September 29 celebrated as) the feast of St Michael the Archangel [ME *mychelmesse*, fr OE *Michaeles mæsse* Michael's mass]

**Michaelmas daisy** *n* any of several (autumn-blooming) ASTERS (leafy-stemmed plants) widely grown in the garden

**Michaelmas term** *n* the university term beginning in October

**Micheas** /'miekiəs/ *n* – see BIBLE table [LL *Michaeas*, fr Gk *Michaias*, fr Heb *Mīkhāyāh* Micah]

**mick** /mik/ *n, chiefly derog* an Irishman [*Mick*, nickname for *Michael*, common Irish forename]

[1]**mickey** /'miki/ *n, chiefly Can* a usu small bottle of alcohol (eg whisky) [perh fr *Mickey*, nickname for *Michael*]

[2]**mickey** *n* [origin unknown] – **take the mickey** *informal* to imitate in a mocking manner; tease – usu + *out of* ⟨*always taking the mickey out of his teachers*⟩

**Mickey Finn** /fin/ *n* an alcoholic drink doctored with a purgative or a hypnotic drug [prob fr the name *Mickey Finn*]

**Mickey Mouse** *adj, informal* trivial, petty [*Mickey Mouse*, cartoon character created by Walt Disney †1966 US film producer]

**mickle** /'mikl/ *adj, chiefly Scot* great, much [ME *mikel*, fr OE *micel* – more at MUCH] – **mickle** *adv, chiefly Scot*

**Micmac** /'mik͵mak/ *n, pl* **Micmacs**, *esp collectively* **Micmac 1** a member of an American Indian people of eastern Canada **2** the ALGONQUIAN language of the Micmac people [Micmac *Migmac*, lit., allies]

**micr-** /miekr-/, **micro-** *comb form* **1a** small; minute ⟨*micro*cosm⟩ **b** used for or involving minute quantities or variations ⟨*micro*barograph⟩ **c** microscopic ⟨*micro*organism⟩ **2** one millionth (10[-6]) part of (a specified unit) ⟨*micro*gram⟩ ⟨*micro*hm⟩ **3** enlarging; magnifying; amplifying ⟨*micro*phone⟩: eg **3a** used in or involving microscopy ⟨*micro*dissection⟩ **b** used in or connected with microphotography ⟨*micro*copy⟩ ⟨*micro*film⟩ **4** of a small or localized area ⟨*micro*climate⟩ ⟨*micro*fauna⟩ *synonyms* see [1]SMALL [ME *micro-*, fr L, fr Gk *mikr-*, *mikro-*, fr *mikros, smikros* small, short; akin to OE *smēal*ic careful, exquisite]

[1]**micro** /'miekroh/ *adj* very small; *esp* microscopic [*micr-*]

[2]**micro** *n* **1** a microcomputer **2** a microprocessor

**microanalysis** /͵miekroh·ə'naləsis/ *n* **1** chemical analysis on a small or minute scale that usu requires special, very sensitive, or small-scale apparatus **2** analysis of a small area or sphere of activity; *esp* detailed analysis of part of a large structure (eg society) – **microanalyst** *n*, **microanalytic, microanalytical** *adj*

**microanatomy** /͵miekroh·ə'natəmi/ *n* HISTOLOGY (biology of the microscopic structure of organisms) – **microanatomical** *adj*

**microbarograph** /͵miekroh'barə͵grahf, -͵graf/ *n* a BAROGRAPH (type of barometer) for recording small and rapid changes in atmospheric pressure [ISV]

**microbe** /'miekrohb/ *n* a microorganism, germ [ISV *micr-* + Gk *bios* life – more at QUICK] – **microbial, microbic** *adj*

**microbiology** /͵miekrəbie'oləji, -kroh-/ *n* the biology of bacteria and other microscopic forms of life [ISV] – **microbiologist** *n*, **microbiological, microbiologic** *adj*, **microbiologically** *adv*

**microcard** /'miekroh͵kahd/ *n* a sensitized card on which printed matter is reproduced photographically in greatly reduced form

**microcephalic** /͵miekrohsi'falik/ *n or adj* (an individual) with an abnormally small head and usu mental defects – **microcephaly** *n*

**microchip** /-͵chip/ *n* CHIP 4

**microcircuit** /-͵suhkit/ *n* INTEGRATED CIRCUIT; *also* a compact electronic circuit constructed from components of small size – **microcircuitry** *n*

**microcirculation** /͵miekroh͵suhkyoo'laysh(ə)n/ *n* the part of the body's CIRCULATORY SYSTEM made up of very fine channels (eg blood capillaries and venules) – **microcirculatory** *adj*

**microclimate** /-͵kliemət/ *n* the essentially uniform local climate of a usu small site or habitat [ISV] – **microclimatic** *adj*

**microclimatology** /͵miekroh͵kliemə'toləji/ *n* the study of microclimates; science of the climates of restricted areas – **microclimatologist** *n*, **microclimatological** *adj*

**microcline** /'miekroh͵klien/ *n* a white to pale yellow, red, or green mineral, KAlSi₃O₈, of the FELDSPAR group that is like the mineral ORTHOCLASE in composition [Ger *mikroklin*, fr *mikr-* micr- + Gk *klinein* to lean – more at LEAN]

**micrococcus** /͵miekroh'kokəs/ *n, pl* **micrococci** /-'kok(s)ie/ a small spherical bacterium; *esp* one of a genus (*Micrococcus*) in which growth forms irregular groups [NL, genus name, fr *micr-* + *coccus*] – **micrococcal** *adj*

**microcode** /'miekroh͵kohd/ *n, computers* code used in MICROPROGRAMMING

**microcomputer** /-kəm'pyoohtə/ *n* a very small computer composed of one or more INTEGRATED CIRCUITS functioning as a unit and typically intended for a single user

**microcopy** /'miekroh͵kopi/ *n* a photographic copy in which graphic matter is greatly reduced in size [ISV] – **microcopy** *vb*

**microcosm** /'miekrə͵koz(ə)m/ *n* **1** a little world; *esp* an individual human being or human nature seen as a miniature model of the world or the universe **2** a whole (eg a community) that is a miniature version of a larger whole [ME, fr ML *microcosmus*, modif of Gk *mikros kosmos*] – **microcosmic** *adj*, **microcosmically** *adv*

**microcosmic salt** *n* a chemical compound, NaNH₄HPO₄.4H₂O, used as a FLUX (substance promoting melting) in testing for the presence of certain metals

**microcrystal** /'miekroh͵kristl/ *n* a crystal visible only under the microscope – **microcrystalline, microcrystallinity** *n*

**microculture** /'miekroh͵kulchə/ *n* a microscopic CULTURE of cells or organisms – **microcultural** *adj*

**microcyte** /'miekroh͵siet/ *n* a small RED BLOOD CELL that appears in the blood, esp in some ANAEMIAS (blood-deficiency diseases) [ISV] – **microcytic** *adj*

**microdissection** /͵miekrohdi'seksh(ə)n/ *n* dissection under the microscope; *specif* dissection of cells and tissues by means of fine needles that are precisely manipulated by a series of levers

**microdot** /'miekrə͵dot/ *n* **1** a photographic reproduction of printed matter reduced to the size of a single dot for security or ease of transmission **2** a small tablet containing a HALLUCINOGENIC drug (eg LSD)

**microeconomics** /͵miekroh·eekə'nomiks, -ekə-/ *n taking sing vb* a study of economics in terms of individual areas of activity (eg a firm, household, or prices) – compare MACROECONOMICS – **microeconomic** *adj*

**microelectrode** /ˌmiekroh·i'lektrohd/ *n* a minute ELECTRODE (metal wire, plate, etc that conducts electric current); *esp* one that is inserted in a living biological cell or tissue in studying its electrical characteristics

**microelectronics** /-iˌlek'troniks, -ˌelek-/ *n taking sing vb* a branch of electronics that deals with or produces miniaturized electronic circuits and components – **microelectronic** *adj*, **microelectronically** *adv*

**microelectrophoresis** /ˌmiekroh·iˌlektrohfə'reesis/ *n* ELECTROPHORESIS (movement of particles in a gas or liquid under the influence of an electric current) in which the movement of single particles is observed under a microscope; *also* electrophoresis in which MICROMETHODS (very small quantities) are used [NL] – **microelectrophoretic, microelectrophoretical** *adj*, **microelectrophoretically** *adv*

**microelement** /ˌmiekroh'eləmənt/ *n* TRACE ELEMENT (chemical element occurring in very small amounts)

**microevolution** /ˌmiekrohˌeevə'loohsh(ə)n, -ˌevə-/ *n* evolutionary change resulting from selective accumulation of minute variations – **microevolutionary** *adj*

**microfauna** /ˌmiekroh'fawnə/ *n*, *pl* **microfaunas, microfaunae** 1 a small or strictly localized fauna (e g of a microhabitat) 2 minute animals; *esp* those invisible to the naked eye ⟨*the soil* ~⟩ [NL] – **microfaunal** *adj*

**microfibril** /ˌmiekroh'fiebril, -'fib-/ *n* a fine small fibre (FIBRIL); *esp* any of the submicroscopic elongated bundles of CELLULOSE that constitute plant cell walls – **microfibrillar** *adj*

**microfiche** /-ˌfeesh/ *n*, *pl* **microfiche, microfiches** /-shiz/ a sheet of microfilm containing rows of greatly reduced images of pages of printed matter; *also* a roll or frame containing such a sheet [Fr, fr *micr-* + *fiche* peg, tag, slide, fr OF, fr *ficher* to stick in – more at FICHU]

**microfilament** /'miekroh,filəmənt/ *n* any of the fine protein filaments found in the CYTOPLASM (jellylike material) in most cells, in bundles or scattered

**microfilaria** /ˌmiekrohfi'leəriə/ *n* a minute larva of a group (Filaroidea) of parasitic roundworms [NL] – **microfilarial** *adj*

¹**microfilm** /'miekrə,film/ *n* a film bearing a photographic record on a reduced scale of graphic matter (e g printing) [ISV]

²**microfilm** *vt* to reproduce on microfilm ⟨~ *a report*⟩ ~ *vi* to make microfilms – **microfilmable** *adj*, **microfilmer** *n*

**microflora** /ˌmiekroh'flawrə/ *n*, *pl* **microfloras, microflorae** /-'flawrie/ 1 a small or strictly localized flora (e g of a microhabitat) 2 minute plants; *esp* those invisible to the naked eye ⟨*aquatic* ~⟩ [NL] – **microfloral** *adj*

**microform** /'miekrə,fawm/ *n* a greatly reduced photographic reproduction of printed matter [*micr-* + *form*]

**microfossil** /ˌmiekroh'fosl/ *n* a fossil that can be studied only microscopically and that may be either a fragment of a larger organism or an entire minute organism

**microfungus** /ˌmiekroh'fung·gəs/ *n* a fungus (e g a mould) with a microscopic FRUITING BODY (spore-producing structure) [NL] – **microfungal** *adj*

**microgamete** /ˌmiekroh'gameet/ *n* the smaller and usu male gamete (reproductive cell) of an organism that is HETEROGAMOUS (produces two kinds of gametes) [ISV]

**microgametocyte** /ˌmiekroh·gə'meetə,siet/ *n* a GAMETOCYTE (cell that divides to form the reproductive cells) producing microgametes [ISV]

**microgram** /'miekrə,gram/ *n* one millionth of a gram [ISV]

**micrograph** /'miekrə,grahf, -,graf/ *n* a graphic reproduction of the image of an object, formed by a microscope [ISV] – **micrograph** *vt*

**microgroove** /'miekroh,groohv/ *n* the fine groove of an EP or LP record

**microhabitat** /ˌmiekroh'habitat/ *n* a small usu distinctly specialized and effectively isolated habitat (e g a decaying tree stump)

**microimage** /ˌmiekroh'imij/ *n* an image (e g on a microfilm) that is greatly reduced in size

**microinjection** /ˌmiekroh·in'jeksh(ə)n/ *n* injection under the microscope; *specif* injection into tissues or individual cells by means of a mechanically controlled small-bore tube – **microinject** *vt*

**microinstruction** /-in'struksh(ə)n/ *n* a computer instruction corresponding to a single machine operation

**microlepidoptera** /ˌmiekrohˌlepi'doptərə/ *n pl* insects that belong to families of minute or medium-sized moths [NL] – **microlepidopterous** *adj*

**microlight** /'miekrəliet/ *n* a single- or two-seat aeroplane with a weight not exceeding 150 kilograms (about 330 pounds) and a wing area not less than 10 square metres (about 11 square yards)

**microlith** /-ˌlith/ *n* a tiny flint blade tool, esp of the Middle STONE AGE (MESOLITHIC) period, sometimes in the form of a geometrical figure (e g a triangle) and often set in a bone or wooden handle [ISV]

**microlithic** /ˌmiekroh'lithik/ *adj* 1 being or resembling a microlith 2 of the people who produced microliths

**microlitre** /'miekroh,leetə/ *n* a unit of capacity equal to one millionth of a litre [ISV]

**micromanipulation** /-mə,nipyoo'laysh(ə)n/ *n* the technique or practice of MICRODISSECTION and microinjection – **micromanipulator** *n*

**micromere** /'miekroh,miə/ *n* a small BLASTOMERE (cell formed by the first divisions of an egg) [ISV]

**micromesh** /'miekroh,mesh/ *adj*, *of hosiery* knitted in such a way as to have a very fine mesh

**micrometeorite** /ˌmiekroh'meeti·ə,riet/ *n* 1 a meteorite so small that it can pass through the earth's atmosphere without becoming intensely heated 2 **micrometeorite, micrometeoroid** /'meetiə,royd/ a very small particle in interplanetary space – **micrometeoritic** *adj*

**micrometeorology** /ˌmiekroh,meeti·ə'roləji/ *n* meteorology that deals with small-scale weather systems ranging up to several kilometres in diameter and confined to the lower TROPOSPHERE (layer of the atmosphere) – **micrometeorologist** *n*, **micrometeorological** *adj*

**micrometer** /mie'kromitə/ *n* 1 an instrument used for measuring minute distances or angular separations between objects seen through a telescope or microscope 2 a measuring instrument having a spindle moved by a finely threaded screw for making precise measurements of length [Fr *micromètre*, fr *micr-* + *-mètre* -meter]

**micromethod** /'miekroh,methəd/ *n* a method (e g of chemical analysis) that requires only very small quantities of material or that involves the use of the microscope

**micrometre** /'miekroh,meetə/ *n* a unit of length equal to one millionth of a metre [ISV]

**micrometry** /mie'kromətri/ *n* measurement with a micrometer [ISV]

**microminiature** /ˌmiekroh'minəchə/ *adj* 1 microminiaturized 2 suitable for use with microminiaturized parts

**microminiaturization** /ˌmiekroh,minəchərie'zaysh(ə)n/ *n* the process of producing microminiaturized things

**microminiaturized** /ˌmiekroh'minəchə,riezd/ *adj* reduced to or produced in a very small size, esp in a size smaller than one considered miniature

**micromorphology** /ˌmiekrohmaw'foləji/ *n* 1 MICROSTRUCTURE (microscopic structure) – used esp with reference to soils 2 (the study of) minute detail of form and structure (MORPHOLOGY), esp as determined by ELECTRON MICROSCOPY – **micromorphologic, micromorphological** *adj*, **micromorphologically** *adv*

**micron** /'miekron/ *n*, *pl* **microns** *also* **micra** a micrometre – not now recommended for technical use [NL, fr Gk *mikron*, neut of *mikros* small – more at MICR-]

**Micronesian** /ˌmiekrə'neezh(y)ən, -zi·ən/ *n* 1 a native or inhabitant of Micronesia 2 a group of AUSTRONESIAN languages spoken in the Micronesian islands [*Micronesia*, islands in the W Pacific Ocean] – **Micronesian** *adj*

**micron·ize, -ise** /'miekrə,niez/ *vt* to pulverize, esp into particles a few micrometres in diameter [*micron* + *-ize*]

**micronucleus** /ˌmiekroh'nyoohkliəs/ *n* a minute nucleus in a cell; *specif* one regarded as primarily concerned with reproductive and genetic functions in most PROTOZOANS (single-celled organisms) provided with CILIA (hairlike structures) – compare MACRONUCLEUS [NL]

**micronutrient** /ˌmiekroh'nyoohtri·ənt/ *n* 1 TRACE ELEMENT (chemical element occurring in very small amounts) 2 an animal- or plant-derived chemical compound (e g a vitamin) essential in minute amounts to the growth and welfare of an animal

**microorganism** /-'awgəniz(ə)m/ *n* an organism of (smaller than) microscopic size [ISV]

**micropalaeontology** /ˌmiekroh,palion'toləji/ *n* the study of microscopic fossils – **micropalaeontological** *also* **micropalaeontologic** *adj*, **micropalaeontologist** *n*

**microparasite** /ˌmiekroh'parə,siet/ *n* a parasitic microorganism – **microparasitic** *adj*

**microphage** /'miekrə,fayj, -,fahzh/ *n* a small PHAGOCYTE (cell that engulfs and destroys foreign matter) [ISV]

**microphone** /'miekrə,fohn/ *n* a device that converts sounds into electrical signals, esp for transmission or recording [ISV] – **microphonic** *adj*

**microphotograph** /,miekroh'fohtəgrahf, -graf/ *n* 1 a reduced photograph that must be magnified for viewing; MICROCOPY 2 PHOTOMICROGRAPH (photograph of a microscopic image) [ISV] – **microphotograph** *vt,* **microphotographer** *n,* **microphotography** *n,* **microphotographic** *adj*

**microphysics** /,miekroh'fiziks/ *n taking sing vb* the physics of molecules, atoms, and ELEMENTARY PARTICLES (minute particles of matter) – **microphysical** *adj,* **microphysically** *adv*

**micropipette, micropipet** /,miekrohpi'pet/ *n* 1 a tube (PIPETTE) for the measurement of minute volumes of liquid 2 a small and extremely fine-pointed pipette used in making MICROINJECTIONS

**micropopulation** /,miekroh,popyoo'laysh(ə)n/ *n* a population of microorganisms

**micropore** /'miekrə,paw/ *n* a very fine pore [ISV] – **microporosity** *n,* **microporous** *adj*

**microprint** /'miekrə,print/ *n* a photographic or photomechanical copy of graphic matter in reduced size – **microprint** *vt*

**microprocessor** /-'prohsesə/ *n* 1 a single INTEGRATED CIRCUIT that functions as the CENTRAL PROCESSING UNIT in a microcomputer 2 a microcomputer

**microprogram** /,miekrə'prohgram/ *n* a ROUTINE (sequence of computer instructions) used in microprogramming

**microprogramming** /,miekrə'prohgraming/ *n* the use of ROUTINES (sequence of computer instructions) stored in memory rather than specialized circuits to control a device (e g a computer)

**microprojector** /,miekrohprə'jektə/ *n* a projector using a COMPOUND MICROSCOPE for projecting on a screen a greatly enlarged image of a microscopic object – **microprojection** *n*

**micropublishing** /,miekroh'publishing/ *n* publishing in greatly reduced photographic form (e g of texts on MICROFICHE sheets) – **micropublisher** *n*

**micropuncture** /,miekroh'pungkchə/ *n* a technique for studying the physiology of microscopic structures, esp very fine tubes (e g kidney tubules), whereby minute amounts of liquid are withdrawn for chemical analysis

**micropyle** /-piel/ *n* 1 a differentiated area of the surface of an egg, through which the sperm enters 2 a minute opening in the outer covering of an OVULE (immature seed) of a flowering plant through which the POLLEN TUBE penetrates to the EMBRYO SAC to fertilize the ovule [ISV *micr-* + Gk *pylē* gate] – **micropylar** *adj*

**microradiograph** /,miekroh'raydioh,grahf, -,graf/ *n* an X-ray photograph showing minute internal structure – **microradiographic** *adj,* **microradiography** *n*

**microscale** /'miekroh,skayl/ *n* a very small scale ⟨*a chemical produced on a* ~⟩

**microscope** /'miekrə,skohp/ *n* 1 an optical instrument consisting of a lens or combination of lenses for making enlarged images of minute objects; *esp* COMPOUND MICROSCOPE 2 an instrument (e g ELECTRON MICROSCOPE) using radiations (e g a beam of electrons) other than light for making enlarged images of minute objects [NL *microscopium,* fr *micr-* + *-scopium* -scope]

**microscopic** /-'skopik/ *also* **microscopical** /-kl/ *adj* 1 of or conducted with the microscope or microscopy 2 resembling a microscope, esp in perception 3a invisible or indistinguishable without the use of a microscope **b** very small, fine, or precise *synonyms* see ¹SMALL – **microscopically** *adv*

**microscopy** /mie'kroskəpi/ *n* the use of or investigation with the microscope – **microscopist** *n*

**microsecond** /'miekroh,sekənd/ *n* one millionth of a second [ISV]

**microseism** /'miekroh,siezəm/ *n* a feeble rhythmically and persistently recurring earth tremor [ISV] – **microseismic** *adj,* **microseismicity** *n*

**microsome** /'miekroh,sohm/ *n* 1 any of various minute structures of the cell, esp the smallest ones that can be observed using a light microscope 2 any of the smallest particles that are separated from broken cells by heavy CENTRIFUGATION (spinning under gravity) and that consist of various fragments of ORGANELLES (specialized cell parts), including RIBOSOMES, ENDOPLASMIC RETICULUM, and MITOCHONDRIA [Ger *mikrosom,* fr *mikr-* micr- + *-som* -some] – **microsomal** *adj*

**microspectrophotometer** /,miekroh,spektrohfoh'tomitə/ *n* a SPECTROPHOTOMETER (instrument for measuring the intensity of light of a particular wavelength) adapted to the examination of light transmitted by a very small specimen (e g a single cell) – **microspectrophotometric** *also* **microspectrophotometrical** *adj,* **microspectrophotometrically** *adv,* **microspectrophotometry** *n*

**microsporangium** /,miekrohspaw'ranjiəm/ *n* a SPORANGIUM (plant organ producing spores) that develops only microspores [NL] – **microsporangiate** *adj*

**microspore** /'miekroh,spaw/ *n* a spore in plants that gives rise to male GAMETOPHYTES (structures producing sex cells) and is generally smaller than the female MEGASPORE [ISV] – **microsporous** *adj*

**microsporidian** /,miekrohspə'ridiən/ *n* any of an order (Microsporidia) of single-celled spore-producing parasites of insects and fishes that typically invade and destroy the cells of their HOST (organism harbouring a parasite) [NL, fr *Microsporidia,* group name, fr *micr-* + *sporidium* small spore, fr *spor-* + *-idium*] – **microsporidian** *adj*

**microsporocyte** /,miekroh'spawrə,siet/ *n* a cell from which microspores are produced

**microsporogenesis** /,miekroh,spawroh'jenəsis/ *n* the formation and maturation of microspores [NL]

**microsporophyll** /,miekroh'spawrəfil/ *n* a SPOROPHYLL (leaflike structure) that develops only microsporangia

**microstructure** /-,strukchə/ *n* the structure of a material (e g an alloy, a mineral, or a biological cell) on a minute scale as revealed by a scientific instrument (e g a microscope) [ISV] – **microstructural** *adj*

**microsurgery** /-'suhjəri/ *n* minute dissection or manipulation usu under a microscope (e g by a MICROMANIPULATOR) of living structures (e g cells) for surgical or experimental purposes – **microsurgical** *adj*

**microswitch** /-,swich/ *n* an electrical switch that can be operated by a small usu delicate movement

**micro-teaching** /'miekroh,teeching/ *n* the teaching of a small group for a short time usu with limited objectives, esp as practice for a trainee teacher in particular teaching skills

**microtechnique** /,miekrohtek'neek/, *chiefly NAm* **microtechnic** /,miekroh'teknik, -tek'neek/ *n* the art of handling and preparing material for microscopic observation and study [ISV]

**microtome** /-,tohm/ *n* an instrument for cutting sections (e g of plant or animal tissues) for microscopic examination [ISV]

**microtone** /-,tohn/ *n* a musical interval smaller than a SEMITONE (smallest interval playable on a piano) – **microtonal** *adj,* **microtonally** *adv,* **microtonality** *n*

**microtubule** /-'tyoohbyoohl/ *n* any of the minute cylindrical structures in cells that are widely distributed in CYTOPLASM (jellylike material) and are made up of protein subunits – **microtubular** *adj*

**microvillus** /,miekroh'viləs/ *n, pl* **microvilli** a microscopic projection of a tissue, cell, or cell ORGANELLE (specialized cell part); *esp* any of the fingerlike outward projections of some cell surfaces [NL] – **microvillar** *adj,* **microvillous** *adj*

**microwave** /'miekrə,wayv/ *n* a comparatively short ELECTROMAGNETIC WAVE; *esp* one between 1 metre and 0.1 metre in wavelength

**microwave oven** *n* an oven in which food is cooked very quickly by the heat produced as a result of the interaction between penetrating microwaves and the substance of the food

**micturate** /'miktyoo,rayt/ *vi, formal* to (want to) urinate [L *micturire,* fr *mictus,* pp of *mingere;* akin to OE *mīgan* to urinate, Gk *omeichein*] – **micturition** *n*

¹**mid** /mid/ *adj* 1 being the part in the middle or midst ⟨*in* ~ *ocean*⟩ – often in combination ⟨mid-*August*⟩ ⟨*in* mid-*sentence*⟩ 2 occupying a middle position ⟨*the* ~ *finger*⟩ 3 *of a vowel* articulated with the arch of the tongue midway between the upper and lower areas of the mouth [ME, fr OE *midde;* akin to OHG *mitti* middle, L *medius,* Gk *mesos*] – **mid** *adv*

²**mid** *prep, poetic* amid

**midair** /-'eə/ *n* a point or region in the air not immediately near the ground ⟨*planes collided in* ~⟩

**midas touch** /'miedəs/ *n, often cap M* the talent for making wealth out of any activity one turns one's hand to [*Midas,* mythical king in Asia Minor who had the power of turning everything he touched to gold]

,**mid-At'lantic** *adj or n* (of) a dialect halfway between American and British English

**midbrain** /-,brayn/ *n* the middle of the three primary divisions of the embryonic brain of VERTEBRATE animals; *also* those parts of the fully differentiated and specialized brain developed from this region

**midday** /-'day/ *n* the middle part of the day; noon

**midden** /'mid(ə)n/ *n* 1 a dunghill 2 a refuse heap; *esp* a heap or stratum of domestic rubbish found on the site of an ancient settlement [ME *midding,* of Scand origin; akin to ON *myki* dung & ON *dyngja* manure pile – more at MUCUS, DUNG]

¹**middle** /'midl/ *adj* 1 equally distant from the extremes; central ⟨*the ~ house in the row*⟩ 2 at neither extreme; intermediate 3 *cap* 3a constituting a division intermediate between those earlier and later or Lower and Upper ⟨Middle *Palaeozoic*⟩ b constituting a period of a language intermediate between one called *Old* and one called *New* or *Modern* ⟨Middle *Dutch*⟩ 4 *of a verb form or voice* typically asserting that one both performs and is affected by the action represented; expressing reflexive or reciprocal action [ME *middel,* fr OE; akin to L *medius*]

²**middle** *n* 1 a middle part, point, or position 2 the central portion of the human body; the waist 3 the position of being among or in the midst of something 4 something intermediate between extremes; a mean

³**middle** *vt* 1 to hit (a shot) accurately with the middle of the bat in cricket ⟨*his timing was all wrong and he couldn't ~ his shots*⟩ 2 to fold in the middle ⟨*~ a sail*⟩

**middle age** *n* the period of life from about 40 to about 60 – **middle-aged** *adj*

**middle-aged spread** *n* an increase in girth, esp round the waist, associated with middle age and usu caused by increased food intake or a decline in physical exercise or both

**Middle Ages** *n pl* the period of European history from about AD 500 to about 1500

**Middle America** *n* 1 the midwestern section of the USA 2 the US MIDDLE CLASS – **Middle American** *n*

**middlebrow** /-,brow/ *n, chiefly derog* a person with conventional and often bourgeois intellectual and cultural interests and activities – **middlebrow** *adj*

**middle C** *n* the musical note that is represented on the first extra line (LEDGER LINE) below the TREBLE CLEF or the first ledger line above the BASS CLEF and has a standardized frequency of 261.63 hertz

**middle-'class** *adj* of the middle class; *esp* BOURGEOIS 2

**middle class** *n taking sing or pl vb,* **middle classes** *n pl* a class occupying a position between the upper class and the lower class; *esp* a fluid mixed socioeconomic grouping composed principally of business and professional people, bureaucrats, and some farmers and skilled workers sharing common social characteristics and values

**middle-,distance** *adj* competing in or being a running race over a distance between that of a sprint and a long-distance race, specif the 800 metres and 1500 metres runs and the 3000 metres steeplechase

**middle distance** *n* a part of a picture or view between the foreground and the background

**middle ear** *n* a small membrane-lined cavity that is separated from the OUTER EAR by the eardrum and that transmits sound waves from the eardrum to the partition between the middle ear and the INNER EAR through a chain of tiny bones

**Middle English** *n* English from about 1150 to 1500

**middle finger** *n* the midmost of the five fingers of the hand

**Middle French** *n* French from about 1300 to 1600

**middle game** *n* the middle phase of a board game; *specif* the part of a chess game after the opening moves when pieces have been brought out for effective use – compare END GAME, OPENING

**Middle Greek** *n* Greek from about 600 to 1500

**middle ground** *n* 1 MIDDLE DISTANCE 2 a standpoint midway between extremes

**Middle High German** *n* HIGH GERMAN from about 1100 to 1500

**Middle Irish** *n* Irish from about 1000 to 1500

**Middle Low German** *n* LOW GERMAN from about 1100 to 1500

**middleman** /-,man/ *n* an intermediary or agent between two parties; *esp* a dealer or agent intermediate between the producer of goods and the retailer or consumer

**middle name** *n* 1 a name between a person's FIRST NAME and surname 2 a quality of character for which a person is well known ⟨*generosity is her ~*⟩

**middle-of-the-'road** *adj* conforming to the majority in taste, attitude, or conduct; *also* neither left-wing nor right-wing in

political conviction – **middle-of-the-roader** *n,* **middle-of-the-roadism** *n*

**middler** /'midlə/ *n, NAm* one belonging to an intermediate group, division, or class (eg in a school)

**middle school** *n* a school or part of a school for pupils aged 8–12 or 9–13

**Middle Scots** *n* the Scots language of the late 15th to early 17th centuries

**middle term** *n, philosophy* the term of a SYLLOGISM (formal deductive argument) that occurs in both premises

**middleweight** /-,wayt/ *n* someone or something of average weight; *specif* a boxer who weighs not more than 11 stone 6 pounds (72.6 kilograms) if professional, or between 71 and 75 kilograms (between about 11 stone 2 pounds and 11 stone 11 pounds) if amateur

**Middle Welsh** *n* Welsh from about 1150 to 1500

¹**middling** /'midling/ *adj* 1 of middle, medium, or moderate size, degree, or quality 2 mediocre, second-rate [ME (Sc) *mydlyn,* prob fr *mid, midde* mid + ²-*ling*] – **middling** *adv,* **middlingly** *adv*

²**middling** *n* 1 any of various commodities of intermediate size, quality, or position 2 *pl but taking sing or pl vb* a granular product of grain milling; *esp* a wheat milling by-product used in animal feeds

**middorsal** /,mid'dawsl/ *adj* situated in the middle part or the central longitudinal line of the back

**middy** /'midi/ *n* 1 a loosely fitting blouse with a sailor collar worn by women and children 2 *informal* a midshipman – no longer in vogue [by shortening & alter. fr *midshipman*]

**midfield** /'mid,feeld, -'-/ *n* 1 the middle portion of a field; *esp* the portion of a playing field (eg in soccer) that is midway between the goals 2 *taking sing or pl vb* the players on a team (eg in lacrosse or soccer) that normally play in midfield – **midfielder** *n*

**midge** /mij/ *n* a tiny mosquitolike fly (eg a CHIRONOMID) [ME *migge,* fr OE *mycg;* akin to OHG *mucka* midge, Gk *myia* fly, L *musca*]

**midget** /'mijit/ *n* 1 a very small person; a dwarf 2 something (eg an animal) much smaller than usual 3 a front-engined single-seat open racing car smaller than standard cars of the type [*midge* + -*et*] – **midget** *adj*

**midgut** /'mid,gut/ *n* the middle part of a digestive tract

**midi** /'midi/ *n* a woman's garment (eg a skirt) that extends to the mid-calf [¹*mid* + -*i* (as in *mini*)]

**midland** /'midlənd/ *n* 1 **midlands** *pl but taking sing vb, also* **midland** *often cap* the interior or central region of a country 2 *cap* 2a the dialect of English spoken in the midland counties of England roughly between Wharfedale, Stratford-on-Avon, Chester, and the Lincolnshire Coast b the dialect of English spoken in the central USA roughly between Tennessee, the Mississippi, the Great Lakes, and the Atlantic – **midland** *adj, often cap*

**midline** /mid'lien, '-,-/ *n* a middle line; *esp* the middle line or plane of (some part of) the body

**midmost** /-,mohst/ *adj* 1 in or near the exact middle 2 most intimate; innermost – **midmost** *adv or n*

**midnight** /'mid,niet/ *n* 1 the middle of the night; *specif* 12 o'clock at night 2 deep or extended darkness or gloom – see also **burn the midnight** OIL – **midnight** *adj,* **midnightly** *adv or adj*

**midnight sun** *n* the sun above the horizon at midnight in the arctic or antarctic summer

**mid-'off** *n* a fielding position in cricket between a third of the way and halfway to the boundary on the OFF SIDE of the pitch, situated in front of the batsman's wicket between EXTRA COVER and the bowler; *also* the fieldsman occupying this position

**mid-on** *n* a fielding position in cricket between a third of the way and halfway to the boundary on the LEG SIDE of the pitch, situated in front of the batsman's wicket between mid-wicket and the bowler; *also* the fieldsman occupying this position

**midpoint** /-,poynt/ *n* 1 a point at or near the centre of an area or midway between the ends of a line 2 a point midway between the beginning and end of something (eg a period of time)

**midrash** /'midrash/ *n, pl* **midrashim** /mid'rashim/ 1 a Jewish work of commentary on a biblical text 2 a collection of midrashim 3 *cap* the midrashic literature written during the first 1000 years of the Christian era [Heb *midhrāsh* exposition, explanation] – **midrashic** *adj, often cap*

**midrib** /-,rib/ *n* the central vein of a leaf

**midriff** /'midrif/ *n* 1 DIAPHRAGM 1 2 the middle part of the human torso **3** a part of a garment that covers the midriff [ME *midrif*, fr OE *midhrif*, fr *midde* mid + *hrif* belly; akin to OHG *href* body, L *corpus*]

**midsection** /'mid‚seksh(ə)n/ *n* a section midway between the extremes; *esp* MIDRIFF 2

**midshipman** /'mid‚shipmən/ *n* – see MILITARY RANKS table

**midships** /-‚ships/ *adv* amidships

**midst** /midst/ *n* **1** the inner or central part or point; the middle, heart ⟨*in the ~ of the forest*⟩ **2** a position near to the members of a group or company ⟨*a traitor in our ~*⟩ **3** the condition of being surrounded or beset ⟨*in the ~ of his troubles*⟩ **4** a period of time about the middle of a continuing act or state ⟨*in the ~ of the celebrations*⟩ [ME *middest*, alter. of *middes*, back-formation fr *amiddes* amid] – **midst** *prep*

**midstream** /-'streem/ *n* **1** the part of a stream towards the middle ⟨*keep the boat in ~*⟩ **2** the middle part of a process ⟨*the speaker was silenced in ~*⟩

**midsummer** /-'sumə/ *n* **1** the middle of summer **2** the summer SOLSTICE (longest day)

**Midsummer Day** /‚--- '-/ *n* (June 24 celebrated as) the feast of the birth of John the Baptist

**midway** /-'way/ *adv* in the middle of the way or distance; halfway

**midweek** /-'week/ *n* the middle of the week – **midweek** *adj*, **midweekly** *adj or adv*

**'mid-‚wicket** *n* a fielding position in cricket about halfway to the boundary on the LEG SIDE of the pitch, situated in front of the batsman's wicket between mid-on and SQUARE LEG; *also* the fieldsman occupying this position

**¹midwife** /'mid‚wief/ *n* **1** a woman who assists other women in childbirth **2** one who or that which helps to produce or bring forth something [ME *midwif*, fr *mid* with (fr OE) + *wif* woman]

**²midwife** *vt* **midwifed**, **midwived** /-‚wievd/; **midwifing**, **midwiving** to assist in producing, bringing forth, or bringing about ⟨*~d a new comedy series*⟩

**midwifery** /'mid‚wifəri/ *n* the art or act of assisting at childbirth; *also* OBSTETRICS (branch of medicine dealing with childbirth)

**midwife toad** *n* either of two rather small toads (*Alytes obstetricans* and *Alytes cisternasi*) of central and SW Europe the male of which carries the strings of eggs laid by the female until they hatch

**midwinter** /-'wintə/ *n* **1** the middle of winter **2** the winter SOLSTICE (shortest day)

**midyear** /‚mid'yiə/ *n* **1** the middle or middle portion of a calendar year **2** *pl, chiefly NAm* (the period of) the set of examinations in the middle of an academic year – **midyear** *adj*

**mien** /meen/ *n, formal* air or bearing, esp as expressive of mood or personality; demeanour ⟨*that ~ of a commercial traveller who has been everywhere* – Arnold Bennett⟩ △ mean [by shortening & alter. (influenced by Fr *mine* appearance) fr ²*demean*]

**mierkat** /'miə‚kat/ *n* MEERKAT (S African mongoose)

**¹miff** /mif/ *n, informal* **1** a brief outburst of bad temper **2** a trivial quarrel [origin unknown]

**²miff** *vt, informal* to make cross or peeved; offend ⟨*~ed at his rival's success*⟩ ⟨*was jolly ~ed by his conduct*⟩

**¹might** /miet/ *past of* MAY – used to express permission or liberty in the past ⟨*asked whether he ~ come*⟩ ⟨*the king ~ do nothing without parliament's consent*⟩, a past or present possibility contrary to fact ⟨*I ~ well have been killed*⟩ ⟨*if he were older he ~ understand*⟩, purpose or expectation in the past ⟨*wrote it down so that I ~ not forget it*⟩, less probability or possibility than *may* ⟨*~ get there before it rains*⟩, a polite request ⟨*you ~ post this letter for me*⟩, or as a polite or ironic alternative to *may* ⟨*~ I ask who is calling?*⟩ ⟨*who ~ you be?*⟩ or to *ought* or *should* ⟨*you ~ at least apologize*⟩ ⟨*he ~ have offered to help*⟩ *usage* see ¹CAN, ¹MAY [ME, fr OE *meahte*, *mihte*; akin to OHG *mahta*, *mohta* could]

**²might** *n* **1** power, authority, or resources wielded individually or collectively ⟨*the growing ~ of the middle class*⟩ **2a** physical strength **b** all the power, energy, or effort of which one is capable ⟨*striving with ~ and main*⟩ [ME, fr OE *miht*; akin to OHG *maht* might, *magan* to be able – more at MAY]

**'might-have-‚been** *n* **1** something desirable that might have happened but did not **2** a person who might have amounted to something but failed to

**mightily** /'miet(ə)l‧i/ *adv* **1** very much ⟨*it amused us ~* – Charles Dickens⟩ **2** *chiefly humorous* in a mighty manner; vigorously ⟨*he strove ~ on our behalf*⟩

**mightn't** /'mietnt/ might not

**¹mighty** /'mieti/ *adj* **1** powerful ⟨*a ~ victor*⟩ **2** accomplished or characterized by might ⟨*a ~ thrust*⟩ **3** imposingly great ⟨*the ~ mountains*⟩ – **mightiness** *n*

**²mighty** *adv, informal* to a great degree; extremely ⟨*a ~ big man*⟩ ⟨*it's ~ kind of you*⟩

**mignonette** /‚minyə'net/ *n* any of a genus (*Reseda* of the family Resedaceae, the mignonette family) of plants with small whitish to yellowish flowers; *esp* a garden plant (*Reseda odorata*) with spikes of fragrant greenish-yellow flowers and conspicuous orange ANTHERS (pollen-bearing structures) [Fr *mignonnette*, fr obs Fr, fem of *mignonnet* dainty, fr MF, fr *mignon* darling – more at MINION]

**migraine** /'meegrayn/ *also* 'mie-/ *n* a (condition marked by) recurrent severe headache usu associated with disturbances of vision, sensation, and movement often on only one side of the body [Fr, fr LL *hemicrania* pain in one side of the head, fr Gk *hēmikrania*, fr *hēmi-* hemi- + *kranion* cranium] – **migrainous** *adj*

*usage* The pronunciation /'meegrayn/ is recommended for BBC broadcasters.

**migrant** /'miegrənt/ *n* **1** a person who moves regularly in order to find work, esp in harvesting crops **2** an animal that moves from one habitat to another **3** *Austr* an immigrant *synonyms* see EMIGRANT [L *migrant-*, *migrans*, prp of *migrare*] – **migrant** *adj*

**migrate** /mie'grayt/ *vi* **1** to move from one country or locality to another **2** to pass usu periodically from one region or climate to another for feeding, breeding, etc **3** to change position in an organism or substance ⟨*filarial worms ~ within the human body*⟩ *synonyms* see EMIGRANT [L *migratus*, pp of *migrare*; akin to Gk *ameibein* to change] – **migration** *n*, **migrational** *adj*, **migrator** *n*

**migratory** /'miegrət(ə)ri/ *adj* **1** of or characterized by migration **2** wandering, roving

**mikado** /mi'kahdoh/ *n, pl* **mikados** – formerly used as a title for the emperor of Japan [Jap, fr *mi* magnificent + *kado* door]

**mike** /miek/ *n, informal* a microphone [by shortening & alter.]

**Mike** – a communications code word for the letter *m*

**mil** /mil/ *n* **1** a unit of length equal to ¹/₁₀₀₀ inch (0.0254 millimetre) used esp for the diameter of wire and formerly in precision engineering **2** a thousand ⟨*found a salinity of 38.4 per ~*⟩ **3** – see *pound* at MONEY table △ mill [L *mille* thousand – more at MILE]

**milady** /mi'laydi/ *n* an Englishwoman of noble or gentle birth – often used as a term of address or reference [Fr, fr E *my lady*]

**milch** /milch/ *adj, of a domestic animal* giving milk; *specif* bred or used primarily for milk production ⟨*~ cows*⟩ [ME *milche*, fr OE *-milce*; akin to OE *melcan* to milk – more at EMULSION]

**milch cow** *n* a source of easily acquired gain ⟨*making industry the ~ of the economy*⟩

**milchig** /'milchik, 'milkik/ *adj* made of, prepared with, or derived from milk or dairy products – used in Jewish cookery; compare FLEISHIG

**¹mild** /mield/ *adj* **1** gentle in nature or manner **2a** not strong or intense in flavour or effect ⟨*a ~ curry*⟩ ⟨*a ~ sedative*⟩ **b** not being or involving what is extreme ⟨*an analysis under ~ conditions*⟩ ⟨*a ~ slope*⟩ **3** not severe; temperate ⟨*a ~ climate*⟩ ⟨*~ symptoms of disease*⟩ [ME, fr OE *milde*; akin to Gk *malthakos* soft, OE *melu* meal – more at MEAL] – **mildly** *adv*, **mildness** *n*

**²mild** *n, Br* a dark-coloured beer not strongly flavoured with hops – compare BITTER

**¹mildew** /'mildyooh/ *n* **1a** any of various plant diseases characterized by a usu whitish growth on the surface of the plant and caused by parasitic fungi (eg of the families Erysiphaceae and Peronosporaceae) – compare DOWNY MILDEW, POWDERY MILDEW **b** a fungus producing mildew **2** a coating or discoloration (eg on paper or leather) caused by the growth of fungi [ME, fr OE *meledēaw* honeydew; akin to OHG *militou* honeydew] – **mildewy** *adj*

**²mildew** *vb* to affect or become affected (as if) with mildew ⟨*~ed old manuscripts*⟩

**mild steel** *n* a tough comparatively easily worked steel with a low carbon content

**mile** /miel/ *n* in an extremely remote place **1** any of various units of distance: eg **1a** an old Roman unit equal to 1000 paces (about 1.48 kilometres) **b** a unit equal to 1760 yards (about 1.61 kilometres) **c** NAUTICAL MILE **2** a race of a mile ⟨*Bannister ran the first 4-minute* ~⟩ **3 mile, miles** pl a large distance or amount ⟨*drove for* ~s *without seeing a soul*⟩ [ME, fr OE *mīl;* akin to OHG *mīla* mile; both fr a prehistoric WGmc word borrowed fr L *milia* miles, fr *milia passuum,* lit., thousands of paces, fr *milia,* pl of *mille* thousand, perh fr a prehistoric compound whose constituents are akin to Gk *mia* (fem of *heis* one) and to Gk *chilioi* thousand, Skt sa*hasra* – more at SAME] – **miles from nowhere**

**mileage** /'mielij/ *n* **1** an allowance for travelling expenses at a certain rate per mile **2** aggregate length or distance in miles: e g **2a** the number of miles travelled over a period of time **b** the distance, or distance covered, in miles ⟨*what sort of* ~ *do these tyres give?*⟩ **c** the average distance in miles a vehicle will travel for an amount of fuel ⟨*gets good* ~⟩ **3** usefulness, profit ⟨*The organisers . . . sought political* ~ *out of this exhibition* – *Nation Review (Melbourne)*⟩

**milecastle** /'miel,kahsl/ *n* any of a series of small forts constructed at regular intervals along a Roman frontier wall

**mileometer, milometer** /mie'lomitə/ *n, chiefly Br* an instrument fitted in a car or other vehicle to record the number of miles it travels; an ODOMETER calibrated in miles

**milepost** /-,pohst/ *n* a post indicating the distance in miles from or to a given point

**miler** /'mielə/ *n* a person or horse that competes in mile races

**miles** /mielz/ *adv* very much ⟨*worked* ~ *better when oiled*⟩

**milestone** /'miel,stohn/ *n* **1** a stone serving as a milepost **2** a crucial stage in the development of something

**milfoil** /'mil,foyl/ *n* **1** YARROW (strong-scented Eurasian plant) **2** WATER MILFOIL (water plant) [ME, fr OF, fr L *millefolium,* fr *mille* + *folium* leaf – more at BLADE; fr its finely-divided leaves]

**miliaria** /,mili'eəriə/ *n* an inflamed condition of the skin that accompanies excessive sweating, is marked by redness, the formation of small raised areas or blisters, and a burning or itching sensation, and that results from the blockage of the ducts of sweat glands in the affected area; *esp* PRICKLY HEAT [NL, fr L, fem of *miliarius*] – **miliarial** *adj*

**miliary** /'milyəri/ *adj* having, made up of, or accompanied by many small projections, blisters, or lesions ⟨~ *tuberculosis*⟩ [L *miliarius* of millet, fr *milium* millet – more at MILLET]

**milieu** /'meelyuh (*Fr* miljø)/ *n, pl* **milieus, milieux** /-lyuh(z) (*Fr* ~)/ ENVIRONMENT, SETTING ⟨*three studies of women, each from a different* ~ – Edmund Wilson⟩ [Fr, fr OF, midst, fr *mi* middle (fr L *medius*) + *lieu* place, fr L *locus*]

**militant** /'militə)nt/ *adj* **1** engaged in warfare or combat **2** aggressively active (e g in a cause); combative ⟨~ *trade unionists*⟩ ⟨*a* ~ *attitude*⟩ – **militant** *n,* **militancy** *n,* **militantly** *adv,* **militantness** *n*

**militarism** /'militə,riz(ə)m/ *n* **1** exaltation of military virtues and ideals **2** a policy of aggressive military preparedness – **militarist** *n,* **militaristic** *adj,* **militaristically** *adv*

**militar·ize, -ise** /'militə,riez/ *vt* **1** to equip with military forces and defences **2** to give a military character to **3** to adapt for military use – **militarization** *n*

¹**military** /'militə)ri/ *adj* **1** (characteristic) of soldiers, arms, or war **2** carried on or supported by armed force ⟨*a* ~ *dictatorship*⟩ **3** of the army or armed forces [MF *militaire,* fr L *militaris,* fr *milit-, miles* soldier] – **militarily** *adv*

²**military** *n* **1** *taking pl vb* soldiers ⟨*the* ~ *are popular with the local girls*⟩ **2** *taking sing or pl vb* the army (as opposed to civilians or police) ⟨*for the present the* ~ *keep order*⟩

**usage** Some people dislike the use of **military** as a noun.

**military academy** *n* **1** a state institution that offers higher military instruction ⟨*the Royal* Military *Academy, Sandhurst*⟩ **2** a private secondary school, esp in the USA with obligatory military uniforms and training

**military band** *n* a band consisting of brass, woodwind, and percussion instruments and playing esp marching and concert music

**Military Cross** *n* a medal awarded for bravery to army officers below the rank of major or to WARRANT OFFICERS

**military law** *n* (an article of) a code of law that applies to all members of the armed forces, in addition to CIVIL LAW, to which they are also subject – compare MARTIAL LAW

**military police** *n* a branch of an army that carries out police functions within the army

**militate** /'militayt/ *vi* to have significant weight or effect ⟨*his boyish appearance* ~d *against his getting an early promotion*⟩

[L *militatus,* pp of *militare* to engage in warfare, fr *milit-, miles* soldier]

**militia** /mi'lish(y)ə/ *n* **1** *taking sing or pl vb* a body of citizens with some military training who are called on to fight in an emergency **2** *NAm* the whole body of male citizens declared by law as being subject to call to military service [L, military service, fr *milit-, miles*] – **militiaman** *n*

**milium** /'milyəm/ *n, pl* **milia** /'mily'ə/ a small whitish lump in the skin due to the retention of secretion in a blocked oil gland outlet [NL, fr L, millet – more at MILLET]

¹**milk** /milk/ *n* **1** a whitish liquid secreted by the MAMMARY GLANDS of female mammals for the nourishment of their young; *esp* cow's milk used as a food by humans **2** a liquid resembling milk in white or creamy appearance: e g **2a** the latex of a plant **b** the juice of a coconut **c** a cosmetic lotion, esp a cleanser [ME, fr OE *meolc, milc;* akin to OHG *miluh* milk] – **cry over spilt milk** to express vain regrets for what cannot be recovered or undone – **milk of human kindness** the compassion or fellow feeling natural to human beings

²**milk** *vt* **1a** to draw milk from the breasts or udder of **b** *of a mammal* to suckle ⟨*a ewe unable to* ~ *her lamb*⟩ **2** to draw something from as if by milking: e g **2a** to induce (a snake) to eject venom **b** to compel or persuade to yield illicit or excessive profit or advantage ⟨*opera stars who* ~ *their audience for applause*⟩ ~ *vi* to draw or yield milk – **milker** *n*

**milk and honey** *n* abundance, luxury – chiefly in *a land of/ flowing with milk and honey* [fr the biblical references to "a land flowing with milk and honey" (Exod 3:8, Num 16:13, Ezek 20:6)]

,**milk-and-'water** *adj* weak, insipid ⟨~ *liberalism* – *Punch*⟩

**milk fever** *n* **1** a feverish disorder that sometimes follows childbirth **2** a disease of cows, goats, or occasionally sheep that have recently given birth that is caused by a drain on the body's mineral reserves during the establishment of the milk flow and characterized by partial or complete loss of consciousness and paralysis

**milkfish** /'milk,fish/ *n, pl* **milkfishes,** *esp collectively* **milkfish** a large active silvery food fish (*Chanos chanos*) that is widely distributed in the warm parts of the Pacific and Indian oceans

**milk float** *n, Br* a light usu electrically-propelled vehicle for carrying esp milk for domestic delivery

**milking machine** /'milking/ *n* a mechanical suction apparatus for milking cows

**milking parlour** *n* PARLOUR 3

**milk leg** *n* a painful swelling of the leg after childbirth, caused by inflammation and clotting in the veins

**milkmaid** /-,mayd/ *n* a female who works in a dairy; a dairymaid

**milkman** /-mən/, *fem* **milkwoman** *n* one who sells or delivers milk

**milk of magnesia** *n* a white suspension of MAGNESIUM HYDROXIDE in water, used as an antacid and mild laxative

**milk pudding** *n* a pudding consisting of rice, tapioca, sago, etc boiled or baked in sweetened milk

**milk run** *n* a regular or frequently travelled journey or course [fr the resemblance in regularity & uneventfulness to the morning delivery of milk]

**milk shake** *n* a thoroughly shaken or blended beverage made of milk, fruit or a flavouring syrup, and often ice cream

**milksop** /-,sop/ *n* a weak and unmanly male [ME, piece of bread soaked in milk, effeminate man, fr *milk* + *sop*]

**milk sugar** *n* LACTOSE

**milk tooth** *n* a temporary tooth of a (young) mammal that will be shed later; *specif* any of four incisors, two canines, and four molars in each jaw of a child

**milk vetch** *n* any of several plants (genus *Astragalus*) of the pea family; *esp* a Eurasian plant (*Astragalus glycyphyllos*) with white to yellow densely clustered flowers [fr the popular belief that it increases the milk yield of goats]

**milkweed** /-,weed/ *n* any of various plants that secrete a milky juice; *esp* any of a genus (*Asclepias* of the family Asclepiadaceae, the milkweed family) of chiefly American plants

**milkweed butterfly** *n* MONARCH 3 (large orange-brown butterfly)

**milkwort** /-,wuht/ *n* any of a genus (*Polygala* of the family Polygalaceae, the milkwort family) of plants and nonwoody shrubs with variously coloured showy flowers [fr the former belief that it increased the milk yield of suckling women]

**milky** /'milki/ *adj* **1** resembling milk in colour or consistency ⟨~ *white teeth*⟩; *also* containing (much) milk ⟨*a* ~ *bedtime* *drink*⟩ **2** cloudy, semi-opaque ⟨*his old* ~ *blue eyes*⟩ ⟨*frequent washing in hard water turns glass* ~⟩ **3** mild, timid – **milkiness** *n*

**Milky Way** *n* **1** a broad irregular band of faint light that stretches completely round the CELESTIAL SPHERE and is caused by the light of the many faint stars forming part of the galaxy of which the sun and the solar system are also a part **2** the galaxy of which the sun and the solar system are a part [ME, trans of L *via lactea*]

**¹mill** /mil/ *n* **1** a building provided with machinery for grinding grain into flour **2a** a machine or apparatus (eg a QUERN) for grinding grain **b** a machine or hand-operated device for crushing or grinding a solid substance (eg coffee beans or peppercorns) **3** a building or collection of buildings with machinery for manufacturing **4** a machine for stamping coins **5** MILLING MACHINE **6** a painful or trying experience that leaves a marked impression on the character (eg by disciplining or hardening) – chiefly *in through the mill* – see also GRIST **to the/one's mill** [ME *mille*, fr OE *mylen;* akin to OHG *muli* mill; both fr a prehistoric NGmc-WGmc word borrowed fr LL *molina, molinum*, fr fem and neut of *molinus* of a mill, of a millstone, fr L *mola* mill, millstone; akin to L *molere* to grind – more at MEAL]

**²mill** *vt* **1** to subject to an operation or process in a mill: eg **1a** to grind into flour, meal, or powder **b** to shape or dress by means of a rotary cutter **c** to mix and condition (eg rubber) by passage between rotating rolls **2** to give a raised rim or a ridged edge to (a coin) **3** to cut grooves in the metal surface of (eg a knob) ~ *vi* **1** to move in a confused swirling mass ⟨*the crowd of shoppers* ~ed *all around him*⟩ **2** to undergo milling

**³mill, mille** *n* a US MONEY OF ACCOUNT equal to one thousandth of a dollar and used esp in calculating taxes △ mil [L *mille* thousand – more at MILE]

**millboard** /-ˌbawd/ *n* strong cardboard suitable for book covers and for panelling in furniture [alter. of *milled board*]

**milldam** /-ˌdam/ *n* a dam to make a millpond; *also* a millpond

**millefiori** /ˌmilifiˈawri/ *adj or n* (made of) ornamental glass usu of floral pattern produced by cutting cross-sections of variously sized and coloured fused bundles of glass rods ⟨*a valuable* ~ *paperweight*⟩ [n It, fr *mille* thousand (fr L) + *fiori*, pl of *fiore* flower, fr L *flor-, flos;* adj fr n]

**millenarian** /ˌmiliˈneəri-ən/ *adj* **1** relating to 1000 years **2** of or having belief in the millennium – **millenarian** *n*, **millenarianism** *n*

**¹millenary** /miˈlenəri/ *n* **1** a group of 1000 units or things **2** 1000 years △ millinery [LL *millenarium*, fr neut of *millenarius* of a thousand, fr L *milleni* one thousand each, fr *mille*]

**²millenary** *adj* **1** (consisting) of 1000 **2** suggesting a millennium [L *millenarius*]

**millennium** /miˈleni-əm/ *n, pl* **millennia** /-niə/, **millenniums 1a** a period of 1000 years **b** (the celebration of) a 1000th anniversary **2a** *the* thousand years mentioned in Revelation 20 during which holiness is to prevail and Christ is to reign on earth **b** a future golden age [NL, fr L *mille* thousand + NL *-ennium* (as in *biennium*)] – **millennial** *adj*

**millepede** /ˈmiliˌpeed/ *n* a millipede

**millepore** /ˈmiliˌpaw/ *n* any of an order (Milleporina of the class Hydrozoa) of marine INVERTEBRATE coral-like animals with chalky skeletons, that form reefs, grow as branching, encrusting or massive shapeless colonies, and produce a free-swimming MEDUSA (umbrella-shaped sperm- and egg-producing individual) [deriv of L *mille* thousand + *porus* pore]

**miller** /ˈmilə/ *n* **1** somebody who owns or works a mill, esp for corn **2** (a tool for use in) a milling machine

**millerite** /ˈmiləˌriet/ *n* SULPHIDE of nickel, NiS, usu occurring as a mineral in the form of hairlike yellow crystals [Ger *millerit*, fr William *Miller* †1880 E mineralogist]

**ˌmiller's-ˈthumb** *n* any of several small freshwater fishes (genus *Cottus*) of Europe and N America; *esp* a common European fish (*Cottus gobio*)

**millesimal** /miˈlesim(ə)l/ *n* the quotient of a unit divided by 1000; any of 1000 equal parts of anything [L *millesimus*, adj, thousandth, fr *mille*] – **millesimal** *adj*, **millesimally** *adv*

**millet** /ˈmilit/ *n* **1** any of various small-seeded cereal grasses (genera *Panicum, Setaria, Pennisetum*, and *Eleusine*) grown for their grain or as fodder; *esp* one (*Panicum miliaceum*) cultivated esp in Europe and Asia for its grain used as a food for humans and in bird feeds **2** the seed of a millet [ME *milet*, fr MF, dim. of *mil*, fr L *milium;* akin to Gk *melinē* millet]

**milli-** /mili-/ *comb form* one thousandth (10⁻³) part of (a

specified unit) ⟨*milli*ampere⟩ ⟨*milli*curie⟩ – compare KILO- [Fr, fr L *milli-* thousand, fr *mille* – more at MILE]

**milliampere** /ˌmiliˈampeə/ *n* one thousandth of an ampere [ISV]

**milliard** /ˈmiliˌahd, ˈmilyahd/ *n* a thousand millions (10⁹) – no longer used technically *usage* see BILLION [Fr, fr MF *miliart*, fr *mili-*, (fr *milion* million) + *-art* -ard]

**milliary** /ˈmilyəri/ *adj* marking the distance of a Roman mile [L *milliarius, miliarius* consisting of a thousand, one mile long, fr *mille* thousand, mile]

**millibar** /ˈmiliˌbah/ *n* a unit of atmospheric pressure equal to ¹/₁₀₀₀ bar [ISV]

**millieme** /miˈlyem/ *n, pl* **milliemes** – see *pound* at MONEY table [Fr *millième* thousandth, fr MF, fr *mille* thousand, fr L]

**milligram** /ˈmiliˌgram/ *n* one thousandth of a gram (about 0.015 grain) [Fr *milligramme*, fr *milli-* + *gramme* gram]

**millilitre** /ˈmiliˌleetə/ *n* one thousandth of a litre (0.002 pint) [Fr, fr *milli-* + *litre*]

**millime** /məˈleem/ *n* – see *dinar* at MONEY table [modif of Ar *mallim*, fr Fr *millième*]

**millimetre** /ˈmiliˌmeetə/ *n* one thousandth of a metre (about 0.039 inch) [Fr *millimètre*, fr *milli-* + *mètre* metre]

**millimetric** /ˌmiliˈmetrik/ *adj* **1** having a length of a millimetre **2** having a wavelength between 1 and 10 millimetres

**millimicro-** *comb form* NANO- (10⁻⁹)

**milliner** /ˈmilinə/ *n* somebody who designs, makes, trims, or sells women's hats [irreg fr *Milan*, city in N Italy; fr the importation of women's finery from Italy in the 16th century] – **millinery** *n*

**milling** /ˈmiling/ *n* a corrugated edge on a coin

**milling machine** /ˈmiling/ *n* a machine tool for shaping metal against rotating cutters

**million** /ˈmilyən/ *n, pl* **millions, million 1** – see NUMBER table **2** *pl* ²MASS 3b ⟨*appealing to the* ~s⟩ **3** million, millions *pl, informal* an indefinitely large number ⟨~s *of cars in that traffic jam*⟩ [ME *milioun*, fr MF *milion*, fr OIt *milione*, aug of *mille* thousand, fr L – more at MILE] – **million** *adj*, **millionth** *adj or n*

**millionaire** /ˌmilyəˈneə/ *n* a person whose assets are worth a million or more monetary units (eg pounds or dollars) [Fr *millionnaire*, fr *million*, fr MF *milion*]

**millionairess** /-ris/ *n* a woman who is a millionaire

**millipede, millepede** /ˈmiliˌpeed/ *n* any of numerous INVERTEBRATE animals (class Diplopoda of the group Myriapoda) related to the centipedes, that have a usu cylindrical body divided into numerous similar segments and pairs of legs on each segment [L *millepeda*, a small crawling animal, fr *mille* thousand + *ped-, pes* foot – more at FOOT]

**millisecond** /ˈmiliˌsekənd/ *n* one thousandth of a second [ISV]

**millivolt** /ˈmiliˌvohlt/ *n* one thousandth of a volt [ISV]

**milliwatt** /ˈmiliˌwot/ *n* one thousandth of a watt [ISV]

**millpond** /ˈmilˌpond/ *n* a pond created by damming a stream to produce a head of water for operating a mill

**millrace** /-ˌrays/ *n* (the current in) a channel in which water flows to and from a mill wheel [ME *milnras*, fr *miln, mille* mill + *ras* race, current]

**millstone** /-ˌstohn/ *n* **1** either of a pair of circular stones that rotate against each other and are used for grinding grain or other substances **2** a heavy or crushing burden

**millstream** /ˈmilˌstreem/ *n* **1** a stream whose flow is utilized to run a mill **2** a millrace

**mill wheel** *n* a waterwheel that drives a mill

**millwright** /-ˌriet/ *n* somebody who plans and builds mills or sets up and maintains their machinery

**milo** /ˈmieloh/ *n, pl* **milos** a small usu early-growing drought-resistant variety of SORGHUM (cereal plant) with compact heads of large yellow, whitish, or pinkish seeds [Sotho *maili*]

**milometer** /mieˈlomitə/ *n* a mileometer

**milord** /miˈlawd/ *n* an Englishman of noble or gentle birth – often used in imitation of foreigners [Fr, fr E *my lord*]

**milpa** /ˈmilpə/ *n* the maize plant [MexSp, fr Nahuatl]

**milt** /milt/ *n* the male reproductive glands of fishes when filled with sperm; *also* the sperm of fishes [prob fr MD *milte* milt of fish, spleen; akin to OE *milte* spleen – more at MELT] – **milty** *adj*

**ˌmilter** /ˈmiltə/ *n* a male fish in breeding condition

**¹mime** /miem/ *n* **1** an actor in a mime; *esp* one who practises the modern art of mime ⟨*the great French* ~ *held the English audience spellbound*⟩ **2** MIMIC 2 **3** an ancient dramatic entertainment representing scenes from life usu in a ridiculous manner **4a** the modern art of portraying a character or telling a story by body movement **b** a performance of mime [L *mimus,* fr Gk *mimos;* akin to Gk *mimeisthai* to imitate]

²**mime** *vi* to act a part with mimic gesture and action, usu without words ~ *vt* **1** to mimic **2** to act out in the manner of a mime – **mimer** *n*

**mimeograph** /'mimiǝ‚grahf, -‚graf/ *n* a duplicator for making many copies that uses a stencil through which ink is pressed [fr *Mimeograph,* a trademark] – **mimeograph** *vt*

**mimesis** /mi'meesis/ *n* imitation, mimicry [LL, fr Gk *mimēsis,* fr *mimeisthai*]

**mimetic** /mi'metik/ *adj* **1** imitative **2** relating to, characterized by, or exhibiting mimicry ⟨~ *colouring of a butterfly*⟩ [LL *mimeticus,* fr Gk *mimētikos,* fr *mimeisthai*] – **mimetically** *adv*

**mimetite** /'mimi‚tiet/ *n* a mineral consisting of an ARSENATE and CHLORIDE of lead, Pb₅(AsO₄)₃ [Ger *mimetit,* fr Fr *mimétèse,* fr Gk *mimētēs* imitator, fr *mimeisthai;* fr its resemblance to pyromorphite]

¹**mimic** /'mimik/ *n* **1** MIME 1 **2** somebody or something that mimics **3** an actor who imitates the appearance, voice, mannerisms, etc of well-known (types of) people in order to entertain

²**mimic** *also* **mimical** /-kl/ *adj* **1a** IMITATIVE 1 **b** imitation, mock ⟨*a* ~ *battle*⟩ **2** of mime or mimicry [L *mimicus,* fr Gk *mimikos,* fr *mimos* mime]

³**mimic** *vt* **-ck-** **1** to imitate slavishly or unintelligently; ape **2** to ridicule by imitation ⟨~ked *his father's mannerisms*⟩ **3** to simulate **4** to resemble by biological mimicry

**mimicry** /'mimikri/ *n* **1** the act or an instance of mimicking **2** the resemblance of one organism to another or to a part of its surroundings that secures it an advantage (e g protection from predators)

**mimosa** /mi'mohzǝ, -sǝ/ *n* **1** any of a genus (*Mimosa*) of tropical and subtropical trees, shrubs, and nonwoody plants of the pea family that have globular heads of small white or pink flowers and many of which have leaves that close up or droop in response to light, touch, etc – compare SENSITIVE PLANT **2** (ornamental shoots from) an acacia tree with sweetly scented yellow flowers in compact globular clusters – not used technically [NL, genus name, fr L *mimus* mime; fr its apparent imitation of animal sensitivity in drooping and closing its leaves when touched]

¹**mina** /'mienǝ/ *n* any of various ancient units of weight (e g in W Asia or Greece); *also* an ancient Greek monetary unit [L, fr Gk *mna,* of Sem origin; akin to Heb *māneh* mina]

²**mina** *n* a myna

**minacious** /mi'nayshǝs/ *adj, formal* minatory [L *minac-, minax,* fr *minari*]

**minaret** /‚minǝ'ret/ *n* a slender tower attached to a mosque and surrounded by one or more projecting balconies from which the summons to prayer is made [Fr, fr Turk *minare,* fr Ar *manārah* lighthouse]

**minatory** /'minǝt(ǝ)ri/ *adj, formal* having a menacing quality; threatening [LL *minatorius,* fr L *minatus,* pp of *minari* to threaten – more at MOUNT]

¹**mince** /mins/ *vt* to cut or chop into very small pieces ~ *vi* to walk with short steps in a prim affected manner ⟨*he* ~d *into the room*⟩ [ME *mincen,* fr MF *mincer,* fr (assumed) VL *minutiare,* fr L *minutia* smallness – more at MINUTIA] – **mincer** *n* – **not mince matters/one's words** to speak honestly and frankly ⟨*not to mince matters, we're ruined*⟩

²**mince** *n* minced meat

**mincemeat** /-‚meet/ *n* a finely chopped mixture of raisins, apples, suet, spices, etc (with brandy) which traditionally used to contain meat – **make mincemeat of** to thrash or defeat soundly and conclusively

*usage* "Minced meat" is called **mince** nowadays, not **mincemeat.**

**mince pie** *n* a sweet usu small and round pie filled with mincemeat, eaten esp at Christmas

**mincing** /'minsing/ *adj* affectedly dainty or delicate ⟨*trying to speak in a small* ~ *treble* – George Eliot⟩ – **mincingly** *adv*

¹**mind** /miend/ *n* **1a** recollection, memory ⟨*keep that in* ~⟩ ⟨*time out of* ~⟩ **b** attention, concentration ⟨*can't keep her* ~ *on her work*⟩ **2** the (capabilities of the) organized conscious and unconscious mental processes of an organism that result in reasoning, thinking, perceiving, etc **3** an intention, desire ⟨*he changed his* ~ *and caught the bus instead*⟩ ⟨*I've a good* ~ *to box his ears*⟩ ⟨*had half a* ~ *to leave early*⟩ **4** the normal condition of the mental faculties ⟨*lost his* ~⟩ **5** an opinion, view ⟨*unwilling to speak his* ~⟩ ⟨*in two* ~s *about the problem*⟩

⟨*though she's just a child, she has a* ~ *of her own*⟩ ⟨*their arguments persuaded me to change my* ~⟩ **6** a disposition, mood ⟨*her state of* ~ *was calm*⟩ **7a** the mental attributes of a usu specified group ⟨*the scientific* ~⟩ ⟨*the European* ~⟩ **b** a person considered as an intellectual being ⟨*one of the finest* ~s *of the academic world today*⟩ **8a** the intellect and rational faculties as contrasted with the emotions ⟨*instead of using his* ~ *he became insanely jealous*⟩ **b** the human spirit and intellect as opposed to the body and the material world ⟨~ *over matter*⟩ **9** a conscious substratum or factor in the universe ⟨*haunted forever by the eternal* ~ – William Wordsworth⟩ [ME, fr OE *gemynd;* akin to OHG *gimunt* memory; both fr a prehistoric EGmc-WGmc compound whose first constituent is represented by OE *ge-* (perfective prefix) and whose second is akin to L *ment-, mens* mind, *monēre* to remind, warn, Gk *menos* spirit, *mnasthai, mimnēskesthai* to remember] – **bear/keep in mind** to think of, esp at the appropriate time; consider – **blow somebody's mind** *slang* to cause somebody to hallucinate **2** to amaze somebody – **cross somebody's mind** to occur to somebody – **on one's mind** occupying or troubling one's thoughts ⟨*she can't work with the problem of the mortgage on her mind*⟩ – **put in mind** to remind ⟨*that puts me in mind of a story my father told*⟩ – see also PIECE **of one's mind,** TIME **out of mind**

²**mind** *vt* **1** to attend to closely ⟨*always* ~s *his own business*⟩ ⟨~ *how you behave!*⟩ **2** to pay attention to or follow (advice, instructions, or orders); mark ⟨~ *what the teacher tells you*⟩ **3a** to be concerned about; care about ⟨*don't* ~ *me; I'll be all right*⟩ ⟨*never* ~ *the rain: it isn't heavy*⟩ ⟨*she didn't* ~ *where she went*⟩ **b** to object to; dislike ⟨*I don't* ~ *going*⟩ **4a** to be careful that ⟨~ *you finish your homework!*⟩ ⟨~ *you don't lose your ticket!*⟩ **b** to be cautious about ⟨~ *the step!*⟩ **5** to give protective care to; LOOK AFTER ⟨~ed *the children while their parents were out*⟩ ⟨*she* ~s *the shop when the shopkeeper has to go out*⟩ **6** *dial Br* to remind ⟨~ *me to tell you about it some day*⟩ **7** *archaic dial* to remember ⟨*I* ~ *the village street sixty years ago*⟩ **8** *obs* to perceive, notice ⟨*I'll fall flat. Perchance he will not* ~ *me* – Shak⟩ ~ *vi* **1a** to be attentive or wary – often + *out* ⟨*it's coming again:* ~ *out!*⟩ **b** to stand clear; move (out of the way) ⟨*please* ~ *: we can't get past with this table*⟩ **2** to be or become concerned; care ⟨*never* ~, *it's nothing serious*⟩ ⟨*"tea or coffee?" "I don't* ~ *"*⟩ – **mind (you)** but take this fact into account; notice this ⟨*I don't blame him,* mind⟩ ⟨*they apologized later,* mind you⟩

'**mind-‚bending** *adj, informal* at the limits of understanding or credibility ⟨*the* ~ *implications of atomic physics*⟩ – **mind-bendingly** *adv,* **mindbender** *n*

'**mind-‚blowing** *adj, informal* **1** of or causing a psychic state similar to that produced by a psychedelic drug **2** mentally or emotionally exhilarating; overwhelming – **mindblower** *n*

'**mind-‚boggling** *adj, informal* causing great surprise or wonder

**minded** /'miendid/ *adj* **1** having a (specified kind of) mind – usu in combination ⟨*narrow*-minded⟩ **2** inclined, disposed *to* ⟨*was not* ~ *to report his losses* – Herts & Essex Observer⟩ – **mindedness** *n*

**minder** /'miendǝ/ *n* **1** one who looks after – usu in combination ⟨*child*minder⟩ **2** *chiefly Br* PRESSMAN 1 **3** *Br* one who acts as a right-hand man and physical protector to someone who operates outside or on the edge of the law: *also* one who is hired to give people physical protection

'**mind-ex‚panding** *adj* PSYCHEDELIC 1a

**mindful** /-f(ǝ)l/ *adj* keeping in mind; aware *of* ⟨~ *of his reputation, he refused*⟩ – **mindfully** *adv,* **mindfulness** *n*

**mindless** /-lis/ *adj* **1** devoid of thought or intelligence; senseless ⟨~ *destruction*⟩ **2** involving or requiring little thought or concentration ⟨*the work is routine and fairly* ~⟩ **3** inattentive, heedless *of* ⟨*spoke the truth* ~ *of criticism*⟩ – **mindlessly** *adv,* **mindlessness** *n*

**mind reader** *n* somebody who can or is thought to be able to perceive another's thought directly – **mind reading** *n*

**mind's eye** *n* the faculty of visual memory or imagination

¹**mine** /mien/ *adj, archaic* my – used before a vowel or *h* ⟨*this treasure in* ~ *arms* – Shak⟩ or sometimes to modify a preceding noun ⟨*O mistress* ~, *where are you roaming?* – Shak⟩ [ME *min,* fr OE *mīn* – more at MY]

²**mine** *pron, pl* **mine** that which or the one who belongs to me – used without a following noun as a pronoun equivalent in meaning to the adjective *my* ⟨*children younger than* ~⟩ ⟨*that brother of* ~⟩ ⟨*friends of* ~⟩ ⟨*the house became* ~⟩

³**mine** *n* **1a** an excavation, esp a system of tunnels and pits, from which mineral substances (e g coal or ore) are taken; *also* such an excavation along with its associated buildings **b** an ore deposit **2** an underground passage beneath an enemy position **3** an encased explosive designed to destroy enemy personnel, vehicles, or ships **4** a rich source *of ⟨a ∼ of information⟩* **5** a firework comprising various smaller fireworks that are scattered into the air with a loud report [ME, fr MF, fr (assumed) VL *mina*, prob of Celt origin; akin to W *mwyn* ore]

⁴**mine** *vi* to dig a mine ⟨*farming land was lost when the government started to ∼ here*⟩ ∼ *vt* **1a** to dig an underground passage to gain access to or cause the collapse of (an enemy position) **b** UNDERMINE 3 **2** to obtain from a mine ⟨∼ *coal*⟩ **3** to burrow in or beneath the surface of ⟨*a larva that* ∼s *leaves*⟩ **4** to place military mines in, on, or under ⟨∼ *a harbour*⟩ **5a** to dig into for ore, coal, etc **b** to process for obtaining a natural constituent ⟨∼ *the air for nitrogen*⟩ – **miner** *n*, **mining** *n*

**minefield** /'mien,fiøld, -,feeld/ *n* **1** an area of land or water where explosive mines have been laid as a defence **2** something that is full of hidden dangers or difficulties

**minelayer** /-,layø/ *n* a vessel or aircraft for laying mines

**mineral** /'min(ø)røl/ *n* **1a** (a synthetic material resembling) a naturally occurring solid homogeneous crystalline inorganic substance; *broadly* any inorganic substance **b** any of various naturally occurring esp homogeneous substances (e g coal, salt, or petroleum) obtained by drilling, mining, etc **2** something neither animal nor vegetable **3** *usu pl, Br* MINERAL WATER [ME, fr ML *minerale*, fr neut of *mineralis* of mines, fr *minera* mine, ore, fr OF *miniere*, fr *mine*] – **mineral** *adj*

**mineral·ize, -ise** /'min(ø)rø,liez/ *vt* **1** to transform (a metal or rock) into an ore **2** to impregnate with or convert into a mineral or an inorganic compound **3** to petrify – **mineralizable** *adj*, **mineralization** *n*, **mineralizer** *n*

**mineral kingdom** *n* the one of the three basic groups of natural objects that includes inorganic objects – compare ANIMAL KINGDOM, PLANT KINGDOM

**mineralogy** /,minø'raløji/ *n* a science dealing with the structure, properties, and classification of minerals [(assumed) NL *mineralogia*, irreg fr ML *minerale* + L *-logia* -logy] – **mineralogist** *n*, **mineralogical** *adj*

**mineral oil** *n* an oil of mineral as opposed to vegetable origin

**mineral water, mineral** *n* water naturally or artificially impregnated with mineral salts or gases (e g CARBON DIOXIDE); *broadly* any effervescent nonalcoholic beverage

**mineral wax** *n* a wax of mineral rather than animal or vegetable origin; *esp* OZOCERITE

**mineral wool** *n* any of various lightweight synthetic fibrous materials used esp in heat and sound insulation

**minestrone** /,mini'strohni/ *n* a soup made from a number of vegetables and usu containing pasta (e g macaroni) [It, aug of *minestra*, fr *minestrare* to serve, dish up, fr L *ministrare*, fr *minister* servant – more at MINISTER]

**minesweeper** /'mien,sweepø/ *n* a ship designed for removing or neutralizing mines – **minesweeping** *n*

**mineworker** /'mien,wuhkø/ *n* a person who works in a mine; a miner

**Ming** /ming/ *n* a Chinese dynasty dated from AD 1368 to 1644 and marked by the restoration of earlier traditions and in the arts by the perfection of established techniques – compare TANG [Chin (Pek) *ming* (*ming*²) luminous]

**mingle** /'ming·gl/ *vt* to bring or mix together or with something else, usu without fundamental loss of identity; intermix ∼ *vi* **1** to become mingled **2** to mix with or go among a group of people ⟨*too shy to* ∼ *at parties*⟩ ⟨∼d *with the crowd*⟩ **synonyms** see ¹MIX **antonym** separate [ME *menglen*, freq of *mengen* to mix, fr OE *mengan*; akin to MHG *mengen* to mix, Gk *massein* to knead]

**ming tree** /ming/ *n* **1** a dwarf tree, usu in a pot; a bonsai tree **2** a small decorative artificial tree made from seeds and twigs [perh fr *Ming*]

**mingy** /'minji/ *adj, informal* mean, stingy [perh blend of ¹*mean* and *stingy*]

**mini** /'mini/ *n, pl* **minis 1** something small of its kind (e g a skirt or car) **2** a woman's skirt or dress with the hemline several inches above the knee ⟨*the* ∼ *was a best-seller*⟩ **3** a minicomputer [*mini-*] – **mini** *adj*

**mini-** /mini-/ *comb form* miniature; small kind of ⟨mini-*dress*⟩ ⟨minicomputer⟩ [*miniature*]

¹**miniature** /'minøchø/ *n* **1a** a copy or representation on a much reduced scale **b** something small of its kind **2** a painting in an illuminated book or manuscript **3** the art of painting miniatures **4** a very small painting (e g a portrait on ivory or metal) [It *miniatura* art of illuminating a manuscript, fr ML, fr L *miniatus*, pp of *miniare* to colour with minium, fr *minium*] – **miniaturist** *n*, **miniaturistic** *adj*

²**miniature** *adj* **1** (represented) on a small or reduced scale ⟨*a ride on the* ∼ *railway at the seaside*⟩ ⟨*a* ∼ *poodle*⟩ **2** of still photography using film 35 millimetres wide or smaller **synonyms** see ¹SMALL

**miniature golf** *n* a golf game played with a putter on a miniature course having tunnels, bridges, sharp corners, and obstacles

**miniatur·ize, -ise** /'minøchø,riez/ *vt* to design or construct as a small copy; reduce in scale – **miniaturization** *n*

**minibus** /'mini,bus/ *n* a small bus for carrying usu between 5 and 10 passengers

**minicab** /-,kab/ *n* a car that serves as a taxicab when hired by telephone but is not permitted to cruise in search of passengers

**minicomputer** /-køm,pyoohtø/ *n* a small and relatively inexpensive computer

**minié ball** /'minyay/ *n* a rifle bullet with a conical head used in the middle of the 19th century [Claude Etienne *Minié* †1879 Fr army officer]

**minify** /'mini,fie/ *vt* to lessen [L *mini*mus smallest + E *-fy*]

**minikin** /'minikin/ *n, archaic* a small or affectedly dainty creature [obs D *minneken* darling] – **minikin** *adj*

**minim** /'minim/ *n* **1** a musical note with the time value of two crotchets or half a semibreve **2** a unit of capacity equal to ¹/₆₀ fluid drachm (about 59.19 cubic millimetres) [L *minimus* least]

**minimal** /'miniml/ *adj* **1** of or being a minimum; constituting the least possible; *specif, of an element in a mathematical set* being less than or equal to every other element in the set **2** *often cap* of or being minimal art – **minimalize** *vt*, **minimally** *adv*

**minimal art** *n* abstract art, esp sculpture, consisting of simple geometric forms executed in an impersonal style

**minimalism** /'minimøliz(ø)m/ *n* MINIMAL ART

**minimalist** /-ist/ *n* **1** one who favours restricting the functions and powers of a political organization or is content with minimum achievement – compare MAXIMALIST **2** a minimal artist

**minimax** /'mini,maks/ *n* the minimum of a mathematical set of maximum values (MAXIMA); *esp* the smallest of a set of maximum possible losses each of which occurs in the most unfavourable outcome of a strategy followed by a participant in a situation governed by the THEORY OF GAMES – compare MAXIMIN [*mini*mum + *ma*ximum]

**minim·ize, -ise** /'minimiez/ *vt* **1** to reduce to a minimum **2** to represent (somebody or something) as less than true value; PLAY DOWN ⟨∼ *losses during war*⟩ – **minimizer** *n*, **minimization** *n* usage Some careful writers feel that minimize is not a matter of degree, and object to expressions such as ⟨greatly minimize the effort⟩. **antonym** maximize

**minim rest** *n* a musical REST (indicating silence) of the same time value as a minim

**minimum** /'minimøm/ *n, pl* **minima, minimums 1** the least quantity or value assignable, admissible, or possible **2** the least element of a mathematical set; *esp* the smallest value assumed by a CONTINUOUS function on a closed interval **3** the lowest degree or amount of variation reached or recorded **4** the time at which a VARIABLE STAR is least bright; *also* the MAGNITUDE (degree of brightness) of a variable star at this time [L, neut of *minimus* smallest; akin to L *minor* smaller] – **minimum** *adj*

**minimum lending rate** *n* the DISCOUNT RATE (annual rate of interest) fixed by a country's central bank (e g the Bank of England) – compare BANK RATE

**minimum wage** *n* a wage fixed by legal authority or by contract as the least that may be paid either to employees generally or to a particular category of employees

**minion** /'minyøn/ *n* **1** a servile attendant ⟨*the* ∼s *of a dictator*⟩ **2** FAVOURITE 1 **3** *derog* a minor official [MF *mignon* darling, fr *mignot* dainty, fr OF, prob of Celt origin]

**miniscule** /'miniskyoohl/ *adj* very small [alter. (influenced by *mini-*) of ²*minuscule*]

¹**minister** /'ministø/ *n* **1** AGENT 1a, 3 **2** an official with spiritual duties in the Christian church: e g **2a** one officiating or assisting the officiant in church worship **b** a clergyman, esp of a Protestant or nonconformist church **3** **minister, minister-general 3a** the superior of any of several religious orders **b** the assistant to the rector or the bursar of a Jesuit community **4** a high

officer of state entrusted with the management of a division of government **5** a diplomatic representative accredited to a foreign state [ME *ministre,* fr OF, fr L *minister* servant; akin to L *minor* smaller] – **ministerial** *adj,* **ministerially** *adv*

²**minister** *vi* **1** to perform the functions of a minister of religion **2** to give aid or service ⟨~ *to the sick*⟩ *usage* see ADMINISTER – **ministrant** *n or adj*

**minister of state** *n* a government minister ranking below a head of department

**minister plenipotentiary** *n, pl* **ministers plenipotentiary** a diplomatic agent ranking below an ambassador but possessing full power and authority

**minister resident** *n, pl* **ministers resident** a diplomatic agent resident at a foreign court or seat of government and ranking below a minister plenipotentiary

**minister without portfolio** *n* a government minister with no specific departmental responsibilities

**ministration** /ˌmini'straysh(ə)n/ *n* ministering, esp in religious matters

**ministry** /'ministri/ *n* **1** service, ministration **2** the office, duties, or functions of a minister **3** the body of ministers of religion; *the* clergy **4** the period of service or office of a minister or ministry **5** *often cap* **5a** the body of ministers governing a state from which a smaller cabinet is sometimes selected **b** the group of ministers constituting a cabinet **6a** a government department presided over by a minister **b** the building in which the business of a ministry is transacted

**minitrack** /'mini,trak/ *n* an electronic system for tracking an earth satellite by radio waves transmitted from it to a chain of ground stations [*mini*mum-weight *track*ing]

**minium** /'mini-əm/ *n* RED LEAD [ME, fr L, cinnabar, red lead, of Iberian origin; akin to Basque *armineá* cinnabar]

**miniver** /'minivə/ *n* a white fur used chiefly for (lining or trimming) robes of state [ME *meniver,* fr OF *menu vair* small vair]

**mink** /mingk/ *n, pl* **minks,** *esp collectively* **mink 1** any of several slender-bodied semiaquatic flesh-eating mammals (genus *Mustela*) that resemble the closely related weasels and have partially webbed feet, a rather short bushy tail, and a soft thick coat **2** the soft fur or pelt of the mink varying in colour from white to dark reddish-brown [ME *mynk*]

**minke whale** /'mingkə/ *n* a small RORQUAL (*Balaenoptera acutorostrata*) of northern seas [prob fr (the name) *Meincke,* reputedly a Norw whaling gunner]

**minnesinger** /'mini,sing-ə, 'minə,zing-ə/ *n* a member of a class of German lyric poets and musicians of the 12th to the 14th centuries △ Meistersinger [Ger, fr MHG, fr *minne* love + *singer*]

**minnow** /'minoh/ *n, pl* **minnows,** *esp collectively* **minnow 1a** *Br* a small dark-coloured freshwater fish (*Phoxinus phoxinus*) related to the carp, that is found in the upper parts of rivers **b** any of various small fish resembling or related to the minnow **2** *Br* something small or insignificant of its kind [ME *menawe;* akin to OE *myne* minnow, Russ *men'* eelpout]

¹**Minoan** /mi'noh-ən/ *adj* of a highly developed BRONZE AGE culture of Crete (3000 BC – 1400 BC) [L *minous* Cretan, of Minos, fr Gk *minōios,* fr *Minōs* Minos, legendary king of Crete]

²**Minoan** *n* a native or inhabitant of ancient Crete

¹**minor** /'mienə/ *adj* **1a** inferior in importance, size, rank, or degree ⟨*a* ~ *poet*⟩ **b** comparatively unimportant ⟨*a* ~ *alteration*⟩ **2** not having attained the age of majority **3a** *esp of a musical scale or mode* having semitones between the second and third, fifth and sixth, and sometimes seventh and eighth steps in the case of the harmonic minor scale, giving the pattern: tone, semitone, tone, tone, semitone, tone, tone/semitone, or, in the case of the melodic minor scale, semitones between the second and third and seventh and eighth steps ascending and between the second and third and fifth and sixth steps descending. Major scales and modes have WHOLE TONES in these positions. **b** being or based on a (specified) minor scale ⟨*in a* ~ *key*⟩ ⟨*mass in B* ~⟩ **c** being a musical interval less by a semitone than a corresponding major interval ⟨~ *third*⟩ – compare AUGMENTED, DIMINISHED, PERFECT **5a d** *of a chord* having an interval of three semitones between the lowest note and the next note above it. Major chords have four semitones in this position. **4** not involving serious risk to life; not serious ⟨*a* ~ *illness*⟩ [ME, fr L, smaller, inferior; akin to OHG *minniro* smaller, L *minuere* to lessen, Gk *meiōn* less]

²**minor** *n* **1** somebody who has not attained the age of majority **2** a minor musical interval, scale, key, or mode **3** a DE-TERMINANT obtained from a given determinant by elim-

inating the row and column in which a given element lies △ miner

**minor axis** *n* the chord of an ellipse that passes through the centre and is perpendicular to the MAJOR AXIS

**minorca** /mi'nawkə/ *n* (any of) a breed of large DOMESTIC FOWL with black, white, or blue plumage and strong graceful appearance, that is widely reared for egg production and competitive show-breeding [*Minorca,* one of the Balearic islands in the Mediterranean]

**minor canon** *n* a canon in the Church of England who usu assists in services but has no vote in the CHAPTER (collective meeting of canons)

**Minorite** /'mienə,riet/ *n* a Franciscan friar [fr *Friar Minor* (Franciscan)]

**minority** /mie'norəti, mi-/ *n* **1a** the period before attainment of the age of majority **b** the state of being a legal minor **2** *taking sing or pl vb* the smaller in number of two groups constituting a whole; *specif* a group having less than the number of votes necessary for control **3** *taking sing or pl vb* a group of people who share common characteristics or interests differing from those of the majority of a population

**minor order** *n usu pl* any of the Roman Catholic or Eastern Orthodox clerical orders that are lower in rank than MAJOR ORDERS

**minor planet** *n* an asteroid

**minor premise** *n* the statement that contains the subject of the conclusion drawn in a SYLLOGISM (a logical exercise of the form "all As are B, C is an A, so C must be B") ⟨*if we assume that all goddesses are immortal, and accept the* ~ *that Venus is a goddess, we conclude that Venus must be immortal*⟩

**minor prophet** *n* any of the Old Testament prophetic books from Hosea to Malachi or their authors

**minor seminary** *n* a Roman Catholic seminary which prepares candidates for a MAJOR SEMINARY

**minor suit** *n* either of the suits of clubs or diamonds that in bridge are of inferior scoring value – compare MAJOR SUIT

**minor term** *n* the term that is the subject of a MINOR PREMISE (eg "Venus" in "Venus is a goddess")

**minster** /'minstə/ *n* a large or important church, often having cathedral status [ME, monastery, church attached to a monastery, fr OE *mynster,* fr LL *monasterium* monastery]

**minstrel** /'minstrəl/ *n* **1** a medieval singer, poet, or musical entertainer **2** any of a troupe of performers, usu with blackened faces, giving a performance of supposedly Negro singing, jokes, dancing, etc [ME *menestrel,* fr OF, official, servant, minstrel, fr LL *ministerialis* imperial household officer, fr L *ministerium* service, fr *minister* servant – more at MINISTER]

**minstrelsy** /-si/ *n* **1** the singing and playing of a minstrel **2** a body of minstrels **3** songs or poems (composed or performed by minstrels) [ME *minstralcie,* fr MF *menestralsie,* fr *menestrel*]

¹**mint** /mint/ *n* **1** a place where coins, medals, or tokens are made **2** a place where something is manufactured or invented ⟨*his mind was a* ~ *of novel ideas*⟩ **3** *informal* a vast sum or amount ⟨*made a* ~ *in the rag trade*⟩ [ME *mynt,* fr OE *mynet* coin, money; akin to OHG *munizza* coin; both fr a prehistoric WGmc word borrowed fr L *moneta* mint, coin, fr *Moneta,* epithet of Juno, Roman goddess in whose temple the Romans coined money]

²**mint** *vt* **1** to make (eg coins) by stamping metal; coin **2** to fabricate, invent ⟨~ *a new word*⟩ – **minter** *n*

³**mint** *adj* **1** unmarred as if fresh from a mint; pristine ⟨~ *coins*⟩ ⟨*secondhand, but never used and in* ~ *condition*⟩ **2** *of a stamp* having the original gum intact

⁴**mint** *n* **1** any of a genus (*Mentha* of the family Labiateae, the mint family) of plants that have whorled leaves and small flowers, and whose foliage has a characteristic strong aromatic taste and smell and is used esp as a flavouring **2** a sweet, chocolate, etc flavoured with mint [ME *minte,* fr OE; akin to OHG *minza* mint; both fr a prehistoric WGmc word borrowed fr L *mentha* mint]

**mintage** /'mintij/ *n* **1** the action, process, or cost of minting coins **2** coins produced in a single period of minting

**mint julep** *n* JULEP 2 (alcoholic drink)

**mint mark** *n* an official mark stamped on a coin to indicate its origin

**minuend** /'minyoo,end/ *n* a number from which another is to be subtracted [L *minuendum,* neut of *minuendus,* gerundive of *minuere* to lessen – more at MINOR]

**minuet** /ˌminyoo'et/ *n* (music for or in the rhythm of) a slow graceful dance in ¾ time [Fr *menuet*, fr obs Fr, tiny, delicate, fr OF, fr *menu* small, fr L *minutus*]

**¹minus** /'mienəs/ *prep* **1** diminished by; less ⟨*seven* ~ *four is three*⟩ **2** without ⟨~ *his hat*⟩ [ME, fr L *minus*, adv, less, fr neut of *minor* smaller – more at MINOR]

**²minus** *n* **1 minus sign, minus** a sign - denoting subtraction (e g in 8 - 6 = 2) or a negative quantity (e g in -10°) **2** a subtracted quantity **3** a negative quantity or quality **4** a deficiency, defect ⟨*crowds are one of the* ~es *of many beauty spots*⟩

**³minus** *adj* **1** less than zero; negative ⟨*a* ~ *quantity*⟩ ⟨*a temperature of* ~ *10°C*⟩ **2** having negative qualities; *esp* involving a disadvantage ⟨*a* ~ *factor was the initial cost*⟩ **3** falling low in a specified range ⟨*a mark of B* ~⟩

**¹minuscule** /'minə,skyoohl/ *n* any of several styles of small joined-up (CURSIVE) handwriting used in ancient and medieval manuscripts; *also* a noncapital letter in any of these styles – compare MAJUSCULE [Fr, fr L *minusculus* rather small, dim. of *minor* smaller]

**²minuscule** *adj* **1** written in minuscules **2** very small *synonyms* see ¹SMALL

**¹minute** /'minit/ *n* **1** the 60th part of an hour of time or of a degree of circular measurement **2** the distance one can cover in a minute ⟨*lived about five* ~s *from the station*⟩ **3** a short space of time; a moment ⟨*I'll be with you in a* ~⟩ **4a** a memorandum **b** *pl* the official record of the proceedings of a meeting [ME, MF, fr LL *minuta*, fr L *minutus* small, fr pp of *minuere* to lessen; (4) ML *minuta*]

**²minute** *vt* **1** to make notes or a brief summary of ⟨*the chairman's secretary* ~d *the proceedings*⟩ **2** to write in or in the form of a minute ⟨~d *a request for more funds*⟩ ~ *vi* to take the minutes of a meeting

**³minute** /mie'nyooht/ *adj* **1** extremely small; tiny **2** of minor importance; petty **3** marked by painstaking attention to detail ⟨*a* ~ *examination*⟩ *synonyms* see ¹SMALL [L *minutus*] – **minutely** *adv*, **minuteness** *n*

**minute bell** *n* (the sound of) a church bell tolled at one minute intervals while a funeral procession is approaching or leaving a church

**minute gun** *n* a gun fired at one minute intervals at funerals, commemoration ceremonies, etc, or as a distress signal

**minute hand** *n* the long hand that marks the minutes on the face of a watch or clock

**minuteman** /-,man/ *n, NAm* a member of a group of armed men pledged to take the field at a minute's notice during and immediately before the American War of Independence

**minute steak** *n* a small thin steak that can be quickly cooked [¹*minute*]

**minutia** /mi'nyoohshyə, mie-/ *n usu pl, pl* **minutiae** /-shi,ee/ a minute or minor detail [L *minutiae* trifles, details, fr pl of *minutia* smallness, fr *minutus*]

**minx** /mingks/ *n* **1** a saucy or flirtatious girl **2** a sly cunning (young) woman [origin unknown]

**mio-** – see MI-

**Miocene** /'mie·ə,seen/ *adj or n* (of or being) an epoch of the TERTIARY geological period between the PLIOCENE and the OLIGOCENE epochs, or the system of rocks formed during this time

**miosis** /mie'ohsis/ *n, pl* **mioses** /-seez/ excessive smallness or contraction of the pupil of the eye [NL, fr Gk *myein* to be closed (of the eyes) + NL *-osis*] – **miotic** *adj*

**miotic** /mie'otik/ *n* something (e g a drug) that causes miosis

**mir** /miə/ *n* a village community in tsarist Russia characterized by joint ownership of the land and cultivation by individual families [Russ]

**mirabile dictu** /mi,rabilay 'diktooh/ *adv* wonderful to relate [L]

**mirabilite** /mi'rabi,liet/ *n* GLAUBER'S SALT [Ger *mirabilit*, fr NL (*sal*) *mirabile*, lit., wonderful salt]

**miracidium** /,mierə'sidiəm/ *n, pl* **miracidia** /-diə/ the free-swimming CILIATED (bearing small hairlike structures used for movement) first-produced larval form in the life cycle of many TREMATODE worms (e g the LIVER FLUKE), that, after hatching from the egg, seeks out and penetrates a suitable snail host in which it develops into a SPOROCYST (saclike larval form) [NL, fr Gk *meirak-*, *meirax* youth, stripling + NL *-idium*] – **miracidial** *adj*

**miracle** /'mirəkl/ *n* **1** an extraordinary event manifesting divine intervention in human affairs **2** an astonishing or unusual event, thing, or accomplishment ⟨*an economic* ~⟩ ⟨~ *drugs*⟩ **3** a person or thing that is a remarkable example or instance

of something ⟨*this watch is a* ~ *of precision*⟩ [ME, fr OF, fr L *miraculum*, fr *mirari* to wonder at – more at SMILE]

**miracle fruit** *n* the fruit of a small shrubby tropical African tree (*Synsepalum dulcificum*) of the sapodilla family, that contains a chemical compound (GLYCOPROTEIN) that causes sour substances to taste sweet; *also* the tree that bears the miracle fruit

**miracle play** *n* a medieval drama based on episodes from the Bible or the life of a saint; *also* MYSTERY PLAY – compare MORALITY PLAY

**miraculous** /mi'rakyooləs/ *adj* **1** of the nature of a miracle; supernatural ⟨*a* ~ *event*⟩ **2** evoking wonder like a miracle; marvellous ⟨*gave proof of a* ~ *memory* – *Time*⟩ **3** (capable of) working miracles ⟨~ *drugs*⟩ [MF *miraculeux*, fr ML *miraculosus*, fr L *miraculum*] – **miraculously** *adv*, **miraculousness** *n*

**mirage** /'mirahzh/ *n* **1** an optical illusion appearing esp as a pool of water or as a reflection of distant objects and caused by the bending or reflection of rays of light by a layer of heated air esp near the ground **2** something illusory and unattainable [Fr, fr *mirer* to look at, fr L *mirari*]

**¹mire** /'mie·ə/ *n* **1** a tract of soft waterlogged ground; a marsh, bog **2** (deep) mud or slush [ME, fr ON *mȳrr*; akin to OE *mōs* marsh – more at MOSS] – **miry** *adj*

**²mire** *vt* **1** to cause to stick fast (as if) in mire; BOG DOWN ⟨~d *in detail and confusion*⟩ **2** to cover or soil with mire ⟨*we were* ~d *up to the knees after our walk*⟩ ~ *vi* to become covered with or stuck in mire; wallow, flounder ⟨*miring in the swamp*⟩

**mirepoix** /miə'pwah/ *n, pl* **mirepoix** a mixture of diced vegetables (e g carrots, celery, and onions) and often ham sautéed and used as a base for brown sauces or as a bed on which to braise meat [Fr, prob fr Charles de Lévis, duc de *Mirepoix* † 1757 Fr diplomat & general]

**mirex** /'miereks/ *n* a chlorine-containing insecticide, $C_{10}Cl_{12}$, used esp against ants [perh fr pis*mire* + *exterminator*]

**mirid** /'mie·ərid, 'mirid/ *n* any of a large family (Miridae) of TRUE BUGS that are mostly plant-feeding [deriv of NL *Miris*, genus of true bugs]

**mirk** /muhk/ *n* murk – **mirky** *adj*

**¹mirror** /'mirə/ *n* **1** a polished or smooth surface (e g of polished metal or silvered glass) that forms images by reflection **2** something that gives a true representation ⟨*art is the* ~ *of life*⟩ [ME *mirour*, fr OF, fr *mirer* to look at, fr L *mirari* to wonder at – more at SMILE] – **mirrorlike** *adj*

**²mirror** *vt* to reflect (as if) in a mirror

**mirror carp** *n* a domesticated variety of the carp with large shiny scales

**mirror image** *n* something that has its parts reversely arranged in comparison with another similar thing or is reversed with reference to an intervening axis or plane

**mirth** /muhth/ *n, chiefly formal* happiness or amusement accompanied by laughter [ME, fr OE *myrgth*, fr *myrge* merry – more at MERRY] – **mirthful** *adj*, **mirthfully** *adv*, **mirthfulness** *n*, **mirthless** *adj*, **mirthlessly** *adv*

**MIRV** /muhv/ *n* an intercontinental missile having multiple warheads which may be directed to separate targets; *also* any of the warheads of such a missile [*multiple independently targeted reentry vehicle*]

**¹mis-** /mis-/ *prefix* **1a** badly; wrongly; unfavourably ⟨mis*judge*⟩ ⟨mis*behave*⟩ ⟨mis*handle*⟩ **b** suspicious; apprehensive ⟨mis*giving*⟩ **2** bad; wrong ⟨mis*deed*⟩ ⟨mis*fit*⟩ **3** opposite or lack of ⟨mis*trust*⟩ ⟨mis*fortune*⟩ **4** not ⟨mis*understand*⟩ [partly fr ME, fr OE; partly fr ME *mes-*, *mis-*, fr OF *mes-*, of Gmc origin; akin to OE *mis-*; akin to OE *missan* to miss]

**²mis-, miso-** *comb form* hatred ⟨miso*gamy*⟩ [Gk, fr *misein* to hate]

**misadventure** /,misəd'venchə/ *n* a MISFORTUNE; *specif* a misfortune due to an action whose results are injurious but unintended ⟨*death by* ~⟩ [ME *mesaventure*, fr OF, fr *mesavenir* to chance badly, fr *mes-* ¹*mis-* + *avenir* to chance, happen, fr L *advenire* – more at ADVENTURE]

**misaligned** /-ə'liend/ *adj* not correctly aligned – **misalignment** *n*

**misalliance** /-ə'lie·əns/ *n* an improper or unsuitable alliance: esp MÉSALLIANCE (unsuitable marriage) [modif of Fr *mésalliance*]

**misallocation** /,mis,alə'kaysh(ə)n/ *n* faulty or unsuitable allocation

**misanthrope** /'miz(ə)n,throhp/, **misanthropist** /mi'zanthrəpist/ *n* one who hates or distrusts people – compare MISOGAMIST, MISOGYNIST [Gk *misanthrōpos* hating mankind, fr *mis-* ²*mis-* + *anthrōpos* human being] – **misanthropy** *n*, **misanthropic** *adj*, **misanthropically** *adv*

**misapply** /,misə'plie/ *vt* to apply wrongly – **misapplication** *n*

**misapprehend** /-apri'hend/ *vt* to apprehend wrongly; misunderstand – **misapprehension** *n*

**misappropriate** /-ə'prohpriayt/ *vt* to appropriate wrongly (e g by theft or embezzlement) – **misappropriation** *n*

**misbecome** /,misbi'kum/ *vt, formal* to be inappropriate or unbecoming to ⟨*it* ~s *you to speak ill of your parents*⟩

**misbegotten** /-bi'gotn/ *adj* 1 having a disreputable or improper origin; ill-conceived ⟨*that* ~ *notion of his*⟩ 2 wretched, contemptible ⟨*a* ~ *scoundrel*⟩ 3 *archaic* illegitimate, bastard

**misbehave** /-bi'hayv/ *vi* to behave badly – **misbehaver** *n*, **misbehaviour** *n*

**misbelief** /,misbi'leef/ *n* (a) false belief

**misbeliever** /,misbi'leevə/ *n* a heretic, infidel

**miscalculate** /-'kalkyoolayt/ *vt* to calculate wrongly – **miscalculation** *n*

**miscall** /,mis'kawl/ *vt* 1 to call by a wrong name; misname 2 *Br dial* to speak ill of; abuse

**miscarriage** /-,karij/ *n* 1 a failure in administration ⟨*a* ~ *of justice*⟩ 2 the expulsion of a human foetus before it is capable of survival outside the womb, esp between the 12th and 28th weeks of pregnancy

**miscarry** /-'kari/ *vi* 1 to suffer miscarriage of a foetus 2 to fail to achieve an intended purpose; go wrong or amiss ⟨*the plan miscarried*⟩

**miscast** /-'kahst/ *vt* **miscast** to cast in an unsuitable role ⟨*they* ~ *her as Juliet last year; she does not intend to be* ~ *again*⟩

**miscegenation** /,mis,eji'naysh(ə)n, ,misijə-/ *n* interbreeding of races, esp between somebody white and somebody nonwhite [L *miscēre* to mix + *genus* race – more at MIX, KIN] – **miscegenational** *adj*

**miscellanea** /,misə'laynyə, -ni-ə/ *n taking pl vb* a miscellaneous collection, esp of literary works [L, fr neut pl of *miscellaneus*]

**miscellaneous** /-nyəs, -ni-əs/ *adj* 1 consisting of diverse items or members; heterogeneous 2 having various characteristics, interests, or capabilities ⟨*as a writer I was too* ~ – George Santayana⟩ [L *miscellaneus*, fr *miscellus* mixed, fr *miscēre*] – **miscellaneously** *adv*, **miscellaneousness** *n*

**miscellany** /mi'seləni/ *n* 1 a mixture of various things 2 a book containing miscellaneous literary pieces [modif of Fr *miscellanées*, pl, fr L *miscellanea*] – **miscellanist** *n*

**mischance** /,mis'chahns/ *n* (a piece of) bad luck [ME *mischaunce*, fr OF *meschance*, fr mes- ¹mis- + *chance*]

**mischief** /'mischif/ *n* 1 a specific injury or damage from a particular agent ⟨*did himself a* ~ *on the barbed wire*⟩ 2 something or esp somebody that causes harm or annoyance 3a often playful action that annoys or irritates, usu without causing or intending serious harm ⟨*told his son to keep out of* ~⟩ **b** the quality or state of being mischievous; mischievousness ⟨*had* ~ *in his eyes*⟩ ⟨*the puppy was full of* ~ *and high spirits*⟩ [ME *meschief*, fr OF, calamity, fr mes- + *chief* head, end – more at CHIEF]

**'mischief-,maker** *n* somebody who deliberately causes trouble between others, esp by spreading gossip and scandal – **mischief-making** *n*

**mischievous** /'mischivəs/ *adj* 1 harmful, malicious ⟨~ *gossip*⟩ 2 able or tending to cause annoyance, unrest, or minor injury 3a playfully provocative; arch ⟨*a* ~ *glance*⟩ **b** disruptively playful ⟨~ *behaviour*⟩ – **mischievously** *adv*, **mischievousness** *n*

**misch metal** /mish/ *n* an alloy of RARE EARTH metals used esp in tracer bullets and as a flint in lighters [Ger *mischmetall*, fr *mischen* to mix + *metall* metal]

**miscible** /'misibl/ *adj, esp of a liquid* capable of being mixed; *specif* capable of being mixed with another liquid in any proportion without separating – often + *with* ⟨*alcohol is* ~ *with water*⟩ [ML *miscibilis*, fr L *miscēre* to mix – more at MIX] – **miscibility** *n*

**misclassify** /,mis'klasi,fie/ *vt* to classify wrongly – **misclassification** *n*

**misconceive** /,miskən'seev/ *vt* to interpret 'wrongly; misunderstand – **misconception** *n*

**¹misconduct** /mis'kondukt/ *n* 1 mismanagement of responsibilities ⟨*serious* ~ *of the company's affairs*⟩ 2 intentional wrongdoing; *specif* deliberate violation of a law or standard ⟨*the doctor was found guilty of professional* ~⟩ 3a bad behaviour **b** adultery

**²misconduct** /,miskən'dukt/ *vt, formal* to conduct (oneself) badly or improperly

**misconstrue** /-kən'strooh/ *vt* to construe wrongly; misinterpret – **misconstruction** *n*

**miscount** /-'kownt/ *vt* to count wrongly ⟨*I* ~ed *the people present*⟩ ~ *vi* to make a wrong count ⟨*there were too few chairs, because I had* ~ed⟩ [ME *misconten*, fr MF *mesconter*, fr mes- + *conter* to count] – **miscount** *n*

**miscreant** /'miskri-ənt/ *n* 1 one who behaves criminally or maliciously 2 *archaic* a misbeliever [ME *miscreaunt*, fr *miscreaunt* unbelieving, fr MF *mescreant*, prp of *mescroire* to disbelieve, fr *mes-* ¹mis- + *croire* to believe, fr L *credere* – more at CREED] – **miscreant** *adj*

**miscreate** /-kri'ayt/ *vt* to create badly or incorrectly ⟨*a higher image, a legitimate hope: she had* ~d *it and deformed it, but it had been there* – Margaret Drabble⟩ – **miscreation** *n*

**¹miscue** /mis'kyooh/ *n* 1a a faulty stroke in billiards or snooker in which the cue slips **b** a faulty stroke in cricket 2 a mistake, slip

**²miscue** *vi* 1 to make a miscue ⟨*both players* ~d *from sheer nerves in the big match*⟩ 2 to answer a wrong cue ⟨*when she* ~d *the other actors improvised and covered up for her*⟩ ~ *vt* to hit in a faulty manner ⟨~d *the shot and was caught at mid-on*⟩

**misdate** /-'dayt/ *vt* to date (e g a letter or occurrence) wrongly

**misdeal** /-'deel/ *vb* **misdealt** /,mis'delt/ to deal (cards) incorrectly ⟨*I'm afraid you've* ~t; *deal again*⟩ ⟨*easy to* ~ *sticky old cards*⟩ – **misdeal** *n*

**misdeed** /-'deed/ *n* a wrong deed; an offence

**misdemeanour** /-di'meenə/ *n* 1 a minor crime formerly technically distinguished from a FELONY 2 a misdeed

**misdescribe** /,misdi'skrieb/ *vt* to describe wrongly – **misdescription** *n*

**misdiagnose** /,mis'die-əg,nohz/ *vt* to diagnose incorrectly – **misdiagnosis** *n*

**misdial** /,mis'diel/ *vb* to dial incorrectly

**misdirect** /-di'rekt, -die-/ *vt* 1 to give a wrong direction to ⟨*asked the way but was* ~ed⟩ ⟨~ *one's energies*⟩ ⟨*a judge must take care not to* ~ *the jury when summing up*⟩ 2 to address (mail) wrongly – **misdirection** *n*

**misdoing** /,mis'dooh-ing/ *n* a misdeed

**misdoubt** /,mis'dowt/ *vt, archaic* 1 to doubt the reality or truth of 2 to suspect, fear – **misdoubt** *n*

**mise-en-scène** /,meez onh 'sen (*Fr* miz ã sɛn)/ *n, pl* **mise-en-scènes** /sen(z) (*Fr* ~)/ 1 the arrangement of actors, props, and scenery on a stage in a theatrical production ⟨*the producer used a model theatre when planning the* ~⟩ 2 the environment or setting in which something takes place ⟨*the ruined chapel was an ideal* ~ *for King Arthur's farewell*⟩ [Fr *mise en scène*, lit., (act of) putting on stage]

**miser** /'miezə/ *n* a mean grasping person; *esp* one who lives miserably in order to hoard his/her wealth **synonyms** see STINGY [L *miser* miserable, wretched] – **miserly** *adj*, **miserliness** *n*

**miserable** /'miz(ə)rəbl/ *adj* 1a wretchedly inadequate or meagre ⟨*a* ~ *hovel*⟩ **b** causing extreme discomfort or unhappiness ⟨*a* ~ *situation*⟩ 2 in a pitiable state of distress or unhappiness ⟨~ *refugees*⟩ 3 shameful, contemptible ⟨*a* ~ *failure*⟩ [ME, fr MF, fr L *miserabilis* wretched, pitiable, fr *miserari* to pity, fr *miser*] – **miserableness** *n*, **miserably** *adv*

**misère** /mi'seə/ *n* a declaration in solo whist and other card games that the declarer will avoid taking any TRICKS (winning combinations of cards) in the next game, playing with no suit as TRUMPS (suit that defeats other suits) [Fr, lit., poverty, misery]

**miserere** /,mizə'reəri/ *n* 1 *cap* the 51st Psalm 2 a vocal plea or lament 3 a misericord [L, be merciful, fr *misereri* to be merciful, fr *miser* wretched; fr the first word of the Psalm]

**misericord, misericorde** /mi'zeri,kawd/ *n* a ledge on the underside of the hinged seat of a choir stall, on which, when the seat is turned up, the occupant can support him-/herself while standing [ML *misericordia* seat in church, fr L, mercy, fr *misericord-, misericors* merciful, fr *misereri* + *cord-, cor* heart – more at HEART]

**misery** /'mizəri/ *n* 1 (a cause of) physical or mental suffering or discomfort 2 great unhappiness and distress 3 *chiefly Br informal* a grumpy or querulous person; *esp* a killjoy [ME *miserie, misere*, fr MF, fr L *miseria*, fr *miser*]

**misfeasance** /mis'feez(ə)ns/ *n* illegal or improper performance of a lawful action [MF *mesfaisance*, fr *mesfaire* to do wrong, fr *mes-* ¹mis- + *faire* to make, do, fr L *facere* – more at DO] – **misfeasor** *n*

**misfield** /-'feeld/ *vb* to make a mistake in fielding (the ball) in cricket, baseball, etc – **misfield** *n*

**misfile** /,mis'fiel/ *vt* to file at the wrong place

**misfire** /-'fie·ə/ *vi* 1 *of a motor vehicle, engine, etc* to have the explosive or propulsive charge fail to ignite at the proper time ⟨*the engine* ~ d⟩ 2 *esp of a firearm* to fail to fire ⟨*the gun* ~ d⟩ 3 to fail to have an intended effect ⟨*as criticism, this essay* ~ s – Stephen Spender⟩ – **misfire** *n*

**misfit** /-ˌfit/ *n* 1 something that fits badly 2 a person poorly adjusted to his/her environment ⟨*social* ~ s⟩

**misfortune** /-'fawchoohn, -chən/ *n* 1 bad luck ⟨*he had the ~ to break his leg*⟩ 2 a distressing or unfortunate incident or event; *also* the unhappy situation that results ⟨~ s *never come singly*⟩ ⟨*she feared that some ~ would befall her*⟩ ⟨*they sympathized with her in her* ~⟩

**misgive** /-'giv/ *vb* **misgave** /mis'gayv/; **misgiven** /mis'giv(ə)n/ to (cause to) be fearful or apprehensive

**misgiving** /-'giving/ *n* a feeling of doubt, suspicion, or apprehension, esp concerning a future event *synonyms* see QUALM

**misgovern** /-'guvən/ *vt* to govern badly – **misgovernment** *n*

**misguidance** /mis'gied(ə)ns/ *n* faulty guidance

**misguide** /-'gied/ *vt* to lead astray; mislead – **misguider** *n*

**misguided** /mis'giedid/ *adj* directed by mistaken ideas, principles, or motives ⟨*well-meaning but ~ benefactors*⟩ – **misguidedly** *adv*, **misguidedness** *n*

**mishandle** /-'handl/ *vt* 1 to treat roughly; maltreat 2 to manage wrongly or ignorantly 3 to handle ineptly; *esp* to drop (a ball passed to one in rugby)

**mishap** /'misˌhap/ *n* an unfortunate accident [ME, fr ¹*mis-* + *hap*]

**mishear** /-'hiə/ *vb* **misheard** /ˌmis'huhd/ *vt* to hear wrongly ~ *vi* to misunderstand what is heard

**mishit** /-'hit/ *vb* **-tt-**; **mishit** to hit (a ball or stroke) in a faulty manner – **mishit** *n*

**mishmash** /'mishˌmash/ *n, informal* a hotchpotch, jumble ⟨*a pretentious ~ of primitive rhythms* – *Time*⟩ [partly redupl of *mash;* partly fr MHG *misch-masch,* redupl of *mischen* to mix]

**Mishmi** /'mishmi/ *n* a TIBETO-BURMAN language of NE India

**Mishnah, Mishna** /'mishnə/ *n* the collection of Jewish traditions chiefly concerned with the law which was compiled about AD 200 and forms the basis of the TALMUD [Heb *mishnāh* instruction, oral law, fr *shānāh* to repeat, learn] – **Mishnaic, Mishnic, Mishnical** *adj*

**misidentify** /ˌmisie'dentiˌfie/ *vt* 1 to identify wrongly ⟨*observers may ~ a star as a spaceship*⟩ 2 to confuse with each other ⟨*field mice and house mice are often* misidentified⟩

**misinform** /ˌmisin'fawm/ *vt* to give untrue or misleading information to – **misinformation** *n*

**misinterpret** /-in'tuhprit/ *vt* 1 to understand wrongly 2 to explain wrongly – **misinterpretation** *n*

**misjudge** /-'juj/ *vt* 1 to estimate wrongly 2 to have an unjust opinion of ~ *vi* to make a mistaken judgment – **misjudgment** *n*

**miskick** /ˌmis'kik/ *vb* to kick (a ball) in a faulty manner ⟨*he* ~ed *and hit the goalpost*⟩ – **miskick** *n*

**Miskito** /mi'skeetoh/ *n, pl* **Miskitos,** *esp collectively* **Miskito** a member, or the language, of a people of Nicaragua and Honduras

**mislay** /mis'lay/ *vt* **mislaid** /mis'layd/ to leave in an unremembered place

**mislead** /-'leed/ *vt* **misled** /mis'led/ to lead in a wrong direction or into a mistaken action or belief ⟨*I was misled by his innocent expression*⟩ – **misleadingly** *adv*

**mislike** /mis'liek/ *vt* 1 *formal* 1a to dislike mildly; not like ⟨*she* ~d *the prospect of a walk, but agreed to go*⟩ b to mistrust ⟨*I* ~d *his unusually polite manner*⟩ 2 *archaic or dial* 2a to displease ⟨*it* ~ s *me that you should go alone*⟩ b to dislike ⟨*they ~ his selfish bullying ways*⟩ – **mislike, misliking** *n*

**mismanage** /-'manij/ *vt* to manage wrongly or incompetently – **mismanagement** *n*

**mismarriage** /ˌmis'marij/ *n* an unsuitable or unhappy marriage

**mismatch** /-'mach/ *vt* to match wrongly or unsuitably, esp in marriage – **mismatch** *n*

**mismate** /ˌmis'mayt/ *vt* to mate unsuitably ⟨*to judge from the puppies, our pedigree dachshund was* ~d *with a dalmatian*⟩

**misname** /-'naym/ *vt* to call by the wrong name

**misnomer** /-'nohmə/ *n* (a use of) a wrong or inappropriate name or designation [ME *misnoumer,* fr MF *mesnommer* to misname, fr *mes-* ¹*mis-* + *nommer* to name, fr L *nominare* – more at NOMINATE]

**miso-** - see MIS-

**misogamist** /mi'sogəmist, mie-/ *n* one who hates marriage [Gk *mis-* ²*mis-*+ *gamos* marriage] – **misogamy** *n*

**misogynist** /mi'soj(ə)n·ist, mie-/ *n* one who hates women – compare MISANTHROPE [Gk *misogynēs,* fr *mis-* + *gynē* woman] – **misogynous** *adj,* **misogyny** *n,* **misogynistic** *adj*

**misology** /mi'soləji, mie-/ *n* a hatred of argument, reasoning, or knowledge [Gk *misologia,* fr *mis-* + *-logia* -logy] – **misologist** *n*

**misoneism** /ˌmisoh'nee·iz(ə)m, ˌmie-/ *n* a hatred, fear, or intolerance of innovation or change [It *misoneismo,* fr *mis-* + Gk *neos* new + It *-ismo* -ism – more at NEW] – **misoneist** *n,* **misoneistic** *adj*

**mispickel** /'mispikl/ *n* ARSENOPYRITE (arsenic and iron mineral) [Ger]

**misplace** /mis'plays/ *vt* 1a to put in the wrong place ⟨~ *a comma*⟩ b to mislay ⟨~d *his keys*⟩ 2a to direct towards a wrong object or outcome ⟨*his trust had been* ~d⟩ ⟨~d *enthusiasm*⟩ b to use on an unsuitable occasion ⟨~d *humour*⟩ – **misplacement** *n*

**misplay** /ˌmis'play/ *n* a wrong or unskilful action, esp in a game; an error – **misplay** *vt*

**misprint** /-'print/ *vt* to print incorrectly – **misprint** *n*

**misprision** /mis'prizh(ə)n/ *n* 1 misconduct or neglect of duty, esp by a public official 2 concealment of treason or other serious crime by somebody who is not actually a participant in the offence [ME, fr MF *mesprison* error, wrongdoing, fr OF, fr *mespris,* pp of *mesprendre* to make a mistake, fr *mes-* ¹*mis-* + *prendre* to take, fr L *prehendere* to seize – more at PREHENSILE]

**misprize** /mis'priez/ *vt, archaic* 1 to despise, scorn 2 to undervalue [MF *mesprisier,* fr *mes-* mis- + *prisier* to appraise – more at PRIZE] – **misprision** *n*

**mispronounce** /-prə'nowns/ *vt* to pronounce wrongly

**mispronunciation** /-prəˌnunsi'aysh(ə)n/ *n* (an instance of) mispronouncing

**misquote** /-'kwoht/ *vt* to quote incorrectly – **misquotation** *n*

**misread** /-'reed/ *vt* **misread** /ˌmis'red/ 1 to read incorrectly ⟨*misread the timetable and missed the train*⟩ 2 to misinterpret (as if) in reading ⟨*totally ~ the lesson of history* – Christopher Hollis⟩

**misremember** /ˌmisri'membə/ *vt* to remember incorrectly or inadequately

**misreport** /-ri'pawt/ *vt* to report falsely – **misreport** *n*

**misrepresent** /-repri'zent/ *vt* to represent falsely; give an untrue or misleading account of ⟨~ed *the facts to suit his purpose*⟩ – **misrepresentation** *n*

¹**misrule** /-'roohl/ *vt* to rule incompetently; misgovern

²**misrule** *n* 1 misruling or being misruled 2 disorder, anarchy

¹**miss** /mis/ *vt* 1a to fail to hit, reach, contact, or attain ⟨*overslept and* ~ed *the bus*⟩ ⟨~ed *her step and fell heavily*⟩ b to fail to respond to or profit by ⟨~ed *her cue and came on stage late*⟩ ⟨~ed *his chance*⟩ 2 to discover or feel the absence of, esp with regret ⟨*he didn't ~ his chequebook for several days*⟩ ⟨*he* ~es *his wife desperately*⟩ 3 to be without or short of; lack – usu in continuous tenses ⟨*it's* ~ing *a couple of screws, but it still works*⟩ ⟨*she was* ~ing *just five pence for the correct fare*⟩ 4 to escape, avoid ⟨*just* ~ed *hitting the other car*⟩ 5 to leave out; OMIT ⟨*left early and had to ~ breakfast*⟩ – often + *out* ⟨~ed *a vital paragraph out*⟩ 6 to fail to understand, sense, or experience ⟨*he* ~ed *the point of the speech*⟩ 7 to fail to perform or attend ⟨*had to ~ school for a week*⟩ ⟨*he's never* ~ed *a day's work*⟩ ~ *vi* 1 to fail to hit something 2 to misfire ⟨*the engine* ~ed⟩ [ME *missen,* fr OE *missan;* akin to OHG *missan* to miss, L *mutare* to change]

**miss out on** *vt* to fail to experience (something desirable)

²**miss** *n* 1a a failure to hit b a failure to attain a desired result 2 a misfire – **give a miss** *chiefly Br* to avoid, bypass, or omit deliberately ⟨*language learners give Russian* a miss – TES⟩

³**miss** *n* 1 *cap* 1a – used as a conventional title of courtesy preceding the name of an unmarried woman or girl except when usage requires the substitution of a title of rank or an honorary or professional title b – used before the name of a place or of a line of activity (e g a sport) or before some epithet to form a title for a usu young unmarried woman viewed or selected as esp outstanding in or representative of the thing indicated ⟨Miss *Know-all*⟩ ⟨Miss *World*⟩ 2 *often cap* – used without a name as a conventional term of address to a young woman ⟨*excuse me,* ~, *are these your gloves?*⟩ 3 *often cap* – used as a term of address to a schoolmistress 4 *informal* 4a a

young girl ⟨*a cheeky young* ~⟩ **b** an unmarried woman; a spinster ⟨*two elderly* ~es⟩ [short for *mistress*]
 **usage** Jane Brown and Ann Brown are, formally speaking, *the* Misses *Brown,* but *the* Miss *Browns* is now more usual.

**missa cantata** /ˌmisə kanˈtahtə/ *n* SUNG MASS [NL]

**missal** /ˈmisl/ *n* a book containing all that is said or sung at mass (both the ORDINARY and the PROPER) for the whole year △ missile [ME *messel,* fr MF & ML; MF, fr ML *missale,* fr neut of *missalis* of the mass, fr LL *missa* mass – more at MASS]

**missel thrush** /ˈmisl/ *n* MISTLE THRUSH

**missense** /ˈmisˌsens/ *n* genetic mutation involving alteration of one or more CODONS (sequences of three chemical BASES that code for AMINO ACIDS) so that one or more different amino acids are specified in protein synthesis – compare NONSENSE [*mis-* + *-sense* (as in *nonsense*)]

**misshape** /ˌmisˈshayp/ *vt* to shape badly; deform – **misshapen** *adj,* **misshapenly** *adv*

**missile** /ˈmisiel; NAm ˈmisl/ *n* an object, esp a weapon thrown or projected, usu so as to strike something at a distance ⟨*stones, artillery shells, bullets, and rockets are* ~s⟩: e g a GUIDED MISSILE **b** BALLISTIC MISSILE △ missive [L, fr neut of *missilis* capable of being thrown, fr *missus,* pp of *mittere* to send, throw

**missilery** *also* **missilry** /ˈmislri/ *n* (the science dealing with the design, manufacture, and use of guided) missiles

**missing** /ˈmising/ *adj* absent ⟨*certain facts are* ~ *from his account*⟩; *also* lost ⟨~ *in action*⟩ – see also GO **missing**
 **usage** Some people dislike the expression go missing.

**missing link** *n* **1** an item needed to form a continuous series **2** *often cap M&L* a hypothetical intermediate form between human beings and their anthropoid ancestors

**¹mission** /ˈmish(ə)n/ *n* **1a** a ministry commissioned by a religious organization to propagate its faith or carry on humanitarian work, usu abroad **b** assignment to or work in a field of missionary enterprise **c(1)** a mission establishment **c(2)** a local church or parish dependent on a larger religious organization for direction or financial support **d** *pl* organized missionary work **e** a course of meetings and services intended to attract those outside the church or strengthen Christian faith **2** *taking sing or pl vb* a body of people sent to perform a service or carry on an activity ⟨*a fact-finding* ~⟩: e g **2a** a group sent to a foreign country to conduct diplomatic or political negotiations **b** a permanent embassy or legation **c** a team of specialists or cultural leaders sent to a foreign country **3** a specific task with which a person or group is charged ⟨*her* ~ *was to find and bring back the escaped prisoner*⟩ **4a** a definite military, naval, or aerospace task ⟨*a bombing* ~⟩ ⟨*a space* ~⟩ **b** a flight operation of an aircraft or spacecraft in the performance of a mission ⟨*a* ~ *to Mars*⟩ **5** a calling, vocation ⟨*felt her* ~ *in life was to heal the sick*⟩ [NL, ML, & L; NL *mission-, missio* religious mission, fr ML, task assigned, fr L, act of sending, fr *missus,* pp of *mittere*]

**²mission** *vt* to carry on a religious mission among or in

**¹missionary** /ˈmishən(ə)ri/ *adj* **1** relating to, engaged in, or devoted to missions **2** characteristic of a missionary

**²missionary** *n* a person undertaking a mission; *esp* one in charge of a religious mission in some remote part of the world

**missionary position** *n* a position for sexual intercourse in which the woman lies on her back with the man above and facing her, regarded as the conventional position [fr its being reputedly advocated as the proper position by missionaries to primitive peoples]

**missioner** /ˈmishənə/ *n* a missionary; *specif* a person engaged in parochial missionary work

**mission-ize, -ise** /ˈmishəˌniez/ *vb* to do missionary work (among) – **missionizer** *n,* **missionization** *n*

**Mississippian** /ˌmisiˈsipiən/ *adj* **1** of Mississippi, its people, or the Mississippi river **2** of or being the geological period of the PALAEOZOIC era in N America that follows the DEVONIAN and precedes the PENNSYLVANIAN and that corresponds to the Lower or earlier subdivision of the CARBONIFEROUS period; *also* of or being the system of rocks formed during this time [*Mississippi,* river & state in USA] – **Mississippian** *n*

**missive** /ˈmisiv/ *n, formal* a written communication; a letter △ missile [MF *lettre missive,* lit., letter intended to be sent]

**misspell** /ˌmisˈspel/ *vt* to spell incorrectly – **misspelling** *n*

**misspend** /-ˈspend/ *vt* **misspent** to spend wrongly or foolishly; squander ⟨*he regretted his* misspent *youth*⟩

**misstate** /-ˈstayt/ *vt* to state incorrectly; give a false account of – **misstatement** *n*

**misstep** /-ˈstep/ *n* **1** a wrong step **2** a blunder

**missus, missis** /ˈmisiz/ *n* **1** *informal or humorous* a wife ⟨*have you met the* ~?⟩ **2** *often cap, chiefly Br informal* – used to address a (married) woman **3** *dial* MISTRESS 1a [alter. of *mistress*]

**missy** /ˈmisi/ *n, chiefly NAm informal* a young girl; a miss

**¹mist** /mist/ *n* **1** water in the form of diffuse particles in the atmosphere, esp near the earth's surface **2** mist, mists *pl* something that dims or obscures ⟨*lost in the* ~s *of time*⟩ **3** a film, esp of tears, before the eyes **4a** a cloud of small particles suggestive of a mist **b** a suspension of a finely divided liquid in a gas [ME, fr OE; akin to MD *mist* mist, Gk *omichlē*]

**²mist** *vi* to be or become misty ~ *vt* to cover (as if) with mist □ often + *over* or *up*

**mistakable, mistakeable** /miˈstaykəbl/ *adj* capable of being mistaken ⟨*without his beard he became* ~ *for his brother*⟩ ⟨*such extravagant praise is* ~; *was it taken as sarcasm?*⟩

**¹mistake** /miˈstayk/ *vb* **mistook** /mistook/; **mistaken** /miˈstaykən/ *vt* **1** to choose wrongly ⟨*mistook her way in the dark*⟩ **2a** to misunderstand the meaning, intention, or significance of ⟨*don't* ~ *me, I mean exactly what I said*⟩ **b** to estimate wrongly ⟨*mistook the strength of the army*⟩ **3** to identify wrongly; confuse with another ⟨*I* mistook *him for his brother*⟩ ~ *vi* to be wrong ⟨*you* mistook *when you thought I laughed at you* – Thomas Hardy⟩ [ME *mistaken,* fr ON *mistaka* to take in error, fr *mis-* + *taka* to take – more at TAKE]

**²mistake** *n* **1** a misunderstanding of the meaning or significance of something **2** a wrong action or statement arising from faulty judgment, inadequate knowledge, or carelessness

**mistaken** /miˈstaykən/ *adj* **1** *of a person* wrong in opinion ⟨*if you think he's honest, you're* ~⟩ **2** *of an action, idea, etc* based on wrong thinking; incorrect ⟨*trusted him in the* ~ *belief that he was honest*⟩ – **mistakenly** *adv*

**mister** /ˈmistə/ *n* **1** – used sometimes in writing instead of the usual *Mr* **2** *often cap* – used without a name as a generalized informal term of direct address to a man who is a stranger ⟨*please,* ~, *I'm lost*⟩ [alter. of ¹*master*]

**mistime** /ˌmisˈtiem/ *vt* to time badly ⟨~d *his remarks and offended his host*⟩ ⟨~d *his cover drive*⟩

**mistle thrush, missel thrush** /ˈmisl/ *n* a large Eurasian thrush (*Turdus viscivorus*) that is distinguished from the SONG THRUSH esp by its greyish-brown upperparts and the larger spots on its underparts [obs *mistle, missel* mistletoe, fr ME *mistel,* fr OE; fr its feeding on mistletoe berries]

**mistletoe** /ˈmislˌtoh/ *n* a European shrub (*Viscum album* of the family Loranthaceae, the mistletoe family) that grows as a parasite on the branches of trees and has thick leaves, small yellowish flowers, and waxy-white glutinous berries; *broadly* any of various plants of the mistletoe family [ME *mistilto* basil, fr OE *misteltān,* fr *mistel* mistletoe, basil + *tān* twig; akin to OHG & OS *mistil* mistletoe, and to OHG *zein* twig]

**mistral** /ˈmistrəl, miˈstrahl (*Fr* mistral)/ *n* a strong cold dry northerly wind of S France *synonyms* see ¹WIND [Fr, fr Prov, fr *mistral* masterful, fr L *magistralis* – more at MAGISTRAL]

**mistranslate** /ˌmistransˈlayt/ *vt* to translate incorrectly – **mistranslation** *n*

**mistreat** /ˌmisˈtreet/ *vt* to treat badly *synonyms* see ¹MISUSE – **mistreatment** *n*

**mistress** /ˈmistris/ *n* **1** a woman in a position of power or authority: e g **1a** the female head of a household ⟨*the* ~ *gave her orders to the housekeeper*⟩ **b** a woman who possesses or controls something ⟨~ *of a large fortune*⟩ ⟨~ *of a successful riding stable*⟩ ⟨*the dog took no notice of his* ~'s *commands*⟩ **c** a woman of the Scottish nobility having a status comparable to that of a master **2** a woman who has achieved mastery of a subject or skill ⟨*she's a* ~ *of fine needlework*⟩ **3** something personified as female that rules or directs ⟨*Britain,* ~ *of the seas for so long, found herself threatened from the air*⟩ **4** a woman with whom a man has a continuing sexual relationship outside marriage **5** *chiefly Br* a female teacher; a schoolmistress **6** *archaic* a sweetheart ⟨*o* ~ *mine where are you roaming?* – Shak⟩ **7** *archaic* – used as a title preceding the name of a married or unmarried woman and now superseded by *Mrs, Miss,* and *Ms* [ME *maistresse,* fr MF, fr OF, fem of *maistre* master – more at MASTER]

**mistress of ceremonies** *n* a woman who acts as hostess at a formal event or for a stage, radio, or television show

**mistrial** /ˌmisˈtrie-əl/ *n* a trial declared void because of some error in the proceedings

**¹mistrust** /misˈtrust/ *n* a lack of trust; distrust *synonyms* see

UNCERTAINTY *antonym* trust – **mistrustful** *adj*, **mistrustfully** *adv*, **mistrustfulness** *n*

**²mistrust** *vt* **1** to have little trust in; be suspicious of ⟨~ed *his neighbours*⟩ **2** to doubt the reliability or effectiveness of ⟨~ed *his own judgment*⟩ **3** to surmise ⟨*your mind* ~ed *there was something wrong* – Robert Frost⟩

**misty** /'misti/ *adj* **1a** obscured by mist ⟨*the* ~ *mountaintop*⟩ **b** consisting of or marked by mist ⟨*a* ~ *haze*⟩ ⟨*a* ~ *day*⟩ **2** not clear to the mind or understanding; indistinct, *vague* ⟨*a* ~ *recollection of the event*⟩ – **mistily** *adv*, **mistiness** *n*

**misunderstand** /,misundə'stand/ *vt* to get the meaning of (something) wrong; interpret incorrectly

**misunderstanding** /-'standing/ *n* **1** a failure to understand; a misinterpretation **2** *euph* a disagreement, dispute ⟨*had a little* ~ *with a traffic warden*⟩

**misusage** /-'yoohsij/ *n* **1** bad treatment; abuse **2** wrong or improper use (e g of words) [MF *mesusage*, fr *mes-* ¹*mis-* + *usage*]

**¹misuse** /mis'yoohz/ *vt* **1** to put to wrong or improper use; misapply ⟨~d *his talents*⟩ **2** to abuse, maltreat ⟨~d *his servants*⟩ [ME *misusen*; partly fr *mis-* + *usen* to use; partly fr MF *mesuser* to disuse, fr OF, fr *mes-* + *user* to use]

  **synonyms Misuse** and **abuse** suggest using something incorrectly, without necessarily implying intention. **Misuse** is the more neutral term, emphasizing the action rather than its result ⟨*it is a pity to* **misuse** *your time in this way*⟩. **Abuse** is stronger in condemnation, suggesting a misuse of privilege or power ⟨**abused** *her friend's hospitality by staying too long*⟩. **Mistreat**, **maltreat**, and **ill-treat** imply treating people or animals badly, even cruelly, either from malice or ignorance. **Mistreat** is the mildest term, often used figuratively; **ill-treat** is less formal than **maltreat**. Compare INJURE *antonym* respect

**²misuse** /mis'yoohs/ *n* incorrect or improper use

**misvalue** /mis'valyooh/ *vt* to value incorrectly

**miswrite** /mis'riet/ *vt* **miswrote** /-'roht/; **miswritten** /-'ritn/ to write incorrectly

**mite** /miet/ *n* **1** any of a large order (Acari or Acarina of the class Arachnida) of small to minute INVERTEBRATE animals related to the spiders and ticks that often infest animals, plants, and stored foods and include carriers of disease **2** a small coin or sum of money **3** a very small object or creature; *esp* a small child [ME, fr OE *mīte*; akin to MD *mite* mite, small copper coin, OHG *meizan* to cut; (2) ME, fr MF, fr MD] – **a mite** *informal* to a small extent; somewhat ⟨*I'm a mite thirsty*⟩

**miter** /'mietə/ *vt or n*, *NAm* (to) mitre

**mithered** /'miedhəd/ *adj*, *dial Br* in a confused and agitated state of mind [alter. of *moidered*, of unknown origin]

**mithridate** /'mithridayt/ *n* an antidote against poison; *esp* a sweetened medicinal preparation held to be effective against all poisons [ML *mithridatum*, fr LL *mithridatium*, fr L, dog-tooth violet (used as an antidote), fr Gk *mithridation*, fr *Mithridatēs* Mithridates] – **mithridatic** *adj*

**mithridatism** /'mithriday,tiz(ə)m/ *n* tolerance to a poison acquired by taking gradually increased doses of it [*Mithridates* VI †63 BC King of Pontus, who reputedly produced this condition in himself] – **mithridatize** *vt*

**miticide** /'mietisied/ *n* something (e g a chemical) that kills mites [*mite* + *-icide* (as in *insecticide*)] – **miticidal** *adj*

**mitigate** /'mitigayt/ *vt* **1** to cause to become less harsh or hostile; mollify ⟨*natural aggressiveness may be* ~d⟩ **2a** to make less severe or painful; alleviate **b** to lessen the seriousness of; *esp* to reduce the blame or responsibility for *synonyms* see RELIEVE *antonym* intensify △ militate [ME *mitigaten*, fr L *mitigatus*, pp of *mitigare* to soften, fr *mitis* soft + *-igare* (akin to L *agere* to drive) – more at AGENT] – **mitigation** *n*, **mitigative** *adj*, **mitigator** *n*, **mitigatory** *adj*

**mitochondrion** /,mietoh'kondri·ən/ *n*, *pl* **mitochondria** /-driə/ any of various round or long specialized cell-parts (ORGANELLES) that are found outside the nucleus of the cell, are rich in fats, proteins, and enzymes, and are the site where activities that produce energy for the cell are carried out [NL, fr Gk *mitos* thread + *chondrion*, dim. of *chondros* grain – more at GRIND] – **mitochondrial** *adj*

**mitogen** /'mietəjən/ *n* a substance that induces mitosis [*mitosis* + *-gen*] – **mitogenic** *adj*, **mitogenically** *adv*, **mitogenicity** *n*

**mitosis** /mie'tohsis/ *n*, *pl* **mitoses** /-seez/ **1** the process, typically involving a series of steps, whereby the nucleus of a cell undergoing CELL DIVISION (splitting of a cell to form new cells) divides to form two new nuclei each with the same number of CHROMOSOMES (strands of gene-carrying material) as the original nucleus **2** CELL DIVISION involving mitosis and resulting in the formation of two new cells □ compare MEIOSIS [NL, fr Gk *mitos* thread] – **mitotic** *adj*, **mitotically** *adv*

**mitrailleuse** /,meetrie'uhz/ *n* a breech-loading machine gun with a number of barrels; *broadly* a machine gun [Fr]

**mitral** /'mietrəl/ *adj* **1** resembling a mitre **2** relating to, being, or adjoining the LEFT ATRIOVENTRICULAR VALVE (valve on the left-hand side of the heart)

**mitral valve** *n* LEFT ATRIOVENTRICULAR VALVE (valve preventing backflow of blood in the heart)

**¹mitre**, *NAm chiefly* **miter** /'mietə/ *n* **1** a tall divided ceremonial hat with two bands hanging at the back that is worn by bishops and abbots **2a(1) mitre joint, mitre** a joint made by cutting the edges or ends of two pieces of wood or other material at an angle so that they form a corner, esp a right-angled corner, when fitted together **a(2)** the sloping surface of an edge or end of a piece cut to fit a mitre joint **b** a diagonal join in sewing resembling a mitre **3 mitre square, mitre** a tool with adjustable arms for drawing lines on, or shaping the surface of, a mitre joint; *esp* such a tool with the arms fixed at 45° [ME *mitre*, fr MF, fr L *mitra* headband, turban, fr Gk]

**²mitre** *vt* **1** to confer a mitre on and thus raise to the rank of abbot or bishop **2a** to match or fit together in a MITRE JOINT **b** to give a sloping surface to the ends of to make a MITRE JOINT **c** to sew together to form a mitre

**mitre box** *n* a device for guiding a handsaw at the proper angle in making a MITRE JOINT in wood

**mitre gear** *n* either of a pair of BEVEL GEARS with axes at RIGHT ANGLES

**mitt** /mit/ *n* **1a** a glove that leaves the fingers or the ends of the fingers uncovered **b** MITTEN 1 **c** a baseball catcher's or first baseman's protective glove made in the style of a mitten **2** *informal* a hand or paw; *specif* a person's hand [short for *mitten*]

**mitten** /'mit(ə)n/ *n* **1** a covering for the hand and wrist that has one section for the fingers and one for the thumb **2** MITT 1a [ME *mitain*, fr MF *mitaine*, fr OF, prob fr *mite* mitten]

**mitzvah** /'mitsvah/ *n*, *pl* **mitzvoth** /'mitsvoht(h), -vohs/, **mitzvahs** **1** a commandment of the Jewish law **2** an act considered in the Jewish religion as being praiseworthy or charitable [Heb *miṣwāh*]

**¹mix** /miks/ *vt* **1a(1)** to combine or blend into one mass **a(2)** to combine with another – often + *in* ⟨*prepare the soup and* ~ *in the herbs*⟩ **b** to bring into close association ⟨~ *business with pleasure*⟩ **2** to prepare by mixing components ⟨~ *a drink at the bar*⟩ **3** to control the balance of (various sounds), esp during the recording of a film, record, etc ~ *vi* **1** to be capable of mixing or becoming mixed ⟨*oil and water will not* ~⟩ **2** to seek or enjoy the fellowship or company of others ⟨*doesn't* ~ *much at parties*⟩ ⟨~es *well with other children*⟩ **3** to interbreed **4** to become actively involved; participate ⟨*decided not to* ~ *in politics*⟩ [ME *mixen*, back-formation fr *mixte* mixed, fr MF, fr L *mixtus*, pp of *miscēre* to mix; akin to Gk *mignynai* to mix] – **mixable** *adj* – **mix it 1** to provoke trouble **2** to fight

  **synonyms Mix**, **mingle**, **blend**, **coalesce**, **merge**, **fuse**: **mix** is the least specific term; it suggests a homogeneous result, but does not necessarily imply that the parts mixed lose their identity. **Mingle**, on the other hand, always implies the keeping of individual characteristics in spite of being mixed ⟨*kindness and spite* **mingle** *strangely in her character*⟩. **Blend** suggests a harmonious mixture, usually for a purpose, where the ingredients shade into each other, and lose their individuality ⟨**blend** *red and white to make pink*⟩. **Coalesce** stresses the gradual formation of something new from the blending of several similar things ⟨*all these impressions* **coalesced** *in her mind to form a charming picture of life at Brent Hall*⟩. **Merge** suggests a total loss of individuality, in the absorption of one thing into the other, or the absorption of all into the whole ⟨*the individual soul will, they say,* **merge** *at death into the world soul*⟩ ⟨*the sky* **merged** *into the sea, so that the horizon was invisible*⟩. **Fuse** suggests the blending, often under pressure or heat, of disparate elements into a new, enduring union ⟨*people from all walks of life,* **fused** *together by a burning desire to set their country free*⟩. Compare ¹JOIN *antonyms* separate, divide

**mix up** *vt* **1** to make untidy or disordered ⟨*his papers were all* mixed up *in a heap on his desk*⟩ **2** to mistake one for another; confuse ⟨*a child who* mixes up *his left and right*⟩ – see also MIX-UP

**²mix** *n* **1** an act or process of mixing **2** a product of mixing; *specif* a commercially prepared mixture of food ingredients ⟨*a cake* ~⟩ **3** a combination, mixture ⟨*the right* ~ *of jobs, people,* *and amenities – The Times*⟩ **4** a combination of recordings; *esp* one having the individual musical sounds (e g drumming and singing) adjusted to provide a pleasing blend

**mixed** /mikst/ *adj* **1** combining features of the capitalist and socialist economic systems ⟨*a ~ economy*⟩ **2** made up of or involving individuals or items of more than one kind: e g **2a** made up of or involving people differing in race, national origin, religion, or class **b** made up of or involving individuals of both sexes ⟨*~ company*⟩ ⟨*a ~ school*⟩ **3** including or accompanied by conflicting or dissimilar elements ⟨*~ emotions*⟩ ⟨*considered technology a ~ blessing*⟩ **4** deriving from two or more races or breeds ⟨*a person of ~ blood*⟩ [ME *mixte*]

,**mixed-a'bility** *adj, of a school, school class, etc* not split up according to academic ability

**mixed bag** *n, informal* a miscellaneous collection; an assortment ⟨*a ~ of sports events*⟩

**mixed bud** *n* a bud that produces a branch and leaves as well as flowers

**mixed farming** *n* the growing of crops and rearing of livestock on the same farm

**mixed grill** *n* a dish of several meats (e g a chop, kidney, and bacon) and vegetables grilled together and served on one plate

**mixed marriage** *n* a marriage between people of different races or religions

,**mixed-'media** *adj* MULTIMEDIA (using several media)

**mixed metaphor** *n* a combination of incongruous metaphors (e g in *iron out bottlenecks*)

**mixed nerve** *n* a nerve containing both SENSORY fibres that transmit stimuli to the brain and spinal cord and MOTOR fibres that carry impulses away from the brain and spinal cord to a muscle, gland, etc

**mixed number** *n* a number (e g $5\frac{2}{3}$) composed of an integer and a fraction

,**mixed-'up** *adj, informal* marked by perplexity, uncertainty, or disorder; confused ⟨*a totally ~ kid*⟩

**mixer** /'miksə/ *n* **1** one who or that which mixes: e g **1a(1)** one whose work is mixing the ingredients of a product **a(2)** an electronic device used to combine signals, esp audio ones (e g dialogue, music, and sound effects), from a number of sources in variable proportions; *also* a person who operates such a device **b** a container, device, or machine for mixing something (e g food or concrete) **c** a game, stunt, or dance used at a get-together to give members of the group an opportunity to meet one another in a friendly and informal atmosphere – called also ICEBREAKER **2** one who or that which mixes with others: e g **2a** a person considered as to his/her sociability ⟨*was shy and a poor ~*⟩ **b** a nonalcoholic beverage (e g ginger ale) intended to be drunk mixed with an alcoholic drink, esp spirits

**mixing valve** /'miksiŋ/ *n* a valve that mixes two sources into one outlet; *esp* a valve mixing hot and cold water

**mixolydian mode** /,miksoh'lidiən/ *n, often cap 1st M* a MODE (fixed arrangement of eight notes) which may be represented on the white keys of the piano on a scale from G to G [trans of Gk *mixolydios harmonia*, fr *mixo-* mixed, semi- + *lydios* Lydian]

**Mixtec** /'mishtek, ,mees(h)-/ *n, pl* **Mixtecs,** *esp collectively* **Mixtec** a member or the language of an American Indian people of Mexico [AmerSp *mixteco*]

**mixture** /'mikschə/ *n* **1a** the act, the process, or an instance of mixing **b(1)** the state of being mixed **b(2)** the relative proportions of constituents; *specif* the proportion of fuel to air produced in a carburettor **2** a product of mixing; a combination: e g **2a** a portion of matter consisting of two or more components in varying proportions that retain their own properties **b** a fabric woven of variously coloured threads **c** a combination of several different kinds (e g of tea or tobacco); a blend [MF, fr OF *misture*, fr L *mixtura*, fr *mixtus*]

'**mix-,up** *n* **1** a state or instance of confusion ⟨*a ~ about who was to meet the train*⟩ **2** a mixture **3** *informal* a conflict, fight

**mizzen, mizen** /'miz(ə)n/ *n* **1** the principal FORE-AND-AFT sail set lengthways in a bow-to-stern direction on a mizzenmast **2** mizzenmast, **mizzen** the mast behind the mainmast in a sailing ship [ME *meson*, fr MF *misaine*, prob deriv of Ar *mazzān* mast]

¹**mizzle** /'mizl/ *vi* to rain in very fine drops; drizzle ⟨*stood bareheaded in the* mizzling *rain*⟩ [ME *misellen*; akin to Flem *mizzelen* to drizzle, MD *mist* fog, mist] – **mizzle** *n*, **mizzly** *adj*

²**mizzle** *vi, chiefly Br informal* to depart suddenly [origin unknown]

¹**mnemonic** /ni'monik, nee-/ *adj* **1** assisting or intended to assist the memory; *also* of mnemonics **2** of memory [Gk *mnēmonikos*, fr *mnēmōn* mindful, fr *mimnēskesthai* to remember – more at MIND] – **mnemonically** *adv*

²**mnemonic** *n* a mnemonic device or code

**mnemonics** /ni'moniks, nee-/ *n taking sing vb* the art of, or a system for, improving the memory

**mo, mo'** /moh/ *n, chiefly Br informal* a very short space of time; a moment ⟨*just popped in for a* mo' – *Southern Evening Echo (Southampton)*⟩ [short for *moment*]

**-mo** /-moh/ *suffix* (→ *n*) – used after numerals or their names to indicate the number of leaves made by folding a sheet of paper ⟨*sixteenmo*⟩ ⟨*16mo*⟩ [duodecimo]

**moa** /'moh-ə/ *n* any of various usu very large extinct flightless birds of New Zealand (family Dinornithidae) including one (*Dinornis giganteus*) about 4 metres (12 feet) in height [Maori]

**Moabite** /'moh-ə,biet/ *n* a member of an ancient Semitic people related to the Hebrews [ME, fr LL *Moabita, Moabites*, fr Gk *Mōabitēs*, fr *Mōab* Moab, ancient kingdom in Syria] – **Moabite, Moabitish** *adj*

¹**moan** /mohn/ *n* **1** a complaint ⟨*the unflagging stream of ~*s *and queries* – *Honey Magazine*⟩ **2** a low prolonged sound of pain or of grief [ME *mone*, fr (assumed) OE *mān*]

²**moan** *vt* **1** to bewail audibly; lament, bemoan ⟨*~ed his cruel fate*⟩ **2** to utter with moans ~ *vi* **1** to complain, grumble ⟨*always ~ing on about something*⟩ **2a** to utter a moan; groan **b** to produce a sound resembling a moan ⟨*the wind ~ed in the trees*⟩ – **moaner** *n*

¹**moat** /moht/ *n* **1** a deep and wide trench usu filled with water, and constructed round the rampart of a fortified place (e g a castle) **2** a channel resembling a moat (e g for confinement of animals in a zoo) [ME *mot, mote* mound, embankment, ditch, fr MF *mote, motte* mound, fr OF – more at MOTTE] – **moatlike** *adj*

²**moat** *vt* to surround as if with a moat

¹**mob** /mob/ *n taking sing or pl vb* **1** the masses, populace **2** a large or disorderly crowd; *esp* one bent on riotous or destructive action **3** a criminal group; a gang **4** *chiefly Br informal* a crowd, bunch **5** *chiefly Austr* a flock, drove, or herd of animals [short for obs *mobile*, fr L *mobile vulgus* fickle crowd] – **mobbish** *adj*

²**mob** *vt* **-bb-** **1** *of a group* to attack, harass ⟨*the prisoner was ~bed by an angry crowd*⟩ **2** to crowd round, esp out of curiosity or admiration ⟨*the actor was ~bed by autograph hunters*⟩

**mob cap** *n* a woman's cap made with a full soft crown and a frill round the edge [prob fr obs *mab*, *mob* slattern, careless dress, fr *Mab*, short for the name *Mabel*]

¹**mobile** /'mohbiel/ *adj* **1** capable of moving or being moved; movable ⟨*a ~ missile launcher*⟩ **2** changing readily in expression or mood ⟨*a ~ face*⟩ **b** adaptable, versatile ⟨*a pupil with a ~ mind*⟩ **3** migratory **4** capable of, having the opportunity for, or undergoing movement into a different social class or from one status to another within the hierarchical social levels of a society ⟨*upwardly ~ middle-class workers*⟩ **5** marked by the use of vehicles for transport ⟨*~ warfare*⟩ **6** of a mobile *synonyms* see MOVABLE [MF, fr L *mobilis*, fr *movēre* to move] – **mobility** *n*

²**mobile** *n* a decorative usu fragile structure with either hanging or balanced components which often either strike each other to give a musical effect or rotate as a result of the action of the wind or by machinery

**mobile home** *n* a caravan

**mobil.ize, -ise** /'mohbiliez/ *vt* **1a** to put into movement or circulation ⟨*~ financial assets*⟩ **b** to release (something stored in the organism) for bodily use **2a** to assemble and make ready e g troops for war duty **b** to marshal (e g resources) for action ⟨*~ support for a proposal*⟩ ~ *vi* to assemble and become ready for war duty – **mobilization** *n*

**Möbius strip** /'muhbi-əs/ *n* a surface having only one side and one edge that can be constructed from a rectangle by holding one end fixed, rotating the opposite end through 180°, and joining it to the first end [August *Möbius* †1868 Ger mathematician]

**mobocracy** /mo'bokrəsi/ *n* **1** rule by the mob **2** *taking sing or pl vb* the mob as a ruling class – **mobocrat** *n*, **mobocratic, mobocratical** *adj*

**mobster** /'mobstə/ *n, chiefly NAm* a member of a criminal gang

**moccasin** /'mokəsin/ *n* **1** a soft leather heelless shoe with the sole brought up the sides of the foot and over the toes where it is joined with a puckered seam to a U-shaped piece lying on top of the foot; *broadly* any shoe with such a puckered seam **2** WATER MOCCASIN (N American snake) [of Algonquian origin; akin to Natick *mokkussin* shoe]

**mocha** /'mokə, 'mohkə/ *n* **1a** a coffee of superior quality; *specif* a coffee with small green or yellow beans, grown in Arabia **b** a flavouring obtained from a strong coffee infusion or from a mixture of cocoa or chocolate with coffee **2** a pliable suede-finished glove leather made from African sheepskins **3** a deep chocolate-brown colour [*Mocha*, seaport in Arabia]

**¹mock** /mok/ *vt* **1** to treat with contempt or ridicule; deride **2** to disappoint the hopes of; delude **3a** to imitate (e g a sound or mannerism) closely; mimic **b** to copy in fun or derision ~ *vi* to jeer, scoff – + *at* synonyms see ²RIDICULE [ME *mocken*, fr MF *mocquer*, fr OF *moquier*] – **mocker** *n*, **mockingly** *adv*

**²mock** *n* **1** one who is an object of derision or scorn **2** a school examination used as a rehearsal or practice for an official examination ⟨*taking his* ~s *next week*⟩

**³mock** *adj* (having the character) of an imitation; simulated, feigned ⟨*the* ~ *solemnity of the parody*⟩

**⁴mock** *adv* in an insincere or pretended manner – usu in combination ⟨mock-*serious*⟩

**,mock-'epic** *adj or n* mock-heroic

**mockers** /'mokəz/ *n pl* [perh modif (influenced by ²*mock*) of Yiddish *makeh* boil, sore, plague, fr Heb *makāh* blow, wound, plague] – **put the mockers on** to bring unhappiness or misfortune upon

**mockery** /'mokəri/ *n* **1** jeering or contemptuous action or speech; derision **2** an object of laughter or derision **3** a deceitful, impertinent, or futile imitation; a travesty ⟨*arbitrary methods that make a* ~ *of justice*⟩ **4** something insultingly or ridiculously unsuitable ⟨*the music was an utter* ~⟩

**¹,mock-he'roic** *adj* ridiculing heroic style, character, or action ⟨*a* ~ *poem*⟩ – **mock-heroically** *adv*

**²mock-heroic** *n* a mock-heroic composition

**mockingbird** /'moking,buhd/ *n* a bird (*Mimus polyglottos*) of esp the S USA that is remarkable for its exact imitations of the calls of other birds

**mock moon** *n* PARASELENE (bright spot in a lunar halo)

**mock orange** *n* an ornamental shrub (*Philadelphus coronarius*) of the saxifrage family with showy fragrant white flowers; *also* any of several similar related shrubs – called also SYRINGA [fr its aroma resembling that of orange blossom]

**mock sun** *n* PARHELION (bright spot in a solar halo)

**mock turtle soup** *n* a soup made from a calf's head in imitation of GREEN TURTLE soup

**'mock-,up** *n* a full-size model or representation chiefly for study, testing, or display ⟨*a* ~ *of desert terrain*⟩ ⟨*a* ~ *of a magazine*⟩

**¹mod** /mod/ *n, usu cap* a Gaelic competitive festival of the arts, esp in singing and recitation, held in Scotland [ScGael *mōd*, fr ON *mōt* meeting; akin to OE *mōt* moot]

**²mod** *n* a modification

**³mod** *n, often cap* one who wears mod clothes; *esp* a member of a group of young people in Britain in the 1960s who dressed in a stylish manner – compare ROCKER 4

**⁴mod** *adj* **1** modern; *esp* bold and free in style, behaviour, or dress **2** *often cap* of mods

**modal** /'mohdl/ *adj* **1** of modality in logic **2** of or being in a musical mode; *specif* being in one of the CHURCH MODES rather than in a major or minor key **3** of general form or structure as opposed to particular substance or content **4** of or constituting a grammatical form or category characteristically indicating distinction of mood **5** of or having a statistical mode [ML *modalis*, fr L *modus*] – **modally** *adv*

**modal auxiliary, modal** *n* an auxiliary verb (e g *can, must, might, may*) that is characteristically used with another verb and expresses a distinction of mood

**modality** /moh'daləti/ *n* **1a** the quality or state of being modal **b** a modal quality or attribute; a form **c** ²MOOD 2b ⟨*"he swims" differs from "does he swim?" in* ~⟩ **2** the classification of logical propositions according to the possibility, impossibility, contingency, or necessity of their content **3** a therapeutic procedure (e g massage) or apparatus used esp in physical therapy

**mod con** /,mod 'kon/ *n, Br informal* a modern convenience; *esp* a household fitting or device designed to increase comfort or save time – chiefly in *all mod cons*

**¹mode** /mohd/ *n* **1a** an arrangement of the eight DIATONIC musical notes of an octave in any of several fixed schemes

which use different patterns of intervals – compare AEOLIAN MODE, CHURCH MODE, DORIAN MODE, IONIAN MODE, LYDIAN MODE, MIXOLYDIAN MODE, PHRYGIAN MODE **b** a rhythmical scheme, esp in 13th- and 14th-century music **2** ²MOOD 2a (form of a verb denoting whether the action is a fact, wish, etc) **3a** *philosophy* ²MOOD 1 **b** the modal form of a logical proposition **4a** a particular form or variety of something **b** a form or manner of expression; a style **5** a way of doing or effecting something ⟨*bicycling is a cheap* ~ *of transport*⟩ **6a** a manifestation, form, or arrangement of being; *specif* a particular form or manifestation of an underlying substance **b** a particular functioning arrangement or condition; a status ⟨*a spacecraft in re-entry* ~⟩ **7** *statistics* **7a** the most frequently occurring value in a set of data **b** the point during a statistical experiment at which the resulting mathematical function (PROBABILITY DISTRIBUTION) reaches a maximum **8** any of various stable vibration patterns of which a vibrating or oscillating body system is capable ⟨*the* ~s *of electromagnetic radiation in a waveguide*⟩ **9** the actual mineral composition of a rock [ME *moede*, fr L *modus* measure, manner, musical mode – more at METE; (3) LL *modus*, fr L]

**²mode** *n, formal* a prevailing fashion or style (e g of dress or behaviour) [Fr, fr L *modus*]

**¹model** /'modl/ *n* **1** structural design ⟨*built his home on the* ~ *of an old farmhouse*⟩ **2** a usu miniature replica of something in relief or three dimensions; *also* a representation of something to be constructed **3** that which is used as a basis for reproducing or copying **4** a person or thing worthy of emulation; an ideal example ⟨*this essay is a* ~ *of conciseness and clarity*⟩ **5** a person or thing that serves as a pattern for an artist; *esp* a person who poses for an artist **6** one who is employed to wear merchandise, esp clothing, in order to display it ⟨*a fashion* ~⟩ ⟨*a male* ~⟩ **7** a type or design of an article (e g a garment or car) ⟨*this year's* ~⟩ **8** a description or analogy used to help visualize something (e g an atom) that cannot be directly observed **9** a system of postulates, data, inferences, or equations presented as a mathematical description of an entity or state of affairs **10** one who poses, esp unclothed, for pictures that are intended to be sexually exciting **11** *euph* a prostitute **12** *obs* a set of plans for a building [MF *modelle*, fr OIt *modello*, fr (assumed) VL *modellus*, fr L *modulus* small measure, fr *modus*]

**²model** *vb* **-ll-** (*NAm* **-l-, -ll-**) *vt* **1** to plan or form after a pattern; shape **2** to shape or fashion in a mouldable material; *broadly* to produce a model of ⟨~ling *aeroplanes*⟩ ⟨*use a computer to* ~ *the city's traffic flow*⟩ **3** to construct or fashion in imitation of a particular model ⟨~led *its constitution on that of the US*⟩ **4** to display, esp by wear or use ⟨~led *hats*⟩ **5** *archaic* to make into an organization (e g an army, government, or parish) ~ *vi* **1** to design or imitate forms; make a pattern ⟨*enjoys* ~ling *in clay*⟩ **2** to work or act as a fashion model – **modeller** *n*

**³model** *adj* **1** being or worthy of being a pattern for others ⟨*a* ~ *student*⟩ **2** being a miniature representation of something ⟨*a* ~ *aeroplane*⟩

**modem** /'mohdem/ *n* an electronic device that converts data from a form understandable by a computer into a form that can be transmitted via a telephone line, radio signal, etc and vice versa (e g to allow communication between distant computers) [*modulator* + *demodulator*]

**¹moderate** /'mod(ə)rət/ *adj* **1a** avoiding extremes of behaviour or expression; practising reasonable restraint ⟨*a* ~ *drinker*⟩ **b** calm, temperate ⟨*a* ~ *climate*⟩ **2** being average or somewhat less than average in quality, amount, or degree ⟨*a pupil of only* ~ *ability*⟩ ⟨*a* ~ *income*⟩ **3** avoiding extreme political or social measures ⟨*a* ~ *candidate*⟩ **4** limited in extent or effect ⟨*had only* ~ *success*⟩ [ME, fr L *moderatus*, fr pp of *moderare* to moderate; akin to L *modus* measure] – **moderately** *adv*, **moderateness** *n*

**²moderate** /'modərayt/ *vt* **1** to lessen the intensity or extremeness of ⟨*the sun* ~d *the chill*⟩ **2** to preside over; act as chairman of ~ *vi* **1** to act as a moderator **2** to decrease in violence, severity, intensity, or volume ⟨*his anger* ~d *when the culprit had been punished*⟩ – **moderation** *n*

**³moderate** /'modərət/ *n* one who holds moderate views or who belongs to a group favouring a moderate course or programme (e g in politics or religion) [¹*moderate*]

**moderate breeze** *n* wind having a speed of 20 to 28 kilometres per hour (about 13 to 18 miles per hour) *synonyms* see ¹WIND

**moderate gale** *n* wind having a speed of 50 to 61 kilometres per hour (about 32 to 38 miles per hour) *synonyms* see ¹WIND

**Moderations** /ˌmodəˈraysh(ə)ns/ *n pl* the first honours examination at Oxford University in classics and some other subjects [*moderator* 2b]

**moderato** /ˌmodəˈrahtoh/ *adv or adj* in a moderate tempo – used as a direction in music [It, fr L *moderatus*]

**moderator** /ˈmodəraytə/ *n* **1** one who arbitrates; a mediator **2** one who presides over an assembly or meeting: e g **2a** the presiding officer of a Presbyterian governing body **b** the officer presiding over certain Oxbridge examinations **3** a substance (e g graphite) used for slowing down neutrons in a NUCLEAR REACTOR in order to control or esp increase the rate at which they collide with and cause the reaction of atomic nuclei – **moderatorship** *n*

**¹modern** /ˈmodən/ *adj* **1a** of or characteristic of a period extending from a particular point in the past to the present time **b** of or characteristic of the present or the immediate past; contemporary **2** involving recent techniques, styles, or ideas; up-to-date **3** *cap* constituting the present or most recent period of a language [LL *modernus*, fr L *modo* just now, fr *modus* measure – more at METE] – **modernly** *adv*, **modernness** *n*, **modernity** *n*

synonyms **Modern**, **contemporary**, and **present-day** may all be applied to the present time. **Present-day** is a neutral term, with the narrowest interpretation of the present. **Modern** may include recent or not so recent time, depending on the subject it qualifies: **modern languages** are simply labelled **modern** in contrast to "ancient" ones. But **modern** usually implies either such a contrast or a change in character or quality ⟨**modern** *engineering techniques*⟩. This implication is lacking from **contemporary**, which stresses rather that something is of the same time as our own ⟨**contemporary** *attitudes to marriage*⟩ and may include modern or old-fashioned attitudes. **Current** and **recent** also apply to the present, and more narrowly than the preceding terms. What is **current** is still viable, but **recent** usually describes the immediate past. **Late** is close in meaning to **recent**, but usually suggests "the most recent of a series". Compare ¹NEW *antonyms* ancient, old-fashioned, out-of-date

**²modern** *n* **1** a person of modern times or modern views **2** a style of printing type distinguished by regularity of shape, precise curves, straight hairline SERIFS, and heavy downstrokes

**Modern English** *n* English since the late 15th century

**Modern French** *n* French since about 1600

**Modern Greek** *n* Greek since about 1500 – called also NEW GREEK

**Modern Hebrew** *n* Hebrew as used in present-day Israel – called also NEW HEBREW

**modernism** /ˈmodəniz(ə)m/ *n* **1** a practice, usage, or expression characteristic of modern times **2** *often cap* a tendency in theology to accommodate traditional religious teaching to contemporary thought, esp to devalue traditional supernatural elements; *specif, cap* such a tendency in Roman Catholicism condemned by Pope Pius X in 1907 **3** the philosophy and practices of modern art; *esp* a search for new forms of expression involving a self-conscious break with the past – **modernist** *n or adj*, **modernistic** *adj*

**modern-ize, -ise** /ˈmodəniez/ *vt* to adapt to modern needs, style, or standards ~ *vi* to adopt modern views, habits, or techniques – **modernizer** *n*, **modernization** *n*

**modern languages** *n taking sing or pl vb* contemporary foreign languages as a subject of academic study

**modern linguist** *n* one who specializes in modern languages

**modern maths** /maths/ *n* mathematics including several new concepts (e g sets, matrices, symmetry, and bases), esp as taught in primary and secondary schools – called also NEW MATHS

**modern pentathlon** *n* a composite athletic contest in which all contestants compete in a 300-metre freestyle swim, a 4000-metre cross-country run, a 5000-metre 30-jump equestrian steeplechase, épée fencing, and target shooting at 25 metres

**modest** /ˈmodist/ *adj* **1** having a moderate estimate of one's abilities or worth; not boastful or self-assertive **2** arising from or characteristic of a modest nature **3** characterized by careful observance of proprieties of dress and behaviour; decent **4** small or limited in size, amount, or aim ⟨*a ~ salary*⟩ *synonyms* see ¹SHY *antonym* immodest [L *modestus* moderate; akin to L *modus* measure] – **modestly** *adv*

**modesty** /ˈmodisti/ *n* **1** freedom from conceit or vanity **2** propriety in dress, speech, or conduct

**modicum** /ˈmodikəm/ *n* a small or limited amount ⟨*a claim without even a ~ of truth in it*⟩ [ME, fr L, neut of *modicus*

moderate, fr *modus* measure]

**modification** /ˌmodifiˈkaysh(ə)n/ *n* **1** the limiting of a statement; a qualification **2** ¹MODE 6a (manifestation or form of being) **3** (the making of) a small or limited change to something ⟨*a ~ of plans*⟩

**modifier** /ˈmodifie-ə/ *n* one who or that which modifies: e g **a** a word or word group that modifies another **b** a gene that modifies the effect of another

**modify** /ˈmodifie/ *vt* **1** to make less extreme; moderate ⟨*persuaded the strikers to ~ their demands*⟩ **2a** to stand in subordinate relation to (a grammatical HEAD) ⟨*in "a hot day in summer"* hot *and* in summer ~ day⟩ **b** to change (a vowel) by UMLAUT **3a** to make minor changes in **b** to make basic changes in often for a definite purpose ⟨*the wing of a bird is an arm modified for flying*⟩ ~ *vi* to undergo change *synonyms* see ¹CHANGE [ME *modifien*, fr MF *modifier*, fr L *modificare* to measure, moderate, fr *modus*] – **modifiability** *n*, **modifiable** *adj*, **modifiableness** *n*

**modillion** /məˈdilyən/ *n* a carved bracket under the projecting part of a classical CORNICE (e g in the Corinthian order of architecture) [It *modiglione*, deriv of L *mutulus*]

**modish** /ˈmohdish/ *adj, chiefly derog* fashionable, stylish ⟨*a ~ hat*⟩ ⟨*a ~ writer*⟩ – **modishly** *adv*, **modishness** *n*

**modiste** /mohˈdeest (*Fr* modist)/ *n* one who makes and sells fashionable dresses or women's hats [Fr, fr *mode* style, mode]

**Mods** /modz/ *n pl, informal* MODERATIONS (exams at Oxford University)

**modular** /ˈmodyoolə/ *adj* **1** of or based on a module or modulus **2** constructed with standardized units or dimensions for flexibility and variety in use – **modularly** *adv*, **modularity** *n*

**modular arithmetic** *n* arithmetic that deals with integers where the numbers are replaced by their remainders after division by the modulus ⟨*in a ~ with modulus 5, 3 multiplied by 4 would be 2*⟩

**modular course** *n* a British educational course based on selection among a number of modules

**modular-ized, -ised** /ˈmodyooləriezd/ *adj* **1** containing or consisting of modules ⟨*~ electronic equipment*⟩ **2a** produced in the form of modules **b** broken up into modules; fragmented ⟨*our cosmetic media and ~ lifestyles – New York Times*⟩ – **modularization** *n*

**modulate** /ˈmodyoolayt/ *vt* **1** to vary in tone; make tuneful ⟨*~ one's voice*⟩ **2** to adjust to or keep in proper measure or proportion; temper **3** to vary the AMPLITUDE (strength of a wave), frequency, or PHASE of (esp a wave used to carry a sound or vision signal) by modulation ~ *vi* **1** to play or sing with modulation **2** to pass by regular melodic or chord progression from one musical key or TONALITY to another [L *modulatus*, pp of *modulari* to play, sing, fr *modulus* small measure, rhythm, dim. of *modus* measure – more at METE] – **modulator** *n*, **modulatory** *adj*, **modulability** *n*

**modulation** /ˌmodyooˈlaysh(ə)n/ *n* **1** a regulating according to measure or proportion; a tempering **2** an inflection of the tone or pitch of the voice; *specif* the use of stress or pitch to convey meaning **3** a change from one musical key or TONALITY to another by regular melodic or chord progression **4** *electronics* **4a** a process of combining two waveforms in such a way that a property of one (e g its amplitude, frequency, or phase) varies as the other waveform varies – used esp of the combining of a RADIO WAVE that carries a signal with the sound or vision signal it carries, in order to transmit that signal **b** the controlled alteration of the frequency or other property of a wave by modulation

**module** /ˈmodyoohl/ *n* **1** a standard or unit of measurement **2** the size of some one structural part taken as a unit of measure by which the proportions of a building are regulated in classical architecture **3** any in a series of standardized units for use together in construction (e g of buildings, computers, or furniture) ⟨*factory-built ~s, assembled on site – Real Estate Review*⟩ **4** an independent unit that is a part of the total structure of a space vehicle **5** a unit or section of an educational course, treating a specific subject or topic [L *modulus*]

**modulo** /ˈmodyooloh/ *prep* with respect to a modulus of ⟨*19 and 54 are congruent ~ 7*⟩ [NL, abl of *modulus*]

**modulus** /ˈmodyooləs/ *n, pl* **moduli** /-li/ **1** a number or quantity that expresses the degree to which a substance or body possesses a physical property (e g the ability to withstand distortion without becoming permanently deformed) ⟨*Young's ~*⟩ **2** *maths* **2a** ABSOLUTE VALUE (value without regard to sign) **b(1)** a number that is used to divide another number in order to find out the remainder (eg in MODULAR ARITHMETIC) **b(2)** the number of different numbers used in a system of MODULAR ARITHMETIC **c** the factor by which a logarithm of a number to one base is multiplied to obtain the logarithm of the number to a new base [NL, fr L, small measure]

**modus operandi** /ˌmohdəs opəˈrandi/ *n, pl* **modi operandi** /ˌmohdi/ a method of procedure [NL]

**modus vivendi** /viˈvendi/ *n, pl* **modi vivendi** /ˌmohdi/ **1** a feasible arrangement or practical compromise, esp between opposed or quarrelling parties **2** a manner of living; a way of life [NL, manner of living]

**mofette, moffette** /mohˈfet (*Fr* mɔfɛt)/ *n* a vent in the earth from which carbon dioxide and some nitrogen and oxygen issue [Fr *mofette* gaseous exhalation, fr It *mofeta*, of Gmc origin]

**Mogadon** /ˈmogəˌdon/ *trademark* – used for NITRAZEPAM (drug used as a hypnotic)

**moggie, moggy** /ˈmogi/*also* **mog** /mog/ *n, Br informal* a cat [prob fr *Mog*, nickname for *Margaret*]

**¹mogul** /ˈmohg(ə)l/ *n* **1** Mogul, Moghul an Indian Muslim of, or descended from, any of several conquering groups of Mongol, Turkish, and Persian origin; *specif* a member of a dynasty that ruled India from the 16th to the 18th century **2** a great or very wealthy person; a magnate △ Mongol [Per *Mughul*, fr Mongolian *Mongol*] – **mogul** *adj, often cap*

**²mogul** *n* a built-up mound of snow causing a bump on a ski slope [prob of Scand origin; akin to Norw dial. *muge* heap, fr ON *mūgi* – more at MOW]

**mohair** /ˈmohˌheə/ *n* (a fabric or yarn made wholly or partly from) the long silky hair of the Angora goat – compare ANGORA **2** [by folk etymology (influenced by *hair*) fr earlier *mocayare*, fr obs It *mocaiarro*, fr Ar *mukhayyar*, lit., choice]

**Mohammedan** /məˈhamid(ə)n/ *adj* MUHAMMADAN (of Muhammad or Islam)

**Mohawk** /ˈmohˌhawk/ *n, pl* **Mohawks,** (*1a*) **Mohawks,** *esp collectively* **Mohawk 1a** a member of an American Indian people of the Mohawk river valley in New York State **b** the Iroquoian language of the Mohawk people **2** *often not cap* a turn in ice-skating from an edge of one foot to the same edge of the other foot in the opposite direction – compare CHOCTAW [of Algonquian origin; akin to Narraganset *Mohowaùuck*, lit., they eat living things]

**Mohegan** /mohˈheegən/ *n, pl* **Mohegans,** *esp collectively* **Mohegan** Mohican

**Mohican** /mohˈheekən, mə-/ *n, pl* **Mohicans,** *esp collectively* **Mohican** (the Algonquian language of) a member of an American Indian people of the upper Hudson river valley

**Moho** /ˈmohˌhoh/ *n the* zone beneath the earth's surface at which studies of seismic waves indicate a transition in the materials making up the earth, and which represents a distinct boundary separating the earth's crust from the underlying mantle [short for *Mohorovicic discontinuity*, fr Andrija *Mohorovičić* †1936 Yugoslav geologist]

**Mohock** /ˈmohˌhok/ *n* a member of a gang of aristocratic ruffians who assaulted or molested people in London streets in the early 18th century [alter. of *Mohawk*] – **Mohockism** *n*

**Mohorovicic discontinuity** /ˌmoh·hə·rohvəchich/ *n the* Moho

**Mohs' scale** /mohz/ *n* an ascending scale of relative hardness for minerals in which 1 represents the hardness of talc and 10, or 15 in the revised version, the hardness of diamond [Friedrich *Mohs* †1839 Ger mineralogist]

**mohur** /ˈmoh·hə/ *n* a former gold coin of India and Persia worth 15 rupees [Hindi *muhr* gold coin, seal, fr Per; akin to Skt *mudrā* seal]

**moidered** /ˈmoydəd/ *adj, dial Br* MITHERED (confused) [origin unknown]

**moidore** /ˈmoydaw/ *n* a former Portuguese gold coin [modif of Pg *moeda de ouro*, lit., coin of gold]

**moiety** /ˈmoyəti/ *n* **1** either of two (approximately) equal parts; a half **2** any of the portions into which something is divided; a component, part **3** either of two complementary social divisions of a tribe [ME *moite*, fr MF *moité*, fr LL *medietat-, medietas*, fr L *medius* middle – more at MID]

**¹moil** /moyl/ *vi* **1** to work hard; drudge – often in *toil and moil* **2** to be in a state of continuous agitation; churn, swirl ~ *vt, dial* to make wet or dirty [ME *moillen* to moisten, make dirty, fr MF *moillier*, fr (assumed) VL *molliare*, fr L *mollis* soft – more at MELT] – **moiler** *n*

**²moil** *n* **1** laborious work; drudgery **2** confusion, turmoil

**Moirai** /ˈmoyrie/ *n pl the* goddesses of fate in Greek mythology [Gk, fr pl of *moira* lot, fate; akin to Gk *meros* part – more at MERIT]

**moiré** /ˈmwahray (*Fr* mware)/, **moire** /ˈmwahray; *also* mwah/ *n* **1** an irregular wavy finish on a fabric **2** a fabric having a wavy watered appearance **3** moiré, moiré pattern a wavy usu shimmering pattern seen when two geometrically regular patterns (eg two sets of parallel lines or two grids) are superimposed, esp at an acute angle [Fr *moiré*, fr *moiré* like watered mohair, fr *moire* watered mohair, fr E *mohair*] – **moiré** *adj*

**moist** /moyst/ *adj* **1** slightly or moderately wet; damp **2** tearful ⟨*she greeted her son with ~ eyes*⟩ **3** of or having high humidity **synonyms** see ¹WET [ME *moiste*, fr MF, fr (assumed) VL *muscidus*, alter. of L *mucidus* slimy, fr *mucus*] – **moistly** *adv,* **moistness** *n*, **moisten** *vb*

**moisture** /ˈmoyschə/ *n* liquid diffused (eg through the air) as vapour or forming a thin film or tiny droplets (eg on a surface) [ME, modif of MF *moistour*, fr *moiste*] – **moistureproof** *adj*

**moistur·ize, -ise** /ˈmoyschəˌriez/ *vt* to add or restore moisture to ⟨~ *the air*⟩ ⟨~ *the skin with cream*⟩ – **moisturizer** *n*

**moke** /mohk/ *n* **1** *Br slang* a donkey **2** *Austr slang* a horse, nag [origin unknown]

**moko** /ˈmohkoh/ *n* a tattoo worn by Maoris; *specif* a tattoo worn on the chin by Maori women [Maori]

**moksha, moksa** /ˈmohkshə/ *n, Hinduism & Buddhism* the release from the repeated cycles of birth, misery, and death (SAMSARA), and liberation from the force controlling destiny (KARMA) together with the attainment of salvation and enlightenment (NIRVANA) – compare DHARMA, KARMA [Skt *mokṣa*; akin to Skt *muñcati* he releases]

**mol** /mohl/ *n* ⁵MOLE (unit of amount of a substance)

**mola** /ˈmohlə/ *n, pl* **molas,** *esp collectively* **mola** SUNFISH [NL, fr L, millstone; fr its shape & rough skin]

**molal** /ˈmohləl/ *adj, chemistry* of or being a solution containing a MOLE (standard amount of a particular substance) of a substance dissolved in 1 kilogram of solvent [⁵*mole* + *-al*]

**molality** /mohˈlaləti/ *n, chemistry* the concentration of a solution measured in terms of the number of MOLES (units of amount of a substance) of a dissolved substance in 1 kilogram of solvent

**¹molar** /ˈmohlə/ *n* a tooth with a rounded or flattened surface adapted for grinding; *specif* any of the teeth towards the back of the jaw in mammals [L *molaris*, fr *molaris* of a mill, grinding, fr *mola* millstone – more at MILL]

**²molar** *adj* **1** (capable of) pulverizing by friction; grinding **2** of, being, or located near the molar teeth

**³molar** *adj* **1** of or containing a mole of a substance ⟨*the ~ volume of a gas*⟩ **2** *chemistry* of or being a solution containing a mole of a substance dissolved in 1 litre of the solution [(1) L *moles* mass – more at ³MOLE; (2) ⁵*mole*]

**molarity** /mohˈlarəti/ *n, chemistry* the concentration of a solution measured in terms of the number of moles of a dissolved substance in 1 litre of the solution

**molasses** /məˈlasiz/ *n* any of three grades of uncrystallized syrup that vary in colour and consistency from light brown to thick dark brown and are separated from raw sugar in sugar manufacture; *esp* the darkest most viscous syrup remaining after all sugar that can be separated by crystallization has been removed [Pg *melaço*, fr LL *mellaceum* grape juice, fr L *mell-, mel* honey – more at MELLIFLUOUS]

**mold** /mohld/ *vt or n, NAm* to mould

**molding** /ˈmohlding/ *n, NAm* a moulding

**¹mole** /mohl/ *n* a dark-coloured permanent spot, mark, or small lump on the human body [ME, fr OE *māl*; akin to OHG *meil* spot]

**²mole** *n* **1** any of numerous small burrowing insect-eating mammals (family Talpidae) with minute eyes, concealed ears, and soft fur; *esp* a widely distributed Eurasian mole (*Talpa europaea*) **2** a machine for tunnelling; *also* the part of such a machine that comes into contact with the material to be moved **3** one who spends a long period of time establishing a position of trust within an institution, in order to secretly further (eg by spying) the interests of a rival government or organization at a later date [ME; akin to MLG *mol*]

**³mole** *n* **1** a massive work formed of masonry and large stones or earth laid in the sea as a pier or breakwater **2** the harbour formed by a mole [MF, fr OIt *molo*, fr LGk *mōlos*, fr L *moles*, lit., mass, exertion; akin to OHG *muodi* weary, Gk *mōlos* exertion]

[4]**mole** *n* an abnormal mass in the uterus, esp when containing foetal tissues [Fr *môle*, fr L *mola*, lit., mill, millstone – more at MILL]

[5]**mole** *also* **mol** /mohl/ *n* the basic SI unit of amount of substance equal to the amount of a substance that contains the same number of entities (eg atoms, molecules, or ions) as there are atoms in 0.012 kilogram of the form of carbon having a MASS NUMBER (number of protons and neutrons in the nucleus of an atom) of 12 [Ger *mol*, short for *molekulargewicht* molecular weight, fr *molekular* molecular + *gewicht* weight]

**mole cricket** /mohl/ *n* any of several large crickets (family Gryllotalpidae) that have the front legs enormously developed for use in digging; *esp* a brown European mole cricket (*Gryllotalpa gryllotalpa*)

**molecular** /məˈlekyoolə/ *adj* 1 of, produced by, or consisting of molecules ⟨~ *oxygen*⟩ 2 of simple or elementary organization 3 CUMULATIVE 1a, 1b – **molecularly** *adv*, **molecularity** *n*

**molecular biology** *n* a branch of biology dealing with the structure, organization, and functioning of the molecules of living matter and including the study of the molecular basis of inheritance, protein synthesis, and tissue differentiation – **molecular biologist** *n*

**molecular formula** *n* a chemical formula that gives the total number of atoms of each chemical element in a molecule – compare STRUCTURAL FORMULA

**molecular weight** *n* the weight of a molecule that may be calculated as the sum of the ATOMIC WEIGHTS of its constituent atoms

**molecule** /ˈmolikyoohl/ *n* 1 the smallest unit of a substance that retains the properties of that substance and is composed typically of two or more atoms of the same or different chemical elements or sometimes of a single stable atom 2 a tiny bit; a particle ⟨*a* ~ *of political honesty* – *Time*⟩ [Fr *molécule*, fr NL *molecula*, dim. of L *moles* mass]

**mole drain** *n* an underground channel made by a MOLE PLOUGH and used esp for draining heavy soils on farms

**mole drainage** *n* the system of draining farmland by MOLE DRAINS

**mole drainer** *n* MOLE PLOUGH

**molehill** /-ˌhil/ *n* a little mound of earth thrown up by a burrowing mole

**mole plough** *n* a subsoil plough that opens an underground channel [[2]*mole*]

**mole rat** *n* any of various small Eurasian and African rodents (esp family Spalacidae) resembling true moles in behaviour or appearance

**moleskin** /ˈmohlˌskin/ *n* 1 the skin of the mole used as fur 2 a heavy durable cotton fabric with a short thick velvety nap on one side used esp for sportswear and work clothes 3 *pl* clothes, esp overalls, made of moleskin

**molest** /məˈlest/ *vt* to annoy, disturb, or attack; *specif* to force unwanted physical sexual advances on (esp a woman or child) [ME *molesten*, fr MF *molester*, fr L *molestare*, fr *molestus* burdensome, annoying, fr *moles* mass] – **molester** *n*, **molestation** *n*

**moll** /mol/ *n* 1 DOLL 2 2 *informal* a gangster's girl friend or mistress 3 *slang* a prostitute [*Moll*, nickname for *Mary*]

**mollie** *also* **molly** /ˈmoli/ *n* any of a genus (*Mollienisia*) of brightly coloured TOPMINNOWS highly valued as aquarium fishes [short for NL *Mollienisia*, genus name, fr Comte François *Mollien* †1850 Fr statesman]

**mollify** /ˈmolifie/ *vt* 1 to lessen the anger or hostility of; soothe 2 to reduce in intensity; assuage, temper [ME *mollifien*, fr MF *mollifier*, fr LL *mollificare*, fr L *mollis* soft – more at MELT] – **mollification** *n*

**mollusc**, *NAm chiefly* **mollusk** /ˈmoləsk/ *n* any of a large phylum Mollusca of INVERTEBRATE animals including snails, oysters, and squids, that have a soft unsegmented body often enclosed in a shell; *broadly* a shellfish [Fr *mollusque*, fr NL *Mollusca*, phylum name, fr L, neut pl of *molluscus* soft, fr *mollis*] – **molluscan** *adj*

**Mollweide projection** /ˈmolˌviedə, ˈmohl-/ *n* a method of representing the earth's surface in which the relative size of areas is accurately shown and the entire surface of the earth is shown in the form of an ellipse with all lines of latitude as parallel straight lines more widely spaced at the equator than at the poles, with the central MERIDIAN imaginary semicircle joining both poles as a straight line half the length of the equator, and with all other meridians as equally spaced ellipses; *also* a map projection or other representation of the earth's surface produced by this method [Karl *Mollweide* †1825 Ger mathematician & astronomer]

[1]**mollycoddle** /ˈmoliˌkodl/ *n* a spoilt or effeminate man or boy; a milksop [*Molly*, nickname for Mary + *coddle*]

[2]**mollycoddle** *vt* to surround with an excessive or absurd degree of indulgence and attention – **mollycoddler** *n*

**mollymawk** /ˈmolimawk/ *n* MALLEMUCK (seabird)

**Molotov cocktail** /ˈmolətof/ *n* a crude hand grenade consisting of a bottle filled with an inflammable liquid (eg petrol) whose wick, usu a saturated rag, is ignited at the moment of hurling [Vyacheslav M *Molotov* b 1890 Russ statesman]

**molt** /mohlt/ *vb or n, NAm* (to) moult

**molten** /ˈmohlt(ə)n/ *adj* 1 liquefied by heat; melted ⟨~ *lava*⟩ 2 *obs* made by melting and casting [ME, fr pp of *melten* to melt] **synonyms** Molten, rather than **melted**, is used of things which melt at very high temperatures. Compare ⟨**molten** *rock/metal*⟩ ⟨**melted** *butter/chocolate*⟩.

**molto** /ˈmoltoh/ *adv* much, very – used in music directions ⟨~ *sostenuto*⟩ [It, fr L *multum*, fr neut of *multus* much]

**molybdate** /moˈlibdayt/ *n* a chemical compound (SALT) containing molybdenum in either of the groups $MoO_4$ or $Mo_2O_7$

**molybdate orange** *n* a brilliant orange pigment consisting of the chromate, molybdate, and usu sulphate of lead

**molybdenite** /məˈlibd(ə)nˌiet/ *n* a greyish-blue mineral, $MoS_2$, that consists of a sulphide of molybdenum and is the chief ore of molybdenum [NL *molybdena*]

**molybdenum** /məˈlibd(ə)nəm/ *n* a hard silvery-white metallic chemical element that is used esp in strengthening and hardening steel and is required in minute quantities by plants and animals [NL, fr *molybdena*, a lead ore, molybdenite, molybdenum, fr L *molybdaena* galena, fr Gk *molybdaina*, fr *molybdos* lead]

**molybdic** /moˈlibdik/ *adj* of or containing molybdenum, esp with one of its higher VALENCIES [NL *molybdenum*]

**molybdous** /moˈlibdəs/ *adj* of or containing molybdenum, esp with one of its lower VALENCIES [NL *molybdenum*]

**mom** /mom/ *n, NAm informal* mum, mother [short for *momma*]

**moment** /ˈmohmənt/ *n* 1 a very brief interval or point of time; an instant 2a present time ⟨*at the* ~ *he is working on a novel*⟩ b a time of excellence or prominence ⟨*he has his* ~s⟩ 3 importance in influence or effect; consequence ⟨*a matter of the greatest* ~⟩ 4 a stage in historical or logical development ⟨*one* ~ *in the history of thought* – T S Eliot⟩ 5a a tendency to produce motion, esp rotational motion about a point or axis b a measure of the tendency to produce rotational motion, equal to the result of multiplying a quantity (eg a force) by its perpendicular distance from a particular axis or point 6 *statistics* 6a the ARITHMETIC MEAN of the sum of specified powers of deviations of observed values from a fixed value ⟨*the second* ~ *about the mean is the variance*⟩ b the EXPECTED VALUE of a power of the deviation of a RANDOM VARIABLE from a fixed value – see also **on the** SPUR **of the moment** [ME, fr MF, fr L *momentum* movement, particle sufficient to turn the scales, moment, fr *movēre* to move]

**momentarily** /ˈmohmənt(ə)rəli, ˌmohmənˈterəli/ *adv* 1 for a moment ⟨*was* ~ *stunned by the blow*⟩ 2 at any moment ⟨~ *expected his coming* – Charlotte Brontë⟩ 3 *chiefly NAm* immediately

*usage* The American English sense of **momentarily** = "immediately" ⟨*we will be landing* **momentarily** *at Kennedy Airport*⟩ is disliked by some speakers of British English, who also prefer to use the rarer word **momently** rather than **momentarily** for the sense "at any moment".

**momentary** /ˈmohmənt(ə)ri/ *adj* 1 lasting a very short time; short-lived, transitory 2 likely to occur at any moment; *also* recurring at every moment ⟨*in* ~ *terror*⟩ **synonyms** see [1]TRANSIENT *antonym* agelong △ momentous – **momentariness** *n*

**momently** /ˈmohməntli/ *adv* 1 from moment to moment ⟨*the danger is* ~ *increasing*⟩ 2 MOMENTARILY 1,2 *usage* see MOMENTARILY

**moment of inertia** *n* a measure of the amount of resistance a body offers to having its rotational speed (ANGULAR VELOCITY) changed; the ratio of the force causing rotation (TORQUE) applied to a body free to rotate about a particular axis to the acceleration thus produced

**moment of truth** *n* 1 the moment of the final sword thrust in a bullfight 2 a moment of crisis or testing on whose outcome much or everything depends

**momentous** /mə'mentəs, moh-/ *adj* of great consequence or significance ⟨*a* ~ *general election*⟩ △ momentary – **momentously** *adv*, **momentousness** *n*

**momentum** /mə'mentəm, moh-/ *n, pl* **momenta** /-tə/, **momentums** a property of a moving body that determines the length of time required to bring it to rest when under the action of a constant force; the result of multiplying the mass of a body by its velocity [NL, fr L, movement]

**momma** /'momə, 'mumə/ *n, NAm* mum, mother [var of *mama*, *mamma*]

**mon** /mon/ *n, chiefly Br* a man

**Mon** /mohn/ *n, pl* **Mons**, *esp collectively* **Mon 1** a member of the dominant ethnic group of Burma and Thailand **2** the Mon-Khmer language of the Mon people

**mon-** /mon-/, **mono-** *comb form* **1** one; single; alone ⟨*monoplane*⟩ ⟨*monodrama*⟩ ⟨*monophobia*⟩ **2** containing one (specified atom or chemical group) in the molecular structure ⟨*monohydrate*⟩ ⟨*monoxide*⟩ [ME, fr MF & L; MF, fr L, fr Gk, fr *monos* alone, single – more at MONK]

**mona** /'mohnə/ *n* a small W African monkey (*Cercopithecus mona*) [NL, prob fr Sp or It, monkey, ape]

**monachal** /'monəkl/ *adj* monastic [MF or LL; MF, fr LL *monachalis*, fr *monachus* monk – more at MONK] – **monachism** *n*

**monad** /'mohnad, 'mo-/ *n* **1** *philosophy* **1a** a fundamental unit or entity; one **b** ATOM 1 (hypothetical minute particle of matter) **c** an elementary indivisible spiritual substance related in a harmonious system with other like substances and forming the basis of the material world – used esp in the philosophy of Leibniz **2** a minute single-celled organism; *esp* a PROTOZOAN (e g of the genus *Monas*) having FLAGELLA (long whiplike structures used for movement) [LL *monad-, monas*, fr Gk, fr *monos*] – **monadism** *n*, **monadic** *adj*

**monadelphous** /,monə'delfəs/ *adj, of the* STAMENS (*male reproductive structures*) *of a flower* united into one group usu forming a tube round the CARPELS (female reproductive structures) – compare DIADELPHOUS, POLYADELPHOUS

**monandrous** /mo'nandrəs/ *adj* **1a** *of a flower* having a single STAMEN (male reproductive structure) **b** *of a plant* having flowers with a single STAMEN **2** of or practising monandry [(1) *mon-* + *-androus*; (2) Gk *monandros*, fr *mon-* + *-andros* having (so many) men – more at -ANDROUS]

**monandry** /mo'nandri/ *n* **1** the state, practice, or custom of having only one husband at a time – compare MONOGAMY, MONOGYNY **2** a monandrous condition of a plant or flower [*monandrous* + ²-*y*]

**monarch** /'monək/ *n* **1** a person who reigns over a kingdom or empire **2** one who or that which occupies a commanding or preeminent position **3** a large N American butterfly (*Danaus plexippus*) that migrates annually and sometimes reaches Europe, and that has orange-brown wings with black veins and borders and a larva that feeds on milkweed – called also MILKWEED BUTTERFLY [LL *monarcha*, fr Gk *monarchos*, fr *mon-* + *-archos* -arch] – **monarchal, monarchial** *adj*

**Monarchian** /mo'nahkiən/ *n* an adherent of either of two anti-Trinitarian groups of the 2nd and 3rd centuries AD teaching that God is one person as well as one being [LL *monarchianus*, fr *monarchia* monarchy, individual rule] – **Monarchianism** *n*

**monarchical** /mo'nahkikl/, **monarchic** *adj* of or characteristic of a monarch or monarchy – **monarchically** *adv*

**monarchism** /'monə,kiz(ə)m/ *n* monarchical government or principles – **monarchist** *n or adj*, **monarchistic** *adj*

**monarchy** /'monəki/ *n* **1** undivided rule or absolute sovereignty by a single person **2** a government or state in which sovereignty is actually or nominally held by a monarch

**monastery** /'monəst(ə)ri/ *n* an esp purpose-built residence for a religious community, esp of ⊙nks [ME *monasterie*, fr LL *monasterium*, fr LGk *monastērion*, fr Gk, hermit's cell, fr *monazein* to live alone, fr *monos* single – more at MONK] – **monasterial** *adj, archaic*

**monastic** /mə'nastik/ *adj* **1** of or being monasteries, monks, or nuns **2** resembling (e g in seclusion or austerity) life in a monastery – **monastic** *n*, **monastically** *adv*, **monasticism** *n*

**monatomic** /,monə'tomik/ *adj* **1a** having or consisting of one atom; *esp* consisting of molecules each of which contains only one atom ⟨*helium and argon are* ~ *gases*⟩ **b** having a thickness equal to the diameter of a constituent atom **2** having a VALENCY of one; UNIVALENT **3** *of a chemical compound* having one atom or chemical group that can be replaced by another in a chemical reaction – **monatomically** *adv*

**monaural** /,mon'awrəl/ *adj* MONOPHONIC 2 (using only one electrical channel to record or reproduce sound) – **monaurally** *adv*

**monaxial** /,mon'aksiəl/ *adj* having or based on a single axis; UNIAXIAL; *specif* having flowers developing on a single axis

**monazite** /'monəziet/ *n* a yellowish- to reddish-brown mineral, (Ce,La)PO$_4$, that is a phosphate of the chemical elements cerium and lanthanum, frequently contains thorium, and is a major source of cerium and often thorium [Ger *monazit*, fr Gk *monazein*; fr its rarity]

**Monday** /'munday, -di/ *n* the 2nd day of the week; the day falling between Sunday and Tuesday [ME, fr OE *mōnandæg*; akin to OHG *mānatag* Monday; both fr a prehistoric WGmc compound (trans of L *lunae dies* day of the moon) whose components are represented by OE *mōna* moon and OE *dæg* day] – **Mondays** *adv*

**monecious** /mə'neeshəs, mo-/ *adj, NAm* MONOECIOUS (having both male and female parts)

**Monel Metal** /'mo'nel/ *trademark* – used for a corrosion-resistant nickel and copper alloy

**monetarism** /'munitə,riz(ə)m/ *n* an economic theory that the most effective way of controlling the economy is by controlling the supply of money – **monetarist** *n or adj*

**monetary** /'munit(ə)ri/ *adj* of money or the mechanisms by which it is supplied to and circulates in the economy [LL *monetarius* of a mint, of money, fr L *moneta*] – **monetarily** *adv*

**monetary unit** *n* the standard unit of value of a currency

**monet·ize, -ise** /'munitiez/ *vt* to coin into money; *also* to establish as legal tender [L *moneta* + E -*ize*] – **monetization** *n*

**money** /'muni/ *n, pl* **moneys, monies 1** something generally accepted as a medium of exchange, a measure of value, or a means of payment; *esp* officially printed, coined, or stamped currency **2** wealth reckoned in terms of money **3** a form or denomination of coin or paper money **4** *informal* **4a** the first, second, and third place winners in a horse or dog race – chiefly in *in the money* or *out of the money* **b** prize money ⟨*his horse took third* ~⟩ **5** *informal* wealthy people ⟨*there's a lot of* ~ *in that town*⟩ – see also for LOVE or/nor money, a (good) RUN for one's money [ME *moneye*, fr MF *moneie*, fr L *moneta* mint, money – more at MINT]

**moneybags** /'muni,bagz/ *n, pl* **moneybags**, *informal derog* a wealthy person

**money box** *n* a container for small personal savings, usu with a slot for the insertion of coins

**money changer** *n* **1** one whose occupation is the exchanging of kinds or denominations of currency **2** a device for dispensing small change

**moneyed, monied** /'munid/ *adj* **1** having much money; wealthy **2** consisting of or derived from money ⟨~ *power*⟩

**moneyer** /'muni-ə/ *n, archaic* an authorized coiner of money; a minter [ME, fr OF *monier*, fr LL *monetarius* master of a mint, coiner, fr *monetarius* of a mint]

**money-grubber** /'muni,grubə/ *n, informal* a person bent on accumulating money, esp by sordid or unscrupulous means – **money-grubbing** *adj or n*

**moneylender** /-,lendə/ *n* one whose business is lending money and charging interest on it

**'money-,maker** *n* **1** one who succeeds in accumulating wealth **2** a product or enterprise that produces much profit – **moneymaking** *adj or n*

**money multiplier** *n* the ratio of a change in bank deposits to a change in reserve assets

**money of account** *n* a denominator of value or basis of exchange which is used in keeping accounts and for which there may not necessarily be an equivalent amount of coin or paper money

**money order** *n, chiefly NAm* POSTAL ORDER

**money spider** *n* a small red or brownish spider supposed to bring luck to the person on whom it crawls

**'money-,spinner** *n, chiefly Br informal* a highly successful money-making product or enterprise – **money-spinning** *adj or n*

**moneywort** /-,wuht/ *n* CREEPING JENNY (European plant of the primrose family) [fr its roundish leaves, resembling small coins]

**monger** /'mung·gə/ *n* **1** a trader, dealer ⟨*alemonger*⟩ **2** one who attempts to stir up or spread something that is usu petty or discreditable ⟨*gossip*monger⟩ ⟨*war*monger⟩ □ usu in combination [ME *mongere*, fr OE *mangere*, fr L *mangon-, mango*, of Gk origin; akin to Gk *manganon* charm, philtre – more at MANGONEL]

**mongo** /'mong·goh/ *n, pl* **mongo** – see *tugrik* at MONEY table [Mongolian]

**Mongol** /'mong,gol, 'mong·gl/ *n* **1** a member of any of the Mongoloid peoples of Mongolia **2** MONGOLIAN 2 **3** a person of Mongoloid racial stock **4** *not cap* a sufferer from DOWN'S SYNDROME (genetic defect causing certain mental and physical abnormalities) – not now used technically △ mogul [Mongolian *Mongol*; (4) fr the partially Mongoloid facial features of a sufferer] – **Mongol** *adj*

¹**Mongolian** /mong'gohliən/ *adj* **1** of, characteristic of, or being Mongolia, the Mongolian People's Republic, the Mongols, or Mongolian **2** *not cap* mongoloid – not now used technically

²**Mongolian** *n* **1a** MONGOL 1 **b** a person of Mongoloid racial stock **c** a native or inhabitant of Mongolia or of the Mongolian People's Republic **2** the Mongolic language of the Mongol people **3** *not cap* MONGOL 4 – not now used technically

**Mongolian gerbil** *n* a gerbil (*Meriones unguiculatus*) of Mongolia and N China that superficially resembles a rat and has a high capacity for temperature regulation

**Mongolic** /mong'golik/ *n* a branch of the Altaic languages including Mongolian and Kalmuck

**mongolism** /'mong·g(ə)l,iz(ə)m/ *n* DOWN'S SYNDROME (genetic defect causing certain mental and physical abnormalities) – not now used technically

**Mongoloid** /'mong·g(ə)loyd/ *adj* **1** Mongoloid, Mongolic of, constituting, or characteristic of a major racial stock native to Asia and including peoples of N and E Asia, Malaysians, Eskimos, and often American Indians **2** *not cap* of or affected with DOWN'S SYNDROME (genetic defect causing certain mental and physical abnormalities) – not now used technically – **Mongoloid** *n*

**mongoose** /'mong,goohs/ *n, pl* **mongooses** any of various ferret-sized short-legged agile mammals (genus *Herpestes* and related genera) of Asia, Africa, and S Europe, that are related to the CIVET CAT, have grey-brown fur and a long furry tail, and that feed on small animals (e g birds and rodents), eggs, and sometimes snakes [Hindi *māgūs*, fr Prakrit *manguso*]

*usage* The plural is **mongooses**, not △ **mongeese**, except in humorous use.

**mongrel** /'mong·grəl, 'mung-/ *n* **1** an individual, esp a dog, resulting from the interbreeding of diverse breeds or strains; *esp* one of unknown ancestry **2** a cross between different types of person or thing [prob fr ME *mong* mixture, short for *ymong*, fr OE *gemong* crowd – more at AMONG] – **mongrel, mongrelly** *adj*, **mongrelism** *n*, **mongrelize** *vt*, **mongrelization** *n*

**mongst** /mungst/ *prep, poetic* amongst

**monied** /'munid/ *adj* moneyed

**monies** /'muniz/ *pl of* MONEY

**moniker, monicker** /'munikə, 'mon-/ *n, slang* a name, nickname [origin unknown]

**moniliasis** /,mohni'lie·əsis, ,mo-/ *n, pl* **moniliases** /-seez/ CANDIDIASIS (fungal infection affecting the mouth, vagina, etc); *specif* ²THRUSH 1 [NL, fr *Monilia*, genus of fungi, fr L *monile* necklace]

**moniliform** /mo'nili,fawm/ *adj, biology* jointed or constricted at regular intervals so as to resemble a string of beads ⟨~ *insect antennae*⟩ ⟨~ *fungi*⟩ [L *monile* necklace – more at MANE] – **moniliformly** *adv*

**monism** /'moh,niz(ə)m, 'mo-/ *n* **1** a doctrine that a complex entity (e g the universe) is basically simple and undifferentiated **2** a doctrine that asserts the identity of mind and matter □ compare DUALISM, PLURALISM [Ger *monismus*, fr *mon-* + *-ismus* -ism] – **monist** *n*, **monistic, monistical** *adj*

**monition** /moh'nish(ə)n/ *n* **1** an admonition, warning **2** a formal notice from an ecclesiastical authority, esp a bishop, requiring a person to refrain from something [ME *monicioun*, fr MF *monition*, fr L *monition-, monitio*, fr *monitus*, pp of *monēre* to warn]

¹**monitor** /'monitə/, *fem* (1aɑb) **monitress** /'monitris/ *n* **1a** a pupil appointed to assist a teacher (e g by keeping order) **b** a person or thing that admonishes or instructs **c** one who or that which monitors or is used in monitoring: e g **c(1)** a television screen used to show the view seen by a television camera **c(2)** a device for observing a biological condition or function ⟨*a heart* ~⟩ **c(3)** the computer programs, circuits, etc that monitor the operation of a computer system **2** **monitor lizard, monitor** any of various large lizards (genus *Varanus* and family

Varanidae) of tropical Asia, Africa, and Australia that are closely related to the iguanas – compare KOMODO DRAGON **3** a small warship having a shallow bottom and heavy firepower for its size [L, one who warns, overseer, fr *monitus*, pp of *monēre* to warn – more at MIND; (2) fr its supposedly giving warning of the presence of crocodiles; (3) *Monitor*, first ship of the type, designed in 1862 for the US navy] – **monitorship** *n*, **monitorial** *adj*

²**monitor** *vt* **1** to check (e g a radio or television signal or programme) by means of a receiver for quality or fidelity or for military, political, or criminal significance **2** to test for intensity of radioactivity **3** to observe or inspect, esp for a special purpose **4** to regulate or control the operation of (e g a machine or process) **5** to check or regulate the volume or quality of (sound) in recording

¹**monitory** /'monit(ə)ri/ *adj, formal* warning, admonitory [L *monitorius*, fr *monitus*]

²**monitory** *n* a letter containing an admonition or warning

**monk** /mungk/ *n* a man who is a member of a religious order and lives in a monastery; *also* a friar [ME, fr OE *munuc*, fr LL *monachus*, fr LGk *monachos*, fr Gk, adj, single, fr *monos* single, alone; akin to OHG *mengen* to lack, Gk *manos* sparse] – **monkhood** *n*

**monkery** /'mungkəri/ *n, derog* **1** monastic life or practice; monasticism **2** a monastic house; a monastery

¹**monkey** /'mungki/ *n* **1** any of the PRIMATE mammals with the exception of human beings and usu the lemurs and tarsiers; *esp* any of the smaller longer-tailed primates as contrasted with the apes **2** a mischievous child; a scamp ⟨*what's the little* ~ *done with my gloves?*⟩ **3** any of various machines, implements, or vessels; *esp* the falling weight of a PILE DRIVER **4** *slang* the sum of 500 pounds or dollars **5** *slang* a desperate desire for or addiction to drugs – often in *monkey on one's back* [prob of LG origin; akin to *Moneke*, name of an ape, prob of Romance origin; akin to OSp *mona* monkey] – **make a monkey of somebody** to make somebody appear ridiculous

²**monkey** *informal vi* **1** to act in an absurd or mischievous manner – usu + *about/around* **2** to meddle, tamper – chiefly in *monkey (around/about) with* to mimic, mock

**monkey business** *n, informal* mischievous or underhand activity

**monkey jacket** *n* a short fitted uniform jacket reaching to the waist; MESS JACKET

**monkey nut** *n* a peanut

**monkeypod** /'mungki,pod/ *n* (the wood of) an ornamental tropical American tree (*Samanea saman*) of the pea family, that has clusters of red and yellow flowers and pods with a sweet pulp that are eaten by cattle – called also RAIN TREE

**monkey pot** *n* **1** any of a genus (*Lecythis* of the family Lecythideae) of S American shrubs or trees that have usu edible nuts, hard heavy wood used in building and sometimes cabinet work, and a woody fruit shaped like a small round bowl; *also* the fruit of a monkey pot **2** an oval cylinder of glass used as a melting pot in the making of FLINT GLASS

'**monkey-,puzzle** *n* a commonly planted S American evergreen conifer tree (*Araucaria araucana* of the family Araucariaceae, the monkey-puzzle family) that has a network of intertwined branches and stiff sharp needlelike leaves – called also CHILE PINE [fr the notion that even a monkey would have difficulty in climbing it]

**monkeyshine** /'mungki,shien/ *n, NAm informal* a prank – often *pl*

**monkey wrench** *n* a large spanner with one fixed and one adjustable jaw at right angles to a straight handle

**monkfish** /'mungk,fish/ *n* **1** any of various edible fish (family Squatinidae) that live on the bottom of the sea, have a flattened body and large winglike PECTORAL FINS (pair of fins just behind the head), and are closely related to the sharks and rays **2** ANGLER FISH [fr the resemblance of its head to a monk's hood]

**Mon-Khmer** /,mohn 'kmeə/ *n* a family of Austroasiatic languages containing several languages of SE Asia including Mon and Khmer

**monkish** /'mungkish/ *adj* **1** of monks **2** *derog* ascetic

**monk's cloth** *n* a coarse heavy fabric made originally of worsted and used for monks' habits but now chiefly of cotton or linen and used for bedspreads, curtains, etc

**monkshood** /'mungks,hood/ *n* a very poisonous Eurasian plant (*Aconitum napellus*) often cultivated for its showy spikes of white or purplish flowers; *also* ACONITUM 1 (poisonous plant of the buttercup family) [fr its hood-shaped flowers]

**¹mono** /'monoh/ *adj* MONOPHONIC 2 (using only one electrical channel to record or reproduce sound)

**²mono** *n, pl* **monos** 1 a monophonic recording (eg a gramophone record) 2 monophonic sound

**³mono** *adj* MONOCHROME 2 – used esp of a black and white television picture

**mono-** – see MON-

**¹monoacid** /,monoh'asid/, **monoacidic** /,monoh-ə'sidik/ *adj* 1 *esp of a chemical* BASE having only one HYDROXYL group capable of reacting as a base in each molecule 2 *of an acid* MONOBASIC 1

**²monoacid** *n* an acid having one acid hydrogen atom

**monoamine** /,monoh'ameen, -ə'meen/ *n* an AMINE, $RNH_2$, that has one carbon-containing chemical group attached to the nitrogen atom; *specif* one (eg NORADRENALIN) that functions as a NEUROTRANSMITTER (substance that transmits nerve impulses) [ISV]

**monoamine oxidase** *n* an enzyme that causes the chemical breakdown of monoamines and is important in the nervous system in deactivating NORADRENALIN and similar monoamines that act as transmitters of nerve impulses, esp in the brain

**monoaminergic** /,monoh,ami'nuhjik/ *adj* using or involving monoamines (eg NORADRENALIN or SEROTONIN) as chemical transmitters of nerve impulses ⟨∼ *mechanisms*⟩ ⟨∼ *nerves*⟩ [*monoamine* + Gk *ergon* work – more at WORK]

**monobasic** /,monoh'baysik/ *adj* 1 *of an acid* having only one hydrogen atom capable of reacting as an acid in each molecule 2 *of a chemical compound* containing one atom of a metal having a VALENCY of one 3 *of a chemical* BASE MONOACID 1 [ISV]

**monocarboxylic** /,monoh,kahbok'silik/ *adj* containing one CARBOXYL group in the molecular structure ⟨*acetic acid is a* ∼ *acid*⟩

**monocarpic** /,monoh'kahpik/ *adj, of a plant* bearing fruit only once and then dying

**monochasium** /,monoh'kayziəm/ *n, pl* **monochasia** /-ziə/ a CYME (type of flower cluster) in which each branch produces one other branch resulting in only one main axis [NL, fr *mon-* + *-chasium* (as in *dichasium*)] – **monochasial** *adj*

**monochord** /'monə,kawd/ *n* an instrument of ancient origin that is used for measuring and demonstrating the mathematical relations of musical notes and consists of a single string stretched over a sounding board and a movable bridge set on a graduated scale [ME *monocorde*, fr MF, fr ML *monochordum*, fr Gk *monochordon*, fr *mon-* + *chordē* string – more at YARN]

**monochromat** /,monə'krohmat/ *n* a person suffering from monochromatism [*mon-* + Gk *chrōmat-, chrōma*]

**monochromatic** /,monəkrə'matik/ *adj* 1 having or consisting of one colour 2 consisting of radiation of a single wavelength or of a very small range of wavelengths ⟨∼ *light*⟩ 3 of or exhibiting monochromatism [L *monochromatos*, fr Gk *monochrōmatos*, fr *mon-* + *chrōmat-, chrōma* colour – more at CHROMATIC] – **monochromatically** *adv*, **monochromaticity** *n*

**monochromatism** /,monə'krohmətiz(ə)m, ,monoh-/ *n* complete COLOUR BLINDNESS in which all colours appear as shades of grey

**¹monochrome** /'monə,krohm/ *n* reproduction or execution in (shades of) one colour, black and white, or shades of grey; *also* a monochrome painting, drawing, or photograph [ML *monochroma*, fr L, fem of *monochromos* of one colour, fr Gk *monochrōmos*, fr *mon-* + *-chrōmos* -chrome] – **monochromist** *n*, **monochromic** *adj*

**²monochrome** *adj* 1 of or executed in (shades of) a single colour 2 BLACK-AND-WHITE 1 ⟨∼ *television*⟩ ⟨*a* ∼ *photograph*⟩ 3 lacking in variety or interest; dull ⟨*universities these days are desperately* ∼ – N Smart⟩

**monocle** /'monəkl/ *n* a device to improve sight consisting of a single lens for one eye [Fr, fr LL *monoculus* having one eye, fr L *mon-* + *oculus* eye – more at EYE] – **monocled** *adj*

**monocline** /'monə,klien/ *n* a fold or bend in rock, in which all the rock layers slope in one direction at a constant angle and on each side of which the land is approx horizontal – **monoclinal** *adj or n*

**monoclinic** /,monə'klinik/ *adj* of or being a crystal or system of crystal structure characterized by three unequal AXES, only two of which are at RIGHT ANGLES to each other [ISV]

**monoclinous** /,monoh'klienəs, '--,--/ *adj, of a plant* having both the male and female reproductive structures (STAMENS and OVARIES) in the same flower – compare DICLINOUS [NL *monoclinus*, fr *mon-* + *-clinus* -clinous]

**monocoque** /'monə,kok/ *n* 1 a type of construction (eg of a fuselage or a rocket body) in which the outer skin carries all or a major part of the stresses 2 a type of vehicle construction (eg of a racing car or railway carriage) in which the body is integral with the chassis [Fr, fr *mon-* + *coque* shell, fr L *coccum* outgrowth on a tree, fr Gk *kokkos* berry] – **monocoque** *adj*

**monocot** /'monə,kot/ *n* a monocotyledon

**monocotyl** /'monə,kotil/ *n* a monocotyledon

**monocotyledon** /,monə,koti'leedn/ *n* a plant with one COTYLEDON (leaf produced by a germinating seed); a member of the group (Monocotyledoneae) of FLOWERING PLANTS comprising all those (eg the grasses, orchids, and lilies) with a single cotyledon and typically long narrow leaves with parallel veins [deriv of NL *mon-* + *cotyledon*] – **monocotyledonous** *adj*

**monocular** /mo'nokyoolə/ *adj* 1 of, involving, or affecting a single eye 2 suitable for use with only one eye [LL *monoculus* having one eye] – **monocularly** *adv*

**monoculture** /'monə,kulchə/ *n* 1 the cultivation of a single crop to the exclusion of other uses of the land 2 a CULTURE (colony of bacteria, viruses, etc grown in a laboratory) that contains a single type of microorganism – **monocultural** *adj*

**monocyclic** /,monə'sieklik/ *adj* 1a *of petals or similar flower parts* arranged in or consisting of a single whorl or circle b *of a plant* living for one year; annual 2 *of a chemical compound* containing one ring arrangement of atoms in the molecular structure 3 having a single annual peak in population ⟨*a population of* ∼ *water fleas in a lake*⟩ [ISV *mon-* + *cyclic*] – **monocycly** *n*

**monocyte** /'monə,siet/ *n* a large mobile WHITE BLOOD CELL that is present in small numbers in the blood and defends the body by enveloping and ingesting harmful or unwanted matter [ISV] – **monocytic** *adj*, **monocytoid** *adj*

**monodist** /'monədist/ *n* a writer, singer, or composer of monodies

**monodrama** /'monə,drahmə/ *n* a dramatic piece for a single actor – **monodramatic** *adj*

**monody** /'monədi/ *n* 1 an ode sung by one voice, esp in a Greek tragedy 2 a poem lamenting someone's death 3 (a composition in) a style of music (eg in 17th-century opera) having one melody with little or no accompaniment [ML *monodia*, fr Gk *monōidia*, fr *monōidos* singing alone, fr *mon-* + *aidein* to sing – more at ODE] – **monodic, monodical** *adj*, **monodically** *adv*, **monodist** *n*

**monoecious**, *NAm also* **monecious** /mə'neeshəs, mo-/ *adj* 1 *esp of primitive animals and plants* having male and female reproductive organs in the same organism; HERMAPHRODITIC 2 having separate female and male flowers on the same plant – compare DIOECIOUS [deriv of Gk *mon-* + *oikos* house – more at VICINITY] – **monoeciously** *adv*, **monoecism** *n*

**monoester** /'monoh,estə/ *n* a chemical compound that contains only one ESTER group (group formed by reaction between an acid and an alcohol); *esp* one containing one or more acid groups that have not reacted to form ester groups

**monoestrous** /mə'neestrəs, mo-/ *adj* experiencing OESTRUS (period when a female mammal is capable of conceiving) once each year; having a single annual breeding period

**monofilament** /,monə'filəmənt/ *n* a single untwisted synthetic filament (eg of nylon)

**monogamy** /mə'nogəmi/ *n* 1 the state, practice, or custom of being married to one person at a time – compare MONANDRY, MONOGYNY 2 *archaic* the practice of marrying only once during a lifetime [Fr *monogamie*, fr LL *monogamia*, fr Gk, fr *monogamos* monogamous, fr *mon-* + *gamos* marriage – more at BIGAMY] – **monogamist** *n*, **monogamous** *adj*, **monogamously** *adv*, **monogamousness** *n*, **monogamic** *adj*

**monogastric** /,monə'gastrik/ *adj* having one digestive cavity ⟨*pigs, chicks, and people are* ∼⟩

**monogenean** /,monə'jeenyən/ *n* any of a subclass (Monogenea of the class Trematoda) of flatworms that ordinarily live as parasites on the surface of a single fish throughout their entire LIFE CYCLE [NL *Monogenea*, group name, fr *mon-* + Gk *genea* race, descent] – **monogenean** *adj*

**monogenesis** /,monə'jenəsis/ *n* unity of origin; development from a single source or common ancestor (eg of all languages from an original language); *esp* the theory or belief that all organisms are descended from a single cell or organism [NL]

**monogenetic** /,monəjə'netik, ,monoh-/ *adj* 1 relating to or involving monogenesis 2 of or being a monogenean

**monogenic** /,monə'jenik/ *adj* of or being an inheritable characteristic controlled by a single gene, esp by either of a pair of genes coding for contrasting forms of that characteristic [ISV] – **monogenically** adv

**monogerm** /'monə,juhm/ adj producing or being a fruit that gives rise to a single plant ⟨a ~ variety of sugar beet⟩ [mon- + germinate]

**monoglot** /'monə,glot/ adj MONOLINGUAL (knowing or using only one language)

**¹monogram** /'monəgram/ n a design usu formed of the interwoven initials of a name [LL monogramma, fr Gk mon- + gramma letter – more at GRAM] – **monogrammatic** adj

**²monogram** vt -mm- to mark with a monogram

**¹monograph** /'monə'grahf, -,graf/ n a learned treatise on a small area of learning; also a written account of a single thing – **monographic** adj

**²monograph** vt to write a monograph on – **monographer**, **monographist** n

**monogyny** /mə'nojəni/ n the state, practice, or custom of having only one wife at a time – compare MONANDRY, MONOGAMY [ISV] – **monogynous** adj

**monohybrid** /,monoh'hiebrid/ adj or n (of or being) an organism or strain of organisms that is HETEROZYGOUS (having two different versions of one gene) for one particular gene or inheritable characteristic

**monohydric** /,monoh'hiedrik/ adj 1 containing one atom of hydrogen that is capable of reacting as an acid 2 monohydroxy

**monohydroxy** /,monoh·hie'droksi/ adj containing one HYDROXYL group in the molecule [ISV monohydroxy-, fr mon- + hydroxy-]

**monolayer** /'monoh,layə/ n a single continuous layer or film that is one cell or one molecule in thickness

**monolingual** /,monoh'ling·gwəl/ adj knowing or using one language ⟨a ~ dictionary⟩ – **monolingual** n

**monolith** /'monə,lith/ n 1 a single large block of stone, often in the form of an obelisk or column 2 a massive structure 3 a complex structure or organization in which individual parts function together as a single powerful whole ⟨the ~ of Russian Communism⟩ [Fr monolithe, fr monolithe consisting of a single stone, fr L monolithus, fr Gk monolithos, fr mon- + lithos stone]

**monolithic** /,monə'lithik/ adj 1a of a monolith b of an INTEGRATED CIRCUIT or a component of such a circuit formed from or produced in or on a single crystal ⟨a ~ silicon chip⟩ 2a cast as a single usu large piece ⟨a ~ concrete wall⟩ b consisting of or constituting a single unit 3a constituting a massive undifferentiated and often rigid whole ⟨a ~ society⟩ b exhibiting or characterized by often rigidly fixed uniformity ⟨~ party unity⟩ – **monolithically** adv

**monologue**, NAm also **monolog** /'monə,log/ n 1 a speech by an actor (as if) alone on stage; also a dramatic sketch performed by one actor – compare SOLILOQUY 2 a literary SOLILOQUY (discourse of personal thoughts, feelings, etc) 3 a long speech monopolizing conversation [Fr monologue, fr mon- + -logue (as in dialogue)] – **monologuist**, **monologist** n

**monomania** /,monoh'maynyə/ n 1 a mental disorder in which the sufferer is entirely preoccupied with one idea or delusion 2 obsessional concentration on a single object or idea [NL] – **monomaniac** n or adj

**monomer** /'monəmə/ n a single unit of a POLYMER (large molecule consisting of many identical repeating units); a chemical compound that can combine to form a polymer [ISV mon- + -mer (as in polymer)] – **monomeric** adj

**monometallic** /,monoh·mi'talik/ adj 1 consisting of or using one metal 2 of monometallism

**monometallism** /,monoh'metl,iz(ə)m/ n the adoption of one metal only as a monetary standard [ISV mon- + -metallism (as in bimetallism)] – **monometallist** n

**monometer** /mə'nomitə/ n a line of verse consisting of a single metrical foot [LL, fr Gk monometros, fr mon- + metron measure – more at MEASURE]

**monomial** /mo'nohmi·əl/ n 1 a mathematical expression consisting of a single term ⟨$3xy^2$ is a ~; $3x + y^2$ is not⟩ 2 a name used in classifying living things that consists of a single term [blend of mon- and -nomial (as in binomial)] – **monomial** adj

**monomolecular** /,monohmə'lekyoolə/ adj only one molecule thick ⟨a ~ film⟩ – **monomolecularly** adv

**monomorphemic** /,monoh·maw'feemik/ adj consisting of only one MORPHEME (smallest linguistic unit) ⟨talk is ~ but talked is not⟩

**mononuclear** /,monoh'nyoohkliə/ adj 1 having only one nucleus ⟨a ~ cell⟩ 2 of a chemical compound MONOCYCLIC 1 (containing one ring arrangement of atoms) [ISV] – **mononuclear** n

**mononuclear phagocyte system** n RETICULOENDOTHELIAL SYSTEM (system of cells and tissues providing defence for the body)

**mononucleate** /,monoh'nyoohkliət, -,ayt/, **mononucleated** adj MONONUCLEAR 1

**mononucleosis** /,monoh,nyoohkli'ohsis/ n INFECTIOUS MONONUCLEOSIS (glandular fever) [NL]

**mononucleotide** /,monoh'nyoohkli·ə,tied/ n a single NUCLEOTIDE, esp as contrasted with a POLYNUCLEOTIDE (compound like DNA that consists of many joined nucleotides); a nucleotide containing one molecule each of its constituent chemical groups

**monophagous** /mə'nofəgəs/ adj feeding on or using a single kind of food; esp feeding on a single kind of plant or animal – **monophagy** n

**monophonic** /,monoh'fonik/ adj 1 having a single melodic line with little or no accompaniment 2 of or being sound reproduction or a system for recording or reproducing sound that uses only one electrical channel between the source of the signal and its final point of use – **monophonically** adv

**monophony** /mə'nofəni/ n monophonic music

**monophthong** /'monəf,thong/ n a simple nongliding vowel sound (e g /i/ in bid) [LGk monophthongos single vowel, fr Gk mon- + phthongos voice, sound] – **monophthongal** adj

**monophyletic** /,monoh·fie'letik/ adj of or belonging to a single stock; specif developed from a single common ancestral form [ISV] – **monophyletism** n, **monophylety** n

**Monophysite** /mo'nofisiet/ n a person who holds the anti-Chalcedonian doctrine that the nature of the incarnate Christ remains altogether divine and not human [ML Monophysita, fr MGk Monophysitēs, fr Gk mon- + physis nature – more at PHYSICS] – **Monophysitism** n, **Monophysite**, **Monophysitic** adj

**monoplane** /'monə,playn/ n an aeroplane with only one main pair of wings

**monoploid** /'monə,ployd/ adj 1 having or being a single set of CHROMOSOMES (strands of gene-carrying material); HAPLOID 2 having or being the basic single set of CHROMOSOMES in a series of organisms that are POLYPLOID (having more than two times the single set of chromosomes as a normal state) [ISV] – **monoploid** n

**monopodial** /,monə'pohdiəl/ adj having or involving the formation of offshoots from a main axis ⟨~ lines of evolution⟩; esp, of a plant having a single main stem or trunk from which side shoots or branches grow [NL monopodium main axis, fr mon- + -podium] – **monopodially** adv

**monopole** /'monə,pohl/ n 1 a hypothetical single concentrated electric charge or MAGNETIC POLE (region of intense magnetism); also a hypothetical particle having such a pole 2 a radio aerial consisting of a single usu straight radiating element

**monopolist** /mo'nopəlist/ n one who has or favours a monopoly – **monopolistic** adj, **monopolistically** adv

**monopol·ize, -ise** /mə'nopəliez/ vt to get a monopoly of; assume complete possession or control of ⟨~ a conversation⟩ – **monopolizer** n, **monopolization** n

**monopoly** /mə'nopəli/ n 1 exclusive ownership or control (e g of a commodity or market) through legal privilege, command of supply, or concerted action 2 exclusive possession or control 3 a commodity controlled by one party 4 a person or group having a monopoly [L monopolium, fr Gk monopōlion, fr mon- + pōlein to sell]

**monopropellant** /,monoh·prə'pelənt/ n a rocket propellant containing both the fuel and the OXIDIZER (substance that supports burning of the fuel) in a single substance

**monopsony** /mə'nopsəni/ n a market in which one buyer has a monopoly [mon- + -opsony (as in oligopsony)]

**monorail** /'monoh,rayl/ n a single rail serving as a track for a wheeled vehicle; also a vehicle travelling on such a track

**monorchid** /mo'nawkid/ n an animal with only one testis or only one descended into the scrotum [irreg fr Gk monorchis, fr mon- + orchis testicle – more at ORCHIS] – **monorchid** adj, **monorchidism** n

**monosaccharide** /,monoh'sakəried/ n a sugar (e g glucose) that cannot be broken down to simpler sugars [ISV]

**monosodium glutamate** /,monə,sohdi·əm 'gloohtəmayt/ n a white chemical compound, $HOOCCH(NH_2)(CH_2)_2COONa$, added to foods, esp meat products, to intensify their natural flavour

**monosome** /'monəsohm/ *n* 1 a CHROMOSOME (strand of gene-carrying material) that remains unpaired during CELL DIVISION in which chromosomes from each parent associate in pairs; *esp* an unpaired X CHROMOSOME (chromosome that paired with another determines an animal's sex) 2 a single RIBOSOME (cell structure where proteins are made) – compare POLYSOME

**monosomic** /,monə'sohmik/ *adj, of a cell or organism* including a monosome and therefore having one less CHROMOSOME than the DIPLOID number (number of chromosomes typical of most mammalian cells) – **monosomic** *n*

**monostable** /'monoh,staybl/ *adj, of an electrical circuit* having one stable state

**monostele** /'monə,steel, ,monə'steeli/ *n* PROTOSTELE (simplest arrangement of water and food-conducting plant tissues) – **monostelic** *adj*, **monostely** *n*

**monostich** /'monə,stik/ *n* a single metrical line; *also* a poem of this length [LL *monostichum*, fr Gk *monostichon*, fr *mon-* + *stichos* line, verse]

**monosyllabic** /,monəsi'labik/ *adj* 1 consisting of one syllable or of monosyllables 2 using or speaking only monosyllables 3 pointedly brief in answering or commenting; terse [Fr *monosyllabique*, fr *monosyllabe*] – **monosyllabically** *adv*, **monosyllabicity** *n*

**monosyllable** /'monə,siləbl/ *n* a word of one syllable [modif of MF or LL; MF *monosyllabe*, fr LL *monosyllabon*, fr Gk, fr neut of *monosyllabos* having one syllable, fr *mon-* + *syllabē* syllable]

**monosymmetric** /,monoh·si'metrik/, **monosymmetrical** /-ikl/ *adj* MONOCLINIC (having or being a particular type of crystal structure)

**monosynaptic** /,monoh·si'naptik/ *adj* having or involving a single SYNAPSE (point where nerve impulses pass from one NERVE CELL to another) – **monosynaptically** *adv*

**monotechnic** /,monoh'teknik/ *n* a institution (e g an art college) that trains people for one occupation only [*mon-* + *-technic* (as in *polytechnic*)]

**monotheism** /'monohthee,iz(ə)m/ *n* the doctrine or belief that there is only one God – **monotheist** *n*, **monotheistic** *also* **monotheistical** *adj*, **monotheistically** *adv*

**Monothelite** /,monə'theliet/ *n* an adherent of the doctrine that Christ had two natures but only one will [ML *Monothelita*, modif of MGk *Monothelētēs*, fr Gk *mon-* + *thelētēs* one who wills, fr *thelein* to will]

**monotint** /'monə,tint/ *n* MONOCHROME

**1monotone** /'monə,tohn/ *n* 1 a succession of speech sounds in one unvaried pitch 2 a single unvaried musical note 3 a tedious sameness or repetition 4 a person unable to produce or to distinguish between musical intervals [Gk *monotonos* monotonous]

**2monotone** *adj* 1 having a uniform colour 2 MONOTONIC 2

**monotonic** /,monə'tonik/ *adj* 1 of or uttered in a monotone 2 *maths* having either of the properties of always increasing or always decreasing ⟨~ *functions*⟩ ⟨*a* ~ *sequence*⟩ – **monotonically** *adv*, **monotonicity** *n*

**monotonous** /mə'not(ə)nəs/ *adj* 1 uttered or sounded in one unvarying tone 2 tediously uniform or repetitive [Gk *monotonos*, fr *mon-* + *tonos* tone] – **monotonously** *adv*, **monotonousness, monotony** *n*

**monotreme** /'monoh,treem/ *n* any of an order (Monotremata) of egg-laying lower mammals comprising the platypus and ECHIDNA [NL *Monotremata*, group name, fr Gk *mon-* + *trēmat-, trēma* hole – more at TREMATODE; fr the single opening, in such mammals, for the genital, urinary, and digestive organs] – **monotrematous** *adj*

**monotrichous** /mə'notrikəs/ *also* **monotrichic** /-ikik/ *adj, of a bacterium* having a single FLAGELLUM (long whiplike structure used for movement)

**monotype** /'monə,tiep/ *n* 1 the only representative of a biological group; *esp* the single type that comprises a monotypic genus or species 2 an impression on paper taken from a painting on glass or metal

**Monotype** *trademark* – used for a keyboard-operated typesetting machine that casts and sets metal type in separate characters

**monotypic** /,monoh'tipik/ *adj* having only a single representative – used esp of a genus with only one species

**monovalent** /,monoh'vaylənt/ *adj* 1 having a VALENCY of one; UNIVALENT 1 2 containing or producing antibodies that act against a single substance [ISV]

**monovular** /mon'ovyoolə, 'ohv-/ *adj, of twins* IDENTICAL 3b (derived from a single egg)

**monoxide** /mo'noksied/ *n* an OXIDE (compound of oxygen and one chemical element or group) containing one atom of oxygen ⟨*carbon* ~⟩ [ISV]

**monozygous** /,monoh'ziegəs/, **monozygotic** /-zie'gotik/ *adj, of twins* IDENTICAL 3b (derived from a single egg)

**Monroe Doctrine** /mən'roh, mun-/ *n* a statement of US foreign policy expressing opposition to extension of European control or influence in the western hemisphere [James *Monroe* †1831 US President]

**monseigneur** /,monse'nyuh/ *n, pl* **messeigneurs** /,mayse-'nyuh/ a French dignitary (e g a prince) – used as a title pre-.ceding a title of office or rank [Fr, lit., my lord]

**monsieur** /mə'syuh/ *n, pl* **messieurs** /me'syuh, mə'syuhz/ *often cap* – used as a title equivalent to *Mr* before the name of a French-speaking man or used without a name as a generalized term of direct address ⟨*how would* ~ *like his hair cut?*⟩ [MF, lit., my lord]

**monsignor** /,monsin'yaw/ *n, pl* **monsignors, monsignori** /-ri/ a high-ranking Roman Catholic priest having a dignity or titular distinction (e g of chamberlain, domestic prelate, or protonotary apostolic) usu conferred by the pope – used as a title preceding the surname or the christian name and surname [It *monsignore*, fr Fr *monseigneur*] – **monsignorial** *adj*

**monsoon** /mon'soohn/ *n* 1 a seasonal wind, esp in the Indian ocean and S Asia, blowing from the SW in summer and the NE in winter 2 the season of the SW monsoon in India and adjacent countries, usu marked by very heavy rains *synonyms* see ¹WIND [obs D *monssoen*, fr Pg *monção*, fr Ar *mawsim* time, season] – **monsoonal** *adj*

**mons pubis** /,monz 'pyoohbis/ *n, pl* **montes pubis** /'monteez/ a rounded raised mass of fatty tissue over the pubic bone and above the vulva of the human female [NL, lit., pubic hill]

**monster** /'monstə/ *n* 1a an animal or plant of (grotesquely) abnormal form or structure b an (imaginary) animal of strange or incredible shape or form that is usu dangerous or horrifying 2 one exceptionally large for its kind ⟨*that spider was a real* ~⟩ 3 something monstrous; *esp* a person of appalling ugliness, wickedness, or cruelty [ME *monstre*, fr MF, fr L *monstrum* omen, supernatural event, monster, fr *monēre* to warn]

**monstrance** /'monstrəns/ *n* a vessel in which the consecrated HOST (holy bread) is exposed for the veneration of the faithful [MF, fr ML *monstrantia*, fr L *monstrant-, monstrans*, prp of *monstrare* to show – more at MUSTER]

**monstrosity** /mon'strosəti/ *n* 1a MONSTER 1a b something deviating wildly from the normal; a freak 2 the quality or state of being monstrous ⟨*the utter* ~ *of the crime*⟩ 3a an object of terrifying size, force, or complexity b an excessively bad or shocking example; a hideous thing ⟨*the old town hall was a red-brick* ~⟩

**monstrous** /'monstrəs/ *adj* 1 having extraordinary often overwhelming size; gigantic 2 having the qualities or appearance of a monster 3a extraordinarily ugly or vicious; horrible ⟨*flew into a* ~ *rage*⟩ b outrageously wrong or ridiculous ⟨*a* ~ *lie*⟩ c shocking, appalling ⟨~ *treatment of political prisoners*⟩ 4 *of an animal or plant* deviating greatly from the natural form or character; abnormal 5 *obs* strange, unnatural – **monstrously** *adv*, **monstrousness** *n*

**mons veneris** /,monz 'venəris/ *n, pl* **montes veneris** /,monteez/ MONS PUBIS [NL, lit., hill of Venus or of venery]

**montadale** /'montə,dayl/ *n* any of a N American breed of white-faced hornless sheep noted for their heavy fleece and good meat production [*Montana*, state of USA + *dale*]

**montage** /'montahzh/ *n* 1a a composite picture made by combining several separate pictures b a literary, musical, or artistic composition made up of various different elements 2a a method of film editing in which the chronological sequence of events is interrupted by juxtaposed or rapidly succeeding shots intended to suggest an association of ideas or convey a narrative b a film sequence using montage [Fr, fr *monter* to mount]

**montagnard** /,montan'yah/ (*Fr* mɔ̃tanjar)/ *n, often cap* 1 (a member of) any of several N American Indian peoples living in the Rocky mountains of Canada 2 (a member of) a people inhabiting the highland region in southern Vietnam bordering on Cambodia [Fr, lit., mountaineer, fr *montagne* mountain] – **montagnard** *adj, often cap*

**montane** /'montayn/ *adj* of, being, or growing or living in mountainous areas, esp the area of relatively moist cool slopes just below the TREE LINE that is characterized by large evergreen trees [L *montanus* of a mountain – more at MOUNTAIN]

**Montanist** /'montǝnist/ *n* an adherent of a heretical Christian sect of the late second century stressing the continuing prophetic gifts of the Holy Spirit [*Montanus*, 2nd-c schismatic in Asia Minor] – **Montanism** *n*

**montan wax** /'montan/ *n* a hard brittle wax obtained usu from LIGNITE (brownish type of coal) and used, esp formerly, in polishes, carbon paper, and electrically insulating materials [L *montanus* of a mountain]

**montbretia** /mon(t)'breesh(y)ǝ, mom–/ *n* a widely grown hybrid plant (*Crocosmia* X *crocosmiflora*) of the iris family, with bright showy yellow or orange flowers [NL, fr A F E Coquebert de *Montbret* †1801 Fr naturalist]

**monte** /'monti/ *n* 1 a card game in which players select any two of four cards exposed in a layout and bet that one of them will be matched before the other as cards are dealt one at a time from the pack 2 THREE-CARD MONTE [Sp, lit., bank, fr It, mountain, heap, bank, fr L *mont-, mons* mountain]

**Monte Carlo** /,monti 'kahloh/ *adj* of or involving the use of random sampling techniques to obtain approximate solutions to mathematical or physical problems, esp in terms of a range of values each of which has a calculated probability of being the solution ⟨~ *methods*⟩ [*Monte Carlo* in Monaco, famous for its gambling casino]

**monteith** /mǝn'teeth/ *n* a large usu silver punch bowl with a scalloped rim [*Monteith*, 17th-c Sc eccentric who wore a cloak with a scalloped hem]

**Montessorian** /,monti'sawri-ǝn/ *adj* of or being a system of teaching young children through free but guided play with special apparatus [Maria *Montessori* †1952 It physician & educator]

**month** /munth/ *n* 1 a measure of time corresponding nearly to the period of the moon's revolution round the earth and amounting to approximately 4 weeks or 30 days or $^1/_{12}$ of a year 2 *pl* an indefinite usu protracted period of time ⟨*he has been gone for* ~s⟩ 3 one ninth of the typical duration of human pregnancy ⟨*she was in her 8th* ~⟩ [ME, fr OE *mōnath;* akin to OHG *mānōd* month, OE *mōna* moon] – **monthlong** *adj*

**¹monthly** /'munthli/ *adv* every month; once a month; by the month

**²monthly** *adj* 1 payable or reckoned by the month 2 done, occurring, or published every month

**³monthly** *n* 1 a monthly periodical 2 *pl, informal* a menstrual period

**Monthly Meeting** *n taking sing or pl vb* a district unit of an organization of Quakers

**month of Sundays** *n, informal* a very long period of time ⟨*won't catch a bus in a* ~⟩

**month's mind** *n* a Roman Catholic requiem mass for a person a month after his/her death

**monticule** /'montikyoohl/ *n* a small mound or hill; *esp* a subordinate cone of a volcano [Fr, fr LL *monticulus,* dim. of L *mont-, mons* mountain – more at MOUNT]

**Montilla** /mon'tilǝ/ *n* a typically dry white wine made in the Córdoba area of Spain that resembles sherry and is usu drunk as an aperitif [Sp, fr *Montilla,* town in S Spain (cf AMONTILLADO)]

**montmorillonite** /,montmǝ'rilǝniet/ *n* (any of a group of clay minerals derived by chemical alteration from) a soft clayey mineral that consists of a SILICATE of aluminium chemically combined with water molecules, has considerable capacity for exchanging part of the aluminium for magnesium and alkalis, and is the chief constituent of FULLER'S EARTH [Fr, fr *Montmorillon,* commune in W France] – **montmorillonitic** *adj*

**monument** /'monyoomǝnt/ *n* 1 a written legal document or record; a treatise 2a a lasting evidence or reminder of someone or something notable or influential b a memorial stone, sculpture, or structure erected to commemorate a person or event 3 a building, structure, or site of historical or archaeological importance 4 a written tribute 5 *NAm* a boundary marker (e g an upright stone) [ME, burial place, legal record, fr L *monumentum,* lit., memorial, fr *monēre* to remind – more at MIND]

**monumental** /,monyoo'mentl/ *adj* 1a of, serving as, or like a monument b occurring or used on a monument ⟨*a* ~ *inscription*⟩ 2 imposing, outstanding ⟨*a* ~ *work*⟩ 3 very great in degree ⟨*the book was a* ~ *failure*⟩ ⟨*their* ~ *arrogance*⟩ – **monumentally** *adv*, **monumentality** *n*

**monumental·ize, -ise** /,monyoo'mentǝliez/ *vt* to establish a lasting memorial or record of

**-mony** /-mǝni/ *comb form* (→ *n*) state or quality of ⟨*acri*mony⟩ ⟨*matri*mony⟩ [MF & L; MF *-monie, -moine,* fr L *-monia, -monium;* akin to L *-mentum* -ment]

**monzonite** /'monzǝniet/ *n* a coarse-grained IGNEOUS rock formed by the solidification of molten material below the earth's surface and composed of the feldspar minerals PLAGIOCLASE and ORTHOCLASE in about equal quantities together with BIOTITE and HORNBLENDE [Fr, fr Mt *Monzoni* in NE Italy] – **monzonitic** *adj*

**moo** /mooh/ *vi or n* (to make) the throat noise characteristic of a cow [imit]

**mooch** /moohch/ *vb, informal vi* 1 to wander aimlessly or disconsolately; *also* to sneak – usu + *around, about,* or *along* 2 *NAm* to sponge, cadge ~ *vt, chiefly NAm* 1 to steal; MAKE AWAY WITH 2 to cadge, beg [prob fr Fr dial. *muchier* to hide, lurk] – **moocher** *n*

**¹mood** /moohd/ *n* 1a a predominant emotion or frame of mind; *also* the evocation of mood, esp in art or literature b the right frame of mind ⟨*you must be in the* ~, *or you'll fall asleep – The Listener*⟩ 2 a fit of often silent anger or bad temper; a sulk ⟨*don't talk to him, he's in a* ~⟩ 3 a prevailing attitude ⟨*politicians who misjudge the* ~ *of the public*⟩ [ME, fr OE *mōd;* akin to OHG *muot* mood, L *mos* will, custom]

**²mood** *n* 1 any of several traditional subclasses of the forms of the SYLLOGISM (statement in logic consisting of two premises and the conclusion drawn from them) 2a a distinct form or set of forms of a verb used to express whether the action or state it denotes is considered a fact, a possibility, or a wish ⟨*the subjunctive* ~⟩ b a similar distinct form or set of verb forms used to express whether the sentence in which it appears conveys a statement, a command, or a question ⟨*the interrogative* ~⟩ 3 MODE 1b [alter. of ¹*mode*]

**¹moody** /'moohdi/ *adj* 1 sullen, gloomy 2 subject to sharply fluctuating moods; temperamental – **moodily** *adv,* **moodiness** *n*

**²moody** *n, slang* a fit of silent anger; a sulk ⟨*she threw a* ~ *and walked out*⟩

**Moog** /'moohg/, **Moog synthesizer** *trademark* – used for a musical synthesizer

**moola, moolah** /'moohlǝ/ *n, slang* money [origin unknown]

**¹moon** /moohn/ *n* 1a the earth's natural satellite that shines by reflecting the sun's light b one complete moon cycle consisting of four phases c a satellite of a planet 2 moonlight ⟨*there is a* ~ *tonight*⟩ 3 something that resembles a moon (e g the crescent-shaped marking at the base of a fingernail) 4 *poetic* a lunar month ⟨*many* ~s *ago*⟩ – **once in a blue moon** very rarely – **over the moon** extremely pleased; overjoyed [ME *mone,* fr OE *mōna;* akin to OHG *māno* moon, L *mensis* month, Gk *mēn* month, *mēnē* moon] – **moonless** *adj,* **moonlet** *n,* **moonlike** *adj*

**²moon** *vi* 1 *informal* to move about listlessly 2 *informal* to spend time in idle gazing or daydreaming 3 *slang* to expose one's bare buttocks to someone as a taunt □ *(1&2)* often + *around* or *about*

**moonbeam** /-,beem/ *n* a ray of light from the moon

**moon blindness** *n* a recurrent inflammation of the eyes that affects horses [fr its being formerly attributed to the moon's influence] – **moon-blind** *adj*

**mooncalf** /-,kahf/ *n* 1 a monster 2 a simpleton

**moon daisy** *n* OXEYE DAISY

**'moon-,faced** *adj* having a very round face

**moonfish** /-,fish/ *n, pl* **moonfish, moonfishes** 1 any of various silvery or yellowish sea fishes with thin deep bodies 2 OPAH

**moonglow** /'moohn,gloh/ *n* moonlight ⟨~ *saturates an empty sky –* Henry Miller⟩

**moonie** /'moohni/ *n, often cap* a member of a religious sect, founded in 1954 by Sun Myung Moon, whose adherents live in communes, donate all their possessions to the movement, and believe that the founder has been given a divine mission to complete the task, originally given to Adam and then to Christ, of uniting the whole world in a perfect sinless family [Sun Myung *Moon* b1920 Korean industrialist & religious leader]

**¹moonlight** /'moohn,liet/ *n* the light of the moon

**²moonlight** *adj* moonlit ⟨*a bright* ~ *night*⟩

**³moonlight** *vi* **moonlighted** to hold a second job in addition to a regular one [back-formation fr *moonlighter* one whose activities are done at night] – **moonlighter** *n*

**moonlit** /-,lit/ *adj* lighted (as if) by the moon

**moonquake** /-,kwayk/ *n* a ground tremor on the moon

**moonrat** /-,rat/ *n* an insect-eating ratlike mammal (*Echinosorex* *gymnurus*) of SE Asia, with a long snout, long naked tail, and whitish-grey fur [fr its whitish colour]

**moonrise** /'moohn,riez/ *n* (the time of) the rising of the moon above the horizon

**moonscape** /'moohn,skayp/ *n* the surface of the moon as seen or as depicted; *also* a landscape similarly barren or devastated

**moonseed** /'moohn,seed/ *n* any of a genus (*Menispermum* of the family Menispermaceae) of twining plants with crescent-shaped seeds and red or black fruits

**moonset** /'moohn,set/ *n* (the time of) the descent of the moon below the horizon

**moonshine** /-,shien/ *n* 1 moonlight 2 empty talk; nonsense 3 *informal* spirits; *esp* illegally distilled whisky

**moonshiner** /-,shienə/ *n, chiefly NAm* a maker or seller of illicit spirits

**moon shot** *n* the launching of a spacecraft to the moon or its vicinity

**moonstone** /-,stohn/ *n* a transparent or milky-white translucent variety of FELDSPAR with a pearly bluish lustre that is used as a gem

**moonstruck** /-,struk/ *adj* affected (as if) by the moon: eg **a** mentally unbalanced **b** romantically sentimental **c** bemused

**moonwards** /'moohnwədz/ *adv* towards the moon – **moon-ward** *adj*

**moony** /'moohni/ *adj* 1 of or like the moon 2 moonlit 3 *informal* inanely dreamy; moonstruck

¹**moor** /maw, mooə/ *n, chiefly Br* an expanse of open rolling uncultivated usu peaty land that is often boggy and is typically overgrown by heathers, grasses, and sedges – compare HEATH [ME *mor*, fr OE *mōr*; akin to OHG *meri* sea – more at MARINE] – **moorland** *n*

²**moor** *vt* to fasten (eg a boat or buoy) with cables, lines, or anchors ~ *vi* 1 to secure a vessel by mooring; anchor 2 to be made fast [ME *moren*; akin to MD *meren, maren* to tie, moor]

**Moor** *n* 1 a member of the mixed Arab and BERBER people that conquered Spain in the 8th century AD 2 BERBER (member of a non-Negro N African people) [ME *More*, fr MF, fr L *Maurus* inhabitant of Mauretania, ancient country in N Africa] – **Moorish** *adj*

**moorage** /'mawrij, 'mooərij/ *n* 1 a charge made for mooring 2 a place to moor

**moorfowl** /'maw,fowl, 'mooə-/ *n, pl* **moorfowl** RED GROUSE

**moorhen** /'maw,hen, 'mooə-/ *n* a small stout blackish common bird (*Gallinula chloropus*) of the RAIL family that has a red beak and nests in reeds and bushes near fresh water, and often in ponds in towns or parks

**mooring** /'mawring, 'mooəring/ *n* 1 an act of fastening a boat, aircraft, etc with ropes or anchors 2a a place where or an object (eg an anchor with a floating buoy) to which a craft can be made fast **b moorings** *pl*, **mooring** a device (eg a rope or chain) by which something, esp a boat or ship, is secured in place ⟨*she may have dragged her* ~s⟩ 3 *pl* principles used as a guide to behaviour ⟨*lose one's* ~⟩

**moose** /moohs/ *n, pl* **moose** 1 a large N American deer (*Alces alces*) that belongs to the same species as the European elk and has very large flattened antlers 2 the European elk [of Algonquian origin; akin to Natick *moos* moose]

¹**moot** /mooht/ *n* 1 an early English local assembly primarily for the administration of justice; esp one held by the freemen of an Anglo-Saxon community 2 a mock court in which law students argue hypothetical cases for practice 3 *obs* argument, discussion [ME, fr OE *mōt*; akin to OE *mētan* to meet – more at MEET]

²**moot** *vt* to put forward for discussion; broach; BRING UP ⟨*the idea was first* ~ed *years ago*⟩

³**moot** *adj* open to question; debatable ⟨*whether he'll succeed is a* ~ *point*⟩

¹**mop** /mop/ *n* 1 an implement consisting of a head made of absorbent material (eg sponge or a bundle of coarse yarn) fastened to a long handle and used esp for cleaning floors 2 something that resembles a mop; *esp* a shock of hair [ME *mappe*, perh deriv of L *mappa* napkin, towel]

²**mop** *vt* -**pp**- 1 to clean by mopping ⟨~ *the floors*⟩ ⟨~ *up the water from the burst pipe*⟩ – often + *up* 2 to wipe as if with a mop ⟨~ped *his brow with a handkerchief*⟩ – **mopper** *n*

**mop up** *vb, informal* 1 to eat greedily; POLISH OFF ⟨*he mopped the rice pudding* up *in no time*⟩ 2 to overcome decisively; trounce 3 to kill (eg stragglers) or take prisoner after a suc-

cessful raid or battle 4 to absorb, take up, or deal with (esp a remnant or remainder) ⟨*mopping up the pool of unemployed graduates – The Economist*⟩ to complete a project or transaction

¹**mope** /mohp/ *vi* to give oneself up to brooding; become listless or dejected [prob fr obs *mop, mope* fool] – **moper** *n*

²**mope** *n* 1 one who mopes 2 *pl but taking sing or pl vb* low spirits; *the* blues 3 *informal* a fit of sulking or low spirits ⟨*she's having a* ~ *in her bedroom*⟩

**moped** /'mohped/ *n* a low-powered motorcycle whose engine can be pedal-assisted (eg for starting) [Sw, fr *mo*tor motor + *ped*al pedal]

**mop fair** *n* an English fair where farmhands and servants were formerly hired [perh fr the implement (eg a mop) said to have been carried by each servant at the fair to show the kind of work he/she could do]

**mopoke** /'mohpohk/ *n* 1 any of several Australian FROG-MOUTHS (nocturnal birds) (esp *Podargus strigoides*) 2 BOOBOOK (type of owl) 3 *Austr* a fool □ called also MOREPORK [imit]

**moppet** /'mopit/ *n, informal, chiefly apprec* a young child; *esp* a little girl [obs *mop* fool, child, fr ME]

'**mop-,up** *n, informal* a concluding action (eg of a battle)

**moquette** /mo'ket/ *n* a carpet or upholstery fabric with a velvety pile [Fr]

**mor** /maw/ *n* a soil humus usu found in forests, that forms a distinct layer of organic matter above the underlying mineral soil [Dan]

**moraine** /mo'rayn/ *n* an accumulation of earth and stones carried and finally deposited by a glacier [Fr] – **morainal, morainic** *adj*

¹**moral** /'morəl/ *adj* 1a of or being principles of right and wrong in behaviour; ethical ⟨~ *judgments*⟩ **b** expressing or teaching a conception of right behaviour ⟨*a* ~ *poem*⟩ **c** conforming to a standard of right behaviour ⟨*a very* ~ *person*⟩ **d** sanctioned by, resulting from, or operative on one's conscience or ethical judgment ⟨*a* ~ *obligation*⟩ ⟨*a* ~ *right*⟩ **e** capable of distinguishing right and wrong ⟨*man is a* ~ *being*⟩ 2 very probable though not proved; virtual ⟨*a* ~ *certainty*⟩ 3 of intangible and usu nonpractical benefit ⟨*a* ~ *victory*⟩ ⟨~ *support*⟩ [ME, fr MF, fr L *moralis*, fr *mor-, mos* custom – more at MOOD] – **morally** *adv*

²**moral** *n* 1 the moral significance or practical lesson (eg of a story); *also* a usu concluding passage pointing out such a lesson 2 *pl* moral practices or teachings; standards of conduct ⟨*a man of loose* ~s⟩

**morale** /mə'rahl, mə'ral/ *n* the mental and emotional condition (eg of enthusiasm, confidence, or loyalty) of an individual or group with regard to the function or tasks at hand ⟨*the* ~ *of the troops was low after the withdrawal*⟩ [modif of Fr *moral* morale, fr *moral*, adj]

**moral hazard** *n* the possibility of loss to an insurance company arising from the possibly dishonest character or circumstances of the insured

**moralism** /'morə,liz(ə)m/ *n* 1a the habit or practice of moralizing **b** a conventional moral attitude or saying 2 an often exaggerated emphasis on moral righteousness (eg in religion or politics)

**moralist** /'morəlist/ *n* 1 somebody who leads a moral life 2 a teacher or student of morals; a philosopher or writer concerned with moral principles and problems 3 *chiefly derog* one concerned with regulating the morals of others – **moralistic** *adj*, **moralistically** *adv*

**morality** /mə'raləti/ *n* 1 a moral speech, statement, or lesson 2 a system or sphere of moral conduct ⟨*Christian* ~⟩ 3 (degree of conformity to standards of) right conduct or moral correctness ⟨*questioned the* ~ *of his act*⟩

**morality play** *n* a form of drama popular esp in the 15th and 16th centuries in which the characters personify moral qualities or abstractions (eg pride or youth) – compare MIRACLE PLAY

**moral·ize, -ise** /'morəliez/ *vt* 1 to interpret morally; draw a moral from ⟨*mistaken attempts to* ~ *the play*⟩ 2 to make moral or morally better ~ *vi* to discourse on morality, esp tediously or sanctimoniously; *esp* to draw attention to moral lapses – **moralizer** *n*, **moralization** *n*

**moral philosophy** *n* ethics

**Moral Rearmament** *n* a worldwide movement for spiritual reform developing out of the OXFORD GROUP during the 1930s and applying its doctrines and techniques esp to problems of international relations

**moral theology** *n* ethics treated as an aspect of theology

**moral tutor** *n* a tutor at the colleges of some British universities who is responsible for guiding and advising the students in his/her care

**morass** /mə'ras/ *n* **1** a marsh, swamp **2** something that ensnares, confuses, or impedes ⟨*a ~ of self-doubt*⟩ [D *moeras*, modif of OF *maresc*, of Gmc origin; akin to OE *mersc* marsh –more at MARSH] – **morassy** *adj*

**moratorium** /,morə'tawri·əm/ *n, pl* **moratoriums, moratoria** /-riə/ **1** a legally authorized period of delay in the performance of a legal obligation or the payment of a debt **2** a suspension of activity ⟨*ordered a ~ on arms sales*⟩ [NL, fr LL, neut of *moratorius* dilatory, fr L *moratus*, pp of *morari* to delay, fr *mora* delay]

**Moravian** /mə'rayvi·ən/ *n* **1** a member of a Protestant denomination arising from a 15th-century religious reform movement in Bohemia and Moravia **2a** a native or inhabitant of Moravia **b** the group of Czech dialects spoken by the Moravians [*Moravia*, region in central Czechoslovakia] – **Moravian** *adj*

**moray eel** /'muri, 'moray; *also* mə'ray/ *n* any of numerous large often brightly coloured eels (family Muraenidae) that have sharp teeth capable of inflicting a savage bite, that occur in warm seas, and that include a Mediterranean eel (*Muraena helena*) valued for food [Pg *moréia*, fr L *muraena*, fr Gk *myraina*]

**morbid** /'mawbid/ *adj* **1a** (characteristic) of disease ⟨*~ anatomy*⟩ **b** affected with or induced by disease ⟨*a ~ condition*⟩ **2** abnormally susceptible to or characterized by gloomy or unwholesome feelings; *esp* having an unnatural preoccupation with death **3** grisly, gruesome ⟨*the ~ details*⟩ ⟨*~ curiosity*⟩ [L *morbidus* diseased, fr *morbus* disease; akin to Gk *marainein* to waste away – more at SMART] – **morbidly** *adv*, **morbidness** *n*

**morbidity** /maw'bidəti/ *n* **1** the quality or state of being morbid **2** the incidence of disease; *esp* the relative incidence of a particular disease or type of disease in a particular place or among a specific group of individuals

**mordacious** /maw'dayshəs/ *adj, formal* **1** biting or sarcastic in style or manner; caustic ⟨*~ wit*⟩ **2** given to biting [L *mordac-, mordax* biting, fr *mordēre* to bite – more at SMART] – **mordacity** *n*

¹**mordant** /'mawd(ə)nt/ *adj* **1** caustic or sharply critical in thought, manner, or style; incisive ⟨*a ~ wit*⟩ **2** acting as a mordant **3** burning, pungent [MF, prp of *mordre* to bite, fr L *mordēre*] – **mordancy** *n*, **mordantly** *adv*

²**mordant** *n* **1** a chemical that fixes a dye in or on a substance by combining with the dye to form an insoluble compound **2** a corroding substance (eg an acid) used in etching

³**mordant** *vt* to treat (eg a fabric) with a mordant

**mordent** /'mawd(ə)nt/ *n* an unnecessary but ornamental musical phrase made by a quick alternation of a principal note with the note immediately above or below it – called also PRALLTRILLER [Ger, fr It *mordente*, fr L *mordent-, mordens*, prp of *mordēre*]

¹**more** /maw/ *adj* **1** greater in quantity or number ⟨*something ~ than she expected*⟩ ⟨*seven is two ~ than five*⟩ **2** additional, further ⟨*three ~ guests arrived*⟩ ⟨*have some ~ tea*⟩ ⟨*what ~ do you want?*⟩ [ME, fr OE *māra;* akin to OE *mā*, adv, more, OHG *mēr*, OIr *mōr* large] – **neither/nothing more or/nor less than** simply, plainly

*usage* One should be careful to avoid ambiguity when using **more** before an adjective. A sentence such as ⟨*here are three* **more** *interesting people for you to meet*⟩ has two meanings.

²**more** *adv* **1a** as an additional amount ⟨*not much ~ to do*⟩ **b** moreover, again ⟨*summer is here once ~*⟩ **2** to a greater degree or extent ⟨*you should practise ~*⟩ ⟨*~ sad than angry*⟩ ⟨*costs ~ than making your own beer – SEU S*⟩ – often used with an adjective or adverb to form the comparative ⟨*much ~ evenly matched*⟩ – **more and more** to a progressively increasing degree – **more often than not** at most times; usually – **more or less 1** to some extent or degree; somewhat ⟨*they were more or less willing to help*⟩ **2** almost, nearly ⟨*it's more or less over*⟩ – **more than** very, exceedingly ⟨*was more than happy*⟩

³**more** *n, pl* **more 1** a greater quantity, amount, or part ⟨*~ than one school has closed*⟩ ⟨*hope to see ~ of her*⟩ ⟨*the ~ the merrier*⟩ **2** an additional amount ⟨*tell me ~*⟩ ⟨*~ than meets the eye*⟩ **3** additional ones ⟨*many ~ were found as the search continued*⟩

*usage* The expression **more** *than one* takes a singular verb.

**moreen** /mo'reen/ *n* a strong fabric of wool, wool and cotton, or cotton that has a plain glossy or watered-silk finish and is used esp in furnishing [prob irreg fr *moiré*]

**moreish** *also* **more-ish** /'mawrish/ *adj, informal* so tasty as to cause a desire for more ⟨*fruity baked puddings are* more-ish *– Good Housekeeping*⟩

**morel** /mo'rel/ *n* any of several large edible fungi (genus *Morchella*); *esp* one (*Morchella esculenta*) with a light yellowish-brown cap [Fr *morille*, of Gmc origin; akin to OHG *morhila* morel]

**morello** /mə'reloh/ *n, pl* **morellos** a cultivated red-skinned SOUR CHERRY used esp in jams [prob modif of Flem *amarelle, marelle*, fr ML *amarellum*, a type of cultivated cherry, fr L *amarus* sour]

**moreover** /maw'rohvə/ *adv* in addition to what has been said – used to introduce new matter

**morepork** /'maw,pawk/ *n* MOPOKE

**mores** /'mawreez/ *n pl* the fixed, morally binding, customs of a particular group; prescribed and accepted conventions or modes of behaviour [L, pl of *mor-, mos* custom – more at MOOD]

¹**moresque** /maw'resk/ *adj, often cap* typical of Moorish art or architecture [Fr, fr Sp *morisco*, fr *moro* Moor, fr L *Maurus*]

²**moresque** *n, often cap* an ornament or decorative motif in Moorish style

**morganatic** /,mawgə'natik/ *adj* of or being a marriage between a member of a royal or noble family and an ordinary person in which the latter, and the children of the marriage, remain unennobled and succeed to no titles or property of the parent of higher rank [NL *matrimonium ad morganaticam*, lit., marriage with morning gift] – **morganatically** *adv*

**morganite** /'mawgəniet/ *n* a rose-coloured variety of BERYL used as a gemstone [J P *Morgan* †1913 US financier]

**morgen** /'mawgən/ *n, pl* **morgen** a Dutch and Southern African unit of land area equal to about 8563 square metres (about 2 acres) [D, lit., morning]

**morgue** /mawg/ *n* **1** a mortuary **2** a collection of reference works and files in a newspaper office **3** *informal* a gloomy dispiriting place

**moribund** /'mori,bund/ *adj* **1** approaching death; dying **2** near to the end of existence; lacking all force or vitality [L *moribundus*, fr *mori* to die – more at MURDER] – **moribundity** *n*

¹**morion** /'mawriən/ *n* a high-crested 16th-century helmet with no visor [MF]

²**morion** *n* a nearly black variety of CAIRNGORM (type of quartz) used as a gemstone [modif of L *mormorion*]

**Morisco** /mə'riskoh/ *n, pl* **Moriscos, Moriscoes** a Moor; *esp* a Spanish Moor [Sp, fr *morisco*, adj, fr *moro* Moor] – **Morisco** *adj*

**Mormon** /'mawmən/ *n* a member of the Church of Jesus Christ of Latter-Day Saints, founded in 1830 in the USA by Joseph Smith, and following precepts contained in their sacred text, the "Book of Mormon" [*Mormon*, alleged 4th-c editor of the "Book of Mormon"] – **Mormonism** *n*

**morn** /mawn/ *n, chiefly poetic* **1** the dawn **2** the morning [ME, fr OE *morgen;* akin to OHG *morgan* morning, L *merus* pure, unmixed]

**mornay sauce** /'mawnay/ *n* a rich creamy cheese sauce [perh fr Philippe de *Mornay* †1623 Fr Huguenot leader]

**morning** /'mawning/ *n* **1a** the dawn **b** the time from sunrise to noon **c** the time from midnight to noon **2** an early period (eg of time or life); *the* beginning **3** a daily newspaper printed at night and available the following morning ⟨*the mad axeman story is in all the ~s*⟩ [ME, fr *morn* + *-ing* (as in *evening*)] – **in the morning** tomorrow morning

**morning-after pill** *n* a drug (eg an OESTROGEN), taken by mouth, that blocks implantation of a fertilized egg in the human womb and so prevents conception [fr its being taken after rather than before intercourse]

**morning coat** *n* a man's tailcoat that is worn on formal occasions during the day

**morning dress** *n* men's dress for formal occasions during the day (eg a wedding) that includes a morning coat, a top hat, and usu striped grey trousers

**morning glory** *n* any of various usu twining plants (esp genus *Ipomoea*) of the bindweed family with showy purplish, blue, pink, or white trumpet-shaped flowers

**Morning Prayer** *n* a daily morning service of the Anglican church

**morning room** *n* a living room for use in the morning

**mornings** /'mawningz/ *adv, chiefly NAm* in the morning; on any morning ⟨~ *we'd go swimming*⟩

**morning sickness** *n* nausea and vomiting that occur esp on rising in the morning during the earlier months of pregnancy

**morning star** *n* a bright planet, specif Venus, seen in the eastern sky before or at sunrise – compare EVENING STAR

**Moro** /'mawroh/ *n, pl* **Moros**, *esp collectively* **Moro** 1 a member of any of several Muslim peoples of the S Philippines 2 any of the AUSTRONESIAN languages of the Moro peoples [Sp, lit., Moor, fr L *Maurus*]

**morocco** /mə'rokoh/ *n* a fine leather made from goatskin tanned with SUMACH and used esp for bookbinding [*Morocco*, country in NW Africa]

**moron** /'mawron/ *n* 1 MENTAL DEFECTIVE 2 *informal* a very stupid person [irreg fr Gk *mōros* foolish; akin to Skt *mūra* foolish] – **moronism** *n*, **moronic** *adj*, **moronically** *adv*, **moronity** *n*

**morose** /mə'rohs/ *adj* 1 having a sullen and gloomy disposition 2 marked by or expressive of gloom ⟨a ~ *little speech on the need for economy*⟩ [L *morosus*, lit., capricious, fr *mor-*, *mos* will – more at MOOD] – **morosely** *adv*, **moroseness** *n*, **morosity** *n*

**¹morph** /mawf/ *n* ²ALLOMORPH (alternative version of a word part) [back-formation fr *morpheme*]

**²morph** *n* 1 any of the variant forms of an animal species that exists in different forms distinguishable by colour, size, etc; *also* an animal or localized group of animals having this form 2 any of the variant forms exhibited by some animals during the course of their LIFE CYCLES [Gk *morphē* form]

**morph-** /mawf-/, **morpho-** *comb form* 1 form ⟨*morphogenesis*⟩ 2 relating to form and ⟨*morphofunctional*⟩ [Ger, fr Gk, fr *morphē*]

**-morph** /-mawf/ *comb form* (→ *n*) one having (such) a form ⟨*isomorph*⟩ [ISV, fr *-morphous* having (such) a form, fr Gk *-morphos*, fr *morphē* form] – **-morphic**, **-morphous** *comb form* (→ *adj*), **-morphy** *comb form* (→ *n*)

**morphactin** /maw'faktin/ *n* any of several synthetic fluorine-containing chemical compounds that tend to suppress growth and produce changes in form and structure in plants [prob fr *morph-* + L *actus*, pp of *agere* to drive, do + E *-in* – more at AGENT]

**morphallaxis** /ˌmawfə'laksis/ *n, pl* **morphallaxes** /-seez/ the regeneration of an organism or of one of its parts by the reorganization and transformation of existing cells and tissues without cell proliferation – compare EPIMORPHOSIS [NL, fr *morph-* + Gk *allaxis* exchange, fr *allassein* to change, exchange, fr *allos* other – more at ELSE]

**morpheme** /'mawfeem/ *n* a meaningful linguistic unit that contains no smaller meaningful parts and can be either a free form (e g *pin*) or a bound form (e g the *-s* of *pins*) – compare LEXEME, PHONEME [Fr *morphème*, fr *morph-* + *-ème* (as in *phonème* phoneme)] – **morphemic** *adj*, **morphemically** *adv*

**morphemics** /maw'feemiks/ *n taking sing vb* 1 the study of morphemes and esp of word structure 2 the structure of a language in terms of morphemes

**morphia** /'mawfi·ə/ *n* morphine [NL, fr L *Morpheus*, god of dreams & sleep]

**morphine** /'mawfeen/ *n* an addictive narcotic drug, $C_{17}H_{19}NO_3$, obtained from opium, that is used esp as a powerful painkiller and sedative [Fr, fr *Morpheus*] – **morphinic** *adj*

**morphinism** /'mawfiniz(ə)m/ *n* addiction to morphine

**morphism** /'mawfiz(ə)m/ *n* HOMOMORPHISM (mathematical function for transforming one set into another)

**-morphism** /-'mawfiz(ə)m/ *comb form* (→ *n*) 1 quality or state of having (such) a form ⟨*heteromorphism*⟩ 2 conceptualization in (such) a form ⟨*anthropomorphism*⟩ [LL *-morphus* -morphous, fr Gk *-morphos*]

**morpho** /'mawfoh/ *n, pl* **morphos** any of a genus (*Morpho*) of large showy tropical American butterflies that typically have a brilliant blue metallic lustre on the upper surface of the wings [NL, genus name, fr Gk *Morphō*, epithet of the goddess Aphrodite]

**morpho-** – see MORPH-

**morphogenesis** /ˌmawfoh'jenəsis/ *n* 1 (the development of form and structure in an organism by) the formation and differentiation of tissues and organs 2 the formation and development of land forms [NL] – **morphogenetic** *adj*, **morphogenetically** *adv*

**morphology** /maw'foləji/ *n* 1 (a branch of biology that deals with) the form and structure of animals and plants 2a a study

and description of word formation in a language, including formation by adding inflections and other suffixes and prefixes, and by compounding **b** the system of word-forming elements and processes in a language 3 (a study of) the structure or form of something ⟨*the ~ of the urban landscape*⟩ ⟨*changes in the ~ of heart muscle*⟩ ⟨*attempted a ~ of the political party – TLS*⟩ *synonyms* see GRAMMAR [Ger *morphologie*, fr *morph-* + *-logie* -logy] – **morphologist** *n*, **morphological** *adj*, **morphologically** *adv*

**morphometry** /maw'fomətri/ *n* the measurement of external form: e g **a** the measurement of anatomical structures (e g the lungs) **b** the measurement of land forms (e g lakes or drainage basins) – **morphometric** *also* **morphometrical** *adj*, **morphometrically** *adv*

**morphophonemics** /'mawfoh·fə'neemiks/ *n taking sing vb* 1 a study of the linguistically significant differences of pronunciation of a single MORPHEME (smallest meaningful unit of language) 2 the distribution of alternative forms (ALLOMORPHS) of a single MORPHEME (smallest meaningful unit of language) 3 the structure of a language in terms of morphophonemics [*morpheme* + *-o-* + *phonemics* ] – **morphophonemic** *adj*, **morphophonemically** *adv*

**morphophonology** /ˌmawfoh·fə'noləji/ *n* morphophonemics

**morris chair** /'moris/ *n* an armchair with an adjustable back and loose cushions [William *Morris* †1896 E writer, artist, & designer]

**morris dance** /'moris/ *n* any of several vigorous traditional English dances performed in the open air that often illustrate a legend (e g that of Robin Hood) or represent a ritual or activity (e g crop harvesting) and are peformed by groups of men wearing costumes usu consisting of white shirt and trousers, flowery hat, bells attached to garters and cross-braces, and often sticks or handkerchiefs which are used in the dances [ME *moreys daunce*, fr *moreys* Moorish (fr *More* Moor) + *daunce* dance] – **morris dancer** *n*, **morris dancing** *n*

**morris man** *n* a man who is a member of a morris dancing team

**morrow** /'moroh/ *n* 1 *formal* the next day 2 *archaic* the morning [ME *morn*, *morwen* morn]

**morse** /maws/ *n* a walrus [Lapp *morša*]

**Morse** /maws/, **Morse code** *n* a signalling code consisting of dots and dashes used to send messages by light or sound signals or esp by radio [Samuel *Morse* †1872 US artist & inventor]

**morsel** /'mawsl/ *n* 1 a small piece of food; a mouthful 2 a small quantity; a scrap ⟨*a last ~ of self-respect*⟩ 3 something usu small or brief that is delectable and pleasing ⟨*the shorter piano pieces include some choice ~* s⟩ [ME, fr OF, dim. of *mors* bite, fr L *morsus*, fr *morsus*, pp of *mordēre* to bite – more at SMART]

**mort** /mawt/ *n* a note sounded on a hunting horn when a deer is killed [prob alter. (influenced by MF *mort* death, fr L *mort-*, *mors*) of ME *mot* horn note, fr MF, word, horn note – more at MOT]

**Mortadella** /ˌmawtə'delə/ *n* a Bologna sausage made from beef, pork, and pork fat and cooked in steam [It, irreg fr L *murtatum* sausage seasoned with myrtle berries, fr *murtus*, *myrtus* myrtle]

**¹mortal** /'mawtl/ *adj* 1 causing or about to cause death; fatal ⟨a ~ *injury*⟩ 2a subject to death; not living forever ⟨~ *man*⟩ **b** humanly conceivable; earthly ⟨*every* ~ *thing*⟩ 3 marked by relentless hostility; implacable ⟨a ~ *enemy*⟩ 4 very great, intense, or severe ⟨~ *fear*⟩ ⟨a ~ *shame*⟩ 5 human ⟨*an all too ~ longing to be a somebody – Time*⟩ 6 of or connected with death ⟨~ *agony*⟩ 7 *informal* very tedious and prolonged ⟨*waited three ~ hours*⟩ [ME, fr MF, fr L *mortalis*, fr *mort-*, *mors* death – more at MURDER]

**²mortal** *n* 1 a human being 2 a person of a specified kind ⟨*what a careless ~ he always was*⟩

**mortality** /maw'taləti/ *n* 1 the quality or state of being mortal 2 the death of large numbers of people, animals, etc 3 the human race; mankind ⟨*take these tears, ~*'s *relief* – Alexander Pope⟩ 4a the number of deaths in a given time, place, or population **b mortality**, **mortality rate** the proportion of deaths to population; DEATH RATE ⟨*infant ~*⟩ **c** the number lost, or the rate of loss or failure

**mortality table** *n* a table showing life expectancy and death rate for people of a given age, job, etc, used esp for insurance purposes

**mortally** /'mawtl·i/ *adv* 1 in a deadly or fatal manner ⟨~ *wounded*⟩ 2 to an extreme degree; intensely ⟨~ *afraid*⟩

**mortal sin** *n* a sin (e g murder) that is deliberately committed and is so serious that according to Christian, esp Roman Catholic, theology it deprives the soul of divine grace – compare VENIAL SIN – **mortal sinner** *n*

¹**mortar** /'mawtə/ *n* 1 a strong usu bowl-shaped vessel (e g of stone) in which substances are pounded or ground with a pestle **2a** a usu muzzle-loading artillery gun whose tube is short in relation to its calibre and that fires projectiles at a relatively low speed and high trajectory **b** any of several similar firing devices [ME *morter*, fr OE *mortere* & MF *mortier*, fr L *mortarium*; akin to Gk *marainein* to waste away – more at SMART; (2) MF *mortier*]

²**mortar** *n* an easily worked building material, usu a mixture of cement and lime with sand and water, that hardens and is used to join bricks, stones, etc together or in plastering [ME *morter*, fr MF *mortier*, fr L *mortarium*]

³**mortar** *vt* to plaster or fix in place with mortar

**mortarboard** /-,bawd/ *n* 1 ¹HAWK 2 (board for holding mortar) **2** an academic cap consisting of a closely fitting crown with a stiff flat square attached on top and often a tassel

¹**mortgage** /'mawgij/ *n* 1 the transfer of the ownership of property, esp a building or land, as security usu for the repayment of a loan on condition that the property becomes redeemed on payment or performance according to stipulated terms **2a** the deed by which a mortgage transfer is made **b** the state of the property so transferred **c** the interest of the mortgagee in such property [ME *morgage*, fr MF, fr OF, fr *mort* dead (fr L *mortuus*, fr pp of *mori* to die) + *gage* security, pledge]

²**mortgage** *vt* 1 to transfer the ownership of (property) by a mortgage **2** to make subject to a claim or obligation; pledge ⟨~d *himself to the navy for seven years*⟩

**mortgagee** /,mawgi'jee/ *n* a person to whom property is mortgaged

**mortgagor** /'mawgijə, ,mawgi'jaw/ *also* **mortgager** /'mawgijə/ *n* a person who mortages his/her property

**mortician** /maw'tish(ə)n/ *n, chiefly NAm* an undertaker [L *mort-, mors* death]

**mortification** /,mawtifi'kaysh(ə)n/ *n* 1 the subjection and denial of bodily needs and desires by abstinence or self-inflicted suffering, esp by Christians to attain a state of grace **2** tissue death or decay; gangrene **3** (a sense of humiliation and shame caused by) something that wounds one's pride or self-respect

**mortify** /'mawtifie/ *vt* 1 to subdue or deaden (e g the body or bodily needs and desires), esp by abstinence or self-inflicted suffering **2** to subject to feelings of shame or acute embarrassment; humiliate **3** *obs* to destroy the strength, vitality, or functioning of ~ *vi* 1 to practise mortification; lead an ascetic life **2** to become gangrenous; decay [ME *mortifien*, fr MF *mortifier*, fr LL *mortificare*, fr L *mort-, mors*]

¹**mortise** *also* **mortice** /'mawtis/ *n* a hole, groove, or slot into or through which some other part fits or passes; *esp* a usu rectangular cavity cut into wood or some other material to receive a wooden projection (TENON) [ME *mortays*, fr MF *mortaise*, perh deriv of Ar *murtazz* fixed in]

²**mortise** *also* **mortice** *n vt* 1 to join or fasten securely; *specif* to join or fasten by a wooden projection (TENON) and mortise **2** to cut or make a mortise in

**mortise lock** *n* a lock that is designed to be fitted into a mortise in the edge of a door

**mortmain** /'mawt,mayn/ *n* 1 a nontransferable possession of lands or buildings by an ecclesiastical or other corporation **2** (the condition of) property or other gifts left to a church or corporation in perpetuity and nontransferably, esp for religious, charitable, or public purposes [ME *morte-mayne*, fr MF *mortemain*, fr OF, fr *morte* (fem of *mort* dead) + *main* hand, fr L *manus* – more at MANUAL]

¹**mortuary** /'mawtyooəri, -chəri/ *n* a room or building in which dead bodies are kept before burial or cremation – called also MORGUE [ME *mortuarie* gift claimed by the church' from the estate of a dead person, funeral, fr ML *mortuarium*, fr L, neut of *mortuarius* of the dead, fr *mortuus*, pp]

²**mortuary** *adj* of or for death or the burial of the dead ⟨*a ~ urn*⟩

**morula** /'mooroolə, 'moryoolə/ *n, pl* **morulae** /-lie/ the embryo of a multicellular animal at a very early stage in its development, consisting of a solid globular mass of cells formed by cleavage of a fertilized egg – compare BLASTULA, GASTRULA [NL, fr L *morum* mulberry] – **morular** *adj,* **morulation** *n*

¹**mosaic** /moh'zayik, mə-/ *n* 1 a form of art or decoration in which small pieces of variously coloured glass, stone, or other material are inlaid to form pictures or patterns **2** a picture or design made in mosaic **3** something resembling a mosaic ⟨*the landscape was a ~ of woods and pastures*⟩ **4a** (a part of) an organism composed of cells with different genetic make-up; CHIMERA 3 **b** any of several virus diseases of plants (e g tobacco) characterized esp by diffuse yellow and green mottling of the foliage **5** PHOTOMOSAIC [ME *musycke*, fr MF *mosaique*, fr OIt *mosaico*, fr ML *musaicum*, alter. of LL *musivum*, fr neut of *musivus* of a muse, artistic, fr L *Musa* muse] – **mosaic** *adj,* **mosaically** *adv*

²**mosaic** *vt* -**ck**- to form into a mosaic

**Mosaic** *adj* of Moses or the institutions or writings attributed to him ⟨~ *law*⟩ [NL *Mosaicus*, fr *Moses* (Heb *Moshēh*), Biblical prophet and lawgiver]

**mosaic gold** *n* a yellow scaly substance that is essentially a SULPHIDE of tin, $SnS_2$, and is used as a pigment and in gilding and bronzing

**mosaicism** /moh'zayisiz(ə)m/ *n* a condition in which patches of tissue of unlike genetic make-up are mingled in an organism

**mosaicist** /moh'zayisist/ *n* a designer or maker of mosaics

**Mosan** /'mohs(ə)n/ *n* a group of American Indian languages of British Columbia and Washington including SALISH and WAKASHAN [*mōs* four (in various Mosan languages)]

**mosasaur** /'mohsəsaw/ *n* any of a genus (*Mosasaurus*) of large extinct marine fish-eating lizards with limbs modified as paddles for swimming [NL *Mosasaurus*, genus name, deriv of L *Mosa* Meuse, river in W Europe (near which the first known species was found) + Gk *sauros* lizard]

**Moselle** /moh'zel/, **Mosel** /~, 'mohzl/ *n* a typically light-bodied white table wine made in the valley of the Moselle; *also* a similar wine made elsewhere [Ger *moselwein*, fr *Mosel* Moselle, river in SW Germany + *wein* wine]

**Moses basket** /'mohziz/ *n* BASSINET (baby's basketlike bed) [fr the basket in which Moses, as an infant, was placed beside a river (Exodus 2:3)]

**mosey** /'mohzi/ *vi, NAm informal* 1 to hurry away; MAKE OFF **2** to walk in an aimless or unhurried manner; saunter – often + *along* or *around* [origin unknown]

**moshav** /moh'shahv/ *n, pl* **moshavim** /,mohshə'veem/ a cooperative settlement of small individual farms in Israel – compare KIBBUTZ [NHeb *mōshābh*, fr Heb, dwelling]

**Moslem** /'mozləm/ *n or adj* (a) Muslim

**Mosotho** /moo'soohtoo/ *n, pl* **Mosothos,** *esp collectively* **Mosotho** a member of the Bantu-speaking people of Lesotho

**mosque** /mosk/ *n* a building used for public worship by Muslims [MF *mosquee*, fr OIt *moschea*, fr OSp *mezquita*, fr Ar *masjid* temple, fr *sajada* to prostrate oneself]

**mosquito** /mo'skeetoh/ *n, pl* **mosquitoes** *also* **mosquitos** any of numerous TWO-WINGED FLIES (family Culicidae) with females that have a PROBOSCIS (projecting tubular mouthpart) adapted to puncture the skin of animals and suck their blood, and that are in some cases carriers of diseases (e g malaria) [Sp, fr *mosca* fly, fr L *musca* – more at MIDGE] – **mosquitoey** *adj*

**mosquito boat** *n, NAm* MOTOR TORPEDO BOAT

**mosquito net** *n* a net or screen of very fine gauze (e g over a bed) for keeping out mosquitoes

**moss** /mos/ *n* 1a any of a class (Musci) of BRYOPHYTES (primitive nonflowering plants) having a very small leafy often tufted stem bearing sex organs at its tip; *also* many of these plants growing together and usu covering a surface (e g a tree or rock) **b** any of various plants resembling moss in appearance or habit of growth (e g SPANISH MOSS or REINDEER MOSS) **2** a mossy growth or covering **3** *chiefly Scot* a bog, swamp; *esp* a peat bog [ME, fr OE *mōs* bog; akin to OHG *mos* moss, L *muscus*] – **mosslike** *adj*

**moss agate** *n* an agate mineral that contains brown, black, or green mosslike or treelike markings and is used as a gemstone

**moss animal** *n* BRYOZOAN (aquatic animal)

**mossback** /-,bak/ *n, NAm* an extremely conservative person; a fogey [*mossback* (old turtle with mossy growth on its back, large sluggish fish)] – **mossbacked** *adj*

**moss green** *n* a yellowish-green colour

**moss-grown** *adj* 1 overgrown with moss; mossy **2** antiquated

**moss rose** *n* an older variety of garden rose (*Rosa centifolia muscosa*) that has a glandular mossy growth on the CALYX (leaflike parts surrounding the flower) and flower stalk and fragrant pink flowers

**moss stitch** *n* a knitting stitch made up of alternate KNIT STITCHES and PURL STITCHES

**'moss-,trooper** *n* a 17th-century raider or freebooter in the marshy border country between England and Scotland – **moss-trooping** *adj*

**mossy** /'mosi/ *adj* 1 covered (as if) with moss 2 resembling moss 3 antiquated, hidebound

**¹most** /mohst/ *adj* 1 the majority of ⟨~ *men*⟩ 2 greatest in quantity or extent ⟨*the* ~ *ability*⟩ [ME, fr OE *mǣst*; akin to OHG *meist* most, OE *māra* more – more at MORE]

**²most** *adv* 1 to the greatest degree or extent ⟨*what I like* ~ *about him*⟩ – often used with an adjective or adverb to form the superlative ⟨*the* ~ *challenging job he ever had*⟩ 2 very ⟨*shall* ~ *certainly come*⟩ ⟨*her argument was* ~ *persuasive*⟩

  *usage* 1 Most should not be used for contrasting only two items, as *in* ⟨△ *I don't know whether Paul or Susan was the most nervous*⟩. 2 The use of most for "very" has been censured by some conservative writers on usage, but is generally accepted today in the case of adjectives and adverbs conveying a "subjective" judgment of feeling and opinion. Compare ⟨*a most beautiful day*⟩ ⟨*some most persuasive arguments*⟩ ⟨△ *a most tall girl*⟩ ⟨*everyone worked* ~ *most quickly*⟩. See MOSTLY

**³most** *n, pl* **most** the greatest quantity, number, or amount ⟨*it's the* ~ *I can do*⟩ ⟨*spends* ~ *of her time in bed*⟩ ⟨~ *became discouraged and left*⟩ ⟨*she made the* ~ *of the fine weather*⟩ – **at most, at the most** 1 as a maximum limit ⟨*took him an hour at most to finish the job*⟩ 2 AT BEST

**⁴most** *adv, archaic, dial, or NAm* almost ⟨~ *everyone was at the drive-in movie*⟩

**-most** /-mohst/ *suffix* (→ *adj*) 1 most; to the highest possible degree ⟨*inner*most⟩ ⟨*ut*most⟩ 2 most towards ⟨*top*most⟩ ⟨*hind*most⟩ [ME, alter. of *-mest* (as in *for*mest foremost)]

**mostest** /'mohstist/ *n, chiefly journalistic* – the utmost in luxury and cachet

**mostly** /'mohstli/ *adv* for the greatest part; mainly; *also* in most cases; usually

  *usage* Mostly (= for the most part) should not replace most (= to the greatest degree) in such sentences as ⟨*the people* most (not △ mostly) *in need of help do not ask for it*⟩.

**mot** /moh/ *n, pl* **mots** /moh(z)/ a pithy or witty saying – compare BON MOT [Fr, word, saying, fr L *muttum* grunt – more at MOTTO]

**MOT** *also* **MoT** /,em oh 'tee/ *n, informal* 1 a compulsory annual roadworthiness test in Britain for motor vehicles older than a certain age 2 a certificate to show that a car has passed a roadworthiness test [*Ministry of Transport*] – **MOT** *vt*

**mote** /moht/ *n* a small particle; a speck; *esp* a particle of dust suspended in the air △ moat [ME *mot*, fr OE; akin to MD & Fris *mot* sand]

**motel** /moh'tel/ *n* a roadside hotel which provides parking and in which the rooms are usu on the ground floor and directly accessible from an outdoor parking area [blend of *motor* and *hotel*]

**motet** /moh'tet/ *n* a choral composition for many voices, sung without accompaniment, on a sacred text [ME, fr MF, dim. of *mot*]

**moth** /moth/ *n* 1 CLOTHES MOTH; *also* the ravages of the clothes moth ⟨*the* ~ *has got into these rugs*⟩ 2 any of numerous usu night-flying insects (order Lepidoptera) with antennae that are often feathery, larvae that are usu plant-eating caterpillars, and with stouter bodies, duller colouring, and proportionately smaller wings than the butterflies [ME *mothe*, fr OE *moththe*; akin to MHG *motte* moth]

**¹mothball** /'moth,bawl/ *n* 1 a ball made formerly of camphor but now often of naphthalene, used to keep moths from clothing 2 *pl* a state of indefinitely long protective storage ⟨*put the ships in* ~s *after the war*⟩; *also* a state of having been rejected as of no further use or interest ⟨*put that idea in* ~s⟩ – compare ON ICE

**²mothball** *vt* to withdraw from use or service and keep in reserve ⟨*several airliners were* ~ed *during the fuel shortage*⟩

**moth bean** *n* a bean (*Phaseolus aconitifolius*) that is cultivated, esp in India, for grazing and soil conditioning and for its cylindrical pods and edible small yellowish-brown seeds; *also* the seed of the moth bean [prob by folk etymology fr Marathi *maṭh*]

**'moth-,eaten** *adj* 1 eaten into by moth larvae ⟨~ *clothes*⟩ 2 *informal* 2a very worn-out or shabby in appearance b antiquated, outmoded

**¹mother** /'mudhə/ *n* 1a a female parent b(1) a woman in authority b(2) an old or elderly woman 2 a source, origin

⟨*necessity is the* ~ *of invention*⟩ [ME *moder*, fr OE *mōdor*; akin to OHG *muoter* mother, L *mater*, Gk *mētēr*, Skt *mātṛ*] – **motherhood** *n*, **motherless** *adj*, **motherlessness** *n*

**²mother** *adj* 1a of or being a mother b bearing the relation of a mother 2 derived (as if) from one's mother 3 acting as or providing parental stock – used without reference to sex

**³mother** *vt* 1a to give birth to b to give rise to; initiate, produce 2 *often derog* to care for or protect like a mother

**⁴mother, mother of vinegar** *n* a slimy membrane composed of yeast and bacterial cells that develops on the surface of alcoholic liquids undergoing vinegar-producing fermentation, and is added to wine or cider to produce vinegar [akin to MD *modder* mud, lees, dregs, MLG *mudde* mud]

**Mother Carey's chicken** /'keəriz/ *n* STORM PETREL (seabird) [origin unknown]

**mother cell** *n* a cell that gives rise to other cells, usu of a different sort

**mother country** *n* a country from which settlers or colonists emigrate

**mothercraft** /'mudhə,krahft/ *n* skill in caring for babies and young children

**Mother Goose rhyme** *n, chiefly NAm* NURSERY RHYME [*Mother Goose*, pretended author of *Mother Goose's Melodies*, a collection of nursery rhymes published in London *ab* 1760]

**motherhouse** /'mudhə,hows/ *n* 1 the convent in which the superior of a religious community lives 2 the original convent of a religious community

**Mothering Sunday** /'mudhəring/ *n* the fourth Sunday in Lent observed in Britain in honour of mothers and motherhood

**'mother-in-,law** *n, pl* **mothers-in-law** the mother of one's husband or wife

**motherland** /-,land/ *n* a fatherland

**motherly** /-li/ *adj* 1 (characteristic) of a mother ⟨~ *advice*⟩ 2 like a mother; maternal ⟨*a kind* ~ *sort of woman*⟩ – **motherliness** *n*

**,mother-'naked** *adj* stark naked

**,mother-of-'pearl** *n* the hard pearly iridescent substance, composed chiefly of CALCIUM CARBONATE, that forms the inner layer of some shells (e g that of an oyster) and that is used to make pearl buttons, as decorative inlay, etc

**mother of vinegar** *n* ⁴MOTHER

**Mother's Day** *n* 1 the second Sunday in May appointed, esp in the USA, for the honouring of mothers 2 MOTHERING SUNDAY

**mother's ruin** *n, humorous* ⁵GIN 1

**mother superior** *n, often cap M&S* the head of a religious community of women

**mother tongue** *n* 1 one's native language 2 a language from which another language derives

**mother wit** *n* natural wit or intelligence

**mothproof** /'moth,proohf/ *vt or adj* (to make) resistant to attack by the larvae of (clothes) moths ⟨~ *wools*⟩ – **mothproofer** *n*

**mothy** /'mothi/ *adj* 1 containing or infested with moths 2 moth-eaten

**motif** /moh'teef/ *n* 1 a thematic element in a work of art, music, or literature; *esp* a dominant or recurring idea or central theme 2 a single or repeated design or colour △ motive [Fr, motive, motif]

**¹motile** /'mohtiel/ *adj* exhibiting or capable of movement [L *motus*, pp] – **motility** *n*

**²motile** *n, psychology* a person whose mental imagery takes the form of inner feelings of action

**¹motion** /'mohsh(ə)n/ *n* 1a a proposal for action; *esp* a formal proposal made in a deliberative assembly b an application made to a court or judge to obtain an order, ruling, or direction 2 an act, process, or instance of changing position; a movement 3 an impulse or inclination of the mind or will ⟨*the* ~s *of humanity to good or evil* – T S Eliot⟩ 4 an act or instance of moving the body or its parts; a gesture ⟨*made a beckoning* ~ *with his hand*⟩ 5 a melodic change of pitch 6a motion, motions *pl* an evacuation of the bowels b the matter evacuated from the bowels at one time; a stool [ME *mocioun*, fr MF *motion*, fr L *motion-, motio* movement, fr *motus*, pp of *movēre* to move] – **motional** *adj*, **motionless** *adj*, **motionlessly** *adv*, **motionlessness** *n* – **go through the motions** to simulate action or perform something halfheartedly or mechanically ⟨*went through the motions of apologizing*⟩ – **(set) in motion** (to cause to begin) moving or functioning

**²motion** *vt* to direct by a motion ⟨~ed *me to a seat*⟩

**motion picture** *n, chiefly NAm* a film, movie **synonyms** see CINEMA

**motion sickness** *n* sickness induced by motion (eg in travel by air, car, or ship) and characterized by nausea – called also TRAVEL SICKNESS

**motivate** /'mohtivayt/ *vt* to provide with a motive or incentive; impel ⟨~d *by fear*⟩ – **motivative** *adj*, **motivator** *n*

**motivation** /,mohti'vaysh(ə)n/ *n* **1** motivating or being motivated **2** a motivating force or influence; an incentive, drive **3** *psychology* a conscious or unconscious driving force that arouses and directs action towards the achievement of a desired goal – **motivational** *adj*

**motivational research** /,mohti'vaysh(ə)nl/, **motivation research** *n* the study of consumer preferences, behaviour, and influences, used in the planning of sales and advertising campaigns

¹**motive** /'mohtiv/ *n* **1** a need, desire, etc that causes a person to act **2** a recurrent phrase or figure that is developed through the course of a musical composition **3** a motif [ME, fr MF *motif*, fr *motif*, adj, moving] – **motiveless** *adj*, **motivic** *adj*

²**motive** *adj* **1** moving or tending to move to action **2** of (the causing of) motion ⟨~ *energy*⟩ [MF or ML; MF *motif*, fr ML *motivus*, fr L *motus*, pp]

**motive power** *n* something (eg water or steam) whose energy is used to impart motion to machinery

**motivity** /moh'tivəti/ *n* the power of (producing) motion

**mot juste** /,moh 'zhoohst/ (*Fr* mo ʒyst) /*n, pl* **mots justes** /~/ the exactly right word or phrasing [Fr]

¹**motley** /'motli/ *adj* **1** multicoloured ⟨*a ~ coat*⟩ **2** composed of varied (disreputable or unsightly) elements ⟨*the ~ crowd*⟩ [ME, perh fr *mot* mote, speck]

²**motley** *n* **1** a woollen fabric of mixed colours made in England between the 14th and 17th centuries **2** the characteristic dress of a jester, that is made of motley **3** a haphazard mixture, esp of incompatible elements

**moto-cross** /'mohtoh ,kros/ *n* the sport of racing motorcycles across country on a closed course that usu includes steep hills, sharp turns, and often mud [*motor* + *cross*-country]

**motoneuron** /,mohtoh'nyooəron/ *n* a motor nerve cell [*motor* + *neuron*]

¹**motor** /'mohtə/ *n* **1** one who or that which imparts motion **2** any of various machines or devices that transform energy into motion: eg **2a** a small compact engine **b** INTERNAL-COMBUSTION ENGINE; *esp* a petrol engine **c** a machine that transforms electrical energy into mechanical energy in the form of rotational movement **3** *chiefly Br* MOTOR VEHICLE; *esp* a car [L, fr *motus*, pp of *movēre* to move] – **motorless** *adj*

²**motor** *adj* **1a** causing or imparting motion **b** of or being a nerve or nerve fibre that conveys nerve impulses from the brain, SPINAL CORD, or a nerve centre (GANGLION) to a muscle, gland, etc to cause contraction, secretion, etc – compare SENSORY **c** of or involving muscles or muscular movement **2** equipped with or driven by a motor **3** *chiefly Br* **3a** of or involving motor vehicles ⟨*the ~ trade*⟩ **b** designed for motor vehicles or motorists ⟨~ *spares*⟩

³**motor** *vi* to travel by motor car; *esp* DRIVE 2a – **motoring** *n*

**Motorail** /'mohtə,rayl/ *trademark* – used for a railway system in which a passenger train also carries the passengers' cars

**motor bike** *n, informal* **1** a motorcycle **2** *NAm* a small usu lightweight motorcycle

**motorboat** /-,boht/ *n* a usu small boat propelled by an internal-combustion engine or an electric motor

**motorcade** /-,kayd/ *n* a procession of motor vehicles

**motor car** *n* **1** a usu 4-wheeled motor vehicle designed for transporting a small number of people and typically propelled by an internal-combustion engine **2** a self-propelled railway carriage

**motorcycle** /-,siekl/ *n* a 2-wheeled motor vehicle that can carry one or sometimes two people astride the engine – **motorcycle** *vi*, **motorcyclist** *n*

**motor home** *n* a vehicle built on a car or van chassis and equipped as a self-contained travelling home

**motor inn** *n* a usu multi-storey city motel – called also MOTOR HOTEL

**motorist** /'mohtərist/ *n* a person who drives a car, esp regularly

**motor·ize, -ise** /'mohtəriez/ *vt* **1** to equip (eg a vehicle) with a motor **2** to provide with motor-driven vehicles ⟨~d *troops*⟩ – **motorization** *n*

**motor lodge** *n* a motel

**motorman** /-mən/ *n* a driver of a motor-driven vehicle, esp a tram or underground train

**motor scooter** *n* a usu 2-wheeled light motor vehicle having a seat so that the driver sits in front of rather than astride the engine

**motor torpedo boat** *n* a small, fast, and manoeuvrable warship propelled by internal-combustion engines and armed with torpedo tubes and antiaircraft guns

**motor unit** *n* a MOTOR nerve cell together with the muscle fibres on which it acts

**motor vehicle** *n* a motor-driven vehicle not operated on rails; *esp* one with rubber tyres and an INTERNAL-COMBUSTION ENGINE for use on highways

**motorway** /-,way/ *n, Br* a high-speed main road with separate carriageways for different directions, each with at least two lanes, and certain restrictions on the types of vehicle and driver allowed on it

**motte** /mot/ *n* the fortified mound of a Norman castle △ moat [Fr, fr OF *mote, motte* mound, fr OProv *mota*]

¹**mottle** /'motl/ *n* **1** a coloured spot or blotch; *esp* one of many on a surface **2** (the irregular arrangement of) spots or blotches on a surface **3** MOSAIC 4b (plant disease) [prob back-formation fr *motley*] – **mottled** *adj*

²**mottle** *vt* to mark with spots or blotches of different (shades of) colour as if stained – **mottler** *n*

**mottled enamel** *n* a mottled or spotted condition of the enamel of the teeth that arises during the time the teeth are hardening and is typically caused by drinking water containing excessive amounts of fluorides

**motto** /'motoh/ *n, pl* **mottoes** *also* **mottos 1** a sentence, phrase, or word inscribed on something as appropriate to or indicative of its character or use ⟨*a Latin ~ on a sundial*⟩ **2** a short expression of a guiding principle; a maxim ⟨*"Never trust a stranger", that's my ~*⟩ **3** (a piece of paper, esp in a Christmas cracker, printed with) a usu humorous or sentimental word or saying [It, fr L *muttum* grunt, fr *muttire* to mutter]

**moue** /mooh/ *n* a little grimace; a pout ⟨*made a coy little ~* – Angus Wilson⟩ [Fr – more at ³MOW]

**mouflon, moufflon** /'moohflonh/ *n* (any of) a race of small wild reddish-brown sheep (*Ovis musimon*) of the mountains of Corsica and Sardinia, the male of which has large curling horns [Fr *mouflon*, fr It dial. *movrone*, fr LL *mufron-, mufro*]

**mouillé** /'mwee·ay, 'mooh·yay/ (*Fr* muje) *adj* pronounced with the tongue touching the HARD PALATE [Fr, lit., moistened, fr pp of *mouiller* to moisten]

**moujik** /'moohzhik/ *n* MUZHIK (Russian peasant)

**moulage** /mooh'lahzh/ *n* (the taking of) an impression (eg of a footprint), esp for use as evidence in a criminal investigation [Fr, moulding, fr MF, fr *mouler* to mould, fr OF *modle* mould]

¹**mould**, *NAm chiefly* **mold** /mohld/ *n* **1** crumbling soft soil suited to plant growth; *esp* soil rich in humus – compare LEAF MOULD **2** *dial & poetic* the earth of the grave **3** *archaic* earth conceived as the substance of the human body ⟨*be merciful great Duke to men of ~* – Shak⟩ [ME *mold, molde*, fr OE *molde*; akin to OHG *molta* soil, L *molere* to grind – more at MEAL]

²**mould**, *NAm chiefly* **mold** *n* **1** distinctive character or type ⟨*need to recruit more men of his ~*⟩ **2** the frame on or round which an object is formed or constructed **3** a cavity or vessel in which a substance (eg a jelly or a metal casting) is shaped **4** a moulded article ⟨*a ~ of ice cream*⟩ **5** a prototype, model **6** a fixed pattern or form ⟨*compresses all these characters into the relentless ~ of the story* – E B Garside⟩ [ME *mold, molde*, fr OF *modle*, fr L *modulus*, dim. of *modus* measure – more at METE]

³**mould**, *NAm chiefly* **mold** *vt* **1** to give shape to ⟨*the wind ~s the waves*⟩ **2** to form in a mould ⟨~ *candles*⟩ **3** to exert a steady formative influence on ⟨*newspapers ~ public opinion*⟩ **4** to fit closely to the contours of; hug **5** to ornament with moulding or carving ⟨~ed *picture frames*⟩ **6** *archaic* to work (dough) into a desired consistency or shape – **mouldable** *adj*, **moulder** *n*

⁴**mould**, *NAm chiefly* **mold** *n* **1** a superficial often woolly fungal growth that forms on damp or decaying matter of plant or animal origin or on living organisms **2** a fungus (eg of the order Mucorales) that produces mould [ME *mowlde*] – **mould** *vi*

**mouldboard** /-,bawd/ *n* a curved iron plate attached to a ploughshare for lifting and turning the soil [¹*mould* + *board*]

**moulder,** *NAm chiefly* **molder** /'mohldə/ *vi* to crumble into dust or decayed fragments, esp gradually; rot, disintegrate [prob fr ¹*mould;* partly influenced in sense by *mould* (to become mouldy)]

**moulding** /'mohlding/ *n* **1** an article produced by moulding **2** a decorative recessed or embossed surface **3** a decorative band or curved strip used for ornamentation or finishing (e g on the top projecting part of a wall or the ceiling of a room)

**mouldy** /'mohldi/ *adj* **1** of, like, or covered with a mould-producing fungus ⟨~ *bread*⟩ **2** old and mouldering; fusty, crumbling ⟨*a dark* ~ *courtyard*⟩ ⟨~ *tradition*⟩ **3** *informal* **3a** miserable, nasty ⟨*a* ~ *old man who snapped at children*⟩ **b** stingy [⁴*mould* + ¹-*y;* (2, 3) influenced by ¹*mould*]

**Mouli** /'moohli/ *trademark* – used for any of various kitchen devices, esp a hand-operated food mill, for grinding, mincing, grating, or pureeing food

**moulin** /'moohlanh *(Fr* mulẽ)/ *n* a nearly cylindrical vertical shaft worn in a glacier by water from melting snow and ice and by rock debris [Fr, lit., mill, fr LL *molinum* – more at MILL]

¹**moult,** *NAm chiefly* **molt** /mohlt/ *vb* to shed or cast off (hair, feathers, shell, horns, or an outer layer) periodically [alter. of ME *mouten,* fr OE -*mūtian* to change, fr L *mutare* – more at MISS]

²**moult,** *NAm chiefly* **molt** *n* the act or process of moulting – compare ECDYSIS

¹**mound** /mownd/ *vt* **1** to form into a mound **2** *archaic* to enclose or fortify with a fence or a ridge of earth [origin unknown]

²**mound** *n* **1a(1)** an artificial bank or hill of earth or stones **a(2) burial mound, mound** such a mound built as a place of burial; ¹BARROW **a(3)** the slightly elevated ground on which a baseball pitcher stands **b** a knoll, hill **2** a heap, pile ⟨*a* ~ *of unanswered letters*⟩ [origin unknown]

**Mound Builder** *n* a member of a prehistoric American Indian people whose extensive earthworks are found from the Great Lakes down the Mississippi valley to the Gulf of Mexico

¹**mount** /mownt/ *n* **1** a high hill; a mountain – usu before an identifying name ⟨Mount *Everest*⟩ **2** *cap* a small area of raised flesh on the palm of the hand, esp at the base of a finger, that is considered by palmists to indicate temperament or traits of character **3** *archaic* a protective earthwork [ME, fr OE *munt* & OF *mont,* fr L *mont-, mons;* akin to ON *mæna* to project, L *minari* to project, threaten]

²**mount** *vi* **1** to increase in amount, extent, or degree ⟨*expenses began to* ~⟩ ⟨*the tension* ~ed⟩ **2** to rise, ascend **3** to get up on or into something above ground level ~ *vt* **1a** to go up; climb **b(1)** to seat or place oneself on ⟨*the speaker* ~ed *the platform*⟩ **b(2)** COVER **6a 2a** to lift up; raise, erect **b(1)** to place (e g artillery) in position **b(2)** to have (e g weapons) as equipment **c(1)** to organize and equip (an attacking force) ⟨~ *an army*⟩ **c(2)** to initiate and carry out (e g an assault or campaign) ⟨~ *a nationwide strike in protest*⟩ **3a** to set (somebody) on a means of conveyance ⟨~ed *his little daughter on a donkey*⟩ **b** to provide with riding animals (e g horses) or vehicles **4** to station for defence or observation or as an escort ⟨~ *guard over the palace*⟩ ⟨~ *a guard of honour*⟩ **5a** to attach to a support, setting, or backing **b** to arrange or assemble for use or display **6a** to prepare (e g a specimen or microscope slide) for examination or display **b** to organize and present for public viewing or performance; stage, produce ⟨~ed *a sumptuous opera*⟩ [ME *mounten,* fr MF *monter,* fr (assumed) VL *montare,* fr L *mont-, mons*] – **mountable** *adj,* **mounter** *n*

³**mount** *n* **1** an act or instance of mounting; *specif* an opportunity to ride a horse in a race **2 mount, mounting** something on which somebody or something is mounted: e g **2a** the material (e g cardboard) on which a picture is mounted **b** a jewellery setting **c(1)** an undercarriage or part on which a motor, piece of artillery, etc rests in service **c(2)** an attachment for an accessory **d** a hinge, card, or transparent envelope for mounting a stamp in a stamp collection **e** a glass microscope slide **3** a horse for riding

**mountain** /'mownt(ə)n, -tayn/ *n* **1** a prominent natural landmass that is higher than a hill **2a** a great heap or pile ⟨*a* ~ *of refuse*⟩; *specif* a large accumulated supply of surplus goods, esp foodstuffs, that is stored to prevent its being sold at a loss ⟨*a butter* ~⟩ – compare LAKE **2 b mountain, mountains** *pl* a vast amount or quantity ⟨*had* ~s *of work to do*⟩ [ME, fr OF *montaigne,* fr (assumed) VL *montanea,* fr fem of *montaneus* of a mountain, alter. of L *montanus,* fr *mont-, mons*]

**mountain ash** *n* any of various trees (genus *Sorbus*) of the rose family with small white flowers, PINNATE leaves, and red or orange-red often poisonous berrylike fruits; *esp* the rowan

**mountain dew** *n* illegally produced spirits, esp whisky

**mountaineering** /ˌmowntə'niəring/ *n* the pastime or technique of climbing mountains and rock faces – **mountaineer** *n*

**mountain lion** *n* a puma

**mountainous** /'mownt(ə)nəs/ *adj* **1** containing many mountains **2** like a mountain; huge – **mountainously** *adv,* **mountainousness** *n*

**mountain sickness** *n* sickness caused by insufficient oxygen in the air at great heights, esp above 3500 metres (about 10000 feet)

**mountainy** *adj* **1** mountainous **2** *chiefly NAm & Irish* living among mountains or in a remote backward area; rustic, uncivilized

**mountebank** /'mownti,bangk/ *n* **1** somebody who sells quack medicines from a platform **2** somebody who engages in unscrupulous trickery or pretence; a charlatan [It *montimbanco,* fr *montare* to mount + *in* in, on + *banco, banca* bench – more at BANK] – **mountebankery** *n*

**Mountie** /'mownti/ *n* a member of the Royal Canadian Mounted Police [*mount*ed policeman]

**mounting** /'mownting/ *n* ³MOUNT **2**

**mounting block** *n* a block, platform with steps, or convenient stone from which a rider may mount a horse

**mourn** /mawn/ *vi* **1** to feel or express grief or sorrow, esp for a death **2** to show the customary signs of grief for a death; *esp* to wear mourning **3** *poetic, of a dove* to murmur mournfully ~ *vt* **1** to feel or express grief or sorrow for ⟨~ed *her pet sparrow*⟩ **2** to utter mournfully [ME *mournen,* fr OE *murnan;* akin to OHG *mornēn* to mourn, Gk *mermēra* care – more at MEMORY] – **mourner** *n,* **mourningly** *adv*

**mournful** /-f(ə)l/ *adj* expressing, causing, or full of sorrow; sorrowful, sad, saddening – **mournfully** *adv,* **mournfulness** *n*

**mourning** /'mawning/ *n* **1** the act or state of somebody who mourns **2a** outward signs (e g black clothes or an armband) of grief for a person's death ⟨*is wearing* ~⟩ **b** a period of time during which signs of grief are conventionally shown

**mourning cloak** *n, NAm* CAMBERWELL BEAUTY (butterfly) [fr its blackish-brown colour]

**mourning dove** *n* a wild dove (*Zenaidura macroura carolinensis*) of the USA, with a long pointed tail, bluish-grey upperparts, and a plaintive call

¹**mouse** /mows/ *n, pl* **mice** /mies/ **1** any of numerous small rodents (esp of the genus *Mus*) with a pointed snout, rather small ears, an elongated body, and a long slender almost hairless tail **2** a timid person; *esp* a shy or very quiet girl or woman **3** *slang* BLACK EYE [ME, fr OE *mūs;* akin to OHG *mūs* mouse, L *mus,* Gk *mys* mouse, muscle]

²**mouse** *vi* **1** to hunt for mice **2** to search or move about stealthily ~ *vt, chiefly NAm* to search for carefully – usu + *out*

**mouse deer** *n* CHEVROTAIN (small Asian and W African mammal)

¹**mouse-ˌear** *n* any of several plants that have soft hairy leaves; *esp* a European HAWKWEED (*Hieracium pilosella*)

**mouse-ear chickweed** *n* any of several usu hairy chickweeds (esp genus *Cerastium*)

**mouser** /'mowsə, -zə/ *n* a catcher of mice and rats; *esp* a cat of a usu specified proficiency at mousing ⟨*an excellent* ~⟩

**mousetrap cheese, mousetrap** *n, Br informal* an inexpensive poor-quality usu Cheddar cheese [fr its being considered fit for use only as bait to trap mice]

**moussaka, mousaka** /mooh'sahkə/ *n* a baked dish, common in Greece and Turkey, consisting of layers of minced meat (e g lamb), aubergine or potato, tomato, and cheese with a cheese or savoury custard topping [NGk *mousakas,* prob fr Turk *mussaka*]

**mousse** /moohs/ *n* a light sweet or savoury cold dish usu containing cream, gelatine, or whipped egg whites [Fr, lit., moss, froth, fr LL *mulsa* hydromel; akin to L *mel* honey – more at MELLIFLUOUS]

**mousseline** /'moohsleen *(Fr* muslin)/ *n* a fine sheer fabric (e g of rayon) that resembles muslin [Fr, lit., muslin – more at MUSLIN]

**mousseline de soie** /~ də 'swah *(Fr* ~ də swa)/ *n, pl* **mousselines de soie** /~/ a silk muslin resembling chiffon but having a crisp finish [Fr, lit., silk muslin]

**mousseline sauce** *n* a light savoury sauce made by adding stiffly whipped cream or egg whites to HOLLANDAISE SAUCE [Fr *sauce mousseline*, lit., muslin sauce]

**moustache,** *NAm chiefly* **mustache** /mə'stahsh, mə'stash/ *n* **1** the hair growing or allowed to grow on somebody's upper lip, and sometimes down the sides of the face, framing the mouth **2** a growth of hair or bristles round the mouth of a mammal [MF *moustache*, fr OIt *mustaccio*, fr MGk *moustaki*, dim. of Gk *mystak-*, *mystax* upper lip, moustache]

**moustachio** /mə'stahshioh/ *n* a mustachio

**Mousterian** /mooh'stiəri-ən/ *adj* of or being a middle Palaeolithic culture of Europe and the Mediterranean area that is dated from before 70 000 BC to 32 000 BC and is characterized by well-made flint tools, considered to be the work of NEANDERTHAL MAN [Fr *moustérien*, fr Le *Moustier*, cave in SW France]

**mousy, mousey** /'mowsi/ *adj* **1** of or like a mouse: e g **1a** quiet, stealthy **b** timid; *also* colourless ⟨*her* ~ *little husband*⟩ **2** *of* hair of a light greyish-brown colour – **mousily** *adv,* **mousiness** *n*

**¹mouth** /mowth/ *n pl* **mouths** /mowdhz/ **1a(1)** the opening through which food passes into the body of an animal and from which vocal sounds are emitted **a(2)** the cavity in the head that in a typical VERTEBRATE animal is bounded externally by the lips and encloses the tongue, gums, and teeth **b** a grimace made with the lips ⟨*made a* ~⟩ **c** a horse's response to pressure on the bit **d** an individual, esp a child, requiring food ⟨*had too many* ~s *to feed*⟩ **2a** voice, utterance ⟨*finally gave* ~ *to his feelings*⟩ **b** MOUTHPIECE 3 **3** something like a mouth, esp in providing entrance or exit: e g **3a** the place where a river enters a larger body of water **b** the surface opening of a cave, volcano, etc **c** the opening of a container **d** an opening in the side of an organ pipe **4** *informal* **4a** a tendency to talk too much ⟨*he's got too much* ~⟩ **b** impertinent language; impudence – compare ¹LIP 5 [ME, fr OE *mūth;* akin to OHG *mund* mouth, L *mandere* to chew, Gk *masasthai* to chew, *mastax* mouth, jaws] – **mouthlike** *adj* – **down in the mouth** dejected, sulky – **keep one's mouth shut** to remain silent – **shoot one's mouth off** *informal* to talk foolishly or indiscreetly – see also **from the** HORSE's **mouth, put** WORDS **into somebody's mouth, take the** WORDS **out of somebody's mouth**

**²mouth** /mowdh/ *vt* **1a** to speak, utter **b** to utter pompously; declaim **c** to repeat without comprehension or sincerity ⟨*always* ~ing *platitudes*⟩ **d** to form (words) soundlessly with the lips ⟨*the librarian* ~ed *the word "quiet"*⟩ **2** to take (food) into the mouth; eat ~ *vi* **1** to talk pompously; rant **2** to make a grimace with the lips – **mouther** *n*

**mouthbreeder** /'mowth,breedə/ *n* any of several fishes that carry their eggs and young in the mouth; *esp* a N African spiny-finned fish (*Haplochromes multicolor*) often kept in aquariums

**mouthed** /mowdhd/ *adj* having a mouth, esp of a specified kind – often in combination ⟨*a large-*mouthed *fish*⟩

**mouthful** /'mowthf(ə)l/ *n* **1a** a quantity that fills the mouth ⟨*was submerged by a wave and got a* ~ *of seawater*⟩ **b** the amount (of food) put into the mouth at one time ⟨*you must learn to pause between* ~s⟩ **2** a small quantity ⟨*a* ~ *of sweet country air* – John Dryden⟩ **3** *informal* **3a** a word or phrase that is very long or difficult to pronounce **b** *chiefly NAm* a very apt or significant comment or statement ⟨*you said a* ~*!*⟩

**mouth hook** *n* either of a pair of hooked mouthparts of the larvae of some flies that function as jaws

**mouth music** *n* a wordless style of singing used by country singers in Ireland and the Scottish highlands

**mouth organ** *n* **1** a panpipe **2** a harmonica

**mouthpart** /-,paht/ *n* a structure or appendage near or forming part of the mouth

**mouthpiece** /-,pees/ *n* **1** something placed at or forming a mouth **2** a part (e g of a musical instrument or of a telephone) that goes in the mouth or is put next to the mouth **3** one who or that which expresses or interprets another's views; a spokesman ⟨Labour Weekly *is the* ~ *of the Labour Party*⟩

**mouth-to-'mouth** *adj* of or being a method of ARTIFICIAL RESPIRATION in which the rescuer places his/her mouth over the victim's mouth and blows air into the lungs forcefully every few seconds to inflate them

**'mouth-,watering** *adj* stimulating or appealing to the appetite, esp in appearance or aroma; appetizing – **mouth-wateringly** *adv*

**mouthy** /'mowdhi/ *adj, informal* **1** excessively talkative; garrulous **2** pompously bombastic

**¹movable, moveable** /'moohvəbl/ *adj* **1** capable of being moved **2** changing date from year to year ⟨~ *holidays*⟩ – **movableness** *n,* **movably** *adv,* **movability** *n*

**synonyms** A **movable** thing is less so than a **mobile** one. A wooden hut which can be reerected elsewhere is **movable**, but a **mobile** *library* is actually on wheels.

**²movable, moveable** *n, usu pl* an item of movable personal property, as distinguished from buildings, land, etc ⟨*they stuffed all the* ~s *into the vans*⟩

**movable feast** *n* an annual church festival (e g Easter) not celebrated on the same date each year

**¹move** /moohv/ *vi* **1a(1)** to go or pass with a continuous motion ⟨~d *into the shade*⟩ **a(2)** to proceed or progress towards a usu specified place or condition ⟨moving *up the executive ladder*⟩ ⟨~d *into second place in the tournament*⟩ – often + *on* ⟨~ *on to the next item*⟩ **b** to go away; depart ⟨*it's time we were moving*⟩ **c(1)** to change one's residence ⟨*they've* ~d *to a bungalow*⟩ **c(2)** to change one's (official) location ⟨*now in a new office after moving*⟩ **d(1)** to transfer a piece (e g in chess) from one position to another ⟨*it's your turn to* ~⟩ **d(2)** *of a piece in a board game* to travel or be capable of travelling to another position ⟨*a bishop* ~s *diagonally*⟩ **2** to pass one's life in a specified environment ⟨~s *in the most fashionable circles*⟩ **3** to change position or posture; stir ⟨*told him to be quiet and not to* ~⟩ **4** to take action; act **5** to operate or function, esp mechanically ⟨*pushed and pushed but the door wouldn't* ~⟩ **6** to make a formal request, application, or appeal ⟨~d *for a postponement*⟩ **7** to change hands by being sold or rented ⟨*goods that were* moving *slowly*⟩ **8** *of the bowels* to discharge faeces; empty **9** *informal* to show marked activity or speed ⟨*after a brief lull things really began to* ~⟩ ~ *vt* **1a** to change the place or position of; transfer, displace **b** to transfer (e g a piece in chess) from one position to another ⟨~d *his castle three squares*⟩ **2a(1)** to cause to go or pass with a continuous motion ⟨~d *the flag slowly up and down*⟩ ⟨*the piano was too heavy to* ~⟩ **a(2)** to take (furniture and possessions) from one residence or location to another **a(3)** to perform this service for ⟨*we're being* ~d *by Richardson and Co*⟩ **b** to cause to operate or function; actuate ⟨*this button* ~s *the whole machine*⟩ **c** to put into activity or rouse up from inactivity **3** to cause (the body or part of the body) to change position or posture ⟨~d *his lips*⟩ **4** to prompt to action ⟨*the report* ~d *the staff to take action*⟩ **5** to affect in such a way as to lead to a (specified) show of emotion ⟨*the story* ~d *her to tears*⟩ **6** to propose formally in a deliberative assembly ⟨~d *that the meeting adjourn*⟩ **7** to cause (the bowels) to empty **8** to cause to change hands through sale or rent ⟨*the new cars were* ~d *very quickly*⟩ [ME *moven*, fr MF *movoir*, fr L *movēre*]

**synonyms Move, influence, sway, affect, touch, impress,** and **strike** can all mean "produce a mental or emotional effect in someone". **Move** suggests that this is strong enough to bring about action or a show of emotion ⟨*moved to tears/to forgiveness/to ask for forgiveness*⟩. **Influence** always implies control or direction, and usually affects thought and actions rather than feelings ⟨*do not let prejudice* **influence** *your judgment*⟩. **Sway** goes further to suggest an irresistible influence, or one that is not resisted ⟨*easily* **swayed** *by tears*⟩. **Affect** is general in meaning and application, but principally applies to the emotions in this context, stressing pity and tenderness. **Touch** is stronger, and suggests pathos, often brief ⟨**touched** *by his kindness, she managed a smile*⟩. **Impress** suggests a deep, lasting, and usually favourable effect on the mind. **Strike**, rather more colloquial, stresses the suddenness or keenness of the impression.

**move in** *vi* **1** to occupy or take possession of a dwelling or place of work **2** to advance progressively in order to take control ⟨*our company can* move in *now the others are bankrupt*⟩ – often + *on* ⟨*police* moved in *on the criminals*⟩

**move on** *vi* to change one's residence or location for another ~ *vt* to cause to leave ⟨*the squatters were* moved on *by the police*⟩

**move out** *vi* to leave a dwelling or place of work

**move over** *vi* to make room

**²move** *n* **1a** the act of moving a piece (e g in chess) **b** the turn of a player to move **2a** a step taken so as to gain an objective; a manoeuvre ⟨*a* ~ *to end the dispute*⟩ **b** a movement ⟨*sat waiting for someone to make the first* ~⟩ **c** a change of residence or official location – **get a move on** to hurry up – usu imper – **on the move 1** in a state of moving about from place to place ⟨*a salesman is constantly* on the move⟩ **2** in a state of moving ahead or making progress ⟨*said that civilization is always* on the move⟩

**movement** /-mənt/ *n* **1a(1)** the act or process of moving; *esp* change of place, position, or posture **a(2)** a particular instance or manner of moving ⟨*her graceful* ~s⟩ **b** a tactical or strategic shifting of a military unit **c** *usu pl* an action, activity ⟨*troop* ~s⟩ **2a** a tendency or trend, specif in prices ⟨*detected a* ~ *towards fairer pricing*⟩ **b(1)** a series of organized activities working towards an objective; *also* an organized effort to promote or attain an end ⟨*the civil rights* ~⟩ **b(2)** a group of people organized to further specific political or religious ends ⟨*the Labour* ~⟩ **3** the moving parts of a mechanism that transmit motion **4a** a melodic change of pitch **b** the rhythmic character or quality of a musical composition **c** a unit or division of a symphony or other extended musical composition, having its own key, rhythmic structure, and themes and forming a separate part marked off, usu by pauses, from other movements **5a** the quality (eg in a painting or sculpture) of representing or suggesting motion **b** the development of the action in a work of literature **c** the quality in literature of having a quickly moving plot or an abundance of incident **6** an act of emptying the bowels

**mover** /'moohvə/ *n* one who or that which moves, removes, or sets something in motion; *specif, chiefly NAm* a removal man

**movie** /'moohvi/ *n* **1** FILM 4a, b ⟨*home* ~s⟩ ⟨*I say* ~ *nowadays rather than film – Encounter*⟩ **2** *pl, chiefly NAm* CINEMA 1a, 2 *synonyms* see CINEMA [*moving picture*]

**moviegoer** /'moohvi,goh·ə/ *n, chiefly NAm* someone who regularly goes to the cinema

**moving** /'moohving/ *adj* **1a** marked by or capable of movement ⟨*a watch with no* ~ *parts*⟩ **b** of or for a change of residence ⟨~ *expenses*⟩ **2a** producing or transferring motion or action ⟨*the* ~ *spirit behind the scheme*⟩ **b** evoking a deep emotional response ⟨*a very* ~ *story of a faithful dog*⟩ – **movingly** *adv*

**moving picture** *n, chiefly NAm* a film, movie *synonyms* see CINEMA

**moving staircase** *n* an escalator

**Moviola** /ˌmoohvi'ohlə/ *trademark* – used for a machine by which film can be viewed for the purpose of cutting and editing

**¹mow** /mow/ *n* **1** a piled-up stack (eg of hay or fodder); *also* a pile of hay or grain in a barn **2** the part of a barn where hay or straw is stored [ME, heap, stack, fr OE *mūga;* akin to ON *mūgi* heap, Gk *mykōn*]

**²mow** /moh/ *vb* **mowed; mown, mown** /mohn/ *vt* **1** to cut down (a crop, esp grass), usu with a scythe, sickle, or machine **2** to cut down the grass of (eg a field) ~ *vi* to cut down a crop, esp grass [ME *mowen,* fr OE *māwan;* akin to OHG *māen* to mow, L *metere* to reap, mow, Gk *aman*] – **mower** *n*

*usage* The past participle when used as part of a verb is usually **mowed** ⟨*I've just* mowed *the lawn*⟩ but when used as an adjective it is usually **mown** ⟨*new*-mown *grass*⟩.

**mow down** *vt* **1** to kill, destroy, or knock down, esp in great numbers or mercilessly **2** to overcome swiftly and decisively; rout

**³mow** /mow/ *n, archaic* a grimace [ME *mowe,* fr MF *moue,* of Gmc origin; akin to MD *mouwe* protruding lip]

**⁴mow** /mow/ *vi, archaic* to make grimaces

**moxa** /'moksə/ *n* a soft woolly material prepared from the dried leaves of various plants, esp an E Asian wormwood (*Artemisia moxa*), that in traditional oriental medicine is formed into small cones or cylinders which are burnt on particular points of the skin to relieve pain and reduce inflammation in the underlying tissues [NL, fr Jap *mogusa*]

**moxie** /'moksi/ *n, NAm informal* **1** energy, pep ⟨*streetcars with so much* ~ *they can run out from under you* – G S Perry⟩ **2** courage [fr *Moxie,* a trademark for a soft drink]

**mozzarella** /ˌmotsə'relə/ *n* a moist white unsalted unripened Italian curd cheese with a mild sour flavour and a smooth texture [It]

**mozzetta** /moh(t)'zetə/ *n* a short cape with a small ornamental hood worn by Roman Catholic priests [It]

**Mr** /'mistə/ *n, pl* **Messrs** /'mesəz/ **1** – used as a conventional title of courtesy before a man's name, except when usage requires the substitution of a title of rank or an honorary or professional title ⟨*spoke to* ~ *Smith*⟩ **2** – used in direct address as a conventional title of respect before a man's title of office ⟨*may I ask one more question,* ~ *Chairman?*⟩ **3** – used instead of *Dr* as a title of courtesy before the name of a surgeon who is a consultant ⟨*Dr Brown will be assisting* ~ *Black in the hysterectomy*⟩ **4** – used before the name of a place or of a line of activity (eg a sport) or before some epithet to form a

title applied to a man viewed or selected as esp outstanding in or representative of the thing indicated ⟨~ *High and Mighty*⟩ ⟨~ *Universe*⟩ **5** a man without any noble, academic, or professional title ⟨*though he was only a* ~, *he was more learned than many PhDs*⟩ [*Mr* fr ME, abbr of *maister* master; *Messrs* abbr of *Messieurs,* fr Fr, pl of *Monsieur*]

**mRNA** *n* MESSENGER RNA

**Mrs** /'misiz/ *n, pl* **Mesdames** /may'dahm/ **1a** – used as a conventional title of courtesy before a married woman's name, except when usage requires the substitution of a title of rank or an honorary or professional title ⟨*spoke to* ~ *Smith*⟩ **b** *informal* – used before the name of a place or of a line of activity (eg a sport) or before some epithet to form a title applied to a married woman viewed or selected as esp outstanding in or representative of the thing indicated **2** *informal* **2a** a wife ⟨*took the* ~ *along to the pub*⟩ **b** a married woman [*Mrs* abbr of ¹*mistress; Mesdames* fr Fr, pl of *Madame*]

**Mrs Grundy** /'grundi/ *n* somebody marked by prudish conventionality in personal conduct [*Mrs Grundy,* offstage character personifying prudery in the play *Speed the Plough* by Thomas Morton †1838 E dramatist]

**Ms** /məz, miz/ *n* – *used instead of Mrs or Miss, esp when marital status is unknown or irrelevant*

*usage* The use of **Ms** shows that the person named is a woman, just as **Mr** indicates a man, but conceals her marital status. It is used with or without her first name ⟨**Ms** (*Sarah*) *Smith*⟩ and is sometimes associated with the use by a married professional woman of her maiden name. In biographical or critical reference to a woman's work, the use of the surname alone is becoming increasingly common ⟨*Frink's new portrait heads*⟩.

**mu** /m(y)ooh/ *n* **1** the 12th letter of the Greek alphabet **2** MICROMETRE [Gk *my;* (2) μ (*mu*), symbol for *micron*]

**muc-** /myoohk-, myoohs-/, **muci-, muco-** *comb form* **1** mucus ⟨*mucoprotein*⟩ **2** mucous and ⟨*mucopurulent*⟩ [L *muc-,* fr *mucus*]

**¹much** /much/ *adj* **more** /maw/; **most** /mohst/ **1a** great in quantity or extent ⟨*not* ~ *money*⟩ ⟨*accept with* ~ *pleasure*⟩ ⟨*nothing* ~ *to do*⟩ ⟨*how* ~ *milk is there?*⟩ – compare SO MUCH **b** excessive, immoderate ⟨*it's a bit* ~ *having to work so late*⟩ **2** *obs* many in number [ME *muche* large, much, fr *michel, muchel,* fr OE *micel, mycel;* akin to OHG *mihhil* great, large, L *magnus,* Gk *megas*] – **too much** *informal* **1** wonderful, exciting – not now in vogue **2** terrible, awful

**²much** *adv* **more; most 1a(1)** to a great degree or extent; considerably ⟨~ *happier*⟩ ⟨*don't* ~ *like it*⟩ ⟨~ *to my surprise*⟩ ⟨*how* ~ *did it cost?*⟩ – compare SO MUCH **a(2)** very – with verbal adjectives ⟨*was* ~ *amused*⟩ **b** frequently, often ⟨~ *married*⟩ **c** BY FAR ⟨~ *the fatter*⟩ ⟨*I'd* ~ *rather not*⟩ ⟨~ *the brightest student*⟩ **2** nearly, approximately ⟨*looks* ~ *the way his father did*⟩ *usage* see ²VERY – **as much** *interj* **1** the same quantity ⟨*give him* as much *again*⟩ **2** that, so ⟨*I thought* as much⟩ – **much as** however much; even though – **much less** and certainly not ⟨*can't even walk,* much less *run*⟩

**³much** *n* **1** a great quantity, amount, or part ⟨*gave away* ~⟩ ⟨~ *of the night*⟩ ⟨*got too* ~ *to do*⟩ – compare SO MUCH **2** something considerable or impressive ⟨*was not* ~ *to look at*⟩ ⟨*the film wasn't up to* ~⟩ ⟨*I don't think* ~ *of that idea*⟩ **3** a relative quantity or part ⟨*I'll say this* ~ *for him*⟩ – **too much for 1** more than a match for **2** beyond the endurance of

**muchness** /'muchnis/ *n* – **much of a muchness** very much the same

**mucic acid** *n* a solid organic chemical acid, $C_4H_4(OH)_4(COOH)_2$, obtained from sugars (LACTOSE and GALACTOSE) present in milk [ISV *muc-* + *-ic*]

**muciferous** /myooh'sifərəs/ *adj* producing or filled with mucus

**mucilage** /'myoohsilij/ *n* **1** any of a group of thick gelatinous substances produced by plants and obtained esp from seaweeds, that contain protein and carbohydrates (POLYSACCHARIDES), are similar to plant gums, and are hard when dry but swell in water to form a slimy mass **2** *NAm* a thick sticky solution (eg of a gum) used esp as an adhesive [ME *muscilage,* fr LL *mucilago* mucus, musty juice, fr L *mucus*]

**mucilaginous** /ˌmyoohsi'lajinəs/ *adj* **1** sticky **2** of, full of, or secreting mucilage [LL *mucilaginosus,* fr *mucilagin-, mucilago*] – **mucilaginously** *adv*

**mucin** /'myoohsin/ *n* any of various MUCOPROTEINS (complex carbohydrate-containing proteins) that occur esp in secretions (eg mucus and saliva) of MUCOUS MEMBRANES [ISV *muc-* + *-in*] – **mucinous** *adj*

**¹muck** /muk/ *n* **1** soft moist farmyard manure **2** slimy dirt or filth **3a** dark highly organic soil **b** mire, mud **4** *informal* a worthless or useless thing; rubbish **5** *Br informal* – used in *Lord Muck* and *Lady Muck* to designate an arrogantly patronizing person [ME *muk*, perh fr OE *-moc;* akin to ON *myki* dung – more at MUCUS] – **mucky** *adj*

**²muck** *vt* to dirty (as if) with muck; soil ~ *vi* to move or load muck (eg in a mine) – **mucker** *n*

**muck about** *vb, chiefly Br informal* **vi** to engage in idle or aimless activity ⟨*stop mucking about and get on with your work*⟩ ~ *vt* to treat discourteously or inconsiderately, esp through incompetence ⟨*not going to be mucked about by these people*⟩ ⟨*stop mucking me about*⟩

**muck in** *vi, Br informal* to share or join in esp a task or sleeping accommodation ⟨*all mucked in together*⟩

**muck out** *vb* to clean up; *esp* to clear a (stable) of manure or filth

**muck up** *vt, chiefly Br informal* **1** to dirty (as if) with muck; soil **2** to bungle, spoil

**mucker** /'mukə/ *n, informal* **1** a disagreeable person **2** a friend, pal [(1) prob alter. (influenced by *muck*) of *fucker;* (2) *muck* (*in*) + ²-*er*]

**muckle** /'mukl/ *adj, Scot & N Eng* much, great [var of *mickle*] – **muckle** *adv or n*

**muckluck** /'mukluk/ *n* MUKLUK (Eskimo boot)

**muckrake** /-,rayk/ *vi* to search out and publicly expose real or apparent misconduct of prominent individuals [obs *muckrake* rake for dung] – **muckraker** *n*

**muckspreader** /'muk,spredə/ *n* an agricultural machine for spreading manure on fields – **muckspreading** *n*

**muco-** – see MUC-

**mucocutaneous** /,myoohkoh·kyoo'taynyəs, -niəs/ *adj* consisting of, affecting, or involving both the skin and MUCOUS MEMBRANES

**¹mucoid** /'myoohkoyd/ *adj* resembling mucus [ISV *muc-* + *-oid*]

**²mucoid** *n* a mucoprotein [ISV]

**mucolytic** /,myoohkə'litik/ *adj* tending to break down or dissolve mucus or similar MUCIN-containing body secretions ⟨~ *enzymes*⟩

**mucopolysaccharide** /,myoohkoh,poli'sakəried/ *n* any of various complex nitrogen-containing POLYSACCHARIDES (carbohydrates composed of many sugar units) that are widely distributed in the body, contain compounds derived from sugars (eg glucose) by the addition of an AMINO group, and are constituents of mucoproteins and blood-group substances [ISV]

**mucoprotein** /'myoohkoh,prohteen, ,--'--/ *n* GLYCOPROTEIN (protein containing one or more carbohydrate groups); *specif* any of various proteins (eg MUCINS) that contain mucopolysaccharides, occur in body fluids and tissues, and have a higher proportion of carbohydrate than glycoproteins

**mucor** /'myoohkaw/ *n* any of a genus (*Mucor*) of moulds with round usu cylindrical or pear-shaped spore-bearing capsules [NL, genus name, fr L, mould, mouldiness; akin to L *mucus*]

**mucosa** /myooh'kohzə/ *n, pl* **-mucosae** /-zie, -zi/, **mucosas** MUCOUS MEMBRANE [NL, fr L, fem of *mucosus* mucous] – **mucosal** *adj*

**mucous** /'myoohkəs/ *adj* **1** covered (as if) with mucus; slimy **2** of or like mucus **3** secreting or containing mucus [L *mucosus,* fr *mucus*]

**mucous membrane** /'membrayn/ *n* a membrane rich in cells or glands that secrete mucus; *specif* one that lines body passages and cavities (eg of the nose and digestive tract) which open directly or indirectly onto the exterior

**mucro** /'myoohkroh/ *n, pl* **mucrones** /myooh'krohneez/ an abrupt sharp end point or tip (eg of a leaf) [NL *mucron-, mucro,* fr L, point, edge; akin to Gk *amyssein* to scratch, sting] – **mucronate** *adj,* **mucronation** *n*

**mucus** /'myoohkəs/ *n* **1** a slippery secretion rich in MUCINS that is produced by MUCOUS MEMBRANES (eg in the nose or mouth), which it moistens and protects **2** any of various slimy or sticky secretions resembling mucus that are produced by INVERTEBRATE animals [L, nasal mucus; akin to ON *myki* dung, Gk *myxa* mucus]

**mud** /mud/ *n* **1** a slimy sticky mixture of solid material with a liquid, esp water; *esp* soft wet earth **2** *informal* abusive and malicious remarks or charges ⟨*so much ~ was thrown at her that she went to live in Aberdeen under an assumed name*⟩ – see also **one's/somebody's** NAME **is mud, drag somebody's** NAME

**through the mud** [ME *mudde,* prob fr MLG; akin to OE *mōs* bog – more at MOSS]

**mudbath** /'mud,bahth/ *n* **1** a bath in heated mud (eg at a spa) for the relief of rheumatism, arthritis, etc **2** a muddy state, occasion, etc ⟨*the goalmouth was a ~*⟩

**mud dauber** *n* any of various wasps (esp family Sphecidae) that construct mud cells in which the female lays an egg and stores live paralysed insects and spiders for the larvae to feed on later

**¹muddle** /'mudl/ *vt* **1** to befog or stupefy, esp with alcohol **2** to mix confusedly in one's mind – often + *up* ⟨*~d up* disinterested *and* uninterested⟩ **3** to confuse ⟨*talk slowly! You're muddling me*⟩ **4** to make a mess of; bungle ~ *vi* **1** to proceed or get along in a confused aimless way – + *along* or *on* **2** to participate in confused activity ⟨*learn to ~ in with the others*⟩ [prob fr obs D *moddelen* to make muddy, fr MD, fr *modde* mud; akin to MLG *mudde*] – **muddler** *n*

**muddle through** *vi* to succeed somehow in spite of incompetence or lack of method and planning

**²muddle** *n* **1** a state of (mental) confusion **2** a confused mess

**muddleheaded** /-'hedid/ *adj* **1** mentally confused **2** inept, bungling – **muddleheadedness** *n*

**¹muddy** /'mudi/ *adj* **1a** full of or covered with mud ⟨~ *shoes*⟩ ⟨*a ~ river*⟩ **b** characteristic or suggestive of mud ⟨*a ~ flavour*⟩ ⟨~ *colours*⟩ **2a** lacking in clarity or brightness; cloudy, dull ⟨*retained only a distorted ~ image of the event*⟩ **b** obscure in meaning; muddled, confused ⟨~ *thinking*⟩ ⟨*a ~ style*⟩ – **muddily** *adv,* **muddiness** *n*

**²muddy** *vt* **1** to make muddy **2** to make cloudy, dull, or confused

**mudfish** /'mud,fish/ *n, pl* **mudfish, mudfishes** any of various fish that live in muddy water or burrow in mud

**mudflap** /'mud,flap/ *n* a flap suspended behind each wheel of a vehicle to prevent mud or splashes being thrown up

**mudflat** /-,flat/ *n,* **mudflats** *n pl* a muddy area of level ground that is covered by water at high tide

**mudguard** /-,gahd/ *n* a metal or plastic guard over each wheel of a bicycle, motorcycle, etc to deflect or catch mud

**mudlark** /-,lahk/ *n* a destitute child in Victorian London; *esp* one who tried to find useful or salable objects in the tidal mud of the Thames

**mudpack** /-,pak/ *n* a face-pack containing FULLER'S EARTH

**mud puppy** *n* any of several large aquatic N American salamanders (genus *Necturus,* esp *Necturus maculosus*) that have bright red external gills and a grey to brown body usu marked with bluish-black spots

**mudskipper** /'mud,skipə/ *n* any of several small GOBIES (genera *Periophthalmus* and *Boleophthalmus*) of Asia and Polynesia that have fleshy modified front fins enabling them to leave the water and move about actively on mud

**mudslinger** /'mud,slingə/ *n* a person who uses offensive epithets, invective, and scandalous allusions, esp against a political opponent – **mudslinging** *n*

**mudstone** /-,stohn/ *n* a SEDIMENTARY rock produced by the consolidation of clay, that is similar to shale but is not easily split into layers

**mud turtle** *n* any of various bottom-dwelling freshwater turtles (eg of the genus *Kinosternon*)

**muesli** /'m(y)oohzli *also* 'mwayzli/ *n* a (breakfast) dish of Swiss origin that consists typically of rolled oats, dried fruit (eg raisins), nuts, and grated apple [Ger *müsli, muesli,* fr *mus* soft food, pap, fr OHF *muos;* akin to OE *mōs* food]

**muezzin** /mooh'ezin/ *n* a Muslim official who calls the faithful to prayer at fixed daily times from the minaret or door of a mosque [Ar *mu'adhdhin*]

**¹muff** /muf/ *n* **1a** a warm cylindrical cloth or fur covering for the hands **b** an earmuff **2** a cluster of feathers on either side of the face of some domestic fowls [D *mof,* fr MF *moufle* mitten, fr ML *muffula*]

**²muff** *n* **1** a bungling performance **2** a failure to hold a ball in attempting a catch **3** *informal* a timid awkward person, esp in sports ⟨*a hopeless ~ at tennis*⟩ [prob fr ¹*muff*]

**³muff** *vt* **1** to handle awkwardly; bungle ⟨~*ed the interview*⟩ **2** to fail to hold (a ball) when attempting a catch

**muffin** /'mufin/ *n* a light round yeast-leavened bun, usu served toasted and buttered [prob fr LG *muffen,* pl of *muffe* cake]

**¹muffle** /'mufl/ *vt* **1** to wrap up so as to conceal or protect; envelop ⟨*he was well ~d up against the cold*⟩ **2a** to wrap or pad with something to dull the sound ⟨~ *the oars*⟩ **b** to deaden the sound of ⟨*the grass ~d their footsteps*⟩ **3** to keep down;

suppress ⟨they ∼d their giggles⟩ [ME *muflen*, perh deriv of MF *moufle* mitten]

²**muffle** *n* a chamber in a furnace or kiln where porcelain, enamel, etc can be fired without direct contact with flames [Fr *moufle*, lit., mitten, fr MF]

**muffler** /'muflǝ/ *n* 1 a warm scarf worn round the neck 2 *NAm* a silencer for a motor vehicle

¹**mufti** /'mufti/ *n* a professional legal expert who interprets Muslim law △ Mahdi [Ar *mufti*]

²**mufti** *n* civilian or ordinary clothes worn by one who is usually in uniform [prob fr ¹*mufti*]

¹**mug** /mug/ *n* 1a a large usu cylindrical drinking cup typically having a flat base, straight sides, and a handle **b** the contents of or quantity contained in a mug ⟨*add a ∼ of milk*⟩ 2 *informal* someone's face or mouth 3 *informal* 3a *chiefly Br* a person who is easily deceived; a sucker **b** *NAm* a ruffian, thug 4 **mug shot, mug** *slang* a photograph of a suspect's face [origin unknown]

²**mug** *vb* -gg- *informal vi* 1 to make faces, esp to attract attention or as part of a stage performance 2 to pose for a photograph ⟨*she ∼s well* – John Wyndham⟩ ∼ *vt* to photograph

³**mug** *vt* -gg- to assault with intent to rob, usu in a public place [back-formation fr *mugger*, prob fr obs *mug* to punch in the face, fr ¹*mug*] – **mugger** *n*

¹**mugger** /'mugǝ/ *n* a common usu harmless freshwater crocodile (*Crocodylus palustris*) of SE Asia – called also MARSH CROCODILE [Hindi *magar*, fr Skt *makara* water monster]

²**mugger** *n* one who grimaces, esp before an audience [²*mug*]

**muggins** /'muginz/ *n, pl* **mugginses, muggins** *informal* a fool, simpleton – often used in address or as a title and esp in reference to oneself ⟨∼ *here lost her passport*⟩ [prob fr the name *Muggins*, influenced in sense by ¹*mug* (cf JUGGINS)]

**muggy** /'mugi/ *adj, of weather* warm, damp, and close [E dial. *mug* drizzle, prob of Scand origin; akin to ON *mugga* drizzle] – **muggily** *adv*, **mugginess** *n*

**mugho pine** /'myoohgoh/ *n* a shrubby spreading pine (*Pinus mugo mughus*) widely cultivated as an ornamental shrub [prob fr Fr *mugho*, fr It *mugo*]

**mug's game** *n, chiefly Br informal* a profitless activity ⟨*saving is widely held to be a ∼* – William Davis⟩ [¹*mug* 3]

**mug shot** *n, slang* MUG 4

**mug up** *vb, Br informal* to study hard; swot [*mug* (to study), of unknown origin]

**mugwort** /-,wuht/ *n* a tall Eurasian plant (esp *Artemisia vulgaris*) of the dandelion family that has small brownish flower heads and is common on waste ground and in hedgerows [ME, fr OE *mucgwyrt*, fr *mucg*- (prob akin to OE *mycg* midge) + *wyrt* wort]

**mugwump** /-,wump/ *n, chiefly NAm* an independent in politics [obs slang *mugwump* important person, fr Natick *mugwomp* captain] – **mugwumpery** *n*

**Muhammadan** /mǝ'hamid(ǝ)n/ *adj* of Muhammad or Islam **synonyms** see MUSLIM [*Muhammad* †632 Arabian prophet & founder of Islam] – **Muhammadan** *n*, **Muhammadanism** *n*

**Muhammadan calendar** *n* a calendar using the phases of the moon, reckoned from the HEGIRA (flight of Muhammad from Mecca) in AD 622, and organized in cycles of 30 years

**Muhammadan era** *n* the period dating from the HEGIRA (flight of Muhammad from Mecca) in AD 622 and measured by the Muhammadan calendar

**Muharram** /mooh'harǝm/ *n* 1 – see MONTH table 2 a Muslim festival held during Muharram [Ar *Muḥarram*]

**mujik** /'mooh-zhik/ *n* MUZHIK

**mukluk** /'mukluk/ *n* a boot usu made of sealskin or reindeer skin and traditionally worn by Eskimos [Eskimo *muklok* large seal]

**mukti** /'mookti/ *n* MOKSHA (salvation from the bondage of finite existence) [Skt, fr *muñcati* he releases]

**muktuk** /'muktuk/ *n* the tough outer flesh of a whale used as a food by Eskimos [Eskimo]

**mulatto** /myooh'latoh/ *n, pl* **mulattoes, mulattos** one of mixed Negro and white ancestry; *esp* the first-generation offspring of a Negro and a white person [Sp *mulato*, fr *mulo* mule, fr L *mulus*]

**mulberry** /'mulb(ǝ)ri/ *n* 1 any of a genus (*Morus*) of trees of the fig family bearing an edible usu purple fruit like a raspberry; *also* the fruit of the mulberry 2 a dark purple or purplish black [ME *murberie, mulberie*, fr OF *moure* mulberry (fr L *morum*, fr Gk *moron*) + ME *berie* berry]

**mulch** /mulch/ *n* a protective covering (e g of sawdust, compost, paper, or plastic) spread or left on the ground esp to reduce evaporation, maintain even soil temperature, prevent erosion, control weeds, or enrich the soil [prob irreg fr E dial. *melch* soft, mild, prob fr OE *melsc* mellow; akin to L *mollis* soft] – **mulch** *vb*

¹**mulct** /mulkt/ *n* a fine, penalty [L *multa, mulcta*]

²**mulct** *vt* 1 to punish by a fine **2a** to defraud, esp of money; swindle **b** to obtain by fraud or swindling

¹**mule** /myoohl/ *n* 1a the offspring of a mating between a (female) horse and an ass – compare HINNY **b** the usu sterile offspring of a mating between animals of different breeds (e g a tigon from a tiger and a lion) 2 a very stubborn person – chiefly in *stubborn as a mule* 3 a machine for simultaneously drawing and twisting fibre into yarn or thread and winding it onto spindles [ME, fr OF *mul*, fr L *mulus;* (3) fr its being a hybrid of two earlier machines]

²**mule** *n* a backless shoe or slipper [MF, a kind of slipper, fr L *mulleus* shoe worn by magistrates]

**mule deer** *n* a long-eared deer (*Odocoileus hemionus* syn *Cariacus macrotis*) of N America

**mule skinner** *n, NAm* a muleteer

**muleta** /m(y)ooh'laytǝ/ *n* a small cloth attached to a short tapered stick that is used by a matador in place of the large cape during the final stage of a bullfight [Sp, crutch, muleta, dim. of *mula* she-mule, fr L, fem of *mulus* mule]

**muleteer** /,myoohlǝ'tiǝ/ *n* one who drives mules [Fr *muletier*, fr *mulet*, fr OF, dim. of *mul* mule]

**muley** /'myoohli/ *adj, of an animal of a type that normally has horns* polled or (naturally) hornless [of Celt origin; akin to IrGael & ScGael *maol* bald, hornless, W *moel*]

**mulga** /'mulgah, -gǝ/ *n, pl* **mulgas, mulga** (the wood of) a shrubby acacia plant (esp *Acacia aneura*) that is widespread in the drier parts of Australia and is often used as fodder; *also* land covered with this plant [native name in Australia]

**mulga wire** *n, Austr informal* a rumour

**muliebrity** /,myoohli'ebrǝti/ *n* the state of being a woman; femininity – compare VIRILITY [LL *muliebritat-, muliebritas*, fr L *muliebris* of a woman, fr *mulier* woman]

**mulish** /'myoohlish/ *adj* unreasonably and inflexibly obstinate; recalcitrant **synonyms** see OBSTINATE [¹*mule* + *-ish*] – **mulishly** *adv*, **mulishness** *n*

¹**mull** /mul/ *vt* to grind or mix thoroughly; pulverize [ME *mullen*, fr *mul, mol* dust, prob fr MD; akin to OE *melu* meal – more at MEAL]

**mull over** *vt* to consider at length; ponder ⟨*mulling over a proposal*⟩

²**mull** *n* a headland or peninsula in Scotland ⟨*the Mull of Kintyre*⟩ [ME (Sc) *mole*, prob fr ON *mūli* projecting crag, snout, muzzle]

³**mull** *vt* to heat, sweeten, and flavour (e g wine or beer) with spices [origin unknown]

⁴**mull** *n, Scot* a snuff-box [var of ¹*mill;* fr its orig containing a mechanism for grinding tobacco]

⁵**mull** *n* a soft fine sheer fabric of cotton, silk, or rayon [by shortening & alter. fr *mulmul* muslin, fr Hindi *malmal*, fr Per]

⁶**mull** *n* 1 a crumbly layer of mixed decaying plant and animal matter (HUMUS) and mineral soil that merges gradually into the mineral soil beneath 2 a finely powdered solid, esp in a suspension [Ger, fr Dan *muld*, fr ON *mold* dust, soil; akin to OHG *molta* dust, soil – more at MOULD]

**mullah** /'mulǝ, 'moolǝ/ *n* a Muslim teacher of theology and sacred law [Turk *molla* & Per & Hindi *mulla*, fr Ar *mawlā*] – **mullahism** *n*

**mullein** *also* **mullen** /'mulǝn/ *n* any of a genus (*Verbascum*) of usu woolly-leaved plants of the foxglove family with spikes of usu yellow flowers [ME *moleyne*, fr AF *moleine*, prob fr OF *mol* soft, fr L *mollis*]

**muller** /'mulǝ/ *n* a stone or piece of wood, metal, or glass used as an instrument for grinding substances (e g powders or pigments) usu on a slab (e g of stone) [alter. of ME *molour*, prob fr *mullen* to grind]

**Müllerian** /moo'liǝri-ǝn, myooh-/ *adj* of or being mimicry that exists between two or more inedible or dangerous species (e g of butterflies) that is a mechanism to reduce predation. The predators learn to recognize and avoid all the related species after feeding on only a small number of any one of the species. [Fritz *Müller* †1897 Ger zoologist]

**mullet** /'mulit/ *n, pl* **mullet**, *esp for different types* **mullets** 1 any of a family (Mugilidae) of valuable food fishes with an elongated rather stout body 2 any of a family (Mullidae) of moderate-sized usu red or golden fishes with two BARBELS (thin sensory projections) on the chin [ME *molet*, fr MF *mulet*, fr L *mullus* red mullet, fr Gk *myllos*; akin to Gk *melas* black, Skt *malina* dirty, black]

**mulley** /'muli/ *adj* MULEY (without horns)

**mulligan stew** /'muligən/ *n* a stew made basically of vegetables and meat or fish [prob fr the name *Mulligan*]

**mulligatawny** /ˌmuligə'tawni/ *n* a rich meat soup of Indian origin seasoned with curry [Tamil *miḷakutaṇṇi*, a strongly seasoned soup, fr *miḷaku* pepper + *taṇṇi* water]

**mulligrubs** /'muligrubz/ *n pl, informal* 1 a despondent, sullen, or ill-tempered mood 2 stomachache, colic [alter. of earlier *mulliegrums*, of unknown origin]

**mullion** /'muli·ən/ *n* a vertical bar placed between panes or panels (e g of windows or doors) or used decoratively (e g between the panels of a screen) – compare TRANSOM [prob alter. of *monial*, fr ME *moynel*, *moniel*, fr MF *moinel*, perh fr *moyen* middle] – **mullion** *vt*

**mullite** /'muliet/ *n* a rare mineral, $3Al_2O_3.2SiO_2$, that is a chemical compound of aluminium and silica and that is resistant to corrosion and heat [*Mull*, island of the Inner Hebrides]

**mullock** /'mulək/ *n* 1 *Austr* mining refuse ⟨~ *heaps*⟩; *also* rock which does not contain gold 2 *dial Br* a state of confusion; a muddle 3 *dial Br & Austr* something devoid of value; rubbish [ME *mullok* rubbish, refuse, fr *mul, mol* dust – more at ¹MULL] – **poke mullock at** *Austr informal* to make fun of; ridicule

**multi-** /multi-/ *comb form* 1a many; multiple; much ⟨multi-*storey*⟩ b more than two ⟨multi*lateral*⟩ ⟨multi*valent*⟩ c more than one ⟨multi*para*⟩ 2 many times over ⟨multi*millionaire*⟩ [ME, fr MF or L; MF, fr L, fr *multus* much, many – more at MELIORATE]

**multicellular** /ˌmulti'selyoolə/ *adj* having or consisting of many cells [ISV] – **multicellularity** *n*

**multicoloured** /-ˌkuləd/ *also* **multicolour** /ˌmulti'kulə, '--,--/ *adj* of various colours; parti-coloured ⟨a ~ *carpet*⟩

**multicomponent** /ˌmultikəm'pohnənt/ *adj* composed of many parts

**multicultural** /ˌmulti'kulchərəl/ *adj* of, being, or designed for a combination of several distinct cultures ⟨a ~ *urban environment*⟩ – **multiculturalism** *n*

**multidentate** /-'dentayt/ *adj* having many teeth

**multidimensional** /ˌmultidi'mensh(ə)nl, -die-/ *adj* of or marked by several dimensions ⟨a ~ *problem*⟩ ⟨~ *calculus*⟩ – **multidimensionality** *n*

**multidirectional** /ˌmultidi'reksh(ə)nl, -die-/ *adj* extending in many directions ⟨~ *efforts to win the election*⟩

**multidisciplinary** /ˌmultidisi'plinəri, -'disəplinri/ *adj* of or using a combination of several scholarly disciplines for a common end ⟨a ~ *approach to child guidance*⟩

**multifaceted** /ˌmulti'fasitid/ *adj* having several distinct facets or aspects ⟨the ~ *problems of foreign policy*⟩

**multifactorial** /ˌmultifak'tawriəl/ *adj* 1 having characteristics or a type of inheritance dependent on a number of genes at different places on the CHROMOSOME (strand of gene-carrying material) 2 **multifactorial, multifactor** /ˌmulti'faktə/ having or involving a variety of elements ⟨a ~ *study*⟩ – **multifactorially** *adv*

**multifamily** /ˌmulti'faməli/ *adj, chiefly NAm* of or designed for use by several distinct families ⟨~ *dwellings*⟩

**multifarious** /-'feəri·əs/ *adj* having or occurring in great variety; diverse ⟨the ~ *duties of a farmer*⟩ [L *multifarius*, fr *multi-* + *-farius* (akin to *facere* to make, do)] – **multifariously** *adv*, **multifariousness** *n*

**multifold** /'multiˌfohld/ *adj* manifold, numerous

**multifont** /ˌmulti'font/ *adj* of, involving, or capable of reading several kinds of printed type ⟨a ~ *OCR machine*⟩ ⟨~ *composition*⟩

**multiform** /-ˌfawm/ *adj* having many forms or appearances [Fr *multiforme*, fr L *multiformis*, fr *multi-* + *-formis* -form] – **multiformity** *n*

**multilaminate** /ˌmulti'laminət/, **multilaminated** /-minaytid/ *adj* having many layers or LAMINAE

**multilateral** /ˌmulti'lat(ə)rəl/ *adj* 1 having many sides 2 participated in by more than two nations or parties ⟨~ *agreements*⟩ 3 *of a school* divided into more than two separately organized sides that offer different courses of study – **multilaterally** *adv*

**multilayered** /-'layəd/, **multilayer** *adj* having or involving several distinct layers, strata, or levels ⟨~ *epidermis*⟩ ⟨~ *tropical rain forest*⟩ ⟨~ *insights*⟩

**multilevel** /ˌmulti'levəl/ *also* **multilevelled** /-'levəld/ *adj* having several levels ⟨*motorways with* ~ *interchanges*⟩

**multilingual** /-'ling·gwəl/ *adj* 1 of, containing, or expressed in several languages ⟨a ~ *sign*⟩ ⟨~ *dictionaries*⟩ 2 using or able to use several languages ⟨a ~ *stewardess*⟩ – **multilingualism** *n*, **multilingually** *adv*

**'multi-ˌman**, *fem* **multi-woman** *n* an employee of a multinational ⟨multi-men *who work in Britain* – *The Economist*⟩

**multimedia** /-'meedi·ə/ *adj* using, involving, or encompassing several media ⟨a ~ *approach to learning*⟩ ⟨a ~ *exhibition*⟩ ⟨~ *resource materials* – *The Australian*⟩

**multimillionaire** /-ˌmilyə'neə/ *n* one whose wealth is estimated at many millions of monetary units (e g pounds or dollars)

**multinational** /-'nash(ə)nl/ *adj* 1 of or involving more than two nations ⟨a ~ *alliance*⟩ ⟨a ~ *society*⟩ 2 having divisions in more than two countries ⟨a ~ *company*⟩ – **multinational** *n*

**multinomial** /ˌmulti'nohmiəl/ *n* a mathematical expression (e g a POLYNOMIAL) consisting of several terms [*multi-* + *-nomial* (as in *binomial*)] – **multinomial** *adj*

**multinuclear** /ˌmulti'nyoohkliə/ *adj* multinucleate

**multinucleate** /ˌmulti'nyoohkliət/, **multinucleated** /-kliaytid/ *adj* having more than two nuclei [ISV]

**multiparous** /mul'tipərəs/ *adj* 1 producing many or more than one offspring at a birth 2 having given birth one or more times previously [NL *multiparus*, fr *multi-* + L *-parus* -parous]

**multipartite** /-'pahtiet/ *adj* 1 divided into several or many parts 2 having numerous members or signatories; multilateral ⟨a ~ *treaty*⟩ [L *multipartitus*, fr *multi-* + *partitus* partite]

**multiparty** /ˌmulti'pahti/ *adj, chiefly NAm* of or involving more than two parties ⟨*our two-party system cloaks a* ~ *reality* – Dean Acheson⟩

**multiphase** /ˌmulti'fayz/ *adj* having various phases; *esp* POLYPHASE

**multiphasic** /-'fayzik/ *adj* having various phases or elements ⟨a ~ *test*⟩

**¹multiple** /'multipl/ *adj* 1 consisting of, including, or involving more than one ⟨~ *births*⟩ 2 many, manifold ⟨~ *achievements*⟩ 3 shared by many ⟨~ *ownership*⟩ 4 having numerous aspects or functions; various 5 *of a fruit* formed by the growing together of the ripening OVARIES (female reproductive parts) of several flowers ⟨a raspberry is a ~ *fruit*⟩ [Fr, fr L *multiplex*, fr *multi-* + *-plex* -fold – more at SIMPLE]

**²multiple** *n* 1a the result of multiplying a quantity by a whole number ⟨35 is a ~ *of 7*⟩ b a group with respect to its divisions or parts ⟨*lay mines in* ~⟩ 2 PARALLEL 4b 3 **multiple, multiple store** *chiefly Br* a chain of retail marketing outlets; CHAIN STORE

**multiple allele** *n* any of more than two genetic characters that form a series (e g A, B, or O types for blood groups) and occur as alternatives at one particular position on a CHROMOSOME (strand of gene-carrying material)

**ˌmultiple-'choice** *adj* 1 having several answers from which one is to be chosen ⟨a ~ *question*⟩ 2 composed of multiple-choice questions ⟨a ~ *test*⟩

**multiple factor** *n* any of a group of unrelated genes that according to the multiple-factor hypothesis control various quantitative hereditary characters (e g size or yield)

**multiple myeloma** *n* a disease of bone marrow that is characterized by the presence of numerous tumours in various bones of the body

**multiple regression** *n* a statistical method for estimating the value of one RANDOM VARIABLE (quantity depending on the result of a statistical experiment) by the use of at least two other random variables whose values are known

**multiple sclerosis** *n* a diseased condition of progressively developing partial or complete paralysis and jerking muscle tremor, resulting from the loss of MYELIN (fatty substance forming an insulating sheath round a nerve) and hardening of patches of nerve tissue in the brain and spinal cord

**multiple shop** *n, Br* CHAIN STORE

**multiple star** *n* several stars in close proximity that appear to form a single system

**multiplet** /'multiplit/ *n* 1 a line composed of two or more closely spaced lines in a spectrum 2 a group of ELEMENTARY PARTICLES (minute particles of matter) that are different in charge but similar in other properties (e g mass) [ISV]

**multiple unit** *n* a train that has one or more carriages containing motors for propulsion and that is used mainly for local services

**,multiple-'valued** *adj, maths* MANY-VALUED

**multiple voting** *n* the illegal act of one person voting in two or more constituencies

¹**multiplex** /'multi,pleks/ *adj* 1 manifold, multiple ⟨*the ~ moods of our human nature* – Herbert Read⟩ 2 being or relating to a system allowing several messages to be transmitted simultaneously by the same circuit or channel [L]

²**multiplex** *vb* to send (messages or signals) by a multiplex system – **multiplexer, multiplexor** *n*

**multiplicable** /,multi'plikəbl/ *adj* capable of being multiplied

**multiplicand** /,multipli'kand/ *n* a number that is to be multiplied by another [L *multiplicandus*, gerundive of *multiplicare*]

**multiplicate** /'multiplikayt/ *adj* multiple [ME, fr L *multiplicatus*, pp]

**multiplication** /,multipli'kaysh(ə)n/ *n* 1 an act, process, or instance of multiplying 2 a mathematical operation that at its simplest is an abbreviated process of adding an integer to itself a specified number of times and that is extended to other numbers in accordance with laws that are valid for integers [ME *multiplicacioun*, fr MF *multiplication*, fr L *multiplication-, multiplicatio*, fr *multiplicatus*, pp of *multiplicare* to multiply]

**multiplication sign** *n* a symbol used to indicate multiplication: **a** the symbol × denoting multiplication **b** DOT 2b

**multiplicative** /,multi'plikətiv/ *adj* 1 tending or having the power to multiply numbers 2 of or characterized by multiplication ⟨~ *inverse*⟩ – **multiplicatively** *adv*

**multiplicity** /,multi'plisəti/ *n* 1 the quality or state of being multiple or various ⟨*the vast ~ of nature*⟩ 2 a great number ⟨*a ~ of errors*⟩ 3 the number of components in a system (e g a group of energy states) [MF *multiplicité*, fr LL *multiplicitat-, multiplicitas*, fr L *multiplic-, multiplex*]

**multiplier** /'multi,plie•ə/ *n* something that multiplies: e g **a** a number by which another number is multiplied **b** an instrument or device for multiplying or intensifying some effect **c** a key-operated machine, or mechanism or circuit on a machine, that multiplies figures and records the products **d** the ratio between the total increase in national income arising from a change in one of the components of aggregate demand (e g investment, government expenditure, or exports) and the change in that component – compare MONEY MULTIPLIER, REGIONAL MULTIPLIER

¹**multiply** /'multiplie/ *vt* 1 to increase in number, esp greatly or in multiples; augment **2a** to combine by multiplication ⟨~ *7 and 8*⟩ **b** to combine with (another number) by multiplication ⟨*7 multiplied by 8 is 56*⟩ ~ *vi* **1a** to become greater in number; spread **b** to breed, propagate 2 to perform multiplication synonyms see ¹INCREASE [ME *multiplien*, fr OF *multiplier*, fr L *multiplicare*, fr *multiplic-, multiplex* multiple] – **multipliable** *adj*

²**multiply** *adv* in a multiple manner; in several ways

**,multi-'ply** *adj* composed of several PLIES (strands or layers)

**multipolar** /,multi'pohlə/ *adj* 1 having several POLES (regions of concentrated magnetization) ⟨*a ~ generator*⟩ 2 of nerve cells having several DENDRITES (cellular extensions) [ISV] – **multipolarity** *n*

**multipotential** /,multipə'tensh(ə)l/ *adj, of a cell* capable of developing into any of several different differentiated cells

**multiprocessing** /,multi'prohsesing/ *n* the processing of several computer programs at the same time; TIME-SHARING; *esp* such processing done by a computer system with several processors sharing a single memory – **multiprocessor** *n*

**multiprogramming** /,multi'prohgraming/ *n* a technique for executing several independent computer programs simultaneously (e g by sequentially taking one instruction from each program)

**multipronged** /-'prongd/ *adj* 1 having several prongs ⟨~ *fishing spears*⟩ 2 having several distinct aspects or elements ⟨*a ~ attack on the problem*⟩

**multipurpose** /-'puhpəs/ *adj* serving several purposes ⟨*a ~ fabric*⟩

**multiracial** /-'raysh(ə)l/ *adj* composed of, involving, or representing various races ⟨~ *organizations*⟩ – **multiracialism** *n*

**multirole** /,multi'rohl/ *adj* having several uses ⟨*a ~ weapon . . . for use in air-to-air ground-to-air and 'ship-to-air weapon systems* – Flight International⟩

**multisense** /'multi,sens/ *adj* having several meanings ⟨~ *words*⟩

**multisensory** /,multi'sensəri/ *adj* relating to or involving several physiological senses (e g sight and sound) ⟨~ *teaching methods*⟩ ⟨~ *experience*⟩

**multistage** /-,stayj/ *adj* 1 having successive operating stages; *esp* having propulsion units that operate in turn ⟨~ *rockets*⟩ 2 conducted in stages ⟨*a ~ investigation*⟩

**,multi-'storey** /-'stawri/ *also* **multistoried** /-'stawrid/ *n or adj* (a building, esp a car park) having several storeys

**multitude** /'multityoohd/ *n* 1 the state of being many 2 a great number; a host ⟨*a ~ of voices*⟩ 3 *chiefly formal* a crowd 4 *chiefly derog* the populace, masses ⟨*politicians who seek the approval of the ~*⟩ [ME, fr MF or L; MF, fr L *multitudin-, multitudo*, fr *multus* much – more at MELIORATE]

**multitudinous** /,multi'tyoohdinəs/ *adj, chiefly formal* 1 comprising a multitude of individuals; populous 2 existing in a great multitude 3 existing in or consisting of innumerable elements or aspects – **multitudinously** *adv*, **multitudinousness** *n*

**multivalent** /,multi'vaylənt/ *adj* 1 POLYVALENT 2 *of chromosomes* represented more than the normal twice in a cell 3 having many values, meanings, or appeals [ISV] – **multivalent** *n*, **multivalence** *n*

**multivalued** /,multi'valyoohd/ *adj* having several or many values; *specif* having three or more TRUTH-VALUES ⟨*a ~ logic*⟩

**multivariate** /,multi'veəriət, -ayt/ *adj* having or involving a number of independent mathematical variables, esp RANDOM VARIABLES (quantities depending on the result of a statistical experiment) [*multi-* + *vari*able + ³-*ate*]

**multiversity** /,multi'vuhsəti/ *n* a very large university with many component schools, colleges, or divisions [*multi-* + *-versity* (as in *university*)]

**multivoltine** /,multi'voltien, -teen/ *adj, of an animal, esp an insect* having several broods or generations each year – compare BIVOLTINE, UNIVOLTINE

**multivolume** /,multi'volyoohm, -'volyoom/, **multivolumed** /-yoohmd, -yoomd/ *adj* comprising several volumes

¹**mum** /mum/ *adj* silent ⟨*keep ~*⟩ [prob imit of a sound made with closed lips] – **mum's the word** keep silent or secret

²**mum** *n, chiefly Br informal* MOTHER 1 [short for *mummy*]

**mumble** /'mumbl/ *vi* to say words in an inarticulate usu subdued voice; mutter ~ *vt* 1 to say in an inarticulate usu subdued voice 2 to chew or bite (as if) with toothless gums [ME *momelen*, of imit origin] – **mumble** *n*, **mumbler** *n*

**mumblety-peg** /'mumblti ,peg, 'mumbli/, **'mumble-the-,peg** *n, NAm* a game in which the players try to flip a knife from various positions so that the blade will stick into the ground [fr the phrase *mumble the peg;* fr the loser's originally having to pull out with his teeth a peg driven into the ground]

**mumbo jumbo** /,mumboh 'jumboh/ *n* 1 an object of superstitious respect and fear 2a elaborate but meaningless ritual **b** involved activity or language that obscures and confuses [*Mumbo Jumbo*, an idol or deity said to have been worshipped in Africa]

**mumetal** /'myooh,metl/ *n* an alloy of nickel with iron, copper, and manganese that is strongly magnetic [$\mu$ (*mu*), symbol for permeability]

**mummer** /'mumə/ *n* 1 a performer in a pantomime 2 one who goes merrymaking in disguise during festivals 3 *derog* an actor [MF *momeur*, fr *momer* to go masked]

**mummery** /'mumən/ *n* 1 a performance by mummers 2 an absurd or pretentious ceremony or performance

**mummify** /'mumifie/ *vt* 1 to embalm and dry (the body of an animal or human being) **2a** to make into or like a mummy ⟨*mummified customs that have long outlasted their usefulness* – W R Inge⟩ **b** to cause to dry up and shrivel ⟨*fruits that have been* mummified *by the hot sunshine*⟩ ~ *vi* to dry up and shrivel like a mummy – **mummification** *n*

**mumming** /'muming/ *n* 1 the practice of performing in a traditional pantomime 2 the custom of going about merrymaking in disguise during festivals [ME *mommyng*, fr *mommen* to act in a pantomime, fr MF *momer* to go masked, act in dumb show]

¹**mummy** /'mumi/ *n* **1a** a body treated for burial with preservatives and linen wrappings in the manner of the ancient Egyptians **b** an unusually well-preserved dead body 2 one who or that which resembles a mummy [ME *mummie* powdered parts of a mummified body used as a drug, fr MF *momie*, fr ML *mumia* mummy, powdered mummy, fr Ar *mūmiyah* bitumen, mummy, fr Per *mūm* wax]

²**mummy** *n, chiefly Br* mother – used esp by or to children [baby talk, var of *mama, mamma*]

**mump** /mump/ *vi* to be sullen or dejected [prob imit; orig senses, to mumble, grimace] – **mumper** *n*

**mumps** /mumps/ *n taking sing or pl vb* an acute infectious virus disease marked by gross swelling of esp the PAROTID GLANDS [fr pl of obs *mump* grimace, fr *mump*, vb]

**mun** /mən; *strong* mun/ *verbal auxiliary, dial Br* **1** must **2** may [ME *mun, mon* must, shall, fr ON *mon* shall; akin to OE *man* he remembers, thinks of, L *ment-, mens* mind]

**munch** /munch/ *vb* to chew (food) with a crunching sound and visible movement of the jaws [ME *monchen*, prob of imit origin] – **muncher** *n*

**mundane** /mun'dayn/ *adj* **1** (characteristic) of this world in contrast to heaven **2** practical and ordinary, esp to the point of dull familiarity [ME *mondeyne*, fr MF *mondain*, fr LL *mundanus*, fr L *mundus* world] – **mundanely** *adv*, **mundaneness, mundanity** *n*

**mung bean** /mung/ *n* (the edible green or yellow seeds of) an erect bushy annual bean (*Phaseolus aureus*) that is widely cultivated in warm regions for forage and as the chief source of bean sprouts [Hindi *mūg*, fr Skt *mudga*]

**mungo** /'mung·goh/ *n, pl* **mungos** reclaimed wool of poor quality; shoddy [origin unknown]

**¹municipal** /myooh'nisipl, ---'--/ *adj* **1** of the internal affairs of a state or nation **2a** of or characteristic of a municipality **b** having local self-government **3** restricted to one locality ⟨*a very ~ variety of dwarf sweet pea* – Osbert Sitwell⟩ [L *municipalis* of a municipality, fr *municip-, municeps* inhabitant of a municipality, lit., undertaker of duties, fr *munus* duty, service + *capere* to take – more at MEAN, HEAVE] – **municipally** *adv*
*usage* The pronunciation /myooh'nisipl/ is recommended for BBC broadcasters.

**municipality** /myooh,nisi'paləti/ *n* (the governing body of) a primarily urban political unit having a legally recognized status and usu powers of self-government

**municipal·ize, -ise** /myooh'nisip(ə)l,iez/ *vt* to invest control or ownership of in a municipality – **municipalization** *n*

**munificent** /myooh'nifis(ə)nt/ *adj, formal* **1** giving or bestowing with great generosity **2** characterized by great liberality or generosity ⟨*a ~ gift*⟩ △ magnificent [back-formation fr *munificence*, fr L *munificentia*, fr *munificus* generous, fr *munus* service, gift] – **munificence** *n*, **munificently** *adv*

**muniment** /'myoohnimənt/ *n usu pl* a document kept as evidence of title or privilege [AF, fr MF, defence, fr ML *munimentum*, fr L, fortification, defence, fr *munire* to fortify]

**munition** /myooh'nish(ə)n/ *n* **1** **munitions** *pl*, **munition** weapons, ammunition **2** *archaic* a rampart, defence [MF, fr L *munition-, munitio*, fr *munitus*, pp of *munire* to fortify, fr *moenia* walls; akin to OE *maere* boundary, L *murus* wall] – **munition** *vt*

**muntin** /'muntin/ *also* **munting** /-tin, -ting/ *n* a central vertical strip separating panes of glass in a sash window or panels in a door [alter. of earlier *montant* vertical dividing bar, fr Fr, fr prp of *monter* to rise – more at MOUNT]

**muntjac** *also* **muntjak** /'munt,jak/ *n* any of several small deer (genus *Muntiacus*) of SE Asia and the E Indies [prob modif of Jav *mindjangan* deer]

**Muntz metal** /munts/ *n* a type of brass usu having 60 per cent copper and 40 per cent zinc, used esp in shipbuilding [George *Muntz* †1857 E metal manufacturer & politician]

**muon** /'myooh·on/ *n* an ELEMENTARY PARTICLE (minute particle of matter) belonging to the family of LEPTONS that is common in the cosmic radiation near the earth's surface and has a mass about 207 times that of the electron [contr of earlier *mu-meson*, fr *mu* (taken as a symbol for *meson*, and used to distinguish it from the short-lived pi-meson, ie pion)] – **muonic** *adj*

**¹mural** /'myooərəl/ *adj* **1** of or resembling a wall **2** attached or applied to a wall surface ⟨*a ~ painting*⟩ [L *muralis*, fr *murus* wall – more at MUNITION]

**²mural** *n* a mural work of art (e g a painting) – **muralist** *n*

**muramic acid** /myoo'ramik/ *n* a sugar, $C_9H_{17}NO_7$, that is found esp in bacterial cell walls and in BLUE-GREEN ALGAE [*mur-* (fr L *murus* wall) + *glucosamide* + *-ic*]

**¹murder** /'muhdə/ *n* **1** the crime of unlawfully and intentionally killing a human being **2** *informal* something very difficult, dangerous, or disagreeable ⟨*it was ~ trying to park in the town centre*⟩ [partly fr ME *murther*, fr OE *morthor*; partly fr ME *murdre*, fr OF, of Gmc origin; akin to OE *morthor*; akin to OHG *mord* murder, L *mort-, mors* death, *mori* to die, Gk *brotos* mortal] – **cry/scream blue murder** *informal* to make a great deal of noise, esp in complaint – **get away with murder** *informal* to do something bad or daring without suffering punishment; act just as one wishes

**²murder** *vt* **1** to kill (a human being) unlawfully and inten-

tionally **2** to slaughter brutally or indiscriminately ⟨*the bombing ~ed most of the civilian population*⟩ **3a** to put an end to ⟨*totalitarian governments ~ truth and freedom*⟩ **b** to mutilate, mangle ⟨*~ a sonata*⟩ *~ vi* to commit murder *synonyms* see ¹KILL

**murderer** /'muhd(ə)rə/, *fem* **murderess** /'muhd(ə)ris, muhdə'res/ *n* a person who murders; *esp* a person who commits the crime of murder

**murderous** /'muhd(ə)rəs/ *adj* **1a** having the purpose or capability of murder ⟨*a ~ intrigue*⟩ ⟨*a murderous-looking knife*⟩ **b** characterized by or causing murder or bloodshed **2** capable of overwhelming ⟨*~ heat*⟩ – **murderously** *adv*, **murderousness** *n*

**murein** /'myooəri·in, -reen/ *n* a chemical compound that is composed of alternating units of two sugars and is characteristic of the cell walls of bacteria and BLUE-GREEN ALGAE [*muramic acid* + *-ein*]

**murex** /'myooəreks/ *n, pl* **murices** /-riseez/, **murexes** any of a genus (*Murex*) of tropical marine snails that have a rough and often spiny shell and that yield a purple dye [NL, genus name, fr L, shellfish yielding a purple dye; akin to Gk *myak-, myax* sea-mussel]

**muriate** /'myooəri·ət, -ayt/ *n* CHLORIDE (chemical compound) [Fr, back-formation fr (*acide*) *muriatique* muriatic acid (hydrochloric acid), fr L *muriaticus* pickled in brine, fr *muria* brine]

**murid** /'myooərid/ *adj* of a family (Muridae) of rodents that comprises the typical mice and rats [deriv of L *mur-, mus* mouse – more at MOUSE] – **murid** *n*

**murine** /'myooərien, -rin/ *adj* of or being a common domestic rat or mouse; *also* of the genus (*Mus*) to which the HOUSE MOUSE belongs [deriv of L *mur-, mus*] – **murine** *n*

**murine typhus** /'myooərin, -rien/ *n* a mild disease that is marked by headache and rash, is caused by a microscopic organism (*Rickettsia mooseri*), is widespread in nature in rodents, and is transmitted to man by the rat flea

**murk** /muhk/ *n* gloom, darkness; *also* fog [ME *mirke*, prob fr ON *myrkr*]

**murky** /'muhki/ *adj* **1** strikingly dark and gloomy ⟨*a ~ night*⟩ **2** of air foggy, misty **3** darkly vague or obscure ⟨*~ official rhetoric*⟩ ⟨*his ~ past*⟩ – **murkily** *adv*, **murkiness** *n*

**¹murmur** /'muhmə/ *n* **1** a half-suppressed or muttered complaint; grumbling **2a** a low indistinct (continuous) sound **b** a subdued or gentle utterance ⟨*the fond ~s of two lovers*⟩ **3** an atypical sound of the heart indicating a functional or structural abnormality [ME *murmure*, fr MF, fr L *murmur* murmur, roar, of imit origin]

**²murmur** *vi* **1** to make a murmur ⟨*the breeze ~ed in the pines*⟩ **2** to complain, grumble *~ vt* to say in a murmur ⟨*~ed an apology for being late*⟩ – **murmurer** *n*

**murmuration** /,muhmə'raysh(ə)n/ *n* **1** the act of murmuring **2** a flock – used with reference to starlings

**murmurous** /'muhmərəs/ *adj* **1** filled with or making murmurs ⟨*the ~ haunt of flies*⟩ **2** low and indistinct – **murmurously** *adv*

**murphy** /'muhfi/ *n, informal* a potato [*Murphy*, a common Irish surname; fr the potato having formerly been the staple food of Ireland]

**murrain** /'murin/ *n* a plague affecting domestic animals or plants [ME *moreyne*, fr MF *morine*, fr *morir* to die, fr L *mori* – more at MURDER]

**murre** /muh/ *n* any of several GUILLEMOTS (large marine diving birds) (genus *Uria*) [origin unknown]

**murrey** /'muri/ *n* a purplish black colour; mulberry [ME, fr MF *moré*, fr ML *moratum*, fr neut of *moratus* mulberry-coloured, fr L *morum* mulberry – more at MULBERRY]

**murther** /'muhdə/ *vb or n, chiefly dial* (to) murder

**Muscadet** /'mooskahday/ *n* a very dry white table wine made near Nantes in NE France [Fr, fr MF, fr OProv, a grape, deriv of *muscat* musky]

**muscadine** /'muskədin, -dien/ *n* a grape (*Vitis rotundifolia*) of the S USA with musky fruits borne in small clusters [prob alter. of *muscatel*]

**muscae volitantes** /,muskie voli'tantayz, -teez, ,musie, ,musee/ *n pl* spots before the eyes, usu in the form of dots, threads, beads, or circles, caused by cells and cell fragments floating in the VITREOUS HUMOUR (liquid inside the eyeball) and lens [NL, lit., flying flies]

**muscarine** /'muskəreen/ *n* a poisonous chemical compound, $C_9H_{21}NO_2$, that occurs in mushrooms, esp FLY AGARIC, and when eaten causes (often severe) disorders of esp the digestive system, heart, and lungs – compare NICOTINE [Ger *muskarin*, fr

NL *muscaria,* specific epithet of *Amanita muscaria* fly agaric] –
**muscarine** *adj*
**muscarinic** /ˌmuskəˈrinik/ *adj* of muscarine or its physiological
effects; *specif* of, being, having, or resembling the actions or
effects produced by stimulation of the PARASYMPATHETIC NER-
VOUS SYSTEM (e g increased action of the sweat glands and gut
and decreased action of the heart) ⟨*atropine blocks the ~
actions of acetylcholine*⟩ – compare NICOTINIC
**muscat** /ˈmuskət, -kat/ *n* any of several cultivated grapes used
in making wine and raisins [Fr, fr Prov, fr *muscat* musky, fr
*musc* musk, fr LL *muscus*]
**muscatel** /ˌmuskəˈtel/ *n* **1** a sweet dessert wine made from
muscat grapes **2** a raisin from muscat grapes [ME *muskadelle,*
fr MF *muscadel,* fr OProv, fr *muscadel* resembling musk, fr
*muscat*]
**muscid** /ˈmusid/ *n* any of a family (Muscidae) of flies that
includes the common housefly [deriv of L *musca* fly] – **muscid**
*adj*
¹**muscle** /ˈmusl/ *n* **1a** a body tissue consisting of variously
modified elongated cells that contract when stimulated and
produce motion **b** an organ of the body that is essentially a
mass of muscle tissue attached at either end to a fixed point
and that by contracting moves or checks the movement of a
body part **2** muscular strength; brawn [MF, fr L *musculus,* fr
dim. of *mus* mouse – more at MOUSE]
²**muscle** *vt, chiefly informal* to push by force or brute strength
⟨*muscling aside American competitors – Punch*⟩
  **muscle in** *vi, informal* to interfere forcibly – usu + *on*
⟨*muscle in on the territory of an unscrupulous gang – The
Bookseller*⟩
'**muscle-ˌbound** /-ˌbownd/ *adj* **1** having some of the muscles
tense and enlarged and of reduced elasticity, sometimes as a
result of excessive exercise **2** lacking flexibility; rigid ⟨*~
government institutions*⟩
**muscled** /ˈmusld/ *adj* having muscles, esp of a specified kind –
often in combination ⟨*hard-muscled arms*⟩
**muscle spindle** *n* a SENSE ORGAN in a muscle that is sensitive
to stretch and consists of small modified striped muscle fibres
**muscovado** /ˌmuskəˈvahdoh/ *n* the raw unrefined sugar
obtained as crystals after sugarcane juice has been evaporated
and the molasses has been drained off [Sp or Pg; Sp (*azúcar*)
*mascabado,* fr Pg (*açúcar*) *mascavado,* fr *açúcar* sugar +
*mascavado,* pp of *mascavar* to adulterate, separate raw sugar,
deriv of L *minus* less + *caput* head]
**muscovite** /ˈmuskəˌviet/ *n* **1** *cap* a native or inhabitant of (the
ancient principality of) Moscow **2** a glasslike mineral,
KAl₃Si₃O₁₀(OH)₂, that is colourless to pale brown [ML or NL
*Muscovia, Moscovia* Moscow, principality & city in Russia; (2)
obs *Muscovy* (*glass*) + *-ite;* fr its former use in Russia for
window panes] – **Muscovite** *adj*
**Muscovy duck** /ˈmuskəvi/ *n* a large crested duck (*Cairina
moschata*) native from Mexico to S Brazil but widely kept in
domestication [prob alter. (influenced by *Muscovy,* the principality of Moscow) of *musk duck*]
**muscul-** /muskyool-/, **musculo-** *comb form* **1** muscle ⟨*muscular*⟩ **2** muscular and ⟨*musculoskeletal*⟩ [LL *muscul-,* fr L
*musculus*]
**muscular** /ˈmuskyoolə/ *adj* **1a** of or constituting muscle **b** of
or performed by the muscles **2** having well-developed
musculature **3** having strength of expression or character;
vigorous – **muscularly** *adv,* **muscularity** *n*
**muscular dystrophy** *n* a hereditary disease characterized by
progressive wasting of muscles
**musculature** /ˈmuskyooləchə/ *n* the muscles of all or a part
of the body [Fr, fr L *musculus*]
¹**muse** /myoohz/ *vi* to become absorbed in thought; *esp* to
engage in daydreaming or idle speculation ~ *vt* to think or
say reflectively [ME *musen,* fr MF *muser* to gape, idle, muse, fr
*muse* mouth of an animal, fr ML *musus*] – **muser** *n*
²**muse** *n* a state of deep thought or dreamy abstraction; BROWN
STUDY
³**muse** *n* **1** *cap* any of the nine sister goddesses in Greek mythology presiding over song and poetry and the arts and sciences
**2** a source of inspiration; *esp* a woman who influences a creative artist **3** *poetic* a poet [ME, fr MF, fr L *Musa,* fr Gk *Mousa;*
prob akin to Gk *mnasthai* to remember]
**musette** /myoohˈzet/ *n* **1** a small bagpipe having a soft sweet
tone **2a** a quiet pastoral air that often has a drone bass and is
adapted to the musette **b** a GAVOTTE danced to the tune of a
musette **3** **musette, musette bag** a small knapsack; *also* a

similar bag with one shoulder strap [Fr, fr MF, dim. of *muse*
bagpipe, fr *muser* to muse, play the bagpipe]
**museum** /myoohˈzeeˑəm/ *n* an institution devoted to the
acquiring, care, study, and display of objects of lasting interest
or value; *also* a place where such objects are exhibited [L
*Museum* library, study, fr Gk *Mouseion,* fr neut of *Mouseios*
of the Muses, fr *Mousa*]
**museum piece** *n* **1** an object valuable and interesting enough
for a museum to display **2** something absurdly old-fashioned
and obsolete
¹**mush** /mush/ *n* **1** a thick porridge made with maize **2** soft and
spongy or shapeless matter **3** weak sentimentality; drivel [prob
alter. of *mash*]
²**mush** *vt, chiefly dial* to reduce to a crumbly mass ~ *vi, of an
aeroplane* to fly in a partly stalled condition with controls ineffective; *also* to fail to gain altitude – **musher** *n*
³**mush** *vi* to travel, esp over snow, with a sledge drawn by
dogs [prob fr AmerF *moucher* to go fast, fr Fr *mouche* fly, fr L
*musca* – more at MIDGE]
¹**mushroom** /ˈmushroohm, -room/ *n* **1a** an enlarged fleshy
fruiting body of a fungus (e g of the class Basidiomycetes) that
consists typically of a stem bearing a flattened cap; *esp* one
that is edible **b** FUNGUS 1 **2** an upstart ⟨*~ aristocrats*⟩ **3** something resembling a mushroom, esp in shape ⟨*a ~ cloud*⟩ ⟨*a
darning ~*⟩ **4** a pale yellowish-brown colour [ME *musseroun,*
fr MF *mousseron,* fr LL *mussirion-, mussirio*]
²**mushroom** *vi* **1** to spring up suddenly or grow or multiply
rapidly ⟨*housing estates that ~ on the outskirts of small
towns*⟩ **2a** *of a bullet* to flatten at the end on impact **b** to well
up and spread out sideways from a central source **3** to pick
wild mushrooms ⟨*go ~ing*⟩
**mushy** /ˈmushi/ *adj* **1** having the consistency of mush; soft ⟨*~
peas*⟩ **2** excessively sentimental; *esp* sickeningly amorous –
**mushily** *adv,* **mushiness** *n*
**music** /ˈmyoohzik/ *n* **1a** the science or art of ordering tones or
sounds in succession and combination to produce a composition having unity and continuity **b** vocal, instrumental, or
mechanical sounds having rhythm, melody, or harmony **2** an
agreeable sound; euphony ⟨*the ~ of the nightingale*⟩ **3** a
musical accompaniment ⟨*a play set to ~*⟩ **4** the score of a
musical composition set down on paper [ME *musik,* fr OF
*musique,* fr L *musica,* fr Gk *mousikē* any art presided over by
the Muses, esp music, fr fem of *mousikos* of the Muses, fr
*Mousa* Muse] – **face the music** to confront and endure the
unpleasant consequences of one's actions
¹**musical** /ˈmyoohzikl/ *adj* **1a** of music **b** having the pleasing
harmonious qualities of music; melodious **2** having an interest
in or talent for music **3** set to or accompanied by music **4** of
musicians or music lovers ⟨*~ organizations*⟩ – **musically** *adv*
²**musical** *n* **1** a film or theatrical production that consists of
songs, dances, and dialogue based on a unifying plot **2** *archaic*
a musicale
**musical box** *n, chiefly Br* a container enclosing an apparatus
that reproduces music mechanically when activated by a
clockwork
**musical chairs** *n taking sing vb* **1** a game in which players
march to music round a row of chairs numbering one less than
the players and scramble for seats when the music stops **2** a
change from one position, situation, or arrangement to
another, esp without significant effect
**musical comedy** *n* MUSICAL 1; *esp* one of a sentimental or
humorous nature
**musicale** /ˌmyoohziˈkahl/ *n* a social entertainment with music as
the leading feature [Fr (*soirée*) *musicale,* lit., musical evening]
**musicality** /ˌmyoohziˈkaləti/ *n* **1** the quality or state of being
musical; melodiousness **2** sensitivity to, knowledge of, or talent
for music
**musical saw** *n* a handsaw made to produce melody by bending the blade with varying tension while sounding it with a
hammer or violin bow
**music box** *n, chiefly NAm* MUSICAL BOX
**music centre** *n, Br* a usu stereophonic system that houses a
record player, a radio, and a cassette tape recorder in a single
unit usu with independently movable loudspeakers
**music drama** *n* an opera in which the action is not interrupted
by formal song divisions (e g recitatives or arias) and the music
is determined solely by dramatic appropriateness
**music hall** *n* (a theatre formerly presenting) entertainments
consisting of a variety of unrelated acts (e g acrobats,
comedians, or singers); VARIETY 4

**musician** /myooh'zish(ə)n/ *n* a composer, conductor, or performer of music; *esp* an instrumentalist – **musicianship** *n*

**musicology** /ˌmyoohzi'koləji/ *n* the study of music as a branch of knowledge or field of research; *esp* the historical study of specific types of music [It *musicologia*, fr L *musica* music + *-logia* -logy] – **musicologist** *n*, **musicological** *adj*

**music stool** *n* a stool usu having an adjustable height and used by a pianist

**¹musing** /'myoohzing/ *n* meditation, reflection

**²musing** *adj* thoughtfully abstracted; meditative – **musingly** *adv*

**musique concrète** /mooh,zeek kong'kret (*Fr* myzik kɔ̃krɛt)/ *n* a collection of recorded natural sounds (e g voices, traffic noise, and bird calls) modified and arranged to form a piece of music [Fr, lit., concrete music]

**musk** /musk/ *n* **1a** (a synthetic substitute for) a substance with a penetrating persistent odour obtained from a sac beneath the abdominal skin of the male musk deer and used as a perfume fixative; *also* a similar substance from another animal **b** the odour of musk; *also* an odour resembling musk esp in heaviness or persistence **2** any of various plants with musky odours [ME *muske*, fr MF *musc*, fr LL *muscus*, fr Gk *moschos*, fr Per *mushk*, fr Skt *muṣka* testicle, fr dim. of *mūṣ* mouse; akin to OE *mūs* mouse]

**musk deer** *n* a small heavy-limbed hornless deer (*Moschus moschiferus*) of central Asiatic uplands, the male of which produces musk

**muskeg** /'mus,keg/ *n* **1** a mossy bog of northern N America, often with tussocks **2** a usu thick deposit of partially decayed vegetable matter of wet northern regions [of Algonquian origin; akin to Ojibwa *mŭskeg* grassy bog]

**musket** /'muskit/ *n* a heavy large-calibre shoulder firearm (e g a flintlock or matchlock) with a smooth bore; *broadly* a shoulder gun carried by infantry [MF *mousquet*, fr OIt *moschetto* arrow for a crossbow, musket, fr dim. of *mosca* fly, fr L *musca* – more at MIDGE]

**musketeer** /ˌmuskə'tiə/ *n* a soldier armed with a musket [modif of MF *mousquetaire*, fr *mousquet*]

**musketry** /'muskitri/ *n* **1** muskets **2** *taking sing or pl vb* musketeers **3a** musket fire **b** the art or science of using small arms esp in battle

**muskmelon** /'musk,melən/ *n* a usu sweet musky-smelling edible melon that is the fruit of the trailing or climbing Asiatic plant (*Cucumis melo*): e g a the cantaloup with reddish-orange flesh **b** WINTER MELON

**Muskogean, Muskhogean** /mu'skohgiən/ *n* a language family of the southeastern USA that includes Muskogee

**Muskogee** /mu'skohgi/ *n*, *pl* **Muskogees**, *esp collectively* **Muskogee 1** a member of an American Indian people of Georgia and E Alabama **2** the language of the Muskogees and of some of the SEMINOLES

**'musk-,ox** *n* a thickset shaggy-coated wild ox (*Ovibos moschatus*) now confined to Greenland and the barren northern lands of N America [fr its strong musky odour]

**muskrat** /-ˌrat/ *n*, *pl* **muskrats**, *esp collectively* **muskrat** an aquatic rodent (*Ondatra zibethica*) of N America that has a long scaly tail, webbed hind feet, and dark glossy brown fur and that has been introduced into Europe [prob by folk etymology fr a word of Algonquian origin; akin to Natick *musquash* muskrat]

**musk rose** *n* a rose (*Rosa moschata*) of the Mediterranean region with flowers having a musky odour

**musk thistle** *n* a Eurasian thistle (*Carduus nutans*) with drooping musky flower heads

**musky** /'muski/ *adj* having an odour of or resembling musk – **muskiness** *n*

**Muslim** /'moozlim, 'muz-/ *n* **1** a follower of the Islamic faith **2** BLACK MUSLIM [Ar *muslim*, lit., one who surrenders (to God)] – **Muslim** *adj*

synonyms **Muslim** is now preferred, rather than the older spelling **Moslem**, for an adherent of Islam (or Muhammadanism), the religion founded by Muhammad. People can be **Muhammadan**, but we tend to speak of **Islamic** art. **Mussulman** is an archaic word for **Muslim**.

**Muslim era** *n* MUHAMMADAN ERA (period of the Muhammadan calendar)

**muslin** /'muzlin/ *n* a plain-woven sheer to coarse cotton fabric [Fr *mousseline*, fr It *mussolina*, fr Ar *mawṣilīy* of Mosul, fr al-*Mawṣil* Mosul, city in Iraq]

**musquash** /'muskwosh/ *n* (the dark glossy brown fur or pelt of) the muskrat [of Algonquian origin; akin to Natick *musquash* muskrat]

**¹muss** /mus/ *n*, *NAm informal* a state of disorder or confusion; a mess [origin unknown] – **mussy** *adj*

**²muss** *vt*, *NAm informal* to make untidy; disarrange, dishevel ⟨*her hairdo was all* ~ed *by the wind*⟩

**mussel** /'musl/ *n* **1** a marine INVERTEBRATE animal (esp genus *Mytilus* of the phylum Mollusca) that has a usu dark elongated hinged shell, is found attached to rocks, and is often used as food **2** a freshwater INVERTEBRATE animal (e g of *Unio*, *Anodonta*, or related genera of the phylum Mollusca) that has a hinged shell with a glossy MOTHER-OF-PEARL lining [ME *muscle*, fr OE *muscelle*; akin to OHG *muscula* mussel; both fr a prehistoric WGmc word borrowed fr (assumed) VL *muscula*, fr L *musculus* muscle, mussel]

**mussel scale** *n* a scale insect (*Lepidosaphes ulmi*) that is a pest of ornamental trees

**Mussulman** *also* **Mussalman** /'muslmən, 'moos-/ *n*, *pl* **Mussulmen** /-mən, -men/, **Mussulmans** a Muslim synonyms see MUSLIM [Turk *müslüman* & Per *musulmān*, modif of Ar *muslim* (pl *muslimūn*)]

**¹must** /məs(t); *strong* must/ *vb*, *pres & past all persons* **must** *va* **1a** be commanded or requested to ⟨*you* ~ *stop*⟩ **b** certainly should; ought by all means to ⟨*I* ~ *read that book*⟩ ⟨*we* mus*t'n't despair*⟩ **2** be compelled by physical, social, or legal necessity to ⟨*man* ~ *eat to live*⟩ ⟨*I* ~ *say you're looking much better*⟩; be required by immediate or future need or purpose to ⟨*we* ~ *hurry if we want to catch the bus*⟩ – past often replaced by *had to* except in reported speech; used in the negative to express the idea of prohibition ⟨*we* ~ *not park here*⟩ **3** WILL **6** ⟨*if you* ~ *go at least wait till the storm is over*⟩; *esp* be unreasonably or perversely compelled to ⟨*why* ~ *you be so stubborn?*⟩ ⟨*in spite of my advice, she* ~ *go and do the opposite*⟩ **4** be logically inferred or supposed to ⟨*it* ~ *be time*⟩ ⟨*they* mus*tn't have arrived*⟩ – compare CANNOT **5** be compelled by fate or by natural law to ⟨*what* ~ *be will be*⟩ **6** was presumably certain to; was bound to ⟨*if he had really been there I* ~ *have seen him*⟩ **7** *dial* may, shall – used chiefly in questions ~ *vi*, *archaic* to be obliged to go ⟨*I* ~ *to Coventry* – Shak⟩ [ME *moste*, fr OE *mōste*, past indic & subj of *mōtan* to be allowed to, have to; akin to OHG *muozan* to be allowed to, have to, OE *metan* to measure – more at METE]

**²must** /must/ *n* something necessary, required, or indispensable; an essential, prerequisite ⟨*a crash helmet is a* ~ *for motorcyclists*⟩

**³must** *n* grape juice before and during fermentation [ME, fr OE, fr L *mustum*, fr neut of *mustus* young, fresh, new]

**⁴must** *n* musk [MF, alter. of *musc* musk]

**⁵must** *n* mould, mustiness [back-formation fr *musty*]

**⁶must** *n* MUSTH (state of frenzy in elephants)

**mustache** /mə'stahsh, mə'stash/ *n*, *chiefly NAm* a moustache

**mustachio** /mə'stahshioh, mə'stashioh/ *n*, *pl* **mustachios** a (large) moustache [Sp & It; Sp *mostacho*, fr It *mustaccio*, *mostaccio*] – **mustachioed** *adj*

**mustang** /'mustang/ *n* the small hardy naturalized horse of the western plains of N America, directly descended from horses brought in by the Spaniards; *also* BRONCO [MexSp *mestengo*, fr Sp, stray, fr *mesteño* strayed, fr *mesta* annual roundup of cattle that disposed of strays, fr ML (*animalia*) *mixta* mixed animals]

**mustard** /'mustəd/ *n* **1** a hot-tasting yellow powder of the seeds of a common mustard used as a seasoning, esp with meat, or in medicine, esp to bring about remedial vomiting **2** any of several plants (*Brassica*, *Sinapis*, and related genera) of the cabbage family with lobed leaves, yellow flowers, and long seed pods **3** *chiefly NAm slang* zest [ME, fr OF *mostarde*, fr *moust* must, fr L *mustum*] – **mustardy** *adj*

**mustard gas** *n* an irritant and blister-inducing oily liquid, $(ClCH_2CH_2)_2S$, used as a poison gas [fr its mustard-like odour]

**mustard plaster** *n* a plaster containing powdered mustard, used in medicine (e g to ease inflammation)

**¹muster** /'mustə/ *vt* **1a** to cause to gather; assemble, convene **b** to call the roll of ⟨*the mate* ~ed *the ship's crew*⟩ **2** to collect or summon in response to a need ⟨*all the courage he could* ~⟩ **3** to amount to; comprise **4** *NAm* to enrol formally to come together; congregate – usu + *in* or *into* ⟨~ed *into the army*⟩ [ME *mustren* to show, muster, fr OF *monstrer*, fr L *monstrare* to show, fr *monstrum* evil omen, monster – more at MONSTER]

**muster out** *vt*, *NAm* to discharge from service

²**muster** *n* **1** an act of assembling; *specif* formal military inspection **2** a critical examination **3** an assembled group; a collection – **pass muster** to be found adequate, esp in passing an inspection or examination ⟨*slipshod work that would never* pass muster⟩

**muster roll** *n* a register of the officers and men in a military unit or ship's company

**musth, must** /must/ *n* a periodic state of frenzy of the bull elephant usu connected with the breeding season [Hindi *mast* intoxicated, fr Per; akin to OE *mete* meat]

**mustn't** /'musnt/ must not

**musty** /'musti/ *adj* **1a** affected by mould, damp, or mildew; mouldy **b** tasting or smelling of damp and decay; fusty ⟨∼ *old leather-bound books*⟩ **2a** trite, stale ⟨*recited a* ∼ *proverb*⟩ **b** antiquated ⟨*the* ∼ *elegance of the old hotel*⟩ [perh alter. (influenced by ³*must*) of earlier *moisty*, fr ME, fr *moist* + *-y*] – **mustily** *adv*, **mustiness** *n*

**mutable** /'myoohtəbl/ *adj* **1** capable of or liable to change or alteration; variable, inconstant **2** capable of or subject to mutation [L *mutabilis*, fr *mutare* to change – more at MISS] – **mutableness** *n*, **mutably** *adv*, **mutability** *n*

**mutagen** /'myoohtəjən/ *n* a substance (e g mustard gas or various radiations) that tends to increase the frequency or extent of mutation [ISV *mutation* + *-gen*] – **mutagenic** *adj*, **mutagenically** *adv*

**mutagenesis** /,myoohtə'jenəsis/ *n* the occurrence or induction of mutation [NL]

**mutagenicity** /,myoohtəjə'nisəti/ *n* the capacity to induce mutations

**mutant** /'myooht(ə)nt/ *adj* of or produced by mutation [L *mutant-, mutans*, prp of *mutare*] – **mutant** *n*

**mutase** /'myoohtayz/ *n* an ENZYME that takes part in a biological reaction involving the rearrangement of the structure of chemical compounds, esp the transfer of electrical charge during OXIDATION-REDUCTION reactions or the transfer of a PHOSPHATE group [ISV *mut-* (fr L *mutare*) + *-ase*]

**mutate** /myooh'tayt/ *vb* to (cause to) undergo mutation [L *mutatus*, pp of *mutare*] – **mutative** *adj*

**mutation** /myooh'taysh(ə)n/ *n* **1** (an instance of) significant and fundamental alteration; change **2** SANDHI (modification of the form or sound of a word); *specif* UMLAUT (alteration of vowel sounds) **3a** a relatively permanent change in the hereditary material of an organism involving either a physical or a biochemical change in the genes or CHROMOSOMES (strands of gene-carrying material) **b(1)** an individual or strain resulting from mutation **b(2)** an animal of a domesticated strain that differs, esp in coat colour, from the WILD TYPE – **mutational** *adj*, **mutationally** *adv*

**mutatis mutandis** /mooh,tahtis mooh'tandis/ *adv* **1** with the necessary changes having been made **2** with the respective differences having been considered [NL]

**mutch** /much/ *n, chiefly Scot* a closely fitting cap often worn by old women or babies [ME (Sc) *much*, fr MD *mutse* cap]

**mutchkin** /'muchkin/ *n* a Scottish unit of liquid capacity equal to about ³/₄ imperial pint (about 0.43 litre) [ME (Sc) *muchekyn*, fr MD *mudseken*]

¹**mute** /myooht/ *adj* **1** unable to speak; dumb **2** characterized by absence of speech: e g **2a** felt but not expressed ⟨*touched her hand in* ∼ *sympathy*⟩ **b** refusing to plead or answer a charge ⟨*the prisoner stands* ∼⟩ **3** *of letters* contributing nothing to the pronunciation of a word ⟨*the* b *in* plumb *is* ∼⟩ [ME *muet*, fr MF, fr OF *mu*, fr L *mutus*; akin to OHG *māwen* to cry out, Gk *mytēs* mute] – **mutely** *adv*, **muteness** *n*

²**mute** *n* **1** a person who cannot or does not speak **2** STOP 7 (type of consonant) **3** a device attached to a musical instrument to reduce, soften, or muffle its tone

³**mute** *vt* **1** to muffle or reduce the sound of **2** to tone down (a colour)

⁴**mute** *vi, of a bird* to pass waste matter from the body [ME *muten*, fr MF *meutir*, short for *esmeutir*, fr OF *esmeltir*, of Gmc origin]

**muted** /'myoohtid/ *adj* **1** being mute; silent, subdued **2** provided with or produced or modified by the use of a mute – **mutedly** *adv*

**mute swan** *n* the common white swan (*Cygnus olor*) of Europe and W Asia that produces no loud notes

**mutilate** /'myoohtilayt/ *vt* **1** to cut off or permanently destroy a limb or essential part of; cripple **2** to impair, damage, or deface radically and usu permanently ⟨*the censors had* ∼d *the script*⟩ [L *mutilatus*, pp of *mutilare*, fr *mutilus* mutilated; akin

to L *muticus* curtailed, docked, OIr *mut* short] – **mutilator** *n*, **mutilation** *n*

**mutineer** /,myoohti'niə/ *n* one who mutinies

**mutinous** /'myoohtinəs/ *adj* **1a** disposed to or in a state of mutiny; rebellious **b** turbulent, unruly ⟨∼ *passions*⟩ **2** of or constituting mutiny – **mutinously** *adv*, **mutinousness** *n*

**mutiny** /'myoohtini/ *n* open resistance to lawful authority; *esp* concerted revolt (e g of a naval crew) against discipline or a superior officer *synonyms* see REBELLION [obs *mutine* to rebel, fr MF (*se*) *mutiner*, fr *mutin* mutinous, fr *meute* revolt, fr (assumed) VL *movita*, fr fem of *movitus*, alter. of L *motus*, pp of *movēre* to move] – **mutiny** *vi*

**mutt** /mut/ *n, informal* **1** a slow-witted, stupid, or pitiful person **2** a dog; *esp* a mongrel [short for *muttonhead*]

**mutter** /'mutə/ *vi* **1** to utter sounds or words indistinctly or in a low voice and with little movement of the lips **2** to utter indistinct or muffled threats or complaints; grumble ∼ *vt* to utter, esp in a low or indistinct manner [ME *muteren*; akin to L *muttire* to mutter, *mutus* mute] – **mutter** *n*, **mutterer** *n*

**mutton** /'mutn/ *n* the flesh of a mature sheep used as food [ME *motoun*, fr OF *moton* ram, wether, of Celt origin; akin to MBret *mout* wether] – **muttony** *adj*

**muttonchops** /-,chops/, **muttonchop whiskers** *n pl* sidewhiskers that are narrow at the temple and broad and round by the lower jaws

**mutton cloth** *n* a plain-knitted usu cotton fabric of loose texture

**muttonhead** /'mut(ə)n,hed/ *n, informal* a slow-witted or stupid person; a blockhead

**mutual** /'myoohtyooəl, -chəl/ *adj* **1a** directed by each towards the other or the others ⟨∼ *affection*⟩ **b** having the same feelings for each other ⟨*they had long been* ∼ *enemies*⟩ **c** shared or enjoyed by two or more at the same time; common ⟨*pursuing their* ∼ *hobby*⟩ **2** of a plan whereby the members of an organization share in the profits and expenses; *specif* of or taking the form of an insurance method in which the policyholders constitute members of the insuring company [ME, fr MF *mutuel*, fr L *mutuus* lent, borrowed, mutual; akin to L *mutare* to change – more at MISS ] – **mutuality** *n*, **mutualize** *vb*, **mutually** *adv*

> *usage* **Mutual** and **reciprocal** each mean "directed by each of two towards the other" ⟨*our* mutual/reciprocal *affection*⟩. In addition, **reciprocal** carries the idea of "reciprocation" on the part of one of the two parties ⟨*he admires her and she has a* reciprocal *respect for him*⟩. Since the 16th century **mutual** has also meant "shared" ⟨*communication between them was cut off for the night by the* mutual *door being locked* – Sir Walter Scott⟩, but today careful writers prefer to express the idea of "shared" by **common**, except in certain expressions such as *our* **mutual** *friend*, where **common** would be ambiguous. Dickens's use of the title *Our* **Mutual** *Friend* has probably made the expression more acceptable.

**mutualism** /'myoohtyooə,liz(ə)m, -chəliz(ə)m/ *n* **1** the doctrine or practice of mutual dependence as an essential condition for individual and social welfare **2** a close relationship (SYMBIOSIS 2) between two organisms from which both benefit – **mutualist** *n*, **mutualistic** *adj*

**mutuel** /'myoohtyooəl, -chəl/ *n, NAm* PARI-MUTUEL (system for betting)

**muumuu** /'mooh,mooh/ *n* a brightly coloured loose often long dress of a type traditionally worn in Hawaii [Hawaiian *mu'umu'u*, fr *mu'umu'u* cut off]

**Muzak** /'myoohzak/ *trademark* – used for recorded background music played in public places (e g airports and hotels)

**muzhik** /'moohzhik/ *n, pl* **muzhiks** *also* **muzhiki** /-ki/ a Russian peasant △ *kulak* [Russ, dim, of *muzh* man, husband]

¹**muzzle** /'muzl/ *n* **1** the projecting jaws and nose of an animal; the snout **2a** a fastening or covering for the mouth of an animal used to prevent eating, biting, or barking **b** something (e g censorship) that restrains free expression **3** the open end or mouth of an implement; *esp* the end of the barrel of a firearm (e g a pistol or rifle) from which the projectile is discharged [ME *musell*, fr MF *musel*, fr dim. of *muse* mouth of an animal, fr ML *musus*]

²**muzzle** *vt* **1** to fit with a muzzle **2** to restrain from expression, esp of criticism; gag ⟨*the forcible muzzling of political dissidents*⟩ – **muzzler** *n*

**muzzle brake** *n* a device at the muzzle of a gun that uses escaping gases to reduce the force of recoil

'**muzzle-,loader** *n* a firearm that is loaded through the muzzle

**muzzy** /'muzi/ *adj* **1** muddled or confused in mind; befuddled

**2a** lacking in clarity and precision ⟨*his conclusions can be ~ and naive – TLS*⟩ **b** dull, gloomy ⟨*a ~ day*⟩ [perh blend of *muddled* and *fuzzy*] – **muzzily** *adv*, **muzziness** *n*

**M-way** *n* a motorway

**my** /mie/ *adj* **1** of me or myself, esp as possessor ⟨*~ car*⟩, agent ⟨*~ promise*⟩, or object of an action ⟨*~ injuries*⟩ – sometimes used with vocatives ⟨*~ child*⟩ ⟨*~ lord*⟩ and in the opening of a letter ⟨*~ dear Mrs Jones*⟩; used attributively **2** – used interjectionally to express surprise and sometimes reduplicated ⟨*~ oh ~!*⟩, in certain fixed exclamations ⟨*~ God!*⟩, and with names of various parts of the body to express doubt or disapproval ⟨*~ foot!*⟩ [ME, fr OE *mīn*, fr *mīn*, suppletive gen of *ic* I; akin to OE *mē* me]

**my-** /mie-/, **myo-** *comb form* **1** muscle ⟨*myograph*⟩ **2** muscular and ⟨*myoneural*⟩ [NL, fr Gk, fr *mys* mouse, muscle – more at MOUSE]

**myalgia** /mie'alj(y)ə/ *n* pain in one or more muscles [NL] – **myalgic** *adj*

**myall** /'mie·awl/ *n* any of several Australian acacias (esp *Acacia pendula*) with hard fragrant wood [native name in Australia]

**myasthenia** /ˌmie·əs'theenyə, -ni·ə/ *n* muscular weakness [NL] – **myasthenic** *adj*

**myasthenia gravis** /'grahvis/ *n* a disease characterized by progressive weakness and exhaustibility of VOLUNTARY MUSCLES (e g of the legs and arms) [NL, lit., grave myasthenia]

**myc-** /miek/, **myco-** *comb form* fungus ⟨*mycology*⟩ ⟨*mycosis*⟩ [NL, fr Gk *mykēt-, mykēs*; akin to Gk *myxa* nasal mucus]

**mycelium** /mie'seelyəm/ *n*, *pl* **mycelia** /-lyə/ the mass of interwoven filaments (HYPHAE) that form esp the nonreproductive portion of a fungus and are often embedded in another body (e g of soil or organic matter or the tissues of an infected organism); *also* a similar mass of filaments formed by a bacterium [NL, fr *myc-* + Gk *hēlos* nail, wart, callus] – **mycelial** *adj*

**Mycenaean** also **Mycenian** /ˌmiesi'nee·ən/ *adj* (characteristic) of the city of Mycenae, its people, or the period (1400 to 1100 BC) of Mycenae's political ascendancy; *broadly* (characteristic) of the late Bronze Age culture of the Aegean and E Mediterranean area [*Mycenae* (Gk *Mykēnai*), ancient city in S Greece] – **Mycenaean** *n*

**mycetoma** /ˌmiesi'tohmə/ *n*, *pl* **mycetomas, mycetomata** /-mətə/ a condition marked by invasion of the deep tissues under the skin with fungi or bacteria; *also* a tumorous mass occurring in such a condition [NL, fr Gk *mykēt-, mykēs*] – **mycetomatous** *adj*

**mycetophagous** /ˌmiesi'tofəgəs/ *adj* feeding on fungi ⟨*~ nematodes*⟩ [Gk *mykēt-, mykēs* + E *-phagous*]

**mycetozoan** /mieˌseetə'zoh·ən/ *n* SLIME MOULD (funguslike organism) [NL *Mycetozoa*, order of protozoans, fr Gk *mykēt-, mykēs* + NL *-zoa*] – **mycetozoan** *adj*

**-mycin** /-'miesin/ *comb form* (→ *n*) substance, esp antibiotic, obtained from bacteria specif of the genus *Streptomyces* ⟨*erythromycin*⟩ [*streptomycin*]

**mycobacterium** /ˌmiekoh·bak'ti·əriəm/ *n* any of a genus (*Mycobacterium*) of bacteria that include numerous forms found in decaying animal and plant matter and many causing diseases (e g tuberculosis and leprosy) in humans and animals [NL, genus name, fr *myc-* + *Bacterium*] – **mycobacterial** *adj*

**mycoflora** /ˌmiekə'flawrə/ *n* the fungi characteristic of a region or special environment [NL]

**mycology** /mie'kolaji/ *n* (the biology of) fungal life or fungi [NL *mycologia*, fr *myc-* + L *-logia* -logy] – **mycologist** *n*, **mycologic** also **mycologic** *adj*, **mycologically** *adv*

**mycophagist** /mie'kofəjist/ *n* an eater of fungi (e g mushrooms) [*mycophagy* (fr *myc-* + *-phagy*) + *-ist*] – **mycophagy** *n*

**mycophagous** /mie'kofəgəs/ *adj* mycetophagous

**mycoplasma** /ˌmiekoh'plazmə/ *n*, *pl* **mycoplasmas, mycoplasmata** /-mətə/ any of a genus (*Mycoplasma*) of minute microorganisms without cell walls that are intermediate in some respects between viruses and bacteria and are mostly parasitic, usu in mammals [NL, genus name, fr *myc-* + *plasma*] – **mycoplasmal** *adj*

**mycorrhiza** /ˌmiekə'riezə/ *n*, *pl* **mycorrhizae** /-zie/, **mycorrhizas** the very close beneficial association of the MYCELIUM (rootlike network of filaments) of a fungus (e g the truffle, *Tuber*) with the roots of a flowering plant (e g an oak or beech tree) [NL, fr *myc-* + Gk *rhiza* root – more at ROOT] – **mycorrhizal** *adj*

**mycosis** /mie'kohsis/ *n*, *pl* **mycoses** /-seez/ infection with or disease caused by a fungus [NL] – **mycotic** *adj*

**mycotoxin** /ˌmiekə'toksin/ *n* a poisonous substance produced by a fungus, esp a mould

**mydriasis** /mie'drie·əsis/ *n* a long-continued or excessive widening of the pupil of the eye [L, fr Gk] – **mydriatic** *adj or n*

**myel-** /mie·əl/, **myelo-** *comb form* bone marrow; spinal cord ⟨*myelencephalon*⟩ [NL, fr Gk, fr *myelos*, fr *mys* mouse, muscle – more at MOUSE]

**myelencephalon** /ˌmie·əlen'sefəlon/ *n* the posterior portion of the hindbrain: **a** MEDULLA OBLONGATA **b** the posterior part of the medulla oblongata that is continuous with the SPINAL CORD [NL] – **myelencephalic** *adj*

**myelin** /'mie·əlin/ *n* a soft white somewhat fatty material that forms a thick insulating sheath round the core of large nerve fibres in VERTEBRATE animals [ISV] – **myelinic** *adj*

**myelinated** /'mie·əliˌnaytid/ *adj*, *of a nerve fibre* having a MYELIN SHEATH

**myelin sheath** *n* the layer of myelin surrounding a myelinated nerve fibre

**myelitis** /ˌmie·ə'lietəs/ *n* inflammation of the SPINAL CORD or of the bone marrow [NL]

**myeloblast** /'mie·ələˌblast/ *n* a large nongranular bone-marrow cell that has a single nucleus and that develops into a myelocyte [ISV] – **myeloblastic** *adj*

**myelocyte** /'mie·ələˌsiet/ *n* a bone-marrow cell; *esp* a granule-containing cell that is capable of movement and gives rise to the granular cells of the blood but is not present in normal blood [ISV] – **myelocytic** *adj*

**myelogenous** /ˌmie·ə'lojinəs/, **myelogenic** /ˌmie·ələ'jenik, -loh-/ *adj* of, originating in, or produced by the bone marrow ⟨*~ sarcoma*⟩ [ISV]

**myelogenous leukemia** *n*, *chiefly NAm* MYELOID LEUKAEMIA

**myeloid** /'mie·əˌloyd/ *adj* **1** of the SPINAL CORD **2** of or resembling bone marrow [ISV]

**myeloid leukaemia** *n* leukaemia characterized by rapid growth of myeloid tissue (e g of the bone marrow and spleen) and by an abnormal increase in the number of bone-marrow cells (e g myelocytes and myeloblasts) in the circulating blood

**myeloma** /ˌmie·ə'lohmə/ *n* a tumour of the bone marrow [NL] – **myelomatous** *adj*

**myelopathy** /ˌmie·ə'lopəthi/ *n* a disease or disorder of the SPINAL CORD or of the bone marrow [ISV] – **myelopathic** *adj*

**myenteric** /ˌmie·ən'terik/ *adj* of the muscular coat of the intestinal wall

**myiasis** /'mie·əsis/ *n*, *pl* **myiases** /-seez/ infestation with fly maggots [NL, fr Gk *myia* fly – more at MIDGE]

**mylonite** /'mieləniet, 'milə-/ *n* a fine-grained rock produced by intense crushing [Gk *mylōn* mill, fr *mylē* – more at MEAL]

**myna, mynah** also **mina** /'mienə/ *n* any of various Asiatic starlings (esp genera *Acridotheres, Gracula*, and *Sturnus*); *esp* a largely black bird (*Gracula religiosa*) easily taught to pronounce words when kept in captivity [Hindi *mainā*, fr Skt *madana*]

**mynheer** /mə'niə/ *n* **1** a Dutch-speaking man **2** *often cap* used as a title equivalent to *Mr* before the name of a Dutch-speaking man, or used without a name as a generalized term of address [D *mijnheer*, fr *mijn* my + *heer* master, sir]

**myo-** /mie·oh-, 'mie·ə-/ – see MY-

**myoblast** /'mie·əˌblast/ *n* an unspecialized cell capable of giving rise to muscle cells [ISV]

**myocardiograph** /ˌmie·oh'kahdiəˌgrahf, -graf/ *n* a recording instrument for making a tracing of the action of the heart muscles

**myocarditis** /ˌmie·oh·kah'dietəs/ *n* inflammation of the myocardium [NL]

**myocardium** /ˌmie·oh'kahdi·əm/ *n* the middle muscular layer of the heart wall [NL, fr *my-* + Gk *kardia* heart – more at HEART] – **myocardial** *adj*

**myofibril** /ˌmie·oh'fiebril, -'fibril/ *n* any of the long thin parallel elements of a muscle cell that can contract [NL *myofibrilla*, fr *my-* + *fibrilla* fibril] – **myofibrillar** *adj*

**myofilament** /ˌmie·oh'filəmənt/ *n* any of the individual filaments of ACTIN or MYOSIN (muscle proteins) that make up a myofibril

**myogenic** /ˌmie·ə'jenik/ *adj* **1** originating in muscle ⟨*~ pain*⟩ **2** taking place or functioning spontaneously in ordered rhythmic fashion because of the natural properties of muscle rather than by reason of specific nervous stimulation ⟨*a ~ heart beat*⟩ [ISV]

**myoglobin** /ˌmie·ə'glohbin, ˌmie·oh-, '--,--/ *n* a red iron-containing protein pigment in muscles that is similar to the haemoglobin found in blood [ISV]

**myoinositol** /ˌmie·oh·i'nohsitol, -tohl/ *n* a chemical compound that is a component of the VITAMIN B COMPLEX and that occurs widely in plants, microorganisms, and higher animals including humans

**myology** /mie'oləji/ *n* a scientific study of muscles [Fr or NL; Fr *myologie*, fr NL *myologia*, fr *my-* + L *-logia* -logy] – **myologic, myological** *adj*

**myoma** /mie'ohmə/ *n*, *pl* **myomas, myomata** /-mətə/ a tumour consisting of muscle tissue [NL] – **myomatous** *adj*

**myoneural** /ˌmie·ə'nyooərəl/ *adj* of both muscle and nerve

**myopathy** /mie'opəthi/ *n* a disorder of muscle tissue or muscles [ISV] – **myopathic** *adj*

**myope** /'mie,ohp/ *n* a person suffering from myopia [Fr, fr LL *myops* myopic, fr Gk *myōps*, fr *myein* to be closed + *ōps* eye, face – more at MYSTERY, EYE]

**myopia** /mie'ohpi·ə/ *n* 1 defective vision of distant objects resulting from a condition in which the visual images come to a focus too far forward in the eye; shortsightedness 2 lack of foresight or discernment [NL, fr Gk *myōpia*, fr *myōp-, myōps*] – **myopic** *adj*, **myopically** *adv*

**myosin** /'mie·əsin/ *n* a fibrous muscle protein that reacts with ACTIN to form ACTOMYOSIN and produce muscular movement [ISV *myos-* (fr Gk *myos*, gen of *mys* mouse, muscle) + *-in*]

**myosis** /mie'ohsis/ *n* MIOSIS (excessive contraction of eye pupil) – **myotic** *adj*

**myosotis** /ˌmie·ə'sohtis/ *n* a forget-me-not [NL, genus name, fr L, mouse-ear, fr Gk *myosōtis*, fr *myos* (gen of *mys* mouse) + *ōt-, ous* ear – more at MOUSE, EAR]

**myotome** /'mie·ə,tohm/ *n* 1 any of a series of hollow cubes formed early in the embryo of a VERTEBRATE animal, from which skeletal musculature is produced 2 the muscles of a body segment, esp in a segmented INVERTEBRATE animal (e g an earthworm) [ISV]

**myotonia** /ˌmie·ə'tohnyə/ *n* (a condition characterized by) involuntary and abnormal contraction of one or more muscles [NL] – **myotonic** *adj*

¹**myriad** /'miri·əd/ *n* 1 ten thousand – used in historical contexts 2 **myriad, myriads** *pl* an indefinitely large number [Gk *myriad-, myrias*, fr *myrioi* countless, ten thousand, pl of *myrios* countless]

²**myriad** *adj* 1 innumerable, countless 2 having innumerable aspects or elements ⟨the ~ *activity of peasant farmers*⟩

**myriapod, myriopod** /'miri·ə,pod/ *n* any of a group (Myriapoda of the phylum Arthropoda) of segmented INVERTEBRATE animals that includes the millipedes and centipedes, having a body made up of numerous similar segments nearly all of which bear true jointed legs [deriv of Gk *myrioi* + *pod-, pous* foot – more at FOOT] – **myriapod, myriopod** *adj*

**myristate** /mi'ristayt, 'mie-, 'mirəstayt, 'mie-/ *n* any of various chemical compounds (SALTS or ESTERS) formed by combination between MYRISTIC ACID and a metal atom, an alcohol, or another chemical group [ISV]

**myristic acid** /mi'ristik, mie-/ *n* a chemical compound, $C_{14}H_{28}O_2$, occurring in most fats [ISV, fr NL *Myristica*, genus of trees, fr LGk *myristikē*, fem of *myristikos* fragrant, fr Gk *myron* perfume]

**myrmec-** /muhmik-/, **myrmeco-** *comb form* ant ⟨*myrmecophagous*⟩ [Gk *myrmēk-, myrmēko-*, fr. *myrmēk-, myrmēx* – more at PISMIRE]

**myrmecology** /ˌmuhmi'koləji/ *n* the scientific study of ants [ISV] – **myrmecologist** *n*, **myrmecological** *adj*

**myrmecophagous** /ˌmuhmi'kofəgəs/ *adj* feeding on ants

**myrmecophile** /'muhmikə,fiel/ *n* an organism that habitually shares an ant nest [ISV] – **myrmecophilous** *adj*, **myrmecophily** *n*

**myrmidon** /'muhmid(ə)n/ *n* 1 *cap* a member of a legendary Greek people from Thessaly who devotedly followed Achilles in the Trojan War 2 a loyal follower; *esp* a subordinate who executes orders unquestioningly or pitilessly [L *Myrmidon-, Myrmido*, fr Gk *Myrmidōn*]

**myrobalan** /mie'robələn, mi-/ *n* 1 the dried bitter fruit of an E Indian tree (genus *Terminalia*) used chiefly in leather tanning and in inks 2 CHERRY PLUM [MF *mirobolan*, fr L *myrobalanus*, fr Gk *myrobalanos*, fr *myron* perfume + *balanos* acorn – more at SMEAR, GLAND]

**myrrh** /muh/ *n* a yellowish-brown to reddish-brown GUM RESIN with a strong smell and a bitter taste, obtained from any of several trees (esp *Commiphora abyssinica* of the family Burseraceae) of E Africa and Arabia; *also* a mixture of myrrh and

LABDANUM (oil and resin from rockroses) [ME *myrre*, fr OE, fr L *myrrha*, fr Gk, of Sem origin; akin to Ar *murr* myrrh]

**myrtle** /'muhtl/ *n* 1 a common S European evergreen bushy shrub (*Myrtus communis*) of the eucalyptus family with usu oval shiny leaves, fragrant white or rosy flowers, and black berries; *also* any of several other chiefly tropical shrubs or trees related to the myrtle 2 *NAm* ¹PERIWINKLE a [ME *mirtille*, fr MF, fr ML *myrtillus*, fr L *myrtus*, fr Gk *myrtos*, prob of Sem origin]

**myself** /mie'self/ *pron* 1 that identical person that is I – used reflexively ⟨*I got* ~ *a new suit*⟩, for emphasis ⟨*I* ~ *will go*⟩, or in absolute constructions ⟨~ *a tourist, I nevertheless avoided other tourists*⟩; sometimes replacing *I* or *me* ⟨*most of my colleagues and* ~ *went – The Times*⟩ 2 my normal self ⟨*I'm not quite* ~ *today*⟩ – compare ONESELF [ME, alter. of *meself*]
**usage** Some people dislike the use of **myself** for unnecessary emphasis ⟨*I* **myself** *don't like it*⟩. See I

**mysost** /'meesawst/ *n* a brown Norwegian whey cheese that has a hard buttery consistency and a mild sweetish taste [Norw, fr *myse* whey + *ost* cheese]

**mystagogue** /'mistəgog/ *n* 1 one who initiates another into a mystical cult 2 one who teaches mystical doctrines [L *mystagogus*, fr Gk *mystagōgos*, fr *mystēs* initiate + *agein* to lead – more at AGENT] – **mystagogy** *n*

**mysterious** /mi'stiəri·əs/ *adj* 1a of or constituting mystery; difficult or impossible to comprehend ⟨the ~ *ways of God*⟩ ⟨*a* ~ *twist of logic*⟩ b exciting wonder or curiosity while baffling efforts at identification ⟨*heard a* ~ *noise each night*⟩ ⟨*a* ~ *stranger*⟩ 2 fond of mystery ⟨*a romantic and* ~ *poet*⟩ – **mysteriously** *adv*, **mysteriousness** *n*

¹**mystery** /'mist(ə)ri/ *n* 1a a religious truth that is disclosed by revelation alone and even so is not fully understandable b(1) any of the 15 events (e g the Nativity, the Crucifixion, or the Assumption) serving as a subject for meditation during the saying of the rosary b(2) *cap* a Christian sacrament; *specif* Communion c(1) a secret religious rite believed (e g in certain ancient religions) to impart enduring bliss c(2) a cult devoted to such rites 2a something not understood or beyond understanding; an enigma ⟨*his disappearance remains a* ~⟩ ⟨*a* ~ *illness*⟩ b the secret or specialized practices peculiar to an occupation or group of people ⟨the mysteries *of the tailor's craft*⟩ c a fictional work dealing usu with the solution of a mysterious crime 3 profound, enigmatic, or secretive quality or character ⟨the ~ *of her smile*⟩ 4 MYSTERY PLAY **synonym** see ¹PROBLEM [ME *mysterie*, fr L *mysterium*, fr Gk *mystērion*, fr (assumed) *mystos* keeping silence, fr Gk *myein* to be closed (of the eyes or lips); (4) Fr *mystère*, fr L *mysterium*]

²**mystery** *n*, *archaic* 1 a trade, craft 2 *taking sing or pl vb* a body of people engaged in a particular trade, business, or profession; a guild [LL *misterium, mysterium*, alter. of *ministerium* service, occupation, fr *minister* servant – more at MINISTER]

**mystery play** *n* a medieval religious drama based on scriptural incidents and usu centring on the life, death, and resurrection of Christ – compare MIRACLE PLAY, MORALITY PLAY [¹*mystery*]

¹**mystic** /'mistik/ *adj* 1 MYSTICAL 2 of mysteries or secret rites; occult 3 of mysticism or mystics 4a mysterious, incomprehensible b obscure, esoteric c arousing a feeling of awe and wonder d possessing magical properties ⟨*a* ~ *potion*⟩ [ME *mistik*, fr L *mysticus* of mysteries, fr Gk *mystikos*, fr (assumed) *mystos*]

²**mystic** *n* a follower or advocate of a mystical way of life; *specif* a person who believes that God or ultimate reality can only be apprehended by direct personal experience (and who orders his/her life towards this goal)

**mystical** /'mistikl/ *adj* 1 having a spiritual meaning or reality that is neither apparent to the senses nor obvious to the intelligence ⟨the ~ *food of the sacrament*⟩ 2a of or resulting from a person's direct experience of God or ultimate reality ⟨the ~ *experience of the Inner Light*⟩ b based on subjective experience (e g intuition or insight) ⟨the ~ *religions of the East*⟩ 3 obscure in meaning; cryptic 4 mystic – **mystically** *adv*

**mysticism** /'mistisiz(ə)m/ *n* 1 the experience of mystical union or direct communion with ultimate reality reported by mystics 2 the belief that direct knowledge of God, spiritual truth, or ultimate reality can be attained through subjective experience (e g intuition or insight) 3 vague speculation; a belief without sound basis

**mystification** /ˌmistifi'kaysh(ə)n/ *n* 1 mystifying or being mystified 2 something intended to mystify

**mystify** /'mistifie/ *vt* 1 to perplex the mind of, esp intentionally; bewilder 2 to cause to appear mysterious or obscure

⟨∼ *an interpretation of a prophecy*⟩ *synonyms* see ¹PUZZLE *antonym* enlighten [Fr *mistifier*, fr *mystère* mystery, fr L *mysterium*] – **mystifier** *n*, **mystifyingly** *adv*

**mystique** /mi'steek/ *n* **1** a mysterious somewhat mystical and reverential atmosphere or quality built up round or assigned to something or someone ⟨*the* ∼ *of the maharishi*⟩ ⟨*the* ∼ *of computers*⟩ **2** a special skill peculiar to an occupation or activity ⟨*the* ∼ *of glass engraving*⟩ [Fr, fr *mystique*, adj, mystic, fr L *mysticus*]

**myth** /mith/ *n* **1** a usu traditional story that embodies popular beliefs or explains a practice, belief, or natural phenomenon **2** a parable, allegory **3a** a person or thing having a merely fictitious or imaginary existence **b** a belief given uncritical acceptance by a group, esp in support of existing institutions or practices ⟨*a* ∼ *of racial superiority*⟩ **4** the whole body of myths [Gk *mythos* tale, speech, myth]

**mythical** /'mithikl/ *also* **mythic** *adj* **1** based on or described in a myth, esp as contrasted with factual history; imaginary **2a** fabricated, invented, or imagined, esp in an arbitrary way or in defiance of facts **b** having qualities suitable to a myth ⟨*a* ∼ *monster*⟩ – **mythically** *adv*

**mythic·ize, -ise** /'mithisiez/ *vt* to treat as or make the basis of a myth; mythologize – **mythicizer** *n*

**mythmaker** /'mith,maykə/ *n* a creator of myths or of mythical situations or lore – **mythmaking** *n*

**mythography** /mi'thogrəfi/ *n* a collection of myths used esp for scholarly purposes [Gk *mythographia*, fr *mythos* + *-graphia* -graphy] – **mythographer** *n*

**mythological** /,mithə'lojikl/ *also* **mythologic** *adj* **1** of or dealt with in mythology or myths **2** lacking factual or historical basis; mythical, fabulous – **mythologically** *adv*

**mytholog·ize, -ise** /mi'tholəjiez/ *vt* to build a myth round ∼ *vi* to relate, classify, and explain myths – **mythologizer** *n*

**mythology** /mi'tholəji/ *n* **1** a body of myths; *esp* the myths dealing with the gods, demigods, and legendary heroes of a particular people and thus involving supernatural elements **2** a branch of knowledge that deals with myths **3** a body of beliefs, usu with little factual foundation, lending glamour or mystique to a person or thing ⟨*there's a whole* ∼ *about The Beatles*⟩ [Fr or LL; Fr *mythologie*, fr LL *mythologia* interpretation of myths, fr Gk, legend, myth, fr *mythologein* to relate myths, fr *mythos* + *logos* speech – more at LEGEND] – **mythologer** *n*, **mythologist** *n*

**mythomania** /,mithoh'maynyə/ *n* an excessive tendency for lying and exaggerating [NL, fr Gk *mythos* + LL *mania*] – **mythomaniac** *n or adj*

**mythopoeia** /,mithə'pee·ə/ *n* a creating of or a giving rise to a myth or myths [LL, fr Gk *mythopoiia*, fr *mythopoiein* to make a myth, fr *mythos* + *poiein* to make – more at POEM] – **mythopoeic, mythopoetic, mythopoetical** *adj*

**mythos** /'miethos, 'mithos/ *n, pl* **mythoi** /-thoy/ **1** a pattern of beliefs expressing, often symbolically, the characteristic or common attitudes in a group or culture **2** a theme, plot [Gk]

**my word** *interj* – used to express surprise or astonishment

**myxoedema** /,miksə'deemə/ *n* an abnormality of the THYROID (gland producing hormones) that causes a thickening and dryness of the skin, dry hair, and loss of mental and physical vigour [NL, fr Gk *myxa* lamp wick, nasal mucus + NL *oedema*]

**myxoma** /mik'sohmə/ *n, pl* **myxomas, myxomata** /-mətə/ a tumour that is made up of soft jellylike CONNECTIVE TISSUE and that is found esp in the limbs and neck [NL, fr Gk *myxa*] – **myxomatous** *adj*

**myxomatosis** /,miksəmə'tohsis/ *n* a condition characterized by the presence of myxomas in the body; *specif* a severe virus disease of rabbits that is transmitted by fleas and has been used in the BIOLOGICAL CONTROL of rabbits [NL, fr *myxomat-, myxoma*]

**myxomycete** /,miksoh'mieseet, ,---'-/ *n* any of a group (Myxomycetes, Myxomycophyta, or Mycetozoa) of very simple organisms, sometimes classified as fungi, that have some plant and some animal characteristics, have a body composed of a creeping mass of cellular material (PROTOPLASM), and reproduce by producing spores – called also SLIME MOULD [deriv of Gk *myxa* + *mykēt-, mykēs* fungus – more at MYC-] – **myxomycetous** *adj*

**myxovirus** /'miksə,vie(ə)rəs/ *n* any of a group of rather large viruses that includes the influenza and mumps viruses [NL, fr Gk *myxa* mucus + NL *virus*; fr its affinity for certain mucins] – **myxoviral** *adj*

# N

**n, N** /en/ *n, pl* **n's, ns, N's, Ns** **1a** the 14th letter of the English alphabet **b** a graphic representation of or device for reproducing the letter *n* **c** a speech counterpart of printed or written *n* **2a** one designated *n,* esp as the 14th in order or class **b** an indefinite number; *esp* a mathematical variable taking only values which are whole numbers **3** something shaped like the letter N **4** the HAPLOID number of CHROMOSOMES (strands of gene-carrying material) found in the sex cells (e g sperms or eggs) that is normally constant for a particular type or species of organism ⟨*in man,* ~ *is 23*⟩ **5** EN (unit of width used by printers)

**-n** – see -EN

**'n'** *also* **'n** /(ə)n/ *conj and* ⟨*fish* 'n' *chips*⟩

**Naafi** /'nafi/ *n* the organization which runs shops and canteens in British military establishments; *also* any of these shops or canteens [*N*avy, *A*rmy, *and A*ir *F*orce *I*nstitutes]

**nab** /nab/ *vt* **-bb-** *informal* **1** to catch or seize in arrest; apprehend **2** to catch hold of; grab [perh alter. of E dial. *nap,* prob of Scand origin (cf KIDNAP)]

**nabob** /'naybob/, *fem* **nabobess** /-'bes/ *n* **1** a provincial governor of the Mogul empire in India **2** *chiefly derog* a person of great wealth or prominence – used originally of an Englishman grown rich in India △ nizam [Hindi & Urdu *nawwāb,* fr Ar *nuwwāb,* pl of *nā'ib* governor]

**nacelle** /na'sel/ *n* a housing for an aircraft or airship engine; *also* the personnel cabin of an airship [Fr, lit., small boat, fr LL *navicella,* dim. of L *navis* ship – more at NAVE]

**nacre** /'nayka/ *n* mother-of-pearl [MF, fr OIt *naccara* drum, nacre, fr Ar *naqqārah* drum] – **nacred** *adj,* **nacreous** *adj*

**NAD** *n* a chemical compound, $C_{21}H_{27}N_7O_{14}P_2$, that occurs in most cells and plays an important role as a COENZYME to activate and assist other ENZYMES in the breakdown of food substances to produce energy [*n*icotinamide-*a*denine *d*inucleotide]

**Na-dene** /nə 'deen/ *also* **Na-déné** /~, nah'deni/ *n* a group of American Indian languages spoken in parts of NW America [*na*- (fr an Athapaskan word-stem basically meaning "people") + *Déné* (a member or the language of an Athapaskan people living in Alaska & NW Canada), fr Fr, fr Déné]

**nadir** /'naydiə, 'nah-/ *n* **1** the point of the heavens that is vertically below the observer – compare ZENITH **2** the lowest point ⟨*the* ~ *of moral degradation*⟩ **antonym** zenith [ME, fr MF, fr Ar *nazīr* opposite]

**NADP** *n* a chemical compound, $C_{21}H_{28}N_7O_{17}P_3$, that occurs esp in RED BLOOD CELLS and plays a role in energy-production similar to NAD but acting often on different food substances [*n*icotinamide-*a*denine *d*inucleotide *p*hosphate]

**naevus** /'neevəs/ *n, pl* **naevi** /-vie/ a pigmented area on the skin developed before birth; a birthmark [L]

**naffing** /'nafing/ *adj or adv, Br euph slang* – used as a meaningless intensive

**naff off** /naf/ *vi, Br euph slang* FUCK OFF – usu in imperative [*naff* perh alter. of *eff*]

**¹nag** /nag/ *n* a horse; *esp* one that is old or in poor condition [ME *nagge;* akin to Du *negge* small horse]

**²nag** *vb* **-gg-** *vi* **1** to find fault or complain incessantly ⟨*driven to drink by a* ~*ging wife*⟩ **2** to be a persistent source of annoyance or discomfort ⟨*a* ~*ging pain*⟩ ~ *vt* **1** to irritate by constant scolding or complaining **2** to badger, worry ⟨*the problem* ~*ged the back of my mind*⟩ **synonyms** see ²SCOLD [prob of Scand origin; akin to ON *gnaga* to gnaw; akin to OE *gnagan* to gnaw] – **nagger** *n,* **nagging** *adj,* **naggingly** *adv*

**³nag** *n, informal* a person, esp a woman, who nags habitually

**Naga** /'nahgə/ *n, pl* **Nagas,** *esp collectively* **Naga** a member of a group of TIBETO-BURMAN peoples in Assam and adjoining parts of Burma

**nagana** /nə'gahnə/ *n* a fatal disease of domestic animals, esp cattle, in tropical Africa caused by a single-celled organism (*Trypanosoma brucei*) and transmitted by tsetse flies [Zulu *u-nakane, ulu-nakane*]

**Nahuatl** /'nah,wahtl, -,wo-/ *n, pl* **Nahuatls,** *esp collectively* **Nahuatl** **1** a group of American Indian peoples of S Mexico and Central America **2** the UTO-AZTECAN language of the Nahuatl people [Sp, fr Nahuatl] – **Nahuatlan** *adj or n*

**Nahum** /'nayhəm/ *n* – see BIBLE table [*Nahum* (Heb *Naḥūm*), 7th-c BC Heb prophet]

**naiad** /'niead/ *n, pl* **naiads, naiades** /'nie•ə,deez/ **1** *often cap* any of the nymphs in classical mythology living in and giving life to lakes, rivers, springs, and fountains **2** the aquatic larva of a mayfly, dragonfly, damselfly, or stone fly **3** any of a genus (*Najas* of the family Najadaceae) of submerged aquatic plants [Fr or L; Fr *naïade,* fr L *naiad-, naias,* fr Gk, fr *nan* to flow – more at NOURISH]

**naice** /nays/ *adj, humorous or derog* affectedly proper or polite [alter. (imitating affected pronunciation) of *nice*]

**naïf** /nah'eef/ *adj* naive [Fr] – **naïf** *n*
> *usage* There is no need to use the French masculine adjective **naïf,** since both masculine and feminine have been anglicized as **naive.**

**¹nail** /nayl/ *n* **1a** a horny sheath protecting the upper end of each finger and toe of most primates (e g humans) **b** a structure (e g a claw) at the end of a digit that corresponds to a nail **2** a slender usu pointed and headed fastener designed to be driven in, esp with a hammer, to join materials, act as a support, etc **3** an old English unit of length equal to $2\frac{1}{4}$ inches (about 57 millimetres) [ME, fr OE *nægl;* akin to OHG *nagal* nail, fingernail, L *unguis* fingernail, toenail, claw, Gk *onyx*] – **hit the nail on the head** to say something that exactly describes a situation or explains the cause of a difficulty – **on the nail** immediately; at once ⟨*cash* on the nail⟩

**²nail** *vt* **1** to fasten (as if) with a nail **2** to fix in steady attention ⟨~*ed his eye on the crack*⟩ **3** to catch, trap ⟨~*ed the thief*⟩ **4** to detect and expose (e g a lie or scandal) so as to discredit **5** *chiefly NAm* to strike, hit ⟨~*ed him in the head with a stone*⟩ □ (*except 1*) *chiefly informal* – **nailer** *n*

**nail down** *vt* **1** to define or establish clearly or decisively **2** to secure a definite promise or decision from

**'nail-,biting** *adj* characteristic of or causing emotional tension or anxiety ⟨*another* ~ *session of Mastermind* – Magnus Magnusson⟩

**nail bomb** *n* an explosive device containing nails and intended to cause mutilation

**nailbrush** /'nayl,brush/ *n* a small firm-bristled brush for cleaning the fingernails

**nail file** *n* a small flat narrow implement (e g of metal or cardboard) with a rough surface used for shaping the fingernails

**nail polish** *n, chiefly NAm* NAIL VARNISH

**nail varnish** *n, chiefly Br* an often coloured coating applied to the nails to give them a smooth or glossy appearance

**nainsook** /'nayn,sook/ *n* a soft lightweight cotton cloth [Hindi *nainsukh,* fr *nain* eye + *sukh* delight]

**naira** /'nierə/ *n* – see MONEY table [native name in Nigeria]

**naive, naïve** /nah'eev, nie-/ *adj* **1** marked by unaffected simplicity; ingenuous, unsophisticated **2a** lacking in worldly wisdom or informed judgment; *esp* credulous **b** not previously subjected to experimentation or a particular experimental procedure ⟨*made the test with* ~ *rats*⟩ **3** PRIMITIVE 3d ⟨~ *art*⟩ **synonyms** see ¹NATURAL [Fr *naïve,* fem of *naïf,* fr OF, inborn, natural, fr L *nativus* native] – **naively** *adv,* **naiveness** *n*

**naïveté, naïveté, naivete** /nah'eevoti, nie-/ *n* naivety [Fr *naïveté,* fr OF, inborn character, fr *naif*]

**naivety** *also* **naïvety** /nah'eev'ti, nie-/ *n* **1** being naive **2** a naive remark or action

**naked** /'naykid/ *adj* **1** having no clothes on; nude **2** devoid of customary or natural covering; bare: e g **2a** *of a knife or sword* not enclosed in a sheath or scabbard **b** exposed to the air or to full view ⟨*a* ∼ *flame*⟩ ⟨*a* ∼ *light*⟩ **c** *of a plant or any of its parts* lacking hairs or enveloping parts **d** lacking foliage or vegetation **e** *of an animal or any of its parts* lacking an external covering (e g of hair, feathers, or shell) **3a** lacking basic comforts or necessities **b** lacking furnishings or ornamentation; unadorned ⟨*a* ∼ *room*⟩ **4** unarmed, defenceless **5** lacking factual confirmation or support ⟨∼ *faith*⟩ **6** not concealed or disguised ⟨*the* ∼ *truth*⟩ **7** unaided by any optical device (e g microscope or telescope) ⟨*visible to the* ∼ *eye*⟩ **synonyms** see ¹BARE *antonym* clothed [ME, fr OE *nacod;* akin to OHG *nackot* naked, L *nudus,* Gk *gymnos*] – **nakedly** *adv,* **nakedness** *n*

**nalidixic acid** /ˌnaylə'diksik/ *n* a synthetic antibacterial drug, $C_{12}H_{12}N_2O_3$, that is used esp in the treatment of infections of the organs and ducts concerned with the formation and release of urine [origin unknown]

**nalorphine** /na'lawfeen/ *n* a drug, $C_{19}H_{21}NO_3$, obtained from morphine, that is used to quicken breathing and counteract poisoning by morphine and morphine-related narcotic drugs (e g sleeping pills) [*N-a*llyl + m*orphine*]

**naloxone** /'naləksohn/ *n* a drug, $C_{19}H_{21}NO_4$, obtained from morphine, that is used similar to nalorphine and is used in the treatment of drug overdoses [*N-a*llyl + hydr*oxy*- + -*one*]

**namby-pamby** /ˌnambi 'pambi/ *adj* **1** marked by insipid sentimentality ⟨∼ *rhymes*⟩ **2** lacking resolution or firmness; weak, soft ⟨∼ *treatment of young offenders*⟩ [*Namby Pamby,* satirical nickname given to Ambrose Philips †1749 E poet, author of sentimental verses on young girls] – **namby-pamby** *n,* **namby-pambyism** *n*

¹**name** /naym/ *n* **1a** a word or phrase whose function is to designate an individual person or thing **b** a word or symbol used in logic to designate **2** a descriptive usu disparaging epithet ⟨*called him* ∼s⟩ **3a** a reputation ⟨*gave the town a bad* ∼ ⟩ **b** a distinguished reputation; fame ⟨*made a* ∼ *for himself in golf*⟩ **c** a famous or notorious person or thing ⟨*the great* ∼s *of show business*⟩ **4** a family, kindred ⟨*was a disgrace to his* ∼ ⟩ **5** mere designation without basis in reality ⟨*a friend in* ∼ *only*⟩ [ME, fr OE *nama;* akin to OHG *namo* name, L *nomen,* Gk *onoma, onyma*] – **drag somebody's name through the mud** to bring somebody's name into disrepute (e g by slander) – **in the name of** by authority of ⟨*open up* in the name of *the law*⟩ – **one's/somebody's name is dirt/mud** one is much disliked or in disgrace – **take God's/the Lord's name in vain** to speak of God without proper reverence or respect; *esp* to blaspheme – **take somebody's name in vain** to speak disrespectfully of somebody, esp in his/her absence – see also **give a DOG a bad name**

²**name** *vt* **1** to give a name to; call **2** to mention or identify by name **3** to nominate for office; appoint ⟨*the king* ∼d *his son to succeed him*⟩ **4** to decide upon; choose ⟨∼ *the day for the wedding*⟩ **5** to mention explicitly; specify ⟨*unwilling to* ∼ *a price*⟩ – **nameable** *adj,* **namer** *n*

³**name** *adj* **1** of or bearing a name ⟨∼ *tapes*⟩ – compare NAMEPLATE **2** giving the name to a literary or theatrical production ⟨*the* ∼ *role*⟩ **3** *chiefly NAm* having an established reputation ⟨*hired a* ∼ *band for the show*⟩

'**name-ˌcalling** *n* the use of abusive language, esp when resorted to in place of reasoned argument

**name day** *n* the day of a church feast (e g a saint's day) whose name corresponds to one's Christian name

'**name-ˌdropping** *n* the practice of seeking to impress others by the studied but apparently casual mention of prominent people as friends or associates – **name-dropper** *n*

**nameless** /-lis, -ləs/ *adj* **1** obscure, undistinguished **2** not known by name; anonymous **3** having no legal right to a name; illegitimate **4a** having no name ⟨*discovered several* ∼ *species of moth*⟩ **b** left purposely unnamed ⟨*a certain person who shall remain* ∼ ⟩ **5** not marked with a name ⟨*a* ∼ *grave*⟩ **6a** incapable of precise description; indefinable ⟨∼ *fears*⟩ **b** too repulsive or distressing to describe ⟨*a* ∼ *horror*⟩ – **namelessly** *adv,* **namelessness** *n*

¹**namely** /'naymli/ *adv* that is to say; TO WIT [ME, especially, at least, to wit, fr ¹*name* + ²-*ly*]

²**namely** *adj, dial Scot* famous, renowned ⟨*Kirkcaldy has always been* ∼ *for its music-making* – *Scottish Field*⟩ [ME, fr ¹*name* + ¹-*ly*]

**name of the game** *n* the essence or true purpose of an activity ⟨*in dieting perseverance is the* ∼⟩

**nameplate** /-ˌplayt/ *n* a plate or plaque bearing a name (e g of a resident)

**namesake** /-ˌsayk/ *n* somebody or something that has the same name as another; *esp* one named after another [prob fr *name's sake* (i e one named for the sake of another's name)]

**nana** /'nanə/ *n, chiefly Br* one's grandmother – used esp by children [prob of baby-talk origin]

**nance** /nans/ *n or adj, chiefly NAm derog* (a) nancy [short for *nancy*]

**nancy** /'nansi/ *n, derog* an effeminate male or male homosexual [*Nancy,* nickname for *Ann(e)* & *Agnes*] – **nancy** *adj*

**NAND** /nand/ *n* an operation in computer LOGIC that produces an output which is the inverse of that of an AND circuit [*not AND*]

**nankeen** /ˌnang'keen/ *n* **1** a durable brownish-yellow cotton fabric originally hand-woven in China **2** *pl* trousers made of nankeen [*Nanjing (Nanking),* city in E China]

**nanna** /'nanə/ *n, Br* a granny – used by or to children [var of *nana*]

**nannoplankton** *also* **nanoplankton** /'naynoh,plangktən, 'nanoh-/ *n* the smallest plankton that consists of bacteria and other organisms that can be passed through nets of very fine mesh silk cloth [NL, fr Gk *nanos, nannos* dwarf + NL *plankton*] – **nannoplanktonic** *adj*

**nanny** *also* **nannie** /'nani/ *n* **1** *chiefly Br* a child's nurse; a nursemaid **2** *Br* a granny – used esp by or to children [prob of baby-talk origin]

**nanny goat** *n, informal* a female domestic goat [*Nanny,* nickname for *Anne*]

**nano-** *comb form* one thousand millionth ($10^{-9}$) part of (a specified unit) ⟨*nanosecond*⟩ [ISV, fr Gk *nanos* dwarf]

**nanometre** /'nanə,meetə/ *n* one thousand millionth of a metre [ISV]

**nanosecond** /'naynoh,sekənd, 'nanoh-/ *n* one thousand millionth of a second [ISV]

**naos** /'nayos/ *n, pl* **naoi** /'nayoy/ the principal chamber of a Greek temple containing the shrine to the divinity – compare CELLA [Gk, temple]

¹**nap** /nap/ *vi* -**pp**- **1** to take a short sleep, esp during the day; doze **2** to be off one's guard ⟨*caught his opponent* ∼*ping*⟩ [ME *nappen,* fr OE *hnappian;* akin to OHG *hnaffezen* to doze] – **napper** *n*

²**nap** *n* a short sleep, esp during the day; a snooze

³**nap** *n* a hairy or downy surface (e g on a woven fabric); a pile [ME *noppe,* fr MD, flock of wool, nap; akin to OE *hnoppian* to pluck, Gk *konis* ashes – more at INCINERATE] – **napless** *adj,* **napped** *adj*

⁴**nap** *vt* -**pp**- to raise a nap on (fabric or leather) – **napper** *n*

⁵**nap** *n* **1** a card game played with hands of five cards in which players bid to name the number of tricks they will take; *also* a bid to win all five tricks **2** a recommended choice (e g of the probable winner of a horse race) [short for *napoleon*]

⁶**nap** *vt* -**pp**- to recommend (a horse) as a possible winner

¹**napalm** /'nay,pahm/ *n* **1** a thickener consisting of a mixture of aluminium soaps used in making jellied petrol **2** petrol jellied with napalm and used esp in incendiary bombs and flame-throwers [*naphthenate* (a compound derived from naphthene) + *palm*itate]

²**napalm** *vt* to attack with napalm

**nape** /nayp/ *n* the back of the neck [ME]

**napery** /'naypəri/ *n, formal* household linen; *esp* table linen [ME, fr MF *naperie,* fr *nappe, nape* tablecloth – more at NAPKIN]

**nap hand** *n* **1** a hand of cards in the game of nap on which a player would be justified in bidding to make NAP (top score) **2** a favourable chance that invites the taking of risks

**naphth-, naphtho-** *comb form* naphthalene ⟨naphth*oquinone*⟩ [ISV, fr *naphthalene*]

**naphtha** /'nafthə/ *n* **1** petroleum **2** any of various often inflammable liquid mixtures of chemical compounds that vaporize readily and are used chiefly as solvents [L, fr Gk, of Iranian origin; akin to Per *neft* naphtha]

**naphthalene** /'nafthəleen, 'nap-/ *n* a chemical compound, $C_{10}H_8$, usu obtained from COAL TAR and used esp in the synthesis of other chemical compounds [alter. of earlier *naphthaline,* irreg fr *naphtha*] – **naphthalenic** *adj*

**naphthene** /'naftheen, 'nap-/ *n* any of a group of chemical compounds (CYCLOALKANES), many of which occur in petroleum [ISV, fr *naphtha* + -*ene*] – **naphthenic** *adj*

**naphthol** /'nafthol, 'nap-/ *n* either of two chemical compounds, $C_{10}H_7OH$, that are derivatives of naphthalene, found in COAL TAR or made synthetically, and used in the manufacture of dyes [ISV]

**naphthylamine** /naf'thiləmeen, nap-/ *n* either of two chemical compounds, $C_{10}H_7NH_2$, that are used esp as dye intermediates [ISV]

**Napierian logarithm** /nə'piəri·ən/ *n* NATURAL LOGARITHM [John *Napier* †1617 Sc mathematician]

**napiform** /'naypifawm/ *adj, esp of a root* globular at the top and tapering off abruptly; turnip-shaped [L *napus* turnip (fr Gk *napy* mustard) + ISV *-iform*]

**napkin** /'napkin/ *n* 1 a usu square piece of material (eg linen or paper) used at table to wipe the lips or fingers and protect the clothes 2 *chiefly Br formal* a nappy *usage* see SERVIETTE [ME *nappekin*, fr *nappe* tablecloth, fr MF, fr L *mappa* napkin, towel]

**napoleon** /nə'pohli·ən/ *n* 1 a French 20-franc gold coin 2 $^5$NAP 1 (card game) [Fr *napoléon*, fr *Napoléon* Napoleon I †1821 Emperor of France]

**Napoleonic** /nə,pohli'onik/ *adj* of or resembling Napoleon I ⟨~ *ambitions*⟩

**nappa** /'napə/ *n* a soft leather made from sheep or goat skin by treatment with mineral salts, and used for gloves, handbags, etc [alter. of *napa*, fr *Napa*, town in California, USA]

**nappe** /nap/ *n* 1 a mountain-forming structure resulting from a large mass thrust over other rocks 2 *maths* SHEET 6 (surface of a geometrical figure); *specif* either of the two sheets of a cone defined in terms of a straight line passing through a fixed point [Fr, tablecloth, sheet, nappe – more at NAPKIN]

**napper** /'napə/ *n, Br humorous* the head [prob fr $^1$*nap* + $^2$-*er*]

**nappy** /'napi/ *n, chiefly Br* a garment for babies that is used to absorb and retain excreta and that is usu drawn up between the legs and fastened at the waist [*napkin* + $^4$-*y*]

**nappy rash** *n* a rash on the part of a baby's body covered by a nappy, caused esp by contact with ammonia from its urine

**naprapath** /'naprəpath/ *n* one who practises naprapathy in the treatment of disease

**naprapathy** /nə'prapəthi/ *n* a system of treatment by manipulation and without the use of drugs that is based on a theory that disease symptoms result from disorder in the ligaments and CONNECTIVE TISSUE [Czech *napra*va correction + E *-pathy*]

**narc, nark** /nahk/ *n, NAm slang* a person (eg a government agent) who investigates narcotics violations [short for *narcotic agent*]

**narcissism** /'nahsi,siz(ə)m/ *n* 1 egotism, egocentrism 2 love of or sexual desire for one's own body [Ger *narzissismus*, fr *Narziss* Narcissus, a youth in Gk mythology who died for love of his own reflection & was turned into a narcissus, fr L *Narcissus*, fr Gk *Narkissos*] – **narcissist** *n or adj*, **narcissistic** *adj*

**narcissus** /nah'sisəs/ *n, pl* **narcissus, narcissuses, narcissi** /-sisie, -sisi/ a daffodil; *esp* one whose flowers are borne on separate stalks [NL, genus name, fr L, fr Gk *Narkissos*]

**narcolepsy** /'nahkə,lepsi/ *n* a condition characterized by brief attacks of deep sleep [ISV, fr Gk *narkē*] – **narcoleptic** *n or adj*

**narcosis** /nah'kohsis/ *n, pl* **narcoses** /-seez/ a state of stupor or unconsciousness produced by narcotic drugs or other chemicals [NL, fr Gk *narkōsis* act of benumbing, fr *narkoun*]

$^1$**narcotic** /nah'kotik/ *n* 1 any of several drugs, esp morphine and its derivatives, that dull the senses, relieve pain, and usu induce profound sleep and that are injected as common drugs of addiction – compare HEROIN, METHADONE, MORPHINE, PETHIDINE 2 *NAm* a drug (eg marijuana or LSD) subject to legal restriction similar to that of addictive narcotics whether in fact physiologically addictive and narcotic or not [ME *narkotik*, fr MF *narcotique*, fr *narcotique*, adj, fr ML *narcoticus*, fr Gk *narkōtikos*, fr *narkoun* to benumb, fr *narkē* numbness – more at SNARE]

$^2$**narcotic** *adj* 1a having the properties of or yielding a narcotic b inducing mental lethargy; soporific 2 of narcotics or narcotic addiction 3 of, involving, or intended for narcotic addicts – **narcotically** *adv*

**narcot·ize, -ise** /'nahkətiez/ *vt* 1 to treat with or subject to a narcotic 2 to put into a state of narcosis ~ *vi* to act as a narcotizing agent [ISV]

**nard** /nahd/ *n* the spikenard plant [ME *narde*, fr MF or L; MF, fr L *nardus*, fr Gk *nardos*, of Sem origin; akin to Heb *nērd* nard]

**narghile, nargileh** /'nahgili/ *n* WATER PIPE 2; *specif* one with a number of flexible tubes for drawing the smoke through water – compare HOOKAH [Per *nārgīla*, fr *nārgīl* coconut (of which the bowls were orig made)]

**naris** /'naris, 'neə-/ *n, pl* **nares** /-reez/ the opening of the nose

or nasal cavity of a VERTEBRATE animal [L; akin to L *nasus* nose – more at NOSE]

$^1$**nark** /nahk/ *n, slang* 1 *Br* a person acting as a decoy or informer; *esp* a police spy sent into a group to report on its activities 2 *chiefly Austr & NZ* someone or something that causes offence or annoyance [prob fr Romany *nak* nose]

$^2$**nark** *vb, Br slang vi* to act as an informer – often + *on* ⟨they'd ~ *on their own mother, some people* – Alan Sillitoe⟩ ~ *vt* to offend, affront ⟨felt really ~ed *by his criticism*⟩

$^3$**nark** *n, NAm slang* NARC (narcotics investigator)

**Narraganset** /,narə'gansit/ *n, pl* **Narragansets,** *esp collectively* **Narraganset** 1 a member of a N American Indian people of Rhode Island 2 an ALGONQUIAN language of the Narraganset people

**narrate** /nə'rayt/ *vt* to recite the details of (a story) [L *narratus*, pp of *narrare*, fr L *gnarus* knowing; akin to L *gnoscere, noscere* to know – more at KNOW] – **narrator** *n*

**narration** /nə'raysh(ə)n/ *n* 1 (a) narrating 2 a story, narrative – **narrational** *adj*

**narrative** /'narətiv/ *n* 1 something (eg a story) that is narrated 2 the art or practice of narration – **narrative** *adj*, **narratively** *adv*

$^1$**narrow** /'naroh/ *adj* 1a of little width, esp in comparison with height or length b of less than standard width c *of a textile* woven in widths less than 450 millimetres (18 inches) 2 limited in size or scope; restricted ⟨a ~ *field of study*⟩ 3 inflexible in attitudes or beliefs; hidebound 4 only just sufficient or successful ⟨won by a ~ *majority*⟩ ⟨a ~ *escape*⟩ 5 *of a speech sound* TENSE 3 6 *formal* meticulous, close ⟨a ~ *search*⟩ [ME *narowe*, fr OE *nearu*; akin to OHG *narwa* scar, *snuor* cord, Gk *narnax* box] – **narrowly** *adv*, **narrowness** *n*

$^2$**narrow** *n*, **narrows** *n pl* a narrow part or (water) passage; *specif* a strait connecting two bodies of water

$^3$**narrow** *vt* 1 to make narrow or narrower; contract 2 to restrict the scope or sphere of; limit ~ *vi* to become narrow or narrower; contract

**narrow boat** *n* a canal barge that is not more than 2.1 metres (about 7 feet) wide

**narrow gauge** /gayj/ *n* a railway gauge narrower than STANDARD GAUGE

**narrow-'minded** /-'miendid/ *adj* lacking tolerance or breadth of understanding; bigoted – **narrow-mindedly** *adv*, **narrow-mindedness** *n*

**narthex** /'nahtheks/ *n* 1 the colonnaded entrance (PORTICO) or inner porch of an Early Christian or Byzantine church 2 an entrance hall at the west end of a church [LGk *narthēx*, fr Gk, giant fennel, cane, casket]

**narwhal** *also* **narwal** /'nahwəl/ *n* an Arctic whale (*Monodon monoceros*) about 6 metres (20 feet) long, the male of which has a long twisted ivory tusk [Norw & Dan *narhval* & Sw *narval*, prob modif of Icel *nárhvalur*, fr ON *nāhvalr*, fr *nār* corpse + *hvalr* whale; fr its colour]

**nary** /'nari, 'neəri/ *adj, chiefly dial* not one single – usu + *a* ⟨they spoke ~ *a word to me*⟩ [alter. of *ne'er a*]

**nas-** /nayz-/, **naso-** *also* **nasi-** *comb form* 1 nose ⟨nasoscope⟩ ⟨nasosinusitis⟩ 2 nasal; nasal and ⟨nasolabial⟩ [L *nasus* nose – more at NOSE]

$^1$**nasal** /'nayzl/ *n* 1 the nosepiece of a helmet 2 a nasal part 3 a nasal speech sound [MF, fr OF, fr *nes* nose, fr L *nasus*]

$^2$**nasal** *adj* 1 of the nose 2a *of a speech sound* 2a(1) uttered through the nose with the mouth passage closed (as in English /m, n, ng/) a(2) uttered with both the mouth and nose passage open and the SOFT PALATE lowered (as in French *en*) b characterized by resonance produced through the nose ⟨spoke in a ~ *tone*⟩ 3 *of a musical sound* having a penetrating unresonant quality – **nasally** *adv*, **nasality** *n*

**nasal·ize, -ise** /'nayzl,iez/ *vb* to speak or say in a nasal manner – **nasalization** *n*

**nascent** /'nas(ə)nt, 'nay-/ *adj, formal* in the process of being born; just beginning to develop ⟨a ~ *rebellion*⟩ [L *nascent-, nascens*, prp of *nasci* to be born – more at NATION] – **nascence, nascency** *n*

**nasopharyngeal** /,nayzoh,farin'jee·əl, -fə'ring·gəl/ *adj* of the nose and PHARYNX (throat) or the nasopharynx

**nasopharynx** /,nayzoh'faringks/ *n* the upper part of the PHARYNX (throat) continuous with the nasal passages [NL]

**nastic** /'nastik/ *adj* of or being a movement of a plant part caused by the disproportionate growth of one surface [Gk *nastos* close-pressed, fr *nassein* to press]

**nasturtium** /nə'stuhsh(ə)m/ *n* any of a genus (*Tropaeolum* of the family Tropaeolaceae, the nasturtium family) of plants with showy spurred flowers and pungent edible seeds; *esp* either of two widely cultivated ornamental plants (*Tropaeolum majus* and *Tropaeolum minus*) [L, a cress, perh fr *nasus* nose + *-turtium* (fr *torquēre* to twist); fr its strong smell]

¹**nasty** /'nahsti/ *adj* **1a** disgustingly filthy ⟨~ *living conditions*⟩ **b** repugnant, *esp* to the smell or taste **2** obscene, indecent **3** mean, tawdry ⟨*a rented flat with cheap and* ~ *furniture*⟩ **4a** harmful, dangerous ⟨*had a* ~ *climb to reach the summit*⟩ ⟨*a* ~ *accident*⟩ **b** disagreeable, dirty ⟨~ *weather*⟩ ⟨*a* ~ *journey*⟩ **5** giving cause for concern or anxiety ⟨*gave his ankle a* ~ *sprain*⟩ ⟨*a* ~ *suspicion*⟩ **6** spiteful, vicious ⟨*lost his temper and was* ~ *to her*⟩ ⟨*trespassers who turn* ~ *when challenged*⟩ *synonyms* see ¹DIRTY *antonym* nice [ME] – **nastily** *adv*, **nastiness** *n*

²**nasty** *n, informal* a very unpleasant or threatening person or thing

**-nasty** /-nasti, -nəsti/ *comb form* (→ *n*) nastic movement of a plant part ⟨*epinasty*⟩ [Ger *-nastie*, fr Gk *nastos*]

**nat** *n, often cap, informal* NATIONALIST **2** ⟨*Scottish Labour party: Yet another gift for the* Nats – *The Economist*⟩

**natal** /'naytl/ *adj* **1** of, present at, or associated with (one's) birth ⟨*a* ~ *star*⟩ **2** *chiefly poetic* native [ME, fr L *natalis*, fr *natus*, pp of *nasci* to be born – more at NATION]

**natality** /nə'taləti/ *n* birthrate

**natant** /'nayt(ə)nt/ *adj* swimming or floating in water ⟨~ *decapods*⟩ [L *natant-*, *natans*, prp of *natare* to swim; akin to L *nare* to swim – more at NOURISH]

**natation** /nay'taysh(ə)n/ *n, formal* the action or art of swimming

**natatorial** /,naytə'tawri·əl/, **natatory** /'naytət(ə)ri/ *adj* **1** of swimming **2** adapted to or characterized by swimming ⟨*a* ~ *leg of an aquatic insect*⟩

**natch** /nach/ *adv, informal* NATURALLY **2** – usu used interjectionally [by shortening & alter.]

**nates** /'nayteez/ *n pl* the buttocks – used technically [L, pl of *natis* buttock; akin to Gk *nōtos*, *nōton* back]

**natheless** /'naythlis/ *adv, archaic* nevertheless, notwithstanding [ME, fr OE *nā thē lǣs* not the less]

**nathless** /'nathlis/ *adv, archaic* natheless

**Natick** /'naytik/ *n* a dialect of the American Indian language Massachuset

**nation** /'naysh(ə)n/ *n* **1** *taking sing or pl vb* **1a** a people with a common origin, tradition, and language and (capable of) constituting a nation-state **b** a community of people possessing a more or less defined territory and government **2** a tribe or federation of tribes (e g of American Indians) *synonyms* see ³RACE [ME *nacioun*, fr MF *nation*, fr L *nation-*, *natio* birth, race, nation, fr *natus*, pp of *nasci* to be born; akin to L *gignere* to beget – more at KIN]

¹**national** /'nash(ə)nl/ *adj* **1** of a nation **2** nationalist **3** belonging to or maintained by the central government **4** of or being a coalition government formed by most or all major political parties – **nationally** *adv*

²**national** *n* **1** a citizen of a specified nation **2a** *pl* a competition that is national in scope **b** *cap* GRAND NATIONAL (horse race) **3** a newspaper sold nationwide

**national assistance** *n, often cap N&A, Br* SUPPLEMENTARY BENEFIT – not now used technically

**National Certificate** *n* a British technician's qualification obtained at either of two levels by part-time study ⟨*an Ordinary* ~ *in Construction*⟩

**national debt** *n* the amount of money owed by the government of a country

**National Diploma** *n* an advanced British technician's qualification, usu in a technical or applied subject, obtained at either of two levels typically by part-time or sandwich-course study

**national forest** *n* a usu forested area of considerable extent that is preserved by government decree from uncontrolled private exploitation

**National Front** *n* an extreme right-wing political party of Britain whose policies are largely based on the assertion of the racial superiority of the indigenous British population over immigrants (e g blacks)

**national grid** *n, Br* **1** a country-wide network of high-voltage cables between major power stations **2** the system of co-ordinates used for map reference by the ORDNANCE SURVEY and other map-producing organizations

**National Guard** *n* a militia force recruited by each state of the USA, equipped by the federal government, and liable to be called up for service by either

**National Health Service, National Health** *n* a system of medical care started in the UK in 1948, by which every person receives free or subsidized medical treatment paid for by taxation

**national income** *n* the total sum of earnings from a nation's current production including wages and salaries of employees, interest, income from rent, and gross trading profits of companies and public utilities measured over some specified time period, usu one year

**national insurance** *n, often cap N&I* a compulsory social-security scheme in the UK funded by contributions from employers, employees, and the government which insures the individual against sickness, retirement, and unemployment

**nationalism** /'nash(ə)nl,iz(ə)m/ *n* loyalty and devotion to a nation; *esp* the exalting of one nation above all others

**nationalist** /-,ist/ *n* **1** an advocate of or believer in nationalism **2** *cap* a member of a political party or group advocating national independence or strong national government – **nationalist, nationalistic** *adj*, **nationalistically** *adv*

**nationality** /,nash(ə)n'aləti/ *n* **1** national character **2a** national status; *specif* a legal relationship involving allegiance on the part of an individual and usu protection on the part of the state **b** citizenship of a particular nation **3** existence as a separate nation **4a** NATION 1a **b** an ethnic group within a larger unit

**national·ize, -ise** /'nash(ə)nl,iez/ *vt* **1** to give a national character to; make national **2** to transfer control or ownership of to the national government △ naturalize – **nationalizer** *n*, **nationalization** *n*

**national park** *n* an area of special scenic, historical, or scientific importance set aside and maintained by the government

**national product** *n* the value of the goods and services produced in a nation during a year

**national service** *n* conscripted service in the British armed forces – **national serviceman** *n*

**national socialism** *n* nazism – **national socialist** *adj*

**National Trust** *n* a charitable trust for the preservation of places of historic interest and natural beauty in England, Wales, and N Ireland

**nationhood** /'naysh(ə)nhood/ *n* NATIONALITY 1,2a,3

¹**nation-,state** /,-- '-/ *n* a sovereign state inhabited by a relatively homogeneous people as opposed to several nationalities

**nationwide** /,naysh(ə)n'wied/ *adj* extending throughout a nation

¹**native** /'naytiv/ *adj* **1** inborn, innate ⟨~ *talents*⟩ **2** belonging to a particular place by birth ⟨~ *to Yorkshire*⟩ **3a** belonging to or being the place of one's birth ⟨~ *language*⟩ ⟨~ *land*⟩ **b** of or being somebody using his/her first language ⟨*a* ~ *speaker*⟩ ⟨~ *fluency*⟩ **4a** grown, produced, or originating in a particular place or in the vicinity; local **b** living or growing naturally in a particular region; indigenous **5** simple, unaffected ⟨~ *charm*⟩ **6** constituting an original substance or source ⟨*the way I must return to* ~ *dust* – John Milton⟩ **7** found in nature, esp in a pure form ⟨*mining* ~ *silver*⟩ **8** *chiefly Austr* having a usu superficial resemblance to a specified British plant or animal [ME *natif*, fr MF, fr L *nativus*, fr *natus*, pp of *nasci* to be born – more at NATION] – **natively** *adv*, **nativeness** *n*

*synonyms* Native, indigenous, endemic, aboriginal, autochthonous: native suggests a birth or immediate origin in the place in question ⟨*a* native *Bristolian*⟩. Indigenous excludes the possibility of earlier introduction or naturalization. It tends to apply to species or races rather than to individuals, and often implies a wider area than native ⟨*kangaroos are* indigenous *to Australia*⟩. Endemic may describe plants or diseases; it implies restriction to a limited area where conditions are particularly favourable. Aboriginal usually applies to people, and describes the earliest known inhabitants of a place ⟨*Indians are the* aboriginal *Americans*⟩. Autochthonous describes plants, rocks, and other things which originate in the place where they are found. Applied to human artefacts or activity, it stresses a freedom from external influences ⟨autochthonous *folk songs*⟩. *antonyms* alien, foreign

²**native** *n* **1** one born or reared in a particular place ⟨*a* ~ *of Yorkshire*⟩ **2a** an original or indigenous inhabitant, esp of a country colonized by Europeans **b** a plant, animal, etc living or growing in a particular locality **3** *Br* an oyster grown in local waters **4** *chiefly humorous* a local resident; *esp* a person who lives in a place permanently as distinguished from a visitor or a temporary resident ⟨*day-trippers who disturb the peace of the* ~ *s*⟩

*usage* The use of **native** to mean "indigenous non-European national" is now considered offensive; but it is acceptable to speak of a **native** *of* a place, or to use the word in the sense "local resident" ⟨*only the* **natives** *[of our village] understand the bus timetable*⟩.

**nativism** /'naytiviz(ə)m/ *n* **1** a policy of favouring native inhabitants as opposed to immigrants **2** the revival or perpetuation of an indigenous culture **3** *psychology* a theory emphasizing that behaviour and personality are innately determined – **nativist** *n or adj*, **nativistic** *adj*

**nativity** /nə'tivəti/ *n* **1** birth; *specif, cap* the birth of Jesus **2** a horoscope [ME *nativite*, fr MF *nativité*, fr ML *nativitat-, nativitas*, fr LL, birth, fr L *nativus*]

**natriuresis** /ˌnaytriyooə'reesis/ *n* excessive loss of CATIONS (atoms with positive electric charge), esp sodium, in the urine [NL, fr *natrium* sodium (fr ISV *natron*) + *uresis* urination, fr Gk *ourēsis*, fr *ourein* to urinate – more at URINE] – **natriuretic** *adj*

**natrolite** /'natrəliet, 'nay-/ *n* a mineral, $Na_2Al_2Si_3O_{10}.2H_2O$, related to ZEOLITE [Ger *natrolith*, fr *natron* (fr Fr) + *-lith* -lite]

**natron** /'nay,tron, -trən/ *n* a mineral SODIUM CARBONATE, $Na_2CO_3.10H_2O$, used in ancient times in embalming, in ceramic pastes, and as a cleansing agent [Fr, fr Sp *natrón*, fr Ar *naṭrūn*, fr Gk *nitron*]

**natter** /'natə/ *vi or n, chiefly Br informal* (to) chatter, gossip [prob imit]

**natterjack** /'natə,jak/ *n* a common brownish-yellow W European toad (*Bufo calamita*) that has short hind legs and moves by running rather than by hopping [origin unknown]

**natty** /'nati/ *adj* neat and trim; spruce ⟨*wearing a ~ dressing gown* – R F Delderfield⟩ [perh alter. of earlier *netty*, fr obs *net* neat, clean, fr ME, fr MF – more at ²NEAT] – **nattily** *adv*, **nattiness** *n*

¹**natural** /'nachərəl/ *adj* **1** based on an inherent moral sense ⟨*~ justice*⟩ **2a** in accordance with or determined by nature ⟨*a more ~ life-style*⟩ **b** based on features that indicate true natural relationships – used esp of biological keys used for the identification of living things **3** related by blood rather than by adoption ⟨*his ~ parents*⟩ **4** following from the nature of the case; warranted by the facts ⟨*a perfectly ~ assumption to make in the circumstances*⟩ **5** innate, inherent ⟨*a ~ talent for art*⟩ **6** of nature as an object of study and research **7** having a specified character or attribute by nature ⟨*a ~ athlete*⟩ ⟨*a ~ blonde*⟩ **8a** happening in accordance with the ordinary course of nature ⟨*death from ~ causes*⟩ **b** developed by human reason alone rather than revelation ⟨*~ religion*⟩ **9** normal, expected ⟨*events followed their ~ course*⟩ **10a** growing without human care; *also* not cultivated ⟨*~ prairie unbroken by the plough*⟩ **b** existing in or produced by nature without human intervention ⟨*~ scenery*⟩ ⟨*~ curiosities*⟩ **11** (as if) in a state of nature unenlightened by culture or morality ⟨*~ man*⟩ **12a** *law* having a physical or real existence ⟨*a corporation is a legal but not a ~ person*⟩ **b** of the physical as opposed to the spiritual world ⟨*~ laws describe phenomena of the physical universe*⟩ **13a** true to nature; lifelike ⟨*painted in ~ colours*⟩ **b** free from affectation or constraint **c** not disguised or altered in appearance or form ⟨*~ hair*⟩ ⟨*furniture with a ~ wood finish*⟩ **14a** (containing only notes that are) neither sharp nor flat **b** having the pitch modified by the NATURAL SIGN **15** *euph* illegitimate ⟨*Monmouth was the ~ son of Charles II*⟩ [ME, fr MF, fr L *naturalis* of nature, fr *natura* nature] – **naturalness** *n*

*synonyms* **Natural, simple, ingenuous, naive, unsophisticated, unaffected,** and **artless** suggest a nature or behaviour free from calculation or deception. **Natural** stresses ease, spontaneity, and unselfconsciousness, contrasting nature with art, and suggesting a lack of artifice, constraint, or effort. **Simple** is opposed to "devious", and may imply either childish ignorance or childlike wisdom and purity of mind ⟨*to be simple is to be great* – R W Emerson⟩. **Ingenuous**, too, suggests a childlike simplicity and candour, and indicates an inability to conceal one's feelings or intentions, without implying a desire to do so. **Naive** implies a lack of artificiality or worldly wisdom which may be praised for its freshness or deplored for its unworldliness; it sometimes suggests ignorance of developments in knowledge or understanding ⟨*a naive patriotism blinded him to his country's faults*⟩. **Unsophisticated** stresses a lack of worldliness or experience in social relations, without making any strong positive statement. **Unaffected**, however, has a positive suggestion of naturalness and praiseworthy simplicity. **Artless** suggests an absence of design, but adds the implication of unawareness of, or indifference to, the effect one is having on other people ⟨*her artless chatter first amused, then bored him*⟩. See SINCERE **antonyms** artificial, unnatural **usage** see OBVIOUS

²**natural** *n* **1a** natural, natural sign a sign placed on the musical stave to indicate that the following note or notes are not sharp or flat **b** a note affected by the NATURAL SIGN **2** a result or combination that immediately wins the stake in a game; *specif* a total of 7 or 11 on the first throw in CRAPS **3a** *informal* one having natural skills, talents, or abilities ⟨*as an actor, he was a ~*⟩ **b** *informal* one who or that which is likely to be particularly suitable or successful **c** *Br slang* one's life ⟨*never worked so hard in all my ~* – Compton Mackenzie⟩ **4** *archaic* one born mentally defective

**natural gas** *n* gas flowing out from the earth's crust through natural openings or bored wells; *esp* a mixture of METHANE and other carbon-containing gases used chiefly as a fuel and raw material

**natural history** *n* **1** a written account of some aspect of nature **2** the natural development of an organism, disease, etc over a period of time **3** the usu amateur study of natural objects (eg plants, animals, or minerals), esp in the field

**naturalism** /'nachərə,liz(ə)m/ *n* **1** action or thought based on natural desires and instincts **2** a theory discounting supernatural explanations of the origin and meaning of the universe **3** realism in art or literature, esp when emphasizing scientific observation of life without idealization of the ugly – **naturalist, naturalistic** *adj*, **naturalistically** *adv*

**naturalist** /'nachərə,list/ *n* **1** a follower or advocate of naturalism **2** a student of NATURAL HISTORY; *esp* a biologist who works outdoors rather than in the laboratory △ naturalist

**natural-ize, -ise** /'nachərə,liez/ *vt* **1a** to introduce into common use or into the language of a community **b** to cause (eg a plant) to become established as if native **2** to make natural **3** to confer the rights of a national on; *esp* to admit to citizenship ~ *vi* to become naturalized △ nationalize – **naturalization** *n*

**natural law** *n* a body of law or a specific principle held to be derived from human beings' innate sense of justice and binding upon human society in the absence of or in addition to positive law

**natural logarithm** *n* a logarithm with $e$ = approx 1.71828 as base – called also NAPIERIAN LOGARITHM

**naturally** /'nachərəli, 'natrəli/ *adv* **1** by nature; by inborn character or ability ⟨*~ timid*⟩ **2** as might be expected ⟨*~, we shall be present at the meeting*⟩ **3a** without artificial aid or treatment ⟨*hair that curls ~*⟩ **b** in a natural manner ⟨*speak ~*⟩ **4** with truth to nature; realistically ⟨*an artist who represents objects ~*⟩

**natural number** *n* the number one (1) or any number (eg 3, 12, or 432) obtainable by repeatedly adding 1 to the number 1 – compare CARDINAL NUMBER

**natural resources** *n pl* industrial materials and capacities (eg mineral deposits and waterpower) supplied by nature

**natural right** *n* a right based on NATURAL LAW

**natural science** *n* any of the sciences (eg physics, chemistry, or biology) that deal with matter, energy, and their interrelations and transformations or with objectively measurable phenomena – **natural scientist** *n*

**natural selection** *n* a natural process that tends to result in the survival of organisms best adapted to their environment and the elimination of organisms carrying undesirable traits that have been produced by genetic mutations – compare STRUGGLE FOR EXISTENCE

**natural sign** *n* NATURAL 1a (musical sign)

**natural theology** *n* theology deriving its knowledge of God from the study of nature, independent of special revelation

**nature** /'naychə/ *n* **1a** the inherent character or constitution of a person or thing; essence **b** disposition, temperament **2a** a creative and controlling force in the universe **b** an inner force or the sum of such forces in an individual **3** a kind or class, usu distinguished by specified fundamental or essential characteristics ⟨*documents of a confidential ~*⟩ ⟨*acts of a ceremonial ~*⟩ **4** the physical constitution or motivating forces of an organism **5** a spontaneous attitude (eg of generosity) ⟨*that no compunctious visitings of ~ shake my fell purpose* – Shak⟩ **6** the external world in its entirety **7** (a way of life resembling) mankind's original or natural condition ⟨*back to ~*⟩ **8** natural scenery **synonyms** see ¹TYPE [ME, fr MF, fr L *natura*, fr *natus*, pp of *nasci* to be born – more at NATION]

**nature reserve** *n* a usu unspoilt area of great botanical or zoological interest (eg because of the rare species it contains) protected from exploitation by human beings

**nature strip** *n, Austr* a grass verge

**nature trail** *n* a walk (e g in a NATURE RESERVE) planned or marked so as to indicate points of interest to the observer of nature

**naturism** /'naychə,riz(ə)m/ *n* nudism – **naturist** *adj or n*

**naturopath** /'naychərə,path, nə'tyooərə-/ *n* one who practices naturopathy in the treatment of disease [back-formation fr *naturopathy*]

**naturopathy** /,naychə'ropəthi/ *n* (a system of) treatment of disease emphasizing stimulation of the natural healing processes and including the use of herbal medicines and some physical treatments (e g manipulation and electrical treatment) [*nature* + *-o-* + *-pathy*] – **naturopathic** *adj*

**naught** /nawt/ *n* **1** *chiefly NAm* nought **2** *chiefly archaic or poetic* **2a** nothing ⟨∼ *ails thee, man!*⟩ **b** nothingness [ME *naught, nought,* fr OE *nāwiht, nōwiht,* fr *nā, nō* no + *wiht* creature, thing – more at WIGHT]

**naughty** /'nawti/ *adj* **1a** badly behaved; wicked ⟨*take those filthy shoes off, you* ∼ *boy!*⟩ ⟨*rather* ∼ *of her not to mention her sources*⟩ – often humorous ⟨"*Get back into bed you* ∼ *man", exclaimed the nurse*⟩ **b** harmlessly mischievous ⟨∼ *teasing*⟩ **2** *chiefly euph or humorous* slightly improper or indecent ⟨∼ *magazines*⟩ ⟨*don't forget to scrub your* ∼ *bits*⟩ **3** *archaic* very wicked *synonyms* see ¹BAD *antonym* well-behaved [*naught* + *-y;* orig senses, inferior, bad] – **naughtily** *adv,* **naughtiness** *n*

**nauplius** /'nawpli·əs/ *n, pl* **nauplii** /'nawpli·ee, -ie/ a first-stage larva of shrimps, prawns, etc that has three pairs of limbs and a single eye and is usu not divided into segments [NL, fr L, a shellfish, fr Gk *nauplios*]

**nausea** /'nawzi·ə, 'nawzhə/ *n* **1** a feeling of discomfort in the stomach accompanied by a distaste for food and an urge to vomit **2** extreme disgust [L, seasickness, nausea, fr Gk *nautia, nausia,* fr *nautēs* sailor] – **nauseant** *n or adj*

**nauseate** /'nawzi,ayt/ *vb* to (cause to) become affected with nausea or disgust – **nauseatingly** *adv*

**nauseous** /'nawzi·əs/ *adj* causing or affected with nausea or disgust – **nauseously** *adv,* **nauseousness** *n*

*usage* Some people dislike the use of **nauseous** to mean **nauseated** (= feeling sick).

**nautch** /nawch/ *n* an entertainment in India performed by professional dancing girls [Hindi *nāc,* fr Skt *nrtya,* fr *nrtyati* he dances]

**nautical** /'nawtikl/ *adj* of or associated with seamen, navigation, or ships [L *nauticus,* fr Gk *nautikos,* fr *nautēs* sailor, fr *naus* ship – more at ²NAVE] – **nautically** *adv*

**nautical mile** *n* any of various units of distance used for sea and air navigation based on the length of a MINUTE (unit of angular measurement) of arc of a GREAT CIRCLE (circle with the same radius as the earth) and differing because the earth is not a perfect sphere: e g **a** a British unit equal to 6080 feet (about 1853.18 metres) **b** an international unit equal to 1852 metres (about 6076.17 feet)

**nautiloid** /'nawtiloyd/ *n* any of a group (Nautiloidea of the class Cephalopoda) of marine INVERTEBRATE animals related to the octopuses and squids that were abundant in the ORDOVICIAN geological period, esp the SILURIAN period, but are now represented by only the nautilus (genus *Nautilus*) – **nautiloid** *adj*

**nautilus** /'nawtiləs/ *n, pl* **nautiluses, nautili** /-lie, -li/ **1** any of a genus (*Nautilus* of the class Cephalopoda) of marine INVERTEBRATE animals related to the octopuses and squids that live in the S Pacific and Indian oceans and have a spiral chambered shell that is pearly on the inside **2** PAPER NAUTILUS (animal related to the nautilus) [NL, genus name, fr L, paper nautilus, fr Gk *nautilos,* lit., sailor, fr *naus* ship]

**Navaho, Navajo** /'navəhoh/ *n, pl* **Navahos, Navajos,** *esp collectively* **Navaho, Navajo** a member of an American Indian people of N New Mexico and Arizona; *also* their language [Sp (*Apache de*) *Navajó,* lit., Apache of Navajó, fr *Navajó,* a pueblo]

**navaid** /'navayd/ *n* a usu electronic device or system (e g a radar beacon) that assists a navigator [*navigation aid*]

**naval** /'nayvl/ *adj* **1** of a navy **2** consisting of or involving warships △ naval [L *navalis,* fr *navis* ship]

**naval architect** *n* one whose profession is the designing of ships

**naval stores** *n pl* products (e g turpentine and pitch) obtained from resinous conifers, esp pines [fr their former use in the construction and maintenance of wooden ships]

**navarin** /'navərin (*Fr* navarɛ̃)/ *n* a lamb and vegetable stew [Fr, irreg fr *navet* turnip]

¹**nave** /nayv/ *n* the hub of a wheel [ME, fr OE *nafu;* akin to OE *nafela* navel]

²**nave** *n* the main body of a church, lying to the west of the CHANCEL (part containing the altar); *esp* the long central space flanked by aisles [ML *navis,* fr L, ship; akin to OE *nōwend* sailor, Gk *naus* ship, Skt *nau*]

**navel** /'nayvl/ *n* **1** a depression in the middle of the abdomen marking the point of former attachment of the UMBILICAL CORD or YOLK STALK **2** the central point ⟨*the blessed Mediterranean ... the* ∼ *of the earth* – Harold Nicholson⟩ △ naval [ME, fr OE *nafela;* akin to OHG *nabalo* navel, L *umbilicus,* Gk *omphalos*]

**navel orange** *n* a seedless orange with a pit at the top enclosing a small secondary fruit

**navicular** /nə'vikyoolə/ *n or adj* (a bone, esp in the ankle) shaped like a boat [L *navicula* boat, dim. of *navis*]

**navigable** /'navigəbl/ *adj* **1** suitable for ships to pass through or along **2** capable of being steered – **navigably** *adv,* **navigability, navigableness** *n*

**navigate** /'navigayt/ *vi* **1** to travel by water and do or assist in doing the work of sailing the vessel **2** to steer a course or determine the course to be steered: e g **2a** to direct the course of an aircraft **b** *of a passenger* to give directions to the driver as to the route to be followed **3** to perform the activities (e g taking sightings and making calculations) involved in navigation ∼ *vt* **1a** to sail over, on, or through **b** to make one's way over or through; traverse **2a** to steer or manage (a boat) in sailing **b** to operate or direct the course of (e g an aircraft) [L *navigatus,* pp of *navigare,* fr *navis* ship + *-igare* (fr *agere* to drive) – more at AGENT]

**navigation** /,navi'gaysh(ə)n/ *n* **1** the act or practice of navigating **2** the science of determining (e g by geometry, astronomy, or radar) position, course, and distance travelled by a ship, aircraft, spacecraft, etc during a journey and hence advising on the best course to be steered or taken **3** ship traffic or commerce – **navigational** *adj,* **navigationally** *adv*

**navigator** /'navigaytə/ *n* **1** one who navigates; *specif* one skilled in the science of navigation **2** a device used to navigate or help navigate

**navvy** /'navi/ *n, Br* an unskilled labourer [by shortening & alter. fr *navigator* (construction worker on a canal, railway, or road)]

**navy** /'nayvi/ *n* **1** a nation's ships of war and support vessels together with the organization needed for maintenance **2** *taking sing or pl vb* the personnel manning a navy **3** **navy blue, navy** a deep dark blue colour (e g that of the British naval uniform) [ME *navie* shipping, fleet fr MF, fr L *navigia* ships, fr *navigare*]

**navy yard** *n, NAm* a naval dockyard

**nawab** /nə'wawb, -'wahb/ *n* **NABOB** **1** (Indian prince) ⟨*the Nawab of Pataudi*⟩ [Hindi & Urdu *nawwāb*]

¹**nay** /nay/ *adv* **1** *formal* not merely this but also; not only so but ⟨*the letter made him happy,* ∼, *ecstatic*⟩ **2** *dial N Eng or archaic* no [ME, fr ON *nei,* fr *ne* not + *ei* ever – more at AYE]

²**nay** *n* **1** a denial, refusal **2a** a negative reply or vote **b** a vote against; *also* a person voting against

**Nazarene** /,nazə'reen/ *n* a native or inhabitant of Nazareth [ME *Nazaren,* fr LL *Nazarenus,* fr Gk *Nazarēnos,* fr *Nazareth,* town in Israel]

**nazi** /'nahtsi/ *n* **1** *cap* a member of the German fascist party controlling Germany from 1933 to 1945 under Adolf Hitler **2** *often cap* one who resembles a German Nazi; a fascist [Ger, by shortening & alter. fr *nationalsozialist,* fr *national* + *sozialist* socialist] – **nazi** *adj, often cap,* **nazify** *vt, often cap,* **nazification** *n, often cap*

**Nazirite, Nazarite** /'nazəriet/ *n* a Jew of biblical times consecrated to God by a vow to avoid drinking wine, cutting the hair, and being defiled by the presence of a corpse [LL *nazaraeus,* fr Gk *naziraios, nazaraios,* fr Heb *nāzīr,* lit., consecrated] – **Naziritism** *n*

**Nazism, Naziism** /'naht,siz(ə)m/ *n* the totalitarian and racialist doctrines of the fascist National Socialist German Workers' party in the Third German Reich, including the totalitarian principle of government, state control of all industry, predominance of groups assumed to be racially superior, and supremacy of the leader [*Nazi* + *-ism*]

**NCO** *n, pl* **NCOs, NCO's** NONCOMMISSIONED OFFICER

**-nd** *suffix* (→ *adj*), *chiefly Br* – used after the figure 2 to indicate the ORDINAL NUMBER *second* ⟨2nd⟩ ⟨72nd⟩

**ne-** /nee-/, **neo-** *comb form* **1a** new; recent ⟨Neocene⟩ **b(1)** new,

subsequent, or revived period or form of ⟨Neo*platonism*⟩ ⟨neo-*Classicism*⟩ **b(2)** in a new, subsequent, or revived form or manner ⟨Neo*platonic*⟩ ⟨Neo*lithic*⟩ **c** NEW WORLD ⟨Neo*tropical*⟩ **2** new chemical compound isomeric with or otherwise related to (a specified compound) ⟨neo*arsphenamine*⟩ – not now in technical use [Gk, fr *neos* new – more at NEW]
**Neanderthal** /nee'andə,tahl, -th(ə)l/ *also* **Neandertal** /-tahl/ *adj* **1** of, like, or being Neanderthal man **2** suggesting a caveman in appearance or behaviour – **Neanderthal** *n*
**Neanderthal man** *n* a prehistoric man (*Homo neanderthalensis*) that lived in the middle of the PALAEOLITHIC period and is known from skeletal remains in Europe, N Africa, and W Asia [*Neanderthal*, valley of the Neander river in W Germany where the remains were first discovered in 1856] – **Neanderthaloid** *adj or n*
**neap** /neep/ *adj or n* (of or being) a NEAP TIDE [adj ME *neep*, fr OE *nēp* being at the stage of neap tide; n fr adj]
**Neapolitan** /,nee·ə'politn/ *n* a native or inhabitant of Naples [L *neapolitanus* of Naples, fr Gk *neapolitēs* citizen of Naples, fr *Neapolis* Naples, city in S Italy] – **Neapolitan** *adj*
**Neapolitan ice cream** *n* ice cream made in layers of different flavours and colours
**neap tide** *n* a tide of minimum height occurring at the 1st and 3rd quarters of the moon
¹**near** /niə/ *adv* **1** in or into a near position or manner ⟨came ~ *to tears*⟩ **2** closely approximating; nearly – often in combination ⟨a near-*perfect performance*⟩ ⟨~ *silk*⟩ ⟨*isn't anywhere* ~ *clever enough*⟩ **3** in a close or intimate manner ⟨~ *related*⟩ **4** *archaic* in a frugal manner [ME *ner*; partly fr *ner* nearer, fr OE *nēar*, comparative of *nēah* nigh; partly fr ON *nær* nearer, compar of *nā-* nigh – more at NIGH] – **as near as makes no difference/matter** practically, virtually ⟨as near a hit as makes no difference⟩ – **near on** *dial* almost, nearly
²**near** *prep* near to ⟨*went too* ~ *the edge*⟩ ⟨*call me* ~er *the time*⟩
³**near** *adj* **1** intimately connected or associated ⟨*he and I are* ~ *relations*⟩ **2a** not far distant in time, space, or degree ⟨*in the* ~ *future*⟩ **b** close, narrow ⟨a ~ *miss*⟩ ⟨a ~ *resemblance*⟩ **3a** being the closer of two ⟨*the* ~ *side*⟩ **b** being the left-hand one of a pair ⟨*the* ~ *wheel of a cart*⟩ **4** direct, short ⟨*the* ~est *road*⟩ **5a** closely resembling a prototype **b** approximating the genuine ⟨~ *silk*⟩ **6** *of light* in that part of the ultraviolet or infrared nearest to the visible spectrum **7** *euph* close, stingy – **nearness** *n*
  *synonyms* Near and close have almost the same meaning, though close is perhaps somewhat "nearer" than near. In certain phrases, usage requires one word rather than the other. Compare ⟨*the* **near** *distance*⟩ ⟨*the* **near** *future*⟩ ⟨a **close** *friend*⟩ ⟨*in* **close** *contact*⟩.
⁴**near** *vb* to approach
**nearby** /-'bie/ *adv or adj* close at hand ⟨*live* ~⟩ ⟨a ~ *café*⟩
**Nearctic** /ni'ahktik/ *adj* of or being the biogeographic subregion that includes Greenland, arctic America, and the parts of N America north of tropical Mexico
**nearest and dearest** *n taking pl vb* – one's family
**near gale** *n* MODERATE GALE
**nearly** /'niali/ *adv* **1** in a close manner or relationship ⟨~ *related*⟩ **2** almost but not quite – not before *any, no, none*, or *never* ⟨*very* ~ *identical*⟩ ⟨~ *a year later*⟩
**near miss** *n* **1** an attempt to hit a target with a weapon, bomb, ball, etc that only narrowly misses ⟨*he aimed for the wicket, but it was a* ~⟩ **2** something that falls just short of complete success ⟨*it was a* ~; *you should pass the exam next time you try*⟩
**near point** *n* the point nearest the eye at which an object is accurately focused on the retina when the lens is fully adjusted – compare FAR POINT
¹**nearside** /'niə,sied/ *adj, chiefly Br* of or being on the left-hand side ⟨*the* ~ *front wheel*⟩
²**nearside** *n, chiefly Br* **1** the side of a vehicle nearest the edge of the road (e g the left-hand side in Britain) ⟨*hit a car parked on his* ~⟩ **2** the left side of an animal or team of harnessed horses, dogs, etc □ usu + *the*; compare OFF SIDE
**nearsighted** /-'sietid/ *adj* able to see near things more clearly than distant ones; MYOPIC – **nearsightedly** *adv*, **nearsightedness** *n*
**near thing** *n* a narrow escape
¹**neat** /neet/ *n, pl* **neat, neats** *archaic* the common domestic ox or cow [ME *neet*, fr OE *nēat*; akin to OHG *nōz* head of cattle, OE *nēotan* to make use of]
²**neat** *adj* **1a** without addition or dilution; straight ⟨~ *brandy*⟩

**b** free from irregularity; smooth **2** elegantly simple ⟨a ~ *outfit*⟩ ⟨a ~ *description*⟩ **3a** precise, well-defined ⟨*not all human problems have a* ~ *solution*⟩ **b** skilful, adroit **4** (habitually) tidy and orderly ⟨a ~ *careful little man*⟩ ⟨*the room was* ~ *and ready for guests*⟩ **5** *chiefly NAm informal* fine, excellent ⟨*we had a* ~ *time at the movies*⟩ [MF *net*, fr L *nitidus* bright, neat, fr *nitēre* to shine; akin to OPer *naiba-* beautiful] – **neatly** *adv*, **neatness** *n*
  *synonyms* Neat, tidy, trim, spruce, dapper, shipshape, and orderly all imply care and orderliness. Neat suggests cleanliness, simplicity, and well-cared for appearance, and attention to detail. Tidy stresses careful arrangement and orderliness. Trim combines neat and tidy to suggest a pleasingly smart appearance, with a neat shape or design, and no detail out of place. Spruce and dapper apply only to people, their appearance, and their clothes. They imply smartness, trimness, and, in the case of dapper, usually fashionableness too. Shipshape suggests things in good condition and in their proper place, as if for the sake of efficiency ⟨*he always kept his affairs/his study* shipshape⟩. Orderly, like shipshape, describes places and things rather than people, and is the weakest and most general term, suggesting simply that everything is in good order.
  *antonyms* untidy, messy; unkempt, dishevelled
³**neat** *adv* without admixture or dilution; straight ⟨*drinks his whisky* ~⟩
**neaten** /'neetn/ *vt* to make neater
**neath** /neeth/ *prep, dial or poetic* beneath
**neat's-foot oil** *n* a pale yellow fatty oil made esp from the bones of cattle and used chiefly as a leather dressing
**neb** /neb/ *n* **1** the beak of a bird or tortoise **2** a small usu pointed end; a tip **3** *chiefly dial* a nose, snout **4** *chiefly N Eng dial* the peak of a cap [ME, fr OE; akin to ON *nef* beak]
**nebuchadnezzar** /,nebookəd'nezə, ,nebyoo-/ *n* a very large champagne bottle that holds 20 times the normal amount (about 16 litres) [*Nebuchadnezzar* (Heb *Nĕbhûkhadhnĕṣṣar*, modif of Bab *Nabû-kudurri-uṣur*) †562 BC king of Babylon]
**nebula** /'nebyoolə/ *n, pl* **nebulas, nebulae** /-lie, -li/ **1** a cloudy patch on the cornea of the eye **2a** any of many immense bodies of very thin gas or dust in interstellar space **b** a galaxy; *esp* one other than the MILKY WAY [NL, fr L, mist, cloud; akin to OHG *nebul* fog, Gk *nephelē, nephos* cloud] – **nebular** *adj*
**nebular hypothesis** *n* a hypothesis in astronomy: the SOLAR SYSTEM has evolved from a hot gaseous nebula
**nebul·ize, -ise** /'nebyooliez/ *vt* to reduce to a fine spray [L *nebula*] – **nebulizer** *n*, **nebulization** *n*
**nebulosity** /,nebyoo'losəti/ *n* **1** being nebulous **2** nebulous matter; *also* NEBULA 2a
**nebulous** /'nebyooləs/ *adj* **1** indistinct, vague **2** of or like a nebula; nebular [L *nebulosus* misty, fr *nebula*] – **nebulously** *adv*, **nebulousness** *n*
**necessarily** /'nesəs(ə)rəli, ,nesə'serəli/ *adv* as a necessary consequence; inevitably ⟨~, *he will have to stay at home*⟩ ⟨*her views were* ~ *coloured by her experiences*⟩
  *usage* The pronunciation /'nesəs(ə)rəli/ is recommended for BBC broadcasters.
¹**necessary** /'nesəs(ə)ri, 'nesə,seri/ *n* an indispensable item; an essential; *esp, pl* items needed to maintain a reasonable or accustomed standard of living
²**necessary** *adj* **1a** inevitable, inescapable **b(1)** logically unavoidable ⟨a ~ *conclusion*⟩ **b(2)** that cannot be denied without contradiction of some other statement ⟨"*all spinsters are unmarried*" *is a* ~ *truth*⟩ **c** determined by a previous state of affairs ⟨a ~ *outcome*⟩ **d** acting under compulsion; not free ⟨a ~ *agent*⟩ **2** essential, indispensable [ME *necessarie*, fr L *necessarius*, fr *necesse* necessary, fr *ne-* not + *cedere* to withdraw – more at NO, CEDE]
  *synonyms* Necessary, needful, requisite, indispensable, essential, and vital all describe someone or something urgently required or desired. Necessary may imply something one cannot do without, or simply something desired more for convenience than completeness. Needful expresses a concrete want or need, but is the weakest term. Requisite stresses the value of what is required to the person or situation requiring it, often suggesting a need imposed for a particular purpose ⟨*the tenacity* requisite *for success*⟩ ⟨*got good marks in the* requisite *subjects*⟩. What is indispensable, essential, or vital cannot be done without. Indispensable often describes something peripheral or only part of a whole ⟨*your presence, as chairman, is* indispensable⟩ ⟨*the presence of the whole committee is* essential *tomorrow*⟩. Vital, influenced by its other meanings, is the most forceful term in this group. Compare ¹LACK
  *antonyms* unnecessary, needless, dispensable.

**necessary condition** *n* **1** a proposition in logic or mathematics whose falsity assures the falsity of another ⟨*they based their argument for Caesar's immortality on the proposition "Caesar was a god", but this ~ being false, they did not prove him immortal*⟩ – compare SUFFICIENT CONDITION **2** a state of affairs that must prevail if another is to occur; a prerequisite ⟨*for foreigners, having a work permit is a ~ for holding a job in Switzerland*⟩

**necessitarianism** /nə,sesi'teəriəniz(ə)m/ *n* the doctrine that all phenomena are causally or logically determined – **necessitarian** *adj or n*

**necessitate** /nə'sesitayt/ *vt* to make necessary or unavoidable – **necessitation** *n*

**necessitous** /nə'sesitəs/ *adj, formal* needy, impoverished – **necessitously** *adv*, **necessitousness** *n*

**necessity** /nə'sesəti/ *n* **1** the quality of being necessary, indispensable, or unavoidable ⟨*the ~ of free speech*⟩ **2** impossibility of a contrary order or condition, esp in a specified sphere ⟨*physical ~*⟩ **3a** something necessary or indispensable ⟨*the daily necessities of life*⟩ **b** a pressing need or desire ⟨*~ is the mother of invention*⟩ **4** *formal* poverty, want [ME *necessite*, fr MF *necessité*, fr L *necessitat-, necessitas*, fr *necesse*] – **of necessity** necessarily

¹**neck** /nek/ *n* **1a** the part of an animal that connects the head with the body; *also* a cut of beef, mutton, etc taken from this part **b** the part of a garment that covers the neck; *also* the neckline **2** a relatively narrow part shaped like a neck: e g **2a(1)** the constricted end of a bottle **a(2)** the slender part of a fruit near its attachment to the plant **b** CERVIX **2** (neck of the womb) **c** the part of a stringed musical instrument extending from the body and supporting the fingerboard and strings **d** a narrow stretch of land **e** STRAIT 1 **f** the part of a tooth between the crown and the root that is just covered by the gum **g** a column of solidified MAGMA (molten rock) of a volcanic pipe or LACCOLITH (dome-shaped mass of magma within layers of rock) **3** a narrow margin ⟨*won by a ~*⟩ [ME *nekke*, fr OE *hnecca;* akin to OHG *hnac* nape, OE *hnutu* nut – more at NUT] – **breathe down somebody's neck 1** to observe somebody carefully and esp so closely as to cause annoyance **2** to be close behind somebody (eg in a race) – **neck of the woods** district, locality – see also PAIN in the neck, UP to one's neck

²**neck** *vt* to reduce the diameter of ~ *vi* **1** to become constricted; narrow **2** *informal* to kiss and caress in sexual play

**neck and neck** *adv* so evenly matched that the lead shifts rapidly from one contestant to another ⟨*the two horses were ~ in the last lap*⟩

**neckband** /'nek,band/ *n* a band at the neckline of a garment (eg to which a shirt collar is attached)

**neckcloth** /'nek,kloth/ *n* a cravat; scarf

**necked** /nekt/ *adj* having a neck, esp of a specified kind – often in combination ⟨*long-necked*⟩

**neckerchief** /'nekə,cheef, -,chif/ *n, pl* **neckerchiefs** *also* **neckerchieves** /-,cheevz/ a square of fabric folded and worn round the neck [ME *nekkerchef*, fr *nekke + kerchef* kerchief]

**necking** /'neking/ *n, informal* kissing and caressing in sexual play

**necklace** /'neklis/ *n* an ornament (eg a chain or string of beads or jewels) worn round the neck ⟨*a pearl ~*⟩ ⟨*a ~ of melon seeds*⟩

**necklet** /'neklit/ *n* **1** a short or closefitting necklace **2** a small label at the neck of a wine bottle, usu showing the vintage

**neckline** /-,lien/ *n* the upper edge of a garment that forms the opening for the neck and head

¹**neck-,rein** *vi, of a horse* to respond to the pressure of a rein on one side of the neck by turning in the opposite direction ~ *vt* to direct (a horse) by pressure of the rein on the neck

**necktie** /-,tie/ *n, chiefly NAm* TIE 5

**necr-** /nekr-/, **necro-** *comb form* **1** corpse; corpses ⟨*necropsy*⟩ ⟨*necrophilia*⟩ **2** conversion to dead tissue ⟨*necrosis*⟩ [LL, fr Gk *nekr-, nekro-*, fr *nekros* dead body – more at NOXIOUS]

**necrolatry** /ne'krolətri/ *n* worship of the dead [LGk *nekrolatreia*, fr Gk *nekr- + -latreia* -latry]

**necrology** /ne'kroləji/ *n* **1** a list of the recently dead **2** an obituary [NL *necrologium*, fr *necr- + -logium* (as in ML *eulogium* eulogy); (2) Fr *nécrologie*, fr NL *necrologium*] – **necrologist** *n*, **necrological** *adj*

**necromancy** /'nekrə,mansi/ *n* **1** the conjuring up of the spirits of the dead in order to predict or influence the future **2** magic, sorcery [alter. of ME *nigromancie*, fr MF, fr ML *nigromantia*, by folk etymology (influenced by L *nigr-, niger* black) fr LL

*necromantia*, fr LGk *nekromanteia*, fr Gk *nekr- + -manteia* -mancy] – **necromancer** *n*, **necromantic** *adj*, **necromantically** *adv*

**necrophagia** /,nekrə'fayj(y)ə/ *n* the act or practice of eating corpses or decaying flesh [NL]

**necrophagous** /ne'krofəgəs, ni-/ *adj* feeding on corpses or decaying flesh ⟨*~ insects*⟩ ⟨*~ savages*⟩

**necrophagy** /ne'krofəji, ni-/ *n* necrophagia

**necrophilia** /,nekrə'fili·ə/ *n* obsession with and usu erotic interest in corpses [NL] – **necrophile, necrophiliac** *adj or n*, **necrophilic** *adj*, **necrophilism** *n*

**necropolis** /ne'kropəlis, ni-/ *n, pl* **necropolises, necropoles** /-leez/, **necropoleis** /-lays/, **necropoli** /-li, -lie/ a cemetery; *esp* a large elaborate cemetery of an ancient city [LL, city of the dead, fr Gk *nekropolis*, fr *nekr- + -polis*]

**necropsy** /'nekropsi/ *n* a postmortem – **necropsy** *vt*

**necrosis** /ne'krohsis, ni-/ *n, pl* **necroses** /-seez/ (localized) death of living tissue [LL, fr Gk *nekrōsis*, fr *nekroun* to make dead, fr *nekros* dead body] – **necrotic** *adj*

**necrot·ize, -ise** /'nekrətiez/ *vi* to undergo necrosis ~ *vt* to cause necrosis [Gk *nekrōtikos* necrotic, fr *nekroun*]

**nectar** /'nektə/ *n* **1** the drink of the Greek and Roman gods; *broadly* a delicious drink **2** a sweet liquid secreted by the nectaries of a plant that is the chief raw material of honey [L, fr Gk *nektar*] – **nectarous** *adj*

**nectarine** /'nektərin, -reen/ *n* (a tree that bears) a smooth-skinned peach [obs *nectarine* like nectar]

**nectary** /'nektəri/ *n* a plant gland that secretes nectar [NL *nectarium*, irreg fr L *nectar + -arium* -ary]

**née, nee** /nay/ *adj* – used to identify a woman by her maiden name ⟨*Mrs Thomas, ~ Wilkinson*⟩ [Fr *née*, fem of *né*, lit., born, pp of *naître* to be born, fr L *nasci* – more at NATION]

¹**need** /need/ *n* **1a** a necessary duty; an obligation ⟨*no ~ to apologize*⟩ ⟨*if ~ be*⟩ **b** reason or grounds for an action or condition ⟨*there's no ~ to worry*⟩ **2a** a lack of something necessary, desirable, or useful ⟨*socks in ~ of mending*⟩; *also* the occasion of such a lack ⟨*when you couldn't buy a side of smoked salmon at ~ – Margaret Drabble*⟩ **b** a physiological or psychological requirement for the well-being of an organism **3** a condition requiring supply or relief ⟨*helped him in his hour of ~*⟩ **4** poverty, want [ME *ned*, fr OE *nied, nēd;* akin to OHG *nōt* distress, need]

²**need** *vb, pr 3 sing* **needs**, (*va*) **need** *vt* **1** to be in need of; require ⟨*the soup ~s salt*⟩ ⟨*my socks ~ mending*⟩ **2** to be constrained; HAVE 2 ⟨*I'll ~ to work hard*⟩ ~ *va* to be under necessity or obligation to – chiefly in negatives and questions ⟨*~ I go?*⟩ ⟨*he ~ not answer*⟩

*usage* The use of *need* with a past participle ⟨⚠ *this* **needs** *changed*⟩ is widely disliked, and should be rephrased as ⟨*this* **needs** *changing*⟩ or ⟨*this* **needs** *to be changed*⟩. *synonyms* see ¹LACK

¹**needful** /'needf(ə)l/ *adj* necessary, requisite *synonyms* see ²NECESSARY *antonym* needless – **needfully** *adv*, **needfulness** *n*

²**needful** *n, informal* **1** something that is necessary or requisite ⟨*do the ~ for an early start*⟩ **2** money ⟨*on the dole for lack of the ~ – Punch*⟩ □ + the

¹**needle** /'needl/ *n* **1a** a small slender usu steel instrument with an eye for thread at one end and a sharp point at the other, used for sewing **b** any of various similar larger instruments without an eye that are used for carrying thread and making stitches (eg in crocheting or knitting) **c(1)** a needle designed to carry sutures when sewing tissues in surgery **c(2)** a slender hollow instrument for introducing material into or removing material from the body **c(3)** a hollow device designed to contain radioactive material **2** a slender usu sharp-pointed indicator on a dial; *esp* MAGNETIC NEEDLE **3a** a slender pointed object resembling a needle: eg **3a(1)** a pointed crystal **a(2)** a sharp pinnacle of rock **a(3)** OBELISK (pointed column) **b** a needle-shaped leaf, esp of a conifer **c** a stylus for playing records **d** a slender pointed rod controlling a fine inlet or outlet (eg in a valve) **4** a beam used to take the load of a wall while supported at each end **5** *Br informal* a feeling of enmity or ill will – chiefly in *get/give the needle* ⟨*gets the ~ if you criticize her work*⟩ [ME *nedle*, fr OE *nǣdl;* akin to OHG *nādala* needle, *nājan* to sew, L *nēre* to spin, Gk *nēn*] – **needlelike** *adj*

²**needle** *vt* **1** to sew or pierce (as if) with a needle **2** to provoke by persistent teasing or gibes ⟨*~d the boy into a fight*⟩ **3** *slang* to strengthen (a beverage) by adding raw alcohol – **needler** *n*, **needling** *n*

**needlecord** /-,kawd/ *n* a fine corduroy with close ribs and a flattish pile

**needlefelt** /'needl,felt/ *n* carpet made on a needleloom instead of being woven by the traditional process, and consequently without pile

**needlefish** /'needl,fish/ *n, pl* **needlefishes**, *esp collectively* **needlefish 1** any of a family (Belonidae) of ferocious long slender tropical fish with bony skeletons and toothed beaks **2** PIPEFISH

**needleloom** /'needl,loohm/ *n* a machine that punches fibre threads into a backing usu treated with adhesive, to make needlefelt carpet

**needle match** *n, Br* a contest between opponents strongly motivated by intense personal rivalry or hostility ⟨*a ~ between neighbouring villages*⟩

**needlepoint** /-,poynt/ *n* **1** lace worked (eg in BUTTONHOLE STITCH) with a needle over a paper or parchment pattern – compare POINT 12, PILLOW LACE **2** embroidery worked on canvas, usu in a simple even stitch (eg CROSS-STITCH or TENT STITCH) across counted threads – compare GROS POINT, PETIT POINT – **needlepoint** *adj*

**needlepunch** /'needl,punch/ *n* needlefelt

**needless** /'needlis/ *adj* not needed; unnecessary ⟨*~ waste*⟩ ⟨*~ to say*⟩ – **needlessly** *adv*, **needlessness** *n*

**needletime** /'needl,tiem/ *n, chiefly Br* the programme time allocated, by agreement with the Musicians' Union, for the broadcasting of music from records

**needle valve** *n* a valve in which the opening is closed by a needle-shaped object

**needlewoman** /-,woomən/ *n* a woman who does needlework, esp skilfully; *esp* a seamstress

**needlework** /-,wuhk/ *n* sewing; *esp* fancywork (eg embroidery)

**needn't** /'neednt/ need not

**needs** /needz/ *adv* of necessity; necessarily ⟨*must ~ be recognized*⟩ [ME *nedes*, fr OE *nēdes*, fr gen of *nēd* need]

**needy** /'needi/ *adj* in want; impoverished ⟨*~ families*⟩ *synonyms* see POOR *antonym* well-to-do – **neediness** *n*

**neep** /neep/ *n, dial Scot* a turnip [ME *nepe*, fr OE *nǣp*, fr L *napus*]

**ne'er** /neə/ *adv, poetic* never

**'ne'er-do-,well** *n* an idle worthless person; a layabout – **ne'er-do-well** *adj*

**nefarious** /ni'feəri-əs/ *adj* flagrantly evil or immoral; iniquitous [L *nefarius*, fr *nefas* crime, fr *ne-* not + *fas* right, divine law; akin to L *fari* to speak] – **nefariously** *adv*, **nefariousness** *n*

**negate** /ni'gayt/ *vt* **1** to deny the existence or truth of **2** to make ineffective or invalid *synonyms* see ABROGATE [L *negatus*, pp of *negare* to say no, deny, fr *neg-* no, not (akin to *ne-* not) – more at NO] – **negator, negater** *n*

**negation** /ni'gaysh(ə)n/ *n* **1a** a denial or refusal **b** a negative statement; *esp* an assertion of the falsity of a given proposition **2a** something that is merely the absence of something actual or positive ⟨*anarchy is the ~ of government*⟩ **b** something opposite to something regarded as positive – **negational** *adj*

**¹negative** /'negətiv/ *adj* **1a** marked by denial, prohibition, or refusal ⟨*a ~ reply*⟩ **b(1)** denoting the absence or the contradiction of something ⟨*nonhuman is a ~ term*⟩ **b(2)** expressing negation ⟨*~ words such as no and not*⟩ **2** lacking positive or agreeable features ⟨*has a very ~ personality*⟩ ⟨*a ~ pessimistic outlook on life*⟩ **3a** numerically less than zero; opposite in sign to a positive number ⟨*÷2 is a ~ number*⟩ **b** extending or generated in a direction opposite to an arbitrarily chosen positive direction, esp clockwise ⟨*~ angle*⟩ **4a** being, relating to, or charged with electricity of which the electron is the elementary unit **b** gaining electrons **c(1)** having lower electric potential and constituting the part towards which the current flows from the external circuit ⟨*the ~ pole*⟩ **c(2)** constituting an ELECTRODE (structure conducting electricity into a device) through which a stream of electrons enters the space between electrodes in an ELECTRON TUBE **5a** not affirming the presence of the organism or condition in question ⟨*a ~ tuberculosis test*⟩ **b** directed or moving away from a source of stimulation ⟨*~ tropism*⟩ **c** less than the pressure of the atmosphere ⟨*~ pressure*⟩ **6** having the light and dark parts of the original photographic subject reversed ⟨*a ~ image*⟩ – **negatively** *adv*, **negativeness, negativity** *n*

**²negative** *n* **1a** a proposition by which something is denied or contradicted; *esp* the one of a pair of propositions in a logical argument in which negation is expressed ⟨*"no pigs have wings" is a ~*⟩ **b** a negative reply; a refusal **2** something that is the opposite or negation of something else **3a** an expression (eg

the word *no*) of negation or denial **b** a negative number **4** the plate of a battery that has the lower electric potential **5** (transparent material bearing) a negative photographic image used for printing positive pictures

**³negative** *vt* **1a** to refuse to accept or approve **b** to reject, veto ⟨*the proposal was ~d by the committee*⟩ **2** to demonstrate the falsity of; disprove **3** to deny the truth, validity, or existence of **4** to neutralize, counteract ⟨*~d the effect of earlier criticism*⟩

**negative feedback** *n* the return of part of the output of a system (eg an electronic or mechanical one) to the input, in order to produce usu corrective changes (eg to reduce distortion in an amplifier)

**negative income tax** *n* a system of subsidy payments to families with incomes below a stipulated level, proposed as a substitute for or supplement to social-security payments

**negative polarity** *n* the quality possessed by a word or expression (eg *either* in "I can't swim either") that is used only in the presence of a negative word

**negative staining** *n* a method of demonstrating the form of small objects (eg bacteria) in microscopy, esp ELECTRON MICROSCOPY, by surrounding them with a stain so that they appear as sharply outlined unstained bright bodies on a coloured ground

**negativism** /'negətiviz(ə)m/ *n* **1** an attitude or system of thought marked by strong mistrust or disbelief of accepted opinions or ideas **2** a tendency to refuse to do, to do the opposite of, or to do something at variance with what is asked – **negativist** *n*, **negativistic** *adj*

**negaton** /'negə,ton/ *n* a negatron [*negative* + *²-on*]

**negatron** /'negətron/ *n* an electron [*negative* + *electron*]

**¹neglect** /ni'glekt/ *vt* **1** to pay insufficient attention to; disregard ⟨*felt the real issues had been ~ed*⟩ **2** to leave undone or unattended to, esp through carelessness ⟨*a problem they'd ~ed to mention*⟩ ⟨*the tenants accused the caretaker of ~ing his duties*⟩ **3** to fail to take proper care of ⟨*they had ~ed their children through ignorance, not cruelty*⟩ ⟨*she always ~s pot plants*⟩ [L *neglectus*, pp of *neglegere, negligere*, fr *nec-* not (akin to *ne-* not) + *legere* to gather – more at NO, LEGEND] – **neglecter** *n*

*synonyms* **Neglect, disregard, overlook,** and **ignore** all mean "give little or no attention to". **Neglect** always suggests a failure to do something one should, whether intentionally or not ⟨**neglected** *to telephone home*⟩. **Disregard** may also imply intentional or unintentional lack of attention to something, but this may be justified ⟨**disregarded** *the jeers of onlookers*⟩. **Overlook** usually suggests an unintentional neglect of something, often through haste or carelessness. If intentional, it suggests leniency ⟨*I will* **overlook** *your insolence on this occasion*⟩. **Ignore** stresses a deliberate disregard of someone or something, to the point of refusing to recognize an acquaintance or something one knows to be true. *antonyms* heed, attend (to), cherish

**²neglect** *n* neglecting or being neglected ⟨*the garden fell into ~*⟩

**neglectful** /-f(ə)l/ *adj* careless, forgetful – **neglectfully** *adv*, **neglectfulness** *n*

**negligee, negligé** /'neglizhay/ *n* a woman's light decorative housecoat, often designed to be worn with a matching nightdress [Fr *négligé*, fr pp of *négliger* to neglect, fr L *neglegere*]

**negligence** /'neglij(ə)ns/ *n* **1** forgetfulness, carelessness **2** failure to exercise the proper care expected of a prudent person

**negligent** /'neglij(ə)nt/ *adj* **1** (habitually or culpably) neglectful **2** pleasantly casual in manner ⟨*conversed with ~ ease*⟩ △ negligible [ME, fr MF & L; MF, fr L *neglegent-, neglegens*, prp of *neglegere*] – **negligently** *adv*

**negligible** /'neglijəbl/ *adj* so small or trivial as to warrant little or no attention; trifling △ negligent, neglectful – **negligibly** *adv*, **negligibility** *n*

**negotiable** /ni'gohshyəbl/; *also* -syəbl USE *the last pron is disliked by some speakers*/ *adj* **1** transferable from one person to another by being delivered with or without endorsement, so that the title passes to the transferee ⟨*~ securities*⟩ **2** capable of being traversed ⟨*a difficult but ~ road*⟩ **3** capable of being dealt with or settled through discussion ⟨*a ~ claim*⟩ ⟨*salary ~*⟩ *usage* see NEGOTIATE – **negotiability** *n*

**negotiate** /ni'gohshiayt; *also* -siayt USE *the last pron is disliked by some speakers*/ *vi* to confer with another in order to reach an agreement or settlement – *vt* **1** to arrange or bring about through discussion ⟨*~ a peace treaty*⟩ **2a** to transfer (eg a BILL OF EXCHANGE) to another by delivery or endorsement **b** to convert into cash or the equivalent value ⟨~ *a cheque*⟩ **3a** to travel successfully along or over ⟨~ *the turn*⟩ **b** to complete or deal with successfully ⟨*the player* ~d *a difficult piece of music*⟩ [L *negotiatus*, pp of *negotiari* to carry on business, fr *negotium* business, fr *neg-* not + *otium* leisure] – **negotiant, negotiator** *n,* **negotiatory** *adj*

**negotiation** /ni,gohshi'aysh(ə)n/ *n* **1** negotiating or being negotiated **2 negotiations** *pl,* **negotiation** discussion of a disputed issue ⟨~ s *over pay have broken down*⟩

**Negress** /'neegris/ *n* a female Negro – chiefly derog and technical **synonyms** see [1]BLACK

**Negrillo** /ni'griloh/ *n, pl* **Negrillos, Negrilloes** a member of any of a group of small Negroid peoples (e g Pygmies) that live in Africa [Sp, dim. of *negro*]

**Negrito** /ni'greetoh/ *n, pl* **Negritos, Negritoes** a member of any of a group of small Negroid peoples that live in Oceania and SE Asia [Sp, dim. of *negro*]

**negritude** /'negri,tyoohd, 'nee-/ *n* **1** the quality of being Negro **2** a consciousness of and pride in the cultural and physical aspects of the African heritage [Fr *négritude*, fr *nègre* Negro + *-i-* + *-tude*]

**Negro** /'neegroh/ *n, pl* **Negroes 1** a member of the esp African branch of the black race of mankind, distinguished from members of other races by physical features without regard to language or culture **2** a person of Negro descent **synonyms** see [1]BLACK [Sp or Pg, fr *negro* black, fr L *nigr-, niger*] – **Negro** *adj, often not cap,* **Negroid** *n or adj, often not cap,* **Negroness** *n*

**negrohead** /'neegroh,hed/ *n* a strong black tobacco that is compressed into flat cakes [fr its colour]

**negrophile** /'neegroh,fiel, -grə-/ *n, often cap* one who is friendly to Negroes and their interests – **negrophilism** *n, often cap*

**negrophobe** /'neegroh,fohb, -grə-/ *n, often cap* one who strongly dislikes or fears Negroes – **negrophobia** *n, often cap*

[1]**negus** /'negəs/ *n, pl* **neguses** – used as a title of the former sovereigns of Ethiopia [Amharic *negūs*, fr Ethiopic *negūša nagašt* king of kings]

[2]**negus** *n* a drink of wine, hot water, sugar, lemon juice, and nutmeg [Francis *Negus* †1732 E soldier & politician, its inventor]

**Nehemiah** /,nee·i'mie·ə/ *n* – see BIBLE table [*Nehemiah* (Heb *Nĕḥemyāh*), 5th-c BC Jewish leader who directed the rebuilding of the walls of Jerusalem]

**Nehemias** /,nee·i'mie·əs/ *n* Nehemiah [LL, fr Heb *Nĕḥemyāh*]

**Nehru** /'neərooh/ *n* a tailored Indian coat that is buttoned down the front and has a stand-up collar ⟨~ *jacket*⟩ [Jawaharlal *Nehru* †1964 Indian statesman]

**neigh** /nay/ *vi* to make the loud prolonged cry characteristic of a horse [ME *neyen,* fr OE *hnǣgan;* akin to MHG *nēgen* to neigh, of imit origin] – **neigh** *n*

[1]**neighbour,** *NAm chiefly* **neighbor** /'naybə/ *n* **1** one living or situated near another **2** a fellow human being ⟨*the misfortune of a ~ who is unknown and far away* – Pius XII⟩ [ME *neighbor, neighebor,* fr OE *nēahgebūr;* akin to OHG *nāhgibūr* neighbour; both fr a prehistoric WGmc compound whose elements are represented by OE *nēah* near & OE *gebūr* dweller]

[2]**neighbour,** *NAm chiefly* **neighbor** *adj* adjacent or relatively near

[3]**neighbour,** *NAm chiefly* **neighbor** *vt* to adjoin or lie relatively near to

**neighbour on** *vt* to be approximately equivalent to

**neighbourhood** /-,hood/ *n* **1** an adjacent or surrounding region; a vicinity **2** an approximate amount, extent, or degree ⟨*cost in the ~ of £300*⟩ **3** *taking sing or pl vb* the neighbours **4a** a district lived in by neighbours and usu having distinguishing characteristics ⟨*a quiet ~*⟩ **b** a comparatively small district (e g of a town or city) usu forming a distinct community ⟨~ *schools*⟩ **5** *maths* **5a** the set of all points whose distances from a given point are not greater than a given (arbitrarily small) positive number **b** an OPEN set containing a given point **6** neighbourly association or feeling **7** proximity, nearness

**neighbouring** /'nayb(ə)ring/ *adj* nearby, adjacent

**neighbourly** /-li/ *n* characteristic of congenial neighbours; *esp* friendly

[1]**neither** /'niedhə 'needhə/ *pron* not the one or the other ⟨~ *of us*⟩ [ME, alter. of *nauther, nother,* fr. OE *nāhwæther, nōther,* fr *nā, nō* not + *hwæther* which of two, whether]

[2]**neither** *conj* **1** not either ⟨~ *here nor there*⟩ ⟨~ *ate, drank, nor smoked*⟩ **2** also not; nor ⟨*he didn't go and ~ did I*⟩

[3]**neither** *adj* not either ⟨~ *hand*⟩ *usage* see [3]EITHER, [1]NOR

[4]**neither** *adv* **1** similarly not; also not ⟨*"I can't swim." "Neither can I"*⟩ ⟨*just as the serf was not permitted to leave the land, so* ~ *was his offspring* – G G Coulton⟩ **2** *chiefly dial* either ⟨*are not to be understood* ~ – Earl of Chesterfield⟩

**nekton** /'nekton/ *n* aquatic animals (e g whales or squid) free-swimming near the surface of the water [Ger *nekton,* fr Gk *nēkton,* neut of *nēktos* swimming, fr *nēchein* to swim; akin to L *nare* to swim – more at NOURISH] – **nektonic** *adj*

[1]**nelly** /'neli/ *n, often cap* a weak-minded or effeminate person; *esp* an effeminate homosexual – often in *nervous Nelly, wet Nelly* [prob fr *Nelly,* nickname for *Helen*]

[2]**nelly** *n* [rhyming slang *Nelly (Duff)* puff, breath, life] – **not on your nelly** *Br slang* certainly not

**nelson** /'nels(ə)n/ *n* a wrestling hold in which leverage is applied against an opponent's arm, neck, and head – compare FULL NELSON, HALF NELSON [prob fr the name *Nelson*]

**Nelsonian** /nel'sohnyən, -niən/ *adj* (characteristic) of Admiral Nelson; *esp* showing calculated disregard of obstacles ⟨*turned an almost ~ blind eye to ... the difficulty* – The Economist⟩ [Horatio, Viscount *Nelson* †1805 E naval hero (who, at the Battle of Copenhagen in 1801, put a telescope to his blind eye and pretended not to see a signal to break off action)]

**nemat-** /'nemət-/, **nemato-** *comb form* **1** thread ⟨nematocyst⟩ **2** nematode ⟨nematology⟩ [NL, fr Gk *nēmat-,* fr *nēmat-, nēma,* fr *nēn* to spin – more at NEEDLE]

**nematic** /ni'matik/ *adj or n* (of or being) the phase of a LIQUID CRYSTAL characterized by having the molecules oriented in parallel lines rather than in layers – compare CHOLESTERIC, SMECTIC [ISV *nemat-* + *-ic*]

**nematoblast** /'nemətəblahst/ *n* a cell (e g in a jellyfish or SEA ANEMONE) that develops into a nematocyst

**nematocide** *also* **nematicide** /'nemətəsied, ni'matəsied/ *n* something that kills nematodes – **nematocidal** *adj*

**nematocyst** /'nemətə,sist/ *n* any of the minute stinging organs of various jellyfishes, SEA ANEMONES, and related animals [ISV]

**nematode** /'nemə,tohd/ *n* any of a class or phylum (Nematoda) of elongated cylindrical worms parasitic in animals or plants or free-living in soil or water – called also ROUNDWORM [deriv of Gk *nēmat-, nēma*]

**nematology** /,nemə'toləji/ *n* a branch of zoology that deals with nematodes – **nematologist** *n,* **nematological** *adj*

**Nembutal** /'nembyoo,tol, -tal/ *trademark* – used for the sedative drug PENTOBARBITONE

**nem con** *adv* no one contradicting **synonyms** see UNANIMOUS [NL *nemine contradicente*]

**nemertean** /ni'muhti·ən/ *n* any of a phylum (Nemertea) of often vividly coloured marine worms, most of which burrow in the mud or sand along seacoasts [deriv of Gk *Nēmertēs* Nemertes, one of the Nereids] – **nemertean** *adj,* **nemertine, nemertinean** *adj or n*

**nemesia** /ni'meezh(y)ə/ *n* any of various S African plants (genus *Nemesia*) of the foxglove family cultivated for their flowers of various colours [NL, genus name, fr Gk, pl of *nemesion* catchfly]

**nemesis** /'nemәsis/ *n, pl* **nemeses** /-seez/ **1a** (an agent of) retribution or vengeance **b** a formidable and usu victorious enemy or opponent **2** downfall, undoing ⟨*drink was his ~*⟩ [L *Nemesis,* goddess of divine retribution, fr Gk, fr *nemesis* retribution, fr *nemein* to distribute]

**nene** /'nay,nay/ *n* a goose (*Branta sandvicensis*) of the Hawaiian islands that was once nearly extinct but has now been bred in captivity and reestablished in the wild [Hawaiian *nēnē*]

**neo-** /'nee·ə-, -oh/ – see NE-

**neoanthropic** /,neeoh·an'thropik/ *adj* belonging to the same species (*Homo sapiens*) as recent man; modern in anatomy or type

**neoarsphenamine** /,neeoh·ahs'fenəmeen/ *n* a synthetic drug, $C_{13}H_{13}As_2N_2NaO_4S$, formerly used to treat syphilis [*neo-* + *arsphenamine* ($C_{12}Cl_2H_{14}As_2$), fr *arsenic* + *phenamine*]

**Neocene** /'nee·əseen/ *adj* of or being the later portion of the TERTIARY geological period including the MIOCENE and PLIOCENE – **Neocene** *n*

**neoclassic** /,neeoh'klasik/ *adj* of or constituting a revival or adaptation of the classical, esp in literature, music, art, or architecture ⟨*the ~ movement at the beginning of the 19th century gave way to ... Romanticism by the 1830s* – Mary Clarke & Clement Crisp⟩ – **neoclassical** *adj,* **neoclassicism** *n,* **neoclassicist** *n or adj*

**neocolonialism** /-kə'lohnyəliz(ə)m, -ni·əl-/ *n* the economic and political policies by which a great power indirectly maintains or extends its influence over other areas or people – **neocolonial** adj, **neocolonialist** n or adj

**neocortex** /ˌneeoh'kawteks/ n the back part of the CEREBRAL CORTEX (area of brain controlling higher-thought ability) that is unique to mammals [NL; fr its being the cortex of the most recently evolved part of the brain] – **neocortical** adj

ˌneo-'Darwinism n, often cap N a theory that explains evolution in terms of NATURAL SELECTION and population genetics and specif denies the possibility of inheriting acquired characteristics – compare LAMARCKISM – **neo-Darwinian** adj or n, often cap N, **neo-Darwinist** n, often cap N

**neodymium** /-'dimi-əm/ n a yellow metallic chemical element of the RARE EARTH group [NL, fr ne- + -dymium (fr didymium)]

**neogenesis** /ˌneeoh'jenəsis, ˌnee-ə-/ n new formation, esp of living tissue; regeneration ⟨~ in rat skin⟩ [NL] – **neogenetic** adj

ˌneo-im'pressionism n, often cap N&I a late 19th-century French art theory and practice characterized by an attempt to make IMPRESSIONISM more precise in form, and by the use of small dots of colour (POINTILLISM) [Fr néo-impressionisme, fr né- ne- + impressionisme impressionism] – **neo-impressionist** adj or n, often cap N&I

ˌNeo-'Latin adj or n 1 (of) NEW LATIN 2 ROMANCE (languages) ⟨Spanish is a ~ language⟩ [ISV]

**neolith** /'nee-ə,lith/ n a Neolithic stone implement [back-formation fr neolithic]

**Neolithic** /ˌnee-ə'lithik/ adj of the last period of the STONE AGE, characterized by polished stone implements

**neologism** /ni'oləjiz(ə)m/ n 1 a new word, usage, or expression 2 NEOLOGY 1 – **neologistic** adj

**neology** /ni'oləji/ n 1 the use of a new word or expression or of an established word in a new sense 2 NEOLOGISM 1 [Fr néologie, fr né- ne- + -logie -logy] – **neological** adj

ˌNeo-Mela'nesian n BÊCHE-DE-MER 2 (S Pacific language) – **Neo-Melanesian** adj

**neomycin** /ˌneeoh'miesin/ n an antibiotic or mixture of antibiotics, $C_{12}H_{26}N_4O_6$, effective against a wide range of microorganisms and obtained from a soil bacterium (Streptomyces fradiae), that is used for surface treatment of local infections or to sterilize the intestine before surgery [ne- + myc- + -in]

**neon** /'neeon/ n 1 a chemical element that is a colourless odourless INERT GAS found in minute amounts in air and used in electric lamps 2a a DISCHARGE LAMP in which the gas contains a large proportion of neon b a sign composed of neon-filled lamps c the illumination provided by lamps or signs using neon ⟨Piccadilly Circus was a blaze of ~⟩ [Gk, neut of neos new – more at NEW] – **neon** adj, **neoned** adj

**neonatal** /ˌneeoh'naytl/ adj of or affecting the newborn, esp the human child during the first month after birth – **neonatally** adv

**neonate** /'nee-ə,nayt/ n a newborn child; esp a child less than a month old [NL neonatus, fr ne- + natus, pp of nasci to be born – more at NATION]

**neoorthodox** /ˌneeoh'awthədoks/ adj of a 20th-century movement in Protestant theology reacting against liberalism and emphasizing various Reformation doctrines based on the Bible – **neoorthodoxy** n

**neophyte** /'nee-ə,fiet/ n 1 a new convert, esp to a religion 2 NOVICE 1 3 formal a beginner [LL neophytus, fr Gk neophytos, fr neophytos newly planted, newly converted, fr ne- + phyein to bring forth – more at BE]

**neoplasia** /ˌneeoh'playzh(y)ə/ n 1 the formation of tumours 2 a tumorous condition [NL]

**neoplasm** /'nee-ə,plaz(ə)m/ n an abnormal growth of tissue; a tumour [ISV] – **neoplastic** adj

**Neoplatonism** /ˌneeoh'playtəniz(ə)m/ n a modified form of PLATONISM (philosophy of Plato) that regards the world as a radiation sent down from a supreme being or God, with whom the soul can unite in a mystical trance – **Neoplatonist** n, **Neoplatonic** adj

**neoprene** /'nee-ə,preen/ n a very strong synthetic rubber that is resistant to deterioration caused by oil, wear, etc [ne- + chloroprene]

ˌneo-scho'lasticism n a movement among Catholic scholars aiming to restate the methods and teachings of medieval SCHOLASTICISM in a manner suited to the intellectual needs of the present

**neostigmine** /ˌnee-ə'stigmeen/ n a synthetic drug containing

the ion $[(CH_3)_2NCO_2C_6H_4N(CH_3)_3]^+$ that is used esp in the diagnosis and treatment of MYASTHENIA GRAVIS (disease causing muscular weakness and exhaustion) [ne- + -stigmine (as in physostigmine)]

**neoteny** /nee'ot(ə)ni/ n 1 attainment of sexual maturity during the larval stage 2 retention of some larval or immature characters in adulthood [NL neotenia, fr ne- + Gk teinein to stretch – more at THIN] – **neotenic** adj

**neoteric** /ˌnee-ə'terik/ adj, formal of recent origin; modern [LL neotericus, fr LGk neōterikos, fr Gk, youthful, fr neōteros, compar of neos new, young – more at NEW]

**Neotropical** /ˌneeoh'tropikl/ also **Neotropic** /-'tropik/ adj of or constituting the biogeographic region that includes S America, the W Indies, and tropical N America [ISV]

**Neozoic** /ˌnee-ə'zoh·ik/ adj or n (of or constituting) the entire geological period from the end of the MESOZOIC to the present time

**Nepalese** /ˌnep(ə)l'eez/ n or adj, pl **Nepalese** a Nepali

**Nepali** /ni'pawli/ n, pl **Nepalis**, esp collectively **Nepali** 1 the INDIC language of Nepal 2 a native or inhabitant of Nepal [Hindi naipālī of Nepal, fr Skt naipālīya, fr Nepāla Nepal, country in Asia] – **Nepali** adj

**nepenthe** /nə'penthi/ n 1 a potion used by the ancients to induce forgetfulness of pain or sorrow 2 formal or poetic something capable of bringing oblivion of grief or suffering [L nepenthes, fr Gk nēpenthes, neut of nēpenthēs banishing pain and sorrow, fr nē- not + penthos grief, sorrow; akin to Gk pathos suffering – more at PATHOS] – **nepenthean** adj

**nephanalysis** /ˌnefə'naləsis/ n 1 the analysis of the clouds and related phenomena over a large area of the earth 2 a map showing cloud patterns and distribution and related phenomena over a large area of the earth [NL, fr Gk nephos cloud + analysis – more at NEBULA]

**nepheline** /'nefəleen/ also **nephelite** /-iet/ n a mineral, $KNa_3Al_4Si_4O_{16}$, that is a usu glassy chemical compound containing sodium, potassium, aluminium, silicon, and oxygen and is common in IGNEOUS rocks [Fr néphéline, fr Gk nephelē cloud – more at NEBULA] – **nephelinic** adj

**nephelinite** /'nefəliniet/ n a fine-grained rock having nepheline as the predominant mineral [ISV, fr nepheline] – **nephelinitic** adj

**nephew** /'nefyooh; also 'nevyooh/ n 1 a son of one's brother or sister or of one's brother-in-law or sister-in-law 2 an illegitimate son of a clergyman ⟨~ s – sons mine! . . . ah God, I know not! – Robert Browning⟩ [ME nevew, fr OF neveu, fr L nepot-, nepos grandson, nephew; akin to OE nefa grandson, nephew, Skt napāt grandson]

**nephogram** /'nefə,gram/ n a photograph of a cloud pattern for meteorological purposes (e g for weather forecasting) [Gk nephos cloud + ISV -gram/]

**nephograph** /'nefə,grahf, -,graf/ n an instrument for taking nephograms

**nephoscope** /'nefəskohp/ n an instrument for observing the direction and speed of movement of clouds [Gk nephos cloud + ISV -scope/]

**nephr-** /nefr-/, **nephro-** comb form kidney; kidneys ⟨nephric⟩ ⟨nephrology⟩ [NL, fr Gk, fr nephros; akin to ME nere kidney]

**nephrectomy** /ni'frektəmi/ n the surgical removal of a kidney [ISV] – **nephrectomized** adj

**nephric** /'nefrik/ adj RENAL (relating to a kidney)

**nephridium** /ni'fridiəm/ n, pl **nephridia** /-diə/ 1 a tubular glandular organ for excreting waste matter characteristic of various INVERTEBRATE animals (e g earthworms) 2 an excretory structure; esp a nephron [NL] – **nephridial** adj

**nephrite** /'nefriet/ n a compact TREMOLITE or ACTINOLITE mineral that is the commoner and less valuable kind of jade and that varies in colour from white to dark green or black [Ger nephrit, fr Gk nephros; fr its formerly being worn as a remedy for kidney diseases]

**nephritic** /ni'fritik/ adj 1 RENAL (relating to a kidney) 2 of or affected with nephritis

**nephritis** /ni'frietəs/ n, pl **nephritides** /ni'fritədeez/ acute or chronic inflammation of the kidney [LL, fr Gk, fr nephros]

**nephrogenic** /ˌnefrə'jenik/ adj 1 originating in the kidney 2 developing into or producing kidney tissue

**nephron** /'nefron/ n a single excretory unit, esp of the kidney of VERTEBRATE animals [Ger, fr Gk nephros]

**nephropathy** /ni'fropəthi/ n an abnormal state of the kidney; esp one associated with or secondary to some other disease [ISV]

**nephrosis** /ni'frohsis/ *n* noninflammatory degeneration of the kidneys chiefly affecting the kidney tubules [NL] – **nephrotic** *adj or n*

**nephrostome** /'nefrəstohm/ *n* the CILIATED (covered with hairlike structures) funnel-shaped opening of a typical nephridium [NL *nephrostoma*, fr *nephr-* + *stoma*]

**ne plus ultra** /ˌnay ploos 'ooltrə/ *n* 1 the highest point or stage capable of being attained; the acme 2 the greatest degree of a quality or state [NL, (go) no more beyond]

**nepotism** /'nepəˌtiz(ə)m/ *n* favouritism shown to a relative (e g by appointment to a political office) [Fr *népotisme*, fr It *nepotismo*, fr *nepote* nephew, fr L *nepot-, nepos* – more at NEPHEW] – **nepotist** *n*

**Neptune** /'neptyoohn/ *n* 1 the ocean poetically personified 2 the planet eighth in order from the sun [L *Neptunus*, Roman god of the sea] – **Neptunian** *adj*

**neptunium** /nep'tyoohni·əm/ *n* a radioactive metallic chemical element that is chemically similar to uranium and is obtained in nuclear reactors as a by-product in the production of plutonium [NL, fr ISV *Neptune*]

**nereid** /'niəri·id/ *n* a sea nymph [L *Nereid-, Nereis*, fr Gk *Nēreid-, Nēreis*, fr *Nēreus* Nereus, a Greek sea god]

**nereis** /'niəri·is/ *n, pl* **nereides** /ni'ree·ədeez/ any of a genus (*Nereis* of the class Polychaeta, phylum Annelida) of usu large greenish marine worms [NL, genus name, fr L, *Nereid*]

**neritic** /ne'ritik/ *adj* of or being the belt or region of shallow water adjoining the seacoast [perh fr NL *Nerita*, genus of marine snails]

**nerol** /'niərol/ *n* a liquid alcohol, $C_{10}H_{18}O$, that has a rose scent and is used esp in perfumery [ISV *ner-* (fr *neroli oil*) + *-ol*]

**neroli oil** /'niərəli/ *n* a fragrant pale yellow ESSENTIAL OIL obtained from the flowers of the orange tree and used esp in cologne and as a flavouring [Fr *néroli*, fr It *neroli*, fr Anna Maria de La Trémoille, princess of *Nerole fl* 1670, its reputed discoverer]

**nerv-** /nuhv-/, **nervi-, nervo-** *comb form* neur- ⟨nerv*ine*⟩ [ME *nerv-*, fr L, fr *nervus*]

**¹nerve** /nuhv/ *n* 1 a sinew, tendon ⟨*strain every* ~⟩ 2 any of the threadlike bands of nervous tissue that connect parts of the nervous system with the other organs, conduct nervous impulses, and are made up of AXONS that conduct away from the NERVE CELL and DENDRITES that conduct to the NERVE CELL, together with protective and supportive structures 3a power of endurance or self-discipline; fortitude, tenacity ⟨*it takes* ~ *to wait for just the right moment*⟩ b (disrespectful) assurance or boldness ⟨*you certainly have a* ~ *to ask such a favour!*⟩ 4a a sore or sensitive subject – esp in hit/touch a nerve ⟨*he hit a* ~ *when he mentioned her divorced husband*⟩ b *pl* feelings of acute nervousness or anxiety ⟨*actors who suffer from first-night* ~s⟩ 5 VEIN 3 6 the sensitive pulp of a tooth [L *nervus* sinew, nerve; akin to Gk *neuron* sinew, nerve, *nēn* to spin – more at NEEDLE]

**²nerve** *vt* 1 to give strength or courage to 2 to prepare (oneself) psychologically *for* – often + *up* ⟨~d *herself up for the confrontation*⟩

**nerve cell** *n* NEURON; *also* CELL BODY

**nerve centre** *n* 1 CENTRE 3 (group of NERVE CELLS with the same function) 2 a source of leadership, control, or energy ⟨*the financial* ~ *of the nation*⟩

**nerve cord** *n* the pair of closely united longitudinal nerves with their GANGLIA (mass of NERVE CELL bodies) that is characteristic of many elongated INVERTEBRATE animals (e g earthworms)

**nerved** /nuhvd/ *adj* 1 veined ⟨*a* ~ *wing*⟩ 2 having veins or nerves, esp of a specified kind or number – often in combination ⟨*fan*-nerved *leaves*⟩

**nerve fibre** *n* a strand (e g an AXON or DENDRITE) of nerve tissue

**nerve gas** *n* a deadly poisonous war gas that interferes with normal nerve transmission and induces intense contraction of the windpipe with resulting inhibition of breathing

**nerve impulse** *n* a surge of electric current that travels along a NERVE FIBRE following stimulation and serves to transmit a record of sensation from the affected nerve ending or an instruction to act to a nerve ending connected with a muscle or gland

**nerveless** /-lis/ *adj* 1 lacking strength or vigour; feeble 2 not affected by fear or agitation; cool ⟨*a flimsy bamboo raft handled by a* ~ *guide – Scottish Field*⟩ – **nervelessly** *adv*, **nervelessness** *n*

**nerve net** *n* a network of NERVE CELLS apparently continuous with one another and conducting impulses in all directions; *also* a primitive nervous system (e g in a jellyfish) consisting of such a network

**'nerve-ˌracking, nerve-wracking** *adj* placing a great strain on the nerves ⟨*a* ~ *ordeal*⟩ *usage* see ¹RACK

**nerve trunk** *n* a bundle of NERVE FIBRES enclosed in a CONNECTIVE TISSUE (loose fibrous supporting tissue) sheath

**nervosity** /nuh'vosəti/ *n* the quality or state of being nervous

**nervous** /'nuhvəs/ *adj* 1 spirited, terse ⟨*a vibrant tight-packed* ~ *style of writing*⟩ 2 of or composed of NERVE CELLS 3a of the nerves; *also* originating in or affected by the nerves b easily excited or agitated; jumpy c timid, apprehensive ⟨*a* ~ *smile*⟩ ⟨*very shy and* ~ *of strangers*⟩ 4 giving cause for nervousness or agitation; uneasy ⟨*a* ~ *situation*⟩ 5 *archaic* sinewy, strong *synonyms* see TIMID – **nervously** *adv*, **nervousness** *n*

**nervous breakdown** *n* (an occurrence of) a disorder characterized by worrying, anxiety, depression, and severe tiredness that stops one from doing one's ordinary work and from coping with one's responsibilities

**nervous system** *n* the system of nerves and nervous tissue that in VERTEBRATE animals includes the brain and spinal cord, nerves, and GANGLIA (mass of NERVE CELL bodies) and that receives and interprets stimuli from the SENSE ORGANS and transmits impulses to muscles, glands, etc

**nervure** /'nuhvyooə/ *n* VEIN 3 [Fr, fr *nerf* sinew, fr L *nervus*]

**nervy** /'nuhvi/ *adj* 1 *informal* suffering from nervousness or anxiety ⟨*she looked so white and* ~ *– Annabel*⟩ 2 *NAm informal* impudent, brash 3 *archaic* sinewy, strong – **nerviness** *n*

**nescience** /'nesi·əns, 'nesh(ə)ns/ *n, formal* lack of knowledge or awareness; ignorance [LL *nescientia*, fr L *nescient-, nesciens*, prp of *nescire* not to know, fr *ne-* not + *scire* to know – more at SCIENCE] – **nescient** *adj*

**ness** /nes/ *n* a cape, headland – usu cap as part of a name [ME *nasse*, fr OE *næss*; akin to OE *nasu* nose – more at NOSE]

**-ness** /-nis/ *suffix adj* (→ *n*) 1 state or quality of ⟨*goodness*⟩; *also* instance of (a specified state or quality) ⟨*a kindness*⟩ 2 degree or amount of ⟨*bigness*⟩ *usage* see -ION, ²-TY [ME *-nes*, fr OE; akin to OHG *-nissa* -ness]

**Nesselrode** /'nesəlrohd/ *n* a mixture of candied fruits and chestnut puree used in frozen puddings and ice cream [Count Karl *Nesselrode* †1862 Russ statesman]

**¹nest** /nest/ *n* 1a a bed or receptacle prepared by a bird for its eggs and young b a place or specially modified structure in which animals live, esp in their immature stages ⟨*an ants'* ~⟩ 2a a usu snug and sheltered place of rest, retreat, or lodging b a den, haunt 3 *taking sing or pl vb* the occupants of a nest ⟨*suppressing the* ~ *of Saracen marauders who had established themselves in the Alpine passes* – R W Southern⟩ 4a a group of similar things ⟨*a* ~ *of giant mountains* – Helen MacInnes⟩ b a hotbed ⟨*a* ~ *of rebellion*⟩ 5 a series of objects made to fit close together or one inside another ⟨*a* ~ *of tables*⟩ 6 an emplaced group of weapons ⟨*a machine-gun* ~⟩ [ME, fr OE; akin to OHG *nest* nest, L *nidus*] – **feather one's nest** to provide for one's own material needs, esp by dishonestly exploiting one's employer

**²nest** *vi* 1 to build or occupy a nest ⟨*birds* ~ *in many places*⟩ 2 to fit compactly together or inside one another ⟨*the chairs stack easily, the tables* ~ *– Time*⟩ ~ *vt* 1 to form a nest for ⟨*an old sweater* ~ed *the lamb by the fire*⟩ 2 to pack or fit compactly together ⟨*she* ~ed *the freezer boxes to make more room on the shelf*⟩ – **nester** *n*

**nest box, nesting box** *n* 1 a box in a henhouse where domesticated fowls lay their eggs 2 a box provided, usu in a park or garden, for wild birds to nest in

**nest egg** *n* 1 a natural or artificial egg left in a nest to induce a fowl to continue to lay there 2 an amount of money saved up as a reserve

**nesting** /'nesting/ *n* bird's-nesting

**nestle** /'nesl/ *vi* 1 to settle snugly or comfortably ⟨*she* ~d *down among the soft cushions*⟩ 2 to lie in an inconspicuous or sheltered position ⟨*a cottage* nestling *in the woods*⟩ 3 *archaic* NEST 1 ~ *vt* 1 to settle, shelter, or enclose (as if) in a nest 2 to press closely and affectionately ⟨~s *her head against his shoulder*⟩ [ME *nestlen*, fr OE *nestlian*, fr *nest*] – **nestler** *n*

**nestling** /'nestling, 'nesling/ *n* a young bird that has not left the nest

**Nestor** /'nestaw/ *n, often not cap* a wise old man or mentor [*Nestor* (Gk *Nestōr*), old wise hero in Gk mythology]

**Nestorian** /ne'stawri·ən/ *adj* 1 of the doctrine ascribed to Nestorius and condemned by the GREEK ORTHODOX church in 431 that divine and human persons remained separate in the incarnate Christ **2** of a church separating from GREEK ORTHODOX Christianity after 431, centring in Persia, and surviving chiefly in the Middle East and the USA [*Nestorius* †*ab*451 patriarch of Constantinople] – **Nestorian** *n*, **Nestorianism** *n*

¹**net** /net/ *n* **1a** an open meshed fabric twisted, knotted, or woven together at regular intervals **b** something made of net: eg **b(1)** a device for catching fish, birds, or insects **b(2)** a net barricade which divides a tennis, badminton, etc court in half and over which a ball or shuttlecock must be hit to be in play **b(3)** (the fabric that encloses the sides and back of) a soccer, hockey, etc goal ⟨*slammed the ball into the back of the* ∼⟩ **c(1)** *usu pl* a practice cricket pitch surrounded by nets ⟨*in the* ∼s *he could maintain an accuracy which seemed beyond him under the tension of actual play* – John Arlott⟩ **c(2)** a period of practice in such a net ⟨*had a good* ∼ *before the match*⟩ **2** a situation in which one is trapped ⟨*caught in the* ∼ *of suspicious circumstances*⟩ **3** something resembling a net in crisscross formation (eg of lines, fibres, or figures) **4** a ball hit into the net in a racket game **5a** a group of communications stations operating under unified control **b** NETWORK 4 [ME *nett*, fr OE; akin to OHG *nezzi* net, L *nodus* knot] – **netless** *adj*, **netlike** *adj*, **netty** *adj*

²**net** *vt* **-tt- 1** to cover or enclose (as if) with a net ⟨∼ *fruit trees to keep off the birds*⟩ **2** to catch (as if) in a net ⟨∼ *a salmon*⟩ **3a** to hit (a ball) into the net for the loss of a point in a game **b** to hit or kick (a ball or puck) into the goal for a score in hockey, soccer, etc – **netter** *n*

³**net**, *chiefly Br* **nett** *adj* **1** free from all charges or deductions: eg **1a** remaining after all deductions (eg for taxes, outlay, or loss) ⟨∼ *earnings*⟩ – compare GROSS **b** excluding all TARE (deduction for weight of container) ⟨∼ *weight*⟩ **2** final, ultimate ⟨*the* ∼ *result*⟩ [ME, clean, bright, fr MF – more at ²NEAT]

⁴**net**, *chiefly Br* **nett** *vt* **-tt- 1a** to make by way of profit; clear **b** to produce by way of profit **2** to get possession of; gain ⟨*succeeded in* ∼*ting more of the goods of this world* – John Wain⟩

⁵**net** *n* a net amount, profit, weight, price, or score

**netball** /-ˌbawl/ *n* a game, usu for women, played between two sides of seven players each who score goals by tossing an inflated ball through a high horizontal ring on a post at each end of a hard court

**net cord** *n* a shot in tennis that hits the top edge of the net but lands correctly in the opponent's court

**nether** /ˈnedhə/ *adj* **1** beneath the earth's surface ⟨*the* ∼ *regions*⟩ **2** *formal* lower, under ⟨*the* ∼ *side*⟩ [ME, fr OE *nithera*, fr *nither* down; akin to OHG *nidar* down, Skt *ni*, Gk *en*, *eni* in – more at IN] – **nethermost** *adj*

**netherworld** /-ˌwuhld/ *n* **1** the world of the dead **2** UNDERWORLD 2 ⟨*the* ∼ *of deceit, subversion, and espionage* – Richard Nixon⟩

**netsuke** /ˈnetsooki, ˈnetski/ *n*, *pl* **netsuke**, **netsukes** a small and often intricately carved toggle (eg of ivory) used to fasten a small pouch or purse to a kimono sash [Jap]

**netting** /ˈneting/ *n* **1** NETWORK 1 **2** the act, process, or right of fishing with a net

¹**nettle** /ˈnetl/ *n* **1** any of a genus (*Urtica* of the family Urticaceae, the nettle family) of widely distributed usu coarse plants covered with stinging hairs **2** any of various plants other than the true nettle – usu in combination ⟨*a dead*nettle *without stinging hairs*⟩ [ME, fr OE *netel*; akin to OHG *nazza* nettle, Gk *adikē*] – **grasp the nettle** to tackle an awkward or unpleasant problem without flinching

²**nettle** *vt* **1** to strike or sting (as if) with nettles **2** to arouse to sharp but short-lived annoyance or anger *synonyms* see IRRITATE *antonym* soothe

**nettle rash** *n* URTICARIA (irritating skin disorder)

¹**net-ˌveined** *adj* having veins arranged in a fine network ⟨*a* ∼ *leaf*⟩ ⟨*a* ∼ *insect wing*⟩ – compare PARALLEL-VEINED

¹**net-ˌwinged** *adj* having wings with a fine network of veins

¹**network** /-ˌwuhk/ *n* **1** a fabric or structure of cords or wires that cross at regular intervals and are knotted or secured at the crossings **2** a system of crisscrossing lines or channels ⟨*a* ∼ *of drainage ditches*⟩ **3** an interconnected chain, group, or system ⟨*a* ∼ *of hotels*⟩ **4 network, net 4a** a group of radio or television stations linked together so that they can broadcast the same programmes if desired **b** a radio or television company that produces programmes for broadcast over such a network

²**network** *vt* **1** to cover (as if) with a network ⟨*suburbs* ∼ed *by railways*⟩ **2** to present on or integrate into a radio or television network ⟨∼ed *programmes*⟩

**Neufchâtel** /ˈnuhˌshatel (*Fr* nœʃatɛl)/ *n* a soft white cheese similar to CREAM CHEESE but containing less fat [Fr, fr *Neufchâtel*, town in France]

**neume, neum** /nyoohm/ *n* any of various symbols used in the notation of early medieval music [ME *newme* group of notes sung to one syllable, fr MF *neume*, fr ML *pneuma, neuma*, fr Gk *pneuma* breath – more at PNEUMATIC] – **neumatic** *adj*

**neur-** /nyooə-/, **neuro-** *also* **neuri-** *comb form* **1** nerve; nervous system ⟨*neural*⟩ ⟨*neurology*⟩ **2** neural; neural and ⟨*neuromuscular*⟩ [NL, fr Gk, nerve, sinew, fr *neuron* – more at NERVE]

**neural** /ˈnyooərəl/ *adj* **1** of or affecting a nerve or the NERVOUS SYSTEM **2** situated in the region of or on the same side of the body as the SPINAL CORD; DORSAL 1 – **neurally** *adv*

**neural arch** *n* the arch of cartilage or bone that extends backwards from the main body of a vertebra of the backbone and encloses the SPINAL CORD – compare CENTRUM

**neural canal** *n* the canal or tube formed by the NEURAL ARCHES of the vertebrae, through which the SPINAL CORD passes – called also SPINAL CANAL

**neuralgia** /nyoo(ə)ˈraljə/ *n* acute spasms of pain radiating along the course of one or more nerves, usu without apparent cause △ neurosis [NL] – **neuralgic** *adj*

**neural spine** *n* a bony structure that projects backwards from the middle of a NEURAL ARCH and provides a surface to which muscles attach

**neural tube** *n* the hollow longitudinal tube that forms in the embryo of a VERTEBRATE animal and later develops into the brain and SPINAL CORD

**neuraminidase** /ˌnyooərəˈminədayz, -ays/ *n* an enzyme that is found esp in microorganisms of the respiratory passages or intestines and that breaks down MUCOPROTEINS (complex compounds of carbohydrate and protein) [*neuramin*ic acid (an amino acid) + *-ide* + *-ase*]

**neurasthenia** /ˌnyooərəsˈtheenyə/ *n* a mental disorder characterized by severe fatigue, depression, feelings of inadequacy, and psychosomatic symptoms; NERVOUS BREAKDOWN – not now used technically [NL] – **neurasthenic** *adj*, **neurasthenically** *adv*

**neurilemma** /ˌnyooəriˈlemə/, **neurolemma** /ˌnyooərə-/ *n* **1** the thin delicate outer sheath surrounding a NERVE FIBRE **2** PERINEURIUM (sheath round a bundle of NERVE FIBRES) [NL, fr *neur-* + Gk *eilēma* covering, coil, fr *eilein* to wind; akin to Gk *eilyein* to wrap – more at VOLUBLE] – **neurilemmal** *adj*

**neuritis** /nyooəˈrietəs/ *n*, *pl* **neuritides** /-ˈrietəˌdeez/, **neuritises** an inflammatory or degenerative condition of a nerve resulting esp in pain, sensory disturbances, and impaired or lost reflexes [NL] – **neuritic** *adj or n*

**neuro-** – see NEUR-

**neuroactive** /ˌnyooərohˈaktiv/ *adj* stimulating nerve tissue

**neurobiology** /ˌnyooəroh-bieˈoləji/ *n* NEUROSCIENCE – **neurobiologist** *n*, **neurobiological** *adj*

**neuroblast** /ˈnyooərəˌblahst/ *n* a cell from which NERVE CELLS develop [ISV, fr *neur-* + *-blast*]

**neuroblastoma** /ˌnyooəroh-blaˈstohmə/ *n*, *pl* **neuroblastomas, neuroblastomata** /-mətə/ a cancerous tumour formed of undeveloped or incompletely developed NERVE CELLS [NL]

**neurochemistry** /ˌnyooərohˈkemistri/ *n* the study of the chemical makeup and activities of nerves, nerve tissue, and NEUROTRANSMITTERS (chemical substances that transmit nerve impulses between nerves) – **neurochemist** *n*, **neurochemical** *adj*

**neuroendocrine** /ˌnyooərohˈendəkrin/ *adj* **1** of or being a hormone that influences the activity of nerves **2** of, being, or functioning in the production of hormones or hormone-like substances by NERVE CELLS; *also* of or being a hormone or hormone-like substance produced by a nerve cell

**neuroepithelial** /ˌnyooərohˌepiˈtheelyəl/ *adj*, *of a cell or tissue* having qualities of or containing both NERVE CELLS and EPITHELIAL cells (cells making up the tissue that covers surfaces)

**neurofibril** /ˌnyooərohˈfiebril/ *n* any of the fine protein fibres made up of bundles of neurofilaments, that are found in a NERVE CELL and are associated with the transport of substances along the length of the cell [NL *neurofibrilla*, fr *neur-* + *fibrilla* fibril] – **neurofibrillary** *adj*

**neurofilament** /ˈnyooəroh.filəmənt/ *n* any of the microscopic threadlike filaments that make up a neurofibril

**neurogenic** /ˌnyooərə'jenik/ *adj* 1 originating in or controlled by nerve tissue ⟨*a ~ heartbeat*⟩ 2 induced, modified, or caused to malfunction by factors originating in the NERVOUS SYSTEM ⟨*a ~ disorder*⟩ ⟨*a ~ kidney*⟩ – **neurogenically** *adv*

**neuroglia** /nyoo(ə)'rogli·ə, ˌnyooərə'glee·ə/ *n* the cells making up the tissue that is intermingled with and supports the NERVE CELLS and NERVE FIBRES in the brain, SPINAL CORD, etc [NL, fr *neur-* + MGk *glia* glue – more at CLAY] – **neuroglial** *adj*

**neurohormonal** /ˌnyooəroh·haw'mohnl/ *adj* 1 (of or being mechanisms) involving both NERVE CELLS and hormonal action 2 of or being a neurohormone

**neurohormone** /'nyooəroh,hawmohn/ *n* a hormone (e g adrenalin) produced by or acting on nerves or nerve tissues [ISV]

**neurohumour** /ˌnyooəroh'hyoohmə/ *n* NEUROTRANSMITTER (substance that transmits nerve impulses between nerves) – **neurohumoural** *adj*

**neurohypophysis** /ˌnyooəroh·hie'pofəsis/ *n* the part of the PITUITARY GLAND that is composed of the rear lobe of the gland and the INFUNDIBULUM (stalk attaching the pituitary gland to the brain) and is concerned with the secretion of various hormones (e g OXYTOCIN and VASOPRESSIN) – compare ADENOHYPOPHYSIS [NL] – **neurohypophyseal, neurohypophysial** *adj*

**neurolemma** /ˌnyooəroh'lemə/ *n* NEURILEMMA

**neuroleptanalgesia** /ˌnyooəroh,leptənəl'jeez(h)yə/, **neuroleptoanalgesia** /-ˌleptoh-anəl-/ *n* the administration of a tranquillizer together with a pain-relieving drug, in order to induce a relaxed sleepy state during which minor surgery (e g the removal of a tooth) can be carried out – compare TWILIGHT SLEEP [NL, fr ISV *neuroleptic* + *analgesic* + NL *-ia* (as in *analgesia*)] – **neuroleptanalgesic** *adj*

**neuroleptic** /ˌnyooərə'leptik/ *n* a tranquillizing drug [Fr *neuroleptique*, fr *neur-* + *-leptique* affecting, fr Gk *lēptikos* seizing, fr *lambanein* to take, seize – more at LATCH] – **neuroleptic** *adj*

**neurologist** /nyooə'roləjist/ *n* a person specializing in neurology; *esp* a medical doctor skilled in the diagnosis and treatment of disease of the NERVOUS SYSTEM

**neurology** /nyoo(ə)'roləji/ *n* the scientific and medical study of the NERVOUS SYSTEM [NL *neurologia*, fr *neur-* + *-logia* -logy] – **neurological, neurologic** *adj*, **neurologically** *adv*

**neuroma** /nyoo'rohmə/ *n*, *pl* **neuromas, neuromata** /-mətə/ a tumour or mass of tissue growing from a nerve and usu consisting of NERVE FIBRES [NL]

**neuromuscular** /ˌnyooəroh'muskyoolə/ *adj* of or involving nerves and muscles ⟨*a ~ junction*⟩ [ISV]

**neuron** /'nyooəron/, **neurone** /'nyooərohn/ *n* a specialized cell that conducts nerve impulses and is the basic functional unit of nerve tissue. A typical neuron consists of a nucleus-containing part (CELL BODY) with one long projecting structure (AXON) that conducts impulses away from the cell body, and numerous short delicate branching projections (DENDRITES) that conduct impulses towards the cell body from other neurons. [NL *neuron*, fr Gk, nerve, sinew – more at NERVE] – **neuronal** *also* **neuronic** *adj*

**neuropathy** /nyoo(ə)'ropəthi/ *n* an abnormal, usu degenerative, state of the nerves or the NERVOUS SYSTEM [ISV] – **neuropathic** *adj*, **neuropathically** *adv*

**neuropharmacology** /ˌnyooəroh,fahmə'koləji/ *n* a branch of physiology dealing with the action of drugs on and in the NERVOUS SYSTEM – **neuropharmacologist** *n*, **neuropharmacologic, neuropharmacological** *adj*

**neurophysiology** /ˌnyooəroh,fizi'oləji/ *n* physiology of the NERVOUS SYSTEM – **neurophysiologist** *n*, **neurophysiological** *also* **neurophysiologic** *adj*, **neurophysiologically** *adv*

**neuropsychiatry** /ˌnyooəroh·sie'kie·ətri/ *n* a branch of medicine concerned with both the psychological and physiological aspects of mental disorder – **neuropsychiatrist** *n*, **neuropsychiatric** *adj*, **neuropsychiatrically** *adv*

**neuropsychic** /ˌnyooəroh'siekik/ *also* **neuropsychical** /-kl/ *adj* relating to both the mind and the NERVOUS SYSTEM as affecting mental processes

**neuropteran** /nyoo(ə)'roptərən/ *n* any of an order (Neuroptera) of insects, including the lacewings and the ANT LIONS, that have biting mouthparts and two pairs of wings covered with a fine network of many veins [deriv of Gk *neur-* + *pteron* wing – more at FEATHER] – **neuropteran** *adj*, **neuropterous** *adj*

**neuroscience** /ˌnyooəroh'sie·əns/ *n* a branch of biology (e g neurophysiology or neurochemistry) that deals with the anatomy, physiology, and biochemistry of nerves and nerve tissue – **neuroscientist** *n*

**neurosecretion** /ˌnyooəroh·si'kreesh(ə)n/ *n* 1 a substance (e g adrenalin) produced and secreted by NERVE CELLS 2 the act or process of producing a neurosecretion [ISV] – **neurosecretory** *adj*

**neurosis** /nyoo(ə)'rohsis/ *n*, *pl* **neuroses** /-seez/ (a) nervous disorder, unaccompanied by disease of the nervous system, in which one or more phobias, compulsions, or obsessions, accompanied usu by anxiety, make normal life difficult – compare PSYCHOSIS △ neuralgia [NL]

**neurospora** /nyoo'rospərə/ *n* any of a genus (*Neurospora* of the family Sphaeriaceae) of fungi which are used extensively in genetic research and some of which are severe pests in bakeries [NL, genus name, fr *neur-* + *spora* spore]

**neurosurgeon** /'nyooəroh,suhjən/ *n* a surgeon specializing in neurosurgery

**neurosurgery** /ˌnyooəroh'suhjəri/ *n* surgery performed on nervous structures (e g nerves, the brain, or the SPINAL CORD) – **neurosurgical** *adj*

¹**neurotic** /nyoo(ə)'rotik/ *adj* 1 of, being, caused by, or affected with (a) neurosis ⟨*a ~ person*⟩ ⟨*~ behaviour*⟩ 2 unduly anxious, worried, or concerned ⟨*he's quite ~ about his front garden*⟩; *also* oversensitive (e g to criticism) – **neurotically** *adv*, **neuroticism** *n*

²**neurotic** *n* 1 a person affected with (a) neurosis 2 an emotionally unstable individual – not used technically

**neurotoxic** /ˌnyooəroh'toksik/ *adj* toxic to the nerves or nerve tissue – **neurotoxicity** *n*

**neurotoxin** /'nyooəroh,toksin/ *n* a poison, esp a poisonous protein (e g in snake venom), that acts on the NERVOUS SYSTEM [ISV]

**neurotransmitter** /ˌnyooəroh·trans'mitə/ *n* a chemical substance (e g NORADRENALIN) that is released at a nerve ending and transmits nerve impulses across a SYNAPSE (point at which nerve impulses pass from one NERVE CELL to another or to a muscle, gland, etc) – **neurotransmission** *n*

**neurotrophism** /ˌnyooəroh'trohfiz(ə)m/ *n* the effect of a nerve in stimulating the growth or preventing the degeneration of the organ (e g a muscle) on which it acts [ISV] – **neurotrophic** *adj*

**neurotropic** /ˌnyooərə,tropik/ *adj* attracted to or growing in nerve tissue ⟨*~ drugs*⟩ ⟨*a ~ virus*⟩ [ISV] – **neurotropism** *n*

**neuston** /'nyoohston/ *n* minute organisms that float or swim in the surface film of water [Ger, fr Gk, neut of *neustos* swimming, fr *nein* to swim – more at NOURISH]

¹**neuter** /'nyoohtə/ *adj* 1a of or being the gender that ordinarily includes most words or grammatical forms referring to things classed as neither masculine nor feminine (e g *it* as opposed to *he/she*) b neither active nor passive; intransitive 2 *of an animal or plant* lacking or having imperfectly developed or nonfunctional reproductive organs or structures ⟨*the worker bee is ~*⟩ [ME *neutre*, fr MF & L; MF *neutre*, fr L *neuter*, lit., neither, fr *ne-* not + *uter* which of two – more at NO, WHETHER]

²**neuter** *n* 1a a word or language form of the neuter gender b the neuter gender 2 a sexually underdeveloped wasp, bee, ant, etc; WORKER 2 3 a castrated animal

³**neuter** *vt* 1 CASTRATE 1 2 to deprive of distinguishing features or of vitality and potency ⟨*a film ~ed by the censor*⟩

¹**neutral** /'nyoohtrəl/ *adj* 1a not engaged on either side; *specif* not politically or ideologically aligned ⟨*a ~ state*⟩ b of a neutral state or power ⟨*~ territory*⟩ 2a neither one thing nor the other; indifferent, indefinite b(1) of or being white, black, or grey; ACHROMATIC (having no hue) b(2) having no definite colour; nearly achromatic 3a NEUTER 2 b *chemistry* neither acid nor alkaline ⟨*a ~ solution*⟩ c(1) having no electrical charge ⟨*a neutron is a ~ atomic particle*⟩ c(2) not electrically live; neither positive nor negative ⟨*the ~ wire in a mains plug is blue*⟩ 4a pronounced with the tongue in the position it has when at rest ⟨*the ~ vowel /ə/*⟩ b *of a speech sound* (e g /ah/) pronounced with the lips neither spread nor rounded; *also, of the lips* in this position [MF, fr (assumed) ML *neutralis*, fr L, of neuter gender, fr *neutr-, neuter*] – **neutrally** *adv*, **neutralness** *n*

²**neutral** *n* 1 a neutral country, person, etc 2 a neutral colour 3 a position (of a gear lever) in which gears are disengaged 4 a neutral electrical conductor

**neutralism** /'nyoohtrəliz(ə)m/ *n* 1 neutrality 2 a policy of strict neutrality, esp in foreign affairs – **neutralist** *n*, **neutralistic** *adj*

**neutrality** /nyooh'traləti/ *n* 1 the quality or state of being neutral in international affairs, involving immunity from invasion by warring states and the withholding of aid from them **2** the state of being electrically or chemically neutral

**neutral-ize, -ise** /'nyoohtrə‚liez/ *vt* **1** to make chemically neutral **2** to counteract the activity or effect of ⟨*propaganda that is difficult to* ∼⟩ ⟨*the phonemic distinction between "Rad" and "Rat" in German is* ∼d⟩ **3** to make electrically neutral by combining equal positive and negative quantities **4** to make (eg a territory or a nation) neutral under international law **5** to make (a colour) black, white, or grey by blending with the COMPLEMENTARY colour ∼ *vi* to undergo neutralization; become neutralized – **neutralizer** *n*, **neutralization** *n*

**neutrino** /nyooh'treenoh/ *n, pl* **neutrinos** an ELEMENTARY PARTICLE (minute particle of matter) that exists in several forms, is a member of the family of LEPTONS, has no electrical charge and probably zero mass, and interacts only slightly with other particles of matter [It, dim. of *neutrone* neutron]

**neutron** /'nyooh‚tron/ *n* an ELEMENTARY PARTICLE (minute particle of matter) that has a mass nearly equal to that of the proton and that together with the proton is present in the nucleus of all known atoms except the hydrogen atom [prob fr *neutral*]

**neutron bomb** *n* a nuclear bomb that produces relatively large amounts of radiation in the form of neutrons and a relatively small blast, and that is designed to destroy life while leaving buildings intact

**neutron star** *n* any of various stars that have a very high density, consist of closely packed neutrons, and result from the collapse of a larger star (SUPERNOVA) after an explosion

**neutrophil** /'nyoohtrə‚fil/, **neutrophile** /-‚fiel/ *n* a neutrophilic cell, tissue, etc; *specif* a WHITE BLOOD CELL present in large numbers in the blood, that has neutrophilic granules in its CYTOPLASM (jellylike material inside a cell and external to the cell nucleus) – compare BASOPHIL, EOSINOPHIL [ISV *neutro*-neutral (fr L *neutr*-, *neuter* neither) + *-phil*]

**neutrophilic** /‚nyoohtrə'filik/ *also* **neutrophil, neutrophile** *adj, of a cell, tissue, etc* staining to the same degree with both acidic and BASIC (alkaline) dyes

**névé** /'nevay (*Fr* neve)/ *n* the granular snow in the process of being compacted into ice, that forms the surface part of the upper end of a glacier; *broadly* a field of granular snow [Fr (Swiss dial.), fr L *niv*-, *nix* snow – more at SNOW]

**never** /'nevə/ *adv* **1** not ever; at no time ⟨∼ *saw him before*⟩ – often in combination ⟨*never-forgotten*⟩ **2** not in any degree; not under any condition ⟨*this will* ∼ *do*⟩ ⟨∼ *mind*⟩ **3** surely not – expressing amazement ⟨*you're* ∼ *18!* – *Daily Mirror*⟩ **4** *nonstandard* – used + a pronoun to deny guilt or responsibility ⟨*"she did it!" "No she* ∼*"*⟩ [ME, fr OE *næfre*, fr *ne* not + *æfre* ever] – **I never** *informal* – used to express amazement ⟨*"that drake of yours has just laid an egg!" "Well, I never!"*⟩

**nevermore** /‚nevə'maw/ *adv* never again ⟨*quoth the raven*, *"Nevermore"* – E A Poe⟩

**never-'never** *n, Br informal* HIRE PURCHASE – + *the*

**never-never land** *n* an ideal or imaginary place

**nevertheless** /‚nevədhə'les/ *adv* in spite of that; yet ⟨*true but* ∼ *unkind*⟩

**nevus** /'neevəs/ *n, pl* **nevi** /'neevee, -vie/ *NAm* NAEVUS (birthmark)

**¹new** /nyooh/ *adj* **1a** having existed a short time; recent ⟨*sociology is a relatively* ∼ *science*⟩ ⟨*the* ∼ *1978 clarets are a disappointment*⟩ **b** not previously used; fresh from the manufacturer ⟨*a* ∼ *car, not a secondhand one*⟩ **2a(1)** having been used or discovered for only a short time; novel ⟨*rice was a* ∼ *crop for the area*⟩ ⟨*a* ∼ *planet may soon be discovered beyond Pluto*⟩ **a(2)** fresh, unfamiliar ⟨*visit* ∼ *places*⟩ **b** different from or replacing a former one of the same category ⟨*a* ∼ *suit from Oxfam*⟩ ⟨*moved into a* ∼ *flat*⟩ **3** having been in the specified condition or relationship for only a short time; unaccustomed – usu + *to* ⟨∼ *to the job*⟩ ⟨∼ *to biochemistry*⟩ **4a** beginning as the repetition of a previous act or thing ⟨*a* ∼ *day*⟩ ⟨*the* ∼ *edition*⟩ **b** being refreshed or regenerated ⟨*awoke a* ∼ *man*⟩ **5** being in a place or condition for the first time ⟨*a* ∼ *member*⟩ ⟨*a* ∼ *mother*⟩ **6** of different origin and usu superior quality ⟨*introducing* ∼ *blood*⟩ **7** *cap* MODERN **3**; *esp* in use after medieval times ⟨New *Greek*⟩ [ME, fr OE *nīwe*; akin to OHG *niuwi* new, L *novus*, Gk *neos*] – **newish** *adj*, **newness** *n*

**synonyms New, novel, original, fresh, newfangled**: *new* is the most general, describing something recently invented, made, or discovered. *Novel* adds to *new* the idea of being strange, odd, or striking ⟨*a novel use for jam jars*⟩. *Original* stresses being the first of its kind, or doing something in a way which has not been done before. *Fresh* implies the qualities of being *new*: youthfulness, brightness, or energy. *Newfangled* (derogatory or humorous) suggests unnecessary or gimmicky novelty. Compare MODERN *antonyms* old, stale

**²new** *n, Austr* an inexperienced person; a novice

**³new** *adv* newly, recently – usu in combination ⟨new-*mown grass*⟩

**New Australian** *n, Austr* a recent immigrant to Australia

**¹newborn** /‚nyooh'bawn/ *adj* **1** recently born; just born **2** born afresh; reborn

**²newborn** *n, pl* **newborn, newborns** a recently born individual; NEONATE

**Newburg** *also* **Newburgh** /'nyooh'buhg/ *adj, esp of shellfish* served with a sauce made of cream, butter, sherry, and egg yolks ⟨*lobster* ∼⟩ ⟨*shrimp* ∼⟩ [origin unknown]

**Newcastle disease** /'nyooh‚kahsl, -‚kasl/ *n* FOWL PEST (virus disease of birds, esp poultry) [*Newcastle* upon Tyne, city in England]

**newchum, new chum** /'nyooh‚chum/ *n, Austr* **1** NEW AUSTRALIAN **2** an inexperienced person; a novice

**newcomer** /'nyooh‚kumə/ *n* **1** a recent arrival **2** a beginner, novice

**New Deal** *n* (the period of) the programme of economic and social reform in the USA introduced by President F D Roosevelt in the 1930s [fr its supposed resemblance to the situation of freshness and equality of opportunity afforded by a fresh deal in a card game] – **New Dealer** *n*, **New Dealism** *n*

**newel** /'nyooh-əl/ *n* **1** an upright post about which the steps of a spiral staircase wind **2** a principal post at each end of the handrail of a staircase [ME *nowell*, fr MF *nouel* stone of a fruit, fr LL *nucalis* like a nut, fr L *nuc*-, *nux* nut – more at NUT]

**New English Bible** *n* a translation of the Bible made by a committee containing representatives of the major British churches and first published in its entirety in 1970

**newfangled** /nyooh'fang-gld/ *adj, chiefly derog* **1** fond of novelty **2** modern and unnecessarily complicated or gimmicky ⟨*those* ∼ *electric calculators*⟩ ⟨∼ *ideas on education*⟩ *synonyms* see ¹NEW *antonym* old-fashioned [ME, fr *newefangel*, fr *new* + OE *fangen*, pp of *fōn* to take, seize – more at PACT] – **newfangledness** *n*

**new-'fashioned** *adj* modern, up-to-date

**Newfoundland** /nyooh'fowndlənd/ *n* (any of) a breed of very large heavy usu black dogs developed in Newfoundland [*Newfoundland*, island of Canada]

**New Greek** *n* MODERN GREEK

**New Hebrew** *n* MODERN HEBREW

**New Jerusalem** /jə'roohsələm/ *n* **1** the dwelling-place of souls redeemed by Christ; *broadly* HEAVEN 2a **2** an ideal earthly community [fr the phrase "the holy city, *new Jerusalem*" (Rev 21:2)]

**New Latin** /'latin/ *n* Latin used after the Middle Ages esp for the writing of scientific texts

**New Left** *n* a political movement developing in Britain in the late 1950s and at its most active in the late 1960s and early 1970s that attracted much support among students, advocated an undogmatic or libertarian interpretation of the works of Marx and Freud, and actively campaigned (eg by means of demonstrations and sit-ins) for radical changes in prevailing political, social, and educational practices – **new leftist** *n, often cap N&L*

**newly** /'nyoohli/ *adv* **1** lately, recently ⟨*a* ∼ *married couple*⟩ **2** in a new form or manner; anew

**Newlyn datum** /'nyoohlin/ *n* ORDNANCE DATUM (value for mean SEA LEVEL)

**newlywed** /-‚wed/ *n or adj* (someone who has) recently married

**new maths** *n* MODERN MATHS

**new moon** *n* **1** the moon's phase when its dark side is towards the earth; *also* the thin crescent moon seen shortly after sunset a few days after the actual occurrence of the new moon phase **2** the first day of the Jewish month

**new penny** *n* PENNY 1a(2)

**news** /nyoohz/ *n taking sing vb* **1** (a report or series of reports of) recent or notable events; new information about something ⟨*have you heard the* ∼*?*⟩ ⟨*there is no* ∼ *of him*⟩ **2a** material reported in a newspaper, news periodical, or news broadcast **b** material that is newsworthy **3** a radio or television broadcast of news – + *the* ⟨*I heard it on the* ∼⟩ [ME *newes*, fr pl of *newe, new* new] – **newsless** *adj*

**news agency** *n* an organization that collects news and sells its reports to newspapers, periodicals, and broadcasting companies

**newsagent** /'nyoohz,ayjənt/ *n, chiefly Br* a shopkeeper who sells newspapers and magazines

**newsboy** /'nyoohz,boy/ *n* a paperboy

**newscast** /'nyoohz,kahst/ *n* a news broadcast [*news* + *broadcast*] – **newscaster** *n*, **newscasting** *n*

**news conference** *n* PRESS CONFERENCE

**news dealer** *n, NAm* a newsagent

**newsflash** /'nyoohz,flash/ *n* a short broadcast news item; *esp* one that interrupts another programme to give brief details of an important piece of news

**newsletter** /'nyoohz,letə/ *n* a printed sheet, pamphlet, or small newspaper containing news or information of interest chiefly to a special group

**newsmagazine** /'nyoohzmagə,zeen, -'---/ *n, chiefly NAm* a magazine or magazine programme devoted chiefly to summarizing and analysing news

**newsman** /'nyoohz,man/, *fem* **newswoman** /-,woomən/ *n* a person who gathers, reports, or comments on the news; a reporter, correspondent

**newsmonger** /'nyoohz,mung·gə/ *n* someone who is active in circulating news; *esp* a gossip

**newspaper** /'nyoohs,paypə/ *n* **1** a paper that is printed and distributed usu daily or weekly and that contains news, articles of opinion, features, and advertising **2** an organization that publishes a newspaper **3** the paper making up a newspaper ⟨*ate fish and chips straight out of the ~*⟩

**newspaperman** /'news,papəmən, -man/, *fem* **newspaperwoman** /,woomən/ *n* a journalist who is employed by a newspaper; *esp* one who writes or edits news for a newspaper

**newspeak** /'nyoohz,speek/ *n, often cap* ambiguous or euphemistic language in which customary meanings are often inverted for propaganda purposes [*Newspeak*, a language "designed to diminish the range of thought," in the novel *Nineteen Eighty-Four* by George Orwell †1950 E writer]

**newsprint** /'nyoohz,print/ *n* cheap paper made chiefly from wood pulp and used mostly for newspapers

**newsreader** /'nyoohz,reedə/ *n* a broadcaster who reads the news

**newsreel** /'nyoohz,reel/ *n* a short film dealing with current events

**newsroom** /'nyoohzroom, -,roohm/ *n* **1** a reading room having newspapers and periodicals **2** a place (eg an office) where news is prepared for publication or broadcast

**news sheet** *n* a newsletter

**newsstand** /'nyoohz,stand/ *n* a place (eg an outdoor stall) where newspapers and periodicals are sold

**New Style** *adj* using or according to the GREGORIAN CALENDAR – compare OLD STYLE

**newsvendor** /'nyoohz,vendə/ *n* one who sells newspapers, esp from a regular pitch in the street

**newsworthy** /'nyoohz,wuhdhi/ *adj* sufficiently interesting to the general public to warrant reporting (eg in a newspaper)

**newsy** /'nyoohzi/ *adj* full of esp inconsequential news ⟨*~ letters from home*⟩ – **newsiness** *n*

**newt** /nyooht/ *n* any of various small semiaquatic amphibians (eg of the genus *Triturus*) that are types of salamander and have a long slender typically rough-skinned body [ME, alter. (by incorrect division of *an ewte*) of *ewte* – more at EFT]

**New Testament** *n* the second part of the Christian Bible containing various versions of the life and death of Jesus (GOSPELS) and other writings of the early Church – see BIBLE table

**newton** /'nyooht(ə)n/ *n* the SI unit of force equal to the force that will give an acceleration of 1 metre per second per second to a mass of 1 kilogram [Sir Isaac *Newton* †1727 E mathematician & scientist]

**Newtonian** /nyooh'tohnyən, -ni-ən/ *adj* of or following Sir Isaac Newton, his discoveries, or his doctrines; *esp* of or based on Newton's laws of motion or gravitation ⟨*~ mechanics*⟩

**new town** *n* any of several towns in Britain built after 1946 in accordance with the principles of TOWN PLANNING so that their various functions (housing, leisure amenities, employment, etc) are related to one another in the most efficient and satisfying manner

**new wave** *n, often cap N&W* **1** *taking sing or pl vb* (the style adopted by) a group of French film-makers active from the late 1950s who rejected many of the techniques of big budget commercial cinema, frequently working on improvised themes using simple equipment in everyday locations; *broadly* any new movement or trend in the arts **2** a type of rock music originating in Britain in the late 1970s [trans of Fr *nouvelle vague*]

**New World** *n* the western hemisphere; *esp* the continental landmass of N and S America – compare OLD WORLD

**New Year** *n* **1** New Year's Day; *also* New Year's Day and the first days of the year **2** ROSH HASHANAH

**New Year's Day** *n* January 1 observed as a public holiday in many countries

**New Year's Honours** *n* the HONOURS LIST published on January 1 each year

**New Zealand** /'zeelənd/ *adj* (typical) of New Zealand [*New Zealand*, country in the SW Pacific]

**New Zealand rug** *n* a partially lined waterproof rug worn by a horse out at grass to keep it warm and dry

**¹next** /nekst/ *adj* **1** immediately preceding or following (eg in place or order) ⟨*the ~ house*⟩ **2** immediately after the present or a specified time ⟨*~ week*⟩ ⟨*he left the very ~ Monday*⟩
*usage* see ¹FIRST [ME, fr OE *nīehst*, superl of *nēah* nigh – more at NIGH]

**²next** *adv* **1** in the time, place, or order nearest or immediately succeeding ⟨*~ we drove home*⟩ ⟨*the ~ closest school*⟩ **2** on the first occasion to come ⟨*when ~ we meet*⟩ – compare WHAT NEXT – **next to 1** immediately following or adjacent to ⟨*sit next to Mary*⟩ ⟨*next to gin I like sherry best*⟩ **2** very nearly; almost ⟨*it was next to impossible to see in the fog*⟩
*synonyms* A person or thing is **next** *to*, **adjacent** *to*, or **contiguous** *to*, or **adjoins** another if nothing intervenes between them ⟨*a field* **next** *to*/**adjacent** *to*/**adjoining** *the road*⟩; but **adjoining** and even more the rarer word **contiguous** must mean that the two actually touch at some point ⟨*a door into the* **adjoining** *room*⟩, which **next** *to* and **adjacent** need not.

**³next** *prep* nearest or adjacent to ⟨*wear wool ~ the skin*⟩

**⁴next** *n* something that is next: eg **a** the next occurrence or item of a kind ⟨*he missed one bus so waited for the ~*⟩ **b** something forthcoming ⟨*to be continued in our ~*⟩

**next-'door** *adj* situated or living in the next building, dwelling; or room ⟨*~ neighbours*⟩

**next door** *adv* in or to the next building, dwelling, or room ⟨*lives next door*⟩ – **next door to** next to

**next friend** *n, law* a person admitted to or appointed by a court to act for the benefit of a person (eg an infant) lacking full legal capacity to act for him-/herself

**next man** *n* anyone else – + *the*; esp in comparisons ⟨*could change a wheel as well as the ~*⟩

**next of kin** *n, pl* **next of kin** a person most closely related (eg by blood, marriage, or adoption) to another person

**nexus** /'neksəs/ *n, pl* **nexuses**, **nexus 1** a connection, a link ⟨*it makes money seem the only social ~ – Nation Review* [*Melbourne*]⟩ **2** a connected group or series [L, fr *nexus*, pp of *nectere* to bind]

**Nez Percé** /,nez 'puhs/ *n* **1** a member of an American Indian people of Idaho, Washington, and Oregon **2** a language of the Nez Percé people [Fr, lit., pierced nose]

**N gauge** *n* a gauge of track in model railways in which the rails are approximately 9 millimetres apart [prob fr *n*ine]

**ngultrum** /en(g)'gooltrəm/ *n* – see MONEY table [native name in Bhutan]

**ngwee** /n'gwee/ *n, pl* **ngwee** – see *kwacha* at MONEY table [native name in Zambia, lit., bright]

**niacin** /'nie-əsin/ *n* NICOTINIC ACID (type of vitamin B) [*nicotinic acid* + *-in*]

**Niagara** /nie'agrə/ *n* an overwhelming flood; a torrent ⟨*a ~ of persuasive eloquence – Yorkshire Post*⟩ [*Niagara* Falls, waterfall of the Niagara River in N America]

**¹nib** /nib/ *n* **1** a bird's bill; a beak **2a** the sharpened point of a quill pen **b** a pen point; *also* each of the two divisions of a pen point **3** a small pointed or projecting part or article ⟨*roasted almond ~*s⟩ [prob alter. of *neb*]

**²nib** *vt* to make into or furnish with a nib

**¹nibble** /'nibl/ *vt* **1a** to bite daintily, gently, or playfully ⟨*she ~*d *his ear affectionately*⟩ **b** to eat or chew in small bits **2** to take away bit by bit ⟨*waves nibbling the shore*⟩ **3** to produce by repeated small bites ⟨*mice had ~*d *a hole in the cheese*⟩ *~ vi* **1** to take gentle, small, or cautious bites **2** to show cautious or qualified interest □ (*vi*) usu + *at* [prob akin to LG *nibbeln* to gnaw] – **nibbler** *n*

**²nibble** *n* **1** an act of nibbling ⟨*can't resist a quick ~ between meals*⟩ **2** *informal* a very small amount (eg of food) ⟨*just give me a ~ of that chocolate cake*⟩

**niblick** /'niblik/ *n* a metal-headed golf club having a deeply slanted face and used for short high shots esp out of sand or long grass – no longer in vogue [origin unknown]

**nibs** /nibz/ *n taking sing vb, informal* an important or self-important person – usu in *his/her nibs* or *His/Her Nibs* [earlier *nabs*, perh alter. of *neb*]

**niccolite** /'nikəliet/ *n* a pale copper-red mineral of metallic lustre that consists essentially of a compound of nickel and arsenic, NiAs, and is an ore of nickel [NL *niccolum* nickel, prob fr Sw *nickel*]

**nice** /nies/ *adj* **1a** showing fastidious or finicky tastes; refined, particular ⟨*an animal ~ about its diet*⟩ **b** possessing, marked by, or demanding delicate discrimination or treatment; fine ⟨*the ~ and subtle ramifications of meaning* – Samuel Johnson⟩ ⟨*a ~ distinction*⟩ **2a** pleasing, agreeable ⟨*a ~ time*⟩ ⟨*it's hard to be ~ to people all the time*⟩ **b** done well; well-executed ⟨*~ shot!*⟩ **3** highly inappropriate or unpleasant – usu used ironically ⟨*a ~ one to talk*⟩ ⟨*got himself in a ~ fix*⟩ **4a** socially acceptable; well-bred ⟨*unpopular with the ~r people in the town*⟩ **b** decent, proper ⟨*not a very ~ joke*⟩ **5** archaic coy, reticent [ME, foolish, wanton, fr OF, fr L *nescius* ignorant, fr *nescire* not to know – more at NESCIENCE] – **nice, nicely** *adv,* **niceness** *n*

*usage* The chief meaning of *nice* has been for some time "pleasing, agreeable"; but for formal writing it is better to confine the word to the meanings "fastidious" and "demanding discrimination" and to replace it elsewhere by **amusing, beautiful, interesting,** etc as appropriate.

**Nicene** /'nieseen/ *adj* of a church council held in Nicaea in AD 325 or the NICENE CREED [ME, fr LL *nicaenus*, fr L *Nicaea* Nicaea, ancient city in Asia Minor]

**Nicene Creed** *n* a Christian creed expanded from a creed issued by the first Nicene Council, beginning "I believe in one God", and used in worship

**nicety** /'niesəti/ *n* **1** the quality or state of being nice **2** an elegant or refined feature ⟨*enjoy the niceties of city life*⟩ **3** a fine point or distinction; a subtlety ⟨*the niceties of English grammar*⟩ **4** careful attention to details; precision **5** the quality of showing or requiring delicacy and discernment ⟨*a question of great ~*⟩ **6** the point at which a thing is at its best ⟨*roasted to a ~*⟩ [ME *nicete*, fr MF *niceté* foolishness, fr *nice*, adj]

**¹niche** /neesh, nich/ *n* **1a** a recess in a wall; *esp* one for a statue **b** something that resembles a niche **2** a place, job, or activity for which a person is best suited ⟨*he's found his ~ at last*⟩ **3** *ecology* **3a** a specialized area in a habitat, supplying the conditions necessary for the existence of a living organism or species – compare MICROHABITAT **b** the ecological role or status of a plant or animal in a community, considered esp with regard to the organism's activities, food consumption, and effects on or relationships with other organisms of the community [Fr, fr MF, fr *nicher* to nest, fr (assumed) VL *nidicare*, fr L *nidus* nest – more at NEST]

**²niche** *vt* to place (as if) in a niche

**Nichrome** /'niekrohm/ *trademark* – used for an alloy of nickel, chromium, iron, and carbon having a high degree of resistance to the flow of an electric current and an ability to withstand high temperatures

**¹nick** /nik/ *n* **1a** a small notch or groove ⟨*file a ~ in the steel*⟩ **b** a small groove on the front of a piece of type **2** the point at which the back wall or either of the side walls meets the floor of a squash court **3** EDGE **4** **4** a break in one of the NUCLEOTIDE chains of a molecule (eg of DNA) composed of two nucleotide chains **5** *Br informal* state of health or repair; condition – esp in *in good/bad nick* **6** *Br slang* a police station or prison – esp in *in the nick* [ME *nyke*, prob alter. of *nocke* nock] – **in the nick of time** at the final critical moment; just before it would be too late

**²nick** *vt* **1a** to make a nick in; notch, chip **b** to cut into or wound slightly ⟨*a bullet ~ed his leg*⟩ **2** to catch at the right point or time **3** *NAm* to jot down; record **4** *NAm* to cut short ⟨*cold weather, which ~ed steel and automobile output – Time*⟩ **5** *chiefly Br informal* to steal, filch ⟨*~ed a fiver from the petty cash*⟩ **6** *Br slang* to arrest ⟨*he ~ed a lot of villains – The Listener*⟩ **7** *NAm informal* to cheat, overcharge ~ *vi, esp of domestic animals* to complement one another genetically and produce superior offspring *synonyms* see ROB

**¹nickel** /'nikl/ *n* **1** a hard silver-white metallic chemical element that has magnetic properties similar to those of iron, is capable of a high polish, is resistant to corrosion, and can be easily worked. Nickel is used chiefly in alloys and as a catalyst to increase the rate at which chemical reactions occur. **2a** the US 5-cent piece regularly containing 25 per cent nickel and 75 per cent copper **b** the sum of five US cents [Sw, fr Ger *kupfernickel* niccolite, prob fr *kupfer* copper + *nickel* goblin; fr the deceptive copper colour of niccolite]

**²nickel** *vt* **-ll-** (*NAm* **-l-, -ll-**) to plate with nickel

**nickelic** /ni'kelik/ *adj* of or containing nickel, esp with a VALENCY higher than two

**nickeliferous** /,nikə'lifərəs/ *adj* containing nickel

**nickelodeon** /,nik(ə)l'ohdi·ən/ *n* **1** an early cinema presenting entertainment for an admission price of usu five cents **2** a jukebox [prob fr ¹*nickel* + -*odeon* (as in *melodeon* music hall, reed organ)]

**nickelous** /'nikələs/ *adj* of or containing nickel, esp with a VALENCY of two

**nickel silver** *n* a silver-white alloy of copper, zinc, and nickel used for making cutlery and articles to be plated with silver

**¹nicker** /'nikə/ *vi* to neigh, whinny [perh alter. of *neigh*]

**²nicker** *n, pl* **nicker**, *Br slang* the sum of one pound sterling [origin unknown]

**nicknack** /'nik,nak/ *n* a knick-knack

**¹nickname** /'niknaym/ *n* **1** an often descriptive name used in place of or in addition to the proper name of a person or thing, esp to express ridicule or familiarity **2** a familiar form of a proper name, esp of a person ⟨*"Bill" is a ~ for "William"*⟩ [ME *nekename* additional name, alter. (by incorrect division of *an ekename*) of *ekename*, fr *eke* also + *name*]

**²nickname** *vt* **1** to misname, miscall **2** to give a nickname to ⟨*~d him "Fatty" because of his weight*⟩ – **nicknamer** *n*

**nicol** /'nik(ə)l/, **nicol prism** *n* a prism consisting of two pieces of the transparent variety of the mineral CALCITE cemented together, that is used esp to obtain a ray of POLARIZED light (light that vibrates only in a restricted number of directions) [William *Nicol* †1851 Sc physicist]

**nicotinamide** /,nikə'tinə,mied, -'tee-/ *n* a vitamin, $C_5H_4N$ $CONH_2$, of the VITAMIN B COMPLEX that is used by the body in a similar way to NICOTINIC ACID [ISV]

**nicotinamide-adenine dinucleotide** *n* NAD

**nicotinamide-adenine dinucleotide phosphate** *n* NADP

**nicotine** /'nikəteen/ *n* a poisonous chemical compound, $C_{10}H_{14}N_2$, that occurs in tobacco, is used as an agricultural insecticide, and causes disorders of the respiratory system, dizziness, increased blood pressure, and disturbances of hearing and vision [Fr, fr NL *nicotiana,* genus name of tobacco plants, fr Jean *Nicot* †1600 Fr diplomat & scholar who introduced tobacco into France]

**nicotinic** /,nikə'tinik/ *adj* **1** of NICOTINIC ACID **2** of nicotine or its physiological effects; *specif* of, being, having, or resembling the actions or effects (eg increased blood pressure and contraction of some muscles) of ACETYLCHOLINE (substance that transmits nerve impulses) on those parts of the nervous system for which nicotine mimics the stimulatory actions of acetylcholine ⟨*tubocurarine blocks the ~ effects of acetylcholine on skeletal muscle*⟩ – compare MUSCARINIC [ISV]

**nicotinic acid** /,nikə'tinik, -'tee-/ *n* a vitamin, $C_6H_5NO_2$, of the VITAMIN B COMPLEX that is found widely in animals and plants, is required by the body to form compounds (eg NAD) important in the production of energy inside cells, and whose lack in the diet results in PELLAGRA – called also NIACIN

**nictitate** /'niktitayt/ *vi* to wink, blink – used technically [alter. of *nictate* (to wink), fr L *nictatus,* pp of *nictare* – more at CONNIVE]

**nictitating membrane** *n* a thin skinlike membrane at the inner angle or beneath the lower lid of the eye in many animals (eg cats and reptiles), that is capable of extending across the eyeball

**nidicolous** /ni'dikələs/ *adj* **1** *of a bird* reared for a time in a nest after hatching **2** sharing the nest of another kind of animal [L *nidus* nest + E -*colous*]

**nidification** /,nidifi'kaysh(ə)n/ *n* the act, process, or technique of building a nest [ML *nidification-, nidificatio,* fr L *nidificatus,* pp of *nidificare* to build a nest, fr *nidus* nest]

**nidus** /'niedəs/ *n, pl* **nidi** /'niedi, -die/, **niduses 1** a nest or breeding place: eg **1a** a nest for the eggs of an insect, spider, etc **b** a cavity or hollow in which plant spores or seeds develop **c** a place or substance in an animal or plant where parasitic organisms (eg bacteria) lodge and multiply; a main or primary site of an infection **2** a place where something originates, develops, or is located [NL, fr L]

**niece** /nees/ *n* a daughter of one's brother or sister or of one's brother-in-law or sister-in-law [ME *nece* granddaughter, niece, fr OF *niece*, fr LL *neptia*, fr L *neptis;* akin to L *nepot-*, *nepos* grandson, nephew – more at NEPHEW]

¹**niello** /ni'eloh/ *n, pl* **nielli** /-li/, **niellos** 1 any of several black enamel-like alloys usu of sulphur with silver, copper, and lead 2 the art or process of decorating metal with incised designs filled with niello 3 a piece of metal or an object decorated with niello [It, fr ML *nigellum*, fr neut of L *nigellus* blackish, dim. of *niger* black]

²**niello** *vt* **niellos; nielloing; nielloed** to inlay or ornament with niello

**Nietzschean** /'neechiən/ *adj* of Nietzsche or his philosophy, esp his doctrine of the SUPERMAN [Friedrich *Nietzsche* †1900 Ger philosopher] – **Nietzschean** *n*

**niff** /nif/ *n, Br informal* an unpleasant smell; a pong [E dial., perh short for *sniff*] – **niffy** *adj*

**nifty** /'nifti/ *adj* 1 very good, excellent, or effective; *esp* cleverly conceived or executed ⟨*a ~ gadget*⟩ 2 *of clothes* stylish, natty ⟨*a ~ little cream linen suit*⟩ [origin unknown] – **niftily** *adv*

**Niger-Congo** /ˌniejə 'kong·goh/ *n* a language family that includes Mande and is spoken in west, central, and southern Africa [*Niger*, river in W Africa + *Congo*, river in central Africa]

**niggard** /'nigəd/ *n* a mean and stingy person; a miser [ME, of Scand origin; akin to ON *hnøggr* niggardly; akin to L *cinis* ashes – more at INCINERATE] – **niggard** *adj*

**niggardly** /'nigədli/ *adj* 1 grudgingly mean about giving or spending 2 provided in meanly limited supply ⟨*~ praise*⟩ *synonyms* see STINGY *antonym* bountiful – **niggardliness** *n*, **niggardly** *adv*

**nigger** /'nigə/ *n* 1 a negro; *broadly* a member of any dark-skinned race – usu taken to be very offensive when used by whites, but may be neutral or even appreciative when used by blacks 2 **nigger, nigger brown** a very dark chocolate brown colour [alter. of earlier *neger*, fr MF *negre*, fr Sp or Pg *negro*, fr *negro* black, fr L *niger*] – **nigger in the woodpile** (one who or that which causes) an unforeseen snag or difficulty

'**nigger-ˌlover** *n, NAm derog* a supporter of Negro rights

**niggle** /'nigl/ *vi* 1 to waste time or effort on minor details 2 to find fault constantly in a trifling way; carp ⟨*she haggles, she ~s, she wears out our patience* – Virginia Woolf⟩ 3 to be a source of petty but persistent irritation; gnaw ~ *vt* to cause petty usu persistent irritation to; bother [origin unknown] – **niggle** *n*, **niggler** *n*, **niggly** *adj*

**niggling** /'nigling/ *adj* 1 persistently troublesome; petty ⟨*filled with all sorts of ~ doubts*⟩ 2 demanding meticulous care – **niggling** *n*, **nigglingly** *adv*

¹**nigh** /nie/ *adv* 1 nearly, almost – often + *well* ⟨*reigned for well ~ sixty years*⟩ or + *on*, *onto*, or *unto* ⟨*~ on fifty years* – William Hardcastle⟩ 2 *poetic* near in place, time, or relation ⟨*my end draws ~* – Alfred Tennyson⟩ [ME, fr OE *nēah*; akin to OHG *nāh*, adv, nigh, prep, nigh, after, ON *nā-* nigh]

²**nigh** *adj* 1 being on the left side ⟨*the ~ horse*⟩ 2 *poetic* close, near

³**nigh** *prep, poetic* near

⁴**nigh** *vt* to approach

**night** /niet/ *n* 1 the period of darkness from dusk to dawn caused by the earth's daily rotation on its axis; *broadly* a period when the sky is dark and the sun is not visible ⟨*in the arctic the ~ lasts half the year*⟩ 2 an evening characterized by a specified event or activity ⟨*the opening ~*⟩ ⟨*Thursday is bingo ~*⟩ 3a darkness b a state or period compared to the darkness of night; *esp* a state of affliction, ignorance, or obscurity c the beginning of darkness; nightfall ⟨*red sky at ~, shepherds' delight*⟩ [ME, fr OE *niht*; akin to OHG *naht* night, L *noct-*, *nox*, Gk *nykt-*, *nyx*] – **make a night of it** to continue celebrations or social activities throughout the evening or night ⟨*let's open another bottle and make a night of it*⟩

**night and day** *adv* all the time; continually

**night blindness** *n* reduced vision or ability to see in faint light (eg at night) – called also NYCTALOPIA – **night-blind** *adj*

**nightcap** /'niet,kap/ *n* 1 a cloth cap worn with nightclothes 2 a usu hot or alcoholic drink taken at bedtime

**nightclothes** /'niet,klohdhz/ *n pl* garments for sleeping in

**nightclub** /'niet,klub/ *n* a place of entertainment open at night that has a floor show, provides music and space for dancing, and usu serves drinks and food

**nightdress** /'niet,dres/ *n* a woman's or girl's loose garment for sleeping in

**night editor** *n* an editor in charge of the final makeup of a morning newspaper

**nightfall** /'niet,fawl/ *n* the close of the day; dusk

**nightglow** /'niet,gloh/ *n* a glow seen in the sky during the night

**nightgown** /'niet,gown/ *n* 1 a loose garment for sleeping in 2 *archaic* a dressing gown

**nighthawk** /'niet,hawk/ *n* any of several American birds (genus *Chordeiles*) with buff to reddish-brown plumage that are active at night; *also* a nightjar

**nightie, nighty** /'nieti/ *n, informal* a nightdress [*night*gown + -*ie* or -*y*]

**nightingale** /'nieting,gayl/ *n* any of several Eurasian and African thrushes (genus *Luscinia*, esp *Luscinia megarhynchos*) noted for the sweet song of the male that is commonly heard at night; *also* any of various other birds that sing at night [ME, fr OE *nihtegale*, fr *niht* + *galan* to sing – more at YELL]

**nightjar** /'niet,jah/ *n* any of many greyish- to reddish-brown insect-eating birds (family Caprimulgidae) that are found in most temperate to tropical regions of the world and are active in the twilight and at night; *esp* a greyish-brown Eurasian nightjar (*Caprimulgus europaeus*) that has a characteristic churring call – called also GOATSUCKER [fr its jarring cry]

**night latch** *n* a door lock whose bolt is operated from the outside by a key and from the inside by a knob

**nightlife** /'niet,lief/ *n* late evening entertainment or social life (eg in nightclubs)

'**night-ˌlight** *n* a light kept burning all night long, esp in a bedroom

¹**nightlong** /'nietlong/ *adj* lasting all night ⟨*~ festivities*⟩

²**nightlong** *adv* throughout the night ⟨*volunteers worked ~ to rescue survivors*⟩

¹**nightly** /'nietli/ *adj* 1 of the night or every night 2 occurring, taken, or done by night or every night ⟨*a ~ bath*⟩ ⟨*a ~ news review*⟩

²**nightly** *adv* every night; *also* at or by night

**nightmare** /'niet,meə/ *n* 1 a frightening dream that usu awakens the sleeper 2 an experience, situation, or object that produces feelings of acute anxiety or terror ⟨*the ~ of nuclear war*⟩ ⟨*a ~ drive through snow and ice*⟩ 3 *archaic* an evil spirit that causes frightening dreams [¹*night* + obs *mare* evil spirit, fr ME, fr OE] – **nightmarish** *adj*, **nightmarishly** *adv*

**night owl** *n* a person who tends to stay up or be most active at night

**nights** /niets/ *adv, informal* in the night repeatedly; on any night ⟨*~ we'd go dancing till late*⟩

**night school** *n* (an educational institution offering) classes often in adult or further education during the evening

**nightshade** /'niet,shayd/ *n* 1 any of various usu poisonous plants (genus *Solanum*) of the potato family: eg 1a a widely distributed weed of cultivated land (*Solanum nigrum*) that bears poisonous black berries – called also BLACK NIGHTSHADE b BITTERSWEET 2 2 DEADLY NIGHTSHADE

**night shift** *n* a shift worked during the night; *also, taking sing or pl vb* the workers employed on this shift

**nightshirt** /'niet,shuht/ *n* a loose shirt for sleeping in

**nightside** /'niet,sied/ *n* the side of a body (eg the earth, the moon, or a planet) not in daylight

**night soil** *n* human excrement collected for fertilizing the soil

**nightstick** /'niet,stik/ *n, NAm* a policeman's truncheon or club

**nighttide** /'niet,tied/ *n* nighttime

**nighttime** /'niet,tiem/ *n* the time from dusk to dawn – **night-time** *adj*

**night watchman** *n* 1 someone who guards or keeps watch over (eg a building) by night 2 a relatively inexpert batsman who is sent in to bat towards the end of a day's play so that a more expert batsman need not face the bowling until the following day

**nighty** /'nieti/ *n* a nightie

**nignog** /'nig,nog/ *n, Br slang* a nigger – sometimes used humorously but usu taken to be very offensive [redupl of *nig*, short for *nigger*]

**nigrescence** /nie'gres(ə)ns/ *n* the process of becoming black or dark [L *nigrescent-*, *nigrescens*, prp of *nigrescere* to become black, fr *nigr-*, *niger* black] – **nigrescent** *adj*

**nigritude** /'nigrityoohd/ *n* intense darkness; blackness [L *nigritudo*, fr *nigr-*, *niger*]

**nigrosine** /'niegrəseen/ *also* **nigrosin** /-sin/ *n, often cap* any of several synthetic black dyes used to colour leather, paper, textiles, plastics, and shoe polish [L *nigr-, niger* + E *-ose* + *-ine, -in*]

**nihilism** /'nie•ə,liz(ə)m, 'ni-/ *n* **1a** a view that rejects all values and beliefs as meaningless or unfounded **b** a doctrine that rejects any objective basis for truth or moral values **2a** a doctrine or belief that social conditions are so bad that the destruction of existing institutions can only lead to improvement regardless of any constructive programme or possibility which may subsequently be introduced **b** *cap* the programme of a 19th-century Russian party advocating revolutionary reform and using terrorism and assassination **3** terrorism [Ger *nihilismus*, fr L *nihil* nothing – more at NIL] – **nihilist** *n or adj*, **nihilistic** *adj*

**nihility** /nie'hiləti/ *n* absence of existence; nullity

**nihil obstat** /,nie•il 'obstat, 'neehil/ *n* **1** the certification by a Roman Catholic censor that a book contains nothing contrary to faith and morals **2** authoritative or official approval [L, nothing hinders]

**-nik** /-nik/ *suffix* (*n or adj* → *n*), *informal* one connected with or characterized by being ⟨*computer*nik⟩ ⟨*nogood*nik⟩ [Yiddish, fr Russ & Pol]

**nil** /nil/ *n* nothing, zero ⟨*a score of two to* ∼⟩ *synonyms* see ¹ZERO [L, nothing, contr of *nihil*, fr OL *nihilum*, fr *ne-* not + *hilum* trifle] – **nil** *adj*

**nilgai** /'nilgie/ *n, pl* **nilgais**, *esp collectively* **nilgai** a large Indian antelope (*Boselaphus tragocamelus*) the male of which is bluish-grey [Hindi *nīlgāw* blue bull (fem *nīlgāī*), fr Skt *nīla* dark blue + *go* bull, cow]

**nill** /nil/ *vb, archaic vi* to be unwilling ⟨*will you* ∼ *you, I will marry you* – Shak⟩ ∼ *vt* to refuse [ME *nilen*, fr OE *nyllan*, fr *ne* not + *wyllan* to wish – more at NO, WILL]

**Nilotic** /nie'lotik/ *adj* of (the inhabitants or languages of) the Nile or the Nile region [L *Niloticus*, fr Gk *Neilōtēs*, fr *Neilos* Nile, river in E Africa]

**nilpotent** /'nil,poht(ə)nt/ *adj*, *maths* equal to zero when raised to some POWER ⟨∼ *matrices*⟩ – compare IDEMPOTENT [L *nil* nothing + *potent-, potens* having power – more at POTENT]

**nim** /nim/ *n* any of various games in which each player in turn draws objects from one or more piles and attempts either to take the last object or to force the opponent to take it [prob fr obs *nim* to take, fr ME *nimen*, fr OE *niman*]

**nimble** /'nimbl/ *adj* **1** quick, light, and easy in movement; deft ⟨∼ *fingers*⟩ **2** quick and clever in thought and understanding; agile ⟨*a* ∼ *mind*⟩ [ME *nimel*, fr OE *numol* holding much, fr *niman* to take; akin to OHG *neman* to take, L *numerus* number, Gk *nemein* to distribute, manage, *nomos* pasture, *nomos* usage, custom, law] – **nimbleness** *n*, **nimbly** *adv*

*synonyms* Nimble, agile, brisk, spry, and sprightly may all describe easy, quick movement. Nimble may apply to mental or physical adroitness, and stresses lightness and rapidity ⟨**nimble** *fingers*⟩. Agile suggests physical grace and dexterity ⟨**agile** *as a mountain goat*⟩. Brisk implies rapidity and energy ⟨*a* **brisk** *walk/walker*⟩. Spry suggests the alacrity which results from good health and vigour, and is often used where such alacrity is unexpected ⟨*surprisingly* **spry** *for her age*⟩. Sprightly implies vitality and vivacity. *antonyms* awkward, ponderous, lethargic

**nimbostratus** /,nimboh'strahtəs/ *n* a low dark grey rainy cloud layer [NL, fr L *nimbus* + NL *stratus*]

**nimbus** /'nimbəs/ *n, pl* **nimbi** /'nimbi, -bie/, **nimbuses 1a** a luminous vapour, cloud, or atmosphere about a god or goddess when on earth **b** a distinctive atmosphere (e g of romance) surrounding a person or thing **2** a circle of radiant light or some other similar mark of status about the head of a drawn or sculptured divinity, saint, or sovereign – compare AUREOLE **3** a cloud from which rain is falling; *also* a large grey raincloud [L, rainstorm, cloud; akin to Pahlavi *namb* mist]

**nimbused** /'nimbəst/ *adj* with or surrounded by a nimbus

**nimiety** /ni'mie•əti/ *n, formal* an excess, a redundancy ⟨*Edwardian* – *made poems drowsier, pictures bigger, . . . meals heavier than ever before* – *TLS*⟩ [LL *nimietas*, fr L *nimius* too much, adj, fr *nimis*, adv]

**niminy-piminy** /,niməni 'piməni/ *adj* affectedly dainty or delicate; mincing ⟨*she had an exquisite* ∼ *ladylike air* – William Golding⟩ [prob alter. of *namby-pamby*]

**Nimrod** /'nimrod/ *n* a great hunter [*Nimrod* (Heb *Nimrōdh*), "a mighty hunter" in the Bible (Gen 10:8–9)]

**nincompoop** /'ningkəm,poohp/ *n* a silly or foolish person; an idiot [alter. (prob influenced by *ninny*) of earlier *nicompoop, nickumpoop*, of unknown origin] – **nincompoopery** *n*

**nine** /nien/ *n* **1** – see NUMBER table **2** the ninth in a set or series **3** something having nine units or members or a denomination

of nine; *esp* the first or last nine holes of an 18-hole golf course **4** *taking pl vb, cap* the Common Market countries between 1973 and 1981 **5** *NAm* a baseball team [ME, fr *nyne*, adj, fr OE *nigon;* akin to OHG *niun* nine, L *novem*, Gk *ennea*] – **nine** *adj or pron*, **ninefold** *adj or adv* – **dressed (up) to the nines** dressed elaborately in special, formal, or party clothes [perh fr the use of nine as a mystic number symbolizing perfection]

**nine days' wonder** *n* something that creates a short-lived sensation

**ninepin** /'nien,pin/ *n* **1** a skittle **2** *pl but taking sing vb* the game of skittles

**nineteen** /nien'teen/ *n* – see NUMBER table [ME *nynetene*, adj, fr OE *nigontīene*, fr *nigon* + *tīen* ten] – **nineteen** *adj or pron*, **nineteenth** *adj or n* – **nineteen to the dozen** very fast and volubly ⟨*chattering away* nineteen to the dozen⟩

**Nineteen Eighty-Four** *n* an era, esp in the future, envisaged as having all aspects of life controlled by an all-seeing and totalitarian government [*Nineteen Eighty-Four*, futuristic novel by George Orwell †1950 E writer (cf BIG BROTHER, NEWSPEAK)]

**nineteenth hole** /,nien'teenth/ *n, humorous* a place where golfers gather after play; *esp* the bar of a golf club [fr its being resorted to after the 18 holes on a standard golf course]

**ninety** /'nienti/ *n* **1** – see NUMBER table **2** *pl* the numbers 90 to 99; *specif* a range of temperatures, ages, or dates within a century characterized by those numbers [ME *ninety*, adj, fr OE *nigontig*, short for *hundnigontig*, fr *hundnigontig*, n, group of 90, fr *hund* hundred + *nigon* nine + *-tig* ¹-ty] – **ninety** *adj or pron*, **ninetyfold** *adj or adv*, **ninetieth** *adj or n*

**ninhydrin** /nin'hiedrin/ *n* an OXIDIZING AGENT, $C_9H_4O_2(OH)_2$, used esp for the detection of proteins or AMINO ACIDS with which a characteristic blue to purple colour is formed on heating [fr *Ninhydrin*, a trademark]

**ninhydrin reaction** *n* a reaction of ninhydrin with an AMINO ACID or related compound in which the intensity of the blue to purple colour that forms corresponds to the quantity of the amino acid, protein, etc present

**ninny** /'nini/ *n, informal* a silly or foolish person; an idiot [perh by shortening & alter. fr *an innocent*]

**ninon** /'neenon, 'nienon (*Fr* nin5)/ *n* a fine smooth sheer fabric originally made of silk [prob fr Fr *Ninon*, nickname for *Anne*]

**ninth** /nienth/ *n* **1** – see NUMBER table **2** *music* **2a** a musical interval between one note and another nine notes away from it counting inclusively in a DIATONIC scale (ordinary 8-note scale) (e g between *doh* and the first repetition of *ray* in sol-fa); *also* a note at this interval (e g *ray* in this case) **b** a chord containing a note which is nine notes from its root – **ninth** *adj or adv*

**niobium** /nie'ohbi•əm/ *n* a shiny whitish-grey metallic chemical element used in alloys [NL, fr L *Niobe*, mythical daughter of Tantalus, fr Gk *Niobē*; fr its occurrence in tantalite]

¹**nip** /nip/ *vb* **-pp-** *vt* **1** to catch hold of and squeeze sharply; pinch ⟨*the dog* ∼*ped his ankle*⟩ **2a** to sever (as if) by pinching sharply – often + *off* ⟨∼ *the young shoots off a rose bush*⟩ **b** to prevent the growth, development, or success of – esp in *nip in the bud* ⟨*her plans to study under Freud in Vienna were* ∼*ped in the bud by the outbreak of war*⟩ **3** to injure or make numb with cold **4** to reduce (part of a garment) in order to emphasize shape – often + *in* ⟨∼*ped in the waist of the dress*⟩ **5** *slang* to snatch, steal ∼ *vi, chiefly Br informal* to go quickly or briefly; hurry ⟨*I'll just* ∼ *out to the shops*⟩ – see also **nip in the** BUD [ME *nippen;* akin to ON *hnippa* to prod, Gk *konis* ashes – more at INCINERATE]

²**nip** *n* **1** something that nips: e g **1a** a sharp stinging cold; frostiness ⟨*there's an autumn* ∼ *in the air*⟩ **b** *chiefly NAm* a pungent flavour; a tang ⟨*cheese with a* ∼⟩ **2** the act or an instance of nipping; a pinch **3** a small portion; a bit

³**nip** *n* a small measure or drink of spirits; *also* ⅓ pint of beer [prob fr *nipperkin* (a small liquor container)]

⁴**nip** *vb* **-pp-** to take nips of (a drink); tipple

**Nip** *n, chiefly derog* a Japanese; *esp* a Japanese soldier [short for *Nipponese*]

**nipa** /'neepə, 'nie-/ *n* **1** (an alcoholic drink made from the fermented juice of) an Australasian creeping palm (*Nipa fruticans*) **2** thatch made of nipa leaves [prob fr It, fr Malay *nipah* nipa palm]

**nip and tuck** *adj or adv, chiefly NAm* NECK AND NECK ⟨*finished the race* ∼⟩ [²*nip* + ²*tuck*]

**nipper** /'nipə/ *n* **1** *pl* any of various devices (e g pincers) for gripping or cutting **2** *chiefly Br informal* a child; *esp* a small boy **3** *Br archaic* a boy employed as a helper by a street hawker or carter

**nipple** /'nipl/ *n* **1** the protuberance of a MAMMARY GLAND (e g a breast) from which milk is drawn **2a** an artificial teat on a baby's feeding bottle **b** a device for regulating the flow of liquid through a hole **3a** a protuberance resembling the nipple of a breast **b** a small projection through which oil or grease is injected into machinery [earlier *neble, nible,* prob dim. of *neb, nib*]

**nipplewort** /'nipl,wuht/ *n* a slender Eurasian plant (*Lapsana communis*) of the daisy family that grows as a weed and has small yellow flowerheads [fr its former use as a remedy for ulcerated nipples]

**Nipponese** /,nipə'neez/ *n or adj, pl* **Nipponese** (a) Japanese [*Nippon* (Japan), fr Jap *Dai Nippon*] – **Nipponese** *n*

**nippy** /'nipi/ *adj* **1** nimble and lively; snappy ⟨*you'd better be ~ if you want to catch the train*⟩ ⟨*a car with a ~ performance*⟩ **2** CHILLY **1** ⟨*a ~ autumn morning*⟩ **3** *NAm* tending to nip ⟨*a ~ dog*⟩ **4** *NAm* pungent, sharp – **nippily** *adv,* **nippiness** *n*

**nirvana** /niə'vahnə, nuh-/ *n, often cap* **1** *Hinduism & Buddhism* ENLIGHTENMENT **3 2** a place or state of relief from pain or anxiety ⟨*spent the night in an alcoholic ~*⟩ [Skt *nirvāṇa,* lit., act of extinguishing, fr *nis-* out + *vāti* it blows – more at WIND]

**Nisan** /'niesan/ *n* – see MONTH table [Heb *Nīsān*]

**nisei** /nee'say, '--/ *n, pl* **nisei** *also* **niseis** *usu cap* a child of immigrant Japanese parents who is born and educated in the USA [Jap, lit., second generation, fr *ni* second + *sei* generation]

**nisi** /'niesie, 'neezi/ *adj* taking effect at a specified time unless previously modified or avoided ⟨*granted decree ~ in his divorce action*⟩ [L, unless, fr *ne-* not + *si* if]

**Nissen hut** /'nis(ə)n/ *n* a prefabricated shelter with a semicircular arching roof of corrugated iron and a concrete floor [Peter *Nissen* †1930 Br mining engineer]

**nisus** /'niesəs/ *n, pl* **nisus** an impulse or effort towards some goal or objective [L, fr *nisus,* pp of *niti* to bear down, strive; akin to L con*nivēre* to close the eyes – more at CONNIVE]

¹**nit** /nit/ *n* the egg of a parasitic insect (e g a louse); *also* the young insect itself [ME *nite,* fr OE *hnitu;* akin to OHG *hniz* nit, Gk *konid-, konis*]

²**nit** *n, chiefly Br informal* a nitwit

**nitid** /'nitid/ *adj* bright, lustrous [L *nitidus* – more at NEAT]

'**nit-,picking** *n* petty and usu unjustified criticism; fault-finding [¹*nit*] – **nitpick** *vi*

**nitr-** /nietr-/, **nitro-** *comb form* **1** nitrate ⟨nitro*bacteria*⟩ ⟨ni-tro*cellulose*⟩ **2** nitrogen ⟨nitr*ide*⟩ **3** containing the NITRO group, $NO_2$, in the molecular structure ⟨nitro*benzene*⟩ [*nitre*]

¹**nitrate** /'nietrayt/ *n* **1** any of various chemical compounds (SALTS OR ESTERS) formed by combination between NITRIC ACID and a metal atom, an alcohol, or another chemical group **2** a nitrate (e g SODIUM NITRATE or POTASSIUM NITRATE) used as a fertilizer [Fr, fr *nitrique*]

²**nitrate** *vt* to treat or combine with NITRIC ACID or a nitrate; *esp* to convert (an organic chemical compound) into a NITRO compound or a nitrate – **nitrator** *n,* **nitration** *n*

**nitrate bacterium** *n* a soil bacterium (e g *Nitrobacter*) that converts NITRITES to nitrates in the process of nitrification – compare NITRITE BACTERIUM

**nitrazepam** /nie'trazi,pam/ *n* a synthetic drug, $C_{15}H_{11}N_3O_3$, that has a molecular structure and actions similar to the tranquillizer DIAZEPAM and is widely used in sleeping pills – compare MOGADON [*nitr-* + *-azepam* (as in *diazepam*)]

**nitre,** *NAm chiefly* **niter** /'nietə/ *n* **1** POTASSIUM NITRATE **2** SODIUM NITRATE, esp when occurring naturally as CHILE SALT-PETRE □ not now used technically [ME *nitre* natron, fr MF, fr L *nitrum,* fr Gk *nitron,* fr Egypt *nṭry*]

**nitric** /'nietrik/ *adj* of or containing nitrogen, esp with a relatively high VALENCY [Fr *nitrique,* fr *nitr-*]

**nitric acid** *n* a corrosive acid, $HNO_3$, used esp as an OXIDIZING AGENT and in making fertilizers, explosives, dyes, etc

**nitric oxide** *n* a colourless poisonous gas, NO, that is obtained from nitrogen or ammonia and reacts in air to produce brown fumes of NITROGEN DIOXIDE gas

¹**nitride** /'nietried/ *n* a compound of nitrogen with one other chemical element ⟨*boron ~*⟩ [ISV]

²**nitride** *vt* to treat (steel) with nitrogen, usu by heating in ammonia gas at about 550°C (1000°F), in order to harden the surface

**nitrification** /,nietrifi'kaysh(ə)n/ *n* the process of nitrifying; *specif* the conversion (e g by bacteria) of AMMONIUM compounds in the soil (e g from dead animal and plant tissue) to nitrites

and the further conversion of nitrites to nitrates that are then used by plants to make proteins – compare NITROGEN CYCLE

**nitrify** /'nietrifie/ *vt* **1** to combine, impregnate, or cause to react with nitrogen or a nitrogen compound **2** to subject (e g AMMONIUM compounds or nitrites) to or produce by nitrification [Fr *nitrifier,* fr *nitr-*]

**nitrile** /'nietriel, -tril, -treel/ *n* any of a group of organic chemical compounds containing the group C≡N [ISV *nitr-* + *-il, -ile* (fr L *-ilis* ¹*-ile*)]

**nitrite** /'nietriet/ *n* any of various chemical compounds (SALTS or ESTERS) formed by combination between NITROUS ACID and a metal atom, an alcohol, or another chemical group

**nitrite bacterium** *n* a soil bacterium (e g *Nitrosomonas*) that converts AMMONIUM compounds to nitrites in the process of nitrification – compare NITRATE BACTERIUM

¹**nitro** /'nietroh/ *adj* being or containing the chemical group $NO_2$ [*nitr-*]

²**nitro** *n, pl* **nitros** any of various NITRATED chemical compounds; *esp* nitroglycerine

**nitro-** – see NITR-

**nitrobacterium** /'nietroh-bak,tiəriəm/ *n, pl* **nitrobacteria** /-ri-ə/ any soil bacterium that is involved in the process of nitrification by which AMMONIUM compounds are converted into compounds that can be used by plants; a NITRATE BACTERIUM or a NITRITE BACTERIUM

**nitrobenzene** /,nietroh'benzeen/ *n* a poisonous oily liquid, $C_6H_5NO_2$, that smells of almonds and is used esp as a solvent, in the manufacture of perfumes, and in making ANILINE (compound used in making dyes, plastics, and drugs) [ISV]

**nitrocellulose** /,nietroh'selyoo,lohs, -,lohz/ *n* CELLULOSE NITRATE (compound used in making explosives, plastics, rayon, and varnishes) [ISV] – **nitrocellulosic** *adj*

**nitrofuran** /,nietroh'fyooəran, -fyoo'ran/ *n* any of several chemical compounds derived from FURAN, that contain a nitro group in their molecular structure and are used to inhibit the growth of bacteria, esp in the treatment of infections of the urinary tract

**nitrogen** /'nietrəj(ə)n/ *n* a colourless tasteless odourless gaseous chemical element that makes up about 78 per cent by volume of the atmosphere and is found in combination with other elements as a constituent of all living things [Fr *nitrogène,* fr *nitr-* + *-gène* -gen] – **nitrogenous** *adj*

**nitrogenase** /nie'trojənayz, -ays/ *n* an enzyme found in various bacteria that carry out NITROGEN FIXATION, that speeds up the rate at which nitrogen from the atmosphere is converted to ammonia

**nitrogen balance** *n* the difference between nitrogen intake and nitrogen loss in the body or the soil

**nitrogen cycle** *n* the continuous circulation of nitrogen and nitrogen-containing compounds between the atmosphere, soil, and living organisms. The cycle involves the processes of NITROGEN FIXATION and NITRIFICATION (conversion of ammonia-containing compounds in the soil into compounds useful to plants) whereby plants obtain nitrogen-containing compounds from which they make proteins, the decay of plants and animals to form ammonia-containing compounds in the soil, and the recycling of nitrogen to the atmosphere by DE-NITRIFICATION.

**nitrogen dioxide** *n* a red-brown highly poisonous gas, $NO_2$, that is formed by the combination of NITRIC OXIDE with oxygen and is used in the manufacture of NITRIC ACID and in rocket fuel to provide oxygen needed for combustion

**nitrogen fixation** *n* **1** the industrial conversion of nitrogen from the atmosphere into nitrogen compounds useful esp as starting materials for making fertilizers or explosives **2** the incorporation of nitrogen from the atmosphere into chemical compounds; *specif* this process performed by soil microorganisms, esp the bacteria rhizobia, in the root NODULES of various plants of the pea family (e g clover), that results in the formation of nitrogen-containing compounds that are used by plants to make proteins

'**nitrogen-,fixer** *n* any of various soil organisms (e g some bacteria and BLUE-GREEN ALGAE) that are involved in NITROGEN FIXATION – **nitrogen-fixing** *adj*

**nitrogen mustard** *n* any of various poisonous compounds that cause blistering of the skin, are related to MUSTARD GAS but contain nitrogen instead of sulphur, and are used in the treatment of some cancers

**nitrogen narcosis** *n* a state of euphoria and exhilaration that occurs, esp in deep-water diving, when nitrogen in normal air is breathed at a higher than normal pressure, and that is dangerous to a diver because his/her ability to think clearly and awareness of danger are impaired

**nitroglycerine** /ˌnietroh'glisəreen, -rin/, *NAm chiefly* **nitroglycerin** /-rin/ *n* an oily explosive liquid, $C_3H_5(NO_3)_3$, used chiefly in making dynamite and, as a weak solution in water, as a drug to dilate the blood vessels (eg in the treatment of angina) [ISV]

**nitroparaffin** /ˌnietroh'parəfin/ *n* any of a class of chemical compounds derived from the ALKANES (series of chemical compounds containing carbon and hydrogen only) by replacing one hydrogen atom with a NITRO group – not now used technically [ISV]

**nitros-** /nietrohs-/, **nitroso-** *comb form* containing the nitroso group NO in the molecular structure ⟨nitrosamine⟩ [NL *nitrosus* nitrous]

**nitrosamine** /nie'trohsə,meen, -min/ *n* any of various often cancer-producing chemical compounds containing the group NNO in the molecular structure

**nitroso** /nie'trohsoh/ *adj* being or containing the chemical group NO

**nitrosobacterium** /nie,trohsohbak'tiəriəm/ *n* NITRITE BACTERIUM [NL, fr *nitrosus* + *-o-* + *bacterium*]

**nitrous** /'nietrəs/ *adj* of or containing nitrogen, esp with a relatively low VALENCY [NL *nitrosus*, fr L, full of natron, fr *nitrum* natron]

**nitrous acid** *n* an unstable acid, $HNO_2$, occurring only in solution or in the form of its compounds (NITRITES)

**nitrous bacterium** *n* NITRITE BACTERIUM

**nitrous oxide** *n* a gas, $N_2O$, that is used as a general anaesthetic, esp in obstetrics and dentistry

**nitty-gritty** /ˌniti 'griti/ *n, informal* the important basic realities ⟨*let's get down to the ~ of the problem*⟩ [origin unknown] – **nitty-gritty** *adj*

**nitwit** /'nit,wit/ *n, informal* a scatterbrained or stupid person ⟨*some ~ has put salt in the sugar bowl!*⟩ [prob fr Ger dial. *nit* not + E *wit*] – **nit-witted** *adj*

¹**nix** /niks/, *fem* **nixie** /-si/ *n* a water sprite of Germanic folklore [Ger, fr OHG *nihhus*; akin to OE *nicor* water monster, Gk *nizein* to wash]

²**nix** *n, informal* nothing *synonyms* see ¹ZERO [Ger *nichts* nothing]

³**nix** *adv, NAm informal* no – used to express disagreement or the refusing of permission; often + *on* ⟨*father said ~ on our plan*⟩

⁴**nix** *vt, NAm informal* to veto, forbid ⟨*the court ~ed the merger*⟩

**nizam** /nie'zahm, ni-, -zam, '--/ *n* any of a line of sovereigns of Hyderabad in India, reigning from 1713 to 1950 △ nabob [Hindi *nizām* order, governor, fr Ar *nizām*] – **nizamate** *n*

¹**no** /noh/ *adv* **1** – used to negate an alternative choice ⟨*whether you like it or ~*⟩ **2** in no respect or degree – used in comparisons ⟨*~ better than before*⟩ **3** – used in answers expressing negation, dissent, denial, or refusal; contrasted with *yes* ⟨*~, I'm not going*⟩ **4** – used like a question-tag demanding assent to the preceding statement ⟨*she's pretty, ~?*⟩ **5** nay ⟨*happy, ~, ecstatic*⟩ **6** – used as an interjection to express incredulity ⟨*"she's 17." "No!"*⟩ **7** *chiefly Scot* not ⟨*it's ~ canny*⟩ [ME, fr OE *nā*, fr *ne* not (akin to ON & OHG *ne* not, L *ne-*, Gk *nē-*) + *ā* always – more at AYE]

²**no** *adj* **1a** not any ⟨*~ money*⟩ ⟨*there's ~ denying*⟩ – often in notices and slogans ⟨*~ parking*⟩ **b** hardly any; very little ⟨*finished in ~ time*⟩ **2a** not a; quite other than a ⟨*he's ~ expert*⟩ **b** – used before a noun phrase to give force to an opposite meaning ⟨*in ~ uncertain terms*⟩ ⟨*it was ~ small achievement*⟩; compare NOT 3 **3** *substandard* any ⟨*haven't got ~ job*⟩ *usage* SEE NO ONE

³**no** *n, pl* **noes, nos** a negative reply or vote; a nay

**No, Noh** /noh/ *n, pl* **No, Noh** a classic Japanese (form of) dance-drama having a heroic theme, a chorus, and highly stylized actions, costumes, and scenery – compare KABUKI [Jap *nō*, lit., talent]

'**no-ac,count** *adj, NAm informal* of no account; trifling, worthless ⟨*his ~ relatives*⟩ – **no-account** *n*

**Noachian** /noh'aykiən/ *adj* **1** of Noah or his time **2** ancient, antiquated ⟨*a . . . grey overcoat of ~ cut* – Thomas Hardy⟩ [Heb *Nōaḥ* Noah, biblical character who built an ark to save his family & animals from a great flood (Gen 5:28–9:29)]

¹**nob** /nob/ *n* **1** a jack of the same suit as the card turned by the dealer in cribbage that scores one point for the holder –

chiefly in *his nob/nobs* ⟨*one for his ~*⟩ **2** *informal* a person's head [prob alter. of *knob*]

²**nob** *n, chiefly Br informal* a wealthy or influential person [perh fr ¹*nob*]

¹**no-'ball** *n* an illegal delivery of the ball in cricket with which the bowler cannot dismiss the batsman and which counts one run to the batsman's side if the batsman does not score a run off it – compare EXTRA

²**no-ball** *interj* – used as a call by an umpire in cricket to indicate that a delivery is a no-ball

³**no-ball** *vt, of an umpire in cricket* to declare (a bowler) to have delivered a no-ball or (a delivery) to be a no-ball ~ *vi, of a bowler in cricket* to bowl a no-ball

**nobble** /'nobl/ *vt, Br* **1** *informal* **1a** to incapacitate (esp a racehorse), esp by drugging **b** to bribe (a jockey) to ride dishonestly **2** *slang* **2a** to win over to one's side, esp by dishonest means **b** to get hold of, esp dishonestly **c** to swindle, cheat **d** to seize, apprehend ⟨*got ~d as he was making off with the loot*⟩ [perh irreg freq of *nab*] – **nobbler** *n*

**nobbut** /'nobət/ *adv, N Eng* no more than; only ⟨*knew him when he was ~ a lad*⟩ [ME *no but*, fr *no* (adv) + *but*]

**nobby** /'nobi/ *adj, informal* smart, stylish [²*nob* + ¹*-y*]

**Nobelist** /noh'belist/ *n* a winner of a Nobel prize

**nobelium** /noh'beeli·əm/ *n* a radioactive metallic chemical element produced artificially from the element CURIUM [NL, fr Alfred *Nobel* †1896 Sw manufacturer, inventor, & philanthropist]

**Nobel prize** /noh'bel/ *n* any of various annual prizes established by the will of Alfred Nobel for the encouragement of people who work for the interests of humanity (eg in the fields of peace, literature, medicine, and physics)

**nobility** /noh'biləti/ *n* **1** the quality or state of being noble in character, quality, or rank **2** *taking sing or pl vb* the people forming the noble class in a country or state; the aristocracy [ME *nobilite*, fr MF *nobilité*, fr L *nobilitat-, nobilitas*, fr *nobilis*]

¹**noble** /'nohbl/ *adj* **1a** gracious and dignified in character or bearing **b** famous, notable ⟨*a ~ victory*⟩ **2** of high birth or exalted rank; aristocratic **3** of fine quality; excellent ⟨*a wine of ~ vintage*⟩ **4** grand or impressive, esp in appearance; imposing, stately ⟨*~ edifice*⟩ **5** having or showing a magnanimous character or high ideals ⟨*a ~ aim, faithfully kept, is as a ~ deed* – William Wordsworth⟩ **6** chemically inert or unreactive; *esp* being a metal (eg gold, silver, or platinum) that tends not to react – compare NOBLE GAS [ME, fr OF, fr L *nobilis* knowable, well known, noble, fr *noscere* to come to know – more at KNOW] – **nobleness** *n*, **nobly** *adv*

²**noble** *n* **1** a person of noble rank or birth **2** a former English gold coin worth $1/3$

**noble gas** *n* any of a group of gases that are chemical elements that do not take part in chemical reactions or that react only very slightly. The group consists of helium, neon, argon, krypton, xenon, and radon. – called also INERT GAS, RARE GAS

**nobleman** /'nohblmən/, *fem* **noblewoman** /-'woomən/ *n* a man of noble rank; a peer

**noblesse** /noh'bles, no-/ *n* **1** noble birth or condition; nobility **2** *taking sing or pl vb* the members of the (French) nobility [ME, fr OF *noblesce*, fr *noble*]

**noblesse oblige** /ˌnohbles o'bleezh, no-/ *n* the obligation of honourable, generous, and responsible behaviour associated with high rank or birth [Fr, lit., nobility obligates]

¹**nobody** /'nohbədi, -ˌbodi/ *pron* not anybody; NO ONE ⟨*~ likes her*⟩ – compare LIKE NOBODY'S BUSINESS

    *usage* Since **nobody** and **no one** are used with a singular verb, it seems logical that they should be followed by a singular pronoun ⟨**nobody** *has finished his work*⟩ and this singular construction should be preferred for formal writing. The plural pronoun ⟨**nobody** *has finished their work*⟩ is often used today, however, to avoid using either *he* for both sexes or the awkward *he or she*. See ELSE

²**nobody** *n* a person of no influence or consequence

**nocent** /'nohs(ə)nt/ *adj* harmful ⟨*a ~ dose*⟩ [ME, fr L *nocent-, nocens*, fr prp of *nocēre* to harm, hurt – more at NOXIOUS]

**nociceptive** /ˌnohsi'septiv/ *adj* **1** *of a stimulus* painful **2** of, induced by, or responding to a nociceptive stimulus – used esp of a reflex action to protect the body from injury or of a specialized structure that receives stimuli [L *nocēre* + E *-i-* + *receptive*]

¹**nock** /nok/ *n* **1** a notch cut at the end of an archer's bow to hold the string **2** a notch in the end of an arrow into which the bowstring fits; *also* the strengthened part of the arrow carrying this notch [ME *nocke* notched tip on the end of a bow; akin to MD *nocke* summit, tip, L *nux* nut – more at NUT]

²**nock** *vt* to make a nock in (e g a bow or arrow); *also* to fit (e g a bowstring) into or by means of a nock

**no-claim bonus, no-claims bonus** *n, Br* a discount offered in esp motor insurance premiums provided no claim has been made under the policy in previous years

**noct-** /'nokt-/, **nocti-, nocto-** *comb form* night ⟨noctambulation⟩ ⟨nocturnal⟩ [L *noct-*, *nocti-*, fr *noct-*, *nox* – more at NIGHT]

**noctiluca** /ˌnoktiˈloohkə/ *n* any of a genus (*Noctiluca* of the order Dinoflagellata) of marine single-celled animals that propel themselves through the water by means of whiplike structures (FLAGELLA) and emit light, often causing phosphorescence of the sea [NL, genus name, fr L, something that shines by night, fr *noct-* + *lucēre* to shine – more at LIGHT]

**noctilucent cloud** /ˌnoktiˈloohs(ə)nt/ *n* a luminous thin usu coloured cloud seen shining at night at a height of about 80 kilometres (50 miles) [*noctilucent* deriv of L *noct-* & *lucent-*, *lucens* lucent]

**noctuid** /'noktyooid/ *n* any of a large family (Noctuidae) of medium-sized often dull-coloured moths with larvae (e g cutworms) that are often destructive agricultural pests [NL *Noctuidae*, group name, fr *Noctua*, genus of moths, fr L, night owl; akin to L *nox* night] – **noctuid** *adj*

**noctule** /'noktyoohl/ *n* a large Eurasian reddish-brown insect-eating bat (*Nyctalus noctula*) [Fr, fr It *nottola*, fr *notte* night, fr L *noct-*, *nox*]

**nocturn** /'noktuhn/ *n* a principal division of MATINS (first of the daily services in the Catholic church) [ME *nocturne*, fr MF, fr ML *nocturna*, fr L, fem of *nocturnus*]

**nocturnal** /nok'tuhnl/ *adj* **1** of or occurring in the night **2** active at night ⟨owls are ∼ birds⟩ [MF or LL; MF, fr LL *nocturnalis*, fr L *nocturnus* by night, fr *noct-*, *nox* night] – **nocturnally** *adv*

**nocturne** /'noktuhn/ *n* a work of art dealing with or suggesting evening or night; *esp* a dreamy pensive composition for the piano [Fr, adj, nocturnal, fr L *nocturnus*]

**nocuous** /'nokyoo-əs/ *adj* harmful, noxious ⟨the ∼ effect of chemical sprays⟩ [L *nocuus*, fr *nocēre* to harm – more at NOXIOUS] – **nocuously** *adv*

¹**nod** /nod/ *vb* **-dd-** *vi* **1** to make a short downward movement of the head (e g in expressing assent or greeting) **2** to lean as though ready to topple **3** to bend or sway gently downwards or forwards ⟨poppies ∼ding in the breeze⟩ **4a** to become drowsy or sleepy ⟨∼ in front of the fire⟩ **b** to make a slip or error in a moment of inattention ⟨even Homer sometimes ∼s⟩ ∼ *vt* **1** to incline (e g the head) in a quick downward movement **2** to bring, summon, or send by a nod ⟨∼ded them into the room⟩ **3** to express with a nod ⟨∼ded their approval⟩ [ME *nodden;* akin to OHG *hnotōn* to shake, L *cinis* ashes – more at INCINERATE] – **nodder** *n*

**nod off** *vi* to fall asleep, esp unintentionally ⟨I'm sorry I didn't hear you ring, I must have nodded off⟩

²**nod** *n* the act or an instance of nodding ⟨gave a ∼ of greeting⟩ – **on the nod** by consensus rather than by taking a vote ⟨accepted the report on the nod⟩

**nodal** /'nohdl/ *adj* of, being, or located at or near a node – **nodally** *adv*, **nodality** *n*

**nodding** /'noding/ *adj* **1** bending downwards or forwards; pendulous, drooping ⟨a plant with ∼ flowers⟩ **2** casual, superficial ⟨a ∼ acquaintance with French literature⟩ **3** of casual or distant acquaintance ⟨on ∼ terms with the neighbours⟩

**noddle** /'nodl/ *n, informal* a person's head ⟨if he'd use his ∼ a bit he'd know that he was the cause – Alan Sillitoe⟩ [ME *nodle* back of the head or neck]

**noddy** /'nodi/ *n* **1** any of several stout-bodied subtropical and tropical terns (genera *Anous* and *Micranous*) **2** *humorous* a silly or foolish person; an idiot [prob short for obs *noddypoll* fool, alter. of *hoddypoll* (fumbling inept person)]

**node** /nohd/ *n* **1a** a thickening or swelling (e g of a rheumatic joint) **b** *anatomy* a small rounded mass of tissue surrounded by tissue of a different kind; *esp* LYMPH NODE **2** either of the two points where the orbit of a planet or comet intersects the ECLIPTIC (apparent path travelled by the sun); *also* either of the points at which a satellite revolving round the earth crosses the plane of the equator **3a** a point at which subsidiary parts originate or converge; *esp* a point at which a TREE DIAGRAM branches **b** a point on a stem at which a leaf or side branch is attached **c** *maths* a point at which a curve intersects itself and at which there are two distinct TANGENTS – compare CUSP **4**

*physics* a point, line, etc on or in a vibrating body (e g a string of a musical instrument) at which the vibration is at a minimum or zero – compare ANTINODE [L *nodus* knot, node – more at NET]

**node of Ranvier** /'ranviə, 'ronhviˌay/ *n* any of the constrictions along the length of the fatty sheath (MYELIN SHEATH) surrounding some NERVE FIBRES [Louis *Ranvier* †1922 Fr histologist]

**nodical** /'nodikl, 'noh-/ *adj* of astronomical nodes

**nodose** /'nohdohs, -'-/ *adj* having numerous or conspicuous swellings or protuberances ⟨∼ antennae⟩ [L *nodosus*, fr *nodus*] – **nodosity** *n*

**nodulation** /ˌnodyoo'laysh(ə)n/ *n* **1** the process of forming nodules, esp bacteria-containing nodules on the roots of a plant **2** a nodule

**nodule** /'nodyoohl/ *n* a small rounded or irregularly shaped mass: e g **a** a small rounded lump of a mineral, or of fragments of mineral or rock, occurring esp in rock of a different type **b** a swelling on the root of a plant, esp one of the pea family (e g clover), that contains NITROGEN-FIXING bacteria that convert nitrogen from the atmosphere into compounds that can be used by the plant [L *nodulus*, dim. of *nodus*] – **nodular** *adj*, **nodulated** *adj*

**nodus** /'nohdəs/ *n, pl* **nodi** /'nohdi, -die/ a difficult or complex situation, esp in the plot of a play or story; *broadly* a complication, difficulty [L, knot, node]

**noel, noël** /noh'el/ *n* **1** a Christmas carol **2** *cap* the Christmas season [Fr *noël* Christmas, carol, fr L *natalis* birthday, fr *natalis* natal]

**noes** /nohz/ *pl of* NO

**noetic** /noh'etik/ *adj, philosophy* of or based on the intellect [Gk *noētikos* intellectual, fr *noein* to think, fr *nous* mind]

**no-'fines** *n taking sing vb, building* concrete made by mixing only coarse AGGREGATE (e g gravel) into the cement without adding any fine material (e g sand)

**nog** /nog/ *n* (an) eggnog

**noggin** /'nogin/ *n* **1** a small mug or cup **2** a small measure of spirits, usu 0.142 litres (¼ pint) **3** *informal* a person's head [origin unknown]

**nogging** /'noging/ *n* rough brick masonry used to fill in the open spaces of a wooden frame [fr gerund of *nog* (to fill in with brickwork), fr *nog* (wooden peg or block)]

**no-'go** *adj* **1** having prohibited or restricted access ⟨a ∼ military zone⟩ **2** impossible, impracticable ⟨tried everything; it's just ∼⟩

**no-,good** *adj, informal* having no worth, use, or chance of success – **no-good** *n*

**Noh** /noh/ *n* NO (classic Japanese dance-drama)

**no-'hoper** *n, chiefly Austr* somebody who has no chance of success

**nohow** /'noh,how/ *adv, chiefly dial or humorous* in no way; not at all ⟨couldn't get that cow out of the ditch ∼⟩

**noil** /noyl/ *n* a short fibre removed during the combing of a textile fibre (e g silk) and often spun separately into yarn [origin unknown]

¹**noise** /noyz/ *n* **1** loud confused shouting or outcry; clamour **2a** (a harsh or unwanted) sound **b** an unwanted signal or disturbance in an electrical circuit **c** ELECTROMAGNETIC RADIATION (e g light or radio waves) that is composed of several frequencies and involves random changes in frequency or strength **d** irrelevant or meaningless information occurring with desired information in the output of a computer **3** *usu pl* a usu trite remark of a specified type ⟨made sympathetic ∼s on hearing of his problem⟩ **4** a much-publicized and often notorious impression; a sensation ⟨I am not the sort of modern writer who wants to make a ∼ – Angus Wilson⟩ **5** *obs* hearsay, gossip; *esp* slander **synonyms** see ²QUIET [ME, fr OF, strife, quarrel, noise, fr L *nausea* nausea] – **noiseless** *adj*, **noiselessly** *adv*

²**noise** *vt* to spread by gossip or hearsay – usu + *about* or *abroad* ⟨the scandal was quickly ∼d abroad⟩

**noisemaker** /'noyzˌmaykə/ *n, NAm* a horn, bell, rattle, etc used to make a noise at parties, football matches, etc – **noisemaking** *n or adj*

**noise pollution** *n* environmental pollution consisting of annoying or harmful noise (e g caused by cars, industrial machinery, or aircraft)

**noisette** /nwah'zet (Fr nwazɛt)/ *n* a small round thick boneless slice of meat, esp lamb, usu from the boned rolled best end of neck or the loin [Fr, hazelnut, fr OF, dim. of *nois, noix* nut, fr L *nux*]

**noisome** /'noys(ə)m/ *adj, formal* **1** noxious, unwholesome **2** *esp of a smell* offensive, repellent [ME *noysome*, fr *noy* annoyance, fr OF *enui, anoi* – more at ENNUI] – **noisomely** *adv*, **noisomeness** *n*

**usage** This word has nothing to do with "noise".

**noisy** /'noyzi/ *adj* **1** making noise ⟨~ *neighbours*⟩ **2** full of or characterized by noise ⟨*a* ~ *office*⟩ – **noisily** *adv*, **noisiness** *n*

**noli me tangere** /ˌnohli may 'tang‑gəray/ *n* a warning against touching or interference [L, do not touch me]

**nolle prosequi** /ˌnoli 'prosikwie/ *n, law* an entry on the record of a legal action stating that the prosecutor or plaintiff will not proceed with part or all of his/her suit or prosecution [L, to be unwilling to pursue]

**noma** /'nohmə/ *n* a spreading gangrene of the lining of the cheek and lips that occurs usu in people suffering from severe weakness (e g from malnutrition) [NL, fr Gk *nomē*, fr *nemein* to spread (of an ulcer), lit., to graze, pasture – more at NIMBLE]

**nomad** /'nohmad/ *n* **1** a member of a people that has no fixed residence but moves from place to place (e g in order to secure grazing for its cattle), usu seasonally and within a well-defined territory **2** somebody who wanders aimlessly from place to place [L *nomad-, nomas*, fr Gk, fr *nemein* to pasture – more at NIMBLE] – **nomad** *adj*, **nomadism** *n*, **nomadic** *adj*

**'no-‚man's-‚land** *n* **1a** an area of waste or unclaimed land **b** an unoccupied area between opposing armies **2** an area of anomalous, ambiguous, or indefinite character ⟨*the* ~ *of the generation gap* – *Psychology Today*⟩

**nombril point** /'nombril/ *n* the centre point of the lower half of a heraldic shield [MF *nombril*, lit., navel]

**nom de guerre** /ˌnom də 'geə (*Fr* nɔ̃ də gɛr)/ *n, pl* **noms de guerre** /~/ a pseudonym [Fr, lit., war name]

**nom de plume** /ˌnom də 'ploohm (*Fr* nɔ̃ də plym)/ *n, pl* **noms de plume** /~/ a pseudonym under which an author writes [Fr *nom* name + *de* of + *plume* pen]

**nome** /nohm/ *n* a province of ancient Egypt [Gk *nomos* district – more at NIMBLE]

**nomen** /'nohmən, -men/ *n, pl* **nomina** /'nominə/ the second of the usu 3 names of an ancient Roman – compare COGNOMEN, PRAENOMEN [L *nomin-, nomen* name – more at NAME]

**nomenclator** /'nohminˌklaytə/ *n* **1** a book containing collections or lists of words **2** somebody who assigns or invents names, esp in a particular field of knowledge **3** *archaic* somebody who announces the names of guests [L, slave who told his master the names of people he met when campaigning for office, fr *nomen* + *calatus*, pp of *calare* to call – more at LOW ]

**nomenclature** /no'menkləchə/ *n* **1** a name, designation **2** the act or an instance of naming, esp within a particular system **3** a system of terms used in a particular science, discipline, or art; *esp* an international system of standardized names used to describe kinds and groups of kinds (e g of animals and plants or chemical compounds) [L *nomenclatura* calling by name, list of names, fr *nomen* + *calatus*, pp] – **nomenclatural** *adj*

**'nominal** /'nominl/ *adj* **1** of or being a grammatical nominal **2a** of or constituting a name **b** bearing the name of a person ⟨~ *shares*⟩ **3a** being something in name only; not real or actual ⟨*the* ~ *head of his party*⟩ – compare TITULAR 1 **b** assigned as a convenient approximation (e g to an actual weight, value, or size) **c** *of an amount of money* negligible, insignificant ⟨*paid only a* ~ *rent*⟩ [ME *nominalle*, fr ML *nominalis*, fr L, of a name, fr *nomin-, nomen* name] – **nominally** *adv*

**²nominal** *n* a word or word group functioning as a noun

**nominalism** /-ˌiz(ə)m/ *n* a philosophical theory that classes of things (e g animal, city, nation) are mere names and have no independent reality inside or outside the mind – **nominalist** *n*, **nominalist, nominalistic** *adj*

**nominal‑ize, ‑ise** /'nominəliez/ *vt, linguistics* to convert into a nominal – **nominalization** *n*

**nominal value** *n* the value indicated on a share certificate, cheque, etc; PAR 1b

**nominal wages** *n pl* wages measured in money as distinct from actual purchasing power – compare REAL WAGES

**nominate** /'nominayt/ *vt* **1** to designate, specify ⟨*an activity* ~d *by the teacher*⟩ **2a** to appoint or recommend for appointment to an office or post **b** to propose as a candidate for election (e g to a political office) **c** to propose for an honour or award ⟨~ *him for player of the year*⟩ **3** to enter (a horse) in a race **4** *formal* to name, call [L *nominatus*, pp of *nominare*, fr *nomin-, nomen* name] – **nominator** *n*

**nomination** /ˌnomi'naysh(ə)n/ *n* **1** the act or process or an instance of nominating ⟨*there were three* ~s *for chairman*⟩ **2** the state of being nominated ⟨*congratulated her on her* ~⟩

**'nominative** /'nominətiv/ *adj* **1** of or being the grammatical nominative **2** appointed by nomination; nominated **3** bearing a person's name ⟨~ *shares*⟩

**²nominative** *n* a grammatical case expressing typically the subject of a verb; *also* a form (e g *he*) in this case

**nominative absolute** *n* a grammatical construction consisting of a noun or noun substitute with a participle or infinitive (e g *John being here* in "John being here, we played snooker")

**nominee** /ˌnomi'nee/ *n* a person who has been nominated [*nominate* + -*ee*]

**nomogram** /'noməˌgram, noh-/, **nomograph** /-ˌgrahf, -ˌgraf/ *n, maths* a graphic device that consists of several lines marked off to scale and arranged in such a way that by using a straightedge to connect known values on two lines an unknown value can be read at the point of intersection with another line [Gk *nomos* law + ISV -*gram* – more at NIMBLE]

**nomological** /ˌnomə'lojikl/ *adj* of, stating, or involving basic physical laws or rules of reasoning ⟨*a* ~ *deductive argument*⟩ [*nomology* (science of physical and logical laws)]

**nomothetic** /ˌnomə'thetik/, **nomothetical** /-kl/ *adj* of, stating, or involving abstract, general, or universal laws [Gk *nomothetikos* of legislation, fr *nomothetēs* lawgiver, fr *nomos* law + -*thetēs* one who establishes, fr *tithenai* to put – more at DO]

**-nomy** /-nəmi/ *comb form* (→ *n*) **1** system of laws or principles governing a (specified) field; science of ⟨*agronomy*⟩ ⟨*astronomy*⟩ **2** management ⟨*economy*⟩ **3** government; rule ⟨*autonomy*⟩ [ME -*nomie*, fr OF, fr L -*nomia*, fr Gk, fr *nemein* to distribute]

**non-** /non-/ *prefix* **1** not; reverse of; absence of ⟨non*conformity*⟩ ⟨non*payment*⟩ ⟨non*existence*⟩ ⟨non*alcoholic*⟩ **2** of little or no consequence; unimportant; worthless ⟨non*issues*⟩ ⟨non*system*⟩ **3** lacking the usual characteristics of the thing specified ⟨non*event*⟩ ⟨non*celebration*⟩ **4** failure to be; refraining from ⟨non*smoker*⟩ ⟨non*violent*⟩ ⟨non*aggression*⟩ **5** proof against; designed to avoid ⟨non*stick*⟩ ⟨non*iron*⟩ ⟨non*flammable*⟩ [ME, fr MF, fr L *non* not, fr OL *noenum*, fr *ne-* not + *oinom*, neut of *oinos* one – more at NO, ONE]

**synonyms** The prefixes **non-**, **in-**, and **un-** all mean "not", but while **non-** expresses simple negation, **in-** and **un-** often express active opposition. Compare ⟨non*moral* (= outside the moral sphere)⟩ ⟨im*moral* (= conflicting with morals)⟩ ⟨non*scientific* (= not connected with science)⟩ ⟨un*scientific* (= slovenly as regards science)⟩. **In-** and **un-** are much alike in meaning, but **in-** attaches itself to obviously Latinate words ⟨in*eligible*⟩ and is rarer than **un-**, which is attached to both Latinate and Germanic words and forms many new combinations ⟨un-*American*⟩.

**nonadditive** /ˌnon'adətiv/ *adj* **1** not equal to the sum of values for the component parts **2** of or being a genetic effect that is not additive – **nonadditivity** *n*

**nonage** /'nohnij, 'nonij/ *n* **1** legal minority **2** a period or state of youth or immaturity [ME, fr MF, fr *non-* + *age*]

---

**nonabrasive** *adj or n*
**nonabsorbable** *adj*
**nonabsorbent** *adj or n*
**nonabsorptive** *adj*
**nonabstainer** *n*
**nonabstract** *adj*
**nonacademic** *adj or n*
**nonacceptance** *n*
**nonaccessible** *adj*
**nonaccountable** *adj*
**nonaccredited** *adj*

**nonachievement** *n*
**nonacid** *adj or n*
**nonacidic** *adj*
**nonactinic** *adj*
**nonaction** *n*
**nonactivated** *adj*
**nonactive** *adj*
**nonadaptive** *adj*
**nonaddict** *n*
**nonaddicted** *adj*
**nonaddicting** *adj*

**nonaddictive** *adj*
**nonadherence** *n*
**nonadhesion** *n*
**nonadhesive** *adj or n*
**nonadjacent** *adj*
**nonadjustable** *adj*
**nonadministrative** *adj*
**nonadmirer** *n*
**nonadmission** *n*
**nonadolescent** *adj or n*
**nonaesthetic** *adj*

**nonaffiliated** *adj*
**nonaffluent** *adj*
**non-African** *adj or n*
**nonaggression** *n*
**nonaggressive** *adj*
**nonagreement** *n*
**nonagricultural** *adj*
**nonalchoholic** *adj or n*
**nonallergenic** *adj*
**nonallergic** *adj*
**nonalphabetic** *adj*

**nonagenarian** /ˌnohnəjiˈneəri·ən, ˌnonə-/ n a person between 90 and 99 years old [L *nonagenarius* containing ninety, fr *nonageni* ninety each, fr *nonaginta* ninety, fr *nona-* (akin to *novem* nine) + *-ginta* (akin to *viginti* twenty) – more at NINE, VIGESIMAL] – **nonagenarian** *adj*

**nonagon** /ˈnonəgən/ n a two-dimensional geometric figure having nine sides; *esp* one that is REGULAR (having nine equal sides and angles) [L *nonus* ninth + E *-gon* – more at NOON]

**nonaligned** /ˌnonəˈliend/ *adj* not allied with other nations, esp any of the superpowers – **nonalignment** *n*

**nonallelic** /ˌnonəˈleelik, -əˈlelik/ *adj, of genes* not coding for the same inheritable characteristic; not behaving as ALLELES (different versions of a particular inheritable characteristic)

**nonappearance** /ˌnonəˈpiərəns/ n failure to appear or attend; *esp* failure to appear in court as a defendant or witness

**nonarrestable offence** n an offence for which an arrest cannot be made without a warrant

**nonassertive** /ˌnonəˈsuhtiv/ *adj* not being or used in a simple positive statement ⟨the ~ word ever in "is he ever late?"⟩

**noncalcareous** /ˌnonkalˈkeəriəs/ *adj* lacking or deficient in lime ⟨~ soils⟩

**noncaloric** /ˌnonkəˈlorik/ *adj* free from or very low in calories

¹**nonce** /nons/ n [ME *nanes*, alter. (by incorrect division of *then anes* in such phrases as *to then anes* for the one purpose) of *anes* one purpose, irreg fr *an* one, fr OE *ān*] – **for the nonce** for the time being or present occasion

²**nonce** *adj, of a word, phrase, etc* occurring, used, or coined only once or for a special occasion

**nonchalant** /ˈnonshələnt/ *adj* giving an impression of easy unconcern or indifference; casual [Fr, fr OF, fr prp of *nonchaloir* to disregard, fr *non-* + *chaloir* to concern, fr L *calēre* to be warm – more at LEE] – **nonchalance** *n*, **nonchalantly** *adv*

**nonchromosomal** /ˌnonkrohməˈsohməl, -ˈzohml/ *adj* 1 not situated on a CHROMOSOME (strand of gene-carrying material) 2 not involving CHROMOSOMES

**noncom** /ˈnonkom/ n, *informal* NONCOMMISSIONED OFFICER

**noncombatant** /nonˈkombət(ə)nt, -kəmˈbat(ə)nt/ n 1 a civilian in wartime 2 a member of the armed forces (e g a chaplain or medical orderly) not used in actual fighting – **noncomba-**tant *adj*

**noncommissioned officer** /nonkəˈmish(ə)nd/ n a subordinate officer (e g a sergeant) in the armed forces appointed from among the personnel who do not hold a commission

**noncommittal** /ˌnonkəˈmitl/ *adj* 1 giving no clear indication of attitude or feeling ⟨a polite but ~ reply⟩ 2 having no clear or distinctive character ⟨the ~ surroundings of a rehearsal room – Osbert Sitwell⟩ *synonyms* see SILENT – **noncommittally** *adv*

**non compos mentis** /ˌnon ˌkompos ˈmentis/ *adj* not of sound mind [L, lit., not having mastery of one's mind]

**nonconcurrence** /ˌnonkənˈkurəns/ n the act or an instance of refusing to concur

**nonconductor** /ˌnonkənˈduktə/ n a substance that conducts heat, electricity, etc, only very slightly under normal conditions

**nonconformance** /ˌnonkənˈfawməns/ n failure or refusal to conform

**nonconformist** /ˌnonkənˈfawmist/ n 1 *often cap* a person who does not conform to an officially recognized national church; *specif* a member of a Protestant body separated from the CHURCH OF ENGLAND 2 one who does not conform to a generally accepted pattern of thought or behaviour – **nonconformism** *n, often cap*, **nonconformist** *adj, often cap*

**nonconformity** /ˌnonkənˈfawməti/ n 1a failure or refusal to conform to an officially recognized national church b *often cap* the ideas and practices of Nonconformist groups, and esp of English Protestant groups separated from the CHURCH OF ENGLAND c *often cap* Nonconformists collectively; *esp* the body of English Nonconformists 2 refusal to conform to an established or conventional creed, rule, or practice; nonconformism 3 absence of correspondence; discrepancy ⟨the striking ~ of his ideas to practice⟩

**noncontributory** /ˌnonkənˈtribyoot(ə)ri/ *adj, of a pension scheme* paid for by the employer only and not requiring contributions from the employee

**noncooperation** /ˌnonkoh.opəˈraysh(ə)n/ n failure or refusal to cooperate; *specif* refusal of a people to cooperate with the government of a country, esp by defiance or boycotting of state institutions – **noncooperationist** *n*, **noncooperative** *adj*, **noncooperator** *n*

---

| | | | |
|---|---|---|---|
| nonalphabetical *adj* | nonbarbiturate *adj or n* | noncarrier *n* | noncollectible *adj* |
| nonanalytic *adj* | nonbasic *adj* | noncash *adj* | noncollector *n* |
| nonanalytical *adj* | nonbearing *adj* | non-Catholic *adj or n* | noncollege *adj* |
| nonanimal *adj or n* | nonbehavioural *adj* | noncausal *adj* | noncollegiate *adj* |
| nonanswer *n* | nonbeing *n* | noncelestial *adj* | noncolloid *n* |
| nonantagonistic *adj* | nonbelief *n* | noncellular *adj* | noncolloidal *adj* |
| nonanthropological *adj* | nonbeliever *n* | noncellulosic *adj* | noncoloured *adj or n* |
| nonantigenic *adj* | nonbelieving *adj* | non-Celtic *adj* | noncolourfast *adj* |
| nonaquatic *adj* | nonbelligerency *n* | noncentral *adj* | noncombat *n* |
| nonaqueous *adj* | nonbelligerent *adj* | noncerebral *adj* | noncombining *adj* |
| nonarable *adj or n* | nonbetting *adj* | noncertificated *adj* | noncombustible *adj or n* |
| nonarbitrary *adj* | nonbibliographic *adj* | noncertified *adj* | noncommercial *adj* |
| nonargument *n* | nonbinding *adj* | nonchargeable *adj* | noncommitment *n* |
| nonaristocratic *adj* | nonbiodegradable *adj* | nonchauvinist *n* | noncommunicable *adj* |
| nonaromatic *adj or n* | nonbiographical *adj* | nonchemical *adj or n* | noncommunicant *n* |
| nonarrival *n* | nonbiological *adj* | non-Christian *adj or n* | noncommunicating *adj* |
| nonascetic *adj or n* | nonbiting *adj* | nonchronological *adj* | noncommunication *n* |
| non-Asian *adj or n* | nonbonded *adj* | nonchurchgoer *n* | noncommunist *adj or n* |
| nonaspirated *adj* | nonbonding *adj* | noncircular *adj* | noncommutative *adj* |
| nonassessable *adj* | nonbreakable *adj* | noncitizen *n* | noncomparability *n* |
| nonassimilable *adj* | nonbreeder *n* | nonclaim *n* | noncomparable *adj* |
| nonassociated *adj* | nonbreeding *adj* | nonclassical *adj* | noncompensating *adj* |
| nonassociative *adj* | nonbureaucratic *adj* | nonclassified *adj* | noncompetent *adj* |
| nonastronomical *adj* | nonburnable *adj* | nonclassroom *adj* | noncompeting *adj* |
| nonathelete *n* | nonbuying *adj* | nonclerical *adj* | noncompetition *n* |
| nonatheletic *adj* | noncabinet *adj* | noncling *adj* | noncompetitive *adj* |
| nonatomic *adj* | noncaking *adj* | nonclinical *adj* | noncompetitor *n* |
| nonattendance *n* | noncampus *adj* | nonclogging *adj* | noncomplementary *adj* |
| nonattender *n* | noncancellable *adj* | nonclotting *adj* | noncompliance *n* |
| nonattributive *adj* | noncancerous *adj* | noncoagulable *adj* | noncomplying *adj* |
| nonauditory *adj* | noncanonical *adj* | noncoagulating *adj* | noncomprehension *n* |
| nonautomated *adj* | noncapital *adj* | noncoercive *adj* | noncompressible *adj* |
| nonautomatic *adj or n* | noncapitalist *adj or n* | noncognitive *adj* | nonconciliatory *adj* |
| nonautomotive *adj* | noncarbohydrate *adj or n* | noncoherent *adj* | nonconlusion *n* |
| nonautonomous *adj* | noncarbonaceous *adj* | noncohesive *adj* | nonconclusive *adj* |
| nonavailability *n* | noncarbonated *adj* | noncoincidence *n* | nonconcurrent *adj* |
| nonbacterial *adj* | noncarcinogenic *adj* | noncoital *adj* | noncondensable *adj* |
| nonbank *adj* | noncarnivorous *adj* | noncollapsible *adj* | noncondensing *adj* |

**noncrossover** /ˌnonˈkrosohvə/ *adj* having or being CHROMOSOMES (strands of gene-carrying material in cells) that have not participated in CROSSING-OVER (interchange of genes or segments of chromosomes) ⟨~ *offspring*⟩

**nondairy** /ˌnonˈdeəri/ *adj* containing no milk or milk products ⟨~ *coffee whitener*⟩

**nondeductible** /ˌnondiˈduktəbl/ *adj* not deductible; *esp* not deductible for income tax purposes – **nondeductibility** *n*

**nondescript** /ˈnondiskript/ *adj* 1 (apparently) belonging to no particular class or kind 2 lacking distinctive or interesting qualities; dull [*non-* + L *descriptus*, pp of *describere* to describe] – **nondescript** *n*

**nondestructive** /ˌnondiˈstruktiv/ *adj* not destructive; *specif* involving no alteration of physical state or arrangement or of chemical constitution ⟨~ *analysis*⟩ – **nondestructively** *adv*, **nondestructiveness** *n*

**nondiapausing** /ˌnonˈdie·ə,pawzing/ *adj*, *esp of an insect* 1 not having a DIAPAUSE (period of suspended development) 2 not in a state of DIAPAUSE

**nondisclosure** /ˌnondisˈklohzhə/ *n* the concealment (eg from an insurance company) of material information

**nondisjunction** /ˌnondisˈjungksh(ə)n/ *n* the failure of two CHROMOSOMES (strands of gene-carrying material in cells) to separate during CELL DIVISION with the result that one daughter cell has both and the other neither of the chromosomes [ISV] – **nondisjunctional** *adj*

**nondistinctive** /ˌnondiˈstingktiv/ *adj*, *of a speech sound* making no difference to meaning; not PHONEMIC

**nondividing** /ˌnondiˈvieding/ *adj*, *of a cell* not undergoing CELL DIVISION

**nondormant** /ˌnonˈdawmənt/ *adj* 1 *of a seed* in such a condition that germination is possible 2 *of a plant* being in active vegetative growth

**nondrying oil** /ˌnonˈdrie·ing/ *n* an oil (eg olive oil) that is unable to solidify when exposed in a thin film to air

¹**none** /nun/ *pron*, *pl* **none** 1 not any; no part or thing ⟨~ *of the money*⟩ ⟨~ *of the telephones are working*⟩ 2 not one person; nobody ⟨*it's* ~ *other than Tom*⟩ ⟨~ *but a fool*⟩ 3 not any such thing or person ⟨*a bad film is better than* ~ *at all*⟩ ⟨*her wits are* ~ *of the brightest*⟩ [ME, fr OE *nān*, fr *ne* not + *ān* one – more at NO, ONE]

**usage** The use of **none** followed by a plural verb and pronouns has been established in English since the 9th century. Since it is, however, disapproved of by some very conservative writers on usage, one may prefer in formal writing to use the singular construction ⟨**none** *of the telephones is working*⟩ where the sense permits it. Compare ⟨**none** (*of them*) *is a better singer than Peter*⟩ ⟨**none** (*of them*) *are better singers than the Welsh*⟩. In any case, there must be consistency throughout the sentence: either ⟨**none** *of them are ready, are they?*⟩ or ⟨**none** *of them is ready, is it?*⟩

²**none** *adj*, *archaic* no; not any

³**none** *adv* 1 by no means; not at all ⟨~ *too soon to begin*⟩ 2 in no way; to no extent ⟨~ *the worse for wear*⟩

⁴**none** /nohn/ *n*, *often cap* NONES 2 [LL *nona*, fr L, 9th hour of the day from sunrise – more at NOON]

**noneconomic** /ˌnoneekəˈnomik, -ekə-/ *adj* not economic; *esp* having no economic importance or significance

**noneffective** /ˌnoniˈfektiv/ *adj* 1 not effective 2 not available for or capable of active military service – **noneffective** *n*

**nonelectrolyte** /ˌnoniˈlektrəliet/ *n* a substance (eg sugar or benzene) that does not appreciably form ions and therefore is a poor conductor of an electric current when in solution

**nonenforceable** /ˌnoninˈfawsəbl/ *adj* not enforceable – **nonenforceability** *n*

**nonentity** /noˈnentiti/ *n* 1 something that does not exist or exists only in the imagination 2 nonexistence 3 a person or thing of little or no importance

**nones** /nohnz/ *n taking sing or pl vb* 1 the ninth day before the IDES according to the ancient Roman calendar; the 7th day of March, May, July, or October, or the 5th day of any other month 2 *often cap* the fifth of the CANONICAL HOURS (seven services at set times of day prescribed by the ROMAN CATHOLIC church) that was originally fixed for 3pm [ME *nonys*, fr L *nonae*, fr fem pl of *nonus* ninth]

**nonesuch** *also* **nonsuch** /ˈnun,such/ *n*, *archaic* a person or thing without an equal; a paragon – **nonesuch** *adj*

**nonetheless** *also* **none the less** /ˌnundhəˈles/ *adv* nevertheless

**ˌnon-euˈclidean** *adj*, *often cap E* not assuming or in accordance with all of Euclid's postulates of geometry

**ˌnon-Euroˈpean** *adj*, *S Afr* not white – **non-European** *n*

---

| | | | |
|---|---|---|---|
| nonconditioned *adj* | noncontrolling *adj* | nondemocratic *adj* | nondivided *adj* |
| nonconductibility *n* | noncontroversial *adj* | nondenominational *adj* | nondivisible *adj* |
| nonconducting *adj* | nonconventional *adj* | nondenominationalism *n* | nondivisional *adj* |
| nonconduction *n* | nonconvergent *adj* | nondepartmental *adj* | nondoctrinaire *adj* |
| nonconductive *adj* | nonconversant *adj* | nondependence *n* | nondocumentary *adj or n* |
| nonconfidence *n* | nonconvertible *adj* | nondependent *adj* | nondogmatic *adj* |
| nonconfidential *adj* | noncorporate *adj* | nondeposition *n* | nondomestic *adj* |
| nonconflicting *adj* | noncorroborative *adj* | nonderivative *adj* | nondomesticated *adj* |
| noncongenital *adj* | noncorrodible *adj* | nondescriptive *adj* | nondrinker *n* |
| nonconjugated *adj* | noncorroding *adj* | nondetachable *adj* | nondrinking *adj* |
| nonconnection *n* | noncorrosive *adj* | nondeteriorative *adj* | nondriver *n* |
| nonconnective *adj* | noncoverage *n* | nondeterministic *adj* | nondurable *adj* |
| nonconscious *adj* | noncreative *adj* | nondetonating *adj* | nondynastic *adj* |
| nonconsecutive *adj* | noncriminal *adj or n* | nondevelopable *adj* | nonearning *adj or n* |
| nonconsensual *adj* | noncritical *adj* | nondevelopment *n* | nonecclesiastical *adj* |
| nonconsenting *adj* | noncrushable *adj* | nondiabetic *adj or n* | nonedible *adj* |
| nonconservation *n* | noncrystalline *adj* | nondialysable *adj* | noneditorial *adj* |
| nonconsolidated *adj* | noncultivated *adj* | nondictatorial *adj* | noneducational *adj* |
| nonconstitutional *adj* | noncultivation *n* | nondidactic *adj* | noneffervescent *adj* |
| nonconstraining *adj* | noncultural *adj* | nondifferentiation *n* | nonelastic *adj* |
| nonconstructive *adj* | noncumulative *adj* | nondiffusible *adj* | nonelect *n* |
| nonconsumable *adj* | noncurrent *adj* | nondiffusing *adj* | nonelected *adj* |
| nonconsumer *n* | noncustomer *n* | nondigestible *adj* | nonelection *n* |
| nonconsuming *adj* | noncyclic *adj* | nondiplomatic *adj* | nonelective *adj* |
| nonconsumption *n* | noncyclical *adj* | nondirectional *adj* | nonelectric *adj* |
| noncontact *n* | nondeciduous *adj* | nondirective *adj* | nonelectrical *adj* |
| noncontagious *adj* | nondecreasing *adj* | nondisciplinary *adj* | nonelectronic *adj* |
| noncontemporary *adj* | nondeductive *adj* | nondiscountable *adj* | noneligible *adj* |
| noncontentious *adj* | nondeferrable *adj* | nondiscretionary *adj* | nonemergency *n* |
| noncontiguous *adj* | nondefining *adj* | nondiscriminating *adj* | nonemotional *adj* |
| noncontinuous *adj* | nondeforming *adj* | nondiscrimination *n* | nonempirical *adj* |
| noncontraband *adj or n* | nondegenerate *adj* | nondiscriminatory *adj* | nonemployee *n* |
| noncontractual *adj* | nondegenerated *adj* | nondiscursive *adj* | nonemployment *n* |
| noncontradiction *n* | nondegradable *adj* | nondisposable *adj* | nonencapsulated *adj* |
| noncontradictory *adj* | nondelegable *adj* | nondisqualifying *adj* | nonending *adj* |
| noncontributing *adj* | nondelegate *n* | nondisruptive *adj* | nonenforcement *n* |
| noncontrollable *adj* | nondelinquent *adj or n* | nondistributed *adj* | nonestablished *adj* |
| noncontrolled *adj* | nondelivery *n* | nondistribution *n* | nonestablishment *n* |

**nonevent** /ˌnoniˈvent/ *n* an event that is (unexpectedly) dull or inconsequential

**nonfat** /ˌnonˈfat/ *adj* lacking fat solids; having fat solids removed ⟨~ *milk*⟩

**nonfeasance** /ˌnonˈfeez(ə)ns/ *n* failure to act, esp when legally obliged to do so [*non-* + obs *feasance* doing, execution – more at MALFEASANCE]

**nonferrous** /ˌnonˈferəs/ *adj* **1** not containing, including, or relating to iron **2** of metals other than iron

**non-ˈfiction** *n* literature based directly on fact; *broadly* literature other than novels and stories

**nonfigurative** /ˌnonˈfig(y)oorətiv/ *adj, of art* not representing anything natural; NONOBJECTIVE 2

**nonflammable** /ˌnonˈflaməbl/ *n* not inflammable; *specif* difficult or impossible to set alight *usage* see INFLAMMABLE – **nonflammability** *n*

**nonflowering** /ˌnonˈflowəring/ *adj* producing no flowers; *specif* lacking a flowering stage in the LIFE CYCLE

**nonhistone** /ˌnonˈhistohn/ *adj* rich in AMINO ACIDS (chemical units from which proteins are formed), esp TRYPTOPHAN, that contain a ring of carbon atoms in their structure ⟨~ *proteins*⟩

**nonidentical** /ˌnonieˈdentikl/ *adj* **1** different **2** of twins FRATERNAL 2

**nonillion** /nohˈnilyən/ *n* – see NUMBER table [Fr, fr L *nonus* ninth + Fr *-illion* (as in *million*) – more at NOON]

**noninductive** /ˌnoninˈduktiv/ *adj* not inductive; *esp* having negligible INDUCTANCE (capacity to induce an electric current)

**nonintervention** /ˌnonintəˈvensh(ə)n/ *n* the state or policy of not intervening ⟨~ *in the affairs of other countries*⟩ – **noninterventionist** *n or adj*

**noninvolvement** /ˌnoninˈvolvmənt/ *n* failure or refusal to become involved or committed

**nonionic** /ˌnonieˈonik/ *adj* not forming IONS (electrically charges atoms); *esp* not dependent on a surface-active ANION (negatively charged ion) for effect ⟨~ *surfactants*⟩

**nonionic detergent** *n* a synthetic detergent that does not produce IONS (electrically charged atoms) in solution in water

**noniron** /ˌnonˈieˌən/ *adj, of a fabric, garment, etc* that does not need to be ironed after washing

**nonjoinder** /ˌnonˈjoyndə/ *n* failure to include a necessary party in a legal action

**nonjudgmental** /ˌnonjuˈjmentl/ *adj* avoiding judgments based on one's personal standards, esp of morality

**nonjuring** /ˌnonˈjoooring/ *adj* being a nonjuror [*non-* + L *jurare* to swear – more at JURY]

**nonjuror** /ˌnonˈjooərə/ *n* a person refusing to take an oath, esp of allegiance; *specif, often cap* a member of the clergy in Britain who refused to take an oath of allegiance to William and Mary or to their successors after the revolution of 1688

**nonlinguistic** /ˌnonlingˈgwistik/ *adj* not consisting of or relating to language

**nonliterate** /ˌnonˈlit(ə)rət/ *adj* having no written language – **nonliterate** *n*

**nonmetal** /ˌnonˈmetl/ *n* a chemical element (e g boron, carbon, or nitrogen) that lacks typical metallic properties and is able to form ANIONS (atoms with a negative electric charge), acidic oxides and acids, and stable chemical compounds with hydrogen

**nonmetallic** /ˌnonmiˈtalik/ *adj* **1** not metallic **2** of or being a nonmetal

**nonmonetary** /ˌnonˈmunit(ə)ri/ *adj* not monetary; not involving money

**nonmoral** /ˌnonˈmorəl/ *adj* lying outside the sphere of morals; amoral

**nonnegative** /ˌnonˈnegətiv/ *adj, of a number* not negative; either positive or zero

**nonnuclear** /ˌnonˈnyookliˌə/ *adj* not having or using nuclear power or weapons ⟨*a* ~ *country*⟩ ⟨*a* ~ *war*⟩

**ˈno-ˌno** *n* something to be avoided or rejected ⟨*what looks at first sight like a genuine* ~, *in fact turns out to be a real eye-opener – Time Out*⟩ [redupl of ³*no*]

**nonobjective** /ˌnonəbˈjektiv/ *adj* **1** not objective **2** *of art* not representing or intended to represent any natural or actual object, figure, or scene; abstract – **nonobjectivism** *n*, **nonobjectivist** *n*, **nonobjectivity** *n*

**non obstante** /ˌnon obˈstanti/ *prep* notwithstanding [L, fr *non* not + *obstante*, abl of *obstans*, prp of *obstare* to stand in the way]

**ˌno-ˈnonsense** *adj* **1** serious, businesslike **2** without trifles or

---

| | | | |
|---|---|---|---|
| **nonenzymatic** *adj* | **nonfilamentous** *adj* | **nonhandicapped** *adj or n* | **noninheritable** *adj* |
| **nonenzymic** *adj* | **nonfilterable** *adj* | **nonhardy** *adj* | **noninjurious** *adj* |
| **nonepiscopal** *adj* | **nonfinancial** *adj* | **nonhazardous** *adj* | **noninjury** *n* |
| **nonequal** *adj or n* | **nonfinite** *adj* | **nonhereditary** *adj* | **noninstinctive** *adj* |
| **nonequilibrium** *n* | **nonfiscal** *adj* | **nonheritable** *adj* | **noninstitutional** *adj* |
| **nonequivalence** *n* | **nonfissile** *adj* | **nonhierarchical** *adj* | **noninstitutionalized** *adj* |
| **nonequivalent** *adj* | **nonfissionable** *adj* | **nonhistorical** *adj* | **noninstructional** *adj* |
| **noneruptive** *adj* | **nonflexible** *adj* | **nonhomogeneous** *adj* | **nonintegral** *adj* |
| **nonessential** *adj or n* | **nonfluency** *n* | **nonhomologous** *adj* | **nonintegrated** *adj* |
| **nonesterified** *adj* | **nonfluid** *adj or n* | **nonhormonal** *adj* | **nonintellectual** *adj or n* |
| **noneventful** *adj* | **nonfluorescent** *adj* | **nonhostile** *adj* | **noninteracting** *adj* |
| **nonexaminable** *adj* | **nonflying** *adj* | **nonhuman** *adj or n* | **nonintercourse** *n* |
| **nonexchangeable** *adj* | **nonfood** *adj or n* | **nonideal** *adj* | **noninterference** *n* |
| **nonexclusive** *adj* | **nonforfeitable** *adj* | **nonidentity** *n* | **nonintersection** *n* |
| **nonexecutive** *adj or n* | **nonforfeiture** *n* | **nonidealogical** *adj* | **nonintoxicant** *adj or n* |
| **nonexempt** *adj* | **nonformation** *n* | **nonimmigrant** *adj or n* | **nonintoxicating** *adj* |
| **nonexistence** *n* | **nonfossiliferous** *adj* | **nonimmune** *adj* | **nonintrusive** *adj* |
| **nonexistent** *adj* | **nonfraternal** *adj* | **nonimportation** *n* | **nonintuitive** *adj* |
| **nonexpendable** *adj* | **nonfraternization** *n* | **noninclusion** *n* | **nonionizing** *adj* |
| **nonexperimental** *adj* | **nonfreezing** *adj or n* | **nonincreasing** *adj* | **nonirradiated** *adj* |
| **nonexpert** *adj or n* | **nonfulfilment** *n* | **nonindependence** *n* | **nonirrigated** *adj* |
| **nonexplanatory** *adj* | **nonfunctional** *adj* | **nonindependent** *adj* | **nonirritant** *adj or n* |
| **nonexploitation** *n* | **nonfunctioning** *adj or n* | **nonindictable** *adj* | **nonirritating** *adj* |
| **nonexploitative** *adj* | **nonfusible** *adj* | **nonindigenous** *adj* | **non-Jew** *n* |
| **nonexploitive** *adj* | **nongaseous** *adj* | **nonindustrial** *adj* | **non-Jewish** *adj* |
| **nonexplosive** *adj or n* | **nongeneric** *adj* | **nonindustrialization** *n* | **nonjoiner** *n* |
| **nonexportation** *n* | **nongenetic** *adj* | **nonindustrialized** *adj* | **nonjudicial** *adj* |
| **nonextant** *adj* | **nongliding** *adj* | **noninfected** *adj* | **nonjury** *adj or n* |
| **nonfactual** *adj* | **nongovernment** *n* | **noninfectious** *adj* | **nonkosher** *adj* |
| **nonfading** *adj* | **nongovernmental** *adj* | **noninfective** *adj* | **nonlaminated** *adj* |
| **nonfatal** *adj* | **nongraduate** *n* | **noninfested** *adj* | **nonleaded** *adj* |
| **nonfattening** *adj* | **nongrammatical** *adj* | **noninflammable** *adj* | **nonleague** *adj* |
| **nonfatty** *adj* | **nongranular** *adj* | **noninflammatory** *adj* | **nonlegal** *adj* |
| **nonfebrile** *adj* | **nongreasy** *adj* | **noninflationary** *adj* | **nonleguminous** *adj* |
| **nonfederal** *adj* | **nongregarious** *adj* | **noninflected** *adj* | **nonlethal** *adj* |
| **nonfederated** *adj* | **nongrowing** *adj* | **noninflectional** *adj* | **nonlexical** *adj* |
| **nonferromagnetic** *adj* | **nongrowth** *n* | **noninformative** *adj* | **nonlife** *n* |
| **nonfictitious** *adj* | **nonhabitable** *adj* | **noninherent** *adj* | **nonlinear** *adj* |

frills ⟨*dressed in a ~ jumper and slacks – Punch*⟩

**nonorgasmic** /ˌnɒnɔːˈgæzmɪk/ *adj* unable to have orgasm – **nonorgasmic** *n*

**nonparametric** /ˌnɒnpærəˈmetrɪk/ *adj* not involving the estimation of PARAMETERS (statistical quantities) of a PROBABILITY DISTRIBUTION ⟨*~ statistical tests*⟩

¹**nonpareil** /ˈnɒnpərəl, ˌnɒnpəˈreɪl/ *adj* having no equal; peerless [MF, fr *non-* + *pareil* equal, fr (assumed) VL *pariculus*, fr L *par* equal]

²**nonpareil** *n* a person or thing of unequalled excellence; a paragon

**nonpartisan** /ˌnɒnˈpɑːtɪzn, -ˌpɑːtɪˈzæn/ *adj* not partisan; *esp* free from party affiliation, bias, or designation ⟨*a ~ approach to the problem*⟩ – **nonpartisanship** *n*

**nonpasserine** /ˌnɒnˈpæsəriːn/ *adj* not being a songbird; *esp* CORACIIFORM (related to the kingfishers, hornbills, etc)

**nonpathogenic** /ˌnɒnpæθəˈdʒenɪk/ *adj* not capable of inducing disease – compare AVIRULENT – **nonpathogenicity** *n*

**nonpersistent** /ˌnɒnpəˈsɪstənt/ *adj* not persistent: e g a decomposed rapidly in the environment (e g by microorganisms) ⟨*~ insecticides*⟩ **b** *of a microorganism or virus* capable of existing in a VECTOR (organism that transmits a disease-causing agent) for only a relatively short time

**nonperson** /ˈnɒnˌpɜːsən/ *n, pl* **nonpersons 1** a person who usu for political or ideological reasons is removed completely from recognition or consideration **2** a person regarded as of no interest or significance ⟨*economically she is a ~ – Observer Magazine*⟩

**non placet** /ˌnɒn ˈplækɛt/ *n* a negative vote [L, it does not please]

¹**nonplus** /ˌnɒnˈplʌs/ *n* a state of bafflement or perplexity; a quandary [L *non plus* no more]

²**nonplus** *vt* **-ss-** (*NAm* **-s-, -ss-**) to cause to be at a loss as to what to say, think, or do; perplex, disconcert

**nonpolar** /ˌnɒnˈpəʊlə/ *adj* not polar; *esp* not having or requiring the presence of electrical poles ⟨*a ~ solvent*⟩

**nonprescription** /ˌnɒnprɪˈskrɪpʃən/ *adj, of a medicine* capable of being bought without a doctor's prescription

**non-ˈpro** *adj or n, informal* not (a) professional; (a) non-professional

**nonproductive** /ˌnɒnprəˈdʌktɪv/ *adj* not productive: e g **a** failing to produce or yield; unproductive ⟨*a ~ oil well*⟩ **b** not directly concerned with production ⟨*the ~ labour of clerks and inspectors*⟩ **c** *of a cough* dry – **nonproductiveness** *n*

**non-ˈprofitmaking,** *chiefly NAm* **nonprofit** *adj* not conducted or maintained for the purpose of making a profit

**nonproliferation** /ˌnɒnprəˌlɪfəˈreɪʃ(ə)n/ *adj* providing for the stoppage of proliferation (e g of nuclear weapons) ⟨*~ treaty*⟩ – **nonproliferation** *n*

**nonprotein** /ˌnɒnˈprəʊtiːn/ *adj* not being or derived from protein ⟨*the ~ part of an enzyme*⟩ ⟨*~ nitrogen*⟩ – **nonproteinaceous** *adj*

**nonprovided school** /ˌnɒnprəˈvaɪdɪd/ *n, archaic* a school built by an independent body but maintained by a British local education authority; VOLUNTARY SCHOOL

**nonreader** /ˌnɒnˈriːdə/ *n* one who does not or cannot read; *esp* a child who is very slow in learning to read

**nonrecombinant** /ˌnɒnriˈkɒmbɪnənt/ *adj* not exhibiting the results of genetic RECOMBINATION (formation of new combinations of genes that did not occur in the parents) ⟨*~ progeny*⟩ – **nonrecombinant** *n*

**nonrefundable** /ˌnɒnriˈfʌndəbl/ *adj* not subject to refunding ⟨*a ~ deposit*⟩

**nonrelativistic** /ˌnɒnˌrelətiˈvistɪk/ *adj* **1** not based on or involving the theory of RELATIVITY ⟨*~ equations*⟩ **2** (of a body) moving at less than a RELATIVISTIC velocity (speed that causes a significant change in the properties of an object in accordance with the theory of RELATIVITY) – **nonrelativistically** *adv*

**nonrepresentational** /ˌnɒnˌreprizenˈteɪʃ(ə)nl/ *adj, of art* not representing anything natural; NONOBJECTIVE **2** – **nonrepresentationalism** *n*

**nonresident** /ˌnɒnˈrezɪd(ə)nt/ *adj* not residing in a particular place (e g a hotel or university hall) – **nonresident** *n*, **nonresidence, nonresidency** *n*

**nonresistance** /ˌnɒnriˈzɪst(ə)ns/ *n* the principles or practice of passive submission to legally established authority even when unjust or oppressive; *also* the principle or practice of not resisting violence by force

**nonresistant** /ˌnɒnriˈzɪst(ə)nt/ *adj* not resistant; *specif* susceptible to the effects of a harmful substance, organism, or

---

| | | | |
|---|---|---|---|
| nonliquid *adj or n* | nonmilitant *adj or n* | nonoperative *adj* | nonpolarizable *adj* |
| nonliterary *adj* | nonmilitary *adj* | nonorganic *adj* | nonpolitical *adj* |
| nonliturgical *adj* | nonmimetic *adj* | nonorthodox *adj* | nonpolluting *adj* |
| nonliving *adj* | nonministerial *adj* | nonoscillatory *adj* | nonporosity *n* |
| nonlocal *adj* | nonmolecular *adj* | nonoverlapping *adj* | nonporous *adj* |
| nonlogical *adj* | nonmoney *adj* | nonowner *n* | nonpossession *n* |
| nonluminous *adj* | nonmotile *adj* | nonoxidizing *adj* | nonpractical *adj* |
| nonlysogenic *adj* | nonmotility *n* | nonpalatal *adj* | nonpractising *adj* |
| nonmagnetic *adj* | nonmotorist *n* | nonpalatalization *n* | nonprecious *adj* |
| nonmalignant *adj* | nonmotorized *adj* | nonparallel *adj* | nonpredatory *adj* |
| nonmalleable *adj* | nonmovable *adj* | nonparalytic *adj* | nonpredicative *adj* |
| nonmanagement *n* | nonmoving *adj* | nonparasitic *adj* | nonpregnant *adj* |
| nonmanagerial *adj* | nonmunicipal *adj* | nonparental *adj* | nonprejudicial *adj* |
| nonmanual *adj* | nonmusical *adj* | nonparliamentary *adj* | nonprescriptive *adj* |
| nonmanufacturing *adj* | nonmutant *adj or n* | nonparticipant *n* | nonpreservable *adj* |
| nonmarine *adj* | nonmyelinated *adj* | nonparticipating *adj* | nonpreservation *n* |
| nonmaritime *adj* | nonnational *adj* | nonparticipation *n* | nonproducer *n* |
| nonmarketable *adj* | nonnative *adj* | nonparty *adj* | nonproducing *adj* |
| nonmatching *adj* | nonnatural *adj* | nonpatrial *adj* | nonprofessional *adj or n* |
| nonmaterial *adj* | nonnavigable *adj* | nonpaying *adj* | nonprogressive *adj or n* |
| nonmaterialistic *adj* | nonnecessity *n* | nonpayment *n* | nonproportional *adj* |
| nonmathematical *adj* | nonnegotiable *adj* | nonpenetrating *adj* | nonpropositional *adj* |
| nonmeasurable *adj* | nonnitrogenous *adj* | nonpensionable *adj* | nonproprietary *adj* |
| nonmeat *adj or n* | nonnormative *adj* | nonperformance *n* | nonprotective *adj* |
| nonmechanical *adj* | nonnucleated *adj* | nonperforming *adj* | nonproven *adj* |
| nonmechanistic *adj* | nonnumeric *adj* | nonperishable *adj* | nonpsychiatric *adj* |
| nonmedical *adj* | nonnumerical *adj* | nonpermanent *adj* | nonpsychological *adj* |
| nonmedicated *adj* | nonnutritive *adj* | nonpermissive *adj* | nonpublic *adj* |
| nonmedicinal *adj* | nonobligatory *adj* | nonpersonal *adj* | nonpungent *adj* |
| nonmember *n* | nonobservance *n* | nonpetroleum *adj* | nonpunishable *adj* |
| nonmembership *n* | nonobvious *adj* | nonphilosophical *adj* | nonpunitive *adj* |
| nonmetered *adj* | nonoccupational *adj* | nonphotosynthetic *adj* | nonquantitative *adj* |
| nonmetric *adj* | nonoccurrence *n* | nonphysical *adj* | nonquota *adj* |
| nonmetrical *adj* | nonofficial *adj* | nonphysiological *adj* | nonracial *adj* |
| nonmetropolitan *adj* | nonoperable *adj* | nonpigmented *adj* | nonracialism *n* |
| nonmicrobial *adj* | nonoperating *adj* | nonplastic *adj or n* | nonradiative *adj* |
| nonmigrant *adj or n* | nonoperation *n* | nonplaying *adj* | nonradical *adj or n* |
| nonmigratory *adj* | nonoperational *adj* | nonpoisonous *adj* | nonradioactive *adj* |

phenomenon (eg an insecticide, pathogen, or extreme environmental condition) – **nonresistant** n

**nonrestrictive** /ˌnonri'striktiv/ adj not restrictive; specif not identifying but describing a modified word or phrase ⟨a ~ clause⟩

**nonrestrictive clause** n a descriptive clause that is not essential to the definiteness of the meaning of what it describes (eg in "the aldermen, who were present, assented")

**nonreturnable** /ˌnonri'tuhnəbl/ adj not returnable; specif not returnable to a shop in exchange for a deposit ⟨~ bottles⟩

**nonrigid** /ˌnon'rijid/ adj not rigid; esp maintaining form by pressure of contained gas ⟨a ~ airship⟩ – **nonrigidity** n

**nonscheduled** /ˌnon'shedyoold, -'sked-/ USE the latter pron is disapproved of by some speakers/ adj licensed to carry passengers or freight by air without a regular schedule ⟨~ airlines⟩

**nonsecretor** /ˌnonsi'kreetə/ n a person of BLOOD GROUP A, B, or AB who does not secrete the ANTIGENS (substances stimulating the production of antibodies) characteristic of these blood groups in bodily liquids (eg saliva)

**nonsectarian** /ˌnonsek'teəri·ən/ adj not affiliated with or restricted to a particular religious sect or denomination

**nonsedimentable** /ˌnon,sedi'mentəbl/ adj not capable of being sedimented under specified conditions (eg of centrifugation)

**¹nonsense** /'nonsəns/ n **1a** words or language having no meaning or conveying no intelligible ideas **b** (an instance of) foolish or absurd language, conduct, or thought ⟨the . . . ~s which are causing the crisis – The Economist⟩ **2a** things of no importance or value; trifles; frills ⟨a plainly cut dress without any ~⟩ **b** frivolous or insolent behaviour ⟨took no ~ from his subordinates⟩ **3** genetic mutation involving alteration of one or more CODONS (sequences of three chemical bases that code for an AMINO ACID) so that they become nonsense codons and usu cause premature termination of the molecular chain in protein synthesis – compare MISSENSE **4** – used interjectionally to express forceful disagreement – **nonsensical** adj, **nonsensically** adv, **nonsensicalness** n

**²nonsense** adj **1** consisting of an arbitrary grouping of speech sounds or symbols ⟨/shrogthinpth/ is a ~ word⟩ **2** of or being a CODON (sequence of three chemical bases that code for an AMINO ACID) that contains genetic nonsense, does not code for any particular AMINO ACID, and is believed to function as a code for beginning or terminating protein synthesis

**nonsense verse** n humorous or whimsically absurd verse often containing invented meaningless words with an evocative sound

**non sequitur** /ˌnon 'sekwitə/ n **1** a conclusion that does not follow from the initial assumptions; specif a fallacy that results from assuming the converse of a logical proposition ⟨"if all women are mortals then all mortals are women" is a ~⟩ **2** a statement that does not follow logically from anything previously said [L, it does not follow]

**nonsignificant** /ˌnonsig'nifikənt/ adj not significant: eg **a** insignificant **b** meaningless **c** statistics having or yielding a value lying within limits between which variation is attributed to chance ⟨a ~ statistical test⟩ – **nonsignificantly** adv

**nonskid** /ˌnon'skid/ adj, of a tyre or road designed or equipped to prevent skidding

**nonslip** /ˌnon'slip/ adj designed to reduce or prevent slipping ⟨~ concrete⟩

**nonsmoker** /ˌnon'smohkə/ n **1** a person who does not smoke **2** a train compartment in which smoking is forbidden – **nonsmoking** adj

**nonsocial** /ˌnon'sohsh(ə)l/ adj not socially oriented; lacking a social component **synonyms** see UNSOCIAL

**nonspecific urethritis** /ˌnonspə'sifik/ n URETHRITIS (inflammation of the canal carrying urine from the bladder) that has no known specific causative agent and that is transmissible by sexual activity

**nonstandard** /ˌnon'standəd/ adj **1** not standard **2** not conforming in pronunciation, grammatical construction, idiom, or word choice to the usage generally characteristic of educated native speakers of a language – compare SUBSTANDARD

**nonstarter** /ˌnon'stahtə/ n **1** one who or that which does not start; esp a horse that is entered for a race but does not run **2** somebody or something that is sure to fail or prove impracticable ⟨the scheme is a non-starter, however plausible it looks theoretically – Conor Cruise O'Brien⟩

**nonsteroid** /ˌnon'steroyd, -'stiə-/ n a chemical compound, esp a drug, that is not a steroid – **nonsteroid, nonsteroidal** adj

**nonstick** /ˌnon'stik/ adj having or being a surface that prevents adherence of food during cooking ⟨a ~ coating in a frying pan⟩ [³stick]

**nonstop** /ˌnon'stop/ adj or adv (done or made) without pausing or stopping ⟨a ~ flight to Tokyo⟩ ⟨it rained ~ for two days⟩

**nonstriker** /ˌnon'striekə/ n the one of the two batsmen at the wicket who is not receiving the bowling

**nonsuch** /'nun,such/ n NONESUCH (person or thing without an equal)

**nonsuit** /ˌnon'sooht/ n a judgment against a plaintiff for failure to prove that he/she has grounds for legal action or failure to institute legal proceedings [ME, fr AF nounsuyte, fr noun- non- + OF siute following, pursuit – more at SUIT] – **nonsuit** vt

**nonsupport** /ˌnonsə'pawt/ n failure to provide support (eg for an estranged wife or a child) despite a court order

**nonswimmer** /ˌnon'swimə/ n one who is unable to swim

**nonsystem** /ˌnon'sistəm/ n a system that lacks effective organization

**nontarget** /ˌnon'tahgit/ adj not being the intended object of action by a particular agent ⟨effect of insecticides on ~ organisms⟩

**nontitle** /ˌnon'tietl/ adj of or being a contest, esp a sports contest, in which a title is not at stake

**nontrivial** /ˌnon'trivi·əl/ adj **1** not trivial **2** of or being a solution to an equation in mathematics in which at least one unknown value is not equal to zero ⟨~ solutions to linear equations⟩

---

| | | | |
|---|---|---|---|
| **nonrandom** adj | **nonreligious** adj | **nonsaline** adj | **nonskilled** adj |
| **nonrated** adj | **nonremovable** adj | **nonscience** n | **nonsocialist** adj or n |
| **nonrational** adj | **nonrenewable** adj | **nonscientific** adj | **nonsolar** adj |
| **nonreactive** adj | **nonrepayable** adj | **nonscientist** n | **nonsolid** adj or n |
| **nonreactivity** n | **nonrepresentative** adj or n | **nonseasonal** adj | **nonsoluble** adj |
| **nonreactor** n | **nonresidential** adj | **nonsecret** adj or n | **nonspeaker** n |
| **nonreader** n | **nonresonant** adj | **nonsecretory** adj | **nonspeaking** adj |
| **nonrealistic** adj | **nonrespondent** adj or n | **nonsecular** adj | **nonspecialist** adj or n |
| **nonreceipt** n | **nonresponder** n | **nonsegregated** adj | **nonspecialized** adj |
| **nonreciprocal** adj | **nonresponse** n | **nonsegregation** n | **nonspecific** adj |
| **nonrecognition** n | **nonrestraint** n | **nonselected** adj | **nonspectacular** adj |
| **nonrecourse** n | **nonrestricted** adj | **nonselective** adj | **nonspectral** adj |
| **nonrecoverable** adj | **nonretractile** adj | **non-self-governing** adj | **nonspeculative** adj |
| **nonrecurrent** adj | **nonretroactive** adj | **nonsensitive** adj | **nonspherical** adj |
| **nonrecurring** adj | **nonreusable** adj | **nonsensuous** adj | **nonspiritual** adj |
| **nonreducing** adj | **nonrevenue** adj | **nonseptate** adj | **nonspontaneous** adj |
| **nonrefillable** adj | **nonreversible** adj | **nonsequential** adj | **nonsporting** adj |
| **nonreflecting** adj | **nonrhetorical** adj | **nonsexist** adj or n | **nonstainable** adj |
| **nonreflective** adj | **nonrotating** adj | **nonsexual** adj | **nonstaining** adj |
| **nonregimented** adj | **nonrubber** adj or n | **nonshrink** adj | **nonstationary** adj |
| **nonregistered** adj | **nonruminant** adj or n | **nonshrinkable** adj | **nonstatistical** adj |
| **nonregulated** adj | **nonrunner** n | **nonsimultaneous** adj | **nonstatutory** adj |
| **nonregulation** n | **nonrural** adj | **nonsinkable** adj | **nonstrategic** adj |
| **nonrelative** n | **nonsalable** adj | **nonskeletal** adj | **nonstriated** adj |

**non troppo** /ˌnon 'tropoh/ *adv or adj* without excess – used to qualify a direction in music [It, lit., not too much]

**non-U** /ˌnon'yooh/ *adj, informal* not characteristic of the upper classes

**nonunion** /ˌnon'yoohnyən/ *adj* **1** not belonging to or connected with a trade union ⟨~ *plumbers*⟩ ⟨*a* ~ *job*⟩ **2** not recognizing or favouring trade unions or their members

**nonvector** /ˌnon'vektə/ *n* an organism (eg an insect) that does not transmit a particular disease-causing agent (eg a virus)

**nonverbal** /ˌnon'vuhbl/ *adj* not verbal: eg **a** other than verbal ⟨~ *factors*⟩ ⟨~ *communication*⟩ **b** involving minimal use of language ⟨~ *tests*⟩ **c** ranking low in verbal skill – **nonverbally** *adv*

**nonviable** /ˌnon'vie-əbl/ *adj* not capable of living, growing, or developing and functioning successfully

**nonviolence** /ˌnon'vie-ələns/ *n* **1** refraining from violence on moral grounds **2** passive resistance or peaceful demonstration for the purpose of securing political ends ⟨*studied the history and techniques of* ~⟩ – **nonviolent** *adj*, **nonviolently** *adv*

**nonvolatile** /ˌnon'volətil/ *adj* not VOLATILE (able to vaporize); *esp* not volatilizing readily

**nonwhite, non-White** /ˌnon'wiet/ *n* a person whose features, esp skin colour, are different from those of Caucasians of NW Europe; *esp* one who has black African ancestors **synonyms** see ¹BLACK – **nonwhite** *adj*

**nonwoven** /ˌnon'wohv(ə)n/ *adj, of a fabric* made without weaving or knitting

**nonzero** /ˌnon'ziəroh/ *adj* having or being a value other than zero; either positive or negative

¹**noodle** /'noohdl/ *n, humorous* **1** a silly or foolish person **2** *NAm* the head [perh alter. of *noddle*]

²**noodle** *n* a narrow flat ribbon of pasta made with egg [Ger *nudel*]

**nook** /nook/ *n* **1** a corner or recess in a room ⟨*sat huddled in the chimney* ~⟩ **2** a small secluded or sheltered place or part [ME *noke, nok* corner, angle, recess]

**nooky** /'nooki/ *n, humorous* SEXUAL INTERCOURSE [perh fr *nook* + ⁴-*y*]

**noon** /noohn/ *n* **1** noon, noonday the middle of the day; midday **2** *poetic* the highest or culminating point ⟨*the* ~ *of his life*⟩ [ME, fr OE *nōn* ninth hour from sunrise, fr L *nona*, fr fem of *nonus* ninth; akin to L *novem* nine – more at NINE]

**no one** *pron* nobody

  *usage* Compare ⟨**no one** (= nobody) *is clever enough*⟩ ⟨**no one** (= no single) *room is big enough*⟩; see NOBODY

**nooning** /'noohning/ *n, dial chiefly NAm* **1** a meal eaten at noon **2** a period at noon for eating or resting

**noontide** /'noohntied/ *n, poetic* **1** noontime **2** the highest or culminating point

**noontime** /'noohntiem/ *n* the time of noon; midday

¹**noose** /noohs/ *n* **1** a loop with a running knot that tightens as the rope is pulled **2** something that snares or binds like a noose [prob fr Prov *nous* knot, fr L *nodus* – more at NET]

²**noose** *vt* **1** to secure by a noose **2** to make a noose in or of

**Nootka** /'nootkə, 'noohtkə/ *n, pl* **Nootkas**, *esp collectively*

**Nootka** a member of an American Indian people of Vancouver Island and NW Washington state; *also* their language

**nopal** /'nohpl/ *n* **1** any of a genus (*Nopalea*) of cacti similar to the PRICKLY PEARS but having red flowers; *esp* one (*Nopalea coccinellifera*) that is cultivated in Mexico as food for the cochineal insect **2** PRICKLY PEAR (type of cactus) [Sp, fr Nahuatl *nopalli*]

ˌ**no-'par, no-par-value** *adj, of a share certificate, bond, etc* having no value indicated ⟨~ *stocks*⟩

**nope** /nohp/ *adv* no – used in writing to represent a casual or American pronunciation [by alter.]

¹**nor** /naw/ *conj* **1** – used to join two sentence elements of the same class or function, and often introduced by *neither* to indicate that what immediately follows is another or a final negated alternative ⟨*neither here* ~ *there*⟩ ⟨*not done by you* ~ *me* ~ *anyone*⟩ **2** also not; neither ⟨*it didn't seem hard,* ~ *was it*⟩ [ME, contr of *nother* neither, nor, fr *nother*, pron & adj, neither – more at NEITHER] – **nor yet** and also not

  *usage* **1** Nor, not or, must follow **neither** ⟨*he* **neither** *wrote* **nor** *telephoned*⟩. After other negative words there is a choice between **nor** and **or** ⟨*he did not write* **nor**/**or** *telephone*⟩ ⟨*not a vessel,* **nor** *a gun,* **nor** *a man, were on the ground to prevent their landing* – W E Gladstone⟩ **2** There are many occasions on which it is perfectly legitimate and very effective to begin a sentence with **nor**.

²**nor** *conj, dial* than [ME, perh fr ¹*nor*]

**NOR** *n* a computer logic circuit that produces an output which is the inverse of that of an OR circuit [*not or*]

**nor'** /naw, nə-/ *n* north – often in combination ⟨*nor'-easter*⟩

**noradrenalin, noradrenaline** /ˌnawə'drenəlin/ *n* a chemical compound, $(OH)_2C_6H_3CH(OH)CH_2NH_2$, that occurs with adrenalin as a hormone, is the major NEUROTRANSMITTER (substance transmitting nerve impulses) released from the nerve endings of the SYMPATHETIC NERVOUS SYSTEM, and has actions similar to adrenalin [ISV *nor-* (a compound derived from another by replacing one or more methyl groups by hydrogen atoms; fr *normal*) + *adrenalin, adrenaline*]

**noradrenergic** /ˌnawrˌadri'nuhjik/ *adj* liberating or activated by (a substance like) noradrenalin ⟨~ *neurones*⟩

¹**Nordic** /'nawdik/ *adj* **1** of a tall, fair, longheaded, blue-eyed physical type characteristic of the Germanic peoples of N Europe, esp Scandinavia **2** of competitive ski events consisting of ski jumping and cross-country racing – compare ALPINE [Fr *nordique*, fr *nord* north, fr OE *north*]

²**Nordic** *n* a person of Nordic physical type or of a supposed Nordic division of the Caucasian race; *esp* one from N Europe

**norepinephrine** /ˌnawepi'nefrin, ˌnawi'pinəfrin/ *n, chiefly NAm* noradrenalin [*nor-* (as in *noradrenalin*) + *epinephrine*]

**Norfolk jacket** /'nawfək/ *n* a man's semifitted belted single-breasted jacket with BOX PLEATS [*Norfolk*, county in E England]

**noria** /'nawriə/ *n* a device consisting of a wheel with buckets attached to its rim, used esp in primitive irrigation systems [Sp, fr Ar *nā'ūrah*]

**norland** /'nawlənd/ *n, chiefly dial* the northland

---

| | | | |
|---|---|---|---|
| **nonstriking** *adj* | **nontechnical** *adj* | **nontropical** *adj* | **nonvintage** *adj* |
| **nonstructural** *adj* | **nontechnological** *adj* | **nontuberculous** *adj* | **nonviolation** *n* |
| **nonstructured** *adj* | **nonteleological** *adj* | **nontypical** *adj* | **nonviral** *adj* |
| **nonsubscriber** *n* | **nontemporal** *adj* | **nonunderstandable** *adj* | **nonvirgin** *adj or n* |
| **nonsubsidized** *adj* | **nontenured** *adj* | **nonuniform** *adj* | **nonvirulent** *adj* |
| **nonsuccess** *n* | **nonterminal** *adj* | **nonuniformity** *n* | **nonviscous** *adj* |
| **nonsugar** *adj or n* | **nonterritorial** *adj* | **nonuniversal** *adj* | **nonvisual** *adj* |
| **nonsuperimposable** *adj* | **nontheatrical** *adj* | **nonuniversity** *adj* | **nonvocal** *adj* |
| **nonsupervisory** *adj* | **nontheistic** *adj* | **nonurban** *adj* | **nonvocational** *adj* |
| **nonsuppression** *n* | **nonthematic** *adj* | **nonurgent** *adj* | **nonvoluntary** *adj* |
| **nonsurgical** *adj* | **nontherapeutic** *adj* | **nonusage** *n* | **nonvoter** *n* |
| **nonsustaining** *adj* | **nonthermal** *adj* | **nonuse** *n* | **nonvoting** *adj or n* |
| **nonsymbiotic** *adj* | **nonthinking** *adj* | **nonuser** *n* | **non-Western** *adj* |
| **nonsymbolic** *adj* | **nonthreatening** *adj* | **nonutilitarian** *adj* | **nonwinner** *n* |
| **nonsymmetric** *adj* | **nontidal** *adj* | **nonutility** *adj or n* | **nonwoody** *adj* |
| **nonsymmetrical** *adj* | **nontotalitarian** *n* | **nonutopian** *adj* | **nonworker** *n* |
| **nonsynchronous** *adj* | **nontoxic** *adj* | **nonvalid** *adj* | **nonworking** *adj* |
| **nonsyntactic** *adj* | **nontoxicity** *n* | **nonvariable** *adj* | **nonyellowing** *adj* |
| **nonsystematic** *adj* | **nontrading** *adj* | **nonvariant** *adj* | |
| **nonsystemic** *adj* | **nontraditional** *adj* | **nonvascular** *adj* | |
| **nontariff** *adj* | **nontransferable** *adj* | **nonvenomous** *adj* | |
| **nontarnishable** *adj* | **nontransparency** *n* | **nonverifiable** *adj* | |
| **nontaxable** *adj* | **nontransparent** *adj* | **nonvibratory** *adj* | |
| **nonteaching** *adj* | **nontransposing** *adj* | **nonviewer** *n* | |

**norm** /nawm/ *n* **1** an authoritative standard; a model **2** a principle or standard of correctness that reflects people's expectation of behaviour, is binding upon the members of a group, and serves to regulate action and judgment **3** the average: e g **3a** a set standard of development or achievement, usu derived from the average achievement of a large group **b** a pattern or trait taken to be typical in the behaviour of a social group **4** *maths* the square root of the sum of the squares of the absolute values of the elements of a MATRIX (set of mathematical elements arranged in rows and columns) or of the components of a VECTOR (quantity having both magnitude and direction) **5** *geology* the theoretical composition of an IGNEOUS (formed by the slow cooling and solidification of molten rock material) rock given in terms of standard minerals [L *norma*, lit., carpenter's square]

**¹normal** /'nawml/ *adj* **1** perpendicular; *esp* perpendicular to a TANGENT (straight line touching a curve at one point only) at the point of its touching **2** conforming to or constituting a norm, rule, or principle; regular, typical **3** occurring naturally ⟨~ *immunity*⟩ **4a** having average intelligence or development **b** free from mental disorder **5a** *of a solution* containing 1 GRAM EQUIVALENT of a dissolved substance per litre of solution **b** *of a* SALT neither basic nor acidic ⟨~ *silver phosphate*⟩ **c** having a structure consisting of atoms arranged in a STRAIGHT CHAIN ⟨~ *pentane*⟩ ⟨~ *butyl alcohol*⟩ **6** *maths & statistics* of, involving, or being a NORMAL CURVE or NORMAL DISTRIBUTION ⟨~ *approximation to the binomial distribution*⟩ [L *normalis*, fr *norma* carpenter's square] – **normally** *adv*, **normality** *n*, **normalcy** *n*

**²normal** *n* **1** a line or plane that is perpendicular to another line, plane, or curve **2** somebody or something that is normal **3** a form or state conforming to or constituting the norm; the standard

**normal curve** *n* the symmetrical bell-shaped curve of a NORMAL DISTRIBUTION

**normal distribution** *n, statistics* a PROBABILITY DENSITY FUNCTION that approximates the distribution of many RANDOM VARIABLES (e g the proportion of outcomes of a particular sort in a large number of independent repetitions of an experiment in which the probabilities remain constant from trial to trial), and that has a symmetrical bell-shaped graph

**normal·ize, -ise** /'nawml,iez/ *vt* **1** to make normal **2** to multiply (e g a VECTOR or mathematical function) by a factor which makes an associated value (e g a norm or INTEGRAL) equal to one – **normalizable** *adj*, **normalization** *n*, **normalizer** *n*

**normal orthogonal** *adj, maths* ORTHONORMAL 1

**normal school** *n* a school for training chiefly elementary teachers, esp in France and formerly in the USA and Canada [trans of Fr *école normale;* fr the first French school of this type being intended to serve as a model]

**Norman** /'nawmən/ *n* **1** a native or inhabitant of Normandy: e g **1a** a member of the Scandinavian people who conquered Normandy in the 10th century **b** a member of the Norman-French people who conquered England in 1066 **2 Norman-French, Norman 2a** the French language of the medieval Normans, as once used in English lawcourts **b** the modern dialect of Normandy **3** a style of architecture characterized, esp in its English form, by semicircular arches and heavy pillars [ME, fr OF *Normant*, fr ON *Northmann-, Northmathr* Norseman, fr *northr* north + *mann-, mathr* man] – **Norman** *adj*

**Normande** /naw'mond (Fr nɔrmãd)/ *adj* cooked with apples, cider, or Calvados ⟨*chicken* ~⟩ [Fr *normande*, fem of *normand* (adj) Norman]

**normative** /'nawmətiv/ *adj* serving as or prescribing a norm; *also* according to a norm [Fr *normatif*, fr *norme* norm, fr L *norma*] – **normatively** *adv*, **normativeness** *n*

**normotensive** /,nawmoh'tensiv/ *adj* having a normal blood pressure for one's age and situation [*normal* + *-o-* + *tension* + *-ive*] – **normotensive** *n*

**normothermia** /,nawmoh'thuhmyə/ *n* normal body temperature [NL, fr *normalis* normal + *-o-* + *-thermia* -thermy] – **normothermic** *adj*

**'norm-,referenced** *adj* being a system of marking GCE O level and CSE examinations in which each of seven grades is awarded to a specified percentage of the candidates – compare CRITERION-REFERENCED

**¹Norse** /naws/ *n* **1** *taking pl vb* the Scandinavians; *specif* the Norwegians **2a** (the older forms of) the language of Norway **b** NORTH GERMANIC (group of Scandinavian languages) [prob fr obs D *noorsch,* adj, Norwegian, Scandinavian, alter. of obs D *noordsch* northern, fr D *noord* north; akin to OE *north*]

**²Norse** *adj* Scandinavian; *esp* of ancient Scandinavia or Norway

**Norseman** /'nawsmən/ *n* a native or inhabitant of ancient Scandinavia

**¹north** /nawth/ *adv* to, towards, or in the north [ME, fr OE; akin to OHG *nord* north, Gk *nerteros* lower, infernal]
*synonyms* Clear divisions of the earth's surface, especially political ones, are often called **north, south, east,** and **west,** while vaguer ones are **northern, southern, eastern,** and **western.** Compare ⟨**South African**⟩ ⟨**Southern England**⟩ ⟨**the North Pole**⟩ ⟨**Northern Europe**⟩ ⟨**East Germany**⟩ ⟨**Eastern countries**⟩.

**²north** *adj* **1** situated towards or at the north ⟨*the* ~ *face of the Eiger*⟩ **2** coming from the north ⟨*a* ~ *wind*⟩

**³north** *n* **1** the direction of the NORTH POLE of the earth; *also* the compass point that corresponds to this direction and is directly opposite to south **2** *often cap* regions or countries lying to the north of a specified or implied point of orientation; *also, taking sing or pl vb* the inhabitants of these regions: e g **2a** the part of England lying north of the Humber **b** the part of the USA lying north of the Ohio river and Maryland; *esp* the states north of the MASON-DIXON LINE (S border of Pennsylvania) which fought against the slave-owning southern states during the American Civil War **3** the left side of a church looking towards the altar from the NAVE (main body of a church) **4** *often cap* **4a** the one of four positions at 90-degree intervals that lies to the north or opposite South **b** a person (e g a bridge player) occupying the North in the course of a specified activity ☐ (2) usu + *the*

**northbound** /'nawth,bownd/ *adj* travelling, heading, or leading north ⟨*the* ~ *carriageway is closed for repair*⟩

**north by east** *adj, adv, or n* (from, towards, or in the direction of) the compass point that is one point east of due north; 11° 15′ clockwise from north

**north by west** *adj, adv, or n* (from, towards, or in the direction of) the compass point that is one point west of due north; 348° 45′ clockwise from north

**'north-,countryman, fem north-countrywoman** *n* an English person from north of the Humber

**¹northeast** /nawth'eest/ *adv* to, towards, or in the northeast ⟨*heading* ~⟩

**²northeast** *n* **1** the compass point midway between north and east; *also* the general direction to which this corresponds **2** *often cap the* regions or countries lying to the northeast of a specified or implied point of orientation; *esp, Br* the northeast of England, esp Northumberland and Durham – **northeastward** *adj or n*, **northeastwards** *adv*

**³northeast** *adj* **1** coming from the northeast ⟨*a* ~ *wind*⟩ **2** situated towards or at the northeast ⟨*the* ~ *corner*⟩

**northeast by east** *adj, adv, or n* (from, towards, or in the direction of) the compass point that is one point east of northeast; 56° 15′ clockwise from north

**northeast by north** *adj, adv, or n* (from, towards, or in the direction of) the compass point that is one point north of northeast; 33° 45′ clockwise from north

**¹northeasterly** /nawth'eestəli/ *adj or adv* situated towards, belonging to, or coming from the northeast; northeast ⟨*in a* ~ *direction*⟩

**²northeasterly, northeaster** /-'eestə/ *n* a strong wind from the northeast [²*northeast* + *-erly* (as in *easterly*)]

**northeastern** /nawth'eest(ə)n/ *adj* **1** *often cap* (characteristic) of a region conventionally designated Northeast **2** northeast [²*northeast* + *-ern* (as in *eastern*)] – **northeasternmost** *adj*

**Northeasterner** /nawth'eestənə/ *n* a native or inhabitant of a northeastern region

**¹northerly** /'nawdhəli/ *adj or adv* situated towards, belonging to, or coming from the north; north ⟨*the* ~ *border*⟩ [²*north* + *-erly* (as in *easterly*)]

**²northerly, NAm also norther** /'nawdhə/ *n* a wind from the north

**¹northern** /'nawdhən/ *adj* **1a** *often cap* (characteristic) of a region conventionally designated North **b** of or constituting a northern dialect, esp that of England north of the Humber **2a** lying or directed towards the north **b** coming from the north ⟨~ *wind*⟩ **3** north of the CELESTIAL EQUATOR *synonyms* see ¹NORTH [ME *northerne*, fr OE; akin to OHG *nordrōni* northern, OE *north* north] – **northernmost** *adj*

**²northern** *n, often cap* **1** British English as spoken north of the Humber **2** the dialect of English spoken in the NE USA roughly between the Mississippi, the Canadian border, and the Atlantic

**Northerner** /'nawdhənə/ *n* a native or inhabitant of the North

**Northernism** /'nawdhəniz(ə)m/ *n* a word, phrase, expression, or pronunciation characteristic of the north of England

**northern lights** *n pl* AURORA BOREALIS

**North Germanic** *n* a group of Germanic languages comprising the Scandinavian languages including Icelandic and Faroese

**northing** /'nawthing/ *n* 1 distance due north in latitude from the preceding point of measurement 2 northerly progress

**northland** /'nawthlənd, -,land/ *n, often cap, poetic* land in the north; the north of a country

**Northman** /'nawthmən/ *n* a Norseman

**,north-north'east** *adj, adv, or n* (from, towards, or in the direction of) the compass point that is midway between north and northeast; 22° 30' clockwise from north

**,north-north'west** *adj, adv, or n* (from, towards, or in the direction of) the compass point that is midway between north and northwest; 337° 30' clockwise from north

**north pole** *n* 1a *often cap N&P* the northernmost point of the earth's axis of rotation; *also* the corresponding point of a celestial body (e g a planet) other than the earth **b** the northernmost point on the CELESTIAL SPHERE (imaginary sphere surrounding earth on whose surface the stars, planets, etc appear to be placed), about which the stars seem to revolve 2 the northward-pointing pole of a magnet

**North Star** *n* POLE STAR

**¹Northumbrian** /naw'thumbri·ən/ *adj* 1 of ancient Northumbria, its people, or their dialect 2 (characteristic) of Northumberland, its people, or their dialect [obs *Northumber* inhabitant of England north of the river Humber, fr ME *Northhumbre*, fr OE *Northhymbre*, pl]

**²Northumbrian** *n* 1 a native or inhabitant of ancient Northumbria 2 a native or inhabitant of Northumberland 3a the OLD ENGLISH dialect of Northumbria **b** the English dialect of modern Northumberland

**¹northward** /'nawthwəd/ *adj* moving or extending northwards

**²northward** *n* the northward direction or part; the north ⟨*sail to the ~*⟩

**northwards** /'nawthwədz/ *adv* towards the north

**¹northwest** /nawth'west/ *adv* to, towards, or in the northwest ⟨*lies 25 miles ~ of London*⟩

**²northwest** *n* 1 the compass point midway between north and west; *also* the general direction to which this corresponds 2 *often cap* *the* regions or countries lying to the northwest of a specified or implied point of orientation; *esp, Br* the northwest of England, esp Lancashire and the Lake District – **northwestward** *adj or n*, **northwestwards** *adv*

**³northwest** *adj* 1 coming from the northwest ⟨*a ~ wind*⟩ 2 situated towards or at the northwest ⟨*the ~ Passage*⟩

**northwest by north** *adj, adv, or n* (from, towards, or in the direction of) the compass point that is one point north of northwest; 326° 15' clockwise from north

**northwest by west** *adj, adv, or n* (from, towards, or in the direction of) the compass point that is one point west of northwest; 303° 45' clockwise from north

**¹northwesterly** /nawth'westəli/ *adv or adj* situated towards, belonging to, or coming from the northwest; northwest

**²northwesterly, northwester** /-'westə/ *n* a strong wind from the northwest [²*northwest* + *-erly* (as in *westerly*)]

**northwestern** /nawth'west(ə)n/ *adj* 1 *often cap* (characteristic) of a region conventionally designated Northwest 2 northwest [²*northwest* + *-ern* (as in *western*)] – **northwesternmost** *adj*

**Northwesterner** /nawth'westənə/ *n* a native or inhabitant of a northwestern region

**nortriptyline** /naw'triptəleen/ *n* an antidepressant drug, $C_{19}H_{21}N$ [*nor-* (as in *noradrenalin*) + *-triptyline* (as in *amitriptyline*)]

**Norway maple** /'naw·way/ *n* a European maple (*Acer platanoides*) with dark green or often reddish or red veined leaves [*Norway*, country in NW Europe]

**Norway rat** *n* BROWN RAT

**Norway spruce** *n* a widely planted spruce (*Picea abies*) that is native to N Europe and has a pyramidal shape, spreading branches, dark leaves, and long pendulous cones

**Norwegian** /naw'weejən/ *n* 1 a native or inhabitant of Norway 2 the Germanic language of the Norwegians [ML *Norvegia, Norwegia* Norway] – **Norwegian** *adj*

**nos-** /nos-/, **noso-** *comb form* disease ⟨*nosology*⟩ [Gk, fr *nosos*]

**¹nose** /nohz/ *n* 1a the part of the face that bears the nostrils and covers the front part of the nasal cavity; *broadly* this part together with the nasal cavity **b** the front part of the head above or projecting beyond the muzzle; a snout, muzzle 2a the sense of smell ⟨*a dog with a good ~*⟩ **b** an aroma, bouquet (e g of wine) 3 the organ of smell in VERTEBRATE animals 4a the projecting part or front end of something (e g a car or aeroplane) **b** the projecting or working end of a tool 5a the nose as a symbol of undue curiosity or interference ⟨*why can't you keep your big ~ out of things?*⟩ **b** instinctive ability; *esp* a knack for detecting what is latent or concealed ⟨*a reporter with a good ~ for a story*⟩ ⟨*a keen ~ for absurdity*⟩ [ME, fr OE *nosu*; akin to OHG *nasa* nose, L *nasus*] – **by a nose** by a very narrow margin ⟨*won by a nose*⟩ – **cut off one's nose to spite one's face** to harm one's own interests by a vengeful action – **follow one's nose** to go on a straight or obvious course – **get up someone's nose** *informal* to irritate somebody intensely – **keep one's nose clean** to stay out of trouble – **keep somebody's/one's nose to the grindstone** to (force somebody to) work unremittingly – **lead by the nose** to have complete control over; dominate – **look down one's nose at** to be disdainful of – **on the nose 1** at or to a target point; exactly, precisely 2 to win only – used of horse or dog racing bets – **pay through the nose** to pay an exorbitant price – **poke one's nose into** to meddle in or interfere with (something which does not concern one) – **put somebody's nose out of joint** to cause somebody offence, esp by gaining something to which he/she feels entitled – **turn one's nose up (at)** to be disdainful or dismissive (of) – **under one's nose** in an obvious place – see also **no** SKIN **off somebody's nose**

**²nose** *vt* 1 to detect (as if) by smell; scent 2 to push (as if) with the nose ⟨*the dog ~d the door open*⟩ 3 to touch or rub with the nose; nuzzle ⟨*the horse ~d him curiously*⟩ ~ *vi* 1 to use the nose in examining, smelling, showing affection, etc; sniff, nuzzle 2a to search or look impertinently; pry – often + *into* ⟨*stop nosing into other people's affairs*⟩ **b** to search or look inquisitively – usu + *about* or *around* ⟨*liked to ~ around junk shops in search of bargains*⟩ 3 to move ahead slowly or cautiously ⟨*the car ~d out into the traffic*⟩

**nose bag** /'nohz ,bag/ *n* a usu canvas bag used for feeding an animal (e g a horse) that is fastened round the head and covers the nose

**noseband** /'nohz,band/ *n* the part of a bridle or halter that passes over a horse's nose

**nosebleed** /'nohz,bleed/ *n* an attack of bleeding from the nose

**nose cone** *n* a protective cone constituting the forward end of a projectile (e g a rocket or missile) or an aircraft

**nosed** /nohzd/ *adj* having a (specified kind of) nose – usu in combination ⟨*snub-nosed*⟩

**nose dive** *n* 1 a downward nose-first plunge of an aircraft or other flying object 2 a sudden dramatic drop ⟨*the nosedive in standards of advocacy by barristers – New Statesman*⟩ – **nose-dive** *vb*

**nosegay** /'nohz,gay/ *n* a small bunch of flowers; a posy [¹*nose* + E dial. *gay* ornament]

**nosepiece** /'nohz,pees/ *n* 1 a piece of armour for protecting the nose 2 the end piece of a microscope to which the lens nearest the specimen is attached 3 the bridge of a pair of glasses

**nosey** /'nohzi/ *adj* nosy

**¹nosh** /nosh/ *vb, informal vt* to chew, munch ~ *vi* to eat [Yiddish *nashn*, fr MHG *naschen* to eat on the sly] – **nosher** *n*

**²nosh** *n, informal* 1 food; *esp* food in sufficient quantities for a meal 2 a meal

**,no-'show** *n* a person who books space on a train, ship, or aeroplane but neither uses nor cancels the booking; *broadly, chiefly NAm* one who fails to show up [¹*no* + *show*, vb (as in *show up*)]

**'nosh-,up** *n, Br informal* a large meal

**,no-'side** *n* the end of a rugby match

**nosing** /'nohzing/ *n* the usu rounded edge of a stair tread that projects over the riser; *also* any of various similar rounded projections [¹*nose* + *-ing*]

**noso-** – see NOS-

**nosology** /no'soləji/ *n* 1 a branch of medical science that deals with the classification of diseases 2 a classification or list of diseases [NL *nosologia*, fr *nos-* + *-logia* -logy] – **nosological, nosologic** *adj*, **nosologically** *adv*

**nostalgia** /no'staljə/ *n* 1 homesickness 2 a wistful or excessively sentimental yearning for something past or irrecoverable [NL, fr Gk *nostos* return home + NL *-algia;* akin to OE ge*nesan* to survive, Skt *nasate* he approaches] – **nostalgic** *adj,* **nostalgically** *adv*

**nostoc** /'nostok/ *n* any of a genus (*Nostoc*) of BLUE-GREEN ALGAE that are able to use atmospheric nitrogen [coined by Theophrastus Paracelsus †1541 Swiss alchemist & physician]

**nostril** /'nostril, nostrəl/ *n* **1** either of the two external openings of the nose, through which air is drawn; *broadly* an external opening of the nose with the adjoining passage on the same side **2** either fleshy side wall of the nose ⟨*wore a jewel in her left* ~⟩ [ME *nosethirl,* fr OE *nosthyrl,* fr *nosu* nose + *thyrel* hole; akin to OE *thurh* through]

**nostrum** /'nostrəm/ *n* **1** a medicine of secret composition recommended by its preparer usu without proof of its effectiveness **2** a facile or questionable remedy or scheme; a panacea ⟨*the party offers no simple ~ for social injustice*⟩ [L, neut of *noster* our, ours, fr *nos* we – more at US]

**nosy, nosey** /'nohzi/ *adj, informal* showing undue curiosity; inquisitive, prying [¹*nose* + ¹*-y*] – **nosily** *adv,* **nosiness** *n*

**nosy parker** /'pahkə/ *n, Br informal* an over-inquisitive or meddlesome person; a busybody [prob fr the name *Parker*]

**not** /not/ *adv* **1** – used to negate a word or word group ⟨~ *thirsty*⟩ ⟨~ *George*⟩ ⟨~ *to complain*⟩; often *n't* after auxiliary verbs ⟨*can't go*⟩ **2** – used to negate a preceding word or word group ⟨*will it rain? I hope* ~⟩ ⟨*are you ready? If* ~*, hurry up*⟩ **3** – used to give force to an opposite meaning ⟨~ *without reason*⟩ ⟨~ *a few of us*⟩; compare NO 1 [ME, alter. of *nought,* fr *nought,* pron – more at NAUGHT] – **not a** not even one – **not at all** you're welcome – used in answer to praise, thanks, or apology ⟨"*sorry to trouble you."* "*Not at all!*"⟩ – **not half 1** not nearly ⟨*not half long enough*⟩ **2** *informal* not at all ⟨*that tie's* not half *bad; where did you get it?*⟩ **3** *slang* very much; totally ⟨*didn't* half *scold us*⟩ ⟨*are you busy?* Not half!⟩ – **not that** yet we must not infer that ⟨*if he refuses,* not that *he will, we must try elsewhere*⟩

**NOT** *n* a logical OPERATOR (symbol denoting an operation to be performed) producing a statement that is the inverse of a given statement [*not*]

**not-** /noht-/, **noto-** *comb form* back; back part ⟨*noto*chord⟩ [NL, fr Gk *nōt-, nōto-,* fr *nōton, nōtos* back – more at NATES]

**nota** /'nohtə/ *pl of* NOTUM (top surface of a segment of an insect's body)

**nota bene** /,nohtə 'benay/ *interj* – used to call attention to something important [L, mark well]

**notabilia** /,nohtə'biliə/ *n pl* things (eg sayings) worthy of note [L, neut pl of *notabilis* notable, fr *notare* to note]

**notability** /,nohtə'biləti/ *n* **1** a distinguished or prominent person; a notable **2** the state or quality of being notable

¹**notable** /'nohtəbl/ *adj* **1** worthy of note; remarkable **2** distinguished, prominent *synonyms* see NOTEWORTHY – **notableness** *n,* **notably** *adv*

²**notable** *n* **1** a prominent person **2** *pl, often cap* a group of people summoned, esp formerly in France, when it was a monarchy, to act as a deliberative body

**notaphily** /noh'tafəli/ *n* the hobby of collecting BANK NOTES [L *nota* mark, token, note + E *-phily* liking for, fr NL *-philia*]

**notarial** /,noh'teəri·əl/ *adj* (characteristic) of a notary; *also* drawn up or executed by a notary – **notarially** *adv*

**notar·ize, -ise** /'nohtə,riez/ *vt, chiefly NAm* to validate (a legal document) as a notary

**notary** /'nohtəri/, **notary public** *n, pl* **notaries, notaries public, notary publics** a public officer appointed to administer oaths and draw up and authenticate documents [ME *notary* clerk, notary public, fr L *notarius* clerk, secretary, fr *notarius* of shorthand, fr *nota* note, shorthand character]

**notate** /noh'tayt/ *vt* to put into notation [back-formation fr *notation*]

**notation** /noh'taysh(ə)n/ *n* **1** a (representation of something by) a system or set of marks, signs, symbols, figures, characters, or abbreviated expressions used in maths, music, etc to express quantities or elements **2** *chiefly NAm* an annotation, note [L *notation-, notatio,* fr *notatus,* pp of *notare* to note] – **notational** *adj*

¹**notch** /noch/ *n* **1a** a V-shaped indentation **b** a slit or cut made to serve as a record **2** a degree, step ⟨*a novel that is* ~*es above the average product*⟩ **3** *NAm* a deep narrow pass; a gap [perh alter. (by incorrect division of *an otch*) of (assumed) *otch,* fr MF *oche*] – **notched** *adj,* **notchy** *adj*

²**notch** *vt* **1** to make a notch in **2a** to mark or record (as if) by a notch – often + *up* ⟨*a man who has* ~ed *up five wives in his*

*life – Nation Review (Melbourne)*⟩ **b** to score, achieve – usu + *up* ⟨*he's hoping to* ~ *up a string of winners – Evening Mail [Birmingham]*⟩

¹**note** /noht/ *vt* **1a** to take due or special notice of ⟨*please* ~ *that payment in full is enclosed*⟩ **b** to notice, observe ⟨*you may have* ~d *my late arrival*⟩ ⟨~d *that he wore a monocle*⟩ **c** to record in writing; make a note of – often + *down* ⟨~d *down her phone number*⟩ **2a** to make special mention of; remark upon ⟨*the speaker* ~d *his outstanding record*⟩ **b** to indicate, show ⟨*records fail to* ~ *what became of him*⟩ [ME *noten,* fr OF *noter,* fr L *notare* to mark, note, fr *nota*] – **noter** *n*

²**note** *n* **1a(1)** a sound having a definite pitch **a(2)** a call, sound; *esp* the musical call of a bird **b** a written symbol used to indicate the duration and pitch of a tone by its shape and position on the musical stave **c** a key of a piano, organ, etc **2a** a characteristic feature (eg of smell or flavour); an element ⟨*the essential* ~s *of his satire* – F R Leavis⟩ **b** a mood, quality ⟨*the talks ended on an optimistic* ~⟩ **c** a quality which reveals an emotion ⟨*a* ~ *of sadness in her voice*⟩ **3a(1)** a memorandum **a(2)** a condensed or informal record **b(1)** a brief comment or explanation ⟨*programme* ~s *for a concert*⟩ **b(2)** a printed comment or reference set apart from the text of a book **c(1)** a written promise to pay a debt **c(2)** a piece of paper money **d(1)** a short informal letter **d(2)** a formal diplomatic communication **e** a scholarly or technical essay shorter than an article and restricted in scope **4a** distinction, reputation ⟨*a figure of international* ~⟩ **b** attention, notice ⟨*took full* ~ *of the proceedings*⟩ **5** *obs* a melody, song [L *nota* mark, character, written note]

**notebook** /'noht,book/ *n* a book for notes or memoranda

**noted** /'nohtid/ *adj* well-known, famous ⟨*a* ~ *authority on tropical diseases*⟩ *synonyms* see NOTEWORTHY – **notedly** *adv,* **notedness** *n*

**notelet** /'nohtlit/ *n* a small folded card with a design on the front, used for writing a short informal letter

**notepad** /'noht,pad/ *n* a pad of paper for notes or memoranda

**notepaper** /'noht,paypə/ *n* writing paper suitable for letters

¹**note-row** *n* TONE-ROW (group of 12 notes in a fixed order which forms the basis of a composition in TWELVE-TONE music) – compare SERIALISM

**noteworthy** /'noht,wuhdhi/ *adj* worthy of or attracting attention; notable ⟨*made* ~ *contributions to nuclear physics*⟩ – **noteworthily** *adv,* **noteworthiness** *n*

*synonyms* **Noteworthy, notable, noted,** and **notorious** should not be confused. **Noteworthy** and **notable** suggest some quality of excellence worthy of being remarked; **notable** often stresses a particular feature which impresses, while **noteworthy** is more often applied to people and their activities ⟨*her* **notable** *good humour*⟩ ⟨*a* **noteworthy** *theologian*⟩. **Noted** implies fame without necessarily connoting worth. **Notorious** implies disreputable fame.

¹**nothing** /'nuthing/ *pron* **1** not any thing; no thing ⟨~ *greasy*⟩ ⟨~ *much to eat*⟩ ⟨*leaves* ~ *to the imagination*⟩ ⟨*eats next to* ~⟩ ⟨*it's* ~ *to do with you*⟩ ⟨*he's* ~ *else but a common crook*⟩ **2a** no part ⟨~ *of the fine lady about her*⟩ **b** something of no consequence ⟨*it means* ~ *to me*⟩ ⟨*thinks* ~ *of walking 20 miles*⟩ ⟨*would be* ~ *without his title*⟩ **3** no truth or value ⟨*there's* ~ *in this rumour*⟩ – compare FOR NOTHING *synonyms* see ¹ZERO [ME, fr OE *nān thing, nāthing,* fr *nān* no + *thing* – more at NONE] – **nothing doing** by no means; definitely not – **nothing for it** no alternative course – **nothing if not** decidedly; ABOVE ALL – **nothing to** not to be compared with

²**nothing** *adv* not at all; in no degree ⟨~ *like as cold*⟩

³**nothing** *n* **1a** something that does not exist **b** NOTHINGNESS 3b **2** someone or something of no or slight importance, value, or size ⟨*a* ~ *of a dress*⟩ ⟨*whisper sweet* ~s⟩

⁴**nothing** *adj* **1** of no account; worthless **2** of no (religious or political) affiliation ⟨*he's a Catholic and I'm* ~⟩

**nothingness** /'nuthingnis/ *n* **1** the quality or state of being nothing: eg **1a** nonexistence **b** utter insignificance or worthlessness **2** something insignificant or worthless **3a** a void, emptiness **b** *philosophy* a state opposed to and devoid of being; *esp* meaninglessness

¹**notice** /'nohtis/ *n* **1a** warning or announcement of a future occurrence ⟨*these rules are subject to change without* ~⟩ **b(1)** notification by one of the parties to an agreement or relation of intention of terminating it at a specified time ⟨*the company gave* ~ *to half its workforce*⟩ ⟨*gave the landlord three weeks'* ~⟩ **b(2)** the condition of being warned or notified – usu in *on notice* **2a** attention, heed ⟨*take no* ~ *of him, he's only teasing*⟩

⟨*his play attracted little public* ~⟩ **b** polite or favourable attention; favour ⟨*she had very little* ~ *from any but him* – Jane Austen⟩ **3** a written or printed announcement ⟨*put a* ~ *in the local paper*⟩ **4** a short critical account or examination (e g of a play); a review [ME, fr MF, acquaintance, fr L *notitia* knowledge, acquaintance, fr *notus* known, fr pp of *noscere* to come to know – more at KNOW] – **take notice of** to observe or treat with special attention

²**notice** *vt* **1** to comment upon; refer to **2** to acknowledge acquaintance with ⟨*were* ~d *only by a curtsey* – Jane Austen⟩ ⟨*scarcely deigned to* ~ *her*⟩ **3** to take notice of; mark ⟨*didn't* ~ *that he left early*⟩ **4** *chiefly NAm* to give a formal notice to **synonyms** see ¹SEE

**noticeable** /'nohtisəbl/ *adj* **1** worthy of notice **2** capable of being noticed; perceptible – **noticeably** *adv*

'**notice-board** *n, chiefly Br* a board on which notices may be (temporarily) displayed

**notifiable** /'nohti,fie-əbl/ *adj, of a disease* required by law to be reported to official health authorities

**notification** /,nohtifi'kaysh(ə)n/ *n* **1** the act or an instance of notifying **2** something in writing that gives notice

**notify** /'nohti,fie/ *vt* **1** to make known; announce ⟨*he notified his intention to sue*⟩; *specif* to report (a case of disease) **2** to give (official) notice to; inform ⟨*if you have any complaints, please* ~ *the manager*⟩ [ME *notifien*, fr MF *notifier* to make known, fr LL *notificare*, fr L *notus* known] – **notifier** *n*

,**no-'tillage** *n* a system of farming that consists of planting a narrow slit trench without tilling or cultivating the soil and with the use of herbicides to suppress weeds

**notion** /'nohsh(ə)n/ *n* **1a(1)** a broad general concept **a(2)** an idea, conception ⟨*had no* ~ *of the poem's meaning*⟩ **a(3)** a usu vague opinion or belief; an impression ⟨*it was his* ~ *that everyone else was wasteful*⟩ **b** a whim, fancy ⟨*a sudden* ~ *to shout "fire!"*⟩ **2** *pl, chiefly NAm* small articles of merchandise (e g haberdashery) **synonyms** see IDEA [L *notion-, notio*, fr *notus*, pp of *noscere*]

**notional** /'nohsh(ə)nl/ *adj* **1** theoretical, speculative ⟨*figures calculated on the lines of a* ~ *profit for the coming year*⟩ **2** existing only in the mind; imaginary **3** of or being a notion or idea; conceptual **4** *of a word* having an actual meaning in a sentence rather than a mere grammatical function ⟨*has is* ~ *in* he has luck, *relational in* he has gone⟩ **5** *chiefly NAm* given to fanciful moods or ideas – **notionally** *adv*, **notionality** *n*

**noto-** – see NOT-

**notochord** /'nohtə,kawd/ *n* a longitudinal flexible rod of cells that forms the supporting axis of the body in the lowest CHORDATES (large group of animals including those with backbones and lower forms without a true skeleton) (e g a lancelet or a lamprey) and in the embryos of the higher VERTEBRATE animals [*not-* + L *chorda* cord – more at CORD] – **notochordal** *adj*

**notoriety** /,nohtə'rie-əti/ *n* **1** the quality or state of being notorious ⟨*a writer who enjoys considerable* ~⟩ **2** a notorious person ⟨*love to have notabilities and* notorieties *under one roof* – TLS⟩ [MF or ML; MF *notorieté*, fr ML *notorietat-, notorietas*, fr *notorius*]

**notorious** /noh'tawri·əs/ *adj* **1** well-known, esp for a specified quality or trait ⟨*copper is a* ~ *conductor of heat*⟩ **2** widely and unfavourably known ⟨*a district* ~ *for crime*⟩ ⟨*a* ~ *gambler*⟩ □ compare INFAMOUS **synonyms** see NOTEWORTHY [ML *notorius*, fr LL *notorium* information, indictment, fr neut of (assumed) LL *notorius* making known, fr L *notus*, pp of *noscere* to come to know – more at KNOW] – **notoriously** *adv*, **notoriousness** *n*

**notornis** /noh'tawnis/ *n, pl* **notornis** any of a genus (*Notornis*) of flightless New Zealand birds [NL, genus name, fr Gk *notos* south + *ornis* bird]

,**no-'trump** *adj* being a bid, contract, or hand in bridge suitable to play without any suit being trumps – **no-trump** *n*

**notum** /'nohtəm/ *n, pl* **nota** /'nohtə/ the top surface of a segment of an insect [NL, fr Gk *nōton* back – more at NATES]

¹**notwithstanding** /,notwidh'standing, -with-/ *prep* IN SPITE OF ⟨*buffaloes or Aztecs* ~ – SEU W⟩ [ME *notwithstonding*, fr *not* + *withstonding*, prp of *withstonden* to withstand]

²**notwithstanding** *adv* nevertheless

³**notwithstanding** *conj* although

**nougat** /'nugət, 'nooh,gah/ *n* a sweetmeat of nuts or fruit pieces in a chewy sugar paste [Fr, fr Prov, fr OProv *nogat*, fr *noga* nut, fr L *nuc-, nux* – more at NUT]

**nought** /nawt/ *n* **1** the arithmetical symbol 0; zero – see NUMBER table **2** *chiefly archaic or poetic* naught **synonyms** see ¹ZERO

**noughts and crosses** *n taking sing or pl vb* a game in which two players alternately put noughts and crosses in usu nine square spaces arranged in a square, in an attempt to get a row of three noughts or three crosses

**noumenon** /'noohmi,non, 'now-/ *n, pl* **noumena** /-nə/ a THING-IN-ITSELF as opposed to a PHENOMENON (thing as it appears) – used in the philosophy of Kant [Ger, fr Gk *nooumenon* that which is apprehended by thought, fr neut of prp passive of *noein* to think, conceive, fr *nous* mind] – **noumenal** *adj*

**noun** /nown/ *n* a word that is the name of a topic for discussion (e g a person, place, thing, substance, or state) [ME *nowne*, fr AF *noun* name, noun, fr OF *nom*, fr L *nomen* – more at NAME]

    **usage** English nouns are often used as adjectives to precede and qualify other nouns. While nobody objects to this practice in moderation, as with the use of **apple** and **family** in ⟨**apple** *dumpling*⟩ ⟨*resigned for* **family** *reasons*⟩, newspaper headlines sometimes carry it to an extreme degree ⟨*Tourist Holiday Coach Crash Disaster*⟩ which should be avoided in general writing.

**noun phrase** *n* **1** a constituent of a sentence (e g "the big bad wolf") consisting of a noun with or without modifiers **2** a constituent of a sentence (e g "what she wanted") functioning like a noun

**nourish** /'nurish/ *vt* **1** to nurture, rear **2** to encourage the growth of; foster ⟨*profits that* ~ *criminal activities*⟩ **3a** to supply with nourishment; feed **b** to cherish, entertain ⟨~ed *a faint hope of success*⟩ [ME *nurishen*, fr OF *noriss-*, stem of *norrir*, fr L *nutrire* to suckle, nourish; akin to Gk *nan* to flow, *noteros* damp, L *nare* to swim, Gk *nein*] – **nourisher** *n*

**nourishing** /'nurishing/ *adj* giving nourishment; nutritious

**nourishment** /'nurishmənt/ *n* **1** food, nutriment; *specif* food that provides the materials necessary for healthy life and growth **2** the act of nourishing or the state of being nourished

**nous** /nows/ *n* **1** mind or reason, esp when regarded as the governing principle of the universe **2** *chiefly Br informal* gumption; COMMON SENSE [Gk *noos, nous* mind]

**nouveau riche** /,noohvoh 'reesh (Fr nuvo riʃ)/ *n, pl* **nouveaux riches** /~/ a person who has recently become rich; *esp* one who is regarded as excessively ostentatious and lacking in refinement; a parvenu [Fr, lit., new rich]

**nouveau roman** /,noohvoh roh'monh (Fr nuvo rɔmã)/ *n* (an example of) a form of fiction originating in France in the 1950s that rejects such traditional novelistic features as coherent plot, simple chronology, and rounded characterization, and usu emphasizes its own fictional nature. It includes detailed descriptions of objects reflecting the (abnormal) mental states of characters, and suggests that reality is only a construct of the mind. [Fr, lit., new novel]

**nouvelle cuisine** /,noohvel kwi'zeen (Fr nuvɛl kyizin)/ *n* a style of cooking originating in France that uses high quality ingredients and emphasizes the natural flavours and textures of the food rather than allowing them to be smothered (e g by heavy rich sauces) – compare CUISINE MINCEUR [Fr, lit., new cooking]

**nouvelle vague** /,noohvel 'vahg (Fr nuvɛl vag)/ *n, often cap N&V* NEW WAVE **1** (cinematic movement) [Fr]

**nova** /'nohvə/ *n, pl* **novae** /'nohvie, -vi/ *also* **novas** a previously faint star that as the result of an internal explosion suddenly becomes very bright and then after a few days or weeks fades away to its former obscurity [NL, fem of L *novus* new] – **novalike** *adj*

**novaculite** /noh'vakyooliet/ *n* a very hard fine-grained silica-containing rock used for WHETSTONES (stones on which blades are sharpened) [L *novacula* razor]

**novation** /noh'vaysh(ə)n/ *n* the substitution of a new legal obligation for an old one (e g by substituting a new contract, creditor, or debtor for a previous one) that is carried out with the consent of all parties concerned [LL *novation-, novatio* renewal, legal novation, fr L *novatus*, pp of *novare* to make new, fr *novus*]

¹**novel** /'novl/ *adj* **1** new and unlike anything previously known **2** original and striking, esp in conception or style ⟨*a* ~ *scheme to collect money*⟩ **synonyms** see ¹NEW [ME, fr MF, new, fr L *novellus*, fr dim. of *novus* new – more at NEW]

²**novel** *n* **1** an invented prose narrative that is usu long and complex and deals esp with human experience and social behaviour through a usu connected sequence of events **2** *the* lite-

rary type constituted by novels ⟨*was the 19th century the great age of the ∼?*⟩ [It *novella*] – **novelistic** *adj*

**novelette** /ˌnovl'et/ *n* **1** a short novel or long short story **2** *Br* a sentimental novel without pretensions to literary merit

**novelettish** /ˌnovl'etish/ *adj* (characteristic) of a novelette; *esp* sentimental

**novelist** /'novəlist/ *n* a writer of novels

**novel·ize, -ise** /'novəliez/ *vt* to convert into the form of a novel ⟨∼ *a play*⟩ – **novelization** *n*

**novella** /no'velə/ *n, pl* **novellas** *also* **novelle** /-li/ **1** a story with a compact and pointed plot **2** a short novel, usu more complex than a short story [It, fr fem of *novello* new, fr L *novellus*]

**novelty** /'nov(ə)lti/ *n* **1** something new and unusual **2** the quality or state of being novel; newness ⟨*the ∼ of solar heating*⟩ ⟨∼ *appeal*⟩ **3** a small manufactured often cheap article intended mainly for personal or household adornment [ME *novelte*, fr MF *noveleté*, fr *novel*]

**¹November** /noh'vembə, nə-/ *n* the 11th month of the year according to the GREGORIAN CALENDAR (standard Western calendar) – see MONTH table [ME *Novembre*, fr OF, fr L *November* (ninth month of the ancient Roman calendar), fr *novem* nine – more at NINE]

**²November** – a communications code word for the letter *n*

**novemdecillion** /ˌnohvemdi'silyən/ *n* – see NUMBER table [L *novemdecim* nineteen (fr *novem* + *decem* ten) + E *-illion* (as in *million*)]

**novena** /noh'veenə/ *n* a Roman Catholic devotion taking place on nine consecutive days and consisting of prayers for the intercession of a particular saint for a special purpose [ML, fr L, fem of *novenus* nine each, fr *novem*]

**novice** /'novis/ *n* **1** a person admitted to probationary membership in a religious order **2** a beginner [ME, fr MF, fr ML *novicius*, fr L, new, inexperienced, fr *novus* – more at NEW]

**novillero** /ˌnohvee'yeəroh/ *n, pl* **novilleros** an aspiring bull-fighter who has not yet attained the rank of matador [Sp, fr *novillo* young bull, fr L *novellus* new – more at NOVEL]

**novitiate** /noh'vishi·ət, -ayt, nə-/ *n* **1** the period or state of being a novice, esp in a religious order **2** a novice **3** the quarters assigned to novices in a religious order [Fr *noviciat*, fr ML *noviciatus*, fr *novicius*]

**novobiocin** /ˌnohvoh'bie·əsin/ *n* an antibiotic drug, $C_{31}H_{36}N_2O_{11}$, that is produced by a bacterium (*Streptomyces spheroides*) [prob fr *nov-* (fr L *novus* new) + *antibiotic* + *streptomycin*]

**novocaine** /'nohvə,kayn/ *n* PROCAINE (drug used in local anaesthetics) [ISV *novo-* (fr L *novus* new) + *cocaine*]

**¹now** /now/ *adv* **1a** at the present time **b** in the immediate past – compare JUST NOW **c** in the time immediately to follow; forthwith ⟨*come in* ∼⟩ ⟨∼ *for tea*⟩ ⟨∼ *to add the flour*⟩ **2** – used with the sense of present time weakened or lost **2a** to introduce an important point or indicate a transition ⟨∼ *if we turn to the next aspect of the problem*⟩ **b** to express command, request, or warning ⟨*oh, come* ∼⟩ ⟨∼, *don't quarrel*⟩ ⟨*be careful* ∼⟩ ⟨∼ *then, what's the matter?*⟩ **3** sometimes – introducing or joining two or more coordinate words or phrases ⟨∼ *one and* ∼ *another*⟩ **4** under the changed or unchanged circumstances ⟨*he'll never believe me* ∼⟩ **5a** at the time referred to ⟨∼ *the trouble began*⟩ **b** up to the present or to the time referred to ⟨*haven't been for years* ∼⟩ [ME, fr OE *nū*; akin to OHG *nū* now, L *nunc*, Gk *nyn*] – **now and again/then** at occasional intervals; from time to time

**²now** *conj* in view of the fact that; since – often + *that* ⟨∼ *that we are here*⟩

**³now** *n* **1** the present time ⟨*been ill up to* ∼⟩ ⟨*goodbye for* ∼⟩ **2** the time referred to ⟨*by* ∼ *the hints and rumours were fairly thick* – *The Economist*⟩

**⁴now** *adj* **1** existing or acting at the present time ⟨*the* ∼ *president*⟩ **2** *informal* excitingly new; up-to-date ⟨∼ *clothes*⟩

**nowadays** /'nowə,dayz/ *adv* in these modern times; today [ME *now a dayes*, fr *¹now* + *a dayes* during the day]

**noway** /'noh,way/, **noways** *adv, formal or archaic* in no way whatever; not at all

**no way** *adv or interj, chiefly NAm informal* – used to express forceful refusal or contradiction ⟨*no pictures in the nude*, ∼ – *Punch*⟩

**Nowell** /noh'el/ *n, archaic* Noel

**¹nowhere** /'noh,weə/ *adv* **1** not anywhere **2** to no purpose or result ⟨*this will get us* ∼⟩ **3** not at all; to no extent ⟨∼ *like ready*⟩ – **nowhere near** not nearly ⟨*you're early; the meal's nowhere near ready*⟩

**²nowhere** *n* **1** a nonexistent place **2** an unknown, distant, or obscure place or state ⟨*rose to fame out of* ∼⟩ – see also MILES from nowhere

**nowheres** /'noh,weəz/ *adv, dial NAm* nowhere

**nowhither** /'noh,widhə/ *adv, archaic* to or towards no place

**nowise** /'noh,wiez/ *adv, archaic* not at all

**nowt** /nowt/ *n, N Eng* nothing, naught ⟨*there's* ∼ *so queer as folk*⟩ [var of *naught*]

**noxious** /'nokshəs/ *adj* **1a** physically harmful or destructive to living things ⟨∼ *industrial wastes*⟩ **b** having a harmful influence on thought or conduct; morally corrupting ⟨∼ *doctrines*⟩ **2** distasteful, objectionable ⟨*a* ∼ *political scandal*⟩ [L *noxius*, fr *noxa* harm; akin to L *nocēre* to harm, *nec-*, *nex* violent death, Gk *nekros* dead body] – **noxiously** *adv*, **noxiousness** *n*

**nozzle** /'nozl/ *n* **1** a projecting part with an opening that usu serves as an outlet: e g **1a** a short tube with a taper or constriction used (e g on a hose or pipe) to speed up or direct a flow of liquid or gas ⟨*fitting a smoke canister to the rear* ∼s – *Flight International*⟩ **b** a part in a rocket engine that accelerates the exhaust gases from the combustion chamber to a high velocity **2** *slang* a nose [dim. of *nose*]

**-n't** /-nt/ *comb form* not ⟨*isn't*⟩ – used to negate verbal auxiliaries

*usage* This contraction should be used only with caution in formal writing.

**nth** /enth/ *adj* **1a** labelled with the letter *n* **b** of or having an unspecified or indefinitely large ORDINAL NUMBER **2** extreme, utmost ⟨*to the* ∼ *degree*⟩ [*n* + *-th*]

**'n-,type** *adj*, of a semiconductor having an excess of electrons – compare P-TYPE [*negative type*]

**nu** /nyooh/ *n* the 13th letter of the Greek alphabet [Gk *ny*, of Sem origin; akin to Heb *nūn* ²nun]

**nuance** /'nyooh,onhs/ (*Fr* nɑ̈:s) *n* **1** a subtle distinction or gradation; a shade ⟨∼s *of meaning that are hard to capture*⟩ **2** a subtle quality; a nicety ⟨*sensitivity to emotional* ∼⟩ [Fr, fr MF, shade of colour, fr *nuer* to make shades of colour, fr *nue* cloud, fr L *nubes*; akin to Gk *nythos* dark] – **nuanced** *adj*

**nub** /nub/ *n* **1** a knob, lump ⟨*a* ∼ *of coal*⟩ **2** a nubbin **3** the gist, crux ⟨*this is the* ∼ *of the matter* – *The Economist*⟩ [alter. of E dial. *knub*, prob fr LG *knubbe*]

**nubbin** /'nubin/ *n, NAm* something (e g an ear of maize) that is small for its kind, stunted, undeveloped, or imperfect [perh dim. of *nub*]

**nubble** /'nubl/ *n* a small knob or lump [dim. of *nub*] – **nubbly** *adj*

**Nubian** /'nyoohbiən/ *n* **1a** a native or inhabitant of Nubia **b** a member of any of the group of Negroid tribes that formed a powerful empire between Egypt and Ethiopia from the 6th to the 14th centuries **2** any of several languages spoken in the central and N Sudan [*Nubia*, region in NE Africa] – **Nubian** *adj*

**nubile** /'n(y)oohbiel/ *adj*, *chiefly humorous*, of a girl of marriageable age; *esp* young and sexually attractive [Fr, fr L *nubilis*, fr *nubere* to marry – more at NUPTIAL] – **nubility** *n*

**nucellus** /nyooh'seləs/ *n, pl* **nucelli** /-li/ the central part of a plant OVULE (immature seed before fertilization) that contains the EMBRYO SAC (female reproductive cell) [NL, fr L *nucella* small nut, fr *nuc-*, *nux* nut] – **nucellar** *adj*

**¹nuchal** /'nyoohkl/ *adj* of or lying in the region of the nape of the neck [ML *nucha* nape, fr Ar *nukhā'* spinal marrow]

**²nuchal** *n* a nuchal anatomical part (e g a scale or bone)

**nucle-** /nyoohkli-/, **nucleo-** *comb form* **1** nucleus ⟨*nucleon*⟩ **2** related to nucleic acid ⟨*nucleoprotein*⟩ [Fr *nuclé-*, *nucléo-*, fr NL *nucleus*]

**¹nuclear** /'nyoohkli·ə/ *adj* **1** of or constituting a cell nucleus **2** of, using, or being the atomic nucleus, atomic energy, the atom bomb, or atomic power

*usage* The pronunciation /'nyoohkli·ə/ rather than /'nyoohkyoolə/ is recommended for BBC broadcasters.

**²nuclear** *n* ATOMIC ENERGY ⟨*if we're going to rely more on* ∼ – Judith Hart⟩

**nuclear disarmament** *n* the reduction or giving up of a country's nuclear weapons

**nuclear family** *n* a family unit that consists of husband, wife, and one or more children and spans two generations – compare EXTENDED FAMILY

**nuclear-free zone** *n* an area in which the use, storage, and transport of all nuclear materials are officially declared prohibited

**nuclear magnetic resonance** *n* the absorption of very high frequency RADIO WAVES by certain atomic nuclei when subjected to a MAGNETIC FIELD; the MAGNETIC RESONANCE of atomic nuclei; *also* a technique for investigating atomic nuclei by observation of this phenomenon

**nuclear membrane** *n* the boundary of a cell nucleus

**nuclear reactor** *n* an apparatus (REACTOR 3b) in which a self-sustaining reaction occurs, involving the breakdown of the nuclei of atoms of uranium, plutonium, etc with the release of large amounts of energy

**nuclear resonance** *n* the absorption of a GAMMA RAY (ELECTROMAGNETIC RADIATION emitted by radioactive atoms) by a nucleus identical to the nucleus that emitted the gamma ray under conditions of MAGNETIC RESONANCE

**nuclear sap** *n* the clear uniform liquid that fills a cell nucleus

**nuclease** /'nyoohkliayz, -ays/ *n* any of various ENZYMES that promote the breakdown of NUCLEIC ACIDS (e g DNA)

**nucleate** /'nyoohkli,ayt, -ət/ *vt* 1 to form into a nucleus; cluster 2 to act as or provide a nucleus for 3 to supply nuclei to ~ *vi* 1 to form a nucleus; cluster 2 to act as a nucleus 3 to begin to form [LL *nucleatus,* pp of *nucleare* to become stony, fr L *nucleus*] – **nucleator** *n,* **nucleation** *n*

**nucleated** /'nyoohkli,aytid/, **nucleate** /-ət, -ayt/ *adj* 1 having a nucleus or nuclei ⟨~ *cells*⟩ 2 **nucleate, nucleated** originating or occurring at nuclei ⟨~ *boiling*⟩ [L *nucleatus,* fr *nucleus* kernel]

**nucleic acid** /nyooh'klayik, -'klee-/ *n* any of various complex acids (e g RNA or DNA) that are composed of a chain of units (NUCLEOTIDES) each of which contains a sugar or derivative of a sugar, PHOSPHORIC ACID, and a chemical BASE containing nitrogen and are found in the cells, esp in the nuclei, of all living things

**nuclein** /'nyoohkli·in/ *n* NUCLEOPROTEIN (principal constituent of hereditary material)

**nucleo-** – see NUCLE-

**nucleocapsid** /,nyoohklioh'kapsid/ *n* the NUCLEIC ACID and surrounding protein coat of a virus

**nucleocytoplasmic** /,nyoohklioh,sietə'plazmik/ *adj* of the nucleus and CYTOPLASM (jellylike material) of a cell

**nucleoid** /'nyoohklioyd/ *n* the DNA-containing area of a PROKARYOTE (having no organized nucleus) cell (e g a bacterium)

**nucleolar organizer** /nyooh'kliələ; *also* ,nyoohkli'ohlə/ *n* NUCLEOLUS ORGANIZER

**nucleolus** /nyooh'klee-ələs, ,nyoohkli'ohləs/ *n, pl* **nucleoli** /-lee, -lie/ a spherical body in the nucleus of cells that are actively synthesizing protein that is associated with a specific part of a CHROMOSOME (strand of gene-carrying material), is probably the site of the synthesis of RIBOSOMES (small specialized cell parts), and contains much RIBOSOMAL RNA [NL, fr L, dim. of *nucleus*] – **nucleolar** *adj*

**nucleolus organizer** *n* the specific part of a CHROMOSOME (strand of gene-carrying material) with which a nucleolus is associated, esp during its reorganization after nuclear division

**nucleon** /'nyoohkli,on/ *n* either of two ELEMENTARY PARTICLES that are found esp in an atomic nucleus: **a** a proton **b** a neutron [ISV] – **nucleonic** *adj*

**nucleonics** /,nyoohkli'oniks/ *n taking sing or pl vb* the physics and technical applications of nucleons, the atomic nucleus, or nuclear energy

**nucleophile** /'nyoohkli·ə,fiel/ *n* a substance (e g a negative ion) with an affinity for atomic nuclei – **nucleophilic** *adj,* **nucleophilicity** *n*

**nucleoplasm** /'nyoohkliə,plaz(ə)m/ *n* the contents of a cell nucleus excluding the CHROMOSOMES (strands of gene-carrying material) [ISV] – **nucleoplasmatic, nucleoplasmic** *adj*

**nucleoprotein** /,nyoohklioh'prohteen/ *n* a complex chemical compound, that consists of a protein (e g a histone) combined with a NUCLEIC ACID (e g DNA) and that is the principal constituent of the hereditary material in CHROMOSOMES (strands of gene-carrying material) [ISV]

**nucleoside** /'nyoohkli·ə,sied/ *n* a chemical compound (e g guanosine or adenosine) that consists of either of two chemical bases (PURINE or PYRIMIDINE) combined with the sugar DEOXYRIBOSE or RIBOSE and is found esp in DNA or RNA – compare NUCLEOTIDE [ISV *nucle-* + *-ose* + *-ide*]

**nucleosynthesis** /,nyoohklioh'sinthəsis/ *n* the production (e g in the sun) of chemical elements from simple components (e g hydrogen nuclei or protons) [NL]

**nucleotidase** /,nyoohkliə'tiedayz, -ays/ *n* an ENZYME that

promotes the breakdown of a nucleotide into a nucleoside and PHOSPHORIC ACID

**nucleotide** /'nyoohkli·ə,tied/ *n* any of several chemical compounds that form the structural units of RNA and DNA and that consist of a nucleoside combined with PHOSPHORIC ACID – compare NUCLEOSIDE [ISV, irreg fr *nucle-* + *-ide*]

**nucleus** /'nyoohkli·əs/ *n, pl* **nuclei** /'nyoohkli,ie, -,ee/ *also* **nucleuses** 1 a small bright dense part of a galaxy or head of a comet 2 a central point, group, or mass about which gathering, concentration, or growth takes place: e g **2a** an ORGANELLE (specialized cell part) that is essential to cell functions (e g reproduction and protein synthesis) and consists of CHROMOSOMES (strands of gene-carrying material) and smaller organelles (e g NUCLEOLI) enclosed in a definite membrane **b** a relatively discrete mass of GREY MATTER or group of NERVE CELLS in the brain or SPINAL CORD **c** a characteristic and stable complex of atoms or groups in a molecule; *esp* a ring ⟨*the naphthalene* ~⟩ **d** the central portion of an atom that has a positive electric charge, comprises nearly all of the atomic mass, and consists of protons and neutrons except in hydrogen which consists of one proton only 3 the peak of greatest prominence in a TONE UNIT [NL, fr L, kernel, dim. of *nuc-, nux* nut – more at NUT]

**nuclide** /'nyoohklied/ *n* a form of atom characterized by the constitution of its nucleus and hence by the number of protons, the number of neutrons, and the energy content [*nucle*us + Gk *eidos* form, species – more at IDOL] – **nuclidic** *adj*

**¹nude** /n(y)oohd/ *adj* 1 lacking something essential to legal validity; *specif, of a contract* not supported by CONSIDERATION (something that makes a promise legally binding) **2a** without clothing; naked **b** without natural covering or adornment; bare **c**(1) of the colour of Caucasian flesh **c**(2) giving the appearance of nudity ⟨*a* ~ *dress*⟩ **d** featuring nudes ⟨*a* ~ *movie*⟩; *also* for nudes ⟨*a* ~ *beach*⟩ **synonyms** see ¹BARE **antonyms** clothed, dressed [L *nudus* naked – more at NAKED] – **nudely** *adv,* **nudeness** *n,* **nudity** *n*

**²nude** *n* **1a** a representation of a nude human figure **b** a nude person 2 the state of being nude ⟨*in the* ~⟩

**nudge** /nuj/ *vt* 1 to touch or push gently; *esp* to catch the attention of or give a hint to by a push of the elbow 2 to approach ⟨*a woman* nudging *forty*⟩ 3 to move (as if) by pushing gently or slowly ⟨nudging *through the tight-packed traffic* – *Sunday Times*⟩ [perh of Scand origin; akin to Icel *nugga* to push, rub, ON *gnaga* to gnaw] – **nudge** *n,* **nudger** *n*

**,nudge-'nudge** *adj* suggestive, salacious [fr the practice of nudging one's listener when telling a risqué story]

**nudibranch** /'n(y)oohdi,brangk/ *n, pl* **nudibranchs** any of a suborder (Nudibranchia of the class Gastropoda, phylum Mollusca) of marine INVERTEBRATE animals related to the snails and whelks that are without a shell in the adult state and without true gills [deriv of L *nudus* + *branchia* gill – more at BRANCHIA] – **nudibranch** *adj,* **nudibranchiate** *adj or n*

**nudism** /'nooh,diz(ə)m, 'nyooh-/ *n* the cult or practice of going nude as much as possible – **nudist** *adj or n*

**Nuffield** /'nufiəld, -feeld/ *adj* of or being any of various modern British school courses (e g in science and languages) embodying the results of research on educational methods [the *Nuffield* Foundation, a charitable trust founded by William Morris, Viscount *Nuffield* †1963 E industrialist & philanthropist]

**nugatory** /'nyoohgət(ə)ri/ *adj, formal* 1 trifling, inconsequential 2 inoperative, invalid [L *nugatorius,* fr *nugatus,* pp of *nugari* to trifle, fr *nugae* trifles]

**nugget** /'nugət/ *n* a solid lump, esp of a precious metal in its natural state [perh dim. of E dial. *nug* lump, block]

**nuggety, nuggetty** /'nugəti/ *adj* 1 composed of or resembling nuggets 2 *Austr & NZ, of a person* thickset, stocky

**nuisance** /'nyoohs(ə)ns/ *n* a person or thing that is annoying, unpleasant, or obnoxious ⟨*found it a* ~ *getting up so early*⟩; *specif* an annoyance that constitutes a legally actionable invasion of the rights of another (e g to fresh air or quiet) [ME *nusaunce,* fr AF, fr OF *nuisir* to harm, fr L *nocēre* – more at NOXIOUS]

**nuke** /nyoohk/ *vt or n, slang* (to destroy with) a nuclear weapon [by shortening & alter.]

**¹null** /nul/ *adj* 1 having no force in law – esp in *null and void* 2 amounting to nothing; nil ⟨*the* ~ *effect of arms embargoes*⟩ 3 without character or distinction ⟨*the intellectually* ~⟩ 4 maths **4a** *of a set* EMPTY 1d (having no elements) **b** having zero as a limit ⟨~ *sequence*⟩ **c** *of a matrix* having all the elements equal to zero **5a** *of an electrical instrument* indicating (e g by a zero reading on a scale) when current or voltage is zero **b** of or being a method of measurement in which an unknown quantity (e g of electric current) is compared with a known quantity of the same kind and found equal by a null instrument [MF *nul*, lit., not any, fr L *nullus*, fr *ne-* not + *ullus* any; akin to L *unus* one – more at NO, ONE] – **null and void** completely invalid

²**null** *n* **1** ZERO 3a(1) **2** a minimum or zero value of an electric current or of a radio signal **3** a meaningless group of letters or characters included in a coded message to hinder interpretation by unauthorized people *synonyms* see ¹ZERO

³**null** *vt* to make null

**nulla** /'nulə/ *n* a zero, nought – used in printing [alter. of ²*null*]

**nullah** /'nulə/ *n, Ind* a gully, ravine [Hindi *nālā*]

**nulla-nulla** /ˌnulə 'nulə/, **nulla** *n* a hardwood club used by Australian aborigines [native name in Australia]

**null hypothesis** *n* a statistical hypothesis to be tested and accepted or rejected in favour of an alternative; *specif* the hypothesis that an observed difference (e g between the MEANS (averages) of two samples) is due to chance alone

**nullify** /'nulifie/ *vt* **1** to make null; *esp* to make legally NULL AND VOID **2** to make worthless, unimportant, or ineffective *synonyms* see ABROGATE [LL *nullificare*, fr L *nullus*] – **nullifier** *n*, **nullification** *n*

**nullipara** /nu'lipərə/ *n* a female that has not borne offspring [NL, fr L *nullus* not any + *-para*] – **nulliparous** *adj*

**nullity** /'nuləti/ *n* **1** the quality or state of being null; *esp* legal invalidity **2** something that is null; *specif* an act or document without legal effect or validity **3** the number of elements in a BASIS of a null-space

'**null-ˌspace** *n* a subspace of a VECTOR SPACE consisting of vectors that under a given LINEAR TRANSFORMATION are equal to zero

**numb** /num/ *adj* **1** devoid of sensation, esp as a result of cold or anaesthesia **2** devoid of emotion ⟨*prisoners . . . ~ from suffering and anguish* – Edgar Lustgarten⟩ [ME *nomen*, fr pp of *nimen* to take – more at NIM] – **numb** *vt*, **numbingly** *adv*, **numbly** *adv*, **numbness** *n*

**numbat** /'numbat/ *n* a small marsupial mammal (*Myrmecobius fasciatus*) that lives in the forests of S and W Australia, is redbrown in colour, and has white stripes across its back, a pointed snout, and a long wormlike sticky tongue that it uses for feeding on termites – called also BANDED ANTEATER [native name in Australia]

¹**number** /'numbə/ *n* **1a(1)** a sum of units; a total **a(2)** COMPLEMENT 1b (usual amount) **a(3)** *taking sing or pl vb* an indefinite, usu large, total ⟨*a growing ~ of MPs believe the government must go to the country*⟩ **a(4)** *pl* a numerous group; many; *also* an instance of numerical superiority ⟨*there is safety in ~ s*⟩ **b(1)** any of an ordered set of standard names or symbols (e g 2, 5, 27th) used in counting or in assigning a position in an order; *esp* NATURAL NUMBER (1, 2, 3, etc) **b(2)** an element (e g 6, -3, ⅝, √7) belonging to an arithmetical system based on the numbers used in counting and subject to specific rules of addition, subtraction, and multiplication – compare INTEGER, RATIONAL NUMBER, ALGEBRAIC NUMBER **b(3)** an element (e g √3, *e*) of the FIELD of REAL NUMBERS that cannot be expressed as the quotient of two integers – compare IRRATIONAL NUMBER, TRANSCENDENTAL NUMBER **b(4)** an element (e g 3 + 2*i*) belonging to a mathematical system obtained by extension of or analogy with the arithmetical system of numbers – compare COMPLEX NUMBER, QUATERNION **2 c** *pl* arithmetic ⟨*teach children their ~ s*⟩ **2** a distinction of word form to denote reference to singular, plural, and in some languages DUAL or TRIAL; *also* a set of forms so distinguished ⟨*Greek has three ~ s*⟩ **3** *pl* **3a** literary metrical structure; metre **b** metrical lines; verses **4a** a word, symbol, letter, or combination of symbols representing a number; *specif* a numeral **b** one or more numerals or digits used to identify or designate ⟨*a car ~*⟩ ⟨*a telephone ~*⟩ **c(1)** a member of a group or sequence designated by esp consecutive numbers; *also* an individual or item (e g a single act in a variety show or a single issue of a periodical) singled out from a group ⟨*a big production ~ closed the show*⟩ **c(2)** a position in a numbered sequence **d** a group of individuals ⟨*he is not of their ~*⟩ **5** numbers *pl but taking sing or pl vb*, **numbers game** a form of US lottery in which an individual bets that a certain combination of three digits will appear in numbers regularly published in newspapers (e g the stock market receipts) **6** *in-*

*formal* **6a** something viewed in terms of the advantage or enjoyment obtained from it ⟨*has a cushy ~ in his father's firm*⟩ ⟨*drives round in a fast little ~*⟩ **b** an article of esp women's clothing ⟨*wearing a chic little black ~*⟩ **c** a person, individual; *esp* an attractive girl ⟨*a red-headed ~ with bedroom eyes* – Raymond Chandler⟩ **7** *informal* insight into a specified person's motives or character ⟨*I've got his ~*⟩ [ME *nombre*, fr OF, fr L *numerus* – more at NIMBLE] – **without number** innumerable ⟨*times without number*⟩

**usage** When a number (*of*) means "an indefinite group" it should take a plural verb ⟨*there are a number of reasons against it*⟩ ⟨*a certain number* [*of them*] *prefer tea*⟩. When **number** is used in a sentence commenting on the size of a total, it takes a singular verb ⟨*the number of visitors increases every year*⟩. See AMOUNT

²**number** *vt* **1** to count, enumerate **2** to include as part of a whole or total ⟨*proud to ~ her among my friends*⟩ **3** to restrict to a definite number; limit – usu pass ⟨*knew that his days on earth were ~* ed⟩ **4** to assign a number to ⟨*~ ed the team members 1 to 10*⟩ ⟨*a ~* ed *road*⟩ **5** to comprise in number; total ⟨*the crowd ~* ed *at least 50 000*⟩ **~** *vi* **1** to be part of a total number ⟨*he ~* s *among my closest friends*⟩ **2** to call off numbers in sequence – **numberable** *adj*

**Number 10** *n, informal* the British government [*Number 10, Downing Street*, official residence in London of the Prime Minister]

'**number-ˌcruncher** *n* a person or machine, esp a powerful computer, that processes large amounts of numerical data – **number-crunching** *adj or n*

**numberless** /'numbəlis/ *adj* innumerable, countless

**number line** *n* a line of infinite lengths whose points correspond to the REAL NUMBERS according to their distance in a positive or negative direction from a point arbitrarily taken as zero

**number one** *n* **1** something that is first in rank, order, or importance ⟨*~ in her list of priorities*⟩ **2** *informal* one's own interests or welfare; oneself ⟨*always thinking of ~*⟩ ⟨*look after ~, that's what I say*⟩ **3** *euph* **3a** an act of urinating **b** urine – used by or to children

**numberplate** /'numbəˌplayt/ *n, chiefly Br* either of a pair of rectangular identifying plates fastened to each end of a vehicle and bearing its registration number

**Numbers** /'numbəz/ *n taking sing vb* – see BIBLE table [fr the census of the Israelites in chapters 1–4]

**number theory** *n* a branch of mathematics dealing with the INTEGERS and their properties

**number two** *n* **1** a principal subordinate; a second-in-command **2** *euph* **2a** an act of defecating **b** faeces – used by or to children

**numbles** /'numblz/ *n, archaic* UMBLES (edible animal entrails) [ME *noumbles, nombles* – more at UMBLES]

**numbskull** /'num,skul/ *n* a numskull

**numen** /'nyoohmen/ *n, pl* **numina** /'nyoohminə/ a divine force or influence often associated with a place or natural object [L, nod, divine will, numen; akin to L *nuere* to nod, Gk *neuein*]

**numerable** /'nyoohm(ə)rəbl/ *adj* capable of being counted – not used technically; compare COUNTABLE

¹**numeral** /'nyoohm(ə)rəl/ *adj* **1** of or expressing numbers **2** consisting of numbers as opposed to letters ⟨*a ~ code*⟩ [MF, fr LL *numeralis*, fr L *numerus*] – **numerally** *adv*

²**numeral** *n* a conventional symbol that represents a NATURAL NUMBER or zero

¹**numerate** /'nyoohmərayt/ *vt* to enumerate [L *numeratus*, pp of *numerare* to count, fr *numerus*]

²**numerate** /'nyoohm(ə)rət/ *adj, Br* **1** marked by an understanding of the scientific approach and by the ability to think quantitatively ⟨*~ graduates required for accountancy*⟩ **2** understanding basic mathematics and able to use numbers in calculation; *also* fond of mathematical calculations ⟨*attempts by excessively ~ people to communicate with the world at large* – Punch⟩ [L *numerus* number + E *-ate* (as in *literate*)] – **numeracy** *n*

**numeration** /ˌnyoohmə'raysh(ə)n/ *n* **1a(1)** the act or process or an instance of counting **a(2)** a system of counting or numbering **b** an act or instance of designating by a number **2** the skill of interpreting numbers written as numerals as if they were written as words – **numerative** *adj*

**numerator** /'nyoohmə,raytə/ *n* **1** the part of a fraction that is above the line; DIVIDEND – compare DENOMINATOR **2** one who or that which numbers

**numerical** /nyooh'merikl/, **numeric** *adj* **1** of numbers ⟨*the ~ superiority of the enemy*⟩ **2** expressed in or involving numbers or a number system ⟨~ *standing in a class*⟩ ⟨*a ~ code*⟩ [L *numerus* + E *-ical, -ic*] – **numerically** *adv*

**numerical analysis** *n* a branch of mathematics concerned with substituting sets of numerical data into mathematical models to obtain approximations to the solutions of equations; *esp* the application and theory of such methods involving computer programs

**numerology** /ˌnyoohmə'roləji/ *n* the study of the occult significance of numbers [L *numerus* + E *-o-* + *-logy*] – **numerologist** *n*, **numerological** *adj*

**numerous** /'nyoohm(ə)rəs/ *adj* consisting of many units or individuals [MF *numereux*, fr L *numerosus*, fr *numerus*] – **numerously** *adv*, **numerousness** *n*

**numerus clausus** /ˌnyoohmərəs 'klowzəs/ *n* a restriction limiting the intake of applicants (e g for a university course) to a fixed maximum number or originally to a percentage from a particular group [NL, lit., closed number]

**numinous** /'nyoohminəs/ *adj* **1** awe-inspiring, mysterious **2** filled with a sense of the presence of divinity **3** appealing to the higher emotions or to the aesthetic sense; spiritual [L *numin-, numen* numen]

**numismatic** /ˌnyoohmiz'matik/ *adj* **1** of numismatics **2** of currency; monetary [Fr *numismatique*, fr L *nomismat-, nomisma* coin, fr Gk, custom, coin; akin to Gk *nomos* custom, law – more at NIMBLE] – **numismatically** *adv*

**numismatics** /ˌnyoohmiz'matiks/ *n taking sing vb* the study or collection of coinage, coins, paper money, medals, tokens, etc – **numismatist** *n*

**nummary** /'numəri/ *adj* of or dealing in coins [L *nummarius*, fr *nummus* coin]

**nummular** /'numyoolə/ *adj, medicine* **1** circular or oval in shape ⟨~ *lesions*⟩ **2** characterized by nummular lesions [Fr *nummulaire*, fr L *nummulus*, dim. of *nummus* coin, fr Gk *nommos* customary; akin to Gk *nomos*]

**numnah** /'numnə/ *n* a saddle-shaped piece of leather, foam, sheepskin, etc placed under a horse's saddle to prevent chafing [Hindi *namdā*, fr Per *namad* carpet, rug]

**numskull, numbskull** /'num,skul/ *n* a slow-witted or stupid person; a dunce [*numb* + *skull*]

**¹nun** /nun/ *n* a woman belonging to a religious order under vows of poverty, chastity, and obedience, usu living in a convent, and often engaged in educational or nursing work [ME, fr OE *nunne*, fr LL *nonna*]

**²nun** *n* the 14th letter of the Hebrew alphabet [Heb *nūn*]

**Nunc Dimittis** /ˌnoongk di'mitis, nungk/ *n* a CANTICLE (religious song) based on the prayer of Simeon in Luke 2:29–32 [L, now lettest thou depart; fr the first words of the canticle]

**nunciature** /'nuns(h)i·əchə/ *n* **1** the office or period of office of a nuncio **2** a papal diplomatic mission headed by a nuncio [It *nunciatura*, fr *nuncio*]

**nuncio** /'nuns(h)ioh/ *n, pl* **nuncios** a papal ambassador to a civil government [obs It (now *nunzio*), fr L *nuntius* messenger, message]

**nuncle** /'nungkl/ *n, chiefly dial* an uncle [by incorrect division of *an uncle*]

**nuncupative** /'nungkyoo,paytiv, nung'kyoohpətiv/ *adj* not written; oral ⟨*a ~ will*⟩ [ML *nuncupativus*, fr LL, so-called, fr L *nuncupatus*, pp of *nuncupare* to name, contr of *nomen capere*, fr *nomen* name + *capere* to take – more at NAME, HEAVE]

**nunnery** /'nunəri/ *n* a convent of nuns

**Nupe** /'noohpay/ *n, pl* **Nupes**, *esp collectively* **Nupe** a member of a black people of W central Nigeria; *also* their KWA language

**¹nuptial** /'nupsh(ə)l/ *adj* **1** of marriage or the marriage ceremony **2** characteristic of or occurring in the breeding season ⟨*a ~ flight*⟩ [L *nuptialis*, fr *nuptiae*, pl, wedding, fr *nuptus*, pp of *nubere* to marry; akin to Gk *nymphē* bride, nymph]

**²nuptial** *n*, **nuptials** *n pl* a wedding

**nuptial mass** *n* a celebration of Communion following a marriage service

**nuptial plumage** *n* the brilliantly coloured plumage assumed by the males of many birds before the start of the annual breeding period – compare ECLIPSE PLUMAGE

**¹nurse** /nuhs/ *n* **1a** a woman who suckles an infant not her own; WET NURSE **b** a woman employed to take care of a young child **2** one who or that which safeguards or fosters **3** one who is skilled or trained in caring for the sick or infirm, esp under the supervision of a physician ⟨*she and her brother are both qualified ~*s⟩ **4a** a member of the worker caste in a society of ants, bees, etc that cares for the young **b** a female mammal

used to suckle the young of another [ME, fr OF *nurice*, fr LL *nutricia*, fr L, fem of *nutricius* nourishing – more at NUTRITIOUS]

**²nurse** *vt* **1a** to nourish at the breast; suckle **b** to take nourishment from the breast of **2** to rear, nurture **3** to encourage the development of; foster ⟨*the policy of . . . nursing authors of promise – TLS*⟩ ⟨*carefully ~*d *his tomatoes*⟩ **4a** to care for and wait on (e g a sick person) **b** to attempt to cure (e g an illness or injury) by appropriate treatment ⟨*stayed at home nursing a bad cold*⟩ **5** to hold in one's mind; refuse to forget ⟨~ *a grievance*⟩ **6a** to handle carefully in order to conserve or prolong ⟨*sat all evening nursing a pint of beer*⟩ ⟨~d *the battered plane back to base*⟩ **b** to hold (e g a baby) lovingly or caressingly ~ *vi* **1a** to suckle an offspring **b** to suck at the breast **2** to act or serve as a nurse [ME *nurshen* to nourish, contr of *nurishen*] – **nurser** *n*

**nursehound** /'nuhs,hownd/ *n* a European dogfish (*Scyliorhinus canicula*) [*nurse* (a shark) + *hound* – more at NURSE SHARK]

**nursemaid** /'nuhs,mayd/ *n* a girl or woman employed to look after children

**nursery** /'nuhs(ə)ri/ *n* **1** a child's bedroom or playroom **2a** a place where small children are looked after in their parents' absence **b** NURSERY SCHOOL **3a** a place or thing that serves to foster or develop ⟨*Florence was the ~ of Renaissance art*⟩ **b** a place where people are trained or educated **4** an area where trees, shrubs, etc are grown for propagation, transplanting, or sale **5** a place where young animals (e g fish) grow or are cared for **6** a handicap race for two-year-old horses, run in Britain after August 1

**nursery class** *n* a class for children aged from three to five attached to a primary school

**nurserymaid** /'nuhs(ə)ri,mayd/ *n* a nursemaid

**nurseryman** /'nuhs(ə)rimən, -,man/ *n* one whose occupation is the cultivation of plants, esp for sale

**nursery rhyme** *n* a short traditional story in rhyme for children

**nursery school** *n* a school for children aged usu from two to five

**nursery slope** *n* a usu gentle ski slope for beginners

**nurse shark** *n* any of various sharks of a widely distributed family (Orectolobidae) [alter. of ME *nusse*]

**nursing** /'nuhsing/ *n* **1** the profession of a nurse ⟨*schools of ~*⟩ **2** the duties of a nurse ⟨*proper ~ is difficult work*⟩

**nursing home** *n* **1** a usu private hospital or home where care is provided for the aged, chronically ill, etc who are unable to care for themselves properly **2** a small and usu private hospital in Britain; *esp* a private maternity hospital

**nursing mother** *n* a mother who is breast-feeding her baby or babies

**nursing officer** *n* a nurse next in rank below a senior nursing officer

**nursling** /'nuhsling/ *n* somebody or something that is solicitously cared for; *specif* a child under the care of a nurse, esp in former times [¹*nurse* + *-ling*]

**¹nurture** /'nuhchə/ *n* **1** training, upbringing **2** food; nourishment **3** all the environmental influences affecting the expression of the innate genetic potentialities of an organism [ME, fr MF *norriture*, fr LL *nutritura* act of nursing, fr L *nutritus*, pp of *nutrire* to nourish, nourish – more at NOURISH]

**²nurture** *vt* **1** to give care and nourishment to ⟨~d *by loving parents*⟩ **2** to educate or develop ⟨~ *your mind with great thoughts* – Benjamin Disraeli⟩ – **nurturer** *n*

**¹nut** /nut/ *n* **1a** (the often edible kernel of) a dry fruit or seed with a hard separable rind or shell **b** a dry non-opening one-seeded fruit usu with a woody wall **2** a difficult person, problem, or undertaking ⟨*he's a tough ~ to crack*⟩ **3** a typically hexagonal usu metal block that has a central hole with an internal screw thread cut on it, and can be screwed onto a piece, esp a bolt, with an external thread to tighten or secure something **4a** the ridge in a stringed instrument (e g a violin) over which the strings pass on the upper end of the fingerboard **b** the end of a violin bow that the player holds **5** a small piece or lump of something ⟨*a ~ of butter*⟩ **6** *pl, informal* nonsense – often used interjectionally **7** *usu pl, chiefly NAm vulg* a testicle **8** *informal* a person's head **9** *informal* **9a** an insane or wildly eccentric person **b** an ardent enthusiast; a freak [ME *nute, note*, fr OE *hnutu*; akin to OHG *nuz* nut, L *nux*] – **nutlike** *adj* – **do one's nut** *informal* to become very agitated or annoyed [*nut* 8]

²**nut** *vi* **-tt-** to gather or seek nuts – chiefly in *go nutting*

**nutation** /nyooh'taysh(ə)n/ *n* **1a** a slight nodding of the earth's axis superimposed on its normal PRECESSION (motion like that of a spinning top) **b** the variation in angle to the vertical of a top-like rotating body; wobble **2** a spontaneous usu irregular spiral movement of a growing stem, tendril, root, etc **3** *formal* the act of nodding the head [L *nutation-, nutatio,* fr *nutatus,* pp of *nutare* to nod, rock, freq of *nuere* to nod – more at NUMEN] – **nutational** *adj,* **nutate** *vi*

‚**nut-'brown** *adj or n* (of) the colour of a ripe hazelnut – used appreciatively, esp of ale or of human complexion

**nutcase** /'nut‚kays/ *n, informal* a nut, lunatic

**nutcracker** /'nut‚krakə/ *n,* **nutcrackers** *n pl* an implement for cracking nuts, usu consisting of two hinged metal arms between which the nut is held and compressed

**nutgrass** /'nut‚grahs/ *n* a ubiquitous grasslike plant (*Cyperus rotundis*) of the sedge family that grows as a weed in Australia, SE Asia, Africa, and other parts of the world [fr its edible nutlike tubers]

**nuthatch** /'nut‚hach/ *n* any of various small tree-climbing birds (family Sittidae) that have a compact body, a short tail, and a long beak used to pick insects from the bark of trees; *esp* a Eurasian nuthatch (*Sitta europaea*) with bluish grey upperparts and a black stripe through the eye [ME *notehache,* fr *note* nut + *hache* axe, fr OF, battle-axe – more at HASH; fr its habit of cracking nuts to eat]

**nuthouse** /'nut‚hows/ *n, slang or humorous* an insane asylum; a madhouse

**nutlet** /'nutlit/ *n* **1a** a small nut **b** a small fruit similar to a nut **2** the stone in each of the fleshy segments that collectively form the fruit of a raspberry, blackberry, etc

**nutmeg** /'nutmeg/ *n* an aromatic seed that is used as a spice and is produced by a tree (*Myristica fragrans* of the family Myristicaceae, the nutmeg family) native to Indonesia; *also* the tree bearing the nutmeg seed [ME *notemuge,* deriv of OProv *noz muscada,* fr *noz* nut (fr L *nuc-, nux*) + *muscada,* fem of *muscat* musky – more at MUSCAT]

**nutria** /'nyoohtri·ə/ *n* **1** a coypu **2** the fur of the coypu [Sp, modif of L *lutra* otter; akin to OE *oter* otter]

**nutrient** /'nyoohtri·ənt/ *n or adj* (something) that provides nourishment [L *nutrient-, nutriens,* prp of *nutrire* to nourish – more at NOURISH]

**nutriment** /'nyoohtrimənt/ *n* something that nourishes or promotes growth [L *nutrimentum,* fr *nutrire*]

**nutrition** /nyooh'trish(ə)n/ *n* nourishing or being nourished; *specif* all the processes by which an organism takes in and utilizes food [MF, fr LL *nutrition-, nutritio,* fr L *nutritus,* pp of *nutrire*] – **nutritional** *adj,* **nutritionally** *adv*

**nutritionist** /nyooh'trishənist/ *n* a specialist in the study of food and nutrition

**nutritious** /nyooh'trishəs/ *adj* nourishing [L *nutricius,* fr *nutric, nutrix* nurse; akin to L *nutrire* to nourish] – **nutritiously** *adv,* **nutritiousness** *n*

**nutritive** /'nyoohtritiv/ *adj* **1** of nutrition **2** nourishing – **nutritively** *adv*

**nutritive ratio** *n* the ratio of digestible protein to other nutrients in a foodstuff

**nuts** /nuts/ *adj, informal* **1** passionately keen or enthusiastic ⟨*she's just ~ about the milkman*⟩ ⟨*he's ~ on ice-hockey*⟩ **2** crazy, mad ⟨*its enough to drive you ~*⟩ [fr pl of ¹*nut*]

**nuts and bolts** *n pl, informal* **1** the working parts or elements ⟨*the ~ of a computer*⟩ **2** the practical workings (e g of a business or enterprise) ⟨*the ~ of municipal government*⟩

¹**nutshell** /'nut‚shel/ *n* the hard external covering enclosing the kernel of a nut – **in a nutshell** in a brief accurate account; concisely expressed

²**nutshell** *vt* to put in a nutshell; précis

**nutter** /'nutə/ *n, chiefly Br informal* a nut, maniac; *also* an insanely eccentric person

**nutty** /'nuti/ *adj* **1** having or producing nuts **2** having a flavour like that of nuts **3** *informal* eccentric, silly; *also* mentally disordered – **nuttiness** *n*

**nux vomica** /‚nuks 'vomikə/ *n, pl* **nux vomica** the poisonous seed of an Asian tree (*Strychnos nux-vomica* of the family Loganiaceae) containing several drugs, esp STRYCHNINE and

BRUCINE; *also* the tree bearing the nux vomica seed [NL, lit., emetic nut]

**nuzzle** /'nuzl/ *vi* **1** to push or rub something with the nose ⟨*the horse ~ d up against him*⟩ **2** to lie close or snug; nestle ~ *vt* **1** to root or rub (as if) with the nose **2** to press closely or snugly ⟨*she ~ d her face into the cushion*⟩ [ME *noselen* to bring the nose towards the ground, fr *nose*]

**nyala** /en'yahlə/ *n, pl* **nyalas,** *esp collectively* **nyala** a SE African antelope (*Tragelaphus angasi*) with vertical white stripes on its sides and shaggy black hair along the underside in the male; *also* a related mountain antelope (*Tragelaphus buxtoni*) [of Bantu origin; akin to Venda *nyala* nyala, Zulu *inxala*]

**nyctalopia** /‚niktə'lohpi·ə/ *n* NIGHT BLINDNESS [LL, deriv of Gk *nykt-, nyx* night + *alaos* blind + *ōps* eye]

**nyctinastic** /‚nikti'nastik/ *adj* of NASTIC movements of plants (e g the opening and closing of flowers) that occur in response to the stimuli of changes in temperature or light intensity occurring during the day and acting on the plant from all directions [ISV *nyctinasty,* fr *nyct-* night (fr L, fr Gk *nykt-, nyx*) + *-nasty*] – **nyctinasty** *n*

**nyctitropic** /‚nikti'tropik, -'trohpik/ *adj* of or being a movement of a plant part at nightfall (e g the closing of a flower or leaf) [ISV *nyct-* + *-i-* + *-tropic*] – **nyctitropism** *n*

**nylon** /'nielon, -lən/ *n* **1** any of numerous strong tough elastic synthetic POLYAMIDE materials that are fashioned into fibres, filaments, bristles, or sheets and used esp in textiles and plastics **2** *pl* stockings made of nylon [coined word]

synonyms **Nylon, polyester,** and **acrylic** are synthetics, with **Dacron** and **Terylene** being trademarks for particular **polyesters** and **Acrilan, Courtelle, Dralon,** and **Orlon** for particular **acrylics;** **acetate** and **rayon** are derived from cellulose, **viscose** being one sort of **rayon.** As fabrics, **nylon** is the strongest, **nylon** and **polyester** are the most resistant to creasing and shrinkage. **Acetate** and **rayon** or **viscose** are pleasanter to wear in hot climates than the others; none is as warm as wool in cold weather, although **acrylic** is the "woolliest" and is used for sweaters and imitation fur. All the others can be used for dresses, but trousers and suits are usually **polyester** and tights are **nylon.** All except **acetate** are used in mixtures, with cotton or wool or with each other.

**nymph** /nimf/ *n* **1** any of the minor female divinities of nature in classical mythology who were mortal but long-lived and who lived in mountains, forests, trees, and waters **2** any of various immature insects; *esp* a larva of an insect (e g a dragonfly or mayfly) with INCOMPLETE METAMORPHOSIS (a gradual change from the larval stage into the mature, but structurally similar, adult) **3** *poetic* a girl – compare SYLPH [ME *nimphe,* fr MF, fr L *nympha* bride, nymph, fr Gk *nymphē* – more at NUPTIAL] – **nymphal** *adj*

**nymphalid** /'nimfəlid/ *n* any of a family (Nymphalidae) of butterflies (e g a CAMBERWELL BEAUTY or fritillary) with the first pair of legs reduced in size in both sexes and useless for walking [NL *Nymphalidae,* group name, deriv of L *nympha* nymph] – **nymphalid** *adj*

**nymphet** /'nimfit/ *also* **nymphette** /nim'fet/ *n* a girl in early adolescence who is sexually desirable [obs *nymphet* young nymph, fr MF *nymphette,* dim. of *nymphe* nymph]

**nympho** /'nimfoh/ *n, pl* **nymphos** *informal* a nymphomaniac

**nympholepsy** /'nimfə‚lepsi/ *n* **1** a demoniac enthusiasm held by the ancients to seize one bewitched by a nymph **2** a frenzy of emotion, usu inspired by something unattainable [*nympholept* fr Gk *nympholēptos* frenzied, lit., caught by nymphs, fr *nymphē* + *lambanein* to seize – more at CATCH] – **nympholept** *n,* **nympholeptic** *adj*

**nymphomania** /‚nimfə'maynyə/ *n* excessive sexual desire in a female – compare SATYRIASIS [NL, fr *nymphae* inner lips of the vulva (fr L, pl of *nympha*) + LL *mania*] – **nymphomaniac** *n or adj,* **nymphomaniacal** *adj*

**Nynorsk** /n(y)ooh'nawsk/ *n* a literary form of Norwegian based on the spoken dialects of Norway – compare BOKMÅL [Norw, lit., new Norwegian]

**nystagmus** /ni'stagməs/ *n* a rapid involuntary oscillation of the eyeballs (e g from dizziness) [NL, fr Gk *nystagmos* drowsiness, fr *nystazein* to doze; akin to Lith *snusti* to doze] – **nystagmic** *adj*

# O

**o, O** /oh/ *n, pl* **o's, os, O's, Os 1a** (a graphic representation of or device for reproducing) the 15th letter of the English alphabet **b** a speech counterpart of printed or written *o* **2** one designated *o*, esp as the 15th in order or class **3** something shaped like the letter O; *esp* nought

**O** /oh/ *interj or n, chiefly poetic* oh

**o-** /oh-/, **oo-** *comb form* egg ⟨*oology*⟩; *specif* ovum ⟨*oogonium*⟩ [Gk *ōi-, ōio-,* fr *ōion* – more at EGG]

**-o-** – used as a connective vowel originally to join word elements of Greek origin and now also to join word elements of Latin or other origin ⟨*milometer*⟩ ⟨*elastomer*⟩ [ME, fr OF, fr L, fr Gk, thematic vowel of many nouns and adjectives in combination]

**¹-o** /-oh/ *suffix* (→ *n or adj*), *informal* (somebody or something) that is, has the qualities of, or is associated with ⟨*cheapo*⟩ ⟨*wino*⟩ ⟨*beano*⟩ [perh fr ¹*oh*]

**²-o** /-oh/ *suffix* (→ *interj*), *informal* – in interjections formed from other parts of speech ⟨*cheerio*⟩ ⟨*righto*⟩ [prob fr ¹*oh*]

**o'** *also* **o** /ə/ *prep* **1** of ⟨*one o'clock*⟩ **2** *chiefly dial* on [ME *o, o-,* contr of *on* & *of*]

**oaf** /ohf/ *n* a clumsy slow-witted person [of Scand origin; akin to ON *alfr* elf – more at ELF] – **oafish** *adj*, **oafishly** *adv*, **oafishness** *n*

**oak** /ohk/ *n, pl* **oaks, oak 1** (the tough hard durable wood of) any of various trees or shrubs (genus *Quercus*) of the beech family usu having lobed leaves and producing acorns as fruits **2** the leaves of an oak used as decoration [ME *ook,* fr OE *āc*; akin to OHG *eih* oak, Gk *aigilōps,* a kind of oak] – **oaken** *adj*

**oak apple** *n* a large round gall produced on oak stems or leaves by a gall wasp (esp *Biorrhiza pallida* or the genus *Andricus*)

**oak-leaf cluster** *n* a bronze or silver cluster of oak leaves and acorns added to various US military decorations to signify a second or subsequent award of the basic decoration – compare BAR

**oakum** /'ohkəm/ *n* loosely twisted hemp or jute fibre impregnated with tar or a tar derivative and used in packing joints (e g of pipes) and stopping up gaps between the planks of a wooden ship [ME *okum,* fr OE *ācumba* tow, fr *ā-* (separative & perfective prefix) + *-cumba* (akin to OE *camb* comb)]

**¹oar** /aw/ *n* **1** a long usu wooden shaft with a broad blade at one end that is used for propelling or steering a boat and that usu rests in a ROWLOCK (U-shaped device) **2** an oarsman [ME *oor,* fr OE *ār*; akin to ON *ār* oar] – **oared** *adj* – **put one's oar in** to interfere

**²oar** *vb, poetic* ¹ROW

**oarfish** /'aw,fish/ *n* any of several silvery sea fishes (genus *Regalecus*) with narrow soft bodies from 6 to 9 metres (about 20 to 30 feet) long, a red fin running the entire length of the back, and red-tipped bony rods rising above the head like a crest

**oarlock** /'aw,lok/ *n, chiefly NAm* ROWLOCK (device for keeping an oar in place)

**oarsman** /'awzmən/ *n* one who rows a boat, esp in a racing crew – **oarsmanship** *n*

**oasis** /oh'aysis/ *n, pl* **oases** /-seez/ **1** a fertile or green area in a dry region **2** something providing relaxation or relief (e g from a dreary routine) [LL, fr Gk]

**Oasis** *trademark* – used for a highly water-absorbent material into which cut flowers, leafy stems, fronds, etc may be inserted for display

**oast** /ohst/ *n* a kiln for drying hops or malt [ME *ost,* fr OE *āst*; akin to MD *eest* kiln, L *aestus* heat, *aestas* summer – more at EDIFY]

**oasthouse** /'ohst,hows/ *n* a usu circular building containing an oast

**oat** /oht/ *n* **1a** *usu pl* any of several grasses (genus *Avena*) with a loosely branched flower head; *esp* a widely cultivated cereal grass (*Avena sativa*) producing grain that is used chiefly as feed for livestock although a small proportion is processed for human consumption **b** *pl* a crop or plot of oats **2** *often pl but taking sing vb* an oat seed ⟨~s *is used to start the calves* ≃ Breeder's Gazette⟩ **3** *archaic* a reed instrument made of an oat straw [ME *ote,* fr OE *āte*] – **sow one's wild oats** to indulge in the wildness and promiscuity of youth, usu before settling down to a steady and sensible way of life

**oatcake** /'oht,kayk/ *n* a usu crisp unleavened biscuit or bread made of oatmeal

**oaten** /'oht(ə)n/ *adj* of or made of oats, oat straw, or oatmeal

**oat grass** *n* **1** WILD OAT **1 2** any of several grasses (genera *Arrhenatherum* and *Danthonia*) of temperate regions in the N and S hemispheres

**oath** /ohth/ *n, pl* **oaths** /ohdhz/ **1a** a solemn usu formal calling upon God or a revered person or thing to witness to the true or binding nature of one's declaration **b** something (e g a promise) formally confirmed by an oath ⟨*an* ~ *of allegiance*⟩ **c** a form of expression used in taking an oath **2** an irreverent use of a sacred name; *broadly* a swearword [ME *ooth,* fr OE *āth*; akin to OHG *eid* oath] – **on/under oath** bound by a solemn promise to tell the truth

**oatmeal** /'oht,meel, -,miəl/ *n* **1** meal made from oats, used esp in porridge; *also, chiefly NAm* oatmeal porridge **2** a greyish beige colour

**ob-, oc-, of-, op-** *prefix* **1** out; forth ⟨*obtrude*⟩ ⟨*offer*⟩; exposed ⟨*obverse*⟩ **2** so as to involve compliance ⟨*obey*⟩ ⟨*observe*⟩ **3** against; in opposition to ⟨*obloquy*⟩ ⟨*opponent*⟩; resisting ⟨*obstinate*⟩ **4** in the way of; hindering ⟨*obstacle*⟩ ⟨*obstruct*⟩ **5** hidden; concealed ⟨*obfuscatory*⟩ ⟨*occult*⟩ **6** inversely ⟨*obovate*⟩ □ usu *oc-* before *c, of-* before *f,* and *op-* before *p* [ME, fr OF, fr L, in the way, against, towards, fr *ob* in the way of, on account of – more at EPI-; (6) NL, prob fr *ob*verse obversely]

**Obadiah** /,ohbə'die-ə/ *n* – see BIBLE table [*Obadiah* (Heb *'Obhadhyāh*), Hebrew prophet]

**¹obbligato** /,obli'gahtoh/ *adj* not to be omitted – used as a direction in music [It, obligatory, fr pp of *obbligare* to oblige, fr L *obligare*]

**²obbligato** *n, pl* **obbligatos** *also* **obbligati** an elaborate, esp melodic, accompaniment, usu played by a single instrument ⟨*a song with violin* ~⟩ △ ostinato

**obcordate** /ob'kawdayt/ *adj, of a leaf* heart-shaped with the notch at the end furthest from the stalk

**obdurate** /'obdyoorət, -joo-/ *adj* **1** stubbornly persistent in wrongdoing; impenitent ⟨*that* ~ *old sinner*⟩ **2** resistant to persuasion or softening influences; inflexible, unyielding ⟨*her* ~ *determination*⟩ [ME, fr L *obduratus,* pp of *obdurare* to harden, fr *ob-* against + *durus* hard – more at DURING] – **obdurately** *adv*, **obdurateness, obduracy** *n*

**obeah** /'ohbi-ə/ *n, often cap* sorcery and magic ritual as practised among blacks, esp of the British W Indies [of African origin; akin to Twi *a¹bi²a³,* a creeper used in making charms]

**obeahman** /'ohbi-əmən/ *n* a man who is expert in the practice of obeah

**obedience** /ə'beedi-əns, oh-/ *n* **1a** an act or instance of obeying **b** the quality or state of being obedient **2** a sphere of jurisdiction, esp of a church

**obedient** /ə'beedi-ənt, oh-/ *adj* submissive to the will or authority of a superior; willing to obey [ME, fr OF, fr L *oboedient-, oboediens,* fr prp of *oboedire* to obey – more at OBEY] – **obediently** *adv*

  *synonyms* Obedient, docile, tractable, biddable, and amenable: obedient implies due acceptance of authority. Docile suggests an inherent disposition to submit without question to control, whether justified or oppressive. Tractable is often used of things as well as people or animals, and stresses ease of handling and manageability. **Biddable**, a rather old-fashioned word, is similar to **docile** in suggesting prompt obedience, but is usually limited to children. **Amenable** suggests an agreeable willingness to listen to and act upon suggestions or requests. *antonyms* disobedient, recalcitrant

**obeisance** /oh'bay(i)səns, -'bee-/ *n* **1** a movement or gesture made as a sign of respect, reverence, or submission; a bow **2** deference, homage [ME *obeisaunce* obedience, obeisance, fr MF *obeissance*, fr *obeissant*, prp of *obeir* to obey] – **obeisant** *adj*, **obeisantly** *adv*

**obelia** /oh'beelyə/ *n* any of a genus (*Obelia* of the class Hydrozoa) of small INVERTEBRATE animals related to the SEA ANEMONES and the jellyfish that live in branching plantlike colonies that bear individuals (HYDROIDS) which feed to sustain the colony and others (MEDUSAE) which are released to reproduce sexually and produce new colonies [NL, genus name, prob deriv of Gk *obelos*]

**obelisk** /'obəlisk/ *n* **1** an upright 4-sided pillar of Egyptian origin, usu made of a single stone, that gradually tapers towards the top and ends in a pyramid **2a** an obelus **b** DAGGER 2 (reference mark) [MF *obelisque*, fr L *obeliscus*, fr Gk *obeliskos*, fr dim. of *obelos*]

**obel·ize, -ise** /'obəliez/ *vt* to designate or annotate with an obelus

**obelus** /'obiləs/ *n, pl* **obeli** /-li/ a symbol – or ÷ chiefly used in ancient manuscripts to mark a passage of doubtful authenticity [LL, fr Gk *obelos* spit, pointed pillar, obelus]

**obese** /oh'bees/ *adj* excessively fat [L *obesus*, fr pp of *obedere* to eat up, fr *ob-* against + *edere* to eat] – **obesity** *n*

**obey** /ə'bay, oh'bay/ *vt* **1** to submit to the commands or guidance of ⟨~s *the teacher*⟩ ⟨~ed *a whim*⟩ **2** to comply with; execute ⟨~ *an order*⟩ ~ *vi* to act obediently [ME *obeien*, fr OF *obeir*, fr L *oboedire*, fr *ob-* towards + *audire* to hear – more at OB-, AUDIBLE] – **obeyer** *n*

**obfuscate** /'obfus,kayt/ *vt* **1a** to darken **b** to make obscure or difficult to understand ⟨*the report* ~d *the principal issues*⟩ **2** to confuse, bewilder [LL *obfuscatus*, pp of *obfuscare*, fr L *ob-* in the way + *fuscus* dark brown – more at DUSK] – **obfuscation** *n*, **obfuscatory** *adj*

**¹obi** /'ohbi/ *n* OBEAH (magic ritual)

**²obi** *n* a broad sash worn with a Japanese kimono [Jap]

**obit** /'obit, 'oh-/ *n* **1** a memorial service held on the anniversary of the death of a founder or benefactor (e g of an institution) **2** *informal* an obituary [ME, fr MF, fr L *obitus* death, fr *obitus*, pp of *obire* to go to meet, die, fr *ob-* in the way + *ire* to go – more at ISSUE]

**obiter dictum** /,obitə 'diktəm/ *n, pl* **obiter dicta** /'diktə/ **1** an incidental observation made by a judge in the course of a case which is not material to his/her judgment and therefore not binding **2** an incidental remark or observation [LL, lit., something said in passing]

**obituary** /ə'bityoo(ə)ri/ *n* a written announcement of a person's death, usu with a short biographical account [ML *obituarium*, fr L *obitus* death] – **obituary** *adj*

**¹object** /'objikt/ *n* **1** something that is (capable of) being sensed physically or examined mentally ⟨*a knobbly* ~⟩ ⟨*an* ~ *of study*⟩ **2a** something or somebody that arouses an emotion or provokes a reaction or response ⟨*a love* ~⟩ ⟨*an* ~ *of derision*⟩ **b** somebody or something that is ridiculous, outlandish, or pathetic in appearance ⟨*looked a real* ~⟩ **3** an end towards which effort, action, or emotion is directed; a motive, goal ⟨*what's the* ~ *of the exercise?*⟩ **4** a thing that forms an element of or constitutes the subject matter of an investigation or science **5** a noun or noun equivalent representing the goal or the result of the action of its verb ⟨*house in* "*we built a house*" *and* her *and* book *in* "*I gave her the book*" *are* ~s⟩; *also* a noun or noun equivalent (e g table in "*on the table*") in a prepositional phrase **6** something of paramount concern ⟨*if money's no* ~ *then buy the coat*⟩ *synonyms* see ¹SUBJECT [ME, fr ML *objectum*, fr L, neut of *obicere* to throw in the way, present, hinder, fr *ob-* in the way + *jacere* to throw – more at JET] – **objectless** *adj*, **objectlessness** *n*

**²object** /əb'jekt/ *vt* to offer in opposition; cite as an objection ⟨~ed *that the statement was misleading*⟩ ~ *vi* **1** to oppose something with words or arguments ⟨~ed *vigorously to the proposal*⟩ **2** to feel dislike or disapproval ⟨*do you* ~ *to my smoking?*⟩ [ME *objecten*, fr L *objectus*, pp of *obicere* to throw in the way, object] – **objector** *n*

*synonyms* **Object, protest, demur, remonstrate**, and **expostulate** may all convey opposition to something, usually expressed. **Object** is the basic term, and may imply expressed or simply felt

aversion. **Protest** suggests strong objections, strongly expressed. **Demur** suggests hesitant or tentative objections, stated mildly or politely. **Remonstrate** and **expostulate** both suggest **protesting** in a way that attempts to convince or persuade against the action deplored. **Remonstrate** suggests a friendly approach and **expostulate** a more earnest one. *antonym* acquiesce *usage* One objects *to* things or *to doing* things, but one cannot correctly **object** *to do* things ⟨△ *they* **objected** *to pay the full amount*⟩.

**object ball** *n* the ball first struck by the CUE BALL in snooker or billiards; *also* any ball struck by the cue ball

**objectify** /əb'jekti,fie/ *vt* **1a** to cause to become an object of perception **b** to make objective **2** EXTERNALIZE 2 – **objectification** *n*

**objection** /əb'jeksh(ə)n/ *n* **1** objecting **2a** a reason or argument presented in opposition; a cause or basis for objecting **b** a feeling of dislike or disapproval ⟨*I've no* ~ *to your smoking*⟩

**objectionable** /əb'jeksh(ə)nəbl/ *adj* unpleasant or offensive – **objectionableness** *n*, **objectionably** *adv*

**¹objective** /əb'jektiv/ *adj* **1a** of an object of action or feeling **b** constituting an object: e g **b(1)** existing independently of the mind **b(2)** belonging to the external world and observable or verifiable esp by scientific methods **b(3)** *of a symptom of disease* perceptible to people other than the affected person **c** concerned with or expressing the nature of external reality rather than personal feelings or beliefs **d(1)** dealing with facts without distortion by personal feelings or prejudices **d(2)** of or being methods that eliminate or are intended to eliminate the subjective by limiting choices to fixed alternatives requiring a minimum of creative interpretation ⟨~ *tests of personality*⟩ **2** derived from sense perception ⟨~ *data*⟩ **3** of or in the case that follows a preposition or a transitive verb *synonyms* see ¹FAIR *antonym* subjective – **objectively** *adv*, **objectiveness** *n*, **objectivity** *n*

**²objective** *n* **1** something towards which efforts are directed; a goal **2** something that is objective; *specif* something outside the mind **3** (a word in) the objective case **4** a strategic position to be attained, or a purpose to be achieved, by a military operation **5** a lens or system of lenses that forms an image of an object

**objective complement** *n* a noun, adjective, or pronoun used in the PREDICATE of a sentence as complement to a verb and referring directly to its DIRECT OBJECT (e g chairman *in* "*we elected him chairman*")

**objective correlative** *n* a situation or chain of events that symbolizes or objectifies a particular emotion and that may be used by a writer to evoke a desired emotional response in the reader

**objective test** *n* a test made up of factual questions to be answered in a word or two or by means of a tick [fr its preventing subjective judgment by the tester]

**objectivism** /əb'jekti,viz(ə)m/ *n* **1** a theory stressing objective reality, esp as distinguished from subjective experience or appearance **2** an ethical theory that moral values are objectively real or possess universal validity **3** the theory or practice of objective art or literature – **objectivist** *n*, **objectivistic** *adj*

**object language** *n* TARGET LANGUAGE

**object lesson** *n* **1** a lesson that takes a material object as its basis **2** something that serves as a concrete illustration of a principle ⟨*successful mixed marriages that are an* ~ *in racial harmony*⟩

**objet d'art** /,obzhay 'dah (*Fr* ɔbʒɛ dar)/ *n, pl* **objets d'art** /~/ a usu small article of some artistic value [Fr, lit., art object]

**objet trouvé** /'troohvay, trooh'vay (*Fr* truve)/ *n, pl* **objets trouvès** /~/ a natural or man-made object found by chance and displayed as having aesthetic value [Fr, lit., found object]

**objurgate** /'objuhgayt/ *vt, formal* to denounce or reproach harshly; castigate [L *objurgatus*, pp of *objurgare*, fr *ob-* against + *jurgare* to quarrel, lit., to take to law, fr *jur-, jus* law + *-igare* (fr *agere* to lead) – more at JUST, AGENT] – **objurgation** *n*, **objurgatory** *adj*

**oblanceolate** /ob'lahnsiəlat, əb-, -'lan-, -layt/ *adj, of a leaf* LANCEOLATE (narrow and tapering at both ends) with the broader part furthest from the stalk

**oblast** /'oblahst/ *n, pl* **oblasts** *also* **oblasti** /-sti/ an administrative subdivision of a constituent republic of the USSR [Russ *oblast* ]

**¹oblate** /'oblayt/ *adj* having the shape of an ellipse revolved about its MAJOR AXIS; flattened at the poles – compare PROLATE [NL *oblatus*, fr *ob-* + *-latus* (as in *prolatus* prolate)] – **oblateness** *n*

²**oblate** *n* **1** a layman living in a monastery under a modified rule and without vows **2** a member of any of several Roman Catholic communities of men or women [ML *oblatus*, lit., one offered up, fr L, pp of *offerre*]

**oblation** /ə'blaysh(ə)n/ *n* **1** the act of making a religious offering; *specif, cap* the act of offering to God the bread and wine used at Communion **2** something offered in worship or devotion; a holy gift offered usu at an altar or shrine [ME *oblacioun*, fr MF *oblation*, fr LL *oblation-*, *oblatio*, fr L *oblatus*, pp of *offerre* to offer]

¹**obligate** /'obligayt, -gət/ *adj* restricted to one particularly characteristic mode of life or action ⟨*an* ~ *parasite*⟩ **2** always happening, irrespective of environmental conditions ⟨~ *parasitism*⟩ – compare FACULTATIVE – **obligately** *adv*

²**obligate** /'obligayt/ *vt* **1a** to bind legally or morally; constrain ⟨*felt* ~d *to abide by the contract*⟩ **b** to make someone gratified or indebted; oblige **2** *NAm* to commit (e g funds) to meet an obligation □ compare OBLIGE [L *obligatus*, pp of *obligare*]

**obligation** /,obli'gaysh(ə)n/ *n* **1** pledging oneself to a course of action **2** something (e g a contract, promise, or demand of conscience) that constrains one to a course of action ⟨*what made him pay up? Moral* ~, *I suppose*⟩ **3** (the amount of) a financial commitment ⟨*unable to meet its* ~s, *the company went into bankruptcy*⟩ **4** something that one is bound (e g by law or conscience) to do or not do; a duty **5** (indebtedness for) a service or favour ⟨*her kindness has put me under an* ~ *to her*⟩

**obligatory** /ə'bligət(ə)ri/ *adj* **1** binding in law or conscience **2** relating to or enforcing an obligation ⟨*a writ* ~⟩ **3** mandatory, compulsory ⟨*religious education is not only permitted but* ~⟩ **4** obligate – **obligatorily** *adv*

**oblige** /ə'bliej/ *vt* **1** to constrain physically, morally, legally, or by force of circumstance ⟨~d *to find money for his taxes*⟩ **2a** to put in one's debt by a favour or service – usu pass ⟨*we're much* ~d *to you for all your help*⟩ **b** to do a favour for ⟨~d *the assembled company with a song*⟩ ~ *vi* to do something as a favour; be of service ⟨*always ready to* ~⟩ □ compare ²OBLIGATE [ME *obligen*, fr OF *obliger*, fr L *obligare*, lit., to bind to, fr *ob-* towards + *ligare* to bind – more at LIGATURE] – **obliger** *n*

**obligee** /,obli'jee/ *n* **1** somebody to whom another is obligated; a creditor **2** somebody who receives a contract or bond

**obliging** /ə'bliejing/ *adj* eager to help; accommodating ⟨*found the shop assistant very* ~⟩ – **obligingly** *adv*, **obligingness** *n*

**obligor** /,obli'gaw/ *n* a person who places him-/herself under a legal obligation

¹**oblique** /ə'bleek/ *adj* **1a**(1) neither perpendicular nor parallel; inclined **a(2)** *of an angle* either acute or obtuse **b** having the central line of symmetry not perpendicular to the base ⟨*an* ~ *cone*⟩ **c** having no RIGHT ANGLE ⟨*an* ~ *triangle*⟩ **2** not straightforward or explicit; indirect ⟨*an* ~ *reference to his colleague's rudeness*⟩ **3** *of a muscle* situated obliquely and esp in VERTEBRATE animals having one end not inserted on bone **4** being an aerial photograph taken with the camera directed horizontally or diagonally downwards [ME *oblike*, fr L *obliquus*, fr *ob-* towards + *-liquus* (akin to *ulna* elbow) – more at ELL] – **obliquely** *adv*, **obliqueness** *n*

²**oblique** *n* **1** something (e g a line) that is oblique **2 oblique muscle**, **oblique** any of several muscles that are oblique; *esp* any of the thin flat muscles forming the middle and outer layers of the side walls of the abdomen **3** SOLIDUS 2 (punctuation mark)

³**oblique** *adv* at a 45° angle ⟨*to the right* ~, *march*⟩

**oblique case** *n* a grammatical case other than the NOMINATIVE or VOCATIVE

**obliquity** /ə'blikwəti/ *n* **1** deviation from sound thinking or moral principles; perversity **2a** (the amount of) deviation from being parallel or perpendicular; (a) divergence **b** the angle between the planes of the earth's equator and orbit round the sun, having an average value of 23°26'30.76" in 1980 and diminishing 0.47" per year ⟨~ *of the ecliptic*⟩ **3** (an instance of) deliberate obscurity of speech or conduct

*synonyms* Obliquity and obliqueness are both formed from oblique, but there is a tendency to prefer obliquity for the senses "moral deviation" and "inexplicitness".

**obliterate** /ə'blitərayt/ *vt* **1** to make illegible or imperceptible (e g by obscuring or wearing away) **2a** to erase utterly from memory **b** to destroy utterly all trace or indication of **c** to cause (e g a body part or a scar) to disappear **d** to cause (e g a duct carrying body fluid) to collapse ⟨*a blood vessel* ~d *by inflammation*⟩ **3** to cancel (a stamp) *synonyms* see ERASE [L

*oblit[t]eratus*, pp of *oblit[t]erare*, fr *ob* in the way of + *lit[t]era* letter] – **obliterator** *n*, **obliteration** *n*

**obliterative** /ə'blit(ə)rətiv/ *adj* inducing or characterized by obliteration: e g a causing or accompanied by closure or collapse of a tube ⟨~ *arterial disease*⟩ **b** tending to make inconspicuous ⟨~ *behaviour*⟩

**oblivion** /ə'blivi-ən/ *n* **1** the state of forgetting or being oblivious; forgetfulness ⟨*the* ~ *of sleep*⟩ **2** the state of being forgotten ⟨*contentedly accepted his own political* ~⟩ **3** official disregarding of political offences; amnesty [ME, fr MF, fr L *oblivion-*, *oblivio*, fr *oblivisci* to forget, perh fr *ob-* in the way + *levis* smooth – more at LIME]

**oblivious** /ə'blivi-əs/ *adj* **1** lacking memory or mindful attention ⟨~ *old age*⟩ **2** lacking conscious knowledge; completely unaware – usu + *of* or *to* ⟨~ *to the risk he ran*⟩ – **obliviously** *adv*, **obliviousness** *n*

*usage* **1** Writers on usage advise **oblivious** *of* rather than *to*. **2** Some people dislike the use of **oblivious** to mean simply "unaware" or "heedless", and prefer to confine its meaning to "forgetful" or "no longer aware". *synonyms* see ABSTRACTED

**oblong** /'oblong/ *adj* deviating from a square or circular form through being longer ⟨*the* ~ *fruit of a lemon tree*⟩; *specif* rectangular but not square [ME, fr L *oblongus*, fr *ob-* towards + *longus* long] – **oblong** *n*

**obloquy** /'obləkwi/ *n* **1** strongly-worded condemnation; abusive language **2** loss of reputation; discredit, disgrace *synonyms* see ²ABUSE [LL *obloquium*, fr *obloqui* to speak against, fr *ob-* against + *loqui* to speak]

**obnoxious** /əb'nokshəs/ *adj* highly offensive or repugnant ⟨*thoroughly* ~ *views on racialism*⟩ [L *obnoxius*, fr *ob* in the way of, exposed to + *noxa* harm – more at NOXIOUS] – **obnoxiously** *adv*, **obnoxiousness** *n*

**obnubilate** /ob'nyoohbilayt/ *vt* **1** to bemuse, stupefy ⟨~ *the patient ... and then wake him up – The Lancet*⟩ **2** *formal* to cloud, obscure [L *obnubilatus*, pp of *obnubilare*, fr *ob-* in the way + *nubilare* to be cloudy, fr *nubilus* cloudy, fr *nubes* cloud – more at NUANCE] – **obnubilation** *n*

**oboe** /'oh,boh/ *n* a woodwind instrument of middle range that has a DOUBLE REED (two flat pieces of cane that when blown across vibrate to produce sound), a conical tube with a moderately flared free end, and a nasal tone [It, fr Fr *hautbois* – more at HAUTBOIS] – **oboist** *n*

**oboe d'amore** /dah'mawray/ *n* an oboe with a pear-shaped free end and sombre tone that has a lower range than the true oboe and is used esp in baroque music [It, lit., oboe of love]

**obol** /'obol/ *n* an ancient Greek coin or weight equal to ¹⁄₆ drachma [L *obolus*, fr Gk *obolos*; akin to Gk *obelos* spit]

**obovate** /o'bohvayt/ *adj*, *of a leaf* egg-shaped with the narrower end nearest the stalk

**obovoid** /o'bohvoyd/ *adj* egg-shaped with the narrower end at the base ⟨*an* ~ *fruit*⟩

**obscene** /əb'seen/ *adj* **1** arousing disgust; repulsive ⟨*dressed in* ~ *rags*⟩ **2** repugnant to morality; *specif* sexually improper; indecent ⟨*vile and* ~ *political doctrines*⟩ ⟨*confiscated various* ~ *publications*⟩ *synonyms* see COARSE *antonym* decent [MF, fr L *obscenus*, *obscaenus*] – **obscenely** *adv*

**obscenity** /əb'senəti/ *n* **1** the quality or state of being obscene **2** an obscene utterance, act, or object

**obscurant** /əb'skyooərənt/, **obscurantic** /,obskyoo'rantik/ *adj* tending to make obscure – **obscurant** *n*

**obscurantism** /,obskyoo'rantiz(ə)m/ *n* **1** opposition to the advance of knowledge or the dissemination of ideas, esp by deliberate concealment **2** an act or instance of obscurantism – **obscurantist** *n* or *adj*

¹**obscure** /əb'skyooə/ *adj* **1** dark, dim **2a** out-of-the-way, remote ⟨*an* ~ *country village*⟩ **b** hard to understand because of complexity or lack of clarity; abstruse ⟨*suffering is permanent,* ~ *and dark* – William Wordsworth⟩ **c** not well-known or widely acclaimed ⟨*an* ~ *Roman poet*⟩ **d** faint, indistinct ⟨*an* ~ *murmur*⟩ **3** being or representing the unstressed vowel /ə/ [ME, fr MF *obscur*, fr L *obscurus*, fr *ob-* in the way + *-scurus* (akin to Gk *keuthein* to conceal) – more at HIDE] – **obscurely** *adv*, **obscureness** *n*

*synonyms* Obscure, abstruse, recondite, enigmatic, cryptic, vague, ambiguous, and equivocal can all mean "difficult to understand". In obscure the meaning may be veiled or hidden in some way. Abstruse and recondite suggest specialized scholarly knowledge or subjects that are difficult for outsiders to penetrate or comprehend. Enigmatic suggests something of significance couched in mysterious terms. Cryptic adds to enigmatic an intention to puzzle. **Vague** stresses the lack of definition or distinctness. What is **ambiguous** may be interpreted in more than one way; an **equivocal** expression is deliberately ambiguous, and often allows of one innocent and one misleading interpretation. *antonyms* obvious, distinct, clear

²**obscure** *vt* **1a** to make dark or dim **b** to make indistinct or unintelligible **2** to conceal (as if) by covering **3** to reduce (a vowel) to the value /ə/ – **obscuration** *n*

**obscurity** /əb'skyooərəti/ *n* **1** the quality or state of being obscure **2** an obscure person or thing *antonym* clarity

**obsequious** /əb'seekwi·əs/ *adj* showing a servile willingness to oblige or admire [ME, fr L *obsequiosus* compliant, fr *obsequium* compliance, fr *obsequi* to comply, fr *ob-* towards + *sequi* to follow – more at SUE] – **obsequiously** *adv*, **obsequiousness** *n*

**obsequy** /'obsikwi/ *n*, **obsequies** *n pl* a funeral ceremony [ME *obsequie*, fr MF, fr ML *obsequiae* (pl), alter. (influenced by L *obsequium*) of L *exsequiae, exequiae* – more at EXEQUIES]

**observable** /əb'zuhvəbl/ *adj* **1** noteworthy **2** capable of being observed; discernible – **observable** *n*, **observably** *adv*

**observance** /əb'zuhv(ə)ns/ *n* **1a** *often pl* a customary practice, rite, ceremony, or prohibition ⟨*Sabbath* ∼s⟩ **b** a rule governing members of a religious order **2** an act of complying with a custom, rule, or law ⟨∼ *of the speed limits*⟩ **3** an act of watching

**observant** /əb'zuhv(ə)nt/ *adj* **1** paying close attention; watchful ⟨∼ *spectators*⟩ **2** careful to observe; mindful *of* ⟨∼ *of local customs*⟩ **3** strictly faithful in esp religious observances ⟨*a pious* ∼ *Jew*⟩ **4** quick to notice; alert – **observantly** *adv*

**observation** /ˌobzə'vaysh(ə)n/ *n* **1** an act or the faculty of observing **2a** an act of recognizing and recording a fact or occurrence, often with the help of scientific instruments ⟨*weather* ∼s⟩ **b** a record so obtained **3** a conclusion based on observing; *broadly* a remark, comment **4** the condition of somebody or something that is observed ⟨*under* ∼ *at the hospital*⟩ [MF, fr L *observation-, observatio*, fr *observatus*, pp of *observare*] – **observational** *adj*, **observationally** *adv*

**observationally adequate** /ˌobzə'vaysh(ə)nəli/ *adj, of a grammar* consistent with the available grammatical data – compare DESCRIPTIVELY ADEQUATE, EXPLANATORILY ADEQUATE

**observation car** *n* a railway carriage, esp in the USA, with large windows and often a partly transparent roof that allows passengers a broad view

**observatory** /əb'zuhvət(ə)ri/ *n* **1** a building or place given over to or equipped for the observation and interpretation of natural phenomena, esp in astronomy; *also* an institution whose chief purpose is the making of such observations **2** a place or structure commanding a wide view; a lookout [prob fr NL *observatorium*, fr L *observatus*]

**observe** /əb'zuhv/ *vt* **1** to act in due conformity with ⟨∼ *rules*⟩ ⟨∼ *a minute's silence*⟩ ⟨*careful to* ∼ *local customs*⟩ **2** to inspect or pay heed to as an augury, omen, or presage **3** to perform or celebrate (e g a ceremony or festival) according to a prescribed or traditional form ⟨∼d *the fast of Ramadan*⟩ **4** to perceive or take note of, esp by concentrated attention ⟨∼d *him stalking through the bushes*⟩ ⟨∼ *what I'm about to do*⟩ **5** to come to realize or know, esp through reflection upon observations **6** to utter as a comment ⟨∼d *that things weren't what they used to be*⟩ **7** to make a scientific observation on or of ∼ *vi* **1a** to take notice; pay attention **b** to make observations; watch **2** to remark, comment [ME *observen*, fr MF *observer*, fr L *observare* to guard, watch, observe, fr *ob-* in the way, towards + *servare* to keep – more at CONSERVE] – **observingly** *adv*

**observer** /əb'zuhvə/ *n* one who observes: e g **a** a representative sent to observe but not participate officially in a gathering **b** one who accompanies the pilot of an aircraft to make observations

**obsess** /əb'ses/ *vt* **1** to preoccupy intensely or excessively **2** *archaic* to harass, beset [L *obsessus*, pp of *obsidēre* to besiege, beset, fr *ob-* against + *sedēre* to sit]

**obsession** /əb'sesh(ə)n/ *n* a persistent and usu disturbing preoccupation with an often unreasonable idea or feeling; *also* an idea or feeling causing such a preoccupation – **obsessional** *adj*, **obsessionally** *adv*

**obsessive** /əb'sesiv/ *adj* **1** excessive to the point of abnormality ⟨*our* ∼ *need for quick solutions* – Adlai Stevenson †1965⟩ **2** of, characterized by, or tending to cause obsession – **obsessive** *n*, **obsessively** *adv*, **obsessiveness** *n*

**obsidian** /əb'sidi·ən/ *n* a usu black VOLCANIC GLASS that fractures in such a way as to give smooth curved surfaces and sharp edges [NL *obsidianus*, fr L *obsidianus lapis*, false MS

reading for *obsianus lapis*, lit., stone of Obsius, fr *Obsius*, a Roman traveller who reputedly discovered it]

**obsolescent** /ˌobsə'les(ə)nt/ *adj* going out of use; becoming obsolete ⟨∼ *machinery*⟩ *synonyms* see ¹OLD [L *obsolescent-, obsolescens*, prp of *obsolescere*] – **obsolescently** *adv*, **obsolescence** *n*

**obsolete** /'obsəleet/ *adj* **1** no longer in use ⟨*an* ∼ *word*⟩ **2** outdated; outmoded ⟨∼ *equipment*⟩ *synonyms* see ¹OLD *antonym* current [L *obsoletus*, fr pp of *obsolescere* to grow old, become disused, prob fr *ob-* towards + *solēre* to be accustomed] – **obsoletely** *adv*, **obsoleteness** *n*

**obstacle** /'obstəkl/ *n* something that hinders or obstructs [ME, fr MF, fr L *obstaculum*, fr *obstare* to stand in the way, fr *ob-* in the way + *stare* to stand]

**obstacle race** *n* a race in which the runners must negotiate contrived obstacles

**obstetric** /əb'stetrik, ob-/, **obstetrical** /-kl/ *adj* of or associated with childbirth or obstetrics [deriv of L *obstetric-, obstetrix* midwife, fr *obstare* to stand in the way, stand in front of] – **obstetrically** *adv*

**obstetrics** /əb'stetriks, ob-/ *n taking sing or pl vb* a branch of medical science dealing with the care and treatment of women before, during, and after childbirth; *also* a corresponding branch of veterinary science – **obstetrician** *n*

**obstinate** /'obstinət/ *adj* **1** clinging stubbornly to an opinion or course of action; not yielding to arguments or persuasion **2** not easily subdued, remedied, or removed ⟨*an* ∼ *fever*⟩ [ME, fr L *obstinatus*, pp of *obstinare* to be resolved, persist, fr *ob-* in the way + *-stinare* (akin to *stare* to stand)] – **obstinately** *adv*, **obstinateness, obstinacy** *n*

*synonyms* Obstinate, stubborn, dogged, pertinacious, mulish, stiff-necked, pigheaded, and bullheaded: **obstinate** suggests an unreasonable adherence to a view or course of action in the face of opposition or argument. **Stubborn** suggests an innate tendency to obstinacy, and a determination not to yield. **Dogged**, the only term which is not necessarily pejorative, suggests unwearying tenacity of purpose even in the face of difficulty. **Pertinacious** (formal) suggests a similar tenacity in pursuing some activity which is annoying to others ⟨*a pertinacious beggar*⟩. **Stiff-necked** suggests inflexibility due to haughtiness. **Mulish, pigheaded, and bullheaded** all imply an irrational obstinacy, as of animals: **mulish** stresses unreasonableness and stubbornness, **pigheaded** implies stupidity and perverseness, while **bullheaded** implies headstrong determination. Compare INFLEXIBLE. *antonyms* pliant, compliant

**obstreperous** /əb'strep(ə)rəs/ *adj* **1** aggressively noisy; clamorous ⟨∼ *merriment*⟩ **2** vociferously defiant; unruly *synonyms* see VOCIFEROUS [L *obstreperus*, fr *obstrepere* to shout against, fr *ob-* against + *strepere* to make a noise; akin to OE *thræft* discord] – **obstreperously** *adv*, **obstreperousness** *n*

**obstruct** /əb'strukt/ *vt* **1** to block or close up by an obstacle ⟨*traffic* ∼ing *the street*⟩ **2** to hinder, impede ⟨*constant interruptions* ∼ *our progress*⟩ **3** to shut off from sight ⟨*a wall* ∼s *the view*⟩ *synonyms* see ¹HINDER [L *obstructus*, pp of *obstruere*, fr *ob-* in the way + *struere* to build – more at STRUCTURE] – **obstructive** *adj or n*, **obstructively** *adv*, **obstructiveness** *n*, **obstructor** *n*

**obstruction** /əb'struksh(ə)n/ *n* **1** obstructing or being obstructed: e g **1a** a condition of being clogged or blocked **b** a delay or attempted delay of business in a deliberative body (e g Parliament) **2** something that obstructs **3** a foul (e g in soccer or hockey) in which a player gets between an opponent and the ball so as to restrict the opponent's playing of the ball

**obstructionism** /əb'strukshə,niz(ə)m/ *n* deliberate interference with the progress or business of a body, esp a legislative body – **obstructionist** *n*, **obstructionistic** *adj*

**obstruent** /'obstrooənt/ *adj, of a speech sound* involving stoppage or friction – **obstruent** *n*

**obtain** /əb'tayn/ *vt* to acquire or attain, usu by effort or request ∼ *vi, formal* to be generally accepted or practised ⟨*the conditions that* ∼ *in most prisons*⟩ [ME *obteinen*, fr MF & L; MF *obtenir*, fr L *obtinēre* to hold on to, possess, obtain, fr *ob-* in the way + *tenēre* to hold – more at THIN] – **obtainable** *adj*, **obtainer** *n*, **obtainment** *n*, **obtainability** *n*

*synonyms* Compare obtain, procure, secure, and effect. **Obtain, procure, and secure** all mean "gain possession of". **Procure** stresses the effort involved ⟨*manage to* **procure** *a rare book*⟩ and **secure** emphasizes the safe possession of something of which one has made certain ⟨**secure** *our seats well in advance*⟩. One can **procure, secure,** or **effect**, but not **obtain**, a state of affairs ⟨**effect** *an entry into the house*⟩.

**obtect** /əb'tekt/ *also* **obtected** *adj, of a pupa* (characterized by being) enclosed in a hard horny case or covering – compare EXARATE [L *obtectus*, pp of *obtegere* to cover over, fr *ob-* in the way + *tegere* to cover – more at THATCH]

**obtest** /ob'test, əb-/ *vb, archaic* to beseech, supplicate [MF *obtester*, fr L *obtestari* to call to witness, beseech, fr *ob-* towards + *testis* witness – more at TESTAMENT] – **obtestation** *n*

**obtrude** /əb'troohd/ *vt* **1** to thrust out; extrude ⟨*the snail slowly* ~d *his horns*⟩ **2** to assert without warrant or request ⟨*not a man to* ~ *his beliefs casually*⟩ ~ *vi* to thrust oneself forward with unwanted assertiveness ⟨*do what we may, our childhood background will* ~⟩ □ compare INTRUDE, PROTRUDE [L *obtrudere* to thrust at, fr *ob-* in the way + *trudere* to thrust – more at THREAT] – **obtruder** *n*, **obtrusion** *n*

**obtrusive** /əb'troohsiv, -ziv/ *adj* **1** thrust out; protruding **2a** forward in manner or conduct; pushing ⟨~ *behaviour*⟩ **b** unduly noticeable or showy □ compare INTRUSIVE *antonym* unobtrusive, shy [L *obtrusus*, pp of *obtrudere*] – **obtrusively** *adv*, **obtrusiveness** *n*

**obtund** /ob'tund/ *vt* to deaden, blunt, or dull ⟨~ed *reflexes*⟩ [ME *obtunden*, fr L *obtundere* – more at OBTUSE] – **obtundent** *adj or n*

**obturate** /'obtyoo(ə),rayt/ *vt* to obstruct or close (an opening, esp the breech of a gun) [L *obturatus*, pp of *obturare*, fr *ob-* in the way + *-turare* (akin to *tumēre* to swell) – more at THUMB] – **obturation** *n*

**obturator** /'obtyooraytə/ *n* something that closes: eg **a** either of two muscles that cover part of the interior or exterior wall of the pelvis **b** something (eg an artificial part) that closes or blocks up an opening (eg a cleft in the roof of the mouth) [NL, fr L *obturatus*, pp]

**obtuse** /əb'tyoohs/ *adj* **1** lacking sensitivity or mental alertness; insensitive, dull **2a(1)** *of an angle* greater than 90°but less than 180° **a(2)** having an obtuse angle ⟨*an* ~ *triangle*⟩ **b** not pointed or acute; blunt **3** *of a leaf* rounded at the end furthest from the stalk *synonyms* see STUPID *antonym* acute [L *obtusus* blunt, dull, fr pp of *obtundere* to beat against, blunt, fr *ob-* against + *tundere* to beat – more at STUTTER] – **obtusely** *adv*, **obtuseness** *n*

¹**obverse** /'obvuhs/ *adj* **1** facing the observer or opponent **2** with the base narrower than the top ⟨*an* ~ *leaf*⟩ **3** constituting a counterpart or complement [L *obversus*, fr pp of *obvertere* to turn towards, fr *ob-* towards + *vertere* to turn – more at WORTH] – **obversely** *adv*

²**obverse** *n* **1a** the side of a coin, medal, or currency note that bears the principal design and lettering; *broadly* a front or principal surface – compare REVERSE **b** the more conspicuous of two possible sides, aspects, cases, or things ⟨*the* ~ *of this situation*⟩ **2a** a counterpart necessarily involved in or answering to a fact or truth **b** *philosophy* a logical proposition that can be inferred directly from another by denying its opposite ⟨"*all* A *is* B" *is the* ~ *of* "*no* A *is not* B"⟩

**obvert** /ob'vuht/ *vt* to turn so as to face towards something [L *obvertere* to turn towards]

**obviate** /'obviayt/ *vt* **1** to anticipate and dispose of in advance ⟨~ *an objection*⟩ **2** to make unnecessary ⟨~ *the need for arriving early*⟩ *synonyms* see PREVENT *antonym* necessitate [LL *obviatus*, pp of *obviare* to meet, withstand, fr L *obviam* in the way] – **obviation** *n*

**obvious** /'obvi-əs/ *adj* **1** evident to the senses or understanding; easily discovered or recognized **2** unsubtle ⟨*the symbolism of the novel was rather* ~⟩ [L *obvius*, fr *obviam* in the way, fr *ob* in the way of + *viam*, acc of *via* way – more at VIA] – **obviously** *adv*, **obviousness** *n*

*usage* Some writers prefer to confine **obvious** and **obviously** to the sense "evident(ly) to the senses" ⟨*it's* **obviously** *too dark*⟩ and to use **natural** and **naturally** for the sense "evident(ly) to the understanding" ⟨*we must* **naturally**/**obviously** *cut down expenses*⟩. *synonyms* see EVIDENT *antonyms* subtle, obscure

**oc-** – see OB-

**ocarina** /,okə'reenə/ *n* a simple wind instrument having an oval body with finger holes and a projecting mouthpiece [It, dim. of *oca* goose, fr LL *auca*, deriv of L *avis* bird – more at AVIARY]

**Occam's razor, Ockham's razor** /'okəmz/ *n* a scientific and philosophical rule that the simplest of competing theories should be preferred to the more complex or that explanations should include as little reference as possible to unknown phenomena [William of *Occam* (or *Ockham*) †1349? E scholastic philosopher]

¹**occasion** /ə'kayzh(ə)n/ *n* **1** a suitable opportunity or circumstance ⟨*a funeral is no* ~ *for laughter*⟩ **2** a state of affairs that provides a ground or reason ⟨*her illness gives no* ~ *for concern*⟩ **3** the immediate or incidental cause as distinguished from the fundamental one ⟨*his insulting remark was the* ~ *of a bitter quarrel*⟩ **4** a time at which something occurs ⟨*on the* ~ *of his son's wedding*⟩ **5** a need arising from a particular circumstance ⟨*had no* ~ *to consult the dictionary*⟩ **6** *pl* one's affairs, business – esp in go about one's lawful occasions **7** a special event or ceremony ⟨*jewels worn only on royal* ~s⟩ ⟨*the wedding was a real* ~⟩ *synonyms* see ¹CAUSE [ME, fr MF or L; MF, fr L *occasion-*, *occasio*, fr *occasus*, pp of *occidere* to fall, fall down, fr *ob-* towards + *cadere* to fall – more at CHANCE] – **on occasion** from time to time

²**occasion** *vt, formal* to cause; BRING ABOUT

**occasional** /ə'kayzh(ə)nl/ *adj* **1** of a particular occasion ⟨*a budget able to meet* ~ *demands as well as regular ones*⟩ **2** acting as the immediate or incidental cause of something **3** composed for a particular occasion ⟨~ *verse*⟩ **4a** appearing or occurring at irregular or infrequent intervals ⟨~ *visitors*⟩ ⟨*takes an* ~ *holiday*⟩ **b** *of a student at a university* not studying for a degree, diploma, etc **5** acting in a specified capacity from time to time ⟨*an* ~ *golfer*⟩ **6** designed for use as the occasion demands ⟨*an* ~ *table*⟩ *synonyms* see PERIODIC

**occasionalism** /ə'kayzh(ə)nl,iz(ə)m/ *n* the doctrine that mind and body are incapable of affecting one another and that their reciprocal action depends upon the intervention of God

**occasionally** /ə'kayzh(ə)nli, ə'kayzhnəli/ *adv* NOW AND AGAIN

**Occident** /'oksid(ə)nt/ *n* WEST **2a** [ME, fr MF, fr L *occident-*, *occidens*, fr prp of *occidere* to fall, set (of the sun)]

**occidental** /,oksi'dentl/ *adj, often cap* of or situated in the Occident; Western – **occidentally** *adv, often cap*

**Occidental** *n* a native or inhabitant of the Occident; *esp* one of European ancestry

**Occidentalism** /,oksi'dentl·iz(ə)m/ *n* the characteristic features of occidental peoples or culture

**occidental·ize, -ise** /,oksi'dentl·iez/ *vb, often cap* to make or become occidental (eg in culture)

**occipital** /ok'sipitl/ *adj* of, situated near, or being the back part of the head or skull – **occipital** *n*, **occipitally** *adv*

**occipital bone** *n* a compound bone that forms the back part of the skull and bears a rounded projection (CONDYLE) by which the skull articulates with the ATLAS (first vertebra of the neck)

**occipital condyle** *n* a surface on the OCCIPITAL BONE by which the skull articulates with the ATLAS (first vertebra of the neck)

**occipital lobe** *n* the back lobe of each CEREBRAL HEMISPHERE (front portion of the brain) that contains the areas that interpret visual impulses

**occiput** /'oksipət/ *n, pl* **occiputs, occipita** /ok'sipitə/ the back part of the head or skull [L *occipit-*, *occiput*, fr *ob-* against + *capit-*, *caput* head – more at HEAD]

**occlude** /ə'kloohd/ *vt* **1** to stop up; block **2** to obstruct, hinder ⟨~d *me from any scientific pursuit* – Michael Bentine⟩ **3** to take up and hold (eg a liquid); SORB **4** *meteorology* to cut off from contact with the surface of the earth and force upwards by the overtaking of the advancing edge of a warm air mass (WARM FRONT) by that of a cold air mass (COLD FRONT) ⟨~d *warm air*⟩ ~ *vi* **1** *of teeth* to fit together with the points on the grinding surfaces of the opposing teeth when the mouth is closed ⟨*his teeth do not* ~ *properly*⟩ **2** to become occluded [L *occludere* to shut up, fr *ob-* in the way + *claudere* to shut, close – more at CLOSE] – **occludent** *adj*, **occlusive** *adj*

**occluded front** *n* OCCLUSION 2

**occlusal** /ə'kloohs(ə)l, -z(ə)l/ *adj* of the grinding or biting surface of a tooth or the occlusion of the teeth

**occlusion** /ə'kloohzh(ə)n/ *n* **1** occluding or being occluded: eg **1a** the complete obstruction of the breath passage in the articulation of a speech sound **b** the bringing of the opposing surfaces of the teeth of the two jaws into contact; *also* the relation between the surfaces when in contact **c** the retention or taking up of gas trapped during solidification of a material **2** *meteorology* the boundary (FRONT) formed by the advancing edge of a cold air mass (COLD FRONT) overtaking that of a warm air mass (WARM FRONT) and lifting the warm air above the earth's surface [prob fr (assumed) NL *occlusion-*, *occlusio*, fr L *occlusus*, pp of *occludere*]

¹**occult** /'okult, -'-/ *vb, astronomy* to conceal or become concealed by occultation [L *occultare*, fr *occultus*, pp] – **occulter** *n*

²**occult** *adj* **1** secret; *esp* esoteric **2** not easily understood; abs-

truse, recondite **3** of the occult **4** *medicine* not manifest or detectable by clinical methods alone ⟨~ *blood loss*⟩; *esp* not present in visible amounts [L *occultus*, fr pp of *occulere* to cover up, fr *ob-* in the way + *-culere* (akin to *celare* to conceal) – more at HELL] – **occultly** *adv*

**³occult** *n* matters regarded as involving the action or influence of supernatural agencies or some secret knowledge of them – + *the*

**occultation** /ˌokul'taysh(ə)n/ *n* **1** the state of being hidden from view or lost to notice ⟨*his fame was already emerging from the* ~ *of changing fashion – TLS*⟩ **2** the shutting off of the light of one celestial body by the intervention of another; *esp* an eclipse of a star or planet by the moon

**occultism** /'okul,tiz(ə)m/ *n* occult theory or practice; belief in or study of the action or influence of supernatural powers – **occultist** *n*

**occupancy** /'okyoopənsi/ *n* **1** the act of taking and holding possession of land, a property, etc **2a** becoming or being an occupant **b** the condition of being occupied **3** the use to which property is put ⟨*industrial* ~⟩

**occupant** /'okyoopənt/ *n* **1** a person who acquires title by taking and holding possession **2** a person who occupies a particular place; *esp* a resident

**occupation** /ˌokyoo'paysh(ə)n/ *n* **1a** an activity in which one engages **b** an activity by which one earns a living; a job – compare BUSINESS **2a** the occupancy of land **b** tenure of an office or position **3a** the act of taking possession or the holding and control of a place or area, esp by a foreign military force; *also* the period of such possession and control **b** *taking sing or pl vb* a military force occupying a country [ME *occupacioun*, fr MF *occupation*, fr L *occupation-*, *occupatio*, fr *occupatus*, pp of *occupare*]

**occupational** /ˌokyoo'paysh(ə)nl/ *adj* **1** of or resulting from a particular occupation ⟨~ *hazards*⟩ **2** of a military occupation ⟨~ *forces*⟩ – **occupationally** *adv*

**occupational therapy** *n* therapy by means of activity; *esp* creative activity prescribed for its effect in promoting recovery or rehabilitation – **occupational therapist** *n*

**occupy** /'okyoopie/ *vt* **1** to engage the attention or energies of ⟨*occupied herself with a hammer and chisel*⟩ **2** to fill up (a portion of space or time) ⟨*ways of* ~ing *a wet afternoon*⟩ **3** to take or maintain possession of **4** to reside in or use as an owner or tenant [ME *occupien* to take possession of, occupy, modif of MF *occuper*, fr L *occupare*, fr *ob-* towards + *-cupare* (akin to *capere* to take, seize) – more at HEAVE] – **occupier** *n*

**occur** /ə'kuh/ *vi* **-rr-** **1** to be found or met with; exist, appear **2** to become the case; happen **3** to come to mind ⟨*didn't it* ~ *to you that he might be late?*⟩ **synonyms** see HAPPEN [L *occurrere*, fr *ob-* in the way + *currere* to run – more at CAR]

**occurrence** /ə'kurəns/ *n* **1** something that takes place; an incident, event ⟨*a startling* ~⟩ **2** the action or process of occurring ⟨*repeated* ~s *of petty theft in the locker room*⟩ – **occurrent** *adj*

synonyms Occurrence, happening, event, incident, episode, and circumstance: occurrence and happening simply describe something that takes place, though happening now has also a related artistic sense. An event may simply happen as a result of something, but it generally suggests an important or significant occurrence. Incident, in contrast, suggests a minor happening, often subordinate to a more important one, but it also frequently describes one distinct event among several ⟨*one incident from the journey stood out in his mind* ... ⟩. Episode is similar, but stresses the separateness and completeness of the incident ⟨*that episode in her life was now closed*⟩. Circumstance, in this context, suggests one of several details which contribute to or help to explain an event. usage The pronunciation /ə'kurəns/ rather than /ə'kuhrəns/ is recommended for BBC broadcasters.

**occurrent** /ə'kurənt/ *n* something that occurs as a brief event rather than persisting through time [L *occurrent-*, *occurrens*, prp of *occurrere*]

**ocean** /'ohsh(ə)n/ *n* **1** (any of the large expanses that constitute) the whole body of salt water that covers nearly three quarters of the surface of the globe **2** *pl, informal* an unlimited amount ⟨*no need to hurry, we've got* ~s *of time*⟩ – see also DROP **in the ocean** [ME *occean*, fr L *oceanus*, fr Gk *Okeanos*, a river believed to encircle the earth, ocean]

**oceanarium** /ˌohsh(ə)n'eəri-əm/ *n, pl* **oceanariums, oceanaria** /-ri-ə/ a large marine aquarium

**oceangoing** /'ohsh(ə)n,goh·ing/ *adj* of or designed for travel on the ocean

**oceanic** /ˌohshi'anik/ *adj* **1a** of, occurring in, or frequenting the ocean, esp the open sea **b** affected by or produced by the ocean **2** vast, immense

**oceanography** /ˌohsh(ə)n'ogrəfi/ *n* a science dealing with oceans and their form, biology, and resources [ISV] – **oceanographer** *n*, **oceanographic** *also* **oceanographical** *adj*, **oceanographically** *adv*

**ocellated** /'osilaytid, oh'selaytid/, **ocellate** /'osilayt, oh'selayt, -lət/ *adj* **1** having ocelli **2** resembling an ocellus – **ocellation** *n*

**ocellus** /oh'seləs, o-/ *n, pl* **ocelli** /-li, -lie/ **1** a minute simple eye in an INVERTEBRATE animal (eg an insect) that consists of little more than a patch of light-sensitive cells **2** a spot of colour encircled by a band of another colour (eg on a peacock's tail feather or the wing of a butterfly) [NL, fr L, dim. of *oculus* eye – more at EYE] – **ocellar** *adj*

**ocelot** /'osə,lot/ *n* a medium-sized American wildcat (*Felis pardalis*) that occurs from Texas to Patagonia and has a tawny yellow or greyish coat dotted and striped with black [Fr, fr Nahuatl *ocelotl* jaguar]

**och** /okh/ *interj, Scot & Irish* – used to express surprise, impatience, or regret [ScGael & IrGael]

**oche** /'oki/ *n* the line on the floor behind which a player must stand when throwing darts at a dartboard; *broadly* the place where a dart player stands when throwing [prob fr (assumed) ME *oche* groove, notch, fr MF]

**ochlocracy** /ok'lokrəsi/ *n* government by the mob; mob rule [Gk & MF; MF *ochlocratie*, fr Gk *ochlokratia*, fr *ochlos* mob + *-kratia* -cracy] – **ochlocrat** *n*, **ochlocratic, ochlocratical** *adj*

**ochone** /ə'khohn/ *interj, Scot & Irish* – used to express sorrow or regret [ScGael & IrGael *ochōn*]

**ochre**, *NAm chiefly* **ocher** /'ohkə/ *n* **1** an earthy usu red or yellow and often impure iron ore used as a pigment **2** the colour of esp yellow ochre [ME *oker*, fr MF *ocre*, fr L *ochra*, fr Gk *ōchra*, fr fem of *ōchros* yellow, pale] – **ochreous** *adj*

**-ock** /-ək/ *suffix* (→ *n*) small or young kind of ⟨*hillock*⟩ ⟨*bullock*⟩ [ME *-oc*, fr OE]

**ocker** /'okə/ *n, often cap, Austr & NZ informal* an Australian; *specif* one who stresses his/her Australian nationality in a boorishly aggressive way [*Ocker*, name (prob nickname for *Oscar*) of a boorish character in an Australian television series broadcast *ab* 1970] – **ockerdom** *n*, **ockerish** *adj*, **ockerism** *n*

**Ockham's razor** /'okəmz/ *n* OCCAM'S RAZOR (rule in philosophy)

**o'clock** /ə'klok/ *adv* **1** according to the clock – used in specifying the exact hour ⟨*the time is three* ~⟩ **2** – used for indicating position or direction as if on a clock dial that is oriented vertically or horizontally ⟨*an aircraft approaching at six* ~⟩ [contr of *of the clock*]

**octa-** /oktə-/, **octo-** *also* **oct-** *comb form* **1** eight ⟨*octane*⟩ ⟨*octoroon*⟩ **2** containing eight atoms, groups of atoms, or chemical equivalents in the molecular structure [Gk *okta-*, *oktō-*, *okt-* (fr *oktō*) & L *octo-*, *oct-*, fr *octo* – more at EIGHT]

**octad** /'oktad/ *n* a group or series of eight [Gk *oktad-*, *oktas* number eight, body of eight men, fr *oktō*]

**octagon** /'oktəgon, -gən/ *n* a 2-dimensional geometric figure having eight sides; *esp* one that is REGULAR (having eight equal sides and angles) [L *octagonum*, fr Gk *oktagōnon*, fr *okta-* + *-gōnon* -gon] – **octagonal** *adj*, **octagonally** *adv*

**octahedral** /ˌoktə'heedrəl/ *adj* **1** having eight flat faces or planes **2** of or formed in octahedrons ⟨~ *crystals*⟩ – **octahedrally** *adv*

**octahedron** /-oktə'heedron, -drən/ *n, pl* **octahedrons, octahedra** /-drə/ a 3-dimensional geometric figure having eight faces; *esp* one that is REGULAR, having eight equal triangular faces [Gk *oktaedron*, fr *okta-* + *-edron* -hedron]

**octal** /'okt(ə)l/ *adj* of, being, or belonging to a system of counting having eight as its BASE

**octameter** /ok'tamitə/ *n* a line of verse consisting of eight metrical units (FEET) [LL, having eight feet, fr LGk *oktametros*, fr *okta-* + *metron* measure – more at MEASURE]

**octane** /'oktayn/ *n* **1** a liquid of the ALKANE series of organic chemical compounds that has the formula $C_8H_{18}$, occurs in petroleum, and exists in several forms (ISOMERS) that have a different arrangement of atoms within a molecule **2** OCTANE NUMBER [ISV]

**octane number** *n* a number that is used as a measure of the quality of a petrol by indicating the fuel's ability to resist KNOCKING (noise resulting from faulty combustion) and that increases as the probability of knocking decreases

**octane rating** *n* OCTANE NUMBER

**octant** /'oktənt/ n **1a** the position or apparent position (ASPECT) of a celestial body when distant from another body by 45° **b** an instrument for measuring altitudes of a celestial body from a moving ship or aircraft **2** any of the eight parts into which a space is divided by three planes each at right angles to the other two [L *octant-, octans* eighth part of a circle, fr *octo*]

**octaploid** /'oktəployd/ adj OCTOPLOID (having eight times the basic number of chromosomes)

**octarchy** /'oktahki/ n a confederacy of Anglo-Saxon kingdoms considered as having eight rulers

**octave** /'oktiv, 'oktayv/ n **1** an 8-day period of observances beginning with a festival day **2a** a group (STANZA) of eight lines of verse; OTTAVA RIMA **b** the first eight lines of esp an Italian sonnet **3a** a musical interval from one note to another eight notes away from it counting inclusively in the DIATONIC scale (ordinary 8-note musical scale) **b** a note separated from a lower note by this interval **c** the harmonic combination of two notes an octave apart **d** the whole series of notes or piano, organ, etc keys within this interval that form the unit of the modern musical scale **4** a group of eight [ME, fr ML *octava,* fr L, fem of *octavus* eighth, fr *octo* eight – more at EIGHT]

**octavo** /ok'tayvoh/ n, pl **octavos 1** the size of a piece of paper cut eight from a sheet **2** a book format in which a folded sheet forms eight leaves; *also* a book in this format [L, abl of *octavus* eighth]

**octet** /ok'tet/ n **1** a musical composition for eight instruments or voices **2** *taking sing or pl vb* a group or set of eight (eg a group of eight musicians performing together) **3** OCTAVE 2b

**octillion** /ok'tilyən/ n – see NUMBER table [Fr, fr MF, fr *oct-* octa- + *-illion* (as in *million*)]

**octo-** – see OCTA-

**October** /ok'tohbə/ n the 10th month of the year according to the GREGORIAN CALENDAR (standard Western calendar) – see MONTH table [ME *Octobre,* fr OF, fr L *October* (eighth month of the original Roman calendar), fr *octo*]

**Octobrist** /ok'tohbrist/ n a member of a moderately liberal political party in tsarist Russia [trans of Russ *oktyabrist;* fr the imperial manifesto issued in October 1905 which the party supported]

**octodecillion** /,oktohdi'silyən/ n – see NUMBER table [L *octodecim* eighteen + E *-illion* (as in *million*)]

**octodecimo** /,oktoh'desimoh/ n EIGHTEENMO (size of paper) [L, abl of *octodecimus* eighteenth, fr *octodecim* eighteen, fr *octo* eight + *decem* ten – more at TEN]

**octogenarian** /,oktəjə'neəri·ən/ n a person between 80 and 89 years old [L *octogenarius* containing eighty, fr *octogeni* eighty each, fr *octoginta* eighty, fr *octo* eight + *-ginta* (akin to vi*ginti* twenty) – more at VIGESIMAL] – **octogenarian** adj

**octoploid** *also* **octaploid** /'oktəployd/ adj having or being eight times the basic (HAPLOID) number of CHROMOSOMES (strands of gene-carrying material) [ISV] – **octoploid** n, **octoploidy** n

**octopod** /'oktə,pod/ n any of an order (Octopoda of the class Cephalopoda, phylum Mollusca) of INVERTEBRATE animals including the octopuses and PAPER NAUTILUSES that have eight arms bearing suckers [deriv of Gk *oktōpod-, oktōpous* scorpion, fr *oktō* octa- + *pod-, pous* foot – more at FOOT] – **octopod** adj, **octopodan** adj or n, **octopodous** adj

**octopus** /'oktəpəs/ n, pl **octopuses, octopi** /-pie/ **1** any of a genus (*Octopus* of the class Cephalopoda, phylum Mollusca) of INVERTEBRATE animals that have eight muscular arms equipped with two rows of suckers **2** something having many radiating branches or far-reaching controlling influence [NL *Octopod-, Octopus,* genus name, fr Gk *oktōpous*]

**octoroon** /'oktə,roohn/ n a person of ⅛ black ancestry; the first-generation offspring of a QUADROON and a white person [*octa-* + *-roon* (as in *quadroon*)]

**octosyllabic** /,oktoh·si'labik, -tə-/ adj **1** consisting of eight syllables **2** composed of lines of verse of eight syllables each [LL *octosyllabus,* fr Gk *oktasyllabos,* fr *okta-* + *syllabē* syllable] – **octosyllabic** n

**octosyllable** /'oktoh,siləbl, -tə-/ n a word or line of eight syllables

**ocul-, oculo-** *comb form* **1** eye ⟨*oculo*motor⟩ ⟨*oculist*⟩ **2** ocular and ⟨*oculo*cardiac⟩ [L *ocul-,* fr *oculus* – more at EYE]

¹**ocular** /'okyoolə/ adj **1** performed or perceived with the eyes ⟨~ *inspection*⟩ **2a** of the eye ⟨~ *muscles*⟩ **b** resembling an eye in form or function ⟨*an* ~ *window*⟩ [LL *ocularis* of the eyes, fr L *oculus* eye]

²**ocular** n an eyepiece

**oculist** /'okyoolist/ n **1** an ophthalmologist **2** OPTICIAN 2 [Fr *oculiste,* fr L *oculus*]

**oculomotor** /,okyooloh'mohtə/ adj **1** moving or tending to move the eyeball **2** of the OCULOMOTOR NERVE

**oculomotor nerve** n either of the 3rd pair of CRANIAL NERVES that pass from the lower surface of the brain through the skull to supply certain muscles of the eye

**od** /od, ohd/ n a mysterious force formerly believed to pervade the universe [Ger (coined by Baron Karl von Reichenbach † 1869 Ger natural philosopher)]

**OD** /,oh 'dee/ n an overdose of a drug [*overdose*] – **OD** vi

**odalisque** /'ohd(ə)l·isk/ n a female slave or concubine in a harem [Fr, fr Turk *odalık*]

**odd** /od/ adj **1a** left over when others are paired or grouped; lacking its match ⟨*an* ~ *shoe*⟩ **b** not matching ⟨~ *socks*⟩ **2a** somewhat more than the specified number – usu in combination ⟨*300-odd pages*⟩ **b** left over as a remainder ⟨*six pounds and a few* ~ *pence*⟩ **3a** not divisible by two without leaving a remainder ⟨*1, 3, and 5 are* ~ *numbers*⟩ **b** marked by an odd number **c** *of a permutation* produced by an odd number of successive transpositions **4** not regular or planned; casual, occasional ⟨*worked at* ~ *jobs*⟩ ⟨*read for the* ~ *hour*⟩ **5** different from the usual or conventional; strange [ME *odde,* fr ON *oddi* point of land, triangle, odd number; akin to OE *ord* point of a weapon] – **oddness** n, **oddish** adj

*usage* When *odd* means "somewhat more than", it should be preceded by a hyphen to avoid ambiguity, since ⟨*300 odd people*⟩ has two meanings. *synonyms* see STRANGE

**oddball** /'od,bawl/ n, *informal* an eccentric or peculiar person – **oddball** adj

**odd bod** /bod/ n, *Br informal* an oddball

**odd colour** n a horse conforming to no fixed colour – **odd coloured** adj

**Odd Fellow** n a member of a major benevolent and fraternal order

**oddity** /'odəti/ n **1** an odd person, thing, event, or trait **2** oddness, strangeness

**odd lot** n a number or quantity other than the usual unit in business transactions; *esp* a quantity of less than 100 shares of stock

**oddly** /'odli/ adv **1** in an odd manner ⟨*behaved* ~⟩ **2** it is odd that ⟨~ *enough, they never met*⟩

**odd man out** n somebody or something that differs in some respect from all the others in a set or group

**oddment** /'odmənt/ n **1** something left over; a remnant **2** pl odds and ends

**odds** /odz/ n *taking sing or pl vb* **1a** an amount by which one thing exceeds or falls short of another ⟨*won the election against considerable* ~⟩ **b** a difference in terms of advantage or disadvantage ⟨*it makes no* ~ *whether you stay for lunch or not*⟩ **2** the probability (expressed as a ratio) that one thing is so or will happen rather than another; chances ⟨*the* ~ *are that he will be dismissed*⟩ ⟨*the* ~ *are 50 to 1 against the newcomer*⟩ **3** the ratio between the amount to be paid off for a winning bet and the amount of the bet ⟨*gave* ~ *of three to one*⟩ **4** *archaic* inequalities – esp in *make odds even* – **at odds (with)** in disagreement (with)

**odds and ends** n pl **1** miscellaneous items **2** miscellaneous remnants or leftovers ⟨~ *of food*⟩

**odds and sods** n pl, *chiefly Br informal* ODDS AND ENDS

**odds-'on** adj **1** (viewed as) having a better than even chance to win ⟨*the* ~ *favourite*⟩ **2** not involving much risk or doubt ⟨*an* ~ *bet*⟩ ⟨*it's* ~ *he won't come*⟩

**odd trick** n each trick in excess of six won by the DECLARER's side at bridge – compare BOOK 7

**ode** /ohd/ n a lyric poem, often addressed to a particular subject, marked by a usu exalted tone, varying length of line, and complexity of verse forms [MF or LL; MF, fr LL, fr Gk *ōidē,* lit., song, fr *aeidein, aidein* to sing; akin to Gk *audē* voice, OHG *farwāzan* to deny]

**-ode** /-ohd/ *comb form* (→ n) **1** way; path ⟨*electro*de⟩ **2** electrode ⟨*dio*de⟩ [Gk *-odos,* fr *hodos* – more at CEDE]

**odeum** /oh'dee·əm, 'ohdi·əm/ n, pl **odea** /-ə/ **1** a small roofed theatre of ancient Greece and Rome, used chiefly for competitions in music and poetry **2** a theatre or concert hall [L & Gk; L, fr Gk *ōideion,* fr *ōidē* song]

**odious** /'ohdi·əs/ adj arousing or deserving hatred or revulsion ⟨*an* ~ *crime*⟩ △ odorous [ME, fr MF *odieus,* fr L *odiosus,* fr *odium*] – **odiously** adv, **odiousness** n

**odium** /'ohdi·əm/ *n, formal* **1** the condition of being generally hated and condemned, usu for despicable conduct **2** the disgrace or shame associated with a despicable act [L, hatred, fr *odisse* to hate; akin to OE *atol* terrible, Gk *odyssasthai* to be angry]

**odium theologicum** /ˌthee·ə'lojikəm/ *n* the bitterness and obduracy typical of controversy about religion [NL, lit., theological hatred]

**odograph** /'odə,grahf, -,graf/ *n* an instrument for automatically plotting (eg on a map) the course and distance travelled by a vehicle [*odo-* (as in *odometer*) + *-graph*]

**odometer** /o'domitə, oh-/ *n* an instrument for measuring the distance travelled (eg by a vehicle) [Fr *odomètre*, fr Gk *hodometron*, fr *hodos* way, road + *metron* measure – more at CEDE, MEASURE]

**odonate** /'ohdənayt, oh'donayt/ *n* any of an order (Odonata) of predatory insects comprising the dragonflies and damselflies [irreg deriv of Gk *odous, odōn* tooth] – **odonate** *adj*

**odont-, odonto-** *comb form* tooth ⟨odont*itis*⟩ ⟨odonto*blast*⟩ [Fr, fr Gk, fr *odont-, odous* – more at TOOTH]

**-odont** /-ə,dont/ *comb form* (→ *adj*) having teeth of (a specified nature) ⟨*meso*dont⟩ [Gk *odont-, odous* tooth]

**odontoblast** /oh'dontəblast, ə-/ *n* any of the elongated outer cells of the soft inner tissue of a tooth containing the nerves and blood vessels, that secrete the hard calcified material comprising most of the tooth [ISV] – **odontoblastic** *adj*

**odontoglossum** /oh,dontə'glosəm, ə-, o-/ *n* any of a genus (*Odontoglossum*) of tropical American orchids widely cultivated for their showy flowers [NL, genus name, fr *odont-* + Gk *glōssa* tongue – more at GLOSS]

**odontoid process** /oh'dontoyd, ə-, o-/ *n* a toothlike projection extending from the AXIS (second vertebra of the neck) on which the ATLAS (first vertebra of the neck) and the head rotate

**odontology** /ˌohdon'toləji, o-/ *n* a science dealing with the structure, development, and diseases of the teeth ⟨*forensic* ∼⟩ [Fr *odontologie*, fr *odont-* + *-logie* -logy] – **odontologist** *n*, **odontological** *adj*

**odontophore** /oh'dontəfaw, o-/ *n* a structure in the mouth of snails, whelks, etc that supports the RADULA (horny band bearing minute teeth) [ISV]

**odorant** /'ohdərənt/ *n* an odorous substance; *esp* one added to a dangerous odourless substance to warn of its presence

**odoriferous** /ˌohdə'rif(ə)rəs/ *adj* **1** yielding a scent or odour; odorous ⟨∼ *spices*⟩ **2** morally offensive ⟨∼ *conduct*⟩ – **odoriferously** *adv*, **odoriferousness** *n*

**odor·ize, -ise** /'ohdəriez/ *vt* to make odorous; scent

**odorous** /'ohd(ə)rəs/ *adj* having an odour: eg **a** fragrant **b** malodorous ɪ**9** odious – **odorously** *adv*, **odorousness** *n*

**odour,** *NAm chiefly* **odor** /'ohdə/ *n* **1** (the sensation resulting from) a quality of something that stimulates the sense of smell **2** *chiefly derog* a characteristic or predominant quality; a savour ⟨*an* ∼ *of sanctity*⟩ **3** repute, favour ⟨*exams as a whole are in bad* ∼ *– Punch*⟩ **synonyms** see ²SMELL [ME *odour*, fr OF, fr L *odor*; akin to L *olēre* to smell, Gk *ozein* to smell, *osmē* smell, odour] – **odourless** *adj*

**odyssey** /'odəsi/ *n* a long wandering or quest usu marked by many changes of fortune ⟨*one man's spiritual* ∼⟩ [the *Odyssey*, ancient Greek epic poem by Homer describing the long wanderings of the legendary hero Odysseus on his way home from the siege of Troy]

**oecumenical** /ˌekyoo'menikl, ˌeekyoo-/ *adj* ecumenical

**oedema,** *NAm chiefly* **edema** /i'deemə/ *n* abnormal accumulation of fluid beneath the skin causing swelling (eg in the ankles and feet) [NL, fr Gk *oidēma* swelling, tumour, fr *oidein* to swell]

**oedipal** /'eedipl, 'ed-/ *adj, often cap* of the OEDIPUS COMPLEX – **oedipally** *adv, often cap*

**Oedipus complex** /'eedipəs, 'edipəs/ *n* (an adult personality disorder resulting from) the sexual attraction that a child develops towards the parent of the opposite sex with accompanying jealousy of the parent of the same sex [*Oedipus* (Gk *Oidipous*), character in Greek mythology who unwittingly killed his father and married his mother]

**oeillade** /uh'yahd (*Fr* œjad)/ *n* an esp amorous or provocative glance [Fr, fr MF, fr *oeil* eye, fr L *oculus* – more at EYE]

**oenology,** *NAm chiefly* **enology** /ee'noləji/ *n* the science of wine and winemaking [Gk *oinos* wine + E *-logy*]

**oenophile,** *NAm chiefly* **enophile** /'eenoh,fiel/ *n* a wine connoisseur [Gk *oinos* + E *-phile*]

**oenophilist** /ee'nofilist/ *n* an oenophile

**o'er** /'oh-ə, aw/ *adv or prep, poetic* over

**Oerlikon** /'uhlikon/ *n* any of several 20 millimetre automatic aircraft or antiaircraft cannon [*Oerlikon*, suburb of Zurich in Switzerland]

**oersted** /'uhstəd/ *n* the cgs unit of MAGNETIC FIELD strength [Hans Christian *Oersted* †1851 Dan physicist]

**oesophag-, oesophago-,** *NAm chiefly* **esophag-, esophago-** *comb form* **1** oesophagus ⟨oesophag*ectomy*⟩ **2** oesophageal and ⟨oesophago*gastric*⟩

**oesophagus** /ee'sofəgəs/ *n, pl* **oesophagi** /-,gie/ a muscular tube that leads from the back of the mouth to the stomach [ME *ysophagus*, fr Gk *oisophagos*, fr *oisein* to be going to carry + *phagein* to eat] – **oesophageal** *adj*

**oestr-** /eestr-, estr-/, **oestro-,** *NAm chiefly* **estr-, estro-** *comb form* (promoting) oestrus ⟨oestro*gen*⟩

**oestradiol** /ˌeestrə'die,ol, ˌestrə-/ *n* the major oestrogenic SEX HORMONE, $C_{18}H_{24}O_2$, in female mammals that is used medically in the treatment of AMENORRHOEA (abnormal absence of menstruation) and menopausal symptoms [ISV *oestra-* (fr *oestrin*) + *di-* + *-ol*]

**oestrin** /'eestrin, 'es-/ *n* an oestrogenic hormone; *esp* oestrone [NL *oestrus* + E *-in*]

**oestriol** /'eestri,ol, 'estri,ol/ *n* an oestrogenic STEROID hormone, $C_{18}H_{24}O_3$, (eg present in the urine of pregnant women) that is a breakdown product of oestradiol and used esp in the treatment of menopausal symptoms [*oestrin* + *tri-* + *-ol*]

**oestrogen** /'eestrəj(ə)n, 'estrə-/ *n* any of a group of STEROID substances that are drugs or natural hormones (eg oestrone) and have functions typical of an oestrogenic hormone [NL *oestrus* + ISV *-o-* + *-gen*]

**oestrogenic** /ˌeestrə'jenik, 'estrə-/ *adj* of, inducing, or constituting the development and maintenance of secondary sex characteristics (eg development of the MAMMARY GLANDS) in female VERTEBRATE animals and initiation of oestrus in lower mammals – **oestrogenically** *adv*

**oestrone** /'eestrohn, 'estrohn/ *n* an oestrogenic STEROID hormone, $C_{18}H_{22}O_2$, that is a derivative of oestradiol and has similar actions and uses [ISV, fr *oestrin*]

**oestrus** /'eestrəs, 'estrəs/ *n* a regularly recurrent state of sexual excitability in the female of most lower mammals when she will copulate with the male and is capable of conceiving; heat [NL, fr L, gadfly, frenzy, fr Gk *oistros* – more at IRE] – **oestral, oestrous, oestrual** *adj*

**oestrus cycle** *n* the series of hormonally controlled changes in the activity of the reproductive organs in a female mammal from the beginning of one period of oestrus to the beginning of the next

**oeuvre** /'uhvə (*Fr* œːvr)/ *n, pl* **oeuvres** /∼/ a substantial body of work constituting the life's work of a writer, artist, or composer [Fr *œuvre*, lit., work, fr L *opera* – more at OPERA]

**of** /əv; *strong* ov/ *prep* **1a** – used to indicate origin or derivation ⟨*a man* ∼ *noble birth*⟩ ⟨*they expect it* ∼ *me*⟩ **b** – used to indicate cause, motive, or reason ⟨*died* ∼ *pneumonia*⟩ ⟨*did it* ∼ *her own free will*⟩ **c** proceeding from; ON THE PART OF ⟨*the approval* ∼ *the minister*⟩ ⟨*the buzzing* ∼ *the bees*⟩ ⟨*very kind* ∼ *him*⟩ **d** BY 4a(3) ⟨*the plays* ∼ *Shaw*⟩ – compare 's 2a(1) composed or made from ⟨*a throne* ∼ *gold*⟩ ⟨*a staff* ∼ *teachers*⟩ ⟨*a family* ∼ *five*⟩ **a(2)** using as a material; OUT OF ⟨*make more* ∼ *eggs, Mum – Woman's Own*⟩ **b** containing ⟨*a cup* ∼ *water*⟩ **c** – used to indicate the mass noun or class that includes the part denoted by the previous word ⟨*an inch* ∼ *rain*⟩ ⟨*a pound* ∼ *sugar*⟩ ⟨*a blade* ∼ *grass*⟩ ⟨*gave* ∼ *his time*⟩ ⟨*the 27th* ∼ *February*⟩ ⟨*a kind* ∼ *grey*⟩ **d** from among ⟨*most* ∼ *the army*⟩ ⟨*one* ∼ *his last poems*⟩ ⟨*the fattest* ∼ *the girls*⟩ ⟨*five* ∼ *us*⟩ ⟨*members* ∼ *the team*⟩ ⟨*she,* ∼ *all people!*⟩ **3a** belonging to (the usu inanimate possessor of a part or property) ⟨*the leg* ∼ *the chair*⟩ ⟨*the colour* ∼ *her dress*⟩ ⟨*the size* ∼ *the wings*⟩ **b** that is or are – used before possessive forms ⟨*a friend* ∼ *John's*⟩ ⟨*that nose* ∼ *his*⟩ **c** characterized by; with, having ⟨*a man* ∼ *courage*⟩ ⟨*an area* ∼ *hills*⟩ ⟨*a woman* ∼ *no importance*⟩ ⟨*suitcases* ∼ *a suitable size*⟩ **d** connected with ⟨*the king* ∼ *England*⟩ ⟨*a teacher* ∼ *English*⟩ ⟨*a smell* ∼ *mice*⟩ ⟨*the results* ∼ *the meeting*⟩ ⟨*the time* ∼ *arrival*⟩ ⟨*the work* ∼ *a moment*⟩ **e** existing or happening in or on ⟨*the University* ∼ *London*⟩ ⟨*the battle* ∼ *Blenheim*⟩ ⟨*my letter* ∼ *the 19th*⟩ **4a** relating to (a topic); concerning ⟨*stories* ∼ *his travels*⟩ ⟨*dreamed* ∼ *home*⟩ ⟨*a picture* ∼ *John*⟩ ⟨*what* ∼ *it?*⟩ **b** in respect to ⟨*slow* ∼ *speech*⟩ ⟨*north* ∼ *the lake*⟩ ⟨*have hopes* ∼ *him*⟩ ⟨*fond* ∼ *chocolate*⟩ ⟨*guilty* ∼ *murder*⟩ ⟨*proud* ∼ *you*⟩

⟨within a mile ~ here⟩ **c** directed towards; done to ⟨love ~ nature⟩ ⟨care ~ guinea pigs⟩ ⟨a drinker ~ beer⟩ ⟨the shooting ~ seals⟩ ⟨ask a question ~ him⟩ **d** – used to show separation or removal ⟨eased ~ pain⟩ ⟨cured him ~ mumps⟩ ⟨cheated him ~ his rights⟩ **5** – used to indicate apposition ⟨the city ~ Rome⟩ ⟨the age ~ eight⟩ ⟨the art ~ painting⟩ ⟨the name ~ Hawkins⟩ ⟨that fool ~ a husband⟩ **6a** informal in, during ⟨died ~ a Monday⟩ ⟨go there ~ an evening⟩ **b** NAm to (a specified hour) ⟨a quarter ~ ten⟩ **7** archaic on ⟨a plague ~ all cowards⟩ – Shak⟩ [ME, off, of, fr OE, adv & prep; akin to OHG aba off, away, L ab from, away, Gk apo]
**usage 1** Of should not be used for have in such sentences as ⟨I might have (not △ of) known⟩. **2** When of expresses the idea of possession by people, one can say ⟨a friend of the family⟩ ⟨a nephew of the king⟩ or ⟨a friend of John's⟩ ⟨some money of the firm's⟩, but the construction with the possessive form is less often used of inanimate things ⟨the crew of a liner (not liner's)⟩. Compare ⟨a picture of John (= representing him)⟩ ⟨a picture of John's (= belonging to him)⟩.

**of-** – see OB-

**ofay** /'oh,fay, -'-/ n, derog a white person – used by blacks [origin unknown]

**¹off** /of/ adv **1a(1)** from a place or position ⟨march ~⟩ ⟨frighten them ~⟩; specif away from land ⟨ship stood ~ to sea⟩ **a(2)** away in space or ahead in time ⟨stood 10 paces ~⟩ ⟨Christmas is a week ~⟩ **b** from a course; aside ⟨turned ~ into a minor road⟩; specif away from the wind **c** into sleep or unconsciousness ⟨dozed ~⟩ **2a** so as to be not supported ⟨rolled to the edge of the table and ~⟩, not in close contact ⟨blew the lid ~⟩ ⟨took his coat ~⟩, or not attached ⟨handle came ~⟩ ⟨cut his ear ~⟩ **b** so as to be divided ⟨surface marked ~ into squares⟩ ⟨a corner screened ~⟩ **c** OUT 2a(2) **3a** to or in a state of discontinuance or suspension ⟨shut ~ an engine⟩ ⟨game was rained ~⟩ ⟨the radio is ~⟩ **b** so as to be completely finished or no longer existent ⟨drink ~ a glass⟩ ⟨finish it ~⟩ ⟨kill them ~⟩ ⟨walk it ~⟩ **c** in or into a state of putrefaction ⟨cream's gone ~⟩ **d** (as if) by heart ⟨know it ~ pat⟩ **4** away from an activity or function ⟨the night shift went ~⟩ ⟨take time ~ for lunch⟩ **5** offstage ⟨noises ~⟩ **6** to a sexual climax ⟨brought him ~⟩ – compare JERK OFF [ME of, fr OE – more at OF] – **off and on** intermittently; ON AND OFF ⟨rained off and on all day⟩ – **off of** nonstandard off, from

**²off** prep **1a** – used to indicate physical separation or distance from ⟨take it ~ the table⟩ ⟨jumped ~ his bicycle⟩ ⟨cut a slice ~ the loaf⟩ ⟨wear it ~ the shoulder⟩ **b** lying or turning aside from; adjacent to ⟨a path ~ the main walk⟩ ⟨a shop just ~ the high street⟩ **c** to seaward of ⟨two miles ~ shore⟩ **d** away from ⟨a week ~ work⟩ ⟨completely ~ the point⟩ – often in combination ⟨off-target⟩ ⟨off-centre⟩ ⟨off-white⟩ **2** – used to indicate the source from which something derives or is obtained ⟨dined ~ oysters⟩ ⟨bought it ~ a friend⟩ ⟨claim it ~ tax⟩ ⟨scoring ~ his bowling⟩ **3a** not occupied in ⟨~ duty⟩ **b** no longer keen on or using ⟨he's ~ drugs⟩ ⟨I've gone ~ science fiction⟩ **c** below the usual standard or level of ⟨~ his game⟩
**usage** In formal writing, **from** should often replace **off** where one thinks of a "source" as in sense **2** ⟨bought it **off** a friend⟩. **Off** is acceptable in this sense only where an alternative or opposite could be **on** ⟨dine **off/on** oysters⟩ ⟨put it **on**/take it **off** the table⟩ **synonyms** see ¹IN

**³off** adj **1a** FAR **3 b** seaward **c** being the right-hand one of a pair ⟨the ~ wheel of a cart⟩ **d(1)** esp of a ball bowled in cricket moving or tending to move in the direction of the LEG SIDE ⟨~ spin⟩ ⟨an ~ cutter⟩ **d(2)** in, on, through, or towards the OFF SIDE of a cricket field ⟨~ drive⟩ **e** situated to one side; adjoining ⟨bedroom with dressing room ~⟩ **2a** started on the way ⟨~ on a spree⟩ **b** not taking place or staying in effect; cancelled ⟨the match is ~⟩ **c** of a dish on a menu no longer being served **3** remote, slight ⟨an ~ chance⟩ **4a** not working; disengaged ⟨he's ~ sick⟩ ⟨reading on his ~ days⟩ **b** slack ⟨~ season⟩ **5a** OFF-COLOUR **1a b** inferior ⟨~ grade of oil⟩ **6** provided ⟨well ~⟩ ⟨how are you ~ for socks?⟩ **7** informal poor, subnormal; esp, chiefly Br rather rude, unkind, or dishonest ⟨his manners were a bit ~⟩

**⁴off** vi to go away; leave ⟨had upped and ~ed with the family chauffeur – Good Housekeeping⟩

**⁵off** n, informal the start, outset; also a starting signal ⟨ready for the ~⟩

**offal** /'ofl/ n **1** the waste or by-product of a process: eg **1a** trimmings of a hide **b** the by-products of milling used esp for

animal feeds **2** the liver, heart, kidneys, etc of a butchered animal, used as food **3** refuse [ME, fr of off + fall]

**¹offbeat** /'of,beet/ n an unaccented (SYNCOPATED) beat of a musical bar

**²offbeat** adj, informal unusual; esp unconventional ⟨~ low price holidays – Evening Argus (Brighton)⟩

**'off-,break** n a slow bowled ball in cricket that turns from the OFF SIDE towards the LEG SIDE when it bounces

**off Broadway** /'brawdway/ adj or n, often cap O (of) a part of the New York professional theatre that is located outside the limits of theatrical Broadway area and stresses fundamental and artistic values

**'off-,chance** n a remote possibility – **on the off chance** in the hope; just in case ⟨looked in on the off chance of finding work⟩ ⟨hung around on the off chance she might turn up⟩

**,off-'colour** adj **1a** not having the correct or standard colour **b** unwell, seedy ⟨feeling a bit ~⟩ **2** chiefly NAm somewhat indecent; risqué ⟨an ~ story⟩

**offcut** /'of,kut/ n a piece (eg of paper, wood, meat, or cloth) that is left after the dividing or trimming of a larger piece

**offence, NAm chiefly offense** /ə'fens/ n **1** something that occasions a sense of outrage ⟨corruption in high places that was an ~ to the public conscience⟩ **2** (an) attack, assault **3** displeasure, resentment ⟨he takes ~ at the slightest criticism⟩ **4a** a sin, misdeed **b** an illegal act; esp one that can be tried without a jury rather than an INDICTABLE OFFENCE (one requiring trial by judge and jury) **5** chiefly NAm ATTACK **7** [ME, fr MF, fr L offensa, fr offensus, pp of offendere] – **offenceless** adj – **take offence** to be offended

**offend** /ə'fend/ vi **1a** to break a moral or divine law; sin – often + against **b** to violate a law or rule; do wrong ⟨~ against the law⟩ **2a** to cause difficulty or discomfort ⟨took off his shoe and removed the ~ing pebble⟩ **b** to cause displeasure, anger, or vexation ⟨thoughtless words that ~ needlessly⟩ ~ vt **1** to cause pain or displeasure to; hurt ⟨colours that ~ the eye⟩ **2** to cause to feel indignation or disgust, usu by violation of what is decent or courteous ⟨she was ~ed by their failure to introduce her to their new friend⟩ [ME offenden, fr MF offendre, fr L offendere to strike against, offend, fr ob- against + -fendere to strike – more at OB-, DEFEND] – **offender** n

**¹offensive** /ə'fensiv/ adj **1a** aggressive, attacking **b** of or designed for attack ⟨~ weapons⟩ **2** arousing physical disgust; repellent ⟨an ~ smell of rotten eggs⟩ **3** causing indignation or outrage ⟨found the film morally ~⟩ – **offensively** adv, **offensiveness** n

**²offensive** n **1** the position or attitude of an attacking party ⟨took the ~⟩ **2** an esp military attack on a large scale

**¹offer** /'ofə/ vt **1a** to present in an act of worship or devotion; sacrifice **b** to utter (eg a prayer) in an act of devotion – often + up ⟨~ed up prayers of thanksgiving⟩ **2a** to present for acceptance, rejection, or consideration ⟨was ~ed a job⟩ ⟨he ~ed me 10,000 for that book⟩ **b** to present in order to satisfy a requirement ⟨candidates for degrees may ~ Welsh as one of their foreign languages⟩ **3a** to propose for consideration; suggest ⟨~ a solution to a problem⟩ **b** to declare one's readiness or willingness ⟨~ed to help me⟩ **4a** to display; PUT UP ⟨~ed stubborn resistance⟩ **b** to threaten ⟨~ed to strike him with her cane⟩ **5a** to make available; afford ⟨the summit ~s a fine panorama⟩ **b** to present (goods) for sale ⟨we ~ a wide range of new and used cars⟩ **6** to present in performance or exhibition **7** to tender as payment; bid ~ vi **1** to present something in an act of worship or devotion; sacrifice **2** to make an offer for consideration, acceptance, etc **3** to present itself; occur ⟨will act when opportunity ~s⟩ **4** to make a proposal of marriage **5** archaic to make an attempt at [(vt 1) ME offren, fr OE offrian, fr LL offerre, fr L, to present, tender, fr ob- towards + ferre to carry; (all other senses) fr OF offrir, fr L offerre – more at BEAR]

**²offer** n **1a** a proposal ⟨accepted the ~ of a job⟩; specif a proposal of marriage **b** an undertaking to do or give something on a specific condition **2** a price named by a prospective buyer; a bid ⟨received a substantial ~ for the bungalow⟩ – **on offer** being offered; specif for sale, esp at a reduced price – **under offer** sold subject to the signing of contracts – used in connection with sales of property

**offering** /'of(ə)ring/ n **1a** the act of one who offers **b** something offered; esp a sacrifice ceremonially offered as a part of worship **c** a contribution to the support of a church or other religious organization **2** something offered for sale or inspection ⟨the latest ~ of a leading novelist⟩

**offertory** /'ofət(ə)ri/ *n* **1** *often cap* **1a** the offering at Communion of bread and wine to God before they are consecrated **b** a verse from a Psalm said or sung at the beginning of the offertory **2** (the collection and presentation of) the offerings of the congregation at public worship [ML *offertorium*, fr *offertus*, pp of LL *offerre*]

¹**offhand** /of'hand/ *adv* without forethought or preparation ⟨*couldn't give the figures* ~⟩

²**offhand** *adj* **1** done or made offhand; impromptu ⟨~ *excuses*⟩ **2** lacking warmth or courtesy; brusque, curt **3** lacking affectation; informal, casual

**offhanded** /of'handid/ *adj* offhand – **offhandedly** *adv*, **offhandedness** *n*

'**off-,hour** *n*, *NAm* off-peak

**office** /'ofis/ *n* **1a** a special duty, charge, or position for a public purpose; a position of authority to exercise a public function and to receive whatever emoluments may belong to it ⟨*hold public* ~⟩ **b** a position with special duties or responsibilities ⟨*was elected to the* ~ *of chairman*⟩ **2** a prescribed form or service of worship; *esp, cap* DIVINE OFFICE **3a** something that should or must be done; a duty ⟨*his various domestic* ~s⟩ **b** an esp beneficial service or action carried out for another ⟨*through her good* ~s *I recovered my belongings*⟩ **4** a place where a particular kind of business is transacted or a service is supplied: e g **4a** a place in which administrative functions and clerical work are performed **b** a room assigned to a person or group of people in a commercial organization or where the work of a particular department in such an organization is carried out ⟨*the manager's* ~⟩ ⟨*drawing* ~⟩ ⟨*inquiry* ~⟩ **c** the place in which a professional person (e g an accountant or solicitor) conducts business; *also, NAm* a doctor's consulting room **d** the headquarters of an enterprise, a company, or an organization or branch of such ⟨*insurance* ~⟩ ⟨*the London* ~⟩ **5a** *cap* a major administrative unit in some governments ⟨*the Foreign* Office⟩ **b** a subdivision of some government departments **6** *pl, chiefly Br* the apartments, attached buildings, or outhouses in which the activities attached to the service of a house are carried on [ME, fr OF, fr L *officium* service, duty, office, fr *opus* work + *facere* to make, do – more at OPERATE, DO]

**office boy,** *fem* **office girl** *n* a boy employed to do odd jobs and run errands in an office

**officeholder** /'ofis,hohldə/ *n* one holding a public office

**office hours** *n pl* the hours during which an office is open for business

¹**officer** /'ofisə/ *n* **1** a policeman **2** one who holds a position with special duties or responsibilities ⟨*the* ~s *of the trade union*⟩ **3a** one who holds a position of authority or command in the armed forces; *specif* one holding by a commission a rank of or above second lieutenant in the army, or its equivalent in other forces **b** the master or any of the mates of a merchant or passenger ship [ME, fr MF *officier*, fr ML *officiarius*, fr L *officium*]

²**officer** *vt* **1** to supply with officers **2** to command or direct as an officer

**officer of arms** *n* any of the officers (e g KING OF ARMS, herald, or pursuivant) of a monarch or government responsible for devising and granting heraldic arms

¹**official** /ə'fish(ə)l/ *n* **1** one who administers esp public or governmental affairs ⟨*government* ~s⟩ ⟨*an* ~ *from the Coal Board*⟩ **2** one who administers the rules of a game or sport, esp as a referee or umpire

²**official** *adj* **1** of an office and its duties ⟨*an* ~ *title*⟩ ⟨*away on* ~ *business*⟩ **2** holding an office **3a** authoritative, authorized ⟨*an* ~ *statement*⟩ **b** prescribed or recognized as authorized; *esp* recognized by a pharmacopoeia ⟨*the* ~ *preparation of a drug*⟩ **4** suitable for or characteristic of a person in office; formal ⟨*an* ~ *welcome*⟩ △ officious – **officially** *adv*

**officialdom** /ə'fishəldəm/ *n* officials as a group

**officialese** /ə,fishə'leez/ *n* the characteristic language of official statements; wordy, pompous, or obscure language

**officialism** /ə'fishəliz(ə)m/ *n* lack of flexibility and initiative combined with excessive adherence to regulations and routine in the behaviour of usu government officials

**Official Receiver** *n* a public official appointed to administer a bankrupt's property

**officiant** /ə'fis(h)yənt/ *n* a person (e g a priest) who officiates at a religious rite

**officiary** *adj* connected with, derived from, or having a title or rank by virtue of holding an office ⟨*the Law Lords are* ~ *nobles, not titular ones*⟩

**officiate** /ə'fishiayt/ *vi* **1** to perform an esp religious ceremony, function, or duty ⟨~ *at a wedding*⟩ **2** to act as an official or in an official capacity (e g at a sporting event) ~ *vt* **1** to serve as a leader or celebrant of (a ceremony) **2** to administer the rules of (a game or sport) esp as a referee or umpire – **officiation** *n*

**officinal** /,ofi'sienl/ *adj* **1** available at a pharmacy without special preparation ⟨~ *medicine*⟩; *also* OFFICIAL 3b **2** medicinal ⟨~ *herbs*⟩ [ML *officinalis* of a storeroom, fr *officina* storeroom, fr L, workshop, fr *opific-, opifex* workman, fr *opus* work + *facere* to do] – **officinal** *n*, **officinally** *adv*

**officious** /ə'fishəs/ *adj* **1** volunteering services that are neither requested nor required; interfering **2** too zealous in the exercise of authority or performance of duty **3** *of a diplomatic agreement* informal, unofficial ⟨*diplomats engaged in* ~ *talks*⟩ **4** *archaic* dutiful, obliging **9** official [L *officiosus*, fr *officium* service, office] – **officiously** *adv*, **officiousness** *n*

**offing** /'ofing/ *n* the part of the deep sea visible from the shore [¹*off* + *-ing*] – **in the offing** about to happen in the near or foreseeable future

**offish** /'ofish/ *adj, informal* inclined to stand aloof; distant [¹*off* + *-ish*] – **offishly** *adv*, **offishness** *n*

,**off-'key** *adj* **1** varying in pitch from the proper tone of a melody **2** irregular, anomalous

'**off-,licence** *n, Br* **1** a licence to sell alcoholic drinks for consumption off the premises **2** a place (e g a shop or part of a pub) having an off-licence – **off-licensee** *n*

**off limits** *adj or adv, chiefly NAm & Austr* out-of-bounds

,**off-'line** *adj* **1** not attached to or controlled by a computer; *esp* temporarily unattached to a computer ⟨~ *equipment*⟩ **2** *of a computer* not linked to or controlling a piece of equipment (e g a terminal) or system with which there is normally a link □ compare ON-LINE – **off-line** *adv*

,**off-'load** *vt* **1** UNLOAD 1,2 **2** to get rid of by transferring ⟨~ed *the blame onto his father*⟩

,**off-off-'Broadway** *adj or n, often cap both Os* (of) an avant-garde theatrical movement in New York – compare FRINGE 3d

,**off-'peak** *adj* of a time of less than usual or maximum demand ⟨~ *train services*⟩ ⟨*electricity at* ~ *prices*⟩

**offprint** /'of,print/ *n* a separately printed excerpt (e g an article from a magazine) – **offprint** *vt*

,**off-'putting** *adj, chiefly Br informal* putting one off; disagreeable, disconcerting – see also PUT OFF

**off sales** *n pl, Br* drinks, esp alcoholic drinks, sold by an off-licence, esp one that is attached to or part of a pub

**offscouring** /'of,skowəring/ *n usu pl* refuse, dregs ⟨*the* ~s *of society*⟩

**offscreen** /,of'skreen/ *adv or adj* **1** out of sight of the film or television viewer **2** in private life

,**off-'season** *n* a time of suspended or reduced activity (e g in business or manufacture)

¹**offset** /'of,set/ *n* **1a(1)** a short shoot that grows out to the side from the base of a plant and produces new shoots and roots **a(2)** a small bulb arising from the base of another bulb **b** an offshoot, esp of a family or race **c** a spur projecting from a range of hills **2a** a horizontal ledge on the face of a wall formed by the wall's becoming thinner above it **b** an abrupt change in the size or outline of an object; *also* the part set off by such change **3** an abrupt bend in an object (e g a pipe or rod), usu to get round an obstacle **4** something that serves to compensate for or balance something else; *specif* either of two balancing items in an account book **5a** a printing process in which an inked impression from a plate is first made on a rubber surface round a cylinder and then transferred to the paper being printed **b** an unintentional transfer of ink (e g from a freshly printed sheet) **6** *archaic* an outset, start

²**offset** /,of'set/ *vb* **-tt-; offset** *vt* **1a** to be placed over against; balance ⟨*credits* ~ *debits*⟩ **b** to serve as a compensation for; make up for ⟨*his speed* ~ *his opponent's greater weight*⟩ **2** to form an offset in ⟨~ *a wall*⟩ **3** to print (e g a book) using the offset process ~ *vi* **1** SET OFF 2 **2** to become marked by offset – used in printing **3** to reduce in quantity or amount ⟨*high taxes should be* ~ *for the poor*⟩

**offset litho** *n* offset printing from plates reproduced photographically (PHOTOLITHOGRAPHS)

**offshoot** /'of,shooht/ *n* **1** a branch growing from the main stem of a plant **2a** a side branch (e g of a mountain range) **b** an indirect or subsidiary branch, descendant, or member

¹**offshore** /of'shaw/ *adv* away from the shore; at a distance from the shore

**²offshore** /'ofshaw/ *adj* **1** coming or moving away from the shore ⟨*an* ~ *breeze*⟩ **2a** situated or carried on at a distance from the shore ⟨~ *fisheries*⟩ **b** distant from the shore; beyond the low-water line

**offshore fund** *n* a form of UNIT TRUST (system of investment) that is registered abroad, usu in countries offering tax advantages

**offside** /ˌofˈsied/ *adv or adj* illegally in advance of the ball or puck in a team game

**off side** *n* **1** *the* part of a cricket field on the opposite side of a line joining the middle stumps to that in which the batsman stands when playing a ball; the right-hand part of the field as viewed by a right-handed batsman looking directly at the bowler – compare LEG SIDE **2 off side, offside** *chiefly Br* **2a** the side of a vehicle furthest from the edge of the road (eg the right-hand side in Britain) **b** the right side of an animal or team of harnessed horses, dogs, etc □ (2) usu + *the*; compare NEARSIDE

**offsider** /ˈofˌsiedə/ *n*, *Austr & NZ informal* an assistant, deputy

**off spin** *n* spin that causes a cricket ball bowled at a slow speed to turn from the OFF SIDE towards the LEG SIDE when it bounces

**off spinner** *n* **1** a bowler who imparts OFF SPIN to a ball; a bowler of OFF-BREAKS **2** OFF-BREAK

**offspring** /'ofˌspring/ *n*, *pl* **offspring** *also* **offsprings 1** the young of a person, animal, or plant; progeny **2** a result, issue [ME *ofspring*, fr OE, fr *of* off + *springan* to spring]

**offstage** /ˌofˈstayj/ *adv or adj* **1** on a part of the stage not visible to the audience **2** in private life ⟨*known* ~ *as a kindly man*⟩ **3** behind the scenes; away from the public gaze ⟨*much of the important work of the conference was done* ~⟩

**offtake** /'ofˌtayk/ *n* **1** the act of taking off: eg **1a** the taking off or purchase of goods **b** the amount of goods purchased during a given period **2** a channel or passage for taking or leading off (eg a liquid or a gas) ⟨~ *of a distilling flask*⟩

**‚off-the-'cuff** *adj or adv*, *informal* said or done without preparation; improvised, impromptu ⟨*an* ~ *remark*⟩ [prob fr the use by a public speaker of notes written on the shirt-cuff]

**‚off-the-'peg** *adj*, *chiefly Br* (of or dealing in clothes) made beforehand to fit standard requirements; *esp* made to fit or suit a wide but standardized range of customers – compare MADE-TO-MEASURE – **off-the-peg** *adv*

**‚off-the-'record** *adj or adv* (given or made) unofficially or in confidence and not for quotation ⟨*an* ~ *remark*⟩

**‚off-the-'shelf** *adj* available as a stock item; not specially designed or custom-made

**‚off-'white** *n or adj* (a) yellowish or greyish white

**off year** *n*, *NAm* **1** a year in which no major (eg presidential) election is held **2** a year of suspended or reduced activity (eg in business or manufacture) ⟨*an* ~ *for arms sales*⟩

**oft** /oft/ *adv*, *poetic* often [ME, fr OE; akin to OHG *ofto* often]

**often** /'ofən, *also* 'oftən/ *adv* **1** at many times **2** in many cases ⟨*they* ~ *die young*⟩ [ME, alter. of *oft*]

**oftentimes** /'of(t)ən‚tiemz/, **ofttimes** /'oftiemz/ *adv* often

**O gauge** *n* a gauge of track in model railways in which the rails are approximately 32 millimetres (1¹⁄₄ inches) apart [²*oh*]

**ogee** /'oh‚jee/ *n* **1** a shallow S-shaped curve; *esp* a moulding in this form **2 ogee arch, ogee** a pointed arch having each side in the form of an ogee [obs *ogee* ogive, modif of Fr *ogive*; fr the use of such mouldings in ogives]

**oggy** /'ogi/ *n*, *dial* CORNISH PASTY – called also TIDDY OGGY, PRIDDY OGGY [origin unknown]

**ogham, ogam** /'ogəm, 'oh‧əm/ *n* a 20-character OLD IRISH alphabet used in commemorative inscriptions in which the symbols consist of notches for vowels or lines for consonants that meet or cut across a straight line (eg the edge of a stone) [IrGael *ogham*, fr MIr *ogom, ogum*] – **oghamist** *n*, **oghamic** *adj*

**ogival** /oh'jievl/ *adj* (having the form) of an ogive or an ogee

**ogive** /'oh‚jiev/ *n* **1a** a GROIN or RIB running diagonally across a Gothic vault **b** a pointed arch or window **2** an ogee-shaped graph that plots the sum of all the frequencies up to and including a given frequency, against the percentage of the total sample at that point [Fr, fr MF *ogive, augive*, perh fr *auge* trough, fr L *alveus*]

**ogle** /'ohgl/ *vb* to glance or stare, esp with marked sexual interest (at) [prob fr LG *oegeln*, fr *oog* eye; akin to OHG *ouga* eye – more at EYE] – **ogle** *n*, **ogler** *n*

**ogre** /'ohgə/, *fem* **ogress** /'ohgris/ *n* **1** a hideous giant of fairy tales and folklore that feeds on human beings; a monster **2** a dreaded person or thing ⟨*the* ~ *of imperialism*⟩ – compare SPECTRE 2 [Fr, perh fr L *Orcus*, god of the underworld] – **ogreish** *adj*

**¹oh** /oh/ *interj* **1** – used to express an emotion (eg surprise, pain, or desire) **2** – used before a name or title when addressing someone ⟨*Oh, Roger, will you come here, please?*⟩ **3** – used to express acknowledgment or understanding of a statement [ME *o*]

**²oh, O** *n* nought *synonyms* see ¹ZERO [*o*; fr the similarity of the symbol for nought (0) to the letter *O*]

**ohm** /ohm/ *n* the SI unit of electrical RESISTANCE (opposition to the flow of an electric current) that is equal to the resistance between two points of a material that conducts electricity when a constant voltage of 1 volt applied to these points produces a current of 1 amp [Georg Simon *Ohm* †1854 Ger physicist] – **ohmic** *adj*, **ohmically** *adv*

**ohmage** /'ohmij/ *n* the resistance of a material or device to the flow of an electric current, expressed in ohms

**ohmmeter** /'ohm‚meetə/ *n* an instrument for indicating electrical RESISTANCE (opposition to the flow of an electric current) directly in ohms [ISV]

**oho** /oh'hoh/ *interj* – used to express various emotions (eg amused surprise, taunting, or exultation) [ME]

**-oic** /-'oh‧ik/ *suffix* (→ *adj*) containing a CARBOXYL group or one of its derivatives ⟨*benzoic acid*⟩ [-*o-* + -*ic*]

**¹-oid** /-oyd/ *suffix* (→ *n*) something resembling (a specified object) or having (a specified quality) ⟨*globoid*⟩ ⟨*asteroid*⟩

**²-oid** *suffix* (→ *adj*) **1** resembling; having the form or appearance of ⟨*petaloid*⟩ ⟨*anthropoid*⟩ **2** *derog* bearing an imperfect resemblance to ⟨*humanoid*⟩ [MF & L; MF -*oïde*, fr L -*oïdes*, fr Gk -*oeidēs*, fr -*o-* + *eidos* appearance, form – more at WISE]

**oidium** /oh'idi‧əm/ *n*, *pl* **oidia** /-di‧ə/ **1a** any of a genus (*Oidium* of the family Moniliaceae) of IMPERFECT FUNGI, many of which are the asexual spore-bearing stages of various POWDERY MILDEWS (fungi parasitic on plants) **b** any of the small asexual spores (CONIDIA) borne in chains by various fungi (eg an oidium) **2** a plant disease (POWDERY MILDEW), esp of grapes, caused by an oidium [NL, fr *o-* + -*idium*]

**oik** /oyk/ *n*, *Br slang* a boorish lout; a yob [origin unknown]

**¹oil** /oyl/ *n* **1** any of numerous smooth greasy substances that burn readily, are liquid or at least easily liquefiable on warming, and are soluble in ether and similar chemical compounds but not in water **2** petroleum ⟨*drilling for* ~ *and natural gas*⟩ **3** a substance (eg a cosmetic preparation) of oily consistency ⟨*bath* ~⟩ **4a** an OIL PAINT used by an artist ⟨*portrait painted in* ~*s*⟩ **b** a painting done in OIL PAINTS **5** *informal* flattery [ME *oile*, fr OF, fr L *oleum* olive oil, fr Gk *elaion*, fr *elaia* olive] – **oil** *adj* – **burn the midnight oil** to work or study far into the night – **pour oil on troubled waters** to attempt to bring a quarrel, argument, etc, to a state of calm and reconciliation, esp by the use of careful and gentle words

**²oil** *vt* to smear, rub over, furnish, or lubricate with oil ~ *vi* **1** to take on fuel oil **2** to change from a solid fat into an oil by melting – **oil somebody's hand/palm** to bribe somebody – see also **oil the** WHEELS

**oil beetle** *n* a BLISTER BEETLE (*Meloe* or a related genus) that emits an oily substance when disturbed

**oilbird** /'oyl‚buhd/ *n* a bird (*Steatornis caripensis*) of northern S America and Trinidad that is related to the nightjar, is active at night, feeds chiefly on the fatty fruits of various palms, and has young that contain much fat from which oil can be extracted and used as a substitute for butter

**oil cake** *n* the solid residue that remains after extracting the oil from seeds (eg linseed), used esp for cattle food

**oilcan** /'oyl‚kan/ *n* a can for oil; *esp* a vessel with a nozzle designed to release oil in a controlled flow (eg for lubricating machinery)

**oilcloth** /'oyl‚kloth/ *n* cloth treated with oil or paint and used for table and shelf coverings

**oil colour** *n* OIL PAINT

**oiled** /oyld/ *adj* **1** lubricated or treated (as if) with oil ⟨~ *paper*⟩ **2** *slang* drunk – often in *well oiled*

**oil engine** *n* an engine that burns a mixture of vaporized oil and air

**oiler** /'oylə/ *n* **1** one (eg a workman) who or that which oils something **2** a receptacle or device for applying oil **3** an oil tanker **4** *pl*, *NAm* oilskins

**oil field** *n* a region rich in petroleum deposits; *esp* one that produces petroleum in commercial quantities

**oil gland** *n* a gland (e g of the skin) that produces an oily secretion; *esp* the UROPYGIAL GLAND that, in birds, produces oil used for preening the feathers

**oil of turpentine** *n* TURPENTINE 2a

**oil of vitriol** *n* concentrated SULPHURIC ACID – not used technically

**oil of wintergreen** *n* an aromatic oily liquid, $C_8H_8O_3$, derived from SALICYLIC ACID, that is present in the leaves of a wintergreen (*Gaultheria procumbens*) and in the bark of SWEET BIRCH and that is used as a flavouring and in medicine as a COUNTER-IRRITANT

**oil paint** *n* paint in which the substance with which the colour or pigment is mixed is a DRYING OIL (e g LINSEED OIL)

**oil painting** *n* **1** the act or art of painting with oil paints **2** a picture painted with oil paints

**oil palm** *n* an African palm tree (*Elaeis guineensis*) with large featherlike leaves, that is cultivated for its fruit whose flesh and seeds yield PALM OIL

**oil pan** *n*, *NAm* the SUMP (reservoir for receiving surplus oil) of an INTERNAL-COMBUSTION ENGINE

**oilseed** /'oyl,seed/ *n* a seed or crop (e g linseed or rape) grown largely for oil

**oil shale** *n* shale from which oil can be extracted

**oilskin** /'oyl,skin/ *n* **1** an oiled waterproof cloth used for coverings and garments **2** an oilskin or plastic raincoat **3** *pl* an oilskin or plastic suit of coat and trousers

**oil slick** *n* a film of oil floating on water

**oilstone** /'oyl,stohn/ *n* a sharpening stone for use with a surface coating of oil

**oil well** *n* a well drilled in the earth from which petroleum is obtained

**oily** /'oyli/ *adj* **1** of or consisting of oil **2** covered or impregnated with oil ⟨~ *rags*⟩ **3** excessively smooth or suave in manner; unctuous, ingratiating – **oilily** *adv*, **oiliness** *n*

**oink** /oyngk/ *n* a noise characteristic of a pig; *also, humorous* a similar human, animal, or mechanical sound [imit] – **oink** *vi*

**ointment** /'oyntmənt/ *n* a soothing or healing substance for applying to the skin – see also FLY **in the ointment** [ME, alter. of *oignement*, fr OF, modif of L *unguentum*, fr *unguere* to anoint; akin to OHG *ancho* butter, Skt *anjati* he salves]

**Ojibwa, Ojibway** /oh'jibway/ *n, pl* **Ojibwas, Ojibways,** *esp collectively* **Ojibwa, Ojibway** a member of an American Indian people originally of Michigan; *also* their ALGONQUIAN language [Ojibwa *ojib-ubway,* a kind of moccasin worn by the Ojibwa]

**¹OK, okay** /oh'kay, '-,-/ *adv, adj, or interj* ALL RIGHT [prob abbr of *oll korrect,* facetious spelling of *all correct*]

**²OK, okay** /oh'kay/ *vt* **OK's, okays; OK'ing, okaying; OK'd, okayed** to approve, authorize

**³OK, okay** /oh'kay/ *n, pl* **OK's, okays** an approval, endorsement

**oka** /'ohkə/ *n* an oke

**okapi** /oh'kahpi/ *n* an African mammal (*Okapia johnstoni*) that is closely related to the giraffe but has a relatively short neck, a coat of solid reddish-chestnut on the body, yellowish-white on the cheeks, and purplish-black and cream rings on the upper parts of the legs [native name in Africa]

**oke** /ohk/ *n* any of three units of weight varying around 1.25 kilograms (about $2^3/_4$ pounds) and used respectively in Greece, Turkey, and Egypt [Fr, NGk, & Turk; Fr *ocque,* fr NGk & Turk; NGk *oka,* fr Turk *okka,* fr Ar *ūqīyah*]

**okeydoke** /,ohki'dohk/, **okeydokey** /-'dohki/ *interj* – used to express assent [redupl of *OK*]

**Okie** /'ohki/ *n* a migrant agricultural worker; *esp* one from Oklahoma in the 1930s [*Oklahoma + -ie*]

**okra** /'ohkrə, 'okrə/ *n* **1** a tall plant (*Hibiscus esculentus*) of the hollyhock family that is cultivated for its edible sticky green pods **2** the pods of the okra used as a vegetable and thickening agent esp in soups, stews, and curries – called also LADY'S FINGERS; compare GUMBO 1 [of African origin; akin to Twi ¹*kulru*¹*ma³* okra]

**okta** /'oktah/ *n* a unit equal to $^1/_8$ of the area of the observable sky used in specifying the amount of cloud cover [alter. of *octa-*]

**¹-ol** /-ol, -ohl/ *suffix* (→ *n*) chemical compound containing a HYDROXYL group; ALCOHOL ⟨glycer*ol*⟩ ⟨phen*ol*⟩ ⟨etha*nol*⟩ [ISV, fr *alcohol*]

**²-ol** *comb form* (→ *n*) -ole

**¹old** /ohld/ *adj* **1a** dating from the remote past; ancient ⟨~ *traditions*⟩ **b** persisting from an earlier time ⟨an ~ *ailment*⟩ **c**

of long standing ⟨an ~ *friend*⟩ **2a(1)** distinguished from something of the same kind by being of an earlier date ⟨many still used the ~ *name*⟩ **a(2)** SENIOR 2 ⟨the Old *Pretender*⟩ **b** *cap* constituting an early period in the development of a language ⟨Old *Irish*⟩ **3** having existed for a specified period of time ⟨a girl three years ~⟩ **4** of or originating in a past era ⟨~ *chronicles record the event*⟩ **5** advanced in years or age ⟨an ~ *man*⟩ ⟨looked ~ at 20⟩ **6** experienced ⟨an ~ *trooper speaking of the last war*⟩ **7** former ⟨his ~ *students*⟩ **8a** showing the effects of time or use; worn, aged ⟨~ *shoes*⟩ **b** *of a land surface or feature* having undergone much erosion and characterized by minimum relief ⟨the wide flattened floor of an ~ *valley*⟩ – compare MATURE 5, YOUTHFUL 5 **c** no longer in use; discarded ⟨~ *rags*⟩ **d** of a greyish or dusty colour ⟨~ *mauve*⟩ **9a** long familiar ⟨the same ~ *story*⟩ ⟨good ~ *Joe*⟩ **b** – used as an intensive ⟨a high ~ *time*⟩ ⟨any ~ *time*⟩ – see also **make old** BONES, CHIP **off the old block, play the old** SOLDIER [ME, fr OE *eald;* akin to OHG *alt* old, L *alere* to nourish, *alescere* to grow, *altus* high, deep] – **oldness** *n*

**synonyms Old, aged, elderly,** and **venerable** can all apply to people. **Old** usually implies advanced years, while **elderly** simply suggests having passed the prime of life. **Aged** suggests extreme old age, and often also infirmity or senility. **Venerable** stresses the respect due to age, and may also be applied to things that have a kind of life, such as trees or languages. In describing inanimate objects, **old** is the general term, suggesting simply that something has existed for a long time. **Olden** is a poetic word suggesting nostalgia for bygone times. **Ancient** describes what belongs to the distant past, **antique** things from a more recent past, which are valued because of this. What is **antiquated,** however, is discredited or out-of-date, and therefore discarded ⟨antique *chairs fetch a high price*⟩ ⟨nobody *pays any attention to his* antiquated *notions*⟩. **Antediluvian** is a humorous exaggeration of **antiquated. Old-fashioned** describes what belongs to the recent past, and is not at this moment in vogue. **Archaic** applies to often primitive survivals from the past ⟨archaic *Greek art*⟩. **Obsolete** and **obsolescent** denote what has passed, or is passing, respectively, from modern use. See ²ELDER. Compare VETERAN. **antonyms** new, modern, recent, fashionable

**²old** *n* **1** old or earlier time – in *of old* ⟨mighty men of ~⟩ **2** one of a specified age – usu in combination ⟨a 3-year-*old*⟩

**old Adam** /'adəm/ *n* the sinful element in man's make-up [*Adam,* the first man & first sinner in the Bible (Gen 2:7–3:24)]

**,old-'age** *adj* of old age

**old age** *n* the final stage of the normal life span; *specif* the period of life after the age of retirement

**old age pension** *n* a state pension paid to retired people – **old age pensioner** *n*

**Old Bailey** /'bayli/ *n* CENTRAL CRIMINAL COURT [the Old *Bailey,* building in London, seat of the Central Criminal Court]

**Old Bill** /bil/ *n taking sing or pl vb, Br slang* the police; *also, taking pl vb* policemen [perh fr Old *Bill,* grousing old soldier in cartoons by Bruce Bairnsfather †1959 Br artist]

**old boy** *n, chiefly Br* **1** *often cap O&B* a former pupil of a particular, esp public, school **2** a fellow, friend – often used as an informal term of address to a male **3** *informal* a usu sprightly or waggish old man

**old boy network** *n, chiefly Br* **1** *the* system of favouritism by which jobs, influence, or information are exchanged between persons of the same social, educational, or professional background; *specif* such a system among former pupils of public schools **2** *taking sing or pl vb* those who operate an old boy network

**Old Bulgarian** *n* Old Church Slavonic

**Old Catholic** *n* a member of any of various national churches having separated from the ROMAN CATHOLIC church since the 18th century and being in communion with the Anglican church

**Old Church Slavonic, NAm Old Church Slavic** *n* a Slavonic language surviving only as the language of the services of the Russian Orthodox Church

**old contemptibles** *n pl, often cap O&C, informal the* British expeditionary force in France in 1914 [fr the alleged description of it by the Kaiser of Germany as a 'contemptible little army'; his phrase *verächtlich klein* really meant 'contemptibly small']

**old country** *n* an emigrant's country of origin; *esp* a European country

**olden** /'ohld(ə)n/ *adj, poetic* of a bygone era **synonyms** see ¹OLD

**Old English** *n* **1a** English of the 7th to 11th centuries **b** English of any period before Modern English 2 BLACK LETTER (style of type or lettering)

**Old English sheepdog** *n* (any of) an English breed of medium-sized sheepdogs with very long shaggy usu blue-grey and white coats

**olde-worlde** /ˌohld ˈwuhld; *often said jocularly as* ˌohldi ˈwuhldi/ *adj* old-world; *esp* excessively or pretentiously so ⟨*modern pubs decorated with* ~ *junk*⟩ [pseudo-antique spelling of *old-world*]

**old face** *n* a style of type distinguished by oblique thickening of curved strokes, slight contrast between light and heavy strokes, and bracketed SERIFS (short lines added to the ends of letters)

**oldfangled** /ˌohldˈfangˌgld/ *adj* old-fashioned – compare NEWFANGLED [*old* + *-fangled* (as in *newfangled*)]

¹**old-ˈfashioned** *adj* **1a** (characteristic) of a past era; outdated ⟨*wears* ~ *spectacles*⟩ **b** clinging to customs of a past era **2** out of date *synonyms* see ¹OLD *antonyms* fashionable, trendy – **old-fashionedly** *adv*

²**old-fashioned** *n* a cocktail usu made with whisky, bitters, sugar, a twist of lemon peel, and a small amount of water or soda

**old-fashioned look** *n* a knowing or quizzical look

**Old French** *n* French of the 9th to 16th centuries; *esp* French from the 9th to the 13th century

**old girl** *n, chiefly Br* **1** *often cap O&G* a former female pupil of a particular, esp public, school **2** a friend – often used as an informal form of address to a female **3** *informal* a usu sprightly or resilient old woman

**Old Glory** *n* the flag of the USA

**old gold** *n or adj* (a) dull brownish-yellow like that of tarnished gold

**old guard** *n taking sing or pl vb, often cap O&G* the conservative members (e g of a political party) who are unwilling to accept new ideas, practices, or conditions

**old hand** *n* VETERAN 1a

**old hat** *adj* **1** old-fashioned **2** lacking in originality; trite

**Old High German** *n* HIGH GERMAN before the 12th century

**Old Icelandic** *n* the Icelandic form of the OLD NORSE language

**oldie** /ˈohldi/ *n, informal* something or someone old; *esp* a popular song from the past ⟨*a radio station specializing in golden* ~s⟩

**Old Ionic** *n* the Greek dialect in which the poems of Homer were written down

**Old Irish** *n* Irish before the 11th century

**oldish** /ˈohldish/ *adj* somewhat old or elderly

**old lady** *n, informal* **1** one's wife **2** one's mother

**Old Latin** *n* Latin before about 75 BC; pre-classical Latin

**old-ˈline** *adj* **1** clinging to traditional policies or practices; conservative **2** *NAm* having a reputation or authority based on seniority; established

**old maid** *n* **1** SPINSTER 2 **2** *informal* a prim fussy person ⟨*he was a real* ~ *about picking up litter*⟩ **3** a simple card game, played with a normal 52-card pack from which one card, usu a queen, has been removed, in which the players try to get rid of their cards in pairs matched by rank as they acquire them, the loser being the player left holding the odd card – **old-maidish** *adj*

**old man** *n* **1** *informal* one's husband or father **2** *informal, cap O&M* one in authority (e g one's employer, manager, or commander) – + *the* **3** *Austr* an adult male kangaroo

**old-man's beard** *n* **1** any of several plants (genus *Clematis*) of the buttercup family having long feathery flower-parts; *esp* TRAVELLER'S JOY **2** a greenish-grey lichen (*Usnea barbata*) that grows in long hairlike strands on the trunks and branches of trees **3** SPANISH MOSS (plant of the pineapple family)

**old master** *n* **1** a superior artist or craftsman of established reputation; *esp* a distinguished European painter of the 16th, 17th, or early 18th century **2** a work by an old master

**Old Nick** /nik/ *n* – used as an informal or humorous name for the devil [prob fr *Nick*, nickname for *Nicholas*]

**Old Norse** *n* the NORTH GERMANIC language of Scandinavia and Iceland before about 1350

**Old North French** *n* the N dialects of Old French and esp those of Normandy and Picardy

**old penny** *n* PENNY 1a(1)

**Old Prussian** *n* a Baltic language used in E Prussia until the 17th century

**Old Red Sandstone** *n* a thick series of rocks of the DEVONIAN geological period, that occur in some parts of Britain and Europe and consist predominantly of red sandstone

**Old Saxon** *n* the language of the Saxons of NW Germany until about the 12th century

**old school** *n taking sing or pl vb* a group of people maintaining the traditional policies and practices of the past

**old school tie** *n* **1a** a tie displaying the colours of an English PUBLIC SCHOOL as worn by former pupils **b** the attitudes of conservatism and upper-class solidarity traditionally attributed to former members of British public schools **2** clannishness among members of an established clique or group

**old soldier** *n* **1** a former or long-serving soldier **2** an experienced person

**old-ˈsquaw** *n, NAm* LONG-TAILED DUCK

**old stager** /ˈstayjə/ *n, chiefly Br* VETERAN 1a

**oldster** /ˈohldstə/ *n, chiefly NAm informal* an old or elderly person

**old style** *n* **1** *cap O&S* a style of reckoning time according to the JULIAN CALENDAR used before the GREGORIAN CALENDAR was introduced **2** *chiefly NAm* OLD FACE (style of type)

**Old Style** *adj, of a date* using or according to the JULIAN CALENDAR

**old sweat** *n, chiefly Br informal* a veteran soldier; *broadly* an experienced person

**Old Testament** *n* a collection of writings forming the Jewish Scriptures and the first part of the Christian Bible – see BIBLE table

**ˈold-ˌtime** *adj* **1** (characteristic) of an earlier period **2** of long standing

**ˌold-ˈtimer** *n* **1** VETERAN 1a **2** something old-fashioned; an antique **3** *chiefly NAm* an oldster

**Old Welsh** *n* Welsh before about 1150

**old wives' tale** *n* a traditional tale or bit of wisdom; *esp* a traditional superstitious notion

**old woman** *n, informal* **1** one's wife or mother **2** *derog* a timid, prim, or fussy person, esp a man

**ˌold-ˈworld** *adj* **1** (characteristic) of the Old World **2** reminiscent of a past age; *esp* quaintly charming or picturesque ⟨*narrow* ~ *streets*⟩

**Old World** *n* EASTERN HEMISPHERE; *specif* Europe, Asia, and Africa

**ole-, oleo-** *comb form* oil ⟨*oleic*⟩ ⟨*oleograph*⟩ [Fr *olé-, oléo-*, fr L *ole-*, fr *oleum* – more at OIL]

**-ole** /-ohl, -ol/ *also* **-ol** /-ol, -ohl/ *comb form* (→ *n*) **1** chemical compound containing a 5-membered ring of atoms, usu not all of which are carbon atoms ⟨*pyrrole*⟩ **2** chemical compound, esp containing an ETHER group ⟨*phenetole*⟩ ⟨*anisole*⟩ [ISV, fr L *oleum*]

**olé** /oh'lay/ *interj* – used as a cry of approval or success, esp at bullfights [Sp *ole, olé*, fr Ar *wa-lláh*, fr *wa-* and + *alláh* God] – **olé** *n or vb*

**oleaginous** /ˌohliˈajinəs/ *adj* **1** resembling, containing, or producing oil ⟨~ *seeds*⟩ **2** *humorous* smoothly ingratiating; unctuous [MF *oleagineux*, fr L *oleagineus* of an olive tree, fr *olea* olive tree, fr Gk *elaia*] – **oleaginously** *adv*, **oleaginousness** *n*

**oleander** /ˌohliˈandə, ˌoli-/ *n* a poisonous evergreen shrub (*Nerium oleander*) of the periwinkle family with fragrant white to red flowers [ML, prob deriv of L *rhododendron*]

**oleandomycin** /ˌohliˌandoh'miesin/ *n* any of several antibiotic substances produced by a bacterium (*Streptomyces antibioticus*) and used to treat bacterial infections in man and farm animals [*oleandr*ose (a sugar of *oleandrin*, a substance found in oleander leaves) + *-o-* + *-mycin*]

**oleaster** /ˌoliˈastə/ *n* any of several plants (genus *Elaeagnus* of the family Elaeagnaceae, the oleaster family); *esp* a large shrub or small tree (*Elaeagnus angustifolia*) with silvery twigs and leaves and sweet-scented yellowish flowers that is cultivated in dry windy regions, esp to provide shelter [L, fr *olea* olive tree]

**oleate** /ˈohliayt/ *n* any of various chemical compounds (SALTS or ESTERS) formed by combination between OLEIC ACID and a metal atom, an alcohol, or another chemical group

**olecranon** /oh'lekrənon, ohli'kraynən/ *n* the end part of the ULNA (bone of the forearm) projecting behind the elbow joint [NL, fr Gk *ōlekranon*, fr *ōlenē* elbow + *kranion* skull – more at ELL, CRANIUM]

**olefin, olefine** /ˈohliˌfin, -ˌfeen/ *n* ALKENE (member of a series of chemical compounds composed of carbon and hydrogen) – not now used technically [ISV, fr Fr (*gaz*) *oléfiant* ethylene, fr L *oleum* oil] – **olefinic** *adj*

**oleic** /oh'lee·ik/ *adj* **1** relating to, derived from, or contained in oil **2** of OLEIC ACID

**oleic acid** *n* a FATTY ACID, $CH_3(CH_2)_7CH=CH(CH_2)_7COOH$, that forms part of many natural fats and oils

**olein** /'ohli·in/ *n* a chemical compound (ESTER) formed by combination between OLEIC ACID and GLYCEROL [Fr *oléine*, fr L *oleum* oil]

**oleo** /'ohlioh/ *n*, *pl* **oleos** 1 an oleograph 2 *NAm* oleomargarine

**oleo-** – see OLE-

**oleograph** /'ohli·ə,grahf, -,graf/ *n* a coloured print made on cloth to resemble an oil painting [ISV *ole-* + *-graph*] – **oleographic** *adj*, **oleography** *n*

**oleomargarine** /,ohlio,mahjə'reen, -,mahgə-/ *n* a fat for cooking and table use that contains oils extracted from beef fat; *broadly*, *NAm* margarine [Fr *oléomargarine*, fr *olé-* + *margarine*]

**oleoresin** /,ohlioh'rezin/ *n* 1 a natural plant product (eg TURPENTINE) consisting of a usu semisolid mixture of oil and RESIN 2 any of various typically liquid preparations consisting of oil and RESIN extracted from plants (eg capsicum and ginger) and used in medicine [ISV] – **oleoresinous** *adj*

**oleum** /'ohli·əm/ *n* a heavy oily strongly corrosive solution of sulphur trioxide in concentrated SULPHURIC ACID – called also FUMING SULPHURIC ACID [L, oil – more at OIL]

**O level** *n* ORDINARY LEVEL

**olfaction** /ol'faksh(ə)n/ *n* 1 the sense of smell 2 the act or process of smelling

**olfactory** /ol'fakt(ə)ri/, **olfactive** /ol'faktiv/ *adj* of or connected with the sense of smell [L *olfactorius*, fr *olfactus*, pp of *olfacere* to smell, fr *olēre* to smell + *facere* to do – more at ODOUR, DO]

**olfactory bulb** *n* OLFACTORY LOBE; *specif* a small bulb-shaped one in higher VERTEBRATE animals (eg humans and other mammals)

**olfactory lobe** *n* an outgrowth from the front of each CEREBRAL HEMISPHERE of the brain in VERTEBRATE animals, whose front part becomes the OLFACTORY NERVE; *specif* this structure in lower vertebrate animals (eg fishes and frogs)

**olfactory nerve** *n* either of the 1st pair of CRANIAL NERVES that conduct stimuli to the brain from the parts of the nose sensitive to smell

**olibanum** /o'libənəm/ *n* frankincense [ME, fr ML, fr Ar *al-lubān* the frankincense]

**olig-** /olig-/, **oligo-** *comb form* few ⟨*oligophagous*⟩ ⟨*oligarchy*⟩ [ML, fr Gk, fr *oligos*; akin to Arm *alkat* scant]

**oligarch** /'oligahk/ *n* a member or supporter of an oligarchy [Gk *oligarchēs*, fr *olig-* + *-archēs* -arch]

**oligarchic** /,oli'gahkik/, **oligarchical** /-kl/ *adj* of or based on an oligarchy

**oligarchy** /'oligahki/ *n* 1 government by a small group 2 a state or organization in which a small group exercises control, esp for corrupt and selfish purposes; *also* a group exercising such control

**Oligocene** /o'ligoh,seen, 'oligoh,seen/ *adj or n* (of or being) a geological epoch of the TERTIARY period between the EOCENE and MIOCENE epochs, or the corresponding system of rocks [ISV]

**oligochaete** /,oligə'keetə, ə'ligə,keetə, -keet, 'oligoh,keet(ə)/ *n* any of a class (Oligochaeta of the phylum Annelida) of HERMAPHRODITIC (having both male and female reproductive systems) ground-living or freshwater segmented worms (eg an earthworm) with relatively few bristles along the body and without a specialized head [deriv of Gk *olig-* + *chaitē* long hair] – **oligochaete, oligochaetous** *adj*

**oligoclase** /'oligoh,klays, o'ligoh,klays/ *n* a common FELDSPAR mineral of the PLAGIOCLASE series of minerals, found in many rocks (eg granite) [Ger *oligoklas*, fr *olig-* + Gk *klasis* breaking, fr *klan* to break – more at HALT]

**oligomer** /ə'ligəmə/ *n* a POLYMER (large molecule composed of many identical repeating units) or intermediate compound formed during the synthesis of a polymer, that contains relatively few repeating structural units [*olig-* + *-mer* (as in *polymer*)] – **oligomeric** *adj*, **oligomerization** *n*

**oligomycin** /,oligoh'miesin/ *n* any of several antibiotic substances produced by a bacterium (eg one similar to *Streptomyces diastatochromogenes*) and used esp in biochemical research to inhibit OXIDATIVE PHOSPHORYLATION (series of energy-producing reactions in cells)

**oligonucleotide** /,oligoh'nyoohkliətied/ *n* a short POLYNUCLEOTIDE (large molecule like DNA composed of many repeating units) usu containing from 2 to 10 NUCLEOTIDES (units making up a polynucleotide)

**oligophagous** /,oli'gofəgəs/ *adj* eating only a few specific kinds of food – **oligophagy** *n*

**oligopoly** /,oli'gopəli/ *n* a market situation in which each of a few producers affects the market without any one of them having decisive control over it [*olig-* + mono*poly*] – **oligopolist** *n*, **oligopolistic** *adj*

**oligopsony** /,oli'gopsəni/ *n* a market situation in which each of a few buyers exerts a disproportionate influence on the market [*olig-* + Gk *opsōnia* purchase of victuals, fr *opsōnein* to purchase victuals, fr *opson* food + *ōneisthai* to buy – more at VENAL]

**oligosaccharide** /,oligoh'sakəried/ *n* a carbohydrate (eg the sugar sucrose) that consists of a small number of linked MONOSACCHARIDE units (simple sugar units like glucose from which more complex carbohydrates are built up) [ISV]

**oligotrophic** /,oligoh'trohfik/ *adj* 1 deficient in plant nutrients ⟨~ *boggy acid soils*⟩ 2 *of a body of water* having abundant dissolved oxygen – compare EUTROPHIC [ISV]

**olio** /'ohlioh/ *n*, *pl* **olios** OLLA PODRIDA (type of stew) [modif of Sp *olla*]

**olivaceous** /,oli'vayshəs/ *adj* OLIVE

[1]**olive** /'oliv/ *n* **1a** an evergreen tree (*Olea europaea*) of the ash family, that is cultivated in the warmer climates of Europe, Africa, and Asia for its small fruit that is an important food and source of oil; *also* the fruit of the olive **b** any of various shrubs and trees resembling the olive **2** a dull yellowish-green colour resembling that of the unripe fruit of the olive tree [ME, fr OF, fr L *oliva*, fr Gk *elaia*]

[2]**olive** *adj* of the colour olive or OLIVE GREEN

**olive branch** *n* **1** a branch of the olive tree, esp when used as a symbol of peace **2** an offer or gesture of conciliation or goodwill

**olive drab** *n* **1a** a wool or cotton fabric of a greyish-olive colour **b** a uniform of this fabric **2** *chiefly NAm* a greyish-olive colour

**olive green** *n* a colour that is greener, lighter, and stronger than olive – **olive green** *adj*

**olivenite** /o'livəniet, 'olivəniet/ *n* an OLIVE GREEN, dull brown, or yellowish mineral, $Cu_2(AsO_4)(OH)$, that is a compound of arsenic and copper [Ger *olivenit*, fr *oliven-*, *olive* olive]

**olive oil** *n* a pale yellow to golden oil obtained from ripe olives and used extensively in cooking and as a SALAD OIL

**olive shell** *n* any of several chiefly tropical marine snails (family Olividae) having an elongated smooth highly polished shell

**olivine** /'oliveen, ,--'-/ *n* an OLIVE GREEN to yellow mineral that is a silicate of magnesium and iron, $(Mg,Fe)_2SiO_4$, and is occasionally incorporated into the materials used to line furnaces – compare PERIDOT [Ger *olivin*, fr L *oliva* olive] – **olivinic, olivinitic** *adj*

**olla** /'olə, 'olyə/ *n* a large bulging widemouthed earthenware vessel often with looped handles that is used (eg in Latin America) esp as a pot for stewing or as a container for water [Sp, fr L, pot – more at OVEN]

**olla podrida** /po'dreedə/ *n*, *pl* **olla podridas** *also* **ollas podridas** a rich seasoned stew of many different meats and vegetables that is a traditional Spanish and Latin American dish [Sp, lit., rotten pot]

**olm** /ohlm, olm/ *n* an eel-like European cave-dwelling aquatic salamander (*Proteus anguinus*) with nonfunctional eyes that are overgrown with skin [Ger, fr OHG]

**ology** /'oləji/ *n*, *humorous or derog* SCIENCE 1a,c [*-ology* (as in *geology*, *psychology*, etc)]

**oloroso** /,ohlə'rohsoh, ,olə-/ *n*, *pl* **olorosos** a golden full-bodied sweet sherry [Sp, fr *oloroso* fragrant, fr *olor* odour, fr L, fr *olēre* to smell]

**olympiad** /ə'limpi,ad/ *n*, *often cap* **1** one of the four-year intervals between Olympian games by which time was reckoned in ancient Greece **2** OLYMPIC GAMES 2 [MF *Olympiade*, fr L *Olympiad-*, *Olympias*, fr Gk, fr *Olympia*, site in S Greece of ancient Olympian games]

[1]**Olympian** /ə'limpi·ən/ *adj* of the ancient Greek region of Olympia

[2]**Olympian** *n* **1** an inhabitant of the ancient Greek region of Olympia **2** *chiefly NAm* a participant in the Olympic Games

[3]**Olympian** *adj* **1** of Mount Olympus in Thessaly in E Greece **2** befitting or characteristic of an Olympian; *esp* lofty, detached

[4]**Olympian** *n* **1** any of the ancient Greek gods or goddesses

dwelling on Olympus **2** a person of lofty detachment or superior attainments

**Olympian Games** *n pl* an ancient Greek festival held every fourth year and made up of contests of sports, music, and literature with the victor's prize a crown of wild olive

¹**Olympic** /ə'limpik/ *adj* ³OLYMPIAN

²**Olympic** *adj* of or executed in the Olympic Games

**Olympic Games** *n taking sing or pl vb, pl* **Olympic Games 1** OLYMPIAN GAMES **2** an international sports contest that is a modified revival of the Olympian Games and is held once every four years in a different host country

**Olympics** /ə'limpiks/ *n taking sing or pl vb, pl* **Olympics** OLYMPIC GAMES – + *the*

**om** /om, awm/ *n* a MANTRA (sacred word) consisting of the sound "om" used esp in Hindu meditation and devotion [Skt]

**-oma** /-'ohmə/ *suffix* (→ *n*) *pl* **-omas, -omata** /-'ohmətə; *also* oh'mahtə/ tumour ⟨*adenoma*⟩ ⟨*fibroma*⟩ [L -*omat*-, -*oma*, fr Gk -*ōmat*-, -*ōma*, fr -*ō*- (stem of causative verbs in -*oun*) + -*mat*-, -*ma*, suffix denoting result – more at -MENT]

**omadhaun** /'omə,down/ *n, Irish* a foolish person [IrGael *amadán*]

**Omaha** /'ohməhah, -haw/ *n, pl* **Omahas,** *esp collectively* **Omaha** a member of an American Indian people of NE Nebraska [Omaha, lit., those going upstream or against the wind]

**omasum** /oh'mays(ə)m/ *n, pl* **omasa** /-sə/ the third chamber of the stomach of a sheep, cow, etc, lying between the RETICULUM and the ABOMASUM [NL, fr L, tripe of a bullock]

**ombre** /'ombə/ *n* a three-handed card game popular in Europe esp in the 17th and 18th centuries [Fr or Sp; Fr *hombre*, fr Sp, lit., man]

**ombré** /'ombray/ *adj, esp of fabrics* having colours or tones that shade into each other; *esp* graduated from light to dark [Fr, pp of *ombrer* to shade, fr It *ombrare*, fr *ombra* shade, fr L *umbra* – more at UMBRAGE] – **ombré** *n*

**ombudsman** /'omboodzmən/ *n, pl* **ombudsmen** /-mən, -men/ a government official (e g in Sweden, Britain, or New Zealand) appointed to receive and investigate complaints made by individuals against government or public bodies [Sw, lit., representative, fr ON *umbothsmathr*, fr *umboth* commission + *mathr* man]

**-ome** /-ohm/ *suffix* (→ *n*) part ⟨*rhiz*ome⟩ – used esp in botanical names [NL -*oma*, fr L, -*oma*]

**omega** /'ohmigə/ *n* **1** the 24th and last letter of the Greek alphabet **2** one who or that which is last (e g in a series or order); an ending – compare ALPHA **2 3 omega minus, omega, omega particle** an ELEMENTARY PARTICLE (particle of matter) having a negative electrical charge and a mass 3276 times the mass of an electron [Gk *ō mega*, lit., large o]

**omelette,** *NAm chiefly* **omelet** /'omlit/ *n* a mixture consisting chiefly of beaten eggs cooked without stirring until set in a shallow usu round pan and often served folded in half over a filling – compare SPANISH OMELETTE [Fr *omelette*, alter. of MF *alumelle*, lit., knife blade, modif of L *lamella*, dim. of *lamina* thin plate]

**omen** /'ohmən/ *n* an occurrence or phenomenon believed to be a sign of some future event; an augury [L *omin-, omen*]

**omentum** /oh'mentəm/ *n, pl* **omenta** /-tə/, **omentums** a fold of PERITONEUM (skin lining the abdomen) connecting or supporting the stomach and other abdominal structures; *also* a fold of peritoneum free at one edge [L, fr *o*- (akin to -*uere* to put on) + -*mentum* -ment – more at EXUVIAE] – **omental** *adj*

**omer** /'ohmə/ *n* **1** an ancient Hebrew unit of dry capacity equal to ¹/₁₀ EPHAH or about 3.5 litres **2** *often cap* a sheaf of barley offered in Jewish Temple worship on the second day of the Passover holiday **3** *cap* a 7-week period between the Jewish holidays of Passover and SHABUOTH [Heb *'ōmer*]

**omicron** /oh'miekrən, 'omikron/ *n* the 15th letter of the Greek alphabet [Gk *o mikron*, lit., small o]

**ominous** /'ominəs/ *adj* being or exhibiting an omen; portentous; *esp* foreboding or foreshowing evil [L *ominosus*, fr *omin-, omen*] – **ominously** *adv*, **ominousness** *n*

**omissible** /oh'misəbl, ə-/ *adj* able to be omitted; not absolutely required or demanded

**omission** /oh'mish(ə)n, ə-/ *n* **1a** apathy towards or neglect of duty; failure to act ⟨*sins of* ∼⟩ **b** something neglected or left undone **2** omitting or being omitted [ME *omissioun*, fr LL *omission-, omissio*, fr L *omissus*, pp of *omittere*]

**omit** /oh'mit, ə-/ *vt* **-tt- 1** to leave out or unmentioned **2** to fail to perform or make use of [ME *omitten*, fr L *omittere*, fr *ob*-towards + *mittere* to let go, send]

**ommatidium** /,omə'tidi·əm/ *n, pl* **ommatidia** /-diə/ any of the parts corresponding to a small simple eye that make up the COMPOUND EYE of an insect, spider, crab, etc [NL, fr Gk *ommat, omma* eye] – **ommatidial** *adj*

**omni-** /omni-/ *comb form* all; universally ⟨*omnidirectional*⟩ [L, fr *omnis*]

¹**omnibus** /'omnibəs/ *n* **1** a book containing reprints of a number of works **2** *formal* BUS 1 [Fr, bus, fr L, for all, dat pl of *omnis*]

²**omnibus** *adj* **1** of or providing for many things at once ⟨*an* ∼ *clause in a bill*⟩ **2** containing or including many miscellaneous items **3a** *of a book* comprising a collection of works, esp by one author, that were previously published individually **b** *of a radio programme* comprising all the episodes of a serial broadcast over a particular period (e g a week)

**omnidirectional** /,omnidi'reksh(ə)nl, -die-/ *adj* involving, present in, or moving in all directions; *esp* receiving or transmitting radio waves equally well in all directions ⟨∼ *antenna*⟩

**omnifarious** /,omni'feəriəs/ *adj* of all varieties, forms, or kinds [LL *omnifarius*, fr L *omni*- + -*farius* (as in *multifarius* having great diversity) – more at MULTIFARIOUS]

**omnificent** /om'nifis(ə)nt/ *adj* unlimited in creative power [L *omni*- + E -*ficent* (as in *magnificent*)]

**omnipotence** /om'nipət(ə)ns/ *n* **1** the quality or state of being omnipotent **2** an agency or force of unlimited power

¹**omnipotent** /om'nipət(ə)nt/ *adj* **1** *often cap* ALMIGHTY 1 **2** having unlimited or very great authority or influence [ME, fr MF, fr L *omnipotent-, omnipotens*, fr *omni*- + *potent-, potens* potent] – **omnipotently** *adv*

²**omnipotent** *n* **1** one who is omnipotent **2** *cap* GOD 1 – usu + *the*

**omnipresent** /,omni'prez(ə)nt/ *adj* present in all places at all times – **omnipresence** *n*

**omnirange** /'omni,raynj/ *n* a system of radio navigation in which any bearing relative to a special radio transmitter on the ground may be chosen and flown by an aircraft pilot

**omniscient** /om'nisi·ənt, om'nish(ə)nt/ *adj* **1** having infinite awareness, understanding, and insight **2** possessed of universal or complete knowledge; all-knowing [NL *omniscient-, omnisciens*, back-formation fr ML *omniscientia* omniscience, fr L *omni*- + *scientia* knowledge – more at SCIENCE] – **omnisciently** *adv*, **omniscience** *n*

**omnium-gatherum** /,omniəm 'gadhərəm/ *n, pl* **omnium-gatherums** a miscellaneous collection (e g of things or people) [L *omnium* (gen pl of *omnis* all) + E *gather* + L -*um*, noun ending]

**omnivora** /om'nivərə/ *n pl* omnivorous animals [NL, fr L, neut pl of *omnivorus*]

**omnivore** /'omni,vaw/ *n* one who or that which is omnivorous; *specif* an omnivorous animal [NL *omnivora*]

**omnivorous** /om'nivərəs/ *adj* **1** feeding on both animal and vegetable substances **2** avidly taking in, and esp reading, everything as if devouring or consuming [L *omnivorus*, fr *omni*- + -*vorus* -vorous] – **omnivorously** *adv*, **omnivorousness** *n*

**omophagous** /oh'mofəgəs/ *adj* feeding on raw flesh [Gk *ōmophagos*, fr *ōmos* raw + *phagein* to eat] – **omophagy** *n*

¹**on** /on/ *prep* **1a(1)** – used to indicate support from below by ⟨*the book is* ∼ *the table*⟩ ⟨*stand* ∼ *one foot*⟩ ⟨*jump* ∼ *a horse*⟩ or contact, juxtaposition, or attachment ⟨*a fly* ∼ *the ceiling*⟩ ⟨*a notice* ∼ *the board*⟩ ⟨*punch him* ∼ *the nose*⟩ ⟨*a dog* ∼ *a lead*⟩ ⟨*we're not* ∼ *the phone*⟩ **a(2)** carried on the person of ⟨*have you a match* ∼ *you?*⟩ **a(3)** very near to, esp along an edge or border ⟨*towns* ∼ *the frontier*⟩ ⟨*Walton-*∼*-Thames*⟩ ⟨*trees* ∼ *each side of the street*⟩ **a(4)** within the limits of (an open area) ⟨∼ *the steppes*⟩ ⟨∼ *page 17*⟩ **b** at the usual standard or level of ⟨∼ *form*⟩ **c(1)** in the direction of ⟨∼ *the right*⟩ ⟨*crept up* ∼ *him*⟩ **c(2)** directed against or towards; IN REGARD TO ⟨*a satire* ∼ *society*⟩ ⟨*keen* ∼ *sports*⟩ ⟨*a plague* ∼ *you*⟩ ⟨*some evidence* ∼ *this matter*⟩ ⟨*unfair* ∼ *me*⟩ ⟨*try it* ∼ *the dog*⟩ **c(3)** having as a topic; about ⟨*a book* ∼ *India*⟩ **c(4)** staked on the success of ⟨*put £1* ∼ *a horse*⟩ **c(5)** connected or in connection with ⟨∼ *a committee*⟩ ⟨*a job* ∼ *The Times*⟩ ⟨*went* ∼ *an errand*⟩ ⟨*sent* ∼ *a course*⟩ ⟨*here* ∼ *business*⟩ ⟨*which side was he* ∼*?*⟩ **c(6)** working at; in charge of ⟨*the man* ∼ *the gate*⟩ **c(7)** engaged in with the hope of achieving ⟨*after two wickets in two balls he's* ∼ *a hat trick*⟩ **2a** having as a basis or source ⟨*know it* ∼ *good authority*⟩ ⟨*swear* ∼ *the Bible*⟩ ⟨*a tax* ∼ *tobacco*⟩ ⟨*prices are down* ∼ *last year*⟩ **b** at the expense of ⟨*a house* ∼ *mortgage*⟩ ⟨*got it* ∼ *the National Health*⟩ ⟨*drinks are* ∼ *the house*⟩ **3a** in the state or process of

⟨~ *fire*⟩ ⟨~ *strike*⟩ ⟨~ *holiday*⟩ ⟨~ *file*⟩ ⟨~ *display*⟩ ⟨~ *offer*⟩ ⟨~ *heat*⟩ ⟨~ *the increase*⟩ **b** in the specified manner ⟨~ *the cheap*⟩ **c** using as a medium ⟨*played it* ~ *the clarinet*⟩; *esp* OVER 4b ⟨*talking* ~ *the telephone*⟩ **d** using by way of transport ⟨*arrived* ~ *foot*⟩ ⟨*left* ~ *the early train*⟩ **e** sustained or powered by ⟨*live* ~ *vegetables*⟩ ⟨*car runs* ~ *petrol*⟩ ⟨~ *the Pill*⟩ ⟨*people* ~ *low incomes*⟩ ⟨*dined out* ~ *the story*⟩; *also* needing (a harmful substance) to continue functioning ⟨~ *heroin*⟩ ⟨~ *3 bottles of port a day*⟩ **4** through contact with; against ⟨*cut himself* ~ *a piece of glass*⟩ **5** OUT OF 2c **6a** at the time of ⟨*came* ~ *Monday*⟩ ⟨*every hour* ~ *the hour*⟩ ⟨*cash* ~ *delivery*⟩ – compare JUST ON **b** immediately after and typically in consequence of ⟨*shot* ~ *sight*⟩ ⟨*swooned* ~ *hearing the news*⟩ **c** in the course of ⟨~ *a journey*⟩ ⟨~ *tour*⟩ ⟨~ *my way*⟩ **d** AFTER 2b ⟨*loss* ~ *loss*⟩ **7** TO 3c – compare CLOSE ON, NEAR ON **8** *chiefly NAm* IN 5b ⟨*ten cents* ~ *the dollar*⟩ **9** *archaic* of [ME *an, on,* prep & adv, fr OE; akin to OHG *ana* on, Gk *ana* up, on] – **on one's own 1** in solitude; alone ⟨*live on one's own*⟩ **2** without assistance or control

**usage 1** The central meaning of **on** is to convey the idea of position or state. It is very commonly used also to convey that of motion, but may be less vivid than **onto** ⟨*jump on/onto the table*⟩. **2** A book **on** *India* is a more serious book than one **about** *India,* which might be a novel. **synonyms** see ¹IN

**²on** *adv* **1** so as to be supported from below ⟨*with no roof* ~⟩, in close contact ⟨*has new shoes* ~⟩, or attached ⟨*sew the buttons* ~⟩ **2a** ahead or forwards in space or time ⟨*went* ~ *home*⟩ ⟨*do it later* ~⟩ ⟨*40 years* ~⟩ ⟨*getting* ~ *for five*⟩ **b** with the specified part forward ⟨*cars crashed head* ~⟩ **c** without interruption ⟨*slept* ~ *and* ~⟩ **3a** in or into operation or a state permitting operation ⟨*switch the light* ~⟩ ⟨*get the potatoes* ~⟩ ⟨*put a record* ~⟩ ⟨*the radio is* ~⟩ – compare TURN ON **b** in or into an activity or function (eg a dramatic role) ⟨*the night shift came* ~⟩ – **on and off** from time to time; intermittently ⟨*rained on and off all day*⟩

**³on** *adj* **1a** LEG 2 ⟨~ *drive*⟩ **b** taking place ⟨*the game is* ~⟩ **c** intended, planned ⟨*has nothing* ~ *for tonight*⟩ **d** being worn as clothing ⟨*sunbathe with nothing* ~⟩ **2a** committed to a bet **b** in favour of a win ⟨*the odds are 2 to 1* ~⟩ **3** *informal* talking dully, excessively, or incomprehensibly – + *about* ⟨*what's he* ~ *about?*⟩ **4** *chiefly Br informal* possible, practicable – usu negative ⟨*you can't refuse, it's just not* ~⟩ **5** *chiefly Br informal* nagging – + *at*

**¹-on** /-on, -ən/ *suffix* (→ *n*) chemical compound ⟨*parathi*on⟩ ⟨*interfer*on⟩ [ISV, alter. of *-one*]

**²-on** /-on/ *suffix* (→ *n*) **1** ELEMENTARY PARTICLE ⟨*electr*on⟩ ⟨*bary*on⟩ **2a** unit; quantum ⟨*phot*on⟩ ⟨*magnet*on⟩ **b** basic operational unit of the genetic material ⟨*cistr*on⟩ ⟨*oper*on⟩ [fr *-on* (in *ion*)]

**³-on** /-on/ *suffix* (→ *n*) NOBLE GAS ⟨*ne*on⟩ [NL, fr *-on* (in *arg*on)]

**onager** /'onəjə/ *n* **1** a small Asiatic wild ass that has a pale-coloured coat and a broad stripe on its back – compare KIANG **2** a heavy catapult used in ancient and medieval times [ME, wild ass, fr L, fr Gk *onagros,* fr *onos* ass + *agros* field – more at ACRE; (2) LL, fr L]

**onanism** /'ohnə,niz(ə)m/ *n* **1** COITUS INTERRUPTUS **2** masturbation [*Onan,* biblical character who "spilled [his seed] on the ground" (Gen 38:9)] – **onanistic** *adj*

**¹once** /wuns/ *adv* **1** one time and no more ⟨*met only* ~⟩ ⟨*shaves* ~ *a week*⟩ **2** even one time; ever ⟨*if* ~ *we lose the key*⟩ **3** at some indefinite time in the past; formerly ⟨*there* ~ *lived a king*⟩ **4** by one degree of relationship [ME *ones,* fr gen of *on* one] – **once again** for the last time; definitively – **once and for all 1** now again as before **2** one more time – **once in a while** from time to time; occasionally – **once more** ONCE AGAIN

**²once** *n* one single time ⟨~ *is enough*⟩ ⟨*just this* ~⟩ – **all at once 1** all at the same time **2** suddenly – **at once 1** at the same time; simultaneously ⟨*both spoke* at once⟩ ⟨*at once firm and gentle*⟩ **2** IMMEDIATELY 2 – **for once/for once in a way** for this occasion only

**³once** *conj* from the moment when; AS SOON AS ⟨~ *he arrives we can start*⟩ ⟨~ *over the wall we're safe*⟩

**once-'over** *n, informal* a swift examination or survey; *esp* a swift comprehensive appraising glance ⟨*gave him the* ~⟩

**oncer** /'wunsə/ *n, Br slang* a £1 note [¹*once* + ²*-er*]

**onchocerciasis** /,ongkohsuh'kie·əsis/ *n, pl* **onchocerciases** /-seez/ infection with or disease caused by parasitic filamentlike FILARIAL worms (genus *Onchocerca*); *esp* a disease of man

caused by a worm (*Onchocerca volvulus*) that is native to Africa but now present in parts of tropical America and is transmitted by several biting flies [NL, fr *Onchocerca,* genus of worms, fr Gk *onkos* barbed hook + *kerkos* tail]

**onchocercosis** /,ongkohsuh'kohsis/ *n, pl* **onchocercoses** /-seez/ onchocerciasis [NL, fr *Onchocerca*]

**oncogene** /'ongkoh,jeen/ *n* a gene (eg in some viruses) that causes cancer

**oncogenesis** /,ongkoh'jenəsis/ *n* the induction or formation of tumours [NL, fr Gk *onkos* mass; akin to Gk *enenkein* to carry – more at ENOUGH]

**oncogenic** /,ongkoh'jenik/, **oncogenous** /-'jeenəs/ *adj* **1** relating to tumour formation **2** tending to cause tumours; carcinogenic – **oncogenically** *adv,* **oncogenicity** *n*

**oncology** /ong'koləji/ *n* a branch of medicine dealing with the study and treatment of cancer and cancerous tumours [Gk *onkos* mass + ISV *-logy*] – **oncologist** *n,* **oncological** *also* **oncologic** *adj*

**oncoming** /'on,kuming/ *adj* **1** coming nearer in time or space; advancing ⟨*the* ~ *year*⟩ ⟨*an* ~ *car*⟩ **2** emergent, rising ⟨*schools needed for the* ~ *generation of children*⟩

**on dit** /on 'dee (Fr כੌ di)/ *n, pl* **on dits** /dee(z) (Fr ~)/ rumour, gossip ⟨*the* ~ *is that a mere paragraph ... pays a hundred quid – Punch*⟩ [Fr, fr *on dit* they say, it is said]

**¹one** /wun/ *adj* **1a** being a single unit or thing ⟨~ *day at a time*⟩ **b** being the first – used postpositively ⟨*on page* ~⟩ **2** being a particular but unspecified instance ⟨*saw her early* ~ *morning*⟩ **3a(1)** being the same; identical ⟨*both of* ~ *species*⟩ ⟨*it's all* ~ *to me where we go*⟩ **a(2)** constituting a unified entity ⟨*all shouted with* ~ *voice*⟩ ⟨*the combined elements form* ~ *substance*⟩ **b** being part of the same whole ⟨*I am* ~ *with the rest of you in this matter*⟩ **4** being some unspecified instance – used *esp* of future time ⟨*will see you* ~ *day soon*⟩ ⟨*we might try it* ~ *Christmas*⟩ **5** being the only individual of an indicated or implied kind ⟨*the* ~ *and only person she wanted to marry*⟩ **6** *chiefly NAm informal* being preeminently what is indicated ⟨~ *fine person*⟩ [ME *on,* fr OE *ān;* akin to OHG *ein* one, L *unus* (OL *oinos*), Skt *eka*] – **one and the same** the very same

**²one** *pron, pl* **ones** **1** a specified person; somebody ⟨*my loved* ~s⟩ ⟨*he's* ~ *who likes his comforts*⟩ **2** an indefinitely indicated person; anybody at all ⟨~ *has a duty to* ~*'s public*⟩ ⟨*they keep* ~ *waiting*⟩ **3** – sometimes used as a third person substitute for a first person pronoun ⟨~*'s whole ministry has been along ecumenical lines* – Donald Coggan, Archbishop of Canterbury⟩ **4** – used to refer to a noun or noun phrase previously mentioned or understood ⟨*two grey shirts and three red* ~s⟩ ⟨*if you want a book about bees, try this* ~⟩ ⟨*the question is* ~ *of great importance*⟩ □ used as subject or object; no plural for senses 2 & 3

**usage 1** In British English, the pronoun **one** should be followed by **one, one's** ⟨*one should do* **one's** *best*⟩ rather than by **he, his** as in American English ⟨*one should do* **his** *best*⟩ although that construction has existed as an alternative since the 15th century. This rule does not, of course, hold good when **one** is a number ⟨**one** *of them is scratching* **his** *nose*⟩ ⟨*only* **one** *in three washes* **her** *hair*⟩. **2** The use of **one,** rather than **you,** to mean "anybody at all" as in sense 2 is to be preferred for formal writing (see YOU); but the use of **one** for "I" as in sense 3 is often laughed at as an affectation. **3** The singular verb should be preferred to the plural in such sentences as ⟨**one** *in every five* **learns** (not **learn**) *French*⟩ ⟨**one** *of the stolen cars was* (not **were**) *recovered*⟩. The plural verb should, however, be preferred to the singular when such a sentence contains **who, which,** or **that** ⟨**one** *of those who* **are** (not **is**) *always grumbling*⟩ ⟨**one** *of the hardest tasks that* **have** (not **has**) *been suggested*⟩, since here the verbs refer to the plurals *those* and *tasks.*

**³one** *n* **1** – see NUMBER table **2** the number denoting unity **3** the first in a set or series ⟨*takes a* ~ *in shoes*⟩ **4a** a single person or thing ⟨*has the* ~ *but needs the other*⟩ **b** a unified entity ⟨*is secretary and treasurer in* ~⟩ ⟨*they all rose up as* ~ *and clamoured for more pay*⟩ **c** a particular example or instance ⟨*they differed* ~ *from the other*⟩ ⟨~ *of the coldest nights this year*⟩ **d** a certain specified person ⟨~ *George Hopkins*⟩ **5** a note or bill for a single unit of currency **6a** a person inclined in the specified direction; an enthusiast ⟨*he's rather a* ~ *for baroque music*⟩ **b** a bold, amusing, or remarkable character ⟨*oh! you are a* ~⟩ **7a** a blow, stroke ⟨*clipped him* ~ *on the ear*⟩ **b** a round of drinks; a drink ⟨*just time for a quick* ~⟩ **c** a remark; *esp* a joke ⟨*have you heard this* ~?⟩ **usage** see ²EACH – **at one** in harmony; in agreement – **for one** even if alone; not to mention others ⟨*I for one will never admit* *defeat*⟩ – **one and all** everyone individually and collectively – **one another** EACH OTHER – **one by one** singly, successively – **one too many 1** extra, unwanted **2** more than a match in wits ⟨*was* one too many *for him*⟩

**-one** /-ohn/ *suffix* (→ *n*) KETONE or related or analogous chemical compound or class of chemical compounds ⟨*acetone*⟩ ⟨*oestrone*⟩ [ISV, alter. of *-ene*]

**one-armed bandit** *also* **one-arm bandit** *n* FRUIT MACHINE [fr the handle pulled to make the wheels spin]

**,one-di'mensional** *adj* lacking depth; superficial ⟨~ *stereotype characters*⟩ – **one-dimensionality** *n*

**,one-'eyed** *adj* **1** having the sight of only one eye **2** narrow in outlook; blinkered **3** *informal* foolish or ill-thought out; COCKEYED 2b

**,one-'handed** *adj* **1** having or using only one hand ⟨*could beat him up* ~⟩ **2a** designed for or requiring the use of only one hand **b** effected by the use of only one hand

**,one-'horse** *adj* **1** drawn or operated by one horse **2** *informal* of little real importance or consequence ⟨*a* ~ *town*⟩

**Oneida** /oh'nieda/ *n*, *pl* **Oneidas** *esp collectively* **Oneida** (the Iroquoian language of) an American Indian people originally of New York [Iroquois *Oneȳóde'*, lit., standing rock]

**oneiric** /oh'nierik/ *adj* of dreams; dreamy [Gk *oneiros* dream; akin to Arm *anurj* dream]

**oneiromancy** /oh'nieramansi/ *n* fortune-telling by means of dreams [Gk *oneiros* + E *-mancy*]

**,one-'legged** *adj* **1** having only one leg **2** lacking an important part or element ⟨*a* ~ *law*⟩

**,one-'man** *adj* of just one person: eg **a** consisting of only one person ⟨*a* ~ *committee*⟩ **b** done, presented, or produced by only one person ⟨*a* ~ *play*⟩ **c** designed for or limited to one person

**oneness** /'wun·nis/ *n* the quality or state or fact of being one: eg **a** singleness **b** integrity, wholeness **c** HARMONY **2 d** sameness, identity **e** unity, union

**one-night stand** *n*, *informal* **1** a performance (eg of a play or concert) given only once in any particular locality **2** (a person with whom one has) a sexual relationship lasting only one night

**,one-'off** *adj*, *chiefly Br* **1** happening or being done only once ⟨*a* ~ *job*⟩ **2** made or intended as a single, individual, and unrepeated item or occurrence ⟨*a* ~ *product*⟩ – **one off** *n*

**,one-on-'one** *adj* MAN-TO-MAN **2**

**,one-'piece** *adj* consisting of or made in a single undivided piece ⟨*a* ~ *swimming costume*⟩ – **one-piecer** *n*

**onerous** /'ohnaras, 'on-/ *adj* **1** involving, imposing, or constituting a burden; troublesome ⟨*an* ~ *task*⟩ **2** having legal obligations that outweigh the advantages ⟨~ *contract*⟩ [ME, fr MF *onereus*, fr L *onerosus*, fr *oner-*, *onus* burden; akin to Skt *anas* cart] – **onerously** *adv*, **onerousness** *n*

**oneself** /wun'self/ *also* **one's self** *pron* **1** a person's self; one's own self – used reflexively ⟨*one should wash* ~⟩, for emphasis ⟨*to do it* ~⟩, or in absolute constructions **2** one's normal self ⟨*not feeling quite* ~⟩

**,one-'sided** *adj* **1a** having or occurring on one side only **b** having one side prominent or more developed **2** limited to one side; partial, biased ⟨*a* ~ *interpretation*⟩ – **one-sidedly** *adv*, **one-sidedness** *n*

**one-sided test** *n* ONE-TAILED TEST

**,one-'star** *adj* of the lowest rank in a system for grading excellence applied to esp hotels, in which the highest standard is usu represented by the fifth rank ⟨*a* ~ *restaurant*⟩

**'one-,step** *n* (a piece of music used for) a ballroom dance in ³⁄₄ time marked by quick walking steps backwards and forwards – **one-step** *vi*

**one-tailed test, one-tail test** *n* a statistical test of a hypothesis, in which all the possible values of the TEST statistic (statistic used in testing a hypothesis) that would lead to rejection of the hypothesis are either greater than a given value or less than some other given value, but not both – compare TWO-TAILED TEST

**onetime** /'wun,tiem/ *adj* former, sometime

**,one-to-'one, one-one** *adj*, *maths* INJECTIVE

**,one-'track** *adj* marked by often narrowly restricted attention to or absorption in one thing only ⟨*a* ~ *mind*⟩

**,one-'two** *n* **1** a combination of two quick blows in rapid succession in boxing; *esp* a left jab followed at once by a hard blow with the right hand **2** a combination of two quick passes between two soccer players

**one up** *adj* being in a position of advantage

**one-upmanship** /'upmanship/ *n* the art or practice of achieving or demonstrating social or professional superiority by means of status symbols or behaviour calculated to impress others – compare GAMESMANSHIP

**,one-'way** *adj* **1** that moves in or allows movement in only one direction ⟨~ *traffic*⟩ **2** one-sided, unilateral ⟨*a* ~ *conversation*⟩ **3** functioning in only one of two or more possible ways **4** *of a fabric* having a nap, pile, or design running in one direction only

**ongoing** /'on,goh·ing/ *adj* **1** being actually in process **2** continuously moving forward; growing, developing

*usage* The use of **ongoing** to mean "in process" ⟨*an* **ongoing** *situation*⟩ is widely disliked as a cliché.

**onion** /'unyan/ *n* **1** an Asian plant (*Allium cepa*) of the lily family that is related to garlic, leeks, and chives and is widely cultivated for its pungent edible bulbs; *also* any of various related plants (genus *Allium*) **2** the bulb of the onion eaten widely as a vegetable [ME, fr MF *oignon*, fr L *union-*, *unio*, perh fr *unus* one] – **know one's onions** *Br slang* to be fully acquainted with all the information, facts, etc concerned with one's work; be experienced – **off one's onion** *slang* mad

**onionskin** /'unyan,skin/ *n* a thin strong paper of very light weight

**onium** /'ohniam/ *adj* being or characterized by a usu complex CATION (group of atoms having positive electrical charge) – often in combination [ISV *-onium* (as in *ammonium*)]

**,on-'line** *adj* **1a** being controlled directly by or in direct communication with a computer ⟨~ *equipment*⟩ **b** *of a computer* in direct communication with a piece of equipment (eg a terminal) or system under computer control ⟨~ *to a page printer* – *British Printer*⟩ **2** of or being a secret code system whose telecommunication machines automatically put into code, transmit, receive, and decode messages in a single instantaneous operation □ (*1*) compare OFF-LINE – **on-line** *adv*

**onlooker** /'on,looka/ *n* one who looks on; *esp* a passive spectator – **onlooking** *adj*

**¹only** /'ohnli/ *adj* **1** unquestionably the best; peerless **2** alone in its class or kind; sole ⟨*an* ~ *child*⟩ ⟨*the* ~ *detergent that contains blue whitener*⟩ [ME, fr OE *ānlīc*, fr *ān* one – more at ONE]

**²only** *adv* **1a** nothing more than; merely ⟨~ *a little one*⟩ ⟨*has* ~ *lost one election* – George Orwell⟩ ⟨*if it would* ~ *rain!*⟩ **b** solely, exclusively ⟨*known* ~ *to him*⟩ **2** nothing other than ⟨*it was* ~ *too true*⟩ **3a** in the final outcome ⟨*will* ~ *make you sick*⟩ **b** with nevertheless the final result ⟨*won the battles*, ~ *to lose the war*⟩ **4** no earlier than ⟨~ *last week*⟩ ⟨*has* ~ *just left*⟩

*usage* **1** In formal writing, **only** should be placed next to the word it modifies. Compare ⟨**only** *John* (= no one else) *saw the lion*⟩ ⟨*John saw* **only** *the lion* (= nothing else)⟩; but the natural place for **only** is often next to the verb ⟨*where beasts were* **only** *slain for sacrifice* – John Dryden⟩ ⟨*a word* **only** *used in Scotland* – Samuel Johnson⟩ and such an arrangement is usually clear enough in speech, where the stress of the sentence helps to convey the meaning. One should be careful over the placement of **only** in writing where ambiguity may occur, and particularly in the writing of incomplete sentences. Does the notice ⟨*This Basin* **Only** *for Cleaning Brushes*⟩ mean that brush-cleaning is the sole use of this basin or that this is the only basin to be so used? **2** The pronunciation /'ohni/ should be avoided in careful speech.

**³only** *conj* **1** but, however ⟨*they look very nice*, ~ *we can't use them*⟩ **2** were it not for the fact that

*usage* The use of **only** as a conjunction should probably be avoided in formal writing.

**,on-'off** *adj* occurring or existing from time to time, esp unpredictably; intermittent ⟨*an* ~ *love affair*⟩

**onomastic** /,ona'mastik/ *adj* **1** (consisting) of a name or names **2** of or being the signature of the author of a letter or document that is written largely in another hand [Gk *onomastikos*, fr *onomazein* to name, fr *onoma* name – more at NAME]

**onomastics** /,ona'mastiks/ *n taking sing or pl vb* the science or study of proper names

**onomatopoeia** /,ona,mata'pee·a/ *n* **1** the naming of a thing or action by a vocal imitation of the sound associated with it (eg in *buzz*, *cuckoo*); *also* a word thus formed **2** the use of words whose sound suggests the sense [LL, fr Gk *onomatopoiia*, fr *onomat-*, *onoma* name + *poiein* to make – more at POET] – **onomatopoeic, onomatopoetic** *adj*, **onomatopoeically, onomatopoetically** *adv*

**Onondaga** /,onan'dahga/ *n*, *pl* **Onondagas** *esp collectively* **Onondaga** (the Iroquoian language of) an American Indian people of New York State and Canada [Iroquois *Onotáge*, village of the Onondaga people]

**onrush** /'on,rush/ *n* 1 a forceful rushing forward or onwards 2 ONSET 1 – **onrushing** *adj*

**onset** /'on,set/ *n* 1 an attack, assault ⟨*withstand the ~ of the army*⟩ 2 a beginning, commencement ⟨*the ~ of winter*⟩ – **onsetting** *adj*

**onshore** /,on'shaw/ *adj* 1 coming or moving towards or onto the shore ⟨*an ~ wind*⟩ **2a** situated on or near the shore **b** domestic ⟨*~ oil production*⟩ – **onshore** *adv*

**onside** /,on'sied/ *adv or adj* not offside; in a position legally to play or receive the ball or puck

**on side** *n* 1 LEG SIDE 2 **on side, onside** *chiefly Br the* left-hand side of a horse, vehicle, etc

**onslaught** /'on,slawt/ *n* a fierce attack [modif of D *aanslag* act of striking; akin to OE *an* on & to OE *slēan* to strike – more at SLAY]

**onstage** /,on'stayj/ *adv or adj* on a part of the stage visible to the audience

**ont-** /ont-/, **onto-** *comb form* 1 *philosophy* being; existence ⟨*ontology*⟩ 2 organism ⟨*ontogeny*⟩ [NL, fr LGk, fr Gk *ont-, ōn*, prp of *einai* to be – more at IS]

**-ont** /-ont/ *comb form* (→ *n*) cell; organism ⟨*diplont*⟩ [Gk *ont-, ōn*, prp]

**on-the-'job** *adj* of something (eg training or experience) learned, gained, or done while working in a job and often under supervision

**on-the-'scene** *adj* being at the place of an action or occurrence ⟨*an ~ witness*⟩

**ontic** /'ontik/ *adj, philosophy* of or having real being or existence ⟨*~ criteria for aesthetic judgments*⟩ – **ontically** *adv*

**¹onto, on to** /'onto; *strong* 'ontooh/ *prep* 1 to a position on 2 in or into a state of awareness about ⟨*put me ~ your methods*⟩ ⟨*I'm ~ you, you bastard*⟩ 3 *maths* – used to indicate a mathematical set each element of which is the image of at least one element of another set ⟨*a function mapping the set* S *~ the set* T⟩ 4 *chiefly Br* in or into contact with ⟨*been ~ him about the drains*⟩; *esp* on at; nagging

**usage** Onto may be spelt as one or two words when it functions as a preposition ⟨*cat jumped* onto/on to *the table*⟩. It must be spelt as two words when on is used as an adverb ⟨*they walked* on *to Keswick*⟩. See ¹ON

**²onto** *adj, maths* SURJECTIVE (having every element in one set the image of an element in another set)

**onto-** – see ONT-

**ontogenesis** /,onto'jenəsis/ *n* ontogeny [NL]

**ontogenetic** /,ontojə'netik/, **ontogenic** /-'jenik/ *adj* 1 of or appearing in the course of ontogeny 2 based on visible structural characteristics [ISV] – **ontogenetically, ontogenically** *adv*

**ontogeny** /on'tojəni/ *n* the (course of) development of an individual organism [ISV]

**ontological** /,ontə'lojikl/ *adj, philosophy* 1 of ontology 2 relating to or based upon being or existence – **ontologically** *adv*

**ontological argument** *n* an argument for the existence of God based upon the logical implication of the term *God* that states that the idea of God implies perfection and that perfection entails the possession of all positive attributes including that of being or existence

**ontology** /on'toləji/ *n, philosophy* 1 a branch of philosophy concerned with the nature of being or existence 2 a particular theory about the nature and categories of being [NL *ontologia*, fr *ont-* + *-logia* -logy] – **ontologist** *n*

**onus** /'ohnəs/ *n* **1a** a burden **b** a disagreeable necessity; an obligation **c** blame, responsibility 2 BURDEN OF PROOF [(1) L – more at ONEROUS; (2) NL *onus probandi* burden of proving]

**onward** /'onwəd/ *adj* directed or moving onward; forward

**onwards** /'onwədz/ *adv* towards or at a point lying ahead in space or time; forwards ⟨*from his childhood ~*⟩

**onychophoran** /,oni'kofərən/ *n* any of a group (Onychophora) of small tropical sluglike animals that have segmented bodies and short stumpy legs [NL *Onychophora*, group name, fr Gk *onych-, onyx* claw + *-phoros* -phore] – **onychophoran** *adj*

**-onym** /-ənim/ *comb form* (→ *n*) 1 name ⟨*pseudonym*⟩ 2 word ⟨*antonym*⟩ [ME, fr L *-onymum*, fr Gk *-ōnymon*, fr *onyma* – more at NAME]

**onyx** /'oniks/ *n* 1 a translucent variety of CHALCEDONY or AGATE (types of quartz) having parallel bands of different colours, typically white and black or white and brown 2 **onyx, onyx**

**marble** ALABASTER 2 [ME *onix*, fr OF & L; OF, fr L *onych-, onyx*, fr Gk, lit., claw, nail – more at NAIL]

**oo-** – see O-

**oocyst** /'oh-əsist/ *n* ZYGOTE (cell formed by the joining of male and female sex cells); *specif* one formed by some single-celled animals [ISV]

**oocyte** /'oh-ə,siet/ *n* a cell that divides to produce the female sex cells; an immature undeveloped egg cell – compare OOTID [ISV]

**oodles** /'oohdlz/ *also* **oodlins** /'oohdlinz/ *n taking sing or pl vb, informal* a great quantity; a lot [perh alter. of ²*huddle*]

**oof** /oohf/ *n, slang* money – no longer in vogue [short for *ooftish*, fr Yiddish *uf tish* on (the) table]

**oogamete** /,oh-əgə'meet, -'gameet/ *n* a female GAMETE (mature reproductive cell); a mature egg cell; *specif* a relatively large immobile female gamete containing reserves of food material

**oogamy** /oh'ogəmi/ *n* sexual reproduction involving the union between a small male GAMETE (mature reproductive cell) that is capable of movement and a large immobile female gamete – **oogamous** *adj*

**OO gauge** *n* a gauge of track in model railways in which the rails are approximately 16.5 millimetres ($5/8$ inch) apart

**oogenesis** /,oh-ə'jenəsis/ *n* the formation and development to maturity of an egg [NL] – **oogenetic** *adj*

**oogonium** /,oh-ə'gohniəm/ *n* 1 a female sexual organ in various algae and fungi 2 a cell that gives rise to oocytes by repeated CELL DIVISION (splitting of a cell to form new cells) [NL] – **oogonial** *adj*

**¹ooh** /ooh *often prolonged*/ *interj* – used to express amazement, pleasure, or agreeable surprise

**²ooh** *vi* to exclaim in amazement, joy, or surprise ⟨*~ing and aahing over the exciting new commercials*⟩ – **ooh** *n*

**oolite** /'oh-ə,liet/ *n* a rock, esp limestone, consisting of small round grains, usu of CALCIUM CARBONATE, cemented together [Fr *oolithe*, fr *o-* + *-lithe* -lite; fr its resembling the roe of fish] – **oolitic** *adj*

**oologist** /oh'oləjist/ *n* one who studies or collects birds' eggs

**oology** /oh'oləji/ *n* the study or collecting of birds' eggs – **oological** *also* **oologic** *adj*, **oologically** *adv*

**oolong** /'ooh,long/ *n* a dark China tea that combines the characteristics of black and green teas as a result of the leaf's being partially fermented before drying [Chin (Pek) *wū lóng* (*wu¹ lung²*), lit., black dragon]

**oompah** /'oompah/ *n* the deep often rhythmical sound of a tuba, euphonium, or similar brass band instrument [īmit]

**oomph** /oom(p)f/ *n, humorous* 1 SEX APPEAL 2 vitality, enthusiasm 3 charisma, glamour [prob imit]

**oophyte** /'oh-ə,fiet/ *n* the GAMETOPHYTE (plant phase that produces male and female reproductive cells) of a moss, fern, or similar lower plant that has alternating sexually and asexually reproducing phases

**oops** /oops, oohps/ *interj* – used to express mild apology, esp for carelessness ⟨*~! I nearly dropped my cup of coffee!*⟩

**'oops-a-,daisy** *interj* 1 – used when helping someone to climb over or onto something 2 – used when someone falls over [alter. of *upsydaisy*]

**oorial** /'ooəriəl/ *n* URIAL (type of sheep)

**oosperm** /'oh-ə,spuhm/ *n* a fertilized egg; ZYGOTE

**oosphere** /'oh-ə,sfiə/ *n* a mature female reproductive cell before fertilization; an unfertilized egg; *esp* one in simple plants (eg mosses, ferns, and algae) [ISV]

**oospore** /'oh-ə,spaw/ *n* an oosperm; *esp* a fertilized spore in some plants (eg fungi and algae) that grows into the phase of the plant that reproduces asexually – compare ZYGOSPORE [ISV]

**ootheca** /,oh-ə'theekə/ *n, pl* **oothecae** /-sie/ a firm-walled and distinctive egg case (eg of a cockroach) [NL, fr *o-* + *theca*] – **oothecal** *adj*

**ootid** /'oh-ətid/ *n* any of the four cells into which an OOCYTE (immature egg cell) divides, that develops into a mature egg cell – compare SPERMATID [irreg fr *o-* + *-id*]

**¹ooze** /oohz/ *n* 1 a soft deposit (eg of mud, slime, or shells and shell debris) on the bottom of a body of water (eg an estuary) 2 a piece of soft wet ground (eg a marsh or bog) [ME *wose*, fr OE *wāse* mire; akin to L *virus* slime – more at VIRUS]

**²ooze** *n* 1 a solution used in the tanning of leather that is made by soaking vegetable material (eg bark) in water 2 the act of oozing 3 something that oozes [ME *wose* sap, juice, fr OE *wōs*; akin to OHG *waso* damp, Gk *hearon* ewer]

**³ooze** *vi* 1 to pass or flow slowly (as if) through small openings or spaces **2a** to move slowly or imperceptibly ⟨*people began oozing forwards*⟩ **b** to dwindle *away* **3a** to exude moisture **b** to exude something in a way suggestive of the emitting of moisture ⟨*a woman oozing with charm*⟩ ∼ *vt* **1** to emit or give out slowly **2** to exude or give off in a way suggestive of the emitting of moisture **3** to display in abundance ⟨*positively* ∼d *vitality*⟩

**ooze leather** *n* leather that is usu made from calfskins by a vegetable tanning process and has a soft suede finish on the flesh side

**oozy** /'oohzi/ *adj* **1** containing, composed of, or resembling ooze **2** exuding moisture; slimy

**op** /op/ *n, informal* OPERATION 3, 5

**op-** - see OB-

**opacity** /oh'pasəti/ *n* **1** the quality or state of a body that makes it unable to be penetrated by rays of light; *broadly* the relative capacity of matter to obstruct the transmission of RADIANT ENERGY **2a** obscurity of sense; unintelligibility ⟨*the* ∼ *of bureaucratic jargon*⟩ **b** the quality or state of being mentally obtuse; dullness **3** an opaque spot on a normally transparent structure (e g the lens of the eye) [Fr *opacité* shadiness, fr L *opacitat-, opacitas*, fr *opacus* shaded, dark]

**opah** /'ohpə/ *n* a large marine fish (*Lampris regius*) with brilliant colours and rich oily red flesh [Ibo *úbà*]

**opal** /'ohp(ə)l/ *n* a transparent to semitransparent silicon mineral, $SiO_2.nH_2O$, that reflects light in a rainbowlike play of colours and that is used in its opalescent forms as a gem [L *opalus*, fr Skt *upala* stone, jewel]

**opalescent** /,ohpl'es(ə)nt, ,ohpə'les(ə)nt/ *adj* reflecting a milky light in a rainbowlike play of colours - **opalescence** *n*

**opaline** /'ohp(ə)l,ien/ *adj* resembling opal, esp in appearance

**¹opaque** /oh'payk/ *adj* **1** exhibiting opacity; not transparent or able to transmit RADIANT ENERGY, esp light **2a** hard to understand or explain; unintelligible **b** obtuse, stupid [L *opacus*] - **opaquely** *adv*, **opaqueness** *n*

**²opaque** *n* something opaque; *esp* an opaque paint for blocking out portions of a photographic negative or print

**op art** /op/ *n* OPTICAL ART - compare POP ART - **op artist** *n*

**ope** /ohp/ *vb, archaic* to open

**¹open** /'ohp(ə)n/ *adj* **1** having no enclosing or confining barrier; accessible on all or nearly all sides ⟨*sheep grazing on the* ∼ *hillside*⟩ **2a(1)** being in a position or adjustment to permit passage; not shut or locked ⟨*an* ∼ *door*⟩ **a(2)** having a barrier (e g a door) so adjusted as to allow passage ⟨*the house was* ∼⟩ **b** having the lips parted ⟨*stood there with his mouth wide* ∼⟩ **3a** completely free from concealment; exposed to general view or knowledge ⟨*their hostilities eventually erupted with* ∼ *war*⟩ **b** exposed or vulnerable to attack or question; subject ⟨∼ *to doubt*⟩ **4a** not covered with a top, roof, or lid ⟨*an* ∼ *car*⟩ ⟨*her eyes were* ∼⟩ **b** having no protective covering; not fastened or sealed ⟨∼ *wiring*⟩ ⟨*an* ∼ *wound*⟩ ⟨*an* ∼ *envelope*⟩ **5** not restricted to a particular group or category of participants ⟨∼ *to the public*⟩ ⟨∼ *housing*⟩: e g **5a** contested by both amateur and professionals **b** *NAm* enterable by a registered voter regardless of political affiliation ⟨*an* ∼ *primary*⟩ **6** fit to be travelled over; presenting no obstacle to passage or view ⟨*the* ∼ *road*⟩ ⟨∼ *country*⟩ **7** having the parts or surfaces laid out in an expanded position; spread out; unfolded ⟨*an* ∼ *book*⟩ **8a(1)** pronounced with a wide opening between the relatively flat tongue and the palate ⟨*back contains an* ∼ *vowel*⟩ **a(2)** formed with the tongue in a lower position than for the other vowel of a pair **b** having clarity and resonance associated with relaxation of the muscles of the throat ⟨*an* ∼ *vocal tone*⟩ **9a** available to follow or make use of ⟨*the only course* ∼ *to us*⟩ **b** not taken up with duties or engagements ⟨*keep an hour* ∼ *on Friday*⟩ **c** not finally decided; subject to further consideration ⟨*leave the matter* ∼⟩ ⟨*an* ∼ *question*⟩ **d** available for a qualified applicant; vacant ⟨*the job is still* ∼⟩ **e** remaining available for use or filling until cancelled ⟨*an* ∼ *order for more items*⟩ **f** available for future purchase ⟨*these items are in* ∼ *stock*⟩ ⟨*an* ∼ *pattern*⟩ **10a** generous in giving; openhanded **b(1)** willing to consider new ideas; unprejudiced ⟨*an* ∼ *mind*⟩ **b(2)** willing to receive and consider or to accept and deal with ⟨*always* ∼ *to suggestions*⟩ **c** free from reserve or pretence; candid and frank **d** accessible to the influx of new factors (e g foreign goods) ⟨*an* ∼ *market*⟩ **11a** having openings, interruptions, or spaces: e g **11a(1)** porous and easily crumbled ⟨∼ *soil*⟩ **a(2)** sparsely distributed; scattered ⟨∼ *population*⟩ **a(3)** having relatively wide spacing between words or lines ⟨∼ *type*⟩ **a(4)** *of a compound word* having components separated by a space in writing or

printing ⟨*laughing jackass is an* ∼ *compound*⟩ **b** not made up of a continuous closed circuit of channels ⟨*the insect circulatory system is* ∼⟩ **12a** *of an organ pipe* not stopped at the top **b** *of a string on a musical instrument* not stopped by the finger **c** *of a note* produced on a musical instrument without fingering the strings, valves, slides, or keys **13** being in operation; *esp* ready for business, patronage, or use ⟨*the shop is* ∼ *from 9 to 5*⟩ ⟨*the new motorway will be* ∼ *next week*⟩ **14a(1)** not having effective regulation of various commercial enterprises ⟨*notorious as an* ∼ *town*⟩ **a(2)** not repressed by legal controls ⟨∼ *gambling*⟩ **b** free from checking or hampering restraints ⟨*an* ∼ *economy*⟩ ⟨*faced with* ∼ *inflation*⟩ **15** having been opened by a first ANTE (initial stake in a card game), bet, or bid ⟨*the bidding is* ∼⟩ **16** *of a mathematical set* having a point such that every NEIGHBOURHOOD of the point contains other points also in the set ⟨*the interior of a sphere is an* ∼ *set*⟩ **17** *Br, of a cheque* payable in cash to the person, organization, etc named on it; not crossed **18** *cap O, Br* of the Open University ⟨*an* Open *student*⟩ [ME, fr OE; akin to OHG *offan* open; both fr a prehistoric NGmc-WGmc word akin to OE *ūp* up] - **open** *adv* - **lay open** to expose: e g **a** to cut ⟨*a blow that laid his head open*⟩ **b** to explain or make known; UNCOVER 1 ⟨*the facts of the case were laid wide* open⟩ - **see also keep one's** EYES **open, with one's** EYES **open**

**²open** *vt* **1a** to change or move (e g a door) from a closed position **b** to permit entry or passage by removing or turning back (e g a barrier), removing (e g a cover), or clearing away (e g an obstruction) **c** to gain access to the contents of ⟨∼ *a parcel*⟩ - often + *up* ⟨∼ed *up the Pharaoh's tomb*⟩ **2a** to make available for or active in a particular use or function ⟨∼ *a new supermarket*⟩; *specif* to establish ⟨∼ed *a new shop*⟩ - often + *up* ⟨∼ *up new land for settlement*⟩ **b** to declare available for use, esp ceremonially ⟨*the Queen* ∼ed *the new suspension bridge*⟩ **3a** to disclose, reveal - often + *up* **b** to make more responsive or enlightened ⟨*must* ∼ *our minds to the needs of minorities*⟩ **c** to bring into view or come in sight of ⟨*sailed on until they* ∼ed *a bay*⟩ **4a** to make one or more openings in ⟨∼ed *the boil*⟩ **b** to loosen and make less compact ⟨∼ *the soil*⟩ **5** to spread out; unfold ⟨∼ed *the umbrella*⟩ **6** to begin, commence ⟨∼ed *the meeting*⟩ **7** to begin (e g the bidding, betting, or play) in a card game **8** to revoke (e g a judgment or decree in a legal action) in order to allow further contest or delay **9a** to initiate (a side's innings) as one of the two opening batsmen **b** to initiate (a side's bowling attack) by bowling one of the first two overs of an innings ∼ *vi* **1** to become open ⟨*the office* ∼ed *early*⟩ **2a** to commence, start ⟨∼ed *with a prayer*⟩ **b** to begin the bidding, betting, or play in a card game ⟨*South* ∼ed *with two clubs*⟩ **3** to become enlightened or responsive **4** to give access ⟨*the rooms* ∼ *onto a hall*⟩ - usu + *into* or *onto*; see also **open** FIRE - **openable** *adj*, **openability** *n*

**open out** *vi* to become less inhibited; *esp* to speak more freely ⟨opened out *a bit after a double brandy*⟩

**open up** *vi* **1** to commence firing **2** to open out **3** to open a door - often as a command ⟨open up, *it's the police!*⟩

**³open** *n* **1** open and unobstructed space: e g **1a** the open air **b** the open water **c** the open country ⟨*get out into the* ∼⟩ **2** *often cap* an open contest, competition, or tournament

**open-'air** *adj* outdoor

**open air** *n* the space where air is unconfined; *esp* OUTDOORS 2

**open-and-'shut** *adj* **1** perfectly simple; obvious **2** easily settled ⟨*an* ∼ *case*⟩

**open book** *n* something completely free from mystery or concealment ⟨*her life is an* ∼⟩

**open-book examination** *n* an examination during which candidates may refer to books

**opencast** /,ohp(ə)n'kahst/ *adj, of a mine or mining* worked from or carried out on the earth's surface by removing material covering the mineral mined for

**open chain** *n, chemistry* an arrangement of atoms in a chain whose ends are not joined to form a ring

**open-'circuit, open-circuited** *adj* **1** of or being an electric circuit that is discontinuous in such a way as to prevent the flow of an electric current **2** being or relating to television in which programmes are broadcast so that they are available to any receivers within range

**open circuit** *n* a connected but incomplete circuit of electrical components through which a current cannot flow

**open city** *n* a city that is not occupied or defended by military forces and that is free from bombardment under international law

**open court** *n* a court to which the public is admitted – chiefly in *in open court*

**open day** *n* a day on which an institution (eg a school or military base) is open to the public and special activities or exhibitions are arranged

**open door** *n* **1** a recognized right of admittance; freedom of access **2** a policy giving opportunity for commercial relations with a country to all nations on equal terms – **open-door** *adj*

,**open-'ended** *adj* **1** not rigorously fixed: eg **1a** adaptable to the developing needs of a situation ⟨*an* ~ *financial policy*⟩ **b** permitting or designed to permit spontaneous and unguided responses ⟨*an* ~ *discussion*⟩ **2** organized to allow for various contingencies; *esp* permitting additional debt to be incurred under the original contract subject to specified conditions ⟨*an* ~ *loan*⟩ – **open-endedness** *n*

**opener** /'ohp(ə)nə/ *n* **1a** an instrument that opens something – usu in combination ⟨*a bottle*-opener⟩ **b** one who opens; *specif* an opening batsman **2** *pl* cards of sufficient value for a player to open the betting in a poker game **3** the first item or event of a series **4** *pl* something serving to begin or introduce

,**open-'eyed** *adj* **1** having the eyes open **2** watchful, discerning

**openhanded** /,ohp(ə)n'handid/ *adj* generous in giving; munificent – **openhandedly** *adv*, **openhandedness** *n*

,**open-'heart** *adj* of or performed on a heart temporarily relieved of its function by a heart-lung machine and surgically opened for inspection and treatment ⟨~ *surgery*⟩

**openhearted** /,ohp(ə)n'hahtid/ *adj* **1** candidly straightforward; frank **2** kind, generous – **openheartedly** *adv*, **openheartedness** *n*

,**open-'hearth** *adj* of, using, or produced in an OPEN-HEARTH FURNACE ⟨*an* ~ *process*⟩

**open-hearth furnace** *n* a gas- or oil-fired steelmaking furnace in which PIG IRON is contained in a shallow HEARTH (floor of the furnace) and heat is radiated down onto the material from the roof

**open house** *n* ready and usu informal hospitality or entertainment for all comers – esp in *keep open house*

**opening** /'ohp(ə)ning/ *n* **1a** an act or instance of making or becoming open **b** an act or instance of beginning; a commencement; *esp* a formal and usu public event by which something new is put officially into operation **2** something open: eg **2a(1)** a breach, aperture **a(2)** an open width; a span **b** a pair of pages that face each other in a book **3** something that constitutes a beginning: eg **3a** a planned series of moves made at the beginning of a game of chess or draughts – compare END GAME, MIDDLE GAME **b** a first performance **4a** a favourable opportunity; a chance **b** an opportunity for employment; a vacancy **5** *NAm* an area without trees or with scattered usu mature trees that occurs as a natural break in a forest

**opening batsman** *n* either of the two batsmen who together take the first turn to bat in a side's innings

**opening bowler** *n* either of the two bowlers who together bowl the first two overs of a side's innings

**opening time** *n*, *Br* the time at which a business, shop, etc opens; *specif* the time set by law at which a pub may open for the sale of alcoholic drinks

**open letter** *n* a letter of protest or appeal that is usu addressed to an individual but is intended for the general public and is printed in a newspaper or periodical

**open loop** *n* a control system for an operation or process in which there is no self-correcting action

**openly** /'ohp(ə)nli/ *adv* in an open manner; *esp* without concealment; frankly

**open market** *n* a market based on free competition and an unrestricted flow of goods (eg between countries)

**open marriage** *n* a form of marriage in which both partners agree to retain a considerable degree of the social and sexual independence they enjoyed when they were single

,**open-'minded** *adj* receptive to arguments or ideas; unprejudiced – **open-mindedly** *adv*, **open-mindedness** *n*

**openmouthed** /,ohp(ə)n'mowdhd/ *adj* **1** having the mouth widely open **2** struck with amazement or wonder **3** clamorous, vociferous – **openmouthedly** *adv*, **openmouthedness** *n*

**openness** /'ohp(ə)n·nis/ *n* the quality or state of being open ⟨*behaved with perfect* ~⟩

**open order** *n* a military formation in which the units are separated by considerable intervals

,**open-'plan** *adj* **1** having few internal dividing walls ⟨*an* ~ *house*⟩ **2** not partitioned off from other areas with different uses ⟨*an* ~ *kitchen*⟩

**open policy** *n* a marine insurance policy in which the value of the goods insured is not specified and must be determined when a loss occurs

,**open-'pollinated** *adj*, *of plants* pollinated by natural agencies (eg wind or insects) without human intervention

**open prison** *n* a prison that has less restrictive security than a conventional prison and to which criminals considered a negligible escape risk (eg those serving short-term sentences) may be sent

**open sandwich** *n* a slice of usu buttered bread covered with any of various savoury cold foods (eg meat, egg, or salad) and usu garnished; *broadly* a sandwich without a top slice of bread

**open scholarship** *n* a scholarship for which any candidate is eligible – compare CLOSED SCHOLARSHIP

**open season** *n* a period during which it is legal to kill or catch game or fish that are protected at other times by law

**open secret** *n* a supposedly secret but generally known matter

**open sesame** /'sezəmi, 'sesəmi/ *n* something that unfailingly brings about a desired end; *specif* a means of gaining access to something which would otherwise be inaccessible [fr *open sesame*, the magical command used by Ali Baba to open the door of the robbers' den in the Ar folktale *Ali Baba and the Forty Thieves*]

**open shop** *n* an establishment in which eligibility for employment is not dependent on membership or nonmembership of a TRADE UNION though there may be an agreement by which a union is recognized as sole bargaining agent – compare CLOSED SHOP, UNION SHOP

**open side** *n* the side of the SCRUM in rugby that is furthest from a touchline – compare BLIND SIDE 2

**open sight** *n* a rear sight of a firearm with an open notch instead of a peephole or a telescope

**open syllable** *n* a syllable ended by a vowel or compound vowel (DIPHTHONG)

**Open University** *n the* nonresidential British university that caters mainly for adults studying part-time, has no formal entrance requirements, and operates mainly through correspondence and broadcasting

**open verdict** *n* a verdict at an inquest that records a death but does not state its cause

**open wagon** *n*, *Br* a railway wagon with no top, a flat bottom, and fixed sides, that is used chiefly for hauling heavy bulk goods

**openwork** /'ohp(ə)n,wuhk/ *n* work (eg in fabric or metal) that shows openings through its substance; work that is perforated or pierced ⟨*wrought-iron* ~⟩ – **open-worked** *adj*

¹**opera** /'op(ə)rə/ *pl of* OPUS

²**opera** /'oprə/ *n* **1** a drama set to music and made up of vocal pieces with orchestral accompaniment and usu other orchestral music (eg an overture); *specif* GRAND OPERA **2** the score of a musical drama **3** the performance of an opera; *also* a theatre where operas are performed **4** the branch of the arts concerned with operas **5** a company performing operas [It, work, opera, fr L, work, pains; akin to L *oper-*, *opus* work] – **operatic** *adj*, **operatically** *adv*

**opera ballet** *n* an opera in which ballet dancing constitutes a principal feature

**operable** /'op(ə)rəbl/ *adj* **1** fit, possible, or desirable to use; practicable **2** suitable for surgical treatment ⟨*an* ~ *cancer*⟩ – **operably** *adv*, **operability** *n*

**opéra bouffe** /,op(ə)rə 'boohf (*Fr* ɔpera buf)/ *n* opera buffa [Fr, fr It *opera buffa*]

**opera buffa** /'boohfə/ *n* a farcical or satirical opera, esp of a form popular in the 18th century [It, lit., comic opera]

**opéra comique** /ko'meek (*Fr* kɔmik)/ *n* COMIC OPERA [Fr]

**opera glass** *n*, **opera glasses** *n pl* small binoculars suitable for use at the opera or theatre

**operagoer** /'oprə,goh·ə/ *n* a person who frequently goes to operas

**opera hat** *n* a man's collapsible top hat

**opera house** *n* a theatre designed for and devoted principally to the performance of operas

**operand** /,opə'rand/ *n* something, esp a quantity, on which an operation is performed (eg in mathematics); *also* the ADDRESS (location) of data to be operated on by a single computer instruction [L *operandum*, neut of gerundive of *operari* to work]

¹**operant** /'op(ə)rənt/ *adj* **1** functioning or tending to produce effects; effective ⟨*an* ~ *conscience*⟩ **2** of the observable or

measurable 3 of or being an operant ⟨~ *conditioning*⟩ ⟨~ *behaviour*⟩ – **operantly** *adv*

²**operant** *n* behaviour (e g bar pressing by a rat to obtain food) that modifies the environment to produce rewarding and reinforcing effects

**opera seria** /'siəri·ə/ *n* an 18th century opera with a heroic or legendary subject [It, lit., serious opera]

**operate** /'opərayt/ *vi* 1 to exert power or influence; act ⟨*factors operating against our success*⟩ 2 to produce an appropriate or desired effect ⟨*the drug* ~d *quickly*⟩ 3a to work, function b to perform surgery – usu + *on* c to carry on a military or naval action or mission 4 to be in action; *specif* to carry out trade or business 5 to follow a course of conduct that is often irregular or dishonest ⟨*crooked gamblers operating in the club*⟩ ~ *vt* 1 to effect; BRING ABOUT 2a to cause to function; work b to put or keep in operation; manage 3 to perform an operation on; *esp* to perform surgery on [L *operatus*, pp of *operari* to work, fr *oper-, opus* work; akin to OE *efnan* to perform, Skt *apas* work]

**operating** /'opərayting/ *adj* of or used for or in operations ⟨~ *expenses*⟩ ⟨*a hospital* ~ *room*⟩

**operating system** *n* the set of computer programs that support and control the running of a computer and its associated equipment (e g by keeping track of the different programs running simultaneously)

**operating table** *n* a high table on which a person lies when undergoing surgery

**operating theatre** *n, Br* a room, usu in a hospital, where surgical operations are carried on

**operation** /,opə'raysh(ə)n/ *n* 1a the act, method, or process of operating b something (to be) done; an activity 2a an exertion of power or influence ⟨*the* ~ *of a drug*⟩ b the quality or state of being functional or operative ⟨*the plant is now in* ~⟩ c a method or manner of functioning ⟨*a machine of very simple* ~⟩ 3 a procedure carried out on a living body with special instruments, usu for the repair of damage or the restoration of health 4 any of various mathematical or logical processes (e g multiplication or addition) carried out to derive one expression from others according to a rule 5 a usu military action, mission, or manoeuvre including its planning and execution 6 a business or financial transaction, esp when speculative or conducted on a large scale 7 a single step performed by a computer in the execution of a program

**operational** /,opə'raysh(ə)nl/ *adj* 1 of or based on operation or an operation ⟨*the* ~ *gap between planning and production*⟩ 2a of, engaged in, or connected with execution of commercial, military, or naval operations b ready for or in condition to undertake a particular function – **operationally** *adv*

**operationalism** /,opə'rayshənl·iz(ə)m/ *n* the theory in the philosophy of science that a concept can only properly be defined in terms of repeatable operations of observation, measurement, etc (e g the concept of weight should be defined in terms of repeatable acts of weighing) – **operationalist** *n*, **operationalistic** *adj*

**operational research** *n, chiefly Br* the application of scientific, esp mathematical, methods to the study and analysis of problems involving complex systems (e g business management, economic planning, and the waging of war)

**operationism** /,opə'rayshəniz(ə)m/ *n* operationalism – **operationist** *n*

**operations research** *n, chiefly NAm* OPERATIONAL RESEARCH

**operations room** *n* a room from which strategic military operations are controlled

¹**operative** /'op(ə)rətiv/ *adj* 1a producing an appropriate effect; efficacious b of the greatest significance or relevance ⟨*she may come – and "may" is the* ~ *word*⟩ 2 exerting force or influence; operating 3a having to do with physical or mechanical operations ⟨~ *skills*⟩ b engaged in or doing work; employed ⟨*an* ~ *craftsman*⟩ 4 based on, consisting of, or using an operation ⟨~ *dentistry*⟩ – **operatively** *adv*, **operativeness** *n*

²**operative** *n* 1 a factory worker 2 *NAm* a secret agent 3 *NAm* PRIVATE DETECTIVE

**operator** /'opə,raytə/ *n* 1a one who operates a machine or device b one who owns or runs a business, organization, etc ⟨*a tour* ~⟩ c one who is in charge of a telephone switchboard 2 a mathematical or logical symbol or expression denoting an operation or process to be performed ⟨*a differential* ~⟩ 3 **operator, operator gene** a piece of genetic material in a cell that controls the function of one or more nearby STRUCTURAL

GENES that are responsible for manufacturing proteins – compare OPERON 4 *informal* a shrewd and skilful person who knows how to circumvent restrictions or difficulties

**operculum** /o'puhkyooləm/ *n, pl* **opercula** /-lə/ *also* **operculums** 1 a lid or covering flap (e g of a spore-containing capsule of a moss) 2 a body structure or part that resembles a lid in form or function: e g 2a a horny or shell-like plate in many snails, whelks, etc that closes the mouth of the shell when the animal is withdrawn b the covering of the gills of a fish [NL, fr L, cover, fr *operire* to shut, cover – more at WEIR] – **opercular** *adj*, **operculate, operculated** *adj*

**operetta** /,opə'retə/ *n* a usu romantic comic opera that includes dancing [It, dim. of *opera*] – **operettist** *n*

**operon** /'opə,ron/ *n* a closely linked combination of genes consisting of an operator and the STRUCTURAL GENES it regulates, that acts as a single functional unit [*operator* + ²-*on*]

**ophicleide** /'ofiklied/ *n* an orchestrated BRASS INSTRUMENT of low range with finger-operated keys for varying the pitch, that was superseded in the 19th century by the tuba [Fr *ophicléide*, fr Gk *ophis* snake + *kleid-, kleis* key – more at CLAVICLE]

**ophidian** /o'fidi·ən/ *adj* of or resembling snakes [deriv of Gk *ophis* snake] – **ophidian** *n*

**ophiology** /,ofi'oləji/ *n* a branch of zoology dealing with snakes [Gk *ophis* + E -*logy*]

**ophite** /'ofiet/ *n* any of various usu green and often mottled rocks (e g serpentine) [L, fr Gk *ophitēs* (*lithos*), lit., serpentine (stone), fr *ophitēs* snakelike, fr *ophis* snake; akin to L *anguis* snake, *anguilla* eel, Gk *enchelys* eel, *echidna* viper, *echinos* hedgehog, OE *igil*]

**ophitic** /o'fitik/ *adj* having or being a texture characteristic of some rocks (e g DOLERITE) in which lath-shaped FELDSPAR crystals are enclosed in a mineral of the PYROXENE group of minerals

**ophiuroid** /,ofhi'yoooəroyd/ *n* BRITTLE STAR (marine animal related to the starfish) [NL *Ophiuroidea*, group name, fr *Ophiura*, genus name, fr Gk *ophis* + *oura* tail – more at SQUIRREL] – **ophiuroid** *adj*

**ophthalm-** /opthalm-, of-/, **ophthalmo-** *comb form* (*eg* ⟨*ophthalmology*⟩; *also* eyeball ⟨*ophthalmitis*⟩ [Gk, fr *ophthalmos*]

**ophthalmia** /op'thalmiə, of-/ *n* inflammation of the eyeball or of the membranes lining the eye and eyelids [ME *obtalmia*, fr LL *ophthalmia*, fr Gk, fr *ophthalmos* eye; akin to Gk *ōps* eye – more at EYE]

> *usage* The pronunciation of **ophthalmia, ophthalmic,** etc with /of-/ rather than /op-/ is recommended for BBC broadcasters.

**ophthalmic** /op'thalmik, of-/ *adj* of or situated near the eye

**ophthalmic optician** *n* an optician qualified to test eyesight and prescribe correctional lenses

**ophthalmologist** /,ofthal'moləjist; *also* op-/ *n* a physician who specializes in ophthalmology – compare OPTICIAN

**ophthalmology** /,ofthal'moləji; *also* op-/ *n* a branch of medicine dealing with the structure, functions, and diseases of the eye – **ophthalmologic** *adj*, **ophthalmologically** *adv*

**ophthalmoscope** /of'thalmə,skohp; *also* op-/ *n* an instrument used to view the RETINA and other structures inside the eye [ISV] – **ophthalmoscopic, ophthalmoscopical** *adj*, **ophthalmoscopy** *n*

**-opia** /-'ohpi·ə/ *comb form* (→ *n*) condition of having (a specified visual defect) ⟨*diplopia*⟩ ⟨*myopia*⟩ [NL, fr Gk -*ōpia*, fr *ōps* eye]

¹**opiate** /'ohpi·ət, -,ayt/ *adj* 1 inducing sleep; narcotic 2 causing dullness or inaction

²**opiate** *n* 1 a preparation of or derived from opium; *broadly* NARCOTIC 1 2 something that induces rest or inaction or quiets uneasiness

**opine** /oh'pien/ *vb, formal vt* to state as an opinion ~ *vi* to express opinions [MF *opiner*, fr L *opinari* to have an opinion]

**opinion** /ə'pinyən/ *n* 1a a view, judgment, or appraisal formed in the mind about a particular matter b approval, esteem – usu used negatively or with adjectives of degree ⟨*I have no great* ~ *of his work*⟩ 2a belief stronger than impression and less strong than positive knowledge b a generally held view ⟨~ *is swinging in her favour*⟩ 3 a formal expression by an expert of his/her judgment or advice ⟨*a medical* ~⟩; *esp* a barrister's written advice to a client on points of law 4 *chiefly NAm* a formal expression (e g by a judge, court, or referee) of the legal reasons and principles upon which a legal decision is based [ME, fr MF, fr L *opinion-, opinio*; akin to L *opinari*]

> *synonyms* Opinion, view, belief, conviction, persuasion, and sentiment all imply a fairly carefully considered idea or judgment

which one considers valid. **Opinion** suggests a conclusion arrived at after some weighing of evidence, but open to debate and suggestion. **View** implies an opinion influenced strongly by feelings or personal bias. **Belief** is unlike **view** or **opinion** in that it is not necessarily formed by an individual for him-/herself; it stresses intellectual acceptance of an idea or dogma, and a strong assurance of its truth. **Conviction** is unshakable **belief**, admitting no possibility of being wrong. **Persuasion**, in this sense, suggests a **belief** strongly influenced by one's feelings and wishes, rather than by intellectual factors. **Sentiment**, usually plural and becoming uncommon in this context, suggests a settled opinion, often influenced by one's feelings or emotion. Compare CERTAINTY, POINT OF VIEW

**opinionated** /ə'pinyə,naytid/ *adj* unduly or stubbornly adhering to one's own opinion or to preconceived notions – **opinionatedly** *adv*, **opinionatedness** *n*

**opinionative** /ə'pinyə,naytiv/ *adj* 1 of or consisting of opinion; doctrinal 2 opinionated – **opinionatively** *adv*, **opinionativeness** *n*

**opisometer** /,opi'somitə/ *n* any of various instruments for measuring distances on a map accurately [Gk *opisō* backwards + E *-meter;* fr the principle of a wheel being rolled forwards on the line to be measured and then backwards along a straight scale]

**opisthobranch** /ə'pisthəbrangk/ *n, pl* **opisthobranchs** any of a large subclass (*Opisthobranchia* of the class Gastropoda, phylum Mollusca) of marine INVERTEBRATE animals that have the gills, when present, behind the heart and the shell reduced or absent [NL *Opisthobranchia*, group name, fr Gk *opisthen* behind + *branchion* gill – more at BRANCHIA] – **opisthobranch** *adj*

**opisthognathous** /,opis'thognəthəs/ *adj* 1 having jaws that slope backwards 2 *of the head of an insect* having the mouthparts directed backwards □ compare HYPOGNATHOUS, ORTHOGNATHOUS, PROGNATHOUS [Gk *opisthen* behind + E *-gnathous*]

**opium** /'ohpi•əm/ *n* 1 an addictive narcotic drug, usu containing morphine, that consists of the dried juice of the unripe seed capsules of the OPIUM POPPY 2 something having an effect like that of opium; *esp* something that inhibits or prevents thought or action ⟨*religion . . . is the* ~ *of the people* – Karl Marx⟩ [ME, fr L, fr Gk *opion*, fr dim. of *opos* sap]

**opium den** *n* a place where opium can be bought and smoked

**opium poppy** *n* a Eurasian poppy (*Papaver somniferum*) cultivated as the source of opium, or for its edible oily seeds or showy flowers

**opossum** /ə'posəm/ *n, pl* **opossums**, *esp collectively* **opossum** 1 any of various American marsupial mammals (family Didelphidae); *esp* a common largely nocturnal and tree-dwelling mammal (*Didelphis virginiana*) of the eastern USA 2 any of several Australian PHALANGERS (tree-dwelling marsupial mammals) [fr *āpäsûm*, lit., white animal (in some Algonquian language of Virginia)]

**opossum shrimp** *n* any of various small aquatic animals (order Mysidacea of the class Crustacea) that resemble shrimps and of which the females carry their eggs in a pouch between the legs

**¹opponent** /ə'pohnənt/ *n* 1 one who or that which takes an opposite position (e g in a debate, contest, or conflict) 2 a muscle that opposes or counteracts and limits the action of another [L *opponent-, opponens*, prp of *opponere* to oppose]

**²opponent** *adj* 1 antagonistic, opposing 2 OPPOSITE 1

**opportune** /,opə'tyoohn, '--,-/ *adj* 1 suitable or convenient for a particular occurrence ⟨*an* ~ *moment*⟩ 2 occurring at an appropriate time ⟨*an* ~ *offer of assistance*⟩ [ME, fr MF *opportun*, fr L *opportunus*, fr *ob-* towards + *portus* port, harbour – more at OB-, FORD] – **opportunely** *adv*, **opportuneness** *n*

**opportunism** /,opə'tyooh,niz(ə)m/ *n* the art, policy, or practice of taking advantage of opportunities or circumstances, esp with little regard for principles or consequences – **opportunist** *n or adj*, **opportunistic** *adj*, **opportunistically** *adv*

**opportunity** /,opə'tyoohnəti/ *n* 1 a set of circumstances that enable something to happen ⟨*the halt provided an* ~ *for rest and refreshment*⟩ 2 a good chance for advancement or progress

   *usage* Correctly, one takes the **opportunity** *for* or *of* doing (a verb) or *to* do (a verb) rather than *of* (a noun) ⟨⚠ *took the* **opportunity** *of his visit to discuss the matter*⟩.

**opposable** /ə'pohzəbl/ *adj* 1 capable of being opposed or resisted 2 capable of being placed opposite and against one or

more of the remaining fingers or toes ⟨*man's* ~ *thumb*⟩ – **opposably** *adv*, **opposability** *n*

**oppose** /ə'pohz/ *vt* 1 to place opposite or against something 2 to place beside something so as to provide resistance, counterbalance, or contrast ⟨*memory and imagination, though we sometimes* ~ *them, are nearly allied* – Benjamin Jowett⟩ 3 to offer resistance to [Fr *opposer*, fr L *opponere* (perf indic *opposui*), fr *ob-* against + *ponere* to place – more at OB-, POSITION] – **opposer** *n*

**opposed** /ə'pohzd/ *adj* set or placed in opposition; contrary ⟨*diametrically* ~ *beliefs*⟩ ⟨*concrete as* ~ *to abstract*⟩

**¹opposite** /'opəzit/ *n* 1 something that is opposed or contrary 2 ANTONYM (word of opposite meaning) 3 the side of a right-angled triangle that joins the adjacent and the hypotenuse
   *usage* One thing is the **opposite** (= noun) *of*, not *to*, another ⟨*his character is the* **opposite** *of hers*⟩, or is **opposite** (= adjective) *to* or *from*, not *of*, another ⟨*they live in the* **opposite** *house to/from ours*⟩.

**²opposite** *adj* 1a situated at the other end or side of an intervening line or space ⟨~ *interior angles*⟩ ⟨~ *ends of a diameter*⟩ b *of plant parts* situated in pairs on an axis (e g the stem of a plant) with each member separated from the other by half the circumference of the axis ⟨~ *leaves*⟩ – compare ALTERNATE 2a 2a occupying an opposing and often antagonistic position ⟨~ *sides of the question*⟩ b diametrically different (e g in nature or character) ⟨*twins, but of* ~ *temperaments*⟩ 3 contrary to one another or to something specified; reverse ⟨*they went off in* ~ *directions*⟩ 4 being the other of a matching or contrasting pair; complementary ⟨*members of the* ~ *sex*⟩ [ME, fr MF, fr L *oppositus*, pp of *opponere*] – **oppositely** *adv*, **oppositeness** *n*

**³opposite** *adv* on or to an opposite side ⟨*she lives* ~⟩

**⁴opposite** *prep* 1 across from and usu facing or on the same level with ⟨*sat* ~ *each other*⟩ 2 in a role complementary to ⟨*played* ~ *the leading man in the comedy*⟩

**opposite number** *n* a member of a system or class (eg a company, institution, or organization) who holds the same relative position as a particular member in a corresponding system or class; a counterpart ⟨*union leaders met their opposite numbers in industry*⟩

**opposition** /,opə'zish(ə)n/ *n* 1 a positioning of one star, planet, etc relative to another such that their LONGITUDES (distances East or West of the earth's axis) differ by 180 degrees 2 the relation between two propositions in logic that have the same subject and predicate but differ in quantity or quality or both (e g in "all dragons are green" and "some dragons are not green") 3 an act of setting opposite or against; the condition of being so set 4 hostile or contrary action or condition 5a something or somebody that opposes; an opponent; *specif, taking sing or pl vb* the body of people opposing something ⟨*the football team's* ~ *were late*⟩ b *taking sing or pl vb, often cap* a political party opposing and prepared to replace the party in power – **oppositional** *adj*

**oppress** /ə'pres/ *vt* 1 to crush or burden by abuse of power or authority; subject to authoritarian rule 2 to burden spiritually or mentally; weigh heavily on [ME *oppressen*, fr MF *oppresser*, fr L *oppressus*, pp of *opprimere*, fr *ob-* against + *premere* to press – more at OB-, PRESS] – **oppressor** *n*

**oppression** /ə'presh(ə)n/ *n* 1 something that oppresses; *esp* (an) unjust or cruel exercise of power or authority ⟨*unfair taxes and other* ~s⟩ 2 a sense of being weighed down in body or mind; depression

**oppressive** /ə'presiv/ *adj* 1 unreasonably harsh or severe ⟨~ *legislation*⟩ 2 tyrannical 3 physically or mentally depressing or overpowering ⟨*an* ~ *climate*⟩ – **oppressively** *adv*, **oppressiveness** *n*

**opprobrious** /ə'prohbri•əs/ *adj, formal* 1 scurrilous and abusive ⟨~ *language*⟩ 2 deserving opprobrium; infamous – **opprobriously** *adv*, **opprobriousness** *n*

**opprobrium** /ə'prohbri•əm/ *n, formal* 1 something that brings disgrace 2 the public disgrace or contempt resulting from shameful behaviour; infamy [L, fr *opprobrare* to reproach, fr *ob* in the way of + *probrum* reproach; akin to L *pro* forwards & to L *ferre* to carry, bring – more at EPI-, FOR, BEAR]

**oppugn** /ə'pyoohn/ *vt, formal* to cast doubt on; CALL IN QUESTION [ME *oppugnen*, fr L *oppugnare*, fr *ob-* against + *pugnare* to fight – more at OB-, PUNGENT] – **oppugner** *n*

**opsimath** /'opsi,math/ *n* a person who begins to learn or study late in life [GK *opsimathēs* late in learning, fr *opsi, opse* late + *manthanein* to learn – more at MATHEMATICAL]

**opsin** /'opsin/ *n* any of various colourless proteins that are formed in the eye with the chemical compound RETINAL by the action of light on a visual pigment (e g RHODOPSIN) [prob back-formation fr *rhodopsin*]

**-opsis** /-'opsis/ *comb form* (→ *n*), *pl* **-opses** /-'opseez/, **-opsides** /-'opsideez/ thing (e g a plant part) resembling ⟨*karyopsis*⟩ [NL, fr Gk, fr *opsis* appearance, vision]

**opslag** /'op,slag/ *n, SAfr* self-sown vegetation [Afrik, fr D]

**opsonin** /'opsənin/ *n* a constituent of BLOOD SERUM that makes foreign cells (e g bacteria) more susceptible to the action of the PHAGOCYTES (cells that engulf and destroy foreign matter) [L *opsonare* to purchase victuals, cater (fr Gk *opsōnein*) + E *-in* – more at OLIGOPSONY] – **opsonic** *adj*

**opson·ize, -ise** /'opsə,niez/ *vt* to treat (bacteria) with opsonin – **opsonization** *n*

**-opsy** /-opsi, -əpsi/ *comb form* (→ *n*) examination ⟨*necropsy*⟩ ⟨*autopsy*⟩ [Gk *-opsia*, fr *opsis*]

**opt** /opt/ *vi* to make a choice; *esp* to decide in favour of something ⟨*has ~ed now for an English life-style – Annabel*⟩ **synonyms** see ¹CHOICE [Fr *opter*, fr L *optare* – more at OPTION]

**opt out** *vi* to choose not to participate in something – often + *of* ⟨*impossible for anyone to opt out of politics* – Brian Crozier⟩

**optative** /'optətiv/ *adj* of or being a grammatical MOOD (category of verb forms) (e g in Greek) that expresses wish or desire – **optative** *n*, **optatively** *adv*

¹**optic** /'optik/ *adj* of vision or the eye [MF *optique*, fr ML *opticus*, fr Gk *optikos*, fr *opsesthai* to be going to see; akin to Gk *opsis* appearance, *ōps* eye – more at EYE

²**optic** *n* **1** any of the lenses, prisms, or mirrors of an optical instrument **2** *Br* a device attached to a bottle, esp one containing spirits, for dispensing an exact measure **3** *humorous* the eye

**optical** /'optikl/ *adj* **1** of the science of optics **2a** of vision; visual ⟨*an ~ illusion*⟩ **b** *astronomy* detectable using optical instruments; visible ⟨*an ~ galaxy*⟩ **c** designed to aid vision ⟨*an ~ instrument*⟩ **3** of or using light ⟨*an ~ telescope*⟩ ⟨*~ microscopy*⟩ **4** of OPTICAL ART – **optically** *adv*

**optical activity** *n* the ability of a substance to rotate the plane of vibration of POLARIZED light to the right or left

**optical art** *n* a style of art characterized by the repeated use of straight or curved lines or geometric patterns designed to create an OPTICAL ILLUSION or visual uncertainty

**optical fibre** *n* a very thin glass or plastic fibre used in FIBRE OPTICS to transmit light

**optical glass** *n* any of various types of glass (e g FLINT GLASS or CROWN GLASS) of well-defined characteristics and high quality used esp for making lenses and prisms

**optical illusion** *n* something that causes the eye to make a false judgment ⟨*thought they could see water but it was only an ~*⟩; *specif* any of various standard figures developed in psychology that appear to have false, unreal, or contradictory properties

**optical rotation** *n* the angle through which the plane of vibration of POLARIZED light that passes through an optically active substance is rotated

**optic axis** *n* a line passing through a lens along which rays of light travel without being deflected

**optic chiasma** /kie'azmə/, **optic chiasm** /'kie·azm/ *n* the X-shaped crossing of fibres of the OPTIC NERVE through which half the fibres originating in each eye pass to the opposite side of the brain

**optic disc** *n* BLIND SPOT (area within the eye that is not sensitive to light)

**optician** /op'tish(ə)n/ *n* **1** a maker of or dealer in optical items and instruments, esp glasses **2** one who examines the eye for defects and prescribes correctional lenses or exercises but not drugs or surgery – compare OPHTHALMOLOGIST

**optic nerve** *n* either of the 2nd pair of CRANIAL NERVES that supply the RETINA (light-sensitive inner layer of the eye) and conduct visual stimuli as nerve impulses back to the brain

**optics** /'optiks/ *n taking sing or pl vb* **1** a branch of science that deals with the nature and properties of light and the effects that it undergoes and produces; *also* a branch of science that deals with similar behaviour of other radiation or particles ⟨*electron ~*⟩ **2** optical properties

**optimal** /'optiml/ *adj* most desirable or satisfactory; optimum – **optimality** *n*, **optimally** *adv*

**optime** /'optimay/ *n* the holder of a second-class or third-class honours degree in mathematics from Cambridge University –

compare WRANGLER [fr the L phrase *optime disputasti* you have argued very well]

**optimism** /'opti,miz(ə)m/ *n* **1** the philosophical doctrine that this world is the best possible world **2** an inclination to emphasize favourable aspects of situations, actions, and events or to expect the best possible outcome [Fr *optimisme*, fr L *optimum*, n, best, fr neut of *optimus* best; akin to L *ops* power – more at OPULENT] – **optimist** *n*, **optimistic, optimistical** *adj*, **optimistically** *adv*

**optim·ize, -ise** /'opti,miez/ *vt* to make as perfect, effective, or functional as possible – **optimizer** *n*, **optimization** *n*

**optimum** /'optiməm/ *n, pl* **optima** /-mə/ *also* **optimums 1** (the amount or degree of) something that is most favourable to some end; *esp* the most favourable condition for the growth and reproduction of an organism **2** the greatest degree attained or attainable under implied or specified conditions [L] – **optimum** *adj*

*usage* Some people dislike the use of **optimum** as an adjective to mean simply "best".

¹**option** /'opsh(ə)n/ *n* **1** an act of choosing **2a** the power or right to choose; freedom of choice **b** (a contract conveying) a right to buy or sell designated stocks, shares, or commodities at a specified price during a stated period **3** something that may be chosen: e g **3a** an alternative course of action ⟨*didn't have many ~s open to him in choosing a career*⟩ **b** an item that is offered in addition to or in place of standard equipment ⟨*a car that includes air-conditioning and a V-8 engine among its ~s*⟩ **synonyms** see ¹CHOICE [Fr, fr L *option-, optio* free choice; akin to L *optare* to choose, Gk *epiopsesthai* to be going to choose]

²**option** *vt* to grant or take an option on

**optional** /'opsh(ə)nl/ *adj* involving an option; not compulsory – **optionally** *adv*

**optometry** /op'tomətri/ *n* the art or profession of examining the eye for defects and prescribing correctional lenses or exercises but not drugs or surgery [Gk *optos* (verbal of *opsesthai* to be going to see) + ISV *-metry* – more at OPTIC] – **optometer** *n*, **optometric** *also* **optometrical** *adj*, **optometrist** *n*

**opulence** /'opyooləns/ *n* **1** wealth, affluence **2** abundance, profusion

**opulent** /'opyoolənt/ *adj* exhibiting or characterized by opulence: e g **a** wealthy ⟨*moved from the middle of town to the ~ suburbs*⟩ **b** amply or plentifully provided or made; luxurious ⟨*the garden produced an ~ display of roses*⟩ ⟨*her figure was more than ample, it was positively ~*⟩ [L *opulentus*, fr. *ops* power, help; akin to L *opus* work] – **opulently** *adv*

**opuntia** /o'punsh(y)ə/ *n* PRICKLY PEAR (type of cactus or its fruit) [NL, fr L, a type of plant, fr fem of *opuntius* of Opus, fr *Opunt-, Opus* Opus, ancient city in Greece]

**opus** /'ohpəs; *also* 'opəs/ *n, pl* **opera** /'opərə/ *also* **opuses** WORK 7; *specif* a musical composition or set of compositions, usu numbered in the order of publication [L *oper-, opus* work – more at OPERATE]

*usage* The pronunciation /'ohpəs/ is recommended for BBC broadcasters.

**opuscule** /o'puskyoohl/ *n* a small, minor, or petty work (e g of literature) [Fr, fr L *opusculum*, dim. of *opus*]

¹**or** /ə; *strong* aw/ *conj* **1a** – used to join two sentence elements of the same class or function and often introduced by *either* to indicate that what immediately follows is another or a final alternative ⟨*either sink ~ swim*⟩ ⟨*red, blue, ~ green*⟩ ⟨*coffee ~ tea ~ whisky*⟩ ⟨*whether you like it ~ not*⟩ **b** – used before the second and later of several suggestions to indicate approximation or uncertainty ⟨*five ~ six days*⟩ ⟨*a place such as Venice ~ Florence ~ somewhere like that – SEU S*⟩ **c** and not – used after a negative ⟨*never drinks ~ smokes*⟩ **d** that is – used to indicate equivalence or clarify meaning ⟨*lessen ~ abate*⟩ ⟨*a heifer ~ young cow*⟩ **e** – used to indicate the result of rejecting a preceding choice ⟨*hurry ~ you'll be late*⟩ **f** – used to introduce an afterthought ⟨*E = mc² – ~ am I boring you?*⟩ **2** – used in logic to connect two sentences to form one complex sentence which is true when at least one of its constituent sentences is true – compare DISJUNCTION **3** *archaic* either **4** *archaic* whether [ME *other, or*, fr OE *oththe*; akin to OHG *eddo* or]

*usage* **1** The use of plural verbs and pronouns after **or** is common, where *X* or *Y* means "either or perhaps both" ⟨*I don't think George or Mary are lying*⟩ but should be avoided in formal writing. See ¹NOR **2** There are many occasions on which it is perfectly legitimate and very effective to begin a sentence with **or**.

²**or** /aw/ *prep or conj, archaic* before [ME, fr *or*, adv, early, before, fr ON ār; akin to OE ǣr early – more at ERE]

³**or** *n* the heraldic colour gold or yellow [MF, gold, fr L *aurum* – more at ORIOLE] – **or** *adj*

**OR** *n* a logical operator equivalent in function to the word *or* ⟨~ *gate in a computer*⟩ [¹ *or*]

¹**-or** /-ə/ *suffix* (→ *n*) one who or that which performs (a specified action) ⟨*grantor*⟩ ⟨*vendor*⟩ [ME, fr OF *-eur, -eor* & L *-or*; OF *-eur*, fr L *-or*; OF *-eor*, fr L *-ator* -or, fr *-atus*, pp suffix + *-or* – more at -ATE]

 *usage* This spelling, rather than **-er**, occurs in some words formed from Latin (*actor*), particularly when no English verb base is involved ⟨*doctor*⟩ ⟨*author*⟩.

²**-or** *suffix* (→ *n*) quality, condition, or state of ⟨*horror*⟩ ⟨*tremor*⟩; *also* instance of (a specified quality or state) ⟨*an error*⟩ – used in *NAm* to replace the British *-our* ⟨*honor*⟩ [ME *-or, -our*, fr OF *-eur*, fr L *-or*]

**ora** /'awrə/ *pl of* ²OS (mouth)

**orache, orach** /'orich/ *n* any of a genus (*Atriplex*) of plants of the goosefoot family that have small flowers, and many of which are weeds of cultivated land; *esp* one (*Atriplex hortensis*) cultivated as a vegetable and eaten like spinach [ME *orage*, fr MF *arrache*, fr (assumed) VL *atrapic-, atrapex*, fr Gk *atraphaxys*]

**oracle** /'orəkl/ *n* **1a** a person (eg a priestess of ancient Greece) through whom a deity is believed to speak **b** a shrine in which a deity reveals hidden knowledge or the divine purpose through such a person **c** an esp obscure answer or decision given by an oracle **2** (a statement by) a person giving wise or authoritative decisions or opinions [ME, fr MF, fr L *oraculum*, fr *orare* to speak – more at ORATION]

**Oracle** *trademark* – used for a service provided by ITV which transmits information (eg the weather or sports results) on usu special channels

**oracular** /o'rakyoolə/ *adj* **1** of or being an oracle **2** resembling an oracle (eg in solemnity or obscurity of expression) [L *oraculum* oracle] – **oracularly** *adv*

¹**oral** /'awrəl, 'o-/ *adj* **1a** uttered by the mouth or in words; spoken **b** handed down or passed on by word of mouth ⟨~ *tradition*⟩ **c** using speech or the lips; *specif* of methods of teaching the deaf relying on lip reading and learning to make speech sounds rather than on SIGNING **2a** of, given through, or affecting the mouth **b** being on or relating to the same surface as the mouth ⟨the ~ *surface of a starfish*⟩ **3** of or characterized by the first stage of sexual development in PSYCHOANALYTIC theory in which gratification is derived from intake (eg of food), by sucking, and later by biting; *also* of or characterized by personality traits (eg passive dependency and aggressiveness) considered typical of fixation at this stage – compare ANAL, GENITAL *usage* see ¹VERBAL [L *or-, os* mouth; akin to OE *ōra* border, L *ora*] – **orality** *n*, **orally** *adv*

²**oral** *n* an oral examination ⟨*passed his ~s and was awarded an O-level in French*⟩

**oral contraceptive** *n* PILL 1b

**oral history** *n* history based on traditions handed down in a community or the memories of those who have taken part in important events which are recorded orally (eg on a tape recorder) rather than in written documents

**oral hygienist** *n, Br* one who assists a dentist, esp in cleaning teeth

**oral sex** *n* stimulation of the sex organs by means of the mouth – compare FELLATIO, CUNNILINGUS

¹**orange** /'orinj/ *n* **1** a spherical fruit with a reddish-yellow leathery aromatic rind and a usu sweet but acid edible pulp rich in vitamin C; *also* any of various rather small evergreen trees (genus *Citrus*, esp *Citrus sinensis* of the family Rutaceae, the orange family) with hard yellow wood, fragrant white flowers, and fruits that are oranges **2** any of several trees or fruits resembling the orange **3** a colour that resembles that of the orange; the colour that lies between red and yellow in the spectrum **4** a drink made from oranges [ME, fr MF, fr OProv *auranja*, fr Ar *nāranj*, fr Per *nārang*, fr Skt *nāraṅga* orange tree, of Dravidian origin; akin to Tamil *naṟu* fragrant] – **orangish** *adj*

²**orange** *adj* **1** of the orange **2** of the colour orange

**Orange** *adj* of or sympathizing with Orangemen – **Orangeism** *n*

**orangeade** /,orinj'ayd/ *n* a beverage of sweetened orange juice mixed with plain or esp with carbonated water [Fr, fr *orange* + *-ade*]

**orange chromide** /'krohmied/ *n* a brilliant orange or yellow red-spotted fish (*Etroplus maculatus*) often kept in tropical aquariums [*Chromide* (any of various small brightly-coloured African fishes), deriv of Gk *chromis*, a type of sea fish]

**orange-flower water** *n* a solution of NEROLI OIL (extract of orange flowers) in water, used esp as a TOILET WATER

**Orangeman** /-mən/ /'orinjmən/ *n* **1** a member of a loyalist society that originated in Ireland and defends the British sovereign and supports the Protestant religion **2** a Protestant Irishman, esp of N Ireland [William III of England, Prince of Orange (fr *Orange*, city in France) †1702 Protestant ruler who deposed the Roman Catholic James II]

**orange peel** *n* a pitted surface (eg on porcelain) like that of an orange skin

**orange pekoe** /'pee,koh/ *n* a BLACK TEA made from the tiny leaf and bud at the end of the stalk, *broadly* Indian or Sri Lankan tea of good quality

**orangery** /'orinj(ə)ri/ *n* a protected place (eg a greenhouse) for growing oranges in cool climates

'**orange-,stick** *n* a thin usu orangewood stick with one pointed end and one rounded end, used in caring for the nails

**orangewood** /'orinj,wood/ *n* the wood of the orange tree used esp in carving and lathe-work

**orangutan, orangoutan** /aw,rang·(y)ooh'tan/, **orangutang** /-'tang/ *n* a largely plant-eating tree-dwelling ANTHROPOID APE (*Pongo pygmaeus*) of Borneo and Sumatra that is about two thirds as large as the gorilla and has brown skin, long sparse reddish brown hair, and very long arms [Malay *orang hutan*, fr *orang* man + *hutan* forest]

**orangy, orangey** /'orinji/ *adj* suggestive of orange; having an orange colour, taste, or tinge

**orate** /aw'rayt/ *vi* **1** to speak in an elevated and often pompous manner; hold forth **2** to give an oration [back-formation fr *oration*]

**oration** /aw'raysh(ə)n/ *n* an elaborate discourse delivered in a formal and dignified manner [L *oration-, oratio* speech, oration, fr *oratus*, pp of *orare* to plead, speak, pray; akin to Russ *orat'* to yell, Gk *ara, arē* prayer]

**orator** /'orətə/ *n* **1** one who delivers an oration **2** one distinguished for his/her skill and power as a public speaker

**Oratorian** /,orə'tawri·ən/ *n or adj* (a member) of the Congregation of the Oratory, a Roman Catholic preaching order founded by St Philip Neri in 1564

**oratorical** /,orə'torikl/ *adj* (characteristic) of an orator or oratory – **oratorically** *adv*

**oratorio** /,orə'tawrioh/ *n, pl* **oratorios** a musical work for choir and soloists performed without action or scenery that is usu based on a scriptural subject and usu composed of RECITATIVES (sections sung in a manner resembling natural speech) by a narrator, elaborate ARIAS by other soloists commenting on the action described, and choruses [It, fr the *Oratorio di San Filippo Neri* (Oratory of St Philip Neri) in Rome, where musical religious services were held in the 16th c]

¹**oratory** /'orət(ə)ri/ *n* **1** a place of prayer; *esp* a private or institutional chapel **2** *cap* an Oratorian congregation, house, or church [ME *oratorie*, fr LL *oratorium*, fr L *oratus*, pp]

²**oratory** *n* **1** the art of speaking in public eloquently or effectively **2a** effective public speaking **b** (public speaking characterized by) highly ornamental or overemotional language [L *oratoria*, fr fem of *oratorius* oratorical, fr *oratus*, pp]

**orb** /awb/ *n* **1** a spherical body; *esp* CELESTIAL SPHERE (imaginary spherical surface on which the planets, stars, etc appear to be projected) **2** a sphere surmounted by a cross symbolizing royal power and justice **3** *poetic* an eye **4** *archaic* something circular; a circle, orbit [MF *orbe*, fr L *orbis* circle, disc, orb; akin to L *orbita* track, rut]

**orbicular** /aw'bikyoolə/ *adj* **1** spherical **2** circular ⟨~ *leaves*⟩ [ME *orbiculer*, fr MF or LL; MF *orbiculaire*, fr LL *orbicularis*, fr L *orbiculus*, dim. of *orbis*] – **orbicularly** *adv*, **orbicularity** *n*, **orbiculate** *adj*

¹**orbit** /'awbit/ *n* **1** the bony socket of the eye **2** a path travelled by one body as it goes round another (eg by the earth about the sun); *also* one complete revolution of a body along such a path **3** a range or sphere of activity or influence ⟨*countries that are within the communist ~*⟩ [L *orbita*] – **orbital** *adj*

²**orbit** *vt* **1** to revolve in an orbit round; circle **2** to send up and make revolve in an orbit ⟨~ *a satellite*⟩ ~ *vi* to travel in circles

**orbital** /'awbitl/ *n* a subdivision of the ENERGY LEVELS of an atom or molecule in which a maximum of two electrons may be found

**orbiter** /'awbitə/ *n* one who or that which orbits; *esp* a spacecraft designed to orbit a moon, planet, etc without landing on its surface

**Orcadian** /aw'kaydi•ən/ *n or adj* (a native or inhabitant) of the Orkney islands [L *Orcades* Orkney islands]

**orchard** /'awchəd/ *n* a usu enclosed area of ground in which fruit trees or occasionally nut trees are planted; *also* the trees in such an area [ME, fr OE *ortgeard*, prob fr L *hortus* garden + OE *geard* yard – more at YARD]

**orchardman** /'awchədmən/ *n* one who works in an orchard

**orchesography** /ˌawki'sografi/ *n, archaic* choreography (dance notation) [Fr *orchésographie*, deriv of Gk *orchēsis* dancing (fr *orcheisthai* to dance) + -*graphia* -graphy]

**orchestra** /'awkistrə/ *n* **1** the circular space at the front of the stage of an ancient Greek theatre used by the chorus **2** the space in front of the stage in a modern theatre that is used by an orchestra **3** *taking sing or pl vb* a group of musicians including esp string players organized to perform ensemble music ⟨a symphony ~⟩ ⟨a 4-piece dance ~⟩ ⟨a chamber ~⟩ [L, fr Gk *orchēstra*, fr *orcheisthai* to dance; akin to Skt *rghāyati* he raves]

**orchestral** /aw'kestrəl/ *adj* **1** of or composed for an orchestra **2** suggestive of an orchestra or its musical qualities – **orchestrally** *adv*

**orchestrate** /'awkiˌstrayt/ *vt* **1a** to compose or arrange (music) for an orchestra **b** to provide with orchestration ⟨~ a ballet⟩ **2** to arrange or combine so as to achieve a maximum effect ⟨~s the elements of his art⟩ – **orchestrator** *n*

**orchestration** /ˌawki'straysh(ə)n/ *n* **1** (the style of) the arrangement of music for performance by an orchestra **2** harmonious organization ⟨develop a world community through ~ of cultural diversities – L K Frank⟩ – **orchestrational** *adj*

**orchid** /'awkid/ *n* **1** a plant or flower of a large family (Orchidaceae, the orchid family) of plants that grow either in soil or on other plants and that usu have showy 3-petalled flowers with an enlarged liplike middle petal **2** a light purplish colour [irreg fr NL *Orchis*]

**orchidectomy** /ˌawki'dektəmi/ *n* the surgical removal of one or both testicles [irreg fr GK *orchis* testicle + E -*ectomy*]

**orchil** /'awchil, 'awkil/ *n* (a violet dye obtained from) any of various lichens (genera *Racella* and *Lecanora*) [ME *orchell*, fr MF *orcheil, orchel*, fr Catal *orxella*]

**orchis** /'awkis/ *n* an orchid; *esp* any of a genus (*Orchis*) of orchids with fleshy roots and a spurred lip [NL, genus name, fr. L, orchid, fr. Gk, testicle, orchid; akin to MIr *uirgge* testicle; fr the shape of the tubers]

**orchitis** /aw'kietəs/ *n* inflammation of the testicles [NL, fr Gk *orchis* testicle]

**ordain** /aw'dayn/ *vt* **1** to invest officially (e g by the laying on of hands) with priestly authority **2a** to establish or order by appointment, decree, or law; enact **b** to destine ⟨his death was ~ed by fate⟩ ~ *vi* to issue an order [ME *ordeinen*, fr OF *ordener*, fr LL *ordinare*, fr L, to put in order, appoint, fr *ordin-, ordo* order] – **ordainer** *n*, **ordainment** *n*

**ordeal** /aw'deel/ *n* **1** a primitive means used to determine guilt or innocence by submitting the accused to dangerous or painful tests believed to be under supernatural control ⟨~ by fire⟩ **2** a severe test, trial, or experience [ME *ordal*, fr OE *ordāl*; akin to OHG *urteil* judgment; both from a prehistoric WGmc compound derived fr a compound verb represented by OHG *irteilen* to judge, distribute, fr *ir-*, perfective prefix + *teilen* to divide, render a verdict; akin to OHG *teil* part – more at DEAL]

¹**order** /'awdə/ *n* **1a** a group of people united in a formal way: e g **1a(1)** a fraternal society with secret membership ceremonies **a(2)** a community under a religious rule; *esp* one (e g of monks or nuns) requiring members to take solemn vows **b** a badge or medal of such a society; *also* a civilian or military decoration ⟨the Order of Merit⟩ **2a** any of the several grades of the Christian ministry **b** *pl* the office of a person in the Christian ministry **3a** a rank, class, or special group in a community or society – often in *higher orders, lower orders* **b** a class of people or things grouped according to quality, value, or natural characteristics: e g **b(1)** a category in the biological classification of living things ranking above a family and below a class **b(2)** the broadest category in soil classification **4a(1)** a rank, level ⟨a statesman of the first ~⟩ **a(2)** a category, class ⟨revolutions are a different ~ of events – John Strachey⟩ **b(1)** an arrangement or sequence of objects or events in time ⟨listed the items in ~ of importance⟩ **b(2)** a sequential arrangement of mathematical elements **c** DEGREE 10a,b **d(1)** the number of times mathematical DIFFERENTIATION is applied successively ⟨derivatives of higher ~⟩ **d(2)** the order of the highest order DERIVATIVE in a DIFFERENTIAL EQUATION **e** the number of columns or rows in a SQUARE MATRIX (arrangement of mathematical elements) **f** the number of elements in a finite mathematical group **5a(1)** a sociopolitical system ⟨was opposed to changes in the established ~⟩ **a(2)** a specified sphere or aspect of a sociopolitical system ⟨the present economic ~⟩ **b** a regular or harmonious arrangement ⟨the ~ of nature⟩ **6a** the customary mode of procedure, esp in debate ⟨point of ~⟩ **b** a prescribed form of a religious service; a rite **7a** the rule of law or proper authority ⟨promised to restore law and ~⟩ **b** a specific rule, regulation, or authoritative direction; a command **8a** a style of building; *esp* any of the classical styles of building ⟨the Doric ~⟩ **b** a column and the part of the building resting upon it (ENTABLATURE) proportioned and decorated according to one of the classical styles **9a** state or condition, esp with regard to functioning or repair ⟨things were in terrible ~⟩ **b** a proper or orderly condition ⟨their passports were in ~⟩ **10a** a written direction to pay money to someone **b** a direction or commission to purchase, sell, or supply goods or to perform work **c** goods or items bought or sold **d** an assigned or requested undertaking – chiefly in *tall order* **11** the style of dress and equipment for a specified purpose ⟨troops reviewed in full marching ~⟩ [MF *ordre*, fr ML & L; ML *ordin-, ordo* ecclesiastical order, fr L, arrangement, group, class; akin to L *ordiri* to lay the warp, begin] – **call to order** to order (a meeting) to observe the customary rules of procedure – **in order 1** arranged in the correct sequence **2** appropriate; fitting **3** functioning properly; working – **in order that** – used to introduce a subordinate clause expressing purpose – **in order to** with the intention or purpose of; so as to – **in short order** quickly – **in the order of**, *NAm* **on the order of** in the approximate range of; about ⟨in the order of five thousand people on the demonstration⟩ – **on order** having been ordered and due for delivery – **order of the day 1** *the* programme of events; agenda **2** *the* prevailing feature or state **3** *the* only course of action or thing available – **out of order 1** not functioning or working properly; broken **2** *informal* not acceptable; not following standard practice – **to order** in accordance with specific instructions, esp those for a personalized article of clothing – see also **put one's HOUSE in order**, **under STARTER's orders**

*usage* The phrase **in order that** is correctly followed by *may* or *might* ⟨spoke slowly **in order that** they might follow him⟩ or sometimes by *shall* or *should*. The use of *can, could, will,* or *would* is to be avoided here.

²**order** *vt* **1** to put in order; arrange **2a** to give an order to; command **b** to destine, ordain **c** to command to go or come to a specified place **d** to give an order for ⟨~ a meal⟩ ~ *vi* **1** to bring about order; regulate **2a** to issue orders; command **b** to give or place an order – **orderer** *n*

**order about/around** *vt* to tell (someone) what to do in an overbearing and bullying manner

**order up** *vt* to summon for active military duty; CALL UP

**order arms** *n* **1** a drill position in which the rifle is held vertically beside the right leg with the butt resting on the ground **2** a command to return the rifle to ORDER ARMS from PRESENT ARMS or to drop the hand from a hand salute [fr the command *order arms*!]

**ordered** /'awdəd/ *adj* characterized by order: e g **a** marked by regularity or self-discipline ⟨led an ~ life⟩ **b** marked by regular or harmonious arrangement of parts ⟨an ~ landscape⟩ **c** *maths* having elements succeeding or arranged according to a rule: **c(1)** PARTIALLY ORDERED **c(2)** TOTALLY ORDERED **c(3)** having a specified first element ⟨a set of ~ pairs⟩

**order in council** *n, often cap O&C* an order made by the British sovereign on the advice of the PRIVY COUNCIL and used to give the force of law to administrative regulations

¹**orderly** /'awdəli/ *adj* **1a(1)** arranged or disposed in some order or pattern; regular ⟨~ rows of houses⟩ **a(2)** not marked by disorder; tidy ⟨keeps an ~ desk⟩ **b** governed by law; regulated ⟨an ~ universe⟩ **c** methodical ⟨an ~ mind⟩ **2** well behaved; peaceful ⟨an ~ crowd⟩ *synonyms* see ²NEAT *antonym* disorderly – **orderliness** *n*, **orderly** *adv*

²**orderly** *n* **1** a soldier assigned to perform various services (e g carrying messages) for a superior officer **2** a hospital attendant who does routine or heavy work (e g cleaning, carrying supplies, or moving patients)

**orderly room** *n* the administration officer of a military unit

**order of magnitude** *n* a range of magnitude extending from some value to ten times that value

**order paper** *n* a programme of the day's business in a parliament or legislative assembly

¹**ordinal** /'awdinl/ *n* **1a** *cap* (a book containing) the forms of service for ordination of priests **b** a book containing directions for Roman Catholic services for each day in the year **2** ORDINAL NUMBER [(1) ME, fr ML *ordinale*, fr LL, neut of *ordinalis;* (2) LL *ordinalis*, fr *ordinalis*, adj]

²**ordinal** *adj* of a specified order or rank in a series **9** ordinary [LL *ordinalis*, fr L *ordin-*, *ordo*]

**ordinal number** *n* a number designating the place (e g first, second, or third) occupied by an item in a sequence – compare CARDINAL NUMBER

**ordinance** /'awdinəns/ *n, formal* **1** an authoritative decree or order; *esp* a public regulation made by a local authority **2** a prescribed usage, practice, or ceremony **9** ordnance [ME, fr MF & ML; MF *ordenance*, lit., art of arranging, fr ML *ordinantia*, fr L *ordinant-*, *ordinans*, prp of *ordinare* to put in order – more at ORDAIN]

**ordinand** /'awdi,nand/ *n* a candidate for ordination [LL *ordinandus*, gerundive of *ordinare* to ordain]

¹**ordinary** /'awdn(ə)ri, 'awd(ə)nri/ *n* **1** *often cap* the parts of the Mass that are fixed throughout the year and do not vary from day to day – compare PROPER **2** the regular or customary condition or course of things – usu in *out of the ordinary* **3** any of the simplest heraldic figures bounded by straight lines (e g the bend or chevron) **4** *archaic* **4a** a bishop or judge having jurisdiction over a specified territory or group in his own right, not by delegation **b** a clergyman appointed formerly in England to attend condemned criminals **5** *archaic Br* a tavern or eating house serving regular meals at a fixed price; *also* a meal served at such a place [ME *ordinarie*, fr AF & ML; AF, fr ML *ordinarius*, fr L *ordinarius*, adj]

²**ordinary** *adj* **1** of a kind to be expected in the normal order of events; routine, usual **2** of unexceptional quality, rank, or ability; commonplace **3** having or being jurisdiction held by virtue of office as opposed to that which is delegated **4** *of a differential equation* involving only two variables and their first DERIVATIVES **5** *chiefly NAm* lacking in refinement; common [ME *ordinarie*, fr L *ordinarius*, fr *ordin-*, *ordo* order] – **ordinarily** *adv*, **ordinariness** *n*

**ordinary degree** *n* PASS DEGREE

**ordinary-language philosophy** *n* an approach to philosophical problems that seeks to resolve perplexity by revealing sources of puzzlement in the misunderstanding of ordinary language

**Ordinary level** *n, often cap L* an examination in any of many subjects that is the lowest of the three levels of the British General Certificate of Education and is taken typically at about the age of 16; *also* a subject taken in this examination – compare ADVANCED LEVEL, SCHOLARSHIP LEVEL

**ordinary seaman** *n* a seaman of some experience but not as skilled as an ABLE SEAMAN; *specif* a British naval rating of the rank below ABLE SEAMAN – see MILITARY RANKS table

**ordinary share** *n* a share in the capital of a company that entitles the holder to a variable dividend on profits after other demands (e g those on other shares) have been met – compare PREFERENCE SHARE, DEFERRED SHARE

**ordinate** /'awdinət/ *n, maths* the coordinate of a point in a CARTESIAN COORDINATE system (one having only an x-axis and a y-axis) obtained by measuring parallel to the y-axis – compare ABSCISSA [NL (*linea*) *ordinate* (*applicata*), lit., line applied in an orderly manner]

**ordination** /,awdi'naysh(ə)n/ *n* ordaining or being ordained, esp as a priest

**ordnance** /'awdnəns/ *n* **1** (the branch of government service dealing with) military supplies (e g weapons, ammunition, and vehicles) **2** cannon, artillery **9** ordinance [ME *ordinaunce*, fr MF *ordenance*, lit., act of arranging]

**ordnance datum** *n* a value for mean SEA LEVEL that is used as a zero point (DATUM) by the ORDNANCE SURVEY in calculating heights above sea level and that is based on the average sea level at Newlyn in Cornwall – called also NEWLYN DATUM

**Ordnance Survey** *n* the national land surveying and mapping organization of Great Britain, Northern Ireland, or the Republic of Ireland; *also* a geographical survey conducted by the Ordnance Survey

**ordo** /'awdoh/ *n, pl* **ordos, ordines** a list of the services and festivals of the Roman Catholic church for each day of the year [ML, fr L, order]

**ordonnance** /'awdənəns (*Fr* ɔrdɔnɑ̃:s)/ *n* the arrangement of the parts (e g of a literary composition) with regard to each other and as a whole **△** ordinance, ordnance [Fr, alter. of MF *ordenance*]

**Ordovician** /,awdo'vishyən/ *adj or n* (of or being) the prehistoric time period between the CAMBRIAN and the SILURIAN or the corresponding system of rocks [L *Ordovices*, ancient people in N Wales]

**ordure** /'awdyooə/ *n* excrement [ME, fr MF, fr *ord* filthy, fr L *horridus* horrid]

**ore** /aw/ *n* **1** a mineral containing a valuable constituent (e g metal) for which it is mined and worked **2** a source from which valuable matter is extracted [ME *or*, fr OE *ār;* akin to OHG *ēr* bronze, L *aes* copper, bronze, Skt *ayas* metal, iron]

**öre** /'uhrə/ *n, pl* **öre** – see *krona, krone* at MONEY table [Sw *öre* & *Dan* & *Norw* *øre*]

**oread** /'awriad, 'oriad/ *n* any of the nymphs of mountains and hills in Greek mythology [L *oread-*, *oreas*, fr Gk *oreiad-*, *oreias*, fr *oreios* of a mountain, fr *oros* mountain – more at RISE]

**oregano** /ori'gahnoh, ə'regənoh/ *n* a bushy plant (*Origanum vulgare*) of the mint family whose leaves are used as a herb in cooking [AmerSp *orégano*, fr Sp, wild marjoram, fr L *origanum* – more at ORIGANUM]

**Oregon grape** *n* a commonly planted evergreen shrub (*Mahonia aquifolium*) of the barberry family that has yellow flowers, bluish black berries, and that is native to the Pacific coast of North America [*Oregon*, state of the USA]

**Oregon pine** /'origən/ *n* **1** DOUGLAS FIR **2** oregon, oregon pine the wood of the Oregon pine

**orfe** /awf/ *n, pl* **orfe** a golden-yellow European freshwater fish (*Idus idus*) kept esp in ponds or aquariums for show [Ger, fr OHG *orvo*, fr L *orphus*, a sea fish, fr Gk *orphos*, *orphōs*]

**orfray** /'aw,fri/ *n* ORPHREY (embroidered band)

**organ** /'awgən/ *n* **1a** a wind instrument consisting of sets of pipes made to sound by compressed air and controlled by keyboards and producing a variety of musical effects; *also* an electronic instrument producing similar sounds **b** REED ORGAN (similar instrument using reeds rather than pipes) **c** any of various similar simpler pipe or reed instruments **2a** a specialized biological structure (e g a heart, kidney, leaf, or stem) consisting of cells and tissues that performs some specific function in an organism **3** a subordinate group or organization that performs specialized functions ⟨*the various* ~s *of government*⟩ **4** a periodical; a journal **5** *euph* the penis [ME, partly fr OE *organa*, fr L *organum*, fr Gk *organon*, lit., tool, instrument; partly fr OF *organe*, fr L *organum;* akin to Gk *ergon* work – more at WORK]

**organ-, organo-** *comb form* **1** organ; organs ⟨organogenesis⟩ **2** organic ⟨organomercurial⟩ [ME, fr ML, fr L *organum*]

**organdie**, *NAm chiefly* **organdy** /'awgəndi/ *n* a very fine transparent muslin with a stiff finish **9** organza, organzine [Fr *organdi*, perh alter. of *organsin* organzine]

**organelle** /,awgə'nel/ *n* a part (e g a mitochondrion) of a cell that has a specialized structure and usu a specific function – compare ORGAN [NL *organella*, fr L *organum*]

¹**organ-,grinder** *n* a street musician who operates a BARREL ORGAN

¹**organic** /aw'ganik/ *adj* **1a** of or arising in a body organ ⟨~ *changes in mood*⟩ **b** affecting the structure of the organism ⟨*an* ~ *disease*⟩ – compare FUNCTIONAL 1b **2a** of or derived from living organisms **b** relating to, produced with, or based on the use of fertilizer of plant or animal origin without employment of chemically formulated fertilizers or pesticides ⟨~ *farming*⟩ ⟨~ *foods*⟩ **3a** of or containing carbon compounds **b** of, being, or dealt with by a branch of chemistry concerned with the carbon compounds of living beings and most other carbon compounds **4a** forming an essential element of a whole; integral ⟨*a work in which the music is incidental rather than* ~⟩ **b** having systematic coordination of parts; organized ⟨*an* ~ *whole*⟩ **c** having the characteristics of an organism; developing in the manner of a living plant or animal ⟨*society is* ~⟩ **5** of or constituting the law by which a government or organization exists – **organically** *adv*

²**organic** *n* an organic substance: e g **a** a fertilizer of plant or animal origin **b** a pesticide whose active component is an organic compound or a mixture of organic compounds

**organicism** /aw'ganisiz(ə)m/ *n* a theory that the organization of a living organism rather than its components constitutes life [ISV] – **organicist** *n*

**organism** /'awgə,niz(ə)m/ *n* **1** a complex structure of inter-dependent and subordinate elements whose relations and properties are largely determined by their function in the whole **2** a living being – **organismic** *also* **organismal** *adj*, **organismically** *adv*

**organist** /'awgənist/ *n* one who plays the organ

**organ·ization, -isation** /,awgənie'zaysh(ə)n/ *n* **1a** organizing or being organized ⟨*a great talent for* ∼⟩ **b** the condition or manner of being organized ⟨*a high degree of* ∼⟩ **2a** an association, society ⟨*tax exemptions for charitable* ∼s⟩ **b** an administrative and functional body (eg a business or a political party); *also, taking sing or pl vb* the personnel of such a structure – **organizational** *adj*, **organizationally** *adv*

**organization and methods** *n* the function of organizing and scheduling business operations, esp with regard to the work that must be performed

**organization man** *n* a person who is totally dedicated to, or over-concerned with, the organization to which he belongs

**organ·ize, -ise** /'awgə,niez/ *vt* **1** to cause to develop an organic structure **2** to arrange or form into a complete or functioning whole; integrate ⟨*trying to* ∼ *her thoughts*⟩ **3a** to set up an administrative structure for **b** to persuade to associate in an organization; *esp* to form (workers) into a trade union **4** to arrange by systematic planning and united effort ⟨∼d *a field trip*⟩ ∼ *vi* **1** to undergo physical or organic structuring and ordering **2** to arrange elements into a whole consisting of interdependent parts **3** to form an association or society; *specif* to form a trade union – **organizable** *adj*

**organ·ized, -ised** /'awgə,niezd/ *adj* **1** having a formal organization to coordinate and carry out activities ⟨∼ *crime*⟩ **2** affiliated by membership of an organization; *esp* having been unionized ⟨∼ *steelworkers*⟩

**organ·izer, -iser** /'awgə,niezə/ *n* **1** one who or that which organizes **2** *biology* INDUCTOR **3** (substance controlling development of tissues)

**organo-** – see ORGAN-

**organochlorine** /aw,ganoh'klaw,reen/ *n* a chlorine-containing pesticide (eg aldrin, DDT, or dieldrin)

**organ of Corti** /'kawti/ *n* a complex structure in the INNER EAR that in mammals is the chief part of the ear by which sound is directly perceived [Alfonso *Corti* †1876 It anatomist]

**organogenesis** /,awgənoh'jenəsis/ *n* the origin and development of bodily organs – compare MORPHOGENESIS [NL] – **organogenetic** *adj*, **organogenetically** *adv*

**organography** /,awgə'nogrəfi/ *n* the descriptive study of the organs of plants or animals

**organoleptic** /,awgənoh'leptik, aw,ganə-/ *adj* **1** affecting or involving the use of one or more of the sense organs ⟨∼ *evaluation of foods*⟩ **2** being, affecting, or relating to qualities (eg taste and smell) of a substance (eg food) that stimulate the sense organs [Fr *organoleptique*, fr *organ-* + Gk *lēptikos* disposed to take, fr *lambanein* to take – more at LATCH] – **organoleptically** *adv*

**organology** /,awgə'noləji/ *n* the study of the organs of plants and animals [ISV] – **organologic, organological** *adj*

**organomercurial** /aw,ganohmuh'kyooəri·əl/ *n* a carbon-containing chemical compound or a pharmaceutical preparation containing mercury

**organometallic** /aw,ganohmə'talik/ *adj* of or being a carbon-containing chemical compound that usu contains one or more metal atoms bonded directly to carbon [ISV] – **organometallic** *n*

**organon** /'awgə,non/ *n, pl* **organa, organons** an instrument for acquiring or ordering knowledge; *specif* a body of principles of scientific or philosophic investigation [Gk, lit., tool – more at ORGAN]

**organophosphate** /aw,ganə'fosfayt/ *n* a carbon-containing chemical compound, esp a war gas or pesticide, containing phosphorus

**organophosphorus** /aw,ganoh'fosfərəs/ *adj or n* (of or being) a phosphorus-containing pesticide (eg MALATHION) – **organophosphorous** *adj*

**organotherapy** /aw,ganoh'therəpi/ *n* the treatment of disease by the use of animal organs or their extracts [ISV] – **organotherapeutic** *adj*

**organum** /'awgənəm/ *n* **1** organon **2** an early style of music of the late Middle Ages that consists of one or more vocal parts accompanying the basic melodic theme; *also* a composition in this style [ML, fr L, organ]

**organza** /aw'ganzə/ *n* a very fine dress fabric resembling

ORGANDIE (stiff muslin) usu made of silk, rayon, or nylon [prob alter. of Fr *organsin* organzine]

**organzine** /'awgən,zeen/ *n* a raw silk thread used in fine fabrics [Fr or It; Fr *organsin*, fr It *organzino*, prob fr *Urgench* town in USSR where it was first manufactured]

**orgasm** /'aw,gaz(ə)m/ *n* (as instance of) intense or paroxysmal emotional or physical excitement; *esp* the climax of sexual excitement that occurs typically as the culmination of sexual intercourse [NL *orgasmus*, fr Gk *orgasmos*, fr *organ* to grow ripe, be lustful; akin to Skt *ūrjā* sap, strength] – **orgasmic** *adj*, **orgastic** *adj*

**orgeat** /'aw,zhah; (*Fr* ɔrʒa)/ *n* a sweet nonalcoholic syrup or drink made with almonds or barley and rose or orange--flower water that is used esp as a cocktail ingredient [Fr, fr MF, fr *orge* barley, fr L *hordeum;* akin to OHG *gersta* barley, Gk *kri*]

**orgiastic** /,awji'astik/ *adj* **1** of or involving orgies **2** characterized by unrestrained emotion [Gk *orgiastikos*, fr *orgiazein* to celebrate orgies, fr *orgia*] – **orgiastically** *adv*

**orgulous** /'awgyooləs/ *adj, archaic* proud, haughty [ME, fr OF *orgueilleus*, fr *orgueil* pride, of Gmc origin; akin to OHG *urguol* distinguished]

**orgy** /'awji/ *n* **1** a secret rite held in honour of an ancient Greek or Roman deity and usu characterized by ecstatic singing and dancing **2** a wild promiscuous or drunken party **3** something that resembles an orgy in lack of control or moderation ⟨*soldiers engaging in an* ∼ *of destruction*⟩ [MF *orgie*, fr L *orgia*, pl, fr Gk; akin to Gk *ergon* work – more at WORK]

**-oria** /-'awri·ə/ *pl of* -ORIUM

**-orial** /-'awri·əl/ *suffix* (→ *adj*) of, belonging to, or connected with ⟨*sensorial*⟩ [ME, fr L *-orius* -ory + ME *-al*]

**oribatid** /o'ribətid/ *n* any of a superfamily (Oribatoidea) of small oval or round nonparasitic mites that have a dark hardened covering and that are abundant in soil and moss [NL *Oribatidae*, group name (coextensive with *Oribatoidea*), fr *Oribata*, genus name, perh fr Gk *oreibatēs* mountain-ranging] – **oribatid** *adj*

**oribi** /'orəbi, 'aw-/ *n, pl* **oribis, oribi** a small graceful tan-coloured antelope (*Ourebia ourebi*) of southern and eastern Africa [Afrik]

**oriel window** /'awri·əl/ *n* a BAY WINDOW projecting from an upper storey and supported by a corbel or bracket [ME *oriel* porch, oriel window, fr MF *oriol* porch]

**¹orient** /'awri·ənt, 'o-/ *n* **1** *cap* EAST 2a,b (eastern lands) **2a** a pearl of great lustre **b** the lustre or sheen of a pearl **3** *archaic* EAST 1b (place where the sun rises) [ME, fr MF, fr L *orient-, oriens*, fr prp of *oriri* to rise – more at RISE]

**²orient** *adj* **1** lustrous, sparkling ⟨∼ *gems*⟩ **2** *archaic* oriental

**³orient** /'awri,ent, 'o-/ *vt* **1a** to cause to face or point towards the east; *specif* to build (a church or temple) with the long axis pointing eastwards and the chief altar at the eastern end **b** to set or arrange in any definite position, esp in relation to the points of the compass **c** to ascertain the bearings of **2a** to adjust to the surroundings or a situation ⟨*helps school leavers* ∼ *themselves in the working environment*⟩ **b** to acquaint with the existing situation or environment ⟨*immigrants who find it hard to* ∼ *themselves*⟩ *usage* see ORIENTATE [Fr *orienter*, fr MF, fr *orient*]

**oriental** /,awri'entl, ,o-/ *adj* **1** *often cap* of or characteristic of the Orient; Eastern **2a** of superior grade, lustre, or value **b** being CORUNDUM or sapphire but simulating another gem in colour **3** *often cap* (having the characteristics) of Orientals **4** *cap* of or constituting the biogeographic region that includes Asia south and southeast of the Himalayas and the Malay group of islands west of WALLACE'S LINE – **orientally** *adv*

**Oriental** *n* **1** a member of any of the peoples of the Orient **2** tobacco from the East; *esp* TURKISH TOBACCO

**oriental carpet** *n* ORIENTAL RUG

**oriental cockroach** *n* a common blackish-brown cockroach (*Blatta orientalis*)

**oriental fruit moth** *n* a small moth (*Cydia molesta*), found in many parts of the world but probably of Japanese origin, whose larva is injurious to the twigs and fruit of orchard trees, esp the peach

**orientalism** /,awri'entəlizm,,o-/ *n, often cap* **1** the characteristic features of oriental peoples or culture **2** scholarship or learning in oriental subjects – **orientalist** *n, often cap*

**oriental·ize, -ise** /,awri'entəliez,,o-/ *vb, often cap* to make or become oriental

**oriental peach moth** *n* ORIENTAL FRUIT MOTH

**Oriental rug** *n* a usu expensive and luxurious handwoven or hand-knotted one-piece rug or carpet made in the Orient

**orientate** /'awri·ən,tayt, 'o-/ *vt, chiefly Br* to orient ~ *vi* to face or turn to the east

 *usage* The chiefly British use of **orientate** as a transitive verb ⟨*found it hard to* **orientate** *themselves*⟩ is disliked by some writers, who prefer to use **orient**.

**orientation** /,awri·ən'taysh(ə)n, ,o-/ *n* 1 orienting or being oriented 2 the state of being oriented; *broadly* arrangement, alignment 3 a usu general or lasting direction of thought, inclination, or interest 4 the change of position by an organism or a part in response to an external stimulus ⟨*the* ~ *of a plant towards the sun*⟩ – **orientational** *adj*, **orientationally** *adv*

**oriented** /'awri·entid,'o-/ *adj* intellectually or emotionally directed ⟨*humanistically* ~ *scholars*⟩

**orienteer** /,awri·en'tiə,o-/ *n* one who engages in orienteering

**orienteering** /,awri·ən'tiəring, ,o-/ *n* a sport in which competitors have to navigate their way across unfamiliar country in the shortest time using only a map and a compass [modif (influenced by *-eer*) of Sw *orientering*, fr *orientera* to orient]

**orifice** /'orifis/ *n* an opening (eg a vent, mouth, or hole) through which something may pass [MF, fr LL *orificium*, fr L *or-*, *os* mouth – more at ORAL] – **orificial** *adj*

**oriflamme** /'ori,flam/ *n* a banner, symbol, or ideal inspiring devotion or courage [ME *oriflamble* the sacred red banner of St Denis (used as the banner of the kings of France in battle), fr MF, fr ML *aurea flamma*, lit., golden flame]

**origami** /,ori'gahmi/ *n* the traditional Japanese art or process of folding paper into complex forms [Jap, fr *ori* to fold + *gami* paper]

**origanum** /ə'rigənəm; *also* ,ori'gahnəm/ *n* OREGANO (type of herb); *also* MARJORAM [ME, fr L, wild marjoram, fr Gk *origanon*]

**origin** /'orijin/ *n* 1 ancestry, parentage 2 a source or starting point ⟨*the* ~ *of the custom is lost in the mist of time*⟩ ⟨*this spring is the* ~ *of the brook*⟩ 3 the more fixed, central, or larger attachment or part of a muscle – compare INSERTION 2a, HEAD 9c 4 *maths* the point of intersection of axes (eg on a graph) where the value of the variables is zero [ME *origine*, prob fr MF, fr L *origin-*, *origo*, fr *oriri* to rise – more at RISE]

 *synonyms* **Origin, inception, source, root,** and **provenance** may all describe the starting-point of something. **Origin** points either to its specific cause, or to the moment when or place where it came into existence. Applied to people, **origin** signifies ancestry or parentage. **Inception** stresses the actual start of a process rather than implying its cause ⟨*at its* **inception**, *the movement consisted only of five members*⟩. **Source** is influenced by its literal sense as the beginning of a watercourse to suggest what provides for the existence, or continued existence, of especially immaterial things ⟨*love was the* **source** *of her unfailing energy*⟩. It may also denote the place from which something has come. **Root** suggests a very deep-lying origin or a fundamental cause ⟨*we must get at the* **root** *of the trouble*⟩. **Provenance** suggests a place where, or the people among whom, an artefact or literary work originated, rather than its cause ⟨*nobody knows the* **provenance** *of these decorated plates, but they are very ancient*⟩.

¹**original** /ə'rijənl/ *n* 1 something from which a copy, reproduction, or translation is made 2 an eccentric person

²**original** *adj* 1 of or constituting an origin or beginning; earliest ⟨*the* ~ *part of the house*⟩ 2a not secondary, derivative, or imitative b being the first instance or source from which a copy, reproduction, or translation is or can be made 3 independent and creative in thought or action; inventive *synonyms* see ¹NEW *antonyms* banal, hackneyed – **originally** *adv*

**originality** /ə,rijə'naləti/ *n* 1 the quality or state of being original 2 freshness of appearance, design, or style 3 the power of independent thought or constructive imagination

**original sin** *n* the state of innate sinfulness held to be possessed by all human beings as a result of Adam's disobedience

**originate** /ə'rijə,nayt/ *vb* to (cause to) begin or come into existence – **origination** *n*, **originator** *n*

**originative** /ə'rijənətiv/ *adj* having ability to originate; creative – **originatively** *adv*

**orinasal** /,awri'nayzl, ,o-/ *adj* NASAL 2a(2) [L *or-*, *os* mouth + E *nasal*] – **orinasal** *n*

**oriole** /'awri,ohl, -əl/ *n* any of a family (Oriolidae) of usu brightly coloured African and Eurasian birds related to the crows [Fr *oriol*, fr L *aureolus*, dim. of *aureus* golden, fr *aurum* gold; akin to Lith *auksas* gold]

**Orion** /ə'rie·ən/ *n* a constellation on the equator represented

on charts by a hunter with a belt and sword – called also *the* HUNTER [*Orion* (Gk *Oriōn*), legendary Boeotian hunter who was placed aong the stars after his death]

**orison** /'oriz(ə)n/ *n, archaic* a prayer △ oration [ME, fr OF, fr LL *oration-*, *oratio*, fr L, oration

**-orium** /-'awri·əm/ *suffix* (→ *n*), *pl* **-oriums, -oria** /-'awri·ə/ ¹ORY ⟨*cremato*rium⟩ [L, fr neut of *-orius* -ory]

**Oriya** /o'ree(y)ə/ *n* the INDIC language of Orissa in India

**orle** /awl/ *n* a border inside but not touching the edge of a heraldic FIELD [MF, lit., border, hem, fr *orler* to put a hem on, deriv of L *ora* border, rim, coast – more at ORAL]

**Orlon** /'awlon/ *trademark* – used for an acrylic fibre *synonyms* see NYLON

**orlop deck, orlop** /'awlop/ *n* the lowest deck in a ship having four or more decks [ME *overlop* deck of a single-decker, fr MLG *overlōp*, lit., something that overleaps]

**Ormazd** /'aw,mazd/ *n* AHURA MAZDA (Supreme Being of Zoroastrianism) [Per *Urmazd*, fr Av *Ahuramazda-*]

**ormer** /'awmə/ *n* ABALONE (type of shellfish); *esp* one (*Haliotis tuberculata*) common in the Channel Islands [Fr dial. (Channel Islands), prob deriv of L *auris maris* ear of the sea]

**ormolu** /'awmə,looh/ *n* golden or gilded brass or bronze used for decorative purposes (eg in mounts for furniture) [Fr *or moulu*, lit., ground gold]

¹**ornament** /'awnəmənt/ *n* 1 something that lends grace or beauty; a decoration or embellishment ⟨*the carved* ~s *of the mouldings*⟩; *also* such parts or additions collectively ⟨*a stone window rich in* ~⟩ 2 a person who enhances or does credit to his/her social group, profession, etc 3 *music* an embellishing note not belonging to the essential harmony or melody [ME, fr OF *ornement*, fr L *ornamentum*, fr *ornare*]

²**ornament** /'awnə,ment/ *vt* to decorate, embellish *synonyms* see DECORATE

**ornamental** /,awnə'mentl/ *adj or n* (of or being) a decorative object, esp a plant cultivated for its appearance – **ornamentally** *adv*

**ornamentation** /,awnəmen'taysh(ə)n/ *n* 1 ornamenting or being ornamented 2 something that ornaments; an embellishment

**ornate** /aw'nayt/ *adj* 1 affectedly elaborate or florid in style 2 elaborately or excessively decorated [ME *ornat*, fr L *ornatus*, pp of *ornare* to furnish, embellish; akin to L *ordinare* to order – more at ORDAIN] – **ornately** *adv*, **ornateness** *n*

**ornery** /'awnəri/ *adj, NAm informal* bad-tempered, cantankerous [alter. of *ordinary*] – **orneriness** *n*

**ornith-, ornitho-** *comb form* bird ⟨*ornithology*⟩ [L, fr Gk, fr *ornith-*, *ornis* – more at ERNE]

**ornithic** /aw'nithik/ *adj* (characteristic) of birds [Gk *ornithikos*, fr *ornith-*, *ornis*]

**ornithine** /'awnithien/ *n* an AMINO ACID, $NH_2(CH_2)_3CH(NH_2)$ COOH, that is important in the production of UREA for the removal of poisonous waste materials (eg urine) in mammals [ISV *ornith*uric acid (an acid of which it is a component, found in the urine of birds) + *-ine*]

**ornithischian** /,awni'thiski·ən/ *n* any of an order (Ornithischia) of plant-eating dinosaurs (eg a stegosaurus) that had a PELVIS (bowl-shaped frame of bones at base of backbone) with four axes of symmetry [NL *Ornithischia*, group name, fr *ornith-* + Gk *ischion* hip joint; fr its birdlike pelvis] – **ornithischian** *adj*

**ornithology** /,awni'tholəji/ *n* a branch of zoology dealing with birds [NL *ornithologia*, fr *ornith-* + *-logia* -logy] – **ornithological** *also* **ornithologic** *adj*, **ornithologically** *adv*, **ornithologist** *n*

**ornithopter** /'awni,thoptə/ *n* an aircraft designed to derive its chief lift and propulsion from flapping wings [Fr *ornithoptère*, fr Gk *ornith-*, *ornis* bird + *pteran* wing]

**ornithorhynchus** /,awnithoh'ringkəs/ *n* DUCKBILLED PLATYPUS (egg-laying mammal) [NL, genus name, fr *ornith-* + Gk *rhynchos* snout]

**ornithosis** /,awni'thohsis/ *n, pl* **ornithoses** /-seez/ PSITTACOSIS (disease of birds) [NL] – **ornithotic** *adj*

¹**oro-** *comb form* mountain ⟨*orology*⟩ [Gk *oros* – more at RISE]

²**oro-** *comb form* 1 mouth ⟨*oropharynx*⟩ 2 oral and ⟨*orofacial*⟩ [L *or-*, *os* – more at ORAL]

**orogenesis** /,awroh'jenəsis/ *n* orogeny [NL] – **orogenetic** *adj*, **orogenetically** *adv*

**orogeny** /o'rojəni/ *n* the process of mountain formation, esp by folding of the earth's crust [ISV] – **orogenic** *adj*, **orogenically** *adv*

**orographic** /orəˈgrafik/ *also* **orographical** /-kl/ *adj* of mountains; *esp* associated with or induced by the presence of mountains ⟨~ *rainfall*⟩ – **orographically** *adv*

**orography** /oˈrogrəfi/ *n* a branch of physical geography that deals with mountains [ISV ¹*oro-* + *geography*]

**orotund** /ˈorətund, ˈoroh-/ *adj* 1 marked by fullness, strength, and clarity of sound; SONOROUS 2 pompous, bombastic □ compare ROTUND [modif of L *ore rotundo*, lit., with round mouth] – **orotundity** *n*

¹**orphan** /ˈawf(ə)n/ *n* 1 a child both of whose parents are dead; *also* a child one of whose parents is dead 2 a young animal that has lost its mother [LL *orphanus*, fr Gk *orphanos*; akin to OHG *erbi* inheritance, L *orbus* orphaned] – **orphan** *adj*, **orphanhood** *n*

²**orphan** *vt* to cause to become an orphan

**orphanage** /ˈawf(ə)n·ij/ *n* an institution for the care of orphans

**orphic** /ˈawfik/ *adj* 1 *cap* of Orpheus or the rites or doctrines ascribed to him 2 mystic, oracular [L *Orphicus*, fr Gk *Orphikos*, fr *Orpheus*, poet & musician in Gk mythology] – **orphically** *adv*

**orphism** /ˈawfiz(ə)m/ *n*, *often cap* a theory or practice in art that developed from cubism about 1912 and is characterized by flowing abstract compositions in often brilliant colour [Fr *orphisme*, fr *Orphée* Orpheus]

**Orphism** /ˈawˌfiz(ə)m/ *n* an ancient Greek mystery religion offering initiates purification of the soul from evil and release from the cycle of rebirth [*Orpheus*, its reputed founder]

**orphrey** *also* **orfray** /ˈawfri/ *n* 1 (a piece of) elaborate embroidery 2 an ornamental border or band, esp on an ecclesiastical vestment [ME *orfrey*, fr MF *orfreis*, fr ML *aurifrigium*, fr L *aurum* gold + *Phrygius* Phrygian – more at ORIOLE]

**orpiment** /ˈawpimənt/ *n* an orange to lemon yellow ARSENIC TRISULPHIDE, As₂S₃, used esp in the manufacture of glass and semiconductors and as a pigment [ME, fr MF, fr L *auripigmentum*, fr *aurum* + *pigmentum* pigment]

**orpine, orpin** /ˈawpin/ *n* a plant (*Sedum telephium*) of the stonecrop family that has fleshy leaves and pink or purple flowers; *broadly* any of a genus (*Sedum*) of plants [ME *rpin*, fr MF, fr *orpiment*]

**Orpington** /ˈawpingt(ə)n/ *n* (any of) an English breed of large deep-chested poultry [*Orpington*, town in Kent, England]

**orra** /ˈawrə, ˈorə/ *adj*, *Scot* 1 left over; odd 2 casual, occasional [origin unknown]

**orrery** /ˈorəri/ *n* a manually operated or clockwork apparatus showing the relative positions and motions of bodies in the solar system [Charles Boyle †1731 4th Earl of *Orrery*]

**orris** /ˈoris/ *n* a European iris (*Iris florentina*) with a fragrant RHIZOME (thick underground stem) that is used esp in perfume and perfumed sachets; *also* the rhizome of the orris [prob alter. of ME *ireos*, fr ML, alter. of L *iris*]

**orrisroot** /ˈorisˌrooht/ *n* the fragrant RHIZOME (thick underground stem) of any of several European irises (e g orris) used esp in perfumery

**ort** /awt/ *n usu pl*, *archaic* a morsel left at a meal; a scrap [ME]

**orth-, ortho-** *comb form* 1 straight; upright; vertical ⟨*ortho*tropic⟩ ⟨*ortho*rhombic⟩ 2 correct; corrective ⟨*ortho*dontics⟩ 3 hydrated or hydroxylated to the highest possible degree ⟨*ortho*phosphoric acid⟩ 4 involving substitution at two neighbouring positions in the BENZENE RING ⟨*ortho*-xylene⟩ – compare META-, PARA- [ME, fr MF, straight, right, true, fr L, fr Gk, fr *orthos* – more at ARDUOUS]

**orthicon** /ˈawthikon/ *n* a television CAMERA TUBE which is similar to but more sensitive than the ICONOSCOPE and in which the original light image is converted into a pattern of electric charges which is then scanned by an electron beam to produce a signal – compare CAMERA TUBE [ISV *orth-* + *icono*scope]

**ortho** /ˈawthoh/ *adj* orthochromatic

**orthocephalic** /ˌawthəsiˈfalik/, **orthocephalous** /-ˈsefələs/ *adj* having a medium ratio of the height to the length or breadth of the skull – compare BRACHYCEPHALIC, DOLICHOCEPHALIC [NL *orthocephalus* orthocephalic person, fr *orth-* + Gk *kephalē* head – more at CEPHALIC] – **orthocephaly** *n*

**orthochromatic** /ˌawthəkrohˈmatik, -thoh-, -krə-/ *adj*, *of a photographic film or emulsion* sensitive to light of all colours except red and orange which reproduce as black; ISOCHROMATIC – compare PANCHROMATIC [ISV]

**orthoclase** /ˈawthəˌklayz, -klays/ *n* a common mineral of the FELDSPAR group consisting of potassium, aluminium, silicon, and oxygen, KAlSi₃O₈, [Ger *orthoklas*, fr *orth-* + Gk *klasis* breaking, fr *klan* to break – more at HALT]

**orthoclastic** /ˌawthəˈklastik/ *adj*, *of a rock, mineral, etc* splitting in directions at right angles to each other ⟨*an* ~ *feldspar*⟩ [Ger *orthoklastisch*, fr *orth-* + Gk *klastos* broken, fr *klan* to break]

**orthodontia** /ˌawthohˈdonsh(y)ə, -thə-/ *n* orthodontics [NL]

**orthodontics** /ˌawthəˈdontiks/ *n taking sing vb* a branch of dentistry dealing with irregularities of the teeth and their correction (e g by means of braces) – **orthodontic** *adj*, **orthodontist** *n*

¹**orthodox** /ˈawthədoks/ *adj* 1a conforming to established, dominant, or official doctrine (e g in religion) b conventional 2 *cap* 2a (consisting) of any of various Eastern churches (e g the Greek Orthodox church and the Russian Orthodox church) that are descended from the churches that separated from the Western church in the 9th century and have characteristic and separate doctrines, liturgy, and forms of organization b of Judaism that adheres to the TORAH (Jewish scripture) as interpreted in the TALMUD (commentary on the Torah) and authoritative rabbinic tradition and seeks to observe all the practices prescribed in it [MF or LL; MF *orthodoxe*, fr LL *orthodoxus*, fr LGk *orthodoxos*, fr Gk *orth-* + *doxa* opinion – more at DOXOLOGY] – **orthodoxly** *adv*

²**orthodox** *n*, *pl* **orthodox** *also* **orthodoxes** 1 one who or that which is orthodox 2 *cap* a member of an Orthodox church or Orthodox Judaism

**orthodoxy** /ˈawthədoksi/ *n* 1 being orthodox 2 an orthodox belief or practice 3 *cap* 3a Eastern Orthodox Christianity b Orthodox Judaism

**orthoepy** /awˈthohəpi/ *n* the study of (correct) pronunciation – used esp in the 17th and 18th centuries to describe attempts to establish standard pronunciations [NL *orthoepia*, fr Gk *orthoepeia*, fr *orth-* + *epos* word – more at VOICE] – **orthoepic** *also* **orthoepical** *adj*, **orthoepically** *adv*, **orthoepist** *n*

**orthogenesis** /ˌawthohˈjenəsis/ *n* 1 evolution of species held to occur in a definite direction independent of external factors (e g NATURAL SELECTION) 2 the theory that the development of society takes place in the same direction and passes through the same stages in every culture despite differing external conditions [NL] – **orthogenetic** *adj*, **orthogenetically** *adv*

**orthogenic** /ˌawthəˈjenik/ *adj* of or devoted to the rehabilitation of emotionally disturbed or mentally retarded children [*orth-* + *-genic*]

**orthognathous** /awˈthognəthəs/ *adj* having the profile of the face roughly vertical; having normally shaped jaws

**orthogonal** /awˈthogənl/ *adj* 1 mutually perpendicular 2 having an INTEGRAL that is zero or sometimes equal to one under specified conditions: e g 2a having the INTEGRAL of the product of any pair of REAL-VALUED functions over a given interval equal to zero b(1) having the SCALAR PRODUCT of any pair of vectors equal to zero b(2) forming an orthogonal pair with a specified vector or function ⟨f *is* ~ *to* g⟩ c having the sum of products of corresponding elements in any two rows or any two columns of a SQUARE MATRIX (arrangement of numbers, letters, etc) equal to one if the rows or columns are the same and equal to zero otherwise; having a TRANSPOSE with which the product equals the IDENTITY MATRIX 3a *of a square matrix* having the TRANSPOSE (rows and columns interchanged) equal to the INVERSE b having a matrix that is orthogonal; preserving the length and distance of a LINEAR TRANSFORMATION 4 composed of mutually orthogonal elements ⟨*an* ~ *basis of a vector space*⟩ 5 statistically independent [MF, fr L *orthogonius*, fr Gk *orthogōnios*, fr *orth-* + *gōnia* angle – more at -GON] – **orthogonally** *adv*, **orthogonality** *n*

**orthograde** /ˈawthəˌgrayd/ *adj* walking with the body upright or vertical

**orthographic** /ˌawthəˈgrafik/ *also* **orthographical** /-kl/ *adj* 1 characterized by perpendicular lines or RIGHT ANGLES 2a of orthography b correctly spelled – **orthographically** *adv*

**orthographic projection** *n* 1 a drawn representation of an object by means of PLAN, SECTION, and ELEVATION where all dimensions are true and not foreshortened by perspective 2a the representation of related views of an object as if they were all in the same plane and projected by orthographic projection b an AZIMUTHAL PROJECTION (map projection) of a hemisphere which is seen in perspective and in which the network of imaginary lines of latitude and longitude is represented as if viewed from infinity

**orthography** /aw'thogrəfi/ *n* **1a** the art of writing words with the proper letters according to standard usage; correct spelling **b** the written representation of the sounds of a language; the manner of spelling **2** the part of language study which deals with letters and spelling and their relationship with the language sounds that they represent [ME *ortografie,* fr MF, fr L *orthographia,* fr Gk, fr *orth-* + *graphein* to write – more at CARVE]

**orthonormal** /ˌawthə'nawml/ *adj, maths* **1** being NORMALIZED and orthogonal ⟨∼ *functions*⟩ **2** being or composed of orthogonal elements of unit length ⟨∼ *basis of a vector space*⟩

**orthopaedic,** *chiefly NAm* **orthopedic** /ˌawthə'peedik/ *adj* **1** of or employed in orthopaedics **2** marked by deformities or crippling [Fr *orthopédique,* fr *orthopédie* orthopaedics, fr *orth-* + Gk *paid-, pais* child] – **orthopaedically** *adv*

**orthopaedics,** *chiefly NAm* **orthopedics** /ˌawthə'peediks/ *n taking sing or pl vb* a branch of medicine dealing with the correction or prevention of skeletal and muscular deformities, esp by surgery **b** paediatrics – **orthopaedist** *n*

**orthophosphate** /ˌawthə'fosfayt/ *n* any of various chemical compounds (SALTS or ESTERS) formed by combination between ORTHOPHOSPHORIC ACID and a metal atom, an alcohol, or another chemical group

**orthophosphoric acid** /ˌawthəfos'forik/ *n* PHOSPHORIC ACID in a form that does not contain water [ISV]

**orthopsychiatry** /ˌawthohsə'kie·ətri/ *n* a branch of psychiatry concerned esp with the prevention of mental and behavioural disorders that occur in young people – **orthopsychiatrist** *n,* **orthopsychiatric** *adj*

**orthopteran** /aw'thoptərən/ *n* any of an order (Orthoptera) of large insects (eg crickets and grasshoppers) that are characterized by biting mouthparts, two pairs of wings or none, and an INCOMPLETE METAMORPHOSIS (gradual change from the larval stage into the mature, but structurally similar, adult) [NL *Orthoptera,* group name] – **orthopteran** *adj,* **orthopterist** *n,* **orthopteroid** *n or adj*

**orthopteron** /aw'thoptərən/ *n, pl* **orthoptera** /-rə/*also* **orthopterons** an orthopteran [NL, sing. of *Orthoptera,* group name, fr *orth-* + Gk *pteron* wing – more at FEATHER]

**orthorhombic** /ˌawthoh'rombik/ *adj* of or constituting a system of crystallization characterized by three unequal axes at RIGHT ANGLES to each other [ISV]

**orthoscopic** /ˌawthə'skopik, -thoh-/ *adj* **1** giving an image in correct and normal proportions **2** giving a flat field of view [ISV *orth-* + *-scopic* (as in *microscopic*)]

**orthotics** /aw'thotiks/ *n taking sing vb* the design and manufacture of medical braces used to control or correct deformed or diseased parts of the body, esp the spine [*orth-* + *-tics* (as in *prosthetics*)]

**orthotropic** /ˌawthə'tropik/ *adj, of a plant or its parts* having a more or less vertical mode of growth ⟨∼ *plant stems*⟩ – compare PLAGIOTROPIC – **orthotropically** *adv,* **orthotropism** *n*

**orthotropous** /aw'thotrəpəs/ *adj, of a plant ovule* growing straight [ISV]

**ortolan** /'awtələn, 'awtl-ən/ *n* a brown and greyish-green European BUNTING (type of bird) (*Emberiza hortulana*) that is about 15 centimetres (6 inches) long and is valued as a table delicacy, esp in France [Fr or It; Fr, fr It *ortolano,* lit., gardener, fr L *hortulanus,* fr *hortulus,* dim. of *hortus* garden – more at YARD]

**Orwellian** /aw'weli·ən/ *adj* (characteristic) of George Orwell or his writings, esp in depicting the way in which people are manipulated by an authoritarian state – compare NEWSPEAK, NINETEEN EIGHTY-FOUR [George *Orwell,* pen-name of Eric Blair †1950 E writer]

¹**-ory** /-(ə)ri/ *suffix* (→ *n*) **1** place of or for ⟨*observatory*⟩ ⟨*refectory*⟩ **2** something that serves for ⟨*directory*⟩ [ME *-orie,* fr L *-orium,* fr neut of *-orius,* adj suffix]

²**-ory** *suffix* (→ *adj*) **1** of or involving ⟨*gustatory*⟩ ⟨*compulsory*⟩ **2** serving for or producing ⟨*justificatory*⟩ [ME *-orie,* fr MF & L; MF, fr L *-orius*]

**oryx** /'oriks/ *n, pl* **oryx, oryxes** any of a genus (*Oryx*) of large straight-horned African antelopes [NL, genus name, fr L, a gazelle, fr Gk, pickaxe, antelope, fr *oryssein* to dig – more at ROUGH]

¹**os** /os/ *n, pl* **ossa** /'osə/ a bone [L *oss-, os* – more at OSSEOUS]

²**os** /ohs/ *n, pl* **ora** /awrə/ a mouth, orifice [L *or-, os* – more at ORAL]

³**os** /ohs/ *n, pl* **osar** /'ohsah/ ESKER [Sw *ås* mountain ridge, fr ON *āss;* akin to Gk *ōmos* shoulder – more at HUMERUS]

**Osage** /oh'sayj/ *n, pl* **Osages,** *esp collectively* **Osage** a member of an American Indian people originally of Missouri; *also* their Siouan language

**Osage orange** *n* an ornamental N American tree (*Maclura pomifera*) of the fig family with shiny oval leaves and hard bright orange wood; *also* its small yellowish orangelike fruit

**Oscan** /'oskən/ *n* a member of a people of ancient Italy that occupied Campania; *also* the language of the Oscans [L *Oscus*] – **Oscan** *adj*

¹**Oscar** /'oskə/ *n* a gold statuette awarded annually by the American Academy of Motion Picture Arts and Sciences for outstanding achievement in the cinema [*Oscar* Pierce, 20th-c US wheat and fruit grower whom the statuette allegedly resembled]

²**Oscar** – a communications code word for the letter *o*

**oscillate** /'osiˌlayt/ *vi* **1a** to swing backwards and forwards like a pendulum **b** to move or travel back and forth between two points **2** to vary between opposing beliefs, feelings, or theories **3** to vary above and below a mid point or average value *synonyms* see ¹SWING △ osculate [L *oscillatus,* pp of *oscillare* to swing, fr *oscillum* swing] – **oscillatory** *adj*

**oscillation** /ˌosi'laysh(ə)n/ *n* **1** the action or fact of oscillating **2** variation, fluctuation **3a** a flow of electricity changing periodically from a maximum to a minimum; *esp* a flow periodically changing direction **4** a single swing (eg of an oscillating body) from one extreme limit to the other – **oscillational** *adj*

**oscillator** /'osiˌlaytə/ *n* **1** one who or that which oscillates **2** a device for producing electrical oscillations in the form of an ALTERNATING CURRENT; *esp* a radio-frequency or audio-frequency signal generator

**oscillogram** /ə'siləgram/ *n* a permanent record made by an oscillograph or oscilloscope [L *oscillare* + ISV *-gram*]

**oscillograph** /ə'siləˌgrahf, -ˌgraf/ *n* an instrument for recording ALTERNATING CURRENT waveforms or other electrical oscillations; *also* an oscillogram [Fr *oscillographe,* fr L *oscillare* + Fr *-graphe* -graph] – **oscillographic** *adj,* **oscillographically** *adv,* **oscillography** *n*

**oscilloscope** /ə'siləˌskohp/ *n* an instrument in which the variations in a fluctuating electrical quantity appear as a visible waveform on a CATHODE-RAY TUBE (instrument that produces images by projecting electrons onto a fluorescent screen); *broadly* an oscillograph [L *oscillare* + ISV *-scope*] – **oscilloscopic** *adj,* **oscilloscopically** *adv*

**oscine** /'osien/ *adj* of or being a suborder of songbirds with vocal chords specialized for singing [deriv of L *oscin-, oscen* bird used in divination, fr *obs-* in front of + *canere* to sing – more at OSTENSIBLE, CHANT] – **oscine** *n*

**oscitance** /'ositəns/ *n, formal* **1** the act of yawning; sleepiness **2** inattentiveness [L *oscitant-, oscitans,* prp of *oscitare* to yawn, fr *os* mouth + *citare* to move] – **oscitancy, oscitation** *n*

**Osco-Umbrian** /ˌoskoh'umbri·ən/ *adj or n* (of) a group of ancient Italian Indo-European languages containing OSCAN and UMBRIAN – **Osco-Umbrian** *adj*

**osculate** /'oskyoˌlayt/ *vt, chiefly humorous* to kiss △ oscillate [L *osculatus,* pp of *osculari,* fr *osculum* kiss, fr dim. of *os* mouth – more at ORAL] – **osculation** *n*

**osculum** /'oskyooləm/ *n* an opening through which a current of water leaves a living sponge [NL, fr L, dim. of *os* mouth]

¹**-ose** /-ohs; *also* -ohz/ *suffix* (→ *adj*) **1** full of; possessing the quality of ⟨*verbose*⟩ ⟨*bellicose*⟩ **2** having; consisting of; resembling ⟨*frondose*⟩ ⟨*ramose*⟩ ⟨*globose*⟩ [ME, fr L *-osus*] – **-osity** (→ *n*)

²**-ose** /-ohz, -ohs/ *suffix* (→ *n*) **1** carbohydrate ⟨*amylose*⟩; *esp* sugar ⟨*fructose*⟩ **2** primary hydrolysis product ⟨*proteose*⟩ ⟨*peptose*⟩ [Fr, fr *glucose*]

**osier** /'ohzhə/ *n* (a pliable twig, used for furniture and basketry, cut from) any of various willows (esp *Salix viminalis*) – compare WITHY [ME, fr MF, fr ML *auseria* osier bed]

**-osis** /-'ohsis/ *suffix* (→ *n*), *pl* **-oses** /-'ohseez/, **-osises** /-'ohsiseez/ **1a** action, process, or condition of ⟨*hypnosis*⟩ ⟨*metamorphosis*⟩ **b** abnormal or pathological condition of ⟨*thrombosis*⟩ **2** increase or formation of ⟨*leucocytosis*⟩ [ME, fr L, fr Gk *-ōsis,* fr *-ō-* (stem of causative verbs in *-oun*) + *-sis*]

**Osmanli** /oz'manli/ *n* **1** a Turk of the western branch of the Turkish peoples **2** Turkish [Turk *osmanlı,* fr *Osman* †1326 founder of the Ottoman Empire]

**osmeterium** /ˌozmə'tiəri·əm/ *n, pl* **osmeteria** /-i·ə/ a forked process that is borne on the first segment behind the head of the larvae of many swallow-tail butterflies and that emits a disagreeable odour and is probably used in defence [NL, fr Gk *osmē* odour + *-tērion,* suffix denoting an instrument]

**osmic** /'ozmik/ *adj* of or derived from osmium, esp with a relatively high VALENCY [ISV]

**osmic acid** *n* OSMIUM TETROXIDE

**osmiridium** /,ozmi'ridi·əm, os-/ *n* IRIDOSMINE (alloy of the metals iridium and osmium) [*osmium* + *iridium*]

**osmium** /'ozmi·əm/ *n* a hard brittle blue-grey or blue-black metallic chemical element of the platinum group with a high melting point that is the heaviest metal known and that is used esp as a catalyst to increase the rate of chemical reactions and in hard alloys [NL, fr Gk *osmē* odour; fr its distinctive pungent smell]

**osmium tetroxide** /te'troksied/ *n* a pale yellow solid chemical compound, $OsO_4$, that has a poisonous irritating vapour and is used in chemical reactions as a catalyst and an OXIDIZING AGENT, and as a stain for biological specimens (e g in ELECTRON MICROSCOPY)

**osmol** /'ozmohl/ *n* a standard unit of OSMOTIC PRESSURE based on the concentration of an ION (electrically charged atom or group of atoms) in a solution [blend of *osmosis* and *mol*] – **osmolal** *adj*, **osmolality** *n*

**osmolar** /oz'mohlə/ *adj*, *of a biological liquid* osmotic [*osmol* + *-ar*] – **osmolarity** *n*

**osmometer** /oz'momitə, os-/ *n* an apparatus for measuring OSMOTIC PRESSURE [*osmo*sis + *-meter*] – **osmometric** *adj*, **osmometry** *n*

**osmoregulation** /,ozmoh,regyoo'laysh(ə)n, ,os-/ *n* the usu automatic regulation of OSMOTIC PRESSURE, esp in the body of a living organism [*osmo*sis + *regulation*] – **osmoregulatory** *adj*

**osmose** /'ozmohs, -mohz, 'os-/ *vi* to diffuse by osmosis [backformation fr *osmosis*]

**osmosis** /oz'mohsis, os-/ *n* **1** the movement of a solvent, esp water, through a skin or membrane that is SEMIPERMEABLE (allows only certain small particles, molecules, etc to pass through) into a solution of higher concentration that tends to equalize the concentrations on the two sides of the membrane **2** a process of absorption or diffusion suggestive of the flow of osmotic action [NL, short for *endosmosis*]

**osmotic** /oz'motik/ *adj* of or having the properties of osmosis – **osmotically** *adv*

**osmotic pressure** /oz'motik, os-/ *n* the pressure produced by or associated with osmosis and dependent on concentration and temperature: e g **a** the maximum pressure that develops in a solution separated from a solvent by a membrane that allows only the solvent to pass through **b** the minimum pressure that must be applied to a solution to prevent osmosis

**osmotic shock** *n* a rapid change in the OSMOTIC PRESSURE (e g by transfer to a medium of different concentration) experienced by a living organism that may cause permanent damage (e g the rupture of cells)

**osmous** /'ozməs/ *adj* of or derived from osmium, esp with a relatively low VALENCY

**osmunda** /oz'mundə/ *n* any of a genus (*Osmunda*) of rather large ferns with fibrous creeping RHIZOMES (thick underground stems) [NL, genus name, fr ML, osmunda, fr OF *osmonde*]

**osprey** /'ospray, -pri/ *n* **1** a large fish-eating hawk (*Pandion haliaetus*) that is dark brown on the back and mostly pure white on the underside **2** a feather trimming used as a decoration for hats [ME *ospray*, fr (assumed) MF *osfraie*, fr L *ossifraga* – more at OSSIFRAGE]

**ossa** /'osə/ *pl of* ¹OS (bone)

**ossein** /'osi·in/ *n* COLLAGEN (fibrous protein) of bones [ISV, fr L *oss-*, *os* bone]

**osseous** /'osi·əs/ *adj* consisting of bone; bony [L *osseus*, fr *oss*, *os* bone; akin to Gk *osteon* bone] – **osseously** *adv*

**Ossianic** /,osi'anik/ *adj* of or resembling the legendary Gaelic bard Ossian, the poems ascribed to him, or the rhythmic grandiloquent style used by James Macpherson in his alleged translations

**ossicle** /'osikl/ *n* a small bone or bony structure (e g any of those in the MIDDLE EAR) [L *ossiculum*, dim. of *oss-*, *os*] – **ossicular, ossiculate** *adj*

**ossification** /,osifi'kaysh(ə)n/ *n* **1a** the natural process of bone formation **b** the hardening (e g of muscular tissue) into a bony substance **2** a mass or particle of ossified tissue **3** a tendency towards or state of being moulded into a rigid, conventional, sterile, or unimaginative condition ⟨*the two party system can be seen as an ∼ of democracy*⟩ – **ossificatory** *adj*

**ossifrage** /'osifrij, -,frayj/ *n* **1** LAMMERGEIER (large Eurasian

vulture) **2** an osprey [L *ossifraga* sea eagle, fr fem of *ossifragus* bone-breaking, fr *oss-*, *os* + *frangere* to break – more at BREAK]

**ossify** /'osi,fie/ *vi* **1** to become bone **2** to become rigid or inflexible in habit or attitude ∼ *vt* to change (e g cartilage) into bone [Fr *ossifier* or (assumed) NL *ossificare*, fr L *oss-*, *os*]

**osso bucco** /,osoh'boohkoh/ *n* an Italian dish of slices of shin of veal including marrowbone braised with tomatoes and white wine [It *ossobucco* marrowbone]

**ossuary** /'osyooəri/ *n* a place or container (e g a vault or urn) for the bones of the dead [LL *ossuarium*, fr L, neut of *ossuarius* of bones, fr OL *ossua*, pl of *oss-*, *os* bone]

**oste-** /'osti-/, **osteo-** *comb form* bone ⟨*osteal*⟩ ⟨*osteomyelitis*⟩ [NL, fr Gk, fr *osteon* – more at OSSEOUS]

**osteal** /'osti·əl/ *adj* of or resembling bone; *also* affecting or involving bone or the skeleton [ISV]

**osteitis** /,osti·ietəs/ *n* inflammation of bone [NL]

**ostensible** /o'stensəbl/ *adj* being such in appearance rather than in reality; professed, declared ⟨*his ∼ frankness covered a devious scheme*⟩ **synonyms** see APPARENT [Fr, fr L *ostensus*, pp of *ostendere* to show, fr *obs-* in front of (akin to *ob-* in the way) + *tendere* to stretch – more at OB-, THIN] – **ostensibly** *adv*

**ostensive** /o'stensiv/ *adj* **1** ostensible **2** of or constituting definition by displaying or pointing to the thing or quality being defined – **ostensively** *adv*

**ostentation** /,osten'taysh(ə)n/ *n* unnecessary display, esp of wealth, luxury, knowledge, etc, intended to impress others or to attract attention [ME *ostentacioun*, fr MF *ostentation*, fr L *ostentation-*, *ostentatio*, fr *ostentatus*, pp of *ostentare* to display ostentatiously, fr *ostentus*, pp of *ostendere*] – **ostentatious** *adj*, **ostentatiously** *adv*, **ostentatiousness** *n*

**osteoarthritis** /,ostiohah'thrietəs/ *n* a long-lasting form of arthritis usu associated with increasing age; degenerative arthritis [NL] – **osteoarthritic** *adj*

**osteoblast** /'ostioh,blast/ *n* a bone-forming cell [ISV] – **osteoblastic** *adj*

**osteoclast** /'ostioh,klast/ *n* any of the large cells in developing bone that are associated with the absorption and destruction of unwanted bone [ISV *oste-* + Gk *klastos* broken, fr *klan* to break – more at HALT] – **osteoclastic** *adj*

**osteocyte** /'ostiə,siet/ *n* a cell that is characteristic of adult bone and is isolated in a cavity of the bone substance

¹**osteoid** /'ostioyd/ *adj* resembling bone [ISV]

²**osteoid** *n* the basic bone tissue before being hardened with calcium

**osteology** /,osti'oləji/ *n* a branch of anatomy dealing with the bones [NL *osteologia*, fr Gk, description of bones, fr *oste-* + *-logia* -logy] – **osteologist** *n*, **osteological** *adj*, **osteologically** *adv*

**osteoma** /,osti'ohmə/ *n*, *pl* **osteomas, osteomata** /-mətə/ a mild nonlethal tumour composed of bone tissue [NL]

**osteomalacia** /,ostiohmə'laysh(y)ə/ *n* a disorder, esp of the elderly, characterized by softening of the bones in the adult and equivalent to RICKETS in young people [NL, fr *oste-* + Gk *malakia* softness, fr *malakos* soft – more at MALAC-]

**osteomyelitis** /,ostiohmie-ə'lietəs/ *n* an infectious inflammatory disease of bone, esp of the bone marrow, marked by local death and separation of tissue [NL]

**osteopath** /'osti·ə,path/ *n* a practitioner of osteopathy

**osteopathy** /,osti'opəthi/ *n* a system of treatment of disease based on the manipulation of bones or other parts of the body supplemented by therapeutic measures (e g use of medicines or surgery) [NL *osteopathia*, fr *oste-* + L *-pathia* -pathy] – **osteopathic** *adj*, **osteopathically** *adv*

**osteophyte** /'osti·ə,fiet/ *n* an abnormal on diseased bony outgrowth – **osteophytic** *adj* [ISV]

**osteoplastic** /,osti·ə'plastik/ *adj* of the surgical replacement of bone – **osteoplasty** *n*

**osteoporosis** /,ostiohpaw'rohsis/ *n* a disease of the bones causing enlargement of the internal cavities in the bones and hence making them thin, brittle, and porous [NL, fr *oste-* + *porosis* porosity, fr L *porus* pore]

**ostinato** /,osti'nahtoh/ *n*, *pl* **ostinatos** a musical figure repeated persistently at the same pitch throughout a composition – compare IMITATION, SEQUENCE △ obbligato [It, obstinate, fr L *obstinatus*]

**ostiole** /'ostiohl/ *n* a small bodily aperture, orifice, or pore [NL *ostiolum*, fr L, dim. of *ostium*]

**ostium** /'osti·əm/ *n*, *pl* **ostia** /'osti·ə/ a mouthlike opening in a body organ [NL, fr L, door, mouth of a river; akin to L *os* mouth – more at ORAL]

**ostler,** *NAm chiefly* **hostler** /'oslə/ *n* a groom or stableman at an inn [ME *osteler, hosteler* innkeeper, ostler, fr *hostel*]

**ostmark** /'ost,mahk (*Ger* ɒstmark)/ *n* – see MONEY table [Ger, lit., East mark]

**ostomy** /'ostəmi/ *n* an operation (eg a colostomy) to create an artificial anus [*colostomy*]

**-ostosis** /-o'stohsis/ *comb form* (→ *n*), *pl* **-ostoses** /-seez/, **-ostosises** /-siseez/ ossification of (a specified part) or to (a specified degree) ⟨*hyper*ostosis⟩ [NL, fr Gk *-ostōsis,* fr *osteon* bone – more at OSSEOUS]

**ostpolitik** /'ostpoli,teek/ *n* the foreign policy of a European country with regard to iron-curtain countries; *specif, cap* a policy of normalizing relations with E European countries, esp Russia and E Germany adopted by W Germany in the 1970s [Ger, fr *ost* east + *politik* policy, politics]

**ostracism** /'ostrə,siz(ə)m/ *n* 1 a method of temporary banishment by popular vote without trial or special accusation practised in ancient Greece 2 exclusion by general consent from common privileges or social acceptance

**ostrac·ize, -ise** /'ostrə,siez/ *vt* 1 to exile by ostracism 2 to exclude from a group by common consent [Gk *ostrakizein* to banish by voting with potsherds, fr *ostrakon* shell, potsherd – more at OYSTER]

**ostracod** /'ostrəkod/ *also* **ostracode** /-,kohd/ *n* any of a subclass (Ostracoda of the class Crustacea) of very small active aquatic INVERTEBRATE animals that have the body enclosed in a shell consisting of two halves hinged together and that have only seven pairs of limbs [deriv of Gk *ostrakon*]

**ostracoderm** /'ostrəkə,duhm/ *n* any of an order (Ostracodermi) of primitive extinct armoured fishes [deriv of Gk *ostrakon* + *derma* skin – more at DERM-] – **ostracoderm** *adj*

**ostrich** /'ostrich, *also* 'ostrij/ *n* 1 a swift-running two-toed flightless bird (genus *Struthio,* esp *Struthio camelus*) of N Africa that has valuable wing and tail plumes and is the largest of existing birds 2 one who attempts to avoid unpleasant realities by refusing to recognize or face up to them [ME, fr OF *ostrusce,* fr (assumed) VL *avis struthio,* fr L *avis* bird + LL *struthio* ostrich, irreg fr Gk *strouthos;* (2) fr the belief that the ostrich when pursued hides its head in the sand and believes itself to be unseen] – **ostrichism** *n*

**Ostrogoth** /'ostrə,goth/ *n* a member of the eastern division of the GOTHS (N German invaders of the Roman Empire in 4th and 5th centuries) [LL *Ostrogothi,* pl. of Gmc origin] – **Ostrogothic** *adj*

**Ostyak** /'ostiak/ *n* an UGRIC language of W Siberia

**ot-, oto-** *comb form* ear ⟨*otitis*⟩; ear and ⟨*oto*laryngology⟩ [Gk *ōt-, ōto-,* fr *ōt-, ous* – more at EAR]

**otary** /'ohtəri/ *n* EARED SEAL [NL *Otaria,* genus name, fr Gk *ōt, ous* ear]

**¹other** /'udhə/ *adj* 1a being the one left of two or more ⟨*held on with one hand and waved with the ~ one*⟩ b being the ones distinct from that or those first mentioned ⟨*taller than the ~ boys*⟩ c SECOND 2 ⟨*every ~ day*⟩ 2a(1) not the same; different ⟨*schools ~ than his own*⟩ a(2) later ⟨*do it some ~ time*⟩ b far, opposite ⟨*lives the ~ side of town*⟩ 3 additional, further ⟨*John and two ~ boys*⟩ 4a recently past ⟨*the ~ evening*⟩ b FORMER 1 ⟨*in ~ times*⟩ [ME, fr OE *ōther;* akin to OHG *andar* other, Skt *antara*]

**usage** Other is correctly followed by *than,* not by *but* or *except* ⟨*in any other country than ours*⟩ ⟨*I could do no other than climb the wall*⟩. See ²ANY

**²other** *pron, pl* **others** *also* **other** 1 the remaining or opposite one ⟨*went from one side to the ~*⟩ ⟨*the ~s came later*⟩ 2 a different or additional one ⟨*some film or ~*⟩ ⟨*some left, but many ~s stayed*⟩ – compare ANOTHER, ONE ANOTHER

**³other** *adv* OTHERWISE – + *than* ⟨*can't get there ~ than by swimming*⟩

**usage** Other *than* should not be used to mean "in other respects than" or "apart from" ⟨⚠ *has a slight headache, but* other *than that he's feeling fine*⟩.

**'other-di,rected** *adj* directed in thought and action primarily by external influences rather than one's own values – **other-directedness** *n*

**otherness** /-nis/ *n* 1 the quality or state of being other or different 2 something that is other or different

**other rank** *n usu pl, chiefly Br* a military person not holding commissioned rank

**otherwhere** /'udhə,weə/ *adv, archaic* elsewhere

**otherwhile** /'udhə,wiel/ *also* **otherwhiles** *adv, archaic* at another time

**¹otherwise** /-,wiez/ *adv* 1 in a different way ⟨*glossed over or ~ handled – Playboy*⟩ 2 in different circumstances ⟨*might ~ have left*⟩ 3 in other respects ⟨*an ~ excellent move – SEU W*⟩ 4 if not; or else ⟨*do what I say, ~ you'll be sorry*⟩ 5 not – used after *and* or *as* to express the opposite ⟨*mothers, whether married or ~*⟩; disapproved of by some people 6 alias ⟨*Chee Soo, ~ Cliff Gibbs – Sportsworld*⟩ [ME, fr OE (*on*) *ōthre wīsan* in another manner]

**²otherwise** *adj* of a different kind ⟨*how can I be ~ than grateful*⟩

**otherworldly** /,udhə'wuldli/ *adj* 1a of a world other than the actual world; transcendental b devoted to preparing for a world to come 2 concerned with spiritual or intellectual matters rather than the real material world – **otherworldliness** *n*

**otic** /'ohtik/ *adj* of or located in the region of the ear [Gk *ōtikos,* fr *ōt-, ous* ear – more at EAR]

**¹-otic** /-'otik/ *suffix* (→ *adj*) 1a of or characterized by (a specified action, process, or condition) ⟨*hypnotic*⟩ ⟨*symbiotic*⟩ b having an abnormal or pathological condition of (a specified kind) ⟨*thrombotic*⟩ ⟨*neurotic*⟩ 2 showing an increase or a formation of ⟨*leucocytotic*⟩ □ often used to form adjectives corresponding to nouns ending in *-osis* [Gk *-ōtikos,* fr *-ōtos,* ending of verbals] – **-otically** *suffix* (→ *adv*)

**²-otic** *comb form* (→ *adj*) having (a specified relationship to) the ear ⟨*periotic*⟩ [Gk *ōtikos*]

**otiose** /'ohshi,ohs, 'ohti-/ *adj, formal* 1 producing no useful result; futile ⟨*an ~ remark*⟩ 2 lacking use or effect; functionless ⟨*a speech full of ~ rhetoric*⟩ 3 *archaic* being at leisure; idle [L *otiosus,* fr *otium* leisure] – **otiosely** *adv,* **otioseness** *n,* **otiosity** *n*

**otitis** /oh'tietəs/ *n* inflammation of the ear [NL]

**oto-** – see OT-

**otocyst** /'ohtə,sist/ *n* STATOCYST (organ controlling balance) [ISV, fr its probable auditory function] – **otocystic** *adj*

**otolaryngology** /,ohtoh,laring'goləji/ *n* a branch of medicine dealing with the ear, nose, and throat [*ot-* + *laryng-* + *-logy*] – **otolaryngologist** *n,* **otolaryngological** *adj*

**otolith** /'ohtoh,lith/ *n* any of many minute aggregations of CALCITE and protein that occur in the internal ear of VERTEBRATE animals or in the otocyst of INVERTEBRATE animals and are the receptors for much of the sense of balance and the perception of the position of the head [Fr *otolithe,* fr *ot-* + *-lithe* -lith] **otolithic** *adj*

**otology** /oh'toləji/ *n* a branch of medicine dealing with the ear – **otological** *adj,* **otologist** *n*

**Otomac** /,ohtə'mahk, -'mak/ *n* a member, or the language, of an extinct people of S Venezuela

**otorhinolaryngology** /,ohtoh,rienoh,laring'goləji/ *n* otorhinolaryngology

**otoscope** /'ohtə,skohp/ *n* an instrument for examining the ear

**ottava** /oh'tahvə/ *adv or adj* at an octave higher or lower than written – used as a direction in music [It, octave, fr ML *octava*]

**ottava rima** /'reemə/ *n* a poetic stanza of eight lines of 10 syllables each in English or 11 syllables each in Italian with a rhyme scheme of *ababbcc* [It, lit., eighth rhyme]

**Ottawa** /'otəwə/ *n, pl* **Ottawas** *esp collectively* **Ottawa** a member of an American Indian people of Michigan and southern Ontario

**otter** /'otə/ *n, pl* **otters,** (*1*) **otters,** *esp collectively* **otter** 1 any of several aquatic fish-eating mammals (genus *Lutra*) that are related to the weasels and minks and have webbed and clawed feet and dark brown fur; *esp* a widely distributed Eurasian otter (*Lutra lutra*) 2 the fur or pelt of an otter 3a a piece of fishing tackle consisting of a submerged board to which baited lines are attached which is drawn slowly through the water by the angler b an otterboard c PARAVANE (device for protecting ships from mines) [ME *oter,* fr OE *otor;* akin to OHG *ottar* otter, Gk *hydōr* water – more at WATER]

**otterboard** /'otə,bawd/ *n* either of two boards that keep the mouth of a trawl net open

**otter hound** *n* a British hound that has a wiry shaggy coat and long drooping ears and is a good but slow water dog with a keen sense of smell [fr its use in hunting otters]

**otter shrew** *n* an insect-eating African mammal (*Potamogale velox*) similar in form to the otter

**otto** /'otoh/ *n* ATTAR (fragrant oil) [by alter.]

**Otto** /'otoh/ *adj* being or having a four-stroke cycle ⟨*an ~ engine*⟩ [Nikolaus *Otto* †1891 Ger technician & inventor]

**ottoman** /'otəmən/ *n* **1** *cap* a Turk **2** a usu heavily upholstered or cushioned box, seat, or couch usu without a back **b** a cushioned footstool **synonyms** see SOFA [Fr *ottomane*, fr fem of *ottoman*, adj]

**Ottoman** *adj* of the Turks or Turkey; Turkish ⟨*the ~ Empire*⟩ [Fr, adj & n, prob fr It *ottomano*, fr Ar *'othmānī*, fr *'Othmān* Othman (Osman) †1326 founder of the Ottoman Empire]

**ouabain** /'wah'bah·in, 'wahbah,een/ *n* a poisonous chemical compound, $C_{29}H_{44}O_{12}$, obtained from several African shrubs or trees of the periwinkle family and used medically as a heart stimulant and in Africa as an arrow poison [ISV, fr Fr *ouabaïo*, an African tree, fr Somali *waba yo*]

**ouakari, uakari** /wə'kahri/ *n* any of a genus (*Cacajao*) of short-tailed South American monkeys [Tupi]

**oubliette** /,oohbli'et/ *n* a dungeon which can only be entered from above [Fr, fr MF, fr *oublier* to forget, fr L *oblitus*, pp of *oblivisci* – more at OBLIVION]

¹**ouch** /owch/ *n, archaic* (a setting for) a precious stone [ME, alter. by incorrect division of *a nouche*) of *nouche*, fr MF, of Gmc origin; akin to OHG *nusca* clasp; akin to OE *nett* net]

²**ouch** *interj* – used esp to express sudden sharp pain [origin unknown]

**oud** /oohd/ *n* a SW Asian and N African musical instrument of the lute family [Ar *'ūd*, lit., wood (cf LUTE)]

¹**ought** /awt/ *verbal auxiliary* – used to express moral obligation ⟨*~ to pay our debts*⟩, advisability ⟨*~ to be boiled for ten minutes*⟩, enthusiastic recommendation ⟨*you ~ to hear her sing*⟩, natural expectation ⟨*~ to have arrived by now*⟩, or logical consequence ⟨*the result ~ to be infinity*⟩; used in the negative to express moral condemnation of an action ⟨*you ~ not to treat him like that*⟩; often used with the perfect infinitive to express unfulfilled obligation ⟨*~ never to have been allowed*⟩ [ME *oughte* (1 & 3 sing. pres indic), fr *oughte*, 1 & 3 sing. past indic & subj of *owen* to own, owe – more at OWE]

usage **1** The negative of **ought** is correctly expressed by **oughtn't** or **ought** *not*, not by △ *didn't/hadn't* **ought**. Many speakers avoid this problem, and the problem of ⟨△ *did/had I* **ought**?⟩ and ⟨△ *I* **ought** *to, didn't I?*⟩, by using **should** instead of **ought** ⟨*you* **shouldn't** *have done it*⟩ ⟨**should** *I go?*⟩ although **ought** expresses a somewhat stronger "obligation" than **should**. **2 Ought** should be followed by *to*, a fact which is sometimes forgotten in such combinations as ⟨△ *he* **ought** *and could have told me*⟩. Young people are beginning to omit *to* ⟨*you* **ought** *go*⟩ but this construction should be avoided in formal writing.

²**ought** *n* a moral obligation; duty ⟨*an ~ implies a can*⟩

³**ought** *n or adj* (a) nought, zero [var of ²*aught*]

**oughtn't** /'awtnt/ ought not

**ouguiya** /ooh'g(w)ee(y)a/ *n, pl* **ouguiya** – see MONEY table [native name in Mauritania]

**Ouija** /'weejə, -ji/ *trademark* – used for a board with the alphabet and other signs marked on it that is used with a movable pointer or upturned glass to seek spiritualistic or telepathic messages

**ouma** /'oohmah/ *n, SAfr* a grandmother [Afrik, fr *ou* old + *ma* mother]

¹**ounce** /owns/ *n* **1a** any of various units of weight based on the ancient Roman unit equal to $^1/_{12}$ Roman pound: e g **1a(1)** a unit of weight equal to $^1/_{16}$ pound (28.349 grams) **a(2)** a unit of TROY WEIGHT or APOTHECARIES' WEIGHT equal to 480 grains (31.1035 grams) **b** a small amount ⟨*an ~ of common sense*⟩ **2** FLUID OUNCE [ME, fr MF *unce*, fr L *uncia* twelfth part, ounce, fr *unus* one – more at ONE]

²**ounce** *n* SNOW LEOPARD [ME *once*, fr OF, alter. (by incorrect division, as if *l'once* the ounce) of *lonce*, fr (assumed) VL *lyncea*, fr L *lync-, lynx* lynx]

**oupa** /'oohpah/ *n, SAfr* a grandfather [Afrik, fr *ou* old + *pa* father]

**our** /'owə, ah/ *adj* of us, ourself, or ourselves, esp as possessors or possessor ⟨*~ throne*⟩, agents or agent ⟨*~ discovery*⟩, or objects or object of an action ⟨*~ being chosen*⟩; of everybody ⟨*~ Saviour*⟩ – used attributively [ME *oure*, fr OE *ūre*; akin to OHG *unsēr* our, OE *ūs* us]

usage The spelling of **ours** meaning "the one belonging to us" as △ **our's** is a common confusion ⟨*the house became* **ours** (not △ **our's**)⟩.

**-our** /-ə/ *suffix* ²-OR

**Our Father** *n* LORD'S PRAYER [fr its opening words]

**Our Lady** *n* VIRGIN MARY

**ours** /'owəz, ahz/ *pron, pl* **ours** that which or the one who belongs to us – used without a following noun as a pronoun

equivalent in meaning to the adjective *our*; compare phrases at ²MINE *usage* see OUR

**ourself** /,owə'self,,ah-/ *pron* myself – used to refer to the single-person subject when *we* is used instead of *I* (e g by a sovereign)

**ourselves** /,owə'selvz,,ah-/ *pron taking pl vb* **1** those identical people that are we – used reflexively ⟨*we're doing it solely for ~*⟩, for emphasis ⟨*we ~ will never go*⟩, or in absolute constructions ⟨*~ no longer young, we can sympathize with the old*⟩; compare ONESELF **2** our normal selves ⟨*not feeling quite ~*⟩

**-ous** /-əs/ *suffix* (→ *adj*) **1** full of; characterized by; possessing the quality of ⟨*clamorous*⟩ ⟨*envious*⟩ **2** having a VALENCY relatively lower than in (specified compounds or ions named with an adjective ending in *-ic*) ⟨*ferrous*⟩ ⟨*mercurous*⟩ [ME; partly fr OF *-ous, -eus, -eux*, fr L *-osus*; partly fr L *-us*, nom sing. masc ending of many adjectives] – **-ously** *adv suffix*

**ousel** /'oohzl/ *n* (type of bird)

**oust** /owst/ *vt* **1** to remove from or dispossess of property or position **2** to take the place of; supplant [AF *ouster*, fr OF *oster*, fr LL *obstare* to ward off, fr L, to stand against, fr *ob-* against + *stare* to stand – more at OB-, STAND]

**ouster** /'owstə/ *n* **1** an illegal or wrongful dispossession or exclusion from property **2** *NAm* expulsion [AF, to oust]

¹**out** /owt/ *adv* **1a** away from the inside or centre ⟨*went ~ into the garden*⟩ **b** from among other things ⟨*separate ~ the bad apples*⟩ **c** away from the shore, the city, or one's homeland ⟨*~ at sea*⟩ ⟨*go ~ to Africa*⟩ ⟨*live ~ in the country*⟩ **d** away from a particular place, esp one's home or business ⟨*~ for lunch*⟩ ⟨*~ on strike*⟩ ⟨*move ~ into lodgings*⟩ – compare OUTSIDE **e(1)** clearly in or into view ⟨*when the sun's ~*⟩ – compare COME OUT ⟨*of a flower in or into full bloom* **e(3)** *of a debutante* in or into society **2a(1)** out of the proper place ⟨*left a word ~*⟩ ⟨*threw his shoulder ~*⟩ **a(2)** amiss in reckoning ⟨*more than 4lb ~* – *Punch*⟩ **b** in all directions from a central point of control ⟨*lent ~ money*⟩ **c** from political power ⟨*voted them ~*⟩ **d** into a state of vexation or disagreement – compare FALL OUT **e** into shares or portions ⟨*parcelled ~ the farm*⟩ **f** out of vogue or fashion **3a** to or in a state of extinction or exhaustion ⟨*burn ~*⟩ ⟨*before the year is ~*⟩ – compare RUN OUT **b** to the fullest extent or degree; completely ⟨*all decked ~*⟩ ⟨*hear me ~*⟩ ⟨*clean ~ the attic*⟩ **c** in or into determined effort ⟨*~ to fight pollution*⟩ **4a** aloud ⟨*cried ~*⟩ ⟨*~ with it!*⟩ **b** *informal* in existence; ever – with a superlative ⟨*the funniest thing ~*⟩; **c** in or into public circulation ⟨*the evening paper came ~ late*⟩ **5** so as to put out of a game ⟨*bowled ~*⟩ **6** – used on a two-way radio circuit to indicate that a message is complete and no reply is expected [ME, fr OE *ūt*; akin to OHG *ūz* out, Gk *hysteros* later, *hybris* arrogance, Skt *ud* up, out] – **out and away** FAR AND AWAY – **be out for** to be trying to get ⟨*he is out for revenge*⟩ – **out of 1a(1)** from within to the outside of ⟨*walked out of the room*⟩ **a(2)** – used to indicate a change in quality, state, or form ⟨*woke up out of a deep sleep*⟩ **b(1)** beyond the range or limits of ⟨*out of sight*⟩ ⟨*lived a mile out of the town*⟩ **b(2)** – used to indicate a position or state away from a qualification or circumstance ⟨*out of practice*⟩ ⟨*out of perspective*⟩ **2a** – used to indicate origin or cause ⟨*came out of fear*⟩ ⟨*did well out of the war*⟩ ⟨*what do I get out of it?*⟩ **b** using as a material; with ⟨*built out of old timber*⟩ **c** having as a mother – used esp of horses ⟨*a colt out of an ordinary mare*⟩ – compare BY **4b(1)** **3** – used to indicate exclusion from or deprivation of ⟨*we're right out of soap*⟩ ⟨*cheated him out of his savings*⟩ ⟨*went out of her mind*⟩ **4** from among; *also* in 5b ⟨*one out of four survived*⟩ – **out of it 1** not part of a group, activity, or fashion **2** hence, away ⟨*get off out of it*⟩

²**out** *vt* to put out; eject

³**out** *adj* **1** located outside; external **2** located at a distance; outlying ⟨*the ~ islands*⟩ **3** not being in operation or power ⟨*the fire's ~*⟩ **4** absent **5** directed or serving to direct outwards ⟨*the ~ tray*⟩ **6** out of the question ⟨*your suggestion's definitely ~*⟩ **7** having had one's turn (e g at batting in cricket, baseball etc) ended by action of the opposing team or by one's own error **8** not being in vogue or fashion; not up-to-date – compare IN

⁴**out** *prep* OUT OF 1a(1) ⟨*jumped ~ the window*⟩

⁵**out** *n* **1** OUTSIDE ⟨*the width of the building from ~ to ~*⟩ **2** one who is out of office or power or on the outside ⟨*a matter of ~s versus ins*⟩ **3** an inadvertent omission from copy in typesetting **4** a way of escaping from an embarrassing or difficult situation ⟨*left his opponent an ~ so that he did not lose too much face*⟩

**out-** *prefix* 1 forth ⟨out*cry*⟩ ⟨out*burst*⟩ ⟨out*rush*⟩ 2 result; product ⟨out*put*⟩ ⟨out*come*⟩ 3 in a manner that goes beyond, surpasses, or excels ⟨out*manoeuvre*⟩ ⟨out*strip*⟩ [¹*out*]

**outage** /'owtij/ *n* a period of interruption or nonoperation (eg of a power supply) [³*out* + *-age*]

**out-and-'out** *adj* being completely as specified at all times, in every part, or from every point of view ⟨*an ~ fraud*⟩ – **out-and-outer** *n*

**outback** /'owt,bak/ *n* isolated rural country, esp of Australia

**outbalance** /,owt'baləns/ *vt* to outweigh in value or importance

**outbid** /,owt'bid/ *vt* **-dd-** to make a higher bid than

¹**outboard** /'owt,bawd/ *adj* 1 situated outboard 2 being a machine bearing, centre, or other support used in conjunction with and outside of a main bearing 3 having, using, or limited to the use of an outboard motor

²**outboard** *adv* 1 in a lateral direction from the hull of a ship or the fuselage of an aircraft 2 in a position closer or closest to either of the wing tips of an aircraft or the sides of a motor vehicle

³**outboard** *n* 1 outboard, **outboard motor** a small portable INTERNAL-COMBUSTION ENGINE with its own propeller and tiller that can be mounted at the stern of a small boat 2 a boat with an outboard motor

**outbound** /'owt,bownd/ *adj* outward bound ⟨*~ traffic*⟩

**outbrave** /owt'brayv/ *vt* to face or resist defiantly

**outbreak** /'owt,brayk/ *n* **1a** a sudden or violent breaking out of activity ⟨*the ~ of war*⟩ **b** a sudden rise in the incidence of a disease ⟨*an ~ of measles*⟩ **c** a sudden increase in numbers of a harmful organism, esp an insect, within a particular area; a plague ⟨*an ~ of locusts*⟩ 2 an uprising, revolt

**outbreed** /owt'breed/ *vt* **outbred** /-'bred/ 1 to subject to outbreeding 2 to breed faster than

**outbreeding** /-,breeding/ *n* the interbreeding of individuals or stocks that are relatively unrelated

**outbuilding** /-,bilding/ *n* a building (eg a stable or a woodshed) separate from but belonging to a main building

**outburst** /-,buhst/ *n* 1 a violent expression of feeling ⟨*an ~ of anger*⟩ 2 a surge of activity or growth ⟨*new ~s of creative thought*⟩ 3 an eruption ⟨*volcanic ~s*⟩

**outcast** /-,kahst/ *n* one who is cast out by society; PARIAH – **outcast** *adj*

¹**outcaste** /'owt,kahst/ *n* 1 a Hindu who has been ejected from his/her hereditary social class (CASTE) for violation of its customs or rules 2 one who has no caste

²**outcaste** *vt* to make (somebody) an outcaste

**outclass** /-'klahs/ *vt* to excel or surpass so decisively as to appear of a higher class

**outcome** /-,kum/ *n* something that follows as a result or consequence

**outcricket** /'owt,krikit/ *n* a side's bowling and fielding, as opposed to its batting ⟨*England's aggressive ~*⟩

¹**outcrop** /-,krop/ *n* 1 (an emergence of) the part of a rock formation that appears at the surface of the ground 2 an outbreak ⟨*the recent ~ of unofficial strikes – The Economist*⟩

²**outcrop** *vi* **-pp-** to project from the surrounding soil ⟨*ledges ~ping from the eroded slope*⟩

¹**outcross** /'owtkros/ *n* the act or result of outcrossing

²**outcross** *vt* to cross with a relatively unrelated individual or strain

**outcry** /-,krie/ *n* 1 a loud cry; a clamour 2 a vehement and usu public expression of anger or disapproval

**outdate** /,owt'dayt/ *vt* to make obsolete

**outdated** /-'daytid/ *adj* outmoded, old-fashioned – **outdatedness** *n*

**outdistance** /-'dist(ə)ns/ *vt* to go far ahead of (eg in a race); outstrip

**outdo** /-'dooh/ *vt* **outdoes** /-'duz/; **outdid** /-'did/; **outdone** /-'dun/ to surpass in action or performance

¹**outdoor** /-,daw/ *also* **outdoors** /-'-/ *adj* 1 of the outdoors 2 performed outdoors ⟨*~ sports*⟩ 3 not enclosed; having no roof ⟨*an ~ restaurant*⟩ [*out* (*of*) *door, out* (*of*) *doors*]

**outdoor relief** *n* public aid administered to the needy not living in institutions, esp in the early 19th century and before

¹**outdoors** /owt'dawz/ *adv* outside a building; in or into the open air

²**outdoors** *n taking sing vb* 1 *the* open air 2 *the* world away from human habitations, esp considered as an area for recreation or adventure ⟨*the lure of the great ~*⟩

**outdraw** /owt'draw/ *vt* **outdrew** /-'drooh/; **outdrawn** /-'drawn/ to draw a handgun more quickly than

¹**outer** /'owtə/ *adj* 1 existing independently of the mind or spirit; objective ⟨*the ~ reality of his life*⟩ **2a** situated farther out ⟨*the ~ limits*⟩ **b** away from a centre ⟨*the ~ planets*⟩ **c** situated or belonging on the outside ⟨*the ~ covering*⟩ [ME, fr ³*out* + *-er*, compar suffix] – **outermost** *adj*

²**outer** *n* (a shot that hits) the ring on a shooting target that is outermost and worth the least score

**outer ear** *n* the outer visible portion of the ear that collects and directs sound waves towards the eardrum by way of a canal which extends inwards through the TEMPORAL BONE (bone of skull covering the area of the temples)

**Outer House** *n* the lower branch of the Court of Session in Scotland

**outer space** *n* space outside the earth's atmosphere; *esp* interstellar space

**outface** /-'fays/ *vt* 1 to cause to waver or submit (as if) by staring 2 to confront unflinchingly; defy

**outfall** /-,fawl/ *n* the outlet of a body of water (eg a river or lake); *esp* the mouth of a drain or sewer

**outfield** /'owt,fiəld, -,feeld/ *n* 1 the part of the cricket field beyond the prepared section on which wickets are laid out; *also* the corresponding part of a baseball field 2 the defensive fielding positions that lie in the outfield; *also, taking sing or pl vb* the players who field in these positions – **outfielder** *n*

**outfighting** /'owt,fieting/ *n* fighting at long range

¹**outfit** /-,fit/ *n* 1 the act of fitting out or equipping (eg for a voyage or expedition) **2a** a complete set of equipment needed for a particular purpose; a kit ⟨*a home brewer's ~*⟩ **b** a set of garments that are worn together for an often specified occasion or activity ⟨*a child's cowboy ~*⟩ 3 *taking sing or pl vb, informal* a group that works as a team; an organization

²**outfit** *vt* **-tt-** to furnish with an outfit; equip

**outfitter** /-,fitə/ *n* one who supplies an outfit or equipment; *esp* a retailer in men's clothing

**outflank** /-'flangk/ *vt* 1 to go round or extend beyond the flank of (an opposing force); outmanoeuvre 2 to gain an advantage over by doing something unexpected – **outflanker** *n*

**outflow** /owt'floh/ *n* 1 a flowing out ⟨*the ~ of currency from the country*⟩ 2 something that flows out – **outflow** *vi*

**outfox** /owt'foks/ *vt* to outwit

**outgas** /'owt,gas, -'-/ *vb* **-ss-** *vt* to remove gases from (a solid) by heating ~ *vi, of a solid* to lose gases as the result of being heated

**outgeneral** /-'jen(ə)rəl/ *vt* **-ll-** (*NAm* **-l-**) to get the better of, esp by using superior military tactics

¹**outgo** /owt'goh/ *vt* **outgoes, outwent** /-went/; **outgone** /-gon/ to go beyond; outdo

²**outgo** *n, pl* **outgoes** *NAm* something that goes out; *specif* expenditure

**outgoing** /'owt,goh-ing; *sense 2* -'--/ *adj* **1a** going away; departing ⟨*an ~ ship*⟩ **b** retiring or withdrawing from a place or position ⟨*the ~ president*⟩ 2 friendly, responsive ⟨*an ~ person*⟩ – **outgoingness** *n*

**outgoings** /'owt,goh-ingz/ *n pl* the expenses or overheads (eg rates and insurance premiums) incurred in running a house, business, etc; expenditures

**outgrow** /-'groh/ *vt* **outgrew** /-'grooh/; **outgrown** /-'grohn/ 1 to grow or increase faster than ⟨*weeds ~ grass*⟩ ⟨*a population ~ing its resources*⟩ 2 to grow too large or too old for ⟨*~ childish habits*⟩

**outgrowth** /-,grohth/ *n* 1 a process or product of growing out ⟨*an ~ of hair*⟩ 2 a consequence, by-product ⟨*crime is often an ~ of poverty*⟩

**outguess** /owt'ges/ *vt* to anticipate the expectations, intentions, or actions of; outwit

**outgun** /owt'gun/ *vt* **-nn-** to surpass in firepower; *broadly* to defeat

**outhaul** /'owt,hawl/ *n* a rope used to haul a sail taut along a supporting pole (SPAR)

,**out-'Herod** /'herəd/ *vt* to exceed in violence or extravagance – chiefly in *out-Herod Herod* [*out-* + *Herod* Antipas *fl*4 BC ruler of Judaea, depicted in medieval mystery plays as a blustering tyrant]

**outhouse** /-,hows/ *n* an outbuilding; *esp, chiefly NAm* an outside toilet

**outing** /'owting/ *n* a short pleasure trip; *esp* one organized for a number of people ⟨*a school ~ to the seaside*⟩

**outlandish** /owt'landish/ *adj* 1 strikingly out of the ordinary;

bizarre ⟨an ~ costume⟩ **2** remote from civilization ⟨an ~ place⟩ **synonyms** see STRANGE [ME, foreign, fr OE ūtlendisc, fr ūtland outlying land, foreign country, fr ūt out + land] – **outlandishly** adv, **outlandishness** n

**outlast** /-'lahst/ vt to last longer than ⟨customs that have long ~ed their usefulness – W R Inge⟩

**¹outlaw** /-,law/ n **1** a person excluded from the benefit or protection of the law **2a** a lawless person; also a fugitive from the law **b** a person or organization under a ban or restriction **3** an animal (eg a horse) that is wild and unmanageable [ME outlawe, fr OE ūtlaga, fr ON ūtlagi, fr ūt out (akin to OE ūt out) + lag-, lög law – more at OUT, LAW] – **outlaw** adj

**²outlaw** vt **1a** to deprive of the benefit and protection of law; declare to be an outlaw **b** to make illegal ⟨the type of legislation which ~ed dueling – Margaret Mead⟩ **2** to place under a ban or restriction ⟨impractical to ~ the old terminology⟩ **3** NAm to remove from legal jurisdiction or enforcement ⟨~ a claim⟩ – **outlawry** n

**¹outlay** /'owt,lay/ vt **outlaid** /-,layd/ to expend (money); LAY OUT

**²outlay** n **1** the act of expending **2** expenditure, payment ⟨~s for national defence⟩

**outlet** /'owtlit, -,let/ n **1a** a place or opening through which something is let out; a vent **b** a means of release or satisfaction for an emotion or drive ⟨sexual ~s⟩ **2a** a market for a commodity **b** an agency (eg a shop or dealer) through which a product is marketed ⟨retail ~s⟩ **3** chiefly NAm POWER POINT [¹out + let, vb]

**outlier** /-,lie-ə/ n something, esp part of a rock formation, separated or lying away from a main or related body

**¹outline** /-,lien/ n **1a** a line or lines bounding the outer limits of an object or figure ⟨the ~ of a triangle⟩ **b** SHAPE 1,2 **2a** a style of drawing in which contours alone are marked with no shading **b** a sketch in outline **3a** a condensed or general treatment of a particular subject ⟨an ~ of world history⟩ **b** a summary of a written work; a synopsis **4** a preliminary account of a project; a plan

**²outline** /'-,-, ,-'-/ vt **1** to draw the outline of **2** to indicate the principal features or different parts of ⟨~d their responsibilities⟩

**outlive** /-'liv/ vt **1** to live longer than ⟨~d most of his friends⟩ **2** to survive the effects of ⟨class differences ~ political change⟩

**outlook** /-,look/ n **1** a view from a particular place ⟨the house has a pleasant ~⟩ **2** an attitude; POINT OF VIEW ⟨his ~ on life⟩ **3** the prospect for the future ⟨the ~ for steel demand in the UK⟩ **synonyms** see ¹VIEW

**outlying** /-,lie·ing/ adj remote from a centre or main point ⟨~ areas⟩

**outmanoeuvre**, NAm **outmaneuver** /-mə'noohvə/ vt **1** to defeat by more skilful manoeuvring **2** to surpass in manoeuvrability

**outmatch** /-'mach/ vt to prove superior to; outdo

**outmoded** /-'mohdid/ adj **1** no longer in fashion **2** no longer acceptable or usable ⟨~ beliefs⟩

**outmost** /'owtmohst, -məst/ adj farthest out; outermost

**outnumber** /-'numbə/ vt to exceed in number

**,out-of-'bounds** adv or adj outside the prescribed boundaries or limits

**,out-of-'date** adj outmoded, obsolete – **out-of-dateness** n

**,out-of-'door, out-of-doors** adj outdoor

**,out-of-'doors** n taking sing vb outdoors – usu + the

**,out-of-'pocket** adj **1** requiring an outlay of cash ⟨~ expenses⟩ **2** having spent or lost more money than one can afford

**,out-of-the-'way** adj **1** off the beaten track; remote ⟨an ~ restaurant⟩ **2** uncommon, unusual ⟨~ information … not found in any other book – John Morris⟩

**outpace** /owt'pays/ vt **1** to surpass in speed **2** to outdo ⟨Japan ~d Western Europe in exporting technology⟩

**outpatient** /-,paysh(ə)nt/ n a patient who is not resident in a hospital but who visits a clinic or dispensary connected with it for diagnosis or treatment – compare INPATIENT

**outperform** /,owtpə'fawm/ vt to do better than ⟨a sports car that ~s them all⟩

**outplay** /-'play/ vt to defeat or play better than in a game

**outpoint** /-'poynt/ vt **1** to sail closer to the wind than (another vessel) **2** to score more points than; esp to defeat (eg in boxing) by scoring more points

**outport** /'owt,pawt/ n **1** a port that is auxiliary to a major

port and generally more able to handle larger vessels **2** a small fishing village – used of such villages in Newfoundland

**outporter** /'owt,pawtə/ n, chiefly Can a native or resident of a Newfoundland fishing village

**outpost** /-,pohst/ n **1** a post or detachment established at a distance from a main body of troops, esp to protect it from surprise attack **2a** an outlying or frontier settlement **b** an outlying branch or position of a main organization, body, or group **3** NAm a military base established by treaty or agreement in another country

**outpouring** /-,pawring/ n **1** the act of pouring out **2** **outpourings** pl, **outpouring** a gushing and emotional stream of expression ⟨~s of grief⟩

**¹output** /-,poot/ n **1** something produced: eg **1a** mineral, agricultural, or industrial production ⟨steel ~⟩ **b** mental or artistic production ⟨literary ~⟩ **c** the amount produced by a person in a given time **d** power or energy produced or delivered by a machine or system (eg for storage or for conversion in characteristics) ⟨solar X-ray ~⟩ **e** the terminal for the output on an electrical device **f** the information fed out by a computer or accounting machine **2** the act, process, or an instance of producing

**²output** vt **-tt-**; **output, outputted** to produce as output

**¹outrage** /-,rayj/ n **1** an act of violence or brutality **2** an act that violates accepted standards of behaviour or taste ⟨an ~ alike against decency and dignity – John Buchan⟩ **3** the anger and resentment aroused by injury or insult [ME, excess, intemperance, violence, fr OF, fr outre beyond, in excess, fr L ultra – more at ULTRA; (3) influenced in sense by out & rage]

**²outrage** vt **1** to violate the standards or principles of ⟨he has ~d respectability past endurance – John Braine⟩ **2** to arouse intense anger or resentment in, usu by some grave offence **3** euph to rape

**outrageous** /owt'rayjəs/ adj **1** wildly and extravagantly unconventional **2a** going beyond all standards of what is right or decent ⟨an ~ disregard of human rights⟩ **b** immoderate, offensive ⟨~ language⟩ ⟨~ manners⟩ – **outrageously** adv, **outrageousness** n

**outrange** /owt'raynj/ vt to surpass in range

**outrank** /-'rangk/ vt **1** to rank higher than **2** to exceed in importance

**outré** /'oohtray (Fr utre)/ adj violating convention or propriety; bizarre [Fr, fr pp of outrer to carry to excess]

**¹outreach** /-'reech/ vt **1a** to reach further than **b** to exceed ⟨the demand ~es the supply⟩ **2** archaic to reach out

**²outreach** /'owt,reech/ n **1** the act of reaching out **2** the extent or limit of reach ⟨the ~ of the pollution⟩ **3** communication with and education of other people, esp in order to convert to a particular religion ⟨Christian ~⟩

**outride** /,owt'ried/ vt **outrode** /-'rohd/; **outridden** /-'rid(ə)n/ **1** to ride better, faster, or farther than; outstrip **2** to ride out (a storm)

**outrider** /-,riedə/ n **1** a mounted attendant or motorcyclist who rides ahead of or beside a carriage or car as an escort **2** NAm a mounted person who herds cattle

**outrigger** /-,rigə/ n **1a** a projecting framework by which a float is attached beside a canoe to give it greater stability; also a canoe so equipped **b** a projecting beam run out from a ship's side to help secure the masts or from a mast to extend a rope or sail **c** a projecting support for a rowlock; also a boat so equipped **2** a member projecting from a main structure to provide additional stability or to support something; esp a projecting frame to support the elevator or tail planes of an aeroplane or the rotor of a helicopter

**¹outright** /-'riet/ adv **1** in entirety; completely ⟨rejected the proposal ~⟩ **2** instantaneously; ON THE SPOT ⟨was killed ~⟩ **3** without accompanying restrictions ⟨purchased the property ~ for cash⟩

**²outright** adj **1** being completely or exactly what is stated ⟨an ~ lie⟩ **2** given without reservation ⟨~ grants for research⟩ **3** made without restrictions ⟨~ purchases⟩ – **outrightly** adv

**outrival** /owt'rievl/ vt **-ll-** (NAm **-l-, -ll-**) to outdo in a competition or rivalry

**outrun** /-'run/ vt **-nn-**; **outran** /-'ran/; **outrun 1** to run faster than; also to keep ahead of ⟨help small presses ~ spiralling costs⟩ **2** to exceed, surpass ⟨his ambitions ~ his abilities⟩

**outscore** /-'skaw/ vt to make a larger score than

**outsell** /-'sel/ vt **outsold** /-'sohld/ **1** to exceed in number of items sold **2** to surpass in selling or salesmanship

**outset** /-,set/ n the beginning, start

**outshine** /-'shien/ *vt* **outshone** /-'shon/, **outshined 1a** to shine brighter than **b** to excel in splendour **2** to outdo, surpass ⟨outshone *most of the other books in quality*⟩

**outshoot** /owt'shooht/ *vt* **outshot** /-'shot/ to surpass in shooting or making shots

¹**outside** /ˌowt'sied, '-,-/ *n* **1a** an external part; the region beyond a boundary **b** the area farthest from an implied point of reference: eg **b(1)** the side of home plate farthest from the batter in baseball **b(2)** the section of a playing area towards the sidelines; *also* a corner **b(3)** the side of a pavement nearer the traffic **2** an outer side or surface **3** an outer manifestation; an appearance **4** the extreme limit of a guess; the maximum ⟨*the crowd numbered 10 000 at the* ∼⟩

²**outside** /'owt,sied/ *adj* **1a** of or being on, near, or towards the outside ⟨*an* ∼ *lavatory*⟩ ⟨*an* ∼ *telephone line*⟩ **b** of or being the outer side of a curve or near the middle of the road or central reservation ⟨*driving in the* ∼ *lane*⟩ **2** outdoor ⟨∼ *workers*⟩ **3** maximum **4a** originating elsewhere ⟨*an* ∼ *broadcast*⟩ ⟨∼ *agitators*⟩ **b** not belonging to one's regular occupation or duties ⟨∼ *interests*⟩ **5** barely possible; remote ⟨*an* ∼ *chance*⟩ **6** made or done from the outside or from a distance ⟨*borrowed a basketball and practised his* ∼ *shot*⟩

³**outside** /owt'sied/ *adv* **1** on or to the outside ⟨*wait* ∼ *in the passage*⟩ – compare OUT 1d **2** outdoors **3** *chiefly Br slang* not in prison – **outside of** *chiefly NAm* outside
**usage** The use of **outside of** for outside ⟨*observers* **outside of** *the industry*⟩ is disliked by many people in Britain and should be avoided in formal writing.

⁴**outside** /owt'sied, '-,-/ *prep* **1** on or to the outside of ⟨*live a mile* ∼ *Cambridge*⟩ **2** beyond the limits of ⟨∼ *my experience*⟩ **3** except, besides ⟨*few interests* ∼ *her children*⟩

**outside half** *n* STAND-OFF 1

**outsider** /owt'siedə/ *n* **1** a person who does not belong to a particular group **2** a competitor who has only an outside chance of winning – **outsiderness** *n*

¹**outsize** /'owt,siez/ *n* an unusual size; *esp* a size larger than the standard

²**outsize** *also* **outsized** *adj* unusually large

**outskirts** *n pl*, **outskirt** *n* a part remote from the centre; *specif* an outer area of a town or city ⟨*lives somewhere on the* ∼ *of Norwich*⟩

**outsmart** /-'smaht/ *vt, chiefly NAm* to get the better of; *esp* to outwit

**outspend** /owt'spend/ *vt* **outspent 1** to exceed the limits of in spending ⟨∼ s *his income*⟩ **2** to spend more than ⟨*he* outspent *the other candidates*⟩

**outspoken** /-'spohkən/ *adj* **1** direct and open in speech or expression; frank **2** spoken or expressed without reserve ⟨*his* ∼ *advocacy of population control*⟩ – **outspokenly** *adv*, **outspokenness** *n*

**outspread** /owt'spred/ *vt* **outspread** to spread out; extend

**outstanding** /-'standing/ *adj* **1** standing out; projecting **2a** unpaid ⟨*left several bills* ∼⟩ **b** continuing, unresolved ⟨*a long* ∼ *problem*⟩ **c** of stocks, shares, bonds, etc publicly issued and sold **3a** standing out from a group; conspicuous **b** marked by eminence and distinction – **outstandingly** *adv*
**usage** Since **outstanding** can mean either "unresolved" or "distinguished" it may be wise to avoid ambiguity by rephrasing such sentences as ⟨*some of the figures are* **outstanding**⟩.

**outstare** /-'steə/ *vt* OUTFACE 1

**outstation** /-,staysh(ə)n/ *n* a remote or outlying station

**outstay** /-'stay/ *vt* **1** to overstay ⟨∼ ed *his welcome*⟩ **2** to surpass in stamina or staying power ⟨∼ ed *his competitors*⟩

**outstretch** /-'strech/ *vt* to stretch out; extend

**outstrip** /-'strip/ *vt* **-pp- 1** to go faster or farther than **2** to get ahead of; leave behind ⟨*has civilization* ∼ ped *the ability of its users to use it?* – Margaret Mead⟩ [*out-* + *obs* **strip** to move fast, fr ME *strypen*]

**outswing** /-,swing/ *n* the swerve of a bowled cricket ball from the LEG SIDE to the OFF SIDE – compare INSWING

**outswinger** /'owt,swing·ə/ *n* **1** a bowled cricket ball having outswing **2** a bowler who uses outswing

**outtalk** /owt'tawk/ *vt* to get the better of by talking (eg in an argument)

**outthink** /owt'thingk/ *vt* **outthought** /-'thawt/ to get the better of by thinking

**outvote** /-'voht/ *vt* to cast more votes than; defeat by a majority of votes ⟨*they can* ∼ *the opposition*⟩

¹**outward** /-wood/ *adj* **1a** situated at or directed towards the outside **b** being or going away from home ⟨*the* ∼ *voyage*⟩ **2** of the body or external appearances ⟨∼ *calm*⟩

²**outward** *n* external form, appearance, or reality

**outward-'bound** *adj* headed in an outward direction (eg away from a home port) ⟨*an* ∼ *ship*⟩

**outwardly** /'owtwədli/ *adv* **1a** on the outside; externally ⟨∼ *visible*⟩ **b** towards the outside **2** in outward state, behaviour, or appearance ⟨*was* ∼ *friendly*⟩ **antonym** inwardly

**outwardness** /'owtwədnis/ *n* **1** the quality or state of being external **2** concern with or responsiveness to outward things

**outwards** /'owtwədz/ *adv* **1** towards the outside **2** *obs* on the outside; externally **antonym** inwards

**outwear** /-'weə/ *vt* **outwore** /-'waw/; **outworn** /-'wawn/ to last longer than ⟨*a fabric that* ∼ s *others*⟩

**outweigh** /-'way/ *vt* to exceed in weight, value, or importance ⟨*the advantages* ∼ *the disadvantages*⟩

**outwit** /-'wit/ *vt* **-tt-** to get the better of by superior cleverness

**outwith** /'owt,widh/ *prep, Scot* outside

**outwork** /-,wuhk/ *n* **1** a minor defensive position constructed outside a fortified area **2** work done for a business or organization off its premises, usu by employees based at home – **outworker** *n*

**outworn** /-'wawn/ *adj* no longer useful or acceptable; outmoded ⟨*an* ∼ *social system*⟩

**ouzel, ousel** /'oohzl/ *n* **1** RING OUZEL (type of thrush) **2** WATER OUZEL (type of waterbird) **3** *obs* the European blackbird [ME *ousel*, fr OE *ōsle* blackbird]

**ouzo** /'oohzoh/ *n* an unsweetened Greek spirit flavoured with aniseed that is usu drunk with water [NGk *ouzon, ouzo*]

**ov-** /ov-, ohv-/, **ovi-, ovo-** *comb form* egg ⟨*oviform*⟩; ovum ⟨*oviduct*⟩ ⟨*ovocyte*⟩ [L *ov-, ovi-*, fr *ovum* – more at EGG]

**ova** /'ohvə/ *pl of* OVUM (egg)

¹**oval** /'ohvl/ *adj* having the shape of an egg; *also* exactly or approximately elliptical [ML *ovalis*, fr LL, of an egg, fr L *ovum*] – **ovally** *adv*, **ovalness** *n*

²**oval** *n* **1** an oval figure or object **2** *chiefly Austr* a sports stadium; *also* an oval field where AUSTRALIAN RULES FOOTBALL is played

**ovalbumin** /ˌoval'byoohmin, ov'albyoomin/ *n* **1** the principal ALBUMIN (type of protein) of white of egg; *esp* the part of egg albumins that can be crystallized **2** dried whites of eggs

**oval window** *n* FENESTRA OVALIS (opening in the ear)

**ovarian** /oh'veəriən/ *also* **ovarial** /-riəl/ *adj* of or involving an ovary

**ovariectomy** /oh,veəri'ektəmi, -,vari-/ *n* the surgical removal of an ovary – **ovariectomized** *adj*

**ovariole** /oh'veəriohl, -'vari-/ *n* any of the tubes of which the ovaries of most insects are composed [(assumed) NL *ovariolum*, dim. of *ovarium*]

**ovariotomy** /oh,veəri'otəmi, -,vari-/ *n* **1** surgical cutting of an ovary **2** ovariectomy

**ovaritis** /ˌohvə'rietəs/ *n* inflammation of an ovary [NL, fr *ovarium*]

**ovary** /'ohvəri/ *n* **1** either of the paired female reproductive organs that produces eggs and, in VERTEBRATE animals, female SEX HORMONES **2** the hollow rounded part at the base of a CARPEL (female reproductive organ) in a flower that contains one or more OVULES (structures that develop into the seeds after fertilization) [NL *ovarium*, fr L *ovum* egg]

**ovate** /'ohvayt/ *adj* **1** shaped like an egg **2** *esp of a leaf* having an ovate outline

**ovation** /oh'vaysh(ə)n/ *n* **1** a ceremony of less importance than a triumph attending the entrance into ancient Rome by a victorious general **2** an expression or demonstration of popular acclaim; *esp* a bout of prolonged and enthusiastic applause ⟨*received a standing* ∼⟩ [L *ovation-, ovatio*, fr *ovatus*, pp of *ovare* to exult; akin to Gk *euoi*, interjection used in bacchic revels]

**oven** /'uv(ə)n/ *n* a chamber used for baking, heating, or drying – see also BUN in the oven [ME, fr OE *ofen*; akin to OHG *ofan* oven, Gk *ipnos*, L *aulla, olla* pot]

**ovenbird** /-,buhd/ *n* any of various S American small brown songbirds (genus *Furnarius*) that build dome-shaped nests of mud [fr the shape of its nest]

**'oven-,ready** *adj, of food* sold ready to be cooked without further preparation

**ovenware** /-,weə/ *n* heat-resistant pots and dishes (eg casseroles) in which food can be cooked in an oven and which are often suitable for use as tableware

¹**over** /'ohvə/ *adv* **1a** across a barrier ⟨*climb* ∼⟩ **b** across an intervening space ⟨*went* ∼ *to the States*⟩; *also* ROUND **5** ⟨*ask*

them ~ for drinks⟩ **c** downwards from an upright position ⟨fell ~⟩ ⟨knocked him ~⟩ **d** across the brim or brink ⟨soup boiled ~⟩ **e** so as to bring the underside up ⟨turned his cards ~⟩ ⟨rolled ~ and ~⟩ **f** so as to be reversed or folded ⟨change the two pictures ~⟩ ⟨bend it ~⟩ **g** from one person or side to another ⟨hand it ~⟩ ⟨won them ~⟩ ⟨went ~ to the enemy⟩ **h** ACROSS 3 ⟨got his point ~⟩ **2a(1)** beyond some quantity or limit ⟨10 or ~⟩ ⟨show ran a minute ~⟩ – often in combination ⟨over*step*⟩ ⟨over*shoot*⟩ **a(2)** in an excessive manner; inordinately – often in combination ⟨over-*optimistic*⟩ ⟨over-*value*⟩ **a(3)** in excess; remaining ⟨there wasn't much ~⟩ ⟨three into seven goes twice and one ~⟩ – compare LEFTOVER **b** till a later time ⟨stay ~ till Monday⟩ **3** so as to cover the whole surface ⟨windows boarded ~⟩ **4a** at an end ⟨the day is ~⟩ **b** – used on a two-way radio circuit to indicate that a message is complete and a reply is expected **5a** discursively through ⟨think it ~⟩ – compare TALK OVER ⟨talk the matter ~⟩ **b** – used to show repetition ⟨10 times ~⟩ ⟨told you ~ and ~⟩ ⟨do it all ~ again⟩ **c** chiefly NAm once more ⟨do one's sums ~⟩ [ME, adv & prep, fr OE *ofer;* akin to OHG *ubar* (prep) above, beyond, over, L *super,* Gk *hyper*] – **over against** as opposed to; in contrast with ⟨*the failure of Christianity* over against *Islam in successive ages – British Book News*⟩ – **over and over** repeatedly

**²over** *prep* **1a** higher than; above ⟨towered ~ his mother⟩ **b** vertically above but not touching ⟨lamp hung ~ the table⟩ **c** – used to indicate movement **c(1)** down upon ⟨hit him ~ the head⟩ **c(2)** down across the edge of ⟨fell ~ the cliff⟩ **d** ACROSS 1a ⟨climbed ~ the gate⟩ ⟨flew ~ the lake⟩ **e** ACROSS 1b **f** so as to cover – used to indicate position upon ⟨laid a blanket ~ the child⟩ ⟨curtains drawn ~ the windows⟩ **g** divided by ⟨6 ~ 2 is 3⟩ **2a** with authority, power, or jurisdiction in relation to ⟨respected those ~ him⟩ **b** – used to indicate superiority, advantage, or preference ⟨a big lead ~ the others⟩ **3** more than ⟨cost ~ £5⟩ – compare OVER AND ABOVE **4a** all through or throughout ⟨showed me all ~ the house⟩ ⟨went ~ his notes⟩ ⟨travelled the world ~⟩ **b** by means of (a medium or channel of communication) ⟨~ the radio⟩ **5a** in the course of; during ⟨~ the past 25 years⟩ ⟨wrote it ~ the weekend⟩ **b** until the end of ⟨stay ~ Sunday⟩ **c** past, beyond ⟨we're ~ the worst⟩ **6a** – used to indicate an object of solicitude or reference ⟨the Lord watches ~ them⟩ ⟨laughed ~ the incident⟩ **b** – used to indicate an object of occupation or activity ⟨sitting ~ their wine⟩ ⟨spent an hour ~ cards⟩ – **over and above** ²BESIDES

**³over** *adj* **1** upper, higher ⟨over*lord*⟩ **2** outer, covering ⟨over*coat*⟩ **3** excessive ⟨~ *imagination*⟩ ⟨over*confidence*⟩ □ often in combination – **over with** finished, completed

**⁴over** *n* any of the divisions of an innings in cricket during which one bowler bowls six or eight balls from the same end of the pitch and which is succeeded by a similar set of balls from the other end bowled by a different bowler [fr the umpire's cry of *over* (ie change to the other end) after the 6th or 8th ball]

**overabundance** /-ə'bund(ə)ns/ *n* an excess, surfeit – **overabundant** *adj*

**overact** /-'akt/ *vb* to perform (a dramatic part) with undue exaggeration

**overactive** /,ohvər'aktiv/ *adj* excessively or abnormally active – **overactivity** *n*

**¹overage** /,ohvər'ayj/ *adj* **1** beyond a specified or usual age; too old **2** older than is normal for one's position, function, or grade [²*over* + *age*]

**²overage** /'ohvərij/ *n* a surplus, excess [³*over* + *-age*]

**¹overall** /,ohvər'awl/ *adv* **1** as a whole; IN TOTO ⟨impressive ~ and in detail⟩ **2** from end to end, esp of a ship

**²overall** /'ohvərəl, -awl/ *n* **1** *pl* a protective garment resembling a boiler suit or dungarees **2** *chiefly Br* a usu loosely fitting protective coat worn over other clothing

**³overall** /,ohvər'awl/ *adj* including everything

**overarching** /,ohvər'ahching/ *adj* **1** forming an arch overhead **2** dominating or embracing everything else

**overarm** /'ohvərahm/ *adj or adv* **1** with the hand brought forwards and down from above shoulder level ⟨~ *bowling*⟩ ⟨serving ~ in tennis⟩ **2** *of a swimming stroke* made with the arm lifted out of the water and stretched forwards over the water in front of the body to begin the stroke

**overawe** /-'aw/ *vt* to restrain or subdue by respect or fear

**overbalance** /,ohvə'baləns/ *vt* to cause to lose balance ~ *vi,* chiefly Br to lose one's balance

**overbear** /-'beə/ *vb* **overbore** /-'baw/; **overborne** *also* **overborn** /-'bawn/ *vt* **1** to bring down by superior weight or force; overwhelm **2a** to domineer over **b** to surpass in importance or relevance; outweigh ~ *vi* to bear fruit or offspring to excess

**overbearing** /-'beəring/ *adj* **1** tending to overwhelm; overpowering **2** harshly and haughtily masterful or arrogant – **overbearingly** *adv*

**overbid** /-'bid/ *vb* **-dd-; overbid** *vi* **1** to bid in excess of value **2** to bid more than the scoring capacity of a hand at cards ~ *vt* to bid beyond or in excess of; *esp* to bid more than the value of (one's hand at cards) – **overbid** *n*

**overbite** /'ohvəbiet/ *n* the projection of the upper front teeth over the lower when the jaws are in contact

**overblow** /,ohvə'bloh/ *vb* **overblew** /-'blooh/; **overblown** /-'blohn/ to blow (a wind instrument) so hard as to produce overtones instead of the note (FUNDAMENTAL) being played

**¹overblown** /,ohvə'blohn/ *adj* inflated, pretentious [¹*blow*]

**²overblown** /'ohvə,blohn/ *adj* past the prime of bloom ⟨~ *roses*⟩ [³*blow*]

**overboard** /-,bawd/ *adv* **1** over the side of a ship or boat into the water **2** to extremes of enthusiasm ⟨went ~ for the plan⟩ **3** into rejection; aside ⟨threw the plan ~⟩

**overbook** /-'book/ *vt* to issue bookings for (eg a hotel) in excess of the space available ~ *vi* to issue bookings in excess of the space available

**overbuild** /-'bild/ *vb* **overbuilt** /-'bilt/ to build (houses) in excess of demand

**¹overburden** /-'buhd(ə)n/ *vt* to place an excessive burden on

**²overburden** /'ohvə,buhd(ə)n/ *n* soil, rock, etc overlying a deposit of useful geological materials (eg coal)

**overbuy** /,ohvə'bie/ *vb* **overbought** /-'bawt/ *vt* to buy in excess of needs or demand ~ *vi* to make purchases beyond one's needs or in excess of one's ability to pay

**overcall** /-'kawl/ *vt* to make a higher bid than (the previous bid or player) in a card game ~ *vi* to bid over an opponent's bid in bridge when one's partner has not bid or doubled – **overcall** *n*

**overcapacity** /,ohvəkə'pasəti/ *n* excessive capacity for production or services in relation to demand

**overcapital·ize, -ise** /-'kapitl,iez/ *vt* **1** to put a nominal value on the capital of (a company) higher than actual cost or fair market value **2** to capitalize beyond what the business or the profit-making prospects warrant or what is legally permitted – **overcapitalization** *n*

**¹overcast** /'ohvə,kahst/ *vt* **overcast 1** to darken, overshadow

---

| | | | |
|---|---|---|---|
| **overaccentuate** *vt* | **overanalytical** *adj* | **overassertive** *adj* | **overbusy** *adj* |
| **overaccumulation** *n* | **overangry** *adj* | **overassertiveness** *n* | **overcapacity** *n* |
| **overachieve** *vb* | **overanimated** *adj* | **overassessment** *n* | **overcareful** *adj* |
| **overachiever** *n* | **overanimatedly** *adv* | **overassist** *vb* | **overcaution** *n* |
| **overadjustment** *n* | **overanimation** *n* | **overattached** *adj* | **overcautious** *adj* |
| **overadorned** *adj* | **overanxiety** *n* | **overattention** *n* | **overcentralization** *n* |
| **overadvance** *vb* | **overanxious** *adj* | **overattentive** *adj* | **overcentalize** *vb* |
| **overadvertise** *vb* | **overappreciation** *n* | **overattentively** *adv* | **overchill** *vt* |
| **overaffect** *vt* | **overappreciative** *adj* | **overattentiveness** *n* | **overcivil** *adj* |
| **overaggressive** *adj* | **overapprehensive** *adj* | **overbake** *vb* | **overcivilized** *adj* |
| **overambitious** *adj* | **overapprehensiveness** *n* | **overbeat** *vt* | **overclaim** *vb* |
| **overambitiously** *adj* | **overargumentative** *adj* | **overbleach** *vt* | **overclassification** *n* |
| **overambitiousness** *n* | **overarousal** *n* | **overboil** *vt* | **overclassify** *vt* |
| **overamplify** *vb* | **overarrange** *vt* | **overborrow** *vb* | **overcommercialization** *n* |
| **overanalysis** *n* | **overassert** *vt* | **overbrave** *adj* | **overcommercialize** *vt* |
| **overanalyse** *vt* | **overassertion** *n* | **overburdensome** *adj* | **overcommon** *adj* |

**2** to sew over (a raw edge) with stitches, esp long slightly slanting widely spaced stitches, to prevent unravelling

²**overcast** *adj* clouded over ⟨*an ~ day*⟩

³**overcast** *n* a covering of clouds over the sky

**overcasting** /-ˌkahsting/ *n* the act or process of stitching a raw edge of fabric to prevent unravelling; *also* the stitching so done

**overcharge** /-ˈchahj/ *vt* **1** to charge too much or too fully **2** to fill too full **3** to exaggerate *~ vi* to make an excessive charge – **overcharge** *n*

**overcloud** /-ˈklowd/ *vb* to cover or become covered with clouds

**overcoat** /-ˌkoht/ *n* **1** a warm usu thick coat for wearing outdoors over other clothing **2** a protective coat (e g of paint)

**overcome** /-ˈkum/ *vb* **overcame** /-ˈkaym/; **overcome** *vt* **1** to get the better of; surmount ⟨*~ difficulties*⟩ **2** to overpower, overwhelm *~ vi* to gain superiority; win [ME *overcomen,* fr OE *ofercuman,* fr *ofer* over + *cuman* to come] – **overcomer** *n*

**overcommit** /ˌohvəkəˈmit/ *vt* **-tt-** to commit excessively: e g a to obligate (e g oneself) beyond the ability for fulfilment **b** to allocate (resources) in excess of the capacity for replenishment – **overcommitment** *n*

**overcompensation** /-ˌkompənˈsaysh(ə)n, -pən-/ *n* excessive compensation; *specif* excessive reaction to a feeling of inferiority, guilt, or inadequacy – **overcompensatory** *adj,* **overcompensate** *vb*

**overconfidence** /ˌohvəˈkonfid(ə)ns/ *n* excess of confidence – **overconfident** *adj,* **overconfidently** *adv*

**overcrowd** /-ˈkrowd/ *vb* to (cause to) be too crowded

**overdevelop** /ˌovədiˈveləp/ *vt* to develop excessively; *esp* to subject (exposed photographic material) to a developing solution for excessive time or at an excessive temperature, concentration, etc – **overdevelopment** *n*

**overdo** /-ˈdooh/ *vt* **overdoes** /-ˈduz/; **overdid** /-ˈdid/; **overdone** /-ˈdun/ **1a** to do in excess **b** to use to excess **c** to exaggerate **2** to cook too much

**overdominance** /ˌohvəˈdominəns/ *n, genetics* the property of having a HETEROZYGOTE (individual having different versions of a gene coding for a particular characteristic) that produces a PHENOTYPE (set of visible characteristics) more extreme or better adapted than either of the HOMOZYGOTES (individuals having identical versions of a particular gene) from which it was formed – **overdominant** *adj*

**overdose** /ˈohvəˌdohs, ˌ--ˈ-/ *vb or n* (to give or take) too great a dose of drugs, medicine, etc – **overdosage** *n*

**overdraft** /-ˌdrahft/ *n* an act of overdrawing at a bank; the state of being overdrawn; *also* the sum overdrawn

**overdraught,** *NAm* **overdraft** /ˈohvəˌdrahft/ *n* a draught or current of air passing over a fire in a furnace

**overdraw** /-ˈdraw/ *vb* **overdrew** /-ˈdrooh/; **overdrawn** /-ˈdrawn/ *vt* **1** to withdraw money from (a bank account) for more than one's balance ⟨*his account was* overdrawn⟩ **2** to exaggerate, overstate *~ vi* to make an overdraft

**overdrawn** /-ˈdrawn/ *adj* having an overdrawn account

¹**overdress** /-ˈdres/ *vb* to dress too elaborately or formally

²**overdress** /ˈohvəˌdres/ *n* a dress worn over another, or over a jumper, blouse, etc

**overdrive** /-ˌdriev/ *n* a speed-changing gear in a motor vehicle that is higher than the normal top gear and is used at high speeds to lower fuel consumption and reduce wear

**overdue** /-ˈdyooh/ *adj* **1a** unpaid when due **b** delayed beyond the proper or an appointed time **2** more than ready or ripe ⟨*colonies that are ~ for independence*⟩ **synonyms** see TARDY

**overeat** /ˌohvərˈeet/ *vb* **overate** /-ˈet, -ˈayt/; **overeaten** /-ˈeet(ə)n/ *vi* to eat to excess *~ vt* to eat too much for (oneself) – **overeater** *n*

**overemphasis** /ˌohvərˈemfəsis/ *n* more emphasis than is necessary or desirable

**overemphas·ize, -ise** /ˌohvərˈemfəsiez/ *vt* to give excessive emphasis to *~ vi* to use too much emphasis

**overestimate** /-ˈestimayt/ *vt* **1** to estimate as being more than the actual size, quantity, or number **2** to place too high a value on; overrate – **overestimate** *n,* **overestimation** *n*

**overexpose** /ˌohvərikˈspohz/ *vt* to expose excessively; *esp* to expose (e g film) to excessive radiation (e g light) – **overexposure** *n*

**overextend** /-ikˈstend/ *vt* to extend or expand beyond a safe or reasonable point; *esp* to commit (oneself) financially beyond what can be paid

**overfatigue** /ˌohvəfəˈteeg/ *n* excessive fatigue, esp when carried beyond the capacity of the individual to recover – **overfatigued** *adj*

**overfeed** /-ˈfeed/ *vb* **overfed** /-ˈfed/ to eat or feed too much

**overfish** /-ˈfish/ *vt* to fish (a fishing ground) so excessively that the numbers of fish are seriously depleted; *also* to catch too many of (a kind of fish) with the same result

**overflight** /-ˌfliet/ *n* a passage over an area in an aircraft

¹**overflow** /ˌohvəˈfloh/ *vb* **overflowed** *vt* **1** to cover (as if) with water; inundate **2** to flow over or beyond the brim, edge, or limit of **3** to cause to overflow *~ vi* to flow over or beyond a brim, edge, or limit ⟨*extra chairs if the meeting ~ s*⟩

²**overflow** /ˈohvəˌfloh/ *n* **1** a flowing over; an inundation **2** something that flows over; a surplus; *also, taking sing or pl vb* the excess members of a group **3** an outlet or receptacle for surplus liquid **4** the generation of a number too large to be stored or displayed in the normal way by a computer or calculator

**overfly** /-ˈflie/ *vt* **overflew** /-ˈflooh/; **overflown** /-ˈflohn/ to fly over; *esp* to pass over in an aircraft

**overfold** /-ˌfohld/ *n* a geological formation in which layers of rock fold upwards into an arch (ANTICLINE) that has one side more steeply sloping than the other

**overgarment** /ˈohvəˌgahmənt/ *n* an outer garment

**overglaze** /ˈohvəˌglayz/ *adj* applied or suitable for applying on top of a fired glaze ⟨*~ enamels*⟩ – **overglaze** *n*

**overgraze** /ˌohvəˈgrayz/ *vt* to allow animals to graze on, to the point of damaging vegetational cover

¹**overground** /ˈohvəˌgrownd/ *adj or adv* on the surface; *specif* not underground ⟨*an ~ pipeline*⟩

²**overground** *n* an overground as opposed to an underground city railway system

**overgrow** /-ˈgroh/ *vb* **overgrew** /-ˈgrooh/; **overgrown** /-ˈgrohn/ *vt* **1** to grow over so as to cover with vegetation **2** to grow beyond or rise above; outgrow *~ vi* **1** to grow excessively **2** to become overgrown – **overgrowth** *n*

---

| | | | |
|---|---|---|---|
| **overcompetitive** *adj* | **overcook** *vt* | **overdependent** *adj* | **overearnest** *adj* |
| **overcomplacency** *n* | **overcool** *adj or vb* | **overdesign** *vt* | **overedit** *vt* |
| **overcomplacent** *adj* | **overcorrect** *adj or vt* | **overdesirous** *adj* | **overeducate** *vt* |
| **overcomplex** *adj* | **overcorrection** *n* | **overdetailed** *adj* | **overeducation** *n* |
| **overcompliance** *n* | **overcostly** *adj* | **overdifferentiation** *n* | **overeffusive** *adj* |
| **overcomplicate** *vt* | **overcount** *vb* | **overdiligent** *adj* | **overelaborate** *adj or vb* |
| **overcomplicated** *adj* | **overcritical** *adj* | **overdiligently** *adv* | **overelaboration** *n* |
| **overcompress** *vt* | **overcriticize** *vb* | **overdilute** *adj or vt* | **overembellish** *vt* |
| **overconcentrate** *vb* | **overcultivate** *vt* | **overdirected** *adj* | **overemotional** *adj* |
| **overconcentration** *n* | **overcultivation** *n* | **overdirection** *n* | **overemphatic** *adj* |
| **overconcern** *n* | **overcurious** *adj* | **overdistant** *adj* | **overenamoured** *adj* |
| **overconfidence** *n* | **overdecorate** *vt* | **overdiversification** *n* | **overencourage** *vt* |
| **overconfident** *adj* | **overdecoration** *n* | **overdiversify** *vb* | **overenergetic** *adj* |
| **overconfidently** *adv* | **overdecorative** *adj* | **overdiversity** *n* | **overenthusiasm** *n* |
| **overconscientious** *adj* | **overdefensive** *adj* | **overdramatic** *adj* | **overenthusiastic** *adj* |
| **overconscious** *adj* | **overdeferential** *adj* | **overdramatize** *vb* | **overequipped** *adj* |
| **overconservative** *adj* | **overdeliberate** *adj* | **overdrink** *vi* | **overevaluation** *n* |
| **overconsiderate** *adj* | **overdelicate** *adj* | **overdry** *adj or vt* | **overexacting** *adj* |
| **overconsume** *vb* | **overdemanding** *adj* | **overeager** *adj* | **overexaggerate** *vb* |
| **overconsumption** *n* | **overdependence** *n* | **overeagerness** *n* | **overexaggeration** *n* |

**overgrown** /ohvə'grohn/ adj **1** grown over or choked with vegetation ⟨an ~ garden⟩ **2** grown too large

¹**overhand** /'ohvə,hand/ adj or adv overarm – **overhanded** adv

²**overhand** n an overarm stroke (eg in tennis)

**overhand knot** n a simple knot often used to prevent the end of a cord from fraying

¹**overhang** /-'hang/ vb overhung /-'hung/ vt **1** to project over **2** to impend over; threaten ~ vi to project so as to be over something

²**overhang** /'ohvə,hang/ n **1** something that overhangs; also the extent by which something overhangs **2** a projection of the roof or upper storey of a building beyond the wall of the lower part

**overhaul** /-'hawl/ vt **1** to examine thoroughly and carry out necessary repairs **2** to overtake [¹over + ¹haul; orig sense, to slacken (a rope), release (a tackle)] – **overhaul** n

¹**overhead** /-'hed/ adv above one's head; aloft

²**overhead** /'ohvə,hed/ adj **1** operating, lying, or coming from above **2** of or being overhead expenses

³**overhead** n **1** overheads pl, overhead a business expense (eg rent, insurance, or heating) not chargeable to a particular part of the work or product – compare FIXED COST **2** a stroke in squash, tennis, etc made above head height; a smash

**overhead projector** n a projector that projects a magnified image of a horizontal transparency (eg one carrying hand-written text) onto a screen via a mirror

**overhead railway** n an urban or interurban railway operating chiefly on an elevated structure

**overhear** /-'hiə/ vb overheard /-'huhd/ to hear (somebody or something) without the speaker's knowledge or intention

**overheat** /-'heet/ vt **1** to heat to excess **2** to excite or stimulate unduly ⟨~ed by political passions⟩ ⟨~ing the economy⟩ ~ vi to become overheated

**overindulge** /,ohvərin'dulj/ vt **1** to indulge in to an excessive degree **2** to indulge (someone) to an excessive degree ~ vi to indulge in something to an excessive degree – **overindulgence** n, **overindulgent** adj

**overinsurance** /,ohvərin'shooərəns, -'shaw-/ n insurance of property for more than its real value – **overinsure** vt

**overissue** /-'ish(y)ooh, -'isyooh/ n an issue of shares, notes, etc exceeding the limit of capital, credit, or authority – **over-issue** vt

**overjoyed** /-'joyd/ adj extremely pleased; elated

¹**overkill** /,ohvə'kil/ vt to obliterate (a target) with more nuclear force than required

²**overkill** /'ohvə,kil/ n **1** the capability of destroying an enemy or target with a force, esp nuclear, larger than is required **2** an excess of something (eg a material, quality, or activity) beyond what is required or suitable for a particular purpose ⟨a propaganda ~⟩ ⟨the satirical ~ in Dickens – John Fowles⟩

**overking** /'ohvə,king/ n a king who is sovereign over inferior kings

**overlaid** /-'layd/ adj having something laid or lying on top; also overlying

¹**overland** /'ohvə,land, ,--'-/ adv or adj by, upon, or across land rather than sea or air ⟨went ~ to Nepal⟩ ⟨an ~ route⟩

²**overland** /'ohvə,land/ vb, Austr to drive (stock) overland for long distances – **overlander** n

**overlap** /-'lap/ vb -pp- vt **1** to extend over and cover a part of **2** to have something in common with; coincide in part with ⟨the baroque period ~s the rococo⟩ ~ vi to coincide partly – **overlap** n

¹**overlay** /-'lay/ vt overlaid /-'layd/ **1** to lay or spread over or across; superimpose **2** to prepare an overlay for **3** OVERLIE 2 ⟨sow overlaid her piglets⟩

   usage Overlay (-laid, -laid) and overlie (-lay, -lain) are as easily confused as the verbs lay and lie. Both are transitive, but compare ⟨she overlaid (= covered) the primer with a thin undercoat⟩ ⟨the sandstone overlies (= lies over) the coal⟩. See ¹LAY

²**overlay** /'ohvəlay/ n something (designed to be) laid over something else: eg **a** an ornamental veneer **b** paper patches added to the packing on a printing press to make a stronger impression **c** a decorative and contrasting design or article placed on top of a plain one **d** a transparent sheet of drawings, designs, etc to be superimposed on another sheet

**overleaf** /-'leef/ adv on the other side of the page ⟨you can read it ~ – Woman's Own⟩

**overlearn** /,ohvə'luhn/ vt to continue to study or practise after attaining proficiency

**overlie** /-'lie/ vt overlying; overlay /-'lay/; overlain /-'layn/ **1** to lie or be situated over **2** to cause the death of (eg a baby) by lying on on usage see ¹OVERLAY

**overload** /,ohvə'lohd/ vt overloaded, overladen /-'laydn/ to load to excess – **overload** n

**overlocking** /-,loking/ n the act, process, or occupation of over-sewing a raw edge of fabric cut to a garment pattern, using a small closely worked machine stitch in order to prevent un-ravelling; also the stitching so done – **overlock** vb, **overlocker** n

**overlong** /,ohvə'long/ adj or adv too long

**overlook** /,ohvə'look/ vt **1a** to look down upon from above **b** to rise above or provide a view of **2a** to fail to notice; miss **b** to ignore **c** to excuse **3** to supervise **4** to look on with the evil eye; bewitch synonyms see ¹NEGLECT antonym notice (for 2) ⚠ oversee

**overlord** /-'lawd/ n **1** a lord who rules over other lords **2** an absolute or supreme ruler ⟨industrial ~s⟩ – **overlordship** n

**overly** /'ohvəli/ adv, chiefly NAm & Scot too, excessively [¹over + ²-ly]

¹**overman** /'ohvəmən, -,man/ n **1** a foreman, overseer **2** SUPERMAN 1 (Nietzsche's ideal man) [(2) trans of Ger übermensch]

²**overman** vt -nn- to have or provide too many workers for ⟨~ a ship⟩

**overmantel** /-,mantl/ n an ornamental often shelved structure above a mantelpiece

**overmaster** /-'mahstə/ vt to overpower, subdue

**overmatch** /,ohvə'mach/ vt **1** to be more than a match for; defeat **2** to match with a superior opponent ⟨a badly ~ed boxer⟩

**overmatter** /'ohvə,matə/ n typeset material that exceeds the space allotted

**overmighty** /-'mieti/ adj unduly powerful; esp exercising or claiming undue political power ⟨the Crown's struggles with ~ subjects⟩

**overmuch** /-'much/ adj or adv too much

---

| | | | |
|---|---|---|---|
| overexcitable adj | overfanciful adj | overidealistic adj | overinvest vb |
| overexcitably adv | overfar adj or adv | overidealize vb | overinvestment n |
| overexcite vt | overfastidious adj | overimaginative adj | overladen adj |
| overexercise vb | overfavour vt | overimpress vt | overlarge adj |
| overexert vt | overfearful adj | overimpressionable adj | overlavish adj |
| overexertion n | overfill vt | overinclined adj | overlend vb |
| overexpand vb | overfond adj | overindustrialization n | overlengthen vt |
| overexpansion n | overfull adj | overindustrialize vb | overliteral adj |
| overexpectant adj | overfund vt | overinflate vt | overliterary adj |
| overexpectation n | overfurnish vt | overinflation n | overloud adj |
| overexpenditure n | overfussy adj | overinfluence vt | overlush adj |
| overexplain vb | overgeneralization n | overinfluential adj | overmagnify vt |
| overexplicit adj | overgeneralize vb | overinform vt | overmanage vb |
| overexploit vt | overgenerous adj | overinsistence n | overmannered adj |
| overexploitation n | overgenerously adv | overinsistent adj | overmany adj |
| overexpressive adj | overglamorize vt | overinsistently adv | overmeasure n |
| overextravagant adj | overhastily adv | overintellectual adj | overmilk vt |
| overexuberant adj | overhasty adj | overintense adj | overmine vt |
| overfamiliar adj | overhunt vt | overintensely adv | overmix vt |
| overfamiliarity n | overhurried adj | overintensity n | overmodest adj |

**overnight** /-'niet/ *adv or adj* **1** on, during, or throughout the evening or night ⟨*stayed away ~*⟩ ⟨*an ~ stay*⟩ **2** suddenly ⟨*became famous ~*⟩ ⟨*~ fame*⟩

**overpage** /,ohvə'payj/ *adv* overleaf

**overpass** /-,pahs/ *n* a flyover; *also* the crossing of two roads, paths, railways, or combinations of these at different levels

**overpay** /-'pay/ *vt* **overpaid** to give excessively high payment to or for – **overpayment** *n*

**overpitch** /-'pich/ *vt* to bowl (a ball) in cricket so as to bounce nearer the batsman's wicket than intended and therefore provide the batsman with an easy shot

**overplay** /-'play/ *vt* **1a** to present (e g a dramatic role) extravagantly; exaggerate **b** to overemphasize **2** to strike a golf ball beyond (a putting green) ~ *vi* to play a role in an exaggerated manner – see also **overplay one's** HAND

**overplus** /-,plus/ *n* a surplus [ME, part trans of MF *surplus*]

**overpopulation** /-,popyoo'laysh(ə)n/ *n* the condition of having a population so dense as to cause environmental deterioration or an impaired quality of life – compare POPULATION EXPLOSION – **overpopulated** *adj*

**overpower** /-'powə/ *vt* **1** to overcome by superior force; defeat **2** to overwhelm – **overpoweringly** *adv*

**overpraise** /,ohvə'prayz/ *vt* to praise excessively

**overprice** /,ohvə'pries/ *vt* to price too high

**[1]overprint** /,ohvə'print/ *vt* to print over with something additional

**[2]overprint** *n* something added (as if) by overprinting; *esp* a printed marking added to a postage stamp, esp to alter the original or to commemorate a special event

**overproduce** /-prə'dyoohs/ *vt* to produce beyond demand, need, or allocation – **overproduction** *n*

**overproof** /-'proohf/ *adj* containing more alcohol than PROOF SPIRIT does

**overprotect** /,ohvəprə'tekt/ *vt* to protect unduly – **overprotection** *n*, **overprotective** *adj*

**overqualified** /,ohvə'kwolifed/ *adj* having more education, training, or experience than a job calls for

**overrate** /-'rayt/ *vt* to rate too highly; overvalue

**[1]overreach** /,ohvə'reech/ *vt* **1** to reach above or beyond **2** to defeat (oneself) by seeking to do or gain too much **3** to get the better of, esp in dealing and bargaining and typically by unscrupulous or crafty methods ~ *vi, of a horse* to strike the toe of the hind foot against the heel or quarter of the forefoot – **overreacher** *n*

**[2]overreach** /'ohvə,reech/ *n* a wound caused by a forefoot being struck by a hind foot

**overreach boot** *n* a protective boot worn by a horse to prevent injury from overreaching

**overreact** /-ri'akt/ *vi* to show an excessive or exaggerated reaction – **overreaction** *n*

**overrepresented** /,ohvə,repri'zentid/ *adj* represented excessively; *esp* having representatives in a proportion higher than the average

**[1]override** /-'ried/ *vt* **overrode** /-'rohd/; **overridden** /-'rid(ə)n/ **1** to ride (e g a horse) too much or too hard **2a** to prevail over; dominate ⟨*fear* overrode *all other emotions*⟩ ⟨*an* overriding *consideration*⟩ **b** to annul; SET ASIDE ⟨*cannot ~ their objections*⟩; *esp* to neutralize the action of (e g an automatic control) **3** to extend or pass over; *esp* to overlap

**[2]override** /'ohvə,ried/ *n* a device or system used to override a control

**overrider** /'ohvə,riedə/ *n, Br* a vertical attachment to the bumper of a motor vehicle for protection in a collision with another vehicle having bumpers at a different height

**overripe** /-'riep/ *adj* passed beyond maturity or ripeness towards decay

**overrule** /-'roohl/ *vt* **1** to prevail over; overcome ⟨*passion ~*d

*reason*⟩ **2** to rule against or set aside, esp by virtue of superior authority ⟨*the chairman ~*d *a point of order*⟩ ⟨*the court of appeal ~*d *the decision of the trial judge*⟩

**[1]overrun** /,ohvə'run/ *vb* **-nn-**; **overran** /'ran/ *vt* **1a** to defeat decisively and occupy the positions of **b** to swarm over; infest **2a** to run or go beyond or past ⟨*the plane* overran *the runway*⟩ **b** to exceed **c(1)** to readjust (set type) by shifting letters or words from one line into another **c(2)** OVERSET **2** (set too much type) **3** to flow over ~ *vi* to go beyond the necessary or desired point in space or time ⟨*don't ~ even by half a minute*⟩

**[2]overrun** /'ohvə,run/ *n* **1** an act or instance of overrunning; *esp* an exceeding of a limit (e g as to estimated cost, space, or time) **2** the amount by which something overruns **3** the slowing down of a vehicle engine owing to a reverse TORQUE (force causing rotation) from the wheels transmitted through the gears

**oversail** /'ohvə,sayl/ *vi* to project beyond what is below ⟨*the ~*ing *storey of a timber building*⟩

**oversea** /'ohvə,see/ *adj or adv* overseas

**[1]overseas** /-'seez/ *adv* beyond or across the seas ⟨*travelled ~*⟩

**[2]overseas** *adj* **1** of transport across the seas **2** of, from, or in places across the seas; foreign ⟨*an ~ travel allowance*⟩ ⟨*~ students here in London*⟩

**overseas student** *n* a student from abroad as contrasted with a home student

**oversee** /-'see/ *vt* **oversaw** /-'saw/; **overseen** /-'seen/ to supervise ⟨*he ~*s *the export department*⟩ △ overlook

**overseer** /-,see-ə/ *n* a superintendent, supervisor

**oversell** /-'sel/ *vt* **oversold** /-'sohld/ **1** to sell too much of; *esp* to sell more of than can be delivered **2** to make excessive claims for; overpraise – **oversell** *n*

**oversensitive** /-'sensətiv/ *adj* unduly or extremely sensitive – **oversensitiveness** *n*

**overset** /-'set/ *vt* **-tt-**; **overset 1a** to disturb mentally or physically; upset **b** to turn or tip over; overturn **2** to set too much type matter for – **overset** *n*

**oversew** /-,soh/ *vt* **oversewed** /-,sohd/; **oversewn** /-,sohn/, **oversewed** to sew over (an edge or two edges placed together), esp with small closely worked often vertical stitches, in order to neaten or make a firm seam

**oversexed** /-'sekst/ *adj* having an abnormally strong sexual drive

**overshadow** /-'shadoh/ *vt* **1** to cast a shadow over; darken **2** to exceed in importance; outweigh

**overshoe** /-,shooh/ *n* a usu rubber shoe worn over another as protection (e g from rain or snow)

**overshoot** /-'shooht/ *vt* **overshot** /-'shot/ to shoot or pass over or beyond, esp so as to miss ⟨*the bullet* overshot *the target*⟩ ⟨*the plane* overshot *the runway*⟩ – **overshoot** *n*

**[1]overshot** /,ohvə'shot/ *adj* **1a** *esp of a dog* having the upper jaw extending beyond the lower **b** *of an upper jaw* projecting beyond the lower jaw **2** driven by the weight of water passing over and flowing from above ⟨*an ~ waterwheel*⟩

**[2]overshot** /'ohvə,shot/ *n* a pattern or weave having WEFT (crosswise) threads that pass two or more WARP (lengthwise) yarns before reentering the fabric

**oversight** /-,siet/ *n* **1** supervision ⟨*has general ~ of the project*⟩ **2** an inadvertent omission or error

**oversimplify** /-'simpli,fie/ *vt* to simplify to such an extent as to bring about distortion, misunderstanding, or error ~ *vi* to engage in undue or extreme simplification – **oversimplification** *n*

**oversized** /'ohvə,siezd/ *also* **oversize** *adj* of a size greater than is common, proper, normal, or average ⟨*~ ears*⟩

**oversleep** /-'sleep/ *vi* **overslept** /-'slept/ to sleep beyond the intended time for waking

| | | | |
|---|---|---|---|
| **overmodestly** *adv* | **overornament** *vt* | **overprompt** *adj* | **overrich** *adj* |
| **overmodify** *vt* | **overparticular** *adj* | **overpromptly** *adv* | **overrighteous** *adj* |
| **overnice** *adj* | **overpeopled** *adj* | **overproud** *adj* | **overroast** *vt* |
| **overnourish** *vt* | **overpessimistic** *adj* | **overpublicize** *vt* | **overromanticize** *vb* |
| **overopinionated** *adj* | **overplan** *vb* | **overrefine** *vt* | **oversalt** *vt* |
| **overoptimism** *n* | **overpowerful** *adj* | **overrefined** *adj* | **oversanguine** *adj* |
| **overoptimist** *n* | **overprecise** *adj* | **overrefinement** *n* | **oversceptical** *adj* |
| **overoptimistic** *adj* | **overprescribe** *vb* | **overregulate** *vt* | **overscrupulous** *adj* |
| **overoptimistically** *adv* | **overprize** *vt* | **overregulation** *n* | **oversecretion** *n* |
| **overorchestrate** *vt* | **overprocess** *vt* | **overreliance** *n* | **overserious** *adj* |
| **overorganize** *vb* | **overprominent** *adj* | **overrespond** *vi* | **oversevere** *adj* |

**overspend** /-'spend/ *vb* **overspent** /-'spent/ *vt* **1** to spend or use to excess; exhaust **2** to spend more than (an allotted amount) ~ *vi* to spend beyond one's means – **overspender** *n*

**overspill** /-,spil/ *n, chiefly Br* the movement of excess urban population into less crowded areas (eg new towns); *also* the excess population itself ⟨*the London* ~⟩

**overspread** /,ohvə'spred/ *vt* **overspread** to spread over or above – **overspread** *n*

**overstate** /-'stayt/ *vt* to state in too strong terms; exaggerate – **overstatement** *n*

**overstay** /-'stay/ *vt* to stay beyond the time or the limits of ⟨~ *one's leave*⟩ ⟨~ *one's welcome*⟩

**oversteer** /-,stiə/ *n* the tendency of a motor vehicle to steer into a sharper turn than the driver intends – **oversteer** *vi*

**overstep** /-'step/ *vt* **-pp-** to exceed, transgress ⟨~ *the limits of good taste*⟩

**overstock** /,ohvə'stok/ *vt* to stock beyond requirements or facilities

**overstrung** /-'strung/ *adj* too highly strung; too sensitive

**overstuff** /-'stuf/ *vt* **1** to stuff too full **2** to cover (eg a chair or sofa) completely and deeply with upholstery

**oversubscribe** /-səb'skrieb/ *vt* to subscribe for more of than is offered for sale or available – usu pass ⟨*the tennis club is* ~d⟩ – **oversubscription** *n*

**oversubtle** /,ohvə'sutl/ *adj* excessively or impracticably subtle

**oversupply** /,ohvəsə'plie/ *n* an excessive supply – **oversupply** *vt*

**overt** /'ohvuht, ,-'-/ *adj* open to view; not concealed ⟨~ *hostilities*⟩ [ME, fr MF *ouvert*, *overt*, fr pp of *ouvrir* to open, fr (assumed) VL *operire*, alter. of L *aperire* – more at WEIR] – **overtly** *adv*, **overtness** *n*

**overtake** /-'tayk/ *vb* **overtook** /-'took/; **overtaken** /-'taykən/ *vt* **1a** to catch up with **b** to catch up with and pass beyond **2** to come upon suddenly ⟨*misfortune overtook them*⟩ ~ *vi, chiefly Br* to catch up with and pass by another vehicle going in the same direction *synonyms* see ¹PASS [ME *overtaken*, fr ¹*over* + *taken* to take]

**overtax** /-'taks/ *vt* **1** to tax too heavily **2** to put too great a burden or strain on

**over-the-'counter** *adj* **1** not traded or effected on an organized securities exchange (eg the stock market) ⟨~ *transactions*⟩; *esp* traded by negotiation between buyers and sellers or their representatives ⟨~ *securities*⟩ **2** *of a drug or medicine* sold lawfully without prescription

¹**overthrow** /-'throh/ *vt* **overthrew** /-'throoh/; **overthrown** /-'throhn/ **1** to overturn, upset **2** to cause the downfall of; ruin

²**overthrow** *n* **1** the act or an instance of overthrowing **2** a return of the ball from a fielder in cricket that eludes the fielders near the wickets and so allows a further run or runs to be scored; *also* a run so scored

**overtime** /-,tiem/ *n* **1** time in excess of a set limit; *esp* working time in excess of a standard day or week **2** the wage paid for overtime – **overtime** *adv*

**overtone** /-,tohn/ *n* **1a** any of the higher tones (HARMONICS) produced simultaneously with the FUNDAMENTAL (principal or lowest note) in a complex musical note – called also PARTIAL, UPPER PARTIAL **b** *physics* HARMONIC 2 (component frequency of a vibration or oscillation) **2** the colour of light reflected (eg by a paint) **3 overtones** *pl*, **overtone** a secondary effect, quality, or meaning; a suggestion ⟨*the unpleasant* ~s *of his speech*⟩ *synonyms* Both **overtone** and **undertone** mean that something has more in it than meets the eye; but an **overtone** is an additional "implication" ⟨*an* **overtone** *of envy in her enthusiasm*⟩ while an **undertone** is something inexplicit and pervasive ⟨*an* **undertone** *of pessimism in the City*⟩.

**overtop** /-'top/ *vt* **-pp-** **1** to rise above the top of **2** to surpass

**overtrack** /,ohvə'trak/ *vt, of a horse* to overtake (the forefeet) with the hind feet

**overtrade** /,ohvə'trayd/ *vi* to trade beyond one's capital ~ *vt* to make (the account of a client) excessively active by frequent purchases and sales, primarily to generate commissions

**overtrain** /,ohvə'trayn/ *vt* to train (eg an athlete) more than is necessary or desirable, esp to the point of loss of efficiency ~ *vi* to engage in excessive training

**overtrick** /-,trik/ *n* a card trick won in excess of the number bid – compare UNDERTRICK

**overtrump** /-'trump/ *vt* to trump with a higher trump card than the highest previously played on the same trick ~ *vi* to play a higher trump card than the highest previously played on the same trick

**overture** /'ohvəchə/ *n* **1a overtures** *pl*, **overture** an initiative towards agreement or action; a proposal ⟨*made* ~s *for peace*⟩ **b** something introductory; a prelude **2a** the orchestral introduction to a musical dramatic work **b** an orchestral concert piece written esp as a single movement in SONATA FORM [ME, lit., opening, fr MF, fr (assumed) VL *opertura*, alter. of L *apertura* – more at APERTURE]

¹**overturn** /,ohvə'tuhn/ *vt* **1** to cause to turn over; upset **2** to overthrow, destroy ~ *vi* TURN OVER

²**overturn** /'ohvə,tuhn/ *n* **1** overturning or being overturned **2** the sinking of surface water and rising of deeper water in a lake or sea that results from the changes in temperature that commonly occur in spring and autumn in temperate regions

**overuse** /,ohvə'joohs/ *n* excessive use – **overuse** *vt*

**overvalue** /,ohvə'valyooh/ *vt* to assign an excessive or fictitious value to – **overvaluation** *n*

**overview** /-,vyooh/ *n* a usu brief general survey; a summary

**overvoltage** /,ohvə'voltij, 'vohlt-/ *n* voltage in excess of the normal operating voltage of a device or circuit

**overweening** /-'weening/ *adj* **1** arrogant, presumptuous **2** immoderate, exaggerated [ME *overwening*, prp of *overwenen* to be arrogant, fr *over* + *wenen* to ween] – **overweeningly** *adv*

¹**overweight** /-,wayt/ *n* **1** weight above what is normal, average, or requisite **2** excessive or burdensome weight

²**overweight** /,ohvə'wayt/ *vt* **1** to give too much weight or consideration to **2** to weight excessively **3** to exceed in weight

³**overweight** *adj* exceeding the expected, normal, or proper weight; *esp* exceeding the body weight normal for one's age, height, and build

**overwhelm** /-'welm/ *vt* **1a** to cover over completely; submerge **b** to overcome by superior force or numbers; crush **2** to overpower with emotion ⟨~ed *by the death of his mother*⟩ [ME *overwhelmen*, fr ¹*over* + *whelmen* to turn over, cover up] – **overwhelmingly** *adv*

**overwind** /-'wiend/ *vt* **overwound** /-'wownd/ to wind (eg a watch) too much

¹**overwinter** /,ohvə'wintə/ *vi* **1** to survive the winter **2** to spend the winter – **overwintering** *adj*

²**overwinter** *adj* occurring during the period spanning the winter

**overwork** /-'wuhk/ *vt* **1** to cause to work too hard, too long, or to exhaustion **2** to make excessive use of ⟨*an* ~ed *and misused term*⟩ ~ *vi* to work too much or too long – **overwork** *n*

**overwrite** /-'riet/ *vb* **overwrote** /-'roht/; **overwritten** /-'ritn/ *vt* to write in inflated or pretentious style ~ *vi* to write too much or pretentiously

**overwrought** /-'rawt/ *adj* **1** extremely excited; *esp* nervously agitated **2** made with too much detail; overdone [fr pp of *overwork*]

**ovi-** /ohvi-/ – see OV-

**ovicide** /'ohvisied/ *n* something that kills eggs; *esp* an insecticide effective against the egg stage [ISV] – **ovicidal** *adj*

**oviduct** /'ohvi,dukt/ *n* a tube that serves for the passage of

---

eggs from an ovary [NL *oviductus*, fr *ov-* + *ductus* duct] – **oviductal** *adj*

**ovine** /'ohvien/ *adj* of or resembling sheep [LL *ovinus*, fr L *ovis* sheep – more at EWE] – **ovine** *n*

**oviparous** /oh'vipərəs/ *adj* producing eggs that develop and hatch outside the mother's body; *also* involving the production of such eggs – compare OVOVIVIPAROUS [L *oviparus*, fr *ov-* + *-parus* -parous] – **oviparously** *adv*, **oviparousness** *n*

**oviposit** /,ohvi'pozit/ *vi*, *esp of an insect* to lay eggs [prob back-formation fr *ovipositor*] – **oviposition** *n*, **ovipositional** *adj*

**ovipositor** /'ohvipozitə/ *n* a specialized organ, esp of an insect, for depositing eggs [NL, fr L *ov-* + *positor* one who or that which places, fr *positus*, pp of *ponere* to place – more at POSITION]

**ovisac** /'ohvisak/ *n* EGG CASE (protective case enclosing eggs) [ISV]

**ovo-** – see OV-

**ovoid** /'ohvoyd/, **ovoidal** /oh'voydl/ *adj* shaped like an egg; OVATE [Fr *ovoïde*, fr L *ovum* egg – more at EGG] – **ovoid** *n*

**ovolo** /'ohvə,loh/ *n*, *pl* **ovolos** a rounded convex moulding [It, dim. of *uovo*, *ovo* egg, fr L *ovum*]

**Ovonics** /oh'voniks/ *n taking sing vb* a branch of electronics that deals with applications of the change from an electrically nonconducting state to a semiconducting state shown by glasses of special composition upon application of a certain minimum voltage [Stanford R *Ov*shinsky *b* 1923 US inventor + electr*onics*] – **ovonic** *adj*

**ovotestis** /,ohvoh'testis/ *n* a GONAD (organ producing sex cells) (eg in some snails) that produces both eggs and sperm [NL]

**ovoviviparous** /,ohvohvi'vipərəs/ *adj* producing eggs that develop within the mother's body and hatch within the mother or immediately after having been laid – compare OVIPAROUS – **ovoviviparity** *n*, **ovoviviparously** *adv*, **ovoviviparousness** *n*

¹**ovulate** /'ovyoolayt, -lət/ *adj* bearing a developing seed

²**ovulate** /'ovyoolayt/ *vi* to produce eggs or discharge them from an ovary – **ovulation** *n*, **ovulatory** *adj*

**ovule** /'ovyoohl, 'oh-/ *n* **1** an outgrowth of the ovary of a SEED PLANT that develops into a seed after fertilization of the egg cell it contains **2** a small egg; *esp* one in an early stage of growth [NL *ovulum*, dim. of L *ovum*] – **ovular** *adj*

**ovum** /'ohvəm/ *n*, *pl* **ova** /'ohvə/ an animal's female GAMETE (reproductive cell) that when fertilized can develop into a new individual; MACROGAMETE [NL, fr L, egg – more at EGG]

**ow** /ow/ *interj* – used esp to express sudden slight pain

**owe** /oh/ *vt* **1** to have or bear (an emotion or attitude) to somebody or something specified ⟨~s *the boss a grudge*⟩ **2a(1)** to be under obligation to pay or repay in return for something given or performed (eg a loan or service) ⟨~s *me five pounds*⟩ **a(2)** to be under obligation to render (eg duty or service) ⟨~s *me a favour*⟩ **b** to be indebted to ⟨~s *the garage for the last service*⟩ **3** to have or enjoy as a result of the action or existence of something or somebody else ⟨~s *his fame to luck*⟩ – *vi* to be in debt ⟨~s *for his house*⟩ **usage** see ¹DUE [ME *owen* to possess, own, owe, fr OE *āgan*; akin to OHG *eigun* (1 & 3 pl pres indic) possess, Skt *īśe* he possesses] – **owing to** because of ⟨*delayed* owing to *a crash*⟩

**owl** /owl/ *n* any of an order (Strigiformes) of BIRDS OF PREY with a large head and eyes, a short hooked bill, strong claws, and more or less nocturnal habits [ME *owle*, fr OE *ūle*; akin to OHG *uwila* owl]

**owlet** /'owlit/ *n* a small or young owl

**owlish** /'owlish/ *adj* resembling or suggesting an owl, esp in having a round face or a wide-eyed stare – **owlishly** *adv*, **owlishness** *n*

¹**own** /ohn/ *adj* **1** belonging to, for, or relating to oneself or itself – usu after a possessive pronoun ⟨*cooked his* ~ *dinner*⟩ **2** immediately related ⟨~ *sister to the queen*⟩ [ME *owen*, fr OE *āgen*; akin to OHG *eigan* own, ON *eiginn*, OE *āgan* to possess – more at OWE] – **be one's own man/woman** to think and act independently

²**own** *vt* **1** to have or hold as property; possess **2** to acknowledge to be true, valid, or as claimed to admit – + *to* **synonyms** see ACKNOWLEDGE *antonym* repudiate – **owner** *n*, **ownership** *n*

**own up** *vi* to confess a fault frankly ⟨*if your ball broke the window... you* own up – *Boy Scout Handbook*⟩

³**own** *pron*, *pl* **own** one belonging to oneself or itself – usu after a possessive pronoun ⟨*a country with oil of its* ~⟩ ⟨*gave out books so that every student had his* ~⟩ – **come into one's**

**own 1** to receive one's rightful property (eg an inheritance) **2** to show one's true worth, ability, etc – **get one's own back** to have revenge – **hold one's own** to maintain one's ground, position, or strength in the face of competition or adversity

**own-'brand** *adj* of or being goods offered for sale under the label or trade name of the retail distributor (eg a chain store)

**owner-occupier** *n*, *Br* a person who lives in a house that he/she owns or is buying – **owner-occupied** *adj*

**own goal** *n* a goal (eg in soccer) hit by a player into his/her own net which therefore counts for the opposing team

**owt** /owt/ *n*, *NEng* anything [var of *aught*]

**ox** /oks/ *n*, *pl* **oxen** /'oks(ə)n/ *also* **ox 1** a domestic species of bovine mammal (*Bos taurus*); *broadly* any bovine mammal **2** an adult castrated male domestic ox [ME, fr OE *oxa*; akin to OHG *ohso* ox, Gk *hygros* wet – more at HUMOUR]

**ox-, oxo-** *comb form* **1** oxygen **2** containing a CARBONYL group in the molecular structure; KETONE ⟨*oxoacetic acid*⟩ [Fr, fr *oxygène*]

**oxalate** /'oksə,layt/ *n* any of various chemical compounds (SALTS or ESTERS) formed by combination between OXALIC ACID and a metal atom, an alcohol, or another chemical group

**oxalic acid** /ok'salik/ *n* a poisonous strong acid, $(COOH)_2$, that occurs in various plants as oxalates and is used esp as a bleaching or cleaning agent and in making dyes [Fr (*acide*) *oxalique*, fr L *oxalis* wood sorrel]

**oxalis** /'ok'sa(h)lis, 'oksəlis/ *n* WOOD SORREL [NL, genus name, fr L, wood sorrel, fr Gk, fr *oxys* sharp – more at OXYGEN]

**oxaloacetate** /,oksəloh'asitayt/, **oxalacetate** /,oksəl'asitayt/ *n* any of various chemical compounds (SALTS or ESTERS) formed by combination between OXALOACETIC ACID and a metal atom, an alcohol, or another chemical group

**oxaloacetic** /,oksəloh-ə'seetik, -'setik/, **oxalacetic** /,oksəlǝ '-seetik, -'setik/ *adj* involving OXALOACETIC ACID or its production

**oxaloacetic acid** *n* an acid, $HO_2CCOCH_2COOH$, that is formed during the biochemical processing (METABOLISM) of carbohydrates to produce energy for a living organism or cell [*oxalic* + *acetic acid*]

**oxalosuccinic acid** /,oksəloh•sək'sinik, ok,saloh-/ *n* an acid, $C_6H_6O_7$, that is formed as an intermediate product in the biochemical processing (METABOLISM) of fats and carbohydrates to produce energy [*oxalic* + *succinic acid*]

**oxazine** /'oksəzeen/ *n* any of several chemical compounds, $C_4H_5NO$, containing a ring structure composed of four carbon atoms, one oxygen atom, and one nitrogen atom [ISV *ox-* + *azine*]

**oxblood** /'oks,blud/ *n* a medium reddish-brown colour

**oxbow** /'oks,boh/ *n* **1** a U-shaped frame forming a collar about a draught ox's neck and supporting the yoke **2a** something (eg a bend in a river) shaped like an oxbow **b oxbow lake, oxbow** a horseshoe-shaped lake formed when a meandering river cuts across an oxbow bend – **oxbow** *adj*

**Oxbridge** /'oks,brij/ *adj or n* (of) the universities of Oxford and Cambridge ⟨*the predominance of graduates of* ~ *in the diplomatic service*⟩ [*Ox*ford + Cam*bridge*]

**oxer** /'oksə/ *n* an obstacle for horses to jump consisting of a hedge, rails, and sometimes a ditch [*ox* + ²*-er*; orig sense, hedge or fence to confine cattle]

**oxeye** /'oks,ei/ *n* any of several plants (eg of the genera *Chrysanthemum*, *Heliopsis*, or *Buphthalmum*) of the daisy family with both DISC FLOWERS (central short flowers) and RAY FLOWERS (outer strap-shaped flowers); *esp* OXEYE DAISY

**oxeye daisy** *n* a leafy-stemmed European plant (*Chrysanthemum leucanthemum*) that has long white strap-shaped RAY FLOWERS and grows esp in grassland – called also MOON DAISY

**oxford** /'oksfəd/ *n*, *NAm* a low shoe laced or tied over the instep [*Oxford*, city in England]

**Oxford accent** *n* an exaggerated form of RP believed to be spoken at Oxford university

**Oxford bags** /'oksfəd/ *n pl* wide-legged trousers

**Oxford down** *n*, *often cap D* (any of) a Down breed of large hornless sheep developed by crossing Cotswolds and Hampshires [*Oxfordshire*, county in England]

**Oxford Group** *n* a movement founded by Frank Buchman in 1921 and stressing the reform of personal and social morality – compare MORAL REARMAMENT

**Oxford movement** *n* a HIGH CHURCH movement within the CHURCH OF ENGLAND begun at Oxford in 1833

**oxidant** /'oksid(ə)nt/ *n* OXIDIZING AGENT – **oxidant** *adj*

**oxidase** /'oksidayz, -ays/ *n* any of various ENZYMES that speed up oxidations; *esp* one able to react directly with molecules of oxygen [ISV] – **oxidasic** *adj*

**oxidation** /,oksi'daysh(ə)n/ *n* 1 the act or process of oxidizing 2 the state or result of being oxidized [Fr, fr *oxider, oxyder* to oxidize, fr *oxide*] – **oxidative** *adj*, **oxidatively** *adv*

**oxidation number** *n* the degree of or potential for oxidation of a chemical element or an atom which is usu expressed as a positive or negative number representing the IONIC or effective electric charge; VALENCY

**oxi,dation-re'duction** *n* a chemical reaction in which one or more electrons are transferred from one atom or molecule to another

**oxidation state** *n* OXIDATION NUMBER

**oxidative phosphorylation** /'oksi,daytiv/ *n* the synthesis of the energy-storing chemical compound ATP, that takes place in the MITOCHONDRIA (specialized cell parts) during the processes (RESPIRATION) by which oxygen is used to provide energy in a living organism or a cell

**oxide** /'oksied/ *n* a chemical compound consisting of oxygen with a chemical element or group [Fr *oxide, oxyde*, fr *ox-* (fr *oxygène* oxygen) + *-ide* (fr *acide* acid)] – **oxidic** *adj*

**oxid·ize, -ise** /'oksi,diez/ *vt* 1 to combine with oxygen 2 to remove hydrogen from, esp by the action of oxygen 3 to change (a chemical compound) by increasing the proportion of the part that has a negative electric charge, or change (an element or ion) from a lower to a higher positive VALENCY; remove one or more electrons from (an atom, ion, or molecule) ∼ *vi* to become oxidized [*oxide* + *-ize*] – **oxidizable** *adj*

**oxidizer** /'oksidiezə/ *n* OXIDIZING AGENT; *esp* one that combines with the fuel used to propel a rocket

**oxidizing agent** /'oksidiezing/ *n* a substance that oxidizes something, esp chemically (e g by gaining electrons) – compare REDUCING AGENT

**oxidoreductase** /,oksidoh·ri'duktayz, -ays/ *n* an ENZYME that speeds up an oxidation-reduction reaction [*oxidation* + *-o-* + *reduction* + *-ase*]

**oxime** /'okseem/ *n* any of various chemical compounds characterized by the grouping C=NOH [ISV *ox-* + *-ime* (fr *imide*)]

**oxlip** /'oks,lip/ *n* a Eurasian primula (*Primula elatior*) similar to the cowslip, but unscented and having larger flowers [(assumed) ME *oxeslippe*, fr OE *oxanslyppe*, lit., ox dung, fr *oxa* ox + *slypa, slyppe* paste – more at SLIP (cf COWSLIP)]

**oxo-** – see OX-

**Oxonian** /ok'sohnyən, -ni·ən/ *n* a student or graduate of Oxford University [ML *Oxonia* Oxford] – **Oxonian** *adj*

**oxpecker** /'oks,pekə/ *n* any of several African birds (genus *Buphagus*) that perch on large animals and feed on ticks – called also TICKBIRD

**oxtail** /'oks,tayl/ *n* the tail of cattle, esp when skinned and used for food (e g in soup)

**oxter** /'okstə/ *n, chiefly Scot & Irish* the armpit [(assumed) ME, alter. of OE *ōxta*; akin to L *axilla* armpit – more at AXIS]

**oxtongue** /-,tung/ *n* any of several plants having rough tongue-shaped leaves: e g **a** a bugloss (genus *Anchusa*) **b** any of several plants (genus *Picris*) of the daisy family; *esp* a Eurasian one (*Picris echioides*) that has yellow flowers and is covered with bristly hairs

**oxy** /'oksi/ *adj* containing or using (additional) oxygen – often in combination ⟨oxy*haemoglobin*⟩ ⟨oxy*hydrogen*⟩ [Fr, fr *oxygène* oxygen]

**oxyacetylene** /,oksi·ə'set(ə)lin, -leen/ *adj* of or using a mixture of oxygen and acetylene, esp for producing a hot flame ⟨*an* ∼ *torch*⟩ [ISV]

**oxyacid** /'oksi,asid/ *n* an acid (e g SULPHONIC ACID) that contains oxygen

**oxygen** /'oksij(ə)n/ *n* a chemical element that is found free as a colourless tasteless odourless gas in the atmosphere of which it forms about 21 per cent by volume or that is found combined in water, in most rocks and minerals, and in numerous ORGANIC compounds. It is capable of combining with all elements except the INERT GASES (e g argon and xenon), is essential for the life of all higher organisms (e g plants and animals), and is required for most combustion processes. [Fr *oxygène*, fr Gk *oxys*, adj, acid, lit., sharp (akin to L *acer* sharp – more at EDGE) + Fr *-gène* -gen fr the former belief that it was present in all acids] – **oxygenless** *adj*, **oxygenic** *adj*, **oxygenicity** *n*

**oxygen acid** *n* an oxyacid

**oxygenate** /'oksijənayt/ *vt* to impregnate, combine, or supply (e g blood) with oxygen – **oxygenation** *n*

**oxygenator** /'oksijənaytə/ *n* something (e g an apparatus for forcing a gas through an organ or tissue) that oxygenates

**oxygen cycle** *n* the cycle whereby oxygen from the atmosphere is converted to CARBON DIOXIDE in animal RESPIRATION (processes providing energy) and regenerated by green plants in PHOTOSYNTHESIS

**oxygen debt** *n* a cumulative lack of oxygen that develops during periods of intense bodily activity and must be made up when the body returns to rest

**oxygen-ize, -ise** /'oksijəniez/ *vt* to oxygenate

**oxygen mask** *n* a device worn over the nose and mouth (e g by aircrew at high altitudes) through which oxygen is supplied from a storage tank

**oxygen tent** *n* a canopy which can be placed over a bedridden person and within which a flow of oxygen-enriched air can be maintained

**oxyhaemoglobin** /,oksi,heemə'glohbin/ *n* HAEMOGLOBIN (red blood pigment) loosely combined with oxygen that it releases to the tissues [ISV]

**oxyhydrogen** /,oksi'hiedrəjən/ *adj* of or using a mixture of oxygen and hydrogen ⟨*an* ∼ *torch*⟩

**oxymoron** /,oksi'mawron/ *n, pl* **oxymora** /-rə/ a combination of contradictory or incongruous words (e g *cruel kindness*, the *wisest fool* in Christendom) [LGk *oxymōron*, fr neut of *oxymōros* pointedly foolish, fr Gk *oxys* sharp, keen + *mōros* foolish – more at MORON]

**oxyphilic** /,oksi'filik/ *also* **oxyphile** /'oksi,fiel/, **oxyphil** /-,fil/ *adj* ACIDOPHILIC [Gk *oxys* acid + E *-phil* – more at OXYGEN] – **oxyphile** *also* **oxyphil** *n*

**oxyphilous** /ok'sifiləs/ *adj, of a plant* living only in an acid environment

**oxysulphide** /,oksi'sulfied/ *n* a SULPHIDE having oxygen atoms in place of some of the sulphur atoms but that nevertheless retains the basic properties of a sulphide

**oxytetracycline** /,oksi,tetrə'sieklien/ *n* an antibiotic, $C_{22}H_{24}N_2O_9$, obtained from a bacterium (*Streptomyces rimosus*) and used in the treatment of a large number of infections including WHOOPING COUGH and pneumonia

**oxytocic** /,oksi'tohsik/ *adj* hastening childbirth; *also* inducing contraction of the muscular wall of the womb [ISV, fr Gk *oxys* sharp, quick + *tokos* childbirth, fr *tiktein* to bear – more at THANE] – **oxytocic** *n*

**oxytocin** /-'tohsin/ *n* a hormone, $C_{43}H_{66}N_{12}O_{12}S_2$, secreted by the PITUITARY GLAND that stimulates contractions of the muscular wall of the womb esp during childbirth and assists the release of milk [ISV, fr *oxytocic*]

**oxytone** /'oksitohn/ *adj* 1 *of a classical Greek word* having an acute accent denoting a rising tone on the last syllable 2 having heavy stress on the last syllable [Fr *oxyton*, fr Gk *oxytonos*, fr *oxys* sharp, acute in pitch + *tonos* tone] – **oxytone** *n*

**oyer and terminer** /,oyər ənd 'tuhminə/ *n* a commission formerly authorizing a British judge to hear and decide a criminal case before a court of ASSIZES [ME, part trans of AF *oyer et terminer*, lit., to hear and determine]

**oyez** /oh'yay, -yes/ *interj* – uttered by a court official or public crier to gain silence and attention before an announcement [ME, fr AF, hear ye, imper pl of *oir* to hear, fr L *audire* – more at AUDIBLE]

**OYO** *n, Austr* a flat owned by the resident [*O*wn *Y*our *O*wn]

**oyster** /'oystə/ *n* 1 any of various often edible marine INVERTEBRATE animals (family Ostreidae of the phylum Mollusca) that have a rough irregular hinged shell and that occur usu in coastal waters or estuaries; *also* any of various similar or related animals 2 something regarded as freely available for one's own benefit or enjoyment ⟨*the world's my* ∼⟩ 3 a small mass of muscle contained in a hollow of the pelvic bone on each side of the back of a fowl 4 a pinkish-white colour, sometimes with a greyish tone [ME, *oistre*, fr MF, fr L *ostrea*, fr Gk *ostreon*; akin to Gk *ostrakon* shell, *osteon* bone – more at OSSEOUS; (2) fr the notion of prising open an oyster to find a pearl inside]

**oyster bed** *n* a place where oysters grow or are cultivated

**oystercatcher** /-,kachə/ *n* any of a genus (*Haematopus*, esp *Haematopus ostralegus*) of wading birds that have stout pink legs, often black and white plumage, and a heavy wedge-shaped orange beak adapted for opening the shells of mussels, cockles, etc

**oyster crab** *n* a crab (*Pinnotheres ostreum*) that lives in the gill cavity of the oyster and gleans food from currents of water passing over the gills

**oyster drill** *n* DRILL 4 (marine snail)

**oyster farm** *n* a stretch of sea bottom where oysters are bred for food

**oystering** /'oystəring/ *n* the act or business of taking oysters for the market or for food

**oysterman** /'oystəmən/ *n* somebody who gathers, opens, breeds, or sells oysters

**oyster plant** *n* salsify [fr the oyster-like flavour of its roots]

**¹Oz** /oz/ *adj, Austr informal* Australian [by shortening & alter.]

**²Oz** *n, Austr informal* Australia

**ozocerite** /ˌohzoh'siəriet/ *n* a waxy substance often found with petroleum that is colourless or white when pure, often smells unpleasant, and is used esp in making candles and waxed paper, in ELECTROTYPING (a printing process), and in insulating [Ger ozokerit, fr Gk *ozein* to smell + *kēros* wax – more at CERUMEN]

**ozokerite** /ˌohzoh'kiəriet/ *n* ozocerite

**ozon-, ozono-** *comb form* ozone ⟨*ozonize*⟩ [ISV, fr *ozone*]

**ozone** /'oh,zohn/ *n* 1 a form of oxygen with three atoms in each molecule, $O_3$, that is a bluish irritating gas with a pungent smell and that is formed naturally in the upper atmosphere by a chemical reaction between oxygen in the air and ultraviolet light from the sun. It can also be generated commercially, and is used esp in sterilizing water and purifying air, and in OXIDATION and bleaching **2** *informal* pure and refreshing air ⟨*a breath of ~ at the seaside*⟩ [Ger *ozon*, fr Gk *ozōn*, prp of *ozein* to smell – more at ODOUR] – **ozonous, ozonic** *adj,* **ozoniferous** *adj,*

**ozonide** /'ohzohnied/ *n* a compound of ozone; *specif* an unstable chemical compound formed by the addition of ozone to the DOUBLE BOND between two carbon atoms in an organic compound

**ozon·ize, -ise** /'ohzohniez/ *vt* **1** to convert (oxygen) into ozone **2** to treat, impregnate, or combine with ozone – **ozonizer** *n,* **ozonization** *n*

**ozonosphere** /oh'zohnəsfiə, -'zonə-/ *n* an atmospheric layer at heights of approximately 30 to 50 kilometres (about 20 to 30 miles) characterized by high ozone content

# P

**p, P** /pee/ *n, pl* **p's, ps, P's, Ps 1a** the 16th letter of the English alphabet **b** a graphic representation of or device for reproducing the letter *p* **c** a speech counterpart of printed or written *p* **2** one designated *p*, esp as the 16th in order or class **3a** a mark or grade rating a pupil's or student's work as passing **b** one who or which is graded or rated with a P **4** something shaped like the letter P *usage* see ³PEE [(3) abbr of *pass*]

**¹pa** /pah/ *n, informal* father [short for *papa*]

**²pa** *n* a Maori village [Maori]

**pa'anga** /pah'ang(g)ə/ *n* – see MONEY table [Tongan, lit., seed]

**PABA** /'pahbə/ *n* PARA-AMINOBENZOIC ACID (substance promoting growth in an organism) [*para-amino-benzoic acid*]

**pabulum** /'pabyooləm/ *n, formal* **1** food **2** intellectual sustenance [L, food, fodder; akin to L *pascere* to feed – more at FOOD]

**paca** /'pakə, 'pahkə/ *n* any of a genus (*Cuniculus*) of large S and Central American burrowing rodents; *esp* a common edible rodent (*Cuniculus paca*) of northern S America that has a brown coat spotted with white and a hide used locally for leather [Pg & Sp, fr Tupi *páca*]

**¹pace** /pays/ *n* **1a** rate of movement ⟨*a ~ of five miles an hour*⟩ ⟨*the favourite set the ~ from the start*⟩ **b** rate of progress; *specif* parallel rate of growth or development ⟨*wages do not keep ~ with inflation*⟩ **c** rate or manner of doing something ⟨*the dizzy social ~ of the jet set*⟩ **d(1)** rate of performance or delivery; tempo **d(2)** rhythmic animation; fluency ⟨*his narrative style has ~*⟩ **2a** a manner of walking; a tread **b** a gait; *esp* a fast 2-beat gait of a horse in which the legs on each side move together **3a** STEP 2a(1) **b** the distance covered by a single step in walking, usu taken to be about 0.75 metre (about 30 inches) **c** an old Roman unit of distance equal to the distance between successive impacts of the same heel (about 1.50 metres or 60 inches) **4** *pl* an exhibition of skills or capacities ⟨*the trainer put the tiger through its ~s*⟩ **5** fast bowling in cricket ⟨*~ was the main weapon*⟩ [ME *pas*, fr OF, step, fr L *passus*, fr *passus*, pp of *pandere* to spread – more at FATHOM] – **go the pace 1** to go at a great speed **2** to live a hectic life ⟨*he believes in going the pace, he's never in bed before 2am*⟩

**²pace** *vi* **1a** to walk with slow or measured tread **b** to move along; proceed **2** *of a horse* to go at a pace ⟨*~*⟩ ~ *vt* **1a** to measure by pacing ⟨*~d out a rough cricket pitch*⟩ – often + *out* or *off* **b** to traverse at a walk ⟨*could hear him pacing the floor*⟩ **2** *of a horse* to cover (a course) by pacing **3a** to set or regulate the pace of ⟨*~s his teaching to his students' abilities*⟩; *specif* to go ahead of (e g a runner or cyclist) as a pacemaker in racing or training **b** to go before; precede **c** to keep pace with

**³pace** /'paysi/ *prep* with due respect to ⟨*I feel, ~ the last speaker, that we should adjourn*⟩ △ vice, vide [L, abl of *pac-*, *pax* peace, permission]

**pace bowler** /pays/ *n* one who bowls the ball fast in cricket

**pace car** *n* a motor car that leads the field of competitors through a warm-up lap but does not participate in the race

**pacemaker** /-,maykə/ *n* **1a** one who or that which sets the pace for another, esp in a race **b** one who or that which takes the lead or sets an example **2a** the SINOATRIAL NODE (small area of tissue in the wall of the heart) or other body part that serves to establish and maintain a rhythmic activity **b** an electronic device implanted in the heart for applying regular electric shocks to stimulate or steady the heartbeat or reestablish the rhythm of a heart that has stopped beating – **pacemaking** *n*

**paceman** /'paysmən/ *n* PACE BOWLER

**pacer** /'paysə/ *n* **1** one who or that which paces; *specif* a horse whose gait is the pace **2** a pacemaker

**pacesetter** /-,setə/ *n* PACEMAKER 1

**pachisi** /pə'cheezi, pah-/ *n* an ancient Indian board game played with dice or cowrie shells and counters on a cross-shaped board in which players attempt to be the first to reach

the home square [Hindi *pacīsī*, fr *pacīs* twenty-five (the highest throw in the game)]

**pachyderm** /'pakiduhm/ *n* any of various NONRUMINANT hoofed mammals (e g an elephant, rhinoceros, or pig), most of which have thick skins and are large [Fr *pachyderme*, fr Gk *pachydermos* thick-skinned, fr *pachys* thick (akin to ON *bingr* heap, Skt *bahu* dense, much) + *derma* skin – more at DERM-] – **pachydermal** *adj*

**pachydermatous** /,paki'duhmətəs/ *adj* **1** of the pachyderms **2** thick, thickened ⟨*~ skin*⟩ [deriv of Gk *pachys* + *dermat-*, *derma* skin] – **pachydermatously** *adv*

**pachytene** /'pakiteen/ *n, genetics* the stage of MEIOSIS (splitting of a cell and its contents into four new cells) in which the paired CHROMOSOMES (strands of gene-carrying material) shorten and thicken and split longitudinally into two strands (CHROMATIDS) on either side of the central part (CENTROMERE) of the chromosome [ISV *pachy-* (fr Gk *pachys*) + *-tene*]

**pacific** /pə'sifik/ *adj* **1a pacific, pacificatory** /pə'sifikət(ə)ri, ,pasi'fikət(ə)ri/ tending to lessen conflict; conciliatory **b** rejecting the use of force as an instrument of policy **2a** having a soothing appearance or effect ⟨*mild ~ breezes*⟩ **b** mild of temper; peaceable **3** *cap* of the Pacific ocean [MF *pacifique*, fr L *pacificus*, fr *pac-*, *pax* peace + *-i-* + *-ficus* -fic – more at PEACE] – **pacifically** *adv*

> **synonyms** Pacific, peaceable, and peaceful should not be confused. Pacific describes people, actions, speeches, ideas, etc which tend to conciliate or preserve the peace ⟨**pacific** policy⟩. Peaceable suggests a peace-loving temperament and a complete absence of any aggressive intention ⟨**peaceable** citizens going about their business⟩. Peaceful describes a state or condition where peace reigns ⟨a **peaceful** scene⟩ or may approach **peaceable** in stressing an absence of violence ⟨**peaceful** demonstrations⟩.
> **antonyms** bellicose, belligerent, aggressive

**pacifier** /'pasifie·ə/ *n* **1** one who or that which pacifies **2** *chiefly NAm* a baby's dummy

**pacifism** /'pasifiz(ə)m/ *n* **1** opposition to war or violence as a means of settling disputes; *specif* refusal to bear arms on moral or religious grounds **2** an attitude or policy of nonresistance [Fr *pacifisme*, fr *pacifique* pacific] – **pacifist** *n*

**pacifist** /'pasifist/ *adj* **1** (characteristic) of pacifism or pacifists **2** strongly and actively opposed to conflict, esp war – **pacifistically** *adv*

**pacify** /'pasifie/ *vt* **1a** to allay the anger or agitation of; soothe ⟨*~ a crying child*⟩ **b** to appease, propitiate **2a** to restore to a tranquil state; settle ⟨*made an attempt to ~ the commotion*⟩ **b** to reduce to a submissive state; subdue ⟨*forces moved in to ~ the country*⟩ [ME *pacifien*, fr L *pacificare*, fr *pac-*, *pax* peace] – **pacifiable** *adj*, **pacification** *n*

**Pacinian corpuscle** /pə'siniən/ *n* an oval capsule that terminates some nerve fibres, esp in the skin of the hands and feet, and is involved in the sensation of pressure [Filippo *Pacini* †1883 It anatomist]

**¹pack** /pak/ *n* **1a** a bundle or bag for goods or equipment carried on the shoulders or back; *specif* a knapsack **b** a usu ordered collection of related objects: e g **b(1)** a number of separate photographic films packed so as to be inserted together into a camera **b(2)** a set of two or three colour films or plates for simultaneous exposure **b(3)** a stack of flat theatrical scenery arranged in sequence **c(1)** a container ⟨*jam in individual ~s*⟩ **c(2)** a compact manufactured article designed to perform a specific function ⟨*a radio power ~*⟩ – compare POWER PACK **2a** the contents of a bundle or bag **b** a large amount or number; a heap ⟨*a ~ of lies*⟩ **c** a full set of playing cards **3a** an act or instance of packing **b** a method of packing ⟨*vacuum ~*⟩ **4** *taking sing or pl vb* **4a** a set of people with a common interest; a clique **b** an organized troop (e g of cub scouts or brownie guides) **c** the forwards in a rugby team, esp when acting together (e g in a scrum) **5** *taking sing or pl vb* **5a** a number of wild or domesticated animals that are kept or naturally group together, esp for hunting ⟨a wolf ~⟩ ⟨a ~ of hounds⟩ **b** an organized group of combat craft ⟨a submarine ~⟩ **6** a concentrated mass (e g of snow); *specif* PACK ICE **7** wet absorbent material (e g gauze) for therapeutic application to the body, esp to fill bleeding cavities temporarily **8** a face-pack **9** material used in packing **10** *chiefly NAm* a packet ⟨a ~ of cigarettes⟩ [ME, of LG or D origin; akin to MLG & MD *pak* pack, MFlem *pac*]

²**pack** *vt* **1a** to stow (as if) in a container, esp for transportation or for carrying with one on a journey ⟨goods ~ed for shipment⟩ ⟨~ your toothbrush⟩ **b** to fill completely ⟨~ed the stadium⟩ **c** to cover, fill, or surround with packing material, esp for protection ⟨~ a joint in a pipe⟩ **2a** to crowd together; assemble in a compact group **b** to increase the density of; compress **3** to gather into tight formation; make a pack of (e g hounds) **4** to cover or surround with a pack **5** to cause or be capable of making or delivering (an impact) ⟨a book that ~s quite a punch⟩ **6** *informal* to bring to an end; finish – usu + *up* or *in* ⟨~ up the assignment⟩ ⟨he's ~ing it all in and cycling round the world⟩ ~ *vi* **1a** to stow goods or equipment for transportation – often + *up* **b** to be suitable for packing ⟨this dress ~s without wrinkling⟩ **2a** to assemble in a group; congregate **b** to crowd together **3** to become built up or compacted in a layer or mass ⟨the ore ~ed into a stony mass⟩ – see also SEND packing – **packable** *adj*, **packer** *n*, **packability** *n*

**pack off** *vt, informal* to send away, esp abruptly or unceremoniously ⟨packed the kids off to school⟩

**pack up** *vi* **1** to leave abruptly ⟨packed up and went⟩ **2** to finish work ⟨pack up and go home⟩ **3** *informal* to cease to function ⟨the engine seems to have packed up⟩

³**pack** *vt* to influence the composition of esp a political body or a meeting so as to bring about a desired result ⟨~ a jury⟩ ⟨they ~ed the meeting and won the vote⟩ [obs *pack* to make a secret agreement, perh alter. of *pact*]

⁴**pack** *adj* able to be broken into several loads for transport ⟨a 105mm ~ howitzer⟩

¹**package** /'pakij/ *n* **1a** a small or moderate-sized pack; a parcel **b** something wrapped or sealed **c** a preassembled unit **2** a wrapper or container in which something is packed **3** something that suggests a package: e g **3a** a group of contract benefits gained through collective bargaining usu between management and union **b(1)** a ready-made computer program or set of programs for carrying out a relatively generalized operation (e g accounting or stock control) that is usu sold as a self-contained immediately usable product **b(2)** an assembly or apparatus complete and ready for installation or use **c package holiday, package** a holiday usu organized by a travel agent or tour operator in which transport and accommodation are provided and included in the basic cost of the holiday **d package deal, package** an offer or agreement involving a number of related items which must be accepted or rejected as a unit; *also* the items offered in a package deal

²**package** *vt* **1** to make into a package **2** to enclose in a package or covering **3** to present (a person or product) in a way that will appeal to an audience – **packager** *n*

**packaging** /'pakijing/ *n* **1** the design and manufacture of materials used for packing goods **2** material used for packing **3** the promotion of the image of a product or of a person in the media ⟨the ~ is great; but the product is rubbish⟩

**pack animal** *n* an animal (e g a donkey) used for carrying packs

**pack drill** *n* a military punishment consisting of marching up and down in full kit

**packed** /pakt/ *adj* **1a** crowded or stuffed – often in combination ⟨an action-packed story⟩ **b** compressed ⟨hard-packed snow⟩ **2** filled to capacity ⟨played to a ~ house⟩

**packet** /'pakit/ *n* **1** a number of letters dispatched at one time – no longer used technically **2** a passenger boat carrying mail and cargo on a regular schedule **3** a small package or parcel **4** *Br informal* a large sum of money ⟨cost a ~⟩ [AF *pacquet*, dim. of *pack*; (2) short for *packet-boat*]

**packhorse** /'pak,haws/ *n* a horse used as a pack animal

**pack ice** *n* sea ice crushed together into a large floating mass

**packing** /'paking/ *n* **1a** the action or process of packing something; *also* a method of packing **b** the processing of food, esp meat, for future sale **2a** material used to pack **b** material used to cover the PLATEN (flat plate) or cylinders of a printing press **3** the fee for packing something ⟨post and ~ 25p⟩

**packing case** *n* a usu wooden crate in which goods are packed for storage or transport

**packinghouse** /'paking,hows/ *n* an establishment in which foodstuffs are processed and packed; *esp* one in which livestock are slaughtered and processed into meat and meat products

**packman** /'pakmən/ *n, archaic* a pedlar

**packsaddle** /-,sadl/ *n* a saddle designed to support loads on the backs of pack animals

**packthread** /-,thred/ *n* strong thread or thin twine used for sewing or tying packages or parcels

**pact** /pakt/ *n* an agreement, treaty; *esp* an international treaty [ME, fr MF, fr L *pactum*, fr neut of *pactus*, pp of *pacisci* to agree, contract; akin to OE *fōn* to seize, L *pangere* to fix, fasten, Gk *pēgnynai*]

¹**pad** /pad/ *n* **1a** a thin flat mat or cushion: e g **1a(1)** a piece of soft stuffed material used as or under a saddle **a(2)** padding used to shape an article of clothing **a(3)** a guard worn to shield body parts against impact; *esp* a padded leg guard worn by a batsman in cricket **a(4)** a piece of usu folded absorbent material (e g gauze) used as a surgical dressing or protective covering **b** a piece of material saturated with ink for inking the surface of a rubber stamp **2a** the foot of an animal **b** the cushioned thickening of the underside of the toes of cats, dogs, etc **3** a large floating leaf of a water plant ⟨a water lily ~⟩ **4** a collection of sheets of paper (e g for writing or drawing on) fastened together at one edge **5a** a flat surface for a vertical takeoff or landing **b** LAUNCHING PAD **6** *informal* somewhere (e g a house or flat) where one lives ⟨has a ~ in a squat in Liverpool⟩ [origin unknown]

²**pad** *vt* **-dd-** **1a** to furnish with a pad or padding **b** to mute, muffle **2** to expand or increase (speech or writing) with superfluous matter ⟨she knew nothing about the essay question, so she padded it with jokes⟩

³**pad** *vb* **-dd-** *vt* to traverse on foot ~ *vi* to walk with a muffled step [perh fr MD *paden* to follow a path, fr *pad* path – more at PATH]

⁴**pad** *n* a horse that moves along at an easy pace [MD *pad* path]

**padded cell** *n* a cell in a mental hospital or prison that has padded walls and floor to prevent a violent patient or prisoner from injuring him-/herself

**padding** /'pading/ *n* **1** material with which something is padded **2** irrelevant or superfluous material used to expand speech or writing ⟨his talk was all ~⟩

**padding stitch** *n* a stitch used in tailoring to fasten the INTERFACING (stiffening material) to the surface layer of lapels, collars, etc, which is almost invisible on the right side and appears in a herringbone pattern underneath

¹**paddle** /'padl/ *n* **1a** a usu wooden implement similar to an oar, but smaller and with a broad flattened blade at one or both ends, used to propel and steer a small craft (e g a canoe) **b** an implement that often has a short handle and a broad flat blade used for stirring, mixing, or hitting **2a** any of the broad boards or blades at the circumference of a paddle wheel or waterwheel **b** any of a series of broad blades attached to a shaft and used for stirring **3** the act or an instance of paddling ⟨went for a ~ in the sea⟩ **4** *NAm* a small flat bat used in various games (e g table tennis) [ME *padell* spade-like tool]

²**paddle** *vi* to go on or through water (as if) by means of a paddle or paddle wheel ~ *vt* **1** to propel (as if) by a paddle **2** to transport in a paddled craft ⟨~d us to the shore in his canoe⟩ – **paddler** *n*

³**paddle** *vi* **1** to walk barefoot or play in shallow water **2** to swim slowly [prob freq of ³*pad*] – **paddler** *n*

**paddleball** /'padl,bawl/ *n* a game for two, three, or four players played on a court with one, three, or four walls using a wood or plastic paddle and a small, firm rubber ball

**paddleboard** /'padl,bawd/ *n* a buoyant surfboard used esp for rescuing swimmers

**paddle steamer** *n* a steam vessel propelled by a pair of PADDLE WHEELS mounted amidships or by a single paddle wheel at the stern

**paddle wheel** *n* a power-driven wheel with paddles, floats, or boards round its circumference used to propel a boat

**paddling pool** /'padling/ *n* an artificial pool or portable, usu plastic, tank containing shallow water for people, esp children, to paddle in

¹**paddock** /'padək/ *n, archaic* a frog or toad [ME *paddok*, fr *pad, pade* toad; akin to ON *padda* toad, MLG *padde*]

²**paddock** *n* **1** a small field that is usu enclosed and is used esp

for pasturing or exercising animals; *esp* an enclosure where racehorses are saddled and paraded before a race 2 an area at a motor-racing track where vehicles (e g cars or motorcycles) are parked and worked on before a race [alter. of ME *parrok*, fr OE *pearroc* fence, enclosure; akin to OHG *pfarrih* enclosure; both fr a prehistoric Gmc word borrowed fr (assumed) VL *parricus* (cf PARK)]

**paddy** /'padi/ *n* 1 rice; *esp* threshed unmilled rice 2 a paddyfield [Malay *padi*]

**Paddy** *n*, 1 *chiefly derog* an Irishman 2 *not cap, chiefly Br informal* (a fit of) temper [*Paddy*, nickname for *Patrick*, a common Irish forename]

**paddyfield** /-,feeld/ *n* a field of wet land in which rice is grown

**paddymelon, pademelon** /'padi,melən/ *n, Austr* a small wallaby (genus *Thylogale*) of Australian coastal scrub [alter. of earlier *paddymalla*, fr native name in Australia]

**paddy wagon** *n, chiefly NAm* BLACK MARIA [prob fr *Paddy* (in the sense "policeman")]

**padishah** /'pahdi,shah/ *n* – used as a title of various Eastern rulers, esp the Shah of Iran [Per *pādshāh*]

**padkos** /'putkos/ *n, SAfr* food to eat on a journey [Afrik, fr *pad* road, path (fr D) + *kos* food (fr D *kost*)]

**padlock** /'padlok/ *n* a portable lock with a hinged or sliding shackle that can be passed through a staple or link (e g of a door, lid, or chain) and then secured [ME *padlok*, fr *pad-* (of unknown origin) + *lok* lock] – **padlock** *vt*

**padre** /'pahdri/ *n* 1 a Christian clergyman; *esp* a priest 2 a military chaplain [Sp or It or Pg, lit., father, fr L *pater* – more at FATHER]

**pad saddle** *n* a felt saddle without a metal frame

**pad saw** *n* KEYHOLE SAW [*pad* (tool handle)]

**padstitch** /'pad,stich/ *n* PADDING STITCH

**padstone** /'pad,stohn/ *n* a stone block fixed in a wall to take the end of a girder or roof truss

**paduasoy** /'padyooə,soy/ *n* a corded silk fabric; *also* a garment made of it [alter. (influenced by *Padua*, city in NE Italy) of earlier *poudesoy*, fr Fr *pou-de-soie*]

**paean** /'pee-ən/ *n* a joyously exultant song or hymn of praise, tribute, thanksgiving, or triumph [L, hymn of thanksgiving esp addressed to the god Apollo, fr Gk *paian, paiōn*, fr *Paian, Paiōn*, epithet of Apollo in the hymn]

**paed-** /ped-, peed/, **paedo-**, /paedo-, *NAm chiefly* ped-, pedo- *comb form* child ⟨paed*iatric*⟩ [Gk *paid-, paido-*, fr *paid-, pais* child, boy – more at FEW]

**paediatrician** /,peediə'trish(ə)n/ *n* a specialist in paediatrics

**paediatrics** /,peedi'atriks/ *n taking sing vb* a branch of medicine dealing with the development, care, and diseases of children △ orthopaedics – **paediatric** *adj*

**paedogenesis** /,peedoh'jenəsis/ *n* reproduction by animals that are still at a young or larval stage in development; NEOTENY 1 [NL] – **paedogenic, paedogenetic** *adj*

**paedologist** /peed'dolǝjist/ *n* a specialist in the study of children

**paedology** /pee'dolǝji/ *n* the scientific study of the growth and development of children – **paedologist** *n*, **paedologic, paedological** *adj*

**paedomorphic** /,peedǝ'mawfik/ *adj* of or involving paedomorphosis or paedomorphism

**paedomorphism** /,peedoh'mawfiz(ǝ)m/ *n* retention in the adult of infantile or juvenile characteristics – compare NEOTENY

**paedomorphosis** /,peedoh-maw'fohsis/ *n* evolutionary development of an organism that involves retention of juvenile characteristics by the adult [NL]

**paedophile** /'peedǝ,fiel, 'peedoh-/ *n or adj* (one) affected with paedophilia

**paedophilia** /,peedoh'fili-ǝ, -dǝ-/ *n* sexual desire directed towards children [NL] – **paedophiliac** *n or adj*

**paella** /pie'elǝ/ *n* a saffron-flavoured Spanish dish containing rice, meat, seafood, and vegetables [Catal, lit., pot, pan, fr MF *paelle*, fr L *patella* small pan – more at PATELLA]

**paeon** /'pee-ǝn/ *n* a unit of poetic metre (FOOT) consisting of four syllables with one long and three short syllables (e g in classical verse) or with one stressed and three unstressed syllables (e g in English verse) [L, fr Gk *paiōn*, fr *paian, paiōn* paean]

**paeony** /'pee-ǝni/ *n* a peony

**pagan** /'paygǝn/ *n* 1 HEATHEN 1; *esp* a follower of a religion having many gods (e g in ancient Rome) 2 someone who has little or no religion and who delights in sensual pleasures and material goods; an irreligious or hedonistic person [ME, fr LL

*paganus*, fr L, country dweller, fr *pagus* country district; akin to L *pangere* to fix – more at PACT] – **pagan, paganish** *adj*, **paganism** *n*, **paganize** *vt*

**¹page** /payj/ *n* **1a(1)** a youth being trained for the medieval rank of knight and in the personal service of a knight **a(2)** a youth attending on a person of rank, esp in the medieval period **b** a boy serving as an honorary attendant at a formal function (e g a wedding) **2** somebody employed (e g in a hotel) to deliver messages or perform personal services for patrons [ME, fr OF, fr OIt *paggio*]

**²page** *vt* **1** to summon by repeatedly calling out or relaying (e g over a public-address system) the name of **2** to summon by a coded signal emitted esp by a short-range radio transmitter

**³page** *n* **1** (a single side of) a leaf of a book, magazine, letter, or manuscript **2a** a written account; a book, writing ⟨*the* ~s *of history*⟩ **b** something (e g an event) worth being recorded in writing ⟨*one of the brightest* ~s *of his life*⟩ **3** a sizable subdivision of computer memory used chiefly for convenience of reference in programming [MF, fr L *pagina;* akin to L *pangere* to fix, fasten]

**⁴page** *vt* to number the sides of the leaves of (e g a book) in a sequence – compare FOLIATE ~ *vi* to turn pages, esp in a haphazard manner – often + *through*

**pageant** /'paj(ǝ)nt/ *n* **1a** a specious or misleading show; pretence ⟨*saw through the hollowness, the sham of the empty* ~ – Oscar Wilde⟩ **b** an ostentatious display **2** a show, exhibition; *esp* an elaborate colourful exhibition or spectacle with a series of tableaux, dramatic presentations, or a procession expressing a common theme [ME *pagyn, padgeant*, lit., scene of a play, fr ML *pagina*, fr L, page]

**pageantry** /'paj(ǝ)ntri/ *n* **1** pageants and the presentation of pageants **2** colourful, rich, or splendid display; spectacle

**page boy** *n* **1** a boy serving as a page **2** a usu shoulder-length hairstyle worn by a woman in which the hair falls straight from the crown, with a fringe on the forehead and the sides and back turned under in a smooth roll

**paginal** /'pajinl/ *adj* of or consisting of pages [LL *paginalis*, fr L *pagina* page]

**paginate** /'pajinayt/ *vt* ⁴PAGE [L *pagina* page]

**pagination** /,paji'naysh(ǝ)n/ *n* **1** the numbers that indicate the sequence of pages (e g of a book) **2** the number or arrangement of pages

**pagoda** /pǝ'gohdǝ/ *n* a many-storeyed usu many-sided tower with elaborately carved upturned projecting roofs at the division of each storey and used esp as a Buddhist or other temple in the Far East △ pergola [Pg *pagode* oriental idol, temple, prob deriv of Skt *bhagavat* blessed]

**pah** /pah/ *interj* – used esp to express contempt or disgust

**Pahlavi** /'pahlǝvi/ *n* **1** the Iranian language of Sassanian Persia, esp as used in classical literature **2** a Semitic script used for writing Pahlavi [Per *pahlawī*, fr *Pahlav* Parthia, fr OPer *Parthava-*]

**paid** /payd/ *past of* PAY

**,paid-'up** *adj* having paid the necessary fees to be a full member of a group or organization; *broadly* showing the characteristic attitudes and behaviour of a specified group to a marked degree ⟨*a* ~ *member of the awkward squad*⟩

**pai-hua** /,bie 'hwah/ *n* a form of written Chinese based on the modern colloquial language [Chin (Pek) *bái huà* (*pai²* *hua⁴*), lit., plain speech]

**pail** /payl/ *n* (the contents of or quantity contained in) an esp wooden or metal bucket [ME *payle, paille*, prob fr OE *pægel*, a small measure of liquid; akin to MD *pegel* gauge, scale] – **pailful** *n*

**paillasse** /'palias, pal'yas/ *n* a palliasse

**paillette** /pal'yet/ *n* a small shiny object (e g a spangle) used to decorate clothing [Fr, fr *paille* straw – more at PALLET]

**¹pain** /payn/ *n* **1a** a basic bodily sensation induced by injury, physical disorder, etc and characterized by physical discomfort (e g pricking, throbbing, or aching) **b** acute mental or emotional distress or suffering; grief **2** *pl* labour pains **3** *pl* trouble, care, or effort taken for the accomplishment of something **4** *informal* one who or that which irks or annoys or is otherwise troublesome ⟨*she's a real* ~⟩ [ME, fr OF *peine*, fr L *poena*, fr Gk *poinē* payment, penalty; akin to Gk *tinein* to pay, *tinesthai* to punish, *timē* price, value, honour] – **painless** *adj*, **painlessly** *adv*, **painlessness** *n* – **on/under pain of** subject to the penalty or punishment of ⟨*ordered not to leave the country on pain of death*⟩ – **pain in the neck** *informal* a source of annoyance; nuisance

²**pain** *vt* **1** to make suffer or cause distress to; hurt ⟨*your silence* ~*s me*⟩ **2** to give or have a sensation of pain **3** *archaic* to suffer

**painful** /'paynf(ə)l/ *adj* **1a** feeling or giving pain **b** irksome, annoying **2** requiring effort or exertion ⟨*a long* ~ *trip*⟩ – **painfully** *adv*, **painfulness** *n*

**painkiller** /-,kilə/ *n* something, esp a drug (e g morphine or aspirin), that relieves pain – **painkilling** *adj*

**painstaking** /'painz,tayking/ *adj* taking pains; expending or showing diligent care and effort – **painstakingly** *adv*

¹**paint** /paynt/ *vt* **1a** to apply colour, pigment, paint, or cosmetics to **b**(1) to apply with a movement resembling that used in painting **b**(2) to treat with a liquid by brushing or swabbing ⟨~ *the wound with iodine*⟩ **2a**(1) to produce in lines and colours on a surface by applying pigments ⟨~ *a watercolour*⟩ **a**(2) to depict by such lines and colours ⟨~ *a landscape*⟩ **b** to decorate or adorn by applying lines and colours **c** to produce or evoke as if by painting ⟨~*s glowing pictures of rural life*⟩ **3** to touch up or cover over (as if) by painting **4** to depict as having specified or implied characteristics ⟨*is neither as black nor as white as he is* ~*ed* – V S Pritchett⟩ ~ *vi* **1** to practise the art of painting **2** to use cosmetics [ME *painten*, fr OF *peint*, pp of *peindre*, fr L *pingere* to tattoo, embroider, paint; akin to OE *fāh* variegated, Gk *poikilos* variegated, *pikros* sharp, bitter]

²**paint** *n* **1** make-up; *esp* make-up (e g rouge) that adds colour to the face **2a**(1) a mixture of a pigment and a suitable liquid which forms a closely adherent coating when spread on a surface in a thin layer **a**(2) the pigment used in this mixture, esp when in the form of a cake which can be mixed with water ⟨*a box of* ~s⟩ **b** an applied coating of paint ⟨*don't scratch the* ~⟩ **3** PINTO (horse with spotted coat) [(3) short for *paint horse*, trans of AmerSp *pinto*] – **painty** *adj*

**paintbrush** /-,brush/ *n* a brush for applying paint

**painted lady** *n* a migratory butterfly (*Vanessa cardui*) with wings mottled in brown, orange, red, and white

**painted woman** *n* an immoral woman; a slut

¹**painter** /'payntə/ *n* one who paints: e g **a** an artist who paints **b** one who applies paint (e g to a building), esp as an occupation

²**painter** *n* a thin rope used for securing or towing a boat [ME *paynter*, prob fr MF *pendoir*, *pentoir* clothesline, fr *pendre* to hang – more at PENDANT]

**painterly** /-li/ *adj* **1** of or typical of a painter; artistic **2** of or being a style of painting that emphasizes colour, tone, and texture rather than line – **painterliness** *n*

**painter's colic** *n* LEAD COLIC (intestinal colic associated with lead poisoning)

**painting** /'paynting/ *n* **1** a product of painting; *esp* an example of the art of painting **2** the art or occupation of painting

**paintwork** /-,wuhk/ *n* paint that has been applied to a surface; *also* a painted surface ⟨*drove into a lamp post and damaged the* ~ *of the car*⟩

¹**pair** /peə/ *n taking sing or pl vb*, *pl* **pairs** *also* **pair** **1a**(1) two corresponding things designed for use together ⟨*a* ~ *of shoes*⟩ **a**(2) two corresponding body parts or members ⟨*a* ~ *of hands*⟩ **b** a single thing made up of two connected corresponding pieces ⟨*a* ~ *of trousers*⟩ **2a** two similar or associated things: e g **2a**(1) two mated animals **a**(2) a couple in love, engaged, or married ⟨*were a devoted* ~⟩ **a**(3) two playing cards of the same value or denomination ⟨*held a* ~⟩ **a**(4) two horses harnessed (e g to a carriage) side by side **a**(5) two members from opposite sides of a deliberative body (e g Parliament) that agree not to vote on a specific issue during a time agreed on, so preserving the relative strengths of the two sides; *also* an agreement not to vote made by two such members **b** a partnership esp of two players in a contest against another partnership ⟨*they took part in the coxless* ~*s in the rowing championships*⟩ **c** a failure to score runs in either innings of a match by a batsman in cricket [ME *paire*, fr OF, fr L *paria* equal things, fr neut pl of *par* equal] *usage* The use of the plural **pair** for **pairs** is now largely dialectal.

²**pair** *vt* **1a** to make a pair of – often + *off* or *up* ⟨~*ed off the animals*⟩ **b** to arrange a voting pair between or for (e g in Parliament) – usu pass **2** to arrange in pairs ~ *vi* **1** to constitute a member of a pair ⟨*a sock that didn't* ~⟩ **2a** to become associated with another – often + *off* or *up* ⟨~*ed up with an old friend*⟩ **b** to become grouped or separated into pairs – often + *off* ⟨~*ed off for the next dance*⟩

**pair of compasses** *n* COMPASS 2b

**pair production** *n* the simultaneous and complete transformation of a pulse of energy derived from gamma rays, X rays, etc into an electron and a POSITRON (particle having a

positive electrical charge and the same mass as an electron) by interaction with the ELECTRIC FIELD near the nucleus of an atom

**paisa** /'piesə/ *n*, *pl* **paise** /-say/, **paisa**, **paisas** – see *rupee*, *taka* at MONEY table [Hindi *paisā*]

**paisley** /'payzli/ *adj*, *often cap* **1** made typically of soft wool and woven or printed with colourful curved teardrop-shaped figures of Indian origin **2** marked by designs, patterns, or figures typically used in paisley fabrics ⟨*a* ~ *print*⟩ [Paisley, town in SW Scotland] – **paisley** *n*

**Paiute** /'pieyooht, -'-/ *n* **1** a member of an American Indian people originally of Utah, Arizona, Nevada, and California **2** the Uto-Aztecan language of the Paiute people

**pajama** /pə'jahmə/ *adj*, *chiefly NAm* pyjama

**pajamas** /pə'jahməz/ *n taking pl vb*, *chiefly NAm* pyjamas

**pakeha** /'pahkə,hah, pah'kee·ə/ *n*, *pl* **pakehas**, *esp collectively* **pakeha** **1** *NZ* someone who is not a Maori; *esp* a New Zealander of European descent **2** *Austr & NZ* a white person; a European [Maori]

**Paki** /'paki/ *n or adj*, *often not cap*, *Br derog* (a) Pakistani

**Pakistani** /,paki'stahni, ,pah-/ *n* **1** a native or inhabitant of Pakistan **2** a descendant of Pakistanis [Hindustani *Pākistānī*, fr *Pākistān*, Pakistan, country in S Asia] – **Pakistani** *adj* *usage* A news broadcaster may speak of ⟨*the* Pakistan *Government*⟩, perhaps because Pakistani would suggest rather "government by Pakistanis".

**pakora** /'pakərə/ *n* an Indian savoury snack consisting of diced vegetables or shell-fish dipped in batter made from chick-pea flour and fried [Hindi *pakoṛā*]

¹**pal** /pal/ *n*, *informal* **1** a close friend **2** – used as a familiar form of address, esp to a stranger [Romany *phral*, *phal* brother, friend, fr Skt *bhrātṛ* brother; akin to OE *brōthor* brother]

²**pal** *vi* -**ll**- to be or become pals; associate as pals – often + *up* or *up with*

¹**palace** /'palis/ *n* **1a** the official residence of a sovereign **b** the official residence of an archbishop or bishop in Britain **2a** a large stately house **b** a large public building ⟨*the Crystal Palace*⟩ **c** a large and often ornate place of public entertainment ⟨*a picture* ~⟩ [ME *palais*, fr OF, fr L *palatium*, fr *Palatium*, the Palatine Hill in Rome where the emperors' residences were built]

²**palace** *adj* **1** of a palace **2** of or involving the intimate circle of a chief executive ⟨*a* ~ *revolution*⟩ ⟨~ *politics*⟩

**paladin** /'palədin/ *n* **1** a champion of a medieval prince **2** an outstanding protagonist of a cause [Fr, fr It *paladino*, fr ML *palatinus* courtier, fr L, palace official – more at PALATINE]

**palae-** /pali-/, **palaeo-**, *NAm chiefly* **pale-**, **paleo-** *comb form* **1** involving or dealing with ancient (e g fossil) forms or conditions ⟨palaeo*botany*⟩ **2** early; primitive; archaic ⟨Palaeo*lithic*⟩ [Gk *palai-*, *palaio-* ancient, fr *palaios*, fr *palai* long ago; akin to Gk *tēle* far off, Skt *carama* last]

**Palaearctic, Palearctic** /,pali'ahktik/ *adj* of or being a BIOGEOGRAPHIC region or subregion (one defined according to the geographical distribution of plants and animals) that includes Europe, Asia north of the Himalayas, N Arabia, and Africa north of the Sahara

**palaeoanthropic** /,palioh·an'thropik/ *adj* of extinct ancestral forms of man more primitive than those belonging to the species (*Homo sapiens*) that includes modern man [*palae-* + Gk *anthrōpos* human being]

**palaeobotany** /,palioh'botəni/ *a* branch of botany dealing with extinct plants by examination of their fossil record [ISV] – **palaeobotanist** *n*, **palaeobotanical palaeobotanic** *adj*, **palaeobotanically** *adv*

**Palaeocene** /'palioh,seen/ *adj or n* (of or being) the earliest epoch of the TERTIARY period or the corresponding system of rocks [ISV]

**palaeoclimate** /'palioh,kliemit/ *n* the climate of past ages – **palaeoclimatic** *adj*, **palaeolclimatology** *n*, **palaeoclimatologist** *n*

**palaeoecology** /,palioh·i'koləji/ *n* a branch of ecology that is concerned with the characteristics of environments of long ago and with their relationships to plants and animals of those times

**palaeoenvironment** /,palioh·in'vierənmənt/ *n* the environment of past ages – **palaeoenvironmental** *adj*

**palaeogeography** /,palioh·ji'ogrəfi/ *n* the geography of ancient times or of a particular past geological period [ISV]

**palaeography** /,pali'ogrəfi/ *n* **1** an ancient manner of writing **2** (the study of) ancient writings and inscriptions [NL *palaeo-*

*graphia*, fr Gk *palaio-* palae- + *-graphia* -graphy] – **palaeographer** *n*, **palaeographic, palaeographical** *adj*, **palaeographically** *adv*

**palaeolith** /'paliə‚lith/ *n* a Palaeolithic stone implement

**Palaeolithic** /‚pali-ə'lithic/ *adj or n* (of or being) the earliest period of the STONE AGE characterized by the development and use of crude chipped stone implements – compare NEOLITHIC [ISV]

**palaeomagnetism** /‚palioh'magnə‚tiz(ə)m/ *n* (the study of) the intensity and direction of residual magnetization in ancient rocks

**palaeontology** /‚palion'toləji/ *n* a science dealing with the life of past geological periods as discovered from fossil remains [Fr *paléontologie*, fr *palé-* palae- + Gk *onta* living things (fr neut pl of *ont-*, *ōn*, prp of *einai* to be) + Fr *-logie* -logy]

**Palaeozoic** /‚pali-ə'zohik/ *adj* of or being an era of geological history which extends from the beginning of the CAMBRIAN to the close of the PERMIAN period, is marked by the final stages in development of nearly all classes of INVERTEBRATE animals except the insects, and in the later epochs of which seed-bearing plants, amphibians, and reptiles first appeared; *also* relating to the system of rocks formed in this era – **Palaeozoic** *n*

**palaeozoology** /‚palioh-zooh'oləji, -zoh-/ *n* a branch of palaeontology dealing with ancient and fossil animals [Fr *paléozoologie*, fr *palé-* palae- + *zoologie* zoology]

**palaestra** /pə'lestrə, -'lee-/ *n, pl* **palaestrae** /-stree/ 1 a school for sports (e g wrestling) in ancient Greece and Rome 2 a gymnasium [L, fr Gk *palaistra*, fr *palaiein* to wrestle; akin to Gk *pallein* to brandish – more at POLEMIC]

**palagi** /pa'lang·i/ *n, pl* **palagi** *NZ* a person of European descent [Maori]

**palais** /'palay, 'pali/, **palais de danse** /~ də 'dahns/ *n, informal* a public dance hall [Fr *palais de danse*, lit., dance palace]

**palanquin** /'palənkeen/ *n* a LITTER (portable, covered, and curtained bed) formerly used in eastern Asia, esp for one person, and usu hung from poles borne on the bearers' shoulders [Pg *palanquim*, fr Jav *pělaňki*, deriv of Skt *palyaňka*, *paryaňka* bed, couch]

**palatable** /'palətəbl/ *adj* 1 agreeable to the palate or taste 2 agreeable to the mind ⟨*did not find the suggestion at all* ~⟩ – **palatableness** *n*, **palatably** *adv*, **palatability** *n*

**palatal** /'palətl/ *adj* 1 *anatomy* of the palate 2 *of a consonant* (e g /y/) pronounced with the front of the tongue near or touching the HARD PALATE – **palatal** *n*, **palatally** *adv*

**palatal-ize, -ise** /'palətəliez/ *vt* to pronounce as or change into a palatal sound – **palatalization** *n*

**palate** /'palət/ *n* 1 the roof of the mouth separating the mouth from the nasal cavity 2a a usu intellectual taste or liking ⟨*a novel too pessimistic for my* ~⟩ b the sense of taste ⟨*drier wines suit my* ~ *better*⟩ 3 flavour – used esp with reference to wine △ *palette, pallet* [ME, fr L *palatum*]

**palatial** /pə'laysh(ə)l/ *adj* 1 of or being a palace 2 suitable for a palace; magnificent [L *palatium* palace] – **palatially** *adv*, **palatialness** *n*

**palatinate** /pə'latinət/ *n* the territory of a palatine

¹**palatine** /'palətien/ *adj* 1 of a palace, esp of a Roman or Holy Roman emperor 2a possessing royal privileges b of a palatine or a palatinate [L *palatinus*, fr *palatium* palace]

²**palatine** *n* 1a a high officer of an imperial palace b a feudal lord (e g a count or bishop) having sovereign power within his domains 2 *cap* a native or inhabitant of the territory in SW Germany formerly ruled by counts palatine [L *palatinus*, fr *palatinus*, adj]

³**palatine** *adj, anatomy* of or lying near the palate [Fr *palatin*, fr L *palatum* palate]

⁴**palatine** *n* either of a pair of bones that are situated behind and between the two bones of the upper jawbone and form the HARD PALATE

**palaver** /pə'lahvə/ *n* 1 a long parley or discussion 2a idle talk b misleading or flowery speech ⟨*after hearing all that* ~ *I forgot what I came for*⟩ 3 a tedious or time-consuming procedure ⟨*all the* ~ *of passports, bookings, customs and so on makes holidays a chore*⟩ [Pg *palavra* word, speech, fr LL *parabola* parable, speech] – **palaver** *vi*

**palazzo** /pə'latsoh, -sə, -'ladzoh, -zə/ *n, pl* **palazzi** /-si/ a large imposing building (e g a museum or palace), esp in Italy [It, fr L *palatium* palace]

¹**pale** /payl/ *adj* 1 deficient in colour or intensity of colour; pallid ⟨*a* ~ *face*⟩ 2 not bright or brilliant; dim ⟨*a* ~ *sun shining through the fog*⟩ 3 feeble, faint ⟨*a* ~ *imitation*⟩ 4 *of a*

*colour* not having much colouring matter; not intense ⟨*a* ~ *pink*⟩ [ME, fr MF, fr L *pallidus*, fr *pallēre* to be pale – more at FALLOW] – **palely** *adv*, **paleness** *n*

²**pale** *vb* to become or make pale

³**pale** *n* 1 an upright post or strip of wood forming part of a fence 2 a territory or district within certain bounds or under a particular jurisdiction 3 a broad vertical band in the centre of a heraldic shield [ME, fr MF *pal* stake, fr L *palus* – more at POLE] – **beyond the pale** in violation of accepted practice or attitudes ⟨*fanning his soup with his hat was quite* beyond the pale⟩

⁴**pale** *n* a palea

**pale-** /payli/, **paleo-** *comb form, chiefly NAm* palae-, palaeo-

**palea** /'paylyə/ *n, pl* **paleae** /-li‚ie/ 1 any of the chaffy scales at the top of the stalk of the flower head of many plants of the daisy family 2 the upper of two scalelike leaves that enclose each flower in a grass – compare ²LEMMA [NL, fr L, chaff – more at PALLET] – **paleal** *adj*

**pale ale** *n, Br* LIGHT ALE

**paleface** /'payl‚fays/ *n* a white person, esp as distinguished from an American Indian

**palette** /'palit/ *n* 1 a thin board which a painter holds and on which he mixes pigments 2a the set of colours put on the palette b(1) a particular range, quality, or use of colour b(2) a comparable range, quality, or use of available elements, esp in another art (e g music) △ palate, pallet [Fr, fr MF, dim. of *pale* spade, shovel, fr L *pala*]

**palette knife** *n* a knife with a flexible steel blade, no cutting edge and a usu rounded end that is used esp for mixing, working, or applying soft substances (e g paint, putty, or icing)

**palfrey** /'pawlfri/ *n, archaic* a saddle horse other than a warhorse; *esp* a light horse suitable for a woman [ME, fr OF *palefrei*, fr ML *palafredus*, fr LL *paraveredus* post-horse for secondary roads, fr Gk *para-* beside, subsidiary + L *verdus* post- horse, fr a Gaulish word akin to W *gorwydd* horse]

**Pali** /'pahli/ *n* the ancient Indian language in which Buddhist scriptures were written [Skt *pāli* row, series of Buddhist sacred texts]

**palimpsest** /'palimpsest/ *n* writing material (e g a parchment or tablet) reused after earlier writing has been erased △ papyrus [L *palimpsestus*, fr Gk *palimpsēstos* scraped again, fr *palin* again + *psēn* to rub, scrape – more at SAND]

**palindrome** /'palindrohm/ *n* 1 a word, verse, or sentence (e g "Able was I ere I saw Elba") or a number (e g 1881) that reads the same backwards or forwards 2 *genetics* a palindromic sequence of the chemical BASES in a molecule of DNA or RNA [Gk *palindromos* running back again, fr *palin* back, again (akin to Gk *polos* axis, pole) + *dramein* to run – more at POLE, DROMEDARY] – **palindromic** *adj*

**paling** /'payling/ *n* a fence made of wooden stakes; *also* stakes for such a fence [³*pale* + *-ing*]

**palingenesis** /‚palin'jenəsis/ *n* 1 rebirth: e g 1a spiritual rebirth through Christian baptism b METEMPSYCHOSIS (the soul's entering a new human or animal body after death) 2 the recurrence of biological characteristics (e g the GILL SLITS in a human embryo) that are derivations from distant ancestral forms rather than adaptations of recent origin [NL, fr Gk *palin* again + L *genesis*] – **palingenetic** *adj*

**palinode** /'palinohd/ *n* 1 a poem in which some statement in a previous poem is withdrawn or disavowed 2 *formal* a retraction, recantation [Gk *palinōidia*, fr *palin* back + *aeidein* to sing – more at ODE]

¹**palisade** /‚pali'sayd/ *n* 1 a fence of stakes, esp for defence 2 a long strong stake pointed at the top and set close with others as a defence [Fr *palissade*, deriv of L *palus* stake – more at POLE]

²**palisade** *vt* to surround or fortify with palisades

**palisade layer** *n* a layer of closely packed cells that contain many CHLOROPLASTS (specialized plant cell parts containing chlorophyll) for photosynthesis and are arranged beneath the upper surface layer of cells in leaves

**palish** /'paylish/ *adj* somewhat pale

¹**pall** /pawl/ *n* 1 PALLIUM (vestment worn by pope or archbishop) 2a a square of linen usu stiffened with cardboard that is used to cover the goblet containing the wine at Holy Communion b a heavy cloth draped over a coffin or tomb 3 something that covers or conceals; *esp* something that produces an effect of gloom ⟨*a* ~ *of thick black smoke*⟩ [ME, cloak, mantle, fr OE *paell*, fr L *pallium*]

²**pall** *vt* to cease to be interesting or attractive ⟨*Do you find*

*London* ~s *in the summer?*⟩ **synonyms** see ²SATIATE [ME *pallen* to become weak or stale, short for *appallen* to become pale – more at APPAL]

**Palladian** /pə'laydi·ən/ *adj* (characteristic) of a style of architecture practised esp in Britain in the 18th century that was based on Greek and Roman models, esp as described or reinterpreted by the 16th-century Italian architect Andrea Palladio – **Palladianism** *n*

¹**palladium** /pə'laydiəm/ *n* **1** *cap* a statue of the Greek goddess Pallas Athena on the preservation of which the safety of Troy was believed to depend **2** *pl* **palladia** /-diə/ something that gives protection; a safeguard [L, fr Gk *palladion*, fr *Pallad-*, Pallas, Gk goddess of wisdom]

²**palladium** *n* a soft easily-worked silver-white metallic chemical element of the platinum group that is used esp in electrical contacts, as a catalyst, and in alloys [NL, fr *Pallad-*, *Pallas*, an asteroid discovered shortly before the element] – **palladous** *adj*

**pallbearer** /'pawl,beərə/ *n* a person who helps to carry the coffin at a funeral or is part of its immediate escort

¹**pallet** /'palit/ *n* **1** a straw-filled mattress **2** a small, hard, or temporary bed △ palate, palette [ME *pailet*, fr (assumed) MF *pailett*, fr *paille* straw, fr L *palea* chaff, straw; akin to Skt *palāva* chaff]

²**pallet** *n* **1** a flat-bladed wooden tool used esp by potters for shaping clay **2** a lever or surface in a clock or watch that receives an impulse from the toothed ESCAPEMENT wheel and sets the BALANCE WHEEL or pendulum in motion **3** a portable platform intended for handling, storing, or moving materials and packages (e g in warehouses) and usu moved by a forklift [MF *palette*, lit., small shovel – more at PALETTE]

**pallet·ize, -ise** /'palitiez/ *vt* to place on, transport, or store by means of pallets – **palletizer** *n*, **palletization** *n*

**pallial** /'paliəl/ *adj* **1** of the CEREBRAL CORTEX (area of brain controlling higher-thought ability) **2** of or produced by the MANTLE (lining of the shell that contains shell-secreting glands) of snails, mussels, etc [NL *pallium*]

**palliasse, pallasse** /'palias, pal'yas/ *n* a thin straw mattress [modif of Fr *paillasse*, fr *paille* straw]

**palliate** /'paliayt/ *vt* **1** to lessen the unpleasantness of (e g a disease) without removing the cause; alleviate **2** to disguise the gravity of (a fault or offence) by excuses or apologies; extenuate **3** to moderate the intensity of ⟨*trying to* ~ *the boredom*⟩ [LL *palliatus*, pp of *palliare* to cloak, conceal, fr *pallium* cloak] – **palliator** *n*, **palliation** *n*

**palliative** /'palyətiv/ *n* something (e g a drug) that palliates – **palliative** *adj*

**pallid** /'palid/ *adj* **1** lacking colour; wan ⟨*a* ~ *countenance*⟩ **2** lacking sparkle or liveliness; dull ⟨*a* ~ *entertainment*⟩ [L *pallidus* – more at PALE] – **pallidly** *adv*, **pallidness** *n*

**pallium** /'pali·əm/ *n, pl* **pallia** /-liə/, **palliums 1a** a draped rectangular cloth worn as a cloak by men of ancient Rome **b** a white woollen vestment worn esp by a pope or archbishop and consisting of a band in the shape of two Ys that meet on the shoulders, and that hang down at the front and back **2** CEREBRAL CORTEX (area of brain controlling higher-thought ability) **3a** the MANTLE (lining of the shell containing shell-producing glands) of snails, mussels, etc **b** the MANTLE (feathers of the back and wings) of a bird [L]

**pall-mall** /,pal'mal/ *n* a 17th century game in which each player, using a mallet, attempts to drive a wooden ball down an alley and through a raised ring in as few strokes as possible; *also* the alley in which it is played [MF *pallemaille*, fr It *pallamaglio*, fr *palla* ball (of Gmc origin; akin to OHG *balla* ball) + *maglio* mallet,fr L *malleus* – more at BALL, MAUL]

**pallor** /'palə/ *n* deficiency of colour, esp of the face; paleness [L, fr *pallēre* to be pale – more at FALLOW]

**pally** /'pali/ *adj, informal* **1** sharing the relationship of pals; intimate ⟨*he was very* ~ *with the local vicar*⟩ **2** willing to be a pal; friendly ⟨*a champion boozer and the* palliest *bloke in the pub* – Alan Sillitoe⟩

¹**palm** /pahm; *NAm* pah(l)m/ *n* **1** any of a family (Palmae) of tropical or subtropical trees, shrubs, or climbing plants with usu a tall unbranched stem or trunk and a crown of large leaves that are fan-shaped or PINNATE (having leaflets arranged in pairs on either side of the stalk) **2** a leaf of the palm as a symbol of victory, distinction, or rejoicing; *also* a branch (e g of laurel) similarly used **3** a symbol of triumph or distinction *also* a victory, triumph **4** an addition to a military decoration in the form of a palm frond, esp to indicate a second award of the

basic decoration [ME, fr OE; akin to OHG *palma* palm tree; both fr a prehistoric NGmc-WGmc word borrowed fr L *palma* palm of the hand, palm tree; fr the resemblance of the tree's leaves to the outstretched hand] – **palmaceous** *adj*, **palmlike** *adj*

²**palm** *n* **1** the concave part of the human hand between the bases of the fingers and the wrist **2** a corresponding part in other mammals, esp monkeys and apes **3** a flat expanded part, esp at the end of a base or stalk (e g the blade of an oar or paddle) **4** a unit of length based on the breadth (e g about 100 millimetres or 4 inches) or length (e g about 200 millimetres or 8 inches) of the hand **5** something (e g a part of a glove) that covers the palm of the hand **6** an act of palming (e g of cards) as performed by a conjuror – see also OIL **somebody's palm** [ME *paume*, fr MF, fr L *palma*; akin to OE *flōr* floor; (4) L *palmus*, fr *palma*]

³**palm** *vt* **1a** to conceal in or with the hand ⟨~ *a card*⟩ **b** to pick up stealthily ⟨*likely to* ~ *small merchandise in a shop*⟩ **2** to impose by fraud ⟨*a second imposter to be* ~ed *upon you* – Sir Walter Scott⟩

**palm off** *vt* to get rid of (something unwanted or inferior) by convincing somebody that it is acceptable – often + *on* ⟨*he* palmed *his old raincoat* off *on the vicar*⟩

**palmar** /'palmə, 'pahmə/ *adj* of or involving the palm of the hand

**palmary** /'palməri/ *adj, formal* outstanding, best [L *palmarius* deserving the palm, fr *palma*]

**palmate** /'palmayt, -mət/ *also* **palmated** /-,maytid/ *adj* resembling a hand with the fingers spread: **a** having lobes radiating from a common point ⟨*a* ~ *leaf*⟩ **b(1)** *of an aquatic bird* having the front toes webbed **b(2)** having the portion farthest from the body broad, flat, and lobed ⟨*a* ~ *antler*⟩ – **palmately** *adv*, **palmation** *n*

**palmatifid** /pal'matifid, pah-/ *adj, of a leaf* split almost to the midrib in a palmate manner [ISV]

**palm civet** *n* any of various tree-dwelling African or Asian CIVET CATS (genera *Nardinia* and *Paradourus*)

**palmer** /'palmə, 'pahmə/ *n* a pilgrim wearing two crossed palm leaves as a sign of a visit to the Holy Land

**palmetto** /pal'metoh/ *n, pl* **palmettos, palmettoes** any of several usu low-growing fan-leaved palms; *esp* CABBAGE PALMETTO [modif of Sp *palmito*, fr *palma* palm, fr L]

**palmist** /'pahmist/ *n* someone who practises palmistry [prob back-formation fr *palmistry*]

**palmistry** /'pahmistri/ *n* the art or practice of reading a person's character or future from the markings on his or her palms [ME *pawmestry*, prob fr *paume* palm + *maistrie* mastery]

**palmitate** /'palmitayt/ *n* any of various chemical compounds (SALTS or ESTERS) formed by combination between PALMITIC ACID and a metal atom, an alcohol, or another chemical group

**palmitic acid** /pal'mitik/ *n* a waxy FATTY ACID, $CH_3(CH_2)_{14}COOH$, occurring in most fats and fatty oils and in several ESSENTIAL OILS and waxes and used in the manufacture of soap and candles [ISV, fr *palmitin*]

**palmitin** /'palmitin/ *n* a chemical compound (ESTER) formed by combination between PALMITIC ACID and glycerol that is found in many natural oils (e g PALM OIL) and fats [Fr *palmitine*, prob fr *palmite* pith of the palm tree, fr Sp *palmitic*]

**palm oil** *n* an edible fat obtained from the flesh of the fruit of several palms and used esp in soap, candles, and lubricating greases

**Palm Sunday** *n* the Sunday before Easter celebrated in commemoration of Christ's triumphal entry into Jerusalem [fr the palm branches strewn in Christ's path]

**palm wine** *n* an alcoholic drink made from the fermented sap of palm trees

**palmy** /'pahmi, 'pahlmi/ *adj* **1** bearing palms or having many palms ⟨~ *shoreline*⟩ **2** marked by prosperity; flourishing ⟨~ *days*⟩

**palmyra** /pal'mie·ərə/ *n* a tall tropical palm (*Borassus flabellifer*) cultivated in Asia for its hard wood, its large fan-shaped leaves used for thatching, and its sap that is rich in sugars [Pg *palmeira*, fr *palma* palm, fr L]

**palolo** /pə'lohloh/ *n* an edible segmented marine worm (*Eunice viridis* of the class Polychaeta) that burrows in the coral reefs of various Pacific islands and forms periodic breeding swarms [Samoan & Tongan]

**palomino** /,palə'meenoh/ *n, pl* **palominos** a light tan or cream coloured horse with a flaxen or white mane and tail, that is usu slender-legged and of Arabian ancestry [AmerSp, fr Sp, like a dove, fr L *palumbinus*, fr *palumbes* ringdove; akin to Gk *peleia* dove, L *pallēre* to be pale – more at FALLOW]

**palp** /palp/ *also* **palpus** /'palpəs/ *n, pl* **palps, palpi** /-pi/ **1** either of a pair of segmented projections on a mouthpart of insects, crabs, shrimps, etc that is usu sensitive to touch or to taste **2** an organ on the head of mussels and related animals and some segmented worms that is sensitive to touch [NL *palpus*, fr L, caress, soft palm of the hand; akin to L *palpare* to stroke, caress] – **palpal** *adj*

**palpable** /'palpəbl/ *adj* **1** capable of being touched or felt; tangible **2** easily perceptible by the mind; manifest ⟨*a ~ falsehood*⟩ *synonyms* see EVIDENT, PERCEPTIBLE *antonyms* **imperceptible, impalpable** [ME, fr LL *palpabilis*, fr L *palpare* to stroke, caress – more at FEEL] – **palpably** *adv*, **palpability** *n*

¹**palpate** /'pal'payt/ *vt* to examine, esp medically, by touch [prob back-formation fr *palpation*, fr L *palpation-, palpatio*, fr *palpatus*, pp of *palpare*] – **palpation** *n*

²**palpate** *adj* having a palp [NL *palpatus*, fr *palpus*]

**palpebral** /'palpibrəl/ *adj* of or located on or near the eyelids [LL *palpebralis*, fr L *palpebra* eyelid; akin to L *palpare*]

**palpitant** /'palpit(ə)nt/ *adj* trembling or throbbing

**palpitate** /'palpitayt/ *vi* **1** to beat rapidly and strongly; throb ⟨*he felt his heart ~ as the beast drew closer*⟩ **2** to tremble [L *palpitatus*, pp of *palpitare*, freq of *palpare* to stroke] – **palpitation** *n*

**palstave** /'pawl,stayv/ *n* a middle BRONZE AGE axe designed to fit into a split wooden handle [Dan *pålstav*, fr ON *pålstafr*, a heavy missile, prob fr *påll* spade, hoe + *stafr* staff]

¹**palsy** /'pawlzi, 'polzi/ *n* **1** paralysis **2** a condition marked by uncontrollable trembling of the body or a part of the body [ME *parlesie*, fr MF *paralisie*, fr L *paralysis*] – **palsied** *adj*

²**palsy** *vt* to affect (as if) with palsy

**palter** /'pawltə, 'poltə/ *vi* **1** to act insincerely or deceitfully; equivocate **2** to haggle – often + *with* [origin unknown] – **palterer** *n*

**paltry** /'pawltri/ *adj* **1** mean, despicable ⟨*a ~ trick*⟩ **2** trivial ⟨*a ~ sum*⟩ [obs *paltry* rubbish, fr E dial. *palt, pelt*] – **paltriness** *n*

**paludal** /pəl'yoohdl, 'palyoodl/ *adj, ecology* of marshes or fens; marshy [L *palud-, palus* marsh; akin to Skt *palvala* pond]

**paludism** /'palyoodiz(ə)m/ *n* malaria – not now used technically [ISV, fr L *palud-, palus*]

**palynology** /,pali'noləji/ *n* a branch of botany dealing with pollen and spores [Gk *palynein* to sprinkle, fr *palē* fine meal – more at POLLEN] – **palynologic, palynological** *adj*, **palynologically** *adv*, **palynologist** *n*

**pampas** /'pampəs/ *n taking sing vb*, **pampa** *n, pl* **pampas** an extensive generally grass-covered plain of temperate S America east of the Andes – compare PRAIRIE, VELD, SAVANNA [AmerSp, pl of *pampa*, fr Quechua & Aymara, plain]

**pampas grass** /'pampəs/ *n* a tall S American grass (*Cortaderia selloana*) that has large feathery silky flower heads and is frequently cultivated as an ornamental plant

**pampean** /pam'pee·ən, 'pampiən/ *adj* of the pampas of S America or their American Indian inhabitants

**pamper** /'pampə/ *vt* **1** to treat with extreme or excessive care and attention ⟨*~ed their guests*⟩ **2** to gratify, humour ⟨*enabled him to ~ his wanderlust – New Yorker*⟩ [ME *pamperen*, prob of D origin; akin to Flem *pamperen* to pamper] – **pamperer** *n*

**pampero** /pam'peəroh/ *n, pl* **pamperos** a strong cold wind from the Andes that sweeps over the pampas [AmerSp, fr *pampa*]

**pamphlet** /'pamflit/ *n* an unbound printed publication usu with a paper cover [ME *pamflet* booklet, fr *Pamphilus seu De Amore* Pamphilus or On Love, popular Latin love poem of the 12th c]

¹**pamphleteer** /,pamflə'tiə/ *n* a writer of pamphlets attacking something or urging a (political) cause

²**pamphleteer** *vi* to write and publish pamphlets

¹**pan** /pan/ *n* **1a(1)** any of various usu broad, shallow, and open receptacles for domestic use (e g a dustpan or bedpan) **a(2)** a metal container or vessel (e g of iron or aluminium) typically having a circular cross section and a long handle that is used on the hob of a cooker or over an open fire to heat or cook food – compare FRYING PAN, SAUCEPAN **b** any of various similar usu metal receptacles: e g **b(1)** the part of the GUNLOCK (firing mechanism) in old guns or pistols that holds a small charge of powder (PRIMING) directly ignited (e g by the spark from the flint) to set off the main charge **b(2)** either of the receptacles in a pair

of scales **b(3)** a round shallow metal container for separating a heavy mineral (e g gold) from lighter waste by washing **2a(1)** a natural hollow or depression in land ⟨*a salt ~*⟩ **a(2)** a similar artificial hollow used for evaporating brine) **b** a drifting fragment of the flat thin ice that forms in bays or along the shore **3** a compacted often clayey layer in soil that is impenetrable to plant roots; hardpan **4** *chiefly NAm* TIN **2b 5** *chiefly Br* the bowl of a toilet – see also FLASH **in the pan** [ME *panne*, fr OE; akin to OHG *phanna* pan; both fr a prehistoric WGmc-NGmc word borrowed fr L *patina*, fr Gk *patanē*; akin to L *patēre* to be open – more at FATHOM]

²**pan** *vb* **-nn-** *vi* **1** to wash earth, gravel, or other materials in a pan in search of precious metal, esp gold **2** to yield precious metal in the process of panning ~ *vt* **1a** to wash (earth, gravel, etc) in a pan for the purpose of separating heavy particles **b** to separate (e g gold) by panning **c** to place in a pan **2** *informal* to criticize severely

**pan out** *vi* to happen as specified; *esp* to succeed ⟨*the signs revealed that the experiment wasn't panning out* – Ronald Reagan⟩

³**pan** /pahn/ *n* (a substance, commonly used for chewing in India, consisting of BETEL NUT and lime wrapped in) a leaf from the climbing pepper plant, betel [Hindi *pān*, fr Skt *parṇa* wing, leaf – more at FERN]

⁴**pan** /pan/ *vb* **-nn-** *vi* **1** to swing the field of view of a camera, esp a television or film camera, across a scene so as to keep a moving object in the picture or obtain a panoramic effect **2** *of a camera* to undergo panning – compare DOLLY, TRACK ~ *vt* to cause (a camera) to pan [*panorama*]

⁵**pan** /pan/ *n* the act or process of panning a film or television camera; the movement of the camera in a panning shot

**pan-** /pan-/ *comb form* **1** all; completely ⟨*panchromatic*⟩ **2a** relating to all of (a specified group) ⟨*Pan-American*⟩ **b** advocating or involving the union of (a specified group) ⟨*Pan-Asian*⟩ **3** whole; general ⟨*panleucopaenia*⟩ of all of (a specified group) ⟨*Pan-American*⟩ [Gk, fr *pan*, neut of *pant-, pas* all, every; akin to Skt *śaśvat* all, every, *śvayati* he swells]

**panacea** /,panə'see·ə/ *n* a remedy for all ills or difficulties; a cure-all – compare PLACEBO [L, fr Gk *panakeia*, fr *pan-* + *akeisthai* to heal, fr *akos* remedy] – **panacean** *adj*

**panache** /pə'nash, pa-/ *n* **1** an ornamental tuft (e g of feathers), esp on a helmet **2** dash or flamboyance in style and action; verve [MF *pennache*, fr OIt *pennacchio*, fr LL *pinnaculum* small wing – more at PINNACLE]

**panada** /pə'nahdə/ *n* a thick sauce or paste of flour or breadcrumbs and water or stock used as a base for a sauce or as a binder for stuffing [Sp, fr *pan* bread, fr L *panis* – more at FOOD]

**panama** /,panə'mah/ *n, often cap* a (man's) lightweight hat of natural-coloured plaited straw from the young leaves of the JIPIJAPA (S American palmlike plant) [AmerSp *panamá*, fr *Panama*, country in Central America]

**panatela, panatella** /,panə'telə/ *n* a long slender straight-sided cigar rounded off at the sealed (mouth) end [Sp *panatela*, fr AmerSp, a long thin biscuit, deriv of L *panis* bread]

**Panatrope** /'panə,trohp/ *trademark* – used for a record player with powerful amplifier used in place of an organ to play background music at a fairground

¹**pancake** /'pan,kayk/ *n* a flat cake made from thin batter and cooked on both sides usu in a frying pan, and often served rolled and stuffed with jam, sugar, and lemon juice, or a savoury mixture

²**pancake** *n* make-up compressed into a flat cake or stick form used esp by actors [fr *Pan-cake*, a trademark]

³**pancake** *vi* to make a PANCAKE LANDING ~ *vt* to cause to pancake

**Pancake Day** *n* SHROVE TUESDAY as marked by the eating of pancakes

**pancake landing** *n* a landing in which an aircraft drops and lands in an approximately horizontal position with little forward motion

**Pancake Tuesday** *n* PANCAKE DAY

**Panchen Lama** /'pahnchən/ *n* the lama next in rank to the DALAI LAMA [*Panchen* fr Chin (Pek) *pan*¹ *ch'an*²]

**panchromatic** /,pankroh'matik, -krə-/ *adj, of a photographic film or emulsion* sensitive to light of all colours in the visible spectrum – compare ORTHOCHROMATIC [ISV]

**pancratium** /pan'krayshiəm/ *n* an ancient Greek athletic contest involving both boxing and wrestling [L, fr Gk *pankration*, fr *pan-* + *kratos* strength – more at HARD]

**pancreas** /'pangkri·əs/ n a large gland of VERTEBRATE animals that is situated beneath the stomach in the first loop of the SMALL INTESTINES and secretes PANCREATIC JUICE and the hormone insulin [NL, fr Gk *pankreas*, fr *pan-* + *kreas* flesh, meat – more at RAW] – **pancreatic** adj

**pancreat-** /'pangkri·ət-/, **pancreato-** comb form pancreas ⟨*pancreatic*⟩ [NL, fr Gk *pankreat-, pancreas*]

**pancreatectomy** /,pangkriə'tektəmi/ n surgical removal of all or part of the pancreas – **pancreatectomized** adj

**pancreatic juice** /,pangkri'atik/ n a clear alkaline liquid secreted by the pancreas into the DUODENUM (part of the intestine) and containing digestive ENZYMES that act on food already partly broken down by the GASTRIC JUICE and saliva

**pancreatin** /pang'kree·ətin, 'pangkri·ə,tin/ n a mixture of ENZYMES from the PANCREATIC JUICE; *also* a preparation containing such a mixture used in medicine

**pancreatitis** /,pangkriə'tietəs/ n, pl **pancreatitides** /-'titədeez/ inflammation of the pancreas [NL]

**pancreozymin** /,pangkrioh'ziemin/ n CHOLECYSTOKININ (hormone regulating the emptying of the GALL BLADDER) [*pancreas* + *-o-* + *zym-* + *-in*]

**panda** /'pandə/ n 1 RED PANDA 2 *also* **giant panda** a large black-and-white mammal (*Ailuropoda melanoleuca*) of W China that resembles a bear but is related to the raccoons and that feeds on bamboo [Fr, fr native name in Nepal]

**panda car** n, Br a small car used by police patrols, esp in urban areas [fr its orig having black-and-white bodywork]

**pandanus** /pan'daynəs/ n, pl **pandani, pandanuses** SCREW PINE (tropical palmlike plant) [NL, genus name, fr Malay *pandan* screw pine]

**pandect** /'pandekt/ n 1 a complete code of the laws of a country or system of law 2 a treatise covering an entire subject [LL *Pandectes*, 6th-c digest of Roman civil law, fr L *pandectes* book that contains everything, fr Gk *pandektēs* all-receiving, all-containing, fr *pan-* + *dektēs* receiver, fr *dechesthai* to receive]

**pandemic** /pan'demik/ n or adj (an outbreak of a disease) occurring over a wide geographical area and affecting an exceptionally high proportion of the population ⟨~ *cholera*⟩ – compare ENDEMIC, EPIDEMIC [adj LL *pandemus*, fr Gk *pandēmos* of all the people, fr *pan-* + *dēmos* people – more at DEMAGOGUE; n fr adj]

**pandemonium** /,pandi'mohnyəm, -ni·əm/ n a wild uproar; tumult [*Pandaemonium*, capital city of Hell in the poem *Paradise Lost* by John Milton †1674 E poet, fr Gk *pan-* + *daimōn* evil spirit – more at DEMON]

¹**pander** /'pandə/ n 1a a go-between in love intrigues b someone who procures clients for a prostitute; a pimp 2 someone who encourages or exploits the weaknesses or vices of others [ME *Pandare* Pandarus, mythical Gk procurer, fr L *Pandarus*, fr Gk *Pandaros*]

²**pander** vi to act as a pander; *esp* to provide gratification for others' desires ⟨*the audience is vulgar and stupid, you've got to ~ to them* – Herman Wouk⟩ – often + *to* – **panderer** n

**pandit** /'pundit/ n a wise or learned man in India – often used as an honorary title [Hindi *paṇḍit*, fr Skt *paṇḍita*]
*synonyms* The original Hindi word should be spelt **pandit** when it means "learned Hindu" ⟨**Pandit** Nehru⟩ but **pundit** as a slightly facetious word for an "authority" ⟨*did what all the* **pundits** *said was impossible*⟩.

**Pandora's box** /pan'dawrəz/ n a prolific source of troubles [fr the Gk myth of a box sent by the gods to Pandora, the first woman, which contained all the ills of mankind]

**pandore** /pan'daw/ n BANDORE (large lutelike musical instrument) [It, fr LL *pandure* 3-stringed lute]

**pandy** /'pandi/ vt, chiefly Scot to punish (a schoolboy) with a blow on the palm of the hand [prob fr L *pande*, imper sing of *pandere* to spread out (the hand) – more at FATHOM]

**pane** /payn/ n 1 a piece, section, or side of something: eg 1a a framed sheet of glass in a window or door b any of the sides of a nut or bolt head 2 any of the sections into which a sheet of postage stamps is cut for distribution [ME *pan, pane* strip of cloth, pane, fr MF *pan*, fr L *pannus* cloth, rag – more at VANE]

**panegyric** /,pani'jirik, -'jierik/ n a flattering oration or piece of writing; *also* formal or elaborate praise [L *panegyricus*, fr Gk *panēgyrikos* of or for a festival assembly, fr *panēgyris* festival assembly, fr *pan-* + *agyris* assembly; akin to Gk *ageirein* to gather – more at GREGARIOUS] – **panegyrical** adj, **panegyrically** adv, **panegyrist** n

¹**panel** /'panl/ n 1a(1) a list of people summoned for service as jurors a(2) *taking sing or pl vb* the group of people so summoned a(3) *taking sing or pl vb* a jury b *taking sing or pl vb* b(1) a group of people selected to render some service (eg as a committee of investigation or arbitration) ⟨*a ~ of experts*⟩ b(2) a group of people who discuss before an audience topics usu of political or social interest b(3) a group of entertainers or guests who appear as contestants in a quiz or guessing game on radio or television 2 a separate or distinct part of a surface: eg 2a(1) a thin usu rectangular board set in a frame (eg in a door) a(2) a usu sunken or raised section of a surface set off by a margin a(3) a flat usu rectangular piece of construction material (eg plywood or precast concrete) usu attached to a frame b a piece of fabric with the pattern or weave running lengthwise ⟨*skirt made with eight ~s*⟩ 3 a thin flat piece of wood on which a picture is painted; *also* a painting on such a surface 4a a flat often insulating support (eg for computer machinery or parts of an electrical device) usu with controls on one face b a usu vertical mount for controls or dials (eg on the dashboard of a car or aircraft) 5 *the* accused – used in Scots Law 6 Br 6a a list of patients formerly insured under the National Health Insurance scheme b a list of doctors in a particular area available for consultation by such patients [ME, piece of cloth, slip of parchment, jury schedule, fr MF, piece of cloth, piece, prob fr (assumed) VL *pannellus*, dim. of L *pannus* cloth]

²**panel** vt -ll- (NAm -l-, -ll-) to furnish or decorate with panels ⟨~ *led the living room*⟩

**panel beater** n a person who beats out the metal bodywork of motor vehicles as an occupation – **panel beating** n

**panel heating** n the heating of rooms by means of panels containing a heat source

**panelling** /'panəling/ n panels joined in a continuous surface; *esp* decorative wood panels so joined to line a room

**panellist** /'panl·ist/ n a member of a discussion or advisory panel or of a radio or television panel

**panel pin** n a short slender nail used in woodwork

**panel truck** n a small light lorry with a fully enclosed body

**panel van** n, Austr a small minibus or station wagon

**pang** /pang/ n 1 a brief piercing spasm of pain 2 a sharp attack of mental anguish ⟨~s *of remorse*⟩ [origin unknown]

**panga** /'pang·gə/ n a broad heavy African knife used as a tool or weapon; a machete [native name in E Africa]

**Panglossian** /pang'glosiən/ adj marked by the view that all is for the best in this best of possible worlds; excessively optimistic [*Pangloss*, optimistic tutor in the satire *Candide* by Voltaire †1778 Fr writer]

**pangolin** /pang'gohlin/ n any of several Asiatic and African anteaters (genus *Manis* of the order Pholidota) having a body that is covered with large overlapping horny scales – called also SCALY ANTEATER [Malay *pěngguling*, fr *guling* rolling over; fr its habit of rolling itself into a ball]

¹**panhandle** /'pan,handl/ n, NAm a narrow strip of land projecting from one territory or state into another or between others ⟨*the Alaska ~ down the Pacific coast of Canada*⟩

²**panhandle** vb, NAm to stop people on the street and ask for food or money (from); beg (from) [back-formation fr *panhandler*, prob fr *panhandle*, n; fr the extended forearm] – **panhandler** n

¹**panic** /'panik/ adj 1 of or arising from a panic ⟨*a wave of ~ buying*⟩ 2 *often cap* of the god Pan; *specif* of or resembling the state of terror he was held to induce [Fr *panique*, fr Gk *panikos*, lit., of, Pan, fr *Pan*, Gk god of woods & shepherds]

²**panic** n 1 a sudden overpowering fright; *esp* a sudden unreasoning terror that spreads rapidly through a group of people or animals 2 a sudden widespread fright concerning financial affairs and resulting in a depression in values, widespread sale of securities, and reduction of the availability of credit *synonyms* see ¹FEAR – **panicky** adj

³**panic** vb -ck- to (cause to) be affected with panic

**panic button** n 1 an emergency control or signalling device; *esp* one used to activate an alarm 2 something setting off a precipitate emergency response

**panic grass** n any of various grasses (*Panicum* or related genera) that grow in warm and tropical regions and of which some are important forage and cereal grasses (eg millet) [ME *panik*, fr MF or L; MF *panic* foxtail millet, fr L *panicum*, fr *panus* swelling, ear of millet]

**panicle** /'panikl/ n 1 a flower head in which the main stem branches to bear flowers on short stalks in succession from the base upwards 2 a pyramidal loosely branched flower cluster [L *panicula*, fr dim. of *panus* swelling] – **panicled** *adj*, **paniculate** *adj*

**'panic-,stricken** *adj* overcome with panic

**Panjabi** /poon'jahbi/ *n or adj* (a) Punjabi

**panjandrum** /pan'jandrəm/ *n*, *pl* **panjandrums** *also* **panjandra** /-drə/ *humorous* a powerful personage or self-important official [Grand *Panjandrum*, burlesque title of an imaginary personage in some nonsense lines by Samuel Foote †1777 E actor & dramatist]

**panleucopaenia**, *chiefly NAm* **panleucopenia** /,pan,-loohkə'peenyə, -,lyooh-, -niə/ *n* an acute usu fatal epidemic virus disease of cats characterized by fever, diarrhoea and dehydration, and extensive destruction of WHITE BLOOD CELLS – called also CAT FLU, DISTEMPER [NL]

**panmictic** /pan'miktik/ *adj*, *genetics* of or exhibiting panmixia [*pan-* + Gk *miktos*, verbal of *mignynai* to mix]

**panmixia** /pan'miksiə/ *n*, *genetics* random mating within a breeding population [NL, fr *pan-* + Gk *mixis* act of mingling, mating, fr *mignynai* to mix – more at MIX]

**panne** /pan/ *n* **1** a silk or rayon velvet with lustrous pile flattened in one direction **2** a heavy silk or rayon satin with high lustre and waxy smoothness [Fr, fr OF *penne*, *panne* fur used for lining, fr L *pinna* feather, wing – more at PEN]

**pannier, panier** /'panyə, 'pani·ə/ *n* **1** a large basket; *esp* either of a pair carried on the back of an animal **2a** a hooped petticoat, esp one giving extra width at the sides and worn in the 18th century **b** drapery that gives extra width to the sides of a skirt at hip level **3** *chiefly Br* either of a pair of bags or boxes fixed on either side of the rear wheel of a bicycle or motorcycle [ME *panier*, fr MF, fr L *panarium*, fr *panis* bread – more at FOOD]

**pannikin** /'panikin/ *n*, *Br* a small metal pan or cup [¹*pan* + *-nikin* (as in *cannikin*)]

**panocha** /pə'nohchə/, **panoche** /-chi/ *n* a coarse Mexican sugar [MexSp *panocha*, dim. of Sp *pan* bread]

**panoply** /'panəpli/ *n* **1a** a full suit of armour **b** ceremonial attire **2a** a magnificent or impressive array ⟨*the full ~ of a military funeral*⟩ **b** a display of all appropriate appurtenances ⟨*has the ~ of science fiction . . . but it is not true science fiction* – Isaac Asimov⟩ [Gk *panoplia*, fr *pan-* + *hopla* arms, armor, pl of *hoplon* tool, weapon – more at HOPLITE] – **panoplied** *adj*

**panopticon** /pan'optikon, kən/ *n* an institution, esp a prison, designed so that all parts of the interior can be seen from one point [*pan-* + Gk *opticon*, neut of *optikos* optic] – **panoptic, panoptical** *adj*, **panoptically** *adv*

**panorama** /,panə'rahmə/ *n* **1a** a large pictorial representation encircling the spectator **b** a picture exhibited a part at a time by being unrolled before the spectator **2a** an unobstructed or complete view of a landscape or area ⟨*from here one has a ~ of the lake with the village in the distance*⟩ **b** a comprehensive presentation or survey of a series of events ⟨*a ~ of American history*⟩ **c** range ⟨*a book in which the author displays the full ~ of his learning*⟩ [*pan-* + Gk *horama* sight, fr *horan* to see – more at WARY] – **panoramic** *adj*, **panoramically** *adv*

**panpipe** /'pan,piep, ,-'-/ *n*, **panpipes** *n pl* a simple wind instrument consisting of a graduated series of short vertical pipes bound together with the mouthpieces in an even row [*Pan*, Gk god of woods & shepherds, its alleged inventor]

**,Pan-'Slavism** *n* a political and cultural movement originally emphasizing the cultural ties between the Slavic peoples but later associated with Russian expansionist policies

**pansy** /'panzi/ *n* **1** a garden plant (*Viola tricolor hortensis*) that is derived from WILD PANSIES and violets and has flowers with rounded velvety petals that are usu variegated in brown, purple, yellow, white, or blue; *also* a flower of the pansy **2** *derog* an effeminate male or male homosexual [MF *pensée*, fr *pensée* thought, fr fem of *pensé*, pp of *penser* to think, fr L *pensare* to ponder – more at PENSIVE]

**¹pant** /pant/ *vi* **1a** to breathe quickly, irregularly, or in a laboured manner **b** to run panting ⟨*~ing along beside the bicycle*⟩ **c** to move with or make a throbbing or puffing sound **2** to long eagerly; yearn ⟨*after a long hot afternoon at the zoo, the children were all ~ing for ice cream*⟩ **3** to throb, pulsate ~ *vt* to utter with panting; gasp ⟨*~ed his apologies for arriving so late*⟩ [ME *panten*, fr MF *pantaisier*, fr (assumed) VL *phantasiare* to have hallucinations, fr Gk *phantasioun*, fr *phantasia* appearance, imagination – more at FANCY]

**²pant** *n* **1a** a panting breath **b** the visible movement of the chest accompanying such a breath **2** a throbbing or puffing sound

**pant-** /pant-/, **panto-** *comb form* all ⟨*pantology*⟩ [MF, fr L, fr Gk, fr *pant-*, *pas* – more at PAN-]

**pantalets, pantalettes** /,pantə'lets/ *n pl* a trouserlike undergarment with a ruffle at the bottom of each leg designed to show beneath the skirt, worn esp by women and children in the early 19th century [alter. of *pantaloons*]

**pantaloon** /,pantə'loohn/ *n* **1** a stock character in the COMMEDIA DELL'ARTE who is usu a skinny old dotard wearing spectacles, slippers, and a tight-fitting combination of trousers and stockings **2** *pl* closely fitting breeches or trousers; *esp* such trousers fastened at the front usu to the waistcoat by means of a panel with buttons and fastened under the instep with straps, and worn esp in the 19th century [MF & OIt; MF *Pantalon*, fr OIt *Pantaleone*, *Pantalone*]

**pantechnicon** /pan'teknikən/ *n*, *Br* a large van, esp for transporting movable possessions (e g furniture) [short for *pantechnicon van*, fr *pantechnicon* (storage warehouse), fr *Pantechnicon*, a building in London established for the sale of works of art but later used as a furniture warehouse, fr *pan-* + Gk *technikon*, neut of *technikos* technical, artistic]

**pantheism** /'panthee·iz(ə)m/ *n* **1** a doctrine that equates God with the forces and laws of nature **2** the worship of all gods of different religions, cults, or peoples indifferently; *also* toleration of such worship (e g at certain periods of the Roman empire) [Fr *panthéisme*, fr *panthéiste* pantheist, fr E *pantheist*, fr *pan-* + *-theist*] – **pantheist** *n*, **pantheistic, pantheistical** *adj*, **pantheistically** *adv*

**pantheon** /'panthi·ən, pan'thee·ən/ *n* **1** a temple dedicated to all the gods **2** a building serving as the burial place of or containing memorials to dead heroes **3** the gods of a people; *esp* the officially recognized gods **4** a group of illustrious persons [ME *Panteon*, a temple at Rome, fr L *Pantheon*, fr Gk *pantheion* temple of all the gods, fr neut of *pantheios* of all gods, fr *pan-* + *theos* god]

**panther** /'panthə/ *n*, *pl* **panthers** *also esp collectively* **panther 1** a leopard; *esp* a black leopard **2** *NAm* a puma [ME *pantere*, fr OF, fr L *panthera*, fr Gk *panthēr*]

**pantie girdle** /'panti/ *n* a woman's girdle shaped like pants

**panties** /'pantiz/ *n pl* pants for women or children; knickers

**pantile** /'pan,tiel/ *n* a roofing tile whose cross section is a flattened S-shape [¹*pan*] – **pantiled** *adj*

**panto** /'pantoh/ *n*, *Br informal* a pantomime

**pantograph** /'pantə,grahf, -,graf/ *n* **1** an instrument consisting of four rigid bars joined in parallelogram form for copying maps or plans on any desired scale; *also* any of various extensible devices of similar construction (e g for use as brackets or gates) **2** a collapsible and adjustable framework mounted on the roof of an electric vehicle (e g a railway locomotive) for collecting current from an overhead wire – compare TROLLEY 1 [Fr *pantographe*, fr *pant-* + *-graphe* -graph] – **pantographic** *adj*

**pantomime** /'pantəmiem/ *n* **1a** any of various dramatic or dancing performances in which a story is told by expressive body or facial movements of the performers; *also* an actor specializing in such performances **b** a British theatrical and musical entertainment of the Christmas season based on any of various nursery tales with stock roles (e g a dame and a principal boy) and topical jokes **2** communication (e g of a story) by body or facial movements esp in drama or dance ⟨*since none of us could speak the language, communication was wholly in ~*⟩ [L *pantomimus*, fr *pant-* + *mimus* mime] – **pantomimist** *n*, **pantomimic** *adj*

**pantothenate** /,pantə'thenayt, pan'tothinayt/ *n* any of various chemical compounds (SALTS or ESTERS) formed by combination between PANTOTHENIC ACID and a metal atom, an alcohol, or another chemical group

**pantothenic acid** /,pantə'thenik/ *n* a thick oily acid, $C_9H_{17}NO_5$, that is a vitamin of the VITAMIN B COMPLEX, is found in all living tissues, and is essential for cell growth [Gk *pantothen* from all sides, fr *pant-*, *pas* all – more at PAN-]

**pantry** /'pantri/ *n* **1** a room or cupboard used for storing provisions or tableware or from which food is brought to the table **2** a room (e g in a hotel or hospital) for preparation of cold foods to order [ME *panetrie*, fr MF *paneterie*, fr OF, fr *panetier* servant in charge of the pantry, irreg fr *pan* bread, fr L *panis* – more at FOOD]

**pants** /pants/ *n pl* **1** *chiefly Br* an undergarment that covers the crotch and hips and that may extend to the waist and partly down each leg **2** *chiefly NAm* trousers [short for *pantaloons*] – **wear the pants** *NAm* WEAR THE TROUSERS

**pantsuit** /'pant,sooht/ *n, chiefly NAm* TROUSER SUIT

**panty hose** /'panti/, **pantihose** *n pl, chiefly NAm* tights

**pantywaist** /'panti,wayst/ *n* 1 a child's garment of former times consisting of short trousers buttoned to a waist 2 *NAm slang* a sissy – **pantywaist** *adj*

¹**panzer** /'panzə/ *adj* of, carried out by, or being a German armoured unit, esp of World War II [Ger, fr *panzer* coat of mail, armour, tank, fr OF *pancière* armour, fr *pance* belly – more at PAUNCH]

²**panzer** *n* a tank; *esp* a German tank of World War II

¹**pap** /pap/ *n* 1 something (e g a rounded hill) shaped like a nipple 2 *chiefly dial* a nipple, teat [ME *pappe*, prob of imit origin]

²**pap** *n* 1 a soft food, esp bread in milk, for infants or invalids 2 something (e g a film, novel, or popular newspaper) lacking solid value or substance 3 *NAm* political patronage [ME, prob of imit origin]

¹**papa** /pə'pah/ *n, chiefly Br formal* father – used formerly, esp in address [Fr (baby talk)]

²**papa** /'papə/ *n, informal* daddy – used esp by children

³**papa** /'pahpə/ *n, NZ* soft rock with a smooth surface that lies under a shallow layer of surface soil [Maori]

**Papa** – a communications code word for the letter *p*

**papacy** /'paypəsi/ *n* 1 the office of pope ⟨*under control of the ~* ⟩ 2 a succession or line of popes 3 the term of a pope's reign 4 *cap* the system of government of the Roman Catholic church having the pope as its supreme head [ME *papacie*, fr ML *papatia*, fr LL *papa* pope – more at POPE]

**papain** /pə'pay·in, pə'pie·in, 'paypə·in/ *n* an ENZYME found in the juice of unripe papaya that speeds up the breakdown of proteins to simpler compounds and is used esp as a tenderizer for meat and in medicine to treat wounds [ISV, fr *papaya*]

**papal** /'paypl/ *adj* of a pope or the Roman Catholic church [ME, fr MF, fr ML *papalis*, fr LL *papa* pope] – **papally** *adv*

**papalagi** /,papə'lang·i/ *n, pl* **papalagi** *NZ* PALAGI (European)

**papal cross** *n* a cross having a long upright shaft and three successively shorter crossbars one above the other

**Papanicolaou test** /,pupə'nikəlow/ *n* PAP SMEAR (smear test for early detection of cancer)

**paparazzo** /pupə'rutsoh/ *n, pl* **paparazzi** /-si/ *chiefly NAm* a news reporter or photographer who doggedly searches for a story that can be sensationalized; *broadly* a journalist [It]

**papaverine** /pə'payvəreen, -rin/ *n* a drug, $C_{20}H_{21}NO_4$, that is obtained from opium, causes the relaxation of SMOOTH MUSCLE (e g of the gut and blood vessels) and is thus used to treat certain types of colic and to relieve spasm in blood vessels (e g in the brain) [ISV, fr L *papaver* poppy]

**papaw** /1 pə'paw, 2 'pawpaw, 'pah-/, **pawpaw** /'pawpaw/ *n* 1 a papaya 2 a N American tree (*Asimina triloba*) of the custard-apple family with purple flowers and a yellow edible fruit; *also* the fruit of the pawpaw [prob modif of Sp *papaya*]

**papaya** /pə'pie·ə/ *n* a tropical American evergreen tree (*Carica papaya* of the family Caricaceae) with large oblong yellow edible fruit; *also* the fruit of the papaya [Sp, of AmerInd origin; akin to Otomac *papai*]

¹**paper** /'paypə/ *n* **1a(1)** a material consisting of closely compacted usu vegetable fibres (e g wood or cloth) in the form of thin sheets **a(2)** other similar material (e g plastic) in sheet form **b** a piece of paper **2a** *often pl* a piece of paper containing a written or printed statement; a document ⟨*naturalization ~s*⟩; *specif* documents carried as proof of identity or status **b** *pl* official documents relating to the cargo, ownership, etc of a ship **c** a piece of paper containing writing or print **d** a formal written composition often designed for publication and often intended to be read aloud ⟨*presented a scholarly ~ at the meeting*⟩ **e** a piece of written schoolwork ⟨*had to write a ~ a week in English class*⟩ **f** an examination paper **3** a paper container or wrapper **4** a newspaper **5** the negotiable notes or instruments of commerce **6** wallpaper **7** *informal* a ticket; *esp* a free pass (to a theatrical performance) [ME *papir*, fr MF *papier*, fr L *papyrus* papyrus, paper, fr Gk *papyros* papyrus]

²**paper** *vt* 1 to cover or line with paper; *esp* to apply wallpaper to 2 *informal* to fill by giving out free passes ⟨*~ the theatre for opening night*⟩ *~ vi* to hang wallpaper – **paperer** *n*

**paper over** *vt* 1 to gloss over, explain away, or patch up (e g major differences) esp in order to maintain an appearance of agreement 2 to hide, conceal

³**paper** *adj* **1a** made of paper, thin cardboard, or papier-mâché ⟨*a ~ bag*⟩ ⟨*a ~ cup*⟩ **b** papery 2 of clerical work or written communication 3 existing only in theory; nominal ⟨*a ~ blockade*⟩ 4 issued as paper money 5 finished with a crisp

smooth surface like that of paper ⟨*~ taffeta*⟩ 6 of or marking a first anniversary ⟨*~ wedding*⟩ 7 *informal* admitted by free passes ⟨*a ~ audience*⟩

**paperback** /-,bak/ *n* a book with a flexible paper binding – compare HARDBACK – **paperback** *adj*

**paperboard** /'paypə,bawd/ *n* cardboard – **paperboard** *adj*

**paperboy** /-,boy/, **papergirl** *n* a young person who delivers or sells newspapers

**paper chase** *n* a game in which some of the players scatter bits of paper as a trail which others try to follow in order to find and catch them

**paper clip** *n* a small clip made from two loops of wire that is used for holding sheets of paper together – **paperclip** *vt*

**paperhanger** /-,hang·ə/ *n* somebody who applies wallpaper to walls as an occupation

**paperhanging** /-,hang·ing/ *n* applying wallpaper

**paper knife** *n* 1 a blunt ornamental knife for slitting envelopes or uncut pages

**papermaker** /'paypə,maykə/ *n* a person, firm, or machine that makes paper – **papermaking** *n*

**paper money** *n* BANK NOTES

**paper mulberry** *n* an Asiatic tree (*Broussonetia papyrifera*) of the fig family, the bark of which was formerly used in paper-making, esp in Japan

**paper nautilus** *n* an INVERTEBRATE animal (genus *Argonauta* of the class Cephalopoda) related to the squids and octopuses that is found in warm tropical seas and the female of which has a delicate papery shell – called also ARGONAUT

**paper profit** *n* an unrealized gain in the value of an asset

**paper qualifications** *n pl* evidence (e g certificates) of having passed one or more examinations

**paper tape** *n* a ribbon of paper used in a computer, telex machine, etc in which a pattern of holes has been punched to represent information or instructions

**paper tiger** *n* one who or that which is outwardly powerful or dangerous but inwardly weak or ineffectual ⟨*had to show that the military commitment was not a ~* ⟩ [trans of a Chin phrase used by Mao Zedong (Mao Tse-tung) †1976 Chin political leader]

**paperweight** /-,wayt/ *n* a usu small heavy ornamental object used to hold down loose papers (e g on a desk)

**paperwork** /-,wuhk/ *n* routine clerical, form-filling, or record-keeping work often incidental to a more important task

**papery** /'payp(ə)ri/ *adj* resembling paper in thinness or fragility ⟨*~ leaves*⟩ ⟨*~ silk*⟩ – **paperiness** *n*

¹**Paphian** /'payfiən/ *adj, formal* of esp illicit sexual love [L *paphius* of Paphos, fr Gk *paphios*, fr *Paphos*, ancient city in Cyprus that was the centre of worship of Aphrodite, Gk goddess of love]

²**Paphian** *n, formal* a prostitute

**papier collé** /,papyay 'kolay, ,paypə/ *n, pl* **papiers collés** a collage [Fr, glued paper]

**papier-mâché** /,papyay 'mashay, mə'shay, 'paypə/ *n* a light strong modelling material made of wastepaper pulped with glue and other additives which is moulded and shaped in layers before being allowed to dry [Fr, lit., chewed paper] – **papier-mâché** *adj*

**papilionaceous** /pə,pilyə'nayshəs/ *adj, of a flower* having petals of irregular shapes and sizes, esp in plants of the pea family [L *papilion-, papilio* butterfly – more at PAVILION]

**papilla** /pə'pilə/ *n, pl* **papillae** /-lie/ a small projecting body part similar to a nipple in form: eg **a** a small area of tissue extending into and nourishing the root of a hair, feather, etc **b** any of the protuberances of the skin often containing organs sensitive to touch **c** any of the small protuberances on the upper surface of the tongue [NL, fr L, nipple; akin to L *papula* pimple, Lith *papas* nipple] – **papillary, papillate, papillose** *adj*

**papilloma** /,papi'lohmə/ *n, pl* **papillomas, papillomata** /-mətə/ 1 a mild nonlethal tumour (e g a wart) caused by over-growth of EPITHELIAL tissue covering an external surface or lining a body cavity 2 an epithelial tumour caused by a virus [NL, fr *papilla* + *-oma*] – **papillomatous** *adj*

**papillon** /'papilon/ *n* (any of) a breed of small slender toy spaniels with large ears having the shape of the wings of a butterfly [Fr, lit., butterfly, fr L *papilion-, papilio*]

**papillote** /'papiloht/ *n* 1 a greased paper wrapper in which food (e g meat or fish) is cooked 2 ²FRILL 1b (paper frill on a chop, cutlet, etc) [Fr, fr *papillon* butterfly]

**papist** /'paypist/ *n, often cap* 1 an advocate of authoritarian government by the Pope 2 *derog* ROMAN CATHOLIC [MF or NL; MF *papiste*, fr *pape* pope; NL *papista*, fr LL *papa* pope] – **papist** *adj*

**papistry** /'paypistri/ *n*, *derog* 1 ROMAN CATHOLICISM 2 the Roman Catholic religion

**papoose** /pə'poohs/ *n* a young child of N American Indian parents [Narraganset *papoòs*]

**papovavirus** /pə'pohvə,vie(ə)rəs/ *n* any of a group of viruses that have an outer protein coating with 42 protuberances resembling knobs and that are associated with or responsible for various growths (eg some warts) of mammals [*pa*pilloma + polyoma + vacuolation + virus]

**pappose** /'papohs/ *adj* having or being a pappus

**pappus** /'papəs/ *n*, *pl* **pappi** /-pi, -pie/ a ring or tuft of light feathery hairs that crowns the fruit in various flowering plants (eg the dandelion) and helps wind dispersal of the fruit [L, fr Gk *pappos* grandfather, old man, down]

**pappy** /'papi/ *n*, *chiefly S & Mid US informal* daddy – used esp by children [*papa* + ⁴-*y*]

**paprika** /'paprikə, pa'preekə/ *n* a mild red condiment consisting of the finely ground dried pods of various cultivated SWEET PEPPERS; *also* a sweet pepper used for making paprika – compare CAYENNE PEPPER [Hung, fr Serb, fr *papar* pepper, fr Gk *peperi*]

**Pap smear** /pap/ *n* a method for the early detection of cancer in which cells (eg from the lining of the cervix) are examined under the microscope using a special staining technique that differentiates diseased tissue – called also PAPANICOLAOU TEST [George N *Papanicolaou* †1962 US (Gk-born) medical scientist]

**Papuan** /'papyooən/ *n* 1 a native or inhabitant of Papua 2 a member of any of the Negroid native peoples of New Guinea and adjacent areas of Melanesia 3 any of a mixed group of languages of New Guinea, New Britain, and the Solomon islands [*Papua*, territory in the SW Pacific] – **Papuan** *adj*

**papule** /'papyoohl/ *n* a small solid usu conical projection from the skin [L *papula*] – **papular** *adj*

**papyrology** /,papi'roləji/ *n* the study of ancient papyrus manuscripts [ISV] – **papyrologist** *n*

**papyrus** /pə'pie-ərəs/ *n*, *pl* **papyruses**, **papyri** /-ri/ 1 a tall grasslike plant (*Cyperus papyrus*) of the sedge family that has dark green stems bearing terminal tufts of leaves and grows in the Nile valley and S Europe 2 the pith of the papyrus plant, esp when cut in strips and pressed into a material for writing on 3 a usu ancient manuscript written on papyrus △ palimpsest [ME, fr L – more at PAPER]

¹**par** /pah/ *n* 1a the established value of the monetary unit of one country expressed in terms of the monetary unit of another country **b** the monetary value assigned to each share in a company, bond, etc 2 a common level; equality – esp in *on a par with* 3a an amount taken as an average or norm **b** an accepted standard; *specif* a usual standard of physical condition or health 4 the standard score (for a good player) for each hole of a golf course; *also* a score equal to par [L, that which is equal, fr *par* equal] – **par** *adj*

²**par** *vt* **-rr-** to score par on (a hole in golf)

¹**para** /'pahrə/ *n*, *pl* **paras**, **para** 1 (a coin representing) any of several monetary units of the Turkish Empire 2 – see *dinar* at MONEY table [Turk, fr Per *pārah*, lit., piece]

²**para** /'parə/ *n*, *informal* a paratrooper

¹**para-** /parə-/, **par-** *prefix* **1a** beside; alongside ⟨para*thyroid*⟩ ⟨par*allel*⟩ **b** beyond ⟨para*normal*⟩ ⟨para*dox*⟩ **2a** having directly opposite positions across the ring structure of BENZENE (chemical compound with six carbon atoms joined in a ring) ⟨para*dichlorobenzene*⟩ **b** involving chemical reaction at a position in a BENZENE RING directly opposite the position of a particular attached atom or chemical group – compare META-, ORTH- **3a** faulty; abnormal ⟨par*aesthesia*⟩ ⟨para*noia*⟩ **b** associated in a subsidiary or auxiliary capacity ⟨para*medical*⟩ **c** closely resembling or related to ⟨para*typhoid*⟩ **4** of the form of a DIATOMIC (composed of two atoms) molecule in which the SPINS (rotation about an axis) of the two constituent atoms are in opposing directions ⟨para*hydrogen*⟩ [ME, fr MF, fr L, fr Gk, fr *para;* akin to Gk *pro* before – more at FOR]

²**para-** *comb form* parachute ⟨para*trooper*⟩ [*parachute*]

**-para** /-pərə/ *comb form* (→ *n*), *pl* **-paras, -parae** /-pərie/ woman delivered of (so many) children ⟨*tri*para⟩ [L, fr *parere* to give birth to – more at PARE]

**para-aminobenzoic acid** /,parə ,aminohben,zoh·ik, ə,meenoh-/ *n* a para-substituted AMINOBENZOIC ACID that is a member of the VITAMIN B COMPLEX, is present in yeast and liver and has an important role in ensuring healthy growth [ISV]

**para-aminosalicylic acid** /,aminoh,sali'silik, ə,meenoh-/ *n* a form of AMINOSALICYLIC ACID that is used in the treatment of tuberculosis

**parabasis** /pə'rabəsis/ *n* an address to the audience by the chorus in a classical Greek comedy [Gk, fr *parabainein* to go aside, step forward, fr *para-* + *bainein* to walk, go – more at COME]

**parabiosis** /,parəbie'ohsis/ *n* anatomical and physiological union of two organisms (eg Siamese twins) so that they share common body parts, blood circulation, etc [NL, fr *para-* + *-biosis*] – **parabiotic** *adj*, **parabiotically** *adv*

**parable** /'parəbl/ *n* a usu short allegorical story illustrating a moral or religious principle *synonyms* see ALLEGORY [ME, fr MF, fr LL *parabola*, fr Gk *parabolē*, fr *paraballein* to compare, fr *para-* + *ballein* to throw – more at DEVIL]

**parabola** /pə'rabələ/ *n* 1 a two-dimensional curve generated by a point moving so that its distance from a fixed point (FOCUS) is equal to its distance from a fixed line (DIRECTRIX); the intersection of a cone with a plane parallel to a straight line on the surface of the cone ⟨*an object flying through the air under the action of gravity traces a ~*⟩ – compare ELLIPSE, HYPERBOLA 2 something bowl-shaped (eg a microphone) [NL, fr Gk *parabolē*, lit., comparison]

**parabolic** /,parə'bolik/ *adj* 1 **parabolic, parabolical** expressed by or being a parable; allegorical 2 of or having the form of a parabola ⟨*~ mirror*⟩ [(1) LL *parabola* parable; (2) NL *parabola*] – **parabolically** *adv*

**parabol·ize, -ise** /pə'rabəliez, 'parəbəliez/ *vt* 1 to explain by means of a parable 2 to shape like a parabola

**paraboloid** /pə'rabəloyd/ *n* a surface or solid generated by the rotation of a parabola about its axis of symmetry – compare ELLIPSOID, HYPERBOLOID – **paraboloidal** *adj*

**paracetamol** /,parə'seetəmol, -'setə-/ *n* (a tablet of) a chemical compound, $HOC_6H_4CH_3CONH$, that is a derivative of ACETANILIDE and is widely used as a painkiller and in the synthesis of other chemical compounds [¹*para-* + *acet-* + *amin-* + *-ol*]

¹**parachute** /'parə,shooht/ *n* 1 a device that folds up and consists of a light fabric canopy connected by strings to a harness and that is used esp for ensuring a safe descent of a person or object from a great height (eg from a flying aeroplane) 2 a device (eg the tufts of a dandelion seed) suggestive of a parachute in form, use, or operation [Fr, fr *para-* (as in *parasol*) + *chute* fall – more at CHUTE] – **parachutist** *n*

²**parachute** *vt* to convey by means of a parachute ~ *vi* to descend by means of a parachute

**Paraclete** /'parəkleet/ *n* the Holy Spirit [ME *Paraclit*, fr MF *Paraclet*, fr LL *Paracletus*, fr Gk *Paraklētos*, lit., advocate, intercessor, fr *parakalein* to invoke, fr *para-* + *kalein* to call – more at LOW]

¹**parade** /pə'rayd/ *n* 1 an ostentatious show; an exhibition ⟨*made a ~ of his superior knowledge*⟩ 2 the (ceremonial) ordered assembly of a body of troops before a superior officer 3 a public procession 4 a place for strolling; a promenade 5 *chiefly Br* a row of shops, esp with a service road 6 *NAm* a place where troops assemble regularly for parade [Fr, fr MF, fr *parer* to prepare – more at PARE]

²**parade** *vt* 1 to cause to manoeuvre or march 2 to exhibit ostentatiously ~ *vi* 1 to march in a procession 2 to promenade 3a SHOW OFF **b** to masquerade ⟨*a myth that ~s as science*⟩ *synonyms* see ¹SHOW – **parader** *n*

**paradichlorobenzene** /,parədie,klawroh'benzeen/ *n* a white chemical compound, $C_6H_4Cl_2$, made by chemically combining BENZENE with chlorine and used chiefly as an agent against clothes moths [ISV]

**paradigm** /'parədiem/ *n* 1 an example or pattern; *esp* an outstandingly clear or typical example 2 a set of all the INFLECTIONS (different forms) of a word [LL *paradigma*, fr Gk *paradeigma*, fr *paradeiknynai* to show side by side, fr *para-* + *deiknynai* to show – more at DICTION] – **paradigmatic** *adj*

**paradisaic** /,parə'diziak/, **paradisaical** /,parədi'zie-əkl/ *adj* paradisiacal [*paradise* + *-aic* (as in *Hebraic*)] – **paradisaical** *adj*, **paradisaically** *adv*

**paradisal** /,parə'diesl/ *adj* paradisiacal

**paradise** /'parədies/ *n* 1 *often cap* **1a** the place or state of perfect happiness enjoyed by Adam and Eve before the first sin; the Garden of Eden **b** an intermediate place or state where the righteous dead await resurrection and judgment **c** HEAVEN 2a 2 a place of bliss, felicity, or delight [ME *paradis*, fr OF, fr LL *paradisus*, fr Gk *paradeisos*, lit., enclosed park, of Iranian origin; akin to Av *pairi-daēza-* enclosure; akin to Gk *peri* round & to Gk *teichos* wall – more at PERI-, DOUGH]

**paradise fish** *n* either of two brilliantly coloured freshwater fishes (*Macropodus opercularis* or *Macropodus chinersis*) from S or SE Asia often kept in aquariums

**paradisiacal** /ˌparədiˈzieˑəkl, -ˈsieˑ, -die-/, **paradisiac** /ˌparəˈdiziak, -ˈdis-/ *adj* of or resembling paradise [LL *paradisiacus*, fr *paradisus*] – **paradisiacally** *adv*

**parados** /ˈparədos/ *n* a bank of earth behind a fortified place or trench, giving protection from firing from the rear [Fr, fr *para-* (as in *parasol*) + *dos* back, fr L *dorsum*]

**paradox** /ˈparəˌdoks/ *n* **1** a tenet contrary to received opinion **2a** a statement (e g "the child is father to the man") that is apparently contradictory or absurd and yet might be true **b** a self-contradictory statement (e g "all generalizations are false") or conclusion **3** something (e g a person, condition, or act) with seemingly contradictory qualities or phases [L *paradoxum*, fr Gk *paradoxon*, fr neut of *paradoxos* contrary to expectation, fr *para-* + *dokein* to think, seem – more at DECENT]

**paradoxical** /ˌparəˈdoksikl/ *adj* **1a** constituting a paradox **b** of a paradox **c** inclined to paradoxes **2** not being the normal or usual kind ⟨~ *pulse*⟩ – **paradoxicalness** *n*

**paradoxically** /ˌparəˈdoksikli/ *adv* **1** in a paradoxical way **2** it is paradoxical that

**paradoxical sleep** *n* a part of the sleep cycle that is characterized by increased electrical activity of the brain, by reduced muscle tone, and, esp in humans, by dreaming and RAPID EYE MOVEMENTS

**paraesthesia**, *NAm chiefly* **paresthesia** /ˌpareesˈtheezyə, -zh(y)ə/ *n* an abnormal sensation of tingling, creeping, etc (e g on the skin) that has no physical cause [NL, fr *para-* + *aesthesia*]

¹**paraffin** /ˈparəˈfin, ˈ---/ *n* **1a** a waxy inflammable substance obtained esp from distillates of wood, coal, petroleum, etc that is a complex mixture of HYDROCARBONS (chemical compounds containing both hydrogen and carbon) and is used chiefly in coating and sealing, in candles, in chemical synthesis, and in drugs and cosmetics **b** any of various mixtures of similar HYDROCARBONS including mixtures that are semisolid or oily **2** a HYDROCARBON of the ALKANE series **3** an inflammable HYDROCARBON oil usu obtained by distillation of petroleum and used esp as a fuel [Ger, fr L *parum* too little (akin to L *paucus* few) + *affinis* bordering on – more at FEW, AFFINITY; fr its not easily entering into compounds with other substances] – **paraffinic** *adj*

²**paraffin** *vt* to treat with paraffin

**paragenesis** /ˌparəˈjenəsis/ *n* **1** the order in which minerals occurring together in rocks have developed **2** the formation of minerals in contact with each other in such a manner as to affect one another's development [NL, fr *para-* + *-graphia* -graphy] – **paragenetic** *adj*, **paragenetically** *adv*

**paragoge** /ˌparəˈgohji/ *n* the addition of a letter or syllable (e g the *b* in *limb*) to the end of a word, esp in the course of language development [LL, fr Gk *paragōgē*, fr *paragesthai* to be derived, be formed, passive of *paragein* to lead past, change (a letter slightly), fr *para-* + *agein* to lead, drive] – **paragogic** *adj*

**paragon** /ˈparəgən/ *n* a model of excellence or perfection [MF, fr OIt *paragone*, lit., touchstone, fr *paragonare* to test on a touchstone, fr Gk *parakonan* to sharpen, fr *para-* + *akonē* whetstone, fr *akē* point; akin to Gk *akmē* point – more at EDGE]

¹**paragraph** /ˈparəˌgrahf, -ˌgraf/ *n* **1a** a subdivision of a written composition that develops a single point or idea and begins on a new line that in English is usu indented **b** a short composition or news item that is complete in one paragraph **2** a sign (e g ¶) used as a reference mark or to indicate the beginning of a paragraph [MF & ML; MF *paragraphe*, fr ML *paragraphus* sign marking a paragraph, fr Gk *paragraphos* line used to mark change of persons in a dialogue, fr *paragraphein* to write alongside, fr *para-* + *graphein* to write – more at CARVE] – **paragraphic** *adj*, **paragraphically** *adv*

²**paragraph** *vt* **1** to write about or express in a paragraph **2** to divide into paragraphs – **paragrapher, paragraphist** *n*

**paragraphia** /ˌparəˈgrahfiə/ *n* a condition, resulting from mental disorder or brain injury, in which words or letters other than those intended are written [NL]

**parainfluenza virus, parainfluenza** /ˌparəˌinflooˈenzə/ *n* any of several viruses that are associated with or responsible for some respiratory infections (e g croup) in children

**parakeet**, *NAm also* **parrakeet** /ˌparəˈkeet, ˈ--ˌ-/ *n* any of numerous usu small slender long-tailed parrots (subfamily Psittacinae) [Sp & MF; Sp *periquito*, fr MF *perroquet* parrot]

**paralanguage** /ˈparəˌlangˑgwij/ *n* optional vocal effects (e g tone of voice) that accompany an utterance and may communicate meaning

**paraldehyde** /pəˈraldihied/ *n* a synthetic drug, $CH(CH_3)OCH(CH_3)OCH(CH_3)O$, used esp as a sedative and hypnotic to control fits (e g in epilepsy) [¹*para-* + *aldehyde*]

**paraleipsis** /ˌparəˈliepsis/ *n pl* **paraleipses** (a) paralipsis

**paralimnion** /ˌparəˈlimnion, -ən/ *n* the shore of a lake extending from the edge of the water to the limit of rooted vegetation [NL, fr *para-* + Gk *limnion*, dim. of *limnē* marshy lake; akin to Gk *limēn* harbour – more at LIMB]

**paralinguistics** /ˌparəlingˈgwistiks/ *n* the study of paralanguage – **paralinguistic** *adj*

**paralipomena** /ˌparəlieˈpominə/ *n taking pl vb* things added to a work as a supplement [LL, fr Gk *paraleipomena*, lit., things left out, fr neut pl of prp passive of *paraleipein* to leave out, fr *para-* + *leipein* to leave – more at LOAN]

**Paralipomenon** /ˌparəlieˈpominən/ *n* – see BIBLE table [LL, fr Gk *Paraleipomenōn*, gen of *Paraleipomena*; fr its forming a supplement to Samuel and Kings]

**paralipsis** /ˌparəˈlipsis/ *n, pl* **paralipses** /-seez/ pretended ignorance for rhetorical emphasis (e g in "not to mention . . ." or "to say nothing of . . .") [LL & Gk; LL *paralipsis, paralipsis*, fr Gk *paraleipsis*, lit., omission, fr *paraleipein* to leave out]

**parallax** /ˈparəlaks/ *n* the apparent displacement or the difference in apparent direction of an object as seen from two different points not on a straight line with the object; *specif* the difference in direction of a planet, star, or other celestial body as measured from two points on the earth or on the earth's orbit round the sun [MF *parallaxe*, fr Gk *parallaxis*, fr *parallassein* to change, fr *para-* + *allassein* to change, fr *allos* other – more at ELSE] – **parallactic** *adj*, **parallactically** *adv*

¹**parallel** /ˈparəlel/ *adj* **1a** extending in the same direction and always being the same distance apart ⟨~ *rows of trees*⟩ **b** everywhere equally distant ⟨*concentric spheres are* ~⟩ **2** having parallel sides ⟨*a* ~ *file*⟩ **3a** of or being an electrical circuit having a number of conductors in parallel **b** arranged in parallel ⟨*a* ~ *computer*⟩ **4a** analogous, comparable **b** *of phrases, sentences, etc* having identical types of word in corresponding positions **c(1)** *of musical keys* having the same first note **c(2)** *of two or more melodies or musical parts* keeping the same distance apart in musical PITCH (highness or lowness of sound) [L *parallelus*, fr Gk *parallēlos*, fr *para* beside + *allēlōn* of one another, fr *allos . . . allos* one . . . another, fr *allos* other – more at PARA-, ELSE]

*usage* One line, surface, etc is **parallel** *to* or *with* another.

²**parallel** *n* **1a** a parallel line, curve, or surface **b** (a line on a map or globe representing) any of the imaginary circles on the surface of the earth that are parallel to the equator and on which all points have the same latitude **c parallels** *pl*, **parallel** a sign ‖ used as the fifth in the series of reference marks **2** somebody or something equal or similar in all essential particulars; a counterpart, analogue **3** a comparison to show resemblance ⟨*drew a* ~ *between the two states*⟩ **4a** the state of being physically parallel; parallelism **b** the arrangement of electrical devices in which all positive connections (e g electrodes or terminals) are joined to one common conductor and all negative ones to another conductor so that each unit is in effect on a parallel branch **c** an arrangement or state that permits several operations or tasks to be performed simultaneously rather than consecutively – often in *in parallel*

³**parallel** *vt* **1** to compare **2a** to equal, match ⟨*no one has* ~ed *my success in business*⟩ **b** to correspond to **3** to make parallel with something else

⁴**parallel** *adv* in a parallel manner or direction

**parallel bars** *n pl* **1** a pair of wooden bars supported horizontally above the floor at the same height or at different heights, usu by a common base, and used for various exercises **2** *taking sing vb* a gymnastics event in which parallel bars are used

**parallelepiped** /ˌparəˌleliˈpieped, ˌparəleˈlepiped/ *n* a POLYHEDRON (three-dimensional geometric figure) whose six faces are parallelograms [Gk *parallēlepipedon*, fr *parallēlos* + *epipedon* plane surface, fr neut of *epipedos* flat, fr *epi-* + *pedon* ground; akin to L *ped-, pes* foot – more at FOOT]

**parallel evolution** *n* PARALLELISM 5

**parallelism** /ˈparəleliz(ə)m/ *n* **1** being parallel **2** a resemblance, correspondence **3** recurrent similarities in grammatical construction introduced for rhetorical effect **4** a theory that mental and physical processes accompany one another but are not causally related **5** the development of similar new characteristics by two or more related organisms in response to similarity of environment

**parallelogram** /ˌparəˈleləgram/ *n* a four-sided two-dimensional geometric figure (QUADRILATERAL) with opposite sides parallel and equal [LL or Gk; LL *parallelogrammum,* fr Gk *parallēlogrammon,* fr neut of *parallēlogrammos* bounded by parallel lines, fr *parallēlos* + *grammē* line, fr *graphein* to write – more at CARVE]

**parallel ruler** *n* an instrument for drawing parallel lines, consisting of two connected movable straight edges

**parallel-ˈveined** *adj, of a leaf* having veins nearly parallel to one another – compare NET-VEINED

**paralogism** /pəˈralədʒiz(ə)m/ *n* an (unintentionally) false argument – compare SOPHISM [MF *paralogisme,* fr LL *paralogismus,* fr Gk *paralogismos,* fr *paralogos* unreasonable, fr *para-* + *logos* speech, reason – more at LEGEND]

**paralyse,** *NAm* **paralyze** /ˈparəliez/ *vt* **1** to affect with paralysis (by injection of an anaesthetic) **2** to make powerless or ineffective **3a** to unnerve **b** to stun, stupefy **4** to bring to an end; prevent, destroy [Fr *paralyser,* back-formation fr *paralysie* paralysis, fr L *paralysis*] – **paralysation** *n,* **paralyser** *n,* **paralysingly** *adv*

**paralysis** /pəˈraləsis/ *n, pl* **paralyses 1** (partial) loss of function, esp when involving motion or sensation in a part of the body **2** loss of the ability to move **3** a state of powerlessness or incapacity to act [L, fr Gk, fr *paralyein* to loosen, disable, fr *para-* + *lyein* to loosen – more at LOSE]

**paralysis agitans** /ˈajitanz/ *n* PARKINSON'S DISEASE (type of nervous illness) [NL, lit., shaking palsy]

**paralytic** /ˌparəˈlitik/ *adj* **1** affected with, characterized by, or resembling paralysis **2** *chiefly Br informal* extremely drunk

**paramagnet** /ˌparəˈmagnit/ *n* a paramagnetic substance [back-formation fr *paramagnetic*]

**paramagnetic** /ˌparəmagˈnetik/ *adj* of or being a substance that has a small positive magnetic susceptibility and thus can be weakly magnetized and that moves towards an applied magnetic field – compare DIAMAGNETIC, FERROMAGNETIC [ISV] – **paramagnetically** *adv,* **paramagnetism** *n*

**paramatta** /ˌparəˈmatə/ *n* a fine lightweight dress fabric of silk and wool or cotton and wool [*Parramatta,* city in SE Australia]

**paramecium, paramoecium** /ˌparəˈmeesyəm/ *n, pl* **paramecia, paramoecia** /-s(h)yə/ *also* **parameciums, paramoeciums** any of a genus (*Paramecium* or *Paramoecium*) of slipper-shaped PROTOZOANS (single-celled animals) that are covered with CILIA (hairlike projections), have an elongated body rounded at the front end, and an oblique funnel-shaped groove bearing the mouth at the tip [NL, genus name, fr Gk *paramēkēs* oblong, fr *para-* + *mēkos* length; akin to Gk *makros* long – more at MEAGRE]

**paramedical** /ˌparəˈmedikl/ *also* **paramedic** *adj* concerned with supplementing the work of medical doctors ⟨~ *technicians*⟩ – **paramedic** *n*

**parameter** /pəˈramitə/ *n* **1** an arbitrary constant whose value characterizes a member of a system (e g a family of curves); *specif* a quantity (e g a mean or variance) that describes a statistical population **2** any of a set of physical properties whose values determine the characteristics or behaviour of something ⟨~ s *of the atmosphere such as temperature, pressure, and density*⟩ **3** *informal* a (limiting) factor or characteristic ⟨*political dissent as a* ~ *of modern life*⟩ ⟨*we must work with the* ~s *of limited time and budget*⟩ [NL, fr *para-* + Gk *metron* measure – more at MEASURE] – **parametric** *also* **parametrical** *adj,* **parametrically** *adv*

    *usage* The vague use of **parameter** to mean variously "limit", "standard", "criterion", or "characteristic" is disliked by some people as jargon. △ perimeter

**parameter·ize, -ise, parametr·ize, -ise** /pəˈramit(ə)riez/ *vt* to express in terms of parameters – **parameterization** *n*

**parametric amplifier** *n* a high-frequency amplifier whose operation is based on time variations in the CAPACITANCE (property of a conductor enabling it to store electric charge) or other circuit parameter

**paramilitary** /ˌparəˈmilit(ə)ri/ *adj* **1** formed on a military pattern, esp as a potential auxiliary military force ⟨*a* ~ *border patrol*⟩ **2** of a paramilitary force ⟨~ *training*⟩

**paramnesia** /ˌparəmˈneez(h)yə, -əm-/ *n* a disorder of the memory involving the recall of events that have not occurred but which the person believes have happened; DÉJÀ VU [NL, fr *para-* + *-mnesia* (as in *amnesia*)]

**paramount** /ˈparəmownt/ *adj* superior to all others; supreme [AF *paramont,* fr OF *par* by (fr L *per*) + *amont* above, fr *a* to (fr L *ad*) + *mont* mountain – more at FOR, AT, MOUNT] – **paramountcy** *n*

**paramour** /ˈparəmooə/ *n* an illicit lover; *esp* a mistress [ME, fr *par amour* by way of love, fr OF]

**paramylum** /pəˈramiləm/ *n* a carbohydrate stored by various PROTOZOANS (single-celled organisms) and algae that resembles starch [NL, fr *para-* + L *amylum* starch – more at AMYL-]

**parang** /ˈparang, ˈpah-/ *n* a heavy straight-edged Malaysian or Indonesian knife used as a tool or weapon [Malay]

**paranoia** /ˌparəˈnoyə/ *n* **1** a mental disorder characterized by systematized delusions of persecution or grandeur **2** a tendency towards excessive or irrational suspiciousness and distrustfulness of others [NL, fr Gk, madness, fr *paranous* demented, fr *para-* + *nous* mind] – **paranoiac, paranoic** *adj or n,* **paranoically** *adv,* **paranoid** *adj or n*

**paranormal** /ˌparəˈnawml/ *adj* not scientifically explainable; supernatural – **paranormally** *adv,* **paranormality** *n*

**parapet** /ˈparəpit, -pet/ *n* **1** a wall, rampart, or elevation of earth or stone to protect soldiers **2** a low wall or balustrade to protect the edge of a platform, roof, or bridge [It *parapetto,* fr *parare* to shield (fr L, to prepare) + *petto* chest, fr L *pectus* – more at PARE, PECTORAL] – **parapeted** *adj*

**paraph** /ˈparəf/ *n* a flourish at the end of a signature, originally intended to prevent forgery [MF, fr L *paragraphus* paragraph]

**paraphernalia** /ˌparəfəˈnaylyə/ *n taking sing or pl vb* **1** personal belongings; *esp* those that former laws allowed a married woman to treat as her own **2** articles of equipment; furnishings **b** accessory items **3** *informal* complicated procedure; rigmarole ⟨*can't bear the* ~ *of getting planning permission*⟩ [ML, deriv of Gk *parapherna* goods a bride brings over and above the dowry, fr *para-* + *phernē* dowry, fr *pherein* to bear – more at BEAR]

[1]**paraphrase** /ˈparəˌfrayz/ *n* **1** a restatement of a text, passage, or work giving the meaning in another form **2** the use or process of paraphrasing in studying or teaching composition [MF, fr L *paraphrasis,* fr Gk, fr *paraphrazein* to paraphrase, fr *para-* + *phrazein* to point out]

[2]**paraphrase** *vb* to make a paraphrase (of) – **paraphrasable** *adj,* **paraphraser** *n*

**paraphrastic** /ˌparəˈfrastik/ *adj* explaining or translating more clearly and amply; having the nature of a paraphrase [Fr *paraphrastique,* fr Gk *paraphrastikos,* fr *paraphrazein*] – **paraphrastically** *adv*

**paraphysis** /pəˈrafisis/ *n, pl* **paraphyses** /-seez/ any of the slender sterile filaments borne among the reproductive organs in mosses, algae, and some fungi [NL, fr Gk, sucker, offshoot, fr *paraphyein* to produce at the side, fr *para-* + *phyein* to bring forth – more at PHYSICS]

**paraplegia** /ˌparəˈpleejə/ *n* paralysis of the lower half of the body, involving both legs, and usually resulting from disease or injury – compare HEMIPLEGIA, QUADRIPLEGIA [NL, fr Gk *paraplēgiē* hemiplegia, fr *para-* + *-plēgia* -plegia] – **paraplegic** *adj or n*

**parapodium** /ˌparəˈpohdiəm/ *n, pl* **parapodia** /-diə/ either of a pair of fleshy projections on the sides of most segments of a POLYCHAETE (having many hairlike bristles) worm that are used esp for movement [NL, fr *para-* + *-podium*] – **parapodial** *adj*

**paraproct** /ˈparəˌprokt/ *n* any of several lobes adjacent to the anus of some insects [[1]*para-* + Gk *prōktos* anus]

**paraprofessional** /ˌparəprəˈfesh(ə)nl/ *n* a trained aide who assists a professional person

**paraprotein** /ˌparəˈprohteen/ *n* any of various abnormal complex proteins (GLOBULINS) found in the liquid portion (SERUM) of the blood that have unique chemical and physical characteristics

**parapsychology** /-sieˈkoləji/ *n* a field of study concerned with the investigation of evidence for the occurrence of psychic phenomena (e g telepathy and clairvoyance) inexplicable by the theories of orthodox psychology [ISV] – **parapsychologist** *n,* **parapsychological** *adj*

**paraquat** /ˈparəkwot, -kwat/ *n* a very poisonous herbicide, containing the chemical group $C_{12}H_{14}N_2{}^{2+}$, used esp as a weedkiller [*para-* + *quater*nary]

**Para rubber** /pəˈrah, ˈpahrə/ *n* natural rubber from S American rubber trees (genus *Hevea,* esp *Hevea brasiliensis*) [*Pará,* state & city in N Brazil]

**parasang** /'parəsang/ *n* any of various ancient Persian units of distance; *esp* one of about 6.5 kilometres (about four miles) [L *parasanga*, fr Gk *parasangēs*, of Iranian origin; akin to Per *farsung* parasang]

**parascending** /'parəsending/ *n* the sport of rising into the air and parachuting down while wearing a specially modified parachute and being towed (e g by a motor vehicle or boat) [blend of *parachute* and *ascending*]

**parascience** /'parə,sie·əns/ *n* enquiry that complements or borrows the methods of scientific research; *specif* enquiry into phenomena inexplicable by orthodox scientific theory – **parascientist** *n*, **parascientific** *adj*

**paraselene** /,parəse'leeni/ *n*, *pl* **paraselenae** /-ni, -nie/ a bright spot seen on circles of light (HALOS) surrounding the moon – compare PARHELION [NL, fr *para-* + Gk *selēnē* moon – more at SELENIUM] – **paraselenic** *adj*

**parasexual** /,parə'seksyooəl, -shəl/ *adj* relating to or being reproduction that results in recombination of genes from different individuals but does not involve MEIOSIS (division of a cell to produce the sex cells) and formation of a ZYGOTE (union of male and female sex cells) by fertilization as in sexual reproduction ⟨*the ~ cycle in some fungi*⟩ – **parasexuality** *n*

**parashah** /'parə,shah/ *n* a passage in Jewish Scripture dealing with a single topic; *specif* a section of the TORAH assigned for weekly reading in synagogue worship [Heb *pārāshāh*, lit., explanation]

**parasite** /'parəsiet/ *n* 1 an organism living in or on another organism in parasitism 2 something that resembles a biological parasite in dependence on something else for existence or support without making a useful or adequate return [MF, fr L *parasitus*, fr Gk *parasitos*, fr *para-* + *sitos* grain, food] – **parasitic** *also* **parasitical** *adj*, **parasitically** *adv*

**parasiticide** /,parə'sietisied/ *n* a substance that destroys parasites [L *parasitus* + E *-cide*] – **parasiticidal** *adj*

**parasitism** /'parəsitiz(ə)m, -sie-/ *n* 1 the behaviour of, or state of being, a parasite 2 an intimate association between organisms of different kinds in which one, the parasite, benefits by obtaining nourishment and shelter at the expense and to the detriment of another, the host 3 parasitosis

**parasit·ize, -ise** /'parəsitiez, -sie-/ *vt* to infest or live on or with as a parasite – **parasitization** *n*

**parasitoid** /'parəsitoyd, -sie-/ *n* an insect, esp a wasp, that develops within the body usu of another insect and eventually kills it – **parasitoid** *adj*

**parasitology** /,parəsi'toləji, -sie-/ *n* a branch of biology dealing with parasites and parasitism, esp among animals [L *parasitus* + ISV *-logy*] – **parasitologist** *n*, **parasitological** *also* **parasitologic** *adj*

**parasitosis** /,parəsi'tohsis, -sie-/ *n*, *pl* **parasitoses** /-seez/ infestation with or disease caused by parasites [NL]

**parasol** /'parəsol/ *n* a lightweight umbrella used, esp by women, as a protection from the sun – compare SUNSHADE [Fr, fr OIt *parasole*, fr *parare* to shield + *sole* sun, fr L *sol* – more at PARAPET, SOLAR]

**¹parasympathetic** /,parəsimpə'thetik/ *adj* of, being, or acting on the PARASYMPATHETIC NERVOUS SYSTEM [ISV]

**²parasympathetic** *n* a parasympathetic nerve

**parasympathetic nervous system, parasympathetic** *n* the part of the AUTONOMIC NERVOUS SYSTEM that contains nerves which produce ACETYLCHOLINE (substance that transmits nerve impulses), and that tends to induce secretion, to increase the tone and contractility of SMOOTH MUSCLE, and to cause the dilation of blood vessels – compare SYMPATHETIC NERVOUS SYSTEM

**parasympathomimetic** /,parə,simpəthohmie'metik, -mi-/ *adj* simulating parasympathetic nervous action in physiological effect [ISV]

**parasynthesis** /,parə'sinthəsis/ *n* the formation of words by adding a prefix, suffix, etc to a compound (e g *brown-haired* from *brown hair* + *-ed*) [NL] – **parasynthetic** *adj*

**parataxis** /,parə'taksis/ *n* the placing of clauses or phrases one after another without connecting words (e g in "Come on, I'm thirsty") [NL, fr Gk, act of placing side by side, fr *paratassein* to place side by side, fr *para-* + *tassein* to arrange – more at TACTICS] – **paratactic, paratactical** *adj*, **paratactically** *adv*

**parathion** /,parə'thie·on/ *n* a very poisonous insecticide, $(C_2H_5O)_2P(S)OC_6H_4NO_2$, used esp in farming [*para-* + *thio*phosphate + *-on*]

**parathyroid** /,parə'thie·əroyd/ *adj* of or produced by the PARATHYROID GLANDS [ISV]

**parathyroidectomy** /,parə,thieroy'dektəmi/ *n* surgical removal of the PARATHYROID GLANDS – **parathyroidectomized** *adj*

**parathyroid gland, parathyroid** /,parə'thie·əroyd/ *n* any of usu four small ENDOCRINE GLANDS that are adjacent to or embedded in the THYROID GLAND and produce a hormone concerned with the biochemical processing of calcium

**paratrooper** /'parə,troohpə/ *n* a member of the paratroops

**paratroops** /'parə,troohps/ *n pl* troops trained and equipped to parachute from an aeroplane [²*para-* + *troops*] – **paratroop** *adj*

*usage* A member of the **paratroops** is correctly called a **paratrooper**, not a △ **paratroop**.

**¹paratyphoid** /,parə'tiefoyd/ *adj* 1 resembling typhoid fever 2 of paratyphoid or its causative organisms ⟨*~ infection*⟩ [ISV]

**²paratyphoid, paratyphoid fever** *n* a disease caused by certain bacteria (SALMONELLAE) that resembles TYPHOID FEVER and is commonly contracted by eating contaminated food

**paravane** /'parəvayn/ *n* a torpedo-shaped underwater protective device, with serrated teeth in its forward end, that is towed underwater from the bow of a ship to sever the moorings of mines

**parboil** /'pah,boyl/ *vt* to boil briefly as a preliminary or incomplete cooking procedure [ME *parboilen* (influenced in meaning by *part*), fr *parboilen* to boil thoroughly, fr MF *parboillir*, fr LL *perbullire*, fr L *per-* thoroughly (fr *per* through) + *bullire* to boil, fr *bulla* bubble – more at FOR]

**¹parbuckle** /'pah,bukl/ *n* a sling of rope that is used for hoisting or lowering a cylindrical object (e g a cask) [alter. (influenced by *buckle*) of earlier *parbunkel*, of unknown origin]

**²parbuckle** *vt* to raise or lower by means of a parbuckle

**¹parcel** /'pahsl/ *n* 1 a tract or plot of land 2a a wrapped bundle; a package b a unit of salable merchandise 3 *chiefly derog* a company, collection, or group of people, animals, or things; a lot ⟨*the whole story was a ~ of lies*⟩ 4 *archaic* a fragment, portion [ME, fr MF, fr (assumed) VL *particella*, fr L *particula* small part – more at PARTICLE]

**²parcel** *adv*, *archaic* partly

**³parcel** *vt* **-ll-** (*NAm* **-l-, -ll-**) 1 to divide into parts; distribute – often + *out* 2 to make up into a parcel; wrap – often + *up* 3 to cover (e g a rope) with strips of canvas

**parcel bomb** *n* an explosive device concealed in a parcel and sent through the post to the intended victim

**parcelling**, *NAm chiefly* **parceling** /'pahsəling/ *n* 1 long narrow tarred strips of canvas wound about a rope to exclude moisture 2 the act of dividing and distributing in portions 3 the act of wrapping into bundles

**parcel post** *n* a postal service handling parcels

**parcenary** /'pahsinəri/ *n* COPARCENARY (joint heirship) [AF *parcenarie*, fr OF *parçonerie*, fr *parçon* portion, fr L *partition-, partitio* partition]

**parcener** /'pahsinə/ *n* COPARCENER (joint heir) [AF, fr OF *parçonier*, fr *parçon*]

**parch** /pahch/ *vt* 1 to roast (e g peas) slightly in a dry heat 2 to make dry or scorched ~ *vi* to become dry or scorched [ME *parchen*]

**Parcheesi** /pah'cheezi/ *trademark* – used for a board game adapted from PACHISI

**parchment** /'pahchmənt/ *n* 1 the skin of an animal, esp of a sheep or goat, prepared for writing on 2 strong, tough, and often somewhat translucent paper made to resemble parchment 3 a manuscript written on parchment; *also* an academic diploma [ME *parchemin*, fr OF, modif of L *pergamena*, fr Gk *pergamēnē*, fr fem of *Pergamēnos* of Pergamum, fr *Pergamon* Pergamum, ancient city in Asia Minor]

**parclose, parclose screen** /'pahklohz/ *n* a screen or railing separating an altar or side chapel from the main body of a church [ME *parclose*, fr MF, enclosure, end, fr fem of *parclos*, pp of *parclore* to enclose]

**pard** /pahd/ *n*, *archaic* a leopard [ME *parde*, fr OF, fr L *pardus*, fr Gk *pardos*]

**pardner** /'pahdnə/ *n*, *dial NAm* a partner, chum [alter. of *partner*]

**¹pardon** /'pahdn/ *n* 1 INDULGENCE 1 2 (an official document granting) a release from the legal penalties of an offence 3 excuse or forgiveness for a fault, offence, or discourtesy – **pardonless** *adj*

**²pardon** *vt* 1 to absolve from the consequences of a fault or crime ⟨*~ed the criminal*⟩ – often used in courteous denial or apology ⟨~ *me: I didn't quite catch what you said*⟩ **2** to allow (an offence) to pass without punishment [ME *pardonen*, fr MF *pardoner*, fr LL *perdonare* to grant freely, fr L *per-* thoroughly + *donare* to give – more at PARBOIL, DONATION] – **pardonable** *adj*, **pardonably** *adv*, **pardonableness** *n*

**usage** Some people dislike the apologetic use of **pardon** or **pardon me** as a genteelism, and prefer to say ⟨*I'm sorry*⟩ or ⟨*what did you say?*⟩

**pardoner** /'pahdənə/ *n* **1** a medieval preacher delegated to raise money for religious works by selling religious INDULGENCES (pardons from sin) **2** one who or that which pardons

**pare** /peə/ *vt* **1** to cut or shave off (the outer surface of) ⟨~ *the skin from an apple*⟩ ⟨~ *an apple*⟩ **2** to diminish gradually (as if) by paring ⟨~ *expenses*⟩ – often + *down* [ME *paren*, fr MF *parer* to prepare, trim, fr L *parare* to prepare, acquire; akin to OE *fearr* bull, ox, L *parere* to give birth to, produce] – **parer** *n*

**paregoric** /ˌpariˈgorik/ *n* a mixture of camphor and opium in alcohol used esp to relieve pain and coughing [Fr *parégorique* mitigating pain, fr LL *paregoricus*, fr Gk *parēgorikos*, fr *parēgorein* to talk over, soothe, fr *para-* + *agora* assembly – more at GREGARIOUS]

**parenchyma** /pəˈrengkimə/ *n* **1** a tissue of higher plants that consists of thin-walled living photosynthetic or storage cells capable of division even when mature and that makes up much of the substance of leaves and roots, the pulp of fruits, and parts of stems and supporting structures **2** the essential and distinctive tissue of an organ or an abnormal growth, as distinguished from its supportive framework [NL, fr Gk, visceral flesh, fr *parenchein* to pour in beside, fr *para-* + *en-* + *chein* to pour – more at FOUND] – **parenchymatous** *also* **parenchymal** *adj*, **parenchymatously** *adv*

**¹parent** /'peərənt/ *n* **1** one who or that which begets or brings forth offspring; *esp* a father or mother **2a** an animal or plant regarded in relation to its offspring ⟨*the identity of the* ~ *plant*⟩ **b** the material or source from which something is derived [ME, fr MF, fr L *parent-*, *parens*, fr prp of *parere* to give birth to] – **parent** *adj*, **parental** *adj*, **parentally** *adv*

**²parent** *vt* to be or act as the parent of; originate, produce

**parentage** /'peərəntij/ *n* **1a** descent from parents or ancestors; lineage ⟨*a woman of noble* ~⟩ **b** derivation, origin ⟨*the rumours about them are of common* ~⟩ **2** the standing or position of a parent; parenthood

**parental generation** /pəˈrentl/ *n* the generation of individuals of distinctively different genetic make-up that are crossed to produce hybrids – compare FILIAL GENERATION

**parenteral** /paˈrentərəl/ *adj* situated or occurring outside the intestine; *esp, of a drug* introduced otherwise than by way of the intestines (eg by injection) [ISV *para-* + *enteral*] – **parenterally** *adv*

**parenthesis** /pəˈrenthəsis/ *n, pl* **parentheses** /-seez/ **1a** an amplifying or explanatory word, phrase, or sentence inserted in a passage from which it is usu set off by punctuation in writing or by intonation in speech **b** a remark or passage that departs from the theme of a discourse; a digression **2** an interlude, interval **3** either or both of the curved punctuation marks ( ) used in writing and printing to enclose a parenthesis or to group a symbolic unit in a logical or mathematical expression – called also BRACKET [LL, fr Gk, lit., act of inserting, fr *parentithenai* to insert, fr *para-* + *en-* + *tithenai* to place – more at DO] – **parenthetic, parenthetical** *adj*, **parenthetically** *adv*

**parenthes·ize, -ise** /pəˈrenthəsiez/ *vt* to make a parenthesis of ~ *vi* to digress

**parenthood** /'peərənt·hood/ *n* the position, function, or standing of a parent

**parenting** /'peərənting/ *n* the caring for and raising of a child

**parent-teacher association** *n* an organization of teachers at a school and the parents of their pupils, that works for the improvement of the school

**parergon** /paˈruhgon/ *n, pl* **parerga** /-gə/ a supplementary or subsidiary work; a piece of work undertaken apart from one's regular employment [L, fr Gk, fr *para-* + *ergon* work]

**paresis** /pəˈreesis, 'parəsis/ *n, pl* **pareses** /-seez/ **1** slight or partial paralysis **2** GENERAL PARESIS (insanity and paralysis resulting from syphilis) [NL, fr Gk, fr *parienai* to let fall, fr *para-* + *hienai* to let go, send – more at JET] – **paretic** *adj or n*

**pareve** /'pahrəvi/ *adj* made without milk, meat, or their derivatives ⟨~ *margarine*⟩ – used in Jewish cookery; compare FLEISHIG, MILCHIG [Yiddish *parev*]

**par excellence** /pah'reks(ə)ləns (*Fr* par ɛksɛlɑ̃:s)/ *adj* being the best example of a kind; without equal – used after a noun ⟨*the dictionary* ~⟩ [Fr, lit., by excellence]

**parfait** /pah'fay/ *n* **1** a rich frozen flavoured dessert that resembles custard and that contains whipped cream and eggs **2** a cold dessert consisting of layers of fruit, syrup, ice cream, and whipped cream [Fr, lit., something perfect, fr *parfait* perfect, fr L *perfectus*]

**parge** /pahj/ *vt* to parget

**¹parget** /'pahjit/ *vt* **-t-**, **-tt-** to coat with plaster, esp ornamentally or for waterproofing [ME *pargetten*, fr MF *parjeter* to throw on top of, fr *par-* thoroughly (fr L *per-*) + *jeter* to throw – more at JET]

**²parget** *n* (plaster used for) plasterwork on walls, esp with raised ornamental figures, commonly found on timber-framed buildings in E and SE England

**pargeting, pargetting** /'pahjiting/ *n* parget

**parhelic circle** /ˌpahˈheelik/ *n* a luminous circle or halo occurring parallel to the horizon at the height of the sun and caused by reflection of the sun's rays by atmospheric ice crystals

**parhelic ring** *n* PARHELIC CIRCLE

**parhelion** /ˌpahˈheelyən/ *n, pl* **parhelia** /-lyə/ any of several bright spots often tinged with colour that often appear on the PARHELIC CIRCLE – called also MOCK SUN; compare ANTHELION [L *parelion*, fr Gk *parēlion*, fr *para-* + *hēlios* sun – more at SOLAR] – **parhelic** *adj*

**pariah** /pəˈrie·ə, 'pari·ə/ *n* **1** a member of a low social class (CASTE) of S India and Burma **2** an outcast [Tamil *paraiyan*, lit., drummer]

**usage** The pronunciation /pəˈrie·ə/ is now preferred except by some old-fashioned speakers.

**Parian** /'peəriən/ *adj* of or being a fine white marble from the Greek island of Paros used extensively for sculpture in ancient times

**Parian ware** /'peəri·ən/ *n* a fine-grained white porcelain usu used for making unglazed classical figures, esp nudes

**paries** /'peəri·eez/, **parietes** /pəˈrie·əteez/ *n pl* the wall of a cavity (eg a honeycomb) or hollow organ [NL *pariet-*, *paries*, fr L, wall; akin to L *sparus* spear – more at SPEAR]

**¹parietal** /pəˈrie·ətl/ *adj* **1a** of the walls of an anatomical part or cavity **b** of or forming the upper rear wall of the skull **2** *of a developing seed or its support* attached to the main wall of the OVARY (female reproductive part) **3** *NAm* of life or regulations within a college

**²parietal** *n* a parietal part (eg a bone or scale)

**parietal bone** *n* either of a pair of MEMBRANE BONES of the roof of the skull

**parietal cell** *n* any of the large oval acid-secreting cells of the stomach lining

**parietal lobe** *n* the middle lobe of each CEREBRAL HEMISPHERE (front and upper portion of the brain); the lobe that contains an area concerned with the interpretation of the body sensations of touch, temperature, etc

**pari-mutuel** /ˌpariˈmyoohtyooəl/ *n* **1** a betting pool in which those who bet on the winners of the first three places share the total amount bet, minus a percentage for the management **2** **pari-mutuel, pari-mutuel machine** TOTALIZATOR (machine used in pari-mutuel betting) [Fr *pari mutuel*, lit., mutual stake]

**paring** /'peəring/ *n* **1** the act of cutting away an edge or surface **2** something pared of ⟨*apple* ~s⟩

**pari passu** /ˌpari 'pasooh, 'pahri/ *adv or adj* at an equal rate or pace [L, with equal step]

**Paris green** /'paris/ *n* a very poisonous bright green powder that is used as an insecticide and pigment [*Paris*, capital city of France]

**parish** /'parish/ *n* **1** (the churchgoers of) the subdivision of a DIOCESE served by a single church or clergyman **2** a unit of local government in rural areas of England, often coinciding with an original ecclesiastical parish [ME *parisshe*, fr MF *parroche*, fr LL *parochia*, fr LGk *paroikia*, fr *paroikos* Christian, fr Gk, stranger, fr *para-* + *oikos* house – more at VICINITY] – **on the parish** receiving financial or other help from a parish

**parishioner** /pəˈrish(ə)nə/ *n* a member or inhabitant of a parish [ME *parisshoner*, prob modif of MF *parrochien*, fr *parroche*]

**parish·'pump** *adj, chiefly Br* having a restricted outlook or limited interest; parochial ⟨*smacked less of a serious schism than of a* ~ *quarrel – TLS*⟩

**parish register** *n* a book containing records of baptisms, marriages, and burials in a parish

**parisyllabic** /ˌparisiˈlabik/ *adj, of a noun* having an equal number of syllables in all grammatical cases [*pari-* equal (fr MF, fr ML, fr L *par*) + *syllabic*]

**¹parity** /'parəti/ *n* **1** the quality or state of being equal or equivalent **2a** equivalence of a commodity price expressed in one currency to its price expressed in another **b** equality of purchasing power established by law between different kinds of money at a given ratio (eg between a gold coin and a number of silver coins to the same value) **3a** the property of an integer with respect to being odd or even ⟨*three and seven have the same* ~⟩ **b(1)** the state of being odd or even that is the basis of a method of detecting errors in computer-coded data **b(2) parity bit, parity** a BIT (unit of computer information) added to an ordered arrangement of bits (eg on magnetic tape) so that the combination has a standardized parity **4** *physics* the property whereby a quantity, esp the WAVE FUNCTION of an ELEMENTARY PARTICLE (minute particle of matter), changes from positive to negative or vice versa or remains unaltered during a particular interaction or reaction [L *paritas*, fr *par* equal]

**²parity** *n* the state or fact of having borne offspring; *also* the number of children previously borne [*-parous* + *-ity*]

**¹park** /pahk/ *n* **1a** an enclosed piece of ground stocked with game and held by royal grant **b** an enclosed area of lawns, woodland, pasture, etc attached to a country house and used as a game reserve or for recreation **2a** an area of land for recreation, usu ornamentally laid out, in or near a city or town **b** an area maintained in its natural state as a public property **3** a level valley between mountain ranges in the western USA **4a** an assigned space for military animals, vehicles, or materials **b** CAR PARK **5a** *Br* a pitch where professional soccer is played ⟨*the best player on the* ~⟩ **b** *NAm* an arena or stadium used for ball games [ME, fr OF *parc* enclosure, fr (assumed) VL *parricus* (cf PADDOCK)] – **parklike** *adj*

**²park** *vt* **1** to enclose in or as a park **2a** to leave or place (a vehicle) for a time, esp at the roadside or in a car park **b** to land or leave (eg an aeroplane) **c** to establish (eg a satellite) in orbit **3** to assemble (eg equipment or stores) in a military dump or park **4** *informal* to set and leave temporarily ⟨~ed *her boyfriend at the bar*⟩ ~ *vi* to park a vehicle – **parker** *n*

**parka** /'pahkə/ *n* **1** a hooded fur garment for wearing in the Arctic, originally by Eskimos **2** an often hooded warm waterproof knee-length coat [Aleut, skin, outer garment, fr Russ, pelt, fr Yurak]

**parkin** /'pahkin/ *n* a moist heavy ginger cake made with oatmeal and treacle [origin unknown]

**parking bay** *n* an area used for parking vehicles

**parking lot** *n, NAm* an outdoor car park

**parking meter** *n* a coin-operated device which registers the payment and displays the time allowed for parking a motor vehicle

**parking orbit** *n* an orbit in which a spacecraft is temporarily placed before being propelled into a new course

**parkinsonism** /'pahkins(ə)n,iz(ə)m/ *n* **1** PARKINSON'S DISEASE **2** a long-lasting nervous disorder that is marked by muscle rigidity but without tremor of resting muscles

**Parkinson's disease** /'pahkins(ə)nz/ *n* a long-lasting progressive nervous disease of later life that is marked by tremor and weakness of resting muscles and by a peculiar gait – called also PARALYSIS AGITANS, SHAKING PALSY [James *Parkinson* † 1824 E physician] – **parkinsonian** *adj*

**Parkinson's Law** *n* an observation in office organization: work expands to fill the time available for its completion [C Northcote *Parkinson* b 1909 E historian]

**parkland** /'pahk,land/ *n* land with clumps of trees and shrubs in cultivated condition suitable for use as a park

**parkway** /-,way/ *n, NAm* a broad landscaped road or highway

**parky** /'pahki/ *adj, Br informal* chilly [prob fr ¹*park* + ¹-*y*]

**parlance** /'pahləns/ *n* (particular) manner of speech and esp choice of words; idiom ⟨*in legal* ~⟩ [MF, fr OF, fr *parler*]

**parlando** /pah'landoh/ *adj or adv* (delivered or performed) in an unsustained style suggestive of speech – used as a direction in music [It, verbal of *parlare* to speak, fr ML *parabolare*]

**parlante** /pah'lahntay/ *adj or adv* parlando [It, prp of *parlare*]

**¹parlay** /'pahli/ *vt, NAm* **1** to bet in a parlay **2** to exploit (a talent, project, etc) successfully △ parley [Fr *paroli*, n, parlay, fr It dial., pl of *parolo*, fr *paro* equal, fr L *par*]

**²parlay** *n, NAm* ACCUMULATOR (system of betting)

**parlement** /(Fr parlmã)/ *n* any of several principal courts of justice existing in France before the revolution of 1789 [Fr]

**¹parley** /'pahli/ *vi* to speak with another; confer; *specif* to dis-

cuss terms with an enemy [MF *parler* to speak, fr ML *parabolare*, fr LL *parabola* speech, parable – more at PARABLE]

**²parley** *n* a conference for discussion of points in dispute; *specif* a conference under truce to discuss terms with an enemy

**parliament** /'pahləmənt, *also* -lyə-/ *n* **1** a formal conference for the discussion of public affairs **2a** *often cap* the supreme legislative body of the UK that consists of the HOUSE OF COMMONS and the HOUSE OF LORDS and that is called together by the sovereign; *also* a similar body in another nation or state ⟨*the third session of Ceylon's second* ~ – *Daily Telegraph*⟩ **b** Parliament as it exists between general elections ⟨*won't get the bill through in this* ~⟩ **3** a parlement [ME, fr OF *parlement*, fr *parler* to speak]

**parliamentarian** /,pahləmən'teəri-ən, -men-, *also* -lyə-/ *n* **1** *often cap* an adherent of the parliament in opposition to the king during the Civil War **2** an expert in parliamentary rules and practice **3** *Br* a Member of Parliament

**parliamentary** /,pahlə'ment(ə)ri, *also* -lyə-/ *adj* **1** of or enacted, done, or ratified by a parliament **2** of or adhering to the parliament as opposed to the king during the Civil War **3** of members of a parliament

**Parliamentary Commissioner for Administration** *n* the central government OMBUDSMAN (investigator of complaints) in the UK

**parliamentary government** *n* a system of government having power vested in a cabinet composed of members of a parliament who are individually and collectively responsible to that parliament for their actions – compare PRESIDENTIAL GOVERNMENT

**parliamentary law** *n* the rules and precedents governing the proceedings of deliberative assemblies

**¹parlour,** *NAm* **parlor** /'pahlə/ *n* **1a** a room in a private house used primarily for the entertainment of guests **b** a room in an inn, hotel, or club for conversation or semiprivate uses **2** any of various business places ⟨*a funeral* ~⟩ ⟨*a beauty* ~⟩ **3** a place for milking cows [ME *parlour*, fr OF, fr *parler* to speak]

**²parlour** *adj* fostered or advocated in comfortable seclusion without consequent action or application to affairs

**parlour car** *n, NAm* a usu luxurious railway passenger carriage with individual seats

**parlour game** *n* an indoor word game, board game, etc

**parlous** /'pahləs/ *adj, formal or humorous* full of uncertainty and danger [ME, alter. of *perilous*] – **parlously** *adv*

**Parmesan** /,pahmi'zan, '---/ *n* a very hard dry strongly flavoured cheese that is often used grated [Fr *Parmesan* of Parma, fr *Parma*, city in N Italy]

**Parnassian** /pah'nasiən/ *adj* **1** of poetry **2** of a school of French poets of the second half of the 19th century that emphasized systematically rhythmical form rather than emotion [(1) L *parnassius* of Parnassus, fr Gk *parnasios*, fr *Parnasos* Parnassus, mountain in Greece sacred to the god Apollo and the Muses; (2) Fr *parnassien*, fr *Le Parnasse contemporain* "The Modern Parnassus" (1866), an anthology of poetry] – **Parnassian** *n*, **Parnassianism, Parnassism** *n*

**parochial** /pə'rohki-əl/ *adj* **1** of a (church) parish **2** limited in range or scope (eg to a narrow area or region); provincial, narrow [ME *parochiall*, fr MF *parochial*, fr LL *parochialis*, fr *parochia* parish – more at PARISH] – **parochially** *adv*

**parochial church council** *n* a predominantly lay body administering the affairs of a Church of England parish and including the vicar, churchwardens, and elected lay members

**parochialism** /pə'rohki-ə,liz(ə)m/ *n* selfish pettiness or narrowness (eg of interests, opinions, or views)

**¹parody** /'parədi/ *n* **1** a literary or musical work in which the style of an author or work is closely imitated for comic or satirical effect – compare CARICATURE **2** a feeble or ridiculous imitation [L *parodia*, fr Gk *parōidia*, fr *para-* + *aidein* to sing – more at ODE] – **parodic** *adj*, **parodist** *n*

**²parody** *vt* **1** to compose a parody on ⟨~ *a poem*⟩ **2** to imitate in the manner of a parody

**parol** /'parəl/ *adj* given by word of mouth ⟨~ *evidence*⟩ – used in law [MF *parole*]

**¹parole** /pə'rohl/ *n* **1** a pledge of one's honour; *esp* the promise of a prisoner of war to fulfil stated conditions in return for his/her release or the granting of privileges **2** a password given only to officers of the guard and of the day **3** a conditional release of a civilian prisoner serving an unexpired sentence **4** the linguistic behaviour of an individual speaker of a language – compare LANGUE, PERFORMANCE **6** [Fr, speech, word, word of honour, fr MF, fr LL *parabola* speech – more at PARABLE]

²**parole** *vt* to put (a prisoner) on parole

**parolee** /pə,roh'lee/ *n* a prisoner released on parole

**paronomasia** /,parənoh'maysyə/ *n* a pun; PLAY ON WORDS [L, fr Gk, fr *paronomazein* to call with a slight change of name, fr *para-* + *onoma* name – more at NAME] – **paronomastic** *adj*

**paronymous** /pə'roniməs/ *adj* 1 CONJUGATE 4 2 formed from a word in another language [Gk *parōnymos*, fr *para-* + *-ōnymos* (as in *homōnymos* homonymous)] – **paronym** *n*

**parotid** /pə'rotid/ *adj* of or situated near the PAROTID GLAND

**parotid gland** /pə'rotid/ *n* either of a pair of large salivary glands situated in humans below and in front of the ear [NL *parotid-, parotis*, fr L, tumour near the ear, fr Gk *parōtid, parōtis*, fr *para-* + *ōt-, ous* ear – more at EAR]

**parotitis** /,parə'tietəs/ *n* inflammation of the PAROTID GLANDS; *also* mumps [NL]

**parous** /'peərəs, 'parəs/ *adj* having borne offspring [-*parous*]

**-parous** /-p(ə)rəs/ *comb form* (→ *adj*) giving birth to; producing (such or so many) offspring ⟨*bi*parous⟩ ⟨*vivi*parous⟩ [L -*parus*, fr *parere* to give birth to, produce]

**Parousia** /pə'roohsiə/ *n* SECOND COMING (of Christ) [Gk, lit., presence, fr *paront-, parōn*, prp of *pareinai* to be present, fr *para-* + *einai* to be – more at IS]

**paroxysm** /'parək,siz(ə)m/ *n* 1 a fit, attack, or sudden increase or recurrence of (disease) symptoms; a convulsion ⟨*a ∼ of coughing*⟩ 2 a sudden violent outburst ⟨*a ∼ of rage*⟩ [Fr & ML; Fr *paroxysme*, fr ML *paroxysmus*, fr Gk *paroxysmos*, fr *paroxynein* to stimulate, fr *para-* + *oxynein* to provoke, fr *oxys* sharp – more at OXYGEN] – **paroxysmal** *adj*

**paroxytone** /pə'roksitohn/ *adj, esp of a Greek word* having an ACUTE accent on the next-to-last syllable [NL *paroxytonus*, fr Gk *paroxytonos*, fr *para-* + *oxytonos* oxytone] – **paroxytone** *n*

¹**parquet** /'pahkay, -ki/ *vt* **parqueting** /'pahkaying/; **parqueted** /'pahkayd/ 1 to provide with a floor of parquet 2 to make of parquetry

²**parquet** *n* 1a a patterned flooring; *esp* such flooring made of parquetry b parquetry 2 *NAm* theatre stalls [Fr, fr MF, small enclosure, fr *parc* park]

**parquetry** /'pahkitri/ *n* work in the form of usu geometrically patterned wood laid or inlaid, esp for floors – compare MARQUETRY

**parr** /pah/ *n,* **parrs,** *esp collectively* **parr** a young salmon actively feeding in fresh water; *also* the young of any of several other fishes [origin unknown]

**parrakeet** /,parə'keet, '--,-/ *n, NAm* a parakeet

**parrel, parral** /'parəl/ *n* a rope loop or sliding collar that holds a SPAR (rigging supporter) to a ship's mast but that allows it to be hoisted, lowered, or turned round to the wind [ME *perell*, alter. of *parail* apparel, short for *apparail*, fr MF *apareil*, fr *apareillier* to prepare – more at APPAREL]

**parricide** /'parisied/ *n* (the act of) one who murders his/her father, mother, or a close relative [L *parricida & parricidium*, fr *parri-* (akin to Gk *pēos* kinsman by marriage) + -*cida & -cidium* – more at -CIDE] – **parricidal** *adj*

¹**parrot** /'parət/ *n* 1 any of numerous widely distributed tropical birds (order Psittaciformes) that have a distinctive stout curved hooked beak, are often crested and brightly multi-coloured, and are excellent mimics 2 a person who parrots another's words [prob irreg fr MF *perrouet*]

²**parrot** *vt* to repeat or imitate (e g another's words) without understanding or thought – **parrotry** *n*

'**parrot-,fashion** *adv, informal* without regard for meaning ⟨*he learnt it ∼*⟩

**parrot fever** *n* PSITTACOSIS (infectious disease of birds)

**parrot fish** *n* any of numerous spiny-finned sea fishes (e g of the families Scaridae and Labridae) that have the teeth in each jaw fused into a cutting plate like a beak

**parry** /'pari/ *vi* to ward off a weapon or blow ∼ *vt* 1 to ward off (e g a blow) 2 to evade, esp by an adroit answer ⟨*∼ an embarrassing question*⟩ [prob fr Fr *parez*, imper of *parer* to parry, fr OProv *parar*, fr L *parare* to prepare – more at PARE] – **parry** *n*

**parse** /pahz/ *vt* 1 to resolve (e g a sentence) into component PARTS OF SPEECH and describe them grammatically 2 to describe (a word in context) grammatically, by stating its PART OF SPEECH and explaining its grammatical relationship to the rest of the phrase or sentence ∼ *vi* to give a grammatical description of a word or group of words [L *pars orationis* part of speech]

**parsec** /'pah,sek/ *n* a unit of measure for distances in space equal to $3.01 \times 10^{16}$ metres (about $3\frac{1}{4}$ light years); the dis-

tance at which the radius of the earth's orbit subtends an angle of one second of arc [*parallax* + *second*]

**Parsi, Parsee** /,pah'see, '-,-/ *n* 1 a ZOROASTRIAN (adherent of a Persian religion) descended from Persian refugees settled principally in Bombay 2 the Iranian dialect of Parsi religious literature; PAHLAVI [Per *pārsī*, fr *Pārs* Persia] – **Parsiism** *n*

**parsimonious** /,pahsi'mohnyəs/ *adj* frugal to the point of stinginess; niggardly *synonyms* see STINGY *antonym* prodigal – **parsimoniously** *adv*

**parsimony** /'pahsiməni/ *n* 1 the quality of being careful with money or resources; thrift 2 the quality or state of being niggardly; stinginess [ME *parcimony*, fr L *parsimonia*, fr *parsus*, pp of *parcere* to spare]

**parsley** /'pahsli/ *n* an originally S European plant (*Petroselinum crispum*) of the carrot family widely cultivated for its leaves which are used as a herb or garnish in cooking [ME *persely*, fr OE *petersilie*, fr (assumed) VL *petrosilium*, alter. of L *petroselinum*, fr Gk *petroselinon*, fr *petros* stone + *selinon* celery]

**parsnip** /'pahsnip/ *n* a European plant (*Pastinaca sativa*) of the carrot family with large leaves and yellow flowers; *also* its long tapered root, some cultivated varieties of which are eaten as a vegetable [ME *pasnepe*, modif (influenced by ME *nepe* turnip) of MF *pasnaie*, fr L *pastinaca*, fr *pastinum* 2-pronged dibble]

**parson** /'pahs(ə)n/ *n* 1 the priest in charge of a parish 2 a clergyman 3 *archaic* RECTOR [ME *persone*, fr OF, fr ML *persona*, lit., person, fr L]

**parsonage** /'pahsənij/ *n* the house provided by a church for its parson

**parson bird** *n* TUI (glossy black New Zealand bird) [fr its black and white plumage resembling a clergyman's garments]

**parson's nose** /'pahs(ə)nz/ *n* the fatty extension of the rump or tail of a cooked fowl

¹**part** /paht/ *n* 1a(1) any of the often indefinite or unequal subdivisions into which something is (regarded as) divided and which together constitute the whole a(2) an essential portion or integral element b an amount equal to another amount ⟨*mix one ∼ of the powder with three ∼s of water*⟩ c an exact fraction of a quantity d a division of a literary work e(1) a vocal or instrumental line or melody in harmony or in music arranged for more than one voice or instrument e(2) (the written music for) a particular voice or instrument in a piece of music f a constituent member of an apparatus (e g a machine); *also* SPARE PART g an organ, member, or other constituent element of a plant or animal body 2 something (e g a task) one gets when something is divided up or apportioned; a share ⟨*yet thine is the better ∼*⟩ ⟨*each must do his ∼*⟩ 3 any of the opposing sides in a conflict or dispute ⟨*took his son's ∼ in the argument*⟩ 4 *pl* an unspecified territorial area ⟨*took off for ∼s unknown*⟩ ⟨*are you from these ∼s?*⟩ 5 a function or course of action performed ⟨*the government's ∼ in the strike*⟩ ⟨*did you take ∼ in the fighting?*⟩ 6 (a written copy of the lines of) an actor's role in a play 7 a constituent of character or capacity; a talent ⟨*a man of many ∼s*⟩ 8 *NAm* PARTING 2 9 *pl, informal* PRIVATE PARTS [ME, fr OF & OE, both fr L *part-, pars*; akin to L *parare* to prepare – more at PARE] – **for one's part** inasmuch as one is concerned – **for the most part** in most cases or respects; mainly – **take something in good/bad part** to respond to something favourably/unfavourably – **in part** in some degree; partially – **on the part of somebody/on somebody's part** by or from somebody – **play a part** 1 to pretend to be something one is not 2 to have something to do with; be instrumental in ⟨*played a part in her promotion*⟩ – **take part (in)** to participate in

²**part** *vi* 1a to separate from or take leave of someone b to take leave of one another 2 to become separated into parts ⟨*the clouds ∼ed and the sun appeared*⟩ 3 to become separated, detached, or broken ⟨*the strands of the rope ∼ed*⟩ 4 *archaic* to go away; depart ∼ *vt* 1a to divide into parts b to separate (the hair) by combing on each side of a line 2a to remove from contact or association; separate ⟨*till death do us ∼*⟩ ⟨*the narrow channel that ∼s England from France*⟩ b to hold (e g combatants) apart 3 *archaic* to divide into shares and distribute; apportion *synonyms* see ¹SEPARATE [ME *parten*, fr OF *partir*, fr L *partire* to divide, fr *part-, pars*]

**part up** *vt, NZ* HAND OVER

³**part** *adv* partly

⁴**part** *adj* PARTIAL 3 ⟨*∼ payment*⟩

**partake** /pah'tayk/ *vb* **partook** /-'took/; **partaken** /-'taykən/ *vi* 1 to take a part or share; participate – usu + *in* or *of* ⟨*he will ∼ in the sports if you push him*⟩ ⟨*she partook of some*

*wine*⟩ **2** to have some of the qualities or attributes *of* ⟨*his speech* partook *of Cockney dialect*⟩ ~ *vt, archaic* to take a share in **synonyms** see ²SHARE [back-formation fr *partaker,* alter. of *part taker*] – **partaker** *n*
**partan** /'paht(ə)n/ *n* a crab [ME (Sc), of Celt origin; akin to ScGael *partan* crab]
**part and parcel** *n* an essential part or element *of*
**parted** /'pahtid/ *adj* **1a** divided into parts **b** cleft so that the divisions reach nearly but not quite to the base – usu in combination ⟨*a 3-*parted *corolla*⟩ **2** *archaic* DEAD 1
**parterre** /pah'teə/ *n* an ornamental garden with paths between the beds [Fr, fr MF, fr *par terre* on the ground]
**part exchange** *n* a business transaction in which an article, esp a secondhand or used article, is given as part payment for a more expensive and usu new article, esp one of the same class, the balance being made up in money
**parthenocarpy** /'pahthinoh,kahpi/ *n* the production of fruits without fertilization or formation of seeds ⟨*bananas set fruit by* ~ *and without pollination*⟩ [ISV, fr Gk *parthenos* virgin + *karpos* fruit – more at HARVEST] – **parthenocarpic** *adj,* **parthenocarpically** *adv*
**parthenogenesis** /,pahthinoh'jenəsis/ *n* reproduction by development of an unfertilized GAMETE (reproductive cell) that occurs esp among lower plants and INVERTEBRATE animals [NL, fr Gk *parthenos* virgin + L *genesis*] – **parthenogenetic** *adj,* **parthenogenetically** *adv*
**Parthian** /'pahthyən/ *adj* (characteristic) of ancient Parthia or its people [*Parthia,* ancient country in SW Asia] – **Parthian** *n*
**Parthian shot** *n* PARTING SHOT [fr the Parthian horsemen's practice of shooting arrows backwards while in real or feigned flight]
¹**partial** /'pahsh(ə)l/ *adj* **1** inclined to favour one party more than the other; biased **2** markedly fond of someone or something – + *to* ⟨~ *to beans*⟩ **3** of a part rather than the whole; not general or total ⟨*found a* ~ *solution to the problem*⟩ **usage** see PARTLY [ME *parcial,* fr MF *partial,* fr ML *partialis,* fr LL, of a part, fr L *part-, pars* part] **partially** *adv*
²**partial** *n, music* OVERTONE 1a
**partial denture** *n* a usu removable artificial replacement of one or more teeth
**partial derivative** *n* the DERIVATIVE of a mathematical FUNCTION of several variable quantities with respect to any one of them and with the remaining variables treated as constants
**partial differential equation** *n* a DIFFERENTIAL EQUATION containing at least one PARTIAL DERIVATIVE
**partial differentiation** *n* the process of finding a PARTIAL DERIVATIVE
**partial fraction** *n* any of the simpler fractions that when summed are equivalent to a QUOTIENT of two POLYNOMIALS
**partiality** /,pahshi'aloti/ *n* **1** the quality or state of being partial; bias **2** a special taste or liking
**partially ordered** /'pahshəli/ *adj* having every pair of elements (eg of a mathematical set) connected by a relation that is REFLEXIVE, TRANSITIVE, and ANTISYMMETRIC
**partial pressure** *n* the pressure exerted by a component gas in a mixture of gases
**partial sum** *n* the sum of a specified number of terms of an infinite mathematical SERIES, starting with the first term and including all terms up to a specified number
**partible** /'pahtəbl/ *adj* capable of being parted or divided up ⟨*bequeathed a* ~ *estate*⟩
**participate** /pah'tisipayt/ *vi* **1** PARTAKE **2 2** to take part *in* or share in something ⟨*always tried to* ~ *in class discussions*⟩ **synonyms** see ²SHARE [L *participatus,* pp of *participare,* fr *particip-, particeps* partaking, fr *part-, pars* part + *capere* to take – more at HEAVE] – **participant** *adj or n,* **participation, participance** *n,* **participative** *adj,* **participator** *n*
**participatory** /pah'tisipətri/ *adj* characterized by or involving participation; *esp* providing the opportunity for individual participation ⟨~ *democracy*⟩
**participle** /'pahti,sipl, pah'tisipl/ *n* a verbal form (eg *singing* or *sung*) in English and other languages that has the function of an adjective and at the same time can be used in compound verb forms [ME, fr MF, modif of L *participium,* fr *particip-, particeps* partaking, sharing; fr its sharing characteristics of both a verb and an adjective] – **participial** *adj*
**particle** /'pahtikl/ *n* **1** a minute subdivision of matter (eg an electron, atom, or molecule) – compare ELEMENTARY PARTICLE **2** a minute quantity or fragment **3** *linguistics* **3a** a minor unit

of speech including all words without INFLECTIONS (different grammatical endings) or all words except nouns and verbs; *esp* FUNCTION WORD **b** AFFIX 1 (part added to form new word) **4** a small wafer distributed to a Roman Catholic at Communion [ME, fr L *particula,* fr dim. of *part-, pars* part]
**particle board** *n* a board made of very small pieces of wood bonded together (eg with a synthetic resin)
**particle physics** *n* a branch of physics dealing with the constitution, properties, and interactions of ELEMENTARY PARTICLES
**parti-coloured** /'pahti/ *adj* showing different colours or tints ⟨~ *threads*⟩ [*parti-* fr obs *party* variegated, fr ME, fr MF *parti* striped, fr OF, fr *parti,* pp of *partir* to divide]
¹**particular** /pə'tikyoolə/ *adj* **1** of or being a single person or thing (among others) ⟨*the* ~ *person I had in mind*⟩ ⟨~ *incidents in the account seem contrived*⟩ **2** of or concerned with details; exact ⟨*gave us a* ~ *account of her day*⟩ **3** worthy of notice; special, unusual ⟨*suffered from measles of* ~ *severity*⟩ ⟨*there was nothing in the letter of* ~ *importance*⟩ **4** of a proposition in logic stating a fact about some but not all members of a specified class ⟨*"some men are wise" is a* ~ *affirmative*⟩ **5a** concerned over or attentive to details; meticulous ⟨*he's a very* ~ *housekeeper*⟩ **b** fastidious **c** hard to please; exacting **synonyms** see ¹SINGLE **antonym** general [ME *particuler,* fr MF, fr LL *particularis,* fr L *particula* small part]
²**particular** *n* **1a** an individual fact, point, circumstance, or detail ⟨*complete in every* ~⟩ **b** a specific item or detail of information or news ⟨*bill of* ~ s⟩ **2a** an individual member of a class in logic **b** a particular proposition in logic – **in particular** particularly, especially
**particular average** *n* accidental partial damage to or loss of an insured ship or cargo affecting only the shipowner or the owner of the cargo – compare GENERAL AVERAGE
**particularism** /pə'tikyooləriz(ə)m/ *n* **1** exclusive or special devotion to a particular interest **2** a political theory that each political group has a right to promote its own interests, esp independence, without regard to the interests of larger groups – **particularist** *n,* **particularistic** *adj*
**particularity** /pə,tikyoo'larəti/ *n* **1a** a minute detail; a particular **b** an individual characteristic; a peculiarity; *also* a singularity **2a** the quality or state of being particular as opposed to universal **b** attentiveness to detail; exactness **c** the quality or state of being fastidious in behaviour or expression
**particular·ize, -ise** /pə'tikyooləriez/ *vt* to state in detail; specify ~ *vi* to go into details – **particularization** *n*
**particularly** /pə'tikyoolәli/ *adv* **1** in a particular manner; in detail **2** to an unusual degree
**usage** The pronunciation /pə'tikyoolɔli/ rather than /pə'tikyooli/ is recommended for BBC broadcasters.
**particulate** /pah'tikyoolət/ *n or adj* (a substance) consisting of minute separate particles [L *particula*]
**particulate inheritance** *n* MENDELIAN INHERITANCE (transmission of hereditary characteristics)
¹**parting** /'pahting/ *n* **1** a place or point where a division or separation occurs **2 parting,** *NAm* **part** the line where the hair is parted
²**parting** *adj* given, taken, or performed at parting ⟨*a* ~ *kiss*⟩
**parting shot** *n* a pointed remark or hostile gesture made in retreat when leaving – called also PARTHIAN SHOT
**parti pris** /,pahti 'pree (Fr parti pri)/ *n, pl* **partis pris** /~/ a preconceived opinion; a prejudice, bias [Fr, lit., side taken]
¹**partisan, partizan** /'pahtizn/ *n* **1** a firm adherent to a party, faction, cause, or person; *esp* one exhibiting blind, prejudiced, and unreasoning allegiance **2a** a member of a historical body of light troops for special missions or raids on enemies **b** a member of a guerrilla band operating behind enemy lines [MF *partisan,* fr OIt *partigiano,* fr *parte* part, party, fr L *part-, pars* part] – **partisan** *adj,* **partisanship** *n*
²**partisan, partizan** *n* a weapon of the 16th and 17th centuries consisting of a broad blade mounted on a long shaft [MF *partisane,* fr OIt *partigiana,* fem of *partigiano*]
**partita** /pah'teetə/ *n* **1** a musical VARIATION **2** a type of musical SUITE [It fr *partire* to divide, fr L – more at PART]
**partite** /'pahtiet/ *adj* **1** divided into a usu specified number of parts – usu in combination ⟨*tri*partite⟩ **2** PARTED 1b ⟨*a* ~ *leaf*⟩ [L *partitus,* fr pp of *partire*]
¹**partition** /pah'tish(ə)n/ *n* **1a** division into parts; *specif, cap* the division of India into India and Pakistan in 1947 **b(1)** separation of a logical class into its constituent elements **b(2)** the separation of a set of things into DISJOINT (mutually exclusive) subsets such

that every element belongs to one subset ⟨*the days of the week are a ∼ of the days of the year*⟩ **2** something that divides; *esp* an interior dividing wall ⟨*could hear them arguing through the* ∼⟩ **3** a part or section of a whole – **partitionist** *n*

²**partition** *vt* **1a** to divide into parts or shares **b** to divide (e g a country) into two or more territorial units having separate political status **2** to divide or separate *off* by a partition ⟨*can we ∼ off part of the room to use as an office?*⟩ – **partitioner** *n*

**partitive** /'pahtətiv/ *adj* **1** serving to part or divide into parts **2** *esp of a noun or case in a grammatical construction* of or denoting a part ⟨*some is a ∼ word*⟩ ⟨*of us in "the three of us" is in the ∼ genitive*⟩ – **partitively** *adv*

**partly** /'pahtli/ *adv* in some measure or degree; partially

> *usage* Some careful writers prefer to use **partly** rather than **partially** for the sense "as concerns one part, not wholly" ⟨*he lives* **partly** *in London and* **partly** *in Paris*⟩ and to confine **partially** to the sense "to a certain extent, not completely" ⟨*was only* **partially** *convinced*⟩.

¹**partner** /'pahtnə/ *n* **1a** an associate, colleague **b** either of a couple who dance together **c** somebody playing with one or more others in a game against an opposing side **d** a person with whom one is having a sexual relationship; a spouse, lover, etc **2** a member of a partnership **3** *pl* a timber frame that strengthens a ship's deck to support a mast [ME *partener*, alter. (influenced by *part*) of *parcener*, fr AF, joint heir – more at PARCENER]

²**partner** *vt* **1** to act as a partner to **2** to provide with a partner

**partnership** /'pahtnə,ship/ *n* **1** the state of being a partner; association **2** (a legal relation between) two or more joint PRINCIPALS (people holding ultimate legal liability) in a business **3** an association involving close cooperation

**part of speech** *n* a class of words (e g nouns or adverbs) distinguished according to the kind of idea they denote and the function they perform in a sentence

**parton** /'pahton/ *n* a hypothetical ELEMENTARY PARTICLE (minute particle of matter) that is held to be a constituent of neutrons and protons and often identified with QUARKS [¹*part* + ²*-on*]

**partridge** /'pahtrij/ *n, pl* **partridges**, *esp collectively* **partridge** any of various typically medium-sized stout-bodied African and Eurasian game birds (*Perdix, Alectoris,* and related genera) with multi-coloured plumage [ME *partrich*, modif of OF *perdris*, modif of L *perdic-, perdix*, fr Gk *perdik-, perdix*]

'**part-,song** *n* a usu unaccompanied song consisting of two or more voice parts with one part carrying the melody

,**part-'time** *adj* involving or working less than customary or standard hours ⟨*a ∼ job*⟩ ⟨∼ *students*⟩ – **part-time** *adv*, **part-timer** *n*

**parturient** /pah'tyooəri·ənt/ *adj* **1a** bringing forth or about to bring forth young **b** of parturition **2** *formal* about to produce something (e g an idea, discovery, or literary work) [L *parturient-, parturiens*, prp of *parturire* to be in labour, fr *parere* to produce – more at PARE]

**parturition** /,pahtyoo'rish(ə)n/ *n* the action or process of giving birth to offspring [LL *parturition-, parturitio*, fr L *parturitus*, pp of *parturire*]

**partway** /,paht'way/ *adv* to some extent; partially, partly

**part work** *n, Br* a regularly published series of magazines devoted to one subject that is designed to be bound together (e g in book form)

**party** /'pahti/ *n* **1a** a person or group taking one side of a question, dispute, or contest **b** *taking sing or pl vb* a group of people organized to carry out an activity or fulfil a function together ⟨*sent out a search* ∼⟩ **2** *taking sing or pl vb* a group of people holding broadly similar views and organized for political involvement **3** a person or group participating in a (legal) action or proceeding; a participant – usu + *to* ⟨*a ∼ to the transaction*⟩ ⟨*is this the guilty* ∼*?*⟩ **4** a (festive) social gathering **5** *informal* a particular individual ⟨*a shameless old* ∼⟩ [ME *partie* part, party, fr OF, fr *partir* to divide – more at PART] – **party** *adj*

**party line** *n* **1** a single telephone line connecting two or more subscribers with an exchange **2** the official principles of a political party ⟨*expelled for voting against the* ∼⟩ – **partyliner** *n*

**party wall** *n* a wall which divides two adjoining properties and in which each owner has a joint interest

**par value** *n* PAR 1b

**parve** /'pahvə/ *adj* PAREVE (made without milk or meat)

**parvenu** /'pahvənyooh/ *n* a person of low social position who

has recently or suddenly acquired wealth or power; an upstart – compare ARRIVISTE [Fr, fr pp of *parvenir* to arrive, fr L *pervenire*, fr *per* through + *venire* to come – more at FOR, COME] – **parvenu, parvenue** *adj*

**parvis** *also* **parvise** /'pahvis/ *n* an enclosed space in front of a church [ME *parvis*, fr MF, modif of LL *paradisus* enclosed park – more at PARADISE]

**pas** /pah/ *n, pl* **pas** /∼, pahz/ a dance step or combination of steps [Fr, fr L *passus* step – more at PACE]

**pascal** /pa'skal, 'paskl/ *n* the SI unit of pressure equal to the pressure produced by a force of one newton applied uniformly over an area of one square metre [Blaise *Pascal* †1662 Fr mathematician & philosopher]

**PASCAL** /'paskl/ *n* a HIGH-LEVEL computer programming language based on Algol that is used esp as a teaching language in computer studies and for business and commercial applications on microcomputers [Blaise *Pascal*]

**Pascal's triangle** /pa'skalz/ *n* a triangular array of numbers consisting of rows that are the coefficients of the expansion of $(a + b)^n$ for successive integers *n* beginning with 0, and that is used in probability theory [Blaise *Pascal*]

**Pasch** /pask/ *n* **1** the Passover **2** Easter [ME *pasche* Passover, Easter, fr OF, fr LL *pascha*, fr LGk, fr Gk, Passover, fr Heb *pesaḥ*, fr *pāsah* to pass over] – **paschal** *adj*

**paschal candle** *n* a large white candle lighted in a church sanctuary, usu during services between HOLY SATURDAY and ASCENSION DAY

**pas de bourrée** /,pah də boo'ray (*Fr* pa də bure)/ *n, pl* **pas de bourrée** /∼/ a sideways walking or running ballet step in which the feet cross each other alternately [Fr, lit., bourrée step]

**pas de chat** /'shah (*Fr* ʃa)/ *n, pl* **pas de chat** a ballet leap which is made with the knees turned outwards and in which each foot in turn is lifted to the opposite knee [Fr, lit., cat's step]

**pas de deux** /,pah də 'duh/ *n, pl* **pas de deux** /∼, duhz/ a dance or set of dance steps for two performers [Fr, lit., step for two]

**pase** /'pahsay/ *n* a movement of the cape by a matador that attracts the bull and encourages it to attack [Sp, lit., feint, fr *pase* let (him) pass, fr *pasar* to pass, fr (assumed) VL *passare*]

**paseo** /pə'sayoh, pah-/ *n, pl* **paseos** a formal entrance march of bullfighters into an arena [Sp, fr *pasear* to walk, fr *paso* step]

**pash** /pash/ *n, chiefly Br* a hero-worshipping adolescent infatuation; a crush ⟨*she had a ∼ on the gym mistress*⟩ [by shortening & alter. fr *passion*]

**pasha** /'pahshə, 'pashə/ *n* a man of high rank or office (e g in Turkey or N Africa) ⟨*Glubb* Pasha⟩ [Turk *paşa*]

**Pashto** /'pushtoh/ *n* the Iranian language of the Pathan people of E Afghanistan and parts of Pakistan [Per *pashtu*, fr Pashto]

**paso doble** /,pahsoh 'dohblay/ *n* (the music for) a modern ballroom dance with two beats to the bar based on a Latin American march step associated with bullfighting [Sp, lit., double step]

**pasqueflower** /'pask,flowə/ *n* any of several low-growing plants (genus *Anemone*, esp *Anemone pulsatilla*) of the buttercup family, with COMPOUND LEAVES and large, usu white or purple, early spring flowers [alter. (influenced by MF *pasque* Easter) of earlier *passeflower*, fr MF *passefleur*, fr *passer* to pass + *fleur* flower, fr L *flor-, flos* – more at BLOW]

**pasquinade** /,paskwi'nayd/ *n* a lampoon, satire; *esp* one posted in a public place [MF, fr It *pasquinata*, fr *Pasquino*, name given to a statue in Rome on which lampoons were posted] – **pasquinade** *vt*

¹**pass** /pahs/ *vi* **1** to move, proceed **2** to go away ⟨*the panic* ∼ed *very quickly*⟩ – often + *off* ⟨*his headache had* ∼ed *off by lunchtime*⟩ **3a** to go by; move past ⟨*waved from the car window as she* ∼ed⟩ **b** *of time* to elapse ⟨*four years* ∼ed *before we met again*⟩ **c** to overtake another vehicle ⟨*we can* ∼ *once we're round this bend*⟩ **4a** to go across, over, or through ⟨*allow no one to* ∼⟩ **b** to go uncensured or unchallenged ⟨*let her remark* ∼⟩ **5** to go from one quality, state, or form to another ⟨∼es *from a liquid to a gaseous state*⟩ **6a** to pronounce a judgment or opinion **b** to be legally pronounced ⟨*judgment* ∼ed *for the plaintiff*⟩ **7** to go from the control or possession of one person or group to that of another ⟨*the throne* ∼ed *to the king's daughter*⟩ **8a** to happen, occur – usu in *bring something to pass, come to pass* **b** to take place as a mutual exchange or transaction ⟨*angry words* ∼ed *between them*⟩ **9a** to become approved by a body (e g a legislature) empowered to sanction or reject ⟨*the proposal* ∼ed⟩ **b** to undergo an inspection, test,

or examination successfully **10a** to be accepted or regarded as adequate or fitting ⟨*it's only a quick repair but it will* ~⟩ **b** to resemble or act the part of someone or something so well as to be accepted – usu + *for* ⟨*would* ~ *for John Travolta in the dark*⟩ ⟨*she* ~es *for 40*⟩ **11** to kick, throw, or hit a ball or puck to a teammate **12** to decline to bid, bet, or play in a card game **13** *chiefly NAm* to identify oneself or accept identification as a white person though having some black ancestry **14** *euph* to go out of existence; *esp* to die – often + *on, away,* or *over;* compare ³PASSING **15** *obs* to make a pass in fencing ~ *vt* **1** to go beyond: eg **1a** to surpass, exceed ⟨~es *all expectations*⟩ **b** to advance or develop beyond ⟨*societies that have* ~ed *the feudal stage*⟩ **2a** to go across, over, or through ⟨~ *a barrier*⟩ **b** to spend (time) ⟨~ed *the holidays at her sister's home*⟩ **3a** to secure the approval of (eg a legislative body) **b** to succeed in satisfying the requirements of (a test, inspection, or examination) **4a** to cause or permit to win approval or legal or official sanction ⟨~ *a law*⟩ **b** to accept (somebody or something) after examination ⟨*I can't* ~ *this bad piece of work*⟩ **5a** to put in circulation, esp illegally ⟨~ *bad cheques*⟩ **b** to transfer from one person to another ⟨*please* ~ *the salt*⟩ **c** to move or place, esp in or for a short time ⟨~ed *his hand across his brow*⟩ ⟨~ *a rope around a tree*⟩ **d** to throw, hit, or kick (a ball or puck), esp to a teammate **6a** to pronounce judicially ⟨~ *sentence*⟩ **b** to utter – esp in **pass a comment, pass a remark 7a** to cause or permit to go past or through a barrier **b** to cause to march or go by in order ⟨ ~ *the troops in review*⟩ **8** to emit or discharge from a body part, esp the bowels or bladder ⟨*told the nurse he was* ~ing *blood*⟩ **9** to hit a ball past (an opponent) in a game (eg tennis) **10** *chiefly NAm* to omit a regularly scheduled declaration and payment of (a dividend) [ME *passen*, fr OF *passer*, fr (assumed) VL *passare,* fr L *passus* step – more at PACE] – **passer** *n* – **in passing** as a relevant digression; parenthetically – see also **pass the** BUCK/MUSTER/**the** TIME **of day**/WATER

**synonyms 1** A person or object in motion **passes** another that is stationary, **passes** or **overtakes** one that is moving in the same direction, but **meets** one going in the opposite direction. **2 Passed** is the past tense of **pass** ⟨*I* **passed** *your house*⟩ and the past participle ⟨*she's* **passed** *her exam*⟩ but **past** is the related adjective ⟨*in* **past** *centuries*⟩, the preposition ⟨*hurried* **past** *the door*⟩, the noun ⟨*life in the* **past**⟩, and the adverb ⟨*the bus went* **past** *without stopping*⟩.

**pass off** *vt* **1** to present (eg for sale) with intent to deceive **2** to give a false identity or character to ⟨*passed herself* off *as a millionaire*⟩ **3** to direct attention away from; pay no heed to ⟨*passed the pains* off *as migraine*⟩ ~ *vi* to take place and be completed ⟨*his stay in France* passed off *smoothly – TLS*⟩
**pass out** *vi* **1** *chiefly Br* to finish a period of (military) training **2** *informal* to lose consciousness to distribute
**pass over** *vt* **1** to ignore in passing ⟨*I will* pass over *this aspect of the book in silence*⟩ **2** to pay no attention to the claims of; disregard ⟨*was passed over for the chairmanship*⟩
**pass up** *vt* to decline, reject
²**pass** *n* a narrow passage over low ground in a mountain range [ME, fr OF *pas,* fr L *passus* step]
³**pass** *n* **1** the act or an instance of passing **2** a usu distressing or bad state of affairs – often in *come to a pretty pass* ⟨*things have come to a pretty* ~ *when you can't buy English butter*⟩ **3a** a written permission to move about freely in a place or to leave or enter it **b** a written leave of absence from a military post or station for a brief period **c** a permit or ticket allowing free travel or admission **4a** a transference of objects by deceptive means, esp SLEIGHT OF HAND **b** a moving of the hands over or along something **5** the passing of an examination ⟨*I got two A-level* ~es⟩ **6** a single complete mechanical operation (eg in manufacturing or data processing) **7a** an act of passing a ball or puck to a teammate (eg in football); *also* a ball or puck so passed **b** a ball hit to the side and out of reach of an opponent in a game, esp tennis **8** an announcement of a decision not to bid, bet, play, or draw an additional card in a card game **9** a single passage or movement of a man-made object (eg an aircraft) over a place or towards a target **10** a sexually inviting gesture or approach – usu in *make a pass at* **11** *archaic* a thrust or lunge in fencing [partly fr ME *passe,* fr MF, fr *passer* to pass; partly fr ¹*pass*]
**passable** /'pahsəbl/ *adj* **1** capable of being passed, crossed, or travelled on ⟨~ *roads*⟩ **2** barely good enough; tolerable – **passably** *adv*
**passacaglia** /ˌpasəˈkahlyə/ *n* **1** (a dance performed to) an old Italian or Spanish dance tune **2** an instrumental musical com-

position in moderately slow time with three beats to the bar, consisting of variations usu played over a repeating bass part [modif of Sp *pasacalle,* fr *pasar* to pass + *calle* street]
**passado** /pa'sahdoh/ *n, pl* **passados, passadoes** *archaic* a thrust in fencing performed with one foot forward [modif of Fr *passade* (fr It *passata*) or It *passata,* fr *passare* to pass, fr (assumed) VL]
¹**passage** /'pasij/ *n* **1** the action or process of passing from one place or condition to another **2a** a way of exit or entrance; a road, path, channel, or course by which something passes **b** a corridor or lobby giving access to the different rooms or parts of a building or set of rooms **3a(1)** a specified act of travelling or passing, esp by sea or air ⟨*a rough* ~⟩ **a(2)** a right to be conveyed as a passenger ⟨*secured a* ~ *to France*⟩ **b** the passing of a legislative measure **4** a right, liberty, or permission to pass **5** a mutual transaction or exchange (eg a negotiation, a quarrel, or lovemaking) ⟨*this* ~ *of arms and wits amused the town –* Robert Browning⟩ **6a** a usu brief portion of a written work or speech **b** a phrase or short section of a musical composition **c** a detail of a work of art (eg a painting) **7** a slow elevated trot performed by a horse in DRESSAGE (test of precise horsemanship), with moments of suspension between the paces **8** the passing of something or the undergoing of a passing ⟨~ *of faeces*⟩ **9** incubation of a disease-causing organism (eg a virus) in culture, another living organism, or a developing egg [ME, fr OF, fr *passer* to pass]
²**passage** *vt* **1** to cause (a horse) to perform a passage **2** to subject (eg a virus) to passage ~ *vi, of a horse* to perform a passage
**passage grave** *n* a megalithic burial chamber of the late Neolithic period covered by a mound and entered through a long passage resembling a tunnel
**passageway** /-ˌway/ *n* a corridor
**passant** /'pas(ə)nt/ *adj, of a heraldic animal* walking with the farther forepaw raised – used after the noun ⟨*leopard* ~⟩ [MF, fr prp of *passer* to pass]
**passband** /-ˌband/ *n* a band of frequencies (eg in an electronic circuit or a light filter) that is transmitted with maximum efficiency
**passbook** /-ˌbook/ *n* **1** a (building society) account-holder's book in which deposits and withdrawals are recorded **2** DOM-PASS (identification document for nonwhite S Africans)
**pass degree** *n* an ordinary first (BACHELOR'S) degree, awarded esp to someone who does not get high enough marks for an HONOURS degree
**passé** /'pahsay, 'pasay/ *adj* **1** past one's prime ⟨*a* ~ *English rose*⟩ **2a** outmoded **b** behind the times [Fr, fr pp of *passer*]
**passed pawn** *n* a chess pawn that has no enemy pawn in front of it on its own or an adjacent vertical line of squares
**passementerie** /pas'ment(ə)ri/ *n* a fancy edging or trimming made of braid, beading, metallic thread, etc [Fr, fr *passement* ornamental braid, fr *passer* to pass]
**passenger** /'pasinjə, -s(ə)n-/ *n* **1** one who travels in, but does not operate, a public or private conveyance **2** *chiefly Br* a member of a group that contributes little or nothing to the functioning or productivity of the group [ME *passager,* fr MF, fr *passager,* adj, passing, fr *passage*]
**passenger pigeon** *n* an extinct but formerly abundant N American migratory pigeon (*Ectopistes migratorius*)
**passe-partout** /ˌpahs pah'tooh/ *n* **1** MASTER KEY **2** (a strong paper gummed on one side and used in) a method of picture framing in which the glass is attached to the backing by strips of gummed cloth or paper [Fr, fr *passe partout* pass everywhere]
**passepied** /ˌpahs'pyay (*Fr* paspje)/ *n* a lively 17th and 18th century dance of French peasant origin resembling the MINUET [Fr *passe-pied,* fr *passer* to pass + *pied* foot, fr L *ped-, pes* – more at FOOT]
**passerby** /ˌpahsə'bie/ *n, pl* **passersby** /ˌpahsəz-/ a person who happens by chance to pass by a particular place
**passerine** /'pasəˌrien/ *adj* **1** of the largest order (Passeriformes) of birds which includes more than half of all living birds and consists chiefly of perching songbirds (eg finches, warblers, and thrushes) **2** of a suborder (Passeres) of passerine birds comprising the true songbirds with specialized vocal apparatus [L *passerinus* of sparrows, fr *passer* sparrow] – **passerine** *n*
**pas seul** /ˌpah 'suhl (*Fr* pa sœl)/ *n* a solo dance or dance figure [Fr, lit., solo step]
**ˌpass-'fail** *n* a system of recording whether a student has passed or failed an examination rather than assigning a class or mark

**passible** /'pasəbl/ *adj* capable of feeling or suffering △ **passable** [ME, fr MF, fr LL *passibilis*, fr L *passus*, pp of *pati* to suffer – more at PATIENT]

**passim** /'pasim/ *adv* HERE AND THERE – used esp in referring to the occurrence of an item in a piece of text [L, fr *passus* scattered, fr pp of *pandere* to spread – more at FATHOM]

¹**passing** /'pahsing/ *adj* **1** going by or past ⟨*a ~ pedestrian*⟩ **2** having a brief duration ⟨*a ~ whim*⟩ **3** superficial **4** of or used in or for passing ⟨*a ~ place in a road*⟩

²**passing** *adv, archaic* to a great degree; exceedingly ⟨*~ fair*⟩

³**passing** *n, euph* an instance of dying; death ⟨*mourned her ~*⟩

**passing note** *n* a melodic but discordant musical note interposed between essential notes of adjacent chords

**passing shot** *n* a stroke in tennis that drives the ball to one side and beyond the reach of an opponent who is at or coming towards the net

**passion** /'pash(ə)n/ *n* **1** *often cap* **1a** the sufferings of Christ between the night of the LAST SUPPER and his death **b** a musical setting of a gospel account of the Passion story **2a** *pl* the emotions, as distinguished from reason **b** intense, driving, or uncontrollable feeling ⟨*driven to paint by a ~ beyond his control*⟩ **c** an outbreak of anger **3a** ardent affection; love **b** (the object of) a strong liking, devotion, or interest ⟨*a ~ for raspberries*⟩ **c** strong sexual desire [ME, fr OF, fr LL *passion-, passio* suffering, being acted upon, fr L *passus*, pp of *pati* to suffer – more at PATIENT] – **passionless** *adj*

*synonyms* Passion, fervour, ardour, enthusiasm, and zeal all suggest intensely felt emotion. Passion suggests an overwhelming or driving emotion which may not be specific, or it may connote love, desire, or rage, all violently felt and expressed. Fervour and ardour both imply heat; that of fervour suggests a steady burning, intense but sustained ⟨*persecution only increased the fervour of his preaching*⟩. Ardour suggests the more fluctuating heat of a flame, which may burn brightly, then die away. It may imply rapturous, violent feeling, vague but intense aspiration, or yearning love ⟨*the ardour of youth*⟩. Enthusiasm may suggest similar emotions, but these are nearly always excited by a particular purpose or cause ⟨*her enthusiasm for the expedition grew daily*⟩. Zeal combines ardour and enthusiasm in a driving passion, expressed in energetic and untiring efforts towards one's goal ⟨*the zeal of a new convert*⟩.

**passional** /'pash(ə)nl/ *adj* of or marked by passion

**passionate** /'pash(ə)nət/ *adj* **1** easily aroused to anger **2** capable of, affected by, or expressing intense feeling or enthusiasm ⟨*a ~ interest in sport*⟩ **3** swayed by or affected with sexual desire – **passionately** *adv*, **passionateness** *n*

**passionflower** /-ˌflowə/ *n* any of a genus (*Passiflora* of the family Passifloraceae, the passionflower family) of chiefly tropical woody climbing or soft stemmed erect plants with usu showy flowers and pulpy often edible berries [fr the fancied resemblance of parts of the flower to the instruments of Christ's crucifixion]

**passionfruit** /-ˌfrooht/ *n* an edible fruit from any of various PASSIONFLOWERS; *esp* GRANADILLA

**Passionist** /'pashənist/ *n* a member of a Roman Catholic order devoted chiefly to missionary work and periods of withdrawal for meditation [It *passionista*, fr *passione* passion, fr LL *passion-, passio*]

**passion play** *n, often cap 1st P* a dramatic representation of the crucifixion of Christ and the events leading up to it

**Passion Sunday** *n* the fifth Sunday in Lent

**Passiontide** /-ˌtied/ *n* the last two weeks of Lent

**Passion Week** *n* **1** HOLY WEEK **2** the second week before Easter

**passivate** /'pasivayt/ *vt* **1** to make (a metal) inactive or less reactive ⟨*~ the surface of steel to prevent corrosion*⟩ **2** to protect (eg a semiconductor device) against failure or contamination by coating with some relatively inert material [*passive + -ate*] – **passivation** *n*

¹**passive** /'pasiv/ *adj* **1a** acted on, receptive to, or influenced by external forces or impressions **b**(1) *of a verb form or* VOICE expressing an action that is done to the grammatical subject of a sentence (eg *was hit* in "the ball was hit") **b**(2) *of a sentence* containing a passive verb form **c** *of a person* lacking in energy, will, or initiative; meekly accepting **d** *esp of an animal* placid ⟨*assured us that the bull was quite ~*⟩ **e** induced by an external agency ⟨*~ exercise of a paralysed limb*⟩ **2a** not active or operative; inert **b** of or characterized by a state of chemical inactivity; *esp* resistant to corrosion **c** not involving expenditure of chemical energy ⟨*~ transport across a cell membrane*⟩ **d** *of an electronic device* using no electrical power for amplifying or controlling an electrical signal ⟨*capacitors and resistors are ~ devices*⟩ – compare ACTIVE 11b **e** operating solely by means of the power of an input signal ⟨*a ~ communication satellite that reflects television signals*⟩ **f** operating by intercepting signals emitted from a target ⟨*a ~ homing missile*⟩ – compare ACTIVE 11a **3a** offering no resistance; submissive ⟨*~ surrender to fate*⟩ **b** existing without being active or open ⟨*~ support*⟩ *synonyms* see INACTIVE *antonym* active [ME, fr L *passivus*, fr *passus*, pp] – **passively** *adv*, **passiveness, passivity** *n*

²**passive** *n* **1** a passive verb form **2** the passive VOICE in a language

**passive immunity** *n* immunity acquired by transfer of antibodies (eg by injection of BLOOD SERUM from an individual with active antibodies) – compare ACTIVE IMMUNITY

**passive resistance** *n* resistance, esp to a government, an occupying power, or particular laws, characterized by nonviolent acts of noncooperation

**passive transfer** *n* a transfer of skin sensitivity from an allergic to a normal person by injection of BLOOD SERUM from the former into the latter, that is used esp for identifying specific allergic substances that cause a high degree of allergic sensitivity

**passkey** /'pahsˌkee/ *n* MASTER KEY

**pass law** *n* any of various S African laws restricting the movements of nonwhites, forcing them to live in certain areas, and requiring them to carry identification at all times – compare DOMPASS

**Passover** /'pahsohvə/ *n* the Jewish celebration commemorating the Hebrews' liberation from slavery in Egypt [fr the exemption of the Israelites from the slaughter of the first-born in Egypt (Exod 12:23-27)]

**passport** /'pahsˌpawt/ *n* **1** an official document issued by a government **a** as proof of identity and nationality to one of its citizens for use when leaving or reentering the country and affording some protection when abroad **b** as a safe-conduct to a foreign citizen passing through its territory **2a** a permission or authorization to go somewhere **b** something that secures admission or acceptance ⟨*education as a ~ to success*⟩ [MF *passeport*, fr *passer* to pass + *port* port, fr L *portus* – more at FORD]

**password** /-ˌwuhd/ *n* **1** a word or phrase that must be spoken by a person before being allowed to pass a guard **2** WATCHWORD 1

¹**past** /pahst/ *adj* **1a** just gone or elapsed ⟨*for the ~ few months*⟩ **b** having gone by; earlier ⟨*~ generations*⟩ ⟨*in years ~*⟩ **2** finished, ended ⟨*winter is ~*⟩ **3** of or being the verb tense that expresses action or state in time gone by **4** preceding, former ⟨*~ president*⟩ *synonyms* see ¹PASS [ME, fr pp of *passen* to pass]

²**past** *prep* **1a** beyond the age of or for ⟨*he's ~ 80*⟩ ⟨*~ playing with dolls*⟩ **b** subsequent to in time ⟨*half ~ two*⟩ **2a** at the farther side of; beyond **b** up to and then beyond ⟨*drove ~ the house*⟩ **3** beyond the capacity, range, or sphere of ⟨*~ belief*⟩ ⟨*wouldn't put it ~ him to cheat*⟩ **4** *obs* more than – **past it** *informal* no longer effective or in one's prime

³**past** *n* **1a** time gone by **b** something that happened or was done in the past ⟨*regret the ~*⟩ **2** the past tense of a language; *also* a verb form (eg *went*) in this tense **3** a past life, history, or course of action; *esp* one that is kept secret ⟨*she has a ~, you know*⟩

⁴**past** *adv* so as to pass by the speaker ⟨*children ran ~*⟩ ⟨*days crawled ~*⟩

**pasta** /'pastə/ *n* any of several (egg or oil-enriched) flour-and-water doughs that are usu shaped and used fresh (eg as ravioli) or dried (eg as spaghetti) [It, fr LL, dough, paste]

¹**paste** /payst/ *n* **1a** a fat-enriched dough used esp for pastry **b** a usu sweet doughy confection ⟨*almond ~*⟩ **c** a smooth preparation of meat, fish, etc used esp for spreading on bread **2** a soft mixture or composition: eg **2a** a preparation of flour or starch and water used as an adhesive **b** clay or a clay mixture used in making pottery or porcelain **3** a brilliant glass of high lead content used in making imitation gems [ME, fr MF, fr LL *pasta* dough, paste]

²**paste** *vt* **1** to stick with paste **2** to cover with something pasted on

³**paste** *vt, informal* to strike hard at [alter. of *baste*]

¹**pasteboard** /-ˌbawd/ *n* board made by pasting together two or more sheets of paper and used esp in bookbinding

²**pasteboard** *adj* **1** made of pasteboard **2** sham, insubstantial

**pastedown** /'paystˌdown/ *n* the outer leaf of an endpaper that is pasted down to the inside of the front or back cover of a book

¹**pastel** /'pastl; *NAm* pas'tel/ *n* **1** (a crayon made of) a paste made of powdered pigment mixed with gum **2** (a) drawing in pastel **3** any of various pale or light colours [Fr, fr It *pastello*, fr LL *pastellus* woad, fr dim. of *pasta* paste] – **pastellist,** *NAm chiefly* **pastelist** *n*

²**pastel** *adj* **1** drawn with pastels **2** pale and light in colour

**pastern** /'pastuhn/ *n* a part of the foot of an animal of the horse family extending from the FETLOCK (joint above the hoof) to the hoof; *also* a corresponding part of the leg in another animal [MF *pasturon*, fr *pasture* pasture, tether attached to a horse's foot]

'**paste-,up** *n* **1** a piece of copy for photographic reproduction consisting of text and artwork in the proper positions **2** DUMMY 5

**pasteur·ization, -isation** /,pahstyoorie'zaysh(ə)n, pa-, -stərie-/ *n* **1** partial sterilization of a substance, esp a liquid (e g milk), at a temperature and for a period of exposure that destroys harmful organisms without major chemical alteration of the substance **2** partial sterilization of perishable food products (e g fruit or fish) with radiation (e g GAMMA RAYS) [Louis *Pasteur* † 1895 Fr chemist]

**pasteur·ize, -ise** /'pahstyooriez, 'pahstə-, 'past-/ *vt* **1** to subject to pasteurization **2** to make bland or innocuous ⟨*a* ~d *description of war*⟩ – **pasteurizer** *n*

**pasticcio** /pa'stichoh/ *n, pl* **pasticci, pasticcios** a pastiche [It, lit., pasty, fr ML *pasticius*, fr LL *pasta* paste]

**pastiche** /pa'steesh/ *n* **1** a literary, artistic, or musical work that imitates the style of previous work **2** a musical, literary, or artistic composition made up of elements borrowed from various sources [Fr, fr It *pasticcio*]

**pasties** /'paystiz/ *n pl* small round coverings for a woman's nipples, worn esp by strippers [²*paste*]

**pastille, pastil** /'past(ə)l, -stil, -steel/ *n* **1** a small cone of aromatic paste, burned to fumigate or scent a room **2** an aromatic or medicated lozenge [Fr *pastille*, fr L *pastillus* small loaf, lozenge; akin to L *panis* bread – more at FOOD]

**pastime** /'pahs,tiem/ *n* something (e g a hobby or game) that amuses and serves to make time pass agreeably [trans of MF *passe-temps*, fr *passer* to pass + *temps* time]

**pasting** /'paysting/ *n, informal* a beating, trouncing [fr gerund of ³*paste*]

**pastis** /pa'stees/ *n* an alcoholic drink flavoured with aniseed [Fr]

**past master** *n* **1** a person who has held the office of master in a guild, society, etc **2** one who is expert or experienced (in a particular activity) [(2) alter. of *passed master*]

**pastor** /'pahstə, 'pastə/ *n* one having responsibility for the spiritual welfare of a group (e g a congregation) [ME *pastour*, fr OF, fr L *pastor* shepherd, fr *pastus*, pp of *pascere* to feed – more at FOOD] – **pastorate, pastorship** *n*

¹**pastoral** /'pahst(ə)rəl/ *adj* **1a(1)** (composed) of shepherds or herdsmen **a(2)** used for or based on livestock rearing **b** of the countryside; not urban **c** portraying rural life, esp in an idealized and conventionalized manner ⟨~ *poetry*⟩ **d** pleasingly peaceful and innocent; idyllic **2a** of or providing spiritual care or guidance, esp of a church congregation **b** of the pastor of a church *synonyms* see RURAL [ME, fr L *pastoralis*, fr *pastor* shepherd, herdsman] – **pastoralism** *n*, **pastorally** *adv*

²**pastoral** *n* **1** pastoral, pastoral letter a letter from a clergyman to the people in his charge; *esp* a letter addressed by a bishop to his diocese **2a** a pastoral literary work **b** an (idealized) depiction of country life **c** a pastorale **3** CROSIER (bishop's staff)

**pastorale** /,pastə'rahli/ *n* **1** an opera of the 16th or 17th centuries having a pastoral plot **2** an instrumental or vocal composition having a pastoral theme [It, fr *pastorale* of herdsmen, fr L *pastoralis*, fr *pastor*]

**Pastoral Epistle** *n* any of the three New Testament letters 1 and 2 Timothy and Titus supposedly written by the apostle Paul that give advice on matters of church government and discipline

**pastoralia** /,pastə'raylyə, -'ahlyə/ *n* the branch of theology that deals with the work of a pastor [L, neut pl of *pastoralis* pastoral]

**pastoralist** /'pahst(ə)rə,list/ *n, Austr* a farmer who keeps grazing animals (e g cattle or sheep)

**pastorate** /'pahstərət/ *n* **1** the office or tenure of office of a pastor **2** *taking sing or pl vb* a body of pastors

**past participle** *n* a participle (e g *finished, eaten, been*) with past, perfect, or passive meaning

**past perfect** *adj* of or being a verb tense (e g *had finished*) that expresses completion of an action at or before a past time – **past perfect** *n*

**pastrami** /pə'strahmi/ *n* a highly seasoned smoked beef prepared esp from shoulder cuts [Yiddish, fr Romanian *pastramă*]

**pastry** /'paystri/ *n* **1** PASTE 1a; *esp* paste when baked (e g for piecrust, flans, and tarts) **2** (an article of) food made with pastry – used esp with reference to sweet baked goods [¹*paste* + *-ry*]

**pasturage** /'pastyoorij, 'pahschərij/ *n* pasture

¹**pasture** /'pahschə/ *n* **1** plants (e g grass) grown for feeding (grazing) animals **2** pasture, pastureland (a plot of) land used for grazing **3** the feeding of livestock; grazing [ME, fr MF, fr LL *pastura*, fr L *pastus*, pp – more at PASTOR]

²**pasture** *vi* to graze on pasture ~ *vt* to feed (e g cattle) on pasture

¹**pasty** /'pasti/ *n* a small pie or pastry case enclosing a usu savoury filling, esp of meat, and baked without a container △ pâté, patty [ME *pastee*, fr MF *pasté*, fr *paste* dough, paste]

²**pasty** /'paysti/ *adj* resembling paste; *esp* pallid and unhealthy in appearance – **pastiness** *n*

**PA system** *n* PUBLIC-ADDRESS SYSTEM

¹**pat** /pat/ *n* **1** a light blow, esp with the hand or a flat instrument **2** a light tapping often rhythmical sound **3** a small mass of something (e g butter) shaped (as if) by patting [ME *patte*, prob of imit origin]

²**pat** *vt* **-tt-** **1** to strike lightly with the open hand or some other flat surface **2** to flatten, smooth, or put into place or shape with light blows ⟨*he* ~ted *his hair into place*⟩ **3** to tap or stroke gently with the hand to soothe, caress, or show approval

³**pat** *adv* in a pat manner; aptly, promptly

⁴**pat** *adj* **1a** exactly suited to the purpose or occasion; apt **b** suspiciously appropriate; contrived ⟨*a* ~ *answer*⟩ **2** learned, mastered, or memorized exactly

**pataca** /pə'tahkə/ *n* – see MONEY table [Pg]

**patagium** /pə'tayji·əm/ *n, pl* **patagia** /-ji·ə/ a wing membrane: e g **a** the fold of skin connecting the forelimbs and hind limbs of some tree-dwelling gliding animals (e g a flying squirrel) **b** the fold of skin in front of the main segments of a bird's wing [NL, fr L, gold edging on a tunic]

'**pat-,ball** *n* slow or feeble play (e g in cricket or tennis)

¹**patch** /pach/ *n* **1** a piece of material used to mend or cover a hole or reinforce a weak spot **2** a tiny piece of black silk or COURT PLASTER worn on the face or neck, esp by women in the 17th and 18th centuries, to hide a blemish or to set off the complexion **3a** a cover (e g a piece of adhesive plaster) applied to a wound **b** a shield worn over the socket of an injured or missing eye **4a** a small piece; a scrap **b** a small area distinct from its surroundings ⟨*damp* ~es *on the wall*⟩ ⟨~es *of fog along the motorway*⟩ **c** a small piece of land usu used for growing vegetables ⟨*a cabbage* ~⟩ **5** a piece of cloth sewn on a garment as an ornament or insignia **6** a temporary connection in a communications system (e g for the purpose of having a three-way telephone conversation) **7** a temporary correction in a faulty computer program **8** *chiefly Br* a usu specified period ⟨*poetry is going through a bad* ~ – Cyril Connolly⟩ **9** *chiefly Br* an area for which a particular individual or unit (e g of police) has responsibility [ME *pacche*, perh fr MF *pece, piece, pieche* piece] – **not a patch on** *informal* not nearly as good as

²**patch** *vt* **1** to mend or cover (a hole or weak spot) with a patch **2** to provide with a patch ⟨*a* ~ed *pair of trousers*⟩ **3a** to make from patchwork **b** to mend or put together, esp in a hasty or shabby fashion – usu + *up* ⟨*attempting to* ~ *up their marriage*⟩ **c** to make a patch in (a computer program); *also* to make a change in (data stored on a computer) without following the standard routine for this procedure **4** to connect (e g circuits) by a PATCH CORD

**patchboard** /-,bawd/ *n* a board which has sets of linked sockets for making temporary circuit connections by means of PATCH CORDS

**patch cord** *n* a wire with a plug at each end that is used to link sockets on a patchboard

**patchouli, patchouly** /'pachooli, pə'choohli/ *n* **1** an E Indian shrubby plant (*Pogostemon cablin*) of the mint family that yields a fragrant ESSENTIAL OIL **2** a heavy perfume made from patchouli oil [Tamil *paccuḷi*]

**patch pocket** *n* a flat pocket attached to the outside of a garment

**patchwork** /-,wuhk/ *n* 1 something composed of miscellaneous or incongruous parts 2 work consisting of pieces of cloth of various colours and shapes sewn together, esp to form a cover (eg for a cushion or bed)

**patchy** /'pachi/ *adj* 1 uneven in quality; incomplete ⟨*the concert was* ~⟩ ⟨*my knowledge of French is* ~⟩ 2 *of certain types of weather* appearing in patches ⟨~ *fog*⟩ – **patchily** *adv*, **patchiness** *n*

**pate** /payt/ *n* 1 (the crown of) the head 2 *chiefly derog* the brain [ME] – **pated** *adj*

**pâté** /'patay/ *n* 1 a savoury pie, esp of meat or fish 2 a rich savoury paste or spread of finely mashed seasoned and spiced food, esp meat or fish △ pasty, patty [Fr, fr OF *pasté,* fr *paste*]

**patella** /pə'telə/ *n, pl* **patellae** /-lie/, **patellas** 1 a thick flat roughly triangular movable bone that forms the front point of the knee and protects the front of the joint – called also KNEECAP 2 an ancient (eg Roman) small pan – used in archaeology [L, fr dim. of *patina* shallow dish] – **patellar, patellate** *adj*

**patelliform** /pə'telifawm/ *adj* 1a resembling a limpet or limpet shell; shaped like a flattened hollow cone b shaped like a patella 2 *botany* disc-shaped with a narrow rim [NL *Patella* genus including the limpet, fr L, small shallow dish]

**paten** /'pat(ə)n/ *n* 1 a plate made usu of precious metal, used to carry the bread at Communion 2 a thin circular metal disc [ME, fr OF *patene,* fr ML & L; ML *patina,* fr L, shallow dish, fr Gk *patanē;* akin to L *patēre*]

¹**patent** /'payt(ə)nt, 'pat(ə)nt; *sense 5* 'payt(ə)nt/ *adj* 1a secured by a patent to the exclusive control and possession of a particular individual or group b protected by a patent; made under a patent ⟨~ *locks*⟩ c protected by a trademark or a TRADE NAME so as to establish proprietary rights like those conveyed by a patent; proprietary ⟨~ *drugs*⟩ 2a of or concerned with the granting of patents, esp for inventions ⟨*a* ~ *lawyer*⟩ b made of PATENT LEATHER ⟨~ *shoes*⟩ 3 *esp of a passage or duct in the body* affording free passage; unobstructed ⟨*a* ~ *opening*⟩ 4 *chiefly botany* spreading out; PATULOUS ⟨~ *branches*⟩ 5 readily visible or intelligible; not hidden or obscure; blatant 6 *chiefly humorous* original and individual as if protected by patent ⟨*a* ~ *way of pickling onions*⟩ [ME, fr MF, fr L *patent-, patens,* fr prp of *patēre* to be open – more at FATHOM; (1,2,&6) orig fr *letters patent* open letter or document conferring a right] – **patency** *n,* **patently** *adv*

    **usage** In British English, the pronunciation /'pat(ə)nt/ is often preferred for **patent** (adjective, noun, and verb) in technical contexts connected with the patenting of inventions, such as ⟨*to file a* **patent**⟩ ⟨the **Patent** *Office*⟩, but /'payt(ə)nt/ is more usual elsewhere.
    **synonyms** see EVIDENT **antonym** latent

²**patent** /'payt(ə)nt, 'pat(ə)nt/ *n* 1 an official document conferring a right or privilege; LETTERS PATENT 2a a formal document securing to an inventor for a specified period the exclusive right to make, use, or sell his/her invention b the monopoly or right so granted c a patented invention 3 a privilege, licence 4 *NAm* a document issued by the government authorizing the grant or sale of public lands; *also* land so sold or granted

³**patent** *vt* to obtain a patent for (an invention) – **patentable** *adj,* **patentability** *n*

**patentee** /,payt(ə)n'tee, ,pa-/ *n* a person to whom a grant is made or a privilege secured by patent

**patent leather** /'payt(ə)nt/ *n* a leather with a hard smooth glossy surface

**patent medicine** /'payt(ə)nt/ *n* a medicine that is made and sold under a patent, trademark, etc

**Patent Office** /'payt(ə)nt, 'pat(ə)nt/ *n* a government office for examining claims to patents and granting patents

¹**pater** /'patə/ *n, often cap* (a) paternoster [ME, by shortening]

²**pater** /'paytə/ *n, chiefly Br humorous* a father [L]

**paterfamilias** /,paytəfə'mili,as/ *n, pl* **patresfamilias** /,pahtrayz-/ 1 a male head of a household 2 the father of a family [L, fr *pater* father + *familias,* archaic gen of *familia* household – more at FATHER, FAMILY]

**paternal** /pə'tuhnl/ *adj* 1 fatherly ⟨~ *benevolence*⟩ 2 received or inherited from one's male parent 3 related through one's father ⟨~ *grandfather*⟩ [L *paternus,* fr *pater*] – **paternally** *adv*

**paternalism** /pə'tuhnəl,iz(ə)m/ *n* a system by which a government or organization deals with its subjects or employees in an authoritarian but benevolent way (eg by supplying all their needs but regulating their conduct) – **paternalist** *n or adj,* **paternalistic** *adj*

**paternity** /pə'tuhnəti/ *n* 1 the quality or state of being a father 2 origin or descent from a father

**paternity test** *n* a test to determine whether a man could be the biological father of a particular child, that is made by comparison of genetic traits (eg blood groups) of the mother, child, and suspected man

**paternoster** /,patə'nostə, ,pah-/ *n* 1 *often cap* LORD'S PRAYER 2 a word formula repeated as a prayer or magical charm 3 a weighted fishing line with a row of hooks [ME, fr ML, fr L *pater noster* our father (the first words of the prayer); (3) fr obs sense, string of beads for counting repetitions of the Lord's Prayer, rosary]

**path** /pahth/ *n, pl* **paths** /pahdhz/ 1 a track formed by the frequent passage of people or animals 2 a track specially constructed for a particular use ⟨garden ~s⟩ – compare BRIDLE PATH 3a a course, route ⟨*the* ~ *of a planet*⟩ b a way of life, conduct, or thought ⟨*his* ~ *through life was difficult*⟩ 4 *maths* 4a the continuous series of positions or configurations that can be assumed in any motion or process of change by a moving or varying system b a sequence of arcs in a network that can be traced continuously without retracing any arc 5 a line of communication over interconnecting NERVE CELLS extending from one organ or nerve centre to another [ME, fr OE *pæth;* akin to OHG *pfad* path]

**path-** /path/, **patho-** *comb form* pathological state; disease ⟨patho*gen*⟩ ⟨patho*gnomonic*⟩ [NL, fr Gk, fr *pathos,* lit., suffering – more at PATHOS]

**-path** /-path/ *comb form* (→ *n*) 1 practitioner of (a specified system of medicine) ⟨*naturo*path⟩ 2 sufferer from disorder of (such a part or system) ⟨*psycho*path⟩ [(1) Ger, back-formation fr *-pathie* -pathy; (2) ISV, fr Gk *-pathēs* (adj) suffering, fr *pathos*]

**Pathan** /pə'tahn/ *n* a member of the principal ethnic group of Afghanistan [Hindi *Paṭhān*]

**pathetic** /pə'thetik/ *adj* 1a PITIFUL 1a ⟨*a* ~ *lost child*⟩ b PITIFUL 1b ⟨*a* ~ *performance*⟩ ⟨~ *attempts to learn German*⟩ 2 marked by sorrow or melancholy; sad [MF or LL; MF *pathetique,* fr LL *patheticus,* fr Gk *pathētikos* capable of feeling, pathetic, fr *paschein* to experience, suffer – more at PATHOS] – **pathetically** *adv*

**pathetic fallacy** *n* the attribution of human characteristics or feelings to inanimate nature (eg in *cruel sea*)

**pathfinder** /'pahth,fiendə/ *n* 1 one who explores untraversed regions to mark out a new route 2 one who discovers new ways of doing things 3 an aircraft that marks (eg with flares) a target area for bombers – **pathfinding** *n or adj*

**pathless** /'pahthlis/ *adj* untrod, trackless – **pathlessness** *n*

**pathogen** /'pathəj(ə)n, -jen/ *n* a bacterium, virus, or other disease-causing agent [ISV] – **pathogenic** *adj,* **pathogenically** *adv,* **pathogenicity** *n*

**pathogenesis** /,pathə'jenəsis/ *n* the origination and development of a disease [NL] – **pathogenetic** *adj*

**pathognomonic** /,pathagnə'monik, ,pathənə-/ *adj* distinctively characteristic of a particular disease ⟨~ *symptoms*⟩ [Gk *pathognōmonikos,* fr *path-* + *gnōmonikos* fit to judge, fr *gnōmon* interpreter]

**pathological** /,pathə'lojikl/, **pathologic** *adj* 1 of pathology 2 altered or caused by disease 3 *informal* having no reasonable foundation; irrational; *also* irrationally habitual ⟨*a* ~ *liar*⟩ ⟨*her* ~ *fear of publicity*⟩ – **pathologically** *adv*

**pathologist** /pə'tholəjist/ *n* a specialist in pathology: eg a one who conducts postmortems to determine the cause of death b one who interprets and diagnoses the changes caused by disease in tissues

**pathology** /pə'tholəji/ *n* 1 the study of the essential nature of diseases, esp the structural and functional changes produced by them 2 something abnormal: 2a the anatomical and physiological deviations from the normal that constitute disease or characterize a particular disease b deviation from an assumed normal state of mentality or morality [NL *pathologia* & MF *pathologie,* fr Gk *pathologia* study of the emotions, fr *path-* + *-logia* -logy]

**pathos** /'paythos/ *n* 1 a quality in experience or in artistic representation evoking pity or compassion – compare BATHOS 2 an emotion of sympathetic pity [Gk, suffering, experience, emotion, fr *paschein* to experience, suffer; akin to Lith *kesti* to suffer]

**pathway** /'pahth,way/ *n* 1 a path, course 2 a sequence of biochemical reactions occurring in a living cell (eg those reactions by which a hormone is synthesized or by which a substance is broken down to yield energy( ⟨*metabolic* ~s⟩

**-pathy** /-pəthi/ *comb form* (→ *n*) **1** feeling; being acted upon ⟨*em*pathy⟩ ⟨*tele*pathy⟩ **2** disorder of (such a part or system) ⟨*neuro*pathy⟩ **3** system of medicine based on (such a factor) ⟨*osteo*pathy⟩ [L *-pathia*, fr Gk *-patheia*, fr *-pathēs* suffering, fr *pathos*]

**patience** /'paysh(ə)ns/ *n* **1** the capacity, habit, or fact of being patient **2** *chiefly Br* any of various card games that can be played by one person; *esp* any that involve the arranging of cards dealt at random in a prescribed pattern

**¹patient** /'paysh(ə)nt/ *adj* **1** bearing pains or hardships calmly or without complaint **2** manifesting forbearance under provocation or strain **3** not hasty or impetuous **4** steadfast despite opposition, difficulty, or adversity **5a** able or willing to bear **b** susceptible, admitting ⟨~ *of one interpretation*⟩ □ (5) + *of* [ME *pacient*, fr MF, fr L *patient-*, *patiens*, fr prp of *pati* to suffer; akin to L *paene* almost, *penuria* need, Gk *pēma* suffering] – **patiently** *adv*

**²patient** *n* **1** a person (or animal) awaiting or undergoing medical care and treatment **2** one who or that which is acted upon

**patina** /'patinə/ *n*, *pl* **patinas**, **patinae** /-nie/ **1a** a usu green film formed naturally on copper and bronze by long exposure to the weather or artificially (eg by acids), and often valued as aesthetically pleasing **b** a surface appearance of something (eg polished wood) that has grown more beautiful, esp with age or use **2** an appearance or aura that is derived from association, habit, or established character ⟨*the mellow* ~ *of a contented old age*⟩ [NL, fr L, shallow dish – more at PATEN]

**patine** /pa'teen/ *vt or n* (to cover with) a patina [n Fr, fr NL *patina*; vb fr n]

**patio** /'pati·oh/ *n*, *pl* **patios** **1** an open inner court characteristic of dwellings in Spain and Latin America **2** a usu paved area adjoining a dwelling, esp one that is adapted to sitting and often eating outdoors [Sp]

**patisserie** /pə'teesəri, -'ti-/ *n* **1** PASTRY 1b (sweet goods made of pastry) **2** an establishment where patisserie is made and sold [Fr *pâtisserie*, fr MF *pastiserie*, deriv of LL *pasta* dough, paste]

**Patna rice** /'patnə/ *n* a long-grained rice suitable for using in savoury dishes [*Patna*, city in NE India]

**patois** /'patwah/ *n*, *pl* **patois** /'patwahz/ **1** a provincial dialect other than the standard or literary dialect **2** JARGON 2 (technical speech) *synonyms* see DIALECT [Fr, fr OF, uncouth or rustic speech, prob fr *patte* paw]

**patr-**, **patri-**, **patro-** *comb form* father ⟨*patr*onymic⟩ [*patr-*, *patri-* fr L, fr *patr-*, *pater*; *patr-*, *patro-* fr Gk, fr *patr-*, *patēr* – more at FATHER]

**patrial** /'paytri·əl/ *adj or n*, *Br* (of or being) a person who has a legal right to reside in the United Kingdom, esp because one of his/her parents or grandparents was born there [ML *patrialis* of one's fatherland, fr L *patria* fatherland – more at EXPATRIATE] – **patriality** *n*

**patriarch** /'paytri,ahk, 'pat-/ *n* **1a** any of the fathers of the human race or of the Hebrew people according to the Bible **b** a man who is father or founder (eg of a race, science, religion, or class of people) ⟨*Samuel Johnson is one of the* ~s *of lexicography*⟩ **c(1)** the oldest member or representative of a group **c(2)** a venerable old man **d** a man who is head of a patriarchy **2a** any of the bishops of the ancient or Orthodox SEES (seats of bishops' authority) of Constantinople, Alexandria, Antioch, and Jerusalem or of the ancient see of Rome, with authority over other bishops **b** the head of any of various Eastern churches **c** a Roman Catholic bishop next in rank to the pope **3** a senior priest of the Mormon church, empowered to give blessings and perform various other rites [ME *patriarche*, fr OF, fr LL *patriarcha*, fr Gk *patriarchēs*, fr *patria* family, clan (fr *patr-*, *patēr* father) + *-archēs* -arch] – **patriarchal** *adj*

**patriarchal cross** /paytri'ahkl, pat-/ *n* a chiefly heraldic cross denoting a cardinal's or archbishop's rank and having two crossbars of which the lower is the longer

**patriarchate** /,paytri'ahkət, -kayt, ,patri-/ *n* **1a** the office, jurisdiction, or time in office of a patriarch **b** the residence or headquarters of a patriarch **2** a patriarchy

**patriarchy** /'paytri,ahki, 'patri-/ *n* a system of social organization marked by the supremacy of the father in the clan or family, the legal dependence of wives and children, and the reckoning of descent and inheritance in the male line

**patriate** /'paytriayt/ *vt* to transfer the control of (its own constitution) to a country [back-formation fr *repatriate*]

**patrician** /pə'trish(ə)n/ *n* **1** a member of any of the original citizen families of ancient Rome **2a** a person of high birth; an aristocrat **b** a person of breeding and cultivation [ME *patricion*, fr MF *patricien*, fr L *patricius*, fr *patres* senators, fr pl of *pater* father] – **patrician** *adj*

**patriciate** /pə'trishi·ət, -,ayt/ *n* **1** the position or dignity of a patrician **2** *taking sing or pl vb* a patrician class

**patricide** /'patri,sied/ *n* **1** one who commits patricide **2** the murder of one's own father [(1) L *patricida* & (2) LL *patricidium*, fr L *patr-* + *-cida* & *-cidium* – more at -CIDE] – **patricidal** *adj*

**patriclinous** /,patri'klienəs/, **patriclinic** /-klinik/ *adj*, *of an animal or plant* showing inherited characteristics of the male parent – compare MATRICLINOUS [Gk *patr-*, *patēr* father + *klinein* to lean]

**patrilineal** /,patri'lini·əl/ *adj* relating to, based on, or tracing descent through the paternal line ⟨~ *society*⟩

**patrimony** /'patriməni/ *n* **1a** property inherited from one's father or ancestor **b** something derived from one's father or ancestors; a heritage **2** an estate or endowment belonging by ancient right to a church [ME *patrimonie*, fr MF, fr L *patrimonium*, fr *patr-*, *pater* father] – **patrimonial** *adj*

**patriot** /'paytri·ət, 'patri-/ *n* one who loves his/her country and (zealously) supports its authority and interests [MF *patriote*, fr LL *patriota*, fr Gk *patriōtēs*, fr *patrios* of one's father, fr *patr-*, *patēr* father] – **patriotism** *n*, **patriotic** *adj*, **patriotically** *adv*

**patristics** /pə'tristiks/ *n taking sing vb* the study of the writings and theology of the authoritative writers of the early Christian church [Ger *patristik*, deriv of L *patr-*, *pater* father] – **patristic**, **patristical** *adj*

**¹patrol** /pə'trohl/ *n* **1a** the action of traversing a district or beat or of going the rounds of a garrison, camp, etc for observation or the maintenance of security ⟨*on* ~⟩ **b** *taking sing or pl vb* a detachment of people employed for reconnaissance, security, or combat **2** *taking sing or pl vb* a subdivision of a scout troop or guide company that has six to eight members

**²patrol** *vb* **-ll-** to carry out a patrol (of) [Fr *patrouiller*, fr MF, to tramp round in the mud, fr *patte* paw – more at PATTEN] – **patroller** *n*

**patrol car** *n* a usu high-performance car used by police to patrol esp motorways

**patrolman** /-mən/ *n*, *NAm* one who patrols; *esp* a policeman assigned to a beat

**patrology** /pə'troləji/ *n* **1** patristics **2** a collection of the works of the authoritative writers of the early Christian church [NL *patrologia*]

**patrol wagon** *n*, *NAm* an enclosed van used by police to carry prisoners; BLACK MARIA

**patron** /'paytrən; *sense 6* pa'tronh/, *fem* **patroness** /'paytrənis, ,paytrə'nes/ *n* **1a** a person chosen, named, or honoured as a special guardian, protector, or supporter **b** a wealthy or influential supporter of an artist or writer **c** a social or financial sponsor of a social function (eg a ball or concert) **2** one who uses his/her wealth or influence to help an individual, institution, or cause **3** a customer **4** the holder of a patronage in the Church of England **5** a master in ancient times who freed his slave but retained some rights over him/her **6** the proprietor of an establishment (eg an inn), esp in France [ME, fr MF, fr ML & L; ML *patronus* patron saint, patron of a benefice, pattern, fr L, defender, fr *patr-*, *pater*; (6) Fr, fr MF] – **patronal** *adj*

**patronage** /'patrənij/ *n* **1** the right to nominate a clergyman for a vacant position (BENEFICE) in the Church of England **2** the support or influence of a patron **3** the granting of favours in a condescending way **4** business or activity provided by patrons ⟨*the new branch library is expected to have a heavy* ~⟩ **5a** the power to make appointments to government jobs **b** the distribution of jobs on the basis of patronage **c** jobs distributed by patronage

**patron·ize**, **-ise** /'patrəniez/ *vt* **1** to act as patron of **2** to adopt an air of condescension towards **3** to be a customer of – **patronization** *n*, **patronizingly** *adv*

**patron saint** *n* **1** a saint regarded as having a particular person, group, church, etc under his/her special care and protection **2** an original leader or prime example ⟨*the* ~ *of anticlericalism*⟩

**patronymic** /,patrə'nimik/ *n* a name derived from that of the father or a paternal ancestor, usu by the addition of an affix (eg *Mac-*) – compare MATRONYMIC [LL *patronymicum*, deriv of Gk *patronymia*, fr *patr-* + *onyma* name – more at NAME] – **patronymic** *adj*

**patsy** /'patsi/ *n*, *NAm informal* one who is easily duped, cheated, or victimized; a sucker [perh fr It *pazzo* fool]

**patten** /'patn/ *n* a sandal or overshoe set on a wooden sole or metal device to keep the foot well clear of the ground [ME *patin*, fr MF, fr *patte* paw, hoof, fr (assumed) VL *patta*, of imit origin]

¹**patter** /'patə/ *vt* to say, speak, or recite (prayers) rapidly or mechanically ~ *vi* to talk glibly and at length [ME *patren*, fr *paternoster*] – **patterer** *n*

²**patter** *n* 1 a specialized and esp criminal jargon 2 the sales talk of a street trader 3 empty chattering talk 4a(1) the rapid-fire talk of a comedian a(2) the talk with which an entertainer accompanies his/her routine b the words of a comic song or of a rapidly spoken usu humorous monologue introduced into such a song

³**patter** *vi* 1 to strike or pat rapidly and repeatedly ⟨*rain* ~ed *against the window pane*⟩ 2 to run with quick light-sounding steps ~ *vt* to cause to patter [freq of ²*pat*]

⁴**patter** *n* a quick succession of slight sounds or pats

¹**pattern** /'pat(ə)n/ *n* 1 a form or model proposed for imitation; an example 2 something designed or used as a model or set of instructions for making things ⟨*a dress* ~⟩ 3 a model for making a mould into which molten metal is poured to form a casting 4 a specimen, sample 5a a usu repeated decorative design (eg on fabric) b a coherent structure of related parts ⟨*the complex* ~ *of a computer program*⟩ 6 a natural or chance configuration ⟨*a frost* ~⟩ ⟨*the* ~ *of events*⟩ 7a the distribution of the shot from a shotgun or the fragments from an exploded shrapnel shell b the grouping made on or round a target by bombs, shells, or bullets 8 the flight path prescribed for an aircraft that is coming in for a landing [ME *patron*, fr MF, fr ML *patronus* – more at PATRON] – **patterned** *adj*

²**pattern** *vt* 1 to make or fashion according to a pattern 2 to furnish, adorn, or mark with a design ~ *vi* to form a pattern

**patterning** /'patəniŋ/ *n* a decoration, composition, or configuration according to a pattern

**patty** *also* **pattie** /'pati/ *n* 1 a little pie or pasty 2 *NAm* a small flat cake of chopped food ⟨*a hamburger* ~⟩ △ **pâté** [Fr *pâté*]

**patulous** /'patyoolǝs/ *adj, chiefly botany* spreading widely from a centre ⟨*a tree with* ~ *branches*⟩ [L *patulus*, fr *patēre* to be open – more at FATHOM] – **patulously** *adv*, **patulousness** *n*

**paua** /'powǝ/ *n* an edible shellfish (*Haliotis iris* of the phylum Mollusca) of New Zealand with a rainbow-coloured shell that is often used as an ornament [Maori]

**paucity** /'pawsǝti/ *n, formal* 1 smallness of number; fewness 2 smallness of quantity; scarceness [ME *paucite*, fr MF or L; MF *paucité*, fr L *paucitat-, paucitas*, fr *paucus* little – more at FEW]

**Pauli exclusion principle** /'powli/ *n* EXCLUSION PRINCIPLE (principle that no two electrons in one atom can be in the same state) [Wolfgang *Pauli* †1958 US (Austrian-born) physicist]

**Pauline** /'pawlien/ *adj* of the apostle Paul, his epistles, or their doctrines or theology [ML *paulinus*, fr L *Paulus* Paul †*ab*67 Christian apostle, fr Gk *Paulos*]

**Paul Jones** /,pawl 'johnz/ *n* a dance during which the couples change partners [prob fr John *Paul Jones* †1792 US naval officer]

**paulownia** /paw'lohni·ǝ/ *n* any of a genus (*Paulownia*) of Chinese trees of the foxglove family; *esp* one (*Paulownia tomentosa*) widely cultivated for its fragrant violet flowers [NL, genus name, fr Anna *Paulovna* †1865 Russ princess]

**paunch** /pawnch/ *n* 1a the belly and its contents b a fat stomach; a potbelly 2 RUMEN (first compartment of the stomach of a cud-chewing animal) [ME, fr MF *panche*, fr L *pantic-, pantex*]

**paunchy** /'pawnchi/ *adj* having a potbelly; fat – **paunchiness** *n*

**pauper** /'pawpǝ/ *n* a very poor person; *specif* a destitute who in former times was supported by charity or from public funds [L, poor – more at FEW] – **pauperism** *n*

**pauper-ize, -ise** /'pawpǝ,riez/ *vt* to reduce to poverty or destitution

¹**pause** /pawz/ *n* 1 a temporary stop 2a CAESURA (break in a line of poetry) b a brief suspension of the voice to indicate the limits and relations of sentences and their parts 3 temporary inaction, esp as caused by uncertainty; hesitation 4 the sign denoting a FERMATA (lengthening of a musical note) 5 a reason or cause for pausing ⟨*a thought that should give one* ~⟩ [ME, fr L *pausa*, fr Gk *pausis*, fr *pauein* to stop; akin to Gk *paula* rest]

²**pause** *vi* 1 to stop temporarily 2 to linger for a time

**pavane** *also* **pavan** /pǝ'van, pǝ'vahn, 'pavǝn/ *n* 1 a stately court dance for couples that was introduced from southern Europe into England in the 16th century 2 music for the pavane; *also* music having the slow rhythm of a pavane with two beats to the bar [MF *pavane*, fr OSp or OIt *pavana*, perh deriv of L *pavon-, pavo* peacock]

**pave** /payv/ *vt* 1 to lay or cover with material (eg stone or concrete) to form a firm level surface for walking or travelling on 2 to cover firmly and solidly as if with paving material 3 to serve as a covering or pavement of [ME *paven*, fr MF *paver*, fr L *pavire* to strike, stamp; akin to OHG *arfūrian* to castrate, L *putare* to prune, reckon, think, Gk *paiein* to strike] – **paver** *n*

**pavé** /'pavay/ *n* 1 a pavement 2 a setting in which jewels are positioned as close together as possible so as to conceal a metal base [Fr, fr pp of *paver* to pave] – **pavé** *adj*

**pavement** /'payvmǝnt/ *n* 1 a paved surface: eg 1a *chiefly Br* a surfaced walk for pedestrians, esp at the side of a road b *NAm* the artificially covered surface of a road 2 something that suggests a pavement or surface of PAVING STONES (eg in flatness, hardness, extent of surface, or compact arrangement of units) ⟨~ *epithelium*⟩ ⟨*a limestone* ~⟩ 3 *chiefly NAm* the material with which something is paved [ME, fr OF, fr L *pavimentum*, fr *pavire*]

**pavement artist** *n* a person who draws pictures, usu in chalk, on the pavement in the hope that passersby will give him/her money

¹**pavilion** /pǝ'vilyǝn, -li·ǝn/ *n* 1 a large often sumptuous tent 2 a part of a building projecting from the rest 3a a light sometimes ornamental structure in a garden, park, or place of recreation that is used for entertainment or shelter b a temporary structure erected at an exhibition by an individual exhibitor 4 the lower faceted part of a cut gem below the GIRDLE (edge grasped by the setting) 5 *chiefly Br* a building on a sports ground with changing and often seating and refreshment facilities ⟨*a cricket* ~⟩ 6 *chiefly NAm* any of several detached or semidetached units into which a building is sometimes divided [ME *pavilon*, fr OF *paveillon*, fr L *papilion-, papilio* butterfly; akin to OHG *fifaltra* butterfly, Lith *peteliške* flighty]

²**pavilion** *vt* to provide or cover with or put in a pavilion

**paving stone** /'payving/ *n* a thin usu rectangular stone or concrete block used for paving

**pavior, paviour** /'payvyǝ/ *n, Br* 1 one who paves 2 a machine or material used for paving [ME *pavier*, fr *paven* to pave]

**pavis, pavise** /'pavis/ *n* a large shield covering the whole body, used in medieval times [ME, fr MF *pavais*, fr OIt *pavese*, prob fr *pavese* of Pavia, fr *Pavia*, city in NE Italy]

**pavlova** /pav'lohvǝ/ *n* a cake made of meringue with a marshmallow centre topped with cream and fruit and eaten esp in Australia [Anna *Pavlova* †1931 Russ ballerina]

**Pavlovian** /pav'lohvyǝn, pav'lofyǝn/ *adj* of Ivan Pavlov or his work and theories on conditioning; *broadly* produced automatically in response to a stimulus; predictable ⟨*a* ~ *reaction*⟩ [Ivan *Pavlov* †1936 Russ physiologist]

**pavonine** /'pavǝnien/ *adj, formal* of or like a peacock; *esp* resembling the bright colours of a peacock's tail [L *pavoninus*, fr *pavon-, pavo* peacock]

¹**paw** /paw/ *n* 1 the foot of a four-legged animal (eg a lion or dog) that has claws; *broadly* the foot of an animal 2 *humorous* a human hand [ME, fr MF *poue*]

²**paw** *vt* 1 to feel or touch clumsily, rudely, or indecently 2 to touch or strike at with a paw 3 to scrape or beat (as if) with a hoof ⟨~ *the ground*⟩ 4 to flail at or grab for wildly ⟨*hands* ~ing *the air*⟩ ~ *vi* 1 to beat or scrape something (as if) with a hoof 2 to touch or strike with a paw

**pawky** /'pawki/ *adj, chiefly Br* artfully shrewd, esp in a humorous way; canny [obs E dial. *pawk* trick (cf JIGGERY-POKERY)]

**pawl** /pawl/ *n* a pivoted tongue or sliding bolt on one part of a machine that is adapted to fall into notches or between teeth on another part (eg a RATCHET WHEEL) so as to permit motion in only one direction [perh modif of D *pal* pawl]

¹**pawn** /pawn/ *n* 1a something delivered to or deposited with somebody as a pledge or security (eg for a loan) b a hostage 2 the state of being pledged – usu in *in pawn* 3 the act of pawning [ME *paun*, modif of MF *pan*]

²**pawn** *vt* to deposit (something) in pledge or as security – **pawner** *n*

³**pawn** *n* 1 any of the eight chessmen of each colour of least value that have the power to move only forward one square at

a time, but with the option of two squares on the first move, to capture only diagonally forward, and to be promoted to any piece except a king when they reach the opposite side of the board **2** one who or that which can be easily manipulated to further the purposes of another [ME *pown*, fr MF *poon*, fr ML *pedon-*, *pedo* foot soldier, fr LL, one with broad feet, fr L *ped-*, *pes* foot – more at FOOT]

**pawnbroker** /-,brohkə/ *n* one who loans money on the security of personal property pledged in his/her keeping – **pawnbroking** *n*

**Pawnee** /paw'nee/ *n, pl* **Pawnees**, *esp collectively* **Pawnee** a member of a N American Indian people originally of Kansas and Nebraska

**pawnshop** /-,shop/ *n* a pawnbroker's shop

**pawn ticket** *n* a receipt given by a pawnbroker to a client for the property pawned

**pawpaw** /'paw,paw/ *n* PAPAW 2 (N American tree or its edible fruit)

**pax** /paks/ *n* **1** a tablet decorated with a sacred figure (e g of Christ) and ceremonially kissed by participants at mass **2** KISS OF PEACE (sign of Christian goodwill) **3** *Br* – used interjectionally by children as an indication that they wish to stop fighting or to be excluded from a game [ME, fr ML, fr L, peace – more at PEACE]

¹**pay** /pay/ *vb* **paid** /payd/, (7) **paid** *also* **payed** *vt* **1a** to make due return to for services rendered or property received ⟨~ *the workers*⟩ **b** to engage for money; hire ⟨*you couldn't* ~ *me to do that*⟩ **2a** to give in return for goods or service ⟨~ *wages*⟩ **b** to discharge indebtedness for; settle ⟨~ *a bill*⟩ **c** to make a disposal or transfer of (money) ⟨~ *money into the bank*⟩ **3** to give or forfeit in retribution ⟨~ *the penalty*⟩ **4** to make compensation for **5** to give, offer, or make freely or as fitting ⟨~ *attention*⟩ ⟨~ *one's respects*⟩ ⟨~ *a visit*⟩ **6a** to be profitable to; be worth the expense or effort to ⟨*it* ~*s shopkeepers to stay open late*⟩ **b** to bring in as a return ⟨*an investment* ~*ing five per cent*⟩ **7** to slacken (e g a rope) and allow to run *out* ~ *vi* **1** to discharge a debt or obligation **2** to be worth the expense or effort ⟨*it* ~*s to advertise*⟩ [ME *payen*, fr OF *paier*, fr L *pacare* to pacify, fr *pac-*, *pax* peace] – **payer** *also* **payor** *n*, **payee** *n* – **the devil/hell to pay** serious trouble as the consequence of an action – **put paid to** *informal* to ruin; WIPE OUT ⟨*this will* put paid to *our chances of winning*⟩ – see also **pay somebody (back) in his/her own** COIN, **pay through the** NOSE

**pay back** *vt* to return punishment to according to what is deserved ⟨pay *him* back *for making me late*⟩

**pay for** *vt* to receive punishment or suffering for ⟨paid for *his night on the town with a hangover*⟩

**pay off** *vt* **1** to pay the whole of (a debt) **2** to dismiss (a worker) with full payment of wages due **3** to pay (someone) to keep silent about an illegal or wrongful act **4** *informal* PAY BACK ~ *vi* to be successful or profitable ⟨*his hunch* paid off⟩ – see also PAYOFF

**pay out** *vt*, *Br* PAY BACK ~ *vi*, *informal* to make a usu large payment of money – see also PAY-OUT

**pay up** *vi* to pay the whole amount owing, esp unwillingly or after the debt is due

²**pay** *n* **1** the status of being paid by an employer; employ ⟨*was in the* ~ *of the enemy*⟩ **2** something paid, esp a salary or wage for work or services done; remuneration

³**pay** *adj* **1** equipped with a coin slot for receiving a fee for use ⟨*a* ~ *phone*⟩ **2** requiring payment **3** containing a sufficient quantity of a desired mineral, metal, etc to be profitably mined ⟨~ *gravel*⟩ ⟨~ *ore*⟩; *broadly, chiefly NAm* containing or leading to something precious or valuable

⁴**pay** *vt* **payed** *also* **paid** to waterproof (a ship's hull) [obs Fr *peier*, fr L *picare*, fr *pic-*, *pix* pitch]

**payable** /'payəbl/ *adj* **1** that may, can, or must be paid **2** profitable

**pay-as-you-'earn** *n* a system of deducting income tax from pay before an employee receives it

**paybed** /-,bed/ *n* a hospital bed the use of which is paid for by the occupant rather than by the state

**payday** /-,day/ *n* a regular day on which wages or salaries are paid

**pay dirt** *n* **1** earth or ore that yields a profit to a miner **2** *chiefly NAm* a useful or remunerative discovery or object

**payload** /-,lohd/ *n* **1** the revenue-producing load that a transport vehicle can carry **2** the explosive charge carried in the warhead of a missile **3** the load (e g instruments) carried in a spacecraft relating directly to the purpose of the flight, as

opposed to the load (e g fuel) necessary for operation; *also* the weight of such a load

**paymaster** /-,mahstə/ *n* an officer or agent whose duty it is to pay salaries or wages; *broadly, chiefly derog* an employer

**paymaster general** *n, often cap P&G* a British government minister who now has only negligible financial duties, but is often made a member of the cabinet and entrusted with special functions

**payment** /-mənt/ *n* **1** the act of paying **2** something that is paid **3** something done or given in return; REQUITAL

**paynim** /'paynim/ *n, archaic* a pagan; *esp* a Muslim [ME *painim*, fr OF *paienime* heathendom, fr LL *paganismus*, fr *paganus* pagan]

**payoff** /-,of/ *n, informal* **1** the act or occasion of paying employees' wages or distributing gains (e g profits or bribe money) **2** a profit, reward; *esp* an amount received by a player in a game **3** the climax of an incident or enterprise; *specif, chiefly NAm* the usu surprise ending of a narrative **4** a decisive fact or factor resolving a situation or bringing about a definitive conclusion

**payola** /pay'ohlə/ *n* an undercover or indirect payment (e g to a disc jockey) for unofficial promotion of a commercial product; *also* the practice of making such payments [prob alter. of *payoff*]

'**pay-,out** *n, informal* **1** PAYOFF 1 **2** (the act of making) a usu large payment of money ⟨*a jackpot* ~ *of £350,000*⟩

'**pay-,packet** *n, Br* an envelope containing a person's pay; *also* the pay itself

**payroll** /-,rohl/ *n* **1** a list of those entitled to be paid and of the amounts due to each **2** the sum necessary to pay those on a payroll **3** *taking sing or pl vb* the people on a payroll

**payslip** /-,slip/ *n, Br* a written statement of one's gross pay, allowances, deductions, and net pay

**pay station** *n, NAm* a public telephone with a coin-box

**PCB** *n* POLYCHLORINATED BIPHENYL

**P-'Celtic** *n* the division of the Celtic languages that includes Welsh, Cornish, and Breton – compare Q-CELTIC [fr the development in these languages of the phoneme *p* from Indo-European *qu*]

**PDQ** *adv, often not cap* immediately [*pretty damned quick*]

**pe** /pay/ *n* the 17th letter of the Hebrew alphabet [Heb *pē*]

**pea** /pee/ *n, pl* **peas 1a** a climbing plant (*Pisum sativum* of the family Leguminosae, the pea family) that is extensively cultivated for its rounded edible protein-rich green seeds that are borne in long green pods; *also* the seed of a pea **b** *pl* the immature pods of the pea with their included seeds **2** (the seed of) any of various usu specified plants (e g a chick-pea or SWEET PEA) related to or resembling the pea [back-formation fr *pease* (taken as a pl), fr ME *pese*, fr OE *pise*, fr L *pisa*, pl of *pisum*, fr Gk *pison*]

**peace** /pees/ *n* **1** a state of tranquillity or quiet: e g **1a** freedom from civil disturbance **b** a state of public order and security maintained by law or custom – chiefly in *breach of the peace*, *keep the peace* **2** freedom from disquieting or oppressive thoughts or emotions ⟨~ *of mind*⟩ **3** harmony in personal relations **4a** a state or period of mutual friendliness between countries **b** a pact or agreement to end hostilities between those who have been at war or in a state of enmity **5** – used interjectionally as a command or request for silence or calm or as a greeting or farewell [ME *pees*, fr OF *pais*, fr L *pac-*, *pax*; akin to L *pacisci* to agree – more at PACT] – **at peace** in a state of quiet or tranquillity – **hold/keep one's peace** to remain silent in spite of having something to say – **keep the peace** to avoid or prevent discord – **make one's peace (with)** to reestablish friendly relations (with); become reconciled (with)

**peaceable** /'peesəbl/ *adj* **1a** disposed to peace; not inclined to dispute or quarrel **b** quietly behaved **2** free from strife or disorder *synonyms* see PACIFIC *antonyms* aggressive, belligerent – **peaceableness** *n*, **peaceably** *adv*

**peace camp** *n* a camp set up outside a military establishment, esp a nuclear missile base, by protesters against military activities

**peace corps** *n* a body of trained personnel sent by the US government as volunteers, esp to assist underdeveloped nations

**peaceful** /-f(ə)l/ *adj* **1** PEACEABLE 1 **2** untroubled by conflict, agitation, or commotion; quiet, tranquil **3** of a state or time of peace **4** devoid of violence or force ⟨*a* ~ *demonstration*⟩ *synonyms* see ²CALM, PACIFIC *antonyms* turbulent, disturbed, violent – **peacefully** *adv*, **peacefulness** *n*

**peaceful coexistence** *n* a state in which countries with different ideologies live together in peace rather than in constant hostility

**peacekeeping** /'pees,keeping/ *n* the preserving of peace; *esp* international enforcement and supervision of a truce between hostile states or communities – **peacekeeper** *n*

**peacemaker** /'pees,maykə/ *n* one who makes peace, esp by reconciling opposing sides – **peacemaking** *n or adj*

**peace offering** *n* a gift or service for the purpose of bringing about peace or reconciliation

**peace pipe** *n* CALUMET (N American Indian pipe)

**peace sign** *n* a sign made by holding the palm outwards and forming a V with the index and middle fingers and used to indicate the desire for peace – compare V SIGN

**peacetime** /-,tiem/ *n* a time when a nation is not at war

**¹peach** /peech/ *n* **1a** a low spreading Chinese tree (*Prunus persica*) of the rose family that is widely grown in temperate areas and has tapering leaves, stalkless usu pink flowers borne in early spring, and an edible fruit **b** the edible fruit of the peach tree, that has a single large stone, sweet juicy yellow or white flesh, and a thin downy reddish to yellow skin **2** a light yellowish-pink colour **3** *informal* a particularly excellent person or thing; *specif* an unusually attractive girl or young woman [ME *peche*, fr MF (the fruit), fr LL *persica*, fr L *persicum*, fr neut of *persicus* Persian, fr *Persia*] – **peachy** *adj*

**²peach** *vt* to inform against; betray ～ *vi* to turn informer 〈～ed *on his accomplices*〉 [ME *pechen*, short for *apechen* to accuse, fr (assumed) AF *apecher*, fr LL *impedicare* to fetter, entangle – more at IMPEACH]

**peach leaf curl** *n* LEAF CURL of the peach tree that is caused by a fungus (*Taphrina deformans*)

**¹peacock** /'pee,kok/ *n* **1** a male peafowl that is distinguished from the female peahen by a crest of upright feathers on the head and by very long loosely webbed tail feathers which are mostly tipped with shimmering eyelike spots and can be erected and spread at will in a large splendidly coloured fan; *broadly* a peafowl **2** a vain person; a show-off [ME *pecok*, fr pe- (fr OE *pēa* peafowl; akin to OHG *pfāwo* peacock; both fr a prehistoric WGmc-NGmc word borrowed fr L *pavon-, pavo* peacock) + *cok* cock] – **peacockish, peacocky** *adj*

**²peacock** *vi* to strut self-importantly ～ *vt, Austr slang* to buy up the best pieces of (land) in an area – no longer in vogue

**peacock blue** *n* a lustrous greenish-blue colour

**peacock butterfly** *n* a butterfly (*Inachis io*) with brownish-red wings marked with large purple eyespots

**peacock ore** *n* BORNITE (red-brown copper-containing mineral)

**pea crab** *n* any of various minute crabs (family Pinnotheridae) that live inside the shells of some oysters, clams, mussels, etc

**peafowl** /-,fowl/ *n* any of several very large ground-living pheasants (family Phasianidae): e g **a** the common peafowl (*Pava cristatus*) of India and Sri Lanka of which the male has a blue and green body and is often reared as an ornamental fowl **b** a Javanese and Burmese peafowl (*Pava muticus*) with a green and bronze body **c** a blue, green, and bronze African bird (*Aropavo congensis*) [*pea-* (as in *peacock*) + *fowl*]

**pea green** *n* a light yellowish-green colour

**peahen** /-,hen/ *n* a female peafowl [ME *pehenne*, fr pe- + *henne* hen]

**pea jacket** *n* a heavy woollen double-breasted jacket worn esp by sailors [by folk etymology fr D *pijjekker*, fr *pij*, a kind of cloth + *jekker* jacket]

**¹peak** /peek/ *vi* to grow pale, thin, or sickly [origin unknown] – **peaked, peaky** *adj*

**²peak** *n* **1** a pointed or projecting part of a garment; *esp* one on the front of a cap **2** a sharp or pointed end **3a(1)** the top of a hill or mountain ending in a point **a(2)** a prominent mountain usu having a well-defined summit **b** something resembling a mountain peak **4a** the upper rearmost corner of a four-cornered sail that is attached to the mast along its edge **b** the narrow part of a ship's bow or stern **5a** the highest level or greatest degree **b** a high point in a course of development, esp as represented on a graph **6** WIDOW'S PEAK (V-shaped hairline) *synonyms* see SUMMIT [perh alter. of *²pike*] – **peaked** *adj*, **peakedness** *n*

**³peak** *vi* to reach a maximum ～ *vt* to cause to come to a peak, point, or maximum

**⁴peak** *adj* at or reaching the maximum of capacity, value, or activity 〈*the factory reached* ～ *productivity*〉 〈～ *traffic hours*〉

**⁵peak** *vt, nautical* **1** to set (e g a spar from which a sail hangs)

nearer the perpendicular **2** to hold (oars) with the blades well raised [*apeak*]

**peak load** *n* maximum demand or density (e g of electricity or traffic)

**peak time** *n* the time of greatest demand for some service (e g television programmes)

**¹peal** /peel/ *n* **1a** the loud ringing of bells **b** a complete set of variations on the order in which a given number of bells can be rung **c** a set of bells tuned to the notes of the major scale for CHANGE RINGING **2** a loud prolonged sound or succession of sounds 〈*heard* ～s *of laughter*〉 [ME, appeal, summons to church, short for *appel* appeal, fr *appelen* to appeal]

**²peal** *vi* to give out peals ～ *vt* to utter or give forth loudly

**³peal** *n, Br* GRILSE (young salmon) [origin unknown]

**pean** /'peen/ *n* the heraldic representation of a black fur with spots of gold [MF *pene*, lit., feather, fr L *penna*]

**¹peanut** /'pee,nut/ *n* **1a** a low-branching widely cultivated plant (*Arachis hypogaea*) of the pea family, that bears showy yellow flowers having a stalklike structure which, after the flower has withered, elongates and pushes into the soil, where the OVARY (seed-bearing structure) ripens and develops into a pod containing one to three seeds **b** the pod or oily edible seed of the peanut **2** *pl* a small and insignificant amount, esp of money

**²peanut** *adj, chiefly NAm* insignificant, petty 〈～ *politics*〉

**peanut butter** *n* a paste made from ground peanuts

**peanut oil** *n* a colourless to yellow fatty oil that is obtained from peanuts and is used chiefly as a SALAD OIL, in margarine, and in soap and pharmaceutical preparations and cosmetics

**pear** /peə/ *n* a large sweet fleshy edible fruit that is borne by a tree (genus *Pyrus*, esp *Pyrus communis*) of the rose family and is typically larger and more rounded at the end furthest from the stalk; *also* a tree that bears pears [ME *pere*, fr OE *peru*, fr L *pirum*]

**¹pearl** /puhl/ *n* **1a** a small dense usu lustrous and often rounded mass of concentric layers of mother-of-pearl, that is formed as an abnormal growth round a foreign particle (e g a grain of sand) in the shell of some oysters, mussels, and related animals, can occur in a variety of colours but is typically milky-white, and is much used as a gem **b** MOTHER-OF-PEARL **2** one who or that which resembles a pearl; *esp* one who or that which is very rare or precious **3** a nearly neutral slightly bluish medium grey colour [ME *perle*, fr MF, fr (assumed) VL *pernula*, dim. of L *perna* haunch, sea mussel; akin to OE *fiersn* heel, Gk *pternē*]

**²pearl** *vt* **1** to set or adorn (as if) with pearls **2** to form (e g barley) into small round grains **3** to give a pearly colour or lustre to ～ *vi* **1** to form drops or beads like pearls **2** to fish or search for pearls – chiefly in *go pearling* – **pearler** *n*

**³pearl** *adj* **1a** of or like pearl **b** made of or decorated with pearls **2** having medium-sized grains 〈～ *barley*〉

**⁴pearl** /puhl/ *n or vt, Br* PICOT (ornamental loop in fabric) [alter. of *purl*]

**pearl danio** *n* a small shiny freshwater fish (*Brachydanio albolineatus*) related to the carp and often kept in tropical aquariums [NL *Danio*, former genus of cyprinid fishes]

**pearl essence** *n* a translucent substance that occurs in the silvery scales of various fish (e g herring) and is used in making artificial pearls, lacquers, and plastics

**pearlite** /'puhliet/ *n* **1** the mixture of FERRITE and CEMENTITE, usu arranged in alternate layers, that occurs in slowly cooled alloys of iron and carbon and is a principal constituent of both steel and CAST IRON **2** PERLITE (greyish glassy material formed from lava) [Fr *perlite*, fr *perle* pearl] – **pearlitic** *adj*

**pearl-ized, -ised** /'puhliezd/ *adj* given a pearly surface or finish 〈～ *cosmetics*〉

**pearl millet** *n* a tall cereal grass (*Pennisetum glaucum*) grown widely in Africa, Asia, and the S USA for its edible seeds and for animal fodder

**pearl onion** *n* a very small usu pickled onion, used esp in appetizers and as a garnish

**pearl oyster** *n* any of various large oysters or related shellfish (esp genera *Pinctada* and *Avicula*) that often produce pearls

**pearlwort** /-,wuht/ *n* any of several very small plants (genus *Sagina*) of the pink family that have usu minute white or green flowers

**¹pearly** /'puhli/ *adj* like, containing, or decorated with pearls or mother-of-pearl

**²pearly** *n, Br* **1** a button made of mother-of-pearl **2** a PEARLY KING or PEARLY QUEEN

**pearly gates** *n pl* **1** *the* gates of heaven **2** *Br slang* teeth [(1) fr the reference in Rev 21:21]

**pearly king,** *fem* **pearly queen** *n* a member of certain cockney families who are traditionally entitled to dress in clothes covered with pearl buttons

**pearly nautilus** *n* NAUTILUS 1 (animal with a spiral shell, related to the octopuses)

**pearmain** /'peə,mayn/ *n, Br* any of several varieties of eating apple [ME *permayn*, a type of pear, fr OF *permain*, perh fr L *Parmensis* of Parma, city in N Italy]

**'pear-,shaped** *adj* having an oval shape tapering at one end

**peasant** /'pez(ə)nt/ *n* 1 a member of a class of usu poor people (e g small landowners or labourers) who farm the land 2 *derog* a usu uneducated person of low social status [ME *paissaunt*, fr MF *paisant*, fr OF, fr *païs* country, fr LL *pagensis* inhabitant of a district, fr L *pagus* country district (cf PAGAN)]

**peasantry** /'pezəntri/ *n* 1 *taking sing or pl vb* peasants as a class 2 the position, rank, or character of a peasant

**pease** /peez/ *also* pees/ *n, chiefly Br archaic* a pea

**peasecod, peascod** /'peezkod/ *n, archaic* a pea pod [ME *pesecod*, fr *pese* pea + *cod* bag, husk – more at CODPIECE]

**pease pudding** *n* a puree of boiled SPLIT PEAS served esp with ham, gammon, or bacon

**peashooter** /-,shoohtə/ *n* a toy blowpipe for shooting peas

**,pea-'souper** /'soohpə/ *also* **pea soup** *n* a heavy fog

**peat** /peet/ *n* (a piece of) partially carbonized vegetable tissue that has been formed by partial decomposition in water of various plants (e g sedge or mosses of the genus *Sphagnum*), that is often found in bogs in many parts of the world, and that is used esp as a fuel for domestic heating and as a soil conditioner [ME *pete*, fr ML *peta*, perh of Celt origin] – **peaty** *adj*

**peat moss** *n* SPHAGNUM (moss that decomposes to form part of peat)

**peat reek** *n* 1 the smoke of a peat fire 2 (the distinctive flavour of) whisky distilled over peat reek

**peau de soie** /'poh də 'swah (*Fr* po də swa)/ *n* a silk or man-made fabric, esp rayon, with a smooth satiny texture and a fine ribbed or grained surface [Fr, lit., skin of silk]

**peavey, peavy** /'peevi/ *n, NAm* a stout lever like a CANT HOOK but with the end armed with a strong spike used esp in handling logs [prob fr the name *Peavey*]

**'pebble** /'pebl/ *n* 1 a small stone; *esp* one rounded and worn smooth by the action of water 2a a transparent and colourless quartz; ROCK CRYSTAL **b** a lens made of this 3 an irregular, crinkled, or grainy surface (e g of leather) [ME *pobble*, fr OE *papolstān*, fr *papol-* (prob imit) + *stān* stone] – **pebbly** *adj*

**²pebble** *vt* 1 to pave or cover with pebbles or something resembling pebbles 2 to grain (e g leather) so as to produce a rough and irregularly indented surface

**pebbledash** /-,dash/ *n* a finish for exterior walls consisting of small pebbles embedded in a plaster base

**pecan** /pi'kan, 'peekan/ *n* 1a a large hickory tree (*Carya illinoensis*) that has roughish bark and hard but brittle wood and is widely grown in the warmer parts of the USA and in Mexico for its nuts **b** the smooth oblong thin-shelled edible nut of the pecan 2 the wood of the pecan tree [of Algonquian origin; akin to Ojibwa *pagân*, a hard-shelled nut]

**peccable** /'pekəbl/ *adj, formal* prone to sin [MF, fr ML *peccabilis*, fr L *peccare*]

**peccadillo** /,pekə'diloh/ *n, pl* peccadilloes, peccadillos a slight or trifling offence [Sp *pecadillo*, dim. of *pecado* sin, fr L *peccatum*, fr neut of *peccatus*, pp of *peccare*]

**peccant** /'pekənt/ *adj, formal* 1 guilty of a moral offence; sinning 2 violating a principle or rule [L *peccant-, peccans*, prp of *peccare* to stumble, sin] – **peccancy** *n*, **peccantly** *adv*

**peccary** /'pekəri/ *n* either of two largely nocturnal American mammals resembling the related pigs: **a** a greyish-black animal (*Tayassu angulatus*) with an indistinct white collar of fur **b** a blackish animal (*Tayassu pecari*) with whitish cheeks [of Cariban origin; akin to Chaima *paquera* peccary]

**peccavi** /pe'kahvi/ *n, pl* peccavis an acknowledgment of sin [L, I have sinned, fr *peccare*]

**'peck** /pek/ *n* 1 a unit of dry capacity equal to 8 quarts (about 9.1 litres) 2 a large quantity or number – esp in *peck of troubles* [ME *pek*, fr OF]

**²peck** *vt* 1a to strike or pierce, esp repeatedly, with the beak or a pointed tool **b** to make by pecking ⟨~ *a hole*⟩ **c** to kiss perfunctorily 2 to pick up with the beak ~ *vi* 1 to strike, pierce, or pick up something (as if) with the beak 2 to eat reluctantly and in small bites ⟨~ *at food*⟩ [ME *pecken*, prob alter. of *piken* to pierce – more at PICK]

**³peck** *n* 1 an impression or hole made by pecking 2 a quick sharp stroke 3 a quick perfunctory kiss

**⁴peck** *vi, of a horse* to stumble (e g on landing from a jump) [alter. of ³*pick* (to pitch, hurl)]

**pecker** /'pekə/ *n* 1 one who or that which pecks; *esp* a woodpecker 2 *chiefly Br* courage – in *keep one's pecker up* 3 *NAm vulg* the penis

**pecking order** /'peking/, **peck order** *n* 1 the natural hierarchy within a flock of birds, esp poultry, in which each bird pecks another lower in the scale without fear of retaliation 2 a social hierarchy

**peckish** /'pekish/ *adj, chiefly Br informal* slightly or agreeably hungry [²*peck* + -*ish*]

**pecksniffian** /pek'snifiən/ *adj* selfish and corrupt behind a display of seeming benevolence; sanctimonious [Seth *Pecksniff*, character in *Martin Chuzzlewit* by Charles Dickens †1870 E novelist]

**Pecorino** /,pekə'reenoh/ *n* a hard pungent Italian cheese made from sheep's milk [It, fr *pecorino* of ewes, fr *pecora* ewe, sheep, fr L *pecora* cattle, pl of *pecor-, pecus* – more at FEE]

**pectate** /'pektayt/ *n* any of various chemical compounds (SALTS or ESTERS) formed by combination between PECTIC ACID and a metal atom, an alcohol, or another chemical group

**pecten** /'pekt(ə)n/ *n, pl* (1) pectines /'pekti,neez/, **pectens,** (2) **pectens** 1 a body part that resembles a comb; *esp* a folded membrane richly supplied with blood vessels that projects inwards from the retina into the chamber of the eyeball of a bird or reptile 2 ¹SCALLOP 1a (shellfish) [NL *pectin-, pecten*, fr L, comb, scallop]

**pectic acid** /'pektik/ *n* any of various water-insoluble PECTIC SUBSTANCES derived from pectins by partial breakdown and containing a large proportion of acid groups

**pectic compound** *n* PECTIC SUBSTANCE

**pectic substance** *n* any of a group of acid POLYSACCHARIDES (carbohydrates composed of many sugar units), including the PECTIC ACIDS and pectins, that contain GALACTURONIC ACID or its derivatives and occur as components of cell walls in plant tissue, esp as the substance binding adjacent cell walls

**pectin** /'pektin/ *n* any of various water-soluble PECTIC SUBSTANCES that are found in some ripe fruits and succulent vegetables and yield a gel which acts as a setting agent in jams; *also* a commercial product rich in pectins [Fr *pectine*, fr *pectique* pectic, fr Gk *pēktikos* coagulating, fr *pēgnynai* to fix, coagulate – more at PACT] – **pectic** *adj*, **pectinaceous** *adj*

**pectinate** /'pektinayt/, **pectinated** /-aytid/ *adj* having narrow parallel projections or divisions like the teeth of a comb ⟨~ *antennae*⟩ [L *pectinatus*, fr *pectin-, pecten* comb; akin to Gk *kten-, kteis* comb, L *pectere* to comb – more at FEE] – **pectination** *n*

**pectinesterase** /,pekti'nestərayz, -ays/ *n* an ENZYME that speeds up the reaction of pectins with water to form PECTIC ACIDS and METHANOL

**pect·ize, -ise** /'pektiez/ *vb* to (cause to) become a jelly

**'pectoral** /'pektərəl/ *n* something worn on the chest

**²pectoral** *adj* of, situated in or on, or worn on the chest [MF or L; MF, fr L *pectoralis*, fr *pector-, pectus* breast]

**pectoral arch** *n* PECTORAL GIRDLE

**pectoral cross** *n* a cross worn on the breast, esp by a high-ranking clergyman

**pectoral fin** *n* either of the fins of a fish, situated one on each side of the body just behind the head, that correspond to the forelimbs of a 4-legged animal

**pectoral girdle** *n* the bone or cartilage arch that supports the front or upper limbs or corresponding fins of a VERTEBRATE animal

**pectoral muscle** *n* any of the muscles that connect the front walls of the chest with the bones of the upper arm and shoulder and of which there are two on each side in human beings

**peculate** /'pekyoolayt/ *vt, formal* to embezzle [L *peculatus*, pp of *peculari*, fr *peculium*] – **peculator** *n*, **peculation** *n*

**'peculiar** /pi'kyoohli·ə, -lyə/ *adj* 1 belonging exclusively to one person or group 2 characteristic of one person or thing only; distinctive 3 different from the usual or normal: 3a special, particular **b** strange, curious **c** eccentric, queer *synonyms* see ¹CHARACTERISTIC, STRANGE [ME *peculier*, fr L *peculiaris* of private property, special, fr *peculium* private property, fr *pecu* cattle; akin to L *pecus* cattle – more at FEE] – **peculiarly** *adv*

**²peculiar** *n* something exempt from ordinary jurisdiction; *esp* a church or parish exempt from the jurisdiction of the diocese in which it is situated

**peculiarity** /pi,kyoohli'arəti/ *n* **1** being peculiar **2** a distinguishing characteristic **3** an oddity, quirk

**pecuniary** /pi'kyoohnyəri/ *adj, formal* **1** consisting of or measured in money **2** of money; monetary [L *pecuniarius*, fr *pecunia* money – more at FEE] – **pecuniarily** *adv*

**ped** /ped/ *n* a natural mass or cluster (e g a granule or crumb) of individual soil particles; a natural soil AGGREGATE [Gk *pedon* ground, earth; akin to L *ped-, pes* foot – more at FOOT]

**ped-, pedo-** *comb form, chiefly NAm* PAED-, PAEDO-

**-ped** /-ped; *also* -pəd/, **-pede** /-peed/ *comb form* (→ *n*) foot ⟨*quadru*ped⟩ ⟨*centi*pede⟩ [L *ped-, pes*]

**pedagogics** /,pedə'gojiks, -'goh-/ *n taking sing vb* pedagogy – **pedagogic, pedagogical** *adj*, **pedagogically** *adv*

**pedagogue** /'pedəgog/ *n* a teacher, schoolmaster – now chiefly derog [ME *pedagoge*, fr MF, fr L *paedagogus*, fr Gk *paidagōgos* slave who escorted children to school, fr *paid-* paed- + *agōgos* leading, fr *agein* to lead – more at AGENT]

**pedagogy** /'pedəgoji, -goji, -goh-/ *n* the art, science, or profession of teaching

**¹pedal** /'pedl/ *n* **1a** a lever pressed by the foot in playing a musical instrument (e g an organ or piano) **b** pedal point, pedal a single note, usu the TONIC or DOMINANT, that is normally sustained in the bass and sounds against changing harmonies in the other parts **2** a lever or other device pressed by the foot to power or activate a machine [MF *pedale*, fr It, fr L *pedalis*, adj]

**²pedal** /'pedl; *sense 1* 'peedl/ *adj* **1** of the foot **2** of or involving a pedal ⟨~ *cycle*⟩ [L *pedalis*, fr *ped-, pes*]

**³pedal** /'pedl/ *vb* **-ll-** (*NAm* **-l-** *also* **-ll-**) *vi* **1** to use or work a pedal **2** to ride a bicycle ~ *vt* to work the pedals of △ peddle

**pedal disc** /'peedl/ *n* the base by which a SEA ANEMONE or similar related animal (POLYP) is attached to the surface on which it lives

**'pedal-,note** *n* **1** PEDAL 1b **2** any of the lowest notes that can be sounded on a brass instrument, being eight notes below the normal usable range [fr the playing of the lowest notes on the organ by means of pedals]

**pedalo** /'pedəloh/ *n, pl* **pedalos, pedaloes** a small pleasure boat that is propelled by paddles turned by pedals

**pedal pushers** *n pl* women's and girls' calf-length trousers

**pedant** /'ped(ə)nt/ *n* **1a** one who parades his/her learning **b** one who is unimaginative or who unduly emphasizes minute details, esp in the presentation or use of knowledge **c** one who strictly adheres to formal rules in teaching **2** *obs* a schoolmaster [MF, fr It *pedante*, perh deriv of L *paedagogus* pedagogue] – **pedantry** *n*, **pedantic** *adj*, **pedantically** *adv*

**peddle** /'pedl/ *vi* to travel about with small goods for sale ~ *vt* **1** to sell or offer for sale from place to place; hawk **2** to deal out or seek to spread (e g ideas or opinions) ⟨*peddling half-digested doctrines to mass audiences*⟩ △ pedal [back-formation fr *peddler*]

**peddler** /'pedlə/ *n* **1** one who peddles drugs; a pusher **2** *NAm* a pedlar

**peddlery** /'pedləri/ *n, archaic* PEDLARY

**-pede** /-peed/ – see -PED

**pederast, paederast** /'pedə,rast, 'pee-/ *n* one who practises anal intercourse with a boy [Gk *paiderastēs*, lit., lover of boys, fr *paid-* paed-+ *erastēs* lover, fr *erasthai* to love – more at EROS] – **pederasty** *n*, **pederastic** *adj*

**pedes** /'peedeez, 'ped-/ *pl of* PES

**¹pedestal** /'pedistl/ *n* **1a** a base supporting a late classic or neoclassic column **b** the base of an upright structure (e g a statue) **2** a base, foundation **3** a position of esteem or idealized respect ⟨*put him on a* ~ *and refused to recognize his faults*⟩ [MF *piedestal*, fr OIt *piedestallo*, fr *pie di stallo* foot of a stall]

**²pedestal** *vt* **-ll-** (*NAm* **-l-, -ll-**) to place on or provide with a pedestal ⟨*desired not to be . . .* ~led, *but to sink into the crowd* – John Buchan⟩

**¹pedestrian** /pi'destri·ən/ *adj* **1** commonplace, unimaginative **2a** going or performed on foot ⟨*a dog will scurry before and behind his* ~ *master* – George Santayana⟩ **b** of or designed for walking ⟨*a* ~ *precinct*⟩ [L *pedestr-, pedester* going on foot, prosaic, fr *pedes* one going on foot, fr *ped-, pes* foot – more at FOOT]

**²pedestrian** *n* a person going on foot; a walker

**pedestrian crossing** *n, Br* a usu marked stretch of road on which pedestrians crossing the road have priority over the traffic in certain circumstances

**pedestrianism** /pi'destriəniz(ə)m/ *n* **1** the practice of walking as exercise or recreation **2** the quality or state of being unimaginative or commonplace

**pedestrian·ize, -ise** /pi'destri·ə,niez/ *vt* to convert (an existing highway for vehicles) to a usu paved area for pedestrians only – **pedestrianization** *n*

**pedicab** /'pedi,kab/ *n* TRISHAW (Oriental covered tricycle); *also* a similar but motorized vehicle [*ped*al + *-i-* + *cab*]

**pedicel** /'pedisel/ *n* **1** a slender supporting attachment of (part of) an organism: e g **1a** a plant stalk that supports a fruiting or spore-bearing organ **b** a narrow attachment of an animal organ or part (e g the narrow stalk joining a spider's abdomen to the rest of its body) **2** a small foot or footlike organ [NL *pedicellus*, dim. of L *pediculus*] – **pedicellate** *adj*

**pedicellaria** /,pedisə'leəriə/ *n, pl* **pedicellariae** /-ri·ie, -ri·ee/ any of various minute pincerlike organs that are borne on the surface of starfishes, sea urchins, etc and keep the surface free from debris and parasites [NL, fr *pedicellus*]

**pedicle** /'pedikl/ *n* a small stalk or stalklike support or attachment; a pedicel [L *pediculus*, fr dim. of *ped-, pes*] – **pedicled** *adj*

**pediculate** /pe'dikyoolət/ *adj* of or belonging to an order (Pediculati) of marine fishes (e g the ANGLER FISH) that have PECTORAL FINS (fins just behind the head) with an elongated base resembling an arm and the front part of the fin on the back (DORSAL fin) modified into a lure to attract prey [deriv of L *pediculus* footstalk] – **pediculate** *n*

**pediculosis** /pi,dikyoo'lohsis/ *n* infestation with lice [NL, fr L *pediculus* louse] – **pediculous, pedicular** *adj*

**pedicure** /'pedikyooə/ *n* **1** *also* **pedicurist** one who practises chiropody **2** (a) treatment for the care of the feet, toes, and toenails [Fr *pédicure*, fr L *ped-, pes* foot + *curare* to take care, fr *cura* care – more at CURE]

**¹pedigree** /'pedigree/ *n* **1** a register recording a line of ancestors **2a** an ancestral line; a lineage **b** the origin and history of something **3a** a distinguished ancestry **b** the recorded purity of breed of an individual or strain [ME *pedegru*, fr MF *pie de grue* crane's foot; fr the shape made by the lines of a genealogical chart] – **pedigreed** *adj*

**²pedigree** *adj* of, being, or producing animals that have recorded purity of breed

**pediment** /'pedimənt/ *n* **1** the triangular piece of wall in the angle formed by the two slopes of a roof in classical architecture; *also* a similar form used as a decoration above doors and windows **2** a broad gently sloping surface of bedrock that is situated at the base of a steeper slope, is often thinly covered with deposited gravel and sand, and occurs in arid regions as a result of the erosion of overlying rock layers [alter. of obs *periment*, prob alter. of *pyramid*; (2) influenced by L *ped-, pes* foot] – **pedimental** *adj*

**pedipalp** /'pedipalp/ *n* either of the second pair of appendages of an ARACHNID (e g a spider) that are borne near the mouth and are often modified for a special (e g sensory) function [NL *pedipalpus*, fr *ped-, pes* foot + *palpus*]

**pedlar, chiefly *NAm* peddler** /'pedlə/ *n* one who travels about offering merchandise for sale (e g along the street or from door to door) [ME *pedlere*, prob alter. of *pedder*, fr *ped* wicker basket]

**pedlary, peddlery** /'pedləri/ *n, archaic* the wares or trade of a pedlar

**pedo-** – see PED-

**¹pedogenesis** /,pedə'jenəsis/ *n, chiefly NAm* PAEDOGENESIS (reproduction by young animals or larvae)

**²pedogenesis** *n* the formation and development of soil [NL, fr Gk *pedon* earth + L *genesis*] – **pedogenic, pedogenetic** *adj*

**¹pedology** /pi'dolǝji/ *n, chiefly NAm* PAEDOLOGY (study of children)

**²pedology** *n* SOIL SCIENCE [Gk *pedon* + ISV *-logy*] – **pedologist** *n*, **pedologic, pedological** *adj*

**pedometer** /pi'domitǝ/ *n* an instrument that records the distance a walker covers by counting the number of steps taken [Fr *pédomètre*, fr L *ped-, pes* foot + Fr *-mètre* -meter – more at FOOT]

**peduncle** /pi'dungkl/ *n* **1** a stalk bearing a flower, flower cluster, or fruit **2a** a narrow or stalklike part by which some larger part or the whole body of an organism is attached; a stalk **b** a band of nerve fibres joining different parts of the brain **3** a narrow stalk by which a tumour or POLYP (small growth) is attached [NL *pedunculus*, dim. of L *ped-, pes*] – **peduncled** *adj*, **peduncular** *adj*

**pedunculate** /pi'dungkyoolət, -ayt/, **pedunculated** /-aytid/ *adj* having, growing on, or being attached by a stalk ⟨*a* ~ *tumour*⟩ [NL *pedunculus*]

**¹pee** /pee/ *vi, euph* to urinate [*piss*]

**²pee** *n, euph* **1** an act of urinating **2** urine

**³pee** *n, pl* **pee** *Br informal* PENNY 1a(2) [*penny*]
**usage** Some people dislike this spoken version of the abbreviation p, and prefer to say **penny** or **pence**.

**¹peek** /peek/ *vi* **1a** to look furtively **b** to peer through a crack or hole or from a place of concealment – often + *in* or *out* **2** to take a brief look; glance [ME *piken*]

**²peek** *n* a peep, glance

**¹peekaboo** /'peekə,booh/ *n* a game for amusing young children in which one repeatedly hides one's face or body and comes back into view, typically exclaiming "Peekaboo!" [¹*peek* + ¹*boo*]

**²peekaboo** *adj, of clothing* **1** trimmed with, or made of material patterned with, small holes **2** made of a sheer or transparent fabric

**¹peel** /peel, piəl/ *vt* **1** to strip off an outer layer of ⟨~ *an orange*⟩ **2** to remove by stripping ⟨~ *the label off the can*⟩ ~ *vi* **1a** to come off in sheets or scales ⟨*old paint* ~ing *from the wall*⟩ **b** to lose an outer layer (e g of skin) ⟨*his face is* ~ing⟩ **2** to take off one's clothes – usu + *off*; see also **keep one's** EYES **peeled** [ME *pelen*, fr MF *peler*, fr L *pilare* to remove the hair from, fr *pilus* hair – more at PILE] – **peelable** *adj*, **peeler** *n*
**peel off** *vi* to break away from a group or formation ⟨*an aircraft peeling off to land*⟩

**²peel** *n* the skin or rind of a fruit

**³peel** *also* **pele** /peel/ *n* a small fortified tower built in the 16th century along the Scottish-English border for defence against raiders [ME *pel* stockade, stake, fr AF, stockade, & MF, stake, fr L *palus* stake – more at POLE]

**⁴peel** *n* a usu long-handled shovel that is used by bakers to carry bread, pies, etc into or out of the oven [ME *pele*, fr MF, fr L *pala*; akin to L *pangere* to fix]

**⁵peel** *vt* to send (another player's ball) through a hoop at croquet [W H *Peel fl* 1870 Br croquet player]

**peeler** /'peelə/ *n, Br archaic* a policeman [Sir Robert *Peel* † 1850 E statesman who founded the Irish constabulary (cf BOBBY)]

**peeling** /'peeling/ *n usu pl* a piece of skin, rind, etc that has been stripped off ⟨*potato* ~s⟩

**¹peen** /peen/ *vt* to flatten, shape, or bend (as if) by hammering with a peen – often + *over*

**²peen, pein** /peen/ *n* a usu hemispherical or wedge-shaped end of the head of a hammer that is opposite the flat face and is used esp for bending, shaping, or cutting the material struck – compare ¹POLL 3 [prob of Scand origin; akin to Norw *penn* peen]

**¹peep** /peep/ *vi* **1** to utter a feeble shrill sound as of a bird newly hatched; cheep **2** to utter the slightest sound ⟨*every time he* ~s, *she jumps to see what's the matter* – Benjamin Spock⟩ [ME *pepen*, of imit origin]

**²peep** *n* **1** a feeble shrill sound; a cheep **2** a slight utterance, esp of complaint or protest ⟨*don't let me hear another* ~ *out of you*⟩

**³peep** *vi* **1** to look cautiously or slyly, esp through a hole; peek **2** to begin to emerge (as if) from concealment; show slightly ~ *vt* to put forth or cause to protrude slightly – often + *out* [ME *pepen*, perh alter. of *piken* to peek]

**⁴peep** *n* **1** the first glimpse or faint appearance ⟨*at the* ~ *of dawn*⟩ **2** a brief or furtive look; a glance

**¹peeper** /'peepə/ *n* one who or that which makes a peeping sound

**²peeper** *n* **1** one who peeps; *specif* a voyeur **2** *usu pl, informal* an eye

**peephole** /-,hohl/ *n* a hole or crevice to peep through

**Peeping Tom** /,peeping 'tom/ *n, often not cap P* a man who secretly looks at people who think they are not being watched (e g women dressing or undressing or courting couples); a voyeur [*Peeping Tom*, legendary E tailor who looked at Lady Godiva riding naked through Coventry and was struck blind] – **Peeping Tomism** *n*

**peep show** *n* **1** an esp erotic entertainment (e g a film) or object (e g a small painting) viewed through a small hole that is usu fitted with a magnifying glass **2** a show featuring erotic entertainment (e g striptease)

**peep sight** *n* a rear sight for a gun having a usu adjustable metal piece pierced with a small hole to peep through in aiming

**peep-,toe, peep-toed** *adj, of a shoe* leaving one or more toes uncovered

**¹peer** /piə/ *n* **1** one who is of equal standing with another; an equal **2a** a member of any of the five ranks (duke, marquess, earl, viscount, or baron) of the British peerage **b** a nobleman **3** *archaic* a companion [ME, fr OF *per*, fr *per*, adj, equal, fr L *par*]

**²peer** *vt, archaic* to rival, match

**³peer** *adj* belonging to the same group in society, esp when membership is determined by age, grade, or status ⟨*a* ~ *group of adolescents*⟩

**⁴peer** *vi* **1** to look closely or curiously; *esp* to look searchingly at something difficult to discern **2** to come slightly into view; peep ⟨*clouds through which the sun* ~ed⟩ *synonyms* see ¹GAZE [perh by shortening & alter. fr *appear*]

**peerage** /'piərij/ *n* **1** *taking sing or pl vb* the body of peers **2** the rank or position of a peer **3** a book containing a list of peers with their family trees, history, and titles

**peeress** /'piəris/ *n* **1** the wife or widow of a peer **2** a woman having in her own right the rank of a peer

**peerless** /-lis/ *adj* matchless, incomparable – **peerlessly** *adv*, **peerlessness** *n*

**¹peeve** /peev/ *vt* to make peevish or resentful; annoy *synonyms* see IRRITATE [back-formation fr *peevish*]

**²peeve** *n* **1** a feeling or mood of resentment **2** a particular grievance; a grudge

**peevish** /'peevish/ *adj* **1** easily upset by and prone to complain about unimportant things; petulant **2** ill-tempered [ME *pevish* spiteful] – **peevishly** *adv*, **peevishness** *n*

**peewit** /'peewit/ *n* a lapwing [imit]

**¹peg** /peg/ *n* **1** a small usu cylindrical pointed or tapered piece of wood, metal, plastic, etc used to pin down or fasten things or to fit into or close holes; a pin **2a** a projecting piece used to hold or support ⟨*a row of* ~s *for hanging coats on*⟩ **b** PITON (metal pin used in mountaineering) **c** something (e g a fact or opinion) used as a support, pretext, or reason ⟨*the strike was simply a* ~ *for their prejudices*⟩ **3a** any of the wooden pins set in the head of a stringed instrument and turned to regulate the pitch of the strings **b** a step or degree, esp in estimation ⟨*our pride in our achievements comes down a* ~ – *TLS*⟩ **4** something (e g a leg) resembling a peg **5** a predetermined level at which something (e g a price) is fixed **6** *pl* peg trousers **7** *Br* a clothespeg **8** *Br* a drink; *esp* a drink of spirits ⟨*poured himself out a stiff* ~ – Dorothy Sayers⟩ **9** *NAm* a throw; *esp* one made in an attempt to get a baseball player out [ME *pegge*, prob fr MD; fr the pegs or pins fixed in a drinking vessel to measure the quantity allowed to each drinker] – **off the peg** mass-produced and ready to wear; not personally tailored ⟨*an off the peg suit*⟩

**²peg** *vt* **-gg-** **1a** to put a peg into **b** to pin down; restrict **c** to fix or hold (e g prices) at a predetermined level ⟨~ *the price of school meals*⟩ **2** to mark with pegs **3** *Br* to fasten (e g wet washed clothes) to a clothesline with a clothespeg – often + *out*
**peg away** *vi, chiefly Br* to work steadily and diligently – often + *at*
**peg out** *vi* **1** to finish a game of croquet by hitting the peg with a ball **2** *chiefly Br informal* to die [(2) prob fr the completion of a game of cribbage by marking the winning points on a pegboard]

**³peg, pegged** *adj* wide at the top and narrow at the bottom ⟨~ *pants*⟩

**pegboard** /-,bawd/ *n* **1** a small board perforated with a pattern of holes into which pegs are stuck in playing or scoring certain games (e g solitaire or cribbage) **2** material (e g fibreboard) pierced at regular intervals with holes into which hooks or pegs may be inserted for the storage or display of articles

**peg leg** *n* an artificial leg; *esp* one fitted at the knee

**pegmatite** /'pegmətiet/ *n* any of various coarse-grained IGNEOUS rocks formed by the solidification of molten material below the earth's surface and occurring usu as veins or vertical wall-like bodies (DYKES) within other rocks; *esp* a coarse-grained granite or granitelike rock composed of quartz and feldspar [Fr, fr Gk *pēgmat-*, *pēgma* something fastened together, fr *pēgnynai* to fasten together – more at PACT] – **pegmatitic** *adj*

**Pehlevi** /'paylovi/ *n* PAHLAVI (Iranian coin)

**peignoir** /'paynwah, ,-'-/ *n* a woman's loose negligee or dressing gown [Fr, lit., garment worn while combing the hair, fr MF *peigner* to comb the hair, fr L *pectinare*, fr *pectin-*, *pecten* comb – more at PECTINATE]

**pein** /peen/ *n* ²PEEN (round head of a hammer)

**pejorative** /pə'jorətiv; *also* 'peej(ə)rətiv/ *adj* depreciatory, dis-

paraging [LL *pejoratus*, pp of *pejorare* to make or become worse, fr L *pejor* worse; akin to L *pessimus* worst, Gk *pedon* ground] – **pejorative** *n*, **pejoratively** *adv*
   *usage* The pronunciation /pə'jorətiv/ is recommended for BBC broadcasters.

**peke** /peek/ *n, often cap, informal* PEKINGESE 2 △ Pom, pug

**Pekin** /pee'kin/ *n* (any of) a breed of large white domestic ducks of Chinese origin used for meat production [*Beijing* (*Peking*, *Pekin*), city in NE China]

**Pekingese, Pekinese** /ˌpeki'neez, ˌpee-/ *n, pl* **Pekingese, Pekinese 1a** a native or inhabitant of Peking **b** the Chinese dialect of Peking; MANDARIN **2** (any of) a Chinese breed of small short-legged dogs with a broad flat face and a long shaggy soft coat

**Peking man** /pee'king/ *n* an extinct early STONE AGE man known from skeletal and cultural remains in cave deposits at Zhoukoutian (Choukoutien) in China that is similar in many details to JAVA MAN

**pekoe** /'peekoh/ *n* a BLACK TEA of superior quality [Chin (Amoy) *pek-ho*]

**pelage** /'pelij/ *n* the outer covering (eg hair, fur, or wool) of a mammal [Fr, fr MF, fr *poil* hair, fr L *pilus* – more at PILE]

**Pelagian** /pe'layji·ən/ *n or adj* (a person) agreeing with Pelagius in denying original sin and consequently in holding that human beings' salvation depends on their own efforts rather than divine grace [*Pelagius* †*ab* 420 Br theologian] – **Pelagianism** *n*

**pelagic** /pe'lajik/ *adj* of, living, or occurring (at moderate depths) in the open sea; oceanic – compare DEMERSAL [L *pelagicus*, fr Gk *pelagikos*, fr *pelagos* sea – more at FLAKE]

**pelargonium** /ˌpelə'gohnyəm, -ni-əm/ *n* any of a genus (*Pelargonium*) of southern African plants of the geranium family having roughly heart-shaped leaves and showy flowers of various shades of red, pink, or white, and including many cultivated as garden plants and houseplants [NL, genus name, irreg fr Gk *pelargos* stork; fr its seed capsules resembling a stork's bill]

**Pelasgian** /pe'lazji·ən, -gi-ən/ *n* a member of an ancient people mentioned by classical writers as early inhabitants of Greece and the eastern islands of the Mediterranean [Gk *pelasgios*, adj, Pelasgian, fr *Pelasgoi* Pelasgians] – **Pelasgian, Pelasgic** *adj*

**pele** /peel/ *n* [3]PEEL (fortified tower)

**pelecypod** /pi'lesipod/ *n* LAMELLIBRANCH (clam, oyster, mussel, or related shellfish) [NL *Pelecypoda*, group name, fr Gk *pelekys* axe + *pod-, pous* foot – more at FOOT]

**pelerine** /'pelǝreen/ *n* a woman's short cape, usu with long ends hanging down in front [Fr, neckerchief, fr *pèlerine*, fem of *pèlerin* pilgrim, fr LL *pelegrinus* – more at PILGRIM]

**pelf** /pelf/ *n, chiefly derog* money, riches [ME, fr MF *pelfre* booty (cf PILFER)]

**pelham** /'pelǝm/ *n* a bit for a horse having a bar mouthpiece and used with a restraining chain (CURB) and two sets of reins [prob fr the name *Pelham*]

**pelican** /'pelikǝn/ *n* any of a genus (*Pelecanus*) of large web-footed birds with a very large bill and a pouch beneath the bill that can be distended for catching and keeping fish [ME, fr OE *pellican*, fr LL *pelecanus*, fr Gk *pelekan*, prob fr *pelekys* axe; fr its long hooked bill]

**pelican crossing** *n* a British pedestrian crossing where the traffic can be stopped by pedestrian-operated lights [irreg fr *pedestrian light controlled crossing*]

**pelisse** /pe'lees/ *n* **1** a long cloak or coat made of fur or lined or trimmed with fur; *esp* one that is part of a hussar's uniform **2** a woman's loose cloak with wide collar and fur trimming [Fr, fr LL *pellicia*, fr fem of *pellicius* made of skin, fr L *pellis* skin – more at FELL]

**pellagra** /pǝ'laygrǝ, -'la-/ *n* a disease associated with a deficiency of NICOTINIC ACID (type of B vitamin) in the diet and marked by inflammation and flaking of the skin, loss of appetite, diarrhoea, and disorders of the CENTRAL NERVOUS SYSTEM △ podagra [It, fr *pelle* skin (fr L *pellis*) + *-agra* (as in *podagra* gout)] – **pellagrous** *adj*

[1]**pellet** /'pelit/ *n* **1** a usu small rounded or spherical body of usu compressed matter (eg food or medicine) **2a** a usu stone ball used as a missile in medieval times **b** a bullet **c** a piece of small shot **d** an imitation bullet (eg of cork, paper, or plastic) for use in a toy gun [ME *pelote*, fr MF, fr (assumed) VL *pilota*, dim. of L *pila* ball – more at PILE] – **pelletal** *adj*

[2]**pellet** *vt* **1** to pelletize **2** to strike with pellets

**pellet·ize, -ise** /'pelitiez/ *vt* to form or compact into pellets ⟨~ *ore*⟩ – **pelletizer** *n*, **pelletization** *n*

**pellicle** /'pelikl/ *n* a thin skin, film, or membrane: eg **a** the outer layer of some PROTOZOA (minute single-celled organisms) **b** a growth (eg of bacteria) on the surface of a liquid culture [MF *pellicule*, fr ML *pellicula*, fr L, dim. of *pellis*] – **pellicular** *adj*

[1]**pellitory** /'pelit(ǝ)ri/, **pellitory-of-Spain** *n* a southern European plant (*Anacyclus pyrethrum*) of the daisy family, whose root was formerly used for various medicinal purposes [ME *peletre*, fr MF *piretre*, fr L *pyrethrum*]

[2]**pellitory, pellitory-of-the-wall** *n* any of a genus (*Parietaria*) of plants of the nettle family with inconspicuous flowers; *specif* a European plant (*Parietaria diffusa*) that grows in cracks in walls and rocks [ME *paritorie*, fr MF *paritaire*, fr LL *parietaria*, fr fem of *parietarius* of a wall, fr L *pariet-, paries* wall]

**pell-mell** /ˌpel 'mel/ *adv* **1** in mingled confusion or disorder **2** in confused haste [MF *pelemele*, fr OF *pesle mesle*, redupl of *mesler* to mix, mingle] – **pell-mell** *adj* or *n*

**pellucid** /pi'l(y)oohsid/ *adj, formal or poetic* **1** allowing light to pass through; transparent or translucent **2** easy to understand [L *pellucidus*, fr *per* through + *lucidus* lucid] – **pellucidly** *adv*, **pellucidness, pellucidity** *n*

**Pelmanism** /'pelmǝniz(ǝ)m/ *n* **1** a system of memory training **2** *often not cap* a card game in which players try to turn up pairs of playing cards spread at random face down on a table by remembering the failed attempts of previous turns [*Pelman* Institute, institute founded in London in 1898 for training the mind]

**pelmet** /'pelmit/ *n, chiefly Br* a decorative length of board or fabric placed above a window to conceal curtain fixtures [prob modif of Fr *palmette* palm-shaped ornament, fr *palme* palm, fr L *palma*]

**peloria** /pi'lawriǝ/ *n* an abnormal regularity of structure occurring in normally irregular flowers [NL, fr Gk *pelōros* monstrous, fr *pelōr* monster; akin to Gk *teras* marvel – more at TERATOLOGY] – **peloric** *adj*

**pelorus** /pi'lawrǝs/ *n* a navigational instrument having two sights mounted on a rotatable ring by which bearings are taken [prob fr *Pelorus*, reputed name of Hannibal's pilot]

**pelota** /pǝ'lotǝ/ *n* **1** any of various Spanish, Basque, or Latin-American ball games played usu with a wickerwork basket strapped to the wrist; *specif* JAI ALAI **2** the ball used in pelota [Sp, fr OF *pelote* little ball – more at PELLET]

[1]**pelt** /pelt/ *n* **1** a skin of an animal with its hair, wool, or fur **2** a skin stripped of hair or wool for tanning [ME, prob back-formation fr *peltry*]

[2]**pelt** *vt* to strip off the skin or pelt of (an animal)

[3]**pelt** *vt* **1** to strike with a succession of blows or missiles ⟨~ ed him with stones⟩ **2** to hurl, throw ⟨hand me anything hard . . . to ~ at her⟩ – Charles Dickens⟩ **3** to beat or dash repeatedly against ⟨hailstones ~ ing the roof⟩ ~ vi **1** of rain, hail, etc to beat incessantly ⟨it's ~ ing with rain⟩ – often + down **2** to move rapidly and vigorously; hurry ⟨the children ~ ed down the road⟩ [ME *pelten*] – **pelter** *n*

[4]**pelt** *n* speed, force – chiefly in (at) full pelt

**peltast** /'peltast/ *n* a foot soldier of ancient Greece [Gk *peltastēs*, fr *peltē* small light shield]

**peltate** /'peltayt/ *adj* shaped like a shield; *specif, of a leaf* having the stem or stalk attached to the under surface instead of at the base or edge [deriv of L *pelta* small shield, fr Gk *peltē*] – **peltately** *adv*

**peltier effect** /'peltiay (Fr pɛltje)/ *n* the phenomenon of the production of heat at one junction and the absorption of heat at the other junction when an electric current is passed round a circuit consisting of two different metals [Jean *Peltier* †1845 Fr physicist]

**peltry** /'peltri/ *n* pelts, furs; *esp* raw unprepared skins [ME, fr AF *pelterie*, fr OF *peleterie*, fr *peletier* furrier, deriv of L *pellis* skin]

**pelvic** /'pelvik/ *adj* of or located in or near the pelvis

**pelvic arch** *n* PELVIC GIRDLE

**pelvic fin** *n* either of the fins of a fish, situated one on each side of the lower surface of the body, that correspond to the hind limbs of a 4-legged animal

**pelvic girdle** *n* the bone or cartilage arch that supports the hind or lower limbs or corresponding fins of a VERTEBRATE animal

**pelvis** /'pelvis/ *n, pl* **pelvises, pelves** /'pelveez/ **1** a basin-shaped structure in the skeleton of many VERTEBRATE animals that is formed by the PELVIC GIRDLE and adjoining bones of the spine 2 the cavity of the pelvis 3 the funnel-shaped cavity of the kidney into which urine is discharged [NL, fr L, basin; akin to OE & ON *full* cup, Gk *pella* wooden bowl]

**pelycosaur** /'pelikəsaw/ *n* any of an order (Pelycosauria) of primitive extinct reptiles of the Carboniferous and Permian geological periods that resembled mammals and often had a sail-like structure on the back [deriv of Gk *pelyc-, pelyx* wooden bowl + *sauros* lizard]

**Pembroke table** /'pembrohk, -brook/ *n* a small 4-legged table with sides that fold down and usu one or two drawers [prob fr *Pembroke,* town in S Wales]

**pemmican** *also* **pemican** /'pemikən/ *n* a concentrated food traditionally made by N American Indians and consisting of lean meat dried, pounded fine, and mixed with melted fat; *also* a similar preparation, usu of beef and dried fruits, used for emergency rations [Cree *pimikân*]

**pemoline** /'peməleen/ *n* a synthetic drug, $C_9H_8N_2O_2$, that is a mild stimulant of the CENTRAL NERVOUS SYSTEM, and has been used in the treatment of fatigue and depression, and experimentally to improve memory [origin unknown]

**pemphigus** /'pemfigəs, pem'fiegəs/ *n* a disease characterized by large blisters on the skin and MUCOUS MEMBRANES lining the mouth, intestines, genitals, etc [NL, fr Gk *pemphig-, pemphix* breath, pustule]

**¹pen** /pen/ *n* **1a** a small enclosure for animals **b** *taking sing or pl vb* the animals in a pen ⟨*a ~ of sheep*⟩ **2** a small place of confinement or storage **3** a dock for a submarine; *esp* a heavily fortified one [ME, fr OE *penn*]

**²pen** *vt* **-nn-** to shut in a pen

**³pen** *n* **1** an implement for writing or drawing with ink: eg **1a** a quill **b** a nib **c** a penholder fitted with a nib **d** FOUNTAIN PEN **e** a ball-point **2a** a writing instrument as a means of expression ⟨*the ~ is mightier than the sword* – Edward Bulwer-Lytton⟩ ⟨*enlisted the ~s of the best writers* – F H Chase⟩ **b** *formal* a writer **3** the horny feather-shaped internal shell of a squid [ME *penne,* fr MF, feather, pen, fr L *penna, pinna* feather; akin to Gk *pteron* wing – more at FEATHER]

**⁴pen** *vt* **-nn-** *formal* to write, compose ⟨*~ a letter*⟩

**⁵pen** *n* a female swan [origin unknown]

**⁶pen** *n, NAm slang* a prison [short for *penitentiary*]

**penal** /'peenl/ *adj* **1** of or involving punishment, penalties, or prisons ⟨*~ servitude*⟩ ⟨*~ taxation*⟩ **2** liable to punishment ⟨*a ~ offence*⟩ **3** used as a place of confinement and punishment ⟨*a ~ colony*⟩ [ME, fr MF, fr L *poenalis,* fr *poena* punishment –more at PAIN] – **penally** *adv*

**penal code** *n* a code of laws concerning crimes and their punishment

**penal·ize, -ise** /'peenl·iez/ *vt* **1** to inflict or impose a penalty on **2** to put at a serious disadvantage *synonyms* see PUNISH – **penalization** *n*

**penal servitude** *n* a former sentence of imprisonment with hard labour

**penalty** /'pen(ə)lti/ *n* **1** a punishment imposed for, or incurred by, committing a crime or public offence **2** a loss or forfeiture to which a person agrees to be subject if specified conditions or stipulations are not fulfilled **3a** disadvantage, loss, or suffering due to some action ⟨*paid the ~ for his heavy drinking*⟩ **b** a disadvantage (eg loss of possession of the ball or an addition to or subtraction from the score) imposed on a team or competitor for violation of the rules of a sport or game **4** *pl* points scored in bridge by the side that defeats the opposing contract **5** (a goal scored with) a PENALTY KICK [ML *poenalitas,* fr L *poenalis*] – **penalty** *adj*

**penalty area** *n* a rectangular area 44 yards (about 40 metres) wide and 18 yards (about 16 metres) deep in front of both goals on a soccer pitch

**penalty box** *n* **1** an area alongside an ice-hockey rink to which penalized players are confined for the duration of their penalty **2** *informal* PENALTY AREA

**penalty corner** *n* a free hit in hockey that is taken from a point on the GOAL LINE 10 yards (about 9 metres) from the goal

**penalty double** *n* a call that increases the value of tricks won and lost in a bridge game, made by DEFENDERS who expect to score penalties by preventing the DECLARERS from making good their bid to win at least a specified number of tricks

**penalty goal** *n* a goal scored from a PENALTY KICK in rugby

**penalty kick** *n* **1** a FREE KICK in rugby **2** a FREE KICK at the goal in soccer that is awarded for any of several offences committed in the PENALTY AREA and that is taken from a point 12 yards (about 11 metres) in front of the goal defended only by the goalkeeper – compare DIRECT FREE KICK, INDIRECT FREE KICK

**penalty shot** *n* a shot at the goal awarded to a team for certain violations by an opponent in any of several games (eg ice hockey)

**¹penance** /'penəns/ *n* **1** an act of self-punishment or religious devotion (eg the saying of prayers) performed to show sorrow or repentance for sin **2** a sacramental rite that is practised in Roman, Orthodox, and some Anglican churches and that consists of private confession, absolution, and a penance directed by the confessor [ME, fr OF, fr ML *poenitentia* penitence, alter. of L *paenitentia* regret, fr *paenitent-, paenitens,* prp of *paenitēre* to be sorry]

**²penance** *vt* to impose penance on

**penannular** /pen'anyoolə/ *adj* having the form of a ring with a small break in the circumference [L *pene, paene* almost + E *annular*]

**Penates** /pə'nahteez, -'nay-/ *n pl* the ancient Roman gods of the household – compare LARES AND PENATES [L – more at PENETRATE]

**pence** /pens, pəns/ *pl of* PENNY

**penchant** /'penchənt, 'pon(h)shonh (*Fr* pãʃã)/ *n* a strong leaning; a liking [Fr, fr prp of *pencher* to incline, fr (assumed) VL *pendicare,* fr L *pendere* to weigh]

**¹pencil** /'pensl/ *n* **1a** an implement for writing, drawing, or marking consisting of or containing a slender cylinder or strip of a solid marking substance (eg graphite) **b** a small roll or stick of a medicated or cosmetic substance **2a** a set of light rays, esp when diverging from or converging to a point **b** a set of straight lines or curves passing through a single point **3** something long and thin like a pencil [ME *pensel* paintbrush, fr MF *pincel,* fr (assumed) VL *penicellus,* fr L *penicillus,* lit., little tail, fr dim. of *penis* tail, penis]

**²pencil** *vt* **-ll-** (*NAm* **-l-, -ll-**) to draw, write, or mark with a pencil – **penciller** *n*

**pencil in** *vt* to include provisionally

**pencilling,** *NAm chiefly* **penciling** /'pensl·ing/ *n* the work of the pencil or brush; *also* a product of this

**pendant** *also* **pendent** /'pend(ə)nt/ *n* **1** something suspended: eg **1a** a piece of jewellery allowed to hang free (eg from a chain round the neck) **b** an electric light fitting suspended from the ceiling **2** a hanging ornament of vaults or ceilings much used in late Gothic architecture **3** the bar or ring of metal on a pocket watch to which the chain is attached **4** a COMPANION PIECE or supplement **5** *chiefly Br* PENNANT 1a (nautical flag) [ME *pendaunt,* fr MF *pendant,* fr prp of *pendre* to hang, fr (assumed) VL *pendere,* fr L *pendēre;* akin to L *pendere* to weigh, estimate, pay, *pondus* weight – more at SPAN]

**pendent, pendant** /'pend(ə)nt/ *adj* **1** supported from above; suspended ⟨*icicles ~ from the eaves*⟩ **2** jutting or leaning over; overhanging ⟨*a ~ cliff*⟩ **3** remaining undetermined; pending [ME *pendaunt*] – **pendency** *n,* **pendently** *adv*

**pendentive** /pen'dentiv/ *n* a triangular concave corner member that supports a circular dome over a square or polygonal space [Fr *pendentif,* fr L *pendent-, pendens,* prp of *pendēre*]

**¹pending** /'pending/ *prep, formal* while awaiting; until [Fr *pendant,* fr prp of *pendre*]

**²pending** *adj* **1** not yet decided or dealt with **2** imminent, impending

**pendragon** /pen'dragən/ *n* the chief leader among the ancient British chiefs [ME, fr W, fr *pen* chief + *dragon* dragon, leader's flag depicting a dragon, leader]

**pendulous** /'pendyoolə/ *adj* **1** suspended so as to swing freely ⟨*branches hung with ~ vines*⟩ **2** inclined or hanging downwards ⟨*~ jowls*⟩ [L *pendulus,* fr *pendere* to weigh] – **pendulously** *adv,* **pendulousness** *n*

**pendulum** /'pendyooləm/ *n* a body suspended from a fixed point so as to swing freely to and fro under the action of gravity and commonly used to regulate movements (eg of clocks) [NL, fr L, neut of *pendulus*] – **pendulor** *adj*

**peneplain** *also* **peneplane** /'peeniplayn, ,-'-/ *n* a large almost flat land surface shaped by erosion [L *paene, pene* almost + E *plain* or *plane* – more at PATIENT]

**penetralia** /,peni'trayli·ə, -lyə/ *n pl* the innermost or most private and hidden parts of a place or thing [L, neut pl of *penetralis* inner, fr *penetrare* to penetrate]

**penetrance** /'penitrəns/ *n* the proportion of individuals possessing a particular gene that show the characteristic associated with that gene; a measure of the frequency with which a gene shows its effect

**penetrate** /'penitrayt/ *vt* **1a** to pass into or through **b** to enter by overcoming resistance; pierce **c** to insert the penis into the vagina of **2a** to see into or through **b** to discover the inner contents or meaning of **3** to diffuse through or into ~ *vi* **1** to pass, extend, pierce, or diffuse into or through something **2** to be absorbed by the mind; be understood ⟨*I heard what he said, but it didn't* ~⟩ [L *penetratus*, pp of *penetrare*; akin to L *penitus* inwards, *Penates* household gods, Lith *peneti* to nourish] – **penetrability** *n*, **penetrable** *adj*, **penetrably** *adv*, **penetrative** *adj*, **penetrativeness** *n*, **penetrator** *n*

**penetrating** /'penitrayting/ *adj* **1** having the power of entering, piercing, or pervading ⟨*a* ~ *shriek*⟩ **2** acute, discerning ⟨~ *insights into life*⟩ – **penetratingly** *adv*

**penetration** /ˌpeni'traysh(ə)n/ *n* **1** the act or process of penetrating: e g **1a** the act of entering a country so that actual establishment of influence is accomplished **b** an attack that penetrates the enemy's territory **2a** the depth to which something penetrates **b** the power to penetrate; *esp* the ability to discern deeply and acutely **3** the process of successfully introducing or increasing sales of a product in an existing market, usu through more intensive marketing effort *synonyms* see DISCERNMENT

**penetrometer** /ˌpeni'tromitə/ *n* an instrument for measuring firmness or consistency (e g of soil) [L *penetrare* + ISV *-meter*]

**'pen-,friend** *n* a person, esp one in another country, with whom a friendship is made through correspondence

**pengö** /'peng·guh/ *n*, *pl* **pengö, pengös** the basic monetary unit of Hungary from 1925 to 1946 [Hung *pengö*, lit., jingling]

**penguin** /'peng·gwin/ *n* any of various erect short-legged flightless aquatic birds (family Spheniscidae) of chiefly cold regions of the southern hemisphere, that have dark backs and white or pale bellies, wings resembling flippers, and webbed feet [perh fr W *pen gwyn* white head]

**penholder** /-ˌhohldə/ *n* **1** a holder or handle for a pen nib **2** a method of gripping a table-tennis bat in which the handle is held like a pen with the blade downwards and in which all shots are made with the same side of the bat

**penicillamine** /ˌpeni'siləmeen/ *n* a chemical compound, $(CH_3)_2C(SH)CH(NH_2)COOH$, derived from penicillins that has the capacity to combine with metal ions, esp copper, to render them inactive and is used esp in the treatment of RHEUMATOID ARTHRITIS, WILSON'S DISEASE (disease resulting from the accumulation of copper in the body), and poisoning by metals (e g copper or lead)

**penicillate** /ˌpeni'silət, -layt/ *adj* having a tuft of fine hairs [deriv of L *penicillus* brush – more at PENCIL] – **penicillately** *adv*, **penicillation** *n*

**penicillin** /ˌpeni'silin/ *n* **1** any of several widely used antibiotics or antibacterial drugs of the general formula $C_9H_{11}N_2O_4R$, that are obtained either from moulds (genus *Penicillium*, esp *Penicillium notatum* or *Penicillium chrysogenum*) or made synthetically, act by interfering with the growth of bacterial cell walls, are relatively nonpoisonous to animals, and are active against a wide range of bacteria – compare AMPICILLIN **2** (a mixture of) any of various chemical compounds (SALTS or ESTERS) derived from a penicillin

**penicillinase** /ˌpeni'silinayz, -ays/ *n* any of various ENZYMES produced by penicillin-resistant bacteria, that break down and inactivate penicillins

**penicillium** /ˌpeni'siliəm/ *n*, *pl* **penicillia** /-liə/ any of a genus (*Penicillium* of the family Moniliaceae) of fungi (e g a BLUE MOULD) that grow chiefly on moist nonliving organic matter (e g cheese) and are used in cheesemaking and as a source of penicillin [NL, genus name, fr L *penicillus*]

**penile** /'peeniel/ *adj* of or affecting the penis

**penillion** /pi'nilyən/ *n* an improvised or traditional Welsh verse sung to a melody played on the harp [W, pl of *penill* verse]

**peninsula** /pə'ninsyoolə/ *n* a piece of land jutting out into or almost surrounded by water; *esp* one connected to a larger body of land or the mainland by an isthmus [L *paeninsula*, fr *paene* almost + *insula* island – more at PATIENT]

**peninsular** /pə'ninsyoolə/ *adj* of a peninsula; *specif, often cap* of Spain and Portugal ⟨*the* Peninsular *War*⟩

**penis** /'peenis/ *n*, *pl* **penes** /-neez/, **penises** the male organ of copulation by which semen is introduced into the female during coitus [L, penis, tail; akin to OHG *faselt* penis, Gk *peos*]

**penis envy** *n* the unconscious desire to be a male that in psychoanalytic theory is attributed to the female

**'penitent** /'penit(ə)nt/ *adj* feeling or expressing humble or regretful pain or sorrow for sins or offences; repentant [ME, fr MF, fr L *paenitent-, paenitens*, fr prp of *paenitēre* to be sorry; akin to L *paene* almost – more at PATIENT] – **penitence** *n*, **penitently** *adv*

synonyms **Penitence, repentance, contrition, compunction,** and **remorse** imply sorrow for having done wrong. **Penitence** and **repentance** add to regret for past faults a desire to avoid them in future; **repentance** suggests more strongly a change of heart and a new beginning. **Contrition** may be a theological term, suggesting that **repentance** is due to an awareness of the love of God, but is often used in a more general sense, to suggest a humble and grieving **penitence. Compunction** and **remorse** imply the sting of a guilty conscience, but while **remorse** suggests a prolonged, often agonized self-reproach for things past, **compunction** implies a merely temporary reaction and often applies to present or future action. It is often used negatively or in a qualified sense ⟨*had little or no* compunction *in lying to his wife*⟩. antonyms impenitent, unrepentant

**²penitent** *n* **1** somebody who repents of sin **2** somebody under church censure but admitted to PENANCE (church rite involving confession and repentance), esp under the direction of a confessor

**penitential** /ˌpeni'tensh(ə)l/ *adj* of penitence or penance – **penitentially** *adv*

**'penitentiary** /ˌpeni'tensh(ə)ri/ *n* **1a** an officer in some Roman Catholic dioceses vested with power from the bishop to absolve in certain special cases **b** *cap* (a cardinal presiding over) a tribunal of the papal court concerned with granting pardons for sin and excusing penitents wholly or partly from penance in this world or the next **2** *NAm* a prison in which offenders against the law are confined for detention or punishment; *specif* a prison for the confinement of people convicted of the more serious crimes [ME *penitenciary*, fr ML *poenitentiarius*, fr *poenitentia* penitence – more at PENANCE]

**²penitentiary** *adj* **1** penitential **2** *NAm* of or incurring confinement in a penitentiary

**penknife** /'pen,nief/ *n* a small pocketknife [fr its original use for mending quill pens]

**penlight, penlite** /'pen,liet/ *n* a small electric torch resembling a fountain pen in size or shape

**penman** /-mən/ *n* **1a** somebody with a specified quality or style of handwriting ⟨*a poor* ~⟩ **b** somebody skilled in penmanship; *esp* a professional copyist or scribe **2** *humorous* an author

**penmanship** /-ship/ *n* **1** the art or practice of writing with the pen **2** (a) quality or style of handwriting

**penna** /'penə/ *n*, *pl* **pennae** /'penie, -nee/ any of the medium-sized feathers (CONTOUR FEATHERS) forming the outer covering of a bird's body, esp as distinguished from down or a showy or conspicuous plume [L, feather, wing – more at PEN] – **pennaceous** *adj*

**pen name** *n* an author's pseudonym

**pennant** /'penənt/ *n* **1a** any of various nautical flags used for identification or signalling **b** a flag or banner that tapers to a point or has a swallowtail **2** *NAm* (a flag denoting the holding of) a championship (e g in a professional baseball league) [alter. (influenced by *pennon*) of *pendant*]

**penni** /'peni/ *n*, *pl* **pennia** /-niə/ **pennis** – see *markka* at MONEY table [Finnish]

**pennies from heaven** *n pl, informal* something desirable, esp money, acquired with little or no effort

**penniless** /'penilis/ *adj* lacking money; poor *synonyms* see POOR

**pennon** /'penən/ *n* **1a** a long usu triangular or swallow-tailed streamer typically attached to the head of a lance as an ensign **b** PENNANT 1a **2** *chiefly poetic* a wing, pinion [ME, fr MF *penon*, aug of *penne* feather – more at PEN]

**pennoncel, penoncel** /'penənsel/ *n* a small pennon borne esp at the head of a lance in late medieval or Renaissance times [ME *penoncell*, fr MF *penoncel*, dim. of *penon*]

**Pennsylvania Dutch** /ˌpens(ə)l'vaynyə, -ni·ə/ *n* **1** a people descended from 18th-century German immigrants to E Pennsylvania **2** a dialect of HIGH GERMAN spoken by the Pennsylvania Dutch – **Pennsylvania Dutchman** *n*

**Pennsylvania German** *n* PENNSYLVANIA DUTCH 2

**Pennsylvanian** /ˌpensəl'vaynyən/ *adj* of or being the N American geological period of the PALAEOZOIC era between the MISSISSIPPIAN and the PERMIAN, that corresponds to the Upper or later division of the CARBONIFEROUS period; *also* the system of rocks formed during this time [*Pennsylvania*, state in NE USA] – **Pennsylvanian** *n*

**penny** /'peni/ *n, pl* **pennies, pence** /pens/ **1a(1)** a former British monetary unit worth £$^1/_{240}$ **a(2)** (a usu bronze coin representing) a British monetary unit in use since 1971 that is worth £$^1/_{100}$ **b** – see *pound* at MONEY table **2** DENARIUS (Roman coin) **3** a trivial amount ⟨*didn't lose a ~ by it*⟩ **4** *NAm* a cent [ME, fr OE *penning, penig*, akin to OHG *pfenning*, a coin] – **a pretty penny** *informal* a large amount of money – **spend a penny** *euph informal* to go to the lavatory [fr the former charge for the use of public toilets] – **the penny drops** the true meaning finally dawns [fr the dropping of a coin activating the mechanism of a slot machine] – **turn up like a bad penny** to keep appearing though unwelcome

synonyms The plural of the British penny is pence when one speaks of a sum of money ⟨*ticket costs 20 pence*⟩ and pennies with reference to the coins themselves ⟨*a heap of pennies*⟩.

**-penny** /-p(ə)ni; *since decimalization also* -peni/ *comb form* (→ *adj*) **1** costing (so many) pence ⟨*nine*penny⟩ **2** being a (specified) nail length ⟨*eight*penny *nail*⟩ [(2) fr the original price per hundred]

**penny arcade** *n, chiefly NAm* AMUSEMENT ARCADE

**pennycress** /'penikres/ *n* any of several usu white- or sometimes purple-flowered plants (genus *Thlaspi*) of the cabbage family; *esp* a white-flowered Eurasian plant (*Thlaspi arvense*) that bears round flat seed pods

**penny dreadful** *n* a novel of violent adventure or crime, originally costing a penny

**penny-'farthing** *n, Br* an early type of bicycle having one small and one large wheel [fr the relative sizes of the old penny and farthing coins]

**'penny-,pinching** *adj* mean, niggardly *synonyms* see STINGY – **penny pincher** *n*, **penny-pinching** *n*

**pennyroyal** /-'royəl/ *n* **1** a European plant (*Mentha pulegium*) of the mint family with bluish-lilac or pink flowers and small leaves that yield an oil that smells strongly of mint and was formerly used as a flavouring and in medicine **2** an aromatic American plant (*Hedeoma pulegioides*) of the mint family [prob by folk etymology fr MF *poullieul*, modif of L *pulegium*]

**pennyweight** /-,wayt/ *n* a unit of troy weight equal to 24 grains (about 1.56 grams)

**,penny-'wise** *adj* prudent only in dealing with small sums or matters – *esp* in *penny-wise and pound-foolish*

**pennywort** /-wuht/ *n* any of various round-leaved plants: eg **a** a European plant (*Umbilicus rupestris*) of the stonecrop family that grows chiefly on rocks and walls and has long spikes of whitish-green to pinkish flowers **b** a plant (*Hydrocotyle vulgaris* of the family Hydrocotylaceae) of marshes and damp meadows that has small pinkish-green flowers and shiny almost circular leaves

**pennyworth** /'penəth, 'peniwəth, -,wuhth/ *n, pl* **pennyworth, pennyworths 1** a penny's worth **2** value for the money spent; a bargain ⟨*I got a good ~*⟩ **3** a small quantity; a modicum

**penology** /pee'noləji/ *n* a branch of criminology dealing with prison management and the treatment of offenders [L *poena* or Gk *poinē* penalty + E -*logy* – more at PAIN] – **penological** *adj*, **penologist** *n*

**penoncel** /'penənsel/ *n* PENNONCEL (small flag)

**pen pal** *n, informal* a pen-friend

**pen pusher** *n* one whose work involves usu boring or repetitive writing at a desk; *specif* CLERK 2a, b

**pensile** /'pensiel/ *adj, esp of a bird's nest* hanging down; pendent; *also, of a bird* building such a nest [L *pensilis*, fr *pensus*, pp of *pendēre* to hang]

**¹pension** /'pensh(ə)n; *sense 2* 'ponhsyonh (*Fr* pãsjɔ̃)/ *n* **1** a fixed sum paid regularly to a person (eg following retirement or as compensation for a wage-earner's death) ⟨*a widow's ~*⟩ – compare OLD AGE PENSION **2a** room and board, esp at a continental European hotel or boarding house **b** a hotel or boarding house, esp in continental Europe [ME, fr MF, fr L *pension-, pensio*, fr *pensus*, pp of *pendere* to pay – more at PENDANT; (2) Fr, fr MF] – **pensionless** *adj*

**²pension** /'pensh(ə)n/ *vt* to grant or pay a pension to
**pension off** *vt* **1** to dismiss or retire from service with a pension ⟨*pensioned off his faithful old servant*⟩ **2** to set aside or dispense with after long use ⟨*pensioned off his old trousers*⟩

**pensionable** /'pensh(ə)nəbl/ *adj* **1** entitled to receive a pension ⟨*a ~ employee*⟩ **2** entitling a person to receive a pension ⟨*~ employment*⟩

**pensionary** /'penshən(ə)ri/ *n* a pensioner; *esp* a hireling – **pensionary** *adj*

**pensione** /,pensi'ohni/ *n* PENSION 2b [It, fr MF *pension*]

**pensioner** /'pensh(ə)nə/ *n* somebody who receives or lives on a pension; *esp* one who receives an OLD AGE PENSION

**pensive** /'pensiv/ *adj* sadly or dreamily thoughtful [ME *pensif*, fr MF, fr *penser* to think, fr L *pensare* to ponder, fr *pensus*, pp of *pendere* to weigh – more at PENDANT] – **pensively** *adv*, **pensiveness** *n*

**penstemon** /pen'steemən/ *n* PENTSTEMON (N American plant)

**penstock** /'pen,stok/ *n* **1** a valve, sluice, or gate for regulating a flow (eg of water) **2** *chiefly NAm* a conduit or pipe for conducting water

**pent** /pent/ *adj* shut up; confined ⟨*a ~ crowd*⟩ – usu + *up* or *in* ⟨*pent-up emotions*⟩ [fr pp of obs *pend* to confine, fr ME *penden*, alter. of *pennen* to pen]

**penta-** /pentə/, **pent-** /pent-/ *comb form* **1** five ⟨*penta*hedron⟩ **2** containing five atoms or groups in the molecular structure ⟨*penta*hydrate⟩ [ME, fr Gk, fr *pente* – more at FIVE]

**pentachlorophenol** /,pentə,klawrə'feenol, -,klorə-, -'feenl/ *n* a chemical compound, $C_6Cl_5OH$, used esp as a wood preservative and fungicide and as a disinfectant [*penta-* + *chlorophenol* (a chlorine derivative of phenol)]

**pentacle** /'pentəkl/ *n* a pentagram [(assumed) ML *pentaculum*, prob fr Gk *pente*]

**pentad** /'pentad/ *n* a group or series of five [Gk *pentad-, pentas*, fr *pente*]

**pentadactyl** /,pentə'daktil/ *adj* having five digits to the hand or foot or five fingerlike parts [L *pentadactylus*, fr Gk *pentadaktylos*, fr *penta-* + *daktylos* finger, toe] – **pentadactylism** *n*

**pentagon** /'pentəgon, -,gon/ *n* a two-dimensional geometric figure having five sides; *esp* one that is REGULAR (having five equal sides and angles) [Gk *pentagōnon*, fr neut of *pentagōnos* pentagonal, fr *penta-* + *gōnia* angle – more at -GON] – **pentagonal** *adj*, **pentagonally** *adv*

**Pentagon** *n taking sing or pl vb* the US military establishment [the *Pentagon* building, headquarters of the US Department of Defense in Arlington, Virginia]

**pentagram** /'pentə,gram/ *n* a 5-pointed star used as a magical symbol [Gk *pentagrammon*, fr *penta-* + -*grammon* (akin to *gramma* letter) – more at GRAM]

**pentamerous** /pen'tamərəs/ *adj* divided into or consisting of five parts; *specif, of a flower* having the petals, SEPALS, and other flower structures arranged in groups, each consisting of (a multiple of) five members [NL *pentamerus*, fr *penta-* (fr Gk) + -*merus* -merous]

**pentameter** /pen'tamitə/ *n* a line of verse consisting of five metrical units ⟨*Gray's ~ "the ploughman homeward plods his weary way", moves slowly with its five steady beats*⟩ [L, fr Gk *pentametros* having five metrical feet, fr *penta-* + *metron* measure – more at MEASURE]

**pentane** /'pentayn/ *n* a liquid chemical compound, $C_5H_{12}$, that is a member of the ALKANE series of organic chemical compounds and occurs in petroleum and natural gas [ISV]

**pentangle** /'pen,tang-gl/ *n* a pentagram

**pentaploid** /'pentəployd/ *adj* having or being five times the single (HAPLOID) set of CHROMOSOMES (strands of gene-carrying material) – **pentaploid** *n*, **pentaploidy** *n*

**pentaprism** /'pentə,priz(ə)m/ *n* a 5-sided prism, esp in a camera, that gives a constant deviation of 90° to light from any direction

**pentarchy** /'pentahki/ *n* a group of five countries or districts each under its own ruler or government [Gk *pentarchia*, fr *penta-* + -*archia* -archy]

**Pentateuch** /'pentə,tyoohk/ *n* the first five books of the Old Testament [LL *Pentateuchus*, fr Gk *Pentateuchos*, fr *penta-* + *teuchos* tool, vessel, book]

**pentathlete** /pen'tathleet/ *n* one who competes in the pentathlon [LGk *pentathlētēs*, fr Gk *pentathlon*]

**pentathlon** /pen'tathlon/ *n* **1** a women's athletic contest in which all contestants compete in the 100 metres hurdles, shot put, high jump, long jump, and 200 metres sprint – compare BIATHLON, DECATHLON **2** MODERN PENTATHLON (men's 5-sport contest) [Gk, fr *penta-* + *athlon* contest]

**pentatonic scale** /,pentə'tonik/ *adj* of, in, or being a musical scale consisting of five tones, specif one in which the tones are arranged like a major scale with the fourth and seventh tones omitted

**pentavalent** /,pentə'vaylənt, pen'tavələnt/ *adj, chemistry* having a VALENCY of five

**pentazocine** /pen'tazəseen/ *n* a synthetic drug, $C_{19}H_{27}NO$, that has the painkilling properties of morphine but is less addictive [*penta-* + *azo* + *-cine* (of unknown origin)]

**Pentecost** /'pentikost/ *n* **1** the Jewish festival of SHABUOTH **2** a Christian festival on the seventh Sunday after Easter commemorating the descent of the Holy Spirit on the apostles [ME, fr OE *pentecosten*, fr LL *pentecoste*, fr Gk *pentēkostē*, lit., fiftieth day, fr *pentēkostos* fiftieth, fr *pentēkonta* fifty, fr *penta-* + *-konta* (akin to L vig*inti* twenty) – more at VIGESIMAL]

**Pentecostal** /,penti'kostl/ *adj* **1** of or suggesting Pentecost **2** of or constituting any of various revivalistic Christian bodies that lay particular emphasis on the gifts of the Holy Spirit (e g faith healing and the ecstatic speaking of esp unintelligible languages) – **Pentecostal** *n*, **Pentecostalism** *n*, **Pentecostalist** *n*

**penthouse** /'pent,hows/ *n* **1** a structure (e g a shed or roof) attached to and sloping from a wall or building **2** a structure or dwelling built on the roof of a (tall) building [alter. (influenced by *house*) of ME *pentis*, fr MF *appentis*, prob fr ML *appenticium* appendage, fr L *appendic-*, *appendix* – more at APPENDIX]

**pentimento** /,penti'mentoh/ *n*, *pl* **pentimenti** /-tee/ a reappearance in a painting of a design which has been painted over [It, repentance, correction, fr *pentire* to repent, fr L *paenitere*]

**pentlandite** /'pentləndiet/ *n* a bronzy-yellow mineral, $(Fe,Ni)_9S_8$, that consists of a nickel iron sulphide and is the principle source of nickel [Fr, fr Joseph *Pentland* †1873 Ir scientist]

**pentobarbital** /,pentə'bahbitl/ *n*, *chiefly NAm* pentobarbitone [*penta-* + *-o-* + *barbital*]

**pentobarbitone** /,pentə'bahbitohn/ *n*, *Br* a barbiturate drug, $C_{11}H_{18}N_2O_3$, used, esp formerly, in sleeping pills, as a sedative, and to prevent convulsions [*penta-* + *-o-* + *barbitone*]

**pentode** /'pentohd/ *n* a THERMIONIC VALVE (device for regulating a flow of electricity) that has an ANODE and a CATHODE to and from which electrons flow and three GRIDS that control the flow of electricity and improve the performance of the valve [ISV]

**pentosan** /'pentəsan/ *n* any of various POLYSACCHARIDES (carbohydrates) composed of many linked pentose units, that occur widely in plants

**pentose** /'pentohs, -tohz/ *n* any of various MONOSACCHARIDES (simple sugars) (e g those in RNA and DNA) that contain five carbon atoms in the molecule [ISV]

**pentoside** /'pentosied/ *n* a GLYCOSIDE (chemical compound derived from a sugar) that yields a pentose when broken down

**Pentothal** /'pentəthal/ *trademark* – used for THIOPENTONE (drug used as a general anaesthetic)

**pentoxide** /pen'toksied/ *n* an OXIDE (compound of oxygen with one other chemical element or group) containing five atoms of oxygen [ISV]

**pentstemon** /,pent'steemən, -'stemən/ **penstemon** /pen-'steemən/ *n* any of a genus (*Penstemon*) of chiefly N American plants of the foxglove family with usu large showy blue, purple, red, yellow, or white flowers [NL *pentstemon*, alter. of *Penstemon*, genus name, fr Gk *penta-* + *stēmōn* thread – more at STAMEN]

**pentyl** /'pentiel, -til/ *n* a chemical group, $C_5H_{11}$, derived from PENTANE by the removal of a hydrogen atom [*pentane* + *-yl*]

**penuche** /pə'noohchi/ *n*, *NAm* fudge made usu of brown sugar, butter, cream or milk, and nuts [MexSp *panocha* raw sugar, fr dim. of Sp *pan* bread, fr L *panis* – more at FOOD]

**penult** /'pi'nult, pe-/ *n* the next to the last member of a series; *esp* the next to the last syllable of a word [L *paenultima*, fr fem of *paenultimus* almost last, fr *paene* almost + *ultimus* last]

**penultima** /pi'nultimə, pen-/ *n* a penult [L *paenultima*]

**¹penultimate** /pi'nultimət, pe-/ *adj* **1** next to the last ⟨the ~ chapter of a book⟩ **2** of a penult ⟨a ~ accent⟩ – **penultimately** *adv*

**²penultimate** *n* a penult

**penumbra** /pi'numbrə/ *n*, *pl* **penumbrae** /-brie/, **penumbras** **1** a region of partial darkness (e g in an eclipse) in a shadow surrounding the UMBRA (region of total darkness) **2** a shaded region surrounding the dark central portion of a sunspot **3** a surrounding or adjoining region in which something exists in a lesser degree; a fringe ⟨the sixteenth century lay in the ~ of the Middle Ages⟩ [NL, fr L *paene* almost + *umbra* shadow – more at PATIENT, UMBRAGE] – **penumbral** *adj*

**penurious** /pi'nyooəri·əs/ *adj*, *formal* **1** marked by or suffering

from penury **2** given to or marked by extreme stinting frugality
**synonyms** see POOR **antonym** affluent – **penuriously** *adv*, **penuriousness** *n*

**penury** /'penyoori/ *n*, *formal* a cramping and oppressive lack of resources, esp money; *esp* severe poverty [ME, fr L *penuria* want – more at PATIENT]

**peon** /'pee·ən/ *n*, *pl* **peons**, **peones** /pay'ohneez/ **1** an Indian or Sri Lankan infantryman, orderly, or other worker **2** a member of the landless agricultural labouring class in Spanish America **3** a drudge, menial [Pg *peão* & Fr *pion*, fr ML *pedon-*, *pedo* foot soldier – more at PAWN]

**peonage** /'pee·ənij/ *n* **1** the condition of a peon **2** the use of labourers bound in servitude because of debt or under a convict lease system

**peony, paeony** /'pee·əni/ *n* any of a genus (*Paeonia* of the family Paeoniaceae, the peony family) of plants widely grown for their very large showy red, pink, or white flowers [ME *piony*, fr MF *pioine*, fr L *paeonia*, fr Gk *paiōnia*, fr *Paiōn* Paeon, mythical physician of the gods]

**¹people** /'peepl/ *n* **1** *taking pl vb* human beings in general **2** *taking pl vb* human beings making up a group or assembly or linked by a common interest ⟨city ~⟩ ⟨academic ~⟩ **3** *taking pl vb* the members of a family or kinship ⟨his ~ have been farmers for generations⟩ **4** *taking pl vb* the mass of a community, esp as distinguished from an elitist class ⟨disputes between the ~ and the nobles⟩ **5** a body of persons that are united by a common culture, tradition, or sense of kinship, that typically have common language, institutions, and beliefs, and that often constitute a politically organized group **6** *taking pl vb* lower animals, usu of a specified kind or situation ⟨squirrels and chipmunks: the little furry ~⟩ **7** *taking pl vb* the citizens of a state who are qualified to vote [ME *peple*, fr OF *peuple*, fr L *populus*] – **of all people** – used to show surprise ⟨the Archbishop of all people said that?⟩

**synonyms People**, rather than **persons**, is now the usual word for a number of human beings ⟨*car will hold six* **people**⟩, except in very formal contexts ⟨*murder by a* **person** *or* **persons** *unknown*⟩ or with reference to the Christian Trinity ⟨*God in three* **Persons**⟩. See ³RACE. *usage* Only in the sense "group united by a common culture" can **people** be treated as a singular noun with a regular plural ⟨*the* **peoples** *of Africa*⟩, but even in the singular it may take a plural verb ⟨*a nomadic* **people** *who follow their herds*⟩.

**²people** *vt* **1** to supply or fill with people **2** to dwell in; inhabit [MF *peupler*, fr OF, fr *peuple*]

**pep** /pep/ *vt or n* **-pp-** (to liven *up* or instil with) brisk energy or initiative and high spirits ⟨the news of his award ~ped him up⟩ [short for *pepper*] – **peppy** *adj*, **peppiness** *n*

**peplos** *also* **peplus** /'peplɔs/ *n* a garment worn by women of ancient Greece that was draped and pinned at the shoulders to resemble a tunic [L *peplus*, fr Gk *peplos*]

**peplum** /'peplɔm/ *n* a short skirt or flounce attached to the waistline of a blouse, jacket, or dress [L, fr Gk *peplos*]

**pepo** /'peepoh/ *n*, *pl* **pepos** a hard-rinded fleshy many-seeded fruit (e g a pumpkin, squash, melon, or cucumber) that is the characteristic fruit of plants of the marrow family [L, a melon – more at PUMPKIN

**¹pepper** /'pepə/ *n* **1a** either of two pungent products from the berries of an E Indian plant that are used whole or ground esp as a condiment: **1a(1)** BLACK PEPPER **a(2)** WHITE PEPPER **b** any of a genus (*Piper* of the family Piperaceae, the pepper family) of tropical mostly climbing shrubs with aromatic leaves; *esp* a woody climbing plant (*Piper nigrum*), widely cultivated in the tropics for its red berries from which BLACK PEPPER and WHITE PEPPER are prepared **2** any of several products similar to pepper that are obtained from close relatives of the pepper plant **3a** CAPSICUM 1; *esp* a tropical American capsicum (*Capsicum frutescens*) whose fruits are HOT PEPPERS or SWEET PEPPERS **b** the usu red or green fruit of a capsicum – compare HOT PEPPER, SWEET PEPPER **c** any of various pungent condiments (e g CAYENNE PEPPER) obtained from the fruit of a capsicum – used with a qualifying term [ME *peper*, fr OE *pipor*; akin to OHG *pfeffar* pepper; both fr a prehistoric WGmc-NGmc word borrowed fr L *piper* pepper, fr Gk *peperi*] – **pepper** *adj*

**²pepper** *vt* **1a** to sprinkle, season, or cover (as if) with pepper **b** to shower with shot or other missiles **2** to sprinkle ⟨~ed his report with statistics⟩ – **pepperer** *n*

**pepper-and-'salt** *adj* having black and white or dark and light colour intermingled in small flecks ⟨a ~ overcoat⟩

**pepperbox** /'pepə,boks/ *n* **1** a late 18th-century pistol with five or six revolving barrels **2** *chiefly NAm* PEPPER POT

**peppercorn** /-,kawn/ *n* a dried berry of the pepper plant

**peppercorn rent** *n* a very small amount of money paid as a nominal rent

**peppered moth** *n* a European moth (*Biston betularia* of the family Geometridae) that typically has white wings with small black specks but also occurs as a solid black form, esp in areas where the air is heavily polluted by industry – compare INDUSTRIAL MELANISM

**pepper mill** *n* a small pot used for grinding peppercorns by hand (e g at table)

**peppermint** /-,mint/ *n* **1a** a plant (*Mentha x piperita*) of the mint family that has dark green tapering leaves and small pink to purplish flowers, and is cultivated for its aromatic oil **b** **peppermint oil** *also* **peppermint** a strong-smelling oil obtained from the flowering tops of a peppermint and used as a flavouring (e g in sweets and toothpaste) and, esp formerly, in medicine (e g to relieve colic) **2** a sweet flavoured with peppermint oil – **pepperminty** *adj*

**pepper pot** *n* **1** a W Indian stew of vegetables and meat or fish highly seasoned usu with the juice of a bitter CASSAVA (tropical plant) **2** *Br* a small usu cylindrical container with a perforated top used for sprinkling ground pepper on food

**peppertree** /'pepə,tree/ *n* a Peruvian evergreen tree (*Schinus molle*) of the sumach family that has clusters of small white flowers and bright red 1-seeded fruits, and is grown as a SHADE TREE in tropical and warm subtropical regions

**peppery** /'pep(ə)ri/ *adj* **1** hot, pungent ⟨*a ~ taste*⟩ **2** hot-tempered, touchy ⟨*a ~ old man*⟩ **3** fiery, stinging ⟨*a ~ speech*⟩

**pep pill** *n, informal* a tablet of a stimulant drug

**pepsin** /'pepsin/ *n* an ENZYME produced by the lining of the stomach that breaks down most proteins to peptides in an acid environment [Ger, fr Gk *pepsis* digestion, fr *pessein*]

**pepsinogen** /pep'sinəjin/ *n* an inactive protein present in the glands of the stomach that is readily converted into pepsin in a slightly acid environment [ISV *pepsin* + *-o-* + *-gen*]

**pep talk** *n* a usu brief, high-pressure, and emotional talk designed esp to encourage an audience (e g a sports team)

**peptic** /'peptik/ *adj* **1** of or promoting digestion; digestive **2** of, producing, or caused by pepsin ⟨*~ breakdown of proteins*⟩ **3** connected with or resulting from the action of digestive juices ⟨*a ~ ulcer*⟩ [L *pepticus*, fr Gk *peptikos*, fr *peptos* cooked, fr *peptein*, *pessein* to cook, digest – more at COOK]

**peptidase** /'peptidayz, -ays/ *n* an ENZYME that breaks down peptides or splits off peptides from the ends of proteins by breaking down PEPTIDE BONDS – compare ENDOPEPTIDASE, EXOPEPTIDASE

**peptide** /'peptied/ *n* a short chain of two or more AMINO ACIDS joined by PEPTIDE BONDS [ISV, fr *peptone*] – **peptidic** *adj*, **peptidically** *adv*

**peptide bond** *n* the chemical bond between the AMINO group of one AMINO ACID and the CARBOXYL (acid) group of another, that links two amino acids in a peptide or protein

**peptidoglycan** /,peptidoh'gliekən/ *n* a large molecule found esp in bacterial cell walls, that is composed of a network of sugar chains and peptide chains [*peptide* + *-o-* + *glycan* (polysaccharide)]

**pept·ize,-ise** /'peptiez/ *vt* to cause to disperse in a medium; *specif* to dissolve so as to form a COLLOIDAL solution (solution containing suspended particles) [prob fr Gk *peptein*] – **peptizer** *n*, **peptization** *n*

**peptone** /'peptohn/ *n* any of various water-soluble (mixtures of) chemical compounds produced by the partial breakdown of proteins [Ger *pepton*, fr Gk, neut of *peptos*]

**pepton·ize, -ise** /'peptəniez/ *vt* to convert into a peptone; *esp* to cause the breakdown or digestion of (a protein) into a peptone by the action of an ENZYME (e g pepsin)

**Pequot** /'pee,kwot/ *n, pl* **Pequots**, *esp collectively* **Pequot** a member, or the Algonquian language, of an American Indian people of SE Connecticut

**per** /pə; *strong* puh/ *prep* **1** with respect to every; for each ⟨*£30 ~ head ~ week*⟩ **2** *commercialese* by the means or agency of; through ⟨*send it ~ rail*⟩ **3** *commercialese* ACCORDING TO 1 ⟨*~ list price*⟩ [L, through, by means of, by – more at FOR]

**per-** *prefix* **1a** through; throughout ⟨*perambulate*⟩ ⟨*pervade*⟩ **b** thoroughly; very ⟨*perfervid*⟩ ⟨*perfect*⟩ **2** to the bad; to destruction ⟨*perjure*⟩ ⟨*perdition*⟩ **3a** containing a large or the largest possible proportion of (a specified chemical element or group) ⟨*perchloride*⟩ ⟨*peroxide*⟩ **b** containing an atom in a high or its highest state of OXIDATION in the molecular structure

⟨*perchloric acid*⟩ [L, through, throughout, thoroughly, to destruction, fr *per*]

[1]**peradventure** /pərəd'venchə, puh-/ *adv, archaic* perhaps, possibly [ME *per aventure*, fr OF, by chance]

[2]**peradventure** *n, archaic* a doubt, chance ⟨*without the vestige of a ~ he was a traitor*⟩

**perambulate** /pə'rambyoolayt/ *vb, formal vt* to travel over or through, esp on foot; traverse to stroll [L *perambulatus*, pp of *perambulare*, fr *per-* through + *ambulare* to walk] – **perambulation** *n*, **perambulatory** *adj*

**perambulator** /pə'rambyoolaytə/ *n, formal* **1** one who perambulates **2** *chiefly Br* a pram

**per annum** /pər 'anəm/ *adv* in or for each year [ML]

**perborate** /pə'bawrayt/ *n* a chemical compound of a BORATE with HYDROGEN PEROXIDE [ISV]

**percale** /pə'kayl, pə'kahl, ,puh-/ *n* a fine closely woven cotton cloth variously finished for clothing, sheeting, and industrial uses [Per *pargālah*]

**percaline** /'puhkəlin, ,puhkə'leen/ *n* a lightweight cotton fabric; *esp* a glossy fabric used for bookbindings [Fr, fr *percale*]

**per capita** /'kapitə/ *adv or adj* per unit of population; by or for each person ⟨*the highest income ~ of any European country*⟩ [ML, by heads]

**perceive** /pə'seev/ *vt* **1** to attain awareness or understanding of **2** to become aware of through the senses; *esp* to see, observe **synonyms** see [1]SEE [ME *perceiven*, fr OF *perceivre*, fr L *percipere*, fr *per-* thoroughly + *capere* to take – more at HEAVE] – **perceivable** *adj*, **perceivably** *adv*, **perceiver** *n*

[1]**per cent** /pə 'sent/ *adv* in or for each hundred ⟨*50 ~ of our workers are married*⟩ [*per* + L *centum* hundred]

[2]**per cent** *n, pl* **per cent** **1** one part in a hundred ⟨*she gave half a ~ of her income to charity*⟩ **2** a percentage ⟨*a large ~ of his income*⟩

**usage** Although some people dislike the use of **per cent** as a noun, it is easier to express "0.5%" in words as ⟨*half a* **per cent**⟩ than as ⟨*point five* **per cent**⟩. A safe alternative is ⟨*half of one* **per cent**⟩.

[3]**per cent** *adj* **1** reckoned on the basis of a whole divided into one hundred parts ⟨*a 10 ~ increase*⟩ **2** of bonds, securities, etc paying interest at a specified per cent

**percentage** /pə'sentij/ *n* **1** a proportion (expressed as per cent of a whole) **2** a share of winnings or profits ⟨*they did him out of his ~*⟩ **3** *informal* an advantage, profit ⟨*no ~ in going around looking like a scarecrow*⟩

**percentile** /pə'sentiel/ *n, statistics* any of 99 values in a FREQUENCY DISTRIBUTION that divides it into 100 parts (INTERVALS), each containing one per cent of the individuals, items, etc under consideration; *also* any of the 100 groups of individuals, items, etc comprising such an interval [prob fr *per cent* + *-ile* (as in *quartile*, n)]

**percents** /pə'sents/ *n pl, Br* stocks that bear a specified rate of interest ⟨*I took out some 10 ~*⟩ [*per cent*]

**per centum** /'sentəm/ *n* PER CENT [*per* + L *centum*]

**percept** /'puhsept/ *n* a mental impression of a perceived object [back-formation fr *perception*]

**perceptible** /pə'septəbl/ *adj* capable of being perceived, esp by the senses ⟨*a ~ change in her tone*⟩ ⟨*the light became increasingly ~*⟩ – **perceptibly** *adv*, **perceptibility** *n*

**synonyms** **Perceptible, sensible, palpable, tangible,** and **appreciable** can all describe what may be apprehended as real by the senses or understanding. **Perceptible** suggests something recognizable in itself, or deduceable from signs or indications ⟨*the shape of a ship just* **perceptible** *in the mist*⟩. It may also suggest something so nearly imperceptible (e g inaudible or invisible) as to be hardly noticeable ⟨*a* **perceptible** *tremor*⟩. **Sensible**, in a sense used only formally today, suggests something more obvious to the senses than what is simply **perceptible**. Both **palpable** and **tangible** include the idea of touch. **Palpable** suggests what may be felt by the fingers, and by extension, what may be felt by the body as a whole ⟨*a* **palpable** *warmth from the sun, even in winter*⟩. **Palpable** also implies something easily perceptible, as if it had a physical existence ⟨*a* **palpable** *coldness in her manner*⟩. Compare EVIDENT. **Tangible** suggests rather something which may be grasped or handled, and so by extension may mean something the intellect can perceive as an entity ⟨*tangible* *advantages*⟩. **Appreciable** describes what is most easily perceptible, and may approximate to *considerable*, but more narrowly it suggests whatever may be weighed, measured, or valued ⟨*an* **appreciable** *change in temperature is one which may be assessed from a thermometer*⟩. Compare [1]MATERIAL, PERSPICUOUS **antonym** imperceptible

**perception** /pə'sepsh(ə)n/ *n* **1a** a result of perceiving; an observation **b** a mental image; a concept, percept **2** the mental interpretation and integration of physical sensations produced by stimuli from the external world **3a** intuitive discernment; insight ⟨~ *into the workings of the criminal mind*⟩ **b** an ability to understand ⟨*men lacking keen* ~⟩ **synonyms** see DISCERNMENT [L *perception-*, *perceptio* act of perceiving, fr *perceptus*, pp of *percipere*] – **perceptional** *adj*

**perceptive** /pə'septiv/ *adj* **1** responsive to sensory stimulus; discerning ⟨*a* ~ *eye*⟩ **2a** capable of or exhibiting keen perception; observant ⟨*a* ~ *scholar*⟩ **b** characterized by sympathetic understanding or insight – **perceptively** *adv*, **perceptiveness, perceptivity** *n*

**perceptual** /pə'septyooəl/ *adj* of or involving perception, esp in relation to immediate sensory experience [L *perceptus* + E -*al*] – **perceptually** *adv*

¹**perch** /puhch/ *n* **1** a roost for a bird **2** *chiefly Br* ROD 2a (unit of length) **3** *informal* **3a** a resting place or vantage point; a seat **b** a prominent position ⟨*his new* ~ *as president*⟩ [ME *perche* pole, stick, roost, fr OF, fr L *pertica* pole]

²**perch** *vt* to place on a perch, height, or precarious spot ~ *vi* to alight, settle, or rest, esp briefly or precariously

³**perch** *n, pl* **perches**, *esp collectively* **perch** **1** a small European freshwater spiny-finned fish (*Perca fluviatilis*) **2** any of numerous fishes (eg of the families Percidae, Centrarchidae, Serranidae) with a bony skeleton that are related to or resemble the European perch [ME *perche*, fr MF, fr L *perca*, fr Gk *perkē*; akin to OHG *faro* coloured, L *porcus*, a spiny fish]

**perchance** /pə'chahns/ *adv, chiefly poetic or humorous* perhaps, possibly [ME *per chance*, fr MF, by chance]

**Percheron** /'puhshərən/ *n* (any of) a breed of powerful rugged draught horses that originated in the Perche region of France [Fr, fr *Perche*, region in N France]

**perchlorate** /pə'klawrayt/ *n* any of various chemical compounds (SALTS or ESTERS) formed by combination between PERCHLORIC ACID and a metal atom, an alcohol, or another chemical group [ISV]

**perchloric acid** /pə'klawrik, -'klorik/ *n* a fuming corrosive strong acid, $HClO_4$, that has the highest proportion of oxygen of any acid of chlorine and is a powerful OXIDIZING AGENT when heated

**percipient** /pə'sipi·ənt/ *adj, formal* perceptive, discerning [L *percipient-*, *percipiens*, prp of *percipere* to perceive] – **percipience** *n*

**percoid** /'puhkoyd/ *also* **percoidean** /pə'koydiən/ *adj* of or belonging to a very large suborder (Percoidea) of spiny-finned fishes with a bony skeleton, including the perches, sunfishes, SEA BASSES, and SEA BREAMS [deriv of L *perca* perch] – **percoid** *n*

**percolate** /'puhkəlayt/ *vt* **1a** to cause (esp a liquid) to pass through a permeable substance (eg a powder), esp in order to extract a soluble constituent **b** to prepare (coffee) in a percolator **2** to be diffused through; permeate ~ *vi* **1** to ooze or trickle through a permeable substance; seep **2** to become percolated **3** to become diffused; spread gradually ⟨*allow the sunlight to* ~ *into our rooms* – Norman Douglas⟩ ⟨*the news finally* ~d *down to us*⟩ [L *percolatus*, pp of *percolare*, fr *per-* through + *colare* to sieve – more at COLANDER] – **percolation** *n*

**percolator** /'puhkəlaytə/ *n* one who or that which percolates; *specif* a coffeepot in which boiling water rising through a tube is repeatedly deflected downwards through a perforated basket containing ground coffee beans to extract their essence

**per contra** /'kontrə/ *adv* **1a** ON THE CONTRARY **b** by way of contrast **2** as a balancing item (OFFSET 4) in a ledger [It, by the opposite side (of the ledger)]

**percuss** /pə'kus/ *vt* to tap sharply; *esp, medicine* to perform percussion on (a body surface) [L *percussus*, pp]

**percussion** /pə'kush(ə)n/ *n* **1a** the striking of a PERCUSSION CAP so as to set off the charge in a firearm **b** the beating or striking of a musical instrument **c** *medicine* the tapping of the surface of a body part (eg the chest) to learn the condition of the parts beneath (eg the lungs) by the resultant sound **2** the striking of sound on the ear **3** *taking sing or pl vb* PERCUSSION INSTRUMENTS that form a section of a band or orchestra [L *percussion-*, *percussio*, stroke, blow, fr *percussus*, pp of *percutere* to beat, fr *per-* thoroughly + *quatere* to shake – more at QUASH] – **percussion** *adj*, **percussive** *adj*

**percussion band** *n* a band usu composed of schoolchildren who play simple PERCUSSION INSTRUMENTS (eg triangles and tambourines)

**percussion cap** *n* CAP 6 (container holding an explosive charge)

**percussion instrument** *n* a musical instrument (eg a drum, xylophone, or maraca) sounded by striking, shaking, or scraping

**percussionist** /pə'kush(ə)nist/ *n* one who plays percussion instruments

**percutaneous** /,puhkyoo'taynyəs, -ni·əs/ *adj* done, effected, or performed through the skin ⟨~ *absorption of an ointment*⟩ – **percutaneously** *adv*

¹**per diem** /'dee·em, 'die·em/ *adv* by the day; for each day [ML]

²**per diem** *adj* **1** based on use or service by the day; daily **2** paid by the day

³**per diem** *n, pl* **per diems** **1** a daily allowance **2** a daily fee

**perdition** /pə'dish(ə)n/ *n, chiefly euph* eternal damnation; Hell [ME *perdicion* utter destruction, damnation, fr LL *perdition-*, *perditio*, fr L *perditus*, pp of *perdere* to destroy, fr *per-* to destruction + *dare* to give – more at PER-, DATE]

**perdurable** /puh'dyooərəbl/ *adj, formal* very durable; eternal [ME, fr OF, fr LL *perdurabilis*, fr L *perdurare* to endure, fr *per-* throughout + *durare* to last – more at DURING] – **perdurably** *adv*, **perdurability** *n*

**père** *also* **pere** /peə/ (*Fr* pɛr)/ *adj* senior – used after the surname of a father to distinguish him from a son of the same name ⟨*Clark* ~ *was an idler with a taste for expensive yachts* - Geoffrey Hulton⟩ [Fr, father, fr L *patr-*, *pater*]

**Père David's deer, Père David deer** *n* a large grey deer (*Elaphurus davidianus*) with long slender antlers now found only in captivity [*Père* Armand *David* †1900 Fr missionary & naturalist]

**peregrinate** /'perigrinayt/ *vb, chiefly poetic or humourous vi* to travel, esp on foot; walk to walk or travel over; traverse [L *peregrinatus*, pp of *peregrinari* to travel abroad, fr *peregrinus* foreign]

**peregrination** /,perigri'naysh(ə)n/ *n*, **peregrinations** *n pl*, *chiefly poetic or humourous* a long and wandering journey, esp in a foreign country

**peregrine** /'perigrin/, **peregrine falcon** *n* a smallish fast-flying falcon (*Falco peregrinus*) found in many parts of the world, that has dark grey wings and back, buff to white underparts, and was formerly much used in falconry [*peregrine*, adj (wandering, widely distributed), fr ML *peregrinus*, fr L, foreign – more at PILGRIM]

**pereion** /pə'rie·ən/ *n, pl* **pereia** /pə'rie·ə/ the THORAX (body part between the head and abdomen) of a lobster, crab, crayfish, etc [NL, fr Gk *peraiōn*, prp of *peraioun* to transport, fr *peraios* situated beyond, fr *pera* beyond]

**peremptory** /pə'rempt(ə)ri, 'perəmpt(ə)ri/ *adj* **1a** putting an end to or precluding a right of action, debate, or delay ⟨*a* ~ *mandamus*⟩ **b** admitting no contradiction or refusal ⟨*a* ~ *conclusion*⟩ ⟨*a* ~ *command*⟩ **2** expressive of urgency or command ⟨*a* ~ *call*⟩ **3** (having an attitude or nature) characterized by imperious or arrogant self-assurance ⟨*how insolent of late he is become, how proud, how* ~ – Shak⟩ ⟨*a* ~ *tone*⟩ ⟨~ *disregard of an objection*⟩ [LL & L; LL *peremptorius*, fr L, destructive, fr *peremptus*, pp of *perimere* to take entirely, destroy, fr *per-* to destruction + *emere* to take – more at REDEEM] – **peremptorily** *adv*, **peremptoriness** *n*

**usage** The pronunciation /pə'rempt(ə)ri/ rather than /'perəmpt(ə)ri/ is recommended for BBC broadcasters. △ perfunctory

**perennate** /'perənayt, pə'renayt/ *vi, of a plant* to live over from one growing season to another; survive for a number of years ⟨*a perennating rhizome*⟩ [L *perennatus*, pp of *perennare*, fr *perennis*] – **perennation** *n*

**perennial** /pə'renyəl, -ni·əl/ *adj* **1** present at all seasons of the year **2** *of a plant* living for more than two and sometimes for several years, usu with new growth or flowers each year ⟨~ *asters*⟩ – compare ANNUAL 3a persistent, enduring **b** continuing without interruption; constant **c** regularly repeated or renewed; recurrent **synonyms** see CONTINUAL **antonym** ephemeral [L *perennis*, fr *per-* throughout + *annus* year – more at ANNUAL] – **perennial** *n*, **perennially** *adv*

**pereon** /pə'reeən/ *n, pl* **perea** /pə'reeə/ a pereion

¹**perfect** /'puhfikt/ *adj* **1** expert, proficient ⟨*practice makes* ~⟩ **2a** entirely without fault or defect; flawless ⟨*a* ~ *crime*⟩ **b** satisfactory in every respect ⟨*the holiday was* ~⟩ **c** corresponding to an ideal standard or abstract concept ⟨*a* ~ *gentleman*⟩ **d** legally valid **3a** accurate, exact ⟨~ *pitch*⟩ ⟨*a* ~ *circle*⟩ **b** lacking in no essential detail; complete **c** absolute, utter ⟨*I*

*felt a ~ fool*⟩ **4** of or being a verb tense that expresses an action or state completed at the time of speaking or at a time spoken of ⟨*went is the ~ tense*⟩ **5a** *of an interval between four, five, or eight musical notes* not altered by having a semitone added to or taken away from the top or bottom note; not AUGMENTED or DIMINISHED ⟨*~ fifth*⟩ ⟨*~ octave*⟩ – compare MINOR 3c **b** *of a musical cadence* passing from a DOMINANT chord to a TONIC chord, giving a feeling of completion **6a** having all organs or parts; *specif, of a flower* having both male and female reproductive structures (STAMENS and CARPELS) **b** *of a fungus* having sexual and asexual reproductive stages; producing both sexual and asexual spores [ME *parfit*, fr OF, fr L *perfectus*, fr pp of *perficere* to carry out, perfect, fr *per-* thoroughly + *facere* to make, do – more at DO] – **perfectness** *n*
*usage* Many people feel that since things either are or are not **perfect** it is illogical to speak of *very* **perfect** or *more* **perfect**, but the word has been used in this way since the 14th century ⟨*to form a more* **perfect** *union – US Declaration of Independence*⟩.

²**perfect** /pə'fekt/ *vt* **1** to make perfect; improve, refine **2** to bring to final form **3** to print the second side or both sides of (a printed sheet) – **perfecter** *n*, **perfectible** *adj*

³**perfect** /'puhfikt/ *n* the PRESENT PERFECT tense of a language; *also* a verb form expressing it (e g **have finished**, as opposed to *had finished*, which is PAST PERFECT)

**perfect binding** *n* bookbinding in which single leaves are held together with adhesive at the spine

**perfectibility** /pə'fektə'biləti/ *n* a capacity for improvement, esp in moral qualities

**perfection** /pə'feksh(ə)n/ *n* **1a** making or being perfect **b** freedom from (moral) fault or defect; flawlessness ⟨*the aim of the Buddhist is to obtain a ~ like the Buddha's*⟩ **c** full development; maturity ⟨*Greek civilization slowly flowered to ~*⟩ **2** (an example of) unsurpassable accuracy or excellence ⟨*the cake was ~*⟩

**perfectionism** /pə'fekshə,niz(ə)m/ *n* **1** the theological doctrine that a state of freedom from sin is attainable on earth **2** a disposition to regard anything short of perfection, esp in one's own work, as unacceptable – **perfectionist** *adj or n*

**perfective** /pə'fektiv/ *adj, of a verb form* (e g in Russian) showing that an action or event is completed before a particular time – compare IMPERFECTIVE – **perfective** *n*, **perfectively** *adv*, **perfectiveness**, **perfectivity** *n*

**perfectly** /'puhfiktli/ *adv* **1** in a perfect manner **2** to an adequate extent; quite ⟨*your dress will be ~ suitable for the party*⟩

**perfect number** *n* an INTEGER (e g 6 or 28) that is equal to the sum of all the integers by which it can be divided without leaving a remainder, including 1 but excluding itself

**perfecto** /pə'fektoh/ *n, pl* **perfectos** a thick cigar that tapers almost to a point at each end [Sp, perfect, fr L *perfectus*]

**perfect participle** *n, linguistics* PAST PARTICIPLE

**perfect pitch** *n, music* ABSOLUTE PITCH 2

**perfect square** *n* an INTEGER (e g 9 or 25) whose SQUARE ROOT is an integer

**perfect year** *n* a standard year of 355 days or a leap year of 385 days in the Jewish calendar

**perfervid** /puh'fuhvid/ *adj, formal* marked by exaggerated emotion; excessively fervent [NL *perfervidus*, fr L *per-* thoroughly + *fervidus* fervid]

**perfidy** /'puhfidi/ *n* being faithless or disloyal; treachery [L *perfidia*, fr *perfidus* faithless, fr *per fidem decipere* to betray, lit., to deceive by trust] – **perfidious** *adj*, **perfidiously** *adv*, **perfidiousness** *n*

**perfoliate** /pə'fohliət, -ayt/ *adj* **1** *of a leaf* having a base that curves completely round the stem so that the stem is enclosed by and appears to pass through the leaf **2** *of the antenna of a beetle or similar insect* having the joints near the tip expanded into flattened plates that appear to encircle the stalk that connects them [NL *perfoliata*, a plant having leaves pierced by the stem, fr L *per* through + *foliata*, fem of *foliatus* foliate] – **perfoliation** *n*

**perforate** /'puhfə,rayt/ *vt* **1** to make a hole through ⟨*an ulcer may ~ the duodenal wall*⟩; *specif* to make a line of holes in or between (e g rows of postage stamps in a sheet) to make separation easier **2** to pass through or into (as if) by making a hole ~ *vi* to penetrate or make a hole in a surface [L *perforatus*, pp of *perforare* to bore through, fr *per-* through + *forare* to bore – more at BORE] – **perforator** *n*

**perforated** /'puhfəraytid/ *also* **perforate** /'puhfərət/ *adj* **1** having a hole or series of holes; *esp, of stamps* having a specified number of perforations in 20 millimetres ⟨*the stamps are ~ 10*⟩ **2** characterized by perforation ⟨*a ~ ulcer*⟩

**perforation** /,puhfə'raysh(ə)n/ *n* **1** the act or process of perforating **2a** a hole or pattern made (as if) by piercing or boring **b** any of the series of holes between rows of postage stamps in a sheet that serve as an aid in separation

**perforce** /pə'faws/ *adv, formal* by force of circumstances [ME *par force* forcibly, fr MF]

**perform** /pə'fawm/ *vt* **1** to do; CARRY OUT ⟨*~ed a small service*⟩ **2a** to do in a formal manner or according to prescribed ritual ⟨*~ a marriage ceremony*⟩ **b** to give a rendering of; present ⟨*they ~ed a new play*⟩ ~ *vi* **1** to carry out an action or pattern of behaviour; act, function **2** to give a performance; play [ME *performen*, fr AF *performer*, alter. of OF *perfournir*, fr *per-* thoroughly (fr L) + *fournir* to complete – more at FURNISH] – **performable** *adj*, **performer** *n*
*synonyms* **Perform, execute, discharge, accomplish, achieve, effect**, and **fulfil** can all mean "carry out or into effect". **Perform** stresses the process rather than the result, and suggests carrying out a prescribed or established procedure with skill and care ⟨**perform** *a dance/an operation*⟩. **Execute** may replace **perform** to imply something requiring extreme care or skill ⟨**executed** *seven backward somersaults in a row*⟩, but it more generally suggests carrying out something planned or intended ⟨**execute** *an escape*⟩. **Discharge** refers to the successful completion of duties or responsibilities ⟨**discharge** *a debt to society*⟩. **Accomplish** stresses the successful completion of something requiring skill or ability. **Achieve** adds to **accomplish** a sense of difficulties overcome and honour gained. **Effect** suggests a powerful, often impersonal force in the thing or people concerned which brings about the desired result ⟨*marches and petitions finally* **effected** *a change in the law*⟩. **Fulfil** implies the realization of something possible, planned, or predicted ⟨**fulfil** *a promise/one's hopes*⟩.

**performance** /pə'fawməns/ *n* **1a** the execution of an action **b** something accomplished; a deed, feat **2** the fulfilment of a claim, promise, etc **3** a presentation to an audience of a (character in a) play, a piece of music, etc ⟨*two ~s a night*⟩ ⟨*gave a brilliant ~ in the title rôle*⟩ **4** the ability to perform or work (efficiently or well) ⟨*good engine ~ requires good tuning*⟩ **5** manner of reacting to stimuli; behaviour ⟨*the ~ of the stock market*⟩ **6** the manifestation of language capacity in actual speech and writing – compare COMPETENCE 2, PAROLE 4 **7** *informal* **7a** a lengthy or troublesome process or activity ⟨*going through the customs was such a ~!*⟩ **b** a display of bad behaviour ⟨*what a spoilt child! I never saw such a ~!*⟩ – **performatory** *adj*

**performative** /pə'fawmətiv/ *n* an expression that serves to effect a transaction or that constitutes the performance of the specified act by virtue of its utterance ⟨*many ~s are contractual ("I bet") or declaratory ("I declare war") utterances* – J L Austin⟩

**performing art** /pə'fawming/ *n* an art (e g music or drama) requiring public performance

¹**perfume** /'puhfyoohm/ *n* **1** a sweet or pleasant smell; a fragrance **2** a pleasant-smelling (liquid) preparation (e g of floral essences) *synonyms* see ²SMELL [MF *perfum*, prob fr OProv, fr *perfumar* to perfume, fr *per-* thoroughly (fr L) + *fumar* to smoke, fr L *fumare* – more at FUME]

²**perfume** /pə'fyoohm, 'puhfyoohm/ *vt* to fill or imbue with a sweet smell

**perfumery** /pə'fyoohm(ə)ri/ *n* **1** (the manufacture of) perfumes **2** a place where perfumes are made or sold

**perfumier** /pə'fyoohmiə/, **perfumer** /pə'fyoohmə/ *n* one who makes or sells perfumes

**perfunctory** /pə'fungkt(ə)ri/ *adj* characterized by routine or superficiality; mechanical, cursory ⟨*a ~ smile*⟩ △ peremptory [LL *perfunctorius*, fr L *perfunctus*, pp of *perfungi* to accomplish, get through with, fr *per-* through + *fungi* to perform – more at FUNCTION] – **perfunctorily** *adv*, **perfunctoriness** *n*

**perfuse** /pə'fyoohz/ *vt* **1** to force a liquid through (an organ or tissue), esp by way of the blood vessels **2** *formal* to suffuse [L *perfusus*, pp of *perfundere* to pour over, fr *per-* through + *fundere* to pour – more at FOUND] – **perfusion** *n*, **perfusive** *adj*

**pergola** /'puhgələ/ *n* an arbour or covered walk made by training climbing plants over a support (e g a trellis); *also* the support itself △ pagoda [It, fr L *pergula* projecting roof, vine arbour, perh fr *pergere* to proceed, come forwards]

¹**perhaps** /pə'haps/ *adv* possibly but not certainly; maybe ⟨*~ I'm mistaken*⟩ – sometimes used in polite requests ⟨*~ you would open it?*⟩ [*per* + *haps*, pl of *hap*]

²**perhaps** *n, informal* something open to doubt or conjecture

**peri** /'piəri/ *n* **1** a supernatural being in Persian folklore descended from fallen angels and excluded from paradise until penance is accomplished **2** a beautiful and graceful girl [Per *perī* fairy, genius, modif of Avestan *pairikā* witch; akin to L *paelex* concubine]

**peri-** /peri-/ *prefix* **1** all; round; about ⟨peri*scope*⟩ ⟨peri*patetic*⟩ **2** near ⟨peri*helion*⟩ ⟨peri*gee*⟩ **3** enclosing; surrounding ⟨peri*toneum*⟩ ⟨peri*style*⟩ [L, fr Gk, round, in excess, fr *peri;* akin to Gk *peran* to pass through – more at FARE]

**perianth** /'peri,anth/ *n* the outer part of a flower, that surrounds the reproductive parts (eg the STAMENS) and consists of the petals and SEPALS, esp when these are not differentiated [NL *perianthium,* fr *peri-* + Gk *anthos* flower – more at ANTHOLOGY]

**periapt** /'periapt/ *n* an amulet, charm [MF or Gk; MF *periapte,* fr Gk *periapton,* fr *periaptein* to fasten round (oneself), fr *peri-* + *haptein* to fasten]

**pericarditis** /,perikah'dietəs/ *n* inflammation of the pericardium [NL]

**pericardium** /-'kahdi•əm, -dyəm/ *n, pl* **pericardia** /-diə/ **1** the membranous sac that surrounds the heart of a VERTEBRATE animal **2** the cavity or space that contains the heart, esp in an insect, snail, centipede, or similar INVERTEBRATE animal [NL, fr Gk *perikardion,* neut of *perikardios* round the heart, fr *peri-* + *kardia* heart – more at HEART] – **pericardial** *adj*

**pericarp** /-,kahp/ *n* the structure that surrounds the seed or seeds of a fruit and consists of the ripened and modified wall of a plant OVARY (seed-bearing organ) [NL *pericarpium,* fr Gk *perikarpion* pod, fr *peri-* + *-karpion* -carp]

**perichondrium** /-'kondri•əm/ *n, pl* **perichondria** /-driə/ the membrane of strong fibrous tissue that surrounds cartilage except at joints [NL, fr *peri-* + Gk *chondros* grain, cartilage – more at GRIND] – **perichondrial** *adj*

**periclase** /'periklays/ *n* naturally occurring MAGNESIUM OXIDE, MgO [Ger *periklas,* fr It *periclasia,* fr Gk *periklasis* act of twisting or breaking round, fr *periklan* to twist or break round, fr *peri-* + *klan* to break]

**pericope** /pə'rikəpi/ *n* a selection from a book: eg **a** LECTION 1 (lesson read in church) **b** a short unit of written narrative or discourse (eg in a New Testament Gospel) [LL, fr Gk *perikopē* section, fr *peri-* + *kopē* act of cutting; akin to Gk *koptein* to cut – more at CAPON]

**pericranium** /-'kraynyəm, -ni•əm/ *n, pl* **pericrania** /-nyə/ the strong fibrous membrane forming the external covering of the skull [NL, fr Gk *perikranion,* neut of *perikranios* round the skull, fr *peri-* + *kranion* skull] – **pericranial** *adj*

**pericycle** /-,siekl/ *n* a thin layer of cells that surrounds the central region (STELE) of water- and food-conducting tissues in many stems and roots [Fr *péricycle,* fr Gk *perikyklos* spherical, fr *peri-* + *kyklos* circle – more at WHEEL] – **pericyclic** *adj*

**pericynthion** /,peri'sinthiən/ *n* PERILUNE (point of a body's orbit closest to the moon) [NL, fr *peri-* + *Cynthia* + *-on* (as in *perihelion*)]

**periderm** /-,duhm/ *n* a typically thick outer protective tissue layer surrounding some plant parts, esp woody and some older roots and stems, that consists of cork (PHELLEM) and associated tissues (PHELLOGEN and PHELLODERM) [NL *peridermis,* fr *peri-* + *-dermis*] – **peridermal, peridermic** *adj*

**peridium** /pi'ridiəm/ *n, pl* **peridia** /-diə/ the outer wall of the spore-bearing structure of many fungi [NL, fr Gk *pēridion,* dim. of *pēra* leather bag]

**peridot** /'peridot, -doh/ *n* a deep yellowish-green transparent variety of the mineral OLIVINE used as a gem [Fr *péridot,* fr OF *peritot*] – **peridotic** *adj*

**peridotite** /,peri'dohtiet/ *n* any of a group of dark coarse-grained IGNEOUS rocks (rocks formed by the solidification of molten rock) composed of minerals, esp OLIVINE, containing iron and magnesium [Fr *péridotite,* fr *péridot*] – **peridotitic** *adj*

**perigee** /'peri,jee/ *n* the point in an orbit (eg of a satellite or vehicle) round the earth that is nearest to the centre of the earth; *also* the point nearest a planet or satellite (eg the moon) reached by any object orbiting it – compare APOGEE [MF, fr NL *perigeum,* fr Gk *perigeion,* fr neut of *perigeios* near the earth, fr *peri-* + *gē* earth] – **perigean** *adj*

**perigynous** /pə'rijinəs/ *adj* **1** *of flower structures* (eg the petals) borne in a ring on the top of the receptacle surrounding an OVARY (seed-bearing structure) **2** *of a flower* having perigynous petals, SEPALS, etc [NL *perigynus,* fr *peri-* + *-gynus* -gynous] – **perigyny** *n*

**perihelion** /,peri'heeli•ən, -lyən/ *n, pl* **perihelia** /-lyə/ the point in the path of a planet, comet, etc that is nearest to the sun – compare APHELION [NL, fr *peri-* + Gk *hēlios* sun – more at SOLAR] – **perihelial, perihelic** *adj*

**perikaryon** /,peri'kariən, -on/ *n, pl* **perikarya** /-kariə/, **perikaryons 1** CELL BODY (nucleus-containing part of a NERVE CELL) **2** the CYTOPLASM (jellylike material inside a cell) surrounding the nucleus of a CELL BODY [NL, fr *peri-* + Gk *karyon* nut, kernel]

**peril** /'perəl, -ril/ *n* **1** exposure to the risk of being injured, destroyed, or lost; danger ⟨*fire put the city in* ~⟩ **2** something that imperils; a risk ⟨*lessen the* ~s *of the streets*⟩ **synonyms** see DANGER [ME, fr OF, fr L *periculum* – more at FEAR]

**perilla** /pə'rilə/ *n* any of a genus (*Perilla*) of plants of the mint family widely distributed in America and Europe, but cultivated mainly in Asia [NL, genus name, perh dim. of *pera* leather bag, wallet, fr Gk *pēra*]

**perilla oil** *n* a light yellow oil obtained from seeds of perillas (esp *Perilla frutescens*) and used in the manufacture of paint, varnish, linoleum, etc, and in oriental countries as an edible oil

**perilous** /'periləs/ *adj* full of or involving peril; hazardous – **perilously** *adv,* **perilousness** *n*

**perilune** /'peri,loohn/ *n* the point in the path of a body orbiting the moon that is nearest to the centre of the moon – compare APOLUNE; called also PERICYNTHION, PERISELENE [*peri-* + L *luna* moon – more at LUNAR]

**perilymph** /-,limf/ *n* the clear liquid in the INNER EAR, that separates the MEMBRANOUS LABYRINTH (part containing the sensory structures concerned with hearing and balance) from the surrounding BONY LABYRINTH and acts as a shock absorber and in the transmission of sound vibrations [ISV]

**perimeter** /pə'rimitə/ *n* **1** (the length of) the boundary of a closed plane figure (eg a square or circle) **2** a line, strip, fence, etc bounding or protecting an area **3** the outer edge or limits of something ⟨*beyond the* ~ *of my field of vision*⟩ △ parameter [Fr *périmètre,* fr L *perimetros,* fr Gk, fr *peri-* + *metron* measure – more at MEASURE]

**per impossibile** /peər ,impo'seebilay/ *adv* by an impossibility [L]

**perimysium** /,peri'miz(h)yəm/ *n, pl* **perimysia** /-z(h)yə/ the sheath of strong elastic tissue that surrounds a bundle of muscle fibres [NL, irreg fr *peri-* + Gk *mys* mouse, muscle – more at MOUSE]

**perinatal** /,peri'naytl/ *adj* (occurring) at about the time of birth

**perineum** /-'nee•əm/ *n, pl* **perinea** /-'nee•ə/ the area between the anus and the rear part of the genitals, esp in the female [NL, fr LL *perinaion,* fr Gk, fr *peri-* + *inein* to empty out; akin to L *ira* ire] – **perineal** *adj*

**perineurium** /,peri'nyooəriəm/ *n, pl* **perineuria** /-riə/ the sheath of tissue that surrounds a bundle of nerve fibres [NL, fr *peri-* + Gk *neuron* nerve – more at NERVE]

¹**period** /'piəri•əd/ *n* **1a** a well-proportioned sentence of several clauses **b** a musical structure or melodic section usu composed of two or more contrasting or complementary phrases and ending with a CADENCE **2a** the full pause at the end of a sentence; *also, chiefly NAm* FULL STOP **b** a stop, end **3a** the (interval of) time that elapses before a cyclic motion or phenomenon begins to repeat itself **b** *maths* a number that does not change the value of a PERIODIC FUNCTION when added to the INDEPENDENT VARIABLE; *esp* the smallest such number **c** (a single occurrence of) menstruation **4a** a chronological division; a stage (of history) **b** a division of geological time longer than an epoch and included in an era – compare AGE 3c, AEON **5** any of the divisions of **a** the school day **b** the playing time of a game **6** *pl, formal* rhetorical language [ME *pariode,* fr MF *periode,* fr ML, L, & Gk; ML *periodus* period of time, punctuation mark, fr L & Gk; L, rhetorical period, fr Gk *periodos* circuit, period of time, rhetorical period, fr *peri-* + *hodos* way – more at CEDE]

²**period** *adj* of or representing a particular historical period ⟨~ *furniture*⟩

**periodic** /,piəri'odik/ *adj* **1** recurring at regular intervals **2** consisting of or containing a series of repeated stages; cyclic ⟨~ *decimals*⟩ ⟨*a* ~ *vibration*⟩ **3** expressed in or characterized by PERIODIC SENTENCES

**synonyms** Periodic, sporadic, intermittent, occasional, fitful, and spasmodic may all suggest recurrence over a period of time. What is **periodic** is usually regular or at least fairly predictable

⟨periodic *epidemics of flu*⟩. **Sporadic**, in contrast, describes what is irregular or unpredictable ⟨**sporadic** *outbursts of violence*⟩. **Intermittent** suggests something that comes and goes, and stresses the break in continuity. What is **occasional** occurs at random and is usually infrequent and unimportant ⟨*an* **occasional** *drink*⟩. **Fitful** stresses variability and suggests brief, sudden, and occasional activity ⟨**fitful** *sunshine of an April day*⟩. **Spasmodic** adds to fitful a heightened contrast between extreme activity and little or none ⟨*has a* **spasmodic** *interest in world peace*⟩. **antonyms** continuous, constant

**periodic acid** /puh·ie'odik/ *n* any of the acids (e g $H_5IO_6$ or $HIO_4$) that have the highest proportion of oxygen of any of the acids of iodine and are strong OXIDIZING AGENTS [ISV *per-* + *iodic*]

¹**periodical** /ˌpiəri'odikl/ *adj* 1 PERIODIC 1 2 *of a magazine or journal* published at fixed intervals (e g weekly or quarterly) – **periodically** *adv*

²**periodical** *n* a periodical publication

**periodical cicada** *n* a cicada (*Cicada septendecim*) of the USA that has a life of 17 years in the north and 13 years in the south, most of which is spent underground as a NYMPH (immature larva with undeveloped wings) with only a few weeks as a winged adult

**periodic function** *n* a mathematical function (e g SINE or COSINE) any of whose possible values recurs at regular intervals

**periodicity** /ˌpiəriə'disəti/ *n* the quality, state, or fact of being regularly recurrent

**periodic law** *n* a law in chemistry on which the PERIODIC TABLE is based: the chemical elements when arranged in the order of their ATOMIC NUMBERS (number of protons in the nucleus of an atom) show a periodic variation in most of their properties

**periodic sentence** *n* a complex sentence that has no subordinate or trailing elements following its principal clause (e g in "yesterday while I was walking down the street, I saw him")

**periodic table** *n* an arrangement of the chemical elements based on the PERIODIC LAW

**periodontal** /ˌperi-oh'dontl/ *adj* (of or affecting tissues) surrounding or covering a tooth – **periodontally** *adv*

**periodontal membrane** *n* a membrane of tissue that covers the CEMENTUM (bony layer covering the roots of a tooth) and attaches a tooth to its socket

**periodontics** /-'dontiks/ *n taking sing or pl vb* a branch of dentistry that deals with diseases of the supporting structures and tissues of the teeth [NL *periodontium*, fr *peri-* + Gk *odont-*, *odous*, *odōn* tooth – more at TOOTH] – **periodontic** *adj*, **periodontist** *n*

**periodontology** /-don'tolaji/ *n* periodontics

**period piece** *n* a piece (e g of fiction, art, furniture, or music) whose special value lies in its evocation of a historical period

**perionychium** /ˌperioh'nikiəm/ *n, pl* **perionychia** /-kiə/ the tissue bordering the root and sides of a fingernail or toenail [NL, fr *peri-* + Gk *onych-*, *onyx* nail – more at NAIL]

**periost-** /periost-/, **perioste-**, **periosteo-** *comb form* periosteum ⟨*periosteomyelitis*⟩ ⟨*periosteoma*⟩ ⟨*periostitis*⟩ [NL *periosteum*]

**periosteal** /ˌperi'ostiəl/ *adj* 1 situated round or produced outside bone 2 of, involving, or affecting the periosteum

**periosteum** /ˌperi'osti·əm/ *n, pl* **periostea** /-stiə/ the membrane of strong fibrous tissue that surrounds all bones except at joints [NL, fr LL *periosteon*, fr Gk, neut of *periosteos* round the bone, fr *peri-* + *osteon* bone – more at OSSEOUS]

**periostitis** /ˌperio'stietəs/ *n* inflammation of the periosteum [NL]

**periostracum** /ˌperi'ostrəkəm/ *n, pl* **periostraca** /-kə/ a horny (CHITINOUS) layer forming the outer covering of the shell of a clam, oyster, scallop, etc [NL, fr *peri-* + Gk *ostrakon* shell]

**periotic** /ˌperi'otik/ *adj* situated round the ear; *specif* being, relating to, or composed of (any of) the typically three bony elements that surround the INNER EAR and (help to) form its capsule [*peri-* + *-otic*]

¹**peripatetic** /ˌperipə'tetik/ *n* 1 *cap* a follower of Aristotle or adherent of Aristotelianism 2 somebody, esp a teacher unattached to a particular school, or something that travels about from place to place (on business) ⟨*she was appointed to teach music in the area as a* ~⟩

²**peripatetic** *adj* 1 *cap* Aristotelian 2 of walking; itinerant [MF & L; MF *peripatetique*, fr L *peripateticus*, fr Gk *peripatētikos*, fr *peripatein* to walk up and down, discourse while pacing (as

did Aristotle(, fr *peri-* + *patein* to tread; akin to Skt *patha* path – more at FIND] – **peripatetically** *adv*, **Peripateticism** *n*

**peripatus** /pə'ripətəs/ *n* a small primitive tropical sluglike animal (phylum Onychophora) that is related to the insects, spiders, centipedes, etc (ARTHROPODS) but has a thin flexible covering and short stumpy unjointed legs [NL, genus name, fr Gk *peripatos* act of walking about, fr *peri-* + *patein* to tread]

**peripeteia** /pə,ripi'tie·ə, -'tee·ə/ *n* a sudden or unexpected reversal of circumstances or situation, esp in a literary work [Gk, fr *peripiptein* to fall round, change suddenly, fr *peri-* + *piptein* to fall – more at FEATHER]

¹**peripheral** /pə'rif(ə)rəl/ *adj* 1 of, involving, or forming a periphery; *also* of minor significance ⟨~ *criticisms of a fine book*⟩ 2 located away from a centre or central portion; external 3a of, affecting, involving, or situated at or near the surface of (a part of) the body of a plant or animal b of, being, or supplying the part of the nervous system other than the brain and SPINAL CORD 4 of, using, or being the outer part of the field of vision ⟨*good* ~ *vision*⟩ 5 auxiliary, supplementary ⟨~ *equipment*⟩ – **peripherally** *adv*

²**peripheral** *n* a device (e g a VDU or printer) connected to a computer to provide communication with the computer or to supply auxiliary functions ⟨e g additional storage⟩

**periphery** /pə'rif(ə)ri/ *n* 1 the external boundary or surface of something, esp as distinguished from its internal regions or centre; the edge ⟨*hovered on the* ~ *of the group*⟩ 2a the external surface of (a part of) the body of a plant or animal b the regions outside the brain and SPINAL CORD (e g the SENSE ORGANS, the muscles, or the viscera) in which nerves terminate [MF *peripherie*, fr LL *peripheria*, fr Gk *periphereia*, fr *peripherein* to carry round, fr *peri-* + *pherein* to carry – more at BEAR]

**periphrasis** /pə'rifrəsis/ *n, pl* **periphrases** /-seez/ (a) use of roundabout phrasing; (a) circumlocution [L, fr Gk, fr *periphrazein* to express periphrastically, fr *peri-* + *phrazein* to point out]

**periphrastic** /ˌperi'frastik/ *adj* 1 of or characterized by periphrasis 2 formed by the use of FUNCTION WORDS or auxiliaries instead of by inflection (e g *more fair* as contrasted with *fairer*) – **periphrastically** *adv*

**periphyton** /pə'rifiton/ *n* organisms (e g some algae) that live underwater attached to parts of rooted aquatic plants [NL, fr Gk *periphytos* (verbal of *periphyein* to grow round, fr *peri-* + *phyein* to bring forth, grow) + *-on* (as in *plankton*) – more at BE] – **periphytic** *adj*

**periplast** /'periplast/ *n* the membrane or outer covering surrounding a cell or single-celled organism

**periproct** 'periprokt/ *n* the well-defined area surrounding the anus of SEA URCHINS and similar related animals [ISV *peri-* + Gk *prōktos* anus]

**peripteral** /pə'riptərəl/ *adj* surrounded by a single row of columns ⟨*a* ~ *temple*⟩ [L *peripteros*, fr Gk, fr *peri-* + *pteron* feather, wing, row of columns]

**perique** /pə'reek/ *n* a rich-flavoured aromatic air-cured Louisiana tobacco used in smoking mixtures [LaF *périque*]

**perisarc** /'perisahk/ *n* the outer usu CHITINOUS (horny) layer of a HYDROID (branching seaweedlike animal) [ISV *peri-* + Gk *sark-*, *sarx* flesh – more at SARCASM]

**periscope** /'periˌskohp/ *n* a tubular optical instrument containing lenses, mirrors, or prisms for seeing objects not in the direct line of sight – compare HYDROSCOPE [ISV]

**periscopic** /-'skopik/ *adj* 1 providing a view all round or on all sides ⟨~ *lens*⟩ 2 of a periscope

**periselene** /-si'leeni/ *n* PERILUNE (point of a body's orbit nearest to the moon) [ISV *peri-* + Gk *selēnē* moon – more at SELENIUM]

**perish** /'perish/ *vt, of cold or exposure* to weaken, numb – usu pass ⟨*we were* ~*ed with cold*⟩ ~ *vi* 1 to be destroyed or ruined ⟨*recollection of a past already long since* ~*ed* – Philip Sherrard⟩ ⟨~ *the thought!*⟩ 2 *chiefly Br* to deteriorate, spoil ⟨*the rubber had begun to* ~⟩ 3 *poetic or journalistic* to die, esp in a terrible or sudden way [ME *perisshen*, fr OF *periss-*, stem of *perir*, fr L *perire*, fr *per-* to destruction + *ire* to go – more at ISSUE]

**perishable** /'perishəbl/ *n or adj* (something, esp food) liable to spoil or decay ⟨*such* ~ *products as fruit, vegetables, butter, and eggs*⟩ – **perishability** *n*

**perisher** /'perishə/ *n, Br informal* an annoying or troublesome person or thing; *esp* a mischievous child

**perishing** /'perishing/ *adj, informal* 1 freezingly cold 2 damnable, confounded ⟨*the* ~ *old blighter wouldn't have it* – Margery Allingham⟩ – **perishingly** *adv*

**perispomenon** /ˌperiˈspohminon/ adj, of a Greek word having a CIRCUMFLEX accent (ˆ) on the final syllable [Gk perispōmenon, n, fr perispan to pronounce or mark with a circumflex accent, draw round, fr peri- + span to draw] – **perispomenon** n

**perissodactyl** /pəˌrisohˈdaktil/ n any of an order (Perissodactyla) of hoofed mammals (e g the horse, tapir, or rhinoceros) that are NONRUMINANT (do not chew the cud) and that usu have an odd number of toes on each foot [NL Perissodactyla, group name, fr Gk perissos excessive, odd in number + daktylos finger, toe] – **perissodactyl** adj

**peristalsis** /ˌperiˈstalsis/ n successive waves of involuntary muscular contraction that pass along the walls of a hollow muscular structure, esp the intestine, and force the contents onwards [NL, fr Gk peristaltikos peristaltic]

**peristaltic** /ˌperiˈstaltik/ adj 1 of, resulting from, or being peristalsis 2 having an action suggestive of peristalsis ⟨a ~ pump⟩ [Gk peristaltikos, fr peristellein to wrap round, fr peri- + stellein to place – more at STALL] – **peristaltically** adv

**peristome** /ˈperistohm/ n 1 the fringe of teethlike projections surrounding the opening of the spore-bearing capsule of a moss 2 the region round the mouth in various INVERTEBRATE animals (e g starfish, earthworms, and some single-celled organisms) [NL peristoma, fr peri- + Gk stoma mouth – more at STOMACH] – **peristomial** adj

**peristyle** /ˈperistiel/ n 1 a colonnade surrounding a building or court 2 an open space enclosed by a colonnade [Fr péristyle, fr L peristylum, fr Gk peristylon, fr neut of peristylos surrounded by a colonnade, fr peri- + stylos pillar – more at STEER]

**perithecium** /ˌperiˈtheesiəm/ n, pl perithecia /-siə/ a spherical, cylindrical, or flask-shaped hollow spore-producing structure (FRUITING BODY) in various ASCOMYCETOUS fungi, that contains the ASCI (spore-containing sacs) and usu opens by a pore at the end or tip [NL, fr peri- + Gk thēkion, dim. of thēkē case – more at TICK] – **perithecial** adj

**periton-, peritone-, peritoneo-** comb form peritoneum ⟨peritonitis⟩ [LL peritoneum]

**peritoneum** /ˌperitohˈnee-əm/ n, pl peritoneums, peritonea /-ˈnee-ə/ 1 the smooth transparent membrane that lines the cavity of the abdomen of a mammal and is folded inwards over the organs (e g the stomach, intestines, and kidneys) of the abdomen and pelvis 2 PLEUROPERITONEUM (membrane like the peritoneum in vertebrate animals other than mammals) [LL, fr Gk peritonaion, neut of peritonaios stretched round, fr peri- + teinein to stretch – more at THIN] – **peritoneal** adj, **peritoneally** adv

**peritonitis** /ˌperitəˈnietəs/ n inflammation of the peritoneum [NL]

**peritrichous** /pəˈritrikəs/ adj 1 of a single-celled organism having FLAGELLA (whiplike structures used for movement) uniformly distributed over the body ⟨a ~ bacterium⟩ 2 of or being a single-celled organism having a spiral line of modified CILIA (hairlike structures) round the mouth [peri- + Gk trich-, thrix hair – more at TRICH-] – **peritrichously** adv

**periwig** /ˈperiwig/ n PERUKE (long curly wig) [modif of MF perruque] – **periwigged** adj

¹**periwinkle** /ˈperiwingkl/ n any of several trailing often woody evergreen plants (genus Vinca of the family Apocynaceae, the periwinkle family): e g **a** a slender-stemmed Eurasian plant (Vinca minor) widely cultivated as a ground cover and for its blue or white flowers **b** a robust European plant (Vinca major) with large blue or white flowers **c** periwinkle, Madagascar periwinkle a commonly cultivated tropical shrub (Vinca rosea) that is the source of several anticancer drugs (e g VINBLASTINE and VINCRISTINE) [ME perwinke, fr OE perwince, fr L pervinca, perh fr per- through + vincire to bind]

²**periwinkle** n any of various small aquatic snails: e g **a** any of a genus (Littorina) of edible marine snails that inhabit seashores; also any of various similar or related marine snails **b** any of several N American freshwater snails [(assumed) ME, alter. of OE pīnewincle, fr L pina, a kind of mussel (fr Gk) + OE -wincle (prob akin to Dan vincle snail shell)]

**perjure** /ˈpuhjə/ vt to make (oneself) guilty of perjury [MF perjurer, fr L perjurare, fr per- to destruction, to the bad + jurare to swear – more at JURY]

**perjurer** /ˈpuhjərə/ n a person guilty of perjury

**perjury** /ˈpuhj(ə)ri/ n the voluntary violation of an oath, esp by a witness

¹**perk** /puhk/ n, chiefly Br a privilege, gain, or profit incidental to regular salary or wages; esp one expected or promised ⟨they mentioned various ~s at the interview, such as the use of one of the firm's cars⟩ [by shortening & alter. fr perquisite]

²**perk** vi, of coffee to percolate [by shortening & alter.]

**perk up** vb, informal, vi to recover one's vigour or cheerfulness, esp after a period of weakness or depression ⟨perked up when the letter arrived⟩ ~ vt 1 to make smart or spruce in appearance; freshen, improve ⟨perk up the outfit with a red scarf⟩ 2 to restore vigour or cheerfulness to ⟨a drink will perk him up⟩ [perch, fr perque perch, fr L pertica pole ME perken to behave jauntily, smarten, perh fr ONF perquer to perch, fr perque perch, fr L pertica pole]

**perky** /ˈpuhki/ adj, informal 1 briskly self-assured; cocky ⟨a ~ salesman⟩ 2 lively, jaunty ⟨she seemed a bit perkier after her holiday⟩ ⟨a ~ polka tune⟩ [perk (up) + ¹-y] – **perkily** adv, **perkiness** n

**perlite** also **pearlite** /ˈpuhliet/ n a usu greyish VOLCANIC GLASS (substance formed from rapidly cooled lava) that appears as if composed of small globular bodies and when expanded by heat forms a lightweight aggregate used esp in concrete and plaster or as a soil conditioner to assist drainage [Fr, fr perle pearl] – **perlitic** adj

**perlocutionary force** /ˌpuhləˈkyooshənri/ n the effect (e g persuading, frightening, or amusing) that happens to be accomplished by an utterance – compare ILLOCUTIONARY FORCE [ML perlocution-, perlocutio act of speaking, fr L per- + locutio speech – more at LOCUTION]

¹**perm** /puhm/ n (the giving of) a PERMANENT WAVE ⟨had a ~⟩

²**perm** vt, Br to give a perm to ⟨had her hair ~ed⟩

³**perm** n, Br PERMUTATION 2; specif any of the possible combinations of teams that can be chosen in the FOOTBALL POOLS

⁴**perm** vt, Br to permute; specif to pick out and combine (a specified number of teams in the FOOTBALL POOLS) in all the possible permutations ⟨~ any 8 from 11⟩

**permafrost** /ˈpuhməˌfrost/ n a layer of permanently frozen ground in very cold regions (e g the Arctic and Antarctic) [permanent + frost]

**permalloy** /puhmˈaloy/ n an alloy of nickel and iron that is easily magnetized and demagnetized [permeability + alloy]

**permanence** /ˈpuhmənəns/ n being permanent; durability

**permanency** /ˈpuhmənənsi/ n 1 permanence 2 something permanent

¹**permanent** /ˈpuhmənənt/ adj 1 continuing or enduring without fundamental or marked change; lasting, stable 2 being a member of the civil service and therefore not subject to replacement according to political circumstances ⟨~ undersecretary at the Home Office⟩ [ME, fr MF, fr L permanent-, permanens, prp of permanēre to endure, fr per- throughout + manēre to remain – more at MANSION] – **permanently** adv, **permanentness** n

²**permanent** n, NAm 1 ¹PERM 2 a long-lasting straightening of the hair that is produced by chemical and mechanical means

**permanent magnet** n a magnet that retains its magnetization after removal of the magnetizing force

**permanent press** n (material subjected to) a treatment for fabric in which a chemical and heat are used for setting the shape and aiding wrinkle resistance

**permanent tissue** n plant tissue in which the cells have completed their growth and differentiation and have reached their final form

**permanent tooth** n any of the second set of teeth of a mammal that follow the MILK TEETH, typically last into old age, and in humans are 32 in number

**permanent wave** n a long-lasting wave set in the hair by chemicals and sometimes heat

**permanent way** n, Br the rails, sleepers, and ballast that make up the track of a railway system

**permanganate** /pəˈmangˌgənət, -ˌnayt/ n a usu dark purple manganese-containing chemical compound (SALT) formed by combination between PERMANGANIC ACID and a metal atom or other chemical group

**permanganic acid** /ˌpuhmanˈganik/ n an unstable strong acid, $HMnO_4$, that occurs chiefly in the form of a purple-coloured solution in water and has strong OXIDIZING properties [ISV]

**permeability** /ˌpuhmi-əˈbiləti/ n 1 being permeable 2 the property of a magnetizable substance that determines the ease with which it becomes a magnet and thus the effect it has on the MAGNETIC FLUX (strength of magnetic forces) operating in the region surrounding it

**permeable** /'puhmi·əbl/ *adj* capable of being permeated; *esp* having pores or openings that permit liquids or gases to pass through ⟨*a ~ membrane*⟩ ⟨*~ limestone*⟩ – **permeableness** *n*, **permeably** *adv*

**permeance** /'puhmiəns/ *n* 1 permeation 2 the permeability of a piece of a magnetizable substance equal to the reciprocal of the magnetic RELUCTANCE (resistance to the passage of a magnetic force)

**permease** /'puhmiayz, -ays/ *n* a substance (e g an ENZYME) that facilitates the transport of another substance across a cell membrane [ISV *perme-* (fr *permeate*) + *-ase*]

**permeate** /'puhmi,ayt/ *vi* to diffuse through or penetrate something ~ *vt* 1 to spread or diffuse through ⟨*a room ~*d *with tobacco smoke*⟩ 2 to pass through the pores or minute spaces of [L *permeatus*, pp of *permeare*, fr *per-* through + *meare* to go, pass; akin to MW *mynet* to go] – **permeant** *adj or n*, **permeation** *n*, **permeative** *adj*

**per mensem** /puh 'mensəm/ *adv* by the month [ML]

**Permian** /'puhmi·ən/ *adj or n* (of or being) the last geological period of the PALAEOZOIC era, or the corresponding system of rocks [*Perm*, region in E Russia]

**per mill** /pə 'mil/ *adv* per thousand [*per* + L *mille* thousand – more at MILE] – **permillage** *n*

**permissible** /pə'misəbl/ *adj* allowable [ME, fr ML *permissibilis*, fr L *permissus*, pp] – **permissibly** *adv*, **permissibility** *n*

**permission** /pə'mish(ə)n/ *n* formal consent; authorization [ME, fr MF, fr L *permission-*, *permissio*, fr *permissus*, pp of *permittere*]

**permissive** /pə'misiv/ *adj* 1 tolerant; *esp* accepting a relaxed social or sexual morality ⟨*the ~ society*⟩ 2 allowing (but not enforcing); optional ⟨*~ legislation*⟩ ⟨*reduced the ~ retirement age from 65 to 60*⟩ ⟨*the provision of Youth Service facilities . . . should become obligatory and not ~ – TES*⟩ [Fr *permissif*, fr L *permissus*, pp] – **permissively** *adv*, **permissiveness** *n*

¹**permit** /pə'mit/ *vb* -tt- *vt* 1 to consent to, usu expressly or formally ⟨*~ access to records*⟩ 2 to give leave; authorize 3 to make possible ⟨*facts ~ no other explanation*⟩ ~ *vi* to give an opportunity; allow ⟨*if time ~*s⟩ ⟨*weather ~*ting⟩ [L *permittere* to let through, permit, fr *per-* through + *mittere* to let go, send] – **permitter** *n*

²**permit** /'puhmit/ *n* a written warrant allowing the holder to do or keep something ⟨*a cheap travel ~*⟩ ⟨*a gun ~*⟩

**permittivity** /,puhmi'tivəti/ *n* (a measure of) the ability of a DIELECTRIC (substance that does not conduct an electric current) to store electrical POTENTIAL ENERGY when placed in an electric field [¹*permit* + *-ive* + *-ity*]

**permutation** /,puhmyoo'taysh(ə)n/ *n* 1 a variation or change (e g in character or condition) brought about by rearrangement of existing elements ⟨*land-owners and peasants . . . in the ~*s of *their tortured interdependence* – P E Mosley⟩ **2a** the act or process of changing or rearranging the order of an ordered set of objects, numbers, letters, etc; the rearrangement of one permutation to form another **b** any of the possible ordered arrangements of a set of objects, numbers, letters, etc – compare COMBINATION [ME *permutacioun* exchange, transformation, fr MF *permutation*, fr L *permutation-*, *permutatio*, fr *permutatus*, pp of *permutare*] – **permutational** *adj*

**permutation group** *n*, *maths* a GROUP whose elements are permutations and in which the result of applying two permutations successively is equivalent to the effect of applying some single permutation ⟨*the set of rotations that map a cube onto itself form a ~*⟩

**permute** /pə'myooht/ *vt* to change the order or arrangement of; *esp* to arrange successively in all possible ways [ME *permuten*, fr MF or L; MF *permuter*, fr L *permutare*, fr *per-* + *mutare* to change – more at MISS]

**pernicious** /pə'nishəs, puh-/ *adj* highly injurious or destructive; deadly [MF *pernicieus*, fr L *perniciosus*, fr *pernicies* ruin, destruction, fr *per-* + *nec-*, *nex* violent death – more at NOXIOUS] – **perniciously** *adv*, **perniciousness** *n*

**pernicious anaemia** *n* a severe form of anaemia marked by a progressive decrease in number and increase in size of the RED BLOOD CELLS and by pallor, weakness, and disturbances of the digestive and nervous systems, and that is associated with reduced ability to absorb VITAMIN $B_{12}$

**pernickety** /pə'nikəti/ *adj*, *informal* 1 fussy about small details; fastidious ⟨*a ~ teacher*⟩ 2 requiring precision and care ⟨*a ~ job*⟩ [perh alter. of *particular*]

**Pernod** /'puhnoh, 'peənoh/ *trademark* – used for a French aperitif with a strong aniseed flavour

**peroneal** /,perə'nee·əl/ *adj* of or near the FIBULA (outer bone of the lower leg) [NL *peroneus*, fr *perone* fibula, fr Gk *peronē*, lit., pin; akin to L *per* through – more at FOR]

**peroral** /,puhr'awrəl/ *adj* occurring through or by way of the mouth ⟨*~ infection*⟩ [ISV, fr L *per* through + *or-*, *os* mouth – more at ORAL] – **perorally** *adv*

**perorate** /'perərayt/ *vi* 1 to deliver a long, pompous, or highly rhetorical oration 2 to make a peroration [L *peroratus*, pp of *perorare* to declaim at length, wind up an oration, fr *per-* through + *orare* to speak – more at ORATION]

**peroration** /,perə'raysh(ə)n/ *n* 1 the concluding part of a discourse, esp an oration 2 a highly rhetorical speech – **perorational** *adj*

**peroxidase** /pə'roksidayz, -ays/ *n* any of a group of ENZYMES that increase the rate at which various substances combine with oxygen provided by peroxides

¹**peroxide** /pə'roksied/ *n* 1 an OXIDE (compound of oxygen with one other chemical element or group) containing a high proportion of oxygen; *esp* a compound containing the peroxy chemical group –O–O– 2 HYDROGEN PEROXIDE – not used technically [ISV] – **peroxidic** *adj*

²**peroxide** *vt* to bleach (hair) with HYDROGEN PEROXIDE – **peroxidation** *n*

**peroxide blonde** *n*, *chiefly derog* a woman with bleached rather than natural blond hair

**peroxisome** /pə'roksisohm/ *n* a specialized structure (ORGANELLE) within a living cell, that contains ENZYMES (e g peroxidase) concerned esp with the decomposition of peroxides [*peroxide* + ³*-some*] – **peroxisomal** *adj*

**peroxy** /pə'roksi/ *adj* being or containing the chemical group – O–O– usu in combination [ISV *per-* + *oxy-*]

¹**perpend** /'puhpənd/ *n* a stone that passes through a wall so that both ends are exposed [ME, fr MF *perpain*]

²**perpend** /pə'pend/ *vb*, *archaic vt* to reflect on carefully; ponder to be attentive; reflect [L *perpendere*, fr *per-* thoroughly + *pendere* to weigh – more at PENDANT]

¹**perpendicular** /,puhpən'dikyoolə/ *adj* **1a** being or standing at RIGHT ANGLES to the plane of the horizon; exactly upright **b** being at RIGHT ANGLES to a given line or plane 2 extremely steep; precipitous 3 *cap* being or built in a late GOTHIC style of architecture prevalent in Britain from the 15th to the 16th century characterized by large windows, FAN VAULTING, and an emphasis on vertical lines – compare DECORATED, EARLY ENGLISH **synonyms** see VERTICAL **antonym** horizontal [ME *perpendiculer*, fr MF, fr L *perpendicularis*, fr *perpendiculum* plumb line, fr *per-* + *pendēre* to hang – more at PENDANT] – **perpendicularly** *adv*, **perpendicularity** *n*

²**perpendicular** *n* a line, plane, or surface at RIGHT ANGLES to the plane of the horizon or to another line or surface

**perpetrate** /'puhpi,trayt/ *vt* to be guilty of performing or doing; commit ⟨*~ a fraud*⟩ ⟨*~ a blunder*⟩ △ perpetuate [L *perpetratus*, pp of *perpetrare*, fr *per-* through + *patrare* to accomplish, perh fr *patr-*, *pater* father] – **perpetrator** *n* **perpetration** *n*

**perpetual** /pə'petyoo(ə)l, -choo(ə)l/ *adj* **1a** continuing or valid forever; everlasting **b** holding something (e g an office) for life or for an unlimited time 2 occurring continually; constant ⟨*a ~ complaint*⟩ 3 *of a plant* blooming continuously throughout the season **synonyms** see CONTINUAL **antonyms** transitory, transient [ME *perpetuel*, fr MF, fr L *perpetuus*, fr *per-* through + *petere* to go to – more at FEATHER] – **perpetually** *adv*

**perpetual calendar** *n* 1 a table for finding the day of the week for any one of a wide range of dates 2 a calendar in which a given date occurs on the same day in any year 3 a display (e g on a frame or stand) that can be adjusted by means of movable words and figures to show the date of any day (in any year)

**perpetual check** *n* an endless succession of CHECKS (challenges to the king) in chess which results in a draw

**perpetuate** /pə'petyoo,ayt, -choo,ayt/ *vt* to make perpetual; cause to last indefinitely ⟨*~ the species*⟩ △ perpetrate [L *perpetuatus*, pp of *perpetuare*, fr *perpetuus*] – **perpetuator** *n*, **perpetuation** *n*

**perpetuity** /,puhpi'tyooh·əti/ *n* 1 (the quality or state of) something that is perpetual; eternity ⟨*bequeathed to them in ~*⟩ 2 (the condition of) an estate limited so that it cannot be disposed of for a period longer than that allowed by law 3 an ANNUITY (regular payment of money) payable for life [ME *perpetuite*, fr MF *perpetuité*, fr L *perpetuitat-*, *perpetuitas*, fr *perpetuus*]

**perphenazine** /pəˈfeenəzeen, -ˈfenə-/ *n* a chemical compound, $C_{21}H_{26}ClN_3OS$, derived from PHENOTHIAZINE that is used as a tranquillizer to control tension, anxiety, and agitation, esp in conditions of severe mental disorder (eg schizophrenia) [blend of *piperazine* and *phen-*]

**perplex** /pəˈpleks/ *vt* **1** to puzzle, confuse ⟨*her attitude* ∼es *me*⟩ ⟨*a* ∼ing *problem*⟩ **2** to complicate *synonyms* see ¹PUZZLE [obs *perplex*, adj, involved, perplexed, fr L *perplexus*, fr *per-* thoroughly + *plexus* involved, fr pp of *plectere* to braid, twine – more at PLY] – **perplexedly** *adv*, **perplexingly** *adv*

**perplexity** /pəˈpleksəti/ *n* **1** (something that causes) the state of being perplexed or bewildered **2** an entanglement [ME *perplexite*, fr OF *perplexité*, fr LL *perplexitat-*, *perplexitas*, fr L *perplexus*]

**perquisite** /ˈpuhkwizit/ *n* **1** something held or claimed as an exclusive right or possession ⟨*concepts . . . not the* ∼s *of any particular groups* – Gilbert Ryle⟩ **2** *formal* a perk △ prerequisite [ME, property acquired by other means than inheritance, fr ML *perquisitum*, fr neut of *perquisitus*, pp of *perquirere* to purchase, acquire, fr L, to search for thoroughly, fr *per-* thoroughly + *quaerere* to seek]

**perron** /ˈperən/ *n* an outdoor stairway leading up to a building entrance; *also* a platform at its top [Fr, fr OF, aug of *perre*, *pierre* rock, stone, fr L *petra*, fr Gk]

**perry** /ˈperi/ *n* an alcoholic drink made from fermented pear juice [ME *peirrie*, fr MF *peré*, fr (assumed) VL *piratum*, fr L *pirum* pear]

**perse** /puhs/ *adj* a dark greyish-blue colour [ME *pers*, fr MF, fr ML *persus*, perh fr L *Persa* Persian]

**per se** /pɜː ˈsay/ *adv* by, of, or in itself; intrinsically [L]

**per second per second** *adv* per second every second – used with reference to a constant rate of acceleration ⟨*each second the velocity increased* $2^{1}/_5$ *ft per second. The acceleration . . .was therefore* $2^{1}/_5$ *ft* ∼ – Geoffrey Dyson⟩

**persecute** /ˈpuhsiˌkyooht/ *vt* **1** to harass in a manner designed to injure or afflict; *specif* to cause to suffer because of race, religion, political beliefs, etc **2** to annoy with persistent or urgent approaches, attacks, pleas, etc; pester △ prosecute [MF *persecuter*, back-formation fr *persecuteur* persecutor, fr LL *persecutor*, fr *persecutus*, pp of *persequi* to persecute, fr L, to pursue, fr *per-* through + *sequi* to follow – more at SUE ] – **persecutor** *n*, **persecution** *n*, **persecutory** *adj*

**perseverance** /ˌpuhsiˈviərəns/ *n* **1** persevering, steadfastness **2** continuance in a state of GRACE (divine favour)

**perseveration** /puhˌsevəˈraysh(ə)n/ *n*, *psychology* continuation of something (eg repetition of a word), usu to an excessive or exceptional degree [L *perseveration-*, *perseveratio*, fr *perseveratus*, pp of *perseverare*] – **perseverate** *vi*

**persevere** /ˌpuhsiˈviə/ *vi* to persist in a state, enterprise, or undertaking in spite of adverse influences, opposition, or discouragement [ME *perseveren*, fr MF *perseverer*, fr L *perseverare*, fr *per-* through + *severus* severe] – **perseveringly** *adv*

**Persian** /ˈpuhsh(ə)n/; *also* -zh(ə)n/ *n* **1** a native or inhabitant of Persia: eg **1a** a member of the ancient Iranian CAUCASIAN people who were the dominant Asian race in the 6th century BC **b** a member of any of the peoples of modern Iran; an Iranian **2a** any of several Iranian languages dominant in Persia at different periods **b** the modern language of Iran and W Afghanistan; FARSI **3** a thin soft silk formerly used esp for linings [*Persia* (now Iran), country in SW Asia] – **Persian** *adj*

**Persian cat** *n* a short-nosed domestic cat with long silky fur

**Persian lamb** *n* **1** the young of the KARAKUL sheep **2** a black very silky tightly curled fur obtained from the skin of Persian lambs

**persiflage** /ˈpuhsiˌflahzh/ *n* frivolous bantering talk [Fr, fr *persifler* to banter, fr *per-* thoroughly + *siffler* to whistle, hiss, boo, fr L *sibilare*, of imit origin]

**persimmon** /puhˈsimən/ *n* **1** any of a genus (*Diospyros*) of American and Asian trees of the ebony family with hard fine wood, oblong leaves, and small bell-shaped white flowers **2** the usu orange several-seeded globular fruit of a persimmon that is edible when fully ripe but usu extremely astringent when unripe [of Algonquian origin; akin to Cree *pasiminan* dried fruit]

**persist** /pəˈsist/ *vi* **1** to go on resolutely or stubbornly in spite of opposition or warning **2** to be insistent in the repetition or pressing of an utterance (eg a question or an opinion) **3** to continue to exist; last, esp beyond a usual, expected, or normal time ⟨*the fine weather* ∼ed *despite the rain farther north*⟩

*synonyms* see CONTINUE *antonyms* cease, give up [MF *persister*, fr L *persistere*, fr *per-* + *sistere* to take a stand, stand firm; akin to L *stare* to stand – more at STAND] – **persister** *n*

**persistent** /pəˈsist(ə)nt/ *adj* **1a** continuing or inclined to persist in a course **b** continuing to exist or recur in spite of interference or treatment ⟨*a* ∼ *cough*⟩ **2** existing for a long or longer than usual time or continuously: eg **2a(1)** *of a plant structure* remaining as part of or attached to the plant beyond the usual period ⟨*a* ∼ *leaf*⟩ **a(2)** *of an animal structure* continuing to be present without change in function or structure; *esp, of a structure characteristic of a young or larval stage* remaining in the adult ⟨∼ *gills*⟩ **a(3)** *of a tooth* continuing to grow throughout life **b** *of a chemical substance* existing or effective in the environment for a long time; *esp* broken down only slowly in the environment ⟨∼ *pesticides*⟩ **c** *of a disease-causing agent (eg a virus)* remaining in an infective state in a carrier organism (VECTOR) for a relatively long time □ compare PERTINACIOUS [L *persistent-*, *persistens*, prp of *persistere*] – **persistence, persistency** *n*, **persistently** *adv*

**persnickety** /pəˈsnikəti/ *adj*, *NAm informal* **1** pernickety **2** snobbish [alter. of *pernickety*]

**person** /ˈpuhs(ə)n/ *n* **1a** an individual human being (considered as having a character of his/her own or as being different from all others) ⟨*you're just the* ∼ *I wanted to see*⟩ **b** a person belonging to a particular occupational category or exercising a particular function – usu in combination ⟨*spokes*person⟩ ⟨*sales*person⟩ ⟨*chair*person⟩ **2** any of the three modes of being in the Trinity as understood by Christians ⟨*God in three* ∼s⟩ **3a** a living human body or its outward appearance ⟨*she was small and neat of* ∼⟩ ⟨*insured against damage to* ∼ *and property*⟩ **b** a human being's clothed body ⟨*unlawful search of the* ∼⟩ ⟨*carrying an offensive weapon about his* ∼⟩ **4** a partnership, corporation, etc with recognized legal rights and duties **5** reference of a segment of discourse to the speaker (FIRST PERSON), to one spoken to (SECOND PERSON), or to someone or something spoken of (THIRD PERSON) as indicated by means of pronouns or by verb inflection [ME, fr OF *persone*, fr L *persona* actor's mask, character in a play, person, prob fr Etruscan *phersu* mask] – **in person** in one's own bodily presence ⟨*he appeared in* person *to introduce his film*⟩

*usage* Some combinations such as *sales*person are now used in the advertising of jobs for which it is no longer legal to specify sex, and others such as *sports*person to avoid the implication that women are excluded. *synonyms* see PEOPLE

**persona** /puhˈsohnə/ *n*, *pl* (*1*) **personae** /-nie/, (*2*) **personas** **1** *pl* the characters in a fictional work (eg a novel or play) ⟨*comic* personae⟩ **2** an individual's social facade or front that, esp in JUNGIAN psychology, reflects the role that the individual is playing in life – compare ANIMA [(1) L; (2) NL, fr L]

**personable** /ˈpuhs(ə)nəbl/ *adj* pleasing in person; attractive – **personableness** *n*

**personage** /ˈpuhs(ə)nij/ *n* **1** a person of rank, note, or distinction; *esp* one distinguished in presence and personal power **2** a dramatic, fictional, or historical character **3** *formal* a human individual; a person

*synonyms* An important person is now called a **VIP** or a **personality** more often than a **personage**; but a **personality** is likely to be a celebrity in the entertainment world, a **VIP** a high official, and a **personage** a member of the royal family.

**persona grata** /puhˌsohnə ˈgrahtə/ *adj* personally acceptable or welcome ⟨*you'll be* ∼ *on the committee with your fund-raising experience!*⟩ [NL, acceptable person]

**personal** /ˈpuhs(ə)nl/ *adj* **1** of or affecting a person; private ⟨*done purely for* ∼ *financial gain*⟩ **2a** done in person without the intervention of another; *also* proceeding from a single person **b** carried on between individuals directly ⟨*a* ∼ *interview*⟩ **3** of the person or body **4** of or referring to (the character, conduct, motives, or private affairs of) an individual, often in an offensive manner ⟨*a* ∼ *insult*⟩ ⟨*don't make* ∼ *remarks*⟩ **5** of PERSONAL PROPERTY ⟨*a* ∼ *estate*⟩ **6** denoting grammatical person [ME, fr MF, fr LL *personalis*, fr L *persona*]

**personal column** *n* a newspaper column containing personal messages, requests, notices, and advertisements which private individuals and organizations pay to have published

**personal equation** *n* (a correction made for) variation (eg in astronomical observation) due to human error

**personal foul** *n* a foul (eg in basketball) involving usu physical contact with or rough tactics against an opponent – compare TECHNICAL FOUL

**personalism** /ˈpuhsənəliz(ə)m/ *n* a doctrine emphasizing the

significance, uniqueness, and supreme value of personality –
**personalist** *n or adj*, **personalistic** *adj*
**personality** /'puhs(ə)n'aləti/ *n* **1** *pl* reference, esp critical, to a
particular person ⟨*let's keep* personalities *out of this debate*⟩ **2**
the totality of an individual's behavioural and emotional tendencies; *broadly* a distinguishing complex of individual or group
characteristics **3a** (somebody having) distinction or excellence
of personal and social traits **b** a person of importance, prominence, renown, or notoriety ⟨*a well-known stage* ~⟩
*synonyms* see PERSONAGE [ME *personalite*, fr LL *personalitat-,
personalitas*, fr *personalis*]
**personality cult** *n* the officially encouraged adulation of a
leader
**personal·ize, -ise** /'puhs(ə)nl,iez/ *vt* **1** PERSONIFY 1 **2** to make
personal or individual; *specif* to mark as the property of a particular person ⟨~d *stationery*⟩ – **personalization** *n*
**personally** /'puhs(ə)nli/ *adv* **1** IN PERSON ⟨*attend to the matter*
~⟩ **2** as a person; in personality ⟨~ *attractive but not very
trustworthy*⟩ **3** for oneself; as far as oneself is concerned ⟨~,
*I don't think much of it*⟩ **4** as directed against oneself in a
personal way ⟨*don't take my remarks about your plan* ~⟩
**personal pronoun** *n* a pronoun (eg *I, you,* or *they*) that expresses a distinction between speaker, spoken to, and spoken of
**personal property** *n* temporary or movable property (eg
goods or money)
**personal tax** *n* DIRECT TAX
**personalty** /'puhs(ə)nlti/ *n* PERSONAL PROPERTY △ personality [AF *personalté*, fr LL *personalitat-, personalitas* person-
ality]
**persona non grata** /puh,sohnə non 'grahtə/ *adj* personally
unacceptable or unwelcome ⟨*after the publication of his book,
he was* ~ *with the Russians*⟩ [NL, person not acceptable]
**personate** /'puhs(ə)nayt/ *vt* **1** to impersonate, represent **2** to
assume (some character or capacity) with fraudulent intent –
**personator** *n*, **personation** *n*, **personative** *adj*
**personification** /pə,sonifi'kaysh(ə)n/ *n* **1** the personifying of an
abstract quality or thing **2** an embodiment, incarnation ⟨*she's
the* ~ *of good sense*⟩
**personify** /pə'sonifie/ *vt* **1** to conceive of or represent as having
human qualities or form **2** to be the embodiment of in human
form ⟨*he was kindness* personified⟩ – **personifier** *n*
**personnel** /,puhsə'nel/ *n taking sing or pl vb* **1** a body of people
employed (eg in a factory, office, or organization) or engaged
on a project **2** a division of an organization concerned with
the employees and their welfare at work [Fr, fr Ger *personale,
personal*, fr ML *personale*, fr LL, neut of *personalis* personal]
*usage* Personnel should not be used with a definite number ⟨△
*six RAF* personnel⟩. △ personal
¹**perspective** /pə'spektiv/ *adj* of, using, or seen in perspective ⟨*a* ~ *drawing*⟩ △ prospective [ME, of sight,
optical, fr ML *perspectivus* of sight, fr L *perspectus*, pp of *perspicere* to look through, see clearly, fr *per-* through + *specere*
to look – more at SPY] – **perspectively** *adv*
²**perspective** *n* **1a** (the technique of accurately representing on
a flat or curved surface) the way in which the relationship of
solid objects to each other in space appears to the eye **b** LINEAR
PERSPECTIVE (representation of space in art by converging
parallel lines) **2a** the aspect of an object of thought from a
particular standpoint ⟨*try to get a different* ~ *on your problem*⟩
**b** (the capacity to discern) the true relationship or relative importance of things ⟨*see events in their historical* ~⟩ ⟨*get things
in* ~⟩ **3** a picture or view giving a distinctive impression of
distance; a vista [MF, fr ML *perspectiva*, fr fem of *perspectivus*]
**Perspex** /'puh,speks/ *trademark* – used for a tough transparent
ACRYLIC plastic
**perspicacious** /,puhspi'kayshəs/ *adj, formal* of acute mental
vision or discernment *synonyms* see SHREWD *antonym* dull [L
*perspicac-, perspicax*, fr *perspicere*] – **perspicaciously** *adv*, **per-
spicaciousness, perspicacity** *n*
**perspicuous** /pə'spikyoo·əs/ *adj, formal* plain to the understanding, esp because of clarity and precision of presentation
⟨*a* ~ *argument*⟩ – compare PERCEPTIBLE [L *perspicuus* transparent, clear, fr *perspicere*] – **perspicuously** *adv*, **perspicuous-
ness, perspicuity** *n*
**perspiration** /,puhspi'raysh(ə)n/ *n* **1** sweating **2** sweat –
**perspiratory** *adj*
**perspire** /pə'spie·ə/ *vi* SWEAT **1a** [Fr *perspirer*, fr MF, fr L *per-*
through + *spirare* to blow, breathe – more at SPIRIT]
**persuade** /pə'swayd/ *vt* **1** to move by argument, reasoning, or

pleading to a belief, position, or course of action ⟨~d *him to
leave*⟩ **2** to cause to feel certain; convince ⟨*the icy roads* ~d
*him of the need to drive carefully*⟩ **3** to get (something) with
difficulty *out of* or *from* ⟨*finally* ~d *an answer out of him*⟩ [L
*persuadēre*, fr *per-* thoroughly + *suadēre* to advise, urge –
more at SUASION] – **persuadable** *adj*, **persuader** *n*
**persuasible** /pə'swaysəbl, -zəbl/ *adj* persuadable [MF, fr L
*persuasibilis* persuasive, fr *persuasus*]
**persuasion** /pə'swayzh(ə)n/ *n* **1a** persuading or being persuaded
**b** persuasiveness ⟨*she has great powers of* ~⟩ **2a** an opinion
held with complete assurance ⟨*despite your arguments I remain
of the same* ~ *as before*⟩ **b** (a group adhering to) a particular
system of religious beliefs **3** a kind, sort ⟨*persons of the same*
~⟩ *synonyms* see OPINION [ME *persuasioun*, fr MF or L; MF
*persuasion*, fr L *persuasion-, persuasio*, fr *persuasus*, pp of *persuadēre*]
**persuasive** /pə'swaysiv, -ziv/ *adj* tending or able to persuade –
**persuasively** *adv*, **persuasiveness** *n*
**pert** /puht/ *adj* **1** impudent and forward; saucy **2** trim and chic;
jaunty ⟨*a* ~ *little hat*⟩ [ME, open, bold, pert, modif of OF
*apert*, fr L *apertus* open, fr pp of *aperire* to open] – **pertly** *adv*,
**pertness** *n*
**pertain** /pə'tayn/ *vi* **1a** to belong *to* as a part, attribute, feature,
function, or right ⟨*the destruction and havoc* ~ing *to war*⟩ **b**
to be appropriate to something ⟨*the new criteria that* ~ *elsewhere do not apply here*⟩ **2** to have reference *to* ⟨*books* ~ing
*to birds*⟩ [ME *perteinen*, fr MF *partenir*, fr L *pertinēre* to reach
to, belong, fr *per-* through + *tenēre* to hold]
**pertinacious** /,puhti'nayshəs/ *adj, formal* adhering resolutely
to an opinion, purpose, or design, often to the point of stubbornness – compare PERSISTENT *synonyms* see OBSTINATE [L *per-
tinac-, pertinax*, fr *per-* thoroughly + *tenac-, tenax* tenacious,
fr *tenēre*] – **pertinaciously** *adv*, **pertinaciousness, pertinacity**
*n*
**pertinent** /'puhtinənt/ *adj* clearly relevant to the matter in
hand ⟨~ *details*⟩ *synonyms* see RELEVANT *antonym* foreign
[ME, fr MF, fr L *pertinent-, pertinens*, prp of *pertinēre*] –
**pertinence, pertinency** *n*, **pertinently** *adv*
**perturb** /pə'tuhb, puh-/ *vt* **1** to disturb greatly in mind; disquiet
**2** to throw into confusion; disorder **3** to cause (a moving object,
celestial body, etc) to deviate from a theoretically regular (orbital)
motion [ME *perturben*, fr MF *perturber*, fr L *perturbare* to
throw into confusion, fr *per-* + *turbare* to disturb – more at
TURBID] – **perturbable** *adj*
**perturbation** /,puhtə'baysh(ə)n/ *n* **1** perturbing or being perturbed **2** a disturbance of the regular and usu elliptic course
of motion of a moving object, esp a celestial body, that is
produced by some force additional to that which causes its
regular motion – **perturbational** *adj*
**pertussis** /pə'tusis/ *n* WHOOPING COUGH [NL, fr L *per-* thoroughly + *tussis* cough]
**Peru balsam** /pə'rooh/ *n* BALSAM OF PERU (aromatic substance
used in perfumes, antiseptics, etc)
**peruke** /pə'roohk/ *n* a long curly wig worn by men in the 17th,
18th, and early 19th centuries [MF *perruque*, fr OIt *parrucca,
perrucca* hair, wig]
**peruse** /pə'roohz/ *vt* **1** *formal* to examine or consider with attention and in detail; study **2** *chiefly humorous* to look over the
contents of (eg a book); read [ME *perusen* to use up, work
through, prob fr L *per-* thoroughly + ME *usen* to use] –
**perusal** *n*, **peruser** *n*
**Peruvian bark** /pə'roohvyən/ *n* CINCHONA 2 (tree bark containing quinine) [NL *Peruvia* Peru, country in S America, fr Sp
*Perú*]
**pervade** /pə'vayd, puh-/ *vt* to become diffused throughout
every part of [L *pervadere* to go through, pervade, fr *per-*
through + *vadere* to go – more at WADE] – **pervasion** *n*, **pervasive** *adj*, **pervasively** *adv*, **pervasiveness** *n*
**perve** /puhv/ *n, chiefly Br derog* a pervert
**perverse** /pə'vuhs, puh-/ *adj* **1** contrary to the evidence or the
direction of the judge on a point of law ⟨~ *verdict*⟩ **2a** obstinate in opposing what is right, reasonable, or accepted;
wrongheaded **b** arising from or indicative of stubbornness or
obstinacy **3** unreasonably opposed to the wishes of others;
uncooperative △ perverted *synonyms* see UNRULY [ME, fr
L *perversus*, fr pp of *pervertere*] – **perversely** *adv*, **perversity,
perverseness** *n*
**perversion** /pə'vuhsh(ə)n, puh-/ *n* **1** perverting or being perverted **2** something perverted; *esp* (an instance of) abnormal
sexual behaviour – **perversive** *adj*

¹**pervert** /pə'vuht/ *vt* **1** to cause to turn aside or away from what is good, true, or morally right; corrupt **2a** to divert to a wrong end or purpose; misuse **b** to twist the meaning or sense of; misinterpret [ME *perverten*, fr MF *pervertir*, fr L *pervertere* to overturn, corrupt, fr *per-* thoroughly + *vertere* to turn – more at WORTH] – **perverter** *n*

²**pervert** /'puhvuht/ *n* a perverted person; *specif* one who practises some form of sexual perversion

**perverted** /pə'vuhtid, puh-/ *adj* **1** CORRUPT 1 **2** characterized by perversion △ perverse – **pervertedly** *adv*, **pervertedness** *n*

**pervious** /'puhvi·əs, -vyəs/ *adj* **1** porous, permeable ⟨~ *soil*⟩ **2** *formal* accessible *to* ⟨~ *to reason*⟩ [L *pervius*, fr *per-* through + *via* way – more at VIA] – **perviousness** *n*

**pes** /peez/ *n pl* **pedes** /'peedez, 'ped-/ the DISTAL (furthest from the body) segment of the hind limb of a VERTEBRATE animal including the TARSUS (ankle) and foot; *also* a footlike anatomical part that serves as a base [NL *ped-, pes*, fr L, foot – more at FOOT]

**Pesach** /'paysahkh/ *n* the Passover [Heb *pesaḥ*]

**pesante** /pe'zantay/ *adv* in a heavy manner – used as a direction in music [It, heavy, fr prp of *pesare* to weigh, fr L *pensare* to weigh, ponder – more at PENSIVE]

**peseta** /ˌpə'saytə/ *n* – see MONEY table [Sp, fr dim. of *peso*]

**pesewa** /pi'saywah/ *n* – see *cedi* at MONEY table [Fante]

**pesky** /'peski/ *adj, NAm informal* troublesome, vexatious [prob irreg fr *pest* + *-y*]

**peso** /'paysoh/ *n, pl* **pesos** **1** a former silver coin of Spain and Spanish America worth eight REALS **2** – see MONEY table **3** the former basic monetary unit of Chile, replaced in 1960 by the ESCUDO [Sp, lit., weight, fr L *pensum* – more at POISE]

**pessary** /'pesəri/ *n* **1** a vaginal SUPPOSITORY (small solid portion of medicine inserted in a body cavity or passage) **2** a device worn in the vagina to support the uterus or prevent conception [ME *pessarie*, fr LL *pessarium*, fr *pessus, pessum* pessary, fr Gk *pessos* oval stone for playing a game like draughts, pessary]

**pessimism** /'pesi,miz(ə)m/ *n* **1** a tendency to stress the adverse aspects of a situation or event or to expect the worst possible outcome **2** the doctrine that this is the worst of all possible worlds [Fr *pessimisme*, fr L *pessimus* worst – more at PEJORATIVE] – **pessimist** *n*, **pessimistic** *adj*, **pessimistically** *adv*

**pest** /pest/ *n* **1** a pestilence **2** a plant or animal capable of causing damage or carrying disease **3** somebody or something that pesters or annoys; a nuisance [MF *peste*, fr L *pestis*]

**Pestalozzian** /ˌpestə'lotsiən/ *adj* of Johann Heinrich Pestalozzi or his educational theories ⟨*the ~ system of education, which makes observation the first approach to learning*⟩ [Johann Heinrich *Pestalozzi* †1827 Swiss educator]

**pester** /'pestə/ *vt* to harass with petty irritations; annoy [modif (influenced by *pest*) of MF *empestrer* to hobble, embarrass, fr (assumed) VL *impastoriare*, fr L *in-* + (assumed) VL *pastoria* hobble, fr L *pastor* herdsman – more at PASTOR]

**pest house** *n, archaic* a hospital for contagious diseases

**pesticide** /'pestisied/ *n* any chemical (e g an insecticide, herbicide, or fungicide) used to destroy insects or other pests (e g bacteria or rodents) of crops, domestic animals, etc

**pestiferous** /pe'stif(ə)rəs/ *adj* **1** dangerous to society; pernicious **2** carrying or spreading infection **3** *humorous* troublesome, annoying [ME, fr L *pestifer* pestilential, noxious, fr *pestis* + *-fer* -ferous] – **pestiferously** *adv*, **pestiferousness** *n*

**pestilence** /'pestiləns/ *n* **1** a virulent and devastating epidemic disease; *specif* BUBONIC PLAGUE **2** something that is destructive or pernicious ⟨*I'll pour this ~ into his ear* – Shak⟩

**pestilent** /'pestilənt/ *adj* **1** destructive of life; deadly **2** morally harmful; pernicious **3** causing displeasure or annoyance; irritating [ME, fr L *pestilent-, pestilens* pestilential, fr *pestis*] – **pestilently** *adv*

**pestilential** /ˌpesti'lensh(ə)l/ *adj* pestilent – **pestilentially** *adv*

¹**pestle** /'pesl/ *n* **1** a usu club-shaped implement for pounding or grinding substances in a MORTAR (bowl) **2** any of various devices for pounding, stamping, or pressing [ME *pestel*, fr MF, fr L *pistillum*; akin to MLG *vīsel* pestle, L *pilum* pestle, javelin, *pinsere* to pound, crush]

²**pestle** *vb* to pound or pulverize (as if) with a pestle

**pestology** /pe'stoləji/ *n* a branch of science dealing with pests, esp insect pests – **pestological** *adj*, **pestologist** *n*

¹**pet** /pet/ *n* **1** a domesticated animal kept for companionship rather than work or food **2a** a pampered and usu spoiled child **b** somebody who is treated with unusual kindness or consideration; a favourite **3** *chiefly Br* darling – used chiefly by women as an affectionate form of address [perh back-formation fr ME *pety* small – more at PETTY]

²**pet** *adj* **1a** kept or treated as a pet **b** for pet animals ⟨*a ~ shop*⟩ **2** expressing fondness or endearment ⟨*a ~ name*⟩ **3** favourite ⟨*his ~ project*⟩

³**pet** *vb* **-tt-** *vt* **1** to stroke in a gentle or loving manner **2** to treat with unusual kindness and consideration; pamper ~ *vi* to engage in amorous embracing, caressing, etc – **petter** *n*

⁴**pet** *n* a fit of peevishness, sulkiness, or anger [origin unknown]

**peta-** /petə-/ *comb form* thousand billion (10¹⁵) [ISV, perh fr Gk *peta-* (in *petannynai* to spread out, *petasma* something spread out) or perh alter. of *penta-*]

**petal** /'petl/ *n* any of the often brightly coloured leaflike segments of a flower that are modified leaves and together make up the COROLLA [NL *petalum*, fr Gk *petalon*; akin to Gk *petannynai* to spread out – more at FATHOM] – **petalled**, *NAm* **petaled** *adj*, **petallike** *adj*

**petaloid** /'petəloyd/ *adj* **1** resembling a flower petal, esp in shape or bright colour **2** consisting of petallike parts

**petalous** /'petələs/ *adj* having petals – usu in combination ⟨*poly*petalous⟩

**petard** /pe'tahd, pi-/ *n* **1** an early military explosive device, used to break down gates, breach walls, etc **2** a firework that explodes with a loud bang [MF, fr *peter* to break wind, fr *pet* expulsion of intestinal gas, fr L *peditum*, fr neut of *peditus*, pp of *pedere* to break wind; akin to Gk *bdein* to break wind] – **hoist with one's own petard** made a victim of, or hurt by, one's own schemes, esp to harm others

**petasus, petasos** /'petəsəs/ *n* a broad-brimmed low-crowned hat worn by ancient Greeks and Romans; *specif* the winged hat of Hermes [L *petasus*, fr Gk *petasos*; akin to Gk *petannynai* to spread out]

**petcock** /'pet,kok/ *n* a small valve in a pipe, cylinder, or boiler for draining off water, steam, or air or for testing the water level [prob fr ¹*pet* + *cock*]

**petechia** /pə'teekiə/ *n, pl* **petechiae** /-ki,ie/ a minute bleeding or blood-filled spot that appears in the skin or MUCOUS MEMBRANE, esp in some infectious diseases (e g TYPHOID FEVER) as a result of the leaking of blood from an underlying blood vessel [NL, fr It *petecchia*, deriv of L *impetigo*] – **petechial, petechiate** *adj*

¹**peter** /'peetə/ *vi* to diminish gradually and come to an end; GIVE OUT – usu + *out* ⟨*novelists whose creative impetus seems largely to have ~ed out – TLS*⟩ [origin unknown]

²**peter** *n, Br slang* a safe [fr the forename *Peter*]

**Peter** *n* – see BIBLE table [*Peter* (LL *Petrus*, fr Gk *Petros*, fr *petra* rock) † *ab* 64 apostle of Christ]

**Peter Pan** /pan/ *n* a man who seems never to grow older or who clings to the irresponsibility of childhood [*Peter Pan*, hero of the play *Peter Pan, or the boy who wouldn't grow up* by Sir James Barrie †1937 Sc novelist & dramatist]

**Peter Pan collar** *n* a usu small flat collar that is attached to a round neck and has rounded ends that meet in front

**Peter principle** *n the* proposition that each member of a hierarchical organization tends to be promoted until he/she reaches a position that is beyond his/her capabilities [Laurence *Peter* b 1919 US (Canadian-born) educator]

**petersham** /'peetəshəm/ *n* **1** a rough heavy woollen cloth used chiefly for men's coats; *also* a coat made of this material **2** a tough corded ribbon used for belts, waistbands, and hatbands [Charles Stanhope, Lord *Petersham* †1851 E colonel]

**Peter's pence** *n taking sing vb* **1** an annual tribute of a penny formerly paid by each householder in England to the pope **2** a voluntary contribution made by Roman Catholics to the pope [fr the tradition that St Peter founded the papal see]

**pethidine** /'pethideen, -din/ *n* a synthetic drug, $C_{15}H_{21}NO_2$, that has actions and uses similar to those of morphine but less sedative effect and that is widely used to relieve pain (e g in childbirth) [blend of *piperidine* and *ethyl*]

**petillant** /'payteeyonh/ (Fr petijah)/ *adj, esp of wine* mildly effervescent [Fr *pétillant*, prp of *pétiller* to effervesce with a crackling sound, fr MF *petiller* to crackle, fr *peter* to break wind – more at PETARD]

**petiolar** /ˌpeti'ohlə/ *adj* of or growing from a petiole

**petiole** /'peti·ohl/ *n* **1** the usu slender stalk that supports the blade of a leaf and by which the leaf is attached to the stem **2** PEDUNCLE (stalk or stalklike part); *specif* a slender waistlike abdominal segment joining the rest of the abdomen to the

THORAX (middle body segment) in some insects (e g wasps) [NL *petiolus*, fr L, small foot, fruit stalk, alter. of *pediculus*, dim. of *ped-*, *pes* foot – more at FOOT] – **petioled, petiolate** *also* **petiolated** *adj*

**petiolule** /'peetiohl,yool/ *n* a stalk of any of the leaflets making up a COMPOUND LEAF [NL *petiolulus*, dim. of *petiolus*]

**¹petit bourgeois** *also* **petty bourgeois** /,peti 'booəzh·wah (*Fr* pəti burzwa)/ *n, pl* **petits bourgeois, petty bourgeois** /-zhwah(z) (*Fr* ~)/ (a member of the) PETITE BOURGEOISIE [Fr, lit., small bourgeois]

**²petit bourgeois** *also* **petty bourgeois** *adj, chiefly derog* characteristic of the PETITE BOURGEOISIE in attitudes or behaviour; *esp* smugly conventional

**¹petite** /pə'teet/ *adj, esp of a woman* having a small trim figure *synonyms* see ¹SMALL [Fr, fem of *petit* small] – **petiteness** *n*

**²petite** *n* a clothing size for small women

**petite bourgeoisie** /pə,teet booəzh·wah'zee (*Fr* pətit burʒ-wazi)/ *also* **petty bourgeoisie** /,peti ~/ *n taking sing or pl vb* the lower middle class (e g small shopkeepers, skilled workers, etc) who own limited wealth and property [Fr, lit., small bourgeoisie]

**petit four** /,peti 'faw (*Fr* pəti fur)/ *n, pl* **petits fours, petit fours** /~ fawz (*Fr* ~)/ a small fancy cake or biscuit, often containing candied fruit and iced [Fr, lit., small oven]

**petitgrain oil** /'petigrayn/ *n* a fragrant yellowish ESSENTIAL OIL (oil occurring naturally in plants) obtained from the leaves and twigs of the Seville orange and other related trees (genus *Citrus*), and used in soap, perfume, and cosmetics [Fr *petit grain* unripe bitter orange, fr *petit* small + *grain* seed]

**¹petition** /pi'tish(ə)n/ *n* 1 an earnest request; an entreaty 2 a formal written request made to a superior or authority (e g a government); *also* a document embodying such a request ⟨the ~ *bore thousands of signatures*⟩ 3 a formal statement of a ground for legal action addressed to a court 4 something asked or requested [ME, fr MF, fr L *petition-, petitio*, fr *petitus*, pp of *petere* to seek, request – more at FEATHER] – **petitionary** *adj*

**²petition** *vb* to make a request by petition (to or for) ⟨the *lobbyists* ~ed *the government*⟩ ⟨they ~ed *for his release*⟩ – **petitioner** *n*

**petitio principii** /pi,tishi·oh prin'kipi·ie, prin'sipi,ie/ *n* a logical fallacy in which a premise is assumed to be true without justification or in which what is to be proved is implicitly taken for granted [ML, lit., postulation of the beginning]

**petit mal** /,peti 'mal/ *n* epilepsy characterized by mild convulsive seizure or muscle spasm and twitching, usu without loss of consciousness; *also* a mild epileptic fit – compare GRAND MAL [Fr, lit., small illness]

**petit point** /,peti 'poynt (*Fr* pəti pwɛ̃)/ *n* TENT STITCH (small diagonal stitch across single threads); *also* embroidery worked on canvas in this stitch – compare GROS POINT [Fr, lit., small point]

**petit pois** /,peti 'pwah (*Fr* pəti pwa)/ *n, pl* **petits pois** a small young slightly sweet green pea [Fr, small pea]

**petr-, petri-, petro-** *comb form* stone; rock ⟨petro*logy*⟩ [NL, fr Gk *petr-, petro-*, fr *petros* stone & *petra* rock]

**Petrarchan sonnet** /pi'trahkən, pe-, pee-/ *n* a sonnet consisting of an eight-line stanza rhyming *abba abba* and a six-line stanza rhyming in any of various patterns (e g *cde cde* or *cdc cdc*) – compare SHAKESPEAREAN SONNET [*Petrarch* (Francesco Petrarca) †1374 It poet]

**petrel** /'petrəl/ *n* any of numerous seabirds (families Procellariidae and Hydrobatidae) that characteristically fly far from land; *esp* a small long-winged sea bird (e g a STORM PETREL) △ petrol [alter. of earlier *pitteral*]

**petri dish** /'peetri, 'petri/ *n* a small shallow dish of thin glass or plastic with a loose cover, used in laboratories esp for cultures of microorganisms (e g bacteria) [*Julius Petri* †1921 Ger bacteriologist]

**petrifaction** /,petri'faksh(ə)n/, **petrification** /,petrifi'kaysh(ə)n/ *n* 1 petrifying or being petrified 2 something petrified

**petrify** /'petrifie/ *vt* 1 to convert into stone or a stony substance; *specif* to convert (organic matter) to a fossilized form by infiltration of dissolved minerals 2a to make lifeless or inactive; deaden ⟨*slogans are apt to* ~ *a man's thinking* – *Saturday Review*⟩ b to stun or paralyse with terror, shock, etc ⟨*is* petrified *of talking in public* – Alan Frank⟩ ~ *vi* to become stone or of stony hardness or rigidity [MF *petrifier*, fr *petr-* + *-ifier* -ify]

**Petrine** /'peetrien/ *adj* 1 of (the doctrines associated with) the apostle Peter 2 of (the reign of) Peter the Great of Russia [LL *Petrus* Peter]

**petro-** *comb form* petroleum; petroleum product ⟨petro*economy*⟩

**¹petrochemical** /,petroh'kemikl/ *adj* involving or obtained from petrochemicals

**²petrochemical** *n* a chemical obtained from petroleum or natural gas – **petrochemistry** *n*

**petrodollar** /-,dolə/ *n* a unit of foreign exchange obtained by a petroleum-exporting country by sales abroad

**petrogenesis** /,petroh'jenəsis/ *n* the formation of rocks [NL] – **petrogenetic** *adj*

**petroglyph** /'petrə,glif/ *n* an ancient or prehistoric carving, painting, or inscription on a rock [Fr *pétroglyphe*, fr *pétr-* petr- + *-glyphe* (as in *hiéroglyphe* hieroglyph)]

**petrography** /pe'trogrəfi/ *n* the description and systematic classification of rocks, esp by examination of small specimens and thin sections [NL *petrographia*, fr *petr-* + L *-graphia* -graphy] – **petrographer** *n*, **petrographic, petrographical** *adj*, **petrographically** *adv*

**petrol** /'petrəl/ *n, chiefly Br* a volatile inflammable liquid mixture of HYDROCARBONS (carbon- and hydrogen-containing compounds) that is blended from several refined products of petroleum, usu contains various additives, and is used chiefly as a fuel for INTERNAL-COMBUSTION ENGINES [Fr *essence de pétrole*, lit., essence of petroleum]

**petrolatum** /,petrə'laytəm/ *n* PETROLEUM JELLY [NL, fr ML *petroleum*]

**petrol bomb** *n* a crude hand grenade consisting of a bottle filled with petrol and having a piece of rag in the neck to act as a fuse when ignited – compare MOLOTOV COCKTAIL

**petroleum** /pə'trohli·əm, -lyəm/ *n* an oily inflammable usu dark brown thick liquid consisting chiefly of a complex mixture of HYDROCARBONS (carbon- and hydrogen-containing compounds), that occurs naturally in certain rock formations, generally in association with natural gas, and that after refining yields petrol, paraffin, NAPHTHA, etc – called also OIL, CRUDE OIL [ML, fr L *petr-* + *oleum* oil – more at OIL]

**petroleum jelly** *n* a semisolid odourless and tasteless mixture of HYDROCARBONS (chemical compounds composed of carbon and hydrogen only) obtained from petroleum and used esp as the basis of ointments, in dressings, and as a lubricant

**petrology** /pe'troləji/ *n* the scientific study of rocks, including their formation, occurrence, structure, and chemical composition [ISV] – **petrologist** *n*, **petrologic, petrological** *adj*, **petrologically** *adv*

**'petrol-,pump** *n, Br* a pump for transferring petrol; *esp* one that measures the amount put into the tank of a motor vehicle at a filling station and displays the price

**petrol station** *n, Br* FILLING STATION

**petronel** /'petrənel/ *n* a portable 16th-century firearm fired with the butt resting against the chest, used esp by cavalry [perh modif of MF *poitrinal, petrinal*, fr *poitrinal* of the chest, fr *poitrine* chest]

**petrosal** /pi'trohs(ə)l/ *adj* of or situated in the region of the petrous portion of the TEMPORAL BONE (bone at the side of the human skull) ⟨~ *nerve*⟩ [NL *petrosa* petrous portion of the temporal bone, fr L, fem of *petrosus*]

**petrous** /'petrəs, 'pee-/ *adj* resembling stone, esp in hardness; *specif* of or being the exceptionally hard and dense portion of the TEMPORAL BONE (bone at the side of the human skull) that encloses and protects the INNER EAR [MF *petreux*, fr L *petrosus*, fr *petra* rock, fr Gk]

**¹petticoat** /'peti,koht/ *n* 1a an outer skirt formerly worn by women and small children b a woman's undergarment hanging from the waist or shoulders; an underskirt or slip 2a a garment characteristic of women, symbolizing the female sex b *chiefly humorous* a woman [ME *petycote* short tunic, petticoat, fr *pety* small + *cote* coat] – **petticoated** *adj*

**²petticoat** *adj, humorous or derog* characteristic of or exercised by women ⟨~ *government*⟩

**pettifog** /'peti,fog/ *vi* -gg- 1 to engage in legal sharp practice 2 to quibble over insignificant details; fuss, bicker [back-formation fr *pettifogger*, prob fr *petty* + obs *fogger*, perh fr *Fugger*, 15th- & 16th-c Ger family of financiers & merchants] – **pettifogger** *n*, **pettifoggery** *n*

**pettifogging** /'peti,foging/ *adj* 1 characteristic of a pettifogger; quibbling 2 petty, trivial

**pettish** /'petish/ *adj* peevish, petulant [prob fr ⁴*pet*] – **pettishly** *adv*, **pettishness** *n*

**pettitoes** /'peti,tohz/ *n pl* 1 the feet of a pig used as food; trotters 2 *archaic* toes; *broadly* FEET [pl of obs *pettytoe* offal, fr MF *petite oye* small goose, goose giblets]

**petty** /'peti/ *adj* 1 having secondary rank or importance; minor, subordinate 2 having little or no importance; small in scale; trivial 3 small-minded [ME *pety* small, minor, alter. of *petit*, fr MF] – **pettily** *adv*, **pettiness** *n*

**petty bourgeois** *n or adj, pl* **petty bourgeois** PETIT BOURGEOIS

**petty bourgeoisie** *n* PETITE BOURGEOISIE

**petty cash** *n* cash kept on hand, esp at a place of work, for payment of minor expenses

**petty larceny** *n* stealing of property below a value specified by law – compare GRAND LARCENY

**petty officer** *n* – see MILITARY RANKS table

**petty officer first class** *n* – see MILITARY RANKS table

**petty officer second class** *n* – see MILITARY RANKS table

**petty officer third class** *n* – see MILITARY RANKS table

**petty sessional division** *n* the area over which a particular MAGISTRATES' COURT has jurisdiction

**petty sessions** *n pl, often cap P&S* MAGISTRATES' COURT – no longer used technically

**petulant** /'petyoolənt/ *adj* characterized by bouts of childish bad temper, often for no real reason; peevish [L or MF; MF, immodest, impudent, fr L *petulant-, petulans;* akin to L *petere* to go to, attack, seek – more at FEATHER] – **petulance** *n*, **petulantly** *adv*

**petunia** /pi'tyoohnyə, -ni·ə/ *n* any of a genus (*Petunia*) of tropical American plants of the potato family grown for their large brightly coloured funnel-shaped flowers [NL, genus name, fr obs Fr *petun* tobacco, fr Tupi *petyn*]

**pew** /pyooh/ *n* 1 a bench fixed in a row for the seating of the congregation in a church; *also* a high compartment with such benches for the accommodation of a group (e g a family) 2 *Br informal* a seat 〈*take a ~*〉 [ME *pewe*, fr MF *puie* balustrade, fr L *podia*, pl of *podium* parapet, podium, fr Gk *podion* base, dim. of *pod-, pous* foot – more at FOOT]

**pewit** /'pee‚wit/ *n* a lapwing [imit]

**pewter** /'pyoohtə/ *n* 1 any of various alloys having tin as the chief component; *esp* a dull alloy of tin and lead formerly widely used for domestic utensils 2 pewter ware 3 a dull bluish-grey colour [ME, fr MF *peutre;* akin to It *peltro* pewter] – **pewter** *adj*

**pewterer** /'pyooht(ə)rə/ *n* one who works with pewter; *esp* one who makes pewter utensils or vessels

**peyote** /pay'ohti, pi-/ *n* 1 any of several cacti (genus *Lophophora*) growing in Mexico and the SW USA; *esp* MESCAL 1 2 MESCAL BUTTON (dried disc-shaped flower top of the mescal cactus); *also* a hallucinogenic drug, esp mescaline, derived from peyote cacti or dried MESCAL BUTTONS [MexSp, fr Nahuatl *peyotl*]

**peyotl** /pay'ohtl/ *n* (a) peyote

**pfennig** /'(p)fenig, -nikh (*Ger* 'pfeniç)/ *n, pl* **pfennigs, pfennige** /'(p)feniɡə (*Ger* pfeniɡə)/ – see *deutsche mark, mark* at MONEY table [Ger, fr OHG *pfenning* – more at PENNY]

**PG** /pee 'jee/ *n or adj* (a film) certified in Britain as suitable for all ages but for which parental guidance is recommended for children under 15 – compare U, 15, 18 [Parental Guidance]

**pH** /pee 'aych/ *n* a number showing the degree of acidity or alkalinity of a solution on a scale of 0 to 14, with 7 representing neutrality, numbers less than 7 increasing acidity, and numbers greater than 7 increasing alkalinity. The pH of a solution is the negative logarithm of the HYDROGEN ION concentration in that solution; *also* the condition of acidity or alkalinity of a solution as represented by its pH number [Ger, fr *potenz* power + *H*, symbol for hydrogen]

**phaeochromocytoma,** *chiefly NAm* **pheochromocytoma** /‚feeoh‚krohmoh·sie'tohmə/ *n, pl* **phaeochromocytomas, phaeochromocytomata** /-mətə/ a tumour, esp in the ADRENAL GLAND, that secretes excess adrenalin or NORADRENALIN into the blood and is usu associated with (bouts of) excessively high blood pressure [NL, fr ISV *phaeochromocyte* chromaffin cell, deriv of Gk *phaios* dusky, grey + *chrōma* colour + *kytos* hollow vessel]

**phaeton** /'fayt(ə)n/ *n* 1 a light open four-wheeled horse-drawn carriage 2a an early open car, a double phaeton having two rows of seats and a triple phaeton having three b an American four-door convertible car of the 1920s and 1930s [*Phaëthon* (Gk *Phaethōn*), character in Gk myth who attempted to drive the chariot of the sun]

**phag-** /fag-/, **phago-** *comb form* eating, devouring 〈phago*cyte*〉 [Gk, fr *phagein* to eat – more at BAKSHEESH]

**phage** /fayj/ *n* BACTERIOPHAGE (virus that destroys bacteria) [by shortening]

**-phage** /-fayj/ *comb form* (→ *n*) one that eats or devours (something specified) 〈*xylo*phage〉 [Gk *-phagos*, fr *phagein*] – **-phagous** *comb form* (→ *adj*)

**phagedaena,** *chiefly NAm* **phagedena** /‚fajə'deenə/ *n* a rapidly spreading ulcer that destroys tissue [L, fr Gk *phagedaina*, fr *phagein* ] – **phagedaenic** *adj*

**-phagia** /-'fayji·ə/, **-phagy** /-fəji/ *comb form* (→ *n*) eating (a specified amount or substance) 〈*dys*phagia〉 〈*micro*phagia〉 [NL *-phagia*, fr Gk, fr *phagein*]

**phagocyte** /'fagə‚siet/ *n* any of various cells (e g a MACROPHAGE or WHITE BLOOD CELL) that characteristically flow round and engulf foreign or harmful material (e g invading bacteria and debris from tissue injury) which is then typically digested within the cell [ISV, fr Gk *phagein* + NL *-cyta* -cyte] – **phagocytic** *adj*, **phagocytically** *adv*

**phagocyt·ize, -ise** *vt* to phagocytose

**phagocytose** /'fagəsietohs, -tohz/ *vt* to take into the cell or consume by phagocytosis [back-formation fr *phagocytosis*]

**phagocytosis** /‚fagəsie'tohsis/ *n, pl* **phagocytoses** /-seez/ the uptake by engulfment, and usu destruction or consumption of solid matter or particles from outside the cell by phagocytes or phagocytic cells (e g amoebas) – compare PINOCYTOSIS, EXOCYTOSIS [NL] – **phagocytotic** *adj*, **phagocytotically** *adv*

**phagosome** /'fagəsohm/ *n* a LYSOSOME (saclike structure in a cell, containing digestive enzymes) that contains materials taken up into the cell esp by phagocytosis and in which the material is usu digested and destroyed [Gk *phagein* + E *-o-* + *-some*]

**Phagun** /'pahgən/ *n* – see MONTH table [Hindi *phāgun*, fr Skt *phālguna*]

**phalange** /'falanj/ *n* PHALANX 2 [Fr]

**phalanger** /fə'lanjə/ *n* any of various small marsupial mammals (family Phalangeridae) of the Australian region, that live in trees and have thick fur and a long frequently prehensile tail – compare FLYING PHALANGER [NL, fr Gk *phalang-, phalanx* bone of the finger or toe]

**phalanstery** /'falənst(ə)ri/ *n* (the buildings housing) a cooperative community; *specif* such an establishment (PHALANX 3b) as proposed by Fourier [Fr *phalanstère*, fr *phalange* phalanx (fr L *phalang-, phalanx*) + *-stère* (as in *monastère* monastery)] – **phalansterian** *adj or n*

**phalanx** /'falangks/ *n, pl* **phalanxes, phalanges** /fə'lanjeez/, (2) **phalanges** 1 *taking sing or pl vb* a battle formation in ancient Greece characterized by close deep ranks and files of infantry joining shields and carrying long spears; *broadly* a body of troops in close array 2 any of the bones of the fingers or toes in human beings or the corresponding parts in other VERTEBRATE animals 3 *taking sing or pl vb* 3a a close-ranked mass of people, animals, or things b a body of people united for a common purpose; *esp* a cooperative agricultural community run on the principles of FOURIERISM (an early variety of communism) [L *phalang-, phalanx*, fr Gk, log, battle line, bone of the finger or toe – more at BALK]

**phalarope** /'falə‚rohp/ *n, pl* **phalaropes,** *esp collectively* **phalarope** any of various small WADING BIRDS (family Phalaropodidae) that resemble sandpipers but have lobed toes and are good swimmers [Fr, fr NL *phalaropod-, phalaropus*, fr Gk *phalaris* coot (akin to Gk *phalios* having a white spot) + *pod-, pous* foot – more at BALD, FOOT]

**phallic** /'falik/ *adj* 1 of or relating to phallicism 〈*a ~ cult*〉 2 of or resembling a phallus 3 relating to or being the stage of psychological development during which a child becomes interested in his/her own genitals – **phallically** *adv*

**phallicism** /'falisiz(ə)m/ *n* the worship of generative power as symbolized by the phallus

**phallus** /'faləs/ *n, pl* **phalli** /'fali, -lie/, **phalluses** (a symbol or representation of) the penis [L, fr Gk *phallos* – more at BLOW]

**-phane** /-fayn/ *comb form* (→ *n*) substance having a specified form, quality, or appearance 〈*hydro*phane〉 [Gk *phanēs* appearing, fr *phainein* to show – more at FANCY]

**phaner-, phanero-** *comb form* visible; obvious 〈*phanero*crystalline〉 [Gk, fr *phaneros* visible, fr *phainein* to show]

**phanerogam** /'fanəroh‚gam/ *n* SPERMATOPHYTE (seed-bearing plant) – no longer used technically [Fr *phanérogame*, deriv of Gk *phaneros* visible + *gamos* marriage – more at BIGAMY] – **phanerogamic, phanerogamous** *adj*

**phanerophyte** /'fanərə‚fiet, fə'nerə-/ *n* a plant that bears dormant buds that survive the winter well above the surface of the ground – compare CHAMAEPHYTE, GEOPHYTE [Gk *phaneros* + ISV *-phyte*]

**Phanerozoic** /ˌfanərəˈzohˌik, fəˌnerə-/ *adj or n* (of, occurring in, or being) a period of geological time that comprises the PALAEOZOIC, MESOZOIC, and CAINOZOIC eras (the last 600 million years), before which fossils are extremely rare [Gk *phaneros* + E [2]*-zoic*]

**phantasm** /ˈfanˌtaz(ə)m/ *n* **1** a product of fantasy; something unreal, illusory, shadowy, or spectral: eg **1a** a deceptive likeness of something; an illusion ⟨*pursuing a ~ of truth*⟩ **b** a ghost, phantom **2** a mental representation of a real object – used in the philosophy of Plato [ME *fantasme*, fr OF, fr L *phantasma*, fr Gk, fr *phantazein* to present to the mind – more at FANCY] – **phantasmal, phantasmic** *adj*

**phantasmagoria** /ˌfantazməˈgawriˌə/ *n* **1** an optical effect by which figures on a screen appear to dwindle into the distance or to rush towards the observer with enormous increase in size **2** a constantly shifting confused succession of things seen or imagined (eg in a dreaming or feverish state) ⟨*a ~ of symbolic persons and animals, divine and diabolical beings, celestial and infernal phenomena* – Edmund Wilson⟩ [Fr *phantasmagorie*, fr *phantasme* phantasm (fr OF *fantasme*) + *-agorie* (prob fr Gk *ageirein* to assemble, collect) – more at GREGARIOUS] – **phantasmagoric, phantasmagorical** *adj*

**phantasy** /ˈfantəsi/ *vb or n, archaic* (to) fantasy

[1]**phantom** /ˈfantəm/ *n* **1a** something (eg a ghost) apparent to the senses but with no physical existence; an apparition **b** something elusive or unreal; a will-o'-the-wisp **c** something existing only in the imagination ⟨*his dreams troubled by ~s of the past*⟩ **2** something existing in appearance only ⟨*a mere ~ of a king*⟩ **3** a representation of something abstract, ideal, or incorporeal ⟨*she was a ~ of delight* – William Wordsworth⟩ **4** an ever-present source of horror or dread ⟨*the ~ of disease*⟩ [ME *fantosme, fantome*, fr MF *fantosme*, modif of L *phantasma*] – **phantomlike** *adv or adj*

[2]**phantom** *adj* **1** like or being a phantom ⟨*a ~ stagecoach*⟩ **2** perceived to be real although having no actual existence outside of the imagination; illusory ⟨*the pain in an amputee's ~ limb*⟩ ⟨*a ~ pregnancy*⟩ **3** fictitious, dummy ⟨*~ voters*⟩

**pharaoh** /ˈfeəroh/ *n, often cap* a ruler of ancient Egypt [LL *pharaon-, pharao*, fr Gk *pharaō*, fr Heb *par'ōh*, fr Egypt *pr-'o*] – **pharaonic** *adj, often cap*

**pharaoh ant** *n* a small red ant (*Monomorium pharaonis*) that is a common household and greenhouse pest

**pharisaic** /ˌfariˈsayˌik/ *adj* **1** *cap* of or resembling the Pharisees **2 pharisaical, pharisaic** marked by hypocritical self-righteousness [LL *pharisaicus*, fr LGk *pharisaikos*, fr Gk *pharisaios* Pharisee]

**pharisaism** /ˈfarisayˌiz(ə)m/ *n* **1** *cap* the doctrines or practices of the Pharisees **2** *often cap* pharisaical character, spirit, or attitude; hypocrisy [NL *pharisaismus*, fr Gk *pharisaios*]

**pharisee** /ˈfariseeə/ *n* **1** *cap* a member of a Jewish nonpriestly sect that came into existence in the 2nd century BC and was noted in Jesus's time for strict adherence to the TORAH (Jewish sacred writings) and to their own oral traditions interpreting it **2** a pharisaical person △ philistine [ME *pharise*, fr OE *farise*, fr LL *pharisaeus*, fr Gk *pharisaios*, fr Aram *pĕrīshayyā*, pl of *pĕrīshā*, lit., separated]

[1]**pharmaceutical** /ˌfahməˈsyoohtikl/ *also* **pharmaceutic** *adj* **1** of or used in drugs, ointments, medicines, etc **2** of or engaged in pharmacy or in the manufacture of medicinal substances [LL *pharmaceuticus*, fr Gk *pharmakeutikos*, fr *pharmakeuein* to administer drugs – more at PHARMACY] – **pharmaceutically** *adv*

[2]**pharmaceutical** *n* a medicinal drug

**pharmaceutics** /ˌfahməˈsyoohtiks/ *n taking sing vb* PHARMACY 1

**pharmacist** /ˈfahməsist/ *n* a person engaged or trained in pharmacy

**pharmaco-** *comb form* medicine; drug ⟨pharmaco*therapy*⟩ ⟨pharmaco*logy*⟩ [Gk *pharmako-*, fr *pharmakon* drug]

**pharmacodynamic** /ˌfahməkohˈdieˈnamik/ *adj* of or concerning the action of drugs on the body – **pharmacodynamics** *n taking sing vb*

**pharmacogenetics** /ˌfahməkohjəˈnetiks/ *n taking sing vb* the study of the interrelation of genetic make-up and response to drugs – **pharmacogenetic** *adj*

**pharmacognosy** /ˌfahməˈkognəsi/ *n* the study of drugs from natural sources, esp plants [ISV, fr Gk *pharmakon* + *-gnōsia* knowledge, fr *gnōsis* – more at GNOSIS] – **pharmacognostic, pharmacognostical** *adj*

**pharmacokinetics** /ˌfahməkohˈkiˈnetiks, -kie-/ *n taking sing vb* the study of the physical and chemical changes undergone by drugs from their absorption by and distribution within the body to their excretion – **pharmacokinetic** *adj*

**pharmacology** /ˌfahməˈkoləji/ *n* **1** the study of drugs, their properties and effects on living things, and their use in the treatment of disease **2** the properties and effects of a usu specified drug ⟨*the ~ of morphine*⟩ – **pharmacologist** *n*, **pharmacologic, pharmacological** *adj*, **pharmacologically** *adv*

**pharmacopoeia**, *NAm also* **pharmacopeia** /ˌfahməkəˈpeeˌə/ *n* **1** a book listing and describing drugs, chemicals, and medicinal preparations; *esp* one issued by an officially recognized authority and serving as a standard **2** a collection or stock of drugs [NL, fr LGk *pharmakopoiia* preparation of drugs, fr Gk *pharmako-* + *poiein* to make – more at POET] – **pharmacopoeial** *adj*

**pharmacy** /ˈfahməsi/ *n* **1** the preparing, preserving, and dispensing of drugs **2a** a place where medicines are made up or dispensed; a dispensary **b** CHEMIST 2 [LL *pharmacia* administration of drugs, fr Gk *pharmakeia*, fr *pharmakeuein* to administer drugs, fr *pharmakon* magic charm, poison, drug; akin to Lith *burti* to practise magic]

**pharyng-** /farinj-/, **pharyngo-** *comb form* pharynx ⟨pharyng*itis*⟩ ⟨pharyngo*logy*⟩ [Gk, fr *pharyng-, pharynx*]

**pharyngal** /fəˈringˌgl/ *adj* pharyngeal

**pharyngeal** /ˌfarinˈjeeˌəl, fəˈrinjiəl/ *adj* **1** relating to or located in (the region of) the pharynx **2** of a consonant produced in the pharynx [NL *pharyngeus*, fr *pharyng-, pharynx*]

**pharyngitis** /ˌfarinˈjietəs/ *n* inflammation of the pharynx [NL]

**pharynx** /ˈfaringks/ *n, pl* **pharynges** /faˈrinjeez/ *also* **pharynxes 1** the part of the digestive tract (ALIMENTARY CANAL) of a VERTEBRATE animal between the cavity of the mouth and the OESOPHAGUS (gullet) **2** a part of the ALIMENTARY CANAL in some INVERTEBRATE animals that follows the cavity of the mouth and may be thickened and muscular, toothed and capable of being turned inside out, or adapted as a sucking organ □ compare LARYNX [NL *pharyng-, pharynx*, fr Gk, throat, pharynx; akin to ON *barki* throat, L *forare* to bore – more at BORE]

**phase** /fayz/ *n* **1** a particular appearance or state in a regularly recurring cycle of changes ⟨*~s of the moon*⟩ **2a** a discernible part or stage in a course, development, or cycle ⟨*the early ~s of his career*⟩ **b** a passing episode with certain characteristics ⟨*the unpleasantness was just a ~*⟩ **c** an aspect or part (eg of a problem) under consideration **3** *physics & electronics* a particular stage of progress reached in a regularly recurring motion or cyclic process with respect to a standard or reference position or assumed starting point; the point to which a rotation, oscillation, or periodic variation has advanced, considered in its relation to a standard or starting position **4** a homogeneous, physically distinct, and mechanically separable portion of matter present in a complex mixture whose constituents have different physical states ⟨*ice in an ice and water mixture constitutes the solid ~*⟩ **5a** an individual or subgroup that is different in appearance or behaviour from the norm of the group to which it belongs; *also* the distinguishing variant characteristic **b** a cyclically recurring variation in the appearance (eg coat or plumage colours) of an animal; *also* an animal in such a phase △ phrase [NL *phasis*, fr Gk, appearance of a star, phase of the moon, fr *phainein* to show (middle voice, to appear) –more at FANCY] – **phasic** *adj* – **out of/in phase 1** (not) synchronized or correlated **2** *of two or more waves* (not) having the same phase; (not) reaching a maximum value simultaneously

[2]**phase** *vt* **1** to adjust so as to be in phase **2a** to conduct or carry out by planned phases **b** to schedule (eg operations) or contract for (eg goods or services) to be performed or supplied as required ⟨*~ a development programme*⟩
  **phase in** *vt* to introduce the practice, production, or use of in gradual stages ⟨phase in *a new model*⟩
  **phase out** *vt* to discontinue the practice, production, or use of in gradual stages ⟨phase out *the old machinery*⟩ – **phaseout** *n, chiefly NAm*

**phase-contrast** *adj* of, employing, or produced by the PHASE-CONTRAST MICROSCOPE

**phase-contrast microscope** *also* **phase microscope** *n* a microscope that translates differences in phase of the light transmitted through or reflected by the object under examination into differences of intensity in the image, and that is used esp in examining unstained biological specimens

**-phasia** /-ˌfayzyə, -zh(y)ə/ *comb form* (→ *n*) speech disorder ⟨*dys*phasia⟩ [NL, fr Gk, speech, fr *phasis* utterance, fr *phanai* to speak, say – more at BAN]

**phasmid** /'fazmid/ *n* any of an order (Phasmida) of plant-eating insects, including STICK INSECTS and LEAF INSECTS, having elongated cylindrical or sometimes flattened bodies and long strong legs, INCOMPLETE METAMORPHOSIS, and usu PARTHENOGENETIC development (development from an unfertilized egg) [NL *Phasmida*, group name, fr *Phasma*, type genus, fr Gk, apparition, fr *phainein* to show – more at FANCY] – **phasmid** *adj*

**phasor** /'fayzə/ *n* a regularly alternating quantity (e g current or voltage) that is represented graphically by a line whose length represents the magnitude and whose direction represents the phase – compare VECTOR [¹*phase* + vecto*r*]

**phat** /*fat*/ *n* FAT 6 (good typesetting copy)

**phatic** /'fatik/ *adj, of conversation* expressing feelings or establishing an atmosphere of sociability rather than communicating ideas [Gk *phatos* spoken, fr *phanai* to speak] – **phatically** *adv*

**pheasant** /'fez(ə)nt/ *n, pl* **pheasants**, *esp collectively* **pheasant** any of numerous large often long-tailed and brightly coloured birds (*Phasianus* and related genera of the family Phasianidae), originally from Asia, many of which are reared as ornamental or game birds; *also* the meat of a pheasant as food [ME *fesaunt*, fr AF, fr OF *fesan*, fr L *phasianus*, fr Gk *phasianos*, fr *phasianos* of the Phasis river, fr *Phasis*, river in Colchis, ancient country in Asia]

**phellem** /'feləm/ *n* a plant tissue on the outside of the roots and stems of woody plants, that is produced by phellogen and consists of a protective layer of dead cork cells whose walls are impregnated with a waxy substance (SUBERIN) that makes them impermeable to water – called also CORK [Gk *phellos* cork + E -*em* (as in *phloem*)]

**phelloderm** /'feloh,duhm/ *n* a layer of thin-walled cells (PARENCHYMA) produced in the roots or stems of woody plants by and to the inside of phellogen [Gk *phellos* + ISV -*derm*]

**phellogen** /'feləjən/ *n* a row of cells in the outer layer of a woody plant stem or root that divides to form phellem to the outside and phelloderm to the inside – called also CORK CAMBIUM [Gk *phellos* + ISV -*gen*]

**phen-** /feen-, fen-/, **pheno-** *comb form* related to or derived from benzene ⟨phen*anthrene*⟩; containing phenyl ⟨pheno*barbitone*⟩ ⟨phen*ol*⟩ [obs *phene* benzene, fr Fr *phène*, fr Gk *phainein* to show – more at FANCY; fr its occurrence in illuminating gas]

**phenacaine** /'feenəkayn, 'fen-/ *n* a synthetic drug, $C_{18}H_{22}N_2O_2HCl$, used as a local anaesthetic, esp for use on the eye [prob fr *phen*etidine + *acet*- + -*caine*]

**phenacetin** /fi'nasətin/ *n* a drug, $CH_3CONHC_6H_4OC_2H_5$, that was formerly widely used to reduce fever and as a painkiller (e g for headache, toothache, and rheumatic pain) – called also ACETOPHENETIDIN [ISV]

**phenacite** /'fenəsiet/ *n* phenakite

**phenakite** /'feenəkiet, 'fen-/ *n* a glassy mineral that consists of a SILICATE of the metallic chemical element beryllium, $Be_2SiO_4$, and is sometimes used as a gemstone [Ger *phenakit*, fr Gk *phenak-, phenax* deceiver; fr its being easily mistaken for quartz]

**phenanthrene** /fi'nanthreen/ *n* a colourless chemical compound, $C_{14}H_{10}$, that occurs in COAL TAR and has the same chemical composition as ANTHRACENE but a different arrangement of atoms [ISV *phen-* + *anthracene*]

**phenazine** /'fenəzeen/ *n* a yellowish chemical compound, $C_6H_4N_2C_6H_4$, that is the parent compound of many AZINE dyes and a few antibiotics [ISV]

**phenelzine** /'fenəlzeen/ *n* a synthetic antidepressant drug, $C_6H_5(CH_2)_2NHNH_2$, that acts on the nervous system by inhibiting the activity of MONOAMINE OXIDASE [*phen*yl + *ethyl* + hydra*zine*]

**phenetic** /fi'netik/ *adj* of or being a classificatory system or procedure, esp in biology, based on the overall observable similarity rather than the evolutionary history of the organisms involved [*phen*otype + -*etic* (as in *genetic*)]

**phenetidine** /fi'netədeen, -din/ *n* any of three liquid chemical compounds, $C_6H_4OC_2H_5NH_2$, that are derivatives of phenetole containing an AMINO group and are used esp in manufacturing dyestuffs [*phen*etole + -*idine*]

**phenetole** /'fenitohl, tol/ *n* a colourless liquid chemical compound consisting of the ETHYL ETHER, $C_6H_5OC_2H_5$, of phenol [ISV *phen-* + *ethyl* + -*ole*]

**phenformin** /fen'fawmin/ *n* a drug, $C_{10}H_{15}N_5$, taken orally in the treatment of DIABETES MELLITUS to reduce blood sugar levels [*phen-* + *form*aldehyde + im*ino*]

**phenmetrazine** /fen'metrəzeen/ *n* a stimulant drug, $C_{11}H_{15}NO$, that depresses the appetite and is used in the treatment of obesity [*phen-* + *methyl* + hydr- + *azine*]

**phenobarbital** /,feenoh'bahbitl/ *n, chiefly NAm* phenobarbitone

**phenobarbitone** /,feenoh'bahbi,tohn/ *n, chiefly Br* a barbiturate, $C_{12}H_{12}N_2O_3$, used esp as a sedative and as an anticonvulsant in the treatment of epilepsy

**phenocopy** /'feenoh,kopi/ *n* a modification in the appearance of an organism that is caused by unusual environmental conditions but resembles a genetically induced change [*pheno*type + *copy*]

**phenocryst** /'fenə,krist, 'fee-/ *n* any of the prominent relatively large crystals that are embedded in a base of fine-grained crystals in some rocks (PORPHYRIES) [Fr *phénocryste*, fr Gk *phainein* to show + *krystallos* crystal – more at FANCY] – **phenocrystic** *adj*

**phenol** /'feenol/ *n* 1 a caustic poisonous acidic chemical compound, $C_6H_5OH$, present in COAL TAR, that is a derivative of benzene containing a HYDROXYL group in place of a hydrogen atom and is used in dilute solution as a disinfectant – called also CARBOLIC ACID 2 any of various acidic chemical compounds analogous to phenol in that they contain one or more HYDROXYL groups attached to a ring of atoms similar to a BENZENE RING [ISV *phen-* + -*ol*]

¹**phenolic** /fi'nolik/ *adj* 1a (having the characteristics of) (a) phenol b containing or derived from (a) phenol 2 of or being a phenolic

²**phenolic, phenolic resin** *n* any of a large group of synthetic plastics that are compounds of a phenol with an ALDEHYDE, and are used esp in electrical insulating materials, varnishes, lacquers, and adhesives, and in making moulded and cast objects

**phenology** /fi'noləji/ *n* (the study of) the relations between climate and periodic biological phenomena (e g bird migration or plant flowering) [*phenom*ena + -*logy*] – **phenological** *adj*, **phenologically** *adv*

**phenolphthalein** /,feenolf'thayli-in, -li-een/ *n* a synthetic chemical compound, $C_{20}H_{14}O_4$, used in medicine as a laxative and in chemical analysis as an acid-alkali INDICATOR, becoming red in alkalis and colourless in acids [ISV *phenol* + *phthalein* (a dye derived from phthalic acid)]

**phenol red** *n* phenolsulphonephthalein

**phenolsulphonephthalein** /,feenol,sulfohn'thali-in, -'thayli-in, -leen/ *n* a red chemical compound, $C_{19}H_{14}O_5S$, used esp as an acid-alkali INDICATOR (substance changing colour in the presence of acids or alkalis) [*phenol* + *sulphone* + *phthalein*]

**phenomenal** /fi'nominl/ *adj* of or being a phenomenon: e g a perceptible by the senses rather than by thought or intuition b concerned with phenomena rather than with hypotheses c extraordinary, prodigious ⟨*a* ~ *success*⟩ – **phenomenally** *adv*

**phenomenalism** /fi'nominəliz(ə)m/ *n* a philosophical theory that limits knowledge to objects that can be perceived by the senses – **phenomenalist** *n*, **phenomenalistic** *adj*, **phenomenalistically** *adv*

**phenomenological** /fi,nominə'lojikl/ *adj* 1 of phenomenology or phenomenalism 2 PHENOMENAL a,b – **phenomenologically** *adv*

**phenomenology** /fi,nomi'noləji/ *n* 1a the philosophical study of objects perceived by the senses as distinct from the study of being (ONTOLOGY) b the description of the formal structure of the objects of awareness and of awareness itself in abstraction from any causal connections with the external world ⟨*the* ~ *of internal time-consciousness*⟩ – used in Husserlian philosophy 2a the description and classification of a related group of phenomena ⟨*the* ~ *of religion*⟩ b an analysis arrived at by phenomenological investigation [Ger *phänomenologie*, fr *phänomenon* phenomenon + -*logie* -logy] – **phenomenologist** *n*

**phenomenon** /fi'nominən/ *n, pl* **phenomena** /-nə/, (3b) **phenomenons** *also* **phenomena** 1 an observable fact or event 2 an object or experience perceived by the senses rather than by thought or intuition – compare NOUMENON, THING-IN-ITSELF 3a a strange or unusual fact or event of some particular, esp scientific, significance ⟨*vandalism is a social* ~⟩ b an exceptional person, thing, or event; a prodigy [LL *phaenomenon*, fr Gk *phainomenon*, fr neut of *phainomenos*, prp of *phainesthai* to appear, fr *phainein* to show – more at FANCY]

**phenothiazine** /,feenoh'thie-əzeen/ *n* 1 a synthetic chemical compound, $C_{12}H_9NS$, used in insecticides and as a worming agent in veterinary medicine **2** any of various chemical compounds (e g CHLORPROMAZINE) derived from phenothiazine that are used as tranquillizers, esp in the treatment of schizophrenia [ISV *phen-* + *thiazine*]

**phenotype** /'feenoh‚tiep/ *n* **1** the visible characteristics of an organism that are produced by the interaction of the organism's genes and environmental factors – compare GENOTYPE **2** a group of organisms sharing a particular phenotype [Ger *phänotypus*, fr Gk *phainein* to show + *typos* type] – **phenotypic** *also* **phenotypical** *adj*, **phenotypically** *adv*

**phenoxy-** /finoksi-/ *comb form* containing the chemical group $C_6H_5O$ in the molecular structure ⟨phenoxy*acetic acid*⟩ [*phenyl* + *oxy-*]

**phentolamine** /fen'toləmeen, -min/ *n* a synthetic drug, $C_{17}H_{19}N_3O$, that blocks some actions of adrenalin (e g the constriction of small blood vessels and relaxation of intestinal muscle) by binding to the cell sites (ALPHA-RECEPTORS) to which adrenalin normally binds [*phen-* + *toluidine* + *amine*]

**phenyl** /'fenil, 'feenil, -niel, -nl/ *adj or n* (being or containing) the chemical group $C_6H_5$, that has a VALENCY of one and is derived from benzene by removal of one hydrogen atom – often in combination [ISV] – **phenylic** *adj*

**phenylalanine** /‚feni'laləneen/ *n* an ESSENTIAL AMINO ACID, $C_6H_5CH_2CH(NH_2)COOH$, that occurs in most proteins, is required by humans for normal development and health, and is converted in the normal body to the amino acid TYROSINE [ISV *phenyl* + *alanine*]

**phenylbutazone** /‚fenil'byoohtə‚zohn, ‚fee-/ *n* a synthetic drug, $C_{19}H_{20}N_2O_2$, used in the treatment of arthritis, gout, etc to relieve pain and reduce inflammation [*phenyl* + *butyric* acid + *pyrazalone* $(C_3H_4N_2O)$]

**phenylephrine** /‚fenil'efreen, -frin/ *n* a synthetic drug, $OHC_6H_4CH(OH)CH_2NHCH_3 \cdot HCl$, that has the physiological actions of NORADRENALIN and is given esp to raise the blood pressure, esp during or after general anaesthesia [*phenyl* + *epinephrine*]

**phenylketonuria** /‚fenil‚keetə'nyooəri·ə, ‚fee-/ *n* an inherited metabolic disease in human beings in which the ENZYME that converts phenylalanine to the amino acid TYROSINE is not active, resulting in the presence of high levels of phenylalanine and abnormal breakdown products of phenylalanine in the body tissues and leading to severe mental deficiency if untreated from birth [*phenyl* + *ketone* + *-uria*] – **phenylketonuric** *adj or n*

**phenylthiocarbamide** /‚fenil‚thie·oh'kahbəmied, ‚fee-/ *n* phenylthiourea [*phenyl* + *thiocarbamide*]

**phenylthiourea** /‚fenil‚thie·ohyoo'ree·ə, ‚fee-/ *n* a chemical compound, $C_6H_5NHCSNH_2$, that has an extremely bitter taste or is tasteless depending on the presence or absence of a particular DOMINANT gene in the taster [*phenyl* + *thiourea*]

**phenytoin** /fi'nitoh·in/ *n* a synthetic drug, $C_{15}H_{12}N_2O_2$, that is used to prevent convulsions esp in the long-term treatment of epilepsy [di*phenyl*hydan*toin*, fr *diphenyl* + *hyd*rogen + all*antoin* (a chemical found in the allantoic liquid of cows)]

**pheochromocytoma** /‚feeoh‚krohmoh·sie'tohmə/ *pl* **pheochromocytomas**, **pheochromocytomata** /-mətə/ *n*, *chiefly NAm* PHAEOCHROMOCYTOMA (type of tumour)

**pheromone** /'ferəmohn/ *n* a chemical substance secreted by an animal that acts as a signal (e g of danger or to attract animals of the opposite sex), stimulating one or more behavioural responses in other individuals of the same species [ISV *phero-* (fr Gk *pherein* to carry) + *-mone* (as in *hormone*) – more at BEAR] – **pheromonal** *adj*

**phew** /fyooh/ *interj* – used to express relief, amazement, or exhaustion

**phi** /fie/ *n* the 21st letter of the Greek alphabet [MGk, fr Gk *phei*]

**phial** /'fie·əl/ *n* a small thin bottle, esp for holding liquid medicine △ philtre [ME, fr L *phiala* shallow bowl, fr Gk *phialē*]

**Phi Beta Kappa** /fie ‚beetə 'kapə/ *n* (a member of) an American national fraternity, founded in 1776, whose membership is based on academic distinction at an American college or university [*Phi Beta Kappa* (*Society*), fr *phi* + *beta* + *kappa*, initials of the society's Gk motto *philosophia biou kybernētēs* philosophy the guide of life]

**phil-** /fil-/, **philo-** *comb form* loving ⟨*philo*gynist⟩; having an affinity for ⟨*philo*progenitive⟩ [ME, fr OF, fr L, fr Gk, fr *philos* dear, friendly]

**philadelphus** /‚filə'delfəs/ *n* any of a genus (*Philadelphus*) of ornamental shrubs of the saxifrage family; *esp* MOCK ORANGE

[NL, genus name, fr Gk *philadelphos* brotherly, fr *phil-* + *adelphos* brother – more at -ADELPHOUS]

**philander** /fi'landə/ *vi*, *of a man* **1** to flirt **2** to have many casual love affairs [obs *philander* lover, philanderer, fr *Philander*, stock name for a lover in early romances, fr Gk *phil-* + *andr-*, *anēr* man] – **philanderer** *n*

**philanthropic** /‚filən'thropik/ *also* **philanthropical** /-kl/ *adj* **1** of or characterized by philanthropy; humanitarian, altruistic **2** dispensing or receiving aid from funds set aside for humanitarian purposes ⟨*a* ∼ *institution*⟩ – **philanthropically** *adv*

**philanthropy** /fi'lanthrəpi/ *n* **1** love of or goodwill towards one's fellow men; *esp* active effort to promote the welfare of others **2** a philanthropic act or gift [LL *philanthropia*, fr Gk *philanthrōpia*, fr *philanthrōpos* loving mankind, fr *phil-* + *anthrōpos* human being] – **philanthropist** *also* **philanthrope** *n*

**philately** /fi'latəli/ *n* stamp collecting; *also* the study of postage stamps and postal history [Fr *philatélie*, fr *phil-* + Gk *ateleia* tax exemption, fr *atelēs* free from tax, fr *a-* + *telos* tax; akin to Gk *telein* to pay, *tlēnai* to bear – more at TOLERATE] – **philatelist** *n*, **philatelic** *adj*, **philatelically** *adv*

**-phile** /-fiel/, **-phil** /-fil/ *comb form* (→ *n or adj*) **1** (person) having a fondness or liking for ⟨*Franco*phile⟩ **2** (one) having a chemical affinity for ⟨*acido*phil⟩ [Fr *-phile* (n) & NL *-philus* (adj), fr Gk *-philos*, fr *philos* dear, friendly]

**Philemon** /fie'leemon/ *n* – see BIBLE table [*Philemon* (Gk *Philēmōn*), companion of the apostle Paul]

**Philharmonic** /‚filə'monik, ‚fil(h)ah-/ *adj* – used as part of the name of a musical society, esp a SYMPHONY ORCHESTRA [Fr *philharmonique*, lit., loving harmony, fr It *filarmonico*, fr *fil-* phil- + *armonia* harmony, fr L *harmonia*]

**philhellene** /'fil‚heleen/, **philhellenic** /‚filhe'leenik, -'lenik/ *adj* admiring or supporting Greece or the Greeks [Gk *philellēn*, fr *phil-* + *Hellēn* Hellene] – **philhellene** *n*, **philhellenism** *n*, **philhellenist** *n*

**-philia** /-'fili·ə/ *comb form* (→ *n*) **1** tendency towards ⟨*haemo*philia⟩ **2** abnormal appetite or liking for ⟨*necro*philia⟩ [NL, fr Gk *philia* friendship, fr *philos* dear] – **-philiac** *comb form* (→ *n or adj*)

**philibeg** /'fili‚beg/ *n* FILIBEG (kilt)

**-philic** /-'filik/, **-philous** /-filəs/ *comb form* (→ *adj*) having a (chemical) affinity for; liking ⟨*photo*philic⟩ ⟨*helio*philous⟩ – compare -PHOBIC [Gk *-philos* loving, fr *philos* dear, friendly]

**Philippians** /fi'lipi·ənz/ *also* /‚fili'pee·ənz/ *n taking sing vb* – see BIBLE table [*Philippi*, ancient town in NE Greece]

**philippic** /fi'lipik/ *n* a speech or declamation full of bitter invective; a tirade [MF *philippique*, fr L & Gk; L *philippica*, *orationes philippicae*, speeches of Cicero against Mark Antony, trans of Gk *philippikoi logoi*, speeches of Demosthenes against Philip II of Macedon, lit., speeches relating to Philip]

**Philippine mahogany** /'filipeen/ *n* any of several Philippine timber trees (family Dipterocarpaceae) with wood resembling that of the true mahoganies; *also* the wood of a Philippine mahogany [*Philippine* islands in E Asia]

**philistine** /'filistien/ *n* **1** *cap* a native or inhabitant of ancient Philistia in SW Palestine **2** *often cap* a person who professes indifference or opposition to intellectual or aesthetic values △ pharisee [(2) trans of Ger *philister* (orig students' slang for a townsman; fr the ancient Philistines being regarded as hostile barbarians by the Israelites] – **philistine** *adj*, **philistinism** *n*

**Phillips curve** /'filips/ *n*, *economics* a graph showing that as unemployment rises inflation should fall [A W H *Phillips b* 1914 Br economist]

**phillumenist** /fi'loohmənist/ *n* a person who collects matchbox labels or books of matches [*phil-* + L *lumen* light – more at LUMINARY]

**philodendron** /‚filə'dendrən/ *n*, *pl* **philodendrons**, **philodendra** /-drə/ any of various plants (esp genus *Philodendron*) of the arum family that are cultivated for their showy foliage [NL, fr Gk, neut of *philodendros* loving trees, fr *phil-* + *dendron* tree – more at DENDR-]

**philogyny** /fi'lojini/ *n*, *formal* fondness for women – compare MISOGYNY [Gk *philogynia*, fr *phil-* + *gynē* woman – more at QUEEN] – **philogynist** *n*

**philology** /fi'loləji/ *n* **1** the study of the historical development of a language or comparison of different languages **2** *chiefly NAm* the study of human language, esp as the vehicle of literature and as a field of study that sheds light on cultural history [Fr *philologie*, fr L *philologia* love of learning and literature, fr Gk, fr *philologos* fond of learning and literature, fr *phil-* + *logos* word, speech – more at LEGEND] – **philologer, philologist, philologian** *n,* **philological** *adj,* **philologically** *adv*

**Philomel** /'filəmel/ *n* – used as a poetic name for the nightingale [L *Philomela,* fr *Philomela* (Gk *Philomēlē*), mythical Gk princess who was changed into a nightingale]

**Philomela** /ˌfilə'meelə/ *n* Philomel

**philoprogenitive** /ˌfiloh-proh'jenətiv/ *adj, formal* **1** producing many offspring; prolific **2** of or characterized by love of offspring [*phil-* + L *progenitus,* pp of *progignere* to beget – more at PROGENITOR] – **philoprogenitiveness** *n*

**philosopher** /fi'losəfə/ *n* **1a** one who seeks wisdom or truth; a thinker **b** a specialist in philosophy **2** a person whose philosophical viewpoint enables him/her to meet trouble with equanimity; *broadly* a wise, calm, or stoical person [ME, modif of MF *philosophe,* fr L *philosophus,* fr Gk *philosophos,* fr *phil-* + *sophia* wisdom, fr *sophos* wise]

**philosophers' stone** *n* an imaginary stone, substance, or chemical preparation believed by alchemists to have the power of changing base metals into gold

**philosophical** /ˌfilə'sofikl/, **philosophic** *adj* **1** of or in accordance with philosophers or philosophy ⟨*a doctrine of* ~ *liberalism*⟩ **2** characterized by the attitude of a philosopher; *specif* calm in the face of trouble – **philosophically** *adv*

**philosoph·ize, -ise** /fi'losəfiez/ *vi* **1** to engage in philosophical reasoning **2** to expound a trite or superficial philosophy; *esp* to moralize ~ *vt* to explain or treat philosophically – **philosophizer** *n*

**philosophy** /fi'losəfi/ *n* **1a** the pursuit of wisdom **b** the rational study of the nature and meaning of existence, reality, knowledge, human perception, moral values, etc **2a** the sciences and humanities exclusive of medicine, law, and theology ⟨*a doctor of* ~⟩ **b** an academic discipline characteristically comprising LOGIC, AESTHETICS, ETHICS, METAPHYSICS, and EPISTEMOLOGY **3a** the philosophical theories or concepts of a specified individual, group, or period ⟨*Kantian* ~⟩ **b** the theory or principles underlying or concerning a specified sphere of activity or thought ⟨*the* ~ *of cooking*⟩ ⟨~ *of science*⟩ **4a** the sum of beliefs and attitudes to life of a specified individual, group, or period ⟨*the vegetarian* ~⟩ **b** equanimity in the face of trouble or stress **5** *archaic* the investigation of natural phenomena; *esp* alchemy, astronomy, and astrology [ME *philosophie,* fr OF, fr L *philosophia,* fr Gk, fr *philosophos* philosopher

**-philous** /-filəs/ *comb form* (→ *adj*) -philic

**philtre,** *NAm* **philter** /'filtə/ *n* a potion or drug held to have the power to arouse love or sexual passion △ filter, phial [MF *philtre,* fr L *philtrum,* fr Gk *philtron;* akin to Gk *philos* dear]

**phimosis** /fie'mohsis/ *n, pl* **phimoses** tightness of the foreskin preventing its retraction [NL, fr Gk *phimōsis,* lit., muzzling, fr *phimos* muzzle]

**phizog** /'fizog/ *n, Br humorous* the face [by shortening & alter. fr *physiognomy*]

**phleb-, phlebo-** *comb form* vein ⟨phleb*itis*⟩ [ME *fleb-,* fr MF, fr LL *phlebo-,* fr Gk *phleb-, phlebo-,* fr *phleb-, phleps;* akin to L *fluere* to flow – more at FLUID]

**phlebitis** /fli'bietəs/ *n* inflammation of a vein [NL] – **phlebitic** *adj*

**phlebogram** /'fleebəgram/ *n* a photograph of a vein or a record of the movement of blood through it (e g by X-ray photography after injection of a substance that does not allow the X rays to pass through it) [ISV]

**phlebography** /fli'bogrəfi/ *n* the making of phlebograms [ISV] – **phlebographic** *adj*

**phlebology** /fli'boləji/ *n* a branch of medicine or physiology concerned with the veins [ISV]

**phlebosclerosis** /ˌfleboh-sklə'rohsis/ *n* hardening of a vein [NL] – **phlebosclerotic** *adj*

**phlebotom·ize, -ise** /fli'botəmiez/ *vt* to draw blood from by phlebotomy; bleed

**phlebotomy** /fli'botəmi/ *n* the letting or taking of blood in the treatment or diagnosis of disease by cutting a vein; VENESECTION [ME *fleobotomie,* fr MF *flebotomie,* fr LL *phlebotomia,* fr Gk, fr *phleb-* + *-tomia* -tomy] – **phlebotomist** *n*

**phlegm** /flem/ *n* **1** the one of the four HUMOURS (bodily fluids believed to determine a person's disposition) in medieval physiology that was believed to cause sluggishness **2** thick mucus secreted in the respiratory passages, esp in abnormal

quantity **3a** dull or apathetic coldness or indifference **b** imperturbability, coolness, composure [ME *fleume,* fr MF, fr LL *phlegmat-, phlegma,* fr Gk, flame, inflammation, phlegm, fr *phlegein* to burn – more at BLACK] – **phlegmy** *adj*

**phlegmatic** /fleg'matik/ *adj* **1** resembling, consisting of, or producing phlegm **2** having or showing a slow and stolid temperament; unexcitable – **phlegmatically** *adv*

**phloem** /'floh·em/ *n* a complex tissue of higher plants that functions chiefly in the conduction of soluble food substances throughout the plant and consists typically of SIEVE TUBES (long tubelike structures composed of interconnecting cells) and their associated COMPANION CELLS supported by thin-walled PARENCHYMA cells and often fibres – compare XYLEM [Ger, fr Gk *phloios, phloos* bark; akin to Gk *phallos* penis – more at BLOW]

**phloem ray** *n* (a portion of) a VASCULAR RAY (band or wedge of nonspecialized tissue) that is located in phloem – compare XYLEM RAY

**phlogistic** /flo'jistik/ *adj* **1** of or containing phlogiston **2** of inflammations and fevers [(1) NL *phlogist*on + E *-ic;* (2) Gk *phlogist*os inflammable + E *-ic*]

**phlogiston** /flo'jist(ə)n/ *n* the hypothetical principle or substance of fire that was thought to be present in all combustible substances and released during combustion [NL, fr Gk, neut of *phlogistos* inflammable, fr *phlogizein* to set on fire, fr *phlog-, phlox* flame, fr *phlegein* to burn]

**phlogopite** /'flogəpiet/ *n* a brown to red form of the mineral MICA [Ger *phlogopit,* fr Gk *phlogōpos* fiery-looking, fr *phlog-, phlox* + *ōps* face – more at EYE]

**phlorizin, phlorhizin** /'flawrəzin, 'flo-, flə'riezin/ *n* a GLUCOSIDE (chemical compound derived from glucose), $C_{21}H_{24}O_{10}$, that is extracted from the bark or root bark of various plants of the rose family (e g the apple, pear, and cherry), produces GLYCOSURIA (excess sugar in the urine) if injected hypodermically, and is used chiefly in producing experimental diabetes in animals [ISV *phlo-* (fr Gk *phloos* bark) + *rhiz-* + *-in*]

**phlox** /floks/ *n, pl* **phlox, phloxes** any of a genus (*Phlox* of the family Polemoniaceae, the phlox family) of American plants widely grown for their pink, red, purple, white, or variegated flowers [NL, genus name, fr L, a flower, fr Gk, flame, wallflower]

**phlyctenule** /flik'tenyool, 'fliktənyoohl/ *n* a small blister or pustule; *esp* one on the CONJUNCTIVA (membrane lining the inner surface of the eyelid) or CORNEA (transparent membrane covering the front of the eye) [NL *phlyctenula,* dim. of *phlyctena* pustule, fr Gk *phlyktaina* blister, fr *phlyzein* to boil over – more at FLUID]

**-phobe** /-ˌfohb/ *comb form* (→ *n or adj*) (one) afraid of or averse to (something specified) ⟨*Franco*phobe⟩ [Gk *-phobos* fearing]

**phobia** /'fohbi-ə, -byə/ *n* an exaggerated and illogical fear of a particular object, class of objects, or situation ⟨*he has a* ~ *about spiders*⟩ [NL, fr LL *-phobia,* fr Gk, fr *-phobos* fearing, fr *phobos* fear, flight; akin to Gk *phebesthai* to flee, be frightened, Lith *bėgti* to flee]

**-phobia** /-fohbi-ə, -byə/ *comb form* (→ *n*) abnormal or illogical fear of ⟨*claustro*phobia⟩

**phobic** /'fohbik/ *adj* **1** of or constituting phobia **2** motivated by or based on withdrawal from an unpleasant stimulus ⟨*a* ~ *response to light*⟩

**-phobic** /-'fohbik/, **-phobous** *comb form* (→ *adj*) lacking (chemical) affinity for ⟨*hydro*phobic⟩; having an aversion for ⟨*Anglo*phobic⟩ – compare -PHILIC [*-phobic* fr Fr *-phobique,* fr LL *-phobicus,* fr Gk *-phobikos,* fr *-phobia; -phobous* fr LL *-phobus,* fr Gk *-phobos*]

**phoebe** /'feebi/ *n* any of several flycatchers (genus *Sayornis,* esp *Sayornis phoebe*) of the USA [alter. of *peewee,* of imit origin]

**Phoebe** /'feebi/ *n* – used as a poetic name for the moon [*Phoebe* (called also Artemis or Diana), Greco-Roman goddess of the moon]

**Phoebus** /'feebəs/ *n* – used as a poetic name for the sun [*Phoebus* (called also Apollo), Greco-Roman god of the sun]

**Phoenician** /fə'neesh(ə)n, -shyən, -'ni-/ *n* **1** a native or inhabitant of ancient Phoenicia **2** the Semitic language of ancient Phoenicia [*Phoenicia,* ancient country in SW Asia] – **Phoenician** *adj*

**phoenix** /'feeniks/ *n* **1** a beautiful mythical bird of the Arabian desert which, according to one account, lived 500 years, burned itself on a pyre, and rose youthfully alive from the ashes to live another period **2** something that appears to rise from its own ashes or be reborn after complete destruction [ME *fenix,* fr OE, fr L *phoenix,* fr Gk *phoinix* purple, crimson, Phoenician, phoenix, date palm, fr *phoinos* bloodred; akin to Gk *phonos* murder, *theinein* to strike – more at DEFEND] – **phoenixlike** *adj*

**phon** /fon/ *n* the unit of loudness on a scale beginning at zero for the faintest audible sound and corresponding to the decibel scale of sound intensity, with the number of phons of a given sound being equal to the intensity in decibels of a pure tone of 1000 hertz frequency judged by the average listener to be equal in loudness to the given sound [ISV, fr Gk *phōnē* voice, sound]

**phon-** /fohn-, fon-/, **phono-** *comb form* sound; voice; speech ⟨phon*ate*⟩ ⟨phono*graph*⟩ [L, fr Gk *phōn-, phōno-,* fr *phōnē* – more at BAN]

**phonate** /foh'nayt/ *vi* to produce vocal sounds, esp speech – **phonation** *n,* **phonatory** *adj*

**¹phone** /fohn/ *n* **1** a telephone **2** *informal* an earphone or headphone [by shortening]

**²phone** *vb* to telephone ⟨*they* ~d *the doctor*⟩ ⟨*he* ~d *in sick*⟩ ⟨*she* ~d *up her neighbour*⟩

**³phone** *n* a single speech sound; a simple vowel or consonant sound [Gk *phōnē*]

**-phone** /-fohn/ *comb form* (→ *n*) **1** sound ⟨*homo*phone⟩ – often in names of musical instruments and sound-transmitting devices ⟨*radio*phone⟩ ⟨*xylo*phone⟩ ⟨*ear*phone⟩ **2** a speaker of (a specified language) ⟨*Anglo*phone⟩ [Gk *-phōnos* sounding, fr *phōnē*] – **-phonic** *comb form* (→ *adj*)

**phone book** *n* TELEPHONE DIRECTORY

**'phone-,in** *n* a broadcast programme in which viewers or listeners can participate by phone

**phonematic** /,fohni'matik/ *adj* phonemic – **phonematically** *adv*

**phoneme** /'fohneem/ *n* any of the smallest speech sounds that are capable of distinguishing words in a given language or dialect ⟨*the* /p/ *of* pat *and the* /f/ *of* fat *are two different* ~s⟩ ⟨*the voiceless* /r/ *of* free *and the voiced* /r/ *of* run *are the same* ~⟩ – compare ALLOPHONE, MORPHEME [Fr *phonème,* fr Gk *phōnēmat-, phōnēma* speech sound, utterance, fr *phōnein* to sound]

**phonemic** /fə'neemik/ *adj* **1** of or using phonemes ⟨*a* ~ *contrast*⟩ **2** constituting distinctive phonemes ⟨*in English* /n/ *and* /ng/ *are* ~ *because they distinguish* sin *from* sing⟩ – **phonemically** *adv*

**phonemics** /fə'neemiks/ *n taking sing vb* **1** the study of phonemes **2** the phonemic system of a language

**phonendoscope** /fə'nendə,skohp/ *n* an instrument for making small sounds, esp in the human body, louder [ISV *phon-* + *end-* + *-scope*]

**phonetic** /fə'netik/ *also* **phonetical** /-kl/ *adj* **1a** of spoken language or speech sounds **b** of the science of phonetics **2** representing the sounds of speech: **2a** *of a language of system of spelling* having all the words spelt as they are pronounced **b** representing speech sounds by one symbol for each distinguishable sound [NL *phoneticus,* fr Gk *phōnētikos,* fr *phōnein* to sound with the voice, fr *phōnē* voice] – **phonetically** *adv*

**phonetic alphabet** *n* **1** a set of symbols used for writing down speech sounds **2** any of various systems of code words used to identify letters of the alphabet in voice communication (e g *golf* for g)

**phonetician** /,fohnə'tish(ə)n, ,fon-/ *n* a specialist in phonetics

**phonetics** /fə'netiks/ *n* **1** *taking sing vb* the study of speech sounds and the processes of speech **2** *taking sing or pl vb* the system of speech sounds of a particular language; *also* the symbols that represent them ⟨*written in* ~⟩

**phonetist** /'fohnətist/ *n* **1** a phonetician **2** an advocate of phonetic spelling

**phoney,** *chiefly NAm* **phony** /'fohni/ *adj, informal* **1** not genuine, real, or true; fake ⟨*a* ~ *name*⟩ **2** *of a person* pretending to be something one is not [origin unknown] – **phoney** *n,* **phoniness** *n*

**-phonia** /-'fohnyə, -ni•ə/ *comb form* (→ *n*) **1** -phony **2** speech disorder; -phasia ⟨*dys*phonia⟩

**phonic** /'fonik/ *adj* **1** of or producing sound; acoustic **2a** of speech sounds **b** of phonics – **phonically** *adv*

**phonics** /'fohniks/ *n taking sing vb* **1** a method of teaching beginners to read by learning how to pronounce letters, letter groups, and syllables **2** *archaic* the science of sound; acoustics

**phono-** – see PHON-

**phonogram** /'fohnə,gram/ *n* **1a** a character or symbol used (e g in shorthand) to represent a spoken sound **b** a sequence of letters sounding the same in many different words **2** a record made by a phonograph [ISV] – **phonogrammic, phonogramic** *adj,* **phonogrammically, phonogramically** *adv*

**phonograph** /'fohnə,grahf, -,graf/ *n* **1** an early device for recording or reproducing sound in which a stylus cuts or follows a groove on a cylinder **2** *chiefly NAm* a gramophone; RECORD PLAYER – **phonographic** *adj*

**phonography** /foh'nogrəfi/ *n* a system of spelling or shorthand based on pronunciation – **phonographer, phonographist** *n,* **phonographic** *adj,* **phonographically** *adv*

**phonolite** /'fohnə,liet/ *n* a fine-grained grey or green rock formed by the cooling and solidification of lava on the earth's surface and consisting essentially of an alkaline FELDSPAR and NEPHELINE [Fr, fr Ger *phonolith,* fr *phon-* + *-lith;* fr its ringing sound when struck] – **phonolitic** *adj*

**phonology** /fə'noləji/ *n* **1** the study of the speech sounds in a language or languages **2** the sound system (PHONETICS and PHONEMICS) of a language at a particular time – **phonologist** *n,* **phonological** *also* **phonologic** *adj*

**phonon** /'fohnon/ *n* a QUANTUM (smallest unit into which a physical quantity can be divided) of energy in the form of vibrations [*phon-* + *²-on*]

**phonoreception** /'fohnoh•ri,sepsh(ə)n/ *n* the perception of vibratory motion of relatively high frequency; *specif* hearing

**phonoreceptor** /'fohnoh•ri,septə/ *n* an animal organ for the perception of sound waves

**phony** /'fohni/ *n or adj, chiefly NAm* (a) phoney

**-phony** /-fəni/ *also* **-phonia** /-'fohnyə/ *comb form* (→ *n*) **1** sound ⟨*tele*phony⟩ ⟨*eu*phony⟩ **2** speech ⟨*dys*phonia⟩ [ME *-phonie,* fr OF, fr L *-phonia,* fr Gk *-phōnia,* fr *-phōnos* sounding – more at -PHONE]

**phooey** /'fooh•i/ *interj* – used to express scorn, disbelief, etc

**-phore** /-faw/ *comb form* (→ *n*) bearer; carrier ⟨*gameto*phore⟩ ⟨*sema*phore⟩ [NL *-phorus,* fr Gk *-phoros,* fr *-phoros* (adj comb form) carrying, fr *pherein* to carry – more at BEAR] – **-phorous** *comb form* (→ *adj*)

**-phoresis** /-fə'reesis/ *comb form* (→ *n*), *pl* **-phoreses** /-seez/ transmission ⟨*electro*phoresis⟩ [NL, fr Gk *phorēsis* act of carrying, fr *phorein* to carry, wear, freq of *pherein*]

**phosgene** /'fozjeen/ *n* a very poisonous colourless gas, $COCl_2$, with a suffocating unpleasant smell, that is a severe respiratory irritant, was used as a war gas in World War I, and is now used in the manufacture of chemicals [deriv of Gk *phōs* light + *-genēs* born; fr its having been originally obtained by the action of sunlight upon equal volumes of chlorine & carbon monoxide]

**phosgenite** /'fozjəniet/ *n* a rare mineral, $Pb_2Cl_2CO_3$, occurring as greyish crystals and consisting of a carbonate and chloride of lead [Ger *phosgenit,* fr *phosgen* phosgene]

**phosph-, phospho-** *comb form* **1** phosphorus ⟨phosph*ide*⟩; phosphorus and ⟨phospho*protein*⟩ **2** phosphate ⟨phospho*fructokinase*⟩ [*phosphorus*]

**phosphatase** /'fosfətayz, -ays/ *n* any of various ENZYMES that accelerate the breakdown and synthesis of organic phosphates that are ESTERS of PHOSPHORIC ACID, and the transfer of phosphate groups to other compounds

**¹phosphate** /'fosfayt/ *n* **1a(1)** any of various chemical compounds (SALTS or ESTERS) formed by combination between PHOSPHORIC ACID and a metal atom, an alcohol, or another chemical group **a(2)** a chemical group derived from PHOSPHORIC ACID by removal of one or more hydrogen atoms, that is characteristic of a phosphate **b** an organic chemical compound of PHOSPHORIC ACID in which the acid unit is bound to nitrogen or a CARBOXYL group (organic acid group) in a way that permits useful energy to be released ⟨*high energy* ~s⟩ **2** *often pl* any of several phosphates or materials containing a phosphate used as fertilizers [Fr, fr *acide phosphorique* phosphoric acid]

**²phosphate** *vt* to coat (zinc alloys or steel) with a thin layer of phosphate

**phosphate rock** *n* a rock that consists largely of CALCIUM PHOSPHATE, usu together with other minerals (e g CALCIUM CARBONATE), and is used in making fertilizers and as a source of phosphorus compounds – called also PHOSPHORITE

**phosphatic** /fos'fatik/ *adj* of or containing PHOSPHORIC ACID or phosphates ⟨~ *fertilizers*⟩

**phosphatide** /'fosfətied/ *n* PHOSPHOLIPID (fatty compound occurring in living cells) [ISV] – **phosphatidic** *adj*

**phosphatidyl** /,fosfə'tiedil, fos'fatidil/ *n* any of several chemical groups, $(RCOO)_2C_3H_5OPO(OH)$, that have a VALENCY of one and are derived from phosphatidic acids

**phosphatidylcholine** /ˌfosfəˌtiedil'kohleen, fosˌfatidil-/ *n* LECITHIN (fatty compound occurring in animals and plants)

**phosphat·ize, -ise** /'fosfətiez/ *vt* **1** to change to a phosphate or phosphates **2** to treat with PHOSPHORIC ACID or a phosphate – **phosphatization** *n*

**phosphaturia** /ˌfosfə'tyooəriə/ *n* the presence of abnormally large amounts of phosphates in the urine [NL, fr ISV *phosphate* + NL -*uria*] – **phosphaturic** *adj*

**phosphene** /'fosfeen/ *n* an impression of light produced by pressure on the eyeball, causing excitation of the retina [deriv of Gk *phōs* light + *phainein* to show – more at FANCY]

**phosphide** /'fosfied/ *n* a compound of phosphorus with one other chemical element or group that is usu more ELECTROPOSITIVE (has a greater tendency to release or lose electrons) than phosphorus [ISV]

**phosphine** *n* (any of various organic chemical compounds derived from) a colourless extremely poisonous inflammable gas, $PH_3$, that has a smell of decaying fish and is used esp to fumigate stored grain [ISV]

**phosphite** /'fosfiet/ *n* any of various chemical compounds (SALTS or ESTERS) formed by combination between PHOSPHOROUS ACID and a metal atom, an alcohol, or another chemical group

**phospho-** – see PHOSPH-

**phosphocreatine** /ˌfosfoh'kree·əteen/ *n* CREATINE PHOSPHATE (compound that acts as an energy source for muscle contraction) [ISV]

**phosphodiesterase** /ˌfosfoh·die'estərayz, -ays/ *n* an ENZYME (e g from snake venom) that inactivates CYCLIC AMP (substance that regulates many processes inside cells) and related compounds containing a phosphate group by splitting one of the two ESTER bonds joining the phosphate group to the rest of the molecule [*phosph-* + *diester* + *-ase*]

**phosphoenolpyruvate** /fosˌfoh·ənolpie'roohvayt/ *n* the negatively charged ion $CH_2=C(OPO_3H_2)COO^-$, that is derived from PHOSPHOENOLPYRUVIC ACID and is formed from PHOSPHOGLYCERIC ACID as an intermediate in the breakdown of carbohydrates in living cells to yield energy

**phosphoenolpyruvic acid** /fosˌfoh·ənolpie'roohvik/ *n* the phosphate, $CH_2=C(OPO_3H_2)COOH$, of the ENOL form of PYRUVIC ACID

**phosphofructokinase** /ˌfosfoh,fruktoh'kienayz, -ˌfrooktoh-, -ays/ *n* an ENZYME that promotes the transfer of a second phosphate group to a compound of FRUCTOSE (a sugar) with one phosphate group in the process by which carbohydrates are broken down in a living cell to yield energy [*phosph-* + *fructo*se + *kinase*]

**phosphoglucomutase** /ˌfosfoh,gloohkoh'myoohtayz, -ays/ *n* an ENZYME found in all plant and animal cells that speeds up the reversible conversion of GLUCOSE-1-PHOSPHATE to GLUCOSE-6-PHOSPHATE in the breakdown of carbohydrates to yield energy or the synthesis of carbohydrates that can be stored in the body [*phosph-* + *gluc-* + *mutase*]

**phosphoglyceraldehyde** /ˌfosfoh·glisə'raldihied/ *n* a phosphate of glyceraldehyde, $CHOCH(OH)CH_2OPO(OH)_2$, that is formed as an intermediate in the breakdown of carbohydrates in living cells from a compound of FRUCTOSE (a sugar) with two phosphate groups

**phosphoglyceric acid** /ˌfosfoh·gli'serik/ *n* either of two forms (ISOMERS) of a phosphate, $HOOCC_2H_3(OH)OPO_3H_2$, of GLYCERIC ACID that are formed as intermediates in photosynthesis and in the breakdown of carbohydrates in living cells to yield energy

**phosphokinase** /ˌfosfoh'kienayz, -ays/ *n* KINASE

**phospholipase** /ˌfosfoh'liepayz, -ays/ *n* an ENZYME that breaks down phospholipids

**phospholipid** /ˌfosfoh'lipid/ *n* a LIPID (fatty compound) containing compounds of PHOSPHORIC ACID that is found in all living cells, esp in membranes – called also PHOSPHATIDE

**phosphonium** /fos'fohniəm/ *n* a chemical group, $PH_4$, having a VALENCY of one, that is analogous to ammonium with the nitrogen atom replaced by a phosphorus atom, and is derived from phosphine [NL

**phosphoprotein** /ˌfosfoh'prohteen/ *n* any of various proteins (e g CASEIN) that contain PHOSPHORIC ACID

**phosphor** *also* **phosphore** /'fosfə/ *n* a phosphorescent substance; *specif* a substance that emits light when subjected to radiation [L *phosphorus*, fr Gk *phōsphoros*, lit., light-bringer, fr

*phōsphoros* light-bearing, fr *phōs* light + *pherein* to carry, bring – more at BEAR]

**phosphor-, phosphoro-** *comb form* phosph- ⟨phosphoro*lysis*⟩

**phosphorate** /'fosfərayt/ *vt* to treat or combine with phosphorus

**phosphor bronze** *n* a hard corrosion-resistant bronze that contains a small amount of phosphorus

**phosphorescence** /ˌfosfə'res(ə)ns/ *n* **1** the emission of light without noticeable heat, caused by the absorption of radiation and continuing after this radiation has stopped; *also* such light **2** the property of shining faintly or glowing in the dark without apparent cause – **phosphoresce** *vi*, **phosphorescent** *adj*

**phosphoretted**, *NAm chiefly* **phosphoreted** /'fosfəretid/ *adj* impregnated or combined with phosphorus [NL *phosphoretum* phoshide, fr *phosphorus*]

**phosphoric** /fos'forik/ *adj* of or containing phosphorus, esp with a relatively high VALENCY

**phosphoric acid** /fos'forik/ *n* **1** an acid, $H_3PO_4$, that becomes liquid on exposure to air and is used esp in preparing phosphates (e g for fertilizers), in rust-proofing metals, and as a flavouring in soft drinks – called also ORTHOPHOSPHORIC ACID **2** any of several forms of phosphoric acid (e g METAPHOSPHORIC ACID or PYROPHOSPHORIC ACID) produced by combination with water

**phosphorism** /'fosfəriz(ə)m/ *n* phosphorus poisoning, esp when exposure to phosphorus has extended over a long period of time

**phosphorite** /'fosfəriet/ *n* PHOSPHATE ROCK – **phosphoritic** *adj*

**phosphorolysis** /ˌfosfə'roləsis/ *n* a reversible reaction analogous to HYDROLYSIS (chemical breakdown of a substance by reaction with water), in which PHOSPHORIC ACID functions in a manner similar to that of water with the formation of a phosphate (e g GLUCOSE-1-PHOSPHATE in the breakdown of liver GLYCOGEN) [NL] – **phosphorolytic** *adj*

**phosphorous** /'fosf(ə)rəs/ *adj* of or containing phosphorus, esp with a relatively low VALENCY

**phosphorous acid** *n* an acid, $H_3PO_3$, that absorbs water from the air and is used esp as a REDUCING AGENT and in making PHOSPHITES

**phosphorus** /'fosf(ə)rəs/ *n* a nonmetallic chemical element with a VALENCY of three or five, that belongs to the nitrogen family and occurs widely, esp as phosphates (e g CALCIUM PHOSPHATE). The two main forms are white phosphorus, which is poisonous, phosphorescent, and very inflammable, and red phosphorus, which is less reactive. [NL, fr Gk *phōsphoros* light-bearing – more at PHOSPHOR]

**phosphorylase** /fos'forilayz, -ays/ *n* any of various ENZYMES that speed up phosphorolysis with the formation of organic PHOSPHATES; *esp* one that promotes the breakdown of GLYCOGEN (form in which carbohydrate is stored in the animal body) to GLUCOSE-1-PHOSPHATE [*phosphoryl* (the radical PO) + *-ase*]

**phosphorylation** /fosˌfori'laysh(ə)n/ *n* the combining of an organic chemical compound with inorganic PHOSPHATE or with a phosphate group transferred from another organic phosphate; *esp* the enzyme-controlled process by which carbohydrates (e g glucose) are converted into their phosphates in metabolic processes (e g the breakdown of carbohydrates to yield energy or the synthesis of carbohydrates that can be stored in the body) – **phosphorylate** *vb*, **phosphorylative** *adj*

**phot** /foht/ *n* the cgs unit of illumination equal to one LUMEN per square centimetre [ISV, fr Gk *phōt-, phōs* light]

**phot-, photo-** *comb form* **1** light; radiant energy ⟨photo*n*⟩ ⟨photo*graphy*⟩ **2** photograph; photographic ⟨photo*engraving*⟩ **3** photoelectric ⟨photo*cell*⟩ [Gk *phōt-, phōto-*, fr *phōt-, phōs* – more at FANCY]

**photic** /'fohtik/ *adj* **1** of or involving light, esp in relation to living organisms **2** penetrated by sunlight; *esp* of or being the zone of a body of water (e g an ocean) that is penetrated by sunlight; EUPHOTIC – **photically** *adv*

**photo** /'fohtoh/ *n, pl* **photos** a photograph

**photoautotrophic** /ˌfohtoh,awtə'trohfik/ *adj, of an organism* (e g a green plant) capable of synthesizing food from inorganic substances (e g carbon dioxide), using energy from light – compare CHEMOAUTOTROPHIC – **photoautotrophically** *adv*

**photobiology** /ˌfohtoh·bie'oləji/ *n* a branch of biology that deals with the effects of radiant energy (e g light) on living things [ISV] – **photobiologist** *n*, **photobiologic, photobiological** *adj*

**photobiotic** /ˌfohtoh·bie'otik/ *adj* requiring light in order to live or thrive

**photocall** /-ˌkawl/ *n* a session at which a person is photographed, typically for the purpose of publicity (e g in the press)

**photocathode** /ˈfohtohˌkathohd/ *n* a CATHODE that emits electrons when exposed to ELECTROMAGNETIC RADIATION, esp light [ISV]

**photocell** /-ˌsel/ *n* PHOTOELECTRIC CELL [ISV]

**photochemical** /ˌfohtoh'kemikl/ *adj* 1 of, being, or resulting from chemical reactions or changes induced by radiant energy, esp light ⟨~ *reactions*⟩ 2 of photochemistry – **photochemically** *adv*

**photochemistry** /-'kemistri/ *n* 1 a branch of chemistry that deals with the effect of radiant energy, esp light, in producing chemical changes 2a photochemical properties ⟨*the ~ of gases*⟩ b photochemical processes ⟨*the ~ of vision*⟩ – **photochemist** *n*

**photochromic** /ˌfohtə'krohmik/ *adj* 1 capable of changing colour on exposure to radiant energy, esp light ⟨~ *glass*⟩ 2 of or using the change of colour shown by a photochromic substance ⟨*a ~ process*⟩ [*phot-* + *chrom-* + *-ic*] – **photochromism** *n*

**photocoagulation** /ˌfohtoh·kohˌagyoo'laysh(ə)n/ *n* a surgical process of coagulating tissue by means of a precisely oriented high-energy light source (e g a laser beam), used esp in the treatment of detached retinas

**photocomposition** /-ˌkompə'zish(ə)n/ *n* the typesetting of reading matter directly on film or photographic paper for reproduction – **photocompose** *vt*, **photocomposer** *n*

**photoconductive** /ˌfohtoh·kən'duktiv/ *adj* having, involving, or operating by photoconductivity

**photoconductivity** /-ˌkonduk'tivəti/ *n* electrical conductivity that is affected by exposure to light or other radiation; *specif* an increase in the ability of a material (e g selenium) to conduct electricity as a result of absorbing radiant energy, esp light

**photocopier** /ˈfohtohˌkopiə/ *n* a machine for making photocopies

**¹photocopy** /ˈfohtohˌkopi, ˈfohtə-/ *n* a copy of graphic matter made by a photographic process [ISV]

**²photocopy** *vb* to make a photocopy (of)

**photocurrent** /ˈfohtohˌkurənt/ *n* an electric current produced by photoelectric effects [*photo*electric *current*]

**photodecomposition** /ˌfohtohˌdeekompə'zish(ə)n/ *n* the chemical breakdown of a substance (e g a pesticide) by means of radiant energy, esp light

**photodetector** /ˌfohtoh·di'tektə/ *n* any of various devices for detecting and measuring the intensity of radiant energy (e g light) by photoelectric action

**photodisintegration** /ˌfohtohˌdisinti'graysh(ə)n/ *n* disintegration of the nucleus of an atom as a result of its absorption of a PHOTON (unit of ELECTROMAGNETIC RADIATION) – **photodisintegrate** *vt*

**photodissociation** /ˌfohtoh·diˌsohsi'aysh(ə)n, -ˌsohshi-/ *n* DISSOCIATION (reversible decomposition of the molecules) of a chemical compound (e g water) by the action of radiant energy, esp light – **photodissociate** *vt*

**photoelectric** /ˌfohtoh·i'lektrik/ *adj* being, involving, or using any of various electrical effects (e g photoconductivity or photoemission) due to the interaction of radiation (e g light) with matter; *esp* being, involving, or using the release of electrons from a surface as a result of its exposure to and absorption of ELECTROMAGNETIC RADIATION (e g ultraviolet radiation) [ISV] – **photoelectrically** *adv*, **photoelectricity** *n*

**photoelectric cell** *n* 1 a device using the electrical effects, esp photoconductivity, of light falling on an electric cell to generate or control an electric current and thus detect and measure the intensity of light – called also PHOTOCELL 2 an instrument (e g a burglar alarm) that is operated by such a device – called also ELECTRIC EYE, MAGIC EYE

**photoelectron** /-i'lektron/ *n* an electron released in photoemission [ISV] – **photoelectronic** *adj*

**photoemission** /-i'mish(ə)n/ *n* the release of electrons from a substance by means of energy supplied by ELECTROMAGNETIC RADIATION, esp light – **photoemissive** *adj*

**photoengraving** /-in'grayving/ *n* 1 a process for making printing blocks by photographing an image on a metal plate and then etching 2a a plate made by photoengraving b a print made from such a plate – **photoengrave** *vt*, **photoengraver** *n*

**photo finish** *n* 1 the finish of a race in which contestants are so close that the winner has to be determined by examination of a photograph of them crossing the finishing line 2 a close contest

**Photofit** /ˈfohtohˌfit/ *trademark* – used for a means of constructing a likeness of a person's face from a combination of photographs of individual features, used esp by the police for purposes of identification ⟨*a ~ picture*⟩; compare IDENTIKIT

**photoflash** /ˈfohtohˌflash/ *n* a flashbulb

**photoflood** /-ˌflud/ *n* an electric lamp using excess voltage to give intense sustained illumination for indoor photography, television, etc

**photofluorogram** /ˌfohtoh'flooərəgram/ *n* a photograph made by photofluorography

**photofluorography** /ˌfohtoh·flooə'rogrəfi/ *n* the photography of the image produced on a fluorescent screen by X rays, used in medical diagnosis and screening – **photofluorographic** *adj*

**photogene** /ˈfohtohˌjen/ *n* AFTERIMAGE [ISV *phot-* + *-gen*]

**photogenic** /ˌfohtə'jenik, -'jeenik/ *adj* 1 produced or caused by light ⟨~ *dermatitis*⟩ 2 producing or generating light; luminescent ⟨~ *bacteria*⟩ 3 looking attractive in photographs – **photogenically** *adv*

**photogram** /ˈfohtəˌgram/ *n* a shadowlike image made without a camera by placing objects between light-sensitive paper and a light source [ISV]

**photogrammetry** /ˌfohtoh'gramətri/ *n* the use of photographs to obtain reliable measurements; *esp* the construction of maps from aerial photographs using stereoscopic equipment [ISV *photogram* photograph (fr *phot-* + *-gram*) + *-metry*] – **photogrammetrist** *n*, **photogrammetric** *adj*

**¹photograph** /ˈfohtəˌgrahf, -ˌgraf/ *n* an exact pictorial reproduction of a person, thing, or scene obtained by use of photography [*phot-* + *-graph*]

**²photograph** *vt* to take a photograph of ~ *vi* to undergo being photographed ⟨*the model ~ed perfectly*⟩ – **photographer** *n*

**photographic** /ˌfohtə'grafik/ *adj* 1 of, obtained by, or used in photography 2 resembling a photograph in exactness or realism 3 *of a person's memory* able to retain visual images in perfect detail; EIDETIC – **photographically** *adv*

**photography** /fə'togrəfi/ *n* the art or process of using a camera to produce images on a sensitized surface (e g a film) by the action of ELECTROMAGNETIC RADIATION (e g light or X rays) and treating the surface chemically to obtain permanent records of the images in the form of photographs

**photogravure** /ˌfohtəgrə'vyooə/ *n* a process for making prints from an INTAGLIO (etched) plate prepared by photographic methods; *also* a print thus produced [Fr, fr *phot-* + *gravure*]

**photoheliograph** /ˌfohtoh'heeli·əˌgrahf, -ˌgraf/ *n* a telescope adapted for photographing the sun

**photoinduced** /ˌfohtoh·in'dyoohst/ *adj* induced by the action of light – **photoinduction** *n*, **photoinductive** *adj*

**photoionization** /ˌfohtohˌie·ənie'zaysh(ə)n, -ni-/ *n* IONIZATION (formation of electrically charged atoms or groups of atoms) (e g in the ionosphere) resulting from collision of atoms or molecules with PHOTONS (units of ELECTROMAGNETIC RADIATION)

**photojournalism** /ˌfohtoh'juhnəliz(ə)m/ *n* journalism which places more emphasis on photographs than on written material – **photojournalist** *n*, **photojournalistic** *adj*

**photokinesis** /ˌfohtoh·ki'neesis, -kie-/ *n* movement or activity of an organism induced by light [NL, fr *phot-* + Gk *kinēsis* motion, fr *kinein* to move] – **photokinetic** *adj*

**photolithography** /ˌfohtohli'thogrəfi/ *n* 1 LITHOGRAPHY (printing process using metal or stone plates) in which photographically prepared plates are used 2 a process in the manufacture of an INTEGRATED CIRCUIT in which a light or electron image of the circuit is projected onto a photosensitive film on the surface of a piece of silicon or similar substance, thus leaving a permanent record of the circuit on the surface [ISV] – **photolithographer** *n*, **photolithograph** *n or vt*, **photolithographic** *adj*

**photolyse**, *NAm chiefly* **photolyze** /ˈfohtəliez/ *vt* to cause to undergo photolysis

**photolysis** /foh'toləsis/ *n* the irreversible breakdown of a chemical compound by the action of radiant energy, esp light [NL] – **photolytic** *adj*, **photolytically** *adv*

**¹photomap** /ˈfohtohˌmap/ *n* a map constructed by adding grid lines, placenames, etc to aerial photographs

**²photomap** *vb* **-pp-** to make a photomap (of)

**¹photomechanical** /ˈfohtoh·mi'kanikl/ *adj* of or involving any of various processes for producing printed matter from a photographically prepared surface [ISV] – **photomechanically** *adv*

²**photomechanical** *n* a piece of finished copy for a book or other publication, consisting typically of typeset proofs and illustrations positioned and mounted for photomechanical reproduction

**photometer** /foh'tomitə/ *n* an instrument for measuring illumination or the intensity of light, usu by comparison with another standard light source [NL *photometrum*, fr *phot-* + *-metrum* -meter]

**photometry** /foh'tomitri/ *n* (a branch of science that deals with) the measurement of the various properties of light (e g intensity of light, illumination, or brightness) [NL *photometria*, fr *phot-* + *-metria* -metry] – **photometric** *adj*, **photometrically** *adv*

**photomicrograph** /,fohtə'miekrə,grahf, -,graf/ *n* a photograph of the image of an object magnified under a microscope [*phot-* + *micr-* + *-graph*] – **photomicrograph** *vt*, **photomicrographic** *adj*, **photomicrography** *n*

**photomicroscope** /,fohtoh'miekrəskohp/ *n* an instrument or system that combines a microscope, camera, and light source, and is used for making photomicrographs – **photomicroscopic** *adj*

**photomontage** /,fohtoh·mon'tahzh/ *n* (the technique of producing) a picture made up of several juxtaposed, overlapping, or superimposed photographs [ISV]

**photomosaic** /,fohtoh·moh'zayik/, **mosaic** *n* **1** a mosaic array of PHOTOEMISSIVE cells in a television CAMERA TUBE (part of a camera where optical images are converted into electrical signals), in which each cell produces an electric charge proportional to the intensity of light falling on it **2** an arrangement of consecutive aerial photographs covering a wide area of ground

**photomultiplier** /,fohtoh'multiplie-ə/ *n* an ELECTRON MULTIPLIER (device for amplifying a current of electrons) that increases the brightness of an electronic image (e g a television picture) by multiplying the number of electrons released by photoelectric emission in successive stages

**photon** /'fohton/ *n* a QUANTUM (smallest possible unit) of ELECTROMAGNETIC RADIATION (e g light) [*phot-* + ²*-on*] – **photonic** *adj*

**photonasty** /'fohtoh,nasti/ *n* movement of a plant part (e g the opening or closing of a flower) induced by changes in the intensity of light [ISV *phot-* + *-nasty*]

**photonegative** /,fohtoh'negətiv/ *adj*, *of an organism or one of its parts* moving or turning away from light

**photonuclear** /,fohtoh'nyoohkliə/ *adj* relating to or caused by ELECTROMAGNETIC RADIATION (e g GAMMA RAYS) striking atomic nuclei

,**photo-'offset** /'ofset/ *n* OFFSET LITHO (photographic printing process)

**photooxidation** /,fohtoh,oksi'daysh(ə)n/ *n* chemical OXIDATION of a compound by the action of radiant energy (e g light) – **photooxidative** *adj*

**photoperiod** /-'piəri·əd/ *n* the length of daylight in every 24 hours or period of light in an artificially regulated environment, esp in relation to its effect on the growth, behaviour, and functioning of a plant or animal – **photoperiodic** *adj*, **photoperiodically** *adv*

**photoperiodism** *n* the response of a plant or animal to the relative lengths of alternating periods of lightness and darkness or day and night

**photophilic** /,fohtə'filik/, **photophilous** /foh'tofiləs/ *adj* thriving in or requiring abundant light ⟨~ *plants*⟩ – **photophily** *n*

**photophobia** /-'fohbi-ə, -byə/ *n* **1** avoidance of or intolerance to light; *esp* painful sensitivity (e g of the eyes) to strong light **2** fear of sunlight or well-lit places [NL]

**photophobic** /,fohtə'fohbik/ *adj* **1a(1)** shunning or avoiding light ⟨~ *organisms*⟩ **a(2)** intolerant of or abnormally sensitive to light; exhibiting photophobia **b** growing best under reduced illumination **2** afraid of strong light

**photophore** /-,faw/ *n* a light-emitting organ; *esp* any of the luminous spots on various marine, mostly deep-sea, fishes [ISV]

**photophosphorylation** /,fohtohfos,fori'laysh(ə)n/ *n* the synthesis of the energy-storing chemical compound ATP from ADP and PHOSPHATE, that occurs in a plant using light absorbed during photosynthesis [*phot-* + *phosphorylation*]

**photopic** /,foh'topik, -'tohpik/ *adj* of or being vision in bright light with light-adapted eyes, that is controlled by the CONES of

the retina and is concerned with the discrimination of colours – compare SCOTOPIC [*photopia* (fr NL, fr *phot-* + *-opia*) + *-ic*] – **photopia** *n*

**photopolymer** /-'polimə/ *n* a light-sensitive plastic used for making printing plates, microfilms, etc

**photopositive** /,fohtoh'pozətiv/ *adj*, *of an organism or one of its parts* moving or turning towards light

**photoprint** /'fohtoh,print/ *n* a reproduction of graphic matter on photographic paper

**photoproduct** /,fohtoh'produkt/ *n* a product of a PHOTOCHEMICAL reaction (chemical reaction induced by light)

**photoproduction** /,fohtoh·prə'duksh(ə)n/ *n* **1** the production of MESONS (particles intermediate in mass between electrons and protons) as a result of the action of PHOTONS (units of ELECTROMAGNETIC RADIATION) on atomic nuclei **2** the production of a substance (e g hydrogen) by a PHOTOCHEMICAL reaction (e g in photosynthetic bacteria)

**photoreactivation** /,fohtoh·ri,akti'vaysh(ə)n, -,ree·aktiv-/ *n* the repair of DNA damaged by ultraviolet radiation by a light-dependent enzyme-controlled reaction – **photoreactivating** *adj*

**photoreception** /,fohtoh·ri'sepsh(ə)n/ *n* perception of electromagnetic waves in the range of visible light; *specif* vision – **photoreceptive** *adj*

**photoreceptor** /-ri'septə/ *n* a cell or organ that receives light stimuli

**photoreconnaissance** /,fohtoh·ri'konis(ə)ns/ *n* reconnaissance by aerial photography

**photoreduction** /,fohtoh·riduksh(ə)n/ *n* chemical REDUCTION of a compound by the action of radiant energy (e g light)

**photorespiration** /,fohtoh·respi'raysh(ə)n/ *n* respiration that occurs in some plants during photosynthesis under conditions of high light intensity and high temperatures, involving the oxidation of GLYCOLIC ACID to produce carbon dioxide

**photosensitive** /-'sensətiv/ *adj* **1** sensitive or sensitized to radiant energy, esp light **2** producing a PHOTOELECTRIC, PHOTOCONDUCTIVE, or PHOTOVOLTAIC effect when subjected to radiant energy – **photosensitivity** *n*

**photosensit·ize, -ise** /-'sensitiez/ *vt* **1** to make sensitive to radiant energy, esp light **2** to make abnormally sensitive to sunlight (e g so as to develop a skin rash) – **photosensitization** *n*, **photosensitizer** *n*

**photoset** /'fohtoh,set/ *vt* **-tt-; photoset** PHOTOCOMPOSE (typeset on film) – **photosetter** *n*

**photosphere** /'fohtə,sfiə/ *n* the visible luminous surface layer of a star, esp the sun – **photospheric** *adj*

**photostat** /'fohtə,stat/ *vt* to make a copy of using a Photostat device; *broadly* to photocopy – **photostat** *n*, **photostatic** *adj*

**Photostat** /'fohtə,stat/ *trademark* – used for a machine for making photographic copies

**photosynthesis** /,fohtoh'sinthəsis/ *n* the synthesis of carbon-containing chemical compounds from carbon dioxide and water using RADIANT ENERGY, esp light; *esp* the formation of carbohydrates in green plants exposed to sunlight, by a series of reactions using light energy absorbed by chlorophyll in the plant tissues [NL] – **photosynthesize** *vb*, **photosynthetic** *adj*, **photosynthetically** *adv*

**phototaxis** /,fohtoh'taksis/ *n* the movement of an organism towards or away from light [NL] – **phototactic** *adj*, **phototactically** *adv*

**phototelegraphy** /,fohtoh·tə'legrəfi/ *n* FACSIMILE **2** (transmission of graphic matter) [ISV]

**phototropism** /foh'totrə,piz(ə)m, ,fohtoh'trohpiz(ə)m/ *n* the turning or curving of an organism, esp a plant, or of one of its parts towards or away from light [ISV] – **phototropic** *adj*, **phototropically** *adv*

**phototube** /'fohtoh,tyoohb/ *n* an ELECTRON TUBE (device in which electrons flow between two electrically conducting plates or wires) in which light or other RADIANT ENERGY hitting the CATHODE (negatively charged plate or wire) causes the release of electrons which are drawn to the ANODE (positively charged plate or wire), thus producing an electric current

**phototypesetting** /,fohtoh'tiepseting/ *n* PHOTOCOMPOSITION (typesetting on film); *esp* photocomposition done on a keyboard or tape-operated composing machine – **phototypesetter** *n*

**phototypography** /-tie'pogrəfi/ *n* a process for composing type on film or paper using photography [ISV] – **phototypographic** *adj*

**photovoltaic** /-vol'tayik/ *adj* of, being, producing, or using the effect that occurs when light or other RADIANT ENERGY falls on the boundary between dissimilar substances in tight contact, resulting in the generation of an ELECTROMOTIVE FORCE (energy causing electric current to flow) ⟨∼ effect⟩ ⟨a ∼ cell⟩ [ISV]

**phragmoplast** /'fragmǝplast/ n the enlarged barrel-shaped bundle of fibres (SPINDLE) that is formed within a plant cell during the later stages of CELL DIVISION (splitting of a cell to form new cells) and is important in the formation of the CELL PLATE (structure forming a wall that divides the cell into two) [ISV phragmo- (fr Gk phragmos fence, fr phrassein to enclose) + -plast]

**phrasal** /'frayzl/ adj (consisting) of a phrase ⟨∼ prepositions⟩ – **phrasally** adv

**phrasal verb** n a verb used idiomatically with an adverb and/or preposition, usu having a meaning distinct from the sum of its parts (e g put up in "they put him up for the night")

**¹phrase** /frayz/ n **1a** a mode or form of speech; diction ⟨a curious turn of ∼⟩ **b** a brief usu idiomatic or pithy expression; esp a catchphrase ⟨good at turning a ∼⟩ **2** a group of musical notes forming a natural unit of melody **3** a group of two or more grammatically related words that do not form a clause; esp a preposition with the words it governs [L phrasis, fr Gk, fr phrazein to point out, explain, tell]

**²phrase** vt **1** to express in words in a particular way; put, word ⟨a politely ∼d rejection⟩ **2** to divide (music) into melodic phrases

**phrase book** n a book containing words and idiomatic expressions of a foreign language and their translation and usu arranged by topic

**phrasemaker** /'frayz,maykǝ/ n **1** one who coins telling phrases **2** one given to making fine-sounding but often meaningless phrases – **phrasemaking** n

**phrase marker** n a tree diagram showing the grammatical structure of a sentence, in which the points of branching (NODES) are labelled with grammatical categories (e g "verb") and the terminal points with MORPHEMES (e g the word "went")

**phraseogram** /'frayzi-ǝ,gram/ n a symbol for a phrase in some shorthand systems [phraseo- (as in phraseology) + -gram]

**phraseograph** /-,grahf, -,graf/ n a phrase for which there is a shorthand symbol

**phraseology** /,frayzi'olǝji/ n **1** a manner of putting together words and phrases; a style **2** choice of words [NL phraseologia, fr Gk phrase-, phrasis + -logia -logy] – **phraseological** adj, **phraseologically** adv

**phrase structure grammar** n a set of rules for replacing symbols by items that can appropriately represent them (e g the set of linguistic rules by which the dog can replace the symbol for the grammatical category "noun phrase")

**phrasing** /'frayzing/ n **1** a style of expression; phraseology **2** the art, act, method, or result of grouping notes into musical phrases

**phratry** /'fraytri/ n **1** a kinship group forming a subdivision of an ancient Greek PHYLE (tribe) **2** a tribal subdivision; specif an intermarried group of several clans with different TOTEMS [Gk phratria, fr phratēr member of the same clan, member of a phratry – more at BROTHER]

**phreatic** /fri'atik/ adj of or being water within the earth, esp below the WATER TABLE (level below which the ground is saturated with water) [Gk phreat-, phrear well]

**phreatophyte** /fri'atǝfiet/ n a deep-rooted plant that obtains its water from the WATER TABLE (level below which the ground is saturated with water) or the layer of soil just above it [Gk phreat-, phrear well + E -o- + -phyte] – **phreatophytic** adj

**phren-** /frin-, fren-/, **phreno-** comb form **1** mind ⟨phrenology⟩ **2** diaphragm ⟨phrenic⟩ [Gk, fr phren-, phrēn diaphragm, mind]

**phrenetic** /fri'netik/ adj frenetic [L phreneticus] – **phrenetically** adv

**phrenic** /'frenik/ adj **1** of the diaphragm dividing the chest and the abdomen **2** of the mind – not now used technically [NL phrenicus, fr phren-]

**phrenitis** /fri'nietǝs/ n ENCEPHALITIS (inflammation of the brain) – not now used technically [NL] – **phrenitic** adj

**phrenology** /fri'nolǝji/ n the study of the conformation of the skull as a supposed indicator of mental faculties and character – **phrenologist** n, **phrenological** adj, **phrenologically** adv

**Phrygian** /'friji-ǝn/ n **1** a native or inhabitant of ancient Phrygia **2** the language of the Phrygians, usu assumed to be Indo-European [Phrygia, ancient country in Asia Minor] – **Phrygian** adj

**phrygian mode** n, often cap P a MODE (fixed arrangement of eight notes) which may be represented on the white keys of the piano on a scale from E to E

**phthalic acid** /'(f)thalik/ n any of three forms of an acid, $C_6H_4(COOH)_2$, derived from benzene and used in various industrial processes (e g the manufacture of dyes and polyester fabrics); specif one whose derivatives are used in insect repellents – compare TEREPHTHALIC ACID [ISV, short for obs naphthalic acid, fr naphthalene]

**phthalic anhydride** n a chemical compound, $C_8H_4O_3$, used esp in making plastics and dyestuffs

**phthalocyanine** /,thaloh'sie-ǝneen, ,fthal-, ,thay-/ n a bright greenish-blue compound, $C_{32}H_{18}N_8$; also any of several compounds of this with metals, that are brilliant blue to green dyes or pigments, used esp in inks and paints [ISV phthalic acid + -o- + cyanine]

**phthiriasis** /thi'rie-ǝsis, thie-/ n infestation with lice, esp CRAB LICE [L, fr Gk phtheiriasis, fr phtheir louse; akin to Gk phtheirein to destroy, Skt kaarati it flows, perishes]

**phthisis** /'thiesis/ n, pl **phthises** /-seez/ a progressive wasting condition; esp tuberculosis of the lungs [L, fr Gk, fr phthinein to waste away; akin to Skt kṣiṇoti he destroys] – **phthisic, phthisical** adj

**¹phut** /fut/ n a dull sound as of something bursting [imit] – **phut** vi

**²phut** adv [partly fr ¹phut; partly fr Hindi phaṭnā to burst, explode] – **go phut** chiefly Br informal to stop functioning; collapse ⟨the steam iron went phut⟩

**phycocyanin** /,fiekoh'sie-ǝnin/ n any of various bluish-green protein pigments in the cells of BLUE-GREEN ALGAE [ISV phyco- (fr Gk phykos) + cyan- + -in]

**phycoerythrin** /,fiekoh'erithrin/ n any of various protein pigments in the cells of RED ALGAE [ISV phyco- + erythr- + -in]

**phycology** /fie'kolǝji/ n the study of algae; ALGOLOGY [Gk phykos seaweed + ISV -logy – more at FUCUS] – **phycologist** n, **phycological** adj

**phycomycete** /,fiekoh'mieseet, -mie'seet/ n any of a large class (Phycomycetes) of highly variable primitive fungi, similar in many respects to algae [deriv of Gk phykos + mykēt-, mykēs fungus – more at MYC-] – **phycomycetous** adj

**phyl-** /fil-/, **phylo-** comb form tribe, race, phylum ⟨phylogeny⟩ [L, fr Gk, fr phylē, phylon; akin to Gk phyein to bring forth – more at BE]

**phylactery** /fi'lakt(ǝ)ri/ n **1** either of two small square leather boxes containing scriptural passages and traditionally worn on the left arm and forehead by Jewish men during morning weekday prayers **2** AMULET (trinket worn as a charm) [ME philaterie, fr ML philaterium, alter. of LL phylacterium, fr Gk phylaktērion amulet, phylactery, fr phylassein to guard, fr phylak-, phylax guard]

**phyle** /'fielee/ n, pl **phylae** /-lie/ **1** a tribe or division of the people in ancient Greece, theoretically based on kinship **2** the largest political subdivision among the ancient Athenians [Gk phylē tribe, phyle]

**phyll-** /fil-/, **phyllo-** comb form leaf ⟨phyllome⟩ [NL, fr Gk, fr phyllon – more at BLADE]

**-phyll** /-fil/ comb form (→ n) leaf ⟨sporophyll⟩ [NL -phyllum, fr Gk phyllon leaf]

**phylloclade** /'filoh,klayd/, **phylloclad** /-,klad/ n a green flattened stem or branch (e g in a cactus) that functions as a leaf – compare CLADODE, PHYLLODE [NL phyllocladium, fr phyll- + Gk klados branch – more at GLADIATOR]

**phyllode** /'filohd/ n a flat expanded leaf stalk that resembles the blade of a leaf and fulfils the same functions – compare CLADODE, PHYLLOCLADE [NL phyllodium, fr Gk phyllōdēs like a leaf, fr phyllon]

**phyllodium** /fi'lohdiǝm/ n, pl **phyllodia** /-diǝ/ a phyllode [NL]

**phylloid** /'filoyd/ n or adj (a part) resembling a leaf

**phyllome** /'filom/ n a leaf or plant part that has evolved from a leaf [ISV] – **phyllomic** adj

**phyllophagous** /fi'lofǝgǝs/ adj feeding on leaves

**phyllopod** /'filoh,pod/ n any of a group (Phyllopoda of the subclass Entomostraca, class Crustacea) of small aquatic INVERTEBRATE animals related to the WATER FLEAS, that typically have leaflike swimming structures that also serve as gills [deriv of Gk phyllon leaf + pod-, pous foot – more at FOOT] – **phyllopod** adj, **phyllopodan** adj or n, **phyllopodous** adj

**phylloquinone** /,fieloh'kwinohn, ,filǝ-/ n VITAMIN $K_1$ [ISV phyll- + quinone]

**phyllotaxy** /'filoh,taksi/, **phyllotaxis** /,filoh'taksis/ n **1** the arrangement of leaves on a stem **2** the study of phyllotaxy and of the laws that govern it [NL *phyllotaxis*, fr *phyll-* + *-taxis*] – **phyllotactic, phyllotactical** *adj*

**-phyllous** /-filəs/ *comb form* (→ *adj*) having (such or so many) leaves, leaflets, or leaflike parts ⟨*di*phyllous⟩ [NL *-phyllus*, fr Gk *-phyllos*, fr *phyllon* leaf – more at BLADE]

**phylloxera** /ˌfilok'siərə/ *n* any of various plant lice (family Phylloxeridae) that are destructive to many plants (e g grapevines) [NL, genus name, fr *phyll-* + Gk *xēros* dry – more at SERENE] – **phylloxeran** *adj or n*

**phylogenesis** /ˌfieloh'jenəsis/ *n, pl* **phylogeneses** /-seez/ phylogeny [NL, fr *phyl-* + *genesis*]

**phylogenetic** /ˌfieloh·jə'netik/, **phylogenic** /-'jenik/ *adj* **1** of phylogeny **2** based on natural evolutionary relationships **3** acquired in the course of phylogenetic development [ISV, fr NL *phylogenesis*] – **phylogenetically, phylogenically** *adv*

**phylogeny** /fi'lojəni/ *n* **1** the evolutionary history of a type of organism or a genetically related group of organisms (e g a race) **2** the history or course of the development of something (e g a word or custom) [ISV]

**phylum** /'filəm/ *n, pl* **phyla** /-lə/ **1** a major division in the classification of plants or animals comprising organisms having a similar basic pattern of organization and composed of one or more CLASSES **2** a group of language families or of languages related more remotely than those of a family or stock; a superfamily ⟨*three families which are related in one ~ known as* Mosan – H A Gleason⟩ [NL, fr Gk *phylon* tribe, race – more at PHYL-]

**-phyre** /-fie-ə/ *comb form* (→ *n*) PORPHYRITIC (having large embedded crystals) rock ⟨*grano*phyre⟩ [Fr, fr *porphyre* porphyry, fr ML *porphyrium*]

**physi-** /fizi-/, **physio-** *comb form* **1** nature ⟨physio*graphy*⟩ **2** physical ⟨physio*therapy*⟩ [L, fr Gk, fr *physis* – more at PHYSICS]

**physiatrics** /ˌfizi'atriks/ *n taking sing vb, NAm* physiotherapy – **physiatrist** *n*, **physiatric, physiatrical** *adj*

¹**physic** /'fizik/ *n* **1a** the medical profession **b** a medicinal preparation (e g a drug); *esp* a laxative **2** *archaic* the art or practice of healing disease △ physique [ME *physik, phisik* natural science, art of medicine, fr OF *fisique*, fr L *physica* (sing.) natural science, fr Gk *physikē*, fr fem of *physikos* of nature – more at PHYSICS]

²**physic** *vt* -ck- *archaic* **1** to treat with or administer medicine to; *esp* to purge **2** to heal, cure

**physical** /'fizikl/ *adj* **1a** having material existence; perceptible, esp through the senses, and subject to the laws of nature ⟨*everything ~ is measurable by weight, motion, and resistance* – Thomas De Quincey⟩ **b** of material things **2a** of or involving NATURAL SCIENCE **b(1)** of or involving physics ⟨*~ chemistry*⟩ **b(2)** characterized or produced by the forces and operations of physics **3a** of or concerned with the body ⟨*~ strength*⟩ ⟨*~ education*⟩ **b** concerned or preoccupied with the body and its needs, as opposed to spiritual matters *synonyms* see ¹MATERIAL [ME, fr ML *physicalis*, fr L *physica* physics] – **physically** *adv*

**physical anthropology** *n* a branch of ANTHROPOLOGY (science of man) concerned with the comparative study of man's physical evolution, variation, and classification, esp through measurement and observation – compare CULTURAL ANTHROPOLOGY – **physical anthropologist** *n*

**physical education** *n* instruction in sports, athletic games, and gymnastics for the development and health of the body

**physical examination, physical** *n* MEDICAL

**physical geography** *n* the branch of geography that deals with the physical features of the earth's surface, including their formation and the changes they undergo as a result of natural processes

**physicalism** /'fizikəliz(ə)m/ *n, philosophy* the view that the laws of physics are basic, and that the laws and concepts of the other sciences are derived from and can be reduced to statements about the fundamental physical properties mass, length, and time – **physicalist** *n*, **physicalistic** *adj*

**physicality** /ˌfizi'kaləti/ *n* intensely physical orientation; predominance of the physical, usu at the expense of the mental, spiritual, or social

**physical jerks** *n pl, chiefly Br humorous* simple physical exercises

**physical science** *n* the NATURAL SCIENCES (e g physics, chemistry, and astronomy) that deal primarily with nonliving matter – compare LIFE SCIENCE – **physical scientist** *n*

**physical therapy** *n, NAm* physiotherapy

**physical training** *n* PHYSICAL EDUCATION

**physician** /fi'zish(ə)n/ *n* a person skilled in the art of healing; a doctor; *esp* a doctor who is not a surgeon [ME *fisicien*, fr OF, fr *fisique* medicine]

**physicist** /'fizisist/ *n* a specialist in physics

**physico-** /fizikoh-/ *comb form* physical ⟨physico*geographical*⟩; physical and ⟨physico*chemical*⟩

**physicochemical** /ˌfizikoh'kemikl/ *adj* of or involving both physics and chemistry or the physical and chemical properties of a substance – **physicochemically** *adv*

**physics** /'fiziks/ *n* **1** *taking sing vb* the science that deals with matter and energy and their interactions in such fields as mechanics, acoustics, optics, heat, electricity, magnetism, radiation, atomic structure, and nuclear phenomena **2** *taking sing or pl vb* the physical properties, processes, and phenomena of something or of a particular system [L *physica*, pl, natural science, fr Gk *physika*, fr neut pl of *physikos* of nature, fr *physis* growth, nature, fr *phyein* to bring forth – more at BE]

**Physiocrat** /'fizioh,krat/ *n* a member of a school of political economists founded in 18th-century France and characterized chiefly by a belief that government policy should not interfere with the operation of natural economic laws and that land is the source of all wealth [Fr *physiocrate*, fr *physi-* + *-crate* -crat] – **physiocratic** *adj, often cap*, **physiocracy** *n*

**physiognomy** /ˌfizi'onəmi/ *n* **1** the art of discovering temperament and character from outward appearance **2** the facial features, esp when held to show qualities of mind or character by their configuration or expression **3** external aspect; *also* inner character or quality revealed outwardly ⟨*the ~ of a political party*⟩ [ME *phisonomie*, fr MF, fr LL *physiognomonia, physiognomia*, fr Gk *physiognōmonia*, fr *physiognōmōn* judging character by the features, fr *physis* nature, physique, appearance + *gnōmōn* interpreter – more at GNOMON] – **physiognomic, physiognomical** *adj*, **physiognomically** *adv*

**physiographic climax** /ˌfiziə'grafik/ *n* an ecological CLIMAX (relatively stable community of plants and animals) that develops in association with a particular geographic environment – compare EDAPHIC CLIMAX

**physiography** /ˌfizi'ogrəfi/ *n* **1** a description of nature or natural phenomena in general **2** PHYSICAL GEOGRAPHY – **physiographer** *n*, **physiographic** *also* **physiographical** *adj*

**physiological** /ˌfizi·ə'lojikl/, **physiologic** *adj* **1** of physiology **2** characteristic of or appropriate to an organism's healthy or normal functioning ⟨*the ~ level of a substance in the blood*⟩ **3** differing in, involving, or affecting physiological properties rather than structural or anatomical features – **physiologically** *adv*

**physiological saline** *n* a solution of a salt or salts that is similar in concentration to blood or the liquids that bathe the body tissues

**physiology** /ˌfizi'oləji/ *n* **1** a branch of biology that deals with the functions and activities of life or of living matter (e g organs, tissues, or cells) and the physical and chemical phenomena involved – compare ANATOMY **2** the physiological activities of (part of) an organism or a particular bodily function ⟨*the ~ of sex*⟩ [L *physiologia* natural science, fr Gk, fr *physi-* + *-logia* -logy] – **physiologist** *n*

**physiotherapy** /ˌfizi·oh'therəpi/ *n* the treatment of disease by physical and mechanical means (e g massage and regulated exercise) [NL *physiotherapia*, fr *physi-* + *therapia* therapy] – **physiotherapist** *n*

**physique** /fi'zeek/ *n* the form or structure of a person's body, esp with regard to size or muscular development; bodily makeup △ physic [Fr, fr *physique* physical, bodily, fr L *physicus* of nature, fr Gk *physikos*

**physostigmine** /ˌfiesoh'stigmeen/ *n* a chemical compound, $C_{15}H_{21}N_3O_2$, obtained from the CALABAR BEAN, that is used in eyedrops to contract the pupil of the eye, and in the form of its compounds to stimulate secretion of digestive juices in disorders of the stomach and intestines – called also ESERINE [ISV, fr NL *Physostigma*, genus of climbing plants whose fruit is the Calabar bean, fr Gk *physa* bladder, bellows + NL *stigma*]

**phyt-** /fiet-/, **phyto-** *comb form* plant ⟨phyto*chemistry*⟩ ⟨phyto*pathology*⟩ [NL, fr Gk, fr *phyton*, fr *phyein* to bring forth – more at BE]

**phytane** /'fietayn/ *n* a chemical compound, $C_{20}H_{42}$, that is found esp in fossilized plant remains from the earliest geological era (PRECAMBRIAN) onwards and in some meteorites

**-phyte** /-ˌfiet/ *comb form* (→ *n*) **1** plant having (a specified characteristic or habitat) ⟨*sapro*phyte⟩ ⟨*xero*phyte⟩ **2** pathological growth ⟨*osteophyte*⟩ [ISV, fr Gk *phyton* plant] – -**phytic** *comb form* (→ *adj*)

**phytoalexin** /ˌfietoh·əˈleksin/ *n* a chemical substance produced by a plant to combat infection by a disease-causing agent (e g a fungus) [*phyt-* + *alexin* (substance combating infection), fr Ger, fr Gk *alexein* to ward off, protect]

**phytochemistry** /ˌfietohˈkemistri/ *n* the chemistry of plants, plant processes, and plant products – **phytochemical** *adj*, **phytochemically** *adv*, **phytochemist** *n*

**phytochrome** /ˈfietəkrohm/ *n* a compound of a protein with a light-sensitive biological pigment, that exists in two forms, is present in traces in many plants, and plays a role in many developmental processes and in initiating flowering when activated by infrared light

**phytogenesis** /ˌfietohˈjenəsis/ *n* the evolution and development of plants [NL] – **phytogenetic** *adj*, **phytogenetically** *adv*

**phytogenic** /ˌfietəˈjenik/ *also* **phytogenous** /ˌfieˈtojənəs/ *adj* of plant origin

**phytogeny** /fieˈtojəni/ *n* phytogenesis

**phytogeography** /ˌfietoh·jiˈografi/ *n* the study of the geographical distribution of plants [ISV] – **phytogeographical**, **phytogeographic** *adj*, **phytogeographically** *adv*

**phytography** /fieˈtografi/ *n* botany dealing with the description of plants, sometimes including plant classification [NL *phytographia*, fr *phyt-* + L *-graphia* -graphy]

**phytohaemagglutinin**, *chiefly NAm* **phytohemagglutinin** /ˌfietoh‚heeməˈgloohtinin/ *n* a protein extracted from the red KIDNEY BEAN that has been used in biochemical research to make cells adhere to each other and to induce structural changes in cells (e g WHITE BLOOD CELLS)

**phytohormone** /ˌfietəˈhawmohn/ *n* a plant hormone or hormone-like substance [ISV]

**phytology** /fieˈtoləji/ *n*, *archaic* botany [NL *phytologia*, fr *phyt-* + L *-logia* -logy] – **phytological** *also* **phytologic** *adj*, **phytologically** *adv*

**phytomenadione** /ˌfietoh‚menəˈdieˈohn/ *n* VITAMIN K₁ [*phyt-* + *menadione*]

**phyton** /ˈfieton/ *n* **1** a structural unit of a plant consisting of a leaf and its associated portion of stem **2** the smallest part of a stem, root, or leaf that when severed may grow into a new plant [NL, fr Gk, plant] – **phytonic** *adj*

**phytopathogen** /ˌfietohˈpathəjən/ *n* an organism that is parasitic on a plant – **phytopathogenic** *adj*

**phytopathology** /ˌfietoh·pəˈtholəji/ *n* the study of plant diseases [ISV] – **phytopathological** *also* **phytopathologic** *adj*

**phytophagous** /fieˈtofəgəs/ *adj*, *esp of an insect* feeding on plants; herbivorous – **phytophagy** *n*

**phytoplankton** /ˌfietohˈplangktən/ *n* plankton consisting of plants – compare ZOOPLANKTON [ISV] – **phytoplanktonic** *adj*

**phytosis** /fieˈtohsis/ *n*, *pl* **phytoses** /-seez/ infection with or a disease caused by parasitic plants [NL]

**phytosociology** /ˌfietoh·sohsiˈoləji/ *n* a branch of ecology that deals with the origin, development, and structure of plant communities in particular geographical areas – **phytosociologist** *n*, **phytosociological**, **phytosociologically** *adv*

**phytotoxic** /-ˈtoksik/ *adj* poisonous to plants – **phytotoxicity** *n*

**phytotoxin** /ˌfietohˈtoksin/ *n* a TOXIN (poisonous substance) produced by a plant

**¹pi** /pie/ *n*, *pl* **pis** /piez/ **1** the 16th letter of the Greek alphabet **2** (the symbol $\pi$ denoting) the ratio of the circumference of a circle to its diameter with a value, to eight decimal places, of 3.14159265 [MGk, fr Gk *pei*, of Sem origin; akin to Heb *pē* pe; (2) fr the initial letter of Gk *periphereia* circumference]

**²pi** *vb or n*, *pl* **pies; pies; piing, pieing; pied** *chiefly NAm* ³,⁴PIE

**³pi** *adj* **1** not intended to appear in final printing ⟨~ *lines*⟩ **2** capable of being inserted only by hand ⟨~ *characters*⟩

**piaffe** /piˈaf/ *vi*, *of a horse* to move at a slow trot, esp in DRESSAGE [Fr *piaffer*, lit., to strut]

**piaffer** /piˈafə/ *n* the act or an instance of piaffing [Fr]

**pial** /ˈpie·əl, ˈpee·əl/ *adj* of the PIA MATER

**pia mater** /ˌpie·ə ˈmahtə, ˈmaytə/ *n* a thin membrane that is the inner of the three membranes (the MENINGES) that surround the brain and backbone – compare DURA MATER, ARACHNOID [ME, fr ML, fr L, tender mother]

**pianism** /ˈpee·əniz(ə)m/ *n* the art or technique of piano playing

**¹pianissimo** /ˌpee·əˈnisimoh/ *adv or adj* very soft – used as a direction in music [It, fr *piano* softly]

**²pianissimo** *n*, *pl* **pianissimi, pianissimos** a passage played, sung, or spoken very softly

**pianist** /ˈpee·ənist/ *n* one who plays the piano; *esp* a skilled or professional performer on the piano

**pianistic** /ˌpee·əˈnistik/ *adj* **1** of or suitable for the piano **2** skilled in piano playing – **pianistically** *adv*

**¹piano** /piˈahnoh, ˈpyah-/ *adv or adj* in a soft or quiet manner – used as a direction in music [It, fr LL *planus* smooth, fr L, level – more at FLOOR]

**²piano** /piˈanoh/ *n*, *pl* **pianos** a musical instrument having steel wire strings that sound when struck by felt-covered hammers operated from a keyboard [It, short for *pianoforte*, fr *piano e forte* soft and loud; fr the variable loudness of its tones]

**piano accordion** *n* an accordion with a small piano-like keyboard for the right hand

**pianoforte** /ˌpyanohˈfawti, pi‚ah-, pi‚a-/ *n*, *formal* a piano [It]

**piano hinge** *n* a hinge that extends along the full length of the parts to be joined

**Pianola** /ˌpee·əˈnohlə/ *trademark* – used for a PLAYER PIANO

**piano stool** *n* a stool for use at a piano, sometimes of adjustable height and with a compartment for sheet music

**piassava** /ˌpiəˈsahvə/ *n* **1** any of several stiff coarse fibres obtained from palms and used esp in making ropes and brushes **2** a palm yielding piassava; *esp* either of two Brazilian palms (*Attalea funifera* and *Leopoldinia piassaba*) [Pg *piassaba*, fr Tupi *piaçaba*]

**piastre**, *NAm* **piaster** /piˈastə/ *n* **1** PIECE OF EIGHT **2** – see *pound* at MONEY table [Fr *piastre*, fr It *piastra* thin metal plate, fr L *emplastra* plaster]

**piazza** /piˈatsə, piˈadzə/ *n*, *pl* **piazzas**, (1) **piazze** /-si/, **piazzas 1** an open square, esp in an Italian town **2** *NAm* a veranda, porch [It, fr L *platea* broad street – more at PLACE]

**pibroch** /ˈpeebrok(h)/ *n* a set of martial or mournful variations for the Scottish Highland bagpipe [ScGael *piobaireachd* pipemusic]

**¹pic** /pik/ *n*, *pl* **pics, pix** /piks/ *informal* **1** *pl* artwork; ART 5 **2** a photograph [short for *picture*]

**²pic** *n* a picador's lance [Sp *pica*, fr *picar* to prick]

**¹pica** /ˈpiekə/ *n* **1** a size of printer's type of approximately 12 POINTS **2** a unit of 4.23 millimetres (about ¹⁄₆ inch) used in measuring typographical material **3** a size of typewriter type providing 10 characters to the linear inch and six lines to the vertical inch [prob fr ML, collection of church rules]

**²pica** *n* the pathological craving to eat inappropriate substances (e g chalk or ashes) [NL, fr L, magpie – more at PIE]

**picador** /ˈpikə‚daw/ *n*, *pl* **picadors, picadores** /ˈpikə‚dawˌrayz/ a horseman who in a bullfight prods the bull with a lance to weaken its neck and shoulder muscles [Sp, fr *picar* to prick, fr (assumed) VL *piccare* – more at PIKE]

**picaninny** /ˌpikəˈnini/ *n*, *chiefly NAm* a piccaninny

**picaresque** /ˌpikəˈresk/ *adj* of rogues; *specif* of or being fiction narrating in loosely linked episodes the career and adventures of a rogue [Sp *picaresco*, fr *picaro*] – **picaresque** *n*

**picaro** /ˈpeekəroh/, *fem* **picara** /-rah/ *n*, *pl* **picaros**, *fem* **picaras** a rogue, Bohemian [Sp *picaro* (fem *picara*)]

**picaroon, pickaroon** /ˌpikəˈroohn/ *n* **1** a picaro **2** a pirate [Sp *picarón*, aug of *picaro*]

**¹picayune** /ˌpikəˈyoohn/ *n* **1a** a small coin of Spanish origin, formerly current in the southern USA **b** HALF DIME **2** *NAm* something trivial [Fr *picaillon* halfpenny, fr Prov *picaioun*, fr *picaio* money, fr *pica* to prick, jingle, fr (assumed) VL *piccare* to prick]

**²picayune** *adj*, *NAm* **1** of little value, paltry **2** petty, small-minded – **picayunish** *adj*

**piccalilli** /ˌpikəˈlili/ *n* a hot relish of chopped vegetables, mustard, and spices [prob alter. of *pickle*]

**piccaninny**, *chiefly NAm* **picaninny, pickaninny** /ˈpikə‚nini, --ˈ--/ *n*, *chiefly derog* a small black child [prob modif of Pg *pequenino* very small; fr *pequeno* small]

**¹piccolo** /ˈpikəloh/ *n*, *pl* **piccolos** a small shrill flute whose range is an OCTAVE higher than that of an ordinary flute [It, short for *piccolo flauto* small flute] – **piccoloist** *n*

**²piccolo** *adj*, *of a musical instrument* smaller than ordinary size ⟨*a* ~ *banjo*⟩ [It, small]

**pice** /pies/ *n*, *pl* **pice** PAISA (coin) [Hindi *paisā*]

**piceous** /ˈpisi·əs, ˈpie-/ *adj* of or resembling pitch; *esp* glossy brownish-black in colour ⟨*an insect with a* ~ *brown abdomen*⟩ [L *piceus*, fr *pic-*, *pix* pitch – more at PITCH]

**pichiciago** /ˌpichisiˈahgoh, -ˈaygoh/, **pichiciego** /-ˈaygoh/ *n*, *pl* **pichiciagos, pichiciegos** a very small S American armadillo (*Chlamyphorus truncatus*) having a protective covering of pinkish plates, and soft white hair on the underparts and sides [AmerSp *pichiciego*, prob fr a native name in S America akin to Araucan *pichi* small thing]

**¹pick** /pik/ *vt* **1** to pierce, penetrate, or break up with a pointed instrument ⟨~ed *the hard clay*⟩; *also* to make (a hole) in this way **2a** to remove bit by bit ⟨~ *meat from bones*⟩ ⟨~ed *hairs off his jacket*⟩ **b** to remove covering or adhering matter from ⟨~ed *the bones clean*⟩ **3a** to gather by plucking ⟨~ *apples*⟩ **b** to choose, select ⟨*tried to ~ the shortest route*⟩ ⟨*she ~ed out the most expensive dress*⟩ **4** to pilfer from; rob ⟨~ *pockets*⟩ **5** to provoke ⟨~ *a quarrel*⟩ **6a** to dig into, esp in order to remove unwanted matter; probe ⟨~ *his teeth*⟩ ⟨~ *his nose*⟩ **b** to pluck with a PLECTRUM or with the fingers ⟨~ *a guitar*⟩ **c** to loosen or pull apart with a sharp point ⟨~ *wool*⟩ **7** to unlock with a device (e g a wire) other than the key ⟨~ *a lock*⟩ ~ *vi* **1** to use or work with a pick **2** to gather or harvest something by plucking – see also **a** BONE **to pick, pick somebody's** BRAINS [ME *piken*; partly fr (assumed) OE *pīcian* (akin to MD *picken* to prick); partly fr MF *piquer* to prick – more at ⁴PIKE]

**pick at** *vt* **1** to find fault with, esp in a petty way **2** to eat sparingly and with little interest; toy with ⟨picking *listlessly at his dinner*⟩

**pick off** *vt* to shoot or bring down one by one ⟨*the sniper* picked off *the enemy troops*⟩

**pick on** *vt* **1** to single out for unpleasant treatment or an unpleasant task **2** to single out for a particular purpose or for special attention

**pick out** *vt* **1** to make clearly visible, esp as distinguished from a background ⟨*the fences were* picked out *in red*⟩ **2** to play the notes of by ear or one by one ⟨*learned to* pick out *tunes on the piano*⟩

**pick over** *vt* to examine in order to select the best or discard the unwanted ⟨picked over *the berries*⟩

**pick up** *vt* **1a** to take hold of and lift up ⟨picked *the baby* up *from its cot*⟩ **b** to gather together; collect ⟨picked up *all the pieces*⟩ **2** to take (passengers or freight) into a vehicle **3a** to acquire casually or by chance ⟨picked up *a valuable antique at a jumble sale*⟩ ⟨picked up *some money doing odd jobs*⟩ **b** to learn bit by bit or incidentally ⟨picking up *a great deal of information in the process*⟩ **c** to obtain, collect ⟨picked up *his clothes at the cleaners*⟩ **d** to accept for the purpose of paying ⟨*the government should* pick up *the bill for the damaged ship*⟩ **e** to become infected with; catch ⟨picked up *a bug*⟩ **4** to enter informally into conversation or companionship with (a previously unknown person) usu with the intention of having sex ⟨*had a brief affair with a girl he* picked up *in a bar*⟩ **5a** to take into custody ⟨*the police* picked up *the fugitive*⟩ **b** to find and follow ⟨picked up *the outlaw's trail*⟩ **c** to bring within range of sight, hearing, or a sensing device ⟨picked up *the planes on the radar*⟩ **6a** to revive **b** to increase ⟨pick up *speed*⟩ **7** to resume after a break; continue ⟨*we'll* pick up *the discussion tomorrow*⟩ **8** *chiefly NAm* to clean up; tidy ~ *vi* **1** to recover or increase speed, vigour, or activity; improve ⟨*after the strike, business* picked up⟩ **2** to put things in order; tidy ⟨*was always* picking up *after her*⟩ **3** to take passengers or freight into a vehicle **4** to resume after a break; continue ⟨*let's* pick up *where we left off*⟩

**²pick** *n* **1** the act or privilege of choosing or selecting; a choice ⟨*take your* ~⟩ **2** *taking sing or pl vb* the best or choicest ⟨*the* ~ *of the herd*⟩ **3** the portion of a crop gathered at one time ⟨*the first* ~ *of peaches*⟩

**³pick** *vt* to throw (a shuttle) across the loom [ME *pykken* to fix, pitch, alter. of *picchen* to pitch]

**⁴pick** *n* **1** a throw of the shuttle across a loom **2** one WEFT (crosswise) thread taken as a unit of fineness of fabric – compare ²COUNT 5

**⁵pick** *n* **1** a heavy wooden-handled iron or steel tool with a head that is pointed at one or both ends and used for breaking up rocks, road surfaces, etc – compare MATTOCK **2a** a toothpick **b** a plectrum [ME *pik*, prob alter. of ¹*pike*]

**pickaback** /'pikə‚bak/ *n, adj, adv, or vt* (a) piggyback

**pickaninny** /'pikə‚nini, ‚--'--/ *n, chiefly NAm* a piccaninny

**pickaxe** /'pik‚aks/ *n* ⁵PICK 1 [alter. (influenced by *axe*) of ME *pikois*, fr OF *picois*, fr *pic* pick, fr L *picus* woodpecker]

**picked** /pikt/ *adj* choice, prime

**¹picker** /'pikə/ *n* a person, machine, or implement that picks something, esp crops [¹*pick*]

**²picker** *n* a person or the part of the loom that threads the shuttle [³*pick*]

**pickerel** /'pik(ə)rəl/ *n, pl* **pickerels,** *esp collectively* **pickerel 1** any of several comparatively small N American fishes (genus *Esox*) – usu with a qualifying term ⟨*grass* ~⟩ **2** *dial chiefly Br* a young or small pike [ME *pikerel*, dim. of *pike*]

**pickerelweed** /'pik(ə)rəl‚weed/ *n* a N American plant (genus *Pontederia*, esp *Pontederia cordata* of the family Pontederiaceae) that grows in shallow ponds and streams and has spikes of blue flowers

**¹picket** /'pikit/ *n* **1** a pointed or sharpened stake, post, or peg **2** *taking sing or pl vb* **2a** a small body of troops detached to guard an army from surprise attack; *also* a group of warships similarly guarding a main fleet **b** a detachment kept ready in camp for such duty **3** a person posted by a trade union at a place of work affected by a strike, esp to dissuade others from breaking the strike; *also* a person posted for a demonstration or protest [Fr *piquet*, fr MF, fr *piquer* to prick – more at PIKE]

**²picket** *vt* **1** to enclose, fence, or fortify with pickets **2a** to guard with a picket **b** to post as a picket **3** to tether **4a** to post pickets at **b** to walk or stand in front of as a picket ~ *vi* to serve as a picket – **picketer** *n*

**picket line** *n* a line of people picketing a business, organization, or institution

**pickings** /'pikingz/ *n pl* something that is picked or picked up: e g **a** leftovers, scraps **b** rewards or perks obtained by dishonest or dubious means ⟨*easy* ~⟩

**¹pickle** /'pikl/ *n* **1** a solution or bath for preserving or cleaning: e g **1a** a brine or vinegar solution in which foods (e g meat, fish, or vegetables) are preserved **b** any of various solutions (e g of acid) used in industrial cleaning or processing **2** food or an article of food (e g an onion) that has been preserved in a brine or vinegar solution; *also* chutney **3** *informal* a difficult or confused situation; a plight, mess ⟨*could see no way out of the* ~ *I was in* – R L Stevenson⟩ **4** *Br informal* a mischievous or troublesome child [ME *pekille*, prob fr MD *pekel, peekel*]

**²pickle** *vt* to treat, preserve, or clean in or with a pickle

**³pickle** *n, Scot* **1** a grain, kernel **2** a small quantity [perh fr Sc *pickle* to trifle, pilfer, fr ME *pikelen*, fr *piken* to pick]

**pickled** /'pikəld/ *adj* **1** preserved in or cured with pickle ⟨~ *herring*⟩ **2** *informal* drunk ⟨*gets thoroughly* ~ *before dinner* – New Yorker⟩

**picklock** /'pik‚lok/ *n* **1** a tool for picking locks **2** a burglar

**'pick-me-‚up** *n* something that stimulates or restores; a tonic

**pickney** /'pikni/ *n, WI* a child [alter. of *piccaninny*]

**'pick-‚off** *n* a sensing device that responds to acceleration (e g of an aeroplane) and produces a signal or exerts a controlling effect (e g by automatically correcting flight stability)

**pickpocket** /-‚pokit/ *n* one who steals from pockets or bags, esp in a public place

**¹pickup** /'pik‚up/ *n* **1** the act or process of picking up: e g **1a** a revival of business activity **b** *NAm* acceleration **2** one who or that which is picked up: e g **2a** a hitchhiker who is given a lift **b** a temporary casual acquaintance; *esp* one made with the intention of having sex **3** a device (e g on a record player) that converts mechanical movements into electrical signals **4a(1)** the reception of sound or an image by a radio or television transmitting apparatus for conversion into electrical signals **a(2)** interference (e g with radio reception) caused by a nearby electrical circuit or system **b** a device (e g a microphone or a television camera) for converting sound or an image into electrical signals **5** a light motor truck having an open body with low sides and tailboard **6** *NAm* **6a** the place where a broadcast originates **b** the electrical system for connecting an outside broadcast to a broadcasting station

**²pickup** *adj* using or comprising local or available personnel, esp without formal organization ⟨*a* ~ *game of cricket*⟩

**Pickwickian** /pik'wiki-ən, -kyən/ *adj* **1** characterized by simplicity and generosity **2** *of a word or expression* intended or taken in a sense other than the obvious or literal one [Samuel *Pickwick*, character in the novel *Pickwick Papers* by Charles Dickens †1870 E novelist]

**picky** /'piki/ *adj, chiefly NAm* fussy, choosy ⟨*a* ~ *eater*⟩

**¹picnic** /'piknik/ *n* **1a** an excursion with food taken along to be eaten in the open; *also* the food taken **b** an informal meal or snack not eaten at the dining table **2** *informal* a pleasant or amusingly carefree experience ⟨*don't expect marriage to be a* ~⟩; *also* an easily accomplished task or feat [Ger or Fr; Ger *picknick*, fr Fr *pique-nique*]

**²picnic** *vi* **-ck-** to have a picnic – **picnicker** *n*

**pico-** /peekoh-, peekə-/ *comb form* one million millionth

$(10^{-12})$ part of (a specified unit) ⟨*pico*gram⟩ [ISV, fr Sp *pico* beak, peak, small bit]

**picoline** /'pikəleen, -lin/ *n* a liquid chemical compound, $C_5H_4N(CH_3)$, found in COAL TAR and used in the manufacture of dyes, plastics, waterproofing agents for fabrics, and insecticides [L *pic-*, *pix* pitch + ISV *-ol* + *-ine* – more at PITCH] – **picolinic** *adj*

**picong** /'pikong/ *n*, *WI* satirical repartee [Sp *picón* mockery, fr *picar* to prick]

**picornavirus** /pee,kawnə'vie(ə)rəs/ *n* any of a group of small viruses comprising the ENTEROVIRUSES (viruses of the stomach and intestine) and RHINOVIRUSES (viruses of the upper respiratory tract) and including those that cause polio and the common cold [*pico-* + *RNA* + *virus*]

[1]**picot** /'peekoh/ *n* any of a series of small ornamental loops forming an edging on ribbon or lace [Fr, lit., small point, fr MF, fr *pic* prick, fr *piquer* to prick – more at PIKE]

[2]**picot** *vt* to finish with an edging of picots

**picotee** /,pikə'tee/ *n* a flower (eg some carnations or tulips) having one basic colour with a margin of another colour [Fr *picoté* pointed, fr *picoter* to mark with points, fr *picot*]

**picr-** /pikr-/, **picro-** *comb form* **1** bitter ⟨*picric acid*⟩ **2** PICRIC ACID ⟨*picrate*⟩ [Fr, fr Gk *pikr-*, *pikro-*, fr *pikros* – more at PAINT]

**picric acid** /'pikrik/ *n* an explosive yellow acid, $C_6H_2(NO_2)_3OH$, used widely in industry, esp in the manufacture of HIGH EXPLOSIVES, and as a antiseptic – called also TRINITROPHENOL [ISV]

**Pict** /pikt/ *n* a member of a possibly non-Celtic people who once occupied Britain, carried on continual border wars with the Romans, and about the 9th century became amalgamated with the Scots [ME *Pictes*, pl, Picts, fr LL *Picti*, perh fr L *picti* painted or tattooed people, fr *pictus*, pp of *pingere* to paint] – **Pictish** *adj or n*

**pictograph** /'piktə,grahf, -,graf/, **pictogram** /-,gram/ *n* **1** an ancient or prehistoric drawing or painting on a rock wall **2** any of the symbols used in a system of picture writing – compare IDEOGRAM, LOGOGRAM **3** a diagram representing statistical data in pictorial form [L *pictus* + E *-o-* + *-graph*] – **pictographic** *adj*

**pictography** /pik'togrəfi/ *n* PICTURE WRITING

**pictorial** /pik'tawri·əl/ *adj* **1** of a painter, a painting, or the painting or drawing of pictures ⟨~ *perspective*⟩ **2** consisting of or illustrated by pictures ⟨~ *records*⟩ ⟨~ *weekly*⟩ **3** suggesting or conveying visual images; vivid [LL *pictorius*, fr L *pictor* painter, fr *pictus*, pp] – **pictorially** *adv*, **pictorialness** *n*

**pictorialism** /pik'tawriəliz(ə)m/ *n* the use or creation of pictures or visual images

**pictorial·ize, -ise** /pik'tawriəliez/ *vt* to make pictorial; illustrate with pictures

[1]**picture** /'pikchə/ *n* **1** a design or representation made by any of various means (eg painting, drawing, or photography) **2a** a description so vivid or graphic as to suggest a mental image or give an accurate idea of something ⟨*the book gives a detailed* ~ *of what is happening*⟩ ⟨*drew an alarming* ~ *of the economic future*⟩ **b** a situation, scene ⟨*a look at the overall political* ~⟩ **3a** the image, copy ⟨*he was the* ~ *of his father*⟩ **b** the perfect example ⟨*he looked the* ~ *of health*⟩ **c** a striking, picturesque, or pretty sight ⟨*her face was a* ~ *when she heard the news*⟩ **4a** a transitory visible image or reproduction ⟨*adjusted the television for a brighter* ~⟩ **b** FILM 4a, b **c** *pl*, *chiefly Br informal* CINEMA 1b, 2 ⟨*what's on at the* ~ s?⟩ **synonyms** see CINEMA [ME, fr L *pictura*, fr *pictus*, pp of *pingere* to paint – more at PAINT]

[2]**picture** *vt* **1** to paint or draw a representation, image, or visual conception of; depict **2** to describe graphically in words **3** to form a mental image of; imagine

**picture book** *n* a book, esp for young children, that consists wholly or chiefly of pictures

**picture card** *n* COURT CARD (jack, queen, or king)

[1]**picture-·frame** *adj*, *of a stage* having a PROSCENIUM ARCH

**picturegoer** /'pikchə,goh·ə/ *n*, *chiefly Br* a cinemagoer

**picture hat** *n* a woman's usu decorated hat with a broad brim

**picture house** *n*, *chiefly Br* CINEMA 2 – no longer in vogue

**picture palace** *n*, *chiefly Br* CINEMA 2 – no longer in vogue

**,picture-·postcard** *adj* of a kind characteristically illustrated on picture·postcards; picturesque ⟨~ *villages*⟩

**picture postcard** *n* a postcard with a picture or photograph, typically of a holiday resort or place of interest, on one side

**picturesque** /,pikchə'resk/ *adj* **1** quaint, charming **2** evoking

striking mental images; vivid ⟨~ *language*⟩ [Fr & It; Fr *pittoresque*, fr It *pittoresco*, fr *pittore* painter, fr L *pictor*, fr *pictus*, pp] – **picturesquely** *adv*, **picturesqueness** *n*

**picture tube** *n* a CATHODE-RAY TUBE having at one end a screen of luminescent material onto which a beam of electrons is projected, producing visible images

**picture window** *n* a large usu single-paned window designed to frame an attractive exterior view

**picture writing** *n* the recording of events or expression of ideas by pictorial symbols; *also* the record or message portrayed

**pictur·ize, -ise** /'pikchəriez/ *vt* to make a picture of or present in pictures; *esp* to make into a film – **picturization** *n*

**picul** /'pikl/ *n* any of various units of weight used in China and SE Asia; *esp* a Chinese unit of about 60.5 kilograms ($133^1/_3$ pounds) [Malay *pikul* to carry a heavy load]

[1]**piddle** /'pidl/ *vi*, *informal* **1** to act or work in an idle or trifling manner – often + *about* **2** to urinate [origin unknown]

[2]**piddle** *n*, *informal* **1** urine **2** an act of urinating

**piddling** /'pidling/ *adj*, *informal* trivial, paltry

**piddock** /'pidək/ *n* an INVERTEBRATE animal (genus *Pholas* or family Pholadidae of the phylum Mollusca) related to the mussels, clams, oysters, etc that bores holes in wood, clay, and rocks [origin unknown]

**pidgin** /'pijin/ *n* a simplified mixed language based on two or more languages and used esp for trade between people with different native languages – compare CREOLE △ pigeon [*Pidgin English*] – **pidginize** *vt*, **pidginization** *n*

**Pidgin English** *n* an English-based pidgin; *esp* one originally used in Chinese ports [Pidgin E, modif of E *business English*]

[1]**pie** /pie/ *n* **1** MAGPIE 1 **2** a variegated animal [ME, fr OF, fr L *pica*; akin to L *picus* woodpecker, OHG *speh*]

[2]**pie** *n* **1** a dish consisting of a sweet or savoury filling (eg fruit or meat) covered or encased by pastry and baked in a container **2a** an affair, business ⟨*had a finger in every* ~⟩ **b** a whole regarded as divisible into shares ⟨*giving the poor a larger share of the economic* ~⟩ [ME] – **pie in the sky** an illusory hope or prospect of future happiness; misplaced optimism – see also **have a FINGER in every pie, eat** HUMBLE PIE

[3]**pie**, *chiefly NAm* **pi** *n* printers' type that is spilt or mixed [origin unknown]

[4]**pie**, *chiefly NAm* **pi** *vt* to spill or throw (type or typeset matter) into disorder

[5]**pie** *n* a former monetary unit of India and Pakistan worth $^1/_{192}$ rupee [Hindi *pāī*, fr Skt *pādikā* quarter]

[6]**pie** *adj* [Maori *pai* good] – **be pie on** *NZ* to be good at or keen on

[1]**piebald** /'pie bawld/ *adj* **1** *esp of a horse* of different colours: **1a** spotted or blotched with black and white **b** SKEWBALD **2** composed of incongruous parts; motley [[1]*pie* + *bald* 3]

[2]**piebald** *n* a piebald horse or other animal

[1]**piece** /pees/ *n* **1a** a part of a whole; *esp* a part detached, cut, or broken from a whole ⟨~ *of string*⟩ **b** a portion marked off ⟨*bought a* ~ *of land*⟩ **2** an object or individual regarded as a unit of a kind or class; an example ⟨*a* ~ *of ripe fruit*⟩ ⟨*fine teak tables copied from antique* ~s⟩ **3** a standard quantity (eg of length, weight, or size) in which something is made or sold **4a** a literary, artistic, dramatic, or musical work **b** a passage to be recited **c** a newspaper or magazine article **5** a gun used for a specified purpose ⟨*an artillery* ~⟩ – compare FOWLING PIECE **6** a coin, esp of a specified value ⟨*a 5-pence* ~⟩ **7** a man used in playing a board game; *esp* a chessman of rank superior to a pawn **8** *slang* a woman ⟨*she looks a nice* ~⟩ [ME, fr OF, fr (assumed) VL *pettia*, of Gaulish origin; akin to Bret *pez* piece] – **go to pieces 1** to lose one's composure; BREAK DOWN **2** to deteriorate utterly; collapse ⟨*the money market* went to pieces⟩ – **in one piece** unharmed – **piece of one's mind** a severe scolding – **to pieces** into fragments or parts ⟨*fell* to pieces *as soon as I picked it up*⟩

[2]**piece** *vt* **1** to repair, renew, or complete by adding pieces; patch – often + *up* **2** to join into a whole – often + *together* ⟨*he* ~d *the story together from the accounts of witnesses*⟩ – **piecer** *n*

**piece by piece** *adv* by degrees; piecemeal

**pièce de résistance** /,pyes də razis'tahn(h)s (*Fr* pjes də rezistã:s)/ *n*, *pl* **pièces de résistance** /~/ **1** the chief dish of a meal **2** an outstanding item; a showpiece [Fr, lit., piece of resistance]

[1]**piece-·dye** *vt* to dye after weaving or knitting

**piece goods** *n pl* cloth fabrics sold from the roll in lengths specified by the customer

**¹piecemeal** /-meel/ *adv* **1** one piece at a time; gradually **2** in pieces or fragments; apart [ME *pece-mele*, fr *pece* piece + *-mele* by a portion at a time, fr OE *-mælum*, fr *mælum*, dat pl of *mæl* appointed time – more at ¹MEAL]

**²piecemeal** *adj* done, made, or accomplished piece by piece or in a fragmentary way

**piece of cake** *n, informal* something easily accomplished ⟨*thought the job would be a* ~⟩

**piece of eight** *n* PESO 1 (Spanish coin)

**piece rate** *n*, **piece-rates** *n pl* a fixed amount paid per unit of piecework; *broadly* a rate of pay based on output rather than time

**piecework** /'pees,wuhk/ *n* work that is paid for at a set rate per unit – compare TIMEWORK – **pieceworker** *n*

**pie chart** *n* a graphical means of showing the composition of a whole (eg the total population), each component (eg racial group) being represented by a sector of a circle, the size of which is proportional to the magnitude of the component [²*pie*]

**piecrust** /'pie,krust/ *n* the baked pastry covering of a pie

**pied** /pied/ *adj* having blotchy markings of two or more colours ⟨*a* ~ *horse*⟩ [ME, fr ¹*pie* + -*ed*]

**pied-à-terre** /,pyay ah 'teə (*Fr* pje a tɛr)/ *n, pl* **pieds-à-terre** /~/ accommodation (eg a flat in a city kept by someone who lives in the country) kept for occasional use [Fr, lit., foot to the ground]

**pied flycatcher** *n* a common European FLYCATCHER (*Ficedula hypoleuca*), the male of which has black and white plumage in summer

**piedmont** /'peedmont/ *adj* lying or formed at the base of mountains ⟨~ *glaciers*⟩ [*Piedmont*, region of Italy at the foot of the Alps] – **piedmont** *n*

**pied piper** /pied/ *n, often cap both Ps* **1** one who offers strong but delusive enticement **2** a leader who makes irresponsible promises [*The Pied Piper of Hamelin*, title & hero of a poem by Robert Browning †1889 E poet]

**pied wagtail** *n* a black and white wagtail (*Motacilla alba yarrellii*) that is a European subspecies of the WHITE WAGTAIL and is common in Britain and often seen in urban areas

**pie-'eyed** *adj, informal* drunk [prob fr ³*pie*]

**pier** /piə/ *n* **1** an intermediate support for the adjacent ends of two bridge spans **2a** a structure extending into navigable water for use as a landing place or as a breakwater **b** a structure of wooden or metal girders supporting a promenade with stalls, amusements, etc, and extending outwards from the shore at a holiday resort **3** a vertical structural support: eg **3a** a short section of wall between two openings **b** a pillar that supports the end of an arch, vault, or lintel **c** an auxiliary mass of masonry used to stiffen a wall; a buttress **4** a structural mount (eg for a telescope) usu of stonework, concrete, or steel [ME *per*, fr OE, fr ML *pera*]

**pierce** /'piəs/ *vt* **1a** to run into or through as a pointed weapon does; stab **b** to enter or thrust into sharply or painfully **2** to make a hole in or through; perforate **3** to force or make a way into or through ⟨*a light* ~d *the darkness*⟩ **4** to penetrate with the eye or mind; discern **5** to penetrate sharply so as to move or touch the emotions of ⟨*grief* ~d *his heart*⟩ **6** to sound sharply through ⟨*a shriek* ~d *the stillness of the night*⟩ **7** of *cold* to penetrate ⟨*the cold* ~d *them to the bone*⟩ ~ *vi* to force a way into or through something [ME *percen*, fr OF *percer*, prob fr (assumed) VL *pertusiare*, fr L *pertusus*, pp of *pertundere* to bore through, fr *per-* through + *tundere* to beat, pound]

**pierced** /piəst/ *adj* **1** having holes; *esp* decorated with perforations **2** having the earlobe punctured for an earring ⟨~ *ears*⟩

**piercing** /'piəsing/ *adj* penetrating: eg **a** loud, shrill ⟨~ *cries*⟩ **b** perceptive ⟨~ *eyes*⟩ **c** penetratingly cold; biting ⟨*a* ~ *winter wind*⟩ **d** cutting, incisive ⟨~ *sarcasm*⟩ – **piercingly** *adv*

**pier glass** *n* a tall mirror; *esp* one designed to occupy the wall space between two windows

**Pierian** /pie'iəriən/ *adj* **1** of the region of Pieria in ancient Macedonia or the Muses who were worshipped there **2** of learning or poetry

**Pierrot** /'piə,roh/ *n* a stock comic character of old French pantomime, usu having a whitened face and wearing loose white clothes [Fr, dim. of *Pierre* Peter]

**pierrot collar** *n* a circular upstanding collar resembling the ruff of a clown's outfit

**pier table** *n* a table designed to be placed against the wall between two windows, often under a PIER GLASS

**pies** /piez/ *pl of* PI *or of* PIE

**pietà** /,pee-ay'tah, ,pyay-/ *n, often cap* a representation (eg a painting or sculpture) of the Virgin Mary mourning over the dead body of Christ [It, lit., pity, fr L *pietat-*, *pietas*]

**pietism** /'pie-ə,tiz(ə)m/ *n* **1** *cap* a religious movement originating in 17th-century Germany and stressing Bible study and personal religious experience rather than the use of the intellect and adherence to prescribed forms **2a** emphasis on personal religious devotion rather than on theological study **b** exaggerated or affected piety; religiosity – **pietist** *n, often cap*, **pietistic, pietistical** *adj*, **pietistically** *adv*

**piety** /'pie-əti/ *n* **1** the quality or state of being pious; devoutness **2** dutifulness, esp to parents ⟨*inspired by filial* ~⟩ **3** an act inspired by piety [Fr *pieté* piety, pity, fr L *pietat-*, *pietas*, fr *pius* dutiful – more at PIOUS]

**piezo-** /pie'eezoh-/ *comb form* pressure ⟨*piezometer*⟩ [Gk *piezein* to press; akin to Skt *pīdayati* he squeezes]

**piezoelectric** /pie,eezoh-i'lektrik/ *adj* of, marked by, or functioning by means of piezoelectricity ⟨*a* ~ *crystal*⟩ ⟨*a cigarette lighter with* ~ *ignition*⟩ [ISV] – **piezoelectrically** *adv*

**piezoelectricity** /pie,eezoh-i,lek'trisəti, -,eelek-/ *n* electricity or a voltage generated as a result of pressure in a crystalline substance (eg quartz) [ISV]

**piezometer** /,pie-i'zomitə/ *n* an instrument for measuring pressure or the compressibility of materials under pressure – **piezometry** *n*, **piezometric** *adj*

**¹piffle** /'pifl/ *vi, informal* to talk or act in a trivial or ineffective way [prob imit]

**²piffle** *n, informal* trivial nonsense

**piffling** /'pifling/ *adj, informal* trivial, derisory

**¹pig** /pig/ *n* **1a** *chiefly Br* any of various short-legged and typically stout-bodied mammals (family Suidae) with a thick bristly skin and a long mobile snout; *esp* a domesticated pig belonging to the same species (*Sus scrofa*) as the European WILD BOAR **b** *NAm* a young pig not yet sexually mature **2a** pork ⟨*roast suck-ing* ~⟩ **b** pigskin **3** an animal related to or resembling the pig – usu in combination ⟨*guinea* ~⟩ **4a** a shaped mass (eg an oblong block) of cast crude metal (eg iron) **b** the mould in which a metal pig is cast **5** a device that is pushed or pulled through a pipeline (eg in an oil refinery) in order to clean or unblock it **6a** *informal* one resembling or suggestive of a pig in habits or behaviour (eg in dirtiness, greed, selfishness, or obstinacy) ⟨*male chauvinist* ~⟩ ⟨*he stood me up, the* ~⟩ **b** *Br informal* something difficult or nasty **7** *slang* a policeman [ME *pigge*] – **make a pig's ear of** *informal* to do awkwardly, messily, or wrongly – **pig in a poke** something offered without being examined or its true nature or worth ascertained ⟨*unwilling to buy a* pig in a poke⟩ [¹*poke*]

**²pig** *vb* **-gg-** *vi, of a sow* to give birth to piglets; farrow ~ *vt* **1** to give birth to (piglets) **2** *informal* **2a** to eat (food, esp more than one's share) greedily ⟨~ged *all the cream cakes*⟩ **b** to overindulge (oneself) with food ⟨*I* ~ged *myself with fish and chips*⟩ – **pig it** to live in squalor

**³pig** *n, chiefly Scot* an earthenware vessel; a crock [ME *pygg*]

**pig bed** *n* a bed of sand in which iron is cast into pigs

**¹pigeon** /'pijin, 'pij(ə)n/ *n* **1** any of a widely distributed family (Columbidae, order Columbiformes) of stout-bodied birds with short legs and smooth compact plumage; *esp* a member of any of many varieties derived from the ROCK DOVE, that are domesticated or live in the wild state in urban areas throughout most of the world **2** CLAY 3 [ME, fr MF *pijon*, fr LL *pipion-*, *pipio* young bird, fr L *pipire* to chirp]

**synonyms** Although technically a **pigeon** and a **dove** are the same bird, **dove** is the word used in poetical and symbolic contexts, and in combination as part of the names of certain pigeons such as the **stock dove** and **turtledove**.

**²pigeon** *n, informal* a matter of special concern; business ⟨*that's not my* ~ *; someone else can deal with it*⟩ [alter. of *pidgin*]

**pigeon breast** *n* a deformity of the chest marked by sharp projection of the breastbone – **pigeon-breasted** *adj*

**¹pigeonhole** /-,hohl/ *n* **1** a hole or small recess for pigeons to nest in **2** any of a set of small open compartments (eg in a desk or wall unit) for letters or documents **3** a neat category which usu fails to reflect actual complexities ⟨*a psychological* ~ *for every misfit*⟩

**²pigeonhole** *vt* **1a** to place (as if) in the pigeonhole of a desk **b** to lay aside; shelve ⟨*plans and reports for the whole project to be* ~d *until there is more money*⟩ **2** to assign to a category; classify

**pigeon step** *n* a step taken by placing one foot immediately in front of the other, heel to toe

,pigeon-'toed *adj* having the toes turned in

**piggery** /'pig(ə)ri/ *n* **1a** a pig-rearing establishment **b** a pigsty **2** dirty, greedy, or nasty behaviour ⟨*male chauvinist* ∼⟩

**piggin** /'pigin/ *n, dial* a small wooden pail with one stave extended upwards as a handle [origin unknown]

**piggish** /'pigish/, **piggy** /'pigi/ *adj* of or resembling a pig, esp in being dirty, greedy, or ill-mannered ⟨*embarrassed by his* ∼ *eating habits*⟩ – **piggishly** *adv*, **piggishness** *n*

**piggy** /'pigi/ *n* a (little) pig – used esp by or to children

[1]**piggyback** /-,bak/ *adv* up on the back and shoulders ⟨*carried the child* ∼ *up the stairs*⟩ [alter. of earlier *a pick back*, *a pick pack*, of unknown origin]

[2]**piggyback** *n* the act of carrying piggyback ⟨*gave his injured friend a* ∼⟩

[3]**piggyback** *adj* **1** up on the shoulders and back ⟨*children love* ∼ *rides*⟩ **2** of or being something carried as an extra load on the back of a vehicle (eg a spacecraft or aircraft)

[4]**piggyback** *vt* to haul (eg a lorry trailer) by rail

**piggy bank** *n* a coin bank often in the shape of a pig

**pigheaded** /pig'hedid/ *adj* obstinate, stubborn **synonyms** see OBSTINATE – **pigheadedness** *n*

**pig iron** *n* impure unrefined iron direct from the BLAST FURNACE

**pig latin** *n, often cap L* a secret language made by systematic mutilation of spoken English (eg *igpay atinLay* for *pig Latin*)

**pig lead** *n* lead cast in oblong blocks or similar shaped masses (PIGS)

**piglet** /'piglit/ *n* a small young pig

[1]**pigment** /'pigmənt/ *n* **1** a substance that colours other materials; *esp* a powdered substance that is mixed with a liquid in which it is relatively insoluble and is used to produce coloured paints, inks, plastics, etc **2** any of various natural coloured substances (eg chlorophyll) in animals and plants, many of which are important in energy-producing reactions (eg respiration) inside cells; *also* any of various colourless substances similar in function and chemical structure to these [L *pigmentum*, fr *pingere* to paint – more at PAINT] – **pigmentary** *adj*

[2]**pigment** /pig'ment/ *vt* to colour (as if) with pigment

**pigmentation** /,pigmen'taysh(ə)n/ *n* **1** coloration with or deposition of pigment in an animal or plant **2** discoloration of body tissue caused by excessive deposition of pigment

**pigmy** /'pigmi/ *n* a pygmy

**pigmy moth** *n* any of various minute often brightly coloured moths (family Nepticulidae) including one (*Johanssonia acetosae*) that is the smallest known moth

**pignut** /'pig,nut/ *n* **1** a common Eurasian plant (*Conopodium majus*) of the carrot family, with edible underground stems (TUBERS) – called also EARTHNUT **2** *chiefly NAm* (the bitter-flavoured hickory nut of) any of several hickory trees (genus *Carya*, esp *Carya glabra*)

**pigpen** /-,pen/ *n, NAm* a pigsty

**pigskin** /-,skin/ *n* (leather made from) the skin of a pig

**pigsticking** /-,stiking/ *n* the sport, formerly practised in India, of hunting WILD BOAR on horseback with a spear – **pigsticker** *n*

**pigsty** /-,stie/ *n* **1** an enclosure with a covered shed for pigs **2** a dirty, untidy, or neglected place

**pigswill** /'pig,swil/ *n* waste food fed to pigs

**pigtail** /-,tayl/ *n* **1** a tight plait of hair, esp when worn singly at the back of the head **2** either of two bunches of hair worn loose or plaited at either side of the head – **pigtailed** *adj*

**pika** /'peekə, 'piekə/ *n* any of various small short-eared mammals (family Ochotonidae) of rocky mountainous regions of Asia and western N America that are related to the rabbits [Tungusic *piika*]

[1]**pike** /piek/ *n* a sharp point or spike; *also* the tip of a spear [ME, fr OE *pīc* pickaxe] – **piked** *adj*

[2]**pike** *n, NW Eng* a mountain or hill, esp in the Lake District, with a peaked summit – used esp in place names [ME, perh of Scand origin; akin to Norw dial. *pīk* pointed mountain]

[3]**pike** *n, pl* **pike**, *esp for different types* **pikes** **1a** a large predatory long-snouted BONY FISH (*Esox lucius*) valued for food and sport and widely distributed in the rivers and lakes of the cooler parts of the N hemisphere **b** any of various freshwater fishes (family Esocidae) related to the pike; *esp* PICKEREL 1 **2** any of various fishes resembling the pike in appearance or habits [ME, fr [1]*pike*; fr the shape of its head]

[4]**pike** *n* a weapon consisting of a long wooden shaft with a pointed steel head that was used by infantrymen until super-

seded by the bayonet [MF *pique*, fr *piquer* to prick, fr (assumed) VL *piccare*, fr *piccus* woodpecker, fr L *picus* – more at PIE] – **pike** *vt*

[5]**pike** *n, NAm* a turnpike

[6]**pike** *n* a body position (eg in diving) in which the hips are bent, the knees are straight, the head is pressed forwards, and the hands touch the toes or clasp the legs behind or just above the knees [prob fr [3]*pike*]

**pikelet** /'pieklit/ *n, dial Br* a crumpet [by shortening & alter. fr earlier *bara-picklet*, fr W *bara pyglyd* pitchy bread]

**pikeman** /'piekmən/ *n* a soldier armed with a pike

**pike perch** *n* any of various freshwater fishes (esp genera *Lucioperca* and *Stizostedion*) of the perch family that resemble pikes

**pikestaff** /-,stahf/ *n* **1** a spiked walking stick for use on slippery ground **2** the wooden shaft of a foot soldier's pike

**pil-** /piel-/, **pili-**, **pilo-** *comb form* hair ⟨*pileous*⟩ ⟨*piliferous*⟩ [L *pilus* – more at PILE]

**pilaf, pilaff** /'pee,laf, 'pi-/ *n* a dish of Oriental origin consisting of seasoned rice and often meat [Per & Turk *pilāu*]

**pilaster** /pi'lastə/ *n* a usu ornamental rectangular column that is embedded in the face of a wall and projects slightly from it – compare [1]PILLAR [MF *pilastre*, fr It *pilastro*, fr ML *pilastrum*, fr L *pila* pillar]

**pilau** /'pilow, 'pee,low/ *n* (a) pilaf

**pilchard** /'pilchəd/ *n* **1** a small fish (*Sardinia pilchardus*) of the herring family resembling the herring and occurring in great schools along the coasts of Europe **2** any of several sardines related to the European pilchard [origin unknown]

[1]**pile** /piel/ *n* **1** a long post or column, usu of timber, steel, or reinforced concrete, driven into the ground to carry a vertical load **2** a wedge-shaped heraldic design, usu placed vertically with the broad end up [ME, dart, stake, fr OE *pīl*; akin to OHG *pfil* dart; both fr a prehistoric WGmc word borrowed fr L *pilum* javelin – more at PESTLE]

[2]**pile** *vt* to drive piles into

[3]**pile** *n* **1a** *taking sing or pl vb* a quantity of things heaped together; a mound ⟨*a* ∼ *of plates*⟩ **b** a heap of wood for burning a corpse or a sacrifice; a pyre **c** a large quantity, number, or amount ⟨*a* ∼ *of stuff still to be read*⟩ ⟨∼*s of friends*⟩ **2** a large imposing building or group of buildings ⟨*a Gothic* ∼⟩ **3** a great amount of money; a fortune ⟨*now that he has made his* ∼, *he can live in luxury*⟩ **4 pile, voltaic pile** a vertical series of alternate discs of two dissimilar metals (eg copper and zinc) separated by discs of cloth or paper moistened with a substance that conducts electricity (ELECTROLYTE) and used formerly for producing an electric current; *also* an early form of battery constructed from piles **5** NUCLEAR REACTOR – see also NIGGER **in the wood pile** [ME, fr MF, fr L *pila* pillar]

[4]**pile** *vt* **1** to lay or place in a pile; stack – often + *up* **2** to heap in abundance; load ⟨∼*d potatoes on his plate*⟩ ⟨*a table* ∼*d high with food*⟩ ∼ *vi* to move or press forwards (as if) in a disorderly crowd ⟨∼*d into a car*⟩ – **pile it on** to exaggerate

**pile up** *vi* **1** to accumulate ⟨*his work* piled up *over the holidays*⟩ **2** to become involved in a pileup of vehicles ∼ *vt* to make into a pile ⟨piled *the boxes* up⟩

[5]**pile** *n* **1** soft hair, down, fur, or wool **2** a soft raised velvety surface on a fabric or carpet consisting of cut threads or loops standing up from the weave [ME, fr L *pilus* hair; akin to L *pila* ball, *pilleus*, *pileus* felt cap, Gk *pilos*]

[6]**pile** *n usu pl* a haemorrhoid [ME, fr L *pila* ball]

**pileate** /'piliət, 'pie-, -ayt/ *adj* **1** *botany* having a pileus **2** **pileated** *also* **pileate** *of a bird* having a crest covering the pileum

**piled** /pield/ *adj* having a pile ⟨*a deep-*piled *rug*⟩

**pile driver** *n* **1** a machine for driving piles into the ground **2** the operator of a pile driver

**pileum** /'pieliəm/ *n, pl* **pilea** /-liə/ the top of a bird's head from the bill to the base of the skull [NL, fr L *pilleum*, *pileum* felt cap, var of *pilleus*, *pileus*]

**pileup** /-,up/ *n* **1** a serious traffic accident in which several motor vehicles crash into each other **2** a jammed tangled mass or pile (eg of motor vehicles or people) resulting from collision

**pileus** /'pieli-əs/ *n, pl* **pilei** /-li,ee, -li,ie/ the typically umbrella-shaped FRUITING BODY (spore-producing body) of many fungi (eg the mushrooms) [NL, fr L *pilleus*, *pileus* felt cap]

**pilfer** /'pilfə/ *vi* to steal stealthily in small amounts or to small value and often again and again ⟨*the mouse that* ∼s *from our pantry*⟩ ∼ *vt* to steal in small quantities **synonyms** see ROB [MF *pelfrer*, fr *pelfre* booty (cf PELF)] – **pilferage** *n*, **pilferer** *n*

**pilgrim** /'pilgrim/ *n* **1** a person making a pilgrimage **2** *chiefly poetic* a traveller, wayfarer [ME, fr OF *peligrin*, fr LL *pelegrinus*, alter. of L *peregrinus* foreigner, fr *peregrinus* foreign, fr *pereger* being abroad, fr *per* through + *agr-*, *ager* land – more at FOR, ACRE]

<sup>1</sup>**pilgrimage** /'pilgrimij/ *n* **1a** a journey to a shrine or sacred place undertaken as an act of devotion, in order to acquire spiritual merit, or as a penance **b** a long journey or search undertaken for sentimental reasons or out of duty **2** the course of life on earth

<sup>2</sup>**pilgrimage** *vi* to go on a pilgrimage

**pili-** /'pieli-/ – see PIL-

**piling** /'pieling/ *n* a structure made of piles; *also* the piles themselves

**Pilipino** /,pilə'peenoh, ,pee-/ *n* the TAGALOG-based language of the Philippines [Pilipino, fr Sp *Filipino* Philippine]

<sup>1</sup>**pill** /pil/ *n* **1a** a small rounded solid mass of a medicine, to be swallowed whole **b** an oral contraceptive; *specif, often cap* a series of pills that usu contain drugs having actions similar to the naturally occurring OESTROGENS (female SEX HORMONES) and PROGESTERONE (hormone produced during pregnancy), one of which is taken daily by a woman over a monthly cycle 〈*she went on the ~ after her fourth child*〉 – usu + *the* **2** something repugnant or unpleasant that must be accepted or endured 〈*the loss of salary was a bitter ~ to swallow*〉 **3** something resembling a pill in size or shape **4** *informal* a disagreeable or tiresome person [L *pilula*, fr dim. of *pila* ball – more at PILE]

<sup>2</sup>**pill** *vt* to dose with pills ~ *vi* to become rough with or mat into little balls of fibre 〈*brushed woollens often ~*〉

<sup>1</sup>**pillage** /'pilij/ *n* **1** the act of looting or plundering, esp in war **2** something taken as booty [ME, fr MF, fr *piller* to plunder, fr *peille* rag, fr L *pilleum, pilleus* felt cap]

<sup>2</sup>**pillage** *vb* to plunder ruthlessly; loot – **pillager** *n*

<sup>1</sup>**pillar** /'pilə/ *n* **1a** a firm upright support for a superstructure; a post **b** a usu ornamental column or shaft; *esp* one standing alone as a monument **2** a chief supporter; a prop 〈*a ~ of the Establishment*〉 **3** a solid mass of coal, rock, or ore left standing to support a mine roof **4** something that resembles a column 〈*a ~ of smoke*〉 ▯ compare PILASTER [ME *piler*, fr OF, fr ML *pilare*, fr L *pila*] – **from pillar to post** from one place or situation to another

<sup>2</sup>**pillar** *vt* to support or decorate (as if) with pillars

**pillar box** *n* a red pillar-shaped public letter box

**pillar-box red** *adj or n* vivid scarlet

**pillbox** /'pil,boks/ *n* **1** a box for pills; *esp* a shallow round box made of pasteboard or of decorated porcelain **2** a small low concrete emplacement for machine guns and antitank weapons **3** a small round brimless hat with a flat crown and straight sides, worn esp by women

**pill bug** *n* WOOD-LOUSE 1 [<sup>1</sup>*pill;* fr its rolling into a ball when disturbed]

<sup>1</sup>**pillion** /'pilyən/ *n* **1** a pad or cushion formerly put behind a saddle for a second rider, usu a woman, to sit on **2** a saddle or seat for a passenger on a motorcycle, motor scooter, or bicycle [ScGael *pillean* or IrGael *pillín*, dim. of *peall* covering, couch]

<sup>2</sup>**pillion** *adv* (as if) on a pillion 〈*ride ~*〉

**pillock** /'pilak/ *n, Br slang* a stupid or objectionable person [E dial. *pill, pilluck, pillick* penis, of Scand origin]

<sup>1</sup>**pillory** /'pilari/ *n* **1** a device for publicly punishing offenders consisting of a wooden frame with holes in which the head and hands can be locked **2** a verbal attack or other means of exposure to public scorn or ridicule [ME, fr OF *pilori*]

<sup>2</sup>**pillory** *vt* **1** to put in a pillory as punishment **2** to expose to public contempt, ridicule, or scorn

<sup>1</sup>**pillow** /'piloh/ *n* **1a** a support for the head of a reclining person; *esp* a usu rectangular cloth bag (e g of cotton) filled with soft but resilient material (e g feathers, down, or foam rubber) **b** something resembling a pillow, esp in form **2** a block or support used esp to equalize or distribute pressure **3** a tightly stuffed cushion or pad used as a support in making PILLOW LACE [ME *pilwe*, fr OE *pyle;* akin to OHG *pfuliwi* pillow; both fr a prehistoric WGmc word borrowed fr L *pulvinus* pillow]

<sup>2</sup>**pillow** *vt* **1** to rest or lay (as if) on a pillow **2** to serve as a pillow for

**pillowcase** /-,kays/ *n* a removable washable cover, esp of linen, cotton, or nylon, for a pillow

**pillow lace** *n* lace worked with bobbins over a padded support – compare NEEDLEPOINT 1, POINT 12

**pillow lava** *n* lava that has solidified, probably under water, in rounded masses, suggestive of pillows

**pillow slip** *n* a pillowcase

**pillow talk** *n* conversation in bed between lovers

**pilo-** /pieloh-/ – see PIL-

**pilocarpine** /,pieloh'kahpeen, -pin/ *n* a chemical compound, $C_{11}H_{16}N_2O_2$, that is obtained from the leaves of the JABORANDI shrub and is used esp in eyedrops to contract the pupil of the eye [ISV, fr NL *Pilocarpus jaborandi*, species of tropical shrubs]

**pilose** /'pie,lohs/ *adj, biology* covered with usu soft hair [L *pilosus*, fr *pilus* hair – more at PILE] – **pilosity** *n*

<sup>1</sup>**pilot** /'pielət/ *n* **1** a coastal navigator who is qualified and usu licensed to guide a ship into and out of a port or in specified waters **2a** a guide, leader **b** a trial run 〈*if local ~s are successful the service will operate nationally*〉 **3** one who handles or is qualified to handle the controls of an aircraft or spacecraft **4** a piece that guides a tool or machine part **5** PILOT LIGHT [MF *pilote*, fr It *pilota*, alter. of *pedota*, fr (assumed) MGk *pēdōtēs*, fr Gk *pēda* steering oars, pl of *pēdon* oar; akin to Gk *pod-, pous* foot – more at FOOT] – **pilotless** *adj*

<sup>2</sup>**pilot** *vt* **1** to act as a guide to; lead or conduct over a usu difficult course **2a** to direct the course of 〈*~ a ship*〉 **b** to act as pilot of 〈*~ a plane*〉

<sup>3</sup>**pilot** *adj* serving as a guide, indicator, activator, or trial 〈*~ holes*〉 〈*~ lamps*〉 〈*a ~ scheme*〉

**pilotage** /'pielətij/ *n* **1** piloting; *specif* the navigation of an aircraft by direct observation of landmarks and use of charts **2** the fee paid to a pilot

**pilot balloon** *n* a small unmanned balloon sent up to show the direction and speed of the wind

**pilot-cloth** *n* a thick blue woollen cloth used esp for seamen's coats

**pilot engine** *n* a locomotive going in advance of a train to make sure that the way is clear

**pilot fish** *n* a small oceanic fish (*Naucrates ductor*) of warm and tropical seas, that is marked with distinctive dark-coloured vertical bands and often swims in the company of a large fish, esp a shark

**pilothouse** /'pielət,hows/ *n* a wheelhouse on a ship

**pilotis** /,peelo'teez/ *n pl* pillars serving as supports of a structure above ground; stilts [Fr, foundation of piles, fr *piloter* to drive piles, fr *pilot* pile, fr *pile*]

**pilot lamp** *n* PILOT LIGHT 1

**pilot light** *n* **1** an indicator light showing whether power is on or where a switch or CIRCUIT BREAKER is located **2** a small permanent flame used to ignite gas at a principal burner (e g on a cooker)

**pilotman** /'pielətmən/ *n, Br* a person who rides on each train as it passes over a section of single track and without whom no train is allowed into the section

**pilot officer** *n* – see MILITARY RANKS table

**pilot whale** *n* BLACKFISH 2 [fr the largest male in a school acting as pilot or leader for the others]

**pilsner** *also* **pilsener** /'pilznə, 'pilsnə/ *n, often cap* a light beer with a strong flavour of hops [Ger, lit., of Pilsen (now Plzen), city in Czechoslovakia]

**Piltdown man** /'pilt,down/ *n* a supposedly very early primitive modern man based on skull fragments that were uncovered in a gravel pit at Piltdown in 1912 and were used in combination with comparatively recent skeletal remains of various animals in the development of an elaborate fraud [*Piltdown*, site in East Sussex in England]

**pilular** /'pilyoolə/ *adj* of or resembling a pill

**pilule** /'pilyoohl/ *n* a little pill [MF, fr L *pilula* pill]

**pilus** /'pieləs/ *n, pl* **pili** /'pieli, -lie/ a hair or hairlike structure (e g of a bacterium) – more at PILE]

**pima cotton** /'peemə, 'pimə/ *n* a cotton that produces fibre of exceptional strength and firmness [*Pima* county in Arizona, USA]

**Piman** /'peemən/ *adj* of or constituting a language family of the UTO-AZTECAN group

**pimento** /pi'mentoh/ *n, pl* **pimentos, pimento 1** PIMIENTO 1 **2** allspice [Sp *pimienta* allspice, pepper, fr LL *pigmenta*, pl of *pigmentum* plant juice, fr L, pigment]

**pi-meson** /'pie ,meez(ə)n/ *n, physics* PION (particle of matter) [<sup>1</sup>*pi* (representing the initial letter of *primary radiation*)]

**pimiento** /pi'myentoh/ *n, pl* **pimientos 1** any of various bluntly conical thick-fleshed SWEET PEPPERS that have a distinctive mild sweet flavour and are used esp as a garnish, as a stuffing for olives, and when ripe as a source of paprika **2** a plant that bears pimientos [Sp, fr *pimienta*]

**pimp** /pimp/ *n* a man who solicits clients for a prostitute or brothel △ poof [origin unknown] – **pimp** *vi*

**pimpernel** /'pimpǝ,nel/ *n* any of several plants (esp genera *Anagallis* and *Lysimachia*) of the primrose family: e g a SCARLET PIMPERNEL **b** YELLOW PIMPERNEL [ME *pimpernele*, fr MF *pimprenelle*, fr LL *pimpinella*, a medicinal herb, perh deriv of L *piper* pepper]

**pimple** /'pimpl/ *n* **1** a small solid inflamed usu pus-containing swelling on the skin **2** a swelling or protuberance like a pimple [ME *pinple*] – **pimpled, pimply** *adj*

**¹pin** /pin/ *n* **1a** a piece of solid material (e g wood or metal) used esp for fastening separate articles together or as a support by which one article may be suspended from another **b** something that resembles a pin, esp in slender elongated form **c(1)** any of the wooden pieces constituting the target in various games (e g skittles and tenpin bowling) **c(2)** the peg at which a quoit is pitched **c(3)** the staff of the flag marking a hole on a golf course **c(4)** a projecting metal bar on an electric plug, which is inserted into a socket **d** a peg for regulating the tension of the strings of a musical instrument **2a(1)** a small slender pointed piece of rigid wire with a rounded or flattened head, used esp for holding things (e g papers or pieces of cloth) together or fastening one thing to another **a(2)** something of little value; a trifle ⟨*doesn't care a ~ for anyone*⟩ **b** an ornament or badge fastened to clothing with a pin **c(1)** a hairgrip **c(2)** a hairpin **c(3)** SAFETY PIN **3** *usu pl, informal* a leg ⟨*wobbly on his ~s*⟩ [ME, fr OE *pinn;* akin to OHG *pfinn* peg] – **pinned** *adj*

**²pin** *vt* **-nn-** **1a** to fasten, join, or secure with a pin **b** to hold fast or immobile ⟨*~ned him to the wall*⟩ **2a** to attach, hang ⟨*~ned his hopes on a miracle*⟩ **b** to assign the blame or responsibility for ⟨*~ the robbery on a night watchman*⟩ **3a** to make (a chess opponent's piece) unable to move without exposing the king to check or a valuable piece to capture **b** *of a wrestler* to hold (an opponent) fast with both shoulders touching the ground; secure a FALL over

**pin down** *vt* **1** to define or identify precisely ⟨*a vague feeling of unease that she couldn't quite pin down*⟩ **2** to compel to state his/her intentions or make a decision **3a** to hold fast; prevent from moving **b** to limit, confine ⟨*didn't want to pin her helpers* down *to set hours*⟩

**piña cloth** /'peenyǝ/ *n* a lustrous transparent cloth of Philippine origin that is woven from silky pineapple fibres [Sp *piña* pinecone, pineapple, fr L *pinea*]

**piña colada** /,peenyǝ kǝ'lahdǝ, ,peenǝ/ *n* a drink made usu from coconut milk, pineapple juice, and rum [Sp, lit., strained pineapple]

**pinafore** /'pinǝ,faw/ *n* **1** an apron, usu with a bib **2** *also* **pinafore dress** a sleeveless usu low-necked dress that is designed to be worn over another garment (e g a blouse or jumper) [²*pin* + *afore*]

**pinaster** /pie'nastǝ, pin-/ *n* a pine tree (*Pinus pinaster*) of the Mediterranean region with large stiff needles arranged in pairs and clusters of long cones [L, a type of pine, fr *pinus* pine]

**piñata, pinata** /peen'yahtǝ/ *n* a decorated pottery jar filled with sweets, fruits, and gifts and hung from the ceiling to be broken as part of Mexican festivities (e g at Christmas or for a birthday party) [Sp *piñata*, lit., pot]

**pinball** /'pin,bawl/ *n* a game in which a small ball is propelled up a sloping board and allowed to roll down across it, scoring points if it hits any of an arrangement of targets on the way

**pinball machine** /'pin,bawl/ *n* an amusement device for playing pinball and automatically recording the score

**pince-nez** /'pans ,nay, 'pins- (*Fr* pɛ̃s ne)/ *n, pl* **pince-nez** /nay(z)/ glasses clipped to the nose by a spring [Fr, fr *pincer* to pinch + *nez* nose, fr L *nasus* – more at NOSE]

**pincer** /'pinsǝ/ *n* **1a** *pl but taking sing or pl vb* a tool having two short handles and two grasping jaws working on a pivot and used for gripping things **b** a claw (e g of a lobster) resembling a pair of pincers; CHELA **2** either of two military forces that converge upon an enemy position from opposite directions [ME *pinceour*, prob deriv of MF *pincier* to pinch] – **pincerlike** *adj*

*synonyms* **Pincers** have rounded jaws with a circular space between them, while the jaws of **pliers** are long and somewhat tapering.

**¹pinch** /pinch/ *vt* **1a** to squeeze between the finger and thumb or between the jaws of an instrument **b** to prune the tip of (a plant or shoot), usu to correct growth or induce branching –

usu + *out* or *back* **c** to squeeze or compress painfully ⟨*the shoes ~ed her toes*⟩ **d** to cause physical or mental pain to ⟨*~ed with cold*⟩ **e(1)** to cause to appear thin or shrunken ⟨*faces ~ed with hunger and fatigue*⟩ **e(2)** to cause to shrivel or wither **2** to subject to strict economy or want; straiten **3** to sail (a ship) too close to the wind **4** *informal* **4a** STEAL 1 **b** ARREST 2 ~ *vi* **1** to compress or squeeze, esp painfully ⟨*my new shoes ~*⟩ **2** to be miserly or frugal ⟨*they have to ~ and save to live*⟩ **3** *of a ship* to sail too close to the wind *synonyms* see ROB [ME *pinchen*, fr (assumed) ONF *pinchier*]

**²pinch** *n* **1a** a critical juncture; an emergency ⟨*when it comes to the ~, he'll let you down*⟩ **b(1)** pressure, stress ⟨*when the ~ of foreign competition came at last* – G M Trevelyan⟩ **b(2)** hardship, privation ⟨*after a year of sanctions, they began to feel the ~*⟩ **2a** an act of pinching; a squeeze **b** as much as may be taken between the finger and thumb ⟨*a ~ of snuff*⟩ **3** a marked thinning of a vein or bed of a mineral – **at a pinch** if necessary; in an emergency – **with a pinch of salt** with doubts as to the truth ⟨*we take what he says* with a pinch of salt⟩

**pinch bar** *n* a crowbar or lever with a split curved end for pulling out nails

**pinchbeck** /'pinch,bek/ *n* **1** an alloy of copper and zinc, used esp to imitate gold in jewellery **2** something counterfeit or sham [Christopher *Pinchbeck* †1732 E watchmaker] – **pinchbeck** *adj*

**pinchcock** /'pinch,kok/ *n* a clamp used (e g in a laboratory) on a flexible tube to regulate the flow of a liquid

**pincher** /'pinchǝ/ *n* **1** one who or that which pinches **2** *pl* PINCERS 1a

**¹pinch-,hit** *vi* **1** to bat in the place of another baseball player, esp in an emergency when a run is particularly needed **2** *NAm* to act or serve in place of another [back-formation fr *pinch hitter*] – **pinch hitter** *n*

**pin curl** *n* a curl produced by securing a dampened curl of hair with a hairgrip or clip

**pincushion** /'pin,koosh(ǝ)n/ *n* a small cushion in which pins may be stuck ready for use in sewing

**¹Pindaric** /pin'darik/ *adj* **1** of the poet Pindar **2** *of a poem* having the complex and irregular metrical structure supposedly characteristic of Pindar [*Pindar* (Gk *Pindaros*) †443 BC Gk lyric poet]

**²Pindaric** *n* **1** a Pindaric ode **2** *pl* loose irregular verses similar to those used in Pindaric odes

**¹pine** /pien/ *vi* **1** to lose vigour, health, or flesh (e g through grief); languish – often + *away* **2** to yearn intensely and persistently, esp for something unattainable; long ⟨*they still ~d for their lost wealth*⟩ [ME *pinen*, fr OE *pīnian*, fr (assumed) OE *pīn* punishment, fr L *poena* – more at PAIN]

**²pine** *n* **1** any of a genus (*Pinus* of the family Pinaceae, the pine family) of coniferous evergreen trees that have long slender needles and some of which are valuable ornamental or timber trees; *also* any of various similar or related coniferous trees **2** the white or yellow usu durable and resinous wood of a pine [ME, fr OE *pīn*, fr L *pinus;* akin to Gk *pitys* pine, L *opimus* fat – more at FAT] – **piny, piney** *adj*

**pineal** /'piniǝl/ *adj* of, involving, or being the PINEAL GLAND [Fr *pinéal*, fr MF, fr L *pinea* pinecone, fr fem of *pineus* of pine, fr *pinus*]

**pineal body** /'pini·ǝl/ *n* PINEAL GLAND

**pineal gland** *n* a small usu cone-shaped gland in the brain of all VERTEBRATE animals with skulls, that is associated with physiological activities connected with light (e g breeding cycles in birds), has the structure of an eye in a few reptiles, and that secretes certain hormones (e g melatonin) in mammals – called also EPIPHYSIS

**pineapple** /'pienapl/ *n* **1a** a tropical plant (*Ananas comosus* of the family Bromeliaceae, the pineapple family) that has stiff spiny-edged leaves and a dense oval to oblong head of small flowers **b** the large edible yellow-fleshed fruit of the pineapple that consists of the segmented but compact succulent ripened flowerhead **2** *slang* **2a** a dynamite bomb **b** a hand grenade [ME *pinappel* pinecone, fr *pin, pine* pine + *appel* apple, fruit]

**pineapple weed** *n* a plant (*Matricaria matricarioides*) of the daisy family that is widely distributed as a weed and has greenish-yellow flowers that smell of pineapple when crushed

**pinecone** /'pien,kohn/ *n* a cone of a pine tree

**pine marten** *n* a slender Eurasian MARTEN (mammal related to the weasel) (*Martes martes*) that has dark brown fur with a yellow patch on the chest and throat

**pinene** /'pieneen/ *n* a liquid TERPENE (compound of hydrogen and carbon found in plant oils), $C_{10}H_{16}$, used in the manufacture of camphor, insecticides, and perfumes [ISV, fr L *pinus*]

**pine nut** *n* the edible seed of any of several chiefly western N American pine trees

**pinery** /'pienəri/ *n* **1** a place (eg a hothouse) where pineapples are grown **2** a forest or plantation of pine trees

**pine-shoot moth** *n* a small moth (*Rhyacionia buoliana*), the caterpillar of which is a serious pest in pine plantations

**pine tar** *n* tar obtained from the wood of the pine tree by a heating process (DESTRUCTIVE DISTILLATION) and used esp in roofing materials and soaps, and in the treatment of skin diseases

**pinetum** /pie'neetəm/ *n, pl* **pineta** /-tə/ a plantation of pine trees; *also* a scientific collection of living coniferous trees [L, fr *pinus*]

**pinewood** /'pien,wood/ *n* **1 pinewood**, *pl* **pinewoods** a wood of pines **2** the wood of the pine tree

**pinfall** /'pin,fawl/ *n* FALL 8c(1)

**pinfeather** /'pin,fedhə/ *n* a feather that is not fully developed; *esp* a feather just emerging through the skin – **pinfeathered** *adj*, **pinfeathery** *adj*

**pinfold** /-,fohld/ *n* a pen for animals; [5]POUND 1a [ME, fr OE *pundfald*, fr *pund*- enclosure + *fald* fold] – **pinfold** *vt*

**ping** /ping/ *n* **1** a sharp ringing sound **2** *NAm* ignition knock; pinking [imit] – **ping** *vi*

**pinger** /'ping-ə/ *n, informal* a device that makes a sharp ringing sound, esp after a preset time

**Ping-Pong** /'ping ,pong/ *trademark* – used for table tennis

**pinguid** /'ping-gwid/ *adj, chiefly humorous* fat and greasy [L *pinguis* fat] – **pinguidity** *n*

**pinguin** /'ping-gwin/ *n* (the plum-shaped edible fruit of) a W Indian plant (*Bromelia pinguin*) of the pineapple family with spiny leaves and reddish flowers [origin unknown]

**pinhead** /'pin,hed/ *n* **1** something very small or insignificant **2** *informal* a slow-witted or stupid person; a blockhead

**pinheaded** /-'hedid/ *adj, informal* lacking intelligence or understanding; dull, stupid – **pinheadedness** *n*

**pinhole** /'pin,hohl/ *n* a small hole made (as if) by or for a pin

**pinhole camera** /'pin,hohl/ *n* a rudimentary photographic camera with a minute aperture and no lens

[1]**pinion** /'pinyən/ *n* **1** the end section of a bird's wing from which the FLIGHT FEATHERS (feathers that support a bird in flight) grow; *broadly, chiefly poetic* a bird's wing **2** a feather, quill; *also* FLIGHT FEATHER [ME, fr MF *pignon*, deriv of L *pinna* feather, wing – more at PEN] – **pinioned** *adj*

[2]**pinion** *vt* **1** to restrain (a bird) from flight, esp by cutting off the pinion of one wing **2a** to disable or restrain by binding the arms **b** to bind fast; shackle

[3]**pinion** *n* **1** a gear with a small number of teeth designed to mesh with a larger toothed wheel or toothed bar (RACK) **2** the smaller of a pair of toothed wheels or smallest of a series of GEAR WHEELS [Fr *pignon*, fr MF *peignon*, fr *peigne* comb, fr L *pecten* – more at PECTINATE]

[1]**pink** /pingk/ *vt* **1** to pierce slightly; stab **2a** to perforate (eg leather) in an ornamental pattern **b** to cut a zigzag or saw-toothed edge on [ME *pinken*]

[2]**pink** *n* a sailing vessel with a narrow overhanging stern [ME, fr MD *pinke*]

[3]**pink** *n* **1** any of a genus (*Dianthus* of the family Caryophyllaceae, the pink family) of plants related to the carnation, that are widely grown for their white, pink, red, or variegated flowers **2** highest degree possible; height ⟨*dressed herself in the ~ of fashion*⟩ [origin unknown] – **in the pink** *informal* in the best of health

[4]**pink** *adj* **1** of the colour pink **2** holding moderately radical political views – **pinkish** *adj*, **pinkishness** *n*, **pinkness** *n*

[5]**pink** *n* **1** a pale red colour (eg that of the human tongue) sometimes having a bluish tinge **2a(1)** the scarlet colour of a fox hunter's coat **a(2)** a fox hunter's scarlet coat **b** *pl* light-coloured trousers formerly worn by army officers **3** a PINKO

[6]**pink** *adv, informal* to a high degree; enormously – **in** *tickled pink*

[7]**pink** *vi, Br, of an internal-combustion engine* to make a series of sharp popping noises because of faulty combustion of the fuel-air mixture; knock [imit]

**pink bollworm** *n* a small dark brown moth (*Pectinophora gossypiella*) whose pinkish larva bores into the flowers and bolls of cotton and is a destructive pest in most cotton-growing regions

**pink elephants** *n pl, humorous* any of various hallucinations arising esp from heavy drinking or use of drugs

**pinkeye** /-,ie/ *n* a highly contagious CONJUNCTIVITIS (inflammation of the membrane lining the eyeball and eyelid) of human beings and various domestic animals

**pink-footed goose** *n* a grey N European goose (*Anser brachyrhynchus*) with a very dark head and pink legs

**pink gin** *n* a drink consisting of gin flavoured with ANGOSTURA BITTERS

**pinkie, pinky** /'pingki/ *n, NAm & dial Br* LITTLE FINGER [prob fr D *pinkje*, dim. of *pink* little finger]

**pinking scissors** *n pl* PINKING SHEARS

**pinking shears** /'pingking/ *n pl* shears with a saw-toothed inner edge on the blades, used in sewing for making a zigzag cut in cloth to prevent fraying [[1]*pink*]

**pinko** /'pingkoh/ *n, pl* **pinkos, pinkoes** *chiefly derog* a person who holds moderately radical political views [[4]*pink* 2 + [1]-*o*]

**pin money** *n* **1a** extra money earned by someone, esp a married woman (eg in a part-time job) **b** (a small sum of) money set aside for the purchase of incidentals **2** a trivial amount of money; peanuts [orig sense, money allotted by a man to his wife, sister, or daughter for her clothes and other personal expenses]

**pinna** /'pinə/ *n, pl* **pinnae** /-nie/, **pinnas 1** a leaflet or primary division of a pinnate leaf or frond **2a** a projecting body part (eg a feather, wing, or fin) **b** the projecting part of the OUTER EAR, that is composed chiefly of cartilage [NL, fr L, feather, wing – more at PEN] – **pinnal** *adj*

**pinnace** /'pinəs/ *n* any of various ship's boats [MF *pinace*, prob fr OSp *pinaza*, fr *pino* pine, fr L *pinus*]

[1]**pinnacle** /'pinəkl/ *n* **1** an upright architectural ornament like a small spire, used esp in Gothic construction to crown a BUTTRESS, roof, etc **2** a structure or formation suggesting a pinnacle; *specif* a lofty mountain peak **3** the highest point of development or achievement ⟨*the ~ of fame*⟩ *synonyms* see SUMMIT [ME *pinacle*, fr MF, fr LL *pinnaculum* gable, fr dim. of L *pinna* wing, battlement]

[2]**pinnacle** *vt* **1** to terminate with a pinnacle **2** to raise (as if) on a pinnacle

**pinnate** /'pinayt, -nət/ *adj* **1** resembling a feather in having similar parts arranged on opposite sides of a central axis or shaft **2** *of a leaf* having leaflets arranged in pairs on either side of a central stem [NL *pinnatus*, fr L, feathered, fr *pinna*] – **pinnately** *adv*, **pinnation** *n*

**pinnati-** *comb form* pinnately ⟨*pinnatisect*⟩ [NL, fr *pinnatus*]

**pinnatifid** /pi'natifid/ *adj, of a leaf* having pinnately arranged lobes with the divisions between the lobes reaching halfway to the central vein (MIDRIB) of the leaf [NL *pinnatifidus*, fr *pinnati-* + L *-fidus* -fid] – **pinnatifidly** *adv*

**pinnatisect** /pi'natisekt/ *adj, of a leaf* having pinnately arranged lobes with the divisions between the lobes reaching almost to the central vein (MIDRIB) of the leaf

**pinniped** /'piniped/ *n* any of a suborder (Pinnipedia) of aquatic flesh-eating mammals (eg a seal or walrus) with all four limbs modified into flippers [deriv of L *pinna* + *ped-, pes* foot – more at FOOT] – **pinniped** *adj*

**pinnula** /'pinyoolə/ *n, pl* **pinnulae** /-lie/ a pinnule [NL, fr L, dim. of *pinna*] – **pinnular** *adj*

**pinnulate** /'pinyoolət, -layt/, **pinnulated** /-aytid/ *adj* having pinnules

**pinnule** /'pinyoohl/ *n* **1** any of the secondary or side branches of a pinnate or feathery organ or structure **2** any of the ultimate divisions or secondary leaflets of a pinnate leaf whose leaflets are also pinnate; a division of a PINNA (primary leaflet of a pinnate leaf) [NL *pinnula*]

**pinny** /'pini/ *n, informal* PINAFORE 1 [by shortening & alter.]

**pinochle** /'pee,nukl/ *n* (the combination of the queen of spades and jack of diamonds in) a card game similar to BEZIQUE played with a 48-card pack containing two each of ace, king, queen, jack, ten, and nine in each suit [prob modif of Ger dial. *binokel*, a game resembling bezique, fr Fr dial. *binocle*]

**pinocytosis** /,pienohsie'tohsis, ,pin-/ *n, pl* **pinocytoses** /-seez/ the uptake by a cell of liquid from its surroundings, by a process involving the folding inwards of a part of the cell membrane to enclose a drop of liquid, and the pinching off of the membrane-surrounded liquid to form a fluid-filled sac or cavity inside the cell – compare PHAGOCYTOSIS, EXOCYTOSIS [NL, fr Gk *pinein* to drink + NL *cyt-* + *-osis* – more at POTABLE] – **pinocytic** *adj*, **pinocytically** *adv*, **pinocytotic** *adj*, **pinocytotically** *adv*, **pinocytose** *vb*

**pinole** /pi'nohli/ *n* (any of various flours resembling) a finely ground flour made from parched corn and used (sweetened) in Mexico and SW USA [AmerSp, fr Nahuatl *pinolli*]

# pin

**piñon** /'pinyohn, 'pinyən, pin'yohn/ *n* (the edible nutlike seed of) any of various low-growing pine trees [AmerSp *piñón*, fr Sp, pine nut, fr *piña* pinecone, fr L *pinea*]

**¹pinpoint** /'pin,poynt/ *vt* **1** to fix, determine, or identify with precision **2** to cause to stand out conspicuously; highlight

**²pinpoint** *adj* **1** extremely small, fine, or precise ⟨*a* ~ *target*⟩ **2** located, fixed, or directed with extreme precision

**³pinpoint** *n* **1** the point of a pin **2** a very small or sharp point or thing ⟨*saw a* ~ *of light at the end of the tube*⟩ ⟨~s *of stinging rain*⟩

**pinprick** /-,prik/ *n* **1** a small puncture made (as if) by a pin **2** a petty irritation or annoyance – **pinprick** *vb*

**pins and needles** *n taking sing or pl vb, informal* a pricking tingling sensation in a limb recovering from numbness

**pinsetter** /'pin,setə/ *n* a person or mechanical device that sets up pins in a bowling alley

**pinstripe** /-,striep/ *n* **1** a very thin stripe, esp on a fabric **2 pinstripes** *pl*, **pinstripe** a suit or trousers with pinstripes, typically light pinstripes on a dark background – **pin-striped** *adj*

**pint** /pient/ *n* **1** either of two units of liquid capacity equal to ⅛ gallon: **1a** a British unit equal to 20 imperial fluid ounces (about 0.568 litre) **b** a US unit equal to 16 US fluid ounces (about 0.473 litre) **2** *chiefly Br* a pint of liquid, esp milk or beer ⟨*two* ~s *today, please*⟩ ⟨*off to the pub for a* ~⟩ [ME *pinte*, fr MF, fr ML *pincta* (assumed) VL, fem of *pinctus*, pp of L *pingere* to paint – more at PAINT; prob fr the use of a painted mark on a vessel to show its capacity]

**pinta** /'pientə/ *n, Br informal* a pint of milk ⟨*likes his daily* ~⟩ [pronunciation spelling of *pint of* (*milk*)]

**pintable** /-,taybl/ *n* PINBALL MACHINE (device for a table game)

**pintail** /-,tayl/ *n, pl* **pintails**, *esp collectively* **pintail** a bird with elongated central tail feathers: **e g a** a slender grey and white DABBLING DUCK (*Anas acuta*), the male of which has a white line on the side of the neck and head **b** any of several grouse in the centre

**'pin-,tailed** *adj* having a tapering tail with the longest feathers in the centre

**pintle** /'pintl/ *n* a usu upright pivot pin on which another part turns [ME *pintel*, lit., penis, fr OE; akin to MLG *pint* penis, OE *pinn* pin]

**¹pinto** /'pintoh/ *n, pl* **pintos** *also* **pintoes** *NAm* a spotted or blotched horse or pony [AmerSp, fr *pinto* spotted, fr obs Sp, fr (assumed) VL *pinctus* painted]

**²pinto** *adj, NAm* pied, mottled

**'pint-,size, 'pint-,sized** *adj, chiefly derog* small

**pin tuck** *n* a very narrow usu ornamental tuck in a garment

**pinup** /'pin,up/ *n* **1** a person whose glamorous qualities make him/her a suitable subject of a photograph pinned up on an admirer's wall **2** a photograph of a pinup; *esp* a photograph of a nude or seminude pinup – **pinup** *adj*

**pinwheel** /-,weel, -,wiəl/ *n* **1** CATHERINE WHEEL **2** *NAm* WINDMILL **2** (toy)

**pinworm** /-,wuhm/ *n* any of various small usu parasitic roundworms (family Oxyuridae) that infect the intestines of VERTEBRATE animals; *esp* one (*Enterobius vermicularis*) parasitic in humans – called also THREADWORM

**piolet** /piə'lay (*Fr* pjɔlɛ)/ *n* ICE AXE [Fr, fr Fr dial. *piola* axe]

**pion** /'pie·on/ *n* an unstable ELEMENTARY PARTICLE (minute particle of matter) of the MESON family of particles, that is primarily responsible for the forces between neutrons and protons in the nucleus of an atom, and that exists in positively and negatively charged forms having a mass about 273 times that of an electron and in a neutral chargeless form with a mass about 264 times that of an electron [contr of *pi-meson*] – **pionic** *adj*

**¹pioneer** /,pie·ə'niə/ *n* **1** a member of a military unit (e g engineers) engaging in light construction and defensive works **2a** a person or group that originates or helps open up a new line of thought or activity or a new method or technical development **b** any of the first people to settle in a territory **3** a plant or animal capable of establishing itself permanently in a bare or barren area [MF *pionier*, fr OF *peonier* foot soldier, fr *peon* foot soldier, fr ML *pedon-, pedo-* – more at PAWN]

**²pioneer** *adj* **1** original, earliest **2** (characteristic) of early settlers or their time

**³pioneer** *vi* to act as a pioneer ⟨~ed *in the development of nuclear reactors*⟩ ~ *vt* **1** to open up or prepare for others to follow; *esp* to settle **2** to originate or take part in the development of

**pious** /'pie·əs/ *adj* **1** marked by or showing reverence and devotion to worship and religious duties; devout **2** sacred or devotional as distinct from the profane or secular **3** dutiful,

loyal **4** marked by sham or hypocritical virtue; sanctimonious [L *pius*; akin to L *piare* to appease] – **piously** *adv*, **piousness** *n*

**¹pip** /pip/ *n* **1** a disorder of a bird marked by the formation of a scale or crust on the tongue; *also* the scale or crust formed in pip **2** *informal* a fit of irritation, low spirits, or disgust – esp in *give somebody the pip* ⟨*gives me the* ~, *the way some of them make a fuss about it* – Dorothy Sayers⟩ [ME *pippe*, fr MD; akin to OHG *pfiffiz* pip; both fr a prehistoric WGmc word borrowed fr (assumed) VL *pipita*, alter. of L *pituita* phlegm, pip; akin to L *opimus* fat – more at FAT]

**²pip** *n* **1a** any of the dots on dice and dominoes that indicate numerical value **b** SPOT 2c (design on playing cards) **2** BLIP (radar image) **3** a small diamond-shaped badge with a starlike motif worn, esp on the shoulder, to indicate any of several ranks (e g second lieutenant, lieutenant, or captain) in the British army; *also* a similar diamond badge worn to indicate rank in other forces (e g the police force) [origin unknown]

**³pip** *vt* **-pp-** *Br informal* to beat (e g a rival or opponent) by a narrow margin – see also **pip at the** POST [orig sense, to blackball (fr ²*pip* in the sense "small ball")]

**⁴pip** *n* a small fruit seed; *esp* one of a several-seeded fleshy fruit (e g an apple) [short for *pippin*]

**⁵pip** *vt* **-pp-** to remove the pips from (e g an orange)

**⁶pip** *vb* **-pp-** *vi* **1** to chirp; ¹PEEP 1 **2** to break through the shell of the egg ⟨*the chicken* ~ped⟩ ~ *vt* to break open (the shell of an egg) in hatching [imit]

**⁷pip** *n* **1** a short high-pitched tone **2** *pl* **2a** *the* series of pips that in Britain indicate to users of coin-box telephones that additional payment will be required for the next unit of time spent talking **b** *the* series of pips that are broadcast as a time signal and that in Britain are usu six in number [imit]

**pipage, pipeage** /'piepij/ *n* **1** (the charge made for) transport by means of pipes **2** material for pipe lines; PIPING 2

**pipal** /'peepl/ *n* a large long-lived fig tree (*Ficus religiosa*) of India [Hindi *pīpal*, fr Skt *pippala*]

**¹pipe** /piep/ *n* **1a** a tubular wind instrument; *specif* a small FIPPLE FLUTE held in and played with one hand, esp while a small drum (TABOR) is played with the other **b** either of two types of tube used in a PIPE ORGAN: **b(1)** FLUE PIPE **b(2)** REED PIPE **c** **pipes** *pl*, **pipe** a bagpipe **d** the sound of a pipe; PIPING 1 **2** a long hollow tube for conducting a liquid, gas, etc or for structural purposes **3a** a tubular or cylindrical object, part, or passage **b** a roughly cylindrical and usu vertical body of ore **c** a cylindrical channel in a volcano through which lava is ejected **4a** a large cask of varying capacity used esp for wine (e g port) and oil **b** any of various units of liquid capacity based on the size of a pipe; *esp* a unit equal to 534 litres (117.46 gallons) **5a** a device for smoking usu consisting of a tube (e g of wood, clay, or plastic) with a small bowl (e g of wood or MEERSCHAUM) at one end in which plant material, esp tobacco, is burned and a mouthpiece at the other end **b** a small quantity of plant material (e g tobacco) held by the bowl of such a pipe ⟨*he lit his* ~⟩ [ME, fr OE *pīpa*; akin to OHG *pfīfa* pipe; both fr a prehistoric WGmc word borrowed fr (assumed) VL *pipa* pipe, fr L *pipare* to peep, of imit origin; (4) ME, fr MF, tube, cask, fr (assumed) VL *pipa*]

**²pipe** *vi* **1a** to play on a pipe **b** to convey orders by signals on a boatswain's pipe **2a** to speak in a high or shrill voice **b** to make a shrill sound ~ *vt* **1a** to play (a tune) on a pipe **b** to utter in the shrill tone of a pipe **2a** to lead, accompany, or announce ceremonially with pipe music **b(1)** to call or direct using the boatswain's pipe **b(2)** to receive aboard or attend the departure of using a boatswain's pipe **3a** to trim (e g an article of clothing) with piping **b** to force (e g cream or icing) through a piping tube or nozzle for a decorative effect **4** to supply or equip with pipes **5a** to convey or supply (as if) by pipes ⟨~ *sewage to the sea*⟩ **b** to transmit (e g music or a television programme) by wire or cable

**pipe down** *vi, informal* to stop talking or making noise

**pipe up** *vi* to begin to play, sing, or speak, esp unexpectedly

**'pipe-,clay** *vt* to whiten or clean with PIPE CLAY

**pipe clay** *n* a fine white clay used esp for making tobacco pipes and for whitening leather

**pipe cleaner** *n* something used to clean the inside of a pipe; *specif* a piece of flexible wire covered with tufted fabric which is used to clean the stem of a tobacco pipe

**pipe cutter** *n* a tool or machine for cutting pipe; *esp* a hand tool consisting of a grasping device and three sharp-edged wheels forced inwards by screw pressure that cut into the pipe as the tool is rotated

**piped music** /piept/ *n* recorded background music in public places

**pipe dream** *n* an illusory or fantastic plan, hope, or story [fr the fantasies brought about by the smoking of opium]

**pipefish** /-,fish/ *n* any of various long slender fishes (*Syngnathus* and related genera) that are related to the SEA HORSES and have a tube-shaped snout and an angular body covered with bony plates

**pipe fitter** *n* a person who installs and repairs piping

**pipe fitting** *n* a piece (eg a coupling or elbow) used to connect pipes or as an accessory to a pipe

**pipeful** /'piepf(ə)l/ *n* a quantity of tobacco smoked in a pipe at one time; PIPE 5b

**pipelike** /'piep,liek/ *adj* like a pipe or piping

**pipeline** /-,lien/ *n* **1** a line of piping with pumps, valves, and control devices for conveying liquids, gases, etc **2a** the processes through which supplies pass from source to user **b** something (eg a social institution) considered as a continuous set of processes which the individual must go through or be subjected to ⟨*children in the educational* ~⟩ ⟨*the housing* ~⟩ **3** *NAm* a direct channel for information

**pipe major** *n* the principal player in a band of bagpipes

**pip emma** *adj, informal* in the afternoon; POST MERIDIEM – no longer in vogue [signallers' terms for *PM*]

**pipe of peace** *n* CALUMET (ceremonial tobacco pipe)

**pipe organ** *n* ORGAN 1a

**piper** /'piepə/ *n* **1** a person who plays on a pipe **2** a maker, layer, or repairer of pipes; PIPE FITTER

**piperazine** /pie'perəzeen/ *n* a synthetic chemical compound, $C_2H_{10}N_2$, used in medicine to treat infection with worms, specif roundworms and threadworms, parasitic in humans and domestic animals and poultry [ISV, blend of *piperidine* and *az*-]

**piperidine** /pi'perə,deen, -din/ *n* a liquid HETEROCYCLIC (containing a ring of atoms, not all of which are carbon) chemical compound, $C_5H_{10}NH$, with a peppery smell like that of ammonia [ISV, blend of *piperine* and *-ide*]

**piperine** /'pipəreen/ *n* a chemical compound, $C_{17}H_{19}NO_3$, that is the chief active sharp-tasting constituent of pepper and is used as a flavouring and as an insecticide [ISV, fr L *piper* pepper]

**piperonal** /'pipəroh,nal, pie'perə,nal/ *n* a chemical compound, $C_7H_5O_2CHO$, with a fragrant smell like that of the plant heliotrope, that is used esp in perfumery and as a flavouring [ISV *piperine* + *-one* + *-al*]

**pipette**, *NAm* **pipet** /pi'pet/ *n* a narrow usu glass tube into which a liquid is drawn (eg for dispensing or measuring) by suction and retained in the tube by closing the upper end [Fr *pipette*, dim. of *pipe* pipe, cask, fr (assumed) VL *pipa, pippa* pipe]

**pipe wrench** *n* any of various devices for gripping and turning a cylindrical object (eg a pipe); *specif* one with two serrated jaws

**pipi** /'peepee/ *n, pl* **pipis**, *esp collectively* **pipi** either of two edible marine smooth-shelled BIVALVES (shellfish with a shell composed of two hinged parts): **a** a New Zealand bivalve (*Mesodesma novae-zelandiae*) **b** an E Australian bivalve (*Plebidonax deltoides*) [Maori]

**piping** /'pieping/ *n* **1a** the music of a pipe **b** a sound, note, or call like that of a pipe **2** a quantity or system of pipes **3a** a narrow decorative trimming consisting of a folded strip of cloth often enclosing a cord that is stitched along seams or edges (eg of clothing or upholstery) **b** a thin cordlike line of icing piped onto a cake

**piping bag** *n* a conical usu polythene bag with a hole at the narrow end to which nozzles are fitted, used in cookery to pipe esp icing

**piping hot** *adj* so hot as to sizzle or hiss; *broadly* very hot

**pipistrelle** /,pipi'strel/ *n* any of a genus (*Pipistrellus*) of insect-eating brownish, grey, or black bats found in most parts of the world; *esp* a common small Eurasian bat (*Pipistrellus pipistrellus*) [Fr, fr It *pipistrello*, alter. of *vispistrello*, fr L *vespertilio* bat]

**pipit** /'pipit/ *n* any of various small typically brown or greyish songbirds (genus *Anthus*) resembling larks [imit]

**pipkin** /'pipkin/ *n* a small usu earthenware pot or pan used esp for cooking [perh fr ¹*pipe* 4 + *-kin*]

**pippin** /'pipin/ *n* **1** any of numerous eating apples with usu yellow or greenish-yellow skins strongly flushed with red **2** *informal* a highly admired or very admirable person or thing – no longer in vogue [ME *pepin*, fr OF]

**pip-'pip** *interj, Br* goodbye – no longer in vogue [prob imit of the sound of a bicycle or car horn]

**pipsissewa** /pip'sisiwə/ *n* any of various evergreen woodland plants (genus *Chimaphila* of the family Pyrolaceae) with fragrant pink or white flowers and leathery leaves that have been used for their diuretic property [Cree *pipisisikweu*, lit., it breaks it (i e a stone in the bladder) into small pieces]

**'pip-,squeak** *n, informal* a small or insignificant person

**piquancy** /'peekənsi, 'peekonh-si/ *n* being piquant

**piquant** /'peekənt/ *adj* **1** agreeably stimulating to the palate; savoury ⟨*a* ~ *sauce*⟩ **2** engagingly provocative; *also* having a lively arch charm ⟨*her* ~ *face*⟩ △ plangent, poignant, pungent [MF, fr prp of *piquer* to prick, sting] – **piquantly** *adv*, **piquantness** *n*

**¹pique** /peek/ *n* (a fit of) resentment resulting from wounded vanity

**²pique** *vt* **1** to arouse anger, irritation, or resentment in; *specif* to offend by slighting **2a** to excite or arouse by a provocation, challenge, or rebuff **b** to pride or congratulate (oneself), esp in respect of a particular accomplishment – + *on* or *upon* ⟨*he* ~s *himself on his skill as a cook*⟩ [Fr *piquer*, lit., to prick – more at PIKE]

**piqué, pique** /'peekay/ *n* a durable ribbed clothing fabric of cotton, rayon, or silk [Fr *piqué*, fr pp of *piquer* to prick, quilt]

**¹piquet** /pi'ket/ *n* a 2-handed card game played with a pack of 32 cards with no cards below the seven [Fr]

**²piquet** *n* PICKET 2 (detachment of soldiers)

**piracy** /'pie-ərəsi/ *n* **1** violence and usu robbery committed against a ship at sea by a private individual; *also* a similar act (eg hijacking) committed against an aircraft in flight **2** the unauthorized use of another person's production, ideas, etc, esp in infringement of a copyright or patent **3** an act (as if) of piracy [ML *piratia*, fr LGk *peirateia*, fr Gk *peiratēs* pirate]

**piragua** /pə'rahgwə/ *n* DUGOUT 1 (canoe) [Sp – more at PIROGUE]

**piranha** /pi'rahn(y)ə/ *n* a small S American fish (genus *Serrasalmo*) capable of attacking and (fatally) wounding human beings and large animals [Pg, fr Tupi]

**¹pirate** /'pie-ərət/ *n* **1** (a ship used by) somebody who commits piracy **2** an unauthorized radio station; *esp* one located on a ship in international waters [ME, fr MF or L; MF, fr L *pirata*, fr Gk *peiratēs*, fr *peiran* to attempt – more at FEAR] – **piratical** *adj*, **piratically** *adv*

**²pirate** *vt* **1** to commit piracy on **2** to take or appropriate by piracy: eg **2a** to reproduce without authorization, esp in infringement of copyright **b** to lure away from another employer by offers of betterment ~ *vi* to commit or practise piracy

**piriform** /'pirifawm/ *adj* PYRIFORM (pear-shaped)

**pirn** /puhn/ *n* **1** QUILL 1a(1) (weaver's reel for yarn) **2** *chiefly Scot* a device resembling a reel; *esp* a fishing reel [ME]

**pirogue** /'peerohg/ *n* DUGOUT 1 (canoe) [Fr, fr Sp *piragua*, of Cariban origin; akin to Galibi *piraua* pirogue]

**pirouette** /,piroo'et/ *n* **1** a rapid whirling about of the body; *specif* a full turn on the toe or ball of one foot in ballet **2** a turn on the haunches performed in dressage, esp by a walking or cantering horse [Fr, lit., teetotum] – **pirouette** *vi*

**pis** /piez/ *pl of* PI (Greek letter)

**pis aller** /,peez a'lay/ *n, pl* **pis allers** /~ a'lay(z)/ a last resource or device; an expedient [Fr, lit., to go worst]

**pisc-, pisci-** *comb form* fish ⟨*pisciculture*⟩ ⟨*piscivorous*⟩ [L *pisci-*, fr *piscis* fish – more at FISH]

**piscary** /'pisk(ə)ri/ *n* **1** the right of fishing in waters belonging to another **2** a place for fishing; FISHERY 2 [(1) ME *piscarie*, fr ML *piscaria*, fr L, neut pl of *piscarius* of fish, fr *piscis*; (2) ML *piscaria*, fr L, fem of *piscarius*]

**piscatory** /'piskət(ə)ri/, **piscatorial** /,piskə'tawriəl/ *adj* of or dependent on fishermen or fishing [L *piscatorius*, fr *piscatus*, pp of *piscari* to fish, fr *piscis*] – **piscatorially** *adv*

**Pisces** /'pieseez/ *n taking sing vb* **1** a constellation of the ZODIAC (imaginary belt in the heavens) lying between Aquarius and Aries and represented as two fishes **2a** the 12th sign of the zodiac in astrology, held to govern the period February 20 - March 20 approx **b** somebody born under this sign [ME, fr L, fr pl of *piscis* fish] – **Piscean** *adj or n*

**pisciculture** /'pisi,kulchə/ *n* the breeding and rearing of fish – **piscicultural** *adj*, **pisciculturist** *n*

**piscina** /pi'seenə/ *n, pl* **piscinae, piscinas** a basin with a drain for disposing of water from ceremonial washing, usu set in a niche in a church wall near the altar [ML, fr L, fishpond, fr *piscis*]

**piscine** /'pisien/ *adj* (characteristic) of fish [L *piscinus,* fr *piscis*]

**piscivorous** /pi'sivərəs/ *adj* feeding on fish

**pish** /pish/ *interj* – used to express impatience, disdain, or contempt

**pisiform** /'pisi,fawm/ *adj, chiefly biology* resembling a pea in size or shape [L *pisum* pea + E -*iform* – more at PEA]

**pisiform bone** *n* a bone on the little finger or ULNAR side of the wrist or CARPUS (joint corresponding to the wrist) in most mammals

**piskie** /'piski/ *n* a pixie

**pismire** /'pis,mie·ə/ *n, dial* an ant [ME *pissemire,* fr *pisse* urine (referring here to the smell of anthills) + *mire* ant, of Scand origin; akin to ON *maurr* ant; akin to L *formica* ant, Gk *myrmēx*]

**pisolite** /'piesoh,liet/ *n* a rock, esp a limestone, composed of small rounded approx pea-sized grains or bodies of rock cemented together [NL *pisolithus,* fr Gk *pisos* pea + -*lithos* -lith] – **pisolitic** *adj*

**¹piss** /pis/ *vi* **1** *vulg* to urinate **2** *slang* to rain heavily – often + *down* ~ *vt* **1** *vulg* to urinate in or on ⟨~ *the bed*⟩ **2** *vulg* to discharge (as if) as urine ⟨*to* ~ *blood*⟩ [ME *pissen,* fr OF *pissier,* fr (assumed) VL *pissiare,* of imit origin]

**piss off** *vi, Br vulg* to go away; depart – usu in imperative ~ *vt, slang* to make annoyed or fed up – often pass

**²piss** *n, vulg* **1** urine **2** an act of urinating

**piss artist** *n, chiefly Br slang* **1** a habitual heavy drinker **2** an annoying or ineffectual person

**pissed** /pist/ *adj, Br slang* drunk

**pissoir** /,pi'swah, '-,-/ *n* a public urinal as found in the street in some European countries [Fr, fr MF, fr *pisser* to urinate, fr OF *pissier*]

**'piss-,up** *n, chiefly Br slang* a heavy drinking session

**pistachio** /pi'stahshi·oh/ *n, pl* **pistachios 1a** a small tree (*Pistacia vera*) of the SUMACH family that bears a hard-shelled nut with a green edible kernel **b** the nut of the pistachio tree **2** the vivid green colour of the pistachio nut [It *pistacchio,* fr L *pistacium* pistachio nut, fr Gk *pistakion,* fr *pistakē* pistachio tree, fr Per *pistah*] – **pistachio** *adj*

**pistareen** /,pistə'reen/ *n* a former Spanish 2-real silver coin circulating in Spain, the West Indies, and the USA at a debased rate [prob modif of Sp *peseta* peseta]

**piste** /peest/ *n* **1** a prepared slope for skiing **2** a rectangular area 14 metres (about 46 feet) by 2.0 metres (about 6 feet 7 inches) on which a fencing bout takes place [Fr, lit., trial, track, fr MF, fr OIt *pista,* fr *pistare* to trample down, pound – more at PISTON]

**pistil** /'pistil/ *n* **1** CARPEL (female reproductive organ of a flowering plant) **2** all the carpels of a single flower collectively, esp when their OVARIES (seed-bearing structures) are united to form a single structure; GYNOECIUM △ pistol, pistole [NL *pistillum,* fr L, pestle – more at PESTLE]

**pistillate** /'pistilət, -,layt/ *adj, of a plant or flower* **1** having pistils but no STAMENS (male reproductive organs); FEMALE 1b **2** bearing pistils; carpellate

**pistol** /'pistl/ *n* a short firearm intended to be aimed and fired with one hand [MF *pistole,* fr Ger, fr MHG dial. *pischulle,* fr Czech *pištal,* lit., pipe; akin to Russ *pischal* arquebus] – **pistol** *vt*

**pistole** /pi'stohl/ *n* a former gold 2-escudo piece of Spain; *also* any of several former European gold coins of approximately the same value [ME]

**pistoleer** /,pistə'liə/ *n* a person, usu a soldier, armed with a pistol

**pistol grip** *n* a handle on a shotgun, rifle, tool, etc shaped like the butt of a pistol to provide a firm grip for the hand

**'pistol-,whip** *vt* to beat with a pistol; *broadly* to assail violently and unrestrainedly

**piston** /'pist(ə)n/ *n* **1** a sliding disc or short cylinder fitting within a cylindrical chamber, along which it moves back and forth by or against fluid pressure **2a** a sliding valve in a cylinder in a brass instrument that is used to lower its pitch **b** a button on an organ keyboard for bringing in a previously chosen combination of stops [Fr, fr It *pistone,* fr *pistare* to pound, fr ML, fr L *pistus,* pp of *pinsere* to crush – more at PESTLE]

**piston pin** *n* GUDGEON PIN (pin linking the piston and CONNECTING ROD in an engine)

**piston ring** *n* a springy split metal ring for sealing the gap between a piston and a cylinder wall

**piston rod** *n* **1** a rod by which a piston is moved or communicates motion **2** CONNECTING ROD

**¹pit** /pit/ *n* **1a(1)** a hole, shaft, or cavity in the ground **a(2)** a mine **b** an area often sunken or depressed below the adjacent floor area: e g **b(1)** an enclosure in which animals or birds are made to fight each other **b(2)** the space at the front of a theatre for the orchestra; ORCHESTRA 2 **b(3)** a sunken area in a garage or workshop floor allowing access to the undersides of motor vehicles **2** Hell – + *the* **3** a hollow or indentation, esp in the surface of a living plant or animal or of one of its parts: e g **3a** a natural hollow in the surface of the body or a body organ or structure **b** any of the indented scars left in the skin by a disease (e g smallpox) characterized by the formation of inflamed pus-filled swellings; a pockmark **c** a pointed depression in the enamel of a tooth **d** a minute depressed area of unthickened tissue in a plant cell wall that has undergone thickening or become woody through LIGNIFICATION **4** pits *pl,* **pit** any of the areas alongside a motor-racing track used for refuelling and repairing the cars during a race – + *the* **5** *chiefly Br* the floor of a theatre auditorium; *esp* the area behind the stalls **6** *pl, informal the* worst imaginable place, person, state of affairs, etc **7** *NAm* an area in a securities or commodities exchange in which members do trading [ME, fr OE *pytt;* akin to OHG *pfuzzi* well]

**²pit** *vb* **-tt-** *vt* **1a** to place, cast, bury, or store in a pit **b** to make pits in; *esp* to scar or mark with pits **2a** to set (e g fighting cocks) to fight (as if) in a cockpit – often + *against* ⟨~ted *the cocks against each other*⟩ **b** to set into opposition or rivalry; oppose ~ *vi* **1** to become marked with pits; *esp* to retain for a time an indentation made by pressure **2** to make a usu brief stop at one's pit during a race for fuel or repairs

**³pit** *n, NAm* a fruit stone [D, fr MD – more at PITH]

**⁴pit** *vt* **-tt-** *NAm* to remove the pit from (a fruit)

**pita** /'peetə/ *n* (the fibre obtained from) any of several fibre-yielding plants (e g an agave or yucca) [Sp & Pg]

**,pit-a-'pat** *n* pitter-patter [imit] – **pit-a-pat** *adv or adj,* **pit-a-pat** *vi*

**¹pitch** /pich/ *n* **1** (any of various thick dark BITUMINOUS substances similar to) a heavy black or dark-coloured sticky substance obtained as a residue in the distillation of tars (e g COAL TAR) or other similar organic materials **2** a resin obtained from any of various conifer trees ⟨*pine* ~⟩ [ME *pich,* fr OE *pic,* fr L *pic-, pix;* akin to L *opimus* fat – more at FAT]

**²pitch** *vt* to cover, smear, or treat (as if) with pitch

**³pitch** *vt* **1** to erect and fix firmly in place ⟨~ *a tent*⟩ **2** to throw, fling ⟨~ *hay onto a wagon*⟩ ⟨~ed *a couple of drunks out of the party*⟩: e g **2a** to throw (a baseball) to a batter **b** to toss (e g coins) so as to fall at or near a mark ⟨~ *pennies*⟩ **c** to put aside or discard by throwing ⟨~ed *his cigarette into the fire*⟩ **3a(1)** to cause to be at a particular level or of a particular quality **a(2)** to set in a particular musical pitch or key **b** to cause to be set at a particular angle; slope ⟨*a* ~ed *roof*⟩ **4** to utter glibly and insincerely ⟨~ *an improbable yarn*⟩ **5** to hit (a golf ball) in a high arc with backspin **6** to bowl (a ball) in cricket to a specified place or in a specified manner ⟨~ed *one outside the off stump*⟩ **7** *chiefly NAm* to sell or advertise, esp in a high-pressure way ~ *vi* **1a** to fall precipitately or headlong **b(1)** *of a ship* to move so that the bow is alternately rising and falling **b(2)** *of an aircraft* to turn about a lateral axis so that the nose rises or falls in relation to the tail **b(3)** *of a missile or spacecraft* to turn about a lateral axis that is both perpendicular to the longitudinal axis and horizontal with respect to the earth **c** *of a horse or mule* to buck **2** to encamp **3** to choose something, usu in a casual way – usu + *on* or *upon* ⟨~ed *on a present for his wife*⟩ **4** to incline downwards; slope **5** to pitch a baseball or golf ball **6** *of a ball, esp a bowled cricket ball* to bounce **synonyms** see ¹THROW [ME *pichen*]

**pitch in** *vi* **1** to begin to work, esp with vigour **2** to contribute to a common endeavour

**pitch into** *vt* to attack, assail

**⁴pitch** *n* **1** pitching; *esp* an up-and-down movement – compare YAW **2a** a slope; *also* the degree of slope **b(1)** the distance between one point on a tooth of a gear and the corresponding point on the next tooth **b(2)** the distance from any point on the thread of a screw to the corresponding point on an adjacent thread measured parallel to the axis **c** the distance advanced by a propeller in one revolution **d** the number of teeth on a gear or of threads on a screw per unit distance **e** the degree to which a blade of a propeller is slanted in relation to the axis of rotation **3a** the relative level, intensity, or extent of some quality or state ⟨*were at a high* ~ *of excitement*⟩ **b(1)** the property of a sound, esp a musical note, that is determined by the frequency of the waves producing it; highness or lowness of sound **b(2)** a standard frequency for tuning instruments **c(1)** the difference in the relative vibration frequency of the human voice that contributes to the total meaning of speech **c(2)** a definite relative pitch that is a significant phenomenon in speech **4** an often high-pressure sales talk or advertisement; *also* a recommendation, boost **5** WICKET 3b **6** the delivery of a baseball by a pitcher to a batter **7** a section of a climb (eg on a rock face) between points where the climber can stand safely **8** *chiefly Br* **8a(1)** an area or place to which a person lays unofficial claim for carrying out business or activities; *esp* the site occupied by a market stall, street performer, or street seller **a(2)** a space for pitching one tent or parking one caravan **b** an area (eg a specially marked-out field) used for playing certain games (eg soccer, cricket, rugby, or hockey) – **pitched** *adj* – **queer somebody's pitch** *informal* to spoil somebody's chances, hopes, or plans

,**pitch-and-'toss** *n* a game in which the player who pitches coins nearest to a mark has first chance at tossing the pitched coins and winning those that fall heads up

,**pitch-'black** *adj* intensely dark or black

**pitchblende** /'pich,blend/ *n* a brown to black lustrous mineral that consists chiefly of a uranium mineral (URANINITE), contains the radioactive chemical element radium, and is the chief ore of uranium [part trans of Ger *pechblende,* fr *pech* pitch + *blende*]

,**pitch-'dark** *adj* extremely dark; pitch-black

**pitched battle** *n* an intense battle; *specif* one fought at a time and place chosen beforehand

[1]**pitcher** /'pichə/ *n* **1a** a large deep usu earthenware vessel with a wide lip and a handle or two ear-shaped handles, for holding and pouring liquids; *broadly* a large jug **b** the contents of or quantity contained in a pitcher **2** a modified leaf of a PITCHER PLANT in which the hollowed stalk and base of the leaf blade form an elongated receptacle [ME *picher,* fr OF *pichier,* fr ML *bicarius* goblet, fr Gk *bikos* earthen jug (cf BEAKER)]

[2]**pitcher** *n* the player who pitches in a game of baseball

**pitcher plant** *n* any of various plants (esp family Sarraceniaceae, the pitcher-plant family) that have leaves modified into pitchers containing liquids in which insects are trapped and digested

[1]**pitchfork** /'pich,fawk/ *n* a long-handled fork that has two or three long somewhat curved prongs and is used esp for pitching hay [ME *pychforke,* alter. (influenced by *pichen* to pitch, throw) of *pikfork,* fr *pik* pick + *fork*]

[2]**pitchfork** *vt* **1** to lift and toss (as if) with a pitchfork ⟨~ed *the hay into the wagon*⟩ **2** to thrust into something (eg a position or office) suddenly or without preparation ⟨*his success* ~ed *him into the sophisticated world of the literary establishment*⟩

**pitch pipe** *n* a small instrument of one or more REED PIPES or FLUE PIPES blown to establish the pitch in singing or in tuning an instrument

**pitchstone** /'pich,stohn/ *n* a glassy rock with a resinous lustre that is formed by the rapid cooling and solidification of molten lava

**pitchy** /'pichi/ *adj* **1a** full of pitch; TARRY **b** of or like pitch **2** pitch-black

**piteous** /'piti·əs/ *adj* causing or deserving pity or compassion **synonyms** see PITIFUL – **piteously** *adv,* **piteousness** *n*

**pitfall** /'pit,fawl/ *n* **1** a trap, snare; *specif* a pit flimsily covered or camouflaged and used to capture and hold animals or humans **2** a hidden or not easily recognized danger or difficulty

[1]**pith** /pith/ *n* **1a** a (continuous) central core of relatively unspecialized spongy tissue in the stems of many plants and in some roots, that probably functions chiefly in the storage of food for the plant **b** the white fibrous tissue surrounding the flesh and directly below the skin of a citrus fruit **c** the soft or spongy interior of a hair, feather, etc **2a** the essential part; the core ⟨*individuality, which was the very* ~ *of liberty* – H J Laski⟩ **b** substantial quality (eg of meaning) ⟨*made a speech that lacked* ~⟩ [ME, fr OE *pitha;* akin to MD & MLG *pit* pith, stone of a fruit]

[2]**pith** *vt* **1a** to kill (eg cattle) by piercing or severing the SPINAL CORD **b** to destroy the SPINAL CORD or CENTRAL NERVOUS SYSTEM of (a frog or other animal used in scientific research), usu by passing a wire or needle up and down the SPINAL CANAL (canal housing the spinal cord) **2** to remove the pith from (a plant part)

**pithead** /'pit,hed; *in mining communities usu* ,pit'hed/ *n* the top of a mining pit or coal shaft; *also* the immediately adjacent ground and buildings

**pithecanthropus** /,pithikan'throhpəs, ,pithi'kanthrəpəs/ *also* **pithecanthrope** /-'throhp/ *n, pl* **pithecanthropi** /-pi, -pie/ *also* **pithecanthropes** /-peez/ any of a former genus (*Pithecanthropus,* now included in *Homo*) of primitive extinct apelike men, including JAVA MAN [NL, fr Gk *pithēkos* ape akin to OHG *bibēn* to tremble, L *foedus* ugly + *anthrōpos* human being] – **pithecanthropine** *adj or n,* **pithecanthropoid** *adj or n*

**pithy** /'pithi/ *adj* **1** consisting of or having much pith **2** having substance and point; tersely convincing **synonyms** see CONCISE **antonyms** wordy, prolix – **pithily** *adv,* **pithiness** *n*

**pitiable** /'piti·əbl/ *adj* **1** deserving or exciting pity; lamentable **2** of a kind to evoke mingled pity and contempt, esp because of inadequacy ⟨*a* ~ *excuse*⟩ **synonyms** see PITIFUL – **pitiably** *adv,* **pitiableness** *n*

**pitiful** /'pitif(ə)l/ *adj* **1a** deserving or arousing pity or commiseration **b** exciting pitying contempt (eg by meanness or inadequacy) **2** *archaic* full of pity; compassionate – **pitifully** *adv,* **pitifulness** *n*

**synonyms** Pitiful, piteous, and pitiable are not always interchangeable. Something piteous seeks, or is likely to, or deserves to arouse, pity ⟨*a piteous cry for help*⟩. Pitiful and pitiable describe the effect of something which actually does excite pity or commiseration, but pitiable especially may also suggest contemptuous pity. Pitiful then suggests inadequacy or inferiority, especially of amount ⟨*pitiful wages*⟩, while pitiable more often applies to people and their condition ⟨*a pitiable husk of the man he once was*⟩.

**pitiless** /'pitilis/ *adj* without pity; merciless – **pitilessly** *adv,* **pitilessness** *n*

**pitman** /-mən/ *n, pl* (1) **pitmen,** (2) **pitmans 1** a male mine worker; *esp* a coal miner **2** *NAm* CONNECTING ROD (rod for transmitting motion in a machine)

**piton** /pi'ton(h) (*Fr* pitɔ̃)/ *n* a spike, wedge, or peg that is driven into a rock or ice surface as a support in mountaineering and usu has an eye through which a rope or CARABINER may be passed [Fr]

**Pitot-static tube** /,peetoh 'statik/ *n* a device consisting of a PITOT TUBE and a STATIC TUBE, that measures both the total pressure and the STATIC pressure (pressure not due to motion) in a stream, esp of air, and is used esp to determine the speed of flow in the stream

**Pitot tube** /'peetoh/ *n* **1** a device for measuring the total pressure in a stream of liquid or gas (eg air) and indirectly its speed of flow, that consists of a tube with a short right-angled bend, whose open end is placed to face the stream and whose other end is attached to a pressure measuring device **2** PITOT-STATIC TUBE [Fr (*tube de*) *Pitot,* fr Henri *Pitot* †1771 Fr physicist]

**pit pony** *n, chiefly Br* a pony used, esp formerly, for pulling trucks in a mine

**pit saw** *n* a handsaw worked by two men, one of whom stands on or above the log being sawn and the other below it, usu in a pit

**pitta bread** /'pitə/ *n* slightly leavened bread, typically flat and oval in shape, with a hollow in the centre [NGk *pitta* bread, cake, pie, fr MGk, fr Gk, pitch]

**pittance** /'pit(ə)ns/ *n* a small amount or allowance; *specif* a meagre wage or remuneration [ME *pitance,* fr OF, piety, pity, fr ML *pietantia,* fr *pietant-, pietans,* prp of *pietari* to be charitable, fr L *pietas* piety, pity]

**pitted** /'pitid/ *adj* marked with pits ⟨*a* ~ *skin*⟩

**pitter-patter** /,pitə 'patə/ *n* a rapid succession of light sounds or beats; a patter [imit] – **pitter-patter** *adv or adj,* **pitter-patter** *vi*

**pitting** /'piting/ *n* the action or process of forming pits (eg in paintwork or a metal surface)

**pituitary** /pi'tyooh·it(ə)ri/ *adj or n* (of or produced by) the PITUITARY GLAND ⟨~ *hormones*⟩ [L *pituita* phlegm – more at PIP; fr the former belief that the pituitary gland secreted phlegm]

**pituitary gland** *n* a small oval ENDOCRINE GLAND (gland that secretes hormones directly into the bloodstream) that is attached by a narrow stalk (the INFUNDIBULUM) to the base of the brain and consists of a front lobe and a rear lobe that secrete many important hormones controlling most basic body functions (eg growth)

**Pituitrin** /pi'tyooh·itrin/ *trademark* – used for an extract of the fresh rear lobe of the PITUITARY GLAND of cattle

**pit viper** *n* any of various venomous snakes (family Crotalidae) chiefly of N and S America, that have a sensory pit on each side of the head and hollow perforated fangs

**¹pity** /'piti/ *n* **1a** sympathetic sorrow for someone suffering, distressed, or unhappy **b** capacity to feel pity **c** a contemptuous feeling of regret aroused by the inferiority or inadequacy of another ⟨*leaves us less with a sense of repugnance... than with a sense of ~ for the man who could think of nothing better* – T S Eliot⟩ **2** something to be regretted ⟨*it's a ~ you can't go*⟩ see also **for pity's** SAKE [ME *pite*, fr OF *pité*, fr L *pietat-*, *pietas* piety, pity, fr *pius* pious]

**²pity** *vb* to feel pity (for) – **pitier** *n*

**pitying** /'piti·iŋ/ *adj* expressing or feeling pity ⟨*a ~ look*⟩ – **pityingly** *adv*

**pityriasis** /,pitə'rie·əsis/ *n* a skin condition of humans or domestic animals marked by dry scaling or scurfy patches [NL, fr Gk, fr *pityron* scurf]

**più** /pyooh/ *adv* more – used to qualify a direction in music [It, fr L *plus*]

**piupiu** /'peeooh,peeooh/ *n, pl* **piupius** *NZ* a traditional Maori skirt made of rolled strips of flax and worn by men and women [Maori]

**¹pivot** /'pivət/ *n* **1** a shaft or pin on which something turns **2a** a person, thing, or factor having a major or central role, function, or effect ⟨*as if the ~ and pole of his life ... was his Mother* – D H Lawrence⟩ **b** a key player or position; *specif* ⁶POST 2b **3** the action of pivoting [Fr]

**²pivot** *vi* to turn (as if) on a pivot ~ *vt* **1** to provide with, mount on, or attach by a pivot **2** to cause to pivot – **pivotable** *adj*

**³pivot** *adj* **1** turning (as if) on a pivot **2** pivotal

**pivotal** /'pivətl/ *adj* **1** of or being a pivot **2** vitally important; crucial – **pivotally** *adv*

**pivot crown** *n, NAm* PIVOT TOOTH

**pivot tooth** *n, NAm* POST CROWN (artificial crown attached to the root of a tooth)

**pix** /piks/ *n taking pl vb, informal* pictures [alter. of *pics*, pl of *pic*]

**pixie, pixy** /'piksi/ *n* a fairy; *specif* a cheerful (mischievous) fairy [origin unknown] – **pixieish** *adj*

**pixilated** /'piksi,laytid/ *adj, chiefly NAm* **1** somewhat unbalanced mentally; *also* bemused **2** drunk [prob alter. of earlier *pixy-led* led astray by pixies, lost, bewildered] – **pixilation** *n*

**pizza** /'peetsə/ *n* a round thin cake of baked bread dough spread with a mixture of tomatoes, cheese, herbs, etc [It, fr (assumed) VL *picea*, fr L, fem of *piceus* of pitch, fr *pic-*, *pix* pitch – more at PITCH]

**pizza pie** *n* a pizza

**pizzazz, pizazz** /pi'zaz/ *n, chiefly NAm informal* the quality of being exciting or attractive [origin unknown]

**pizzeria** /,peetsə'rie/ *n* an establishment where pizzas are made or sold [It, fr *pizza*]

**pizzicato** /,pitsi'kahtoh/ *n, adv, or adj, pl* **pizzicati** /-ti/ (a note or passage played) by means of plucking instead of bowing – used as a direction in music [It, pp of *pizzicare* to pinch, pluck]

**pizzle** /'pizl/ *n* **1** the penis of an animal, esp a bull **2** a whip made of a bull's penis [prob fr Flem *pezel*; akin to LG *pesel* pizzle]

**PL/1** *n* a general-purpose HIGH-LEVEL computer programming language [*Programming Language One*]

**placable** /'plakəbl/ *adj* easily placated; tolerant, tractable – **placably** *adv*, **placability** *n*

**¹placard** /'plakahd/ *n* a notice for display or advertising purposes, usu printed on or fixed to a stiff backing material; a poster [ME *placquart* sealed official document, fr MF, fr *plaquier* to plate – more at PLAQUE]

**²placard** *vt* **1a** to cover (as if) with placards **b** to post in a public place **2** to give public notice of (as if) by means of placards

**placate** /plə'kayt/ *vt* to soothe or mollify, esp by concessions; appease [L *placatus*, pp of *placare* – more at PLEASE] – **placation** *n*, **placative** *adj*, **placatory** *adj*

**¹place** /plays/ *n* **1a** physical environment; a space **b** physical surroundings; atmosphere **2a** an indefinite region or expanse; an area **b** a building or locality used for a usu specified purpose ⟨*a ~ of amusement*⟩ ⟨*a ~ of worship*⟩ **3a** a particular region or centre of population **b** a house, dwelling ⟨*invited them to his ~ for the evening*⟩ **4** a particular part of a surface or body; a spot **5** relative position in a scale or series: eg **5a** a particular part in a piece of writing; *esp* the point at which a reader has temporarily stopped ⟨*can't find my ~*⟩ **b** an important or valued position ⟨*there was never much of a ~ in his life for women*⟩ **c** degree of prestige ⟨*put her in her ~*⟩ **d** a (numbered) point in an argument, explanation, etc ⟨*in the first ~, you're wrong*⟩ **6** a leading place, esp second or third, in a competition

**7a** a proper or designated niche ⟨*thought that a woman's ~ was in the home*⟩ ⟨*put it back in its ~*⟩ **b** an appropriate moment or point ⟨*this is not the ~ to discuss legal liability*⟩ **8a** an available seat or accommodation **b** an empty or vacated position **c** PLACE SETTING ⟨*lay another ~ for our guest*⟩ **d** *chiefly Br* an available vacancy ⟨*got a university ~*⟩ **9** the position of a figure in relation to others of a row or series; *esp* the position of a digit within a numeral ⟨*in 316 the figure 1 is in the tens ~*⟩ **10a** remunerative employment; a job; *esp* public office **b** prestige accorded to one of high rank; status ⟨*an endless quest for preferment and ~* – *Time*⟩ **c** a duty accompanying a position of responsibility ⟨*it was not his ~ to sack the employee*⟩ **11** a public square [ME, fr MF, open space, fr L *platea* broad street, fr Gk *plateia* (*hodos*), fr fem of *platys* broad, flat; akin to Skt *prthu* broad, L *planta* sole of the foot] – **give place to** to be followed and superseded by ⟨*valves gave place to transistors*⟩ – **go places** to be on the way to success – **in place of** so as to replace – **place in the sun** a favourable place or situation – **take place** to happen; COME ABOUT

**²place** *vt* **1** to distribute in an orderly manner; arrange ⟨*~ these documents in their correct order*⟩ **2a** to put in, direct to, or assign to a particular place ⟨*~d her on the right of the host*⟩ ⟨*could always ~ the dart exactly where he wanted to*⟩ **b** to present for consideration ⟨*a question ~d before the group*⟩ **c** to put in a particular state ⟨*~ a performer under contract*⟩ **d** to cause (the voice) to produce free and well resonated singing or speaking tones **3** to appoint to a position ⟨*~d her in charge of the class*⟩ **4** to find employment or a home for **5a** to assign to a position in a series or category; rank **b** to estimate ⟨*~d the value of the estate too high*⟩ **c** to identify by connecting with an associated context ⟨*couldn't quite ~ her face*⟩ **6a** to determine the place of (a contestant) in a competition ⟨*was ~d third in the championships*⟩ **b** to assign to any of the leading positions as the result of a competition **7** to put, lay ⟨*the teacher ~s a great deal of stress on correct spelling*⟩ **8a** to give (an order) to a supplier **b** to give an order for (eg a bet) ~ *vi* to come in one of the top places in a competition, esp a race; *specif* to come in second or third in a horse race – **placeable** *adj*

**placebo** /plə'seeboh/ *n, pl* **placebos 1** the Roman Catholic evening service (VESPERS) for the dead **2a(1)** a medication that has no physiological effect on a disease or disorder and is prescribed more for the mental relief of the patient – compare PANACEA **a(2)** an inactive substance against which the usefulness of another substance (eg a drug) is tested in a controlled investigation **b** something tending to soothe or gratify ⟨*children whose parents buy them off with monetary ~s*⟩ [L, I shall please, fr *placēre* to please; (1) ME, fr L (fr the opening word of the first antiphon in the service)]

**placebo effect** *n* an improvement in the condition of a sick person that occurs in response to treatment but is more connected with mental factors than with the specific treatment

**place card** *n* a small card inscribed with the name of a guest and set at the place he/she is to occupy at table during a formal dinner

**placed** /playst/ *adj* **1** having been put in a place ⟨*a ~ bet*⟩ **2** *chiefly Br* having finished in a leading place, esp second or third place, at the end of a competition, esp a horse race

**¹placekick** /'plays,kik/ *n* a kick at a ball (eg in rugby) placed or held in a stationary position on the ground

**²placekick** *vt* **1** to kick (a ball) from a stationary position **2** to score by means of a placekick – **placekicker** *n*

**placeman** /-mən/ *n* a political appointee to a public office, esp in 18th-century Britain

**place mat** *n* a tablemat for one person's plate at table

**placement** /'playsmənt/ *n* an act or instance of placing: eg **a** an accurately hit ball (eg in tennis) that an opponent cannot return **b** the assignment of a person to a suitable place (eg a job or a class in school)

**'place-,name** *n* the name of a geographical locality (eg a town or field)

**placenta** /plə'sentə/ *n, pl* **placentas, placentae** /-tie/ **1** the mass of tissue in all mammals except MONOTREMES and marsupials that unites the foetus to the mother's womb, is formed by the interlocking of the membranes of the foetus with the lining of the womb, and is supplied with a network of blood vessels through which oxygen and nourishment pass from the mother's blood to that of the foetus **2a** an area or surface of a plant on which a spore-producing capsule (SPORANGIUM) is borne **b** the part of the OVARY (seed-producing structure) of a FLOWERING

PLANT to which the OVULES (immature seeds before fertilization) are attached [NL, fr L, flat cake, fr Gk *plakount-, plakous,* fr *plak-, plax* flat surface – more at PLEASE] – **placental** *adj or n*

**placentation** /ˌplasen'taysh(ə)n/ *n* **1a** the development of the placenta and (manner of) attachment of the foetus to the uterus during pregnancy **b** the particular type of form and structure of a placenta **2** the arrangement of OVULES (immature seeds before fertilization) in a plant OVARY (seed-producing structure) or the way in which they are attached to the ovary

¹**placer** /'playsə/ *n* one who or that which places: e g **a** a person who deposits or arranges **b** any of the winners in a competition

²**placer** *n* a deposit of sediment (e g in the bed of a stream) containing particles of valuable minerals, esp gold [Sp, fr Catal, underwater plain, fr *plaza* place, fr L *platea* broad street – more at PLACE]

**place setting** *n* a set of dishes, glasses, and cutlery for one person to use at table

**place value** *n* the value of the position of a digit in a numeral ⟨*in 425 the location of the digit 2 has a* ~ *of ten*⟩

**placid** /'plasid/ *adj* serenely free of interruption or disturbance; quiet ⟨~ *summer skies*⟩ ⟨*a* ~ *disposition*⟩ **synonyms** see ²CALM **antonym** ruffled [L *placidus,* fr *placēre* to please – more at PLEASE] – **placidly** *adv,* **placidness** *n,* **placidity** *n*

**placket** /'plakit/ *n* a slit in a garment, esp a skirt, for a fastening or for access to a pocket [origin unknown]

**placoid** /'plakoyd/ *adj* of or being a toothlike scale with an enamel-tipped spine, characteristic of the body covering of fish with cartilage skeletons [Gk *plak-, plax* flat surface]

**plagal** /'playgl/ *adj* **1** *of a* CHURCH MODE (*musical scale*) having the KEYNOTE (note on which the mode is based) on the fourth scale step – compare AUTHENTIC 3 **2** *of a musical cadence* passing from a SUBDOMINANT chord to a TONIC chord [ML *plagalis,* deriv of Gk *plagios* oblique, sideways, fr *plagos* side; akin to L *plaga* net, region, Gk *pelagos* sea – more at FLAKE]

**plage** /plahzh/ *n* a bright region on the sun caused by the light from gas clouds and often associated with a SUNSPOT [Fr, beach, luminous surface, fr It *piaggia* beach, fr LL *plagia,* fr Gk *plagios* oblique]

**plagi-** /'playji-/, **plagio-** *comb form* slanting; inclined; oblique ⟨*plagiotropism*⟩ [Gk, fr *plagios*]

**plagiarism** /'playj(y)əˌriz(ə)m/ *n* **1** plagiarizing **2** something plagiarized – **plagiarist** *n,* **plagiaristic** *adj*

**plagiar·ize, -ise** /'playj(y)əˌriez/ *vt* to appropriate and pass off (the ideas or words of another) as one's own – *vi* to commit literary theft; present as new and original an idea or product derived from an existing source [*plagiary + -ize*] – **plagiarizer** *n*

**plagiary** /'playj(y)əri/ *n* **1** plagiarism **2** *archaic* a person who plagiarizes [L *plagiarius,* lit., plunderer, fr *plagium* hunting net, fr *plaga* net]

**plagioclase** /'playji·əˌklays, -ˌklayz/ *n* any of a series of rock-forming FELDSPAR minerals, usu containing calcium or sodium [Ger *plagioklas,* fr Gk *plagios + klasis* breaking, fr *klan* to break – more at HALT]

**plagioclimax** /ˌplayjioh'kliemaks/ *n* a mature or stable stage reached in the development of a plagiosere

**plagiosere** /'playjiəˌsiə/ *n* a sequence of ecological changes (SUCCESSION) in the development of a plant community that deviates from its natural course as a result of human activity (e g the constant mowing of fields), natural disaster, or other external intervention [*plagi- + ²sere*]

**plagiotropic** /ˌplayjioh'trohpik, -'tropik/ *adj, of a plant or its parts* growing in a direction away from the vertical ⟨~ *side branches*⟩ [ISV *plagi- + -tropic*] – **plagiotropically** *adv,* **plagiotropism** *n*

¹**plague** /playg/ *n* **1a** a disastrous evil or affliction; a calamity **b** a large destructive influx ⟨*a* ~ *of locusts*⟩ **2** any of several epidemic virulent diseases that cause many deaths; *esp* a highly infectious fever that occurs in several forms and is caused by a bacterium (*Pasteurella pestis*) **3a** a cause of irritation; a nuisance **b** a sudden unwelcome outbreak ⟨*a* ~ *of burglaries*⟩ [ME *plage,* fr MF, fr LL *plaga,* fr L, blow; akin to L *plangere* to strike – more at PLAINT]

²**plague** *vt* **1** to infest or afflict (as if) with disease, calamity, or natural evil **2a** to cause worry or distress to; hamper, burden **b** to disturb or annoy persistently – **plaguer** *n*

**plaguesome** /'playgs(ə)m/ *adj* **1** troublesome **2** pestilential

**plaguey, plaguy** /'playgi/ *adj, informal* causing irritation or annoyance; troublesome – **plaguey** *adv,* **plaguily** *adv*

**plaice** /plays/ *n, pl* **plaice** any of various flatfishes; *esp* a large European flatfish (*Pleuronectes platessa*) valued as food, with an oval body that is brown with conspicuous orangish spots on the upper side and whitish underneath [ME *plaice,* fr OF *plaïs,* fr LL *platensis,* prob fr Gk *platys* broad, flat]

**plaid** /plad/ *n* **1** a rectangular length of tartan worn over the left shoulder as part of Highland dress **2** a fabric, esp TWILLED (diagonally woven) woollen fabric, with a tartan pattern **3a** TARTAN 1 **b** a pattern of unevenly spaced repeated stripes crossing at right angles [ScGael *plaide*] – **plaid** *adj,* **plaided** *adj*

¹**plain** /playn/ *vi, archaic* to complain [ME *plainen,* fr MF *plaindre,* fr L *plangere* to lament – more at PLAINT]

²**plain** *n* **1a** an extensive area of level or rolling treeless country **b** a broad unbroken expanse **2** KNIT STITCH [ME, fr OF, fr L *planum,* fr neut of *planus* flat, level, clear – more at FLOOR]

³**plain** *adj* **1** lacking ornament; undecorated ⟨*a* ~ *and simple dress*⟩ **2** free of added substances; pure **3** free of impediments to view; unobstructed **4a(1)** evident to the mind or senses; obvious ⟨*it's perfectly* ~ *that they will resist*⟩ **a(2)** clear ⟨*made his intentions* ~⟩ **b** free from deceitfulness or subtlety; candid, blunt **5** lacking special distinction or affectation; ordinary **6** characterized by simplicity; not complicated ⟨~ *home cooking*⟩ **7** not rich or elaborately prepared or decorated; made without or not containing additional ingredients or essential seasonings: e g **7a** made with small quantities of fat and sugar ⟨~ *cake mixture*⟩ **b** *of flour* not containing a raising agent **8** unremarkable either for physical beauty or for ugliness ⟨*a* ~ *woman with a face as homely as her house*⟩ **9** *archaic* even, level **synonyms** see EVIDENT – **plainly** *adv,* **plainness** *n*

⁴**plain** *adv* in a plain manner; clearly, simply ⟨*always spoke* ~⟩; *also* totally, utterly ⟨*it's just* ~ *daft*⟩

**plainchant** /-ˌchahnt/ *n* plainsong [Fr *plain-chant,* lit., plain song]

**plain clothes** *n* ordinary civilian dress as opposed to uniform; *esp* the clothes of a police detective who does not wear uniform while on duty – often attrib in *plain-clothes man* ⟨~ *men were watching every exit*⟩

**plain dealing** *n* straightforward honesty ⟨*a businessman noted for his* ~⟩

¹**plain-ˌlaid** *adj, of a rope* consisting of three strands twisted together from left to right

**Plains** /playnz/ *adj* of or being N American Indians of the Great Plains or their culture

**plain sailing** *n* easy progress along an unobstructed course (e g of action) ⟨*once that is solved the rest will be* ~⟩ [alter. (influenced by ³*plain*) of *plane sailing* (a simple method of navigation based on the premise that the earth is flat)]

    *usage* This is now the established spelling of this expression.

**plainsman** /'playnzmən/ *n* an inhabitant of plains

**plainsong** /-ˌsong/ *n* **1** the nonmetrical MONOPHONIC (having a single melodic line) usu MODAL music of the medieval church; *esp* GREGORIAN CHANT **2** a liturgical chant of any of various Christian rites

**plainspoken** /-'spohkən/ *adj* candid, frank – **plainspokenness** *n*

**plain stitch** *n* KNIT STITCH

**plaint** /playnt/ *n* **1** a protest, complaint **2** *archaic* a lamentation, wail [ME, fr MF, fr L *planctus,* fr *planctus,* pp of *plangere* to strike, beat one's breast, lament; akin to OHG *fluokhōn* to curse, Gk *plēssein* to strike]

**plaintext** /-ˌtekst/ *n* the intelligible form (e g the original form) of a text in code

**plaintiff** /'playntif/ *n* a person who commences a civil legal action [ME *plaintif,* fr MF, fr *plaintif,* adj]

**plaintive** /'playntiv/ *adj* expressive of suffering or woe; melancholy, mournful [ME *plaintif,* fr MF, fr *plaint*] – **plaintively** *adv,* **plaintiveness** *n*

**plain weave** *n* a simple weave in which the crosswise (WEFT) yarns pass alternatively over and under the lengthwise (WARP) yarns – **plain-weave** *adj,* **plain-woven** *adj*

¹**plait** *also* **plat** /plat/ *n* **1** a pleat **2** a length of plaited material, (e g hair or straw); *specif* a pigtail [ME *pleit,* fr MF, fr (assumed) VL *plictus,* fr *plictus,* pp of L *plicare* to fold – more at PLY]

²**plait** *also* **plat** *vt* **1** to pleat **2a** to form (three or more strands) into a plait ⟨~ *straws*⟩ **b** to make by plaiting **c** to do up (the hair) by interweaving three or more strands – **plaiter** *n*

¹**plan** /plan/ *n* **1** a drawing or diagram drawn on a plane: e g **1a** a top or horizontal view of an object **b** a large-scale map of

a small area **2a** a method for achieving an end ⟨*working hard at a ~ to avoid work*⟩ **b** an often customary method of doing something; a procedure ⟨*the usual ~ is to both arrive and leave early*⟩ **c** a detailed formulation of a programme of action ⟨*the ~ called for increasing the bet whenever he won*⟩ **d** a goal, aim ⟨*her ~ was to get a degree in engineering*⟩ **3** an orderly arrangement of parts of an overall design or objective [Fr, plane, foundation, ground plan; partly fr L *planum* level ground, fr neut of *planus* level; partly fr Fr *planter* to plant, fix in place, fr LL *plantare* – more at FLOOR, PLANT] – **planless** *adj*, **planlessly** *adv*, **planlessness** *n*

²**plan** *vb* **-nn-** *vt* **1** to arrange the parts of; design **2** to devise or project the realization or achievement of ⟨*~ a programme*⟩ **3** to have in mind; intend ~ *vi* to make plans – **planner** *n*
**usage** In formal writing, **plan** to do something is a better construction than **plan** on doing it.

¹**plan-** /playn-/, **plano-** *comb form* moving or able to move about; mobile ⟨plano*blast*⟩ ⟨plano*gamete*⟩ [prob fr NL, fr Gk, wandering, fr *planos*; akin to Gk *planasthai* to wander – more at PLANET]

²**plan-, plano-** *comb form* **1** flat ⟨plano*sol*⟩; flat and ⟨plano-*concave*⟩ **2** flatly ⟨plano*spiral*⟩ [L *planus*]

**planar** /'playnə, -nah/ *adj* of or lying in a plane; two-dimensional – **planarity** *n*

**planarian** /plə'neəri·ən/ *n* any of several small mostly aquatic FREE-LIVING (nonparasitic) flatworms (family Planariidae or order Tricladida of the class Turbellaria) that have elongated bodies bearing CILIA (small hairlike structures used for movement) [NL *Planaria*, type genus of the family, fr fem of LL *planarius* lying on a flat surface, fr L *planum* flat surface]

**planation** /play'naysh(ə)n/ *n* the condition or process of becoming flattened; *esp* mechanical erosion (e g by waves or glacial action) that produces smoothed or flattened surfaces

**planchet** /'plahnchit/ *n* a plain metal disc before stamping as a coin [dim. of *planch* (flat plate), fr ME *plaunche* plank, fr MF *planche*]

**planchette** /plahn'shet/ *n* a small triangular or heart-shaped board supported with casters at two points and a vertical pencil at a third and believed to produce writing of telepathic or spiritualistic origin when lightly touched by the fingers; *also* a similar board without a pencil [Fr, fr dim. of *planche* plank, fr MF, fr L *planca*]

¹**plane, plane tree** /playn/ *n* any of a genus (*Platanus* of the family Platanaceae, the plane-tree family) of N American and Eurasian trees with scaly bark, large PALMATELY lobed leaves, and flowers in spherical heads [ME, fr MF, fr L *platanus*, fr Gk *platanos*; akin to Gk *platys* broad – more at PLACE]

²**plane** /playn/ *vt* **1a** to make smooth or even; level **b** to make smooth, flat, or even with a plane ⟨*~d the sides of the door*⟩ **2** to remove by planing – often + *away, off,* or *down* ~ *vi* **1** to work with a plane **2** to do the work of a plane [ME *planen*, fr MF *planer*, fr LL *planare*, fr L *planus* level – more at FLOOR] – **planer** *n*

³**plane** *n* a tool with a sharp blade protruding from the base of a flat metal or wooden stock, for smoothing or shaping a wood surface [ME, fr MF, fr LL *plana*, fr *planare*]

⁴**plane** *n* **1a** maths a surface such that a straight line joining any of its points lies wholly in the surface **b** a flat or level physical surface **2** a level of existence, consciousness, or development ⟨*on the intellectual ~*⟩ **3a** any of the main supporting surfaces of an aeroplane **b** an aeroplane [L *planum*, fr neut of *planus* level; (3b) by shortening]

⁵**plane** *adj* **1** having no elevations or depressions; flat **2a** of or dealing with geometric planes **b** lying in a plane ⟨*a ~ curve*⟩ □ compare PLAIN SAILING **synonyms** see ³LEVEL [L *planus*]

⁶**plane** *vi* **1a** to fly while keeping the wings motionless **b** to fly without using engine power **c** *of a vessel or vessel's hull* to skim across the surface of the water so that the resistance to motion is reduced and high speeds attained **2** to travel by aeroplane [Fr *planer*, fr *plan* plane; fr the plane formed by the wings of a soaring bird]

**plane geometry** *n* a branch of elementary geometry that deals with two-dimensional figures

**planer** /'playnə/ *n* a smooth-faced usu wooden block used for levelling type in a CHASE (steel or iron frame)

**planet** /'planit/ *n* **1a** any of the seven celestial bodies, sun, moon, Venus, Jupiter, Mars, Mercury, and Saturn that in ancient belief have motions of their own among the fixed stars **b** any of the bodies except a comet, meteor, or satellite that revolve round the sun in the solar system **2** STAR 2a(1) [ME

*planete,* fr OF, fr LL *planeta,* modif of Gk planēt-, *planēs,* lit., wanderer, fr *planasthai* to wander; akin to ON *flana* to rush around]

**plane table** *n* a surveying instrument used for plotting lines directly from observations, that consists essentially of a drawing board mounted on a tripod together with an ALIDADE (instrument for determining the direction of an object)

**planetarium** /,plani'teəri·əm/ *n, pl* **planetariums, planetaria** /-riə/ **1** a model of the solar system **2a** an optical device to project various celestial images and effects **b** a building or room housing such a projector

**planetary** /'planit(ə)ri/ *adj* **1a** of or being a planet **b** having a motion like that of a planet; *specif, of an electron* revolving round the nucleus of an atom **2a** of or belonging to the earth; terrestrial **b** global, worldwide **3** having or consisting of an EPICYCLIC TRAIN (cluster of GEAR WHEELS that revolve round a central gear) **4** *poetic* erratic, wandering

**planetary nebula** *n* a very hot star surrounded by a vast cloud of tenuous gases

**planetesimal** /,plani'tesim(ə)l/ *n* any of numerous small solid celestial bodies that may have existed at an early stage of the development of the SOLAR SYSTEM [*planet* + *-esimal* (as in *infinitesimal*)]

**planetesimal hypothesis** *n* a hypothesis in astronomy: the planets have evolved by union and fusion of planetesimals

**planetoid** /'planitoyd/ *n* **1** a body resembling a planet **2** ASTEROID (small planet) – **planetoidal** *adj*

**plane tree** *n* ¹PLANE

**planet wheel** *n* a GEAR WHEEL in an EPICYCLIC TRAIN (cluster of gear wheels that revolve round a central gear) that revolves round the wheel with which it comes into working contact

**planform** /'plan,fawm/ *n* the shape of an object (e g an aircraft) as seen from above

**plangent** /'planj(ə)nt/ *adj* **1** loudly reverberating **2** having an expressive, esp plaintive, quality △ piquant, poignant, pungent [L *plangent-, plangens,* prp of *plangere* to strike, lament] – **plangency** *n*, **plangently** *adv*

**planimeter** /plə'nimitə/ *n* an instrument for measuring the area of a plane figure by tracing its boundary line [Fr *planimètre,* fr L *planum* plane + Fr *-mètre* -meter]

**planimetric** /,plani'metrik/ *adj* **1** of or made by means of a planimeter ⟨*~ measurements*⟩ **2** *of a map* containing only planimetry

**planimetry** /plə'nimətri/ *n* **1** the representation of features (e g rivers, coasts, or roads) on a map which have been measured as though they existed only in a flat plane **2** the science of the measurement of plane surfaces [Fr *planimétrie,* fr ML *planimetria,* fr L *planus* flat + *-metria* -metry]

**planish** /'planish/ *vt* to toughen and finish (metal) by hammering lightly [MF *planiss-,* stem of *planir* to make smooth, fr *plan* level, fr L *planus*] – **planisher** *n*

**planisphere** /'plani,sfiə/ *n* a representation of a sphere on a plane surface; *esp* a polar projection of the CELESTIAL SPHERE and the stars on a plane surface so as to show celestial phenomena at any given time [ML *planisphaerium,* fr L *planum* plane + *sphaera* sphere] – **planispheric** *adj*

¹**plank** /plangk/ *n* **1a** a long heavy thick piece of wood; *specif* one 50 to 100 millimetres (2 to 4 inches) thick and at least 200 millimetres (about 8 inches) wide **b** an object made of a plank or planking **c** planking **2a** an article in a political platform **b** an item, esp a principal item, of a policy or programme [ME, fr ONF *planke,* fr L *planca*] – **walk the plank** to be forced (e g by pirates) to walk, esp blindfold, along a board laid over the side of a ship until one falls into the sea

²**plank** *vt* **1** to cover or floor with planks **2** *NAm* to cook and serve on a wooden board, usu with an elaborate garnish **3** *informal* to set down or deposit, esp roughly; *specif* to lay out (money) on the spot – usu + *down*

**planking** /'plangking/ *n* **1** the act or process of covering or fitting with planks **2** a quantity of planks

**plankter** /'plangktə/ *n* a planktonic organism [Gk *planktēr* wanderer, fr *plazesthai* to wander]

**plankton** /'plangktən/ *n* the floating or weakly swimming usu minute animal and plant organisms of a body of water – compare PHYTOPLANKTON, ZOOPLANKTON [Ger, fr Gk, neut of *planktos* drifting, fr *plazesthai* to wander, drift, passive of *plazein* to drive astray; akin to L *plangere* to strike – more at PLAINT] – **planktonic** *adj*

**planned parenthood** *n* the planned control (e g by contraception) of the number of children born to a person

**planning** /'planing/ *n* the act or process of making or carrying out plans; *esp* the establishment of goals, policies, and procedures for a social or economic unit ⟨*town* ~ ⟩ ⟨*business* ~ ⟩

**plano-** /'playnoh-/ – see PLAN-

,**plano-con'cave** *adj* flat on one side and concave or curving inwards on the other ⟨~ *lens*⟩

,**plano-con'vex** *adj* flat on one side and convex or curving outwards on the other ⟨~ *mirror*⟩

**planography** /plə'nografi/ *n* a process (e g LITHOGRAPHY) for printing from a plane surface – **planographic** *adj*

**plan position indicator** *n* a radar display device that shows the position of radar-reflecting objects (e g aircraft and ships) as if they were seen from above – called also PPI

**¹plant** /plahnt/ *vt* **1a** to put in the ground, soil, etc for growth ⟨~ *seeds*⟩ **b** to set or sow (land) with seeds or plants **c** to implant ⟨~ *the idea in their minds*⟩ **2a** to establish, institute **b** to place (animals) in a new locality **c** to stock with animals ⟨~ed *the stream with trout*⟩ **3** to place firmly or forcibly ⟨~ed *a hard blow on his chin*⟩ **4** to position secretly; *specif* to conceal in order to observe or deceive ⟨~ed *a microphone in the hotel room*⟩ ~ *vi* to plant something [ME *planten*, fr OE *plantian*, fr LL *plantare* to plant, fix in place, fr L, to plant, fr *planta* plant] – **plantable** *adj*

  **plant out** *vt* to transplant (e g seedlings or a house plant) from a pot, seed tray, etc to open ground

**²plant** *n* **1a** a tree, shrub, vine, herb, etc that is or can be planted; *esp* a soft- or fleshy-stemmed nonwoody plant smaller than a shrub or tree **b** any of a kingdom (Plantae) of living things (e g a moss, fern, conifer, or FLOWERING PLANT) that typically synthesize their food from simple inorganic substances (e g water and carbon dioxide), have cell walls composed of CELLULOSE, and respond slowly to stimulation, and that typically lack the power of locomotion and an obvious nervous system or SENSE ORGANS **2a** the buildings, machinery, apparatus, and fixtures used in carrying on a trade or an industrial business **b** a factory or workshop for the manufacture of a particular product **c** the total facilities available for production or service **d** the buildings and other physical equipment of an institution **3** an act of planting **4** something or someone planted ⟨*left muddy footprints as a* ~ *to confuse the police*⟩ **5** a play in snooker by which one of two red balls is driven by the CUE BALL to strike the other [ME *plante*, fr OE, fr L *planta*] – **plantlike** *adj*

**Plantagenet** /plan'taj(ə)nit/ *adj* of the English royal house that ruled from 1154 to 1399 [*Plantagenet*, nickname of the family adopted as surname] – **Plantagenet** *n*

**¹plantain** /'plantayn, -tin/ *n* any of a genus (*Plantago* of the family Plantaginaceae, the plantain family) of short-stemmed plants bearing dense spikes of minute greenish or brownish flowers [ME, fr OF, fr L *plantagin-, plantago,* fr *planta* sole of the foot; fr its broad leaves]

**²plantain** *n* **1** a tropical plant (*Musa paradisiaca*) of the banana plant family **2** the angular greenish starchy fruit of the plantain that is similar to a banana and is used cooked as a staple food in the tropics [Sp *plántano* plane tree, banana tree, fr ML *plantanus* plane tree, alter. of L *platanus* – more at PLANE]

**plantar** /'plantə/ *adj* of, on, or supplying the sole of the foot [L *plantaris*, fr *planta* sole – more at PLACE]

**plantation** /plahn'taysh(ə)n, plan-/ *n* **1** a usu large group of plants, esp trees, under cultivation **2** a settlement in a new country or region; a colony **3a** a place that is planted or under cultivation **b** an agricultural estate, usu worked by resident labour

**planter** /'plahntə/ *n* **1** someone who cultivates plants: e g **1a** a farmer **b** someone who owns or operates a plantation ⟨*a tea* ~ ⟩ **2** someone who settles or founds a new colony **3** a container in which ornamental plants are grown **4** a planting machine or tool

**planter's punch** *n* a punch of rum, lime or lemon juice, sugar, water, and sometimes bitters

**plant food** *n* **1** FOOD 1b **2** fertilizer

**plantigrade** /'planti,grayd/ *adj* walking or designed for walking on the sole of the foot with the heel touching the ground ⟨*human beings are* ~ *animals*⟩ – compare DIGITIGRADE [Fr, fr L *planta* sole + Fr *-grade*] – **plantigrade** *n*

**planting** /'plahnting/ *n* an area where plants are grown for commercial or decorative purposes

**plant kingdom** *n* one of the three basic groups of natural objects that includes all living and extinct plants – compare ANIMAL KINGDOM, MINERAL KINGDOM

**plant louse** *n* an aphid or other small insect (e g a JUMPING PLANT LOUSE) parasitic on plants

**plantocracy** /plahn'tokrəsi/ *n taking sing or pl vb* a ruling class of plantation owners (e g in the West Indies) [*planter* + *-o-* + *-cracy*]

**planula** /'planyoolə/ *n, pl* **planulae** /-lie/ the very young usu flattened oval or oblong free-swimming CILIATED (bearing small hairlike structures used for movement) larva of a COELENTERATE (e g a jellyfish, coral, or sea anemone) [NL, fr L *planus* level, flat – more at FLOOR] – **planular** *adj,* **planuloid** *adj*

**plaque** /plak, plahk/ *n* **1a** an ornamental brooch; *esp* the badge of an honorary order **b** a flat thin piece (e g of metal) used for decoration **c** a commemorative or identifying inscribed tablet **2a** a localized abnormal patch in or esp on a body part or surface **b** a film of mucus and bacteria on the surface of a tooth – compare TARTAR **3** a clear area in a culture of bacteria produced by destruction of the bacterial cells (e g by a virus) [Fr, fr MF, metal sheet, fr *plaquier* to plate, fr MD *placken* to piece, patch; akin to MD *placke* piece, MHG *placke* patch]

**¹plash** /plash/ *n* a shallow or muddy pool [ME *plasche*, fr OE *plæsc*; akin to MD *plasch, plas* pool, prob of imit origin]

**²plash** *vt* to interweave (branches and twigs) to form a hedge; *also* to form (a hedge) thus [ME *plashen*, fr MF *plaissier*, fr OF, fr *plais* hedge, prob deriv of L *plectere* to entwine, braid (cf PLEACH)]

**³plash** *n* a splashing sound ⟨*the* ~ *of oars*⟩ [prob imit]

**⁴plash** *vt* to break the surface of (water); splash ~ *vi* to cause a splashing or spattering effect [perh fr D *plassen*, fr MD, of imit origin]

**¹plashy** /'plashi/ *adj* marshy, boggy [¹*plash*]

**²plashy** *adj* splashy, plashing [³*plash*]

**-plasia** /-playzyə, -zh(y)ə/, **-plasy** *comb form* (→ *n*) development; formation ⟨*hyper*plasia⟩ [NL *-plasia,* fr Gk *plasis* moulding, fr *plassein* to mould]

**plasm** /'plaz(ə)m/ *n* plasma [LL *plasma* something moulded]

**plasm-** /plazm-/, **plasmo-** *comb form* plasma; cytoplasm ⟨plasmo*dium*⟩ ⟨plasmo*lysis*⟩ [Fr, fr NL *plasma*]

**-plasm** /-,plaz(ə)m/ *comb form* (→ *n*) structural material of a living organism (e g a cell or tissue) ⟨*endo*plasm⟩ [Ger *-plasma,* fr NL *plasma*]

**plasma** /'plazmə/ *n* **1** a green faintly translucent variety of CHALCEDONY (type of quartz) used as a gemstone **2** the liquid part of blood, LYMPH, or milk as distinguished from suspended material (e g cells or fat globules) **3** PROTOPLASM (living material inside a cell and its nucleus) **4** a gas at a very high temperature (e g in the atmospheres of stars) that contains only electrically charged particles and is composed of approximately equal numbers of electrons and positively charged ions [NL, fr LL, something moulded, fr Gk, fr *plassein* to mould – more at PLASTER; (1) Ger, fr LL] – **plasmatic** *adj*

**plasma cell** *n* a WHITE BLOOD CELL that is usu found near the site of a fairly mild long-lasting inflammation or allergic reaction

**plasmagel** /'plazmə,jel/ *n* firm jellylike PROTOPLASM (living material inside a cell); *esp* the ECTOPLASM (outer firm layer of jellylike material) of a cell (e g an amoeba) that uses the interconversion of plasmagel and plasmasol as a means of movement

**plasmagene** /'plazmə,jeen/ *n* a particle or piece of DNA or RNA that exists outside the cell nucleus in some cells, and that is inherited and produces a genetic effect in the same way as, but independently of, a gene or small CHROMOSOME (strand of gene-carrying material) in the cell nucleus [ISV] – **plasmagenic** *adj*

**plasmalemma** /,plazmə'lemə/ *n* PLASMA MEMBRANE 1 [NL, fr *plasma* + Gk *lemma* husk – more at LEMMA]

**plasma membrane** *n* **1** the very thin semipermeable membrane that surrounds a cell and is composed chiefly of fat and protein **2** TONOPLAST (membrane round an air- or liquid-filled cavity in a cell)

**plasmapheresis** /,plazmə'ferəsis/ *n* a process in which blood taken from the body of a patient or donor is separated into RED BLOOD CELLS and plasma and the red blood cells are returned to the person's bloodstream. The process is used for the removal of poisonous substances from blood plasma or to obtain plasma for use in blood transfusions. [NL, fr *plasma* + Gk *aphairesis* taking off, removal – more at APHAERESIS]

**plasmasol** /'plazmə,sol/ *n* relatively liquid PROTOPLASM (living material inside a cell); *esp* the ENDOPLASM (inner fluid zone) of a cell (e g an amoeba) that uses the interconversion of plasmasol and plasmagel as a means of movement

**plasma torch** n an electrical device that heats a gas to form a plasma for high-temperature operations (e g melting metal)

**plasmid** /'plazmid/ n a plasmagene; *specif* a small strand of genetic material in a bacterium, that exists and reproduces independently of the bacterium's CHROMOSOMES (strands of gene-carrying material) [*plasma* + ²-*id*]

**plasmin** /'plazmin/ n an ENZYME that breaks down the FIBRIN (insoluble fibrous protein) of blood clots

**plasminogen** /plaz'minəjən/ n the substance found in blood plasma from which plasmin is formed

**plasmo-** – see PLASM-

**plasmodesm** /'plazmə,dez(ə)m/ n plasmodesma

**plasmodesma** /,plazmə'dezmə/ n, *pl* **plasmodesmata** /-mətə/, **plasmodesmas** any of the strands of CYTOPLASM (jellylike material inside a cell) that pass through minute openings in the walls of some plant cells and provide living bridges between adjacent cells [NL, fr *plasma* + Gk *desmat-*, *desma* bond, fr *dein* to bind – more at DIADEM]

**plasmodium** /plaz'mohdi•əm/ n, *pl* **plasmodia** /-diə/ 1 (an organism, esp a stage of a SLIME MOULD consisting of) a mobile mass of living matter that contains many nuclei and results from the fusion of amoebalike cells with a single nucleus but itself is not differentiated into separate cells; *broadly* SYNCYTIUM (fused mass of cells, containing many nuclei) 2 an individual malaria parasite (genus *Plasmodium*) [NL, fr *plasm-* + *-odium* thing resembling, fr Gk *-ōdēs* like]

**plasmogamy** /plaz'mogəmi/ n the fusion of the CYTOPLASM (jellylike material inside a cell but outside the cell nucleus) of two or more cells without or as distinguished from the fusion of cell nuclei [ISV]

**plasmolyse** /'plazməliez/ vb to subject to or undergo plasmolysis

**plasmolysis** /plaz'moləsis/ n the shrinking of the CYTOPLASM (jellylike material inside a cell) away from the wall of a living cell, esp a plant cell, due to water loss by EXOSMOSIS [NL, fr *plasm-* + *-lysis*] – **plasmolytic** *adj*, **plasmolytically** *adv*

**-plast** /-plast, -plahst/ *comb form* (→ n) organized particle or subcellular body or granule; cell ⟨*proto*plast⟩ [MF -*plaste* thing moulded, fr LL -*plastus*, fr Gk -*plastos*, fr *plastos* moulded, fr *plassein* to mould]

**¹plaster** /'plahstə/ n 1 a medicated or protective dressing that consists of a film of cloth, plastic, etc often spread with a medicated substance; STICKING PLASTER 2 a pastelike mixture (e g of lime, water, and sand) that hardens on drying and is used esp for coating walls, ceilings, and partitions 3 PLASTER CAST 2 [ME, fr OE, fr L *emplastrum*, fr Gk *emplastron*, fr *emplassein* to plaster on, fr *en-* + *plassein* to mould, plaster; akin to L *planus* level, flat – more at FLOOR] – **plastery** *adj*

**²plaster** vt 1 to overlay or cover with plaster; coat 2 to apply a plaster to 3a to cover over or conceal as if with a coat of plaster ⟨*she* ~ed *over unhappy memories*⟩ b to smear (something) thickly (on); coat ⟨*he* ~ed *butter on his bread*⟩ ⟨*she* ~ed *her face with makeup*⟩ c to cause to lie flat or stick to another surface ⟨~ed *his hair down*⟩ ⟨*the rain* ~ed *his shirt to his body*⟩ 4 to treat with PLASTER OF PARIS 5a to fasten something to or place something on, esp conspicuously or in quantity ⟨*walls* ~ed *with posters*⟩ b to affix to or place on something, esp conspicuously or in quantity ⟨~ed *posters all over the walls*⟩ 6 *informal* to inflict heavy damage, injury, or casualties on, esp by a concentrated or unremitting attack; strike heavily and effectively ~ *vi* to apply plaster – **plasterer** n

**plasterboard** /-,bawd/ n a board used in large sheets as a backing or as a substitute for plaster on walls and consisting of several piles of fibreboard, paper, or felt usu bonded to a hardened GYPSUM plaster core

**plaster cast** n 1 a sculpture cast in PLASTER OF PARIS 2 a rigid dressing of gauze impregnated with plaster of paris for immobilizing a diseased or broken body part

**plastered** /'plahstəd/ adj, *informal* drunk

**plastering** /'plahst(ə)ring/ n 1 a coating (as if) of plaster 2 *informal* a decisive defeat

**plaster of paris** /'paris/ n, *often cap 2nd P* a white powder, $2CaSO_4.H_2O$, made usu by partly dehydrating the mineral GYPSUM, that when mixed with water forms a quicksetting paste used chiefly for casts and moulds; *also* the plaster formed by mixing this with water [*Paris*, capital city of France]

**plasterwork** /-,wuhk/ n plastering applied as a finish on architectural constructions

**¹plastic** /'plastik; *also* 'plahstik/ adj 1 formative, creative ⟨~ *forces in nature*⟩ 2a(1) capable of being moulded or modelled

⟨~ *clay*⟩ a(2) supple, pliant b *biology* capable of growing or developing under or adapting to varying conditions 3 relating to, composed of, or producing 3-dimensional forms or movement; sculptural 4 made or consisting of a plastic 5 capable of being bent, stretched, etc continuously and permanently in any direction without breaking – compare ELASTIC 6 of, involving, or being PLASTIC SURGERY 7 *chiefly derog* formed by or adapted to an artificial or conventional standard; synthetic ⟨*takes a positive effort of will ... to avoid* ~ *food,* ~ *living, and* ~ *entertainment* – L E Sissman⟩ [L *plasticus* of moulding, fr Gk *plastikos*, fr *plassein* to mould, form]

  *synonyms* Plastic, pliable, pliant, ductile, malleable, adaptable: these may apply to things, and by extension, to people, regarded as material to be shaped or modified in some way. **Plastic** suggests the qualities of clay or wax, soft enough to take impressions, hard enough to retain them. What is **pliant** or **pliable** may be bent without breaking. Applied to people, **pliant** suggests someone ready to accommodate change or people's wishes, while **pliable** suggests someone easily dominated or influenced. Something **ductile** may be drawn out like some metals, or made to flow like water, while **malleable** suggests something which can be beaten or pressed into shape with, or as if by, tools. What is **adaptable** can change itself to suit different circumstances. **Flexible** and **supple** are related to this group in their ability to be bent or twisted without harm. They suggest in people an ability or willingness to adapt; in the case of **supple** this may approach complaisance or even servility. Compare ¹ELASTIC *antonyms* rigid, stiff, brittle *usage* The pronunciation /'plastik/ is recommended for BBC broadcasters.

**²plastic** n a plastic substance; *specif* any of numerous synthetic organic chemical POLYMERS (large molecules composed of many identical repeating units), that can be moulded or cast into objects, drawn into thin filaments, or stretched into sheets or films when soft

**-plastic** /-plastik/ *comb form* (→ *adj*) 1 developing; forming ⟨*thrombo*plastic⟩ 2 of (something designated by a term ending in *-plasm, -plast, -plasty, -plasia,* or *-plasy*) ⟨*homo*plastic⟩ ⟨*neo*plastic⟩ [Gk *-plastikos*, fr *plassein*]

**plastically** /'plastikli; *also* 'plah-/ adv 1 in a plastic manner 2 with respect to plastic qualities

**plastic art** n 1 art (e g sculpture or bas-relief) characterized by modelling; three-dimensional art 2 art concerned with representing three-dimensional things; *specif* any of the visual arts (e g painting, sculpture, or film), esp as distinguished from those that are written or meant to be heard (e g poetry or music)

**Plasticine** /'plastəseen; *also* 'plah-/ *trademark* – used for a modelling substance made in various colours that remains plastic for a long period

**plasticity** /plas'tisəti, plahs-/ n 1 being plastic; *esp* capacity for being moulded or altered 2 the ability of a material to retain a shape produced by bending, stretching, etc without breaking or returning to its former shape – compare ELASTICITY

**plastic-ize, -ise** /'plastisiez; *also* 'plah-/ vt 1 to make plastic 2 to treat with a plastic ⟨*a* ~d *mattress cover*⟩ – **plasticization** n

**plastic-izer, -iser** /'plasti,siezə, 'plahs-/ n one who or that which plasticizes; *specif* a chemical added, esp to rubbers and plastics, to give flexibility, workability, or stretchability

**plastic surgeon** n a specialist in PLASTIC SURGERY

**plastic surgery** n a branch of surgery concerned with the repair, restoration, or cosmetic improvement of part of the body chiefly by the transfer and grafting of tissue

**plastid** /'plastid/ n any of various specialized structures (ORGANELLES) occurring in most plant and some animal cells, that typically contain pigment and function as centres of photosynthesis in plants and in the storage of starch, oil, and protein [Ger, fr Gk *plastos* moulded] – **plastidial** *adj*

**plastogene** /'plastəjeen/ n a PLASMAGENE (piece of genetic material) in a plastid [*plastid* + -o- + -*gene*]

**plastron** /'plastrən/ n 1a a metal breastplate formerly worn under the HAUBERK (chain armour) b a quilted pad worn in fencing to protect the chest, waist, and the side on which the weapon is held 2 the part of the shell of a tortoise or turtle that covers the underside of the body, and consists typically of nine symmetrically placed bones overlaid by horny plates 3 a false shirt or blouse front; DICKEY 1 4 a thin film of air or air bubbles surrounding some aquatic insects and held in place by water-repellent hairs [MF, fr OIt *piastrone*, aug of *piastra* thin metal plate – more at PIASTRE] – **plastral** *adj*

**-plasty** /-,plahsti/ *comb form* (→ *n*) replacement or formation of (something specified) by means of plastic surgery ⟨*osteo*plasty⟩ ⟨*rhino*plasty⟩ [Fr *-plastie*, fr LGk *-plastia* moulding, fr Gk *-plastēs* moulder, fr *plassein* to mould]

**-plasy** /-playzi/ *comb form* (→ *n*) -plasia

¹**plat** /plat/ *vt or n* **-tt-** (to) plait

²**plat** *n*, *NAm* a plan or map of a piece of land with actual or proposed features (e g plots); *also* the land represented [prob alter. of *plot*]

³**plat** *vt* **-tt-** to make a plat of; map

**platan** /'plat(ə)n/ *n* a plane tree [ME, fr L *platanus*]

**plat du jour** /,plah doo 'zhooə (*Fr* pla dy ʒuːr)/ *n*, *pl* **plats du jour** /~/ a dish featured by a restaurant on a particular day [Fr, lit., dish of the day]

¹**plate** /playt/ *n* **1a** a smooth flat thin usu rigid piece of material **b(1)** forged, rolled, or cast metal in sheets usu thicker than 6 millimetres (¹/₄ inch) **b(2)** a very thin layer of metal deposited on a surface of another metal by plating **c** any of the broad metal pieces used in armour; *also* armour of such plates **d(1)** an (external) scale or flat rigid layer or structure of bone, horn, etc forming part of an animal body; *esp* SCUTE **d(2)** the thin under portion of the forequarter of beef; *esp* the fatty back part **e** any of the huge movable segments into which the earth's crust is divided **f** a racehorse's shoe **2** precious metal; *esp* silver bullion **3a** domestic utensils and tableware made of or plated with gold, silver, or base metals **b** a more or less flat vessel that is typically circular or sometimes oval and from which food is eaten or served **c** the contents of a plate; a plateful **d(1)** a prize given to the winner of certain competitions (e g horse races) **d(2)** a horse race in which the contestants compete for a fixed prize irrespective of the number of competitors **e** a dish or pouch passed in taking collections (e g in church) **f** a flat glass dish or plate (e g a PETRI DISH) used chiefly for growing cultures of microorganisms **4a** a prepared surface from which printing is done **b** a sheet of material (e g glass) coated with a light-sensitive photographic emulsion **c** a typically flat thin piece of metal that conducts an electric current and forms (part of) a component in an electrical circuit; *esp* an ELECTRODE that is immersed in the electrically conducting liquid (ELECTROLYTE) in a rechargeable battery (e g a car battery) **d** a flat piece or surface bearing letters or a design; *specif* NUMBERPLATE **5** a horizontal structural part (e g a timber) that supports esp the trusses of a roof or the rafters **6a** a device for correcting irregularities of the teeth **b** the part of a denture that fits to the mouth; *broadly* a denture **7** a full-page book illustration, often on different paper from the text pages **8** *NAm* **8a** a complete main course served on a plate **b** food and service supplied to one person ⟨*a dinner at £5 a* ~⟩ **9** *NAm* the ANODE (metal plate, wire, etc to which electrons flow) of an ELECTRON TUBE (valve or similar device in which there is a controlled flow of electrons between two points) [ME, fr OF, fr *plate*, fem of *plat* flat, fr (assumed) VL *plattus*, prob fr Gk *platys* broad, flat – more at FLAT; (2) ME, partly fr OF *plat*, piece of silver, & partly fr OSp *plata* silver, fr (assumed) VL *plattus* flat; (3) ME, fr MF *plat* dish, plate, fr *plat* flat] – **platelike** *adj* – **have a lot/enough on one's plate** to be (fully) occupied often with a variety of tasks, problems, etc – **on a plate** *informal* so as not to require effort ⟨*handed the job to him* on a plate⟩

²**plate** *vt* **1** to cover or equip with plate: e g **1a** to arm with armour plate **b** to cover (metal) with a thin adherent layer of silver, chrome, etc; *also* to deposit (e g a layer) on a surface **2** to make a printing plate (e g a stereotype) from **3** to fix or secure with a plate

¹**plateau** /'platoh/ *n*, *pl* **plateaus, plateaux** /-ohz/ **1a** a usu extensive relatively flat land area raised above adjacent land on at least one side **b** a similar undersea feature **2a** a region of little or no change in a graph or graphical representation **b** a relatively stable level, period, or condition ⟨*a price* ~ *interrupting an inflationary spiral*⟩ [Fr, fr MF, platter, fr *plat* flat]

²**plateau** *vi* to reach a level, period, or condition of stability

**plateful** /-f(ə)l/ *n* as much or as many as a plate will hold

**plate glass** *n* rolled, ground, and polished sheet glass

**platelayer** /-,layə/ *n*, *Br* a workman who lays and repairs railway lines; TRACK CHARGEMAN

**platelet** /-lit/ *n* BLOOD PLATELET (minute particle in the blood important in blood clotting)

**platemaker** /'playt,maykə/ *n* a machine for making printing plates, esp OFFSET printing plates – **platemaking** *n*

¹**plate-,mark** *n* HALLMARK (official mark on gold, silver, etc)

**platen** /'plat(ə)n/ *n* **1** a flat plate (e g of metal); *esp* one that exerts or receives pressure (e g in a printing press) **2** the roller of a typewriter [MF *plateine*, fr *plate*]

**plate powder** *n* a preparation (e g of whitening and rouge) used for cleaning silver or plated articles

**plater** /'playtə/ *n* **1** one who or that which plates **2a** a horse that runs chiefly in SELLING RACES **b** an inferior racehorse

**plateresque** /,platə'resk/ *adj*, *often cap* of or being a 16th-century Spanish architectural style characterized by elaborate ornamentation suggestive of silverplate [Sp *plateresco*, fr *platero* silversmith, fr *plata* silver]

**plate tectonics** *n taking sing vb* the study of the formation of the major structures (e g the continents) of the earth's surface by the movement and interaction of the plates of the earth's crust – **platetectonic** *adj*, **platetectonically** *adv*

**platform** /'platfawm/ *n* **1** a declaration of the principles on which a group of people stand; *esp* a declaration of principles and policies adopted by a political party or a candidate **2a(1)** a horizontal flat surface, usu higher than the adjoining area; *esp*, *Br* a raised surface at a railway station to facilitate access to trains **a(2)** a raised floor or stage (e g for speakers or performers) **a(3)** a raised metal structure secured to the sea bed by posts and serving as a base for the extraction of oil **b** a place or opportunity for public discussion **3a** a layer (e g of leather) between the inner sole and outer sole of a shoe **b** a shoe having such a sole **4** *chiefly Br* the area next to the entrance or exit of a bus [MF *plate-forme* diagram, map, lit., flat form]

**platform balance** *n* PLATFORM SCALE

**platform scale** *n* a weighing machine with a flat platform on which objects are weighed

**platin-, platino-** *comb form* platinum; platinum and ⟨*platino-chloride*⟩ ⟨platin*iridium*⟩ [NL *platinum*]

**platina** /'platinə, plə'teenə/ *n* platinum; *esp* crude naturally occurring platinum [Sp]

**plating** /'playting/ *n* **1** the act or process of plating **2a** a coating of metal plates **b** a thin coating of metal

**platinic** /plə'tinik/ *adj* of or containing platinum, esp with a VALENCY of four

**platin·ize, -ise** /'platiniez/ *vt* to coat, treat, or combine with platinum or a compound of platinum ⟨*a* ~d *electrode*⟩ – **platinization** *n*

**platinoid** /'platinoyd/ *n* an alloy of copper, nickel, and zinc having a high degree of resistance to the passage of an electric current

**platinous** /'platinəs/ *adj* of or containing platinum, esp with a VALENCY of two

**platinum** /'platinəm/ *n* **1** a heavy precious silvery-white metallic chemical element that is soft and easily worked, has a high melting point, and is extremely resistant to corrosion, and that is used esp as a catalyst to speed up the rate of chemical reactions and for jewellery **2** a light metallic-grey colour [NL, fr Sp *platina*, fr dim. of *plata* silver – more at PLATE] – **platinum** *adj*

**platinum black** *n* a soft dull black powdered form of platinum used as a catalyst to speed up the rate of chemical reactions

**platinum blond** *n* a pale silvery-blond colour that in human hair is usu produced by bleach and a bluish rinse; *also* a person having hair of this colour

**platinum blonde** *n* PLATINUM BLOND; *also* a person, esp a woman, with hair of this colour

**platitude** /'platityoohd/ *n* **1** being dull or insipid; triteness **2** a banal, trite, or stale remark, esp when presented as if it were original and significant [Fr, fr *plat* flat, dull]

**platitudinal** /,plati'tyoohdinl/ *adj* platitudinous

**platitudinarian** /,plati,tyoohdi'neəriən/ *n* a person who is in the habit of using platitudes

**platitudin·ize, -ise** /,plati'tyoohdiniez/ *vi* to utter platitudes [*platitudin*ous + *-ize*]

**platitudinous** /-nəs/ *adj* having the characteristics of a platitude; full of platitudes ⟨~ *remarks*⟩ [*platitude* + *-inous* (as in *multitudin*ous)] – **platitudinously** *adv*

**platonic** /plə'tonik/ *adj* **1** *cap* (characteristic) of Plato or Platonism **2** of or being a close relationship between two people in which sexual desire is absent or has been repressed or sublimated **b** nominal, theoretical [L *platonicus*, fr Gk *platōnikos*, fr *Platōn* Plato †347 BC Gk philosopher] – **platonically** *adv*

**platonic love** *n*, *often cap P* love conceived by Plato as ascending from feeling for the individual to contemplation of the universal and ideal

**Platonic solid** *n* REGULAR SOLID (having all faces equal)

**Platonism** /'playtə,niz(ə)m/ *n* the philosophy of Plato stressing that actual things and ideas (e g of truth or beauty) are mere copies of transcendent ideas which are the objects of true knowledge – **Platonist** *n*, **Platonistic** *adj*

**platoon** /plə'toohn/ *n taking sing or pl vb* **1** a subdivision of a military company normally consisting of two or more sections or squads **2** a group of people sharing a common characteristic or activity ⟨*a ~ of waiters*⟩ [Fr *peloton* small detachment, lit., ball, fr *pelote* little ball – more at PELLET]

**Plattdeutsch** /'plat,doych/, ,plaht-/ *n* a colloquial language of N Germany comprising several LOW GERMAN dialects [Ger, fr D *Platduitsch*, lit., Low German, fr *plat* flat, low + *duitsch* German]

**platteland** /'plutə,lunt/ *n*, *SAfr* BACKVELD (rural areas) [Afrik, fr D, lit., flatland]

**platter** /'platə/ *n* **1a** a large often oval plate used esp for serving meat **b** a main course on a plate; PLATE **8a 2** *NAm* a gramophone record [ME *plater*, fr AF, fr MF *plat* plate] – **platterful** *n*

**platy** /'playti/ *adj* resembling a plate; *also* consisting of plates or flaky layers – used chiefly of soil, rock, or mineral formations

**platyhelminth** /,plati'helminth/ *n* any of a PHYLUM (Platyhelminthes) of soft-bodied flatworms (e g the planarians, flukes, and tapeworms) [deriv of Gk *platys* broad, flat + *helminth-*, *helmis* worm – more at HELMINTH] – **platyhelminthic** *adj*

**platypus** /'platipəs/ *n*, *pl* **platypuses** *also* **platypi** /-pi, -pie/ a small primitive aquatic egg-laying mammal (*Ornithorhynchus anatinus*) of Australia and Tasmania, that has a fleshy bill resembling that of a duck, dense fur, webbed feet, and a broad flattened tail – called also DUCKBILLED PLATYPUS [NL, fr Gk *platypous* flat-footed, fr *platys* broad, flat + *pous* foot – more at PLACE, FOOT]

**platyrrhine** /'platirien/ *adj* of or being any of a division (Platyrrhina) of American monkeys characterized by having nostrils far apart and 36 teeth – compare CATARRHINE [NL *Platyrrhina*, group name, fr Gk *platyrrhin-*, *platyrrhis* broadnosed, fr *platys* + *rhin-*, *rhis* nose] – **platyrrhiny** *n*

**plaudit** /'plawdit/ *n* **1** an act or round of applause **2 plaudits** *pl*, **plaudit** enthusiastic approval ⟨*received the ~s of the critics*⟩ [L *plaudite* applaud, pl imper of *plaudere* to applaud]

**plausibility** /,plawzə'biləti/ *n* **1** being plausible **2** something plausible

**plausible** /'plawzəbl/ *adj* **1** apparently fair, reasonable, or valid but often specious ⟨*a ~ pretext*⟩ **2** superficially pleasing or persuasive ⟨*a swindler . . . , then a quack, then a smooth, ~ gentleman* – R W Emerson⟩ **3** appearing worthy of belief; convincing ⟨*his argument was both powerful and ~*⟩ [L *plausibilis* worthy of applause, fr *plausus*, pp of *plaudere* to applaud] – **plausibleness** *n*, **plausibly** *adv*

**¹play** /play/ *n* **1a** the conduct, course, or action of a game **b** a particular act or manoeuvre in a game (e g the action in which a baseball batter is put out) **c** the action in which cards are played after bidding in a card game **d** the moving of a piece in a board game (e g chess) **2a** recreational activity; *esp* the spontaneous activity of children **b** absence of serious or harmful intent; jest ⟨*said it in ~*⟩ **c** the act or an instance of playing on words or speech sounds **d** gaming, gambling **3a** operation, activity ⟨*bringing other forces into ~*⟩ **b** light, quick, transitory, or fitful movement ⟨*the gem presented a dazzling ~ of colours*⟩ ⟨*the ~ of sunlight and shadows through the trees*⟩ **c** free or unimpeded motion (e g of a part of a machine); *also* the length or measure of such motion ⟨*give the rope more ~*⟩ **d** scope or opportunity for action **4a** the dramatized representation of an action or story on stage **b** a script for a play; a dramatic composition **5** *chiefly NAm* **5a** an act, way, or manner of proceeding; a manoeuvre ⟨*that was a ~ to get your fingerprints* – Erle Stanley Gardner⟩ **b** a move or series of moves calculated to arouse friendly feelings – usu + *make* ⟨*made a big ~ for the blonde*⟩ [ME, fr OE *plega*; akin to OE *plegan* to play, MD *pleyen*] – **in/into play 1** in/into a condition or position to be legitimately played ⟨*the ball was in play*⟩ **2** in/into operation or consideration – **out of play** not IN PLAY

**²play** *vi* **1a** to engage in sport or recreation **b(1)** to behave aimlessly; toy, trifle ⟨*don't ~ with your food*⟩ **b(2)** to deal or behave frivolously, mockingly, or playfully – often + *around* or *about* ⟨*be serious, and stop ~ing with me*⟩ **b(3)** to deal in a light speculative manner ⟨*liked to ~ with ideas*⟩ **b(4)** to make use of double meaning or of the similarity of sound of two words for stylistic or humorous effect – usu in *play on words* **2a** to take advantage ⟨*~ing on fears*⟩ **b** to move or operate in a lively,

irregular, or intermittent manner ⟨*watch the light ~ing on the water*⟩ ⟨*a faint smile ~s on her lips*⟩ **c** to move or function freely within prescribed limits ⟨*a piston rod ~s within cylinders*⟩ **d** to discharge, eject, or fire repeatedly or so as to make a stream ⟨*hoses ~ing on a fire*⟩ **3a(1)** to perform music ⟨*~ on a violin*⟩ **a(2)** to sound in performance ⟨*the organ is ~ing*⟩ **a(3)** to reproduce or emit (recorded) sounds ⟨*his radio is ~ing*⟩ **b(1)** to act in a dramatic production **b(2)** to be presented at a place of entertainment (e g a theatre) **c** to be suitable for dramatic performance **d** to act with special consideration so as to gain favour, approval, or sympathy – usu + *up to* **4a** to engage or take part in a game **b** to perform (e g in a sport) in a specified manner or position ⟨*the fullbacks are ~ing deep*⟩ **c** to play a card or move a piece during one's turn in a game **d** to gamble **e(1)** to behave or conduct oneself in a specified way ⟨*~ safe*⟩ ⟨*the pitch will ~ well*⟩ **e(2)** to feign a specified state or quality ⟨*~ dead*⟩ **e(3)** to take part in or assent to some activity; co-operate ⟨*~ along with his scheme*⟩ **e(4)** to act so as to prove advantageous to another – chiefly in *play into the hands of* **5** *euph* to have sexual relations; *esp* to have promiscuous or illicit sexual relations – chiefly in *play around* ~ *vt* **1a(1)** to engage in or occupy oneself with ⟨*~ football*⟩ **a(2)** to engage in as if in a game **a(3)** to deal with, handle, or manage ⟨*decided to ~ the dispute another way*⟩ – often + *it* ⟨*trying to ~ it cool*⟩ **a(4)** to exploit, manipulate ⟨*~ the stock market*⟩ **b** to pretend to engage in ⟨*children ~ing cops and robbers*⟩ **c(1)** to perform or execute for amusement or to deceive or mock ⟨*~ a trick*⟩ **c(2)** to wreak ⟨*~ havoc*⟩ **2a(1)** to put on a performance of (a play) **a(2)** to act in the character or part of **a(3)** to act or perform in ⟨*~ed leading theatres*⟩ **b** to perform or act the part of ⟨*~ the fool*⟩ **3a(1)** to contend against in a game **a(2)** to use as a contestant in a game ⟨*the selectors did not ~ him*⟩ **a(3)** to perform the duties associated with (a certain position) ⟨*~ed fullback*⟩ **b(1)** to make bets on ⟨*~ the horses*⟩ **b(2)** to operate on the basis of ⟨*~ a hunch*⟩ **c** to put into action in a game; *esp* to remove (a playing card) from one's hand and place usu face up on a table in one's turn either as part of a scoring combination or as one's contribution to a trick **d** to catch or pick up (a batted ball); field ⟨*~ed the ball bare-handed*⟩ **e** to direct the course of (e g a ball); hit ⟨*~ed a wedge shot to the green*⟩; *also* to cause (a ball or puck) to rebound ⟨*~ed the ball off the backboard*⟩ **4a** to perform (music) on an instrument ⟨*~ a waltz*⟩ **b** to perform music on ⟨*~ the violin*⟩ **c** to perform music of (a specified composer) **d(1)** to cause (e g a radio or tape recorder) to emit sounds **d(2)** to cause the recorded sounds of (e g a record or a MAGNETIC TAPE) to be reproduced **5a** to discharge, fire, or set off with continuous effect ⟨*~ed the hose on the burning building*⟩ **b** to cause to move or operate lightly and irregularly or intermittently ⟨*~ed her torch along the fence*⟩ **c** to allow (a hooked fish) to become exhausted by pulling against a line – **playable** *adj*, **playability** *n* – **play with oneself** to masturbate – **to play with** at one's disposal ⟨*a lot of funds to play with*⟩ – see also **play** BALL/**by** EAR/FAST **and** LOOSE/**second** FIDDLE/**the** FIELD/**with** FIRE/**to the** GALLERY/**the** GAME/**into the** HANDS **of**/HOOKY/**a** PART/POLITICS/**the old** SOLDIER/**for** TIME/TRUANT

**play back** *vt* to listen to or look at material on (a usu recently recorded disc or tape)

**play down** *vt* to cause to seem less important; minimize – compare PLAY UP

**play off** *vt* **1** to decide the winner of (a competition or match) or break (a tie) by a play-off **2** to set in opposition for one's own gain ⟨*survived by* playing *his enemies* off *against each other*⟩

**play on** *vi*, *of a batsman in cricket* to hit the ball into one's own wicket

**play out** *vt* **1** to finish; USE UP **2** to unreel, unfold ⟨play out *a length of rope*⟩

**play up** *vt* **1** to give special emphasis or prominence to ⟨*the press* played up *the divorce story*⟩ **2** *Br* to cause pain or distress to ⟨*my corns have been* playing *me up again*⟩ ~ *vi* to behave in a disobedient or annoying manner; ACT UP

**playa** /'plah·yə/ *n* the flat bottom of an undrained desert basin that becomes at times a shallow lake [Sp, lit., beach]

**playact** /'play,akt/ *vi* **1a** to take part in theatrical performances, esp as a professional **b** to make believe; pretend **2** to behave in a misleading or insincere manner ~ *vt* to dramatize; ACT OUT **1a** [back-formation fr *playacting*]

**playback** /-,bak/ *n* **1** the action of reproducing recorded sound or pictures, often immediately after recording **2** a device enabling one to play back recorded material

**playback head** *n* a tape-recorder head used for playing back – compare HEAD 19b

**playbill** /'play,bil/ *n* a poster advertising a play

**playboy** /-,boy/ *n* a usu rich man who lives a life devoted chiefly to the pursuit of pleasure

**played out** *adj* 1 worn out or used up 2 tired out; spent

**player** /'playə/ *n* one who or that which plays: e g **a** one who plays a game **b** a person who plays a musical instrument **c** an actor **d** a mechanical device for automatically playing a musical instrument (e g a piano)

**player piano** /'playə/ *n* a piano containing a mechanical piano player

**playfellow** /-,feloh/ *n* a playmate

**playful** /-f(ə)l/ *adj* 1 inclined to play; frolicsome, sportive ⟨*a* ~ *kitten*⟩ 2 humorous, jocular ⟨*the* ~ *tone of his voice*⟩ – **playfully** *adv*, **playfulness** *n*

**playgoer** /'play,goh-ə/ *n* one who frequently attends plays

**playground** /-,grownd/ *n* 1 a piece of land, often next to a school or in a public park, that is set aside for children to play on 2 an area favoured for amusement or recreation, esp as giving scope for a specified activity ⟨*that town was a gambling* ~⟩ ⟨*a climber's* ~⟩

**playgroup** /-,groohp/ *n, chiefly Br* a supervised group of children below school age who play together regularly

**playhouse** /-,hows/ *n* 1 a theatre 2 *chiefly NAm* WENDY HOUSE

**playing card** /'playing/ *n* any of a set of usu 52 thin rectangular pieces of cardboard or plastic that are identical on one side and marked on the other to show one of 13 ranks in one of 4 suits, and are used in playing any of numerous games

**playing field** *n*, **playing fields** *n pl* a field that is used for playing organized games and is often divided into several separate pitches

**playlet** /'playlit/ *n* a short play

**playlist** /'play,list/ *n* a list of records to be played on a radio programme

**playmate** /-,mayt/ *n* a companion in play

**'play-,off** *n* a final sports contest or series of contests (e g between teams or contestants that have drawn or tied) to determine a winner

**play on words** *n* a pun

**playpen** /-,pen/ *n* a portable usu collapsible enclosure in which a baby or young child may play safely

**playroom** /'play,roohm, -room/ *n* a room set aside for children to play in

**playschool** /'play,skoohl/ *n, chiefly Br* NURSERY SCHOOL – not used technically

**playsuit** /-,s(y)ooht/ *n* a garment, esp dungarees, for children to play in

**,play-the-'ball** *n* the method in RUGBY LEAGUE of restarting play after a tackle by allowing the tackled player to heel the ball back to a teammate

**plaything** /-,thing/ *n* 1 a toy 2 a person treated as lightly and carelessly as a toy ⟨*are men the* ~*s of fate?*⟩

**playtime** /'play,tiem/ *n* a time for play or recreation, esp for children

**playwright** /-,riet/ *n* a writer of plays [¹*play* + obs *wright* maker – more at WRIGHT]

**plaza** /'plahzə/ *n* a public square in a city or town [Sp, fr L *platea* broad street – more at PLACE]

**plea** /plee/ *n* 1a an allegation made by someone in support of his/her case in a court of law **b** an accused person's answer to a charge or indictment ⟨*a* ~ *of guilty*⟩ 2 something offered by way of excuse or justification ⟨*she left early with the* ~ *of a headache*⟩ 3 an earnest entreaty or appeal ⟨*their* ~ *for understanding must be answered*⟩ 4 *archaic* a legal suit or action ⟨*Court of Common Pleas*⟩ **synonyms** see ²EXCUSE [ME *plaid, plai*, fr OF *plait, plaid*, fr ML *placitum*, fr L, decision, decree, fr neut of *placitus*, pp of *placēre* to please, be decided – more at PLEASE]

**plea bargaining** *n* the pleading of guilty, by agreement with the prosecutor, to a lesser charge in exchange for the modification of or dropping of part of a more serious charge – **plea bargain** *vi*

**pleach** /pleech/ *vt* to interlace, entwine ⟨~*ed hedge*⟩ [ME *plechen*, fr ONF *plechier*, fr L *plexus*, pp of *plectere* to entwine, braid – more at PLY]

**plead** /pleed/ *vb* **pleaded, pled** /pled/ *vi* 1 to argue a case as an advocate in court 2a to make an allegation in an action or other legal proceeding; *esp* to answer the previous pleading of the other party by denying facts stated in it or by alleging new facts **b** *of an advocate* to address a court 3 to make a plea of a specified nature in answer to a legal charge ⟨~ *not guilty*⟩ 4a to urge reasons for or against something **b** to entreat, appeal, or implore earnestly ⟨~*ed with him not to go*⟩ ~ *vt* 1 to maintain (e g a case) in court 2 to allege as a legal plea ⟨*it does no good to* ~ *ignorance*⟩ 3 to offer as a plea usu in defence, apology, or excuse ⟨*sorry I'm late – I* ~ *pressure of work and flat tyres*⟩ [ME *plaiden* to institute a lawsuit, fr OF *plaidier*, fr *plaid* plea] – **pleadable** *adj*, **pleader** *n*, **pleadingly** *adv*

    **usage** In strict legal use, one **pleads** *guilty* or *not guilty*, but does not **plead** *innocent*.

**pleading** /'pleeding/ *n* 1 advocacy of a case in a court of law 2 any of the formal usu written allegations and counter allegations made alternately by the parties in a legal action or proceeding 3 (the act of making) an earnest request ⟨*her* ~*s went unnoticed*⟩

**pleasance** /'plez(ə)ns/ *n* 1 a quiet area of a garden attached to a great house; *broadly, archaic* a place for rest or recreation 2 *archaic* a feeling of pleasure; delight

**pleasant** /'plez(ə)nt/ *adj* 1 having qualities that tend to give pleasure; agreeable ⟨*a* ~ *surprise*⟩ ⟨*a* ~ *day*⟩ 2 having pleasing manners, behaviour, or appearance ⟨*a* ~ *person*⟩ ⟨*you might at least have tried to be* ~ *to my mother*⟩ [ME *plesaunt*, fr MF *plaisant*, fr prp of *plaisir* to please] – **pleasantly** *adv*, **pleasantness** *n*

**pleasantry** /'plez(ə)ntri/ *n* 1 an agreeable remark made esp in order to be polite ⟨*exchanged the usual* pleasantries⟩ 2 a humorous act or remark; a little joke △ pleasantness

**please** /pleez/ *vi* 1 to afford or give pleasure or satisfaction ⟨*he is eager to* ~⟩ ⟨*we try to* ~⟩ 2 to like, wish, choose ⟨*do as you* ~⟩ ⟨*stay as long as you* ~⟩ 3 to be willing – usu imper; used (1) to express a polite request ⟨*coffee,* ~⟩ ⟨~ *come in*⟩ (2) to turn an apparent question into a request ⟨*can you shut it,* ~?⟩ (3) to express polite acceptance ⟨*more tea? Please!*⟩ (4) to make polite a request for attention ⟨~, *Sir, I don't understand*⟩ 4 *archaic* to have the kindness ⟨*will you* ~ *to enter the carriage* – Charles Dickens⟩ ~ *vt* 1 to give pleasure or satisfaction to; gratify ⟨*nothing ever* ~*s him*⟩ 2 *formal* to be the will or pleasure of ⟨*may it* ~ *your Majesty*⟩ [ME *plesen*, fr MF *plaisir*, fr L *placēre*; akin to L *placare* to placate, OE *flōh* flat stone, Gk *plak-, plax* flat surface] – **if you please** – used to indicate surprise or indignation ⟨*and then, if you please, he had the cheek to ask for his money back*⟩ – **please oneself** to do as one likes; follow one's own desires

**pleasing** /'pleezing/ *adj* giving pleasure; agreeable ⟨*he found the sun's warmth* ~⟩ – **pleasingly** *adv*, **pleasingness** *n*

**pleasurable** /'plezh(ə)rəbl/ *adj* pleasant, enjoyable – **pleasurableness** *n*, **pleasurably** *adv*, **pleasurability** *n*

**¹pleasure** /'plezh-ə/ *n* 1a a state or feeling of happiness or satisfaction ⟨*have great* ~ *in opening this new supermarket*⟩ **b** a source of happiness or satisfaction ⟨*it's always a* ~ *to see her*⟩ 2a frivolous or sensual gratification ⟨*a life of* ~⟩ **b** enjoyment, recreation ⟨*are you here on business or for* ~?⟩ 3 *archaic or formal* desire, inclination ⟨*wait upon his* ~ – Shak⟩ [ME *plesure*, alter. of *plesir*, fr MF *plaisir*, fr *plaisir* to please]

    **synonyms** Pleasure, delight, joy, delectation, enjoyment: **pleasure** is the most general and least forceful term ⟨*the* **pleasure** *of your company*⟩. **Delight** suggests a keener and an evident **pleasure**, which is often fleeting, and may take one by surprise ⟨*her suggestion was greeted with* **delight**⟩. **Joy** suggests a deeper, more lasting and intensely felt **delight**, and is frequently linked with spiritual happiness or pureminded pleasures ⟨*and all its aching* **joys** *are now no more, and all its dizzy raptures* – W Wordsworth⟩. **Delectation** and **enjoyment** both stress the reaction to pleasure rather than conveying a feeling. **Enjoyment** suggests the conscious savouring of what pleases one, while **delectation** stresses rather the provision of entertainment or amusement ⟨*derived much* **enjoyment** *from his books*⟩ ⟨*read a few passages for the* **delectation** *of his guests*⟩. Compare JOYFUL **antonyms** pain, sorrow, suffering **usage** The idea of "I am glad to do this" is correctly expressed by ⟨*I have the* **pleasure** *of* . . .⟩ or ⟨*I have* **pleasure** *in* . . .⟩; one can reply politely, when thanked ⟨*it's a* **pleasure**⟩ or ⟨*my* **pleasure**⟩. But since **pleasure** may be understood to mean "wish" or "desire", it can sound somewhat imperious to say ⟨*it is my* **pleasure** *to* . . .⟩ though one could properly ask ⟨*is it your* **pleasure** *that I sign the agenda as correct?*⟩

**²pleasure** *vt, archaic* to give (sexual) pleasure to

**pleasure principle** *n* a tendency postulated by psychoanalytic theory: an individual's behaviour is directed towards immediate satisfaction of instinctual drives and immediate relief from pain or discomfort

**¹pleat** /pleet/ *vt* to fold; *esp* to arrange in pleats ⟨~ *a skirt*⟩ [ME *pleten*, fr *pleit*, *plete* plait] – **pleater** *n*

**²pleat** *n* a flattened fold in cloth made by doubling material over on itself and usu securing it at the top; *also* something resembling such a fold ⟨*paper* ~s⟩ [ME *plete*] – **pleated** *adj*, **pleatless** *adj*

**pleb** /pleb/ *n, chiefly derog* a plebeian – **pleb** *adj*

**plebby** /'plebi/ *adj, chiefly Br informal* PLEBEIAN 2

**plebe** /pleeb/ *n, NAm informal* a new recruit at a US military or naval academy [short for *plebeian*]

**¹plebeian** /pli'bee·ən/ *n* 1 a member of the ancient Roman plebs 2 a member of the common people [L *plebeius* of the common people, fr *plebs* common people; akin to Gk *plēthos* throng, *plēthein* to be full – more at FULL] – **plebeianism** *n*

**²plebeian** *adj* 1 of plebeians 2 crude or coarse in manner or style; common – **plebeianly** *adv*

**plebiscite** /'plebi‚siet/ *n* a vote by which the people of an entire country or district express an opinion for or against a proposal, esp on a choice of government or ruler [Fr *plébiscite*, fr L *plebis scitum* law voted by the comitia, lit., decree of the common people] – **plebiscitary** *adj*

**plebs** /plebz/ *n, pl* **plebes** /'pleebeez/ the common people of ancient Rome [L]

**plecopteran** /pli'koptərən/ *n* STONEFLY [NL *Plecoptera*, group name, fr Gk *plekein* to braid + *pteron* wing – more at FEATHER] – **plecopteran** *adj*

**plectognath** /'plektognath/ *n* any of an order (Plectognathi) of BONY FISHES (e g a filefish) that usu have the body covered with bony plates or spines [deriv of Gk *plektos* twisted (fr *plekein* to braid) + *gnathos* jaw – more at PLY, GNATH-] – **plectognath** *adj*

**plectrum** /'plektrəm/ *n, pl* **plectra** /-trə/, **plectrums** a small thin piece of plastic, metal, etc used to pluck the strings of a stringed instrument (e g a guitar, lute, or zither) [L, fr Gk *plēktron*, fr *plēssein* to strike – more at PLAINT]

**pled** /pled/ *past of* PLEAD

**¹pledge** /plej/ *n* 1 something that is delivered by one person to another as security for an obligation (e g a debt or an undertaking of action) and that is liable to forfeiture in case of failure 2 the state of being held as a security or guarantee ⟨*his watch is in* ~⟩ 3 a token or sign of something else (e g love or favour) 4 TOAST 3 5 a binding promise or agreement to do or forbear ⟨*under* ~ *of secrecy*⟩ [ME, security, fr MF *plege*, fr LL *plebium*, fr (assumed) LL *plebere* to pledge] – **sign/take the pledge** to make a solemn undertaking to abstain from alcoholic drink

**²pledge** *vt* 1 to make a pledge of; *specif* to deposit as security for fulfilment of a contract or obligation 2 to drink the health of 3 to bind by a pledge 4 to give a promise of ⟨*to* ~ *allegiance to the flag*⟩ – **pledger**, **pledgor** *n*

**pledgee** /ple'jee/ *n* a person to whom a pledge is given

**pledget** /'plejit/ *n* a compress or pad used to apply medication or absorb discharges (e g from a wound) [origin unknown]

**-plegia** /-'pleeji·ə/ *comb form* (→ *n*) paralysis ⟨*hemi*plegia⟩ [NL, fr Gk *-plēgia*, fr *plēssein* to strike]

**pleiad** /'plie·əd/ *n* a group of usu seven illustrious or brilliant people or things [Fr *Pléiade*, group of 7 16th-c Fr poets, fr MF, group of 7 poets of ancient Alexandria, fr Gk *Pleiad-*, *Pleias*, fr sing. of *Pleiades*]

**Pleiades** /'plie·ə‚deez/ *n pl* a conspicuous cluster of stars in the constellation Taurus that includes seven stars visible to the average naked eye [L, fr Gk]

**plein air** /‚playn 'eə (Fr plɛn ɛr)/ *adj* of or being painting done out of doors which attempts to capture the atmospheric effects of outdoor daylight – used esp of the French Impressionists [Fr, open air] – **pleinairist** *n*

**pleio-, pleo-, plio-** *comb form* more ⟨pleio*tropic*⟩ ⟨*Plio*cene⟩ [Gk *pleiōn, pleōn* – more at PLUS]

**pleiotaxy** /'plie·ə‚taksi/ *n* development of more than the normal number of WHORLS (circular arrangement of similar flower parts round the stem) of petals, SEPALS, etc [ISV]

**pleiotropic** /‚plie·ə'trohpik, -'tropik/ *adj, of a gene* having more than one effect on the PHENOTYPE (organism's visible characteristics) (e g affecting several organ systems at once) – **pleiotropically** *adv*, **pleiotropy** *n*

**Pleistocene** /'pliestə‚seen, -stoh-/ *adj or n* (of or being) the earlier epoch of the QUATERNARY or its system of rocks [Gk *pleistos* most (akin to Gk *pleiōn* more) + ISV *-cene*]

**plenary** /'pleenəri/ *adj* 1 complete in every respect; absolute,

unqualified ⟨~ *power*⟩ 2 fully attended or constituted by all entitled to be present ⟨*a* ~ *session*⟩ [LL *plenarius*, fr L *plenus* full – more at FULL]

**plenary indulgence** *n* a remission of the entire temporal punishment for sin

**plenipotentiary** /‚plenipə'tensh(ə)ri/ *n or adj* (a person, esp a diplomatic agent) invested with full power to transact business ⟨*Ambassador Extraordinary and* Plenipotentiary⟩ [ML *plenipotentiarius*, deriv of LL *plenipotent-, plenipotens* having or conferring full power, fr L *plenus* full + *potent-, potens* powerful]

**plenitude** /'plenityoohd/ *n, formal* 1 the quality or state of being full; completeness 2 a great sufficiency; abundance [ME, fr MF or L; MF, fr L *plenitudo*, fr *plenus* full]

**plenteous** /'plentyəs/ *adj, formal or poetic* 1 fruitful, productive ⟨*a* ~ *harvest*⟩ – usu + in or of ⟨*the seasons had been* ~ *in corn* – George Eliot⟩ 2 plentiful ⟨~ *grace with thee is found* – Charles Wesley⟩ **synonyms** see PLENTIFUL [ME *plentevous, plenteous*, fr OF *plentiveus*, fr *plentif* abundant, fr *plenté* plenty] – **plenteously** *adv*, **plenteousness** *n*

**plentiful** /'plentif(ə)l/ *adj* 1 containing or yielding plenty ⟨*a* ~ *land*⟩ 2 characterized by, constituting, or existing in plenty – **plentifully** *adv*, **plentifulness** *n*

**synonyms** Plentiful, plenteous, ample, abundant, and copious may all suggest "more than enough, but not too much". Plentiful is generally used with concrete things, and suggests a comparison with a need or demand ⟨plentiful *food and drink*⟩ ⟨*a* plentiful *supply of matches*⟩. Plenteous is a poetic or formal synonym for plentiful. Ample suggests something between *enough* and plentiful; it often implies a generous supply for a particular need ⟨ample *reward for all her trouble*⟩ ⟨ample *room for one, but not for two*⟩. Abundant is usually preferred to plentiful to describe abstracts ⟨abundant *praise*⟩. With concrete objects, it describes natural rather than man-made things ⟨abundant *vegetation*⟩. Copious suggests abundant flow or volume ⟨copious *tears*⟩ ⟨*a* copious *vocabulary*⟩. Otherwise it is linked with such expressions as *supply of* or *store of* to suggest great abundance ⟨*a* copious *crop of tomatoes*⟩. Compare PROFUSE **antonyms** scarce, scanty, few

**¹plenty** /'plenti/ *n* 1a a full or more than adequate amount or supply ⟨*had* ~ *of time to finish the job*⟩ ⟨*there's* ~ *more*⟩ b a large number or amount ⟨*he's in* ~ *of trouble*⟩ 2 the quality or state of being copious; plentifulness ⟨*years of* ~⟩ [ME *plente*, fr OF *plenté*, fr LL *plenitat-, plenitas*, fr L, fullness, fr *plenus* full – more at FULL]

**²plenty** *adj, chiefly archaic, dial Scot, or NAm informal* plentiful in amount, number, or supply; ample ⟨~ *midges on the moor*⟩ ⟨~ *work to be done* – *Time*⟩

**³plenty** *adv, informal* 1 quite, abundantly ⟨~ *warm enough*⟩ 2 *chiefly NAm* to a considerable or extreme degree; very ⟨~ *hungry*⟩

**plenum** /'pleenəm/ *n, pl* **plenums, plena** /-nə/ 1a a space or all space every part of which is full of matter b a condition in which the pressure of the air in an enclosed space is greater than that of the outside atmosphere; *also* an enclosed space in which this condition exists 2 a general assembly of all members of a body, esp a legislative body [NL, fr L, neut of *plenus* full]

**pleochroism** /plee'okroh‚iz(ə)m/ *n* the property of a crystal of showing different colours when viewed by light that has been POLARIZED so as to vibrate parallel to three different axes – compare DICHROISM [ISV *pleochroic* (fr *pleio-* + Gk *chrōs* skin, colour) + *-ism* – more at GRIT] – **pleochroic** *adj*

**pleomorphism** /‚plee·oh'maw‚fiz(ə)m/ *n* 1 the occurrence of more than one distinct form in the life cycle of a plant 2 the quality or state of having or assuming various forms; polymorphism [ISV] – **pleomorphic** *adj*

**pleon** /'plee·on/ *n* the abdomen of a shrimp, crab, lobster, etc [NL, fr Gk *pleōn*, prp of *plein* to sail, float – more at FLOW; fr its bearing the swimming limbs]

**pleonasm** /'plee·ə‚naz(ə)m/ *n* the use of more words than are necessary to convey the intended sense (e g in *the man he said*); redundancy; *also* an instance of this [LL *pleonasmus*, fr Gk *pleonasmos*, fr *pleonazein* to be excessive, fr *pleiōn, pleōn* more – more at PLUS] – **pleonastic** *adj*, **pleonastically** *adv*

**pleophagous** /pli'ofəgəs/ *adj* 1 eating a variety of foods; polyphagous 2 *of a parasite* not restricted to a single kind of HOST (organism harbouring a parasite)

**pleopod** /'plee·ə‚pod/ *n* an abdominal limb of a shrimp, crab, lobster, etc [Gk *plein* to sail, float + E *-o-* + *-pod*; fr its use in swimming]

**plerocercoid** /‚pliəroh'suhkoyd/ *n* the solid elongated infective larva of some tapeworms that is usu parasitic in the muscles of fishes [Gk *plērēs* full + *kerkos* tail – more at FULL]

**plesiosaur** /'pleesi·ə,saw/ *n* any of a suborder (Plesiosauria) of extinct marine reptiles of the MESOZOIC period that had flattened bodies and limbs modified into paddles [deriv of Gk *plēsios* close (fr *pelas* near) + *sauros* lizard – more at FELT]

**plethora** /'plethərə/ *n* **1** an abnormal condition in which there is an excess of blood in the body – not now used technically **2** an excess, superfluity ⟨*a ~ of regulations*⟩ [ML, fr Gk *plēthōra*, lit., fullness, fr *plēthein* to be full – more at FULL] – **plethoric** *adj*

**plethysmogram** /plə'thizməgram, pleth-/ *n* a tracing made by a plethysmograph

**plethysmograph** /plə'thizmə,grahf, pleth-, -,graf/ *n* a medical instrument for determining and registering variations in the size of an organ or limb and in the amount of blood present or passing through it [ISV, fr Gk *plēthysmos* increase, fr *plēthynein* to increase, fr *plēthys* mass, quantity, fr *plēthein* to be full] – **plethysmographic** *adj*, **plethysmographically** *adv*, **plethysmography** *n*

**pleur-** /plooər-/, **pleuro-** *comb form* **1a** pleura ⟨*pleuropneumonia*⟩; pleura and ⟨*pleuroperitoneum*⟩ **b** pleural and ⟨*pleurocerebral*⟩ **2** side, lateral ⟨*pleurodont*⟩ ⟨*pleurodynia*⟩ [(1) NL, fr *pleura;* (2) Gk, fr *pleura*]

**pleura** /'plooərə/ *n*, *pl* **pleurae** /-rie/, **pleuras** either of the two delicate SEROUS MEMBRANES (membranes that secrete watery fluid) that lines each half of the chest cavity of mammals and birds and is folded back over the surface of the lung of the same side [Gk, rib, side] – **pleural** *adj*

**pleurisy** /'plooərəsi/ *n* inflammation of the pleura, usu accompanied by fever, painful and difficult breathing, coughing, and oozing of liquid into the pleural cavity [ME *pluresie*, fr MF *pleuresie*, fr LL *pleurisis*, alter. of L *pleuritis*, fr Gk, fr *pleura* side] – **pleuritic** *adj*

**pleurodont** /'plooəroh,dont/ *adj*, *of a tooth* consolidated with the inner surface of the jaw (e g in a lizard) and not implanted in a socket; *also, of an animal* having pleurodont teeth – compare ACRODONT [Gk *pleura* side + ISV *-odont*]

**pleuron** /'plooəron/ *n* a side part of a segment in the middle region (THORAX) of an insect [NL, fr Gk, rib, side]

**pleuroperitoneum** /,plooəroh·peritə'nee·əm/ *n* the membrane lining the body cavity and covering the surface of the enclosed organs of VERTEBRATE animals (e g fish) that have no diaphragm [NL]

**pleuropneumonia** /,plooərohnyooh'mohnyə, -ni·ə/ *n* **1** combined inflammation of the pleura and lungs **2** a short-lived feverish and often fatal respiratory disorder of bovine animals, esp cattle caused by MYCOPLASMAS (minute bacterialike organisms) [NL]

**pleuston** /'ploohston, -stən/ *n* free-floating living organisms forming a matlike layer on or near the surface of a body of fresh water [(assumed) Gk *pleustos* (verbal of *plein* to sail, float) + ISV *-on* (as in *plankton*)] – **pleustonic** *adj*

**plexiform** /'pleksifawm/ *adj* of, being, or having the form or characteristics of a plexus [NL *plex*us + E *-iform*]

**Plexiglas** /'pleksi,glahs/ *trademark* – used for plastic sheets and moulding powders

**plexor** /'plexə/ *n* a small rubber-headed hammer used for testing reflexes and PERCUSSING (tapping) the chest to aid medical diagnosis [NL, fr Gk *plēxis* stroke, fr *plēssein* to strike]

**plexus** /'pleksəs/ *n* **1** a network of interlacing blood vessels or nerves **2** an interwoven combination of parts or elements in a structure or system [NL, fr L, braid, network, fr *plexus*, pp of *plectere* to braid – more at PLY]

**pliable** /'plie·əbl/ *adj* **1a** supple enough to bend easily or repeatedly without breaking; flexible **b** yielding readily to the wishes or commands of others; compliant **2** adjustable to varying conditions; adaptable *synonyms* see [1]PLASTIC *antonym* obstinate [ME, fr MF, fr *plier* to bend, fold – more at PLY] – **pliableness** *n*, **pliably** *adv*, **pliability** *n*

**pliancy** /'plie·ənsi/ *n* the quality or state of being pliant

**pliant** /'plie·ənt/ *adj* **1** PLIABLE 1a **2** easily influenced; yielding *synonyms* see [1]PLASTIC – **pliantly** *adv*, **pliantness** *n*

**plica** /'pliekə/ *n*, *pl* **plicae** /'pliesie/ a fold or folded part; *esp* a groove or fold of skin [ML, fr L *plicare* to fold – more at PLY] – **plical** *adj*

**plicate** /'pliekayt/ *adj* **1** folded lengthways like a fan ⟨*a ~ leaf*⟩ **2** having the surface folded, pleated, or marked with parallel ridges ⟨*~ wing cases*⟩ [L *plicatus*, pp of *plicare*] – **plicately** *adv*, **plicateness** *n*

**plication** /pli'kaysh(ə)n, plie-/ *n* **1** the act or process of folding; the state of being folded **2** a fold

**plié** /'plee·ay/ *n* the action in ballet of bending the knees outwards while holding the back straight [Fr, fr pp of *plier* to bend]

**pliers** /'plie·əz/ *n pl* a pair of pincers with long jaws for holding small objects or for bending and cutting wire; *broadly* PINCERS 1a *synonyms* see PINCER [[1]*ply* + [2]*-er* + [1]*-s*]

[1]**plight** /pliet/ *vt*, *archaic* to put or give in pledge; engage ⟨*~ one's troth*⟩ [ME *plighten*, fr OE *plihtan* to endanger, fr *pliht* danger; akin to OHG *pflegan* to take care of] – **plighter** *n*

[2]**plight** *n* a condition; *specif* an unpleasant or difficult state; a predicament ⟨*the ~ of these poor refugees*⟩ [ME *plit*, fr AF, fr (assumed) VL *plictus* fold – more at PLAIT]

**plimsoll** /'plims(ə)l, -sol, -sohl/ *n*, *Br* a shoe with a flat rubber sole and canvas upper, worn esp for playing sports [prob fr the supposed resemblance of the upper edge of the rubber to the Plimsoll line on a ship]

**Plimsoll line** *n* a set of load-line markings on the side of a ship indicating the levels to which it may legally be loaded in various seasons and waters [Samuel *Plimsoll* †1898 E leader of shipping reform]

**Plimsoll mark** *n* PLIMSOLL LINE

**plink** /plink/ *vb or n* (to make or cause to make) a short tinkling metallic sound [imit] – **plinker** *n*

**plinth** /plinth/ *n* **1** the lowest part of the base of a column **2** a usu square block serving as a base (e g of a pedestal) **3** a course of masonry forming a continuous foundation or base [L *plinthus*, fr Gk *plinthos*]

**plio-** – see PLEIO-

**Pliocene** /'plie·oh,seen/ *adj or n* (of or being) the latest epoch of the TERTIARY period or its system of rocks

**Pliofilm** /'plie·ə,film/ *trademark* – used for a glossy membrane made of rubber and used chiefly for water-resistant and packaging materials

**plissé, plisse** /'pleesay/ *n* **1** a textile finish that consists of permanently puckered designs **2** a fabric usu of cotton, rayon, or nylon with a plissé finish [Fr *plissé*, fr pp of *plisser* to pleat, fr MF, fr *pli* fold, fr *plier* to fold – more at PLY]

**plod** /plod/ *vb* **-dd-** *vi* **1a** to walk heavily or slowly; trudge **b** to proceed slowly or tediously ⟨*the film just ~s along*⟩ **2** to work laboriously and monotonously ⟨*~ding through stacks of unanswered letters*⟩ ~ *vt* to tread slowly or heavily along or over ⟨*~ded the streets all day, looking for work*⟩ [imit] – **plod** *n*, **plodder** *n*, **ploddingly** *adv*

**-ploid** /-ployd/ *comb form* (→ *adj*) having a CHROMOSOME NUMBER that bears (such) a relationship to or is (so many) times the HAPLOID number of the reproductive cells ⟨*poly*ploid⟩ – compare -SOMIC [ISV, fr *diploid & haploid*] – **-ploid** *comb form* (→ *n*)

**ploidy** /'ploydi/ *n* degree of repetition of the HAPLOID number of unpaired CHROMOSOMES (strands of gene-carrying material) [fr such words as *diploidy*, *hexaploidy*]

[1]**plonk** /plongk/ *vt*, *informal* to plunk

[2]**plonk** *n*, *chiefly Br slang* cheap or inferior wine [short for earlier *plink-plonk*, perh modif of Fr *vin blanc* white wine]

**plonkie** /'plongki/ *n*, *slang* an alcoholic

**plop** /plop/ *vb* **-pp-** *vi* **1** to fall, drop, or move suddenly with a sound like that of something dropping into water **2** to allow one's body to drop heavily ⟨*~ped into a chair*⟩ ~ *vt* to set, drop, or throw heavily [imit] – **plop** *n*

**plosion** /'plohzh(ə)n/ *n* the release of obstructed breath that occurs in one kind of articulation of STOP consonants (e g *p* or *k*) [fr *explosion*]

[1]**plosive** /'plohsiv, -ziv/ *adj* characterized by plosion

[2]**plosive** *n* a plosive consonant; STOP 7

[1]**plot** /plot/ *n* **1** a small piece of land, esp one used or designated for a specific purpose ⟨*a vegetable ~*⟩ ⟨*a building ~*⟩ **2** the plan or main story of a literary work **3** a secret plan for accomplishing a usu evil or unlawful end; an intrigue **4** *NAm* a graphic representation (e g a chart) **5** *NAm* GROUND PLAN [ME, fr OE] – **plotless** *adj*, **plotlessness** *n*

[2]**plot** *vb* **-tt-** *vt* **1a** to make a plan or map of **b** to mark or note (a ship's position) (as if) on a map or chart **2** to lay out (land) in plots **3a** to assign a position to (a point) by means of CO-ORDINATES (numbers defining location) (e g on a graph) **b** to draw (a curve) according to the positions of plotted points **c** to represent (an equation) by means of a curve so constructed **4** to plan or contrive, esp secretly ⟨*he ~ted his revenge*⟩ **5** to invent or devise the plot of (a literary work) ~ *vi* **1** to form a plot;

scheme ⟨they ~ted to overthrow the king⟩ **2** to be located by means of coordinates ⟨the data ~ at a single point⟩

**Plotinism** /ploh'tieniz(ə)m, 'plohtiniz(ə)m/ *n* the doctrines of the NEOPLATONIC philosopher Plotinus [*Plotinus* †270 Roman philosopher] – **Plotinist** *n*

**plotter** /'plotə/ *n* **1** a person who plots **2** an instrument that produces a graphical representation of an input (e g a varying voltage)

¹**plough,** *NAm* **plow** /plow/ *n* **1a** an implement used to cut, lift, and turn over soil, esp in preparing ground for sowing **b** any of various devices operating like a plough **2** ploughed land **3** *cap* URSA MAJOR [ME, fr OE *plōh,* a unit of land; akin to OHG *pfluog* plough] – **put/set one's hand to the plough** to begin a serious or difficult task with the firm intention of completing it

²**plough,** *NAm* **plow** *vt* **1a** to turn, break up, or work (as if) with a plough **b** to make (e g a furrow) with a plough **2** to cut into, open, or make furrows or ridges in (as if) with a plough – often + *up* **3** to cleave the surface of or move through (water) ⟨whales ~ing the ocean⟩ **4** chiefly Br slang **4a** to give a failing mark to (a student), esp in a university examination **b** to fail to pass (an examination) – no longer in vogue ~ *vi* **1a** to use a plough **b** of land to bear or allow ploughing **2** to force a way, esp violently ⟨the car ~ed into a group of spectators⟩ **3** to proceed steadily and laboriously; plod ⟨had to ~ through a summer reading list⟩ **4** chiefly Br slang to fail an examination – **ploughable** *adj,* **plougher** *n*

**plough back** *vt* to reinvest (profits) in an industry

**ploughboy** /'plow,boy/ *n* one, esp a boy, who leads the team drawing a plough

**ploughhead** /'plow,hed/ *n* the CLEVIS (U-shaped fastener securing the tow bar) of a plough

**ploughman** /-mən/ *n* one who guides a plough; *broadly* a farm labourer

**ploughman's lunch** /-mənz/ *n, chiefly Br* a cold lunch consisting of bread, cheese, and usu pickled onions that is often served in a pub

**plough pan** *n* a layer of earth at the bottom of the furrow compacted by repeated ploughing at the same depth

**ploughshare** /-,sheə/ *n* the part of a plough that cuts the furrow [ME *plowghschare,* fr *plowgh* plough + *schare* ³share]

**plouter, plowter** /'plowtə/ *vi* **1** to potter **2** Scot to splash about; wade [prob imit]

**plover** /'pluvə/ *n, pl* **plovers,** *esp collectively* **plover** any of numerous wading birds (family Charadriidae) that have a short hard-tipped bill and usu a stout compact build [ME, fr MF, fr (assumed) VL *pluviarius,* fr L *pluvia* rain – more at PLUVIAL]

**ploy** /ploy/ *n* a tactic intended to embarrass or frustrate an opponent; *broadly* something devised or contrived; a device ⟨may have issued his threat merely as a bargaining ~⟩ – NY Times⟩ [orig sense, activity, occupation; prob fr *employ*]

¹**pluck** /pluk/ *vt* **1** to pull or pick off or out ⟨she ~ed out a grey hair⟩ **2** to remove something (e g hairs) from (as if) by plucking ⟨~ one's eyebrows⟩; *esp* to remove the feathers from (e g a chicken) **3** to move or separate forcibly ⟨~ed the child from the middle of the street⟩ **4** to pick, pull, or grasp at; *also* to play (a stringed musical instrument) in this manner ~ *vi* to make a sharp pull *at;* tug sharply *at* ⟨~ed at the folds of her skirt⟩ [ME *plucken,* fr OE *pluccian;* akin to MHG *pflücken* to pluck] – **plucker** *n*

²**pluck** *n* **1** an act or instance of plucking or pulling **2** the heart, liver, and lungs of a slaughtered animal, esp as an item of food **3** courageous readiness to fight or continue against odds; dogged resolution

**plucky** /'pluki/ *adj* having courage; spirited *synonyms* see ¹BRAVE – **pluckily** *adv,* **pluckiness** *n*

¹**plug** /plug/ *n* **1a** a piece used to fill a hole; a stopper **b** an obtruding or obstructing mass of material resembling a stopper ⟨a volcanic ~⟩ **2** a flat compressed cake of tobacco, esp chewing tobacco; *also* a piece cut from this for chewing **3** a small core or segment removed from a larger object **4** something inferior; *esp, W US* an inferior, aged or unsound horse; *also* a quiet steady horse usu of light or moderate weight **5** a fire hydrant **6** SPARKING PLUG **7** an artificial angling lure used primarily for casting and made with one or more sets of joined hooks **8a** any of various electrical devices resembling or functioning like a plug; *esp* a device having usu three pins projecting from an insulated case for making electrical connection with a suitable socket **b** an electrical socket **9** *informal* a piece of favourable publicity (e g for a commercial product) usu

incorporated in general matter ⟨gave his book a ~ on the radio⟩ [D, fr MD *plugge;* akin to MHG *pfloc* plug]

²**plug** *vb* **-gg-** *vt* **1a** to block, close, or secure (as if) by inserting a plug **b** to furnish with plugs **2** *informal* to hit with a bullet; shoot **3** *informal* to advertise or publicize insistently and usu favourably ~ *vi* **1a** to become plugged – usu + *up* **b** of a golf ball to become impacted in the surface (e g of sand in a bunker) on landing **2** to work doggedly and persistently ⟨~ged away at his homework⟩ – **plugger** *n*

**plug in** *vi* to establish an electric circuit by inserting a plug to attach or connect (an electrical device) to a power point

**plughole** /'plug,hohl/ *n* a hole into which a plug fits; *specif* an opening in a sink, basin, or bath for the drainage of water

**plum** /plum/ *n* **1a** any of numerous trees and shrubs (genus *Prunus*) of the rose family with globular to oval usu edible smooth-skinned fruits with oblong stones; *esp* one (*Prunus domestica*) that is widely cultivated for its fruit **b** the edible fruit of a plum **2** any of various trees with edible fruits resembling plums; *also* the fruit of such a tree **3** a raisin when used in a pudding, cake, etc ⟨~ cake⟩ **4** something excellent or superior; *esp* an opportunity or position offering exceptional advantages ⟨her part in the play was a real ~⟩ ⟨a ~ job⟩ **5** a dark reddish-purple colour [ME, fr OE *plūme;* akin to OHG *pflūmo* plum tree; both fr a prehistoric WGmc word borrowed fr L *prunum* plum, fr Gk *proumnon*] – **plumlike** *adj*

**plumage** /'ploohmij/ *n* the entire covering of feathers of a bird [ME, fr MF, fr OF, fr *plume* feather – more at PLUME] – **plumaged** *adj*

¹**plumb** /plum/ *n* **1** a lead weight attached to a cord and used to indicate a vertical line **2** any of various weights (e g a sinker for a fishing line or a lead for sounding) [ME, fr (assumed) OF *plomb,* fr OF *plon* lead, fr L *plumbum*] – **out of plumb** not exactly vertical

²**plumb** *adv* **1** straight down or up; vertically **2** *informal* exactly, precisely ⟨his house is ~ in the middle of the island⟩ **3** chiefly dial NAm or informal to a complete degree; absolutely ⟨"you're ~ crazy", she remarked, with easy candor – Harper's Weekly⟩

³**plumb** *vt* **1** to measure the depth of with a plumb **2** to examine minutely and critically, esp so as to achieve complete understanding ⟨~ing the book's complexities⟩ **3** to adjust or test by a plumb line **4** to supply with plumbing ~ *vi* to work as a plumber – see also **plumb the** DEPTHS of [(*vt* 4 & *vi*) back-formations fr plumber]

**plumb in** *vt* to install by connecting with a supply of water ⟨plumb in a new sink⟩

⁴**plumb** *adj* **1** exactly vertical or true **2** of a cricket wicket flat and allowing little or no horizontal or vertical deviation of the bowled ball ⟨could bat all day on such a ~ pitch⟩ **3** *informal* downright, complete *synonyms* see VERTICAL

**plumb-** /plumb-/, **plumbo-** *comb form* lead ⟨plumb*ism*⟩ [L *plumb-,* fr *plumbum*]

**plumbaginous** /plum'bajinəs/ *adj* resembling, consisting of, or containing graphite

**plumbago** /plum'baygoh/ *n, pl* **plumbagos 1** graphite **2** any of a genus (*Plumbago*) of shrubs, woody climbers, and nonwoody plants of the thrift family that have spikes of showy flowers and are widely found in warm climates [L *plumbagin-, plumbago* lead ore, a type of plant, fr *plumbum*]

**plumb bob** *n* the metal weight of a PLUMB LINE

**plumbeous** /'plumbi-əs/ *adj* consisting of or resembling lead; *esp* of a leaden grey colour [L *plumbeus,* fr *plumbum*]

**plumber** /'plumə/ *n* **1** a person who installs, repairs, and maintains piping and fittings involved in the distribution and use of water in a building **2** *obs* a dealer or worker in lead [ME, fr MF *plombier,* fr L *plumbarius,* fr *plumbarius* producing or working in lead, fr *plumbum*]

**plumbic** /'plumbik/ *adj* of or containing lead, esp when having a VALENCY of four

**plumbiferous** /plum'bifərəs/ *adj* containing lead

**plumbing** /'pluming/ *n* **1** the act of using a plumb **2** a plumber's occupation or trade **3** the apparatus (e g pipes and fixtures) involved in the distribution and use of water in a building

**plumbism** /'plumbiz(ə)m/ *n* LEAD POISONING, esp when chronic

**plumb line** *n* **1** a line (e g of cord) that has at one end a weight (e g a PLUMB BOB) and is used esp to determine verticality, depth of water, etc **2** a line directed to the CENTRE OF GRAVITY of the earth; a vertical line

**plumbous** /'plumbəs/ *adj* of or containing lead, esp when having a VALENCY of two

¹**plume** /ploohm/ n 1 a feather of a bird: eg 1a a large conspicuous or showy feather b CONTOUR FEATHER c a cluster of distinctive feathers 2 an ornament consisting usu of a large or showy feather, a cluster of feathers, or a tuft of horsehair, worn esp on a hat or helmet or in the hair 3 something resembling a feather (eg in shape, appearance, or lightness): eg 3a a feathery or featherlike plant part b an elongated and usu open and mobile column or band (eg of smoke, exhaust gases, or blowing snow) c a fluffy or feathery animal structure; esp a full bushy tail [ME, fr MF, fr L pluma (small soft) feather – more at FLEECE] – **plumy** adj – **dress in/wear borrowed plumes** to parade ostentatiously possessions, qualifications, etc which are not one's own

²**plume** vt 1 to provide or deck with plumes 2 to indulge (oneself) in pride with an obvious or vain display of self-satisfaction 3a of a bird to preen and arrange the feathers of (itself) b to preen and arrange (feathers)

**plumed** /ploohmd/ adj having or adorned (as if) with a plume – often in combination ⟨a white-plumed egret⟩

¹**plummet** /'plumit/ n a plumb; also PLUMB LINE [ME plomet, fr MF plombet ball of lead, fr plomb lead, fr (assumed) OF – more at PLUMB]

²**plummet** vi 1 to fall perpendicularly ⟨the plane ~ed to earth⟩ 2 to drop sharply and abruptly ⟨prices ~ed⟩

**plummy** /'plumi/ adj 1 full of plums ⟨a rich ~ cake⟩ 2 of the voice rich and mellow often to the point of affectation 3 informal choice, desirable ⟨got a ~ role in the film⟩

**plumose** /'ploohmohs/ adj 1 having feathers or plumes; feathered 2 feathery 3 having a main shaft bearing small filaments ⟨the ~ antennae of an insect⟩ [L plumosus, fr pluma feather] – **plumosely** adv

¹**plump** /plump/ vi to drop, sink, or come in contact suddenly or heavily ⟨~ed down in the chair⟩ ~ vt to drop, cast, or place suddenly or heavily [ME plumpen, of imit origin]
**plump for** vt to decide on out of several choices or courses of action ⟨plumped for beer rather than wine⟩

²**plump** adv 1 with a sudden or heavy drop 2 without qualification; directly

³**plump** n (the sound of) a sudden plunge, fall, or blow

⁴**plump** adj having a full rounded usu pleasing form; slightly fat ⟨a ~ woman⟩ ⟨a ~ chicken⟩ [MD, dull, blunt] – **plumpish** adj, **plumpness** n

⁵**plump** vb to make or become plump – often + up or out
**plump up** vt to cause to fill or swell out ⟨plumped up the pillows when she made the bed⟩

¹**plumply** /'plumpli/ adv in a plump way ⟨a ~ pretty girl⟩

²**plumply** adv in a wholehearted manner and without hesitation or circumlocution; forthrightly [²plump]

**plum pudding** n a rich boiled or steamed pudding containing dried fruits (eg raisins) and spices

**plumule** /'ploohmyoohl/ n 1 the primary bud of a plant embryo that consists of leaves and a main stem and that develops into the shoot 2 a down feather [NL plumula, fr L, dim. of pluma feather] – **plumulose** adj

¹**plunder** /'plundə/ vt 1 to pillage, sack 2 to take, esp by force (eg in war); steal ~ vi to commit robbery or looting [Ger plündern, fr MHG plundern, fr plunder household goods, clothes] – **plunderer** n

²**plunder** n 1 an act of plundering; pillaging 2 something taken by force, theft, or fraud; loot

**plunderage** /'plundərij/ n 1 an act or instance of plundering; esp embezzlement of goods on board ship 2 goods obtained by plunderage

¹**plunge** /plunj/ vt 1a to cause to penetrate or enter quickly and forcibly into something b to sink (a potted plant) in the ground or a prepared bed 2 to cause to enter a thing, state, or course of action, usu suddenly, unexpectedly, or violently ⟨the room was ~d into darkness⟩ ~ vi 1 to thrust or throw oneself (as if) into water ⟨~d into the crowd to look for the child⟩ 2a to be pitched or thrown headlong or violently forwards and downwards ⟨the car stopped abruptly and he ~d through the windscreen⟩; also to move oneself in such a manner b to act with reckless haste; enter suddenly or unexpectedly ⟨the firm ~d into debt⟩ 3 to descend or dip suddenly 4 informal to bet or gamble heavily and recklessly [ME plungen, fr MF plonger, fr (assumed) VL plumbicare, fr L plumbum lead – more at PLUMB]

²**plunge** n an act or instance of plunging; a dive; also a swim – **take the plunge** to embark determinedly on an esp frightening or dangerous enterprise from which one had previously held back

**plunger** /'plunjə/ n one who or that which plunges: eg a a device (eg a piston in a pump) that acts with a plunging or thrusting motion b a rubber suction cup on a handle used to free plumbing from blockages c informal a reckless gambler or speculator

**plunging fire** /'plunjing/ n direct fire from a superior elevation resulting in the projectiles striking the target at a steep angle

**plunging neckline** n a low-cut neckline on a woman's garment

**plunk** /plungk/ vt 1 to pluck or hit so as to produce a hollow, metallic, or harsh sound 2 informal to set down suddenly; plump ~ vi 1 to make a plunking sound ⟨~ing away at a double bass⟩ 2 informal to drop abruptly; dive [imit] – **plunk** n, **plunker** n
**plunk down** vb, informal vi to drop abruptly; settle into position ~ vt 1 to put down usu firmly or abruptly ⟨plunked his money down on the counter⟩ 2 to settle (oneself) into position ⟨plunked himself down on the bench⟩

**pluperfect** /plooh'puhfikt/ adj PAST PERFECT (verb tense) [modif of LL plusquamperfectus, lit., more than perfect] – **pluperfect** n

**plural** /'plooərəl/ adj 1 linguistics of or being a word form (eg we, houses, cattle, are) denoting more than one, or in some languages more than two or more than three, people, things, or instances 2 of, consisting of, or containing more than one or more than one kind or class ⟨a ~ society⟩ [ME, fr MF & L; MF plurel, fr L pluralis, fr plur-, plus more – more at PLUS] – **plural** n, **plurally** adv, **pluralize** vt, **pluralization** n

**pluralism** /'plooərə,liz(ə)m/ n 1 the quality or state of being plural 2 the holding of two or more offices or positions (eg benefices) at the same time 3 philosophy a theory that there is more than one kind of ultimate reality – compare DUALISM, MONISM 4a the existence in a society of several independent groups or institutions (eg government and trade unions) which together regulate most aspects of corporate life ⟨the emergence of free trade unions has led to a new ~ in some Communist countries⟩ b a state of society in which members of social groups, esp diverse ethnic, racial, or religious groups, exist autonomously in a common civilization and develop their traditional cultures or special interests within it – **pluralist** adj or n, **pluralistic** adj, **pluralistically** adv

**plurality** /plooə'raləti/ n 1a the state of being plural or numerous b a large number or quantity; a multitude 2 PLURALISM 2; also a benefice held by pluralism 3 chiefly NAm 3a an excess of votes over those cast for an opposing candidate in an election b a number of votes cast for the winning candidate in an election in which more than two candidates are competing that is greater than the number cast for any other candidate but not more than half the total votes cast – compare MAJORITY 3

**pluri-** /plooəri-/ comb form having or being more than one; several; multi- ⟨pluriaxial⟩ [L, fr plur-, plus]

**pluriliteral** /,plooəri'lit(ə)rəl/ adj, of a Hebrew word having more than three letters in the root [pluri- + L litera, littera letter]

¹**plus** /plus/ prep 1 increased by; with the addition of ⟨four ~ five⟩ ⟨the debt ~ interest⟩ 2 and also ⟨job needs experience ~ patience⟩ [L, adv, more, fr neut of plur-, plus, adj, more; akin to Gk pleiōn more, L plenus full – more at FULL]
**usage** Since plus means "with the addition of", its presence should not in formal writing affect the question of whether a following verb is singular or plural: the plurality of the verb depends on that of the first item mentioned. Compare ⟨his earnings (plural) plus his pension come to £80⟩ ⟨his pension (singular) plus his earnings comes to £80⟩.

²**plus** n, pl pluses also plusses 1 plus sign, plus a sign + denoting addition (eg in 3 + 5 = 8) or a positive quantity (eg in +5%) 2 an added quantity 3 a positive quantity or quality 4 a surplus

³**plus** adj 1 greater than zero; positive 2 additional and welcome ⟨another ~ factor is its nearness to the shops⟩ 3a falling high in a specified range ⟨got B ~ for his essay⟩ b of an exceptional or unanticipated degree ⟨she had glamour ~⟩ 4 having a positive electrical charge

⁴**plus** conj and moreover ⟨~ he has to watch what he says – Punch⟩

**plus fours** n pl loose wide trousers gathered on a band just below the knee and now worn mainly by golfers [fr the extra four inches of length allowed for looseness]

**¹plush** /plush/ *n* a fabric with an even pile longer and less dense than that of velvet [MF *peluche*, deriv of L *pilus* hair]

**²plush** *adj* **1** (made) of or resembling plush **2** luxurious, showy – **plushly** *adv*, **plushness** *n*

**plushy** /'plushi/ *adj* **1** having the texture of or covered with plush **2** PLUSH 2 – **plushiness** *n*

**pluteus** /'ploohtiəs/ *n* the free-swimming larva of a SEA URCHIN or BRITTLE STAR (marine animal related to the starfish) [NL, fr L, parapet, low wall]

**Pluto** /'ploohtoh/ *n* the planet ninth in order and furthest from the sun [L *Pluton-, Pluto,* god of the underworld, fr Gk *Ploutōn*]

**plutocracy** /plooh'tokrəsi/ *n* (government by) a controlling class of rich people [Gk *ploutokratia,* fr *ploutos* wealth + *-kratia* -cracy] – **plutocrat** *n,* **plutocratic** *adj,* **plutocratically** *adv*

**pluton** /'ploohton/ *n* a typically large mass of IGNEOUS rock formed from the slow cooling and solidification of molten rock that has been forced between layers of the earth [prob backformation fr *plutonic*]

**plutonian** /plooh'tohnyən, -ni•ən/ *also* **plutonic** /plooh'tonik/ *adj, often cap* (characteristic) of the underworld; infernal [L *plutonius,* fr Gk *ploutonios,* fr *Ploutōn* Pluto, god of the underworld]

**plutonic** /plooh'tonik/ *adj, of a rock* formed by the slow cooling and solidification of molten rock deep within the earth and crystalline throughout

**plutonium** /plooh'tonyəm, -ni•əm/ *n* a radioactive metallic chemical element similar chemically to uranium that is formed by radioactive decay of the chemical element neptunium and found in minute quantities in the mineral pitchblende, that undergoes slow disintegration to form URANIUM 235, and that is used in nuclear weapons and as a fuel for NUCLEAR REACTORS [NL, fr *Pluton-, Pluto,* the planet Pluto]

**¹pluvial** /'ploohvi•əl/ *adj* **1a** of rain **b** characterized by abundant rainfall **2** resulting from the action of rain ⟨~ *erosion*⟩ ⟨~ *lakes*⟩ [L *pluvialis,* fr *pluvia* rain, fr fem of *pluvius* rainy, fr *pluere* to rain – more at FLOW]

**²pluvial** *n* a prolonged geological period of heavy rainfall ⟨*the ~s of the early Pleistocene epoch*⟩

**¹ply** /plie/ *vt* to twist together ⟨~ *two single yarns*⟩ [ME *plien* to fold, fr MF *plier,* fr L *plicare;* akin to OHG *flehtan* to braid, L *plectere,* Gk *plekein*]

**²ply** *n* **1a** a strand in a yarn, wool, etc ⟨*four-ply wool*⟩ **b** any of several layers (e g of cloth) usu sewn or laminated together **2a** (any of the veneer sheets forming) plywood **b** a layer of paper or paperboard

**³ply** *vt* **1a** to use or wield diligently or effectively ⟨*busily ~ing his axe*⟩ **b** to practise or perform diligently ⟨~ *ing his trade*⟩ **2** to keep furnishing or supplying something to ⟨*plied them with drinks*⟩ **3** to go or travel over or on regularly ⟨*the boat plies the river*⟩ ~ *vi* **1** to apply oneself or work steadily ⟨*oars ~ing against the current*⟩ **2** *of a boatman, taxi driver, etc* to wait regularly in a particular place for custom – esp in *ply for hire* **3** to go or travel regularly ⟨*a steamer ~ing between opposite shores of the lake*⟩ [ME *plien,* short for *applien* to apply]

**Plymouth Brethren** /'pliməth/ *n pl* a strongly puritanical Christian religious body founded about 1830 in Plymouth that rejects creeds, ritual, and an institutional ministry [*Plymouth,* city in SW England]

**Plymouth Rock** *n* (any of) an American breed of medium-sized domestic fowls [*Plymouth Rock* in Massachusetts, USA, on which the Pilgrim Fathers are supposed to have landed in 1620]

**plywood** /'plie,wood/ *n* a light structural material consisting of thin sheets of wood glued or cemented together with the grains of adjacent layers arranged crosswise usu at right angles

**-pnea,** *NAm chiefly* **-pnea** /-pnee•ə/ *comb form* (→ *n*), *chiefly NAm* -PNOEA

**pneum-** /nyoohm-/, **pneumo-** *comb form* **1** air; gas ⟨*pneumothorax*⟩ **2a** lung ⟨*pneumectomy*⟩ **b** pulmonary and ⟨*pneumogastric*⟩ **3** respiration ⟨*pneumograph*⟩ **4** pneumonia ⟨*pneumococcus*⟩ [NL; partly fr Gk *pneum-* (fr *pneuma*), partly fr Gk *pneumōn* lung]

**pneuma** /'nyoohmə/ *n* soul, spirit [Gk]

**pneumat-** /nyoohmat-/, **pneumato-** *comb form* **1** spirit ⟨*pneumatology*⟩ **2** air; vapour; gas ⟨*pneumatics*⟩ **3** respiration ⟨*pneumatometer*⟩ [Gk, fr *pneumat-, pneuma*]

**pneumatic** /nyooh'matik/ *adj* **1** of or using gas (e g air or wind): **1a** moved or worked by air pressure **b(1)** adapted for holding or inflated with compressed air ⟨*a ~ tyre*⟩ **b(2)** having air-filled cavities **2** of the pneuma; spiritual **3** *informal* voluptuous,

shapely ⟨*the ~ woman of his dreams – Time Out*⟩ [L *pneumaticus,* fr Gk *pneumatikos,* fr *pneumat-, pneuma* air, breath, spirit, fr *pnein* to breathe – more at SNEEZE] – **pneumatically** *adv*

**pneumatic drill** *n, chiefly Br* a device driven by compressed air which causes a tool (e g a chisel for breaking up road surfaces) to strike repeatedly

**pneumaticity** /,nyoohmə'tisəti/ *n* a condition marked by the presence of air cavities ⟨~ *of bird bones*⟩

**pneumatics** /nyooh'matiks/ *n taking sing vb* a science that deals with the mechanical properties of gases

**pneumatology** /,nyoohmə'toləji/ *n* **1** the doctrine of the HOLY SPIRIT **2** the study of spiritual beings or phenomena [NL *pneumatologia,* fr Gk *pneumat-, pneuma* + NL *-logia* -logy]

**pneumatolysis** /,nyoohmə'toləsis/ *n* the process by which pneumatolytic minerals are formed [NL]

**pneumatolytic** /,nyoohmətə'litik/ *adj, esp of a mineral or an ore* formed by hot vapours or superheated liquids under pressure [ISV]

**pneumatometer** /,nyoohmə'tomitə/ *n* **1** an instrument for measuring the force exerted by the lungs in breathing **2** SPIROMETER (instrument for measuring air entering and leaving the lungs)

**pneumatophore** /'nyoohmətoh,faw, nyoo'matohfaw, -tə-/ *n* **1** a muscular gas-containing sac that serves as a float on a SIPHONOPHORE colony (jellyfishlike marine animal) (e g a PORTUGUESE MAN-OF-WAR) **2** a root in a marsh plant often functioning as a respiratory organ [ISV] – **pneumatophoric** *adj*

**pneumectomy** /nyoo'mektəmi/ *n* the surgical removal of lung tissue [ISV]

**pneumobacillus** /,nyoohmoh•bə'siləs/ *n, pl* **pneumobacilli** /-li/ a bacterium (*Klebsiella pneumoniae*) associated with inflammations (e g pneumonia) of the respiratory tract [NL]

**pneumococcus** /,nyoohmoh'kokəs/ *n, pl* **pneumococci** /-'kok(s)i/ a bacterium (*Diplococcus pneumoniae*) that causes a short-lived and often fatal pneumonia [NL] – **pneumococcal** *also* **pneumococcic** *adj*

**pneumoconiosis** /-,koni'ohsis/ *n, pl* **pneumoconioses** /-seez/ a crippling disease of the lungs, esp of miners, caused by the habitual inhalation of irritant mineral or metallic particles – compare SILICOSIS [NL, fr *pneum-* + Gk *konis* dust – more at INCINERATE]

**pneumogastric** /-'gastrik/ *adj* **1** of the lungs and stomach **2** VAGAL (relating to the vagus nerve)

**pneumograph** /'nyoohmə,grahf, -,graf/ *n* an instrument for recording movements of the THORAX (part of the body between neck and abdomen) and volume change during breathing [ISV]

**pneumonectomy** /,nyoohmə'nektəmi/ *n* excision of (one or more lobes of) a lung [Gk *pneumōn* + ISV *-ectomy*]

**pneumonia** /nyooh'mohnyə, -ni•ə/ *n* a serious disease of the lungs caused by infection or irritants and characterized by localized or widespread inflammation [NL, fr Gk, fr *pneumōn* lung, alter. of *pleumōn* – more at PULMONARY]

**pneumonic** /nyooh'monik/ *adj* **1** of the lungs; pulmonic, pulmonary **2** of or affected with pneumonia [NL *pneumonicus,* fr Gk *pneumonikos,* fr *pneumōn*]

**pneumothorax** /,nyoohmoh'thawraks/ *n* an abnormal state in which gas, esp air, is present in the cavity between the lung and the chest wall and which occurs spontaneously as a result of disease or injury or is induced as a therapeutic measure to collapse the lung [NL]

**-pnoea,** *NAm chiefly* **-pnea** /-pnee•ə/ *comb form* breath; breathing ⟨*apnoea*⟩ [NL, fr Gk *-pnoia,* fr *pnoia,* fr *pnein* to breathe]

**po** /poh/ *n, pl* **pos** *Br informal* CHAMBER POT [Fr *pot* (*de chambre*)]

**¹poach** /pohch/ *vt* to cook (e g fish or an egg) in simmering liquid [ME *pochen,* fr MF *pocher,* fr OF *pochier,* lit., to put into a bag, fr *poche* bag, pocket, of Gmc origin; akin to OE *pocca* bag – more at POKE]

**²poach** *vt* **1** to trample or cut up (e g turf) (as if) with hoofs **2a** to trespass on ⟨*a field ~ed too frequently by the amateur – TLS*⟩ **b** to take (game or fish) illegally **c** to take or acquire by unfair or underhand means ~ *vi* **1** *of land* to become soft or muddy and full of holes when trampled on **2a** to trespass for the purpose of stealing game; *also* to take game or fish illegally **b** to trespass on or upon ⟨*what happens to a poet when he ~es upon a novelist's preserves* – Virginia Woolf⟩ [MF *pocher,* of Gmc origin; akin to ME *poken* to poke] – **poacher** *n*

**poacher** /'pohchə/ n a pan or dish used in poaching food; *esp* a covered pan containing a metal plate with shallow cups for cooking eggs over steam

**pochard** /'pohchəd/ n any of numerous heavy-bodied diving ducks (genera *Aythya* or *Netta*) with a large head and with feet and legs placed far back under the body; *esp* a common African and Eurasian duck (*Aythya ferina*) the male of which has a chestnut head and grey upperparts [origin unknown]

**pochette** /po'shet/ n a small envelope-shaped handbag, usu without straps; CLUTCH BAG [Fr, dim. of *poche* pocket]

¹**pock** /pok/ n (a spot resembling) a pustule in a rash-producing disease (eg smallpox) [ME *pokke*, fr OE *pocc;* akin to MLG & MD *pocke* pock, L *bucca* cheek, mouth] – **pocky** *adj*

²**pock** *vt* to mark (as if) with pocks; pit, scar

¹**pocket** /'pokit/ n 1 a small bag that is sewn or inserted in a garment so that it is open at the top or side ⟨*coat* ~⟩ 2 a supply of money; means ⟨*has houses to suit all* ~s⟩ 3 a receptacle, container: eg 3a any of several openings at the corners or sides of a billiard table into which balls are propelled b a superficial pouch in some animals 4a a small isolated area or group ⟨~s *of unemployment*⟩ b a cavity (eg in the earth) containing a deposit (eg of gold or water) c AIR POCKET 5 *chiefly SAfr* (the amount contained in) a bag ⟨*bought a* ~ *of grapefruit for 49 cents* – *Weekend Argus Magazine* (*Cape Town*)⟩ 6 *NAm* a small handbag [ME *poket*, fr ONF *pokete*, dim. of *poke* bag, of Gmc origin; akin to OE *pocca* bag] – **pocketful** n – **in one's pocket** in one's control or possession – **in pocket** in the position of having made a profit – **out of pocket** having suffered a financial loss

²**pocket** *vt* 1a to put or enclose (as if) in one's pocket ⟨~ed *his change*⟩ b to appropriate to one's own use; steal ⟨~ed *the money he had collected for charity*⟩ 2 to accept; PUT UP WITH ⟨~ *an insult*⟩ 3 to suppress; SET ASIDE ⟨~ed *his pride*⟩ 4 to drive (a ball) into a pocket of a billiard table 5 *NAm* to veto (a bill) by failing to sign until the legislature has adjourned ⟨*the President managed to* ~ *the controversial new bill*⟩

³**pocket** *adj* 1 small enough to be carried in the pocket ⟨*a* ~ *camera*⟩ 2 small, miniature ⟨*a* ~ *submarine*⟩

**pocket battleship** n a small battleship built so as to come within treaty limitations of tonnage and armament

**pocket billiards** n usu taking sing vb ²POOL 2

**pocketbook** /-ˌbook/ n 1 a pocket-size container for (paper) money and personal papers; a wallet 2 *NAm* 2a a small, esp paperback, book that can be carried in the pocket b a purse c a strapless handbag

**pocket borough** n an English constituency controlled by an individual person or family before parliamentary reform in 1832

**pocket-'handkerchief** n a handkerchief

**pocketknife** /-ˌnief/ n a knife that has one or more blades that fold into the handle and that can be carried in the pocket

**pocket money** n money for small personal expenses, esp as given to a child each week

'**pocket-ˌsize, pocket-sized** adj POCKET 1

¹**pockmark** /'pok.mahk/ n a mark or pit caused by smallpox; *also* any similar scar or depression

²**pockmark** *vt* to cover (as if) with pockmarks; pit, scar

**poco** /'pohkoh/ adv slightly, somewhat – used to qualify a direction in music ⟨~ *allegro*⟩ [It, little, fr L *paucus* – more at FEW]

**poco a poco** /ˌpohkoh ah 'pohkoh/ adv little by little; gradually – used as a direction in music [It]

**pococurante** /ˌpohkoh·kyoo'ranti/ adj indifferent, apathetic [It *poco curante* caring little, fr *poco* little + *curante,* prp of *curare* to care] – **pococurante** n, **pococuranteism, pococurantism** n

¹**pod** /pod/ n 1 an elongated usu dry seed vessel or fruit, esp of the pea, bean, or a related plant, that is composed of one or more CARPELS (female reproductive organs of plants) 2 an egg case of any of several insects, esp a grasshopper or locust 3 a streamlined compartment under the wings or fuselage of an aircraft, used as a container (eg for fuel); *broadly* a protective container or housing ⟨*a submarine with its reactor in an external* ~⟩ 4 a detachable compartment (eg for personnel, a power unit, or an instrument) on a spacecraft [prob alter. of *cod* bag – more at CODPIECE] – **podded** adj

²**pod** vb -dd- vi to produce pods ~ vt to remove (eg peas) from the pod

³**pod** n taking sing or pl vb a small group of animals (eg seals) packed closely together [origin unknown]

**-pod** /-pod/ comb form (→ n) foot; part resembling a foot ⟨*pleopod*⟩ [Gk *-podos*, fr *pod-, pous* foot – more at FOOT]

**podagra** /pə'dagrə/ n GOUT 1 ⚠ pellagra [ME, fr L, fr Gk, fr *pod-, pous* foot + *agra* hunt, catch; akin to L *agere* to drive – more at AGENT] – **podagral** adj

**poddy** /'podi/ n, Austr a bottle-fed calf [*poddy* (fat, pot-bellied), fr ¹*pod* + ¹*-y*]

**podesta** /po'destə/ n 1 a chief magistrate in a medieval Italian town or republic 2 a chief executive of an Italian commune during the Fascist regime 3 a subordinate judge or magistrate in some modern Italian towns [It *podestà*, lit., power, fr L *potestat-, potestas,* irreg fr *potis* able – more at POTENT]

**podge** /poj/ n, chiefly Br informal a chubby person; a fatty [prob alter. of *pudge,* of unknown origin]

**podgy** /'poji/ adj short and plump; chubby

**podiatry** /po'die·ətri/ n, NAm chiropody [Gk *pod-, pous* foot + E *-iatry*] – **podiatric** adj, **podiatrist** n

**podite** /'podiet/ n a limb segment of an insect, spider, crab, or related animal [ISV *pod-* (fr Gk *pod-, pous* foot) + *-ite*] – **poditic** adj

**podium** /'pohdi·əm/ n, pl **podiums, podia** /-diə/ 1 a low wall serving as a foundation or terrace wall: eg 1a one round the arena of an ancient amphitheatre, serving as a base for the tiers of seats b the stone base supporting the columns of a classical structure (eg a Roman temple) 2 a small raised platform or dais; *esp* one for an orchestral conductor [L – more at PEW]

**-podium** /-pohdium/ comb form (→ n), pl **-podia** -pod ⟨*pseudo*podium⟩ [NL, fr Gk *podion,* dim. of *pod-, pous* foot – more at FOOT]

**podophyllin** /ˌpodoh'filin, ˌpohdə'fielin, -doh-/ n a bitter irritant resin obtained from the underground stem (RHIZOME) of the mayapple and used esp as a paint in the treatment of warts [ISV, fr NL *Podophyllum,* genus of plants including the mayapple]

**podsol** /podsol/ n podzol

**podzol** /'podzol/ n any of a group of soils that develop in a moist climate, esp under coniferous forest or heathland, and have an upper grey layer from which humus and iron and aluminium chemical compounds have LEACHED (become washed out) by the rain) and a lower dark layer that is enriched by these leached substances [Russ] – **podzolize** vb, **podzolization** n, **podzolic** adj

**poem** /'poh·im/ n 1 an individual work of poetry 2 a creation, experience, or object suggesting a poem ⟨*the interior was a* ~ *of chinoiserie*⟩ [MF *poeme,* fr L *poema,* fr Gk *poiēma,* fr *poiein* to make, create]

**poesy** /'poh·izi, -si/ n 1 a poem or body of poems 2 the art or composition of poetry [ME *poesie,* fr MF, fr L *poesis,* fr Gk *poiēsis,* lit., creation, fr *poiein*]

**poet** /'poh·it/, fem **poetess** n 1 somebody who writes poetry 2 a creative artist of great imaginative and expressive gifts and special sensitivity to his/her medium ⟨*a* ~ *of the piano*⟩ usage see -ESS [ME, fr OF *poete,* fr L *poeta,* fr Gk *poiētēs* maker, poet, fr *poiein* to make, create; akin to Skt *cinoti* he heaps up]

**poetaster** /ˌpoh·i'tastə/ n an inferior poet [NL, fr L *poeta* + *-aster* -aster]

**poetic** /poh'etik/, **poetical** /-kl/ adj 1a (characteristic) of poets or poetry b having the qualities associated with poetry 2 written in verse – **poetically** adv

**poeticism** /poh'etisiz(ə)m/ n 1 an archaic, trite, or strained expression in poetry 2 poetic quality

**poetic·ize, -ise** /poh'etisiez/ vt to give a poetic quality to

**poetic justice** n an outcome in which vice is punished and virtue rewarded in a manner peculiarly or ironically appropriate

**poetic licence** n LICENCE 3

**poetics** /poh'etiks/ n, pl **poetics** 1 a treatise on poetry or aesthetics 2 taking sing or pl vb poetic theory or practice

**poet·ize, -ise** /'poh·itiez/ vi to compose poetry ~ vt to poeticize – **poetizer** n

**poet laureate** /'lawri·ət/ n, pl **poets laureate, poet laureates** 1 a distinguished poet honoured for achievement in his/her art 2 a poet appointed for life by the sovereign as a member of the British royal household and expected to compose poems for state occasions

**poetry** /'poh·itri/ n 1a metrical writing; verse b a poet's compositions; poems 2 writing that is arranged to formulate a concentrated imaginative awareness of experience through meaning, sound, and rhythm 3 a quality of beauty, grace, and great feeling ⟨~ *in motion*⟩

**po-faced** /poh/ *adj, Br informal* having a foolishly solemn or humourless expression [*po* + *faced*]

**pogey** /'pohgi/ *n, Can informal* DOLE 3 [origin unknown]

**pogonology** /,pohgə'noləji/ *n* the study of beards [NL *pogonologia*, fr Gk *pŏgŏn* beard]

**pogonophoran** /,pohgə'nofərən/ *n* any of a phylum or class (Pogonophora) of marine worms of uncertain biological classification that superficially resemble the bristly segmented worms (POLYCHAETES) but have some features characteristic of more highly developed animals [NL *Pogonophora*, group name, fr Gk *pŏgŏnophora*, neut pl of *pŏgŏnophoros* wearing a beard, fr *pŏgŏn* beard + *pherein* to carry, bear] – **pogonophoran** *adj*

**pogo stick** /'pohgoh/ *n* a pole with a strong spring at the bottom and two footrests on which a person stands and jumps up and down or along [fr *Pogo*, a trademark]

**pogrom** /'pogrəm/ *n* an organized massacre, esp of Jews [Yiddish, fr Russ, lit., devastation]

**pohutukawa** /pə'hoohtə,kah·wə/ *n* an evergreen New Zealand tree (*Metrosideros excelsa*) of the myrtle family that bears brilliant red flowers – called also CHRISTMAS TREE [Maori]

**¹poi** /poy/ *n, pl* **poi, pois** a Hawaiian food made from the root of the TARO (tropical plant) cooked, pounded, and kneaded to a paste and often allowed to ferment [Hawaiian & Samoan]

**²poi** *n, pl* **poi, pois 1** a ball of flax suspended on a thong of flax and swung by Maori women in certain dances **2** a dance performed with a poi [Maori]

**-poiesis** /-poy'eesis/ *comb form* (→ *n*), *pl* **-poieses** /-seez/ production; formation ⟨*erythro*poiesis⟩ ⟨*mytho*poiesis⟩ [NL, fr Gk *poiēsis* creation – more at POESY] – **-poietic** *comb form* (→ *adj*)

**poignant** /'poynyənt/ *adj* **1a** painfully affecting the feelings; distressing **b** deeply affecting; touching **2** designed to make an impression; cutting ⟨~ *satire*⟩ △ piquant, plangent, pungent *antonym* dull (eg of sensation or reaction) [ME *poinaunt*, fr MF *poignant*, prp of *poindre* to prick, sting, fr L *pungere* – more at PUNGENT] – **poignancy** *n*, **poignantly** *adv*

**poikilotherm** /,poy'kilothuhm/ *n* a living organism (eg a frog) with a variable body temperature that is usu slightly higher than the temperature of its environment; a cold-blooded organism [Gk *poikilos* variegated (akin to L *pingere* to paint – more at PAINT) + ISV *-therm*] – **poikilothermic** *adj*, **poikilothermism** *n*

**poilu** /'pwahlooh/ *n* a French private soldier; *esp* one in the front line during World War I [Fr, fr *poilu* hairy, fr MF, fr *poil* hair, fr L *pilus* – more at PILE]

**poinciana** /,poynsi'ahnə/ *n* any of a genus (*Poinciana*) of ornamental tropical trees or shrubs of the pea family with bright orange or red flowers; *also* FLAMBOYANT (tropical tree) [NL, genus name, fr De *Poinci*, 17th-c governor of part of the French West Indies]

**poind** /poynd/ *vt* to take forceful legal possession of (eg a debtor's property); IMPOUND; *esp* DISTRAIN – used in Scots law [ME (Sc) *punden, pynden*, fr OE *pyndan* to dam up, fr *pund*-enclosure]

**poinsettia** /poyn'seti·ə/ *n* any of a genus (*Euphorbia*) of plants of the spurge family bearing flower clusters opposite brightly coloured BRACTS (leaflike structures); *esp* one (*Euphorbia pulcherrima*) commonly grown as a house or garden plant [NL, fr Joel R *Poinsett* †1851 US diplomat]

**¹point** /poynt/ *n* **1a(1)** an individual detail; an item **a(2)** a distinguishing detail ⟨*tact is one of her strong* ~s⟩ **b** the most important essential in a discussion or matter ⟨*missed the whole* ~ *of the joke*⟩ **c** cogency **2** an end or object to be achieved; a purpose ⟨*did not see what* ~ *there was in continuing the discussion*⟩ **3a(1)** a geometric element that has a position in space but no size and that does not extend in any direction ⟨*a moving* ~ *traces a line*⟩ **a(2)** a geometric element determined by an ordered set of COORDINATES (numbers defining location) ⟨*a* ~ *on a graph*⟩ **b(1)** a narrowly localized place having a precisely indicated position ⟨*walked to a* ~ *50 yards north of the building*⟩ **b(2)** a particular place; a locality ⟨*have come from distant* ~s⟩ **c(1)** an exact moment ⟨*at this* ~ *he was interrupted*⟩ **c(2)** a time interval immediately before something indicated; *the* verge ⟨*at the* ~ *of death*⟩ **d(1)** a particular step, stage, or degree in development ⟨*had reached the* ~ *where nothing seemed to matter any more*⟩ **d(2)** a definite position in a scale ⟨*boiling* ~⟩ **4a** the terminal usu sharp or narrowly rounded end of something; a tip **b** a weapon or tool having such a part and used for stabbing or piercing **c** the contact or discharge extremity of an electric device (eg a SPARKING PLUG

or contact breaker) **5a** a projecting usu tapering piece of land **b(1)** the tip of a projecting body part **b(2)** TINE 2 (branch of an antler) **b(3)** *pl* (the markings of) the extremities of an animal, esp when of a different colour from the rest of the body **b(4)** *usu pl* the tip of the toes – used in ballet **6** a short musical phrase; *esp* a phrase in music characterized by COUNTERPOINT (combination of different melodies) **7a** a very small mark **b(1)** PUNCTUATION MARK; *esp* FULL STOP **b(2)** a dot, stroke, or other diacritic used (eg in Hebrew or Arabic) to indicate vowel sounds or (eg in phonetic script) to modify sounds **b(3)** DECIMAL POINT – used chiefly in articulating decimal fractions **8** a lace for tying parts of a garment (eg a bodice) together, used esp from the 13th to the 16th centuries **9** any of usu 11 divisions of a heraldic shield that determine the position of a CHARGE (figure) **10** any of the 32 evenly spaced directions marked at 11° 15′ intervals on the circle of a compass; *also* the angular difference between two such successive points **11** *taking sing or pl vb* a small detachment ahead of an advance guard or behind a rear guard **12a** lace worked with a needle; NEEDLEPOINT 1 **b** lace imitating needlepoint worked with bobbins; PILLOW LACE **13** any of 12 triangular spaces marked off on each side of a backgammon board **14** a unit of measurement: e g **14a(1)** a unit of counting in the scoring of a game or contest **a(2)** a unit used in evaluating the strength of a bridge hand **b(1)** a unit used in quoting prices (eg of shares, bonds, and commodities) or value ⟨*the dollar has fallen several* ~s⟩ **b(2)** *pl* a percentage of the face value of a loan often added as a placement fee or service charge **c** a unit of 0.351 millimetre (about ¹/₇₂ inch) used to measure the body size of printing type and in computerized composition to measure set width, line length, and column depth **15** the action of pointing: e g **15a** the rigidly intent attitude of a gundog, usu with one front paw raised, marking game for a hunter ⟨*the dog came to a* ~⟩ **b** the action in dancing of extending one leg and stretching the foot so that only the tips of the toes touch the floor **16** (the position of) a defensive player in various team games, esp lacrosse **17** a close fielding position in cricket more or less in line with the stumps on the OFF SIDE; *also* the fieldsman occupying this position **18** a number thrown on the first roll of the dice in CRAPS which the player attempts to repeat before throwing a seven **19** *chiefly Br* POWER POINT **20** *pl, Br* a device made of usu 2 movable rails and necessary connections and designed to turn a locomotive or train from one track to another [ME; partly fr OF, puncture, small spot, point in time or space, fr L *punctum*, fr neut of *punctus*, pp of *pungere* to prick; partly fr OF *pointe* sharp end, fr (assumed) VL *puncta*, fr L, fem of *punctus*, pp – more at PUNGENT] – **beside the point** unrelated, irrelevant – **in point of** with regard to; in the matter of ⟨*in point of law*⟩ ⟨*in point of fact you're wrong*⟩ – **make a point of** to take particular care to ⟨*always makes a point of locking every door*⟩ – **score points off somebody** to outwit (somebody), esp by making clever but snide or humiliating comments or replies – **stretch a point** to allow something which is normally forbidden; make an exception ⟨*just this once we'll stretch a point and let you stay out until midnight*⟩ – **to the point** relevant, pertinent

**²point** *vt* **1** to provide with a point; sharpen ⟨~*ing a pencil with a knife*⟩ **2** to scratch out the old mortar from the joints of (eg a brick wall) and fill in with new material **3a(1)** to mark the pauses or grammatical divisions in; punctuate **a(2)** to separate (a decimal fraction) from an integer by a decimal point – usu + *off* **b(1)** to mark (eg psalms) with signs for chanting **b(2)** to mark (eg Hebrew words) with points **4** *of a gundog* to indicate the presence and place of (game) by a point **5a** to cause to be turned in a specified direction ⟨~ *a gun*⟩ ⟨~ed *the boat upstream*⟩ **b** to stretch out (the foot or toes of an extended leg) in dancing ~ *vi* **1a** to indicate the fact or probability of something specified ⟨*everything* ~s *to a bright future*⟩ **b** to indicate the position or direction of something, esp by extending a finger ⟨~ *at the map*⟩ **c** to point game ⟨*a dog that* ~s *well*⟩ **2a** to lie extended, aimed, or turned in a particular direction ⟨*a directional arrow that* ~ed *north*⟩ **b** to execute a point in dancing **3** *of a sailing vessel* to sail close to the wind – see also **point the** FINGER **(at)**

**point out** *vt* to direct somebody's attention to ⟨*point out a mistake*⟩

**point up** *vt* to give added force, emphasis, or piquancy to ⟨*point up a remark*⟩

**point-'blank** *adj* **1** so close to a target that a missile fired will travel in a straight line to the mark **2** direct, blunt ⟨*a* ~ *refusal*⟩ [prob fr ²*point* + ²*blank* (in the sense "centre of a target")] – **point-blank** *adv*

**point d'appui** /ˌpwahn daˈpwee (Fr pwɛ̃ dapɥi)/ n, pl **points d'appui** /~/ a base, esp for a military operation [Fr, lit., point of support]

**'point-ˌduty** n, Br regulation of traffic by a policeman or policewoman stationed at a particular point (e g a road junction) and using hand signals

**pointe** /pwant (Fr pwɛ̃:t)/ n a ballet position in which the body is balanced on the extreme tip of the toe [Fr, lit., point]

**pointed** /ˈpoyntid/ adj 1 having a point 2a pertinent; TO THE POINT b aimed at a particular person or group 3 conspicuous, marked ⟨~ indifference⟩ – **pointedly** adv, **pointedness** n

**pointer** /ˈpoyntə/ n 1 one who or that which points out; specif a rod or stick used (e g by a speaker or teacher) to draw attention to something (e g writing on a blackboard) 2 a large strong slender smooth-haired gundog that hunts by scent and indicates the presence of game by pointing 3 a useful suggestion or hint; a tip

**Pointers** /ˈpoyntəz/ n pl the two stars in URSA MAJOR, a line through which points to the POLE STAR

**pointillism** /ˈpwantiˌliz(ə)m, ˈpoyn-, -tiˌyiz(ə)m/ n the technique in art of applying small separate strokes or dots of pure colour to a picture surface so that from a distance they appear to fuse together with an effect of increased luminosity ⟨the ~ of Seurat⟩ [Fr pointillisme, fr pointiller to stipple, fr point spot] – **pointillist** also **pointilliste** n or adj

**point lace** n POINT 12; esp NEEDLEPOINT 1

**pointless** /-lis/ adj devoid of meaning, relevance, or purpose; senseless ⟨a ~ remark⟩ – **pointlessly** adv, **pointlessness** n

**point of honour** n a matter which one considers to have a serious effect on one's honour or reputation

**point of inflection, inflexion** n, maths a point on a curve at which the shape of the curve changes from being convex to concave; a point where the first and second DERIVATIVES of the function describing the curve are both zero

**point of no return** n 1 the point in a long-distance journey (e g by an aircraft over an ocean) beyond which the remaining supplies, esp fuel, will be insufficient for a return to the starting point with the result that the journey must be continued 2 a critical point (e g in a course of action) at which turning back or reversal is not possible

**point of order** n a question relating to procedure in an official meeting

**ˌpoint-of-ˈsale** adj of or being advertising or promotional material accompanying a product at its place of distribution, esp in a retail shop

**point of view** n 1 a position from which something is considered or evaluated; a standpoint, viewpoint 2 an opinion ⟨always glad to hear your ~⟩
    synonyms Point of view, standpoint, and viewpoint all mean "position from which something is considered". They are often overused in contexts such as ⟨inconvenient from the cleaning point of view⟩, which could be more concisely rephrased as ⟨inconvenient for cleaning⟩. See ¹VIEW

**point shoe** n a ballet shoe with a block; BLOCK 4

**pointsman** /ˈpoyntsmən/ n 1 a policeman on point-duty 2 Br a person in charge of railway points

**point source** n a source of radiation (e g light) that is concentrated at a point and considered to have no extension into space

**point system** n a printer's system of measurement based on the point

**ˌpoint-to-ˈpoint** n a usu cross-country steeplechase principally for amateur riders – **point-to-pointer** n

**¹poise** /poyz/ vt 1a to balance; esp to hold or carry in equilibrium ⟨walked along gracefully with a water jar ~d on her head⟩ b to hold supported or suspended without motion in a steady position 2 to hold or carry in a particular way 3 to put into readiness; brace ~ vi 1 to make oneself ready for something, esp by changing position ⟨he ~d for the attack⟩ 2 to hang (as if) suspended; hover [ME poisen to weigh, ponder, fr MF pois-, stem of peser, fr L pensare – more at PENSIVE]

**²poise** n 1 a stably balanced state; an equilibrium ⟨a ~ between widely divergent impulses – F R Leavis⟩ 2a easy self-possessed assurance of manner; composure b a particular way of carrying oneself; bearing, carriage [ME poyse weight, heaviness, fr MF pois, fr L pensum, fr neut of pensus, pp of pendere to weigh – more at PENDANT]

**³poise** /pwahz/ n a unit of VISCOSITY (property of a gas or liquid by which it resists forces to make it flow) in the centimetre-gram-second system; the viscosity of a liquid or gas that would require a sideways force equal to 1 dyne to move a square-centimetre area of either of two parallel layers of liquid or gas one centimetre apart with a velocity of 1 centimetre per second relative to the other layer with the space between the layers being filled with the liquid or gas [Fr, fr Jean Louis Marie Poiseuille †1869 Fr physician & anatomist]

**poised** /poyzd/ adj 1 marked by balance or equilibrium 2 marked by easy composure of manner or bearing 3 in a state of readiness ⟨~ for flight⟩ ⟨~ for action⟩

**¹poison** /ˈpoyz(ə)n/ n 1a a substance that through its chemical action kills, injures, or impairs an organism b something destructive, harmful, or abhorrent 2 a substance that inhibits the activity of another substance or the course of a chemical reaction or process ⟨a catalyst ~⟩ ⟨nuclear fission ~s⟩ [ME, fr OF, drink, poisonous drink, poison, fr L potion-, potio drink – more at POTION]

**²poison** vt 1a to injure or kill with poison b to treat, taint, or impregnate with poison 2a to exert a harmful influence on; corrupt ⟨~ed their minds with propaganda⟩ b to cause to turn against ⟨~ed her mind against me⟩ 3a to inhibit or prevent the activity of (e g a catalyst) b to inhibit or prevent the course or occurrence of (e g a chemical reaction) – **poisoner** n

**³poison** adj 1 poisonous ⟨a ~ plant⟩; venomous ⟨a ~ tongue⟩ 2 impregnated with poison; poisoned ⟨a ~ arrow⟩

**poison gas** n a poisonous gas or a liquid or solid giving off poisonous vapours designed (e g in chemical warfare) to kill, injure, or disable by inhalation or contact

**poison ivy** n (any of several plants related to) a climbing plant (Rhus toxicodendron) of the sumach family that is common esp in the eastern and central USA, has greenish flowers and white berries, and produces an oil causing an intensely itching skin rash

**poisonous** /ˈpoyz(ə)nəs/ adj having the properties or effects of poison; venomous – **poisonously** adv

**poison-pen letter** n a usu anonymous letter written with malicious intent to frighten or offend

**Poisson distribution** /ˈpwusonh/ n, statistics a PROBABILITY DISTRIBUTION that is often used to model the number of outcomes of discrete events (e g traffic accidents or atomic disintegrations) that occur in a continuum, and in which the probability of the event happening is small but the number of times at which the event can happen is large, and which can be used as an approximation to the BINOMIAL DISTRIBUTION [Siméon Poisson †1840 Fr mathematician]

**¹poke** /pohk/ n, chiefly dial NAm a bag, sack [ME, fr ONF – more at POCKET]

**²poke** vt 1a(1) to prod, jab ⟨~d him in the ribs and grinned broadly⟩ a(2) to stir the coals or logs of (a fire) so as to promote burning b to produce by piercing, stabbing, or jabbing ⟨~ a hole⟩ 2 to cause to project ⟨~d her head out of the window⟩ 3 informal to hit, punch ⟨~d him in the nose⟩ 4 vulg, of a man to have sexual intercourse with ~ vi 1 to make a prodding, jabbing, or thrusting movement, esp repeatedly – often + at 2 to become stuck out or forwards; protrude 3 vulg, of a man to have sexual intercourse – see also poke FUN at/MULLOCK at/one's NOSE into [ME poken; akin to MD poken to poke]
    **poke about/around** vi 1 to look about or through something in a random manner; rummage ⟨poked about in her handbag for her keys⟩ 2 to move or act slowly or aimlessly; potter ⟨just poked about at home all day⟩

**³poke** n 1 a quick thrust; a jab 2 informal a blow with the fist; a punch 3 vulg an act of sexual intercourse

**pokeberry** /ˈpohkˌberi/ n (the berry of the) pokeweed

**poke bonnet** n a woman's bonnet with a projecting brim at the front

**¹poker** /ˈpohkə/ n a metal rod for poking a fire

**²poker** n any of several card games in which a player bets that the value of his/her hand is greater than that of the hands held by others and in which each subsequent player has to either equal or raise the bet or drop out, the winner being the player holding the highest hand at the end of the betting [prob modif of Fr poque, a card game similar to poker]

**poker dice** n 1 (any of) a set of usu five dice each of which carries the representation of the six highest playing cards 2 any of several gambling games played with poker dice

**poker face** n an inscrutable face that reveals no hint of a person's thoughts or feelings [²poker; fr the need of the poker player to conceal the true quality of his hand] – **poker-faced** adj

**pokerwork** /-ˌwuhk/ n the art of decorating wood or other material by burning designs into it with a heated point; *also* decorative work done in this way

**pokeweed** /'pohk,weed/ *n* a coarse American plant (*Phytolacca americana* of the family Phytolaccaceae) with white flowers, dark purple juicy berries, and a poisonous root [*poke* by shortening & alter. fr *puccoon*]

**pokey** /'pohki/ *n, NAm slang* a jail [origin unknown]

**pokie** /'pohki/ *n, Austr informal* ONE-ARMED BANDIT [by shortening & alter. fr *poker machine* (a one-armed bandit displaying card symbols)]

**poky** *also* **pokey** /'pohki/ *adj, informal* **1** small and cramped **2** *chiefly NAm* annoyingly slow [²*poke*] – **pokily** *adv*, **pokiness** *n*

**Polack** /'pohlak/ *n, archaic or derog* a Pole ⟨*he smote the sledded* ~s *on the ice* – Shak⟩ [Polish *Polak*]

**Poland China** *n* (any of) an American breed of large white-marked black pigs [*Poland*, country in Europe + *China*, country in Asia]

**polar** /'pohlə/ *adj* **1a** of, coming from, or characteristic of a geographical pole or the region round it **b** passing over a planet's north and south poles ⟨*a satellite in a* ~ *orbit*⟩ ⟨*a* ~ *satellite*⟩ **2** *physics* of one or more poles (e g of a magnet) **3** serving as a guide in the manner of the POLE STAR **4** completely opposite in nature, tendency, or action **5** *chemistry, of a compound, crystal, or molecule* exhibiting polarity; *esp* having a DIPOLE (pair of equal but opposite electrical charges or magnetic poles) **6** resembling a pole or axis round which all else revolves; pivotal **7** of or expressed in POLAR COORDINATES ⟨~ *equations*⟩; *also* of or being a system using polar coordinates [NL *polaris*, fr L *polus* pole]

**polar bear** *n* a large creamy-white bear (*Ursus maritimus*) that inhabits arctic regions

**polar body** *n* a cell that separates from an OOCYTE (immature egg) during MEIOSIS (division of a cell to produce the reproductive cells) and contains a nucleus but very little CYTOPLASM (jellylike material outside the nucleus)

**polar circle** *n* either of the two parallels of latitude each at a distance from a pole of the earth equal to about 23 degrees 27 minutes: **a** ARCTIC CIRCLE **b** ANTARCTIC CIRCLE

**polar coordinate** *n, maths* either of two numbers that locate a point in a plane by its distance along a line from a fixed point and the angle this line makes with a fixed line – compare CARTESIAN COORDINATE

**polar front** *n* the boundary between the cold air of a polar region and the warmer air of lower latitudes

**polarimeter** /,pohlə'rimitə/ *n* **1** an instrument for determining the amount of polarization of light or the proportion of polarized light in a partially polarized ray **2** an instrument for measuring the amount of OPTICAL ROTATION (angle through which polarized light can be rotated) produced by an optically active substance (e g a sugar solution) [ISV, fr *polarization*] – **polarimetry** *n*, **polarimetric** *adj*

**Polaris** /pə'lahris, poh-/ *n* POLE STAR [NL, fr *polaris* polar]

**polariscope** /poh'lari,skohp/ *n* **1** an instrument for studying the properties of or examining substances in polarized light **2** POLARIMETER 2 [ISV, fr *polarization*]

**polarity** /pə'larəti, poh-/ *n* **1** the quality or condition of a body that exhibits opposite or contrasted properties or powers in opposite or contrasted parts or directions **2** attraction towards a particular object or in a specific direction **3** the particular state of having either a positive or negative electrical charge **4** (an instance of) diametric opposition

**polar·ization, -isation** /,pohlərie'zaysh(ə)n/ *n* **1** the action of polarizing or state of being or becoming polarized: e g **1a**(1) the action or process of affecting radiation, esp light, so that the vibrations of the wave assume a definite form (e g being confined to vibrations in one plane) **a**(2) the state of radiation affected by this process **b** the deposition of gas on one or both ELECTRODES (structure that conducts electricity into or out of a device) during ELECTROLYSIS (chemical decomposition of a substance by an electric current) that increases the electrical resistance and sets up an opposing voltage **c** MAGNETIZATION **2a** division into two opposites **b** the concentration about opposing extremes of groups or interests formerly ranged on a continuum

**polar·ize, -ise** /'pohləriez/ *vt* **1** to cause (e g light waves) to vibrate in a definite pattern **2** to give electrical or magnetic polarity to **3** to divide into opposing factions or groupings ~ *vi* to become polarized [Fr *polariser*, fr NL *polaris* polar] – **polarizable** *adj*, **polarizability** *n*

**polar nucleus** *n* either of the two nuclei of an EMBRYO SAC of

a SEED PLANT that are destined to form ENDOSPERM (nutritive tissue)

**Polaroid** /'pohləroyd/ *trademark* **1** – used esp for a light-polarizing material used esp in sunglasses and lamps to prevent glare and in various optical devices **2** – used for a camera that produces a finished photographic print very soon after the picture has been taken

**polder** /'poldə, pohl-/ *n* an area of low land reclaimed from a body of water (e g the sea), esp in the Netherlands [D]

¹**pole** /pohl/ *n* **1a** a long slender usu cylindrical object (e g a length of wood) **b** a shaft which extends from the front axle of a wagon between two draught animals (e g horses) and by which the wagon is drawn **c** the upper part of a ship's mast **2** ROD 2a (unit of length) **3** the most favourable front-row or inside position on the starting line of a race, esp a motor or horse race [ME, fr OE *pāl* stake, pole, fr L *palus* stake; akin to L *pangere* to fix – more at PACT] – **under bare poles** *of a ship* with furled sails – **up the pole** *chiefly Br informal* **1** slightly mad; crazy **2** misguided, mistaken

²**pole** *vt* **1** to push or propel (e g a boat) along with a pole or poles **2** to support (e g runner beans) on poles ~ *vi* **1** to propel oneself or something, esp a boat, with a pole or poles **2** to use ski poles to move more quickly over snow ⟨~d *down the hill*⟩ – **poler** *n*

**pole on** *vt, Austr informal* to cadge or scrounge from

³**pole** *n* **1** either extremity of an axis of a sphere, or of a body, esp the earth, resembling a sphere **2a** either of two related opposites **b** something serving as a guiding influence or centre of attraction ⟨*the pivot and* ~ *of his life ... was his mother* – D H Lawrence⟩ **3a** either of the two terminals of an electric cell, battery, or dynamo **b** any of two or more regions in a magnetized body at which the magnetism is concentrated **4** either of two anatomically or physiologically differentiated areas at opposite ends of an organism or cell **5** the fixed point in a system of POLAR COORDINATES that serves as the ORIGIN (position where values are zero) [ME *pool*, fr L *polus*, fr Gk *polos* pivot, pole; akin to Gk *kyklos* wheel – more at WHEEL] – **poles apart** having nothing in common; totally unrelated

**Pole** *n* a native or inhabitant of Poland [Ger, of Slav origin; akin to Polish *Polak* Pole]

¹**poleaxe** /'pohl,aks/ *n* **1** a battle-axe with short handle and often a hook or spike opposite the blade; *also* one with a long handle used as an ornamental weapon **2** an axe used, esp formerly, in slaughtering cattle [ME *polax, pollax*, fr *pol, polle* poll + *ax* axe]

²**poleaxe** *vt* to attack, strike, or fell (as if) with a poleaxe

**polecat** /'pohl,kat/ *n, pl* **polecats**, *esp collectively* **polecat 1** an African and Eurasian flesh-eating mammal (*Mustela putorius*) of which the ferret is considered a domesticated variety **2** *NAm* SKUNK 1 [ME *polcat*, prob fr MF *poul, pol* cock + ME *cat*; prob fr its preying on poultry]

**polemic** /pə'lemik, po-, poh-, -'lee-/ *n* **1** an aggressive attack on or refutation of the opinions or principles of another **2 polemics** *taking sing or pl vb,* **polemic** the art or practice of disputation or controversy [Fr *polémique*, fr MF, fr *polemique* controversial, fr Gk *polemikos* warlike, hostile, fr *polemos* war; akin to OE eal*felo* baleful, Gk *pallein* to brandish] – **polemic, polemical** *adj,* **polemically** *adv,* **polemicist** *n*

**polemic·ize, -ise** /pə'lemisiez, -'lee-/ *vi* to polemize

**polem·ize, -ise** /'polimiez/ *vi* to engage in controversy; dispute aggressively – **polemist** *n*

**polenta** /po'lentə, poh-, pə-/ *n* a porridge made with maize meal, semolina, or farina [It, fr L, crushed grain]

**polestar** /'pohl,stah/ *n* **1** a directing principle; a guide **2** a centre of attraction

**Pole Star** *n* the star in the constellation URSA MINOR that lies very close to the north CELESTIAL POLE so that it seems to remain almost motionless in the sky with all the other stars revolving round it

**pole vault** *n* (an athletic field event consisting of) a jump for height over a crossbar with the aid of a long pole – **pole-vault** *vi,* **pole-vaulter** *n*

¹**police** /pə'lees/ *n* **1** the department of government concerned primarily with maintenance of public order, law enforcement, and the prevention and detection of crime **2a** *taking sing or pl vb* POLICE FORCE **b** *taking pl vb* policemen and policewomen **3a** *taking sing or pl vb* an organized body having similar functions to a police force but within a more restricted sphere ⟨*military* ~⟩ ⟨*railway* ~⟩ **b** *pl* the members of such a body **4a** the action or process of cleaning and putting in order **b** *taking pl*

*vb* military personnel detailed to perform this function [MF, government, fr LL *politia*, fr Gk *politeia*, fr *politeuein* to be a citizen, engage in political activity, fr *politēs* citizen, fr *polis* city, state; akin to Skt *pur* city]

²**police** *vt* 1 to control, regulate, or keep in order by use of police ⟨~d *the football match*⟩ 2 to make clean and put in order 3a to supervise the operation, execution, or administration of, esp in order to prevent or detect violation of rules ⟨*UN officials* ~d *the first democratic elections*⟩ b to exercise such supervision over the policies and activities of 4 to perform the functions of a police force in or over

**police action** *n* a localized military action undertaken without formal declaration of war by regular forces against people held to be violators of international peace and order

**police dog** *n* a dog trained to assist the police (e g in tracking criminals or detecting drugs)

**police force** *n taking sing or pl vb* a body of trained people entrusted by a government with maintenance of public order, enforcement of laws, and prevention and detection of crime

**policeman** /-mən/, *fem* **policewoman** *n* 1 a member of a police force 2 an instrument (e g a flat piece of rubber on the end of a glass rod) for removing solids from a vessel (e g a beaker)

**policeman's helmet** *n* HIMALAYAN BALSAM (plant native to the Himalayas)

**police state** *n* a state or country characterized by repressive governmental control of political, economic, and social life, usu enforced by an esp secret police, in place of regular operation of administrative and judicial organs of the government according to publicly known legal procedures

**police station** *n* the headquarters of a local police force

¹**policy** /'polisi/ *n* 1 management or procedure based primarily on material interest ⟨*it's bad* ~ *to smoke*⟩ 2a a definite course or method of action selected from among alternatives and in the light of given conditions ⟨*your best* ~ *would be to follow my original suggestion*⟩ b an overall plan, esp of a governmental body, embracing general goals and procedures and intended to guide and determine present and future decisions ⟨*foreign* ~⟩ 3 *archaic* prudence or wisdom in the management of affairs; sagacity [ME *policie* government, policy, fr MF, government, regulation, fr LL *politia* – more at POLICE]

²**policy** *n* (a document embodying) a contract of insurance [alter. of earlier *police*, fr MF, certificate, fr OIt *polizza*, modif of ML *apodixa* receipt, fr MGk *apodeixis*, fr Gk, proof, fr *apodeiknynai* to demonstrate – more at APODICTIC]

**policyholder** /-,hohldə/ *n* a person, company, etc holding an insurance policy

**poling board** /'pohling/ *n* any of the vertical planks that support the sides of narrow trenches during excavation

**polio** /'pohli·oh/ *n* POLIOMYELITIS

**poliomyelitis** /,pohli·oh,mie·ə'lietis/ *n* an acute infectious virus disease, esp of children, characterized by fever, inflammation of the nerve cells of the SPINAL CORD, paralysis of nerves, and wasting of skeletal muscles and often resulting in permanent disability and deformity [NL, fr Gk *polios* grey + *myelos* marrow – more at FALLOW, MYEL-] – **poliomyelitic** *adj*

**poliovirus** /,pohlioh'vie·ərəs/ *n* a virus that occurs in several forms and is the causative agent of human poliomyelitis [NL, fr *polio*myelitis + *virus*]

**polis** /'polis/ *n, pl* **poleis** /'polays/ an ancient Greek city-state; *broadly* a state or society, esp when characterized by a sense of community [Gk – more at POLICE]

**-polis** /-pəlis/ *comb form* (→ *n*) city ⟨*megalo*polis⟩ [LL, fr Gk, fr *polis*]

¹**polish** /'polish/ *vt* 1 to make smooth and glossy, usu by rubbing; burnish ⟨~ed *up the handle of the big front door* – W S Gilbert⟩ 2 to smooth or refine in manners or condition 3 to bring to a highly developed, finished, or refined state; perfect; *also* to work at in order to bring back to a previously attained, higher level ⟨*gave a* ~ed *performance*⟩ ⟨~ed *up her French before the holiday*⟩ ~ *vi* to become smooth or glossy (as if) by rubbing [ME *polisshen*, fr OF *poliss-*, stem of *polir*, fr L *polire*] – **polisher** *n*

**polish off** *vt, informal* 1 to dispose of rapidly or completely 2 to kill

²**polish** *n* 1a shine, lustre b freedom from rudeness or coarseness; refinement 2 the action or process of polishing ⟨*give the table a good* ~⟩ 3 a preparation that is used to produce a gloss and often a colour for the protection and decoration of a surface ⟨*furniture* ~⟩ ⟨*nail* ~⟩

¹**Polish** /'pohlish/ *adj* (characteristic) of Poland, the Poles, or Polish [*Pole* + *-ish*]

²**Polish** *n* the Slavonic language of the Poles

**politburo** /'polit,byoooroh, -'-,--/ *n, pl* **politburos** *often cap* the principal policy-making and executive committee of a Communist party [Russ *politbyuro*, fr *politicheskoye byuro* political bureau]

**polite** /pə'liet/ *adj* 1 showing or characterized by correct social usage; refined ⟨~ *society*⟩ 2 marked by consideration, tact, or deference; courteous [L *politus*, fr pp of *polire* to polish, refine] – **politely** *adv*, **politeness** *n*

**politesse** /,poli'tes/ *n* formal politeness; decorousness [Fr, fr MF, cleanness, fr OIt *pulitezza*, fr *pulito*, pp of *pulire* to polish, clean, fr L *polire*]

**politic** /'politik/ *adj* 1a shrewd and skilful in managing, negotiating, or dealing (e g in business) b devious, unscrupulous 2 expedient, prudent ⟨*a* ~ *decision*⟩ *synonyms* see SUAVE [ME *politik*, fr MF *politique*, fr L *politicus*, fr Gk *politikos*, fr *politēs* citizen – more at POLICE]

**political** /pə'litikl/ *adj* 1a of (a) government b of or concerned with the making as distinguished from the administration of government policy 2a of or involving politics, esp party politics b adept at, sensitive to, or engrossed in politics ⟨*highly* ~ *students*⟩ 3 defined in political terms ⟨*a* ~ *unit*⟩ 4 involving or charged or concerned with acts against a government or a political system ⟨~ *criminals*⟩ [L *politicus*] – **politically** *adv*

**political economy** *n* 1 a 19th-century social science comprising the modern science of economics 2 a modern social science dealing with the interrelationship of political and economic processes – **political economist** *n*

**political levy** *n* a levy that trade-union members may pay over and above their union subscriptions and that is used for political purposes, esp affiliation to the Labour party

**political science** *n* a social science concerned chiefly with the description and analysis of political and governmental institutions and processes – **political scientist** *n*

**politician** /,poli'tish(ə)n/ *n* a person experienced in the art or science of government or party politics; *esp* one actively engaged in conducting the business of a government

**politic·ize, -ise** /pə'litisiez/ *vi* to discuss politics ~ *vt* to give a political tone or character to – **politicization** *n*

**politick** /'polətik/ *vi* to engage in political discussion or activity [back-formation fr *politicking*, n, fr *politics* + *-ing*] – **politicker** *n*

**politico** /pə'litikoh/ *n, pl* **politicos** *also* **politicoes** *informal* a politician [It *politico* or Sp *politico*, derivs of L *politicus* political]

**politico-** *comb form* political and ⟨politico-*diplomatic*⟩ [L *politicus*]

**politics** /'politiks/ *n taking sing or pl vb* 1a the art or science of government b the art or science concerned with guiding or influencing governmental policy c the art or science concerned with winning and holding governmental control 2 political actions, practices, or policies 3a political affairs or business; *specif* competition between competing interest groups or individuals for power and leadership in a group, esp a government ⟨*office* ~⟩ b political life, esp as a principal activity or profession c political activities characterized by artful and often dishonest practices 4 the political opinions or sympathies of a person or group ⟨*what are her* ~?⟩ 5 the total complex of relations between members of a society; *esp* the usu conflicting interactions between leaders and led and the influences and controls exerted 6 POLITICAL SCIENCE [Gk *politika*, fr neut pl of *politikos* political]

*usage* **Politics** usually takes a plural verb when it means "political sympathies" ⟨*her* **politics** *are nothing to do with you*⟩ but a singular verb in the other senses ⟨**politics** *is a controversial topic*⟩ ⟨**politics** *was my chosen career*⟩.

**polity** /'poləti/ *n* 1 a politically organized unit 2a the form or constitution of a politically organized unit b the form of government of a religious denomination △ policy [LL *politia* – more at POLICE]

**polka** /'polkə/ *n* (music for or in the rhythm of) a lively dance of Bohemian origin having two beats to the bar and a basic pattern of hop-step-close-step [Fr & Ger, fr Czech *půlka* half-step, fr *půl* half] – **polka** *vi*

**polka dot** /'polkə, 'pohkə/ *n* any of many regularly distributed usu small circular spots forming a pattern on a fabric – **polka-dot, polka-dotted** *adj*

¹**poll** /pohl/ *n* 1 the head 2 the prominent hairy top or back of

the head **3** the broad or flat end of the head of a striking tool (eg a hammer) – compare PEEN **4a** the casting or recording of votes **b polls** *pl,* **poll** the place where votes are cast or recorded ⟨*at the* ~s⟩ **c** the number of votes recorded ⟨*a heavy* ~⟩ **5** a survey conducted by questioning or canvassing people selected at random or by quota – compare GALLUP POLL [ME *pol, polle,* fr MLG; (4–5) fr the idea of counting heads and hence votes]

²**poll** *vt* **1a** to cut off or cut short the hair or wool of; crop, shear **b** to cut off or cut short (eg wool) **2a** to remove the top of (eg a tree); *specif* to pollard **b** to cut off or cut short the horns of (cattle) **3** to receive and record the votes of **4** to receive (votes) in an election ⟨~ed *5,000 votes in the local election*⟩ **5** to question or canvass in a poll **6** to cast (a vote) in an election **7** *chiefly NAm* to request each member of to declare his/her vote individually ⟨~ *the assembly*⟩ ~ *vi* to cast one's vote at a poll – **pollee** *n,* **poller** *n*

³**poll** *n* a polled animal [prob fr obs *poll,* adj, naturally hornless, short for *polled*]

**pollack, pollock** /'polək/ *n, pl* **pollack, pollock** a N Atlantic food fish (*Pollachius pollachius*) related to and resembling the cods but darker; *also* a coley [Sc *podlok,* of unknown origin]

¹**pollard** /'poləd/ *n* **1** a hornless animal of a usu horned kind **2** a tree cut back to the main stem to promote the growth of a dense head of leaves **3** finely ground bran obtained from wheat during milling [²*poll* + *-ard*]

²**pollard** /'poləd, 'polahd/ *vt* to make a pollard of (a tree)

**polled** /pohld/ *adj* hornless

**pollen** /'polən/ *n* a mass of minute granules produced by the ANTHER (part of the male reproductive organ) of the flower of a FLOWERING PLANT and serving to fertilize the OVULES (structures which develop into seeds) [NL *pollin-, pollen,* fr L, fine flour, powder; akin to L *pulvis* dust, Gk *palē* fine meal] – **pollinic** *adj*

**pollen analysis** *n* the identification and the determination of frequency of POLLEN GRAINS (eg in the various layers of peat in a peat bog) as a means of dating esp fossil remains and determining the vegetation and climate of past ages; *broadly* PALYNOLOGY

**pollenate** /'polənayt/ *vt* to pollinate – **pollenation** *n*

**pollen basket** *n* a smooth area on each hind leg of a bee that is edged by a fringe of stiff hairs and serves to collect and transport pollen – called also CORBICULA

**pollen count** *n* an index representing the amount of pollen in the air, available as a warning to people allergic to pollen

**pollen grain** *n* any of the small grainlike spores that occur in pollen and give rise to the male reproductive cells of a SEED PLANT

**pollen·izer, -iser, pollin·izer, -iser** /'polənizə/ *n* **1** a plant that is a source of pollen **2** a pollinator [*pollenize,* var of *pollinize*]

**pollen mother cell** *n* a cell that divides to form four cells which develop into POLLEN GRAINS

**pollenosis** /,polə'nohsis/ *n* POLLINOSIS (type of HAY FEVER)

**pollen sac** *n* any of the pouches of the ANTHER (part of the male reproductive organ) of a SEED PLANT in which pollen is formed

**pollen tube** *n* a tube that is formed by a POLLEN GRAIN in contact with the STIGMA (part of the female reproductive organs) of a flowering plant, passes down the STYLE (long slender structure supporting the stigma), and conveys the sperm nuclei to the EMBRYO SAC of the OVARY (female reproductive structure)

**pollex** /'poleks/ *n, pl* **pollices** /'poliseez/ the first digit of the forelimb; the thumb [NL *pollic-, pollex,* fr L, thumb, big toe] – **pollical** *adj*

**pollin-** /'polən-/, **pollini-** *comb form* pollen ⟨pollin*ate*⟩ [NL *pollin-, pollen*]

**pollinate** /'polə,nayt/ *vt* to place pollen on the STIGMA (female reproductive organ of a plant) of, and so fertilize

**pollination** /,polə'naysh(ə)n/ *n* the transfer of pollen from a STAMEN (male reproductive organ of a plant) to the STIGMA (female reproductive organ) prior to fertilization of an OVULE (structure that develops into a seed)

**pollinator** /'polənaytə/ *n* **1** something (eg a person, an animal, or the wind) that pollinates flowers **2** a pollenizer

**polliniferous** /,polə'nif(ə)rəs/ *adj* **1** bearing or producing pollen **2** adapted for the purpose of carrying pollen

**pollinium** /pə'lini·əm/ *n, pl* **pollinia** /-niə/ a cohering mass of POLLEN GRAINS (eg produced by many orchids) often with a stalk bearing a sticky disc that clings to insects [NL, fr *pollin-* + *-ium*]

**pollin·ize, -ise** /'poləniez/ *vt* to pollinate [ISV]

**pollin·izer, -iser** /'poləniezə/ *n* a pollenizer

**pollinose** /'polənohs/ *adj, of an insect* covered with pollen

**pollinosis, pollenosis** /,polə'nohsis/ *n* HAY FEVER caused by allergic sensitivity to specific pollens [NL *pollinosis,* fr *pollin-* + *-osis*]

**polliwog, pollywog** /'poliwog/ *n, NAm & dial Br* a tadpole [alter. of ME *polwygle,* prob fr *pol* head + *wiglen* to wiggle]

**pollock** /'polək/ *n* POLLACK (type of fish)

**pollster** /'pohlstə/ *n* one who conducts a poll or compiles data obtained by a poll

**poll tax** *n* a tax of a fixed amount per person levied on adults and often, esp formerly, payable as a requirement for voting

**pollutant** /pə'l(y)oohtənt/ *n* something that pollutes

**pollute** /pə'looht/ *vt* **1** to make morally impure; defile **2** to make physically impure or unclean; to befoul, dirty **3** to contaminate (an environment), esp with man-made waste *synonyms* see CONTAMINATE [ME *polluten,* fr L *pollutus,* pp of *polluere,* fr *por-* (akin to L *per* through) + *-luere* (akin to L *lutum* mud, Gk *lyma* dirt, defilement)] – **polluter** *n,* **pollutive** *adj*

**pollution** /pə'loohsh(ə)n/ *n* **1** emission of semen at other times than in SEXUAL INTERCOURSE **2a** the action of polluting; the condition of being polluted **b** material that pollutes

**Pollux** /'poləks/ *n* one of the Dioscuri [L, modif of Gk *Polydeukēs*]

**Pollyanna** /,poli'anə/ *n* an irrepressible optimist [*Pollyanna,* heroine of the novel *Pollyanna* by Eleanor Porter †1920 US fiction-writer] – **Pollyannaish, Pollyannish** *adj*

**polo** /'pohloh/ *n* **1** a game of oriental origin played by teams of usu four players on ponies using mallets with long flexible handles to drive a wooden ball into the opponents' goal; *also* any of several games in which horses are replaced by vehicles (eg canoes or bicycles) **2** WATER POLO [Balti, ball] – **poloist** *n*

**polonaise** /,polə'nayz/ *n* **1** a short-sleeved elaborate dress with a fitted waist and loops of material drawn up at the sides and back to reveal a decorative underskirt **2** (music in moderate time with three beats to the bar for) a stately Polish processional dance popular in 19th-century Europe [Fr, fr fem of *polonais* Polish, fr *Pologne* Poland, fr ML *Polonia*]

**polo neck** *n, chiefly Br* (a jumper with) a very high closely fitting collar that is worn rolled over

**polonium** /pə'lohnyəm, -ni·əm/ *n* a radioactive metallic chemical element that is similar chemically to the elements tellurium and bismuth, occurs esp in the mineral pitchblende and radium-lead residues, and decays radioactively to form an ISOTOPE (form in which an atom can occur) of lead [NL, fr ML *Polonia* Poland; fr its discovery by the Polish-born chemist Marie Curie]

**polony** /pə'lohni/ *n* a dry sausage of partly cooked meat, esp pork; *also* a cooked sausage made from soya and meat and eaten cold [alter. of *bologna (sausage)*]

**poltergeist** /'poltə,giest/ *n* a noisy usu mischievous ghost believed to be responsible for unexplained noises and physical damage [Ger, fr *poltern* to knock + *geist* spirit, fr OHG – more at GHOST]

**poltroon** /pol'troohn/ *n* a spiritless coward [MF *poultron,* fr OIt *poltrone,* fr aug of *poltro* colt, deriv of L *pullus* young of an animal – more at FOAL]

¹**poly** /'poli/ *n, pl* **polys** GRANULOCYTE (type of WHITE BLOOD CELL) [short for *polymorphonuclear leucocyte*]

²**poly** *n, pl* **polys** *Br informal* a polytechnic

**poly-** *comb form* **1a** many; several; much; multi- ⟨poly*phonic*⟩ ⟨poly*gyny*⟩ **b** excessive; abnormally great; hyper- ⟨poly*phagia*⟩ **2a** containing two or more (specified ions or chemical groups) in the molecular structure ⟨poly*sulphide*⟩ **b** polymeric; polymer of (a specified monomer) ⟨poly*ethylene*⟩ ⟨poly*adenylic acid*⟩ [ME, fr L, fr Gk, fr *polys;* akin to OE *full* full]

**polyacrylamide** /,poli·ə'kriləmied/ *n* a polyamide of ACRYLIC ACID (type of liquid chemical compound used in the production of plastics, rubber, etc)

**polyacrylamide gel** /,poli·ə'kriləmied/ *n* polyacrylamide in a soft jellylike form that is used esp for ELECTROPHORESIS (movement of particles under the influence of an electric field)

**polyadelphous** /,poli·ə'delfəs/ *adj* **1** of or being STAMENS (male reproductive organs of a plant) united into three or more groups **2** *of a flower* having stamens united into groups □ compare DIADELPHOUS, MONADELPHOUS [deriv of Gk *polyadelphos* having many brothers, fr *poly-* + *adelphos* brother]

**polyamide** /,poli'amied, -mid/ *n* **1** a chemical compound characterized by more than one AMIDE group; *esp* one composed of repeated amide subunits **2** a synthetic fibre made from polyamide [ISV]

**polyandry** /'poli‚andri/ *n* **1** the state or practice of having more than one husband or male mate at one time – compare POLYGAMY, POLYGYNY **2** the condition in a flower of having many STAMENS (male reproductive organs) [Gk *polyandros,* adj, having many men or husbands, fr *poly-* + *andr-, anēr* man, husband – more at ANDR-] – **polyandrous** *adj*

**polyanthus** /-'anthəs/ *n, pl* **polyanthuses, polyanthi** /-thi, -thie/ **1** any of various cultivated hybrid primroses **2** a narcissus (*Narcissus tazetta*) having small white or yellow flowers [NL, fr Gk *polyanthos* blooming, fr *poly-* + *anthos* flower – more at ANTHOLOGY]

**polybasite** /‚poli'baysiet, pə'libəsiet/ *n* an iron-black metallic-looking ore, $(Ag,Cu)_{16}Sb_2S_{11}$, containing the chemical elements silver, copper, sulphur, and antimony [Ger *polybasit,* fr *poly-* + *basi-* base]

**polycarbonate** /‚poli'kahbənayt, -nət/ *n* any of various tough transparent plastics characterized by high impact strength and high softening temperature

**polychaete** /-‚keet/ *n or adj* (any) of a class (Polychaeta of the phylum Annelida) of chiefly marine segmented worms with many bristles borne on paired locomotory structures (PARAPODIA) which project from each segment of the worm – compare OLIGOCHAETE [deriv of Gk *polychaitēs* having much hair, fr *poly-* + *chaitē* long hair – more at CHAETA] – **polychaetous** *adj*

**polychasium** /‚poli'kayziəm/ *n, pl* **polychasia** /-ziə/ a CYME (type of flower cluster) in which each main flower stem produces more than two branches [NL, fr *poly-* + *-chasium* (as in *dichasium*)]

**polychlorinated biphenyl** /‚poli'klawri‚naytid/ *n* any of several chemical compounds that are produced by replacing the hydrogen atoms in BIPHENYL with chlorine, have various industrial applications, and are poisonous environmental pollutants which tend to accumulate in animal tissues

**polychromatic** /-kroh'matik/ *adj* **1** showing a variety or a change of colours; multicoloured **2** of or being radiation that is composed of more than one wavelength [Gk *polychrōmatos,* fr *poly-* + *chrōmat-, chrōma* colour – more at CHROMATIC]

**polychrome** /-‚krohm/ *adj* relating to, made with, or decorated in several colours ⟨~ *pottery*⟩ [Gk *polychrōmos,* fr *poly-* + *chrōma*] – **polychromy** *n*

**polycistronic** /‚polisi'stronik/ *adj* containing the genetic information of a number of CISTRONS (groups of genes controlling protein structure) ⟨~ *messenger RNA*⟩

**polycondensation** /‚polikonden'saysh(ə)n, -dən-/ *n* a chemical reaction (CONDENSATION) leading to the formation of a compound of high MOLECULAR WEIGHT [ISV]

**polyconic projection** /‚poli'konik/ *n* a composite map projection made up of several CONIC PROJECTIONS of adjacent areas of the earth's surface

**polycot** /'poli‚kot/ *n* a polycotyledon

**polycotyl** /'poli‚kotl/ *n* a polycotyledon

**polycotyledon** /‚polikoti'leedən/ *n* a plant (e g a conifer) having more than two COTYLEDONS (first leaves developed by the embryo of a SEED PLANT) [NL] – **polycotyledonous** *adj*

**polycrystalline** /-'kristl‚ien/ *adj* **1** consisting of variously oriented crystals **2** composed of more than one crystal – **polycrystal** *n*

**polycyclic** /‚poli'sieklik, -'siklik/ *adj* having more than one cyclic component: e g **a** *of a plant* having more than one ring or WHORL (circular arrangement of similar parts) **b** having two or more fused rings of atoms in the molecule ⟨~ *naphthalene*⟩ [ISV]

**polycythaemia** /-sie'theemi-ə/ *n* a condition marked by an abnormal increase in the number of circulating RED BLOOD CELLS; *specif* POLYCYTHAEMIA VERA [NL, fr *poly-* + *cyt-* + *-haemia,* var of *-aemia*] – **polycythaemic** *adj*

**polycythaemia vera** /‚polisie‚theemia 'viərə/ *n* polycythaemia of unknown cause that is characterized by increase in total blood volume and accompanied by nosebleeds, widening of the circulatory blood vessels, and enlargement of the spleen [NL, true polycythaemia]

**polydactyl** /-'daktil/ *adj* having abnormally many DIGITS (fingers or toes); *broadly* having numerous digits [Gk *polydaktylos,* fr *poly-* + *daktylos* digit] – **polydactyl** *n,* **polydactylism** *n,* **polydactyly** *n*

**polydactylous** /‚poli'daktiləs/ *adj* polydactyl

**polydaemonism** /‚poli'deemaniz(ə)m/ *n* belief in or worship of a multitude of demons or demonic powers

**polydipsia** /‚poli'dipsiə/ *n* excessive thirst [NL, fr *poly-* + Gk *dipsia* thirst]

**polydisperse** /‚polidi'spuhs/ *adj* of or characterized by particles of varied sizes evenly dispersed throughout a medium [*poly-* + L *dispersus* dispersed, fr pp of *dispergere* to disperse] – **polydispersity** *n*

**polyelectrolyte** /‚poli-i'lektrəliet/ *n* a substance of high MOLECULAR WEIGHT (e g a protein) that is an ELECTROLYTE (nonmetallic substance that conducts electricity)

**polyembryony** /‚poli'embriəni/ *n* **1** the condition of having several embryos **2** the production (e g by certain plants and parasitic insects) of two or more embryos from one fertilized ovum [ISV *poly-* + *embryon-* + *-y*] – **polyembryonic** *adj*

**polyene** /'poli-een/ *n* a chemical compound containing many DOUBLE BONDS (forces which hold two atoms together); *esp* one having the double bonds in a long straight chain [ISV] – **polyenic** *adj*

**polyester** /-'estə/ *n* **1** a complex chemical compound (POLYMER) in which the repeated subunits are ESTERS (compounds formed by the combination of an acid and an alcohol) and which is used esp in making fibres or plastics **2** a synthetic fibre made from polyester *synonyms* see POLYTHENE, NYLON [ISV] – **polyesterification** *n*

**polyethylene** /-'ethi‚leen/ *n* polythene

**polygamic** /‚poli'gamik/ *adj* polygamous – **polygamical** *adj,* **polygamically** *adv*

**polygamous** /pə'ligəməs/ *adj* **1a** of or practising polygamy **b** having more than one mate at one time ⟨*baboons are* ~⟩ **2** bearing both HERMAPHRODITE (having both male and female reproductive organs) and UNISEXUAL (having either male or female reproductive organs, but not both) flowers on the same plant [Gk *polygamos,* fr *poly-* + *-gamos* -gamous] – **polygamously** *adv*

**polygamy** /pə'ligəmi/ *n* **1** the state or practice of being married to more than one person at a time; *esp* marriage in which the husband has more than one wife – compare POLYANDRY, POLYGYNY **2** the state of being polygamous – **polygamist** *n,* **polygamize** *vi*

**polygene** /'poli‚jeen/ *n* any of a group of genes that collectively control the inheritance of a quantitative characteristic or modify the expression of a qualitative characteristic [ISV] – **polygenic** *adj*

**polygenesis** /-'jenəsis/ *n* origin from more than one ancestral line or stock [NL] – **polygenesist** *n*

**polygenetic** /‚polijə'netik/ *adj* **1** having many distinct sources **2** POLYPHYLETIC (originating from more than one ancestral line) – **polygenetically** *adv*

**polyglandular** /‚poli'glandyoolə/ *adj* of or involving several glands ⟨~ *therapy*⟩ [ISV]

**¹polyglot** /-‚glot/ *n* **1** one who is polyglot **2** *cap* a book, esp a Bible, containing versions of the same text in several languages **3** a mixture or confusion of languages [Gk *polyglōttos,* adj, polyglot, fr *poly-* + *glōtta* tongue, language – more at GLOSS] – **polyglottal** *adj*

**²polyglot** *adj* **1a** speaking or writing several languages; MULTILINGUAL **2 b** composed of numerous linguistic groups ⟨*a* ~ *population*⟩ **2** containing matter in several languages ⟨*a* ~ *sign*⟩ **3** composed of elements from different languages – **polyglottism, polyglotism** *n*

**polygon** /'poligən, -gon/ *n* **1** a closed two-dimensional geometric figure bounded by straight lines **2** a closed figure on a sphere bounded by arcs of GREAT CIRCLES (circles having the same centre as the sphere) [LL *polygonum,* fr Gk *polygōnon,* fr neut of *polygōnos* many-sided, fr *poly-* + *gōnia* angle – more at -GON] – **polygonal** *adj,* **polygonally** *adv*

**polygonum** /pə'ligənəm/ *n* any of a genus (*Polygonum*) of plants (e g bistort) of the dock family with thickened stem joints and small usu white, red, or green flowers [NL, genus name, fr Gk *polygonon* knotgrass, fr *poly-* + *gony* knee, joint – more at KNEE]

**polygraph** /-‚grahf, -‚graf/ *n* an instrument for recording variations of the pulse, blood pressure, etc simultaneously; *broadly* LIE DETECTOR – **polygraphic** *adj*

**polygynous** /pə'lijinəs/ *adj* **1** of or practising polygyny **2** *of a plant* having many OVARIES (female reproductive organs containing the seeds)

**polygyny** /pə'lijini/ *n* the state or practice of having more than one wife or female mate at one time – compare POLYANDRY, POLYGAMY

**polyhedral angle** /‚poli'heedrəl/ *n* a portion of space partly enclosed by three or more planes that intersect at a vertex

**polyhedron** /,poli'heedrən/ *n, pl* **polyhedrons, polyhedra** /-drə/ a solid three-dimensional geometric figure bounded by plane faces [NL] – **polyhedral** *adj*

**polyhedrosis** /,polihee'drohsis/ *n, pl* **polyhedroses** /-seez/ any of several virus diseases of insect larvae characterized by dissolution of tissues and accumulation of polyhedral granules in the resultant fluid [NL, fr *polyhedron*]

**polyhydroxy** /,polihie'droksi/ *adj, of a chemical compound* containing more than one HYDROXYL group in the molecule [*poly-* + *hydroxyl*]

**polymath** /-,math/ *n* a person of encyclopedic or varied learning; *broadly* one who has a wide range of accomplishments [Gk *polymathēs* very learned, fr *poly-* + *manthanein* to learn – more at MATHEMATICAL] – **polymath, polymathic** *adj*, **polymathy** *n*

**polymer** /'polimə/ *n* a chemical compound or mixture of compounds formed by polymerization and consisting essentially of repeating structural units [ISV, back-formation fr *polymeric*]

**polymerase** /'polimərayz, -ays/ *n* an ENZYME that speeds up the formation of polymers; *specif* any of several enzymes that take part in the formation of DNA or RNA [*polymer* + *-ase*]

**polymeric** /,poli'merik/ *adj* **1** of or constituting a polymer **2** of, being, or involving genes that collectively control one or more hereditary traits [ISV, fr Gk *polymerēs* having many parts, fr *poly-* + *meros* part – more at MERIT] – **polymerically** *adv*, **polymerism** *n*

**polymer·ization, -isation** /,polimərie'zaysh(ə)n/ *n* **1** a chemical reaction in which two or more small molecules combine to form larger molecules that contain repeating structural units of the original molecules – compare ASSOCIATION 5 **2** reduplication of parts in a big organism [ISV]

**polymer·ize, -ise** /'poliməriez/ *vb* to subject to or undergo polymerization

**polymorph** /'polimawf/ *n* **1** (any of the several forms of) a polymorphic organism **2** any of the crystalline forms of a polymorphic substance **3** GRANULOCYTE (type of WHITE BLOOD CELL) [ISV]

**polymorphic** /-'mawfik/ *adj* having, assuming, or occurring in various forms, characters, or styles [Gk *polymorphos*, fr *poly-* + *-morphos* -morphous] – **polymorphically** *adv*, **polymorphism** *n*

**polymorphonuclear** /,poli,mawfoh'nyoohkli-ə/ *adj* having an irregularly shaped or multi-lobed nucleus – **polymorphonuclear** *n*

**polymorphonuclear leucocyte** *n* GRANULOCYTE (type of WHITE BLOOD CELL)

**polymorphous** /,poli'mawfəs/ *adj* polymorphic – **polymorphously** *adv*

**polymyxin** /,poli'miksin/ *n* any of several antibiotics obtained from a soil bacterium (*Bacillus polymyxa*) and used to treat severe infections by bacteria, esp PSEUDOMONADS [ISV, fr NL *polymyxa* (specific epithet of *Bacillus polymyxa*), fr *poly-* + Gk *myxa* mucus – more at MUCUS]

**Polynesian** /,poli'neez(h)yən, -s(h)yən/ *n* **1** a native or inhabitant of Polynesia **2** a group of AUSTRONESIAN languages spoken in Polynesia [*Polynesia*, island group in central & S Pacific, fr *poly-* + Gk *nēsos* island] – **Polynesian** *adj*

**polyneuritis** /-nyooə'rietəs/ *n* inflammation or degeneration of several nerves at the same time, caused usu by alcoholism, poisons, infectious disease, or vitamin deficiency (e g of VITAMIN B₁) [NL]

**¹polynomial** /-'nohmyəl/ *n, maths* a sum of two or more algebraic terms each of which consists of a constant multiplied by one or more VARIABLES raised to a nonnegative integral power $\langle a + bx + cx^2 \text{ is } a \sim \rangle$ [*poly-* + *-nomial* (as in *binomial*)]

**²polynomial** *adj* (composed) of or expressed as one or more polynomials $\langle \sim functions \rangle \langle \sim equations \rangle$

**polynucleotide** /-'nyoohkli-ətied/ *n* a complex chemical compound (POLYMER) composed of a chain of linked repeating NUCLEOTIDES; *esp* NUCLEIC ACID (e g RNA or DNA) [ISV]

**polynya** /,polə'nyah/ *n* an area of open water in sea ice [Russ *polyn'ya*]

**polyoestrous** /,poli'eestrəs/ *adj* having more than one period of OESTRUS (sexual excitement and preparedness) in a year

**polyoma virus, polyoma** /,poli'ohmə/ *n* a virus of rodents that is associated with various kinds of tumours [NL *polyoma*, fr *poly-* + *-oma*]

**polyonymous** /,poli'onimәs/ *adj* having or known by various names [Gk *polyōnymos*, fr *poly-* + *onoma, onyma* name]

**polyp** /'polip/ *n* **1** a SEA ANEMONE, coral, or related animal that has typically a hollow cylindrical body closed and attached at one end and opening at the other by a central mouth surrounded by tentacles armed with stinging organs; *also* the usu stationary and non-sexually-reproducing phase of animals belonging to the same group – compare MEDUSA **2** a mass of tissue (e g a tumour) of usu abnormally enlarged cells that projects from a MUCOUS MEMBRANE (e g of the nose) [MF *polype* octopus, nasal tumour, fr L *polypus*, fr Gk *polypous*, lit., having many feet, fr *poly-* + *pous* foot – more at FOOT] – **polypoid** *adj*, **polypous** *adj*

**polypary** /'polip(ə)ri/ *n* the common structure or tissue in which the polyps of certain compound organisms (e g corals) are embedded

**polypeptide** /-'peptied/ *n* a long chain of AMINO ACIDS (chemical compounds forming subunits of proteins) [ISV, fr *poly-* + *peptide*] – **polypeptidic** *adj*

**polypetalous** /,poli'petələs/ *adj* having or consisting of separate petals [NL *polypetalus*, fr *poly-* + *petalum* petal]

**polyphagia** /-fayjyə/ *n* an abnormal desire to overeat, esp as a symptom of illness [Gk, fr *polyphagos*]

**polyphagous** /pə'lifəgəs/ *adj* feeding on or utilizing many kinds of food [Gk *polyphagos* eating too much, fr *poly-* + *-phagos* -phagous] – **polyphagy** *n*

**polyphase** /'poli,fayz/ *adj* having, using, or producing two or more phases $\langle a \sim machine \rangle \langle a \sim electric\ current \rangle$ [ISV]

**polyphasic** /,poli'fayzik/ *adj* consisting of two or more phases

**polyphenol** /,poli'feenol/ *n* a PHENOL (type of chemical compound) containing more than one HYDROXYL group [ISV] – **polyphenolic** *adj*

**polyphone** /'poli,fohn/ *n* a symbol or sequence of symbols (e g English *ea*) that can represent more than one linguistically distinctive sound

**polyphonic** /-'fonik/, **polyphonous** /pə'lifənəs/ *adj* **1** of or marked by polyphony – compare HOMOPHONIC **2** being a polyphone – **polyphonically, polyphonously** *adv*

**polyphony** /pə'lifəni/ *n* a style of musical composition in which two or more independent but related voice parts sound against one another [Gk *polyphōnia* variety of tones, fr *polyphōnos* having many tones or voices, fr *poly-* + *phōnē* voice – more at BAN]

**polyphyletic** /,polifi'letik/ *adj* of more than one stock; *specif* derived from more than one ancestral line [ISV, fr Gk *polyphylos* of many tribes, fr *poly-* + *phylē* tribe – more at PHYL-] – **polyphyletically** *adv*, **polyphyleticism** *n*

**¹polyploid** /-ployd/ *adj* having or being a multiple greater than two of the basic (HAPLOID) number of CHROMOSOMES (strands of gene-carrying material) [ISV] – **polyploidy** *n*

**²polyploid** *n* a polyploid cell, individual, or generation

**polypnea** /po'lipnee-ə/ *n, medicine* rapid breathing; panting [NL, fr *poly-* + *-pnea*] – **polypneic** *adj*

**polypod** /'poli,pod/ *adj, of an insect larva* having many legs or leglike structures [Gk *polypod-, polypous* having many feet – more at POLYP] – **polypod** *n*

**polypody** /pə'lipədi/ *n* a widely distributed fern (*Polypodium vulgare*) that has creeping ROOTSTOCKS (underground stems) [ME *polypodie*, fr L *polypodium*, fr Gk *polypodion*, fr *polypod-, polypous* having many feet]

**polypropylene** /,poli'prohpileen/ *n* any of various plastics or fibres that can be softened and shaped with heat (are THERMOPLASTIC), are POLYMERS (chemical compounds containing repeating structural units) of PROPYLENE, and are used for making moulded articles *synonyms* see POLYTHENE

**polypus** /'polipəs/ *n, pl* **polypi** /-pie/ POLYP 2 (projecting mass of tissue) [L]

**polyrhythm** /-,ridh(ə)m/ *n* the simultaneous combination of contrasting rhythms in a musical composition – **polyrhythmic** *adj*, **polyrhythmically** *adv*

**polyribosome** /,poli'riebəsohm/ *n* a cluster of RIBOSOMES (specialized cell parts) linked together by a molecule of MESSENGER RNA and forming the site of protein synthesis in a cell – **polyribosomal** *adj*

**polysaccharide** /-'sakəried/ *n* a carbohydrate that can be broken down into two or more molecules of MONOSACCHARIDES (simple sugars); *esp* any of the more complex carbohydrates (e g cellulose, starch, or glycogen) [ISV]

**polysaprobic** /,polisə'prohbik/ *adj* living in a medium that is rich in decomposable animal or plant matter and is nearly free from dissolved oxygen [ISV]

**polysemous** /,poli'seemәs, pə'lisimәs/ *adj* having many

meanings [LL *polysemus*, fr Gk *polysēmos*, fr *poly-* + *sēma* sign] – **polysemy** *n*

**polysepalous** /,poli'sepələs/ *adj* having two or more separate SEPALS (leaflike structures surrounding developing flower bud)

**polysome** /'polisohm/ *n* a polyribosome

**polysomic** /,poli'sohmik/ *adj* having one or a few CHROMOSOMES (strands of gene-carrying material in a cell) present in greater or smaller number than the rest [ISV] – **polysomic** *n*

**polysorbate** /,poli'sawbayt/ *n* any of several EMULSIFIERS (substances used to stabilize oil-and-water mixtures) used in the preparation of some medicines or foods

**polystyrene** /-'stie·əreen/ *n* a POLYMER (chemical compound containing repeating structural units) of STYRENE; *esp* a rigid transparent plastic of good physical and electrical insulating properties used esp in moulded products, foams, and sheet materials *synonyms* see POLYTHENE

**polysulphide** /,poli'sulfied/ *n* a chemical compound (SULPHIDE) containing two or more atoms of sulphur in the molecule [ISV]

**polysyllabic** /-si'labik/, **polysyllabical** /-kl/ *adj* 1 having more than three syllables 2 characterized by polysyllabic words [ML *polysyllabus*, fr Gk *polysyllabos*, fr *poly-* + *syllabē* syllable] – **polysyllabically** *adv*

**polysyllable** /-,siləbl/ *n* a polysyllabic word [modif of ML *polysyllaba*, fr fem of *polysyllabus*]

**polysynaptic** /,polisi'naptik/ *adj* involving two or more SYNAPSES (point at which impulses pass from one NERVE FIBRE to another) in the CENTRAL NERVOUS SYSTEM ⟨~ *reflexes*⟩ – **polysynaptically** *adv*

**polysyndeton** /,poli'sindətən/ *n* the repetition of conjunctions in close succession (e g in *we have ships and men and money and stores*) [NL, fr LGk, neut of *polysyndetos* using many conjunctions, fr Gk *poly-* + *syndetos* bound together, conjunctive – more at ASYNDETON]

**polysynthetic** /,polisin'thetik/ *adj, of a language* combining many linguistic parts into one word with appropriate changes; having few free linguistic forms – compare AGGLUTINATION [LGk *polysynthetos* much-compounded, fr Gk *poly-* + *synthetos* compounded, fr *syntithenai* to put together – more at SYNTHESIS]

¹**polytechnic** /-'teknik/ *adj* relating to or devoted to instruction in many technical arts or applied sciences [Fr *polytechnique*, fr Gk *polytechnos* skilled in many arts, fr *poly-* + *technē* art – more at TECHNICAL]

²**polytechnic** *n* a polytechnic institution; *specif* any of a number of British institutions offering full-time, sandwich, and part-time courses in various subjects but with a bias towards the vocational

**polytene** /'politeen/ *adj* of, being, or having CHROMOSOMES (strands of gene-carrying material in cells) each of which consists of many strands with the corresponding sections in contact [ISV *poly-* + ¹-*tene*] – **polyteny** *n*

**polytetrafluoroethylene** /-tetrə,flooəroh'ethileen/ *n* a POLYMER (chemical compound containing repeating structural units) of TETRAFLUOROETHYLENE; *esp* a tough translucent plastic, $(CF_2CF_2)_x$, that is resistant to chemicals, has good non-stick properties, and is used esp for linings (e g of cooking utensils), for insulation, and for artificial body parts (e g hip joints)

**polytheism** /-thi,iz(ə)m/ *n* belief in or worship of more than one god [Fr *polytheisme*, fr LGk *polytheos* polytheistic, fr Gk, of many gods, fr *poly-* + *theos* god] – **polytheist** *adj or n*, **polytheistic** *adj*

**polythene** /'politheen, 'polətheen/ *n* a POLYMER (chemical compound containing repeating structural units) of ethylene; *esp* any of various lightweight plastics, $(CH_2CH_2)_x$, that are resistant to chemicals and moisture, have good insulating properties, and are used esp in packaging, insulation, and making moulded articles (e g bowls and buckets) [contr of *polyethylene*]

*synonyms* Of the best known synthetic materials beginning with **poly-**, **polythene** (or **polyethylene**) is flexible and is most familiar in the form of sheet, tubing, and coating for cables; **polypropylene** is tougher than **polythene** and can be used for rigid objects such as safety helmets; **polystyrene** is the only fully transparent material mentioned here, is rigid, and makes the outer casing of large domestic appliances such as refrigerators; **polyurethane** makes the squashy foam in mattresses and upholstery; **polyvinyl chloride** is important in the manufacture of imitation leather; and **polyester** is chiefly spun into fibres for fabrics.

**polytocous** /pə'litəkəs/ *adj* producing many eggs or young at one time [Gk *polytokos*, fr *poly-* + *tiktein* to beget – more at THANE]

**polytonality** /-toh'naləti/ *n* the simultaneous use of two or more musical keys – **polytonal** *adj*, **polytonally** *adv*

**polytrophic** /,poli'trohfik/ *adj, esp of microorganisms* deriving nourishment from more than one animal or plant substance

**polytype** /'politiep/ *n* a crystal structure occurring in various forms – **polytypism** *n*

**polytypic** /,poli'tipik/ *adj* 1 *of a species of living thing* having different races in different geographical areas 2 of or being a polytype

**polyunsaturated** /-un'sachooraytid/ *adj, of a fat or oil* rich in double and triple chemical BONDS (forces that hold atoms together)

**polyurethane** /-'yooəri,thayn/ *n* any of various POLYMERS (chemical compounds containing repeating structural units) that are used esp in flexible and rigid foams, paints, and resins *synonyms* see POLYTHENE [ISV]

**polyuria** /,poli'yooəriə/ *n* excessive secretion of urine [NL]

**polyvalent** /-'vaylənt/ *adj* 1a having a VALENCY greater usu than two b having variable VALENCY 2a *of a vaccine, antibody, etc* effective against, sensitive towards, or counteracting more than one agent (e g a toxic substance or an antigen) b *of chromosomes* MULTIVALENT 2 [ISV] – **polyvalence** *n*

**polyvinyl** /,poli'vienl/ *adj* of or being a POLYMERIZED (made up of repeated structural units) vinyl chemical compound, resin, or plastic – often in compound words [ISV]

**polyvinyl chloride** /-'vienl/ *n* a colourless plastic, $(CH_2CHClCH_2CHCl)$ *x*, that is characterized by chemical inertness and used esp as a rubber substitute (e g in raincoats and wire covering) *synonyms* see POLYTHENE

**polyzoan** /-'zoh·ən/ *n* BRYOZOAN (aquatic animal that superficially resembles seaweed) [NL *Polyzoa*, phylum name, fr *poly-* + -*zoa*] – **polyzoan** *adj*

**polyzoarium** /,polizoh'eəriəm/ *n, pl* **polyzoaria** /-riə/ a colony of BRYOZOANS (aquatic animals that superficially resemble seaweeds); *also* the supporting skeleton of such a colony [NL, fr *Polyzoa*]

**polyzoic** /,poli'zoh·ik/ *adj* 1 composed of many ZOOIDS (individuals forming a compound organism) 2 producing many SPOROZOITES (reproductive spores of single-celled organisms)

¹**Pom** /pom/ *n, sometimes not cap, informal* POMERANIAN 2 △ peke, pug

²**Pom** *n, sometimes not cap, Austr & NZ informal* a pommy

**pomace** /'pumis/ *n* something (e g apples) crushed to a pulpy mass (e g to extract juice for cider-making) [prob fr ML *pomacium* cider, fr LL *pomum* apple, fr L, fruit]

**pomaceous** /po'mayshəs/ *adj* 1 of apples 2 of or resembling a pome [NL *pomaceus*, fr LL *pomum* apple]

**pomade** /pə'mahd, po-/ *n* a perfumed ointment for the hair or scalp [MF *pommade* ointment formerly made from apples, fr It *pomata*, fr *pomo* apple, fr LL *pomum*] – **pomade** *vt*

**pomander** /po'mandə, pə-/ *n* a mixture of aromatic substances enclosed in a perforated bag or box and used to scent clothes or linen, or carried in former times as a guard against infection or unpleasant smells; *also* an orange stuck with cloves used for a similar purpose [ME, modif of MF *pome d'ambre*, lit., apple or ball of amber]

**pomatum** /pə'maytəm/ *n* pomade [NL, fr LL *pomum* apple]

**pome** /pohm/ *n* a fleshy fruit (e g an apple) consisting of an outer thickened fleshy layer and a central core with the seeds enclosed in a capsule [ME, fr MF *pome, pomme* apple, pome, ball, fr LL *pomum* apple, fr L, fruit]

**pomegranate** /'pomi,granət, 'pom,granət/ *n* a thick-skinned several-celled reddish fruit that is about the size of an orange and contains many seeds each surrounded by a tart edible crimson pulp; *also* a widely cultivated tree of N Africa and W Asia (*Punica granatum* of the family Punicacea) that bears pomegranates [ME *poumgarnet*, fr MF *pomme grenate*, lit., seedy apple]

*usage* The pronunciation /'pomi,granət/ rather than /'pom,granət/ is recommended for BBC broadcasters.

**pomelo** /'pomiloh/ *n, pl* **pomelos** 1 SHADDOCK (fruit resembling a grapefruit) 2 a grapefruit [alter. of earlier *pompelmous*, fr D *pompelmoes*]

**Pomeranian** /,pomə'raynyən, -ni·ən/ *n* 1 a native or inhabitant of Pomerania 2 (any of) a breed of very small compact long-haired dogs [*Pomerania*, region in N Europe] – **Pomeranian** *adj*

**Pomfret cake** /'pumfrit, 'pom-/ *n* PONTEFRACT CAKE (liquorice sweet) [*Pomfret*, earlier form of *Pontefract*]

**pomiferous** /po'mif(ə)rəs/ *adj* bearing pomes [L *pomifer* fruit-bearing, fr *pomum* fruit + *-fer* -ferous]

**¹pommel** /'puməl, 'po-/ *n* 1 the knob on the hilt of a sword 2 the raised part at the front and top of a saddle 3 either of a pair of removable rounded or U-shaped handles on a POMMEL HORSE [ME *pomel*, fr MF, fr (assumed) VL *pomellum* ball, knob, fr dim. of LL *pomum* apple]

**²pommel** /'puməl/ *vt* -ll- (*NAm* -l-, -ll-), to pummel [¹*pommel*]

**pommel horse** *n* (a men's gymnastic event using) a leather-covered rectangular or cylindrical form that has two handles on the top, is supported in a horizontal position by an adjustable frame, and is used for swinging and balancing feats

**Pommy, Pommie** /'pomi/ *n, sometimes not cap, Austr & NZ chiefly derog* a British person; *esp* a British immigrant [prob short for *pomegranate*, prob alter. (referring to the redness of the fruit and British complexions) of rhyming slang *Jimmy Grant* immigrant]

**pomology** /po'moləji, poh-/ *n* the science and practice of fruit growing [NL *pomologia*, fr L *pomum* fruit + *-logia* -logy] – **pomologist** *n*, **pomological** *adj*, **pomologically** *adv*

**pomp** /pomp/ *n* 1 a show of magnificence; splendour 2 ostentatious or specious display [ME, fr MF *pompe*, fr L *pompa* procession, pomp, fr Gk *pompē* act of sending, escort, procession, pomp, fr *pempein* to send, escort]

**pompadour** /'pompə,dooə, -,daw/ *n* 1 a woman's hairstyle, popular in the early 18th century, in which the hair is turned back, often over a pad, into a loose full roll around the face 2 *NAm* a man's hairstyle in which the hair is combed into a high mound curving out over the forehead [Marquise de *Pompadour* †1764 mistress of Louis XV of France]

**¹pom-pom** /'pom ,pom/ *n* an automatic gun of 20 to 40 millimetres (about ⁴/₅ inch to 1³/₅ inches) mounted on ships in pairs, fours, or eights [imit]

**²pom-pom** *n* an ornamental ball or tuft used esp on clothing, hats, etc [alter. of *pompon*]

**pompon** /'pompon(h)/ *n* a chrysanthemum or dahlia with small rounded flower heads [Fr, pom-pom, fr MF *pompe* tuft of ribbons]

**pomposity** /pom'posəti/ *n* 1 pompous demeanour, speech, or behaviour 2 a pompous gesture, habit, or act

**pompous** /'pompəs/ *adj* 1 self-important, pretentious ⟨a ~ politician⟩ 2 excessively elevated or ornate ⟨~ rhetoric⟩ 3 *archaic* (suggestive) of pomp; magnificent – **pompously** *adv*, **pompousness** *n*

**¹ponce** /pons/ *n, Br informal* 1 a pimp 2 a man who behaves in an effeminate manner △ poof [perh fr ¹*pounce* or ²*pounce*]

**²ponce** *vi, Br informal* 1 to act as a ponce; pimp 2 to act in a frivolous, showy, or effeminate manner – usu + *around* or *about*

**poncho** /'ponchoh/ *n, pl* **ponchos** 1 a cloak resembling a blanket with a slit in the middle for the head 2 a garment (e g a waterproof one) resembling a poncho [AmerSp, fr Araucanian *pontho* woollen fabric]

**poncy, poncey** /'ponsi/ *adj, Br informal* (characteristic) of a ponce

**pond** /pond/ *n* a body of usu fresh water smaller than a lake [ME *ponde* artificially confined body of water, alter. of *pounde* enclosure – more at POUND] – **pond** *vi*

**ponder** /'pondə/ *vt* 1 to weigh in the mind; assess ⟨~ed *their chances of success*⟩ 2 to review mentally; think over ⟨~ed *the events of the day*⟩ ~ *vi* to think or consider, esp quietly, soberly, and deeply [ME *ponderen*, fr MF *ponderer*, fr L *ponderare* to weigh, ponder, fr *ponder-, pondus* weight – more at PENDANT] – **ponderer** *n*

*synonyms* Compare **ponder, cogitate, debate,** and **deliberate. Pondering** and **cogitating** must be, and **debating** and **deliberating** can be, done by one person alone. **Ponder** suggests prolonged and sober meditation, often over a matter of human or moral concern ⟨**pondered** *over the failure of his marriage*⟩. **Cogitate** (*formal*) expresses rather the objective evaluation of something ⟨**cogitate** *on the best means of escape*⟩. Both **debate** and **deliberate** imply a choice between recognizable alternatives ⟨**debated/deliberated** *whether to tell her*⟩ but **deliberate** has a stronger suggestion of lengthy consideration. *usage* Correctly, one **ponders** *on* or *over* a topic rather than *as to* it.

**ponderable** /'pond(ə)rəbl/ *adj* capable of being weighed or appraised; appreciable [LL *ponderabilis*, fr L *ponderare*]

**ponderosa pine** /,pondə'rohsə/ *n* a tall pine (*Pinus ponderosa*) of N W America that has long needles and is grown for its wood; *also* its strong reddish straight-grained wood [NL *ponderosa*, specific epithet of *Pinus ponderosa*, species name, fr L, fem of *ponderosus* heavy]

**ponderous** /'pond(ə)rəs/ *adj* 1 unwieldy or clumsy because of weight and size 2 oppressively or unpleasantly dull; pedestrian ⟨~ *prose*⟩ [ME, fr MF *pondereux*, fr L *ponderosus*, fr *ponder-, pondus* weight] – **ponderously** *adv*, **ponderousness** *n*

**pondok** /pon'dok/ *n, SAfr* a crude hut or shack ⟨*possible to convert a cluster of* ~s *into a community* – *Weekend Argus* (*Cape Town*)⟩ [Afrik, fr Malay *pondók* hut, shelter made of leaves]

**pondokkie** /pon'doki/ *n, SAfr* a pondok [Afrik, dim. of *pondok*]

**pond skater** *n* any of various long-legged TRUE BUGS (family Gerridae) that move about on the surface of the water

**pond snail** *n* any of various aquatic snails (genus *Limnaea*) that live in ponds

**pondweed** /-,weed/ *n* any of a genus (*Potamogeton* of the family Potamogetonaceae, the pondweed family) of aquatic plants with jointed usu rooting stems, floating or submerged leaves, and spikes of greenish flowers

**pone** /pohn/ *n* CORN PONE (corn bread) [of Algonquian origin; akin to Delaware *äpân* baked]

**pong** /pong/ *vi* or *n, Br informal* (to emit) an unpleasant smell; stink [origin unknown]

**pongee** /pon'jee/ *n* a thin soft beige or tan fabric of Chinese origin woven from raw silk; *also* an imitation of this fabric in cotton or rayon [Chin (Pek) *běnjī* (*pen³ chi¹*), fr *běn* (*pen³*) own + *jī* (*chi¹*) loom]

**pongid** /'ponjid/ *n* ANTHROPOID APE (tailless manlike ape) [deriv of Kongo *mpungu* ape] – **pongid** *adj*

**poniard** /'ponyəd/ *vt* or *n* (to stab with) a small dagger with a slender blade [n MF *poignard*, fr *poing* fist, fr L *pugnus* fist – more at PUNGENT; vb fr n]

**pons** /ponz/ *n, pl* **pontes** /'ponteez/ a broad mass of NERVE FIBRES on the lower front surface of the brain of man and lower mammals [NL, short for *pons Varolii*]

**pons asinorum** /,ponz asi'nawrəm/ *n* a critical test of ability imposed on the inexperienced or ignorant [NL, lit., asses' bridge (name orig applied to the proposition that the base angles of an isosceles triangle are equal, considered to be a stumbling-block for students of geometry)]

**pons Varolii** /,ponz və'rohli•ee, -li•ie/ *n* the pons [NL, lit., bridge of Varoli, fr Costanzo *Varoli* †1575 It surgeon & anatomist]

**Pontefract cake** /'pontifrakt/ *n* a small flat circular liquorice sweet [*Pontefract*, town in W Yorkshire in England, where it was orig produced]

**Pontic** /'pontik/ *adj* of the Black sea [L *ponticus*, fr Gk *ponti-kos*, fr *Pontos* the Black Sea, Pontus (ancient country in Asia Minor)]

**pontifex** /'pontifeks/ *n, pl* **pontifices** /pon'tifiseez/ a member of the council of priests in ancient Rome [L *pontific-, pontifex*, prob fr *pont-, pons* bridge + *facere* to make – more at FIND, DO]

**pontifex maximus** /'maksiməs/ *n* the pope [L, chief pontifex]

**pontiff** /'pontif/ *n* 1 a pontifex 2 a bishop; *specif* the pope [Fr *pontif*, fr L *pontific-, pontifex*]

**¹pontifical** /pon'tifikl/ *adj* 1a of a pontiff or pontifex b celebrated with distinctive ceremonies by a high-ranking church dignitary (e g a bishop or cardinal) ⟨~ *mass*⟩ 2 pretentiously dogmatic [L *pontificalis*, fr *pontific-, pontifex*] – **pontifically** *adv*

**²pontifical** *n* 1 *pl* the ceremonial robes of a bishop; *specif* the robes worn by a bishop, cardinal, etc celebrating a pontifical mass 2 a book containing the forms for sacraments and rites performed by a bishop

**¹pontificate** /pon'tifikət/ *n* the state, office, or term of office of the pope [L *pontificatus* office of a pontifex, fr *pontific-, pontifex*]

**²pontificate** /pon'tifikayt/ *vi* 1a to officiate as a pontiff b to celebrate pontifical mass 2 to deliver oracular utterances or dogmatic opinions [ML *pontificatus*, pp of *pontificare*, fr L *pontific-, pontifex*] – **pontificator** *n*, **pontification** *n*

**pontil** /'pontil/ *n* PUNTY (rod used in glassblowing) [Fr]

**pontine** /'pontien/ *adj* of the PONS (mass of NERVE FIBRES in the brain) [ISV *pont-* (fr NL *pont-, pons*) + *-ine*]

**Pont l'Evêque** /,ponh lay'vek (*Fr* pɔ̃ levɛk)/ *n* a semisoft square cheese firmer, yellower, and having less surface mould than Camembert but with a similar flavour [*Pont l'Evêque*, town in NW France]

**ponton** /'pontən, pon'toohn/ *n* a pontoon

**pontonier** /ˌpontə'niə/ *n* a person engaged in constructing a pontoon bridge [Fr *pontonnier*, fr *ponton*]

¹**pontoon** /pon'toohn/ *n* **1** a flat-bottomed boat (eg a lighter); *esp* a flat-bottomed boat or portable float used in building a floating temporary bridge **2** an esp inflatable float used to raise a submerged vessel; CAISSON 2b **3** a float, esp of an aircraft [Fr *ponton*, floating bridge, punt, fr L *ponton-*, *ponto*, fr *pont-*, *pons* bridge

²**pontoon** *n* a gambling card game in which the object is to be dealt cards scoring more than those of the dealer up to but not exceeding 21 [prob alter. of *vingt-et-un*]

**pontoon bridge** *n* a bridge whose deck is supported on pontoons

**pony** /'pohni/ *n* **1** a small horse; *esp* a member of any of several breeds of very small stocky horses 14.2 hands and under in height noted for their gentleness and endurance **2** *NAm* CRIB 7a (literal translation used esp surreptitiously by students) **3** *informal* **3a** a small liqueur glass **b** a small measure of spirits **4** *usu pl*, *slang* a racehorse **5** *Br slang* the sum of £25 [prob fr obs Fr *poulenet*, dim. of Fr *poulain* colt, fr ML *pullanus*, fr L *pullus* young of an animal, foal – more at FOAL]

**ponytail** /-ˌtayl/ *n* a hairstyle in which the hair is drawn back tightly and tied at the back of the head

**pony trekking** *n* the activity of riding ponies long distances across country in a group and usu at a slow steady pace

**pooch** /poohch/ *n*, *chiefly NAm slang* a dog [origin unknown]

**pood** /poohd/ *n* a Russian unit of weight equal to about 16.4 kilograms (36.11 pounds) [Russ *pud*, fr ON *pund* pound – more at POUND]

**poodle** /'poohdl/ *n* (any of) a breed of active intelligent dogs with a thick curly coat that is typically clipped and shaved into an elaborate pattern [Ger *pudel*, short for *pudelhund*, fr *pudeln* to splash (fr *pudel* puddle, fr LG) + *hund* dog (fr OHG *hunt*) – more at PUDDLE, HOUND]

**poof, pouf** /poohf, poof/ *n*, *Br derog* an effeminate male or male homosexual △ ponce, pimp [perh fr *poof* (interj used to express contempt), or perh alter. of ²*puff*]

**poofter, pooftah** /'poohftə/ *n*, *Br & Austr derog* a poof [by alter.]

**pooh** /pooh/ *interj* – used to express contempt, disapproval, or distaste at an unpleasant smell

**pooh-bah** /bah/ *n*, *often cap P&B* a person holding many public or private offices [*Pooh-Bah*, character bearing the title Lord-High-Everything-Else in the comic opera *The Mikado* by W S Gilbert †1911 E librettist & poet]

ˌ**pooh-'pooh** *vb* to express contempt (for) [*pooh*]

**pooka** /'poohkə/ *n*, *Irish* a hobgoblin [IrGael *púca*, fr or akin to OE *púca* puck]

¹**pool** /poohl/ *n* **1a** a small and relatively deep body of usu fresh water (eg a still place in a stream or river) **b** something resembling a pool (eg in depth or shape) ⟨~s *of light*⟩ **c** a small body of standing liquid; a puddle ⟨*lay in a* ~ *of blood*⟩ **2** SWIMMING POOL [ME, fr OE *pōl*; akin to OHG *pfuol* pool]

²**pool** *n* **1a** the combined stakes contributed by the players in a betting game **b** all the money bet by a number of people on a particular event **2** any of various games played with esp 15 numbered balls on an oblong billiard table with six pockets **3** a combination of the interests or property of different parties that is made to further a joint undertaking by subjecting each party to the same controls and a common liability: eg **3a** a common fund (eg of the profits of different companies) or combination of interests for a common commercial enterprise; *esp*, *chiefly NAm* one for speculating in or manipulating the market price of securities or commodities (eg grain) **b** an association or agreement between business organizations for the purpose of gaining control of a market by driving out competition **4a** the whole quantity of a particular material present in the body and available for METABOLISM (life-supporting processes) **b** a body product (eg blood) collected from many donors and stored for later use **5** a facility, service, or group of people providing a service to which a number of people (eg the members of a business organization) have access ⟨*a typing* ~⟩ ⟨*a car* ~⟩ **6** *pl* FOOTBALL POOLS [Fr *poule*, lit., hen, fr OF, fem of *poul* cock – more at PULLET; perh fr a hen being set as the target and prize in a game]

³**pool** *vt* to contribute to a common stock (eg of resources or effort)

**poolroom** /'poohlroohm, -room/ *n*, *NAm* a usu public room for the playing of pool

¹**poop** /poohp/ *n* an enclosed superstructure at the stern of a ship above the main deck [MF *poupe*, fr L *puppis*]

²**poop** *vt* **1** *of a wave* to break over the stern of (a vessel) **2** *of a vessel* to receive (a sea or wave) over the stern

³**poop** *vb*, *chiefly NAm informal vt* to put out of breath; *also* to tire out ~ *vi* to become exhausted □ usu + *out* [origin unknown]

⁴**poop** *vb*, *informal vt* to blow (the horn of a vehicle) ~ *vi* to poop one's horn [imit]

**poop deck** *n* a partial deck above a ship's main stern deck

**poor** /pooə, paw/ *adj* **1a** lacking material possessions **b** of or characterized by poverty **2a** less than adequate; meagre ⟨*a* ~ *harvest*⟩ **b** small in worth **3** exciting pity ⟨~ *old soul!*⟩ **4a** inferior in quality, value, or workmanship ⟨*in* ~ *health*⟩ ⟨*a* ~ *essay*⟩ ⟨*a* ~ *tennis player*⟩ **b** humble, unpretentious ⟨*in my* ~ *opinion*⟩ **5** *of land* barren, unproductive [ME *poure*, fr OF *povre*, fr L *pauper*; akin to L *pau*cus little and to L *parere* to produce, *parare* to acquire – more at FEW, PARE] – **poorish** *adj*, **poorly** *adv*, **poorness** *n*

synonyms **Poor, impoverished**, and **poverty-stricken** all imply lack of sufficient money or possessions. **Poor** is the most general word. It usually implies habitual or continuous poverty, though that poverty may be relative, simply connoting a lack of those comforts considered desirable by society ⟨*too poor to run a car*⟩. **Poverty-stricken** vividly conveys the suffering of true poverty, while **impoverished** stresses its outward appearance in pinched faces and shabby dwellings. **Penurious, indigent, needy,** and **destitute** stress need. **Penurious** (formal) suggests the cramping effect of poverty and need. **Indigent** and **needy** are interchangeable in meaning "in urgent want", but **indigent** is more formal. **Destitute** is the strongest of the four, suggesting people totally without resources, often as a result of some misfortune ⟨*many people were destitute after the earthquake*⟩. **Penniless, impecunious,** and **hard up** do not suggest so much actual need as a lack of money, and this is often only temporary ⟨*the penniless lad from Wales is now a minister in the government*⟩. **Impecunious** and **hard up** both suggest habitual lack of money: the former is formal and the latter informal. **Deprived** and **underprivileged** mean what they say, and are euphemisms sometimes substituted for **poor**. antonyms rich, affluent, well-off, well-to-do

**poor box** *n* a box (eg in a church) for alms for the poor

**Poor Clare** /kleə/ *n* a member of an austere order of nuns founded in Assisi by St Clare in 1212, under the direction of St Francis

**poorhouse** /-ˌhows/ *n* WORKHOUSE 1

**poor law** *n* a law that in former times provided for or regulated the public relief or support of the poor

**poorly** /'pooəli, 'pawli/ *adj*, *informal* somewhat ill; indisposed

**poor relation** *n* somebody or something regarded as inferior or subordinate among a group of comparable people or things ⟨*this wine is a* ~ *of champagne*⟩

ˌ**poor-'spirited** *adj* lacking zest, confidence, or courage – **poor-spiritedly** *adv*, **poor-spiritedness** *n*

**poor white** *n*, *chiefly derog* a member of an inferior or underprivileged white social group, esp in the S USA and in S Africa

**poove** /poohv/ *n*, *Br derog* a poof [by alter.]

¹**pop** /pop/ *vb* **-pp-** *informal vt* **1** to strike or knock sharply; hit ⟨~*ped him one on the jaw*⟩ **2** to push, put, or thrust suddenly ⟨~*ped a sweet into his mouth*⟩ **3** to cause to explode or burst open **4** to shoot at **5** to take (drugs) orally or by injection ⟨*he* ~*ped pills*⟩ **6** *Br* to pawn ~ *vi* **1a** to go, come, or enter suddenly or quickly ⟨*just* ~*ped out to do some shopping*⟩ **b** to escape or break away from something (eg a point of attachment) usu suddenly or unexpectedly ⟨*was highly embarrassed when her button* ~*ped*⟩ **2** to make or burst with a sharp explosive sound **3** *of eyes* to protrude from the sockets ⟨*eyes* ~*ping in astonishment*⟩ **4** to shoot ⟨~ *at rabbits*⟩ [ME *poppen*, of imit origin]

**pop off** *vi*, *informal* **1** to leave suddenly **2** to die unexpectedly

**pop up** *vi* to occur or appear suddenly or unexpectedly; CROP UP

²**pop** *n*, *informal* **1** a popping sound **2** a flavoured fizzy drink **3** *Br* PAWN 2

³**pop** *adv*, *informal* like or with a pop; suddenly

**⁴pop** n, chiefly NAm informal a father [short for poppa]

**⁵pop** adj popular: eg **a** of pop music ⟨~ singer⟩ **b** of or constituting a mass culture widely disseminated through the mass media ⟨~ society⟩ **c** of POP ART ⟨~ painter⟩

**⁶pop** n **1** POP MUSIC **2** POP ART

**pop art** n, often cap P&A art in which commonplace objects and elements from popular culture and the mass media (eg advertising material and comic strips) are used as subject matter and are often physically incorporated in the work ⟨~ . . . extends from Warhol's rows of Coca-Cola bottles to supplying the Monà Lisa with a mustache – Harold Rosenberg⟩ – compare OP ART – **pop artist** n

**popcorn** /-ˌkawn/ n (the popped kernels of) a variety of maize (Zea mays everta) whose kernels burst open on exposure to heat to form a white starchy mass

**pope** /pohp/ n **1** often cap the bishop of Rome as head of the ROMAN CATHOLIC church **2** someone who holds a position of absolute authority **3** a priest of an Eastern Christian church **4** RUFF (freshwater fish) [ME, fr OE pāpa, fr LL papa, fr Gk pappas, papas, title of bishops, lit., papa; (3) Russ pop, fr OSlav popŭ, deriv of Gk pappas, papas] – **popedom** n

**popery** /'pohp(ə)ri/ n, derog ROMAN CATHOLICISM; esp its teachings, government, and forms of worship

**pope's nose** n PARSON'S NOSE (fatty rump of a cooked fowl)

**'pop-ˌeyed** adj having staring or bulging eyes (eg as a result of surprise or excitement)

**popgun** /-ˌgun/ n a toy gun that shoots a cork or pellet and produces a popping sound; also an inadequate or inefficient firearm

**popinjay** /'popinˌjay/ n a strutting supercilious person [ME papejay parrot, fr MF papegai, papejai, fr Ar babghā']

**popish** /'pohpish/ adj, derog of popery – **popishly** adv

**poplar** /'poplə/ n **1** (the wood of) any of a genus (Populus) of slender quick-growing trees (eg an aspen) of the willow family **2a** TULIP TREE **b** TULIPWOOD 1 [ME poplere, fr MF pouplier, fr pouple poplar, fr L populus]

**poplin** /'poplin/ n a strong esp cotton fabric in plain weave with fine crosswise ribs [Fr papeline]

**popliteal** /pop'liti·əl, ˌpopli'tee·əl/ adj of the back part of the leg behind the knee joint [NL popliteus, fr L poplit-, poples ham of the knee]

**pop music** n modern commercially promoted popular music that is usu simple and simple and has a strong beat

**popover** /'popˌohvə/ n **1** a child's garment (eg a pinafore) that is put on by being pulled over the head **2** Br an individual YORKSHIRE PUDDING often served with roast beef

**poppa** /'popə/ n, NAm informal a father [alter. of papa]

**poppadom, poppadum** /'popədom/ n a crisp wafer-thin pancake of deep-fried dough eaten chiefly with Indian food [Tamil-Malayalam pappaṭam]

**popper** /'popə/ n somebody or something that pops; eg **a** chiefly Br PRESS-STUD **b** chiefly NAm a utensil in which popcorn is prepared

**poppet** /'popit/ n **1** a valve that rises up and down from its seat **2** chiefly Br informal a lovable or appealing person or animal [ME popet doll, puppet – more at PUPPET]

**poppie** /'popi/ n, SAfr informal a girlfriend [Afrik, fr pop doll + -ie, dim. suffix]

**popping crease** /'poping/ n either of the lines that are drawn perpendicularly across a cricket pitch 4 feet (about 1.22 metres) in front of each wicket and behind which the batsman must have a foot or his/her bat on the ground to avoid being run out or stumped – compare BOWLING CREASE [prob fr ¹pop (in the sense "to strike")]

**poppy** /'popi/ n **1** any of several genera (Papaver and related genera of the family Papaveraceae, the poppy family) of plants with usu red, orange, or yellow flowers and seeds contained in capsules. The poppy family includes the OPIUM POPPY and several other plants that are cultivated for their ornamental value. **2** a strong reddish orange colour [ME popi, fr OE popæg, popig, modif of L papaver]

**poppycock** /-ˌkok/ n, informal empty talk; nonsense [D dial. pappekak, lit., soft dung, fr D pap pap + kak dung]

**popsy** /'popsi/ n, Br informal a girlfriend – no longer in vogue [pop (short for poppet) + -s + -y]

**populace** /'popyooləs/ n taking sing or pl vb **1** the common people; the masses **2** the whole population [MF, fr It popolaccio rabble, pejorative of popolo the people, fr L populus]

**popular** /'popyoolə/ adj **1** of the general public **2** suited to the needs, means, tastes, or understanding of the general public;

esp not very expensive or highbrow ⟨sold at ~ prices⟩ ⟨a ~ history of the war⟩ **3** widespread, prevalent ⟨a ~ misconception⟩ **4** commonly liked or approved ⟨a very ~ girl⟩ [L popularis, fr populus the people, a people] – **popularity** n, **popularly** adv

**popular front** n, often cap P&F a working coalition of progressive or left-wing political parties against a common opponent

**popular·ize, -ise** /'popyoolə,riez/ vt to make popular: eg **a** to cause to be liked or esteemed **b** to present in a generally understandable or interesting form – **popularizer** n, **popularization** n

**popular sovereignty** n a doctrine in political theory that government is created by and subject to the will of the people

**populate** /'popyoolayt/ vt **1** to have a place in; occupy, inhabit **2** to provide with inhabitants; people [ML populatus, pp of populare to people, fr L populus people]

**population** /ˌpopyoo'laysh(ə)n/ n **1a** taking sing or pl vb the whole number of people or inhabitants in a country or region ⟨the entire ~ mourned the death of the president⟩ ⟨what's the ~ of Tokyo?⟩ **b** the total number or quantity of things in an area ⟨the tractor ~ of our farms⟩ **c** the total number of particles in a particular ENERGY LEVEL – used esp with reference to atoms in a laser **2** the act or process of populating **3a** taking sing or pl vb a body of people having a quality or characteristic in common ⟨the Jewish ~ of London⟩ **b(1)** the group of organisms inhabiting a particular area **b(2)** a group of members of a species that regularly interbreed in one area **4** a set (eg of individual people or items) from which samples are taken for statistical measurement [LL population-, populatio, fr L populus people]

**population explosion** n a vast and usu rapid increase in the size of a living population, esp due to an increase in life expectancy and an increase in the birthrate – compare OVERPOPULATION

**populist** /'popyoolist/ n **1** a member of a political party claiming to represent the common people **2** a believer in the rights, wisdom, or virtues of the common people [L populus the people] – **populism** n, **populist** also **populistic** adj

**populous** /'popyooləs/ adj densely populated [L populosus, fr populus people] – **populously** adv, **populousness** n

**'pop-ˌup** adj of or having a device that causes its contents to spring up or stand out in relief ⟨a ~ toaster⟩ ⟨a ~ book⟩

**porbeagle** /'pawˌbeegl/ n a small shark (Lamna nasus) of the N Atlantic and Pacific oceans with a pointed nose and crescent-shaped tail [Cornish porgh-bugel]

**porcelain** /'paws(ə)lin/ n **1a** hard fine-grained nonporous translucent white ceramic ware made from a mixture of KAOLIN, QUARTZ, and FELDSPAR fired at a high temperature – called also HARD-PASTE PORCELAIN **b** translucent ceramic ware made from a mixture of refined clay and ground glass fired at a low temperature – called also SOFT-PASTE PORCELAIN **2** porcelain ware [MF porcelaine cowrie shell, porcelain, fr It porcellana, prob fr porcello vulva, lit., little pig, fr L porcellus, dim. of porcus pig, vulva – more at FARROW] – **porcelainlike** adj, **porcelaneous, porcellaneous** adj

**porcelain·ize, -ise** /'pawsəliniez/ vt to fire a VITREOUS (containing glass) coating on (eg steel)

**porch** /pawch/ n **1** a covered usu projecting entrance to a building **2** NAm a veranda **3** obs a portico [ME porche, fr OF, fr L porticus portico, fr porta gate – more at FORD]

**porcine** /'pawsien/ adj of or like pigs; esp obese [L porcinus, fr porcus pig]

**porcupine** /'pawkyoopien/ n any of various relatively large rodents having stiff sharp bristles mingled with the hair and constituting an African and Eurasian ground-living family (Hystricidae) and an American tree-dwelling family (Erethizontidae) [ME porkepin, fr MF porc espin, fr OIt porcospino, fr L porcus pig + spina spine, prickle]

**¹pore** /paw/ vi **1** to gaze intently ⟨~ over a microscope⟩ **2** to read studiously or attentively **3** to reflect or meditate steadily □ usu + on, over, or upon △ pour [ME pouren]

**²pore** n **1** a minute opening, esp in an organism; esp one by which matter passes through a membrane (eg the skin) **2** a small space between solid parts or particles (eg in soil) which allows liquid to pass through or be absorbed [ME, fr MF, fr L porus, fr Gk poros passage, pore – more at FARE] – **pored** adj

**pore fungus** n a fungus (family Boletaceae or Polyporaceae) having the spore-bearing surface within tubes or pores

**porgy** /'pawgi/ n, pl **porgies**, esp collectively **porgy** a blue-spotted crimson spiny-finned food fish (*Pagrus pagrus*) of the coasts of Europe and America; *also* any of various related fishes (family Sparidae) [partly fr earlier *pargo*, deriv of Gk *phagros* sea bream; partly fr earlier *scuppaug*, fr Narraganset *mishcùppaúog*]

**poriferan** /paw'rif(ə)rən/ *n* SPONGE 1 (type of aquatic organism) [deriv of L *porus* pore + *-fer* -ferous] – **poriferan, poriferal** *adj*

**pork** /pawk/ *n* 1 the flesh of a pig used as food 2 *NAm slang* government money, jobs, or favours used by politicians as patronage [ME, fr OF, pig, fr L *porcus* – more at FARROW]

**pork barrel** *n, chiefly NAm* a government project or appropriation yielding rich patronage benefits

**porker** /'pawkə/ *n* PIG 1a; *esp* a young pig fattened for food 〈*50 weaners are bought for finishing as* ∼ s – *Farmers Weekly*〉

**porkpie hat** /ˌpawk'pie/ *n* a man's hat with a low crown, flat top, and usu a turned-up brim 〈*shiny suits, draped jackets, skinny ties, porkpie hats, collarless jackets . . . all had a flavour of the coffee-bar decade* – *The Observer*〉 [fr its shape]

**porky** /'pawki/ *adj* 1 of or resembling pork 2 *informal* fat, fleshy 〈*a* ∼ *young man*〉

**porn** /pawn/ *n, informal* pornography

**porno** /'pawnoh/ *n, informal* pornography

**pornographer** /paw'nogrəfə/ *n* one who produces or deals in pornography

**pornography** /paw'nogrəfi/ *n* 1 the depiction of erotic behaviour (e g in pictures or writing) intended to cause sexual excitement 2 material (e g books, photographs, or films) that depicts erotic behaviour and is intended to cause sexual excitement [Gk *pornographos*, adj, writing of prostitutes, fr *pornē* prostitute + *graphein* to write; akin to Gk *pernanai* to sell, *poros* journey – more at FARE, CARVE] – **pornographic** *adj*, **pornographically** *adv*

**porose** /'pawrohs/ *adj* divided into or forming a continuous series of pores

**porosity** /paw'rosəti/ *n* 1 the quality or state of being porous 2 the ratio of the volume of spaces between the particles of a material to the volume of its mass

**porous** /'pawrəs/ *adj* 1a having or full of pores or spaces b containing channels or tubes 〈*hardwood is* ∼〉 2 able to let liquids through – **porously** *adv*, **porousness** *n*

**porphyria** /paw'firi·ə/ *n* a usu hereditary abnormality of the biochemical processing of porphyrin characterized esp by discoloured and usu red urine, extreme sensitivity to light, and phases of mental derangement [NL, fr ISV *porphyrin*]

**porphyrin** /'pawfirin/ *n* any of various metal-free derivatives of PYRROLE (type of liquid chemical compound) obtained esp from the pigments chlorophyll or haemoglobin [ISV, fr Gk *porphyra* purple]

**porphyritic** /ˌpawfi'ritik/ *adj* 1 of porphyry 2 *of a rock* having distinct crystals (e g of FELDSPAR) in a relatively fine-grained base [ML *porphyriticus*, fr Gk *porphyritikos*, fr *porphyrītēs* (*lithos*) porphyry]

**porphyroid** /'pawfiroyd/ *n* a METAMORPHIC rock (rock formed from another by the action of heat or pressure) with porphyritic texture [*porphyry* + *-oid*]

**porphyropsin** /ˌpawfi'ropsin/ *n* a purple pigment in the RODS (specialized cells in the retina of the eye) of freshwater fishes that resembles RHODOPSIN [Gk *porphyra* purple + E *-opsin* (as in *rhodopsin*)]

**porphyry** /'pawfiri/ *n* 1 a rock consisting of crystals of the mineral FELDSPAR embedded in a compact dark red or purple mass of surrounding rock 2 an IGNEOUS rock (rock formed from the solidification of molten rock) of porphyritic texture [ME *porfurie*, fr ML *porphyrium*, alter. of L *porphyrites*, fr Gk *porphyrītēs* (*lithos*), lit., purple stone, fr *porphyra* purple]

**porpoise** /'pawpəs/ *n* any of several small TOOTHED WHALES (*Phocaena* and related genera) which live together in large groups; *esp* a blunt-snouted usu largely black whale (*Phocaena phocaena*) of the N Atlantic and Pacific about 2 metres (6 feet) long [ME *porpoys*, fr MF *porpois*, fr ML *porcopiscis*, fr L *porcus* pig + *piscis* fish – more at FARROW, FISH]

**porrect** /pə'rekt/ *adj, biology* extended forwards 〈*an insect with* ∼ *antennae*〉 [L *porrectus*, pp of *porrigere* to stretch out, fr *por-* forwards + *regere* to direct – more at PORTEND, RIGHT]

**porridge** /'porij/ *n* 1 a soft food made by boiling a cereal product, esp oatmeal, in milk or water until thick; *broadly* something resembling porridge in consistency 2 *Br slang* time spent in prison [alter. of *pottage*]

**porringer** /'porinjə/ *n* a small bowl or dish for one person from which esp soft or liquid foods (e g porridge or soup) are

eaten; *specif* a small covered cylindrical silver vessel of the 16th or 17th century with vertical scroll handles [alter. of ME *poteger, potinger*, fr AF *potageer*, fr MF *potager* of pottage, fr *potage* pottage]

**¹port** /pawt/ *n* 1 a town or city with a harbour where ships, hovercraft, etc may take on or discharge cargo or passengers 2 **port, port of entry** a place (e g a harbour or airport) where goods and people may be permitted to pass into or out of a country subject to clearing through customs [ME, fr OE & OF, fr L *portus* – more at FORD]

**²port** *n* 1 an opening (e g in machinery) which allows liquid or gas to enter or escape 2a an opening in a ship's side for loading and unloading cargo b PORTHOLE 1 c the means by which a computer or microprocessor communicates with a terminal, LINE PRINTER, disk drive, etc 3 a hole in an armoured vehicle or fortification through which guns may be fired 4 *chiefly Scot* a gate or gateway (e g of a walled town or fortress) [ME *porte*, fr MF, gate, door, fr L *porta* passage, gate; akin to L *portus* port]

**³port** *n* 1 a position in arms drill in which, in response to the command *port arms*, the weapon (e g a rifle) is held diagonally across the body for inspection 2 *archaic* the manner in which one bears oneself; bearing, deportment [ME, fr MF, fr *porter* to carry, fr L *portare*] – **port** *vt*

**⁴port** *adj or n* (of or at) the left side of a ship or aircraft when facing forwards – compare STARBOARD [prob fr ¹*port* or ²*port*]

**⁵port** *vt* to turn or put (a helm) to the left – used chiefly as a command

**⁶port** *n* a fortified sweet wine of rich taste and aroma made in Portugal; *also* a similar wine made elsewhere [*Oporto*, city in NW Portugal]

**¹portable** /'pawtəbl/ *adj* capable of being carried or moved about 〈*a* ∼ *typewriter*〉 [ME, fr MF, fr LL *portabilis*, fr L *portare* to carry – more at FARE] – **portably** *adv*, **portability** *n*

**²portable** *n* something (e g a television set or typewriter) that is portable

**¹portage** /'pawtij/ *n* 1a the carrying of boats or goods overland from one body of water to another b the route followed in portage; *also* a place where portage is necessary 2 *archaic* the cost of carrying; porterage [ME, act or cost of carrying, cargo, fr MF, fr *porter* to carry]

**²portage** *vi* to move gear over a portage ∼ *vt* to carry over a portage

**Portakabin** /'pawtəˌkabin/ *trademark* – used for a portable prefabricated hut (e g for use on building sites)

**¹portal** /'pawtl/ *n* 1 **portal, portals** *pl* a door, entrance; *esp* a grand or imposing one 2 the approach or entrance to a bridge or tunnel 3 a structural frame consisting of two uprights connected at the top by a third horizontal piece 4 a communicating part or area of an organism; *specif* the point at which something (e g a disease-causing agent) enters the body [ME, fr MF, fr ML *portale* city gate, porch, fr neut of *portalis* of a gate, fr L *porta* gate – more at ²PORT]

**²portal** *adj* 1 of the transverse opening on the underside of the liver where most of the vessels enter 2 of or being a PORTAL VEIN or a PORTAL SYSTEM [NL *porta* transverse opening in the liver, fr L, gate]

**portal system** *n* a system of veins that begins and ends in capillaries or SINUSOIDS (minute spaces or passages for blood in the tissues of an organ)

**portal vein** *n* a vein that transfers blood from one part of the body to another without passing through the heart; *esp* the vein carrying blood from the digestive organs and spleen to the liver

**portamento** /ˌpawtə'mentoh/ *n, pl* **portamenti** /-ti/ a continuous gliding movement from one note to another by the voice, a trombone, or a bowed stringed instrument [It, lit., act of carrying, fr *portare* to carry, fr L]

**port arms** *n* a military drill position in which the rifle is held diagonally in front of the body with the muzzle pointing upwards to the left; *also* a command to assume this position [fr the command *port arms!*]

**portative** /'pawtətiv/ *adj, archaic* portable [ME *portatif*, fr MF, fr L *portatus*, pp of *portare*]

**portative organ** *n* a small portable organ carried in processions in medieval times and supplied with air by bellows

**portcullis** /pawt'kulis/ *n* a usu iron or wood grating hung over the gateway of a fortified place and lowered between grooves to prevent passage [ME *port colice*, fr MF *porte coleice*, lit., sliding door]

**port de bras** /ˌpaw də 'brah (*Fr* pɔr də bra)/ *n* the technique and practice of arm movement in ballet [Fr, lit., bearing of the arm]

**Porte** /pawt/ *n* the government of the Ottoman empire [Fr, short for *Sublime Porte*, lit., sublime gate; fr the gate of the sultan's palace where justice was administered]

**porte cochere** /ˌpawt ko'sheə (*Fr* pɔrt kɔʃɛr)/ *n* **1** a passageway through a building or wall designed to let vehicles pass from the street to an inner courtyard **2** a roofed structure extending from the entrance of a building over an adjacent driveway and sheltering those getting in or out of vehicles [Fr *porte cochère*, lit., coach door]

**portend** /paw'tend/ *vt* **1** to give an omen or anticipatory sign of; bode **2** to indicate, signify *synonyms* see FORETELL [ME *portenden*, fr L *portendere*, fr *por-* forwards (akin to *per* through) + *tendere* to stretch – more at FOR, THIN]

**portent** /'pawt(ə)nt, -tent/ *n* **1** something foreshadowing a coming event; an omen **2** prophetic indication or significance **3** a marvel, prodigy [L *portentum*, fr neut of *portentus*, pp of *portendere*]

**portentous** /paw'tentəs/ *adj* **1** of or constituting a portent **2** eliciting amazement or wonder; prodigious **3** self-consciously weighty; pompous △ pretentious – **portentously** *adv*, **portentousness** *n*

**¹porter** /'pawtə/, *fem* **portress** /-tris/ *n*, *chiefly Br* a gatekeeper or doorkeeper, esp of a large building, who usu regulates entry and answers enquiries [ME, fr OF *portier*, fr LL *portarius*, fr L *porta* gate – more at PORT]

**²porter** *n* **1** a person who carries burdens; *specif* somebody employed to carry luggage (e g in a hotel or railway station) **2** a heavy dark brown beer brewed from browned or charred malt **3** *NAm* a railway employee who waits on passengers; *esp* a sleeping-car attendant [ME *portour*, fr MF *porteour*, fr LL *portator*, fr L *portatus*, pp of *portare* to carry – more at FARE; (2) short for *porter's beer*]

**porterage** /'pawt(ə)rij/ *n* (the charge made for) the work performed by a porter

**porterhouse** /-ˌhows/, **porterhouse steak** *n* a large steak cut from the back end of the sirloin above the ribs and containing part of the fillet [arch. *porterhouse* public house selling porter and other drinks, chop-house]

**portfolio** /pawt'fohli·oh/ *n, pl* **portfolios 1** a hinged cover or flexible case for carrying documents, paintings, etc; *also* the contents of such a case **2** the office and functions of a government minister or member of a cabinet ⟨*was given the ~ of Northern Ireland affairs*⟩ **3** the securities held by an investor (e g an individual or bank) [It *portafoglio*, fr *portare* to carry (fr L) + *foglio* leaf, sheet, fr L *folium* – more at BLADE]

**porthole** /'pawt,hohl/ *n* **1** **porthole**, **port** a sealed or sealable usu round window in the side of a ship, aircraft, spacecraft, etc; *also* a round window (e g in a washing machine) **2** ²PORT 1 (opening in a machine to allow the passage of liquids or gases) **3** a port through which to shoot [²*port*]

**portico** /'pawtikoh/ *n, pl* **porticoes, porticos** a colonnade or covered veranda, usu at the entrance of a building and characteristic of classical architecture [It, fr L *porticus* – more at PORCH]

**portiere** /ˌpawti'eə/ *n* a curtain hanging across a doorway [Fr *portière*, fr OF, fem of *portier* porter, doorkeeper]

**¹portion** /'pawsh(ə)n/ *n* **1** an individual's part or share of something: e g **1a** a share of an estate received by gift or inheritance; *esp* a share of a parents' estate in the form of a sum of money paid to a child out of a settlement **b** a helping of food **c** *archaic* a dowry **2** an individual's lot or fate **3** a limited part or quantity taken from a whole [ME, fr OF, fr L *portion-, portio*; akin to L *part-, pars* part]

**²portion** *vt* to divide into portions; distribute – often + *out*

**portionless** /-lis/ *adj* having no portion; *esp* having no dowry or inheritance

**Portland cement** /'pawtlənd/ *n* a cement capable of setting underwater made by finely grinding together lime and clay and then roasting the mixture in a kiln [fr its resemblance to Portland stone]

**Portland stone** *n* a limestone much used in building [Isle of *Portland*, peninsula in Dorset, England]

**portly** /'pawtli/ *adj* **1** heavy or rotund of body; stout **2** *archaic* dignified, stately [³*port* + ¹*-ly* ] – **portliness** *n*

**¹portmanteau** /pawt'mantoh/ *n, pl* **portmanteaus, portmanteaux** /-tohz/ a trunk for a traveller's belongings that opens into two equal parts [MF *portemanteau*, fr *porter* to carry + *manteau* cloak – more at PORT, MANTLE]

**²portmanteau** *adj* combining more than one use or quality ⟨*another typical ~ horror flic – The Observer*⟩

**portmanteau word** *n* BLEND 2a (word formed by combining other words)

**port of call** *n* **1** a port where ships customarily stop during a voyage for supplies, repairs, or transfer of cargo **2** a stop included in an itinerary

**port of entry** *n* **1** a place where foreign goods may be cleared through a customs house **2** ¹PORT 2 (harbour, airport, etc, where people may enter a country)

**¹portrait** /'pawtrit, -trayt/ *n* **1** a painting, drawing, photograph, sculpture, or other representation of an individual; *esp* one depicting the face **2** a vivid description in words [MF, fr pp of *portraire*]

**²portrait** *adj* oblong with the vertical dimension greater than the horizontal ⟨*a ~ page*⟩

**portraitist** /'pawtritist, 'pawtraytist/ *n* an artist, photographer, etc, who specializes in portraits

**portraiture** /'pawtrichə/ *n* **1** the art or technique of making portraits; portrayal **2** a portrait

**portray** /paw'tray/ *vt* **1** to make a picture of; depict **2a** to describe in words **b** to play the part of (a character) in a play or film [ME *portraien*, fr MF *portraire*, fr L *protrahere* to draw forth, reveal, expose, fr *pro-* forth + *trahere* to draw – more at PRO-, DRAW] – **portrayer** *n*

**portrayal** /paw'tray(ə)l/ *n* **1** the act or process of portraying; representation **2** a portrait

**portress** /'pawtris/ *n* a female porter

**Port Royalist** *n* a member or adherent of a 17th-century French Jansenist lay community noted for its logicians and educators [Fr *port-royaliste*, fr *Port-Royal*, a convent near Versailles in France]

**Port Salut** /ˌpaw sa'looh (*Fr* pɔr saly)/ *n* a pale yellow mild-flavoured cheese made originally by Trappist monks in France [Fr *port-salut, port-du-salut*, fr *Port du Salut*, Trappist abbey in NW France]

**Portuguese** /ˌpawchoo'geez, ˌpawtyoo'geez/ *n, pl* **Portuguese 1** a native or inhabitant of Portugal **2** the ROMANCE language of esp Portugal and Brazil [Pg *português*, adj & n, fr *Portugal*, country in SW Europe] – **Portuguese** *adj*

**Portuguese man-of-war** *n* any of a genus (*Physalia* of the order Siphonophora, class Hydrozoa) of INVERTEBRATE animals that resemble the related jellyfish, are composed of a collection (COLONY) of organisms, and have very long stinging tentacles and a large bluish bladderlike sac with a broad crest on the upper side, by means of which the colony floats at the surface of the sea

**posada** /pə'sahdə/ *n* an inn – used with reference to inns in Spanish-speaking countries [Sp, fr *posar* to lodge, fr LL *pausare*]

**¹pose** /pohz/ *vt* **1a** to put or set in place **b** to place (e g a model) in a studied attitude **2a** to put or set forth; offer, present ⟨*this attitude ~s a threat to our hopes for peace*⟩ **b** to present for attention or consideration ⟨*let me ~ a question*⟩ ~ *vi* **1** to assume a posture or attitude, usu for artistic purposes **2** to affect an attitude or character; posture ⟨*~d as an honest man*⟩ [ME *posen*, fr MF *poser*, fr (assumed) VL *pausare* (influenced in meaning by L *pos-*, perfect stem of *ponere* to put, place) fr LL, to stop, rest, pause, fr L *pausa* pause]

**²pose** *n* **1** a sustained posture; *esp* one assumed for artistic purposes **2** an attitude or mode of behaviour assumed deliberately and usu for effect ⟨*kept up a ~ of innocence*⟩

**¹poser** /'pohzə/ *n* a puzzling or baffling question [*pose* (to puzzle), short for earlier *appose*, fr ME *apposen*, alter. of *opposen* to confront with, fr MF *opposer* – more at OPPOSE]

**²poser** *n* a poseur [¹*pose*]

**poseur** /poh'zuh/ *n* an affected or insincere person [Fr, lit., poser, fr *poser* to pose]

**¹posh** /posh/ *adj, informal* **1** very fine; splendid ⟨*a ~ new car*⟩ **2** *chiefly derog* socially exclusive or fashionable; *broadly* upper-class ⟨*a ~ Knightsbridge address*⟩ ⟨*the ~ Sunday papers*⟩ [perh fr earlier slang *posh* money, dandy]

**²posh** *adv, informal* in a posh accent ⟨*anyone who talks ~ is a non-starter in the media – Punch*⟩

**posit** /'pozit/ *vt* to assume or affirm the existence of; postulate [L *positus*, pp]

**¹position** /pə'zish(ə)n/ *n* **1** the statement of a proposition or thesis **2** an opinion; POINT OF VIEW ⟨*made her ~ on the issue* *clear*⟩ **3** a market commitment in securities or commodities; *also* the inventory of a market trader **4a(1)** the place occupied by somebody or something ⟨*took her ∼ at the head of the queue*⟩ ⟨*house in an attractive ∼ overlooking the sea*⟩ ⟨*left the chess pieces in ∼ overnight*⟩ **a(2)** the proper place – esp in *in/into/out of position* **a(3)** a place occupied by troops for strategic reasons ⟨*stormed the enemy ∼*s⟩ **b** a disposition or attitude of (a part of) the body ⟨*rose to a standing ∼*⟩ **5a** a condition, situation ⟨*is now in a ∼ to make important decisions on his own*⟩ ⟨*your question puts me in a very difficult ∼*⟩ **b** social or official rank or status **c** a situation that confers advantage or preference ⟨*jockeying for ∼*⟩ **6** the arrangement of the notes of a musical chord **7** the part of a field or playing area in which a player generally operates ⟨*what ∼ do you play?*⟩ **8** *formal* a post, job *usage* see SITUATION [MF, fr L *position-, positio*, fr *positus*, pp of *ponere* to lay down, put, place, fr (assumed) OL *posinere*, fr *po-* away (akin to Gk *apo-*) + L *sinere* to lay, leave – more at SITE]

²**position** *vt* to put in a proper or specified position

**positional** /pə'zish(ə)nl/ *adj* **1** of or fixed by position ⟨*∼ astronomy*⟩ **2** involving little movement ⟨*∼ warfare*⟩ **3** dependent on position ⟨*the front-articulated /k/ in* key *and the back-articulated /k/ in* cool *are ∼ variants*⟩

**positional notation** *n* a system (e g the ARABIC NUMERALS) of expressing numbers in which the figures are arranged in succession, the position of each figure has a PLACE VALUE, and the number is equal to the sum of each figure multiplied by its place value (e g $256 = (2 \times 100) + (5 \times 10) + (6 \times 1)$)

¹**positive** /'pozətiv/ *adj* **1a** formally laid down or imposed; prescribed ⟨*∼ laws*⟩ **b** expressed clearly or peremptorily ⟨*her answer was a ∼ no*⟩ **c** fully assured; confident ⟨*∼ that he is right*⟩ **2a** of or constituting the simple form of an adjective or adverb that expresses no degree of comparison **b(1)** independent of changing circumstances; not conditioned or relative **b(2)** of or constituting a motion or device that is definite, unyielding, constant, or certain in its action ⟨*a ∼ system of levers*⟩ **3** incontestable ⟨*∼ proof*⟩ **4** utter ⟨*a ∼ disgrace*⟩ **5** real, active ⟨*a ∼ influence for good in the community*⟩ **6a** capable of being constructively applied; helpful ⟨*∼ advice*⟩ **b** concentrating on what is good or beneficial; optimistic ⟨*has a ∼ attitude towards his illness*⟩ **7a** having or expressing actual existence or quality as distinguished from deprivation or deficiency ⟨*∼ change in temperature*⟩ **b** not speculative; empirical **8** having the light and dark parts similar in tone to those of the original photographic subject **9a** extending or generated in a sense or direction arbitrarily chosen to be positive ⟨*∼ rotation of the earth*⟩ ⟨*∼ x-axis*⟩ **b** directed or moving towards a source of stimulation ⟨*a ∼ response to light*⟩ **10** numerically greater than zero ⟨*+2 is a ∼ integer*⟩ **11a(1)** of, being, or charged with electricity of which the proton is the elementary unit. A positive charge predominates in a glass body after it has been rubbed with silk. **a(2)** losing electrons **b** having higher electric potential and constituting the part from which the current flows to the external circuit ⟨*the ∼ terminal of a discharging storage battery*⟩ **c** being an electron-collecting ELECTRODE (structure which conducts electricity into or out of a system) of an electron tube **12a** marked by or indicating acceptance, approval, or affirmation **b** affirming the presence of something sought or suspected to be present ⟨*the test for glandular fever proved ∼*⟩ **13** of a lens converging light rays and forming a real inverted image **14** *chiefly NAm*, of a government economically or esp socially active and effective *synonyms* see ¹SURE *antonym* doubtful [ME, fr OF *positif*, fr L *positivus*, fr *positus*] – **positively** *adv*, **positiveness** *n*, **positivity** *n*

²**positive** *n* something positive: e g **a** the positive degree or form (e g of an adjective or adverb) in a language **b** something of which an affirmation can be made; reality **c** a positive photograph or a print from a negative **d** a positive number

**positive discrimination** *n* a bias in favour of a particular individual or group of people precisely because they are often the object of prejudice and discrimination ⟨*in order to secure ∼ for female entry, half the "lottery places" will be reserved for girls – TES*⟩

**positive law** *n* law established and recognized by governmental authority – compare NATURAL LAW

**positive organ** *n* **1** a small esp medieval PIPE ORGAN – compare PORTATIVE ORGAN **2** CHOIR ORGAN

**positive polarity** *n* the quality possessed by a word or expression (e g *rather* in "I *rather* like Brahms") that is used only in an affirmative context

**positivism** /'pozitiviz(ə)m/ *n* **1a** a theory deriving from Auguste Comte that theology and philosophical speculation are earlier imperfect modes of knowledge and that genuine knowledge is based on the scientific observation of natural phenomena **b** LOGICAL POSITIVISM (philosophical system stressing that statements are only meaningful if they can be verified by observation) **2** the quality or state of being positive [Fr *positivisme*, fr *positif* positive + *-isme* -ism] – **positivist** *adj or n*, **positivistic** *adj*

**positron** /'pozitron/ *n* a positively charged ELEMENTARY PARTICLE (minute particle of matter) that has the same mass and magnitude of electrical charge as the electron and when brought together with it brings about mutual annihilation [*positive* + *-tron* (as in *electron*)]

**positronium** /ˌpozi'trohnyəm, -ni-əm/ *n* a short-lived system that is suggestive of an atom and is similar to the hydrogen atom and consists of a positron and an electron bound together [*positron* + *-ium*]

**posology** /pə'soləji/ *n* a branch of medicine specializing in the study of the quantities in which drugs should be administered [Fr *posologie*, fr Gk *posos* how much + Fr *-logie* -logy] – **posological** *adj*

**posse** /'posi/ *n taking sing or pl vb* **1** posse, **posse comitatus** a body of people summoned by a sheriff, esp in N America, to assist in preserving the public peace usu in an emergency **2** a large group often with a common interest [ML *posse comitatus*, lit., power or authority of the county]

**possess** /pə'zes/ *vt* **1** to make the owner or holder – + *of* or *with*; usu pass ⟨*was ∼ed of dogged determination*⟩ **2a** *law* to have possession of **b** to have and hold as property; own **c** to have as a characteristic, knowledge, or skill **3a** to take into one's possession **b** to influence so strongly as to direct the actions; control, dominate ⟨*whatever ∼ed her to act like that?*⟩ **c** *of a demon, evil spirit, etc* to enter into and control **4** to maintain (oneself, one's mind, etc) in a constant state (e g of peace or patience) **5** to have SEXUAL INTERCOURSE with (a woman) [ME *possessen*, fr MF *possesser* to have or take possession of, fr L *possessus*, pp of *possidēre*, fr *potis* able, in power + *sedēre* to sit – more at POTENT, SIT] – **possessor** *n*

**possessed** /pə'zest/ *adj* **1** influenced or controlled by something (e g an evil spirit or a passion) **2** mad, crazed **3** self-possessed, calm – **possessedly** *adv*, **possessedness** *n*

*usage* One is **possessed** *of* something that one merely "owns", but **possessed** *by* or *with* a passion ⟨**possessed** *by a sudden fury*⟩.

**possession** /pə'zesh(ə)n/ *n* **1a** the act of having or taking into control **b** *law* ownership; *also* control or occupancy (e g of property) without regard to ownership **c** control of the ball, puck, etc by a player or team **2a** something owned, occupied, or controlled **b** *pl* wealth, property **c** a territory subject to a foreign nation **3** domination by something (e g an evil spirit, a passion, or an idea) – **possessional** *adj*

¹**possessive** /pə'zesiv/ *adj* **1** manifesting possession or the desire to own or dominate ⟨*a ∼ mother*⟩ **2** of or being the grammatical possessive – **possessively** *adv*, **possessiveness** *n*

²**possessive** *n* a grammatical case expressing ownership or a relation corresponding to ownership; *also* a form (e g *my*) in this case – compare GENITIVE

**possessive adjective** *n* an adjective (e g *my*) expressing possession

**possessive pronoun** *n* a pronoun (e g *mine*) that derives from a PERSONAL PRONOUN and expresses possession

**possessory** /pə'zes(ə)ri/ *adj* **1** of, arising from, or having the nature of possession ⟨*a ∼ interest*⟩ **2** having possession **3** characteristic of a possessor

**posset** /'posit/ *n* a comforting hot drink of sweetened and spiced milk curdled with ale or wine, formerly used as a remedy for colds; *also* a dessert made with cream, eggs, sugar, and usu lemon [ME *poshet, possot*]

**possibility** /ˌposə'biləti/ *n* **1** the condition or fact of being possible **2a** something possible **b** a candidate, competitor, etc who is reasonably likely to be selected, win, etc **3 possibilities** *pl*, **possibility** potential or prospective value ⟨*the room had great possibilities*⟩

¹**possible** /'posəbl/ *adj* **1** within the limits of ability, capacity, or realization **2** capable of being done or occurring according to nature, custom, or manners **3** that may or may not occur ⟨*it is ∼ but not probable that he will win*⟩ **4** having a specified potential use, quality, etc ⟨*a ∼ housing site*⟩ [ME, fr MF, fr L *possibilis*, fr *posse* to be able, fr *potis*, *pote* able + *esse* to be – more at POTENT, IS]

*usage* Since things are either possible or impossible, some people dislike such expressions as ⟨*even more* **possible**⟩.

²**possible** *n* **1** something possible ⟨*politics is the art of the* ~⟩ **2** somebody or something that may be selected for a specified role, task, etc ⟨*a* ~ *for the first eleven*⟩

**possibly** /'posǝbli/ *adv* **1** it is possible that; maybe ⟨~ *there is life on another planet*⟩ ⟨*he may* ~ *have caught a later train*⟩ **2** – used as an intensifier with *can* or *could* ⟨*you can't* ~ *eat all that cake*⟩ ⟨*I'll do all I* ~ *can to finish it on time*⟩

**possum** /'pos(ǝ)m/ *n* **1** OPOSSUM **1** (American marsupial mammal) – not used technically **2** *Austr* OPOSSUM **2** (Australian marsupial mammal) – **play possum** to pretend to be ignorant, asleep, dead, etc in order to deceive somebody [fr the opossum's habit of pretending to be dead when threatened with danger]

¹**post** /pohst/ *n* **1** a piece of timber, metal, etc fixed firmly in an upright position, esp as a stay or support **2** a pole that marks the starting or finishing point of a horse race **3** a metallic fitting attached to an electrical device (eg a storage battery) for convenience in making connections **4** a goalpost [ME, fr OE; akin to OHG *pfosto* post; both fr a prehistoric WGmc word borrowed fr L *postis;* akin to Gk *pro* before and to Gk *histasthai* to stand – more at FOR, STAND] – **pip at the post** to beat at the very last minute (eg in a race or competition) ⟨*the favourite was* pipped at the post⟩ – see also **from** PILLAR **to post**

²**post** *vt* **1** to fasten to a wall, board, etc in a public place – often + *up* **2a** to publish, announce, or advertise (as if) by use of a placard, poster, etc **b** to enter (a name) on a published list **c** to publish the name of (a ship) as missing or lost

³**post** *n* **1** *chiefly Br* **1a** an official postal system ⟨*put that memo in the internal* ~⟩; *also* a means of posting (eg a postbox) ⟨*I'll take it to the* ~⟩ **b** the letters, parcels, etc handled by a postal system; mail **c** a single collection or delivery of mail ⟨*what time is the last* ~?⟩; *also* the postal matter that makes up one delivery ⟨*today's* ~ *is on the mat*⟩ **d** postage ⟨~ *and packing 25p*⟩ **2** *archaic* **2a** any of a series of stopping-places along a route in former times, where travellers or messengers could rest, change horses, etc, and where letters could be passed to a fresh rider; *also* the distance between two such places **b** a rider who carried mail from one such place to the next – see also **by** RETURN **of post** [MF *poste* relay station, courier, fr OIt *posta* relay station, fr fem of *posto,* pp of *porre* to place, fr L *ponere* – more at POSITION]

⁴**post** *vi* **1** to travel with post-horses **2** *of a rider* to rise from the saddle and return to it in rhythm with a horse's trot **3** *archaic* to ride or travel with haste; hurry ~ *vt* **1** to send by post ⟨~ *a letter*⟩ – sometimes + *off* **2a** to transfer or carry from a BOOK OF ORIGINAL ENTRY (book in which transactions are initially recorded) to a ledger **b** to make transfer entries in (a ledger) **3** to provide with the latest news; inform ⟨*kept her* ~ed *on the latest gossip*⟩

⁵**post** *adv* with post-horses; express

⁶**post** *n* **1a** the place at which a soldier is stationed; *esp* a sentry's beat or station **b** a station or task to which one is assigned **c** the place at which a body of troops is stationed; a camp **2a** an office or position to which a person is appointed; a job ⟨*obtained a* ~ *in the civil service*⟩ **b** (the position of) a player in basketball who provides the focal point of the attack **3** a settlement; TRADING POST **4** *Br* either of two army bugle calls giving notice of the hour for retiring at night [MF *poste,* fr OIt *posto,* fr pp of *porre* to place]

⁷**post** *vt* **1** to station ⟨*guards were* ~ed *at the doors*⟩ **2** *chiefly Br* to assign to a unit or location (eg in the military or civil service)

**post-** *prefix* **1a** after; subsequent; later ⟨*post*date⟩ **b** posterior; following after ⟨*post*script⟩ ⟨*post*consonantal⟩ **2a** subsequent to; later than ⟨*post*operative⟩ ⟨*post-Pleistocene*⟩ **b** situated behind ⟨*post*orbital⟩ [ME, fr L, fr *post,* adv & prep; akin to Skt *paśca* behind, after, Gk *apo* away from – more at OF]

**postage** /'pohstij/ *n* **1** postage, post the fee for a postal service **2** markings or stamps representing a postal fee

**postage-due stamp** *n* an adhesive or imprinted stamp that is applied by a post office to mail bearing insufficient postage and that indicates a fee to be paid by the addressee immediately before delivery

**postage meter** *n, NAm* FRANKING MACHINE

**postage stamp** *n* an adhesive stamp or imprinted stamp for use on mail as evidence of prepayment of postage

**postal** /'pohstl/ *adj* **1** of or being a system for the conveyance of written and printed material, parcels, etc between a large number of users **2** conducted by post ⟨~ *vote*⟩ – **postally** *adv*

**postal order** *n, Br* an order issued by a post office for payment of a specified sum of money usu at another post office

**postal union** *n* an association of national postal services setting up uniform regulations and practices for international mail

**postaxial** /pohst'aksiǝl/ *adj* located behind an AXIS (central line of symmetry) of the body; *esp* of the back of a limb of a VERTEBRATE animal – **postaxially** *adv*

**postbag** /-,bag/ *n, Br* **1** a mailbag **2** a single batch of post; letters

**postbox** /-,boks/ *n* a secure receptacle for the posting of outgoing mail; *also, NAm* LETTER BOX **b**

**postboy** /-,boy/ *n* **1** POSTILION (rider on a horse pulling a carriage) **2** *chiefly Br* a boy or man who deals with post

**postbus** /'pohst,bus/ *n* a bus in a rural area that both delivers the post and carries passengers

**postcard** /-,kahd/ *n* a card that can be posted without an enclosing envelope; *esp* PICTURE POSTCARD

**post chaise** /shayz/ *n* a usu closed 4-wheeled carriage seating two to four people

**postclassical** /-'klasikl/, **postclassic** *adj* of or being a period (eg in art, literature, or civilization) following a classical one

**postcode** /-,kohd/, **postal code** *n* a combination of letters and numbers that is used in the postal address of a place in the UK to assist sorting – compare ZIP CODE

**postcolonial** /,pohst-kǝ'lohniǝl/ *adj* of or being the period following a colony's achieving independence

**post-com'munion** *n, often cap P&C* the part of the Mass following the taking of Communion [ML *postcommunion-, postcommunio,* fr L *post-* + LL *communio* communion]

**postconsonantal** /,pohst-konsǝ'nantl/ *adj* immediately following a consonant

**post crown** *n* an artificial crown attached to the root of a tooth by a usu metallic pin

**postdate** /-'dayt/ *vt* **1a** to mark (a letter, cheque, etc) with a date later than the actual one – compare BACKDATE **b** to give a later date to (an event) than the actual date of occurrence **2** to follow in time

**postdiluvian** /,pohst-di'l(y)oohviǝn/ *n* of or being the period after the flood described in the Bible

**postdoctoral** /pohst'doktǝrǝl/ *also* **postdoctorate** /-tǝrǝt/ *adj* of or engaged in advanced academic or professional work beyond a doctor's degree ⟨*a* ~ *fellowship*⟩ ⟨~ *scholars*⟩

**postembryonic** /,pohstembri'onik/ *also* **postembryonal** /-brie-ǝnl/ *adj* succeeding the embryonic stage ⟨~ *development*⟩

¹**post-,entry** *adj* of or being a CLOSED SHOP in which an employer employs only people who are or agree to become union members – compare PRE-ENTRY

**poster** /'pohstǝ/ *n* a bill or placard for display often in a public place; *specif* one that is decorative or pictorial [²*post*]

**poste restante** /,pohst 'restont (*Fr* post rɛstãt)/ *n, chiefly Br* letters that are intended for collection from a post office; *also* the department or branch of a post office that handles such letters [Fr, lit., waiting mail] – **poste restante** *adv*

¹**posterior** /po'stiǝri-ǝ/ *adj* **1** coming later in time; subsequent **2** situated behind or towards the back: eg **2a** *of a human body or its parts* of, near, or on the back; DORSAL **b** *of an animal part* of or near the hind end; CAUDAL **c** *of a plant part* on the same side as or facing the main stem; SUPERIOR **6b** – compare ANTERIOR [L, compar of *posterus* coming after, fr *post* after – more at POST-]

²**posterior** *n* the rear parts of the body; *specif* the buttocks

**posteriority** /po,stiǝri'orǝti/ *n, formal or journalistic* the quality or state of being later or subsequent

**posterity** /po'sterǝti/ *n* **1** *taking sing or pl vb* all the descendants of one ancestor **2** all future generations [ME *posterite,* fr MF *posterité,* fr L *posteritat-, posteritas,* fr *posterus* coming after]

**postern** /'postuhn, 'poh-/ *n, archaic* a back door or gate [ME *posterne,* fr OF, alter. of *posterle,* fr LL *posterula,* dim. of *postera* back door, fr L, fem of *posterus*] – **postern** *adj*

**poster paint** *n* an opaque watercolour paint made with a gum or glue binder

**post exchange** *n, NAm* a shop at a military base that sells goods and offers services to military personnel and authorized civilians – called also PX; compare NAAFI

**postexilic** /,pohsteg'zilik/ *adj* of or of the period of Jewish history between the end of the exile in Babylon in 538 BC and AD 1

**postfix** /'pohst,fiks/ *n* SUFFIX – compare PREFIX [*post-* + *-fix* (as in *prefix*)]

,**post-'free** *adj, chiefly Br* with the postage prepaid or post-paid

**postglacial** /,pohst'glaysh(ə)l, -siəl/ *adj* occurring after an age of glaciation (e g the PLEISTOCENE) [ISV]

[1]**postgraduate** /pohst'gradyooət/ *adj, of a person or course* engaged in or dealing with studies beyond the first or bachelor's degree ⟨a ~ student⟩

[2]**postgraduate** *n* a student continuing higher education after completing a first degree

**posthaste** /-'hayst/ *adv* with all possible speed

**post hoc** /,pohst 'hok/ *n* the fallacy in logic of assuming that one particular event (e g getting wet feet) always causes another particular event (e g getting a cold) simply because, on some past occasion, the first preceded the second [NL *post hoc, ergo propter hoc* after this, therefore because of this]

**posthole** /'pohst,hohl/ *n* a hole sunk in the ground to hold a fence post

**post horn** *n* a simple straight or coiled brass or copper wind instrument without valves or keys but with a cupped mouthpiece used esp by guards of mail coaches in the 18th and 19th centuries

'**post-,horse** *n* a horse formerly kept at an inn for use esp by travellers or mail carriers

**posthumous** /'postyooməs/ *adj* **1** born after the death of the father **2** published after the death of the author or composer **3** following or occurring after death ⟨~ fame⟩ [LL *posthumus,* alter. of L *postumus* late-born, posthumous, fr superl of *posterus* coming after – more at POSTERIOR] – **posthumously** *adv*

**posthypnotic** /,pohst·hip'notik/ *adj* (characteristic) of the period following a hypnotic trance – used esp of suggestions made during hypnosis that remain or become effective after the end of the trance [ISV]

**postiche** /po'steesh/ *n* **1** a woman's decorative hairpiece; *also* a wig; TOUPEE **2** **2** an imitation, sham [Fr, fr Sp *postizo,* fr *postizo* false, artificial]

**postie** /'pohsti/ *n, chiefly Scot, Can, & Austr informal* a postal worker; *esp* a postman [³*post* (in the sense "courier, postman") + -*ie*]

**postilion, postillion** /po'stilyən/ *n* a person who rides on the near horse of one of the pairs attached to a coach or POST CHAISE and acts as a guide to all the horses, esp when there is no coachman [MF *postillon* mail carrier using post-horses, fr It *postiglione,* fr *posta* post]

**Postimpressionism** /,pohstim'preshəniz(ə)m/ *n* any of various theories or practices of art originating among French artists (e g Cezanne and Gauguin) in the last quarter of the 19th century that, in revolt against the naturalist tendency of IMPRESSIONISM, stress form or subjective feeling (e g composition or the expression of the artist's individual feelings) [Fr *postimpressionisme,* fr *post-* + *impressionisme* impressionism] – **Postimpressionist** *adj or n,* **Postimpressionistic** *adj*

[1]**posting** /'pohsting/ *n* the act of transferring an entry from an informal record to the formal account in a ledger; *also* the resulting entry [⁴*post*]

[2]**posting** *n* an appointment to a post or command [⁷*post*]

**postirradiation** /,pohsti,raydi'aysh(ə)n/ *adj* occurring after irradiation ⟨~ sickness⟩

**postlude** /'pohstloohd/ *n* **1** a final or concluding piece of music; *esp* one (VOLUNTARY) played on the organ at the end of a church service **2** a closing phase (e g of an epoch or literary work) [*post-* + *-lude* (as in *prelude*)]

**postman** /-mən/, *fem* **postwoman** *n* a person who delivers the post

**postman's knock** *n* a children's game in which the pretence of delivering a letter to a named player is rewarded with a kiss from that player

**postmark** /-,mahk/ *vt or n* (to mark with) a cancellation mark showing the post office and date of posting of a piece of mail

**postmaster** /-,mahstə/, *fem* **postmistress** *n* somebody who has charge of a post office – **postmastership** *n*

**postmaster general** *n, pl* **postmasters general** a minister or other official in charge of a national post office

**postmenopausal** /,pohstmenə'pawzl/ *adj* **1** having undergone menopause **2** occurring after menopause

**post meridiem** /mə'ridi·əm/ *adj* after noon [L]

**postmillennial** /-mi'leni·əl/ *adj* **1** of or following the period after the MILLENNIUM **2** of or believing in postmillennialism

**postmillennialism** /,pohst·mi'leniəliz(ə)m/ *n* the belief that Christ will return only after the MILLENNIUM – **postmillennialist** *n*

[1]**postmortem** /-'mawtəm/ *adj* **1** occurring after death **2** following the event ⟨a ~ discussion of the game⟩ [L *post mortem* after death]

[2]**postmortem** *n* **1** *also* **postmortem examination** an examination of a body after death to determine the cause of death or the character and extent of changes produced by disease **2** an analysis or discussion of an event after it is over

**postnasal** /pohst'nayzl/ *adj* lying or occurring behind the nose

**postnatal** /-'naytl/ *adj* subsequent to birth; *also* of a newborn child ⟨~ care⟩ [ISV] – **postnatally** *adv*

**postnuptial** /-'nupsh(ə)l/ *adj* made or occurring after marriage or mating – **postnuptially** *adv*

,**post-'obit** /-'obit, -'ohbit/ *adj* occurring or taking effect after death [L *post obitum* after death]

**post office** *n* **1** a national organization or government department or agency responsible for a postal system; *specif, cap* P&O the corporation that fulfils this function in the UK **2** a local branch of a national post office that deals with the mail for a particular area and that, in the UK, also acts as an agency for certain government departments (e g in making family-allowance payments) **3** *NAm* POSTMAN'S KNOCK

**post-office box** *n* a rented compartment in a post office for the keeping of mail that is not to be delivered but is to be collected by the renter

**postoperative** /-'op(ə)rətiv/ *adj* occurring after a surgical operation [ISV] – **postoperatively** *adv*

**postorbital** /pohst'awbitl/ *adj, anatomy* situated behind the eye socket

**postpaid** /-'payd/ *adv* with the postage paid by the sender and not chargeable to the receiver

**postpartum** /-'pahtəm/ *adj* following birth ⟨~ period⟩ [NL *post partum* after birth] – **postpartum** *adv*

**postpituitary** /,pohstpi'tyooh·it(ə)ri/ *adj* arising in or derived from the rear lobe of the PITUITARY GLAND

**postpone** /pə'spohn, ,pohs(t)'pohn/ *vt* **1** to move to a later time; defer **2** to place after in order of precedence, preference, or importance [L *postponere* to place after, postpone, fr *post-* + *ponere* to place – more at POSITION] – **postponable** *adj,* **postponement** *n,* **postponer** *n*

**postposition** /,pohstpə'zish(ə)n/ *n* the placing of a grammatical element after a word to which it is related in a sentence; *also* such a grammatical element (e g -*wards* in *homewards* or *elect* in "president *elect*") [Fr, fr *postposer* to place after, fr L *postponere* (perf indic *postposui*)] – **postpositional** *adj,* **postpositionally** *adv*

**postpositive** /-'pozətiv/ *adj* placed after or at the end of another word ⟨*errant* in "knight errant" is a ~ adjective⟩ – **postpositively** *adv*

**postprandial** /-'prandi·əl/ *adj, formal or humorous* following a meal

,**post-Re'naissance** *adj* of or being the period since the Renaissance, esp in contrast to medieval times

**post road** *n* a road along which mail was formerly conveyed

**postscript** /'pohs(t),skript/ *n* **1** a note or series of notes added at the end of a completed article, book, or esp letter **2** a subordinate or supplementary part [NL *postscriptum,* fr L, neut of *postscriptus,* pp of *postscribere* to write after, fr *post-* + *scribere* to write – more at SCRIBE]

**postsynaptic** /,pohstsi'naptik, -sie-/ *adj* **1** occurring after or having gone through the process of genetic SYNAPSIS (stage in the division of a cell) **2** occurring in or being the part of a NERVE CELL by which an impulse is conveyed away from a SYNAPSE – **postsynaptically** *adv*

**posttension** /,pohst'tensh(ə)n/ *vt* to apply tension to (reinforcing steel) after concrete has set

**postulant** /'postyoolənt/ *n* a person requesting or petitioning for something (e g admission); *esp* a person admitted to a religious house with a view to becoming a NOVICE [Fr, petitioner, candidate, postulant, fr MF, fr prp of *postuler* to demand, solicit, fr L *postulare*] – **postulancy** *n*

[1]**postulate** /'postyoo,layt/ *vt* **1** to demand as of right or necessity; *also* to take for granted – often + *that* **2a** to assume or claim to be existent or true; depend on or start from the assumption that **b** to take as a postulate or AXIOM (e g in logic or mathematics) **3** to put forward (a candidate for an office) for the approval of a higher authority – used in ecclesiastical law [L *postulatus,* pp of *postulare,* fr (assumed) *postus,* pp of L *poscere* to ask; akin to OHG *forsca* question, Skt *pṛcchati* he asks] – **postulation** *n,* **postulational** *adj*

[2]**postulate** /'postyoolət/ *n* **1** a hypothesis advanced as an

essential basis or PREMISE in a process of reasoning **2** a statement (e g in logic or mathematics) that is accepted without proof [ML *postulatum,* fr neut of *postulatus,* pp of *postulare* to assume, fr L, to demand]

**postulator** /'postyoolaytə/ *n* a Roman Catholic official who presents a plea that someone should be given the title "blessed" or made a saint – compare DEVIL'S ADVOCATE

**postural** /'poschərəl/ *adj* of, involving, or caused by posture

¹**posture** /'poschə/ *n* **1a** the manner of holding the body, whether habitual or assumed for a special purpose; bearing ⟨*erect* ∼⟩ **b** the disposition of the body; a pose **2** the relative position or organization of the parts of a whole **3** a state or condition at a given time, esp in relation to other people or things ⟨*put the country in a* ∼ *of defence*⟩ **4** a frame of mind or an attitude taken up; a stance ⟨*his* ∼ *of moral superiority*⟩ [Fr, fr It *postura,* fr L *positura,* fr *positus,* pp of *ponere* to place – more at POSITION]

²**posture** *vt* to position or dispose (someone's limbs) in a particular way; pose ∼ *vi* **1** to assume a posture; *esp* to strike a pose for effect **2** to assume an artificial or insincere attitude; attitudinize – **posturer** *n*

**postvocalic** /,pohstvoh'kalik/ *adj* immediately following a vowel [ISV]

**postwar** /,pohst'waw/ *adj* of or being the period after a war, esp World War I or II

**posy** /'pohzi/ *n* **1** a small bouquet of flowers; a nosegay **2** *archaic* a brief sentiment, motto, or legend, esp when inscribed inside a ring [alter. of *poesy*]

¹**pot** /pot/ *n* **1a(1)** any of various usu rounded vessels (e g of metal or earthenware) used for holding liquids or solids, esp domestically in cooking; *also* any of various technical or industrial vessels or enclosures resembling a household pot ⟨*the* ∼ *of a still*⟩ **a(2)** a handmade vessel, often ornamental, made from baked clay ⟨*she makes* ∼s⟩ ⟨*she throws* ∼s *as a hobby*⟩ **b** a drinking vessel (e g of pewter) used esp for beer **c** the contents of or quantity contained in a pot; a potful **2** CHAMBER POT **3** CHIMNEY POT **4** an enclosed framework for catching fish or lobsters **5** a random or casual shot; a potshot **6a** the total of the bets at stake at one time **b** one round in a poker game **c** *NAm* the common fund of a group **d** pots *pl,* **pot** a large amount (e g of money) **7** *Br* a shot in billiards, snooker, etc in which a ball goes into a pocket **8** *pl, dial Br* a pit or depression in the ground or in the bed of a stream **9** *informal* a trophy; CUP **4a** ⟨*won lots of* ∼s *in her time*⟩ **10** *informal* a potbelly **11** *slang* an intoxicating drug, usu smoked, made from parts of the hemp plant; *specif* marijuana [ME, fr OE *pott;* akin to MLG *pot* pot; (11) perh of different origin] – **go to pot** *informal* to get out of condition or order; deteriorate, collapse

²**pot** *vb* **-tt-** *vt* **1a** to place (e g a plant) in a pot **b** to place in a sealable pot, jar, or tin for preservation ⟨∼ted *chicken*⟩ **2** to shoot (e g an animal) for food with a potshot **3** to make or shape (earthenware) as a potter does **4** to embed (e g electronic components) in a container with an insulating or protective material (e g plastic) **5** to send (a ball) into a pocket in billiards, snooker, etc **6** *informal* to sit (a young child) on a potty ∼ *vi* **1** to take a potshot **2** to make or shape earthenware as a potter does ⟨*she doesn't weave now, she* ∼s⟩

³**pot** *n* POTENTIOMETER **2** (device used in electronic circuits)

¹**potable** /'pohtəbl/ *adj, formal or humorous* drinkable; *also* suitable or good for drinking [LL *potabilis,* fr L *potare* to drink; akin to L *bibere* to drink, Gk *pinein*] – **potability** *n*

²**potable** *n, formal or humorous* a liquid that is suitable for drinking

**potage** /po'tahzh/ *n* a thick soup – compare POTTAGE [MF, fr OF, pottage]

**pot ale** *n* the residue of fermented WORT (solution of malt and water) left in a still after whisky has been distilled off

**potash** /'potash/ *n* **1a** POTASSIUM CARBONATE, esp as found in wood ashes **b** POTASSIUM HYDROXIDE **2** potassium or a potassium-containing chemical compound, esp as used in agriculture or industry [sing. of *pot ashes,* trans of obs D *potaschen;* fr its being orig obtained by leaching wood ashes & evaporating the lye in iron pots]

**potash alum** *n* ALUM

**potassium** /pə'tasyəm, -si·əm/ *n* a silver-white soft light metallic chemical element of the ALKALI METAL group that has a low melting point, is highly reactive, and occurs chiefly in the minerals CARNALLITE and SYLVITE [NL, fr *potassa* potash, fr E *potash*] – **potassic** *adj*

**potassium-argon dating** *n* a method of dating archaeo-

logical or geological material (e g minerals) based on the radioactive decay of potassium to argon that has taken place

**potassium bromide** *n* a chemical compound, KBr, with a salty taste that is used for making photographic emulsions and as a sedative

**potassium carbonate** *n* a chemical compound, $K_2CO_3$, that in solid form will absorb water from the air to form a strongly alkaline solution and that is used in making glass and soap

**potassium chlorate** *n* a chemical compound, $KClO_3$, that is a powerful OXIDIZING AGENT and is very commonly used in making matches, fireworks, and explosives

**potassium chloride** *n* a chemical compound, KCl, that occurs as the mineral SYLVITE and in the sea and SALT LAKES, and is used esp as a fertilizer

**potassium cyanide** *n* a very poisonous chemical compound, KCN, used esp in extracting gold and silver from their ores

**potassium dichromate** *n* an orange-red chemical compound, $K_2Cr_2O_7$, used esp in dyeing and as an OXIDIZING AGENT

**potassium hydroxide** *n* a chemical compound, KOH, that in solid form will absorb water from the air to form a strongly alkaline and caustic liquid. It is used chiefly in making liquid soaps and detergents

**potassium metabisulphite** *n* a white chemical compound, $K_2S_2O_5$, that is used as an antimicrobial preservative (e g in the food industry, esp fruit preserving) and as a REDUCING AGENT to stabilize drug solutions

**potassium nitrate** *n* a chemical compound, $KNO_3$, that occurs naturally in fertile soils as a product of the action of bacteria on ammonium compounds, is made commercially from POTASSIUM HYDROXIDE and NITRIC ACID, and is a strong OXIDIZING AGENT. It is used as a fertilizer and in making gunpowder and preserving meat.

**potassium permanganate** *n* a dark purple chemical compound, $KMnO_4$, used as an OXIDIZING AGENT and disinfectant

**potassium phosphate** *n* any of various PHOSPHATES of potassium; *esp* any of the three ORTHOPHOSPHATES

**potassium sodium tartrate** *n* ROCHELLE SALT (chemical compound used as a mild purgative)

**potassium sulphate** *n* a chemical compound, $K_2SO_4$, that is obtained from the minerals KAINITE and LANGBEINITE, is made commercially from SULPHURIC ACID and POTASSIUM CHLORIDE, and is used esp in fertilizers

**potation** /poh'taysh(ə)n/ *n, formal or humorous* **1** a usu alcoholic drink or brew **2** an act or instance of drinking; *also* the portion, usu of alcohol, taken in one such act – often used to imply drinking too much ⟨*his* ∼s *left him unsteady on his feet*⟩ [ME *potacioun,* fr MF *potation,* fr L *potation-, potatio* act of drinking, fr *potatus,* pp of *potare* to drink]

**potato** /pə'taytoh/ *n, pl* **potatoes 1** SWEET POTATO **2** an erect S American plant (*Solanum tuberosum* of the family Solanaceae, the potato family) widely cultivated in temperate regions for its edible starchy tubers; *also* a potato tuber eaten as a vegetable [Sp *batata,* fr Taino]

**potato beetle** *n* COLORADO BEETLE

**potato blight** *n* any of several destructive fungus diseases of the potato; *specif* LATE BLIGHT

**potato chip** *n* **1** a strip of potato fried in deep fat **2** *NAm* CRISP **2**

**potato crisp** *n, chiefly Br* CRISP **2**

**potato moth** *n* POTATO TUBERWORM

**potato tuberworm** *n* a small greyish brown moth (*Phthorimaea operculella*), found esp in the Mediterranean region, whose larva invades the leaves and bores in the stems esp of potato and tomato plants and often overwinters in potato tubers

**pot-au-feu** /,pot oh 'fuh (*Fr* pɔtofø)/ *n, pl* **pot-au-feu** /∼/ a French dish of meat boiled with vegetables; *also* the pot in which this dish is cooked [Fr, lit., pot on the fire]

**potbellied stove** *n* a stove with a rounded or bulging body

**potbelly** /-'beli/ *n* **1** a protruding, fat, or swollen belly **2** potbelly, potbelly stove POTBELLIED STOVE – **potbellied** *adj*

**potboiler** /-,boylə/ *n* a usu inferior work (e g of art or literature) produced chiefly to make money

¹**pot-,bound** *adj, of a potted plant* with little or no space for further growth, as the roots are so densely matted in a pot too small for them

**potboy** /-,boy/ *n* a boy who serves drinks in a pub or inn

**pot cheese** *n, NAm* COTTAGE CHEESE (soft white cheese)

**poteen** *also* **potheen** /po'cheen, po'teen/ *n* Irish whiskey illegally distilled; *broadly* any distilled alcoholic drink made at home [IrGael *poitīn*, dim. of *pota* pot, fr E *pot*]

¹**potent** /'poht(ə)nt/ *adj, of a heraldic cross* with flat bars like the top of a crutch across the ends of the arms [obs *potent* crutch, fr ME, modif of MF *potence* crutch, gibbet]

²**potent** *adj* **1** having or exerting great force, authority, or influence; powerful **2** persuasive and forceful in influencing thought or opinion; cogent ⟨*a* ~ *argument*⟩ **3** effective in bringing about a particular result ⟨*a* ~ *factor in causing delinquency*⟩: e g **3a** chemically or medicinally effective, esp in small doses ⟨*a* ~ *drug*⟩ **b** producing a powerful reaction, esp unexpectedly; strong ⟨*this whisky is* ~ *stuff*⟩ ⟨*the play gave a* ~ *account of unemployment and was deeply moving*⟩ **4** able to have sexual intercourse because capable of maintaining an erection of the penis [ME (Sc), fr L *potent-, potens*, fr prp of (assumed) L *potēre* to be powerful, fr L *potis, pote* able; akin to Goth *brūthfaths* bridegroom, Gk *posis* husband, Skt *pati* master] – **potency** *also* **potence** *n*, **potently** *adv*

**potentate** /'poht(ə)n,tayt/ *n* a person with great power; *esp* a ruler

¹**potential** /pə'tensh(ə)l/ *adj* **1** existing as a possibility but not yet active; capable of coming into being or developing further ⟨~ *benefits*⟩ ⟨~ *musical ability*⟩ **2** expressing possibility; *specif* of or constituting a verb phrase that expresses possibility (e g in "it may rain") [ME, fr LL *potentialis*, fr *potentia* potentiality, fr L, power, fr *potent-, potens*] – **potentially** *adv*

²**potential** *n* **1** something that can develop or become actual; possible or prospective capacity or value ⟨*a* ~ *for violence*⟩ ⟨*the computer's* ~ *in business*⟩ **2a** any of various mathematical functions from which the intensity or velocity at any point in a field may be readily calculated **b** the work required to move a unit positive electrical charge from a reference point (e g infinity) to a point in question **c** POTENTIAL DIFFERENCE *synonyms see* CAPABILITY

**potential difference** *n* the voltage difference between two points that represents the work involved or the energy released in the transfer of a unit quantity of electricity from one point to another

**potential divider** *n* a chain of RESISTORS (devices that oppose the flow of an electric current) that can be tapped at any point to provide a voltage that is a definite fraction of the total across the chain – called also VOLTAGE DIVIDER

**potential energy** *n* the energy that a piece of matter has because of its position or because of the arrangement of parts

**potentiality** /pə,tenshi'aləti/ *n* **1** the ability to develop or come into existence **2** POTENTIAL 1

**potentiate** /pə'tenshi,ayt/ *vt* to make (more) effective; *specif* to make (two drugs) more effective by administering them together – **potentiator** *n*, **potentiation** *n*

**potentilla** /,poht(ə)n'tilə/ *n* any of a large genus (*Potentilla*) of plants and shrubs (e g a CINQUEFOIL) of the rose family that have 5-petalled usu yellow flowers and leaves that are PINNATE (having leaflets arranged in pairs on each side of the stalk) or PALMATE (having lobes radiating from a common point) [NL, genus name, fr ML, garden heliotrope, fr L *potent-, potens* powerful]

**potentiometer** /pə,tenshi'omitə/ *n* **1** an instrument for measuring ELECTROMOTIVE FORCE (force driving a current round an electric circuit) **2** a POTENTIAL DIVIDER with three terminals that is used to provide variable resistances in an electronic circuit (e g to control volume in a radio) – called also POT [ISV *potential* + *-o-* + *-meter*] – **potentiometric** *adj*, **potentiometrically** *adv*

**potful** /-f(ə)l/, **pot** *n* as much or as many as a pot will hold

**pothead** /'pot,hed/ *n, slang* a person who smokes marijuana

**potheen** /po'cheen, po'teen/ *n* POTEEN (illegally distilled whiskey)

¹**pother** /'podhə/ *n* **1a** a noisy disturbance; a commotion **b** needless agitation or controversy over a trivial matter; fuss **2** a choking cloud of dust or smoke **3** a display of grief; mental turmoil [origin unknown]

²**pother** *vb* to (cause to) fuss or worry

**potherb** /'pot,huhb/ *n* any of various plants whose leaves or stems are cooked as greens; *also* a herb (e g parsley) used to season food

**pothole** /'pot,hohl/ *n* **1** a circular hole formed by the wearing away of the rock in a riverbed by the grinding action of stones or gravel whirled round by the water **2** a natural vertically descending hole in the ground or in the floor of a cave; *also* a network of these, usu linked by caves **3** an unwanted hole in a road surface – **potholed** *adj*

**potholing** /'pot,hohling/ *n* the recreation of exploring pothole systems – **potholer** *n*

**pothook** /-,hook/ *n* **1** a curved S-shaped hook for hanging pots and kettles over an open fire or for lifting a hot cooking pot **2** a written mark or character resembling a pothook

**pothouse** /'pot,hows/ *n, Br archaic or derog or NAm* a pub

**pothunter** /-,huntə/ *n, chiefly derog* **1** a person who shoots animals indiscriminately for food, without regard for the sporting aspects of hunting **2** an amateur archaeologist – **pothunting** *n*

**potion** /'pohsh(ə)n/ *n* **1** a dose of medicine or poison in liquid form **2** a drink mixed with the intention of producing a specified effect ⟨*a love* ~⟩ [ME *pocioun*, fr MF *potion*, fr L *potion-, potio* drink, potion, fr *potus*, pp of *potare* to drink (cf POISON)]

**potlatch** /'pot,lach/ *n* a ceremonial feast of the Indians of the northwest coast of N America marked by the host's lavish distribution of gifts requiring some return in kind [Chinook Jargon, fr Nootka *patshatl* giving] – **potlatch** *vb*

**potluck** /-'luk/ *n* **1** food that is available, esp for an unexpected guest, without any special preparations being made **2** whatever luck or chance may bring – esp in *take potluck*

**pot marigold** *n* an orange-flowered plant (*Calendula officinalis*) of the daisy family, grown esp for ornament

**potoroo** /,pohtə'rooh/ *n, pl* **potoroos** RAT KANGAROO [native name in New South Wales in Australia]

**pot plant** *n* a plant grown in a flowerpot, usu for ornament; *also* a houseplant

**potpourri** /,pohpə'ree, poh'pooəri/ *n* **1** a mixture of dried flowers, herbs, and spices that is usu kept in a jar and used for its fragrance **2** a miscellaneous collection, esp of writings or music; a medley ⟨*a* ~ *of songs and sketches*⟩ [Fr *pot pourri*, lit., rotten pot]

**pot roast** *n* a joint of meat cooked in a covered pot by braising, usu on the top of a cooker – **pot-roast** *vt*

**potsherd** /-,shuhd/ *n* a fragment of pottery – used esp in archaeology [ME *pot-sherd*, fr *pot* + *sherd* shard]

**potshot** /-,shot/ *n* **1** a shot taken in a casual manner or at an easy target; *esp* one taken at game without regard to the rules of sportsmanship **2** a critical remark made in a random manner, in the hope of hitting a sensitive spot [fr the notion that such a shot is unsportsmanlike and worthy only of somebody wishing to fill a cooking pot]

**pot still** *n* a device (⁶STILL 2), used esp in the distillation of Irish GRAIN WHISKY and Scotch MALT WHISKY, in which the heat of the fire is applied directly to the pot containing the fermenting grain or malt (MASH)

**potstone** /'pot,stohn/ *n* a more or less impure STEATITE (soft soapy mineral) used, esp in prehistoric times to make cooking vessels

**pottage** /'potij/ *n* a thick soup of vegetables or a stew of vegetables and meat – compare POTAGE [ME *potage*, fr OF, fr *pot* pot, of Gmc origin; akin to OE *pott* pot]

**potted** /'potid/ *adj* **1** planted or grown in a pot ⟨~ *palms*⟩ **2** *chiefly Br* abridged or summarized, usu in a simplified or popular form ⟨~ *biographies*⟩ ⟨*another* ~ *history of World War II*⟩ **3** *chiefly NAm slang* drunk; high

¹**potter** /'potə/ *n* a person who makes pottery [ME *pottere*, fr OE, fr *pott* pot]

²**potter** *vi* **1** to waste time in aimless or unproductive activity; *also* to spend time in a leisurely but agreeable way – often + *around* or *about* ⟨*he loves* ~*ing about in boats*⟩ **2** to move or travel in a leisurely or random fashion ⟨*avoided the motorways und* ~*ed along country lanes*⟩ [prob freq of E dial. *pote* to poke, fr ME *poten*, fr OE *potian*] – **potterer** *n*

**potter's field** *n* a public burial place for paupers, unknown people, and criminals [fr the mention in Mt 27:7 of the purchase of a potter's field for use as a graveyard]

**potter's wheel** *n* a usu horizontal disc that revolves on a vertical spindle so that a potter can shape clay on it

**pottery** /'pot(ə)ri/ *n* **1** a place where CERAMICS (articles of baked clay) are made and fired **2a** the art or craft of the potter **b** the business of making pottery **3a** articles of baked clay; *esp* earthenware as distinguished from porcelain and STONEWARE **b** coarse or hand-made ware made from baked clay

**pottle** /'potl/ *n* **1** a container holding half a gallon (about 2.27 litres) **2** *archaic* a measure equal to half a gallon [ME *potel*, fr OF, fr *pot*]

**potto** /'potoh/ *n, pl* **pottos** any of several African primates (genera *Arctocebus* and *Perodicticus*) related to the lorises of S Asia; *esp* a nocturnal primate (*Perodicticus potto*) that has rudimentary index fingers and a very short tail, lives in the forests of W Africa, and moves slowly through the trees feeding on insects and fruit [of Niger-Congo origin; akin to Wolof *pata*, a tailless monkey]

**Pott's disease** /pots/ *n* a tuberculosis of the spine that is characterized by softening and crumbling of the bone and often results in a hunchback deformity [Percivall *Pott* †1788 E surgeon]

**¹potty** /'poti/ *adj, chiefly Br informal* 1 trivial, insignificant 2 slightly crazy ⟨*that noise is driving me* ∼⟩ 3 foolish, silly ⟨*a* ∼ *idea*⟩ 4 having a great interest in or liking for the specified person or thing ⟨∼ *about steam engines*⟩ [prob fr ¹*pot*] – **pottiness** *n*

**²potty** *n, informal* CHAMBER POT; *esp* one for a small child [¹*pot* + ⁴-*y*]

**¹pouch** /powch/ *n* **1a** a small drawstring bag carried on the person **b** an arrangement of cloth that resembles a large loose pocket **2** a bag for storing or transporting goods; *specif* a lockable bag for mail or diplomatic dispatches **3** an anatomical structure resembling a pouch: eg **3a** a pocket of skin in the abdomen of female marsupial mammals (eg the kangaroo and the opossum) for carrying their young **b** a pocket of skin in the cheeks of some rodents used for storing food **c** a loose fold of skin under the eyes **4** *chiefly Scot* a pocket [ME *pouche*, fr MF, of Gmc origin; akin to OE *pocca* bag] – **pouched** *adj*

**²pouch** *vt* **1** to put (as if) into a pouch **2** to form (as if) into a pouch ⟨*his face was* ∼ed *and lined from fatigue*⟩ ∼ *vi* to form a pouch

**pouchy** /'powchi/ *adj* having, tending to have, or resembling a pouch ⟨∼ *insomniac eyes* – Graham Greene⟩

**pouf** /poof, poohf/ *n* POOF (male homosexual)

**pouffe, pouf** *also* **pouff** /poohf/ *n, chiefly Br* **1** a bouffant arrangement of the hair over a pad; *broadly* a soft loose roll of hair **2** a part of a dress gathered in a bunch or padded out **3** a large firmly stuffed usu cylindrical cushion that is used as a low seat or footrest [Fr *pouf* something inflated, of imit origin] – **pouffed, poufed** *adj*

**Poujadism** /pooh'zhah,diz(ə)m/ *n* advocacy of the political rights and interests of the lower middle class [Fr *Poujadisme*, fr Pierre *Poujade* b1920 Fr publisher & politician] – **Poujadist** *adj or n*

**poulard** /'poohlahd/ *n* a young hen that has been spayed to make it grow fatter [Fr *poularde*, fr MF *pollarde*, fr *polle*, *poule* hen]

**¹poult** /pohlt/ *n* a young domestic fowl; *esp* a young turkey [ME *polet*, *pulte* young fowl – more at PULLET]

**²poult, poult-de-soie** /pohlt də 'swah (*Fr* pu də swa)/ *n* a PLAIN-WEAVE silk fabric with slight crosswise ribs [Fr *pou-de-soie*, *poult-de-soie*]

**poulterer** /'pohlt(ə)rə/ *n* one who deals in poultry, poultry products, or game [alter. of ME *pulter*, fr MF *pouletier*]

**¹poultice** /'pohltis/ *n* a soft mass (eg of bread or mustard), usu heated and sometimes medicated, spread on cloth and applied to inflamed or injured parts (eg sores) [ML *pultes* pap, fr L, pl of *pult-, puls* porridge]

**²poultice** *vt* to apply a poultice to

**poultry** /'pohltri/ *n* domestic fowl (eg chickens) kept for the eggs or meat they produce [ME *pultrie*, fr MF *pouleterie*, fr OF, fr *pouletier* poulterer, fr *polet* young fowl – more at PULLET]

**poultryman** /'pohltrimən/ *n* **1** somebody who keeps domestic fowls, esp on a commercial scale, for the production of eggs or meat **2** a poulterer

**¹pounce** /powns/ *n, archaic* the claw or talon of a bird of prey [ME, talon, sting, prob by shortening & alter. fr *ponson*, *punson* pointed tool or weapon – more at PUNCHEON]

**²pounce** *vi* **1** to swoop on and seize something (as if) with talons **2** to make a sudden approach or assault; *also* to seize on something eagerly ⟨*she* ∼d *on the idea with relief*⟩

**³pounce** *n* an act of pouncing

**⁴pounce** *n* **1** a fine powder formerly sprinkled on wet ink to stop it running **2** a fine powder of charcoal for making stencilled patterns [Fr *ponce* pumice, fr LL *pomic-, pomex*, alter. of L *pumic-, pumex* – more at FOAM] – **pounce** *vt*

**'pouncet-,box** /'pownsit/ *n* a perforated box formerly used for carrying perfume or powder (eg for powdering hair) [prob fr (assumed) MF *poncette* small pounce bag]

**¹pound** /pownd/ *n, pl* **pounds** *also* **pound** **1** any of various units of mass and weight: eg **1a** a unit used by English-speaking peoples that is equal to 16 standard (AVOIRDUPOIS) ounces

(0.453 592 37 kilogram) **b** a unit that is equal to 12 TROY ounces (weight system for precious stones and metals) (0.373 242 kilogram) **2a** **pound, pound sterling** the basic monetary unit of the UK, consisting of one hundred pence **b** any of numerous basic monetary units of other countries □ (2) see MONEY table [ME, fr OE *pund*; akin to ON *pund* pound; both fr a prehistoric Gmc word borrowed fr L *pondo* pound; akin to L *pondus* weight – more at PENDANT]

**²pound** *vi, Br* to check the weight of coins by weighing an amount that should equal one pound in weight

**³pound** *vt* **1** to reduce to powder or pulp by beating or crushing ⟨∼ *the meat to a paste*⟩ **2a** to strike heavily or repeatedly ⟨∼ed *the door with his fists*⟩ **b** to inculcate by insistent repetition; drive ⟨*tried to* ∼ *the facts into his memory*⟩ **3** to move along heavily or persistently ⟨∼ed *the pavements looking for work*⟩ ⟨*a policeman* ∼s *his beat*⟩ ∼ *vi* **1** to strike heavy repeated blows ⟨∼ing *angrily on the table*⟩ ⟨∼ed *at the enemy with heavy artillery*⟩ **2** to move with or make a dull heavy repetitive sound ⟨*his heart was* ∼ing *with fear*⟩ ⟨*went* ∼ing *down the road after him*⟩ [alter. of ME *pounen*, fr OE *pūnian*]

**pound away** *vi* to work hard and continuously – often + *at* or *on*

**pound out** *vt* to produce (as if) by striking repeated heavy blows ⟨*pounded out a story on the typewriter*⟩; *also* to produce rapidly and easily, often without much care ⟨*he pounds out 20 novels a year*⟩

**⁴pound** *n* an act or sound of pounding

**⁵pound** *n* **1a** an enclosure for animals; *esp* a public enclosure for stray or unlicensed animals ⟨*a dog* ∼⟩ **b** a base for holding personal property until redeemed by the owner ⟨*a car* ∼⟩ **2** a place or state of confinement – chiefly in *in pound* **3** an enclosure within which fish are kept or caught; *esp* the inner compartment of a fish trap or POUND NET [ME, enclosure, fr OE *pund-*]

**⁶pound** *vt* **1** to confine (esp animals) in an enclosure **2** *archaic* IMPOUND 1b, 2

**¹poundage** /'powndij/ *n* **1a** a fee, tax, or charge of so much per pound sterling **b** the proportion of the takings of a business paid in wages **2a** a charge per pound of weight **b** weight expressed in pounds

**²poundage** *n* **1** the act of impounding or confining in a pound **2** a fee for the release of an impounded animal

**poundal** /'powndl/ *n* an imperial unit of force that gives a mass of one pound an acceleration of one foot per second per second [*pound* + -*al* (as in *quintal*)]

**pound cake** *n* a rich cake made with equal weights of fat, sugar, flour, and eggs [fr the original recipe prescribing a pound of each of the chief ingredients]

**pounder** /'powndə/ *n* something (eg a tool) that pounds

**-pounder** /-'powndə/ *comb form (adj → n)* **1** one having a specified weight or value in pounds ⟨*caught a ten-*pounder *with his new fishing rod*⟩ **2** a gun firing a projectile of a specified weight ⟨*the artillery were using 25-*pounders⟩

**pound net** *n* a fish trap consisting of netting arranged in such a way that the fish are directed into an enclosure with a narrow entrance

**pound sterling** *n* ¹POUND 2a

**¹pour** /paw/ *vt* **1a** to cause to flow in a stream ⟨∼ *the dirty water down the sink*⟩ **b** to dispense (a beverage) into a container ⟨∼ *me a whisky*⟩ **2a** to supply or produce freely or copiously ⟨*he* ∼ed *money into the firm*⟩ **b** to speak or express volubly or at length ⟨∼ed *out his woes*⟩ ⟨∼ed *scorn on the suggestion*⟩ ∼ *vi* **1a** to move or issue with a continuous flow; stream ⟨*people* ∼ed *out of the offices at the end of the day*⟩ ⟨*blood* ∼ing *down her face*⟩ **b** to come or go in great numbers; flood ⟨*letters came* ∼ing *in from all over the country*⟩ ⟨*books started to* ∼ *off the presses*⟩ **2** to rain hard – often + *down* or *in pour with rain* **3** to pour a beverage, esp tea into cups ⟨*shall I* ∼?⟩ [ME *pouren*] – **pourable** *adj*, **pourer** *n*, **pouringly** *adv* – **pour it on** to praise or admire something effusively – see also **pour OIL on troubled waters**

**²pour** *n* **1** the action of pouring **2a** an amount of something poured ⟨*a* ∼ *of concrete*⟩ **b** a heavy fall of rain; a downpour

**pourboire** /'pooə,bwah, 'paw-* (*Fr* purbwar)/ *n* a tip, gratuity [Fr, fr *pour boire* for drinking]

**pourparler** /pooə'pahlay/ *n* an informal discussion preliminary to negotiations [Fr, fr MF, fr *pourparler* to discuss, fr *pour* for, before + *parler* to speak]

**pourpoint** /'pooə,poynt/ *n* a close-fitting garment (DOUBLET) for a man, padded and quilted and worn mainly from the 14th to the 17th century [ME *purpoint,* fr MF *pourpoint,* fr OF *porpoint* quilted, embroidered]

**pour point** *n, physics* the lowest temperature at which a substance flows under specified conditions

**pousse-café** /'poohs ka‚fay (*Fr* puskafe)/ *n* a liqueur or small glass of brandy drunk esp with coffee after dinner [Fr, lit., coffee chaser]

**poussin** /pooh'sanh (*Fr* pusĕ)/ *n* a chicken of four to six weeks old that has been reared esp for food and weighs only up to 500 grams (approx 1 pound) [Fr, fr LL *pullicenus* young chicken, dim. of L *pullus* young bird, young of an animal – more at FOAL]

**¹pout** /powt/ *n, pl* **pout,** *esp for different types* **pouts** any of several large-headed fishes (e g a BULLHEAD or EELPOUT) of the cod family [prob fr (assumed) ME *poute,* a fish with a large head, fr OE *-pūte;* akin to ME *pouten* to pout, Skt *budbuda* bubble]

**²pout** *vi* **1** to show real or mock displeasure by thrusting out the lips or wearing a sullen expression **2** *esp of lips* to protrude ∼ *vt* to cause to protrude ⟨∼ed *her lips*⟩ [ME *pouten*]

**³pout** *n* **1** an act or expression of pouting **2** *pl* a fit of pique – usu + *the*

**pouter** /'powtə/ *n* **1** somebody who pouts **2** a domestic pigeon of a breed having a crop that can be inflated to an immense size

**poverty** /'povəti/ *n* **1a** the state of being extremely poor and lacking the money or means to exist adequately **b** the renunciation, by a member of a religious order, of the right to own property as an individual **2** lack of fertility in the soil **3** *formal* a weakness or lack in the qualities or elements needed or desired; a deficiency, dearth ⟨*a* ∼ *of ideas and images*⟩ ⟨*the* ∼ *of our critical vocabulary*⟩ [ME *poverte,* fr OF *poverté,* fr L *paupertat-, paupertas,* fr *pauper* poor – more at POOR]

**'poverty-‚stricken** *adj* very poor; destitute *synonyms* see POOR

**poverty trap** *n* a situation in which a poor family is caught when its earned income increases above a certain level, so that it loses SOCIAL SECURITY and other state benefits and is thus worse off financially than it was on a lower earned income

**pow** /pow/ *n, informal* a sound or exclamation imitating that of a blow or explosion [imit]

**powan** /'powən/ *n, pl* **powans,** *esp collectively* **powan** a freshwater foodfish (*Coregonus lavaretus*) related to the salmons and trouts that occurs in some Scottish lochs [origin unknown]

**¹powder** /'powdə(r)/ *n* **1** matter reduced to a mass of dry loose particles (e g by crushing or grinding) **2** a preparation in the form of fine particles, esp for medicinal or cosmetic use ⟨*face* ∼⟩ **3** any of various fine-grained dry solid explosives used chiefly in firearms and blasting; *esp* gunpowder ⟨*keep one's* ∼ *dry*⟩ **4** fine dry light snow ⟨∼ *isn't good for skiing*⟩ [ME *poudre,* fr OF, fr L *pulver-, pulvis* dust – more at POLLEN] – **take a powder** *NAm slang* to escape or disappear quickly

**²powder** *vt* **1a** to sprinkle or cover (as if) with powder **b** to apply cosmetic powder to ⟨∼ *one's nose*⟩ **2** to reduce or convert to powder ∼ *vi* **1** to become powder **2** to apply cosmetic powder – **powderer** *n*

**powder blue** *n* a pale blue colour [fr its being orig composed of powdered smalt]

**powder horn** *n* a flask for carrying gunpowder; *esp* one made of the horn of an ox or cow

**powder keg** *n* **1** a small usu metal cask for holding gunpowder or blasting powder **2** an explosive place or situation ⟨*the gas leak was the ∼ that started the fire*⟩ ⟨*the problem of race is a potential* ∼⟩

**powder metallurgy** *n* a branch of science, or an art, concerned with producing powdered metals, or with producing metallic objects by compressing powdered metal to the desired shape and then heating it to just below the melting point in order to solidify and strengthen it

**powder monkey** *n* one who carries or has charge of explosives (e g in blasting operations); *esp* a boy who in former times carried gunpowder from the magazine to the gunners on board ship

**powder puff** *n* **1** a small usu fluffy pad for applying cosmetic or talcum powder to the skin **2** *informal* a weak or ineffectual shot, esp in tennis

**powder room** *n, euph* a women's toilet in a restaurant, large shop, or similar public place

**powdery** /'powdəri/ *adj* **1a** resembling or consisting of powder

⟨∼ *snow*⟩ **b** easily reduced to powder; crumbling **2** covered (as if) with powder

**powdery mildew** *n* a disease of cereals, grasses, roses, gooseberries, etc caused by a parasitic fungus (family Erysiphaceae) and characterized by a mass of powdery white spores (CONIDIA) on usu the stems and leaves of an infected plant; *also* any of the fungi (e g of the genus *Oidium*) causing this disease

**¹power** /'pow‚ə/ *n* **1a** possession of control, authority, or influence over others **b** one having such power; *specif* a sovereign state **c** a controlling group; the establishment – often in *the powers that be* **2a(1)** the ability to act or produce an effect **a(2)** the capacity to be acted on or to undergo an effect **b** legal or official authority, capacity, or right ⟨*the police had no* ∼ *to intervene*⟩ **3a** physical might **b** mental or moral incisiveness and effectiveness; vigour ⟨*the* ∼ *and insight of his analysis*⟩ **c** political control or influence ⟨*the party in* ∼⟩ ⟨*the balance of* ∼⟩ **4a** *pl* the sixth of the nine orders of angelic beings in the CELESTIAL HIERARCHY ranking immediately below VIRTUES and above PRINCIPALITIES **b** a good or evil spirit; *also, usu pl* an unearthly force believed to be able to influence people's fate ⟨*the* ∼s *of darkness*⟩ **5a** the number of times a given number is (to be) multiplied by itself ⟨*the cube is the third* ∼ *of a number*⟩ **b** the letter or number indicating such a power; EXPONENT 1 **c** CARDINAL NUMBER 2 **6a** a source or means of supplying energy; *esp* electricity **b** propelling or driving force supplied by electrical or mechanical energy; MOTIVE POWER **c** the amount of work done or energy emitted or transferred per unit of time **7** MAGNIFICATION 2 **8** *statistics* the probability of correctly rejecting the NULL HYPOTHESIS **9** *informal* a large number or quantity ⟨*the walk did him a* ∼ *of good*⟩ [ME, fr OF *poeir,* fr *poeir* to be able, fr (assumed) L *potēre* to be powerful – more at POTENT]

**²power** *vt* **1** to supply with power, esp motive power **2** to make (one's way) in a powerful and vigorous manner ⟨∼ed *his way to the top*⟩ ∼ *vi* to move in a powerful and vigorous manner ⟨∼ing *down the back straight*⟩

**³power** *adj* driven by a motor ⟨a ∼ *saw*⟩ ⟨a ∼ *mower*⟩

**powerboat** /'powə‚boht/ *n* a motorboat; *esp* a fast motorboat designed for racing

**power cut** *n* a failure or reduction in the supply of electric power to an area ⟨*whole village was blacked out in the* ∼ *last night*⟩

**'power-‚dive** *vi* to make a power dive ∼ *vt* to cause to powerdive

**power dive** *n* a dive of an aircraft when accelerated by the power of the engine

**powerful** /'powəf(ə)l/ *adj* having great power, prestige, or influence – **powerfully** *adv*

**power function** *n* a function of the probability of rejecting a statistical NULL HYPOTHESIS

**powerhouse** /-‚hows/ *n* **1a** POWER STATION **b** a source of influence, inspiration, or energy **2** *informal* a dynamic person with great physical energy or a forceful personality

**powerless** /-lis/ *adj* **1** devoid of strength or resources; helpless **2** lacking the authority or capacity to act ⟨*the police were* ∼ *to intervene*⟩ – **powerlessly** *adv,* **powerlessness** *n*

**power of attorney** *n* **1** the legal power authorizing a person to act for another person, temporarily or permanently, in certain specified ways (e g to sign cheques or act as agent) **2** the official legal document giving power of attorney

**power pack** *n* a unit for converting a power supply (e g mains electricity) to a voltage suitable for an electronic or electrical circuit or device

**power plant** *n* **1** POWER STATION **2** an engine and related parts supplying the moving or impelling power for a machine (e g a rocket or car) or process

**power play** *n* a concentrated attack in ice hockey by one team that has an extra player on the ice because the opposing team has a player temporarily suspended from play

**power point, point** *n, chiefly Br* a socket in a wall containing a set of TERMINALS connected to the electric mains, into which an electrical device can be plugged

**power politics** *n taking sing or pl vb* international politics characterized by attempts to advance national interests through threats of the use of military or economic power [trans of Ger *machtpolitik*]

**power series** *n* an infinite series whose terms are successive integral POWERS of a variable multiplied by CONSTANTS and that takes the form $a + bx + cx^2 + dx^3 + ex^4 + \ldots$

**power set** *n, maths* the set of all subsets of a given set

**power station** n an electricity generating station

**power take-off** n a supplementary mechanism (e g on a tractor) enabling the engine power to be used to operate a separate apparatus (e g a pump or saw)

¹**powwow** /'pow,wow/ n 1 an American Indian MEDICINE MAN 2 an American Indian ceremony (e g for victory in war) 3 *informal* a meeting for discussion [of Algonquian origin; akin to Natick *pauwau* conjurer]

²**powwow** vi to hold a powwow

¹**pox** /poks/ n, pl **pox, poxes 1a** a virus disease (e g CHICKEN POX) characterized by spots containing pus **b** *informal* syphilis **c** *archaic* smallpox 2 *archaic slang* a plague, curse – usu + *on* ⟨a ~ on him⟩ □ (1b&c) usu + *the* [alter. of *pocks*, pl of *pock*]

²**pox** vt, *archaic* to infect with a pox, esp syphilis

**poxvirus** /'poks,vie-ərəs/ n any of a group of animal viruses (e g the virus causing smallpox) having a covering of small tubules and threads that gives a characteristic fluffy appearance

**poxy** /'poksi/ adj, slang foul, worthless ⟨the son of a ~ bitch – Punch⟩ [pox + -y]

**pozzolana** /,potsə'lahnə/ n volcanic ash used in making HYDRAULIC cement (cement that hardens under water) [It *pozzolana, pozzuolana*, fr fem of *pozzolano, pozzuolano* of Pozzuoli, fr *Pozzuoli*, town near Naples in Italy] – **pozzolanic** adj

**pozzuolana** /,potswə'lahnə/ n pozzolana

**PPI** n PLAN POSITION INDICATOR (type of radarscope)

**praam** /pram, prahm/ n ¹PRAM (small boat)

**practicable** /'praktikəbl/ adj 1 capable of being put into practice or carried out; feasible ⟨a ~ plan⟩ 2 capable of being used; usable ⟨the road was ~ despite the weather conditions⟩ – **practicableness** n, **practicably** adv, **practicability** n

> synonyms Since both **practicable** and **practical** can mean "capable of being used or carried out", a plan, method, or suggestion may be both **practicable** and **practical**; but with **practicable** the emphasis is on sheer possibility, while **practical** emphasizes usefulness and effectiveness. Compare ⟨it wasn't **practicable** to open the window, because it was locked⟩ ⟨it wasn't **practical** to open the window, because of the rain⟩. antonym impracticable

¹**practical** /'praktikl/ adj 1 actively engaged in some course of action or occupation ⟨a ~ farmer⟩ 2 of or manifested in practice or action ⟨a ~ question, not a theoretical one⟩ ⟨for all ~ purposes⟩ 3a capable of being put to use or account; useful ⟨he had a ~ knowledge of French⟩ **b** adapted or suitable for actual use ⟨the table is ~ though not beautiful⟩ ⟨a ~ outfit for the occasion⟩ **4a(1)** having the inclination or capacity for action as opposed to speculation or abstraction **a(2)** having or indicating a realistic and down-to-earth approach rather than a theoretical one in dealing with problems or situations **b(1)** qualified by practice or practical training ⟨a good ~ mechanic⟩ **b(2)** designed to supplement theoretical training by experience ⟨a ~ course in navigation⟩ 5 concerned with voluntary action and moral decisions ⟨~ reason⟩ 6 being or having the specified position or role in practice or effect, if not in name ⟨a ~ atheist, though brought up as a Christian⟩ ⟨~ headmaster, though called assistant⟩ synonyms see PRACTICABLE, USEFUL antonyms impractical, unpractical [LL *practicus*, fr Gk *praktikos*, fr *prassein* to pass over, fare, do; akin to Gk *peran* to pass through – more at FARE] – **practicalness** n, **practicality** n

²**practical** n an examination requiring demonstration of some practical skill ⟨a zoology ~⟩

**practical arts** n pl arts (e g woodworking) that serve ordinary or material needs – often + *the*

**practical joke** n a trick or prank played on someone for the amusement derived from his/her discomfiture – **practical joker** n

**practically** /'praktikli/ adv 1 in a practical manner ⟨talked ~ about the problem⟩ 2 almost, nearly ⟨~ everyone went to the party⟩ ⟨~ finished⟩

**practice**, NAm also **practise** /'praktis/ n **1a** actual carrying out or performance, as opposed to theory; application ⟨ready to carry out in ~ what he advocated in principle⟩ **b** a repeated or customary action; a habit ⟨he made a ~ of going to bed early⟩ **c** the usual way something is done by a specified group or at a specified place or time ⟨it is wise to conform to local ~ s⟩ **d** the established method of conducting legal proceedings **e** dealings or conduct involving artifice or intrigue – esp in *sharp practice* **2a** regular or repeated exercise in order to acquire proficiency; also an instance of such exercise ⟨today's choir ~ is cancelled⟩ **b** proficiency or experience gained through regular or repeated exercise ⟨out of ~⟩ ⟨had several years ~ of

*nursing*⟩ **3a** the continuous exercise of a profession, esp law or medicine **b** the work, business, and connections of a professional person (e g a doctor) regarded as a unit, esp in relation to its value or quality ⟨a very busy but efficient ~⟩ ⟨sold her ~ for a good price⟩ synonyms see ¹HABIT [fr *practise*, vb, by analogy to *advice:advise*]

**practice teaching** n, *chiefly NAm* TEACHING PRACTICE

**practise**, NAm chiefly **practice** /'praktis/ vt **1a** to perform or work at repeatedly so as to become proficient ⟨~d the drums every day⟩ **b** to train (others) by repeated exercises ⟨~ pupils in penmanship⟩ **2a** to put into practice; apply; CARRY OUT ⟨~s what he preaches⟩ **b** to make a habit or practice of ⟨~ politeness⟩ **c** to be professionally engaged in ⟨~ medicine⟩ ~ vi 1 to do repeated exercises for proficiency ⟨~s every day⟩ 2 to pursue a profession, esp medicine or law, actively ⟨a practising doctor⟩ 3 to take advantage of someone ⟨he ~d on their credulity with huge success – TLS⟩ **4** *archaic* to intrigue, plot ⟨he will ~ against thee by poison – Shak⟩ [ME *practisen*, fr MF *practiser*, fr *practique, pratique* practice, fr LL *practice*, fr Gk *praktikē*, fr fem of *praktikos*] – **practiser** n

**practised**, NAm chiefly **practiced** /'praktist/ adj 1 experienced, skilled 2 learned by practice; esp perfected in order to deceive or beguile ⟨a ~ smile⟩

**practitioner** /prak'tish(ə)nə/ n **1a** one who practises a profession, esp law or medicine ⟨a legal ~⟩ **b** one who practises a skill or art rather crudely ⟨a ~ of fiction⟩ ⟨a ~ of witchcraft⟩; also one who practises a rather dubious skill or art 2 an authorized CHRISTIAN SCIENCE healer [alter. of earlier *practician*, fr ME (Sc) *pratician*, fr MF *practicien*, fr *pratique* practice]

**praedial, predial** /'preedi-əl/ adj, *formal* of land or its products [ML *praedialis*, fr L *praedium* estate, land, fr *praed-, praes* surety, bondsman]

**praemunire** /,preemyoo'nie-əri/ n the offence against the English Crown of asserting that the pope had supremacy in England [ME *praemunire facias*, fr ML, that you cause to warn; fr prominent words in the writ instructing a sheriff to summon a person accused of the offence]

**praenomen** /pree'nohmen/ n, pl **praenomens, praenomina** /-'nomina/ the first of the usu 3 names of an ancient Roman – compare COGNOMEN, NOMEN [L, fr *prae-* pre- + *nomen* name – more at NAME]

**praesidium** /pri'sidi-əm, -'zidi-/ n, pl **praesidiums, praesidia** /-diə/ PRESIDIUM (Communist executive committee)

**praetor**, chiefly NAm **pretor** /'preetə/ n a magistrate in ancient Rome ranking below a CONSUL and having chiefly judicial functions [ME *pretor*, fr L *praetor*, fr *praeire* to go ahead, lead the way, fr *prae-* pre- + *ire* to go – more at ISSUE] – **praetorship** n, **praetorial** adj

**praetorian** /pree'tawri-ən/ adj 1 of a praetor 2 *often cap* of, forming, or resembling the Roman imperial bodyguard – **praetorian** n, *often cap*

**pragmatic** /prag'matik/ adj **1a** dealing with historical events only in so far as they can teach practical lessons **b** concerned with immediate practicalities or expediency, often to the exclusion of intellectual, moral, or aesthetic considerations ⟨~ men of power have had no time or inclination to deal with ... social morality – K B Clark⟩ 2 also **pragmatical** relating to or in accordance with philosophical pragmatism 3 also **pragmatical** *archaic* **3a** meddlesome, officious **b** opinionated, dogmatic [L *pragmaticus* skilled in law or business, fr Gk *pragmatikos*, fr *pragmat-, pragma* deed, fr *prassein* to do – more at PRACTICAL] – **pragmatic** n, **pragmatically** adv

**pragmatics** /prag'matiks/ n 1 *taking sing or pl vb* a branch of SEMIOTICS (study of signs and symbols) dealing with the relation between signs or linguistic expressions and those who use them 2 a branch of linguistics dealing with the contexts in which people use language and the behaviour of speakers and listeners

**pragmatic sanction** n a solemn decree of a sovereign on a matter of primary importance (e g the regulation of the succession) that has the force of fundamental law

**pragmatism** /'pragmə,tiz(ə)m/ n 1 a practical approach to problems and affairs ⟨tried to strike a balance between principles and ~⟩ 2 an American philosophical movement founded by C S Peirce and William James and based on the assertion that the meaning or truth of a concept depends on its practical consequences, and that the function of thought is to guide action – **pragmatist** adj or n, **pragmatistic** adj

**prairie** /'preəri/ n an extensive area of level or rolling almost treeless grassland in N America – compare PAMPAS, VELD,

SAVANNA [Fr, fr (assumed) VL *prataria*, fr L *pratum* meadow; akin to L *pravus* crooked, MIr *rāth* earthworks]

**prairie chicken** *n* a grouse (*Tympanuchus cupido*) that lives mainly in the eastern part of the N American prairie and the male of which has an orange air sac on each side of its throat that it inflates during courtship displays

**prairie dog** *n* a stout yellow-brown burrowing rodent (genus *Cynomys*, esp *Cynomys ludovicianus*) that is related to the marmots, has a sharp barklike call, and lives in colonies in the N American prairie

**prairie oyster** *n* a whole raw egg, or egg yolk, seasoned (e g with salt, pepper, and WORCESTER SAUCE) and swallowed whole, esp as a remedy for a hangover

**prairie schooner** *n* a COVERED WAGON used by American pioneers in cross-country travel

**¹praise** /prayz/ *vt* **1** to express a favourable judgment of; commend **2** to glorify (e g God or a god), esp for the perfection of qualities or attributes (e g mercy) [ME *praisen*, fr MF *preisier* to prize, praise, fr LL *pretiare* to prize, fr L *pretium* price – more at PRICE] – **praiser** *n*

**²praise** *n* **1** an expression of approval; commendation ⟨*won high ~ for his efforts*⟩ **2** WORSHIP 1

**praiseworthy** /-,wuhdhi/ *adj* worthy of praise; laudable, commendable – **praiseworthily** *adv*, **praiseworthiness** *n*

**Prakrit** /'prahkrit/ *n* any or all of the ancient or modern INDIC languages or dialects other than Sanskrit [Skt *prākṛta*, fr *prākṛta* natural, vulgar]

**praline** /'prahleen/ *n* a confection of nuts, esp almonds, caramelized in boiling sugar; *also* something, esp a powder or paste, made from this [Fr, fr Count Plessis-*Praslin* †1675 Fr soldier whose cook invented the confection]

**pralltriller** /'prahl,trilə/ *n* MORDENT (ornamental alternation of musical notes) [Ger, fr *prallen* to rebound + *triller* trill, fr It *trillo*]

**¹pram, praam** /pram, prahm/ *n* **1** a flat-bottomed Dutch cargo boat **2** a small lightweight almost flat-bottomed boat with a broad stern and a usu squared-off bow, used mainly as a tender to a larger boat [D *praam*; akin to MLG *prām* pram]

**²pram** /pram/ *n, chiefly Br* a 4-wheeled carriage for one or two babies that is pushed by a person on foot [by shortening & alter. fr *perambulator*]

**¹prance** /prahns/ *vi* **1** *of a horse* to spring from the hind legs or move by doing this **2** to ride on a prancing horse **3** to walk or move in a gay, lively, or haughty manner ⟨*prancing up and down, sublimely pleased with himself* – Norman Douglas⟩ ~ *vt* to cause (a horse) to prance [ME *prauncen*] – **prancer** *n*, **prancingly** *adv*

**²prance** *n* an act or instance of prancing; *specif* a prancing movement

**prandial** /'prandyəl/ *adj, formal or humorous* of a meal [L *prandium* late breakfast, lunch]

**¹prang** /prang/ *vb, chiefly Br slang* to have an accident (with); (cause to) crash ⟨*the pilot ~ed his aeroplane*⟩ – no longer in vogue [prob imit]

**²prang** *n, chiefly Br slang* an accident or crash, esp involving a car or aircraft – no longer in vogue

**¹prank** /prangk/ *n* a playful or mischievous act; a trick ⟨*undergraduate ~s*⟩ [obs *prank* to play tricks] – **prankish, pranksome** *adj*

**²prank** *vb, formal vt* to dress or adorn gaily or showily ⟨*field was ~ed with flowers*⟩ ~ *vi* to show oneself off [prob fr D *pronken* to strut; akin to MHG *gebrunkel* glitter of metal]

**prankster** /'prangkstə/ *n* one who plays pranks

**prase** /prayz/ *n* a CHALCEDONY (kind of quartz) that is translucent and leek green [Fr, fr L *prasius*, fr Gk *prasios*, fr *prasios*, adj, leek green, fr *prason* leek; akin to L *porrum* leek]

**praseodymium** /,prayzi·oh'dimi·əm/ *n* a yellowish-white metallic chemical element of the RARE EARTH group that occurs in minerals such as MONAZITE, is soft and easily worked, and is used chiefly in making special alloys and glass [NL, alter. of *praseodidymium*, irreg fr Gk *prasios*, adj + NL *didymium*]

**prat** /prat/ *n, Br slang* a foolish or contemptible person [prob fr slang *prat* buttocks]

**¹prate** /prayt/ *vi* to talk idly and excessively; chatter ⟨*he ~d on about his new car*⟩ [ME *praten*, fr MD; akin to MLG *pratten* to pout] – **prater** *n*, **pratingly** *adv*

**²prate** *n* empty or meaningless talk; prating

**pratfall** /'prat,fawl/ *n, NAm slang* **1** a fall on the buttocks **2** a humiliating mishap or blunder [*prat* (buttocks) + *fall*]

**pratie** /'praydi/ *n, chiefly Irish* a potato [by alter.]

**pratincole** /'prating,kohl/ *n* any of a genus (*Glareola*) of European, African, and Asian brownish short-legged SHOREBIRDS that have long wings and forked tails and that hunt dragonflies, grasshoppers, etc on the wing [deriv of L *pratum* meadow + *incola* inhabitant, fr *in-* + *colere* to cultivate – more at PRAIRIE, WHEEL]

**pratique** /'prateek/ *n* clearance given to an incoming ship by the health authority of a port [Fr, lit., practice – more at PRACTICE]

**¹prattle** /'pratl/ *vi* to chatter in an artless or childish manner ~ *vt* to say in a prattling manner; *esp* to babble [LG *pratelen;* akin to MD *praten* to prate] – **prattler** *n*, **prattlingly** *adv*

**²prattle** *n* idle or childish talk; chatter

**prau** /prow/ *n* PROA (canoe-like S Pacific boat)

**prawn** /prawn/ *n* any of numerous widely distributed edible 10-legged INVERTEBRATE animals (e g of the genera *Pandalus* and *Peneus*, class Crustacea) that resemble large shrimps [ME *prane*]

**prawning** /'prawning/ *n* fishing for or with prawns – **prawner** *n*

**praxis** /'praksis/ *n, pl* **praxes** /'prakseez/ *formal* **1** the exercise or practice of an art, science, or skill **2** customary practice or conduct [ML, fr Gk, doing, action, fr *prassein* to pass through, practise – more at PRACTICAL]

**pray** /pray/ *vt* **1a** to entreat earnestly; *esp* to call devoutly on (God or a god) ⟨*I ~ God we may be saved*⟩ **b** to wish or hope fervently ⟨*we all hope and ~ it won't happen*⟩ **2** *archaic or formal* to request courteously ⟨*~ tell me*⟩ – often used to introduce a question, request, or plea **3** *archaic* to get or bring by praying ⟨*they ~ed his soul into heaven*⟩ ~ *vi* to address God or a god with adoration, confession, supplication, or thanksgiving; engage in prayer [ME *prayen*, fr OF *preier*, fr L *precari*, fr *prec-, prex* request, prayer; akin to OHG *frāgēn* to ask, Skt *pṛcchati* he asks]

**¹prayer** /preə/ *n* **1a(1)** an address (e g a petition) to God or a god in word or thought ⟨*said a ~ for the success and safety of the voyage*⟩ **a(2)** a set order of words used in praying ⟨*repeat a ~*⟩ **b** an earnest request or devout wish **2** the action or practice of praying to God or a god ⟨*kneeling in ~*⟩ **3** **prayers** *pl, also* **prayer** a religious service consisting chiefly of prayers ⟨*~s are at 9:15*⟩ ⟨*family ~s*⟩ **4** something prayed for **5** *informal* a slight chance ⟨*tried hard but didn't have a ~*⟩ [ME, fr OF *preiere*, fr ML *precaria*, fr L, fem of *precarius* obtained by entreaty, fr *prec-, prex*]

**²prayer** /'prayə/ *n* a person who prays; a suppliant [ME *prayere*, fr *prayen* to pray + *-er*]

**prayer book** *n* a book containing prayers and often other forms and directions for worship; *specif, often cap P&B* the official SERVICE BOOK of the Anglican church

**prayerful** /'preəf(ə)l/ *adj* **1** inclined to prayer; devout **2** earnest, sincere – **prayerfully** *adv*, **prayerfulness** *n*

**prayer mat** *n* a small Oriental rug used by Muslims to kneel on when praying

**prayer meeting** *n* a religious meeting at which prayers are offered; *specif, chiefly NAm* a Protestant service of worship usu held on a week night

**prayer rug** *n* PRAYER MAT

**prayer shawl** *n* TALLITH (Jewish shawl)

**prayer wheel** *n* a revolving cylinder, usu of wood or metal, that contains written prayers and that is used in praying, esp by Tibetan Buddhists

**praying mantid** /'praying/ *n* PRAYING MANTIS

**praying mantis** /'praying/ *n* a large green flesh-eating insect (MANTIS) (*Mantis religiosa*) that holds its forelegs up as if in prayer; *broadly* a mantis

**pre-** /,pree-, pri-/ *prefix* before in time, position, rank, or order: e g a earlier than; prior to ⟨*Precambrian*⟩ ⟨*prehistoric*⟩; *specif* immediately preceding ⟨*preadolescence*⟩ ⟨*prematch nerves*⟩ **b** preparatory or prerequisite to ⟨*premedical*⟩ ⟨*prejournalism*⟩ **c** in advance; beforehand ⟨*prepay*⟩ ⟨*prefabricate*⟩ **d(1)** situated in front of; anterior to ⟨*preaxial*⟩ ⟨*premolar*⟩ **d(2)** front; anterior ⟨*preabdomen*⟩ **e** ahead or before (in rank or degree) ⟨*preeminence*⟩ [ME, fr OF & L; OF, fr L *prae-*, fr *prae* in front of, before – more at FOR]

**preach** /preech/ *vi* **1** to deliver a sermon **2** to urge acceptance or abandonment of an idea or course of action; *specif* to exhort in an officious, tiresome, or highly moral manner ~ *vt* **1** to set forth in a sermon ⟨*~ the gospel*⟩ **2** to advocate earnestly ⟨*~ed revolution*⟩ **3** to deliver (e g a sermon) publicly [ME *prechen*, fr OF *prechier*, fr LL *praedicare*, fr L, to proclaim publicly, fr *prae-* pre- + *dicare* to proclaim – more at DICTION ] – **preacher** *n*, **preachingly** *adv*

**preachy** /'preechi/ *adj, NAm informal* marked by or given to moralizing – **preachily** *adv*, **preachiness** *n*

**preadaptation** /ˌpree·adap'taysh(ə)n/ *n* (the possession by an organism or group of organisms of) heritable characteristics that are not adapted to the ancestral environment but favour survival in some other environment

**preadaptive** /ˌpree·ə'daptiv/, **preadapted** /-daptid/ *adj* of or characterized by preadaptation

**preagricultural** /ˌpree·agri'kulchərəl/ *adj* existing or occurring before human beings practised agriculture

**preamble** /'preeˌambl/ *n* **1** an introductory statement; *specif* the introductory part of a legislative bill, statute, or constitution that usu states the reasons for and intended effect of the legislation **2** an introductory or preliminary circumstance, fact, etc [ME, fr MF *preambule*, fr ML *preambulum*, fr LL, neut of *praeambulus* walking in front of, fr L *prae-* + *ambulare* to walk]

**preamplifier** /-'amplifie·ə/ *n* an amplifier used to amplify a relatively weak signal (e g from a microphone or gramophone pickup), and often to reduce distortion by making the signal more uniform, before feeding it to the main amplifier

**prearrange** /-ə'raynj/ *vt* to arrange beforehand ⟨*at a* ~d *signal*⟩ – **prearrangement** *n*

**preatomic** /-ə'tomik/ *adj* of a time before the use of the ATOM BOMB and ATOMIC ENERGY

**preaxial** /pree'aksiəl/ *adj* located in front of an AXIS (central line of symmetry) of the body; *esp* of the front side of the axis of a limb of a VERTEBRATE animal – **preaxially** *adv*

**prebend** /'prebənd/ *n* **1** a money allowance (STIPEND) paid by a cathedral or COLLEGIATE CHURCH (e g in the Church of England until the 19th century) to a member of its CHAPTER (body of canons) **2** PREBENDARY [ME *prebende*, fr MF, fr ML *praebenda*, fr LL, subsistence allowance granted by the state, fr L, fem of *praebendus*, gerundive of *praebēre* to offer, fr *prae-* + *habēre* to hold – more at GIVE] – **prebendal** *adj*

**prebendary** /'prebənd(ə)ri/ *n* **1** a clergyman receiving a prebend **2** a member of the body of canons (CHAPTER) of a cathedral

**prebind** /ˌpree'biend/ *vt* **prebound** /-'bownd/ **1** to bind (a book) in durable materials, esp for library use **2** to give (a book) a durable original binding

**prebiological** /ˌpreebie·ə'lojikl/ *also* **prebiologic** *adj* of or being (chemical) substances that existed before life began; *also* of (chemical) substances held to have been involved in originating life

**prebiotic** /-bie'otik/ *adj* prebiological

**Precambrian** /-'kambri·ən/ *adj or n* (of or being) the earliest era of geological history equivalent to the ARCHAEOZOIC and PROTEROZOIC eras or the corresponding system of rocks [*pre-* + *Cambrian*]

**precancel** /ˌpree'kansl/ *vt* to cancel (a postage stamp) before use – **precancellation** *n*

**precancerous** /ˌpree'kansərəs/ *adj* showing changes associated with the later development of cancer ⟨~ *tissue*⟩ [ISV]

**precarious** /pri'keəri·əs/ *adj* **1** dependent on uncertain premises or basic ideas; dubious ⟨a ~ *argument*⟩ ⟨~ *generalizations*⟩ **2a** dependent on chance circumstances, unknown conditions, or uncertain developments ⟨*makes a* ~ *living*⟩ **b** characterized by a lack of security or stability; perilous **3** *archaic* depending on the will or pleasure of another ⟨*tenure of the land was* ~⟩ [L *precarius* obtained by entreaty, uncertain – more at PRAYER] – **precariously** *adv*, **precariousness** *n*

**precast** /ˌpree'kahst/ *adj* being concrete that is cast in the form of a structure element (e g a panel or beam) before being placed in final position

**precative** /'prekətiv/ *adj* of or being a verb form expressing a wish; *broadly, formal* precatory [LL *precativus* precatory, beseeching, fr L *precatus*, pp of *precari* to pray – more at PRAY]

**precatory** /'prekət(ə)ri/ *adj, formal* expressing a wish or request [LL *precatorius*, fr L *precatus*, pp]

**precaution** /pri'kawsh(ə)n/ *n* **1** care taken in advance; the use of foresight ⟨*warned of the need for* ~⟩ **2** a measure taken beforehand to avoid possible harmful or undesirable consequences; a safeguard [Fr *précaution*, fr LL *praecaution-*, *praecautio*, fr L *praecautus*, pp of *praecavēre* to guard against, fr *prae-* + *cavēre* to be on one's guard – more at HEAR] – **precautionary** *adj*

**precava** /ˌpree'kayvə/ *n, pl* **precavae** /-vie/ SUPERIOR VENA

CAVA (main vein returning blood from the head and forelimbs to the heart) [NL] – **precaval** *adj*

**precede** /pri'seed/ *vt* **1** to be superior to in rank, dignity, or importance **2** to be, go, or come ahead or in front of **3** to be earlier than **4** to cause to be preceded; preface ⟨*he* ~d *his address with a welcome to the visitors*⟩ ~ *vi* to go or come before △ proceed [ME *preceden*, fr MF *preceder*, fr L *praecedere*, fr *prae-* pre-+ *cedere* to go – more at CEDE]

**precedence** /'presid(ə)ns/ *also* **precedency** /-d(ə)nsi/ *n* **1** the fact of preceding in time **2a** the right to superior honour on a ceremonial or formal occasion **b** the order of ceremonial or formal preference **3** priority of importance ⟨*this job must take* ~ *over that one*⟩

   **synonyms** Where **precedence** and **priority** refer to the right of going first, **precedence** is generally used in matters of etiquette and protocol, while **priority** relates to time ⟨*what has priority must be dealt with first*⟩ ⟨*priority of birth decides who shall be the heir*⟩.

**¹precedent** /pri'seed(ə)nt, 'presid(ə)nt/ *adj* preceding in time, order, arrangement, or significance [ME, fr MF, fr L *praecedent-*, *praecedens*, prp of *praecedere*]

**²precedent** /'presid(ə)nt/ *n* **1** an earlier occurrence of something similar **2** something done or said that may serve as an example or rule to justify a similar later act or statement; *specif* a judicial decision or form of proceeding that serves as a rule for future decisions in similar or analogous cases

**preceding** /pri'seeding/ *adj* that comes immediately before in time or place ⟨*the* ~ *day*⟩ ⟨~ *paragraphs*⟩

**precentor** /pri'sentə/ *n* **1** a person who leads the singing of a choir or congregation **2** the officer, usu a clergyman, responsible for directing choral services in a cathedral or COLLEGIATE CHURCH [LL *praecentor*, fr L *praecentus*, pp of *praecinere* to sing before, fr *prae-* + *canere* to sing – more at CHANT] – **precentorial** *adj*, **precentorship** *n*

**precept** /'preesept/ *n* **1** a command or principle intended as a general rule of conduct; a maxim **2** a writ or warrant issued by a person or authority to a subordinate official **3** *Br* an order to collect payment of rates [ME, fr L *praeceptum*, fr neut of *praeceptus*, pp of *praecipere* to take beforehand, instruct, command, fr *prae-* + *capere* to take – more at HEAVE] – **preceptive** *adj*

**preceptor** /pri'septə/ *n* **1** *fem* **preceptress** /-tris/ a doctor who gives practical training to medical students; *broadly, formal* an instructor, teacher **2** the head of a preceptory of Knights TEMPLARS (religious military order) – **preceptorship** *n*

**preceptorial** /ˌpreesep'tawriəl/ *adj* of or making use of preceptors

**preceptory** /pri'septəri/ *n* a subordinate house or community of the Knights TEMPLARS (religious military order)

**precess** /pri'ses/ *vb* to (cause to) progress with a movement of precession [back-formation fr *precession*]

**precession** /pri'sesh(ə)n/ *n* a slow motion of the axis of rotation of a spinning body (e g a top) round another line intersecting it so as to describe a cone △ procession [NL *praecession-*, *praecessio*, fr ML, act of preceding, fr L *praecessus*, pp of *praecedere* to precede] – **precessional** *adj*

**precession of the equinoxes** *n* the slow westward shift of the EQUINOCTIAL points along the ECLIPTIC (apparent path of the sun round the earth), which is caused by the action of sun and moon on the protuberant matter about the earth's equator. This causes the two times in the year when day and night are of equal length to occur slightly earlier in each successive year. The shift, which takes 25800 years to return to its starting point, has resulted in the signs of the zodiac no longer coinciding with the constellations after which they were named.

**ˌpre-'Chellean** /'shelian/ *adj* of an early PALAEOLITHIC culture preceding the ABBEVILLIAN and characterized by crudely flaked stone hand axes

**ˌpre-'Christian** *adj* of or being a time before the beginning of the Christian era

**precinct** /'preesingkt/ *n* **1 precincts** *pl*, **precinct** an enclosure bounded by the walls of a building or other walls; *esp* such an enclosure round a church or cathedral **2** *pl* the region immediately surrounding a place; the environs **3 precincts** *pl*, **precinct** the boundary ⟨*a ruined tower within the* ~s *of the squire's grounds* – T L Peacock⟩ **4** *Br* an open space closed permanently or at stated times to motor vehicles and often providing access to rows of shops ⟨*a shopping* ~⟩ **5** *NAm* a part of a territory with definite bounds or functions often established for administrative purposes; a district: e g **5a** a subdivision of a county, town, city, or ward for election purposes **b** a division of a city for police control [ME, fr ML *praecinctum*, fr L, neut of *praecinctus*, pp of *praecingere* to gird about, fr *prae-* pre-+ *cingere* to gird – more at CINCTURE]

**preciosity** /,pres(h)i'osəti/ *n* 1 fastidious or excessive refinement (e g in language) 2 an instance of preciosity

**¹precious** /'preshəs/ *adj* 1 of great value or high price ⟨a ~ stone⟩ ⟨~ metals such as gold and silver⟩ 2 highly esteemed or cherished; dear ⟨his friendship was ~ to her⟩ 3 excessively refined; affected 4 worthless – used as an intensive ⟨you can keep your ~ Costa Brava – I prefer Blackpool!⟩ [ME, fr OF *precios*, fr L *pretiosus*, fr *pretium* price – more at PRICE] – **preciousness** *n*

**²precious** *adv, chiefly derog* very, extremely ⟨has ~ little to say⟩

**³precious** *n* a dear one; darling ⟨my ~⟩

**preciously** /'preshəsli/ *adv* 1 in a precious manner 2 precious

**precipice** /'presipis/ *n* 1 a very steep, perpendicular, or over-hanging surface (e g of a rock or mountain) 2 the brink (e g of a disaster); *the* very edge [MF, fr L *praecipitium*, fr *praecipit-, praeceps* headlong, fr *prae-* + *caput* head – more at HEAD]

**precipitable** /pri'sipitəbl/ *adj* capable of being precipitated

**¹precipitant** /pri'sipit(ə)nt/ *adj* unduly hasty or sudden; precipitate – **precipitance, precipitancy, precipitantness** *n*, **precipitantly** *adv*

**²precipitant** *n* a precipitating agent; *esp* one that causes the formation of a precipitate

**¹precipitate** /pri'sipitayt/ *vt* 1 to throw violently; hurl ⟨the impact of the collision ~d one car into a basement⟩ 2 to bring about suddenly, unexpectedly, or too soon ⟨the failure of government policy ~d a general election⟩ 3a *chemistry* to cause to separate from solution or suspension **b** to cause (vapour) to condense and fall (e g as rain or snow) ~ *vi* 1 *chemistry* to separate from solution or suspension 2 to fall as rain, snow, etc [L *praecipitatus*, pp of *praecipitare*, fr *praecipit-, praeceps*] – **precipitator** *n*, **precipitative** *adj*

**²precipitate** /pri'sipitət/ *n* a substance separated from a solution or suspension by chemical or physical change, usu taking the form of an insoluble (crystalline) solid [NL *praecipitatum*, fr L, neut of *praecipitatus*]

**³precipitate** /pri'sipitət/ *adj* 1 exhibiting violent or undue haste ⟨a ~ departure⟩; *also* lacking due care or consideration ⟨~ remarks offended them⟩ 2 falling, flowing, or rushing steeply – **precipitately** *adv*, **precipitateness** *n*

**precipitation** /pri,sipi'taysh(ə)n/ *n* 1 the quality or state of being precipitate; rash haste 2 an act, process, or instance of precipitating; *esp* the process of forming a chemical precipitate 3 something precipitated: e g 3a a deposit on the earth of hail, mist, rain, sleet, or snow; *also* the quantity of water deposited **b** a chemical precipitate

**precipitin** /pri'sipitin/ *n* an ANTIBODY (substance produced by the body to fight disease) that forms an insoluble precipitate when mixed with its ANTIGEN (foreign substance that activates the body's defence mechanism) [ISV, fr *precipitate*]

**precipitinogen** /pri,sipi'tinəjən/ *n* an ANTIGEN (foreign substance that activates the body's defence mechanism) stimulating the production of a specific precipitin – **precipitinogenic** *adj*

**precipitous** /pri'sipitəs/ *adj* 1 precipitate 1 **2a** resembling a precipice, esp in being dangerously steep or perpendicular ⟨a ~ slope⟩ ⟨a ~ staircase⟩ **b** having precipitous sides ⟨a ~ gorge⟩ [Fr *précipiteux*, fr MF, fr L *precipitium* precipice] – **precipitously** *adv*, **precipitousness** *n*

**¹précis** /'praysee/ *n, pl* **précis** a concise summary of essential points, statements, or facts [Fr, fr *précis* precise]

**²précis** *vt* **précising** /'praysi-ing/, **précised** /'praysid/ to make a précis of; summarize

**precise** /pri'sies/ *adj* 1 exactly or sharply defined or stated ⟨~ images⟩ ⟨~ details⟩ 2 highly exact ⟨a ~ mind⟩ 3 strictly conforming to a rule, code, or convention; punctilious 4 distinguished from every other; very ⟨at just that ~ moment⟩ [MF *precis*, fr L *praecisus*, pp of *praecidere* to cut off, fr *prae-* + *caedere* to cut – more at CONCISE] – **precisely** *adv*, **preciseness** *n*

**precisian** /pri'sizh(ə)n/ *n* 1 a person who stresses or practises scrupulous adherence to a strict standard, esp of religious observance or morality 2 ¹PURITAN 1 – **precisianism** *n*

**¹precision** /pri'sizh(ə)n/ *n* 1 the quality or state of being precise; exactness **2a** the degree of refinement and accuracy with which an operation is performed or a measurement stated **b** the accuracy (e g in BINARY or decimal places) with which a number can be represented, usu expressed in terms of computer words – compare DOUBLE PRECISION – **precisionist** *n*

**²precision** *adj* 1 adapted for extremely accurate measurement or operation ⟨~ instruments⟩ 2 marked by precision of execution ⟨~ bombing⟩

**preclinical** /,pree'klinikl/ *adj* 1 of or occurring in a period of an illness before symptoms appear 2 of or being the period of theoretical study undergone by a medical student before he/she encounters patients – **preclinical** *n*

**preclude** /pri'kloohd/ *vt* 1 to make ineffectual or impracticable; exclude ⟨his confident manner ~d all doubt or suspicion⟩ 2 to make (something) impossible for (someone); prevent ⟨his busy timetable ~d him from extending his stay⟩ ⟨his busy timetable ~d extending his stay⟩ **synonyms** see PREVENT [L *praecludere* to block up, prevent, fr *prae-* + *claudere* to close – more at CLOSE] – **preclusion** *n*, **preclusive** *adj*, **preclusively** *adv*

**precocial** /pri'kohsh(ə)l/ *adj* capable of a high degree of independent activity (e g feeding or seeing) from birth ⟨ducklings are ~⟩; *also* having precocial young – compare ALTRICIAL [NL *praecoces* precocial birds, fr L, pl of *praecoc-, precox*]

**precocious** /pri'kohshəs/ *adj* 1 developing or occurring exceptionally early or prematurely; *esp, of a plant or plant part* flowering, fruiting, or developing before the usual time 2 showing mature qualities at an unusually early age [L *praecoc-, praecox* early ripening, precocious, fr *prae-* + *coquere* to cook, ripen – more at COOK] – **precociously** *adv*, **precociousness, precocity** *n*

**precognition** /,preekog'nish(ə)n/ *n* clairvoyance relating to a future event or state [LL *praecognition-, praecognitio*, fr L *praecognitus*, pp of *praecognoscere* to know beforehand, fr *prae-* + *cognoscere* to know – more at COGNITION] – **precognitive** *adj*

**precolonial** /,preekə'lohnyəl/ *adj* of or being the time before colonial status

**pre-Co'lumbian** *adj* of or being a time before the arrival of Columbus in America

**preconceive** /,preekən'seev/ *vt* to form (e g an opinion or idea) prior to actual knowledge or experience ⟨~d notions⟩

**preconception** /,preekən'sepsh(ə)n/ *n* 1 a preconceived idea 2 a prejudice

**preconcert** /,preekən'suht/ *vt* 1 to settle by prior agreement 2 to organize beforehand; prearrange ⟨her little plans and ~ed speeches had all left her⟩ – George Eliot⟩

**¹precondition** /,preekən'dish(ə)n/ *n* a prerequisite

**²precondition** *vt* to put in a proper or desired condition or frame of mind in advance

**precon-ize, -ise** /'preekə,niez/ *vt* 1 *of the pope* to approve the appointment of (a clergyman) to some high office (e g that of a bishop) 2 *formal* to publicly proclaim, commend, or summon [ML *praeconizare* to proclaim publicly, fr L *praecon-, praeco* one who makes public announcements, perh fr *praedicare* to proclaim publicly – more at PREACH] – **preconization** *n*

**preconscious** /,pree'konshəs/ *n or adj* (the memories, thoughts, etc) not present in consciousness but capable of being readily recalled – **preconsciously** *adv*

**preconsonantal** /,preekonsə'nantl/ *adj* immediately preceding a consonant

**precook** /,pree'kook/ *vt* to cook partially or entirely before final cooking or reheating

**precopulatory** /,pree'kopyoolətri/ *adj* preceding copulation ⟨~ behaviour⟩

**precritical** /,pree'kritikl/ *adj* prior to the development of critical capacity

**precursor** /pri'kuhsə/ *n* **1a** one who or that which precedes and signals the approach of another; a forerunner **b** a predecessor 2 a substance from which another substance is formed ⟨pepsinogen is the ~ of the enzyme pepsin⟩ [L *praecursor*, fr *praecursus*, pp of *praecurrere* to run before, fr *prae-* pre- + *currere* to run – more at CAR]

**precursory** /pri'kuhs(ə)ri/, **precursive** /-siv/ *adj* having the character of a precursor; preliminary

**predacious, predaceous** /pri'dayshəs/ *adj* living by preying on other animals; predatory – **predaciousness, predacity** *n*

**predate** /,pree'dayt/ *vt* to antedate

**predation** /pri'daysh(ə)n/ *n* 1 the act of preying or plundering; depredation 2 a way of life of certain animals in which food is primarily obtained by the killing and consuming of other animals; *also* the extent of predation in an animal population ⟨the level of ~⟩ [L *praedation-, praedatio*, fr *praedatus*, pp of *praedari*]

**predation pressure** *n* the effects of predation on a natural animal community, esp with respect to the survival of the prey

**predator** /'predətə/ n one who or that which preys, destroys, or devours; *specif* an animal that lives by predation

**predatory** /'predət(ə)ri/ adj **1a** of or carrying out plunder or robbery **b** showing a disposition to injure or exploit others for one's own gain **2** *of an animal* living by predation; predacious; *also* adapted to predation – **predatorily** adv

**predawn** /,pree'dawn/ n the time just before dawn

**predecease** /,predi'sees/ vt to die before (another person) – **predecease** n

**predecessor** /'preedi,sesə/ n **1** one who or that which precedes; *esp* the previous occupant of a position or office to which another has succeeded **2** an ancestor [ME *predecessour*, fr MF *predecesseur*, fr LL *praedecessor*, fr L *prae-* pre- + *decessor* retiring governor, fr *decessus*, pp of *decedere* to depart, retire from office – more at DECEASE]

**pre-'decimal** adj of a period before the introduction of decimal currency – **pre-decimalization** n

**predestinarian** /,preedesti'neəri•ən/ n a person who believes in predestination [*predestin*ation + *-arian*] – **predestinarian** adj, **predestinarianism** n

**¹predestinate** /,pree'destinət/ adj destined, fated, or determined beforehand [ME, fr L *praedestinatus*, pp of *praedestinare*]

**²predestinate** /,pree'destinayt/ vt **1** to predestine **2** *archaic* to predetermine [ME *predestinaten*, fr L *praedestinatus*, pp]

**predestination** /,preedesti'naysh(ə)n/ n **1** predestinating or being predestinated **2** the doctrine that God irrevocably destines some people for salvation

**predestine** /,pree'destin/ vt to destine, decree, determine, appoint, or settle beforehand; *esp* to foreordain to an earthly or eternal destiny by divine decree [ME *predestinen*, fr MF or L; MF *predestiner*, fr L *praedestinare*, fr *prae-* + *destinare* to determine – more at DESTINE]

**predetermine** /,preedi'tuhmin/ vt **1** to determine, arrange, or settle beforehand ⟨*at a* ~d *signal*⟩ **2** to impose a direction or tendency on beforehand [LL *praedeterminare*, fr L *prae-* + *determinare* to determine] – **predetermination** n

**predeterminer** /,preedi'tuhminə/ n an adjective or adverb (e g *both* or *twice*) that occurs before the DETERMINER (e g *the* or *her*) in a noun phrase

**prediabetes** /,preedie•ə'beetis, -teez/ n (the condition of a person with) diabetes that is not fully developed; *also* the period during which this condition lasts – **prediabetic** adj or n

**predial** /'preedyəl/ adj PRAEDIAL (of land)

**¹predicable** /'predikəbl/ n something that may be predicated; *esp* any of the five types of predicate in Aristotelian logic [ML *praedicabile*, fr neut of *praedicabilis*]

**²predicable** adj capable of being asserted [ML *praedicabilis*, fr LL *praedicare* to predicate]

**predicament** /pri'dikəmənt/ n **1** the character, status, or classification assigned by a predication; *specif* CATEGORY 1 **2** a condition, state; *esp* a difficult, perplexing, or trying situation [ME, fr LL *praedicamentum*, fr *praedicare*]

**¹predicate** /'predikət/ n **1** something that is affirmed or denied of the subject in a logical proposition ⟨*in "paper is white"*, *whiteness is the* ~⟩ **2** *linguistics* the part of a sentence or clause that expresses what is said of the subject ⟨*in "paper is white"*, *"is white" is the* ~⟩ [LL *praedicatum*, fr neut of *praedicatus*]

**²predicate** /'predikayt/ vt, *chiefly formal* **1** to affirm, declare **2a** to assert to be a quality or property – usu + *of* ⟨~s *intelligence of man*⟩ **b** to make (a logical term) the predicate of a proposition **3** to imply **4** *chiefly NAm* to base – usu + *on* or *upon* ⟨*his theory is* ~d *on recent findings*⟩ ⟨*China's ... modernisation programme is* ~d *on cheap Japanese loans – The Observer*⟩ △ **predict** [LL *praedicatus*, pp of *praedicare* to assert, predicate logically, preach, fr L, to proclaim publicly, assert – more at PREACH]

**predicate nominative** n a noun or pronoun in the nominative or common case (e g *king* in "he became *king*") that refers to the same thing or person as the subject and completes the meaning of a linking verb such as *be* or *become*

**predication** /,predi'kaysh(ə)n/ n an act or instance of predicating: e g **a** the expression of action, state, or quality by a grammatical predicate **b** the affirmation of a predicate in logic

**predicative** /pri'dikətiv/ adj **1** of or being a predicate **2** joined to a modified noun by a linking verb such as *be* or *become* ⟨*red in "the dress is red" is in the* ~ *position*⟩ – compare ATTRIBUTIVE – **predicatively** adv

**predicatory** /'predikətri, ,predi'kaytəri, '--,--/ adj of preaching [LL *praedicatorius*, fr *praedicatus*, fr *praedicare* to preach]

**predict** /pri'dikt/ vt to declare in advance; *esp* to foretell on the basis of observation, experience, or scientific reason ~ vi to make a prediction **synonyms** see FORETELL △ **predicate** [L *praedictus*, pp of *praedicere*, fr *prae-* pre- + *dicere* to say – more at DICTION] – **predictor** n

**predictable** /pri'diktəbl/ adj **1** capable of being predicted; *esp* irritatingly foreseeable ⟨*her reaction was so* ~⟩ **2** *derog, of a person* habitually behaving in a predictable way – **predictably** adv, **predictability** n

**prediction** /pri'diksh(ə)n/ n **1** an act of predicting **2** something that is predicted; a forecast – **predictive** adj, **predictively** adv

**predigest** /,preedi'jest, -die-/ vt to subject to predigestion

**predigestion** /,preedi'jeschən, -die-/ n **1** the partial breakdown or digestion of food by artificial means, for use esp in illness or conditions of impaired digestion **2** presentation of something (e g a book) in a simplified form

**predilection** /preedi'leksh(ə)n, pre-/ n a liking, taste, or preference ⟨*has a* ~ *for plain chocolate*⟩ [Fr *prédilection*, fr ML *praedilectus*, pp of *praediligere* to love more, prefer, fr L *prae-* + *diligere* to love – more at DILIGENT]

**predispose** /,preedi'spohz/ vt **1** to incline, esp in advance ⟨*a good teacher* ~s *children to learn*⟩ **2** to make susceptible ⟨~ *the audience to laughter*⟩ ~ vi to bring about susceptibility ⟨*smoking* ~s *to cancer*⟩ □ usu + *to* or *towards*

**predisposition** /,preedispə'zish(ə)n/ n a condition of being predisposed; an inclination ⟨*a hereditary* ~ *to disease*⟩

**prednisolone** /pred'nisə,lohn/ n a synthetic steroid drug, $C_{21}H_{28}O_5$, that has the actions of a GLUCOCORTICOID (hormone produced by the ADRENAL GLAND) and is used esp to reduce inflammation in the treatment of arthritis and to suppress allergic and similar reactions produced by the body's immune system [blend of *prednisone* and *-ol*]

**prednisone** /pred'nisohn/ n a synthetic steroid drug, $C_{21}H_{26}O_5$, with similar actions and uses to prednisolone [prob fr *pregnane* ($C_{21}H_{36}$) + *diene* (compound containing two double bonds) + cort*isone*]

**predominant** /pri'dominənt/ adj having superior strength, influence, or authority; prevailing [MF, fr ML *praedominant-*, *praedominans*, prp of *praedominari* to predominate, fr L *prae-* + *dominari* to rule, govern – more at DOMINATE] – **predominance, predominancy** n, **predominantly** adv

**predominate** /pri'dominayt/ vi **1** to exert controlling power or influence; prevail **2** to hold advantage in numbers or quantity ~ vt to exert control over; dominate [ML *praedominatus*, pp of *praedominari*] – **predomination** n

**pre-'eclampsia** /e'klampsi•ə/ n a serious abnormal condition that develops in late pregnancy and is characterized by a sudden rise in blood pressure and OEDEMA (accumulation of watery liquid in body tissues)

**preemergence** /,pree•i'muhj(ə)ns/, **preemergent** /,pree•i'muhj(ə)nt/ adj used or occurring before emergence of seedlings above ground ⟨~ *weed control*⟩

**preeminent** /pri'eminənt/ adj having the greatest rank, dignity, or importance; outstanding [LL *praeeminent-*, *praeeminens*, fr L, prp of *praeeminēre* to be outstanding, fr *prae-* + *eminēre* to stand out – more at EMINENT] – **preeminence** n, **preeminently** adv

**preempt** /pri'empt/ vt **1** to acquire (e g land) by preemption **2** to seize on to the exclusion of others; take for oneself ⟨*the movement was then* ~ed *by a lunatic fringe*⟩ **3** to take the place of; replace ⟨*favourite TV programme was* ~ed *by the special coverage of a football match*⟩ **4** to invalidate or render useless by taking action or appearing in advance ⟨*the government's decision to build an airport* ~ed *the council's plans*⟩ ~ vi to make a preemptive bid in bridge [back-formation fr *preemption*] – **preemptor** n

**preemption** /pri'empsh(ə)n/ n **1a** the right of purchasing before or in preference to others **b** the purchase of something under this right **2** a prior seizure or appropriation [ML *praeemptus*, pp of *praeemere* to buy before, fr L *prae-* pre- + *emere* to buy – more at REDEEM]

**preemptive** /pri'emptiv/ adj **1a** of preemption **b** having power to preempt **2** of or being a bid in bridge that is higher than necessary and is designed to prevent bids by the opponents **3** giving a shareholder first option to purchase new stock in an amount proportionate to his/her existing holdings ⟨*a* ~ *right*⟩ **4** marked by a seizing of the initiative, esp in order to prevent or delay intended action by others ⟨*a* ~ *attack that disabled the enemy*⟩ – **preemptively** adv

**¹preen** /preen/ n, *dial chiefly Br* **1** a pin **2** a brooch [ME *prene*, fr OE *prēon*; akin to MHG *pfrieme* awl]

**²preen** *vt, chiefly Scot* to pin

**³preen** *vt* **1a** *of a bird* to trim, arrange, and oil (the feathers) using the beak; *also* to trim, arrange, and oil the feathers of (itself or a part of the body) **b** *of a mammal* to clean (itself, the fur, or a part of the body) esp by licking ⟨*huge sea elephants loll and ~ themselves – Time*⟩ **2** to dress or smarten (oneself) up **3** to pride or congratulate (oneself) on an achievement ~ *vi* **1** to smarten oneself, esp in a vain way ⟨~ *ing in front of the mirror*⟩ **2** to appear to be congratulating oneself; gloat ⟨*couldn't help ~ing after he had controlled the meeting successfully*⟩ **3** *of a bird* to trim, arrange, and oil the feathers; *broadly, of an animal* to clean the fur or other body covering [ME *preinen*] – **preener** *n*

**preen gland** *n* UROPYGIAL GLAND (oil-secreting gland in birds, used in preening)

**pre-'entry** *adj* of or being a CLOSED SHOP in which an employer employs only people who are already union members – compare POST-ENTRY

**preexilic** /ˌpree·igˈzilik/, **preexilian** /-ˈzilyən/ *adj* previous to the exile of the Jews to Babylon in about 600 BC

**preexist** /ˌpree·igˈzist/ *vi* to exist earlier or before ~ *vt* to antedate

**preexistence** /ˌpree·igˈzist(ə)ns/ *n* existence in a former state or previous to something else : e g **a** existence of the soul before its union with the body **b** Christ's existence before his incarnation – **preexistent** *adj*

**prefab** /ˈpreefab/ *n* a prefabricated building or other structure; *specif* a small prefabricated house of a type put up extensively in Britain to cope with the housing shortage in the years immediately following World War II – **prefab** *adj*

**prefabricate** /priˈfabrikayt/ *vt* **1** to fabricate the parts of (e g a building) at a factory so that construction consists mainly of assembling standardized parts; *also* to fabricate (a part of a building or other structure) in this way **2** to produce artificially or synthetically – **prefabrication** *n*, **prefabricator** *n*

**¹preface** /ˈprefəs/ *n* **1** *often cap* a prayer of thanksgiving serving as an introduction to the main part of the Mass in most Christian services, esp in the Roman Catholic liturgy **2** the introductory remarks of a speaker or writer; *esp* the foreword of a book **3** something that precedes or heralds; a preliminary [ME, fr MF, fr ML *prephatia*, alter. of L *praefation-*, *praefatio* foreword, fr *praefatus*, pp of *praefari* to say beforehand, fr *prae-* pre- + *fari* to say – more at BAN]

**²preface** *vt* **1** to introduce by or provide with a preface ⟨~s it with a reasoned and sagacious introduction – Anthony Powell⟩ **2** to be a preliminary or preface to **3** to stand in front of ⟨*a porch ~s the entrance*⟩ *usage* see ¹PREFIX – **prefacer** *n*

**prefatorial** /ˌprefəˈtawriəl/ *adj* prefatory – **prefatorially** *adv*

**prefatory** /ˈprefət(ə)ri/ *adj* **1** of or being a preface ; introductory **2** located in front [L *praefatus*, pp] – **prefatorily** *adv*

**prefect** /ˈpreefekt/ *n* **1** any of various high officials or magistrates of differing functions and ranks in ancient Rome **2** a chief officer or chief magistrate (e g the chief administrative official of a department in France or Italy) **3** a senior pupil in a secondary school who usu has some authority over other pupils [ME, fr MF, fr L *praefectus*, fr pp of *praeficere* to place at the head of, fr *prae-* + *facere* to make – more at DO]

**prefect apostolic** *n* a Roman Catholic clergyman, esp a priest, with jurisdiction over a district of a missionary territory – **prefecture apostolic** *n*

**prefecture** /ˈpreefekchə/ *n* **1** the (term of) office of a prefect **2** the official residence of a prefect **3** the district governed by a prefect – **prefectural** *adj*

**prefer** /priˈfuh/ *vt* **-rr-** **1** to choose or esteem above another; like better ⟨~s *sports to reading*⟩ **2** to give (a creditor) priority **3** to bring or lay (charges) against someone **4** to bring forward or submit for consideration **5** *archaic* to promote or advance to a rank or position **6** *archaic* to put or set forward or before someone; recommend [ME *preferren*, fr MF *preferer*, fr L *praeferre* to put before, prefer, fr *prae-* + *ferre* to carry – more at BEAR] – **preferrer** *n*

   *usage* **Prefer** and **preferable** are best followed by *to*, as in ⟨*I prefer swimming to riding*⟩ ⟨*our method is* **preferable** *to yours*⟩; but since *to* sounds absurd where it is followed by a *to* infinitive ⟨⚠ *I* **prefer** *to swim to to ride*⟩ it should there be replaced by *rather than* ⟨*I* **prefer** *to swim rather than to ride*⟩ or the whole sentence rephrased ⟨*I'd rather swim than ride*⟩. The use of *than* alone after **prefer** or **preferable** ⟨*I prefer to swim than to ride*⟩ should be avoided in formal writing. *synonyms* see ¹CHOICE

**preferable** /ˈpref(ə)rəbl/ *adj* that is to be preferred; more desirable – **preferableness, preferability** *n*

   *usage* **1** Since things either are or are not **preferable**, some people dislike such expressions as *more* **preferable**. **2** The pronunciation /ˈpref(ə)rəbl/ rather than /prəˈfuhrəbəl/ is recommended for BBC broadcasters. See PREFER *synonyms* see ¹CHOICE

**preferably** /ˈpref(ə)rəbli/ *adv* as is to be preferred; as would be best or most desirable ⟨*the box should ~ be lined with straw*⟩

**preference** /ˈpref(ə)rəns/ *n* **1a** preferring or being preferred **b** the power or opportunity of choosing **2** one who or that which is preferred; a choice ⟨*which is your ~?*⟩ **3** the act, fact, or principle of giving advantages or consideration to some over others ⟨*give ~ to candidates with a maths O level*⟩ **4** priority in the right to demand and receive settlement of an obligation [Fr *préférence*, fr ML *praeferentia*, fr L *praeferent-*, *praeferens*, prp of *praeferre*] – for **preference** as being the more desirable; preferably ⟨*use red wine for preference*⟩

**preference share** *n* a share in the capital of a company that entitles the holder to a fixed dividend before anything is paid to the holders of ORDINARY SHARES – compare DEFERRED SHARE, ORDINARY SHARE

**preferential** /ˌprefəˈrensh(ə)l/ *adj* **1** showing preference ⟨*received ~ treatment*⟩ **2** employing or creating a preference in trade relations **3** designed to permit expression of voting preference among candidates ⟨*a ~ primary*⟩ – **preferentially** *adv*

**preferment** /priˈfuhmənt/ *n* **1a** advancement or promotion in rank, office, or station **b** a position or appointment, esp ecclesiastical, that brings social or financial advancement **2** priority in right, esp to receive payment or to buy property on equal terms with others **3** the act of bringing something (e g charges) forward

**preferred stock** /priˈfuhd/ *n, chiefly NAm* PREFERENCE SHARES

**prefiguration** /ˌpreefigəˈraysh(ə)n/ *n* **1** prefiguring or being prefigured **2** something that prefigures something else

**prefigure** /ˌpreeˈfigə/ *vt* **1** to show, suggest, or announce by a type, image, or likeness that comes before; foreshadow **2** to picture or imagine beforehand; foresee [ME *prefiguren*, fr LL *praefigurare*, fr L *prae-* pre- + *figurare* to shape, picture, fr *figura* figure] – **prefigurative** *adj*, **prefigurement** *n*

**¹prefix** /ˈpreefiks/ *vt* **1** to fix or appoint beforehand **2** to attach as a prefix ⟨~ *a syllable to a word*⟩ **3a** to add to the beginning ⟨~ed *a brief introduction to the article*⟩ **b** to add something to the beginning of ⟨~ed *his speech with a few complimentary remarks*⟩ [ME *prefixen*, fr MF *prefixer*, fr *pre-* + *fixer* to fix, fr *fix* fixed, fr L *fixus* – more at FIX]

   *usage* Some careful writers prefer to use **preface**, rather than **prefix**, in the sense "provide with a beginning" ⟨*prefaced his speech with a few complimentary remarks*⟩.

**²prefix** *n* **1** an AFFIX (e g *un* in *unhappy*) appearing at the beginning of a word – compare INFIX, SUFFIX **2** a title (e g Mr or Lord) used before a person's name [NL *praefixum*, fr L, neut of *praefixus*, pp of *praefigere* to fasten before, fr *prae-* + *figere* to fasten – more at DYKE] – **prefixal** *adj*, **prefixally** *adv*

**preflight** /ˌpreeˈfliet/ *adj* preparing for or preliminary to flight

**preform** /ˌpreeˈfawm/ *vt* **1** to form or shape beforehand **2** to bring to approximate shape and size [L *praeformare*, fr *prae-* + *formare* to form, fr *forma* form] – **preform** *n*

**preformation** /ˌpreefawˈmaysh(ə)n/ *n* **1** previous formation **2** the now discredited theory that every egg and sperm cell contains a fully formed miniature version of the adult organism and that development consists merely in increase in size – compare EPIGENESIS

**prefrontal** /ˌpreeˈfruntl/ *adj* in or at the front of or involving the frontmost part of a frontal anatomical structure; *esp* being or occurring in or near the front part of a FRONTAL BONE or the forehead or of a FRONTAL LOBE of the brain – **prefrontal** *n*

**preganglionic** /ˌpreegang·gliˈonik/ *adj* leading into a GANGLION (solid mass of nerve cells); *specif* of or being a usu MYELINATED (covered with a fatty insulating sheath) nerve or nerve fibre that originates in the spinal cord and ends in a ganglion

**preggers** /ˈpregəz/ *adj, Br informal* pregnant [*pregnant* + *-ers* (as in *crackers*)]

**preglacial** /ˌpreeˈglays(h)yəl/ *adj* occurring before a period of glaciation

**pregnable** /ˈpregnəbl/ *adj, formal* vulnerable to capture ⟨*a ~ fort*⟩ [modif of ME *prenable*, fr MF – more at IMPREGNABLE] – **pregnability** *n*

**pregnancy** /ˈpregnənsi/ *n* **1** the condition of being pregnant;

GESTATION 2 an instance of being pregnant 3 *formal* 3a fertility of mind; inventiveness **b** richness in ideas; profundity ⟨*the* ∼ *of Shakespeare's language*⟩

**pregnant** /'pregnənt/ *adj* 1 carrying unborn young within the body 2 containing the germ of future events; having important consequences ⟨*the* ∼ *years of the prewar era*⟩ 3 full, teeming – usu + *with* ⟨*nature* ∼ *with life*⟩ 4 *chiefly formal* rich in significance or implication; meaningful, profound ⟨*the* ∼ *phrases of the Bible* – Edmund Wilson⟩ ⟨*a* ∼ *pause*⟩ 5 *formal* full of ideas, wit, or resourcefulness; inventive ⟨*all this has been said ... by great and* ∼ *artists* – *TLS*⟩ 6 *obs* open, receptive ⟨*your own most* ∼ *and vouchsafed ear* – Shak⟩ [ME, fr L *praegnant-, praegnans,* alter. of *praegnas,* fr *prae-* pre- + -*gnas* (akin to *gignere* to produce) – more at KIN] – **pregnantly** *adv*

**preheat** /‚pree'heet/ *vt* to heat beforehand; *esp* to heat (an oven) to a designated temperature before using for cooking – **preheater** *n*

**prehensile** /pri'hensiel, ‚pree-/ *adj* adapted for seizing or grasping, esp by wrapping round ⟨*a* ∼ *tail*⟩ [Fr *préhensile,* fr L *prehensus,* pp of *prehendere* to grasp, fr *prae-* + -*hendere* (akin to ON *geta* to get) – more at GET] – **prehensility** *n*

**prehension** /pri'hensh(ə)n/ *n* 1 the act of taking hold, seizing, or grasping – used technically 2 *chiefly formal* mental understanding; comprehension

**prehistorian** /‚preehi'stawriən/ *n* an archaeologist who specializes in prehistoric man and prehistoric culture

**prehistoric** /‚preehi'storik/, **prehistorical** /-kl/ *adj* of or existing in times before written history – **prehistorically** *adv*

**prehistory** /‚pree'histəri/ *n* 1 the study of prehistoric man 2 a history of the events leading up to a situation or occurrence 3 the prehistoric period of man's evolution

**prehominid** /‚pree'hominid/ *n* any of the extinct manlike primates that are often classified as a family (Prehominidae) [deriv of L *pre-* + *homin-, homo* human being] – **prehominid** *adj*

**preignition** /‚pree·ig'nish(ə)n/ *n* the premature detonation of the fuel-air mixture in the cylinder of an INTERNAL-COMBUSTION ENGINE

**preincubate** /pree'ingkyoobayt/ *vt* to incubate beforehand; *esp* to incubate (e g a preparation of cells or tissue) prior to the incubation period of major interest in an experiment – **preincubation** *n*

**preindustrial** /‚pree·in'dustriəl/ *adj* of or occurring in a period prior to the development of large-scale industry

**prejudge** /‚pree'juj/ *vt* to pass judgment on prematurely or before a full and proper examination [MF *prejuger,* fr L *praejudicare,* fr *prae-* + *judicare* to judge – more at JUDGE] – **prejudger** *n*, **prejudgment** *n*

**¹prejudice** /'prejoodis, -jə-/ *n* 1 disadvantage or damage resulting from some judgment or action of another in disregard of one's rights; *esp* detriment to one's legal rights or claims – chiefly in *without prejudice (to)* 2a(1) preconceived judgment or opinion **a**(2) an opinion for or against something formed without just grounds or before sufficient knowledge; a bias **b** an instance of such judgment or opinion **c** an irrational attitude of hostility directed against an individual, group, or race [ME, fr OF, fr L *praejudicium* previous judgment, damage, fr *prae-* + *judicium* judgment – more at JUDICIAL]

   *usage* One has a **prejudice** *against* or, more rarely, *in favour of* something or somebody, but the use of *to* should be avoided here ⟨△ *a strong prejudice to eating snails*⟩.

**²prejudice** *vt* 1 to injure or damage by some judgment or action (e g in a case of law) 2 to cause to have an unreasonable bias

**prejudiced** /'prejədist/ *adj* having a prejudice or bias for or esp against

**prejudicial** /prejə'dish(ə)l/, **prejudicious** /-'dishəs/ *adj* 1 tending to injure or impair; detrimental *to* 2 leading to prejudiced judgments or opinions – **prejudicially** *adv*, **prejudicialness** *n*, **prejudiciously** *adv*

**prelacy** /'prelasi/ *n* 1 the office of a prelate 2 church government by bishops

**prelapsarian** /‚preelap'seəriən/ *adj* characteristic of or belonging to the time or state before the fall of man [*pre-* + L *lapsus* slip, fall – more at LAPSE]

**prelate** /'prelət/ *n* an ecclesiastic (e g a bishop or abbot) of high rank [ME *prelat,* fr OF, fr ML *praelatus,* lit., one receiving preferment, fr L (pp of *praeferre* to prefer), fr *prae-* + *latus,* pp of *ferre* to carry – more at TOLERATE, BEAR] – **prelatic, prelatical** *adj*

**prelate nullius** /'nooliəs/ *n* a Roman Catholic prelate who is usu a titular bishop and who has ordinary jurisdiction over a district independent of any diocese [NL *nullius (dioeceseos)* of no (diocese)]

**prelature** /'preləchə/ *n* 1 PRELACY 1 2 *taking sing or pl vb* a body of prelates

**prelaunch** /'pree‚lawnch/ *adj* preparing for or preliminary to a launch (e g of a spacecraft)

**prelect** /pri'lekt/ *vi, formal* to discourse publicly; lecture [L *praelectus,* pp of *praelegere,* fr *prae-* + *legere* to read – more at LEGEND] – **prelection** *n*

**prelibation** /‚preelie'baysh(ə)n/ *n, formal* a foretaste [L *praelibation-, praelibatio,* fr *praelibatus,* pp of *praelibare* to taste beforehand, fr *prae-* + *libare* to pour as an offering, taste – more at LIBATION]

**prelim** /'preelim/ *n* 1 a preliminary 2 *pl, Br* FRONT MATTER

**¹preliminary** /pri'limin(ə)ri/ *n* something that precedes or is introductory or preparatory: e g **a** a preliminary scholastic examination **b** *pl, Br* prelims **c** a minor match preceding the main event (e g of a boxing programme) [Fr *préliminaires,* pl, fr ML *praeliminaris,* adj, preliminary, fr L *prae-* pre- + *limin-, limen* threshold – more at LIMB]

**²preliminary** *adj* preceding and preparing for the main discourse or business; introductory ⟨*held a* ∼ *discussion to set up the agenda of the conference*⟩ – **preliminarily** *adv*

**preliterate** /‚pree'lit(ə)rət/ *adj* of times before the use of writing; not yet using writing as a cultural medium ⟨*ancient* ∼ *cultures*⟩ – **preliterate** *n*

**¹prelude** /'prelyoohd/ *n* 1 an introductory or preliminary performance, action, or event; an introduction 2a a musical section or movement introducing the theme or chief subject (e g of a fugue or suite) or serving as an introduction to an opera or oratorio **b** an opening VOLUNTARY (piece of music) **c** a separate concert piece, usu for piano or orchestra and based entirely on a short MOTIVE (recurring theme) [MF, fr ML *praeludium,* fr L *praeludere* to play beforehand, fr *prae-* + *ludere* to play – more at LUDICROUS] – **preludial** *adj*

**²prelude** *vt* 1 to serve as prelude to; foreshadow 2 to introduce with a prelude – **preluder** *n*

**prelusive** /pri'l(y)oohsiv/, **prelusory** /pri'l(y)oohzəri/ *adj, formal* constituting or having the form of a prelude; introductory [L *praelusus,* pp of *praeludere*] – **prelusively** *adv*

**premalignant** /‚preemə'lignənt/ *adj* PRECANCEROUS (likely to become cancerous) – **premalignancy** *n*

**preman** /‚pree'man, '-‚-/ *n, pl* **premen** /-men/ any of various primates (e g PEKING MAN) that are direct ancestors of man; PREHOMINID

**premarital** /‚pree'maritl/ *adj, esp* of sexual relations occurring before marriage ⟨∼ *sex*⟩

**premature** /'premə̈chə, ‚premə'tyooə, 'premə‚tyooə/ *adj* 1 happening, arriving, existing, or performed before the proper or usual time; *esp, of a human baby* born after a pregnancy lasting less than 37 weeks 2 *informal* acting before the proper or appropriate time ⟨*was a bit* ∼ *in claiming he'd won*⟩ □ compare IMMATURE [L *praematurus* too early, fr *prae-* + *maturus* ripe, mature] – **premature** *n*, **prematurely** *adv*, **prematureness, prematurity** *n*

**premaxilla** /‚preemak'silə/ *n, pl* **premaxillae** /-li/ either of the pair of bones that form the front part of the upper jaw of most VERTEBRATE animals and lie in front of the MAXILLAE [NL] – **premaxillary** *adj or n*

**premed** /‚pree'med/ *adj or n, informal* (of) a premedical student or course of study

**premedian** /‚pree'meedi·ən/, **premedial** /-di·əl/ *adj* lying in front of the middle of the body or a body part ⟨*a* ∼ *vein in the wing of an insect*⟩

**premedical** /‚pree'medikl/ *adj* preceding and preparing for the professional study of medicine

**premedication** /‚preemedi'kaysh(ə)n/ *n* the drugs given to a patient to prepare him/her for an anaesthetic preceding surgery

**premeditate** /pri'meditayt, ‚pree-/ *vt* to think over and plan in the mind beforehand ∼ *vi* to think, consider, or deliberate beforehand [L *praemeditatus,* pp of *praemeditari,* fr *prae-* + *meditari* to meditate] – **premeditative** *adj,* **premeditator** *n*

**premeditated** /pri'meditaytid, ‚pree-/ *adj* characterized by or resulting from conscious intent; showing forethought and planning ⟨∼ *murder*⟩ – **premeditatedly** *adv*

**premeditation** /pri‚medi'taysh(ə)n/ *n* an act or instance of premeditating; *specif* consideration or planning of an act beforehand as evidence (e g in law) of intent to commit that act

**premeiotic** /ˌpreemie'otik/ *adj* of, occurring in, or typical of a stage prior to MEIOSIS ⟨~ *DNA synthesis*⟩ ⟨~ *tissue*⟩

**premenstrual** /ˌpree'menstrooəl/ *adj* of or occurring just before the start of a menstrual period – **premenstrually** *adv*

**premenstrual tension** *n* a syndrome characterized by irritability, headaches, etc that occurs in some women during the days preceding menstruation

¹**premier** /'premyə, 'premi·ə/ *adj* **1** first in position, rank, or importance; principal **2** first in time; earliest; *specif* being the holder of the earliest-created title in a rank of nobility ⟨*England's* ~ *duke*⟩ [ME *primier*, fr MF *premier* first, chief, fr L *primarius* of the first rank – more at PRIMARY]

²**premier** *n* PRIME MINISTER [Fr, fr *premier*, adj]

¹**premiere** /'premiə, 'premi·eə/ *n* a first public performance or showing ⟨*the* ~ *of a play*⟩ [Fr *première*, fr fem of *premier* first]

²**premiere, premier** *vt* to give a first public performance of ~ *vi* **1** to have a first public performance **2** to appear for the first time as a star performer

**premiership** /'premyəˌship, -mi·ə-/ *n* **1** the position or office of a premier **2** *Austr* a sports league

**premillenarianism** /ˌpreemilə'neəri·əniz(ə)m/ *n* premillennialism – **premillenarian** *adj or n*

**premillennial** /ˌpreemi'leni·əl/ *adj* **1** coming before the MILLENNIUM (period of peace and happiness following Christ's return) **2** holding or relating to premillennialism – **premillennially** *adv*

**premillennialism** /ˌpreemi'leni·əliz(ə)m/ *n* the view that Christ will return and rule over a period of a thousand years' peace and happiness on earth – compare POSTMILLENNIALISM – **premillennialist** *n*

¹**premise** /'premis/ *n* **1** *Br also* **premiss 1a** a proposition stated or assumed as a basis of argument or inference; *specif* either of the first two propositions of a SYLLOGISM (pair of statements in logic) from which the conclusion is drawn **b** something assumed or taken for granted; a presupposition **2** *Br also* **premiss** *pl* matters previously stated; *specif* the preliminary and explanatory part of a legal document (DEED) **4)** **3** *pl* **3a** a piece of land with the buildings on it **b** a building or part of a building, usu with any accompanying rights, grounds, etc [(1) ME *premisse*, fr MF, fr ML *praemissa*, fr L, fem of *praemissus*, pp of *praemittere* to place ahead, fr *prae-* pre- + *mittere* to send; (2-3) ME *premisses*, fr ML *praemissa*, fr L, neut pl of *praemissus*; (3) fr its being identified in the premises of a deed of conveyance]

²**premise** *vt* **1a** to state beforehand as an introduction or postulate **b** to assert as a premise in an argument **2** to presuppose or imply as preexistent; postulate

¹**premium** /'preemyəm, -mi·əm/ *n* **1a** a reward or recompense for a particular act **b** a sum over and above a fixed price or remuneration paid chiefly as an inducement or incentive; a bonus ⟨*willing to pay a* ~ *for immediate delivery*⟩ **c** a sum in advance of or in addition to the nominal value of something ⟨*bonds callable at a* ~ *of six per cent*⟩ **d** something given free or at a reduced price with the purchase of a product or service **e** the excess of one futures contract price over that of another – compare DISCOUNT 1c **2** the sum paid for a contract of insurance **3** a high value or a value in excess of that normally expected ⟨*put a* ~ *on accuracy*⟩ [L *praemium* booty, profit, reward, fr *prae-* + *emere* to take, buy – more at REDEEM]

²**premium** *adj, chiefly NAm* of exceptional quality or amount ⟨*paid a* ~ *price*⟩ ⟨*wine made from* ~ *grapes*⟩

**premium bond, Premium Savings Bond** *n* a British government bond that is issued in units of one pound and that instead of earning interest is entered into a monthly or weekly draw for money prizes

**premix** /ˌpree'miks/ *vt* to mix far in advance of use ⟨~ *ed concrete*⟩ – **premix** *n*

¹**premolar** /ˌpree'mohlə/ *adj* situated in front of or preceding the molar teeth; *specif* of or being a premolar tooth

²**premolar** *n* any of the teeth of a mammal that resemble the molars, have two roots, and are located in the cheek region in front of the true molars and behind the canines when the latter are present

**premonish** /pri'monish/ *vb, archaic vt* to forewarn ~ *vi* to give warning in advance [*pre-* + *monish* (to warn), fr ME *monisshen*, alter. of *monesten*, fr OF *monester*, fr (assumed) VL *monestare*, fr L *monēre*]

**premonition** /ˌpremə'nish(ə)n, ˌpree-/ *n* **1** a previous notice or warning; a forewarning ⟨*a* ~ *of the troubles that lay in store*⟩ **2** an anticipation of an event without conscious reason; a

presentiment ⟨*felt a* ~ *of danger*⟩ [MF, fr LL *praemonition-, praemonitio*, fr L *praemonitus*, pp of *praemonēre* to warn in advance, fr *prae-* + *monēre* to warn – more at MIND]

**premonitory** /pri'monit(ə)ri/ *adj* giving warning ⟨*a* ~ *symptom*⟩ – **premonitorily** *adv*

**Premonstratensian** /ˌpreeˌmonstrə'tensh(ə)n/ *n* a member of a religious order founded by St Norbert at Prémontré near Laon in France in 1120 [ML *praemonstratensis*, fr *praemonstratensis* of Prémontré, fr *Praemonstratus* Prémontré, abbey in N France]

**premorse** /pri'maws/ *adj, biology* having an abrupt but irregular or ragged end as if bitten off ⟨*a* ~ *root*⟩ [L *praemorsus*, pp of *praemordēre* to bite off in front, fr *prae-* + *mordēre* to bite – more at SMART]

**premune** /ˌpree'myoohn/ *adj* exhibiting premunition [back-formation fr *premunition*]

**premunition** /ˌpreemyooh'nish(ə)n/ *n* resistance or immunity to a disease resulting either from the existence of the disease-causing agent in an inactive state in the organism or previous infection by the agent [L *praemunition-, praemunitio* advance fortification, fr *praemunitus*, pp of *praemunire* to fortify in advance, fr *prae-* + *munire* to fortify – more at MUNITION]

**prename** /'preeˌnaym/ *n* a forename

**prenatal** /ˌpree'naytl/ *adj* occurring, existing, or being in a stage before birth – **prenatally** *adv*

**prenominate** /pree'nominayt/ *vt, obs* to mention previously [LL *praenominatus*, pp of *praenominare*, fr L *prae-* + *nominare* to name – more at NOMINATE] – **prenominate** *adj*, **prenomination** *n*

**prenotion** /ˌpree'nohsh(ə)n/ *n, archaic* a preconception [L *praenotion-, praenotio*, fr *prae-* + *notio* idea, conception – more at NOTION]

**prentice** /'prentis/ *n, archaic* an apprentice, learner [ME *prentis*, short for *apprentis*] – **prentice** *adj*

**preoccupancy** /ˌpree'okyoopənsi/ *n* **1** an act or the right of taking possession before another **2** the state of being preoccupied

**preoccupation** /priˌokyoo'paysh(ə)n, ˌpree-/ *n* **1** preoccupying or being preoccupied **2a** complete mental absorption **b** something that causes such absorption [L *praeoccupation-, praeoccupatio* act of seizing beforehand, fr *praeoccupatus*, pp of *praeoccupare* to seize beforehand, fr *prae-* + *occupare* to seize, occupy]

**preoccupied** /ˌpree'okyoopied/ *adj* **1** lost in thought; engrossed **2** already occupied *synonyms* see ABSTRACTED

**preoccupy** /ˌpree'okyoopie/ *vt* **1** to engage or engross the attention of to the exclusion of other things **2** to take possession of or occupy in advance or before another [*pre-* + *occupy*]

**preoperative** /ˌpree'op(ə)rətiv/ *adj* occurring in the period preceding a surgical operation – **preoperatively** *adv*

**preorbital** /ˌpree'awbitl/ *adj* **1** occurring before entering orbit **2** situated in front of the hollow or bony cavity (ORBIT) of the eye

**preordain** /ˌpreeaw'dayn/ *vt* to decree or determine in advance – **preordainment, preordination** *n*

**preovulatory** /ˌpree'ovyoolətri/ *adj* occurring in or typical of the period immediately preceding ovulation

**ˌpre-'owned** *adj, euph* secondhand

¹**prep** /prep/ *n, Br* homework [short for *preparation*]

²**prep** *n* PREPARATORY SCHOOL

³**prep** *vt* **-pp-** *NAm* to prepare (eg a patient) for operation or examination

**prepack** /ˌpree'pak/ *vt* to prepackage

**prepackage** /ˌpree'pakij/ *vt* to package (eg food or a manufactured article) before offering for sale to the consumer

**preparation** /ˌprepə'raysh(ə)n/ *n* **1** the action or process of making something ready for use, service, or consumption or of getting ready for some occasion, test, or duty **2** a state of being prepared; readiness **3** *usu pl* a preparatory act or measure ⟨*made his* ~ *s for the journey*⟩ **4** something that is prepared; *esp* a medicine or medicinal substance ⟨*a* ~ *for colds*⟩ [ME *preparacion*, fr MF *preparation*, fr L *praeparation-, praeparatio*, fr *praeparatus*, pp of *praeparare*]

**preparative** /pri'parətiv/ *n* something that prepares the way for or serves as a preliminary to something else

¹**preparatory** /pri'parət(ə)ri/, **preparative** *adj* preparing or serving to prepare for something; introductory – **preparatorily, preparatively** *adv*

²**preparatory** *adv* by way of preparation; in a preparatory manner – usu + *to* ⟨*took a deep breath* ~ *to drinking*⟩

**preparatory school** *n* **1** *Br* a private school preparing pupils aged from about eight to thirteen primarily for public schools **2** *NAm* a usu private school preparing pupils primarily for college

**prepare** /pri'peə/ *vt* **1a** to make ready beforehand for some purpose, use, or activity ⟨~ *food for dinner*⟩ ⟨~ *children for school*⟩ **b** to put into a suitable frame of mind for something ⟨~d *her gradually for the shocking news*⟩ **2** to work out the details of; plan in advance ⟨preparing *his strategy for the coming campaign*⟩ **3a** to put together; compound ⟨~ *a prescription*⟩ **b** to draw up in written form ⟨~ *a report*⟩ ~ *vi* to get ready; make preparations ⟨preparing *for a career in teaching*⟩ [ME *preparen*, fr MF *preparer*, fr L *praeparare*, fr *prae-* pre-+ *parare* to procure, prepare – more at PARE] – **preparer** *n*

**prepared** /pri'peəd/ *adj* subjected to a special process or treatment – **preparedly** *adv*

**preparedness** /pri'peədnis, -'peəridnis/ *n* the quality or state of being prepared; *specif* a state of adequate preparation in case of war

**prepay** /,pree'pay/ *vt* **prepaid** to pay (the charge on) in advance ⟨*carriage* prepaid⟩ – **prepayment** *n*

**prepense** /pri'pens/ *adj* planned beforehand; premeditated – used in law, usu after a noun ⟨*malice* ~⟩ [alter. (influenced by *pre-*) of earlier *purpensed*, fr ME, pp of *purpensen* to deliberate, premeditate, fr MF *purpenser*, fr OF, fr *pur-* for + *penser* to think – more at PURCHASE, PENSIVE] – **prepensely** *adv*

**preplant** /,pree'plahnt/ *also* **preplanting** *adj* occurring or used before planting a crop ⟨~ *soil fertilization*⟩

**preponderance** /pri'pond(ə)rəns/ *n* **1** a superiority in weight, power, influence, or strength **2** a superiority or excess in number or quantity

**preponderant** /pri'pond(ə)rənt/, **preponderate** /-rət/ *adj* **1** having superior weight, force, or influence; predominant **2** occurring in greater number or quantity – **preponderantly**, **preponderately** *adv*

**preponderate** /pri'pondərayt/ *vt, archaic* to outweigh ~ *vi* **1a** to be greater in weight **b** to descend or incline downwards **2** to predominate in influence, power, or importance **3** to predominate in number or frequency [L *praeponderatus*, pp of *praeponderare*, fr *prae-* + *ponder-*, *pondus* weight – more at PENDANT] – **preponderation** *n*

**preposition** /,prepə'zish(ə)n/ *n* a word or word group (eg *at*, *under*, or *on top of*) that combines with a noun, pronoun, or noun equivalent to form a phrase (eg *at the table*, *under the table*, or *on top of the table*) linking the noun (eg *the table*) in some way to the rest of the sentence – see "Ten Vexed Points" △ proposition [ME *preposicioun*, fr L *praeposition-*, *praepositio*, lit., act of placing in front, fr *praepositus*, pp of *praeponere* to put in front, fr *prae-* pre- + *ponere* to put – more at POSITION] – **prepositional** *adj*, **prepositionally** *adv*

**prepositive** /pri'pozətiv/ *adj*, *of a word or word part* placed before the word described or combined with ⟨*the* ~ *adjective* mere⟩ [LL *praepositivus*, fr L *praepositus*] – **prepositively** *adv*

**prepossess** /,preepə'zes/ *vt* **1** to cause to be preoccupied with an idea, belief, or attitude **2** to prejudice, esp in favour of something or someone

**prepossessing** /,preepə'zesing/ *adj* tending to create a favourable impression; attractive – **prepossessingly** *adv*, **prepossessingness** *n*

**prepossession** /,preepə'zesh(ə)n/ *n* **1** an opinion or impression formed beforehand; a prejudice **2** an exclusive concern with one idea or object; a preoccupation

**preposterous** /pri'post(ə)rəs/ *adj* so contrary to nature, reason, or common sense as to be outrageous; *also* ridiculous *synonyms* see LAUGHABLE [L *praeposterus*, lit., with the hindside in front, fr *prae-* + *posterus* hinder, following – more at POSTERIOR] – **preposterously** *adv*, **preposterousness** *n*

**prepotency** /,pree'poht(ə)nsi/ *n* **1** unusual ability of an individual or strain to transmit its inheritable characters to offspring because of being pure-breeding for numerous DOMINANT genes (genes that suppress the effect of other genes coding for alternative forms of the same characteristics) **2** *formal* the quality or state of being prepotent; predominance

**prepotent** /,pree'poht(ə)nt/ *adj* **1** exhibiting genetic prepotency **2** *formal* **2a** having exceptional power, authority, or influence; preeminent **b** exceeding others in power [ME, fr L *praepotent-*, *praepotens*, fr *prae-* + *potens* powerful – more at POTENT] – **prepotently** *adv*

**preprandial** /,pree'prandyəl/ *adj, chiefly formal or humorous* of or suitable for the time just before a meal ⟨*a* ~ *drink*⟩

**preprint** /,pree'print/ *n* **1** a printing of a speech or paper before its formal delivery; *esp* an issue of a technical paper, often in preliminary form, before its publication in a journal – compare OFFPRINT **2** something (eg an advertisement) printed before the rest of the publication in which it is to appear – **preprint** *vt*

**preprofessional** /,preeprə'fesh(ə)nl/ *adj* of the period preceding specific study for or practice of a profession

**prep school** /prep/ *n* PREPARATORY SCHOOL

**prepuberal** /,pree'pyoohbərəl/ *adj* of prepuberty – **prepuberally** *adv*

**prepuberty** /,pree'pyoohbəti/ *n* the period immediately before puberty – **prepubertal** *adj*, **prepubertally** *adv*

**prepubescence** /,preepyooh'bes(ə)ns/ *n* prepuberty – **prepubescent** *adj*

**prepublication** /,preepubli'kaysh(ə)n/ *adj* of a period before the official publication date of a book ⟨~ *price*⟩

**prepuce** /'pree,pyoohs/ *n* the foreskin; *also* a similar fold surrounding the clitoris [ME, fr MF, fr L *praeputium*, fr *prae-* + *-putium* (akin to Belorussian *potka* penis)] – **preputial** *adj*

**prequel** /'preekwəl/ *n, informal* a book, film, etc that portrays the events, characters, etc that lead up to those described in an already existing work – compare SEQUEL [*pre-* + *-quel* (as in *sequel*)]

**[1]Pre-'Raphaelite** *n* **1a** a member of the PRE-RAPHAELITE BROTHERHOOD **b** an artist or writer influenced by this brotherhood **2** a modern artist dedicated to restoring early Renaissance ideals or methods **3** an Italian painter active before the time of Raphael's fame and influence [*Raphael* (Raffaello Santi) †1520 It painter] – **Pre-Raphaelitism** *n*

**[2]Pre-Raphaelite** *adj* of or suggesting the Pre-Raphaelites or their works; *specif* suggesting the dreamy medievalism of the Pre-Raphaelites

**Pre-Raphaelite Brotherhood** *n* a group of artists formed in England in 1848 which aimed to restore the artistic principles and practices regarded as characteristic of Italian art before Raphael and whose work is characterized esp by religious subject matter, elaborate detail, and the use of bright colour

**prerecord** /,preeri'kawd/ *vt* to record (eg a radio or television programme) in advance of presentation or use

**pre-regi'stration** *n* a special registration (eg for returning students) before an official registration period – **pre-register** *vi*

**[1]pre-re'lease** *vt* to release (eg a film or record) before the official date – **pre-release** *adj*

**[2]pre-release** *n* something that is pre-released; *also* a public showing of a film before its official date of release

**prerequisite** /pri'rekwizit/ *n* a requirement that must be satisfied in advance ⟨*a* ~ *for entry to a career in medicine*⟩ △ perquisite – **prerequisite** *adj*

**prerevolutionary** /,preerevə'l(y)oohshənri/ *adj* of or existing in the time before a revolution

**prerogative** /pri'rogətiv/ *n* **1** an exclusive or special right, power, or privilege: eg **1a** one belonging to an office or an official body **b** one belonging to a person, group, or class of individuals **c** one possessed by a nation as an attribute of sovereignty **2** the discretionary power of a sovereign or head of state ⟨*the* ~ *of the President to pardon criminals*⟩ [ME, fr MF & L; MF, fr L *praerogativa*, Roman century voting first in the comitia, privilege, fr fem of *praerogativus* voting first, fr *prae-* + *rogare* to ask – more at RIGHT] – **prerogatived** *adj*

**presa** /'presah/ *n, pl* **prese** /-say/ a mark or cue (eg :S:) indicating the point of entry of the successive voice parts of a CANON (musical composition) [It, lit., act of taking, fr *prendere* to take, fr L *prehendere* to grasp – more at PREHENSILE]

**[1]presage** /'presij/ *n* **1** something that foreshadows or portends a future event; an omen **2** an intuition or feeling of what is going to happen in the future **3** warning or indication of the future [ME, fr L *praesagium*, fr *praesagire* to forebode, fr *prae-* + *sagire* to perceive keenly – more at SEEK] – **presageful** *adj*

**[2]presage** /'presij, pri'sayj/ *vt* **1** to give an omen or warning of; foreshadow, portend **2** to forecast, predict **3** to have a presentiment of ~ *vi* to make or utter a prediction *synonyms* see FORETELL – **presager** *n, obs*

**presanctified** /,pree'sangktified/ *adj, of bread or wine used in the Mass* consecrated at a previous service

**presby-** /prezbi-/, **presbyo-** *comb form* old age ⟨presby*opia*⟩ [NL, fr Gk *presby-* elder, fr *presbys* old man]

**presbyopia** /,prezbi'ohpyə/ *n* a condition of deteriorating visual ability occurring in older people, in which loss of elasticity of the lens of the eye results in its inability to bring near objects into sharp focus [NL, fr *presby-* + *-opia*] – **presbyopic** *adj or n*

**presbyter** /'prezbitə/ *n* **1** a member of the governing body of an early Christian church **2** ELDER 3b (officer of a Presbyterian church) [LL, elder, priest – more at PRIEST] – **presbyterate** *n*

**presbyterial** /ˌprezbi'tiəri·əl/ *adj* of presbyters or a presbytery

¹**Presbyterian** /ˌprezbi'tiəri·ən/ *adj* **1** *often not cap* characterized by a graded system of elected representative ecclesiastical bodies (e g presbyteries) exercising legislative and judicial powers **2** of or constituting a Protestant Christian church that is presbyterian in government and traditionally CALVINISTIC in doctrine – **Presbyterianism** *n*

²**Presbyterian** *n* a member of a Presbyterian church

**presbytery** /'prezbit(ə)ri/ *n* **1** the part of a church reserved for the officiating clergy **2** *taking sing or pl vb* a ruling body in presbyterian churches consisting of the ministers and representative elders from congregations within a district **3** the jurisdiction of a presbytery **4** the house of a Roman Catholic parish priest [ME & LL; ME *presbytory* part of church reserved for clergy, fr LL *presbyterium* group of presbyters, part of church reserved for clergy, fr Gk *presbyterion* group of presbyters, fr *presbyteros* elder, priest – more at PRIEST]

¹**preschool** /'preeˌskoohl/ *adj* of or being the period in a child's life up to the age (e g of five in Britain) of first attendance at primary school

²**preschool** *n* a kindergarten; NURSERY SCHOOL

**prescience** /'presi·əns, -sh(ə)ns, -shi·əns/ *n* foreknowledge of events: **a** divine omniscience **b** human anticipation of the course of events; foresight [ME, fr LL *praescientia*, fr L *praescient-*, *praesciens*, prp of *praescire* to know beforehand, fr *prae-* + *scire* to know – more at SCIENCE] – **prescient** *adj*, **presciently** *adv*

**prescientific** /ˌpreesie·ən'tifik/ *adj* (having the characteristics) of a period before the rise of modern science

**prescind** /pri'sind/ *vb*, *formal vt* to separate in the mind; abstract ~ *vi* to withdraw one's attention □ usu + *from* [L *praescindere* to cut off in front, fr *prae-* + *scindere* to cut – more at SHED]

**prescribe** /pri'skrieb/ *vi* **1** to claim a title to something by right of prescription – usu + *to* or *for* **2** to lay down a rule; dictate **3** to write or give medical prescriptions **4** to become by prescription invalid or unenforceable ~ *vt* **1a** to lay down as a guide, direction, or rule of action; ordain **b** to specify with authority **2** to designate or order the use of as a remedy ⟨~d *a course of injections*⟩ △ proscribe [L *praescribere* to write at the beginning, dictate, order, fr *prae-* + *scribere* to write – more at SCRIBE; (*vi* 1) ME *prescriben*, fr ML *prescribere*, fr L *praescribere* to write at the beginning] – **prescriber** *n*

**prescript** /'pri'skript, 'preeˌskript/ *n or adj* (something) prescribed as a rule [ME, fr L *praescriptus*, pp]

**prescription** /pri'skripsh(ə)n/ *n* **1a** the establishment of a claim to something (e g a right) by use and enjoyment of it over a long period **b** the right or title acquired by such possession **2** the action of laying down authoritative rules or directions **3a** a written direction for a therapeutic or corrective agent ⟨*got his spectacles on* ~⟩; *specif* one for the preparation and use of a medicine **b** a prescribed medicine **4** (a claim founded on) ancient or long-standing custom **5** a prescript [partly fr ME *prescripcion* establishment of a claim, fr MF *prescription*, fr LL *praescription-*, *praescriptio*, fr L, preamble, regulation, limitation of subject matter, fr *praescriptus*, pp of *praescribere*; partly fr L *praescription-*, *praescriptio* regulation]

**prescriptive** /pri'skriptiv/ *adj* **1** serving to prescribe **2** established by, founded on, or arising from prescription or long-standing custom **3** authoritarian as regards language use ⟨*a* ~ *dictionary*⟩ – compare DESCRIPTIVE **4** – **prescriptively** *adv*, **prescriptivism** *n*, **prescriptivist** *n*

**preselect** /ˌpreesi'lekt/ *vt* to choose in advance, usu on the basis of a particular criterion – **preselection** *n*

**preselector** /ˌpreesi'lektə/ *n* a system of gears (e g of a motor vehicle transmission) by which a gear can be selected before it is actually engaged

**presence** /'prez(ə)ns/ *n* **1** the fact or condition of being present ⟨*requested his* ~ *at the meeting*⟩ **2a** the immediate vicinity near the specified person ⟨*never looked at ease in my* ~⟩ **b** the vicinity of one of superior, esp royal, rank ⟨*bowed before withdrawing from the* ~⟩ **3** one who or that which is present: e g **3a** the actual person or thing that is present ⟨*a fiery column*

*charioting his Godlike* ~ – John Milton⟩ **b** something present of a visible or concrete nature ⟨*a* ~ *on the radar screen*⟩ **c** a number of people seen as representatives who are engaged in playing an influential role, esp in the political, economic, or cultural life of another country ⟨*the withdrawal of the American* ~ *in Vietnam*⟩ ⟨*wanted to establish a British* ~ *in a largely foreign-controlled industry*⟩ **4a(1)** a personal magnetism that attracts and holds the attention of others **a(2)** a usu dignified or stately bearing or appearance **b** a quality of poise or distinction in a person, esp a performer, that enables him/her to impress or have a strong effect on others ⟨*an actor with considerable* ~⟩ **5** something (e g a ghost) felt or believed to be present

**presence chamber** *n* the room where a great personage (e g a sovereign) receives those entitled to come into his/her presence

**presence of mind** *n* the ability to retain one's self-possession and act calmly or quickly in an emergency or an unforeseen situation

¹**present** /'prez(ə)nt/ *n* something presented; a gift [ME, fr OF, fr *presenter*] – **make somebody a present of** to give to somebody as a present; *also* to allow somebody to gain without effort ⟨*made the opposition a present of a goal*⟩

²**present** /pri'zent/ *vt* **1a** to bring or introduce into the presence of someone; *esp* to introduce socially **b** to bring (e g a play) before the public ⟨*we proudly* ~ *Tom Jones*⟩ **2** to give or bestow formally ⟨~ed *a gold watch to him on his retirement*⟩ **3** to lay (e g a charge) before a court **4** to nominate (a clergyman) to a BENEFICE (ecclesiastical office) **5a** to offer so as to be seen or viewed; show, exhibit ⟨~ *a bedraggled appearance*⟩ **b** to offer for approval or consideration ⟨~ *this report again next week in greater detail*⟩ **6** to aim, point, or direct (e g a weapon) so as to face something or in a particular direction **7** to act as a presenter of (e g a television or radio programme) **8** *archaic* to act the part of; perform ~ *vi* **1** to present a weapon **2** to come forward for medical examination ⟨*a patient rarely* ~s *during the vesicular phase* – A B Wade⟩ – usu + *with* ⟨*she* ~s *with abdominal pains*⟩ **3** to be seen, esp in a particular form; appear ⟨*a tumour that* ~s *as an axillary mass*⟩ □ (*vi 2&3*) used in medicine *synonyms* see ¹GIVE [ME *presenten*, fr OF *presenter*, fr L *praesentare*, fr *praesent-*, *praesens*, adj] – **present oneself** to be present; appear ⟨*was told to* present *herself at the stage door at 9:30*⟩

**present with** *vt* **1** to give to, esp formally ⟨presented *him with a gold watch on his retirement*⟩ **2** to allow to gain without effort ⟨presented *the opposition* with *a goal*⟩

³**present** /pri'zent/ *n* PRESENT ARMS ⟨*his gun held at the* ~⟩

⁴**present** /'prez(ə)nt/ *adj* **1** now existing or in progress ⟨*under the* ~ *system of government*⟩ **2a** in or at an often specified place ⟨*is everyone* ~?⟩ ⟨*he wasn't* ~ *at the meeting*⟩ **b** existing in something mentioned or under consideration ⟨*methane and air had to be* ~ *in the right quantities for combustion to take place*⟩ **c** vividly felt, remembered, or imagined – usu + *to* or *in* ⟨*the events of a decade ago are still* ~ *to our minds*⟩ **3** constituting the one actually being discussed, dealt with, or considered ⟨*as far as the* ~ *writer is concerned*⟩ **4** of or being the verb tense that expresses action or state in the present time and is also sometimes used to refer to action in the past or to future events **5** *archaic* attentive, immediate **6** *obs* attentive [ME, fr OF, fr L *praesent-*, *praesens*, fr prp of *praeesse* to be before one, fr *prae-* pre- + *esse* to be – more at IS] – **presentness** *n*

⁵**present** /'prez(ə)nt/ *n* **1** the present tense of a language; *also* a verb form (e g *goes*) in this tense **2** the present time **3** *pl*, *formal* the present words or statements; *specif* the document (e g a royal proclamation) in which these words are used – **at present** now

**presentable** /pri'zentəbl/ *adj* **1** capable of being presented **2** fit to be seen or inspected, esp by the critical **3** fit (e g in dress or manners) to appear in company ⟨*must make myself* ~ *for dinner*⟩ – **presentableness** *n*, **presentably** *adv*, **presentability** *n*

**present arms** /pri'zent/ *n* **1** a deferential saluting position in which the firearm is held vertically in front of the body **2** a command to assume the position of present arms or to give a hand salute [fr the command *present arms!*]

**presentation** /ˌprezən'taysh(ə)n/ *n* **1a** the act of presenting **b** the act, power, or privilege, esp of a patron, of applying to the appropriate ecclesiastical authorities for the institution of someone nominated to a BENEFICE (ecclesiastical office) **2** something presented: eg **2a** a symbol or image that represents something **b** something offered or given; a gift **c** something set forth for consideration or notice **d** a descriptive or persuasive account (e g by a salesman of a product) **e** the manner in which something is set forth, laid out, or presented ⟨*his ~ of the argument was masterly*⟩ ⟨*the ~ of the final dish is important in cookery*⟩ **3** the position in which the foetus lies in the womb during labour with respect to the mouth of the womb **4** an immediate object of perception, knowledge, or memory – **presentational** *adj*

**presentationism** /ˌprezənˈtaysh(ə)niz(ə(m/ *n* the theory that the mind is directly aware of items in the external world – compare REPRESENTATIONALISM

**presentative** /priˈzentətiv/ *adj* known, knowing, or capable of being known directly rather than through reflection

**present-ˈday** /ˈprez(ə)nt/ *adj* current, contemporary **synonyms** see ¹MODERN

**presentee** /ˌprezənˈtee/ *n* one who is presented or to whom something is presented

**presenter** /priˈzentə/ *n* one who presents; *specif* a person who introduces and provides comments on a radio or television programme

**presentient** /priˈsensh(ə)nt, -ti-ənt, -zen-/ *adj, formal* having a presentiment [L *praesentient-, praesentiens*, prp of *praesentire*]

**presentiment** /priˈzentimənt/ *n* a feeling that something will or is about to happen; a premonition [Fr *pressentiment*, fr MF, fr *pressentir* to have a presentiment, fr L *praesentire* to feel beforehand, fr *prae-* + *sentire* to feel – more at SENSE] – **presentimental** *adj*

**presently** /ˈprez(ə)ntli/ *adv* **1** before long; soon ⟨*he'll be back ~*⟩ **2** *chiefly NAm & Scot* at the present time; now **3** *archaic* immediately ⟨*dispatch it ~, the hour draws on* – Shak⟩

*usage* The use of **presently** to mean "now" ⟨*he's* **presently** *writing his memoirs*⟩ is now coming back into Southern British English from America, though disapproved of by some people. The sense has always been current in Scotland, and was once used south of the Border too.

**presentment** /priˈzentmənt/ *n* **1** the act of presenting a formal statement to an authority; *specif* a statement made on oath by a jury of a matter of fact within their own knowledge **2** an act of offering at the proper time and place a document (e g a BILL OF EXCHANGE) that calls for acceptance or payment by another **3a** the act of presenting to view or notice **b** something set forth, presented, or exhibited **c** the aspect or form in which something is presented

**present participle** /ˈprez(ə)nt/ *n* a participle (e g *dancing, being*) with present or active meaning

**present perfect** *adj* of or being a verb tense (e g *have finished*) that expresses completion of an action at or before the time of speaking – **present perfect** *n*

**preservationist** /ˌprezəˈvaysh(ə)nist/ *n* a conservationist

¹**preservative** /priˈzuhvətiv/ *adj* having the power of preserving

²**preservative** *n* something that preserves or has the power of preserving; *specif* a substance (e g an ANTIOXIDANT) added to something (e g a food product) to protect against decay, discoloration, or spoilage

¹**preserve** /priˈzuhv/ *vt* **1** to keep safe from injury, harm, or destruction; protect **2a** to keep alive, intact, or free from decay **b** to maintain ⟨*~s her habitual calm at all times*⟩ **3a** to keep or save from decomposition **b** to can, pickle, or similarly prepare (a perishable food) for future use **c** to make a preserve of (fruit) **4** to keep and protect (e g land or game) for private, esp sporting, use ~ *vi* **1** to make preserves **2** to withstand preserving (e g by canning) ⟨*some vegetables do not ~ well*⟩ [ME *preserven*, fr MF *preserver*, fr ML *praeservare*, fr LL, to observe beforehand, fr L *prae-* + *servare* to keep, guard, observe – more at CONSERVE] – **preservable** *adj*, **preservation** *n*, **preserver** *n*

²**preserve** *n* **1** a preparation (e g a jam or jelly) consisting of fruit preserved by cooking whole or in pieces with sugar **2** an area restricted for the protection and preservation of natural resources (e g animals or trees); a reserve; *esp* one used primarily for regulated hunting or fishing – compare RESERVATION 2a, RESERVE 2b **3** something (e g a sphere of activity) regarded as being reserved for certain people ⟨*polo is the ~ of the rich*⟩

**preset** /ˌpreeˈset/ *vt* **-tt-**; **preset** to set beforehand – **preset** *adj*, **presettable** *adj*

**preshrunk** /ˌpreeˈshrunk/ *adj* of or being material (e g a textile fabric) subjected to a shrinking process during manufacture, usu to reduce later shrinking

**preside** /priˈzied/ *vi* **1** to occupy the place of authority; act as president or chairman ⟨*~ at a public meeting*⟩ **2** to exercise guidance, authority, or control ⟨*~d over the tea tray* – Adrian

Bell⟩ **3** to perform as featured or chief instrumentalist – usu + *at* ⟨*~d at the organ*⟩ **4** to be prominent ⟨*the* presiding *genius of the company*⟩ ⟨*a tall tree ~s at the gate*⟩ [L *praesidēre* to guard, preside over, lit., to sit in front of, sit at the head of, fr *prae-* + *sedēre* to sit – more at SIT] – **presider** *n*

**presidency** /ˈprezid(ə)nsi/ *n* **1a** the office of president **b** a governmental institution in some countries (e g the USA) comprising the office of president and various associated administrative and policy-making agencies **2** the term during which a president holds office **3** *formal* the action or function of one who presides; superintendence

**president** /ˈprezid(ə)nt/ *n* **1** an official chosen to preside over a meeting or assembly **2** an appointed governor of a subordinate political unit in some countries **3a** an elected official serving as both head of state and chief political executive in a republic having a PRESIDENTIAL GOVERNMENT **b** an elected official having the position of head of state but usu only minimal political powers in a republic having a PARLIAMENTARY GOVERNMENT **c** the presiding officer of a governmental body in some countries **4** *chiefly NAm* the chief officer of an organization (e g a business corporation or university), usu entrusted with the direction and administration of its policies [ME, fr MF, fr L *praesident-, praesidens*, fr prp of *praesidēre*] – **presidential** *adj*, **presidentially** *adv*, **presidentship** *n*

**presidential government** *n* a system of government in which executive power is vested in a president who is elected separately from the law-making body – compare PARLIAMENTARY GOVERNMENT

**presidial** /priˈsidiəl, -ˈzi-/ *adj* **1** of a president **2** of a province [LL *praesidialis* of a provincial governor, fr L *praesid-, praeses* guard, governor, fr *praesidēre*; (2) Fr *présidial*, fr MF, alter. of *presidal*, fr LL *praesidalis*]

**presidiary** /priˈsidiəri, -ˈzi-/ *adj* of, having, or constituting a garrison [L *praesidarius*, fr *praesidium* defence, garrison, fr *praesid-, praeses*]

**presidio** /priˈsidioh/ *n, pl* **presidios** a garrisoned place; *esp* a military post or fortified settlement in areas currently or originally under Spanish control [Sp, fr L *praesidium*]

**presidium, praesidium** /priˈsidi-əm, -ˈzi-/ *n, pl* **presidia** /-diə/, **presidiums, praesidia, praesidiums** a permanent executive committee selected, esp in Communist countries, to act for a larger, esp governmental, body [Russ *prezidium*, fr L *praesidium* garrison]

**presignify** /ˌpreeˈsignifie/ *vt* to intimate or signify beforehand [L *praesignificare*, fr *prae-* + *significare* to signify]

**ˌpre-Soˈcratic** *adj* of Greek philosophers before Socrates – **pre-Socratic** *n*

¹**press** /pres/ *n* **1a** a crowd of people or crowded condition; a throng **b** an act of thronging or crowding forwards or together **2a** an apparatus or machine by which pressure is applied (e g for shaping material, extracting liquid, or compressing something) **b** a building containing presses; *also* a place of business using presses **3** a cupboard; *esp* a large one for books or clothes **4a** an action of pressing or pushing; pressure **b** an aggressive defence in basketball in which tight marking of the opposing team is employed **5a** PRINTING PRESS **b** the act or process of printing **c** a printing or publishing establishment **6a** *taking sing or pl vb, often cap* **6a(1)** the newspapers and magazines collectively **a(2)** *the* journalists collectively **b** comment or notice in newspapers, magazines, television interviews, etc ⟨*is getting a good ~*⟩ **7** a device for keeping sporting gear (e g a tennis racket) from warping when not in use **8** a lift in weight-lifting in which the weight is raised to shoulder height and then smoothly extended overhead without assistance from the legs – compare CLEAN 2, JERK 3, SNATCH [ME *presse*, fr OF, fr *presser* to press]

²**press** *vt* **1** to push firmly and steadily against; squeeze ⟨*~ed her arm with a meaningful glance*⟩ **2** to assail, harass – esp in **hard-pressed 3a** to squeeze out the juice or contents of **b** to squeeze with apparatus or instruments to a desired density, flatness, smoothness, or shape ⟨*~ flowers*⟩ ⟨*use a steam iron to ~ the pleats*⟩ **c** to iron ⟨*~ed his trousers*⟩ **4a** to exert influence on; constrain **b** to try hard to persuade; entreat **5** to move by means of pressure **6a** to lay stress or emphasis on ⟨*~ing his point at the meeting as far as he dared*⟩ **b** to insist on or request urgently ⟨*~ed her for an answer*⟩ **7** to follow through (a course of action) ⟨*~ed his claim*⟩ **8** to clasp in affection or courtesy ⟨*~ed his hand*⟩ **9** to make copies of (a gramophone record) from a MATRIX (mould) ~ *vi* **1** to crowd closely; mass **2** to force or push one's way ⟨*~ing through the*

*crowd*⟩ **3** to seek urgently; contend ⟨~ing *for salary increases*⟩ **4** to require haste or speed in action ⟨*time is* ~ing⟩ **5** to exert pressure **6** to take or retain a desired shape or condition (eg smoothness) by being pressed [ME *pressen*, fr MF *presser*, fr L *pressare*, fr *pressus*, pp of *premere* to press; akin to L *prelum* press] – **presser** *n*

**press on** *vi* **1** to continue on one's way **2** to proceed in an urgent or resolute manner ⟨*the firm is* pressing on *with its plans for expansion*⟩

³**press** *vt* **1** to force into service, esp in an army or navy **2a** to take by authority, esp for public use; commandeer **b** to take and force into any usu emergency service [alter. (influenced by ²*press*) of obs *prest* to enlist by giving pay in advance, fr *prest* loan of money, advance on wages, fr ME, fr MF, deriv of L *praestare* to supply, pay, fr *prae-* pre- + *stare* to stand]

⁴**press** *n* compulsory enlistment into service, esp in a navy

**press agent** *n* an agent employed to establish and maintain good public relations through publicity [¹*press*]

**press box** *n* a space reserved for reporters (eg at a sports stadium)

**press button** *n* PUSH BUTTON – **press-button** *adj*

**press conference** *n* an interview given by a public figure to journalists by appointment

**press cutting** *n, Br* a paragraph or article cut from a newspaper or magazine

**press gallery** *n* a place set aside for the press, esp in a parliamentary assembly

¹**press-,gang** *n taking sing or pl vb* a detachment of men under command of an officer empowered to force men into military or naval service [⁴*press*]

²**press-gang** *vt* to force into service (as if) by a press-gang ⟨*was* ~ed *into playing cricket in a charity match*⟩

**pressie, prezzie** /'prezi/ *n, informal* a present [by alter.]

¹**pressing** /'presing/ *adj* **1** urgently important; critical **2** earnest, insistent ⟨*a* ~ *invitation*⟩ – **pressingly** *adv*

²**pressing** *n* one or more gramophone records reproduced at one time from a single MATRIX (mould)

**pressman** /-mən; *sense 2 or* -,man/ *n* **1** an operator of a press; *esp* the operator of a printing press **2** *fem* **presswoman** *Br* a journalist; *esp* a newspaper reporter

**pressmark** /'pres,mahk/ *n, chiefly Br* CALL NUMBER (code assigned to a book to indicate its place in a library) [¹*press 3*]

**press of canvas** *n* PRESS OF SAIL

**press office** *n* an office of an organization, esp a government department, from which information concerning the organization's activities is released to the press

**press of sail** *n* the greatest amount of sail that a ship can use

**pressor** /'presə/ *adj* raising or tending to raise blood pressure; *also* tending to constrict the blood vessels [LL, one who or that which presses, fr L *pressus*, pp of *premere* to press – more at PRESS]

**press proof** *n* the last proof to be examined before a piece of text or illustrative material is printed or plated

**press release** *n* a prepared statement released to the news media

**pressroom** /'pres,roohm, -room/ *n* a room in a printing office containing the printing presses

**pressrun** /'pres,run/ *n* a continuous operation of a printing press producing a specific number of copies; *also* the number of copies printed

¹**press-,stud** *n, chiefly Br* a metal fastener consisting essentially of a ball and socket that fasten together, esp to join two sides of a garment opening, when one is pressed into the other

¹**press-,up** *n* an exercise performed face down by raising and lowering the body with the straightening and bending of the arms while keeping the back and legs straight and supporting the body on the hands and toes

¹**pressure** /'preshə/ *n* **1a** the oppression of physical or mental distress ⟨*the* ~ *of family anxieties*⟩ **b** trouble or difficulty resulting from social or economic constraints ⟨*under severe financial* ~⟩ **2** (the state resulting from) the application of force to something by something else in direct contact with it; compression **3** *physics* the force or thrust exerted over a surface divided by the area over which it acts; force per unit area **4** the stress of matters demanding attention ⟨*people who work well under* ~⟩ **5** any of several forces (eg predation) that tend to reduce a population of living organisms and thus influence the course of evolution by NATURAL SELECTION **6** atmospheric pressure **7** the touch sensation aroused by moderate compression of an external body part or surface **8** influence or com-

pulsion directed towards achieving a particular end ⟨*the unions put* ~ *on the government to increase wages*⟩ **9** repeated persistent attack; harassment ⟨*the English batsmen were under* ~ *from the Australian bowlers*⟩ **10** *archaic* an impression, stamp [L *pressura* action of pressing, pressure, fr *pressus*, pp of *premere* to press; (1) ME, fr LL *pressura*, fr L]

²**pressure** *vt* **1** to apply pressure to **2** *chiefly NAm* to pressurize

**pressure cabin** *n* a pressurized cabin

**pressure cooker** *n* a metal vessel with an airtight lid in which superheated steam under pressure produces a temperature greater than that of boiling water for quick cooking or preserving of food – **pressure-cook** *vb*

**pressure gauge** *n* a gauge for indicating the pressure of a gas or liquid

**pressure group** *n taking sing or pl vb* a group organized to influence public, esp governmental policy by active promotion and propaganda of a cause (eg by lobbying and demonstrating)

**pressure point** *n* a point where a blood vessel runs near a bone and can be compressed (eg to check bleeding) by the application of pressure against the bone

**pressure suit** *n* an inflatable suit for high-altitude or space flight to protect the body from low pressure

'**pressur-,ize, -ise** /'preshəriez/ *vt* **1** to maintain near-normal atmospheric pressure in (eg an aircraft cabin) during high-altitude or space flight **2** to apply pressure to ⟨*the team* ~d *the opponents' goal and eventually scored*⟩; *specif* to coerce ⟨*the prisoner's hunger strike* ~d *the authorities into action*⟩ – **pressurizer** *n*, **pressurization** *n*

**presswork** /'pres,wuhk/ *n* the operation, management, or product of a printing press; *esp* the actual transfer of ink from printing surface to paper

**Prestel** /pre'stel, '--/ *trademark* – used for a service provided by British Telecom which transmits information (eg the weather, news, or sports results) on a television screen to subscribers who call it up on the telephone

**presternum** /,pree'stuhnəm/ *n* the front or upper segment of the STERNUM (breastbone) of a mammal; MANUBRIUM [NL]

**prestidigitation** /,presti,diji'taysh(ə)n/ *n, formal or humorous* conjuring; SLEIGHT OF HAND [Fr, fr *prestidigitateur* prestidigitator, fr *preste* nimble, quick (fr It *presto*) + L *digitus* finger – more at TOE] – **prestidigitator** *n*

¹**prestige** /pre'steezh, pre'steej/ *n* **1** high standing or esteem in the eyes of others **2** superiority or desirability in the eyes of society in general resulting from associations of social rank or material success [Fr, fr MF, conjuror's trick, illusion, fr LL *praestigium*, fr L *praestigiae*, pl, conjuror's tricks, irreg fr *praestringere* to tie up, blindfold, fr *prae-* + *stringere* to bind tight – more at STRAIN]

²**prestige** *adj* giving prestige or esteem ⟨*a* ~ *event*⟩ ⟨*a* ~ *executive suite*⟩

**prestigeful** /pre'steezhf(ə)l, -'steej-/ *adj* PRESTIGIOUS 1

**prestigious** /pre'stijəs/ *adj* **1** having or conferring prestige **2** *archaic* of or marked by illusion, conjuring, or trickery [L *praestigiosus*, fr *praestigiae*] – **prestigiously** *adv*, **prestigiousness** *n*

*usage* Although **prestigious** is derived from the Latin *praestigiae* = "conjuror's tricks", its chief meaning today is that associated with "prestige" ⟨*a career in pure science is still more socially* **prestigious**, *in Britain, than one in engineering* – The Times⟩ and the word would probably be misunderstood if used in its earlier sense.

**prestissimo** /pre'stisimoh/ *adv or adj* faster than presto – used as a direction in music [It, superl of *presto*]

¹**presto** /'prestoh/ *adv or adj* at a rapid tempo – used as a tempo direction in music [It, quick, quickly, fr L *praestus* ready, fr *praesto*, adv, on hand; akin to L *prae* before – more at FOR]

²**presto** *n, pl* **prestos** a presto musical passage or movement

³**presto** *interj* HEY PRESTO

¹**prestress** /,pree'stres/ *vt* to introduce internal stresses into (eg a structural beam) to counteract stresses that will result from an applied load ⟨~ *concrete by incorporating cables under tension*⟩

²**prestress** *n* **1** the process of prestressing **2** the stresses introduced in prestress **3** the condition of being prestressed

**presumable** /pri'zyoohməbl/ *adj* capable of being presumed; probable

**presumably** /pri'zyoohməbli/ *adv* as is presumable; it is presumable that ⟨~ *Nick will marry Liz*⟩

**presume** /pri'zyoohm/ *vt* **1** to undertake without leave or justification; dare ⟨*I wouldn't ~ to tell you how to do your job*⟩ **2** to suppose or assume, esp with some degree of certainty **3** to suppose to be true pending proof to the contrary ⟨*~d innocent until proved guilty*⟩ **4** to take for granted; imply ~ *vi* **1** to act or proceed on a presumption; take something for granted **2** to take liberties **3** to take advantage, esp in an unscrupulous manner – usu + *on* or *upon* ⟨*don't ~ on his kindness*⟩ [ME *presumen*, fr LL & MF; LL *praesumere* to dare, fr L, to anticipate, assume, fr *prae-* + *sumere* to take; MF *presumer* to assume, fr L *praesumere* – more at CONSUME] – **presumer** *n*

 **synonyms** Both **presume** and **assume** can mean "suppose", but **presume** is used particularly where one supposes something naturally from the evidence ⟨*Dr Livingstone, I* **presume**?⟩ and **assume** takes something temporarily for granted without proof, as a basis for argument ⟨**assuming**/*let's* **assume** *you don't marry; what will the tax position be?*⟩

**presuming** /pri'zyoohming/ *adj* presumptuous – **presumingly** *adv*

**presumption** /pri'zumpsh(ə)n, pri'zumsh(ə)n/ *n* **1** presumptuous attitude or conduct; effrontery **2a** an attitude or belief based on reasonable evidence or grounds; an assumption **b** the ground, reason, or evidence for presuming something **3** a legal inference as to the existence or truth of a fact not known for certain [ME *presumpcioun*, fr OF *presumption*, fr LL & L; LL *praesumption-*, *praesumptio* presumptuous attitude, fr L, assumption, fr *praesumptus*, pp of *praesumere*]

**presumptive** /pri'zum(p)tiv/ *adj* **1** giving grounds for reasonable opinion or belief ⟨*~ evidence*⟩ **2** based on probability or presumption ⟨*heir ~*⟩ **3a** being a tissue, cell, or region of cells in an embryo that, in the normal course of development, will form a particular tissue, organ, or structure **b** being a presumptive tissue, region, etc that develops into the specified tissue or organ ⟨*~ neural tissue*⟩ △ presumptuous – **presumptively** *adv*

**presumptuous** /pri'zum(p)choo-əs, -tyoo-əs/ *adj* overstepping due bounds; taking liberties [ME, fr MF *presumptueux*, fr LL *praesumptuosus*, irreg fr *praesumptio*] – **presumptuously** *adv*, **presumptuousness** *n*

**presuppose** /,preesə'pohz/ *vt* **1** to suppose beforehand **2** to require logically as a preexisting fact; imply [ME *presupposen*, fr MF *presupposer*, fr ML *praesupponere* (perf indic *praesupposui*), fr L *prae-* + ML *supponere* to suppose – more at SUPPOSE] – **presupposition** *n*

**presynaptic** /,preesi'naptik/ *adj* situated or occurring just before a SYNAPSE (point at which nerve impulses pass from one nerve fibre to another) – **presynaptically** *adv*

**pret-a-porter** /,pret ah 'pawtay/ *adj, of a garment* off-the-peg [Fr *prêt à porter* ready to wear]

**pretax** /,pree'taks/ *adj* existing before tax has been taken into account ⟨*~ earnings*⟩

**preteen** /,pree'teen/ *adj or n* (of or being) a child not yet in his/her teens

**pretence**, *NAm chiefly* **pretense** /pri'tens/ *n* **1** a claim made or implied; *esp* one not supported by fact ⟨*made no ~ to learning*⟩ **2a** mere ostentation; pretentiousness ⟨*a man entirely free of pomp and ~*⟩ **b** a false act or assertion **3** an outward and often insincere or inadequate show; a semblance ⟨*struggling to maintain some ~ of order in the meeting*⟩ **4** professed rather than real intention or purpose; pretext – esp in *false pretences* **5** false show; simulation ⟨*saw through his ~ of indifference*⟩ [ME, fr MF *pretensse*, fr (assumed) ML *praetensa*, fr LL, fem of *praetensus*, pp of L *praetendere*]

**¹pretend** /pri'tend/ *vt* **1** to represent oneself falsely as being, possessing, or performing; profess ⟨*does not ~ that he is a psychiatrist*⟩ **2a** to make believe; feign ⟨*he ~ed deafness*⟩ **b** to claim, represent, or assert falsely ⟨*~ing an emotion he could not really feel*⟩ **3** to venture, presume ⟨*I do not ~ to understand the theory fully*⟩ ~ *vi* **1** to feign an action, part, or role (as if) in play ⟨*she was only ~ing*⟩ **2** to lay claim ⟨*did not ~ to high office*⟩ [ME *pretenden*, fr L *praetendere* to stretch out, extend in front, allege as an excuse, fr *prae-* pre- + *tendere* to stretch – more at THIN]

 **synonyms Pretend, assume, affect, simulate, feign, fake**, and **sham** all mean "put on a deceptive or false appearance". **Assume** suggests a mild, often generous deception ⟨**assumed** *an unconcerned air, in order not to worry her*⟩. **Affect** more strongly suggests falseness: one may **affect** something in order to mislead; to improve one's image; to be in the fashion; or because one admires something ⟨*he* **affects** *a brogue in the country, but speaks without*

*an accent in town*⟩. **Pretend** may involve assumption of a false identity, not undertaken too seriously ⟨*Daddy's* **pretending** *to be a lion*⟩. It may also imply an (often sustained) profession of what is false ⟨**pretended** *to be enjoying the play*⟩. **Simulate** and **feign** are often interchangeable in suggesting an imitation of something in order to deceive. **Simulate** stresses the likeness of an appearance or action ⟨**simulated** *the hoot of an owl as a signal*⟩. **Feign** often implies craftiness ⟨**feigned** *a retreat, then encircled the enemy*⟩. **Fake** is a less formal alternative to either ⟨**faked** *death as the bear sniffed round him*⟩. **Sham** suggests a rather obvious pretence ⟨*actors* **shamming** *dead on the stage*⟩. Compare DISSEMBLE

**²pretend** *adj* make-believe – used esp by children

**pretended** /pri'tendid/ *adj* professed but not genuine ⟨*~ affection*⟩ – **pretendedly** *adv*

**pretender** /pri'tendə/ *n* one who pretends: eg **a** one who lays claim to something; *specif* a claimant to a throne who is held to have no just title **b** one who makes a false or hypocritical show ⟨*a ~ to spirituality* – E L Lawrence⟩

**¹pretension** /pri'tensh(ə)n/ *n* **1** a claim; *also* an effort to establish a claim **2** a claim or right to attention or esteem because of merit or superiority **3** vanity, pretentiousness [ML *praetension-*, *praetensio*, fr LL *praetensus*, pp] – **pretensionless** *adj*

**²pretension** /,pree'tensh(ə)n/ *vt* to prestress [*pre-* + *²tension*]

**pretentious** /pri'tenshəs/ *adj* making usu unjustified or excessive claims (eg of value or standing) ⟨*the ~ fraud who assumes a love of culture that is alien to him* – Richard Watts⟩ △ portentous [Fr *prétentieux*, fr *prétention* pretension, fr ML *praetention-*, *praetentio*, fr L *praetentus*, pp of *praetendere*] – **pretentiously** *adv*, **pretentiousness** *n*

**preter-** /preetə-/ *comb form* beyond; more than ⟨*preterhuman*⟩ [L *praeter* past, by, beyond, fr *prae* before – more at FOR]

**preterite** /'pretərit/ *adj or n* (of or being) a verb tense that expresses action in the past without reference to duration, continuance, or repetition [adj ME *preterit*, fr MF, fr L *praeteritus*, fr pp of *praeterire* to go by, fr *praeter* beyond, past + *ire* to go – more at ISSUE; n fr adj]

**preterm** /,pree'tuhm/ *adj* before a term; *specif* occurring, born, or giving birth before the full time of a normal pregnancy has elapsed ⟨*~ labour*⟩

**preterminal** /,pree'tuhminl/ *adj* occurring in the period preceding death

**pretermit** /,preetə'mit/ *vt* **-tt-** *formal* **1** to let pass without mention or notice; omit **2** to leave undone; neglect [L *praetermittere*, fr *praeter* by, past + *mittere* to let go, send – more at SMITE] – **pretermission** *n*

**preternatural** /,preetə'nachərəl/ *adj, formal* **1** exceeding what is natural or regular; extraordinary ⟨*wits trained to ~ acuteness by the debates* – G L Dickinson⟩ **2** lying beyond or outside normal experience; supernatural ⟨*~ phenomena*⟩ [ML *praeternaturalis*, fr L *praeter naturam* beyond nature] – **preternaturally** *adv*, **preternaturalness** *n*

**pretest** /'pree,test/ *n* a preliminary test serving for exploration rather than valuation – **pretest** *vt*

**pretext** /'preetekst/ *n* a false reason given to disguise the real reason for an action or state of affairs; an excuse **synonyms** see APOLOGY [L *praetextus*, fr *praetextus*, pp of *praetexere* to allege as a pretext, lit., to weave in front, fr *prae-* + *texere* to weave – more at TECHNICAL]

**pretor** /'preetə/ *n, chiefly NAm* PRAETOR (Roman magistrate) – **pretorian** *adj*

**pretreat** /,pree'treet/ *vt* to treat beforehand – **pretreatment** *n or adj*

**prettify** /'pritifie/ *vt* to make pretty or depict prettily, esp in an inappropriate or lacklustre way; *also* to soften, palliate ⟨*attempts to ~ criminal violence*⟩ – **prettification** *n*

**¹pretty** /'priti/ *adj* **1a** attractive or aesthetically pleasing, esp because of delicacy or grace, but less than beautiful ⟨*a ~ girl*⟩ ⟨*a ~ piece of porcelain*⟩ **b** appearing or sounding pleasant or nice but lacking strength, force, manliness, purpose, or intensity ⟨*~ words that make no sense* – Elizabeth Barrett Browning⟩ **2** miserable, terrible ⟨*a ~ mess you've got us into*⟩ **3** moderately large; considerable ⟨*a very ~ profit*⟩ **4** *archaic Scot* stout, brave – see also **a pretty** PENNY **synonyms** see BEAUTIFUL **antonym** plain [ME *praty*, *prety* artful, dainty, fr OE *prættig* tricky, fr *prætt* trick; akin to ON *prettr* trick] – **prettily** *adv*, **prettiness** *n*, **prettyish** *adj*

**²pretty** *adv* **1a** in some degree; rather ⟨*~ comfortable*⟩; *esp* somewhat excessively ⟨*felt ~ sick*⟩ **b** very – used as an intensive to emphasize *much* or *nearly* ⟨*~ nearly ready*⟩ **2** *chiefly dial or informal* in a pretty manner; prettily, neatly ⟨*talking ~*

*to his new girl⟩ ⟨please park ∼⟩* – **sitting pretty** in a highly favourable or satisfying position

³**pretty** *vt, informal* to make pretty – usu + *up ⟨curtains to ∼ up the room⟩*

⁴**pretty** *n, archaic* a pretty person or thing; *esp* a dear or pretty child or young woman – esp in *my pretty*

'**pretty-,pretty** *adj* pretty in an insipid or inappropriate way

**pretty well** *adv* very nearly; almost

**pretzel** /'pretsl/ *n* a brittle salted biscuit typically having the form of a loose knot [Ger *brezel*, deriv of L *brachiatus* having branches like arms, fr *brachium* arm – more at BRACE]

**prevail** /pri'vayl/ *vi* **1** to gain ascendancy through strength or superiority; triumph – often + *against* or *over* **2** to be or become effective or effectual **3** to be frequent; predominate ⟨*the west winds that ∼ in the mountains*⟩ **4** to be or continue in use or fashion; persist ⟨*a custom that still ∼*s⟩ [ME *prevailen*, fr L *praevalēre*, fr *prae-* pre- + *valēre* to be strong – more at WIELD]

  **prevail on/upon/with** *vt* to persuade ⟨prevailed on *him to sing*⟩

**prevailing** /pri'vayling/ *adj* **1** having superior force or influence **2a** most frequent ⟨∼ *winds*⟩ **b** generally current; common ⟨*the ∼ fashion*⟩ – **prevailingly** *adv*

**prevalence** /'prevələns/ *n* **1** the quality or state of being prevalent **2** the degree to which something is prevalent; *esp* the percentage of a population that is affected with a particular disease at a given time

**prevalent** /'prevələnt/ *adj* generally or widely occurring, accepted, practised, or favoured; widespread [L *praevalent-, praevalens* very powerful, fr prp of *praevalēre*] – **prevalently** *adv*

**prevaricate** /pri'varikayt/ *vi* to speak or act evasively so as to hide the truth; equivocate △ procrastinate [L *praevaricatus*, pp of *praevaricari* to straddle, collude, fr *prae-* + *varicus* having the legs spread apart, fr *varus* bent, bow-legged; prob akin to OE *wōh* crooked, L *vacillare* to sway, *vagus* wandering] – **prevaricator** *n*, **prevarication** *n*

**prevenient** /pri'veenyənt, -ni•ənt/ *adj, formal* antecedent, anticipatory [L *praevenient-, praeveniens*, prp of *praevenire*] – **preveniently** *adv*

**prevent** /pri'vent/ *vt* **1** to deprive of power or possibility of acting or succeeding in a purpose **2** to keep from happening or existing ⟨*steps to ∼ war*⟩ **3** to hold or keep back; hinder, stop – often + *from* **4** *archaic* **4a** to meet or satisfy in advance **b** to arrive before **5** *archaic* to go before with spiritual guidance ⟨*O let thy grace ... ever ∼, accompany, and follow me* – Thomas Ken⟩ [ME *preventen* to anticipate, fr L *praeventus*, pp of *praevenire* to come before, anticipate, forestall, fr *prae-* + *venire* to come – more at COME] – **preventable** *also* **preventible** *adj*, **preventer** *n*, **preventability** *n*

  **synonyms** Prevent, preclude, obviate, and forestall can all mean "hinder or stop something happening". The first two may also mean "stop someone from doing something". **Prevent** suggests the taking of active measures, or implies the existence of some insurmountable obstacle ⟨*the guard/a high wall* prevented *them from entering*⟩. **Preclude** suggests that conditions or measures already taken make something or some action impossible ⟨**precluded** *from making the visit by a lack of transport*⟩. **Obviate** suggests making something unnecessary by taking anticipatory measures, especially to avoid difficulty or unpleasantness ⟨*the use of travellers' cheques* **obviates** *the need to carry large sums of money*⟩. **Forestall** suggests anticipatory action to make something powerless or useless ⟨**forestalled** *his attempt to speak of it by quickly changing the subject*⟩. Compare ¹HINDER **antonym** permit **usage** Somebody can **prevent** me from doing something, or **prevent** my doing it ⟨*we tried to* **prevent** *him from drinking*⟩. In formal writing it is best to avoid the construction **prevent** me doing it ⟨*we tried to* **prevent** *him drinking*⟩, although this is common in spoken English.

**prevention** /pri'vensh(ə)n/ *n* the act of preventing or hindering ⟨*crime ∼*⟩

¹**preventive** /pri'ventiv/, **preventative** /-tətiv/ *n* something that prevents; *esp* something used to prevent disease

  **usage** Preventive and preventative (noun and adjective) mean exactly the same thing, but **preventive** is the more usually recommended form.

²**preventive, preventative** *adj* **1** devoted to or concerned with prevention ⟨∼ *steps against soil erosion*⟩ ⟨∼ *medicine*⟩ **2** undertaken to forestall anticipated hostile action – **preventively** *adv*, **preventiveness** *n*

**preventive detention** *n, Br* a prolonged term of imprisonment of 5-14 years for habitual criminals over the age of 30

**preverbal** /,pree'vuhbl/ *adj* **1** occurring before the verb **2** having not yet acquired the faculty of speech ⟨*a ∼ child*⟩

¹**preview** /'pree,vyooh/ *vt* **1a** to see beforehand **b** to view or show in advance of public presentation **2** to write or broadcast a preview of

²**preview** *n* **1** an advance showing or performance (e g of a film or play) **2** a brief view or foretaste of something that is to come; *esp* a brief descriptive notice giving details of a programme soon to be broadcast, a film soon to be released, etc **3** *also* **prevue** *chiefly NAm* a film or television trailer

**previous** /'preevyəs, -vi•əs/ *adj* **1** going before in time or order **2** *informal* acting too soon; premature ⟨*she was a bit ∼ when she said she'd got the job*⟩ [L *praevius* leading the way, fr *prae-* pre- + *via* way – more at VIA] – **previously** *adv*, **previousness** *n* – **previous to** before; PRIOR TO

**previous question** *n* **1** a motion in the House of Commons that the pending question be not put, which if passed has the effect of delaying a vote and enabling the debate to continue **2** a motion in the House of Lords and the US legislature that the question be put, which if passed has the effect of ensuring the debate is ended and a vote taken immediately

**prevision** /,pree'vizh(ə)n/ *n, formal* **1** foresight, prescience **2** a forecast, prognostication [LL *praevision-, praevisio*, fr L *praevisus*, pp of *praevidēre* to foresee, fr *prae-* + *vidēre* to see – more at WIT] – **previsional, previsionary** *adj*

**prevocalic** /,preevə'kalic, -voh-/ *adj* immediately preceding a vowel [ISV]

**prevocational** /,preevoh'kaysh(ə)nl/ *adj* given or required before admission to a vocational college or school

**prewar** /,pree'waw/ *adj* of or being the period preceding a war, esp World War I or II

¹**prey** /pray/ *n* **1a** an animal taken by a predator as food – compare BIRD OF PREY **b** one who or that which is helpless or unable to resist attack; a victim ⟨*was ∼ to his own appetites*⟩ **2** the act or habit of preying ⟨*a beast of ∼*⟩ [ME *preie*, fr OF, fr L *praeda*; akin to L *prehendere* to grasp, seize – more at PREHENSILE]

²**prey** *vi* **1** to make plundering raids ⟨*pirates ∼ed on the coast*⟩ **2a** to seize and devour prey ⟨*kestrels ∼ upon mice*⟩ **b** to live by extortion, deceit, or exerting undue influence ⟨*confidence tricksters ∼ing on elderly women*⟩ **3** to have an injurious, destructive, or wasting effect ⟨*troubles that ∼ on one's mind*⟩ □ usu + *on* or *upon* [ME *preyen*, fr OF *preier*, fr L *praedari*, fr *praeda*] – **preyer** *n*

**prezzie** /'prezi/ *n, informal* a present [by alter.]

**prial** /'prie•əl/ *n* THREE OF A KIND (three playing cards of the same value) in the games of BRAG and CRIBBAGE and their variants [alter. of *pair royal*]

**priapic** /prie'aypik, -'apik/ *adj* phallic [L *Priapus*, god of male generative power, fr Gk *Priapos*]

**priapism** /'prie•ə,piz(ə)m/ *n* continuous abnormal often painful erection of the penis

¹**price** /pries/ *n* **1a** the quantity of one thing that is exchanged or demanded in barter or sale for another **b** the amount of money given or asked for the sale of something **2** the terms for the sake of which something is done or undertaken: e g **2a** an amount sufficient to bribe someone ⟨*believed every man had his ∼*⟩ **b** a reward for the catching or killing of a person ⟨*a man with a ∼ on his head*⟩ **3** the cost at which something is obtained ⟨*the ∼ of freedom is eternal vigilance*⟩ **4** *archaic* value, worth ⟨*her ∼ is far above rubies* – Prov 31:10(AV)⟩ [ME *pris*, fr OF, fr L *pretium* price, money; akin to Skt *prati-* against, in return – more at PROS-]

²**price** *vt* **1** to set a price on **2** to find out the price of – **pricer** *n*

'**price-,cutting** *n* the practice of reducing prices, esp to a level designed to undermine competition

**-priced** /-priest/ *comb form* (→ *adj*) set at (such) a price ⟨*low-priced merchandise*⟩

**price-earnings ratio** *n* a measure of the value of ORDINARY SHARES determined as the ratio of their market price to their earnings per share

**price index** *n* a number expressing the level of a group of commodity prices relative to the level of the prices of the same commodities during an arbitrarily chosen base period and used to indicate changes in the level of prices from one period to another – **price indexing** *n*

**priceless** /'prieslis/ *adj* **1a** having a value beyond any price; invaluable **b** costly because of rarity or quality; precious **2** having worth in terms of other than market value ⟨*a pair of* *well-worn comfortable walking shoes is* ~〉 **3** *informal* particularly amusing, odd, or absurd 〈*told me this* ~ *story*〉 **synonyms** SEE INVALUABLE

**'price-,ring** *n taking sing or pl vb* a group of traders acting in agreement to maintain prices

**price support** *n* artificial maintenance of prices (e g of a raw material) at some predetermined level, usu through government action

**price tab** *n* PRICE TAG

**price tag** *n* **1** a label on merchandise showing the price at which it is offered for sale **2** price, cost 〈*the* ~ *of private education is becoming prohibitive*〉

**price war** *n* a period of commercial competition characterized by the repeated cutting of prices below those of competitors

**pricey** *also* **pricy** /'priesi/ *adj, chiefly Br informal* dear, expensive

**¹prick** /prik/ *n* **1** a mark or shallow hole made by a pointed instrument **2** a sharp projecting organ or part (e g a thorn) of a plant or animal **3** an instance of pricking or the sensation of being pricked: e g **3a** a nagging or sharp feeling of remorse, regret, or sorrow **b** a slight sharply localized discomfort 〈*the* ~ *of a needle*〉 **4** *vulg* the penis **5** *vulg* a disagreeable or contemptible person [ME *prikke,* fr OE *prica;* akin to MD *pric* prick] – **kick against the pricks** to struggle against irksome controls, esp futilely [fr *prick* in the obs sense "goad for oxen"]

**²prick** *vt* **1** to pierce slightly with a sharp point **2** to affect with anguish, grief, or remorse 〈*doubts began to* ~ *him*〉 **3** to ride, guide, or urge on (as if) with spurs; goad 〈*desperation* ~ed *him on to greater efforts*〉 **4** to mark, distinguish, or note by means of a small mark **5** to trace or outline with punctures **6** *of an animal* to cause (the ears) to be or stand erect ~ *vi* **1a** to prick something or cause a pricking sensation **b** to feel discomfort as if from being pricked **2** *archaic* **2a** to urge a horse with the spur **b** to ride fast – see also **prick up one's** EARS

**prick out** *vt* to transplant (seedlings) from the place of germination to a more permanent position (e g a flower bed)

**pricked** /prikt/ *adj, of wine* acetified through exposure to the air or age; vinegary [trans of Fr *piqué,* fr *piquer* to prick]

**pricker** /'prikə/ *n* **1** one who or that which pricks **2** a prickle, thorn

**pricket** /'prikit/ *n* **1** (a candlestick having) a spike on which a candle is stuck **2** a male deer, esp a male FALLOW DEER, two years old – compare BROCKET [ME *priket,* fr *prikke;* (2) fr its straight unbranched antlers]

**¹prickle** /'prikl/ *n* **1** a fine sharp part or projection; *esp* a sharp pointed part arising from the outer layer of a plant stem, leaf, etc **2** a prickling or tingling sensation [ME *prikle,* fr OE *pricle;* akin to OE *prica* prick]

**²prickle** *vt* **1** to prick slightly **2** to produce prickles in ~ *vi* to cause or feel a prickling or stinging sensation; tingle

**prickly** /'prik(ə)li/ *adj* **1** full of or covered with prickles; *esp* distinguished from a similar or related kind of animal or esp plant by the presence of prickles **2** marked by prickling; stinging 〈*a* ~ *sensation*〉 **3a** troublesome, vexatious 〈~ *issues*〉 **b** easily irritated 〈*had a* ~ *disposition*〉 – **prickliness** *n*

**prickly heat** *n* a skin rash marked by red spots and intense itching and tingling, that is caused by inflammation round the sweat ducts

**prickly pear** *n* (the pulpy pear-shaped edible fruit of) any of a genus (*Opuntia*) of cacti with yellow flowers and jointed flat or cylindrical stems usu studded with small swellings bearing spines or prickly hairs

**prickly poppy** *n* any of a genus (*Argemone,* esp *Argemone mexicana*) of plants of the poppy family with prickly leaves and white or yellow flowers

**prickteaser** /'prik,teezə/ *n, derog slang* COCKTEASER (sexually provocative woman) – **pricktease** *vb*

**pricy** /'priesi/ *adj* pricey

**priddy oggy** /'pridi/ *n* OGGY (Cornish pasty) [*priddy* (prob alter. of *pratie*) + *oggy,* of unknown origin]

**pride** /pried/ *n* **1** the quality or state of being proud: e g **1a** excessive self-esteem; conceit **b** a reasonable or justifiable self-respect **c** delight or elation arising from some act, possession, or relationship 〈*parental* ~〉 **2** proud or disdainful behaviour or treatment **3** the highest pitch; the prime 〈*in the* ~ *of one's life*〉 **4** a source of pride; *esp, taking sing or pl vb* the best in a group or class 〈*this pup is the* ~ *of the litter*〉 **5** *taking sing or pl vb* a group of lions [ME, fr OE *prȳde,* fr *prūd* proud – more at PROUD] – **prideful** *adj*

**synonyms Pride, conceit, vanity,** and **vainglory** all suggest an excessive awareness of or belief in one's own excellence or superiority. **Pride** in this sense is contrasted with "humility", and expresses itself in disdainfulness or haughty arrogance. Compare PROUD. **Conceit** and **conceited** imply an exaggerated opinion of one's own ability or worth. **Vanity** and **vain** suggest an excessive desire for admiration, total self-centredness, and too great a concern for trifles, especially for one's appearance. **Vainglory** and **vainglorious** suggest the expression of pride in boastfulness or display 〈*vainglorious old colonels, dripping with medals*〉. **antonyms** humility, modesty

**pride of place** *n* the highest or first position 〈*gave* ~ *in the show to an enormous home-grown marrow*〉

**pride on, pride upon** *vt* to be proud of (oneself) because of 〈*prided himself on his generosity*〉

**prie-dieu** /'pree ,dyuh/ *n, pl* **prie-dieux** /~/ **1** a kneeling bench designed for use by a person at prayer and fitted with a raised shelf on which the elbows or a book may be rested **2** a low armless upholstered chair with a high straight back [Fr, lit., pray God]

**prier** /'priə/ *n* one who pries; *esp* an inquisitive person

**priest** /preest/ *n* a person authorized to perform the sacred rites of a religion, esp as an intermediary agent between man and God; *specif* a clergyman ranking below a bishop and above a deacon (e g in the Anglican, Orthodox, and Roman Catholic churches) [ME *preist,* fr OE *prēost,* modif of LL *presbyter,* fr Gk *presbyteros* elder, priest, compar of *presbys* old man]

**priestess** /'pree'stes, 'preestis/ *n* a female priest of a non-Christian religion

**priest hole, priest's hole** *n* a secret room or place of concealment for a priest (e g in an English house during the persecution of Roman Catholic priests)

**priesthood** /'preest·hood/ *n* **1** the office or character of a priest **2** *taking sing or pl vb* the whole body of priests

**priest in charge** *n* a parish priest in the Church of England who serves at the pleasure of the ORDINARY (clergyman having certain jurisdictional powers)

**priestly** /'preestli/ *adj* **1** of a priest or the priesthood **2** characteristic of or suitable to a priest – **priestliness** *n*

**'priest-,ridden** *adj* controlled or oppressed by priests

**prig** /prig/ *n* one who is excessively self-righteous or affectedly precise about observing proprieties (e g of speech or manners) [arch. *prig* fop, unpleasant person, prob fr *prig* tinker, thief, of unknown origin] – **priggery** *n,* **priggish** *adj,* **priggishly** *adv,* **priggishness, priggism** *n*

**prill** /pril/ *vt* to convert (a solid) into granules or pellets (e g by melting and letting molten drops solidify); *also* to make (a granular or crystalline material) fluid or free-flowing [perh fr E dial. *prill* a running stream, alter. of ³*purl*] – **prill** *n*

**¹prim** /prim/ *vt* **-mm-** to give a prim or demure expression to 〈~*ming her thin lips after every mouthful* – John Buchan〉 [origin unknown]

**²prim** *adj* **-mm-** **1a** stiffly formal and proper **b** prudish **2** neat, trim 〈~ *hedges*〉 – **primly** *adv,* **primness** *n*

**prima ballerina** /'preemə/ *n* the principal female dancer in a ballet company [It, leading ballerina]

**primacy** /'prieməsi/ *n* **1** the state of being first (e g in importance, order, or rank); preeminence 〈*the* ~ *of artistry over mechanical skill*〉 **2** the office, rank, or preeminence of a PRIMATE (high-ranking bishop)

**prima donna** /,preemə 'donə/ *n* **1** a principal female singer (e g in an opera company) **2** an extremely sensitive, vain, or temperamental person [It, lit., first lady]

**primaeval** /prie'meevl/ *adj, chiefly Br* primeval

**'prima facie** /,preemə 'fayshi/ *adv* at first view; on the first appearance 〈*his arguments appear* ~ *true*〉 [L]

**²prima facie** *adj* **1** true, valid, or sufficient at first impression; apparent 〈*the theory gives a* ~ *solution* – R J Butler〉 **2** legally sufficient to establish a fact or a case unless disproved 〈~ *evidence*〉

**¹primal** /'prieml/ *adj* **1** original, primitive 〈~ *innocence*〉 **2** first in importance; fundamental 〈*our* ~ *concern*〉 [ML *primalis,* fr L *primus* first – more at PRIME] – **primality** *n*

**²primal** *n* a reexperiencing of some disturbing or frustrating experience from the earliest years of life, esp within the context of PRIMAL THERAPY

**³primal** *vi* **-ll-** (*NAm* **-l-, -ll-**) to experience a primal – **primaller** *n*

**primal therapy** *n* a form or technique of psychotherapy that aims to take a patient back to a very early frustrating experience so that by reliving it he/she may unblock the suppressed rage or frustration that lies at the bottom of his/her personal and social problems

**primarily** /'priem(ə)rəli; *also* prie'merəli/ *adv* **1** chiefly; FOR THE MOST PART ⟨*has now become ~ industrial*⟩ **2** in the first place; originally

     *usage* The pronunciation /'priem(ə)rəli/ is recommended for BBC broadcasters.

¹**primary** /'priem(ə)ri/ *adj* **1a** first in order of time or development; primitive ⟨*the ~ stage of civilization*⟩ **b** of (geological formations of) the PALAEOZOIC and earlier periods **2a** of first rank, importance, or value; principal ⟨*the ~ purpose*⟩ **b** basic, fundamental ⟨*security is a ~ need*⟩ **c** of or being an industry that produces raw materials ⟨*mining is a ~ industry*⟩ **d** of a Latin, Greek, or Sanskrit verb tense expressing present or future time **e** of or being the strongest degree of stress in speech ⟨*the first syllable of* basketball *carries ~ stress*⟩ **3a** direct, firsthand ⟨*~ sources of information*⟩ **b** not derivable from other colours, odours, or tastes **c** preparatory to something else in a continuing process ⟨*~ instruction*⟩ **d** of or at a PRIMARY SCHOOL ⟨*~ education*⟩ **e** belonging to the first group in a series of successive groups formed by division, combination, or branching ⟨*~ nerves*⟩ **f** of or being the electrical current or the circuit round which it flows, that induces a current in a neighbouring circuit in an INDUCTION COIL, TRANSFORMER, etc **g** directly derived from ores ⟨*~ metals*⟩ **h** of or being the sequence of chemical compounds making up a large biological molecule (e g DNA); *esp* of or being the AMINO ACID sequence in a protein ⟨*the ~ structure of a protein*⟩ **4** *chemistry* **4a** characterized by or resulting from the replacement of one of two or more replaceable atoms or chemical groups in a molecule by another atom or group ⟨*a ~ phosphate*⟩ **b**(1) being or containing a carbon atom united to one other carbon atom ⟨*a ~ compound*⟩ **b**(2) being a chemical group attached to a primary carbon atom **c** *of an* AMINE having the nitrogen atom attached to one carbon atom and two hydrogen atoms; containing the group $NH_2$ **5a** of, involving, or derived directly from a PRIMARY MERISTEM ⟨*~ tissue*⟩ ⟨*~ growth*⟩ ⟨*a ~ stem*⟩ **b** of or being the first-formed water- or food-conducting tissue (XYLEM or PHLOEM) of a plant, that develops from PROCAMBIUM **6** of or involved in the production of organic substances (e g sugars) by means of photosynthesis carried out by green plants or bacteria ⟨*~ productivity*⟩ [LL *primarius* basic, primary, fr L, principal, fr *primus* first]

²**primary** *n* **1** *usu pl* something that stands first in rank, importance, or value; a fundamental **2a** a planet as distinguished from its satellites **b** the brighter component of a DOUBLE STAR **3** *primary, primary feather* any of the usu nine or ten strong feathers on the joint of a bird's wing furthest from the body **4** *primary colour, primary* any of a set of three colours from which all other colours of the spectrum can be obtained by suitable combinations, but which themselves cannot be made by mixing other colours: **4a** any of the three bands of red, green, and bluish-violet light, that when mixed in equal proportions give WHITE LIGHT (light containing all colours of the spectrum) **b** any of the three coloured pigments red, yellow, and blue, or magenta, yellow, and cyan **5** a US election in which qualified voters nominate or express a preference for a particular candidate or group of candidates for political office, choose party officials, or select delegates for a party convention; *also, NAm* CAUCUS (closed political meeting) **6** *primary school, primary* a school for pupils usu aged between five and eleven

**primary cell** *n* a CELL (device for producing an electric current) that converts chemical energy into electrical energy by irreversible chemical reactions and that cannot be recharged by passing an electric current through it – compare STORAGE CELL

**primary coil** *n* the electrical COIL through which the primary current passes in an INDUCTION COIL, TRANSFORMER, etc

**primary consumer** *n* HERBIVORE (plant-eating animal) – compare SECONDARY CONSUMER, TERTIARY CONSUMER

**primary meristem** *n* any of the MERISTEMS (plant tissues capable of dividing to form new cells and tissues) that are derived directly from cells in the plant embryo and that are active in producing new cells throughout the plant's life

**primary root** *n* the root of a plant that develops first and originates from the RADICLE (root of a seedling)

**primary syphilis** *n* the first stage of syphilis, that is marked by the development of a deep ulcer (CHANCRE) and the spread

of the causative bacterium (SPIROCHAETE) throughout the tissues of the body

**primary tooth** *n* MILK TOOTH

**primate** /'priemayt *or* (*esp in sense 1*) -mət/ *n* **1** *often cap* a bishop who has precedence in a province, group of provinces, or nation **2** any of an order (Primates) of mammals, including human beings, the apes, monkeys, and related forms (e g lemurs and TARSIERS), that have hands or feet adapted for grasping and a relatively large brain [ME *primat*, fr OF, fr ML *primat-*, *primas* archbishop, fr L, leader, fr *primus* first] – **primateship** *n*, **primatial** *adj*

**primatology** /ˌpriemə'toləji/ *n* the study of primates, esp those other than recent man – **primatologist** *n*, **primatological** *adj*

¹**prime** /priem/ *n* **1** *often cap* the second of the CANONICAL HOURS (prescribed services of Christian worship), that was originally held at 6 am **2** the earliest stage **3** the most active, thriving, or successful stage or period ⟨*in the ~ of his life*⟩ **4** the chief or best individual or part; *the* pick ⟨*the ~ of the flock, and choicest of the stall* – Alexander Pope⟩ **5** *prime number, prime* a positive integer except the number one (1) that has no factor except itself and 1 **6** the first note or tone of a musical scale; TONIC **2 7** the symbol ′ used in mathematics as a distinguishing mark (e g in denoting DERIVATIVES of a function) [ME, fr OE *prīm*, fr L *prima hora* first hour]

²**prime** *adj* **1** first in time; original **2** of or being a prime number ⟨*a ~ factor*⟩ – compare RELATIVELY PRIME **3a** first in rank, authority, or significance; principal **b** *of meat, esp beef* of the highest grade or best quality regularly sold **4** not deriving from something else; primary [ME, fr MF, fem of *prin* first, fr L *primus;* akin to L *prior* former, first] – **primely** *adv*, **primeness** *n*

³**prime** *vt* **1** to fill, load; *esp* to fill or ply (a person) with alcohol **2** to prepare (a firearm or charge) for firing by supplying with priming or a primer **3** to apply a first coat (e g of paint or oil) to (a surface), esp in preparation for painting **4** to put into working order by filling or charging with something ⟨*~ a pump with water*⟩ **5** to instruct beforehand; coach ⟨*~d the witness*⟩ **6** to stimulate **7** to harvest (tobacco leaves) by picking a few leaves at a time as they ripen *~ vi* to become prime [prob fr ¹*prime*]

⁴**prime** /preem/ *n* a prize (e g of points or money) awarded in a bicycle road race to the first rider to reach a predetermined intermediate point (e g the top of a hill) [Fr, premium, bonus, fr E *premium*]

**prime cost** *n* the combined total of raw material and direct labour costs incurred in production

**prime meridian** *n* a MERIDIAN (imaginary semicircle passing through both geographical poles) from which longitude is measured; *specif* the line of 0° longitude which runs through the original site of the Royal Observatory at Greenwich and from which other longitudes are calculated east and west

**prime minister** *n, often cap P&M* **1** the chief minister of a ruler or state **2** the official head of a cabinet or ministry; *esp* the chief executive of a parliamentary government – **prime ministerial** *adj*, **prime ministership** *n*, **prime ministry** *n*

**prime mover** *n* **1** God as the creator and first cause of the universe **2a** an initial source of motive power (e g a windmill, waterwheel, turbine, or INTERNAL-COMBUSTION ENGINE) designed to receive and modify force and motion as supplied by some natural source and apply them to drive machinery **b** a powerful tractor or truck, usu with all-wheel drive **3** the original or most influential force in a development or undertaking ⟨*he was a ~ in the reform of the constitution*⟩

¹**primer** /'priemə/ *n* **1** a small book for teaching children to read **2** a small introductory book on a subject [ME, fr ML *primarium*, fr LL, neut of *primarius* primary]

²**primer** *n* **1a** a device, esp a PERCUSSION CAP, used for igniting a charge **b** a molecule (e g of DNA) whose presence is required for the formation of more molecules of the same kind **2** material used in priming a surface

**prime rate, prime interest rate** *n* an interest rate at which preferred customers can borrow from banks and which is the lowest commercial interest rate available at a particular time and place

**primero** /pri'meəroh/ *n* a card game popular in the 16th and 17th centuries, from which the game of BRAG was partly derived [modif of Sp *primera*, fr fem of *primero* first, fr L *primarius* principal]

**prime time** *n* the peak television viewing time, for which the highest rates are charged for advertisers

**primeval**, *Br also* **primaeval** /prie'meevl/ *adj* **1** of the earliest ages ⟨*vestigial traces of* ~ *forest*⟩ **2** existing in or persisting from the beginning (e g of a solar system or universe) ⟨*a* ~ *gas cloud*⟩ [L *primaevus*, fr *primus* first + *aevum* age – more at AYE] – **primevally** *adv*

**priming** /'prieming/ *n* **1** the act of one who or that which primes **2** the explosive used for igniting a charge **3** a category of FLUE-CURED tobacco consisting of the small leaves pulled from the very bottom of the plant stalk

**primipara** /prie'mipərə/ *n, pl* **primiparas, primiparae** /-rie/ **1** a woman who is pregnant for the first time **2** a woman who has had only one child [L, fr *primus* first + *-para*] – **primiparity** *n*, **primiparous** *adj*

¹**primitive** /'primətiv/ *adj* **1a** not derived; original, primary **b** assumed as a basis; *esp* axiomatic ⟨~ *concepts*⟩ **2a** of the earliest age or period; primeval ⟨*the* ~ *church*⟩ **b** *biology* **b(1)** PRIMORDIAL 1b **b(2)** closely approximating to an early ancestral type; little evolved ⟨~ *mammals*⟩ **c** belonging to or characteristic of an early stage of development; crude, rudimentary ⟨~ *technology*⟩ **d** of or constituting the assumed parent speech of related languages ⟨~ *Germanic*⟩ **3a** elemental, natural ⟨*the noble savage endowed with* ~ *virtue* – Oscar Handlin⟩ **b** of or produced by a relatively simple people or culture ⟨~ *art*⟩ **c** lacking in sophistication or subtlety; simple, crude **d(1)** self-taught, untutored ⟨~ *craftsmen*⟩ **d(2)** produced by a self-taught artist ⟨*a* ~ *painting*⟩ [ME *primitif*, fr L *primitivus*, fr *primitus* originally, fr *primus* first – more at PRIME] – **primitively** *adv*, **primitiveness, primitivity** *n*

²**primitive** *n* **1a** something primitive; *specif* a primitive concept, term, or proposition **b** a basic simple word not formed with any prefixes, suffixes, etc **2a(1)** an artist of an early period of a culture or artistic movement; *esp* an artist of the period preceding the Renaissance **a(2)** a later imitator or follower of such an artist **b(1)** a self-taught artist **b(2)** an artist whose work is marked by directness and naiveté **c** a work of art produced by a primitive artist **3a** a member of a primitive people **b** an unsophisticated person

**Primitive Methodist** *n* a member of a former Methodist sect that broke away from the main body of the church in 1810

**primitivism** /'primitiviz(ə)m/ *n* **1** belief in the superiority of a simple way of life close to nature or without the acquisitions of modern civilization **2** the style of art of primitive peoples or primitive artists – **primitivist** *n or adj*, **primitivistic** *adj*

**primo** /'preemoh/ *n, pl* **primos** the first or leading part (e g in a duet or trio) [It, fr *primo* first, fr L *primus*]

**primogenitor** /ˌpriemoh'jenətə/ *n* an ancestor, forefather [LL, fr L *primus* + *genitor* begetter, fr *genitus*, pp of *gignere* to beget – more at KIN]

**primogeniture** /ˌpriemoh'jenichə/ *n* **1** the state or fact of being the firstborn of the children of the same parents **2** the principle by which right of inheritance or succession belongs to the eldest son [LL *primogenitura*, fr L *primus* + *genitura* birth, fr *genitus*, pp]

**primordial** /prie'mawdyəl/ *adj* **1a** first created or developed; primeval **b** *biology* earliest formed in the development of an individual or structure **2** fundamental, primary ⟨~ *human joys* – Sir Winston Churchill⟩ [ME, fr LL *primordialis*, fr L *primordium* origin, fr neut of *primordius* original, fr *primus* first + *ordiri* to begin – more at PRIME, ORDER] – **primordially** *adv*

**primordial soup** *n* the liquid mixture of chemical molecules (e g AMINO ACIDS, fats, and sugars) from which life on earth is thought to have originated

**primordium** /prie'mawdyəm/ *n, pl* **primordia** /-diə/ a part or organ in its earliest form or stage of development when first identifiable as a particular structure [NL, fr L]

**primp** /primp/ *vt* to dress, adorn, or arrange in a careful or finicky manner ~ *vi* to dress or groom oneself carefully ⟨~ s *for hours before going to a party*⟩ [perh alter. of ¹*prim*]

**primrose** /'primrohz/ *n* **1** any of several plants (genus *Primula* of the family Primulaceae, the primrose family) with large tufted usu crinkled leaves and showy variously coloured flowers; *esp* one (*Primula vulgaris*) that is common throughout Europe and bears pale yellow flowers in early spring **2** a pale yellow colour [ME *primerose*, fr MF, fr OF, prob fr *prime* first + *rose* rose ]

**primrose path** *n* **1** a path of ease or pleasure, esp sensual pleasure ⟨*himself the* ~ *of dalliance treads* – Shak⟩ **2** a path of least resistance; *esp* one leading to disaster

**primula** /'primyoolə/ *n* a (cultivated) primrose [ML, fr *primula veris*, lit., firstling of spring]

**primum mobile** /ˌpriemoom 'mohbili/ *n, pl* **primum mobiles** /-leez/ the outermost of the concentric spheres that made up the universe in medieval astronomy, which carried the spheres of the fixed stars and the planets round with it in its daily revolution [ME, fr ML, lit., first moving thing]

**primus** /'priemus/ *n, often cap* the presiding bishop of the Scottish EPISCOPAL church [ML, one who is first, magnate, fr L, first – more at PRIME]

**Primus** /'priemus/ *trademark* – used for a portable oil-burning stove used chiefly for cooking (e g when camping)

**primus inter pares** /ˌpriemus intə 'peəreez, 'pahriz/ *n* first among equals [L]

**prince** /prins/ *n* **1** the ruler of a principality or state **2** a male member of a royal family; *esp* a son or grandson of a sovereign **3** any of various noblemen **4** a person of high rank or of high standing in his class or profession ⟨*a merchant* ~⟩ ⟨*a* ~ *among poets*⟩ [ME, fr OF, fr L *princip-, princeps* leading person, chief, lit., one who takes the first part, fr *primus* first + *capere* to take – more at HEAVE] – **princeship** *n*

**Prince Albert** /'albət/ *n, chiefly NAm* a long double-breasted FROCK COAT [Prince *Albert* Edward (later Edward VII king of England) †1910, who set the fashion of wearing it]

**prince charming** *n* a suitor who fulfils the dreams of his beloved; *also* a man whose charm towards women is often untrustworthy [*Prince Charming*, hero of the fairy tale *Cinderella* by Charles Perrault †1703 Fr writer]

**prince consort** *n, pl* **princes consort** the husband of a reigning female sovereign – used only after the title has been specifically conferred by the sovereign

**princedom** /'prinsdəm/ *n* **1** the rank, office, or territory of a prince **2** *pl* PRINCIPALITY 3 (order of angels) ⟨~ s *and powers*⟩

**prince imperial** *n* the male heir to an emperor's throne

**princeling** /'prinsling/, **princelet** /'prinslit/ *n* a petty or insignificant prince

**princely** /'prinsli/ *adj* **1** of a prince; royal **2** befitting a prince; noble, magnificent ⟨~ *manners*⟩ ⟨*a* ~ *sum*⟩ – **princeliness** *n*, **princely** *adv*

**Prince of Wales** /waylz/ *n* the male heir to the British throne – used only after the title has been specifically conferred by the sovereign

**prince's-'feather** *n* a showy plant (*Amaranthus hybridus hypochondriacus*) of the amaranth family often cultivated for its dense spikes of usu red flowers

¹**princess** /ˌprin'ses *as an ordinary word, usu* 'prinses *or* 'prinsəs *before a name*/ *n* **1** a female member of a royal family; *esp* a daughter or granddaughter of a sovereign **2** the wife or widow of a prince **3** a woman having in her own right the rank of a prince **4** a woman or something personified as female that is outstanding in a specified respect ⟨*a* ~ *of a violinist*⟩ ⟨*a winding* ~ *of a river*⟩

²**princess, princesse** /prin'ses, 'prinses/ *adj* closely fitting at the top, flared from the hips to the hemline, and having GORES (triangular pieces) or panels ⟨*dress with* ~ *line*⟩ [Fr *princesse* princess, fr *prince*]

**princess royal** *n, pl* **princesses royal** the eldest daughter of a sovereign – used only after the title has been specifically conferred by the sovereign

¹**principal** /'prinsipl/ *adj* **1** most important, consequential, or influential; chief **2** of or constituting principal or a principal *usage* see PRINCIPLE [ME, fr OF, fr L *principalis*, fr *princip-, princeps*] – **principally** *adv*

²**principal** *n* **1** a person who has controlling authority or is in a leading position: e g **1a** the head of an educational institution (e g a college) **b** one who employs another to act for him/her subject to general control and instruction; *specif* the person from whom an agent's authority derives **c** the chief or an actual participant in a crime **d** the person primarily or ultimately liable on a legal obligation **e** a leading performer (e g in a play, opera, or group of musicians) **2** a matter or thing of primary importance: e g **2a(1)** a sum of money invested to accumulate interest, due as a debt, or used as a fund **a(2)** the original amount of an estate, bequest, etc, as distinct from any income derived from it **b** a main rafter of a roof – **principalship** *n*

**principal boy** *n* the role of the hero in British pantomime, traditionally played by a girl

**principal clause** *n* a main clause (e g in a sentence)

**principal diagonal** *n* the diagonal in a SQUARE MATRIX (array of mathematical elements) that runs from upper left to lower right

**principality** /ˌprinsi'paləti/ *n* **1** the state, office, or authority of a prince **2** the territory or jurisdiction of a prince; the country that gives title to a prince **3** *pl* the seventh of the nine orders of angelic beings in the CELESTIAL HIERARCHY ranking immediately below POWERS and above ARCHANGELS

**principal parts** *n pl* that series of verb forms from which all the other forms of a verb can be derived, including in English the infinitive, the past tense, and the PAST PARTICIPLE

**principium** /prin'kipiəm, -'sip-/ *n, pl* **principia** /-piə/ a fundamental principle ⟨*Bertrand Russell's "Principia Mathematica"*⟩ [L, beginning, basis]

**principle** /'prinsipl/ *n* **1a** a universal and fundamental law, doctrine, or assumption ⟨*the* ~s *of physics*⟩ **b(1)** a rule or code of conduct **b(2)** habitual devotion to principles ⟨*a man of* ~⟩ **b(3)** the underlying idea or philosophy ⟨*he objects to the* ~ *of the thing, not the method*⟩ **c** the laws or facts of nature underlying the working of an artificial device ⟨*the* ~ *of the internal-combustion engine*⟩ **2** a primary source; a fundamental element ⟨*the ancients emphasized the opposing* ~s *of heat and cold, moisture and dryness*⟩ **3** an underlying faculty or attribute ⟨*such* ~s *of human nature as greed and curiosity*⟩ **4** a constituent (e g a chemical) that has or imparts a characteristic quality – compare BITTER PRINCIPLE [ME, modif of MF *principe*, fr L *principium* beginning, fr *princip-*, *princeps* one taking the first part – more at PRINCE] – **in principle** with respect to the underlying idea or philosophy – **on principle** because of the principle involved rather than the details

*usage* Principle can be only a noun, and a person can never be a **principle**. Principal can be either an adjective ⟨*the* **principal** *reason*⟩ or a noun ⟨*the* **principal** *of the college*⟩ ⟨*receive interest on our* **principal**⟩.

**principled** /'prinsipəld/ *adj* showing, based on, or characterized by principle – often in combination ⟨*high*-principled⟩

**principle of proximity** *n* an observation in linguistics: a verb may agree with the nearest noun or pronoun rather than with the grammatical subject (e g in "one in five are French") – see "Ten Vexed Points"

**prink** /pringk/ *vb* to primp [prob alter. of ²*prank*] – **prinker** *n*

¹**print** /print/ *n* **1a** a mark made by pressure; an impression **b** something impressed with a print or formed in a mould **2** a device or instrument for impressing or forming a print **3** printed state or form **4** printed matter **5** printed letters; type – compare SMALL PRINT **6a(1)** a copy made by printing **a(2)** a reproduction of an original work of art (e g a painting) made by a photographic process **a(3)** an original work of art reproduced from a wooden block or an engraved stone or metal plate and produced by, under the supervision of, or with the permission of the artist who designed it **b** cloth with a pattern applied by printing; *also* an article of such cloth **c** a photographic copy; *esp* one made from a negative [ME *preinte*, fr OF, fr *preint*, pp of *preindre* to press, fr L *premere* – more at PRESS] – **out of/in print** (no longer) available from the publisher

²**print** *vt* **1a** to impress something in or on **b** to stamp (e g a mark) in or on something **2a** to make a copy of by impressing paper against an inked printing surface **b(1)** to impress (e g wallpaper) with a design or pattern **b(2)** to impress (a pattern or design) on something **c** to publish in print **3** to write each letter separately rather than joining them together **4** to make (a positive picture) on a sensitized photographic surface from a negative or positive ~ *vi* **1a** to work as a printer **b** to produce printed matter **2** to write using unjoined letters

**printable** /'printəbl/ *adj* **1** capable of being printed or of being printed from or on **2** considered fit to publish – **printability** *n*

**printed circuit** *n* an electronic circuit in which the components are connected by conductive material deposited in thin continuous paths on an insulating surface rather than by wires

**printed matter** *n* matter printed by any of various mechanical processes that may be posted at a special rate

**printer** /'printə/ *n* one who or that which prints: e g **a** a person whose work is printing **b** a device used for printing; *esp* a machine for printing from photographic negatives **c** a device (e g a LINE PRINTER) that produces printout

**printer's devil** *n* an apprentice in a PRINTING OFFICE

**printer's mark** *n* IMPRINT b(2)

**printery** /'printəri/ *n* PRINTING OFFICE

**printing** /'printing/ *n* **1** reproduction in printed form **2** the art, practice, or business of a printer **3** IMPRESSION 4c (all the copies printed at one time) **4** *pl* paper to be printed on

**printing office** *n* an establishment where printing is done

**printing press** *n* a machine that produces printed copies

**printless** /'printlis/ *adj* making, bearing, or taking no imprint

**printmaking** /'print,mayking/ *n* the design and production of prints, esp by an artist – **printmaker** *n*

**printout** /'print,owt/ *n* a printed record produced automatically (e g by a computer) – **print out** *vt*

¹**prior** /'prie·ə/ *n* **1** the deputy head of a monastery, ranking next below the abbot **2** the head (of a house) of any of various religious communities [ME, fr OE & MF, fr ML, fr LL, administrator, fr L, former, superior] – **priorate** *n*, **priorship** *n*

²**prior** *adj* **1** earlier in time or order **2** taking precedence (e g in importance) [L, former, superior, compar of OL *pri* before; akin to L *priscus* ancient, *pristinus* primitive, *prae* before – more at FOR] – **prior to** *formal* before in time; IN ADVANCE OF

**prioress** /'prie·əris, -res/ *n* a nun corresponding in rank to a prior

**priority** /prie'orəti/ *n* **1a(1)** being prior **a(2)** precedence in date or position of publication – used with reference to the names of TAXA (biological groups) **b** superiority in rank, position, or privilege **2a** something meriting prior attention **b** *pl* the relative importance one attaches to each of a number of things ⟨*get one's* priorities *right*⟩ **3** *obs* legal precedence in exercise of rights *synonyms* see PRECEDENCE

**priory** /'prie·əri/ *n* (the church of) a religious house under a prior or prioress

**prise** /priez/ *vt, chiefly Br* ⁵PRIZE

**prisere** /'priesiə/ *n* the succession of vegetational stages that occurs in passing from bare earth or water to a CLIMAX community (stable group of plants fully adjusted to their environment) [¹*primary* + *sere*]

**prism** /'priz(ə)m/ *n* **1** a 3-dimensional figure (POLYHEDRON) having two equal ends which are polygons lying in parallel planes connected by sides which are parallelograms – compare PRISMATOID, PRISMOID **2a** a transparent body that is bounded in part by two nonparallel flat surfaces and is used to deviate or disperse a beam of light **b** a prism-shaped piece of decorative glass (e g in a chandelier) **3** a form of a crystal that has the flat surfaces (FACES) parallel to one AXIS (fixed line used to characterize a crystal); *esp* one whose faces are parallel to the vertical axis [LL *prismat-*, *prisma*, fr Gk, lit., anything sawn, fr *priein* to saw]

**prismatic** /priz'matik/ *adj* **1** of, like, or being a prism ⟨~ *crystals*⟩ **2** formed, dispersed, or refracted (as if) by a prism ⟨~ *effects*⟩ ⟨~ *colours*⟩ **3** highly coloured; brilliant **4** *of a crystal* having the type of symmetry characteristic of a prism ⟨~ *crystals*⟩ – **prismatically** *adv*

**prismatoid** /'prizmətoyd/ *n* a 3-dimensional figure (POLYHEDRON) that has all of its VERTICES (points where edges meet) in two parallel planes, but the number of whose vertices in each plane is not necessarily equal. Prismatoids may be pyramids. – compare PRISM, PRISMOID – **prismatoidal** *adj*

**prismoid** /'prizmoyd/ *n* a prismatoid having an equal number of VERTICES (points where edges meet) in each of two parallel planes – compare PRISM, PRISMATOID – **prismoidal** *adj*

**prison** /'priz(ə)n/ *n* **1** a state of confinement or captivity **2** a place of confinement; *esp* a public building or institution in which people are confined for safe custody while on trial for a criminal offence or for punishment after trial and conviction ⟨*in* ~⟩ [ME, fr OF, fr L *prehension-*, *prehensio* act of seizing, fr *prehensus*, pp of *prehendere* to seize – more at PREHENSILE] – **prison** *vt*

**prisoner** /'priz(ə)nə/ *n* a person kept under involuntary confinement or imprisonment; *esp* somebody on trial or in prison

**prisoner of war** *n* a person captured in war; *esp* a member of the armed forces of a nation who is taken by the enemy in war

**prisoner's base** *n* a game in which players on each of two teams try to tag and imprison players of the other team who have ventured out of their home territory

**prissy** /'prisi/ *adj* prim and prudish, esp regarding sexual matters [prob blend of *prim* and *sissy*] – **prissily** *adv*, **prissiness** *n*

**pristine** /'pristeen, -tien/ *adj* **1** belonging to the earliest period or state ⟨*the hypothetical* ~ *lunar atmosphere*⟩ **2** free from impurity or decay; fresh and clean as if new [L *pristinus* – more at PRIOR] – **pristinely** *adv*

*usage* Some people dislike the use of **pristine** to mean "fresh and clean", but it is becoming common ⟨*the* **pristine**, *air-conditioned new building* – The Times⟩

**prithee** /'pridhee/ *interj, archaic* – used to express a wish or request [alter. of (*I*) *pray thee*]

**privacy** /'privəsi; *also* 'prie-/ *n* **1** being apart from the company or observation of others; seclusion **2** freedom from undesirable intrusions; *esp* avoidance of publicity [ME *privacie*, fr *privat* private]

**privatdocent, privatdozent** /ˌpriˌvaht·doht'sent/ *n* an unsalaried university lecturer or teacher in a German-speaking country paid directly from students' fees [Ger *privatdozent*, fr *privat* private + *dozent* teacher]

**¹private** /'prievit/ *adj* **1a** intended for or restricted to the use of a particular person, group, etc ⟨*a ~ park*⟩ **b** belonging to or concerning an individual person, company, or interest ⟨*a ~ house*⟩ **c(1)** restricted to the individual or arising independently of others ⟨*my ~ opinion is that the whole scheme's ridiculous*⟩ **c(2)** independent of the usual institutions ⟨*~ study*⟩ **d** not general in effect ⟨*a ~ statute*⟩ **e** of or receiving medical treatment in Britain for which fees are charged and in which the patient has more privileges than a patient being treated under the NATIONAL HEALTH SERVICE **f** of or administered by a private individual or organization as opposed to a governmental institution or agency ⟨*a ~ pension scheme*⟩ **2a(1)** not holding public office or employment ⟨*a ~ citizen*⟩ **a(2)** not related to one's official position; personal ⟨*~ correspondence*⟩ **b** having the rank of a private ⟨*a ~ soldier*⟩ **3a(1)** withdrawn from company or observation; sequestered ⟨*a ~ retreat*⟩ **a(2)** not seeking the companionship or confidence of others ⟨*she was a very ~ person*⟩ **b** not (intended to be) known publicly; secret [ME *privat*, fr L *privatus*, fr pp of *privare* to deprive, release, fr *privus* private, set apart; akin to L *pro* for – more at FOR] – **privately** *adv*, **privateness** *n*

**²private** *n* **1** – see MILITARY RANKS table **2** *pl, slang* the genitals – **in private** without the presence or knowledge of others; confidentially

**private bar** *n, Br* SALOON BAR

**private bill** *n* a legislative bill affecting a particular individual, class, or locality rather than the public at large – compare HYBRID BILL, PUBLIC BILL

**private company** *n* a company that has a limited number of shareholders and whose shares are not offered to the general public – compare PUBLIC COMPANY

**private detective** *n* one who is employed by a person or organization other than the state to prevent crime (e g by catching shoplifters) or to investigate someone's activities (e g in divorce cases)

**private enterprise** *n* FREE ENTERPRISE

**privateer** /ˌprievə'tiə/ *n* **1** an armed private ship commissioned to be used against the commerce or warships of an enemy **2** the commander or any of the crew of a privateer – **privateer** *vi*

**private eye** *n, informal* PRIVATE DETECTIVE

**private first class** *n* – see MILITARY RANKS table

**private hotel** *n* a usu unlicensed hotel catering esp for resident guests accepted at the proprietor's discretion

**private investigator** *n* PRIVATE DETECTIVE

**private law** *n* a branch of law concerned with the duties and rights of ordinary private people and their relations with one another – compare PUBLIC LAW

**private means** *n pl* income arising from investments or capital rather than from wages or a salary

**private member's bill** *n, Br* a parliamentary bill introduced by a member of parliament who does not hold a government appointment

**private parts** *n pl, euph* the genitals

**private practice** *n, Br* the practice of a professional person carried on independently of an organization; *esp* the practice of a doctor or dentist outside the NATIONAL HEALTH SERVICE

**private school** *n, Br* a school that is supported by the fee-paying parents of pupils, not by the government

**private secretary** *n* a secretary employed to assist with a person's individual and confidential business matters

**private sector** *n* the part of the economy that is not owned or directly controlled by the state – compare PUBLIC SECTOR

**private treaty** *n* a sale of property on terms determined by negotiation between the seller and buyer – compare AUCTION

**privation** /prie'vaysh(ə)n/ *n* **1** an act or instance of depriving; deprivation **2** being deprived; *esp* lack of the usual necessities of life [ME *privacion*, fr MF *privation*, fr L *privation-*, *privatio*, fr *privatus*, pp of *privare* to deprive – more at PRIVATE]

**privative** /'privətiv/ *adj, linguistics* consisting in, marked by, or affirming the lack or absence of a quality ⟨*a-, un-, non- are ~ prefixes*⟩ – **privative** *n*

**privat-ization, -isation** /ˌprievətie'zaysh(ə)n/ *n* **1** the avoiding of involvement in anything beyond one's immediate interests **2** the restoration of a nationalized body to private ownership – **privatize** *vt*

**privet** /'privit/ *n* an ornamental shrub (*Ligustrum vulgare*) of the ash family with evergreen leaves and small white flowers widely planted for hedges; *broadly* any of various similar related shrubs [origin unknown]

**¹privilege** /'priv(i)lij/ *n* **1** a right, immunity, or advantage granted exclusively to a particular person, class, or group; a prerogative; *esp* such an advantage attached to a position or office **2** the possession of privileges, esp those conferred by rank or wealth [ME, fr OF, fr L *privilegium* law for or against a private person, fr *privus* private + *leg-, lex* law – more at LEGAL]

**²privilege** *vt* to grant a privilege to

**privileged** /'priv(i)lijd/ *adj* **1** having or enjoying one or more privileges ⟨*~ classes*⟩ **2a** not subject to disclosure in a court ⟨*a ~ communication*⟩ **b** exempt *from*

**privily** /'privəli/ *adv, archaic* in a private or secret manner

**privity** /'privəti/ *n* **1** joint, usu secret, knowledge of a private matter **2** the relation between people who have a legal interest in the same transaction (e g a contract or lease) [ME *privite*, fr OF, fr ML *privitat-*, *privatas*, fr L *privus* private]

**¹privy** /'privi/ *adj* **1** sharing in a secret – + *to* ⟨*~ to the conspiracy*⟩ **2** *archaic* private, withdrawn, secret [ME *prive*, fr OF *privé*, fr L *privatus* private]

**²privy** *n* **1** a small building containing a bench with a hole in it that is used as a toilet **2** *NAm* TOILET 1a

**privy council** *n* **1** *cap P&C* an advisory council nominally chosen by the British monarch and usu functioning through its committees **2** *archaic* a secret or private council

**privy councillor** *n, often cap P&C* a member of a privy council

**privy purse** *n, often cap both Ps* an allowance for the monarch's private expenses

**¹prize** /priez/ *n* **1** something offered or striven for in competition or in a contest of chance **2** something exceptionally desirable or precious [ME *pris* prize, price – more at PRICE]

**²prize** *adj* **1a** awarded or worthy of a prize ⟨*a ~ pupil*⟩ **b** awarded as a prize ⟨*a ~ medal*⟩ **2** outstanding of a kind ⟨*raised ~ pigs*⟩ ⟨*a ~ idiot*⟩

**³prize** *vt* **1** to estimate the value of; rate **2** to value highly; esteem [ME *prisen*, fr MF *prisier*, fr LL *pretiare*, fr L *pretium* price, value – more at PRICE]

**⁴prize** *n* something taken by force, stratagem, or threat; *esp* a ship or other property lawfully captured at sea in time of war [ME *prise*, fr OF, act of taking, fr *prendre* to take, fr L *prehendere* – more at PREHENSILE]

**⁵prize, *Br* also prise** /priez/ *vt* **1** to press, force, or move with a lever **2** to open, obtain, or remove with difficulty ⟨*tried to ~ information out of him*⟩ [E dial. *prize, prise*, lever, fr ME *prise*, fr OF, act of taking, grasp]

**prizefight** /'priez,fiet/ *n* a professional boxing match, esp in the 18th and 19th centuries – **prizefighter** *n*, **prizefighting** *n*

**prize money** *n* **1** a part of the proceeds of a captured ship formerly divided among the officers and men taking the prize **2** money offered as a prize

**prizewinner** /'priez,winə/ *n* one who or that which wins a prize or deserves to do so – **prizewinning** *adj*

**Prjevalski's horse** /ˌpuhzhi'vulskiz/ *n* PRZEWALSKI'S HORSE (Mongolian wild horse)

**¹pro** /proh/ *n, pl* **pros 1** an argument or piece of evidence in favour of a particular proposition or view ⟨*an appraisal of the ~s and cons*⟩ **2** a person who favours or supports a particular proposition or view [ME, fr L, prep, for]

**²pro** *adv* in favour or affirmation ⟨*much has been written ~ and con*⟩ [²*pro-*]

**³pro** *prep* for; IN FAVOUR OF 1 ⟨*he's very ~ the Common Market*⟩ [L – more at FOR]

**⁴pro** *n or adj, pl* **pros** *informal* (a) professional

**⁵pro** *n, pl* **pros** *slang* a prostitute

**¹pro-** *prefix* **1a** earlier than; prior to; before ⟨*prologue*⟩ **b** rudimentary; PROT- ⟨*pronucleus*⟩ **2a** situated in front of or at the front of; anterior to ⟨*procephalic*⟩ ⟨*proventriculus*⟩ **b** front; anterior ⟨*prothorax*⟩ **3** projecting ⟨*prognathous*⟩ [ME, fr OF, fr L, fr Gk, before, forwards, forth, for, fr *pro* – more at FOR]

**²pro-** /proh-/ *prefix* **1** taking the place of; substituting for ⟨*procathedral*⟩ ⟨*procaine*⟩ ⟨*proproctor*⟩ **2** favouring; supporting; championing ⟨*pro-American*⟩ **3** onwards; forwards ⟨*progress*⟩ ⟨*propel*⟩ [L *pro* in front of, before, for – more at FOR]

**proa** /'proh·ə/ *n* a fast Malay boat shaped like a canoe and equipped with oars, a large triangular sail, and a framework (OUTRIGGER) attached along one or both sides to stabilize it – called also PRAU [Malay *pěrahu*]

**proactive** /proh'aktiv/ *adj, psychology* involving modification by a factor which precedes that which is modified ⟨ ~ *inhibition of memory*⟩ – compare RETROACTIVE [L *pro-* forwards]

**pro-am** /,proh 'am/ *n* a competition in which amateurs are matched against professional players, esp in golf [*pro*fessional + *am*ateur]

**probabilism** /'probəbəliz(ə)m/ *n* 1 a doctrine that certainty is unattainable, esp in the sciences, and that probable conclusions must be sufficient to guide belief and action 2 a theological theory that moral dilemmas may be resolved by any of several justifiable decisions even though an opposing decision is or appears better justified [Fr *probabilisme*, fr L *probabilis* probable] – **probabilist** *adj or n*

**probabilistic** /,probəbə'listik/ *adj* 1 of probabilism 2 of or based on probability

**probability** /,probə'biləti/ *n* 1 being probable 2 something (eg an occurrence or circumstance) that is probable 3a(1) a measure of the likelihood that a given event will occur, usu expressed as a fraction between 0 (impossible) and 1 (certain), and usually based on the ratio of the number of times the event occurs in a test series to the total number of trials in the series ⟨*the ~ of tossing a coin and getting a head is* $^1/_2$⟩ **a(2)** the chance that a given event will occur ⟨*there is a high ~ they will get married*⟩ **b** a branch of mathematics concerned with the study of probabilities ⟨~ *theory*⟩ 4 a logical relation between statements such that the truth of one implies the probable truth of the other

**probability density** *n, statistics* PROBABILITY DENSITY FUNCTION; *also* a particular value of a probability density function

**probability density function** *n, statistics* 1 PROBABILITY FUNCTION 2 a function of a continuous RANDOM VARIABLE (quantity depending on the result of a statistical experiment) whose INTEGRAL over an interval gives the probability that its value will fall within the interval

**probability distribution** *n, statistics* 1 PROBABILITY FUNCTION 2 PROBABILITY DENSITY FUNCTION

**probability function** *n, statistics* a function of a discrete RANDOM VARIABLE (quantity depending on the result of a statistical experiment) that gives the probability that a specified value will occur

¹**probable** /'probəbl/ *adj* 1 supported by evidence strong enough to establish likelihood but not proof ⟨*a ~ hypothesis*⟩ 2 likely to be or become true or real ⟨~ *events*⟩ [ME, fr MF, fr L *probabilis*, fr *probare* to test, approve, prove – more at PROVE] – **probably** *adv*

   *usage* An event that is likely to happen is **probable**, but one cannot correctly say it is ⟨⚠ **probable** *to happen*⟩.

²**probable** *n* one who or that which is probable; *esp* somebody who will probably be selected (eg for a representative team) ⟨*she's a ~ for the new post*⟩

**probable cause** *n* reasonable grounds for supposing that the bringing of a legal action is or was justified

**proband** /'proh,band/ *n* SUBJECT 3b(2) (individual being studied in an experiment) [L *probandus*, gerundive of *probare*]

**probang** /'proh,bang/ *n* a slender flexible rod with a sponge on one end used esp for removing obstructions from the OESOPHAGUS (tube carrying food from the mouth to the stomach) [alter. (prob influenced by ¹*probe*) of earlier *provang* (so named by its inventor), of unknown origin]

¹**probate** /'prohbayt, -bət/ *n* the judicial determination of the validity of a will; *also* an official copy of a will certified as valid [ME *probat*, fr L *probatum*, neut of *probatus*, pp of *probare*]

²**probate** *vt, NAm* to establish (a will) by probate

**probate court** *n* a court that has jurisdiction chiefly over the probate of wills and administration of deceased people's estates

**probation** /prə'baysh(ə)n, proh-/ *n* 1a subjection of an individual to a period of testing to ascertain fitness (eg for a job) **b** a method of dealing with (young) offenders by which sentence is suspended subject to regular supervision by a probation officer 2 the state or a period of being subject to probation – **probational** *adj*, **probationally** *adv*, **probationary** *adj*

**probationer** /prə'baysh(ə)nə/ *n* 1 a person (eg a newly admitted student nurse) whose fitness for a post is being tested during a trial period 2 an offender on probation

**probation officer** *n* an officer appointed to supervise the conduct of convicted offenders on probation

**probative** /'prohbətiv/ *adj, formal* serving to prove; substantiating

¹**probe** /prohb/ *n* 1 a slender surgical instrument for examining a cavity 2a a slender pointed metal conductor (eg of electricity or sound) that is connected to a measuring or monitoring device and that is temporarily connected to or inserted in the device or quantity to be monitored **b** a device used to penetrate or send back information, esp from interplanetary space **c** a pipe on the receiving aircraft that is thrust into the DROGUE (funnel-shaped device on the end of the refuelling hose) of the delivering aircraft in air refuelling 3a the action of probing **b** a tentative exploratory advance or survey **c** *chiefly journalistic* a penetrating or critical investigation; an inquiry [ML *proba* examination, fr L *probare* to try, test, prove]

²**probe** *vt* 1 to examine (as if) with a probe 2 *chiefly journalistic* to investigate thoroughly ~ *vi* to make an exploratory investigation – **prober** *n*

**probenecid** /proh'benəsid/ *n* a synthetic drug, $HO_2C_6H_4SO_2N((CH_2)_2CH_3)_2$, that acts on the function of the kidney tubules and is used to increase the concentration of some drugs (eg penicillin) in the blood by inhibiting their excretion and also to increase the excretion of URATES (chemical compounds normally produced in urine) in the treatment of gout [irreg fr *propyl* + *benz*oic *acid*]

**probit** /'prohbit/ *n, statistics* a unit of measurement of probability based on deviations from the average of a NORMAL DISTRIBUTION [*probability* un*it*]

**probity** /'prohbəti/ *n, formal* adherence to the highest principles and ideals; uprightness [MF *probité*, fr L *probitat-, probitas*, fr *probus* honest – more at PROVE]

¹**problem** /'probləm/ *n* 1a a question raised for inquiry, consideration, or solution **b** a proposition, esp in mathematics or physics, stating something to be done 2 somebody or something that is difficult to deal with, understand, or resolve ⟨*social ~*s⟩ [ME *probleme*, fr MF, fr L *problema*, fr Gk *problēmat-, problēma*, lit., something thrown forwards, fr *proballein* to throw forwards, fr *pro-* forwards + *ballein* to throw – more at PRO-, DEVIL]

   *synonyms* Problem, mystery, enigma, riddle, puzzle, and conundrum can all mean "something difficult to solve or understand". **Problem** is the most general term, suggesting a predicament, or something perplexing that has to be resolved. **Mystery** originally meant "something beyond human understanding", but now also implies something which has never been explained or fully understood. **Enigma** suggests a tantalizing **mystery**, full of contradictions or ambiguity. A **riddle** is rather like an **enigma**, but stresses that a solution is possible. A **puzzle** is a problem, usually intricate, that may be solved by following up clues and fitting them together with skill and ingenuity. A **conundrum** is a problem which invites speculation rather than solution. All these words except the last may also be applied to people, with similar connotations. Compare ¹PUZZLE *usage* Some people dislike the use of **problem** to mean "source of distress" ⟨*he has a weight* **problem**⟩.

²**problem** *adj* 1 dealing with a problem of human conduct ⟨*a ~ play*⟩ 2 difficult to deal with; presenting a problem ⟨*a ~ child*⟩

**problematic** /,problə'matik/, **problematical** /-kl/ *adj* 1a difficult to solve or decide; puzzling **b** not definite or settled ⟨*their future remains ~*⟩ **c** open to question or debate; questionable 2 of a proposition in logic asserted as possible – **problematically** *adv*

**problem page** *n* a page or column in a magazine in which readers' personal problems are discussed

**proboscidean, proboscidian** /,prohbə'sidi-ən/ *n* any of an order (Proboscidea) of large mammals comprising the elephants and extinct related forms [NL *Proboscidea*, order me, fr L *proboscid-, proboscis*] – **proboscidean** *adj*

**proboscis** /prə'bosis/ *n, pl* **proboscises** *also* **proboscides** /-sideez/ 1 a long flexible snout (eg the trunk of an elephant) 2 any of various elongated or extendable tubular projecting mouth-parts of an INVERTEBRATE animal (eg a butterfly) that are used esp for sucking 3 *humorous* the human nose, esp when prominent [L, fr Gk *proboskis*, fr *pro-* + *boskein* to feed; akin to Lith *gauja* herd]

**proboscis monkey** *n* a large monkey (*Nasalis larvatus*) of Borneo with a long fleshy nose

**procaine** /'prohkayn, -'-/ *n* a synthetic drug, $H_2NC_6H_4CO_2(CH_2)_2N(C_2H_5)_2$, that is used as a local anaesthetic [ISV ²*pro-* + co*caine*]

**procambium** /proh'kambiəm/ *n* the part of a plant MERISTEM (region of cells dividing continually to produce new cells) that is just behind the growing tip of stems and roots and that forms the cells that will diversify to produce the primary VASCULAR (food-and water-conducting) tissues and CAMBIUM (meristem that produces secondary vascular tissues) [NL] – **procambial** *adj*

**procaryote** /ˌproh'kari·oht/ *n* PROKARYOTE (simple organism)

**procathedral** /ˌprohkə'theedrəl/ *n* a parish church used as a cathedral

**procedural** /prə'seej(ə)rəl, -dyoorəl, -dyə-/ *adj* of procedure, esp of courts or other bodies administering the law – **procedurally** *adv*

**procedure** /prə'seejə, proh-/ *n* **1** a particular way of acting or of accomplishing something **2a** a series of ordered steps **b** a formalized series of steps taken in initiating and carrying out a legal action, conducting parliamentary business, etc **3** an established method of doing things ⟨*a stickler for ~*⟩ [Fr *procédure*, fr MF, fr *proceder*]

**proceed** /prə'seed, proh-/ *vi* **1** to arise from a source; originate ⟨*this trouble ~ed from a misunderstanding*⟩ **2** to continue after a pause or interruption **3** to begin and carry on an action, process, or movement **4** to move along a course; advance [ME *proceden*, fr MF *proceder*, fr L *procedere*, fr *pro-* forwards + *cedere* to go – more at PRO-, CEDE]

**proceed to** *vt* – used to reinforce a following verb, esp ironically ⟨*then* proceeded *to* lecture *me on how it should be done*⟩

**proceeding** /prə'seeding, proh-/ *n* **1** a procedure **2** *pl* events, goings-on ⟨*through his drunken brain the whole memory of the evening's ~s rushed back* – Liam O'Flaherty⟩ **3** *pl* legal action ⟨*divorce ~s*⟩ **4** *pl* an official record of things said or done **5 proceeding** *formal*, **proceedings** *pl* an affair, transaction

**proceeds** /'prohseedz/ *n pl* **1** the total amount brought in ⟨*the ~ of a sale*⟩ **2** the net amount received (eg for a cheque) after deduction of any discount or charges

**procephalic** /ˌprohsi'falik/ *adj* relating to, forming, or situated on or near the front of the head

**procercoid** /proh'suhkoyd/ *n* the solid first parasitic larva of some tapeworms that develops usu in the body cavity of a COPEPOD (minute shellfish) [*pro-* + Gk *kerkos* tail]

**¹process** /'prohses/ *n* **1a** a moving forwards, esp as part of a progression or development ⟨*the historical ~*⟩ **b** something going on; a proceeding **2a** a natural phenomenon marked by gradual changes that lead towards a particular result ⟨*the ~ of growth*⟩ **b** a series of actions or operations designed to achieve an end; *esp* a continuous operation or treatment (eg in manufacture) **3a** a whole course of proceedings in a legal action **b** a summons, writ **4** a prominent or projecting part of a living organism or anatomical structure ⟨*a bone ~*⟩ [ME *proces*, fr MF, fr L *processus*, fr *processus*, pp of *procedere*]

**²process** *vt* **1** to subject to a special process or treatment (eg in the course of manufacture) **2** to take appropriate action on ⟨*~ an insurance claim*⟩

**³process** *adj* **1** treated or made by a special process, esp one involving artificial production or modification **2** made by or used in a mechanical or photographic duplicating process

**⁴process** /prə'ses/ *vi, chiefly Br* to move in a procession [back-formation fr *procession*]

**processible, processable** /'prohsesəbl/ *adj* suitable for processing; capable of being processed – **processibility, processability** *n*

**procession** /prə'sesh(ə)n/ *n* **1** a group of individuals or objects moving along in an orderly way, esp as part of a ceremony or demonstration **2** a succession, sequence

**¹processional** /prə'sesh(ə)nl/ *n* **1** a book containing hymns, prayers, etc for a procession **2** a musical composition (eg a hymn) designed for a procession

**²processional** *adj* of or moving in a procession – **processionally** *adv*

**processor** /'prohsesə/ *n* **1** one who or that which processes ⟨*food ~*⟩ **2a(1)** a computer **a(2)** the part of a computer system that operates on data – called also CENTRAL PROCESSING UNIT **b** a computer program that puts another program into a form acceptable to the computer

**process printing** *n* a method of printing from HALFTONE plates, in usu three or more colours, so that nearly any shade may be reproduced

**procès-verbal** /proh,say vuh'bal (*Fr* prɔ̃ɛ vɛrbal)/ *n, pl* **procès-verbaux** /vuh'boh (*Fr* vɛrbo)/ an official written record; *specif* a

written statement in support of a charge in French law [Fr, lit., verbal trial]

**proclaim** /prə'klaym, proh-/ *vt* **1** to declare publicly and usu officially; announce **2** to give outward indication of; show **3** to praise or glorify openly or publicly; extol [ME *proclamen*, fr MF or L; MF *proclamer*, fr L *proclamare*, fr *pro-* before + *clamare* to cry out – more at PRO-, CLAIM] – **proclaimer** *n*

**proclamation** /ˌproklə'maysh(ə)n/ *n* **1** proclaiming or being proclaimed **2** an official public announcement [ME *proclamacion*, fr MF *proclamation*, fr L *proclamation-, proclamatio*, fr *proclamatus*, pp of *proclamare*]

**proclimax** /proh'kliemaks/ *n* an ecological community that resembles a CLIMAX (community in the final stage of adjustment to its environment) in stability and permanence but is not primarily the product of climate

**proclitic** /proh'klitik/ *adj, of a word or word part* without independent accent and pronounced with the following word as a single unit of sound ⟨*at in "at home" is ~*⟩ [NL *procliticus*, fr Gk *pro-* + LL *-cliticus* (as in *encliticus* enclitic)] – **proclitic** *n*

**proclivity** /prə'klivəti, proh-/ *n*, **proclivities** *n pl* an inclination or predisposition towards something, esp something reprehensible [L *proclivitas*, fr *proclivis* sloping, prone, fr *pro-* forwards + *clivus* hill – more at PRO-, DECLIVITY]

**proconsul** /ˌproh'konsl/ *n* **1** a governor or military commander of an ancient Roman province **2** an administrator in a modern dependency or occupied area, usu with wide powers [ME, fr L, fr *pro consule* for a consul] – **proconsular** *adj*, **proconsulate** *n*, **proconsulship** *n*

**procrastinate** /proh'krastinayt, prə-/ *vi, formal* to delay intentionally and reprehensibly in doing something necessary △ prevaricate [L *procrastinatus*, pp of *procrastinare*, fr *pro-* forwards + *crastinus* of tomorrow, fr *cras* tomorrow] – **procrastinator** *n*, **procrastination** *n*

**procreant** /'prohkriənt/ *adj, formal* producing young

**procreate** /ˌprohkri'ayt/ *vb, formal* **1** *vt* to beget or bring forth (young); propagate ~ *vi* to produce young; reproduce [L *procreatus*, pp of *procreare*, fr *pro-* forth + *creare* to create – more at PRO-, CREATE] – **procreation** *n*, **procreative** *adj*, **procreator** *n*

**procrustean** /proh'krustyən, -ti·ən/ *adj, often cap, formal* seeking to enforce or establish conformity (eg to a policy or doctrine) by arbitrary and often violent means [*Procrustes* (Gk *Prokroustēs*, lit., stretcher), mythical robber of ancient Greece who forced his victims to fit a certain bed by stretching them or lopping off their legs]

**procrustean bed** *n, often cap P* a scheme or pattern into which someone or something is arbitrarily forced

**procryptic** /proh'kriptik/ *adj* of or being a protective and concealing pattern or shade of colouring, esp in insects [*pro-* (as in *protect*) + *cryptic*]

**proctodaeum** /ˌproktə'dee·əm/ *n, pl* **proctodaea** /-'dee·ə/, **proctodaeums** the posterior and anal part of the digestive tract formed in the embryo of a VERTEBRATE animal by an infolding of the outer body wall [NL, fr Gk *prōktos* anus + *hodos* way – more at CEDE]

**proctology** /prok'toləji/ *n* a branch of medicine dealing with the structure and diseases of the anus, rectum, and lower part of the LARGE INTESTINE [Gk *prōktos* anus + E *-logy*] – **proctologist** *n*, **proctologic, proctological** *adj*

**proctor** /'proktə/ *n* a supervisor, monitor: **a** a person appointed to maintain student discipline at Oxford and Cambridge **b** *NAm* an invigilator [ME *procutour* procurator, proctor, alter. of *procuratour*] – **proctor** *vb*, **proctorship** *n*, **proctorial** *adj*

**procumbent** /proh'kumbənt/ *adj* **1** being or having stems that trail along the ground without rooting **2** *formal* lying face down [L *procumbent-, procumbens*, prp of *procumbere* to fall or lean forwards, fr *pro-* forwards + *-cumbere* to lie down – more at HIP]

**procuration** /ˌprokyoo'raysh(ə)n/ *n* **1a** the act of appointing another as one's agent or attorney **b** the authority vested in such an agent or attorney **2a** the action of obtaining something (eg supplies); procurement **b** the offence of procuring women for prostitution [ME *procuratioun* act of taking care, management, fr MF *procuration*, fr L *procuration-, procuratio*, fr *procuratus*, pp of *procurare*]

**procurator** /'prokyoo,raytə/ *n* **1** a person authorized by another to manage his/her affairs; an agent, attorney **2** an administrator of the Roman empire entrusted with the financial management of a province – **procuratorial** *adj*

,procurator-'fiscal *n, often cap P&F* a local public prosecutor in Scotland

procure /prə'kyooə/ *vt* 1 to get and provide (esp women) to act as prostitutes 2 *formal* to obtain, esp by particular care and effort 3 *formal* to achieve; BRING ABOUT ~ *vi* to procure women **synonyms** see OBTAIN [ME *procuren* to contrive, obtain, fr LL *procurare*, fr L, to take care of, fr *pro-* for + *cura* care] – **procurable** *adj*, **procurance, procurement** *n*

procurer /prə'kyooərə/, *fem* **procuress** /prə'kyooəris/ *n* somebody who procures women for prostitution

¹prod /prod/ *vb* **-dd-** *vt* 1 to poke or jab (as if) with a pointed instrument 2 to incite to action; stir ~ *vi* to make a prodding or jabbing movement, esp repeatedly [perh alter. of E dial. *brod* to goad, fr or akin to ON *broddr* spike] – **prodder** *n*

²prod *n* 1 a pointed instrument used to prod 2 a prodding action; a jab 3 an incitement to act

Prod *n, Irish & Scot derog* a Protestant [by shortening & alter.]

¹prodigal /'prodigl/ *adj* 1 recklessly extravagant or wasteful 2 *formal* yielding abundantly; lavish ⟨~ *of new ideas*⟩ **synonyms** see PROFUSE **antonyms** sparing, frugal [L *prodigus*, fr *prodigere* to drive away, squander, fr *pro-, prod-* forth + *agere* to drive – more at PRO-, AGENT] – **prodigally** *adv*, **prodigality** *n*

²prodigal *n* 1 one who spends or gives lavishly and foolishly 2 *also* **prodigal son** a repentant sinner or reformed spendthrift [(2) fr the prodigal son in a biblical parable (Luke 15:11–32)]

prodigious /prə'dijəs/ *adj* 1 causing amazement or wonder 2 extraordinary in bulk, quantity, or degree; enormous – **prodigiously** *adv*, **prodigiousness** *n*

prodigy /'prodiji/ *n* 1a something extraordinary, inexplicable, or marvellous **b** an exceptional instance ⟨*a* ~ *of patience*⟩ 2 a person, esp a child, with extraordinary talents △ progeny [L *prodigium* omen, monster, fr *pro-, prod-* + *-igium* (akin to *aio* I say) – more at ADAGE]

prodromal /'prodrəml, proh'drohml/, **prodromic** /proh-'dromik/ *adj* precursory, premonitory; *esp* marked by prodromes

prodrome /'proh,drohm/ *n, pl* **prodromata** /,proh'drohmətə/, **prodromes** a warning symptom of an impending disease [Fr, lit., precursor, fr Gk *prodromos*, fr *pro-* before + *dromos* running – more at PRO-, DROMEDARY]

¹produce /prə'dyoohs/ *vt* 1 to offer to view or notice; exhibit 2 to give birth or rise to 3 to extend in length, area, or volume ⟨~ *a side of a triangle*⟩ 4 to act as a producer of (esp a film or play) 5 to give being, form, or shape to; *esp* to manufacture 6 to (cause to) accumulate ⟨~*s a good rate of interest*⟩ ~ *vi* to bear, make, or yield something **synonyms** see ¹MAKE [ME (Sc) *producen*, fr L *producere*, fr *pro-* forwards + *ducere* to lead – more at TOW] – **producible** *adj*

²produce /'prodyoohs/ *n* 1 agricultural products; *esp* fresh fruits and vegetables as distinguished from grain and other staple crops 2 the offspring usu of a female animal

produced /prə'dyoohst/ *adj* disproportionately elongated ⟨*a* ~ *leaf*⟩

producer /prə'dyoohsə/ *n* one who or that which produces: e g **a** an individual or entity that grows agricultural products or manufactures articles **b** a furnace or apparatus that produces gas to be used for fuel by circulating air or a mixture of air and steam through a layer of coke **c** a living organism (e g a green plant) that produces its own chemical compounds from simple substances (e g CARBON DIOXIDE and nitrogen) and is often a food source for other organisms – compare CONSUMER **b** **d(1)** one who has responsibility for the administrative aspects of the production of a film (e g casting, schedules, and esp finance) **d(2)** *Br* one who has responsibility for the artistic and technical aspects of a play or broadcast

producer gas *n* a manufactured fuel gas made in a producer and consisting chiefly of CARBON MONOXIDE, hydrogen, and nitrogen

producer goods *n pl* goods (e g tools and raw materials) that are used in manufacturing and only indirectly for human wants

producing manager *n* one who is responsible for the administration of a theatre company

product /'prodəkt, -dukt/ *n* 1 the result of the multiplying together of two or more numbers or expressions 2 something produced by a natural or artificial process; *specif* a result of a combination of incidental causes or conditions ⟨*a typical* ~ *of an arts education*⟩ ⟨*heart disease is thought to be a* ~ *of stress and bad diet*⟩ 3 the amount, quantity, or total produced 4 a

salable or marketable commodity ⟨*tourism should be regarded as a* ~⟩ 5 CONJUNCTION 4 (sentence in logic true only if its components are) [(1) ME, fr ML *productum*, fr L, something produced, fr neut of *productus*, pp of *producere*; (2–5) L *productum*]

production /prə'duksh(ə)n/ *n* 1a something produced; a product **b(1)** a literary or artistic work **b(2)** a work presented on the stage or screen or over the air 2a the act or process of producing **b** the creation of exchange value; *esp* the making of goods available for human wants 3 the total output, esp of a commodity or an industry – **productional** *adj*

production line *n* LINE 6h

production manager *n* one who is responsible for the administration of a theatrical production

productive /prə'duktiv/ *adj* 1 having the quality or power of producing, esp in abundance ⟨~ *fishing waters*⟩ 2 effective in bringing about; being the cause of ⟨*laws that are* ~ *of such hardship*⟩ 3a yielding results or benefits ⟨*a* ~ *programme of education*⟩ **b** yielding or devoted to the satisfaction of wants or the creation of utilities 4 continuing to be used in the formation of new words or constructions ⟨un- *is a* ~ *prefix*⟩ 5 *of a cough* raising mucus or sputum (e g from the lungs) – **productively** *adv*, **productiveness** *n*

productivity /,prodək'tivəti, -duk-/ *n* 1 being productive; *also* rate of production ⟨*a* ~ *agreement*⟩ 2 the rate of production of chemical substances by utilization of energy from the sun by producer organisms (e g green plants) during photosynthesis

proem /'proh·em/ *n* 1 a preface or introduction, esp to a book or speech 2 a prelude [ME *proheme*, fr MF, fr L *prooemium*, fr Gk *prooimion*, fr *pro-* + *oimē* song] – **proemial** *adj*

proenzyme /,proh·'enziem/ *n* ZYMOGEN (substance capable of being transformed into an ENZYME) [ISV]

prof /prof/ *n, informal* a professor

profanation /,profə'naysh(ə)n/ *n* (a) profaning

*synonyms* Profanation, desecration, blasphemy, and sacrilege: profanation is the mildest term, suggesting a lack of proper respect which outrages those who hold something sacred. Desecration especially suggests the defilement, often wilful and malicious, of some sacred place by improper use. Sacrilege is the strongest term, implying contemptuous violation of what is held to be sacred. Blasphemy implies gross irreverence in thought, word, or deed, especially towards God.

profanatory /prə'fanət(ə)ri/ *adj* tending to profane; desecrating

¹profane /prə'fayn/ *vt* 1 to treat (something sacred) with abuse, irreverence, or contempt; desecrate 2 to debase by an unworthy or improper use – **profaner** *n*

²profane *adj* 1 not concerned with religion or religious purposes 2 not holy because unconsecrated, impure, or defiled; unsanctified 3 debasing or defiling what is holy; irreverent 4a not among those initiated (e g into religious rites) **b** *formal* not possessing esoteric or expert knowledge [ME *prophane*, fr MF, fr L *profanus*, fr *pro-* before + *fanum* temple – more at PRO-, FEAST] – **profanely** *adv*, **profaneness** *n*

*synonyms* Profane, secular, lay, and temporal may all mean "not dedicated to religious ends or uses". Profane, not derogatory in this sense, simply contrasts with "sacred" ⟨profane *love is the love between man and woman, compared to the love between God and humanity*⟩. Secular contrasts the world with the church or the religious life ⟨secular *drama*⟩ ⟨secular *education*⟩. Lay describes people and their activities, comparing them to (those of) the clergy. It may also denote domestic or manual workers within a religious order, as contrasted with those engaged in theological studies. Temporal is opposed to "spiritual", and usually describes those in authority ⟨*the lords* temporal, *in the House of Lords, are those who are not leaders of the church*⟩. antonyms sacred, spiritual

profanity /prə'fanəti/ *n* 1a being profane **b** (the use of) profane language 2 a profane utterance; a curse

profess /prə'fes/ *vt* 1 to receive formally into a religious community following a NOVITIATE (period of probation) 2a to declare or admit openly or freely; affirm **b** to declare falsely; pretend 3 to confess one's faith in or allegiance to 4 to be a professor of (an academic discipline) ~ *vi* to make a profession or avowal **synonyms** see ASSERT [(1) ME *professen*, fr *profes*, adj, having professed one's vows, fr OF, fr LL *professus*, fr L, pp of *profiteri* to profess, confess, fr *pro-* before + *fateri* to acknowledge; (2–4 & *vi*) L *professus*, pp – more at CONFESS]

professed /prə'fest/ *adj* 1 openly and freely admitted or declared ⟨*a* ~ *atheist*⟩ 2 professing to be qualified ⟨*a* ~ *solicitor*⟩ 3 pretended, false ⟨~ *misery*⟩

**professedly** /prə'fesidli/ *adv* **1** by profession or declaration; avowedly **2** with pretence; allegedly

**profession** /prə'fesh(ə)n/ *n* **1** the act of taking the vows of a religious community **2** an act of openly declaring or claiming a faith, opinion, etc; a protestation ⟨~s *of hatred*⟩ **3** an avowed religious faith **4a** a calling requiring specialized knowledge and often long and intensive academic preparation ⟨*the medical and legal* ~s⟩ – compare BUSINESS **b** a principal calling, vocation, or employment ⟨*men who make it their* ~ *to hunt the hippopotamus* – J G Frazer⟩ **c** *taking sing or pl vb* the whole body of people engaged in a particular calling

**¹professional** /prə'fesh(ə)nl/ *adj* **1a** (characteristic) of a profession **b** engaged in one of the learned professions **c(1)** characterized by or conforming to the technical or ethical standards of a profession ⟨~ *conduct*⟩ **c(2)** characterized by conscientious workmanship ⟨*a sound* ~ *novel*⟩ ⟨*did a really* ~ *job on the garden*⟩ **2a** participating for gain or livelihood in an activity or field of endeavour often engaged in by amateurs **b** engaged in by professionals ⟨~ *football*⟩ **3** *chiefly derog* following a line of conduct as though it were a profession ⟨*a* ~ *agitator*⟩ ⟨*a* ~ *Irishman*⟩ **4** *euph, of a breaking of rules, esp in sport* intentional – **professionally** *adv*

**²professional** *n* **1** one who engages in a pursuit or activity professionally **2** *informal* one with sufficient experience or skill in an occupation or activity to resemble a professional ⟨*a real* ~ *when it comes to croquet*⟩

**professionalism** /prə'fesh(ə)nl,iz(ə)m/ *n* **1** the esp high and consistent conduct, aims, or qualities that characterize a profession or a professional person ⟨*the* ~ *of most school orchestras*⟩ **2** the following for gain or livelihood of an activity (eg golf) often engaged in by amateurs

**professional·ize, -ise** /prə'feshənəliez/ *vt* to give a professional character to – **professionalization** *n*

**professor** /prə'fesə/ *n* **1** someone who professes, avows, or declares something (eg a faith or opinion) **2a** a staff member of the highest academic rank at a university; *esp* the head of a university department **b** somebody who teaches or professes special knowledge of an art, sport, or occupation requiring skill ⟨*Madame Chores,* ~ *of dancing*⟩ **c** *NAm* a teacher at a university, college, or sometimes secondary school – **professorial** *adj*, **professorially** *adv*

**professorate** /prə'fesərət/ *n* **1** the office, term of office, or position of a professor **2** *taking sing or pl vb* PROFESSORIATE 1

**professoriate, professoriat** /prə,profə'sawri·ət/ *n* **1** *taking sing or pl vb* a body of professors **2** a professorship [modif of Fr *professorat*, fr *professeur* professor, fr L *professor*, fr *professus*]

**professorship** /prə'fesəship/ *n* the office, duties, or position of a professor

**proffer** /'profə/ *vt* to present for acceptance; tender [ME *profren*, fr AF *profrer*, fr OF *poroffrir*, fr *por-* forth (fr L *pro-*) + *offrir* to offer – more at PRO-]

**proficient** /prə'fish(ə)nt/ *adj* well advanced or expert in an art, skill, branch of knowledge, etc [L *proficient-, proficiens*, prp of *proficere* to go forwards, accomplish, fr *pro-* forwards + *facere* to make – more at PRO-, DO] – **proficiency** *n*, **proficient** *n*, **proficiently** *adv*

**synonyms** *Proficient, skilful, skilled, adept, expert:* **proficient** suggests greater than average competence in a given field, due to training and practice ⟨*a* **proficient** *pianist/linguist*⟩. **Adept** implies a natural aptitude and cleverness improved by practice ⟨*adept at fielding the ball/answering awkward questions*⟩. **Skilled** suggests mastery of a trade or craft, while **skilful** adds to a competence derived from training a natural dexterity or creative ingenuity. Someone who is **expert** is exceptionally proficient or adept, combining skill with experience ⟨*expert at cleaning fish*⟩. All these adjectives may be applied to actions as well as to people. *antonyms* unskilful, inexpert

**¹profile** /'prohfiel/ *n* **1** a representation of something in outline; *esp* the human face seen from the side – compare ¹SILHOUETTE 1 **2** an outline seen or represented in sharp relief; a contour **3** a side or sectional elevation: eg **3a** a drawing showing a vertical section of the ground **b** a vertical section of a soil from the ground surface to the underlying unweathered material (eg rock) **c** a temporary guide, usu of small boards, to determine the position of the foundations of a building **4** a set of data often in graphic form portraying the significant features of something ⟨*a company's earnings* ~⟩ **5** a concise written or spoken biographical sketch [It *profilo*, fr *profilare* to draw in outline, fr *pro-* forwards (fr L) + *filare* to spin, fr LL – more at FILE]

**²profile** *vt* **1** to represent in profile or by a profile; produce a profile of (eg by drawing or writing) **2** to shape the outline of by passing a cutter round – **profiler** *n*

**¹profit** /'profit/ *n* **1** a valuable return; a gain **2** the excess of returns over expenditure **3a** net income, usu for a given period of time **b** **profit rate, profit** the ratio of net income for a given year to the amount of capital invested or to the value of sales **4** the compensation for the assumption of risk in business enterprise, as distinguished from wages or rent [ME, fr MF, fr L *profectus* advance, profit, fr *profectus*, pp of *proficere*] – **profitless** *adj*

**²profit** *vi* to derive benefit; gain – usu + *from* or *by* ⟨~ed *greatly from these lessons*⟩ ~ *vt* to be of service to; benefit ⟨*it will not* ~ *you to start an argument*⟩

**profitable** /'profitəbl/ *adj* producing financial or other gains or profits *synonyms* see BENEFICIAL *antonyms* unprofitable, wasted – **profitableness** *n*, **profitably** *adv*, **profitability** *n*

**profit and loss** *n* a summary account used at the end of an accounting period in which income and expenditure and the resulting net profit or loss are shown

**profiteer** /,profi'tiə/ *n* somebody who makes an unreasonable profit, esp on the sale of scarce and essential goods – **profiteer** *vi*

**profiterole** /'profitə,rohl, ,---'-, prə'fitə,rohl/ *n* a small hollow ball of cooked CHOUX PASTRY that is filled with a sweet or savoury preparation; *esp* one filled with whipped cream and covered with a chocolate sauce [Fr, fr *profiter* to profit]

**profit margin** *n* the amount by which a business's net income exceeds its outgoings

**profit sharing** *n* a system or process under which employees receive a part of the profits of an industrial or commercial enterprise

**profit system** *n* FREE ENTERPRISE

**¹profligate** /'profligət/ *adj* **1** utterly dissolute; immoral **2** wildly extravagant; prodigal [L *profligatus*, fr pp of *profligare* to strike down, fr *pro-* forwards, down + *-fligare* (akin to *fligere* to strike); akin to Gk *thlibein* to squeeze] – **profligacy** *n*, **profligately** *adv*

**²profligate** *n* a person given to wildly extravagant and usu grossly self-indulgent expenditure

**pro forma** /,proh 'fawmə/ *adj* **1** made or carried out in a perfunctory manner or as a formality **2** provided in advance to prescribe form or describe items ⟨~ *invoice*⟩ [L]

**profound** /prə'fownd/ *adj* **1a** having intellectual depth and insight **b** difficult to fathom or understand **2a** extending far below the surface **b** coming from, reaching to, or situated at a depth; deep-seated ⟨*a* ~ *sigh*⟩ **3a** characterized by intensity of feeling or quality **b** all encompassing; complete ⟨~ *sleep*⟩ [ME, fr MF *profond* deep, fr L *profundus*, fr *pro-* before + *fundus* bottom – more at PRO-, BOTTOM] – **profoundly** *adv*, **profoundness** *n*

**profundity** /prə'fundəti/ *n* **1a** intellectual depth **b** something profound or difficult to understand **2** the quality or state of being very profound or deep [ME *profundite*, fr MF *profundité*, fr L *profunditat-, profunditas* depth, fr *profundus*]

**profuse** /prə'fyoohs/ *adj* **1** liberal, extravagant ⟨~ *in their thanks*⟩ **2** greatly abundant; bountiful ⟨*a* ~ *harvest*⟩ [ME, fr L *profusus*, pp of *profundere* to pour forth, fr *pro-* forth + *fundere* to pour – more at FOUND] – **profusely** *adv*, **profuseness** *n*

**synonyms** *Profuse, lavish, prodigal, luxuriant, lush,* and **exuberant** may all suggest unrestrained abundance. **Profuse** conjures up an image of something being poured out in a stream ⟨*profuse apologies*⟩. **Lavish** suggests profusion so great as to be extravagant or munificent, but it may also suggest immoderation ⟨*a* **lavish** *feast*⟩ ⟨*lavish use of our natural resources*⟩. **Prodigal,** in formal use, suggests "yielding abundantly" ⟨*a conference* **prodigal** *of resolutions*⟩. But in general use, **prodigal** implies a reckless squandering or lavish giving which may exhaust one's resources ⟨**prodigal** *with his money*⟩ ⟨*we cannot afford to be* **prodigal** *with our use of oil*⟩. **Luxuriant** and **lush** are often applied to vegetation, but may equally describe whatever is produced in splendid abundance ⟨*luxuriant hair*⟩. **Lush** suggests a soft rich luxuriance, while **luxuriant** often implies a richness of variety ⟨*a* **luxuriant** *imagination*⟩ ⟨*the* **lush** *era of the Nineties*⟩. **Exuberant** implies a vigorous, even rampant vitality and abundance, and usually describes people, their emotions, or their activities. *antonyms* scant, scanty

**profusion** /prə'fyoohzh(ə)n/ *n* **1** being profuse **2** a large or lavish amount

**progamete** /proh'gameet, -gə'meet/ *n* a cell giving rise to

GAMETES (reproductive cells): e g **a** OOCYTE (female gamete) **b** SPERMATOCYTE (male gamete) [ISV]

**progenitor** /ˌproh'jenitə/ n **1a** a direct ancestor; a forefather **b** a biologically ancestral form **2** a precursor, originator ⟨∼s *of socialist ideas – TLS*⟩ [ME, fr MF *progeniteur*, fr L *progenitor*, fr *progenitus*, pp of *progignere* to beget, fr *pro-* forth + *gignere* to beget – more at KIN ]

**progeny** /'projini/ n **1** *taking sing or pl vb* **1a** descendants, children **b** the offspring of animals or plants **2** an outcome, product **3** *taking sing or pl vb* a body of followers, disciples, or successors △ prodigy [ME *progenie*, fr OF, fr L *progenies*, fr *progignere*]

**progestational** /ˌprohje'staysh(ə)nl/ adj preceding pregnancy or gestation; *esp* of, inducing, or constituting the modifications of the female mammalian system associated with ovulation and CORPUS LUTEUM (hormone-producing body present in the ovary during pregnancy) formation ⟨∼ *hormones*⟩

**progesterone** /proh'jestə,rohn/ n a STEROID progestational hormone, $C_{21}H_{30}O_2$, that is secreted by the CORPUS LUTEUM (structure present in the ovary during pregnancy), causes proliferation of the wall of the uterus, and inhibits uterine contractions [*progestin* + *sterol* + *-one*]

**progestin** /proh'jestin/ n a progestational drug or hormone; *esp* progesterone [*pro-* + *gestation* + *-in*]

**progestogen** /proh'jestəjin/ n any of a group of STEROID substances that are drugs or natural hormones (e g progesterone) and have the functions typical of a progestational hormone [*progestational* + *-ogen* (as in *oestrogen*)]

**proglottid** /proh'glotid/ n a segment of a tapeworm containing both male and female reproductive organs [NL *proglottis*] – **proglottidean** adj

**proglottis** /proh'glotis/ n, pl **proglottides** /-'glotideez/ a proglottid [NL *proglottid-, proglottis*, fr Gk *proglōttis* tip of the tongue, fr *pro-* + *glōtta* tongue – more at GLOSS]

**prognathous** /prog'naythəs/, **prognathic** /prog'nathik/ adj having the jaws projecting beyond the upper part of the face [¹*pro-* + *-gnathous*] – **prognathism** n

**prognosis** /prog'nohsis/ n, pl **prognoses** /-seez/ **1** the prospect of recovery as anticipated from the usual course of disease or peculiarities of a particular case **2** *formal* a forecast, prognostication [LL, fr Gk *prognōsis*, lit., foreknowledge, fr *progignōskein* to know before, fr *pro-* + *gignōskein* to know – more at KNOW]

**prognostic** /prog'nostik/ n, *formal* **1** something that foretells; a portent **2** a prognostication, prophecy [ME *pronostique*, fr MF, fr L *prognosticum*, fr Gk *prognōstikon*, fr neut of *prognōstikos* foretelling, fr *progignōskein*] – **prognostic** adj

**prognosticate** /prog'nosti,kayt/ vt, *formal* **1** to foretell from signs or symptoms; predict **2** to indicate in advance; presage *synonyms* SEE FORETELL – **prognosticator** n, **prognosticative** adj, **prognostication** n

**prograde** /ˌproh'grayd/ adj, of orbital or rotational movement in the same direction as neighbouring celestial bodies ⟨∼ *orbit of a satellite*⟩ – compare RETROGRADE [L *pro-* forwards + *gradi* to go – more at PRO-, GRADE]

**¹program** /'prohgram, -grəm/ n **1a** a plan for the programming of a mechanism (e g a computer) **b** a sequence of coded instructions that can be stored in a mechanism (e g a computer) or that is part of an organism **2** *chiefly NAm* a programme

**²program** /'prohgram/ vt **-mm-** (*NAm* **-mm-, -m-**) **1** to work out a sequence of operations to be performed by (a mechanism, esp a computer); provide with a program **2** *chiefly NAm* to programme – **programmable** adj, **programmability** n

**programmatic** /ˌprohgrə'matik/ adj **1** of or being PROGRAMME MUSIC **2** of, like, or having a programme – **programmatically** adv

**¹programme**, *NAm chiefly* **program** /'prohgram/ n **1a** a brief usu printed (pamphlet containing a) list of the features to be presented, the people participating, etc (e g in a public performance or entertainment) **b** the performance of a programme **c** a radio or television broadcast characterized by some feature (e g a presenter, a purpose, or a theme) giving it coherence and continuity **2** a systematic plan of action ⟨*a rehousing* ∼⟩ **3** a curriculum **4** a prospectus, syllabus **5** matter for PROGRAMMED INSTRUCTION [Fr *programme* agenda, public notice, fr Gk *programma*, fr *prographein* to write before, fr *pro-* before + *graphein* to write]

**²programme**, *NAm chiefly* **program** vt **1a** to arrange or provide a programme of or for **b** to enter in a programme **2** to cause to conform to a preestablished pattern (e g of thought or

behaviour); condition ⟨*our visions of marriage have been* ∼d *by Hollywood*⟩ – **programmable** adj, **programming** n, **programmability** n

**programmed**, *NAm also* **programed** /'prohgramd/ adj **1** of learning by means of PROGRAMMED INSTRUCTION **2** (in the form) of PROGRAMMED INSTRUCTION

**programmed instruction** n instruction given in small steps, with each requiring a correct response by the learner before going on to the next step

**programme music** n music that is intended to suggest images or incidents

**programmer**, *NAm also* **programer** /'prohgramə/ n one who or that which programmes: e g **a** one who prepares and tests programs for mechanisms **b** a person or device that programs a mechanism (e g a computer) **c** somebody who prepares educational programmes

**¹progress** /'prohgres/ n **1a** an official or ceremonial journey; *esp* a monarch's tour of his/her dominions **b** an expedition, journey, or march through a region ⟨*balls, dinners and crowds of beautiful women attended his* ∼ *– Time*⟩ **2** a forward or onward movement (e g to an objective or goal); an advance **3** a gradual improvement; *esp* the progressive development of humanity [ME, fr L *progressus* advance, fr *progressus*, pp of *progredi* to go forth, fr *pro-* forwards + *gradi* to go – more at PRO-, GRADE] – **in progress** occurring; GOING ON

**²progress** /prə'gres/ vi **1** to move forwards; proceed **2** to develop to a higher, better, or more advanced stage ∼ vt **1** to oversee and ensure the satisfactory progress or running of (e g a project) ⟨*the editor must* ∼ *articles from conception to publication*⟩ **2** to ascertain and attempt to bring forward the delivery or completion date of ⟨*mature man to* ∼ *outgoing and internal orders – Evening News*⟩

**progress chaser** n, *chiefly Br* a person who is employed by a business to ensure that deadlines are met (e g for orders from suppliers or to customers)

**progression** /prə'gresh(ə)n/ n **1** a sequence of numbers in which each term is related to its predecessor by a uniform law – compare ARITHMETIC PROGRESSION, GEOMETRIC PROGRESSION, HARMONIC PROGRESSION **2a** the action or process of progressing; an advance **b** a continuous and connected series; a sequence **3a** a succession of musical notes or chords (in harmony) **b** SEQUENCE 2c (repetition of musical phrase getting higher or lower) – **progressional** adj

**progressionist** /prə'greshənist/ n a person who believes in progress; *esp* one who believes in the continuous progress of the human race

**¹progressive** /prə'gresiv/ adj **1a** of or characterized by progress or progression **b** making use of or interested in new ideas, findings, or opportunities **c** of or being an educational theory marked by emphasis on the individual child, informality of classroom procedure, and encouragement of self-expression **2** moving forwards or onwards continuously or in stages; advancing **3** increasing in extent or severity ⟨*a* ∼ *disease*⟩ **4** *often cap* of political Progressives **5** of or being a verb form (e g am working, were coming) that expresses action or state in progress at the time of speaking or a time spoken of **6** increasing in rate as the base increases ⟨*a* ∼ *tax*⟩ – **progressively** adv, **progressiveness** n, **progressivism** n, **progressivist** n or adj, **progressivistic** adj

**²progressive** n **1** one who is progressive **2** one who believes in moderate political change, esp social improvement, by governmental action; *esp, cap* a member of a political party that advocates these beliefs **3** a progressive tense or verb form

**Progressive Conservative** adj of or being a major Canadian political party traditionally advocating economic nationalism and close ties with the UK and the Commonwealth – **Progressive Conservative** n

**progressive jazz** n modern jazz characterized by complex experimentation in harmony and rhythm

**progressivism** /prə'gresiviz(ə)m/ n **1** the principles or beliefs of progressives **2** *cap* the political and economic doctrines advocated by Progressives **3** the theories of progressive education – compare ESSENTIALISM 1 – **progressivist** n or adj, **progressivistic** adj

**proguanilr** /proh'gwahnil/ n a synthetic drug, $Cl_6H_4C(NH)_3C(NH)_2CH(CH_3)_2$, used esp for PROPHYLAXIS (preventive treatment) against malaria [iso*propyl* + *guan*ine + *-il*, deriv of L *-ilis* -ile]

**prohibit** /prə'hibit, proh-/ vt **1** to forbid by authority **2a** to prevent from doing something **b** to preclude [ME *prohibiten*, fr

L *prohibitus*, pp of *prohibēre* to hold away, prevent, fr *pro-* forwards + *habēre* to hold]

**usage** One **prohibits** an action, or **prohibits** somebody *from* performing it ⟨*they were* **prohibited** *from striking*⟩ but one cannot correctly **prohibit** somebody *to* do something ⟨⚠ *they were* **prohibited** *to strike*⟩.

**prohibition** /ˌproh·hi'bish(ə)n/ *n* **1** the act of prohibiting by authority **2** an order to restrain or stop **3** *often cap* the forbidding by law of the manufacture, transport, and sale of alcohol for general consumption **4** a judicial order forbidding a lower court from proceeding in a case beyond its jurisdiction

**prohibitionist** /ˌproh·hi'bishənist/ *n* one who favours the prohibition of the sale or manufacture of alcoholic drink

**prohibitive** /prə'hibətiv, proh-/, **prohibitory** /-t(ə)ri/ *adj* **1** tending to prohibit or restrain **2** tending to rule out the use or acquisition of something ⟨*the running expenses seemed* ∼⟩ – **prohibitively** *adv*, **prohibitiveness** *n*

¹**project** /'projekt; *also* proh-/ *n* **1** a specific plan or design; a scheme **2** a planned undertaking: eg **2a** a piece of research arranged to a definite plan or scheme **b** a large undertaking, esp a public works scheme **c** a task or problem engaged in usu by a group of pupils, esp to supplement and apply classroom studies [ME *proiecte*, modif of MF *pourjet*, fr *pourjeter* to throw out, spy, plan, fr *pour-* (fr L *porro* forwards) + *jeter* to throw – more at JET]

²**project** /prə'jekt/ *vt* **1a** to devise in the mind; design **b** to plan, figure, or estimate for the future ⟨∼ *expenditures for the coming year*⟩ **2** to throw forwards or upwards, esp by mechanical means ⟨*the fountain* ∼ed *a thin column of water high into the air*⟩ **3** to present or transport in imagination ⟨*a book that tries to* ∼ *how the world will look in 2000*⟩ **4** to cause to protrude **5** to cause (light or an image) to fall into space or on a surface ⟨∼ *a beam of light*⟩ ⟨∼ *a picture onto a screen*⟩ **6** to reproduce (e g a point, line, or area) on a surface by motion in a prescribed direction **7a** to cause (one's voice) to be heard at a distance **b** to communicate vividly, esp to an audience **c** to present or express (oneself) in a manner that wins approval ⟨*you must learn to* ∼ *yourself better if you want the job*⟩ **8** to attribute (something in one's own mind) to a person, group, or object ⟨*a nation is an entity on which one can* ∼ *many of the worst of one's instincts – TLS*⟩ ∼ *vi* **1** to jut out: protrude **2** to attribute something in one's own mind to a person, group, or object [partly modif of MF *pourjeter*; partly fr L *projectus*, pp of *proicere* to throw forwards, fr *pro-* + *jacere* to throw] – **projectable** *adj*

¹**projectile** /prə'jektiel/ *n* **1** a body projected by external force and continuing in motion by its own INERTIA; *esp* a missile (eg a bullet or shell) fired from a weapon **2** a self-propelling weapon (e g a rocket)

²**projectile** *adj* **1** projecting or impelling forwards ⟨*a* ∼ *force*⟩ **2** capable of being thrust forwards

**projection** /prə'jeksh(ə)n/ *n* **1a** a systematic representation of latitude and longitude on a flat surface upon which features from the curved surface of the earth, the CELESTIAL SPHERE (imaginary sphere surrounding the earth on whose surface the planets, stars, etc appear to be placed), etc may be mapped **b** (a graphic reproduction formed by) the process or technique of reproducing a spatial object on a flat or curved surface by projecting its points **2** the act of throwing or shooting forwards; ejection **3** the forming of a plan; scheming **4a** a jutting out **b** a part that juts out **c** a representation of a building or architectural element **5** the act of perceiving a subjective mental image as objective; *also* something so perceived **6** the attribution of one's own ideas, feelings, or attitudes to other people or to objects, esp as a defence against feelings of guilt or inadequacy **7** the display of films or slides by projecting an image from them onto a screen **8** an estimate of future possibilities based on a current trend – **projectional** *adj*

**projectionist** /prə'jekch(ə)nist/ *n* one who operates a film projector or television equipment

**projective** /prə'jektiv/ *adj* **1** of, produced by, or involving geometric projection **2** of a technique designed to analyse an individual's personality structure by the study of responses to standard stimuli (e g the inkblots of the RORSCHACH TEST) that are ambiguous and thus allow the individual to project his/her own meaning or motives onto the stimulus – **projectively** *adv*

**projective geometry** *n* a branch of geometry that deals with the properties of solids that are unaltered by projection

**projector** /prə'jektə/ *n* **1** an apparatus for projecting films or

pictures onto a surface **2** an imagined line from an object to a surface along which projection takes place

**projet** /'prozhay (*Fr* prɔjɛ)/ *n* a draft of a proposed measure or treaty [Fr, fr MF *pourjet* plan]

**prokaryote, procaryote** /proh'kari,oht/ *n* any of a group of minute organisms (e g a bacterium or a BLUE-GREEN ALGA) that do not have a distinct nucleus – compare EUKARYOTE [*pro-* + *kary-* + *-ote* (as in *zygote*)] – **prokaryotic** *adj*

**prolactin** /proh'laktin/ *n* a protein hormone produced by the front lobe of the PITUITARY GLAND that is important in the reproduction of mammals and that stimulates milk production [²*pro-* + *lact-* + *-in*]

**prolamin** /'prohləmin, proh'lamin/, **prolamine** /'prohləmeen, proh'lameen, -min/ *n* any of various simple proteins found esp in seeds [ISV *proline* + *ammonia* + *-in, -ine*]

**prolan** /'prohlan/ *n* either of two GONADOTROPHIC (controlling or stimulating the SEX GLANDS) hormones: **a** FOLLICLE-STIMULATING HORMONE **b** LUTEINIZING HORMONE [Ger, fr L *proles* offspring]

**prolapse** /'proh,laps/ *n* the falling down or slipping of a body part (e g the womb) from its usual position [NL *prolapsus*, fr LL, fall, fr L *prolapsus*, pp of *prolabi* to fall or slide forwards, fr *pro-* forwards + *labi* to slide – more at PRO-, SLEEP] – **prolapse** *vi*

**prolate** /'proh,layt/ *adj* elongated in the direction of a line joining the poles ⟨*a* ∼ *spheroid*⟩ – compare OBLATE [L *prolatus* (pp of *proferre* to bring forward, extend), fr *pro-* forwards + *latus*, pp of *ferre* to carry]

**prole** /prohl/ *n or adj, derog* (a) proletarian

**proleg** /'proh,leg/ *n* a fleshy leg that occurs on an abdominal segment of some insect larvae but does not occur in the adult

**prolegomenon** /ˌprohle'gominən, ˌpro-/ *n, pl* **prolegomena** /-nə/ an introductory section, esp to a learned work [Gk, neut prp passive of *prolegein* to say beforehand, fr *pro-* before + *legein* to say] – **prolegomenous** *adj*

**prolepsis** /proh'lepsis/ *n, pl* **prolepses** /-seez/ anticipation: e g **a** the application of an adjective to a noun in anticipation of its becoming applicable (e g in "tan one's body *brown* in the sun") **b** *formal* the representation of a future act or development as already existing or accomplished [Gk *prolēpsis*, fr *prolambanein* to take beforehand, fr *pro-* before + *lambanein* to take – more at LATCH] – **proleptic** *adj*

**proletarian** /ˌprohli'teəri·ən/ *n or adj* (a member) of the proletariat [L *proletarius*, fr *proles* offspring, fr *pro-* forth + *-olescere* (fr *alescere* to grow) – more at OLD]

**proletarian·ize, -ise** /ˌprohli'teəriəniez/ *vt* to reduce to a proletarian status or level – **proletarianization** *n*

**proletariat** /ˌprohli'teəri·ət/ *n taking sing or pl vb* **1** the lowest social or economic class of a community **2** WORKING CLASS; *esp* the class of industrial workers who lack their own means of production and hence sell their labour to earn a living [Fr *prolétariat*, fr L *proletarius*]

¹**proliferate** /prə'lifərayt/ *vi* **1** to grow by rapid production of new parts, cells, buds, or offspring **2** to increase in number or quantity as if by proliferating; multiply ∼ *vt* to cause to grow by proliferating [back-formation fr *proliferation*, fr Fr *prolifération*, fr *proliférer* to proliferate, fr *prolifère* proliferous, fr L *proles* + *-fer* *-ferous*] – **proliferation** *n*, **proliferative** *adj*, **proliferatively** *adv*

²**proliferate** /prə'lif(ə)rət/ *adj, formal* increased in number or quantity [back-formation fr *proliferation*]

**proliferous** /prə'lif(ə)rəs/ *adj* **1** *of a plant* reproducing freely by vegetative means (e g by putting out runners or side-shoots) **2** *of an animal* undergoing proliferation; *specif* producing a cluster of branchlets from a larger branch ⟨*a* ∼ *coral*⟩ – **proliferously** *adv*

**prolific** /prə'lifik/ *adj* **1** producing young or fruit (freely) **2** marked by abundant inventiveness or productivity ⟨*a* ∼ *writer*⟩ [Fr *prolifique*, fr L *proles* offspring] – **prolificacy, prolificity, prolificness** *n*, **prolifically** *adv*

**proline** /'prohleen, -lin/ *n* an AMINO ACID, $C_4H_8NCOOH$, that forms part of many proteins and that can be synthesized by animals [Ger *prolin*, contr of *pyrrolidin* pyrrolidine (a derivative of pyrrole)]

**prolix** /'proh,liks/ *adj* **1** unduly prolonged or repetitious ⟨*a* ∼ *speech*⟩ **2** given to using more words than are needed in speaking or writing; long-winded [ME, fr MF & L; MF *prolixe*, fr L *prolixus* extended, copious, fr *pro-* forwards + *liquēre* to be fluid – more at LIQUID] – **prolixity** *n*, **prolixly** *adv*

**prolocutor** /proh'lokyootə/ *n* **1** the chairman of the lower house of a CONVOCATION (assembly) of the Anglican church 2 *formal* a presiding officer; a chairman [L, spokesman, fr *pro-* for + *locutor* speaker, fr *locutus,* pp of *loqui* to speak]

**prologue**, *NAm also* **prolog** /'prohlog/ *n* 1 the preface or introduction to a literary work 2 (the actor delivering) a speech, often in verse, addressed to the audience at the beginning of a play 3 an introductory or preceding event or development □ compare EPILOGUE [ME *prolog,* fr OF *prologue,* fr L *prologus* preface to a play, fr Gk *prologos* part of a Greek play preceding the entry of the chorus, fr *pro-* before + *legein* to speak – more at PRO-, LEGEND]

**prolong** /prə'long/ *vt* 1 to lengthen in time; continue 2 to lengthen in space ⟨~ *a line*⟩ [ME *prolongen,* fr MF *prolonguer,* fr LL *prolongare,* fr L *pro-* forwards + *longus* long] – **prolonger** *n*

**prolongation** /ˌprohlong'gaysh(ə)n, 'prol-/ *n* 1 an extension or lengthening in time or duration 2 an expansion or continuation in spatial extent

**prolusion** /prə'loohzh(ə)n, -'lyooh-/ *n, formal* 1 a preliminary trial or exercise; a prelude 2 an introductory and often tentative discourse [L *prolusion-, prolusio,* fr *prolusus,* pp of *proludere* to play beforehand, fr *pro-* before + *ludere* to play – more at LUDICROUS] – **prolusory** *adj*

**prom** /prom/ *n* 1 PROMENADE CONCERT 2 *Br* PROMENADE 2 3 *NAm* a formal dance given by a high-school or college class

¹**promenade** /'promə,nahd, ,--'-/ *n* 1 a leisurely stroll or ride taken for pleasure, usu in a public place and often as a social custom 2 a place for strolling; *esp, Br* a paved walk along the seafront at a resort – compare PARADE 3a a ceremonious opening of a formal ball consisting of a march in which all the guests participate b a figure in a SQUARE DANCE in which couples move anticlockwise in a circle [Fr, fr *promener* to take for a walk, fr L *prominare* to drive forwards, fr *pro-* forwards + *minare* to drive – more at AMENABLE]

²**promenade** *vi* 1 to take or go on a promenade 2 to perform a promenade in a dance ~ *vt* 1 to walk about in or on 2 to display (as if) by promenading around ⟨~d *his new bicycle in front of his friends*⟩ – **promenader** *n*

**promenade concert** *n* a concert at which some of the audience can stand or walk about

**promenade deck** *n* an upper deck or an area on a deck of a passenger ship where passengers may stroll

**promethazine** /proh'methəzeen/ *n* a drug, $C_{17}H_{21}N_2S$, used to treat allergies [*pro*pyl + *di*methylamine + *phenothiazine*]

**Promethean** /prə'meethyən, -thi·ən/ *adj* daringly original or creative [*Prometheus* (Gk *Promētheus*), demigod in Gk myth who stole fire from heaven and gave it to mankind, and taught mankind various arts & sciences]

**promethium** /prə'meethyəm/ *n* a metallic chemical element of the RARE EARTH group obtained by the radioactive decay of uranium [NL, fr *Prometheus*]

**prominence** /'prominəns/ *n* 1 being prominent or conspicuous 2 something prominent; a projection ⟨*a rocky* ~⟩ 3 a large mass of gas arising from the lower solar atmosphere

**prominent** /'prominənt/ *adj* 1 projecting beyond a surface or line; protuberant 2a readily noticeable; conspicuous b widely and popularly known; leading [L *prominent-, prominens,* fr prp of *prominēre* to jut forwards, fr *pro-* forwards + *-minēre* (akin to *mont-, mons* mountain) – more at MOUNT] – **prominently** *adv*

**promiscuity** /ˌpromi'skyooh·əti/ *n* 1 a miscellaneous mixture or mingling of people or things 2 promiscuous sexual behaviour

**promiscuous** /prə'miskyoo·əs/ *adj* 1 composed of a mixture of people or things 2 not restricted to one class or person; indiscriminate ⟨*a* ~ *and unprincipled attack on radicalism* – A M Schlesinger⟩; *esp* not restricted to one sexual partner 3 casual, irregular ⟨~ *eating habits*⟩ [L *promiscuus,* fr *pro-* forth + *miscēre* to mix – more at PRO-, MIX] – **promiscuously** *adv,* **promiscuousness** *n*

¹**promise** /'promis/ *n* 1 a declaration that one will or will not do something specified 2 grounds for expectation usu of success, improvement, or excellence ⟨*show* ~⟩ 3 something that is promised – see also A LICK and a promise [ME *promis,* fr L *promissum,* fr neut of *promissus,* pp of *promittere* to send forth, promise, fr *pro-* forth + *mittere* to send]

²**promise** *vt* 1 to pledge oneself to do, bring about, or provide (something for) ⟨~ *aid*⟩ ⟨*but you* ~d *me*⟩ 2 to assure ⟨*it can be done, I* ~ *you*⟩ 3 to betroth 4 to suggest beforehand; indicate ⟨*dark clouds* ~ *rain*⟩ ~ *vi* 1 to make a promise 2 to give grounds for expectation, esp of something good

**usage** Some people dislike the use of **promise** about present or past facts ⟨*I* **promise** *you it was at least eight feet long*⟩, and feel that the word should refer only to the future.

**promised land** *n* a place or condition believed to promise final satisfaction or realization of hopes [fr God's promise to Abraham that his descendants should possess the land of Canaan (Gen 12:7)]

**promisee** /ˌpromi'see/ *n* a person to whom a promise is made

**promising** /'promising/ *adj* full of promise; likely to succeed or to yield good results – **promisingly** *adv*

**promisor** /ˌpromi'saw, 'promisə/ *n* a person who makes a promise

**promissory** /'promis(ə)ri/ *adj* containing or conveying a promise [ML *promissorius,* fr L *promissus,* pp]

**promissory note** *n* a written signed promise to pay, either on demand or at a fixed or determinable future time, a sum of money to a specified individual or to the bearer

**promo** /'promoh/ *n, pl* **promos** *chiefly Austr informal* an advertising promotion [short for *promotion*]

**promontory** /'promənt(ə)ri/ *n* 1a a high point of land or rock projecting into a body of water; a headland b a prominent mass of land (eg a bluff) overlooking or projecting into a lowland 2 a bodily prominence or projection [L *promunturium, promonturium;* prob akin to *prominēre* to jut forth – more at PROMINENT]

**promote** /prə'moht/ *vt* 1a to advance in station, rank, or honour; raise b to change (a pawn) into a more valuable piece in chess by moving to the eighth RANK (horizontal line of squares) c to assign to a higher division of a sporting competition (eg a football league) – compare RELEGATE d to advance (a pupil) to the next higher form 2a to contribute to the growth or prosperity of; further ⟨~ *international understanding*⟩ b to help bring (eg an enterprise) into being; launch c to present (eg merchandise) for public acceptance through advertising and publicity [L *promotus,* pp of *promovēre,* lit., to move forwards, fr *pro-* forwards + *movēre* to move] – **promotable** *adj,* **promotability** *n*

**promoter** /prə'mohtə/ *n* one who or that which promotes: eg a a person who takes the financial and organizing responsibilities for setting up a public event or entertainment (eg a boxing match or concert) b a person engaged in the formation of a company c a substance that in very small amounts is able to increase the activity of a catalyst in a chemical reaction

**promotion** /prə'mohsh(ə)n/ *n* 1 the act or fact of being raised in position or rank 2a the act of furthering the growth or development of something, esp sales or public awareness b something (eg a price reduction or free sample) intended to promote esp sales of merchandise – **promotional** *adj*

**promotive** /prə'mohtiv/ *adj* tending to further or encourage – **promotiveness** *n*

¹**prompt** /'prompt/ *vt* 1 to move to action; incite ⟨*curiosity* ~ed *him to ask the question*⟩ 2 to assist (someone acting or reciting) by saying the next words of something forgotten or imperfectly learnt 3 to serve as the inciting cause of; urge ⟨~s *serious anxiety about unemployment*⟩ [ME *prompten,* fr ML *promptare,* fr L *promptus* prompt] – **prompter** *n*

²**prompt** *adj* of or for prompting actors ⟨*the* ~ *copy*⟩

³**prompt** *adj* 1a ready and quick to act as occasion demands b punctual ⟨~ *in arriving at the scene of the accident*⟩ 2 performed readily or immediately ⟨~ *assistance*⟩ [ME, fr MF or L; MF, fr L *promptus* ready, prompt, fr pp of *promere* to bring forth, fr *pro-* forth + *emere* to take – more at REDEEM] – **promptly** *adv,* **promptness** *n*

⁴**prompt** *n* 1a the act or an instance of prompting; a reminder b something that prompts 2 (the contract fixing) a limit of time given for payment of an account for goods purchased [(1) ¹*prompt;* (2) ³*prompt*]

**promptbook** /'prompt,book/ *n* a copy of a play with directions for performance used by a theatre prompter

**promptitude** /'prompti,tyoohd/ *n, formal* the quality or habit of being prompt; promptness [ME, fr MF or LL; MF, fr LL *promptitudo,* fr L *promptus*]

**prompt side** *n* the side of the stage (usu to the actor's left in Britain and to his/her right in the USA) where the prompter is

**promulgate** /'prom(ə)l,gayt/ *vt* 1 to make known by open declaration; proclaim 2a to make known or public the terms of (a proposed law) b to put (a law) into action or force [L *promulgatus,* pp of *promulgare*] – **promulgator** *n,* **promulgation** *n*

**pronate** /proh'nayt/ *vb* to (cause to) assume a position of pronation [LL *pronatus*, pp of *pronare* to bend forwards, fr L *pronus*]

**pronation** /proh'naysh(ə)n/ *n* **1** rotation of the hand and forearm so that the palm faces backwards or downwards; *also* a corresponding movement of the foot and leg – compare SUPINATION **2** the position resulting from pronation

**pronator** /proh'naytə/ *n* a muscle affecting pronation [NL, fr LL *pronatus*]

**prone** /prohn/ *adj* **1** having a tendency or inclination; disposed to ⟨*a man is ~ to error*⟩ ⟨*is ~ to overlook such things*⟩ **2a** having the front or lower surface downwards; prostrate **b** lying flat on the ground [ME, fr L *pronus* bent forwards, tending; akin to L *pro* forwards – more at FOR] – **prone, pronely** *adv*, **proneness** *n*

   *usage* **Prone** is now coming to be used, like **prostrate**, to mean simply "lying flat"; but careful writers prefer to confine the meaning of both **prone** and **prostrate** to "lying face downwards" and to use **supine** for "lying face upwards".

**pronephros** /proh'nefros/ *n, pl* **pronephroi** /-froy/ either member of the anterior pair of the three pairs of embryonic kidneys of higher VERTEBRATE animals that functions only in the adults of some fishlike animals (e g lampreys) and in larval fishes and amphibians – compare MESONEPHROS, METANEPHROS [NL, fr Gk *pro-* + *nephros* kidney] – **pronephric** *adj*

**¹prong** /prong/ *n* **1** any of the slender sharp-pointed parts of a fork **2** a slender pointed or projecting usu branching part: e g **2a** a fang of a tooth **b** a point of an antler **3** a subdivision of an argument, attacking force, etc [ME *pronge, prange* fork; perh akin to MHG *pfrengen* to press]

**²prong** *vt* to stab, pierce, or break up (as if) with a prong

**pronged** /prongd/ *adj* having or divided into prongs; *esp* having more than one attacking force, each coming from a different direction – usu in combination ⟨*a 3-pronged attack*⟩

**pronghorn** /'prong,hawn/, **pronghorn antelope** *n, pl* **pronghorns,** *esp collectively* **pronghorn** a cud-chewing mammal (*Antilocapra americana*) of treeless parts of western N America that resembles an antelope

**pronominal** /,proh'nominl, prə-/ *adj* of, like, or being a pronoun [LL *pronominalis*, fr L *pronomin-, pronomen*] – **pronominally** *adv*

**pronoun** /'prohnoun/ *n* a word that is used as a substitute for a noun or noun equivalent and that refers to a previously named or understood person or thing [ME *pronom*, fr L *pronomin-, pronomen*, fr pro- for + *nomin-, nomen* name – more at PRO-, NAME]

**pronounce** /prə'nowns/ *vt* **1** to declare officially or ceremoniously ⟨*the priest ~d them man and wife*⟩ **2** to declare authoritatively or as an opinion ⟨*doctors ~d him fit to resume duties*⟩ **3a** to utter the sounds of ⟨*~ these words*⟩; *esp* to say correctly ⟨*I can't ~ his name*⟩ **b** to show in print the sound of (a written word) ⟨*both dictionaries ~ clique the same*⟩ ~ *vi* **1** to pass judgment; declare one's opinion definitely or authoritatively – often + *on* or *upon* **2** to produce speech sounds ⟨*she ~s abominably!*⟩ [ME *pronouncen*, fr MF *prononcier*, fr L *pronuntiare*, fr pro- forth + *nuntiare* to report, fr *nuntius* messenger – more at PRO-] – **pronounceable** *adj*, **pronouncer** *n*

**pronounced** /prə'nownst/ *adj* strongly marked; decided ⟨*a ~ stutter*⟩ – **pronouncedly** *adv*

**pronouncement** /prə'nownsmənt/ *n* **1** a usu formal declaration of opinion **2** an authoritative announcement

**pronouncing** /prə'nownsing/ *adj* of or indicating pronunciation ⟨*a ~ dictionary*⟩

**pronto** /'prontoh/ *adv, informal* without delay; quickly [Sp, fr L *promptus* prompt]

**pronucleus** /proh'nyoohkliəs/ *n* the nucleus of either a mature sperm or a mature egg before fertilization [NL] – **pronuclear** *adj*

**pronunciamento** /prə,nunsi·ə'mentoh/ *n, pl* **pronunciamentos, pronunciamentoes** a proclamation, pronouncement; *esp* an edict or declaration (e g made by the leaders of a revolt or coup d'état in a Spanish-speaking country) announcing a change of government [Sp *pronunciamiento*, fr *pronunciar* to pronounce, fr L *pronuntiare*]

**pronunciation** /prə,nunsi'aysh(ə)n/ *n* the act or manner of pronouncing words or speech sounds [ME *pronunciacion*, fr MF *prononciation*, fr L *pronuntiation-, pronuntiatio*, fr *pronuntiatus*, pp of *pronuntiare*] – **pronunciational** *adj*

   *usage* This word should be neither pronounced nor spelt like *pronounce*.

**pro-oestrus** /,proh 'eestrəs/ *n* a period immediately preceding OESTRUS (period of sexual receptivity) in female animals characterized by physiological changes preparing for pregnancy

**¹proof** /proohf/ *n* **1a** evidence that compels acceptance of a truth or a fact **b** the process or an instance of establishing the truth or validity of a statement **2** an act, effort, or operation designed to establish or discover a fact or the truth; a test **3** evidence operating to determine the finding or judgment of a tribunal **4a** a sample printing of a piece of text, or of an engraving, etching, etc, made for examination or correction **b** a test photographic print **5** a test of the quality of an article or substance **6** the alcoholic content of a beverage compared with the standard for PROOF SPIRIT [ME, alter. of *preove*, fr OF *preuve*, fr LL *proba*, fr L *probare* to test, prove – more at PROVE]

**²proof** *adj* **1** designed for or successful in resisting or repelling; impervious – often in combination ⟨*waterproof*⟩ ⟨*soundproof*⟩ **2** used in proving or testing or as a standard of comparison **3** of standard strength, quality, or alcoholic content ⟨*duty charged on the ~ gallon*⟩

**³proof** *vt* **1** to make a proof of **2** to proofread **3** to give a resistant quality to; make (something) proof *against* – **proofer** *n*

**proofread** /'proohf,reed/ *vt* to read and mark corrections on (a proof) [back-formation fr *proofreader*] – **proofreader** *n*

**proof spirit** *n* a mixture of alcohol and water containing a standard amount of alcohol, in Britain 57-1% by volume and in the USA 50% by volume – used as a standard of comparison for the alcoholic strength of beverages

**¹prop** /prop/ *n* **1** a rigid usu auxiliary vertical support (e g a pole) ⟨*pit ~*⟩ **2** a source of strength or support ⟨*his son was his chief ~ in his old age*⟩ **3** PROP FORWARD (forward player in rugby) [ME *proppe*, fr MD, stopper; akin to MLG *proppe* stopper]

**²prop** *vb* -pp- *vt* **1** to support by placing something under or against **2** to support by placing against something ~ *vi, Br, Austr, & SAfr, esp of a horse* to refuse to jump an obstacle □ (*vt*) often + *up*

   **prop up** *vt* to give nonmaterial (e g moral or financial) support to ⟨*government propping up ailing industries*⟩

**³prop** /prop/ *n* an article or object used in a play or film other than painted scenery or costumes [short for *property*]

**⁴prop** /prop/ *n, informal* a propeller

**¹propaedeutic** /,prohpi'dyoohtik/ *n* preparatory study or instruction [Gk *propaideuein* to teach beforehand, fr pro- before + *paideuein* to teach, fr *paid-, pais* child – more at PRO-, FEW]

**²propaedeutic** *adj* needed as preparation for learning or study

**propaganda** /,propə'gandə/ *n* **1** *cap* an administrative division of the Roman Catholic church having jurisdiction over missionary territories and the training of priests for these **2** (the usu organized spreading of) ideas, information, or rumour designed to promote or damage an institution, movement, person, etc [NL, fr *Congregatio de propaganda fide* Congregation for propagating the faith, organization established in 1622 by Pope Gregory XV]

**propagandism** /,propə'gandiz(ə)m/ *n* the action, practice, or art of propagating doctrines or of spreading or employing propaganda – **propagandist** *n or adj*, **propagandistic** *adj*, **propagandistically** *adv*

**propagand·ize, -ise** /,propə'gandiez/ *vt* to subject to propaganda ~ *vi* to carry on propaganda

**propagate** /'propə,gayt/ *vt* **1** to cause to continue or increase by sexual or asexual reproduction **2** to pass down (e g a characteristic) to offspring **3a** to cause to spread out and affect a greater number or area; disseminate **b** to publicize ⟨*~ the Gospel*⟩ **c** to transmit (esp energy) in the form of a wave ~ *vi* **1** to multiply sexually or asexually **2** to increase, extend [L *propagatus*, pp of *propagare* to set slips, propagate, fr *propages* slip, offspring, fr pro- before + *pangere* to fasten – more at PRO-, PACT] – **propagable** *adj*, **propagative** *adj*

**propagation** /,propə'gaysh(ə)n/ *n* the act or action of propagating: e g **a** an increase (e g of a type of organism) in numbers **b** the spreading of something (e g a belief) abroad or into new regions; dissemination **c** an enlargement or extension (e g of a crack) in a solid body – **propagational** *adj*

**propagator** /'propə,gaytə/ *n* one who or that which propagates; *specif* a usu heated and covered soil tray for the rapid germination of seeds

**propagule** /'propəgyoohl/ *n* a structure (e g a cutting, seed, or spore) that propagates a plant [NL *propagulum*, fr L *propages* slip]

**propane** /'prohpayn/ *n* a heavy inflammable gas, $C_3H_8$, that is a member of the ALKANE series of chemical compounds, is found in crude petroleum and NATURAL GAS, and is used esp as a fuel and in chemical synthesis [ISV, fr *prop*ionic + *-ane*]

**proparoxytone** /,prohpar'oksitohn/ *adj* having or characterized by an acute accent or by stress on the last syllable but two in a word ⟨independently *is* ∼⟩ [Gk *proparoxytonos*, fr *pro-* + *paroxytonos* paroxytone] – **proparoxytone** *n*

**propel** /prə'pel/ *vt* **-ll- 1** to drive forwards or onwards by means of a force that imparts motion **2** to urge on; motivate *synonyms* see [1]PUSH [ME *propellen*, fr L *propellere*, fr *pro-* before + *pellere* to drive – more at FELT]

**propellant** *also* **propellent** /prə'pelənt/ *n* something that propels: e g **a** an explosive for propelling projectiles **b** fuel plus OXIDIZER (explosive substance) used by a rocket engine **c** a gas in a pressurized container for expelling the contents when the pressure is released

**propellent, propellant** /prə'pelənt/ *adj* capable of propelling

**propeller** *also* **propellor** /prə'pelə/ *n* one who or that which propels; *specif* SCREW PROPELLER

**propeller shaft** *n* a shaft that transmits mechanical power (e g from an engine gearbox to the driving axle or from an aircraft's or ship's engine to the propeller)

**propelling pencil** /prə'peling/ *n*, *Br* a usu metal or plastic pencil whose lead is moved forwards by a screw device

**propensity** /prə'pensəti/ *n*, *formal* a natural inclination or tendency [arch. *propense* inclined, fr L *propensus*, pp of *propendēre* to lean or incline towards, fr *pro-* before + *pendēre* to hang – more at PENDANT]

[1]**proper** /'propə/ *adj* **1** suitable, appropriate **2** appointed for the LITURGY (form of church service) of a particular day **3** belonging to one; own **4** represented heraldically in natural colour **5** belonging characteristically *to* a species or individual; peculiar ⟨*ailments* ∼ *to tropical climates* – George Santayana⟩ **6** being strictly so-called ⟨*the borough is not part of the city* ∼⟩ **7a** strictly accurate; correct **b** strictly decorous; genteel ⟨*a very prim and* ∼ *gentleman*⟩ **8** being a mathematical subset that does not contain all the elements of the inclusive set from which it is derived **9** *informal* very good; excellent **10** *chiefly Br* thorough, complete ⟨*I felt a* ∼ *Charlie!*⟩ **11** *archaic dial* becoming, handsome *synonyms* see [3]FIT *antonym* improper [ME *propre* proper, own, fr OF, fr L *proprius* own] – **properness** *n*

[2]**proper** *n* the parts of the mass that vary according to the particular day or time

[3]**proper** *adv*, *chiefly dial* in a thorough manner; completely

**proper adjective** *n* an adjective that is formed from a PROPER NOUN and that is usu capitalized in English

**properdin** /proh'puhdin/ *n* a protein from SERUM (watery liquid part of blood) that participates in destruction of bacteria, neutralization of viruses, and disintegration of red blood cells [prob fr [1]*pro-* + L *perd*ere to destroy + E *-in* – more at PERDITION]

**proper fraction** *n* a fraction in which the number above the line (NUMERATOR) is less than or of lower degree than the number below the line (DENOMINATOR)

**properly** /'propəli/ *adv* in a proper manner: e g **a** in a fit manner; suitably ⟨*not* ∼ *dressed for the occasion*⟩ **b** strictly in accordance with fact; correctly ⟨∼ *speaking*⟩ **c** *chiefly Br* to the full extent; completely

**proper name** *n* PROPER NOUN

**proper noun** *n* a noun (e g *Janet, London* rather than *woman, city*) that designates a particular being or thing and is usu capitalized in English

**propertied** /'propətid/ *adj* possessing property, esp land

**property** /'propəti/ *n* **1a** a quality, attribute, or power inherent in something **b** an attribute common to all members of a class **2a** something owned or possessed; *specif* a piece of REAL ESTATE **b** ownership ⟨∼ *is theft* – P J Proudhon⟩ **c** something to which a person has a legal title **3** *formal* [3]PROP (object used in play or film) *synonyms* see [1]QUALITY [ME *proprete*, fr MF *propreté*, fr L *proprietat-*, *proprietas*, fr *proprius* own] – **propertyless** *adj*

**property right** *n* a legal right or interest in or against specific property

**property tax** *n* a tax levied on property (e g land, buildings, or movable articles)

**prop forward, prop** *n* (the position of) either of the two players in rugby on either side of the HOOKER (central forward) in the front row of the SCRUM

**prophage** /'prohfayj/ *n* a form of a BACTERIOPHAGE (virus that infects bacteria) in which it is harmless to the HOST (organism harbouring a parasite), is usu integrated into the genetic material of the host, and reproduces when the host does [[1]*pro-* + *phage*]

**prophase** /'prohfayz/ *n* **1** the initial stage of MITOSIS (division of a cell and its nucleus to produce two new cells) in which CHROMOSOMES (strands of gene-carrying material) are CONDENSED (become visible by thickening and contracting) from the resting form and split into paired CHROMATIDS (strands of a chromosome) **2** the initial phase of MEIOSIS (division of a cell and its nucleus to produce the sex cells) in which the chromosomes become visible, corresponding pairs of chromosomes come together and become shortened and thickened, individual chromosomes become visibly double as paired chromatids, CHIASMATA (areas where sections of chromosomes are interchanged) occur, and the nuclear membrane disappears – compare DIAKINESIS, DIPLOTENE, LEPTOTENE, PACHYTENE, ZYGOTENE [ISV [1]*pro* + *phase*] – **prophasic** *adj*

**prophecy** *also* **prophesy** /'profisi/ *n* **1** the function or vocation of a prophet; (the capacity to utter) an inspired declaration of divine will and purpose **2** a prediction of an event [ME *prophecie*, fr OF, fr LL *prophetia*, fr Gk *prophēteia*, fr *prophētēs* prophet]

**prophesy** /'profisie/ *vt* **1** to utter (as if) by divine inspiration **2** to predict with assurance or on the basis of mystic knowledge ∼ *vi* **1** to speak as if divinely inspired **2** to make a prediction **3** *archaic* to give instruction in religious matters; preach *synonyms* see FORETELL [ME *prophesien*, fr MF *prophesier*, fr OF, fr *prophecie*] – **prophesier** *n*

**prophet** /'profit/, *fem* **prophetess** /tes, -'tes/ *n* **1** a person who utters divinely inspired revelations; *specif, often cap* the writer of any of the prophetic books of the Old Testament **2** a person gifted with more than ordinary spiritual and moral insight **3** a person who foretells future events; a predictor ⟨*a weather* ∼⟩ **4** a spokesman for a doctrine, movement, etc ⟨*a* ∼ *of socialism*⟩ [ME *prophete*, fr OF, fr L *propheta*, fr Gk *prophētēs*, fr *pro* for + *phanai* to speak – more at FOR, BAN]

**prophetic** /prə'fetik/, **prophetical** /-kl/ *adj* **1** (characteristic) of a prophet or prophecy **2** foretelling events; predictive – **prophetically** *adv*

**Prophets** /'profits/ *n pl* the second part of the Jewish scriptures

[1]**prophylactic** /,profi'laktik/ *adj* **1** guarding or protecting from or preventing disease **2** *formal* tending to prevent or ward off; preventive ⟨*an ancient* ∼ *symbol*⟩ [Gk *prophylaktikos*, fr *prophylassein* to keep guard before, fr *pro-* before + *phylassein* to guard, fr *phylak-*, *phylax* guard] – **prophylactically** *adv*

[2]**prophylactic** *n* something prophylactic: e g **a** a prophylactic drug **b** *chiefly NAm* a contraceptive device; *specif* a condom

**prophylaxis** /,profi'laksis/ *n*, *pl* **prophylaxes** /-seez/ measures designed to preserve health (e g of the body or of society) and prevent the spread of disease [NL, fr Gk *prophylaktikos*]

**propinquity** /prə'pingkwəti/ *n*, *formal* **1** nearness of relationship; kinship **2** nearness in place or time; proximity [ME *propinquite*, fr L *propinquitat-*, *propinquitas* kinship, proximity, fr *propinquus* near, akin, fr *prope* near – more at APPROACH]

**propionate** /'prohpi-ənayt/ *n* any of various chemical compounds (SALTS or ESTERS) formed by combination between PROPIONIC ACID and a metal atom, an alcohol, or another chemical group [ISV]

**propionic acid** /,prohpi'onik/ *n* a rancid-smelling FATTY ACID, $CH_3CH_2COOH$, found in milk and in liquids obtained from the distillation of wood, coal, and petroleum and used esp in making flavourings and perfumes [ISV [1]*pro-* + Gk *piōn* fat; akin to L *opimus* fat – more at FAT]

**propitiate** /prə'pishi,ayt/ *vt* to gain or regain the favour or goodwill of; appease [L *propitiatus*, pp of *propitiare*, fr *propitius* propitious] – **propitiable** *adj*, **propitiator** *n*

**propitiation** /prə,pishi'aysh(ə)n/ *n* **1** the act of propitiating **2** something that propitiates; *specif* an atoning sacrifice

**propitiatory** /prə'pishiət(ə)ri/ *adj* intended to propitiate; expiatory

**propitious** /prə'pishəs/ *adj* **1** favourably disposed; benevolent ⟨*the fates are* ∼⟩ **2** boding well; auspicious ⟨∼ *sign*⟩ **3** tending to favour; opportune ⟨*a* ∼ *moment for the revolt to break out*⟩ [ME *propicious*, fr L *propitius*, fr *pro-* for + *petere* to seek – more at PRO-, FEATHER] – **propitiously** *adv*, **propitiousness** *n*

**propjet** /'prop,jet/ *n* TURBOPROP (jet engine driving a propeller)

**proplastid** /proh'plastid/ *n* a minute body in the CYTOPLASM (jellylike material) of a plant cell from which a PLASTID (specialized cell part containing pigment) is formed [ISV]

**propolis** /'propəlis/ *n* a brownish material of waxy consistency collected by bees from the buds of trees and used as a glue (e g to strengthen the hive) [L, fr Gk, fr *pro-* for + *polis* city – more at PRO-, POLICE]

**propone** /prə'pohn/ *vt, Scot* 1 to propose, propound 2 to bring or put forward (a defence) [ME (Sc) *proponen* – more at PROPOUND]

**proponent** /prə'pohnənt/ *n* one who argues in favour of something; an advocate [L *proponent-, proponens,* prp of *proponere*]

¹**proportion** /prə'pawsh(ə)n/ *n* 1 the relation of one part to another or to the whole with respect to magnitude, quantity, or degree; a ratio 2 the harmonious relation of parts to each other or to the whole; balance, symmetry 3 a statement of equality of two ratios in which the first of the four terms divided by the second equals the third divided by the fourth (e g in 4/2 = 10/5) 4a a proper or equal share ⟨*each did his ~ of the work*⟩ b a quota, percentage 5 *pl* size, dimensions [ME *proporcion,* fr MF *proportion,* fr L *proportion-, proportio,* fr *pro* for + *portion-, portio* portion – more at FOR]

*usage* Some people dislike the use of *a proportion* to mean simply "some" ⟨*a proportion of the students are French*⟩, and prefer to confine **proportion** to situations involving the idea of "percentage" ⟨*the greater proportion of the students are French*⟩ or to replace the word by **some, a few, most,** etc.

²**proportion** *vt* 1 to adjust (a part or thing) in proportion to other parts or things 2 to make the parts of harmonious or symmetrical

¹**proportional** /prə'pawsh(ə)nl/ *adj* 1a proportionate – usu + *to* ⟨*a is ~ to b*⟩ b having the same or a constant ratio 2 regulated or determined in proportionate amount or degree ⟨*a ~ system of immigration quotas*⟩ – **proportionally** *adv,* **proportionality** *n*

²**proportional** *n* a number or quantity in a proportion

**proportionalist** /prə'pawshənəlist/ *n* a person who advocates PROPORTIONAL REPRESENTATION

**proportional representation** *n* an electoral system designed to represent in a legislative body each political group or party in proportion to the number of votes cast for it in an election

**proportional tax** *n* a tax in which the tax rate remains constant regardless of the amount of the tax base

¹**proportionate** /prə'pawsh(ə)nət/ *adj* in due proportion – **proportionately** *adv*

²**proportionate** /prə'pawsh(ə),nayt/ *vt* to make proportionate; proportion

**proposal** /prə'pohzl/ *n* 1 an act of putting something forward for consideration 2a a proposed idea or plan of action; a suggestion b an offer of marriage 3 an application for insurance

*synonyms* Both **proposal** and **proposition** can mean a "suggestion", but an offer of marriage is a **proposal** (not a **proposition**) and an invitation to sex outside marriage is a **proposition** (not a **proposal**).

**propose** /prə'pohz/ *vi* 1 to form or put forward a plan or intention ⟨*man ~*s, *but God disposes*⟩ 2 to make an offer of marriage ~ *vt* 1a to present for consideration or adoption ⟨*~d terms for peace*⟩ b to establish as an aim; intend ⟨*~d to spend the summer in study*⟩ 2a to recommend to fill a place or vacancy; nominate ⟨*agreed to ~ him for membership*⟩ b to nominate (oneself) for an insurance policy c to offer as a toast ⟨*~ the health of the bridesmaids*⟩ [ME *proposen,* fr MF *proposer,* fr L *proponere* (perf indic *proposui*) – more at PROPOUND]

**proposer** /prə'pohzə/ *n* a person who proposes; *esp* one who applies for insurance

¹**proposition** /,propə'zish(ə)n/ *n* 1a something offered for consideration or acceptance; *specif* a proposal of sexual intercourse b a formal mathematical statement to be proved; a theorem 2 *philosophy* an expression, in language or signs, of something that can be asserted as either true or false 3 a project, situation, or individual requiring to be dealt with ⟨*he's a nasty ~*⟩ ⟨*the firm is not a paying ~*⟩ △ preposition *synonyms* see PROPOSAL – **propositional** *adj*

²**proposition** *vt* to make a proposal to; *specif* to propose sexual intercourse to

**propound** /prə'pownd/ *vt* 1 to produce (a will or similar document) to a court of law or before the proper authority so as to establish validity 2 *formal* to offer for discussion or considera-

tion [alter. of earlier *propone,* fr ME (Sc) *proponen,* fr L *proponere* to display, propound, fr *pro-* before + *ponere* to put, place – more at PRO-, POSITION] – **propounder** *n*

**propraetor, propretor** /proh'preetə/ *n* a PRAETOR (senior magistrate) of ancient Rome sent out to govern a province [L *propraetor,* fr *pro-* (as in *proconsul*) + *praetor*]

**propranolol** /proh'pranəlol/ *n* a synthetic drug, $C_{16}H_{21}NO_2$, that blocks the action of the hormone adrenalin on BETA-RECEPTORS in the heart and is used esp in the treatment of abnormal heart rhythms and to lower high blood pressure [*propyl* + *propanol* (propyl alcohol) + *-ol*]

¹**proprietary** /prə'prie-ət(ə)ri/ *n* 1 a body of proprietors 2 PATENT MEDICINE [ME *proprietarie* owner, fr LL *proprietarius,* fr *proprietarius,* adj]

²**proprietary** *adj* 1 (characteristic) of a proprietor ⟨*~ rights*⟩ 2 made and marketed under a patent, trademark, etc ⟨*a ~ process*⟩ 3 privately owned and managed ⟨*a ~ clinic*⟩ [LL *proprietarius,* fr L *proprietas* property – more at PROPERTY]

**proprietary colony** *n* a colony granted to a proprietor with full prerogatives of government

**proprietary company** *n, Austr* PRIVATE COMPANY

**proprietor** /prə'prie-ətə/, *fem* **proprietress** /-tris/ *n* 1 a person who has the legal right or exclusive title to something; an owner 2 a person having an interest (e g control or present use) less than absolute and exclusive right [alter. of ¹*proprietary*] – **proprietorship** *n,* **proprietorial** *adj*

**propriety** /prə'prie-əti/ *n, formal* 1 the quality or state of being proper; fitness 2 the standard of what is socially or morally acceptable in conduct or speech, esp between the sexes; decorum 3 *pl* the conventions and manners of polite society [ME *propriete,* fr MF *propriété* property, quality of a person or thing – more at PROPERTY]

**proprioception** /,prohpri-ə'sepsh(ə)n/ *n* the reception of stimuli produced within the organism [*proprioceptive* + *-ion*]

**proprioceptive** /,prohpriə'septiv/ *adj* of or being stimuli arising within the organism [L *proprius* own + E *-ceptive* (as in *receptive*)]

**proprioceptor** /,prohpri-ə'septə/ *n* a SENSE ORGAN receiving and excited by proprioceptive stimuli

**prop root** *n* a root that serves as a prop or support to the plant; *specif* an aerial root that grows down from the stem, trunk, or a branch into the ground

**proptosis** /prop'tohsis/ *n* forward projection or displacement, esp of the eyeball [NL, fr LL, falling forwards, fr Gk *proptōsis,* fr *propiptein* to fall forwards, fr *pro-* + *piptein* to fall – more at PRO-, FEATHER]

**propulsion** /prə'pulsh(ə)n/ *n* 1 the action or process of propelling 2 something that propels [L *propulsus,* pp of *propellere* to propel]

**propulsive** /prə'pulsiv/ *adj* having power to or tending to propel [L *propulsus*]

**propyl** /'prohpil, -piel/ *n* a chemical group, $C_3H_7$, with a VALENCY of one, that is derived from the gas PROPANE [ISV, fr *propionic* + *-yl*] – **propylic** *adj*

**propylaeum** /,propə'lee-əm, ,proh-/ *n, pl* **propylaea** /-'lee-ə/ a vestibule or gateway of architectural importance in front of a Greek temple precinct [L, fr Gk *propylaion,* fr *pro-* before + *pylē* gate]

**propylene** /'propileen/ *n* an inflammable gas, $C_3H_6$, obtained from petroleum and used chiefly in the synthesis of other chemical compounds

**propylene glycol** *n* a thick liquid, $CH_3CHOHCH_2OH$, that is used esp as an antifreeze and solvent and in brake fluids

**pro rata** /,proh 'rahtə/ *adv* in proportion; proportionally [L] – **pro rata** *adj*

**prorate** /,proh'rayt, '-,-/ *vt* to divide, distribute, or assess proportionately ~ *vi* to make a pro rata distribution [*pro rata*] – **proration** *n*

**prorogue** /prə'rohg, ,proh-/ *vt* 1 to terminate a session of (e g a parliament) by royal prerogative 2 *formal* to defer, postpone ~ *vi* to suspend or end a legislative session [ME *prorogen,* fr MF *proroguer,* fr L *prorogare,* fr *pro-* before + *rogare* to ask – more at PRO-, RIGHT] – **prorogation** *n*

**pros-** /pros/ *prefix* 1 near; towards ⟨*proselyte*⟩ 2 in front ⟨*prosencephalon*⟩ 3 replacement; substitute ⟨*prosthesis*⟩ [LL, fr Gk, fr *proti, pros* face to face with, towards, in addition to, near; akin to Skt *prati-* near, towards, against, in return, Gk *pro* before – more at FOR]

**prosaic** /proh'zayik, prə-/ *adj* 1a characteristic of prose as distinguished from poetry b dull, unimaginative 2 belonging to the everyday world; commonplace [LL *prosaicus*, fr L *prosa* prose] – **prosaically** *adv*

**prosaism** /'prohzay,iz(ə)m, 'prohzi-/ *n, formal* **1** a prosaic manner, style, or quality **2** *usu pl* a prosaic expression

**prosaist** /proh'zayist/ *n, formal* a prosaic person [L *prosa* prose]

**proscenium** /proh'seenyəm, prə-, -ni-əm/ *n* the stage of an ancient Greek or Roman theatre [L, fr Gk *proskēnion* front of the building forming the background for a dramatic performance, stage, fr *pro-* + *skēnē* building forming the background for a dramatic performance – more at SCENE]

**proscenium arch** *n* the arch in a conventional theatre through which the spectator sees the stage

**prosciutto** /prə'shootoh/ *n, pl* **prosciutti** /-ti/, **prosciuttos** smoked spiced Italian ham, usu served in very thin slices [It, alter. of obs *presciutto*, fr *pre-* + *-sciutto*, fr L *exsuctus* dried up, sucked out, pp of *exsugere* to suck out, fr *ex-* + *sugere* to suck]

**proscribe** /proh'skrieb/ *vt* **1a** to put outside the protection of the law **b** to outlaw, exile; *specif* to outlaw by publishing the name of (a person) in ancient Rome **2** to condemn or forbid as harmful; prohibit △ prescribe [L *proscribere* to publish, proscribe, fr *pro-* before + *scribere* to write – more at SCRIBE] – **proscriber** *n*

**proscription** /prə'skripsh(ə)n, proh-/ *n* **1** proscribing or being proscribed **2** an imposed restraint or restriction; a prohibition [ME *proscripcion*, fr L *proscription-, proscriptio*, fr *proscriptus*, pp of *proscribere*] – **proscriptive** *adj*, **proscriptively** *adv*

**¹prose** /prohz/ *n* **1a** ordinary nonmetrical language **b** a literary medium distinguished from poetry esp by its greater irregularity and variety of rhythm and its closer correspondence to the patterns of everyday speech **2** a prosaic style, quality, character, or condition; ordinariness ⟨the ~ of daily existence⟩ [ME, fr MF, fr L *prosa*, fr fem of *prorsus, prosus*, straightforward, being in prose, contr of *proversus*, pp. of *provertere* to turn forwards, fr *pro-* forwards + *vertere* to turn – more at PRO-, WORTH]

**²prose** *vi* **1** to write prose **2** to write or speak in a dull prosaic manner ~ *vt* to turn (e g a poem) into prose

**³prose** *adj* **1** of or written in prose **2** matter-of-fact, prosaic ⟨dry, ~ people of superior intelligence – Mary McCarthy⟩

**prosector** /proh'sektə/ *n* one who makes dissections for anatomical demonstrations [deriv of LL *prosector* anatomist, fr L *prosectus*, pp of *prosecare* to cut away, fr *pro-* forth + *secare* to cut – more at PRO-, SAW] – **prosectorial** *adj*

**prosecute** /'prosikyooht/ *vt* **1a** to institute and pursue legal proceedings against for a criminal offence ⟨~d *them for fraud*⟩ **b** to institute legal proceedings with reference to ⟨~ *a claim*⟩ **2** *formal* to pursue; FOLLOW THROUGH ⟨determined to ~ the investigation⟩ **3** *formal* to engage in; CARRY OUT ~ *vi* to institute and carry on a legal suit or prosecution △ persecute [ME *prosecuten*, fr L *prosecutus*, pp of *prosequi* to pursue – more at PURSUE] – **prosecutable** *adj*

**prosecuting attorney** /'prosikyoohting/ *n* a lawyer who conducts proceedings in a court on behalf of the government in the USA; DISTRICT ATTORNEY

**prosecution** /prosi'kyoohsh(ə)n/ *n* **1** prosecuting; *specif* the formal institution of a criminal charge, leading to a final judgment **2** *taking sing or pl vb* the party by whom criminal proceedings are instituted or conducted – compare DEFENCE

**prosecutor** /'prosikyoohtə/ *n* a person who institutes or conducts an official prosecution before a court

**proselyte** /'prosiliet/ *n* a new convert; *esp* a convert to Judaism [ME *proselite*, fr LL *proselytus* convert to Judaism, alien resident, fr Gk *prosēlytos*, fr *pros* near + *-ēlytos* (akin to *elthein* to go); akin to Gk *elaunein* to drive – more at PROS-, ELASTIC]

**proselytism** /'prosili,tiz(ə)m/ *n* **1** the act of becoming or condition of being a proselyte; religious conversion **2** the act or process of proselytizing

**proselyt·ize, -ise** /'prosili,tiez/, *NAm chiefly* **proselyte** *vt* to make a convert of ~ *vi* to make or try to make converts, esp to a religion – **proselytizer** *n*, **proselytization** *n*

**prosencephalon** /prosin'sefələn/ *n* FOREBRAIN (uppermost or frontmost of the major divisions of the brain) – compare MESENCEPHALON [NL] – **prosencephalic** *adj*

**prosenchyma** /pros'engkimə/ *n, pl* **prosenchymata** /-engk-'kiemətə, -'kim-/, **prosenchymas** a plant tissue composed of elongated pointed cells often having thickened cell walls, that occurs esp in the woody parts of a plant specialized for conduction of water and food and for mechanical support [NL] – **prosenchymatous** *adj*

**prose poem** *n* a work in prose that has some of the qualities of a poem – **prose poet** *n*

**prosimian** /proh'simiən/ *n* any of a suborder (Prosimii) of lower primates including the tree-shrews, the lemurs, and the lorises [NL *Prosimii*, suborder name, fr *¹pro-* + L *simia* ape – more at SIMIAN]

**prosit** /'prohzit/ *interj* – used to wish good health, esp before drinking; compare CHEERS [Ger, fr L *prosit* may it be beneficial, fr *prodesse* to be useful – more at PROUD]

**prosobranch** /'prosəbrangk/ *n, pl* **prosobranchs** any of a subclass (Prosobranchia of the class Gastropoda, phylum Mollusca) of chiefly marine INVERTEBRATE animals (e g limpets and whelks) that have the loop of visceral nerves twisted into a figure eight and typically have a spiral shell closed by a lid (OPERCULUM), separate sexes, and gills positioned in front of the heart [NL *Prosobranchia*, group name, fr *proso-* in front (fr Gk *prosō* forwards) + *branchia* gill]

**prosody** /'prosədi/ *n* **1** the study of versification; *esp* the systematic study of metre – compare METRICS **2** a particular system, theory, or style of versification **3** the stress and intonation patterns in language – compare SUPRASEGMENTAL [ME, fr L *prosodia* accent of a syllable, fr Gk *prosōidia* song sung to instrumental music, accent, fr *pros* in addition to + *ōidē* song – more at PROS-, ODE] – **prosodist** *n*, **prosodic, prosodical** *adj*, **prosodically** *adv*

**prosopopoeia** /,prosəpə'pee-ə/ *n* a figure of rhetoric in which an imaginary or absent person is represented as speaking or acting; *esp* PERSONIFICATION **1** [L, fr Gk *prosōpopoiia*, fr *prosōpon* mask, person (fr *pros-* + *ōps* face) + *poiein* to make – more at EYE, POET]

**¹prospect** /'prospekt/ *n* **1a** an extensive view; *also* a place that commands an extensive view **b** something spread out as a view; a scene **2** the outlook or aspect of a building **3a** a mental picture of something to come; a vision **b** something that is awaited or expected; a possibility – often in *in prospect* ⟨has a fine career in ~⟩ **c** the act of looking forward; anticipation **d** *pl* **d(1)** financial expectations **d(2)** chances **4a** a place showing signs of containing a mineral deposit **b** a partly developed mine **c** the mineral yield of a tested sample of ore or gravel **5a** a potential client or customer **b** a likely candidate for some appointment, job, or position *synonyms* see *¹*VIEW [ME, fr L *prospectus* view, prospect, fr *prospectus*, pp of *prospicere* to look forwards, exercise foresight, fr *pro-* forwards + *specere* to look – more at PRO-, SPY]

**²prospect** /prə'spekt/ *vb* to explore (an area), esp for mineral deposits – **prospector** *n*

**prospective** /prə'spektiv/ *adj* **1** likely to come about; expected ⟨the ~ benefits of this law⟩ **2** likely to be or become ⟨a ~ mother⟩ △ perspective – **prospectively** *adv*

**prospectus** /prə'spektəs/ *n* a printed statement giving details of an organization or enterprise (e g a university, business, or forthcoming publication), distributed to prospective buyers, investors, or participants [L, prospect]

**prosper** /'prospə/ *vi* **1** to succeed in an enterprise or activity; *esp* to achieve economic success **2** to become strong and flourishing ~ *vt, archaic* to cause to succeed or thrive ⟨may the gods ~ our city⟩ [ME *prosperen*, fr MF *prosperer*, fr L *prosperare* to cause to succeed, fr *prosperus* favourable]

**prosperity** /pro'sperəti, prə-/ *n* the condition of being successful or thriving; *esp* economic well-being

**prosperous** /'prosp(ə)rəs/ *adj* **1** marked by success or wellbeing; *esp* financially successful **2** *archaic* auspicious, favourable [ME, fr MF *prospereux*, fr *prosperer* to prosper + *-eux* -ous] – **prosperously** *adv*

**prost** /prohst/ *interj* PROSIT

**prostaglandin** /,prostə'glandin/ *n* any of a group of related chemical compounds derived from FATTY ACIDS, that occur widely in body tissues (e g semen and lung and brain tissue) and function as locally acting hormones in the control of various processes. The group includes compounds that affect the nerve system, regulate blood flow and lower blood pressure, and induce labour and abortion by stimulating the muscles of the womb [*prosta*te *gland* + *-in;* fr its occurrence in the sexual glands of animals]

**prostate** /'prostayt/ *also* **prostatic** /pro'statik, prəs-/ *adj* of or being the PROSTATE GLAND △ prostrate

**prostatectomy** /,prostə'tektəmi/ *n* surgical removal of the PROSTATE GLAND

**prostate gland, prostate** *n* a small mass of muscular and glandular tissue in male mammals, that is situated round the neck of the bladder and secretes an alkaline liquid that makes up most of the volume of semen [NL *prostata*, fr Gk *prostatēs*, fr *proïstanai* to put in front, fr *pro-* before + *histanai* to cause to stand – more at PRO-, STAND]

**prostatism** /'prostətiz(ə)m/ *n* disease of the PROSTATE GLAND; *esp* a disorder resulting from obstruction of the bladder neck by an enlarged prostate gland

**prostatitis** /,prostə'tietəs/ *n* inflammation of the PROSTATE GLAND [NL]

**prosthesis** /'prosthəsis; *sense 1 or* -'thee-/ *n, pl* **prostheses** /-seez/ 1 an artificial part (eg a limb or tooth) to replace a missing part of the body 2 PROTHESIS (addition of a sound to the beginning of a word) [NL, fr Gk, addition, fr *prostithenai* to add to, fr *pros-* in addition to + *tithenai* to put – more at PRO-, DO]

**prosthetic** /pros'thetik/ *adj* 1 of a prosthesis or prosthetics 2 of or being a nonprotein group of a CONJUGATED PROTEIN (compound of a protein and a nonprotein group) – **prosthetically** *adv*

**prosthetics** /pros'thetiks/ *n taking sing or pl vb* the branch of surgery or dentistry concerned with the artificial replacement of missing parts

**prosthodontics** *n taking sing or pl vb* dentistry concerned with the replacement of missing teeth and adjacent tissues by artificial parts; dental prosthetics [NL *prosthodontia*, fr *prosthesis* + -*odontia*]

¹**prostitute** /'prosti,tyooht/ *vt* 1 to offer (oneself or another person) for sexual purposes in exchange for money 2 to put to a corrupt or unworthy use; debase ⟨~ *one's talents*⟩ [L *prostitutus*, pp of *prostituere* to expose publicly, offer for sale, prostitute, fr *pro-* before + *statuere* to set up, place – more at PRO-, STATUTE] – **prostitutor** *n*

²**prostitute** *n* a woman or man who engages in sexual activities in return for payment

**prostitution** /,prosti'tyoohsh(ə)n/ *n* 1 the act or practice of engaging in sexual activities in return for payment 2 the state of being prostituted; debasement

**prostomium** /proh'stohmyəm, -mi·əm/ *n, pl* **prostomia** /-miə/ the portion of the head of various worms and MOLLUSCS that is situated in front of the mouth [NL, fr Gk *pro-* + *stoma* mouth – more at STOMACH] – **prostomial** *adj*

¹**prostrate** /'prostrayt/ *adj* 1a lying full-length face downwards as a token of adoration or submission b extended in a horizontal position; flat 2a lacking in vitality or will; overcome ⟨*a whole continent* ~ *and impoverished* – Andrew Shonfield⟩ b physically exhausted 3 *of a plant* trailing on the ground; PROCUMBENT 1 ⟨*a* ~ *shrub*⟩ *usage* see PRONE △ **prostate** [ME *prostrat*, fr L *prostratus*, pp of *prosternere*, fr *pro-* before + *sternere* to spread out, throw down – more at STREW]

²**prostrate** /pro'strayt/ *vt* 1 to throw or put into a prostrate position 2 to put (oneself) in a humble and submissive posture or state ⟨*the whole town had to* ~ *itself in official apology* – Claudia Cassidy⟩ 3 to reduce to submission, helplessness, or exhaustion; overcome ⟨~d *with grief*⟩

**prostration** /pro'straysh(ə)n/ *n* 1a the act of assuming a prostrate position b the state of being in a prostrate position; abasement 2a complete physical or mental exhaustion; collapse b the process of being made powerless or the condition of powerlessness ⟨*the country suffered economic* ~ *after the war*⟩

**prostyle** /'prohstiel/ *adj, of a building* having pillars or columns in front, forming a PORTICO [L *prostylos*, fr Gk *pro-* + *stylos* pillar – more at STEER]

**prosy** /'prohzi/ *adj* 1 having the characteristics of prose 2 *of speech, writing, or manner* dull, tedious, and wearisome – compare PROLIX – **prosily** *adv*, **prosiness** *n*

**Prot** /prot/ *n, Irish derog* a Protestant

**prot-** /proht-/, **proto-** *comb form* 1 first in time; earliest; original ⟨proto*lithic*⟩ ⟨proto*nymph*⟩ ⟨proto*type*⟩ 2 first-formed; primary ⟨proto*xylem*⟩ 3 *cap* of or being the recorded or assumed language that is ancestral to (a specified language or group of related languages or dialects) ⟨Proto-*Indo-European*⟩ [ME *protho-*, fr MF, fr LL *proto-*, fr Gk *prōt-*, *prōto-*, fr *prōtos;* akin to Gk *pro* before – more at FOR]

**protactinium** /,prohtak'tini·əm/ *n* a shiny metallic radioactive chemical element of relatively short life [NL, fr *prot-* + *actinium;* fr its disintegrating into actinium]

**protagonist** /proh'tagənist, prə-/ *n* 1 one who takes the leading part in a drama, novel, or story 2 a leader or notable supporter of a cause 3 a player, competitor, or contender in a sport or game [Gk *prōtagōnistēs*, fr *prōt-* prot- + *agōnistēs*

competitor at games, actor, fr *agōnizesthai* to compete, fr *agōn* contest, competition at games – more at AGONY]

*usage* The **protagonist** of anything is, correctly, the "leader", and there can be only one, so that one should not properly speak of *the main* **protagonist** or of *several* **protagonists**. The use of the word to mean "supporter" ⟨*she's an enthusiastic* **protagonist** *of devolution*⟩ probably arose from a misunderstanding of the derivation by those who supposed that since an **antagonist** is "against" something, a **protagonist** must be "for" it; but the word is in fact formed from *prot-* = "first", not from *pro-* = "following".

**protamine** /'prohtəmeen, -min/ *n* any of various simple proteins that are strong chemical BASES, typically contain much ARGININE (an amino acid), and occur associated with DNA and RNA (eg in the sperm of fish) [ISV *prot-* + *amine*]

**protandrous** /proh'tandrəs/ *adj* of or being a hermaphrodite plant or animal in which the male sex organs mature and produce reproductive cells before the female organs – compare PROTOGYNOUS [*prot-* + -*androus*] – **protandry** *n*

**pro tanto** /proh 'tantoh/ *adv* for so much; to a certain extent [LL]

**protasis** /'prohtəsis/ *n, pl* **protases** /-seez/ 1 the introductory part of a classical drama – compare CATASTROPHE, EPITASIS 2 the subordinate clause of a conditional sentence (eg "If I were you" in "If I were you, I'd go") – compare APODOSIS [LL, fr Gk, premise of a syllogism, conditional clause, fr *proteinein* to stretch out before, put forwards, fr *pro-* + *teinein* to stretch – more at THIN] – **protatic** *adj*

**prote-, proteo-** *comb form* protein ⟨proteo*lysis*⟩ [ISV, fr Fr *protéine*]

**protea** /'prohti·ə/ *n* any of a genus (*Protea* of the family Proteaceae) of evergreen shrubs of the southern hemisphere often grown for their flowers that are clustered in dense flower heads and have showy coloured BRACTS (modified leaves) [NL, genus name, fr L *Proteus* Proteus; fr the widely-differing forms of various species]

**protean** /'prohtee·ən/ *adj* 1 readily assuming different shapes or roles 2 displaying great diversity or variety △ **protein** [*Proteus* (fr L, fr Gk *Prōteus*), mythological sea-god with the power of assuming different shapes]

**protease** /'protiayz, -ays/ *n* an ENZYME that breaks down proteins [ISV *prote-* + -*ase*]

**protect** /prə'tekt/ *vt* 1 to cover or shield from injury or destruction; guard 2 to shield or foster (eg a home industry) by a PROTECTIVE TARIFF *synonyms* see DEFEND [L *protectus*, pp of *protegere*, fr *pro-* in front + *tegere* to cover – more at PRO-, THATCH] – **protective** *adj*, **protectively** *adv*, **protectiveness** *n*

**protectant** /prə'tektənt/ *n* something that protects

**protection** /prə'teksh(ə)n/ *n* 1 protecting or being protected 2 something that protects 3 the freeing of the producers of a country from foreign competition in their home market by restrictions (eg high duties) on foreign competitive goods 4a safety from threatened violence achieved by making payments b money extorted by racketeers posing as a protective association 5 insurance coverage

**protectionist** /prə'tekshənist/ *n* an advocate of government economic protection for domestic producers through restrictions on foreign competitors – **protectionism** *n*, **protectionist** *adj*

**protective coloration** /prə'tektiv/ *n* coloration by which an animal blends with its natural surroundings and is made less visible to predators

**protective custody** *n* detention of a person by the state actually or allegedly for his/her own safety

**protective tariff** *n* a tariff intended primarily to protect domestic producers rather than to yield revenue – compare REVENUE TARIFF

**protector** /prə'tektə/, *fem* **protectress** /-tris/ *n* 1a one who or that which protects; a guardian; *specif* a man who maintains a woman as his mistress b a device used to prevent injury; a guard 2 *often cap* 2a one having the care of a kingdom until the sovereign comes of age; a regent b the executive head of the Commonwealth of England, Scotland, and Ireland from 1653 to 1659 – **protectorship** *n*

**protectorate** /prə'tekt(ə)rət/ *n* 1a government by a protector b *often cap* the government of England, Scotland, and Ireland under the Cromwells from 1653 to 1659 c the rank, office, or period of rule of a protector 2a the relationship of superior authority assumed by one power or state over a dependent one which it partly controls but has not formally annexed b the dependent political unit in such a relationship

**protégé**, *fem* **protégé** /'protə,zhay, 'proh-, -tay- (*Fr* prɔteʒe)/ *n* a person under the protection, guidance, or patronage of an influential person, usu for the purpose of furthering his/her career [Fr, fr pp of *protéger* to protect, fr L *protegere*]

**protein** /'prohteen/ *n* **1** any of numerous extremely complex organic chemical compounds that consist of one or more chains of linked AMINO ACIDS, are essential constituents of all living cells, and are synthesized from raw materials by plants but must be built up from separate amino acids obtained from proteins in the diet by humans and other animals **2** food (eg meat, fish, cheese, and lentils) rich in protein [Fr *protéine*, fr LGk *prōteios* primary, fr Gk *prōtos* first – more at PROT-]

**proteinaceous** /,prohti'naysh(ə)s/ *adj* of, like, or being protein

**proteinase** /'prohti,nayz, -,nays/ *n* an ENZYME that breaks down proteins; *specif* ENDOPEPTIDASE (one that splits proteins into smaller chains of AMINO ACIDS) [ISV]

**proteinuria** /,prohti'nyooəriə/ *n* the abnormal presence of protein in the urine, that is usu a sign of kidney disease – compare ALBUMINURIA [NL, fr ISV *protein* + NL *-uria*] – **proteinuric** *adj*

**pro tem** /,proh 'tem/ *adv* for the time being [short for *pro tempore*, fr L]

**proteo-** – see PROTE-

**proteolysis** /,prohti'oləsis/ *n* the breakdown of proteins or PEP-TIDES (chains of two or more linked AMINO ACIDS) with the formation of simpler (soluble) products [NL] – **proteolytic** *adj*

**proteose** /'prohtiohs, -ohz/ *n* any of various water-soluble protein derivatives formed by the partial breakdown of proteins [ISV]

**proteranthous** /,prohtə'ranthəs, prot-/ *adj* having flowers appearing before the leaves [Gk *proteros* + *anthos* flower – more at ANTHOLOGY] – **proteranthy** *n*

**Proterozoic** /,prohtərə'zoh·ik/ *adj or n* (of or being) an era of geological history equivalent to the later division of the PRE-CAMBRIAN and preceding the PALAEOZOIC era, that is marked by rocks containing a few fossils of algae and soft-bodied INVERTEBRATE animals (eg ANNELID worms); *also* (of or being) the system of rocks formed in this era [Gk *proteros* former, earlier (fr *pro* before) + ISV *-zoic* – more at FOR]

**¹protest** /'prohtest/ *n* **1** a formal or serious declaration of opinion and usu of dissent: eg **1a** *law* a sworn declaration that a note or bill has been duly presented and that payment has been refused **b** a formal declaration of dissent from an act or resolution of esp a legislature **c** a formal declaration of dis-approval ⟨*reprieved in response to international* ~s⟩ **2** the act or an instance of protesting; *esp* a usu organized public demonstration of disapproval ⟨*staged a* ~ *against the war*⟩ **3** a complaint, objection, or display of unwillingness, usu to an idea or a course of action ⟨*went to the dentist under* ~⟩ **4** an objection (eg against an opponent) made to an official or governing body of a sport **5** a statement made by the master of a ship and attested by a consul, notary, or justice of the peace, of the circumstances in which the ship or cargo was damaged

**²protest** /prə'test/ *vt* **1** to make formal or solemn declaration or affirmation of ⟨~ ed *his innocence*⟩ **2** *law* to execute or have executed a formal protest against (eg a BILL OF EXCHANGE or PROMISSORY NOTE) **3** *NAm* to make a formal protest against ⟨~ing *the war*⟩ **4** *NAm* to offer objection to or remonstrate against ⟨*unwilling to* ~ *the cost of his ticket*⟩ ~ *vi* to express disagreement, object strongly, or make a protest *synonyms* see ASSERT, ²OBJECT [ME *protesten*, fr MF *protester*, fr L *protestari*, fr *pro-* forth + *testari* to call to witness – more at PRO-, TESTAMENT] – **protester, protestor** *n*

**protestant** /'protistənt/ *n* **1** *cap* an adherent of any of those Christian churches that separated from the Roman Catholic communion at the Reformation or subsequently **2** one who makes or enters a protest [MF, one who protests (*specif* one of the German dissenters from an anti-Lutheran edict of the Diet of Spires in 1529), fr L *protestant-*, *protestans*, prp of *protestari*] – **Protestantism** *n*

**Protestant** *adj* concerning Protestants, their churches, or their religion

**protestation** /,prote'staysh(ə)n, proh-, -ti-/ *n* **1** the act of pro-testing **2** a solemn declaration or avowal

**proteus** /'prohtios/ *n, pl* **protei** /'prohti,ee, -ie/ any of a genus (*Proteus*) of bacteria including forms found in decaying organic matter and others associated with disorders of the stomach and intestines [NL, genus name, fr L, Proteus – more at PRO-TEAN]

**prothalamion** /,prohthə'laymi·ən/ *n, pl* **prothalammia** /-miə/ a song or poem in celebration of a forthcoming marriage [NL, fr Gk *pro-* + *-thalamion* (as in *epithalamion*)]

**prothalamium** /,prohthə'laymi·əm/ *n, pl* **prothalamia** /-miə/ *n*, a prothalamion

**prothallium** /proh'thalyəm, -li·əm/ *n, pl* **prothallia** /-liə/ a prothallus [NL] – **prothallial** *adj*

**prothallus** /proh'thaləs/ *n, pl* **prothalli** /-li, -lie/ the small typically flat green plant body that develops from an asexually produced spore of a fern or related plant and bears sex organs that produce the reproductive cells; the GAMETOPHYTE (plant stage that bears cells for sexual reproduction) of a fern, horse-tail, etc; *also* a small structure of a conifer or related plant corresponding to this [NL, fr *pro-* + *thallus*]

**prothesis** /'prothəsis/ *n, pl* **protheses** /-seez/ the addition of a sound to the beginning of a word (eg in Old French *estat* from Latin *status*) [LL, alter. of *prosthesis,* fr Gk, lit., addition – more at PROSTHESIS] – **prothetic** *adj*

**prothetely** *n* the precocious development or manifestation of one or more structures or characteristics associated with a later stage of development (eg the presence of pupal struc-tures in an insect larva) – compare HYSTEROTELY [perh fr Gk *protithenai* to put before (fr *pro-* + *tithenai* to put) + *telein* to complete, perfect, fr *telos* end – more at DO, WHEEL] – **prothetelic** *adj*

**prothonotary** /,proht(h)ə'noht(ə)ri, ,proh't(h)onət(ə)ri/ *n* PRO-TONOTARY

**prothoracic gland** /,prohthaw'rasik/ *n* either of a pair of glands in some insects that secrete a hormone that controls moulting

**prothorax** /,proh'thawraks/ *n* the front segment of the THORAX (middle body part between the head and abdomen) of an insect [NL *prothorac-, prothorax,* fr *¹pro-* + *thorax*] – **prothoracic** *adj*

**prothrombin** /proh'thrombin/ *n* a protein present in blood plasma that is produced in the liver in the presence of vitamin K and is converted into THROMBIN as part of the process of blood clotting [ISV]

**protist** /'prohtist/ *n* any of a large group or kingdom (*Protista*) of chiefly single-celled organisms including the PROTOZOANS and most single-celled algae, and, according to various classifications, some or all of the fungi, bacteria, and more complex algae [deriv of Gk *prōtistos* very first, primal, fr superl of *prōtos* first – more at PROT-] – **protistan** *adj or n*

**protium** /'prohtyəm/ *n* the ordinary and lightest form (ISOTOPE) of hydrogen containing one proton in the atomic nucleus – compare DEUTERIUM, TRITIUM [NL, fr Gk *prōtos* first]

**proto-** – see PROT-

**protochordate** /,prohtoh'kawdayt/ *n* any of a major group (Protochordata) of marine animals including the SEA SQUIRTS, ACORN WORMS, and LANCELETS, that have a NOTOCHORD (sup-porting rod analogous to a backbone) but do not possess a skull or SPINAL COLUMN; a CHORDATE animal (animal with a notochord) other than a VERTEBRATE [NL *Protochordata,* divi-sion name]

**protocol** /'prohtəkol/ *n* **1** an original draft of a diplomatic document (eg a treaty) **2** the summary or minutes of a diplo-matic conference or congress stating what took place **3** a treaty attached to another treaty as an amendment, adding extra provisions, changing the emphasis, etc **4** a code of conduct or etiquette prescribing how those taking part should behave on official or ceremonial occasions; *also* the observance of proto-col **5** *NAm* the plan of a scientific experiment or treatment [MF *prothocole,* fr ML *protocollum,* fr LGk *prōtokollon* first sheet of a papyrus roll bearing details of its manufacture or contents, fr Gk *prōt-* prot- + *kollan* to glue together, fr *kolla* glue; akin to MD *helen* to glue]

**protogalaxy** /'prohtoh,galəksi/ *n* a hypothetical cloud of gas believed to have condensed into the present-day galaxies and stars

**protogynous** /proh'tojinəs, prət-/ *adj* of or being a herma-phrodite plant or animal in which the female sex organs mature and produce reproductive cells before the male organs – com-pare PROTANDROUS [ISV *prot-* + *-gynous*] – **protogyny** *n*

**protohistory** /,protoh'histəri/ *n* the study of man in the times that immediately precede adequately documented history [ISV]

**protohuman** /,protoh'hyoohmən/ *adj or n* (of or resembling) a primitive ancestor of humans (eg a humanlike PRIMATE)

**protolanguage** /'protoh,lang·gwij/ *n* an assumed or recorded ancestral language

**protolithic** /ˌprohtə'lithik/ *adj* of the earliest period of the STONE AGE; EOLITHIC

**protomartyr** /ˌprohtoh'mahtə/ *n* the first martyr in a cause – used esp with reference to the first Christian martyr, St Stephen [ME *prothomartir*, fr MF, fr LL *protomartyr*, fr LGk *prōtomartyr-*, *prōtomartys*, fr Gk *prōt-* + *martyr-*, *martys* martyr]

**proton** /'prohton/ *n* an ELEMENTARY PARTICLE (minute particle of matter) that carries a single positive electrical charge and that together with the neutron is a constituent of the nucleus of all known atoms, with the exception of the hydrogen atom of which it forms the entire nucleus – compare ELECTRON [Gk *prōton*, neut of *prōtos* first – more at PROT-] – **protonic** *adj*

**protonate** /'prohtənayt/ *vt* to add a proton to ~ *vi* to acquire an additional proton – **protonation** *n*

**protonema** /ˌprohtə'neemə/ *n*, *pl* **protonemata** /-mətə/ the branching threadlike structure that is produced by the germination of a moss spore and from which side buds develop that grow into the moss plants [NL *protonemat-*, *protonema*, fr *prot-* + Gk *nēma* thread – more at NEMAT-] – **protonematal** *adj*

**protonotary** /ˌprohtə'noht(ə)ri, proh'tonət(ə)ri/, **prothonotary** /-t(h)ə-, 't(h)o-/ *n* **1** a chief clerk of any of various courts of law, an office abolished in 1837 **2** the principal registrar and chief administrative officer in the SUPREME COURTS of some Australian states [ME *prothonotarie*, fr LL *protonotarius*, fr *prot-* + L *notarius* notary]

**protonotary apostolic** *n*, *pl* **protonotaries apostolic** a Roman Catholic bishop who is a member of the chief college of prelates in the papal CURIA (governing body of the Roman Catholic church)

**protonymph** /'prohtoh,nimf/ *n* any of various mites in their first developmental stage – **protonymphal** *adj*

**protopathic** /ˌprohtə'pathik/ *adj* **1** being or relating to the reception of rather coarse stimuli only (e g pain, heat, and cold) by RECEPTORS (cells or groups of cells that receive stimuli) in the skin or the nerves supplying such receptors ⟨~ *sensitivity*⟩ **2** of or being a nerve or RECEPTOR in the skin that responds only to rather coarse stimuli □ compare EPICRITIC [ISV, fr MGk *prōtopathēs* affected first, fr Gk *prōt-* prot- + *pathos* experience, suffering – more at PATHOS]

**protophloem** /ˌprohtoh'floh•em/ *n* the first-formed PHLOEM (food-conducting tissue) of a plant that develops from PROCAMBIUM

**protoplanet** /ˌprohtoh,planit/ *n* a hypothetical whirling gaseous mass within a giant cloud of gas and dust that rotates round a sun and is believed to give rise to a planet

**protoplasm** /'prohtə,plaz(ə)m/ *n* **1** the living material of a cell and its nucleus consisting of a complex of organic and inorganic substances (e g proteins and salts in solution) **2** CYTOPLASM (protoplasm of a cell outside the nucleus) [Ger *protoplasma*, fr *prot-* + NL *plasma*] – **protoplasmic** *adj*

**protoplast** /'prohtə,plast/ *n* **1** something formed first; a prototype **2** a living mass of protoplasm including a nucleus, considered as a single unit; *specif* a plant or bacterial cell without its surrounding cell wall [MF *protoplaste*, fr LL *protoplastus* first man, fr Gk *prōtoplastos* first formed, fr *prōt-* prot- + *plastos* formed, fr *plassein* to mould – more at PLASTER] – **protoplastic** *adj*

**protostar** /'prohtoh,stah/ *n* a hypothetical cloud of dust and atoms in space believed to develop into a star

**protostele** /'prohtə,steel, ˌprohtə'steeli/ *n* the simplest arrangement of the food- and water-conducting tissues of a plant that occurs in the roots of many plants and in the stems of some ferns and CLUB MOSSES and consists of a solid longitudinal rod of XYLEM (water-conducting tissue) surrounded by PHLOEM (food-conducting tissue) – **protostelic** *adj*

**prototrophic** /ˌprohtə'trofik/ *adj* deriving nourishment from inorganic sources ⟨*sulphur bacteria are* ~⟩ [ISV] – **prototroph** *n*, **prototrophy** *n*

**prototype** /'prohtə,tiep, -toh-/ *n* **1** an original model on which something is patterned or based, or from which it derives – compare ARCHETYPE **2** a first full-scale and usu operational form of a new type or design of a construction (e g an aeroplane) [Fr, fr Gk *prōtotypon*, fr neut of *prōtotypos* archetypal, fr *prōt-* + *typos* type] – **prototypical, prototypic** *adj*

**protoxylem** /ˌprohtə'zieləm/ *n* the first-formed XYLEM (water-conducting tissue) of a plant that develops from PROCAMBIUM and consists of narrow relatively thin-walled cells capable of stretching

**protozoan** /ˌprohtə'zoh•ən/ *n* any of a phylum or subkingdom (Protozoa) of minute single-celled animals varying in structure and physiology, that often have complex life cycles, occur in almost every kind of habitat, and include some that are serious parasites of human beings and domestic animals [NL *Protozoa*, phylum name, fr *prot-* + *-zoa*] – **protozoal, protozoan, protozoic** *adj*

**protozoology** /ˌprohtohzooh'oləji, -zoh-, -tə-/ *n* a branch of zoology dealing with protozoans [NL *Protozoa* + ISV *-logy*] – **protozoologist** *n*, **protozoological** *adj*

**protozoon** /ˌprohtə'zoh•on/ *n*, *pl* **protozoa** /-'zoh-ə/ a protozoan [NL, fr sing. of *Protozoa*]

**protract** /prə'trakt/ *vt* **1** to prolong in time or space **2** to lay down the lines and angles of with scale and protractor; plot **3** to extend forwards or outwards [L *protractus*, pp of *protrahere*, lit., to draw forwards, fr *pro-* forwards + *trahere* to draw – more at PRO-, DRAW]

**protractile** /prə'traktiel/ *adj* capable of being thrust out ⟨~ *jaws*⟩ [L *protractus*]

**protraction** /prə'traksh(ə)n/ *n* **1** protracting or being protracted **2** the drawing to scale of an area of land

**protractor** /prə'traktə/ *n* **1a** one who or that which protracts, prolongs, or delays **b** a muscle that extends a body part or draws it out or away from the body – compare RETRACTOR **2** an instrument that is used for marking out or measuring angles in drawing

**protrude** /prə'troohd/ *vt* **1** to cause to project or stick out **2** *archaic* to thrust forwards ~ *vi* to jut out from the surrounding surface or context ⟨*a handkerchief* protruding *from his breast pocket*⟩ □ compare INTRUDE, OBTRUDE [L *protrudere*, fr *pro-* + *trudere* to thrust – more at THREAT] – **protrusible** *adj*

**protrusion** /prə'troohzh(ə)n/ *n* **1** protruding or being protruded **2** something that protrudes [L *protrusus*, pp of *protrudere*]

**protrusive** /prə'troohsiv/ *adj* prominent, protuberant ⟨*a* ~ *jaw*⟩ – **protrusively** *adv*, **protrusiveness** *n*

**protuberance** /prə'tyooohb(ə)rəns/ *n* **1** being protuberant **2** something that is protuberant

**protuberant** /prə'tyooohb(ə)rənt/ *adj* thrusting or projecting out from a surrounding or adjacent surface, often as a rounded mass; prominent [LL *protuberant-*, *protuberans*, prp of *protuberare* to bulge out, fr L *pro-* forwards + *tuber* hump, swelling] – **protuberantly** *adv*

**proud** /prowd/ *adj* **1** feeling or showing pride: e g **1a** having or displaying excessive self-esteem **b** much pleased; exultant **c** having proper self-respect **2a** marked by stateliness; magnificent **b** giving reason for pride; glorious ⟨*the* ~est *moment in her life*⟩ **3** vigorous, spirited ⟨*a* ~ *steed*⟩ **4** projecting slightly from a surrounding surface; protuberant [ME, fr OE *prūd*, prob fr OF *prod*, *prud*, *prou* capable, good, valiant, fr LL *prode* advantage, advantageous, back-formation fr L *prodesse* to be advantageous, fr *pro-*, *prod-* for, in favour + *esse* to be – more at PRO-, IS] – **proudly** *adv* – **do proud** to give cause for pride or gratification to

synonyms **Proud**, **arrogant**, **haughty**, **disdainful**, and **supercilious** can all mean "feeling or showing a sense of one's own superiority, and scorn for what is inferior". **Proud** may suggest a proper pride, but in this context usually implies a lofty dignity or imposing manner which conveys contempt or conceit. **Arrogant** suggests a domineering attitude which seeks more consideration than its due ⟨arrogant *young men elbowed them off the pavement*⟩. **Haughty** suggests an innate consciousness of one's own superior worth, often due to birth or position, that manifests itself in scornfulness, not always concealed ⟨*passed by with a* haughty *look*⟩. **Disdainful** stresses manner rather than temperament, but also suggests (sometimes justifiable) contempt for something considered unworthy ⟨*waved the tray away with a* disdainful *smile*⟩. **Supercilious** adds to disdainful an aloofness amounting to rudeness. Compare [1]PRIDE
antonyms humble, self-effacing, unassuming

**proud flesh** *n* GRANULATION TISSUE (tissue that forms on the surface of a healing wound)

**proudhearted** /prowd'hahtid/ *adj* proud in spirit; haughty

**proustite** /'proohstiet/ *n* a mineral, $Ag_3AsS_3$, consisting of a sulphide of silver and arsenic that occurs as scarlet grains and is a minor source of silver [Fr, fr Joseph *Proust* †1826 Fr chemist]

**provable, proveable** /'proohvəbl/ *adj* capable of being proved – **provably** *adv*, **provability** *n*

**prove** /proohv/ *vb* **proved**; **proved**, **proven** /'proohv(ə)n/ *vt* **1a** to test the quality of; try out ⟨*the exception* ~s *the rule*⟩ **b** to test for conformity to a standard; *esp* to subject to a technical testing process **2a** to establish the truth or validity of by evidence or demonstration ⟨~d *her innocence*⟩ ⟨*young people need to* ~ *themselves as competent adults*⟩ **b** to check the correctness of ⟨e g an arithmetic operation⟩ **3** to ascertain the genuineness of; verify *specif* to obtain PROBATE of (a will) **4** *archaic* to experience ⟨*we will all the pleasures* ~ – Christopher Marlowe⟩ ~ *vi* **1** to turn out, esp after trial or test ⟨*the new drug* ~d *to be very effective*⟩ **2** *of bread dough* to rise and become aerated through the action of yeast [ME *proven*, fr OF *prover*, fr L *probare* to test, approve, prove, fr *probus* good, honest, fr *pro-* for, in favour + *-bus* (akin to OE *bēon* to be)] – **prover** *n*

*usage* The past participle when used as part of a verb is now usually **proved** ⟨*he's proved his point*⟩ but **proven** is becoming common in adjectival use ⟨*has a* **proven** *record of successful management*⟩.

**provenance** /'provənəns/ *n* an origin, source – used esp with reference to works of art or literature *synonyms* see ORIGIN [Fr, fr *provenir* to come forth, originate, fr L *provenire*, fr *pro-* forth + *venire* to come – more at PRO-, COME]

**Provençal** /ˌprovonh'sahl (*Fr* prɔvãsal)/ *n* **1** a native or inhabitant of Provence **2** a ROMANCE language of SE France [MF, fr *provençal* of Provence, fr *Provence*, region in SE France] – **Provençal** *adj*

**provender** /'provində/ *n* **1** dry food for domestic animals; feed **2** *chiefly humorous* food, victuals [ME, fr MF *provende, provendre*, fr ML *provenda*, alter. of *praebenda* subsistence allowance – more at PREBEND]

**provenience** /pro'veenyəns, -niəns/ *n, chiefly NAm* provenance [L *provenient-, proveniens*, prp of *provenire*]

**proventriculus** /ˌprohven'trikyooləs/ *n, pl* **proventriculi** /-li, -lie/ **1** the thin-walled chamber in front of the GIZZARD (chamber where food is ground up) of a bird, that constitutes the true stomach and contains glands that secrete digestive juices **2** the thick-walled muscular gizzard of an insect that is lined with horny teeth or plates for grinding food; *also* a corresponding part of the digestive tract of a crab, lobster, etc **3** the thin-walled sac in front of the gizzard of an earthworm; CROP [NL]

**proverb** /'provuhb/ *n* a brief pithy saying embodying a truth or widely held belief (e g "absence makes the heart grow fonder") – compare ADAGE [ME *proverbe*, fr MF, fr L *proverbium*, fr *pro-* ¹*pro-* + *verbum* word]

**'pro-ˌverb** *n* a form of the verb *do* used to avoid repetition of a full verb ⟨*the word* do *in "act as I do" is a* ~⟩ [²*pro-* + *verb*]

**proverbial** /prə'vuhbyəl, -bi-əl/ *adj* **1** of or resembling a proverb **2** that has become a proverb or byword ⟨*France is* ~ *as the land of good food and wine*⟩ – **proverbially** *adv*

**Proverbs** /'provuhbz/ *n taking sing vb* – see BIBLE table

**provide** /prə'vied/ *vi* **1** to make adequate provision or preparation for something ⟨*we* ~d *for winter by buying warm clothes*⟩ ⟨~ *against future loss*⟩ **2** to make a proviso or stipulation ⟨*the constitution. . .* ~s *for an elected president*⟩ **3** to supply what is needed for sustenance or support ⟨~s *for a large family*⟩ ~ *vt* **1** to state, stipulate ⟨*he* ~d *in his will that he should be buried in unconsecrated ground*⟩ **2a** to supply, afford ⟨*curtains* ~ *privacy*⟩ ⟨*a string quartet* ~d *the entertainment*⟩ **b** *archaic* PROVIDE WITH ⟨*take the goods the gods* ~ *thee* – John Dryden⟩ [ME *providen*, fr L *providēre*, lit., to see ahead, fr *pro-* forwards + *vidēre* to see – more at PRO-, WIT]

**provide with** *vt* to equip or furnish (a person) with (something) ⟨*the school* provided *the children* with *pencils*⟩

**provided** /prə'viedid/ *conj* providing [pp of *provide*]

**providence** /'provid(ə)ns/ *n* **1a** often *cap* the care or superhuman guidance or care – compare FATE **b** *cap* God or Nature conceived as the power sustaining and guiding human destiny **2** being provident [ME, fr MF, fr L *providentia*, fr *provident-, providens*]

**provident** /'provid(ə)nt/ *adj* **1** showing foresight in providing for the future; prudent **2** frugal, thrifty [L *provident-, providens*, fr prp of *providēre*] – **providently** *adv*

**providential** /ˌprovi'densh(ə)l/ *adj* **1** of or determined by providence **2** occurring (as if) by an intervention of providence; opportune ⟨*a* ~ *escape*⟩ – **providentially** *adv*

**provident society** *n* FRIENDLY SOCIETY (savings association)

**provider** /prə'viedə/ *n* one who or that which provides; *esp* one who provides for his/her family

**providing** /prə'vieding/ *conj* on condition; if and only if – often + *that* ⟨*you may come* ~ *that you pay for yourself*⟩ [prp of *provide*]

*usage* **Providing** and **provided** both imply a clear stipulation for some condition to be fulfilled, and should not be used merely for "if" ⟨⚠ *it wouldn't have happened* **providing** *he'd known the truth*⟩. Writers on usage recommend the use of **provided**, rather than **providing**, in formal writing, but both have been established in English since the 15th century ⟨*always* **providing** *our leisure is not circumscribed by duty* – George Eliot⟩.

**province** /'provins/ *n* **1a** an area of the Roman empire outside Italy and under the jurisdiction of a governor **b** an administrative district or division of a country **c** *pl* all of a country except the metropolis – usu + *the* **2a** *Christianity* an area in a country, under the jurisdiction of an archbishop or METROPOLITAN (Eastern Orthodox prelate) **b** a territorial and administrative unit of a religious order **3** an area characterized by homogeneous geographical, geological, or ecological features **4a** a branch of learning or thought; a field of activity **b** a person's proper business, function, or activity; a sphere [Fr, fr L *provincia*]

**¹provincial** /prə'vinsh(ə)l/ *n* **1** the head of a province of a Roman Catholic religious order **2** one living in or coming from a province **3a** a person of local or restricted interests or outlook **b** a person lacking urban polish or refinement

**²provincial** *adj* **1** of or coming from a province **2a** limited in outlook; narrow-minded **b** lacking the polish of urban society; unsophisticated – **provincialize** *vb*, **provincially** *adv*, **provinciality** *n*

**provincialism** /prə'vinshəliz(ə)m/ *n* **1** a dialectal or local word, phrase, or idiom **2** being provincial

**proving ground** /'proohving/ *n* **1** a place designed for testing equipment or making scientific experiments **2** a place where something new is tried out ⟨*this* ~ *of social experiment*⟩

**provirus** *n* a noninfectious form of a virus that reproduces itself inside a cell and is transmitted along with the genetic material of the host cell from one generation to the next [NL] – **proviral** *adj*

**¹provision** /prə'vizh(ə)n/ *n* **1a** the act or process of providing **b** that which is provided **2** a measure taken beforehand; a preparation ⟨*no* ~ *for replacements*⟩ **3** *pl* a stock of necessary materials or supplies; *esp* food **4** a condition, proviso, or stipulation [ME, fr MF, fr LL & L; LL *provision-, provisio* act of providing, fr L, foresight, fr *provisus*, pp of *providēre* to see ahead]

**²provision** *vt* to supply with provisions

**provisional** /prə'vizh(ə)nl/ *adj* serving for the time being; temporary; *specif* requiring later confirmation ⟨*gave her* ~ *consent*⟩ *synonyms* see ¹TRANSIENT – **provisionally** *adv*

**¹Provisional** *adj* of or being the wing of the IRA that uses violence and terrorism to achieve its ends

**²Provisional** *n* a member of the Provisional IRA

**proviso** /prə'viezoh/ *n, pl* **provisos, provisoes 1** an article or clause (e g in a statute or a contract) that introduces a condition, qualification, or exception **2** a conditional stipulation; a provision [ME, fr ML *proviso quod* provided that]

**provisory** /prə'viez(ə)ri/ *adj* **1** containing or subject to a proviso; conditional **2** provisional

**provitamin** *n* a substance that can be converted in an organism into a specific vitamin

**¹Provo** /'prohvoh/ *n* a member of a militant Dutch antiauthoritarian and antiestablishment group [D, short for *provocateur* one who provokes, fr Fr, fr *provoquer*]

**²Provo** /'provoh, 'prohvoh/ *n, informal* a member of the Provisional wing of the IRA [by shortening & alter. fr *Provisional*]

**provocation** /ˌprovə'kaysh(ə)n/ *n* **1** the act of provoking; incitement **2** something that provokes, usu to anger or irritation [ME *provocacioun*, fr MF *provocation*, fr L *provocation-, provocatio*, fr *provocatus*, pp of *provocare*]

**provocative** /prə'vokətiv/ *adj* acting or tending to provoke, excite, or stimulate ⟨*a* ~ *statement*⟩ ⟨*a* ~ *low-cut dress*⟩ – **provocative** *n*, **provocatively** *adv*, **provocativeness** *n*

**provoke** /prə'vohk/ *vt* **1** to incite to anger; incense ⟨*enough to* ~ *a saint*⟩ **2** to stir up; evoke ⟨*his candour* ~d *a storm of controversy* – *TLS*⟩ **3** to cause (a person) to behave in a certain way **4** to provide the needed stimulus for **5** *archaic* to arouse, stir *synonyms* see IRRITATE *antonym* mollify [ME *provoken*, fr MF *provoquer*, fr L *provocare*, fr *pro-* forth + *vocare* to call – more at PRO-, VOICE]

**provoking** /prə'vohking/ *adj* causing mild anger; annoying – **provokingly** *adv*

**provolone** /ˌprohvə'lohni/ *n* a hard smooth yellow cheese of Italian origin that is made from cows' milk curds that have been heated and kneaded, moulded into various shapes, hung in strings to cure, and often lightly smoked [It, aug of *provola*, a kind of cheese]

**provost** /'provəst/ *n* 1 the head of the assembly of canons (CHAPTER) in a cathedral or other church; *specif* one who is also the parish priest in a parish of which the cathedral is the church 2 the chief magistrate of a Scottish BURGH (town) 3a the head of certain British colleges and schools b *NAm* a high-ranking university administrative officer [ME, fr OE *profost* & OF *provost*, fr ML *propositus*, alter. of *praepositus*, fr L, one in charge, director, fr pp of *praeponere* to place at the head – more at PREPOSITION]

**provost court** *n* a military court usu for the trial of minor offences within an occupied territory

**provost marshal** /prə'voh/ *n* an officer who supervises military police

**prow** /prow/ *n* 1 the bow of a ship – compare STEM 2 a pointed projecting front part [MF *proue*, prob fr OIt dial. *prua*, fr L *prora*, fr Gk *prōira*]

**prowess** /'prowis/ *n* 1 distinguished gallantry; *esp* military valour and skill 2 outstanding ability ⟨*her* ~ *at the piano*⟩ [ME *prouesse*, fr OF *proesse*, fr *prou* valiant – more at PROUD]

¹**prowl** /prowl/ *vb* to move about or roam over (a place) in a stealthy or predatory manner ⟨*submarines were* ~*ing along the coast*⟩ ⟨*they* ~*ed the garden*⟩ [ME *prollen*] – **prowler** *n*

²**prowl** *n* an act or instance of prowling

**prowl car** *n*, *NAm* a police car

**proximal** /'proksim(ə)l/ *adj*, *anatomy* next to or nearest the centre or point of attachment or origin – compare DISTAL [L *proximus*] – **proximally** *adv*

**proximal convoluted tubule** *n* the coiled tubular part of a NEPHRON (urine-secreting unit in a kidney) that leads away from the BOWMAN'S CAPSULE (structure where water and dissolved substances are filtered from the blood) and that is concerned esp with the transfer back into the blood of some of the water, sugar, and sodium and chloride ions removed by filtration, so that the blood retains the correct composition and only unwanted substances remain in the urine

**proximate** /'proksimət/ *adj*, *formal* 1a very near; close b soon to be forthcoming; imminent 2 next preceding or following ⟨*interested in* ~, *rather than ultimate, goals*⟩; *specif* next in a chain of cause and effect ⟨*the* ~ *cause of the accident*⟩ [L *proximatus*, pp of *proximare* to approach, fr *proximus* nearest, next, superl of *prope* near – more at APPROACH] – **proximately** *adv*

**proxime accessit** /,proksimay ak'sesit/ *n*, *pl* **proxime accesserunt** /ak'sesəroont/ a runner-up to the winner in a competitive examination [L, he has come next]

**proximity** /prok'siməti/ *n*, *formal* being close in space, time, or association; nearness [MF *proximité*, fr L *proximitat-, proximitas*, fr *proximus*]

**proximity fuse** *n* an electronic fuse that detonates an explosive device (e g a projectile or mine) when activated by the proximity of a target

**proximo** /'proksimoh/ *adj* of or occurring in the next month after the present – compare ULTIMO [L *proximo mense* in the next month]

**proxy** /'proksi/ *n* 1a authority or power to act or vote for another b a document giving such authority; *specif* a POWER OF ATTORNEY authorizing a specified person to vote on behalf of absent shareholders at a company meeting 2 a person authorized to act for another [ME *procucie*, contr of *procuracie*, fr AF, fr ML *procuratia*, alter. of L *procuratio* procuration] – **proxy** *adj* – **by proxy** through the agency of a deputy

**prude** /proohd/ *n* one who affects extreme modesty or propriety, esp in sexual matters [Fr, good woman, prudish woman, short for *prudefemme* good woman, fr OF *prode femme*]

**prudence** /'proohd(ə)ns/ *n* 1 discretion or shrewdness in the management of affairs ⟨*the hard* ~ *of statesmen* – G M Trevelyan⟩ 2 skill and good judgment in the use of resources ⟨*wealth due to* ~ *during prosperous times*⟩ 3 caution or circumspection with regard to danger or risk ⟨*conservative from* ~ – T S Eliot⟩

**prudent** /'proohd(ə)nt/ *adj* characterized by, arising from, or showing prudence [ME, fr MF, fr L *prudent-, prudens*, contr of *provident-, providens* – more at PROVIDENT] – **prudently** *adv*

**prudential** /prooh'densh(ə)l/ *adj* 1 of or proceeding from prudence 2 exercising prudence, esp in business matters – **prudentially** *adv*

**prudery** /'proohd(ə)ri/ *n* 1 the characteristic quality or state of a prude 2 a prudish act or remark

**prudish** /'proohdish/ *adj* marked by prudery – compare PRIGGISH – **prudishly** *adv*, **prudishness** *n*

**pruinose** /'prooh·inohs/ *adj*, *botany* covered with whitish dust or bloom ⟨~ *stems*⟩ [L *pruinosus* covered with hoarfrost, fr *pruina* hoarfrost]

¹**prune** /proohn/ *n* 1 a plum dried or capable of drying without fermentation 2 *Br informal, chiefly humorous* a silly person [ME, fr MF, plum, fr L *prunum* – more at PLUM]

²**prune** *vt* 1 to cut off or cut back parts of (e g a shrub) to obtain a better shape or more abundant growth 2a to reduce by eliminating superfluous matter ⟨~d *the text*⟩ b to remove as superfluous ⟨~ *away all ornamentation*⟩ c to effect a reduction in ⟨~ *the budget*⟩ ~ *vi* to cut away what is unwanted [ME *prouynen*, fr MF *proignier*, prob alter. of *provigner* to layer, fr *provain* layer, fr L *propagin-, propago*, fr *pro-* forwards + *pangere* to fix – more at PRO-, PACT] – **pruner** *n*

**pruning hook** /'proohning/ *n* a pole with a curved blade for pruning plants

**prurient** /'prooəri·ənt/ *adj* 1 having an unhealthily strong or abnormal interest in sexual matters 2 arousing lascivious thoughts or desires [L *prurient-, pruriens*, prp of *prurire* to itch, crave, be wanton; akin to L *pruna* glowing coal, Skt *ploṣati* he singes] – **prurience** *n*, **pruriently** *adv*

**pruriginous** /prooh'rijinəs/ *adj* resembling, caused by, affected with, or being prurigo

**prurigo** /proo(ə)'riegoh/ *n* a persistent inflammatory skin disease marked by raised itching spots [NL, fr L *prurigin-, prurigo* itch, fr *prurire*]

**pruritic** /proo(ə)'ritik/ *adj* of or marked by itching

**pruritus** /proo(ə)'rietəs/ *n* (any of various conditions or skin disorders marked by) an intense sensation of itching [L, fr *pruritus*, pp of *prurire*]

**Prussian blue** /'prush(ə)n/ *n* 1 any of numerous blue iron pigments 2 a dark blue chemical compound of iron and cyanide, $Fe_4[Fe(CN)_6]_3.xH_2O$, used in chemistry as a test for FERRIC iron 3 a strong greenish-blue colour [*Prussia*, former kingdom & state in N Germany, where the pigment was discovered in 1704]

**Prussianism** /'prushəniz(ə)m/ *n* the practices or policies (e g the advocacy of militarism) held to be typically Prussian

**prussian-ize, -ise** /'prushəniez/ *vt*, *often cap* to make Prussian in character or principle (e g in authoritarian control or rigid discipline)

**prussic acid** /'prusik/ *n* HYDROCYANIC ACID [part trans of Fr *acide prussique*, fr *acide* acid + *prussique* of Prussian blue]

¹**pry** /prie/ *vi* 1 to inquire in an overinquisitive or impertinent manner *into* 2 to look closely or inquisitively at someone's possessions, actions, etc ⟨~*ing neighbours*⟩ [ME *prien*]

²**pry** *vt*, *chiefly NAm* ⁵PRIZE [by alter.]

**pryer** /'prie·ə/ *n* a prier

**Przewalski's horse** /,puhzhə'valskiz/ *n* a wild horse of Central Asia that has a dun-coloured coat with a short erect brown mane and no forelock [Nikolai *Przhevalski* †1888 Russ soldier & explorer]

**psalm** /sahm/ *n* a sacred song or poem used in worship; *esp* any of the biblical hymns collected in the Book of Psalms [ME, fr OE *psealm*, fr LL *psalmus*, fr Gk *psalmos*, lit., twanging of a harp, fr *psallein* to pluck, play a stringed instrument]

**psalmbook** /'sahm,book/ *n*, *archaic* a psalter

**psalmist** /'sahmist/ *n* a writer or composer of (biblical) psalms

**psalmody** /'sahmədi, 'salmədi/ *n* 1 the act, practice, or art of singing psalms in worship 2 a collection of psalms [ME *psalmodie*, fr LL *psalmodia*, fr LGk *psalmōidia*, lit., singing to the harp, fr *psalmos* + *aidein* to sing – more at ODE]

**Psalms** /sahmz/ *n taking sing vb* – see BIBLE table

**psalter** /'sawltə/ *n* a collection of psalms for use in church services; *also, often cap* the Book of Psalms [ME, fr OE *psalter* & OF *psaltier*, fr LL *psalterium*, fr LGk *psaltērion*, fr Gk, psaltery]

**psalterium** /sawl'tiəriəm/ *n*, *pl* **psalteria** OMASUM (third compartment of the stomach of a cow, sheep, etc) [NL, fr LL, psalter; fr the resemblance of the folds to the pages of a book]

**psaltery** *also* **psaltry** /'sawlt(ə)ri/ *n* an ancient musical instrument resembling the zither [ME *psalterie*, fr MF, fr L *psalterium*, fr Gk *psaltērion*, fr *psallein* to play on a stringed instrument]

**psammite** /'samiet/ *n* a sandstone [Fr, fr Gk *psammos* sand] – **psammitic** *adj*

**p's and q's** /ˌpeez ən(d) 'kyoohz/ *n pl* behaviour, manners – esp in *to mind one's p's and q's* [fr the phrase *mind one's p's and q's*, prob alluding to the difficulty a child learning to write may have in distinguishing between *p* and *q*]

**psephite** /'seefiet/ *n* a coarse rock (eg a CONGLOMERATE or BRECCIA) composed of pebbles or rock fragments [Fr *pséphite*, fr Gk *psēphos* pebble] – **psephitic** *adj*

**psephology** /se'foləji/ *n* the scientific study of elections, involving statistical analysis of results and voting patterns [Gk *psēphos* pebble, ballot, vote; fr the use of pebbles by the ancient Greeks in voting] – **psephologist** *n*, **psephological** *adj*

**pseud** /s(y)oohd/ *n, chiefly Br informal* one who is considered intellectually or socially pretentious [*pseud-*] – **pseud, pseudy** *adj*

**pseud-** /soohd-, syoohd-/, **pseudo-** *comb form* false; sham; spurious ⟨pseud*axis*⟩ ⟨pseudo*science*⟩ ⟨pseudo*podium*⟩ ⟨pseudo*intellectual*⟩ [ME, fr LL, fr Gk, fr *pseudēs*]

**pseudepigrapha** /ˌs(y)oohdi'pigrəfə/ *n pl, often cap* pseudonymous or anonymous Jewish religious writings of the period 200 BC to 200 AD; *esp* such writings (eg the Psalms of Solomon) not officially included in any Scriptures [NL, fr Gk, neut pl of *pseudepigraphos* falsely inscribed, fr *pseud-* + *epigraphein* to inscribe – more at EPIGRAM]

**pseudepigraphy** /ˌs(y)oohdi'pigrəfi/ *n* the ascription of false names of authors to works [Gk *pseudepigraphos*]

**pseudo** /'s(y)oohdoh/ *adj* not genuine: **a** spurious **b** pretentious [ME, fr *pseudo-*]

**pseudoallele** /ˌs(y)oohdoh-ə'leel/ *n* any of two or more closely linked genes that usu function in an identical manner as a single member of a pair of ALLELES (genes producing alternative versions of a particular characteristic) but occasionally undergo rearrangement by CROSSING-OVER to produce two genes that are noticeably different – **pseudoallelic** *adj*, **pseudoallelism** *n*

**pseudocarp** /'s(y)oohdoh,kahp/ *n* ACCESSORY FRUIT

**pseudocoel** /'s(y)oohdə,seel/ *n* a fluid-filled body cavity between the BODY WALL and the digestive tract in some INVERTEBRATE animals (eg NEMATODE worms)

**pseudocoelomate** /ˌs(y)oohdoh'seeləmayt/ *n or adj* (an animal) having a body cavity that is a pseudocoel [*pseud-* + *coelomate*]

**pseudocyesis** /ˌs(y)oohdohsie'eesis/ *n* FALSE PREGNANCY (psychosomatic state in which some signs of pregnancy occur) [NL, fr *pseud-* + *cyesis* pregnancy, fr Gk *kyēsis*, fr *kyein* to be pregnant – more at CAVE]

**pseudohermaphroditism** /ˌs(y)oohdoh-huh'mafrədietiz(ə)m/ *n* the congenital abnormality of having the internal sexual organs of one sex but external genitals that are either of the other sex or have characteristics of both sexes [ISV]

**pseudomonad** /ˌs(y)oohdoh'mohnad, -nəd/ *n* any of a genus (*Pseudomonas*) of short rod-shaped bacteria many of which produce a greenish fluorescent water-soluble pigment and including many that live on dead or decaying organic matter in soil or water and some that cause diseases in plants or animals [NL *Pseudomonad-, Pseudomonas*, genus name, fr *pseud-* + *monad-, monas* monad]

**pseudomonas** /ˌs(y)oohdoh'mohnəs/ *n, pl* **pseudomonades** /-nədeez/ a pseudomonad [NL, genus name, fr *pseud-* + *monad-, monas* monad]

**pseudomorph** /'s(y)oohdə,mawf, -doh-/ *n* **1** a mineral having a crystal form typical of another mineral type rather than of its own type **2** a deceptive or irregular form [prob fr Fr *pseudomorphe*, fr *pseud-* + *-morphe* -morph] – **pseudomorphic, pseudomorphous** *adj*, **pseudomorphism** *n*

**pseudomycelium** /ˌs(y)oohdoh·mie'seeliəm/ *n* an association of some bacteria or yeast cells in which the cells cling together in chains resembling small MYCELIA (networks of rootlike filaments in fungi) [NL] – **pseudomycelial** *adj*

**pseudonym** /'s(y)oohdə,nim/ *n* a fictitious name; *esp* one used by an author [Fr *pseudonyme*, fr Gk *pseudōnymos* bearing a false name]

**pseudonymous** /s(y)ooh'doniməs/ *adj* having or using a fictitious name ⟨*a* ~ *report*⟩; *also* being a pseudonym [Gk *pseudōnymos*, fr *pseud-* + *onoma, onyma* name] – **pseudonymously** *adv*, **pseudonymousness** *n*

**pseudopod** /'s(y)oohdə,pod/ *n* a pseudopodium [NL *pseudopodium*] – **pseudopodal, pseudopodial** *adj*

**pseudopodium** /ˌs(y)oohdə'pohdi·əm/ *n, pl* **pseudopodia** /-di·ə/ **1** a temporary protrusion of the CYTOPLASM (jellylike material inside a cell) of an amoeba or related single-celled animal, or of an amoeba-like cell (eg a WHITE BLOOD CELL), that is used for movement or for engulfing food or

other substances **2** a slender leafless branch of the GAMETOPHYTE (plant that produces reproductive cells) in various mosses, that often bears buds from which new plants will develop [NL]

**pseudopregnancy** /ˌs(y)oohdoh'pregnənsi/ *n* **1** FALSE PREGNANCY (psychosomatic state in which some signs of pregnancy occur) **2** a state resembling pregnancy that occurs in various mammals, usu after an infertile copulation, and during which OESTRUS (period of sexual excitement when a mammal can conceive) does not occur – **pseudopregnant** *adj*

**pseudorandom** /ˌs(y)oohdoh'randəm/ *adj* being or involving numbers that are selected by a definite computational process (eg one involving a computer) but that satisfy one or more standard tests for statistical randomness

**pseudoscorpion** /ˌs(y)oohdoh,skawpiən/ *n* any of a group (Pseudoscorpiones of the class Arachnida) of minute INVERTEBRATE animals that resemble the related scorpions but have no tail sting [NL *Pseudoscorpiones*, group name, fr *pseud-* + L *scorpion-, scorpio* scorpion]

**pshaw** /(p)shaw/ *interj* – used to express irritation, disapproval, contempt, or disbelief

**psi** /(p)sie/ *n* the 23rd letter of the Greek alphabet [LGk, fr Gk *psei*]

**psilocybin** /ˌsielə'siebin/ *n* a hallucinogenic chemical compound, $C_{12}H_{17}N_2O_4P$, obtained from a mushroom (*Psilocybe mexicana*) [NL *Psilocybe*, genus name + *-in*]

**psilomelane** /sie'lomilayn/ *n* a mineral that consists of an oxide of manganese together with potassium, sodium, and barium and is an important source of manganese [Gk *psilos* bare + *melan-, melas* black]

**psilophyte** /siela,fiet/ *n* any of an order (Psilophytales) of extinct simple rootless plants of Europe and E Canada that have horizontal underground stems (RHIZOMES) and forked branches and that include the oldest known land plants with water- and food-conducting tissues [NL *Psilophyton*, genus of plants, fr Gk *psilos* bare, mere + *phyton* plant – more at PHYT-] – **psilophytic** *adj*

**psittaceous** /si'tayshəs/ *adj* **1** psittacine **2** *formal or humorous* resembling a parrot ⟨~ *chatter*⟩ [L *psittacus* parrot]

**psittacine** /'(p)sitə,sien, -,seen, -sin/ *adj* relating to the parrot [L *psittacinus*, fr *psittacus* parrot, fr Gk *psittakos*]

**psittacosis** /ˌ(p)sitə'kohsis/ *n* a severe infectious disease of birds that is caused by a RICKETTSIA (parasitic microorganism) (*Miyagawanella psittaci*) and is transmissible to human beings in whom it usu causes a serious pneumonia [NL, fr L *psittacus*] – **psittacotic** *adj*

**psocid** /'sohsid/ *n* any of an order (Psocoptera syn Corrodentia) of minute soft-bodied often winged primitive insects (eg a BOOK LOUSE) [deriv of NL *Psocus*, genus of lice]

**psoriasis** /(p)so'rie·əsis, (p)sə-/ *n* a persistent skin condition characterized by red patches covered by continuously peeling white scales on a part or all of the body [NL, fr Gk *psōriasis*, fr *psōrian* to have the itch, fr *psōra* itch; akin to Gk *psēn* to rub] – **psoriatic** *adj or n*

**psych, psyche** /siek/ *vt, chiefly NAm informal* **1** to psychoanalyse **2a** to anticipate correctly the intentions or actions of **b** to analyse or work *out* (a problem or course of action) ⟨*I* ~ed *it all out by myself*⟩ **3a** to make psychologically uneasy; intimidate, scare; *esp* to cause to lose resolve ⟨*pressure doesn't* ~ *me* – Jerry Quarry⟩ – often + *out* **b** to make (oneself) psychologically ready for performance – usu + *up* ⟨~ed *himself up for the race*⟩ [by shortening]

**psych-** /siek-/, **psycho-** *comb form* **1** psyche ⟨psycho*gnosis*⟩ **2a** mind, mental processes and activities ⟨psycho*logy*⟩ ⟨psycho*analysis*⟩ ⟨psycho*active*⟩ **b** using psychoanalytical methods ⟨psycho*therapy*⟩ **c** brain ⟨psycho*surgery*⟩ **d** mental and ⟨psycho*somatic*⟩ [Gk, fr *psychē* breath, principle of life, life, soul; akin to Gk *psychein* to breathe, blow, cool, Skt *babhasti* he blows]

**psychasthenia** /ˌsiekəs'theenyə, siekasthə'nie·ə/ *n* an incapacity to resolve doubts or uncertainties or to resist phobias, obsessions, or compulsions that one knows is irrational – not now in technical use [NL] – **psychasthenic** *adj or n*

**psyche** /'sieki/ *n* the mind or soul; that which makes up the self [Gk *psychē*]

**psychedelic** /ˌsiekə'delik/ *adj* **1a** of or being drugs (eg LSD) capable of producing altered states of consciousness usu involving changed mental and sensory awareness and the experiencing of hallucinations **b** produced by or associated with the use of psychedelic drugs ⟨*a* ~ *experience*⟩ **2** imitating or reproducing effects (eg distorted or bizarre images or sounds, or bright swirling colours) resembling those produced by psychedelic drugs ⟨*a ~ light show*⟩ [Gk *psychē* soul + *dēloun* to show] – **psychedelically** *adv*

**psychiatry** /sie'kie·ətri/ *n* a branch of medicine that deals with mental, emotional, or behavioural disorders – compare PSYCHOLOGY [prob fr (assumed) NL *psychiatria*, fr *psych-* *-iatria* -iatry] – **psychiatrist** *n*, **psychiatric** *adj*, **psychiatrically** *adv*

¹**psychic** /'siekik/ *also* **psychical** *adj* **1** of or originating in the psyche **2** lying outside the sphere of physical science or knowledge; immaterial, moral, or spiritual in origin or force **3** *of a person* sensitive to nonphysical or supernatural forces and influences; having extraordinary or mysterious sensitivity, perception, or understanding (eg clairvoyance) [Gk *psychikos* of the soul, fr *psychē* soul] – **psychically** *adv*

²**psychic** *n* **1** a psychic person **2** MEDIUM 2e

**psychical research** /'siekikl/ *n* scientific investigation into apparent psychic phenomena

**psycho** /'siekoh/ *n, pl* **psychos** *informal* a psychopath – **psycho** *adj*

**psychoactive** /-'aktiv/ *adj, of a drug* affecting the mind or behaviour

**psychoanalyse**, *NAm chiefly* **psychoanalyze** /-'anəliez/ *vt* to treat by means of psychoanalysis

**psychoanalysis** /-ə'naləsis/ *n* a method of analysing unconscious mental processes and treating mental disorders that aims to bring such processes into consciousness by allowing the patient to talk freely about him-/herself, esp his/her early childhood experiences and dreams [ISV]

**psychoanalyst** /,siekoh'anəlist/ *n* a practitioner of psychoanalysis

**psychoanalytical** /,siekoh·anə'litikl/, **psychoanalytic** *adj* of or employing psychoanalysis or its principles and techniques – **psychoanalytically** *adv*

**psychobiography** /,siekoh·bie'ogrəfi/ *n* biography concentrating on the psychological development of its subject – **psychobiographical** *adj*

**psychobiology** /,siekoh·bie'oləji/ *n* the study of mental processes and behaviour in relation to other biological processes [ISV] – **psychobiologist** *n*, **psychobiological** *adj*

**psychodrama** /'siekoh,drahmə/ *n* an improvised dramatization of events from a patient's life designed to afford insight into and resolution of personal conflicts; *broadly* the playing of roles as a technique of psychotherapy or education – **psychodramatic** *adj*

**psychodynamics** /-die'namiks/ *n* the psychology of mental or emotional forces or processes and their effects on behaviour and mental states; *also* explanation or interpretation (eg of behaviour) in terms of these forces – **psychodynamic** *adj*, **psychodynamically** *adv*

**psychogenesis** /,siekoh'jenəsis/ *n* **1** (the study of) the origin and development of mental functions, traits, or states **2** development from mental as distinguished from physical origins [NL] – **psychogenetic** *adj*

**psychogenic** /,siekoh'jenik, -kə-/ *adj, esp of an illness, symptoms, etc* originating in the mind or in mental or emotional conflict – **psychogenically** *adv*

**psychokinesis** /,siekohki'neesis/ *n* the apparent production of movement in physical objects by the power of the mind without physical contact – compare TELEKINESIS [NL, fr *psych-* + Gk *kinēsis* motion – more at KINESIS] – **psychokinetic** *adj*

**psycholinguistics** /-ling'gwistiks/ *n taking sing vb* the study of the interrelation between the use of language and the minds of speaker and hearer – **psycholinguist** *n*, **psycholinguistic** *adj*

**psychological** /,siekə'lojikl/, *NAm also* **psychologic** *adj* **1a** of, concerned with, or used in psychology **b** or, arising in, affecting, or concerning the mind **2** directed towards or intended to affect the will or the mind ⟨*~ warfare*⟩ – **psychologically** *adv*

**psychological hedonism** *n* the Freudian theory that conduct is entirely motivated by the pursuit of pleasure or the avoidance of pain

**psychological moment** *n the* point in time when words or actions are most likely to produce the desired effect; *the* appropriate time to do or say anything

**psychologism** /sie'kolǝjiz(ǝ)m/ *n* the application of psychological conceptions and methods to the interpretation of historical events or logical thought

**psycholog·ize, -ise** /sie'kolǝjiez/ *vt* to explain or interpret in psychological terms ~ *vi* to study or use psychology

**psychology** /sie'kolǝji/ *n* **1** the science or study of the mind, mental processes, and behaviour in humans and animals – compare PSYCHIATRY **2a** the mental or behavioural characteristics of an individual or group **b** the study of mind and behaviour in relation to a particular field of knowledge or activity ⟨*the ~ of learning*⟩ **3** a school or tendency in psychology ⟨*the ~ of C G Jung*⟩ [NL *psychologia*, fr *psych-* + *-logia* -logy] – **psychologist** *n*

**psychometrics** /,siekoh'metrik/ *n taking sing vb* (the branch of psychology concerned with) the measurement of mental capacities and attributes, esp by the use of psychological tests (eg intelligence tests) and the application of statistical techniques

**psychometry** /sie'komǝtri/ *n* **1** the supposed divination of facts concerning an object or its owner through contact with or proximity to the object **2** the measurement of mental states and processes; psychometrics – **psychometrist** *n*, **psychometric** *adj*

**psychomotor** /,siekoh'mohtǝ/ *adj* of or being muscular action directly proceeding from mental activity ⟨*a ~ seizure*⟩ [ISV]

**psychoneurosis** /-nyoo(ǝ)'rohsis/ *n* a neurosis; *esp* one based on emotional conflict in which an impulse that has been blocked seeks expression in a disguised response or symptom [NL] – **psychoneurotic** *adj or n*

**psychopath** /'siekǝpath/ *n* a person suffering from a severe emotional and behavioural disorder characterized by abnormal egocentricity, lack of a sense of social responsibility, and usu by the pursuit of immediate gratification through often violent acts; *broadly* a dangerously violent mentally ill person [ISV] – **psychopathic** *adj*, **psychopathy** *n*

**psychopathology** /,siekohpǝ'tholǝji/ *n* (the study of) the psychological and behavioural aberrations occurring in mental disorders [ISV *psych-* + *pathology*] – **psychopathologist** *n*, **psychopathological** *adj*

**psychopharmacology** /-fahmǝ'kolǝji/ *n* the study of the actions and effect of drugs on the mind and behaviour – **psychopharmacologist** *n*, **psychopharmacological** *adj*

**psychophysical** /,siekoh'fizikl/ *adj* of psychophysics; *also* sharing mental and physical qualities – **psychophysically** *adv*

**psychophysics** /,siekoh'fiziks/ *n taking sing vb* a branch of psychology that deals with the relationship between the physical attributes of a stimulus and the characteristics of the sensation or perception it produces [ISV] – **psychophysicist** *n*

**psychophysiology** /,siekoh·fizi'olǝji/ *n* the physiology of psychological phenomena and mental processes [ISV] – **psychophysiological** *adj*, **psychophysiologist** *n*

**psychosexual** /-'seksy(oo)ǝl, -sh(ǝ)l/ *adj* of or concerning the mental, emotional, and behavioural aspects of sexual development or activity – **psychosexuality** *n*, **psychosexually** *adv*

**psychosis** /sie'kohsis/ *n, pl* **psychoses** /-seez/ (a condition of) severe mental derangement (eg schizophrenia) that results in marked alteration of behaviour and personality and distorted or lost contact with reality – compare NEUROSIS [NL] – **psychotic** *adj or n*, **psychotically** *adv*

**psychosocial** /-'sohsh(ǝ)l/ *adj* relating social conditions to mental health ⟨*~ medicine*⟩ – **psychosocially** *adv*

**psychosomatic** /-sǝ'matik/ *adj* of or resulting from the interaction of psychological and physical factors; *esp* of or being a physical symptom or disorder produced or aggravated by mental or emotional factors (eg stress) ⟨*~ medicine*⟩ ⟨*~ illnesses*⟩ [ISV] – **psychosomatically** *adv*

**psychosurgery** /-'suhjǝri/ *n* brain surgery used to treat mental disorders – **psychosurgical** *adj*

**psychotherapy** /,siekoh'therǝpi/ *n* treatment of mental, emotional, or psychosomatic disorders by psychological methods; *esp* such treatment by analytical psychology rather than behaviour therapy [ISV] – **psychotherapist** *n*, **psychotherapeutic** *adj*

**psychotogen** /sie'kotǝjǝn/ *n, NAm* something (eg a drug) that induces a state of severe mental derangement [*psychot*ic + *-o-* + *-gen*] – **psychotogenic** *adj*

¹**psychotomimetic** /sie,kotoh·mi'metik, -mie-/ *adj* of, involving, or inducing changes in behaviour and personality resembling those characteristic of a psychotic state ⟨*~ drugs*⟩ [*psychot*ic + *-o-* + *mimetic*] – **psychotomimetically** *adv*

²**psychotomimetic** *n* a psychotomimetic agent (eg a drug)

**psychotropic** /siekǝ'trohpik/ *adj, of a drug* acting on the mind; PSYCHOACTIVE

**psychro-** *comb form* cold ⟨psychro*meter*⟩ ⟨psychro*philic*⟩ [Gk, fr *psychros*, fr *psychein* to cool – more at PSYCH-]

**psychrometer** /sie'kromitə/ *n* a HYGROMETER (device for measuring atmospheric humidity) consisting essentially of two similar thermometers with the bulb of one being kept wet so that the cooling that results from evaporation makes it register a lower temperature than the dry one and with the difference between the readings constituting a measure of the dryness of the atmosphere – called also WET-AND-DRY-BULB HYGROMETER [ISV] – **psychrometry** *n*, **psychrometric** *adj*

**psychrophilic** /,siekroh'filik/ *adj* thriving at a relatively low temperature ⟨~ *bacteria*⟩

**psylla** /'silə/ *n* any of various PLANT LICE (family Psyllidae) including economically important plant pests [NL, genus name, fr Gk, flea; akin to L *pulex* flea, Skt *pluṣi*]

**psyllid** /'silid/ *n* a psylla [deriv of NL *Psylla*] – **psyllid** *adj*

**ptarmigan** /'tahmigən/ *n, pl* **ptarmigans,** *esp collectively* **ptarmigan** any of various grouse (genus *Lagopus*) of northern regions with completely feathered feet and plumage that turns white in winter [modif (influenced by *pter-*) of ScGael *tàrmachan*]

**P T boat** *n, NAm* MOTOR TORPEDO BOAT [*patrol torpedo*]

**PTC** *n* PHENYLTHIOCARBAMIDE [*phenylthiocarbamide*]

**pter-** /ter-/, **ptero-** *comb form* wing ⟨ptero*dactyl*⟩ ⟨ptero*pod*⟩ [NL, fr Gk, fr *pteron* wing, feather – more at FEATHER]

**pterid-** /terid-/, **pterido-** *comb form* fern ⟨pterid*oid*⟩ ⟨pterido*logy*⟩ [Gk *pterid-*, *pteris;* akin to Gk *pteron* wing, feather]

**pteridine** *n* a yellow nitrogen-containing chemical compound, $C_6H_4N_4$, with a structure composed of two joined rings of atoms, that is a structural constituent of various naturally occurring compounds including the vitamin FOLIC ACID and various animal pigments (e g those in the wings of some butterflies) [ISV *pter-* (fr Gk *pteron*) + *-id* + *-ine;* fr its being a factor in the pigments of butterfly wings]

**pteridology** /,teri'dolǝji/ *n* the study of ferns – **pteridologist** *n*, **pteridological** *adj*

**pteridophyte** /'teridoh,fiet, -dǝ-/ *n* any of a division (Pteridophyta) of plants including the ferns, horsetails, and CLUB MOSSES that reproduce by means of spores and have water- and food-conducting tissue, roots, stems, and leaves but lack flowers or seeds [deriv of Gk *pterid-*, *pteris* fern + *phyton* plant – more at PHYT-] – **pteridophytic, pteridophytous** *adj*

**pteridosperm** /'teridoh,spuhm/ *n* SEED FERN (extinct plant with fernlike leaves) [ISV]

**pterin** *n* any of a group of chemical compounds that contain the ring structure characteristic of pteridine and are widespread as pigments, esp in insects [ISV *pter-* (fr Gk *pteron* wing) + *-in*]

**pterodactyl** /,terǝ'daktil/ *n* any of an order (Pterosauria) of extinct flying reptiles of the Jurassic and Cretaceous periods that had a featherless membranous wing that extended from the side of the body along the arm to the end of the greatly enlarged fourth digit [NL *Pterodactylus,* genus of reptiles, fr Gk *pteron* wing + *daktylos* finger – more at FEATHER] – **pterodactyloid** *adj,* **pterodactylous** *adj*

**pteropod** /'terǝ,pod/ *n* SEA BUTTERFLY (usu shell-less marine animal related to the snails) [NL *Pteropoda,* group name, fr *pter-* + *-poda*] – **pteropod** *adj,* **pteropodan** *adj or n*

**pterosaur** /'terǝ,saw/ *n* a pterodactyl [deriv of Gk *pteron* + *sauros* lizard]

**pteroylglutamic acid** /,teroh·il·glooh'tamik/ *n* FOLIC ACID (vitamin of the B group)[ISV *pteroyl*(the radical)$C_{13}H_{11}N_6O(CO)$ + *glutamic*]

**pterygoid** /'terigoyd/ *adj* **1** (of or being a wing-shaped structure) lying in the region of the lower part of the bat- or butterfly-shaped bone (SPHENOID bone) at the base of the skull of a VERTEBRATE animal **2** of or supplying the PTERYGOID PROCESS [NL *pterygoides,* fr Gk *pterygoeidēs,* lit., shaped like a wing, fr *pteryg-, pteryx* wing; akin to Gk *pteron* wing – more at FEATHER] – **pterygoid** *n*

**pterygoid bone** *n* a horizontally placed bone or group of bones of the upper jaw or roof of the mouth in most lower VERTEBRATE animals (e g fishes)

**pterygoid process** *n* either of two bony structures that extend downwards from either side of the central wedge-shaped body of the SPHENOID bone (butterfly-shaped bone at the base of the skull) in humans and other mammals

**pterygote** /'terǝgoht/ *n or adj* (any) of a subclass (Pterygota) of insects that includes all the winged forms and many advanced wingless forms (e g fleas and lice) [NL *Pterygota,* subclass name, fr Gk, neut pl of *pterygōtos* winged, fr *pteryg-, pteryx*]

**pteryla** /'terǝlǝ/ *n, pl* **pterylae** /-lie/ any of the regions of a bird's skin on which feathers grow and which, together with the areas of naked skin in between, form a particular pattern for each different species and are used in the classification of birds [NL, fr Gk *pteron* + *hylē* wood, forest]

**PTFE** *n* POLYTETRAFLUOROETHYLENE (a plastic) [*polytetrafluoroethylene*]

**ptochocracy** /toh'kokrǝsi/ *n* rule or government by the poor [Gk *ptōchos* poor + E *-cracy*]

**Ptolemaic** /,toli'mayik/ *adj* **1** of Ptolemy or the PTOLEMAIC SYSTEM **2** of the Graeco-Egyptian Ptolemies ruling Egypt from 323 BC to 30 BC [(1) *Ptolemy* (Claudius *Ptolemaeus*) † *ab*168 Egyptian astronomer & geographer; (2) Gk *Ptolemaikos,* fr *Ptolemaios* Ptolemy, name of 14 kings of Egypt]

**Ptolemaic system** /,tolǝ'mayik/ *n* the theory of planetary motions according to which the sun, moon, and planets revolve round a stationary earth – compare COPERNICAN [*Ptolemy* the astronomer].

**Ptolemaist** /,tolǝ'mayist/ *n* an adherent of the Ptolemaic system

**ptomaine** /'tohmayn/ *n* any of various nitrogen-containing often poisonous organic chemical compounds that are formed by the action of bacteria on proteins in decaying animal matter [It *ptomaina,* fr Gk *ptōma* fall, fallen body, corpse, fr *piptein* to fall – more at FEATHER]

**ptomaine poisoning** *n* food poisoning caused by bacteria or bacterial products

**ptosis** /'tohsis/ *n, pl* **ptoses** /-seez/ a sagging or slipping down of an organ or part; *esp* a drooping of the upper eyelid [NL, fr Gk *ptōsis* act of falling, fr *piptein*]

**ptyalin** /'tie·ǝ,lin/ *n* an ENZYME found in the saliva of many animals that breaks down starch into sugar [Gk *ptyalon* saliva, fr *ptyein* to spit – more at SPEW]

**ptyalism** /'tie·ǝliz(ǝ)m/ *n* an excessive flow of saliva [NL *ptyalismus,* fr Gk *ptyalismos,* fr *ptyalizein* to salivate, fr *ptyalon*]

**'p-,type** *adj,* of a semiconductor having an excess of positively charged current carriers – compare N-TYPE [*positive type*]

**pub** /pub/ *n, chiefly Br* PUBLIC HOUSE 1

**pubby** /'pubi/ *adj* having the atmosphere of a pub; *specif* informal and friendly

**pub crawl** *n, Br informal* a tour of several pubs in succession with a pause for drinking at each

**puberty** /'pyoohbǝti/ *n* **1** the period marking the onset of sexual maturity at which an animal becomes capable of reproducing and which is marked by the maturing of the genitals, the development of SECONDARY SEX CHARACTERISTICS, and by the first occurrence of menstruation in human females and other female higher primates (e g chimpanzees) **2** the age at which puberty occurs **3** the condition of being at puberty [ME *puberte,* fr L *pubertas,* fr *puber* pubescent] – **pubertal** *adj*

**puberulent** /pyoo'beryoolǝnt/ *adj* covered with minute fine hairs [L *puber* pubescent + E *-ulent* (as in *pulverulent*)]

**pubes** /'pyoohbeez/ *n, pl* **pubes 1** the pubic region **2** PUBIC HAIR [NL, fr L, manhood, body hair, pubic region; akin to L *puber* pubescent]

**pubescence** /pyooh'bes(ǝ)ns/ *n* **1** being pubescent **2** a pubescent covering or surface

**pubescent** /pyooh'bes(ǝ)nt/ *adj* **1** arriving at or having reached puberty **2** covered with fine soft short hairs – compare HISPID, VILLOUS [L *pubescent-, pubescens,* prp of *pubescere* to reach puberty, become covered as with hair, fr *pubes*]

**pubic** /'pyoohbik/ *adj* of or situated in or near the region of the pubis or the PUBIC HAIR

**pubic hair** *n* the hair that appears at puberty round the genitals

**pubis** /'pyoohbis/ *n, pl* **pubes** /-beez/ the lower front bone of the three principal bones composing either half of the pelvis [NL *os pubis,* lit., bone of the pubic region]

**¹public** /'publik/ *adj* **1a** of or affecting all the people or the whole area of a nation or state ⟨~ *law*⟩ **b** of or being in the service of the community or nation ⟨*an eminent figure in* ~ *life*⟩ ⟨~ *affairs*⟩ **2** general, popular ⟨~ *sentiment*⟩ ⟨*increasing* ~ *awareness*⟩ **3** of national or community concerns as opposed to private affairs; social, impersonal ⟨*confessional poetry replaced more* ~ *forms*⟩ **4** devoted to the general or national welfare; humanitarian ⟨*the Greek philosophers thought as* ~ *men*⟩ **5a** accessible to or shared by all members of the community ⟨*a* ~ *park*⟩ **b** capitalized in shares that can be freely traded on the open market ⟨*the company has gone* ~⟩ **6a** exposed to general view; open ⟨*a* ~ *quarrel*⟩ **b** well-known, prominent ⟨*rock stars and* ~ *figures*⟩ [ME *publique,* fr MF, fr L *publicus,* prob alter. (influenced by *pubes* grown-up, adult) of *poplicus,* fr *populus* the people] – **publicness** *n*

²**public** *n taking sing or pl vb* **1** the people as a whole; populace **2** a group or section of people having common interests or characteristics ⟨*the motoring* ~⟩ ⟨*a film star's concern for his* ~⟩ – **in public** in the presence, sight, or hearing of strangers – see also **wash one's dirty** LINEN **in public**

**public-address system** *n* an apparatus including a microphone and loudspeakers, used to address a large audience

**publican** /'publikən/ *n* **1a** a Jewish tax collector for the ancient Romans **b** a collector of taxes or tribute **2** *chiefly Br* the licensee of a public house [ME, fr MF, fr L *publicanus* tax farmer, fr *publicum* public revenue, fr neut of *publicus*]

**public assistance** *n, NAm* SUPPLEMENTARY BENEFIT

**publication** /ˌpubliˈkaysh(ə)n/ *n* **1** the act or process of publishing **2** a published work [ME *publicacioun,* fr MF *publication,* fr LL *publication-, publicatio,* fr L *publicatus,* pp of *publicare* to make public, publish]

**public bar** *n, Br* a plainly furnished and often relatively cheap bar in a public house – compare SALOON BAR

**public bill** *n* a legislative bill affecting the public at large rather than a particular individual, class, or locality – compare HYBRID BILL, PRIVATE BILL

**public company** *n* a company whose shares are offered to the general public – compare PRIVATE COMPANY

**public convenience** *n, Br* public facilities provided by local government

**public corporation** *n* a corporation created by act of Parliament and responsible for running a nationalized service or industry

**public domain** *n* **1** the status in law of property rights that belong to the community at large, are unprotected by copyright or patent, and are subject to appropriation by anyone **2** *NAm* land owned directly by the government

**public enemy** *n* a person, esp a wanted criminal, who is a danger to the public while at liberty and whose notoriety is usu widely publicized

**public health** *n* the field of community health care, being the responsibility of the government or local authority and involving preventive medicine, sanitation, hygiene in public places, etc

**public house** *n* **1** *chiefly Br* an establishment where alcoholic drinks are sold to be drunk on the premises **2** *NAm* a hostelry; INN **1a**

**publicist** /'publisist/ *n* **1** one who publicizes; *specif* PRESS AGENT **2** an expert or commentator on public affairs

**publicity** /puˈblisəti/ *n* **1a** a technique or device designed to attract public interest **b(1)** information with news value issued as a means of gaining public attention or support **b(2)** paid advertising **c** the dissemination of information or promotional material **2** public attention or acclaim **3** *formal* the quality or state of being public ⟨*the* ~ *of an open court*⟩

**public·ize, -ise** /'publisiez/ *vt* to give publicity to

**public law** *n* **1** a law applicable to the general public **2** a branch of law concerned with the relations of the State with individuals and the activities, rights, and duties of the government and its departments and agencies – compare PRIVATE LAW

**public lending right** *n, often cap P,L,&R* the right of authors to receive a royalty payment on issues of their books from public libraries

**publicly** /'publikli/ *adv* **1** in a manner observable by or in a place accessible to the public; openly **2a** by the people generally ⟨~ *owned industry*⟩ **b** by a government ⟨~ *provided medical care*⟩

**public opinion** *n* the opinions, views, or beliefs held by the general public, esp on an issue of national importance

**public orator** *n* the official spokesman of an English university who delivers addresses on official occasions

**public prosecutor** *n* an official appointed to conduct criminal prosecutions on behalf of the state

**public relations** *n taking sing or pl vb* the business of creating goodwill among the public towards a person, organization, or institution; *also* the degree of understanding and goodwill achieved

**public sale** *n, NAm* AUCTION 1

**public school** *n* **1** an independent usu single-sex school in Britain that is typically a large fee-paying boarding school which prepares pupils from about the age of 13 for higher education **2** *NAm & Scot* STATE SCHOOL

**public sector** *n* the part of the economy owned or controlled by the state – compare PRIVATE SECTOR

**public sector borrowing requirement** *n* the difference between the revenue of the public sector and its expenditure

**public servant** *n* a government official or employee

**public service** *n* **1** the business of supplying a commodity (eg electricity or gas) or service (eg transport) to any or all members of a community **2** a service rendered in the public interest **3** governmental employment; *esp* CIVIL SERVICE

**public speaking** *n* **1** the act or process of making speeches in public **2** the art or science of effective spoken communication with an audience ⟨*took a course in* ~⟩

ˌ**public-'spirited** *adj* motivated by concern for the welfare of the community – **public-spiritedness** *n*

**public trustee** *n, often cap P&T, NAm* an official appointed by the government to act as a trustee (eg in relation to the investment of charitable funds)

**public utility** *n, chiefly NAm* a business organization providing a public amenity (eg supplying water, gas, or electricity) and subject to special governmental regulation; *also* an amenity so provided

**public works** *n pl* works (eg schools, roads, and docks) constructed for public use or enjoyment, esp when financed and owned by the government

**publish** /'publish/ *vt* **1a** to make generally known **b** to announce publicly **2a** to place before the public; disseminate **b** to produce or release for publication; *specif* to print **c** to issue the work of (an author) ~ *vi* **1** to put out an edition ⟨*the local paper didn't* ~ *yesterday*⟩ **2** to have one's work accepted for publication ⟨*a* ~*ing scholar*⟩ [ME *publishen,* modif of MF *publier,* fr L *publicare,* fr *publicus* public] – **publishable** *adj*

**publisher** /'publishə/ *n* one who publishes; *esp* a person or company whose business is publishing

**publishing** /'publishing/ *n* the business or profession of the commercial production and issuing of literature, information, musical scores or sometimes recordings, or art ⟨*newspaper* ~⟩ ⟨*microfilm* ~⟩

**puccoon** /pəˈkoohn/ *n* any of several American plants that yield a red or yellow dye [fr *puccoon* (in some Algonquian language of Virginia)]

**puce** /pyoohs/ *n* a brownish-purple colour [Fr, lit., flea, fr L *pulic-, pulex* – more at PSYLLA]

¹**puck** /puk/ *n* a mischievous sprite [ME *puke,* fr OE *pūca;* akin to ON *pūki* devil]

²**puck** *n* a rubber disc used as the object to be driven into the goal in ice hockey [E dial. *puck* to poke, hit, alter. of E ²*poke*]

¹**pucker** /'pukə/ *vb* to (cause to) become wrinkled or irregularly creased [prob irreg fr ¹*poke*]

²**pucker** *n* a crease or wrinkle in a normally even surface

**puckish** /'pukish/ *adj* impish, whimsical [¹*puck*] – **puckishly** *adv,* **puckishness** *n*

**pud** /pood/ *n, Br informal* (a) pudding

**pudding** /'pooding/ *n* **1** a sausage or sausagelike mixture of minced meat, cereal, etc: eg **1a** BLACK PUDDING **b** WHITE PUDDING **2** any of various sweet or savoury dishes of soft to spongy or fairly firm consistency that are made with a mixture of ingredients including a cereal or farinaceous material (eg rice, tapioca, or esp flour) and are cooked by boiling, steaming, or baking ⟨*sponge* ~⟩ ⟨*steak and kidney* ~⟩ **3** the sweet or dessert course of a meal **4** *informal* a small podgy person [ME]

**pudding stone** *n* CONGLOMERATE (rock composed of pebbles, stones, etc embedded in a cement)

¹**puddle** /'pudl/ *n* **1** a small pool of liquid; *esp* a small pool of usu dirty or muddy rainwater (eg in a road) **2a** an earthy mixture (eg of clay, sand, and gravel) worked while wet into a compact mass that becomes impervious to water when dry and is used for lining artificial lakes **b** a thin mixture of soil and water for dipping the roots of plants in before transplanting [ME *podel;* akin to LG *pudel* puddle, OE *pudd* ditch]

²**puddle** *vi* to dabble or wade around in a puddle ~ *vt* **1** to make (a liquid) muddy **2a** to work (a wet mixture of earth or concrete) into a dense impervious mass **b** to subject (iron) to the process of puddling **3a** to compact (soil), esp by working when too wet **b** to dip the roots of (a plant) in a thin mud before transplanting – **puddler** *n*

**puddling** /'pudling, 'pudl·ing/ *n* the process of converting crude PIG IRON into WROUGHT IRON by heating and stirring in a furnace in the presence of OXIDIZING substances

**puddly** /'pudli/ *adj* having many puddles

**pudenda** /pyooh'dendə/ *n taking pl vb* the external genital organs of a human being, esp a woman [L, fr neut pl of *pudendus*, gerundive of *pudēre* to be ashamed] – **pudendal** *adj*
**pudendum** /pyooh'dendəm/ *n*, *pl* **pudenda** the pudenda [NL, sing. of L *pudenda*]
**pudgy** /'puji/ *adj* podgy [origin unknown] – **pudginess** *n*
**pueblo** /'pwebloh, poo'ebloh/ *n*, *pl* **pueblos 1a** the communal dwelling of an American Indian village of Arizona, New Mexico, and adjacent areas consisting of contiguous flat-roofed stone or clay houses in groups sometimes several storeys high **b** an American Indian village of the SW USA **2** a small town or village in Spanish America [Sp, village, lit., people, fr L *populus*]
**puerile** /'pyooəriel/ *adj* **1** juvenile **2** not befitting an adult; childish, silly ⟨~ *remarks*⟩ *synonyms* see [1]YOUNG [Fr or L; Fr *puéril*, fr L *puerilis*, fr *puer* boy, child; akin to Gk *pais* boy, child – more at FEW] – **puerilely** *adv*, **puerilism** *n*, **puerility** *n*
**puerperal** /pyooh'uhp(ə)rəl/ *adj* of or occurring during childbirth or the period immediately following ⟨~ *depression*⟩ [L *puerpera* woman in childbirth, fr *puer* child + *parere* to give birth to – more at PARE]
**puerperal fever** *n* an often serious condition that results from infection of some part of the female reproductive organs, typically the site of the placenta, following childbirth or abortion and is characterized usu by fever
**puerperal sepsis** *n* PUERPERAL FEVER
**puerperium** /pyooə'piəriəm/ *n*, *pl* **puerperia** /-riə/ the period, usu lasting five or six weeks, immediately following labour and childbirth during which the womb returns to its normal size and condition [L, fr *puerpera*]
[1]**puff** /puf/ *vi* **1a**(1) *of air* to blow in short gusts **a**(2) to exhale or blow forcibly ⟨~ed *into a blowpipe to shape the molten glass*⟩ **b** to breathe hard and quickly; pant **c** to emit small whiffs or clouds (e g of smoke or steam) **2a** to become distended; swell – usu + *up* **b** to appear (as if) in a puff ⟨*the chute* ~ed *out behind the plane*⟩ ~ *vt* **1a** to emit, propel, blow, or expel (as if) by puffs; waft **b** to draw on (a pipe, cigar, or cigarette) with intermittent exhalations of smoke **2a** to distend (as if) with air or gas; inflate **b** to make proud or conceited – usu + *up* ⟨*extravagant praise* ~ed *up his ego*⟩ **c** to praise extravagantly and usu with exaggeration; *also* to advertise by this means **3** *chiefly Br informal* to cause to be out of breath ⟨*the walk* ~ed *him*⟩ [ME *puffen*, fr OE *pyffan*, of imit origin]
**puff out** *vt* **1** to extinguish by blowing ⟨puff *the candles* out⟩ **2** to cause to enlarge, esp by filling or inflating with air ~ *vi* to become enlarged with air
[2]**puff** *n* **1a** an act or instance of puffing; a whiff **b** a slight explosive sound accompanying a puff **c** a perceptible cloud (e g of smoke) emitted in a puff **d** DRAW 1a ⟨*take a* ~ *on his pipe*⟩ **2** a light round hollow pastry usu made of puff pastry and often filled with jam or cream **3a** a slight swelling; a protuberance **b** a fluffy mass: e g **b**(1) POUFFE 1 **b**(2) POWDER PUFF **b**(3) *NAm* a quilted bed cover; an eiderdown **4** a commendatory notice or review **5** an enlarged region of a CHROMOSOME (strand of gene-carrying material) (e g in the salivary glands of a FRUIT FLY) that is associated with the intensely active genes involved in RNA synthesis **6** *chiefly Br* BREATH 2a ⟨*sat down until he got his* ~ *back*⟩ **7** *slang* a poof – **puffiness** *n*, **puffy** *adj*
**puff adder** *n* a large venomous African viper (*Bitis arietans*) that inflates its body and hisses loudly when disturbed
**puffball** /-ˌbawl/ *n* any of various spherical and often edible fungi (esp family Lycoperdaceae) that discharge ripe spores in a smokelike cloud when pressed or struck
**puffed** /puft/ *adj*, *chiefly Br informal* out of breath
**puffed sleeve** *n* a short full sleeve gathered at the upper and lower edges
**puffer** /'pufə/ *n* **1** a person or thing that puffs **2** GLOBEFISH; *broadly* any of various similar fishes (order Plectognathi)
**puffery** /'pufəri/ *n*, *informal* flattering publicity; exaggerated commendation, esp for promotional purposes
**puffin** /'pufin/ *n* any of several seabirds (genera *Fratercula* and *Lunda*) that have a short neck and a deep grooved multi-coloured laterally compressed beak [ME *pophyn*]
**puff pastry** *n* a light flaky pastry made with a rich dough containing a large quantity of butter
[1]**pug** /pug/ *n* **1** (any of) a breed of small sturdy compact dog of Asiatic origin with a close coat, tightly curled tail, and broad wrinkled face **2** PUG NOSE △ peke, Pom [obs *pug* hobgoblin, monkey, perh alter. of [1]*puck*]
[2]**pug** *vt* -**gg**- **1** to plug or pack with a substance (e g clay or

mortar) esp for deadening sound **2** to work and mix (e g clay) when wet, esp to make more homogeneous and easier to handle [perh alter. of [2]*poke*]
[3]**pug** *n*, *informal* a boxer [by shortening & alter. fr *pugilist*]
[4]**pug** *n* a footprint; *esp* a print of a wild mammal [Hindi *pag* foot]
[5]**pug** *vt* to track by means of footprints ⟨~ *a tiger*⟩
**puggaree, pugaree, puggree** /'pug(ə)ri/ *n* a light turban or scarf wrapped round a sun helmet [Hindi *pagṛī* turban]
**pugilism** /'pyoohji,liz(ə)m/ *n*, *formal* boxing [L *pugil* boxer; akin to L *pugnus* fist – more at PUNGENT] – **pugilistic** *adj*
**pugilist** /'pyoohjilist/ *n*, *formal* a fighter; *esp* a professional boxer
**pugmark** /'pug,mahk/ *n* [4]PUG
**pug mill** *n* a machine in which materials (e g clay and water) are mixed or kneaded into a desired consistency [[2]*pug*]
**pugnacious** /pug'nayshəs/ *adj* having a belligerent nature; quarrelsome, combative [L *pugnac-*, *pugnax*, fr *pugnare* to fight – more at PUNGENT] – **pugnaciously** *adv*, **pugnaciousness**, **pugnacity** *n*
**pug nose** *n* a nose with a slightly concave bridge and flattened nostrils [[1]*pug* ] – **pug-nosed** *adj*
**puisne** /'pyoohni/ *adj* lower in rank – used esp of judges of the HIGH COURT other than the lord chancellor, Lord Chief Justice, and President of the Family Division [MF *puisné* younger – more at PUNY] – **puisne** *n*
**puissance** /'pyooh·is(ə)ns, 'pwis(ə)ns, pyoo(h)'is(ə)ns; *in showjumping* 'pweesahnhs (*Fr* pɥisãːs)/ *n* **1** a showjumping competition involving the jumping of very high fences **2** *formal or poetic* strength, power [ME, power, fr MF, fr OF, fr *puissant* powerful, fr *poeir* to be able, be powerful – more at POWER] – **puissant** *adj*, **puissantly** *adv*
**puke** /pyoohk/ *vb*, *slang* to vomit – often + *up* [perh imit] – **puke** *n*
**pukeko** /poo'kekoh, 'poohkekə/ *n*, *pl* **pukekos** a GALLINULE (water bird related to the rails) (*Porphyrio melanotus*) of Australia and New Zealand that has black, blue, and white plumage and a red beak [Maori]
**pukka** /'pukə/ *adj* **1** genuine, authentic; *also* first-class **2** *chiefly Br humorous* stiffly formal or proper; *specif* reminiscent of the rigid social manners supposed to characterize the British in India during the Raj [Hindi *pakkā* cooked, ripe, solid, fr Skt *pakva*; akin to Gk *pessein* to cook – more at COOK]
[1]**puku** /'poohkooh/ *n*, *pl* **pukus** a brown antelope (*Kobus vardoni*) that is found in the African savanna [native name in Africa]
[2]**puku** *n*, *NZ* the stomach [Maori]
**pul** /poohl/ *n*, *pl* **puls, puli** /-li, -lee/ – see *afghani* at MONEY table [Per *pūl*]
**pula** /'p(y)oohlə/ *n*, *pl* **pula** – see MONEY table [native name in Botswana]
**pulchritude** /'pulkri,tyoohd/ *n*, *formal or humorous* physical beauty [ME, fr L *pulchritudin-*, *pulchritudo*, fr *pulchr-*, *pulcher* beautiful]
**pulchritudinous** /ˌpulkri'tyoohdinəs/ *adj*, *formal or humorous* having pulchritude; beautiful
**pule** /pyoohl/ *vi* to whine, whimper [prob imit] – **puler** *n*
**puli** /'pooli/ *n*, *pl* **pulik** /-ik/, **pulis** /-iz, -eez/ (any of) a Hungarian breed of intelligent medium-sized sheepdog with a long usu shaggy coat [Hung]
**pulicide** /'pyoohlisied/ *n* an agent used for destroying fleas [blend of L *pulic-*, *pulex* flea and E *-cide*]
**Pulitzer prize** /'poolitsə/ *n* any of various annual prizes (e g for outstanding literary or journalistic achievement) established by the will of Joseph Pulitzer [Joseph *Pulitzer* †1911 US newspaper publisher]
[1]**pull** /pool/ *vt* **1a** to draw out from the skin ⟨~ *feathers from a cock's tail*⟩ **b** to pluck from a plant or by the roots ⟨~ *flowers*⟩ ⟨~ *turnips*⟩ **c** to extract ⟨~ *a tooth*⟩ **2a** to exert force upon so as to cause or tend to cause motion towards the force; tug at **b** to stretch (e g cooling humbug mixture) repeatedly **c** STRAIN 2b ⟨~ *a tendon*⟩ **d** to hold back (a horse) from winning a race **e** to work (an oar) by drawing back strongly **f** to draw (e g beer or cider) from the barrel, esp by pulling a pump handle ⟨~ *a pint*⟩ **3** to hit (e g a ball in cricket or golf) towards the left from a right-handed swing or towards the right from a left-handed swing **4** to draw apart; rend, tear **5** to print (e g a proof) by impression **6** to bring (a weapon) into the open in readiness for use – usu + *on* ⟨~ed *a knife on me*⟩ **7** *informal* to draw the support or attention of; attract **8** *informal* to commit, per-

petrate ⟨~ *a robbery*⟩ **9** *informal* **9a** to carry out with daring and imagination ⟨~ed *another financial coup*⟩; *also* to accomplish the seduction of ⟨*spends his weekends* ~ing *birds*⟩ **b** to do, perform, or say with a deceptive intent ⟨*been* ~ing *these tricks for years*⟩ ~ *vi* **1a** to use force in drawing, dragging, or tugging **b** to move, esp through the exercise of mechanical energy ⟨*the car* ~ed *out of the driveway*⟩ **c** to draw hard or suck in smoking or drinking ⟨~ed *at his pipe*⟩ **d** *of a horse* to strain against the bit **e** to row **2** to draw a gun **3** to be capable of being pulled ⟨*soft wool* ~s *easily*⟩ [ME *pullen*, fr OE *pullian*] – **puller** *n* – **pull oneself together** to regain one's self-possession – see also **pull oneself up by one's own** BOOTSTRAPS, **pull a** FAST **one/one's** FINGER **out/somebody's** LEG/**one's** PUNCHES/RANK **on somebody/the** RUG **(out) from under somebody/one's** SOCKS **up, pull up** STAKES, **pull out all the** STOPS, **pull** STRINGS/**one's** WEIGHT

*synonyms* **Pull, draw, drag, haul, tug, yank, tow: pull** is the general term, often qualified by adverbs or phrases ⟨**pull** *hard/it over here*⟩. **Draw** suggests a smoother motion in the direction of the person or thing pulling ⟨*six horses* **draw** *the carriage*⟩⟨**drew** *the child closer*⟩. **Drag** implies resistance, and drawing something slowly or heavily behind one ⟨**drag** *logs to the water*⟩. **Haul** implies steady, forceful pulling or dragging ⟨**hauled** *him into the boat*⟩. It is often used for the transporting of heavy loads ⟨*trains* **hauling** *coal*⟩. **Tug** implies energetic, brief pulls, without necessarily producing movement as a result ⟨*stop* **tugging**! *I'm not coming*⟩. **Yank** (informal) suggests one good, productive pull. **Tow** suggests pulling along something without its own means of locomotion, especially with a rope or something similar ⟨*horses* **towing** *barges down the canal*⟩. Compare ¹PUSH

**pull away** *vi* **1** to draw oneself back or away; withdraw **2** to move off or ahead ⟨pulled away *from the leaders on the last lap*⟩

**pull down** *vt* **1** to demolish, destroy **2a** to bring to a lower level; reduce **b** to depress in health, strength, or spirits

**pull in** *vt* **1** to check, restrain ⟨pull in *one's emotions*⟩ **2** to arrest ⟨*police* pulled *the burglars* in⟩ **3** *informal* to acquire as payment or profit ⟨pulls in *£10000 a year*⟩ ~ *vi* **1** *esp of a train or road vehicle* to arrive at a destination or stopping place **2** *of a vehicle or driver* to move to the side of or off the road in order to stop – see also PULL-IN

**pull off** *vt* to carry out or accomplish despite difficulties

**pull out** *vi* **1** *esp of a train or road vehicle* to leave, depart **2** to withdraw **a** from a military position **b** from a joint enterprise or agreement **3** *of an aircraft* to resume horizontal flight after a dive ⟨pulled out *at 400 feet*⟩ **4** *of a motor vehicle or driver* **4a** to move into a stream of traffic (eg from a side turning or the side of the road) **b** to move out from behind a vehicle (eg when preparing to overtake)

**pull over** *vi, of a driver or vehicle* to move towards the side of the road, esp in order to stop

**pull round** *vt* to restore to good health or spirits ~ *vi* to regain one's health or spirits

**pull through** *vb* to help through or survive a dangerous or difficult situation (eg illness)

**pull together** *vi* to work in harmony towards a common good; cooperate

**pull up** *vt* **1** to bring to a stop; halt **2** *informal* to reprimand, rebuke ⟨*her manager* pulled *her* up *for her carelessness*⟩ ~ *vi* **1a** to check oneself ⟨*the doctor told him to* pull up *and take a rest*⟩ **b** to come to a halt; stop **2** to draw even with or gain on others (eg in a race)

**²pull** *n* **1a** the act or an instance of pulling; *also* the force exerted by such an act **b(1)** a deep draught of liquid ⟨*took a long* ~ *of his beer*⟩ **b(2)** an inhalation of smoke (eg from a cigarette) **c** the effort expended in moving ⟨*a long* ~ *uphill*⟩ **d** force required to overcome resistance to pulling ⟨*trigger* ~⟩ **e** an attacking stroke in cricket, made by hitting the ball to the LEG SIDE with a horizontal bat **2a** advantage ⟨*the* ~ *of a classical education*⟩; *also* special influence exerted to obtain a privilege or advantage **3** PROOF **4a** – used in printing **4** a device for pulling something, or for operating by pulling ⟨*drawer* ~⟩ **5** a force that attracts, compels, or influences; an attraction

**pullback** /'pool‚bak/ *n* a pulling back; *esp* an orderly withdrawal of troops from a position or area

**pullet** /'poolit/ *n* a young hen; *specif* a hen of the domestic fowl less than a year old [ME *polet* young fowl, fr MF *poulet*, fr OF, dim. of *poul* cock, fr LL *pullus*, fr L, young of an animal, chicken, sprout – more at FOAL]

**pulley** /'pooli/ *n* **1** a small wheel with a grooved rim, used singly with a rope or chain to change the direction and point of application of a pulling force, and in various combinations to increase the applied force, esp for lifting weights; *also* the simple machine constituted by such a pulley with ropes **2** a wheel used to transmit power or motion by means of a belt, rope, or chain passing over its rim [ME *pouley*, fr MF *poulie*, prob deriv of Gk *polos* axis, pole]

**'pull-‚in** *n, chiefly Br* a place where vehicles may pull in and stop; *also* a roadside café

**Pullman** /'poolmən/ *n* **1** a railway passenger carriage with particularly comfortable furnishings, esp for night travel **2** a fast train made up of Pullmans [George M *Pullman* †1897 US inventor]

**'pull-‚on** *n* a garment (eg a hat) that has no fastenings and is pulled onto the head or body – **pull-on** *adj*

**pullout** /'pool‚owt/ *n* something that can be pulled out: eg **a** a larger leaf in a book or magazine that when folded is the same size as the ordinary pages **b** a removable section of a magazine or newspaper ⟨*see this week's handy TV guide* ~⟩

**pullover** /-‚ohvə/ *n* a garment for the upper body, esp a jumper, that is put on by being pulled over the head – **pullover** *adj*

**pullthrough** /-‚throoh/ *n* a device for cleaning the bore (eg of a rifle barrel or a woodwind instrument) that consists of a length of cord with a weight at one end and a loop for a piece of cleaning material at the other

**pullulate** /'pulyoo‚layt/ *vi* **1a** to germinate, sprout **b** to breed or produce rapidly and abundantly **2** *formal* to swarm, teem – often + *with* [L *pullulatus*, pp of *pullulare*, fr *pullulus*, dim. of *pullus* chicken, sprout] – **pullulation** *n*

**'pull-‚up** *n* **1** a conditioning exercise performed by raising oneself while hanging by the hands until the chin is level with the support **2** *chiefly Br* pull-in

**pulmonary** /'poolmən(ə)ri, 'pul-/, **pulmonic** /-'monik/ *adj* **1** of, functioning like, or associated with the lungs **2** pulmonate **3** carried on by the lungs [L *pulmonarius*, fr *pulmon-, pulmo* lung; akin to Gk *pleumōn* lung]

**pulmonary artery** *n* an artery that conveys deoxygenated blood from the heart to the lungs

**pulmonary valve** *n* the heart valve between the right VENTRICLE (lower chamber of the heart) and the PULMONARY ARTERY that stops blood flowing back into the right ventricle

**pulmonary vein** *n* a valveless vein that returns oxygenated blood from the lungs to the heart

**¹pulmonate** /'poolmənət, 'pul-/ *adj* **1** having lungs or organs resembling lungs **2** of a large order (Pulmonata of the class Gastropoda, phylum Mollusca) of INVERTEBRATE animals comprising most land snails and slugs and many freshwater snails that are characterized by having a lung or similar breathing organ [L *pulmon-, pulmo* lung]

**²pulmonate** *n* a pulmonate slug or snail

**¹pulp** /pulp/ *n* **1a(1)** the soft succulent part of fruit, usu formed from the MESOCARP (middle layer of the fruit wall) **a(2)** stem pith when soft and spongy **b** a soft mass of vegetable matter (eg of apples) from which most of the water has been extracted by pressure **c** the soft sensitive tissue that fills the central cavity of a tooth **d** a material used in making paper and cellulose products, and prepared by chemical or mechanical means from various materials (eg rags or wood) **2** pulverized ore mixed with water **3** a soft moist shapeless mass, esp when produced by crushing or beating ⟨*smashed his face to a* ~⟩ **4** a magazine or book cheaply produced on rough paper and containing sensational material [MF *poulpe*, fr L *pulpa* flesh, pulp] – **pulpiness** *n*, **pulpy** *adj*

**²pulp** *vt* **1** to reduce to pulp; cause to appear pulpy **2** to remove the pulp from **3** to produce or reproduce (written matter) in pulp form ~ *vi* to become pulp or pulpy – **pulper** *n*

**pulpal** /'pulpl/ *adj* of pulp, esp of a tooth ⟨*a* ~ *abscess*⟩ – **pulpally** *adv*

**pulp canal** *n* ROOT CANAL (channel in the root of a tooth)

**pulp cavity** *n* the central cavity of a tooth containing the dental pulp

**pulp chamber** *n* the part of the PULP CAVITY lying in the crown of a tooth

**pulpit** /'pool‚pit/ *n* **1** a raised platform or high reading desk in church from which a sermon is preached or a service conducted **2** *the* clergy as a profession [ME, fr LL *pulpitum*, fr L, staging, platform]

**pulpwood** /-‚wood/ *n* a wood (eg of aspen, hemlock, pine, or spruce) used in making pulp for paper

**pulque** /'poolkay, -ki/ *n* a Mexican alcoholic drink made from the fermented juice of MAGUEY plants [MexSp]

**pulsar** /'pul,sah/ *n* a source in the sky, thought to be a rotating NEUTRON STAR, of uniformly pulsating radio waves characterized by a short interval (e g .033 or 3.5 seconds) between pulses – compare QUASAR [*pulse* + *-ar* (as in *quasar*)]

**pulsate** /pul'sayt/ *vi* 1 to exhibit a pulse or pulsation; beat 2 to throb or move rhythmically; vibrate [L *pulsatus,* pp of *pulsare,* fr *pulsus,* pp of *pellere*]

**pulsatile** /'pulsətiel/ *adj* marked by pulsation

**pulsation** /pul'saysh(ə)n/ *n* 1 rhythmical throbbing or vibrating (e g of an artery); *also* a single beat or throb 2 a periodically recurring alternate increase and decrease of a quantity (e g pressure, volume, or voltage)

**pulsator** /pul'saytə/ *n* a device (e g attached to a cow's milking machine) that works with a throbbing movement (e g alternating suction and release on cow's teats)

**pulsatory** /'pulsət(ə)ri, pul'saytəri/ *adj* capable of or characterized by pulsation; throbbing ⟨~ *organ*⟩

¹**pulse** /puls/ *n* the edible seeds of any of various crops (e g peas, beans, or lentils) of the pea family; *also* a plant yielding pulse [ME *puls,* fr OF *pouls* porridge, fr L *pult-, puls;* akin to L *pollen* fine flour – more at POLLEN]

²**pulse** /puls/ *n* **1a** a regular throbbing caused in the arteries by the contractions of the heart; *also* a single movement of such throbbing **b** the number of beats of a pulse in a specific period of time **2a** an underlying sentiment or opinion, or an indication of it ⟨*felt the* ~ *of the political nation at Westminster*⟩ **b** a feeling of excitement or liveliness; vitality ⟨*new industry has quickened the* ~ *of the people*⟩ **3a** a rhythmical beating, vibrating, or sounding **b** a single beat or throb; *specif* a beat or stress in music or poetry **4a** a short-lived variation of a quantity (e g of electrical current or voltage) whose value is normally constant **b** an ELECTROMAGNETIC WAVE or a sound wave of brief duration [ME *puls,* fr MF *pouls,* fr L *pulsus,* lit., beating, fr *pulsus,* pp of *pellere* to drive, push, beat – more at FELT]

³**pulse** *vi* to pulsate, throb ~ *vt* **1** to drive (as if) by a pulsation **2** to cause to pulsate **3a** to produce or modulate (e g ELECTROMAGNETIC WAVES) in the form of pulses ⟨~d *waves*⟩ **b** to cause (an apparatus) to produce pulses – **pulser** *n*

'**pulse-,jet** *n* a JET ENGINE in which combustion, and hence thrust, occurs in regular pulses, between which pressure builds up in the firing chamber

**pulsimeter** /pul'simitə/ *n* an instrument for measuring esp the force and rate of a person's pulse

**pulsometer** /pul'somitə/ *n* a pump with valves for raising water by steam and atmospheric pressure, without the intervention of a piston [ISV]

**pulverable** /'pulv(ə)rəbl/ *adj* capable of being pulverized

**pulver·ize, -ise** /'pulvəriez/ *vt* **1** to reduce (e g by crushing, beating, or grinding) to very small particles **2** to annihilate, demolish ~ *vi* to become pulverized [MF *pulveriser,* fr LL *pulverizare,* fr L *pulver-, pulvis* dust, powder – more at POLLEN] – **pulverizable** *adj,* **pulverizer** *n,* **pulverization** *n*

**pulverulent** /pul'ver(y)oolənt/ *adj* **1** consisting of, or reducible to, fine powder **2** *formal* being or looking dusty; crumbly [L *pulverulentus* dusty, fr *pulver-, pulvis*]

**pulvillus** /pul'viləs/ *n, pl* **pulvilli** /-li, -lie/ any of the lobed hairy adhesive pads on the feet of flies [NL, fr L, dim. of *pulvinus* cushion]

**pulvinated** /'pulvinaytid/ *adj* having a convex profile – used chiefly of an architectural frieze [L *pulvinatus,* fr *pulvinus*]

**pulvinus** /pul'vienəs/ *n, pl* **pulvini** /-ni, -nie/ a mass of large thin-walled plant cells surrounding a strand of VASCULAR TISSUE (circulatory and transporting tissue) at the base of a stalk, and functioning in the movements of leaves or leaflets [NL, fr L, cushion]

**puma** /'pyoohmə/ *n, pl* **pumas,** *esp collectively* **puma** a powerful tawny brown BIG CAT (*Felis concolor*), formerly widespread in the Americas but now extinct in many areas [Sp, fr Quechua]

¹**pumice** /'pumis/ *n* a volcanic rock full of cavities and very light in weight, used esp in powder form for smoothing and polishing [ME *pomis,* fr MF, fr L *pumic-, pumex* – more at FOAM ] – **pumiceous** *adj*

²**pumice** *vt* to dress or polish with pumice

**pumicite** /'pumisiet/ *n* pumice

**pummel** /'puml/ *vt* **-ll-** (*NAm* **-l-, -ll-**) to pound or strike repeatedly, esp with the fists [alter. of *pommel*]

¹**pump** /pump/ *n* **1a** a device that raises, transfers, or compres-

ses liquids or gases; *also* one that reduces the density of gases, esp by suction or pressure, or both **b** a mechanism (e g the SODIUM PUMP) for pumping atoms, ions, or molecules **2** the heart **3** an act or the process of pumping [ME *pumpe, pompe,* fr MLG *pumpe* or MD *pompe,* prob fr Sp *bomba,* of imit origin]

²**pump** *vt* **1a** to raise (e g water) with a pump **b** to draw fluid from with a pump – often + *out* **2** to pour out or inject (as if) with a pump ⟨~ed *money into the economy*⟩ ⟨~ *new life into the classroom*⟩ **3** to question persistently and exhaustively ⟨~ed *her for information*⟩ **4** to move (something) rapidly up and down, as if working a pump handle ⟨~ed *his hand warmly*⟩ **5a** to inflate by means of a pump or bellows – usu + *up* ⟨~ed *up his bicycle tyres*⟩ **b** to supply with air by means of a pump or bellows ⟨*to* ~ *an organ*⟩ **6** to transport (e g ions) against a concentration gradient by the expenditure of energy **7a** to raise (atoms or molecules) to a higher ENERGY LEVEL by exposure to usu ELECTROMAGNETIC RADIATION at a particular frequency so that the radiation can be reemitted at another frequency, resulting in AMPLIFICATION (increased intensity) or sustained OSCILLATION **b** to expose (e g a laser, semiconductor, or crystal) to radiation in the process of pumping ~ *vi* **1** to work a pump; raise or move a liquid or gas with a pump **2** to move in a manner that resembles the action of a pump handle **3** to spurt out intermittently

³**pump** *n* **1** a low shoe without fastenings that grips the foot chiefly at the toe and heel **2** *Br* a gym shoe, plimsoll [origin unknown]

**pumped storage** *n* a hydroelectric system in which electricity is generated during periods of greatest consumption by the use of water that has been pumped into a reservoir at a higher altitude during periods of low consumption

**pumpernickel** /'pumpə,nikl, 'poom-/ *n* a dark coarse slightly sour-tasting bread made from wholemeal rye [Ger]

**pumpkin** /'pum(p)kin/ *n* **1** the very large edible usu round deep yellow fruit of a type of vegetable marrow; *also* a usu hairy prickly plant that bears pumpkins **2** *Br* (the large fruit of) any of various cultivated squashes derived from a natural species (*Cucurbita maxima*) [alter. of earlier *pumpion,* modif of Fr *popon, pompon* melon, pumpkin, fr L *pepon-, pepo,* fr Gk *pepōn,* fr *pepōn* ripened; akin to Gk *pessein* to cook, ripen – more at COOK]

**pump priming** *n* government investment expenditure designed to induce a self-sustaining expansion of economic activity

**pump room** *n* a room at a spa in which the water is distributed and drunk

¹**pun** /pun/ *vt* **1** to consolidate (e g earth, concrete, or hardcore) by repeated ramming or pounding **2** to drive a metal rod repeatedly through (wet concrete) to distribute cement and aggregate evenly [ME *pounen* – more at ²POUND]

²**pun** *n* a witticism involving the use of a word with more than one meaning, or of words having the same, or nearly the same, sound but different meanings [prob short for obs *punnet, pundigrion,* perh alter. of It *puntiglio* fine point, quibble – more at PUNCTILIO]

³**pun** *vi* **-nn-** to make puns

**puna** /'poohnə/ *n* **1** a treeless windswept tableland or basin in the higher Andes **2** MOUNTAIN SICKNESS [AmerSp, fr Quechua]

¹**punch** /punch/ *vt* **1a** to strike, esp with a hard and quick thrust of the fist **b** to drive or push forcibly (as if) by a punch **c** to hit (a ball) with less than a full swing (e g of a bat or racket) **2** to emboss, cut, perforate, or make (as if) with a punch **3** *NAm* to drive, herd ⟨~ *cattle*⟩ ~ *vi* to punch something [ME *punchen* to prod, prick, fr MF *poinçonner* to prick, stamp, fr *poinçon* puncheon] – **puncher** *n*

**punch in** *vi, NAm* CLOCK IN

**punch out** *vi, NAm* CLOCK OUT

²**punch** *n* **1** the action of punching **2** a blow (as if) with the fist **3** effective energy or forcefulness ⟨*an opening paragraph with a lot of* ~⟩ ⟨*a minority group with no political* ~⟩ – **punchless** *adj* – **beat somebody to the punch** *informal* to act or speak before somebody; preempt somebody ⟨*wanted to tell them the news but the others* beat us to the punch⟩ – **pull one's punches** *informal* to refrain from using all the force at one's disposal; *esp* to refrain from criticizing as severely as one might

³**punch** *n* **1** a tool esp for perforating, embossing, or cutting, usu in the form of a short rod of steel shaped in any of several ways at one end; *also* a short tapering steel rod for driving the heads of nails below a surface **2** a steel die, faced with a letter

in relief, that is forced into a softer metal to form an incised matrix from which foundry type is cast **3** a device for cutting holes or notches in paper or cardboard [prob short for *puncheon*]

⁴**punch** *n* a hot or cold drink usu composed of wine or spirits, fruit, spices, water, and sometimes tea; *also* a similar drink composed of nonalcoholic liquids – compare CUP 6 [perh fr Hindi *pãc* five, fr Skt *pañca;* akin to Gk *pente* five; fr the number of ingredients]

**Punch-and-Judy show** /ˌpunch ən 'joohdi/ *n* a traditional puppet show in which the little hook-nosed humpback Punch fights comically with his wife Judy

'**punch-ˌbag** *n* **1** an inflated or stuffed bag or ball which is punched with the fists as a form of exercise or training **2** someone victimized as a butt or stooge ⟨*the prevailing view of woman as a work-horse, cook and procreative* ~ *– British Book News*⟩

**punchball** /'punchˌbawl/ *n* baseball adapted to playing in small areas and marked by the use of a rubber ball hit with a closed fist instead of a bat

'**punch-ˌball** *n, Br* a punch-bag

**punch bowl** *n* a large bowl in which a drink, esp punch, is mixed and served

'**punch-ˌdrunk** *adj* **1** suffering brain damage from many minute brain haemorrhages, as a result of repeated head blows received in boxing **2** behaving as if punch-drunk; dazed, confused [²*punch*]

**punched card, punch card** *n* a card in which a pattern of holes or notches has been cut to represent information or instructions, and which is used in data processing

¹**puncheon** /'punchən/ *n* **1a** a short upright timber for a frame, esp to carry a load (e g a roof) **b** a split log or heavy slab with the face smoothed **2** ³PUNCH; *esp* a die used by goldsmiths, cutlers, and engravers [ME *ponson* pointed tool or weapon, king post (perh fr its being marked by the builder with a pointed tool), fr MF *poinçon*, fr (assumed) VL *punction-, punctio* pointed tool, fr *punctiare* to prick, fr L *punctus*, pp of *pungere* to prick – more at PUNGENT]

²**puncheon** *n* **1** a large cask of varying capacity **2** any of various units (e g of 70 or 120 gallons) of liquid capacity [ME *poncion*, fr MF *ponchon, poinçon*, of unknown origin]

**Punchinello** /ˌpunchi'neloh/ *n, pl* **punchinellos** a short fat humpbacked clown or buffoon in Italian puppet shows [modif of It dial. *polecenella*, dim. of It *pulcino* chicken, fr LL *pullicenus*, dim. of L *pullus*]

**punching bag** /'punching/ *n, chiefly NAm* a punch-bag

**punch line** *n* a sentence or phrase, esp a joke, that forms the climax to a speech or dialogue and makes the point – compare FEED-LINE

**punch press** *n* a press equipped with cutting, shaping, or combination dies for working on material (e g metal)

'**punch-ˌup** *n, chiefly Br informal* a usu spontaneous fight or brawl, esp with the bare fists

**punchy** /'punchi/ *adj* having punch; forceful

**punctate** /'pung(k)tayt/ *adj* **1** marked with minute spots or depressions ⟨*a* ~ *leaf*⟩ **2** occurring in dots or points ⟨~ *skin lesions*⟩ [NL *punctatus*, fr L *punctum* point – more at POINT] – **punctation** *n*

**punctilio** /pung(k)'tilioh/ *n, pl* **punctilios** **1** a minute detail of conduct in a ceremony or in observance of a code **2** careful observance of forms (e g in social conduct) [It & Sp; It *puntiglio* point of honour, scruple, fr Sp *puntillo*, fr dim. of *punto* point, fr L *punctum*]

**punctilious** /pung(k)'tili·əs/ *adj* strict or precise in observing the details of codes of conduct, conventions, or duties **synonyms** see CAREFUL – **punctiliously** *adv*, **punctiliousness** *n*

**punctual** /'pung(k)chooəl, -tyoo-/ *adj* **1** *maths* relating to or having the nature of a point **2** (habitually) arriving, happening, performing, etc at the exact or agreed time; prompt ⟨*a* ~ *businessman*⟩ [ML *punctualis*, fr L *punctus* pricking, point, fr *punctus*, pp of *pungere* to prick – more at PUNGENT] – **punctually** *adv*, **punctualness** *n*, **punctuality** *n*

**punctuate** /'pung(k)chooˌayt, -tyoo-/ *vt* **1** to mark or divide (written matter) with PUNCTUATION MARKS **2** to break into or interrupt at intervals ⟨*the steady click of her needles* ~d *the silence –* Edith Wharton⟩ ~ *vi* to use PUNCTUATION MARKS [ML *punctuatus*, pp of *punctuare* to point, provide with punctuation marks, fr L *punctus* point] – **punctuator** *n*

**punctuation** /ˌpung(k)choo'aysh(ə)n, -tyoo-/ *n* **1** punctuating or being punctuated **2** the act or practice of inserting standardized marks or signs in written matter to clarify the meaning and separate structural units; *also* a system of punctuation

**punctuation mark** *n* any of various standardized marks or signs (e g a comma) used in punctuation

¹**puncture** /'pung(k)chə/ *n* **1** an act of puncturing **2** a perforation (e g a hole or narrow wound) made by puncturing; *esp* a small accidental hole in a pneumatic tyre **3** a minute natural depression in a body part [L *punctura*, fr *punctus*, pp of *pungere*]

²**puncture** *vt* **1** to pierce with a pointed instrument or object **2** to cause a puncture in **3** to make useless or deflate as if by a puncture ⟨*failures* ~d *his confidence*⟩ ~ *vi* to become punctured

**punctured** /'pungkchəd/ *adj* PUNCTATE

**pundit** /'pundit/ *n* **1** a learned man; a teacher; *specif* PANDIT (learned Hindu) **2** one who gives opinions in an authoritative manner; an authority, critic **synonyms** see PANDIT [Hindi *pandit*, fr Skt *pandita*, fr *pandita* learned] – **punditry** *n*

**pungency** /'punjənsi/ *n* the quality or state of being pungent

**pungent** /'punj(ə)nt/ *adj* **1** *of a leaf or leaflet* having a stiff and sharp point **2** sharply painful; *also* poignant **3a** sharply incisive; caustic ⟨*a* ~ *denunciation*⟩ **b** to the point; highly expressive ⟨~ *prose*⟩ **4** having a strong sharp smell or taste; *esp* acrid △ piquant, plangent, poignant **antonym** bland [L *pungent-, pungens*, prp of *pungere* to prick, sting; akin to L *pugnus* fist, *pugnare* to fight, Gk *pygmē* fist] – **pungently** *adv*

¹**Punic** /'pyoohnik/ *adj* of Carthage or the Carthaginians [L *punicus*, fr *Poenus* inhabitant of Carthage, modif of Gk *Phoinix* Phoenician]

²**Punic** *n* the Phoenician dialect of ancient Carthage

**punish** /'punish/ *vt* **1a** to impose a penalty on for a fault, offence, or violation **b** to inflict a penalty for (an offence) **2** *informal* to treat roughly, harshly, or damagingly ⟨*to* ~ *an engine*⟩ ~ *vi* to inflict punishment [ME *punisshen*, fr MF *puniss-*, stem of *punir*, fr L *punire*, fr *poena* penalty – more at PAIN] – **punishable** *adj*, **punisher** *n*, **punishability** *n*

**synonyms** Punish, chastise, chasten, castigate, discipline, penalize: punish implies a penalty for wrongdoing, such as a fine, imprisonment, or the infliction of pain. Chastise now usually implies corporal punishment, but may be used for a severe rebuke. In either case, chastisement is intended to correct wrong behaviour. Chasten stresses this intention, and often suggests an exposure to suffering which humbles and improves someone. Castigate (formal) suggests punishment by a severe and caustic, often public, rebuke. Discipline implies taking minor or severe measures to improve someone's conduct. Penalize is the least forceful term, simply noting the payment of a fine, or forfeiture of a privilege, as a punishment for breaking rules. Compare ²REPRIMAND

**punishment** /-mənt/ *n* **1** the act of punishing **2a** retributive suffering, pain, or loss **b** a penalty inflicted on an offender through judicial procedure **3** *informal* severe, rough, or damaging treatment ⟨*the contender took plenty of* ~ *in the last round*⟩

**punitive** /'pyoohnətiv/ *adj* inflicting or intended to inflict punishment ⟨*take* ~ *action*⟩ ⟨*a* ~ *rate of taxation*⟩ [F *punitif*, fr ML *punitivus*, fr L *punitus*, pp of *punire*] – **punitively** *adv*, **punitiveness** *n*

**punitive damages** *n pl* damages awarded in excess of normal compensation to the plaintiff to punish a defendant for a particularly reprehensible wrong

**Punjabi** /pun'jahbi, poon-/ *n* **1** a native or inhabitant of the Punjab region of NW India and Pakistan **2** the Indic language of the Punjab [Hindi *pañjābī*, fr *pañjābī* of Punjab, fr Per, fr *Pañjāb* Punjab] – **Punjabi** *adj*

¹**punk** /pungk/ *n* **1a** a movement among young people of the 1970s and 1980s in Britain, characterized by a violent rejection of established society and expressed through PUNK ROCK and the wearing of aggressively outlandish clothes and hairstyles **b** PUNK ROCK **c** somebody following punk styles in music, dress, etc **2** *chiefly NAm informal* someone considered worthless, degraded, or inferior; *esp* a petty criminal **3** *archaic* a prostitute [origin unknown]

²**punk** *adj* **1** of or resembling the style or fashion of punk or PUNK ROCK **2** *chiefly NAm slang* of very poor quality; inferior, worthless

³**punk** *n* **1** a dry spongy substance prepared from fungi (genus *Fomes*) and used to ignite fuses, esp of fireworks **2** *chiefly NAm* wood useful for tinder; TOUCHWOOD [perh alter. of *spunk*]

**punkah** /'pungkə/ *n* a fan used esp formerly in India consisting of a cloth-covered frame suspended from the ceiling and swung to and fro by means of a cord [Hindi *pākhā*]

**punk rock** *n* a style of rock music characterized by a driving tempo, crude or obscene lyrics, and an aggressive delivery – **punk rocker** *n*

**punner** /'punə/ *n* **1** a heavy-headed tool used for punning or compacting **2** a metal rod used for punning concrete

**punnet** /'punit/ *n, chiefly Br* a small basket or tray, made from thin woven pieces of wood or plastic or from reinforced card, in which soft fruits (eg strawberries) and vegetables are sold [origin unknown]

**punster** /'punstə/ *n* one who is given to punning

**¹punt** /punt/ *n* a long narrow flat-bottomed boat with square ends, usu propelled with a pole [(assumed) ME, fr OE, fr L *ponton-, ponto* – more at PONTOON]

**²punt** *vt* to propel (eg a punt) with a pole; *also* to convey in a punt ∼ *vi* to propel a punt; go punting

**³punt** *vi* **1** to play against the banker in a gambling game **2** *Br* to gamble [Fr *ponter*, fr *ponte* point in some games, play against the banker, fr Sp *punto* point, fr L *punctum* – more at POINT]

**⁴punt** *vt* to kick (a football) by means of a punt ∼ *vi* to punt a ball [perh fr E dial. *punt* to push with force]

**⁵punt** *n* the act or an instance of kicking a football with the top or tip of the foot after dropping it from the hands and before it hits the ground: eg **a** a kick used by a goalkeeper in soccer to clear the ball **b** a kick used in American or Canadian football to give the opposing team possession of the ball away from the line of scrimmage

**¹punter** /'puntə/ *n* **1** *chiefly Br* someone who gambles; *esp* someone who bets against a bookmaker **2** *slang* a con-man's victim or potential victim **3** *slang* a prostitute's client; *broadly* a client, patron [³*punt* + ²*-er*]

**²punter** *n* someone who uses a punt in boating [²*punt* + ²*-er*]

**³punter** *n* a player who punts a ball [⁴*punt* + ²*-er*]

**punty** /'punti/ *n* a metal rod used for fashioning hot glass [Fr *pontil*, prob fr It *puntello*, dim. of *punto* point, fr L *punctum*]

**puny** /'pyoohni/ *adj* slight or inferior in size, strength, or importance; weak △ pusillanimous [MF *puisné* younger, lit., born afterwards, fr *puis* afterwards + *né* born] – **punily** *adv*, **puniness** *n*

**¹pup** /pup/ *n* a puppy; *also* one of the young of various animals (eg a seal or rat) [short for *puppy*] – **sell somebody a pup** to cheat somebody by selling him/her something worthless

**²pup** *vi* **-pp-** to give birth to pups

**pupa** /'pyoohpə/ *n, pl* **pupae** /-pie/, **pupas** the intermediate usu inactive form of an insect (eg a bee, moth, or beetle) that undergoes METAMORPHOSIS (change of structure and way of life) that occurs between the larva and the adult, is usu enclosed in a cocoon or case, and undergoes internal changes by which larval structures are replaced by those typical of the adult [NL, fr L *pupa* girl, doll] – **pupal** *adj*

**puparium** /pyoo'peəriəm/ *n, pl* **puparia** /-riə/ the outer shell of a pupa formed from the larval skin [NL, fr *pupa*] – **puparial** *adj*

**pupate** /pyooh'payt/ *vi* to become a pupa; pass through a pupal stage – **pupation** *n*

**¹pupil** /'pyoohpl/ *n* **1** a child or young person at school or receiving tuition; *also* anyone receiving tuition **2** someone who has been taught or influenced by a famous or distinguished person; a disciple ⟨*was a ∼ of Michelangelo*⟩ **3** a boy up to the age of 14 or girl up to the age of 12 who is in the care of a guardian – used in Roman & Scots law [ME *pupille* minor ward, fr MF, fr L *pupillus* male ward (fr dim. of *pupus* boy) & *pupilla* female ward, fr dim. of *pupa* girl, doll, puppet]

*synonyms* In British English, a **pupil** is a schoolchild and a **student** is a young adult at a university; but the American English use of **student** for those too young for college ⟨*high school* **students**⟩ is coming into British English. A person of any age being directly instructed by a professor, barrister, musician, or painter is his/her **pupil**. **Scholar** as a word for a schoolchild may have dropped out of use because of the danger of confusion with the word's other senses "learned person" and "holder of a scholarship".

**²pupil** *n* the usu round opening in the iris of the eye that varies in size to regulate the amount of light passing to the retina [MF *pupille*, fr L *pupilla*, fr dim. of *pupa* doll; fr the tiny image of oneself seen reflected in another's eye] – **pupilar, pupillary** *adj*

**pupillage, pupilage** *chiefly NAm* /'pyoohpilij/ *n* the state or period of being a pupil; *specif, Br* a training period served as unpaid assistant to a barrister

**pupil teacher** *n* a young person who in former times taught in an elementary school while concurrently receiving education

**pupiparous** /pyooh'pip(ə)rəs/ *adj* **1** producing mature larvae that are ready to pupate at birth **2** of a division (Pupipara) of two-winged flies with pupiparous larvae [NL *pupa* + E *-i-* + *-parous*]

**¹puppet** /'pupit/ *n* **1a** a small-scale figure (eg of a person or animal) usu with a cloth body and hollow head that fits over and is moved by the hand **b** a marionette **2** someone whose acts are controlled by an outside force or influence **3** POPPET 1 (type of valve) [ME *popet*, fr MF *poupette*, dim. of (assumed) *poupe* doll, fr L *pupa*] – **puppetry** *n*

**²puppet** *adj* controlled by an outside force or influence ⟨*the invaders installed a ∼ president*⟩

**puppeteer** /,pupi'tiə/ *n* **1** someone who manipulates puppets **2** someone who manipulates people

**puppy** /'pupi/ *n* **1** **puppy, puppy dog** a young dog; *specif* one less than a year old **2** a conceited or ill-mannered young man [ME *popi*, fr MF *poupée* doll, toy, fr (assumed) *poupe* doll] – **puppyish** *adj*

**puppy fat** *n* temporary plumpness in children and adolescents

**puppy love** *n* short-lived romantic affection felt by an adolescent for one of the opposite sex

**pup tent** *n* a small shelter tent, usu without a groundsheet or sidewalls

**Purana** /poo'rahnə/ *n, often cap* any of a class of Hindu sacred writings that date chiefly from AD 300 to AD 750 and are made up of traditional lore, including popular myths and legends [Skt *purāṇa*, fr *purāṇa* ancient, fr *purā* formerly; akin to OE *fore*] – **Puranic** *adj*

**Purbeck marble** /'puhbek/ *n* PURBECK STONE of fine quality that can be highly polished

**Purbeck stone** *n* a hard limestone that is quarried in the Purbeck Hills in Dorset and used for building

**purblind** /'puh,bliend/ *adj* **1** partly blind **2** lacking in vision, insight, or understanding; obtuse **3** *obs* wholly blind [ME *pur blind*, fr *pur* purely, wholly, fr *pur* pure] – **purblindly** *adv*, **purblindness** *n*

**¹purchase** /'puhchəs/ *vt* **1a** *law* to acquire (eg an estate) by means other than descent or inheritance **b** to obtain by paying money or its equivalent; buy **c** to obtain by labour, danger, or sacrifice ⟨*∼d life at the expense of honour*⟩ **2** to move or raise by a device (eg a lever or pulley) **3** to constitute the means for buying ⟨*a pound seems to ∼ less each year*⟩ ∼ *vi* to purchase something [ME *purchacen*, fr OF *purchacier* to seek to obtain, fr *por-, pur-* for, forwards (modif of L *pro-*) + *chacier* to pursue, chase] – **purchasable** *adj*, **purchaser** *n*

**²purchase** *n* **1** an act or instance of purchasing **2** something obtained by payment of money or its equivalent **3a(1)** mechanical advantage or leverage gained by use of a device (eg a pulley) **a(2)** an apparatus or device by which such advantage is gained **a(3)** an effective hold or position for leverage; *broadly* a secure hold or place to stand **b** an advantage used in applying power or influence in any effort

**purchase tax** *n* a tax levied on the sale of goods and services that is usu calculated as a percentage of the purchase price – compare VALUE-ADDED TAX

**purdah** /'puhdah, -də/ *n* the system of secluding women from public observation practised among Muslims and some Hindus, esp formerly in India; *also* a screen used for this purpose [Hindi *parda*, lit., screen, veil, fr Per]

**pure** /pyooə/ *adj* **1a(1)** unmixed with any other matter; unadulterated ⟨*∼ gold*⟩ **a(2)** free from contamination or corruption ⟨*∼ food*⟩ **a(3)** spotless; *specif* free from moral fault **a(4)** chaste **b** *of a musical sound* in tune and free from harshness or roughness **c** *of a vowel* not joined to another; MONOPHTHONGAL **2a** sheer, unmitigated ⟨*∼ folly*⟩ ⟨*∼ delight*⟩ **b** *of an esp scientific subject* not practical or applied; abstract, theoretical **c** *esp of art or literature* not directed towards exposition of reality; *esp* nonobjective ⟨*∼ art is often concerned only with form and colour*⟩ **3a(1)** free from anything that vitiates, weakens, or pollutes ⟨*the ∼ religion of our fathers*⟩ ⟨*taste in music was ∼*⟩ **a(2)** containing nothing that does not properly belong ⟨*the ∼ and original text*⟩ **b(1)** of pure blood and unmixed ancestry **b(2)** *biology* breeding true for one or more inheritable characteristics; HOMOZYGOUS **c** ritually clean [ME *pur*, fr OF, fr L *purus;* akin to Skt *punāti* he cleanses, MIr *ūr* fresh, green] – **pureness** *n*

**pureblood** /-,blud/, **pure-'blooded** *adj* of unmixed ancestry; purebred – **pureblood** *n*

**purebred** /-,bred/ *adj* bred from members of a recognized breed, strain, or kind, over many generations, without mixture of other blood – **purebred** *n*

**pure democracy** *n* democracy in which power is exercised directly by the people rather than through representatives

¹**puree, purée** /'pyooəray/ *n* a thick pulp (eg of fruit or vegetable), usu produced by rubbing cooked food through a sieve or blending it in a liquidizer; *also* a thick soup made from pureed vegetables [Fr *purée*, fr MF, fr fem of *puré*, pp of *purer* to purify, strain, fr L *purare* to purify, fr *purus*]

²**puree, purée** *vt* **pureeing; pureed** to reduce to a pulp, esp by rubbing through a sieve

**pure line** *n* a genetically uniform strain of organisms produced as a result of inbreeding and selection

**purely** /'pyooəli/ *adv* **1** without addition, esp of anything harmful **2** simply, merely ⟨*read ~ for relaxation*⟩ **3** in a chaste or innocent manner **4** wholly, completely ⟨*a selection based ~ on merit*⟩

**purfle** /'puhfl/ *vt* to ornament the border or edges of (eg a violin or building) [ME *purfilen*, fr MF *porfiler*, fr (assumed) VL *profilare*, fr L *pro-* forwards + LL *filare* to spin – more at FILE] – **purfle, purfling** *n*

**purgation** /puh'gaysh(ə)n/ *n* the act or result of purging

¹**purgative** /'puhgətiv/ *adj* purging or tending to purge [ME *purgatif*, fr MF, fr LL *purgativus*, fr L *purgatus*, pp]

²**purgative** *n* a medicine that causes evacuation of the bowels; a strong laxative

**purgatorial** /,puhgə'tawriəl/ *adj* **1** cleansing of sin; expiatory **2** of purgatory

**purgatory** /'puhgət(ə)ri/ *n* **1** an intermediate state after death for purification achieved by expiation; *specif* a place or state of punishment in which, according to ROMAN CATHOLIC doctrine, the souls of those who die in God's grace may make amends for past sins and so become fit for heaven **2** *informal* a place or state of temporary suffering or misery ⟨*the return trip was absolute ~*⟩ [ME, fr AF or ML; AF *purgatorie*, fr ML *purgatorium*, fr LL, neut of *purgatorius* purging, fr L *purgatus*, pp of *purgare*]

¹**purge** /puhj/ *vt* **1a** to clear of guilt **b** to free from moral or spiritual impurity **2a** to cause evacuation from (eg the bowels) **b(1)** to make free of an unwanted substance (eg an impurity or a foreign material) ⟨*~ a cabin of gas*⟩ ⟨*~ the body of toxic substances*⟩ **b(2)** to free (eg a boiler) of sediment or relieve (eg a steam pipe) of trapped air by bleeding **c(1)** to rid (eg a nation or party) of unwanted or undesirable members, often summarily or by force **c(2)** to get rid of (eg undesirable people) by means of a purge **3** *law* to relieve oneself of (a legal offence or sentence) by atonement ~ *vi* **1** to become purged **2** to have or produce frequent evacuations of the bowels **3** to cause purgation [ME *purgen*, fr OF *purgier*, fr L *purigare*, *purgare* to purify, purge, fr *purus* pure + *-igare* (akin to *agere* to drive, do) – more at ACT] – **purger** *n*

²**purge** *n* **1a** an act or instance of purging **b** the removal of elements or members regarded as undesirable, esp as treacherous or disloyal **2** something that purges; *esp* a purgative

**puri** /'pooəri/ *n, pl* **puris** a deep-fried wheaten cake eaten esp with Indian curries [Hindi, fr Skt *pūri*]

**purification** /,pyooərifi'kaysh(ə)n/ *n* the act or an instance of purifying or of being purified

**purificator** /'pyooərifi,kaytə/ *n* a purifier; *specif* a linen cloth used to wipe the chalice after celebration of Communion

**purificatory** /,pyoo(ə)rifi'kaytəri, -tri/ *adj* serving, tending, or intended to purify

**purify** /'pyooərifie/ *vt* to make pure: **a** to clear from material defilement or imperfection **b** to free from guilt or moral or spiritual blemish **c** to free from undesirable or extraneous chemical elements ~ *vi* to grow or become pure or clean [ME *purifien*, fr MF *purifier*, fr L *purificare*, fr L *purus* + *-ificare* -ify] – **purifier** *n*

**Purim** /'pooərim, pooh'reem/ *n* a Jewish holiday celebrated on the 14th of ADAR in commemoration of the deliverance of the Jews from the massacre plotted by Haman [Heb *pūrīm*, lit., lots; fr the casting of lots by Haman (Esth 9:24–26)]

**purine** /'pyooəreen, -rin/ *n* **1** a chemical compound, $C_5H_4N_4$, that is a BASE and the parent of chemical compounds of the URIC-ACID group of excretory products **2** a derivative of purine; *specif* a base (eg ADENINE or GUANINE) that is a constituent of DNA or RNA – compare PYRIMIDINE [Ger *purin*, fr L *purus* pure + NL *uricus* uric, fr E *uric*]

**purism** /'pyooəriz(ə)m/ *n* **1** rigid adherence to or insistence on

purity or correctness, esp in the use of words **2** an example of purism

**purist** /'pyooərist/ *n* someone who adheres strictly and often excessively to a method, technique, or tradition; *esp* someone preoccupied with the protection of a language from the use of foreign or altered forms or meanings – **puristic** *adj*

¹**puritan** /'pyooərit(ə)n/ *n* **1** *cap* a member of a 16th- and 17th-century mainly CALVINIST Protestant group in England and New England opposing as unscriptural the ceremonial worship of the Church of England and the institution of bishops **2** someone who practises or preaches a rigorous or severe moral code; *esp* someone who denounces as immoral generally accepted practices or pleasures [LL *puritas* purity + E *-an*]

²**puritan** *adj, often cap* of puritans, the Puritans, or puritanism

**puritanical** /,pyooəri'tanikl/ *adj* **1** puritan **2** of or characterized by a rigid morality; severe, austere ⟨*~ censors of literature*⟩ ⟨*~ approach to food*⟩ – **puritanically** *adv*

**puritanism** /'pyooəritə,niz(ə)m/ *n* **1** *cap* the beliefs and practices characteristic of the Puritans **2** strictness and austerity, esp in matters of religion or conduct

**purity** /'pyooərəti/ *n* **1** pureness **2** freedom from dilution with white; SATURATION 4a [ME *purete*, fr OF *pureté*, fr LL *puritat-*, *puritas*, fr L *purus* pure]

**Purkinje cell** /puh'kinji/ *n* any of numerous NERVE CELLS that occupy the middle layer of the outer part (CORTEX) of the CEREBELLUM (division of the brain) and are characterized by a large globular body with massive branchlike processes (DENDRITES) directed outwards and a single slender nerve fibre (AXON) directed inwards [Johannes *Purkinje* †1869 Czech physiologist]

**Purkinje fibre** *n* any of the modified heart muscle fibres that make up a network of conducting tissue in the MYOCARDIUM (muscular wall of the heart) [Johannes *Purkinje*]

¹**purl** /puhl/ *n* **1** a thread of twisted gold or silver wire used for embroidering or edging **2** PURL STITCH **3** the intertwist of thread that knots a stitch, usu along an edge ⟨*place the ~ of the stitch on the cut edge of the buttonhole* – *Singer Sewing Book*⟩ **4** *Br* an ornamental edging of small loops or picots on lace, ribbon, or braid [obs *pirl* to twist]

²**purl** *vt* **1** to decorate, edge, or border with gold or silver thread **2** to knit in PURL STITCH **3** to edge with loops; picot ~ *vi* to do knitting in purl stitch

³**purl** *n* a gentle murmur or movement (eg of purling water) [perh of Scand origin; akin to Norw *purla* to ripple]

⁴**purl** *vi, of a stream or brook* to flow in eddies with a soft murmuring sound

**purler** /'puhlə/ *n, chiefly Br informal* a heavy headlong fall (eg from a horse) – esp in *come*/*take a purler* [*purl* (to whirl, capsize, upset) alter. of obs *pirl* to twist]

**purlieu** /'puhlyooh/ *n, pl* **purlieus 1a** a frequently visited place; a haunt **2** *pl* environs, neighbourhood; *also* outlying region **3** *pl, formal* confines, bounds [ME *purlewe* land severed from an English royal forest by inspecting the boundary on foot, fr AF *puralé* inspection of a boundary by walking round it, fr OF *puraler* to go through, fr *pur-* for, through + *aler* to go – more at PURCHASE, ALLEY]

**purlin** /'puhlin/ *n* a horizontal beam in a roof that is supported by roof trusses and that itself supports the common rafters [origin unknown]

**purloin** /puh'loyn, pə-/ *vt, formal or humorous* to take dishonestly; steal, pilfer **synonyms** see ROB [ME *purloinen* to put away, render ineffectual, fr AF *purloigner*, fr OF *porloigner* to put off, delay, fr *por-* forwards + *loing* at a distance, fr L *longe*, fr *longus* long] – **purloiner** *n*

**purl stitch** *n* a basic knitting stitch that is usu made by inserting the right needle through a loop on the left needle from the front to the back, bringing the yarn from the front of the work round the right needle in an anticlockwise direction, and pulling it through the first loop to form a new loop. It produces a raised pattern on the back of the work. – compare KNIT STITCH [¹*purl*]

**puromycin** /,pyooərə'miesin/ *n* an antibiotic, $C_{22}H_{29}N_7O_5$, that is obtained from a bacterium (*Streptomyces alboniger*) and is used esp as a potent inhibitor of protein synthesis in microorganisms and mammalian cells [*purine* + *-o-* + *-mycin*]

¹**purple** /'puhpl/ *adj* **1** of the colour purple **2** highly rhetorical; ornate, overelaborate ⟨*~ prose*⟩ **3** *poetic* noble, royal [ME *purpel*, alter. of *purper*, fr OE *purpuran* of purple, gen of *purpure* purple colour, fr L *purpura*, fr Gk *porphyra*]

²**purple** *n* **1a** a colour falling about midway between red and

blue in hue **b(1)** cloth or a garment of such colour; *esp* a purple robe worn as an emblem of rank or authority **b(2)** the scarlet robe of a cardinal **c(1)** an INVERTEBRATE animal (e g of the genus *Purpura* of the phylum Mollusca) that is related to the snails and whelks and yields a purple dye, esp the TYRIAN PURPLE of ancient times **c(2)** a pigment or dye that colours purple **2** imperial, regal, or very high rank ⟨*born to the* ∼⟩

**³purple** *vb* to make or become purple

**purple heart** *n* **1** a light blue tablet containing the drug PHENOBARBITONE, and formerly often prescribed as a hypnotic or sedative and often abused by addicts **2** *cap P&H* a US military decoration awarded to any member of the armed forces wounded in action

**purple loosestrife** *n* a European and US marsh plant (*Lythrum salicaria*) of the henna family, that has a long spike of purple flowers

**purple passage** *n* a piece of obtrusively ornate writing [trans of L *pannus purpureus* purple patch; fr the traditional splendour of purple cloth as contrasted with more shabby materials]

**purple patch** *n* PURPLE PASSAGE

**purplish** /'puhplish/ *adj* having a tinge of purple; somewhat purple

**¹purport** /'puhpawt, -pət/ *n, formal* conveyed, professed, or implied meaning; import; *also* the substance, gist [ME, fr AF, content, tenor, fr *purporter* to contain, fr OF *porporter* to convey, fr *por-* forwards + *porter* to carry – more at PURCHASE, PORT]

**²purport** /pə'pawt, puh'pawt, 'puhpət/ *vt* to seem or be intended to seem; profess ⟨*a book that* ∼*s to be an objective analysis*⟩

usage Since **purport** means "seem" rather than "claim", it should not properly be used as in ⟨⚠ *she* **purports** *to have* (= says she has) *found the document in an old trunk*⟩. See PURPORTED

**purported** /puh'pawtid, pə-/ *adj* reputed, rumoured – **purportedly** *adv*

usage Writers on usage advise against the use of **purported** ⟨*produced a document* **purported** *to have been found in an old trunk*⟩ and suggest that it should be replaced by the verb **purport** in the active ⟨*produced a document* **purporting** (or *that* **purports**) *to have been found in an old trunk*⟩.

**¹purpose** /'puhpəs/ *n* **1** the object for which something exists or is done; the intention **2** resolution, determination ⟨*his* ∼ *is fixed; you can't dissuade him*⟩ [ME *purpos*, fr OF, fr *purposer* to purpose, fr L *proponere* (perf indic *proposui*) to propose – more at PROPOSE] – **on purpose** by intent; deliberately – **to the purpose** relevant; TO THE POINT – see also **to all INTENTS and purposes**

**²purpose** *vt, formal* to have as one's intention

**,purpose-'built** *adj, chiefly Br* designed to meet a specific need ⟨*a* ∼ *conference centre*⟩

**purposeful** /-f(ə)l/ *adj* **1** full of determination ⟨*a* ∼ *man*⟩ **2** having a purpose or aim ⟨∼ *activities*⟩ – **purposefully** *adv*, **purposefulness** *n*

**purposeless** /'puhpəslis/ *adj* having no purpose; aimless – **purposelessly** *adv*, **purposelessness** *n*

**purposely** /-li/ *adv* with a deliberate or express purpose

**purposive** /'puhpəsiv/ *adj, formal* **1** serving or effecting a useful function though not necessarily as a result of deliberate design ⟨*a work of art may be without a purpose, yet* ∼⟩ **2** having or tending to fulfil a conscious purpose or design; purposeful – **purposively** *adv*, **purposiveness** *n*

**purpura** /'puhpyoorə/ *n* any of several abnormal conditions characterized by patches of purplish discoloration on the body resulting from tiny blood vessels bleeding into the skin and MUCOUS MEMBRANES [NL, fr L, purple colour] – **purpuric** *adj*

**purpure** /'puhpyooə/ *n, heraldry* the colour purple [ME, fr OE, purple]

**purr** /puh/ *vi* **1** to make the low vibrating murmur characteristic of an apparently contented or pleased cat; *also* to move with this sound ⟨*car* ∼*ed along*⟩ **2** to speak in a manner that resembles a purr, esp in expressing satisfaction or pleasure ∼ *vt* to say with esp malicious satisfaction [imit] – **purr** *n*, **purringly** *adv*

**¹purse** /puhs/ *n* **1** a small flattish bag for money; *also* a wallet with a compartment for holding change **2a** resources, funds **b** a sum of money offered as a prize or present; *also* the total amount of money offered in prizes for a given event **3** *NAm* a handbag [ME *purs*, fr OE, modif of ML *bursa*, fr LL, oxhide, fr Gk *byrsa*] – **purselike** *adj*

**²purse** *vt* to draw together (e g the lips) into folds or wrinkles; to pucker, knit

**'purse-,proud** *adj* proud because of one's wealth, esp in the absence of other distinctions

**purser** /'puhsə/ *n* **1** an official on a ship responsible for documents and accounts and on a passenger ship also for the comfort and welfare of passengers **2** an official on an airliner responsible esp for the comfort and welfare of passengers [ME, fr *purs* purse + ² *-er*]

**purse seine** *n* a large net (SEINE) designed to be set round a school of fish by two boats and so arranged that, after the ends have been brought together, the bottom can be closed – **purse seiner** *n*

**purse strings** *n pl* control over expenditure ⟨*who holds the* ∼ *in your house?*⟩

**purslane** /'puhslin/ *n* a fleshy-leaved trailing plant (*Portulaca oleracea* of the family Portulacaceae, the purslane family) with tiny yellow flowers; *broadly* any of several related usu fleshy-leaved plants [ME, fr MF *porcelaine*, fr LL *porcillagin-, porcillago*, alter. of L *porcillaca*, alter. of *portulaca*]

**pursuance** /pə'syooh·əns/ *n, formal* a carrying out or into effect (e g of a plan or order); prosecution ⟨*in* ∼ *of her duties*⟩

**pursuant to** /pə'syooh·ənt/ *prep* in carrying out; in conformance to; according to

**pursue** /pə'syooh/ *vt* **1** to follow in order to overtake, capture, kill, or defeat **2** to find or use measures to obtain or accomplish; seek ⟨∼ *a goal*⟩ **3a** to proceed along ⟨∼*s a northern course*⟩ **b** to act or continue in accordance with (e g a plan or policy) **4a** to engage in ⟨∼ *a hobby*⟩ **b** to follow up ⟨∼ *an argument*⟩ ⟨*police* ∼*d the enquiry*⟩ **5** to continue to afflict; haunt ⟨*was* ∼*d by horrible memories*⟩ ∼ *vi* to go in pursuit [ME *pursuen*, fr AF *pursuer*, fr OF *poursuir*, fr L *prosequi*, fr *pro-* forwards + *sequi* to follow – more at PRO-, SUE]

**pursuer** /pə'syooh·ə/ *n* **1** somebody or something that pursues **2a** a plaintiff **b** a prosecutor □ (2) used in Scots law

**pursuit** /pə'syooht/ *n* **1** the act of pursuing **2** an activity that one regularly engages in (e g as a pastime or profession); an occupation **3** a bicycle race over usu 3 to 5 kilometres (about 1¾ to 3 miles) in which usu two competitors at a time start on opposite sides of a track and pursue each other round it [ME, fr OF *poursuite*, fr *poursuir*]

**pursuit plane** *n* FIGHTER b

**pursuivant** /'puhsiv(ə)nt; *also* -swi-/ *n* an OFFICER OF ARMS ranking below a herald but having similar duties [ME *pursevant* attendant of a herald, fr MF *poursuivant*, lit., follower, fr prp of *poursuir, poursuivre* to pursue]

**pursy** /'puhsi/ *adj* **1** short-winded, esp because of fatness **2** fat [ME, fr AF *pursif*, alter. of MF *polsif*, fr *poulser, polser* to beat, push, pant – more at PUSH] – **pursiness** *n*

**purulence** /'pyooərələns/ *n* the quality or state of being purulent; *also* pus

**purulent** /'pyooərələnt/ *adj* **1** containing, consisting of, or being pus ⟨*a* ∼ *discharge*⟩ **2** accompanied by the formation of pus [L *purulentus*, fr *pur-, pus* pus]

**purvey** /pə'vay, puh-/ *vt* to supply; *esp* to supply (e g provisions) in the course of business [ME *purveien*, fr MF *porveeir*, fr L *providēre* to provide]

**purveyance** /pə'vayəns, puh-/ *n* the act or process of purveying something, esp provisions

**purveyor** /pə'vayə, puh-/ *n* **1** someone who purveys **2** a victualler, caterer

**purview** /'puh,vyooh/ *n* **1** the body or enacting part of a statute as distinguished from the preamble **2** *formal* the range or limit of authority, responsibility, or concern **3** *formal* range of vision, understanding, or cognizance [ME *purveu*, fr AF *purveu est* it is provided (opening phrase of a statute)]

**pus** /pus/ *n* thick opaque usu yellowish-white liquid matter formed by SUPPURATION and composed of exuded matter containing WHITE BLOOD CELLS, tissue debris, and microorganisms [L *pur-, pus* – more at FOUL]

**Pus** /poos/ *n* – see MONTH table [Hindi *pūs*, fr Skt *puṣya*]

**Puseyism** /'pyoohzi,iz(ə)m/ *n, derog* TRACTARIANISM [Edward Bouverie *Pusey* †1882 E theologian] – **Puseyite** *n*

**¹push** /poosh/ *vt* **1a** to apply a force to (something) in order to cause movement away from the person or thing applying the force **b** to move (something) away or forwards by applying such a force ⟨*to* ∼ *a car uphill*⟩ **2a** to cause (something) to change in quantity or extent as if under pressure ⟨*scarcity of labour* ∼*ed up wages*⟩ **b** to exert influence on (someone) to do something; pressurize ⟨∼ *her to take up music*⟩ **3a** to develop (e g an idea or argument), esp to an extreme degree **b** to urge or press the advancement, adoption, or practice of ⟨~ed *a bill in the legislature*⟩ ⟨~es *his protégés in the firm*⟩; *specif* to make aggressive efforts to sell ⟨*a drive to* ~ *tinned foods*⟩ **4** to force towards or beyond the limits of capacity or endurance ⟨*grinding poverty* ~ed *them to breaking point*⟩ **5** to hit (a ball) towards the right from a right-handed swing or towards the left from a left-handed swing **6** *informal* to approach in age or number ⟨*the old man was* ~ing 75⟩ **7** *slang* to engage in the illicit sale of (drugs) ~ *vi* **1** to press against something with steady force (as if) in order to move it away **2** to press forwards energetically against obstacles or opposition ⟨*explorers* ~ed *out into the Antarctic*⟩ **3** to exert oneself continuously, vigorously, or obtrusively to gain an end ⟨*unions* ~ing *for higher wages*⟩ [ME *pusshen*, fr OF *poulser* to beat, push, fr L *pulsare*, fr *pulsus*, pp of *pellere* to drive, strike – more at FELT] – **be pushed 1** to be too busy ⟨*would love to stop and chat but I'm rather pushed this afternoon*⟩ **2** to find it difficult ⟨*you'll be pushed to improve on that record*⟩ – **be pushed for** to be almost unable to find enough (time, money, etc) ⟨*I'm a bit pushed for time at the moment*⟩ – see also **push one's** LUCK

**synonyms** Push, shove, thrust, impel, and propel all mean "use **force** to move something away or aside". **Push** implies physical contact with what is moved, and often suggests a continuous, steady motion ⟨**push** *one's bicycle up a hill*⟩. **Shove**, somewhat informal, stresses exertion, or may connote rudeness, roughness, or haste ⟨**shoved** *it into his pocket*⟩. It may also imply pushing something along a surface, as in the game of shove-halfpenny. **Thrust** suggests a sudden, often violent **push**, sometimes directed with such force as to pierce or enter the object aimed at ⟨**thrust** *a book into her hand*⟩ ⟨**thrust** *the dagger into his heart*⟩. **Propel** suggests driving something forward from behind, especially by mechanical power ⟨**propelled** *by steam*⟩ ⟨*the wind* **propelled** *them along the promenade*⟩. **Impel** has a similar meaning, but is more usual in a figurative sense, for which it is often preferred to **propel**. Compare ¹PULL

**push around** *vt* to impose on contemptuously; bully
**push in** *vi* to join a queue at a point in front of others already waiting, esp by pushing or jostling
**push off** *vi, informal* to go away, esp hastily or abruptly ⟨*we pushed off home*⟩ ⟨*told him to push off*⟩
**push on** *vi* to continue on one's way, esp despite obstacles or difficulties; proceed

²**push** *n* **1** a vigorous effort to attain an end; a drive: **1a** a military assault or offensive **b** an advance that overcomes obstacles **2a** an act of pushing; a shove **b(1)** a physical force steadily applied in a direction away from the body exerting it ⟨*the* ~ *of the water against the wharf*⟩ **b(2)** a nonphysical pressure; an influence, urge ⟨*the* ~ *and pull of conflicting emotions*⟩ **c** vigorous enterprise or energy **3a** an exertion of influence to promote another's interests ⟨*his father's* ~ *took him to the top*⟩ **b** stimulation to activity; a boost, impetus ⟨*the war gave weather forecasts a tremendous* ~⟩ **4** *informal* a time for action; an emergency ⟨*when it came to the* ~ *I forgot my lines*⟩ **5** *Br informal* dismissal – esp in *get/give the push* ⟨*he'll get the* ~ *if he's late again*⟩ – **at a push** *chiefly Br* if really necessary; if forced by special conditions
ˈ**push-ˌbike** *n, Br informal* a pedal bicycle
ˈ**push-ˌbutton** *adj* **1** operated by means of a push button **2** characterized by the use of long-range weapons rather than physical combat ⟨~ *warfare*⟩
**push button** *n* a small button or knob that when pushed operates or triggers something, esp by closing an electric circuit
**pushcart** /ˈpooshˌkaht/ *n* a handcart
**pushchair** /-ˌcheə/ *n, Br* a light folding chair on wheels in which a young child may be pushed
**pushdown list** /ˈpooshˌdown/ *n* STACK 8 (store of data in a computer)
**pushdown stack** *n* STACK 8 (store of data in a computer)
**pushed** /poosht/ *adj, informal* having difficulty in finding enough time, money, etc ⟨*you'll be* ~ *to finish that by tonight*⟩
**pusher** /ˈpooshə/ *n* **1** a utensil used by a child for pushing food onto a spoon or fork **2** an aircraft engine with the propeller mounted behind; *also* an aircraft with such an engine **3** *slang* one who sells drugs illegally
**pushful** /ˈpooshf(ə)l/ *adj* pushing – **pushfulness** *n*
**pushing** /ˈpooshing/ *adj* marked by energetic ambition and self-confidence; *also* tactlessly or aggressively self-assertive
**pushover** /-ˌohvə/ *n, informal* **1** an opponent who is easy to defeat or a victim who is capable of no effective resistance **2**

someone unable to resist a usu specified attraction or appeal; a sucker ⟨*he's a* ~ *for blondes*⟩ **3** something accomplished without difficulty; a cinch
**pushpin** /ˈpooshˌpin/ *n* a pin that has a roughly cylindrical head and that is easily inserted into or withdrawn from a surface (eg a map) with the fingers
ˌ**push-ˈpull** *adj* of or being an arrangement of two similar electronic devices (eg valves or transistors) such that an alternating input causes them to send electric current through a load alternately ⟨*a* ~ *circuit*⟩ – **push-pull** *n*
**pushrod** /-ˌrod/ *n* a rod put into action by a CAM to open or close a valve in an INTERNAL-COMBUSTION ENGINE
ˈ**push-ˌstart** *vt* to start (a motor vehicle) by pushing it along to turn the engine – **push-start** *n*
**Pushtu** /ˈpushtooh/ *n or adj* the language of the Pathans; PASHTO
ˈ**push-ˌup** *n, chiefly NAm* a press-up
**pushy** /ˈpooshi/ *adj, informal* aggressive often to an objectionable degree; forward, self-assertive – **pushily** *adv*, **pushiness** *n*
**pusillanimity** /ˌpyoohsiləˈniməti/ *n, formal* the quality or state of being pusillanimous; cowardliness
**pusillanimous** /ˌpyoohsiˈlaniməs/ *adj, formal* lacking courage and resolution; contemptibly timid △ **puny** [LL *pusillanimis*, fr L *pusillus* very small (dim. of *pusus* small child; akin to L *puer* child) + *animus* spirit – more at PUERILE, ANIMATE] – **pusillanimously** *adv*
¹**puss** /poos/ *n, informal* **1** a cat – used chiefly as a pet name or calling name **2** a girl ⟨*a saucy little* ~⟩ [origin unknown]
²**puss** *n, slang* the face [IrGael *pus* mouth, fr MIr *bus*]
**puss moth** *n* a grey and white moth (*Cerura vinula*), which, as a caterpillar, is green with a reddish-brown saddle and has its last pair of PROLEGS modified into fleshy horns, each containing a whiplike filament
¹**pussy** /ˈpoosi/ *n* **1** a catkin of the pussy willow **2** *informal* a cat – used chiefly as a pet name
²**pussy** /ˈpusi/ *adj* full of or resembling pus
³**pussy** /ˈpoosi/ *n, vulg* the female genitals; VULVA [earlier *puss* (perh of LG or Scand origin) + -*y*; akin to ON *püss* pocket, pouch, LG *püse* vulva, OE *pusa* bag, Gk *byein* to stuff, plug]
**pussycat** /-ˌkat/ *n* a cat – used chiefly by or to children
**pussyfoot** /-ˌfoot/ *vi* **1** to tread or move warily or stealthily **2** to avoid committing oneself (eg to a course of action or an opinion) – **pussyfooter** *n*
**pussy willow** *n* any of various willows having large cylindrical grey silky catkins
**pustulant** /ˈpustyoolənt/ *n* something (eg a chemical compound) that induces pustule formation – **pustulant** *adj*
**pustular** /ˈpustyoolə/ *adj* **1** of or resembling pustules **2** pustulate
**pustulate** /ˈpustyoolət, -ˌlayt/, **pustulated** *adj* covered with pustules
**pustulation** /ˌpustyooˈlaysh(ə)n/ *n* **1** the act of producing pustules; the state of being covered with pustules **2** a pustule
**pustule** /ˈpustyoohl/ *n* **1** a small raised spot on the skin containing pus and having an inflamed base; PIMPLE 1 **2** a small often distinctively coloured elevation or spot (eg on a plant) resembling a blister or pimple [ME, fr L *pustula* – more at FOG]
¹**put** /poot/ *vb* -**tt**-; **put** *vt* **1a** to place or move into a specified position or relationship ⟨~ *the book on the table*⟩ ⟨~ *the cat out*⟩ ⟨~ *a thief in prison*⟩ ⟨~ *a child to bed*⟩ **b(1)** to send (eg a weapon or missile) into or through something; thrust **b(2)** to throw (eg a shot or weight) with an overhand pushing motion, esp as an athletic contest **c** to bring into a specified condition ⟨~ *a rule into effect*⟩ ⟨~ *the matter right*⟩ ⟨~ *her on a diet*⟩ **2a** to cause to endure or undergo; subject ⟨~ *him to death*⟩ ⟨~ *me to a lot of expense*⟩ ⟨~ *it to the test*⟩ **b** to impose, establish ⟨~ *a tax on luxuries*⟩ ⟨~ *an end to the argument*⟩ ⟨*this'll* ~ *hair on your chest*⟩ **3a** to formulate for judgment or decision ⟨~ *the question*⟩ ⟨~ *the motion*⟩ ⟨~ *it to him frankly*⟩ **b** to express, state ⟨~ting *it mildly*⟩ **4a** to turn into language or literary form ⟨~ *his feelings into words*⟩ **b** to translate ⟨~ *the poem into English*⟩ **c** to adapt, set ⟨*lyrics* ~ *to music*⟩ **5a** to devote, apply ⟨~ *himself to winning back their confidence*⟩ ⟨~ *her mind to the problem*⟩ **b** to assign ⟨~ *them to work*⟩ **c** to cause to perform an action; urge ⟨~ *the horse at the fence*⟩ **d** to impel, incite ⟨~ *them into a frenzy*⟩ **6a** to repose, rest ⟨~s *his faith in reason*⟩ **b** to invest ⟨~ *his money into steel*⟩ **7a** to give as an estimate ⟨~ *her age at about 40*⟩; *also* to imagine as being ⟨~ *yourself in my place*⟩ **b**

to attach, attribute ⟨~s *a high value on his friendship*⟩ **c** to impute ⟨~ *the blame on her partner*⟩ **8** to write, inscribe ⟨~ *a question mark at the end*⟩ ⟨~ *their names to what they wrote* – Virginia Woolf⟩ **9** to bring together with one of the opposite sex for breeding ⟨~ *a mare to a stallion*⟩ **10** to bet, wager ⟨~ *five pounds on the favourite*⟩ ~ *vi*, *of a ship* to take a specified course ⟨~ *back to port*⟩ [ME *putten;* akin to OE *putung* instigation, MD *poten* to plant] – **putter** *n* – **not put it past somebody** to think somebody capable of or likely *to* ⟨*would not put it past him to cheat*⟩ – **put it across somebody** *Br* to trick or deceive somebody – compare PUT ACROSS – **put it there** – used as an invitation to shake hands

**put about** *vi*, *of a ship* to change direction; go on another tack ~ *vt* **1** to cause (a ship) to change course or direction **2** to spread abroad ⟨*put false news or gossip*⟩

**put across** *vt* to convey (the meaning or significance of something) effectively or forcefully

**put aside** *vt* SET ASIDE

**put away** *vt* **1a** to place for storage when not in use ⟨*put the knives away in the drawer*⟩ **b** to discard, renounce ⟨*to put grief away is disloyal to the memory of the dead*⟩ **2** to save (money) for future use **3a** to confine, esp in a mental institution **b** to kill; *esp* PUT DOWN **4** *informal* to eat or drink up; consume ⟨*used to* put away *a bottle without blinking*⟩ **5** *archaic* to divorce

**put back** *vi* to return to port ⟨*had to* put back *because of foul weather*⟩

**put by** *vt* to lay aside; save

**put down** *vt* **1** to bring to an end; suppress, check ⟨*put down a riot*⟩ **2** to kill (e g a sick or injured animal) painlessly **3a** to put in writing ⟨*put it* down *on paper*⟩ **b** to enter in a list (e g of subscribers) ⟨*put me* down *for £5*⟩ **4** to pay as a deposit **5a** to place in a category ⟨*I put him* down *as an eccentric*⟩ **b** to attribute – + *to* ⟨*put it* down *to inexperience*⟩ **6** to store or set aside (e g bottles of wine) for future use **7** *informal* **7a** to disparage, belittle ⟨*mentioned his poetry only to* put it down⟩ **b** to humiliate, snub ⟨*put him* down *with a sharp retort*⟩ **8** *informal* to consume ⟨*putting* down *helping after helping* – Carson McCullers⟩ ~ *vi*, *of an aircraft or pilot* to land – see also PUT-DOWN

**put forth** *vt* **1a** to assert, propose **b** to make public, issue **2** to bring into action; exert **3** to produce or send out by growth ⟨put forth *leaves*⟩ ~ *vi* to embark

**put forward** *vt* **1** to bring into prominence ⟨*have no wish to* put *myself* forward⟩ **2** to propose ⟨put forward *a theory*⟩

**put off** *vt* **1a** to disconcert ⟨*was* put off *by the sudden noise and missed the target*⟩ **b** to repel, disgust ⟨*put off by the smell of drains*⟩ **c** to dissuade ⟨*so keen it was impossible to* put *her* off⟩ **2a** to postpone ⟨*decided to* put off *their departure*⟩ **b** to get rid of or persuade to wait, esp by excuses or evasions ⟨*put his creditors off for another few days*⟩ **3** to take off; rid oneself of – see also PUT-OFF

**put on** *vt* **1a** to dress oneself in; don **b** to make part of one's appearance or behaviour **c** to feign, assume ⟨*put a saintly manner on*⟩ **2** to cause to act or operate; apply ⟨*put on more speed*⟩ **3** to come to have an increased amount of ⟨*put on weight*⟩ **4** to stage, produce ⟨*put on a play*⟩ **5** to bet (a sum of money) **6** to bring to or cause to speak on the telephone ⟨*is your father there? Put* him *on, then*⟩ **7 put on, put upon** *chiefly Br* to be a trouble to ⟨*you're sure I won't be* putting on *you if I stay for dinner?*⟩ **8** *chiefly NAm informal* to mislead deliberately, esp for amusement ⟨*the interviewer ... must be put down – or possibly,* put on – Melvin Maddocks⟩ – see also PUT-ON

**put out** *vt* **1** to exert, use ⟨put out *considerable effort*⟩ **2** to extinguish ⟨put *the fire* out⟩ **3** to publish, issue **4** to produce for sale **5a** to disconcert, embarrass **b** to annoy, irritate **c** to inconvenience ⟨*don't* put *yourself* out *for us*⟩ **6** to cause to be out (e g in baseball or cricket) **7** to give or offer (a job of work) to be done by someone else outside the premises ~ *vi* to set out from shore

**put over** *vt* **1** PUT ACROSS **2** *NAm* to delay, postpone

**put through** *vt* **1** to carry into effect or to a successful conclusion ⟨put through *a number of reforms*⟩ **2a** to make a telephone connection for **b** to obtain a connection for (a telephone call) **3** to cause to suffer (e g pain or unhappiness)

**put together** *vt* **1** to create as a united whole; construct **2** to add, combine

**put up** *vt* **1** to put away (a sword) in a scabbard; sheathe **2** to flush (game) from cover ⟨put up *some partridges*⟩ **3** to nominate for election **4** to offer up (e g a prayer) **5** to offer for

public sale ⟨puts *her possessions* up *for auction*⟩ **6** to give food and shelter to; accommodate **7** to build, erect **8** to make a display of; show ⟨*desperate as he was, he* put up *a brave front*⟩ **9** to wage; CARRY ON ⟨put up *a struggle against considerable odds*⟩ **10a** to contribute, pay ⟨put up *the money for the venture*⟩ **b** to offer as a prize or stake **11** to increase the amount of; raise ~ *vi* **1** to lodge, shelter ⟨*we'll* put up *here for the night*⟩ **2** to offer oneself as a candidate in an election – usu + *for*

**put up to** *vt* to incite, instigate ⟨*they* put him up to *playing the prank*⟩

**put up with** *vt* to tolerate with resignation; endure ⟨*can't* put up with *the noise much longer*⟩

²**put** *n* **1** a throw made with an overhand pushing motion; *specif* the act or an instance of putting the shot **2** an option to sell a specified amount of a security (e g a stock) or commodity (e g wheat) at a fixed price, at or within a specified time – compare ²CALL 3d

³**put** *adj* – **stay put** to remain in the same position, condition, or situation

,**put-and-'take** *n* any of various games of chance played with a TEETOTUM, or with dice, in which players contribute to and take from a pool according to the instructions on the top or dice

**putative** /'pyoohtətiv/ *adj, formal* **1** commonly accepted or supposed ⟨*her* ~ *father*⟩ **2** assumed to exist or to have existed [ME, fr LL *putativus*, fr L *putatus*, pp of *putare* to think – more at PAVE] – **putatively** *adv*

'**put-,down** *n, informal* a humiliating remark; a snub

**putlog** /'put,log/ *n* a piece of timber between a wall and the uprights of a scaffold that ties a single row of uprights to the wall and supports the scaffolding planks [prob alter. of earlier *putlock*, perh fr ³*put + lock*]

'**put-,off** *n, informal* **1** the act or an instance of evasion or delay; an excuse **2** an act or statement calculated to repel or dissuade ⟨*couldn't decide whether his statement was a* ~ *or a come-on*⟩

¹,**put-'on** *adj* pretended, assumed

²'**put-,on** *n, chiefly NAm informal* an instance of deliberately misleading somebody ⟨*couldn't decide whether the question was serious or just a* ~⟩; *also, chiefly NAm* a parody, spoof ⟨*a kind of* ~ *of every pretentious film ever made* – C A Ridley⟩

**Putonghua** /,poohtong'hwah/ *n* a modern language of China based on Mandarin as spoken in Peking – used instead of *Mandarin* as the name for the official language of China [Chin *putonghua* (*p'u-t'ung-hua*) common language]

**putrefaction** /,pyoohtri'faksh(ə)n/ *n* **1** the decomposition of animal or plant matter; *esp* the breakdown of proteins by bacteria and fungi, typically in the absence of oxygen, causing the formation of foul-smelling products **2** the state of being putrefied; corruption [ME *putrefaccion*, fr LL *putrefaction-, putrefactio*, fr L *putrefactus*, pp of *putrefacere*] – **putrefactive** *adj*

**putrefy** /'pyoohtrifie/ *vb* to make or become putrid [ME *putrefien*, fr MF & L; MF *putrefier*, fr L *putrefacere*, fr *putrēre* to be rotten + *facere* to make – more at DO]

**putrescent** /,pyooh'tres(ə)nt/ *adj* **1** undergoing putrefaction; becoming putrid **2** of putrefaction [L *putrescent-, putrescens*, prp of *putrescere* to grow rotten, incho of *putrēre*] – **putrescence** *n*, **putrescible** *adj*

**putrescine** /pyooh'treseen, -sin/ *n* a slightly poisonous chemical compound (PTOMAINE), $C_4H_{12}N_2$, that occurs widely in small quantities in living things, and is found esp in putrid flesh [ISV, fr L *putrescere*]

**putrid** /'pyoohtrid/ *adj* **1a** in a state of putrefaction; rotten **b** (characteristic) of putrefaction; *esp* foul-smelling **2a** morally corrupt **b** *slang* very unpleasant or worthless [L *putridus*, fr *putrēre* to be rotten, fr *puter, putris* rotten; akin to L *putēre* to stink] – **putridly** *adv*, **putridness** *n*, **putridity** *n*

**putsch** /pooch/ *n* a secretly plotted and suddenly executed attempt to overthrow a government **synonyms** see REBELLION [Ger]

**putt** /put/ *n* a gentle golf stroke made to roll the ball towards or into the hole on a PUTTING GREEN [alter. of ²*put*] – **putt** *vb*

**puttee** /'puti, pu'tee/ *n* **1** a long cloth strip wrapped spirally round the leg from ankle to knee, esp as part of an army uniform **2** GAITER 1b [Hindi *paṭṭī* strip of cloth, fr Skt *paṭṭikā*]

¹**putter** /'putə/ *n* **1** a golf club used in putting **2** a person who putts

²**putter** /'putə/ *vi, NAm* to potter [by alter.] – **putterer** *n*

**putting green** /'puting/ *n* a smooth grassy area at the end of a

golf fairway containing the hole into which the ball must be played
**putto** /'pootoh/ *n, pl* **putti** /-ti/ a figure of a chubby Cupid-like boy, esp in Renaissance painting [It, lit., boy, fr L *putus*]
[1]**putty** /'puti/ *n* **1** a pasty substance consisting of hydrated lime and water, used as a finishing coat on plaster **2a** a doughlike cement, usu made of WHITING and boiled LINSEED OIL, used esp in fastening glass in window sashes and stopping crevices in woodwork **b** any of various substances resembling such cement in appearance, consistency, or use: eg **b(1)** an acid-resistant mixture of FERRIC OXIDE and boiled LINSEED OIL **b(2)** a mixture of red and white lead and boiled linseed oil used to seal joints of pipes **3** someone who is easily manipulated ⟨*is ~ in her hands*⟩ [Fr *potée*, lit., potful, fr OF, fr *pot* – more at POTAGE]
[2]**putty** *vt* to use putty on or apply putty to
[1]**put-,up** *adj, informal* arranged or contrived secretly beforehand ⟨*the vote was obviously a ~ job*⟩
[2]**put-u,pon** *adj* imposed upon; taken advantage of
**puy** /pwee (*Fr* pɥi)/ *n* any of the hills of volcanic origin common in the Auvergne region of France [Fr, fr L *podium* balcony, parapet – more at PEW]
[1]**puzzle** /'puzl/ *vb* **puzzling** /'puzling, 'puzl·ing/ *vt* to offer or represent to (a person or his/her mind) a problem difficult to solve or a situation difficult to resolve; perplex ⟨*a schoolmaster ~d by a hard sum* – R W Emerson⟩; *also* to exert (eg oneself) over such a problem or situation ⟨*they ~d their brains to find a solution*⟩ ~ *vi* to be uncertain as to action, choice, or meaning ⟨*we ~d for days about whether to go*⟩ ⟨*~d all night over her remarks*⟩ [origin unknown] – **puzzler** *n*
   *synonyms* Puzzle, perplex, mystify, bewilder, confound, and baffle may all describe mental confusion and disturbance. What puzzles one may do so because it is unusual or odd, or because it presents an intricate problem. Perplex in addition suggests anxiety ⟨*her absence puzzled him, but her continuing silence perplexed him even more*⟩. Perplex also frequently conveys uncertainty over the solution of (usually personal) problems. Mystify implies intentional obscuring and concealment in order to puzzle, and extreme puzzlement on the part of the one puzzled ⟨*mystified by her cryptic remarks*⟩. Bewilder suggests great perplexity and confusion of mind ⟨*bewildered by the conflicting opinions put forward on every side*⟩. Confound adds to bewilder an astonishment so great as to paralyse actually or mentally ⟨*and Satan stood . . . confounded* – Milton⟩. Baffle suggests an intention to outwit or frustrate, resulting in great perplexity or mystification ⟨*baffled by his sudden disappearance*⟩. Compare [1]PROBLEM *antonym* clarify
   **puzzle out** *vt* to find (a solution or meaning) by means of mental effort
[2]**puzzle** *n* **1** the state of being puzzled; perplexity **2a** something that puzzles **b** a question, problem, or contrivance designed for testing ingenuity *synonyms* see [1]PROBLEM
**puzzlement** /'puzəlmənt/ *n* the state of being puzzled; perplexity
**PVC** *n* POLYVINYL CHLORIDE (type of plastic)
**py-** /pie·/-, **pyo-** *comb form* pus ⟨*pyaemia*⟩ ⟨*pyorrhoea*⟩ [Gk, fr *pyon* pus – more at FOUL]
**pya** /pyah, pi'ah/ *n* – see *kyat* at MONEY table [Burmese]
**pyaemia** /pie'eemyə, -mi·ə/ *n* blood poisoning accompanied by multiple abscesses [NL] – **pyaemic** *adj*
**pycnidium** /pik'nidiəm/ *n, pl* **pycnidia** /-diə/ an asexual usu flask-shaped FRUITING BODY containing spores (CONIDIA) and occurring in various fungi [NL, fr Gk *pyknos* dense; akin to Gk *pyka* thickly, Albanian *puth* kiss] – **pycnidial** *adj*
**pycnogonid** /pik'nogənid, ˌpiknə'gonid/ *n* SEA SPIDER [deriv of Gk *pyknos* + *gony* knee – more at KNEE]
**pycnometer** /pik'nomitə/ *n* a standard vessel, often provided with a thermometer, for measuring and comparing the densities of liquids or solids [Gk *pyknos* + ISV *-meter*]
**pye** /pie/ *n* [3]PIE (spilt type)
[1]**pye-,dog** /pie/ *n* a half-wild dog common in and around Asian villages [prob by shortening & alter. fr *pariah dog*]
**pyel-** /pie·əl-/, **pyelo-** *comb form* pelvis of the kidney ⟨*pyelography*⟩ [NL, pelvis, fr Gk *pyelos* trough; akin to Gk *plein* to sail – more at FLOW]
**pyelitis** /ˌpie·ə'lietis/ *n* inflammation of the lining of the PELVIS (expanded portion of the tube carrying urine to the bladder) of the kidney [NL]
**pyelonephritis** /ˌpie·əloh·ne'frietəs/ *n* inflammation of both the lining of the PELVIS (expanded portion of the tube carrying urine to the bladder) and the tissue of the kidney [NL] – **pyelonephritic** *adj*

**pygidium** /pie'jidi·əm, -'gidi-/ *n, pl* **pygidia** /-diə/ the end structure (eg a tail) or end part of the body of various INVERTEBRATE animals [NL, fr Gk *pygidion*, dim. of *pygē* rump; akin to L *pustula* pustule] – **pygidial** *adj*
**pygmaean, pygmean** /pig'mee·ən/ *adj* (characteristic) of the Pygmies; Pygmy [L *pygmaeus*]
**pygmoid** /'pigmoyd/ *adj* resembling or having the characteristics of the Pygmies
**pygmy, pigmy** /'pigmi/ *n* **1** *cap* a member of a people of equatorial Africa under 1.5 metres (about 5 feet) in height **2** someone who is insignificant or inferior in the specified sphere or way ⟨*a political ~*⟩ **3** *derog* a very short person; a dwarf [ME *pigmei* member of a legendary race of dwarfs, fr L *pygmaeus* of a pygmy, dwarfish, fr Gk *pygmaios*, fr *pygmē* fist, measure of length – more at PUNGENT] – **pygmy** *adj*, **pygmyish** *adj*
**pygmyism** /'pigmi,iz(ə)m/ *n* a stunted or dwarfed condition
**pygmy shrew** *n* a very small Eurasian shrew (*Sorex minutus*)
**pygostyle** /'piegə,stiel/ *n* a plate of bone that forms the rear end of the SPINAL COLUMN in most birds [deriv of Gk *pygē* rump + *stylos* pillar]
**pyjama** /pə'jahmə/ *adj* of or designed for pyjamas
**pyjamas**, *NAm chiefly* **pajamas** /pə'jahməz/ *n pl* **1** loose lightweight trousers traditionally worn in the East **2** a suit of loose lightweight jacket and trousers for sleeping in [Hindi *pājāma*, fr Per *pā* leg + *jāma* garment] – **pyjama** *adj*
**pyknic** /'piknik/ *adj* characterized by shortness of stature, broadness of girth, and powerful muscularity; ENDOMORPHIC **2** [ISV, fr Gk *pyknos* dense, stocky – more at PYCNIDIUM] – **pyknic** *n*
**pylon** /'pielon, -lən/ *n* **1a** either of two towers with sloping sides flanking the entrance to an ancient Egyptian temple **b** a monumental mass flanking an entranceway or approach **2** a tower for supporting either end of a wire, esp electricity power cables, over a long span; *broadly* any of various towerlike structures **3** a projection (eg a post or tower) marking a prescribed course of flight for an aircraft **4** a rigid structure on the outside of an aircraft for supporting something (eg an engine, fuel tank, or bomb) [Gk *pylōn* gateway, fr *pylē* gate]
**pyloric** /pie'lorik, -'lawrik/ *adj* of the pylorus; *also* of or situated in or near the back part of the stomach
**pylorus** /pie'lawrəs/ *n, pl* **pylori** /-ri/ the opening from the stomach into the intestine of VERTEBRATE animals [LL, fr Gk *pylōros*, lit., gatekeeper, fr *pylē*]
**pyo-** – see PY-
**pyoderma** /ˌpieoh'duhmə/ *n* a bacterial skin inflammation characterized by pus-filled spots or pimples [NL] – **pyodermic** *adj*
**pyogenic** /ˌpie·ə'jenik/ *adj* producing pus ⟨*~ bacteria*⟩; characterized by pus production [ISV]
**pyorrhoea** /ˌpie·ə'riə/ *n* inflammation, accompanied by the formation of pus, of the sockets of the teeth leading usu to loosening of the teeth [NL] – **pyorrhoeal** *adj*
**pyr-** /pie·ər-/, **pyro-** *comb form* **1** fire; heat ⟨*pyrometer*⟩ ⟨*pyrheliometer*⟩ **2** produced (as if) by the action of heat ⟨*pyroelectricity*⟩ ⟨*pyrolysis*⟩ **3** fever ⟨*pyrogen*⟩ [ME, fr MF, fr LL, fr Gk, fr *pyr* – more at FIRE]
**pyracantha** /ˌpiera'kanthə/ *n* any of a genus (*Pyracantha*) of Eurasian thorny evergreen or half-evergreen shrubs of the rose family with clusters (CORYMBS) of white flowers and red berries [NL, genus name, fr Gk *pyrakantha*, a tree, fr *pyr-* + *akantha* thorn – more at ACANTH-]
**pyralid** /'pirəlid/ *n* any of a very large mixed family (Pyralidae) of moths, most of which are small, slender, and long-legged [deriv of L *pyralis*, fly supposed to live in fire, fr Gk, fr *pyr* fire] – **pyralid** *adj*
**pyralidid** /'pirəlidid/ *n* a pyralid [deriv of L *pyralis*] – **pyralidid** *adj*
[1]**pyramid** /'pirəmid/ *n* **1a** an ancient massive structure found esp in Egypt having typically a square ground plan, smooth or stepped outside walls in the form of four triangles that meet in a point at the top, and inner burial chambers **b** a structure or object of similar form **2** a three-dimensional figure having a base that is a polygon and other faces which are triangles with a common vertex **3** a crystal form having nonparallel faces that meet at a point **4** an anatomical structure resembling a pyramid: eg **4a** any of the conical masses that project from the MEDULLA (central portion) of the kidney into the kidney PELVIS (expanded portion of the tube carrying urine to the bladder) **b** either of two large bundles of NERVE FIBRES from the outer portion of the forebrain (CEREBRUM) that reach the

MEDULLA OBLONGATA (rear portion of the brain) and are continuous with the PYRAMIDAL TRACTS of the SPINAL CORD **5 a** nonphysical structure or system (e g a social or organizational hierarchy) conceived as having the form of a triangle or pyramid with a broad supporting base and narrowing gradually to an apex ⟨*the socioeconomic* ∼ ⟩ [L *pyramid-, pyramis,* fr Gk] – **pyramidal** *adj,* **pyramidally** *adv,* **pyramidical** *adj*

²**pyramid** *vi* **1** to speculate (e g on an exchange) by using paper profits as margin for additional transactions **2** to increase rapidly and progressively step by step from a broad base ∼ *vt* **1** to arrange or build up as if on the base of a pyramid **2** to use (e g profits) in speculative pyramiding **3** to increase the impact of (e g a tax assessed at the production level) on the ultimate consumer by treating as a cost that is subject to markup ⟨*they* ∼ *every cost, with middlemen, tariffs, taxes, and overheads* – D D Eisenhower⟩

**pyramidal tract** /pi'ramidl/ *n* any of four columns of NERVE FIBRES carrying impulses away from the brain that run in pairs on each side of the SPINAL CORD, and are continuations of the pyramids of the MEDULLA OBLONGATA (rear portion of the brain)

**pyramid selling** *n* a fraudulent financial system whereby agents for the sale of a product are induced to recruit an infinite series of other agents on an ever-dwindling commission

**pyran** /'pieran, -'-/ *n* either of two chemical compounds, $C_5H_6O$, that contain five carbon atoms and one oxygen atom arranged in a ring structure [ISV *pyr-* + *-an*]

**pyranoid** /'pirənoyd, 'pie-/ *adj* derived from or related to the pyrans

**pyranose** /'pirənohs, 'pie-/ *n* a MONOSACCHARIDE (simple sugar) containing a pyranoid ring [ISV *pyran* + *-ose*]

**pyranoside** /pi'ranəsied, pie-/ *n* a GLYCOSIDE (chemical compound derived from a sugar) containing the pyranoid ring

**pyrargyrite** /pie'rahjəriet, pi'rah-/ *n* a dark red or black mineral, $Ag_3SbS_3$, consisting of silver antimony sulphide that occurs either in the form of a mass or in crystals and is a source of silver [Ger *pyrargyrit,* fr Gk *pyr-* + *argyros* silver – more at ARGENT]

**pyre** /'pie·ə/ *n* a heap of combustible material for burning a dead body as part of a funeral rite; *broadly* a pile of material to be burned ⟨*a* ∼ *of dead leaves*⟩ [L *pyra,* fr Gk, fr *pyr* fire – more at FIRE]

**pyrene** /'piereen/ *n* the stone or kernel of a fruit (DRUPELET); *broadly* a small hard nutlet [NL *pyrena,* fr Gk *pyrēn* stone of a fruit; akin to Gk *pyros* wheat – more at FURZE]

**Pyrenean mountain dog** /,pirə'nee·ən/ *n* (any of) a breed of large heavy-coated white dogs [*Pyrenees,* mountain range along the border between France & Spain]

**pyrenoid** /'pierənoyd/ *n* any of the protein bodies in the CHROMATOPHORES (pigment-containing cell parts) of various lower organisms (e g some algae) that act as centres for storing starch [ISV, fr NL *pyrena*]

**pyrethrin** /pie'reethrin/ *n* either of two oily liquid insecticides, $C_{21}H_{28}O_3$ and $C_{22}H_{28}O_5$, that occur esp in pyrethrum flowers [ISV, fr L *pyrethrum*]

**pyrethroid** /pie'reethroyd/ *n* any of various synthetic chemical compounds that are related to the pyrethrins and resemble them in insecticidal properties [*pyrethr*in + *-oid*] – **pyrethroid** *adj*

**pyrethrum** /pie'reethrəm/ *n* **1** any of several chrysanthemums with finely divided often aromatic leaves, including ornamental plants as well as ones that yield pyrethrin **2** an insecticide consisting of the dried heads of any of several African and Eurasian chrysanthemums [L, pellitory, fr Gk *pyrethron,* fr *pyr* fire]

**pyretic** /pie'retik/ *adj* of fever; febrile [NL *pyreticus,* fr Gk *pyretikos,* fr *pyretos* fever, fr *pyr*]

**Pyrex** /'piereks/ *trademark* – used for glass and glassware that is resistant to heat, chemicals, and electricity

**pyrexia** /pie'reksi·ə/ *n* abnormal rise of body temperature; fever [NL, fr Gk *pyressein* to be feverish, fr *pyretos*] – **pyrexial, pyrexic** *adj*

**pyrheliometer** /pə,heeli'omitə/ *n* an instrument for measuring the radiant energy from the sun that is received at the earth [ISV] – **pyrheliometric** *adj*

**pyridine** /'pierideen, -din/ *n* a toxic water-soluble inflammable liquid chemical BASE, $C_5H_5N$, with a pungent smell, that is obtained by distillation of bone oil or from coal, is the parent of many naturally occurring carbon-containing chemical compounds, and is used as a solvent and in the manufacture of medicines and waterproofing agents [*pyr-* + *-id* + *-ine*]

**pyridoxal** /,piri'doksəl/ *n* a vitamin, $C_8H_9NO_3$, of the VITAMIN $B_6$ group, that is an ALDEHYDE and is converted in the body into its active phosphate essential in the formation, conversion, and breakdown of AMINO ACIDS [ISV, fr *pyridoxine*]

**pyridoxamine** /,piri'doksəmeen/ *n* a vitamin, $C_8H_{12}N_2O_2$, of the VITAMIN $B_6$ group, that is an AMINE with the actions and uses in the body of pyridoxal [ISV *pyridox*ine + *amine*]

**pyridoxine** *also* **pyridoxin** /,piri'dokseen, -sin/ *n* a vitamin, $C_8H_{11}NO_3$, of the VITAMIN $B_6$ group, found esp in cereals and convertible in the body into pyridoxal and pyridoxamine [*pyrid*ine + *ox-* + *-ine*]

**pyriform** /'piri,fawm/ *adj, esp of a plant or animal part* pear-shaped ⟨∼ *apparatus in the egg of a mite*⟩ [NL *pyriformis,* fr ML *pyrum* pear (alter. of L *pirum*) + L *-iformis* -iform – more at PEAR]

**pyrimethamine** /,piri'methəmeen/ *n* a synthetic drug, $C_{12}H_{13}ClN_4$, that acts in opposition to FOLIC ACID (type of vitamin B) and is used in the preventative treatment of malaria and of TOXOPLASMOSIS (disease caused by a parasitic microorganism) [*pyrim*idine + *ethyl* + *amine*]

**pyrimidine** /pie'rimideen, -din/ *n* **1** a chemical compound, $C_4H_4N_2$, that is a weak BASE and has a penetrating odour **2** a derivative of pyrimidine; *specif* a base (e g cytosine, thymine, or uracil) that is a constituent of DNA or RNA – compare PURINE [ISV, alter. of *pyridine*]

**pyrite** /'pie·əriet/ *n* IRON PYRITES (type of mineral) [L *pyrites*]

**pyrites** /pie'rieteez, pi-/ *n, pl* **pyrites** any of various metallic-looking sulphur-containing minerals of which IRON PYRITES is the commonest [L, flint, fr Gk *pyritēs* of or in fire, fr *pyr* fire] – **pyritic** *adj*

**pyro-** – see PYR-

**pyrocatechol** /,pieroh'katəkol, -rə-/ *n* a chemical compound (PHENOL), $C_6H_4(OH)_2$, usu made synthetically and used esp as a photographic developer and in the synthesis of carbon-containing chemical compounds [ISV *pyr-* + *catechol* ($C_{15}H_{14}O_6$), fr *catechu* + *-ol*]

**pyrochemical** /,pieroh'kemikl/ *adj* relating to or involving chemical activity at high temperatures – **pyrochemically** *adv*

**pyroclastic** /,pieroh'klastik, -rə-/ *adj* formed from fragments resulting from volcanic action

**pyroelectricity** /,pieroh·ilek'trisəti, -elek-/ *n* a state of electrical POLARIZATION (orientation of opposite electrical charges) produced (e g in crystals) by a change of temperature [ISV] – **pyroelectric** *adj*

**pyrogallic acid** /,pieroh'galik/ *n* pyrogallol [ISV]

**pyrogallol** /,pieroh'galol/ *n* a poisonous chemical compound (PHENOL), $C_6H_4(OH)_3$, with weak acid properties that is used esp in photographic developers and in dye manufacture [ISV *pyrogall*ic (acid) + *-ol*]

**pyrogen** /'pieroh,jen, -rə-/ *n* a fever-producing substance (e g formed by a bacterium) [ISV]

**pyrogenic** /,pieroh'jenik/, **pyrogenous** /pie'rojinəs/ *adj* **1** producing or produced by heat or fever **2** *of a rock* IGNEOUS (formed by the slow cooling and solidification of molten rock material) [ISV] – **pyrogenicity** *n*

**pyroligneous** /,pieroh'ligni·əs/ *adj* obtained by DESTRUCTIVE DISTILLATION (decomposition by heat) of wood [Fr *pyroligneux,* fr *pyr-* + *ligneux* woody, fr L *lignosus,* fr *lignum* wood – more at LIGNEOUS]

**pyroligneous acid** /,pie·əroh'lignəs/ *n* an acid reddish-brown aqueous liquid containing chiefly ACETIC ACID, METHANOL, wood oils, and tars

**pyrolusite** /,pieroh'loohsiet/ *n* a mineral, $MnO_2$, consisting of manganese dioxide that is of an iron-black or dark steel-grey colour and metallic lustre, is usu soft, and is the most important source of manganese [Ger *pyrolusit,* fr Gk *pyr-* + *lousis* washing, fr *louein* to wash – more at LYE]

**pyrolysate,** *NAm also* **pyrolyzate** /pie'roləzayt/ *n* a product of pyrolysis

**pyrolyse,** *NAm chiefly* **pyrolyze** /'pierəliez/ *vt* to subject to pyrolysis – **pyrolysable** *adj,* **pyrolyser** *n*

**pyrolysis** /pie'roləsis/ *n* chemical change brought about by the action of heat [NL] – **pyrolytic** *adj,* **pyrolytically** *adv*

**pyromania** /,pierə'maynyə, -ni·ə/ *n* a compulsive urge to start fires [NL] – **pyromaniac** *n,* **pyromaniacal** *adj*

**pyrometallurgy** /,pieroh'metəluhji, -mi'taləji/ *n* chemical metallurgy depending on heat action (e g roasting and smelting) [ISV] – **pyrometallurgical** *adj*

**pyrometer** /pie'romitə/ *n* an instrument for measuring temperatures, esp when beyond the range of mercury thermometers,

usu by the increase of electric resistance in a metal, by the
generation of electric current in a THERMOCOUPLE, or by the
increase in intensity of light radiated by an incandescent body
[ISV] – **pyrometry** *n*, **pyrometric** *adj*, **pyrometrically** *adv*

**pyromorphite** /ˌpiərəˈmawfiet/ *n* a mineral, $Pb_5(PO_4)_3Cl$, consisting of a phosphate and chloride of lead and occurring in
green, yellow, brown, grey, or white crystals or masses [Ger
*pyromorphit*, fr Gk *pyr-* + *morphē* form]

**pyronine** /ˈpieroneen, -nin/ *n* any of several dyes of the
XANTHENE group used chiefly to stain biological specimens
for examination under the microscope [ISV *pyr-* + *-on* + *-ine*]

**pyroninophilic** /ˌpiərəˌneenəˈfilik/ *adj, of a plant or animal
tissue, cell, etc* staining selectively with pyronines ⟨~ *cells*⟩

**pyrope** /ˈpieˌrohp/ *n* a deep red garnet containing magnesium
and aluminium that is frequently used as a gem [ME *pirope*, a
red gem, fr MF, fr L *pyropus*, a red bronze, fr Gk *pyrōpos*, lit.,
fiery-eyed, fr *pyr-* + *ōp-*, *ōps* eye – more at EYE]

**pyrophoric** /ˌpiərəˈforik/ *adj* 1 igniting spontaneously 2 *of an
alloy* emitting sparks when scratched or struck, esp with steel
[NL *pyrophorus*, fr Gk *pyrophoros* fire-bearing, fr *pyr-* +
*-phoros* -phorous]

**pyrophosphate** /ˌpiərəˈfosfayt/ *n* any of various chemical
compounds (SALTS OR ESTERS) formed by combination between PYROPHOSPHORIC ACID and a metal atom, an alcohol, or
another chemical group – **pyrophosphatic** *adj*

**pyrophosphoric acid** /ˌpierəfosˈforik/ *n* an acid, $H_4P_2O_7$,
formed when ORTHOPHOSPHORIC ACID is heated, or prepared in
the form of SALTS by heating acid salts of orthophosphoric
acid [ISV]

**pyrophyllite** /ˌpiərəˈfiliet, pieˈrofiliet/ *n* a white or greenish
mineral, $AlSi_2O_5(OH)$, that consists of a silicate of aluminium, resembles the mineral talc, occurs in a layered
form or in compact masses, and is used in pottery [Ger
*pyrophyllit*, fr Gk *pyr-* + *phyllon* leaf – more at BLADE]

**pyrosulphuric acid** /ˌpierohˈsulˈfooərik/ *n* an unstable acid,
$H_2S_2O_7$, usu handled commercially as a thick oily liquid, and
converted to SULPHURIC ACID when mixed with water

¹**pyrotechnic** /ˌpieˈərəˈteknik/ *also* **pyrotechnical** *adj* of pyrotechnics [Fr *pyrotechnique*, fr Gk *pyr* fire + *technē* art] – **pyro-
technically** *adv*

²**pyrotechnic** *n* **1a** a firework **b** any of various similar devices
(e g for igniting a rocket or producing an explosion) **2** a combustible substance used in a firework

**pyrotechnics** /ˌpieˈərəˈtekniks/ *n pl* **pl 1** *taking sing or pl vb* the
art of making or the manufacture and use of fireworks **2** a
brilliant or spectacular display (e g of oratory or extreme virtuosity) ⟨*his verbal* ~ *are entertaining* – *TLS*⟩ – **pyro-
technist** *n*

**pyroxene** /ˈpierokˌseen, -ˈ--/ *n* any of a group of minerals that
are constituents of IGNEOUS rocks (rocks formed by the slow
cooling and solidification of molten rock material), contain calcium, sodium, magnesium, iron, or aluminium in silicon-based
chemical compounds, occur often in thin flat layers, and vary
in colour from white to dark green or black [Fr *pyroxène*, fr
Gk *pyr-* + *xenos* stranger] – **pyroxenoid** *adj or n*

**pyroxenite** /pieˈroksiniet/ *n* a coarse-grained rock that is
composed essentially of pyroxene – **pyroxenitic** *adj*

**pyroxylin** /pieˈərˈroksilin/ *n* **1** an inflammable mixture of
CELLULOSE NITRATES, usu with a low nitrogen content, that is
less explosive than GUNCOTTON, is soluble in a mixture of ether
and ethanol or other solvents, and is used esp in making
plastics and coatings (e g lacquers) **2** a pyroxylin product [ISV
*pyr-* + Gk *xylon* wood]

**pyrrhic** /ˈpirik/ *n* a unit of poetic metre (FOOT) consisting of two
short or unstressed syllables [L *pyrrhichius*, fr Gk (*pous*)
*pyrrhichios*, fr *pyrrhichē*, a kind of dance] – **pyrrhic** *adj*

**Pyrrhic victory** *n* a victory won at excessive cost [*Pyrrhus* †
272 BC king of Epirus whose army sustained heavy losses in
defeating the Romans]

**Pyrrhonism** /ˈpirəniz(ə)m/ *n* **1** the sceptical doctrines of Pyrrho
and his followers **2** total or radical scepticism [Fr *pyrrhonisme*,
fr *Pyrrhon* Pyrrho, 4th-c BC Gk philosopher, fr Gk *Pyrrhōn*] –
**Pyrrhonist** *n*

**pyrrhotite** /ˈpirətiet/, **pyrrhotine** /ˈpirəteen, -tien/ *n* a bronze-
coloured mineral, FeS, of metallic lustre that consists of iron
sulphide and is attracted by a magnet [modif of Ger *pyrrhotin*,
fr Gk *pyrrhotēs* redness, fr *pyrrhos* red, fr *pyr* fire – more at
FIRE]

**pyrrole** *also* **pyrrol** /ˈpirohl, -ˈ-/ *n* a toxic liquid chemical compound, $C_4H_5N$, that is the parent compound of many biologically important substances (e g bile pigments, PORPHYRINS, and
chlorophyll); *broadly* a derivative of pyrrole [Gk *pyrrhos* red] –
**pyrrolic** *adj*

**pyruvate** /ˈpieˈroohvayt/ *n* any of various chemical compounds
(SALTS or ESTERS) formed by combination between PYRUVIC
ACID and a metal atom, an alcohol, or another chemical
group

**pyruvic acid** /pieˈroohvik/ *n* an acid, $CH_3COCOOH$, that is
an intermediate in the biochemical processing (METABOLISM) of
carbohydrates and can be formed either from GLYCOGEN
(starchlike food storage substance) or from glucose [ISV *pyr-* +
L *uva* grape – more at UVULA; fr its importance in fermenta-
tion]

**Pythagoras' theorem** /pieˈthagərəs(iz)/ *n, chiefly Br* a theorem
in geometry: the square of the length of the hypotenuse of a
right-angled triangle equals the sum of the squares of the
lengths of the other two sides [*Pythagoras* † *ab* 500 BC Gk
philosopher & mathematician]

**Pythagoreanism** /pieˌthagəˈree-əniz(ə)m/ *n* the doctrines and
theories of Pythagoras and his followers consisting mainly of
belief in the ultimate mathematical nature of the world, the
mystical significance of numbers, and the possibility of the soul
achieving union with the divine – **Pythagorean** *n*

**Pythiad** /ˈpithiad/ *n* the 4-year period between celebrations of
the Pythian games [Gk *Pythia*, the Pythian games, fr neut pl
of *pythios*]

**Pythian** /ˈpithiən/ *adj* **1** of Delphi or its oracle of Apollo **2** of
the games celebrated at Delphi every four years in ancient
times [L *pythius* of Delphi, fr Gk *pythios*, fr *Pythō* Pytho,
former name of Delphi, ancient town in Greece]

**python** /ˈpieth(ə)n/ *n* a large nonvenomous snake (e g a boa that
kills its prey by constriction); *esp* any of a genus (*Python*) that
includes the largest living snakes [L, monstrous serpent killed
by Apollo, fr Gk *Pythōn*] – **pythonine** *adj*

**pythoness** /ˈpiethənes, -is, -ˈes/ *n* **1** a woman who practises
divination **2** a prophetic priestess of Apollo [ME *Phitonesse*,
fr MF *pithonisse*, fr LL *pythonissa*, fr Gk *Pythōn*, spirit of
divination, fr *Pythō*, seat of the Delphic oracle] – **pythonic** *adj*

**pyuria** /ˌpieˈyooəriˈə/ *n* (a condition characterized by) pus in the
urine [NL]

**pyx** /piks/ *n* **1** a container in which the bread used at Communion is kept; *esp* a small round metal receptacle used for
carrying Communion to the sick **2** a box used in a mint
for the deposit of sample coins reserved for testing weight
and fineness [ME, fr ML *pyxis*, fr L, box, fr Gk – more at
BOX]

**pyxidium** /pikˈsidiˈəm/ *n, pl* **pyxidia** /-diə/ **1** a CAPSULAR fruit
that bursts open at maturity so that the upper part falls off
like a cap **2** CAPSULE 2b (structure containing the spore of a
moss) [NL, fr Gk *pyxidion*, dim. of *pyxis*]

**pyxis** /ˈpiksis/ *n, pl* **pyxides** /ˈpiksideez/ PYXIDIUM 1 [NL, fr L,
box]

# Q

**q, Q** /kyooh/ *n, pl* **q's, qs, Q's, Qs 1a** the 17th letter of the English alphabet **b** a graphic representation of or device for reproducing the letter *q* **c** a speech counterpart of printed or written *q* **2** one designated *q*, esp as the 17th in order or class **3** something shaped like the letter Q

**Q** *n* a source usu put forward by biblical critics for the material common to the gospels of Matthew and Luke and not derived from that of Mark [Ger *q*uelle source]

**qadi, cadi** /'kahdi, 'kaydi/ *n* a Muslim judge who interprets and administers the religious law of Islam [Ar *qāḍī*, fr *qaḍā* to judge]

**qat** /kaht, kat/ *n* KAT (shrub whose leaves are chewed as a drug)

**QC** *n* QUEEN'S COUNSEL

**,Q-'Celtic** *n* the branch of the Celtic languages that includes IRISH GAELIC, SCOTTISH GAELIC, and Manx – called also GOIDELIC; compare P-CELTIC [fr the retention in these languages of the Indo-European phoneme *qu*]

**Q fever** *n* a mild disease characterized by high fever, chills, and muscular pains, that is caused by a RICKETTSIA (microscopic organism) (*Coxiella burnetii*), and is transmitted by drinking raw milk, by contact, or by ticks [*q*uery; fr its cause being orig unknown]

**qindar, qintar** /kin'dah/ *n, pl* **qindarka** /kin'dahkə/ – see *lek* at MONEY table [Albanian]

**qoph** /koof, kof (*Hebrew* kɔf)/ *n* the 19th letter of the Hebrew alphabet [Heb *qōph*]

**'Q-,ship** *n* an armed ship, used chiefly in World War I, disguised as a merchant or fishing ship and used to decoy enemy submarines into surfacing within range of the guns [*q*uery]

**QSO** *n* QUASAR (starlike celestial object) [*q*uasi-*s*tellar *o*bject]

**qt** /kyooh 'tee/ *n often cap* Q&T, *slang* [*q*uie*t*] – **on the qt** secretly; ON THE QUIET

**qua** /kway, kwah/ *prep* in the capacity or character of; as ⟨*disliked the chairman not ~ chairman but ~ person*⟩ [L, which way, as, fr abl sing. fem of *qui* who – more at WHO]

**'quack** /kwak/ *vi* to make the characteristic cry of a duck [imit] – **quack** *n*

**²quack** *n* **1** an ignorant impostor in medicine **2** *informal* CHARLATAN 2 **3** *chiefly Br & Austr informal* a medical doctor; *esp* GENERAL PRACTITIONER [short for *quacksalver*] – **quackish** *adj*

**³quack** *adj* (characteristic) of a quack; *esp* pretending to cure diseases ⟨*~ medicines*⟩

**quackery** /'kwakəri/ *n* the practices or pretensions of a quack

**quack grass** *n, NAm* COUCH GRASS [alter. of *quick grass*, alter. of *quitch grass*]

**quacksalver** /'kwak,salvə/ *n, archaic* a charlatan, quack [obs D (now *kwakzalver*), prob fr *quacken* to quack, prattle + *salf* salve]

**'quad** /kwod/ *n* QUADRANGLE 2; *specif* one in a university college

**²quad** *n* a type-metal space block, used in printing,that is one EN or more in width [short for *quadrat*]

**³quad** *vt* **-dd-** to fill out (e g a typeset line) with blank spaces

**⁴quad** *n* a quadruplet

**⁵quad** *adj*, of sound or its recording or reproduction quadraphonic

**quadr-** – see QUADRI-

**Quadragesima** /,kwodrə'jesimə/ *n* the first Sunday in Lent [LL, fr L, fem of *quadragesimus* fortieth, fr *quadraginta* forty – more at QUARANTINE; fr its being approximately 40 days before Easter]

**quadrangle** /'kwodrang·gl/ *n* **1** a quadrilateral **2** a four-sided enclosure surrounded by buildings [ME, fr MF, fr LL *quadr(i)angulum*, fr L, neut of *quadr(i)angulus* quadrangular, fr *quadri-* + *angulus* angle] – **quadrangular** *adj*

**quadrant** /'kwodrənt/ *n* **1a** an instrument consisting commonly of a graduated arc of 90° used, esp formerly, in astronomy, navigation, etc for measuring altitudes and other angles **b** a device or mechanical part shaped like or suggestive of the quadrant of a circle **2a** an arc of 90° that is one quarter of the circumference of a circle **b** the area of one quarter of a circle that is bounded by a quadrant and two radii at RIGHT ANGLES to one another **3a** any of the four parts into which a plane is divided by two axes lying at RIGHT ANGLES to each other in that plane **b** any of the four quarters into which something is divided by two real or imaginary lines that intersect each other at RIGHT ANGLES [ME, fr L *quadrant-, quadrans* fourth part; akin to L *quattuor* four – more at FOUR] – **quadrantal** *adj*

**quadraphonic** *also* **quadrophonic** /,kwodrə'fonik/ *adj* of or being sound or a system for recording or reproducing sound that uses four electrical channels between the source of the signal and its final point of use [irreg fr *quadri-* + *-phonic*] – **quadraphonics** *also* **quadrophonics** *n taking sing or pl vb*

**quadraphony** *also* **quadrophony** /kwo'drofəni/ *n* quadraphonic sound reproduction

**quadrat** /'kwodrət, 'kwodrat/ *n* **1** ²QUAD (space block in printing) **2a** a usu square plot of land used as a sample area for the ecological investigation of the plants, or sometimes animals, of a region **b** a metal frame or similar apparatus used to delimit an area selected for biological investigation [alter. of ²*quadrate*]

**'quadrate** /'kwodrət, 'kwodrayt/ *adj* **1** (approximately) square **2** of or being a quadrate bone [ME, fr L *quadratus*, pp of *quadrare* to make square, fit; akin to L *quattuor*]

**²quadrate** *n* **1** an approximately square or cubical area, space, or object **2 quadrate, quadrate bone** either of a pair of bones or sometimes cartilage structures, one on each side of the skull, to which the lower jaw is hinged in birds, reptiles, fish, and amphibians

**³quadrate** /kwo'drayt/ *vi, archaic* to agree, correspond – usu + *with*

**'quadratic** /kwo'dratik, kwə-/ *adj, maths* of or involving (mathematical terms of) the second DEGREE, ORDER, or POWER – **quadratically** *adv*

**²quadratic** *n, maths* a quadratic equation, curve, expression, etc

**quadrature** /'kwodrəchə/ *n* **1** *maths* the process of finding a square equal in area to a given surface or figure **2a** an astronomical configuration in which two celestial bodies (e g the sun and the moon) form an angle of 90° with a third body, esp the earth **b** either of two points on an orbit in a middle position between CONJUNCTION and OPPOSITION **3** *electronics* a difference in PHASE of one quarter cycle or 90° between two waves (e g the current and voltage in an ALTERNATING CURRENT) [L *quadratura* square, act of squaring, fr *quadratus*, pp]

**quadrennial** /kwo'dreni·əl/ *adj* **1** consisting of or lasting for four years **2** occurring every four years – **quadrennial** *n*, **quadrennially** *adv*

**quadrennium** /kwo'dreni·əm/ *n, pl* **quadrenniums, quadrennia** /-ni·ə/ a period of four years [L *quadriennium*, fr *quadri-* + *annus* year – more at ANNUAL]

**quadri-** /kwodri-/ **quadr-, quadru-** *comb form* **1a** four ⟨quadri*lateral*⟩ **b** square ⟨quadr*ic*⟩ **2** fourth ⟨quadri*centennial*⟩ [ME, fr L; akin to L *quattuor* four]

**quadric** /'kwodrik/ *adj, maths* quadratic ⟨*a ~ surface*⟩ – used for an equation, expression, etc having more than two variables [ISV] – **quadric** *n*

**quadricentennial** /,kwodrisen'teni·əl/ *adj or n* (of) a QUATERCENTENARY (400th anniversary)

**quadriceps** /'kwodri,seps/ *n* a muscle that is attached in four places at one end; *specif* the large muscle of the front of the thigh that acts to extend and straighten the leg at the knee joint [NL, fr *quadri-* + *-ceps* (as in *biceps* biceps)]

**quadrifid** /'kwodrifid/ *adj* divided or deeply cleft into four parts ⟨*a ~ petal*⟩ [L *quadrifidus*, fr *quadri-* + *-fidus* -fid]

**quadriga** /kwo'dreegə/ *n, pl* **quadrigae** /kwo'dreejee/ a chariot drawn by four horses abreast [L, sing. of *quadrigae* team of four, contr of *quadrijugae*, fem pl of *quadrijugus* yoked four abreast, fr *quadri-* + *jungere* to yoke, join – more at JOIN]

¹**quadrilateral** /ˌkwodri'lat(ə)rəl/ *adj* having four sides [prob fr (assumed) NL *quadrilateralis*, fr L *quadrilaterus*, fr *quadri-* + *later-, latus* side]

²**quadrilateral** *n* a two-dimensional geometric figure having four angles and four straight sides

**quadrilingual** /ˌkwodri'ling-gwəl/ *adj* of, containing, or expressed in four languages; *also* using or able to use four languages

**quadrille** /kwə'dril/ *n* **1** a 4-handed variant of OMBRE played with a pack of 40 cards and popular esp in the 18th century **2** a SQUARE DANCE for four couples, made up of five or six FIGURES, chiefly in ⁶⁄₈ and ²⁄₄ time; *also* the music for this dance [Fr, group of knights engaged in a carousel, variant of ombre, fr Sp *cuadrilla* troop, fr It *quadriglia* band, troop, company, fr *cuadra, quadra* square]

**quadrillion** /kwo'drilyən/ *n* **1** *Br* a million million million millions (10²⁴) **2** *chiefly NAm* a thousand million millions (10¹⁵) □ see NUMBER table [Fr, fr MF, fr *quadri-* + *-illion* (as in *million*)]

**quadripartite** /ˌkwodri'pahtiet/ *adj* **1** consisting of or divided into four parts **2** shared or participated in by four parties or people ⟨*a ~ agreement*⟩ [ME, fr L *quadripartitus*, fr *quadri-* + *partitus*, pp of *partire* to divide, fr *part-, pars* part]

**quadriplegia** /ˌkwodri'pleej(y)ə/ *n* paralysis of both arms and both legs – compare HEMIPLEGIA, PARAPLEGIA [NL, fr *quadri-* + *-plegia*] – **quadriplegic** *adj or n*

**quadrisyllable** /ˌkwodri'siləbl/ *n* a word of four syllables – **quadrisyllabic** *adj*

¹**quadrivalent** /ˌkwodri'vaylənt/ *adj* **1** having a VALENCY of four; TETRAVALENT 1 **2** of or being a quadrivalent [ISV]

²**quadrivalent** *n* a group of four CHROMOSOMES (strands of gene-carrying material in the nucleus of a cell) temporarily held together during the first stages of MEIOSIS (division of a cell into four new cells)

**quadrivial** /kwo'driviəl/ *adj* **1** of the quadrivium **2** having four ways or roads meeting in a point

**quadrivium** /kwo'drivi-əm/ *n* a group of studies consisting of arithmetic, music, geometry, and astronomy, and forming the division of the seven liberal arts studied after the trivium in medieval universities – compare TRIVIUM [LL, fr L, crossroads, fr *quadri-* + *via* way – more at VIA]

**quadroon** /kwo'droohn/ *n* a person of one-quarter black ancestry; *esp* the first-generation offspring of a mulatto and a white person [modif of Sp *cuarterón*, fr *cuarto* fourth, fr L *quartus*; akin to L *quattuor* four]

**quadrophonic** /ˌkwodrə'fonik/ *adj* quadraphonic ⟨*~ sound*⟩

**quadrophony** /kwo'drofəni/ *n* QUADRAPHONY

**quadru-** – see QUADRI-

**quadrumana** /kwo'droohmənə/ *n taking pl vb* monkeys, apes, and other PRIMATES excluding man, considered as a group distinguished by hand-shaped feet [NL, fr *quadri-* + L *manus* hand – more at MANUAL] – **quadrumanal, quadrumanous** *adj*, **quadrumane** *adj or n*

**quadruped** /'kwodroo,ped/ *n* an animal with four legs [L *quadruped-, quadrupes*, fr *quadruped-, quadrupes*, adj, having four feet, fr *quadri-* + *ped-, pes* foot – more at FOOT] – **quadruped, quadrupedal** *adj*

¹**quadruple** /'kwodroopl, kwo'droohpl/ *vb* to make or become four times as great or as many

²**quadruple** *n* **1** an amount four times as great as another **2** a combination or group of four

³**quadruple** *adj* **1** having four units or members **2** four times as great or as many **3** *music* marked by four beats per bar ⟨*~ time*⟩ [MF or L; MF, fr L *quadruplus*, fr *quadri-* + *-plus* multiplied by – more at DOUBLE] – **quadruply** *adv*

**quadruplet** /'kwodrooplit, kwo'droohplit/ *n* **1** any of four offspring born at one birth **2** a combination of four of a kind **3** a group of four musical notes performed in the time of three notes of the same value [fr ³*quadruple*, by analogy to *double: doublet*]

¹**quadruplicate** /kwo'droohplikət/ *adj* **1** consisting of or existing in four corresponding or identical parts or examples ⟨*~ invoices*⟩ **2** being the fourth of four things exactly alike ⟨*file the ~ copy*⟩ [L *quadruplicatus*, pp of *quadruplicare* to quad-

ruple, fr *quadruplic-, quadruplex* fourfold, fr *quadri-* + *-plic-, -plex* fold – more at SIMPLE]

²**quadruplicate** /kwo'droohplikayt/ *vt* **1** to make quadruple or fourfold **2** to prepare in quadruplicate – **quadruplication** *n*

³**quadruplicate** /kwo'droohplikət/ *n* **1** any of four things exactly alike; *specif* any of four identical copies **2** four copies all alike – + *in* ⟨*typed in ~*⟩

**quadruplicity** /ˌkwodroo'plisəti/ *n* the state of being quadruple or quadruplicate [L *quadruplic-, quadruplex* fourfold + E *-ity*]

**quaere** /'kwiəri/ *n, archaic* a query [L, imper of *quaerere* to seek, question]

**quaestor** /'kweestə, -staw/ *n* any of numerous ancient Roman officials concerned chiefly with financial administration [ME *questor*, fr L *quaestor*, fr *quaestus*, pp of *quaerere*]

¹**quaff** /kwof, kwahf/ *vb, chiefly humorous or poetic* to drink (a beverage) deeply in long draughts ⟨*~ed his ale*⟩ [origin unknown] – **quaffer** *n*

²**quaff** *n* a long draught of a beverage

**quag** /kwag, kwog/ *n* a marsh, bog [origin unknown] – **quaggy** *adj*

**quagga** /'kwagə/ *n* a recently extinct wild zebra (*Equus quagga*) of southern Africa that has a brown back and striped head, neck, and forequarters [obs Afrik (now *kwagga*), fr Hottentot *qua-ha*, of imit origin]

**quagmire** /'kwag,mie·ə, 'kwog-/ *n* **1** soft miry land that shakes or yields under the foot **2** a predicament from which it is difficult to extricate oneself

**quahog** /'kwah,hog/ *n* a thick-shelled edible N American clam (*Mercenaria mercenaria*) [Narraganset *poquaûhock*, fr *pohkeni* dark, closed + *hogki* shell]

**quaich, quaigh** /kwayk, kwaykh/ *n, chiefly Scot* a small shallow drinking cup with two handles [ScGael *cuach*]

¹**quail** /kwayl/ *n, pl* **quails**, *esp collectively* **quail 1** any of various short-tailed plain-coloured Eurasian birds (esp genus *Coturnix*) that resemble but are usu smaller than the related partridge; *esp* a migratory game bird (*Coturnix coturnix*) common in Europe **2** any of various small American game birds (order Galliformes) related to the Eurasian quail [ME *quaille*, fr MF, fr ML *quaccula*, of imit origin]

²**quail** *vi* **1** to give way or fail ⟨*his courage never ~ed*⟩ **2** to recoil in dread or terror; cower ⟨*the strongest ~ before financial ruin* – Samuel Butler †1902⟩ *synonyms* see ¹RECOIL [ME *quailen* to curdle, fr MF *quailler*, fr L *coagulare* – more at COAGULATE]

**quaint** /kwaynt/ *adj* **1a** unusual or different in character or appearance; odd ⟨*figures of fun, ~ people* – Herman Wouk⟩ **b** pleasingly or strikingly old-fashioned or unfamiliar, esp in manner or dress **2** *archaic* **2a** made or executed with skill, ingenuity, or cunning ⟨*~ with many a device in India ink* – Herman Melville⟩ **b** beautiful, elegant ⟨*a body so fantastic, trim, and ~* – William Cowper⟩ *synonyms* see STRANGE [ME *cointe* skilled, elegant, fastidious, strange, fr OF, fr L *cognitus*, pp of *cognoscere* to know – more at COGNITION] – **quaintly** *adv*, **quaintness** *n*

¹**quake** /kwayk/ *vi* **1** to shake or vibrate, usu from shock or instability **2** to tremble or shudder, esp inwardly from fear *synonyms* see ¹SHAKE [ME *quaken*, fr OE *cwacian*; akin to OE *cweccan* to shake, vibrate] – **quaky** *adj*

²**quake** *n* **1** an instance of shaking or trembling **2** *informal* an earthquake

**quaker** /'kwaykə/ *n* **1** one who or that which quakes **2** *cap* a member of a Christian sect, the Society of Friends, that stresses INNER LIGHT, rejects sacraments and an ordained ministry, and opposes war – called also FRIEND – **Quakerish** *adj*, **Quakerism** *n*, **Quakerly** *adj*

**Quaker gun** *n, NAm* a dummy piece of artillery usu made of wood [fr the Quakers' opposition to war]

**quale** /'kwayli, 'kwahli/ *n, pl* **qualia** /-liə/ a property (e g redness) considered apart from the things having that property; a universal [L, neut of *qualis* of what kind]

**qualifiable** /'kwoli,fie·əbl/ *adj* capable of being qualified or modified

**qualification** /ˌkwolifi'kaysh(ə)n/ *n* **1** a restriction in meaning or application; a limiting modification ⟨*this statement stands without ~*⟩ ⟨*their pleasure was complete, with only one ~*⟩ **2a** a quality or skill that fits a person (e g for a particular task or appointment) ⟨*the applicant with the best ~s*⟩ **b** a condition that must be complied with (e g for the attainment of a privilege) ⟨*a ~ for membership*⟩ [ML *qualification-, qualificatio*, fr *qualificatus*, pp of *qualificare*]

**qualified** /'kwolifid/ *adj* **1a** fitted (e g by training or experience) for a usu specified purpose; competent **b** complying with the specific requirements or conditions (e g for appointment to an office or employment); eligible **2** limited or modified in some way ⟨~ *approval*⟩ – **qualifiedly** *adv*

**qualifier** /'kwoli,fie·ə/ *n* one who or that which qualifies: e g **a** somebody or something that satisfies requirements or meets a specific standard **b** a grammatical modifier **c** a preliminary heat or contest

**qualify** /'kwolifie/ *vt* **1a** to reduce from a general to a particular, restricted, or more exact form; modify ⟨qualified *his statement to cover only teenagers*⟩ **b** to make less harsh or strict; moderate **c** to alter the strength or flavour of **d** *linguistics* MODIFY 2a **2** to characterize by naming an attribute; describe ⟨*cannot* ~ *it as ... either glad or sorry* – T S Eliot⟩ **3a** to fit by training, skill, or ability for a special purpose **b** to render legally capable or entitled ⟨*residence* qualifies *you for membership*⟩ ~ *vi* **1** to be fit (e g for an office) ⟨qualifies *for the job by virtue of his greater experience*⟩ **2** to reach an accredited level of competence ⟨*has just* qualified *as a solicitor*⟩ **3a** to exhibit a required degree of ability or achievement in a preliminary contest ⟨qualified *earlier today for the semifinals*⟩ **b** to fire a score that makes one eligible for the award of a marksmanship badge [MF *qualifier*, fr ML *qualificare*, fr L *qualis*]

**qualitative** /'kwolitətiv/ *adj* of or involving quality or kind – **qualitatively** *adv*

**qualitative analysis** *n* chemical analysis designed to identify the components of a substance or mixture – compare QUANTITATIVE ANALYSIS

¹**quality** /'kwoləti/ *n* **1a** peculiar and essential character; nature ⟨*differences in the* ~ *of the two personalities*⟩ ⟨*the* ~ *of mercy is not strained* – Shak⟩ **b** an inherent feature; a property ⟨*had a* ~ *of stridence, dissonance* – Roald Dahl⟩ **2a** degree of excellence; grade, level ⟨*a decline in the* ~ *of applicants*⟩ ⟨*goods of the first* ~⟩ **b** superiority in kind ⟨*proclaimed the* ~ *of his wife* – Compton Mackenzie⟩ **3a** high social position ⟨*a man of* ~⟩; broadly, archaic social status, rank ⟨*your name, your* ~ – Shak⟩ **b** *taking sing or pl vb, chiefly humorous* the aristocracy ⟨*the* ~ *will sit in the front row*⟩ **4** a distinguishing attribute; a characteristic ⟨*the star* ~ *he radiates*⟩ ⟨*listed all her good qualities*⟩ **5** *philosophy* the character of a logical proposition as affirmative or negative **6a** musical timbre **b** the identifying character of a vowel sound; timbre **7** the attribute of an elementary sensation that makes it fundamentally unlike any other sensation **8** *archaic* capacity, role ⟨*in the* ~ *of reader and companion* – Joseph Conrad⟩ [ME *qualite*, fr OF *qualité*, fr L *qualitat-, qualitas*, fr *qualis* of what kind; akin to L *qui* who – more at WHO]

  **synonyms** Quality, attribute, characteristic, property, and trait can all mean "distinguishing inherent feature". People or things can have **qualities, attributes,** or **characteristics; quality** often applies to what is really true ⟨*boy has many fine* **qualities**⟩, whereas an **attribute** is less clearly known and may be merely ascribed ⟨*wisdom is an* **attribute** *of the goddess Athene*⟩. **Characteristic** applies particularly to what is typical of a group ⟨*reptilian* **characteristics**⟩. Things, but not people, can have **properties,** the basic qualities that make them behave in a particular way ⟨*the* **properties** *of a dye*⟩. People, but not usually things, can have **traits,** minor peculiarities of habit or temperament ⟨*her concern for her canary is one of her most attractive* **traits**⟩.

²**quality** *adj* **1** concerned with or displaying excellence ⟨~ *goods*⟩ **2** *of a newspaper* aiming to appeal to an educated readership ⟨*the* ~ *Sundays*⟩

**quality control** *n* all the activities (e g design analysis and sampling of the final product with inspection for defects) designed to ensure adequate quality in manufactured products

**qualm** /kwahm, kwawm/ *n* **1** a sudden and brief attack of illness, faintness, or nausea **2** a sudden feeling of anxiety or apprehension **3** a scruple or feeling of uneasiness about a point of conscience, honour, or propriety [origin unknown] – **qualmy** *adj*

  **synonyms** Qualm, misgiving, scruple, compunction, reservation, and demur all mean "consideration that inhibits action". **Qualms** and **misgivings** can both arise from fear ⟨*felt* **qualms** *about crossing the narrow bridge*⟩, but while **misgiving** applies particularly to lack of confidence and fear of mistakes ⟨*a* **misgiving** *that he had been making a fool of himself* – G B Shaw⟩, **qualm** often entails a personal aversion to what offends taste or morals ⟨*few little girls can squash insects and kill rabbits without a* **qualm** – Rose Macaulay⟩. **Scruple** and **compunction** are specifically moral, **scruple** involving

an offence to one's principles ⟨*religious* **scruples**⟩ and the weaker **compunction** including also mild remorse for what one has already done ⟨*feel no* **compunction** *about having left him all alone*⟩. A **reservation** is a specific objection to some part of what is proposed, while **demur** implies a positive act of objecting ⟨*paid the bill without* **demur**⟩.

**qualmish** /'kwahmish, 'kwawmish/ *adj* feeling qualms; nauseated – **qualmishly** *adv*, **qualmishness** *n*

**quandary** /'kwond(ə)ri/ *n* a state of perplexity or doubt; a dilemma [perh based on L *quando* when]

**quango** /'kwang·goh/ *n, pl* **quangos** an autonomous body (e g the Race Relations Board in Britain) set up by a government and having statutory powers in a specific field [*quasi-* autonomous *non-*governmental *organization*; or *quasi* non-governmental *organization*; or *quasi-*autonomous *national* governmental *organization*]

**quanta** /'kwontə/ *pl of* QUANTUM

**quantal** /'kwontl/ *adj, physics* of a QUANTUM

**quantasome, quantosome** /'kwontə,sohm/ *n* any of the tiny regularly arranged chlorophyll-containing particles that occur in the CHLOROPLASTS of plant cells and may constitute the functional units of photosynthesis [prob fr *quanta* (pl of *quantum*) + ³*-some*]

**quantification** /,kwontifi'kaysh(ə)n/ *n* the operation of quantifying – **quantificational** *adj,* **quantificationally** *adv*

**quantifier** /'kwontifie·ə/ *n* **1** *philosophy* a term that specifies the universal, particular, or singular character of a logical proposition **2** *linguistics* a word referring to a noun, esp a DETERMINER (e g *five, many*), expressive of quantity; *esp* one (e g *many, several, lots of*) other than a number

**quantify** /'kwontifie/ *vt* **1** *philosophy* to specify the logical quantity of **2** to determine, express, or measure the quantity of [ML *quantificare*, fr L *quantus* how much] – **quantifiable** *adj*

**quantitative** /'kwontitətiv/ *adj* **1** of or expressible in terms of quantity **2** of or involving the measurement of quantity or amount **3** based on quantity; *specif, of classical verse* based on the relative duration of sequences of sounds – compare ACCENTUAL – **quantitatively** *adv,* **quantitativeness** *n*

**quantitative analysis** *n* chemical analysis designed to determine the amounts or proportions of the components of a substance or mixture – compare QUALITATIVE ANALYSIS

**quantity** /'kwontəti/ *n* **1a** an indefinite amount or number **b** a known, measured, or estimated amount ⟨*precise quantities of four ingredients*⟩ **c** the total amount or number **d** **quantities** *pl,* **quantity** a considerable amount or number ⟨*wept like anything to see such* quantities *of sand* – Lewis Carroll⟩ **2a** the aspect in which a thing is measurable in terms of the degree of magnitude **b** the number, value, etc subjected to a mathematical operation **c** a factor to take into account or be reckoned with ⟨*an unknown* ~ *as military leader*⟩ **3** the relative duration of a speech sound or sound sequence; *specif* the relative length or brevity of a prosodic syllable (e g in Greek and Latin) **4** *philosophy* the character of a logical proposition as universal, particular, or singular *usage* see AMOUNT [ME *quantite*, fr OF *quantité*, fr L *quantitat-, quantitas*, fr *quantus* how much, how large; akin to L *quam* how, as, *quando* when, *qui* who – more at WHO]

**quantity surveyor** *n* somebody who estimates or measures quantities (e g for builders) – **quantity surveying** *n*

**quantity theory, quantity theory of money** *n* a theory in economics: changes in the price level tend to vary directly, and in the value of money inversely, with the amount of money in circulation and the speed of its circulation

**quant·ized, -ised** /'kwontiezd/ *adj, physics* **1a** existing in or subdivided into quanta; restricted to taking or occurring in discrete values ⟨~ *energy*⟩ ⟨*the* ~ *properties of an atomic particle*⟩ **b** having properties (e g energy) that are subdivided into quanta ⟨*an atom is a* ~ *system*⟩ **2** calculated or expressed in terms of QUANTUM MECHANICS [*quantum* + *-ize* ] – **quantize** *vt,* **quantization** *n,* **quantizer** *n*

**quantosome** /'kwontə,sohm/ *n* QUANTASOME

**quantum** /'kwontəm/ *n, pl* **quanta** /-tə/ **1** any of the very small discrete increments or parcels that form the smallest units into which many physical quantities (e g energy and momentum) can be subdivided, and by which the value of a quantity increases or decreases **2** *formal* **2a** a quantity, amount **b** a portion, part [L, neut of *quantus* how much]

**quantum electrodynamics** *n* a branch of physics dealing with the application of QUANTUM MECHANICS to the interactions between particles having electrical charge and ELECTRO-MAGNETIC RADIATION

**quantum mechanics** *n* a branch of physics based on a general mathematical theory developed to deal with the physical behaviour of atoms and particles of matter (e g their interactions with other particles or radiation), for which the laws of classical mechanics were found to be inapplicable – **quantum mechanical** *adj*, **quantum mechanically** *adv*

**quantum number** *n* any of a set of numbers that are INTEGERS or half integers, that serve to define the state of a quantized system (e g an atom) or a particle (e g an electron) within such a system, and each of which indicates the value of a property (e g energy) of the system or particle

**quantum theory** *n* a theory in physics based on the concept of the subdivision of energy, esp RADIANT ENERGY (e g light), into discrete increments or quanta

**quarantinable** /'kworən‚teenəbl/ *adj* subject to or constituting grounds for quarantine ⟨*a ~ disease*⟩

¹**quarantine** /'kworən‚teen/ *n* **1a** a period during which a ship arriving in port, and suspected of carrying contagious disease, is held in isolation from the shore **b** a regulation placing a ship in quarantine **c** a place where a ship is detained during quarantine **2a** (the period of) a restraint on the activities or communication of people, or the transport of goods or animals, designed to prevent the spread of disease or pests **b** a place in which people, animals, vehicles, etc under quarantine are kept **3** a state of enforced isolation [It *quarantina* period of 40 days, fr MF *quarantaine*, fr OF, fr *quarante* forty, fr L *quadraginta*, fr *quadra-* (akin to *quattuor* four) + *-ginta* (akin to vi*ginti* twenty) – more at FOUR, VIGESIMAL]

²**quarantine** *vt* **1** to detain in or exclude by quarantine **2** to isolate from normal relations or communication ⟨*~ an aggressor*⟩ *~ vi* to establish or declare a quarantine

**quark** /kwahk/ *n* a hypothetical particle of matter that carries a fractional electrical charge, is postulated to exist in several forms, and is thought to be a constituent of known ELEMENTARY PARTICLES (e g the proton, neutron, or other minute particle of matter) [coined by Murray Gell-Mann *b*1929 US physicist (later associated by him with the nonce-word *quark* in *Finnegan's Wake* by James Joyce '1941 Ir writer)]

¹**quarrel** /'kworəl/ *n* a short heavy square-headed bolt or arrow, esp for a crossbow [ME, fr MF & OF; MF, square of glass, fr OF, square-headed arrow, building stone, fr (assumed) VL *quadrellum*, dim. of L *quadrum* square; akin to L *quattuor* four – more at FOUR]

²**quarrel** *n* **1** a reason for dispute or complaint ⟨*have no ~ with his reasoning*⟩ **2** a usu verbal conflict between antagonists; a dispute [ME *querele*, fr MF, complaint, fr L *querela*, fr *queri* to complain]

*synonyms* Quarrel, wrangle, bicker, squabble, spat, and tiff all refer to a more or less angry dispute. Quarrel is the most serious word, often implying a dispute that entails lasting estrangement. Wrangle suggests a prolonged noisy dispute between stubborn adversaries. The other words apply to merely petty quarrels over trifles: bickering involves petulant verbal sparring on a somewhat childish level, squabbling is noisy but without much ill feeling, spat is an informal word for a short lively dispute arising perhaps from sudden ill temper, and a tiff, which may arise from hurt feelings ⟨*a lovers' tiff*⟩, is ill-humoured but trivial and temporary.

³**quarrel** *vi* **-ll-** (*NAm* **-l-**, **-ll-**) **1** to find fault with ⟨*the teacher invariably found something to ~ with in her essays*⟩ **2** to contend or dispute actively; argue ⟨*~led frequently with her superiors*⟩; *also* to cease friendly relations; FALL OUT – **quarreller** *n*

**quarrelsome** /-səm/ *adj* inclined or quick to quarrel, esp in a petty manner; contentious – **quarrelsomely** *adv*, **quarrelsomeness** *n*

¹**quarry** /'kwori/ *n* **1** the animal pursued in hunting; *specif* game hunted with hawks **2** the intended victim; prey [ME *querre* entrails of game given to the hounds, fr MF *cuiree*, fr OF, prob alter. (influenced by *cuir* leather & *curer* to cleanse, disembowel) of *coree* entrails, fr LL *corata* (pl), fr L *cor* heart]

²**quarry** *n* **1** an open excavation for obtaining bulk civil engineering materials (e g stone, sand, or slate) **2** a source from which useful material, esp information, may be extracted ⟨*the archives were an invaluable ~*⟩ [ME *quarey*, alter. of *quarrere*, fr MF *quarriere*, fr (assumed) OF *quarre* squared stone, fr L *quadrum* square]

³**quarry** *vt* **1** to dig or take (as if) from a quarry ⟨*~ marble*⟩ **2** to make a quarry in ⟨*~ a hill*⟩ *~ vi* to dig or delve (as if) in a

quarry ⟨*~ing in the largely unexplored Italian mines – TLS*⟩ – **quarrier** *n*

**quarrying** /'kwori‚ing/ *n* the business, occupation, or act of extracting useful material (e g building stone) from quarries

**quarryman** /'kworimən/ *n* a worker in a quarry; a quarrier

**quarry tile** *n* a hardwearing unglazed floor tile

**quart** /kwawt/ *n* either of two units of liquid capacity equal to 2 pints: **a** a British unit equal to about 1.136 litres **b** a US unit equal to about 0.946 litre [ME, one quarter of a gallon, fr MF *quarte*, fr OF, fr fem of *quart*, adj, fourth, fr L *quartus;* akin to L *quattuor* four – more at FOUR]

**quartan** /'kwawtn/ *adj* of or being attacks of a fever, esp malaria, that recur at approx 72-hour intervals [ME *quarteyne*, fr OF (*fievre*) *quartaine* quartan fever, fr L (*febris*) *quartana*, fr *quartanus* of the fourth, fr *quartus*] – **quartan** *n*

¹**quarter** /'kwawtə/ *n* **1** any of four equal parts into which something is divisible **2a** any of various units (e g of capacity, weight, length, or area) equal to or derived from one fourth of some larger unit **b** a quarter of either a US or a British hundredweight **3** the fourth part of a measure of time: e g **3a** any of a set of four 3-month divisions of a year ⟨*business was up during the third ~*⟩ **b** a school or college term of about 12 weeks, esp in America **c** a quarter of an hour – used in the designation of a point of time ⟨*a ~ past three*⟩ **d** a fourth part of the moon's period of revolution round the earth **4** (a coin worth) a quarter of a dollar, esp a US or Canadian dollar; *also, chiefly NAm* 25 cents **5a**(1) a limb of a 4-legged animal with the adjacent parts; *esp* a fourth part of the carcass of a slaughtered animal including a leg **a(2)** a hindquarter **b** a teat together with the part of a cow's udder that it drains ⟨*milk from all four ~*s⟩ **6a** the region or direction lying towards or round any of the four CARDINAL POINTS of the compass; *broadly* any compass point or direction ⟨*the wind is in that ~*⟩ **b(1)** a person or group not specifically identified ⟨*had financial help from many ~*s⟩ **b(2)** a point, direction, or place not specifically identified ⟨*did little trade in that ~*⟩ **7a** a division or district of a town or city ⟨*the Chinese ~*⟩ **b** *taking sing or pl vb* the inhabitants of such a quarter **8a quarters** *pl*, **quarter** an assigned station or post ⟨*battle ~*s⟩ **b** *pl* living accommodation; lodgings ⟨*show you to your ~*s⟩; *esp* accommodation for military personnel or their families **9** merciful consideration of an opponent; *specif* the clemency of not killing a defeated enemy ⟨*gave him no ~*⟩ **10** the side of a horse's hoof between the toe and the heel **11a** any of the four or more divisions of a heraldic shield that are marked off by horizontal and vertical lines, and used as distinct fields **b** a CHARGE occupying the first quarter of a heraldic field **12** the part of a ship's side towards the stern; *also* any direction to the rear of ABEAM and from a specified side ⟨*light on the port ~*⟩ **13** either side of the upper of a shoe or boot, from heel to vamp **14** any of the four equal periods into which the playing time of certain games (e g American football) is divided [ME, fr OF *quartier*, fr L *quartarius*, fr *quartus* fourth]

²**quarter** *vt* **1a** to divide into four equal or nearly equal parts **b** to separate into either more or fewer than four parts ⟨*~ an orange*⟩ **2** to provide with lodging or shelter; *esp* to assign (a member of the armed forces) to accommodation – often + *on* ⟨*~ed his men on the inhabitants*⟩ **3** *esp of a gundog* to crisscross (an area) in many directions in search of game, or in order to pick up an animal's scent **4a** to arrange or bear (e g different coats of arms) in heraldic quarters on one shield **b** to add (a coat of arms) to others on one heraldic shield **c** to divide (a heraldic shield) with vertical or horizontal lines into four or more sections **5** *archaic* to divide (esp a traitor's body) into four parts, esp after hanging or other means of execution ⟨*hung, drawn, and ~ed*⟩ *~ vi* **1** to lodge, dwell **2** to change from one quarter to another ⟨*the moon ~*s⟩ **3** to strike on a ship's quarter ⟨*the wind was ~ing*⟩

³**quarter** *adj* consisting of or equal to a quarter

**quarterage** /'kwawt(ə)rij/ *n* a quarterly payment, tax, wage, or allowance

¹**quarterback** /'kwawtə‚bak/ *n* an offensive back in American or Canadian football who usu lines up behind the centre and directs the offensive play of the team

²**quarterback** *vt* to direct the offensive play of (e g a football team)

‚**quarter-'bound** *adj, of a book* bound in two materials, with the better material (e g leather) on the spine only – **quarterbinding** *n*

**quarter day** *n* the day which begins one quarter of the year and on which a quarterly payment often falls due: eg a *Eng & Irish law* **a(1)** March 25; LADY DAY **a(2)** June 24; MIDSUMMER DAY **a(3)** September 29; Michaelmas **a(4)** December 25; Christmas **b** *Scot* **b(1)** February 2; Candlemas **b(2)** May 15; Whitsunday **b(3)** August 1; Lammas **b(4)** November 11; Martinmas

**quarterdeck** /-,dek/ *n* **1** the stern area of a ship's upper deck **2** *taking sing or pl vb, chiefly Br* the officers of a ship or navy – compare LOWER DECK

**¹quarterfinal** /,kwawtə'fienl/ *adj* of, participating in, or being a quarterfinal or quarterfinals

**²quarterfinal** *n* a match whose winner goes through to the semifinals of a knock-out tournament; *also, pl* a round made up of such matches – **quarterfinalist** *n*

**quarter horse** *n* an alert stocky muscular horse developed in the USA and capable of high speed for short distances and of great endurance [fr its high speed over distances up to a quarter of a mile]

**quarter hour** *n, chiefly NAm* **1** QUARTER 3c (point of time) **2** any of the quarter points of an hour

**¹quartering** /'kwawtəring/ *n* **1a** the division of a heraldic shield into four or more sections that usu contain COATS OF ARMS brought into a family by marriage **b** a quarter of a shield, or the coat of arms on it **2** a line of usu noble or distinguished ancestry

**²quartering** *adj* lying at right angles

**quarter light** *n, Br* a small usu triangular panel in a motor vehicle side window that can usu be opened for ventilation

**¹quarterly** /'kwawtəli/ *adv* **1** in heraldic quarters **2** at 3-monthly intervals

**²quarterly** *adj* **1** computed for or payable at 3-monthly intervals ⟨*a ~ premium*⟩ **2** recurring, issued, or spaced at 3-monthly intervals **3** divided into four, or a specified number of, heraldic quarters

**³quarterly** *n* a periodical published at 3-monthly intervals

**Quarterly Meeting** *n* an organizational unit of the Society of Friends usu composed of several MONTHLY MEETINGS (district units)

**quartermaster** /-,mahstə/ *n* **1** a petty officer or seaman who attends to a ship's compass, tiller or wheel, and signals **2** an army officer who provides clothing, subsistence, and quarters for a body of troops

**quartern** /'kwawtən/ *n* a quarter of various measures (eg a pint, gill, or peck) [ME *quarteron*, fr OF, quarter of a pound, quarter of a hundred, fr *quartier* quarter]

**quarter note** *n, NAm* CROTCHET 1 (musical note)

**quarter-'phase** *adj, of an electrical supply or system* (eg a *motor*) TWO-PHASE

**quarter rest** *n, NAm* a musical rest of the same time value as a crotchet

**quartersawn** /'kwawtə,sawn/, **quartersawed** /-sawd/ *adj, of boards and planks* sawn from quartered logs so that the ANNUAL RINGS are nearly at right angles to the wide face

**quarter sessions** *n pl, often cap Q&S* **1** a former English local court, with limited chiefly criminal jurisdiction, held quarterly and now replaced by the CROWN COURT **2** a local court with criminal jurisdiction and sometimes administrative functions in some states of the USA

**quarterstaff** /-,stahf/ *n, pl* **quarterstaves** /-,stayvz, -,stahvz/ *a* long stout staff formerly used as a weapon and wielded with one hand in the middle and the other between the middle and the end

**quarter tone** *n* **1** a musical interval of half a semitone **2** a note at an interval of one quarter tone

**quartet** *also* **quartette** /kwaw'tet/ *n* **1** a musical composition for four instruments or voices **2** *taking sing or pl vb* a group or set of four; *esp* a group of four musicians performing together [It *quartetto*, fr *quarto* fourth, fr L *quartus* – more at QUART]

**quartic** /'kwawtik/ *adj, maths* of or involving (mathematical terms of) the fourth DEGREE, ORDER, or POWER [L *quartus* fourth] – **quartic** *n*

**¹quartile** /'kwawtiel/ *n, statistics* any of three values in a FREQUENCY DISTRIBUTION that divide it into four parts (INTERVALS), each containing one quarter of the individuals, items, etc under consideration; *also* any of the four groups of individuals, items, etc comprising such an interval [ISV, fr L *quartus*]

**²quartile** *adj* **1** of a quartile **2** *of the apparent position of two heavenly bodies* separated by 90° ⟨*~ aspect*⟩ – used in astrology

**quarto** /'kwawtoh/ *n, pl* **quartos** **1** the size of a piece of paper cut four from a sheet **2** a book format in which a folded sheet

forms four leaves; *also* a book in this format **3** *Br* a size of paper usu 10 × 8 inches (about 25 × 20 centimetres) – not used technically [L, abl of *quartus* fourth]

**¹quartz** /kwawts/ *n* a crystalline mineral consisting of silicon dioxide, $SiO_2$, that is a major constituent of many rocks (eg granite and sandstone) and occurs in colourless varieties (eg ROCK CRYSTAL) and coloured forms (eg amethyst and citrine) [Ger *quarz*, fr MHG] – **quartziferous** *adj*, **quartzose** *adj*

**²quartz** *adj* controlled by the oscillations of a quartz crystal ⟨*a ~ watch*⟩

**quartz glass** *n* a glass made of high purity SILICA prepared from quartz and noted for its transparency to ultraviolet radiation

**,quartz-'halogen lamp** *n* QUARTZ-IODINE LAMP

**,quartz-'iodine lamp** *also* **quartz lamp** *n* a light bulb used (eg in some car headlights and film projectors) to give a very bright light, that consists of a quartz envelope containing a tungsten filament and iodine vapour which reacts with any tungsten that vaporizes, thus preventing it from blackening the inside of the envelope

**quartzite** /'kwawtsiet/ *n* **1** a compact granular rock composed of quartz and derived from sandstone by heat that caused recrystallization of the sandstone into quartz grains **2** a hard sandstone composed of quartz grains held together by a SILICA cement [ISV] – **quartzitic** *adj*

**quasar** /'kwaysah/ *n* any of various unusually bright probably very distant starlike celestial objects that are characterized by a large RED SHIFT – compare PULSAR [*quasi*-stellar radio source]

**quash** /kwosh/ *vt* **1a** to nullify; *esp* to nullify by judicial action ⟨*~ an indictment*⟩ **b** to reject (a legal document) as invalid **2** to suppress or extinguish summarily and completely; subdue ⟨*~ a rebellion*⟩ △ squash [ME *quassen*, fr MF *casser*, *quasser* to annul, fr LL *cassare*, fr L *cassus* void, without effect; akin to L *carēre* to be without – more at CASTE; (2) partly fr ME *quashen* to smash, fr MF *quasser*, *casser*, fr L *quassare* to shake violently, shatter, fr *quassus*, pp of *quatere* to shake; akin to OE *hūdenian* to shake]

**quasi** /'kwahzi, 'kwayzie, -sie/ *adj* having some resemblance to ⟨*a ~ corporation*⟩

**quasi-** *comb form* to some degree; partly; seemingly ⟨*quasi-officially*⟩ ⟨*quasi-stellar object*⟩ [L *quasi* as if, as it were, approximately, fr *quam* as + *si* if – more at QUANTITY, SO]

**quasi contract** *n* an obligation imposed by law to transfer or return money or property or make payment as if a contract to do so existed, in order to prevent the unjust enrichment of one at another's expense

**,quasi-'judicial** *adj* ⌐ having a partly judicial character, esp by virtue of the authority to conduct inquiries, exercise discretion, and make decisions in the general manner of courts ⟨*~ bodies*⟩ **2** essentially judicial in character but not proceeding from a court of law ⟨*~ decisions*⟩ ⟨*a ~ review*⟩ – **quasi-judicially** *adv*

**,quasi-'legislative** *adj* having a partly legislative character by possession of the right to make rules and regulations having the force of law

**Quasimodo** /,kwahzi'mohdoh/ *n* LOW SUNDAY [ML *quasi modo geniti infantes* as newborn babes (opening words of the introit for Low Sunday)]

**,quasi-'stellar object** *n* a quasar

**quassia** /'kwoshə/ *n* a bitter drug obtained from the heartwood of any of various tropical trees (family Simaroubaceae) and used, esp formerly, as a tonic and remedy for roundworms in children, and as an insecticide; *also* a tree from which quassia is extracted [NL, genus name, fr *Quassi* 18th-c Surinam Negro slave who discovered its medicinal value]

**quatercentenary** /,kwatəsen'teenəri, -'tenəri/ *n* a 400th anniversary or its celebration [L *quater* four times + E *centenary*]

**¹quaternary** /kwə'tuhnəri/ *adj* **1a** of or consisting of four units or members **b** of, being, or belonging to a system of numbers having 4 as its base **2** *cap* of or being the geological period from the end of the TERTIARY period to the present time, or the system of rocks of this period **3** characterized by or resulting from the substitution of four atoms or groups in a molecule; *esp* being or containing an atom united by four bonds to four carbon atoms – compare QUATERNARY AMMONIUM COMPOUND [L *quaternarius*, fr *quaterni* four each]

**²quaternary** *n* **1** a member of a group of four **2** *cap* the Quaternary period or system of rocks

**quaternary ammonium compound** *n* any of numerous chemical compounds that are strong alkalis, are derived from ammonium by replacement of the four hydrogen atoms with carbon-containing chemical groups, and are used esp in detergents, disinfectants, and drugs

**quaternion** /kwə'tuhnyən, -ni-ən/ *n* **1** a set of four parts, things, or people **2** a generalized COMPLEX NUMBER that contains one REAL part and three IMAGINARY parts [ME *quaternyoun*, fr LL *quaternion-*, *quaternio*, fr L *quaterni* four each, fr *quater* four times; akin to L *quattuor* four – more at FOUR]

**quaternity** /kwə'tuhnəti/ *n* a union of a group or set of four; *specif* four persons in one Godhead – compare TRINITY [LL *quaternitas*, fr L *quaterni* four each]

**quatrain** /'kwotrayn/ *n* a stanza of four lines [Fr, fr MF, fr *quatre* four, fr L *quattuor*]

**quatrefoil** /'katrə,foyl/ *n* **1** a stylized figure or ornament in the form of a leaf or flower with four lobes **2** a design enclosed by four joined FOILS [ME *quaterfoil* set of four leaves, fr MF *quatre* + ME *-foil* (as in *trefoil*)]

**quattrocento** /,kwatroh'chentoh/ *n, often cap the* 15th century in Italy, esp with reference to its literature and art [It, lit., four hundred, fr *quattro* four (fr L *quattuor*) + *cento* hundred – more at CINQUECENTO]

**quattuordecillion** /,kwotəwaw,də'silion/ *n* – see NUMBER table [L *quattuordecim* fourteen (fr *quattuor* four + *decem* ten) + E *-illion* (as in *million*) – more at TEN]

**¹quaver** /'kwayvə/ *vi* **1** to tremble, shake ⟨~ing *inwardly*⟩ **2** to speak or sing in a trembling voice ~ *vt* to utter in a quavering voice [ME *quaveren*, freq of *quaven* to tremble] – **quaveringly** *adv*, **quavery** *adj*

**²quaver** *n* **1** a musical note with the time value of half a crotchet **2** a musical trill **3** a tremulous sound

**quaver rest** *n* a musical REST (indicating silence) of the same time value as a quaver

**quay** /kee/ *n* an artificial landing place beside navigable water for loading and unloading ships [alter. of earlier *key*, fr ME, fr MF *cai*, of Celt origin; akin to Corn *kē* hedge, fence; akin to OE *hecg* hedge]

**quayage** /'kee-ij/ *n* **1** a charge for use of a quay **2** space on or for quays **3** a system of quays

**quayside** /-,sied/ *n* land forming or bordering a quay ⟨*met them on the* ~⟩

**quean** /kween/ *n* **1** a disreputable woman; *specif* a prostitute **2** *chiefly Scot* a woman; *esp* one who is young or unmarried [ME *quene*, fr OE *cwene*; akin to OE *cwēn* woman, queen]

**queasy** *also* **queazy** /'kweezi/ *adj* **1a** causing nausea **b** suffering from nausea; *also* of weak digestion **2a** overscrupulous, squeamish ⟨*a* ~ *conscience*⟩ **b** ill at ease [ME *coysy*, *qwesye* unsettled, hazardous] – **queasily** *adv*, **queasiness** *n*

**Quebec** /kwi'bek/ *n* – a communications code word for the letter *q*

**Quebecois, Québecois** /,kwibe'kwah, ,ki-/ *n, pl* **Quebecois, Québecois** a native or inhabitant of Quebec; *specif* a French-speaking one [Fr *Québecois*, fr *Québec* Quebec, city & province in Canada]

**quebracho** /kay'brahchoh/ *n, pl* **quebrachos 1** any of several trees of southern S America with hard wood: eg **1a** a tree (*Aspidosperma quebracho*) of the periwinkle family that occurs in Argentina and Chile and whose dried bark was formerly used to relax the air passages of the lungs (eg in the treatment of asthma) **b** a tree (*Schinopsis lorentzii*) of the sumach family that occurs esp in Argentina and has dense wood rich in TANNINS (substances used in tanning and dyeing) **2** the wood of a quebracho [AmerSp, alter. of *quiebracha*, fr Sp *quiebra* it breaks + *hacha* ax]

**Quechua** /'kechwə/ *n, pl* **Quechuas**, *esp collectively* **Quechua 1** a member of an American Indian people of central Peru **2a** the language of the Quechua people, widely spoken by other American Indian peoples of Peru, Bolivia, Ecuador, Chile, and Argentina **b** a language family comprising the Quechua language only [Sp, fr Quechua *kkechúwa* plunderer, robber] – **Quechuan** *adj or n*

**Quechumaran** /,kechoomə'ran/ *n* KECHUMARAN (American language family) [*Quechua* + Aymara + *-an*]

**¹queen** /kween/ *n* **1** the wife or widow of a king **2** a female monarch **3** a woman, or something personified as a woman, that is preeminent in a specified respect ⟨*a beauty* ~⟩ ⟨*Paris,* ~ *of cities*⟩ **4** the most powerful piece of each colour in a set of chessmen, that has the power to move any number of squares in any direction **5** a playing card marked with a stylized figure of a queen and ranking usu below the king **6** the fertile fully developed female in a colony of bees, ants, or termites,

whose function is to lay eggs **7** a mature female cat kept esp for breeding **8** *cap, Br informal the* British national anthem – used when the reigning British monarch is a woman **9** *slang* a usu flamboyantly effeminate aging male homosexual – used esp by male homosexuals – see also **turn queen's** EVIDENCE [ME *quene*, fr OE *cwēn* woman, wife, queen; akin to Goth *qens* wife, Gk *gynē* woman, wife]

**²queen** *vi, of a pawn* to become a queen in chess ~ *vt* to promote (a pawn) to a queen in chess – **queen it** *of a woman* to behave in a domineering or arrogant manner – often + *over*; compare LORD IT

**Queen Anne** /an/ *adj* of or having the characteristics of **a** a style of furniture that was prevalent in Britain esp during the first half of the 18th century, and is marked by extensive use of upholstery, marquetry, and Oriental fabrics **b** a style of English building of the early 18th century characterized by restrained classic detail and the use of red brickwork [*Queen Anne* of Britain †1714 (reigned 1702–1714)]

**Queen Anne's lace** *n* WILD CARROT

**queen bee jelly** *also* **queen jelly** *n* ROYAL JELLY

**queen consort** *n, pl* **queens consort** the wife of a reigning king

**queen dowager** *n* the widow of a king

**queen mother** *n* a QUEEN DOWAGER who is mother of the reigning sovereign

**queen post** *n* either of two vertical posts connecting the principal rafters of a timber roof truss with its tie beam – compare KING POST

**queen regnant** *n, pl* **queens regnant** a queen reigning in her own right

**Queen's Bench, Queen's Bench Division** *n* a division of the HIGH COURT hearing both civil and criminal cases – used when the reigning British monarch is a woman

**Queensberry rules** /'kweenzb(ə)ri/ *n* a set of boxing rules sponsored by the 8th Marquess of Queensberry in 1867 that remain the basic rules of boxing [John Sholto Douglas, 8th Marquess of *Queensberry* †1900]

**Queen's Counsel** *n* any of a number of senior barristers who have been appointed counsel to the Crown as a mark of professional distinction, and who take precedence in court over other barristers – used when the reigning British monarch is a woman

**Queen's English** *n* – used instead of *King's English* when the reigning British monarch is a woman

**queen's evidence** *n* **1** evidence given for the Crown by an accomplice in a crime against the other people charged with that crime **2** an accused person who gives queen's evidence □ used when the reigning British monarch is a woman; compare STATE'S EVIDENCE

**queen's shilling** *n, often cap Q&S* – used instead of *king's shilling* when the reigning British monarch is a woman

**queen substance** *n* a substance (PHEROMONE) that is secreted by queen bees, is consumed by worker bees, and inhibits the development of their ovaries

**queen truss** *n* a roof truss framed with QUEEN POSTS

**¹queer** /kwiə/ *adj* **1a** differing in some odd way from what is usual or normal **b(1)** eccentric, unconventional **b(2)** mildly insane; touched **c** unreasonably absorbed; CRAZY **2d 2** questionable, suspicious ⟨~ *goings-on*⟩ **3** *informal* not quite well; queasy, faint **4** *derog* homosexual *synonyms* see STRANGE [perh fr Ger *queh* athwart, oblique, perverse] – **queerish** *adj*, **queerly** *adv*, **queerness** *n*

**²queer** *vt, informal* **1** to spoil the effect or success of ⟨~ *one's plans*⟩ **2** to put into an embarrassing or disadvantageous situation – see also **queer somebody's** PITCH

**³queer** *n* somebody who is queer; *esp, derog* a usu male homosexual

**queer street** *n, often cap Q&S* a condition of financial embarrassment

**quelea** /'kweeliə/ *n* a tiny brownish African WEAVERBIRD (*Quelea quelea*) that lives in very large groups and is destructive to crops [NL, genus name, prob fr a native name in Africa]

**quell** /kwel/ *vt* **1** to overwhelm thoroughly and reduce to submission or passivity ⟨~ *a riot*⟩ **2** to quiet, pacify ⟨~ *fears*⟩ [ME *quellen* to kill, quell, fr OE *cwellan* to kill; akin to OHG *quellen* to torture, kill, *quāla* torment, Gk *belonē* needle] – **queller** *n*

**quench** /kwench/ *vt* **1a** to put out (eg a fire or light) **b** to put out the light or fire of ⟨~ *glowing coals with water*⟩ **c** to cool (eg hot metal) suddenly by immersion in oil, water, etc; *broadly* to cause to lose heat or warmth ⟨*you have* ~ed *the warmth of France toward you* – Alfred Tennyson⟩ **2a** to bring (something immaterial) to an end typically by satisfying, damping, cooling, or decreasing ⟨*the praise that* ~es *all desire to read the book* – T S Eliot⟩ **b** to terminate (as if) by destroying; eliminate ⟨~ *a rebellion*⟩ **c** to relieve or satisfy with liquid ⟨~ed *his thirst at a wayside spring*⟩ [ME *quenchen*, fr OE *-cwencan*; akin to OE *-cwincan* to vanish, OFris *quinka*] – **quenchable** *adj*, **quencher** *n*, **quenchless** *adj*

**quenelle** /kə'nel/ *n* a small ball of a seasoned meat or fish mixture (eg of pike) that is fried or poached in stock or water and used as a garnish or served in a sauce [Fr, fr Ger *knödel* dumpling, fr MHG, dim. of *knode* knot, fr OHG *knodo, knoto* – more at KNOT]

**quercetin** /'kwuhsitin/ *n* a yellow chemical compound, $C_{15}H_{10}O_7$, that occurs in many plants and was formerly used to strengthen CAPILLARIES (tiny blood vessels) in cases (eg high blood pressure) where bleeding from the capillaries was thought likely [ISV, fr L *quercetum* oak forest, fr *quercus* oak – more at FIR]

**querist** /'kwiərist/ *n* somebody who inquires [L *quaerere* to ask]

**quern** /kwuhn/ *n* a primitive hand mill for grinding grain [ME, fr OE *cweorn*; akin to OHG *quirn* mill, OSlav *žrūny*]

**querulous** /'kwer(y)ooləs/ *adj* **1** habitually complaining **2** fretful, whining ⟨*a* ~ *voice*⟩ [L *querulus*, fr *queri* to complain] – **querulously** *adv*, **querulousness** *n*

**¹query** /'kwiəri/ *n* **1** a question, inquiry **2** a question in the mind; a doubt **3** a QUESTION MARK, esp as used to question the accuracy of a text [alter. of earlier *quere*, fr L *quaere*, imper of *quaerere* to seek, question]

**²query** *vt* **1** to put as a question ⟨*"what's wrong?"* she queried⟩ **2** to question the accuracy of (eg a statement) **3** to mark with a query **4** *chiefly NAm* to ask questions of

**¹quest** /kwest/ *n* **1** a jury of an inquest **2** an act or instance of seeking: **2a** (the object of) a pursuit, search ⟨*went in* ~ *of gold*⟩ **b** an adventurous search or journey undertaken by a knight in medieval romance for a chivalrous purpose [ME, search, pursuit, investigation, inquest, fr MF *queste* search, pursuit, fr (assumed) VL *quaesta*, fr L, fem of *quaestus*]

**²quest** *vi* **1** *of a dog* **1a** to search for a trail or game **b** to bay **2** to go on a quest ⟨~ing *after gold*⟩ ~ *vt, chiefly poetic* to search for – **quester** *n*

**¹question** /'kwesch(ə)n/ *n* **1a(1)** a command or interrogative expression used to elicit information or a response, or to test knowledge ⟨*unable to answer the exam* ~⟩ **a(2)** an interrogative sentence or clause **b** a subject or concern that is uncertain or in dispute; an issue ⟨*the devolution* ~⟩; *broadly* a problem, matter ⟨*the* ~ *of buying a new car*⟩ ⟨*it's only a* ~ *of time*⟩ **c(1)** a subject or point of discussion or debate or a proposition to be voted on in a meeting ⟨*the* ~ *before the House*⟩ **c(2)** the bringing of such to a vote ⟨*put the matter to the* ~⟩ **d** the specific point at issue ⟨*a remark that was beside the* ~⟩ **2a** an act or instance of asking; an inquiry ⟨*could not have withstood close* ~⟩ **b** judicial interrogation **c** torture as part of an examination to elicit a confession **d(1)** objection, dispute ⟨*true beyond* ~⟩ **d(2)** room for doubt or objection ⟨*little* ~ *of his skill*⟩ **d(3)** chance, possibility ⟨*no* ~ *of escape*⟩ [ME, fr MF, fr L *quaestion-, quaestio*, fr *quaesitus, quaestus*, pp of *quaerere* to seek, ask] – **call in(to) question** to cast doubt upon – **in question** under discussion – **out of the question** impossible, preposterous

*usage* **1** When the word **question** is followed by an actual "question" ⟨*the* **question** *how to raise enough money*⟩ ⟨*any* **question** *whether she is reliable*⟩ it is better not to say **question** *of* or **question** *as to* ⟨*any* **question** *of/as to whether she is reliable*⟩; but when **question** is followed by a noun it must be linked to that noun by something. Here, **question** *of* is correct when **question** means "problem" or "matter" ⟨*it's a* **question** *of money*⟩ and **question** *as to* when **question** means "doubt" ⟨*is there any* **question** *as to her reliability?*⟩ **2** Since **question** can mean either "doubt" or "possibility" the word often gives rise to ambiguity. Does ⟨*there's no* **question** *that such films are being rented by children*⟩ mean that they certainly are, or certainly are not, being rented? It may be clearer in such cases to use *no* **question** *but that* for "no doubt that", or indeed to avoid **question** here altogether.

**²question** *vt* **1** to ask a question of or about ⟨*to* ~ *the absence of a committee member*⟩ **2** to interrogate intensively; cross-examine ⟨~ *her as to her whereabouts*⟩ **3a** to doubt,

dispute ⟨*the accuracy of these statistics may be* ~ed⟩ **b** to subject (facts or phenomena) to analysis; examine ⟨*Magi who* ~ed *the stars*⟩ ~ *vi* to ask questions; inquire – **questioner** *n*

**questionable** /'kweschənəbl/ *adj* **1** open to doubt or challenge; not certain or exact ⟨*water of* ~ *purity*⟩ ⟨*a* ~ *decision*⟩ **2** of doubtful morality, wisdom, or propriety; shady ⟨~ *motives*⟩ *antonyms* unquestionable, authoritative – **questionableness** *n*, **questionably** *adv*

**questionless** /'kweschənlis/ *adj* **1** indubitable, unquestionable **2** unquestioning

**question mark** *n* **1** a punctuation mark ? used at the end of a sentence to indicate a direct question, and also used to indicate the writer's ignorance (eg in "Omar Khayyám, ? – ?1123") **2** an inverted question mark used at the beginning of a question in Spanish **3** something unknown, unknowable, or uncertain ⟨*their future remains a* ~⟩

**'question-,master** *n* someone who puts questions during a quiz

**questionnaire** /,kweschə'neə; *also* ,kes-/ *n* **1** (a form having) a set of questions to be asked of a number of people to obtain statistically useful information **2** a survey made by the use of a questionnaire [Fr, fr *questionner* to question, fr MF, fr *question, n*]

**'question-,tag** *n* an interrogative phrase inviting the listener's response to the statement to which it is appended (eg *doesn't he* in "He likes his job, doesn't he?")

**question time** *n* a period in a session of a parliamentary body during which members may put to a minister questions on matters concerning his/her department

**quetzal** /'ketsl/ *n, pl* **quetzals, quetzales** /ket'sahlays/ **1** a Central American bird (*Pharomachrus mocino*) that has a rounded hairlike crest on the head, brilliant blue, green, red, and gold-tinged plumage, and the male of which has exceptionally long upper tail feathers **2** – see MONEY table [AmerSp, fr Nahuatl *quetzaltototl*, fr *quetzalli* brilliant tail feather + *tototl* bird]

**¹queue** /kyooh/ *n* **1** a pigtail **2** a waiting line, esp of people or vehicles one behind the other **3** WAITING LIST ⟨*a housing* ~⟩ **4** an ordered arrangement of items of data, jobs to be performed (eg by a computer) [Fr, lit., tail, fr L *cauda, coda*] – **jump the queue 1** to move in front of others in a queue **2** to obtain an unfair advantage over others who have been waiting longer

**²queue** *vb,* **queuing, queueing** *vt* to arrange or form in a queue ~ *vi* to line up or wait in a queue – **queuer** *n*

**'queue-,jump** *vi* to join a queue at a point in front of (some of) those already waiting; PUSH IN – **queue-jumper** *n*

**¹quibble** /'kwibl/ *n* **1** an evasion of or shift from the point; an equivocation **2** a minor objection or criticism [prob dim. of obs *quib* quibble, prob fr L *quibus*, dat & abl pl of *qui* who, which]

**²quibble** *vi* **1** to make minute verbal distinctions; equivocate **2a** to cavil, carp **b** to bicker – **quibbler** *n*

**quiche** /keesh/ *n* a pastry shell filled with a rich savoury egg and cream custard and various other ingredients (eg ham, cheese, or vegetables) – compare FLAN [Fr, fr Ger dial. (Lorraine) *küche*, dim. of *kuchen* cake, fr OHG *kuocho* – more at CAKE]

**Quiche** /'ki,chay, ki'chay/ *n, pl* **Quiches,** *esp collectively* **Quiche 1** a member of an American Indian people of Guatemala **2** the MAYAN language of the Quiche

**¹quick** /kwik/ *adj* **1** (capable of) acting with speed: eg **1a(1)** fast in understanding, thinking, or learning; mentally agile ⟨*a* ~ *mind*⟩ ⟨~ *thinking*⟩ **a(2)** reacting to stimuli with speed and keen sensitivity **a(3)** aroused immediately and intensely ⟨~ *tempers*⟩ **b(1)** fast in development or occurrence ⟨*a* ~ *succession of events*⟩ **b(2)** done or taking place with rapidity ⟨*gave them a* ~ *look*⟩ **c** marked by speed, readiness, or promptness of physical movement ⟨*walked with* ~ *steps*⟩ **d** inclined to hastiness ⟨*too* ~ *to criticize*⟩ **e** capable of being easily and speedily prepared ⟨*a* ~ *and tasty dinner*⟩ **2** *archaic* not dead; living, alive **3** *archaic* not stagnant; running, flowing **4** *archaic* fiery, glowing **5** *archaic* at the stage of pregnancy at which the movement of the foetus can be felt ⟨~ *with child*⟩ *synonyms* see ¹FAST *antonyms* slow, lingering, sluggish [ME *quik*, fr OE *cwic* alive; akin to ON *kvikr* living, L *vivus* living, *vivere* to live, Gk *bios, zōē* life] – **quickly** *adv*, **quickness** *n*

**²quick** *adv* in a quick manner ⟨*ran as* ~ *as I could*⟩ – often *imper* ⟨~ *! The cat's eating the fish*⟩

*usage* The use of **quick** as an adverb has been established in English since the 14th century ⟨*the latter* **quick** *up flew, and kicked the beam* – John Milton⟩, but is today considered less formal than **quickly**.

Quick is particularly used with verbs of motion, but both alternatives are usually possible ⟨*come* **quick/quickly**⟩ ⟨*it'll cook* **quicker**/*more* **quickly**⟩.

³**quick** *n* **1** *taking pl vb* living beings ⟨*the* ~ *and the dead*⟩ **2a** a painfully sensitive spot or area of flesh; *esp* that under a fingernail or toenail **b** the inmost sensibilities ⟨*hurt to the* ~ *by the remark*⟩ **c** the very centre of something; the heart [(2) prob of Scand origin; akin to ON *kvika* sensitive flesh, fr *kvikr* living]

**quick assets** *n pl* the cash, ACCOUNTS RECEIVABLE, and other current assets readily available, excluding inventories

**quick bread** *n* bread made with a raising agent (e g BAKING POWDER or BAKING SODA) that allows immediate baking of the dough or batter mixture

**quicken** /'kwikən/ *vt* **1a** to make alive; revive **b** to enliven, stimulate **2** to make more rapid; hasten, accelerate ⟨~ed *her steps*⟩ **3a** to make (a curve) sharper **b** to make (a slope) steeper **4** *archaic* to kindle or make burn more brightly ~ *vi* **1** to come to life; *esp* to enter into a phase of active growth and development ⟨*seeds* ~ing *in the soil*⟩ **2** to reach the stage of gestation at which foetal motion is felt **3** to become more rapid ⟨*her pulse* ~ed *at the sight*⟩ *antonyms* deaden, arrest – **quickener** *n*

**quickfire** /-,fie·ə/ *adj* coming or operating quickly; *esp* sharp and lively ⟨*the* ~ *patter of the auctioneer*⟩

,**quick-'freeze** *vt* **quick-froze; quick-frozen** to freeze (food for preservation) rapidly in order to avoid the formation of large ice crystals and minimize cell rupture and accompanying loss of natural juices and flavour

**quickie** /'kwiki/ *n, informal* something done or made in a hurry

**quicklime** /-,liem/ *n* LIME 2a (calcium oxide obtained by heating shells, limestone, etc)

**quicksand** /-,sand/ *n* (a deep mass of) loose wet sand into which heavy objects readily sink

**quickset** /-,set/ *n, chiefly Br* plant cuttings set in the ground to grow, esp in a hedgerow; *also* a hedge or thicket, esp of hawthorn, grown from quickset

¹**quicksilver** /-,silvə/ *n* the chemical element mercury

²**quicksilver** *adj* changeable in mood or rapid in movement; MERCURIAL 3

**quickstep** /-,step/ *n* **1** a spirited march tune, usu accompanying a march in quick time **2** (a piece of music for) a ballroom dance that is a fast foxtrot characterized by a combination of short rapid steps

,**quick-'tempered** *adj* easily angered; irascible

**quickthorn** /-,thawn/ *n* hawthorn

**quick time** *n* a rate of marching of about 120 steps in one minute

,**quick-'witted** *adj* quick in perception and understanding; mentally alert *synonyms* see INTELLIGENT *antonym* slow-witted – **quick-wittedly** *adv*, **quick-wittedness** *n*

**Quicunque vult** /,kwee,koongkway 'voolt/ *n* ATHANASIAN CREED [L, whoever wishes; fr the opening words of the creed]

¹**quid** /kwid/ *n, pl* **quid** *also* **quids** *Br informal* the sum of one pound sterling [perh fr L *quid* what, anything, something] – **quids in** *Br informal* in the state of having made a usu large profit ⟨*if we sell them at £5 each, we'll be* quids in⟩

²**quid** *n* a cut or wad of something, esp tobacco, for chewing [E dial., cud, fr ME *quide*, fr OE *cwidu*, *cwudu* – more at CUD]

**quiddity** /'kwidəti/ *n, formal* **1** a trifling point; a quibble **2** that which makes something what it is; the essence [ML *quidditas* essence, lit., whatness, fr L *quid* what, neut of *quis* who – more at WHO]

**quidnunc** /'kwid,nungk/ *n* somebody who wants to know all the latest news or gossip; a busybody [L *quid nunc* what now?]

**quid pro quo** /,kwid proh 'kwoh/ *n* something given or received in exchange for something else [L, something for something]

**quiescent** /kwi'es(ə)nt/ *adj* **1** causing no trouble or symptoms ⟨~ *gallstones*⟩ **2** *formal* at rest; inactive [L *quiescent-, quiescens*, prp of *quiescere* to become quiet, rest, fr *quies*] – **quiescence** *n*, **quiescently** *adv*

¹**quiet** /'kwie·ət/ *n* the quality or state of being quiet; tranquillity [ME, fr L *quiet-, quies* rest, quiet – more at WHILE] – **on the quiet** without telling anyone; discreetly, secretly

²**quiet** *adj* **1a** marked by little or no motion or activity; calm ⟨*a* ~ *day at the office*⟩ ⟨*business had been very* ~ *recently*⟩ **b** gentle, reserved ⟨*a* ~ *temperament*⟩ **c** not disturbed; not interfered with ⟨~ *reading*⟩ **d** enjoyed in peace and relaxation ⟨*a*

~ *cup of tea*⟩ **e** informal and usu involving small numbers of people ⟨*a* ~ *wedding*⟩ **2a** free from noise or uproar; still ⟨*a* ~ *little village in the Cotswolds*⟩ **b** unobtrusive, conservative ⟨~ *clothes*⟩ **3a** secluded ⟨*a* ~ *nook*⟩ **b** private, discreet ⟨*can I have a* ~ *word with you?*⟩ [ME, fr MF, fr L *quietus*, fr pp of *quiescere*] – **quietly** *adv*, **quietness** *n*

*synonyms* Quiet, still, silent, noiseless, and hushed can all mean "without sound". Quiet is a relative word, and may describe merely the absence of customary bustle ⟨a quiet *street*⟩. Still and silent are stronger, still emphasizing complete freedom from agitation and silent applying particularly to an absence of speech. Noiseless and hushed describe situations in which an expected noise is not made ⟨crept away with noiseless *steps*⟩, hushed suggesting that something has been deliberately made quiet ⟨discussed his illness in hushed *tones*⟩. Compare ²CALM *antonym* noisy

³**quiet** *adv* in a quiet manner ⟨*a quiet-running engine*⟩

⁴**quiet** *vt* to calm, soothe ⟨*did nothing to* ~ *her fears*⟩ ~ *vi, chiefly NAm* to become quiet – usu + *down* – **quieter** *n*

**quieten** /'kwie·ətn/ *vb, chiefly Br* to make or become quiet – often + *down*

**quietism** /'kwie·ə,tiz(ə)m/ *n* **1** a system of religious mysticism teaching that perfection and spiritual peace are attained by annihilation of the will and passive absorption in contemplation of God and divine things **2** a passive withdrawn attitude or policy towards the world or worldly affairs – **quietist** *adj or n*

**quietude** /'kwie·ətyoohd/ *n, formal* the state of being quiet; repose [MF, fr LL *quietudo*, fr L *quietus*]

**quietus** /kwie'eetəs, -'aytəs/ *n* **1** final settlement (e g of a debt); *broadly* anything that conclusively settles or represses ⟨*gave a* ~ *to the rumour*⟩ **2** removal from activity; *esp* death [ME *quietus est*, fr ML, he is quit, formula of discharge from obligation]

**quiff** /kwif/ *n, Br* a prominent forelock; *specif* a flat curl on the forehead or a tuft of hair turned up over the forehead [origin unknown]

¹**quill** /kwil/ *n* **1a(1)** a bobbin, spool, or spindle on which WEFT yarn is wound **a(2)** a hollow shaft often surrounding another shaft, used in various mechanical devices **b** a roll of dried bark ⟨*cinnamon* ~s⟩ **2a(1)** the hollow horny central shaft of a feather **a(2)** a feather; *esp* any of the large stiff feathers of a bird's wing or tail **b** any of the hollow sharp spines of a porcupine, hedgehog, etc **3** something made from or resembling the quill of a feather; *esp* a pen for writing **4** a float for a fishing line [ME *quil* hollow reed, bobbin; akin to MHG *kil* large feather]

²**quill** *vt* **1** to wind (thread or yarn) on a quill **2** to make a series of small rounded ridges in (cloth)

¹**quilt** /kwilt/ *n* **1a** a thick warm top cover for a bed consisting of padding held in place between two layers of cloth by lines of stitching – compare EIDERDOWN, DUVET **b** a thinnish cover for a bed that resembles a quilt in design (e g in the pattern of stitching); a bedspread **2** something that is quilted or resembles a quilt [ME *quilte* mattress, quilt, fr OF *cuilte*, fr L *culcita* mattress]

²**quilt** *vt* **1a** to fill, pad, or line like a quilt ⟨*a* ~ed *jacket*⟩ **b(1)** to stitch, sew, or cover with lines or patterns like those used in quilts **b(2)** to stitch (designs) through layers of cloth **c** to fasten between two pieces of material **2** to stitch or sew together in layers with padding in between ~ *vi* to make quilts or quilted work – **quilter** *n*

**quilting** /'kwilting/ *n* **1** the process of quilting **2** material that is quilted, or used for making quilts

**quim** /kwim/ *n, vulg* the female genitals [origin unknown]

**quin** /kwin/ *n, Br* a quintuplet

**quin-** /kwin-/, **quino-** *comb form* **1** cinchona; cinchona bark ⟨quin*ine*⟩ **2** quinone ⟨quin*oid*⟩ [Sp *quina* – more at QUININE]

**quince** /kwins/ *n* the round to pear-shaped fruit of a central Asian tree (*Cydonia oblonga*) of the rose family, that resembles an acid hard-fleshed yellow apple and is used for marmalade, jelly, and preserves; *also* the tree that bears quinces [ME *quynce* quinces, pl of *coyn, quyn* quince, fr MF *coin*, fr L *cotoneum*, *cydoneum* (*malum*) Cydonian (apple), fr Gk *kydōnion*, fr *Kydōnia* Cydonia, ancient city in Crete]

**quincentenary** /,kwinsen'teenəri, -'tenəri/ *n* a 500th anniversary or its celebration [L *quinque* five + E *centenary*]

**quincuncial** /,kwin'kunsh(ə)l/ *adj* **1** of or arranged in a quincunx **2** *of a bud, flower, etc* having five members (e g petals or leaves) regularly overlapped in such a way that two are exterior, two are interior, and one has one edge exterior and one interior – **quincuncially** *adv*

**quincunx** /'kwin,kungks/ *n* **1** an arrangement of five things (e g marks on a playing card or dice) with one at each corner and one in the middle of a square or rectangle **2** a quincuncial arrangement of plant parts [L *quincunc-, quincunx,* lit., five twelfths, fr *quinque* five + *uncia* twelfth part – more at FIVE, OUNCE]

**quincunxial** /kwin'kungksh(ə)l/ *adj* quincuncial

**quindecillion** /ˌkwində'siliən/ *n* – see NUMBER table [L *quindecim* fifteen (fr *quinque* five + *decem* ten) + E *-illion* (as in *million*) – more at TEN]

**quinidine** /'kwini,deen/ *n* a drug, $C_{20}H_{24}N_2O_2$, that is used in treating irregularities of heart rhythm, and that occurs naturally with, and has the same molecular composition as quinine [ISV, fr *quinine*]

**quinine** /'kwineen, -'-/ *n* **1** a bitter-tasting chemical compound, $C_{20}H_{24}N_2O_2$, obtained from the dried bark of the CINCHONA tree, that is used as a bitter in tonic water, and has been widely used, esp in the form of its compounds, as a drug to reduce fever, relieve pain, and in the treatment of malaria [Sp *quina* cinchona, short for *quinaquina,* fr Quechua]

¹**quinoid** /'kwinoyd/ *n* a QUINONOID compound

²**quinoid** *adj* quinonoid

**quinol** /'kwinol/ *n* HYDROQUINONE (chemical used as a photographic developer)

**quinoline** /'kwinə,leen, -lin/ *n* **1** a pungent oily liquid, $C_9H_7N$, that is present in small amounts in COAL TAR, is obtained usu from ANILINE, and is used in the manufacture of many drugs and dyes **2** any of various chemical compounds derived from quinoline [ISV *quin-* + *-ol* + *-ine*]

**quinone** /'kwi'nohn, '--/ *n* **1** a chemical compound, $C_6H_4O_2$, that is derived from benzene and is used in photography and the manufacture of dyes **2** any of a related group of usu yellow, orange, or red compounds, including several that are biologically important in energy-producing reactions inside cells [ISV *quinine* + *-one*]

**quinonoid** /'kwinə,noyd, kwi'nohnoyd/ *adj* resembling or derived from quinone

**Quinquagesima** /ˌkwingkwə'jesimə/ *n* the Sunday before Lent [ML, fr L, fem of *quinquagesimus* fiftieth, fr *quinquaginta* fifty, fr *quinque* + *-ginta* (akin to *viginti* twenty – more at VIGESIMAL); fr its being approximately fifty days before Easter]

**quinque-** /kwingkwi-, kwinkwi-/, **quinqu-** *comb form* five ⟨*quinquennium*⟩ [L, fr *quinque* – more at FIVE]

**quinquennial** /kwing'kweni-əl, kwin-/ *adj* **1** consisting of or lasting for five years **2** occurring every five years – **quinquennial** *n*, **quinquennially** *adv*

**quinquennium** /kwing'kweni-əm, kwin-/ *n, pl* **quinquenniums, quinquennia** /-ni-ə/ a period of five years [L, fr *quinque-* + *annus* year – more at ANNUAL ]

**quinquereme** /ˌkwingkwi'reem/ *n* an ancient galley with five banks of oars [MF, fr L *quinqueremis,* fr *quinque-* + *remus* oar]

**quinquevalent** /ˌkwingkwi'vaylənt, kwin'kwevələnt/ *also* **quinquivalent** /ˌkwingkwi'vaylənt/ *adj, chemistry* having a VALENCY of five; PENTAVALENT

**quinsy** /'kwinzi/ *n* a severe inflammation of the tonsils, throat, or adjacent parts accompanied by swelling of the affected parts and fever [ME *quinesie,* fr MF *quinancie,* fr LL *cynanche,* fr Gk *kynanchē,* fr *kyn-, kyōn* dog + *anchein* to strangle – more at HOUND, ANGER]

**quint** /kwint/ *n, NAm* a quintuplet

**quintain** /'kwintin/ *n* **1** an object to be tilted at; *esp* a post with a revolving crosspiece that has a target at one end and a sandbag at the other end, used in medieval military exercises **2** the exercise of tilting at a quintain [ME *quintaine,* fr MF, fr L *quintana* street in a Roman camp separating the fifth maniple from the sixth where military exercises were performed, fr fem of *quintanus* fifth in rank, fr *quintus* fifth]

**quintal** /'kwintl/ *n* **1** an imperial unit of weight equal to 100 pounds; HUNDREDWEIGHT 2b **2** a metric unit of weight equal to 100 kilograms (about 220.5 pounds) [ME, fr MF, fr ML *quintale,* fr Ar *quintār,* fr LGk *kentēnarion,* fr LL *centenarium,* fr L, neut of *centenarius* consisting of a hundred – more at CENTENARY]

**quintessence** /kwin'tes(ə)ns/ *n* **1** the fifth and highest essence in ancient and medieval philosophy that forms the heavenly bodies and permeates all nature **2** the pure and concentrated essence of something; the most significant or typical element in a whole ⟨*the ~ of the book is missed in the film*⟩ **3** the most perfect example or embodiment (e g of a quality or class) ⟨*the*

*~ of pride*⟩ [ME, fr MF *quinte essence,* fr ML *quinta essentia,* lit., fifth essence (fr its being additional to the four elements of air, earth, fire, and water)] – **quintessential** *adj*

**quintet** *also* **quintette** /kwin'tet/ *n* **1** a musical composition for five instruments or voices **2** *taking sing or pl vb* a group or set of five: e g **2a** a group of five musicians performing together **b** a basketball team [*quintet* fr It *quintetto,* fr *quinto* fifth, fr L *quintus; quintette* fr Fr, fr It *quintetto*]

**quintic** /'kwintik/ *adj, maths* of or involving (mathematical terms of) the fifth DEGREE, ORDER, or POWER [L *quintus* fifth] – **quintic** *n*

**quintillion** /kwin'tilyən/ *n* – see NUMBER table [L *quint*us + E *-illion* (as in *million*)] – **quintillion** *adj,* **quintillionth** *adj or n*

¹**quintuple** /'kwintyoopl, kwin'tyoohpl/ *adj* **1** having five units or members **2** five times as great or as many **3** *music* marked by five beats per bar [MF, fr LL *quintuplex,* fr L *quintus* fifth (akin to L *quinque* five) + *-plex* -fold – more at FIVE, SIMPLE] – **quintuple** *n*

²**quintuple** *vb* to make or become five times as great or as many

**quintuplet** /'kwintyooplit, kwin'tyoohplit/ *n* **1** a combination of five of a kind **2** any of five offspring born at one birth **3** a group of five musical notes performed in the time of three or four notes of the same value [fr ¹*quintuple,* by analogy to *double : doublet*]

¹**quintuplicate** /kwin'tyoohplikət/ *adj* **1** consisting of or existing in five corresponding or identical parts or examples ⟨*~ invoices*⟩ **2** being the fifth of five things exactly alike ⟨*file the ~ copy*⟩ [LL *quintuplicatus,* pp of *quintuplicare* to quintuple, fr *quintuplic-, quintuplex* quintuple]

²**quintuplicate** *n* **1** any of five things exactly alike; *specif* any of five identical copies **2** five copies all alike – + *in* ⟨*typed in ~*⟩

³**quintuplicate** /-,kayt/ *vt* **1** to make quintuple or fivefold **2** to prepare in quintuplicate

¹**quip** /kwip/ *n* a witty or sarcastic observation or response usu made on the spur of the moment [earlier *quippy,* perh fr L *quippe* indeed, to be sure (often ironical), fr *quid* what – more at QUIDDITY] – **quipster** *n*

²**quip** *vi,* **-pp-** to make quips

**quipu** /'keepooh, 'kwipooh/ *n* a device made of a main cord with smaller knotted cords attached, used by the ancient Peruvians (e g for calculating or recording information) [Sp *quipo,* fr Quechua *quipu*]

¹**quire** /kwie·ə/ *n* **1** a set of folded sheets (e g of a book) fitting one within another **2** a collection of 24 or sometimes 25 sheets of paper of the same size and quality; one twentieth of a ream [ME *quair* four sheets of paper folded once, collection of sheets, fr MF *quaer,* fr (assumed) VL *quadernum,* alter. of L *quaterni* four each, set of four – more at QUATERNION]

²**quire** *vb or n* (to) choir

**quirk** /kwuhk/ *n* **1a** an abrupt twist or curve (e g in drawing or writing) **b** an odd or peculiar trait (e g of character or behaviour); an idiosyncrasy **c** an accident, vagary ⟨*by some ~ of fate*⟩ **2** a groove separating an architectural moulding (e g a bead) from adjoining members [origin unknown] – **quirkish** *adj,* **quirky** *adj,* **quirkily** *adv,* **quirkiness** *n*

¹**quirt** /kwuht/ *n, NAm* a riding whip with a short handle and a leather lash [MexSp *cuarta*]

²**quirt** *vt, NAm* to strike or drive with a quirt

**quisling** /'kwizling/ *n* a traitor who collaborates with the invaders of his/her country, esp by serving in a puppet government [Vidkun *Quisling* †1945 Norw politician who collaborated with the Germans in World War II] – **quislingism** *n*

¹**quit** /kwit/ *adj* released from obligation, charge, or penalty; *esp* free – + *of* [ME *quite, quit,* fr OF *quite*]

²**quit** *vb,* **-tt-; quitted,** *NAm chiefly* **quit** *vt* **1a** to depart from or out of ⟨*ready to ~ the building at a moment's notice*⟩ **b** to leave the company of ⟨*~ted her without a backward glance*⟩ **c** to relinquish, abandon, or give over (e g a way of thinking, acting, or living); stop ⟨*~ moaning!*⟩ **d** to give up (an action, activity, or employment); leave ⟨*~ a job*⟩ **2** *archaic* to set free; relieve, release ⟨*~ oneself of fear*⟩ **3** *archaic* to make full payment of; pay up ⟨*~ a debt*⟩ **4** *archaic* to conduct (oneself) in a usu specified way ⟨*Elizabeth ~s herself well before her people – Newsweek*⟩ ⟨*the youths ~ themselves like men*⟩ *~ vi* **1** to cease doing something; *specif* to give up one's job **2** *of a tenant* to vacate occupied premises ⟨*the landlord gave them notice to ~*⟩ **3** *informal* to admit defeat; give up *synonyms* see ¹GO [ME

*quiten, quitten,* fr MF *quiter, quitter,* fr OF, fr *quite* free of, released, lit., at rest, fr L *quietus* quiet, at rest]

**quitch** /kwich/, **quitch grass** *n* COUCH GRASS [(assumed) ME *quicche,* fr OE *cwice;* akin to OHG *quecca* couch grass, OE *cwic* living – more at QUICK]

**quitclaim** /'kwit,klaym/ *n* a legal document by which one person renounces his/her right to some title, claim, or possession in favour of another [ME *quite-claim,* fr MF *quiteclame,* fr *quiteclamer,* lit., to declare free, fr OF, fr *quite* ¹quit + *clamer* to declare, claim] – **quitclaim** *vt*

**quite** /kwiet/ *adv or adj* **1** wholly, completely ⟨*not ~ all*⟩ ⟨*~ the best shop*⟩ ⟨*~ sure*⟩ ⟨*~ different*⟩ – often used interjectionally to express agreement **2** more than usually; rather ⟨*took ~ a time*⟩ ⟨*I really ~ enjoy it*⟩ ⟨*~ a lot of people*⟩ – sometimes used informally to express appreciation ⟨*that was ~ some party!*⟩ **3** *chiefly Br* to only a moderate degree ⟨*~ good but not perfect*⟩ [ME, fr *quite,* adj, quit] – **quite so** JUST SO 2

**quitrent** /'kwit,rent/ *n* a fixed rent payable to a feudal superior in place of the performing of services; *specif* a fixed rent due from a SOCAGE tenant [ME *quiterent,* fr *quite, quit* ¹quit + *rent*]

**quits** /kwits/ *adj* on even terms as a result of repayment of a debt or retaliation for an injury [ME, quit, prob fr ML *quittus,* alter. of L *quietus* at rest] – **call it quits 1** CALL IT A DAY **2** to acknowledge that neither side has an advantage – **double or quits** with the stake to be either doubled or cancelled

**quittance** /'kwit(ə)ns/ *n* **1a** discharge or release from a debt or obligation **b** a document that is evidence of quittance **2** recompense, requital

**quitter** /'kwitə/ *n* a person or animal that quits; *esp* someone who gives up too easily; a defeatist

**quittor** /'kwitə/ *n* an inflamed condition of the feet, esp of horses and asses, that chiefly affects the cartilage, is accompanied by the discharge of pus, and is caused by injury (eg bruising) or infection [ME *quiture* pus, prob fr OF, act of boiling, fr L *coctura,* fr *coctus,* pp of *coquere* to cook – more at COOK]

¹**quiver** /'kwivə/ *n* a case for carrying or holding arrows; *also* the arrows in a quiver [ME, fr OF *quivre,* of Gmc origin; akin to OE *cocer* quiver, OHG *kohhari*]

²**quiver** *vb* to (cause to) shake or vibrate with a slight rapid trembling motion *synonyms* see ¹SHAKE [ME *quiveren,* prob fr *quiver* agile, quick, fr (assumed) OE *cwifer*]

³**quiver** *n* the act or action of quivering; a tremor

**qui vive** /,kee 'veev/ *n* [Fr *qui-vive,* fr *qui vive?* long live who?, challenge of a French sentry] – **on the qui vive** on the alert; on the lookout

**quixote** /'kwiksət/ *n, often cap* a quixotic person [Don *Quixote*] – **quixotism, quixotry** *n*

**quixotic** /kwik'sotik/, **quixotical** /-ikl/ *adj* idealistic to an impractical degree; *esp* marked by rash lofty romantic ideas or extravagantly chivalrous action [Don *Quixote,* hero of the novel *Don Quixote de la Mancha* by Miguel de Cervantes Saavedra †1616 Sp novelist] – **quixotically** *adv*

¹**quiz** /kwiz/ *n, pl* **quizzes 1** a test of knowledge: eg **1a** a public test usu of general knowledge, esp as a television or radio entertainment ⟨*a ~ programme*⟩ **b** *NAm* an informal test given by a teacher to a student or class **2** *archaic* a joke, hoax **3** *archaic* **3a** an eccentric person **b** a quizzical person [origin unknown]

²**quiz** *vt* **-zz- 1** *NAm* to test (a student or class) informally **2** *chiefly journalistic* to question closely **3** *archaic* to make sport of; mock; *also* to look mockingly at (eg with an eyeglass) – **quizzer** *n*

**quiz master** *n* a question-master

**quizzical** /'kwizikl/ *adj* **1** marked or characterized by gentle mockery or questioning ⟨*a ~ glance*⟩ **2** *archaic* slightly eccentric; odd – **quizzicality** *n,* **quizzically** *adv*

**quizzing glass** /'kwizing/ *n* a single round usu magnifying lens on a ribbon or cord or mounted on a handle

**quod** /kwod/ *n, Br slang* prison [perh by shortening & alter. fr *quadrangle*]

**quodlibet** /'kwodli,bet/ *n* **1** a philosophical or theological point put forward for disputation; *also* a disputation on such a point **2** a whimsical combination of familiar melodies or texts [ME, fr ML *quodlibetum,* fr L *quodlibet,* neut of *quilibet* any whatever, fr *qui* who, what + *libet* it pleases, fr *libēre* to please – more at WHO, LOVE]

¹**quoin** /koyn; *also* kwoyn/ *n* **1a** the solid exterior angle of a

building **b** any of the blocks forming a quoin and distinguishing it from the adjoining surfaces **2** a wooden or expandable metal block used by printers to lock up a FORME within a CHASE (frame) [alter. of ¹*coin*]

²**quoin** *vt* **1** to equip (a type forme) with quoins **2** to provide with quoins ⟨*~ed walls*⟩

¹**quoit** /koyt; *also* kwoyt/ *n* **1** a ring (eg of rubber or iron) used in a throwing game **2** *pl but taking sing vb* a game in which quoits are thrown at an upright pin in an attempt to ring the pin or come as near to it as possible [ME *coite*]

²**quoit** *vt* to throw like a quoit

**quokka** /'kwokə/ *n* a small short-tailed wallaby (*Setonix brachyurus*) of W Australia [native name in Australia]

**quondam** /'kwondam, -dəm/ *adj* former, sometime ⟨*a ~ friend*⟩ [L, at one time, formerly, fr *quom, cum* when; akin to L *qui* who – more at WHO]

**Quonset** /'kwonsit/ *trademark* – used in N America for a prefabricated shelter similar to a NISSEN HUT

**quorate** /'kwawrət, -rayt/ *adj, formal* being or having a quorum ⟨*is this meeting ~?*⟩

**quorum** /'kwawrəm/ *n* the number (eg a majority of officers or members of a body) that when duly assembled is constitutionally competent to transact business [ME, quorum of justices of the peace, fr L, of whom, gen pl of *qui* who; fr the wording of the commission formerly issued to justices of the peace]

**quota** /'kwohtə/ *n* **1** a proportional part or share; *esp* the share or proportion to be either contributed or received by an individual or body ⟨*most factories fulfilled their production ~*⟩ **2** the number or amount constituting a proportional share **3** a numerical limit set on some class of people or things ⟨*an immigration ~*⟩ [ML, fr L *quota pars* how great a part]

**quotable** /'kwohtəbl/ *adj* **1** fit for or worth quoting **2** made with permission for publication (eg in a newspaper) ⟨*were the Minister's remarks ~ or off the record?*⟩

**quotation** /kwoh'taysh(ə)n/ *n* **1a** something that is quoted; *esp* a passage or phrase quoted from printed literature **b** the use in art, esp music, of material from earlier work by someone else or oneself ⟨*the ~ from Berlioz was immediately recognizable*⟩ **2a** the act or process of quoting **b**(1) the naming or publishing of current bids and offers for or prices of shares, securities, commodities, etc **b**(2) the bids, offers, or prices so named or published; *esp* the highest bid and lowest offer for a particular security in a given market at a particular time **3** an estimate of the cost of a service or commodity ⟨*Buying a carpet? Get a ~ from us*⟩ **4** a hollow printer's QUADRAT (block) larger than 24 points square

**quotation mark** *n* either of a pair of punctuation marks " and " or ' and ' used to indicate the beginning and end of a direct quotation

¹**quote** /kwoht/ *vt* **1a** to repeat (a passage or phrase previously spoken or written, esp by another) in writing or speech, usu with an acknowledgment **b** to repeat a passage or phrase from, esp in substantiation or illustration ⟨*to ~ the Scriptures*⟩ **2** to give in illustration ⟨*~ cases*⟩ **3a** to name (the current or recent buying or selling price) of a commodity, stock, share, etc **b** to make an estimate of or give exact information on (the price of a commodity or service) **4** to set off by quotation marks *~ vi* **1** to say or write again something already said or written by another – often used to inform a hearer or reader that matter following is quoted ⟨*the Prime Minister said, and I ~, "We have beaten inflation"*⟩ **2** to name one's price [ML *quotare* to mark the number of, number references, fr L *quotus* of what number or quantity, fr *quot* how many, (as) many as; akin to L *qui* who – more at WHO]

²**quote** *n, informal* **1** a quotation **2** QUOTATION MARK – often used, esp orally, to indicate the beginning of a direct quotation ⟨*the Prime Minister said ~ we have beaten inflation unquote*⟩

**quoth** /kwohth/ *vb past, archaic* said – chiefly in the first and third persons with a subject following ⟨*~ he*⟩ [ME, past of *quethen* to say, fr OE *cwethan;* akin to OHG *quedan* to say]

¹**quotidian** /kwoh'tidiən/ *adj* **1** occurring or recurring every day; *specif* of or being attacks of a fever, esp malaria, that recur at approx 24-hour intervals **2** *formal* **2a** belonging to each day; everyday ⟨*~ routine*⟩ **b** commonplace, ordinary ⟨*~ drabness*⟩ [ME *cotidian,* fr MF, fr L *quotidianus, cotidianus,* fr *quotidie* every day, fr *quot* (as) many as + *dies* day – more at DEITY]

²**quotidian** *n* a fever, esp malaria, characterized by attacks that recur at approx 24-hour intervals

**quotient** /'kwohsh(ə)nt/ *n* **1** the result of the division of one number or mathematical expression by another **2** the ratio, usu multiplied by 100, between a score achieved in a test and a measurement on which that score might be expected largely to depend – compare INTELLIGENCE QUOTIENT **3** *nonstandard* a quota, share; *also* a level ⟨*Princess Alexandra's high fashion ~ – New York Times*⟩ [ME *quocient,* modif of L *quotiens* how many times, fr *quot* how many]

**Qur'an, Quran** /kaw'rahn/ *n* KORAN (Muslims' sacred book)

**qursh** /kooəsh/ *n, pl* **qursh** – see *riyal* at MONEY table [Ar *qirsh*]

R

# R

r, R /ah/ *n, pl* r's, rs, R's, Rs **1a** the 18th letter of the English alphabet **b** a graphic representation of or device for reproducing the letter *r* **c** a speech counterpart of printed or written *r* **2** one designated *r*, esp as the 18th in order or class **3** something shaped like the letter R

¹-r /-ə/ *suffix* – used to form the comparative degree of adjectives and adverbs of one syllable, and of some adjectives and adverbs of two or more syllables, that end in *e* ⟨true*r*⟩ ⟨free*r*⟩; compare -ER 1

²-r *suffix* -ER 2 – used with nouns that end in *e* ⟨old-time*r*⟩ ⟨teenage*r*⟩ ⟨dine*r*⟩

¹**rabbet** /'rabit/ *n* a channel, groove, or recess cut out of an edge or surface; *specif* one intended to receive another piece (eg a panel) [ME *rabet*, fr MF *rabat* act of beating down, fr OF *rabattre* to beat down, reduce – more at REBATE]

²**rabbet** *vt* **1** to cut a rabbet in **2** to unite the rabbeted edges of ~ *vi* to become joined by a rabbet

**rabbet joint** *n* a joint formed by fitting together rabbeted boards or timbers

**rabbi** /'rabie/ *n, pl* **rabbis 1** master, teacher – used by Jews as a respectful term of address **2** a Jew qualified to expound and apply Jewish law **3** a Jew trained and ordained for professional religious leadership; *specif* the official leader of a Jewish congregation [LL, fr Gk *rhabbi*, fr Heb *rabbī* my master, fr *rabh* master + -*ī* my]

**rabbin** /'rabin/ *n* a rabbi [Fr]

**rabbinate** /'rabinət/ *n* **1** the office or tenure of a rabbi **2** the whole body of rabbis

**rabbinic** /rə'binik/, **rabbinical** /-ikl/ *adj* **1** of rabbis or their writings **2** of or preparing for the rabbinate **3** comprising or belonging to any of several sets of Hebrew characters simpler than the square Hebrew letters – **rabbinically** *adv*

**Rabbinic Hebrew** *n* the Hebrew used esp by medieval rabbis

**rabbinism** /'rabi,niz(ə)m/ *n* rabbinic teachings and traditions

¹**rabbit** /'rabit/ *n, pl* **rabbits, (1) rabbits,** *esp collectively* **rabbit 1** a small long-eared mammal (*Oryctolagus cuniculus*) that is related to the hares but differs from them in producing naked young and in its burrowing habits **2** the fur of a rabbit **3** *NAm* HARE 2 **4** *Br informal* an unskilful player (eg in golf, cricket, or tennis) [ME *rabet*, prob fr Walloon *robett*, *robete*, fr MD *robbe*] – **rabbity** *adj*

²**rabbit** *vi* **1** to hunt rabbits **2** *Br informal* to talk aimlessly or inconsequentially – often + *on* ⟨*just sit back and let him ~ on*⟩ [(2) rhyming slang *rabbit (and pork)* talk] – **rabbiter** *n*

**rabbit fever** *n* TULARAEMIA (infectious disease of rodents, humans, and some domestic animals)

**rabbitfish** /'rabit,fish/ *n* CHIMAERA (marine fish with a long tapering tail); *esp* a chimaera (*Chimaera monstrosa*) of the Atlantic and Mediterranean [fr its rabbit-like nose]

**rabbit killer** *n, NZ* a blow directed at someone's throat

**rabbit punch** *n* a short chopping blow delivered to the back of the neck or the base of the skull [fr the manner in which a rabbit is stunned before being killed]

**rabbitry** /'rabitri/ *n* a place where domestic rabbits are kept or bred

¹**rabble** /'rabl/ *n taking sing or pl vb* **1** a disorganized or disorderly crowd of people; a mob **2** *derog or humorous the* common people; *the* lowest class of society [ME *rabel* pack of animals]

²**rabble** *n* an iron bar with the end bent, used for stirring or moving material in a furnace; *esp* one used to stir or skim molten PIG IRON during its conversion in a furnace to WROUGHT IRON [Fr *râble* fire shovel, fr ML *rotabulum*, alter. of L *rutabulum*, fr *rutus*, pp of *ruere* to dig up – more at RUG]

³**rabble** *vt* to stir or skim with a rabble – **rabbler** *n*

'**rabble-,rouser** *n* one who stirs up (eg to hatred or violence) the common people; a demagogue

**Rabelaisian** /,rabi'layzyən, -zh(y)ən/ *adj* (characteristic) of Rabelais or his works; *specif* marked by coarse robust humour, extravagance of caricature, or bold naturalism [François *Rabelais* †1553 Fr humorist & satirist]

**Rabi** /'rubi/ *n* – see MONTH table [Ar *rabī'*]

**rabic** /'rabik/ *adj* of rabies

**rabid** /'rabid; *sense 2 also* 'raybid/ *adj* **1a** extremely violent; furious **b** unreasoning or fanatical in an opinion or feeling ⟨*a ~ racialist*⟩ **2** affected with rabies [L *rabidus* mad, fr *rabere*] – **rabidly** *adv*, **rabidness** *n*, **rabidity** *n*

**rabies** /'raybeez, -biz/ *n, pl* **rabies** a short-lasting usu fatal virus disease of the nervous system of warm-blooded animals, that is usu transmitted through the bite of a rabid animal and is characterized by extreme fear of water and by convulsions [NL, fr L, madness, fr *rabere* to rave – more at RAGE]

**raccoon, racoon** /rə'koohn/ *n, pl* **raccoons, racoons,** *esp collectively* **raccoon, racoon 1** (the fur of) a small flesh-eating mammal (*Procyon lotor*) of N America that is chiefly grey, has a bushy tail ringed with black bands, and lives chiefly in trees **2** any of several animals resembling or related to the raccoon [*äräkhun* (in some Algonquian language of Virginia)]

¹**race** /rays/ *n* **1a** a strong or rapid current of water, esp in the sea or a river **b** a heavy or choppy sea **c** (the current flowing in) a watercourse used industrially (eg to turn the wheel of a mill) **2a** a contest of speed (eg in running or riding) **b** *pl* a meeting in which several races (eg for horses) are run ⟨*go for a day at the ~s*⟩ **c** a contest or rivalry for an ultimate prize or position ⟨*the ~ for the league championship*⟩ **3** a track or channel in which something rolls or slides; *specif* a groove for the balls in a BALL BEARING **4** *archaic* **4a** a set course (eg of the sun or moon) or duration of time **b** the course of life ⟨*ere his ~ was run*⟩ [ME *ras*, fr ON *rās;* akin to OE *ræs* rush, L *rorarii* skirmishers, Gk *erōē* rush]

²**race** *vi* **1** to compete in a race **2** to go or move at top speed or out of control ⟨*his pulse was* racing⟩ **3** *of a motor, engine, etc* to revolve too fast under a diminished load ~ *vt* **1** to have a race with ⟨*~d her brother to the garden gate*⟩ **2a** to enter in a race ⟨*always ~s his horses at Chepstow*⟩ **b** to drive at high speed **c** to transport or propel at maximum speed **3** to accelerate (eg an engine) without a working load or with the transmission disengaged

³**race** *n taking sing or pl vb* **1a** a family, tribe, people, or nation belonging to the same stock **b** a group or kind of people united by community of interests, habits, or characteristics ⟨*the English ~*⟩ **2a** an actually or potentially interbreeding group within a species; *also* a category (eg a subspecies) in the classification of living things that represents such a group **b** a particular breed of plants or animals **c** a division of human beings possessing traits (eg skin colour or shape of head) that are transmitted genetically and sufficiently distinct to characterize it as a particular human type ⟨*the Caucasian ~*⟩ **d** any large distinct division of living creatures ⟨*the human ~*⟩ **3a** the division of mankind into races ⟨*the brotherhood of man independent of colour, creed, or ~*⟩ **b** the fact or condition of belonging to or being a race **4** distinctive flavour, taste, or strength (eg of wine) **5** *obs* inherited temperament or disposition [MF, generation, fr OIt *razza*]

**synonyms** The use of **race** and **racial** in the strict anthropological sense (2c) ⟨*the Mongoloid* race⟩ has led to much abuse and misunderstanding, so that it is now safer to avoid the use of these words except with reference to physical characteristics or, in the popular sense (1), where a sovereign state is involved ⟨*the British* race⟩. Available alternatives are **nation** and **national** ⟨*the French* nation⟩, which emphasize common customs and loyalties without necessarily implying political statehood ⟨*the Gipsy* nation⟩; **people**, which implies neither distinct physical traits nor statehood ⟨*primitive* peoples⟩; **ethnic**, which may suggest distinct physical traits but does not imply statehood ⟨*a natural* **ethnic** *frontier*⟩ ⟨**ethnic** *minorities in Britain*⟩; and **community**, which often applies to an identifiable group within a larger society ⟨*the London Jewish* **community**⟩ ⟨**community** *relations*⟩.

'**race-,card** *n* the programme of events at a horse-race meeting; *also* the printed list of this (e g showing runners, riders, trainers, and owners)

**racecourse** /-,kaws/ *n* a place where or the track on which races, esp horse races, are held

**racegoer** /'rays,gohə/ *n* someone who goes to horse-race meetings

**racehorse** /'rays,haws/ *n* a horse bred or kept for racing

**racemate** /ray'seemayt, rə-, 'rasi-/ *n* a racemic chemical compound or mixture

**raceme** /ray'seem, rə-/ *n* an INFLORESCENCE (e g that of the lily of the valley or the foxglove) in which the flowers are borne on short stalks of about equal length, along a long central stem, with the oldest flowers at the base and the youngest at the tip of the stem [L *racemus* bunch of grapes (cf RAISIN)]

**racemic** /rə'seemik, -'se-/ *adj* of or being a chemical compound or mixture that is composed of equal amounts of DEXTROROTATORY and LAEVOROTATORY forms of the same compound, and has no OPTICAL ACTIVITY [Fr *racémique*, fr L *racemus*; fr the occurrence of such a compound in the juice of grapes]

**racem·ization, -isation** /,rasimie'zaysh(ə)n/ *n* the action or process of changing from a chemical compound that has OPTICAL ACTIVITY into a racemic compound or mixture – **racemize** *vb*

**racemose** /'rasimohs/ *adj* having or growing in the form of a raceme [L *racemosus* full of clusters, fr *racemus*]

**racemose gland** *n* a gland having branching ducts that end in small sacs (ACINI) lined with secreting cells

**racer** /'raysə/ *n* a person, animal, or thing (e g a boat or car) that races or is used for racing

**race riot** *n* a riot caused by racial dissensions

**race suicide** *n* the gradual extinction of a race through deliberate restriction of the birth rate

**racetrack** /'rays,trak/ *n* a usu oval closed track on which races (e g between cars or runners) are held

**raceway** /'rays,way/ *n, NAm* 1 a channel for a current of water (e g a millrace) 2 a racetrack; *esp* a track for HARNESS RACING

**rachi-** /rayki-, raki-/, **rachio-** *comb form* spine ⟨rachi*tic*⟩ [Gk *rhachi-*, fr *rhachis*; akin to Gk *rhachos* thorn, Lith *ražas* stubble]

**rachis** /'raykis/ *n, pl* **rachises** *also* **rachides** /'rakideez,'ray-/ 1 the backbone; SPINAL COLUMN 2 an elongated central supporting structure; e g **2a(1)** the long main stem or axis of a flower-bearing shoot, spike, etc of a plant **a(2)** an extension of the stalk of a COMPOUND LEAF (leaf made up of two or more leaflets) that bears the leaflets **b** the part of the shaft of a feather that bears the BARBS [NL *rachid-, rachis*, modif of Gk *rhachis*]

**rachitis** /ra'kietəs/ *n* rickets [NL, fr Gk *rhachitis* disease of the spine, fr *rhachis*] – **rachitic** *adj*

**rachmanism** /'rakmə,niz(ə)m/ *n, often cap, Br* the unscrupulous intimidation and exploitation of tenants by a landlord [Peter *Rachman* †1962 Br (Polish-born) landlord]

**racial** /'raysh(ə)l/ *adj* 1 of or based on a race 2 existing or occurring between races ⟨~ *harmony*⟩ – **racially** *adv*

**racialism** /'rayshə,liz(ə)m/ *n* 1 racial prejudice or discrimination 2 RACISM 1 – **racialist** *adj or n,* **racialistic** *adj*

**racing** /'raysing/ *n* the pursuit or sport of competing in or organizing esp horse races

**racism** /'raysiz(ə)m/ *n* 1 a belief that race is the primary determinant of human traits and capacities and that racial differences produce an inherent superiority of a particular race 2 RACIALISM 1 – **racist** *n or adj*

¹**rack, wrack** /rak/ *n, poetic* a wind-driven mass of high often broken clouds [ME *rak*, prob of Scand origin; akin to Sw dial. *rak* wreck; akin to OE *wrecan* to drive – more at WREAK]
  *usage* Compare the spellings **rack** and **wrack**. Clouds are usually **rack** (rather than **wrack**) and they **rack** (rather than **wrack**). It is, correctly, a luggage **rack**, and **rack** of lamb, and one **racks** wine. One **racks** (but also sometimes **wracks**) one's brains, and finds things **nerve-racking** (but also sometimes **nerve-wracking**). It is **wrack** *and* **ruin** (but also sometimes **rack** *and* **ruin**). Seaweed is **wrack**.

²**rack, wrack** *vi, poetic* of clouds to fly or scud in high wind

³**rack** *also* **wrack** *n* 1 a framework for holding hay, silage, etc for livestock 2 an instrument of torture on which the victim's body is stretched – usu + *the* 3 a framework, stand, or grating

on or in which articles are placed ⟨*a luggage* ~⟩ ⟨*a plate* ~⟩ **4a** a bar with teeth on one surface for meshing with a toothed wheel (e g a PINION or WORM GEAR) **b** a notched bar used as a ratchet to engage with the locking member of a mechanism (e g a PAWL or DETENT) [ME, prob fr MD *rec* framework; akin to OE *reccan* to stretch, Gk *oregein* – more at RIGHT] – **on the rack** under great mental or emotional stress

⁴**rack** *also* **wrack** *vt* 1 to torture on the rack 2 to cause to suffer torture, pain, or anguish ⟨~ed *by headaches*⟩ **3a** to stretch or strain considerably ⟨~ed *his brains*⟩ **b** to raise (rents) oppressively **c** *of a landlord* to harass or oppress (a tenant) with high rents or extortions 4 to work or treat (material) on a rack 5 to work by a mechanism using a rack and a toothed wheel (e g a PINION or WORM GEAR) so as to extend or contract 6 to bind (e g parallel ropes of a tackle) together – **racker** *n*
  **rack up** *vt, NAm* to score ⟨racked up *30 points in the first half*⟩

⁵**rack** *vt* to draw off (e g wine) from the LEES (dregs) [ME *rakken*, fr OProv *arraca*]

⁶**rack** *n* 1 the neck and spine of a forequarter of veal, pork, or esp mutton 2 the front rib section of lamb used for chops or as a roast [perh fr ³*rack*]

⁷**rack, wrack** *n* destruction – chiefly in *rack and ruin* [see *wrack*]

¹**racket** *also* **racquet** /'rakit/ *n* 1 a lightweight implement that consists of a netting (e g of gut or nylon) stretched in an oval or round open frame with a handle attached and that is used for striking the ball in any of various games (e g tennis, squash, or badminton) 2 *pl but taking sing vb* a game for two or four players played with a ball and rackets on a 4-walled court 3 a snowshoe shaped like a racket [MF *raquette*, fr It *racchetta*, fr Ar *rāhah* palm of the hand]

²**racket** *n* 1 a loud, confused, and disturbing noise; a clamour, din 2 the strain of exciting or trying experiences ⟨*getting too old to stand the* ~⟩ 3 *informal* **3a** a fraudulent scheme, enterprise, or activity **b** a usu illegal enterprise made workable by bribery or intimidation **c** an easy and lucrative means of livelihood ⟨*writing's a real* ~⟩ **d** a usu specified occupation or business ⟨*he's in the publicity* ~⟩ 4 *archaic* social whirl or excitement [prob imit]

³**racket** *vi* 1 to engage in an active, esp a debauched, social life – usu + *about* or *round* 2 to move with or make a racket

**racketeer** /,raki'tiə/ *n* one who extorts money or advantages by threats of violence, by blackmail, or by illegal interference with business or employment – **racketeer** *vb*

**rackety** /'rakiti/ *adj* 1 noisy, rowdy 2 enjoying social excitement or debauchery

**rack railway, rack and pinion railway** *n* a railway having between its rails a rack that meshes with a gear wheel or pinion on the locomotive for pulling it up steep gradients and braking it when going down

'**rack-,rent** *vt* to subject to rack rent

**rack rent** *n* 1 an excessive or unreasonably high rent 2 *Br* the highest rent that can be earned on a property [⁴*rack*]

'**rack-,renter** *n* one who pays or exacts rack rent

**racon** /'raykon/ *n* RADAR BEACON [radar bea*con*]

**raconteur** /,rakon'tuh/ *n* one who excels in telling anecdotes [Fr, fr MF, fr *raconter* to tell, fr OF, fr re- + *aconter, acompter* to tell, count – more at ACCOUNT]

**racoon** /rə'koohn/ *n* a raccoon

**racquet** /'rakit/ *n* ¹RACKET

¹**racy** /'raysi/ *adj* 1 full of zest or vigour 2 having a strongly marked quality; piquant ⟨*a* ~ *flavour*⟩ 3 risqué, suggestive [³*race* 4 + ¹-*y*] – **racily** *adv,* **raciness** *n*

²**racy** *adj* having a body fitted for racing; long-bodied and lean [partly fr ¹*racy;* partly fr ²*race* + ¹-*y*]

**rad** /rad/ *n* a unit of absorbed dose of ionizing radiation (e g x RAYS) equal to an energy of 100 ergs per gram of irradiated material [short for *radiation*]

**radar** /'raydah/ *n* an electronic device that generates ultrahigh frequency RADIO WAVES and locates objects in the vicinity by analysis of the radio waves reflected back from them [*radio detection and ranging*]

**radar beacon** *n* a radar transmitter that upon receiving a radar signal emits a signal which reinforces the normal reflected signal or which introduces a code into the reflected signal, esp for identification purposes

**radarscope** /'raydah,skohp/ *n* an OSCILLOSCOPE used to display radar signals

**raddle** /'radl/ *n* RED OCHRE (natural red pigment) [prob alter. of *ruddle*] – **raddle** vt

**raddled** /'radld/ *adj* dilapidated; *esp* showing the haggardness of old age and debauchery [origin unknown]

**radi-** /raydi-/ – see RADIO-

¹**radial** /'raydyəl/ *adj* **1** (having parts) arranged like rays or radii from a central point ⟨*the ~ form of a starfish*⟩ **2a** relating to, placed like, or moving along a radius **b** characterized by divergence from a centre **3** of or situated near the RADIUS (bone in the human forearm) ⟨*the thumb is on the ~ side of the hand*⟩ **4** developing uniformly round a central axis [ML *radialis*, fr L *radius* ray] – **radially** *adv*

²**radial** *n* **1** any of a system of radial lines **2** a radial body part (eg an artery) **3 radial, radial tyre** a pneumatic tyre in which the internal cords are laid at a right angle to the centre line of the tread

**radiale** /,raydi'ahli/ *n, pl* **radialia** /-liə/ a bone or cartilage of the wrist that articulates with the RADIUS (bone in the human forearm); *specif* the small boat-shaped bone (NAVICULAR) in the human wrist [NL, fr ML, neut of *radialis*]

**radial engine** *n* an INTERNAL-COMBUSTION ENGINE with cylinders arranged radially round the CRANKSHAFT (shaft for transmitting the power) like the spokes of a wheel

**radial symmetry** *n* the condition of having similar parts regularly arranged round a central line dividing a body symmetrically – **radially symmetrical** *adj*

**radian** /'raydyən/ *n* a unit of angular measurement that is equal to the angle between two radii of a circle that subtend an arc of the circumference equal to the length of the radius [*radi*us + *-an*]

¹**radiant** /'raydyənt/ *adj* **1a** radiating rays or reflecting beams of light **b** vividly bright and shining; glowing **2** marked by or expressing love, confidence, or happiness ⟨*a ~ smile*⟩ **3a** emitted or transmitted by radiation ⟨*~ energy*⟩ **b** of or emitting RADIANT HEAT **4** relating to or exhibiting biological radiation *synonyms* see BRIGHT [ME, fr L *radiant-, radians*, prp of *radiare*] – **radiance, radiancy** *n*, **radiantly** *adv*

²**radiant** *n* something that radiates: eg **a** the apparent originating point in the heavens of a meteor shower **b** a point or object from which light emanates **c** the part of a gas or electric heater that glows with the heat

**radiant energy** *n* energy in the form of ELECTROMAGNETIC WAVES (eg heat, light, or RADIO WAVES)

**radiant flux** *n* the rate of emission or transmission of RADIANT ENERGY

**radiant heat** *n* heat transmitted by radiation as contrasted with that transmitted by conduction or CONVECTION (circulation of heat in a liquid or gas by movement of the constituent molecules)

**radiant heating** *n* PANEL HEATING (system of heating buildings by radiators)

¹**radiate** /'raydi,ayt/ *vi* **1** to send out rays (as if) of light; shine brightly **2a** to issue in rays **b** to evolve by biological radiation **3** to proceed in a direct line from or towards a centre ~ *vt* **1** to send out (as if) in rays **2** to disseminate as if from a centre ⟨*the universities ~ learning*⟩ [L *radiatus*, pp of *radiare*, fr *radius* ray]

²**radiate** /-ət/ *adj* having rays or radial parts: eg **a** having RAY FLOWERS (small strap-shaped flowers in the flower heads of some plants of the daisy family) **b** characterized by radial symmetry – **radiately** *adv*

**radiation** /,raydi'aysh(ə)n/ *n* **1a** the action or process of radiating; *esp* the process of emitting RADIANT ENERGY in the form of waves or particles **b** the combined processes of emission, transmission, and absorption of RADIANT ENERGY **2a** something that is radiated **b** energy radiated in the form of waves or particles; *esp* ELECTROMAGNETIC RADIATION (eg light) or emission from radioactive sources (eg ALPHA RAYS) **3** a radial arrangement **4** biological evolution in a group of organisms that is characterized by spreading into different environments and by divergence of structure as a result of adaptation to different conditions – **radiational, radiative** *adj*

**radiation sickness** *n* sickness that results from exposure to ionizing radiation (eg X rays) and is commonly marked by fatigue, nausea, vomiting, loss of teeth and hair, and in more severe cases by damage to blood-forming tissue with decrease in RED BLOOD CELLS and WHITE BLOOD CELLS often leading to leukaemia

**radiator** /'raydi,aytə/ *n* something that radiates: eg **a** a room heater (with a large surface area for radiating heat); *specif* one

through which hot water or steam circulates as part of a central-heating system **b** a device with a large surface area used for cooling an INTERNAL-COMBUSTION ENGINE by means of water circulating through it **c** a transmitting aerial

¹**radical** /'radikl/ *adj* **1** of or proceeding from a root: eg **1a** of or growing from the root or the base of a stem – compare CAULINE **b** of or being a linguistic form from which others have derived **c** relating to or involving a mathematical root **d** designed to remove the root of a disease or all diseased tissue ⟨*~ surgery*⟩ **2** essential, fundamental **3a** marked by a considerable departure from the usual or traditional; extreme **b** affecting or involving the basic nature or composition of something; thoroughgoing ⟨*~ changes*⟩ **c** tending or disposed to make extreme changes in existing views, habits, conditions, or institutions **d(1)** of or being a political group associated with views, practices, and policies of extreme change **d(2)** advocating extreme measures to attain a political end ⟨*the ~ right*⟩ [ME, fr LL *radicalis*, fr L *radic-, radix* root – more at ROOT] – **radicalness** *n*

²**radical** *n* **1** a basic principle; a foundation **2** ROOT 6 (basic word from which others are formed) **3** someone who is a member of a radical party or holds radical views **4a** a single replaceable atom of the reactive atomic form of a chemical element **b** a group of atoms that is replaceable in a molecule by a single atom, that is capable of remaining unchanged during a series of chemical reactions, or that may have a definite transitory existence in the course of a reaction **5a** a mathematical expression involving RADICAL SIGNS **b** RADICAL SIGN

**radical chic** *n, often cap R&C, chiefly derog* fashionable and usu superficial left-wing radicalism

**radicalism** /'radikəliz(ə)m/ *n* **1** the quality or state of being radical **2** the doctrines or principles of radicals

**radical-ize, -ise** /'radikəliez/ *vt* to make radical, esp in politics – **radicalization** *n*

**radically** /'radik(ə)li/ *adv* **1** in origin or essence ⟨*~ different*⟩ **2** in a radical or extreme manner

**radical sign** *n* the sign $\sqrt{}$ placed before a mathematical expression to denote that the SQUARE ROOT is to be calculated, or some other root corresponding to an index number placed over the sign

**radicand** /'radikand, ,--'-/ *n* the quantity after a RADICAL SIGN [L *radicandum*, neut of *radicandus*, gerundive of *radicari* to take root, fr *radic-, radix* root]

**radices** /'raydi,seez/ *pl of* RADIX

**radicle** /'radikl/ *n* **1** the lower part of the main central region of a plant embryo or seedling that includes the embryonic root and sometimes also the stem of the seedling (HYPOCOTYL) **2** the rootlike beginning of an anatomical vessel or part **3** RADICAL 4a, 4b △ **radical** [L *radicula*, dim of *radic-, radix* root] – **radicular** *adj*

**radii** /'raydi-ee, 'raydi-ie/ *pl of* RADIUS

¹**radio** /'raydi,oh/ *n, pl* **radios 1a** the system of wireless transmission and reception of signals by means of ELECTROMAGNETIC WAVES **b** the use of such a system for the transmission of electrical signals which correspond to and are reproduced as sounds **2** a radio receiver **3a** a radio transmitter (eg in an aircraft) **b** a radio broadcasting organization or station ⟨*Radio London*⟩ **c** the radio broadcasting industry **d** the medium of radio communication [short for *radiotelegraphy*]

²**radio** *adj* **1** of or operated by radiant energy **2** of electric currents or phenomena of frequencies between about 15000 and 10¹¹ hertz **3a** of, used in, or transmitted or received by a radio **b** specializing in radio or associated with the radio industry ⟨*~ engineer*⟩ **c(1)** transmitted by radio ⟨*~ broadcast*⟩ **c(2)** making or participating in radio broadcasts ⟨*a ~ star of the forties*⟩ **d** controlled or directed by or using radio

³**radio** *vt* **1** to send or communicate by radio **2** to send a radio message to ~ *vi* to send or communicate something by radio

**radio-, radi-** *comb form* **1** radial ⟨*radiosymmetrical*⟩ **2a** RADIANT ENERGY; radiation ⟨*radiodermatitis*⟩ **b** radioactive ⟨*radioelement*⟩ ⟨*radionuclide*⟩ **c** using ionizing radiation ⟨*radiotherapy*⟩ **d** radioactive ISOTOPES of (a specified chemical element) ⟨*radiocarbon*⟩ **e** radio ⟨*radiotelegraphy*⟩ [Fr, fr L *radius* ray]

**radioactive** /,raydioh'aktiv/ *adj* of, caused by, or exhibiting radioactivity [ISV] – **radioactively** *adv*

**radioactivity** /,raydioh·ak'tivəti/ *n* the property possessed by some chemical elements (eg uranium) of spontaneously emitting ALPHA RAYS or BETA RAYS and sometimes also GAMMA RAYS by the disintegration of the nuclei of atoms [ISV]

**radio astronomy** *n* astronomy dealing with RADIO WAVES received from outside the earth's atmosphere – **radio astronomer** *n*

**radioautograph** /ˌraydioh'awtəgrahf, -graf/ *n* AUTORADIOGRAPH (image produced by radioactivity) – **radioautographic** *adj*, **radioautography** *n*

**radio beacon** *n* a radio transmitter usu capable of transmitting equally in all directions in a horizontal plane used as a navigational aid, esp for aircraft

**radiobiology** /ˌraydioh·bie'oləji/ *n* a branch of biology dealing with the effects of radiation on living organisms or the use of radioactive materials in biological and medical investigation – **radiobiologist** *n*, **radiobiological, radiobiologic** *adj*, **radiobiologically** *adv*

**radio car** *n* a motor vehicle equipped with radio communication

**radiocarbon** /-'kahbən/ *n* radioactive carbon; *esp* CARBON 14 [ISV]

**radiocarbon dating** *n* CARBON DATING (means of dating objects containing some carbon)

**radiocast** /'raydioh,kahst/ *vt, NAm* to broadcast by radio [*radio-* + broad*cast*] – **radiocaster** *n*

**radiochemistry** /-'kemistri/ *n* a branch of chemistry dealing with radioactive substances and phenomena and including the use of labelled chemical elements or atoms to trace the course of chemical reactions – **radiochemical** *adj*, **radiochemically** *adv*, **radiochemist** *n*

**radio compass** *n* a direction finder used in navigation

**radioecology** /ˌraydioh·i'koləji/ *n* the study of the effect of radiations or radioactive substances on natural communities – **radioecologist** *n*, **radioecological** *adj*

**radioelement** /-'eləmənt/ *n* a radioactive chemical element [ISV]

**radio frequency** *n* a frequency (e g of ELECTROMAGNETIC WAVES) intermediate between audio frequencies and infrared frequencies used esp in radio and television transmission

**radio galaxy** *n* a GALAXY (star system) containing a source from which radio energy is detected

**radiogenic** /-'jenik/ *adj* produced by radioactivity

**radiogram** /'raydi·ə,gram, -dioh-/ *n* 1 a radiograph 2 a telegram sent by radio 3 *Br* a combined radio receiver and record player

**radiograph** /'raydi·ə,grahf, -,graf, -dioh-/ *n* a picture produced on a sensitive surface by a form of radiation other than light; *specif* an X-ray or gamma-ray photograph – **radiograph** *vt*, **radiographic** *adj*, **radiographically** *adv*

**radiographer** /ˌraydi'ogrəfə/ *n* one who works with sources of radiation (e g X rays), esp in medicine: e g **a** one who makes or interprets radiographs, esp for the purpose of medical diagnosis **b** one who administers RADIOTHERAPY (e g in the treatment of cancer) – **radiography** *n*

**radioimmunoassay** /ˌraydioh,imyoonoh'asay, -i,myoohnoh-, -a'say/ *n* IMMUNOASSAY (technique for identifying and measuring the concentration of a protein, sugar, etc) of a substance (e g insulin) that has been radioactively labelled

**radioisotope** /ˌraydioh'iesətohp/ *n* a radioactive ISOTOPE (form in which an atom can occur) [ISV] – **radioisotopic** *adj*, **radioisotopically** *adv*

**radiolabel** /ˌraydioh'laybl/ *vt* -ll- (*NAm* -l-, -ll-) LABEL 2

**radiolarian** /ˌraydioh'leəri·ən/ *n* any of a large order (Radiolaria) of marine single-celled organisms (PROTOZOANS) having a skeleton of silica and radiating retractable threadlike PSEUDOPODIA (cellular extensions used for locomotion and feeding) [deriv of LL *radiolus* small sunbeam, fr dim. of L *radius* ray – more at RAY]

**radiolocation** /ˌraydioh·loh'kaysh(ə)n/ *n* the detection or determination of the position and course of distant objects by radar

**radiological** /ˌraydiə'lojikl/, **radiologic** *adj* 1 of radiology 2 of nuclear radiation – **radiologically** *adv*

**radiologist** /ˌraydi'oləjist/ *n* a specialist in the use of radiant energy, esp in medical diagnosis and treatment

**radiology** /ˌraydi'oləji/ *n* the study and use of radioactive substances and high-energy radiations; *esp* the use of RADIANT ENERGY (e g X rays and the chemical element radium) in the diagnosis and treatment of disease

**radiolucency** /raydioh'loohs(ə)nsi/ *n* the quality or state of being penetrable by radiation (e g X rays) – **radiolucent** *adj*

**radiolysis** /ˌraydi'oləsis/ *n* the breakdown of a chemical compound by the action of radiation [NL] – **radiolytic** *adj*

**radioman** /'raydioh,man/ *n* a radio operator or technician

**radiometer** /ˌraydi'omitə/ *n* an instrument for measuring the intensity of RADIANT ENERGY (e g X rays) or ACOUSTIC energy – **radiometry** *n*

**radiometric** /ˌraydioh'metrik/ *adj* 1 relating to, using, or measured by a radiometer 2 of or relating to the measurement of geological time by means of the rate of disintegration of radioactive elements [ISV] – **radiometrically** *adv*

**radiomimetic** /ˌraydiohmi'metik, -mie-/ *adj, esp of chemical compounds* producing effects on living tissue similar to those of ionizing radiation (e g X rays) [ISV]

**radionuclide** /ˌraydioh'nyoohklied/ *n* a radioactive NUCLIDE (type of atom characterized by the makeup of its nucleus)

**radiopaque** /ˌraydioh'payk/ *adj* being relatively impenetrable to various forms of radiation (e g X rays)

**radiopharmaceutical** /ˌraydioh·fahmə'syoohtikl/ *n* a radioactive drug used for diagnostic or therapeutic purposes

**radiophone** /'raydiə,fohn/ *n* an apparatus for the production of sound by RADIANT ENERGY

**radiophonic** /ˌraydi·ə'fonik, -dioh-/ *adj* of or being sounds that are electrically produced ⟨*the BBC* Radiophonic *Workshop*⟩ – **radiophonically** *adv*

**radioprotective** /ˌraydioh·prə'tektiv/ *adj* serving to protect or aiding in protecting against the harmful effect of radiations ⟨~ *drugs*⟩ – **radioprotection** *n*

**radioscopy** /ˌraydi'oskəpi/ *n* direct observation of objects impenetrable to light by means of some other form of RADIANT ENERGY (e g X rays) [ISV] – **radioscopic** *adj*

**radiosensitive** /ˌraydioh'sensətiv/ *adj* sensitive to the effects of radiation, esp ionizing radiation (e g X rays) ⟨~ *cancer cells*⟩ – **radiosensitivity** *n*

**radiosonde** /'raydioh,sond/ *n* a miniature radio transmitter that is carried (e g by an unmanned balloon) into the atmosphere and is equipped with instruments for broadcasting (e g by means of signals that are precise in pitch and vibration) the humidity, temperature, and pressure [ISV]

**radio spectrum** *n* the region of the ELECTROMAGNETIC SPECTRUM usu including frequencies below 300000 megahertz in which radio or radar transmission and detection techniques may be used

**radio star** *n* a source of RADIO WAVES in space that is of very small dimensions and emits relatively strong radiation

**radiostrontium** /ˌraydioh'strontiəm/ *n* the chemical element strontium in a radioactive form; *esp* STRONTIUM 90 [NL]

**radiosymmetrical** /ˌraydioh·si'metrikl/ *adj* RADIALLY SYMMETRICAL

**radiotelegraph** /ˌraydioh'teligrahf, -graf/ *n* a radio apparatus enabling telegraph messages to be sent and received [ISV] – **radiotelegraphic** *adj*, **radiotelegraphy** *n*

**radiotelemetry** /ˌraydioh·tə'lemətri/ *n* TELEMETRY (measurement and transmission of pressure, temperature, speed, etc by radio) – **radiotelemetric** *adj*

**radiotelephone** /-'telifohn/ *n* an apparatus for enabling telephone messages to be sent by radio (e g from a moving vehicle) [ISV] – **radiotelephony** *n*

**radio telescope** *n* a radio receiver connected to a large often dish-shaped aerial for recording and measuring RADIO WAVES from stars, planets, etc

**radiotherapy** /raydioh'therəpi/ *n* the treatment of disease (e g cancer) by means of X rays or radioactive substances [ISV] – **radiotherapist** *n*

**radiothorium** /ˌraydioh'thawriəm/ *n* a radioactive form (ISOTOPE) of the chemical element thorium that has the MASS NUMBER (number of protons and neutrons in the nucleus of an atom) 228 [NL]

**radiotracer** /'raydioh,traysə/ *n* a radioactive TRACER (labelled chemical element or atom used to trace the course of chemical and biological reactions)

**,radio-'ulna** *n* a bone in the forelimb of an amphibian (e g a frog) that represents the fused RADIUS and ULNA bones of higher forms [NL]

**radio wave** *n* an ELECTROMAGNETIC WAVE of radio frequency

**radish** /'radish/ *n* the strong-tasting fleshy typically dark red root of a plant (*Raphanus sativus*) of the mustard family usu eaten raw as a salad vegetable; *also* the plant that produces radishes [ME, alter. of OE *rædic*, fr L *radic-, radix* root, radish –more at ROOT]

**radium** /'raydyəm/ *n* an intensely radioactive shining white metallic chemical element that resembles the element barium chemically, occurs in combination in minute quantities in minerals (e g pitchblende or carnotite), emits ALPHA PARTICLES and GAMMA RAYS to form the gaseous element radon, and is used chiefly in luminous materials and in the treatment of cancer [NL, fr L *radius* ray]

**radium therapy** *n* radiotherapy

[1]**radius** /'raydi-əs/ *n, pl* **radii** /'raydi-ee, 'raydi-ie/ *also* **radiuses** **1a** the bone on the thumb side of the human forearm; *also* a corresponding part of the forelimb of amphibians, reptiles, birds, and mammals **b** the third and usu largest vein of an insect's wing **2** (the length of) a straight line extending from the centre of a circle or sphere to the circumference or surface – compare DIAMETER **3a** the length of a radius **b** the circular area defined by a stated radius ⟨*within a ~ of 30 miles*⟩ **c** a bounded or circumscribed area ⟨*the hospital serves a wide ~*⟩ ⟨*alerted all police cars within a 2-mile ~*⟩ **4** a part (e g a spoke of a wheel) that extends like a ray from a central point **5** the distance from a centre line or point to an axis of rotation **6** an imaginary radial plane dividing the body of a RADIALLY SYMMETRICAL animal (e g a starfish) into similar parts [L, ray, radius]

[2]**radius** *vt* to give a rounded edge to (e g a machine part)

**radius of curvature** *n* the RECIPROCAL of the curvature of a curve

**radius of gyration** *n* the SQUARE ROOT of the quotient of a MOMENT OF INERTIA of a body and its mass

**radius vector** *n* **1** the length of a line segment from a fixed point (e g the origin in a system of POLAR COORDINATES) to a variable point **2** an imaginary straight line joining the centre of an attracting body (e g the sun) with that of a body (e g a planet) in orbit around it

**radix** /'raydiks/ *n, pl* **radices** /'raydi,seez/, **radixes 1** BASE 5d(1) **2** the root of a plant **3** an anatomical RADICLE; *esp* a root of a nerve arising from the lower surface of the brain or the SPINAL CORD [L, root]

**radix point** *n* a dot (e g a decimal point) separating INTEGRAL (whole) and fractional parts of a number

**radome** /'ray,dohm/ *n* a housing sheltering a radar antenna, esp on an aircraft [*radar dome*]

**radon** /'raydon/ *n* a heavy radioactive stable gaseous chemical element formed by disintegration of the element radium [ISV, fr *radium*]

**radula** /'radyoolə/ *n, pl* **radulae** /-lie/ *also* **radulas** a horny band covered with minute teeth that is found in snails, whelks, etc and is used to tear up food and draw it into the mouth [NL, fr L, scraper, fr *radere* to scrape – more at RAT] – **radular** *adj*

**raffia, raphia** /'rafi-ə/ *n* the fibre of the raffia palm, used for tying plants and for making baskets, hats, and table mats [Malagasy *rafia*]

**raffia palm** *n* a palm tree (*Raphia ruffia*) of Madagascar that has enormous fan-shaped leaves and the leafstalks of which yield raffia

**raffinose** /'rafinohs/ *n* a slightly sweet sugar, $C_{18}H_{32}O_{16}$, obtained commercially from cottonseed meal and present in many plant products [Fr, fr *raffiner* to refine, fr *re-* + *affiner* to make fine, fr *a-* ad- (fr L *ad-*) + *fin* fine]

**raffish** /'rafish/ *adj* **1** flashily vulgar **2** carelessly unconventional and somewhat disreputable [*raff* (jumble, rubbish, disreputable person), fr ME *raf*, perh fr MF *raffe*, *rafle* act of snatching, sweeping] – **raffishly** *adv*, **raffishness** *n*

[1]**raffle** /'rafl/ *vt or n* (to dispose of by means of) a lottery in which the prizes are usually goods ⟨~ *a turkey*⟩ – sometimes + *off* [ME *rafle*, a dice game, fr MF]

[2]**raffle** *n, chiefly nautical* rubbish; *specif* a tangle of ropes [prob fr Fr *rafle* act of snatching, sweeping, fr MF *raffe*, *rafle*, fr MHG *raffen* to snatch; akin to OE *hreppan* to touch, *hearpe* harp – more at HARP]

[1]**raft** /rahft/ *n* **1a** a collection of logs or timber fastened together so that they can be transported by water **b** a flat usu wooden structure designed to float on water and used as a vessel or platform **2** a floating cohesive mass (e g of seaweed or insect eggs) **3** a collection of aquatic animals, esp waterfowl, resting on the water **4** a usu reinforced concrete foundation slab laid on soft ground to take the weight of a building [ME *rafte* rafter, raft, fr ON *raptr* rafter]

[2]**raft** *vt* **1a** to transport in the form of or by means of a raft **b** to cross (e g a lake or river) by raft **2** to make into a raft ~ *vi* to travel by raft – **raftsman** *n*

[3]**raft** *n, chiefly NAm* a large collection or quantity ⟨*assembled a ~ of facts and figures – New Yorker*⟩ [alter. (influenced by [1]*raft*) of *raff* (jumble)]

[1]**rafter** /'rahftə/ *n* any of the sloping usu parallel beams that form part of the framework of a roof [ME, fr OE *ræfter;* akin to ON *raptr* rafter]

[2]**rafter** *vb, chiefly Can, vi of ice* to pile up in large slabs, esp to a great height ~ *vt* to cause to rafter

[3]**rafter** *n* one who manoeuvres logs into position and binds them into rafts [[2]*raft*]

[1]**rag** /rag/ *n* **1a** a waste piece of cloth, esp when in poor or ragged condition **2** something resembling a rag; *esp* a scrap or unevenly shaped fragment of something ⟨*a ~ of cloud*⟩ **3** the pithy parts of a citrus fruit **4** shredded tobacco used esp for cigarettes **5** *chiefly derog* a newspaper [ME *ragge*, fr (assumed) OE *ragg*, fr ON *rögg* tuft, shagginess – more at RUG] – **lose one's rag** *informal* to lose one's temper – **red rag to a bull** *informal* something that causes uncontrollable anger – see also CHEW **the rag**

[2]**rag** *n* any of various hard rocks used in building ⟨*Kentish ~*⟩ [origin unknown]

[3]**rag** *vb* **-gg-** *chiefly Br informal vt* **1** to scold **2** to torment, tease ~ *vi* to indulge in horseplay; behave noisily ⟨*Evans and Jones were ~ging in the corridor*⟩ □ no longer in vogue [origin unknown]

[4]**rag** *n, chiefly Br* **1** a series of processions and stunts organized by students to raise money for charity ⟨~ *week*⟩ **2** *informal* an outburst of boisterous fun; a prank – no longer in vogue

[5]**rag** *n* (a composition or dance in) ragtime [short for *ragtime*]

**raga** /'rahgə/ *n* **1** any of the ancient traditional melodic patterns in Indian music **2** an improvisation based on a traditional raga – compare TALA [Skt *rāga*, lit., colour, tone]

**ragamuffin** /'ragə,mufin/ *n* a ragged often disreputable person, esp a child [*Ragamoffyn*, a demon in the poem *Piers Plowman* by William Langland †1400 E poet]

**rag-and-bone man** *n, chiefly Br* a usu travelling dealer in things of low value (e g old clothes, newspapers, and furniture)

**ragbag** /'rag,bag/ *n* **1** a bag in which scraps of fabric are stored **2** *informal* a miscellaneous collection ⟨*a ~ of prejudices*⟩ **3** *informal* a dishevelled or slovenly person

**rag bolt** *n* a bolt that has barbs on the part between its head and its thread to grip the material in which it is set [[1]*rag* (in the sense "jagged projection on cast metal")]

**rag doll** *n* a stuffed cloth doll

[1]**rage** /rayj/ *n* **1a** violent and uncontrolled anger **b** a fit or bout of such anger **2** violent action (e g of the wind or sea) **3** an intense feeling; a passion **4** *informal* a fashionable enthusiasm; *also* an object of such enthusiasm ⟨*enormous hats were all the ~*⟩ **5** *archaic* insanity **synonyms** see [1]ANGER [ME, fr MF, fr LL *rabia*, fr L *rabies* rage, madness, fr *rabere* to be mad; akin to Skt *rabhas* violence]

[2]**rage** *vi* **1** to be in a rage **2** to be violently stirred up or in tumult ⟨*the wind ~d outside*⟩ **3** to be unchecked in violence or destructive effect ⟨*smallpox was raging*⟩ ⟨*the controversy still ~s*⟩

**ragged** /'ragid/ *adj* **1** roughly unkempt; shaggy **2** having an irregular edge or outline ⟨*a ~ shoreline*⟩ **3** torn or worn to tatters **4** wearing tattered clothes **5a** straggly **b** executed or performed in an irregular, faulty, or uneven manner ⟨*a rambling, ~ ... book – TLS*⟩ **c** *of a sound* harsh, dissonant – **raggedly** *adv*, **raggedness** *n*

**ragged robin** *n* a Eurasian plant (*Lychnis flos-cuculi*) of the pink family with ragged pink flowers

**ragged school** *n, Br* an early charity school that taught children from impoverished families

**raggedy** /'ragidi/ *adj, informal* ragged

**raggle-taggle** /'ragl ,tagl/ *adj* unkempt, ragged ⟨~ *gypsies*⟩ [irreg fr *ragtag*]

**ragi, ragee, raggee** *also* **raggy** /'rahgee, 'ra-/ *n* an E Indian cereal grass (*Eleusine coracana*) yielding a main food crop in the Orient; *also* the seeds of ragi used for food [Hindi *rāgī*]

**raging** /'rayjing/ *adj* **1** causing great pain or distress ⟨~ *toothache*⟩ **2** violent, wild **3** *informal* extraordinary, tremendous ⟨*a ~ success*⟩

**raglan** /'raglən/ *n* a loose overcoat with raglan sleeves [F J H Somerset, Baron *Raglan* †1855 E field marshal]

**raglan sleeve** *n* a sleeve that extends to the neckline with slanted seams from under the arm to the neck

**ragman** /'rag,man, -mən/ *n* RAG-AND-BONE MAN

**Ragnarök** /'rahgnərok/ *n* a final conflict between the gods and the powers of evil that according to Norse mythology will result in the destruction of the world [ON *ragna rök*, lit., destined end of the gods]

**ragout** /'ragooh, -'-/ *n* **1** a well-seasoned stew, esp of meat and vegetables, cooked in a thick sauce **2** a mixture, mélange [Fr *ragoût*, fr *ragoûter* to revive the taste, fr *re-* + *a-* ad- (fr L *ad-*) + *goût* taste, fr L *gustus;* akin to L *gustare* to taste – more at CHOOSE] – **ragout** *vt*

**ragpicker** /'rag,pikə/ *n* one who deals in rags and refuse for a livelihood

**ragtag and bobtail** *also* **rag, tag, and bobtail** /,rag ,tag ən(d) 'bobtayl/ *n, derog* (the) rabble [¹*rag* + ¹*tag*]

**ragtime** /'rag,tiem/ *n* **1** a rhythm characterized by strong SYNCOPATION (temporary displacement of the regular rhythmic accent) in the melody with a regularly accented accompaniment **2** music or dance having ragtime rhythm, popular esp in the 1920s [prob fr *ragged* + *time*]

**rag trade** *n, informal* the clothing trade, comprising the design, manufacture, and selling of clothes

**ragweed** /'rag,weed/ *n* any of various chiefly N American plants (genus *Ambrosia*) of the daisy family whose pollen is a major cause of hay fever

**ragworm** /'rag,wuhm/ *n* any of various marine segmented worms (family Nereidae of the class Polychaeta) that have pairs of bristly flat appendages used for locomotion and are used as bait by sea anglers

**ragwort** /'rag,wuht/ *n* any of several plants (genus *Senecio*) of the daisy family that have bright yellow flowers and are common weeds of cultivated land

**rah** *also* **ra** /rah/ *interj, chiefly NAm* hurrah – used esp to cheer on a team

¹**raid** /rayd/ *n* **1a** a hostile invasion for a limited or specified object ⟨*a cattle* ∼⟩ **b** a surprise attack by a small force **c** AIR RAID **d** an act of robbery ⟨*a bank* ∼⟩ **2** a sudden invasion by the police (e g in search of criminals or stolen goods or to suppress illegal activities) **3** an attempt by professional operators to depress stock-exchange prices by concerted selling **4** *chiefly humorous* a brief foray outside one's usual sphere, esp to obtain something ⟨*a* ∼ *on the local antique shops*⟩ [Sc dial., fr OE *rād* ride, raid – more at ROAD]

²**raid** *vt* to make a raid on ⟨*who's been* ∼ing *the larder?*⟩ ∼ *vi* to conduct or take part in a raid

**raider** /'raydə/ *n* one who or that which raids: e g **a** a fast lightly armed ship operating against merchant shipping **b** one who commits a robbery

¹**rail** /rayl/ *n* **1a** an esp horizontal bar, usu supported by posts, which serves as a guard, a barrier (e g across a balcony), or a support on or from which something (e g a curtain) is hung **b** a horizontal structural member or support (e g in a door) **c** an electrical conductor maintained at a constant voltage and used (e g on a printed circuit board) to supply a number of circuit elements with power at a fixed voltage **2a** RAILING 1a **b** a light structure serving as a guard at the outer edge of a ship's deck **c** **rails** *pl*, **rail** either of the fences on each side of a horse-racing track ⟨*found himself hemmed in on the* ∼*s at the finish*⟩ **3a** either of a pair of lengths of rolled steel forming a guide and running surface (e g a railway) for wheeled vehicles **b** the railway ⟨*always travels by* ∼⟩ [ME *raile*, fr MF *reille* ruler, bar, fr L *regula* ruler, fr *regere* to keep straight, direct, rule – more at RIGHT] – **be/go off the rails** *informal, of a person* **1** to be or become mentally disturbed; behave strangely **2** to be or become misguided or mistaken

²**rail** *vt* to enclose or separate with a railing; fence – often + *off*

³**rail** *n, pl* **rails**, *esp collectively* **rail** any of numerous wading birds (family Rallidae) that are structurally related to the cranes but are of small or medium size and have short rounded wings, a short tail, and usu very long toes which enable them to run on soft wet ground [ME *raile*, fr MF *raale*]

⁴**rail** *vi* to utter angry complaints or abuse – often + *against* or *at* ⟨∼ed *against his fate*⟩ **synonyms** see ²SCOLD [ME *railen*, fr MF *railler* to mock, fr OProv *ralhar* to babble, joke, fr (assumed) VL *ragulare* to bray, fr LL *ragere* to neigh] – **railer** *n*

**railcar** /'rayl,kah/ *n* a self-propelled railway carriage – called also MOTOR CAR

**rail fence** *n* a fence made of posts and split rails

**railhead** /'rayl,hed/ *n* **1** a point on a railway at which military supplies are unloaded for distribution **2** the farthest point reached by a railway; *also* the point at which goods are transferred to or from road transport

**railing** /'rayling/ *n* **1a** a usu vertical rail in a fence or similar barrier **b** **railings** *pl*, **railing** a barrier consisting of a rail and supports **2** (material for making) rails

**raillery** /'rayl(ə)ri/ *n* (a piece of) good-humoured teasing or ridicule [Fr *raillerie*, fr MF, fr *railler* to mock]

¹**railroad** /'rayl,rohd/ *n, NAm* a railway

²**railroad** *vt* **1a** to push through hastily or without due consideration ⟨∼ *a bill through the legislature*⟩ **b** to hustle (an unwilling person) into taking action or making a decision **2** *NAm* to transport by railway **3** *NAm* to convict with undue haste and by means of false charges or insufficient evidence – **railroader** *n*

**railway** /'rayl,way/ *n, chiefly Br* a line of track consisting of usu two parallel rails that are fixed to sleepers embedded in a layer of ballast and that provide the support on which vehicles, esp trains, with flanged wheels run to transport goods and passengers; *also* such a track and its assets (e g ROLLING STOCK and buildings) constituting a single property

**railwayman** /'raylwaymən/ *n, Br* a railway worker

**raiment** /'raymənt/ *n, poetic* clothing, attire ⟨*the heroine garbed in flowing* ∼ – *New York Times*⟩ [ME *rayment*, short for *arrayment*, fr *arrayen* to array]

¹**rain** /rayn/ *n* **1a** water falling in drops condensed from vapour in the atmosphere; *also* the descent of such water **b** water that has fallen as rain; rainwater **c** **rain, rainfall** a fall of rain; a rainstorm **2** *pl* the rainy season **3** rainy weather **4** a heavy fall or flow of liquid or solid particles or objects ⟨*a* ∼ *of petals*⟩ ⟨*a steady* ∼ *of fire from the helicopters*⟩ [ME *reyn*, fr OE *regn, rēn;* akin to OHG *regan* rain]

²**rain** *vi* **1** *of rain* to fall as water in drops from the clouds **2** to send down rain ⟨*it's* ∼ing⟩ **3** to fall in profusion ⟨*congratulations* ∼ed *on his head*⟩ ∼ *vt* **1** to cause to fall; pour or send down **2** to bestow abundantly; shower ⟨∼ed *presents on her*⟩ – **rain off**, *NAm* **rain out** *vt* to interrupt or prevent (e g a sporting fixture) by rain – usu pass ⟨*the match was* rained off⟩

**rainbird** /'rayn,buhd/ *n* any of numerous birds (esp of the family Cuculidae) whose cries are popularly believed to indicate oncoming rain

**rainbow** /'raynboh/ *n* **1** a series of concentric arcs each containing a concentric sequence of colours (e g red, orange, yellow, green, blue, indigo, and violet) that is formed in the sky opposite the sun by the REFRACTION, reflection, and INTERFERENCE of light rays (e g from the sun) in raindrops, spray, or mist **2** an array of bright colours

'**rainbow-,coloured** *adj* coloured like a rainbow; *broadly* of many colours

**rainbow trout** *n* a large plump-bodied trout (*Salmo gairdneri*) of Europe and western N America that typically is greenish above and white on the belly with a pink, red, or lavender stripe along each side of the body and with profuse black dots

**rain check** *n, NAm* an assurance that an offer that cannot at present be accepted will remain open; *esp* an assurance that a customer can take advantage of a sale later if the item or service offered is not available (e g by being sold out) ⟨*if it's OK with you, I'll take a* ∼ *on that*⟩ [orig referring to the stub of a ticket for an outdoor event, kept by a spectator to get free admission to a later performance if the event is interrupted by rain]

**raincoat** /-,koht/ *n* a coat made from waterproof or water-resistant material

**raindrop** /'rayn,drop/ *n* a drop of rain

**rainfall** /-,fawl/ *n* **1** RAIN 1c **2** the amount of rain or snow, usu measured by the depth in millimetres or inches, that has fallen in a given area during a given time

**rain forest** *n* a dense tropical woodland with an annual rainfall of at least 2500 millimetres (about 100 inches) and containing tall broad-leaved evergreen trees forming a continuous canopy

**rain gauge** *n* an instrument for measuring the quantity of rainfall

**rainmaking** /'rayn,mayking/ *n* the action or process of producing or attempting to produce rain by artificial means – **rainmaker** *n*

**rainproof** /-,proohf/ *vt or adj* (to make) impervious to rain

**rain shadow** *n* an area of lighter rainfall in the shelter of a mountain range

**rainstorm** /'rayn,stawm/ *n* a storm of or with rain

**rain tree** *n* MONKEYPOD [fr the belief that it exudes water from its leaflets]

**rainwater** /'rayn,wawtə/ *n* water fallen as rain that has not taken up matter dissolved from the soil and is therefore soft

**rainwear** /'rayn,weə/ *n* waterproof or water-resistant clothing

**rainy** /'rayni/ *adj* **1** having or characterized by heavy rainfall ⟨*the* ~ *season*⟩ ⟨*a* ~ *region*⟩ **2** bringing rain ⟨~ *clouds*⟩ **3** wet with rain ⟨~ *streets*⟩

**rainy day** *n* a future period of usu financial want or need ⟨*save something for a* ~⟩

**¹raise** /rayz/ *vt* **1** to cause or help to rise to an upright or standing position **2a** to awaken, arouse **b** to stir up; incite ⟨~ *a rebellion*⟩ **c** to cause (hunted game) to come out from concealment **d** to recall (as if) from death **e** to establish radio communication with ⟨*can't* ~ *Melbourne*⟩ **3a** to set upright by lifting or building **b** to lift higher **c** to place higher in rank or dignity; elevate **d** to heighten, invigorate ⟨~ *the spirits*⟩ **e** to end or suspend the operation or validity of ⟨~ *a siege*⟩ **4a** to get together for a purpose; collect, levy ⟨~ *funds*⟩ ⟨~ *an army*⟩ **b** to grow, cultivate ⟨~ *cotton*⟩ **c** to rear; BRING UP ⟨~d *five children*⟩ ⟨~s *chickens*⟩ **6a** to give rise to; provoke ⟨~ *a commotion*⟩ ⟨*didn't* ~ *a laugh*⟩ **b** to give voice or expression to ⟨~ *a cheer*⟩ **7** to bring up for consideration or debate ⟨~ *an issue*⟩ **8a** to increase the strength, intensity, degree, or pitch of ⟨~ *the temperature*⟩ **b** to cause to rise in level or amount ⟨~ *the rent*⟩ **c(1)** to increase the amount of (a poker bet) **c(2)** to bet more than (a previous better) **d(1)** to make a higher bridge bid in (a partner's suit) **d(2)** to increase the bid of (one's partner) **9** to make light and porous, esp by adding yeast ⟨~ *dough*⟩ **10** to multiply (a quantity) by itself a number of times so as to produce a specified power ⟨*2* ~d *to the power 3 equals 8*⟩ **11** to bring in sight on the horizon by approaching ⟨~ *land*⟩ **12a** to bring up the surface texture (NAP) of (cloth), esp by brushing **b** to cause (e g a blister) to form on the skin **13** to pronounce (a vowel sound) with the tongue unusually near the roof of the mouth **14** *chiefly NAm* to increase the face value of fraudulently ⟨~ *a cheque*⟩ ~ *vi* **1** to increase a bet or bid – see also **raise an** EYEBROW/**a** FINGER/ HELL/**the** ROOF **2** *dial* to rise [ME *raisen*, fr ON *reisa* – more at REAR] – **raiser** *n*

*usage* **1 Raise (raised, raised)** should not be confused with **rise (rose, risen)**. While **raise** is chiefly transitive ⟨**raise** *the dead*⟩ with only specialized or dialect intransitive senses, **rise** is intransitive only ⟨*prices* **rose**⟩. **2** The use of **raise** for ''rear'' ⟨**raise** *a family*⟩ ⟨**raise** *horses*⟩ ⟨*where were you* **raised**?⟩ was originally an Americanism and is still thought less formal than **breed** (for animals) or **bring up** (for children) in British English. *synonyms see* ¹LIFT *antonym* lower

**²raise** *n* **1** an act of raising or lifting **2** an increase in amount: e g **2a** an increase of a bet or bid **b** *chiefly NAm* an increase in wages or salary; a rise

**raised** /rayzd/ *adj* **1a** done in such a way that some parts of the design stand out from the rest **b** *of a textile* having a surface texture (NAP) produced by brushing **2** leavened with yeast rather than with BAKING POWDER

**raised beach** *n* a beach formed by sea or lake and now above the present water level as a result of either local movements of the earth's crust or lowering of the sea level

**raised pie** *n* a tall pie made with a special type of pastry that is moulded into shape before cooking and retains this shape without the support of a container during cooking

**raisin** /'rayz(ə)n/ *n* a dried grape, usu of a special type [ME, fr MF, grape, fr L *racemus* cluster of grapes or berries]

**raising agent** /'rayzing/ *n* LEAVEN 1 (e g yeast or BAKING POWDER)

**raison d'être** /,rayzon(h) 'detrə (*Fr* rezɔ̃ dɛtr)/ *n* a reason or justification for existence [Fr]

**raj** /rahj/ *n* RULE 3; *specif, cap* British rule in India ⟨*the* Raj *is over* – Roy Hattersley⟩ [Hindi *rāj*, fr Skt *rājya;* akin to Skt *rājan* king]

**Rajab** /rə'jab/ *n* – see MONTH table [Ar]

**rajah, raja** /'rahjə/ *n* **1** an Indian or Malay prince or chief **2** a person bearing a Hindu title of nobility □ compare RANI, MAHARAJAH [Hindi *rājā,* fr Skt *rājan* king – more at ROYAL]

**Rajasthani** /,rahjə'stahni/ *n* the language of Rajasthan, which belongs to the INDIC subdivision of the INDO-EUROPEAN language family [Hindi *Rājasthānī,* fr *Rājasthān* Rajasthan (Rajputana), region in NW India] – **Rajasthani** *adj*

**Rajput, Rajpoot** /'rahjpoot/ *n* a member of a landowning and military class (CASTE) of N India who claim descent from KSHATRIYAS (Hindus of an upper caste) [Hindi *rājpūt,* fr Skt *rājaputra* king's son, fr *rājan* king + *putra* son – more at FEW]

**¹rake** /rayk/ *n* **1** a long-handled implement equipped with pro-

jecting prongs to gather material (e g grass) or for loosening or levelling the surface of the ground; *also* any of several implements similar in shape or use (e g a tool used to draw together the money or chips on a gaming table) **2** a machine, usu with rotating pronged wheels, for gathering hay [ME, fr OE *racu;* akin to OHG *rehho* rake]

**²rake** *vt* **1** to gather, loosen, or level (as if) with a rake **2** to search through thoroughly **3** to sweep the length of, esp with gunfire **4** to glance over rapidly; scan – **raker** *n*

**rake in** *vt, informal* to earn or gain (money) rapidly or abundantly ⟨raked in *a fortune*⟩

**rake up** *vt, informal* **1** to uncover, revive ⟨raked up *an old grievance*⟩ **2** to find or collect, esp with difficulty ⟨*managed to* rake up *enough money for the rent*⟩

**³rake** *vi* to incline from the vertical [origin unknown]

**⁴rake** *n* **1** inclination from the vertical; *esp* the overhang of a ship's bow or stern **2** the angle of inclination from the horizontal; a slope – used esp with reference to a theatre stage **3** the angle between the top cutting surface of a tool and a plane at right angles to the surface of the work **4** the degree to which a wing is swept-back

**⁵rake** *n* a dissolute man, esp in fashionable society; a libertine [short for arch. *rakehell* dissolute person, fr ²*rake* + *hell*]

**rakehelly** /'rayk,heli/ *adj* rascally, dissolute

**'rake-,off** *n, informal* a percentage or share (e g of a profit made by questionable means) taken or received [²*rake* + *off;* fr the use of a rake by a croupier to collect the operator's profits in a gambling casino]

**¹rakish** /'raykish/ *adj* (characteristic) of a rake; dissolute – **rakishly** *adv,* **rakishness** *n*

**²rakish** *adj* **1** *of a ship, boat, etc* having a smart stylish appearance suggestive of speed **2** heedless of convention or formality; dashing, jaunty ⟨*wore his hat at a* ~ *angle*⟩ [prob fr ³*rake;* fr the raking masts of pirate ships] – **rakishly** *adv,* **rakishness** *n*

**rale** /rahl/ *n* an abnormal wheezing sound heard in the chest that accompanies the normal sounds of breathing, due esp to liquid in the lungs [Fr *râle,* fr *râler* to rattle]

**¹rallentando** /,ralən'tandoh/ *adv or adj* with a gradual decrease in speed – used as a direction in music; compare RITARDANDO, RITENUTO [It, lit., slowing down, fr *rallentare* to slow down again, fr *re-* + *allentare* to slow down, fr LL, fr L *al-* ad-+ *lentus* slow, pliant]

**²rallentando** *n, pl* **rallentandos** *also* **rallentandi** /-di/ a gradual decrease in the speed at which music is played

**ralline** /'ralien, 'ralin/ *adj* of or resembling birds of the rail family [ML *rallus* rail, fr MF *raale*]

**¹rally** /'rali/ *vt* **1a** to bring together for a common purpose **b** to recall to order or unity **2a** to arouse for action ⟨rallied *his wits to face this problem*⟩ **b** to rouse from depression or weakness ~ *vi* **1** to come together again to renew an effort ⟨*the* soldiers rallied *at the top of the pass*⟩ **2** to join in a common cause ⟨*thousands will* ~ *to the new party*⟩ **3** to recover, rebound ⟨*began to* ~ *after his long illness*⟩ **4** to engage in a rally [Fr *rallier,* fr OF *ralier,* fr *re-* + *alier* to unite – more at ALLY] – **rallyer** *n*

**²rally** *n* **1a** a mustering of scattered esp military forces to renew an effort **b** a summoning up of strength or courage after weakness or dejection **c** a recovery of price after a decline **d** a renewed offensive **2** a mass meeting intended to arouse enthusiasm among supporters (e g of a political party) **3** a series of strokes exchanged between players (e g in tennis) before a point is won **4** *also* **rallye** a contest of driving and navigation skills in which competitors drive their cars over a course of several stages, often with some of the distance on public roads, with the object of maintaining a specified average speed between checkpoints over a route often unknown before the start of the run [(4) Fr *rallye,* fr E ¹*rally*]

**³rally** *vt* to ridicule or tease in a good-humoured way *synonyms* see ²RIDICULE [Fr *railler* to mock – more at RAIL]

**rallycross** /'rali,kros/ *n* a motor sport in which specially adapted saloon cars race round a short circuit consisting partly of paved surfaces and partly of unpaved surfaces (e g grass and mud) – compare AUTOCROSS [²*rally* + *-cross* (as in *cyclo-cross*)]

**¹ram** /ram/ *n* **1a** a male sheep **b** *cap* ARIES (constellation and zodiac sign) **2a** BATTERING RAM **b** a warship with a heavy metal-pointed beam at the front for piercing an enemy ship **3** any of various parts for exerting pressure or for driving or forcing something by impact: e g **3a** the plunger of a press driven by the pressure exerted by a liquid or a FORCE PUMP that draws or forces liquid through valves **b** the weight that strikes the blow in a machine (PILE DRIVER) that drives heavy posts into the ground [ME, fr OE *ramm;* akin to OHG *ram*]

²**ram** *vb* **-mm-** *vi* to strike with violence; crash ⟨*her car* ~med *into a tree*⟩ ~ *vt* **1** to force down or in by driving, pressing, or pushing ⟨~ *fence posts into the ground*⟩ ⟨~med *his hat down over his ears*⟩ **2a** to make (eg earth) firm and compact by pounding **b** to cram, crowd ⟨*toys* ~med *into the cupboard*⟩ **3** to force passage or acceptance of ⟨~ *home an idea*⟩ **4** to strike against violently and usu head-on – see also **ram something down somebody's** THROAT [ME *rammen,* prob fr *ram,* n] – **rammer** *n*

**Ramadan, Ramadhan** /'ramədan, -dahn, ,--'-/ *n* – see MONTH table [Ar *Ramaḍān*]

**ramate** /'raymayt, 'ram-/ *adj* having branches [L *ramus* branch]

¹**ramble** /'rambl/ *vi* **1a** to move aimlessly from place to place **b** to walk for pleasure, esp without a planned route **2** to talk or write in a desultory or long-winded wandering fashion **3** to grow or extend irregularly ⟨*a rambling old house*⟩ to wander over; roam [perh fr ME *romblen,* freq of *romen* to roam] – **ramblingly** *adv*

²**ramble** *n* a leisurely walk taken purely for pleasure and often without a planned route

**rambler** /'ramblə/ *n* **1** one who rambles **2** any of various climbing roses with rather small, often double, flowers in large clusters

**rambouillet** /,rombooh'yay, ram-/ (*Fr* răbuje)/ *n, often cap* a large sturdy breed of sheep developed in France [*Rambouillet,* town in N France]

**rambunctious** /ram'bungkshəs/ *adj, NAm informal* rumbustious, unruly [prob alter. of *rumbustious*] – **rambunctiously** *adv,* **rambunctiousness** *n*

**rambutan** /ram'boohtn/ *n* a bright red spiny Malayan fruit closely related to the litchi; *also* a tree (*Nephelium lappaceum* of the family Sapindaceae) that bears this fruit [Malay, fr *rambut* hair]

**ramekin, ramequin** /'ram(i)kin/ *n* **1** a preparation of cheese with breadcrumbs, puff pastry, or eggs baked in an individual mould **2** an individual baking and serving dish [Fr *ramequin,* fr LG *ramken,* dim. of *ram* cream, fr MLG *rōm*]

**ramentum** /rə'mentəm/ *n, pl* **ramenta** /-tə/ a thin brownish scale on a leaf or young shoot of a fern [NL, fr L, a shaving, fr *radere* to scratch, scrape – more at RAT]

**ramie** /'raymee, 'ramee/ *n* an Asian woody plant (*Boehmeria nivea*) of the nettle family; *also* the strong shiny flexible flaxlike fibre yielded by the stem of this plant [Malay *rami*]

**ramification** /,ramifi'kaysh(ə)n/ *n* **1a** the act or process of branching out **b** the arrangement of branches (eg on a plant) **2a** a branch, subdivision **b** a branched structure; an offshoot **3** a usu extended or complicated consequence ⟨*the* ~s *of a problem*⟩

**ramiform** /'rami,fawm, 'ray-/ *adj* resembling or constituting branches; branched [L *ramus* branch + E -*iform*]

**ramify** /'ramifie/ *vt* **1** to cause to branch **2** to separate into divisions ~ *vi* **1** to split up into branches or constituent parts **2** to send forth branches or extensions [MF *ramifier,* fr ML *ramificare,* fr L *ramus* branch; akin to L *radix* root – more at ROOT]

**ramjet** /'ram,jet/ *n* a jet engine that uses the flow of compressed air produced by the forward movement of the aeroplane, rocket, etc to burn the fuel [²*ram* + *jet*]

**ramose** /'raymohs/ *adj* consisting of or having branches ⟨*a* ~ *sponge*⟩ [L *ramosus,* fr *ramus* branch] – **ramosely** *adv*

¹**ramp** /ramp/ *vi* **1a** of a heraldic animal to stand or advance menacingly, with forelegs or arms raised **b** *esp of an animal* to move or act furiously; rush *around* **2** *esp of a plant* to climb or spread vigorously [ME *rampen,* fr OF *ramper* to climb, crawl, rear, of Gmc origin; akin to OHG *rimpfan* to wrinkle – more at RUMPLE]

²**ramp** *n* **1** a short usu vertical bend, slope, or curve where a handrail or the top course of a wall changes its direction **2** a sloping way: eg **2a** a sloping floor, walk, or roadway leading from one level to another **b** a stairway for entering or leaving an aircraft **3** APRON 2g (paved part of an airport) [Fr *rampe,* fr *ramper*]

¹**rampage** /ram'payj/ *vi* to rush about wildly or violently [Sc, perh irreg fr ¹*ramp*]

²**rampage** /ram'payj, '--/ *n* violent or uncontrolled behaviour – chiefly in *on the rampage* – **rampageous** *adj,* **rampageously** *adv,* **rampageousness** *n*

**rampant** /'rampənt/ *adj* **1a** rearing on the hind legs with fore-legs extended **b** *of a heraldic animal* standing on one hind foot with one foreleg raised above the other and the head in profile **2a** characterized by wildness or extravagance (eg of opinion or action) ⟨*a* ~ *militarist*⟩ **b** spreading or growing unchecked ⟨*a* ~ *crime wave*⟩ **3** having sides that spring from different levels ⟨*a* ~ *arch*⟩ [ME, fr MF, prp of *ramper* to crawl, rear] – **rampancy** *n,* **rampantly** *adv*

**rampart** /'rampaht/ *n* **1** a broad embankment raised as a for-tification (eg round a fort or city) and usu surmounted by a low wall (PARAPET) **2** a protective barrier; a bulwark ⟨*a great* ~ *of mountains*⟩ **3** a wall-like ridge (eg of rock fragments, earth, or debris) [MF *rampart, rempart,* fr *ramparer, remparer* to fortify, strengthen, fr *re-* + *emparer* to defend, protect, deriv of L *ante* before + *parare* to prepare]

**rampion** /'rampyən/ *n* a European flower (*Campanula rapun-culus*) of the harebell family whose fleshy root is sometimes eaten with the leaves in salads [prob modif of MF *raiponce,* fr OIt *raponzo,* prob fr *rapa, rapo* turnip, fr L *rapa, rapum*]

¹**ramrod** /'ramrod/ *n* **1** a thin strong rod for ramming home the charge into a firearm from the discharging end of the barrel **2** a cleaning rod for the barrel of rifles and other small firearms **3** one who or that which is unyielding or rigid; *esp* a strict disciplinarian

²**ramrod** *adj* marked by rigidity, severity, or stiffness

**ramshackle** /'ramshakl/ *adj* carelessly or loosely constructed and in need of repair; rickety [alter. of earlier *ransackled,* fr pp of obs *ransackle,* freq of *ransack*]

**ramshorn** /'ramz,hawn/ *n* a snail (genus *Planorbis*) often used as a scavenger in an aquarium

**ramsons** /'ramsənz, -zənz/ *n taking sing vb* a Eurasian plant (*Allium ursinum*) of the lily family closely related to and smell-ing like garlic; *also* the bulbous root of ramsons, sometimes used in salads [ME *ramsyn,* fr OE *hramsan,* pl of *hramsa* wild garlic; akin to OHG *ramusia* garlic]

**ramus** /'rayməs, 'ram-/ *n, pl* **rami** /-mi, -mie/ a projecting or elongated part or branch (eg a branch of a nerve) [NL, fr L, branch – more at RAMIFY]

**ran** /ran/ *past of* RUN

¹**ranch** /rahnch/ *n* **1** a large farm for raising horses, beef cattle, or sheep, esp in N America and Australia **2** *chiefly NAm* a farm or area devoted to a particular crop or animal ⟨*a poultry* ~⟩ ⟨*an orange* ~⟩ [MexSp *rancho* small ranch, fr Sp, camp, hut & Sp dial., small farm, fr OSp *ranchear* (*se*) to take up quarters, fr MF (*se*) *ranger* to take up a position, fr *ranger* to set in a row – more at RANGE]

²**ranch** *vi* to own or live or work on a ranch ~ *vt* **1** to work as a rancher on **2** to raise on a ranch – **rancher** *n*

**ranchman** /'rahnchmən/ *n* one who owns or works on a ranch

**rancid** /'ransid/ *adj* **1** having a rank smell or taste **2** offensive [L *rancidus,* fr *rancēre* to be rotten] – **rancidity, rancidness** *n*

**rancour,** *NAm* **rancor** /'rangkə/ *n* bitter deep-seated ill will or hatred *synonyms* see ENMITY, VINDICTIVE [ME *rancour,* fr MF *ranceur,* fr LL *rancor* rancidity, rancour, fr L *rancēre*] – **ran-corous** *adj,* **rancorously** *adv*

¹**rand** /rand/ *n, pl* **rand** – see MONEY table [the *Rand,* gold-mining district in S Africa]

²**rand** *n* a strip, usu of leather, put on a shoe before the LIFTS (layers in the heel) are attached [ME, border, fr OE; akin to OHG *rant* edging, rim of a shield, ON *rönd* rim, shield, OE *rima* rim – more at RIM]

¹**random** /'randəm/ *n* [ME, impetuosity, fr MF *randon,* fr OF, fr *randir* to run, of Gmc origin; akin to OHG *rinnan* to run – more at RUN] – **at random** without definite aim, direction, rule, or method

²**random** *adj* **1** lacking a definite plan, purpose, or pattern **2a** marked by absence of bias **b** relating to, having, or being statistical elements or events with an ungoverned or unpredict-able outcome, but with definite probability of occurrence ⟨~ *processes*⟩ **c** being or relating to a statistical sample drawn from a population each member of which has equal probability of occurring in the sample ⟨*a table of* ~ *numbers*⟩; *also* characterized by procedures designed to obtain such samples ⟨~ *sampling*⟩ – **randomly** *adv,* **randomness** *n*

,**random-'access** *adj* permitting access to stored data in any order the user desires ⟨*a* ~ *computer memory*⟩

**random-ize, -ise** /'randəmiez/ *vt* to arrange (eg samples or experimental treatments) so as to simulate a chance distribu-tion, reduce interference by irrelevant variables, and yield unbiased statistical data – **randomizer** *n,* **randomization** *n*

**randomized block** *n* an experimental design (e g in horticulture) in which different treatments are distributed in random order in a block or plot

**random variable** *n* a statistical variable that can take on a defined range of values which are governed by a PROBABILITY DISTRIBUTION ⟨*the number of spots showing if two dice are thrown is a* ∼⟩

**random walk** *n* a statistical process consisting of a sequence of steps each of whose characteristics (e g magnitude and direction) are determined by chance

**randy** /'randi/ *adj* 1 *informal* sexually aroused; lustful, lecherous 2 *chiefly Scot* rowdy, boisterous [prob fr obs *rand* to rant, fr obs D *randen, ranten*]

**rang** /rang/ *past of* RING

**¹range** /raynj/ *n* 1a(1) a series of things in a line; a row a(2) a large connected group of mountains **b** a number of individual people, objects, or products forming a distinct class or series **c** a variety, cross-section ⟨*a good* ∼ *of people here*⟩ 2 a usu solid-fuel fired cooking stove that has one or more ovens and a flat metal, esp iron, top with one or more areas for heating pans 3a an open region over which livestock may roam and feed, esp in N America **b** the region throughout which a kind of living organism or community naturally lives or occurs 4a(1) the distance to which a projectile can be propelled **a(2)** the distance between a weapon and target **b** the maximum distance a vehicle can travel without refuelling **c** a place where shooting (e g with bows, guns, or missiles) is practised; *also* a place where golf drives are practised 5a the space or extent included, covered, or used; the scope **b** the extent of pitch within a melody or within the capacity of a voice or instrument ⟨*the E flat is below my* ∼⟩ 6a a sequence, series, or scale between limits ⟨*a wide* ∼ *of patterns*⟩ **b** the limits of a series; the distance or extent between possible extremes **c** the difference between the least and greatest values of a mathematical function, sequence, or series 7a the set of values a function may take on – compare DOMAIN 4 **b** the class of admissible values of a variable 8 LINE 11 ⟨*advertising their new* ∼ *of garden furniture*⟩ [ME, row of persons, fr OF *renge*, fr *rengier* to range]

**²range** *vt* 1a to set in a row or in the proper order ⟨*troops were* ∼d *on either side of the palace gates*⟩ **b** to place among others in a specified position or situation ⟨∼d *himself with the radicals in his party*⟩ 2a to rove over or through ⟨*ranging the plains*⟩ **b** to sail or pass along 3 to graze (livestock) on a range 4 to determine or give the elevation necessary for (a gun) to propel a projectile to a given distance ∼ *vi* 1a to roam at large or freely ⟨*ranging around the remote countryside*⟩ ⟨*the talk* ∼d *over current topics*⟩ **b** to move over an area so as to explore it 2 to take a position 3 *esp of printing type* to correspond in direction or line; align ⟨*the lines should* ∼ *right*⟩ 4 to extend in a specified direction 5 *of a gun or projectile* to have a specified range ⟨*the gun* ∼s *over 3 miles*⟩ 6 to change or differ within specified limits ⟨*their ages* ∼d *from 5 to 65*⟩ 7 *of an organism* to live or occur in or be native to a specified region [ME *rangen*, fr MF *ranger*, fr OF *rengier*, fr *renc, reng* line, place, row – more at RANK]

**range finder** *n* 1 an instrument used in gunnery to determine the distance of a target 2 a device in a camera that indicates when the object is in focus by comparing images of the object from two different angles

**ranger** /'raynjə/ *n* 1a the keeper of a British royal park or forest **b** an officer who patrols a N American national park or forest 2a a member of any of several organized bodies of armed men in the USA who range over a usu specified region, esp to enforce the law **b** a soldier in the US army specially trained in close-range fighting and in raiding tactics 3 *often cap* a private in an Irish combat regiment 4 *cap* a member of the most senior section of the British Guide movement for girls aged from 14 to 19

**ranging rod** /'raynjing/ *n* a rod usu painted with alternate red and white stripes, used in surveying to mark a straight line

**rangy** /'raynji/ *adj* 1a *of an animal* long-limbed and long-bodied ⟨∼ *cattle*⟩ **b** *of a person* tall and slender 2 having room for ranging; spacious [¹·²*range* + ¹-*y*] – **ranginess** *n*

**rani, ranee** /rah'nee, '--/ *n* a Hindu queen or princess; *esp* the wife of a rajah – compare MAHARANI [Hindi *rānī*, fr Skt *rājnī*, fem of *rājan* king – more at ROYAL]

**¹rank** /rangk/ *adj* 1a luxuriantly or excessively vigorous in growth ⟨∼ *vegetation*⟩ **b** covered with rank vegetation 2 offensively gross or coarse; foul ⟨∼ *language*⟩ 3a shockingly conspicuous; flagrant ⟨*lecture him on his* ∼ *disloyalty*⟩ **b** complete – used as

an intensive ⟨*a* ∼ *outsider*⟩ 4 offensive in smell or flavour; *esp* rancid [ME, fr OE *ranc* overbearing, strong; akin to OE *riht* right – more at RIGHT] – **rankly** *adv*, **rankness** *n*

**²rank** *n* 1a a row, line, or series of people or things ⟨∼s *of trees*⟩ b(1) *taking sing or pl vb* a line of soldiers ranged side by side b(2) *pl* RANK AND FILE 1 ⟨*rose from the* ∼s *to become a major*⟩ ⟨*was reduced to the* ∼s *for misconduct*⟩ **c** any of the eight rows of squares that extend across a chessboard, as opposed to the FILES, which extend up and down 2 **ranks** *pl*, **rank** an orderly arrangement; a formation; *esp* a military formation ⟨*they broke* ∼s *and fled*⟩ 3a a degree or position in a hierarchy or order; *specif* an official position in the armed forces **b** a social class 4a a level of relative excellence ⟨*writing of the very first* ∼⟩ **b** high social position ⟨*the privileges of* ∼⟩ 5 the order according to some statistical characteristic (e g a score in a test) 6 any of a series of classes of coal based on increasing alteration of the original vegetable matter, increasing carbon content, and increasing fuel value 7 the number of rows in a mathematical matrix 8 *Br* a place where taxis wait to pick up passengers ⟨*a cab* ∼⟩ [MF *renc, reng*, of Gmc origin; akin to OHG *hring* ring – more at RING] – **close ranks** to unite in a concerted stand, esp to meet a challenge – **pull rank on somebody** to assert one's authority over somebody, esp in order to get something one wants

**³rank** *vt* 1 to arrange in lines or in a regular formation 2 to determine the relative position of; rate 3 *NAm* to outrank ⟨*a captain* ∼s *a lieutenant*⟩ ∼ *vi* 1 to form or move in ranks 2 to take or have a position in relation to others

**rank and file** *n taking sing or pl vb* 1 the body of other ranks of an armed force, as distinguished from the officers 2 the individuals who constitute the body of an organization, society, or nation, as distinguished from the leading or principal members ⟨∼ *members of the orchestra*⟩ – **rank and filer** *n*

**rank correlation** *n, statistics* a measure of mutual relationship (CORRELATION) depending on rank

**ranker** /'rangkə/ *n* one who serves or has served in the ranks; *esp* a commissioned officer promoted from the ranks

**Rankine** /'rangkin/ *adj* relating to, conforming to, or being an absolute-temperature scale on which water freezes at 491.69° and boils at 671.69° under standard conditions [William *Rankine* †1872 Sc engineer & physicist]

**ranking** /'rangking/ *adj, chiefly NAm* having a high or the highest position: e g a foremost ⟨∼ *poet*⟩ **b** next to the chairman in seniority ⟨∼ *committee member*⟩

**rankle** /'rangkl/ *vi* 1 to cause continuing anger, irritation, or deep bitterness 2 to feel anger and irritation ∼ *vt, archaic* to cause irritation or bitterness in [ME *ranclen* to fester, fr MF *rancler*, fr OF *draoncler, raoncler*, fr *draoncle, raoncle* festering sore, fr (assumed) VL *dracunculus*, fr L, dim. of *draco* serpent – more at DRAGON]

**ransack** /'ransak/ *vt* to search in a disordered but thorough manner; *also* to rob or plunder in the course of such a search [ME *ransaken*, fr ON *rannsaka*, fr *rann* house + *-saka* (akin to OE *sēcan* to seek)] – **ransacker** *n*

**¹ransom** /'ransəm/ *n* 1 a price paid or demanded for the release of a captured or kidnapped person 2 the act of ransoming [ME *ransoun*, fr OF *rançon*, fr L *redemption-, redemptio* – more at REDEMPTION]

**²ransom** *vt* 1 to deliver or redeem, esp from sin or its consequences 2 to free from captivity or punishment by paying a price – **ransomer** *n*

**¹rant** /rant/ *vi* to talk in a noisy, excited, and usu empty manner ∼ *vt* to declaim noisily, excitedly, and usu emptily [obs D *ranten, randen*] – **rantingly** *adv*

**²rant** *n* 1 a high-sounding extravagant usu empty speech 2 high-sounding extravagant usu empty language

**ranter** /'rantə/ *n* 1 one who rants 2 *often cap* 2a a member of a Christian sect that arose in the 1640s and held the ANTINOMIAN view that there is no obligation to follow moral law **b** *derog* PRIMITIVE METHODIST (a member of an early breakaway Methodist sect)

**ranula** /'ranyoolə/ *n* a liquid-filled pouch (CYST) formed under the tongue by obstruction of a channel arising from a gland [NL, fr L, swelling on the tongue of cattle, fr dim. of *rana* frog]

**ranunculus** /rə'nungkyooləs/ *n, pl* **ranunculuses, ranunculi** /-li/ any of a large widely distributed genus (*Ranunculus*) of plants of the buttercup family including the buttercups and crowfoots [NL, genus name, fr L, tadpole, crowfoot, dim. of *rana* frog]

**¹rap** /rap/ *n* **1** a sharp blow or knock; *also* the short sharp sound made by such a blow ⟨*heard a ~ on the door*⟩ **2** a sharp rebuke or criticism **3** *informal* **3a** the responsibility for or adverse consequences (e g blame or punishment) of an action ⟨*I ended up taking the ~*⟩ **b** *chiefly NAm* CHARGE 6; *esp* a criminal charge ⟨*had to bribe the jury to beat the ~*⟩ [ME *rappe*, prob of imit origin]

**²rap** *vb* **-pp-** *vt* **1** to strike with a sharp blow **2** to express or communicate (e g a message) by means of sharp taps – usu + *out* **3** to utter (e g a remark or command) abruptly and forcibly – usu + *out* **4** to train (a horse) to jump more carefully by abruptly raising a fence bar during the jump so that the bar hits the horse **5** *journalistic* to criticize sharply ⟨*judge ~s police*⟩ **6** *chiefly NAm slang* to arrest, hold, or sentence on a criminal charge ~ *vi* **1** to strike a quick sharp blow **2** to make the short sharp sound of a rap – see also **rap somebody over the** KNUCKLES

**³rap** *n, informal* the least bit (e g of care or consideration) ⟨*doesn't care a ~*⟩ [arch. *rap* counterfeit coin in Ireland, smallest coin, prob fr IrGael *ropaire*]

**⁴rap** *n, chiefly NAm slang* talk, conversation [perh by shortening & alter. fr *repartee*]

**⁵rap** *vi* **-pp-** *chiefly NAm slang* to talk freely and frankly ⟨*a place where they could meet and ~ congenially ... with people ... with similar interests and problems*⟩

**rapacious** /rə'payshəs/ *adj* **1** excessively grasping or covetous ⟨*in an age of unscrupulous plunder he was among the most ~ – TLS*⟩ **2** *of an animal* living on prey **3** ravenous, voracious ⟨*a ~ appetite*⟩ [L *rapac-, rapax*, fr *rapere* to seize] – **rapaciously** *adv*, **rapaciousness, rapacity** *n*

    **synonyms** Both **rapacious** and **voracious** mean "greedy"; but **rapacious**, derived from the Latin for "seize", is used especially of greed for money ⟨*a* **rapacious** *landlord*⟩ and is more derogatory, because crueller, than **voracious**, from the Latin for "devour".

**¹rape** /rayp/ *n* a European plant (*Brassica napus*) of the cabbage family grown as animal feed and for its seeds which yield rapeseed oil [ME, fr L *rapa, rapum* turnip, rape; akin to OHG *rāba* turnip, rape, Gk *rhapys* turnip]

**²rape** *vt* **1** to despoil **2** to commit rape on **3** *archaic* to seize and take away by force [ME *rapen*, fr L *rapere*] – **rapist** *n*

**³rape** *n* **1** an act or instance of robbing or despoiling or carrying away a person by force ⟨*the ~ of the countryside*⟩ ⟨*the ~ of the Sabine women*⟩ **2** (an instance of) the crime of forcing somebody, esp a woman, to have sexual intercourse against her/his will **3** an outrageous violation (e g of a principle or institution) ⟨*a ~ of Justice*⟩

**⁴rape** *n* the remains of grapes (e g skins and pips) after they have been pressed [Fr *râpe* grape stalk, prob of Gmc origin]

**rapeseed** /'rayp,seed/ *n* the seed of the rape plant

**rapeseed oil, rape oil** *n* an oil obtained from rapeseed and turnip seed and used chiefly as a cooking oil and lubricant

**raphe, rhaphe** /'ray,fee/ *n* **1** the seamlike union of the two halves of a part or organ (e g the tongue) appearing externally as a ridge or furrow **2a** the part of the stalk of an inverted plant ovary that is united in growth to the outside covering and forms a ridge along the body of the OVULE (immature seed before fertilization) **b** the median line of one of the two membranes enclosing a DIATOM (microscopic alga) [NL, fr Gk *rhaphē* seam, fr *rhaptein* to sew – more at RHAPSODY]

**raphia** /'rafi•ə/ *n* raffia

**raphide** /'rafied/ *n* one of the needle-shaped crystals usu of calcium OXALATE that develop as metabolic by-products in plant cells [Fr & NL; Fr *raphide*, fr NL *raphides*, pl, modif of Gk *rhaphides*, pl of *rhaphid-, rhaphis* needle, fr *rhaptein* to sew]

**rapid** /'rapid/ *adj* **1** occurring with speed; happening within a short time ⟨*~ growth*⟩ **2** moving or acting with speed; swift ⟨*a ~ reader*⟩ **3** characterized by speed ⟨*a ~ stream*⟩ **synonyms** see ¹FAST *antonym* sluggish [L *rapidus* seizing, sweeping, rapid, fr *rapere* to seize, sweep away; akin to OE *refsan* to blame] – **rapidly** *adv*, **rapidity** *also* **rapidness** *n*

**rapid eye movement** *n* a rapid movement of the eyes that is associated with certain phases of sleep during which dreams are particularly common

**rapid-'fire** *adj* **1** (adapted for) firing shots in rapid succession **2** *esp of speech* proceeding with or characterized by rapidity, liveliness, or sharpness ⟨*~ interrogation*⟩

**rapids** /'rapidz/ *n pl*, **rapid** *n* a part of a river where the current is fast and the surface is usu broken by rocks

**rapid transit** *n* fast passenger transport (e g by underground railway) in urban areas

**rapier** /'raypi•ə/ *n* a straight two-edged sword with a narrow pointed blade [MF (*espee*) *rapiere*]

**rapine** /'rapien/ *n, formal or archaic* pillage, plunder [ME *rapyne*, fr L *rapina*, fr *rapere* to seize, rob]

**rapparee** /,rapə'ree/ *n* a 17th-century Irish bandit or soldier who was not part of the regular army [IrGael *rāpaire*]

**rappee** /ra'pee/ *n* a strong snuff made from dark tobacco leaves [Fr (*tabac*) *râpé*, lit., grated tobacco]

**rappel** /ra'pel/ *vi* **-ll-** (*NAm* **-l-, -ll-**) ABSEIL (descend steep rock face by rope) [Fr, lit., recall, fr OF *rapel*, fr *rapeler* to recall, fr *re-* + *apeler* to appeal, call – more at APPEAL] – **rappel** *n*

**rappen** /'rahpən, 'ra-/ *n, pl* **rappen** /~/ the Swiss centime [Ger, lit., raven; akin to OHG *hraban* raven – more at RAVEN]

**rapport** /ra'paw/ *n* a sympathetic or harmonious relationship [Fr, fr *rapporter* to bring back, refer, fr OF *raporter* to bring back, fr *re-* + *aporter* to bring, fr L *apportare*, fr *ad-* + *portare* to carry – more at FARE]

**rapporteur** /,rapaw'tuh/ *n* a person responsible for preparing and presenting reports (e g from a committee to a higher body) [Fr, fr *rapporter* to bring back, report]

**rapprochement** /ra'proshmonh/ *n* the reestablishment of cordial relations, esp between nations [Fr, fr *rapprocher* to bring together, fr MF, fr *re-* + *approcher* to approach, fr OF *aprochier*]

**rapscallion** /rap'skalyən/ *n, archaic or humorous* a rascal [alter. of earlier *rascallion*, fr ¹*rascal*]

**rapt** /rapt/ *adj* **1** lifted up and carried away (e g by a supernatural force) ⟨*~ into future times, the bard began* – Alexander Pope⟩ **2** transported with emotion; enraptured **3** wholly absorbed; engrossed △ wrapped [ME, fr L *raptus*, pp of *rapere* to seize – more at RAPID] – **raptly** *adv*, **raptness** *n*

**raptor** /'raptə/ *n* a bird of prey [deriv of L *raptor* plunderer, fr *raptus*]

**raptorial** /rap'tawri•əl/ *adj* **1** *esp of a bird* living off prey; predacious **2** *of birds' feet* adapted to seize prey **3** relating to or being a bird of prey

**¹rapture** /'rapchə/ *n* **1a** a state or experience of being carried away by overwhelming emotion **b** a mystical experience in which the spirit is exalted to a knowledge of divine things **2** an expression or manifestation of ecstasy, passion, or extreme delight ⟨*went into ~s over the new car*⟩ [L *raptus*, pp] – **rapturous** *adj*, **rapturously** *adv*, **rapturousness** *n*

**²rapture** *vt*, *archaic* to enrapture

**rara avis** /,rahrə 'ayvis, ,reərə/ *n, pl* **rara avises, rarae aves** /,rahrie 'ayveez, ,reərie/ a rare person or thing; a rarity [L, rare bird]

**¹rare** /reə/ *adj*, *of meat* cooked so that the inside is still red ⟨*~ roast beef*⟩ [alter. of earlier *rere*, fr ME, fr OE *hrēre* boiled lightly; akin to OE *hrēran* to stir, OHG *hruoren*]

**²rare** *adj* **1** marked by wide separation of component particles; thin ⟨*a ~ atmosphere*⟩ **2** marked by unusual quality, merit, or appeal; distinctive ⟨*to show ~ tact*⟩ **3** seldom occurring or found; uncommon ⟨*a ~ moth*⟩ **4** *informal* very great or extreme ⟨*gave her a ~ fright*⟩ [ME, fr L *rarus*] – **rareness** *n*

    **synonyms** Uncommon and perhaps valuable things are **rare** ⟨*a* **rare** *bird/coin*⟩. Common useful things that we are short of, perhaps temporarily, are **scarce** ⟨*potatoes were* **scarce** *last winter*⟩. **Rare**, but not **scarce**, can mean "infrequent" ⟨*one of my* **rare** *visits to Paris*⟩.

**rarebit** /'reəbit/ *n* WELSH RAREBIT

**rare earth** *n* **1** any of a group of similar OXIDES of metals or a mixture of such oxides occurring together in widely distributed but relatively scarce minerals **2** RARE-EARTH ELEMENT

**rare-earth element** *n* any of a series of metallic elements of which the OXIDES are classed as RARE EARTHS and which include the elements with ATOMIC NUMBERS from 58 to 71, as well as usu the chemical element lanthanum and sometimes the elements yttrium and scandium

**rarefaction** /,reəri'faksh(ə)n/ *n* **1** the action or process of rarefying **2** the quality or state of being rarefied **3** a state or region of minimum pressure in a medium traversed by longitudinal waves (e g sound waves) [Fr or ML; Fr *raréfaction*, fr ML *rarefaction-, rarefactio*, fr L *rarefactus*, pp of *rarefacere* to rarefy] – **rarefactional, rarefactive** *adj*

**rarefied** *also* **rarified** /'reərified/ *adj* **1** of or interesting to a select group; esoteric, abstruse **2** very high or exalted (e g in rank) ⟨*moved in ~ political circles*⟩

**rarefy** *also* **rarify** /'reərifie/ *vt* **1** to make rare, thin, porous, or less dense **2** to make more spiritual, refined, or abstruse ~ *vi* to become less dense [ME *rarefien, rarifien*, fr MF *rarefier*, modif of L *rarefacere*, fr *rarus* rare + *facere* to make – more at DO]

**rare gas** *n* NOBLE GAS

**rarely** /'reəli/ *adv* **1** not often; seldom **2** with rare skill; excellently **3** in an extreme or exceptional manner *usage* see ¹SELDOM

**raring** /'reəring/ *adj* full of enthusiasm or eagerness ⟨~ *to go*⟩ [fr prp of E dial. *rare* to rear, alter. of ¹*rear*]

**rarity** /'reərəti/ *n* **1** the quality, state, or fact of being rare **2** one who or that which is rare

¹**rascal** /'rahskəl/ *n* **1** an unprincipled or dishonest person **2** *chiefly humorous* a mischievous person or animal [ME *rascaile* rabble, one of the rabble, prob fr ONF *rasque* mud]

²**rascal** *adj, archaic* of, forming, or befitting the rabble; low

**rascality** /rah'skaləti/ *n* **1a** the character or actions of a rascal; knavery **b** a rascally act **2** *taking sing or pl vb, archaic* the rabble

**rascally** /'rahskəli/ *adj* (characteristic) of a rascal – **rascally** *adv*

**raschel** /rah'shel/ *n* a WARP-KNITTED (with the yarns running lengthwise) fabric, usu with openwork patterns – compare TRICOT [*Raschel* (*machine*), a kind of loom, fr Ger *Raschelmaschine*, fr *Rachel* (Elisa Félix) †1858 Fr actress]

**rase** /rayz/ *vt* to raze, demolish

¹**rash** /rash/ *adj* acting with, marked by, or proceeding from undue haste or lack of deliberation or caution *synonyms* see ¹ADVENTURE *antonyms* circumspect, prudent [ME (northern) *rasch* quick; akin to OHG *rasc* fast] – **rashly** *adv*, **rashness** *n*

²**rash** *n* **1** an outbreak of spots on the body **2** a large number of instances in a short period ⟨*a* ~ *of arrests*⟩ [obs Fr *rache* scurf, fr OF *rasche*, fr (assumed) VL *rasica*, fr *rasicare* to scratch, fr L *rasus*, pp of *radere* to scrape, shave]

**rasher** /'rashə/ *n* a thin slice of bacon or ham [perh fr obs *rash* to cut, fr ME *rashen*]

**rasorial** /rə'sawriəl/ *adj, of a bird* habitually scratching the ground in search of food [deriv of LL *rasor* scraper, fr L *rasus*, pp of *radere* to scrape, shave]

¹**rasp** /rahsp/ *vt* **1** to rub with something rough; *specif* to file with a rasp **2** to grate on; irritate **3** to utter in a grating tone ~ *vi* **1** to scrape **2** to produce a grating sound [ME *raspen*, fr (assumed) MF *rasper*, of Gmc origin; akin to OHG *raspōn* to scrape together] – **rasper** *n*, **raspingly** *adv*

²**rasp** *n* **1** a coarse file with cutting points instead of lines **2** something used for rasping **3** a rasping sound, sensation, or effect

**raspatory** /'raspət(ə)ri/ *n* a rasp used by surgeons [ML *raspatorium*, fr *raspare*, pp of *raspare* to rasp, of Gmc origin]

**raspberry** /'rahzb(ə)ri/ *n* **1** any of various usu red edible berries similar to blackberries; *also* a widely cultivated shrub (genus *Rubus*, esp *Rubus idaeus*) of the rose family that bears raspberries **2** *slang* a rude sound made by sticking the tongue out and blowing noisily [E dial. *rasp* (raspberry) + E *berry;* (2) rhyming slang *raspberry* (*tart*) fart]

**raspings** /'rahspingz/ *n pl* dried crisp breadcrumbs

**raspy** /'rahspi/ *adj, esp of a noise* harsh, grating

**rasse** /'rasi, ras/ *n* a small S Asian CIVET CAT (*Viverricula indica*) [Jav *rasé*]

**Rasta** /'raztə/ *n or adj* (a) Rastafarian

**Rastafarian** /,rastə'feəri·ən, ,rastəfə'rie·ən, ,raztə-/ a follower of a religious and political movement among black W Indians which looks for the deliverance of the black race and the establishment of a homeland in Ethiopia, and incorporates a puritan ethic, elements of Old Testament religion, and veneration of Haile Selassie, the former Emperor of Ethiopia [*Ras Tafari*, title of Haile Selassie †1975 Emperor of Ethiopa] – **Rastafarian** *adj*, **Rastafarianism** *n*

**Rastaman** /'raztəmən, 'ras-/ *n* a Rastafarian

**raster** /'rastə/ *n* the pattern of lines whose intensity is controlled to form an image on a television picture tube [Ger, fr L *raster, rastrum* rake, fr *radere* to scrape]

¹**rat** /rat/ *n* **1a** any of numerous rodents (*Rattus* and related genera) differing from the related mice by their considerably larger size and by structural details (e g of the teeth) **b** any of various similar rodents **2** *informal* **2a** a contemptible or wretched person; *specif* one who betrays or deserts his/her party, friends, or workmates **b** *chiefly NAm* an informer **3** *pl, informal* – used as an exclamation of annoyance [ME, fr OE *ræt;* akin to OHG *ratta* rat, L *rodere* to gnaw, *radere* to scrape, shave] – **ratlike** *adj* – **smell a rat** to become aware of something suspicious; have a suspicion of something wrong

²**rat** *vi* **-tt-** **1** to catch or hunt rats **2** *informal* to betray, desert,

or inform *on* one's associates

**rata** /'rahtə/ *n* either of two New Zealand trees (*Metrosideros robusta* and *Metrosideros lucida*) of the eucalyptus family that bear bright red flowers and yield a hard dark red wood; *also* the wood of a rata [Maori]

**ratable** /'raytəbl/ *adj* rateable – **ratably** *adv*

**ratafia** /,ratə'fiə/ *n* **1** a liqueur flavoured with fruit kernels and bitter almonds **2** a small sweet almond-flavoured biscuit or cake – compare MACAROON [Fr]

**ratal** /'raytl/ *n* the amount on which rates are assessed

**rataplan** /,ratə'plan, '--,-/ *n* a repeated drumming sound ⟨*a rolling* ~ *of drums – Time*⟩ [Fr, of imit origin]

**rat-a-tat** /,rat ə 'tat/ *n* a sharp repeated knocking or tapping sound [imit]

**,rat-a-tat-'tat** *n* a rat-a-tat

**ratatouille** /,ratə'tooh·i/ (*Fr* ratatu:j)/ *n* a vegetable dish typically containing tomatoes, aubergines, courgettes, onions, and peppers cooked lightly in olive oil and then stewed slowly in a vegetable stock until most of the liquid has evaporated [Fr, fr *touiller* to stir, fr L *tudiculare*, fr *tudes* hammer]

**ratbag** /'rat,bag/ *n, slang* an unpleasant or disagreeable person

**rat-bite fever** *n* either of two feverish bacterial diseases of human beings usu transmitted by the bite of a rat

**ratcatcher** /'rat,kachə/ *n* **1** one who (catches and) destroys vermin, esp rats **2** unorthodox foxhunting dress, usu consisting of a HACKING JACKET and fawn breeches

**ratch** /rach/ *n* **1** a catch mechanism (PAWL or DETENT) for holding or propelling a RATCHET WHEEL **2** *chiefly NAm* a notched bar with which a catch mechanism (PAWL) engages to prevent reversal of motion [Ger *ratsche*, fr *ratschen* to rattle, fr MHG *ratzen;* akin to MHG *razzeln* to rattle]

**ratchet** /'rachit/ *n* **1** a mechanism that consists of a bar or wheel having inclined teeth into which a catch mechanism (PAWL) drops so that motion to the wheel or bar can be imparted, governed, or prevented and that is used in a hand tool (e g a brace or screwdriver) to allow effective motion in one direction only **2** *NAm* RATCHET WHEEL [alter. (influenced by *ratch*) of earlier *rochet*, fr Fr, alter. of MF *rocquet* lance head, of Gmc origin; akin to OHG *rocko* distaff – more at ROCK]

**ratchet wheel** *n* a toothed wheel held in position or turned by a special catch mechanism (PAWL)

¹**rate** /rayt/ *vt, archaic* to scold angrily [ME *raten*]

²**rate** *n* **1** reckoned value; a valuation ⟨*appraised him at a low* ~⟩ **2a** a fixed ratio between two things **b** a charge, payment, or price fixed according to a ratio, scale, or standard **c rates** *pl,* **rate** *Br* a tax levied by a local authority **3a** a quantity, amount, or degree of something measured per unit of something else **b** an amount of payment or charge based on another amount; *specif* the amount of premium per unit of insurance *synonyms* see ²TAX [ME, fr MF, fr ML *rata*, fr L (*pro*) *rata* (*parte*) according to a fixed proportion] – **at any rate** anyway; IN ANY CASE

³**rate** *vt* **1** to consider, regard ⟨*was* ~d *an excellent pianist*⟩ **2a** to set an estimate on; value, esteem ⟨*black is* ~d *very high this season*⟩ **b** to determine or assign the relative rank or class of; grade **c** to estimate the normal capacity or power of (e g a machine) **3** to fix the amount of premium to be charged per unit of insurance on **4** to have a right to; deserve ⟨*now* ~s *his own show*⟩ **5** *informal* to think highly of; consider to be good ⟨*doesn't* ~ *Spurs' chances of avoiding relegation*⟩ ~ *vi* to be evaluated of a specified level ⟨~s *as the best show ever staged in London*⟩

**-rate** /-rayt/ *comb form* (→ *adj*) being of the specified level of quality ⟨*fifth-rate*⟩

**rateable, ratable** /'raytəbl/ *adj* capable of or susceptible to being rated, estimated, or apportioned

**rateable value** *n, Br* the estimated value of a property on which annual rate payments are calculated

**rate-capping** *n, Br* restriction by central government legislation of the level of rates which a local authority can levy, esp in order to prohibit rate increases intended to finance special expenditure which the government finds economically or politically unacceptable

**ratel** /'raytl/ *n* an Afro-Asian nocturnal badgerlike mammal (genus *Mellivora*) that is related to the weasels, lives in a burrow, and feeds on small animals, fruit, and honey [Afrik, lit., rattle, fr MD – more at RATTLE]

**ratemeter** /'rayt,meetə/ *n* an instrument that indicates the counting rate of an electronic counter

**rate of exchange** *n* the amount of one currency that will buy a given amount of another – compare EXCHANGE

**rate of interest** *n* the percentage, usu on an annual basis, that is paid for the use of money belonging to another

**ratepayer** /'rayt,payə/ *n* a taxpayer; *also, Br* a person liable to pay rates

**rater** /'raytə/ *n* 1 one who rates; *specif* a person who estimates or determines a rating 2 one who or that which has a specified rating or class – usu in combination ⟨*fifth*-rater⟩

**rate support grant** *n, Br* a grant paid by the central to a local government authority to finance a proportion of its expenditure

**rath** /rahth/ *n* an early Irish usu circular earthwork serving as a stronghold or residence [IrGael *rāth*]

**rathe** /raydh/ *adj, archaic* coming or blooming early in the year or season ⟨*bring the* ~ *primrose that forsaken dies* – John Milton⟩ [ME, quick, fr OE *hræth*, alter. of *hræd*; akin to OHG *hrad* quick]

**rather** /'rahdhə/ *adv* 1 more readily or willingly; sooner ⟨*left* ~ *than cause trouble*⟩ ⟨*I'd* ~ *not go*⟩ – often used interjectionally, esp by British speakers, to express enthusiastic affirmation ⟨*"will you come?" "Rather!"*⟩ 2 more properly, reasonably, or truly ⟨*my father, or* ~ *my stepfather*⟩ ⟨*ran* ~ *than walked*⟩ 3 to some degree; somewhat ⟨*it's* ~ *warm*⟩ ⟨~ *a cold day*⟩ ⟨~ *too big*⟩ ⟨*I* ~ *thought so*⟩ ⟨~ *like a potato*⟩; *esp* somewhat excessively ⟨*it's* ~ *far for me*⟩ ⟨~ *a pity*⟩ 4 on the contrary; instead ⟨*was nothing bettered, but* ~ *grew worse* – Mk 5:26 (AV)⟩ [ME, fr OE *hrathor*, compar of *hrathe* quickly; akin to OHG *rado* quickly, OE *hræd* quick]

  *usage* Would **rather** and **had rather** are equally correct ways of expressing a preference. *I'd* **rather**, *he'd* **rather**, etc stand for either.

**rathskeller** /'rahts,kelə (Ger ratskelər)/ *n, chiefly NAm* a restaurant or beer cellar modelled after the cellar of a German town hall [obs Ger (now *ratskeller*), restaurant in the basement of a town hall, fr *rat* council + *keller* cellar]

**ratify** /'ratifie/ *vt* to approve and sanction formally; confirm ⟨~ *a treaty*⟩ [ME *ratifien*, fr MF *ratifier*, fr ML *ratificare*, fr L *ratus* determined, fr pp of *reri* to calculate – more at REASON] – **ratification** *n*

**ratiné** /'ratinay/, **ratine** /ra'teen/ *n* 1 a lumpy yarn of various fibres made by twisting a thick and a thin yarn together under tension 2 a rough bulky fabric, usu woven loosely in PLAIN WEAVE from ratiné yarns – compare RATTEEN [Fr *ratiné*, fr pp of *ratiner* to make a nap on, fr *ratine* ratteen]

**rating** /'rayting/ *n* 1 a classification according to grade 2a a relative estimate or evaluation; standing ⟨*the school has a good academic* ~⟩ b an estimate of an individual's or business's credit and responsibility 3 a stated operating limit of a machine expressible in power units (eg kilowatts for a direct-current generator) or in characteristics (eg voltage) 4 *pl* any of various indexes which list television programmes, new records, etc in order of popularity – usu + *the* 5 *chiefly Br* ORDINARY SEAMAN (seaman of lowest rank)

**ratio** /'rayshioh/ *n, pl* **ratios** 1 the indicated division of one mathematical expression by another 2 the relationship in quantity, number, or degree between things or between one thing and another thing; proportion [L, computation, reason – more at REASON]

**ratiocinate** /,rati'osinayt/ *vi, formal* to reason logically or formally [L *ratiocinatus*, pp of *ratiocinari* to reckon, fr *ratio*] – **ratiocinator** *n*

**ratiocination** /,rati,osi'naysh(ə)n/ *n, formal* 1 the process of logical thinking; reasoning 2 a reasoned train of thought – **ratiocinative** *adj*

**ratio decidendi** /,ratioh daysi'dendi/ *n, law* reason or ground for a judicial decision [L]

¹**ration** /'rash(ə)n/ *n* 1a a food allowance for one day b *pl* food, provisions 2 a share or amount which one permits oneself or which one is permitted ⟨*the petrol* ~⟩ ⟨*had used his* ~ *of television time*⟩ [Fr, fr L *ration-, ratio* computation, reason]

²**ration** *vt* 1 to supply with or put on rations 2a to distribute (esp things in short supply) in fixed quantities – often + *out* ⟨~ed *out sugar and flour*⟩ b to limit (a person or commodity) to a fixed ration ⟨*sugar was strictly* ~ed⟩ ⟨*must* ~ *you to two cups per day*⟩ c to use sparingly

¹**rational** /'rash(ə)nl/ *adj* 1a having reason or understanding ⟨*man is a* ~ *creature*⟩ b relating to, based on, or compatible with reason; reasonable ⟨*a* ~ *explanation*⟩ ⟨~ *behaviour*⟩ 2a involving only multiplication, division, addition, and subtraction a finite number of times b of, involving, or being (a

mathematical expression containing) a RATIONAL NUMBER [ME *racional*, fr L *rationalis*, fr *ration-, ratio*] – **rationally** *adv*, **rationalness** *n*

²**rational** *n* something rational; *specif* RATIONAL NUMBER

**rationale** /,rashə'nahl/ *n* 1 an explanation of controlling principles of opinion, belief, practice, or phenomena 2 an underlying reason; a basis [L, neut of *rationalis*]

**rational function** *n* 1 POLYNOMIAL 2 a function that is the quotient of two POLYNOMIALS

**rational horizon** *n* HORIZON 1b(2)

**rationalism** /'rash(ə)nə,liz(ə)m/ *n* 1 reliance on reason for establishment of religious truth 2a a theory that reason or the intellect is a source of knowledge superior to and independent of sense perception b a view that reason is or should be decisive in solving problems or making moral choices – **rationalist** *n*, **rationalist, rationalistic** *adj*, **rationalistically** *adv*

**rationality** /,rashə'naləti/ *n* 1 the quality or state of being rational 2 the quality or state of being compatible with reason; reasonableness 3 *usu pl* something (eg an opinion, belief, or practice) that is rational

**rational·ize, -ise** /'rash(ə)nəliez/ *vt* 1 to free (a mathematical expression) from parts that are IRRATIONAL NUMBERS ⟨~ *a denominator*⟩ 2 to bring into accord with reason or cause to seem reasonable: eg 2a to substitute a natural for a supernatural explanation of ⟨~ *a myth*⟩ b to attribute (eg one's actions) to rational and creditable motives, without analysis of true, esp unconscious, motives, in order to provide plausible but untrue reasons for conduct ⟨~d *his dislike of his brother*⟩ 3 to increase the efficiency of (eg an industry), esp by the more economical use of resources ~ *vi* to provide plausible but untrue reasons for one's actions, opinions, etc – **rationalizer** *n*, **rationalization** *n*

**rational number, rational** *n* a number (eg 2, $^5/_2$, $-^1/_2$) that can be expressed as the result of dividing one integer by another – compare IRRATIONAL NUMBER, SURD

**ratite** /'ratiet/ *n* a bird with a flat breastbone; *esp* any of a superorder (Ratitae) of birds (eg an ostrich, an emu, a moa, or a kiwi) that have small or rudimentary wings and no keel-like part or ridge in the breastbone [deriv of L *ratitus* marked with the figure of a raft, fr *ratis* raft] – **ratite** *adj*

**rat kangaroo** *n* any of various small kangaroos (*Bettongia, Potorous,* and related genera) that are no larger than a rabbit – called also POTOROO

**ratline** /'ratlin/ *n* any of the short horizontal ropes attached to the ropes or cables steadying the mast of a ship, so as to form the steps of a rope ladder [origin unknown]

**rat mite** *n* a widely distributed mite (*Bdellonyssus bacoti*) that usu feeds on rodents but may cause skin disease in and transmit the disease typhus to human beings

**rato** /'raytoh/ *n, pl* **ratos** JATO (takeoff using extra rocket power) [*r*ocket-*a*ssisted *t*akeoff]

¹**ratoon** /ra'toohn/ *n* 1 a new shoot that develops from the root or crown of a perennial plant (eg sugarcane) after cropping 2 a crop (eg of bananas) produced on ratoons [Sp *retono,* fr *retonar* to sprout, fr *re-* (fr L) + *otonar* to grow in autumn, fr *otono* autumn, fr L *autumnus*]

²**ratoon** *vi* 1 to sprout or spring up from the root ⟨*some cottons* ~ *freely*⟩ 2 to grow or produce (a crop) from or on ratoons

**rat race** *n* a fiercely competitive and wearisome activity; *specif* the struggle to maintain one's position in a career or survive the pressures of modern urban life ⟨*abandoned the* rat race *and retired to the country*⟩

**ratsbane** /'rats,bayn/ *n, archaic* something poisonous to rats

**rattail** /'rat,tayl/ *n* 1 a horse's tail with little or no hair 2 *usu pl* something resembling the tail of a rat ⟨*her wet hair hung in* ~s⟩

**rat-tail file** *n* a slender tapered file of circular cross section

**rattan** /rə'tan/ *n* 1a a climbing palm (esp of the genera *Calamus* and *Daemonorops*) with very long tough stems b a part of the stem of a rattan used esp for walking sticks and wickerwork 2 a rattan cane or walking stick [Malay *rotan*]

**rat-tat** /,rat 'tat/ *n* a rat-a-tat

**ratteen** /ra'teen/ *n, archaic* a coarse fabric [Fr *ratine*]

**ratter** /'ratə/ *n* a person or animal that catches rats; *specif* a rat-catching dog or cat

¹**rattle** /'ratl/ *vi* 1 to make a rapid succession of short sharp sounds ⟨*the windows* ~d *in the wind*⟩ 2 to chatter incessantly and aimlessly – often + *on* 3 to move with a clatter or rattle ~ *vt* 1 to say or perform in a brisk lively fashion – often + *off* ⟨~d *off a long list of examples*⟩ 2 to cause to make a

rattling sound **3** *informal* to upset to the point of loss of poise and composure ⟨*he looked severely* ∼d⟩ [ME *ratelen;* akin to MD *ratel* rattle, OE *hratian* to rush – more at CARDINAL]

²**rattle** *n* **1** a rattling sound **2** a device that produces a rattle: eg **2a** a child's toy consisting of loose pellets in a hollow container that rattles when shaken **b** a device that consists of a springy tongue in contact with a revolving ratchet wheel which is rotated or shaken to produce a loud noise and is used esp by football fans **3** the sound-producing organ on a rattlesnake's tail **4** a throat noise caused by air passing through mucus and heard esp at the approach of death

**rattler** /'ratlə/ *n* **1** something that rattles **2** *chiefly NAm* a rattlesnake

**rattlesnake** /-ˌsnayk/ *n* any of various poisonous American snakes (family Crotalidae, genera *Sistrurus* and *Crotalus*) with horny interlocking joints at the end of the tail that make a sharp rattling sound when shaken

**rattletrap** /'ratlˌtrap/ *n, informal* a noisy old vehicle, esp a car

¹**rattling** /'ratling/ *adj, informal* **1** lively, brisk ⟨*moved at a* ∼ *pace*⟩ **2** extremely good; excellent □ no longer in vogue – **rattlingly** *adv*

²**rattling** *adv, informal* to an extreme degree; very – chiefly in *rattling good* ⟨*a* ∼ *good yarn*⟩

**rattly** /'ratli/ *adj* likely to rattle; making a rattle

'**rat-ˌtrap** *n, informal* **1** a dirty dilapidated structure **2** a hopeless situation

**ratty** /'rati/ *adj* **1a** infested with rats **b** (suggestive) of a rat **2** *Br informal* irritable ⟨*felt* ∼ *as hell*⟩ **3** *NAm informal* shabby, unkempt

**raucous** /'rawkəs/ *adj* **1** disagreeably harsh or strident; hoarse ⟨∼ *voices*⟩ **2** boisterously disorderly ⟨*a* ∼ *mining town*⟩ [L *raucus* hoarse; akin to OE *rēon* to lament – more at RUMOUR] – **raucously** *adv,* **raucousness** *n*

**raunchy** /'rawnchi/ *adj* **1** lewd, smutty ⟨∼ *jokes*⟩; *also* LUSTY **2** ⟨*a group with a confident* ∼ *sound*⟩ **2** *chiefly NAm* slovenly, dirty ⟨*a* ∼ *panhandler*⟩ [origin unknown] – **raunchily** *adv,* **raunchiness** *n*

**raupo** /'rowpoh/ *n, NZ* BULRUSH **b** [Maori]

**rauwolfia** /row'woolfiə/ *n* any of a large widespread genus (*Rauwolfia*) of tropical somewhat poisonous trees and shrubs of the periwinkle family, that yield RESERPINE and other similar substances that have a physiological effect; *also* a drug extracted from the root of an Indian rauwolfia (*Rauwolfia serpentina*) that contains reserpine [NL, genus name, fr Leonhard *Rauwolf* †1596 Ger botanist]

¹**ravage** /'ravij/ *n* **1** an act or practice of ravaging ⟨*secure from* ∼ *by fire*⟩ **2 ravages** *pl,* **ravage** damage resulting from ravaging; violently destructive effect ⟨*the* ∼s *of time*⟩ [Fr, fr MF, fr *ravir* to ravish – more at RAVISH]

²**ravage** *vt* to wreak havoc on; deal with destructively and often violently; devastate ∼ *vi* to wreak havoc △ ravish – **ravagement** *n,* **ravager** *n*

¹**rave** /rayv/ *vi* **1a** to talk irrationally (as if) in delirium **b** to declaim wildly **c** to talk with extreme enthusiasm ⟨∼d *about her beauty*⟩ **2** to make a wild or violent sound; storm ⟨*the iced gusts still* ∼ *and beat* – John Keats⟩ ∼ *vt* to utter in madness or frenzy [ME *raven,* prob fr MF *raver, resver* to wander, be delirious] – **raver** *n*

²**rave** *n* **1** an act or instance of raving **2** an extravagantly favourable review ⟨*the play opened to* ∼ *notices*⟩ **3** *slang* a wild exciting period, experience, or event ⟨*the party was a real* ∼⟩

¹**ravel** /'ravl/ *vb* **-ll-** (*NAm* **-l-, -ll-**) *vt* **1a** to separate or undo the texture of; unravel **b** to undo the intricacies of; disentangle **2** to entangle, confuse – often + *up* ∼ *vi* **1** to become unwoven, untwisted, or unwound; fray **2** *of a road surface* to break up; crumble □ (*vt 1*) usu + *out* [D *rafelen,* fr *rafel* loose thread; akin to OE *ræfter* rafter] – **raveller** *n,* **ravelment** *n*

²**ravel** *n* an act or result of ravelling: eg **a** something tangled **b** something ravelled out; *specif* a loose thread

**ravelin** /'rav(ə)lin/ *n* a detached triangular temporary fortification, usu situated between two bastions [MF, fr OIt *ravellino,* alter. of *rivellino,* dim. of *riva* bank, fr L *ripa*]

**ravelling** /'ravling, 'ravlˈing/ *n* RAVEL b

¹**raven** /'rayv(ə)n/ *n* a very large glossy black bird (*Corvus corax*) of the crow family, that is found in N Europe, Asia, and N America and has a large black beak, shaggy feathers at the throat, and a wedge-shaped tail [ME, fr OE *hræfn;* akin to OHG *hraban* raven, L *corvus,* Gk *korax,* L *crepare* to rattle, crack]

²**raven** *adj* of the black colour or glossy sheen of the raven ⟨∼ *hair*⟩

³**raven** /'rav(ə)n/ *vt* **1** to devour greedily **2** to despoil ⟨*men . . .* ∼ *the earth, destroying its resources* – New Yorker⟩ ∼ *vi* **1** to feed greedily **2** to prowl about for food; prey **3** to plunder [MF *raviner* to rush, take by force, fr *ravine* rapine] – **ravener** *n*

**ravenous** /'rav(ə)nəs/ *adj* **1** rapacious, voracious ⟨∼ *wolves*⟩ **2** fiercely eager for food, satisfaction, or gratification ⟨*a* ∼ *appetite*⟩ – **ravenously** *adv,* **ravenousness** *n*

**raver** /'rayvə/ *n, chiefly Br slang* an energetic and uninhibited person who enjoys a hectic social life; *also* a sexually uninhibited or promiscuous person [¹*rave* + ²*-er*]

'**rave-ˌup** *n, chiefly Br slang* a wild party

**ravin** /'ravin/ *n* **1a** an act or habit of preying **b** something seized as prey ⟨*red in tooth and with* ∼ – Alfred Tennyson⟩ **2** *archaic* plunder, pillage [ME, fr MF *ravine*]

**ravine** /rə'veen/ *n* a narrow steep-sided valley that is smaller than a canyon and is usu formed by the action of running water [Fr, fr MF, rapine, rush, fr L *rapina* rapine]

¹**raving** /'rayving/ *n,* **ravings** *n pl* irrational, incoherent, wild, or extravagant utterance or declamation

²**raving** *adj* **1** talking wildly or irrationally ⟨*a* ∼ *lunatic*⟩ **2** *informal* extreme, marked ⟨*a* ∼ *beauty*⟩ ⟨*a* ∼ *homosexual*⟩

**ravioli** /ˌravi'ohli/ *n* little cases of pasta containing a savoury filling (eg of meat or cheese); *also* a dish consisting of ravioli in a tomato sauce [It, fr It dial., pl of *raviolo,* lit., little turnip, dim. of *rava* turnip, fr L *rapa* – more at RAPE]

**ravish** /'ravish/ *vt* **1** to seize and take away by violence **2** to overcome with emotion (eg joy or delight) ⟨∼ed *by the beauty of the scene*⟩ **3** to rape, violate △ ravage [ME *ravisshen,* fr MF *raviss-,* stem of *ravir,* fr (assumed) VL *rapire,* alter. of L *rapere* to seize, rob – more at RAPID] – **ravisher** *n,* **ravishment** *n*

**ravishing** /'ravishing/ *adj* unusually attractive, pleasing, or striking; entrancing – **ravishingly** *adv*

¹**raw** /raw/ *adj* **1** not cooked **2a(1)** in or nearly in the natural state; not processed or purified ⟨∼ *fibres*⟩ ⟨∼ *sewage*⟩ **a(2)** not diluted or blended ⟨∼ *spirits*⟩ **b** unprepared or imperfectly prepared for use **c** not in a polished, finished, or processed form ⟨∼ *data*⟩ ⟨*hem this* ∼ *edge to stop it fraying*⟩ **3a** having the surface abraded or chafed ⟨∼ *skin*⟩ **b** very irritated ⟨*a* ∼ *sore throat*⟩ **4a** lacking experience, training, etc; new ⟨*a* ∼ *recruit*⟩ **b** marked by absence of refinements **5** disagreeably damp or cold ⟨*a* ∼ *morning*⟩ **6** *NAm* vulgar, coarse ⟨*a* ∼ *joke*⟩ [ME, fr OE *hrēaw;* akin to OHG *hrō* raw, L *crudus* raw, *cruor* blood, Gk *kreas* flesh] – **rawly** *adv,* **rawness** *n*

²**raw** *n* a raw place or state – **in the raw 1** in the natural or crude state ⟨*life in the raw*⟩ **2** naked ⟨*slept in the raw*⟩

**rawboned** /ˌraw'bohnd/ *adj* having little flesh; gaunt; *specif* having a heavy or clumsy frame that seems inadequately covered with flesh

**raw deal** *n* an instance of unfair treatment

**rawhide** /'rawˌhied/ *n* **1** untanned cattle skin **2** a whip of untanned hide

**rawinsonde** /'rawwinˌsond/ *n* a balloon carrying a device that can be tracked by radar and that is used to determine the speed and direction of winds in the atmosphere [*radar* + *wind* + *radiosonde*]

**raw material** *n* material whether crude or processed that can be converted by manufacture, processing, or combination into a new and useful product ⟨*wheat, which is the finished product of the farmer, is* ∼ *for the flour mill*⟩; *broadly* something with a potential for improvement, development, or elaboration ⟨*problems are often the* ∼ *of discoveries*⟩

**raw score** *n* an individual's actual score in a test before any statistical treatment or adjustment

**raw sienna** /si'enə/ *n* SIENNA (naturally occurring brownish-yellow earthy substance) used in its natural state as a pigment; *also* the light brown to brownish-yellow or orange colour of this – compare BURNT SIENNA

**raw umber** /'umbə/ *n* UMBER (naturally occurring brown earthy substance) used in its natural state as a pigment; *also* the yellowish- to greenish-brown colour of this – compare BURNT UMBER

¹**ray** /ray/ *n* any of numerous sea fishes (order Hypotremata) that have a skeleton composed of cartilage, a flat body with the eyes on the upper surface, a much-reduced tail region, and typically a slender whiplike tail [ME *raye,* fr MF *raie,* fr L *raia*]

²**ray** *n* **1a** any of the lines of light that appear to radiate from a bright object **b** a narrow beam of RADIANT ENERGY (e g light or X rays) **c** a stream of typically radioactive particles travelling in the same line – compare ALPHA RAY, BETA RAY, COSMIC RAY **d** a straight line representing the direction in which a wave (e g of light) is travelling **2** light cast by rays; radiance **3** a thin line suggesting a ray **4** *maths* **4a** any of a group of lines diverging from a common centre **b** a straight line extending from a point in one direction only **5a** any of the cartilage or bony rods that support the fin of a fish **b** any of the arms or radiating parts of a starfish or similar animal **6a** a branch or flower stalk of an UMBEL (flower head in which all branches arise from the same point) **b** a wedge-shaped area of plant tissue: **b(1)** MEDULLARY RAY **b(2)** VASCULAR RAY **c** RAY FLOWER 1 **7** a slight indication or trace (e g of intelligence or hope) [ME, fr MF *rai*, fr L *radius* rod, ray]

³**ray** *vi* **1a** to shine (as if) in rays **b** to issue as rays **2** to extend like the radii of a circle; radiate ∼ *vt* **1** to emit in rays; radiate ⟨*eyes that* ∼ *out intelligence* – Thomas Carlyle⟩ **2** to decorate or mark with rays

⁴**ray, re** /ray, ree/ *n* the 2nd note of the scale in the SOL-FA method of representing the musical scale [ME *re*, fr ML – more at GAMUT]

**rayed** /rayd/ *adj* having ray flowers

**ray floret** *n* RAY FLOWER 1

**ray flower** *n* **1** any of the small strap-shaped flowers that are clustered together to make up the whole or a part (e g an outer ring) of the flower head of a dandelion, daisy, or related plant – compare DISC FLOWER **2** a flower head (e g of a dandelion) consisting entirely of ray flowers

**rayless** /'raylǝs/ *adj* **1** having, admitting, or emitting no rays; *esp* dark, gloomy **2** lacking ray flowers – **raylessness** *n*

**rayon** /'rayon, -ǝn/ *n* **1** any of a group of textile fibres made by forcing and drawing CELLULOSE (constituent of woody or fibrous plant tissue) through minute holes **2** a rayon yarn or fabric *synonyms* see NYLON [irreg fr ²*ray*]

**raze, rase** /rayz/ *vt* **1** to destroy (e g a town or building) completely; demolish *specif* to lay level with the ground **2** *archaic* to erase △ raise [ME *rasen* to scratch, scrape, fr MF *raser*, fr (assumed) VL *rasare*, fr L *rasus*, pp of *radere* to scrape, shave] – **razer** *n*

**razoo** /rǝ'zooh/ *n, Austr & NZ* a small sum of money – used in negative phrases ⟨*never gave them a brass* ∼ – *Coast to Coast (Sydney)*⟩ [origin unknown]

**razor** /'rayzǝ/ *n* a sharp-edged cutting implement for shaving or cutting hair, esp of the face [ME *rasour*, fr OF *raseor*, fr *raser* to scrape, shave] – **razor** *vt*

**razorback** /'rayzǝbak/ *n* **1** RORQUAL (type of whale) **2** a semi-iwild pig of the USA, with a narrow body and ridged back

'**razor-,backed, razorback** *adj* having a sharp narrow back ⟨*a* ∼ *horse*⟩

**razorbill** /'rayzǝ,bil/ *n* a N Atlantic auk (*Alca torda*) that has a compressed sharp-edged beak and plumage that is black above and white below

**razor clam** *n, NAm* razor-shell

'**razor-,shell** *n* any of numerous marine INVERTEBRATE animals (family Solenidae of the phylum Mollusca) having a long narrow curved thin shell consisting of two halves hinged together

¹**razz** /raz/ *n, NAm informal* RASPBERRY 2 [by shortening & alter.]

²**razz** *vt, NAm informal* to heckle, deride ⟨*the fans* ∼*ed the visiting players*⟩

**razzle** /'razl/ *n, chiefly Br slang* a binge – usu in *on the razzle* [short for *razzle-dazzle*]

**razzle-dazzle** /,--'--, '--,--/ *n, informal* razzmatazz [irreg redupl of *dazzle*]

**razzmatazz** /'razmǝ,taz, ,--'-/ *n, informal* **1** noisy, colourful, and often gaudily showy atmosphere or activity ⟨*the* ∼ *of professional sport*⟩ **2** DOUBLE-TALK 2 [prob alter. of *razzle-dazzle*]

**r colour** *n* an acoustic effect of a simultaneously articulated /r/ imparted to a vowel (e g in a common NAm pronunciation of *bird*) – **r-coloured** *adj*

¹**re** /ray, ree/ *n, music* ⁴RAY [ML – more at GAMUT]

²**re** /ree/ *prep, law & commercialese* WITH REGARD TO; concerning [L, abl of *res* thing – more at REAL]

**re-** /ri-, ,ree-/ *prefix* **1a** again, anew ⟨*reborn*⟩ ⟨*reprint*⟩ **b(1)** again in a new, altered, or improved way ⟨*rehash*⟩ ⟨*rewrite*⟩ ⟨*rehouse*⟩ **b(2)** repeated, new, or improved version of ⟨*retread*⟩

⟨*rebroadcast*⟩ ⟨*remake*⟩ **2** back, backwards ⟨*recall*⟩ ⟨*retract*⟩ [ME, fr OF, fr L *re-, red-* back, again, against]

'**re** /ǝ/ *vb* are ⟨*you're right*⟩

**reabsorb** /,ree-ǝb'zawb; *also* -bs-/ *vt* to take up (something previously secreted) ⟨*sugars* ∼*ed in the kidney*⟩; *also* RESORB 2

¹**reach** /reech/ *vt* **1** to stretch out; extend ⟨∼ *out your hand to her*⟩ **2a** to touch or grasp by extending a part of the body (e g a hand) or an object ⟨*couldn't* ∼ *the apple*⟩ **b** to pick up and draw towards one; take ⟨∼*ed down my hat*⟩ **c(1)** to extend to ⟨*the shadow* ∼*ed the wall*⟩ **c(2)** to get up to or as far as; come to ⟨*took two days to* ∼ *the mountains*⟩ ⟨*they hoped to* ∼ *an agreement*⟩ **d(1)** to make an impression on ⟨*a programme designed to* ∼ *backward children*⟩ **d(2)** to contact; communicate with ⟨∼*ed him by phone at the office*⟩ **3** *informal* to hand over; pass ⟨∼ *me my hat*⟩ ∼ *vi* **1a** to make a stretch (as if) with one's hand ⟨∼ *for some money*⟩ ⟨∼*ed towards the book on the top shelf*⟩ **b** to strain after something ⟨∼*ing above our nature does no good* – John Dryden⟩ **2a** to project, extend ⟨*his land* ∼*es to the river*⟩ **b** to arrive at or come to something ⟨*as far as the eye could* ∼⟩ **3** to sail on a reach [ME *rechen*, fr OE *rǣcan*; akin to OHG *reichen* to reach, Lith *raižytis* to stretch oneself repeatedly] – **reachable** *adj*, **reacher** *n*

**synonyms** Reach, gain, attain, achieve, accomplish, and compass can all mean, literally or figuratively, "arrive at a point by effort". Reach is the most general, but often emphasizes progress towards a goal ⟨*will soon reach Cambridge*⟩ ⟨*team reached the finals*⟩. Both gain and attain often stress the difficulty of reaching one's goal ⟨*gradually gained their confidence*⟩, and both attain and achieve imply pride in reaching an important point through skill ⟨*attain the stratosphere*⟩ ⟨*achieve a distinguished position*⟩. Accomplish chiefly implies triumphant completion ⟨*accomplish one's mission*⟩. Compass is not used of "arriving" in the literal sense; it may suggest crafty circumvention or encirclement ⟨*he compassed their ruin*⟩.

²**reach** *n* **1a** the action or an act of reaching ⟨*made a* ∼ *for his gun*⟩ **b** the distance or extent of reaching or of ability to reach **c** range; *specif* comprehension ⟨*an idea well beyond his* ∼⟩ **2** a continuous stretch or expanse; *esp* a straight uninterrupted portion of a river or canal **3** the tack sailed by a vessel with the wind blowing more or less from the side **4** *pl* groups or sections of those involved in a usu specified activity or occupation; echelons ⟨*the higher* ∼*es of academic life*⟩

'**reach-me-,down** *n or adj, chiefly Br* (a garment) passed on from another; (a) cast-off

**react** /ri'akt/ *vi* **1** to exert a reciprocal or counteracting force or influence – often + *on* or *upon* **2a** to respond to a stimulus **b** to have a particular physiological response or reaction to a drug, course of medical treatment, etc **3** to act in opposition to a force or influence – usu + *against* **4** to move or tend in a reverse direction **5** to undergo chemical reaction ∼ *vt* to cause to react chemically [NL *reactus*, pp of *reagere*, fr L *re-* + *agere* to act – more at AGENT]

**reactance** /ri'akt(ǝ)ns/ *n, electronics* the part of the total opposition (IMPEDANCE) to the flow of an ALTERNATING CURRENT in a circuit, that is due to CAPACITANCE or INDUCTANCE or both, but not due to the resistance of the material along which the current is conducted, measured in ohms

**reactant** /ri'akt(ǝ)nt/ *n* a substance that takes part in a chemical reaction; *specif* a substance that is altered in the course of reacting chemically with another

**reaction** /ri'aksh(ǝ)n/ *n* **1a** (a) reacting **b** tendency towards a former and usu outmoded political or social condition, system, or order **2** mental or physical response to or activity aroused by a stimulus: e g **2a** the response of tissues to a foreign substance (e g a drug or infective agent) **b** a mental or emotional response to an individual's circumstances ⟨*an anxiety* ∼⟩ **3** *physics* the force exerted by something subjected to the action of a force, that is equal in strength and acts in the opposite direction to the applied force **4a** a chemical transformation or change; the interaction of chemical entities (e g atoms or molecules) to form one or more new substances **b** a process involving change in the nucleus of an atom resulting from the interaction of the nucleus with another nucleus or atomic particle – **reactional** *adj*, **reactionally** *adv*

**usage** In the scientific senses, a stimulus has a **reaction** on or upon something which in its turn has a **reaction** to or reacts against the stimulus. When **reaction** means merely "response to circumstances" it is used with to ⟨*what was their reaction to his proposals?*⟩ or with from where it is strong enough to mean virtually "backlash" ⟨*took to crime as a reaction from his strict upbringing*⟩.

¹**reactionary** /ri'akshǝn(ǝ)ri/ *also* **reactionist** /-ist/ *adj* relat-

ing to, marked by, or favouring political or social reaction; *broadly* opposed to change – **reactionaryism, reactionism** *n*

²**reactionary** *also* **reactionist** *n* a reactionary person

**reaction engine** *n* an engine (eg a JET ENGINE) that develops thrust by expelling a stream of gas

**reactivate** /ri'aktivayt/ *vb* to make or become active again – **reactivation** *n*

**reactive** /ri'aktiv/ *adj* **1a** of or marked by reaction ⟨∼ *symptoms*⟩ **b** tending to or liable to react readily ⟨*highly* ∼ *chemicals*⟩ **2** of or marked by reactance **3a** readily responsive to a stimulus **b** occurring as a result of or reaction to something, esp stress or emotional upset ⟨∼ *depression*⟩ – **reactively** *adv*, **reactiveness** *n*, **reactivity** *n*

**reactor** /ri'aktə/ *n* **1** one who or that which reacts **2** *electronics* a device (eg a coil of wire) in an electrical circuit that introduces reactance into the circuit (eg for dimming a light); *esp* INDUCTOR **3a** a vat for an industrial chemical reaction **b** an apparatus in which a self-sustaining CHAIN REACTION involving atomic nuclei is started and controlled; *specif* NUCLEAR REACTOR

¹**read** /reed/ *vb* **read** /red/ *vt* **1a(1)** to look at or otherwise sense (eg letters or symbols, words, or a collection of words) with understanding of what is being communicated ⟨*can't* ∼ *his handwriting*⟩ ⟨*to* ∼ *a book*⟩ ⟨∼ *music*⟩ ⟨∼ *braille*⟩ **a(2)** to study the movements of (eg lips) with understanding of what is being expressed ⟨∼ *semaphore*⟩ **a(3)** to utter aloud the printed or written words of ⟨∼ *them a story*⟩ **b** to learn or find out from written or printed matter ⟨*had* ∼ *that the operation was dangerous*⟩ **2a** to interpret the meaning or significance of ⟨∼ *palms*⟩ ⟨*can* ∼ *the situation in two ways*⟩ **b** to foretell, predict ⟨*able to* ∼ *his fortune*⟩ **3a** to learn the nature of by observing outward expression or signs ⟨∼s *him like a book*⟩ **b** to interpret the action of or in so as to anticipate what will happen or what needs doing ⟨*a good canoeist* ∼s *the rapids*⟩ ⟨*the captain must be able to* ∼ *the game*⟩ **4a** to attribute a meaning to (eg something read); interpret ⟨*how do you* ∼ *this passage?*⟩ **b** to attribute (a meaning) to something read or considered ⟨∼ *a nonexistent meaning into her words*⟩ **5** to use as a substitute for or in preference to another written or printed word, character, etc ⟨∼ '*hurry*' *for* '*harry*'⟩ **6** to indicate ⟨*the thermometer* ∼s *zero*⟩ **7** to interpret (a musical work) in performance **8a** *of a computer* **8a(1)** to sense the meaning of (coded information recorded or stored on punched cards, in a computer memory, etc) **a(2)** to take (information) from storage **b** to read the coded information on (eg tape or a punched card) ∼ *vi* **1a** to perform the act of reading words; read something **b(1)** to learn about something by reading – usu + *up* ⟨∼ing *up on astronomy*⟩ **b(2)** to pursue a course of study; *specif, Br* to study a subject in order to qualify – + *for* ⟨*to* ∼ *for the Bar*⟩ **c(1)** to deliver aloud (as if) by reading; *specif* to utter interpretively ⟨∼s *Shakespeare with moving simplicity*⟩ **c(2)** to grant a reading to (a legislative bill) **d(1)** to study (a subject, esp for a degree ⟨∼ *law*⟩ **d(2)** to read works of (an author or type of literature) ⟨∼s *science fiction mainly*⟩ **e(1)**

to copy-edit **e(2)** to proofread **f(1)** to receive and understand (a message) by radio **f(2)** to understand, comprehend ⟨∼ *his thoughts*⟩ **2** to have particular qualities that affect comprehension when read ⟨*Hebrew* ∼s *from right to left*⟩ ⟨*a passage that* ∼s *differently in older versions*⟩ – see also **read between the** LINES, **read the** RIOT ACT [ME *reden* to advise, interpret, read, fr OE *rǣdan;* akin to OHG *rātan* to advise, Gk *arariskein* to fit – more at ARM]

**read out** *vt* **1a** to read aloud **b** to produce a readout of **2** *NAm* to expel from an organization (eg a political party) (as if) by a public reading of notice of dismissal

²**read** /reed/ *n* **1** something (eg a book) for reading ⟨*his latest novel is a pretty dreary* ∼⟩ **2** the action or an instance of reading **3** *chiefly Br* a period of reading ⟨*had a* ∼ *and went to bed early*⟩

³**read** /red/ *adj* instructed by or informed through reading ⟨*widely* ∼ *in contemporary literature*⟩

**readable** /'reedəbl/ *adj* able to be read easily: eg **a** legible **b** pleasurable or interesting to read – **readableness** *n*, **readably** *adv*, **readability** *n*

**reader** /'reedə/ *n* **1a** a person who reads ⟨*she's a slow* ∼⟩ **b** one appointed to read to others: eg **b(1)** LAY READER **b(2)** LECTOR (person who reads the lesson in church) **c(1)** one who reads and corrects proofs; a proofreader **c(2)** one who evaluates manuscripts **c(3)** one who reads periodicals to discover items of special interest or value **d** one employed to read and record the indications of meters **2** a member of the staff of a British university between the ranks of lecturer and professor **3a** a device for projecting a readable image of transparent film (eg microfilm) **b** a device that reads coded information (eg that on a tape or punched cards) **4** an educational book or anthology

**readership** /'reedəˌship/ *n* **1a** the quality or state of being a reader **b** the office, duties, or position of university reader **2** *taking sing or pl vb* a collective body of readers; *esp* the readers of a particular publication (eg a newspaper or magazine) or author

**readily** /'redəli/ *adv* in a ready manner: eg **a** without hesitating, willingly ⟨*he* ∼ *accepted advice*⟩ **b** without much difficulty; easily ⟨*for reasons that anyone could* ∼ *understand*⟩

**reading** /'reeding/ *n* **1** the act of reading **2a** material read or for reading ⟨*his biography makes fine* ∼⟩ **b** the extent to which a person has read ⟨*a man of wide* ∼⟩ **c** an event at which a play, poetry, etc is read to an audience **d** an act of formally reading a bill that constitutes any of three successive stages of approval by a legislature, *specif* Parliament **3a** a form or version of a particular passage in a text ⟨*the generally accepted* ∼⟩ **b** the value indicated or data produced by an instrument ⟨*examined the thermometer* ∼⟩ **4a** a particular interpretation of something (eg a statute) ⟨*what is your* ∼ *of the situation?*⟩ **b** a particular performance of something (eg a musical work)

**reading desk** *n* a desk designed to support a book in a convenient position for a reader, esp a standing reader

---

| | | | |
|---|---|---|---|
| **reabsorption** *n* | **readdress** *vt* | **reannex** *vt* | **reassemble** *vb* |
| **reaccede** *vi* | **readjourn** *vb* | **reannexation** *n* | **reassembly** *n* |
| **reaccept** *vt* | **readjournment** *n* | **reappear** *vi* | **reassert** *vt* |
| **reacceptance** *n* | **readjust** *vb* | **reappearance** *n* | **reassertion** *n* |
| **reaccession** *n* | **readjustable** *adj* | **reapplication** *n* | **reassess** *vt* |
| **reacclaim** *vt* | **readjustment** *n* | **reapply** *vb* | **reassessment** *n* |
| **reacclimatize** *vb* | **readmission** *n* | **reappoint** *vt* | **reassign** *vt* |
| **reaccommodate** *vt* | **readmit** *vb* | **reappointment** *n* | **reassignment** *n* |
| **reaccredit** *vt* | **readmittance** *n* | **reapportion** *vt* | **reassimilate** *vb* |
| **reaccreditation** *n* | **readopt** *vt* | **reapportionment** *n* | **reassimilation** *n* |
| **reaccumulation** *n* | **readoption** *n* | **reappraisal** *n* | **reassort** *vt* |
| **reaccustom** *vt* | **reaffirm** *vt* | **reappraise** *vt* | **reassortment** *n* |
| **reachieve** *vt* | **reaffirmation** *n* | **reappropriate** *vt* | **reassume** *vt* |
| **reachievement** *n* | **reaffix** *vt* | **reapprove** *vt* | **reassumption** *n* |
| **reacidify** *vt* | **reallocate** *vt* | **reargue** *vt* | **reattach** *vb* |
| **reacquaint** *vt* | **reallocation** *n* | **reargument** *n* | **reattachment** *n* |
| **reacquaintance** *n* | **reallot** *vt* | **rearousal** *n* | **reattack** *vb* |
| **reacquire** *vt* | **reallotment** *n* | **rearouse** *vt* | **reattain** *vt* |
| **reacquisition** *n* | **realter** *vb* | **rearrange** *vt* | **reattainment** *n* |
| **reactuate** *vt* | **realteration** *n* | **rearrangement** *n* | **reattempt** *vt or n* |
| **readapt** *vb* | **reanaesthetize** *vt* | **rearranger** *n* | **reauthorize** *vt* |
| **readaptation** *n* | **reanalysis** *n* | **rearrest** *vt or n* | **reawake** *vb* |
| **readd** *vt* | **reanalyse** *vt* | **reascend** *vb* | **reawaken** *vb* |
| **readdict** *vt* | **reanimate** *vt* | **reascent** *n* | |
| **readdiction** *n* | **reanimation** *n* | **reassemblage** *n* | |

**reading room** *n* a room (eg in a library, museum, or club) with facilities for reading or study

**readout** /'reed,owt/ *n* **1** the process of removing information from storage (eg in a computer memory) for display in an understandable form (eg a printout) **2** the information removed from storage for display **3** a device (eg a display) that is used to give a readout **4** *NAm* the radio transmission of data or pictures from a space vehicle by means of playback of a tape recording

¹**ready** /'redi/ *adj* **1a** prepared mentally or physically for some experience or action **b** prepared for immediate use ⟨*dinner is* ~⟩ **2a(1)** willingly disposed; inclined ⟨~ *to agree to his proposal*⟩ **a(2)** likely to do the specified thing ⟨~ *to cry with vexation*⟩ **b(1)** spontaneously prompt ⟨*always has a* ~ *answer*⟩ ⟨*a* ~ *wit*⟩ **b(2)** forward or presumptuously eager ⟨*he is very* ~ *with his criticism*⟩ **3** notably dexterous, adroit, or skilled ⟨*a* ~ *craftsman*⟩ **4** immediately available ⟨*had little* ~ *cash*⟩ [ME *redy;* akin to OHG *reiti* ready, Goth *garaiths* arrayed, Gk *arariskein* to fit – more at ARM] – **readiness** *n*

²**ready** *vt* to make ready

³**ready** *n*, **readies** *n pl*, *informal* READY MONEY 1; *broadly* money ⟨*where did he get the* ~?⟩ – **at/to the ready** prepared or available for immediate use or action; *specif, of a gun* prepared and in the position for immediate aiming and firing

⁴**ready** *adv* in advance; beforehand ⟨*food that is bought* ~ *cooked*⟩

,**ready-'made** *adj* **1** made beforehand; *esp* off-the-peg ⟨~ *suits*⟩ **2** lacking originality or individuality ⟨~ *opinions*⟩ **3** readily available ⟨*her illness provided a* ~ *excuse*⟩ – **ready-made** *n*

**ready money** *n* **1** immediately available cash **2** payment on the spot

**ready reckoner** *n*, *Br* an arithmetical table (eg a list of numbers multiplied by a fixed per cent) or set of tables for aid in calculating

,**ready-to-'wear** *adj*, *of a garment* off-the-peg

,**ready-'witted** *adj* quick-witted

**reafforest** /,ree-ə'forəst/ *vt*, *chiefly Br* to renew the forest cover of by seeding or planting – **reafforestation** *n*

**reagent** /ri'ayj(ə)nt/ *n* a chemical substance that takes part in or brings about a particular chemical reaction and is used esp in detecting or measuring a component, in preparing a product, or in developing photographs [NL *reagent-, reagens,* prp of *reagere* to react – more at REACT]

**reaggregate** /ree'agrigayt/ *vt* to reform into an aggregate or a whole ⟨~ *the subunits of a complex molecule*⟩ – **reaggregate,** **reaggregation** *n*

¹**real** /reel, riəl/ *adj* **1** relating to fixed, permanent, or immovable property (eg lands or tenements) **2a** not artificial, fraudulent, illusory, or apparent; genuine; *also* being precisely what the name implies ⟨~ *economic growth equals apparent growth less the current inflationary increment*⟩ **b(1)** occurring in fact ⟨*a story of* ~ *life*⟩ **b(2)** of practical or everyday concerns or activities ⟨*left university to live in the* ~ *world*⟩ **c** having objective independent existence ⟨*unable to believe that what he saw was* ~⟩ **d** formed by light rays converging at a point ⟨*a* ~ *image*⟩ – compare VIRTUAL **2 e** *maths* **e(1)** belonging to the set of REAL NUMBERS ⟨*the* ~ *roots of an equation*⟩ **e(2)** concerned with or containing REAL NUMBERS ⟨~ *analysis*⟩ **f** measured by purchasing power ⟨~ *income*⟩ **g** complete, great – used chiefly for emphasis ⟨*a* ~ *surprise*⟩ ⟨*considered him a* ~ *idiot*⟩ *synonyms* see GENUINE *antonyms* apparent, factitious, imaginary [ME, relating to things (in law), fr MF, fr ML & LL; ML *realis* relating to things (in law), fr LL, actual, fr L *res* thing, fact; akin to Skt *rai* property] – **realness** *n*

²**real** *n* **1** reality; that which is real – used chiefly in philosophy **2** *NAm* a real thing; *esp* REAL NUMBER – **for real 1** seriously; IN EARNEST ⟨*they were fighting* for real⟩ **2** genuine ⟨*couldn't believe the threats were* for real⟩

³**real** *adv*, *informal* very ⟨*there was only one word for him. He was* ~ *cool* – H M McLuhan⟩

⁴**real** /ray'ahl/ *n*, *pl* **reals, reales** /-lays/ **1** a former monetary unit of Spain and its possessions **2** a coin representing one real [Sp, fr *real* royal, fr L *regalis* – more at ROYAL]

**real estate** *n*, *chiefly NAm* REAL PROPERTY

**realgar** /ri'algə/ *n* an orange-red mineral consisting of a compound of arsenic and sulphur [ME, fr ML, fr Catal, fr Ar *rahj al-ghār* powder of the mine]

**realia** /ri'ahliə, ri'ayliə/ *n pl* objects or activities used to relate classroom teaching to real life [LL, neut pl of *realis* actual]

**realign** /,ree-ə'lien/ *vt* to align again; *esp* to reorganize or make new groupings of – **realignment** *n*

**realism** /'ree,liz(ə)m, 'riə-/ *n* **1** concern for fact or reality and rejection of impractical theory or dogma **2** *philosophy* **2a** a doctrine that classes and universals exist independently of the mind **b** the doctrine or assumption that objects of sense perception exist independently of the mind **3** fidelity in art and literature to nature or to real life and to accurate representation without idealization or distortion – **realist** *adj or n*, **realistic** *adj*, **realistically** *adv*

**reality** /ri'aləti/ *n* **1** the quality or state of being real **2a(1)** a real event, entity, or state of affairs ⟨*his dream became a* ~⟩ **a(2)** the totality of real things and events ⟨*trying to escape from* ~⟩ **b** *philosophy* something that exists necessarily but without causal or logical dependence on anything else

**realization** /,riəli'zaysh(ə)n/ *n* **1** the action of realizing; the state of being realized **2** something realized

**real·ize, -ise** /'reeliez, 'riə-/ *vt* **1a** to convert into actual fact; accomplish ⟨*finally* ~d *his goal*⟩ **b** to cause to seem real; make appear real ⟨*a book in which the characters are carefully* ~d⟩ **2a** to convert into actual money ⟨~ *assets*⟩ **b** to bring or get by sale, investment, or effort; gain ⟨*the house will* ~ *several thousand*⟩ ⟨~d *a large profit on the deal*⟩ **3** to conceive vividly as real; be fully aware of ⟨*he did not* ~ *the risk he was taking*⟩ **4** to play or write (music) in full (eg from a figured bass) [Fr *réaliser,* fr *réal* real] – **realizable** *adj*

**real life** *n* life as it is actually experienced, esp as opposed to fiction or fantasy

**really** /'reeli, 'riəli/ *adv* **1a** in reality, actually ⟨*did he* ~ *say that?*⟩ ⟨*not very difficult* ~⟩ **b** without question; thoroughly ⟨~ *cold weather*⟩ ⟨~ *hates him*⟩ **2** more correctly – used to give force to an injunction ⟨*you should* ~ *have asked me first*⟩

**realm** /relm/ *n* **1** a kingdom **2 realms** *pl*, **realm** a sphere, domain ⟨*within the* ~s *of possibility*⟩ **3** a primary marine or terrestrial biogeographic division of the earth's surface [ME *realme,* fr OF, modif of L *regimen* rule – more at REGIMEN]

**real number** *n*, *maths* a number (eg a SQUARE ROOT of a positive number, an integer, or pi) that does not include a part that is a multiple of the square root of minus one – compare COMPLEX NUMBER, IMAGINARY NUMBER

**real part** *n* the part of a COMPLEX NUMBER that does not include the IMAGINARY NUMBER

**realpolitik** /ray'ahlpoliteek, ray'al-/ *n* politics based on opportunistic and material factors rather than on moral or ethical objectives and usu involving the flouting of civil liberties [Ger, fr *real* practical + *politik* politics]

**real presence** *n*, *often cap R&P* the doctrine that Christ's body and blood are actually present in the Eucharist

**real property** *n* property in buildings and land

**real tennis** *n* a game played with a racket and ball in an irregularly shaped indoor court divided by a net; the original form of tennis – called also ROYAL TENNIS

'**real-,time** *adj* **1** being or involving the almost instantaneous processing, presentation, or use of data by a computer ⟨~ *control of an industrial chemicals plant*⟩ **2** being or involving data processed by real-time methods

**realtor** *n* an estate agent who is a member of the American National Association of Real Estate Boards

**realty** /'reelti, 'riəl-/ *n*, *NAm* real property △ reality [*real* + -*ty* (as in *property*)]

,**real-'valued** *adj*, *of a mathematical function* taking on only REAL NUMBERS for values

**real wages** *n pl* wages measured in terms of actual purchasing power – compare NOMINAL WAGES

¹**ream** /reem/ *n* **1** a quantity of paper equal to 20 quires or variously 480, 500, or 516 sheets **2 reams** *pl*, **ream**, *informal* a great amount (eg of something written or printed) ⟨*composed* ~s *of poetry*⟩ [ME *reme,* fr MF *raime,* fr Ar *rizmah,* lit., bundle]

²**ream** *vt* **1a** to widen the opening of (a hole); countersink **b** to enlarge or finish (a hole) with a reamer **c** to remove by reaming **2** *NAm* to press the juice from (a citrus fruit) with a lemon squeezer **3** *NAm slang* to cheat, victimize [perh fr (assumed) ME dial. *remen* to open up, fr OE dial. *rēman;* akin to OE *rÿman* to open up, *rūm* roomy – more at ROOM]

³**ream** *vt*, *Scot & N Eng* to skim (cream) from the surface of milk [ME *remen,* fr *rem* cream, froth, fr OE *rēam* cream; akin to MLG *rōm* cream]

**reamer** /'reemə/ *n* **1** a rotating finishing tool with cutting edges used to enlarge or shape a hole **2** *NAm* LEMON SQUEEZER

**reap** /reep/ *vt* **1a(1)** to cut (a crop) usu with a sickle, scythe, or COMBINE HARVESTER **a(2)** to clear (eg a field) of a crop by reaping **b** to gather by reaping; harvest **2** to obtain or win, esp as the reward for effort ⟨*to ~ lasting benefits from study*⟩ ~ *vi* to reap something [ME *repen*, fr OE *reopan*; akin to OE *rāw* row – more at ROW] – **reaper** *n*

**reaphook** /'reep,hook/ *n* a sickle

¹**rear** /riə/ *vt* **1** to erect by building; construct **2** to raise upright **3a(1)** to look after and educate (a child) **a(2)** to breed and keep (an animal) for use or market **b** to cause (eg plants) to grow ~ *vi* **1** to rise to a height **2** *esp of a horse* to rise up on the hind legs *synonyms* see ¹LIFT [ME *reren*, fr OE *rǣran*; akin to ON *reisa* to raise, OE *rīsan* to rise] – **rearer** *n*

²**rear** *n* **1** the back part of something: eg **1a** the unit (eg of an army) or area farthest from the enemy **b** the part of something located opposite its front ⟨*the ~ of a house*⟩ **c** *informal* the buttocks **2** the space or position at the back ⟨*moved to the ~*⟩ [prob fr *rear-* (in such terms as *rearguard*)] – **bring up the rear** to be or come last

³**rear** *adj* at the back ⟨*a ~ window*⟩

⁴**rear** *adv* towards or from the rear – usu in combination ⟨*a rear-driven car*⟩

**rear admiral** *n* – see MILITARY RANKS table

¹**rearguard** /'riə,gahd/ *adj* of or being vigorous resistance, esp in the face of defeat ⟨*fought a ~ action against automation*⟩

²**rearguard** *n* a military detachment detailed to protect the rear of a main body or force, esp during a retreat [ME *reregarde*, fr MF, fr OF, fr *rere* backward, behind (fr L *retro*) + *garde* guard – more at RETRO-]

**rearm** /,ree'ahm/ *vb* to arm (eg a nation or military force) again, esp with new or better weapons – **rearmament** *n*

**rearmost** /'riə,mohst/ *adj* farthest in the rear; last

**rearview mirror** /'riə,vyooh/ *n* a mirror (eg in a motor car) that gives a view of the area behind a vehicle

¹**rearward** /'riə,wood/ *n* the rear; *esp* the rear division (eg of an army) ⟨*to ~ of the main column*⟩ [ME *rerewarde*, fr AF; akin to OF *reregarde* rearguard]

²**rearward** *adj* at, near, or towards the rear [²*rear* + -*ward*] – **rearwardly** *adv*

**rearwards** /'riə,woodz/, *NAm chiefly* **rearward** *adv* at or towards the rear; backwards

¹**reason** /'reez(ə)n/ *n* **1a** a statement offered in explanation or justification ⟨*gave ~s that were quite satisfactory*⟩ **b** a rational ground or motive ⟨*a good ~ to act soon*⟩ **c** a sufficient ground of explanation or of logical defence; *esp* something that supports a conclusion or explains a fact ⟨*outlined the ~s behind his client's action*⟩ **d** that which makes some phenomenon intelligible; a cause ⟨*wanted to know the ~ for earthquakes*⟩ **2a(1)** the power of comprehending, inferring, or thinking, esp in an orderly rational way; intelligence **a(2)** proper exercise of the mind **a(3)** sanity [ME *resoun*, fr OF *raison*, fr L *ration-, ratio* reason, computation; akin to Goth *garathjan* to count, L *reri* to calculate, think, Gk *arariskein* to fit – more at ARM] – **it stands to reason** it is obvious or logical – **within reason** within reasonable limits – **with reason** with good cause

*synonyms* Reason, understanding, discernment, judgment, and intuition all mean "the power by which we reach truth or knowledge". Reason implies the orderly process of arriving at logical conclusions. Understanding stresses mental grasp of what is perceived, and the ability to apply concepts to it. Discernment emphasizes discrimination in the selection of what is relevant or valuable, to which judgment adds the idea of reaching sound conclusions about things. Intuition, by contrast, is the spontaneous perception of the underlying nature of things without evident rational thought. See ¹CAUSE *usage* We speak of the reason *of* or *for* something, or the reason *that* something happens, and it is perfectly legitimate also to speak either of the reason something happens or the reason *why* something happens. Sentences such as ⟨*the reason he failed was due to/attributed to/on account of his health*⟩ are disapproved of by some people, who feel that the idea of "explanation" should not be expressed twice in the same sentence. The construction ⟨*the reason was because . . .*⟩ is disapproved of for the same

reason, although it has been established in English since the 17th century ⟨*the Reason why so few Marriages are Happy is because Young Ladies spend their time in making Nets not in making Cages* – Jonathan Swift⟩. See ¹BECAUSE

²**reason** *vi* **1** to use the faculty of reason so as to arrive at conclusions; think **2** to talk or argue with another so as to influence his/her actions or opinions ⟨*can't ~ with them*⟩ ~ *vt* **1** to persuade or influence by the use of reason ⟨*~ed myself out of such fears*⟩ **2** to discover, formulate, or conclude by the use of reason ⟨*a carefully ~ed analysis*⟩ – **reasoner** *n*

**reasonable** /'reez(ə)nəbl/ *adj* **1a** in accord with reason ⟨*a ~ theory*⟩ **b** not extreme or excessive ⟨*~ requests*⟩ **c** moderate, fair ⟨*a ~ boss*⟩ ⟨*a ~ price*⟩ **d** inexpensive **2a** having the faculty of reason; rational **b** possessing sound judgment; sensible – **reasonableness** *n*, **reasonably** *adv*

**reasoning** /'reez(ə)ning/ *n* **1** the use of reasons; *esp* the drawing of inferences or conclusions through the use of reason **2** an instance of the use of reason; an argument

**reasonless** /'reezənləs/ *adj* **1a** not reasoned; senseless ⟨*~ hostility*⟩ **b** not based on or supported by reasons ⟨*a ~ accusation*⟩ **2** *archaic* not having the faculty of reason ⟨*a ~ brute*⟩ – **reasonlessly** *adv*

**reassurance** /,ree-ə'shooərəns,-'shawrəns/ *n* **1** reassuring or being reassured **2** reinsurance

**reassure** /,ree-ə'shooə, -'shaw/ *vt* **1** to assure anew ⟨*~d him that the work was satisfactory*⟩ **2** to restore confidence to ⟨*I was ~d by his promise*⟩ **3** to reinsure – **reassuringly** *adv*

**Réaumur** /,rayoh'myooə/ *adj* relating to, conforming to, or being a scale of temperature on which the water freezes at 0° and boils at 80° under standard conditions [René Antoine Ferchault de *Réaumur* †1757 Fr physicist]

**reave** /reev/ *vb* **reaved, reft** /reft/ *archaic vi* to plunder, rob ~ *vt* **1a** to deprive of; rob **b** to seize **2** to carry or tear away [ME *reven*, fr OE *rēafian* – more at BEREAVE] – **reaver** *n*

**rebarbative** /ri'bahbətiv/ *adj, formal* repellent, unattractive [Fr *rébarbatif*, fr MF, fr *rebarber* to be repellent, fr *re-* + *barbe* beard, fr L *barba* – more at BEARD] – **rebarbatively** *adv*

¹**rebate** /'reebayt/ *vt* **1a** to make a rebate of **b** to give a rebate to **2** *archaic* to reduce the force or activity of; diminish **3** *archaic* to reduce the sharpness of; blunt ~ *vi* to give rebates [ME *rebaten* to deduct, reduce, fr MF *rabattre* to beat down again, fr OF, fr *re-* + *abattre* to beat down, fr *a-* (fr L *ad-*) + *battre* to beat, fr L *battuere* – more at BATTLE] – **rebater** *n*

²**rebate** *n* a return of part of a payment; an abatement

³**rebate** /'rabit, 'reebayt/ *vt or n* RABBET [by alter.]

**rebbe** /'rebə/ *n* a Jewish spiritual leader or teacher; a rabbi [Yiddish, fr Heb *rabbī* rabbi]

**rebec, rebeck** /'reebek/ *n* a medieval usu 3-stringed musical instrument that has a pear-shaped body and slender neck and is played with a bow [MF *rebec*, alter. of OF *rebebe*, fr OProv *rebeb*, fr Ar *rebāb*]

¹**rebel** /'rebl/ *adj* **1a** opposing or taking arms against a government or ruler **b** of rebels ⟨*the ~ camp*⟩ **2** disobedient, rebellious [ME, fr OF *rebelle*, fr L *rebellis*, fr *re-* + *bellum* war, fr OL *duellum* – more at DUEL]

²**rebel** *n* one who rebels or participates in a rebellion

³**rebel** /ri'bel/ *vi* -ll- **1a** to oppose or disobey (one in) authority or control **b** to renounce and resist by force the authority of one's government **2a** to act in or show opposition or dissent ⟨*~led against the conventions of polite society*⟩ **b** to feel or exhibit anger or revulsion ⟨*~led at the injustice of life*⟩

**rebellion** /ri'belyən/ *n* **1** opposition to (one in) authority or dominance **2a** open, armed, and usu unsuccessful defiance of or resistance to an established government **b** an instance of such defiance or resistance

*synonyms* Rebellion, insurrection, uprising, revolt, mutiny, revolution, coup d'état, and putsch all mean "armed outbreak against authority". A rebellion, insurrection, uprising, or revolt usually fails in its objective; but a rebellion is commonly a war between the central government of a country and some part of that country, and is strong enough to constitute a real problem to the authorities; while an insurrection or uprising is more localized, uprising particularly suggesting suddenness, and revolt often imply-

---

| | | | |
|---|---|---|---|
| **rebait** *vt* | **rebiddable** *adj* | **reboil** *vb* | **rebutton** *vt* |
| **rebalance** *vt* | **rebind** *vt* | **rebook** *vb* | **rebuy** *vt* |
| **rebaptism** *b* | **reblend** *vb or n* | **rebottle** *vt* | |
| **rebaptize** *vt* | **rebloom** *vi* | **rebranch** *vi* | |
| **rebid** *vb* | **reboard** *vt* | **rebury** *vt* | |

ing a rebellion by a section of the population rather than by an area ⟨*the Peasants'* **Revolt**⟩. A **mutiny** is a local insurrection usually by some part of the armed forces. The successful overthrow and replacement of an established government is **revolution** or, if achieved by a small group, a **coup d'état**. A **putsch** is a secretly planned attempt at revolution.

**rebellious** /ri'belyəs/ *adj* **1a** given to or engaged in rebellion ⟨∼ *troops*⟩ **b** relating to or characteristic of a rebel or rebellion ⟨*a* ∼ *speech*⟩ **2** resisting treatment or management; refractory – **rebelliously** *adv*, **rebelliousness** *n*

**rebirth** /,ree'buhth/ *n* **1a** a new or second birth – compare REINCARNATION, METEMPSYCHOSIS **b** spiritual renewal or regeneration **2** a renaissance, revival ⟨*a* ∼ *of nationalism*⟩

**reboant** /'rebohənt/ *adj, chiefly poetic* loudly echoing; reverberant [L *reboant-, reboans*, prp of *reboare* to resound, fr *re-* + *boare* to cry aloud, roar, fr Gk *boan*, of imit origin]

**rebore** /,ree'baw/ *vt* to bore again; *specif* to enlarge and renew the BORE (hole in which a piston moves) of a cylinder in (a car engine or other INTERNAL-COMBUSTION ENGINE) – **rebore** *n*

**reborn** /,ree'bawn/ *adj* (as if) born again; regenerated, revived; *specif* spiritually renewed

¹**rebound** /ri'bownd/ *vi* **1** to spring back (as if) on collision or impact with another body; *also* RECOIL 3 **2** to recover from setback or frustration ∼ *vt* to cause to rebound [ME *rebounden*, fr MF *rebondir*, fr OF, fr *re-* + *bondir* to bound – more at BOUND]

    **synonyms** Compare **rebound**, **redound**, and **resound**. Both **rebound** and **redound** can mean figuratively "bounce back" ⟨*their hatred* **rebounds/redounds** *on themselves*⟩, but careful writers prefer to confine **redound** to the sense "contribute to" ⟨*your behaviour will* **redound** *to your credit*⟩, while distinguishing it from **resound** meaning figuratively "reverberate" ⟨*her name will* **resound** *through the ages*⟩.

²**rebound** /'ree,bownd; *also* ri'bownd/ *n* **1a** the action of rebounding; a recoil **b** an upward leap or movement; a recovery ⟨*a sharp* ∼ *in prices*⟩ **2a** a basketball, soccer ball, or hockey puck that rebounds **b** the act of gaining possession of a rebound (e g in basketball) – **on the rebound** (whilst) in an unsettled or emotional state resulting from setback, frustration, or crisis ⟨*on the rebound from an unhappy love affair*⟩

**rebroadcast** /,ree'brawd,kahst/ *vt* **rebroadcast 1** to broadcast again (a radio or television programme being simultaneously received from another source) **2** to repeat (a broadcast) at a later time – **rebroadcast** *n*

**rebuff** /ri'buf/ *vt* to refuse or check sharply; snub △ rebut [MF *rebuffer*, fr OIt *ribuffare* to reprimand] – **rebuff** *n*

**rebuild** /ree'bild/ *vb* **rebuilt** /-bilt/ *vt* **1a** to make extensive repairs to; reconstruct ⟨∼ *a war-torn city*⟩ **b** to restore to a previous state ⟨∼ *inventories*⟩ **2** to make extensive changes in; remodel ⟨∼ *society*⟩ ∼ *vi* to build again ⟨*planned to* ∼ *after the fire*⟩

¹**rebuke** /ri'byoohk/ *vt* **1a** to criticize sharply; reprimand **b** to serve as a rebuke to ⟨*his humility* ∼s *me*⟩ **2** *archaic* to turn back or keep down; check [ME *rebuken*, fr ONF *rebuker*] – **rebuker** *n*

²**rebuke** *n* an expression of strong disapproval; a reprimand

**rebus** /'reebəs/ *n* a representation of words or syllables by pictures of objects or by symbols whose names resemble the intended words or syllables in sound; *also* a riddle made up of such pictures or symbols [L, by things, abl pl of *res* thing – more at REAL]

**rebut** /ri'but/ *vb* **-tt-** *vt* **1** to beat back or check; repel ⟨*unable to* ∼ *this despairing mood*⟩ **2a** to refute by formal legal argument **b** to expose the falsity of; refute ∼ *vi* to make or furnish an answer or counter proof *usage* see REFUTE △ rebuff [ME *rebuten*, fr OF *reboter*, fr *re-* + *boter* to butt – more at BUTT] – **rebuttable** *adj*

**rebuttal** /ri'but(ə)l/ *n* **1** the act of rebutting, esp in a legal action **2** an argument or proof that rebuts

¹**rebutter** /ri'butə/ *n* the answer made by the defendant in the third round of allegations and counter-allegations (PLEADING) in a legal action to the plaintiff's SURREJOINDER [AF *rebuter*, fr OF *reboter* to rebut]

²**rebutter** *n* something that rebuts; a refutation

**recalcitrant** /ri'kalsitrənt/ *adj* **1** persistently defiant of authority **2** difficult to handle or control; refractory **3** resistant *synonyms* see UNRULY *antonym* amenable [LL *recalcitrant-, recalcitrans*, prp of *recalcitrare* to be stubbornly disobedient, fr L, to kick back, fr *re-* + *calcitrare* to kick, fr *calc-, calx* heel

– more at CALKIN] – **recalcitrance** *n*, **recalcitrant**·*n*

**recalculate** /,ree'kalkyoolayt/ *vt* to calculate again, esp in order to discover the source of an error or formulate new conclusions – **recalculation** *n*

**recalescence** /,reekə'lesəns/ *n* an increase in the temperature of iron or a similar metal, that occurs as the metal cools through a range of temperatures in which a change in crystal structure occurs [L *recalescere* to grow warm again, fr *re-* + *calescere* to grow warm, incho of *calēre* to be warm – more at LEE]

¹**recall** /ri'kawl/ *vt* **1a** to call or summon back ⟨*was* ∼ed *to active duty*⟩ ⟨∼ed *their ambassador*⟩ **b** to bring back to mind; think of again ⟨∼s *his early years*⟩ **c** to remind one of ⟨*a playwright who* ∼s *the Elizabethan dramatists*⟩ **2** to cancel, revoke **3** *poetic* to restore, revive – **recallable** *adj*, **recaller** *n*, **recallability** *n*

²**recall** /ri'kawl, 'ree,kawl/ *n* **1** a call to return ⟨*a* ∼ *of workers after a layoff*⟩ **2** remembrance of what has been learned or experienced; recollection ⟨*had almost perfect visual* ∼⟩ **3** the act of revoking or the possibility of being revoked ⟨*this matter is past* ∼⟩ **4** the return to a dealer of a product (e g a car) specified as defective by the manufacturer for the dealer to make repairs **5** the ability (e g of an information retrieval system) to retrieve stored material **6** *NAm* the right or procedure by which an elected representative may be removed by his/her constituency or constituency party

**recanal·ization, -isation** /ree,kanəlie'zaysh(ə)n/ *n* the process of rejoining a cut, torn, etc body tube (e g the duct that conveys semen)

**recant** /ri'kant/ *vt* to withdraw or repudiate (a statement or belief) formally and publicly; renounce ∼ *vi* to make an open confession of error; *esp* to disavow a religious or political opinion or belief [L *recantare*, fr *re-* + *cantare* to sing – more at CHANT] – **recantation** *n*

¹**recap** /'ree,kap/ *vt* **-pp-** *NAm* to partially retread (a worn pneumatic tyre) [*re-* + ²*cap*] – **recappable** *adj*

²**recap** *n, NAm* a recapped tyre

³**recap** /ri'kap, 'ree,kap/ *vb* **-pp-** to recapitulate [by shortening]

⁴**recap** /'ree,kap/ *n* RECAPITULATION 1

**recapital·ization, -isation** /ree,kapitəlie'zaysh(ə)n/ *n* a reorganization of the capital structure of a business enterprise – **recapitalize** *vt*

**recapitulate** /,reekə'pityoolayt/ *vt* to repeat the principal points or stages of (e g an argument or discourse); summarize ∼ *vi* to sum up an argument or discourse [LL *recapitulatus*, pp of *recapitulare* to restate by heads, sum up, fr L *re-* + *capitulum* division of a book – more at CHAPTER]

**recapitulation** /,reekəpityoo'laysh(ə)n/ *n* **1** a concise summary **2** the process, occurring during the development of an embryo, of passing through successive stages that resemble the series of types through which the ancestors of the organism evolved **3** *music* the last of usu three parts of a movement written in SONATA FORM in which the main themes are repeated, usu in the TONIC key or main tonality – compare DEVELOPMENT 1, EXPOSITION 2b(1)

¹**recapture** /ri'kapchə, 'ree,kapchə/ *n* **1a** the act of retaking **b** an instance of being retaken **2** *NAm* a government seizure under law of earnings or profits beyond a fixed amount

²**recapture** *vt* **1a** to capture again **b** to experience again ⟨*to* ∼ *the atmosphere of the past*⟩ **2** *NAm* to take (e g a portion of earnings or profits above a fixed amount) by law or through negotiations under law

**recast** /,ree'kahst/ *vt* **recast** to cast again ⟨∼ *a gun*⟩ ⟨∼ *a play*⟩; *also* to remodel, refashion ⟨∼s *his political image to fit the times*⟩ – **recast** *n*

¹**recce** /'reki/ *n, informal* a preliminary investigation or exploration (e g of a territory); a reconnaissance [by shortening & alter. fr *reconnaissance*]

²**recce** *vb* **recceing; recced, recceed** *informal* to reconnoitre [by shortening & alter.]

¹**recede** /ri'seed/ *vi* **1a** to move back or away; withdraw **b** to slant backwards ⟨*a receding chin*⟩ **2** to grow less, smaller, or more distant; diminish ⟨*fears that demand will* ∼⟩ ⟨*hope* ∼d⟩ *antonyms* proceed, advance, protrude (for 1b) [L *recedere* to go back, fr *re-* + *cedere* to go – more at CEDE]

²**recede** /,ree'seed/ *vt* to restore (e g land) to a former possessor [*re-* + *cede*]

¹**receipt** /ri'seet/ *n* **1** the act or process of receiving ⟨*in* ∼ *of a large salary*⟩ ⟨*please acknowledge* ∼ *of the goods*⟩ **2 receipts** *pl*, **receipt** something (e g goods or money) received – ⟨*took*

*the day's* ~s *to the bank*⟩ **3** a written acknowledgment of having received goods or money **4** *archaic* a recipe [ME *receite,* fr ONF, fr ML *recepta,* prob fr L, neut pl of *receptus,* pp of *recipere* to receive]

²**receipt** *vt* to give a receipt for or acknowledge, esp in writing, the receiving of; *esp* to mark (e g a bill) with a receipt

**receivable** /ri'seevəbl/ *adj* **1** capable of being received **2** liable for payment ⟨*accounts* ~⟩

**receivables** /ri'seevəblz/ *n pl* amounts of money owed to a company and thus part of its assets

**receive** /ri'seev/ *vt* **1a** to come into possession of; acquire ⟨~ *a gift*⟩ **b** to accept for consideration; give attention to ⟨*had to* ~ *their unwanted attentions*⟩ ⟨~ *a petition*⟩ **2a** to act as a receptacle or container for ⟨*the cistern* ~s *water from the roof*⟩ **b** to assimilate through the mind or senses ⟨~ *new ideas*⟩ **3a** to permit to enter; admit **b** to welcome, greet; *also* to entertain **c** to act in response to ⟨*how did she* ~ *the offer?*⟩ ⟨*well* ~d *on his tour*⟩ **4** to accept as authoritative or true; believe ⟨~d *wisdom*⟩ **5a** to take the force or pressure of; bear ⟨*these pillars* ~ *the weight of the roof*⟩ **b** to take (a mark or impression) from the weight of something ⟨*some clay* ~s *clear impressions*⟩ **c** to be provided with; experience ⟨~d *his early education at home*⟩ **d** to suffer the hurt or injury of ⟨~ *a broken nose*⟩ **6** to be the player who returns (the service of his/her opponent) in tennis, squash, etc **7** to convert (an incoming signal, esp RADIO WAVES) into a form suitable for human perception or for further electronic processing (e g amplification) ~ *vi* **1** to be a recipient **2** to be at home to visitors ⟨~s *on Tuesdays*⟩ **3** to receive an incoming signal, esp RADIO WAVES **4** *chiefly Br* to buy and sell articles which have been stolen; act as an intermediary for thieves [ME *receiven,* fr ONF *receivre,* fr L *recipere,* fr re- + *capere* to take – more at HEAVE]

**Received Pronunciation** *n* a prestigious form of nonlocal British English pronunciation used by many educated British people, esp in the south, and usu by the BBC

**Received Standard** *n, NAm* Received Pronunciation

**received text** *n* TEXTUS RECEPTUS

**receiver** /ri'seevə/ *n* **1** one who receives: e g **1a** a person appointed by a court to hold in trust and administer property under litigation **b** a person appointed to administer the affairs of a business that is being wound up **c** a person who knowingly receives stolen goods; a fence **2** *chemistry* a vessel to receive and contain something (e g gases); *specif* one that collects the pure or concentrated liquid produced by DISTILLATION **3a** a radio, television, or other part of a communications system that receives the signal **b** the part of a telephone that contains the mouthpiece and earpiece

**receiver general** *n, pl* **receivers general** a public officer who receives the taxes in each area and forwards them to the Treasury

**receivership** /ri'seevəship/ *n* **1** the office or function of a receiver **2** the state of being in the hands of a receiver

**receiving end** *n* the position of being a recipient, esp a victim – usu in *on the receiving end*

**recension** /ri'sensh(ə)n/ *n* **1** a critical revision of a text **2** a text established by critical revision [L *recension-, recensio* enumeration, fr *recensēre* to review, fr re- + *censēre* to assess,

tax]

**recent** /'rees(ə)nt/ *adj* **1a** of a time not long past ⟨*the* ~ *election*⟩ **b** having lately come into existence; new, fresh ⟨~ *snow*⟩ **2** *cap* of or being the present or post-Pleistocene geological epoch – called also HOLOCENE **synonyms** see ¹MODERN **antonym** ancient [MF or L; MF, fr L *recent-, recens;* akin to Gk *kainos* new] – **recentness, recency** *n*

**recently** /'reesəntli/ *adv* during a recent period of time; lately

**receptacle** /ri'septəkl/ *n* **1** an object that receives and contains something; a container **2a** a cavity between cells in a plant or animal that contains substances (e g oils) secreted by the adjacent cells **b** the end of the flower stalk of a FLOWERING PLANT on which the floral structures (e g petals and stamens) are borne **c** a modified branch bearing spore-producing capsules or cases in a plant (e g a fern, alga, or lichen) that reproduces by means of spores rather than seeds **3** *chiefly NAm* an electrical socket [L *receptaculum,* fr *receptare* to receive, fr *receptus,* pp of *recipere* to receive]

**receptaculum** /,reesep'takyooləm/ *n, pl* **receptacula** /-lə/ RECEPTACLE 2 [NL, fr L]

**reception** /ri'sepsh(ə)n/ *n* **1** receiving or being received: e g **1a** admission ⟨*his* ~ *into the church*⟩ **b** a response, reaction ⟨*the play met with a mixed* ~⟩ **c** the receiving of a radio or television broadcast, esp with reference to the quality of sound or picture ⟨*good* ~ *on VHF*⟩ **2** a formal social gathering during which guests are received **3** *Br* an office or desk where visitors or clients (e g to an office, factory, or hotel) are received on arrival ⟨*ask at* ~⟩ [ME *recepcion,* fr MF or L; MF *reception,* fr L *reception-, receptio,* fr *receptus,* pp of *recipere*]

**reception class** *n* a class for newly entered children in a school

**receptionist** /ri'sepshənist/ *n* one employed (e g in a hotel or office or by a doctor or dentist) to greet and assist callers or clients

**reception room** *n* **1** a room used primarily for banquets and receptions in a hotel **2** a room in which guests can be entertained in a private house; *esp* a sitting room or dining room – used esp by estate agents **3** WAITING ROOM

**receptive** /ri'septiv/ *adj* **1** able or inclined to receive; *esp* open and responsive to ideas, impressions, or suggestions ⟨*a* ~ *mind*⟩ **2a** of a nerve, nerve ending, etc *that receives stimuli* in a state of readiness to receive and transmit stimuli **b** of or concerned with the reception of stimuli; SENSORY – **receptively** *adv,* **receptiveness, receptivity** *n*

**receptor** /ri'septə/ *n* a receiver: e g **a** a cell or group of cells that receives stimuli which are then transmitted as nerve impulses; *esp* a nerve ending (e g in the skin) or SENSE ORGAN (e g a taste bud) that receives information about temperature, light, sound, etc from the environment **b(1)** a chemical group on the surface of a cell, that provides a site for a particular antibody or a virus to attach to; *broadly* a chemical structure (e g on an ENZYME) that provides a site of attachment **b(2)** a chemical structure in or on the surface of a cell, to which a hormone, NEUROTRANSMITTER, etc binds, triggering off a reaction (e g transmission of a nerve impulse) inside the cell – compare ALPHA-RECEPTOR, BETA-RECEPTOR

¹**recess** /ri'ses, 'reeses USE *the last pron is disliked by some speakers*/ *n* **1** *usu pl* a hidden, secret, or secluded place ⟨*illum-*

| | | | |
|---|---|---|---|
| **recalibrate** *vt* | **reclothe** *vt* | **recompression** *n* | **reconsolidate** *vb* |
| **recapitalization** *n* | **recock** *vt* | **recomputation** *n* | **reconsolidation** *n* |
| **recapitalize** *vb* | **recodification** *n* | **recompute** *vt* | **reconsult** *vb* |
| **recatalogue** *vt* | **recodify** *vt* | **reconceive** *vb* | **reconsultation** *n* |
| **recaution** *vt* | **recolonization** *n* | **reconcentrate** *vb* | **recontact** *vb or n* |
| **recentralization** *n* | **recolonize** *vt* | **reconcentration** *n* | **recontaminate** *vt* |
| **recentrifuge** *vt* | **recolour** *vt* | **reconception** *n* | **recontamination** *n* |
| **recertification** *n* | **recomb** *vt* | **reconceptualization** *n* | **recontest** *vt* |
| **recertify** *vt* | **recombine** *vb* | **reconceptualize** *vt* | **recontract** *vb* |
| **rechallenge** *vt* | **recommence** *vb* | **recondensation** *n* | **reconvene** *vb* |
| **rechannel** *vt* | **recommencement** *n* | **recondense** *vb* | **reconvict** *vt* |
| **rechart** *vt* | **recommission** *n* | **reconduct** *vt* | **reconviction** *n* |
| **recharter** *vt* | **recommit** *vt* | **reconfine** *vt* | **reconvince** *vt* |
| **recheck** *vb or n* | **recommitment** *n* | **reconnect** *vt* | **recook** *vt* |
| **rechoreograph** *vt* | **recommittal** *n* | **reconnection** *n* | **recopy** *vt* |
| **rechristen** *vt* | **recompare** *vt* | **reconquer** *vt* | **recross** *vb* |
| **recirculate** *vb* | **recomparison** *n* | **reconquest** *n* | **recross** *vb* |
| **recirculation** *n* | **recompilation** *n* | **reconsecrate** *vt* | **recrown** *vt* |
| **reclassification** *n* | **recompile** *vt* | **reconsecration** *n* | **recultivate** *vt* |
| **reclassify** *vt* | **recompound** *vt* | **reconsign** *vt* | **recut** *vt* |
| **reclean** *vt* | **recompress** *vt* | **reconsignment** *n* | |

*inating the ~es of American politics – TLS⟩ ⟨the dark ~es of the mind⟩* **2a** an indentation, cleft ⟨*a deep ~ in the hill*⟩ **b** an alcove, niche ⟨*a ~ lined with books*⟩ **3a** a suspension of usual business or activity (e g of a legislative body or law court) usu for a period of rest or relaxation ⟨*a parliamentary ~*⟩ – often *+ in* ⟨*Parliament is in ~*⟩ **b** *NAm* a break between school classes **4** INTAGLIO 1c *synonyms* see ¹HOLIDAY [L *recessus,* fr *recessus,* pp of *recedere* to recede]

²**recess** /ri'ses/ *vt* **1** to put into a recess; *esp* to conceal in a recess ⟨*~ed lighting*⟩ **2** to make or build a recess in **3** *chiefly NAm* to interrupt for a recess ~ *vi, chiefly NAm* to take a recess

¹**recession** /ri'sesh(ə)n/ *n* **1** the act or action of receding; a withdrawal **2** a departing procession (e g of clergy and choir at the end of a church service) **3** a period of reduced economic activity – **recessionary** *adj*

²**recession** /ˌree'sesh(ə)n/ *n* the act of restoring to a former possessor [re- + cession]

¹**recessional** /ri'sesh(ə)nl/ *adj* **1** of a withdrawal **2** of a parliamentary recess

²**recessional** *n* a hymn or piece of music played at the conclusion of a church service, during which the clergy and choir withdraw

¹**recessive** /ri'sesiv/ *adj* **1** tending to go back; receding **2a** being the one of a pair of genes coding for alternative forms of a particular inheritable characteristic (e g eye colour) whose effect is shown if the other member of the pair codes for the same version of the characteristic (e g blue eyes) but is suppressed if the other gene codes for a contrasting version of the characteristic (e g brown eyes) **b** being an inheritable characteristic coded for by a recessive gene ⟨*blue eyes are ~*⟩ □ (2) compare DOMINANT – **recessively** *adv,* **recessiveness** *n*

²**recessive** *n* **1** a recessive gene or inherited characteristic **2** an organism possessing one or more recessive characteristics

**recharge** /ˌree'chahj/ *vt* to charge again; *esp* to renew the active materials in (a storage battery) – **recharge** *n,* **recharger** *n,* **rechargeable** *adj*

**réchauffé** /ray'shohfay (*Fr* reʃofe)/ *n* **1** a warmed-up dish of cooked food, esp leftover food **2** a rehash [Fr, fr pp of *réchauffer* to reheat, fr ré- re- + *chauffer* to warm, fr MF *chaufer* – more at CHAFE]

**recherché** /rə'sheəshay (*Fr* rəʃɛrʃe)/ *adj* **1a** chosen with care; exquisite, choice ⟨*a ~ stock of snuff*⟩ **b** exotic, rare ⟨*discusses all manner of words – common, ~, and slang – New Yorker*⟩ **2** pretentious, affected ⟨*his ~ highbrow talk*⟩ [Fr, fr pp of *rechercher* to seek out, fr MF *recherchier* – more at RESEARCH]

**recidivist** /ri'sidivist/ *n* one who relapses, specif into a previous pattern of criminal behaviour [Fr *récidiviste,* fr *récidiver* to relapse, fr ML *recidivare,* fr L *recidivus* recurring, fr *recidere* to fall back, fr re- + *cadere* to fall – more at CHANCE] – **recidivism,** *n,* **recidivist, recidivistic** *adj*

**recipe** /'resipi/ *n* **1** a set of instructions for making something (e g a food dish) from a given list of ingredients **2** a procedure for doing or attaining something ⟨*a ~ for success*⟩ **3** *archaic* PRESCRIPTION 3a [L, take, imper of *recipere* to take, receive – more at RECEIVE]

**recipient** /ri'sipi-ənt/ *n* one who or that which receives; a receiver [L *recipient-, recipiens,* prp of *recipere*] – **recipient** *adj*

¹**reciprocal** /ri'siprəkl/ *adj* **1a** *esp of a mathematical function* inversely related to another; increasing as the other decreases or vice versa **b** *genetics* of, being, or resulting from crosses between two strains in which the male parent of one strain is crossed with the female of the second strain and vice versa **2** shared, felt, or shown by both sides; mutual ⟨*~ love*⟩ ⟨*agreed to extend ~ privileges to each other's citizens*⟩ **3** serving to reciprocate; given, shown, felt, or done in return ⟨*the ~ devastation of nuclear war*⟩ ⟨*did not expect ~ benefit*⟩ **4** marked by or based on reciprocity ⟨*~ trade agreements*⟩ *synonyms* see MUTUAL [L *reciprocus* returning the same way, alternating, irreg fr re- + *pro-*] – **reciprocally** *adv*

²**reciprocal** *n* **1** something in a reciprocal relationship to another **2a** either of any two numbers (e g ²/₃, ³/₂) which when multiplied together give one ⟨*the ~ of 2 is 0.5*⟩ **b** the number obtained by dividing one by a particular number ⟨*the ~ of 10 is 0.1*⟩

**reciprocal pronoun** *n* a pronoun (e g *each other*) used to denote mutual action or cross relationship between the members comprised in a plural subject

**reciprocate** /ri'siprə,kayt/ *vt* **1** to give and take mutually ⟨*the two countries ~d pledges of friendship*⟩ **2** to return in kind or

degree ⟨*~ a compliment gracefully*⟩ ~ *vi* **1** to make a return for something ⟨*he stroked the cat and it ~d by purring*⟩ **2** to move forwards and backwards alternately ⟨*a reciprocating valve*⟩ – **reciprocator** *n*

**reciprocating engine** /ri'siprə,kayting/ *n* an engine in which the to-and-fro motion of a piston is transformed into circular motion of the crankshaft

**reciprocation** /ri,siprə'kaysh(ə)n/ *n* **1a** a mutual exchange **b** a return in kind or similar value **2** an alternating motion – **reciprocative** *adj*

**reciprocity** /ˌresi'prosəti/ *n* **1** the quality or state of being reciprocal; mutual dependence, action, or influence **2** a mutual exchange of privileges; *specif* a recognition by one of two countries or institutions of the validity of licences or privileges granted by the other

**recital** /ri'sietl/ *n* **1a** the act or an instance of reciting **b** a detailed account; an enumeration ⟨*the ~ of his troubles*⟩ **c** a discourse, narration ⟨*a colourful ~ of a night on the town*⟩ **2a** a concert given by an individual musician or dancer or by a dance troupe **b** a public performance by music or dance pupils – **recitalist** *n*

**recitation** /ˌresi'taysh(ə)n/ *n* **1** the act of enumerating ⟨*a ~ of relevant details*⟩ **2** the act or an instance of reading or repeating aloud, esp before an audience

**recitative** /ˌresitə'teev/ *n* a rhythmically free declamatory style for singing a narrative text; *also* a passage delivered in this style [It *recitativo,* fr *recitare* to recite, fr L] – **recitative** *adj*

**recitativo** /ˌresitə'teevoh/ *n, pl* **recitativi** /-ee/, **recitativos** (a) recitative [It]

**recite** /ri'siet/ *vt* **1** to repeat from memory or read aloud, esp before an audience **2a** to relate in full ⟨*~s dull anecdotes*⟩ **b** to enumerate, detail ⟨*~d a catalogue of offences*⟩ **3** *NAm* to repeat or answer questions about (a lesson) ~ *vi* **1** to repeat or read aloud something memorized or prepared **2** *NAm* to reply to a teacher's question about a lesson [ME *reciten* to state formally, fr MF or L; MF *reciter* to recite, fr L *recitare,* fr re- + *citare* to summon – more at CITE] – **reciter** *n*

**reck** /rek/ *vt archaic or poetic* **1** to take account of; worry about ⟨*he little ~ed what the outcome might be*⟩ **2** to matter to; concern ⟨*what ~s it me that I shall die tomorrow?*⟩ [ME *recken* to take heed, fr OE *reccan;* akin to OHG *ruohhen* to take heed]

**reckless** /'reklis/ *adj* marked by lack of proper caution; careless of consequences ⟨*~ driving*⟩ ⟨*~ courage*⟩ *synonyms* see ¹ADVENTURE *antonyms* calculating, cautious, prudent ⚠ feckless – **recklessly** *adv,* **recklessness** *n*

**reckon** /'rekən/ *vt* **1a** to count ⟨*~ the days till Christmas*⟩ – often *+ up* **b** to estimate, compute ⟨*~ the height of a building*⟩ **c** to determine by reference to a fixed basis ⟨*the Gregorian calendar is ~ed from the birth of Christ*⟩ **2** to regard or think of in a specified way; consider ⟨*she is ~ed the leading expert*⟩ **3** *chiefly dial* to suppose, think ⟨*I ~ they're not coming*⟩ **4** *informal* to think highly of ⟨*the boys ~ him because he's one of the lads*⟩ ~ *vi* **1** to make a calculation **2** to judge **3** *chiefly dial* to suppose, think **4** to accept something as certain; place reliance ⟨*I'm ~ing on your support*⟩ *synonyms* see RELY ON [ME *rekenen,* fr OE *-recenian* (as in *gerecenian* to narrate); akin to OE *reccan* to take heed]

**reckon with** *vt* to take into consideration, esp because formidable

**reckon without** *vt* to fail to consider; ignore

**reckoner** /'rekənə/ *n* **1** one who reckons **2** a non-electrical aid to reckoning (e g an abacus) **3** *chiefly N Eng* a calculator

**reckoning** /'rekəning/ *n* **1** the act or an instance of reckoning: e g **a** an account, bill **b** a computation **c** calculation of a ship's position **2** a settling of accounts ⟨*day of ~*⟩ **3** a summing up; an appraisal

**reclaim** /ri'klaym/ *vt* **1a** to recall from wrong or improper conduct; reform **b** to tame, subdue **2a** to rescue from an undesirable state **b** to make available or suitable for human use by changing natural conditions ⟨*~ed marshland*⟩ **3** to obtain from a waste product or by-product; recover [ME *reclamen,* fr OF *reclamer* to call back, fr L *reclamare* to cry out against, fr re- + *clamare* to cry out – more at CLAIM] – **reclaimable** *adj*

**re-claim** /ˌree'klaym/ *vt* to demand or obtain the return of

**reclamation** /ˌreklə'maysh(ə)n/ *n* the act or process of reclaiming: e g **a** reformation, rehabilitation **b** restoration to use; recovery [MF, fr L *reclamation-, reclamatio,* fr *reclamatus,* pp of *reclamare*]

**réclame** /ˌray'klahm (*Fr* reklɑ:m)/ *n* **1** public acclaim; vogue **2**

a gift for dramatization or publicity; showmanship [Fr, advertising, publicity, fr *réclamer* to appeal, fr OF *reclamer*]

**recline** /ri'klien/ *vt* **1** to cause or permit to incline backwards ⟨~d *the seat a little*⟩ **2** to place in a recumbent position; lean, rest ⟨~s *her head on the pillow*⟩ ~ *vi* **1** to lean or incline backwards **2** to repose, lie [ME *reclinen*, fr MF or L; MF *recliner*, fr L *reclinare*, fr *re-* + *clinare* to bend – more at LEAN]

**¹recluse** /ri'kloohs/ *adj* marked by withdrawal from society; solitary [ME, fr OF *reclus*, lit., shut up, fr LL *reclusus*, pp of *recludere* to shut up, fr L *re-* + *claudere* to close – more at CLOSE] – **reclusive** *adj*, **reclusion** *n*

**²recluse** *n* a person who leads a secluded or solitary life; a hermit

**recognition** /,rekəg'nish(ə)n/ *n* **1** recognizing or being recognized: eg **1a** acknowledgment; *esp* formal acknowledgment of the political existence of a government or state **b** perception of something as identical with something already known in fact or by description ⟨~ *of a former friend*⟩ ⟨~ *of a fine claret*⟩ **2** special notice or attention ⟨*a writer who has received much* ~⟩ **3** the sensing and coding of printed or written data by a machine ⟨*optical character* ~⟩ ⟨*machine* ~ *of handwritten characters*⟩ [L *recognition-*, *recognitio*, fr *recognitus*, pp of *recognoscere* to recognize]

**recogn·izance** *also* **-isance** /ri'kogniz(ə)ns/ *n, law* **1** a bond entered into before a court or magistrate requiring a person to do something (eg appear in court) **2** the sum pledged as surety for the performance of such an obligation △ **reconnaissance** [alter. of ME *reconissaunce*, fr MF *reconoissance* recognition, fr *reconoistre* to recognize]

**recogn·ize, -ise** /'rekəgniez/ *vt* **1a** to perceive to be something or somebody previously known ⟨~d *the word*⟩ **b** to perceive clearly; realize ⟨~d *his own inadequacy*⟩ **2** to acknowledge or take notice of in some definite way: eg **2a** to show appreciation of (eg by praise or a reward) ⟨~ *an act of bravery with the award of a medal*⟩ **b** to acknowledge acquaintance with ⟨~ *an old crony with a nod*⟩ **c** to admit the fact of ⟨~s *his obligation*⟩ **3** to acknowledge formally: eg **3a** to admit as being lord or sovereign **b** to admit as being of a particular status ⟨~d *him as legitimate representative*⟩ **c** *chiefly NAm* to allow or call upon to speak in a meeting or debate; give the floor to **d** to acknowledge the de facto existence or the independence of (eg a government or state) [modif of MF *reconoiss-*, stem of *reconoistre*, fr L *recognoscere*, fr *re-* + *cognoscere* to know – more at COGNITION] – **recognizable** *adj*, **recognizably** *adv*, **recognizer** *n*, **recognizability** *n*

*usage* The pronunciation /'rekəgniez/ rather than /'rekəniez/ is recommended for BBC broadcasters.

**¹recoil** /ri'koyl/ *vi* **1a** to fall back under pressure ⟨*the troops* ~ed *before the enemy onslaught*⟩ **b** to shrink back physically or emotionally (eg in horror, fear, or disgust) **2a** to spring back into an uncompressed position; rebound ⟨*the spring* ~ed⟩ **b** *esp of a firearm* to move backwards sharply when fired **3** to return with an adverse effect to a source or starting point –often + *on* or *upon* ⟨*their hatred* ~ed *on themselves*⟩ [ME *reculen*, fr OF *reculer*, fr *re-* + *cul* backside, fr L *culus*]

*synonyms* Recoil, shrink, cower, quail, cringe, flinch, wince, and blench all mean "draw back through fear or distaste". Recoil often suggests disgust and horror ⟨**recoiled** *at the sight of a snake*⟩. Shrink, cower, quail, and cringe imply huddling or crouching, but figuratively shrink may indicate sensitiveness or scrupulousness ⟨*when it came to telling the truth about himself he* **shrank** *from the task with all the horror of a well-bred English gentleman* – Virginia Woolf⟩, while the others are somewhat discreditable ⟨*I am never known to* **quail** *at the fury of a gale* – W S Gilbert⟩, cower suggesting abject fear of something menacing and cringe implying servility. Flinch, wince, and blench imply an involuntary starting back, flinch being chiefly associated with fear of pain, wince often suggesting sensitiveness ⟨*she* **winced** *at the blasphemy*⟩, and blench being somewhat discreditable, implying cowardice and perhaps, by confusion with the other verb blench (= "whiten"), the idea of turning white. *antonyms* confront, defy

**²recoil** /'ree,koyl, ri'koyl/ *n* **1** the act or action of recoiling; *esp* the backwards movement of a gun on firing **2** reaction ⟨*the* ~ *from the rigours of Calvinism* – Edmund Wilson⟩ – **recoiler** *n*

**recoilless** /'ree,koyl·ləs, ri'koyl·ləs/ *adj* having a minimum of recoil

**,recoil-'operated** *adj, of a firearm* using the movement of parts in recoil to operate the mechanism of ejection, reloading,

and firing

**recoin** /,ree'koyn/ *vt* to coin again or anew – **recoinage** *n*

**recollect** /,rekə'lekt/ *vt* **1** to bring back to the level of conscious awareness; remember ⟨*trying to* ~ *a forgotten address*⟩ **2** to recall to (oneself) something temporarily forgotten **3** to bring (oneself) back to a state of composure or concentration ~ *vi* to call something to mind [ML *recollectus*, pp of *recolligere*, fr L, to gather again]

**recollection** /,rekə'leksh(ə)n/ *n* **1a** self-possessed tranquillity of mind; composure **b** religious contemplation **2a** the action or power of recalling to mind **b** something recalled to the mind *synonyms* see MEMORY

**recombinant** /,ree'kombinənt/ *adj* **1** exhibiting genetic recombination ⟨~ *progeny*⟩ **2** of or being DNA prepared in the laboratory by combining pieces of DNA from several different species of organisms – **recombinant** *n*

**recombination** /,reekombi'naysh(ə)n/ *n* the formation in offspring of new combinations of genes that did not occur in the parents, by processes (CROSSING-OVER and INDEPENDENT ASSORTMENT) whereby sections of the gene-carrying material (CHROMOSOMES) become interchanged, and genes coding for different forms of inheritable characteristics (eg blue or brown eyes and tallness or shortness) combine randomly – **recombinational** *adj*

**recommend** /,rekə'mend/ *vt* **1a** to declare to be worthy of acceptance or trial; praise ⟨~ed *the medicine*⟩ **b** to endorse as fit, worthy, or competent ⟨~s *her for the position*⟩ **2** to make acceptable ⟨*has other points to* ~ *it*⟩ **3** to advise ⟨~ *that the matter be dropped*⟩ **4** *archaic* to entrust, commit ⟨~ed *his soul to God*⟩ [ME *recommenden* to praise, fr ML *recommendare*, fr L *re-* + *commendare* to commend] – **recommendable** *adj*, **recommendatory** *adj*, **recommender** *n*

**recommendation** /,rekəmen'daysh(ə)n/ *n* **1a** the act of recommending **b** something (eg a course of action) recommended **2** something that recommends or expresses commendation

**¹recompense** /'rekəmpens/ *vt* **1** to give something to by way of compensation (eg for a service rendered or damage incurred) ⟨~d *him for his losses*⟩ **2** to make or amount to an equivalent or compensation for ⟨*a pleasure that* ~s *our trouble*⟩ [ME *recompensen*, fr MF *recompenser*, fr LL *recompensare*, fr L *re-* + *compensare* to compensate]

**²recompense** *n* an equivalent or a return for something done, suffered, or given; a compensation ⟨*offered in* ~ *for injuries*⟩

**recompose** /,reekəm'pohz/ *vt* **1** to compose again; rearrange **2** to restore to composure – **recomposition** *n*

**reconcilable** /,rekən'sieləbl/ *adj* capable of being reconciled – **reconcilableness, reconcilability** *n*

**reconcile** /'rekənsiel/ *vt* **1a** to restore to friendship or harmony ⟨~d *the factions*⟩ **b** to settle, resolve ⟨~ *differences*⟩ **2** to make consistent or compatible ⟨~ *an ideal with reality*⟩ **3** to cause to submit to or accept ⟨*was* ~d *to hardship*⟩ [ME *reconcilen*, fr MF or L; MF *reconcilier*, fr L *reconciliare*, fr *re-* + *conciliare* to conciliate] – **reconcilement** *n*, **reconciler** *n*

**reconciliation** /,rekən,sili'aysh(ə)n/ *n* reconciling or being reconciled [ME, fr L *reconciliation-*, *reconciliatio*, fr *reconciliatus*, pp of *reconciliare*] – **reconciliatory** *adj*

**recondite** /'rekəndiet, ri'kon-/ *adj* **1** difficult to understand or penetrate; deep, abstruse ⟨*a* ~ *subject*⟩ **2** of or dealing with something little known or obscure ⟨*the* ~ *literature of the Middle Ages*⟩ **3** *archaic* hidden from sight; concealed ⟨*produced some* ~ *flasks of wine* – T L Peacock⟩ [L *reconditus*, pp of *recondere* to conceal, fr *re-* + *condere* to store up, fr *com-* + *-dere* to put – more at DO] – **reconditely** *adv*, **reconditeness** *n* *usage* The pronunciation /ri'kondiet/ is recommended for BBC broadcasters. *synonyms* see ¹OBSCURE

**recondition** /,reekən'dish(ə)n/ *vt* **1** to restore to good condition (eg by replacing parts) **2** to condition (eg a person or his/her attitudes) anew; *also* to reinstate (a learned response) in an organism

**reconfirm** /,reekən'fuhm/ *vt* to confirm again; *also* to establish more strongly – **reconfirmation** *n*

**reconnaissance** /ri'konəs(ə)ns/ *n* a preliminary survey to gain information; *esp* an exploratory military survey, esp of enemy territory △ **recognizance** [Fr, lit., recognition, fr MF *reconoissance*, fr *reconoistre* to recognize]

**reconnoitre**, *NAm* **reconnoiter** /,rekə'noytə/ *vb* to make a reconnaissance (of) [obs Fr *reconnoître*, lit., to recognize, fr MF *reconoistre* – more at RECOGNIZE]

**reconsider** /,reekən'sidə/ *vb* to consider (something) again with a view to changing or reversing ⟨*to* ~ *a decision*⟩ – **reconsideration** *n*

**reconstitute** /ˌree'konstityooht, -chooht/ *vt* to constitute again or anew; *esp* to restore to a former condition by adding water ⟨~ *powdered milk*⟩ – **reconstitution** *n*

**reconstruct** /ˌreekən'strukt/ *vt* **1** to construct again: eg **1a** to rebuild ⟨*to* ~ *a ruined bridge*⟩ **b** to reorganize, reestablish ⟨~ ing *society during the postwar period*⟩ **c** to rehabilitate ⟨*to* ~ *a twisted personality*⟩ **2** to build up a mental image of (eg the past, a crime, or a battle) from the available evidence – **reconstructible** *adj*, **reconstructive** *adj*, **reconstructor** *n*

**reconstruction** /ˌreekən'struksh(ə)n/ *n* **1a** reconstructing or being reconstructed **b** *often cap* the reorganization and reestablishment of the seceded states in the Union after the American Civil War **2** something reconstructed

**reconversion** /ˌreekən'vuhsh(ə)n/ *n* conversion back to a previous state

**reconvert** /ˌreekən'vuht/ *vt* to cause to undergo reconversion

**reconvey** /ˌreekən,vay/ *vt* to convey back to a previous position or owner – **reconveyance** *n*

¹**record** /ri'kawd/ *vt* **1a(1)** to put down in writing; *esp* to commit to writing so as to furnish authentic written evidence **a(2)** to deposit an authentic official copy of ⟨~ *a deed*⟩ **b** to state or indicate (as if) for a record ⟨*spoke in favour of the bill but also said he wanted to* ~ *certain reservations*⟩ **c(1)** to register permanently by mechanical means ⟨*earthquake shocks* ~ ed *by a seismograph*⟩ **c(2)** to indicate, read ⟨*the thermometer* ~ ed *25°*⟩ **2** to give evidence of ⟨*the intensity of the explosion is* ~ ed *on the charred tree trunks*⟩ **3** to convert (eg sound) into a permanent form fit for reproduction ⟨*Aida was the last opera she* ~ ed *before she died*⟩ ~ *vi* to record something [ME *recorden*, lit., to recall, fr OF *recorder*, fr L *recordari*, fr *re-* + *cord-*, *cor* heart – more at HEART] – **recordable** *adj*

²**record** /'rekawd, 'rekəd/ *n* **1** the state or fact of being recorded **2** something that records or on which information, evidence, etc has been recorded: eg **2a** something that recalls, relates, or commemorates past events or facts **b** an official document that records the acts of a public body or officer **c** an authentic official copy of a document deposited with a legally designated officer **d** the official copy of the papers used in a law case **3a(1)** a body of known or recorded facts regarding something or someone ⟨*a criminal* ~⟩ ⟨*a fine* ~ *as manager*⟩ **a(2)** a list of previous convictions for offences or crimes ⟨*they refused to employ him because he has a* ~⟩ **b** a performance, occurrence, or condition that goes beyond or is extraordinary among others of its kind; *specif* the best recorded performance in a competitive sport **4a** a flat usu plastic disc with a spiral groove whose undulations represent recorded sound for reproduction on a gramophone **b** the sound recorded on a gramophone record; RECORDING 2 – **for the record** to be reported as official ⟨*just for the record I think the President is a fool*⟩ – **off the record** not for publication; spoken privately ⟨*my remarks were* off the record *and not to be printed*⟩ – **on record** in or into the status of being known, published, or documented ⟨*he is* on record *as saying this*⟩

³**record** /'rekawd, 'rekəd/ *adj* surpassing others of the kind

**record deck** *n* the apparatus, including a turntable and stylus, on which a gramophone record is played

**recorded delivery** /ri'kawdid/ *n* a postal service available in the UK in which a record is made of the delivery of a posted item – **recorded delivery** *adv*

**recorder** /ri'kawdə/ *n* **1** a person who records **2** *often cap* **2a** a barrister of at least five years' standing who formerly presided over a court of QUARTER SESSIONS **b** a barrister or solicitor of at least 10 years' standing who sits as a circuit judge or as a part-time judge in the CROWN COURT **3** any of a group of end-blown flutes ranging from SOPRANINO to bass and having a conical tube, eight finger holes, and a mouthpiece like a whistle [(3) prob fr ¹*record* in the arch. senses "to get by heart, practise (a tune)"]

**recording** /ri'kawding/ *n* **1** RECORD 4a **2** something (eg sound on a television programme) that has been recorded electronically

**recording head** *n* a tape-recorder head used for recording – compare HEAD 19b

**recordist** /ri'kawdist/ *n* one who records sound (eg on MAGNETIC TAPE)

**record player** /'rekawd, -kəd/ *n* a gramophone that is electrically driven and that reproduces sounds electronically

¹**recount** /ri'kownt/ *vt* to relate in detail; narrate [ME *re-*

*counten*, fr MF *reconter*, fr *re-* + *conter*, *compter* to count, relate –more at COUNT] – **recounter** *n*

²**recount** /ˌree'kownt/ *vt* to count again [*re-* + *count*]

³**recount** /'ree,kownt/ *n* a second or fresh count, esp of votes

**recoup** /ri'koohp/ *vt* **1** to withhold rightfully part of (a sum legally claimed) **2a** to get an equivalent for (eg losses); make up for **b** to reimburse, compensate ⟨~ *a person for losses*⟩ **3** to regain ⟨*an attempt to* ~ *his fortune*⟩ ~ *vi* to make up for something lost [Fr *recouper* to cut back, fr OF, fr *re-* + *couper* to cut – more at COPE] – **recoupable** *adj*, **recoupment** *n*

**recourse** /ri'kaws/ *n* **1a** a turning to someone or something for help or protection ⟨*to have* ~ *to the law*⟩ **b** a source of help or strength; a resort ⟨*the only* ~ *was prayer*⟩ **2** the right to demand payment from the maker or endorser of a negotiable document (eg a cheque) [ME *recours*, fr MF, fr LL *recursus*, fr L, act of running back, fr *recursus*, pp of *recurrere* to run back – more at RECUR]

*usage* **Recourse, resort,** and **resource** are similar in one meaning, but used in different constructions; **recourse** and **resource** (in this sense) being only nouns and **resort** a noun or verb. To *have* **recourse** *to,* to *have* **resort** *to,* and to *resort to* all mean "to turn to when needed". The person or thing that one turns to is a **resource** ⟨*flight was my only* **resource**⟩ or a **resort** ⟨*in the last* **resort**⟩⟨*as a last* **resort**⟩. It is a common confusion to use **resource** instead of one of the others ⟨*we shall never succeed without* **recourse**/**resort** (but not △ **resource**) *to the law*⟩ ⟨*in the last* **resort** (but not △ **resource**) *we shall fight*⟩.

**recover** /ri'kuvə/ *vt* **1** to get back; regain **2a** to bring back to normal position or condition ⟨*stumbled, then* ~ ed *himself*⟩ **b** to regain possession or normal use of ⟨*quickly* ~ ed *his senses*⟩ **3a** to make up for ⟨~ *increased costs through higher prices*⟩ **b** to obtain by legal action **4a** to obtain (a valuable or useful material) from an ore, a waste product, or a by-product **b** to save from loss and restore to usefulness; reclaim **5** *archaic* to rescue, deliver **6** *archaic* to reach ~ *vi* **1** to regain a normal position or condition (eg of health) ⟨~ ing *from a cold*⟩ **2** to obtain a final legal judgment in one's favour [ME *recoveren*, fr MF *recoverer*, fr L *recuperare*; akin to L *recipere* to receive – more at RECEIVE] – **recoverable** *adj*, **recoverability** *adj*, **recoverer** *n*

**re-cover** /ˌree'kuvə/ *vt* to cover again; provide with a new cover

**recovery** /ri'kuv(ə)ri/ *n* (an instance) of recovering: eg **a** a return to normal health **b** a regaining of balance or control (eg after a stumble or mistake) **c** an economic upturn (eg after a depression) **d** the obtaining of a legal right to something by verdict or judgment

**recovery room** *n* a hospital room equipped for dealing with postoperative emergencies

**recreant** /'rekriənt/ *adj, formal or poetic* **1** cowardly **2** unfaithful to duty or allegiance; disloyal [ME, fr MF, fr prp of *recroire* to renounce one's cause in a trial by battle, surrender, fr *re-* + *croire* to believe, fr L *credere* – more at CREED] – **recreant** *n*

¹**recreate** /'rekri·ayt/ *vb, chiefly formal vt* to refresh or enliven, esp by means of entertainment or relaxation ⟨*might not choose to* ~ *themselves on a scenic railway – Blackwood's*⟩ ~ *vi* to take recreation [L *recreatus*, pp] – **recreative** *adj*

²**recreate** /ˌreekri'ayt/ *vt* to create again: eg **a** to reproduce exactly ⟨~ d *an old frontier town for the film*⟩ **b** to visualize or create (something which exists or has existed) in the imagination ⟨*recreating their youth in old age*⟩ – **recreatable** *adj*, **recreation** *n*, **recreative** *adj*

**recreation** /ˌrekri'aysh(ə)n/ *n* refreshment of strength and spirits after work ⟨*I . . . consider intervals of* ~ *and amusement as desirable for everybody* – Jane Austen⟩; *also* a means of refreshment or diversion; a pastime ⟨*her favourite* ~ *was spying on her neighbours*⟩ [ME *recreacion*, fr MF *recreation*, fr L *recreation-*, *recreatio* restoration to health, fr *recreatus*, pp of *recreare* to create anew, restore, refresh, fr *re-* + *creare* to create] – **recreational** *adj*

**recreation ground** *n* an open space (eg a field) on which games can be played, usu provided by the local council for public use

**recreation room** *n* a room, esp in an institution (eg a hospital), used for recreational and social activities

**recriminate** /ri'krimi,nayt/ *vi* **1** to make a retaliatory charge against an accuser **2** to indulge in bitter mutual accusations [ML *recriminatus*, pp of *recriminare*, fr L *re-* + *criminari* to accuse – more at CRIMINATE] – **recrimination** *n*, **recriminative** *adj*, **recriminatory** *adj*

**recrudesce** /ˌreekrooh'des/ *vi, formal, of something undesirable, esp a disease* to break out or become active again *synonyms* see ¹RETURN [L *recrudescere*, lit., to become raw again, fr *re-* + *crudescere* to become raw, fr *crudus* raw – more at RAW]

**recrudescence** /ˌreekrooh'desəns/ *n, formal* a new outbreak (e g of a disease or problem) after a period of abatement or inactivity; a renewal – **recrudescent** *adj*

**¹recruit** /ri'krooht/ *n* a newcomer to a field or activity; *specif* a newly enlisted member of the armed forces [Fr *recrute, recrue* fresh growth, new levy of soldiers, fr MF, fr *recroistre* to grow up again, fr L *recrescere*, fr *re-* + *crescere* to grow – more at CRESCENT]

**²recruit** *vt* **1a(1)** to enlist recruits for (e g an army, regiment, or society) **a(2)** to enlist (a person) as a recruit **b** to secure the services of; engage, hire **2a** to replenish ⟨*it was from gifts bestowed upon him ... that he* ~ed *his finances* – Charles Dickens⟩ **b** to restore or increase the health, vigour, or intensity of ⟨*come down here ... to* ~ *yourself after an excess of work* – G B Shaw⟩ ~ *vi* to enlist new members – **recruiter** *n*, **recruitment** *n*

**recrystall·ize, -ise** /ˌree'kristl·iez/ *vb* to crystallize again or repeatedly; cause new crystals to form (in) – **recrystallization** *n*

**rect-** /rekt-/, **recto-** *comb form* rectum ⟨rect*al*⟩ [NL *rectum*]

**rectal** /'rekt(ə)l/ *adj* relating to, affecting, or near the rectum – **rectally** *adv*

**rectangle** /'rektang·gl/ *n* a 2-dimensional 4-sided figure having opposite sides that are equal in length and parallel, and all four of whose angles are RIGHT ANGLES; *esp* one that is not a square [ML *rectangulus* having a right angle, fr L *rectus* right + *angulus* angle – more at RIGHT, ANGLE]

**rectangular** /rek'tang·gyoolə/ *adj* **1** shaped like a rectangle ⟨*a* ~ *area*⟩ **2a** crossing, lying, or meeting at a RIGHT ANGLE ⟨~ *axes*⟩ **b** having edges, surfaces, or faces that meet at RIGHT ANGLES; having faces or surfaces shaped like rectangles ⟨*volume of a* ~ *solid*⟩ ⟨~ *blocks*⟩ – **rectangularity** *n*, **rectangularly** *adv*

**rectangular coordinate** *n, maths* CARTESIAN COORDINATE

**rectifiable** /'rekti·fie·əbl/ *adj* **1** able to be rectified **2** *maths* having finite length ⟨*a* ~ *curve*⟩ – **rectifiability** *n*

**rectifier** /'rekti·fie·ə/ *n* one who or that which rectifies; *esp* an electrical device used to convert ALTERNATING CURRENT (e g from the mains) into DIRECT CURRENT (e g for use in a radio or amplifier)

**rectify** /'rekti·fie/ *vt* **1** to set right; remedy ⟨*to* ~ *mistakes*⟩ **2** to purify (e g alcohol), esp by processes involving repeated DISTILLATION **3** to correct by removing errors; adjust ⟨~ *the calendar*⟩ **4** *maths* to determine the length of (an arc or curve) **5** to convert (ALTERNATING CURRENT) to DIRECT CURRENT [ME *rectifien*, fr MF *rectifier*, fr ML *rectificare*, fr L *rectus* right, straight] – **rectification** *n*

**rectilinear** /ˌrekti'lini·ə/ *adj* **1** moving in, being in, or forming a straight line ⟨~ *motion*⟩ **2** characterized by straight lines [LL *rectilineus*, fr L *rectus* + *linea* line] – **rectilinearly** *adv*

**rectitude** /'rekti,tyoohd/ *n* **1** moral integrity, uprightness, or correctness; righteousness **2** the quality or state of being correct in judgment or procedure [ME, fr MF, fr LL *rectitudin-, rectitudo*, fr L *rectus* straight, right]

**rectitudinous** /ˌrekti'tyoohdinəs/ *adj, formal* **1** characterized by rectitude **2** piously self-righteous

**recto** /'rektoh/ *n, pl* **rectos 1** the side of a leaf (e g of a manuscript) that is to be read first **2** a right-hand page – contrasted with *verso* [NL *recto (folio)* the page being straight]

**recto-** – see RECT-

**rector** /'rektə/ *n* **1a** a Church of England clergyman in charge of a parish where TITHES were once payable directly to him – compare VICAR **b** a clergyman (e g of the Episcopal church in the USA) in charge of a parish **2** a Roman Catholic priest directing a church with no pastor or one whose pastor has other duties **3** the head of a university, college, or school, esp of one of old foundation or in Scotland [ML, fr L, governor, ruler, fr *rectus*, pp of *regere* to direct, rule – more at RIGHT] – **rectorate** *n*, **rectorial** *adj*, **rectorship** *n*

**rectory** /'rekt(ə)ri/ *n* **1** a benefice held by a rector **2** a rector's residence

**rectrix** /'rektriks/ *n, pl* **rectrices** /-seez/ any of the long stiff feathers of a bird's tail that are important in controlling flight direction [NL, fr L, fem of *rector* governor, ruler]

**rectum** /'rektəm/ *n, pl* **rectums, recta** /-tə/ the end part of the intestine of a VERTEBRATE animal from the SIGMOID FLEXURE to the anus [NL, fr *rectum intestinum*, lit., straight intestine]

**rectus** /'rektəs/ *n, pl* **recti** /-tie/ any of several straight muscles; *esp* either of the two long muscles of the abdomen [NL, fr *rectus musculus* straight muscle]

**recumbency** /ri'kumbənsi/ *n* the state of leaning, resting, or reclining; repose; *also* a recumbent position

**recumbent** /ri'kumbənt/ *adj* **1a** in an attitude suggestive of repose; leaning, resting ⟨*comfortably* ~ *against a tree*⟩ **b** lying down **c** representing a person lying down ⟨*a* ~ *statue*⟩ **2** *of a plant or esp animal structure* resting on the surface to which it is attached **3** *of or being* a fold in rock that has been pushed over to such an extent that the rock layers are practically horizontal and parallel to those of the surrounding rock □ compare INCUMBENT [L *recumbent-, recumbens*, prp of *recumbere* to lie down, fr *re-* + *-cumbere* to lie down (akin to L *cubare* to lie, recline) – more at HIP] – **recumbently** *adv*

**recuperate** /ri'k(y)oohpə,rayt/ *vt* to get back; regain ⟨~ *financial losses*⟩ ~ *vi* to regain a former state or condition; *esp* to recover health or strength [L *recuperatus*, pp of *recuperare* – more at RECOVER] – **recuperation** *n*

**recuperative** /ri'kyoohpərətiv/ *adj* **1** of recuperation ⟨~ *powers*⟩ **2** aiding in recuperation; restorative

**recur** /ri'kuh/ *vi* **-rr-** to occur again: e g **a** to come up again for consideration; confront one again ⟨*knew the difficulties would only* ~⟩ **b** to come back to one's mind; enter one's thoughts again **c** to occur repeatedly or after an interval *synonyms* see ¹RETURN [ME *recurren* to return, fr L *recurrere*, lit., to run back, fr *re-* + *currere* to run – more at CAR] – **recurrence** *n*

**recurrent** /ri'kurənt/ *adj* **1** running or turning back in a direction opposite to a former course – used esp of various nerves and branches of vessels carrying blood, LYMPH, etc in the arms and legs **2** returning or happening repeatedly or periodically ⟨~ *complaints*⟩ [L *recurrent-, recurrens*, prp of *recurrere*] – **recurrently** *adv*

**recurring decimal** /ri'kuhring/ *n, chiefly Br* a decimal in which a particular digit or sequence of digits repeats itself indefinitely at some stage after the DECIMAL POINT

**recursion** /ri'kuhsh(ə)n/ *n* **1** a return **2** the repeated application of a particular mathematical procedure to the previous result to determine either a sequence of numbers or a more accurate approximation to a SQUARE ROOT, fraction, etc [LL *recursion-, recursio*, fr *recursus*, pp of *recurrere* to run back]

**recursive** /ri'kuhsiv/ *adj* **1** of or involving mathematical recursion **2** of or being a procedure that can repeat itself: e g **2a** being a prescribed method that recurs indefinitely or until a specified condition is met ⟨*a* ~ *rule in a grammar*⟩ **b** being a computer program that calls itself into operation or calls other programs which in turn recall the original – **recursively** *adv*, **recursiveness** *n*

**recurved** /ri'kuhvd/ *adj, of a plant or animal structure* curved backwards or inwards

**recusancy** /'rekyooz(ə)nsi/, **recusance** /-əns/ *n* refusal to accept or obey established authority; *specif* the refusal of Roman Catholics to attend services of the Church of England, which was a statutory offence from about 1570 until 1791 [*recusant*, n, fr L *recusant-, recusans*, prp of *recusare* to refuse, fr *re-* + *causari* to give a reason, plead, fr *causa* cause, reason] – **recusant** *n or adj*

**recycle** /ˌree'siekl/ *vt* **1** to pass through a series of changes or treatments so as to return to a previous stage in a cyclic process ⟨*to* ~ *tax revenue into the economy*⟩; *specif* to process (waste paper, glass, sewage, etc) for conversion back into a useful product **2** to recover, reclaim ~ *vi* **1** to return to an earlier point in a countdown **2** *esp of an electronic device* to return to an original condition so that operation can begin again – **recyclable** *adj*, **recycler** *n*

**¹red** /red/ *adj* **-dd- 1a** of the colour red **b** having red as a distinguishing colour **2a(1)** flushed, esp with anger or embarrassment **a(2)** *esp of a complexion* ruddy, florid **a(3)** of a coppery hue ⟨*the* ~ *skin of the American Indian*⟩ **b** bloodshot ⟨*eyes* ~ *from crying*⟩ **c** *of hair or the coat of an animal* in the colour range between a medium orange and russet or bay ⟨*flaming thatch of* ~ *hair*⟩ **d** tinged with red; reddish ⟨~ *sky*⟩ **3** heated to redness; glowing **4** *cap* of a Communist country, esp the USSR **5** failing to show a profit ⟨*a* ~ *financial statement*⟩ – compare BLACK **6** *informal or derog* **6a** inciting or endorsing radical social or political change, esp by force **b** *often cap* extremely left-wing; *esp* communist – see also **red RAG to a**

**bull** [ME, fr OE *rēad;* akin to OHG *rōt* red, L *ruber* & *rufus,* Gk *erythros*] – **redly** *adv*

²**red** *n* **1** a colour whose hue resembles that of blood or of the ruby or is that of the long-wave extreme of the visible spectrum **2** something that is of a red or reddish colour: e g **2a** an animal with a reddish coat **b** red wine **c** a red traffic light meaning "stop" **3a** a pigment or dye that colours red **b** a shade or tint of red **4** the condition of being financially in debt or of showing a loss – chiefly in *in/out of the red;* compare BLACK **6 5** *often cap, chiefly derog* a person of extreme left-wing political views; *esp* a communist – **redness** *n* – **see red** to become suddenly enraged

**redact** /ri'dakt/ *vt* **1** to select or adapt for publication; edit **2** *formal* to draw up, frame [back-formation fr *redaction*]

**redaction** /ri'daksh(ə)n/ *n* **1** an act or instance of redacting **2** a work that has been redacted; an edition, version [Fr *rédaction,* fr LL *redaction-, redactio* act of reducing, compressing, fr L *redactus,* pp of *redigere* to bring back, reduce, fr *re-, red-* re- + *agere* to lead – more at AGENT] – **redactional** *adj*

**redactor** /ri'daktə/ *n* one who redacts; *esp* an editor

**red admiral** *n* a butterfly (*Vanessa atalanta*) that is common in both Europe and N America, has broad orange-red bands on the front wings, and feeds on nettles in the larval stage

**red alert** *n* the final stage of alert in which enemy attack appears imminent

**red alga** *n* any of many algae (division Rhodophyta) that are seaweeds with a predominantly red colour

**redan** /ri'dan/ *n* a fortification consisting of two parapets forming a projecting angle and open to the rear [Fr, alter. of *redent,* fr *re-* + *dent* tooth, fr L *dent-, dens*]

**red ant** *n* any of various reddish ants (e g the PHARAOH ANT)

**red-backed shrike** *n* a Eurasian bird (*Lanius collurio*) that is a type of SHRIKE of which the male has a chestnut-coloured back and a grey crown

'**red-,baiting** *n, often cap R, chiefly NAm* the act of unfairly attacking, persecuting, or denouncing as a communist

**red blood cell, red cell** *n* any of the HAEMOGLOBIN-containing cells that carry oxygen to the tissues and are responsible for the red colour of the blood of VERTEBRATE animals – called also ERYTHROCYTE; compare WHITE BLOOD CELL

**red blood corpuscle, red corpuscle** *n* RED BLOOD CELL

,**red-'blooded** *adj* full of spirit and vigour; virile

**redbreast** /'red,brest/ *n* a bird with a reddish breast; *esp* a robin

,**red-breasted mer'ganser** *n* a Eurasian and N American merganser (type of duck) (*Mergus serrator*) the male of which has a dark chestnut breast band separated from the greenish-black head by a conspicuous white collar

**redbrick** /'red,brik/ *n or adj* (an English university) founded between 1800 and World War II [fr the common use of red brick in the buildings of recently founded universities]

**redbud** /'redbud/ *n* any of several N American trees (genus *Cercis,* esp *Cercis canadensis*) of the pea family with heart-shaped or roundish leaves and usu pale rosy-pink flowers

**red campion** /'kampi·ən/ *n* a red-flowered Eurasian campion (*Silene dioica*)

**redcap** /'redkap/ *n* **1** *Br* a military policeman **2** *NAm* a railway porter

**red card** *n* a red-coloured card held up by a soccer referee to indicate the sending-off of a player – not used in English domestic soccer since 1981; compare YELLOW CARD

**red carpet** *n* a greeting or reception marked by ceremonial courtesy – usu in *roll out the red carpet* [fr the traditional laying down of a red carpet for important guests to walk on]

,**red-'carpet** *adj* marked by ceremonial courtesy ⟨~ *treatment*⟩

**red cedar** *n* (the fragrant close-grained red wood of) a N American juniper tree (*Juniperus virginiana*)

**red cell** *n* RED BLOOD CELL

**red cent** *n, chiefly NAm* a trivial amount; a penny, whit ⟨*not worth a* ~⟩

**red clover** *n* a Eurasian clover (*Trifolium pratense*) with spherical heads of reddish-purple flowers, that is widely cultivated for hay and forage

**redcoat** /'red,koht/ *n* a British soldier, esp during the late 18th and early 19th centuries when scarlet jackets were worn

**red coral** *n* any of various GORGONIAN corals (genus *Corallium,* esp *Corallium nobile*) with hard pinkish to red skeletons used for jewellery and ornaments

**red corpuscle** *n* RED BLOOD CELL

**Red Cross** *n* a red Greek cross on a white background used as the emblem of the International Red Cross

**redcurrant** /,red'kurənt/ *n* (the small red edible fruit of) a widely cultivated European currant bush (*Ribes rubrum*)

**red curtain** *n* the political and ideological barrier between the USSR and the socialist countries of eastern Europe

**redd** /red/ *vt* **redded, redd** *chiefly NAm & Scot* to set in order; make tidy [ME *redden* to clear, prob alter. of *ridden* – more at RID]

**red deer** *n* a large deer (*Cervus elaphus*) that is the common deer of temperate Europe and Asia and has a reddish-brown coat in summer

**redden** /'red(ə)n/ *vt* to make red or reddish to become red; *esp* to blush

**reddish** /'redish/ *adj* having a tinge of red; somewhat red ⟨~ *orange*⟩ – **reddishness** *n*

**reddle** /'redl/ *n* RED OCHRE [alter. of *ruddle*]

¹**rede** /reed/ *vt, archaic or dial* **1** to give counsel to; advise **2** to interpret, explain [ME *reden* – more at READ]

²**rede** *n, archaic or dial* counsel, advice

**redecorate** /,ree'dekərayt/ *vb* to decorate (something) anew; *specif* to paint or paper (the interior of a building) anew – **redecoration** *n,* **redecorator** *n*

**redeem** /ri'deem/ *vt* **1a** to buy back full possession of; repurchase; *esp* to buy back (something used as security in return for a loan) by repaying the money loaned ⟨*to* ~ *a pawned ring*⟩ **b** to get or win back ⟨~ed *his losses of the previous night's gambling*⟩ **2** to free from what distresses or harms: e g **2a** to free from captivity by payment of ransom **b** to extricate from or help to overcome something detrimental ⟨*new interests that* ~ed *his life from futility*⟩ **c** to release from blame or debt; clear ⟨*hoped to* ~ *himself by these heroics*⟩ **d** to free from the consequences of sin **3a** *law* to recover possession of by fulfilling an obligation; free (something) from another's right of retention, esp by payment of a debt **b(1)** to remove the obligation of (e g a bond) by making a stipulated payment ⟨*the government* ~ *savings bonds on demand*⟩; *specif* to convert (paper money) into coin **b(2)** to convert (trading stamps, tokens, etc) into money or goods **c** to make good; fulfil ⟨~ed *his promise*⟩ **4a** to atone for; expiate ⟨*to* ~ *an error*⟩ **b(1)** to offset the bad effect of ⟨*flashes of wit* ~ed *a dreary speech*⟩ **b(2)** to make worthwhile; retrieve ⟨*no efforts of his could* ~ *such a hopeless undertaking*⟩ [ME *redemen,* modif of MF *redimer,* fr L *redimere,* fr *re-, red-* re- + *emere* to take, buy; akin to Lith *imti* to take] – **redeemable** *adj*

**redeemer** /ri'deemə/ *n* a person who redeems; *specif, cap* Jesus

**redefine** /,reedi'fien/ *vt* to define (a concept) again; reexamine or reevaluate, esp with a view to change ⟨*had to* ~ *their terms in order to deal with the problem*⟩ – **redefinition** *n*

**redemption** /ri'dempsh(ə)n, -'demsh(ə)n/ *n* redeeming or being redeemed; *also* something that redeems [ME *redempcioun,* fr MF *redemption,* fr L *reemption-, redemptio,* fr *redemptus,* pp of *redimere* to redeem] – **redemptional** *adj*

**redemptive** /ri'demptiv/ *adj* relating to or bringing about redemption

**Redemptorist** /ri'demptərist/ *n* a member of the Congregation of the Most Holy Redeemer founded by St Alphonsus Liguori in 1732 and devoted to preaching [Fr *rédemptoriste,* fr LL *redemptor* redeemer, fr L, contractor, fr *redemptus*]

**redemptory** /ri'dempt(ə)ri/ *adj* serving to redeem

**redeploy** /,reedi'ploy/ *vb* to transfer (e g troops or workers) from one area or activity to another – **redeployment** *n*

**redescribe** /,reedis'krieb/ *vt* to describe anew or again; *esp* to give a new and more complete description to (a category in the classification of living things)

**redesign** /,reedi'zien/ *vt* to revise in appearance, function, or content – **redesign** *n*

**redevelop** /,reedi'veləp/ *vt* to design, develop, or build again; *specif* to renovate (a deteriorating or depressed urban area) – **redeveloper** *n*

**redevelopment** /,reedi'veləpmənt/ *n* the act or process of redeveloping; *esp* the improvement of an urban area considered as being below certain minimum standards

**red fescue** /'feskyooh/ *n* a European and N American grass (*Festuca rubra*) that is used for lawns and pasture and has long creeping RHIZOMES (underground stems), erect stems, and spikes of usu pinkish or purplish flowers

**red fox** *n* the common fox (*Vulpes vulpes*) that is found throughout Europe and is typically reddish-brown in colour

**red giant** *n* a star that has low surface temperature and a diameter that is large relative to the sun

**red grouse** *n* a dark reddish-brown grouse (*Lagopus lagopus scoticus*) that is important as a game bird and is found esp on the moors of N England and Scotland – called also MOORFOWL

**Red Guard** *n* a member of a militant youth organization in China (1965-1971) formed to preserve popular revolutionary and ideological enthusiasm for the Communist regime and to bring about the CULTURAL REVOLUTION

**red gum** *n* (the hard reddish wood of or the reddish-brown gum yielded by) any of several Australian eucalyptus trees

**red-'handed** *adv or adj* in the act of committing a crime or misdeed ⟨*caught* ~⟩

**redhead** /'red,hed/ *n* a person with red hair – **redheaded** *adj*

**red heat** *n* the state of being red-hot; *also* the temperature at which a substance is red-hot

**red herring** *n* **1** a herring cured by salting and slow smoking to a dark brown colour **2** something irrelevant that distracts attention from the real issue ⟨*what appear to be clues in Agatha Christie's thrillers are often* ~s⟩ [(2) fr the practice of drawing a red herring across a trail to confuse hunting dogs]

**red-'hot** *adj* **1** glowing with heat; extremely hot **2a** exhibiting or marked by intense emotion; ardent ⟨~ *passion*⟩ **b** sensational; *specif* salacious ⟨*this* ~ *story of a Regency love affair*⟩ **c** full of energy, vigour, or enterprise ⟨*our new boss seems* ~⟩ ⟨*a* ~ *band*⟩ **d** arousing enthusiasm; currently extolled ⟨*a* ~ *favourite for the Grand National*⟩ **3** fresh, new ⟨~ *news*⟩

**red-hot poker** *n* any of various S African plants (genus *Kniphofia*) of the lily family with tall erect spikes of yellow flowers changing to bright red towards the top

**redia** /'reedi-ə/ *n, pl* **rediae** /'reedi-ee/, **redias** a larval form in the LIFE CYCLE of many parasitic flatworms (e g the LIVER FLUKE) that is produced by an earlier saclike larval form (SPOROCYST), lives as a parasite in a snail, oyster, etc, and itself produces either another generation of rediae or a CERCARIA (final larval stage that develops into an adult) [NL, fr Francesco *Redi* †1698? It naturalist] – **redial** *adj*

**Red Indian** *n* an American Indian of N America – not used technically

**redingote** /'reding,goht/ *n* a fitted outer garment: eg a an overcoat with a large collar worn, esp by men, in the 18th and 19th centuries **b** a woman's lightweight coat open at the front below the waist [Fr, modif of E *riding coat*]

**red ink** *n* **1** a business loss; a deficit **2** the condition of showing a business loss [fr the use in financial statements of red ink to indicate a loss]

**redintegrate** /ri'dintigrayt/ *vt, archaic* to restore to a former, esp sound, state [ME *redintegraten*, fr L *redintegratus*, pp of *redintegrare*, fr *re-, red-* re- + *integrare* to make complete – more at INTEGRATE]

**redintegration** /ri,dinti'graysh(ə)n/ *n* **1** *psychology* the arousal of a behavioural or emotional response by a part of the complex of stimuli that originally aroused that response **2** *archaic* restoration to a former state – **redintegrative** *adj*

**redirect** /,reedi'rekt, -die'rekt/ *vt* to change the course or direction of – **redirection** *n*

**¹rediscount** /,reedis'kownt/ *vt* to discount again (e g commercial paper) – **rediscountable** *adj*

**²rediscount** *n* **1** the act or process of rediscounting **2** negotiable paper that is rediscounted

**redistribute** /reedis'tribyoot/ *vt* to alter the distribution of; reallocate – **redistributive, redistributory** *adj,* **redistribution** *n*

**redistrict** /,ree'distrikt/ *vb, NAm vt* to divide anew into districts; *specif* to revise the legislative districts of ~ *vi* to revise legislative districts

**redivivus** /,redi'vievəs/ *adj, formal* brought back to life; reborn [LL, fr L, renovated]

**red jasmine** *n* a widely cultivated plant (*Plumeria rubra*) of the periwinkle family, that is a type of frangipani and has large clusters of fragrant pink, red, or purple flowers

**red kite** *n* a European bird of prey (*Milvus milvus*) that is a type of kite and has a long deeply forked chestnut tail

**red lead** /led/ *n* an orange-red to brick-red lead oxide, $Pb_3O_4$, used in glass and ceramics, as a paint pigment, and in the plates that are immersed in the acid of a car battery

**redleg** /'red,leg/ *n, WI derog* a POOR WHITE, esp in Barbados

**red-legged partridge** *n* a common W European partridge (*Alectoris rufa*) with bright red legs and bill

**red-letter day** *n* a day of special significance; *esp* one memorable as being particularly happy [fr the practice of marking holy days in red letters in church calendars]

**red light** *n* **1** a red warning light, esp on a road or railway, commanding traffic to stop **2** a cautionary sign; a deterrent ⟨*saw her warning as a* ~ *to potential troublemakers*⟩

**red-light district** *n* a district in which brothels are numerous

**red man** *n, chiefly derog* a N American Indian

**red maple** *n* a common maple tree (*Acer rubrum*) of N America that grows chiefly on moist soils, has reddish twigs, and yields a lighter and softer wood than the SUGAR MAPLE

**red meat** *n* dark-coloured meat (e g beef or lamb) – compare WHITE MEAT

**red mite** *n* EUROPEAN RED MITE (bright to brownish-red spiderlike animal)

**red mulberry** *n* (the edible purple fruit of) a mulberry tree (*Morus rubra*) of forests of eastern and central N America with soft but durable wood

**red mullet** *n* MULLET 2 (type of fish)

**'red-,neck** *n, derog* a white member of the rural labouring class of the southern USA – **red-neck** *adj*

**redo** /,ree'dooh/ *vt* **redoes** /-'duz/; **redoing** /-'dooh-ing/; **redid** /-'did/; **redone** /-'dun/ **1** to do over again **2** *informal* to decorate (e g a room or building) anew

**red ochre** *n* a red earthy HAEMATITE (iron oxide mineral) used as a pigment

**redolent** /'redələnt/ *adj* **1** full of a specified fragrance; scented ⟨*air* ~ *of seaweed*⟩ **2** evocative, suggestive ⟨*a city* ~ *of antiquity*⟩ [ME, fr MF, fr L *redolent-, redolens,* prp of *redolēre* to emit a scent, fr *re-, red-* + *olēre* to smell – more at ODOUR] – **redolence** *n,* **redolently** *adv*

**redouble** /ri'dubl; *sense 2* ,ree-/ *v* **a** to make greater, more numerous, or more intense ⟨~ *our efforts*⟩ ⟨*the enemy* ~⟩ **d** *their attack*⟩ **1** to become redoubled **2** to double an opponent's DOUBLE (increase in value of tricks won or lost) in bridge – **redouble** *n*

**redoubt** /ri'dowt/ *n* **1** a small usu temporary enclosed defensive structure **2** a secure place; a stronghold ⟨*withdrew to an Alpine* ~⟩ ⟨*faith was her last* ~⟩ [Fr *redoute,* fr It *ridotto,* fr ML *reductus* secret place, fr L, withdrawn, fr pp of *reducere* to lead back – more at REDUCE]

**redoubtable** /ri'dowtəbl/ *adj* **1** causing fear or alarm; formidable ⟨*a* ~ *adversary*⟩ **2** inspiring or worthy of awe or reverence; illustrious [ME *redoutable,* fr MF, fr *redouter* to dread, fr *re-* + *douter* to doubt] – **redoubtably** *adv*

**redound** /ri'downd/ *vi, formal* **1** to have a direct effect; lead or contribute *to* ⟨*can only* ~ *to our advantage*⟩ **2** to rebound *on* or *upon* ⟨*the President's behaviour* ~s *on his Party*⟩ **synonyms** see ¹REBOUND [ME *redounden* to overflow, flow back, fr MF *redonder,* fr L *redundare,* fr *re-, red-* re- + *unda* wave – more at WATER]

**redox** /'ree,doks/ *adj* of or involving OXIDATION-REDUCTION (chemical reaction involving the transfer of electrons from one atom, molecule, etc to another) [*reduction* + *oxidation*] – **redox** *n*

**red panda** *n* a long-tailed Himalayan flesh-eating mammal

| | | | |
|---|---|---|---|
| **redate** *vt* | **redeposit** *vt or n* | **rediscuss** *vt* | **redraft** *vt or n* |
| **rededicate** *vt* | **redescend** *vb* | **redispose** *vt* | **redraw** *vt* |
| **rededication** *n* | **redesignate** *vt* | **redisposition** *n* | **redrawer** *n* |
| **redelegate** *vt* | **redetermination** *n* | **redissolve** *vb* | **redream** *vt* |
| **redeliver** *vt* | **redetermine** *vt* | **redistil** *vt* | **redrill** *vt* |
| **redelivery** *n* | **redial** *vb* | **redistillation** *n* | **redry** *vb* |
| **redemand** *vt* | **redifferentiation** *n* | **redivide** *vb* | **redub** *vt* |
| **redemandable** *adj* | **redigest** *vt* | **redivision** *n* | **redye** *vt* |
| **redemocratize** *vt* | **redigestion** *n* | **redock** *vb* | |
| **redemonstrate** *vt* | **rediscover** *vt* | **redomesticate** *vt* | |
| **redemonstration** *n* | **rediscovery** *n* | **redon** *vt* | |

(*Ailurus fulgens*) that is related to and closely resembles the American raccoon and has long chestnut fur and a black-ringed tail

**red-'pencil** *vt, informal* to censor

**red pepper** *n* 1 CAYENNE PEPPER 2 the ripe fruit of certain CAPSICUM plants

**red pine** *n* 1 a N American pine tree (*Pinosa resinosa*) with scaly reddish bark 2 the hard but not durable wood of the red pine that consists chiefly of SAPWOOD

**redpoll** /'red,pol/ *n* any of several small finches (genus *Acanthis*) that resemble the closely related linnet, and the males of which usu have a red or rosy crown [¹*poll*]

**red poll** *n, often cap R&P* (any of) a British breed of large red hornless dairy and beef cattle [³*poll*]

¹**redress** /ri'dres/ *vt* **1a** to set right; remedy ⟨∼ *social wrongs*⟩ **b** to remove the cause of (a grievance or complaint) **c** to exact reparation for; avenge ⟨*these wrongs must be* ∼ed *in blood*⟩ **2** to adjust evenly; make stable or equal again ⟨∼ *the balance of power*⟩ [ME *redressen*, fr MF *redresser*, fr OF *redrecier*, fr re- + *drecier* to make straight – more at DRESS] – **redresser** *n*

²**redress** *n* **1** an act or instance of redressing; the putting right of what is wrong **2** means or possibility of seeking a remedy ⟨*we are without* ∼ *in this matter*⟩ **3** compensation for wrong or loss; reparation

**red salmon** *n* (the reddish flesh of) a SOCKEYE salmon

**redshank** /'red,shangk/ *n* a common Eurasian and African WADING BIRD (*Tringa totanus*) that has long pale red legs and feet and a reddish bill

**red shift** *n* a shift in the wavelengths of the ELECTROMAGNETIC RADIATIONS (visible light, radio waves, etc) emitted by a celestial body when seen from a distant point (e g the earth), from their normal positions in the SPECTRUM (array of the components of electromagnetic radiation ordered according to wavelength) towards longer wavelengths, that is a consequence of the DOPPLER EFFECT or of the gravity of the body

**red sindhi** /'sindi/ *n* (any of) an Indian breed of rather small red dairy cattle with a hump on the back, that are extensively used for crossbreeding with European stock in tropical areas [*sindhi* (one from Sind, region in S Pakistan), fr Ar *Sindi*]

**redskin** /'red,skin/ *n, chiefly derog* a N American Indian

**red snapper** *n* any of various reddish fishes (esp genus *Lutjanus*), including many important as food, that are common in warm seas

**red snow** *n* snow coloured red by airborne dusts or esp by a growth of algae (e g of the genus *Chlamydomonas*) that contain red pigment and live in the upper layer of snow; *also* an alga causing red snow

**red spider, red spider mite** *n* any of several small web-spinning mites (family Tetranychidae) that attack crop plants; *also* an infestation of these ⟨∼ *is usually only serious in hot dry summers – Popular Gardening*⟩

**red spruce** *n* a spruce tree (*Picea rubens*) of eastern N America that has hairy shoots and brown or purplish bark, and is an important source of timber and PULPWOOD (soft wood used for making paper)

**red squirrel** *n* a reddish-brown Eurasian squirrel (*Sciurus vulgaris*) that is native to British woodlands but is gradually being replaced by the GREY SQUIRREL

**red star** *n* a star having a very low surface temperature and a red colour

**redstart** /'red,staht/ *n* a small European songbird (*Phoenicurus phoenicurus*) with chestnut underparts and tail [*red* + obs *start* handle, tail, fr ME *stert*, fr OE *steort* tail]

**red tape** *n* excessively complex bureaucratic routine or procedure that results in delay or inaction [fr the red tape formerly used to bind legal documents in Britain]

**red tide** *n* sea water discoloured and made poisonous to many forms of marine life by the presence of large numbers of red-coloured single-celled algae (esp of the genera *Gonyaulax* and *Gymnodinium*)

**reduce** /ri'dyoohs/ *vt* **1a** to draw together or cause to converge; consolidate ⟨∼ *all the questions to one*⟩ **b** to diminish in size, amount, volume, extent, or number; make less ⟨∼ *taxes*⟩ ⟨∼ *the likelihood of war*⟩ ⟨∼ *the sauce by boiling*⟩ **2** to bring or force to a specified state or condition ⟨*was* ∼d *to tears of frustration*⟩ **3** to force to capitulate ⟨∼d *Alexandria after a lengthy siege*⟩ **4a** to bring to a systematic form or character ⟨∼ *natural events to laws*⟩ **b** to put down in written or printed form ⟨∼ *an agreement to writing*⟩ **5** to correct (e g a fracture of a bone) by bringing the displaced or broken parts back into

their normal positions **6a** to lower in grade or rank; demote ⟨∼d *to the ranks*⟩ **b** to lower in condition or status; downgrade ⟨*living in* ∼d *circumstances*⟩ **7a** to diminish in strength, density, or value **b** to lower the price of ⟨*shoes* ∼d *in the sale*⟩ **8a(1)** to change the denominations or form of without changing the value ⟨∼ *fractions to a common denominator*⟩ **a(2)** to construct a geometrical figure similar to but smaller than (a given figure) **b** to transpose from one form into another esp more simple or basic form; convert ⟨∼d *the complicated instructions to simple language*⟩ **9** to break down (e g by crushing or grinding); pulverize **10** to convert (e g an ore) to a metal by removing nonmetallic elements **11** *chemistry* **11a** to cause to lose oxygen atoms; remove oxygen from **b** to combine with or subject to the action of hydrogen; add hydrogen atoms to **c** to add one or more electrons to (an atom, molecule, ion, etc) **12** to change (a stressed vowel) to an unstressed vowel **13** *archaic* to restore to righteousness; save ∼ *vi* **1a** to become diminished or lessened; *esp, chiefly NAm* to lose weight by dieting **b** to become concentrated or consolidated ⟨*let the stock* ∼ *to half its volume*⟩ **c** to become reduced ⟨*ferric iron* ∼s *to ferrous iron*⟩ **2** to become converted or transposed from one form into another □ (*vt 11*) compare OXIDIZE [ME *reducen* to lead back, fr L *reducere*, fr re- + *ducere* to lead – more at TOW] – **reducer** *n*, **reducible** *adj*, **reducibility** *n*, **reducibly** *adv*

**usage** One is **reduced** to doing something ⟨*she was* **reduced** *to* apologizing⟩ (not △ *to apologize*⟩).

**reducing agent** /ri'dyoohsing/ *n* a substance that reduces an atom, chemical compound, etc, usu by donating electrons – compare OXIDIZING AGENT

**reductant** /ri'duktənt/ *n* REDUCING AGENT

**reductase** /ri'duktayz/ *n* any ENZYME that increases the rate at which a biochemical reaction involving the chemical reduction of a compound occurs

**reductio ad absurdum** /ri,dukti-oh ad ab'suhdəm/ *n* proof of the falsity of a proposition by revealing the absurdity of its logical consequences [LL, lit., reduction to the absurd]

**reduction** /ri'duksh(ə)n/ *n* **1** reducing or being reduced **2a** something made by reducing; *esp* a reproduction (e g of a picture) in a smaller scale **b** the amount by which something is reduced **3** the process, occurring during REDUCTION DIVISION, whereby the CHROMOSOMES (strands of gene-carrying material) of a cell divide into two equal groups, so that the cells resulting from the division each contain half the number of chromosomes of the original cell [ME *reduccion* restoration, fr MF *reduction*, fr LL & L; LL *reduction-, reductio* reduction (in a syllogism), fr L, restoration, fr *reductus*, pp of *reducere*] – **reductional** *adj*, **reductive** *adj*

**reduction division** *n* the first division of MEIOSIS (splitting of a cell and its contents, ultimately into four new cells) in which two cells or cell nuclei are produced, each containing half the number of chromosomes of the original cell; *also* meiosis

**reduction gear** *n* a combination of gears used to cause a reduction in rotational speed (e g between a marine turbine and a ship's propeller)

**reductionism** /ri'dukshə,niz(ə)m/ *n* a procedure or theory that reduces complex data or phenomena to simple terms; *esp* oversimplification ⟨*to explain the roof of the Sistine Chapel either in terms of the interest rates of the Florentine banks in 1500 or in terms of Michelangelo's toilet training is crass* ∼⟩ – **reductionist** *n or adj*, **reductionistic** *adj*

**redundancy** /ri'dundənsi/ *also* **redundance** *n* **1** being redundant **2** that part of anything which is superfluous or nonessential; *specif* the part of a message that can be eliminated without loss of essential information **3** *chiefly Br* dismissal of a person from a job, specif because he/she is no longer required

**redundant** /ri'dundənt/ *adj* **1a** exceeding what is necessary or normal; superfluous; *specif* needlessly repeating an already expressed idea; tautological ⟨*from in "from thence" is* ∼⟩ **b** characterized by or containing an excess; *specif* using more words than necessary; verbose ⟨*a* ∼ *literary style*⟩ **2** serving as a backup so as to prevent failure of an entire system (e g a spacecraft) in the event of failure of a single component **3** *chiefly Br* unnecessary, unfit, or esp no longer required for a job **antonym** concise (for 1b) [L *redundant-, redundans*, prp of *redundare* to overflow – more at REDOUND] – **redundantly** *adv*

**reduplicate** /ri'dyoohplikayt/ *also* -'dooh-/ *vt* **1** to make or perform again; copy, repeat **2** to form (a word) by reduplication – *vi* to undergo reduplication [LL *reduplicatus*, pp of *reduplicare*, fr L re- + *duplicare* to double – more at DUPLICATE] – **reduplicate** *adj*

**reduplication** /ri,dyoohpli'kaysh(ə)n; *also* -,dooh-/ *n* **1** an act or instance of doubling or reiterating **2a** the formation of a derived or inflected form by doubling (part of) a word, with or without partial modification **b** a word or form (eg *hocus-pocus* or *dilly-dally*) produced by reduplication – **reduplicative** *adj*, **reduplicatively** *adv*

**reduviid** /ri'dyoohvi·id/ *n* any of a large and widely distributed family (Reduviidae) of blood-sucking insects including the ASSASSIN BUGS [deriv of L *reduvia* hangnail] – **reduviid** *adj*

**red water, red-water fever** *n* any of various diseases of cattle marked by the presence of blood or RED BLOOD CELLS in the urine

**red wine** *n* (a) wine with a predominantly red colour derived during fermentation from the natural pigment in the skins of dark-coloured grapes

**redwing** /'red,wing/ *n* a Eurasian thrush (*Turdus iliacus*) with red patches beneath its wings

**redwood** /'red,wood/ *n* (the brownish light red wood of) a commercially important Californian timber tree (*Sequoia sempervirens*) of the pine family that often reaches a height of 100 metres (about 300 feet)

**red worm** *n* **1** BLOODWORM (reddish segmented worm used as bait for fishing); *esp* a small reddish aquatic worm (genus *Tubifex*) **2** STRONGYLE (roundworm parasitic in horses)

**reecho** /,ree'ekoh/ *vb* **reechoes; reechoing; reechoed** *vi* to repeat or return an echo; reverberate ∼ *vt* to echo back; repeat

**reed** /reed/ *n* **1a** any of various tall grasses (esp genera *Phragmites* or *Arundo*) with slender often prominently jointed stems, that grow esp in wet areas **b** the stem of a reed **c** a person or thing too weak to rely on; somebody or something easily swayed or overcome **2** a growth or mass of reeds; *specif* reeds for thatching **3** an ancient Hebrew unit of length equal to 6 CUBITS (about 3 metres or 9 feet) **4a** a thin elastic tongue or flattened tube (eg of cane, wood, or plastic) fastened over an air opening in a musical instrument (eg a clarinet, organ pipe, or accordion) and set in vibration by an air current **b** a woodwind instrument having a reed ⟨the ∼s of an orchestra⟩ **5** a device on a loom resembling a comb and used to space the lengthways yarns (WARP 1a) evenly **6** *architecture* REEDING 1 (semicircular moulding) **7** *poetic* an arrow [ME *rede*, fr OE *hrēod*; akin to OHG *hriot* reed, Lith *krutèti* to stir]

**reedbuck** /'reed,buk/ *n, pl* **reedbuck** *also* **reedbucks** any of a genus (*Redunca*) of fawn-coloured African antelopes of which the females are hornless

**reed bunting** *n* a common black, brown, and white Eurasian BUNTING (type of bird) (*Emberiza schoeniclus*) that frequents marshy places

**reeding** /'reeding/ *n, architecture* **1** a narrow semicircular convex moulding that is usu one of several set parallel as architectural decoration **2** decoration consisting of a series of reedings

**reedit** /,ree'edit/ *vt* to edit again; make a new edition of

**reedling** /'reedling/ *n* BEARDED TIT (long-tailed European bird common in reedy areas)

**reedmace** /'reed,mays/ *n* any of a genus (*Typha* of the family Typhaceae) of tall reedy marsh plants with brown furry spikes of tiny closely packed flowers

**reed organ** *n* a keyboard wind instrument in which the wind acts on a set of reeds to produce sound

**reed pipe** *n* an organ pipe producing its tone by vibration of a beating reed in an air current – compare FLUE PIPE

**reeducate** /,ree'edyookayt, -'ejoo-/ *vt* to train again; *esp* to rehabilitate (eg a disabled person) through education – **reed-**

ucation *n*, **reeducative** *adj*

**reed warbler** *n* any of several Eurasian warblers (genus *Acrocephalus*, esp *Acrocephalus scirpaceus*) that frequent marshy places

**reedy** /'reedi/ *adj* **1** full of, covered with, or made of reeds **2** resembling reeds; *esp* slender, frail **3** having the tonal quality of a reed instrument; *esp* thin and high

**¹reef** /reef/ *n* **1** a part of a sail taken in or let out in regulating the area exposed to the wind **2** reduction in sail area by reefing [ME *riff*, fr ON *rif*]

**²reef** *vt* to reduce the area of (a sail) exposed to the wind by rolling up or taking in a portion ∼ *vi* to reduce the area of a sail by taking in a reef

**³reef** *n* **1** a chain of rocks or ridge of sand at or near the surface of water **2** a deposit of ore; a lode [D *rif*, prob of Scand origin; akin to ON *rif* reef of a sail] – **reefy** *adj*

**¹reefer** /'reefə/, **reefer jacket** *n* a close-fitting usu double-breasted jacket of thick cloth [²reef (prob in the sense "to fold closely") + ²-*er*]

**²reefer** *n* a marijuana cigarette [perh fr ¹*reef* (in the sense "something rolled up"), or perh modif of MexSp *grifo* (one who smokes) marijuana]

**reef knot** *n* a symmetrical knot made of two HALF-KNOTS tied in opposite directions and commonly used for joining two pieces of string, cord, etc

**¹reek** /reek/ *n* **1** a strong or disagreeable smell **2** *chiefly Scot & N Eng* smoke, vapour [ME *rek* smoke, fr OE *rēc;* akin to OHG *rouh* smoke]

**²reek** *vi* **1** to emit smoke or vapour **2a** to give off or become permeated with a strong or offensive smell – often + *of* ⟨the whole place ∼ed *of tobacco*⟩ **b** to give a strong impression of some usu undesirable quality or feature – + *of* or with ⟨an area that ∼s *of poverty*⟩ to give off; exude ⟨a man who ∼s charm⟩ – **reeker** *n*, **reeky** *adj*

**¹reel** /reel, riəl/ *n* **1** a revolvable device on which something flexible is wound: eg **1a** a small wheel at the butt of a fishing rod for winding the line **b** a spool with a projecting rim (eg for photographic film or magnetic tape) **c** *chiefly Br* a small spool for sewing thread **2** a quantity of something wound on a reel [ME, fr OE *hrēol;* akin to ON *hræll* weaver's reed, Gk *krekein* to weave]

**²reel** *vt* **1** to wind (as if) on a reel **2** to put into a specified place or condition by winding ⟨∼ *in the line*⟩ ∼ *vi* to turn a reel – **reelable** *adj*, **reeler** *n*

**reel off** *vt* **1** to tell, repeat, or state readily and without pause ⟨reeled off *all the facts and figures*⟩ **2** to chalk up, usu as a series ⟨reeled off *six wins in succession*⟩

**³reel** *vi* **1a** to turn or move round and round ⟨the constellations ∼ *and dance like fireflies* – P B Shelley⟩ **b** to be giddy; be in a whirl ⟨her mind was ∼ing⟩ **2** to waver or fall back (eg from a blow); recoil ⟨a fierce attack that sent the enemy ∼ing⟩ **3** to walk or move unsteadily (eg from dizziness or intoxication) [ME *relen*, prob fr ¹*reel*]

**⁴reel** *n* a reeling motion

**⁵reel** *n* (the music for) a lively esp Scottish-Highland or Irish dance in which two or more couples perform a series of circular figures and winding movements [prob fr ⁴*reel*]

**reel-to-'reel** *adj* of or using MAGNETIC TAPE passing between two reels that are unconnected and not in a cassette or cartridge ⟨a ∼ tape recorder⟩

**reemploy** /,ree·im'ploy/ *vt* to employ again; *esp* to hire back ⟨the tribunal ordered the company to ∼ the sacked men⟩ – **reemployment** *n*

**reenact** /,ree·i'nakt/ *vt* to act or perform again; *specif* to repeat

| | | |
|---|---|---|
| **reelect** *vt* | **reenergize** *vt* | **reenthrone** *vt* | **reexamination** *n* |
| **reelection** *n* | **reenforce** *vt* | **reentrance** *n* | **reexamine** *vt* |
| **reeligible** *adj* | **reenforcement** *n* | **reequip** *vt* | **reexchange** *vt* |
| **reembodiment** *n* | **reengage** *vb* | **reequipment** *n* | **reexhibit** *vt* |
| **reembody** *vt* | **reengagement** *n* | **reerect** *vt* | **reexhibition** *n* |
| **reemerge** *vi* | **reengineer** *vt* | **reerection** *n* | **reexperience** *vt* |
| **reemergence** *n* | **reengrave** *vt* | **reescalate** *vb* | **reexploration** *n* |
| **reemergent** *adj* | **reenlarge** *vt* | **reescalation** *n* | **reexplore** *vt* |
| **reemission** *n* | **reenlighten** *vt* | **reestablish** *vt* | **reexport** *vt or n* |
| **reemit** *vt* | **reenlightenment** *n* | **reestablishment** *n* | **reexportation** *n* |
| **reemphasis** *n* | **reenlist** *vb* | **reestimate** *vt or n* | **reexporter** *n* |
| **reemphasize** *vt* | **reenlistment** *n* | **reevaluate** *vt* | |
| **reenchant** *vt* | **reenrol** *vb* | **reevaluation** *n* | |
| **reendow** *vt* | **reenslave** *vt* | **reevoke** *vt* | |

or reconstruct the actions of (an earlier event or incident) ⟨*agreed to* ~ *the crime*⟩ – **reenactment** *n*

**reenter** /ˌreeˈentə/ *vb* to enter again

**reentrant** /ˌreeˈentrənt/ *n or adj* (an angle, point, etc) directed or pointing inwards ⟨*a* ~ *angle*⟩

**reentry** /ˌreeˈentri/ *n* **1** *law* the act or an instance of taking possession again; *esp* the retaking of possession by a lessor of leased premises on the tenant's failure to fulfil the conditions of the lease **2** a second or new entry ⟨*a* ~ *visa*⟩; *esp* the return to and entry of the earth's atmosphere by a spacecraft **3** a playing card that will enable a player to regain the lead

¹**reeve** /reev/ *n* **1** a local administrative agent of an Anglo-Saxon king **2** a medieval English manor officer responsible chiefly for overseeing the discharge of feudal obligations **3** the council president in some Canadian municipalities [ME *reve*, fr OE *gerēfa*, fr *ge-* (associative prefix) + *-rēfa* (akin to OE *-rōf* number, group, OHG *ruova*)]

²**reeve** *vt* **rove** /rohv/, **reeved 1** to pass (eg a rope) through a hole or opening **2** to fasten by passing through a hole or round something **3** to pass a rope through (eg a block) [origin unknown]

³**reeve** *n* the female of the RUFF (Eurasian bird) [prob alter. of *ruff*]

¹**ref** /ref/ *n, informal* a sports referee

²**ref** *vb* **-ff-** *informal* to act as referee (of)

**refashion** /ˌreeˈfash(ə)n/ *vt* to make again; remodel, alter

**refect** /riˈfekt/ *vt, archaic* to refresh with food or drink [L *refectus*, pp]

**refection** /riˈfeksh(ə)n/ *n, formal* **1** refreshment of mind, spirit, or body; nourishment **2a** the taking of refreshment **b** a portion of food, drink, or both taken together; a repast [ME *refeccioun*, fr MF *refection*, fr L *refection-*, *refectio*, fr *refectus*, pp of *reficere* to restore, fr *re-* + *facere* to make – more at DO]

**refectory** /riˈfekt(ə)ri/ *n* a dining hall in an institution (eg a monastery or college) [LL *refectorium*, fr L *refectus*, pp]

**refectory table** *n* a long narrow dining table with heavy legs

**refer** /riˈfuh/ *vb* **-rr-** *vt* **1a(1)** to think of, regard, or classify within a general category or group ⟨*his tribe cannot be* ~ *red to this common stock*⟩ **a(2)** to explain in terms of a general cause ⟨~*s their depression to the weather*⟩ **b** to allot to a specified place, stage, or period ⟨*to* ~ *the fall of Rome to 410 AD*⟩ **c** to experience (eg pain) as coming from or located in a different area from the actual source ⟨*the pain in appendicitis may be* ~*red to any area of the abdomen*⟩ ⟨~*red pain*⟩ **2a** to send or direct for treatment, aid, information, or decision ⟨~ *a patient to a specialist*⟩ ⟨~*s students to his other works*⟩ ⟨~ *a case to arbitration*⟩ **b** to direct for testimony as to character or ability ⟨~ *the company to a former employer*⟩ ~ *vi* **1a** to have relation or connection; relate *to* ⟨*the numbers* ~ *to notes at the foot of the page*⟩ **b** to direct attention, usu by clear and specific mention; allude *to* ⟨*no one* ~*red to yesterday's quarrel*⟩ ⟨*the numbers* ~ *to footnotes*⟩ **2** to have recourse *to;* glance briefly for information ⟨~*red frequently to his notes while speaking*⟩ **synonyms** see ASCRIBE [ME *referren*, fr L *referre* to bring back, report, refer, fr *re-* + *ferre* to carry – more at BEAR] – **referable** *adj*, **referral** *n*

¹**referee** /ˌrefəˈree/ *n* **1** a person to whom a thing is referred: eg **1a** one to whom a legal matter is referred for investigation and report or for settlement **b** one who reviews an esp technical paper before publication **c** REFERENCE 4a **2** an official who supervises the play and enforces the laws in any of several sports (eg football and boxing) – compare UMPIRE

²**referee** *vb* to act as a referee (in or for)

¹**reference** /ˈref(ə)rəns/ *n* **1a** the act of referring or consulting ⟨~ *to a map will make the position clear*⟩ ⟨*a manual designed for ready* ~⟩ **b** the seeking of information; consultation ⟨*books more suitable for* ~ *than for reading*⟩ **2** an alluding to, bearing on, or connection with a specified matter; relation ⟨*ability has little* ~ *to age*⟩ – often in *in/with reference to* ⟨*with* ~ *to your recent letter*⟩ **3** something that refers: eg **3a** an allusion, mention **b** something that refers a reader or consulter to another source of information (eg a book or passage) **4** one referred to or consulted: eg **4a** a person to whom inquiries as to character or ability can be made **b** a statement of the qualifications of a person seeking employment or appointment given by somebody familiar with him/her **c** a source of information (eg a book or passage) to which a reader or enquirer is referred **d** a standard for measuring, evaluating, etc

²**reference** *vt* to provide (eg a book) with references to authorities and sources of information

³**reference** *prep* with reference to – used esp in business language ⟨~ *your memo of the 23rd*⟩

**reference book** *n* **1** a book (eg a dictionary, encyclopedia, or atlas) intended primarily for consultation rather than for consecutive reading **2** *SAfr* DOMPASS (identification document for non-white S Africans)

**reference group** *n* a group to which an individual aspires or belongs that influences his/her attitudes and behaviour by providing a source of comparison and a set of values, standards, and approved norms

**reference library** *n* a library where books may be consulted but not borrowed

**reference mark** *n* a conventional sign (eg *, †, or ‡) used to direct the reader's attention, esp to a footnote

**referendum** /ˌrefəˈrendəm/ *n, pl* **referendums** *also* **referenda** /-də/ **1** the principle or practice of allowing the electorate to vote on a measure proposed by a parliament or other lawmaking body or arising from public opinion **2** a vote on a measure submitted to the electorate [NL, fr L, neut of *referendus*, gerundive of *referre* to refer]

**referent** /ˈref(ə)rənt/ *n* the thing that a symbol (eg a word or sign) stands for [L *referent-*, *referens*, prp of *referre*] – **referent** *adj*

**referential** /ˌrefəˈrensh(ə)l/ *adj* containing or constituting a reference ⟨*symbols are inherently* ~⟩ – **referentially** *adv*

¹**refill** /ˌreeˈfil/ *vb* to make or become full again – **refillable** *adj*

²**refill** /ˈreeˌfil/ *n* **1** a fresh or replacement supply for a device ⟨*a* ~ *for a ball-point pen*⟩ **2** a replenishment (eg for a drink) ⟨*can I give you a* ~?⟩

**refinance** /ˌreeˈfienans/ *vb* to renew or reorganize financing (of)

**refine** /riˈfien/ *vt* **1** to free from impurities; make pure ⟨~ *sugar*⟩ **2** to improve or perfect by pruning or polishing ⟨~ *a poetic style*⟩ **3** to reduce in vigour or intensity by pruning, polishing, or purifying ⟨*most of the nutritive value of the food was* ~*d away*⟩ **4** to free from imperfection, esp from what is coarse, vulgar, or uncouth; elevate ~ *vi* **1** to become pure or perfected **2** to make improvement by introducing subtleties or distinctions [*re-* + ⁴*fine*] – **refiner** *n*

**refined** /riˈfiend/ *adj* **1** free from impurities **2** fastidious, cultivated

**refinement** /riˈfienmənt/ *n* **1** the action or process of refining **2** the quality or state of being refined; cultivation **3a** a refined feature or method ⟨*pursued the delicate art of suggestion to its furthest* ~*s* – Maurice Bowra⟩ **b** a highly refined distinction; a subtlety ⟨~*s of logic*⟩ **c** a contrivance or device intended to improve or perfect ⟨*this new model has many* ~*s*⟩

**refinery** /riˈfien(ə)ri/ *n* a plant where raw materials (eg oil or sugar) are refined or purified

**refit** /ˌreeˈfit/ *vb* **-tt-** *vt* to fit out or supply again; *esp* to renovate and modernize (eg a ship) ~ *vi* to obtain repairs or fresh supplies or equipment ⟨*the fleet returned to* ~⟩ – **refit** *n*

**reflation** /ˌreeˈflaysh(ə)n/ *n* an expansion in the volume of available money and credit in the economy, esp as a result of government policy [*re-* + *-flation* (as in *deflation, inflation*)] – **reflate** *vb*, **reflationary** *adj*

**reflect** /riˈflekt/ *vt* **1** to send or throw (light, sound, etc) back or at an angle ⟨*a mirror* ~*s light*⟩ **2** *anatomy & botany* to bend or fold back ⟨*petals* ~*ed at the tops*⟩ ⟨*the peritoneum is* ~*ed inwards over the intestines*⟩ **3** to give back or show as an image, likeness, or outline; mirror ⟨*the clouds were* ~*ed in the water*⟩ **4** to cause to be attributed ⟨*his attitude* ~*s little credit on his judgment*⟩ **5** to make manifest or apparent; show ⟨*the pulse* ~*s the condition of the heart*⟩ **6** to come to remember or realize; consider ⟨*liked her before I* ~*ed that she was a member of the opposing team*⟩ ~ *vi* **1** to throw back light, sound, etc **2a** to think quietly and calmly **b** to express a thought or opinion resulting from reflection **3a** to tend to bring reproach or discredit ⟨*an investigation that* ~*s on all the members of the department*⟩ **b** to tend to bring about a specified appearance or impression ⟨*an act which* ~*s favourably on her*⟩ □ (*vi 2 & 3*) usu + *on* or *upon* [ME *reflecten*, fr L *reflectere* to bend back, fr *re-* + *flectere* to bend]

**reflectance** /riˈflekt(ə)ns/ *n* REFLECTION FACTOR

**reflecting telescope** /riˈflekting/ *n* REFLECTOR 2

**reflection**, *Br also* **reflexion** /riˈfleksh(ə)n/ *n* **1** the act or an instance of reflecting something (eg light, sound, or heat) **2** the production of an image (as if) by a mirror ⟨*the eye sees not itself but by* ~ – Shak⟩ **3** *anatomy & botany* the action of bending or folding back; *also* a reflected part **4** something produced by reflecting: eg **4a** an image given back (as if) by a reflecting surface **b** an effect produced by or related to a specified influence or cause ⟨*a high crime rate is a ~ of an unstable society*⟩ **5** an often obscure or indirect criticism; a reproach ⟨*the book was suppressed as a ~ on the regime*⟩ **6** a thought, idea, or opinion formed or a remark made as a result of serious thought or consideration ⟨Reflections *on the Revolution in France* – Edmund Burke⟩ **7** consideration of some subject matter, idea, or purpose ⟨*on ~ it didn't seem such a good plan*⟩ **8** *maths* a transformation of a figure with respect to a reference line (AXIS), producing a MIRROR IMAGE of the figure [ME, fr LL *reflexion-, reflexio* act of bending back, fr L *reflexus*, pp of *reflectere*] – **reflectional** *adj*

**reflection factor** *n* a measure of the ability of a surface to reflect light or other RADIANT ENERGY (e g heat), that is equal to the ratio of the rate of flow of energy reflected from the surface to the rate of flow of energy falling on the surface

**reflective** /ri'flektiv/ *adj* **1** capable of reflecting light, an image, sound waves, etc **2** marked by reflection; thoughtful, deliberative **3** of or caused by reflection ⟨*the ~ glare of the snow*⟩ – **reflectively** *adv*, **reflectiveness** *n*

**reflectivity** /ˌriˌflek'tivəti, ˌreeflek-/ *n* **1** being reflective; reflectiveness **2** a measure of the ability of a surface to reflect light or other RADIANT ENERGY, equal to the REFLECTION FACTOR of a layer of material sufficiently thick for any increase in its thickness to make no difference to the reflection factor

**reflector** /ri'flektə/ *n* **1** a surface or object that reflects light, heat, sound, etc; *specif* a small usu red piece of metal or plastic fixed on the back of a bicycle, car, etc to reflect the headlights of following traffic **2** a telescope that uses a mirror that reflects light rays as its principal focussing element rather than a lens – compare REFRACTOR

**¹reflex** /'reefleks/ *n* **1a** reflected heat, light, or colour **b** a mirrored image ⟨*to cut across the ~ of a star* – William Wordsworth⟩ **c** a reproduction or reflection that corresponds to some usu specified original **2** a word or word element found in a language in a form determined by development from an earlier stage of the language **3a** an automatic involuntary response to a stimulus, that involves the passage of a nerve impulse along a REFLEX ARC and does not reach the level of consciousness ⟨*tested the patient's ~es*⟩ **b** the process that culminates in a reflex response and comprises the reception and transmission of, and reaction to a stimulus **c** *pl* the power of acting or responding with adequate speed ⟨*a pilot needs good ~es*⟩ **d** an (automatic or mechanical) way of thinking or behaving ⟨*lying became a natural ~ for him*⟩ [L *reflexus*, pp of *reflectere* to reflect]

**²reflex** *adj* **1** bent, turned, or directed back; reflected ⟨*a stem with ~ leaves*⟩ **2** directed back on the mind or its operations; introspective **3** occurring as an (automatic) reaction or response **4** *of an angle* greater than 180° but less than 360° **5** of, being, or produced by a reflex without intervention of consciousness ⟨*~ action*⟩ [L *reflexus*, pp] – **reflexly** *adv*

**reflex arc** *n* the complete nerve pathway involved in a reflex, that includes a specialized cell or group of cells that receives a stimulus which is then passed, in the form of a nerve impulse, to a nerve centre outside the brain, and from there outwards to a muscle, gland, or other organ that effects a response

**reflex camera** *n* a camera in which the image formed by the lens is reflected onto a ground-glass screen or is seen through the viewfinder for focussing and composition

**reflexed** /'reeflekst, ri'flekst/ *adj* bent or curved backwards or downwards ⟨*~ petals*⟩ ⟨*~ leaves*⟩ [L *reflexus* + E *-ed*]

**¹reflexive** /ri'fleksiv/ *adj* **1** directed or turned back on itself **2** of or being a (mathematical) relation (e g is equal to) such that *x*\**x* where \* denotes the relation **3a** of or being (a member of) a class of pronouns (e g "himself") which refer back to the subject of a clause or sentence **b** of or being a verb whose action is directed back on the doer or the grammatical subject (e g in "he perjured himself") **4** of a (physiological) reflex [ML *reflexivus*, fr L *reflexus*, pp] – **reflexively** *adv*, **reflexiveness**, **reflexivity** *n*

**²reflexive** *n* a reflexive verb or pronoun

**refluent** /'reflooənt/ *adj* flowing back [L *refluent-, refluens*, prp of *refluere* to flow back, fr *re-* + *fluere* to flow – more at FLUID] – **refluence** *n*

**¹reflux** /'ree,fluks/ *n* **1** a flowing back; an ebb **2** refluxing or being refluxed ⟨*a ~ condenser*⟩ [ME, fr ML *refluxus*, fr L *re-* + *fluxus* flow – more at FLUX]

**²reflux** *vb* to (cause to) flow back or return; *esp, chemistry* (to heat so as) to form vapours that cool and condense, and return to be heated again

**refocus** /ˌree'fohkəs/ *vb* **-ss-, -s-** *vt* **1** to focus again **2** to change the emphasis or direction of ⟨*had ~sed his life*⟩ *~ vi* **1** to focus something again **2** to change emphasis or direction

**reforest** /ˌree'forist/ *vt* to reafforest – **reforestation** *n*

**reforge** /ˌree'fawj/ *vt* to forge again [ME *reforgen*, fr MF *reforgier*, fr *re-* + *forgier* to forge]

**¹reform** /ri'fawm/ *vt* **1** to amend or alter for the better; improve ⟨*~ the political system*⟩ **2** to put an end to (an evil) by enforcing or introducing a better method or course of action **3** to induce or cause to abandon evil ways ⟨*~ a drunkard*⟩ *~ vi* to become changed for the better [ME *reformen*, fr MF *reformer*, fr L *reformare*, fr *re-* + *formare* to form] – **reformable** *adj*, **reformability** *n*, **reformative**, **reformatory** *adj*

**²reform** *n* **1** amendment of what is defective or corrupt ⟨*educational ~*⟩ **2** (a measure intended to bring about) a removal or correction of an abuse, a wrong, or errors

**³reform** *adj* relating to or favouring reform ⟨*a ~ movement*⟩

**ˌre-'form** *vt* to form again *~ vi* to take form again ⟨*the ice ~ed on the lake*⟩

**reformation** /ˌrefə'maysh(ə)n/ *n* **1** reforming or being reformed **2** *cap* the 16th-century religious movement marked ultimately by the rejection of papal authority and some Roman Catholic doctrines and practices and by the establishment of the Protestant churches △ Renaissance, Restoration – **reformational** *adj*

**reformatory** /ri'fawmət(ə)ri/ *n, chiefly NAm* a penal institution to which young or first offenders or women are sent for reform – no longer used technically in Br

**reformed** /ri'fawmd/ *adj* **1** changed for the better ⟨*a ~ character*⟩ **2** *cap* Protestant; *specif* of or being a Calvinist Protestant church or the Calvinist Protestant churches

**reformer** /ri'fawmə/ *n* **1** somebody who works for or urges reform **2** *cap* a leader of the Protestant Reformation

**reformism** /ri'fawmiz(ə)m/ *n* a doctrine, policy, or movement of reform – **reformist** *n*

**Reform Judaism** /ri'fawm/ *n* a liberalizing and modernizing branch of the Jewish religion

**reform school** *n, chiefly NAm* a reformatory for young offenders – no longer used technically in Br

**refract** /ri'frakt/ *vt* **1** to subject to or cause to undergo refraction **2** to determine the refracting power of (e g a lens) [L *refractus*, pp of *refringere* to break open, break up, refract, fr *re-* + *frangere* to break – more at BREAK]

**refracting telescope** /ri'frakting/ *n* REFRACTOR

**refraction** /ri'fraksh(ə)n/ *n* **1a** the deflection or deviation of a wave (e g a beam of light) from one straight path to another when passing from one medium (e g air) into another (e g glass) in which the speed of transmission of the wave is different **b** the amount of deviation of a wave undergoing refraction **2** the change in the apparent position of a celestial body due to bending of the light rays coming from it as they pass through the atmosphere; *also* the correction to be applied to the apparent position of a body because of this

**refractive** /ri'fraktiv/ *adj* **1** *of a substance, lens, etc* having power to cause refraction **2** relating or due to refraction – **refractively** *adv*, **refractiveness**, **refractivity** *n*

**refractive index** *n* a measure of the amount by which a substance refracts a wave, esp of light, equal to the ratio of the speed of transmission (VELOCITY) of the wave in a reference medium or vacuum to its velocity in the substance

**refractometer** /ˌreefrak'tomitə/ *n* an instrument for measuring the REFRACTIVE INDEX of a substance [ISV] – **refractometry** *n*, **refractometric** *adj*

**refractor** /ri'fraktə/ *n* a telescope that uses a lens that refracts light rays as its principal focussing element rather than a mirror – compare REFLECTOR 2

¹**refractory** /ri'frakt(ə)ri/ *adj* 1 resisting control or authority; stubborn, unmanageable 2a resistant to treatment or cure ⟨*a ~ cough*⟩ **b** temporarily unresponsive to a stimulus ⟨*a ~ nerve*⟩ **c** immune, insusceptible ⟨*after recovery they were ~ to infection*⟩ 3 difficult to melt, corrode, draw into a wire, etc ⟨*~ metals*⟩; *esp* capable of enduring high temperatures without alteration of the physical, chemical, or structural properties *synonyms* see UNRULY *antonyms* malleable, amenable [alter. of *refractary*, fr L *refractarius*, irreg fr *refragari* to oppose, fr *re-* + *-fragari* (as in *suffragari* to support with one's vote) – more at SUFFRAGE] – **refractorily** *adv*, **refractoriness** *n*

²**refractory** *n* a material capable of withstanding high temperatures; *esp* one (e g firebrick) used for lining a furnace, kiln, etc

**refractory period** *n* the brief resting period, immediately following the response to a stimulus, in which a muscle, nerve, etc is unable to respond to further stimulation

**refractory phase** *n* REFRACTORY PERIOD

¹**refrain** /ri'frayn/ *vt*, *archaic* to curb, restrain ~ *vi* to keep oneself *from* doing, feeling, or indulging in something, esp from following a passing impulse [ME *refreynen*, fr MF *refrener*, fr L *refrenare* to bridle, hold back, restrain, fr *re-* + *frenum* bridle] – **refrainment** *n*

²**refrain** *n* a regularly recurring phrase or verse, esp at the end of each stanza or division of a poem or song; a chorus; *also* the musical setting of a refrain [ME *refreyn*, fr MF *refrain*, fr *refraindre* to resound, fr L *refringere* to break up, refract]

**refrangible** /ri'franjəbl/ *adj* capable of being refracted [irreg fr L *refringere* to refract] – **refrangibleness, refrangibility** *n*

**refresh** /ri'fresh/ *vt* 1 to restore strength or vigour to (e g by food or rest); revive 2 to freshen up; renovate 3a to restore or maintain by renewing supply; replenish ⟨*the waiter ~ed our glasses*⟩ **b** to arouse, stimulate ⟨*let me ~ your memory*⟩ 4 to renew (information stored in a computer) [ME *refresshen*, fr MF *refreschir*, fr OF, fr *re-* + *freis* fresh – more at FRESH]

**refresher** /ri'freshə/ *n* 1 something (e g a drink) that refreshes 2 **refresher, refresher course** a course of instruction designed esp to keep one abreast of developments in one's professional field

**refreshing** /ri'freshing/ *adj* serving to refresh; *esp* agreeably stimulating because of freshness or newness – **refreshingly** *adv*

**refreshment** /ri'freshmənt/ *n* 1 refreshing or being refreshed 2a something (e g food or drink) that refreshes **b** *pl* assorted foods, esp as suitable and sufficient for a light meal

¹**refrigerant** /ri'frijərənt/ *adj* 1 causing cooling or freezing 2 *medicine* lessening heat or fever

²**refrigerant** *n* something refrigerant: e g **a** a medication for reducing body heat **b** a substance used in refrigeration; *specif* one (e g a Freon) with the property of changing easily from a liquid to a gas, that is used in a refrigerator, freezer, etc to remove heat energy and transfer it to the surroundings

**refrigerate** /ri'frijərayt/ *vt* to make or keep cold or cool; *specif* to freeze or chill (e g food) for preservation [L *refrigeratus*, pp of *refrigerare*, fr *re-* + *frigerare* to cool, fr *frigor-, frigus* cold – more at FRIGID] – **refrigeration** *n*

**refrigerator** /ri'frijəraytə/ *n* something that refrigerates or keeps cool; *specif* an insulated cabinet or room for keeping items, esp food or drink, cool

**refringent** /ri'frinj(ə)nt/ *adj* of or causing refraction; refractive [L *refringent-, refringens*, prp of *refringere* to refract] – **refringence, refringency** *n*

**reft** /reft/ *past of* REAVE

**refuel** /,ree'fyooh·əl/ *vb* **-ll-** (*NAm* **-l-, -ll-**) to provide with or take on additional fuel

**refuge** /'refyoohj/ *n* 1 (a place that provides) shelter or protection from danger or distress ⟨*a mountain ~*⟩ ⟨*seek ~ in flight*⟩ 2 a person, thing, or course of action that offers protection or is resorted to in difficulties ⟨*patriotism is the last ~ of a scoundrel* – Samuel Johnson⟩ [ME, fr MF, fr L *refugium*, fr *refugere* to run away, flee, fr *re-* + *fugere* to flee – more at FUGITIVE]

**refugee** /,refyoo'jee/ *n* one who flees for safety, esp to a foreign country to escape danger or avoid political, religious, or racial persecution [Fr *réfugié*, pp of (*se*) *réfugier* to take refuge, fr L

*refugium*]

**refugium** /ri'fyoohjiəm/ *n*, *pl* **refugia** /-jiə/ an area of relatively unaltered climate inhabited by plants and animals during a period of climatic change (e g a glaciation) affecting the surrounding regions, in which the surviving plants and animals are remnants of otherwise extinct forms [NL, fr L, refuge]

**refulgence** /ri'fulj(ə)ns/ *n*, *formal* radiance, brilliance [L *refulgentia*, fr *refulgent-, refulgens*, prp of *refulgēre* to shine brightly, fr *re-* + *fulgēre* to shine – more at FULGENT] – **refulgent** *adj*

¹**refund** /ri'fund/ *vt* 1 to return (money) in restitution, repayment, or balancing of accounts 2 to pay (somebody) back [ME *refunden*, fr MF & L; MF *refonder*, fr L *refundere*, lit., to pour back, fr *re-* + *fundere* to pour – more at FOUND] – **refundable** *adj*, **refundability** *n*

²**refund** /'ree,fund/ *n* 1 the act of refunding 2 a sum refunded

³**refund** /,ree'fund/ *vt* to fund (a debt) again [*re-* + *fund*]

**refurbish** /,ree'fuhbish/ *vt* to brighten or freshen up (e g a house); renovate – **refurbisher** *n*, **refurbishment** *n*

**refusal** /ri'fyoohzl/ *n* 1 the act or an instance of refusing, denying, or being refused 2 the opportunity or right of refusing or accepting before others – compare FIRST REFUSAL

¹**refuse** /ri'fyoohz/ *vt* 1 to express one's unwillingness to accept ⟨*~ a gift*⟩ ⟨*~ a promotion*⟩ 2a to show or express unwillingness to do or comply with ⟨*the engine ~d to start*⟩ **b** to deny ⟨*they were ~d admittance to the game*⟩ 3 *of a horse* to decline to jump or leap over ⟨*~d the water jump*⟩ ~ *vi* to withhold acceptance, compliance, or permission [ME *refusen*, fr MF *refuser*, fr (assumed) VL *refusare*, fr L *refusus*, pp of *refundere* to pour back] – **refusable** *adj*, **refuser** *n*

²**refuse** /'refyoohs/ *n* worthless or useless material; rubbish, garbage [ME, fr MF *refus* rejection, fr OF, fr *refuser*]

**refusenik, refusnik** /ri'fyoohznik/ *n* a Soviet Jew who has been refused permission to emigrate, esp to Israel [part trans of Russ *otkáznik*, fr *otkazát'* to refuse]

**refute** /ri'fyooht/ *vt* 1 to prove wrong by argument or evidence; show to be false or erroneous ⟨*I ~d him easily*⟩ ⟨*I ~d his claim*⟩ 2 to deny the truth or accuracy of ⟨*~d the election returns which showed him the loser*⟩ [L *refutare*, fr *re-* + *-futare* to beat – more at BEAT] – **refutable** *adj*, **refutably** *adv*, **refuter** *n*, **refutation** *n*

*usage* To **refute** or **rebut** a statement is, correctly, to "disprove" it, not merely to "deny" it, although **refute** is now quite commonly used in this second meaning. One can **refute** a person as well as a statement, but compare ⟨*no, I* **refute** *you* (= prove you wrong); *here's my evidence*⟩⟨*no, I* **refute** *you* (= contradict you); *it was Tuesday*⟩.

**regain** /ri'gayn/ ,ree-/ *vt* to gain or reach again; recover

¹**regal** /'reegl/ *adj* 1 of or suitable for a king or queen 2 stately, splendid [ME, fr MF or L; MF, fr L *regalis* – more at ROYAL] – **regally** *adv*, **regality** *n*

²**regal** *n* a small portable organ used from the 15th to the 17th century [MF *regale*, perh fr fem of *regal* royal]

**regale** /ri'gayl/ *vt* 1 to entertain sumptuously 2 to give pleasure or amusement to ⟨*~d us with stories of her exploits*⟩ [Fr *régaler*, fr MF, fr *regale* feast, fr *re-* + *gale* pleasure, merry-making – more at GALLANT]

**regalia** /ri'gaylyə/ *n taking sing or pl vb* 1a (the) emblems or symbols indicative of royalty **b** decorations or insignia indicative of an office or order ⟨*the mayor was wearing her full ~*⟩ 2 special dress; *esp* finery ⟨*unrecognizable in his Sunday ~*⟩ [ML, fr L, neut pl of *regalis* royal]

¹**regard** /ri'gahd/ *n* 1 a gaze, look 2a attention, consideration ⟨*due ~ should be given to all facets of the question*⟩ **b** (a) protective interest; care ⟨*ought to have more ~ for his health*⟩ 3a a feeling of respect and affection; esteem ⟨*her hard work won her the ~ of her colleagues*⟩ **b** *pl* friendly greetings ⟨*give him my ~s*⟩ 4 an aspect to be taken into consideration; a respect ⟨*is a small school, and is fortunate in this ~*⟩ 5 *archaic* appearance 6 *obs* an intention [ME, fr MF, fr OF, fr *regarder*] – **in/with regard to** with respect to; concerning

²**regard** *vt* 1 to pay attention to; take into consideration or account 2 to look steadily at 3 to relate to; concern 4a to contemplate and appraise, usu in a specified way or from a specified point of view ⟨*he is highly ~ed as a mechanic*⟩ ⟨*~ed the prospect with horror*⟩ **b** to consider, esteem ⟨*would ~ it an honour*⟩ [ME *regarden*, fr MF *regarder* to look back at, regard, fr OF, fr *re-* + *garder* to guard, look at] – **as regards** in so far as it concerns; IN REGARD TO

*synonyms* Regard, respect, esteem, and admire all mean "recognize the worth of somebody or something". **Regard** is the weakest, needing in this sense a qualifying phrase or adverb ⟨*regard him with approval*⟩. **Respect** often implies suitable deference towards a senior or superior, which need not entail liking. **Esteem** implies a warmer feeling of lasting and pleasurable respect ⟨*esteem the work of a fine scholar*⟩. **Admire** is the strongest word, implying a not always judicious pleasure and wonder, often freely expressed and perhaps combined with the desire to imitate or possess. *usage* When **regard** means "consider" it is correctly used as in ⟨*he regarded them highly/with admiration/as his superiors*⟩ but not as in ⟨⚠ *he regarded them his superiors*⟩ or ⟨⚠ *he regarded them to be his superiors*⟩.

**regardant** /ri'gahd(ə)nt/ *adj, of a heraldic animal* looking backwards over the shoulder [ME, fr MF, prp of *regarder*]

**regardful** /ri'gahdf(ə)l/ *adj* 1 heedful, observant 2 respectful – **regardfully** *adv*, **regardfulness** *n*

**regarding** /ri'gahding/ *prep* concerning; WITH REGARD TO

¹**regardless** /ri'gahdlis/ *adj* heedless, careless – **regardlessly** *adv*, **regardlessness** *n* – **regardless** of despite; IN SPITE OF

²**regardless** /ri'gahdlis/ *adv* despite everything ⟨*went ahead with their plans ∼*⟩

**regatta** /ri'gatə/ *n* (a meeting for) a series of rowing, speedboat, or sailing races [It]

**regelation** /ˌreeji'laysh(ə)n/ *n* the freezing again of water derived from the melting of ice, when the high pressure that caused the ice to melt is relieved – **regelate** *vi*

**regency** /'reej(ə)nsi/ *n* 1 the office, jurisdiction, period of rule, or government of a regent or body of regents 2 *taking sing or pl vb* a body of regents

**Regency** *adj* of or resembling the styles (eg of furniture or dress) prevalent during the regency of George, Prince of Wales (1811–20)

¹**regenerate** /ri'jenərət/ *adj* 1 formed or created again 2 spiritually reborn or converted 3 restored to a better, higher, or more worthy state [ME *regenerat*, fr L *regeneratus*, pp of *regenerare* to regenerate, fr *re-* + *generare* to beget – more at GENERATE] – **regeneracy** *n*, **regenerate** *n*, **regenerately** *adv*, **regenerateness** *n*

²**regenerate** /ri'jenərayt/ *vi* 1 to become regenerate or regenerated 2 *of a body, body part, or tissue* to undergo renewal, restoration, or regrowth (eg after injury) ∼ *vt* 1a to subject to spiritual or moral renewal or revival b to change radically and for the better 2a to generate or produce anew; *esp* to replace (a body part or tissue) by new growth b to produce from a derivative or modified form, esp by chemical treatment ⟨∼d *cellulose*⟩ 3 to restore to original strength or properties 4 to increase the amplification of (an electrical signal) by causing part of the power in the output circuit to act on the input circuit – **regenerable** *adj*, **regenerative** *adj*, **regeneration** *n*

**regenerator** /ri'jenəraytə/ *n* 1 one who or that which regenerates 2 a device used esp with hot-air engines or gas furnaces in which incoming air or gas is heated by contact with masses (eg of brick) previously heated by outgoing hot air or gas

**regent** /'reej(ə)nt/ *n* 1 somebody who rules or reigns; a governor 2 somebody who governs a kingdom in the minority, absence, or disability of the sovereign [ME, fr MF or ML; MF, fr ML *regent-, regens*, fr L, prp of *regere* to rule – more at RIGHT] – **regent, regental** *adj*

**reggae** /'regay/ *n* popular music of W Indian origin that is characterized by a strongly accented subsidiary beat [Jamaican E, fr *rege rege* rags]

**regicide** /'reji,sied/ *n* 1 somebody who kills a king 2 the killing of a king [deriv of L *reg-, rex* king + *-cida* & *-cidium* – more at ROYAL, -CIDE] – **regicidal** *adj*

**regime** *also* **régime** /ray'zheem/ *n* 1a REGIMEN 1 b a regular pattern of occurrence or action (eg of seasonal rainfall) 2a a form of management or government ⟨*a socialist ∼*⟩ b a government in power ⟨*predicted that the new ∼ would fall*⟩ c a period of rule ⟨*during the Stalin ∼*⟩ [Fr *régime*, fr L *regimin-, regimen*]

**regimen** /'rejimən/ *n* 1 a systematic plan (eg of diet, exercise, or medical treatment) adopted esp to achieve some end (eg improved health) 2 government, rule [ME, fr L *regimin-, regimen* rule, fr *regere* to rule]

¹**regiment** /'rejimənt/ *n* 1 *taking sing or pl vb* a permanent military unit consisting usu of a number of companies, troops, batteries, or sometimes battalions 2 *taking sing or pl vb* a large number or group 3 *archaic* (governmental) rule [ME, government, area governed, fr MF, fr LL *regimentum*, fr L *regere*] – **regimental** *adj*, **regimentally** *adv*

²**regiment** /'reji,ment/ *vt* 1 to form into or assign to a regiment 2 to subject to strict and stultifying organization or control ⟨∼ed *the whole office*⟩ – **regimentation** *n*

**regimentals** /ˌreji'mentlz/ *n pl* 1 the uniform of a regiment 2 military dress

**Regina** /ri'jienə/ *n* CROWN 5b – used, when a queen is ruling, in British lawsuits ⟨*in the action ∼ v Richardson*⟩ [L, queen, fem of *reg-, rex* king]

**region** /'reej(ə)n/ *n* 1a an administrative area, division, or district b *pl* PROVINCES 1c 2a an indefinite area of the world or universe ⟨*few unknown ∼s left on earth*⟩ b a broadly uniform geographical or ecological area ⟨*desert ∼s*⟩ 3 an indefinite area surrounding a specified body part ⟨*a pain in the ∼ of the heart*⟩ 4 an extent of a surface or in a body or 3-dimensional space ⟨*the ∼ of growth in a plant*⟩ 5 a sphere of activity or interest; a field ⟨*the abstract ∼ of higher mathematics*⟩ 6 any of the zones into which the atmosphere is divided according to height or into which the sea is divided according to depth 7 *maths* an open connected set together with none, some, or all of the points on its boundary [ME, fr MF, fr L *region-, regio*, fr *regere* to rule] – **in the region of** about, approximately

**regional** /'reejənl/ *adj* 1 (characteristic) of a region 2 affecting a particular region; localized – **regionally** *adv*

**regionalism** /'reejənl,iz(ə)m/ *n* 1a consciousness of and loyalty to a particular region b development of an administrative system based on one or more such regions 2 a characteristic feature (eg of speech) of a geographical area – **regionalist** *n or adj*, **regionalistic** *adj*

**regional·ize, -ise** /'reejənl,iez/ *vt* to divide into (administrative) regions or districts – **regionalization** *n*

**regional multiplier** *n* a MULTIPLIER used to calculate the specific regional effect of an increase in autonomous expenditure in that area

**regisseur, régisseur** /ˌrayzhi'suh (*Fr* reʒisœːr)/ *n* a director responsible for staging a theatrical work (eg a ballet) [Fr *régisseur*, fr *régir* to direct, rule, fr L *regere*]

¹**register** /'rejistə/ *n* 1 a written record containing (official) entries of items, names, transactions, etc ⟨∼ *of births, marriages, and deaths*⟩ ⟨*a hotel ∼*⟩ 2a a roster of qualified or available individuals ⟨*a civil service ∼*⟩ ⟨*the electoral ∼*⟩ b a school attendance record 3a an organ STOP (set of pipes) b (a part of) the range of a human voice or musical instrument ⟨*out of my ∼*⟩ 4 the language style and vocabulary appropriate to particular circumstances or subject matter 5a a movable plate regulating admission of air, esp to solid fuel in a fire b a grille, often with shutters, for admitting heated air or for ventilation 6 registering or being registered 7a an automatic device registering numbers, quantities, or other information – compare CASH REGISTER b a number or quantity so registered 8 a condition of correct alignment or proper relative position (eg of the plates used in colour printing) – often in *in/out of register* 9 a device (eg in a computer) for storing and working on small amounts of data [ME *registre*, fr MF, fr ML *registrum*, alter. of LL *regesta*, pl, register, fr L, neut pl of *regestus*, pp of *regerere* to bring back, fr *re-* + *gerere* to bear]

²**register** *vt* 1a to make or secure official entry of in a register ⟨∼ed *the birth of their daughter*⟩ b to enrol formally, esp as a voter or student c to record automatically; indicate ⟨*the dial ∼s speed*⟩ d to make a (mental) record of; note 2 to make or adjust (eg a printing plate) so as to correspond exactly 3 to secure special protection for (a letter, parcel, etc) by prepayment of a fee 4 to convey an impression of; express ⟨*her face ∼ed horror when she read the telegram*⟩ 5 to achieve, win ⟨∼ed *an impressive victory*⟩ ∼ *vi* 1a to enrol one's name in a register ⟨∼ed *at the hotel*⟩ b to enrol one's name officially as a voter c to enrol formally, esp as a student 2a to correspond exactly b *of printed matter* to be in correct alignment or register

| **regalvanize** *vt* | **regerminate** *vb* | **reglue** *vt* | **regrind** *vt* |
|---|---|---|---|
| **regather** *vb* | **regermination** *n* | **regrade** *vt* | **regrow** *vb* |
| **regauge** *vt* | **regild** *vt* | **regraft** *vt or n* | **regrowth** *n* |
| **regear** *vt* | **reglaze** *vt* | **regrant** *vt* | |

**3** to make or convey an impression ⟨*the name didn't* ∼⟩ –
**registrable** *adj*
³**register** *n* a registrar [prob alter. of ME *registrer*]
**registered** /'rejistəd/ *adj* qualified or approved formally or
officially
**register office** *n* REGISTRY OFFICE
**register ton** *n* a unit of internal capacity for ships equal to
100 cubic feet (about 2.83 cubic metres)
**registrar** /ˌreji'strah, '--,-/ *n* **1** an official recorder or keeper of
records ⟨*the* ∼ *of births, marriages, and deaths*⟩: e g **1a** a
senior administrative officer of a university **b** a court official
who deals with certain administrative and legal matters and
may act as a subordinate judge **2** the grade of British hospital
doctor senior to SENIOR HOUSE OFFICER that is held by a doctor
in training; *also* a doctor holding this post [alter. of ME *registrer*, fr MF *registreur*, fr *registrer* to register, fr ML *re-
gistrare*, fr *registrum* register]
**registration** /ˌreji'straysh(ə)n/ *n* **1** registering or being registered **2** an entry in a register **3a** the art or act of selecting
organ STOPS (sets of pipes) **b** the combination of organ STOPS
used in a particular performance
**registration document** *n, chiefly Br* a document kept with a
motor vehicle that gives the REGISTRATION NUMBER, make,
engine size, etc and details of the current ownership – compare
LOGBOOK 2
**registration number** *n, Br* an identifying combination of
letters and numbers assigned to a motor vehicle
**registry** /'rejistri/ *n* **1** REGISTRATION 1 **2** a place of registration;
*specif* REGISTRY OFFICE
**registry office** *n, Br* a place where births, marriages, and
deaths are recorded and civil marriages are conducted
**regius professor** /'reejəs/ *n* a holder of a professorship
founded by royal subsidy at a British university, esp Oxford or
Cambridge [NL, royal professor]
**reglet** /'reglit/ *n* **1** a flat narrow architectural moulding **2** a
strip of wood or plastic used like a strip of metal (LEAD 2c) to
separate lines of type [Fr *réglet*, fr MF *reglet* straightedge, fr
*regle*, fr L *regula* – more at RULE]
**regnal** /'regnəl/ *adj* of a reign; *specif* calculated from a monarch's accession to the throne ⟨*in his eighth* ∼ *year*⟩ [ML *reg-
nalis*, fr L *regnum* reign – more at REIGN]
**regnant** /'regnənt/ *adj* **1** exercising rule; reigning ⟨*a queen* ∼⟩
**2** of widespread occurrence; prevalent [L *regnant-, regnans*, prp
of *regnare* to reign, fr *regnum*]
**regolith** /'regəlith/ *n* MANTLEROCK (loose soil, rock fragments,
etc covering the earth's solid rock) [Gk *rhēgos* blanket + E
*-lith*]
**regrate** /ri'grayt/ *vt* to buy up (commodities) with the intention
of reselling in or near the same place at a profit; *also* to sell
(commodities bought in this way), usu at retail [ME *regraten*,
fr MF *regrater*] – **regrater** *n*
¹**regress** /'ree,gres/ *n* **1** REGRESSION 2a **2** the act of reasoning
backwards from a conclusion **3** *formal* an act of going or
coming back [ME, fr L *regressus*, fr *regressus*, pp of *regredi* to
go back, fr *re-* + *gradi* to go – more at GRADE]
²**regress** /ri'gres/ *vi* **1** to undergo or exhibit regression, decline,
or backwards movement, esp to an earlier state or condition **2**
*chiefly statistics* to tend to approach or revert to a MEAN (average) ∼ *vt* to induce, esp by hypnosis, a state of psychological
regression in – **regressor** *n*
**regression** /ri'gresh(ə)n/ *n* **1** the act or an instance of regressing; *esp* (a) retrograde movement **2a** a trend or shift towards
a lower, less perfect, or earlier state or condition **b** progressive
decline of a diseased condition **c(1)** gradual loss of specialization and function by a body part or organ, esp as a physiological change accompanying aging ⟨∼ *of the ovaries after
the menopause*⟩ **c(2)** gradual loss of memory and acquired
skills **d** *psychology* reversion to the mental or behavioural level
of a child, esp in order to escape existing problems and
anxieties **3** an evolutionary process involving increasing simplification of body structure **4** (the statistical analysis of) a
mathematical relationship between two or more correlated
variables that is often determined directly from observed data
and is used esp to predict values of one variable when given
values of the other ⟨*linear* ∼⟩ – compare MULTIPLE REGRESSION
**5** *astronomy* retrograde motion, esp of the orbits of celestial
bodies
**regressive** /ri'gresiv/ *adj* **1** tending to regress or produce regression **2** being, characterized by, showing, or developing in
the course of physiological, psychological, or evolutionary

regression **3** decreasing in rate as the base increases ⟨*a* ∼
*tax*⟩ – **regressively** *adv*, **regressiveness** *n*
¹**regret** /ri'gret/ *vt* **-tt-** **1** to mourn the loss or death of **2** to be
very sorry about ⟨∼s *his mistakes*⟩ [ME *regretten*, fr MF *re-
greter*, fr OF, fr *re-* + *-greter* (of Scand origin; akin to ON
*grāta* to weep) – more at GREET]
²**regret** *n* **1** the emotion arising from a wish that some matter
or situation could be other than it is; *esp* grief or sorrow tinged
esp with disappointment, longing, or remorse **2a** an expression
of distressing emotion (e g sorrow or disappointment) **b** *pl* a
conventional expression of disappointment, esp on declining
an invitation ⟨*couldn't come to tea, and sent her* ∼s⟩ – **regretful** *adj*, **regretfulness** *n*
**regretfully** /ri'gretfəli/ *adv* **1** in a regretful manner **2** *nonstandard* REGRETTABLY ⟨*the obvious requirement of increased
security . . . has* ∼ *created the necessity of making an appointment* – *Decanter*⟩
   *usage* The increasingly common use of **regretfully**, rather than
   **regrettably**, to mean "it is regrettable that" is widely disliked.
**regrettable** /ri'gretəbl/ *adj* other than as one would wish;
unwelcome
**regrettably** /ri'gretəbli/ *adv* **1** in a regrettable manner; to a
regrettable extent ⟨*a* ∼ *steep decline in wages*⟩ **2** it is regrettable that ⟨∼, *we had failed to consider alternatives*⟩
**regroup** /ˌree'groohp/ *vt* to form into a new grouping; *specif*
to alter the tactical formation of (military forces) ∼ *vi* **1** to
reorganize (e g after a setback) for renewed activity **2** to alter
the tactical formation of a military force
¹**regular** /'regyoolə/ *adj* **1a** belonging to a religious order ⟨*the*
∼ *clergy*⟩ – compare SECULAR **b** being an officially qualified
or approved member of a specified profession ⟨*a* ∼ *solicitor*⟩
**2a** formed, built, arranged, or ordered harmoniously, symmetrically, or according to some rule, principle, or type ⟨∼
*verse*⟩ ⟨*girl with* ∼ *features*⟩ **b(1)** *of a polygon* having sides
of equal length and angles of equal size **b(2)** *of a polyhedron*
having faces that are identical regular polygons with identical
angles between them – compare REGULAR SOLID **c** *of a flower*
having the petals, sepals, or other flower parts arranged in a
RADIALLY SYMMETRICAL manner **d** *of a crystal or crystal system*
CUBIC **2 3a** steady or uniform in course, practice, or occurrence; habitual, usual, or constant ⟨∼ *habits*⟩ ⟨*a* ∼ *visitor*⟩ **b**
recurring or functioning at fixed or uniform intervals ⟨*a* ∼
*income*⟩ **c** defecating or having menstrual periods at normal
intervals **4a** constituted, conducted, or done in conformity
with established or prescribed usages, rules, or discipline ⟨*a* ∼
*meeting of the council*⟩ **b(1)** complete, absolute ⟨*a* ∼ *fool*⟩
⟨*the office was a* ∼ *madhouse*⟩ **b(2)** *chiefly NAm* thinking or
behaving in an acceptable manner ⟨*wanted to prove he was a*
∼ *guy*⟩ **c** *of a word, esp a verb* conforming to the normal
manner of INFLECTION (change according to grammatical
function) ⟨*walk, paint, and dance are* ∼ *verbs*⟩; *specif* WEAK
**7 5** of or being (a member of) a permanent standing army ⟨*a*
∼ *soldier*⟩ [ME *reguler*, fr MF, fr LL *regularis* regular, fr L,
of a bar, fr *regula* rule – more at RULE] – **regularize** *vt*, **re-
gularization** *n*, **regularity** *n*
²**regular** *n* **1a** a member of the regular clergy **b** a soldier in a
regular army **2** one who is usu present or participating; *esp*
one who habitually visits a particular place ⟨*bought drinks for
all the* ∼s⟩
**regularly** /'regyoolǝli/ *adv* in a regular manner; *esp* habitually
   *usage* The pronunciation /'regyoolǝli/ rather than /'regyooli/ is
   recommended for BBC broadcasters.
**regular solid** *n* any of the five regular POLYHEDRONS (solid
figures with flat faces meeting at straight lines) ⟨*a cube is a*
∼⟩ – called also PLATONIC SOLID
**regular year** *n* a standard year of 354 days or a leap year of
384 days in the JEWISH CALENDAR
**regulate** /'regyoo,layt/ *vt* **1** to govern or direct according to
rule **2** to bring order, method, or uniformity to ⟨∼ *one's habits*⟩ **3a** to fix or adjust the time, amount, degree, or rate of
⟨∼ *the pressure of a tyre*⟩ **b** to fix or adjust (e g an appliance)
to ensure correct functioning [LL *regulatus*, pp of *regulare*, fr
L *regula*] – **regulator** *n*, **regulative, regulatory** *adj*
¹**regulation** /ˌregyoo'laysh(ə)n/ *n* **1** regulating or being regulated **2a** an authoritative rule dealing with details or procedure
⟨*safety* ∼s *in a factory*⟩ **b** a rule or order having the force of
law ⟨*EEC* ∼s⟩
²**regulation** *adj* conforming to regulations; official ⟨∼ *haircut*⟩
**regulator gene** /'regyoolaytə/, **regulatory gene** /'reg-

yoolət(ə)ri, ‚regyoo'laytəri/ *n* a gene carrying information that codes for a substance that controls (eg by repressing) the function of other genes – compare STRUCTURAL GENE

**regulo** /'regyooloh/ *n, chiefly Br* the temperature in a gas oven expressed as a specified number ⟨*meat cooked on* ∼ *4*⟩ [fr *Regulo*, a trademark for a thermastatic device]

**regulus** /'regyooləs/ *n, pl* **reguluses, reguli** /-li/ the impure metal formed beneath the slag in smelting ores [ML, metallic antimony, fr L, petty king, fr *reg-, rex* king – more at ROYAL]

**regurgitate** /ri'guhji‚tayt/ *vi* to become thrown or poured back ∼ *vt* 1 to vomit or pour back or out (as if) from a cavity ⟨∼ *food*⟩ 2 to reproduce in speech or writing with little or no alteration ⟨∼d *everything the teacher said*⟩ [ML *regurgitatus*, pp of *regurgitare*, fr L *re-* + LL *gurgitare* to engulf, fr L *gurgit-, gurges* whirlpool – more at VORACIOUS] – **regurgitative** *adj*

**regurgitation** /ri‚guhji'taysh(ə)n/ *n* an act of regurgitating: eg **a** the bringing up into the mouth of incompletely digested food by some birds and animals in feeding their young **b** the backward flow of blood through a defective heart valve

**rehabilitate** /‚ree(h)ə'bilitayt/ *vt* **1a** to restore to a former capacity; reinstate **b** to restore to good repute; reestablish the good name of **2a** to restore to a former state (eg of efficiency, sound condition, or solvency) ⟨∼ *slum areas*⟩ **b** to restore to a condition of health or useful and constructive activity (eg after illness or imprisonment) [ML *rehabilitatus*, pp of *rehabilitare*, fr L *re-* + LL *habilitare* to habilitate] – **rehabilitator** *n*, **rehabilitative** *adj*, **rehabilitation** *n*

**¹rehash** /‚ree'hash/ *vt* to present or use again in another form without substantial change or improvement

**²rehash** /'ree‚hash, ‚-'-/ *n* something presented in a new form without change of substance ⟨*a book that was just a* ∼ *of stale ideas*⟩

**rehear** /‚ree'hiə/ *vt* **reheard** /-'huhd/ to hear (a trial or lawsuit) over again – **rehearing** *n*

**rehearsal** /ri'huhsl/ *n* **1** a practice exercise; a trial **2** a practice session, esp of a play, concert, etc preparatory to a public appearance – **in rehearsal** being practised prior to performance in public

**rehearse** /ri'huhs/ *vt* **1** to present an account of; narrate, relate ⟨∼ *a familiar story*⟩ **2** to recount in order; enumerate ⟨*had* ∼d *their grievances in a letter to the governor*⟩ **3a** to hold a rehearsal of; practise **b** to train or make proficient by rehearsal ⟨∼d *each participant several times*⟩ **4** to perform or practice as if in a rehearsal ∼ *vi* to engage in a rehearsal of a play, concert, etc [ME *rehersen*, fr MF *rehercier*, lit., to harrow again, fr *re-* + *hercier* to harrow, fr *herce* harrow – more at HEARSE] – **rehearser** *n*

**¹reheat** *vt* to heat (eg cooked food) again

**²reheat** /‚ree'heet/, **reheating** *n* the injection of fuel into the tailpipe of a TURBOJET ENGINE to obtain extra thrust by combustion with uncombined air in the exhaust gases

**rehoboam** /‚ree-ə'boh-əm/ *n* a wine bottle, esp for champagne, that contains six times the amount of a standard bottle (about 4.8 litres or 8½ pints) – compare JEROBOAM [*Rehoboam* fl *ab* 925 BC king of Judah]

**rehouse** /‚ree'howz, -'hows/ *vt* to house again or anew; *esp* to

establish in a new or different housing unit of a better quality

**rehydrate** /‚ree'hiedrayt, '---/ *vt* to restore fluid lost in dehydration to – **rehydratable** *adj*, **rehydration** *n*

**Reich** /riekh/ *n* the German empire ⟨*the third* ∼⟩ [Ger, empire, kingdom, fr OHG *rīhhi* – more at RICH]

**reichsmark** /'riekhs‚mahk/ *n, pl* **reichsmarks** *also* **reichsmark** the German mark from 1925 to 1948 [Ger, fr *reichs* (gen of *reich* empire, kingdom) + *mark*]

**reify** /'ree‑ifie/ *vt* to regard (something abstract) as a material thing [L *res* thing + E *-ify*] – **reification** *n*, **reificatory** *adj*

**¹reign** /rayn/ *n* **1a** royal authority; sovereignty ⟨*under the* ∼ *of the Stuart kings*⟩ **b** the dominion, sway, or influence of one resembling or likened to a monarch ⟨*the* ∼ *of the military dictators*⟩ **2** the time during which somebody (eg a monarch) or something reigns [ME *regne*, fr OF, fr L *regnum*, fr *reg-, rex* king – more at ROYAL]

**²reign** *vi* **1a** to possess or exercise sovereign power; RULE **1a b** to hold office as head of state although possessing little governing power ⟨*the queen* ∼s *but does not rule*⟩ **2** to exercise authority in the manner of a monarch **3** to be predominant or prevalent ⟨*chaos* ∼ed *in the classroom*⟩

**reign of terror** *n* a period that is marked by ruthless violence committed by those in power against their suspected enemies and that produces widespread terror [*Reign of Terror*, a period (1793-4) of the French Revolution marked by mass executions of political suspects]

**reimburse** /‚ree·im'buhs/ *vt* **1** to pay back to somebody; repay ⟨∼ *travel expenses*⟩ **2** to make restoration or repayment to ⟨∼ *an interviewee for her travelling expenses*⟩ [*re-* + obs *imburse* to put in the pocket, pay, fr MF *embourser*, fr OF *emen-* + *borser* to get money – more at DISBURSE] – **reimbursable** *adj*, **reimbursement** *n*

**reimpression** /‚ree·im'presh(ə)n/ *n* REPRINT a (further printing of a book)

**¹rein** /rayn/ *n*, **reins** *pl* **1a** a long line fastened usu to both sides of the bit of a bridle by which a rider or driver controls an animal **b** a similar device used to restrain children and attached to a harness on the body **2a** a restraining influence; check ⟨*regulations impose* ∼s *on personal freedom*⟩ **b** controlling or guiding power ⟨*the* ∼s *of government*⟩ [ME *reine*, fr MF *rene*, fr (assumed) VL *retina*, fr L *retinēre* to restrain – more at RETAIN] – **draw rein** to stop a horse one is riding; PULL UP – **give (free) rein to** to allow to proceed or function freely ⟨*gave rein to his imagination*⟩

**²rein** *vt* to check or stop (as if) by pulling on reins – often + *in* or *back* ⟨∼ed *in his horse*⟩ ⟨*couldn't* ∼ *his impatience*⟩

**'rein-‚back** *n* a backwards walk by a horse with the legs moving in diagonal pairs

**reincarnate** /‚ree'inkahnayt, ‚--'--/ *vt* **1** to incarnate again; give a new form or fresh embodiment to **2** to cause (a person or his/her soul) to be reborn in another (human) body after death – usu pass; compare TRANSMIGRATE – **reincarnate** *adj*, **reincarnation** *n*, **reincarnationist** *n*

**reindeer** /'rayn‚diə/ *n* any of several deer (genus *Rangifer*) that inhabit northern Europe, Asia, and N America, have large branching antlers in both the male and female, and are often domesticated, esp in Lapland [ME *reindere*, fr ON *hreinn* rein-

| | | | |
|---|---|---|---|
| **rehandle** *vt* | **reimposition** *n* | **reinform** *vt* | **reinstitutionalization** *n* |
| **rehang** *vt* | **reimprison** *vt* | **reinfuse** *vt* | **reinstitutionalize** *vt* |
| **reharden** *vb* | **reinclude** *vt* | **reinfusion** *n* | **reinstruct** *vt* |
| **reharness** *vt* | **reinclusion** *n* | **reinhabit** *vt* | **reinstruction** *n* |
| **reheel** *vt* | **reincorporate** *vt* | **reinject** *vt* | **reinter** *vt* |
| **rehem** *vt* | **reincorporation** *n* | **reinjection** *n* | **reinterment** *n* |
| **rehinge** *vt* | **reincur** *vt* | **reinjure** *vt* | **reinterrogate** *vt* |
| **rehire** *vt* | **reindex** *vt* | **reinjury** *n* | **reinterrogation** *n* |
| **rehospitalize** *vt* | **reindict** *vt* | **reink** *vt* | **reinterview** *vt* |
| **rehumanize** *vt* | **reindictment** *n* | **reinnervate** *vt* | **reintroduce** *vt* |
| **rehypnotize** *vt* | **reinduce** *vt* | **reinnervation** *n* | **reintroduction** *n* |
| **reidentification** *n* | **reinduction** *n* | **reinoculate** *vt* | **reinvade** *vt* |
| **reidentity** *vt* | **reindustrialize** *vt* | **reinoculation** *n* | **reinvasion** *n* |
| **reignite** *vt* | **reindustrialization** *n* | **reinsert** *vt* | **reinvestigate** *vb* |
| **reimmerse** *vt* | **reinfect** *vt* | **reinsertion** *n* | **reinvestigation** *n* |
| **reimmersion** *n* | **reinfection** *n* | **reinspect** *vt* | **reinvite** *vt* |
| **reimplant** *vt* | **reinfest** *vt* | **reinspection** *n* | **reinvoke** *vt* |
| **reimplantation** *n* | **reinfestation** *n* | **reinstall** *vt* | **reinvolve** *vt* |
| **reimport** *vt* | **reinfiltrate** *vb* | **reinstallation** *n* | **reinvolvement** *n* |
| **reimportation** *n* | **reinfiltration** *n* | **reinstitute** *vt* | |
| **reimpose** *vb* | **reinflame** *vt* | **reinstitution** *n* | |

deer + ME *deer*]

**reindeer lichen** *n* REINDEER MOSS

**reindeer moss** *n* a grey lichen (*Cladonia rangiferina*) that grows in upright tufts, forms extensive patches in arctic and north-temperate regions, constitutes a large part of the food of reindeer, and is sometimes eaten by human beings

**reinforce** /ˌree·inˈfaws/ *vt* **1** to strengthen by additional assistance, material, or support; make stronger or more pronounced ⟨~ *the elbows of a jacket*⟩ ⟨*claimed that the media* ~ d *violent impulses*⟩ **2** to strengthen or increase by fresh additions ⟨~ *the regular troops*⟩ ⟨*were reinforcing their scrum*⟩ **3** to stimulate (an experimental subject) with a reward or other reinforcer following a correct or desired response or performance; *also* to encourage (a response) with a reinforcer [*re-* + *inforce,* alter. of *enforce*] – **reinforceable** *adj*

**reinforced concrete** /ˌree·inˈfawst, '--,-/ *n* concrete in which metal (eg steel) is embedded for strengthening

**reinforcement** /ˌree·inˈfawsmənt/ *n* **1** reinforcing or being reinforced **2** something that reinforces; *esp, pl* additional troops

**reinforcer** /ˌree·inˈfawsə/ *n* one who or that which reinforces; *specif* a stimulus (eg a reward or the removal of discomfort) that follows a desired response and is used in conditioning to encourage the establishment of the response

**reins** /raynz/ *n pl, archaic* (the region of) the kidneys [ME, fr MF & L; MF, fr L *renes*]

**reinsman** /ˈraynzmən/ *n, NAm, Austr, & NZ* a jockey; *also* a HARNESS RACING driver

**reinstate** /ˌree·inˈstayt/ *vt* to place again (eg in possession or in a former position); restore to a previous state ⟨*demanded that she* ~ *her employees*⟩ – **reinstatement** *n*

**reinsurance** /ˌree·inˈshooərəns, -ˈshaw-/ *n* insurance by another insurer of all or a part of a risk previously assumed by an insurance company

**reinsure** /ˌree·inˈshooə, -ˈshaw-/ *vb* to insure (a risk or person) by reinsurance – **reinsurer** *n*

**reintegrate** /reeˈintigrayt/ *vt* to integrate again into an entity; restore to unity [ML *reintegratus,* pp of *reintegrare* to renew, reinstate, fr L *re-* + *integrare* to integrate] – **reintegration** *n,* **reintegrative** *adj*

**reinterpret** /ˌree·inˈtuhprit/ *vt* to interpret again; *specif* to give a new or different interpretation to – **reinterpretation** *n*

**reinvent** /ˌree·inˈvent/ *vt* **1** to make (something already invented) as if for the first time ⟨*realized they were* ~ing *a machine that had been designed a century before*⟩ **2** to remake or redo completely – **reinvention** *n*

**reinvest** /ˌree·inˈvest/ *vt* **1** to invest again or anew ⟨~ed *the clichés with meaning*⟩ **2** to invest (eg earnings or investment income) rather than take or distribute as dividends or profits ~ *vi* to make a second investment – **reinvestment** *n*

**reinvigorate** /ˌree·inˈvigərayt/ *vt* to give renewed or fresh vigour to ⟨*a long walk* ~s *the mind*⟩ – **reinvigorator** *n,* **reinvigoration** *n*

**reissue** /ˌree·ish(y)ooh, -ˈisyooh/ *vt* to issue again; *esp* to cause to become available again – **reissue** *n*

**reiterate** /ˌree·itərayt/ *vt* to say or do over again or repeatedly, sometimes with wearying effect [L *reiteratus,* pp of *reiterare* to repeat, fr *re-* + *iterare* to iterate] – **reiterate** *n,* **reiterative** *adj,* **reiteratively** *adv,* **reiterativeness** *n,* **reiteration** *n*
    *usage* **Reiterate** and **iterate** (a rarer word) both mean **repeat,** but suggest continual wearisome repetition. None of these words should properly be followed by **again.**

**Reiter's syndrome** /ˈrietəz/ *n* a medical disorder of uncertain cause that is characterized esp by arthritis, and soreness and inflammation of the membranes lining the eye socket and the URETHRA (canal carrying urine from the bladder) [Hans *Reiter* †1969 Ger physician]

¹**reject** /riˈjekt/ *vt* **1a** to refuse to accept, consider, submit to, take for some purpose, or use ⟨*thought about her suggestion and then* ~ed *it*⟩ ⟨~ *a manuscript*⟩ ⟨~ed *the mouldy grain as unfit for use*⟩ **b** to refuse to accept or admit; rebuff ⟨*parents who* ~ *their children*⟩ ⟨*the underprivileged feel* ~ed *by society*⟩ **2** to eject (eg from the mouth or stomach); *esp* VOMIT 1 **3** to fail to accept (eg a skin graft or transplanted organ) as part of the organism because of immunological differences *antonyms* select, accept, choose [ME *rejecten,* fr L *rejectus,* pp of *reicere,* lit., to throw back, fr *re-* + *jacere* to throw – more at JET] – **rejecter, rejector** *n,* **rejection** *n,* **rejective** *adj*

²**reject** /ˈreejekt/ *n* a rejected person or thing; *esp* a substandard article of merchandise

**rejection slip** *n* a printed slip enclosed with a rejected manu-

script returned by a publisher to an author

**rejig** /ˌreeˈjig/ *vt* **-gg-** to rearrange or reequip (eg a factory) so as to perform different work; *broadly* to adjust, reorganize ⟨*recommended* ~ging *the timetable* – *TES*⟩

**rejoice** /riˈjoys/ *vt* to give joy to; gladden ~ *vi* to feel or express joy or great delight [ME *rejoicen,* fr MF *rejoiss-,* stem of *rejoir,* fr *re-* + *joir* to rejoice, fr L *gaudēre* – more at JOY] – **rejoicer** *n,* **rejoicingly** *adv*
    **rejoice in** *vt* to have, possess – usu used ironically ⟨*rejoices in the name of Higginbottom*⟩

**rejoin** /riˈjoyn/ *vi* to answer to a legal charge ~ *vt* **1** to join again ⟨~ed *his battalion*⟩ **2** to say often sharply or critically in response *synonyms* see ²ANSWER [ME *rejoinen* to answer to a legal charge, fr MF *rejoin-,* stem of *rejoindre,* fr *re-* + *joindre* to join – more at JOIN]

**rejoinder** /riˈjoyndə/ *n* **1** the answer made by the defendant in the second round of allegations and counter-allegations (PLEADING) in a legal action to the plaintiff's first reply **2** (an esp sharp or critical answer to) a reply [ME *rejoiner,* fr MF *rejoindre* to rejoin]

**rejuvenate** /ˌree·joohvəˌnayt, ri-/ *vt* **1a** to make young or youthful again; reinvigorate **b** to restore to an original or new state ⟨~ *old cars*⟩ **2a** to cause (a stream or river) to increase erosive activity, esp as a result of an increase in the height of the surrounding land **b** to cause (land) to develop features, esp greater relief, characteristic of an earlier stage in a cycle of erosion ~ *vi* to cause or undergo rejuvenation [*re-* + L *juvenis* young – more at YOUNG] – **rejuvenator** *n,* **rejuvenation** *n*

**rejuvenescence** /riˌjoohvəˈnes(ə)ns/ *n* a renewal of youthfulness or vigour; rejuvenation [ML *rejuvenescere* to become young again, fr L *re-* + *juvenescere* to become young, fr *juvenis*] – **rejuvenescent** *adj*

**rekindle** /riˈkindl/ *vt* to kindle again ~ *vi* to ignite anew ⟨*in case the fire* ~s⟩ – **rekindler** *n*

¹**relapse** /riˈlaps, 'reeˌlaps/ *n* the act or an instance of relapsing or backsliding; *esp* a recurrence of symptoms of a disease after a period of improvement [L *relapsus,* pp of *relabi* to slide back, fr *re-* + *labi* to slide – more at SLEEP]

²**relapse** /riˈlaps/ *vi* **1** to slip or fall back into a former worse state **2** to sink, subside ⟨~ *into deep thought*⟩

**relapsing fever** /riˈlapsing/ *n* a short-lasting epidemic disease that is marked by recurring high fever lasting five to seven days and is caused by a SPIROCHAETE (bacterium with a spirally twisted shape) (genus *Borrelia*) transmitted by the bites of lice and ticks

**relate** /riˈlayt/ *vt* **1** to give an account of; tell **2** to show or establish logical or causal connection between ⟨~ *poverty and crime*⟩ ~ *vi* **1** to have relationship or connection ⟨*can't see how the two things* ~⟩ **2** to have or establish a relationship ⟨*the way a child* ~s *to a psychiatrist*⟩ **3** to respond, esp favourably ⟨*can't* ~ *to that kind of music*⟩ □ (*vi*) usu + *to synonyms* see ¹JOIN [L *relatus* (pp of *referre* to carry back), fr *re-* + *latus,* pp of *ferre* to carry – more at TOLERATE, BEAR] – **relatable** *adj,* **relater** *n*

**related** /riˈlaytid/ *adj* **1** connected by reason of an established or discoverable relation **2** connected by common ancestry or sometimes by marriage **3** of musical notes, chords, and tonalities having close harmonic connection – **relatedly** *adv,* **relatedness** *n*

**relation** /riˈlaysh(ə)n/ *n* **1** the act of telling or recounting **2** an aspect or quality (eg resemblance) that connects two or more things or parts as being, belonging, or working together or as being of the same kind; *specif* a property (eg one expressed by *is equal to, is less than,* or *is the brother of*) that holds between an ORDERED pair of objects **3a(1)** a person connected by blood, marriage, or adoption; RELATIVE 3a **a(2)** a person legally entitled to a share of the property of a person who has died without making a valid will **b** relationship by blood, marriage, or adoption; kinship **4** reference, respect, or connection ⟨*size bears little* ~ *to ability*⟩ – often in *in/with relation to* **5** **relations** *pl,* **relation** the attitude or stance which two or more people or groups assume towards one another; interaction ⟨*race* ~s⟩ **6** *pl* **6a** dealings, affairs ⟨*foreign* ~s⟩ **b** communication, contact ⟨*broke off all* ~s *with his family*⟩ **c** *euph* SEXUAL INTERCOURSE *synonyms* see ¹RELATIVE – **relational** *adj,* **relationally** *adv*

**relationship** /riˈlaysh(ə)nship/ *n* **1** the state or character of being related or interrelated; connection ⟨*show the* ~ *between two things*⟩ **2** (a specific instance or type of) kinship **3** a state of affairs existing between those having relations or dealings *(had a good ~ with his family)* **synonyms** see ¹RELATIVE

¹**relative** /'relətiv/ *n* **1** a word referring grammatically to a preceding word, phrase, sentence, etc (ANTECEDENT) **2** something having or a term expressing a relation to, connection with, or necessary dependence on another thing **3a** a person connected with another by blood, marriage, or adoption **b** an animal or plant related to another by common descent

**synonyms** A person connected to another by ancestry, marriage, or adoption is a **relative** or **relation** *(spend Christmas with my relatives)*. The fact or degree or way of being so connected is a **relationship** *(there's no relationship between Peter Jones and Jack Jones)*. **Relationship** is extended to other kinds of human connection *(ours is a purely platonic relationship)*, but more abstract connections may be better called a **relation** *(the close relation between Blake's painting and his poetry)*. Actual dealings or contact are **relations** *(the relations between landlord and tenant)*.

²**relative** *adj* **1** *also* **relatival** introducing a subordinate clause qualifying a preceding word, phrase, sentence, etc (ANTECEDENT) that has been either expressed or implied *(the ~ pronoun who in "the man who told me")*; *also* introduced by such a connective *(a ~ clause)* **2** relevant, pertinent to *(matters ~ to world peace)* **3a** not absolute or independent; comparative *(the ~ isolation of life in the country)* **b** existing in, expressing, or having connection with or reference to something else *(~ density)* *(supply is ~ to demand)* **4** of major and minor musical keys and scales having the same KEY SIGNATURE **5** *maths & statistics* expressed as the ratio of the specified quantity (eg an error in measuring) to the total magnitude (eg the value of a measured quantity) or to the mean of all the quantities involved *(~ error)* *(~ frequency)* – **relativeness** *n* – **relative to** in relation to; WITH REGARD TO

**relative density** *n* the ratio of the density of a substance to the density of another substance (eg pure water or hydrogen) taken as a standard, when both densities are measured under the same conditions

**relative humidity** *n* the amount of WATER VAPOUR actually present in the air expressed as a percentage of the amount present when the air is saturated with water vapour at the same temperature

**relatively** /'relətivli/ *adv* **1** in a relative manner **2** comparatively, somewhat *(a ~ good piece of work)* **usage** see ¹COMPARATIVE

**relatively prime** *adj, maths* having no common factor except the number one (1) *(12 and 25 are ~)*

**relativism** /'reləti,viz(ə)m/ *n, philosophy* a theory that knowledge and moral principles are relative and have no objective standard – **relativist** *n*

**relativistic** /,reləti'vistik/ *adj* **1** of or characterized by relativity or relativism **2** *physics* moving at or being a velocity that causes a significant change in properties (eg mass) in accordance with the theory of relativity *(a ~ electron)* – **relativistically** *adv*

**relativity** /,relə'tivəti/ *n* **1** the quality or state of being relative **2** the state of being dependent for existence on or determined in nature, value, or quality by relation to something else **3a** *also* **special theory of relativity** a theory which is based on the two postulates (1) that the speed of light in a vacuum is constant and independent of the source or observer and (2) that the laws of physics, as expressed mathematically, are the same in all systems, leading to the assertion that mass and energy are equivalent and that mass, dimension, and time will change with increased velocity **b** *also* **general theory of relativity** an extension of this theory to include gravitation and related acceleration phenomena

**relator** /ri'laytə/ *n* **1** one who relates; a narrator **2** *law* a private person without LOCUS STANDI (right to appear before a tribunal) at whose suggestion or information an action is commenced by the ATTORNEY GENERAL

**relax** /ri'laks/ *vt* **1** to make less tense or rigid; slacken *(~ed her muscles)* **2** to make less severe or stringent *(~ immigration laws)* **3** to lessen the intensity, zeal, or energy of *(~ed his concentration)* **4** to relieve from nervous tension ~ *vi* **1** to become lax, weak, or loose; rest **2** to become less intense or severe **3** *of a muscle or muscle fibre* to stop contracting **4** to cast off inhibition, nervous tension, or anxiety *(couldn't ~ in crowds)* **5** to seek rest or recreation [ME *relaxen* to make less compact, fr L *relaxare*, fr *re-* + *laxare* to loosen, fr *laxus* loose – more at SLACK] – **relaxer** *n*

**relaxant** /ri'laks(ə)nt/ *n* a substance, esp a drug, that produces relaxation; *specif* one that relieves muscular tension – **relaxant** *adj*

**relaxation** /,reelak'saysh(ə)n, ,relaks-/ *n* **1** relaxing or being relaxed **2** a relaxing state, activity, or pastime; a diversion *(one of my favourite ~s is fishing)* **3** the lengthening that characterizes muscle fibres or muscles that are completely relaxed **4** the attainment by a chemical, physical, etc system of an equilibrium state following the abrupt removal of some influence (eg light, high temperature, or stress)

**relaxed** /ri'lakst/ *adj* **1** freed from or lacking in precision or stringency **2** set or being at rest or at ease **3** easy of manner; informal **antonyms** strict, formal – **relaxedly** *adv*, **relaxedness** *n*

**relaxin** /ri'laksin/ *n* a hormone of the CORPUS LUTEUM (hormone-producing mass of tissue present in the ovary during pregnancy) that makes birth easier by causing relaxation of the ligaments of the pelvis

¹**relay** /'ree,lay/ *n* **1a** a fresh supply (eg of horses) placed in readiness to relieve other so that a traveller may proceed without delay **b** a number of people who relieve others in some work *(worked in ~s round the clock)* **2** a race between teams in which each team member successively covers a specified portion of the course **3** an electrical device for remote or automatic control that is operated by variation in the current, voltage, etc of an electric circuit and that operates in turn other devices (eg switches) in the same or a different circuit **4** SERVOMOTOR (mechanism that converts a small force into a larger force) **5** a combination of a radio receiver and a transmitter that is used to receive broadcast radio and television signals and retransmit them **6** the act of passing something (eg a message or ball) along in stages; *also* such a stage **7** something, esp a message, that is relayed

²**relay** /'ree,lay, ri'lay/ *vt* **relayed** **1** to arrange in or provide with relays **2** to pass along by relays *(news was ~ed to distant points)* **3** to control or operate by a relay **4a** to retransmit (a radio or television signal) by means of a relay **b(1)** to broadcast (a radio or television transmission), esp from a specified place *(this programme is being ~ed by satellite from the USA)* **b(2)** to send (a signal) by electronic means [ME *relayen*, fr MF *relaier*, fr OF, fr *re-* + *laier* to leave – more at DELAY]

³**relay** *vt* **relaid** /-'layd/ to lay again *(~ track)*

¹**release** /ri'lees/ *vt* **1a** to set free from restraint, confinement, or servitude **b** *of a cell, tissue, etc* to allow (eg a hormone) to pass from the place of origin or storage into the bloodstream, digestive tract, etc **2** to relieve from something that confines, burdens, or oppresses *(was ~d from her promise)* **3** to give up in favour of another; relinquish *(~ a claim to property)* **4** to give permission for publication, performance, exhibition, or sale of; *also* to publish, issue *(the commission ~d its findings)* **5** to operate or move (eg a handle or catch) in order to allow a mechanism free movement *(~d the safety catch)* *(~d the hand brake)* **antonyms** detain (eg a prisoner), check (eg thoughts or feelings) [ME *relesen*, fr OF *relessier*, fr L *relaxare* to relax] – **releaseable** *adj*, **releasably** *adv*, **releasability** *n*

²**release** *n* **1** relief or deliverance from sorrow, suffering, or trouble **2a** discharge from obligation or responsibility **b** (a document effecting) relinquishment or conveyance of a legal right or claim **3** the act or an instance of freeing or being freed *(an early ~ from jail)* **4** a device (eg a handle) adapted to release a mechanism as required **5a** (the act of permitting) performance, publication, or issue *(the record became a best seller immediately on ~)* **b** matter (eg information) released; *esp* a statement prepared for the press **c** a newly issued film, gramophone record, etc

| | | | |
|---|---|---|---|
| **rejudge** *vt* | **relacquer** *vt* | **relicense** *vt* | **reloan** *vt or n* |
| **rejuggle** *vt* | **relandscape** *vt* | **relight** *vb* | **relock** *vb* |
| **rejustify** *vt* | **relaunch** *vt or n* | **relink** *vb* | **relubricate** *vt* |
| **rekey** *vt* | **relearn** *vb* | **reliquefy** *vb* | **relubrication** *n* |
| **rekeyboard** *vt* | **relend** *vt* | **relist** *vt* | |
| **reknit** *vb* | **relet** *vt* | **reload** *vt* | |
| **relabel** *vt* | **reletter** *vt* | **reloader** *n* | |

,re-'lease *vt* to lease again

**releaser** /ri'leesə/ *n* one who or that which releases; *specif* a usu naturally occurring stimulus, esp in organisms more primitive than humans, that serves as the initiator of a specific behavioural response (eg the migration of birds in response to changing day length)

**relegate** /'relə,gayt/ *vt* 1 to assign or move to an inferior or insignificant place or status ⟨~d *his old clothes to the scrap heap*⟩ ⟨~d *him to the furthest recesses of her mind*⟩; *specif* to demote to a lower division of a sporting competition (eg a football league) – compare PROMOTE 2 *formal* 2a to assign to an appropriate place or situation on the basis of classification or appraisal **b** to submit or refer to somebody or something for appropriate action △ regulate [L *relegatus*, pp of *relegare*, fr *re-* + *legare* to send with a commission – more at LEGATE] – **relegation** *n*

**relent** /ri'lent/ *vi* 1 to become less severe, harsh, or strict, usu from reasons of humanity 2 to slacken; LET UP *synonyms* see [1]YIELD [ME *relenten* to melt, dissolve, fr (assumed) ML *relentare* to soften, fr L *re-* + *lentare* to bend, fr *lentus* flexible, slow]

**relentless** /ri'lentlis/ *adj* persistent, unrelenting – **relentlessly** *adv*, **relentlessness** *n*

**relevant** /'reliv(ə)nt/ *adj* 1 having significant and demonstrable bearing on the matter at hand 2 applicable to the practicalities of everyday living and esp work ⟨*are traditional university courses any longer* ~?⟩ [ML *relevant-*, *relevans*, fr L, prp of *relevare* to raise up – more at RELIEVE] – **relevance, relevancy** *n*, **relevantly** *adv*

synonyms **Relevant, pertinent, germane, apposite, applicable, apt, material,** and **apropos** all mean "relating to the matter in hand". **Relevant** and **pertinent** imply a logical connection with the matter, **pertinent** particularly applying to what may help in solving a problem ⟨*gave some* **pertinent** *advice*⟩. **Germane** adds the idea of being so close to the subject as to be inherent in it ⟨*explaining some point of Hibernian scholarship* **germane** *to her minstrelsy* – Michael Innes⟩. **Apposite, applicable,** and **apt** apply to what is both relevant and appropriate; **apposite** often suggesting felicitousness ⟨**apposite** *quotations from the classics*⟩, **applicable** suggesting that something can usefully be brought to bear ⟨*rule is scarcely* **applicable** *to your circumstances*⟩, and **apt** emphasizing the use of clever contrivance to meet the occasion ⟨*words were* **apt** *and well chosen* – Osbert Sitwell⟩. What is **material** is not only relevant but actually needed to complete a task ⟨**material** *evidence*⟩. What is **apropos** is not only relevant but timely ⟨*his arrival at this moment was particularly* **apropos**⟩. *antonyms* irrelevant, extraneous

**reliable** /ri'lie-əbl/ *adj* suitable or fit to be relied on; dependable – **reliableness** *n*, **reliably** *adv*, **reliability** *n*

**reliance** /ri'lie-əns/ *n* 1 the act of relying; the condition or attitude of one who relies; dependence ⟨~ *on military power to achieve political ends*⟩ 2 something or somebody relied on – **reliant** *adj*, **reliantly** *adv*

**relic** /'relik/ *n* 1 a part of the body of, or some object associated with, a saint or martyr that is preserved as an object of reverence 2 something left behind after decay, disintegration, or disappearance ⟨~s *of ancient cities*⟩ 3 something surviving from the past; *esp* an outmoded custom, belief, or practice 4 *informal* an old or decrepit person 5 *pl*, *archaic* the remains of a dead body; a corpse [ME *relik*, fr OF *relique*, fr ML *reliquia*, fr LL *reliquiae*, pl, remains of a martyr, fr L, remains, fr *relinquere* to leave behind – more at RELINQUISH]

**relict** /'relikt/ *n* 1 a group of plants or animals, or a particular organism, that is a surviving remnant of an otherwise extinct form ⟨~ *species*⟩ 2 a geological or geographical feature (eg a rock, mountain, or glacier) remaining after other associated parts have disappeared or substantially altered 3 *archaic* a widow △ relic [*relict*, adj (residual), fr L *relictus*, pp of *relinquere* to leave behind; (3) LL *relicta*, fr L, fem of *relictus*, pp]

**relief** /ri'leef/ *n* 1 a payment made by a feudal tenant to his lord on succeeding to an inherited estate 2a(1) removal or lightening of something oppressive, painful, or distressing ⟨*sought* ~ *from asthma by moving to the coast*⟩ a(2) a feeling of happiness or comfort brought about by the removal of such a burden ⟨~ *swept through me*⟩ **b** aid in the form of money or necessities, esp for the poor ⟨*a* ~ *fund*⟩ **c(1)** military assistance to an endangered or surrounded post or force **c(2)** liberation of a besieged city, castle, etc ⟨*the* ~ *of Mafeking*⟩ **d** a means of breaking or avoiding monotony or boredom; a

diversion ⟨*read Beano for light* ~⟩ 3 release from a post or from the performance of a duty ⟨~ *of a sentry*⟩ 4 one who takes over the post or duty of another ⟨*a* ~ *driver*⟩ 5 legal remedy or redress 6a a method of sculpture in which forms and figures stand out from a surrounding flat surface – compare BAS-RELIEF, HIGH RELIEF **b** a piece of sculpture done in relief **c** projecting detail, ornament, or figures in sculpture 7 sharpness of outline due to contrast ⟨*a roof in bold* ~ *against the sky*⟩ 8 the differences in height of a land surface; *also* the representation of this on a map [ME, fr MF, fr OF, fr *relever* to raise, relieve]

**relief map** *n* a map showing the form and height of the land surface **a** graphically by using shading, HACHURES (lines of shading to indicate differences in slope), contours, etc **b** by means of a three-dimensional model constructed typically to scale

**relief printing** *n* LETTERPRESS 1a (printing from raised letters)

**relieve** /ri'leev/ *vt* 1a to free from a burden; give aid or help to **b** to set free from an obligation, condition, or restriction – often + *of* 2 to bring about the removal or alleviation of; mitigate ⟨*attempts to* ~ *poverty in the Third World*⟩ 3a to release from a post, station, or duty – often + *of* **b** to take the place of ⟨*sent him to* ~ *the sentry*⟩ 4 to remove or lessen the monotony of ⟨*his red robes* ~d *the drabness of the scene*⟩ 5 to raise (eg figures or letters) in relief 6 to give relief to (oneself) by urinating or defecating 7 *informal* to deprive *of*; rob ⟨*pickpockets swiftly* ~d *him of his wallet*⟩ ~ *vi* 1 to bring or give relief 2 to release one from a legal obligation or restriction [ME *releven*, fr MF *relever* to raise, relieve, fr L *relevare*, fr *re-+ levare* to raise – more at LEVER] – **relievable** *adj*, **reliever** *n*

synonyms **Relieve, alleviate, lighten, mitigate, assuage, allay, soothe,** and **comfort** all mean "lessen a burden". **Relieve** suggests positive action leading to a lasting cure; in contrast to **alleviate**, which is merely temporary and does not remove the cause. **Lighten** implies a refreshing abatement of oppression ⟨*lighten my task by employing an extra clerk*⟩. To **mitigate** is to reduce the intensity of something bad ⟨**mitigate** *the barbarity of the law*⟩. **Assuage** suggests that a burden is offset with something pleasant ⟨*cool breezes that* **assuage** *the torment of heat*⟩. **Allay** suggests a pacifying or laying at rest ⟨**allay** *their fears*⟩. **Soothe** adds the idea of a reassuring gentleness ⟨**soothe** *a screaming baby*⟩ and **comfort** is even more personal, implying kind sympathy and consolation. *antonym* intensify

**relieved** /ri'leevd/ *adj* experiencing or showing relief, esp from anxiety or pent-up emotions – **relievedly** *adv*

**religio-** *comb form* religion ⟨religio*centric*⟩; religion and ⟨religio*philosophical*⟩

**religion** /ri'lij(ə)n/ *n* 1a(1) the (organized) service and worship of a god, gods, or the supernatural a(2) personal commitment or devotion to religious faith or observance **b** the state of being a member of a religious order under monastic vows ⟨*a nun in her twentieth year of* ~⟩ 2 an institutionalized system or personal set of religious attitudes, beliefs, and practices ⟨*the Christian* ~⟩ 3 a cause, principle, or interest upheld or followed with great seriousness and zeal ⟨*sport is his* ~⟩ [ME *religioun*, fr L *religion-*, *religio* reverence, religion, prob fr *religare* to tie back – more at RELY ON]

**religionist** /ri'lijənist/ *n* a person adhering (zealously) to a religion – **religionism** *n*

**religiose** /ri'liji,ohs/ *adj* excessively, obtrusively, or sentimentally religious – **religiosity** *n*

[1]**religious** /ri'lijəs/ *adj* 1 of or showing faithful devotion to an acknowledged ultimate reality or deity; *specif* pious, godly ⟨*a* ~ *man*⟩ 2 of, being, or concerned with (the beliefs or observances of a) religion 3 committed or dedicated to the service of a deity or deities ⟨*the* ~ *life*⟩ 4 scrupulously and conscientiously faithful or zealous ⟨~ *in his observance of the rules*⟩ [ME, fr OF *religieus*, fr L *religiosus*, fr *religio*] – **religiously** *adv*, **religiousness** *n*

[2]**religious** *n*, *pl* **religious** a member of a religious order under monastic vows [ME, fr OF *religieus*, fr *religieus*, adj]

**reline** /,ree'lien/ *vt* to renew the lining of (eg a garment or set of brakes)

**relinquish** /ri'lingkwish/ *vt* 1 to renounce, abandon; GIVE UP 3b ⟨~ed *their claims to the estate*⟩ 2a to stop holding physically; release ⟨*slowly* ~ed *his grip on the bar*⟩ **b** to give over possession or control of; yield ⟨*few leaders willingly* ~ *power*⟩ [ME *relinquisshen*, fr MF *relinquiss-*, stem of *relinquir*, fr L *relinquere* to leave behind, fr *re-* + *linquere* to leave – more at

LOAN] – **relinquishment** n

**reliquary** /'relikwəri/ n a container or shrine in which sacred relics are kept [Fr *reliquaire*, fr ML *reliquiarium*, fr *reliqua* relic – more at RELIC]

**reliquiae** /ri'likwi,ee/ n pl remains of the dead; *esp* relics [L – more at RELIC]

¹**relish** /'relish/ n 1 characteristic, pleasing, or piquant flavour or quality 2 enjoyment of or delight in something that satisfies one's tastes, inclinations, or desires ⟨*eat with* ~⟩ 3 a strong liking; an inclination ⟨*had little* ~ *for the prospect*⟩ 4 something that adds an appetizing or savoury flavour; *esp* a highly seasoned sauce (e g of pickles or mustard) usu eaten with plain food [alter. of ME *reles* taste, fr OF, something left behind, release, fr *relessier* to release]

²**relish** vt 1 to add relish to 2 to be pleased or gratified by; enjoy, like ⟨*didn't* ~ *the prospect of her interview with the headmaster*⟩; *specif* to eat or drink with pleasure – **relishable** adj

**relive** /,ree'liv/ vt to live over again; *esp* to experience again in the imagination

**relocate** /,reeloh'kayt/ vt to locate again; establish in, lay out in, or move to a new place ~ vi to move to a new place – **relocation** n

**relucent** /ri'loohs(ə)nt/ adj, archaic or poetic bright, shining [L *relucent-, relucens*, pp of *relucēre* to shine back, fr *re-* + *lucēre* to shine – more at LIGHT]

**reluctance** /ri'luktəns/ also **reluctancy** /-si/ n 1 the quality or state of being reluctant 2 physics the property of a piece of magnetizable substance to oppose or resist the passage of a MAGNETIC FLUX (force causing magnetization)

**reluctant** /ri'luktənt/ adj disinclined to; averse, unwilling ⟨~ *to condemn him*⟩ [L *reluctant-, reluctans*, prp of *reluctari* to struggle against, fr *re-* + *luctari* to struggle – more at LOCK] – **reluctantly** adv

**relume** /ri'lyoohm/ vt, poetic to rekindle [irreg fr LL *reluminare*, fr L *re-* + *luminare* to light up – more at ILLUMINATE]

**rely on, rely upon** vt 1 to have confidence in; trust ⟨*her husband was a man she could* rely on⟩ 2 to be dependent on ⟨*they* rely on *the spring for water*⟩ [ME *relien* to rally, fr MF *relier* to connect, rally, fr L *religare* to tie back, fr *re-* + *ligare* to tie –more at LIGATURE]

*synonyms* Rely on, count on, reckon on, bank on, depend on, and trust all mean "place full confidence in". Rely on suggests an objective judgment, based on previous experience particularly of the truthfulness or ability of the one relied on. The less formal count on, reckon on, and bank on are close to rely on in meaning, but may in addition involve the fulfilment of a future promise; count on sometimes entails actual "counting" ⟨*can* count on *at least 500 new members*⟩, reckon on may entail consequent planning ⟨*the king scarcely knew on what members of his cabinet he could* reckon⟩ – T B Macaulay⟩, and bank on suggests the safety of money in a bank. Depend on, by emphasizing that one relies on another for strength and support, often suggests a lack in one's own strength or forethought. To trust is to place one's confidence without misgiving but as the result of faith rather than factual evidence.

**rem** /rem/ n a unit of ionizing radiation equal to the dosage that will cause the same biological effect as one RÖNTGEN of X-ray or gamma-ray radiation [röntgen equivalent *man*]

**REM** n RAPID EYE MOVEMENT ⟨REM *sleep*⟩

**remain** /ri'mayn/ vi 1a to be something or a part not destroyed, taken, or used up ⟨*only a few ruins* ~⟩ b to be something yet to be shown, done, or treated ⟨*it* ~s *to be seen*⟩ 2 to stay in the same place or with the same person or group; *specif* to stay behind 3 to continue to be ⟨~ *calm under attack*⟩ ⟨*the fact* ~s *that nothing can be done*⟩ synonyms see ³STAY [ME *remainen*, fr MF *remaindre*, fr L *remanēre*, fr *re-* + *manēre* to remain – more at MANSION]

¹**remainder** /ri'mayndə/ n 1 a future interest in property that arises and is dependent on the termination of a previous interest created at the same time 2a *taking sing or pl vb* a remaining

group, part, or trace b *maths* b(1) the number left after a subtraction b(2) the undivided part of the number to be divided (DIVIDEND) after division that is less or of lower degree than the dividing number (DIVISOR) 3 a book sold at a reduced price by the publisher after sales have fallen off [ME, fr AF, fr MF *remaindre* to remain]

²**remainder** vt to dispose of (copies of a book) as remainders

**remains** /ri'maynz/ n pl 1 a remaining part or trace ⟨*threw away the* ~ *of the meal*⟩ 2 writings left unpublished at a writer's death ⟨*literary* ~⟩ 3 a dead body

¹**remake** /,ree'mayk/ vt **remade** /-'mayd/ to make anew or in a different form

²**remake** /'ree,mayk/ n something that is remade; *esp* a new version of a film

**reman** /,ree'man/ vt **-nn-** to man again or anew

¹**remand** /ri'mahnd/ vt 1a to send back (a case) to another court for further action b to adjourn (a case) for further enquiries 2 to return (a person) to custody pending trial or for further detention [ME *remaunden* to send back, fr MF *remander*, fr LL *remandare* to send back word, fr L *re-* + *mandare* to order – more at MANDATE]

²**remand** n the state of being remanded – esp in *on remand*

**remand home** n, Br a temporary centre for usu juvenile offenders waiting to appear in court or for a court decision to come into effect – not now in technical use; compare COMMUNITY HOME

**remanence** /'remənəns/ n the magnetism remaining in a magnetized substance when the force that caused its magnetization has become zero

**remanent** /'remənənt/ adj 1 of, being, or characterized by remanence 2 formal residual, remaining [ME, fr L *remanent-, remanens*, prp of *remanēre* to remain]

¹**remark** /ri'mahk/ vt 1 to express as an observation or comment; say 2 formal to take notice of; observe ~ vi to notice something and make a comment or observation *on* or *upon* it *synonyms* see ¹SEE [Fr *remarquer*, fr MF, fr *re-* + *marquer* to mark – more at ²MARQUE]

²**remark** n 1 mention or notice of that which deserves attention ⟨*her behaviour could hardly escape* ~⟩ ⟨*worthy of special* ~ *in a social history* – G M Trevelyan⟩ 2 a casual expression of an opinion or judgment; an observation ⟨*heartily sick of his snide* ~s⟩

**remarkable** /ri'mahkəbl/ adj worthy of being or likely to be noticed, esp as being uncommon or extraordinary – **remarkableness** n

**remarkably** /ri'mahkəbli/ adv 1 to a remarkable degree ⟨~ *clever*⟩ 2 it is remarkable that ⟨~, *he never came*⟩

**remarque** /ri'mahk/ n 1 a scribble or sketch done on the margin of an engraved plate or stone and removed before the main run of prints is taken 2 (a proof taken from) a plate or stone bearing a remarque [Fr *remarque* remark, note, fr MF, fr *remarquer*]

**rematch** /'ree,mach/ n a second match between the same contestants or teams – **rematch** vt

**remedial** /ri'meedi-əl, -dyəl/ adj 1 intended as a remedy ⟨~ *treatment*⟩ 2 of or being teaching (methods or equipment) designed to help slow learners ⟨~ *reading courses*⟩ – **remedially** adv

¹**remedy** /'remədi/ n 1 a medicine, application, or treatment that relieves or cures a disease 2 something that corrects or counteracts an evil or deficiency ⟨*a prison sentence is the only* ~ *for your actions*⟩ 3 the legal means to recover a right or to prevent a wrong or obtain redress for it [ME *remedie*, fr AF, fr L *remedium*, fr *re-* + *mederi* to heal – more at MEDICAL] – **remediless** adj

²**remedy** vt to provide or serve as a remedy for; relieve – **remediable** adj

**remember** /ri'membə/ vt 1 to bring to mind or think of again ⟨~s *the old days*⟩ 2a to keep in mind for attention or consideration ⟨~ *me in your prayers*⟩ b to give or leave (somebody) a present, tip, etc ⟨*was* ~ed *in the will*⟩ 3 to retain in

the memory ⟨~ *the facts until the test is over*⟩ **4** to convey
greetings from ⟨~ *me to your mother*⟩ **5** to record, commemorate ⟨*history has not* ~ed *their names*⟩ ~ *vi* **1** to exercise
or have the power of memory **2** to have a recollection or
remembrance **antonym** forget [ME *remembren,* fr MF *re-
membrer,* fr LL *rememorari,* fr L *re-* + LL *memorari* to be
mindful of, fr L *memor* mindful – more at MEMORY] – **re-
memberable** *adj,* **rememberer** *n,* **rememberability** *n*
**remembrance** /ri'membrəns/ *n* **1** the state of bearing in mind
⟨*occupation troops kept alive their* ~ *of the defeat*⟩ **2a** the ability to remember; memory **b** the period over which one's
memory extends **3** an act of recalling to mind ⟨ ~ *of the offence
angered him all over again*⟩ **4** a memory of a person, thing, or
event ⟨*had only a dim* ~ *of that night*⟩ **5a** something that
serves to keep in or bring to mind; a reminder **b** a commemoration, memorial **c** a greeting or gift recalling or expressing friendship or affection
   *usage* The pronunciation /ri'membrəns/ rather than /ri'membərəns/ is
   recommended for BBC broadcasters.  △ reminder **synonyms** see
   MEMORY **antonym** forgetfulness
**Remembrance Day** *n* REMEMBRANCE SUNDAY
**remembrancer** /ri'membrənsə/ *n* one who or that which reminds; *esp, cap* any of several English officials originally having
the duty of bringing a matter to the attention of the proper
authority
**Remembrance Sunday** *n* the Sunday closest to November
11 set aside in commemoration of fallen Allied servicemen and
of the end of hostilities in 1918 and 1945 – compare VETERANS
DAY
**remex** /'reemeks/ *n, pl* **remiges** /'reməjeez/ a large stiff feather
of the wing of a bird [NL *remig-, remex,* fr L, oarsman, fr
*remus* oar + *agere* to drive – more at ROW, AGENT] – **remigial**
*adj*
**remilitar·ize, -ise** /,ree'militəriez/ *vt* to equip again with military forces and installations – **remilitarization** *n*
**remind** /ri'miend/ *vt* to cause to remember or call something
to mind ⟨*the view* ~ed *him of his old home*⟩ ⟨~ *me to ring my
mother*⟩ – **reminder** *n*
   **remind of** *vt* to appear to (someone) to be similar to ⟨*he
   reminds me of my brother*⟩
**remindful** /ri'miendf(ə)l/ *adj, formal* **1** mindful **2** tending to
remind; suggestive, evocative
**reminisce** /,remi'nis/ *vi* to indulge in reminiscence [back-for-
mation fr *reminiscence*]
**reminiscence** /,remi'nis(ə)ns/ *n* **1** the action of recalling particulars and ideas believed to have been known in a previous
existence – used in Platonic philosophy; called also ANAMNESIS
**2** the process or practice of thinking or telling about past experiences **3a** a remembered experience **b** *usu pl* an account of
a memorable experience ⟨*published the* ~s *of the old settler*⟩ **4**
something that recalls or is suggestive of something else
**synonyms** see MEMORY
**reminiscent** /,remi'nis(ə)nt/ *adj* **1** of the character of, or relating to, reminiscence **2** marked by or given to reminiscence **3**
tending to remind one (e g *of* something seen or known before);
suggestive ⟨*a technology* ~ *of the Stone Age*⟩ [L *reminiscent-,
reminiscens,* prp of *reminisci* to remember, fr *re-* + *-minisci*
(akin to L *ment-, mens* mind) – more at MIND] – **reminiscently**
*adv*
**remint** /,ree'mint/ *vt* to make (old or worn coin that has been
melted down) into new coin
**remiss** /ri'mis/ *adj* **1** negligent in the performance of work or
duty; careless ⟨*he would be* ~ *if he failed to report the accident*⟩
**2** showing neglect or inattention; lax ⟨*service was* ~ *in most of
the hotels*⟩ [ME, fr L *remissus,* fr pp of *remittere* to send back,
relax] – **remissly** *adv,* **remissness** *n*
**remissible** /ri'misəbl/ *adj* capable of being forgiven ⟨~ *sins*⟩
– **remissibly** *adv*
**remission** /ri'mish(ə)n/ *n* **1** the act or process of remitting **2** a
state or period during which something (e g the symptoms of a
disease) is remitted **3** reduction of a prison sentence, esp because of the prisoner's good behaviour
**¹remit** /ri'mit/ *vb* **-tt-** *vt* **1a** to release someone from the guilt
or penalty of ⟨~ *sins*⟩ **b** to refrain from inflicting or exacting
⟨~ *a tax*⟩ ⟨~ *the penalty of loss of pay*⟩ **c** to give relief from
(suffering) **2a** to desist from (an activity) **b** to let (e g attention
or diligence) slacken; relax **3** to submit or refer for consideration, judgment, decision, or action; *specif* to return (a case) to
a lower court **4** to put back into a former state or condition **5**
to postpone, defer **6** to send (money) to a person or place, esp

in payment of a demand, account, or draft ~ *vi* **1a** to lessen
in force or intensity; moderate **b** *of a disease or abnormality* to
become less severe for a temporary period **2** to send money
(e g in payment) [ME *remitten,* fr L *remittere* to send back, fr
*re-* + *mittere* to send – more at SMITE] – **remitment** *n* **remitt-
able** *adj,* **remitter** *n*
**²remit** /ri'mit; *also* 'reemit/ *n* **1** an act of remitting **2a** something remitted to another person or authority for consideration
or judgment; *also* the area of responsibility or concern assigned
to a person or authority ⟨*teachers stepping outside their* ~⟩ **b**
a proposal submitted (e g to a committee) for decision or
action
**remittal** /ri'mitl/ *n* remission
**remittance** /ri'mit(ə)ns/ *n* **1a** a sum of money remitted **b** a
document by which money is remitted **2** sending of money (e g
to a distant place)
**remittance man** *n* a person living abroad on money sent from
home, esp in the days of the British Empire
**remittent** /ri'mit(ə)nt/ *adj* marked by alternating periods of
diminished and increased severity – used of a disease, esp a
fever, or its symptoms [L *remittent-, remittens,* prp of *remittere*]
– **remittently** *adv*
**remnant** /'remnənt/ *n* **1a** a usu small part or trace remaining
**b** remnant, remnants *pl* a small surviving group **2** an unsold
or unused end of a piece of fabric [ME, contr of *remenant,* fr
MF, fr prp of *remenoir* to remain, fr L *remanēre* – more at
REMAIN]
**remodel** /,ree'modl/ *vt* **-ll-** (*NAm* -l-, -ll-) to alter the structure
of; reconstruct ⟨~ *an old house*⟩
**remold** /,ree'mohld/ *vt, chiefly NAm* to remould – **remold** *n*
**remonet·ize, -ise** /ree'munitiez/ *vt* to restore to use as legal
tender ⟨~ *silver*⟩ – **remonetization** *n*
**remonstrance** /ri'monstrəns/ *n* **1** an act or instance of re-
monstrating **2** *archaic* a representation, demonstration; *specif*
a document formally stating points of opposition or grievance
**remonstrant** /ri'monstrənt/ *adj, formal* vigorously objecting
or opposing – **remonstrant** *n,* **remonstrantly** *adv*
**remonstrate** /'remən,strayt, ri'mon-/ *vt, formal* to say or plead
in protest, reproof, or opposition ~ *vi* to present and urge
reasons in opposition; expostulate, protest – often + *with*
**synonyms** see ²OBJECT [ML *remonstratus,* pp of *remonstrare* to
demonstrate, fr L *re-* + *monstrare* to show – more at MUSTER]
– **remonstrator** *n,* **remonstration** *n,* **remonstrative** *adj,* **re-
monstratively** *adv*
**remora** /'remərə/ *n* any of several fishes (*Echeneis* and related
genera) of warm seas that have a sucking disc on the top of
the head by means of which they cling to and are transported
by larger fishes (e g sharks), ships, etc [L, lit., delay, fr *remorari*
to delay, fr *re-* + *morari* to delay – more at MORATORIUM; fr a
former belief that the fish could hold ships back]
**remorse** /ri'maws/ *n* **1** a deep and bitter distress arising from
a sense of guilt for past wrongs **2** pity, compassion – usu neg
**synonyms** see ¹PENITENT [ME, fr MF *remors,* fr ML *remorsus,*
fr LL, act of biting again, fr L *remorsus,* pp of *remordēre* to
bite again, fr *re-* + *mordēre* to bite – more at SMART]
**remorseful** /ri'mawsf(ə)l/ *adj* motivated or marked by remorse
– **remorsefully** *adv,* **remorsefulness** *n*
**remorseless** /ri'mawslis/ *adj* **1** having no remorse; merciless
⟨~ *cruelty*⟩ **2** persistent, indefatigable – **remorselessly** *adv,*
**remorselessness** *n*
**remote** /ri'moht/ *adj* **1** far removed in space, time, or relation
⟨*the* ~ *past*⟩ ⟨*comments* ~ *from the truth*⟩ **2** out-of-the-way,
secluded **3** acting on or controlling something or being controlled indirectly or from a distance ⟨*a computer with a hundred*
~ *terminals*⟩ **4** not arising from a direct or close action **5** small
in degree; slight ⟨*a* ~ *possibility*⟩ **6** distant in manner; aloof
[L *remotus,* fr pp of *removēre* to remove] – **remotely** *adv,* **remoteness** *n*
**remote control** *n* control over an operation (e g of a machine
or weapon) exercised from a distance, usu by means of an
electrical circuit or radio waves; *also* a device by which this is
carried out
**¹remould,** *NAm chiefly* **remold** /,ree'mohld/ *vt* **1** to mould or
shape again or anew **2** to refashion the tread of (a worn tyre)
**²remould,** *NAm chiefly* **remold** /'ree,mohld/ *n* a remoulded
tyre
**¹remount** /,ree'mownt/ *vt* **1** to mount again ⟨~ *a picture*⟩ **2**
to provide (e g a unit of cavalry) with replacement horses ~ *vi*
to mount again [ME *remounten;* partly fr *re-* + *mounten* to
mount; partly fr MF *remonter,* fr *re-* + *monter* to mount]

²**remount** /'ree,mownt, ,-'-/ *n* a fresh riding horse; *esp* one used as a replacement for one which is exhausted

**removable** /ri'moohvəbl/ *adj* capable of being removed – **removably** *adv,* **removableness, removability** *n*

¹**removal** /ri'moohvl/ *n* the act or process of removing; the fact of being removed; *specif, Br formal* a change of residence ⟨*our* ~ *to Hampton Wick*⟩

²**removal** *adj, Br* of or for the transfer of furniture and possessions from one residence to another ⟨~ *expenses*⟩ ⟨*a* ~ *van*⟩

**removalist** /ri'moohvəlist/ *n, Austr* a person who owns or works for a removal company

¹**remove** /ri'moohv/ *vt* **1** to change the location, position, station, or residence of ⟨~ *soldiers to the front*⟩ **2** to move by lifting, pushing aside, or taking away or off ⟨~s *his hat in church*⟩ **3** to dismiss from office **4** to get rid of; eliminate ⟨~ *a tumour surgically*⟩ ~ *vi* **1** to be capable of being removed **2** *formal* to change location, station, or residence ⟨*removing from the city to the suburbs*⟩ **3** *archaic* to go away [ME *removen*, fr OF *removoir*, fr L *removēre*, fr *re-* + *movēre* to move] – **remover** *n*

²**remove** *n* **1a** a distance or interval separating one person or thing from another ⟨*poems that work best at a slight* ~ *from the personal*⟩ **b** a degree or stage of separation ⟨*a repetition, at many* ~s, *of the theme of his first book*⟩ **2** a form intermediate between two others in some British schools

**removed** /ri'moohvd/ *adj* **1a** distant in degree of relationship **b** of a younger or older generation ⟨*a second cousin's child is a second cousin once* ~⟩ **2** separate or remote in space, time, or character

**REM sleep** *n* PARADOXICAL SLEEP (sleep in which the brain is very active)

**remunerate** /ri'myoohnə,rayt/ *vt* **1** to pay an equivalent for ⟨*his services were generously* ~d⟩ **2** to pay an equivalent to for a service, loss, or expense; recompense [L *remuneratus,* pp of *remunerare* to recompense, fr *re-* + *munerare* to give, fr *muner-, munus* gift – more at MEAN] – **remunerator** *n,* **remuneratory** *adj*

**remuneration** /ri,myoohnə'raysh(ə)n/ *n* **1** an act or fact of remunerating **2** something that remunerates; recompense, pay

**remunerative** /ri'myoohnərətiv/ *adj* **1** serving to remunerate **2** providing remuneration; profitable – **remuneratively** *adv,* **remunerativeness** *n*

**renaissance** *also* **renascence** /ri'nays(ə)ns, ri'nesohns/ *n* **1** *cap* **1a** the transitional movement in Europe between medieval and modern times beginning in the 14th century in Italy, lasting into the 17th century, marked by a surge of intellectual activity stimulated by a revival of classical influence, and expressed in a flowering of the arts and literature and by the beginnings of modern science △ Reformation, Restoration **b** the period of the Renaissance **c** the NEOCLASSIC style of architecture prevailing during the Renaissance **2** *often cap* a movement or period of vigorous artistic and intellectual activity **3** a rebirth, revival [Fr *renaissance* fr MF, rebirth, fr *renaistre* to be born again, fr L *renasci,* fr *re-* + *nasci* to be born – more at NATION]

**Renaissance man** *n* a person of wide interests and expertise; *specif* a person equally at home in the arts and sciences

**renal** /'reenl/ *adj* of, involving, or located in the region of the kidneys [Fr or LL; Fr *rénal,* fr LL *renalis,* fr L *renes* kidneys]

**renascent** /ri'nays(ə)nt/ *adj, formal* becoming active or vigorous again [L *renascent-, renascens,* prp of *renasci* to be born again]

**renature** /ree'naychə/ *vt* to restore (e g a protein or NUCLEIC ACID whose properties have been altered by heat, acid, etc) to an original or normal condition, esp of activity or function [*re* + *-nature* (as in *denature*)] – **renaturation** *n*

**rend** /rend/ *vb* **rent** /rent/ *vt* **1** to remove from place by violence; wrest **2** to split or tear apart or in pieces (as if) by violence **3** to tear (the hair or clothing) as a sign of anger, grief, or despair **4a** to tear mentally or emotionally **b** to pierce with sound ~ *vi* **1** to perform an act of tearing or splitting **2** to become torn or split *synonyms* see ²TEAR [ME *renden,* fr OE *rendan;* akin to OFris *renda* to tear, Skt *randhra* hole]

¹**render** /'rendə/ *vt* **1a** to melt down; extract by melting ⟨~ *lard*⟩ **b** to treat so as to convert into useful materials (e g industrial fats and oils) **2a** to convey to another; deliver **b** to give up; yield **c** to deliver for consideration, approval, or information: e g **c(1)** HAND DOWN 3 (give the opinion of a court) **c(2)** to agree on and report (a verdict) **3a** to give in return or

retribution **b** to give back; restore **c** to give in acknowledgment of dependence or obligation; pay **d** to do (a service) for another **4a(1)** to cause to be or become; make ⟨*enough rain to* ~ *irrigation unnecessary*⟩ **a(2)** to impart **b(1)** to reproduce or represent by artistic or verbal means; depict **b(2)** to give a performance of **b(3)** to produce a copy or version of ⟨*the documents are* ~ed *in the original French*⟩ **b(4)** to perform the motions of ⟨~ *a salute*⟩ **c** to translate **5** to direct the execution of; administer ⟨~ *justice*⟩ **6** to apply a coat of plaster or cement directly to (brickwork, stone, etc) [ME *rendren,* fr MF *rendre* to give back, yield, fr (assumed) VL *rendere,* alter. of L *reddere,* partly fr *re-* + *dare* to give & partly fr *re-* + *-dere* to put – more at DATE, DO] – **renderable** *adj,* **renderer** *n*

²**render** *n* a return, esp in goods or services, due from a feudal tenant to his lord

**rendering** /'rend(ə)ring/ *n* **1** a material usu made of cement, sand, and a small percentage of lime and applied to form a protective or decorative covering for exterior walls **2** *Br* a rendition

¹**rendezvous** /'rondi,vooh/ *n, pl* **rendezvous 1a** a place appointed for assembling or meeting **b** a place to which people customarily come; a haunt ⟨*these cafés are popular* ~ *for the rich and beautiful*⟩ **2** a meeting at an appointed place and time **3** the process of bringing two spacecraft together [MF, fr *rendez vous* present yourselves]

²**rendezvous** *vi* **rendezvouses** /-voohz/; **rendezvousing** /-vooh·ing/; **rendezvoused** /-voohd/ to come together at a rendezvous

**rendition** /ren'dish(ə)n/ *n* the act or result of rendering: e g **a** a translation **b** a performance, interpretation [obs Fr, fr MF, alter. of *reddition,* fr LL *reddition-, redditio,* fr L *redditus,* pp of *reddere*]

**rendzina** /ren'jeenə/ *n* a dark greyish-brown to black CALCIUM CARBONATE- containing soil developed from chalk, limestone, etc in grassy or formerly grassy areas of high to moderate humidity [Russ, fr Polish *redzina* rich limy soil]

¹**renegade** /'renigayd/ *n* **1** a deserter from one faith, cause, or allegiance to another **2** an individual who rejects lawful or conventional behaviour [Sp *renegado,* fr ML *renegatus,* fr pp of *renegare* to deny, fr L *re-* + *negare* to deny – more at NEGATE]

²**renegade** *adj* **1** having deserted a faith, cause, or religion for a hostile one **2** having rejected tradition; unconventional

**renege** *also* **renegue** /ri'neeg, ri'nayg/ *vt* to deny, renounce ~ *vi* **1** REVOKE (fail to follow suit in cards) **2** to go back on a promise or commitment – usu + *on* ⟨~d *on his contract*⟩ [ML *renegare*] – **reneger** *n*

**renegotiable** /,reeni'gohsh(y)əbl/ *adj* subject to renegotiation

**renegotiate** /,reeni'gohshiayt/ *vt* to negotiate again; *esp* to readjust by negotiation so as to eliminate or recover excessive profits – **renegotiation** *n*

**renew** /ri'nyooh/ *vt* **1** to make as if new; restore to freshness, vigour, or perfection ⟨*as we* ~ *our strength in sleep*⟩ **2** to make new spiritually; regenerate **3a** to restore to existence; revive **b** to make extensive changes in; rebuild **4** to make or do again **5** to begin again; resume **6** to replace, replenish ⟨~ *water in a tank*⟩ **7a** to grant or obtain an extension of or on (e g a subscription, lease, or licence) **b** to grant or obtain a further loan of ⟨~ *a library book*⟩ ~ *vi* **1** to become (as) new **2** to begin again; resume **3** to make a renewal (e g of a lease) – **renewer** *n*

**renewable** /ri'nyooh·əbl/ *adj* capable of being renewed; *esp* capable of being replaced by natural processes or correct management practices ⟨*sun, wind, and waves are* ~ *sources of energy*⟩ – **renewably** *adv,* **renewability** *n*

**renewal** /ri'nyooh·əl/ *n* **1** renewing or being renewed **2** something (e g a subscription to a magazine) renewed **3** something used for renewing; *specif* an expenditure that improves existing fixed assets

**reni-** /reeni-, reni-/, **reno-** *comb form* kidney ⟨*renipuncture*⟩ [L *renes* kidneys]

**reniform** /'reni,fawm, 'ree-/ *adj* shaped like a kidney ⟨~ *leaves*⟩ [NL *reniformis,* fr *reni-* + *-formis* -form]

**renin** /'reenin, 'renin/ *n* an ENZYME secreted by the kidneys whose action in breaking down proteins in the blood results in the release of ANGIOTENSIN (hormone that influences the water balance of the body) [ISV, fr L *renes*]

**renitent** /'renit(ə)nt, ri'niet(ə)nt/ *adj, formal* **1** resisting physical pressure **2** resisting constraint or compulsion; recalcitrant [Fr or L; Fr *rénitent,* fr L *renitent-, renitens,* prp of *reniti* to struggle against, fr *re-* + *niti* to strive] – **renitency** *n*

**rennet** /'renit/ *n* **1a** the contents of the stomach of an unweaned animal, esp a calf **b** the membrane lining the stomach, esp the fourth stomach (ABOMASUM), of a young calf or related animal, used for curdling milk **c** a prepared extract from the stomach or stomach lining of a young animal, that contains the ENZYME rennin and is used for curdling milk in making cheese and junket **2a** rennin **b** any preparation containing rennin or a substance having the action of rennin on milk [ME, fr (assumed) ME *rennen* to cause to coagulate, fr OE *gerennan*, fr *ge-* together + (assumed) OE *rennan* to cause to run; akin to OHG *rennen* to cause to run, OE *rinnan* to run –more at RUN]

**rennin** /'renin/ *n* an ENZYME occurring in the digestive juice of a young calf or related mammal that causes the solidification of milk by converting the soluble milk protein CASEINOGEN into an insoluble compound (CASEIN), and that is extracted esp from the membrane lining the fourth stomach of a calf and used in making cheese and junket [*rennet* + ¹ *-in*]

**¹renounce** /ri'nowns/ *vt* **1** to give up, refuse, or resign, usu by formal declaration ⟨~ *his errors*⟩ **2** to refuse to follow, obey, or recognize any further; repudiate ⟨~ *the authority of the church*⟩ **3** to play a card which is not trumps when unable to follow with a card from (the suit led); *broadly* to fail to follow with a card from (the suit led) *antonym* claim [ME *renouncen*, fr MF *renoncer*, fr L *renuntiare*, fr *re-* + *nuntiare* to report, fr *nuntius* messenger] – **renouncable** *adj*, **renouncement** *n*, **renouncer** *n*

**²renounce** *n* failure to follow suit in a card game

**renovate** /'renə,vayt/ *vt* **1** to restore to life, vigour, or activity; revive ⟨*the party was* ~d *by a new spirit of unity*⟩ **2** to restore to a former or improved state (eg by cleaning, repairing, or rebuilding) [L *renovatus*, pp of *renovare*, fr *re-* + *novare* to make new, fr *novus* new – more at NEW] – **renovator** *n*, **renovation** *n*

**renown** /ri'nown/ *n* a state of being widely acclaimed; fame [ME, fr MF *renon*, fr OF, fr *renomer* to make famous, fr *re-* + *nomer* to name, fr L *nominare*, fr *nomin-*, *nomen* name – more at NAME]

**renowned** /ri'nownd/ *adj* having renown; celebrated, famous

**¹rent** /rent/ *n* **1** property (eg a house) rented or for rent **2a** a usu fixed periodical payment made by a tenant or occupant of property to the owner for the possession and use of it; *esp* an agreed sum paid at fixed intervals by a tenant to his/her landlord for the use of land, a house, a flat, etc **b** the amount paid by a hirer of personal property to the owner for its use **3** the portion of the income of an economy (eg of a nation) attributable to land as a means of production in addition to capital and labour [ME *rente*, fr OF, income from a property, fr (assumed) VL *rendita*, fr fem of *renditus*, pp of *rendere* to yield – more at RENDER] – **for rent** available for use or service in return for payment

**²rent** *vt* **1** to take and hold under an agreement to pay rent **2** to grant the possession and use of for rent – often + *out* ~ *vi* **1** to be for rent (*at or for* a specified rental) **2a** to obtain the possession and use of a place or article for rent **b** to allow the possession and use of property or rent *synonyms* see ²HIRE – **rentable** *adj*, **rentability** *n*

**³rent** *past of* REND

**⁴rent** *n* **1** an opening or split made (as if) by rending **2** an act or instance of rending [E dial. *rent* to rend, fr ME *renten*, alter. of *renden*]

**¹rental** /'rentl/ *n* **1a** an amount paid or collected as rent **b** income from rents **2** an act of renting ⟨*Bloggs for car* ~s⟩ **3** a business that rents something **4** *NAm* something (eg a house) that is rented

**²rental** *adj* **1a** of rent **b** available for rent **2** dealing in property available for renting ⟨*a* ~ *agency*⟩

**rent control** *n* government regulation of the amount charged as rent for housing, and often also control of the practice of eviction

**rente** /ronht (*Fr* rãt)/ *n* **1** annual income under French law resembling an ANNUITY (sum paid at regular intervals in return for an investment) **2a** interest payable by the French and other European governments on government securities **b** a government security yielding rente [Fr, income, rent]

**renter** /'rentə/ *n* one who or that which rents: eg **a** the leaseholder or tenant of property **b** a distributor of cinema films

**rentier** /'ronti,ay, 'ronh- (*Fr* rãtje)/ *n* **1** one who owns rentes **2** a person who receives a fixed income (eg from land or shares); *also* a person who supplies capital in return for interest and

dividends but otherwise takes no part in the running of a firm [Fr, fr OF, fr *rente*]

**'rent-,roll** *n* a register of a person's or company's lands, buildings, etc showing the rents due and the total paid by each tenant

**rent strike** *n* a refusal by a group of tenants to pay rent (eg in protest against high rates)

**rent tribunal** *n* a board appointed to fix the rent payable for premises within certain limits

**renumber** /,ree'numbə/ *vt* to number again or differently

**renunciation** /ri,nunsi'aysh(ə)n/ *n* the act or practice of renouncing; a repudiation; *specif* self-denial practised for religious reasons [ME, fr L *renuntiation-*, *renuntiatio*, fr *renuntiatus*, pp of *renuntiare* to renounce] – **renunciative**, **renunciatory** *adj*

**renvers** /ron'veə (*Fr* rãveʀ)/ *n*, *pl* **renvers** a movement in DRESSAGE (test of precise horsemanship) in which the horse moves forward with its haunches bent to the side away from the line of advance – compare TRAVERS [deriv of MF *renverser* to turn back, fr *re-* + *enverser* to invert, fr OF, fr *envers* upside down, fr L *inversus* inverse]

**reoffer** /,ree'ofə/ *vt* to offer (an issue of shares, bonds, etc) for public sale

**reopen** /,ree'ohp(ə)n/ *vt* **1** to open again **2a** to take up again; resume ⟨~ *discussion*⟩ **b** to resume discussion or consideration of ⟨~ *a contract*⟩ **3** to begin again ~ *vi* to open again ⟨*school* ~s *in September*⟩

**¹reorder** /,ree'awdə/ *vt* **1** to arrange in a different way **2** to order again ~ *vi* to place a reorder

**²reorder** *n* an order for goods like a previous order placed with the same supplier

**reorgan·ization, -isation** /ree,awgənie'zaysh(ə)n, -ni-/ *n* reorganizing or being reorganized; *esp* the financial or administrative reconstruction of a business concern or group of companies – **reorganizational** *adj*

**reorgan·ize, -ise** /ri'awgəniez/ *vb* to organize (something) again or anew – **reorganizer** *n*

**reorient** /,ree'awriənt, -ent/, **reorientate** /-'awriəntayt/ *vt* to change the outlook or attitude of – **reorientation** *n*

**¹rep** /rep/ *n*, *NAm slang* a reputation

**²rep, repp** *n* a PLAIN-WEAVE fabric with raised rounded crosswise ribs [Fr *reps*, modif of E *ribs*, pl of *rib*]

**³rep** *n* a representative; *esp*, *chiefly Br informal* SALES REPRESENTATIVE

**⁴rep** *vi* **-pp-** *chiefly Br informal* to act as a SALES REPRESENTATIVE

**⁵rep** *n*, *informal* a repertory theatre or company

**repackage** /,ree'pakij/ *vt* to package again or anew; *specif*, *chiefly NAm* to put into a more efficient or attractive form ⟨~ *a candidate's public image*⟩ – **repackager** *n*

**¹repair** /ri'peə/ *vi*, *formal* to betake oneself; go ⟨~ed *to his home*⟩ [ME *repairen*, fr MF *repairier* to go back to one's country, fr LL *repatriare*, fr L *re-* + *patria* native country – more at EXPATRIATE]

**²repair** *vt* **1** to restore by replacing a part or putting together what is torn or broken; mend ⟨~ *a shoe*⟩ **2** to restore to a sound or healthy state; renew ⟨~ *his strength*⟩ **3** to make good; compensate for; remedy ⟨*will* ~ *his earlier failure*⟩ ~ *vi* to make repairs [ME *repairen*, fr MF *reparer*, fr L *reparare*, fr *re-* + *parare* to prepare – more at PARE] – **repairable** *adj*, **repairer** *n*, **repairability** *n*

     **synonyms** Material things are **repairable** ⟨*these shoes aren't repairable*⟩; *antonym* **unrepairable**. Loss, damage, injury, etc are **reparable**; *antonym* **irreparable**.

**³repair** *n* **1a** the act or process of repairing **b** an instance or result of repairing **c** the replacement of old or damaged cells or tissues by new growth **2a** relative condition with respect to soundness or need of repairing ⟨*the car is in reasonably good* ~⟩ **b** the state of being in good or sound condition ⟨*the machinery is all out of* ~⟩

**repairman** /ri'peəman/ *n* someone employed to repair mechanisms

**repand** /ri'pand/ *adj*, *of a plant or animal part* having a slightly wavy edge ⟨*a* ~ *leaf*⟩ [L *repandus* bent backwards, fr *re-* + *pandus* bent; akin to ON *fattr* bent backwards]

**reparable** /'rep(ə)rəbl/ *adj* capable of being repaired *synonyms* see ²REPAIR

**reparation** /,repə'raysh(ə)n/ *n* **1a** the act of making amends, offering to pay the penalty, or giving satisfaction for a wrong or injury **b** something done or given as amends or satisfaction

**2 reparations** *pl, also* **reparation** the payment of damages; *specif* compensation in money or materials payable by a defeated nation for damages to or expenditures sustained by another nation as a result of hostilities with the defeated nation [ME, fr MF, fr LL *reparation-, reparatio,* fr L *reparatus,* pp of *reparare*]

**reparative** /ri'parətiv/ *adj* **1** of or effecting repair **2** serving to make amends

**repartee** /,repah'tee/ *n* **1a** a quick and witty reply **b** a succession or interchange of clever remarks; amusing and usu light sparring with words **2** adroitness and cleverness in reply; skill in repartee *synonyms* see WIT [Fr *repartie,* fr *repartir* to retort, fr MF, fr *re-* + *partir* to divide – more at PART]

**¹repartition** /,repah'tish(ə)n/ *n* distribution [prob fr Sp *repartición,* fr *repartir* to distribute, fr *re-* + *partir* to divide, fr L *partire* – more at PART]

**²repartition** *n* a second or additional dividing or distribution [*re-* + *partition*]

**repass** /,ree'pahs/ *vi* to pass again, esp in the opposite direction; return ~ *vt* **1** to pass through, over, or by again ⟨~ *the house*⟩ **2** to cause to pass again **3** to adopt again ⟨~ed *the resolution*⟩ [ME *repassen,* fr MF *repasser,* fr OF, fr *re-* + *passer* to pass] – **repassage** *n*

**repast** /ri'pahst/ *n, formal* a meal [ME, fr MF, fr OF, fr *repaistre* to feed, fr *re-* + *paistre* to feed, fr L *pascere* – more at FOOD]

**repatriate** /,ree'patri,ayt, ri-, -'pay-/ *vt* to restore or return to the country of origin, allegiance, or citizenship ⟨~ *prisoners of war*⟩ [LL *repatriatus,* pp of *repatriare* to go back to one's country – more at REPAIR] – **repatriate** *n,* **repatriation** *n*

**repay** /ri'pay, ,ree-/ *vb* **repaid** /-payd/ *vt* **1a** to pay back; refund ⟨~ *a loan*⟩ **b** to give or inflict in return or retaliation ⟨~ *evil for evil*⟩ **2** to make a return payment to; compensate **3** to reward; recompense ⟨*a company which* ~s *hard work*⟩ ~ *vi* to make return payment, compensation, or retaliation – **repayable** *adj,* **repayment** *n*

**repeal** /ri'peel/ *vt* **1** to withdraw or annul by authoritative act; *esp* to revoke (a law) **2** to abandon, renounce [ME *repelen,* fr MF *repeler,* fr OF, fr *re-* + *apeler* to appeal, call] – **repeal** *n,* **repealable** *adj*

**¹repeat** /ri'peet/ *vt* **1a** to say or state again **b** to say through from memory; recite **c** to say after another ⟨~ *these words after me*⟩ **2a** to make, do, or perform again ⟨~ *an experiment*⟩ **b** to cause to appear or be broadcast again; reproduce ⟨*a programme* ~ed *on tape*⟩ **c** to go through or experience again **3** to express or present (oneself) again in the same words, terms, or form ~ *vi* **1** to say, do, or accomplish something again; *esp, NAm* to vote illegally by casting more than one vote at an election **2** *of food* to continue to be tasted intermittently after being swallowed – often + *on* ⟨*onions always* ~ *on me*⟩ **3** to occur more than once; recur ⟨*the first 3 figures* ~⟩ **4** *of a firearm* to be capable of being fired several times without manual reloading **5** *of a clock or watch* to strike the time to the last hour or quarter hour when a spring is pressed *usage* see REITERATE [ME *repeten,* fr MF *repeter,* fr L *repetere,* fr *re-* + *petere* to go to, seek – more at FEATHER] – **repeatable** *adj,* **repeatability** *n*

**²repeat** *n* **1** the act of repeating **2a** something repeated; a repetition; *specif* a television or radio programme that has previously been broadcast at least once **b** a musical passage to be repeated in performance; *also* a sign placed before and after such a passage

**repeated** /ri'peetid/ *adj* **1** renewed or recurring again and again ⟨~ *changes of plan*⟩ **2** said, done, or presented again

**repeatedly** /ri'peetidli/ *adv* again and again

**repeater** /ri'peetə/ *n* one who or that which repeats: e g **a** someone who relates or recites **b** a watch or clock with a striking mechanism that will indicate the time to the last hour or quarter when a spring is pressed **c** a firearm having a magazine that holds a number of cartridges which are loaded into the firing chamber automatically **d** *NAm* someone who votes illegally by casting more than one vote in an election

**repeating decimal** /ri'peeting/ *n* RECURRING DECIMAL

**repechage** /,repi'shahzh, '--,-/ *n* a heat (e g of a rowing race) in which losers from earlier heats are given another chance to qualify for the next round or the final [Fr *repêchage* second chance, reexamination for a candidate who has failed, fr *repêcher* to fish out, rescue, fr *re-* + *pêcher* to fish, fr L *piscari,* fr *piscis* fish]

**repel** /ri'pel/ *vb* **-ll-** *vt* **1** to drive back; repulse **2** to turn away; reject ⟨~led *the insinuation*⟩ **3a** to drive away; discourage ⟨*foul words and frowns must not* ~ *a lover* – Shak⟩ **b** to be incapable of sticking to, mixing with, taking up, or holding ⟨*a fabric that* ~s *moisture*⟩ **c** to (tend to) force away or apart by mutual action at a distance ⟨*two like electric charges* ~ *one another*⟩ **4** to cause aversion in; disgust ~ *vi* to cause aversion [ME *repellen,* fr L *repellere,* fr *re-* + *pellere* to drive – more at FELT] – **repeller** *n*

*synonyms* Disgusting things **repel** (not △ **repulse**) one, and are **repellent** or (stronger) **repulsive**, causing one to feel **repulsion**. Fabrics that **repel** moisture are **repellent** (not △ **repulsive**). One **repels** or (stronger) **repulses** an invader, who undergoes a **repulse**.

**¹repellent** *also* **repellant** /ri'pelənt/ *adj* **1** serving or tending to drive away or ward off – often in combination ⟨*a mosquito-repellent spray*⟩ **2** arousing aversion or disgust; repulsive [L *repellent-, repellens,* prp of *repellere*] – **repellently** *adv*

**²repellent** *also* **repellant** *n* something that repels; *esp* a substance used to drive away insects

**¹repent** /ri'pent/ *vi* **1** to turn from sin and amend one's life **2a** to feel regret or remorse **b** to change one's mind ~ *vt* **1** to cause to feel regret or remorse **2** to feel sorrow, regret, or remorse for *synonyms* see ¹PENITENT [ME *repenten,* fr OF *repentir,* fr *re-* + *pentir* to be sorry, fr L *paenitēre* – more at FENITENCE] – **repentance** *n,* **repenter** *n*

**²repent** /'reepənt/ *adj, of a plant part* trailing or growing along the ground; creeping ⟨*a* ~ *stem*⟩ [L *repent-, repens,* prp of *repere* to creep – more at REPTILE]

**repentant** /ri'pent(ə)nt/ *adj* **1** experiencing repentance; penitent **2** expressive of repentance – **repentantly** *adv*

**repercussion** /,reepə'kush(ə)n/ *n* **1** an echo, reverberation **2a** an action or effect given or exerted in return; a reciprocal action or effect **b** a widespread, indirect, or unforeseen effect of an act, action, or event [L *repercussion-, repercussio,* fr *repercussus,* pp of *repercutere* to drive back, fr *re-* + *percutere* to beat – more at PERCUSSION] – **repercussive** *adj*

**repertoire** /'repə,twah/ *n* **1a** a list or supply of items (e g plays, operas, roles, or songs) that a company or person has prepared and is capable of performing **b** a range of skills, techniques, or expedients ⟨*part of the* ~ *of a halfback*⟩; *broadly* an amount, supply ⟨*an endless* ~ *of summer clothes*⟩ **2a** the complete list or supply of works available for performance ⟨*our modern orchestral* ~⟩ **b** the complete list or range of skills, techniques, or ingredients used in a particular field, occupation, or practice ⟨*the* ~ *of literary criticism*⟩ **c** a list or stock of capabilities ⟨*the instruction* ~ *of a computer*⟩ [F *répertoire,* fr LL *repertorium*]

**repertory** /'repət(ə)ri/ *n* **1** a place where something may be

---

| | | | |
|---|---|---|---|
| **renail** *vt* | **reoccur** *vi* | **repave** *vt* | **repolymerize** *vt* |
| **rename** *vt* | **reoccurrence** *n* | **repeg** *vt* | **repopularization** *n* |
| **renationalization** *n* | **reoil** *vb* | **rephase** *vt* | **repopularize** *vt* |
| **renationalize** *vt* | **reoperate** *vb* | **rephotograph** *vt* | **repopulate** *vt* |
| **renest** *vt* | **reorchestrate** *vt* | **repin** *vt* | **repopulation** *n* |
| **renominate** *vt* | **reorchestration** *n* | **replan** *vt* | **repot** *vt* |
| **renomination** *n* | **reordination** *n* | **replaster** *vt* | **repressurize** *vt* |
| **renotification** *n* | **reoutfit** *vt* | **replot** *vt* | **reprice** *vt* |
| **renotify** *vt* | **reoxidation** *n* | **replumb** *vt* | **repropose** *vb* |
| **reobserve** *vt* | **reoxidize** *vb* | **repolarization** *n* | **reprovision** *n* |
| **reobtain** *vt* | **repack** *vb* | **repolarize** *vb* | **republish** *vt* |
| **reobtainable** *adj* | **repaint** *vt or n* | **repolish** *vt* | **repurchase** *vt or n* |
| **reoccupation** *n* | **repaper** *vt* | **repoll** *vt* | **repurify** *vt* |
| **reoccupy** *vt* | **repattern** *vt* | **repolymerization** *n* | |

found; a repository **2a** a repertoire **b(1)** a company that presents several different plays alternately in the course of a season at one theatre; *also* a theatre housing such a company **b(2)** the production and presentation of plays by a repertory company ⟨*acting in* ~⟩ [LL *repertorium* list, fr L *repertus*, pp of *reperire* to find, fr *re-* + *parere* to produce – more at PARE] – **repertory** *adj*

**répétiteur** /ri,peti'tuh/ *n* someone who coaches opera singers [Fr, fr L *repetitus*, pp]

**repetition** /,repi'tish(ə)n/ *n* **1** the act or an instance of repeating or being repeated **2** a reproduction, copy [L *repetition-, repetitio*, fr *repetitus*, pp of *repetere* to repeat] – **repetitional** *adj*

**repetitious** /,repi'tishəs/ *adj* characterized or marked by repetition; *esp* tediously repeating – **repetitiously** *adv*, **repetitiousness** *n*

**repetitive** /ri'petətiv/ *adj* REPETITIOUS – **repetitively** *adv*, **repetitiveness** *n*

**rephrase** /ree'frayz/ *vt* to phrase again; put in different words, esp to make the meaning clearer

**repine** /ri'pien/ *vi, formal* to feel or express dejection or discontent [*re-* + ¹*pine*] – **repiner** *n*

**replace** /ri'plays/ *vt* **1** to restore to a former place or position ⟨~ *cards in a file*⟩ **2** to take the place of, esp as a substitute or successor **3** to put something new in the place of ⟨~ *a worn carpet*⟩ *usage* see ²SUBSTITUTE *synonyms* see DISPLACE – **replaceable** *adj*, **replacer** *n*

**replacement** /ri'playsmənt/ *n* **1** replacing or being replaced; substitution **2** one who or that which replaces; *esp* a person assigned to a military unit to replace a loss or complete a quota

**replant** /,ree'plahnt/ *vt* **1** to plant again or anew **2** to provide with new plants

**replate** /'reeplayt/ *n* a change of the printing plate for a page of a newspaper during the printing of an edition, esp to include late news – **replate** *vb*

¹**replay** /,ree'play/ *vt* to play again

²**replay** /'reeplay/ *n* **1a** an act or instance of replaying **b** the playing of a tape (eg a videotape) **2** a repetition, reenactment ⟨*don't want a* ~ *of our old mistakes*⟩ **3** a match (eg in soccer) played because an earlier match between the same sides has been tied

**replenish** /ri'plenish/ *vt* **1** to fill with vigour or power; nourish **2a** to stock or fill up again ⟨~ed *his glass*⟩ **b** to make good; replace **3** *archaic* to supply fully; perfect [ME *replenisshen* to fill, inhabit, fr MF *repleniss-*, stem of *replenir* to fill, fr OF, fr *re-* + *plein* full, fr L *plenus* – more at FULL] – **replenisher** *n*, **replenishment** *n*

**replete** /ri'pleet/ *adj* **1** fully or abundantly provided or filled **2** abundantly fed; sated [ME, fr MF & L; MF *replet*, fr L *repletus*, pp of *replēre* to fill up, fr *re-* + *plēre* to fill – more at FULL] – **repleteness** *n*

**repletion** /ri'pleesh(ə)n/ *n* **1** eating or being fed to excess **2** the condition of being filled up or overcrowded **3** gratification of a need or desire; satisfaction

**replevin** /ri'plevin/ *n* the recovery by a person of goods that are claimed to have been wrongfully taken or detained, subject to the person pledging to try the matter in court and to return the goods if defeated in the action; *also* a writ granting this [ME, fr AF *replevine*, fr *replevir* to give security, fr OF, fr *re-* + *plevir* to pledge, fr (assumed) LL *plebere*]

**replevy** /ri'plevi/ *vt* to take or get back by a writ for replevin [AF *replevir*]

**replica** /'replikə/ *n* **1** a close reproduction or exact copy, esp by the maker of the original **2** a copy, duplicate [It, repetition, fr *replicare* to repeat, fr LL, fr L, to fold back – more at REPLY]

**replicase** /'replikayz, -ays/ *n* an ENZYME that promotes the replication of RNA in a virus whose genetic material is RNA; the RNA POLYMERASE of an RNA-containing virus [*replic*ation + *-ase*]

¹**replicate** /'repli,kayt/ *vt* **1a** to duplicate or repeat exactly ⟨~ *a statistical experiment*⟩ ⟨*DNA* ~s *itself*⟩ **b** to reproduce or make an exact copy of; cause to undergo replication ⟨*DNA* ~s *itself*⟩ **2** to fold or bend back or over ⟨*a* ~d *leaf*⟩ ~ *vi* to undergo replication; produce a replica of itself ⟨*viruses* ~ *only under certain conditions*⟩ [LL *replicatus*, pp of *replicare*] – **replicable** *adj*, **replicability** *n*, **replicative** *adj*

²**replicate** /'replikət/ *adj* **1** duplicate, repeated **2** folded over or back on itself ⟨~ *leaves*⟩

**replication** /,repli'kaysh(ə)n/ *n* **1a** an answer, reply **b(1)** an answer to a reply; a rejoinder **b(2)** the reply made by the PLAINTIFF (person bringing an action) in answer to the DEFENDANT's (person against whom the action is brought) initial plea, answer, or opposing claim in a legal action – not now used technically **2** an echo, reverberation **3a** a copy, reproduction **b** the action or process of reproducing **c** the process by which a complex molecule, virus, or cell structure (eg a MITOCHONDRION) is exactly reproduced or duplicated; *esp* the process by which an exact copy of a molecule of genetic material (DNA or RNA) is produced within a living cell **4** performance of an experiment or procedure more than once; *esp* repetition of a complete experiment under the same conditions or the performance of an experiment on several samples at one time and place

¹**reply** /ri'plie/ *vi* **1a** to respond in words or writing **b** to echo, resound **c** to make a legal replication **2** to do something in response; *specif* to return gunfire or an attack ~ *vt* to give as an answer *synonyms* see ²ANSWER [ME *replien*, fr MF *replier* to fold again, fr L *replicare* to fold back, fr *re-* + *plicare* to fold – more at PLY] – **replier** *n*

²**reply** *n* something said, written, or done in answer or response

¹**report** /ri'pawt/ *n* **1a** (an account spread by) common talk; (a) rumour **b** character or reputation ⟨*a man of good* ~⟩ **2a** a usu detailed account or statement ⟨*a news* ~⟩ **b** an account or statement of a judicial opinion or decision **c** a usu formal record of the proceedings of a meeting or inquiry **d** a statement of a pupil's performance at school, usu issued every term to the pupil's parents or guardian **3** a loud explosive noise [ME, fr MF, fr OF, fr *reporter* to report, fr L *reportare*, fr *re-* + *portare* to carry – more at FARE]

²**report** *vt* **1** to give information about; relate **2a** to convey news of **b** to relate the words or sense of (something said) **c** to make a written record or summary of **d** to watch for and present the newsworthy aspects or developments of, in writing or for broadcasting **3a(1)** to give a formal or official account or statement of ⟨*the treasurer* ~ed *a balance of 12*⟩ **a(2)** to return or present (a matter referred for consideration) with conclusions or recommendations **b** to announce or relate as the result of examination or investigation ⟨~ed *no sign of disease*⟩ **c** to announce the presence, arrival, or sighting of **d** to make known to the relevant authorities ⟨~ *a fire*⟩ **e** to make a charge of misconduct against; complain about ⟨*I'll* ~ *you to the headmaster*⟩ ~ *vi* **1a** to give an account **b** to present oneself ⟨~ *at the main entrance*⟩ **c** to account for oneself as specified ⟨~ed *sick on Friday*⟩ **2** to make, issue, or submit a report **3** to act in the capacity of a news reporter – **reportable** *adj*

**report out** *vt* to return after consideration, and often with revision, to a legislative body for action ⟨*after much debate the committee reported the bill out*⟩

**reportage** /,repaw'tahzh, ri'pawtij/ *n* **1a** the act or process of reporting news **b** something (eg news) that is reported **c** a typical journalistic style of reporting news **2** writing intended to give a usu factual account of observed or documented events [Fr, fr *reporter* to report]

**report card** *n* **1** *Br* a card imposing punishment on a pupil at school **2** *NAm* REPORT 2d

**reportedly** /ri'pawtidli/ *adv* according to report; reputedly

**reported speech** /ri'pawtid/ *n* the report of something said or written by one person grammatically adapted for inclusion in something said or written by another (eg *he was sorry* in *he said he was sorry*)

**reporter** /ri'pawtə/ *n* one who or that which reports: eg **a** a person who makes a shorthand report of a speech or proceeding; *specif, often cap* COURT REPORTER **b(1)** someone employed by an organization such as a newspaper, magazine, or news agency to gather and write news **b(2)** someone who broadcasts news – **reportorial** *adj*, **reportorially** *adv*

**report stage** *n* the stage in the British legislative process before the THIRD READING of a bill in Parliament, concerned esp with amendments and details

**reposal** /ri'pohzl/ *n, obs* the act or state of reposing

¹**repose** /ri'pohz/ *vt, formal* **1** to place (eg confidence or trust) in someone or something usu specified **2** to entrust for control, management, or use [ME *reposen* to replace, fr L *reponere* (perf indic *reposui*)]

²**repose** *vt, informal* to lay at rest ⟨~ *oneself on a couch*⟩ ~ *vi* **1** *formal* **1a** to lie resting **b** to lie dead ⟨*reposing in state*⟩ **c** to remain still **2** *formal* to take rest **3** *formal* to rest for support; lie ⟨*a bowl* ~d *on the table*⟩ **4** *archaic* to reply [ME *reposen*,

fr MF *reposer*, fr OF, fr LL *repausare*, fr L *re-* + LL *pausare* to stop – more at PAUSE]

[3]**repose** *n, formal* **1a** the state of resting after exertion or strain; *esp* rest in sleep **b** eternal or heavenly rest ⟨*pray for the ~ of a soul*⟩ **2a** a place of rest **b** calm, tranquillity **c** a restful effect (eg of a painting or colour scheme) **3** cessation or absence of activity, movement, or animation ⟨*the appearance of his face in ~*⟩ **4** composure of manner; poise

**reposeful** /ri'pohzl(ə)l/ *adj, formal* conducive to ease and relaxation – **reposefully** *adv*, **reposefulness** *n*

**reposit** /ri'pozit/ *vt, formal* **1** to deposit, store **2** to put back in place; replace [L *repositus*, pp of *reponere* to replace, fr *re-* + *ponere* to place – more at POSITION]

[1]**reposition** /,reepə'zish(ə)n, ,repə-/ *n, formal* repositing or being reposited

[2]**reposition** *vt* to change the position of

**repository** /ri'pozət(ə)ri/ *n* **1** a place, room, or container where something is deposited or stored; depository **2** a side altar in a Roman Catholic church where the consecrated Host is set aside from Maundy Thursday until Good Friday **3** one who or that which contains or stores something nonmaterial ⟨*considered the book a ~ of knowledge*⟩ **4** a person to whom something is confided or entrusted

synonyms A **repository** may be smaller than a **depository**: perhaps a mere box. Things are usually put into a **depository** for storage, but may be merely dumped in a **repository** ⟨*cupboard was a repository of old jam jars and broken crockery*⟩.

**repossess** /,reepə'zes/ *vt* **1a** to regain possession of **b** to resume possession of (eg goods being bought by hire purchase) because of nonpayment of instalments due **2** *formal* to restore to a state of possessing – usu + *of* – **repossession** *n*

[1]**repoussé** /rə'poohsay/ *adj* **1** *esp of sheet metal* ornamented with raised patterns made by hammering or pressing on the reverse side **2** formed with parts of the surface raised (in RELIEF) [Fr, pp of *repousser* to press back, fr MF, fr *re-* + *pousser* to push, thrust, fr OF *poulser* – more at PUSH]

[2]**repoussé** *n* repoussé work

**repp** /rep/ *n* [2]REP (fabric)

**reprehend** /,repri'hend/ *vt, formal* to voice disapproval of; censure [ME *reprehenden*, fr L *reprehendere*, lit., to hold back, fr *re-* + *prehendere* to grasp – more at PREHENSILE]

**reprehensible** /,repri'hensəbl/ *adj* deserving reprehension; blameworthy – **reprehensibleness** *n*, **reprehensibly** *adv*, **reprehensibility** *n*

**reprehension** /,repri'hensh(ə)n/ *n, formal* the act of reprehending; censure [ME *reprehensioun*, fr MF or L; MF *reprehension*, fr L *reprehension-*, *reprehensio*, fr *reprehensus*, pp of *reprehendere*]

**reprehensive** /,repri'hensiv/ *adj, formal* serving to reprehend; conveying reprehension or reproof

**represent** /,repri'zent/ *vt* **1** to convey a mental impression of; present ⟨*a book which ~s the character of Tudor England*⟩ **2** to serve as a sign or symbol of ⟨*the snake ~s Satan*⟩ **3** to portray or exhibit in art; depict **4** to act the part or role of **5a(1)** to take the place of in some respect **a(2)** to act for or in the place of, usu by legal right **b** to serve, esp in a legislative body, by delegated authority usu resulting from election ⟨*~s Leeds East*⟩ **6** to attribute a specified character or identity to ⟨*~s himself as a friend of the workingman*⟩ **7a** to give one's impression and judgment of; state or describe in a manner intended to affect action or judgment; advocate **b** to point out in protest or remonstrance **8** to serve as a specimen, model, example, or instance of **9** to form a mental impression of **10** to correspond in essence; constitute ⟨*~s a flagrant breach of the rules*⟩ *~ vi* to make representations against something; protest [ME *representen*, fr MF *representer*, fr L *repraesentare*, fr *re-* + *praesentare* to present] – **representable** *adj*, **representer** *n*

,**re-pre'sent** *vt* to present again or anew – **re-presentation** *n*

**representation** /,reprizen'taysh(ə)n/ *n* **1** one who or that which represents: eg **1a** an artistic likeness or image **b(1)** **representations** *pl*, **representation** a statement or account made to influence opinion or action ⟨*the minister was not moved by their ~s*⟩ **b(2)** an assertion of fact on the faith of which a contract is entered into, and to which legal liability may be attached **c** a usu formal protest ⟨*a ~ in parliament*⟩ **2** the act or action of representing or the state of being represented: eg **2a(1)** the action or fact of one person standing in place of another so as to have the other's rights and obligations **a(2)** the substitution of an individual or class or individuals in place of a person (eg a child or children for a deceased parent) **b** the action of representing or the fact of being represented, esp in a legislative body **3** the body or number of people representing a constituency **4** the analysis of a linguistic entity (eg a word or sentence) into its component units

**representational** /,reprizen'taysh(ə)nl/ *adj* of representation, esp realistic representation in art

**representationalism** /,reprizen'tayshn·liz(ə)m/ *n* the theory that perceived objects are only representations formed in the mind and not the real objects existing in the external world – **representationalist** *n*

[1]**representative** /,repri'zentətiv/ *adj* **1** serving to represent ⟨*a painting ~ of strife*⟩ **2a** standing or acting for another, esp through delegated authority **b** of or based on representation of the people in government or lawmaking, usu by election **3** serving as a typical or characteristic example ⟨*a ~ area*⟩ **4** of representation or representationalism – **representatively** *adv*, **representativeness**, **representativity** *n*

[2]**representative** *n* **1** a typical example of a group, class, or quality; a specimen **2** someone who represents another or others: eg **2a(1)** someone who represents a constituency (eg as a member of a parliament) **a(2)** a member of the Australian or US HOUSE OF REPRESENTATIVES or a US state legislature **b** someone who represents another as agent, deputy, substitute, or delegate **c** someone who represents a business organization; *esp* SALES REPRESENTATIVE **d** someone who represents another as successor or heir

**representative peer** *n* a peer elected by the Irish or Scottish peers to represent them in the HOUSE OF LORDS

**repress** /ri'pres/ *vt* **1a** to hold in check; curb ⟨*injustice was ~ed*⟩ **b** to put down by force; subdue ⟨*~ an insurrection*⟩ **2a** to hold in by self-control ⟨*~ed a laugh*⟩ **b(1)** to prevent the natural or normal expression, activity, or development of ⟨*~ed his anger*⟩ **b(2)** to exclude (eg a feeling) from consciousness by psychological repression **3** to inactivate (a gene) reversibly by inhibiting or blocking normal action *~ vi* to take repressive action synonyms see SUPPRESS [ME *repressen*, fr L *repressus*, pp of *reprimere* to check, fr *re-* + *premere* to press – more at PRESS] – **repressible** *adj*, **repressibility** *n*, **repressive** *adj*, **repressively** *adv*, **repressiveness** *n*

,**re-'press** *vt* to press again ⟨*~ a record*⟩ ⟨*~ trousers*⟩

**repression** /ri'presh(ə)n/ *n* **1a** repressing or being repressed ⟨*~ of unpopular opinions*⟩ **b** an instance of repressing ⟨*racial ~s*⟩ **2a** a psychological process by which unacceptable desires or impulses are excluded from conscious awareness **b** an item so excluded – **repressionist** *adj*

**repressor** /ri'presə/ *n* one who or that which represses; *esp* a substance, esp a protein, produced by the action of a REGULATOR GENE, that indirectly inhibits the function of a gene responsible for the synthesis of a protein by interacting with and repressing the activity of its controlling OPERATOR [NL]

[1]**reprieve** /ri'preev/ *vt* **1** to delay or remit the punishment of (eg a condemned prisoner) **2** to give temporary relief or rest to [perh fr MF *repris*, pp of *reprendre* to take back]

[2]**reprieve** *n* **1a** reprieving or being reprieved **b** a formal temporary suspension of the execution of a sentence, esp a death sentence; *also* a remission of a sentence **2** an order or warrant for a reprieve **3** a temporary remission (eg from pain or trouble)

[1]**reprimand** /'repri,mahnd/ *n* a severe and usu formal reproof [Fr *réprimande*, fr L *reprimenda*, fem of *reprimendus*, gerundive of *reprimere* to check]

[2]**reprimand** /'--,-, ,--'-/ *vt* to criticize sharply or censure formally, usu from a position of authority

[1]**reprint** /ree'print/ *vt* to print again; make a reprint of *~ vi* to be printed as a reprint – **reprinter** *n*

[2]**reprint** *n* a reproduction of printed matter: eg **a** a subsequent impression of a book already published that preserves the same text as the previous impression **b** OFFPRINT (separately printed excerpt) **c** matter (eg an article) that has appeared in print before

**reprisal** /ri'priezl/ *n* **1a** the act or practice in international law of resorting to force short of war in retaliation for damage or loss suffered **b** an instance of such action **2** the usu forcible retaking of something (eg territory) **3** **reprisals** *pl*, **reprisal** something (eg a sum of money) given or paid in restitution **4** **reprisals** *pl*, **reprisal** a retaliatory act; retaliation [ME *reprisail*, fr MF *reprisaille*, fr OIt *ripresaglia*, fr *ripreso*, pp of *riprendere* to take back, fr *ri-* re- (fr L *re-*) + *prendere* to take, fr L *prehendere* – more at PREHENSILE]

¹**reprise** /ri'preez; *sense 1 also* ri'priez/ *n* **1 reprises** *pl*, **reprise** a deduction or charge made yearly out of a manor or estate **2** a recurrence or resumption of an action **3** a dance step of French origin that was popular in the 16th and 17th centuries **4a** a musical repetition: **4a(1)** the repetition of the first section (EXPOSITION) preceding the middle section (DEVELOPMENT)in SONATA FORM **a(2)** RECAPITULATION (third section returning to the original theme in SONATA FORM) **b** a repeated performance; a repetition [ME, fr MF, lit., action of taking back, fr OF, fr *reprendre* to take back, fr *re-* + *prendre* to take, fr L *prehendere*]

²**reprise** /ri'priez/ *vt, archaic* **1** to take back; *esp* to recover by force **2** to compensate [MF *reprise* action of taking back]

**repro** /'reeproh/ *n, pl* **repros 1** a clear sharp proof made esp from a LETTERPRESS (raised and inked) printing surface to serve as photographic copy for a printing plate **2** REPRODUCTION 2; *esp* a copy of a work of art [short for *reproduction*]

¹**reproach** /ri'prohch/ *n* **1a** a cause or occasion of blame, discredit, or disgrace ⟨*the poverty of millions is a constant* ∼⟩ **b** discredit, disgrace ⟨*their methods brought* ∼ *on them*⟩ **2** the act or action of reproaching or disapproving ⟨*was beyond* ∼⟩ **3** an expression of rebuke or disapproval **4** *obs* someone subjected to censure or scorn [ME *reproche*, fr MF, fr OF, fr *reprochier* to reproach, fr (assumed) VL *repropiare*, fr L *re-* + *prope* near – more at APPROACH] – **reproachful** *adj*, **reproachfully** *adv*, **reproachfulness** *n*

²**reproach** *vt* **1** to make (something) a matter of reproach **2** to express disappointment and displeasure with (a person) for conduct that is blameworthy or in need of improvement; upbraid **3** to bring into discredit – **reproachable** *adj*, **reproacher** *n*, **reproachingly** *adv*

¹**reprobate** /'reprə,bayt/ *vt, formal* **1** to condemn strongly as unworthy, unacceptable, or evil ⟨reprobating *the laxity of the age*⟩ **2** to condemn or predestine to eternal damnation; exclude from salvation **3** to refuse to accept; reject [ME *reprobaten*, fr LL *reprobatus*, pp of *reprobare* – more at REPROVE] – **reprobation** *n*, **reprobative**, **reprobatory** *adj*

²**reprobate** /'reprəbayt/ *adj* **1a** condemned or predestined to eternal damnation **b** morally dissolute; unprincipled **2** *formal* expressing or involving reprobation **3** *archaic* rejected as valueless or not standing up to a test; condemned

³**reprobate** *n* someone who is reprobate

**reprocess** /ree'prohses/ *vt* to treat or process again (so as to be suitable for reuse)

**reproduce** /,reeprə'dyoohs/ *vt* to produce again: e g **a(1)** to produce (new living things of the same kind) by a sexual or asexual process **a(2)** to cause to undergo reproduction by a sexual or asexual process **b** to cause to exist again or anew ⟨∼ *water from steam*⟩ **c** to imitate closely ⟨*sound-effects that* ∼ *the sound of thunder*⟩ **d** to present (e g a play) again **e** to make an image or copy of ⟨∼ *a face on canvas*⟩ **f** to bring back to mind; recall **g** to translate (a recording) into sound or an image ∼ *vi* **1** to undergo reproduction in a usu specified manner ⟨*the picture* ∼s *well*⟩ **2** to produce new individuals or offspring – **reproducer** *n*, **reproducible** *adj*, **reproducibility** *n*

**reproduction** /,reeprə'duksh(ə)n/ *n* **1** the act or process of reproducing; *specif* the process, either sexual or asexual, by which plants and animals give rise to new individuals – compare SEXUAL REPRODUCTION, ASEXUAL REPRODUCTION **2** something (e g a painting) that is reproduced; a copy

**reproductive** /,reeprə'duktiv/ *adj* of, involved in, or taking part in, or capable of reproduction – **reproductively** *adv*, **reproductiveness** *n*

**reproductive fitness** *n* the capacity for successful breeding as measured by the number of survivors of a species or variety from generation to generation

**reproductive isolation** *n* the isolation of a breeding population (e g by geographical barriers) from the others of a species leading to the formation of new races within the species because of the subsequent reduced intermixing of genetic strains

**reprogram** /ree'prohgram/ *vb* **-mm-** *vt* to alter the functioning of (e g a computer) by introducing a new program; *also* to rewrite a program for ∼ *vi* to introduce a new program or rewrite an existing one

**reprography** /ri'progrəfi/ *n* the science or practice of reproducing graphic matter (e g by photocopying) [*repro*duction + *-graphy*] – **reprographic** *adj*

**reproof** /ri'proohf/ *n* criticism for a fault; a rebuke [ME *reprof*, fr MF *reprove*, fr OF, fr *reprover* to reprove]

**reproportion** /,reeprə'pawsh(ə)n/ *vt* to change the proportions of

**reprove** /ri'proohv/ *vt* **1** to call attention to the remissness of, usu with a kindly intent to correct or assist ⟨∼ *a child's bad manners*⟩ **2** to express disapproval of; censure ⟨∼ *a child for his bad manners*⟩ **3** *obs* to disprove, refute ∼ *vi* to express rebuke or reproof [ME *reproven*, fr MF *reprover*, fr LL *reprobare* to disapprove, condemn, fr L *re-* + *probare* to test, approve – more at PROVE] – **reprover** *n*, **reprovingly** *adv*

**reptant** /'rept(ə)nt/ *adj, biology* crawling, trailing, or creeping along the ground [L *reptant-, reptans,* prp of *reptare* to creep, fr *reptus*, pp]

**reptile** /'reptiel/ *n* **1** any of a class (Reptilia) of air-breathing cold-blooded VERTEBRATE animals including the alligators and crocodiles, lizards, snakes, turtles, and extinct related forms (e g the dinosaurs), that have a bony skeleton, a body usu covered with scales or bony plates, and most of which reproduce by laying eggs **2** a grovelling or despicable person [ME *reptil*, fr MF or LL; MF *reptile* (fem), fr LL *reptile* (neut), fr neut of *reptilis* creeping, fr L *reptus*, pp of *repere* to creep; akin to OHG *reba* tendril]

¹**reptilian** /rep'tilyən/ *adj* **1** of, resembling, or having the characteristics of the reptiles **2** mean, despicable

²**reptilian** *n* REPTILE 1

**republic** /ri'publik/ *n* **1a** (a nation or other political unit having) a government in which the head of state is not a monarch and is usu a president **b** (a nation or other political unit having) a government in which supreme power rests in the people and is exercised by their elected representatives governing according to law **c** a usu specified republican government ⟨*the French Fourth* Republic⟩ **2** a constituent political and territorial unit of the USSR or Yugoslavia **3** *formal* a body of people freely and equally engaged in a common activity ⟨*the* ∼ *of art*⟩ [Fr *république*, fr MF *republique*, fr L *respublica*, fr *res* thing, wealth + *publica*, fem of *publicus* public – more at REAL, PUBLIC]

¹**republican** /ri'publikən/ *adj* **1a** of or like a republic **b** favouring, supporting, or advocating a republic **c** belonging or appropriate to one living in or supporting a republic ⟨∼ *simplicity*⟩ **2** *cap* of or constituting a political party of the USA that is usu primarily associated with business, financial, and some agricultural interests and is held to favour a restricted governmental role in social and economic life – compare DEMOCRATIC

²**republican** *n* **1** someone who favours or supports a republican form of government **2** *cap* **2a** a member of a political party advocating republicanism **b** a member of the US Republican party

**republicanism** /ri'publikəniz(ə)m/ *n* **1** adherence to or sympathy for a republican form of government **2** the principles or theory of republican government **3** *cap* the principles, policy, or practices of the US Republican party

**republican-ize, -ise** /ri'publikəniez/ *vt* to make republican in character, form, or principle

**republication** /,reepubli'kaysh(ə)n, ri,pub-/ *n* **1** republishing or being republished **2** something that has been republished

**republic of letters** *n* **1** authors in general **2** writings having excellence of form or expression, or of universal interest; literature

**republish** /ree'publish/ *vt* to publish again or anew – **republishable** *adj*, **republisher** *n*

**repudiate** /ri'pyoohdi,ayt/ *vt* **1** to refuse to have anything to do with; disown **2a** to refuse to accept; *esp* to reject as unauthorized or as having no binding force **b** to reject as untrue or unjust ⟨∼ *a charge*⟩ **3** to refuse to acknowledge or pay ⟨∼ *a debt*⟩ **4** *archaic* to divorce or separate formally from (a woman) [L *repudiatus*, pp of *repudiare* to divorce, reject, fr *repudium* divorce] – **repudiator** *n*

**repudiation** /ri,pyoohdi'aysh(ə)n/ *n* repudiating or being repudiated; *esp* the refusal of public authorities to acknowledge or pay a debt – **repudiationist** *n*

**repugn** /ri'pyoohn/ *vt, informal* to strive against; OPPOSE ∼ *vi*, *archaic* to offer opposition, objection, or resistance [ME *repugnen*, fr MF & L; MF *repugner*, fr L *repugnare*]

**repugnance** /ri'pugnəns/, **repugnancy** /-si/ *n* **1** strong dislike, aversion, or antipathy **2** *formal* **2a** the quality or fact of being contradictory or incompatible **b** an instance of contradiction or incompatibility

**repugnant** /ri'pugnənt/ *adj* **1** arousing strong dislike or aversion **2** *formal* incompatible, inconsistent **3** *archaic* antagonistic *antonym* congenial [ME, opposed, contradictory, incompatible, fr MF, fr L *repugnant-, repugnans,* prp of *repugnare* to fight against, fr *re-* + *pugnare* to fight – more at PUNGENT] – **repugnantly** *adv*

¹**repulse** /ri'puls/ *vt* **1** to drive or beat back; repel ⟨~ *the invading army*⟩ **2** to repel by discourtesy, coldness, or denial **3** to cause repulsion in *synonyms* see REPEL [L *repulsus,* pp of *repellere* to repel]

²**repulse** *n* **1** a rebuff, rejection **2** the action of repelling an assailant; the fact of being repelled; repulsion

**repulsion** /ri'pulsh(ə)n/ *n* **1** repulsing or being repulsed **2a** a force (eg between like electric charges or like magnetic poles) tending to produce separation **b** the result of such a force; the state of being repelled or separated **3** a feeling of strong aversion; repugnance

**repulsive** /ri'pulsiv/ *adj* **1** tending to repel or reject; cold, forbidding **2** serving or able to repulse **3** arousing strong aversion or disgust *synonyms* see REPEL – **repulsively** *adv,* **repulsiveness** *n*

**reputable** /'repyootəbl/ *adj* held in good repute; well regarded – **reputably** *adv,* **reputability** *n*

    *usage* The pronunciation /'repyootəbl/ rather than /rə'pyoohtəbl/ is recommended for BBC broadcasters.

**reputation** /,repyoo'taysh(ə)n/ *n* **1a** overall quality or character as seen or judged by others **b** recognition by other people of some characteristic or ability ⟨*has the* ~ *of being clever*⟩ **2** a place in public esteem or regard; good name

¹**repute** /ri'pyooht/ *vt* to believe, consider – usu pass ⟨*is* ~d *to be the oldest specimen*⟩ ⟨*is* ~d *honest*⟩ [ME *reputen,* fr MF *reputer,* fr L *reputare* to reckon up, think over, fr *re-* + *putare* to reckon – more at PAVE]

²**repute** *n* **1** the specified character, quality, or status; reputation ⟨*a person of ill* ~⟩ **2** the state of being favourably known or spoken of

**reputed** /ri'pyoohtid/ *adj* **1** having a favourable repute; reputable **2** being such according to general or popular belief ⟨*the* ~ *father of the child*⟩

**reputedly** /ri'pyoohtidli/ *adv* according to reputation or general belief

¹**request** /ri'kwest/ *n* **1** the act or an instance of asking for something **2** something asked for **3** the condition or fact of being requested ⟨*available on* ~⟩ **4** *formal* the state of being sought after; demand ⟨*a book in great* ~⟩ [ME *requeste,* fr MF, fr (assumed) VL *requaesta,* fr fem of *requaestus,* pp of *requaerere* to require]

²**request** *vt* **1** to make a request to or of ⟨~ed *her to write a paper*⟩ **2** to ask as a favour or privilege ⟨*he* ~s *to be excused*⟩ **3** to ask for ⟨~ed *a brief delay*⟩ **4** *obs* to ask (a person) to come or go to a thing or place – **requester, requestor** *n*

    *usage* One can **request** something *from* or *of* somebody ⟨*she* **requested** *information from us*⟩ but not, correctly, **request** somebody *for* something ⟨⚠ *she* **requested** *them for information*⟩ or **request** *for* somebody to do something ⟨⚠ *she* **requested** *for them to be quiet*⟩. The verb **request** should not be used with *for,* unlike the noun **request** ⟨*a* **request** *for information*⟩. *synonyms* see ASK

**request stop** *n* a point at which a public transport vehicle stops only by previous arrangement or when signalled

**requiem** /'rekwi·əm, -,em/ *n* **1** a mass for the dead **2a** a solemn chant for the repose of the dead **b** something that resembles a solemn funeral chant in tone or function ⟨"Requiem *for a Nun*" – William Faulkner⟩ **3** *often cap* **3a** a musical setting of the mass for the dead **b** a musical composition in honour of the dead [ME, fr L (first word of the introit of the requiem mass), acc of *requies* rest, fr *re-* + *quies* quiet, rest – more at WHILE]

**requiescat** /,rekwi'eskat/ *n* a prayer for the repose of a dead person [L, may he/she rest, fr *requiescere* to rest, fr *re-* + *quiescere* to be quiet, fr *quies*]

**require** /ri'kwie·ə/ *vt* **1** to claim or demand by right and authority **2a** to call for as suitable or appropriate ⟨*the occasion* ~s *formal dress*⟩ **b** to call for as necessary or essential; have a compelling need for ⟨*all living beings* ~ *food*⟩ **3** to impose an obligation or command on; compel **4** *chiefly Br* to feel or be obliged; need *to* ⟨*one does not* ~ *to be a specialist* – Elizabeth Bowen⟩ [ME *requeren,* fr MF *requerre,* fr (assumed) VL *requaerere* to seek for, need, require, alter. of L *requirere,* fr *re-* + *quaerere* to seek, ask]

    *usage* Some people dislike the chiefly British use of an infinitive verb after **require**, as in sense 4. *synonyms* see ²DEMAND, ¹LACK **5** *archaic* to request

**requirement** /ri'kwie·əmənt/ *n* **1** the condition of being necessary **2** *usu pl* something one wants or needs

¹**requisite** /'rekwizit/ *adj* necessary, required ⟨*make the* ~ *payment*⟩ *synonyms* see ²NECESSARY *antonym* optional [ME, fr L *requisitus,* pp of *requirere*] – **requisiteness** *n*

²**requisite** *n* something that is required or necessary; *broadly* an article of the specified sort ⟨*toilet* ~s⟩

**requisition** /,rekwi'zish(ə)n/ *n* **1** the act of formally requesting someone to perform an action **2a** the act of requiring something to be supplied **b** a demand or application made usu with authority: eg **b(1)** a demand made by military authorities on civilians for needs (eg supplies) **b(2)** a written request for something authorized but not made available automatically **3** *formal* the state of being in demand or use [MF or ML; MF, fr ML *requisition-, requisitio,* fr L, act of searching, fr *requisitus*] – **requisition** *vt*

**requital** /ri'kwietl/ *n, formal* **1** requiting or being requited **2** something given in return, compensation, or retaliation

**requite** /ri'kwiet/ *vt, formal* **1a** to make return for; give something in return for; repay **b** to make retaliation for; avenge **2a** to make suitable return to (for a benefit or service); reward **b** to compensate sufficiently for (an injury) [*re-* + obs *quite* to quit, pay, fr ME *quiten* – more at QUIT] – **requiter** *n*

**reradiate** /,ree'raydiayt/ *vt* to radiate again or anew; *esp* to emit (energy) in the form of radiation after previously absorbing radiation of the same or a different wavelength ⟨*at night the sea* ~s *heat absorbed during the day*⟩ – **reradiation** *n*

**reredos** /'riə,dos, 'riəri,dos, 'reərə-/ *n* a usu ornamented wood or stone screen or partition wall behind an altar [ME, fr AF *areredos,* fr MF *arrere* behind + *dos* back, fr L *dorsum* – more at ARREARS]

¹**rerun** /,ree'run/ *vt* **-nn-; reran** /-'ran/; **rerun** to run again or anew

²**rerun** *n* the act or action or an instance of rerunning; a repetition; *esp* a presentation of recorded material (eg a film or tele-

---

| | | | |
|---|---|---|---|
| **rerack** *vt* | **reseason** *vt* | **reslate** *vt* | **restartable** *adj* |
| **reraise** *vt* | **reseat** *vt* | **resmooth** *vt* | **restimulate** *vt* |
| **reread** *vt* | **resecrete** *vt* | **resoak** *vt* | **restimulation** *n* |
| **rerecord** *vt* | **resecure** *vt* | **resocialization** *n* | **restock** *vt* |
| **reregister** *vb* | **resegregate** *vb* | **resocialize** *vt* | **restraighten** *vb* |
| **reregistration** *n* | **resegregation** *n* | **resolder** *vt* | **restrengthen** *vt* |
| **rerelease** *vt or n* | **resell** *vb* | **resole** *vt* | **restring** *vt* |
| **reremind** *vt* | **resentence** *vt* | **resolidification** *n* | **restuff** *vt* |
| **rereview** *vt* | **reservice** *vt* | **resolidify** *vb* | **resublime** *vb* |
| **reroll** *vt* | **resettle** *vb* | **resow** *vb* | **resubmission** *n* |
| **reroller** *n* | **resettlement** *n* | **respecification** *n* | **resubmit** *vb* |
| **reroof** *vt* | **resew** *vt* | **respecify** *vt* | **resubscribe** *vi* |
| **reroute** *vt* | **resharpen** *vt* | **respray** *vt or n* | **resummon** *vt* |
| **resample** *vt* | **reshave** *vt* | **respring** *vb* | **resupply** *vt* |
| **resay** *vt* | **reshingle** *vt* | **resprout** *vb* | **resurvey** *vt or n* |
| **reschedule** *vt* | **reshoe** *vt* | **restabilize** *vt* | **resuspend** *vt* |
| **reschool** *vt* | **reshoot** *vb* | **restaff** *vt* | **resuspension** *n* |
| **rescreen** *vt* | **reshoulder** *vt* | **restamp** *vt* | **resynthesis** *n* |
| **resculpt** *vt* | **resight** *vt* | **restandardization** *n* | **resynthesize** *vt* |
| **reseal** *vt* | **resilver** *vt* | **restandardize** *vt* | **resystematize** *vt* |
| **resealable** *adj* | **resite** *vt* | **restart** *vb or n* | |

vision programme) after its first run

**resale** /'reesayl/ *n* the act of selling again, usu to a different person, organization, etc – **resale** *adj*

**resale price maintenance** *n* the fixing by a manufacturer of a minimum price at which its goods may be sold to the public by a retailer, distributor, etc

**rescale** /ˌree'skayl/ *vt* to plan, establish, or formulate on a new and usu smaller scale

**rescind** /ri'sind/ *vt* **1a** to annul, cancel; TAKE BACK ⟨*refused to ~ his harsh order*⟩ **b** to revoke (a contract) by restoring to the opposite party what was received from him/her **2** to make (e g a legislative act) void by order of the enacting authority or a superior authority; repeal [L *rescindere* to annul, fr *re- + scindere* to cut – more at SHED] – **rescinder** *n*, **rescindment** *n*

**rescission** /ri'sizh(ə)n/ *n* an act of rescinding [LL *rescission-, rescissio,* fr L *rescissus,* pp of *rescindere*]

**rescissory** /ri'sisəri/ *adj* serving or tending to rescind

**rescript** /'ree.skript/ *n* **1** a written answer of a Roman emperor or of a pope to a legal inquiry or petition **2** an official or authoritative order, decree, edict, or announcement **3** an act or instance of rewriting [L *rescriptum,* fr neut of *rescriptus,* pp of *rescribere* to write in reply, fr *re- + scribere* to write – more at SCRIBE]

**rescue** /'reskyooh/ *vt* to free from confinement, danger, or harm; save deliver ⟨*tried to ~ the drowning man*⟩: e g **a** to take (e g a prisoner) usu forcibly from (legal) custody **b** to recover (e g property) by force **c** to free (e g a place under siege) by armed force [ME *rescuen,* fr MF *rescourre,* fr OF, fr *re- + escourre* to shake out, fr L *excutere,* fr *ex- + quatere* to shake – more at QUASH] – **rescue** *n*, **rescuer** *n*

**rescue mission** *n* a religious mission in a city seeking to convert and rehabilitate down-and-outs

**¹research** /ri'suhch, 'reesuhch USE *the last pron is disliked by some speakers*/ *n* **1** careful or systematic search or inquiry **2** scientific or scholarly inquiry; *esp* study or experiment aimed at the discovery, interpretation, reinterpretation, or application of (new) facts, theories, or laws [MF *recerche,* fr *recerchier* to investigate thoroughly, fr OF, fr *re- + cerchier* to search – more at SEARCH]

*usage* The pronunciation /ri'suhch/, for both noun and verb, is recommended for BBC broadcasters.

**²research** *vt* **1** to search or investigate thoroughly ⟨*~ a problem*⟩ **2** to engage in research on or for ⟨*~ a book*⟩ ⟨*~ the life of Chaucer*⟩ ~ *vi* to perform research – **researchable** *adj*, **researcher** *n*, **researchist** *n, chiefly NAm*

**reseau, réseau** /'rezoh (*Fr* rezo)/ *n, pl* **reseaux, reseaus** /'rezoh(z) (*Fr* ~)/ **1** a regular network of lines superimposed on a photograph of stars to help in taking measurements **2** a net background or foundation in lace **3** a screen with minute elements of three colours in a regular geometric pattern used for taking colour photographs [Fr *réseau,* fr OF *resel,* dim. of *rais* net, fr L *retis, rete* – more at RETINA]

**resect** /ri'sekt/ *vt* to perform resection on [L *resectus,* pp of *resecare* to cut off, fr *re- + secare* to cut – more at SAW] – **resectable** *adj,* **resectability** *n*

**resection** /ri'seksh(ə)n/ *n* the surgical removal of part of an organ or structure (e g the intestines)

**¹reseda** /'residə/ *n* any of a genus (*Reseda* of the family Resedaceae) of European, esp Mediterranean, plants including mignonette, that have spikes of small whitish, yellow, or greenish flowers [NL, genus name, fr L, a plant used to reduce tumours]

**²reseda** *n* a greyish-green colour [Fr *réséda,* fr *réséda* reseda plant]

**reseed** /ˌree'seed/ *vt* **1** to sow seed on again or anew **2** to maintain (itself) by self-sown seed ~ *vi* to maintain itself by self-sown seed

**resemblance** /ri'zembləns/ *n* **1a** the quality or state of resembling; *esp* correspondence in appearance or superficial qualities **b** a point of likeness **2** a representation, image **3** *archaic* characteristic appearance *antonyms* difference, distinction

**resemble** /ri'zembl/ *vt* **1** to be like or similar to **2** *archaic* to represent as like [ME *resemblen,* fr MF *resembler,* fr OF, fr *re- + sembler* to be like, seem, fr L *similare* to copy, fr *similis* like – more at SAME] – **resemblant** *adj*

**resent** /ri'zent/ *vt* to harbour or express ill will or bitterness at *synonyms* see VINDICTIVE [Fr *ressentir* to feel strongly about, fr OF, fr *re- + sentir* to feel, fr L *sentire* – more at SENSE] – **resentful** *adj,* **resentfully** *adv,* **resentfulness** *n*

**resentment** /ri'zentmənt/ *n* a feeling of bitterness or persistent hurt and indignation at something regarded as an insult, injury, or injustice

*usage* One feels **resentment** *at* or *against* something. The use of *to* here ⟨*the* **resentment** *I feel to their proposal*⟩ is to be avoided.

**reserpine** /'resəpin/ *n* a chemical compound, $C_{33}H_{40}N_2O_9$, obtained esp from the root of RAUWOLFIA plants and used esp in the treatment of mildly raised blood pressure and formerly as a tranquillizer [Ger *reserpin,* prob irreg fr NL *Rauwolfia serpentina,* a species of rauwolfia]

**reservation** /ˌrezə'vaysh(ə)n/ *n* **1** an act of reserving something: e g **1a** a clause in a deed by which some right or interest is retained in property being transferred to another; *also* the right or interest so reserved **b** the specifying of conditions or limits to complete disclosure ⟨*answered without ~*⟩ **c** an arrangement to have something (e g a hotel room or a seat on a plane) held for one's use; *also* a promise, guarantee, or record of such a transaction **2** something reserved: e g **2a** a tract of public land set aside; *specif* one designated by treaty for the use of American Indians – compare RESERVE 2b, PRESERVE 2 **b** a strip of land separating carriageways; CENTRAL RESERVATION **3a** a limiting condition ⟨*agreed, but with ~s*⟩ **b** a specific doubt or objection ⟨*had ~s about the results*⟩ **4** *chiefly NAm* an area in which hunting is not permitted; *esp* one set aside as a secure breeding place *synonyms* see QUALM

**¹reserve** /ri'zuhv/ *vt* **1a** to hold in reserve; keep back ⟨*~ grain for seed*⟩ **b(1)** *of a religious superior* to retain power of absolution of (a kind of sin) to oneself **b(2)** to set aside (a portion of the consecrated bread and wine) at Communion for future use **c** to hold over for a future time or place defer ⟨*~ one's judgment on a plan*⟩ **d** to make legal reservation of **2** to set aside or apart for a particular reason or for one's own or another's use; book ⟨*~ a hotel room*⟩ *synonyms* see ¹KEEP [ME *reserven,* fr MF *reserver,* fr L *reservare,* lit., to keep back, fr *re- + servare* to keep – more at CONSERVE]

**²reserve** *n* **1** something retained for future use or need a stock **2** something reserved or set aside for a particular use or reason: e g **2a(1)** **reserves** *pl,* **reserve** a military force withheld from action for later decisive use **a(2)** the military forces of a country not part of the regular services; *also* a reservist **b** a tract (e g of public land) set apart for the protection and preservation of natural resources or (rare) plants and animals ⟨*a nature ~*⟩; *also* an area used primarily for regulated hunting or fishing – compare RESERVATION 2a, PRESERVE 2 **3** an act of reserving; qualification ⟨*accepted without ~*⟩ **4a** restraint, closeness, or caution in one's words and actions; reticence, shyness **b** forbearance from making a full explanation, complete disclosure, or candid expression of one's views **5** **reserves** *pl,* **reserve 5a** money or its equivalent kept in hand or set apart, usu to meet liabilities **b** the LIQUID resources (assets readily converted into cash) of a nation for meeting international payments **6** a player or participant who has been selected to substitute for another if the need should arise (e g through injury) **7** *archaic* a secret – **in reserve** held back ready for future or special use

**reserve bank** *n* a central bank holding reserves of other banks

**reserved** /ri'zuhvd/ *adj* **1** restrained in speech and behaviour **2** kept or set apart or aside for future or special use *synonyms* see SILENT *antonym* expansive – **reservedly** *adv,* **reservedness** *n*

**reserved power** *n* a political power reserved by a constitution to the exclusive jurisdiction of a specified political authority

**reserve price** *n* a price announced at an auction as the lowest that will be considered

**reservist** /ri'zuhvist/ *n* a member of a military reserve

**reservoir** /'rezə.vwah/ *n* **1** a place where something is kept in store: e g **1a** an artificial lake where water is collected and kept in quantity for use **b** a part of an apparatus in which a liquid or gas is held **2** a sac or cavity in an organism containing a body liquid or secretion **3** an available but unused extra source or supply; a reserve ⟨*a large untapped ~ of educated people*⟩ **4a** an organism in which a parasite that causes disease in some other species lives and multiplies without causing much damage **b** an organism of no economic significance within which a disease-causing agent (e g a virus) of economic or medical importance flourishes ⟨*foxes can be a ~ for rabies*⟩ [Fr *réservoir,* fr MF, fr *reserver* to reserve]

**reset** /ˌree'set/ *vt* **-tt-; reset 1** to set again or anew ⟨*~ type*⟩ ⟨*~ a diamond*⟩ **2** to change the reading of ⟨*~ a mileometer*⟩ – **resettable** *adj*

**res gestae** /ˌrayz 'gestie/ *n taking pl vb* facts which are immediately relevant to the subject matter of legal proceedings and are usu admissible as evidence [L, things done]

**resh** /raysh/ *n* the 20th letter of the Hebrew alphabet [Heb *rēsh*]

**reshape** /ˌree'shayp/ *vt* to give a new form or orientation to – **reshaper** *n*

**reship** /ˌree'ship/ *vb* -**pp**- *vt* to ship again: **a** to transfer from one ship to another **b** to put on board a second time ~ *vi* to embark on a ship again or anew; *specif* to sign again for service on a ship – **reshipment** *n*, **reshipper** *n*

**reshuffle** /ˌree'shufl/ *vt* **1** to shuffle (eg cards) again **2** to reorganize by the redistribution of (existing) elements ⟨*the cabinet was* ~d *by the Prime Minister*⟩ – **reshuffle** *n*

**reside** /ri'zied/ *vi* **1a** to be in residence as the holder of an office **b** to dwell permanently or continuously; occupy a place as one's legal home **c** to make one's home for a time ⟨*the King* ~d *at Lincoln*⟩ **2a** to be present as an element or quality; inhere **b** to be vested as a right ⟨*such powers* ~ *solely in the trustees*⟩ [ME *residen*, fr MF or L; MF *resider*, fr L *residēre* to sit back, remain, abide, fr *re-* + *sedēre* to sit – more at SIT] – **resider** *n*

**residence** /'rezid(ə)ns/ *n* **1a** the act or fact of dwelling in a place **b** the act or fact of living in or regularly attending some place for the discharge of a duty or the enjoyment of a benefit **2** a dwelling; *esp* one that is large or impressive **3a** the period during which one lives in a place ⟨*after a* ~ *of 30 years*⟩ **b** a period of active and esp full-time study, research, or teaching at a college or university **4** the persistence of a substance in a suspended or dissolved form in a particular place or medium ⟨*the* ~ *time of a pollutant in the atmosphere*⟩ **5** *chiefly NAm* housing or a unit of housing provided for students – **in residence 1** serving in a regular capacity ⟨*a poet* in residence *at a university*⟩ **2** actually living in a usu specified place ⟨*the Queen is* in residence *at Windsor*⟩

**residency** /'rezid(ə)nsi/ *n* **1** a usu official place of residence ⟨*the governor's* ~⟩ **2** *NAm* a period of advanced training as a medical specialist

¹**resident** /'rezid(ə)nt/ *adj* **1a** living in a place, esp for some length of time; residing **b** serving in a regular or full-time capacity ⟨*the* ~ *engineer for a highway department*⟩; *also* IN RESIDENCE ⟨~ *poet*⟩ **2** present, inherent **3** not migratory ⟨*a* ~ *species of thrush*⟩ [ME, fr L *resident-, residens,* prp of *residēre*]

²**resident** *n* **1** someone who lives in a place **2** a diplomatic agent ranking below an ambassador or HIGH COMMISSIONER and residing at a foreign court or seat of government; *esp* one exercising authority in a protected state as representative of the protecting power **3** *NAm* a physician serving a residency

**residential** /ˌrezi'densh(ə)l/ *adj* **1a** used as a residence or by residents ⟨~ *accommodation*⟩ **b** providing living accommodation for students ⟨*a* ~ *college*⟩ **c** involving residence ⟨*a* ~ *course*⟩ **2** given over to private housing as distinct from industry or commerce ⟨*a* ~ *neighbourhood*⟩ **3** of residence or residences – **residentially** *adv*

**residentiary** /ˌrezi'denshəri/ *n* an ecclesiastic who is bound to be in residence for a certain time

¹**residual** /ri'zidyooəl/ *adj* **1** of, being, or remaining as a residue **2** remaining in a body cavity after the maximum normal expulsion has occurred ⟨~ *urine*⟩ – compare RESIDUAL AIR **3** *of a deposit, soil, etc* formed by the weathering and disintegration of rock previously existing on the same site **4** leaving a residue that remains active or effective in the air, soil, etc for some time ⟨~ *insecticides*⟩ – **residually** *adv*

²**residual** *n* a remainder, residuum: eg **a** *statistics* the difference between a result obtained by observation and one obtained by computation from a formula, or between the MEAN (average) of a set of observations and any one of them **b** a product or substance remaining as a residue

**residual air** *n* the volume of air remaining in the lungs after the maximum amount has been forcibly exhaled

**residual power** *n* power held to remain at the disposal of a governmental authority after delegation of specified powers to other authorities

**residual volume** *n* RESIDUAL AIR

**residuary** /ri'zidyooəri/ *adj* of or constituting a residue

**residuary legatee** *n* a person who inherits what remains of an estate after specific bequests and charges have been met

**residue** /'rezidyooh/ *n* something that remains after a part, is taken, separated, or designated; a remnant, remainder: eg **a** that part of a deceased person's estate remaining after the discharge of debts and the payment of all bequests specified in a will **b** the remainder after subtracting a multiple of a MODULUS from an integer ⟨*2 and 7 are* ~s *of 12 modulo 5*⟩; *esp* the smallest nonnegative instance of such a residue **c(1)** a substance remaining after chemical processing (eg distillation) or treatment esp to extract something useful or valuable **c(2)** an insecticide, herbicide, etc or a breakdown product of this that remains active, usu as a harmful pollutant, in the environment for some time after use **d** a structural unit (eg a chemical group) that is a constituent of a usu complex chemical molecule ⟨*amino acid* ~s *left after breakdown of protein*⟩ [ME, fr MF *residu,* fr L *residuum,* fr neut of *residuus* left over, fr *residēre* to remain]

**residuum** /ri'zidyooəm/ *n, pl* **residua** /-yooə/ something residual: eg **a** the residue from a person's estate **b** a residual product (eg from the distillation of petroleum) [L]

**resign** /ri'zien/ *vt* **1** to renounce voluntarily; *esp* to relinquish (eg a right or position) by a formal act ⟨*will* ~ *her seat before the next election*⟩ **2** to reconcile, consign; *esp* to give (oneself) over without resistance ⟨~ed *himself to his fate*⟩ ~ *vi* to give up one's office or position [ME *resignen,* fr MF *resigner,* fr L *resignare,* lit., to unseal, cancel, fr *re-* + *signare* to sign, seal – more at SIGN] – **resigner** *n*

**resignation** /ˌrezig'naysh(ə)n/ *n* **1a** an act or instance of resigning something **b** a formal notification of resigning ⟨*handed in his* ~⟩ **2** the quality or state of being resigned; submissiveness

**resigned** /ri'ziend/ *adj* marked by or expressing submission to something regarded as inevitable ⟨*a* ~ *look on his face*⟩ – **resignedly** *adv*, **resignedness** *n*

**resile** /ri'ziel/ *vi* to recoil, retract; *esp* to return resiliently to a prior position [LL & L; LL *resilire* to withdraw, fr L, to recoil]

**resilience** /ri'zilyəns/, **resiliency** /-si/ *n* **1** the ability of a body to recover its original form after deformation (eg by applied pressure or stretching) **2** an ability to recover quickly from or adjust easily to misfortune, change, or disturbance

**resilient** /ri'zilyənt/ *adj* characterized or marked by resilience: eg **a** capable of withstanding shock without permanent deformation or rupture **b** tending to recover easily from misfortune or change [L *resilient-, resiliens,* prp of *resilire* to jump back, recoil, fr *re-* + *salire* to leap – more at SALLY] – **resiliently** *adv*

¹**resin** /'rezin/ *n* **1a** any of various solid and usu brittle or thick sticky substances (eg amber) that are obtained from secretions of, or are exuded by, plants (eg fir and pine trees), are usu transparent or translucent and yellowish to brown, are capable of being melted and are insoluble in water, and are used chiefly in varnishes, printing inks, plastics, etc and in medicine **b** ROSIN (brittle amber-coloured to black resin) **2a** any of a large class of synthetic materials that have some of the physical properties of natural resins but are different chemically, and that are used chiefly as plastics **b** any of various products made from a natural resin or another natural plant product (eg rubber) [ME, fr MF *resine,* fr L *resina,* fr Gk *rhētinē* pine resin]

²**resin** *vt* to treat with resin

**resinate** /'rezinayt/ *vt* to impregnate or flavour with a resin or resinous product ⟨*retsina is a* ~d *wine*⟩

**resin canal** *n* a canal or tubular space in the bark, wood, etc of some plants, esp conifers, that is lined with cells that secrete resin and ESSENTIAL OILS

**resin duct** *n* RESIN CANAL

**resiniferous** /ˌrezi'nif(ə)rəs/ *adj* producing or secreting resin

**resinify** /re'zinifie/ *vt* to convert into or treat with resin – **resinification** *n*

¹**resinoid** /'rezinoyd/ *adj* resembling resin; resinous

²**resinoid** *n* **1** a (somewhat) resinous or resinlike substance **2** any of various synthetic THERMOSETTING (becoming permanently rigid when heated) resins

**resinous** /'rezinəs/ *adj* of, resembling, containing, or derived from resin

¹**resist** /ri'zist/ *vt* **1** to withstand the force or effect of **2** to strive against; oppose ⟨~ed *the enemy valiantly*⟩ **3** to refrain from ⟨*could never* ~ *a joke*⟩ ~ *vi* to exert force in opposition [ME *resisten,* fr MF or L; MF *resister,* fr L *resistere,* fr *re-* + *sistere* to take a stand; akin to L *stare* to stand – more at STAND] – **resistible** *adj,* **resistibility** *n*

²**resist** *n* something (eg a protective coating) applied to a surface to cause it to resist or prevent the action of a particular substance (eg an acid or dye) on it

**resistance** /ri'zist(ə)ns/ *n* **1** an act or instance of resisting; opposition **2** the ability to resist; *esp* the inherent capacity of a plant, animal, species, etc to resist adverse circumstances (eg disease, malnutrition, or poisons) ⟨*wheat strains with high ~ to fungal infections*⟩ **3** an opposing or retarding force **4a** the opposition offered by a body (eg an electrical component), circuit, or substance to the passage through it of a steady electric current; *also* the measure of resistance equal to the ratio of the voltage across a conductor to the current flowing through it **b** a source of resistance **5** *taking sing or pl vb, often cap* an underground organization of a conquered country engaging in sabotage and secret operations against occupation forces and collaborators

  *usage* Resistance should not be followed by an infinitive verb ⟨*their strong resistance to being* (not ⚠ *to be*) amalgamated⟩.

**¹resistant** /ri'zist(ə)nt/ *adj* capable of or offering resistance – often in combination ⟨*heat-*resistant *paint*⟩

**²resistant** *n* one who or that which resists

**resister** /ri'zistə/ *n, chiefly NAm* one who or that which resists; *esp* one who actively opposes the policies of a government

**resistive** /ri'zistiv/ *adj* resistant – **resistively** *adv*, **resistiveness** *n*

**resistivity** /ˌrezis'tivəti/ *n* **1** capacity for resisting or opposing something; resistance **2** (a measure of) the ability of a substance (eg copper) to resist the passage through it of an electric current, equal to the electrical resistance of a unit volume (eg a cubic metre) of the substance – compare CONDUCTIVITY

**resistless** /ri'zistlis/ *adj* **1** impossible to resist; irresistible **2** unable to resist – **resistlessly** *adv*, **resistlessness** *n*

**resistor** /ri'zistə/ *n* a component having electrical resistance; *specif* one included in an electrical circuit to provide a known resistance

**resit** /ˌree'sit/ *vt* **-tt-**; **resat** *Br* to take (an examination) again after failing – **resit** *n*

**res judicata** /ˌrayz yoohdi'kahtə, joohdi-, reez/ *n* a matter finally decided by a court and not subject to being raised or contested in court again by the same parties unless the decision is amended on appeal to a higher court [L, judged matter]

**resojet engine** /'rezohjet/ *n* a JET ENGINE that consists of a continuously open air inlet, a device for diffusing the air, a combustion chamber, and an exhaust nozzle, has fuel admitted continuously, and has resonance established within the engine so that there is a pulsating thrust produced by the intermittent flow of hot gases [*resonance* + *jet* + *engine*]

**resoluble** /ri'zolyoobl, 'rezəlyoobl/ *adj* capable of being resolved [LL *resolubilis*, fr L *resolvere* to resolve]

**resolute** /'rezəl(y)ooht/ *adj* **1** firmly resolved; determined **2** bold, unwavering [L *resolutus*, pp of *resolvere*] – **resolutely** *adv*, **resoluteness** *n*

**resolution** /ˌrezə'loohsh(ə)n, -'lyoohsh(ə)n/ *n* **1** the act or process of reducing to simpler form: eg **1a** the act of analysing a complex notion into its constituents; reduction **b** the act of making a firm decision; determination **c** the act of finding out something (eg the answer to a problem); solving **d** the passing of a voice part from a discordant (DISSONANT) to a harmonious sounding (CONCORDANT or CONSONANT) note or the progression of a chord from discord to agreeable harmony **e** the separating of a chemical compound or mixture into its constituents; *specif* the separation of a RACEMIC compound or mixture into its two forms **f(1)** the division of an element of poetry or verse into its component parts **f(2)** the substitution in Greek or Latin PROSODY (systems of verse construction) of two short syllables for a long syllable **g** the analysis of a vector into two or more vectors of which it is the sum **h** RESOLVING POWER; *also* the act or process of making adjacent or closely spaced parts, objects, events, etc distinguishable **2** the natural subsidence of a disease process or symptom and the return of the affected tissue to a normal condition; *esp* the subsidence of inflammation (eg in a lung) **3a** something that is resolved; *esp* a statement of firm intent ⟨*my New Year* ~s⟩ **b** firmness of resolve; steadfastness **4** a formal expression of opinion, will, or intent voted by an official (eg legislative) body or assembled group

**¹resolve** /ri'zolv/ *vt* **1a** to break up or separate into constituent parts ⟨*the prism* ~d *the light into a play of colour*⟩; *also* to change by disintegration **b** to reduce by analysis ⟨~ *the problem into simple elements*⟩ **c** to separate adjacent parts, images, etc of and make distinguishable or independently visible **d** to separate (a chemical compound or mixture) into the constituents; *specif* to separate (a RACEMIC compound or mixture) into the two component forms **2** to cause the resolution or subsi-

dence of (eg an inflammation) **3a** to deal with successfully; settle ⟨~ *doubts*⟩ ⟨~ *a dispute*⟩ **b** to bring to a satisfactory conclusion ⟨*the illness* ~d *itself*⟩ **c** to find an answer to **d** to make clear or understandable; explain **e** to find a mathematical solution of **f** to express (eg a vector) as the sum of two or more components, esp in assigned directions **4** to reach a firm decision about ⟨~ *to get more sleep*⟩ ⟨~ *disputed points in a text*⟩ **5** to declare or decide by a formal resolution and vote **6** *music* to make (eg voice parts) progress from discord (DISSONANCE) to agreeable harmony (CONSONANCE or CONCORDANCE) **7** to work out the resolution of (eg a play) **8** *obs* to dissolve, melt ~ *vi* **1** to become separated into constituent parts; *also* to become reduced by dissolving or analysis **2** to form a resolution; determine ⟨*he* ~d *against overeating at Christmas*⟩ **3** *music* to progress from discord to agreeable harmony [L *resolvere* to unloose, dissolve, fr *re-* + *solvere* to loosen, release – more at SOLVE] – **resolvable** *adj*, **resolver** *n*

**²resolve** *n* **1** something that is resolved **2** fixity of purpose; resoluteness **3** a legal or official decision; *esp* a formal resolution

**¹resolvent** /ri'zolv(ə)nt/ *adj* having power to resolve ⟨*a ~ drug*⟩ [L *resolvent-*, *resolvens*, prp of *resolvere*]

**²resolvent** *n* **1** a drug or other agent capable of reducing inflammation **2** a solvent **3** a means of solving or helping to solve something

**resolving power** /ri'zolving/ *n* **1** the ability of an instrument or system to distinguish between objects, events, etc that are very close in time or space: eg **1a** the ability of a microscope, telescope, etc or of the eye to form distinct and separate images of objects separated by small distances **b** the ability of a SPECTROMETER (device for splitting light, sound, etc into its components) to separate and distinguish between nearly identical wavelengths or particles of nearly the same energy or mass **2** the ability of a photographic film or plate to reproduce the fine detail of an optical image

**resonance** /'rezənəns/ *n* **1a** the quality or state of being resonant **b(1)** (a) strong vibration set up in a mechanical or electrical system by the stimulus of a relatively small periodic vibration of (nearly) the same frequency as the natural frequency of vibration of the system **b(2)** the state of adjustment of a mechanical or electrical system that results in resonance **2a** the intensification and enrichment of a musical tone by added vibration **b** a quality imparted to speech sounds by a buildup esp of vibrations in the mouth and throat and in some cases also in the nostrils **3** the sound produced by tapping on a hollow body part, esp the chest (eg to find out the condition of the lungs) **4** a phenomenon shown by a molecule, ion, or chemical group to which two or more possible structures differing only in the distribution of electrons can be assigned, that gives rise to a stable structure intermediate among the assigned structures **5** the enhancement of an atomic, nuclear, or particle reaction resulting from an increase in the energy of the particles in the atom or atomic nucleus **6** any of various extremely short-lived ELEMENTARY PARTICLES (minute particles of matter) that appear as intermediates in interactions between other elementary particles

**resonant** /'rezənənt/ *adj* **1** continuing to sound; echoing **2a** capable of inducing resonance **b** relating to or exhibiting resonance **3a** intensified and enriched by resonance **b** marked by grand or pompous language ⟨*a new and more* ~ *sort of headline* – H G Wells⟩ – **resonant** *n*, **resonantly** *adv*

**resonate** /'rezə,nayt/ *vi* **1** to produce or exhibit resonance **2** to respond as if by resonance ⟨*a child learning to talk* ~s *to his family*⟩ ~ *vt* to make resonant [L *resonatus*, pp of *resonare* to resound – more at RESOUND]

**resonator** /'rezənaytə/ *n* something that resounds or resonates: eg **a** a device for increasing the resonance of a musical instrument **b** a device that resonates in response to waves (eg sound waves) or vibrations of a particular frequency and can therefore detect that frequency when in combination with others

**resorb** /ri'sawb/ *vt* **1** to swallow or suck in again; reabsorb **2** to break down and incorporate (a previously differentiated tissue or structure) into the surrounding tissue ~ *vi* to undergo resorption [L *resorbēre*, fr *re-* + *sorbēre* to suck up – more at ABSORB]

**resorcinol** /ri'zawsinol/ *also* **resorcin** /ri'zawsin/ *n* a chemical compound, $C_6H_4(OH)_2$ that is a PHENOL, is obtained from various natural resins or made artificially, and is used esp in making dyes and resins, and in lotions and ointments for the treatment of various skin conditions (eg acne) [ISV *res-* (fr L *resina* resin) + *orcin* (a phenol, $CH_3C_6H_3(OH)_2$) + *-ol*]

**resorption** /ri'sawpsh(ə)n/ *n* resorbing or being resorbed ⟨~ *of the root of a tooth*⟩ [L *resorptus*, pp of *resorbēre*] – **resorptive** *adj*

¹**resort** /ri'zawt/ *n* **1a** one who or that which is looked to for help; a refuge, resource ⟨*saw him as a last* ~⟩ **b** recourse ⟨*have* ~ *to force*⟩ **2a** a frequently visited place; a haunt **b** an attractively situated town or village providing accommodation and recreation for holidaymakers *usage* see RECOURSE [ME, fr MF, resource, recourse, fr *resortir* to rebound, resort, fr OF, fr *re-* + *sortir* to escape, sally] **3** *formal* frequent, habitual, or general visiting ⟨*a place of popular* ~⟩

²**resort** *vi, formal* to go, esp frequently or in large numbers; repair

**resort to** *vt* to have recourse to ⟨*resort to force*⟩

**resound** /ri'zownd/ *vi* **1** to become filled with sound; reverberate **2a** to sound loudly **b** to produce a sonorous or echoing sound ⟨*let the trumpet* ~⟩ **3** to become renowned ⟨*a name to* ~ *for ages* – Alfred Tennyson⟩ ~ *vt* **1** to extol loudly or widely; celebrate **2** to echo, reverberate *synonyms* see ¹REBOUND [ME *resounen*, fr MF *resoner*, fr L *resonare*, fr *re-* + *sonare* to sound; akin to L *sonus* sound – more at SOUND]

**resounding** /ri'zownding/ *adj* **1a** producing or characterized by resonant sound; resonating **b** impressively sonorous **2** vigorously emphatic; unequivocal ⟨*a* ~ *success*⟩ – **resoundingly** *adv*

¹**resource** /ri'zaws, ri'saws; *also* 'reesaws USE *the last pron is disliked by some speakers*/ *n* **1a** *usu pl* **1a(1)** an available means of support or provision **a(2)** a natural source of wealth or revenue – compare NATURAL RESOURCES **b** *pl* calculable wealth **2** a source of information or expertise **3** something to which one has recourse in difficulty an expedient **4** a possibility of relief or recovery ⟨*lost without* ~⟩ **5** a means of occupying one's spare time **6** the ability to deal with a difficult situation; resourcefulness *usage* see RECOURSE [Fr *ressource*, fr OF *ressourse* relief, resource, fr *resourdre* to relieve, lit., to rise again, fr L *resurgere* – more at RESURRECTION]

²**resource** *vt* to equip or supply with resources

**resourceful** /-f(ə)l/ *adj* skilful in handling situations; capable of devising expedients; enterprising – **resourcefully** *adv*, **resourcefulness** *n*

¹**respect** /ri'spekt/ *n* **1** a relation *to* or concern with something usu specified; reference – in *in respect to, with respect to* ⟨*with* ~ *to your last letter*⟩ **2** particular attention; consideration ⟨*performed without* ~ *to rhythm*⟩ **3a** high or special regard; esteem **b** the quality or state of being esteemed ⟨*achieving* ~ *among connoisseurs*⟩ **c** *pl* expressions of respect or deference ⟨*paid his* ~s⟩ **4** an aspect, detail ⟨*a good plan in some* ~s⟩ [ME, fr L *respectus*, lit., act of looking back, fr *respectus*, pp of *respicere* to look back, regard, fr *re-* + *specere* to look – more at SPY] – **in respect of 1** from the point of view of **2** in payment of

²**respect** *vt* **1a** to consider worthy of high regard; esteem **b** to refrain from interfering with ⟨~ *the sovereignty of a state*⟩ **c** to show consideration for ⟨~ *a person's privacy*⟩ **2** to have reference to; concern *synonyms* see ²REGARD *antonyms* despise, misuse – **respecter** *n* – **as respects** with respect to; IN REGARD TO

¹**respectable** /ri'spektəbl/ *adj* **1** worthy of respect; estimable **2** decent or conventional in character or conduct; proper **3a** acceptable in size or quantity ⟨~ *amount*⟩ **b** fairly good; tolerable **4** fit to be seen; presentable ⟨~ *clothes*⟩ – **respectableness** *n*, **respectably** *adv*, **respectability** *n*

²**respectable** *n* a respectable person

**respectful** /-f(ə)l/ *adj* marked by or showing respect or deference – **respectfully** *adv*, **respectfulness** *n*

**respecting** /ri'spekting/ *prep* **1** in view of; considering **2** with regard to; concerning

**respective** /ri'spektiv/ *adj* of each; particular, separate ⟨*their* ~ *homes*⟩ – **respectiveness** *n*

*usage* The proper use of **respective** and **respectively** is to clarify the relationships between two groups. In ⟨*he and I sat by our respective telephones* (= he by his and I by mine)⟩ **respective** is necessary, since otherwise we might be sitting together surrounded by a group of telephones; but in ⟨*he was educated at Harrow and Trinity respectively*⟩ **respectively** is unnecessary, since only one man is involved, and it should be omitted or replaced by *both*. ⚠ respectable, respectful

**respectively** /ri'spektivli/ *adv* **1** as distinct from others; separately ⟨*could not recognize the solutions as salty or sour,* ~⟩ **2** in the order given ⟨*Mary and Anne were* ~ *12 and 16*

*years old*⟩

**respectworthy** /ri'spekt,wuhdhi/ *adj* deserving respect

**respell** /,ree'spel/ *vt* to spell again or in another way, esp according to a phonetic system

**respirable** /'respirəbl, ri'spie·ərəbl/ *adj* fit for breathing; *also* capable of being taken in by breathing ⟨~ *particles of ash*⟩

**respiration** /,respi'raysh(ə)n/ *n* **1a** the physical process (e g breathing) by which air or dissolved gases from an organism's surroundings are taken into the body and brought into contact with the blood or other liquid circulating in the organism ⟨*most fishes use gills in* ~⟩ **b** a single complete act of breathing **2** the physical and chemical processes by which an organism's cells and tissues are supplied with the oxygen needed for life-supporting processes and by which carbon dioxide formed in energy-producing reactions inside the cells is removed **3** any of the various chemical processes, occurring in all living cells, by which food substances (e g glucose and fats) are broken down to yield energy, and that in most animals and plants involves the use of oxygen and the production of carbon dioxide as a waste product – **respirational, respiratory** *adj*

**respirator** /'respi,raytə/ *n* **1** a device worn over the mouth or nose to prevent the breathing in of poisonous gases, harmful dusts, etc **2** a device for providing ARTIFICIAL RESPIRATION, esp over a long period

**respiratory pigment** /'respirət(ə)ri, ri'spirət(ə)ri, ri'spie·ərət(ə)ri/ *n* any of various permanently or intermittently coloured complex proteins that function in the respiration of living cells: **a** a protein (e g haemoglobin) that loosely combines with and transports oxygen in the blood or other circulating liquid or that functions in its transfer from there to cells and tissues **b** a protein (e g a CYTOCHROME) that functions in the transfer of electrons between chemical compounds in energy-producing reactions inside cells

**respiratory quotient** *n* the ratio of the volume of CARBON DIOXIDE given off in respiration to that of the oxygen used

**respiratory system** *n* a system of organs carrying out the function of respiration which, in mammals, reptiles, birds, etc, consists typically of the lungs and their nervous and circulatory systems and the channels by which these are connected with the outer air

**respire** /ri'spie·ə/ *vi* **1** to breathe; *specif* to alternately inhale and exhale air **2** *of a cell or tissue* to take up oxygen and produce CARBON DIOXIDE during respiration to breathe [ME *respiren*, fr L *respirare*, fr *re-* + *spirare* to blow, breathe – more at SPIRIT]

¹**respite** /'respit, 'respiet/ *n* **1** a period of temporary delay; *esp* a formal delay in the execution of a sentence; a reprieve **2** an interval of rest or relief [ME *respit*, fr OF, fr ML *respectus*, fr L, act of looking back – more at RESPECT]

²**respite** *vt, formal* **1** to grant respite to **2** to put off; delay

**resplendent** /ri'splend(ə)nt/ *adj* shining brilliantly; characterized by splendour ⟨*the Queen sat* ~ *on her throne*⟩ [L *resplendent-, resplendens*, prp of *resplendēre* to shine back, fr *re-* + *splendēre* to shine – more at SPLENDID] – **resplendently** *adv*, **resplendence** *n*

¹**respond** /ri'spond/ *vi* **1** to write or speak in reply; make an answer ⟨~ *to the appeal for aid*⟩ **2a** to react in response ⟨~ *to a stimulus*⟩ **b** to show favourable reaction ⟨~ *to surgery*⟩ to reply *synonyms* see ²ANSWER [MF *respondre*, fr L *respondēre* to promise in return, answer, fr *re-* + *spondēre* to promise – more at SPOUSE]

²**respond** *n* a pillar or pier partly embedded in a wall and supporting an arch or occurring at the end of a colonnade or arcade

¹**respondent** /ri'spond(ə)nt/ *n* **1** someone who responds: e g **1a** someone who defends a thesis in answer to objections **b(1)** a defendant in legal proceedings started by petition or appeal; *esp* a person against whom a petition is brought in a divorce case **c** a person who replies to a poll **2** a reflex action that occurs in response to a specific external stimulus [L *respondent-, respondens*, prp of *respondēre*]

²**respondent** *adj* making response; responsive: e g **a** being a respondent at law **b** of or being an action that is a respondent; *esp* of, being, or resulting from the psychological conditioning of an animal to perform a particular reflex action (e g salivation) in response to a specific external stimulus (e g the ringing of a bell)

**responder** /ri'spondə/ *n* one who or that which responds; *esp* the part of a TRANSPONDER (radio device that automatically transmits in response to a received signal) that transmits a radio signal

**response** /ri'spons/ *n* **1** an act of responding **2** something constituting a reply or reaction: eg **2a** a verse, phrase, or word sung or said by the congregation or choir after or in reply to the minister in a religious service **b** a change in the biochemical, physiological, or physical activity of an organism or any of its parts resulting from stimulation **c** the ratio of the power produced by an electrical system to the power put into the system **d** a bid made in bridge on the basis of a partner's bid [ME & L; ME *respounse*, fr MF *respons*, fr L *responsum* reply, fr neut of *responsus*, pp of *respondēre*]

**responsibility** /ri͵sponsə'biləti/ *n* **1** the quality or state of being responsible: eg **1a** moral or legal obligation **b** reliability, trustworthiness **2** something or someone that one is responsible for; a burden, concern

**responsible** /ri'sponsəbl/ *adj* **1a** liable to be required to justify **b(1)** liable to be called to account as the agent or primary cause ⟨*the woman ~ for the job*⟩ **b(2)** being the reason or cause ⟨*mechanical defects were ~ for the accident*⟩ **2a** able to answer for one's own conduct; trustworthy **b** able to discriminate between right and wrong and therefore accountable for one's actions ⟨*legally ~*⟩ **3** marked by or involving responsibility or liability ⟨*~ financial policies*⟩ ⟨*a ~ job*⟩ **4** *esp* of the British cabinet politically answerable; *esp* required to submit to the electorate if defeated by the legislature – **responsibleness** *n*, **responsibly** *adv*

*usage* The use of **responsible** with reference to impersonal causes, as in sense 1b(2), is accepted in American English but disliked by some users of British English, who feel that only a person or human group can be **responsible** *for* something.

**responsions** /ri'sponsh(ə)nz/ *n pl* an examination formerly required to qualify for entry as an undergraduate at Oxford university

**responsive** /ri'sponsiv/ *adj* **1** giving response; constituting a response; answering ⟨*a ~ glance*⟩ ⟨*~ aggression*⟩ **2** quick to respond or react appropriately or sympathetically; sensitive **3** using responses ⟨*~ worship*⟩ – **responsively** *adv*, **responsiveness** *n*

**responsor** /ri'sponsə, -saw/ *n* a radio or radar device that receives the signal transmitted by a TRANSPONDER (device that automatically transmits in response to a received signal) – compare INTERROGATOR

**responsory** /ri'spons(ə)ri/ *n* a set of phrases and responses sung or said after a reading in church

**responsum** /ri'sponsəm/ *n, pl* **responsa** /-sə/ a written decision from a rabbi or Jewish scholar in response to a submitted question or problem [NL, fr L, reply, formal opinion of a legal adviser]

**res publica** /͵rayz 'pooblikə, ͵reez 'publikə/ *n* the commonwealth, state, or republic [L – more at REPUBLIC]

**ressentiment** /rə'sontimonh (*Fr* rəsãtimã)/ *n* resentment expressed indirectly, esp in scorn for values of a dominant individual or class [Fr, resentment, fr *ressentir* to resent]

**¹rest** /rest/ *n* **1** repose, sleep; *specif* a body state characterized by minimal biochemical, physical, and mental activity **2a** freedom or a break from activity or labour **b** a state of motionlessness or inactivity **3** a place for resting, lodging, or taking refreshment ⟨*sailor's ~*⟩ **4** peace of mind or spirit; tranquillity **5a** (a character representing) silence of a fixed duration in music **b** a brief pause in reading **6** something (eg an armrest) used for support; *esp* a pole with a usu cross-shaped support at one end on which a snooker or billiards player rests his/her cue when playing a ball too far away to be reached using the hand as a support **7** *euph* the repose of death [ME, fr OE, rest, bed; akin to OHG *rasta* rest, *ruowa* calm, Gk *erōē* respite] – **at rest** resting or reposing, esp in sleep or death

**²rest** *vi* **1** to relax by lying down; *esp* to sleep **2** to cease from action or motion; desist from labour or exertion **3** to be free from anxiety or disturbance **4** to be set or lie fixed or supported ⟨*a column ~s on its pedestal*⟩ **5** to be based or founded ⟨*the verdict ~ed on several sound precedents*⟩ **6** to depend for action or accomplishment ⟨*the answer ~s with him*⟩ **7** of farmland to remain idle or uncultivated **8** to voluntarily stop introducing evidence in a law case ⟨*the defence ~s*⟩ **9** *euph* to lie dead ⟨*~ in peace*⟩ ~ *vt* **1** to give rest to **2** to set at rest **3** to place on or against a support **4a** to cause to be firmly based or founded ⟨*~ed all hope in his son*⟩ **b** to stop voluntarily from presenting evidence pertinent to (a case at law) – **rester** *n*

**³rest** *n* a projection or attachment on the side of the breastplate of medieval armour for supporting the butt of a lance [ME *reste*, lit., stoppage, short for *areste*, fr MF, fr OF, fr *arester* to arrest]

**⁴rest** *n taking sing or pl vb* a collection or quantity that remains over; the remainder ⟨*ate the ~ of the chocolate*⟩ [ME, fr MF *reste*, fr *rester* to remain, fr L *restare*, lit., to stand back, fr *re- + stare* to stand – more at STAND]

**restage** /͵ree'stayj/ *vt* to present again on the stage

**restate** /͵ree'stayt/ *vt* to state again or in a different way (eg more emphatically) – **restatement** *n*

**restaurant** /'rest(ə)ronh, -ront, -rənt/ *n* a place where refreshments, esp meals, are sold, usu to be eaten on the premises [Fr, fr prp of *restaurer* to restore, fr L *restaurare*]

*usage* The pronunciation /'rest(ə)ronh/ is recommended for BBC broadcasters.

**restaurant car** *n, Br* DINING CAR

**restauranteur** /͵rest(ə)ron'tuh/ *n* a restaurateur [by alter.]

**restaurateur** /͵rest(ə)rə'tuh, ͵resto-/ *n* the manager or proprietor of a restaurant [Fr, fr LL *restaurator* restorer, fr L *restauratus*, pp of *restaurare*]

**restful** /'restf(ə)l/ *adj* **1** marked by, affording, or suggesting rest and repose; soothing ⟨*a ~ colour scheme*⟩ **2** at rest; quiet, tranquil *synonyms* see COMFORTABLE – **restfully** *adv*, **restfulness** *n*

**rest home** *n* a home for old people

**resting** /'resting/ *adj* **1a** of or characterized by dormancy or lack of growth; *esp* being or undergoing a period of dormancy before germination ⟨*a ~ spore*⟩ ⟨*bulbs in the ~ stage*⟩ **b** not physiologically active ⟨*a ~ nerve cell*⟩ **2** of a cell or cell nucleus not currently undergoing or concerned with CELL DIVISION **3** *euph, esp* of an actor or actress out of work

**restitute** /'restityooht/ *vb, formal vt* to hand back; refund ⟨*compelled to ~ the territory*⟩ ~ *vi* to make restitution [L *restitutus*, pp]

**restitution** /͵resti'tyoohsh(ə)n/ *n* **1** the act of restoring or condition of being restored: eg **1a** the returning of something (eg property) to its rightful owner **b** the making good of or giving a compensation for an injury **2** a legal action serving to cause restoration of a previous state (eg by returning goods or money) **3** the restoration of something to a former state, shape, or position [ME, fr OF, fr L *restitution-, restitutio*, fr *restitutus*, pp of *restituere* to restore, fr *re- + statuere* to set up – more at STATUTE]

**restive** /'restiv/ *adj* **1** stubbornly resisting control; refractory **2** marked by restlessness or unease; fidgety [ME, *restif* (of animals) stationary, refusing to move, fr MF, fr *rester* to stop behind, remain] – **restively** *adv*, **restiveness** *n*

**restless** /-lis/ *adj* **1** giving no rest ⟨*a ~ night*⟩ **2** continuously agitated; unquiet ⟨*the ~ ocean*⟩ **3** characterized by or indicating unrest, esp of mind ⟨*~ pacing*⟩; *also* changeful, discontented – **restlessly** *adv*, **restlessness** *n*

**rest mass** *n, physics* the mass of a body when it is at rest relative to the observer

**restoration** /͵restə'raysh(ə)n/ *n* **1** the act of restoring or condition of being restored: eg **1a** a bringing back to a former position or condition; reinstatement ⟨*the ~ of the monarch*⟩ **b** a handing back of something; restitution **c** a restoring to an original or undamaged condition ⟨*the ~ of a painting*⟩ **d** the replacing of missing teeth or crowns **2** something that is restored; *specif* a representation or reconstruction of the original form (eg of a fossil or a building) **3** *cap* **3a** the reestablishment of the monarchy in England in 1660 under Charles II ⚠ Reformation, Renaissance **b** the period in English history during the reign of Charles II but sometimes also including the reign of James II ⟨*Restoration drama*⟩

**¹restorative** /ri'stawrətiv/ *adj* of restoration; *esp* having power to restore health or vigour – **restoratively** *adv*, **restorativeness** *n*

**²restorative** *n* something that serves to restore to consciousness, vigour, or health

**restore** /ri'staw/ *vt* **1** to give back; return ⟨*~ the book to its owner*⟩ **2** to bring back into existence or use **3** to bring back to or put back into a former or original (undamaged) state ⟨*~ a painting*⟩ **4** to put again in possession of something (eg territory or rights) ⟨*newly ~d to health*⟩ [ME *restoren*, fr OF *restorer*, fr L *restaurare* to renew, rebuild, alter. of *instaurare* to renew – more at STORE] – **restorable** *adj*, **restorer** *n*

**restrain** /ri'strayn/ *vt* **1a** to prevent *from* doing something ⟨*~ed the boy from jumping*⟩ **b** to limit, repress, or keep under control; check ⟨*he found it hard to ~ his anger*⟩ **2** to deprive of liberty; *esp* to place under arrest [ME *restraynen*, fr MF

**restraindre**, fr L *restringere* to restrain, restrict, fr *re-* + *stringere* to bind tight – more at STRAIN] – **restrainable** *adj*, **restrainer** *n*

**synonyms** Restrain, check, curb, bridle, and inhibit all mean "hold back from doing something". **Restrain** implies the use of either force or persuasion, often for the good of the one restrained or with a moderating effect. **Check, curb,** and **bridle,** from their association with horsemanship, suggest the restraining of a forward impetus, **curb** implying a more drastic restraint than **check** ⟨*curb the power of a monarch*⟩ and **bridle** indicating a steady holding back from excess, particularly of the emotions and passions. **Inhibit** implies prohibition rather than prevention, and suggests that free activity is discouraged by moral or social means. *antonyms* impel, incite, activate, abandon (oneself)

**restrained** /ri'straynd/ *adj* characterized by restraint; without excess or extravagance; subdued – **restrainedly** *adv*

**restraint** /ri'straynt/ *n* **1a** restraining or being restrained **b** a means of restraining; a restraining force or influence **2** control over the expression of one's emotions or thoughts; moderation of one's behaviour; self-restraint [ME, fr MF *restrainte*, fr *restraindre*]

**restrict** /ri'strikt/ *vt* **1** to confine within bounds; restrain **2** to regulate or limit as to use or distribution [L *restrictus*, pp of *restringere*]

**restricted** /ri'striktid/ *adj* **1** subject or subjected to restriction: eg **1a** not general; limited ⟨*the decision had a ~ effect*⟩ **b** available only to particular groups or for a particular purpose **c** not intended for general circulation or release ⟨*a ~ document*⟩ – compare CONFIDENTIAL, SECRET, TOP SECRET **d** subject to control, esp by law ⟨*in Britain the sale of cigarettes is ~*⟩ **2** narrow and shut in; confined ⟨*a very ~ space*⟩ – **restrictedly** *adv*

**restricted area** *n* **1** *Br* an area in which there is a speed limit or parking restrictions for vehicles **2** *NAm* an area from which certain groups, esp military personnel, are excluded

¹**restriction** /ri'striksh(ə)n/ *n* **1** something that restricts: eg **1a** a regulation that restricts or restrains ⟨*speeds ~s for motorists*⟩ **b** a limitation on the use or enjoyment of something (eg a facility) **2** restricting or being restricted

²**restriction** *adj* of, resulting from the action of, or being a RESTRICTION ENZYME

**restriction endonuclease** *n* RESTRICTION ENZYME

**restriction enzyme** *n* any of various ENZYMES that promote the breaking of DNA strands into fragments at specific sites, and are extensively used in genetic research

**restrictionism** /ri'strikshəniz(ə)m/ *n* a policy or philosophy advocating restriction (e g of trade) – **restrictionist** *adj or n*

**restrictive** /ri'striktiv/ *adj* **1** restricting or tending to restrict ⟨*~ regulations*⟩ **2** identifying rather than describing a modified word or phrase ⟨*a ~ clause*⟩ – **restrictive** *n*, **restrictively** *adv*, **restrictiveness** *n*

**restrictive practice** *n, Br* **1** a practice by the members of a trade union that limits the flexibility of management (eg by hindering the efficient and economic running of a business) **2** a trading agreement (e g as to conditions of sale or quantities to be manufactured) that is against the public interest

**restrike** /'ree,striek/ *n* a coin or medal struck from an original die at some time after the original issue

**rest room** *n, NAm* public toilet facilities in a hotel, restaurant, or similar public place

**restructure** /,ree'strukchə/ *vt* to change the make up, organization, or pattern of ⟨*~ local government*⟩ *~ vi* to restructure something

¹**result** /ri'zult/ *vi* **1** to proceed or arise as a consequence, effect, or conclusion, usu *from* something specified ⟨*injuries ~ing from skiing*⟩ **2** to have a usu specified outcome or result ⟨*errors that ~ in tragedy*⟩ **3** *law* to return property *to* its original owner or his/her heirs after a period during which it has been controlled by somebody else; REVERT 2 [ME *resulten*, fr ML *resultare*, fr L, to rebound, fr *re-* + *saltare* to leap – more at SALTATION]

²**result** *n* **1** something that results as a consequence, outcome,

or conclusion; *also* a beneficial or tangible effect **2** something obtained by calculation or investigation ⟨*showed us the ~ of the calculations*⟩ **3a** *pl* a candidate's level of performance in an examination ⟨*her ~s in maths were better than last year*⟩; *also* (official) notification of this **b** the outcome of a sporting contest; *esp* a win ⟨*Brighton will have to play above themselves to bring home a ~ from any of their final away games*⟩ **c** the broadcast or published listing of sports results – **resultful** *adj*, **resultfulness** *n*, **resultless** *adj*

¹**resultant** /ri'zult(ə)nt/ *adj* derived or resulting from something else, esp as the total effect of many causes – **resultantly** *adv*

²**resultant** *n* something that results; an outcome; *specif* the single vector that is the sum of a given set of vectors

**resume** /ri'zyoohm/ *vt* **1** to take up or assume again; reoccupy ⟨*~d her place in society*⟩ ⟨*~d his seat by the fire* – Thomas Hardy⟩ **2** to return to or begin again after interruption ⟨*~d her work*⟩ ⟨*~d working*⟩ **3** to take back to oneself ⟨*he will ~ his title*⟩ **4** to summarize, recapitulate *~ vi* to begin again after an interruption ⟨*the meeting will ~ after lunch*⟩ [ME *resumen*, fr MF or L; MF *resumer*, fr L *resumere*, fr *re-* + *sumere* to take up, take – more at CONSUME]

**résumé, resume, resumé** /'rezyoo,may/ *n* a summary: e g **a** a summing up (e g of a speech or narrative, often prior to its continuation ⟨*a ~ of the discussion so far*⟩ **b** *NAm* CURRICULUM VITAE (details of a person's career, qualifications, etc) [Fr *résumé*, fr pp of *résumer* to resume, summarize]

**resumption** /ri'zumpsh(ə)n/ *n* an act or instance of resuming; a recommencement [ME, fr MF or LL; MF *resomption*, fr LL *resumption-*, *resumptio*, fr L *resumptus*, pp of *resumere*]

**resupinate** /ri'syoohpinət/ *adj, of a plant part* inverted in position; *also* appearing twisted so as to be upside down [L *resupinatus*, pp of *resupinare* to bend back to a supine position, fr *re-* + *supinus* supine] – **resupination** *n*

**resupine** /ri'syoohpien/ *adj* SUPINE 1a (lying on the back) [L *resupinus*, back-formation fr *resupinare*]

**resurface** /ree'suhfis/ *vt* to provide with a new or fresh surface *~ vi* to come again to the surface (e g of water); *broadly* to appear or show up again

**resurge** /ri'suhj/ *vi* to rise or surge up again [L *resurgere*] – **resurgent** *adj*

**resurgence** /ri'suhj(ə)ns/ *n* a rising again into life, activity, or influence ⟨*a ~ of nationalist feelings in Wales and Scotland*⟩

**resurrect** /,rezə'rekt/ *vt* **1** to raise from the dead **2** to bring back into use or view; revive [back-formation fr *resurrection*]

**resurrection** /,rezə'reksh(ə)n/ *n* **1a** *cap* the rising of Christ from the dead **b** *often cap* the rising again to life of all the human dead before the LAST JUDGMENT **c** the state of being risen from the dead **2** a resurgence, revival [ME, fr LL *resurrection-, resurrectio* act of rising from the dead, fr *resurrectus*, pp of *resurgere* to rise from the dead, fr L, to rise again, fr *re-* + *surgere* to rise – more at SURGE] – **resurrectional** *adj*

**resurrectionist** /,rezə'reksh(ə)nist/ *n* BODY SNATCHER

**resuscitate** /ri'susə,tayt/ *vt* to revive from apparent death or from unconsciousness; *also* to revitalize *~ vi* to revive; COME TO [L *resuscitatus*, pp of *resuscitare*, lit., to stir up again, fr *re-* + *suscitare* to stir up, fr *sub-, sus-* up + *citare* to put in motion, stir – more at SUB-, CITE] – **resuscitative** *adj*, **resuscitation** *n*

**resuscitator** /ri'susitaytə/ *n* one who or that which resuscitates; *specif* an apparatus used to restore the breathing of a partially asphyxiated person

**ret** /ret/ *vb* **-tt-** *vt* to soak (e g flax) to loosen the fibre from the woody tissue *~ vi* to become retted [ME *reten*, fr MD]

**retable** /ri'taybl/ *n* a raised shelf or ledge above a church altar for the altar cross, the altar lights, and flowers [Fr, fr Sp *retablo*, deriv of L *retro-* + *tabula* board, tablet]

¹**retail** /'ree,tayl; *sense 2 often* ri'tayl/ *vb* **1** to sell in small quantities directly to the ultimate consumer (eg for personal or household use) **2** to tell of; recount *~ vi* to be sold at retail ⟨*gin ~ing at £6.50 per bottle*⟩ [ME *retailen*, fr MF *retaillier* to cut back, divide into pieces, fr OF, fr *re-* + *taillier* to cut –

| | | | |
|---|---|---|---|
| **retabulate** *vt* | **retexture** *vt* | **retitle** *vt* | **retransmit** *vt* |
| **retackle** *vt* | **rethread** *vt* | **retrain** *vb* | **retraverse** *vt* |
| **retaste** *vt* | **retie** *vt* | **retransfer** *vt* | **retrim** *vt* |
| **reteach** *vt* | **retighten** *vb* | **retransform** *vt* | **retune** *vt* |
| **retest** *vt or n* | **retime** *vt* | **retransformation** *n* | **returf** *vt* |
| **retestify** *vb* | **retint** *vt* | **retransmission** *n* | **retype** *vt* |

more at TAILOR] – **retailer** n

²**retail** /'reetayl/ n the sale of commodities or goods in small quantities to ultimate consumers – compare WHOLESALE

³**retail** adj of or engaged in the sale of commodities at retail ⟨~ trade⟩

⁴**retail** adv in small quantities; from a retailer

**retailing** /'reetayling/ n the activities involved in the selling of goods to ultimate consumers for personal or household consumption

**retail price index** n a price index showing changes in the cost of living in Britain from month to month which is based on the shop prices of a range of selected essential commodities

**retain** /ri'tayn/ vt 1a to keep in possession or use b to keep in one's pay or employment; specif to engage the services of (eg a barrister) by paying a retainer c to keep in mind or memory 2a to keep relatively unaltered; preserve ⟨an area that ~s its rural character⟩ b to (be able to) hold or contain ⟨a well to ~ water⟩ ⟨lead ~s heat⟩ synonyms see ¹KEEP antonyms relinquish, give up [ME reteinen, retainen, fr MF retenir, fr L retinēre to hold back, keep, restrain, fr re- + tenēre to hold – more at THIN]

**retained object** n an object in a DITRANSITIVE (having two objects) passive construction that corresponds to either the direct or the indirect object in the equivalent active construction (eg me in a book was given me and book in I was given a book)

¹**retainer** /ri'taynə/ n 1 a fee paid to a lawyer or professional adviser for advice or services or to ensure that he/she will act on one's behalf if needed 2 a fee paid regularly to a freelance journalist to ensure that his/her services will be available when required [ME reteiner act of withholding, fr reteinen + AF -er (as in weyver waiver)]

²**retainer** n 1 one who or that which holds or retains 2a someone who serves a person of high rank b an old and trusted domestic servant [retain + ²-er]

**retaining wall** n a wall built to hold back a mass of earth, water, etc

¹**retake** /,ree'tayk/ vt retook /-took/; retaken /-'taykən/ 1 to take or receive again 2 to recapture 3 to photograph again; record (eg an item for broadcasting) again

²**retake** /'reetayk/ n an act or instance of filming, photographing, or recording again ⟨the camera has run out of film. We'll have to do a ~!⟩

**retaliate** /ri'tali,ayt/ vt to repay (eg an injury) in kind; requite ~ vi to return like for like; also to get revenge ⟨was careful to give her no opportunity to ~⟩ [LL retaliatus, pp of retaliare, fr re- + talio legal retaliation] – **retaliative** adj, **retaliatory** adj, **retaliation** n

¹**retard** /ri'tahd/ vt to slow down, esp by preventing or hindering advance, completion, or accomplishment; impede synonyms see ¹HINDER antonyms accelerate, advance, further [L retardare, fr re- + tardus slow] – **retardant** adj or n, **retarder** n

²**retard** n a holding back or slowing down; a retardation, delay

**retardate** /ri'tahdayt, -dət/ n, chiefly NAm a mentally retarded person – **retardate** adj

**retardation** /,reetah'daysh(ə)n, ri,tah'daysh(ə)n/ n 1 an act or instance of retarding 2 the extent to which something is retarded 3 the holding over in music of a note from one chord into the next, in which it does not belong, so that it is raised a degree to fit into the new chord 4a an abnormal slowness of thought or action; also less than normal intellectual ability usu characterized by an IQ of less than 70 b abnormally slow mental development

**retarded** /ri'tahdid/ adj slow or limited in intellectual or emotional development or academic progress

**retch** /rech/ vb (to make an effort) to vomit [(assumed) ME rechen to spit, retch, fr OE hrǣcan to spit, hawk; akin to L crepare to rattle – more at RAVEN] – **retch** n

**rete** /'reeti/ n, pl retia /'reeshyə, 'reetyə/ 1 a network; esp a network (PLEXUS) of blood vessels or nerves 2 an anatomical part resembling or including a network [NL, fr L, net – more at RETINA]

**retell** /ree'tel/ vt retold /-'tohld/ to tell again or in another form

**retelling** /ree'teling/ n a new version of a story ⟨a ~ of a Greek legend⟩

**retene** /'reeteen, 'reeten/ n a chemical compound, $C_{18}H_{18}$, obtained esp from pine tar and fossil plant resins [Gk rhētinē

resin]

**retention** /ri'tensh(ə)n/ n 1a the act of retaining; the state of being retained b abnormal and often painful retaining of a liquid (eg urine) or a secretion in a body cavity 2a power to retain; retentiveness b an ability to retain things in the mind; memory [ME retencioun, fr L retention-, retentio, fr retentus, pp of retinēre to retain – more at RETAIN]

**retentive** /ri'tentiv/ adj able or tending to retain; esp retaining knowledge easily ⟨a ~ mind⟩ – **retentively** adv, **retentiveness** n

**retentivity** /,reeten'tivəti/ n the capacity for retaining; specif the power to retain magnetism after the action of the magnetizing force has ceased

¹**rethink** /,ree'thingk/ vb rethought /-'thawt/ to think about again; esp to reconsider with a view to changing

²**rethink** /'reethingk/ n a revision or fresh appraisal, esp of official policy or planning ⟨a government ~⟩

**retiarius** /,reeti'eəriəs, ,reeshi-, -ahriəs/ n, pl retiarii /-ri-ee/ an ancient Roman gladiator armed with a net and a trident [L, fr rete net]

**reticence** /'retis(ə)ns/ n 1 the character or state of being reticent; reserve, restraint 2 an instance of being reticent

**reticent** /'retis(ə)nt/ adj 1 inclined to be silent or reluctant to speak; shy, reserved 2 restrained in expression, presentation, or appearance; self-effacing ⟨the room has an aspect of ~ dignity – A N Whitehead⟩ synonyms see SILENT antonyms frank [L reticent-, reticens, prp of reticēre to keep silent, fr re- + tacēre to be silent – more at TACIT] – **reticently** adv

**reticle** /'retikl/ n a system of fine lines, dots, cross hairs, or wires in the focus of the eyepiece of an optical instrument used to assist observation and measurement [L reticulum network]

**reticular** /ri'tikyoolə/ adj 1 reticulate; esp of or forming a reticulum 2 intricate

¹**reticulate** /ri'tikyoolət/ adj 1 resembling a net; esp having veins, fibres, or lines crossing ⟨a ~ leaf⟩ 2 of or constituting evolutionary change and species formation that is dependent on the genetic RECOMBINATION resulting from the interbreeding of previously separated and genetically different populations [L reticulatus, fr reticulum] – **reticulately** adv

²**reticulate** /ri'tikyoo,layt/ vt 1 to divide, mark, or arrange so as to form a network 2 to distribute (eg electricity, water, or goods) by a network ~ vi to become reticulated [back-formation fr reticulated, adj (reticulate)]

**reticulation** /ri,tikyoo'laysh(ə)n/ n a reticulated formation; a network; also something reticulated

**reticule** /'retikyoohl/ n 1 a reticle 2 a decorative bag closed with a drawstring carried as a handbag by women in the 18th and 19th centuries [Fr réticule, fr L reticulum network, network bag, fr dim. of rete net

**reticulocyte** /ri'tikyooloh,siet, -lə-/ n a young RED BLOOD CELL that has no nucleus, and is produced esp during active regeneration of lost blood [NL reticulum + ISV -cyte] – **reticulocytic** adj

**reticuloendothelial** /ri,tikyoolooh,endoh'theeliəl/ adj of or being the RETICULOENDOTHELIAL SYSTEM [NL reticulum + endothelium]

**reticuloendothelial system** n a widespread system of cells arising from the MESENCHYME (embryonic tissue layer forming blood, bone, cartilage, etc) and comprising most of the body's PHAGOCYTES (cells that engulf and destroy bacteria and particles of foreign matter) except for the WHITE BLOOD CELLS – compare MACROPHAGE

**reticulose** /ri'tikyooloohs/ adj reticulate

**reticulum** /ri'tikyooləm/ n 1 the second stomach of a RUMINANT (cud-chewing animal) (eg a cow) in which folds of the lining membrane form 6-sided cells – called also HONEYCOMB 2 a reticular formation; a network; esp supporting and interconnecting tissue composed of RETICULUM CELLS [NL, fr L, network]

**reticulum cell** n any of the branched reticuloendothelial cells that join together to form an intricate supporting and interconnecting network branching through and between other tissues and organs

**retiform** /'reetifawm, 're-/ adj composed of crossing lines and spaces; reticular [NL retiformis, fr L rete net + -iformis -iform]

**retin-** /retin-/, **retino-** comb form retina ⟨retinitis⟩ ⟨retinoscopy⟩

**retina** /'retinə/ n, pl retinas, retinae /-nie/ the light-sensitive membrane that lines the back of the eye, receives the image formed by the lens, is the immediate instrument of vision, and is connected with the brain by the OPTIC NERVE [ME *rethina*, fr ML *retina*, prob fr L *rete* net; akin to Gk *erēmos* lonely, solitary, Lith *rètis* sieve] – **retinal** *adj*

**retinaculum** /ˌreti'nakyooləm/ *n, pl* **retinacula** /-lə/ a connecting or retaining band or body; *specif* a hook or group of bristles on the front wings of some moths that join the wings together by interlocking with a group of bristles on the hind wings [NL, fr L, halter, cable, fr *retinēre* to hold back – more at RETAIN] – **retinacular** *n*

**retinal** /'retinal, ˌ-'-'-/ *n* a yellowish to orange chemical compound, $C_{19}H_{27}CHO$, that is an ALDEHYDE, is derived from vitamin A, and that in combination with proteins forms the pigments of the light-receiving parts (RODS and CONES) of the retina [*retin-* + $^3$-al]

**retinene** /'retineen/ *n* retinal

**retinitis** /ˌreti'nietəs/ *n* inflammation of the retina often leading to blindness [NL]

**retinitis pigmentosa** /reti,nietəs pigmen'tohzə/ *n* a hereditary disease causing a gradual degeneration of the retina and subsequent loss of vision [NL, pigmentary retinitis; fr its being characterized by the occurrence of black pigment in the retina]

**retinol** /'retinol/ *n* the chief and typical vitamin A, $C_{20}H_{29}OH$ [*retin-* + $^1$-*ol*; fr its being the source of retinal]

**retinopathy** /ˌreti'nopəthi/ *n* any of various noninflammatory disorders of the retina including some that are major causes of blindness

**retinue** /'reti,nyooh/ *n* a group of attendants or aides accompanying an important personage (eg a head of state) [ME *retenue*, fr MF, fr fem of *retenu*, pp of *retenir* to retain]

**retinula** /ri'tinyoolə/ *n, pl* **retinulae** /-lie/ *also* **retinulas** the light receptor of a single unit of the COMPOUND EYE of an insect, spider, crab, or other ARTHROPOD corresponding to the retina in the eye of a VERTEBRATE animal [NL, dim. of ML *retina*] – **retinular** *adj*

**retire** /ri'tie-ə/ *vi* 1 to withdraw from action or danger; retreat (~ *from the scene of the crime*) 2 to withdraw, esp for rest or seclusion 3 to recede; FALL BACK 4a to give up one's position or occupation; end one's working or professional career **b** to withdraw from a sporting contest, esp an innings at cricket, because of injury 5 to go to bed ~ *vt* 1 to withdraw: eg **1a** to order (a military force) to withdraw from the enemy **b** to withdraw (eg currency or shares) from circulation; recall **c** to withdraw from normal use or service 2 to cause to retire from a position or occupation (*a policy of* retiring *teachers at* 60) 3 to dismiss or end the turn of (a batter or a batting side) in baseball [MF *retirer*, fr *re-* + *tirer* to draw – more at TIRADE]
*synonyms* An army may **retire** as a matter of strategy, but it **retreats** when things are going badly.

**retired** /ri'tie-əd/ *adj* 1 remote from the world; secluded (*a* ~ *village*) 2 withdrawn from one's position or occupation; having ended one's working or professional career 3 received by or due to someone in retirement (~ *pay*) – **retiredly** *adv*, **retiredness** *n*

**retiree** /ri,tie-ə'ree/ *n, NAm* a person who has retired from his vocation, profession, or employment

**retirement** /ri,tie-əmənt/ *n* **1a** an act of retiring; the state of being retired **b** withdrawal from one's position or occupation or from active working life **c** the age at which one normally retires (*reached* ~ *but was asked to work another year*) 2 a place of seclusion or privacy *synonyms* see SOLITUDE

**retiring** /ri'tie-əring/ *adj* characterized by a love of privacy or solitude; reserved, shy – **retiringly** *adv*, **retiringness** *n*

**retool** /ˌree'toohl/ *vt* to equip (esp a factory) with new tools

$^1$**retort** /ri'tawt/ *vt* 1 to fling back or return aggressively (~ *an insult*) **2a** to reply sharply or quickly to **b** to say or exclaim in reply 3 to answer (eg an argument) by a counter argument ~ *vi* 1 to answer back sharply or tersely 2 to return an argument or charge 3 to retaliate *synonyms* see $^2$ANSWER [L *retortus*, pp of *retorquēre*, lit., to twist back, hurl back, fr *re-* + *torquēre* to twist – more at TORTURE]

$^2$**retort** *n* a terse, witty, or cutting reply; *esp* one that turns the first speaker's words against him/her – **retortion** *n*

$^3$**retort** *n* a vessel in which substances are distilled or decomposed by heat [MF *retorte*, fr ML *retorta*, fr L, fem of *retortus*, pp; fr its bent shape]

$^4$**retort** *vt* to treat (eg oil shale) by heating in a retort

$^1$**retouch** /ˌree'tuch/ *vt* 1 to rework in order to improve; TOUCH UP 2 to alter (eg a photographic negative) to produce a more desirable appearance 3 to colour (a new growth of hair) or

match previously dyed, tinted, or bleached hair ~ *vi* to make or give retouches [Fr *retoucher*, fr MF, fr *re-* + *toucher* to touch] – **retoucher** *n*

$^2$**retouch** /'ree,tuch/ *n* the act, process, or an instance of retouching; *esp* the retouching of a new growth of hair

**retrace** /ˌree'trays/ *vt* to trace again or back (~d *his footsteps*) [Fr *retracer*, fr MF *retracier*, fr *re-* + *tracier* to trace]

**retract** /ri'trakt/ *vt* 1 to draw back or in (*most cats can* ~ *their claws*) **2a** to withdraw; TAKE BACK (~ *a confession*) **b** to refuse to admit or abide by (~ *a promise*) ~ *vi* 1 to draw back (*she* ~ed *in horror*) 2 to recant or disclaim something [ME *retracten*, fr L *retractus*, pp of *retrahere* – more at RETREAT; (2) MF *retracter*, fr L *retractare*, freq of *retrahere*] – **retractable** *adj*

**retractile** /ri'traktiel/ *adj* capable of being drawn back or in (*a cat's* ~ *claws*) – **retractility** *n*

**retraction** /ri'traksh(ə)n/ *n* 1 an act of recanting; *specif* a statement made by one retracting 2 an act of retracting; the state of being retracted

**retractor** /ri'traktə/ *n* one who or that which retracts: eg **a** a surgical instrument for holding open the edges of a wound **b** a muscle that draws in an organ or body part – compare PROTRACTOR

**retral** /'reetrəl, 'retrəl/ *adj* situated at or towards the back; rear [L *retro* back – more at RETRO-] – **retrally** *adv*

**retranslate** /ˌreetrans'layt, -trahns-, -tranz-, -trahnz-/ *vt* to translate (a translated text) into another language, esp that of the original text; *also* to give a fresh form to ~ *vi* to retranslate something – **retranslation** *n*

$^1$**retread** /ˌree'tred/ *vt* to renew the tread of (a worn tyre)

$^2$**retread** /'ree,tred/ *n* (a tyre with) a new tread

ˌre-'tread *vt* **retrod; retrodden, retrod** to tread again

$^1$**retreat** /ri'treet/ *n* **1a(1)** an act or process of withdrawing, esp from what is difficult, dangerous, or disagreeable (*half way up the mountain bad weather forced a hasty* ~) **a(2)** the process of receding from a position or state attained (*the* ~ *of a glacier*) (*the slow* ~ *of an epidemic*) **b(1)** the usu forced withdrawal of troops from an enemy or from an advanced position **b(2)** a signal for retreating **c** a bugle call sounded at about sunset 2 a place of privacy or safety; a refuge 3 a period of usu group withdrawal for prayer, meditation, and study [ME *retret*, fr MF *retrait*, fr pp of *retraire* to withdraw, fr L *retrahere*, lit., to draw back, fr *re-* + *trahere* to draw – more at DRAW]

$^2$**retreat** *vi* 1 to make a retreat; withdraw 2 *NAm* to slope backwards; recede (*a* ~ing *chin*) ~ *vt* to draw or lead back; *specif* to move (a piece) back in chess *synonyms* see RETIRE – **retreater** *n*

**retreatant** /ri'treet(ə)nt/ *n* a person who is on a religious retreat

**retrench** /ri'trench/ *vt* **1a** to cut down; reduce (~ *company expenditure*) **b** to cut out; excise (~ *offending paragraphs from an article*) 2 to cut off; remove 3 *Austr, NZ, & WI* to make (a worker) redundant ~ *vi* to make retrenchments; *specif* to economize [obs Fr *retrencher* (now *retrancher*), fr MF *retrenchier*, fr *re-* + *trenchier* to cut]

**retrenchment** /ri'trenchmənt/ *n* 1 a curtailment, reduction; *specif* a cutting of expenses 2 *Austr, NZ, & WI* redundancy

**retribution** /ˌretri'byoohsh(ə)n/ *n* 1 requital for an insult or injury; retaliation – often in *exact retribution* 2 the dispensing or receiving of reward or punishment – used esp for divine judgment 3 something given or exacted in recompense; *esp* punishment [ME *retribucioun*, fr MF *retribution*, fr LL *retribution-*, *retributio*, fr L *retributus*, pp of *retribuere* to pay back, fr *re-* + *tribuere* to pay – more at TRIBUTE] – **retributory** *adj*

**retributive** /ri'tribyootiv/ *adj* of or marked by retribution (~ *justice*) – **retributively** *adv*

**retrieval** /ri'treevl/ *n* an act or process of retrieving

$^1$**retrieve** /ri'treev/ *vi, of a dog or breed of dog* to bring in game (*a dog that* ~s *well*); *also* to bring back an object thrown by a person ~ *vt* 1 *of a dog or breed of dog* to find and bring in (killed or wounded game) 2 to call to mind again 3 to get back again; recover (~d *the keys he left on the bus*) **4a** to rescue, save (~ *a young girl from moral ruin*) **b** to return (eg a ball or shuttlecock that is difficult to reach) successfully 5 to restore, revive (*his writing* ~s *past glories*) 6 to remedy ill effects of; put right (~ *the situation*) 7 to get and bring back; *esp* recover (eg computerized information) from storage [ME *retreven*, modif of MF *retrouver* to find again, fr *re-* + *trouver* to find, prob fr (assumed) VL *tropare* to compose – more at TROUBADOUR] – **retrievable** *adj*, **retrievably** *adv*, **retrievability** *n*

²**retrieve** *n* an act, process, or possibility of retrieving; retrieval ⟨*beyond* ~⟩

**retriever** /ri'treevə/ *n* one who or that which retrieves; *specif* any of several breeds of vigorous active medium-sized dog that have a heavy water-resistant coat and are used esp for retrieving game

**retro-** *prefix* **1a** back towards the past ⟨retro*spect*⟩ ⟨retro*grade*⟩ **b** backwards ⟨retro*cede*⟩ ⟨retro*flex*⟩ **2** situated behind ⟨retro*sternal*⟩ ⟨retro*choir*⟩ [ME, fr L, fr *retro*, fr *re-* + *-tro* (as in *intro* within) – more at INTRO-]

¹**retroaction** /'retroh,aksh(ə)n/ *n* retroactive operation (eg of a law or tax) [*retroactive* + *-ion*]

²**retroaction** *n* a reciprocal action; reaction [*retro* + *action*]

**retroactive** /,retroh'aktiv/ *adj* extending in scope or effect to a prior time; *esp* made effective as of a date prior to enactment, proclamation, or imposition ⟨*a* ~ *liability for tax*⟩ [Fr *retroactif*, fr L *retroactus*, pp of *retroagere* to drive back, reverse, fr *retro-* + *agere* to drive – more at AGENT] – **retroactively** *adv*, **retroactivity** *n*

**retrocede** /,retroh'seed/ *vi* to go back; recede ~ *vt* to cede back (eg a territory) [*vi* L *retrocedere*, fr *retro-* + *cedere* to go, cede – more at CEDE; *vt* Fr *rétrocéder*, fr ML *retrocedere*, fr L *retro-* + *cedere* to cede] – **retrocession** *n*

**retrochoir** /'retroh,kwie·ə/ *n* the part of a large church or cathedral behind the HIGH ALTAR

**retrofire** /'retroh,fie·ə/ *vb*, *of a retro-rocket* to (cause to) become ignited – **retrofire** *n*

**retrofit** /-'fit/ *vt* to equip (eg an aircraft) with new parts or equipment not available at the time of manufacture

**retroflex** /'retrəfleks/, **retroflexed** *adj* **1** turned or bent abruptly backwards **2** *of a speech sound* produced with the tongue tip turned up or curled back just under the HARD PALATE ⟨~ *vowel*⟩ [ISV, fr NL *retroflexus*, fr L *retro-* + *flexus*, pp of *flectere* to bend]

**retroflexion**, *chiefly NAm* **retroflection** /,retrə'fleksh(ə)n/ *n* **1** the act or process of bending back **2** the state of being bent back; *esp* the bending back of an organ (eg the womb) upon itself **3** the action or process of producing a retroflex speech sound ⟨*an 'r' produced with little* ~⟩

**retrogradation** /,retroh-grə'daysh(ə)n/ *n* the action or process of retrograding

¹**retrograde** /'retrəgrayd/ *adj* **1a** *of orbital or rotational movement* in a direction contrary to neighbouring celestial bodies ⟨~ *spin of a satellite*⟩ ⟨~ *motion of a planet*⟩ – compare PROGRADE **b** moving or directed backwards ⟨*a* ~ *step*⟩ **c** ordered in a manner that is opposite to normal; inverse, reverse ⟨*a* ~ *alphabet*⟩ **2** tending towards or resulting in a worse state **3** marked by retrogression **4** relating to or affecting a period immediately prior to an event with sudden and dramatic consequences ⟨*suffering from* ~ *amnesia and unable to recall what led up to the accident*⟩ [ME, fr L *retrogradus*, fr *retro-* + *gradi* to go] – **retrogradely** *adv*

²**retrograde** *vb* to turn back; reverse ~ *vi* **1a** to move back; recede ⟨*a glacier* ~s⟩ **b** to give a résumé (eg of a narrative); summarize **2** to decline to a worse condition; degenerate [L *retrogradi*, fr *retro-* + *gradi* to go – more at GRADE] – **retrogradation** *n*

**retrogress** /,retrə'gres/ *vi* to revert, regress, or decline from a better to a worse state [L *retrogressus*, pp of *retrogradi*]

**retrogression** /,retrə'gresh(ə)n/ *n* **1** an esp orbital retrograde motion; a regression **2** a reversal in development or condition; *esp* a passing from a higher to a lower or from a more to a less specialized state or type in the course of development (eg of an organism)

**retrogressive** /,retrə'gresiv/ *adj* characterized by retrogression: eg **a** moving or directed backward **b** causing or showing a decline from a better to a worse state ⟨~ *government policies*⟩ – **retrogressively** *adv*

**retrolental** /,retroh'lentl/ *adj* situated or occurring behind a lens (eg of the eye) [*retro-* + L *lent-*, *lens* lens]

**retrolingual** /,retroh'ling-gwəl/ *adj* situated behind or near the base of the tongue ⟨~ *salivary glands*⟩

**retropack** /'retroh,pak/ *n* an assembly of retro-rockets

'**retro-,rocket** *n* an auxiliary rocket on an aircraft, spacecraft, etc that produces thrust in a direction opposite to, or at an oblique angle to the direction of flight in order to slow the craft down or change its direction

**retrorse** /ri'traws/ *adj* bent backwards or downwards ⟨~ *hairs*⟩ ⟨~ *thorns*⟩ – compare ANTRORSE [L *retrorsus*, contr of *retroversus* – more at RETROVERSION] – **retrorsely** *adv*

¹**retrospect** /'retraspekt/ *n* **1** a survey or consideration of past events **2** *archaic* reference to or regard for a precedent or authority *synonyms* see MEMORY [*retro-* + *-spect* (as in *prospect*)] – **in retrospect** in considering the past or a past event; looking back in time

²**retrospect** *adj* retrospective

³**retrospect** *vi* to engage in retrospection; reflect ~ *vt* to look back on in thought [L *retrospectus*, pp of *retrospicere* to look back at, fr *retro-* + *specere* to look – more at SPY]

**retrospection** /,retrə'speksh(ə)n/ *n* the act or process or an instance of looking back over the past

¹**retrospective** /,retrə'spektiv/ *adj* **1a(1)** of or given to retrospection **a(2)** based on memory ⟨*a* ~ *report*⟩ **b** being a retrospective ⟨*a* ~ *exhibition*⟩ **2** relating to or affecting things past; RETROACTIVE – **retrospectively** *adv*

²**retrospective** *n* an exhibition showing the development of an artist's work over a period of years

**retroussé** /rə'troohsay/ *adj*, *esp of a nose* turned up, esp at the end [Fr, fr pp of *retrousser* to tuck up, fr MF, fr *re-* + *trousser* to truss, tuck up]

**retroversion** /,retroh'vuhsh(ə)n/ *n* **1** the act or process of turning back or regressing **2** the bending backwards of a body part or organ, esp the womb [L *retroversus* turned backwards, fr *retro-* + *versus*, pp of *vertere* to turn – more at WORTH]

**retry** /ree'trie/ *vt* to try again; *specif* to give new judicial trial to – **retrial** *n*

**retsina** /ret'seenə/ *n* a Greek resin-flavoured white wine [NGk, deriv of Gk *rhētinē* resin]

¹**return** /ri'tuhn/ *vi* **1a** to go back or come back again ⟨~ *home*⟩ **b** to go back in thought, conversation, or practice; revert ⟨*soon* ~ed *to her old habits*⟩ **2** to pass back to an earlier possessor ⟨*the estate* ~ed *to a distant branch of the family*⟩ **3** *formal* to reply, retort ~ *vt* **1a** to state officially, esp in answer to a formal demand ⟨~ed *details of her income*⟩ **b** to elect (a candidate) (eg to Parliament) **c** to declare as an official (eg legal) judgment ⟨*the jury* ~ed *him not guilty*⟩ ⟨~ *a verdict of guilty*⟩ **2a** to restore to a former or proper place, position, or state ⟨~ *the gun to its holster*⟩ **3** to bring in (eg a profit); yield **4a** to give or perform in return; repay ⟨~ *a compliment*⟩ **b** to give or send back, esp to an owner **5** to cause (eg a wall or decorative moulding) to continue in a different direction (eg at a right angle) **6** to lead (a specified suit or specified card of a suit) in response to a partner's earlier lead, esp in bridge **7** to play (a ball or shuttlecock) hit, esp served, by an opponent **8** *obs* to retort [ME *retournen*, fr MF *retourner*, fr *re-* + *tourner* to turn – more at TURN] – **returner** *n*

**synonyms** Return, revert, recur, and **recrudesce** all mean "go or come back". **Return**, the most general, implies either going or coming back to an earlier place or state. **Revert** often emphasizes a return to a lower or worse condition ⟨*people* reverted *to savagery*⟩, although one may also **revert** to a former topic of conversation. **Recur** and the formal **recrudesce** both mean "arise again" or "happen again" ⟨*symptoms may* recur *at any time*⟩, **recrudesce** being confined to the recurring of something undesirable, particularly a disease, after a period of quiescence.

²**return** *n* **1a** the act or process of coming back to or from a place or condition **b** a regular or frequent returning; recurrence ⟨*the* ~ *of the tide*⟩ ⟨*the* ~ *of leaves in spring*⟩ **2a(1)** the delivery of a legal order (eg a writ) to the proper officer or court **a(2)** the endorsed certificate of an official stating his action in the execution of a legal order **b** a (financial) account or formal report **c(1)** **returns** *pl*, **return** a report of the results of balloting ⟨*election* ~s⟩ **c(2)** an official declaration of the election of a candidate **c(3)** *chiefly Br* an election **d(1)** a formal statement on a required legal form showing taxable income, allowable deductions and exemptions, and the assessment of the tax due **d(2)** a list of taxable property **3a** the continuation, usu at a right angle, of the facade of a building or of a moulding or series of mouldings **b** a turn, bend, or winding back (eg in a stream or trench) **c** a means for conveying something (eg water) back to its starting point **4a(1)** **returns** *pl*, **return** the profit from labour, investment, business, etc; yield **a(2)** *pl* results ⟨*showing* ~s *from his long hours of study*⟩ **b** the rate of profit in a process of production per unit of capital employed **5a** the act of returning something to a former place, condition, or owner; restitution **b** something returned: eg **b(1)** *pl* unsold publications (eg newspapers) returned to the publisher for a cash or credit refund **b(2)** *pl* mail received in answer

to a questionnaire or advertising appeal **6a** something given in repayment or reciprocation **b** an answer, retort **7** a lead in a suit previously led by one's partner in a card game **b** the action of returning a ball or shuttlecock **8** *also* **return ticket** *Br* a ticket bought for a journey to a place and back again – compare SINGLE – **by return (of post)** by the next returning post – **in return** in compensation or repayment – **no returns** it is not to be done in return – used by children ⟨*a pinch and a punch and no returns*⟩

³**return** *adj* **1a** marked or formed by a change of direction or alignment ⟨*a ∼ facade*⟩ **b** doubled back on itself ⟨*a ∼ flue*⟩ **2** played, delivered, or given in return; *specif* taking place on the grounds of the team that played away in the previous encounter **3** used or followed on returning ⟨*the ∼ road*⟩ **4** permitting return ⟨*a ∼ valve*⟩ ⟨*a ∼ ticket*⟩ **5** of or causing a return to a place or condition

**returnable** /ri'tuhnəbl/ *adj* **1** legally required to be returned, delivered, or argued at a specified time or place ⟨*a writ ∼ on the date indicated*⟩ **2a** able to return or be returned (eg for reuse) ⟨*∼ bottles*⟩ **b** requiring to be returned

**return crease** *n* any of the four lines on a cricket pitch at right angles to the BOWLING CREASE and POPPING CREASE and 4 feet 4 inches (1.32 metres) from the middle stump, from inside which the ball must be bowled

**returnee** /,reetuh'nee/ *n, chiefly NAm* someone who returns; *esp* one returning to the USA after military service overseas

**returning officer** /ri'tuhning/ *n, Br* a public official who presides over an election count and declares the result

**retuse** /ri'tyoohs/ *adj, esp of a leaf* having a rounded or blunt tip (APEX) with a slight notch – compare EMARGINATE, OBCORDATE [L *retusus* blunted, fr pp of *retundere* to pound back, blunt, fr *re-* + *tundere* to beat, pound – more at STINT]

**reunion** /ree'yoohnyən/ *n* **1** an act of reuniting; the state of being reunited **2** a gathering of people (eg relatives or associates) after a period of separation

**reunionist** /ri'yoohnyənist/ *n* an advocate of reunion (eg of sects or parties) – **reunionistic** *adj*

**reunite** /,reeyoo'niet/ *vt* to bring together again ⟨*∼ brother and sister*⟩ to come together again; rejoin [ML *reunitus*, pp of *reunire*, fr L *re-* + LL *unire* to unite – more at UNITE]

¹**reuse** /,ree'yoohz/ *vt* to use again, esp after reclaiming or reprocessing ⟨*the need to ∼ scarce resources*⟩ – **reusable** *adj*, **reuser** *n*

²**reuse** /ree'yoohs/ *n* further or repeated use

¹**rev** /rev/ *n* a revolution (eg of a motor)

²**rev** *vb* **-vv-** *vt* **1** to increase the number of revolutions per minute of (esp an engine) – often + *up* ⟨*∼ up the engine*⟩ ⟨*the sound of a motormower revving its engine*⟩ **2** to cause to undergo revving ∼ *vi* to operate at an increased speed of revolution – usu + *up*
  **rev up** *vt* **1** to make more active and effective **2** *informal* to increase the speed of ⟨*∼ production*⟩

**revalidate** /ree'validayt/ *vt* to make valid again – **revalidation** *n*

**revalor·ize, -ise** /ree'valəriez/ *vt* to revalue (assets or currency) – **revalorization** *n*

**revaluate** /ree'valyooayt/ *vt* to revalue; *specif* to increase the value of (currency) [back-formation fr *revaluation*] – **revaluation** *n*

**revalue** /,ree'valyooh/ *vt* **1** to value (eg currency) anew **2** to make a new valuation of; reappraise

**revamp** /,ree'vamp/ *vt* **1** to renovate, reconstruct **2** to revise without fundamental alteration [*re-* + ²*vamp* (in the sense "to mend, renovate")] – **revamp** *n*

**revanche** /ri'vahnsh/ *n* revenge; *esp* a usu political policy designed to recover lost territory or status [Fr, fr MF, alter. of *revenche* revenge, fr *revengier, revenchier* to revenge]

¹**revanchist** /ri'vahnshist/ *n* someone who advocates a policy of revanche

²**revanchist** *adj* of a policy of revanche – **revanchism** *n*

¹**reveal** /ri'veel/ *vt* **1** to make known through divine inspiration **2** to make known (something secret or hidden) ⟨*∼ a secret*⟩ **3**

to open up to view; display ⟨*the uncurtained window* ∼ed *a cluttered room*⟩ [ME *revelen*, fr MF *reveler*, fr L *revelare* to uncover, fr *re-* + *velare* to cover, veil, fr *velum* veil] – **revealable** *adj*, **revealer** *n*, **revealment** *n*
  **synonyms** Reveal, tell, disclose, discover, impart, divulge, and betray can all mean "make known what has been hidden". **Reveal** indicates a process rather like unveiling, and may apply to supernatural or divine knowledge, or to what is indicated by evidence ⟨*the painting reveals the painter*⟩. **Tell** applies chiefly to the simple giving of necessary or helpful information, particularly in words ⟨*tell her the news*⟩. **Disclose**, and the rarer, more formal (in this sense) **discover**, suggest the uncovering to public knowledge of what has perhaps for good reasons been hidden ⟨*did not disclose his true objective*⟩. **Impart** and **divulge** involve the sharing of information with a small circle ⟨*imparted what she knew to the police*⟩, **divulge** suggesting also some indiscretion or breach of confidence. **Betray**, when it is voluntary, goes further than **divulge** in implying the violation of trust, but also like **reveal** applies to indication by involuntary signs, adding the idea of displaying what one would rather conceal ⟨*a quivering of the lips betrayed his secret amusement*⟩. **antonyms** conceal, hide

²**reveal** *n* the side of an opening (eg for a window) between a frame and the outer surface of a wall; *also* an upright piece (JAMB) forming the side of an opening [alter. of earlier *revale*, fr ME *revalen* to lower, fr MF *revaler*, fr *re-* + *val* valley – more at VALE]

**revealing** /ri'vieling, -'vee-/ *adj* **1** full of import; significant **2** exposing something usu concealed from view ⟨*a ∼ dress*⟩

**revegetate** /ree'vejitayt/ *vt* to provide (barren or denuded land) with a new plant cover – **revegetation** *n*

**reveille** /ri'vali, -'ve-/ *n* **1** a bugle call at about sunrise signalling the first military parade or assembly of the day; *also* the assembly so signalled **2** a call or signal to rise in the morning [modif of Fr *réveillez*, imper pl of *réveiller* to awaken, fr *re-* + *eveiller* to awaken, fr (assumed) VL *exvigilare*, fr L *ex-* + *vigilare* to keep watch, stay awake – more at VIGILANT]

¹**revel** /'revl/ **-ll-**, *NAm* **-l-**, **-ll-** *vi* **1** to take part in a revel; carouse **2** to take intense satisfaction *in* ⟨*∼ in show jumping*⟩ [ME *revelen*, fr MF *reveler*, lit., to rebel, fr L *rebellare*] – **reveller** *n*

²**revel** *n*, **revels** *n pl* a usu riotous party or celebration

**revelation** /,revə'laysh(ə)n/ *n* **1a** an act of revealing or communicating divine truth **b** something that is revealed by God to man **2** Revelation, Revelations *taking sing vb* – see BIBLE table **3a** an act of revealing or making known; revealment **b** something that is revealed; *esp* a sudden and illuminating disclosure [ME, fr MF, fr LL *revelation-, revelatio*, fr L *revelatus*, pp of *revelare* to reveal]

**revelator** /'revəlaytə/ *n* one who or that which reveals; *esp* one who reveals the will of God

**revelatory** /'revələt(ə)ri, ,revə'layt(ə)ri/ *adj* of revelation; serving to reveal something

**revelry** /'revlri/ *n* exuberant festivity or merrymaking

**revenant** /'revinənt/ *n* someone who returns (as if) from the dead [Fr, fr prp of *revenir* to return] – **revenant** *adj*

¹**revenge** /ri'venj/ *vt* **1** to inflict a like injury in return for (an injury, insult, humiliation, etc) **2** to avenge (eg oneself) usu by retaliating in kind or degree [ME *revengen*, fr MF *revengier*, fr OF, fr *re-* + *vengier* to avenge – more at VENGEANCE] – **revenger** *n*

²**revenge** *n* **1** an act or instance of retaliating in order to get even **2** a desire for revenge ⟨*saw ∼ in his eyes*⟩ **3** an opportunity for getting satisfaction or requital **synonyms** see VINDICTIVE – **revengeful** *adj*

**revenue** /'revənyooh/ *n* **1** the total income derived from an investment before tax and other deductions are made; the gross income from an investment **2** the yield of sources of income (eg taxes or rates) that a political unit (eg a nation or local authority) collects and receives into its treasury for public use **3** the total income produced by a given source ⟨*a property expected to yield a large annual ∼*⟩ **4** a government department concerned with the collection of the national revenue [ME, fr MF, fr *revenir* to return, fr L *revenire*, fr *re-* + *venire* to come

– more at COME]

**revenue bond** n a bond issued by a public agency authorized to build, acquire, or improve a revenue-producing property (e g a toll road or a water system) and payable solely out of revenue derived from such property

**revenue stamp** n a stamped or printed paper affixed to something (e g a cigar box) as evidence of payment of a tax, import duty, etc

**revenue tariff** n a tariff intended wholly or primarily to produce public revenue – compare PROTECTIVE TARIFF

**reverb** /ri'vuhb, 'ree¸vuhb/ n (a device for producing) an electronic echo effect in recorded music [short for *reverberation*]

**reverberate** /ri'vuhbə¸rayt/ vt **1a** to echo repeatedly and sonorously ⟨~ *the rhythm*⟩ **b** to reflect or return (light, sound, heat, etc) **2** to subject to the action of a reverberatory ~ vi **1** to be reflected **2** to continue (as if) in a series of echoes; resound **3** to produce a continuing strong effect ⟨*the scandal* ~d *round Whitehall*⟩ [L *reverberatus*, pp of *reverberare* to strike back, repel, fr *re-* + *verberare* to lash, fr *verber* rod – more at VERVAIN] – **reverberant** adj, **reverberate** adj, **reverberative** adj, **reverberatory** adj

**reverberation** /ri¸vuhbə'raysh(ə)n/ n **1** an instance of reverberating; the state of being reverberated **2a** something (e g a loud noise) that is reverberated **b** an effect that resembles an echo

**reverberatory** /ri'vuhb(ə)rətri/, **reverberatory furnace** n a furnace or kiln in which heat is radiated onto the material (e g iron ore) to be treated from the low curved roof so that the source of heat and the material are not in contact

¹**revere** /ri'viə/ vt to regard with devotion or deep, esp religious, respect [L *revereri*, fr *re-* + *vereri* to fear, respect – more at WARY]

    **synonyms Revere, reverence, venerate, worship, adore,** and **idolize** all mean "honour deeply and respectfully". **Revere** stresses deference, awe, and treasuring affection, and is directed particularly towards people ⟨revere *the memory of Gandhi*⟩. **Reverence** directs a similar feeling more often towards things and places. **Venerate** entails loving deference towards what is felt to have intrinsic worth, particularly when it is also old ⟨venerate *an ancient tradition*⟩. **Worship** in the strict sense involves unquestioning participation in set religious forms, but when the object is not divine may suggest lack of judgment in the worshipper ⟨*silly mothers who* **worship** *spoilt children*⟩. **Adore** is close to this second sense of **worship,** but may emphasize a more personal and rapturous love ⟨*child* **adores** her *pony*⟩. **Idolize** carries to excess the idea of **adoring** ⟨*girls* **idolizing** a *pop star*⟩.

²**revere** n REVERS (facing on a garment) [by alter.]

¹**reverence** /'rev(ə)rəns/ n **1** honour or respect felt or shown; deference; esp respect shown to something sacred **2a** a gesture (e g a bow) denoting respect **b** a deep bow performed in a court dance or ballet **3** the state of being revered ⟨*hold in* ~⟩ **4** someone held in reverence – used preceded by *your* or *his* to address or refer to a priest ⟨*his* ~ *the Archdeacon*⟩

²**reverence** vt to regard or treat with reverence ⟨~d *the memory of their old teacher*⟩ **synonyms** see ¹REVERE – **reverencer** n

¹**reverend** /'rev(ə)rənd/ adj **1** worthy of reverence; revered **2** cap being a member of the clergy – used as a title usu preceded by *the* and followed by a title or a full name ⟨*the* Reverend *Mr Smith*⟩ ⟨*the* Reverend *John Smith*⟩ [ME, fr MF, fr L *reverendus*, gerundive of *revereri* to revere]

    **usage Reverend,** and its abbreviation **Rev,** should not correctly be used without *the*, nor without the first name or initials or *Mr, Dr,* etc ⟨△ **Reverend** Brown will say a few words⟩. – compare REVEREND

²**reverend** n, *informal* a member of the clergy – often used as an informal form of address

**Reverend Mother** n the Mother Superior of a convent – used esp as a form of address

**reverent** /'rev(ə)rənt/ adj expressing or characterized by reverence – compare REVEREND [ME, fr L *reverent-, reverens,* prp of *revereri*] – **reverently** adv

**reverential** /¸revə'rensh(ə)l/ adj **1** expressing or having the quality of reverence ⟨~ *awe*⟩ **2** inspiring reverence – **reverentially** adv

**reverie, revery** /'revəri/ n **1** a daydream **2** the condition of being lost in thought or dreamlike fantasy [Fr *rêverie,* fr MF, delirium, fr *resver, rever* to wander, be delirious]

**revers** /ri'viə/ n, pl **revers** /ri'viəz/ a wide turned-back or applied facing along each of the front edges of a garment; *specif* a lapel, esp on a woman's garment [Fr, lit., reverse, fr

MF, fr *revers,* adj]

**reversal** /ri'vuhsl/ n **1** an act or the process of reversing: e g **1a** a change or overthrow of a legal proceeding or judgment, esp on appeal **b** a movement in an opposite direction or appearance in an opposite or inverted position; *also* the causing of such a movement or appearance **2** a conversion of a photographic positive into a negative or vice versa **3** a change for the worse ⟨*his condition suffered a* ~⟩ **usage** see REVERSION

**reversal film** n photographic film (e g colour transparency film) that typically gives a positive image without an intermediate negative

¹**reverse** /ri'vuhs/ adj **1a** opposite or contrary to a previous or normal condition **b** having the front turned away from an observer or opponent **2** relating to, commanding, or facing the rear of a military force **3** acting, operating, or arranged in a manner contrary to the usual ⟨~ *order*⟩ **4** effecting reverse movement ⟨~ *gear*⟩ **5** so made that the part normally printed is left unprinted and vice versa; *specif* so made that the part normally black is white and vice versa ⟨~ *photoengraving*⟩ [ME *revers,* fr MF, fr L *reversus,* pp of *revertere* to turn back –more at REVERT] – **reversely** adv

²**reverse** vt **1a** to turn or change completely about in position or direction ⟨~ *a sheet of paper*⟩ ⟨~ *the order of words*⟩ **b** to turn upside down; invert **2** to annul: e g **2a** to overthrow, set aside, or make void (a legal decision) by a contrary decision **b** to change to the contrary ⟨~ *a decision*⟩ **1** to turn or move in the opposite direction **2** to put a mechanism (e g an engine) into reverse – see also **reverse the** CHARGES **3a** to cause to go in the opposite direction; *esp* to cause (e g an engine) to perform an action in the opposite direction **b** to cause (e g a motor car) to go backwards – **reverser** n

³**reverse** n **1** the opposite of something; the contrary **2** an act or instance of reversing **3** a misfortune, reversal **4** the back part of something: e g **4a** the back cover of a book **b** the side of a coin, medal, or currency note that does not bear the principal design and lettering – compare OBVERSE **5a** a gear that reverses something; *also* the whole mechanism brought into play when such a gear is used **b** movement in reverse – **in reverse** in an opposite manner or direction; backwards

**reverse dive** n a dive made from a standing position facing the water with backward rotation of the body – compare BACK DIVE, FORWARD DIVE, INWARD DIVE

¹**reversible** /ri'vuhsəbl/ adj capable of being reversed or of reversing: e g **a** capable of going through a sequence (e g of changes) either backwards or forwards ⟨*a* ~ *chemical reaction*⟩ **b(1)** having two finished, often contrasting, usable sides ⟨~ *fabric*⟩ **b(2)** wearable with either side out ⟨~ *coat*⟩ – **reversibly** adv, **reversibility** n

²**reversible** n a reversible cloth or article of clothing

**reversing thermometer** /ri'vuhsing/ n a thermometer for registering temperature in deep water in which the thermometer inverts at a specified depth and causes a column of mercury to break in such a way that the original temperature can still be read when the thermometer is returned to the surface

**reversion** /ri'vuhsh(ə)n/ n **1a** that part of a legal estate which remains in the control of its owner after he/she has made a grant of a lesser estate from it **b** a future interest in property left in the control of someone who has made a temporary grant of all or part of it or his/her successor **2** the right of inheritance or future possession or enjoyment **3** the sum to be paid on death of the holder of a life-insurance policy **4** the process of reverting **5a** a return towards an ancestral type or condition; reappearance of an ancestral character **b** a product of reversion; *specif* an organism showing ancestral rather than parental characteristics; a throwback **6** *chiefly NAm* an act or instance of turning the opposite way; the state of being so turned; a reversal [ME, fr MF, fr L *reversion-, reversio* act of returning, fr *reversus,* pp]

    **usage Reversion** is connected with the verb **revert,** and should not be confused with **reversal,** connected with **reverse** ⟨the reversal (not △ **reversion**) of this economic policy⟩.

**reversionary** /ri'vuhshən(ə)ri/ adj of, constituting, or involving a reversion, esp a legal reversion

**reversioner** /ri'vuhsh(ə)nə/ n a person who has or is entitled to a reversion

**revert** /ri'vuht/ vi **1a** to return, esp to a lower or worse condition ⟨*many* ~ed *to savagery*⟩ **b** to go back in thought or conversation ⟨~ed *to the subject of finance*⟩ **2** to return to the proprietor or his/her heirs after an interest granted away has expired **3** to return to an ancestral type **synonyms** see ¹RETURN [ME *reverten,* fr MF *revertir,* fr L *revertere,* vt to turn back & *reverti,* vi to return, come back, fr *re-* + *vertere, verti* to turn – more at WORTH] – **reverter** *n,* **revertible** *adj*

**revertant** /ri'vuht(ə)nt/ *n* a mutant organism, strain, or gene that has regained a former capability (eg to produce a particular protein or to use a particular nutrient) by a further mutation

**reverted** /ri'vuhtid/ *adj* turned or curled back or the wrong way ⟨*a ~ leaf*⟩

**reverter** /ri'vuhtə/ *n* a reversion of a legal estate [ME, fr AF *reverter* to return, fr OF *revertir* to return, revert]

**revery** /'revəri/ *a* reverie

**revet** /ri'vet/ *vt* **-tt-** to face (an embankment, wall, etc) with a material (eg masonry) [Fr *revêtir,* lit., to clothe again, dress up, fr L *revestire,* fr *re-* + *vestire* to clothe – more at VEST]

**revetment** /ri'vetmənt/ *n* **1** a facing (eg of stone or concrete) to retain an embankment **2** RETAINING WALL; *esp* a barricade to provide shelter (eg against bomb splinters)

¹**review** /ri'vyooh/ *n* **1** revision ⟨*prices are subject to ~*⟩ **2a** a formal military inspection **b** a military ceremony honouring a person or event **3** a general survey (eg of current affairs) **4** an act of inspecting or examining **5** a judicial reexamination (eg of the proceedings of a lower court or tribunal by a higher) **6a** a critical evaluation (eg of a book or play) **b** (a section of) a magazine or newspaper devoted chiefly to reviews and essays **7** a retrospective view or survey (eg of one's life) **8** a revue **9** *chiefly NAm* the act of revising *usage* see REVUE [MF *revue,* fr *revoir* to look over, fr *re-* + *voir* to see – more at VIEW]

²**review** *vt* **1** to view again **2** to examine or study again; *esp* to reexamine judicially **3** to look back on; take a retrospective view of ⟨*~ the past year*⟩ **4a** to go over or examine critically or thoughtfully ⟨*~ed the results of the study*⟩ **b** to give a critical evaluation of ⟨*~ a novel*⟩ **5** to hold a review of ⟨*~ troops*⟩ *~ vi* **1** to examine material again; make a review **2** to write reviews **3** *NAm* to revise ⟨*~ for a test*⟩ [(vt 1 & 2) *re-* + *view*; (other senses) ¹*review*]

**review copy** *n* a free copy of a book sent by its publisher to a magazine or newspaper to be reviewed

**reviewer** /ri'vyooh-ə/ *n* someone who reviews; *esp* a writer of critical reviews

**revile** /ri'viel/ *vt* to subject to harsh verbal abuse; berate to use abusive language; rail *synonyms* see ²SCOLD [ME *revilen,* fr MF *reviler* to despise, fr *re-* + *vil* vile] – **revilement** *n,* **reviler** *n*

**revisal** /ri'viezl/ *n* the act of revising; revision

¹**revise** /ri'viez/ *vt* **1** to look over again in order to correct or improve ⟨*~ a manuscript*⟩ **2a** to make an amended, improved, or up-to-date version of ⟨*~ a dictionary*⟩ **b** to provide with a new arrangement of scientific classification ⟨*revising the alpine ferns*⟩ **3** *chiefly Br* to refresh knowledge of (eg a subject) esp in preparation for an examination ⟨*busy revising his Latin verbs*⟩ *~ vi, chiefly Br* to refresh one's knowledge of a subject, esp in preparation for an examination ⟨*revising for my O levels*⟩ [Fr *reviser,* fr L *revisere* to look at again, fr *revisus,* pp of *revidēre* to see again, fr *re-* + *vidēre* to see – more at WIT] – **revisable** *adj,* **reviser, revisor** *n*

²**revise** *n* **1** the act of revising; revision **2** a printing proof taken from matter that incorporates changes marked in a previous proof

**Revised Standard Version** *n* a revised English translation of the Bible descended from the REVISED VERSION and published in the USA in 1946 and 1952

**Revised Version** *n* a British revision of the AUTHORIZED VERSION of the Bible published in 1881 and 1885

**revision** /ri'vizh(ə)n/ *n* **1** the action or an act of revising ⟨*~ of a manuscript*⟩ ⟨*~ for an examination*⟩ **2** a revised version – **revisionary** *adj*

**revisionism** /ri'vizhə,niz(ə)m/ *n* **1** advocacy of revision (eg of a doctrine or policy) **2** *chiefly derog* (a movement in Marxist socialism favouring) an evolutionary rather than a revolutionary transition to socialism

**revisionist** /ri'vizhənist/ *adj, chiefly derog* advocating revisionism – **revisionist** *n*

**revital-ize, -ise** /,ree'vietl,iez/ *vt* to give new life or vigour to; revive ⟨*circumstances which have ~d the disarmament movement*⟩ – **revitalization** *n*

**revival** /ri'vievl/ *n* **1** reviving or being revived: eg **1a** renewed

attention to or interest in something **b** a new presentation or production (eg of a play) **c(1)** a period of renewed religious fervour **c(2)** an often emotional evangelistic meeting or series of meetings **d** restoration of an earlier fashion, style, or practice **e** revitalization **2** restoration of force, validity, or effect (eg to a contract)

**revivalism** /ri'vievəliz(ə)m/ *n* **1** the spirit or methods characteristic of religious revivals **2** a tendency or desire to revive things of the past

**revivalist** /ri'vievəlist/ *n* **1** a person who conducts religious revivals; *specif* a clergyman who travels about to conduct revivals **2** someone who revives or restores something disused (eg a custom or style)

**revivalistic** /ri,vievə'listik/, **revivalist** *adj* of revivalists or religious revivals

**revive** /ri'viev/ *vi* to return to consciousness or life; become active or flourishing again *~ vt* **1** to restore to consciousness or life; reanimate **2** to restore from a depressed, inactive, or unused state; bring back ⟨*~ a Broadway musical*⟩ **3** to renew in the mind; recall ⟨*~d memories of the war*⟩ [ME *reviven,* fr MF *revivre,* fr L *revivere* to live again, fr *re-* + *vivere* to live – more at QUICK] – **revivable** *adj*

**reviver** /ri'vievə/ *n* one who or that which revives; *esp, humorous* an intoxicating drink

**revivify** /,ree'vivifie/ *vt* to give new life to; revive [Fr *révivifier,* fr LL *revivificare,* fr L *re-* + LL *vivificare* to vivify] – **revivification** *n*

**reviviscence** /,revi'vis(ə)ns, ri'vivis(ə)ns/ *n, formal* reviving or being revived [L *reviviscere* to come to life again, fr *re-* + *viviscere* to come to life, incho of *vivere* to live] – **reviviscent** *adj*

**revocable** *also* **revokable** /'revə'kəbl, ri'vohkəbl/ *adj* capable of being revoked ⟨*a ~ clause in a standard contract*⟩ [ME, fr MF, fr L *revocabilis,* fr *revocare*]

**revocation** /,revə'kaysh(ə)n/ *n* an act or instance of revoking [ME, fr MF, fr L *revocation-, revocatio,* fr *revocatus,* pp of *revocare*]

¹**revoke** /ri'vohk/ *vt* **1** to bring or call back **2** to annul; rescind ⟨*~ a will*⟩ *~ vi* to fail to follow suit in a card game (eg bridge) when able to do so, in violation of the rules [ME *revoken,* fr MF *revoquer,* fr L *revocare,* fr *re-* + *vocare* to call – more at VOICE] – **revoker** *n*

²**revoke** *n* an act or instance of revoking in a card game

¹**revolt** /ri'vohlt/ *vi* **1** to renounce allegiance or subjection to a government, law, established social conditions, etc; rebel – usu + *against* ⟨*trade unionists ~ing against rising unemployment*⟩ **2a** to experience disgust or shock at ⟨*~ at the carnage*⟩ **b** to turn away in disgust or abhorrence *~ vt* to cause to turn away or recoil with disgust or loathing; nauseate [MF *revolter,* fr OIt *rivoltare* to overthrow, fr (assumed) VL *revolvitare,* freq of L *revolvere* to revolve, roll back] – **revolter** *n*

²**revolt** *n* **1** a renouncing of allegiance (eg to a government or party) *esp* a determined armed uprising; **2** a movement or expression of vigorous opposition *synonyms* see REBELLION – **in revolt** in the process or state of rebelling

**revolting** /ri'vohlting/ *adj* extremely offensive; nauseating

**revolute** /'revəlyooht, -looht/ *adj, botany* rolled backwards or downwards ⟨*a leaf with ~ margins*⟩ [L *revolutus,* pp]

**revolution** /,revə'loohsh(ə)n/ *n* **1a(1)** the action by a celestial body of going round in an orbit; *also* the time taken by a celestial body to make one complete revolution **a(2)** the apparent movement of a celestial body round the earth **a(3)** the rotation of a celestial body on its axis **b** completion of a course (eg of years); *also* the period marked out by the regular succession of a measure of time or by a succession of similar events **c(1)** a progressive motion of a body round a centre or axis so that any line of the body remains parallel to and returns to its initial position; ROTATION 1a(1) – compare SOLID OF REVOLUTION **c(2)** motion of any figure about a centre or axis **c(3)** one complete turn; ROTATION 1b **2a** a sudden or far-reaching change ⟨*The Structure of Scientific Revolutions* – Thomas S Kuhn⟩ **b** a fundamental change in political organization; *esp* the overthrow or renunciation of one government or ruler and the substitution of another by the governed ⟨*the French Revolution*⟩ **c** activity or movement designed to

---

| | | | |
|---|---|---|---|
| **rewarm** *vt* | **reweave** *vt* | **reweld** *vb* | **rewin** *vb* |
| **rewash** *vb* | **rewed** *vb* | **rewet** *vt* | **rewrap** *vt* |
| **rewater** *vt* | **reweigh** *vt* | **rewiden** *vb* | |

effect fundamental changes in the socioeconomic situation or in some aspect of social, cultural, or intellectual life ⟨*a cultural* ~⟩ *synonyms* see REBELLION [ME *revolucioun*, fr MF *revolution*, fr LL *revolution-, revolutio*, fr L *revolutus*, pp of *revolvere*] – **of revolution** *of a solid shape* formed by the rotation of a plane figure or curve about an axis ⟨*ellipsoid* of revolution⟩

**¹revolutionary** /ˌrevəˈloohshən(ə)ri/ *adj* **1a** of or being a revolution ⟨~ *war*⟩ **b** tending to or promoting revolution ⟨*a* ~ *speech*⟩; *also* radical, extremist ⟨*a* ~ *outlook*⟩ **2** completely new and different ⟨*a* ~ *new soap-powder*⟩ – **revolutionarily** *adv*, **revolutionariness** *n*

**²revolutionary** *n* someone who advocates or is engaged in a revolution

**Revolutionary calendar** *n* the calendar of the first French republic adopted in 1793, dated from September 22, 1792, and divided into 12 months of 30 days with 5 extra days in a regular year

**revolutionist** /ˌrevəˈloohshənist/ *n, chiefly NAm* a revolutionary – **revolutionist** *adj*

**revolution·ize, -ise** /ˌrevəˈloohshəniez/ *vt* **1** to overthrow the established government of **2** to imbue with revolutionary doctrines **3** to change fundamentally or completely ⟨~ *industrial relations*⟩ ~ *vi* to undergo revolution – **revolutionizer** *n*

**¹revolve** /riˈvolv/ *vt* **1** to turn over at length in the mind; ponder ⟨~ *a scheme*⟩ **2a** to cause to go round in an orbit **b** to cause to turn round (as if) on an axis; rotate ~ *vi* **1** to recur ⟨*the seasons* ~d⟩ **2** to be considered in turn ⟨*all sorts of ideas* ~d *in his head*⟩ **3a** to move in a curved path round a centre or axis **b** to turn or roll round (as if) on an axis **4** to be centred on a specified theme or main point ⟨*the dispute* ~d *around wages*⟩ [ME *revolven*, fr L *revolvere* to roll back, cause to return, fr *re- + volvere* to roll – more at VOLUBLE] – **revolvable** *adj*

**²revolve** *n* something that revolves or is able to revolve; *specif, Br* a device used on a stage to allow a set or piece of scenery to be rotated

**revolver** /riˈvolvə/ *n* **1** one who or that which revolves **2** a handgun with a revolving cylinder of several chambers each holding one cartridge and allowing several shots to be fired in succession without reloading

**revolving** /riˈvolving/ *adj* tending to revolve or recur; *esp* recurrently available

**revolving charge account** *n* a CHARGE ACCOUNT (customer's account to which the purchase of goods is charged) under which payment is made in monthly instalments and includes a CARRYING CHARGE (extra charge on the goods purchased)

**revolving credit** *n* a credit which may be used repeatedly up to the limit specified after partial or total repayments have been made

**revolving fund** *n* a fund set up for specified purposes with the proviso that repayments to the fund may be used again for these purposes

**revue, review** /riˈvyooh/ *n* a theatrical production consisting typically of brief loosely connected often satirical sketches, songs, and dances [Fr, *revue*, fr MF, review – more at REVIEW] *usage* To avoid confusion it is better not to use the spelling **review**, which has many other meanings, for the theatrical performance.

**revulsion** /riˈvulsh(ə)n/ *n* **1** an act or instance of pulling back or away; withdrawal **2a** a sudden or violent reaction or change ⟨*the puzzling* ~s *of his moods*⟩ **b** a feeling of utter distaste or repugnance [L *revulsion-, revulsio* act of tearing away, fr *revulsus*, pp of *revellere* to pluck away, fr *re- + vellere* to pluck – more at VULNERABLE] – **revulsive** *adj*

**rewake** /ˌreeˈwayk/ *vb* **rewaked, rewoke** /ˈwohk/; **rewaked, rewoken, rewoke** *vt* to waken again ~ *vi* to become awake again

**rewaken** /ˌreeˈwaykən/ *vb* to rewake

**¹reward** /riˈwawd/ *vt* **1** to give a reward to or for **2** to recompense ⟨*persistence at length* ~ed *with success*⟩ [ME *rewarden*, fr ONF *rewarder* to regard, reward, fr *re- + warder* to watch, guard, of Gmc origin; akin to OHG *wartēn* to watch – more at WARD] – **rewardable** *adj*, **rewarder** *n*

**²reward** *n* something that is given in return for good or evil done or received ⟨*put great effort into it, but got scant* ~ *for his pains*⟩; *esp* something offered or given for some service, effort, or achievement ⟨*offered a* ~ *for finding the lost puppy*⟩

**rewarding** /riˈwawding/ *adj* **1** yielding a reward; personally satisfying ⟨*a very* ~ *experience*⟩ **2** offered by way of reward; serving as a reward ⟨*a* ~ *smile of thanks*⟩

**rewind** /ˌreeˈwiend/ *vt* **rewound** /ˈwownd/ to wind again; *esp*

to wind (film, tape, etc) back onto a spool – **rewind** *n*

**rewire** /ˌreeˈwie·ə/ *vt* to provide (eg a house) with new electric wiring ~ *vi* to replace old or defective electric wiring – **rewirable** *adj*

**reword** /ˌreeˈwuhd/ *vt* **1** to repeat in the same words **2** to alter the wording of; *also* to restate in different words

**rework** /ˌreeˈwuhk/ *vt* to treat again or anew: eg **a** to revise ⟨~ *a musical composition*⟩ **b** to reprocess (eg used material) for further use

**¹rewrite** /ˌreeˈriet/ *vb* **rewrote** /-ˈroht/; **rewritten** /-ˈritn/ *vt* to make a revision of (eg a story); cause to be revised: eg **a** to put (contributed material) into proper form for publication **b** to alter (previously published material) for use in another publication ~ *vi* to revise something previously written – **rewriter** *n*

**²rewrite** /ˈreeˌriet/ *n* **1** a piece of writing (eg a news story) which is the result of rewriting **2** an act or instance of rewriting

**rewrite rule** *n* a rule in a GENERATIVE GRAMMAR (description of a language in terms of ordered rules) that specifies how a single symbol may be expanded ⟨*the* ~ *that allows a noun phrase to be rewritten as determiner plus noun*⟩

**Rex** /reks/, *fem* **Regina** /riˈjienə/ *Br* **1** – used following the first name as a title of a reigning monarch ⟨*Elizabeth* Regina⟩ **2** – used in legal cases (eg criminal prosecutions) where the crown or state is a party to the action ⟨Regina *v Button (1966)*⟩ [L *rex* king, *regina* queen]

**Rexine** /ˈrekseen/ *trademark* – used for a strong artificial leather used esp for bookbinding

**reynard** /ˈrenəd, ˈray-, -nahd/ *n, often cap* a fox – used esp in stories as a name for the fox [ME *Renard*, name of the fox who is hero of the 13th-c Fr poem *Roman de Renart*, fr MF *Renart, Renard*]

**rezone** /ˌreeˈzohn/ *vt* to alter the zoning of

**R factor** *n* a factor that is present in some bacteria, is a basis of resistance to usu more than one antibiotic, and can be passed from one bacterium to another by CONJUGATION (process of sexual reproduction involving a one-way transfer of genetic material) [resistance]

**Rh** /ˌahr ˈaych/ *adj* of or being an RH FACTOR (substance present in RED BLOOD CELLS) ⟨~ *antigens*⟩ ⟨~ *sensitization in pregnancy*⟩

**rhabdocoele** /ˈrabdəˌsiəl, -ˌseel/ *n* a TURBELLARIAN (free-living aquatic flatworm) (order Rhabdocoela) with an unbranched intestine [deriv of Gk *rhabdos* rod + *koilos* hollow – more at CAVE]

**rhabdom** /ˈrabdom, -dəm/ *n* any of the minute light-sensitive rodlike structures in the RETINULAE (structural units) in the COMPOUND EYES of insects, crabs, spiders, or other ARTHROPODS [LGk *rhabdōma* bundle of rods, fr Gk *rhabdos* rod]

**rhabdome** /ˈrabdohm/ *n* a rhabdom

**rhabdomere** /ˈrabdəmiə/ *n* a division of a rhabdom [blend of *rhabdom* and *-mere*]

**rhadamanthine** /ˌradəˈmanthien/ *adj, often cap, formal* rigorously just or uncompromising [*Rhadamanthus*, mythical judge of souls in the underworld, fr L, fr Gk *Rhadamanthos*]

**Rhaeto-Romanic** /ˌreetoh rohˈmanik/ *n* any of a group of ROMANCE (Latin-based) languages of E Switzerland and the Tyrol including ROMANSH [L *Rhaetus* of Rhaetia, ancient Roman province + E *Romanic*]

**rhamnaceous** /ramˈnayshəs/ *adj* of or being the buckthorn family (Rhamnaceae) of trees and shrubs [deriv of Gk *rhamnos* buckthorn]

**rhamnose** /ˈramnohs, -nohz/ *n* a sugar, $CH_3(CHOH)_4CHO$, that occurs combined in many plants [ISV, fr NL *Rhamnus*, genus of the buckthorn, fr Gk *rhamnos* buckthorn; fr its being produced from a plant of this genus]

**rhaphe** /ˈrayˌfee/ *n, biology* RAPHE (seamlike join or ridge)

**rhapsodic** /rapˈsodik/ *adj* **1** resembling or characteristic of a rhapsody **2** extravagantly emotional; rapturous – **rhapsodical** *adj*, **rhapsodically** *adv*

**rhapsodist** /ˈrapsədist/ *n* **1** a professional reciter of EPIC poems (long poems telling stories esp of legendary heroes), esp in ancient Greece **2** one who writes or speaks rhapsodically

**rhapsod·ize, -ise** /ˈrapsədiez/ *vi* to speak or write in a rhapsodic manner ⟨~ *about a new book*⟩

**rhapsody** /ˈrapsədi/ *n* **1** a portion of an EPIC poem (long poem telling stories esp of legendary heroes) suitable for recitation **2a(1)** a highly emotional utterance or literary composition **a(2)** an effusively rapturous or extravagant expression of ideas **b**

rapture, ecstasy **3** a musical composition of irregular form suggesting improvisation **4** *archaic* a miscellaneous collection [L *rhapsodia*, fr Gk *rhapsōidia* recitation of selections from epic poetry, rhapsody, fr *rhaptein* to sew, stitch together (akin to OHG *worf* scythe handle, Gk *rhepein* to bend, incline) + *ōidē* song – more at ODE ]

**rhatany** /'ratəni/ *n* the dried root of either of two S American shrubs (*Krameria triandra* and *Krameria argentea*, family Krameriaceae) used medically as an ASTRINGENT (substance that constricts or contracts tissue); *also* a shrub that yields rhatany [Sp *ratania* & Pg *ratânhia*, fr Quechua *ratánya*]

**rhea** /'riə/ *n* any of several large tall flightless S American birds (order Rheiformes) that resemble the African ostrich but are smaller and have three rather than two toes, and that have a fully feathered head and neck, an undeveloped tail, and pale grey to brownish feathers that droop over the rump and back [NL, genus of birds, prob fr L *Rhea*, mother of the god Zeus, fr Gk]

**rhematic** /ri'matik/ *adj* of the formation of words ⟨*the* ∼ *instinct*⟩ [Gk *rhēmatikos*, fr *rhēmat-*, *rhēma* word]

**rhenium** /'reeniəm/ *n* a rare heavy metallic chemical element that resembles manganese, is obtained either as a powder or as a silver-white hard metal, and is used esp in catalysts and THERMOCOUPLES (devices for measuring temperature differences) [NL, fr L *Rhenus* Rhine, river in W Europe]

**rheo-** *comb form* flow; current ⟨rheo*stat*⟩ [Gk *rhein* to flow – more at STREAM]

**rheology** /ri'oləji/ *n* a science dealing with the deformation and flow of matter [ISV] – **rheologist** *n*, **rheological** *adj*, **rheologically** *adv*

**rheophile** /'ree-əfiel/ *adj* rheophilic [ISV]

**rheophilic** /,ree-ə'filik/ *also* **reophil** /'ree-əfil/ *adj* preferring or living in flowing water ⟨∼ *fauna*⟩

**rheostat** /'riəstat/ *n* a RESISTOR (device which offers resistance to an electric current) for regulating a current by means of variable resistances – **rheostatic** *adj*

**rheotaxis** /,ree-ə'taksis/ *n* a TAXIS (movement of an organism in response to a stimulus) in which current flow (e g of water) is the directive factor

**rhesus baby** *n* a baby born with a disease (ERYTHROBLASTOSIS FOETALIS) of the blood caused by the presence of antibodies in its mother's RH-NEGATIVE blood which act on and destroy the cells of its own blood, which is RH-POSITIVE

**rhesus factor** /'reesəs/ *n* RH FACTOR (substance present in RED BLOOD CELLS)

**rhesus monkey** *n* a small pale brown Indian monkey (*Macaca mulatta*) extensively used in medical research [NL *Rhesus*, genus of monkeys, fr L, a mythical king of Thrace, fr Gk *Rhēsos*]

**rhesus-'negative** *adj* RH-NEGATIVE

**rhesus-'positive** *adj* RH-POSITIVE

**rhetoric** /'retərik/ *n* **1** the art of speaking or writing effectively; *specif* the study of principles and rules of composition formulated by critics of ancient times **2a** skill in the effective use of speech **b** insincere or exaggerated language; *esp* language calculated to produce an effect **3** verbal communication; discourse [ME *rethorik*, fr MF *rethorique*, fr L *rhetorica*, fr Gk *rhētorikē*, lit., art of oratory, fr fem of *rhētorikos* of an orator, fr *rhētōr* orator, rhetorician, fr *eirein* to say, speak – more at WORD]

**rhetorical** /ri'torikl/ *also* **rhetoric** *adj* **1a** of or concerned with rhetoric **b** used for rhetorical effect **2** given to use of rhetoric; using lofty or pompous language – **rhetorically** *adv*, **rhetoricalness** *n*

**rhetorical question** *n* a question asked merely for effect with no answer expected

**rhetorician** /,retə'rish(ə)n/ *n* **1** rhetorician, rhetor **1a** a master or teacher of rhetoric **b** an orator **2** a writer or speaker who is (over) eloquent, or who uses grand or pompous language

**rheum** /roohm/ *n* **1** a watery discharge from the MUCOUS MEMBRANES, esp those lining the eyes or nose **2** *archaic* tears [ME *reume*, fr MF, fr L *rheuma*, fr Gk, lit., flow, flux, fr *rhein* to flow – more at STREAM] – **rheumy** *adj*

**¹rheumatic** /rooh'matik, roo-/ *adj* of, being, characteristic of, or affected with rheumatism [ME *rewmatik* subject to rheum, fr L *rheumaticus*, fr Gk *rheumatikos*, fr *rheumat-*, *rheuma*] – **rheumatically** *adv*

**²rheumatic** *n* someone suffering from rheumatism

**rheumatic fever** *n* an acute disease that occurs chiefly in children and young adults and is characterized by fever, and by inflammation and pain in and around the joints, the mem-

brane (PERICARDIUM) surrounding the heart and the heart valves

**rheumaticky** /rooh'matiki, roo-/ *adj*, *informal* rheumatic

**rheumatics** /rooh'matiks, roo-/ *n pl*, *informal* rheumatism

**rheumatism** /'roohmə,tiz(ə)m/ *n* **1** any of various conditions characterized by inflammation or pain esp in the muscles and joints **2** RHEUMATOID ARTHRITIS [L *rheumatismus* flux, rheum, fr Gk *rheumatismos*, fr *rheumatizesthai* to suffer from a flux, fr *rheumat-*, *rheuma* flux]

**rheumatoid** /'roohmə,toyd/ *adj* characteristic of or affected with rheumatism or RHEUMATOID ARTHRITIS [ISV, fr *rheumatism*]

**rheumatoid arthritis** *n* a disease of unknown cause and progressively worsening course that is characterized by painful inflammation and swelling of joint structures, esp of the leg and hip

**rheumatology** /,roohmə'toləji/ *n* a branch of medicine dealing with rheumatic diseases – **rheumatologist** *n*

**Rh factor** /,ahr 'aych/ *n* any of several substances present in the RED BLOOD CELLS of certain monkeys and most humans that are used to define blood groups and can, esp during pregnancy and blood transfusions, provoke intense and sometimes fatal antibody-producing reactions in the blood when incompatible factors are mixed [*rh*esus monkey (in which it was first detected)]

**rhin-** /rien-/, **rhino-** *comb form* nose ⟨rhino*ceros*⟩; nose and ⟨rhino*laryngology*⟩ [NL, fr Gk, fr *rhin-*, *rhis*]

**rhinal** /'rienl/ *adj* of the nose; nasal

**rhine** /rien/ *n*, *dial Br* a wide drainage ditch or watercourse [earlier *royne*, prob alter. of ME *rune* watercourse, fr OE *ryne* flow, watercourse; akin to OE *rinnan* to run]

**-rhine** /-rien/ – see -RRHINE

**rhinencephalon** /,rienen'sefəlon/ *n*, *pl* **rhinencephalons**, **rhinencephala** /-lə/ the part of the forebrain concerned chiefly with the sense of smell [NL] – **rhinencephalic** *adj*

**rhinestone** /-,stohn/ *n* a colourless artificial gemstone made of glass, paste, or quartz [*Rhine*, river in W Europe]

**Rhine wine** /rien/ *n* usu white wine made from grapes grown in the Rhine valley; *esp* hock

**rhinitis** /rie'nietəs/ *n* inflammation of the MUCOUS MEMBRANE that lines the nose and nasal passages [NL]

**¹rhino** /'rienoh/ *n*, *chiefly Br slang* money – no longer in vogue [origin unknown]

**²rhino** *n*, *pl* **rhinos**, *esp collectively* **rhino** a rhinoceros

**rhino-** – see RHIN-

**rhinoceros** /rie'nos(ə)rəs/ *n*, *pl* **rhinoceroses** /-seez/ *also* **rhinoceri** /-rie/, *esp collectively* **rhinoceros** any of various large powerful plant-eating very thick-skinned hoofed African or Asian mammals (family Rhinocerotidae) that have one or two heavy upright horns on the snout [ME *rinoceros*, fr L *rhinocerot-*, *rhinoceros*, fr Gk *rhinokerōt-*, *rhinokerōs*, fr *rhin-* + *keras* horn – more at HORN] – **rhinocerotic** *adj*

**rhinoceros beetle** *n* any of various large chiefly tropical beetles (of *Dynastes* and closely related genera) having projecting horns on the THORAX (central body section) and head

**rhinopharyngitis** /,rienoh,farin'jietəs/ *n* inflammation of the MUCOUS MEMBRANE lining the nose, nasal passages, and PHARYNX (muscular tube joining the mouth to the upper portion of the digestive tract) [NL]

**rhinoscope** /'rienə,skohp/ *n* an instrument used for examination of the nasal passages [ISV] – **rhinoscopy** *n*

**rhinosporidium** /,rienoh·spə'ridiəm/ *n* any of a genus (*Rhinosporidium*) of microorganisms related to the fungi that are found in some nasal POLYPS (small outgrowths or tumours) in man and in horses [NL, genus name, fr *rhin-* + *sporidium* small spore]

**rhinovirus** /'rienoh,vie(ə)rəs/ *n* any of a group of very small RNA-containing viruses (PICORNAVIRUSES) that are associated with disorders (e g colds) of the nose and throat [NL]

**rhiz-** /riez-/, **rhizo-** *comb form* root ⟨*Rhizobium*⟩ ⟨rhizo*carpous*⟩ [NL, fr Gk, fr *rhiza* – more at ROOT]

**-rhiza, -rrhiza** /-riezə/ *comb form* (→ *n*), *pl* **rhizae** /-si/, **rhizas** root; part resembling or connected with a root ⟨*coleo*rhiza⟩ ⟨*mycor*rhiza⟩ [NL, fr Gk *rhiza*]

**rhizanthous** /rie'zanthəs/ *adj* producing flowers apparently directly from the root [ISV *rhiz-* + Gk *anthos* flower – more at ANTHOLOGY]

**rhizobial** /rie'zohbiəl/ *adj* of or produced by a rhizobium ⟨*a* ∼ *enzyme*⟩

**rhizobium** /rie'zohbiəm/ *n*, *pl* **rhizobia** /-biə/ any of a genus

(*Rhizobium*) of small soil bacteria that form nodules on the roots of peas, beans, and other LEGUMINOUS plants and within which they convert atmospheric nitrogen into nitrogen-containing chemical compounds [NL, genus name, fr *rhiz-* + Gk *bios* life – more at QUICK]

**rhizocarp** /'riezoh,kahp/ *n* a plant with permanent underground parts but stems and leaves that die back each year [ISV] – **rhizocarpic, rhizocarpous** *adj*

**rhizocephalan** /,riezoh'sefələn/, **rhizocephalid** /-'sefəlid/ *n* any of an order (Rhizocephala of the class Crustacea) of marine INVERTEBRATE animals related to the barnacles, comprising specially adapted forms that live as parasites on crabs and HERMIT CRABS [deriv of Gk *rhiza* root + *kephalē* head – more at ROOT, CEPHALIC]

**rhizogenesis** /,riezoh'jenəsis/ *n* root development [NL]

**rhizogenic** /,riezoh'jenik/, **rhizogenetic** /-jə'netik/ *adj* producing roots ⟨~ *tissue*⟩

**rhizoid** /'riezoyd/ *n* a rootlike structure – **rhizoidal** *adj*

**rhizomatous** /rie'zohmətəs/ *adj* having or resembling a rhizome [ISV, fr NL *rhizomat-, rhizoma*]

**rhizome** /'riezohm/ *n* a somewhat elongated usu horizontal underground plant stem that is often thickened by deposits of reserve food material, produces shoots above and roots below, and is distinguished from a true root in having buds and usu scalelike leaves [NL *rhizomat-, rhizoma*, fr Gk *rhizōmat-, rhizōma* mass of roots, fr. *rhizoun* to cause to take root, fr *rhiza* root] – **rhizomic** *adj*

**rhizomorphous** /,riezoh'mawfəs/ *adj* shaped like a root [ISV]

**rhizoplane** /'riezoh,playn/ *n* the external surface of roots together with closely adhering soil particles and debris

**rhizopod** /'riezohpod/ *n* any of a subclass (Rhizopoda) of usu creeping PROTOZOANS (single-celled microorganisms) (e g an amoeba) that have lobed rootlike PSEUDOPODS (temporary projections enabling movement, feeding, etc) [deriv of Gk *rhiza* root + *pod-, pous* foot – more at FOOT] – **rhizopodal** *adj*, **rhizopodous** *adj*

**rhizopus** /'riezohpəs/ *n* any of a genus (*Rhizopus*) of mould fungi including bread mould and some important pests of fruit and vegetables [NL, genus name, fr *rhiz-* + Gk *pous* foot]

**rhizosphere** /'riezoh,sfiə/ *n* soil that surrounds and is affected by the roots of a plant [ISV] – **rhizospheric** *adj*

**rhizotomy** /rie'zotəmi/ *n* the surgical operation of cutting the front or back roots of SPINAL NERVES (e g for the relief of otherwise incurable pain) [ISV]

**Rh-'negative** *adj* lacking RH FACTOR in the RED BLOOD CELLS

**rho** /roh/ *n* the 17th letter of the Greek alphabet [Gk *rhō*, of Sem origin; akin to Heb *rēsh* resh]

**rhod-** /rohd-/, **rhodo-** *comb form* rose; rose-red ⟨*rhodium*⟩ ⟨*rhodolite*⟩ [NL, fr L, fr Gk, fr *rhodon* rose]

**rhodamine** /'rohdəmeen/ *n*, *often cap* any of a group of yellowish-red to blue fluorescent dyes; *esp* a brilliant bluish-red dye used esp in colouring paper and as a biological stain [ISV *rhod-* + *amine*]

**Rhode Island Red** /rohd/ *n* (any of) an American breed of general-purpose domestic poultry having a long heavy body, smooth yellow or reddish legs, and rich brownish-red plumage [*Rhode Island*, state of the USA]

**Rhode Island White** *n* (any of) an American breed of domestic poultry resembling Rhode Island Reds but having pure white plumage

**Rhodesian man** /roh'deezh(ə)n, rə-/ *n* an extinct African man (*Homo rhodesiensis* or *Africanthropus rhodesiensis*) having long bones of modern type, a skull with prominent brow ridges and large face but with a human palate and teeth, and a simple but relatively large brain [*Rhodesia*, region (now forming the countries Zambia & Zimbabwe) in S Africa]

**Rhodesian Ridgeback** /'rij,bak/ *n* (any of) an African breed of powerful long-bodied hunting dogs having a dense rough short tan coat with a characteristic crest of reversed hair along the spine

**Rhodes scholar** /rohdz/ *n* the holder of any of numerous scholarships founded under the will of Cecil Rhodes that can be used at Oxford University for two or three years and are open to candidates from the Commonwealth and the USA [Cecil *Rhodes* †1902 E statesman & financier in S Africa] – **Rhodes scholarship** *n*

**rhodium** /'rohdyəm/ *n* a white hard metallic chemical element that usu has a VALENCY of three, is resistant to attack by acids, occurs in platinum ores, and is used in alloys with platinum [NL, fr Gk *rhodon* rose; fr the colour of a solution of salts containing it]

**rhodochrosite** /,rohdoh'krohsiet, roh'dokrəsiet/ *n* a rose red mineral consisting essentially of the chemical compound manganese carbonate, $MnCO_3$ [G *rhodocrosit*, fr Gk *rhodochrōs* rose-coloured, fr *rhod-* + *chrōs* colour; akin to Gk *chrōma* colour – more at CHROMATIC]

**rhododendron** /,rohdə'dendrən/ *n* any of a genus (*Rhododendron*) of widely cultivated shrubs and trees of the heather family that have clusters of showy red, purple, pink, or white flowers; *esp* one (e g *Rhododendron ponticum*) with leathery evergreen leaves as distinguished from a deciduous azalea [NL, genus name, fr L, oleander, fr Gk, fr *rhod-* + *dendron* tree – more at DENDR-]

**rhodolite** /'rohdəliet/ *n* a pink or purple garnet used as a gem

**rhodonite** /'rohdəniet/ *n* a pale red mineral that consists essentially of the chemical compound manganese silicate, $MnSiO_3$, and is used as an ornamental stone [Ger *rhodonit*, fr Gk *rhodon* rose]

**rhodoplast** /'rohdəplast/ *n* any of the reddish CHROMATOPHORES (pigment-containing cell parts) that occur in RED ALGAE (e g seaweed) [ISV]

**rhodopsin** /roh'dopsin/ *n* a red light-sensitive pigment in the RODS (light-receiving cells) in the retina of marine fishes and most higher VERTEBRATE animals that is important in vision in dim light – compare IODOPSIN [ISV *rhod-* + Gk *opsis* sight, vision + ISV *-in* – more at OPTIC]

**rhodora** /roh'dawrə/ *n* any of a genus (*Rhodora*) of N American shrubs of the heather family that have delicate pink flowers [NL, genus name, fr L, a plant]

**rhomb** /rom/ *n* 1 a rhombus 2 a rhombohedron [MF *rhombe*, fr L *rhombus*]

**rhomb-** /romb-/, **rhombo-** *comb form* rhombus ⟨*rhombencephalon*⟩ ⟨*rhombohedron*⟩ [MF, fr L, fr Gk, fr *rhombos*]

**rhombencephalon** /,romben'sefəlon/ *n* the parts of the brain of a VERTEBRATE animal that develop from the hindmost portion of the embryonic brain; *also* HINDBRAIN 1a – compare MESENCEPHALON [NL]

**rhombic** /'rombik/ *adj* 1 shaped like a rhombus 2 ORTHORHOMBIC

**rhombohedron** /,romboh'heedrən/ *n*, *pl* **rhombohedrons, rhombohedra** /-drə/ a PARALLELEPIPED (three-dimensional geometric figure) whose faces are rhombuses [NL] – **rhombohedral** *adj*

**¹rhomboid** /'romboyd/ *n* a parallelogram that is not a rhombus [MF *rhomboïde*, fr L *rhomboides*, fr Gk *rhomboeidēs* resembling a rhombus, fr *rhombos*]

**²rhomboid, rhomboidal** /rom'boydl/ *adj* shaped somewhat like a rhombus or rhomboid

**rhombus** /'rombəs/ *n*, *pl* **rhombuses, rhombi** /-bi/ an equilateral parallelogram; *esp* one that is not a square [L, fr Gk *rhombos*]

**rhonchus** /'rongkəs/ *n*, *pl* **rhonchi** /-ki, -kie/ a whistling or snoring sound heard on listening to the chest (e g with a stethoscope) when the air channels are partly obstructed (e g in asthma) [LL, snoring, fr Gk *rhonchos*, fr *rhenchein* to snore, wheeze; akin to OIr *srennim* I snore]

**rhotac·ize, -ise** /'rohtəsiez/ *vt* to change to an /r/ sound to introduce superfluous /r/ sounds into speech, esp before consonants [Gk *rhōtakizein*, fr Gk *rhō* rho] – **rhotacism** *n*

**rhotic** /'rohtik/ *adj* denoting or speaking a dialect in which /r/ sounds are pronounced both at the ends of words and before consonants [*rho* + ¹*-otic*]

**Rh-'positive** *adj* containing RH FACTOR in the RED BLOOD CELLS

**rhubarb** /'roohbahb/ *n* 1 any of several plants (genus *Rheum*) of the dock family having large leaves with thick reddish succulent stems that are edible when cooked 2 the bitter dried underground stem and roots of any of several rhubarbs grown in China and Tibet and used esp as a laxative 3 *chiefly Br* – used esp by actors to suggest the sound of a crowd, background conversation, etc 4 *chiefly Br informal* nonsense, rubbish 5 *chiefly NAm* a heated or noisy dispute [ME *rubarbe*, fr MF *reubarbe*, fr ML *reubarbarum*, alter of *rha barbarum*, lit., foreign rhubarb, fr LL *rha* rhubarb (fr Gk) + L *barbarus* foreign, barbarous]

**rhumb** /rum/ *n* any of the 32 points of the mariner's compass [Sp *rumbo* rhumb, rhumb line]

**rhumba** /'rumbə/ *n* a rumba

**rhumb line** *n* an imaginary line on the surface of the earth that makes equal oblique angles with all MERIDIANS (imaginary semicircles passing through both poles) so that it forms a spiral coiling round the poles but never reaching them, and that is the course sailed by a ship following a single compass direction – called also LOXODROME [Sp *rumbo*]

**¹rhyme** /riem/ *n* **1a** correspondence in the sound of (the last syllable of) words, esp those at the end of lines of verse **b** a word that provides a rhyme for another ⟨*wanted a ~ for* fate⟩ **c** correspondence of sounds other than at the end of words: eg **c(1)** ALLITERATION (similar sounds at the beginning of neighbouring words) **c(2)** INTERNAL RHYME (rhyming of words within a line, sometimes with one at the end) **2a** rhyming verse; *also* a composition in rhyming verse **b** poetry ⟨*tales in prose or ~*⟩ [alter. of ME *rime*, fr OF, prob deriv of L *rhythmus* rhythm] – **rhymeless** *adj*

**²rhyme** *vi* **1** to make rhymes; *also* to compose rhyming verse **2a** *of a word or verse* to end in syllables that rhyme **b** to constitute a rhyme ⟨*date ~s with* fate⟩ *~ vt* **1** to put (eg a piece of prose) into rhyme **2** to cause to rhyme; use as (a) rhyme

**rhyme or reason** *n* good sense; reasonableness, logic – esp in *without rhyme or reason*

**rhyme royal** *n* a stanza of seven 10-syllable lines with a rhyme scheme of *ababbcc*

**rhyme scheme** *n* the pattern of rhymes in a stanza or a poem

**rhymester** /'riemstə/ *n* a poet; *esp* a dull or mediocre one

**rhyming dictionary** /'rieming/ *n* a dictionary that groups words according to the rhymes of their endings

**rhyming slang** *n* slang in which the word actually meant is replaced by a rhyming phrase of which only the first element is usu pronounced (eg "head" becomes "loaf of bread" and then "loaf")

**rhynchocephalian** /ˌringkoh-siˈfaylyən/ *n* any of an order (Rhynchocephalia) of mostly extinct lizardlike reptiles whose only surviving member is the TUATARA of New Zealand [deriv of Gk *rhynchos* beak, snout + *kephalē* head]

**rhynchophoran** /ringˈkofərən/, **rhynchophore** /'ringkəfaw/ *n* any of a group (Rhynchophora) of beetles with the head usu prolonged as a snout; a weevil [deriv of Gk *rhynchos* + *pherein* to bear]

**rhyolite** /'rie-əliet/ *n* a fine-grained acid volcanic rock that is similar to granite but formed from lava on the earth's surface [Ger *rhyolith*, fr Gk *rhyax* stream, stream of lava (fr *rhein* to flow) + Ger *-lith* -lite] – **rhyolitic** *adj*

**rhythm** /'ridh(ə)m/ *n* **1a** a pattern of recurrent alternation of strong and weak or long and short elements in the flow of sound and silence in speech **b** a particular example or form of rhythm; ¹METRE 1a ⟨*iambic ~*⟩ **2a** the aspect of music concerning the regular recurrence of a pattern of stress and length of notes **b** a characteristic rhythmic pattern ⟨*rumba ~*⟩; *also* ¹METRE 2 (the basic rhythmic pattern per measure) **c** rhythm, **rhythm section** *taking sing or pl vb* the group of instruments in a band (eg drums, piano, or bass) supplying the rhythm **3** movement or fluctuation marked by a regular recurrence of elements (eg pauses or emphases) **4** a regularly recurrent quantitative change in a variable biological process ⟨*the diurnal ~*⟩ **5** the effect created by the interaction of the elements in a play, film, or novel that leads to the development of the action ⟨*even as the emotional ~ catches hold, the mood is continually jolted by meaningless digressions – Time*⟩ **6** RHYTHM METHOD [MF & L; MF *rhythme*, fr L *rhythmus*, fr Gk *rhythmos*, fr *rhein* to flow – more at STREAM]

**rhythm and blues** *n* popular music with elements of blues and Negro folk music

**rhythm band** *n, chiefly NAm* a band, usu composed of school children, who play simple percussion instruments (eg sleigh bells, tambourines, or pairs of sticks)

**rhythmic** /'ridhmik/, **rhythmical** /-kl/ *adj* **1** of or involving rhythm **2** moving or progressing with a pronounced or flowing rhythm **3** regularly recurring – **rhythmically** *adv*

**rhythmicity** /ridh'misəti/ *n* the state of being rhythmic or of responding rhythmically

**rhythmics** /'ridhmiks/ *n taking sing or pl vb* the science or theory of rhythms

**rhythmist** /'ridhmist/ *n* one who studies or has a feeling for rhythm

**rhythm·ize, -ise** /'ridhmiez/ *vt* to order or compose rhythmically – **rhythmization** *n*

**rhythm method** *n* a method of birth control depending on not having sexual intercourse on those days in the woman's menstrual cycle when pregnancy is most likely to occur

**ria** /riə/ *n* a long narrow coastal inlet caused by the submergence of a river valley [Sp *ría*, fr *rio* river, fr L *rivus*]

**¹rial** /ri'ahl, 'rie·əl/ *n* – see MONEY table [Per, fr Ar *riyāl* riyal]

**²rial** /ree'awl, -'ahl/ *n* RIYAL

**rialto** /ri'altoh/ *n, pl* **rialtos** *chiefly NAm* an exchange, marketplace [*Rialto,* island & district in Venice in Italy]

**¹rib** /rib/ *n* **1a** any of the paired curved rods of bone or cartilage that stiffen the body walls of most VERTEBRATE animals and protect the heart, lungs, etc **b** a cut of meat, esp beef, that includes a rib **c** *chiefly humorous* a woman; *esp* a wife **2** something resembling a rib in shape or function: eg **2a(1)** any of the curved members of the frame of a ship that run upwards and outwards from keel to deck **a(2)** a light supporting strut in an aircraft wing that runs parallel to the fuselage **b** any of the stiff strips supporting an umbrella's fabric **c** an arched support or ornamental band in Romanesque and Gothic VAULTING (arched structure usu forming a ceiling or roof) **3** an elongated ridge: eg **3a(1)** a vein of an insect's wing **a(2)** any of the primary veins of a leaf **b** any of the ridges in a knitted or woven fabric; *also* ribbing [ME, fr OE; akin to OHG *rippi* rib, Gk *erephein* to roof over; (1c) fr the account of Eve's creation from Adam's rib (Gen 2:21–22)]

**²rib** *vt* **-bb-** **1** to provide or enclose with ribs ⟨*~bed vaulting*⟩ **2** to form a pattern of vertical ridges in by alternating knit stitches and purl stitches – **ribber** *n*

**³rib** *vt* **-bb-** *informal* to poke fun at; tease [prob fr ¹*rib;* fr the tickling of the ribs to cause laughter] – **ribber** *n*

**¹ribald** /'ribəld/ *n* a ribald person [ME, fr OF *ribaut, ribauld* wanton, rascal, fr *riber* to be wanton, of Gmc origin; akin to OHG *riban* to be wanton, lit., to twist; akin to Gk *rhiptein* to throw]

**²ribald** *adj* **1** crude, offensive ⟨*~ language*⟩ **2** characterized by coarse or indecent humour ⟨*a ~ youth*⟩ **synonyms** see COARSE – **ribaldry** *n*

**riband** /'ribənd/ *n* a ribbon used esp as a decoration; *also* ¹RIBBON 1c [ME, alter. of *riband*]

**ribbing** /'ribing/ *n* an arrangement or collection of ribs; *esp* a knitted pattern of ribs

**¹ribbon** /'ribən/ *n* **1a** a length of narrow closely woven fine fabric (eg of silk or rayon) usu used for decorating or fastening garments, tying up the hair, etc **b** a narrow length of fabric used for tying packages **c** a piece of usu multicoloured ribbon worn as a military decoration or in place of a medal **2** a long narrow strip resembling a ribbon; *esp* a strip of inked fabric or plastic used in a typewriter **3** *pl* reins for controlling an animal **4** *pl* tatters, shreds ⟨*his coat was in ~*s⟩ [ME *riban*, fr MF *riban, ruban*] – **ribbonlike** *adj*

**²ribbon** *vt* **1a** to adorn with ribbons **b** to cover (as if) with ribbons ⟨*a face ~ed with tears*⟩ **2** to divide or tear into ribbons

**ribbon development** *n* building, esp housing, running in a continuous line along a main road

**ribbonfish** /-ˌfish/ *n* any of various long thin sea fishes (eg an OARFISH)

**ribbon worm** *n* NEMERTEAN (marine burrowing worm)

**rib cage** *n* the bony enclosing wall of the chest consisting chiefly of the ribs and their connections

**ribgrass** /'rib,grahs/ *n, chiefly NAm* RIBWORT (type of plant)

**riboflavin, riboflavine** /ˌrieboh'flayvin/ *n* a yellow chemical compound, $C_{17}H_{20}N_4O_6$, that is a vitamin of the VITAMIN B COMPLEX, is found esp in green vegetables, milk, eggs, liver, and yeast, and is the essential active component (COENZYME) of various ENZYMES concerned with the breakdown of fats, carbohydrates, etc and the production of energy in living cells – called also VITAMIN $B_2$, VITAMIN G [ISV *ribose* + L *flavus* yellow – more at BLUE]

**ribonuclease** /ˌreboh'nyoohkliayz, -ays/ *n* an ENZYME that speeds up the breakdown of RNA [*ribonucle*ic (acid) + *-ase*]

**ribonucleic acid** /ˌriebohnyooh'klee·ik, -'klayik/ *n* RNA [*ribose* + *nucleic acid*]

**ribonucleoprotein** /ˌrieboh,nyoohklioh'prohteen/ *n* a NUCLEOPROTEIN that contains RNA [*ribonucle*ic + *-o-* + *protein*]

**ribonucleoside** /ˌrieboh'nyoohkliəsied/ *n* a NUCLEOSIDE that contains ribose [*ribose* + *nucleoside*]

**ribonucleotide** /ˌrieboh'nyoohkli·ətied/ *n* a NUCLEOTIDE that contains ribose and occurs esp as a constituent of RNA [*ribose* + *nucleotide*]

**ribose** /'riebohs, -bohz/ *n* a sugar, $CH_2OH(CHOH)_3CHO$, that is a PENTOSE (one containing five carbon atoms in the molecule) and is obtained esp from RNA and riboflavin [ISV, fr *ribonic* *acid* (an acid, $HOCH_2(CHOH)_3COOH$, derived from ribose), deriv of *arabinose*]

**ribosomal RNA** /ˌriebə'sohml/ *n* the part of RNA that is a fundamental structural element of the ribosomes – called also RRNA

**ribosome** /'riebəsohm/ *n* any of the minute granules containing RNA and protein that occur in cells and are the sites where proteins are synthesized [*ribo*nucleic (acid) + *-some*] – **ribosomal** *adj*

**ribwort** /'rib‚wuht/, **ribwort plantain** *n* an African and Eurasian plantain (*Plantago lanceolata*) with long narrow ribbed leaves

**rice** /ries/ *n, pl* **rice** a cereal grass (*Oryza sativa*) widely cultivated in warm climates for its seed that is an important food; *also* the seed of rice [ME *rys*, fr OF *ris*, fr OIt *riso*, fr Gk *oryza, oryzon*]

**rice paper** *n* a thin edible material resembling paper and made from the pith of various trees, esp the rice-paper tree [fr its resemblance to paper made from rice straw]

**rice-paper tree** *n* a small Asiatic tree or shrub (*Tetrapanax papyriferum*) of the ivy family whose pith is made into rice paper

**rice polishings** *n pl* the inner bran layer of rice when rubbed off in milling or polishing

**ricer** /'riesə/ *n, chiefly NAm* a kitchen utensil in which soft foods (e g potato) are pressed through a perforated container to produce strings about the diameter of a rice grain – **rice** *vt*

**ricercar** /ˈreechəkah/, **ricercare** /ˌreechə'kahray/ *n, pl* **ricercari** /-ri/, **ricercars** any of various forms of instrumental music esp of the 16th and 17th centuries, usu in the style of a FUGUE [It, fr *ricercare* to seek again, fr *ri-* re- (fr L *re-*) + *cercare* to seek, fr LL *circare* to go about; fr the disguising of the subjects by various alterations]

**rich** /rich/ *adj* 1 having abundant possessions, esp material and financial wealth 2a having high worth, value, or quality ⟨*a ~ crop*⟩ b well supplied or endowed; abundant ⟨*~ in natural talent*⟩ 3 lavishly impressive; sumptuous 4a vivid and deep in colour ⟨*a ~ red*⟩ b full and mellow in tone and quality ⟨*a ~ voice*⟩ c pungent ⟨*~ odours*⟩ 5 highly productive or remunerative; giving a high yield ⟨*a ~ mine*⟩ 6a having abundant plant nutrients ⟨*~ soil*⟩ b(1) (of food that is) highly seasoned, fatty, oily, or sweet ⟨*~ foods*⟩ ⟨*a ~ diet*⟩ b(2) concentrated ⟨*a ~ blend of juices*⟩ c high in the combustible component; containing more petrol than normal ⟨*a ~ fuel mixture*⟩ 7 pure or nearly pure ⟨*~ lime*⟩ 8a *informal* highly amusing, *also* laughable b full of import; significant ⟨*~ allusions*⟩ **antonyms** poor, plain (for 6b(1)) [ME *riche*, fr OE *rīce;* akin to OHG *rīhhi* rich, OE *rīce* kingdom, OHG *rīhhi;* all fr prehistoric Gmc words borrowed fr Celt words akin to OIr *rī* (gen *rīg*) king – more at ROYAL] – **richen** *vt*, **richness** *n*

**Richard Roe** /ˌrichəd 'roh/ *n* a fictitious name for a person or party involved in legal proceedings, whose true name is unknown or withheld – compare JOHN DOE

**riches** /'richiz/ *n pl* things that make one rich; wealth [ME, sing. or pl, fr *richesse*, lit., richness, fr OF, fr *riche* rich, of Gmc origin; akin to OE *rīce* rich]

**richly** /'richli/ *adv* 1 in a rich manner 2 in full measure; amply ⟨*praise ~ deserved*⟩

**Richter scale** /'riktə, 'rikhtə/ *n* a scale for expressing the magnitude of a seismic disturbance (e g an earthquake) in terms of the energy dissipated in it, with 1.5 indicating the smallest earthquake that can be felt, 4.5 an earthquake causing slight damage, and 8.5 a devastating earthquake [Charles *Richter b* 1900 US seismologist]

**ricin** /'riesin, 'risin/ *n* a poisonous protein in the bean of the CASTOR-OIL PLANT [L *ricinus* castor-oil plant]

**ricinoleic acid** /ˌrisinoh'lee‑ik, -'layik, ˌrisi'nohli‑ik/ *n* an oily FATTY ACID, $C_{18}H_{34}O_3$, that occurs in CASTOR OIL and forms chemical compounds (ESTERS) that are important in the manufacture of rubber and plastics [L *ricin*us + E *oleic*]

**¹rick** /rik/ *n* a stack (e g of hay) in the open air [ME *reek*, fr OE *hrēac;* akin to ON *hraukr* rick]

**²rick** *vt* to pile (e g hay) in ricks

**³rick** *vt* to wrench or sprain (e g one's ankle) [perh fr ME *wrikken* to move unsteadily]

**rickets** /'rikits/ *n taking sing vb* a disease, chiefly affecting children, that is characterized esp by soft and deformed bones and that is caused by failure to assimilate and use calcium and phosphorus usu due to a lack of sunlight or of VITAMIN D [origin unknown]

**rickettsia** /ri'ketsi‑ə/ *n, pl* **rickettsias, rickettsiae** /-si‚ee/ any of a family (Rickettsiaceae) of rod-shaped microorganisms similar to bacteria, that live as parasites in cells and cause various diseases (e g typhus) [NL, genus of microorganisms, fr Howard T *Ricketts* †1910 US pathologist] – **rickettsial** *adj*

**rickety** /'rikiti/ *adj* 1 suffering from rickets 2a feeble in the joints ⟨*a ~ old man*⟩ b shaky, unsound ⟨*a ~ chair*⟩

**rickey** /'riki/ *n, NAm* a cocktail containing a spirit, esp gin, and lime juice, sugar, and SODA WATER [prob fr the name *Rickey*]

**rickrack, ricrac** /'rik‚rak/ *n* a flat braid woven to form zigzags and used esp as trimming on clothing [redupl of ⁴*rack*]

**rickshaw, ricksha** /'rik‚shaw/ *n* a small covered 2-wheeled vehicle pulled by one or more people, originally used in Japan but now found in many parts of Asia [alter. of *jinrikisha*]

**¹ricochet** /'rikəshay/ *also* -shet/ *n* (the sound of) the glancing rebound of a projectile (e g a bullet) off a hard or flat surface [Fr]

**²ricochet** *vi* **ricocheting** /-'shaying/, **ricocheted** /-‚shayd/, **ricochetting** /-‚sheting/, **ricochetted** /-‚shetid/ to rebound one or more times

**ricotta** /ri'kotə/ *n* a soft white bland Italian cheese that resembles COTTAGE CHEESE and is made from the whey of sheep's milk [It, fr fem of pp of *ricuocere* to cook again, fr L *recoquere*, fr *re-* + *coquere* to cook – more at COOK]

**rictus** /'riktəs/ *n* **1a** (the width of the) opening of a bird's mouth b the (width of the) gap of an open mouth (e g of a person or fish) 2 an unnatural gaping grin or grimace [NL, fr L, open mouth, fr *rictus*, pp of *ringi* to open the mouth; akin to OSlav *regnǫti* to gape] – **rictal** *adj*

**rid** /rid/ *vt* **-dd-;** **rid** *also* **ridded** to make free; relieve, disencumber ⟨*~ himself of his troubles*⟩ [ME *ridden* to clear, fr ON *rythja;* akin to L *ruere* to dig up – more at RUG] – **get rid of** to free or disencumber oneself of

**riddance** /'rid(ə)ns/ *n* 1 the act of ridding 2 deliverance or relief from something oppressive or objectionable – often in *good riddance*

**-ridden** /ˌrid(ə)n/ *comb form* (→ *adj*) 1 afflicted or excessively concerned with ⟨*conscience-ridden*⟩ 2 excessively full of or supplied with ⟨*slum-ridden*⟩ [fr pp of ¹*ride*]

**¹riddle** /'ridl/ *n* 1 a short and esp humorous verbal puzzle; a conundrum 2 a mystifying problem or fact ⟨*the ~ of her disappearance*⟩ 3 something or someone difficult to understand **synonyms** see ¹PROBLEM [ME *redels, ridel*, fr OE *rǣdelse* opinion, conjecture, riddle; akin to OE *rǣdan* to interpret – more at READ]

**²riddle** *vb* **riddling** /-ridl‑ing/ *vt* to find the answer to ⟨*~ me this*⟩ ~ *vi* to speak in or propound riddles – **riddler** *n*

**³riddle** *n* a coarse sieve (e g for sifting grain or gravel) [ME *riddil*, fr OE *hriddel;* akin to L *cribrum* sieve, *cernere* to sift – more at CERTAIN]

**⁴riddle** *vt* 1 to separate (e g grain from chaff) with a riddle; sift 2 to cover with holes ⟨*he was ~d with bullets*⟩ 3 to spread through, and so damage or afflict; permeate – usu pass + *with* ⟨*the state was ~d with poverty* – Thomas Wood⟩ ⟨*~d with errors*⟩

**¹ride** /ried/ *vb* **rode** /rohd/; **ridden** /'rid(ə)n/ *vi* **1a** to sit and travel mounted on an animal b to travel on or in a vehicle c to be carried (e g in a litter or on people's shoulders) 2 to be sustained ⟨*rode on a wave of popularity*⟩ **3a** to lie moored or anchored ⟨*a ship ~s at anchor*⟩ b to sail; be borne along ⟨*the little boat rode before the breeze*⟩ c to appear to float ⟨*the moon rode in the sky*⟩ 4 to become supported on a point or surface 5 to travel over a surface ⟨*the car ~s smoothly*⟩ 6 to project, overlap – usu + *over* 7 of a racecourse to be in a specified condition ⟨*the course will ~ very hard today*⟩ **8a** to be placed as a bet ⟨*his money is riding on the favourite*⟩ b *of a bet or winnings* to remain placed on a horse, dog, etc in another race 9 to improvise freely on a jazz theme while keeping in rhythm 10 *informal* to continue without interference ⟨*let it ~*⟩ ~ *vt* **1a** to travel mounted on and in control of ⟨*~ a bike*⟩ b to move with or float on ⟨*~ the waves*⟩ **2a** to traverse by car, horse, or other conveyance ⟨*rode the byways of Sussex*⟩ b to ride a horse, bicycle, etc in ⟨*~ a race*⟩ 3 *of a jockey* to weigh in at prior to a race ⟨*Bill ~s 112 pounds*⟩ 4 to survive without great damage or loss; outlast – usu + *out* ⟨*rode the storm*⟩ ⟨*rode out the gale*⟩ 5 *esp of a male animal* to mount in copulation 6 to obsess, oppress ⟨*ridden by anxiety*⟩ 7 to recoil from or give with (a punch) to soften the impact 8 to keep in partial

engagement by resting a foot continuously on the pedal ⟨~ the clutch⟩ **9** chiefly NAm to give a ride to; carry, convey **10a** NAm to harass persistently; nag **b** NAm to tease, rib [ME *riden*, fr OE *rīdan;* akin to OHG *rītan* to ride]
**ride in** vt to prepare (a horse) for a competition by riding and exercising
**ride on** vt to depend or be countingent on
**ride up** vi to move upwards away from the correct or usual position ⟨my skirt rides up whenever I walk⟩
²**ride** n **1** a trip on horseback or in a vehicle **2** a road or path used for horse riding **3** any of various mechanical devices (eg a BIG WHEEL) for riding on at a fairground **4** the quality of travel comfort in a vehicle ⟨gives a rough ~⟩ – **take somebody for a ride 1** informal to deceive or cheat somebody **2** chiefly NAm slang to take somebody away in a car in order to murder him/her
**rident** /ˌrīed(ə)nt/ adj, archaic laughing with joy [L rident-, ridens, prp of rīdēre to laugh]
**rider** /ˈrīedə/ n **1** one who or that which rides; specif somebody who rides a horse **2** something added by way of qualification or amendment: eg **2a** a clause appended to a legal document, esp a legislative bill at its THIRD READING in the British Parliament **b** a statement (eg a recommendation for mercy) appended to a jury's verdict **3a** something (eg a seam of coal or turn of rope) overlying and often strengthening something else of a like nature **b** something (eg a piece of wood or metal) linking or moving along parts of a tool or piece of machinery (eg a harrow or balance) – **riderless** adj
¹**ridge** /ˌrij/ n **1** an elongated part that is raised above a surrounding surface: eg **1a** an elevated body part (eg along the backbone) **b(1)** a range of hills or mountains **b(2)** an elongated elevation of land (eg or an ocean bottom) **c** the raised part between furrows on ploughed land **2** the line along which two upward-sloping surfaces meet; specif the top of a roof at the intersection of two opposite slopes **3** an elongated area of high barometric pressure – compare TROUGH [ME rigge, fr OE hrycg; akin to OHG hrukki ridge, back, L cruc-, crux cross, curvus curved – more at CROWN] – **ridged** adj
²**ridge** vt **1** to form into a ridge or ridges **2** Br to plant (eg potatoes) in ridges ~ vi to form ridges
**ridgeling, ridgling** /ˈrijling/ n a male animal, esp a horse, having one or both testicles undescended into the scrotum [perh fr ¹ridge; fr the supposition that the undescended testicle remains near the animal's back]
**ridgepiece** /-ˌpees/ n a horizontal beam in a roof that supports the upper ends of the rafters
**ridgepole** /-ˌpohl/ n **1** a ridgepiece **2** the horizontal pole at the top of certain tents
**ridger** /ˈrijə/ n one who or that which ridges; esp an implement (eg a plough) that throws earth into ridges
**ridgeway** /-ˌway/ n, Br a path or road along the ridge of a hill
¹**ridicule** /ˈridikyoohl/ n scornful words or actions; derision, mockery [Fr or L; Fr, fr L ridiculum jest]
²**ridicule** vt to mock; make fun of – **ridiculer** n
   **synonyms** Ridicule, deride, mock, taunt, gibe, twit, and rally all mean "make an object of laughter". One may **ridicule** or **deride** somebody or something that is not present ⟨ridicule the government's financial policy⟩, **deride** perhaps carrying a stronger sense of bitterness and contempt. All the other words entail a direct attack. **Mock** stresses a scorn which is often expressed by derisive mimicry. **Taunt** implies cruel sarcasm and insult. **Gibe** applies to a scoffing and jeering which is nevertheless less offensive than **taunt**. **Twit** and **rally** involve a quite good-natured joking attack, **twit** usually implying that one draws attention to something mildly embarrassing ⟨twitted him about his ignorance of French⟩.
**ridiculous** /riˈdikyooləs/ adj arousing or deserving ridicule; absurd, preposterous **synonyms** see LAUGHABLE [L ridiculosus (fr ridiculum jest, fr neut of ridiculus) or ridiculus, lit., laughable, fr rīdēre to laugh; akin to Skt vrīdate he is ashamed] – **ridiculously** adv, **ridiculousness** n
¹**riding** /ˈrieding/ n **1** often cap any of the three former administrative districts of Yorkshire **2** an administrative or electoral district of a Commonwealth dominion (eg Canada) [ME, alter. of (assumed) OE thriding, fr ON thrithjungr third part, fr thrithi third; akin to OE thridda third – more at THIRD]
²**riding** n the action, state, or art of one who rides ⟨a ~ school⟩
**ridotto** /riˈdotoh/ n, pl **ridottos** a public entertainment consisting of music and dancing, often in fancy costumes, that was popular in 18th-century England [It, retreat, place of

entertainment, redoubt]
**riel** /ˈree-əl/ n – see MONEY table [Khmer]
**riem** /reem/ n, SAfr a soft pliable strip of rawhide or leather; a thong [Afrik, lit., strap, belt, fr MD rieme]
**Riemann integral** /ˈreemən/ n, maths DEFINITE INTEGRAL [G F B Riemann †1866 Ger mathematician]
**riempie** /ˈreempi/ n, SAfr a narrow leather thong used esp in furniture construction [Afrik riempje, dim. of riem]
**Riesling** /ˈreezling/ n (the grape variety used to make) a typically medium-dry white TABLE WINE [Ger]
**rifampicin** /riˈfampisin/ n an antibiotic, $C_{43}H_{58}N_4O_{12}$, that acts against some viruses and bacteria, esp by inhibiting their ability to make RNA (compound essential for the production of proteins) [blend of rifamycin (an antibiotic produced from a bacterium, from which it is derived) and piperazine]
**rife** /rief/ adj **1** prevalent, esp to a rapidly increasing degree ⟨fear was ~ in the city⟩ **2** abundant, common **3** copiously supplied; abounding – usu + with ⟨the city was ~ with rumours⟩ [ME ryfe, fr OE rȳfe; akin to ON rifr abundant] – **rife, rifely** adv, **rifeness** n
**riff** /rif/ n (a piece based on) a constantly repeated phrase in jazz or rock music, typically played as a background to a solo improvisation [prob by shortening & alter. fr refrain] – **riff** vi
**Riff** n, pl **Riffs, Riffi** /ˈrifee/, **Riff** a BERBER (pale-skinned people) of the Rif mountains in N Morocco
¹**riffle** /ˈrifl/ n **1** (the sound made during) the act or process of shuffling or leafing through something **2** Nam **2a** a rocky area in shallow water **b** a shallow stretch of rough water in a stream **3** NAm a ripple on water; RIPPLE 1 [perh alter. of ruffle]
²**riffle** vb **riffling** /ˈrifling/ vi, NAm to form, flow, or move in riffles ~ vt **1** to ruffle slightly ⟨the wind ~d the waters⟩ **2a** to leaf through rapidly; specif to leaf through (eg a pile of papers) by running a thumb along the edge of the leaves **b** to shuffle (playing cards) by separating the pack into two parts and riffling with the thumbs so that the cards become mixed together
**riffle through** vt to leaf or thumb cursorily through ⟨riffled through the files⟩
³**riffle** n **1** (any of) a serious of blocks, rails, etc laid on the bottom of a sluice to make grooves to catch and retain a mineral (eg gold) **2** a groove formed by riffles [prob fr ¹riffle]
⁴**riffle** vt to run through a riffle or over a series of riffles ⟨~ ground ore⟩
**riffler** /ˈriflə/ n any of several small filing or scraping tools [Fr rifloir, fr rifler to file, rifle]
**riff-raff** /ˈrifˌraf/ n taking sing or pl vb **1a** disreputable people **b** the rabble **2** refuse, rubbish [ME riffe raffe, fr rif and raf every single one, fr MF rif et raf completely, fr rifler to plunder + raffe act of sweeping – more at ²RAFFLE]
¹**rifle** /ˈriefl/ vt **rifling, rifl-ing** /ˈrief-ling/ **1** to ransack, esp in order to steal some or all of the contents ⟨~d the safe⟩ **2** to steal and carry away ⟨till time shall ~ every youthful grace – Alexander Pope⟩ ⟨~d merchandise worth about £1000⟩ [ME riflen, fr MF rifler to scratch, file, plunder, of Gmc origin; akin to obs D riffelen to scrape] – **rifler** n
²**rifle** vt to cut spiral grooves into the interior surface of (a cylindrical object) [Fr rifler to scratch, file]
³**rifle** n **1** a shoulder firearm with a rifled barrel designed to cause a bullet to spin and thus improve its stability through the air, and hence improve the accuracy **2** pl, often cap a body of soldiers armed with rifles – **rifleman** n
⁴**rifle** vt to propel (eg a ball) with great force or speed [³rifle]
**riflebird** /ˈrieflˌbuhd/ n any of several BIRDS OF PARADISE
**rifle range** n a place set aside for shooting practice using rifles
**riflery** /ˈrief(ə)lri/ n, chiefly NAm the practice of shooting at targets with a rifle
**riflescope** /ˈrieflˌskohp/ n, chiefly NAm a telescopic sight for a rifle
**rifling** /ˈriefling/ n **1** the act or process of making spiral grooves, esp in the barrel of a gun **2** a system of spiral grooves in the interior surface of the barrel of a gun designed to cause a projectile to spin, and thus make it more accurate
¹**rift** /rift/ n **1a** a fissure, crack **b** a geological FAULT or fracture in the earth's crust **2** an opening made by tearing or splitting apart ⟨a ~ in the clouds⟩ **3** a breach, estrangement ⟨suffered a ~ in their relations⟩ [ME, of Scand origin; akin to Dan & Norw rift fissure, ON rīfa to rive – more at RIVE]
²**rift** vt to tear apart; split
³**rift** n, chiefly NAm a shallow or rocky place in a stream [prob alter. of E dial. riff reef, fr D rif]

**rift valley** *n* a long valley formed by the subsidence of land between at least two FAULTS or fractures in the earth's crust

**¹rig** /rig/ *n, chiefly Br* RIDGELING (male animal with undescended testicles) [ME (northern), back, ridge, fr OE *hrycg*]

**²rig** *vt* **-gg-** 1 to fit out (eg a ship) with rigging 2 to clothe; dress up – usu + *out* ⟨~ged *out in a long lilac dress*⟩ 3 to equip or fit for a particular use – often + *out* ⟨*a plane* ~ged *for remote control*⟩ **b** to put together, esp for temporary use – usu + *up* [ME *riggen*]

**³rig** *n* 1 the distinctive shape, number, and arrangement of sails and masts of a ship 2 an outfit of clothing worn for an often specified occasion or activity ⟨*in ceremonial* ~⟩ 3 tackle, equipment, or machinery fitted for a specified purpose ⟨*a drilling* ~⟩ ⟨*an oil* ~⟩ ⟨*a CB* ~⟩ 4 *chiefly NAm* a horse-drawn carriage

**⁴rig** *vt* **-gg-** to manipulate, influence, or control for dishonest purposes ⟨~ *an election*⟩ [*rig*, n (ridicule, trick, swindle), of unknown origin]

**rigadoon** /ˌrigəˈdoohn/ *n* a rigaudon

**rigatoni** /ˌrigəˈtohni/ *n* pasta in the form of short, ridged, and sometimes curved tubes [It, pl, fr *rigato* furrowed, fluted, fr pp of *rigare* to furrow, flute, fr *riga* line, of Gmc origin; akin to OHG *rīga* line – more at ROW]

**rigaudon** /riˈgohdonh/ *n* a lively dance of the 17th and 18th centuries; *also* the music for this dance [Fr]

**rigger** /ˈrigə/ *n* **1a** somebody who rigs ships **b** somebody who constructs or works on oil rigs 2 a ship having a specified rig ⟨*square*-rigger⟩ 3 OUTRIGGER 1c (support for a rowlock)

**rigging** /ˈriging/ *n* 1 lines and chains used aboard a ship, esp for controlling sails and supporting masts and spars – compare RUNNING RIGGING, STANDING RIGGING 2 a network similar to a ship's rigging (eg in theatrical scenery)

**¹right** /riet/ *adj* 1 in accordance with what is morally good, just, or proper ⟨~ *conduct*⟩ **2a** in accordance with a rule **b** conforming to facts or truth; correct ⟨*the* ~ *answer*⟩ 3 suitable, appropriate ⟨*the* ~ *woman for the job*⟩ 4 *maths* straight ⟨*a* ~ *line*⟩ **5a** of, situated on, or being the side of the body that is away from the heart **b** located nearer to the right hand than to the left ⟨*the* ~ *pocket*⟩; *esp* located on the right hand when facing in the same direction as an observer ⟨*stage* ~⟩ **c** located on the right when facing downstream ⟨*the* ~ *bank of a river*⟩ **d** being the side of a fabric that should show or be seen when made up 6 having the vertex directly above the centre of the base ⟨*a* ~ *cone*⟩ ⟨*a* ~ *pyramid*⟩ 7 of or constituting the principal or more prominent side of an object 8 acting or judging in accordance with truth or fact; not mistaken ⟨*time proved him* ~⟩ 9 in a correct, proper, or healthy state ⟨*put things* ~⟩ ⟨*not in his* ~ *mind*⟩ 10 conforming to or influencing what is socially favoured or acceptable ⟨*knew all the* ~ *people*⟩ 11 *often cap* of, adhering to, or constituted by the Right, esp in politics 12 *chiefly Br informal* real, utter ⟨*a* ~ *idiot*⟩ 13 *N Eng, Austr, & NZ* ready, prepared ⟨*are you* ~?⟩ **antonyms** wrong, left [ME, fr OE *riht*; akin to OHG *reht* right, L *rectus* straight, right, *regere* to lead straight, direct, rule, *rogare* to ask, Gk *oregein* to stretch out] – **rightness** *n* – **see somebody right** to protect and reward or provide for somebody – see also **right as** RAIN, **get on the right** SIDE **of**

**²right** *n* 1 qualities (eg adherence to duty) that together constitute the ideal of moral conduct or merit moral approval 2 a power, privilege, interest, etc to which one has a just claim ⟨*has no* ~ *to say that*⟩ **2a** right, rights *pl* a legal claim to (the contents of) land or property ⟨*mineral* ~s⟩ **b** *pl* a financial interest in a product or enterprise ⟨*has bought the film* ~s *of the novel*⟩ 3 something that one may legitimately claim as due 4 the cause of truth or justice ⟨*trust that* ~ *may prevail*⟩ **5a** (a blow struck with) the right hand ⟨*gave him a hard* ~ *on the jaw*⟩ **b** the location or direction of the right side ⟨*can just see the Tower of London on your* ~⟩ **c** the part on the right side 6 the quality or state of being factually or morally correct ⟨*be in the* ~⟩ 7 *taking sing or pl vb, often cap* **7a** those who hold conservative or traditional political, social, or economic views **b** *the* members of a European legislative body holding conservative political views and occupying the right of a legislative chamber **8a** a privilege given stockholders to subscribe pro rata to a new issue of securities, generally below market price **b** *usu pl* the negotiable certificate signifying such privilege – compare RIGHTS ISSUE [ME, fr OE *riht*, fr *riht*, adj] – **rightless** *adj* – **by rights** with reason or justice; properly – **in one's own right** by virtue of one's own qualifications or attributes – **to rights** into proper order

**³right** *adv* 1 in a right, proper, or correct manner ⟨*treat him* ~⟩ ⟨*knew he wasn't doing it* ~⟩ 2 in the exact location or position ⟨~ *at his fingertips*⟩ ⟨~ *in the middle of the floor*⟩ 3 in a direct line or course; straight ⟨*go* ~ *home*⟩ 4 all the way; completely ⟨*blew* ~ *out of the window*⟩ 5 directly, immediately ⟨~ *after lunch*⟩ 6 according to fact or truth; truly ⟨*guessed* ~⟩ 7 on or to the right ⟨*looked left and* ~⟩ 8 to a great degree; very ⟨*entertained them* ~ *royally*⟩ – often used in titles ⟨~ *worshipful*⟩ – **right away** *informal* immediately; at once

*usage* Both **right** and **rightly** can mean "correctly" ⟨*if I remember right(ly)*⟩, but **right** is commoner than **rightly** for the meaning "so as to be satisfactory" ⟨*I guessed* **right**⟩ ⟨*it isn't fastened* **right**⟩. **Rightly**, but not **right**, is used before a verb to mean "as is right" ⟨*he* **rightly** *refused* (= he did right to refuse)⟩. **Right**, but not **rightly**, can mean "exactly" or "straight" ⟨*sent it* **right** *back*⟩ ⟨**right** *in the corner*⟩, and is the only antonym of *left*.

**⁴right** *vt* 1 to avenge ⟨*vows to* ~ *the injustice done to his family*⟩ **2a** to adjust or restore to the proper state or condition; correct ⟨*helps to* ~ *the imbalance of his previous work*⟩ **b** to bring or restore to an upright position ⟨~ *a capsized boat*⟩ 3 *archaic* **3a** to do justice to; redress the injuries of ⟨*so just is God to* ~ *the innocent* – Shak⟩ **b** to justify, vindicate ~ *vi* to become upright – **righter** *n*

**right angle** *n* the angle subtended by a quarter of the circumference of a circle; an angle of 90° – **right-angled, right-angle** *adj*

**right ascension** *n, astronomy* the distance along the CELESTIAL EQUATOR (circle round the imaginary sphere representing the universe) between the VERNAL EQUINOX (point marking the time of equal day and night in spring) and the point where a line drawn from the CELESTIAL POLE through a given celestial object cuts the celestial equator. The distance is measured eastwards, usu in hours, minutes, and seconds and is used, along with DECLINATION (distance north or south of the equator), to give reference points for celestial objects.

**right atrioventricular valve** /ˌaytriohvenˈtrikyoolə/ *n* the heart valve, consisting of three flaps, that is situated on the right-hand side of the heart between the right ATRIUM (upper chamber) and the right VENTRICLE (lower chamber) and that stops blood flowing back from the ventricle to the atrium – called also TRICUSPID VALVE; compare LEFT ATRIOVENTRICULAR VALVE

**right circular cone** *n* CONE 2a (2)

**right circular cylinder** *n* CYLINDER 1b(2)

**righteous** /ˈriechəs/ *adj* 1 acting in accordance with divine or moral law; free from guilt or sin **2a** morally right or justified ⟨*a* ~ *decision*⟩ **b** arising from an outraged sense of justice ⟨~ *indignation*⟩ [alter. of earlier *rightuous*, alter. of ME *rightwise*, *rightwos*, fr OE *rihtwīs*, fr *riht*, n, right + *wīs* wise] – **righteously** *adv*, **righteousness** *n*

**rightful** /ˈrietf(ə)l/ *adj* 1 just, equitable ⟨*a* ~ *proposal*⟩ **2a** having a just or legally established claim; legitimate ⟨*the* ~ *owner*⟩ **b** held by right or just claim; legal ⟨~ *authority*⟩ 3 fitting, proper ⟨*thought his* ~ *place was behind a desk*⟩ – **rightfully** *adv*, **rightfulness** *n*

**right hand** *n* **1a** the hand on the right-hand side of the body **b** a reliable or indispensable person **2a** the right side **b** a place of honour

**right-'hand** *adj* 1 situated on the right 2 right-handed 3 chiefly or constantly relied on ⟨~ *man*⟩

**right-'handed** *adj* 1 using the right hand preferentially or more easily than the left; *also* swinging from right to left ⟨*a* ~ *batsman*⟩ 2 relating to, designed for, or done with the right hand 3 having the same direction or course as the hands of a watch when viewed from the front; clockwise – used of a twist, rotary motion, or spiral curve (eg of a screw) as viewed from a given direction with respect to the axis of rotation – **right-handed** *adv*, **right-handedly** *adv*, **right-handedness** *n*

**right-'hander** *n* 1 a blow struck with the right hand 2 a right-handed person

**right-'ho** /hoh/ *interj, chiefly Br* righto

**right honourable** *adj, often cap R&H* entitled to great honour – used as a title for PRIVY COUNCILLORS and certain other dignitaries

**rightism** /ˈrieˌtiz(ə)m/ *n, often cap* advocacy of or adherence to) the doctrines of the Right – **rightist** *n or adj, often cap*

**rightly** /ˈrietli/ *adv* 1 in accordance with right conduct; fairly, justly 2 in the right manner; properly, suitably 3 according to truth or fact; correctly **4** *informal* with certainty; exactly ⟨*I can't ~ say*⟩ *usage* see ³RIGHT *antonym* wrongly

**right-'minded** *adj* thinking and acting according to just or honest principles ⟨*a ~ citizen*⟩ – **right-mindedness** *n*

**righto** /ˌriet'oh/ *interj, chiefly Br* – used to express assent or agreement [¹*right* + ²-*o*]

**right of common** *n, law* COMMON 4

**right of search** *n* the right granted by international law to a nation at war to stop and search neutral vessels on the high seas to ascertain whether they are liable to seizure

**right-of-'way** *n, pl* **rights-of-way 1** a legal right of passage over another person's property **2a** the course along which a right-of-way exists **b** the strip of land over which a public road, railway, electricity cable, etc is built or installed **3a** a precedence in passing accorded to one vehicle over another by custom, decision, or statute **b** the right to take precedence over others ⟨*gave the bill the ~ in Parliament*⟩

**right on** *interj, informal* – used to express agreement or approval; no longer in vogue

**Right Reverend** *adj* – used as a title for high ecclesiastical officials, esp Anglican bishops

**rights issue** *n* an issue of new shares available to existing shareholders only

**right triangle** *n, chiefly NAm* a triangle having a RIGHT ANGLE; a right-angled triangle

**rightward** /ˈrietwood/ *adj* towards or on the right

**rightwards** /-woodz/, *chiefly NAm* **rightward** *adv* towards or on the right

**right whale** *n* any of several large WHALEBONE WHALES (family Balaenidae) having very long whalebone plates instead of teeth, a large head, and usu no fin on the back [fr its having been considered the right whale to hunt]

**right wing** *n taking sing or pl vb* **1** *often cap R&W* the conservative division of a group or party **2** *cap R&W* RIGHT 7a – **right-wing** *adj*, **right-winger** *n*

**righty-ho** /ˌrieti'hoh/ *interj, chiefly Br* righto

**rigid** /ˈrijid/ *adj* **1a** deficient in or devoid of flexibility ⟨*a ~ pay policy*⟩ ⟨*a ~ bar of metal*⟩ **b** fixed or unyielding in appearance ⟨*his face ~ with pain*⟩ **2a** inflexibly set in opinions or habits **b** strictly maintained ⟨*adheres to a ~ schedule*⟩ **3** firmly inflexible rather than lax or indulgent ⟨*a ~ disciplinarian*⟩ **4** precise and accurate in procedure ⟨*was subject to a ~ examination*⟩ **5a** having the gas containers enclosed within compartments of a fixed fabric-covered framework ⟨*a ~ airship*⟩ **b** having the outer shape maintained by a fixed framework *synonyms* see ¹STIFF *antonyms* lax, elastic [MF or L; MF *rigide*, fr L *rigidus*, fr *rigēre* to be stiff] – **rigidify** *vb*, **rigidity** *n*, **rigidize** *vb*, **rigidly** *adv*, **rigidness** *n*

**rigmarole** /ˈrigmə.rohl/ *n* **1** confused or nonsensical talk **2** an absurd and complex procedure [alter. of obs *ragman roll* long list, catalogue]

**rigor** /ˈrigə *also* 'riegaw; *sense 4* 'rigə/ *n* **1** a chill or sense of chilliness accompanied by muscle contraction and convulsive shuddering or tremor (eg in the chill preceding a fever) **2** rigidity or stiffness of a body or tissue: eg **2a** uncontrolled rigidity and contraction of a muscle (eg in some fevers) **b** the temporary rigidity of muscle tissue that occurs some time after death **c** a state of temporary rigidity that occurs in some animals after a sudden shock, and during which the animal is incapable of responding to stimuli **3** an inert state assumed by some plants during conditions unfavourable for growth **4** *NAm* rigour [L, lit., stiffness]

**rigorism** /ˈrigə.riz(ə)m/ *n* rigid observance of doctrines or practice – **rigorist** *n or adj*, **rigoristic** *adj*

**rigor mortis** /ˈmawtis/ *n* the state, occurring some time after death, in which the muscles of the body become temporarily rigid [NL, stiffness of death]

**rigorous** /ˈrigərəs/ *adj* **1** manifesting, exercising, or favouring rigour; very strict ⟨*~ standards of hygiene*⟩ **2a** marked by extremes of temperature or climate **b** harsh, severe ⟨*a ~ jury*⟩ **3a** scrupulously accurate; precise, painstaking **b** having mathematical or logical rigour △ vigorous – **rigorously** *adv*, **rigorousness** *n*

**rigour** /ˈrigə/ *n* **1a(1)** harsh inflexibility in opinion, temper, or judgment; severity **a(2)** the quality of being unyielding or inflexible; strictness **a(3)** severity of life; austerity **b** *usu pl* an act or instance of strictness, severity, or cruelty **2 rigours** *pl*, **rigour** a condition that makes life difficult, challenging, or painful; *esp* extremity of cold ⟨*the ~s of a Highland winter*⟩ **3** strict mathematical or logical precision [ME, fr MF *rigueur*, fr

L *rigor*, lit., stiffness, fr *rigēre* to be stiff]

**rigout** /ˈrigowt/ *n, informal* a complete outfit of clothing

**Riksmål, Riksmaal** /ˈriksmol/ *n* BOKMÅL (literary form of Norwegian) [Norw, fr *rik* kingdom + *mål* speech, fr ON *māl*]

**rile** /riel/ *vt* **1** to make angry or resentful; annoy **2** *NAm* ROIL 1 *synonyms* see IRRITATE [alter. of *roil*]

**¹rill** /ril/ *n, chiefly poetic* a small brook [D *ril* or LG *rille*; akin to OE *rīth* rivulet]

**²rill, rille** /ril/ *n* any of several long narrow valleys on the moon's surface [Ger *rille*, lit., channel made by a small stream, fr LG, rill]

**¹rim** /rim/ *n* **1** an outer usu curved or circular edge or border **2** the outer ring of a wheel not including the tyre **3** the frame of a pair of glasses [ME, fr OE *rima*; akin to ON *rimi* strip of land, Gk *ērema* gently, Lith *remti* to support] – **rimless** *adj*

**²rim** *vt* **-mm-** **1** to serve as a rim for; border **2** to run round the rim of ⟨*putts that ~ the cup*⟩

**¹rime** /riem/ *n* **1** FROST 1c **2** an accumulation of granular ice tufts on the sides of exposed objects facing the wind, that is formed from supercooled fog or cloud [ME *rim*, fr OE *hrīm*; akin to ON *hrīm* frost, Latvian *kreims* cream] – **rimy** *adj*

**²rime** *vt* to cover (as if) with rime

**rimmed** /rimd/ *adj* having a rim – usu in combination ⟨*dark*-rimmed *glasses*⟩ ⟨*red*-rimmed *eyes*⟩

**rimose** /ˈriemohs/, **rimous** /ˈrieməs/ *adj* having numerous clefts, cracks, or fissures ⟨*~ tree bark*⟩ [L *rimosus*, fr *rima* slit, crack – more at ROW]

**rimrock** /ˈrim.rok/ *n* a vertical rock face (eg the wall of a canyon) formed by erosion of less resistant rock layers; *also* the rock layer forming such a face

**rimu** /ˈree.mooh/ *n* a large New Zealand coniferous tree (*Dacrydium cupressinum* of the family Podocarpaceae) with reddish-brown to yellowish-brown wood used for furniture and general construction; *also* the wood of this tree [Maori]

**¹rind** /riend/ *n* **1** the bark or outer tissue layer of a tree or plant **2** a usu hard or tough outer layer of fruit, cheese, bacon, etc [ME, fr OE; akin to OHG *rinda* bark, OE *rendan* to rend] – **rinded** *adj*

**²rind** *vt* to remove the rind or bark from

**rinderpest** /ˈrində.pest/ *n* a short-lasting infectious fever, esp of cattle, that is caused by a virus and is marked by inflammation and ulceration of MUCOUS MEMBRANES esp of the intestines [Ger, fr *rinder*, pl, cattle + *pest* pestilence]

**¹ring** /ring/ *n* **1** a circular band for holding, connecting, hanging, moving, or fastening, or for identification ⟨*a key ~*⟩ ⟨*a curtain ~*⟩ ⟨*a towel ~*⟩ ⟨*birds carrying ~s on their legs*⟩ **2** a circlet, usu of precious metal, worn on the finger **3a** a circular line, figure, or object ⟨*a smoke ~*⟩ **b** an encircling arrangement ⟨*a ~ of suburbs*⟩ **c** a circular or spiral course **4a** an often circular space, esp for exhibitions or competitions; *esp* such a space at a circus **b** a square enclosure in which boxers or wrestlers fight **5** any of the concentric bands that revolve round certain planets (eg Saturn and Uranus) **6** GIRDLE 1d (band made by removing bark from a tree) **7** a ringlike or circular marking indicating growth or age: eg **7a** ANNUAL RING (one year's growth of wood in a stem or tree trunk) **b** a ridge or marking on a fish scale representing one year's growth; ANNULUS 2b **8** *taking sing or pl vb* an exclusive combination of people working together for a selfish and often corrupt purpose ⟨*a drug ~*⟩ ⟨*a spy ~*⟩ **9** a closed chain of atoms in a molecule **10** a mathematical GROUP that is CLOSED under two BINARY operations (eg addition and multiplication) in which the first operation is COMMUTATIVE and the second operation is ASSOCIATIVE and DISTRIBUTIVE relative to the first **11a** *pl* a pair of usu rubber-covered metal rings suspended from a ceiling or crossbar to a height of approximately 2.5 metres (8 feet) above the floor and used for hanging, swinging, and balancing feats **b** *pl but taking sing or pl vb* a gymnastics event in which the rings are used **12** boxing, esp as a profession – usu + *the* ⟨*retired after 9 years in the ~*⟩ ⟨*ended his ~ career*⟩ **13** an electric element or gas burner in the shape of a circle used as a source of heat for cooking – compare GAS RING [ME, fr OE *hring*; akin to OHG *hring* ring, L *curvus* curved – more at CROWN] – **ringlike** *adj* – **run rings round somebody** to surpass or outdo somebody, esp in a way which makes him/her appear foolish

**²ring** *vb* **ringed** *vt* **1** to place or form a ring round; encircle ⟨*police ~ed the building*⟩ **2a** to attach a ring having identifying information, esp a number, to the leg of (a bird) **b** to put a ring through the nose of (a bull or other animal) so that it can be led **3 ring, ringbark** GIRDLE 3 (cut a ring of bark from a tree) **4** to throw a ring over (a peg) in a game (eg quoits) ~ *vi* **1** to move in a ring or rings **2** to form or take the shape of a ring

³**ring** *vb* **rang** /rang/; **rung** /rung/ *vi* **1** to sound resonantly or sonorously ⟨*the doorbell* rang⟩ ⟨*cheers* rang *out*⟩ **2a** to be filled with resonant sound; resound ⟨*the halls* rang *with laughter*⟩ **b** to feel the sensation of being filled with a continuous humming sound ⟨*his ears* rang⟩ **3** to sound a bell as a summons ⟨~ *for the waiter*⟩ **4a** to be filled with talk or report ⟨*the whole land* rang *with his fame*⟩ **b** to sound repeatedly ⟨*their praises* rang *in his ears*⟩ **5** chiefly Br to telephone – often + *up* ~ *vt* **1** to cause to ring, esp by striking **2** to sound (as if) by ringing a bell ⟨~ *a merry peal*⟩ **3** to announce (as if) by ringing ⟨~ *an alarm*⟩ – often + *in* or *out* ⟨~ *in the new year*⟩ **4** chiefly Br to telephone – usu + *up* – **ring false/true** to sound or appear false/true – see also **ring a** BELL/the CHANGES, **ring down the** CURTAIN [ME *ringen*, fr OE *hringan*; akin to MD *ringen* to ring, Lith *krankti* to croak]

**ring off** *vi*, chiefly Br to terminate a telephone conversation; HANG UP

**ring up** *vt* **1** to record (eg a sale) by means of a cash register **2** to record, achieve ⟨rang up *many social triumphs*⟩ [fr the bell that rings when a sum is recorded by a cash register]

⁴**ring** *n* **1** a set of bells **2** a clear resonant sound made by vibrating metal; *also* a similar sound **3** resonant tone; sonority **4** a loud sound continued, repeated, or reverberated **5** a sound or character suggestive of a particular quality or feeling ⟨*the speech had a familiar* ~⟩ **6a** an act or instance of ringing **b** a telephone call ⟨*give me a* ~ *in the morning*⟩

**ring binder** *n* a loose-leaf binder in which split metal rings attached to a metal back hold perforated sheets of paper

**ringbolt** /-,bohlt/ *n* an EYEBOLT with a ring through its loop

**ringbone** /-,bohn/ *n* a bony outgrowth on the PASTERN (part of leg above the hoof) of a horse usu causing lameness – **ringboned** *adj*

**ring circuit** *n* a circuit for supplying electricity in which the supply cables form a continuous closed loop beginning and ending at the power source; *specif* one used (eg in a house) for supplying electricity from the mains

**ringdove** /-,duv/ *n* a woodpigeon [fr the white patch on each side of its neck]

**ringed** /ringd/ *adj* **1** encircled or marked (as if) with rings **2** composed or formed of rings

**ringed plover** *n* a common small active European plover (*Charadrius hiaticula*) with orange legs and a broad black band across its white breast

**ringent** /'rinj(ə)nt/ *adj* having two distinct lips separated like an open mouth – used esp of the COROLLA (grouped arrangement of petals) of some flowers [L *ringent-, ringens*, prp of *ringi* to open the mouth – more at RICTUS]

¹**ringer** /'ring-ə/ *n* **1** one who or that which rings; *esp* somebody who rings bells **2** *informal* one who or that which strongly resembles another – esp in *dead ringer* ⟨*she's a dead* ~ *for the Prime Minister*⟩ **3** NAm *informal* a horse entered in a race under false pretences (eg claiming a false identity or record); *broadly* an impostor

²**ringer** *n* one who or that which encircles or puts a ring round something; *esp* a quoit that lodges so as to surround a peg

**Ringer** *n*, *informal* RINGER'S SOLUTION

**Ringer's solution, Ringer solution** *n* a solution that contains chloride, sodium, potassium, calcium, bicarbonate, and phosphate IONS (electrically charged atoms or groups of atoms) in water and that is used in physiological experiments to provide a medium similar in content and concentration to the liquid of many animal tissues [Sydney *Ringer* †1910 E physician]

**ring finger** *n* the third finger esp of the left hand, counting the INDEX FINGER as the first, on which the wedding ring is usually worn

**ringgit** /'ring-git/ *n* – see MONEY table [Malay]

**ringhals** /'ring,hals/ *n* a poisonous African snake (*Haemachates haemachatus*) that has a coloured ring round its neck and spits its venom at the eyes of its victim [Afrik *rinkals* (formerly *ringhals*), fr *ring* ring + *hals* neck]

**ringing** /'ring·ing/ *adj* **1** clear and rich in tone; resounding ⟨a ~ *baritone*⟩ **2** vigorously unequivocal; outspoken ⟨a ~ *condemnation of immorality*⟩ – **ringingly** *adv*

**ringleader** /-,leedə/ *n* a leader of a group that engages in objectionable or unlawful activities

**ringlet** /'ringlit/ *n* **1** a long lock of hair curled in a spiral **2**

*archaic* a small ring or circle

**ring main** *n*, Br a domestic wiring circuit in which a number of sockets or other power points are connected to the mains by supply cables that form a closed loop (RING CIRCUIT)

**ringmaster** /-,mahstə/ *n* a person in charge of performances in a ring (eg of a circus)

¹**ring-,necked, ring-neck** *adj*, of an animal, esp a bird having a ring of colour about the neck – **ringneck** *n*

**ring-necked pheasant** *n* any of various pheasants with white neck rings that have been widely introduced in temperate regions as game birds and that are varieties of, or hybrids of varieties of, the common Eurasian pheasant (*Phasianus colchicus*)

**ring ouzel** /'oohz(ə)l/ *n* a European thrush (*Turdus torquatus*) the male of which is black with a broad white bar across the breast

¹**ring-,porous** *adj*, of a woody plant or its wood having more numerous and usu larger water-conducting vessels in the first-formed part of an ANNUAL RING (ring of wood corresponding to a year's growth) than in the later part, with a resulting more or less distinct boundary between wood (SPRINGWOOD) formed in the earlier part of a growing season and that (SUMMERWOOD) formed in the later part of a season – compare DIFFUSE-POROUS

¹**ring-,pull** *n* a built-in device for opening a tin (eg of drink) consisting of a ring that when pulled removes a hermetically sealed tab or lid

**ring road** *n*, Br a road round a town or town centre designed to relieve traffic congestion

¹**ringside** /-,sied/ *n* **1** the area surrounding a ring, esp a boxing or wrestling ring **2** a place that affords a close view

²**ringside** *adj or adv* at the ringside ⟨a ~ *seat*⟩ ⟨*sitting* ~⟩

**ring spot** *n* **1** a diseased area on a plant consisting of often concentric rings of yellowish, purplish, or dead tissue **2** a plant disease characterized by ring spots

¹**ring-,tailed** *adj*, of an animal having a tail marked with rings of differing colours

**ringworm** /'ring,wuhm/ *n* any of several contagious fungal diseases of human beings and domestic animals that affect the outer layer of the skin (eg of the head and neck), the hair, and nails and that is characterized by ring-shaped patches of discoloured often dry skin covered with scales or blisters

**rink** /ringk/ *n* **1a** a smooth extent of ice marked off for curling or ice hockey **b** (a building containing) a surface of ice for ice-skating **c** an enclosure for roller-skating **2** part of a bowling green being used for a match **3** *taking sing or pl vb* a team in bowls or curling [ME (Sc) *rinc* area in which a contest takes place, fr MF *renc* place, row – more at RANK]

¹**rinse** /rins/ *vt* **1** to cleanse by flushing with liquid (eg water) – often + *out* ⟨~ *out the mouth*⟩ **2a** to cleanse (eg from soap used in washing) with clean water ⟨~ *clothes*⟩ **b** to treat (the hair) with a rinse **3** to remove (dirt or impurities) by washing lightly or in water only [ME *rincen*, fr MF *rincer*, fr (assumed) VL *recentiare*, fr L *recent-, recens* fresh, recent] – **rinser** *n*

²**rinse** *n* **1** an act or the process of rinsing **2a** liquid used for rinsing **b** a solution that temporarily tints the hair ⟨a blue ~⟩

¹**riot** /'rie·ət/ *n* **1** unrestrained revelry **2a** public violence, disorder, or commotion **b** a violent public disorder; *specif, law* a disturbance of the peace by three or more people assembled together and acting with a common unlawful intent **3** a profuse and random display ⟨*the woods were a* ~ *of colour*⟩ **4** one who or that which is wildly funny ⟨*the new comedy is a* ~⟩ **5** *archaic* wanton behaviour; debauchery [ME, fr OF, dispute] – **run riot 1** to act wildly or without restraint **2** to grow or spread profusely

²**riot** *vi* to participate in a riot – **rioter** *n*

**riot act** *n* [the *Riot Act*, British law of 1715 (repealed in 1973) providing for the dispersal of a riotous or unlawful crowd upon command of legal authority] – **read somebody the riot act** to reprimand or warn somebody severely

**riot gun** *n* a small firearm, esp a short-barrelled shotgun, used to disperse rioters rather than to inflict serious injury or death

**riotous** /'rie·ətəs/ *adj* **1** participating in a riot **2a** wild and disorderly **b** exciting, exuberant ⟨*the party was a* ~ *success*⟩ – **riotously** *adv*, **riotousness** *n*

¹**rip** /rip/ *vb* **-pp-** *vt* **1a** to tear or split apart or open, esp in a violent manner **b** to saw or split (wood) along the grain **2** to slit roughly or slash (as if) with a sharp blade **3** to remove by force; tear – + *out* or *off* ⟨~ped *out the panelling and replastered the walls*⟩ ~ *vi* **1** to become ripped; rend ⟨*his coat* ~ped *on the barbed wire*⟩ **2** to rush along; career ⟨~ped *past the finishing post*⟩ **3** to start or proceed without restraint ⟨*let*

*it ~⟩ synonyms* see ²TEAR [prob fr Flem *rippen* to strip off roughly] – **let rip** to (allow to) proceed with abandon
**rip into** *vt* to criticize or abuse violently
**rip off** *vt* **1** to rob; *also* to steal **2** to defraud – see also RIP-OFF

²**rip** *n* a rough or violent tear

³**rip** *n* **1** a body or stretch of water, esp in the sea, made rough **1a** by the meeting of opposing tides, currents, or winds **b** by passing over ridges on the bottom **2** RIPTIDE (strong surface current flowing from the shore) [perh fr ²*rip*]

⁴**rip** *n, informal* **1** a worn-out worthless horse **2** a dissolute person; a lecher **3** a mischievous usu young person □ no longer in vogue [perh by shortening & alter. fr *reprobate*]

**riparian** /rie'peəri·ən/ *adj* of, relating to, or living or occurring on the bank of a natural body of water, esp a river ⟨~ *species*⟩ [L *riparius* – more at RIVER]

**riparian right** *n* a right (eg access to or use of the shore, bed, and water) of somebody owning riparian land

**rip cord** *n* **1** a cord by which the gasbag of a balloon may be opened for a limited distance to release the gas quickly and so cause immediate descent **2** a cord or wire for releasing a parachute from its pack

**rip current** *n* RIPTIDE (strong surface current flowing from the shore)

**ripe** /riep/ *adj* **1** fully grown and developed; mature **2** mature in knowledge, understanding, or judgment **3** of advanced years ⟨lived to a ~ old age⟩ **4a** fully arrived; propitious ⟨the time seemed ~ for the experiment⟩ **b** fully prepared; ready for ⟨monopoly capitalism ~ for public ownership – New Statesman⟩ **5** brought by aging to full flavour or the best state; mellow ⟨~ cheese⟩ **6** ruddy, plump, or full like ripened fruit ⟨~ and mobile lips⟩ **7** euph smutty, indecent ⟨the ~ language that his predecessors would never have dared to use – Annabel⟩ *antonyms* unripe, green [ME, fr OE *rīpe;* akin to OE *rīpan* to reap – more at REAP] – **ripely** *adv*, **ripeness** *n*

**ripen** /'riepən/ *vb* to make or become ripe – **ripener** *n*

**ripieno** /ri'pyenoh/ *n, pl* **ripieni** /-ni/, **ripienos** *music* all the instruments or musical parts except those of the soloist or soloists; *also* a passage played by the ripieno players – used esp with reference to 17th- and 18th-century orchestral music and to brass-band music ⟨the ~ cornet only plays when the whole band is playing⟩ [It, lit., filled up]

¹**rip-,off** *n, informal* **1** an act or instance of stealing; theft **2** an instance of financial exploitation; *esp* the charging of an exorbitant price **3** a usu illegal or poor-quality imitation or copy (eg of a film or book)

**riposte** /ri'pohst, -post/ *n* **1** a fencer's quick return thrust following a PARRY **2** a piece of retaliatory banter; a retort **3** a usu rapid retaliatory manoeuvre or measure *synonyms* see ²ANSWER [Fr, modif of It *risposta*, lit., answer, fr *rispondere* to respond, fr L *respondēre*] – **riposte** *vi*

**ripper** /'ripə/ *n* **1** one who or that which rips (eg a machine used to break up rock, ore, etc) **2** *chiefly Austr informal* an excellent example or instance of its kind

**ripping** /'riping/ *adj* extremely good; excellent ⟨a ~ yarn⟩ – no longer in vogue [prob fr prp of ¹*rip*] – **ripping, rippingly** *adv*

¹**ripple** /'ripl/ *vb* **rippling** /'ripling, 'ripl·ing/ *vi* **1a** to become gently ruffled or covered with small waves **b** to flow in small waves or undulations **2** to flow with a light rise and fall of sound or inflection ⟨laughter ~d across the auditorium⟩ **3** to proceed with an undulating motion or so as to cause ripples ⟨the canoe ~d through the water⟩ **4** to spread irregularly outwards, esp from a central point ~ *vt* **1** to stir up small waves on **2** to impart a wavy motion or appearance to ⟨rippling his muscles⟩ **3** to utter or play with a slight rise and fall of sound [perh freq of ¹*rip*] – **rippler** *n*

²**ripple** *n* **1** a small wave or succession of small waves **2a ripple mark, ripple** any of a series of small ridges produced, esp on sand, by the action of wind, a current of water, or waves **b** a sound like that of rippling water ⟨a ~ of laughter⟩ **3** a small periodic fluctuation or variation in an otherwise steady current or voltage **4** *NAm* RIFFLE 2b (shallow stretch of rough water)

**riprap** /'rip,rap/ *n, NAm* a foundation or sustaining wall of loose stones; *also* stone used for riprap [obs *riprap* sound of rapping, redupl of ¹*rap*] – **riprap** *vt*

¹**rip-,roaring** *adj, informal* noisily excited or exciting; exuberant ⟨a ~ wave of musical. . . achievement – TES⟩

**ripsaw** /'rip,saw/ *n* a coarse-toothed saw having teeth only slightly bent to alternate sides that is designed to cut wood in

the direction of the grain – compare CROSSCUT SAW

**ripsnorter** /'rip,snawtə/ *n, chiefly NAm informal* somebody or something exceptionally powerful, unusual, or exciting ⟨the finale was a ~⟩ – **ripsnorting** *adj*

**riptide** /'rip,tied/ *n* a strong usu narrow surface current flowing outwards from a shore that results from the return flow of waves and wind-driven water – called also RIP, RIP CURRENT

**Ripuarian** /,ripyoo'eəri·ən/ *adj* of or being a group of FRANKS (Germanic peoples) settling in the 4th century on the Rhine near Cologne [ML *Ripuarius*]

**Rip van Winkle** /van 'wingkl/ *n* **1** a person who has hopelessly outdated ideas or attitudes **2** somebody who sleeps a lot [*Rip Van Winkle*, character who fell asleep for 20 years in a story by Washington Irving †1859 US writer]

¹**rise** /riez/ *vi* **rose** /rohz/; **risen** /'riz(ə)n/ **1a** to assume an upright position, esp from lying, kneeling, or sitting **b** to get up from sleep or from one's bed **2** to return from death **3** to take up arms ⟨~ in rebellion⟩ **4a** to respond warmly or readily; applaud – usu + *to* ⟨the audience rose to his verve and wit⟩ **b** to react or respond *to* offensive words or behaviour, esp by showing annoyance or anger ⟨despite the innuendos, he didn't ~⟩ ⟨didn't ~ to their taunts⟩ **5** to end a session; adjourn ⟨Parliament rose for the summer recess⟩ **6** to appear above the horizon ⟨the sun rose⟩ **7a** to move upwards; ascend ⟨fish rose to the surface⟩ **b** to increase in height or volume ⟨the river rose after the heavy rains⟩ **8** to extend above other objects or people ⟨houses rose out of the trees⟩ ⟨a ridge rising to 1500 metres⟩ **9a** to become cheered or encouraged ⟨his spirits rose⟩ **b** to increase in fervour or intensity ⟨his anger rose as he thought about the insult⟩ **10a** to attain a higher office or rank ⟨a colonel who rose from the ranks⟩ **b** to increase in amount or number **11a** to occur; TAKE PLACE ⟨a dispute rose between them⟩ **b** to come into being; originate ⟨the Rhine ~s in Switzerland⟩ **12** to follow as a consequence; result ⟨a problem rising from his proposal⟩ **13** to show oneself equal to a challenge ⟨~ to the occasion⟩ – see also GORGE **rises (at)** *usage* see ¹RAISE [ME *risen*, fr OE *rīsan;* akin to OHG *rīsan* to rise, L *oriri* to rise, *rivus* stream, Gk *ornynai* to rouse]

²**rise** *n* **1** an act of rising or a state of being risen: e g **1a** a movement upwards; an ascent **b** emergence (e g of the sun) above the horizon **c** the upward movement of a fish to seize food or bait **2** development, emergence ⟨the ~ of microtechnology gave industry a new lease of life⟩ **3** the vertical height of something; elevation **4a** an increase in amount, number, or intensity **b** an increase in price, value, rate, or sum; *specif, chiefly Br* an increase in pay **c** an increase in rank or status **5a** an upward slope or gradient ⟨a ~ in the road⟩ **b** a spot higher than surrounding ground **6** a rising-pitch intonation in speech – **get/take a rise out of** to provoke to annoyance by teasing – **give rise to** to cause to appear or happen; produce

**riser** /'riezə/ *n* **1** one who or that which rises (e g from sleep) ⟨a late ~⟩ **2** the upright part between two consecutive stair treads

**risible** /'rizəbl/ *adj, formal* **1** inclined or susceptible to laughter **2** arousing or provoking laughter; funny, ludicrous **3** associated with or used in laughter ⟨the ~ faculties⟩ △ visible [LL *risibilis*, fr L *risus*, pp of *ridēre* to laugh – more at RIDICULOUS] – **risibility** *n*, **risibly** *adv*

¹**rising** /'riezing/ *n* an insurrection, uprising ⟨the Easter Rising⟩

²**rising** *adv* approaching a specified age; nearly ⟨he's ~ fifty⟩

**rising trot** *n* a trot on horseback executed by rising in the saddle at alternate beats

¹**risk** /risk/ *n* **1** possibility of loss, injury, or damage; a peril **2** a dangerous element or factor; a hazard, threat ⟨a great ~ to security⟩ **3a** the chance of loss or the perils to the subject matter of an insurance contract; *also* the degree of probability of such loss **b** a person or thing that is a specified hazard to an insurer ⟨a poor ~ for insurance⟩ **c** an insurance hazard from a specified cause or source ⟨war ~⟩ *synonyms* see DANGER [Fr *risque*, fr It *risco*] – **risky** *adj*, **riskily** *adv*, **riskiness** *n* – **at risk** in danger – **on risk** *of* an insurer having assumed and accepting liability for a risk

²**risk** *vt* **1** to expose to hazard or danger ⟨~ed his life⟩ **2** to incur the risk or danger of ⟨~ed breaking his neck⟩ – **risker** *n*

**risk capital** *n* capital invested in a new enterprise

**risorgimento** /ri,sawji'mentoh/ *n, pl* **risorgimentos** a time of renewal or renaissance; a revival; *specif, often cap* the 19th-century movement for Italian political unity [It, lit., rising again, fr *risorgere* to rise again, fr L *resurgere* – more at

RESURRECTION]

**risotto** /ri'zotoh, -'so-/ *n, pl* **risottos** an Italian dish of rice cooked in meat stock and flavoured (e g with onion and green pepper) [It, fr *riso* rice]

**risqué** /'reeskay, 'ri-/ *adj* verging on impropriety or indecency [Fr, fr pp of *risquer* to risk, fr *risque*]

**rissole** /'risohl/ *n* a small fried cake or ball of cooked minced food, esp meat [Fr, fr MF *roissole*, fr (assumed) VL *russeola*, fr L *russeus* reddish, fr *russus* red]

**ritard** /ri'tahd/ *n* a ritardando

**ritardando** /ˌritah'dandoh/ *adv, adj, or n, pl* **ritardandos** (with) a gradual slackening in tempo – used as a direction in music [It, fr L *retardandum*, gerund of *retardare* to retard]

**rite** /riet/ *n* **1a** a prescribed form of words or actions for a ceremony **b** a ceremonial act or action **2a** the characteristic form of service or worship of a church or group of churches **b** a division of the Christian church using a distinctive form of service or worship [ME, fr L *ritus*; akin to OE *rīm* number, Gk *arithmos* number – more at ARITHMETIC]

**ritenuto** /ˌreete'n(y)oohtoh, ˌrita'nyoohtoh/ *adv, adj, or n, pl* **ritenutos** (with) an immediate slackening of tempo – used as a direction in music – compare RALLENTANDO, RITARDANDO [It, pp of *ritenere* to hold back, retain, fr L *retinēre*]

**rite of passage** *n* a ritual associated with a crisis or a change of status (e g puberty, marriage, or death) in the life of an individual [trans of Fr *rite de passage*]

**ritornello** /ˌritaw'neloh/ *n, pl* **ritornelli** /-'neli/, **ritornellos 1** a short recurrent instrumental passage in a vocal composition **2** a passage played by the full orchestra in a classical concerto before the entrance of the soloist or soloists, often repeated later with variations by the soloist or orchestra [It, dim. of *ritorno* return, fr *ritornare* to return]

**¹ritual** /'richooəl, -tyoo-/ *adj* **1** of rites or a ritual; ceremonial ⟨*a* ∼ *dance*⟩ **2** according to religious law or social custom ⟨∼ *purity*⟩ – **ritually** *adv*

**²ritual** *n* **1** the established form for a ceremony; *specif* the order of words prescribed for a religious ceremony **2a** ritual observance; *specif* a system of rites **b** a ceremonial act or action; *broadly* any formal and customary act or series of acts

**ritualism** /'richooəˌliz(ə)m, -tyoo-/ *n* **1** (excessive devotion to) the use of ritual **2** the study of ritual, esp religious rites – **ritualist** *n*, **ritualistic** *adj*, **ritualistically** *adv*

**ritual·ize, -ise** /'richooəˌliez, -tyoo-/ *vi* to practise ritualism ∼ *vt* to convert into a ritual ⟨*the tendency to* ∼ *violence*⟩ – **ritualization** *n*

**ritzy** /'ritsi/ *adj, informal* ostentatiously smart; fashionable, chic [*Ritz* hotels, chain of international luxury hotels founded by César *Ritz* †1918 Swiss hotelier] – **ritziness** *n*

**rivage** /'rivij/ *n, archaic* a bank, shore [ME, fr MF, fr *rive* bank, shore, fr L *ripa*]

**¹rival** /'rievl/ *n* **1** any of two or more individuals, teams, etc competing for a single goal **2** one who or that which equals another in desirable qualities; a peer **3** *obs* an associate, companion [MF or L; MF, fr L *rivalis* one using the same stream as another, rival in love, fr *rivalis* of a stream, fr *rivus* stream – more at RISE]

**²rival** *adj* having comparable pretensions or claims; competing

**³rival** *vt* **-ll-** (*NAm* **-l-, -ll-**) **1** to be in competition with; contend with **2** to strive to equal or excel **3** to possess qualities or abilities that approach or equal (those of another)

synonyms **Rival, match, emulate, compete, contend** and **vie** can all mean "try to equal or surpass". **Rival** and **match** may suggest merely the fact of being in competition, **rival** often in addition entailing an effort to reach the same level as another ⟨*strove to rival her brother as a pistol shot*⟩, and **match** often carrying the idea of being pitted against another in an encounter ⟨*troops whom none could* **match** *in battle*⟩. **Emulate** implies the effort to equal another by imitation ⟨*a simplicity* **emulated** *without success by numerous modern poets* – T S Eliot⟩. **Compete** and **contend** imply a struggle, not necessarily in an organized contest ⟨*the dinosaurs could not* **compete** *successfully with the smaller mammals*⟩, **contend** emphasizing effort and determination ⟨*a grey stone castle, for whose keep Bruces and Comyns and Macdowalls* **contended** – John Buchan⟩. **Vie** is close to **compete**, but less forceful.

**rivalry** /'riev(ə)lri/ *n* an instance of rivalling; the state of being a rival

**rive** /riev/ *vb* **rived** ; **riven** /'riv(ə)n/ *also* **rived** *vt* **1a** to wrench open or tear apart or to pieces **b** to split with force or violence; cleave ⟨*a tree* ∼n *by lightning*⟩ **2** to rend with distress or dispute ⟨*her heart was* ∼n *by the news*⟩ ⟨*a council still* ∼n *over*

*the housing issue*⟩ ∼ *vi* to become split [ME *riven*, fr ON *rīfa*; akin to L *ripa* shore, Gk *ereipein* to tear down, OE *rāw* row]

**river** /'rivə/ *n* **1** a natural stream of water of considerable volume **2a** a flow that matches a river in volume ⟨*a* ∼ *of lava*⟩ **b river, rivers** *pl* a copious or overwhelming quantity ⟨∼s *of blood*⟩ **3** a white streak running through printed matter and caused by wide spacing occurring at the same place in several lines [ME *rivere*, fr OF, fr (assumed) VL *riparia*, fr L, fem of *riparius* riparian, fr *ripa* bank, shore] – **sell down the river** to be disloyal to; betray [fr the selling of slaves in the USA to plantations further down the Mississippi river, where harsher conditions prevailed]

**riverbed** /'rivəˌbed/ *n* the channel occupied by a river

**riverine** /'rivərien/ *adj* **1** of, formed by, or resembling a river **2** living or situated on the banks of a river

**riverside** /'rivəˌsied/ *n* the side or bank of a river

**¹rivet** /'rivit/ *n* a metal pin with a head at one end, used to unite two or more pieces by passing the shaft through a hole in each piece and then beating or pressing down the plain end so as to make a second head [ME *rivette*, fr MF *river* to be attached]

**²rivet** *vt* **1** to fasten (as if) with rivets **2** to hammer or flatten the end or point of (e g a metal pin, rod, or bolt) so as to form a head **3** to fix firmly ⟨*was* ∼ed *to the spot*⟩ **4** to attract and hold (e g the attention) completely ⟨*another part of the room soon* ∼ed *her gaze* – Thomas Hardy⟩ – **riveter** *n*

**riviera** /ˌrivi'eərə/ *n, often cap* a coastal region, usu with a mild climate, in which many resorts are situated ⟨*the Cornish* Riviera⟩; *specif* the Mediterranean coast extending from SE France to NW Italy [the *Riviera*, region in SE France and NW Italy]

**rivière** /ˌrivi'eə/ *n* a necklace of precious stones (e g diamonds), usu having one large stone at the centre [Fr, lit., river, fr OF *rivere*]

**rivulet** /'rivyoolit/ *n* a small stream; a brook [It *rivoletto*, dim. of *rivolo*, fr L *rivulus*, dim. of *rivus* stream – more at RISE]

**¹riyal** /ri'yahl/ *n* – see MONEY table [Ar *riyāl*, fr Sp *real* real]

**²riyal** *n* RIAL (unit of currency)

**RNA** *n* a chemical compound (NUCLEIC ACID) that occurs in living cells as long strands chemically similar to and containing the same genetic information as a single strand of DNA but with a RIBOSE sugar in place of DEOXYRIBOSE, and URACIL instead of THYMINE. RNA occurs in various forms that are essential for the production of proteins and important in the regulation of chemical activities inside living cells. – compare MESSENGER RNA, RIBOSOMAL RNA, TRANSFER RNA [ribonucleic acid]

**RNA polymerase** *n* an enzyme that promotes the synthesis of RNA

**RNase** /ˌahren'ayz/, **RNAase** /ˌahren'ayayz/ *n* RIBONUCLEASE (enzyme that breaks down RNA) [*RNA* + *-ase*]

**¹roach** /rohch/ *n, pl* **roach**, *esp for different types* **roaches** (any of various fishes related to) a silver-white European freshwater fish (*Rutilus rutilus*) of the carp family that has a greenish back and reddish fins [ME *roche*, fr MF]

**²roach** *vt, NAm* ²HOG **1** (cut a horse's mane) [origin unknown]

**³roach** *n* a concave or convex curve in the edge of a sail

**⁴roach** *n, NAm* **1** a cockroach **2** *slang* the butt of a marijuana cigarette

**road** /rohd/ *n* **1** road, roads *pl*, roadstead a relatively sheltered stretch of water near the shore where ships may ride at anchor **2a** an open way, usu covered with tarmac or concrete, for the passage of vehicles, people, and animals **b** road, roadway the part of such a way reserved for vehicles **3** a route, path ⟨*on the* ∼ *to wisdom*⟩ **4** *NAm* a railway [ME *rode*, fr OE *rād* ride, journey; akin to OE *rīdan* to ride] – **roadless** *adj* – **hit the road** *informal* to start on a journey

synonyms **Road** and **street** both mean "thoroughfare". A more or less long-distance highway between towns is decidedly a **road** rather than a **street**, often called after the place it goes to ⟨*the Bath* **Road**⟩ ⟨*the Great North* **Road**⟩, with the exception of the names of the great Roman roads in Britain ⟨*Watling* **Street**⟩. A thoroughfare in a town, between two lines of buildings, is a **street** ⟨*Regent* **Street**⟩, but the name **road** is often retained in suburbs or where a road leading out of town has become built up ⟨*the Old Kent* **Road**⟩.

**road agent** *n, NAm* a highwayman who formerly operated esp on stagecoach routes in remote districts

**roadbed** /-ˌbed/ *n* **1a** the bed on which the sleepers, rails, and ballast of a railway rest **b** (the upper surface of) the ballast on which the sleepers rest **2a** the foundation of a road prepared for surfacing **b** *NAm* the part of the surface of a road travelled by vehicles

**roadblock** /-,blok/ *n* **1** a road barricade set up by an army, the police, etc to halt or slow the progress of traffic (eg in order to catch a criminal) **2** *chiefly NAm* an obstruction in a road **3** *chiefly NAm* an obstacle to progress or success – **roadblock** *vt*

**road hog** *n, informal* a reckless driver of a motor vehicle who obstructs or intimidates others

**roadholding** /-,hohlding/ *n, chiefly Br* the ability of a moving vehicle to remain stable on the road

**roadhouse** /-,hows/ *n* an inn situated usu on a main road in a country area; *also, NAm* a nightclub situated usu outside city limits

**roadie** /'rohdi/ *n, informal* ROAD MANAGER

**roadman** /'rohdmən, -,man/ *n* one who mends or builds roads

**road manager** *n* somebody responsible for the organization of travel and equipment for entertainers, esp rock musicians, who are on tour

**road metal** *n* broken stone used in making and repairing roads or ballasting railways

**road roller** *n* a machine equipped with heavy wide smooth rollers for compacting road surfaces during construction

**roadrunner** /-,runə/ *n* a largely ground-living fast-running American bird (*Geococcyx californianus*) of the cuckoo family with a small crest and with brown and white plumage

**road show** *n* (a performance given by) a group of touring entertainers, esp pop musicians

**roadside** /'rohd,sied/ *n* the strip of land beside a road; the side of a road ⟨*a* ~ *café*⟩

**roadstead** /'rohd,sted/ *n* ROAD 1 (sheltered stretch of water)

**roadster** /'rohdstə/ *n* **1** a horse or sturdy bicycle for riding on roads **2** an open sports car that seats usu two people – no longer in vogue

**road tax** *n* a tax paid on road vehicles usu once or twice a year

**road test** *n* a test of a vehicle under practical operating conditions on the road – **road test** *vt*

**roadway** /-,way/ *n* a road; *specif* ROAD 2b

**roadwork** /-,wuhk/ *n* **1** conditioning for an athletic contest (eg a boxing match) consisting mainly of long runs **2** *pl, Br* (the site of) the repair or construction of roads

**roadworthy** /-,wuhdhi/ *adj, of a vehicle* fit for use on the road – **roadworthiness** *n*

**roam** /rohm/ *vi* **1** to go aimlessly from place to place; wander **2** to travel unhindered through a wide area ⟨*cattle* ~*ing in search of water*⟩ ~ *vt* to range or wander over ⟨~*ed the streets*⟩ [ME *romen* – **roam** *n*, **roamer** *n*

**¹roan** /rohn/ *adj, esp of a horse or cow* having a coat of a usu reddish-brown base colour that is muted and lightened by some white hairs [MF, fr OSp *roano*]

**²roan** *n* **1** (the colour of) an animal (eg a horse) with a roan coat **2** a sheepskin tanned with powder made from the leaves of the sumach tree and coloured and finished to imitate MOROCCO leather

**¹roar** /'raw/ *vi* **1a** to utter or emit a roar **b** to sing or shout with full force **2a** to make or emit a loud reverberating or rumbling **b** to laugh loudly and deeply **3** to be boisterous or disorderly – usu + *about* **4** *of a horse suffering from roaring* to make a loud rasping noise in breathing **5** *journalistic* to make one's way vigorously ⟨*Botham* ~*s to* 100 *in* 70 *minutes*⟩ ~ *vt* **1** to utter with a roar ⟨~*ed his commands*⟩ **2** to cause (oneself) to become by roaring ⟨~*ed himself hoarse*⟩ [ME *roren*, fr OE *rārian*; akin to OHG *rērēn* to bleat, Skt *rāyati* he barks] – **roarer** *n*

**²roar** *n* **1** the deep prolonged cry characteristic of certain wild animals, esp lions **2** a loud deep cry or call (eg of pain, anger, or laughter) **3** a loud continuous confused sound ⟨*the* ~ *of conversation in the bar*⟩

**¹roaring** /'rawring/ *n* noisy breathing in a horse noticeable esp during exertion and caused by paralysis of muscles of the larynx or inflammation and thickening of the membrane lining the larynx

**²roaring** *adj* **1** making or characterized by a sound resembling a roar; loud ⟨~ *thunder*⟩ **2** marked by energetic or successful activity; booming ⟨*did a* ~ *trade*⟩

**³roaring** *adv, informal* extremely, thoroughly – esp in *roaring drunk*

**roaring forties** *n pl* either of two areas of ocean between latitudes 40° and 50° N and S noted for stormy westerly winds

**¹roast** /rohst/ *vt* **1a** to cook by exposing to dry heat (eg in an oven or over a fire) or by surrounding with hot embers or coals **b** to dry and brown slightly by exposure to heat ⟨~ *coffee*⟩ **2** to heat (eg an ore) in air at a temperature too low for melting in order ro remove impurities or unwanted material, cause reaction with oxygen, etc; *esp* to heat (a sulphur-containing metal ore) in order to remove sulphur and thus produce a product more suitable for further refining **3** to heat to excess ⟨*the sun* ~*ed the sand dunes*⟩ **4** *informal* to criticize severely ⟨*critics* ~*ed his early novels*⟩ ~ *vi* **1** to cook food by roasting **2** to undergo being roasted [ME *rosten*, fr OF *rostir*, of Gmc origin; akin to OHG *rōsten* to roast]

**²roast** *n* **1a** a piece of roasted meat; *also* a piece of meat suitable for roasting **b** food formed into a solid shape resembling meat and roasted ⟨*a nut* ~⟩ **2** *NAm* a party at which food is roasted and served, esp in the open air

**³roast** *adj, esp of meat* that has been roasted ⟨~ *beef*⟩

**roaster** /'rohstə/ *n* **1** a device for roasting **2** an animal (eg a pig or chicken) or vegetable (eg a potato) suitable for roasting

**¹roasting** /'rohsting/ *adj, informal* extremely hot

**²roasting** *n, informal* a severe scolding

**rob** /rob/ *vb* **-bb-** *vt* **1** to take something away from (a person or place) without right; *esp* to take personal property from by violence or threat **2** to deprive of something due, expected, or desired ⟨*a slip that* ~*bed him of first place*⟩ **3** *nonstandard* to take away as loot; steal ~ *vi* **1** to commit robbery [ME *robben*, fr OF *rober*, of Gmc origin; akin to OHG *roubōn* to rob – more at BEREAVE] – **robber** *n*

**synonyms Rob** differs from the numerous other verbs meaning "commit theft", since in its strict use one **robs** a person or a place, particularly by violence or threats ⟨**rob** *a bank*⟩, while one **steals** the possessions of another. **Purloin** is a formal word for **steal**. **Pilfer, filch,** and the informal **snitch** refer to furtive petty stealing, **pilfer** suggesting progressive stealing in small amounts ⟨*had been* **pilfering** *regularly from the till*⟩ while **filch** and **snitch** may imply a quick snatching. **Swipe, pinch, lift,** and **nick** (*Br*) are all informal or slang words for petty casual stealing, and may all play down the offence to the point where what is taken seems a lawful perquisite ⟨*I* **swiped** *these knives from our canteen*⟩.

**robber fly** *n* any of numerous predatory flies (family Asilidae) with piercing mouthparts, that feed on other insects and usu have long powerful legs and a slender but strongly built body covered with bristly hairs

**robbery** /'robəri/ *n* the act or practice of robbing; *specif* theft accompanied by violence or threat

**¹robe** /rohb/ *n* **1** robe, robes a long flowing outer garment; *esp* one used for ceremonial occasions or as a symbol of office or profession **2** *chiefly NAm* a woman's dressing gown [ME, fr OF, robe, booty, of Gmc origin; akin to OHG *roubōn* to rob]

**²robe** *vt* to clothe or cover (as if) with a robe to put on a robe; *broadly* to dress

**robin** /'robin/ *n* **1** a small plump European bird (*Erithacus rubecula*) that is closely related to the thrushes and has a brownish-olive back and an orange-red throat and breast **2** a large N American thrush (*Turdus migratorius*) with a dull reddish breast and underparts [short for *robin redbreast*]

**robin redbreast** *n* a robin – used esp in stories or to children [ME, fr *Robin*, nickname for *Robert*]

**robot** /'rohbot/ *n* **1a** a (fictional) usu humanoid machine that walks and talks **b** an automatic apparatus or device that performs functions ordinarily done by or ascribed to human beings or operates with what appears to be almost human intelligence ⟨*cars built by* ~*s*⟩ **2** a person who is efficient or clever but lacking in human warmth or sensitivity **3** a mechanism guided by automatic controls; *specif, SAfr* a set of traffic lights [Czech (formed by Karel Čapek †1938 Czech writer, in his play *RUR*), fr *robota* work; akin to OHG *arabeit* trouble, L *orbus* orphaned] – **robotism** *n*

**robotics** /roh'botiks, rə-/ *n taking sing vb* a field of interest concerned with the construction, maintenance, and behaviour of robots

**robust** /roh'bust, '--/ *adj* **1a** having or exhibiting vigorous health, strength, or stamina, vigorous **b** firm in purpose or outlook; resilient **c** strongly formed or constructed; sturdy **2** earthy, rude ⟨*a tale full of* ~ *humour*⟩ **3** requiring strenuous exertion ⟨~ *work*⟩ **4** full-bodied ⟨*a* ~ *red wine*⟩ **antonyms** frail, feeble [L *robustus* oaken, strong, fr *robor-, robur* oak, strength] – **robustly** *adv*, **robustness** *n*

**robusta coffee** /roh'bustə/ *n* (the seed of) a coffee tree (*Coffea canephora*) that is indigenous to Central Africa but has been introduced elsewhere (e g in Java) [NL *robusta*, specific epithet of *Coffea robusta*, syn of *Coffea canephora*]

**robustious** /roh'buschəs/ *adj, archaic* robust **2** vigorous, boisterous – **robustiously** *adv,* **robustiousness** *n*

**roc** /rok/ *n* a mythical bird of Arabian legend held to be of great size and strength and to inhabit the Indian ocean area [Ar *rukhkh*]

**rocambole** /'rokəmbohl/ *n* a European leek (*Allium scorodoprasum*) whose bulb is used for flavouring in cooking [Fr, fr Ger *rockenbolle*, fr *rocken, roggen* rye + *bolle* bulb]

**Rochelle salt** /ro'shel/ *n* a chemical compound (SALT), $KNaC_4H_4O_6.4H_2O$, of potassium, sodium, and TARTARIC ACID that is used in baking powder and, esp formerly, as a laxative, and whose crystals are used for their PIEZOELECTRIC property (property of producing an electric charge when subjected to pressure) in various acoustic devices sensitive to vibration (e g microphones) – called also POTASSIUM SODIUM TARTRATE [La *Rochelle*, city in W France]

**roche moutonnée** /,rosh moohto'nay/ *n, pl* **roches moutonnées** a long rounded rock mound shaped and ridged by the movement of an ice sheet [Fr, lit., fleecy rock]

**rochet** /'rochit/ *n* a white linen vestment resembling a surplice with close-fitting sleeves worn esp by bishops and other high-ranking clergy [ME, fr MF, fr OF, fr (assumed) OF *roc* coat, of Gmc origin; akin to OHG *roc* coat]

**¹rock** /rok/ *vt* **1a** to move gently back and forth (as if) in a cradle **b** to wash (ore or gravel containing a valuable mineral) in a rocking device **2a** to cause to sway or move violently **b(1)** to daze, stun ⟨∼ed *him with a hard right*⟩ **b(2)** *chiefly journalistic* to disturb, upset ⟨*news of the disaster* ∼ed *the population*⟩ ∼ *vi* **1** to become moved rapidly or violently backwards and forwards (e g under impact); shake **2** to move rhythmically back and forth **3** to dance to or play rock music – see also **rock the** BOAT *synonyms* see ¹SHAKE [ME *rokken*, fr OE *roccian;* akin to OHG *rucken* to cause to move]

**²rock** *n* **1** a rocking motion **2 rock and roll, rock 'n' roll** /,rok (ə)n 'rohl/, **rock** a style of popular music prevalent esp in the 1950s and characterized by a heavy beat, much repetition of simple phrases, and often country, folk, and blues elements; *also* a style of dancing to such music **3** any of several styles of popular music derived form rock and roll which are usu played on electronically amplified instruments and characterized esp by a persistent heavily accented beat

**³rock** *n* **1** a large mass of stone forming a cliff, promontory, or peak **2** a large solid mass of stony or mineral material **3** (any of the naturally formed aggregates or masses of mineral matter that make up) the solid part of the earth's crust **4a** something like a rock in firmness; a firm or solid foundation or support **b rock, rocks** *pl* something that threatens or causes disaster ⟨*our enterprise was perilously near the* ∼s⟩ **5 rock,** *NAm chiefly* **rock candy** a coloured and flavoured sweet usu produced in the form of a cylindrical stick ⟨*a stick of Brighton* ∼⟩ **6** ROCK SALMON **7** *NAm* a stone or small piece of stony material **8** *slang* a gem; *esp* a diamond **9** *usu pl, vulg* a testicle [ME *rokke,* fr ONF *roque,* fr (assumed) VL *rocca*] – **rocklike** *adj* – **on the rocks 1** in or into a state of ruin or destruction ⟨*their marriage was* on the rocks⟩ **2** with ice cubes ⟨*Scotch* on the rocks⟩

**rockabilly** /'rokə,bili/ *n* rock music with a strong country-and-western influence [²*rock* + hill*billy* ]

**,rock-'bottom** *adj* being the lowest possible ⟨∼ *off-season rates*⟩

**rock bottom** *n* the lowest, most fundamental, or most degraded part or level

**rockbound** /-,bownd/ *adj* surrounded or strewn with rocks; rocky ⟨∼ *shores*⟩

**rock bun** *n* ROCK CAKE

**rock cake** *n* a small cake that has a rough irregular surface, is made from a stiff fairly plain cake mixture, and contains currants and sometimes spice

**rock crystal** *n* transparent colourless quartz

**rock dove** *n* a bluish-grey wild pigeon (*Columba livia*) of Europe and Asia that is the ancestor of the domestic pigeons and of the wild pigeons that live in towns and cities – called also ROCK PIGEON

**rock eel** *n* ROCK SALMON; *esp* a dogfish

**rocker** /'rokə/ *n* **1a** either of the two curved pieces of wood or metal on which an object (e g a cradle or ROCKING CHAIR) rocks **b** something mounted on rockers; *specif* ROCKING CHAIR **c** any object (with parts) resembling a rocker (e g a skate with a curved blade) **2** a device that works with a rocking motion **3** a

rock and roll musician or fan **4** a member of a group of young people in Britain in the 1960s who dressed in leather jackets, rode motorcycles, and waged war on the mods – compare HELL'S ANGEL, ³MOD – **off one's rocker** *informal* crazy, mad

**rocker arm** *n* a centre-pivoted lever to push an engine valve down

**rockery** /'rokəri/ *n* a natural or usu artificial bank of rocks and earth where ROCK PLANTS are grown

**¹rocket** /'rokit/ *n* any of numerous plants of the cabbage family: e g **a** a Mediterranean plant (*Eruca sativa*) with yellowish-white flowers, whose larger leaves are sometimes used when young in salad **b** any of various plants (genera *Sisymbrium* and *Barbarea*) with usu yellow flowers and somewhat coarse often deeply cut leaves that grow as weeds in most parts of the world [MF *roquette,* fr OIt *rochetta,* dim. of *ruca* garden rocket, fr L *eruca*]

**²rocket** *n* **1a** a firework consisting of a case partly filled with a combustible material fastened to a guiding stick and projected through the air by the rearward discharge of the gases released in burning **b** such a device used as an incendiary weapon or as a propelling unit (e g for a lifesaving line or whaling harpoon) **2** a JET ENGINE that carries with it everything necessary for its operation, is thus independent of the oxygen in the air, and is used esp for the propulsion of a missile (e g a bomb) or a vehicle (e g an aircraft) **3** a rocket-propelled bomb, missile, or vehicle **4** *chiefly Br informal* a sharp reprimand [It *rocchetta,* lit., small distaff, fr dim. of *rocca* distaff, of Gmc origin; akin to OHG *rocko* distaff] – **rocketeer** *n*

**³rocket** *vt* **1** to convey by means of a rocket **2** to attack with rockets ⟨∼ed *the enemy troops*⟩. ∼ *vi* **1** to rise or increase rapidly or spectacularly ⟨*a slump caused by* ∼ing *prices*⟩ **2** to travel with the speed of a rocket

**rocket bomb** *n* **1** an aerial bomb designed for release at low altitude and equipped with a rocket apparatus for giving it added momentum **2** a rocket-propelled bomb launched from the ground

**rocketry** /'rokitri/ *n* the study of, experimentation with, or use of rockets

**rocket ship** *n* a rocket-propelled craft capable of navigation beyond the earth's atmosphere

**rockfall** /'rok,fawl/ *n* a mass of falling or fallen rocks

**rockfish** /'rok,fish/ *n* **1** any of various fishes that live among rocks **2** ROCK SALMON; *esp* WOLFFISH (N Atlantic food fish)

**rock garden** *n* a garden laid out among rocks or decorated with rocks and adapted for the growth of particular kinds of plants (e g alpines); *also* a small rockery within a larger garden

**rocking chair** /'roking/ *n* a chair mounted on rockers

**rocking horse** *n* a toy horse mounted on rockers

**rockling** /'rokling/ *n, pl* **rockling,** *esp for different types* **rocklings** any of several rather small elongated marine fishes of the cod family (Gadidae)

**rock lobster** *n* SPINY LOBSTER (edible lobsterlike shellfish)

**rock maple** *n* SUGAR MAPLE (maple tree from which syrup and sugar are derived)

**rock 'n' roll** /,rok (ə)n 'rohl/ *n* ²ROCK 2

**rock oil** *n* petroleum

**rockoon** /ro'koohn/ *n* a small rocket containing equipment for scientific research that is carried to a high altitude by a balloon and then fired [²*rock*et + ball*oon*]

**rock pigeon** *n* ROCK DOVE (wild pigeon)

**rock plant** *n* a small plant (e g an alpine plant) that grows among rocks or in rockeries

**'rock-,ribbed** *adj, NAm* **1** rocky ⟨*the* ∼ *coast of Maine*⟩ **2** firmly orthodox in beliefs or moral conduct

**rockrose** /-,rohz/ *n* any of various woody plants or shrubs (family Cistaceae, the rockrose family) often grown for their showy white, yellow, or pink flowers

**rock salmon** *n, Br* (the flesh of) any of several common food fishes; *esp* (the flesh, when prepared for sale, of) a dogfish or WOLFFISH – not used as a scientific name

**rock salt** *n* COMMON SALT (sodium chloride) occurring in solid form as a mineral; *also* salt artificially prepared in large crystals or masses – called also HALITE

**rockshaft** /-,shahft/ *n* a shaft (e g in a steam engine) that rocks on its bearings instead of revolving

**rockskipper** /'rok,skipə/ *n* any of several BLENNIES (scaleless fish)

**rock tripe** *n* any of various dark leathery lichens (e g of the genus *Umbilicaria*) that are widely distributed on rocks in northern and alpine areas and are sometimes used as emergency food

**rock wool** *n* MINERAL WOOL made by blowing a jet of steam through molten rock or slag and used chiefly for heat and sound insulation

¹**rocky** /'roki/ *adj* **1a** full or consisting of rocks **b** resembling rock,esp in hardness **2** firmly maintained; steadfast **3** full of obstacles; difficult [³*rock*] – **rockiness** *n*

²**rocky** *adj* unsteady, tottering [¹*rock*]

¹**rococo** /rə'kohkoh, rə-/ *adj* **1a** of a style of architecture and decoration, esp of 18th-century Europe, characterized by asymmetrical curved forms and elaborate ornamentation **b** of an 18th-century musical style marked by light gay ornamentation **2** excessively ornate or florid □ compare BAROQUE [Fr, irreg fr *rocaille* rock-work, fr *roc* rock, alter. of MF *roche*, fr (assumed) VL *rocca*]

²**rococo** *n* rococo work or style

**rod** /rod/ *n* **1a(1)** a straight slender stick **a(2)** a stick or bundle of twigs used for punishment **a(3)** a slender pole with a line and usu a reel attached for fishing **b(1)** a slender bar (eg of wood or metal) **b(2)** a wand or staff carried as a sign of office, power, or authority **2a** a unit of length equal to $5\frac{1}{2}$ yards (about 5 metres) **b** a unit of square measure equal to 30.25 square yards (about 25.3 square metres) **3** punishment, esp by beating with a cane – + *the* **4** any of the rod-shaped light-sensitive cells in the retina of the eye that are responsible for black-and-white vision and vision in dim light – compare CONE **5** a rod-shaped bacterium **6** an angler **7** *NAm slang* a pistol [ME, fr OE *rodd;* akin to ON *rudda* club] – **rodless** *adj*, **rodlike** *adj*

**rode** /rohd/ *past of* RIDE

**rodent** /'rohd(ə)nt/ *n* any of an order (Rodentia) of relatively small gnawing mammals including mice, rats, squirrels, and beavers, that have a single pair of incisor teeth with a chisel-shaped edge in the upper jaw [deriv of L *rodent-, rodens,* prp of *rodere* to gnaw – more at RAT] – **rodent** *adj*

**rodenticide** /roh'denti,sied/ *n* something, esp a poison, that kills, repels, or controls rodents

**rodent ulcer** *n* a cancer of the deepest layer of skin cells that appears as an ulcer on the surface of the skin, esp on the face, and spreads slowly outwards destroying other tissue; *also* such an ulcer [L *rodent-, rodens* gnawing]

**rodeo** /'roh'dayoh, 'rohdi,oh/ *n, pl* **rodeos 1** ROUNDUP **1a(1)** (gathering together of cattle) **2a** a public performance or contest featuring cowboy skills (eg riding unbroken horses and handling unruly animals) **b** a performance or contest resembling a rodeo [Sp, fr *rodear* to surround, fr *rueda* wheel, fr L *rota* – more at ROLL]

**rodomontade** /,rohdəmon'tayd, -'tahd/ *n* **1** a bragging speech **2** vain boasting or bluster; bombast [MF, fr It *Rodomonte,* boastful character in *Orlando Innamorato* by Matteo Boiardo †1494 It poet] – **rodomontade** *adj*

**roe** /roh/ *n* **1a roe, hard roe** the eggs of a female fish, esp when still enclosed in the membrane of the ovary **b roe, soft roe** the sperm of a male fish, esp when still enclosed in the testis **2** the eggs or ovaries of a lobster, crab, etc; CORAL [ME *roof;* akin to OHG *rogo* roe, Lith *kurkulai* frog's eggs]

**roebuck** /'roh,buk/ *n, pl* **roebucks,** *esp collectively* **roebuck** a (male) ROE DEER

**roe deer** *n* a small Eurasian deer (*Capreolus capreolus*) that has erect cylindrical antlers forked at the top, is reddish-brown in summer and greyish in winter, has a white rump patch, and is noted for its nimbleness and grace [ME *ro,* fr OE *rā;* akin to OHG *rēh* roe deer, OIr *rīabach* dappled]

**roentgen** /'rontgən, 'rentgən, - jən, -tyən (Ger rœntgən)/ *adj or n* RÖNTGEN

**roentgenogram** /'rontgənəgram, 'rent-, -'jən-, -'tyən-/, **roentgenograph** /-grahf, -graf/ *n* RÖNTGENOGRAM (X-ray photograph)

**roentgenography** /,rontgə'nografi, ,rent-, -jən-, -tyən-/ *n* RÖNTGENOGRAPHY (X-ray photography) – **roentgenographic** *adj* – **roentgenographically** *adv*

**roentgenology** /,rontgə'noləji, rent-, -jən-, -tyən-/ *n* RÖNTGENOLOGY (study and use of X rays) – **roentgenologist** *n*, **roentgenologic, roentgenological** *adj*, **roentgenologically** *adv*

**roentgenoscope** /'rontgənoh,skohp, ,rent-, -jən-, -tyən-/ *n* RÖNTGENOSCOPE (device for directly viewing X-ray images without using photography) – **roentgenoscopic** *adj*, **roentgenoscopy** *n*

**roentgen ray** *n, often cap 1st R* RÖNTGEN RAY (X ray)

**rogation** /roh'gaysh(ə)n/ *n,* **rogations** *n pl* the religious observance of the ROGATION DAYS marked esp by solemn supplication [ME *rogacion* litany, supplication, fr LL *rogation-, rogatio,* fr L, questioning, fr *rogatus,* pp of *rogare* to ask – more at RIGHT]

**Rogation Day** /roh'gaysh(ə)n/ *n* any of the days of prayer, esp for the harvest, observed on the three days before ASCENSION DAY and by Roman Catholics also on April 25

¹**roger** /'rojə/ *vt, slang* to have sexual intercourse with [obs *roger* penis, fr the forename *Roger*]

²**roger** *interj* – used esp in radio and signalling to indicate that a message has been received and understood [fr *Roger,* former communications codeword for the letter *r* (here standing for *received*)]

¹**rogue** /rohg/ *n* **1** a wilfully dishonest or corrupt person, esp a man; a scoundrel **2** a mischievous person; a scamp **3** an animal or esp a plant exhibiting a chance and usu inferior biological variation or a deviation from the typical characteristics of the breed or variety **4** a rogue animal **5** *archaic* a tramp, vagrant [perh fr obs *roger* beggar, vagabond, perh fr L *rogare* to ask] – **roguish** *adj*, **roguishly** *adv*, **roguishness** *n*

²**rogue** *vt* **roguing, rogueing** to weed out (inferior, diseased, or nontypical plants) from a crop or a field

³**rogue** *adj* **1** *of an animal* having a vicious and destructive nature and usu living away from the herd ⟨*a* ∼ *elephant*⟩ **2** deviating from the norm, esp in an unruly or troublesome manner ⟨∼ *politicians who refuse to toe the party line*⟩

**roguery** /'rohg(ə)ri/ *n* **1** an act characteristic of a rogue **2** mischievous behaviour

**rogues' gallery** *n* a collection of pictures of people arrested as criminals; *broadly* a collection of rebellious or troublesome people

**roil** /royl/ *vt* **1a** to make (a liquid) muddy or opaque by stirring up sediment **b** to stir up; agitate ⟨*the fine powder was* ∼*ed by the waves*⟩ **c** to disturb, perturb ⟨*their emotions were* ∼*ed by the news*⟩ **2** to annoy, rile [origin unknown] – **roily** *adj*

**roister** /'roystə/ *vi* to engage in noisy revelry [arch. *roister* roisterer, fr MF *rustre* boor, ruffian, fr *ruste* rude, rough, fr L *rusticus* rustic] – **roisterer** *n*, **roisterous** *adj*

**role, rôle** /rohl/ *n* **1a** a character or part assumed by an actor or actress in a film, play, etc **b** a socially expected behaviour pattern, usu determined by an individual's status in a particular society ⟨*her* ∼ *was principally that of mediator*⟩ △ roll [Fr *rôle,* lit., roll, fr OF *rolle*]

**role playing** *n* the act of behaving in a way typical of somebody else or of a stereotype, either deliberately, for educational or therapeutic purposes, or unconsciously

¹**roll** /rohl/ *n* **1a** a written document that may be rolled up; a scroll; *specif* a document bearing an official or formal record ⟨*the* ∼s *of Parliament*⟩ **b** a list of names or related items; a catalogue **c** an official list (eg of members of a school or class or of people entitled to vote) **2** something that is rolled up to resemble a cylinder or ball eg **2a** a quantity (eg of fabric or paper) rolled up to form a single cylindrical package **b** any of various food preparations rolled up for cooking or serving; *specif* a small shaped piece of bread – compare SAUSAGE ROLL, SWISS ROLL **c** a cylindrical twist of tobacco **2** a hollow or solid cylinder for use in a ROLLING MILL (machine for rolling metal into plates) **3** ROLLER **1a** (1) (revolving cylinder having various uses) **4** *NAm* paper money folded or rolled into a wad [ME *rolle,* fr OF, fr L *rotula,* dim. of *rota* wheel; akin to OHG *rad* wheel, Skt *ratha* wagon]

²**roll** *vt* **1a** to propel forwards by causing to turn over and over on a surface **b** to cause (something fixed) to revolve (as if) on an axis **c** to cause to move in a circular manner ⟨*he* ∼*ed the sweet around in his mouth*⟩ **d** to form into a mass by revolving and compressing ⟨∼*ed the dough into a ball*⟩ **e** to impel or carry forwards with an easy continuous motion **2a** to put a wrapping round; enfold, envelop ⟨*lying snugly* ∼*ed in blankets*⟩ **b** to wrap round on itself or something else; shape into a ball or roll ⟨∼*ed his own cigarettes*⟩ – often + *up* **3a** to press, spread, or level with a roller; make thin, even, or compact ⟨∼*ed oats*⟩ **b** to extend; spread out – often + *out* ⟨∼ *out the red carpet*⟩ **4a** to move on rollers or wheels ⟨∼*ed the pram down the road*⟩ **b** to cause to begin operating or moving ⟨∼ *the cameras*⟩ **5a** to sound with a full reverberating tone ⟨∼*ed out the words*⟩ **b** to make a continuous beating sound on; sound a roll on ⟨∼*ed their drums*⟩ **c** to utter with a trill ⟨∼*ed his r's*⟩ **d** *music* to play (a chord) by sounding the notes in close succession rather than simultaneously **6** *NAm informal* to

rob (a drunk, sleeping, or unconscious person), usu by going through the pockets ~ *vi* **1a** to travel along a surface with a rotary motion **b(1)** to turn over and over ⟨*the children* ~ed *in the grass*⟩ **b(2)** to luxuriate *in* an abundant supply; wallow ⟨~ing *in money*⟩ **2a** to move onwards in a regular cycle or succession elapse, pass ⟨*the months* ~ *on*⟩ **b** to (partially) revolve or rotate ⟨*eyes* ~ing *in terror*⟩ **c** to revolve on an axis **3a** to flow with an undulating motion ⟨*the waves* ~ed *in*⟩ **b** to extend in broad undulations ⟨~ing *hills*⟩ **4a** to become carried on a stream ⟨*rubble and branches* ~ed *down the swollen river*⟩ **b** to move on wheels ⟨*the train* ~ed *into the station*⟩ **5a** to make a deep reverberating sound ⟨*the thunder* ~ed⟩ **b** to trill **6a** to rock from side to side ⟨*the ship heaved and* ~ed⟩ **b** to walk with a swinging gait; sway **c** to move so as to reduce the impact of a blow – usu + *with* ⟨~ *with the punch*⟩ **7a** to take the form of a cylinder or ball – often + *up* **b** to undergo rolling as specified ⟨~s *easily*⟩ ⟨~ed *out flat*⟩ **8a** to get underway; begin to move or operate ⟨*let the cameras* ~⟩ **b** to move forward; develop and maintain impetus ⟨*hoped to get the business* ~ing⟩ **9a** to bowl **b** to perform a somersault – see also **keep the** BALL **rolling,** HEADS **will roll**
  **roll back** *vt* to cause to retreat or withdraw; push back
  **roll in** *vi* to come or arrive in large quantities ⟨*money came rolling in*⟩
  **roll up** *vt, chiefly NAm* to increase by successive accumulations; accumulate ⟨*rolled up a large majority*⟩ ~ *vi* **1** to turn up at a destination, esp unhurriedly ⟨*he rolled up at nine o'clock eventually*⟩ **2** to arrive in a vehicle **3** – used interjectionally to urge people to come and join an audience or participate, esp at fairs or circuses
³**roll** *n* **1a** a sound produced by rapid strokes on a drum **b** a rhythmic and usu sonorous flow of speech **c** a rolling sound ⟨*the* ~ *of cannon*⟩ **d** a chord in which the notes are played in close succession rather than simultaneously **e** a trill of some birds (e g a canary) **2** (an action or process involving) a rolling movement ⟨*a* ~ *of the dice*⟩: e g **2a** a swaying movement of the body (e g in walking or dancing) **b** a side-to-side movement (e g of a ship) **c** a flight manoeuvre in which a complete revolution about the lengthways axis of an aircraft is made with the horizontal direction of flight being approximately maintained; *also* the angular motion of a spacecraft about its lengthways axis **d** a somersault
**rollback** /'rohl,bak/ *n* the act or an instance of rolling back
**roll bar** *n* a metal bar in a car that is designed to strengthen the frame and act as overhead protection should the car roll over
**roll call** *n* (a time set aside for) the calling out of a list of names (e g for checking attendance)
**rolled gold** *n* metal (e g brass) coated with a thin layer of gold
¹**roller** /'rohlə/ *n* **1a(1)** a revolving cylinder over or on which something is moved or which is used to press, shape, smooth, or apply something **a(2)** a hair curler **b** a cylinder or rod on which something (e g a blind) is rolled up **2a** a long heavy wave, esp moving towards the coast **3** one who or that which rolls
²**roller** *n* any of numerous mostly brightly coloured birds (family Coraciidae) found in most parts of the world, whose plumage is predominantly blue and violet and that are noted for performing aerial somersaults and dives in their courtship display **2** a canary having a song in which the notes are soft and run together [Ger, fr *rollen* to roll, reverberate, fr MF *roller*, fr (assumed) VL *rotulare*, fr L *rotula*]
**roller bearing** *n* a bearing in which the rotating part turns on rollers held in a cylindrical housing
**roller blind** *n* BLIND 1b
**roller coaster** *n* an elevated railway (e g in a fun fair) constructed with curves and inclines on which the cars roll
**roller skate** *n* a metal frame holding usu four small wheels that is fitted to the sole of a shoe and allows the wearer to glide over hard surfaces; *also* a shoe with such a set of wheels attached – **roller–skate** *vi*, **roller skater** *n*
**roller towel** *n* a continuous towel hung from a roller
**Rolle's theorem** /rolz, rohlz/ *n* a theorem in calculus: if a curve is CONTINUOUS, crosses the x-axis at two points, and has a tangent at every point on the curve between those two points, the tangent to the curve is parallel to the x-axis somewhere between the two points [Michel *Rolle* †1719 F mathematician]
**roll film** *n* a strip of film for still-camera use wound on a reel
**rollick** /'rolik/ *vi* to move or behave in a carefree boisterous manner; frolic [perh blend of *romp* and *frolic*] – **rollick** *n*
¹**rollicking** /'roliking/ *adj* boisterously carefree

²**rollicking** *n, Br informal* a severe scolding [prob alter. of *bollocking*]
**rolling** /'rohling/ *adj* developing by stages with undiminished impetus ⟨~ *devolution in Northern Ireland* – John Timpson⟩
**rolling mill** *n* an establishment or machine in which metal is rolled into plates and bars
**rolling pin** *n* a long usu wooden cylinder for rolling out dough
**rolling stock** *n* **1** the wheeled vehicles owned and used by a railway **2** *NAm* the road vehicles owned and used by a company
**rolling stone** *n* a person who leads a wandering or unsettled life
**rollmop** /'rohl,mop/ *n* a herring fillet rolled up and pickled by being marinated in spiced vinegar or brine [Ger *rollmops*, fr *rollen* to roll + *mops* simpleton, pugnosed dog, fr LG]
**roll neck** *n* a loose high collar, esp on a jumper, that is worn rolled over
**roll of honour** *n* a list of people deserving honour: e g **a** a list of students achieving academic distinction **b** a list of citizens who have served in the armed forces
'**roll-,on** *n* **1** a woman's elasticated girdle without fastenings **2** a liquid preparation (e g deodorant or lip-gloss) that is applied by means of a rolling ball in the neck of the container
**roll on** *interj, Br* – used to urge on a specified desired event ⟨*roll on summer!*⟩
**roll-,on roll-'off** *adj* allowing vehicles to drive on or off ⟨*a* ~ *ship*⟩
**rollout** /'rohl,owt/ *n* the public introduction or unveiling of a new aircraft
**roll-over arm** *n* a fully upholstered chair or sofa arm curving outwards from the seat
**rolltop desk** /'rohl,top/ *n* a writing desk with a sliding cover often of parallel slats fastened to a flexible backing
'**roll-,up** *n, Br informal* a hand-rolled cigarette
¹**roly-poly** /,rohli 'pohli/ *n* **1** a dish, esp a pudding, consisting of suet pastry with a filling (e g jam), rolled, and baked or steamed **2** *informal* a plump person [redupl of *roly*, fr ²*roll* + ³*-y*]
²**roly-poly** *adj, informal* short and plump; rotund
**Romaic** /roh'mayik/ *n* the commonly spoken language of modern Greece [NGk *Rhōmaiikos*, fr Gk *Rhōmaïkos* Roman, fr *Rhōmē* Rome] – **Romaic** *adj*
¹**Roman** /'rohmən/ *n* **1** a native or inhabitant of ancient or modern Rome **2** *not cap* roman letters or type **3** *chiefly derog* ROMAN CATHOLIC [ME, fr OE *Roman* & OF *Romain*, fr L *Romanus*, adj & n, fr *Roma* Rome]
²**Roman** *adj* **1** (characteristic) of Rome or the people of Rome; *specif* characteristic of the ancient Romans ⟨~ *fortitude*⟩ **2** *not cap, of a letter or number* not slanted; perpendicular **3** of the SEE (diocese) of Rome or the Roman Catholic church
**roman à clef** /roh,monh a 'klay (*Fr* rɔmɑ̃ a kle)/ *n, pl* **romans à clef** /~/ a novel in which real people or actual events are fictionally disguised [Fr, lit., novel with a key]
**Roman calendar** *n* a calendar of ancient Rome preceding the JULIAN CALENDAR and having 12 months with the days of the month reckoned backwards from fixed points – compare CALENDS
**Roman candle** *n* a cylindrical firework that discharges balls or stars of fire at intervals
¹**Roman Catholic** *n* a member of the Roman Catholic church
²**Roman Catholic** *adj* of the body of Christians headed by the pope and having a hierarchy of priests and bishops under the pope, a form of service centred on the Mass, and a body of dogma formulated by the church as the infallible interpreter of revealed truth; *specif* of the Western rite of this church marked by a formerly Latin form of service *usage* see CATHOLIC – **Roman Catholicism** *n*
¹**romance** /roh'mans, rə-/ *n* **1a(1)** a medieval tale, usu in verse, dealing with chivalric love and adventure **a(2)** a prose narrative dealing with imaginary characters involved in usu heroic, adventurous, or mysterious events that are remote in time or place **a(3)** a love story **b** such literature as a class **2** something that lacks any basis in fact **3** an emotional attraction or aura attaching to an enthralling or heroic era, adventure, or pursuit ⟨*the* ~ *of sailing*⟩ **4** LOVE AFFAIR **5** *cap* the Romance languages [ME *romauns*, fr OF *romans* French, something written in French, fr L *romanice* in the Roman manner, fr *romanicus* Roman, fr *Romanus*]

²**romance** *vi* **1** to exaggerate or invent detail or incident; fantasize **2a** to entertain romantic thoughts or ideas **b** *of a man and a woman* to spend time together in a romantic way (eg dancing or kissing) ⟨*spent all evening* romancing⟩

³**romance** *n* a short instrumental piece of music in ballad style [Fr, fr Sp, short poem set to music, fr OSp, lit., Spanish, fr L *romance*]

**Romance** *adj* of or being the languages developed from Latin

**romancer** /rə'mansə, roh-/ *n* **1** a writer of romance **2** somebody who is prone to romancing

**Roman collar** *n* CLERICAL COLLAR; *specif* one worn esp by Roman Catholic clergy that shows through a gap in the upright shirt neck at the front

**Romanesque** /ˌrohmə'nesk/ *adj or n* (of) a style of architecture developed in Italy and W Europe between the ROMAN and the GOTHIC styles and characterized in its development after 1000 AD by the use of the round arch and vault, decorative arcading, and elaborate mouldings – compare NORMAN 3

**roman-fleuve** /rohˌmonh 'fluhv (*Fr* rəmã flœːv)/ *n, pl* **romans-fleuves** /~/ a novel in the form of a long and leisurely chronicle of a family or community [Fr, lit., river novel]

**Roman holiday** *n* an entertainment gained at the expense of others' suffering [fr the bloody combats staged as entertainment in ancient Rome]

**Romanian, Rumanian** *also* **Roumanian** /roo'maynyən, roh-, rə-, -ni·ən/ *n* **1** a native or inhabitant of Romania **2** the ROMANCE language of the Romanians [*Romania* (*Rumania, Roumania*), country in E Europe] – **Romanian** *adj*

**Romanic** /roh'manik/ *adj* **1** of the ROMANCE language **2** descended or derived from the Romans – **Romanic** *n*

**Romanism** /'rohməˌniz(ə)m/ *n* ROMAN CATHOLICISM, esp when considered extreme in its expression or ritual

**Romanist** /'rohmənist/ *n* **1** a specialist in or student of the language, culture, or law of ancient Rome **2** *chiefly derog* ROMAN CATHOLIC – **Romanist, Romanistic** *adj*

**roman·ize, -ise** /'rohməniez/ *vt* **1** *often cap* to make Roman or ROMAN CATHOLIC **2** to write or print (eg a language) in the Roman alphabet ⟨~ *Chinese*⟩ – **romanization** *n, often cap*

**roman law** *n, often cap R* the legal system of the ancient Romans, which forms the basis of many modern legal codes

**Roman nose** *n* a nose with a prominent slightly aquiline bridge

**roman numeral** *n, often cap R* a numeral in a system of notation based on the ancient Roman system using the symbols i for "one", v for "five", x for "ten", l for "fifty", c for "hundred", d for "five hundred", and m for "thousand"

**Romano** /roh'mahnoh/ *n* a hard Italian cheese that is sharper in flavour than Parmesan [It, Roman, fr L *Romanus*]

**Romans** /'rohmənz/ *n taking sing vb* – see BIBLE table

**Romansh, Romansch** /roh'mahnsh/ *n* the Rhaeto-Romanic dialects spoken in the Grisons in E Switzerland and in adjacent parts of Italy [Romansh *romonsch*]

**Roman snail** *n* a European edible snail (*Helix pomatia*)

¹**romantic** /rə'mantik, roh-/ *adj* **1a** of or resembling a ROMANCE (medieval tale of chivalry) **b** consisting of or resembling a romance ⟨*a* ~ *short story*⟩ **2** having no basis in real life; imaginary **3** impractical or fantastic in conception or plan; quixotic, visionary ⟨*a* ~ *get-rich-quick scheme*⟩ **4a** marked by the imaginative or emotional appeal of the heroic, adventurous, remote, or mysterious **b** *often cap* (having the characteristics) of literary or artistic ROMANTICISM **c** of or being music of the 19th century characterized by an emphasis on subjective emotional qualities and freedom of form; *also* of or being a composer of this music – compare CLASSICAL **5a** having an inclination for romance **b** marked by or constituting strong feeling, esp love; ardent [Fr *romantique*, fr obs *romant* romance, fr OF *romans*] – **romantically** *adv*

²**romantic** *n* **1** a romantic person **2** *cap* a romantic writer, artist, or composer

**romanticism** /roh'mantiˌsiz(ə)m, rə-/ *n* **1** the quality or state of being romantic **2** *often cap* **2a(1)** a literary, artistic, and philosophical movement originating in the 18th century in reaction against NEOCLASSICISM, characterized chiefly by an emphasis on the emotions and aspirations of the individual and marked, esp in English literature, by emphasis on sensibility and the use of autobiographical material, an exaltation of nature, and an interest in the remote and exotic **a(2)** an expression of romanticism in an art form **b** adherence to or practice of romantic ideas or assumptions – **romanticist** *n, often cap*

**romantic·ize, -ise** /roh'mantiˌsiez, rə-/ *vt* to give a romantic character to ~ *vi* **1** to hold romantic ideas **2** to present incidents or people in a romantic and usu misleading way – **romanticization** *n*

**Romany** /'rohməni/ *n* **1** a Gipsy **2** the INDIC language of the Gipsies [Romany *romani*, adj, gipsy, fr *rom* gipsy man, fr Skt *ḍomba* man of a low caste of musicians] – **Romany** *adj*

**romaunt** /rə'mawnt/ *n, archaic* ROMANCE 1a(1) [ME, fr MF *romant*]

**romeldale** /'romlˌdayl/ *n, often cap* (any of) an American breed of sheep yielding a heavy fleece of fine wool and producing a quickly maturing high-grade lamb for market [blend of *Romney* (*Marsh*), *Rambouillet*, and *Corriedale*]

¹**Romeo** /'rohmi·oh, -myoh/ *n, pl* **Romeos** a romantic male lover [*Romeo*, hero of Shakespeare's play *Romeo and Juliet*]

²**Romeo** – a communications code word for the letter *r*

**Romish** /'rohmish/ *adj, chiefly derog* ROMAN CATHOLIC – **Romishly** *adv*, **Romishness** *n*

**Romney Marsh** /'romni, 'rumni/ *n* (any of) a British breed of hardy long-woolled meat-producing sheep adapted esp to damp or marshy regions [*Romney Marsh*, pasture tract in SE England]

¹**romp** /romp/ *n* **1** a person, esp a girl, who is fond of romping; a tomboy **2** a boisterous or bawdy entertainment or form of play; a frolic **3** an effortless winning pace [partly alter. of *ramp* (act of ramping), fr ¹*ramp*; partly alter. of *ramp* (bold woman), fr ME *rampe*, perh fr *rampen* to ramp, rage]

²**romp** *vi* **1** to play in a boisterous manner **2** to proceed in an animated or lighthearted manner **3** to win easily ⟨~ *home with a good lead*⟩ [alter. of ¹*ramp*] – **romper** *n*

**rompers** /'rompəz/ *n pl*, **romper** *n* a one-piece child's garment combining a top or bib and short trousers

**rondavel** /'rondəˌvel, ˌron'dahvl/ *n, SAfr* a circular one-roomed often prefabricated hut in the grounds of a house, used esp as a guest room or for storage [Afrik *rondawel*]

**rondeau** /'rondoh/ *n, pl* **rondeaux** /'rondoh(z)/ **1a** a form of verse, divided into three stanzas, that uses only two rhymes throughout and consists usu of 15 lines of 8 or 10 syllables each. The opening words of the first line of the first stanza serve as the refrain of the second and third stanzas. **b** a poem in the form of a rondeau **2** a vocal form from the 13th to the 15th centuries with a single melodic line and a two-part refrain **3** RONDO 1 [MF *rondeau, rondel*]

**rondel** /'rondl/ *n* **1** ROUNDEL 1 (circular figure or object) **2a** a special form of rondeau using only two rhymes and consisting usu of 14 lines of 8 or 10 syllables divided into three stanzas in which the first two lines of the first stanza serve as the refrain of the second and third stanzas **b** a poem in this form **c** RONDEAU 1 □ (2) called also ROUNDEL [ME, fr OF, lit., small circle – more at ROUNDEL]

**rondo** /'rondoh/ *n, pl* **rondos 1** *also* **rondeau** an instrumental composition typically with a refrain recurring four or more times in the TONIC (keynote of the scale) and with three or more couplets in contrasting keys **2** the musical form of a rondo used esp for a movement in a concerto or sonata [It *rondò*, fr MF *rondeau*]

**roneo** *vt* **roneos; roneoing; roneoed** to copy on a Roneo machine

**Roneo** /'rohnioh/ *trademark* – used for a duplicating machine that uses stencils

¹**röntgen, roentgen, rontgen** /'rontgən, 'rent-, -jən, -tyən (*Ger* rœntgən)/ *adj* of or using X rays ⟨~ *examinations*⟩ [ISV, fr Wilhelm Conrad *Röntgen* (*Roentgen*) †1923 Ger physicist]

²**röntgen, roentgen, rontgen** *n* a unit of IONIZING radiation (eg X rays or gamma rays) equal to the amount that produces positively or negatively charged IONS (electrically charged atoms or groups of atoms) carrying a charge of $2.58 \times 10^4$ coulombs in air

**röntgenogram** /'rontgenəgram, rent-, -'jən-, -'tyən-/, **röntgenograph** /-grahf, -graf/ *n* an X-ray photograph [ISV]

**röntgenography** /ˌrontgə'nografi, ˌrent-, -jən-, -tyən-/ *n* photography by means of X rays [ISV] – **röntgenographic** *adj*, **röntgenographically** *adv*

**röntgenology** /ˌrontgə'noləji, rent-, -jən-, -tyən-/ *n* radiology that deals with the use of X rays for diagnosis or treatment of disease [ISV] – **röntgenologic, röntgenological** *adj*, **röntgenologically** *adv*, **röntgenologist** *n*

**röntgenoscope** /'rontgənoh,skohp, ,rent-, -jən-, -tyən-/ *n* FLUOROSCOPE (device for directly viewing X-ray images without using photography) – **röntgenoscopic** *adj*, **röntgeno-**

scopy *n*

**röntgen ray** *n, often cap 1st R* X RAY

**roo** /rooh/ *n, pl* **roos**, *esp collectively* **roo** *Austr informal* a kangaroo

**rood** /roohd/ *n* **1** a cross or crucifix symbolizing the cross on which Jesus died; *specif* a large crucifix on a beam or screen in a medieval church at the entrance to the CHANCEL (area near the altar) **2** a British unit of land area equal to a ¹/₄ acre (about 1011.7 square metres) [ME, fr OE *rōd* rod, rood; akin to OHG *ruota* rod, OSlav *ratište* shaft of a lance]

**rood screen** *n* a usu wooden screen separating the CHANCEL (area of a church near the altar) from the main body of the church

¹**roof** /roohf, roof/ *n, pl* **roofs** *also* **rooves** /roohvz/ **1a** the upper usu rigid cover of a building b a dwelling, home ⟨*why not ... share the same* ~ – Virginia Woolf⟩ **2a(1)** *the* highest point or level of a specified area; *the* summit ⟨*on the* ~ *of the Himalayas*⟩ **a(2)** an upper limit; a ceiling ⟨*prices have hit the* ~⟩ **b** something resembling a roof in form or function ⟨*the* ~ *of the cave*⟩ **3a** the concave structure that forms the top of the cavity of the mouth **b** a covering structure of any of various parts of the body ⟨~ *of the skull*⟩ **4** the top of a covered vehicle [ME, fr OE *hrōf;* akin to ON *hrōf* roof of a boathouse, OSlav *stropŭ* roof] – **roofed** *adj*, **roofless** *adj*, **rooflike** *adj* – **go through the roof 1** *of prices* to increase dramatically **2** HIT THE ROOF – **hit the roof** *informal* to give vent to extreme anger

²**roof** *vt* **1** to cover (as if) with a roof **2** to serve as a roof over – **roofer** *n*

**roof garden** *n* **1** a garden on a flat roof **2** a restaurant at the top of a building, usu with facilities for music and dancing

**roofing** /'roohfing/ *n* material for a roof

**roof rack** *n, chiefly Br* a metal frame fixed on top of a car roof, for carrying things

**roof rat** *n* BLACK RAT

¹**rooftop** /'roohf,top, 'roof-/ *n* a roof; *esp* the outer surface of a usu flat roof ⟨*sunning themselves on the* ~⟩

²**rooftop** *adj* happening or situated on a rooftop ⟨*a* ~ *drama*⟩

**rooftree** /-,tree/ *n* **1** RIDGEPIECE (supporting beam in a roof) **2** *poetic* ROOF 1a

**rooinek** /'rooinek, 'roy-/ *n, SAfr chiefly derog or humorous* a British person; *esp* a British immigrant [Afrik, fr *rooi* red + *nek* neck]

¹**rook** /rook/ *n* a common European and Asian bird (*Corvus frugilegus*) with black plumage, that nests in colonies and is similar to the related CARRION CROW but has a bare grey face [ME, fr OE *hrōc;* akin to OE *hræfn* raven – more at RAVEN]

²**rook** *vt* to defraud by cheating (eg at cards) or swindling [fr ¹*rook* in the sense "cheat, swindler"]

³**rook** *n* a piece in chess that can be moved either horizontally or vertically across any number of consecutive unoccupied squares – called also CASTLE [ME *rok,* fr MF *roc,* fr Ar *rukhkh,* fr Per]

**rookery** /'rookəri/ *n* **1a** the nests or breeding place of a colony of rooks, usu built in the branches of a tree; *also* a colony of rooks **b** a breeding ground or haunt of various birds (eg penguins) or mammals (eg seals) that live in colonies; *also* a colony of such birds or mammals **2** *chiefly NAm* a crowded dilapidated tenement or maze of dwellings

**rookie** /'rooki/ *n, informal* **1** *chiefly NAm* a raw recruit, esp in the armed forces; *also* a novice **2** NAm a new inexperienced competitor in a professional sport [perh alter. of *recruit*]

¹**room** /roohm, room/ *n* **1a** an extent of space occupied by or sufficient or available for something ⟨*houseplants that take up very little* ~⟩ ⟨*in the country where there is* ~ *to run and play*⟩ ⟨*make* ~ *for me to squeeze by*⟩ **b** the scope, possibility, or necessity for something to be done ⟨*there is* ~ *for argument and discussion*⟩ ⟨*there is no* ~ *for indecision*⟩ **2a** a part of the inside of a building that is partitioned off from other similar parts usu by walls, ceiling, and floor **b** such a part used as a separate lodging ⟨*has* ~s *in the Albany*⟩ **3** *taking sing or pl vb* the people in a room ⟨*the whole* ~ *burst out laughing*⟩ [ME, fr OE *rūm;* akin to OHG *rūm* room, L *rur-, rus* open land] – **roomful** *n*

²**room** /roohm/ *vt* to accommodate with lodgings ~ *vi, NAm* to occupy a room or rooms, often paying rent; lodge

**-roomed** *comb form* (→ *adj*) having a specified number or kind of rooms ⟨*a six-roomed house*⟩

**roomer** /'roohmə/ *n, NAm* a lodger

**rooming house** /'roohming, 'room-/ *n, chiefly NAm* LODGING HOUSE

**roommate** /'roohm,mayt, 'room-/ *n* any of two or more people sharing the same room (eg in a university hall)

**room service** *n* a service provided by some hotels by which a guest can have certain items (eg food and drinks) brought to his/her room

**roomy** /'roohmi/ *adj* **1** having ample room; spacious **2** *of a female mammal* having a large or well-proportioned body suited for breeding – **roominess** *n*

**roorback** /'rooə,bak/ *n, NAm* a defamatory falsehood published for political effect [fr an attack on the US politician James K Polk in 1844 purporting to quote from a book by a fictitious Baron von *Roorback*]

**roose** /roohz/ *vt, dial N Eng & Scot* to praise [ME *rusen* to boast of, praise, fr ON *hrōsa*]

¹**roost** /roohst/ *n* **1a** a support on which birds rest **b** a place where birds customarily roost **2** a group of birds (eg fowl) roosting together **3** temporary sleeping accommodation [ME, fr OE *hrōst;* akin to MD *roest* roost, OSlav *krada* pile of wood] – **rule the roost** to be in charge ⟨*you can see she* rules the roost *in that household*⟩ – see also COME HOME to roost

²**roost** *vi, esp of a bird* to settle down for rest or sleep; perch

**rooster** /'roohstə/ *n, chiefly NAm* an adult male domestic fowl; a cock

¹**root** /rooht/ *n* **1a** the usu underground part of a FLOWERING PLANT that provides anchorage and support for the plant, absorbs water and dissolved mineral salts from the soil, may function as a food storage organ, and differs from a stem esp in lacking buds and leaves **b** an underground plant part (eg a true root or a bulb, tuber, or rootstock), esp when fleshy and edible; *also, pl, Br* ROOT CROPS **2a** the end of a nerve nearest the brain and SPINAL CORD **b** the part of an organ or physical structure (eg a hair, tooth, or nail) by which it is attached to or embedded in the body **3a** something that is a basis or an underlying cause (eg of a condition or quality) ⟨*the love of money is the* ~ *of all evil* – 1 Tim 6:10 (AV)⟩ **b** one or more of the originators of a group of descendants **c** the essential core; the heart ⟨*get to the* ~ *of the matter*⟩ **d** *pl* a feeling of belonging, established through close familiarity or family ties with a particular place ⟨*the need for* ~s⟩ ⟨~s *in Scotland*⟩ **4a** a number that, when multiplied by itself a stated number of times, gives another stated number ⟨*2 is the fourth* ~ *of 16*⟩ **b** a number that, when substituted for one variable, satisfies a particular equation ⟨*3 is a* ~ *when* $x^2 - 5x + 6 = 0$⟩ **5a root, roots** *pl* the lower part; the base ⟨*the* ~s *of the mountains*⟩ **b** the part by which an object is attached to or embedded in something else **6** the basis from which a word is derived (eg by sound change, compounding, or the adding of prefixes or suffixes) **7** the tone from whose overtones a chord is composed; the lowest note of a chord in normal position **8** *Austr vulg* an act of sexual intercourse; *also* a woman considered for her part in sexual intercourse **synonyms** see ORIGIN [ME, fr OE *rōt,* fr ON; akin to OE *wyrt* root, L *radix,* Gk *rhiza*] – **rooted** *adj,* **rootedness** *n,* **rootless** *adj,* **rootlike** *adj* – **take root 1** to become rooted **2** to become fixed or established

²**root** *vt* **1** to enable to develop roots **2** to fix or implant (as if) by roots ⟨*fear* ~ed *him to the spot*⟩ **3** *Austr vulg* to have sexual intercourse with ~ *vi* **1** to grow roots or take root **2** to have an origin or base **3** *Austr vulg* to have sexual intercourse – **root out** *vt* to get rid of or destroy completely; extirpate ⟨*root out the cause of racial prejudice*⟩

³**root** *vi* **1** *esp of a pig* to turn up or dig in the earth with the snout; grub **2** to poke or dig about ⟨~ed *in the desk for paper clips*⟩ ~ *vt* to dig up or discover and bring to light; unearth – usu + *out* ⟨~ed *out the truth*⟩ [ME *wroten,* fr OE *wrōtan;* akin to OHG *ruozzan* to root]

⁴**root** *vi, chiefly NAm* to lend vociferous or enthusiastic support to someone or something – usu + *for* ⟨*noisily* ~ing *for the team*⟩ ⟨~ed *for the new plan*⟩ [perh alter. of ²*rout*] – **rooter** *n*

**rootage** /'roohtij/ *n* **1** a developed system of roots **2** the process of taking root **3** the state of being rooted

**root and branch** *adv* so as to leave no remnant; completely ⟨*destroyed the the evil* ~⟩ – **root-and-branch** *adj*

**root beer** *n, chiefly NAm* a sweetened effervescent drink flavoured with extracts of roots and herbs

**root canal** *n* the narrow part of the PULP CAVITY (central cavity of a tooth containing blood vessels and nerves) lying in the root of a tooth

**root cap** *n* a cap of loosely arranged thin-walled cells that covers and protects the growing tissue at the tip of a root

**root crop** *n* a crop (eg turnips or SUGAR BEET) grown for its enlarged fleshy edible roots

**root graft** n 1 a plant graft in which the stock onto which a branch, shoot, etc is grafted is a root or piece of a root 2 a naturally formed join between roots of compatible plants

**root hair** n a thin-walled hairlike outgrowth from a cell of the EPIDERMIS (outer protective layer of cells) near the tip of a root, that absorbs water and dissolved minerals from the soil

**roothold** /'rooht,hohld/ n 1 the anchoring of a plant into the soil by the growing and spreading of roots 2 a place where plants may obtain a roothold

**root knot** n a plant disease caused by parasitic NEMATODE worms that produces characteristic enlargements on the roots and stunts the growth of the plant

**rootle** /'rooohtl/ vi, Br ³ROOT [freq of ³root]

**rootlet** /'roohtlit/ n a small root or branch of a root

**root-,mean-'square** n the SQUARE ROOT of the ARITHMETIC MEAN (average) of the squares of a set of numbers

**root-mean-square deviation** n, statistics STANDARD DEVIATION

**root nodule** n NODULE b (bacteria-containing swelling on a plant root)

**root pressure** n the pressure, chiefly OSMOTIC PRESSURE, that develops in the root of a plant and by which water passes into the water-containing tissue (XYLEM) and rises into the stem from the root

**root rot** n a plant disease characterized by a decay of the roots

**rootstock** /-,stok/ n 1 a RHIZOME (underground stem that produces buds and shoots) or rhizome-like underground part of a plant 2 a stock for grafting consisting of a root or a piece of root; broadly ¹STOCK 2b

**rooty** /'roohti/ adj full or composed of roots ⟨~ soil⟩

**¹rope** /rohp/ n 1a a strong thick cord composed of strands of cotton, hemp, flax, wire, etc twisted or braided together b a long slender strip of material used as or resembling rope c a hangman's noose – often + the 2 a row or string of things united (as if) by braiding, twining, or threading ⟨splendid ~ of pearls⟩ 3 pl special methods or procedures ⟨show him the ~s⟩ [ME, fr OE rāp; akin to OHG reif hoop] – **give somebody (enough) rope** to give somebody (enough) freedom of action ⟨give him enough rope and he'll ruin the whole enterprise⟩

**²rope** vt 1a to bind, fasten, or tie with a rope or cord; also to attach (oneself or others) to a rope, esp in mountaineering – often + up b to enclose, separate, or divide by a rope ⟨~ off the street⟩ 2 to persuade (one who is unwilling or reluctant) into a group or activity; inveigle – usu + in ⟨~d in several celebrities to publicize the cause⟩ 3 NAm to lasso ~ vi to put on a rope for climbing; also to climb down or up on a rope – **roper** n

**ropedancer** /-,dahnsə/ n a person who dances, walks, or performs acrobatic feats on a rope high in the air – **ropedancing** n

**rope ladder** n a ladder with rope sides and rope, wood, or metal rungs

**ropewalk** /-,wawk/ n a long covered walk, building, or room in which ropes are made

**ropewalker** /-,wawkə/ n an acrobat who walks along a rope high in the air

**ropeway** /-,way/ n 1 a fixed cable or a pair of fixed cables between supporting towers from which apparatuses for carrying passengers or goods are suspended; CABLE RAILWAY 2 an aerial cable, in the shape of a circle, that is moved by a stationary engine and used to transport goods (eg logs and ore)

**ropy, ropey** /'rohpi/ adj 1a capable of being drawn out into a thread; VISCOUS b having a gelatinous or slimy quality from bacterial or fungal contamination ⟨~ milk⟩ ⟨~ flour⟩ 2 resembling rope in texture or appearance 3 Br informal 3a inadequate or poor in quality; shoddy b somewhat unwell – **ropiness** n

**roque** /rohk/ n a form of croquet played in the USA on a hard-surfaced court surrounded by a bank [alter. of croquet]

**Roquefort** /'rok(ə),faw, (Fr rɔkfɔ:r)/ trademark – used for a strong-flavoured crumbly French cheese with bluish-green veins that is made from the curds of ewes' milk and ripened in limestone caves

**roquelaure** /'rokəlaw/ n a knee-length cloak worn esp in the 18th and 19th centuries [Fr, fr the Duc de Roquelaure †1738 Fr marshal]

**roquet** /'rohki/ vt, of a croquet ball or of the player who strikes it to hit (another ball) [prob alter. of croquet] – **roquet** n

**rorqual** /'rawkwəl/ n any of a genus (Balaenoptera) of large WHALEBONE WHALES (eg a FIN WHALE) having the skin of the throat marked with deep longitudinal furrows [Fr, fr Norw rorhval fr ON reytharhvalr, fr reythr rorqual + hvalr whale]

**Rorschach** /'rawshahk, -shahkh (Ger rɔ:rʃax)/ adj of, used in connection with, or resulting from the Rorschach test

**Rorschach test** n, psychology a PROJECTIVE test in which a person's reactions to standard inkblot designs are interpreted in an attempt to see what they may reveal about his/her state of mind or personality [Hermann Rorschach †1922 Swiss psychiatrist]

**rosaceous** /roh'zayshəs/ adj 1 of or belonging to the rose family of plants that includes many fruit trees and shrubs (eg the apple, peach, plum, blackberry, and raspberry) in addition to the roses 2 of or like a rose, esp in having a COROLLA composed of five symmetrically arranged and similarly shaped petals [NL Rosaceae, family name, fr rosa rose + -aceae]

**rosaniline** /roh'zanilien, -lin, -leen/ n 1 a chemical compound, $C_{20}H_{21}N_3O$, from which many dyes are derived 2 FUCHSINE (red dye) [L rosa rose + ISV aniline]

**rosarian** /roh'zeəriən/ n one who specializes in the cultivation of roses

**rosary** /'rohz(ə)ri/ n 1 a string of beads used in counting prayers, esp the prayers of the Roman Catholic rosary, while they are being recited 2 often cap a series of prayers in Roman Catholicism consisting of meditation on usu five sacred mysteries during recitation of 5 to 15 groups of 10 HAIL MARYS, each of which begins with the LORD'S PRAYER and ends with a GLORIA [ML rosarium, fr L, rose garden, fr neut of rosarius of roses, fr rosa rose]

**rosary pea** n 1 an E Indian climbing plant (Abrus precatorius) of the pea family that produces JEQUIRITY BEANS and has a root that is used as a substitute for liquorice 2 JEQUIRITY BEAN 1 [fr its seed being used for beads in rosaries and necklaces]

**¹rose** /rohz/ past of RISE

**²rose** /rohz/ n 1a any of a genus (Rosa of the family Rosaceae, the rose family) of widely cultivated usu prickly shrubs with showy 5-petalled, usu fragrant, and often double flowers; also the flower of a rose b any of several roselike flowering plants (eg the CHRISTMAS ROSE) 2 something resembling a rose in form: eg 2a(1) a circular design on something (eg a lute) a(2) COMPASS CARD (circular card marked with points of the compass) b(1) a form in which gems, esp diamonds, are cut that usu has a flat circular base and triangular facets rising to a point b(2) a gem with a rose cut c a perforated outlet for water (eg from a shower or watering can) d a circular fitting that anchors the flex of a light bulb to a ceiling 3 a pale to dark pinkish colour [ME, fr OE, fr L rosa; akin to Gk rhodon rose] – **roselike** adj

**³rose** adj 1a of a rose b containing or used for roses c flavoured, scented, or coloured with or like roses 2 of the colour rose

**rosé** /roh'zay, '--/ n a light pink table wine made from red grapes by removing the skins after fermentation has begun; also a similar wine made by mixing red and white wine [Fr, fr rosé pink, fr rose rose, fr L rosa]

**roseate** /'rohzi·ət/ adj 1 resembling a rose, esp in colour 2 of an attitude or philosophy marked by unrealistic optimism ⟨the ~ internationalism of prewar days⟩ [L roseus rosy, fr rosa] – **roseately** adv

**roseate spoonbill** n a SPOONBILL (storklike bird) (Ajaia ajaja) that has chiefly pink plumage and is found from the S USA to Patagonia

**roseate tern** n a graceful tern (Sterna dougallii) that has a deeply forked tail with very long outer feathers

**rosebay willowherb** /,rohzbay 'wiloh,huhb/ n a tall Eurasian and N American plant (Epilobium angustifolium) of the fuschia family that has long spikes of pinkish purple flowers

**rose beetle** n ROSE CHAFER

**rosebud** /'rohz,bud/ n 1 the bud of a rose 2 a young pretty girl or woman

**rosebush** /-,boosh/ n a shrubby rose plant

**rose chafer** /'chayfə/ n a common metallic green European beetle (Cetonia aurata) that, as a larva, feeds on plant roots and, as an adult, on leaves and flowers (eg of roses)

**'rose-,coloured** adj 1 having a rose colour 2 representing a person, situation, etc in a promising or overoptimistic light; roseate ⟨a ~ impression of country life⟩ ⟨views the world through ~ spectacles⟩

**rose comb** n a flat rather broad comb of a DOMESTIC FOWL, that has numerous small rounded elevations on the upper surface and ends in a fleshy spike at the rear

**rose geranium** *n* any of several pelargoniums grown for their fragrant 3- to 5-lobed leaves and small pink flowers

**rosehip** *n* ¹HIP (ripened fruit of a rose)

**rosella** /roh'zelə/ *n* **1** any of several brightly coloured Australian parakeets (genus *Platycercus*) **2** *Austr* a sheep that has shed most of its wool [irreg fr *Rosehill*, district in SE Australia]

**rose mallow** *n* **1** any of several hibiscuses with large rose-coloured flowers **2** *NAm* a hollyhock

**rosemary** /'rohzməri/ *n* a fragrant shrubby Eurasian plant (*Rosmarinus officinalis*) of the mint family that has pale lilac flowers and leathery evergreen leaves and is used as a herb in cooking and as the source of an oil used in perfumes [ME *rosmarine*, fr L *rosmarinus*, fr *ror-, ros* dew (akin to ON *rās* race) + *marinus* of the sea; – more at RACE, MARINE]

**rose of Jericho** /'jerikoh/ *n* an Asian plant (*Anastatica hierochuntica*) of the cabbage family that rolls up when dry and unfolds when moistened [ME, fr *Jericho*, ancient city in Palestine]

**rose of Sharon** /'sharən/ *n* a Eurasian Saint-John's-wort (*Hypericum calycinum*) often grown for its large yellow flowers [Plain of *Sharon*, region in Palestine]

**rose oil** *n* a fragrant oil obtained from roses and used chiefly in perfumery and flavouring

**roseola** /roh'zee•ələ/ *n* a rose-coloured rash of spots or a disease marked by such rash: eg **a** GERMAN MEASLES **b** *also* **roseola infantum** /in'fantəm/ a mild virus disease of children characterized by fever lasting three days followed by a rash of rose-coloured spots [NL, fr L *roseus* rosy, fr *rosa* rose] – **roseolar** *adj*

**roset** /'rohzət/ *n, chiefly Scot* resin [alter. of ME *rosin*]

**'rose-,tinted** *adj* rose-coloured

**rosette** /roh'zet, rə-/ *n* **1** an ornament usu made of material gathered or pleated so as to resemble a rose and worn as a badge, trimming, or prize **2** a stylized rose usu carved or moulded in relief and used as a decorative motif in architecture **3** a structure (eg a swirl of fur) or colour marking on an animal suggestive of a rosette **4** a cluster of leaves growing in crowded circles or spirals from the base of the stem (eg in the dandelion), or from the top of a stem, branch, or stalk (eg in many tropical palms) **5** any of several plant diseases characterized by the grouping of the leaves in dense clusters [Fr, lit., small rose, fr OF, fr *rose*, fr L *rosa*]

**rosewater** /'rohz,wawtə/ *adj* **1** having the scent of rose water **2** affectedly nice or delicate

**rose water** *n* a solution of ROSE OILS in water, used as a perfume

**rose window** *n* a circular window filled with tracery radiating from its centre

**rosewood** /-,wood/ *n* the dark red or purplish wood of any of various tropical trees (eg of the genus *Dalbergia* of the pea family), that is streaked and variegated with black and is used for furniture; *also* a tree that yields rosewood

**Rosh Hashanah** /,rosh hə'shahnə, -'sha-/ *n* the Jewish New Year, observed on the first, and often also on the second, of the month of TISHRI [LHeb *rōsh hashshānāh*, lit., beginning of the year]

**Rosicrucian** /,rohzi'kroohsh(y)ən/ *n* **1** an adherent of a 17th- and 18th-century movement devoted to esoteric wisdom and emphasizing psychic and spiritual enlightenment **2** a member of any of several organizations held to be descended from the Rosicrucians [Christian *Rosenkreutz* (NL *Rosa Crucis*), reputed 15th-c founder of the movement] – **Rosicrucian** *adj*, **Rosicrucianism** *n*

**rosily** /'rohzəli/ *adv* **1** with a rosy colour or tinge **2** cheerfully, optimistically

**¹rosin** /'rozin/ *n* a translucent amber-coloured to almost black brittle resin that is the residue from the distillation of turpentine from pine trees and is used esp in making varnish, soap, and soldering flux and for rubbing on violin bows [ME, modif of MF *resine* resin] – **rosinous** *adj*

**²rosin** *vt* to rub or treat (eg the bow of a violin) with rosin

**rostellar** /ro'stelə/ *adj* of or having the form of a rostellum

**rostellate** /ro'stelət/ *adj* having a rostellum

**rostellum** /ro'steləm/ *n, pl* **rostella** /-lə/ a small part resembling a beak: eg **a** the projecting sterile top of the female part of the flowers of some orchids **b** a sucking beaklike mouthpart of an insect (eg a louse or aphid) **c** a small rounded hooked

projection from the head of a tapeworm [NL, fr L, dim. of *rostrum* beak]

**¹roster** /'rostə/ *n* **1a** a list or register of personnel; *esp* one that gives the order in which a duty is to be performed **b** *taking sing or pl vb* the people listed on a roster **2** an itemized list [D *rooster*, lit., gridiron; fr the parallel lines]

**²roster** *vt* to place on a roster

**rostrum** /'rostrəm/ *n, pl* **rostrums, rostra** /'rostrə/ **1a** a stage or raised place for public speaking **b** a raised platform on a stage (eg for conducting an orchestra) **2** the beaklike prow of an ancient Roman ship **3a** the beak of a bird **b** a body part (eg an insect's snout or beak or the projecting part at the front of the shell of a lobster, prawn, etc) that resembles a bird's beak [L, beak, ship's beak, fr *rodere* to gnaw – more at RAT; (1) L *Rostra* (pl), a stage in Rome ornamented with prows of captured ships] – **rostral, rostrate, rostrated** *adj*

**rosy** /'rohzi/ *adj* **1a** of the colour rose **b** having a rosy complexion; blooming – often in combination ⟨rosy-cheeked *youngsters*⟩ **2** characterized by or tending to encourage optimism ⟨*things are looking* ~⟩ ⟨*rather a* ~ *picture of the future*⟩ – **rosiness** *n*

**¹rot** /rot/ *vb* **-tt-** *vi* **1a** to undergo decomposition from the action of bacteria or fungi – sometimes + *down* **b** to become unsound or weak (eg from chemical or water action) **2a** to go to ruin; perish ⟨*without patriotism the nation will* ~⟩ **b** to become morally corrupt; degenerate ~ *vt* to cause to decompose or deteriorate with rot – sometimes + *down* [ME *roten*, fr OE *rotian*; akin to OHG *rōzzen* to rot, L *rudus* rubble – more at RUDE]

**²rot** *n* **1a** rotting or being rotten decay **b** something rotten or rotting **2a** any of several parasitic diseases, esp of sheep, marked by wasting and death of tissue **b** a plant disease marked by breakdown and decay of tissues and caused usu by fungi or bacteria **3** nonsense, rubbish – often used interjectionally **4** *archaic* a wasting disease accompanied by rotting of tissue

**rota** /'rohtə/ *n* **1** a tribunal of the governing body of the Roman Catholic church (papal CURIA) exercising jurisdiction esp in matrimonial cases appealed from a court in a diocese **2** *chiefly Br* **2a** a list specifying a fixed order of rotation (eg of people or duties) **b** an ordered succession ⟨*meals were served on a* ~ *basis*⟩ [L, wheel – more at ROLL]

**rotameter** /'rohtə,meetə/ *n* a gauge that consists of a graduated glass tube containing a free float and used for measuring the flow of a liquid or gas [L *rota* wheel + E *-meter*]

**Rotarian** /roh'teəri•ən/ *n* a member of the Rotary Club

**¹rotary** /'roht(ə)ri/ *adj* **1a** turning on an axis like a wheel ⟨*a* ~ *clothes line*⟩ **b** proceeding about an axis ⟨~ *motion*⟩ **2** having a principal part that turns on an axis ⟨*a* ~ *cutter*⟩ **3** characterized by rotation **4** of or being a press in which paper is printed by being rotated in contact with a curved printing surface that is attached to a cylinder [ML *rotarius*, fr L *rota* wheel]

**²rotary** *n* **1** a rotary machine **2** *NAm* a traffic roundabout

**Rotary Club** *n* an organization of business and professional men devoted to serving the community and advancing world peace

**rotary cultivator** *n* an implement with blades or claws that revolve rapidly and till or break up the soil

**rotary engine** *n* **1** any of various engines (eg a turbine) in which power is applied to parts (eg vanes) that can move only in a circular path **2** a RADIAL ENGINE in which the cylinders revolve round a stationary crankshaft

**rotary plough** *n* ROTARY CULTIVATOR

**rotary-wing aircraft** *n* ROTORCRAFT (helicopter or similar aircraft)

**¹rotate** /'rohtayt/ *adj, of a flower* with the petals or SEPALS flat and spreading or radiating like the spokes of a wheel [L *rota* wheel]

**²rotate** /roh'tayt/ *vi* **1** to turn or revolve round an axis or a centre; *specif* to move in such a way that all particles follow circles with a common ANGULAR VELOCITY about a common axis **2a** to take turns at performing an act, function, or operation **b** to perform a series of actions or functions in a particular order ~ *vt* **1** to cause to turn round an axis or centre; revolve **2** to cause (a crop or crops) to grow in rotation **3** to order in a recurring sequence; alternate **4** to exchange (individuals or units) with other personnel [L *rotatus*, pp of *rotare*, fr *rota* wheel – more at ROLL] – **rotatable** *adj*, **rotative, rotatory** *adj*

**rotation** /roh'taysh(ə)n/ *n* **1a(1)** rotating (as if) on an axis or centre **a(2)** an act or instance of rotating something **b** one complete turn; the angular displacement required to return a rotating body or figure to its original orientation **2a** recurrence in a regular order ⟨*the ~ of the seasons*⟩ **b** the growing of different crops in succession in one field, usu in a regular sequence **3** the turning of a limb or other body part about its long axis, as if on a pivot – **rotational** *adj*

**rotator** /roh'taytə/ *n* something that rotates or causes rotation: eg **a** a muscle that partially rotates a body part on its axis **b** a rotating planet or galaxy

¹**rote** /roht/ *n* ³CROWD 1 (stringed instrument) [ME, fr OF, of Gmc origin; akin to OHG *hruozza* crowd]

²**rote** *n* **1** unthinking use of the memory through repetition or habit ⟨*learn by ~*⟩ **2** routine or repetition carried out habitually and/or unthinkingly ⟨*a joyless sense of order, ~, and commercial hustle* – L L King⟩ synonyms see ¹HEART [ME, custom, practice]

**rotenone** /'rohti,nohn/ *n* an insecticide, $C_{23}H_{22}O_6$, extracted from the roots of various tropical plants (esp genera *Derris* and *Lonchocarpus*) [ISV, fr Jap *roten* derris]

**rotgut** /'rot,gut/ *n, NAm slang* alcoholic spirits of low quality

**roti** /'rohti/ *n, pl* **roti** a flat cake of unleavened bread [Hindi *roṭī* bread]

**rotifer** /'rohtifə/ *n* any of a class or phylum (Rotifera) of minute but many-celled aquatic INVERTEBRATE animals whose front end is modified into a retractable disc bearing circles of strong CILIA (hairlike structures used for movement) that give the appearance of rapidly revolving wheels [deriv of L *rota* wheel + *-fer*]

**rotisserie** /roh'tisəri, -'tee-/ *n* **1** a restaurant specializing in roast and barbecued meats **2** an appliance fitted with a spit on which food is rotated in front of or over a source of heat, esp for roasting [Fr *rôtisserie*, fr MF *rostisserie*, fr *rostir* to roast – more at ROAST]

**rotl** /'rotl/ *n* any of various units of weight of Mediterranean and Near Eastern countries, usu of slightly less than 0.5 kilogram (about 1 pound) [Ar *raṭl*]

**rotogravure** /,rohtohgrə'vyooə/ *n* PHOTOGRAVURE (printing process using photography) in which the impression is produced by a rotary press [L *rota* + E *-o-* + *gravure*]

**rotor** /'rohtə/ *n* **1** a part that revolves in a machine; *esp* the rotating part of an electrical machine (eg a motor or generator) **2** a complete system of more or less horizontal blades that supplies all or a major part of the force supporting an aircraft (eg a helicopter) in flight [contr of *rotator*]

**rotorcraft** /'rohtə,krahft/ *n* an aircraft (eg a helicopter) supported in flight partially or wholly by rotating winglike parts (AEROFOILS) – called also ROTARY-WING AIRCRAFT

**rotovate** /'rohtə,vayt/ *vt* to loosen or break up (soil or a region covered with soil) using a ROTARY CULTIVATOR *vi* to use a ROTARY CULTIVATOR [back-formation fr *rotovator*]

**rotovator** /'rohtə,vaytə/ *trademark* – used for a ROTARY CULTIVATOR

**rotten** /'rot(ə)n/ *adj* **1** rotting or having rotted; putrid **2** morally or politically corrupt **3** *informal* extremely unfortunate, unpleasant, or inferior ⟨*it was a ~ show* – M J Arlen⟩ **4** *informal* marked by illness, discomfort, or unsoundness ⟨*feeling ~*⟩ [ME *roten*, fr ON *rotinn*; akin to OE *rotian* to rot] – **rottenly** *adv*, **rottenness** *n*

**rotten borough** *n* an election district that has many fewer voters than other comparable election districts – used esp with reference to certain English constituencies before the Reform Bill of 1832

**rottenstone** /-,stohn/ *n* a much weathered limestone containing silica, that is used for polishing

**rotter** /'rotə/ *n, chiefly humorous* a thoroughly objectionable person ⟨*the little ~ was fibbing*⟩

**rottweiler** /'rot,vielə/ *n, often cap* (any of) a German breed of tall black-and-tan shorthaired working dogs [Ger, fr *Rottweil*, town in SW Germany]

**rotund** /roh'tund/ *adj* **1** rounded **2** marked by grandiloquence or fullness of sound or cadence; high-flown, sonorous ⟨*a master of ~ phrase*⟩ **3** *chiefly euph* markedly plump; obese ☐ compare OROTUND [L *rotundus* – more at ROUND] – **rotundity, rotundness** *n*, **rotundly** *adv*

**rotunda** /roh'tundə/ *n* **1** a round building; *esp* one covered by a dome **2** a large round room or hall [It *rotonda*, fr L *rotunda*, fem of *rotundus*]

**roturier** /roh'tyooəri,ay/ *n* a member of the common people [MF, fr *roture* tenure of land by a common person, deriv of L

*ruptura* breaking – more at RUPTURE]

**rouble, ruble** /'roohbl/ *n* – see MONEY table [Russ *rubl'*]

**rouche** /roohsh/ *n* RUCHE (gathered fabric trimming) – **rouched** *adj*, **rouching** *n*

**roué** /'rooh·ay/ *n* a debauched man; a rake; *esp* one past his prime [Fr, lit., broken on the wheel, fr pp of *rouer* to break on the wheel, fr ML *rotare*, fr L, to rotate; fr an implication that such a person deserves this punishment]

**rouen** /'rooh·onh (Fr rwã)/ *n, often cap* (any of) a breed of domestic ducks resembling wild mallards in colouring [*Rouen*, city in N France]

¹**rouge** /roohzh/ *n* **1** any of various red-coloured cosmetics for colouring the lips or esp the cheeks **2** a red powder consisting essentially of FERRIC OXIDE used as a pigment and in polishing glass, metal, or gems [Fr, fr MF, fr *rouge* red, fr L *rubeus* reddish – more at RUBY]

²**rouge** *vt* **1** to apply rouge to **2** to cause to redden ~ *vi* to use rouge

¹**rough** /ruf/ *adj* **1** having a surface marked by irregularities, ridges, or projections: eg **1a** not smooth **b** covered with or made up of coarse hair or bristles ⟨*~ sheep*⟩ ⟨*a face ~ with two days' beard*⟩ **c(1)** having a broken, uneven, or bumpy surface ⟨*~ terrain*⟩ **c(2)** difficult to travel through or penetrate; wild ⟨*into the ~ woods* – P B Shelley⟩ **2a** turbulent, stormy ⟨*~ seas*⟩ **b(1)** characterized by harshness, violence, or force ⟨*a ~ breed of men*⟩ **b(2)** requiring strenuous effort ⟨*tasks that are ~ to perform*⟩ ⟨*had a ~ day*⟩ **3** coarse or rugged in character or appearance: eg **3a** harsh to the ear; grating **b** crude in style or expression **c** ill-mannered, rude **d** marked by a lack of refinement or grace; uncouth **4a** crude, unfinished ⟨*~ carpentry*⟩ **b** executed or ventured hastily, tentatively, or approximately ⟨*a ~ draft*⟩ ⟨*a ~ estimate*⟩ ⟨*~ justice*⟩ **5** *Br informal* **5a** unfortunate and hard to bear ⟨*what ~ luck!*⟩ – often + *on* ⟨*it's rather ~ on his wife*⟩ **b** exhausted or unwell, esp through lack of sleep or heavy drinking ⟨*had a fantastic time but felt really ~ the next morning*⟩ [ME, fr OE *rūh*; akin to L *ruga* wrinkle, Gk *oryssein* to dig, ON *rögg* tuft – more at RUG] – **roughish** *adj*, **roughness** *n*

synonyms **Rough, rugged, scabrous, harsh, jagged**, and **uneven** can all mean "not smooth or even". **Rough** applies to an irregular surface with bristles, ridges, or projections ⟨**rough** *stone*⟩. **Rugged** applies to a rough land surface ⟨**rugged** *mountains*⟩. **Scabrous** and **harsh** are now necessarily unpleasant, **scabrous** implying a repulsive and perhaps obscene scaliness or scabbiness ⟨**scabrous** *paint*⟩ and **harsh** describing a coarse texture unpleasant to the touch, or to any sense ⟨**harsh** *cognac*⟩. **Jagged** particularly describes sharply uneven edges ⟨*a* **jagged** *coastline*⟩. **Uneven** implies fluctuation or lack of uniformity ⟨*a book of* **uneven** *quality*⟩. antonyms smooth, sleek

²**rough** *n* **1** uneven ground covered with high grass, brush, and stones; *specif* the ground bordering a golf fairway, where the grass and other plants are left uncut **2** the rugged or disagreeable side or aspect ⟨*nature in the ~*⟩ **3a** something in a crude, unfinished, or preliminary state **b** broad outline; general terms ⟨*discussed in ~*⟩ **c** a hasty preliminary drawing or layout **4** a hooligan, ruffian **5** a rough part; *specif* the side of a sports racket on which the binding round the top and bottom string is not smooth and continuous ⟨*call ~ or smooth*⟩ **6** *Br slang* uncouth but sexually attractive men – esp in *a bit of rough* – **take the rough with the smooth** to put up with the less agreeable aspects of something because there are more agreeable aspects to compensate

³**rough** *adv, chiefly Br* in want of material comforts; without proper lodging – esp in *live rough* and *sleep rough*

⁴**rough** *vt* **1a** to roughen **b** to turn up (eg cloth, hair, or feathers) against the grain **2** to roughen (a horse's shoes) to prevent slipping – **rougher** *n* – **rough it** to live under harsh or primitive conditions

**rough off** *vt* to prepare (a horse) for rest at grass (eg by reducing exercise and diet)

**rough out** *vt* **1** to shape or plan in a preliminary way **2** to outline

**rough up** *vt, informal* to subject to violence; manhandle; BEAT 1a ⟨*was roughed up and pushed into the street*⟩

**roughage** /'rufij/ *n* coarse bulky food (eg bran) that is relatively high in fibre and low in digestible nutrients and that, by its bulk, stimulates contraction of the intestine and moves the contents onwards

,**rough-and-'ready** *adj* crudely or hastily constructed or conceived; no more than adequate; makeshift

,**rough-and-'tumble** *n* disorderly unrestrained fighting or

struggling; *broadly* rough, rowdy, or disorganized living –
**rough-and-tumble** *adj*
**rough book** *n* a book used for making rough or preparatory
notes for schoolwork
**rough breathing** *n* a mark ɔ used in Greek over some initial
vowels or over ρ to show pronunciation with an *h*-sound (AS-
PIRATION) – compare SMOOTH BREATHING
¹**roughcast** /'rufˌkahst/ *n* 1 a rough model 2 a plaster of lime
mixed with shells or pebbles used for covering buildings 3 a
rough surface or finish (eg of a plaster wall)
²**roughcast** *vt* **roughcast** 1 to plaster (eg a wall) with roughcast 2 to shape or form roughly
**rough diamond** *n* a person without social graces but of an
upright or amiable nature
ˌ**rough-'dry** *vt* to dry (laundry) without ironing or pressing –
**rough-dry** *adj*
**roughen** /'ruf(ə)n/ *vt* to make rough or rougher ⟨*hands were
~ed by toil*⟩ ~ *vi* to become rough
ˌ**rough-'hew** *vt* **rough-hewed; rough-hewn, rough-hewed** 1
to hew (eg timber) coarsely without smoothing or finishing 2
to form crudely
ˌ**rough-'hewn** *adj* 1 in a rough, unsmoothed, or unfinished
state; crudely formed ⟨*~ beams*⟩ 2 lacking refinement; rugged
⟨*attractive, in a ~ kind of way* – Jan Speas⟩
¹**roughhouse** /'rufˌhows/ *n, informal* an instance of brawling
or excessively boisterous play
²**roughhouse** *vb, informal vt* to treat in a boisterously rough
manner ~ *vi* to engage in a roughhouse
**rough lemon** *n* 1 a hybrid lemon that forms a large spreading
thorny tree, bears rough-skinned almost globular acid fruit,
and is mainly important as a rootstock for other citrus trees 2
the fruit of a rough lemon
**roughly** /'rufli/ *adv* 1 in a rough manner: eg **1a** with insolence
or violence ⟨*treated the prisoner ~*⟩ **b** in primitive fashion;
crudely ⟨*~ dressed timbers*⟩ 2 without claim to completeness
or exactness; approximately ⟨*~ 20 per cent*⟩
**roughneck** /'rufˌnek/ *n* 1 a person who handles the heavy
equipment on the floor of a drilling rig 2 *chiefly NAm informal*
a rough or rowdy person; a ruffian, tough
**roughrider** /'rufˌriedə/ *n* a person who is accustomed to riding
unbroken or little-trained horses
¹**roughshod** /'rufˌshod/ *adj* 1 *of a horse* wearing roughened
shoes 2 marked by force without justice or consideration ⟨*a
tyrant's ~ rule*⟩
²**roughshod** *adv* – **ride roughshod over** to treat forcefully
and without justice or consideration
**rough shooting** *n* the sport of shooting game (eg pigeons or
rabbits) on unprepared ground with no BEATERS (people who
flush the game out of hiding)
ˌ**rough-'spoken** *adj* crude or uncouth in speech
ˈ**rough-ˌstuff** *n, Br informal* violent behaviour; violence
**roulade** /ˌrooh'lahd/ *n* 1 a florid vocal embellishment sung to
one syllable 2 a roll of food; *esp* a rolled and cooked slice of
usu stuffed meat [Fr, lit., act of rolling]
**rouleau** /'roohˌloh/ *n, pl* **rouleaux** /'roohˌloh(z)/, **rouleaus** 1 a
little roll; *esp* a roll of coins in paper 2 a decorative piping or
rolled strip used esp as a trimming for a garment [Fr, fr MF
*rolel*, dim. of *role* roll]
¹**roulette** /rooh'let/ *n* 1 a gambling game in which players bet
on which red or black numbered compartment of a revolving
wheel a small ball rolled round on it in the opposite direction
will come to rest in **2a** any of various toothed wheels or discs
(eg for producing rows of dots on engraved plates or for perforating paper) **b** tiny slits between rows of stamps in a sheet
that are made by a roulette and serve as an aid in separation –
compare PERFORATION [Fr, lit., small wheel, fr OF *roelete*, dim.
of *roele* small wheel, fr LL *rotella*, dim. of L *rota* wheel – more
at ROLL]
²**roulette** *vt* to mark or perforate with a roulette
**Roumanian** /roo'maynyən, roh-, rə-, -ni-ən/ *n or adj* (a) Romanian
¹**round** /rownd/ *adj* **1a(1)** having every part of the surface or
circumference equally distant from the centre **a(2)** cylindrical
⟨*a ~ peg*⟩ **b** more circular or semicircular than angular;
rounded ⟨*a ~ face*⟩ ⟨*a ~ arch*⟩ 2 well filled out; plump ⟨*~
cheeks*⟩ **3a** complete, full ⟨*a ~ dozen*⟩ **b(1)** expressed as an
integer; having no fractional or decimal part ⟨*1.9, or 2 in ~
figures*⟩ **b(2)** expressed as a multiple of 10 **c** substantial in
amount; ample ⟨*a good ~ sum*⟩ 4 direct in expression; outspoken, unvarnished ⟨*a ~ oath*⟩ ⟨*a ~ tale*⟩ **5a** moving in or

forming a ring or circle – compare ROUND DANCE **b** following a
roughly circular route ⟨*a ~ tour of the Cotswolds*⟩ **c** inclusive
of outward and return journeys ⟨*the ~ voyage took six
months*⟩ **6a** brought to completion or perfection; finished **b**
presented with lifelike fullness or vividness 7 delivered with a
swing of the arm ⟨*a ~ blow*⟩ – used esp in sport **8a** having
full or unimpeded resonance or tone; sonorous **b** pronounced
with rounded lips 9 *of handwriting* curved rather than angular
10 having or performed with the back rounded ⟨*a ~ canter*⟩
[ME, fr OF *roont*, fr L *rotundus*; akin to L *rota* wheel – more
at ROLL] – **roundish** *adj*, **roundness** *n*
²**round** *adv* **1a** in a circular or curved path ⟨*danced ~ and ~*⟩
**b** with revolving or rotating motion ⟨*wheels go ~*⟩ **c** in circumference ⟨*a tree five feet ~*⟩ **d** in, along, or through a circuitous or indirect route ⟨*the road goes ~ by the lake*⟩ **e** in an
encircling position ⟨*a field with a fence all ~*⟩ **2a** on or to all
sides ⟨*handed the sweets ~*⟩ **b** in close from all sides so as to
surround ⟨*the children crowded ~*⟩ **c** near, about **d** here
and there in various places **3a** in rotation or recurrence ⟨*your
birthday will soon be ~ again*⟩ **b** from beginning to end;
through ⟨*all the year ~*⟩ **c(1)** in or to the other or a specified
direction ⟨*turn ~*⟩ ⟨*talk her ~*⟩ **c(2)** TO 4 **c(3)** in the specified
order or relationship ⟨*got the story the wrong way ~*⟩ 4 about,
approximately ⟨*~ 1900*⟩ 5 to a particular person or place ⟨*invite them ~ for drinks*⟩ – **round about** 1 approximately; MORE
OR LESS 2 in a ring round; on all sides
³**round** *prep* **1a** so as to revolve or progress about (a centre) **b**
so as to encircle or enclose ⟨*seated ~ the table*⟩ **c** so as to
avoid or get past; beyond the obstacle of ⟨*went ~ the lake*⟩
⟨*got ~ his objections*⟩ ⟨*lives just ~ the corner*⟩ **d** near to; about
**2a** in all directions outwards from ⟨*looked ~ him*⟩ **b** here and
there in or throughout ⟨*travel ~ Europe*⟩ 3 so as to have a
centre or basis in ⟨*a movement organized ~ the idea of service*⟩
4 continuously during; throughout *usage* see ²AROUND
⁴**round** *n* **1a** something (eg a circle, curve, or ring) that is round
**b(2)** a ring or circle of people or things 2 ROUND DANCE 3 a
short vocal form in which each voice enters, in turn, at the
same pitch and sings the same tune, which is repeated continuously **4a** a rung of a ladder or chair **b** a rounded moulding
**5a** a circling or circuitous path or course **b** motion in a circle
or a curving path **6a** a route or circuit habitually traversed (eg
by a milkman or policeman) **b** round, **rounds** *pl* a series of
professional visits made by a doctor to patients in their homes;
*also* such visits made by a hospital doctor to patients in hospital **c** rounds *pl*, **round** a series of customary social calls
⟨*doing the ~s of his friends*⟩ 7 a set of alcoholic drinks served
at one time to each person in a group ⟨*I'll buy the next ~*⟩ 8
a recurring sequence or set of actions or events ⟨*a pay ~*⟩ ⟨*a
~ of talks*⟩ 9 a period of time that recurs in fixed succession
⟨*the daily ~*⟩ **10a** a single shot fired by a weapon **b** a unit of
ammunition consisting of the parts necessary to fire one shot
**11a** any of a series of units of action in a game or sport (eg
covering a prescribed time or distance, or giving each player
one turn) **b** a division of a tournament in which each contestant plays one other 12 a prolonged burst (eg of applause) 13 a
cut of beef between the rump and the lower leg **14a** a sandwich
made with two whole slices of bread **b** a single slice of bread
or toast – **in the round** 1 in solid sculptured form and unattached to a background 2 in both good and bad aspects; AS
A WHOLE 3 with the audience surrounding a central stage
⟨*theatre in the round*⟩
⁵**round** *vt* **1a** to make round or rounded **b(1)** to make (the
lips) round and protruded **b(2)** to pronounce (eg the vowel
/ooh/) with lip rounding **2a** to go round **b** to pass part of the
way round (eg a bend) ⟨*the ship ~ed the headland*⟩ 3 to bring
to completion or perfection – often + *off* or *out* 4 to express
as a round number – often + *off*, *up*, or *down* ⟨*11.3572 ~ed
off to three decimal places becomes 11.357*⟩ 5 *archaic* to encircle, encompass ~ *vi* **1a** to become round, plump, or smooth
in outline **b** to reach fullness or completion – usu + *off* or *out*
2 to follow a winding or circular course; bend ⟨*~ing into the
home stretch*⟩
**round on** *vt* to turn against with unexpected vehemence;
retort unexpectedly to
**round up** *vt* 1 to collect (cattle) by means of a roundup 2 to
gather in or bring together from various quarters – see also
ROUNDUP
¹**roundabout** /'rowndəˌbowt/ *n, Br* 1 a merry-go-round; *also*
a rotatable platform that is an amusement in a children's
playground 2 a road junction formed round a central island

about which traffic moves in one direction only; *also* a paved or planted circle in the middle of this

²**roundabout** *adj* circuitous, indirect ⟨*had to take a* ~ *route*⟩ – **roundaboutness** *n*

**round angle** *n* an angle of 360°

**round bracket** *n, chiefly Br* PARENTHESIS 3

**round dance, round** *n* **1** a folk dance in which participants form a ring and move in a prescribed direction **2** a ballroom dance in which couples progress round the room with circular or revolving movement

**rounded** /'rowndid/ *adj* **1** made round; smoothly curved **2** fully developed; mature ⟨*a* ~ *mellow view of life*⟩ – compare WELL-ROUNDED – **roundedness** *n*

**roundel** /'rowndl/ *n* **1** a round figure or object: eg **1a** a circular panel, window, or niche **b** a circular mark identifying the nationality of an aircraft, esp a warplane **2a** RONDEL **2 b** an English modification of this □ (*l*) called also RONDEL [ME, fr OF *rondel*, fr *roont* round – more at ROUND]

**roundelay** /'rowndi,lay/ *n* **1** a simple song with a refrain **2** a poem with a refrain recurring frequently or at fixed intervals, as in a RONDEL [modif (influenced by ⁴*lay*) of MF *rondelet*, dim. of *rondel*]

**rounder** /'rowndə/ *n* **1a** *pl but taking sing vb* a game with bat and ball that is played esp in Britain and resembles baseball **b** a unit of scoring in rounders, when a run has been made round all four bases after one hit **2** a machine or tool for making edges or surfaces round **3** a boxing or wrestling match lasting a specified number of rounds – usu in combination ⟨*a 10-rounder*⟩

¹**roundhead** /'rownd,hed/ *n* **1** *cap* **1a** PURITAN 1 **b** a supporter of Parliament in its contest with Charles I – compare CAVALIER **2** a BRACHYCEPHALIC (roundheaded) person [fr the Puritans' cropping their hair short in contrast to the Cavaliers]

²**roundhead** *adj, of a screw or bolt* having a hemispherical head

**roundheaded** /,rownd'hedid/ *adj* having a round head; *specif* BRACHYCEPHALIC – **roundheadedness** *n*

**roundhouse** /'rownd,hows/ *n* **1** a circular building for housing and repairing locomotives **2** a cabin or apartment on the rear part of a quarterdeck **3** *NAm* a blow in boxing delivered with a wide swing **4** *archaic* LOCKUP (temporary prison)

**round lot** *n* the standard unit of trading in shares, usu amounting to 100 shares of stock

**roundly** /'rowndli/ *adv* **1** in a round or circular form or manner **2a** in a thorough wholehearted way ⟨*set* ~ *to the task*⟩ **b** in a blunt or severe manner ⟨~ *rebuked him*⟩

**round robin** *n* **1a** a written petition or protest on which the signatures are arranged in a circle so that no name heads the list **b** a statement signed by several people **c** a document circulated among the members of a group for consideration and comment **2** ROUND TABLE **3** a charitable collection, esp among a group of friends or associates **4** a tournament in which every contestant plays every other contestant in turn [fr the name *Robin*]

,**round-'shouldered** *adj* having the shoulders stooped or rounded

**roundsman** /'rowndzmən/ *n* **1** a person who makes rounds; *specif* one (eg a milkman) who takes, orders, sells, or delivers goods on an assigned route **2** *NAm* a supervisory police officer

**round table** *n* a meeting or conference of several people on equal terms – **round-table** *adj*

,**round-the-'clock** *adj* lasting or continuing 24 hours a day; constant

**round trip** *n* a trip to a place and back again, usu over the same route

**roundup** /-,up/ *n* **1a(1)** the act or activity of collecting cattle by riding round them and driving them in **a(2)** *taking sing or pl vb* the men and horses so engaged **b** a gathering in of scattered people or things ⟨*a* ~ *of all suspects*⟩ **2** a compilation or summary of various items of news ⟨*a sports* ~⟩

**roundworm** /-,wuhm/ *n* a NEMATODE worm

**roup** /roohp/ *n* a virus disease of poultry in which soft whitish lesions form on the mouth, throat, and eyes [origin unknown]

¹**rouse** /rowz/ *vi* **1** to cease to sleep; awaken **2** to become stirred; come to life from a state of torpor or apathy ~ *vt* **1** to stir or startle (game) from cover **2a** to stir up; excite, provoke ⟨*was* ~d *to fury*⟩ **b** to bring out of sleep, inactivity, or apathy; awaken **c** to evoke (eg feelings or memories); CALL UP [ME *rousen* (of a bird) to shake the feathers] – **rouser** *n*

²**rouse** *n* **1** *archaic* carousing **2** *obs* a drink, toast [alter. (by incorrect division of *to drink carouse*) of *carouse*]

**rouseabout** /'rowsə,bowt/ *n, Austr* **1** a handyman on a sheep farm **2** a labourer

**rousing** /'rowzing/ *adj* **1** giving rise to enthusiasm; stirring ⟨*a* ~ *chorus*⟩ **2** brisk, lively ⟨*a* ~ *business*⟩

**Rousseauism** /roo'soh-iz(ə)m/ *n* **1** the philosophical, educational, and political doctrines of Jean Jacques Rousseau **2** a return to or glorification of a simpler and more primitive way of life [Jean Jacques *Rousseau* †1778 Fr philosopher] – **Rousseauist** *n*, **Rousseauistic** *adj*

**roustabout** /'rowstə,bowt/ *n* **1** a circus worker who erects and dismantles tents, cares for the grounds, and handles animals and equipment **2** *chiefly NAm* **2a** a deckhand **b** a dock labourer **3** *chiefly NAm or Austr* an unskilled or semiskilled labourer, esp in an oil field or refinery [*roust*, alter. of *rouse*]

**rouster** /'rowstə/ *n* ROUSTABOUT 2

¹**rout** /rowt/ *n* **1** a disorderly crowd of people; a throng, mob **2a** a disturbance, clamour **b** *law* a disturbance of the peace by three or more people assembled together with a common unlawful purpose which they have not yet put fully into effect **3** *archaic* a fashionable social gathering [ME *route*, fr MF, troop, defeat, fr (assumed) VL *rupta*, fr L, fem of *ruptus*, pp of *rumpere* to break – more at BEREAVE]

²**rout** *vi, dial chiefly Br, of cattle* to low loudly; bellow [ME *rowten*, fr ON *rauta*; akin to OE *rēotan* to weep, L *rudere* to roar]

³**rout** *vi* **1** to poke about with the snout; root ⟨*pigs* ~ing *in the earth*⟩ **2** to search haphazardly – often + *about* ~ *vt* to gouge out or make a furrow in (eg wood or metal); *specif* to cut away (eg blank parts) from a printing surface (eg an engraving) with a router [alter. of ³*root*]

**rout out** *vt* **1** to cause to emerge (eg from bed or hiding), esp by force ⟨*Norman's been in bed long enough – go and* rout *him out*⟩ **2** to hunt for and produce; uncover ⟨routed out *some old photographs*⟩ ⟨routed out *the truth*⟩

⁴**rout** *n* **1** a state of wild confusion; *specif* a confused retreat ⟨*charging tanks put the infantry to* ~⟩ **2a** a disastrous defeat; a debacle **b** a headlong flight [MF *route* troop, defeat]

⁵**rout** *vt* **1** to disorganize completely; wreak havoc among **2** to put to headlong flight – often + *out* **3** to defeat decisively or disastrously ⟨*their party was* ~ed *at the polls*⟩

¹**route** /rooht/ *n* **1a** a regularly travelled way; a road ⟨*the trunk* ~ *north*⟩ **b** a means of access; a path ⟨*the* ~ *to social success*⟩ **2** a line of travel; a course ⟨*rivers that have changed their* ~⟩ **3a** an established or selected course of travel; an itinerary **b** ROUND 6a [ME, fr OF, fr (assumed) VL *rupta* (*via*), lit., broken way, fr L *rupta*, fem of *ruptus*, pp]

²**route** *vt* **1a** to send or arrange to be sent by a selected route; direct ⟨*was* ~d *along the scenic coast road*⟩ **b** to divert in a specified direction ⟨*all business was* ~d *through his colleague*⟩ **2** to prearrange and direct the order and execution of (a series of operations)

**routeman** /-,man/ *n, NAm* ROUNDSMAN 1

**route march** *n* a usu long and tiring march, esp as part of a military unit's training

¹**router** /'rowtə/ *n* something that routs: eg **a** a plane for cutting a groove **b** a machine with a cutter set on a revolving spindle for milling out the surface of wood or metal

²**router** /'roohtə/ *n* a person who routes

¹**routine** /rooh'teen/ *n* **1a** a regular course of procedure ⟨*if industrial action becomes an accepted* ~⟩ **b** habitual or mechanical performance of an established procedure ⟨*women in revolt against household* ~⟩ **2** a customary form of speech or verbal formula ⟨*the usual sales* ~⟩ **3** a set piece of entertainment, often repeated ⟨*a dance* ~⟩ **4** a sequence of instructions for a computer for performing a particular task [Fr, fr MF, fr *route* travelled way]

²**routine** *adj* **1** commonplace or repetitious in character; ordinary **2** of or in accordance with established procedure ⟨~ *business*⟩ **synonyms** see USUAL – **routinely** *adv*

**routin-ize, -ise** /rooh'teeniez, 'roohtiniez/ *vt, NAm* **1** to habituate to a routine **2** to reduce to or organize as routine – **routinization** *n*

**roux** /rooh/ *n, pl* **roux** a cooked mixture of fat and flour used as a thickening agent in a sauce [Fr, fr (*beurre*) *roux* browned (butter)]

¹**rove** /rohv/ *vi* **1** to move aimlessly or idly; roam, stray – often + *about* **2** *esp of the eyes* to stray and change direction, without concentration ~ *vt* to wander through or over [ME *roven* to

shoot arrows at random targets, perh alter. of *raven* to stray, wander]

**²rove** *n* an act or instance of wandering

**³rove** *past of* REEVE

**⁴rove** *vt* to join (textile fibres) with a slight twist and draw out into roving [origin unknown]

**rove beetle** *n* any of numerous often predatory active beetles (family Staphylinidae) having a long body and very short wing covers, beneath which the wings are folded transversely [perh fr ¹*rove*]

**¹rover** /'rohvə/ *n* a pirate ⟨*tales of the sea* ~s⟩ [ME, fr MD, fr *roven* to rob; akin to OE *rēafian* to rob – more at BEREAVE]

**²rover** *n* **1a** *usu pl* a randomly chosen or long-distance target in archery **b** *pl but taking sing vb* an informal archery contest, held usu in rough country, in which any suitable object is used as a target, and the archer whose arrow lands nearest chooses the next target **2** a person who roves; a wanderer [ME, fr *roven* to shoot arrows at random targets]

**¹roving** /'rohving/ *adj* **1** not restricted as to location or area of concern ⟨*a* ~ *reporter*⟩ **2** inclined to ramble or stray ⟨*a* ~ *fancy*⟩ [¹*rove*]

**²roving** *n* a slightly twisted roll or strand of textile fibres [⁴*rove*]

**roving eye** *n* promiscuous sexual interests

**¹row** /roh/ *vi* **1** to propel a boat by means of oars **2** to move (as if) by the propulsion of oars ~ *vt* **1a** to propel (as if) with oars **b** to be equipped with (a specified number of oars) **c(1)** to participate in (a rowing match) **c(2)** to compete against in rowing **c(3)** to occupy (a specified position as oarsman) in a rowing crew ⟨~s *bow in the first boat*⟩ **2** to transport in a boat propelled by oars [ME *rowen*, fr OE *rōwan;* akin to MHG *rüejen* to row, L *remus* oar] – **rower** *n*

**²row** /roh/ *n* **1** an act or instance of rowing a boat **2** a trip in a rowing boat

**³row** /roh/ *n* one after another; successively **1** a number of objects or people arranged in a line, esp a straight one ⟨*a* ~ *of bottles*⟩; *also* the line along which such objects or people are arranged ⟨*planted the seeds in parallel* ~s⟩ **2** a way, street; *esp* a narrow street between continuous lines of buildings [ME *rawe;* akin to OE *rāw* row, OHG *rīga* line, L *rima* slit] – **in a row**

**⁴row** /row/ *n* **1** excessive or unpleasant noise; a racket, commotion **2** a noisy quarrel or stormy dispute [origin unknown]

**⁵row** /row/ *vi* to have a row; engage in a quarrel

**rowan** /'roh·ən/ *n* a small Eurasian tree (*Sorbus aucuparia*) of the rose family that has flat-topped clusters (CORYMBS) of white flowers, followed by small red berries; *also* the berry of a rowan [of Scand origin; akin to ON *reynir* rowan; akin to OE *rēad* red – more at RED]

**rowboat** /'roh,boht/ *n, chiefly NAm* ROWING BOAT

**¹rowdy** /'rowdi/ *adj* coarse or boisterous in behaviour; rough **synonyms** see VOCIFEROUS [perh irreg fr ⁵*row*] – **rowdily** *adv*, **rowdiness** *n*, **rowdyish** *adj*

**²rowdy** *n* a rowdy person; a tough

**rowdyism** /'rowdi,iz(ə)m/ *n* rowdy characteristics or behaviour ⟨*sought a cure for football* ~⟩

**¹rowel** /'rowəl/ *n* a revolving disc with sharp points along the edge, at the end of a spur [ME *rowelle*, fr MF *rouelle* small wheel, fr OF *roele* – more at ROULETTE]

**²rowel** *vt* **-ll-** (*NAm* **-l-, -ll-**) to goad (as if) with a rowel

**row house** /roh/ *n, NAm* a terraced house

**rowing** /'roh·ing/ *n* the sport of racing in rowing boats

**rowing boat** /'roh·ing/ *n* a small boat designed to be rowed

**rowlock** /'rolək; *also* (*not tech*) 'roh,lok/ *n, chiefly Br* a usu U-shaped device fastened to, or let into, the rim of a boat, so as to hold an oar and provide a pivot for its action [prob alter. of *oarlock*]

**¹royal** /'roy(ə)l/ *adj* **1a** of monarchical ancestry ⟨*the* ~ *family*⟩ **b** of, from, or subject to the crown ⟨*the* ~ *estates*⟩ **c** in the crown's service ⟨Royal *Air Force*⟩ **2** suitable for or worthy of royalty; regal, magnificent ⟨~ *acclaim*⟩ ⟨*the* ~ *gift of such poets* – Kathleen Raine⟩ **3a** of superior size, magnitude, or quality ⟨*a patronage of* ~ *dimensions* – J H Plumb⟩ **b** established or chartered by the crown **4** of or being a part (eg a sail or spar) of the rigging of a sailing ship next above the TOPGALLANT (part near the top of the mast) [ME *roial*, fr MF, fr L *regalis*, fr *reg-, rex* king; akin to OIr *rí* (gen *ríg*) king, Skt *rājan*, L *regere* to rule – more at RIGHT] – **royally** *adv*

**²royal** *n* **1** a stag of 8 years or more having antlers with at least 12 points **2** a small sail immediately above the TOPGALLANT sail (sail near the top of the mast) **3** a size of paper usu 25 × 20 inches (635 × 508 millimetres) **4** *informal* a person of royal blood

*usage* Some people dislike the use of **royal** as a noun meaning "royal person".

**royal antler** *n* the third point (TINE) above the base of a stag's antler

**Royal Assent** *n the* formal acceptance by the monarch of a bill passed through the British parliament, which thus transforms it into an act

**royal blue** *n* a rich purplish-blue colour

**Royal Commission** *n* a committee of inquiry appointed by the Crown

**royal flush** *n* a poker hand containing the ten, jack, queen, king, and ace of the same suit

**royalism** /'royə,liz(ə)m/ *n* support or advocacy of rule by monarchs

**royalist** /'royəlist/ *n* **1** *often cap* a supporter of a monarch or of rule by monarchs: eg **1a** CAVALIER **2 b** TORY **3 2** *NAm informal* a reactionary magnate – **royalist** *adj*

**royal jelly** *n* a highly nutritious substance secreted by the honeybee that is fed to the very young larvae and to all the larvae that will develop into queen bees in a colony

**royal poinciana** /,poynsi'ahnə/ *n* FLAMBOYANT (flowering tree)

**royal prerogative** *n the* constitutional rights of the monarch

**royal purple** *n* a dark reddish-purple colour

**royal road** *n* the most direct way *to* a condition or object of study

**royal tennis** *n* REAL TENNIS [by alter.]

**royalty** /'royəlti/ *n* **1a** royal status or power; sovereignty **b** a right or perquisite of a sovereign (eg a percentage paid to the crown of the gold or silver taken from mines) **2** regal character or bearing; nobility **3** *taking sing or pl vb* **3a** people of royal blood, collectively or singly **b** a privileged class of a specified type ⟨*economic* ~⟩ **4** a right of jurisdiction granted to an individual or corporation by a sovereign **5a** a share of the product or profit kept by the grantor of esp an oil or mining lease **b** a payment made to an author or composer for each copy of his/her work sold, or to an inventor for each article sold under a patent [ME *roialte*, fr MF *roialté*, fr OF, fr *roial*]

**rozzer** /'rozə/ *n, Br slang* a policeman [origin unknown]

**RPG** *n* a HIGH-LEVEL computer language (one closer to English than the code recognized by a computer) that generates programs from the user's specifications and is used esp to produce business reports [*r*eport *p*rogram *g*enerator]

**-rrhagia** /-'rayj(y)ə/ *comb form* (→ *n*) abnormal or excessive discharge or flow ⟨*menorrhagia*⟩ [NL, fr Gk, fr *rhēgnynai* to break, burst; akin to OSlav *rĕzati* to cut]

**-rrhine, -rhine** /-,rien/ *comb form* (→ *adj*) having (such) a nose ⟨*platyrrhine*⟩ [ISV, fr Gk *-rrhin-, -rrhis*, fr *rhin-, rhis* nose]

**-rrhiza** /-'riezə/ – see -RHIZA

**-rrhoea**, *chiefly NAm* **-rrhea** /-'riə/ *comb form* (→ *n*) flow; discharge ⟨*leucorrhoea*⟩ [ME *-ria*, fr LL *-rrhoea*, fr Gk *-rrhoia*, fr *rhoia*, fr *rhein* to flow – more at STREAM]

**rRNA** *n* RIBOSOMAL RNA

**¹rub** /rub/ *vb* **-bb-** *vi* **1a** to move along a surface with pressure **b(1)** to move with friction so as to become worn down or sore **b(2)** to cause vexation or anger **2** to be able to be marked or damaged by rubbing ⟨*velvet* ~s *easily*⟩ ~ *vt* **1** to subject to pressure and friction, esp with a back-and-forth motion **2** to cause (a body) to move with pressure and friction along a surface so as to smooth or wear down – sometimes + *down* **3** to treat in any of various ways by rubbing ⟨~ *the rust from old rifles*⟩ ⟨~*bed liniment into his skin*⟩ **4** to bring into reciprocal back-and-forth or rotary contact ⟨~ *two sticks together*⟩ – see also **rub** SHOULDERS **with, rub up the wrong** WAY [ME *rubben;* akin to Icel *rubba* to scrape]

**rub along** *vi, chiefly Br* **1** to continue coping with a usu difficult situation; GET BY ⟨*in spite of financial difficulties, he is rubbing along*⟩ **2** to remain on friendly terms – often + *together*

**rub in** *vt* **1** to harp on (eg something unpleasant or embarrassing); emphasize **2** to blend (fat) with flour by rubbing together with the fingertips to form a crumbly mixture

**rub off** *vi* **1** to disappear as the result of rubbing **2** to exert an influence through contact or example ⟨*ideas* rub off *on* *them*⟩ ~ *vt* to remove by rubbing ⟨rub off *the marks on the table*⟩

**rub out** *vt* **1** to remove (eg pencil marks) with a rubber; *broadly* to obliterate by rubbing **2** *chiefly NAm slang* to kill, murder ⟨*somebody* rubbed *him out . . . with a twenty-two* – Raymond Chandler⟩ ~ *vi* to disappear as the result of rubbing

**rub up** *vt* to revive or refresh knowledge of; revise ⟨rub up *Latin verbs*⟩

²**rub** *n* **1a** an unevenness of surface (eg of the ground in bowls) **b** *the* obstacle, difficulty **c** something grating to the feelings (eg a gibe or harsh criticism) **2** the application of friction and pressure ⟨*an alcohol* ~⟩ – **rub of the green** (*the* hypothetical cause of) a piece of good or bad luck [fr the use of the phrase in golf to describe any accidental interference with a ball]

**rubato** /rooh'bahtoh/ *n, pl* **rubatos** expressive fluctuation of speed within a musical phrase [It, pp of *rubare* to rob, of Gmc origin]

¹**rubber** /'rubə/ *n* **1a** something that rubs **b**(1) an instrument or object used in rubbing, polishing, or cleaning ⟨*a board* ~⟩ **b**(2) *Br* a small piece of rubber or plastic used for rubbing out esp pencil marks on paper, card, etc **b**(3) STABLE RUBBER (towel for horses) **c** something that prevents rubbing or chafing **2a** an elastic substance that is obtained by coagulating the milky juice of the RUBBER TREE or any of various other tropical plants (eg a RUBBER PLANT), consists essentially of many repeating ISO-PRENE units, and is prepared as sheets and then dried **b** any of various synthetic rubberlike substances **c** a natural or synthetic rubber modified by chemical treatment to increase its useful properties (eg toughness and resistance to wear) and used esp in tyres, electrical insulation, and waterproof materials **3** something made of or resembling rubber: eg **3a** *NAm* a rubber overshoe **b** *NAm slang* a condom [¹*rub* + ²*-er*; (2) fr its use in erasers] – **rubber** *adj*, **rubberlike** *adj*

²**rubber** *n* **1** a contest won by the side that takes a majority of an odd number of games (eg two out of three) **2** an extra game played to determine the winner of a tied match – + *the* [origin unknown]

**rubber band** *n* a continuous band of rubber used for holding together or securing small objects

**rubber cement** *n* an adhesive consisting typically of VUL-CANIZED rubber dispersed in an organic chemical solvent (eg toluene)

**rubber cheque** *n, informal* a cheque returned by the bank as not good [fr its coming back like a bouncing rubber ball]

**rubber·ize, -ise** /'rubəriez/ *vt* to coat or impregnate with rubber or a rubber solution

¹**rubberneck** /'rubə,nek/ *also* **rubbernecker** *n, chiefly NAm derog* **1** an over-inquisitive person **2** a tourist, sightseer; *esp* one on a guided tour

²**rubberneck** *vi, chiefly NAm* **1** *informal* to show exaggerated attention or curiosity; be agog **2** *derog* to engage in sightseeing

'**rubber-,necked** *adj, of a horse* bending only the neck in response to the rein

**rubber plant** *n* a plant that yields rubber; *esp* a tall tropical Asian tree (*Ficus elastica*) of the fig family, that has glossy leathery leaves and is frequently dwarfed and grown as a houseplant

,**rubber-'stamp** *vt* **1** to imprint with a rubber stamp **2** to approve, endorse, or dispose of as a matter of routine, or at the dictate of another

**rubber stamp** *n* **1** a stamp of rubber for making imprints **2** a person who unthinkingly imitates others, or assents to their actions or policies without discussion **3a** a stereotyped copy or expression ⟨*the usual rubber stamps of criticism* – H L Mencken⟩ **b** a routine endorsement or approval

**rubber tree** *n* a S American tree (*Hevea brasiliensis*) of the spurge family that is cultivated in plantations and is the chief source of natural rubber

**rubbery** /'rubəri/ *adj* resembling rubber (eg in elasticity, texture, or smell)

**rubbing** /'rubing/ *n* an image of a raised, incised, or textured surface obtained by placing paper over it and rubbing the paper with a marking substance (eg chalk) ⟨*a brass* ~ *from an old church*⟩; *also* the act or activity of making rubbings

¹**rubbish** /'rubish/ *n* **1a** useless waste matter; refuse **b** worthless or rejected articles or material; trash **2** something that is worthless or makes no sense; NONSENSE **1a** – often used inter-

jectionally [ME *robys*] – **rubbishy** *adj*

²**rubbish** *vt, chiefly Austr informal* **1** to condemn as worthless; *also* to criticize severely ⟨*party leaders* ~ed *the other side's manifesto*⟩ **2** to litter with rubbish

**rubble** /'rubl/ *n* **1a** broken fragments (eg of stone or rock) produced by the collapse or destruction of a building ⟨*fortifications knocked into* ~ – C S Forester⟩ **b** a jumbled mass or collection of usu broken or worthless things **2a** the weathered surface layer of rock **b** rough broken stones or bricks used in coarse masonry or in filling courses of walls; *also* rubblework **3** rough stone as it comes from the quarry [ME *robyl*]

**rubblework** /'rubl,wuhk/ *n* masonry of unsquared or roughly squared stones that are irregular in size and shape

**rubdown** /'rub,down/ *n* a brisk rubbing of the body, usu with a towel or cloth

**rube** /roohb/ *n, NAm informal* an unsophisticated rustic; a bumpkin [*Rube*, nickname for *Reuben*]

¹**rubefacient** /,roohbi'faysh(ə)nt/ *adj* causing redness, esp of the skin [L *rubefacient-*, *rubefaciens*, prp of *rubefacere* to make red, fr *rubeus* reddish + *facere* to make – more at RUBY, DO]

²**rubefacient** *n* a substance applied externally that produces redness of the skin; *specif* COUNTERIRRITANT

**rubefaction** *n* **1** the act or process of causing redness, esp of the skin **2** redness of the skin caused by a rubefacient

**Rube Goldberg** /,roohb 'gohld,buhg/ *adj, NAm* HEATH ROB-INSON [Reuben (*Rube*) L *Goldberg* †1970 US cartoonist]

**rubella** /rooh'belə/ *n* GERMAN MEASLES [NL, fr L, fem of *rubellus* reddish, fr *ruber* red – more at RED]

**rubellite** /'roohbə,liet/ *n* a pink to red variety of the mineral TOURMALINE used as a gem [L *rubellus* reddish]

**rubeola** /rooh'bee·ələ/ *n* measles [NL, fr neut pl of (assumed) NL *rubeolus* reddish, fr L *rubeus* – more at RUBY] – **rubeolar** *adj*

**rubescent** /rooh'bes(ə)nt/ *adj* becoming or tending to red [L *rubescent-*, *rubescens*, prp of *rubescere* to grow red, incho of *rubēre* to be red]

**Rubicon** /'roohbikən/ *n* a bounding or limiting line; *esp* one that, when crossed, commits a person irrevocably [L *Rubicon-*, *Rubico*, river in N Italy forming part of the boundary between Cisalpine Gaul and Italy, whose crossing by Julius Caesar in 49 BC began a civil war]

**rubicund** /'roohbikənd/ *adj, chiefly formal or humorous* ruddy [L *rubicundus*, fr *rubēre* to be red; akin to L *rubeus* reddish] – **rubicundity** *n*

**rubidium** /rooh'bidi·əm/ *n* a highly reactive soft silvery metallic chemical element of the ALKALI METAL group (group of elements including sodium and potassium) that occurs in small amounts in many minerals and bursts into flame spontaneously in air [NL, fr L *rubidus* red, fr *rubēre*; fr the two red lines in its spectrum]

**rubiginous** /rooh'bijinəs/ *adj* of a rusty red colour [L *robiginous*, *rubiginosus* rusty, fr *robigin-*, *robigo* rust; akin to L *rubēre*]

**Rubik's cube, Rubik cube** /'roohbik/ *n* a puzzle consisting of a usu plastic cube having each face divided into nine small coloured or distinctively marked square segments and rotatable about a central square, that must be restored to an initial condition in which each face shows nine identical squares [Ernö *Rubik b* 1944 Hung designer]

**ruble** /'roohbl/ *n* a rouble

**rubric** /'roohbrik/ *n* **1** a heading (eg in a book or manuscript) written or printed in a distinctive colour or style **2a**(1) a name, title; *specif* the title of a statute **a**(2) a heading under which something is classed; a category ⟨*all falling under the same general* ~⟩ **b** an authoritative rule; *esp* a rule for the conduct of church ceremonial **c** an explanatory or introductory commentary; a gloss **3** an established rule or custom [ME *rubrike* red ochre, heading in red letters of part of a book, fr MF *rubrique*, fr L *rubrica*, fr *rubr-*, *ruber* red] – **rubric, rubrical** *adj*, **rubrically** *adv*

**rubricate** /'roohbri,kayt/ *vt* **1** to write or print as a rubric **2** to provide with rubrics – **rubricator** *n*, **rubrication** *n*

¹**ruby** /'roohbi/ *n* **1a** a precious stone that is a deep red variety of the natural or synthetic mineral CORUNDUM **b** something (eg a watch bearing) made of ruby or a substitute material **2a** the dark red colour of the ruby **b** something resembling a ruby in colour [ME, fr MF *rubis*, *rubi*, irreg fr L *rubeus* reddish; akin to L *ruber* red – more at RED]

²**ruby** *adj* **1** *of port* having a bright red colour as a result of relatively short maturation in barrel **2** of, marking, or being a 40th anniversary ⟨~ *wedding*⟩

**ruby glass** *n* glass of a deep red colour containing the chemical element selenium, an oxide of copper, or a chloride of gold

**ruby spinel** *n* SPINEL 1 (mineral used as a gem)

**ruby-throated hummingbird** *n* a hummingbird (*Archilochus colubris*) of eastern N America, the male of which has a red throat with metallic reflections

**ruche, rouche** /roohsh/ *n* a pleated, fluted, or gathered strip of fabric used for trimming [Fr *ruche*, fr ML *rusca* bark of a tree, of Celt origin] – **ruched** *adj*

**ruching, rouching** /'roohshing/ *n* 1 a ruche 2 ruched trimming

**¹ruck** /ruk/ *n* 1 an indistinguishable mass; a jumble ⟨*a ~ of minor transactions*⟩ 2a *the* main body of competitors, well behind the leaders **b** *the* usual run of people or things; *the* generality ⟨*his verse compares well with the general ~ of poets of his day* – Bonamy Dobrée⟩ 3 a situation in RUGBY UNION in which one or more players from each team close round the ball when it is on the ground and try to kick the ball out to their own team – compare MAUL [ME *ruke* pile of combustible material, of Scand origin; akin to ON *hraukr* rick – more at RICK]

**²ruck** *vb or n* (to) wrinkle, crease – often with *up* ⟨*the page was wet and ~ed up*⟩ [n of Scand origin (akin to ON *hrukka* wrinkle); vb fr n]

**rucksack** /'ruk,sak/ *n* a lightweight bag that is carried on the back by straps fastening over the shoulders, and that is used typically by walkers and climbers [Ger, fr *rucken* (alter. of *rücken* back) + *sack* sack]

> **synonyms** The modern backpacker carries a **rucksack** (*NAm* a **backpack**). The **knapsack** or **haversack** was an earlier and less developed equivalent, used particularly by soldiers and sometimes having only one strap.

**ruckus** /'rukəs/ *n*, *chiefly NAm informal* a ruction [prob blend of *ruction* and *rumpus*]

**ruction** /'ruksh(ə)n/ *n*, *informal* 1 a violent dispute 2 a disturbance, uproar [perh by shortening & alter. fr *insurrection*]

**rudbeckia** /rud'beki·ə/ *n* any of a genus (*Rudbeckia*) of N American plants of the daisy family, that are grown for their showy flower heads having usu yellow to golden strap-shaped flowers surrounding a dark brownish to black centre [NL, genus name, fr Olof *Rudbeck* †1702 Sw scientist]

**rudd** /rud/ *n* a European freshwater fish (*Scardinius erythrophthalmus*) of the carp family that resembles the roach [prob fr arch. *rud* redness, fr ME *rude*, fr OE *rudu* – more at RUDDY]

**rudder** /'rudə/ *n* 1 a flat piece or structure of wood or metal, hinged vertically to a ship's stern, which can be turned at an angle in the water to change the course of a moving ship 2 a movable auxiliary AEROFOIL, usu attached to the fin, that controls an aircraft's direction of flight in the horizontal plane [ME *rother*, fr OE *rōther* paddle; akin to OE *rōwan* to row] – **rudderless** *adj*

**rudderpost** /'rudə,pohst/ *n* 1 a rudderstock 2 an additional sternpost to the rear of the propeller, to which the rudder is attached

**rudderstock** /'rudə,stok/ *n* the shaft of a rudder

**¹ruddle** /'rudl/ *n* RED OCHRE (natural red earthy substance), esp when used for marking sheep [dim. of E dial. *rud* red ochre, fr ME *rude* redness]

**²ruddle** *vt* to mark or colour (esp sheep) (as if) with RED OCHRE

**ruddock** /'rudək/ *n* a robin [ME *ruddok*, fr OE *rudduc;* akin to OE *rudu* red]

**ruddy** /'rudi/ *adj* 1 having a healthy reddish colour; rosy ⟨*~ faces*⟩ 2 red, reddish ⟨*a ~ sky*⟩ ⟨*the ~ duck*⟩ 3 *Br euph* BLOODY 6 ⟨*a ~ lie*⟩ [ME *rudi*, fr OE *rudig*, fr *rudu* redness; akin to OE *rēad* red – more at RED] – **ruddily** *adv*, **ruddiness** *n*

**rude** /roohd/ *adj* 1a being in a primitive, rough, or unfinished state; lacking subtlety; crude ⟨*~ wooden implements*⟩ **b** in the natural state; raw ⟨*~ cotton*⟩ ⟨*~ passions*⟩ **c** simple, elemental ⟨*landscape done in ~ whites, blacks, deep browns* – Richard Harris⟩ 2 lacking refinement, propriety, or cultivation: eg 2a offensive in manner or action; discourteous **b** vulgar, indecent **c** ignorant, unlearned **d** uncivilized, savage 3 robust, vigorous ⟨*the ~ health of their children* – Joseph Conrad⟩ 4 sudden and unpleasant; abrupt ⟨*a ~ awakening*⟩ [ME, fr MF, fr L *rudis;* akin to L *rudus* rubble, *ruere* to fall – more at RUG] – **rudely** *adv*, **rudeness** *also* **rudery** *n*

**ruderal** /'roohdərəl/ *adj*, *of a plant* growing where the natural cover of vegetation has been disturbed by human activity; *esp* growing on waste ground or among debris ⟨*~ weeds of old fields and roadsides*⟩ [NL *ruderalis*, fr L *ruder-, rudus* rubble] – **ruderal** *n*

**rudiment** /'roohdimənt/ *n* 1 *usu pl* a basic principle or element or a fundamental skill ⟨*the ~s of mathematics*⟩ 2a *usu pl* something as yet unformed or undeveloped; an embryo, beginning ⟨*the ~s of a plan*⟩ ⟨*lacked even the ~s of politeness*⟩ **b** an imperfectly developed body part or organ: **b(1)** one in its earliest stage of development or just beginning to develop; PRIMORDIUM **b(2)** a structure whose development was arrested at an early stage and so deficient in size or structure as to be entirely unable to perform its normal function **b(3)** the nonfunctional remains of a part that was complete and functional only at an earlier stage in the organism's development or in an ancestor; VESTIGE [L *rudimentum* beginning, fr *rudis* raw, rude] – **rudimental** *adj*

**rudimentary** /,roohdi'ment(ə)ri/ *adj* 1 basic, fundamental ⟨*these ~ truths*⟩ 2 of a primitive kind; crude ⟨*the equipment of these past empire-builders was ~* – A J Toynbee⟩ 3 being or having the character of a rudiment; imperfectly or incompletely developed or represented only by a vestige ⟨*the ~ tail of a hyrax*⟩ – **rudimentarily** *adv*, **rudimentariness** *n*

**¹rue** /rooh/ *vt* to feel penitence, remorse, or bitter regret for ⟨*I ~ the day when I made you mine*⟩ [ME *ruen*, fr OE *hrēowan;* akin to OHG *hriuwan* to regret]

**²rue** *n*, *archaic* 1 deep regret; bitter sorrow 2 compassion, pity

**³rue** *n* a strong-scented woody plant (*Ruta graveolens*) of the orange family that has bitter leaves formerly used in medicine [ME, fr MF, fr L *ruta*, fr Gk *rhytē*]

**rueful** /'roohf(ə)l/ *adj* 1 arousing pity or compassion; pitiable ⟨*~ squalid poverty*⟩ 2 mournful, regretful; *also* feigning sorrow ⟨*troubled her with a ~ disquiet* – W M Thackeray⟩ – **ruefully** *adv*, **ruefulness** *n*

**rufescent** /rooh'fes(ə)nt/ *adj*, *formal* reddish [L *rufescent-, rufescens*, prp of *rufescere* to become reddish, fr *rufus* red – more at RED] – **rufescence** *n*

**¹ruff, ruffe** /ruf/ *n* a small freshwater European perch (*Gymnocephalus cernua*) [ME *ruf*]

**²ruff** *n* 1 a wheel-shaped stiff frill worn as a collar by men and women of the late 16th and early 17th centuries 2 a fringe or frill of long hairs or feathers growing round or on the neck of a bird or other animal 3 *fem* **reeve** a common Eurasian sandpiper (*Philomachus pugnax*), the male of which has a large ruff of erectable feathers on the neck during the breeding season [prob back-formation fr *ruffle*] – **ruffed** *adj*

**³ruff** *n* the act of trumping in cards [MF *roffle* card-game resembling whist]

**⁴ruff** *vt* to play a trump on (a card previously led or played) ~ *vi* to take a trick with a trump

**ruffian** /'rufi·ən/ *n* a brutal and lawless person [MF *rufian*] – **ruffian** *adj*, **ruffianism** *n*, **ruffianly** *adj*

**¹ruffle** /'rufl/ *vt* 1a to disturb the smoothness of; roughen **b** to trouble, vex ⟨*~d his composure*⟩ 2 to erect (eg feathers) in or like a ruff 3a to flip through (eg pages) **b** to shuffle ⟨*~ playing cards*⟩ 4 to make into a ruffle ~ *vi* to become ruffled ⟨*their dispositions ~ perceptibly* – Life⟩ [ME *ruffelen;* akin to LG *ruffelen* to crumple]

**²ruffle** *n* 1 a state or cause of annoyance or perturbation 2 a commotion, brawl 3 a surface unevenness or disturbance (eg a ripple or crumple) 4a a strip of fabric gathered or pleated on one edge **b** ²RUFF 2 – **ruffly** *adj*

**³ruffle** *n* a low vibrating drumbeat less loud than a roll [arch. *ruff* drumbeat, of imit origin]

**rufous** /'roohfəs/ *adj*, *esp of an animal* reddish brown [L *rufus* red – more at RED]

**rug** /rug/ *n* 1 a piece of thick heavy fabric that is smaller than a carpet, usu has a nap or pile, and is used as a floor covering or for decoration (eg on a wooden floor or on top of a carpet) 2 a floor mat made of an animal skin ⟨*a bearskin ~*⟩ 3 a woollen blanket that often has fringes on two opposite edges and is used as a covering; *esp* TRAVELLING RUG 4 a blanket for an animal (eg a horse or cow) [(assumed) ME, rag, tuft, of Scand origin; akin to ON *rögg* tuft; akin to L *ruere* to rush, fall, dig up, Skt *ravate* he breaks up] – **pull the rug (out) from under somebody** to remove support or assistance from somebody

**ruga** /'roohgə/ *n usu pl*, *pl* **rugae** /'roohjee, -gee/ an anatomical fold or wrinkle, esp of the membrane lining of an internal organ [NL, fr L, wrinkle – more at ROUGH] – **rugal** *adj*,

**rugate** *adj*

**rugby** /'rugbi/ *n, often cap* a football game, played with an oval football, that features kicking, sideways hand-to-hand passing, and tackling, and in which forward passing is prohibited [*Rugby* School in Warwickshire, England, where the game allegedly originated]

**Rugby League** *n* the form of rugby that is played by teams of 13 players each, features a 6-man scrum and PLAY-THE-BALL, and can be played professionally

**Rugby Union** *n* the form of rugby that is played by teams of 15 players each, features an 8-man scrum, and is restricted to amateurs

**rugged** /'rugid/ *adj* **1** having a rough uneven surface or outline; craggy ⟨*~ mountains*⟩ **2** having or being strong often irregular features ⟨*a ~ face*⟩; *also* marked with furrows **3a** austere, stern; *also* uncompromising ⟨*~ individualism*⟩ **b** lacking gentleness or refinement; unpolished ⟨*~ manners*⟩ **4a** strongly built or constituted; sturdy ⟨*those that survive are stalwart, ~ men* – L D Stamp⟩ **b** involving a severe test of ability or stamina **synonyms** see ¹ROUGH [ME, fr (assumed) ME *rug* rag, tuft] – **ruggedly** *adv*, **ruggedness** *n*

**rugger** /'rugə/ *n, Br informal* rugby [by alter.]

**rugose** /'rooh,gohs/ *adj* **1** full of wrinkles **2** *of a leaf* having the veins sunken and the spaces between raised ⟨*~ leaves of the sage*⟩ [L *rugosus*, fr *ruga* wrinkle] – **rugosely** *adv*, **rugosity** *n*

**rugulose** /'roohgyooiohs/ *adj* finely wrinkled [NL *rugula*, dim. of L *ruga* wrinkle]

**rug up** *vt* -gg- to cover (a horse) with a rug or rugs

¹**ruin** /'rooh·in/ *n* **1** physical, moral, economic, or social collapse; downfall **2** *ruin, ruins pl* **2a** the state of being wrecked or decayed ⟨*the city lay in ~s*⟩ **b** the remains of something destroyed ⟨*the ~s of the ancient world*⟩ **3** a cause of destruction or downfall ⟨*whisky was his ~*⟩ **4** the action of destroying, laying waste, or wrecking ⟨*the ~ of modern drama* – T S Eliot⟩ **5** someone or something that is ruined; *esp* a ruined person or structure [ME *ruine*, fr MF, fr L *ruina*; akin to L *ruere* to fall – more at RUG] – **ruinate** *adj*, **ruinate** *vt*, **ruination** *n*

**synonyms Ruin, destruction, demolition, havoc, devastation, wreck,** and **damage** can all mean "the causing of or result of disaster". **Ruin** implies making something totally useless by collapse or downfall, but without putting an end to its existence. By contrast, the result of **destruction** may be that what is destroyed is no longer there at all ⟨*destruction of a city by bombing*⟩. **Demolition** is the often deliberate smashing or tearing down of something into fragments. **Havoc** and **devastation** involve widespread laying waste, particularly of an area, to the point of desolation ⟨*earthquake caused appalling havoc and loss of life*⟩, **devastation** being perhaps the stronger word of the two. **Wreck** is the serious and often irreparable injury of something, particularly by violence. **Damage**, the weakest of these words, is merely harm from injury ⟨*car suffered only slight damage*⟩.

²**ruin** *vt* **1** to reduce to ruins; devastate **2a** to damage irreparably ⟨*a mural ~ed by vandals*⟩ **b** to bankrupt, impoverish ⟨*~ed by speculation*⟩ **3** to subject to frustration, failure, or disaster ⟨*~ed his chances of promotion*⟩ **4** *archaic or poetic* to seduce and thus cause the downfall of (a woman) ⟨*a ~ed woman*⟩ *~ vi, archaic or poetic* to fall into ruins – **ruiner** *n*

**ruinous** /'rooh·inəs/ *adj* **1** dilapidated, ruined **2** causing or tending to inflict ruin; disastrous ⟨*wages that are ~ to employers*⟩ – **ruinously** *adv*, **ruinousness** *n*

¹**rule** /roohl/ *n* **1a** a principle regulating conduct or action; *also* such a principle specifically prescribed **b** the laws or regulations prescribed by the founder of a religious order for observance by its members **c** an established procedure, custom, or habit ⟨*errors that are the exception rather than the ~*⟩ ⟨*you may be allowed to do that, but it goes against our ~*⟩ **d** a legal precept or doctrine **2a(1)** a statement that generally holds good; a usu valid generalization **a(2)** a generally prevailing quality, state, or form ⟨*fine weather was the ~ yesterday*⟩ **b** a standard of judgment; a criterion **c** a regulating principle, esp of a system ⟨*the basic ~s of grammar*⟩ **3a** the exercise of authority or control; dominion **b** a period during which a specified ruler or government exercises control **4a** a strip, or set of jointed strips, of material marked off in units and used for measuring or marking off lengths **b** a metal strip with a type-high face that prints a linear design; *also* the design so printed [ME *reule*, fr OF, fr L *regula* straightedge, rule, fr *regere* to lead straight – more at RIGHT] – **as a rule** for the most part; generally

²**rule** *vt* **1a** to exert control, direction, or influence on ⟨*the superstitions that ~ primitive minds*⟩ **b** to exercise control over, esp by curbing or restraining ⟨*~d her appetites firmly*⟩ **2a** to exercise power or firm authority over; govern ⟨*the Speaker ~d the House judiciously*⟩ **b** to be preeminent in; command, dominate ⟨*an actor who ~s the stage*⟩ **3** to lay down authoritatively, esp judicially ⟨*the judge ~d the witness out of order*⟩ **4a(1)** to mark with lines drawn (as if) along the straight edge of a ruler **a(2)** to mark (a line) on something with a ruler *~ vi* **1a** to exercise supreme authority **b** to be first in importance or influence; predominate ⟨*the physical did not ~ in her nature* – Sherwood Anderson⟩ **2** to exist in a specified state or condition; prevail **3** to lay down a legal rule or make a judicial decision

**rule out** *vt* **1a** to exclude, eliminate **b** to deny the possibility of; decide to be irrelevant ⟨*rule out further discussion*⟩ **2** to make impossible; prevent ⟨*heavy rain ruled out the picnic*⟩

**ruleless** /'roohl·lis/ *adj* not restrained or regulated by law

**rule of the road** *n* a customary practice (eg driving on a particular side of the road or yielding the right of way) developed in the interests of safety and often reinforced by law; *esp* any of the rules making up a code governing ships in matters relating to mutual safety

**rule of thumb** *n* a method or principle based on experience and common sense rather than technical knowledge or theory [fr the use of the thumb to make rough measurements of length]

**ruler** /'roohlə/ *n* **1** a person who rules; *specif* a sovereign **2** a worker or machine that rules paper **3** a smooth-edged strip of material that is usu marked off in units (eg centimetres) and is used for guiding a pen or pencil in drawing lines or for measuring – **rulership** *n*

¹**ruling** /'roohling/ *n* an official or authoritative decision, decree, statement, or interpretation (eg by a judge on a point of law)

²**ruling** *adj* **1a** exerting power or authority ⟨*the ~ party*⟩ **b** chief, predominating ⟨*a ~ passion*⟩ **2** generally prevailing; currently in existence ⟨*the ~ feeling in the group was against it*⟩

¹**rum** /rum/ *adj* **-mm-** *chiefly Br informal* **1** queer, strange ⟨*writing is a ~ trade . . . and what is all right one day is all wrong the next* – Angela Thirkell⟩ **2** causing wary curiosity; mystifying ⟨*she's a ~ customer*⟩ [prob fr earlier *rome* fine, excellent, perh fr Romany *rom* gipsy man] – **rumly** *adv*, **rumness** *n*

²**rum** *n* a spirit distilled from a fermented cane product (eg molasses) [prob short for obs *rumbullion*, of unknown origin]

**Rumanian** /roo'maynyən, roh-, rə-, -ni·ən/ *n or adj* (a) Romanian

**rumba, rhumba** /'rumbə/ *n* a ballroom dance of Cuban Negro origin with a basic pattern of step-close-step and marked by the delaying of the transfer of weight and pronounced hip movements; *also* the music for this dance – compare MAMBO, SAMBA, CONGA [AmerSp] – **rumba** *vi*

¹**rumble** /'rumbl/ *vi* **1** to make a low heavy rolling sound ⟨*thunder rumbling in the distance*⟩ **2** to travel with a low reverberating sound ⟨*wagons ~d into town*⟩ **3** to speak in a deep rolling tone; *also, of the stomach* to produce deep rolling sounds ⟨*stomach ~d with hunger*⟩ **4** *NAm slang* to engage in a street fight *~ vt* **1** to utter or emit in a low rolling voice **2** *Br informal* to reveal or discover the true character of; SEE THROUGH ⟨*~d their game*⟩ [ME *rumblen*; akin to MHG *rummeln* to rumble] – **rumbler** *n*

²**rumble** *n* **1a** a rumbling sound (eg of thunder) **b** low-frequency noise from a record deck, caused by the transmission of mechanical vibrations from the turntable to the pickup **2a** widespread expression of dissatisfaction or unrest; rumblings **b** *NAm slang* a street fight, esp between gangs of youths

**rumble seat** *n, NAm* DICKEY 2b

**rumbling** /'rumbling, 'rumbl·ing/ *n* **1** RUMBLE 1 **2 rumblings** *pl,* **rumbling** the beginning of a general but unarticulated expression of dissatisfaction ⟨*widespread ~s about government spending*⟩

**rumbustious** /rum'buschəs/ *adj, chiefly Br informal* marked by irrepressible or boisterous exuberance; unruly [alter. of *robustious*] – **rumbustiousness** *n*

**rum butter** *n* butter that has been sweetened and flavoured with rum, usu served with sweet puddings – compare BRANDY BUTTER

**rumen** /'roohmen/ *n, pl* **rumina** /'roohminə/, **rumens** the large first compartment of the stomach of a ruminant mammal (e g a cow) in which food is partially broken down by the action of microorganisms, esp bacteria, and from which it can be regurgitated into the mouth for further chewing [NL *rumin-, rumen,* fr L, gullet] – **ruminal** *adj*

¹**ruminant** /'roohminənt/ *n* a ruminant mammal

²**ruminant** *adj* **1a** that chews the cud **b** of, being, or belonging to a group of hoofed mammals (e g sheep, cattle, giraffes, deer, and camels) that chew the cud and have a complex 3- or 4-chambered stomach **2** given to or engaged in meditation; meditative ⟨*a ~ attitude of repose*⟩ – **ruminantly** *adv*

**ruminate** /'roohmi,nayt/ *vt* **1** to go over in the mind repeatedly and often thoughtfully or slowly **2** to chew repeatedly for an extended period ~ *vi* **1** to chew again what has already been chewed slightly and swallowed; chew the cud **2** to engage in contemplation; reflect, muse – sometimes + *on, over,* or *about* [L *ruminatus,* pp of *ruminari* to chew the cud, muse upon, fr *rumin-, rumen* gullet; akin to Skt *romantha* chewing the cud] – **ruminator** *n,* **ruminative** *adj,* **ruminatively** *adv,* **rumination** *n*

¹**rummage** /'rumij/ *n* **1** a thorough search, esp among a jumbled assortment of objects **2a** *chiefly NAm* JUMBLE **2 b** *NAm* a miscellaneous or confused accumulation [obs *rummage* act of packing cargo, modif of MF *arrimage*]

²**rummage** *vt* **1** to make a thorough search of (an untidy or congested place); ransack ⟨*~d the attic*⟩ **2** to uncover by searching – usu + *out* ⟨*~ out some old magazines*⟩ ~ *vi* **1** to make a thorough search or investigation **2** to engage in an indiscriminate or haphazard search, usu leaving a mess as a result – **rummager** *n*

**rummage sale** *n, chiefly NAm* JUMBLE SALE

**rummer** /'rumə/ *n* a tall often elaborately etched or engraved drinking glass typically having the shape of a large goblet and used esp for wine [Ger or D; Ger *römer,* fr D *roemer*]

¹**rummy** /'rumi/ *adj, informal* queer, odd ⟨*were still feeling a little ~ from our trip up the escalator* – *New Yorker*⟩ [¹*rum* + ¹-*y*]

²**rummy** *n, NAm informal* a drunkard [²*rum* + ⁴-*y*]

³**rummy** *n* any of several card games for two or more players in which each player tries to assemble groups of three or more cards of the same rank or in sequence, usu in the same suit, and to be the first to declare all his/her cards for a score [perh fr ¹*rummy*]

¹**rumour,** *NAm chiefly* **rumor** /'roohmə/ *n* **1** talk or opinion, often of doubtful accuracy, widely disseminated but with no identifiable source **2** a current story or assertion that has not been verified ⟨*the ~ has it that he will resign*⟩ [ME *rumour,* fr MF, fr L *rumor;* akin to OE *rēon* to lament, Gk *ōryesthai* to howl]

²**rumour,** *NAm chiefly* **rumor** *vt* to tell or spread by rumour – usu pass

'**rumour-,monger** *n* one who spreads (malicious) rumour – **rumour-mongering** *n*

**rump** /rump/ *n* **1a** the upper rounded part of the hindquarters of a mammal **b** a person's buttocks **c** the part of a bird's back near the tail **2** a cut of beef between the LOIN and ROUND **3** a small or inferior remnant of something larger (e g a parliament continuing after the departure or expulsion of a majority of its members) [ME, of Scand origin; akin to Icel *rumpr* rump; akin to MHG *rumph* torso]

¹**rumple** /'rumpl/ *n* a fold, wrinkle

²**rumple** *vt* **1** to wrinkle, crumple ⟨*~d sheets*⟩ **2** to make unkempt; tousle ⟨*~ his hair*⟩ ~ *vi* to become rumpled [D *rompelen;* akin to OHG *rimpfan* to wrinkle, L *curvus* curved]

**rumpus** /'rumpəs/ *n, chiefly informal* a usu noisy commotion [perh alter. of *rumble*]

**rumpus room** *n, NAm* a room, usu in the basement of a house, that is used for recreation (e g hobbies and games)

¹**run** /run/ *vb* **-nn-;** **ran** /ran/; **run** *vi* **1a** to go faster than a walk; *specif* to go steadily by springing steps so that both feet leave the ground for an instant in each step **b** *of a horse* to move at a fast gallop or with short fast strides – compare CANTER, GALLOP, TROT, WALK **c** to flee, escape ⟨*dropped his gun and ran*⟩ **2a** to go without restraint ⟨*let his chickens ~ loose*⟩ ⟨*~ about barefoot*⟩ **b** to sail in the same direction as the wind, as distinct from REACHING or sailing CLOSE-HAULED – compare REACH 3, BEAT 5 **3a** to hasten with a specified often distressing purpose ⟨*~ and fetch the doctor*⟩ ⟨*~s to his mother at every little difficulty*⟩ **b** to make a quick, easy, or casual trip or visit ⟨*~ up to town for the day*⟩ **4** to contend in a race; *also*

to finish a race in the specified place ⟨*ran third*⟩ **5a** to move (as if) on wheels ⟨*the train* ran *past the signal*⟩ ⟨*a chair that ~s on castors*⟩ **b** to pass or slide freely or cursorily ⟨*a rope ~s through the pulley*⟩ ⟨*a thought* ran *through my mind*⟩ **6** to sing or play quickly ⟨*~ up the scale*⟩ **7a** to go back and forth; ply ⟨*the ferry ~s between Harwich and the Hook*⟩ ⟨*made the trains ~ on time*⟩ **b** *of fish* to migrate or move in schools; *esp* to ascend a river to spawn **8** to function, operate ⟨*don't touch the engine while it's ~*ning⟩ ⟨*the engine ~s on petrol*⟩ ⟨*everything's ~*ning *smoothly at the office*⟩ **9a** to continue in force or operation ⟨*the lease has two more years to ~*⟩ **b** to accompany as a legal obligation or right ⟨*a right-of-way that ~s with the land*⟩ **c** to continue to accumulate or become payable ⟨*interest on the loan ~s from July 1st*⟩ **10** to pass, esp by negligence or indulgence, into a specified state ⟨*~ wild*⟩ ⟨*~ to waste*⟩ ⟨*money* ran *low*⟩ **11a(1)** to flow, course ⟨*~*ning *water*⟩ **a(2)** to become by flowing ⟨*the water* ran *cold*⟩ **a(3)** to discharge liquid ⟨*made my nose ~*⟩ ⟨*left the tap ~*ning⟩ **a(4)** to reach a specified state by discharging liquid ⟨*the well* ran *dry*⟩ **b** to melt ⟨*butter started to ~*⟩ **c** to spread, dissolve ⟨*colours guaranteed not to ~*⟩ **d** to discharge pus or serum ⟨*a ~*ning *sore*⟩ **12a** to develop rapidly in some specific direction; *esp* to throw out an elongated shoot **b** to have a tendency; be prone ⟨*if your tastes ~ that way*⟩ ⟨*they ~ to big noses in that family*⟩ **13a** to lie or extend in a specified position, direction, or relation to something ⟨*the boundary line ~s east*⟩ ⟨*the road ~s through a tunnel*⟩ **b** to extend in a continuous range ⟨*the numbers ~ from 3 to 57*⟩ ⟨*shades ~ from white to dark grey*⟩ **c** to be in a certain form or expression ⟨*the letter ~s as follows*⟩ **14a** to occur persistently ⟨*musical talent ~s in his family*⟩ ⟨*a note of despair ~s through the narrative*⟩ **b** to continue to be as specified ⟨*profits were ~*ning *high*⟩ **c** to play or be featured continuously (e g in a theatre or newspaper) ⟨*the musical* ran *for six months*⟩ **15a** to spread quickly from point to point ⟨*chills* ran *up his spine*⟩ **b** to be current; circulate ⟨*speculation* ran *rife on who would win*⟩ **16** to ladder ⟨*stockings guaranteed not to ~*⟩ **17** *chiefly NAm* STAND 11 ⟨*~ for President*⟩ ~ *vt* **1a** to bring to a specified condition (as if) by running ⟨*ran himself to exhaustion*⟩ **b** to go in pursuit of; hunt ⟨*dogs that ~ deer*⟩ ⟨*ran the rumour to its source*⟩ **c** to drive, chase ⟨*~ him out of town*⟩ **d** to enter, register, or enrol as a contestant in a race **e** to put forward as a candidate for office **2a** to drive (livestock), esp to a grazing place **b** to provide pasturage for (livestock) **3a** to cover, accomplish, or perform (as if) by running ⟨*ran 10 miles*⟩ ⟨*ran a great race*⟩ ⟨*~ errands for his mother*⟩ ⟨*disease must ~ its course*⟩ ⟨*ran the whole gamut of emotions*⟩ **b** to slip through or past ⟨*~ a blockade*⟩ **4a** to cause or allow to penetrate or enter ⟨*ran a splinter into his toe*⟩ **b** to stitch **c** to cause to lie or extend in a specified position or direction ⟨*~ a wire in from the aerial*⟩ ⟨*~ a line through a word*⟩ **d** to cause to collide ⟨*ran his head into a post*⟩ **e** to smuggle ⟨*~ guns*⟩ **5** to cause to pass lightly, freely, or cursorily ⟨*ran his eye down the list*⟩ ⟨*ran a comb through her hair*⟩ **6a(1)** to cause or allow (a vehicle or vessel) to go ⟨*~ his car off the road*⟩ ⟨*~ the ship aground*⟩ **a(2)** to cause to travel along a regular route ⟨*~ an extra train on Saturdays*⟩ **a(3)** to own and drive ⟨*she ~s an old banger*⟩ **a(4)** to convey in a vehicle ⟨*can I ~ you home?*⟩ **b** to operate ⟨*~ a lathe*⟩ ⟨*~ your razor off the mains*⟩ **c** to manage, control ⟨*~ a factory*⟩ ⟨*who's ~*ning *this outfit?*⟩ **7** to be full of; flow with ⟨*streets* ran *blood*⟩ **8a** to cause to move or flow in a specified way or into a specified position ⟨*~ cards into a file*⟩ **b(1)** to cause to pour out liquid ⟨*~ the hot tap*⟩ **b(2)** to fill from a tap ⟨*~ a hot bath*⟩ **9a** to melt and cast in a mould ⟨*~ bullets*⟩ **b** to subject to a treatment or process ⟨*~ a problem through a computer*⟩ **10** to make oneself liable to ⟨*~ risks*⟩ ⟨*~ the chance of being recognized*⟩ **11** to permit (e g charges) to accumulate before settling ⟨*~ an account at the grocer's*⟩ **12a** RUN OFF **1b** ⟨*a book to be ~ on lightweight paper*⟩ **b** to carry in a printed medium; print ⟨*paper* ran *a story about the royal baby*⟩ **13** to play a winning first card from (a single suit) in successive rounds of a game **14** to score by running between the wickets in cricket ⟨*an all-*run *four*⟩ **15** to make (a golf ball) roll forwards after hitting the ground [ME *ronnen,* alter. of *rinnen,* vi (fr OE *iernan, rinnan* & ON *rinna*), & of *rennen,* vt, fr ON *renna;* akin to OHG *rinnan,* vi, to run, OE *rīsan* to rise] – **run to earth/ground** to find after a lengthy search – see also **run** FOUL **of, run like the** CLAPPERS, **run round in** CIRCLES, **run** RINGS **round somebody, run** RIOT/**to** SEED/SHORT **(of)**

**run across** *vt* to meet with or discover by chance

**run after** *vt* **1** to pursue, chase; *esp* to seek the company of **2** to follow; TAKE UP WITH ⟨*run after new theories*⟩

**run against** *vt* **1** to meet suddenly or unexpectedly **2** to work or take effect unfavourably to

**run along** *vi* to go away; depart – often used as an order or request

**run away** *vi* **1a** to take to flight **b** to flee from home; *esp* to elope **2** to run out of control; stampede, bolt – see also RUNAWAY

**run away with** *vt* **1** to take away in haste or secretly; *esp* to steal **2** to believe too easily ⟨*don't* run away with *the idea that you needn't go*⟩ **3** to carry beyond reasonable limits ⟨*his imagination* ran away with *him*⟩ **4** to outshine the others in achieving ⟨*she* ran away with *the prize*⟩

**run down** *vt* **1a** to knock down, esp with a motor vehicle **b** to run against and cause to sink **2a** to chase to exhaustion or until captured **b** to find by searching ⟨run down *a book in the library*⟩ **3** to disparage ⟨*don't* run *him* down; *he's an honest fellow*⟩ **4** to allow the gradual decline or closure of ⟨*the lead mines are being gradually* run down⟩ ~ *vi* **1** to cease to operate because of the exhaustion of power ⟨*that battery* ran down *weeks ago*⟩ **2** to decline in physical condition – see also RUNDOWN, RUN-DOWN

**run in** *vt* **1a** to make (typeset matter) continuous, without a paragraph or other break **b** to insert as additional matter **2** to bring gradually to full operation ⟨run *a new play* in⟩ ⟨ran *her new car* in⟩ **3** *informal* to arrest, esp for a minor offence

**run into** *vt* **1a** to merge with **b** to mount up to ⟨*her yearly income often* runs into *six figures*⟩ **2a** to collide with **b** to encounter, meet ⟨ran into *an old friend the other day*⟩

**run off** *vt* **1a** to recite or compose rapidly or glibly **b** to produce with a printing press or copier ⟨ran off *a few copies*⟩ **c** to decide (e g a race) by a runoff **2** to drain off (a liquid) **3** *NAm* to steal (e g cattle) by driving away ~ *vi* RUN AWAY 1

**run off with** *vt* RUN AWAY WITH 1

**run on** *vi* **1** to keep going without interruption ⟨*the opera* ran on *for four hours*⟩ **2** to talk or narrate at length ⟨ran on *for hours about his gardening*⟩ ~ *vt* **1** to continue (written material or typeset text) without a break or a new paragraph **2** to place or add (e g an entry in a dictionary) at the end of a paragraphed item **3** to be concerned with; dwell on ⟨*her mind keeps* running on *the past*⟩ – see also RUN-ON

**run out** *vi* **1a** to come to an end ⟨*time* ran out⟩ **b** to become exhausted or used up ⟨*the petrol* ran out⟩ **2** to finish a course or contest in the specified position ⟨ran out *the winner*⟩ **3** *of a horse* to evade a fence by turning aside ~ *vt* **1** to dismiss (a batsman in cricket who is outside his CREASE and attempting a run) by breaking the wicket with the ball **2a** to fill the measure of (a typeset line) **b** to set (the first line of a paragraph) so that it projects further to the left than the following lines **3** to exhaust (oneself) by running **4** *chiefly NAm* to compel to leave ⟨run *him* out *of town*⟩

**run out of** *vt* to use up the available supply of

**run out on** *vt* to desert

**run over** *vi* **1** to overflow **2** to exceed a limit ⟨*meetings that* run over *into the next day*⟩ ~ *vt* **1** to glance over, repeat, or rehearse quickly **2** to injure or kill with a motor vehicle ⟨ran *the dog* over⟩ – see also RUNOVER

**run through** *vt* **1** to pierce with a weapon (e g a sword) **2** to squander **3a** to carry out or rehearse (without pausing) **b** to deal with rapidly and usu perfunctorily – see also RUN-THROUGH

**run to** *vt* **1** to extend to ⟨*the book* runs to *500 pages*⟩ **2a** to afford **b** *of money* to be enough for ⟨*his salary won't* run to *a car*⟩

**run up** *vi* to grow rapidly ~ *vt* **1** to increase (a price) by bidding **2** to make (esp a garment) quickly **3a** to erect hastily **b** to hoist (a flag) **4** to accumulate or incur (debts)

**run up against** *vt* to encounter (e g a difficulty)

**run upon** *vt* to meet; COME ACROSS

²**run** *n* **1a** an act or the activity of running; continued rapid movement **b** a quickened gallop; *broadly* the gait of a runner **c** (a school of fish) migrating or ascending a river to spawn **d** a running race ⟨*a mile* ~⟩ **e** a unit of scoring in cricket achieved typically by each batsman running the full length of the wicket **f** the basic scoring unit in baseball achieved by a batter reaching the home base safely after having touched all the bases in turn **2a** the curved rear part of a ship's hull where it narrows in below the waterline towards the stern **b** the direction in which something (e g a vein of ore or the grain of wood) lies **c(1)** the horizontal distance covered by a flight of steps **c(2)** the horizontal distance from the WALL PLATE (support for roof rafters) to an imaginary line equally distant from

the sides of a building **d** general tendency or direction ⟨*watching the* ~ *of the stock market*⟩ **3** a continuous series or unbroken course, esp of identical or similar things ⟨*a* ~ *of bad luck*⟩: e g **3a** a rapid passage up or down a musical scale **b** a succession of rapid small dance steps, each taking the same time to perform **c** an unbroken series of performances or showings of plays, films, etc ⟨*a long West End* ~⟩ **d** a set of consecutive measurements, readings, or observations **e** a persistent and heavy commercial or financial demand ⟨*a* ~ *on the pound*⟩ **f** three or more playing cards, usu of the same suit, in consecutive order of rank **4** the quantity of work turned out in a continuous operation ⟨*a newspaper press* ~⟩ **5** the average or prevailing kind or class ⟨*the general* ~ *of students*⟩ – compare RUN-OF-THE-MILL **6a** the distance covered in a period of continuous journeying ⟨*a regularly travelled course or route* ⟨*lorries on the Far East* ~⟩ **b(1)** a regularly travelled course or route ⟨*lorries on the Far East* ~⟩ **b(2)** a short excursion in a car ⟨*went for a Sunday* ~⟩ **c** a news reporter's regular territory **d** the distance a golf ball travels after touching the ground **e** freedom of movement in or access to a place ⟨*has the* ~ *of the house*⟩ **7a** the period during which a machine or plant is in continuous operation **b** the use of machinery for a single set of processing procedures ⟨*a computer* ~⟩ **8a** a way, track, etc frequented by animals **b** an enclosure for domestic animals where they may feed or exercise **c** an inclined passageway **9a** an inclined course (e g for skiing or tobogganing) **b** *also* **runway** a support or channel (e g a track, pipe, or trough) along which something runs **10** a ravel in hosiery or knitting; LADDER 2 ⟨*have a* ~ *in my stocking*⟩ **11** a defect in a coat of paint caused by excessive flow **12** *NAm* a brook, rivulet **13** *pl, informal* diarrhoea – + *the* ⟨*his illness gave him the* ~s⟩ – **a (good) run for one's money** the profit, enjoyment, etc to which one feels legitimately entitled – **in the long run** in the course of a sufficiently long time, trial, or experience – **in the short run** in the immediate future – **on the run 1** in haste; without pausing **2** in hiding or running away, esp from lawful authority

³**run** *adj, of a fish* having migrated (for spawning) ⟨*a fresh* ~ *salmon*⟩

**runabout** /'runə,bowt/ *n, informal* a light motor car, aeroplane, or motorboat

**runagate** /'runəgayt/ *n, archaic* **1** a fugitive, runaway **2** a vagabond [alter. of obs *renegate*, fr ML *renegatus* – more at RENEGADE]

**runaround** /'runə,rownd/ *n, chiefly NAm* delaying action, esp in response to a request ⟨*getting the* ~ *from the pay board*⟩

¹**runaway** /'runə,way/ *n* **1** a fugitive **2** something (e g a horse) that is running out of control

²**runaway** *adj* **1** fugitive **2** accomplished as a result of running away ⟨*a* ~ *marriage*⟩ **3** won by a long lead; decisive ⟨*a* ~ *victory*⟩ **4** out of control ⟨~ *inflation*⟩

**runcible spoon** /'runsəbl/ *n* a sharp-edged fork with three broad curved prongs [coined with indefinite meaning by Edward Lear †1888 E writer & painter]

**runcinate** /'runsinət, -,nayt/ *adj, of a leaf* deeply lobed with the lobes pointing down towards the stalk ⟨*the* ~ *leaves of the dandelion*⟩ [L *runcinatus*, pp of *runcinare* to plane off, fr *runcina* plane]

**rundlet** /'rundlit/ *n* **1** an old unit of liquid capacity equal to about 68 litres (15 gallons) **2** *archaic* a small barrel; a keg [ME *rondelet*, fr MF, dim. of *rondel* small circle – more at ROUNDEL]

**rundown** /'run,down/ *n* **1** the running down of something ⟨*the* ~ *of the steel industry*⟩ **2** an item-by-item report; a résumé

,**run-'down** *adj* **1** in a state of disrepair **2** in poor health; worn-out **3** *NAm* completely unwound ⟨*a* ~ *clock*⟩

**rune** /roohn/ *n* **1** any of the characters of an alphabet probably derived from Latin and Greek and used, esp in carved inscriptions, by the Germanic peoples from about the 3rd to the 13th centuries **2** a magical or mysterious utterance or inscription **3** a Finnish or Old Norse poem [ON & OE *rūn* mystery, runic character, writing; akin to OHG *rūna* secret discussion; (3) Finn *runo*, of Gmc origin; akin to ON *rūn*] – **runic** *adj*

¹**rung** /rung/ *past part of* RING

²**rung** *n* **1a** a crosspiece between the legs of a chair **b** any of the crosspieces of a ladder **2** a level or stage in something that can be ascended ⟨*the bottom* ~ *of the social scale*⟩ [ME, fr OE *hrung*; akin to OE *hring* ring – more at RING]

¹**run-,in** *n* **1** the final part of a race(track) **2** *NAm* a quarrel

**runless** /'runlis/ *adj* scoring no runs or marked by the scoring of no runs ⟨*a* ~ *period of play*⟩

¹**runlet** /'runlit/ n a rundlet

²**runlet** n a runnel

**runnel** /'runl/ n a small stream; a brook [alter. of ME *rinel*, fr OE *rynel*; akin to OE *rinnan* to run – more at RUN]

**runner** /'runə/ n **1a** one who runs **b** an entrant for a race (e g an athlete or horse) who actually competes in it **2a** a bank or stockbroker's messenger **b** one who smuggles or distributes illegal or contraband goods – usu in combination ⟨a *dope*-runner⟩ **3** a straight piece on which something slides: e g **3a** a longitudinal piece attached to a sledge or ice skate to allow sliding **b** a groove or bar along which a drawer or sliding door slides **4a** STOLON 1a (horizontal stem from the base of a plant that buds to produce new plants) **b** a plant that forms or spreads by means of runners **5a** a long narrow carpet (e g for a hall or staircase) **b** a narrow decorative cloth for a table or dresser top **6** a cricketer who runs in place of a teammate who is batting but cannot run because of injury **7 runner bean, runner** *chiefly Br* (the long green edible pod of) a widely cultivated originally tropical American high-climbing bean (*Phaseolus coccineus*) with large usu bright red flowers **8** *Br informal* one who or that which is given acceptance or favour ⟨a *theory with the chance of being a* ~⟩

,**runner-'up** n, pl **runners-up** *also* **runner-ups** a competitor other than the outright winner whose attainment still merits a prize; *esp* the second-placed competitor

¹**running** /'runing/ n **1a** an act or the action of running **b** the state of competing, esp with a good chance of winning – in *in/out of the running* **2** management, operation ⟨the ~ *of a small business*⟩ ⟨the ~ *of a company car*⟩

²**running** adj **1** runny **2a** having stages that follow in rapid succession ⟨a ~ *battle*⟩ **b** made during the course of a process or activity ⟨a ~ *commentary*⟩ ⟨~ *repairs*⟩ **3** being part of a continuous length ⟨*cost of timber per* ~ *metre*⟩ **4** cursive, flowing ⟨*written in a* ~ *hand*⟩ **5a** initiated or performed while running or with a running start ⟨a ~ *jump*⟩ **b** designed or used for races on foot ⟨a ~ *track*⟩

³**running** adv in succession ⟨*for three days* ~⟩

**running board** n a footboard, esp at the side of a car

**running gear** n the working parts of a machine (e g a locomotive)

**running head** n a headline repeated on consecutive pages (e g of a book)

**running knot** n a knot that slips along the rope or line round which it is tied

**running light** n any of the lights carried by a moving ship, aeroplane, car, etc, esp at night, that indicate size, position, and direction of movement

**running martingale** n a device for checking the upward movement of a horse's head that consists of a strap fastened to the GIRTH (strap encircling the body), passing between the forelegs, and forking to end in two rings through which the reins pass

**running mate** n a candidate standing for a subordinate place in a US election; *esp* the candidate for vice-president of the USA

**running powers** n pl the right to run trains over the tracks of another railway

**running rigging** n rigging that is used primarily in setting, furling, and otherwise handling sails and movable spars, or in handling cargo, and that usu runs through blocks or pulleys

**running shed** n, *Br* a building for housing and repairing railway vehicles

**running stitch** n a small even sewing stitch run in and out of cloth (e g for gathering)

**running title** n the title or SHORT TITLE of a book printed at the top of left-hand text pages or sometimes of all text pages

**runny** /'runi/ adj having a tendency to run ⟨a ~ *nose*⟩

**runoff** /'run,of/ n **1** the portion of the rainfall that ultimately reaches streams; *esp* the water from rain or melted snow that flows over the surface of the land to streams instead of draining away into the soil **2** a final decisive race, contest, or election

,**run-of-the-'mill** adj average, commonplace [²run 4; orig referring to ungraded goods of varying quality produced in a textile mill or sawmill]

¹**run-'on** adj continuing without pause from one line of verse into the next

²**run-,on** n something (e g a dictionary entry) run on

**runover** /'run,ohvə/ n typeset matter that exceeds the allotted space

'**run-re,sist** adj, *Br, of hosiery* knitted in such a way that the fabric will resist the tendency to ladder

**runround** /'run,rownd/ n matter typeset in condensed form to fit round something else

**runt** /runt/ n **1** an animal unusually small of its kind; *esp* the smallest of a litter of pigs **2** *chiefly Scot* a hardened stalk or stem of a plant **3** *derog* a puny person [origin unknown] – **runty** adj, **runtiness** n

'**run-,through** n **1** a cursory reading, summary, or rehearsal ⟨*give it a quick* ~⟩ **2** a sequence of actions performed for practice

'**run-,up** n **1** (the track or area provided for) an approach run to provide momentum (e g for a jump or throw) **2** *Br* a period that immediately precedes an action or event ⟨*the* ~ *to the last election*⟩

**runway** /'run,way/ n **1** a beaten path made by or for animals **2** an artificially surfaced strip of ground on an airfield for the landing and takeoff of aeroplanes **3** RUN 9b **4** a strip of ground on which athletes run up to the takeoff or throwing point in jumping events (e g the POLE VAULT or LONG JUMP) and the javelin

**rupee** /rooh'pee/ n – see MONEY table [Hindi *rūpaiyā*, fr Skt *rūpya* coined silver]

**rupestrine** /rooh'pestreen/ adj living among, inhabiting, or growing on rocks [deriv of L *rupes* rack; akin to L *rumpere* to break]

**rupiah** /rooh'pee·ə, rooh'pie·ə/ n, pl **rupiah, rupiahs** – see MONEY table [Hindi *rūpaiyā*]

**rupicolous** /rooh'pikələs/, **rupicoline** /-lien, -leen/ adj rupestrine [L *rupes* rock + -*cola* inhabitant – more at WHEEL]

¹**rupture** /'rupchə/ n **1a** the tearing apart of a tissue ⟨~ *of the heart muscle*⟩ ⟨~ *of an intervertebral disk*⟩ **b** a hernia **2a** a breaking apart or bursting; a breach ⟨~ *of friendly relations between the two nations*⟩ **b** the state of being broken apart or burst [ME *ruptur*, fr MF or L; MF *rupture*, fr L *ruptura* fracture, fr *ruptus*, pp of *rumpere* to break – more at BEREAVE]

²**rupture** vt **1a** to part by violence; break, burst **b** to create or induce a breach of ⟨*even at the expense of* rupturing *Arab unity* – Denis Healey⟩ **2** to produce a rupture in ⟨*the blow* ~d *his spleen*⟩ ~ vi to have or undergo a rupture

**rural** /'rooərəl/ adj of the country, country people or life, or (training in) agriculture [ME, fr MF, fr L *ruralis*, fr *rur-, rus* open land – more at ROOM] – **rurally** adv, **rurality** n

synonyms **Rural, rustic, bucolic,** and **pastoral** all mean "relating to the country". **Rural** is the general word for places that are neither towns nor totally wild (the North Pole is scarcely **rural**) and suggests agricultural communities ⟨**rural** *schools*⟩ ⟨a **rural** *constituency*⟩. **Rustic** and **bucolic** suggest a clumsy lack of sophistication ⟨**bucolic** *humour*⟩ ⟨*heavy* **rustic** *boots*⟩ but **rustic** rather than **bucolic** can also apply to the pleasingly primitive ⟨a **rustic** *cabin by the lake*⟩. **Pastoral** expresses nostalgia for the idyllic peace of the country.

**rural dean** n a priest who supervises one district of a DIOCESE (bishop's district)

**Ruritanian** /,rooəri'taynyən, -ni·ən/ adj (characteristic) of an imaginary Central European country used as a setting for contemporary cloak-and-dagger court intrigues [*Ruritania*, fictional kingdom in the novel *The Prisoner of Zenda* by Anthony Hope (Sir Anthony Hope Hawkins) †1933 E writer]

**ruse** /roohz/ n a wily trick [Fr, fr MF, fr *ruser* to dodge, deceive]

¹**rush** /rush/ n any of various often tufted marsh plants (e g of the genus *Juncus* of the family Juncaceae, the rush family) with cylindrical often hollow stems that are used for the seats of chairs and for plaiting mats [ME, fr OE *risc*; akin to MHG *rusch* rush, L *restis* rope] – **rushy** adj

²**rush** vi to move forward, progress, or act quickly or eagerly or without preparation ~ vt **1** to push or impel on or forward with speed or violence **2** to perform or finish in too short a time or at too high a speed ⟨~ed *his breakfast*⟩ **3** to urge to an excessive speed ⟨*never* ~ *a watch repairer*⟩ **4** to run against in attack, often with an element of surprise; charge **5** *NAm* to lavish attention on; court [ME *russhen*, fr MF *ruser* to put to flight, repel, deceive, fr L *recusare* to refuse – more at RECUSANCY] – **rusher** n

³**rush** n **1a** a rapid and violent forward motion **b** an onslaught, attack **c** a sudden onset of emotion ⟨a *quick* ~ *of sympathy*⟩ **2a** a surge of activity; *also* busy or hurried activity ⟨*the bank holiday* ~⟩ **b** a burst of productivity or speed **c rush hour, rush** a period of the day when travel to or from work is at a peak **3** a great movement of people, esp in search of wealth – compare GOLD RUSH **4** *usu pl* the unedited print of a film scene

processed directly after shooting **5** *slang* FLASH 10 (sensation produced by a narcotic drug)

**⁴rush** *adj* requiring or marked by special speed or urgency ⟨~ orders⟩

**rush candle** *n* a rushlight

**rushlight** /'rush,liet/ *n* a candle that consists of the pith of a rush dipped in grease

**rusk** /rusk/ *n* a piece of sliced bread baked again until dry and crisp; *also* a similar commercially made light dry biscuit [modif of Sp & Pg *rosca* coil, twisted roll]

**Russ** /rus/ *n, pl* **Russes**, *esp collectively* **Russ** *archaic* a Russian [Russ *Rus'*] – **Russ** *adj*

**russet** /'rusit/ *n* **1** a reddish to yellowish brown **2** any of various winter eating apples with russet rough skins [ME, fr OF *rousset*, fr *rousset*, adj, russet, fr *rous* russet, fr L *russus* red; akin to L *ruber* red – more at RED] – **russet** *adj*

**Russia leather** *n* leather used esp for bookbinding and made by tanning various kinds of skin with willow, birch, or oak bark and then rubbing the flesh side with a birch oil [*Russia*, country in E Europe]

**Russian** /'rush(ə)n/ *n* **1** a native or inhabitant of Russia; *broadly* a native or inhabitant of the USSR **2** a SLAVONIC language of the Russians – **Russian** *adj*

> *usage* The people of the USSR should correctly be called **Soviets** rather than **Russians**, except for those who actually live in Russia, one of its constituent republics.

**russian·ize, -ise** /'rushəniez/ *vt, often cap* to russify – **russianization** *n*

**Russian roulette** *n* **1** an act of bravado consisting of spinning the cylinder of a revolver loaded with one cartridge, pointing the muzzle at one's own head, and pulling the trigger **2** a potentially risky or suicidal venture

**Russian salad** *n* a salad of cold diced cooked vegetables (e g carrot and potato) in a mayonnaise sometimes containing chilli sauce, chopped pickles, and pimientos

**Russian wolfhound** *n* BORZOI

**russify** /'rusifie/ *vt, often cap* to make Russian in nature – **russification** *n*

**Russky, Russki** /'ruski/ *n or adj, derog or humorous* (a) Russian [Russ *Russkii*, fr *Rus'*], old name for Russia]

**Russo-** /rusoh-/ *comb form* **1** Russian nation, people, or culture ⟨Russo*phobia*⟩ **2** Russian; Russian and ⟨Russo-*Japanese*⟩

**Russophile** /'rusoh,fiel/ *n or adj* (one who is) markedly friendly to Russia or Russian culture

**Russophobe** /'rusoh,fohb/ *n* one who greatly fears or dislikes Russia or Russian culture or customs – **Russophobe** *adj*, **Russophobia** *n*

**¹rust** /rust/ *n* **1a** the brittle reddish coating of FERRIC OXIDE formed on iron, esp when chemically attacked by moist air **b** a comparable coating produced on another metal **c** something resembling rust **2** corrosive or injurious influence or effect **3** (a fungus causing) any of numerous destructive diseases of plants produced by fungi (order Uredinales) and characterized by reddish-brown pustules **4** a reddish-brown to orange colour [ME, fr OE *rūst;* akin to OE *rēad* red – more at RED]

**²rust** *vi* **1** to form rust; become oxidized ⟨*iron* ~s⟩ **2** to degenerate, esp through lack of use or advancing age ⟨*most men would . . . have allowed their faculties to* ~ – T B Macaulay⟩ **3** to become reddish brown as if with rust ⟨*the leaves slowly* ~*ed*⟩ **4** to be affected with a rust fungus ~ *vt* **1** to cause (a metal) to form rust ⟨*keep up your bright swords, for the dew will* ~ *them* – Shak⟩ **2** to impair or corrode by time, inactivity, or misuse ⟨*skills* ~*ed by retirement*⟩ **3** to cause to become rust-coloured

**¹rustic** /'rustik/ *also* **rustical** /-kl/ *adj* **1** (characteristic) of the country **2a** made of the rough limbs of trees ⟨~ *furniture*⟩ **b** finished by rusticating ⟨a ~ *joint in masonry*⟩ **3a** characteristic of country people ⟨~ *features*⟩ **b** lacking in social graces or refinement **4** appropriate to the countryside (e g in plainness or sturdiness) ⟨*heavy* ~ *boots*⟩ **synonyms** see RURAL [ME *rustik*, fr MF *rustique*, fr L *rusticus*, fr *rus* open land – more at ROOM] – **rustically** *adv*, **rusticity** *n*

**²rustic** *n* **1** a person born and bred in a rural area **2** a coarse, unsophisticated, or simple person ⟨*you can't expect these* ~s *to understand James Joyce*⟩

**rusticate** /'rusti,kayt/ *vi* to go into or reside in the country; follow a rural life ~ *vt* **1** to suspend (a student) from college or university **2** to cut a groove, channel, etc in (e g the edges of stone blocks) to make the joints conspicuous ⟨a ~*d stone wall*⟩ **3** to send into the country **4** to impart a rustic character to –

**rusticator** *n*, **rustication** *n*

**¹rustle** /'rusl/ *vi* **1a** to make or cause a rustle **b** to move with a rustling sound **2** *NAm* to act or move with energy or speed **3** *chiefly NAm* to steal cattle or horses ~ *vt* **1** to cause to make a rustle ⟨*the wind* ~d *the leaves*⟩ **2** *chiefly NAm* to steal (e g cattle) [ME *rustelen*, of imit origin; (2, 3) prob influenced in meaning by *hustle*] – **rustler** *n*

**rustle up** *vt, informal* to produce (e g food) adeptly or at short notice

**²rustle** *n* a quick succession or confusion of faint sounds ⟨*the* ~ *of dry leaves blown by the wind*⟩

**rustless** /'rustlis/ *adj* **1** without rust **2** *chiefly Br* rustproof

**rust mite** *n* any of various small mites that burrow in the surface of leaves or fruits, usu producing brown or reddish patches

**rustproof** /'rust,proof/ *adj* incapable of rusting; (treated to be) able to resist rust

**rusty** /'rusti/ *adj* **1** affected (as if) by rust; *esp* stiff (as if) with rust ⟨*the creaking of* ~ *hinges*⟩ **2** inept and slow through lack of practice or advanced age **3a** of the colour rust **b** dulled in colour by age and use; shabby ⟨a ~ *old suit of clothes*⟩ **4** outmoded **5** hoarse, croaking ⟨*my voice is a bit* ~ *this morning*⟩ – **rustily** *adv*, **rustiness** *n*

**¹rut** /rut/ *n* **1a** an annually recurrent state of readiness to copulate that occurs in some mammals, esp the male deer **b** the corresponding period in the female, when she is able to conceive; OESTRUS, HEAT **2** *the* period during which rut normally occurs [ME *rutte*, fr MF *rut* roar, fr LL *rugitus*, fr L *rugitus*, pp of *rugire* to roar; akin to OE *rēoc* wild, MIr *rucht* roar]

**²rut** *vi* **-tt-** *of an animal, esp a male deer* to be in a state of rut

**³rut** *n* **1a** a track worn by habitual passage, esp of wheels on soft or uneven ground **b** a groove or furrow **2** an established practice; *esp* a tedious routine ⟨*the common* ~ ⟩ ⟨*get into a* ~ ⟩ [perh modif of MF *route* way, route] – **rutty** *adj*, **ruttiness** *n*

**⁴rut** *vt* **-tt-** to make a rut in

**rutabaga** /,roohtə'baygə, ,roo-, -'begə/ *n, chiefly NAm* SWEDE **2** (type of turnip) [Sw dial. *rotabagge*, fr *rot* root + *bagge* bag]

**ruth** /roohth/ *n, archaic* **1** pity, compassion **2** sorrow for one's own faults; remorse [ME *ruthe*, fr *ruen* to rue]

**Ruth** /roohth/ *n* – see BIBLE table [*Ruth* (Heb *Rūth*), ancestress of King David]

**ruthenic** /rooh'thenik/ *adj* of or derived from the chemical element ruthenium, esp with a relatively high VALENCY

**ruthenious** /rooh'theeniəs/ *adj* of or derived from ruthenium, esp with a relatively low VALENCY

**ruthenium** /rooh'theenyəm, -niəm/ *n* a hard brittle greyish rare metallic element occurring in platinum ores, and used in hardening platinum alloys [NL, fr ML *Ruthenia* Russia (where it was first found)]

**rutherford** /'rudhəfəd/ *n* a unit of radioactivity equal to the quantity of a NUCLIDE (particular kind of atom) required to produce one million disintegrations per second [Ernest *Rutherford* †1937 Br (NZ-born) physicist]

**rutherfordium** /,rudhə'fawdyəm, -di-əm/ *n* an artificially produced radioactive chemical element of ATOMIC NUMBER 104 [Ernest *Rutherford*]

**ruthful** /'roohthf(ə)l/ *adj, archaic* **1** full of sorrow or compassion **2** causing sorrow or pity – **ruthfully** *adv*, **ruthfulness** *n*

**ruthless** /'roohthlis/ *adj* showing no pity or compassion; cruel – **ruthlessly** *adv*, **ruthlessness** *n*

**rutilant** /'roohtilənt/ *adj, formal* having a reddish or golden glow [ME *rutilaunt*, fr L *rutilant-, rutilans*, pp of *rutilare* to be reddish, fr *rutilus* reddish; akin to L *ruber* red – more at RED]

**rutile** /'roohtil, -,tiel/ *n* a usu reddish-brown lustrous mineral that consists of TITANIUM DIOXIDE, $TiO_2$, usu with a little iron [Ger *rutil*, fr L *rutilus* reddish]

**ruttish** /'rutish/ *adj* lustful [¹*rut* + *-ish*] – **ruttishly** *adv*, **ruttishness** *n*

**-ry** /-ri/ – see -ERY ⟨*wizard*ry⟩ ⟨*citizen*ry⟩ [ME *-rie*, fr OF, short for *-erie* -ery]

**rya** /'ree-ə/ *n* (the weave typical of) a Scandinavian handwoven rug with a deep resilient comparatively flat pile [*Rya*, village in SW Sweden]

**¹rye** /rie/ *n* **1** a hardy cereal grass (*Secale cereale*) that is widely grown for its grain, often on soils that are unfavourable for other cereals, and that is used for livestock feed and for making rye bread and rye whisky **2** the seeds of rye, from which a wholemeal flour for bread-making is made **3 rye bread**, *NAm also* **rye** bread made wholly or in part rye flour and usu containing caraway seeds **4 rye whisky,** *NAm also* **rye** a whisky distilled from rye or from rye and malt [ME, fr OE *ryge;* akin to OHG *rocko* rye, Lith *rugys*]

²**rye** *n* a male gipsy [Romany *rai* gentleman, fr Skt *rājan* king – more at ROYAL]

**ryegrass** /'rie,grahs/ *n* any of several grasses (genus *Lolium*) that grow in Europe, Asia, and N Africa and produce flower heads consisting of a zig-zag stalk bearing unstalked flowers; *esp* two (*Lolium perenne* and *Lolium multiflorum*) that are highly valued as pasture plants for their vigorous growth, palatability, and nutritional content [alter. of *raygrass*, fr obs *ray* darnel]

**ryot** /'rie·ət/ *n* an Indian peasant or tenant farmer [Hindi *raiyat*, fr Per, fr Ar *ra'īyah* flock, herd]

# S

**s, S** /es/ *n, pl* **s's, ss, S's, Ss 1a** the 19th letter of the English alphabet **b** a graphic representation of or device for reproducing the letter *s* **c** a speech counterpart of printed or written *s* **2** one designated *s*, esp as the 19th in order or class **3** something shaped like the letter S

**¹-s** /-s *after voiceless consonant sounds other than* s, sh, ch; z *after vowel sounds & voiced consonant sounds other than* z, zh, j; iz *after* s, sh, ch, z, zh, j/ *suffix* (→ *n pl*) **1a** – used to form the plural of most nouns that do not end in *s, z, sh,* or *ch* or in *y* after a consonant ⟨*head*s⟩ ⟨*book*s⟩ ⟨*boy*s⟩ ⟨*belief*s⟩ **b** – used to form the plural of proper nouns that end in *y* after a consonant ⟨*Mary*s⟩ **c** – used with or without a preceding apostrophe to form the plural of abbreviations, numbers, letters, and symbols used as nouns ⟨*MC*s⟩ ⟨*4*s⟩ ⟨*the 1940*'s⟩ ⟨*£*s⟩ ⟨*B*'s⟩ **2** *chiefly NAm* – used to form adverbs denoting usual or repeated action or state ⟨*always at home Sunday*s⟩ ⟨*morning*s *he stops by the newsstand*⟩ □ *(1)* compare **¹-ES 1** [(1) ME -*es, -s,* fr OE -*as,* nom & acc pl ending of some masc nouns; akin to OS -*os*; (2) ME -*es, -s,* pl ending of nouns, fr -*es,* gen sing. ending of nouns (functioning adverbially), fr OE -*es*]

> **usage** The spelling of plural nouns with **-s** and an apostrophe ⟨*a pound of △ tomato's*⟩ is a common confusion. The apostrophe is used for the plural of only abbreviations, numbers, letters, and symbols ⟨*the 1880's*⟩.

**²-s** *suffix* (→ *vb*) – used to form the third person singular present of most verbs that do not end in *s, z, sh,* or *ch* or *y* after a consonant ⟨*fall*s⟩ ⟨*take*s⟩ ⟨*play*s⟩; compare **²-ES** [ME (Northern & N Midland) -*es,* fr OE (Northumbrian) -*es, -as,* prob fr OE -*es, -as,* 2 sing. pres indic ending – more at -EST]

**¹'s** /*like* **¹-s**/ *vb* **1** ⟨ *she's here*⟩ **2** has ⟨*he's seen them*⟩ **3** does – used in questions ⟨*what's he want?*⟩

**²'s** *pron* us – + let ⟨*let's*⟩

**-'s** *suffix* (→ *n or pron*) – used to form the possessive of singular nouns ⟨*boy*'s⟩, of plural nouns not ending in *s* ⟨*children*'s⟩, of some pronouns ⟨*anyone*'s⟩, and of word groups functioning as nouns ⟨*the man in the corner*'s *hat*⟩ or pronouns ⟨*someone else*'s⟩ [ME -*es, -s,* gen sing. ending, fr OE -*es;* akin to OHG -*es,* gen sing. ending, Gk -*oio, -ou,* Skt -*asya*]

> **usage -'s** commonly forms the possessive of animates ⟨*John's leg*⟩ ⟨*the cat's* (but not △ *the table's*) *leg*⟩ and is used with periods of time ⟨*a day's work*⟩ and in certain fixed phrases ⟨*out of harm's way*⟩ ⟨*get your money's worth*⟩. Some people dislike its use elsewhere as a journalistic spacesaver ⟨*London's traffic*⟩.

**sabadilla** /ˌsabəˈdilə/ *n* a Mexican plant (*Schoenocaulon officinale*) of the lily family; *also* its seeds that are used as a source of the drug VERATRINE [Sp *cebadilla,* dim. of *cebada* barley, fr *cebo* feed, fr L *cibus* food]

**Sabaoth** /səˈbayoth/ *n* armed hosts – used in the biblical title *Lord of Sabaoth* for God [LL, fr Gk *sabaōth,* fr Heb *şĕbāōth, pl of şābā* army]

**sabbat** /ˈsabat, -bat/ *n, often cap* a secret midnight assembly of witches held, esp in medieval and Renaissance times, to renew allegiance to the devil through mystic rites and orgies [Fr, lit., sabbath, fr L *sabbatum*]

**¹Sabbatarian** /ˌsabəˈteəriən/ *n* **1** a person who observes the Sabbath on Saturday in exact conformity with the fourth commandment **2** an adherent of Sabbatarianism ⟨*a strict* ~ *who wouldn't even wash the car on the Sabbath*⟩ [L *sabbatarius,* fr *sabbatum* sabbath]

**²Sabbatarian** *adj* **1** of the Sabbath **2** of Sabbatarians or Sabbatarianism

**Sabbatarianism** /ˌsabəˈteəri.ə.niz(ə)m/ *n* the avoidance of work and suppression of enjoyment on the Sabbath

**sabbath** /ˈsabəth/ *n* **1** *often cap* the seventh day of the week observed from Friday evening to Saturday evening as a day of rest and worship by Jews and some Christians **2** *often cap* Sunday observed among Christians as a day of rest and wor-

ship **3** *often cap* some other biblical period (eg a year) of rest **4** a time of rest **5** a sabbat [ME *sabat,* fr OF & OE, fr L *sabbatum,* fr Gk *sabbaton,* fr Heb *shabbāth,* lit., rest]

**¹sabbatical** /səˈbatikl/, **sabbatic** *adj* **1** of the sabbath ⟨~ *laws*⟩ **2** of or being a sabbatical ⟨~ *leave*⟩ ⟨*a* ~ *year*⟩ ⟨~ *president of the college union – TES*⟩ [LL *sabbaticus,* fr Gk *sabbatikos,* fr *sabbaton*]

**²sabbatical** *n* a leave, often with pay, granted usu every seventh year (eg to a university teacher) typically for rest, travel, or research **synonyms** see **¹HOLIDAY**

**sabbatical year** *n, often cap S* a year of rest for the land, observed every seventh year in ancient Judea

**saber** /ˈsaybə/ *vt or n, NAm* (to) sabre

**sabin** /ˈsaybin/ *n* a unit of absorption of sound waves equivalent to the absorption by one square foot of a surface that absorbs all sound striking it [Wallace C W *Sabine* †1919 US physicist]

**Sabine** /ˈsabien/ *n* (the ITALIC language of) a member of an ancient people of the Apennines NE of Latium [ME *Sabin,* fr L *Sabinus*] – **Sabine** *adj*

**¹sable** /ˈsaybl/ *n, pl* **sables,** (*2*) **sables,** *esp collectively* **sable 1** the heraldic colour black **2a** (the valuable dark brown fur of) a mammal (*Martes zibellina*) that is related to the martens and weasels, is found in the forests of N Asia, and feeds on small animals and eggs **b** (the fur of) any of various animals related to the sable **3** *poetic* the colour black [ME (senses 1, 2a, 3), fr MF (senses 1, 2a), fr MLG *sabel* (sense 2a), fr MHG *zobel,* of Slav origin; akin to Russ *sobol'* sable or its fur]

**²sable** *adj* **1** of the colour black – used poetically or in heraldry **2** *poetic* dark, gloomy

**sable antelope** *n* a large black antelope (*Hippotragus niger*) that lives in herds in the forests of S Africa and that has large parallel curved horns, an erect mane, and long hair at the throat

**sabot** /ˈsaboh/ *n* **1** a wooden shoe worn in various European countries **2** a thrust-transmitting carrier that positions a smaller projectile in a larger gun barrel or launching tube and that prevents the escape of gas ahead of the missile so as to increase the speed of the projectile on firing [Fr, fr MF, alter. of *savate* old shoe]

**¹sabotage** /ˈsabəˌtahzh/ *n* **1** destruction of an employer's property (eg tools or materials) or the hindering of manufacturing by discontented workers **2** destructive or obstructive action carried on by a civilian enemy agent in order to hinder military activity **3a** an act or process tending to hamper or hurt **b** deliberate subversion (eg of a plan or project) [Fr, fr *saboter* to clatter with sabots, botch, sabotage, fr *sabot*]

**²sabotage** *vt* to practise sabotage on

**saboteur** /ˌsabəˈtuh/ *n* one who commits sabotage [Fr, fr *saboter*]

**sabra** /ˈsabrə/ *n, often cap* a native-born Israeli [NHeb *şabrāh,* lit., prickly pear]

**¹sabre,** *NAm chiefly* **saber** /ˈsaybə/ *n* **1** a cavalry sword with a curved blade, thick back, and guard **2** (the sport of) fencing with) a light fencing or duelling sword having an arched guard that covers the back of the hand and a tapering flexible blade with a full cutting edge along one side – compare ÉPÉE, FOIL [Fr *sabre,* modif of Ger dial. *sabel,* fr MHG, of Slav origin; akin to Russ *sablya* sabre]

**²sabre,** *NAm chiefly* **saber** *vt* to strike or kill with a sabre

**sabre rattling** *n* blustering display of military power

**sabretache** /ˈsabəˌtash, ˈsay-/ *n* a flat leather case worn suspended on the left from a waist belt by men of some cavalry regiments [Fr, fr Ger *säbeltasche,* fr *säbel* sabre + *ta:che* pocket]

**sabretooth** /ˈsaybəˌtoohth/ *n* SABRE-TOOTHED TIGER

**sabre-toothed tiger** *n* any of numerous extinct big cats (eg genus *Smilodon*) with long curved upper canines

**sabreur** /sa'bruh/ *n* one who carries or fences with a sabre [Fr, fr *sabrer* to strike with a sabre, fr *sabre*]

**sabulous** /'sabyooləs/ *n* sandy, gritty [L *sabulosus*, fr *sabulum* sand]

**sac** /sak/ *n* a (fluid-filled) pouch within an animal or plant 〈*a synovial* ~〉 [Fr, lit., bag, fr L *saccus* – more at SACK] – **saclike** *adj*

**saccade** /sa'kahd/ *n* a small rapid jerky movement of the eye, esp as it jumps from fixation on one point to another (eg in reading) [Fr, twitch, jerk, fr MF, fr *saquer* to pull, draw] – **saccadic** *adj*

**saccate** /'sakayt, -kət/ *adj* having the form of a sac or pouch 〈*a* ~ *corolla*〉 [NL *saccatus*, fr L *saccus* bag]

**facchar-, facchari-, faccharo-** *comb form* sugar 〈*saccharo-meter*〉 〈*saccharide*〉 [L *saccharum*, fr Gk *sakcharon*, fr Pali *sakkharā*, fr Skt *śarkarā* gravel, sugar]

**faccharase** /'sakərayz, -rays/ *n* INVERTASE (enzyme that breaks down the sugar SUCROSE into simpler sugars) [ISV]

**faccharate** /'sakərayt/ *n* a chemical compound of a sugar usu with a metal; *esp* a chemical compound of sucrose and a metal

**faccharide** /'sakəried/ *n* a SIMPLE SUGAR, combination of simple sugars, or POLYMERIZED sugar

**faccharify** /sa'karifie/ *vt* to break down (eg a complex carbohydrate) into SIMPLE SUGARS – **saccharification** *n*

**faccharimeter** /,sakə'rimitə/ *n* a device for measuring the amount of sugar in a solution; *esp* a POLARIMETER used for this purpose [ISV] – **saccharimetry** *n*

**faccharin** /'sak(ə)rin, --'-/ *n* a chemical compound, $C_7H_5NO_3S$, that is unrelated to the carbohydrates, is several hundred times sweeter than cane sugar, is non-fattening, and is used as a sugar substitute by diabetics and in slimming diets [ISV]

**faccharine** /'sak(ə)rin, -reen/ *adj* 1 of, like, or containing sugar 〈~ *taste*〉 2 excessively sweet; mawkish 〈~ *flavour*〉 〈~ *sentiment*〉 3 ingratiatingly or affectedly polite or friendly [L *saccharum* sugar] – **saccharinity** *n*

**faccharoidal** /,sakə'roydl/ *adj* having or being a fine granular texture like that of lump sugar 〈~ *marble*〉

**faccharometer** /,sakə'romitə/ *n* a saccharimeter; *esp* a HYDROMETER with a special scale for use as a saccharimeter

**faccharomyces** /,sakəroh'mieseez/ *n* any of a genus (*Saccharomyces* of the family Saccharomycetaceae) of usu single-celled yeasts that typically reproduce asexually by BUDDING (outgrowth of a parent cell to form a new cell) [NL, genus name, fr *facchar-* + *-myces* fungus, fr Gk *mykēs* – more at MYC-]

**faccharose** /'sakərohz, -rohs/ *n* sucrose

**faccular** /'sakyoolə/ *adj* resembling a sac 〈~ *ovaries*〉

**facculate** /'sakyoolət, -,layt/, **facculated** /-,laytid/ *adj*, *anatomy* having or formed of a series of saclike expansions – **facculation** *n*

**faccule** /'sakyoohl/ *n* a little sac; *specif* the smaller of the two connected chambers in the sensory structures of the INNER EAR from which the COCHLEA arises – compare UTRICLE [NL *sacculus*, fr L, dim. of *saccus* bag – more at SACK]

**facculus** /'sakyooləs/ *n*, *pl* **facculi** /-li/ a saccule [NL]

**facerdotal** /,sasə'dohtl/ *adj* 1 of priests or a priesthood 2 of or suggesting sacerdotalism [ME, fr MF, fr L *sacerdotalis*, fr *sacerdot-, sacerdos* priest, fr *sacer* sacred + *-dot-, -dos* (akin to *facere* to make) – more at SACRED, DO] – **sacerdotally** *adv*

**facerdotalism** /,sasə'dohtəliz(ə)m/ *n* religious belief emphasizing the powers of priests as essential mediators between God and humans – **sacerdotalist** *n*

**fachem** /'saych(ə)m, 'sach(ə)m/ *n* 1 a N American Indian chief 2 *NAm* a political leader [Narraganset & Pequot *sachima*] – **sachemic** *adj*

**fachet** /'sashay/ *n* 1 a small usu plastic bag or packet; *esp* one holding just enough liquid (eg shampoo or sugar) for use at one time 2 a small bag containing a perfumed powder used to scent clothes and linens [Fr, fr OF, dim. of *sac* bag, fr L *saccus*] – **facheted** *adj*

**¹fack** /sak/ *n* 1 a usu rectangular large bag (eg of paper or canvas) 2 the amount contained in a sack; *esp* a fixed amount of a commodity used as a unit of measure 3 a garment without shaping: eg 3a a loosely fitting dress b a loose coat or jacket; *esp* one worn by men in the 19th century 4 *informal* dismissal from employment – usu in *get/give the sack* 5 *chiefly NAm informal* a bed [ME *sak* bag, sackcloth, fr OE *sacc*; akin to

OHG *sac* bag; both fr a prehistoric Gmc word borrowed fr L *saccus* bag & LL *saccus* sackcloth, both fr Gk *sakkos* bag, sackcloth, of Sem origin; akin to Heb *śaq* bag, sackcloth; (4) prob fr the notion of a dismissed workman going away with his tools or clothes in a sack] – **hit the sack** *informal* to go to bed

**²fack** *vt* 1 to place in a sack 2 *informal* to dismiss from a job – **sacker** *n*

**³fack** *n* any of various dry white wines imported to England from Spain and the Canary Islands during the 16th and 17th centuries [modif of MF *sec* dry, fr L *siccus*; akin to OHG *sīhan* to filter, Gk *hikmas* moisture]

**⁴fack** *n* the plundering of a place captured in war [MF *sac*, fr OIt *sacco*, lit., bag, fr L *saccus*]

**⁵fack** *vt* 1 to plunder (eg a town) after capture 2 to strip (a place) of valuables; loot – **sacker** *n*

**fackbut** /'sak,but/ *n* the renaissance trombone [MF *saque-boute*, lit., hooked lance, fr OF, fr *saquer* to pull + *bouter* to push – more at BUTT]

**fackcloth** /'sak,kloth/ *n* 1 sacking 2 a garment of sackcloth worn as a sign of mourning or penitence [¹*sack*]

**fackful** /'sakf(ə)l/ *n*, *pl* (1) **fackfuls, facksful**, (2) **fackfuls** 1 the amount a sack will hold 2 **fackful, facksful** *pl*, *informal* a considerable quantity 〈*a* ~ *of songs*〉 〈*collected* ~s *of fines*〉

**facking** /'saking/ *n* material for sacks; *esp* a coarse fabric (eg hessian)

**fack race** *n* a race in which each contestant has his/her legs enclosed in a sack tied or held up at the waist, and progresses by jumping and, if permitted, by shuffling or hobbling

**facque** /sak/ *n* SACK 3 [by alter. (pseudo-Fr spelling)]

**¹facr-, facro-** *comb form* sacred; holy 〈*sacrosanct*〉 [ME *sacr-*, fr MF & L; MF, fr L, fr *sacr-, sacer* – more at SACRED]

**²facr-, facro-** *comb form* 1 sacrum 2 sacral and 〈*sacroiliac*〉 [NL, fr *sacrum*]

**¹facral** /'saykrəl/ *adj* of or lying near the SACRUM (part of the SPINAL COLUMN that connects with or forms part of the pelvis)

**²facral** *adj* holy, sacred

**facrament** /'sakrəmənt/ *n* 1 a formal religious act (eg baptism) functioning as a sign or symbol of a spiritual reality; *esp* one believed to have been instituted or recognized by Jesus 2 *cap* the bread and wine used at Communion; *specif* the consecrated bread [ME *sacrement, sacrament*, fr OF & LL; OF, fr LL *sacramentum*, fr L, oath of allegiance, obligation, fr *sacrare* to consecrate]

**¹facramental** /,sacrə'mentl/ *adj* (having the character) of a sacrament – **sacramentally** *adv*

**²facramental** *n* a sacrament-like action or object of devotion in Roman Catholic practice

**facramentalism** /,sakrə'mentəliz(ə)m/ *n* belief in or use of sacramental rites, acts, or objects; *specif* belief that the sacraments bring about and are necessary for salvation – **sacramentalist** *n*

**Sacramentarian** /,sakrəmen'teəriən/ *n* 1 one who interprets sacraments as merely visible symbols 2 one who believes in sacramentalism – **Sacramentarian** *adj*, **Sacramentarianism** *n*

**facrarium** /sa'kreəriəm/ *n*, *pl* **facraria** /-riə/ **1a** SANCTUARY 1b (sacred part of church) **b** SACRISTY **c** PISCINA (water basin near altar) 2 an ancient Roman shrine or sanctuary in a temple or a home holding sacred objects [ML, fr L (sense 2), fr *sacr-, sacer* sacred]

**facred** /'saykrid/ *adj* **1a** dedicated or set apart for the service or worship of a god or gods 〈*a tree* ~ *to the gods*〉 **b** devoted exclusively to one service or use (eg of a person or group) 〈*a fund* ~ *to charity*〉 **c** dedicated as a memorial 〈~ *to his memory*〉 **2a** worthy of religious veneration; holy **b** commanding reverence and respect 3 of religion; not secular or profane 〈~ *music*〉 [ME, fr pp of *sacren* to consecrate, fr OF *sacrer*, fr L *sacrare*, fr *sacr-, sacer* holy, cursed; akin to L *sancire* to make sacred, Hitt *saklais* rite] – **sacredly** *adv*, **sacredness** *n*

**facred baboon** *n* HAMADRYAD 2b [fr its veneration by the ancient Egyptians]

**facred cow** *n* someone or something granted unreasonable immunity from criticism [fr the veneration of the cow by the Hindus]

**facred mushroom** *n* 1 any of various hallucinogenic mushrooms: eg **1a** one (eg genus *Psilocybe*) found in N and S America and used esp in some American Indian ceremonies **b** one (*Amanita muscaria*) found in Europe and Asia that may have been used in the religious cults of the ancient Hindus and the Zoroastrians; FLY AGARIC **2** MESCAL BUTTON (dried top of the small MESCAL cactus)

¹**sacrifice** /'sakrifies/ *n* **1** an act of offering to a god; *esp* the killing of a victim on an altar **2** something offered in sacrifice **3a** destruction or surrender of one thing for the sake of another of greater worth or importance **b** something given up or lost ⟨*the ~ s made by parents*⟩ [ME, fr OF, fr L *sacrificium*, fr *sacr-, sacer* + *facere* to make – more at DO]

²**sacrifice** *vt* **1** to offer as a sacrifice **2** to give up or lose for the sake of an ideal or end **3** to sell at a loss *~ vi* to offer up or perform rites of a sacrifice – **sacrificer** *n*

**sacrificial** /ˌsakri'fish(ə)l/ *adj* of or involving sacrifice – **sacrificially** *adv*

**sacrilege** /'sakrilij/ *n* **1** a technical violation (eg improper reception of a sacrament) of what is sacred **2** gross irreverence towards somebody or something sacred *synonyms* see PROFANATION [ME, fr OF, fr L *sacrilegium*, fr *sacrilegus* one who steals sacred things, fr *sacr-, sacer* + *legere* to gather, steal – more at LEGEND] – **sacrilegious** *adj*, **sacrilegiously** *adv*, **sacrilegiousness** *n*

**sacristan** /'sakristən/ *n* a person in charge of the sacristy and ceremonial equipment; *also* a sexton [ME, fr ML *sacristanus*, fr *sacrista*]

**sacristy** /'sakristi/ *n* a room in a church where sacred vessels and vestments are kept and where the clergy put on their vestments [ML *sacristia*, fr *sacrista* sacristan, fr L *sacr-, sacer*]

**sacro-** – see SACR-

¹**sacroiliac** /ˌsaykroh'iliak, ˌsakroh-/ *adj* of or being the region where the sacrum and ILIUM (part of the pelvis) join [ISV]

²**sacroiliac** *n* (the firm fibrous cartilage of) the sacroiliac region

**sacrosanct** /'sakrəsangkt/ *adj* accorded the highest reverence and respect; *also* regarded with unwarranted reverence ⟨*~ institutions that have outlived their usefulness*⟩ [L *sacrosanctus*, prob fr *sacro sanctus* hallowed by a sacred rite] – **sacrosanctity** *n*

**sacrum** /'saykrəm/ *n, pl* **sacra** /-krə/ the part of the SPINAL COLUMN that is directly connected with or forms a part of the pelvis and in human beings consists of five fused vertebrae [NL, fr LL *os sacrum* last bone of the spine, lit., holy bone, fr L *os* bone + *sacrum*, neut of *sacer* sacred]

**sad** /sad/ *adj* **-dd-** **1a** affected with or expressing grief or unhappiness **b(1)** causing or associated with grief or unhappiness ⟨*~ news*⟩ **b(2)** deplorable, regrettable ⟨*a ~ decline in standards*⟩ ⟨*~ to say*⟩ **2** of a dull sombre colour **3** *of baked goods* ¹HEAVY 9b [ME, fr OE *sæd* sated; akin to OHG *sat* sated, L *satis* enough] – **sadness** *n*

**sadden** /'sadn/ *vb* to make or become sad

**saddhu** /'sudooh/ *n* SADHU (Indian holy man)

¹**saddle** /'sadl/ *n* **1a(1)** a usu padded and leather-covered seat secured to the back of a horse, donkey, etc for the rider to sit on **a(2)** a part of a harness for a draught animal (eg a horse pulling a carriage) comparable to a saddle that is used to keep in place the strap that passes under the animal's tail **b** a seat in certain types of vehicle (eg a bicycle or agricultural tractor); *specif* one to be straddled **2** something like a saddle in shape, position, or function **3** a ridge connecting two peaks **4a** a large cut of meat from a sheep, hare, rabbit, deer, etc consisting of both sides of the unsplit back of a carcass including both loins **b** the rear part of a male fowl's back extending to the tail **5** a coloured saddle-shaped marking on the back of an animal [ME *sadel*, fr OE *sadol;* akin to OHG *satul* saddle] – **saddleless** *adj* – **in the saddle** in control

²**saddle** *vt* **1** to put a saddle on **2** to burden, encumber ⟨*got ~ d with all the paperwork*⟩

**saddleback** /-ˌbak/ *n* any of several animals with saddle-shaped markings on the back; *esp* a medium-sized black pig with a white band crossing the back

**saddlebag** /-ˌbag/ *n* **1** a pouch or bag on the back of a horse behind the saddle; *also* either of a pair laid across behind the saddle **2** a pouch or bag hanging behind the saddle of a bicycle or motorcycle; *also* either of a pair hanging over the rear wheel

**saddle blanket** *n* a saddlecloth

**saddlebow** /-ˌboh/ *n* the arch in or the pieces forming the front of a saddle

**saddlecloth** /-ˌkloth/ *n* a piece of cloth, leather, etc placed under a horse's saddle to prevent chafing

**saddleflap** /'sadlˌflap/ *n* SKIRT 1b (flap on saddle hiding bars for stirrups)

**saddle horse** /-ˌhaws/ *n* a horse suited or trained for riding

**saddle point** *n* a point at which the value of a FUNCTION of two mathematical variable quantities is a maximum with respect to one quantity and a minimum with respect to the other

**saddler** /'sadlə/ *n* one who makes, repairs, or sells leather equipment (eg saddles) for horses

**saddlery** /'sadləri/ *n* **1** the trade, articles of trade, or shop of a saddler **2** a set of the equipment used for sitting on and controlling a riding horse

**saddle seat** *n* a slightly concave chair seat (eg of a WINDSOR CHAIR), sometimes with a thickened ridge at the centre front

**saddle soap** *n* a mild oily soap used for cleansing and conditioning leather

**saddle sore** *n* **1** a sore developing on the back of a horse at points of pressure from a badly fitting or badly adjusted saddle **2** an irritation or sore on parts of the rider due to chafing by the saddle

¹**saddle-ˌstitched** *adj* fastened by staples through the fold ⟨*a ~ magazine*⟩

**saddletree** /-ˌtree/ *n* the frame of a saddle

**Sadducee** /'sadyooˌsee/ *n* a member of a Jewish aristocratic and priestly party emerging in the 2nd century BC and being noted in Jesus' time for rejecting various beliefs (eg in resurrection and angels) of the Pharisees [ME *saducee*, fr OE *sadduce*, fr LL *sadducaeus*, fr Gk *saddoukaios*, fr LHeb *ṣāddūqī*] – **Sadducean** *adj*, **Sadduceeism** *n*

**sadhe** /'sahdi, 'tsahdi/ *n* the 18th letter of the Hebrew alphabet [Heb *ṣādhē*]

**sadhu, saddhu** /'sudooh/ *n* an Indian ascetic usu wandering holy man [Skt *sādhu*, fr *sādhu* straight, good]

**sadiron** /'sadˌie-ən/ *n* a flatiron that is pointed at both ends [fr *sad* in the obs sense "compact, heavy"]

**sadism** /'saydiz(ə)m/ *n* **1** a sexual perversion in which pleasure is obtained by inflicting physical or mental pain on others – compare MASOCHISM **2** delight in inflicting pain [ISV, fr Marquis (really Count) de *Sade* †1814 Fr writer] – **sadist** *adj or n*, **sadistic** *adj*, **sadistically** *adv*

**sadly** /'sadli/ *adv* **1** in a sad manner **2** as is sad; it is sad that ⟨*~, someone has stolen my umbrella*⟩

**sadomasochism** /ˌsaydoh'masəkiz(ə)m/ *n* an abnormal condition in which sadism and masochism occur together in the same person [ISV *sad*ism + *-o-* + *masochism*] – **sadomasochist** *n*, **sadomasochistic** *adj*

**sad sack** *n, NAm informal* an inept person

**sae** /ˌesˌay'ee/ *n* a stamped addressed envelope

**Safar** /sə'fah/ *n* – see MONTH table [Ar *ṣafar*]

¹**safari** /sə'fahri/ *n* (the caravan and equipment of) a hunting or scientific expedition, esp in E Africa ⟨*went on ~ to study the habits of the hyena*⟩ [Ar *safarī* of a trip] – **safari** *vi*

²**safari** *adj* made of lightweight material, esp cotton, and typically having two breast pockets, a belt, and sometimes epaulettes ⟨*a ~ suit*⟩

**safari park** *n* a large open space stocked with usu big-game animals (eg lions) so that visitors can observe them in surroundings similar to their natural habitat

¹**safe** /sayf/ *adj* **1** freed from harm or risk ⟨*~ and sound*⟩ **2** secure from threat of danger, harm, or loss **3** providing safety from danger **4a** not threatening or entailing danger ⟨*is your dog ~?*⟩ **b** unlikely to cause controversy ⟨*keeping to ~ subjects*⟩ **5a** not liable to take risks; cautious **b** trustworthy, reliable **6** being a constituency where the MP was elected with a large majority ⟨*a ~ Labour seat*⟩ – compare MARGINAL *antonyms* dangerous, unsafe [ME *sauf*, fr OF, fr L *salvus* safe, healthy; akin to L *salus* health, safety, *salubris* healthful, *solidus* solid, Gk *holos* whole, safe] – **safe, safely** *adv*, **safeness** *n*

²**safe** *n* **1** a place or receptacle for the safe storage of valuables **2** a receptacle, esp a cupboard, for the temporary storage of fresh and cooked foods that typically has at least one side of wire mesh to allow ventilation while preventing flies from entering

**safeblower** /-ˌbloh·ə/ *n* a safecracker who uses explosives – **safeblowing** *n*

**safebreaker** /-ˌbraykə/ *n* a safecracker – **safebreaking** *n*

**ˌsafe-'conduct** *n* (a document authorizing) protection given a person passing through a military zone or occupied area [ME *sauf conduit*, fr OF, safe conduct]

**safecracker** /-ˌkrakə/ *n* one who breaks open safes to steal – **safecracking** *n*

**safe-deposit box** *n* a box (eg in the vault of a bank) for safe storage of valuables

¹**safeguard** /-,gahd/ *n* **1** a pass, safe-conduct **2a** a precautionary measure or stipulation **b** a technical device for the prevention of accidents [ME *saufgarde*, fr MF *saufegarde*, fr OF, fr *sauve* safe + *garde* guard]

²**safeguard** *vt* **1** to provide a safeguard for **2** to make safe; protect **synonyms** see DEFEND

**safekeeping** /-'keeping/ *n* keeping safe or being kept safe ⟨*left it with her for ~*⟩

**safelight** /-,liet/ *n* a darkroom lamp with a filter that produces light of a colour to which the photographic film or paper being handled is insensitive

**safe period** *n* the time during or near the menstrual period when conception is least likely to occur

**safety** /'sayfti/ *n* **1** the condition of being safe from causing or suffering hurt, injury, or loss **2 safety catch, safety** a device (eg on a gun, a mine, or a machine) designed to prevent accidental use **3** a billiard or snooker shot made with no attempt to score or so as to leave the balls in an unfavourable position for the opponent; *also* the playing of such shots [ME *saufte*, fr MF *sauveté*, fr OF, fr *sauve*, fem of *sauf* safe]

**safety belt** *n* a belt fastening a person to an object to prevent falling or injury

**safety curtain** *n* a fireproof curtain which can isolate the stage from the auditorium in case of fire

**safety-deposit box** *n* SAFE-DEPOSIT BOX

**safety glass** *n* **1** transparent material that is prepared by sandwiching a sheet of transparent plastic between sheets of clear glass and is used esp for windows (eg in cars) likely to be subjected to shock or impact **2** glass that is strengthened by TEMPERING and that when broken shatters into relatively safe rounded granules

**safety helmet** *n* CRASH HELMET

**safety lamp** *n* a miner's lamp constructed to avoid ignition of inflammable gas, usu by enclosing the flame in fine wire gauze

**safety match** *n* a match capable of being ignited only on a specially prepared surface

**'safety-,net** *n* **1** a net designed to safeguard people working or performing in high places **2** SAFEGUARD 2a ⟨*the ~ of unemployment benefit – Sunday Times Magazine*⟩

**safety pin** *n* a pin in the form of a clasp with a guard covering its point when fastened

**safety razor** *n* a razor provided with a guard for the blade to prevent cutting the skin when in use

**safety valve** *n* **1** an automatic escape or pressure-relief valve (eg for a steam boiler) **2** an outlet for pent-up energy or emotion ⟨*a ~ for life's frustrations*⟩

**safflower** /'sa,flowə/ *n* (a red dye prepared from the large orange or red flower heads of) a widely grown SW Asian and N African plant (*Carthamus tinctorius*) of the daisy family with seeds rich in oil that is used in the manufacture of soft margarines, cooking oil, and salad oil [MF *saffleur*, fr OIt *saffiore*, fr Ar *asfar* a yellow plant]

**saffron** /'safron, 'safrən/ *n* **1** a purple-flowered crocus (*Crocus sativus*) **2** the deep orange aromatic pungent dried STIGMAS (parts of the female reproductive organs in flowers) of saffron used to colour and flavour foods and formerly as a dyestuff and in medicine **3** orange-yellow [ME, fr OF *safran*, fr ML *safranum*, fr Ar *za'farān*]

**safranine, safranin** /'safrənin, -neen/ *n* **1** any of various usu red synthetic dyes that are made from certain chemical BASES **2** any of various mixtures of safranine compounds used in dyeing and to colour certain structures in biological specimens in preparation for viewing under a microscope [ISV, fr Fr or Ger *safran* saffron]

**safrole** /'safrohl/ *n* a colourless or yellow oily chemical compound, $C_3H_5C_6H_3O_2CH_2$, that is the principal component of sassafras oil and is used chiefly for perfuming and flavouring [ISV, fr Fr or Ger *safran*]

¹**sag** /sag/ *vb* -**gg**- *vi* **1** to droop, sink, or settle (as if) from weight, pressure, or loss of tautness **2a** to lose firmness or vigour ⟨*spirits ~ging from overwork*⟩ **b** to decline from a thriving state ⟨*~ging industrial production*⟩ **3** to fail to stimulate or retain interest ⟨*~ged a bit in the last act*⟩ ~ *vt* to cause to sag; leave slack in [ME *saggen*, prob of Scand origin; akin to Sw *sacka* to sag]

²**sag** *n* **1a** a sagging part ⟨*the ~ in a rope*⟩ **b** a drop or depression in the land below a surrounding area **2** an instance or amount of sagging ⟨*~ is inevitable in a heavy unsupported span*⟩ **3** a temporary economic decline (eg in the price of a commodity)

**saga** /'sahgə/ *n* **1** a medieval Icelandic narrative dealing with historic or legendary figures and events **2** a modern heroic narrative resembling the Icelandic saga **3** a long detailed account ⟨*had to endure the ~ of her American holiday*⟩ **4** ROMAN-FLEUVE (long novel about a social group) [ON – more at SAW]

**sagacious** /sə'gayshəs/ *adj* **1** *formal* of keen and farsighted judgment ⟨*~ judge of character*⟩ **2** *formal* prompted by or indicating acute discernment ⟨*~ purchase of stock*⟩ **3** *obs* acute in perception with the senses **synonyms** see SHREWD [L *sagac-, sagax;* akin to L *sagire* to perceive keenly – more at SEEK] – **sagaciously** *adv*, **sagaciousness, sagacity** *n*

**sagamore** /'sagəmaw/ *n* **1** a subordinate chief of the Algonquian Indians of the N Atlantic coast of America **2** SACHEM 1 (Indian chief) [Abnaki *sagimau*, lit., he prevails over]

¹**sage** /sayj/ *adj* **1** *formal* wise on account of reflection and experience **2** *formal* proceeding from or indicating wisdom and sound judgment ⟨*~ counsel*⟩ **3** *archaic* grave or solemn in expression [ME, fr OF, fr (assumed) VL *sapius*, fr L *sapere* to taste, have good taste, be wise; akin to OE *sefa* mind, Oscan *sipus* knowing] – **sagely** *adv*, **sageness** *n*

²**sage** *n* **1** somebody (eg a great philosopher) renowned for wise teachings **2** a venerable man of sound judgment

³**sage** *n* **1** a plant (*Salvia officinalis*) of the mint family whose greyish-green aromatic leaves are used esp in flavouring meat **2 sagebrush, sage** any of several N American undershrubs (genus *Artemisia*, esp *Artemisia tridentata*) of the daisy family that cover large areas of plains in the W USA [ME, fr MF *sauge*, fr L *salvia*, fr *salvus* healthy – more at SAFE; fr its use as a medicinal herb]

**sage cheese** *n* a cheese (eg Derby) flecked with green and flavoured with sage

**sage green** *adj or n* greyish green

**saggar, sagger** /'sagə/ *n* a box made of fireclay in which delicate ceramic pieces are baked [prob alter. of *safeguard*]

**sagitta** /sə'gitə/ *n* the perpendicular distance from the centre of a CHORD (straight line joining two points on a curve) to the arc it subtends – no longer used technically [NL, fr L, arrow]

**sagittal** /'sajitl/ *adj* **1** of the join between the PARIETAL BONES that stretches from the front to the back of the top of the skull **2** of, situated in, or being (a plane parallel to) the middle plane or midline of the body [L *sagitta* arrow] – **sagittally** *adv*

**Sagittarius** /,saji'teəri·əs/ *n* **1** a large constellation of the ZODIAC (imaginary belt in the heavens) lying across the MILKY WAY between Scorpius and Capricornus and represented as a centaur shooting an arrow **2a** the 9th sign of the zodiac in astrology, held to govern the period November 22 - December 22 approx **b** somebody born under this sign [L, lit., archer, fr *sagitta*] – **Sagittarian** *adj or n*

**sagittate** /'saji,tayt/ *adj*, of a plant or animal part, esp a leaf shaped like an arrowhead [L *sagitta* arrow]

**sago** /'saygoh/ *n, pl* **sagos** a dry powdered starch prepared from the pith of a SAGO PALM and used as a food (eg in a milk pudding) and as textile stiffening [Malay *sagu* sago palm]

**sago palm** *n* any of various tall Indian and Malaysian palms (genus *Metroxylon*) that yield sago

**saguaro** /sə'gwahroh/ *n, pl* **saguaros** a treelike cactus (*Carnegiea gigantea*) of SW USA and Mexican deserts with a tall (sparsely branched) trunk of up to 20 metres (about 60 feet), white flowers, and an edible fruit [MexSp]

**sahib** /'sah·hib, 'sah·eeb/ *n* – used, esp among the indigenous population in colonial India, when addressing or speaking of a European man [Hindi *ṣāhib*, fr Ar]

**said** /sed/ *adj* aforementioned [pp of *say*]

**usage** Writers on usage advise that the adjective **said** should be confined to legal contexts ⟨*the said Simpson*⟩ and not used generally as in ⟨*the said pub*⟩.

**saiga** /'seigə/ *n* an antelope (*Saiga tatarica*) that lives on the steppes of the Volga and Caspian Sea, is heavy and somewhat sheeplike in build, and has a swollen snout [Russ *saiga*]

¹**sail** /sayl/ *n, pl* **sails,** (*1b*) **sail** *also* **sails 1a(1)** an expanse of fabric which is spread to catch or deflect the wind as a means of propelling a ship, SAND YACHT, etc **a(2)** the sails of a ship ⟨*crowded on more ~*⟩ **b** a ship equipped with sails ⟨*a French fleet of 60 ~*⟩ **2** something like a sail in function or form ⟨*the ~s of a windmill*⟩ **3** a voyage by ship ⟨*a five-day ~ from the nearest port*⟩ [ME, fr OE *segl*; akin to OHG *segal* sail, L *secare* to cut – more at SAW] – **sailed** *adj* – **set sail** to begin a voyage ⟨*set sail for America*⟩ – **under sail** of a sailing vessel in motion with sails set – see also **take the** WIND **out of somebody's sails**

²**sail** *vi* **1a** to travel in a boat or ship **b** to make journeys in or manage a sailing boat for pleasure **2a** to travel on water, esp by the action of wind on sails **b** to move without visible effort or in a stately manner ⟨~ed *gracefully into the room* – L C Douglas⟩ **3** to begin a journey by water ⟨~ *with the tide*⟩ ~ *vt* **1** to travel over (a body of water) in a ship ⟨~ *the seven seas*⟩ **2** to direct or manage the operation of (a ship or boat) – **sailable** *adj*
  **sail into** *vt* to attack vigorously or sharply ⟨sailed into *his dinner*⟩ ⟨sailed into *me for being late*⟩
**sailboard** /-,bawd/ *n* a flat buoyant board that is equipped with a sail, CENTREBOARD (retractable stabilizer), and rudder and is used in the sport of wind-surfing
**sailboat** /-,boht/ *n, chiefly NAm* SAILING BOAT – **sailboater** *n*, **sailboating** *n*
**sailcloth** /-,kloth/ *n* a heavy canvas used for sails, tents, or upholstery; *also* a lightweight canvas used for clothing
**sailfish** /-,fish/ *n* any of a genus (*Istiophorus*) of large marine fishes related to the swordfish but having teeth, scales, and a very large sail-like fin along the back that can be lowered to give increased speed or raised to prevent undue rolling and yawing
**sailing** /'sayling/ *n* **1** the technical skills of managing a ship or boat **2** the sport of handling a SAILING BOAT **3** a departure from a port, esp of a scheduled passenger vessel
**sailing boat** *n* a boat fitted with sails for propulsion
**sailing ship** *n* a ship fitted with sails for propulsion
**sailor** /'saylə/ *n* **1a** a seaman, mariner **b** a member of a ship's crew other than an officer **2** a traveller by water; *esp* one considered with reference to any tendency to seasickness ⟨*it was a rough crossing – lucky we're all good* ~s⟩
**sailor collar** *n* a broad collar that has a square flap across the back and tapers to a V in the front
**sailor hat** *n* a stiff straw hat with a low flat crown and straight circular brim
**sailplane** /'sayl,playn/ *n* a glider designed to rise in an upward air current – **sailplane** *vi*, **sailplaner** *n*
**sainfoin** /'san,foyn/ *n* a Eurasian red or pink-flowered plant (*Onobrychis viciifolia*) of the pea family widely grown for hay and pasture on chalk and dry soils because it has long strong roots that can penetrate considerable depths in search of water [Fr, fr MF, fr *sain* healthy (fr L *sanus*) + *foin* hay, fr L *fenum*]
¹**saint** /saynt; *before a name usu* s(ə)nt/ *n* **1** a person officially recognized through CANONIZATION as being outstandingly holy and so worthy of veneration **2a** any of the spirits of the departed in heaven **b** ANGEL 1a ⟨Saint *Michael the Archangel*⟩ **3** any of (various Christian groups regarding themselves as) God's chosen people **4** a person of outstanding piety or virtue [ME, fr MF, fr LL *sanctus*, fr L, sacred, fr pp of *sancire* to make sacred – more at SACRED] – **saintly** *adj*, **saintliness** *n*, **sainthood** *n*, **saintlike** *adj*
²**saint** *vt* to recognize or designate as a saint; *specif* CANONIZE
**Saint Agnes' Eve** /s(ə)nt 'agnis(iz)/ *n* the night of January 20 when a girl is traditionally held to see her future husband in a dream [*St Agnes* †304 virgin martyr]
**Saint Andrew's cross** /'androohz/ *n* **1** a cross consisting of two intersecting diagonal bars **2** a cross formed by two white diagonals on a blue field (e g on a flag) [*St Andrew* †*ab* AD 60, one of the twelve apostles]
**Saint Andrew's Day** *n* November 30 observed in honour of St Andrew, the patron saint of Scotland
**Saint Anthony's cross** /'antəniz; *also* 'anth-/ *n* TAU CROSS (T-shaped cross) [*St Anthony* †356 Egyptian monk]
**Saint Anthony's fire** *n* any of several inflammations or gangrenous conditions (e g ERYSIPELAS or ERGOTISM) of the skin
**Saint Bernard** /'buhnəd/ *n* (any of) a Swiss alpine breed of tall powerful working dogs used, esp formerly, in aiding lost travellers [fr the hospice of Grand *St Bernard* in Switzerland, where such dogs were first bred]
**Saint David's Day** /'dayvidz/ *n* March 1 observed in honour of St David, the patron saint of Wales [*St David* †601 W bishop]
**sainted** /'sayntid/ *adj* **1** of or suitable to a saint **2** saintly, pious **3** entered into heaven; dead ⟨*my* ~ *mother*⟩ – often used in exclamations ⟨*oh my* ~ *aunt!*⟩
**Saint Elmo's fire** /'elmohz/ *n* a flamelike electrical discharge sometimes seen in stormy weather at prominent points (e g on a ship, aeroplane, or large building) [*St Elmo* (*Erasmus*) †303 It bishop & patron saint of sailors]

**Saint George's cross** /'jawjiz/ *n* a cross formed by red horizontal and vertical stripes on a white field (e g on a flag) [*St George* †*ab* 303 Christian martyr]
**Saint George's Day** *n* April 23 observed in honour of St George, the patron saint of England
**Saint-John's-wort** /jonz/ *n* any of a genus (*Hypericum* of the family Hypericaceae, the Saint-John's-wort family) of plants and shrubs with often showy usu 5-petalled yellow flowers [*St John* the Baptist *fl ab* 27 prophet]
**Saint Luke's summer** /loohk/ *n, Br* INDIAN SUMMER [*St Luke* †*ab* 74 evangelist, whose feast day is 18 October]
**Saint Martin's summer** /'mahtin/ *n* INDIAN SUMMER when occurring in November [*Saint Martin*, whose feast day is 11 November (cf MARTINMAS)]
**Saint Patrick's Day** /'patriks/ *n* March 17 observed in honour of St Patrick, the patron saint of Ireland [*St Patrick* † *ab* 461 Christian missionary]
**saint's day** /'saynts/ *n* a day in a church calendar on which a saint is commemorated
**Saint Swithin's Day** /'swidh(ə)nz/ *n* July 15 that traditionally indicates 40 days of rain if rainy or 40 dry days if dry [*St Swithin* †862 E bishop]
**Saint Valentine's Day** /'valəntienz/ *n* February 14 observed in honour of St Valentine and as a time for sending valentines [*St Valentine* † *ab* 270 It priest]
**Saint Vitus's dance** /'vietəs(iz)/ *n* CHOREA (disorder of the CENTRAL NERVOUS SYSTEM) [*St Vitus*, 3rd-c Christian child martyr]
**saith** /seth, sayth/ *archaic pres 3 sing of* SAY
**saithe** /sayth/ *n, pl* **saithe** COLEY (food fish) [of Scand origin; akin to ON *seithr* coalfish]
**Saiva** /'shievə, 'sievə/ *n* a member of a major Hindu sect devoted to the cult of the god Siva [Skt *Saiva*, fr *Siva* Siva] – **Saivism** *n*
¹**sake** /sayk/ *n* [ME, dispute, guilt, purpose, fr OE *sacu* guilt, action at law; akin to OHG *sahha* action at law, cause, OE *sēcan* to seek – more at SEEK] – **for God's/goodness/heaven's/pity's sake** – used in protest or appeal ⟨for God's sake *stop that noise*⟩ – **for the sake of, for somebody's/something's sake 1** for the purpose of ⟨for the sake of *argument*⟩ **2** so as to get, keep, or improve ⟨for *conscience* sake⟩ ⟨*study Latin* for *its own* sake⟩ **3** so as to help, please, or honour ⟨*to go to the seaside* for the sake of *the children*⟩ ⟨for *old times'* sake⟩
²**sake, saki** /'sahki/ *n* a Japanese alcoholic drink of fermented rice, usu served hot [Jap *sake*]
**saker** /'saykə/ *n* a large falcon (*Falco cherrug*) that has dark plumage and winters in the Balkans, Asia Minor, and Egypt [ME *sagre*, fr MF *sacre*, fr Ar *ṣaqr*]
**saki** /'sahki/ *n* any of several monkeys (genera *Pithecia* and *Chiropotes*, family Cebidae) that live in the forests of S America, have thick curly hair and usu a long bushy tail, and feed on fruit [Fr, fr Tupi *sagui*]
**Sakti** /'s(h)ahkti/ *n* SHAKTI (cosmic energy in Hinduism) – **Saktism** *n*
¹**sal** /sal/ *n* SALT 1d – used in pharmacology [L – more at SALT]
²**sal** *n* (the wood of) an Indian timber tree (*Shorea robusta*) [Hindi *sāl*, fr Skt *śāla*]
¹**salaam** /sə'lahm/ *n* **1** a ceremonial greeting in E countries **2** an obeisance performed by bowing very low and placing the right palm on the forehead [Ar *salām*, lit., peace]
²**salaam** *vb* to perform a salaam (to)
**salable, saleable** /'saylabl/ *adj* fit for sale; capable of being sold – **salability** *n*
**salacious** /sə'layshəs/ *adj* **1** arousing or appealing to sexual desire; lewd ⟨*a collection of* ~ *poems*⟩ **2** lecherous, lustful [L *salac-, salax* fond of leaping, lustful, fr *salire* to leap – more at SALLY] – **salaciously** *adv*, **salaciousness** *n*
**salad** /'saləd/ *n* **1a** (mixed) raw vegetables (e g lettuce, watercress, or tomato), often with a dressing, served as a side dish or with meat, fish, cheese, etc as a main course ⟨*ham* ~⟩ **b** (a dish consisting of) raw or (cold) cooked foods often cut into small pieces and combined with a dressing ⟨*seafood* ~⟩ ⟨*fruit* ~⟩ ⟨*potato* ~⟩ **2** a vegetable or herb eaten raw (in salad); *esp* lettuce [ME *salade*, fr MF, fr OProv *salada*, fr *salar* to salt, fr *sal* salt, fr L – more at SALT]
**salad cream** *n* a dressing for salad that is similar to mayonnaise and is usu made commercially and bottled
**salad days** *n pl* time of youthful inexperience or indiscretion ⟨*my* ~ *when I was green in judgment* – Shak⟩

**salad oil** *n* an edible vegetable oil (e g olive oil) suitable for using in salad dressings

**salad onion** *n* SPRING ONION

**salamander** /'salə,mandə, ,--'--/ *n* **1** a mythical animal having the power to endure fire without harm **2** an elemental being held to inhabit fire **3** any of numerous amphibians (order Caudata) superficially resembling lizards but scaleless and covered with a soft moist skin and breathing by external gills in the larval stage **4** an article used in connection with fire; *esp* a metal (e g iron) plate that is heated and held over food (e g puddings or pastry) to brown the top [ME *salamandre*, fr MF, fr L *salamandra*, fr Gk] – **salamandrine** *adj*

**salami** /sə'lahmi/ *n*, *pl* **salamis** a highly seasoned sausage, esp one containing pork, that may be either smoked or fresh and often contains garlic [It, pl of *salame* salami, fr *salare* to salt, fr *sale* salt, fr L *sal*]

**sal ammoniac** /,sal ə'mohniak/ *n* AMMONIUM CHLORIDE [ME *sal armoniak*, fr L *sal ammoniacus* – more at AMMONIA]

**salariat** /sə'leəriat/ *n taking sing or pl vb* the class or body of salaried people, usu as distinguished from wage earners [Fr, fr *sal*aire salary (fr L *salarium*) + *-ariat* (as in *prolétariat* proletariat)]

**salary** /'saləri/ *n* a fixed usu monthly payment for regular services, esp of a nonmanual kind – compare WAGE [ME *salar-ie*, fr L *salarium* money for the purchase of salt, pension, salary, fr neut of *salarius* of salt, fr *sal* salt – more at SALT] – **salaried** *adj*

**salbutamol** /sal'byoohtə,mol/ *n* a synthetic drug, $(HO)(HOCH_2)C_6H_3CHOHCH_2NHC(CH_3)_3$, used in the treatment of asthma to relax the muscle of the walls of the BRONCHIOLES (small air-conducting tubes) of the lungs and make breathing easier [*sal* + *butyl* + *amin-* + *-ol*]

**salchow** /'salkow/ *n* a jump in ice-skating from the inside backward edge of one skate with a turn in the air and a return to the outside backward edge of the other skate [Ulrich *Salchow* †1949 Sw skating champion]

**sale** /sayl/ *n* **1** the act or an instance of selling; *specif* the transfer of ownership of and title to property or goods from one person to another for a price **2a** opportunity of selling or being sold; demand ⟨*counting on a large ~ for the new product*⟩ **b sale, sales** *pl* quantity sold ⟨*average total ~s rose in the last quarter*⟩ **3** an event at which goods are offered for sale ⟨*an antiques ~*⟩ **4** public disposal to the highest bidder **5** a selling of goods at bargain prices **6** *pl* **6a** operations and activities involved in promoting and selling goods or services ⟨*manager in charge of ~s*⟩ **b** gross receipts obtained from selling [ME, fr OE *sala*, fr ON – more at SELL] – **on/for sale** available for purchase

**saleable** /'saylabl/ *adj* salable

**sale of work** *n*, *Br* a sale of goods made by members of a club or society in order to raise money

**sale or return** *n* an arrangement by which a dealer pays only for the goods he/she sells and may return what is unsold

**salep** /'saləp/ *n* the starchy dried tubers of various orchids (esp genus *Orchis*) used for food [Fr or Sp, fr Ar dial. *saḥlab*, alter. of Ar (*khuṣy ath-*) *tha'lab*, lit., testicles of the fox]

**saleratus** /,salə'raytəs/ *n*, *NAm* a raising agent used in baking consisting of potassium or sodium bicarbonate [NL *sal aeratus* aerated salt]

**saleroom** /'saylroohm, -room/, *NAm chiefly* **salesroom** /'saylz-/ *n*, *chiefly Br* a place where goods are displayed for sale, esp by auction

**sales** /saylz/ *adj* of, engaged in, or used in selling ⟨*~ promotion*⟩

**salesclerk** /-,klahk/ *NAm* -,kluhk/ *n*, *chiefly NAm* SHOP ASSISTANT

**salesgirl** /-,guhl/ *n* a female SHOP ASSISTANT

**Salesian** /sə'leezh(ə)n, say-/ *n* a member of the Society of St Francis de Sales, a Roman Catholic religious order founded by St John Bosco in Turin in Italy in the 19th century that is devoted chiefly to education [St Francis de *Sales* †1622 Fr bishop]

**saleslady** /-,laydi/ *n* a female SHOP ASSISTANT

**salesman** /-mən/, *fem* **saleswoman** *n* a salesperson – **salesmanship** *n*

**salesperson** /-,puhs(ə)n/ *n* a person employed to sell goods or services (e g in a shop or within an assigned territory)

**sales representative** *n* a person who travels, usu in an assigned territory, to win orders for his/her firm's goods

    *synonyms* A person who travels to get orders for goods is today

usually called a **sales representative** or merely a **representative**, or informally in Britain a **rep** or **sales rep**. **Traveller** and **commercial traveller** are old-fashioned and somewhat lowly in their implications, suggesting a humble pedestrian with a bag of samples rather than a smart executive in a large car. **Salesperson, salesman**, and **saleswoman** may be avoided in Britain because they can also mean that one stands behind a counter in a shop.

**sales resistance** *n* unwillingness on the part of a potential customer or market to purchase a product; *also* resistance to sales talk

**salesroom** /'saylz,roohm, -room/ *n*, *NAm* a saleroom

**sales talk** *n* **1** talk intended to sell, esp by praising what is for sale **2** persuasive argument intended to convert to a standpoint

**sales tax** *n* PURCHASE TAX

**sali-** *comb form* salt ⟨sali*ferous*⟩ [L, fr *sal* – more at SALT]

**salic** /'salik, 'saylik/ *adj* SIALIC [by alter.]

**Salic** *also* **Salique** /'saylik, 'salik/ *adj* of or being a Frankish people that settled on the Ijssel river early in the 4th century [MF or ML; MF *salique*, fr ML *Salicus*, fr LL *Salii* Salic Franks]

**salicin** /'salisin/ *n* a bitter drug, $C_6H_{11}O_5OC_6H_4CH_2OH$, found in the bark and leaves of several willows and poplars and used in medicine like SALICYLIC ACID [Fr *salicine*, fr L *salic-, salix* willow – more at SALLOW]

**Salic law** /'salik/ *n* the legal code of the Salic Franks; *also* a rule held to derive from this code excluding females from succession to a throne

**salicornia** /,sali'kawniə/ *n* any of a genus (*Salicornia*) of plants of the goosefoot family that have fleshy pointed stems, no leaves, inconspicuous flowers, and that are typically found on SALT MARSHES and seashores [NL, genus name, fr Fr *salicorne* glasswort, deriv of L *sali-* + *cornu* horn]

**salicylate** /sə'lisilayt/ *n* any of various chemical compounds (SALTS or ESTERS) formed by combination between SALICYLIC ACID and a metal atom, an alcohol, or another chemical group

**salicylic acid** /,sali'silik/ *n* an acid, $HOC_6H_4COOH$, from which chemical compounds (e g aspirin) are made that are used to relieve pain and fever and in the treatment of rheumatism [ISV, fr *salicyl* (the radical $HOC_6H_4CO$), fr Fr *salicyle*, fr *salicine*]

**¹salient** /'saylyənt, -li·ənt/ *adj* **1** *of an animal* moving by leaps or springs; *specif* of or being a salientian ⟨*a ~ amphibian*⟩ **2** pointing upwards or outwards ⟨*a ~ angle*⟩ **3a** projecting beyond a line or level **b** standing out conspicuously ⟨*~ characteristics*⟩ [L *salient-, saliens*, prp of *salire* to leap – more at SALLY] – **saliently** *adv*, **salience, saliency** *n*

**²salient** *n* something (e g a promontory) that projects outwards or upwards from its surroundings; *esp* an outwardly projecting part of a fortification, trench system, or line of defence

**salientian** /,sayli'ensh(ə)n/ *n* any of an order (Salientia) of amphibians comprising the frogs and toads, that lack a tail as adults and have long hind limbs suited to leaping and swimming [deriv of L *salient-, saliens*] – **salientian** *adj*

**salina** /sə'lienə/ *n* **1** a hollow from which water has evaporated leaving a deposit of salt **2** a salt marsh, lake, spring etc [Sp, fr L *salinae* saltworks, fr fem pl of *salinus*]

**¹saline** /'say,lien/ *adj* **1** (consisting) of, containing, or resembling salt ⟨*a ~ solution*⟩ ⟨*a ~ taste*⟩ **2** *esp* of a laxative containing SALTS of potassium, sodium, or magnesium [ME, fr (assumed) L *salinus*, fr *sal* salt – more at SALT] – **salinity** *n*

**²saline** *n* **1** a SALT of potassium, sodium, or magnesium that acts as a laxative **2** a saline solution; *esp* one similar in its concentration of IONS (electrically charged atoms) to body fluids

**salinometer** /,sali'nomitə/ *n* an instrument (e g a HYDROMETER) for measuring the amount of salt in a solution [ISV *saline* + *-o-* + *-meter*]

**Salique** /'saylik, 'salik/ *adj* SALIC

**Salish** /'saylish/ *n* **1** a language stock of the MOSAN group (PHYLUM) of languages, spoken in NW USA and W Canada **2** *taking pl vb* the peoples speaking Salish dialects – **Salishan** *adj*

**saliva** /sə'lievə/ *n* a slightly alkaline liquid mixture of water, protein, salts, and often enzymes that is secreted into the mouth by SALIVARY GLANDS and that lubricates ingested food and often begins the breakdown of starches in the food [L – more at SALLOW]

**salivary** /'salivəri, sə'lievəri/ *adj* of saliva or the glands that secrete it; *esp* producing or carrying saliva

**salivary chromosome** *n* any of the very large strands of CHROMOSOMAL material that consist of many pairs of identical strands (CHROMATIDS) that have undergone repeated duplication, and are typical of the salivary gland cells of various insects

**salivary gland** *n* any of the glands that open into or near the mouth and secrete saliva

**salivate** /'salivayt/ *vi* **1** to have an (excessive) flow of saliva **2** to show great or excessive eagerness or excitement ⟨salivating *at the prospect of huge profits*⟩ – **salivation** *n*

**Salk vaccine** /sawlk/ *n* a vaccine against polio consisting of inactivated polio virus [Jonas *Salk* b1914 US physician]

**sallet** /'salit/ *n* a light 15th-century helmet with or without a visor and with a projection over the neck [ME, fr MF *sallade*]

**salley, sally** /'sali/ *n, chiefly dial* a sallow

**¹sallow** /'saloh/ *n* any of various Eurasian broad-leaved willows (eg *Salix cinerea*) some of which are important sources of charcoal [ME, fr OE *sealh;* akin to OHG *salha* sallow, L *salix* willow]

**²sallow** *adj* of a sickly yellowish colour ⟨*a ~ complexion*⟩ [ME *salowe,* fr OE *salu;* akin to OHG *salo* murky, L *saliva* spittle] – **sallowish** *adj,* **sallowness** *n*

**¹sally** /'sali/ *n* **1** a rushing forth; *esp* a sortie of troops from a besieged position **2a** a brief outbreak ⟨*a ~ of rage*⟩ **b** a witty or penetrating remark; *esp* one made in banter or as provocation in argument **3** a short excursion, *esp* off the beaten track; a jaunt [MF *saillie,* fr OF, fr *saillir* to rush forwards, fr L *salire* to leap; akin to Gk *hallesthai* to leap]

**²sally** *vi* **1** to rush out suddenly **2** to set out (eg on a journey) – usu + *forth*

**Sally Army** *n, Br informal* SALVATION ARMY [by shortening & alter.]

**Sally Lunn** /,sali 'lun/ *n* a slightly sweetened bread bun made with yeast [*Sally Lunn,* 18th-c E baker]

**sally port** *n* a gate or passage in a fortified place for use by troops making a sortie

**salmagundi** /,salmə'gundi/ *n* **1** a dish of chopped meats, anchovies, eggs, and vegetables often arranged in rows for contrast and dressed with a salad dressing **2** a mixture composed of many usu unrelated elements [Fr *salmigondis*]

**salmi** /'salmi/ *n* a dish consisting of partly roasted game stewed in a rich wine sauce [Fr *salmis,* short for *salmigondis*]

**salmon** /'samən/ *n, pl* **salmon,** *esp for different types* **salmons 1a** a large soft-finned game fish (*Salmo salar*) of the N Atlantic that has pink flesh and is highly valued as a food fish; *also* any of various related soft-finned fishes (family Salmonidae) **b** a fish (eg a barramunda) resembling a salmon **2** orangy-pink [ME *samon,* fr MF, fr L *salmon-, salmo*]

**salmonella** /,salmə'nelə/ *n, pl* **salmonellae** /-lie/, **salmonellas, salmonella** any of a genus (*Salmonella*) of rod-shaped bacteria that typically are capable of movement and cause diseases, esp food poisoning, in human beings and other warm-blooded animals [NL, genus name, fr Daniel E *Salmon* †1914 US veterinarian]

**salmonellosis** /,salməne'lohsis/ *n, pl* **salmonelloses** /-seez/ infection with or disease (eg food poisoning) caused by salmonellae [NL]

**salmonid** /'samənid, 'sal-/ *n* any of a family (Salmonidae) of elongated soft-finned fishes (eg a salmon or trout) that have the last vertebra upturned [NL *Salmonidae* group name, fr *Salmon-, Salmo,* genus name, fr L *salmo* salmon] – **salmonid** *adj*

**salmon leap** *n* FISH LADDER

**salmonoid** /'salmənoyd/ *n* any of a suborder (Salmonoidea) of fishes that includes the salmon; *esp* a salmonid – **salmonoid** *adj*

**salmon trout** *n* SEA TROUT

**salon** /'salonh/ *n* **1** an elegant reception room or living room **2** a fashionable gathering of literary figures, artists, statesmen, etc held at the home of a prominent person and common in the 17th and 18th centuries **3a** a hall for exhibiting art **b** *cap* an exhibition, esp in France, of works of art by living artists **4** a stylish business establishment or shop ⟨*a beauty ~*⟩ [Fr]

**saloon** /sə'loohn/ *n* **1** a public apartment or hall (eg a ballroom, exhibition room, or shipboard social area) **2** a railway carriage with no compartments **3 saloon car, saloon** an enclosed car having no partition between the driver and passengers **4a saloon bar, saloon** a comfortable, well-furnished, and often relatively expensive bar in a pub – compare PUBLIC BAR **b** *NAm* a room or establishment in which alcoholic beverages are sold and consumed [Fr *salon,* fr It *salone,* aug of

*sala* hall, of Gmc origin; akin to OHG *sal* hall; akin to Lith *sala* village]

**saloop** /sə'loohp/ *n* SALEP (food product from orchids)

**Salopian** /sə'lohpi·ən/ *n or adj* (a native or inhabitant) of Shropshire [*Salop,* alternative name of Shropshire]

**salp** /salp/ *n* a salpa

**salpa** /'salpə/ *n* a transparent barrel-shaped or spindle-shaped free-swimming INVERTEBRATE marine animal (esp genus *Salpa* of the family Salpidae, class Thaliacea) that is related to the SEA SQUIRTS and is abundant in warm seas [NL, genus name, fr L, a kind of stockfish, fr Gk *salpē*]

**salpicon** /'salpikən/ *n* any of various mixtures of finely diced meat, poultry, fish, or vegetables seasoned, flavoured, and incorporated into a thick sauce [Fr, fr Sp *salpicón,* fr *sal* salt (fr L) + *picar* to prick, mince, chop]

**salping-, salpingo-** *comb form* salpinx ⟨salping*itis*⟩ ⟨salping*ectomy*⟩ [NL, fr salping-, salpinx]

**salpingian** /sal'pinjiən/ *adj* of a salpinx

**salpingitis** /,salpin'jietəs/ *n* inflammation of a FALLOPIAN TUBE (tube connecting an ovary to the womb) or EUSTACHIAN TUBE (tube connecting the MIDDLE EAR to the throat) [NL]

**salpinx** /'salpingks/ *n, pl* **salpinges** /sal'pinjeez/ **1** EUSTACHIAN TUBE (tube connecting the MIDDLE EAR to the throat) **2** FALLOPIAN TUBE (tube connecting an ovary to the womb) [NL *salping-, salpinx,* fr Gk, trumpet]

**salsify** /'salsifie, -fi/ *n* (the long tapering edible root of) a European plant (*Tragopogon porrifolius*) of the daisy family – called also OYSTER PLANT [Fr *salsifis,* modif of It *sassefrica,* fr LL *saxifrica,* any of various herbs, fr L *saxum* rock + *fricare* to rub – more at SAXIFRAGE, FRICTION]

**¹salt** /sawlt, solt/ *n* **1a** SODIUM CHLORIDE, NaCl, occurring naturally esp as a mineral deposit and dissolved in sea water and used esp for seasoning or preserving – called also COMMON SALT **b** any of numerous chemical compounds that result from replacement of (part of) the HYDROGEN ION of an acid by a metal atom or other chemical group **c** *pl* **c(1)** a mixture of SALTS of usu sodium, potassium, or magnesium (eg EPSOM SALTS) used as a laxative **c(2)** SMELLING SALTS **2a** an ingredient that imparts savour, piquancy, or zest ⟨*the ~ of humour*⟩ **b** sharpness of wit **3** an experienced sailor ⟨*a tale worthy of an old ~*⟩ **4** a saltcellar [ME, fr OE *sealt;* akin to OHG *salz* salt, L *sal,* Gk *hals* salt, sea] – **saltlike** *adj* – **earn one's salt** to work hard and honestly – **salt of the earth** a person or group of people having or embodying praiseworthy or essential values or qualities [fr Christ's reference to his disciples in Mt 5:13] – **worth one's salt** worthy of respect, esp because competent or effective – see also **with a** PINCH **of salt**

**²salt** *vt* **1** to treat, provide, season, or preserve with COMMON SALT or brine **2** to give flavour or piquancy to (eg a story) **3** to enrich (eg a mine) fraudulently by the secret introduction of valuable matter (eg mineral ores) **4** to sprinkle (as if) with salt ⟨*~ing the icy roads*⟩ ⟨*snowflakes ~ed the countryside*⟩ – **salter** *n*

**salt away** *vt* to put by in reserve; save ⟨salted *his money away*⟩

**salt out** *vb* to precipitate or separate (a dissolved substance) from a solution by the addition of salt

**³salt** *adj* **1a** saline, salty **b** being or inducing a taste similar to that of COMMON SALT that is one of the four basic taste sensations – compare BITTER, SOUR, SWEET **2** cured or seasoned with salt; salted ⟨*~ pork*⟩ **3** containing, overflowed by, or growing in salt water ⟨*a ~ pond*⟩ **4** sharp, pungent ⟨*a ~ wit* – John Buchan⟩ – **saltness** *n*

**⁴salt** *adj, obs* lustful, lewd [by shortening & alter. fr *assaut,* fr ME *a sawt,* fr MF *a saut,* lit., on the jump]

**saltant** /'salt(ə)nt/ *adj, of an organism* exhibiting saltation [L *saltant-, saltans,* prp of *saltare* to leap, dance]

**saltarello** /,saltə'reloh/ *n, pl* **saltarellos** an Italian dance characterized by lively hop steps [It, fr *saltare* to leap, fr L]

**saltation** /sal'taysh(ə)n/ *n* **1a** the direct transformation of one form of an organism into another that is suggested by some evolutionary theories **b** mutation – used esp with reference to changes of form in bacteria and fungi **2** *formal* the action or process of leaping or jumping [L *saltation-, saltatio* dancing, dance, fr *saltatus,* pp of *saltare* to leap, dance, fr *saltus,* pp of *salire* to leap – more at SALLY]

**saltatorial** /,saltə'tawriəl/ *adj* of, marked by, or adapted for leaping ⟨*~ legs of a grasshopper*⟩

**saltatory** /'saltət(ə)ri/ *adj, formal* proceeding by abrupt leaps rather than by smooth transitions; discontinuous

**saltbush** /-,boosh/ *n* any of various shrubby plants, esp an ORACHE, of the goosefoot family that thrive in dry alkaline soil and some of which are important grazing plants in dry regions

**saltcellar** /-,selə/ *n* a cruet for salt; *esp* a small open dish or a shaker with one or more holes in the top used for salt at table [alter. (influenced by *cellar*) of ME *salt saler*, fr *salt* + *saler* cruet for salt, fr MF, fr L *salarius* of salt – more at SALARY]

**salt dome** *n* a dome-shaped arch in layered SEDIMENTARY rock (rock formed from deposited material that has accumulated and hardened) that has a mass of ROCK SALT as its core

**salted** /'sawltid, 'soltid/ *adj, of an animal* immune to a contagious disease because of prior infection and recovery

**saltern** /'sawltən, 'soltən/ *n* a place where salt is manufactured (e g by boiling) [OE *sealtern*, fr *sealt* salt + *ærn* house; akin to ON *rann* house]

**salt flat** *n* a salt-encrusted flat area resulting from evaporation of a former body of water

**salt gland** *n* a gland (e g of a marine bird) capable of excreting a concentrated salt solution

**saltings** /'sawltingz, 'soltingz/ *n pl*, **salting** *n, chiefly Br* a marshy area flooded regularly by tides

**saltire** /'saltie·ə/ *n* a diagonal heraldic cross [ME *sautire*, fr MF *saultoir* X-shaped animal barricade that can be jumped over by people, saltire, fr *saulter* to jump, fr L *saltare* – more at SALTATION]

**salt lake** *n* a landlocked body of water (e g the Dead Sea) that has become increasingly salty through evaporation

**salt lick** *n* LICK 3 (place where animals go to lick salt)

**salt marsh** *n* flat land that is frequently flooded by seawater and supports a characteristic community of plants able to survive under these conditions; *also* an inland marsh in a very dry region in which the water contains a lot of salt

**saltpan** /-,pan/ *n* a natural or artificial basin for producing salt by evaporation of salt water

**saltpetre**, *NAm* **saltpeter** /-'peetə/ *n* 1 POTASSIUM NITRATE 2 SODIUM NITRATE [alter. of earlier *salpeter*, fr ME, fr MF *salpetre*, fr ML *sal petrae*, lit., salt of the rock]

**saltus** /'saltəs/ *n* a sudden transition (e g to a conclusion in logic); a jump [NL, fr L, leap, fr pp of *salire* to leap]

**saltwater** /-'wawtə/ *adj* of, living in, or being salt water

**saltwort** /'sawltwuht, 'solt-/ *n* any of a genus (*Salsola*, esp *Salsola kali*) of plants of the goosefoot family that have prickly leaves and small greenish flowers and grow esp in salty habitats

**salty** /'sawlti, 'solti/ *adj* 1 of, seasoned with, or containing salt 2 having a usu strong taste of salt 3 smacking of the sea or nautical life **4a** piquant, witty **b** earthy, coarse – **saltily** *adv*, **saltiness** *n*

**salubrious** /sə'l(y)oohbri·əs/ *adj* 1 favourable to or promoting health or well-being ⟨*a ~ climate*⟩ 2 RESPECTABLE 1,2 ⟨*not a very ~ district*⟩ [L *salubris* – more at SAFE] – **salubriously** *adv*, **salubriousness**, **salubrity** *n*

**saluki** /sə'loohki/ *n* (any of) an old N African and Asian breed of tall slender keen-eyed hunting dogs having long narrow heads, long silky ears, and a smooth silky coat [Ar *salūqīy* of Saluq, fr *Salūq* Saluq, ancient city in Arabia]

**salutary** /'salyoot(ə)ri/ *adj* 1 promoting health; curative 2 having a beneficial effect; remedial ⟨*~ advice*⟩ [MF *salutaire*, fr L *salutaris*, fr *salut-*, *salus* health] – **salutarily** *adv*, **salutariness** *n*

**salutation** /,salyoo'taysh(ə)n/ *n* **1a** an expression of greeting, goodwill, or courtesy by word or gesture **b** *pl* regards 2 the word or phrase of greeting (e g *Gentlemen* or *Dear Sir*) that conventionally comes immediately before the body of a letter or speech – **salutational**, **salutatory** *adj*

**salutatory** /sə'loohtət(ə)ri, -'lyooh-/ *n* an address of welcome given by a graduating student in an American college

**¹salute** /sə'l(y)ooht/ *vt* **1a** to address with expressions of greeting, goodwill, or respect **b** to give a sign of friendship, respect, or courtesy to **2a** to honour by a conventional military or naval ceremony **b** to show respect and recognition to (a military superior) by assuming a prescribed position (e g by raising the hand to the side of the head) **c** to praise ⟨~d *her courage*⟩ 3 *archaic* to become apparent to (one of the senses) ~ *vi* to make a salute [ME *saluten*, fr L *salutare*, fr *salut-*, *salus* health, safety, greeting – more at SAFE] – **saluter** *n*

**²salute** *n* 1 a greeting, salutation **2a** a sign, token, or ceremony expressing goodwill, compliment, or respect ⟨*the festival was a ~ to the arts*⟩ **b** an act of saluting a military superior; *also* the

position (e g of the hand or weapon) or the entire attitude of a person saluting a superior

**salutiferous** /,salyoo'tifərəs/ *adj, formal* salutary [L *salutifer*, fr *salut-*, *salus* + *-i-* + *-fer* -ferous]

**Salvadorean**, **Salvadorian** /,salvə'dawriən/, **Salvadoran** /,salvə'dawrən/ *n* a native or inhabitant of El Salvador [El *Salvador*, country in Central America] – **Salvadorean**, **Salvadoran**, **Salvadorian** *adj*

**¹salvage** /'salvij/ *n* **1a** compensation paid to those who save property from loss or damage **b** the act of saving a ship or its cargo from the perils of the sea or of rescuing lives or property after a shipwreck **c** the act of saving or rescuing property in danger (e g from fire) **2a** property saved from calamity (e g a wreck or fire) **b** something of use or value extracted from waste material or debris [Fr, fr MF, fr *salver* to save – more at SAVE]

**²salvage** *vt* to rescue or save (e g from wreckage or ruin) – **salvageable** *adj*, **salvager** *n*, **salvageability** *n*

**Salvarsan** /'salvəsan/ *trademark* – used for ARSPHENAMINE (drug formerly used to treat syphilis)

**salvation** /sal'vaysh(ə)n/ *n* 1 (an agent or means which brings about) deliverance from the power and effects of sin 2 liberation from ignorance or illusion 3 deliverance from danger, difficulty, or destruction [ME, fr OF, fr LL *salvation-*, *salvatio*, fr *salvatus*, pp of *salvare* to save – more at SAVE] – **salvational** *adj*

**Salvation Army** *n* an international religious and charitable group organized on military lines and founded in E London in 1865 by William Booth for performing welfare and esp missionary work among the poor and destitute

**salvationism** /sal'vaysha,niz(ə)m/ *n* religious teaching emphasizing the saving of the soul

**Salvationist** /sal'vayshənist/ *n* 1 a soldier or officer of the SALVATION ARMY 2 *often not cap* an evangelist – **salvationist** *adj, often cap*

**¹salve** /salv, sahv/ *n* 1 a medicinal usu soothing ointment for application to wounds or sores 2 a soothing influence or agency ⟨*a ~ to their hurt feelings*⟩ [ME, fr OE *sealf*; akin to OHG *salba* salve, Gk *olpē* oil flask]

**²salve** *vt* 1 to apply a salve to or remedy (as if) with a salve 2 to quiet, assuage ⟨~ *a troubled conscience*⟩

**³salve** *vt* to save from loss or destruction; salvage ⟨*returned to the wreck to supervise the salving of the cargo – TLS*⟩ [back-formation fr *salvage*] – **salvor** *n*

**salver** /'salvə/ *n* a tray; *esp* an ornamental tray (e g of silver) on which food or drinks are served or letters and visiting cards are presented [modif of Fr *salve*, fr Sp *salva* sampling of food to detect poison, tray, fr *salvar* to save, sample food to detect poison, fr LL *salvare* to save – more at SAVE]

**salvia** /'salvi·ə/ *n* any of a large and widely distributed genus (*Salvia*) of plants or shrubs of the mint family; *esp* one (*Salvia splendens*) grown for its scarlet or purple flowers [NL, genus name, fr L, sage – more at SAGE]

**salvific** /sal'vifik/ *adj, formal* having the intent or power to save or redeem ⟨*the ~ life and death of Jesus*⟩ [LL *salvificus*, fr L *salvus* safe + *-ficus* -fic]

**¹salvo** /'salvoh/ *n, pl* **salvos**, **salvoes 1a** a simultaneous discharge of two or more guns or missiles in military or naval action or as a salute **b** the release at one moment of several bombs or missiles (e g from an aircraft) **c** a successive discharge of one gun or missile after another in a battery **d** the bombs or projectiles released in a salvo 2 a sudden or emphatic burst (e g of cheering, applause, or approbation) [It *salva*, fr Fr *salve*, fr L, hail!, imper of *salvēre* to be healthy, fr *salvus* healthy – more at SAFE]

**²salvo** *vb* **salvos**; **salvoing**; **salvoed** *vt* to release a salvo of ~ *vi* to fire a salvo

**³salvo** *n, pl* **salvos 1a** an unstated reservation; a proviso **b** a dishonest quibble or evasion 2 a means of safeguarding one's reputation or preserving one's self-respect; a salve [ML *salvo jure* with the right reserved]

**sal volatile** /,sal və'latili/ *n* a strong-smelling solution of AMMONIUM CARBONATE dissolved in alcohol or AMMONIA WATER, used as SMELLING SALTS [NL, lit., volatile salt]

**salwar** /'sulwah/ *n* a pair of trousers with wide legs gathered at the ankle, traditionally worn by Punjabi women [Per *Shalwār*, *shulwār*]

**samara** /sə'mahrə/ *n* a dry 1-seeded INDEHISCENT (not splitting open to release the seed) fruit with one or more winglike projections, that is produced by various trees (e g the ash, maple, and sycamore) – called also KEY [NL, fr L, seed of the elm]

**Samaritan** /sə'marit(ə)n/ *n* **1a** a native or inhabitant of ancient Samaria **b** a descendant of Samaritans **2a** *often not cap* somebody who selflessly gives aid to those in distress **b** a member of an organization that offers help to those in despair [ME, fr LL *samaritanus*, n & adj, fr Gk *samaritēs* inhabitant of Samaria, fr *Samaria*, district & city in ancient Palestine fr the parable of the good Samaritan, Lk 10:30–37] – **samaritan** *adj, often cap*

**samarium** /sə'meəri·əm/ *n* a pale grey metallic chemical element used esp in alloys that form permanent magnets [NL, fr Fr *samarskite*]

**samarskite** /sə'mahskiet/ *n* a black or brownish-black mineral that is a complex mixture of many chemical elements and is a source of some RARE-EARTH ELEMENTS and uranium [Fr, fr Colonel von *Samarski*, 19th-c Russ mine official]

**samba** /'sambə/ *n* (the music for) a Brazilian dance of African origin characterized by a dip and spring upwards at each beat of the music – compare MAMBO, RUMBA, CONGA [Pg] – **samba** *vi*

**sambal** /'sumbul/ *n* any of various side dishes or relishes (e g of fish or vegetables) flavoured with onions, herbs, spices, and coconut and served esp with curries [Malay]

**sambar, sambur** /'sahmbə, 'sam-/ *n* a large Asian deer (*Cervus unicolor*) having strong 3-pointed antlers and long coarse hair on the throat [Hindi *sābar*, fr Skt *śambara*]

¹**sambo** /'samboh/ *n, often cap* **1** somebody of three-quarters Negro ancestry **2** *derog* a Negro [AmerSp *zambo* Negro, mulatto]

²**sambo** *n* an international style of wrestling employing judo techniques [Russ, fr *samozashchita bez oruzhiya* self-defence without weapons]

**Sam Browne belt** /ˌsam 'brown/ *n* a leather belt formerly worn by British and other army officers, supported by a light strap passing over the right shoulder [Sir *Samuel* James *Browne* †1901 Br army officer]

¹**same** /saym/ *adj* **1** being one single thing, person, or group; identical ⟨*wear the* ~ *shoes for a week*⟩ – often used as an intensive ⟨*born in this very* ~ *house*⟩ **2** being the specified one or ones – + *as* or *that* ⟨*made the* ~ *mistake as last time*⟩ **3** corresponding so closely as to be indistinguishable ⟨*two brothers have the* ~ *nose*⟩ – see also ALL **the same, in the same** BOAT, ONE **and the same** [ME, fr ON *samr*; akin to OHG *sama* same, L *similis* like, *simul* together, at the same time, *sem-* one, Gk *homos* same, *hama* together, *hen-, heis* one]

*synonyms* **Same, very,** and **identical** may mean, and **selfsame** must mean, that the items under consideration are really one, and not two or more different but like things ⟨*they take their children to the* **same/selfsame** *doctor*⟩ ⟨*it's the* **same/selfsame** *book I borrowed from you*⟩ ⟨*there's the* **very** *man I mentioned*⟩ ⟨*their dresses were* **identical**⟩. **Similar** means that two or more different items are alike in certain respects ⟨*they live in a house* **similar** *to ours*⟩. **Equivalent** and **equal** mean that two or more different items correspond in value, number, size, etc ⟨*barter involves the exchange of one thing for another of* **equivalent** *value*⟩ ⟨*receive* **equal** *pay for* **equal** *work*⟩. *usage* Writers on usage recommend that **same** should be followed by *as* rather than by *that* ⟨*the* **same** *shoes as/that I wore yesterday*⟩.

²**same** *pron, pl* **same 1** *the* same thing, person, or group ⟨*do the* ~ *for you*⟩ ⟨*happy Christmas!* Same *to you!*⟩ **2** *commercialese* something previously mentioned ⟨*ordered a drink and refused to pay for* ~⟩

³**same** *adv* in the same manner – + *the* ⟨*two words spelt the* ~⟩

**samekh** /'sahmekh/ *n* the 15th letter of the Hebrew alphabet [Heb *sāmekh*]

**sameness** /'saymnis/ *n* **1** the quality or state of being the same; identity, similarity **2** monotony, uniformity

**samey** /'saymi/ *adj, informal* lacking variety; monotonous

**Samian ware** /'saymiən/ *n* a very common fine glossy red earthenware pottery produced mainly in Roman Gaul in the first three centuries AD [L *samius* of Samos, fr Gk *samios*, fr *Samos*, Gk island]

**samisen** /'sami,sen/ *n* a 3-stringed Japanese musical instrument resembling a banjo [Jap, fr Chin (Pek) *sānxián* [*san*¹ *hsien*²], fr *sān* (*san*¹) three + *xián* (*hsien*²) string]

**samite** /'samiet, 'say-/ *n* a rich medieval silk fabric interwoven with gold or silver and used for clothing [ME *samit*, fr MF, fr ML *examitum, samitum*, fr MGk *hexamiton*, fr Gk, neut of *hexamitos* of six threads, fr *hexa-* + *mitos* thread]

**samiti** /'sumiti/ *n* a usu political organization, esp of workers, in India [Hindi, committee, meeting]

**samizdat** /səmiz'dat/ *n* a system in the USSR by which literature suppressed by the government is clandestinely typed, printed, or photocopied and distributed; *also* such literature [Russ, lit., self-publishing]

**samlet** /'samlit/ *n* PARR (young salmon) [irreg fr *salmon* + *-let*]

**Samoan** /sə'moh·ən/ *n* **1** a native or inhabitant of Samoa **2** the Polynesian language of the Samoans [*Samoa*, group of islands in the Pacific Ocean] – **Samoan** *adj*

**samosa** /sə'mohsə/ *n, pl* **samosa, samosas** a small triangular pastry case filled with spiced minced meat, vegetables, etc and deep-fried in butter [Hindi]

**samovar** /'saməvah, ˌ--'-/ *n* a metal urn with a tap at its base and an interior charcoal-fired heating tube, that is used, esp in Russia, to boil water for tea [Russ, fr *samo-* self + *varit'* to boil]

**Samoyed** *also* **Samoyede** /samoy'ed; *sense 3* sə'moyed/ *n* **1** a member of a people of the coastal regions of N USSR and NW Siberia **2** any of a group of URALIC languages spoken by the Samoyeds **3** (any of) a Siberian breed of medium-sized deep-chested thick-coated white or cream-coloured sledge dogs [Russ *samoed*] – **Samoyed, Samoyedic** *adj*

**samp** /samp/ *n, NAm* (a boiled porridge made from) coarsely ground maize [Narranganset *nasaump* corn mush]

**sampan** /'sam,pan/ *n* a flat-bottomed oar-propelled boat used in rivers and harbours in the Far East [Chin (Pek) *s(h)ānbǎn* (*s(h)an*¹ *pan*³), fr *s(h)ān* (*s(h)an*¹) three + *bǎn* (*pan*³) board, plank]

**samphire** /'sam,fie·ə; *also* -fə/ *n* **1** a European rock plant (*Crithmum maritimum*) of the carrot family, that grows round seacoasts and has fleshy green leaves that are sometimes eaten boiled and pickled **2** GLASSWORT (plant that grows in salt marshes) [alter. of earlier *sampiere*, fr MF (*herbe de*) *Saint Pierre*, lit., St. Peter's herb]

¹**sample** /'sahmpl/ *n* **1** a representative part or a single item serving to show the character or quality of a larger whole or group; a specimen **2** a subset of a statistical POPULATION (complete set of individuals, objects, etc) whose properties are studied to gain information about the whole *synonyms* see EXAMPLE [ME, fr MF *essample*, fr L *exemplum* – more at EXAMPLE]

²**sample** *vt* to take a sample of or from

³**sample** *adj* intended as an illustration or example ⟨~ *questions*⟩

¹**sampler** /'sahmplə/ *n* a decorative piece of needlework typically having letters or verses embroidered on it in various stitches as an example of skill

²**sampler** *n* **1** one who or that which collects, prepares, or examines samples **2** *NAm* a collection of representative specimens or selections ⟨*a* ~ *of nineteen poets*⟩

**sample space** *n, statistics* a set consisting of all the possible outcomes of a statistical experiment

**sampling** /'sahmpling/ *n* **1** a statistical sample ⟨*ask a* ~ *of people why they didn't buy one client's product* – Vance Packard⟩ **2** the act, process, or technique of selecting a suitable sample; *specif* the .act, process, or technique of selecting a representative subset of a statistical POPULATION (complete set of individuals, objects, etc) in order to determine the characteristics of or quantities describing the whole population

**samsara** /sam'sahrə/ *n* the indefinitely repeated Hindu cycle of birth, misery, and death caused by KARMA (fate) [Skt *saṁsāra*, lit., passing through]

**samsce** /'samzoh/ *n* a pale yellow Danish cheese with a firm texture, mild slightly sweet flavour, and a few medium-sized holes [*Samsoe, Samsø*, island in Denmark]

**Samson** /'samsən/ *n* a man of great strength [*Samson* (Heb *Shimshōn*), Heb hero famed for his strength]

**Samuel** /'samyəl, 'samyooəl/ *n* – see BIBLE table [*Samuel* (fr LL, fr Gk *Samouel*, fr Heb *Shěmū'ēl*), 11th-c BC Heb leader]

**samurai** /'sam(y)oo,rie/ *n, pl* **samurai 1** a military retainer of a Japanese feudal baron **2** the warrior aristocracy of Japan [Jap]

**sanatarium** /ˌsanə'teəriəm/ *n, pl* **sanatariums, sanataria** /-riə/ *NAm* a sanatorium [by alter. (influenced by *sanitarium*)]

**sanative** /'sanətiv/ *adj, formal* having the power to cure or heal; curative [ME *sanatif*, fr MF, fr LL *sanativus*, fr L *sanatus*, pp of *sanare* to cure, fr *sanus* healthy]

**sanatorium** /ˌsanə'tawri·əm/ *n, pl* **sanatoriums, sanatoria**

/-riə/ **1** an establishment (eg a health farm) that provides therapy together with a controlled diet, exercise, etc and sometimes medical treatment **2** an establishment for the treatment of people suffering from long-term illnesses and requiring much care **3** *Br* a room, esp in a boarding school, where sick people are looked after; SICK BAY [NL, fr LL, neut of *sanatorius* curative, fr *sanatus*]

**sanbenito** /ˌsanbə'neetoh/ *n, pl* **sanbenitos** a Spanish Inquisition garment that was either yellow with red crosses for the penitent or black with painted devils and flames for the impenitent condemned to an AUTO-DA-FÉ (burning of heretics) [Sp *sambenito*, fr *San Benito* St Benedict †*ab* 543 It monk who introduced a scapular resembling the garment]

**sanctification** /ˌsangktifi'kaysh(ə)n/ *n* **1** an act of sanctifying **2a** the state of being sanctified **b** the state of growing in divine grace as a result of Christian commitment after baptism or conversion

**sanctifier** /'sangktifie·ə/ *n* one who or that which sanctifies; *specif, cap* HOLY SPIRIT

**sanctify** /'sangkti‚fie/ *vt* **1** to set apart for a sacred purpose or for religious use; consecrate **2** to free from sin; purify **3** to give moral or social sanction to **4** to make productive of holiness or piety ⟨*keep the sabbath day to* ~ *it* – Deut 5:12 (AV)⟩ [ME *sanctifien*, fr MF *sanctifier*, fr LL *sanctificare*, fr L *sanctus* sacred – more at SAINT]

**sanctimonious** /ˌsangkti'mohnyəs, -ni·əs/ *adj* **1** pretending piousness; hypocritically devout **2** assured of one's own righteousness or goodness; self-righteous **3** *obs* endowed with sanctity; holy – **sanctimoniously** *adv*, **sanctimoniousness** *n*

**sanctimony** /'sangktiməni/ *n* **1** assumed or hypocritical holiness **2** *obs* holiness [MF *sanctimonie*, fr L *sanctimonia*, fr *sanctus* holy]

**¹sanction** /'sangksh(ə)n/ *n* **1** a formal (ecclesiastical) decree **2** something (eg a moral principle) that makes an oath or rule binding **3** a penalty attached to an offence as a means of enforcing the law **4a** a consideration, principle, or influence (eg of conscience) that determines moral action or judgment **b** a mechanism of social control for enforcing a society's standards ⟨*in some societies shame may act as the principal* ~ *against wrongdoing*⟩ **c** official permission or authoritative ratification; approbation **5** *usu pl* an economic or military measure adopted to force a nation to change some policy or to comply with international law [MF or L; MF, fr L *sanction-, sanctio*, fr *sanctus*, pp of *sancire* to make holy – more at SACRED]

**²sanction** *vt* **1** to make valid or binding, usu by a formal procedure; ratify **2** to give effective or authoritative approval or consent to

**sanctity** /'sangktəti/ *n* **1** holiness of life and character; godliness **2a** the quality or state of being holy or sacred ⟨*the* ~ *of marriage*⟩ **b** *pl* sacred objects, obligations, or rights [ME *saunctite*, fr MF *saincteté*, fr L *sanctitat-, sanctitas*, fr *sanctus* holy]

**sanctuary** /'sangktyoo(ə)ri, -chəri/ *n* **1** a consecrated place: eg **1a** the ancient temple at Jerusalem or its HOLY OF HOLIES (sacred inner chamber) **b** the most sacred part of a religious building: eg **b(1)** the part of a Christian church in which the altar is placed **b(2)** the room in a Protestant church in which services of worship are held **c** a place (eg a church or a temple) for worship **2a** a place of refuge and protection **b(1)** a place where birds or animals are given special care or protection ⟨*a donkey* ~⟩ **b(2)** a refuge for wildlife, esp endangered wildlife, where predators are controlled and hunting is illegal **c** the immunity from punishment by law formerly extended to somebody taking refuge in a church or other sacred building [ME *sanctuarie*, fr MF *sainctuarie*, fr LL *sanctuarium*, fr L *sanctus* holy]

**sanctum** /'sangktəm/ *n, pl* **sanctums** *also* **sancta** /-tə/ **1** a sacred place **2** a place (eg a study or office) that is kept completely private ⟨*an editor's* ~⟩ [LL, fr L, neut of *sanctus* holy]

**sanctum sanctorum** /sangk'tawrəm/ *n* **1** HOLY OF HOLIES **2** *humorous* SANCTUM 2 [LL]

**Sanctus** /'sangktəs/ *n* a hymn of adoration sung or said before the prayer of consecration in the service of communion [ME, fr LL *Sanctus, sanctus, sanctus* Holy, holy, holy, opening of a hymn sung by the angels in Isa 6:3]

**Sanctus bell** *n* a bell rung by the server at several points (eg at the Sanctus) during the Roman Catholic Mass

**¹sand** /sand/ *n* **1a** a loose grainy material resulting from the disintegration of esp quartz rocks, that consists of rock or mineral particles smaller than gravel but coarser than silt, is a major constituent of cement, concrete, and glass, and is used as an abrasive, in making moulds for casting metal, and for lining furnaces; *specif* such material composed of particles between 0.02 and 2 millimetres (about 0.00079 and 0.079 inch) in diameter **b** soil containing 85 per cent or more of sand and a maximum of 10 per cent of clay; *broadly* sandy soil **2 sands** *pl*, **sand** an area of sand; a beach **3 sands** *pl*, **sand** the sand in an hourglass; *also* the moments of a lifetime measured (as if) with an hourglass ⟨*the* ~s *of this government run out very rapidly* – H J Laski⟩ **4** a yellowish-grey colour **5** *NAm informal* firm resolution; determination [ME, fr OE; akin to OHG *sant* sand, L *sabulum*, Gk *psammos* & *ammos* sand, *psēn* to rub] – **sand** *adj*

**²sand** *vt* **1** to sprinkle (as if) with sand ⟨~*ing the roads*⟩ **2** to cover or choke with sand ⟨*currents that have* ~ed *a harbour*⟩ – often + *up* **3** to smooth or dress by grinding or rubbing with an abrasive (eg sandpaper) – often + *down*

**sandal** /'sandl/ *n* **1** a shoe consisting of a sole held on to the foot by straps or thongs **2** a strap to hold on a slipper or low shoe [ME *sandalie*, fr L *sandalium*, fr Gk *sandalion*, dim. of *sandalon* sandal]

**sandalwood** /-‚wood/ *n* **1a** an Indo-Malayan semiparasitic tree (*Santalum album* of the family Santalaceae, the sandalwood family) with compact close-grained fragrant yellowish HEARTWOOD (hard central wood of a tree) **b** the heartwood of the sandalwood tree, much used in ornamental carving and cabinetwork **2** any of various trees yielding wood similar to true sandalwood; *also* the fragrant wood of such a tree [earlier *sandal*, fr ME, fr MF, fr ML *sandalum*, fr LGk *santalon*, deriv of Skt *candana*, of Dravidian origin; akin to Tamil *cāntu* sandalwood tree]

**sandalwood oil** *n* any of several ESSENTIAL OILS (class of natural plant oils) obtained from sandalwood trees; *esp* a pale yellow somewhat sticky fragrant liquid obtained from a sandalwood (*Santalum album*) and used chiefly in perfumes and soaps

**sandarac** *also* **sandarach** /'sandə‚rak/ *n* **1** sandarac tree, sandarac **1** a large N African tree (*Tetraclinis articulata*) of the pine family, with a hard durable fragrant wood much used in building; *also* any of several related Australian trees **2** a brittle faintly aromatic translucent RESIN obtained esp from the African sandarac tree and used chiefly in making varnish and as incense [L *sandaraca* red colouring, fr Gk *sandarakē* realgar, red pigment from realgar]

**¹sandbag** /'sand‚bag/ *n* a bag filled with sand or soil and used in esp temporary fortifications or constructions, as ballast, as a weapon, or as flood protection

**²sandbag** *vt* **-gg- 1** to barricade, stop up, or weight with sandbags **2a** to hit or stun with a sandbag **b** *NAm* to coerce by crude means – **sandbagger** *n*

**sandbank** /-‚bangk/ *n* a large deposit of sand, esp in a river or coastal waters

**sandbar** /-‚bah/ *n* a ridge of sand built up by currents in a river or sea

**sandblast** /'sand‚blahst/ *vt or n* (to treat with) a high-speed jet of sand propelled by air or steam (eg for engraving, cutting, or cleaning glass or stone) – **sandblaster** *n*

**¹sand-‚blind** *adj, archaic* having poor eyesight; PURBLIND [ME, prob fr (assumed) ME *samblind*, fr OE *sam-* half (akin to OHG *sāmi-* half) + *blind* – more at SEMI-]

**sandbox** /'sand‚boks/ *n* a box or receptacle containing loose sand: eg **a** a shaker formerly used for sprinkling sand on wet ink **b** a box carried on a train from which sand may be scattered on the rails to prevent slipping **c** *NAm* a box that contains sand for children to play in

**¹sand-‚cast** *vt* to make (a casting) by pouring metal into a mould made of sand – **sand casting** *n*

**sandcastle** /-‚kahsl/ *n* a model of a castle made in damp sand by children, esp at the seaside

**sand crack** *n* a crack in the wall of a horse's hoof, often causing lameness

**sand dollar** *n* any of numerous flat circular INVERTEBRATE animals (order Clypeastroidea of the class Echinoidea) related to the SEA URCHINS, that live chiefly on sandy bottoms in shallow water

**sand eel** *n* any of various silvery eel-like sea fishes (family Ammodytidae) that have a single fin set in a groove along the back, live in large schools, and are often found buried or burrowing in sand – called also SAND LANCE

**sander** /'sandə/ *n* one who or that which sands: eg **a** (a lorry carrying) a device for spreading sand on newly surfaced or icy roads **b** a machine or device that smooths, polishes, or scours by means of abrasive material, usu in the form of a disc or belt

**sanderling** /'sandəling/ *n* a small plump sandpiper (*Calidris alba*) with largely grey-and-white plumage [perh irreg fr *sand* + *-ling*]

**sand flea** *n* 1 CHIGOE 1 (tropical flea) 2 a sandhopper

**sand fly** *n* any of various small biting flies (esp family Psychodidae) that transmit diseases

**sandfly fever** *n* a short-lasting virus disease that is characterized by fever, headache, pain in the eyes, and general nonspecific feelings of illness, and that is transmitted by the bite of a SAND FLY (*Phlebotomus papatasii*)

**sandglass** /'sand‚glahs/ *n* an instrument (eg an hourglass) for measuring time by the running of sand

**sand grouse** *n* any of numerous birds (family Pteroclidae) of dry parts of Europe, Asia, and Africa, that have long pointed wings and tail, grey or brown plumage, and resemble the closely related pigeons in structure but have downy young capable of leaving the nest shortly after hatching

**sandhi** /'sandi/ *n* the modification of a speech sound according to context ⟨*the change of a* to an *before a vowel is an example of* ~⟩ [Skt *saṁdhi*, lit., placing together]

**sandhog** /'sand‚hog/ *n, chiefly NAm* a labourer who works on underwater construction projects (eg tunnels) in an air-filled watertight cabin

**sandhopper** /'sand‚hopə/ *n* any of numerous flattened shrimplike INVERTEBRATE animals (family Talitridae of the order Amphipoda, class Crustacea) that live on beaches and leap like fleas – called also BEACH FLEA

**sand lance** *n* SAND EEL (eel-like fish)

**sand lizard** *n* a common grey to brown European lizard (*Lacerta agilis*) that is 15 to 20 centimetres (about 6 to 8 inches) in length

**sand martin** *n* a small martin (*Riparia riparia*) of the N hemisphere that has brown upperparts and white underparts and that usu nests in colonies in holes bored into banks of sand

**sand painting** *n* a ceremonial design made by Navaho and Pueblo American Indian tribes using various materials (eg coloured sands) on a flat surface of sand or buckskin

¹**sandpaper** /-‚paypə/ *n* paper to which a thin layer of sand has been glued for use in smoothing paintwork, wood, etc; *broadly* any abrasive paper (eg glasspaper) – **sandpapery** *adj*

²**sandpaper** *vt* to rub (as if) with sandpaper

**sandpiper** /-‚piepə/ *n* any of numerous small WADING BIRDS (suborder Charadrii) of the N hemisphere, having long slender legs and distinguished from the related plovers chiefly by the longer and soft-tipped bill [fr its shrill piping cry]

**sandpit** /-‚pit/ *n, chiefly Br* an enclosure containing sand for children to play in

**sand pump** *n* a pump used for clearing excavations, tunnels, etc of wet sand

**sandshoe** /-‚shooh/ *n, chiefly Br* a plimsoll

**sand smelt** *n* SILVERSIDES (small fish)

**sandspout** /'sand‚spowt/ *n* a column of sand raised by a desert whirlwind

**sandstone** /-‚stohn/ *n* a SEDIMENTARY (formed by the accumulation of deposited rock fragments) rock consisting of sand grains, usu composed of quartz, held together by a cement (eg SILICA or CALCIUM CARBONATE)

**sandstorm** /-‚stawm/ *n* a windstorm driving clouds of sand, esp in a desert

**sand trap** *n, chiefly NAm* a depression containing sand on a golf course; a bunker

¹**sandwich** /'san(d)wij, -wich/ *n* **1a** two slices of usu buttered bread that contain a layer of meat, cheese, fish, or various sweet or savoury fillings; *also* a bread roll stuffed with a filling – compare OPEN SANDWICH **b** a sponge cake with a layer of filling **2** something resembling a sandwich in being layered or having a filling [John Montagu, 4th Earl of *Sandwich* †1792 E diplomat, for whom this food was devised so that he could eat without leaving the gaming-table]

²**sandwich** *vt* **1** to make (as if) into a sandwich; *esp* to insert or enclose *between* two things of a different quality or character **2** to create room for – often + *in* or *between* ⟨~ *a rest between engagements*⟩ ⟨*can* ~ *you in between 4:30 and 5:00*⟩

³**sandwich** *adj* **1** of or used for sandwiches ⟨~ *bread*⟩ **2** *Br* of a SANDWICH COURSE ⟨~ *students*⟩ ⟨*the* ~ *method of a study* – *The New Polytechnics*⟩

**sandwich board** *n* either of two boards hung in front of and behind the body by straps from the shoulders and used esp to display advertisements

**sandwich course** *n* a British vocational course during which a student spends alternate periods of several months in college and in employment

**sandwich man** *n* somebody who advertises a business by wearing SANDWICH BOARDS

**sandwich tern** *n* a European tern (*Sterna sandvicensis*) that has whitish plumage, a black-topped head, long wings, and a long black bill with a yellow tip [*Sandwich*, town in Kent, England]

**sandworm** /'sand‚wuhm/ *n* any of several large segmented worms (class Polychaeta) that burrow in sand and are often used as bait by fishermen; *esp* LUGWORM

**sandwort** /'sand‚wuht/ *n* any of several usu low-growing plants (esp genera *Minuartia*, *Arenaria*, *Honkenya*, and *Moehringia*) of the pink family, that grow in tufts usu in dry sandy regions

**sandy** /'sandi/ *adj* **1** consisting of, containing, or covered with sand **2** resembling sand in colour or texture – **sandiness** *n*

**sand yacht** *n* a light wheeled vehicle that is propelled by sails and is used for recreation and racing on sand

**sane** /sayn/ *adj* **1** mentally sound; *esp* able to anticipate and assess the effect of one's actions **2** proceeding from a sound mind; rational ⟨*a* ~ *assessment of the consequences*⟩ **antonyms** insane, mad [L *sanus* healthy, sane] – **sanely** *adv*, **saneness** *n*

**Sanforized** /'sanfəriezd/ *trademark* – used for fabrics that are shrunk by a mechanical process before being manufactured into articles (eg clothing)

**sang** /sang/ *past of* SING

**sangaree** /‚sang·gə'ree/ *n* **1** a sweetened iced drink of wine or sometimes of ale, beer, or spirits garnished with nutmeg **2** sangria [Sp *sangria*]

**sangfroid** /‚song'frwah/ *n* self-possession or coolness, esp under strain [Fr *sang-froid*, lit., cold blood]

**sangria, sangria** /sang'gree-ə/ *n* a usu cold punch made of red wine, fruit juice, and SODA WATER [Sp *sangria*, lit., bleeding, fr *sangre* blood, modif of L *sanguin-*, *sanguis*]

**sanguinary** /'sang·gwin(ə)ri/ *adj, formal* **1** bloodthirsty, murderous ⟨~ *hatred*⟩ **2** accompanied or characterized by bloodshed; bloody ⟨*a bitter and* ~ *war*⟩ **3** readily punishing with death ⟨~ *laws*⟩ [L *sanguinarius*, fr *sanguin-*, *sanguis* blood] – **sanguinarily** *adv*

¹**sanguine** /'sang·gwin/ *adj* **1** having blood as the predominating HUMOUR (body fluid believed in medieval physiology to determine a person's disposition); *also* having the bodily form and temperament held to be characteristic of such predominance and marked by sturdiness, high colour, and cheerfulness **2** confident, optimistic **3** *formal* **3a** (consisting) of blood **b** SANGUINARY 1 **c** ruddy ⟨*a* ~ *complexion*⟩ [ME *sanguin*, fr MF, fr L *sanguineus*, fr *sanguin-*, *sanguis*] – **sanguinity** *n*

²**sanguine** *n* (a pencil producing) a bloodred colour

**sanguineous** /sang'gwiniəs/ *adj, formal* **1** bloodred **2** of or involving bloodshed; bloodthirsty **3** of or containing blood [L *sanguineus*]

**sanguinolent** /sang'gwinələnt/ *adj, formal* of, containing, or tinged with blood ⟨~ *sputum*⟩ [L *sanguinolentus*, fr *sanguin-*, *sanguis*]

**Sanhedrin** /'sanidrin, san'heedrin, -'hedrin/ *n taking sing or pl vb* the supreme council and tribunal of the Jews before 70 AD headed by the High Priest and having religious, civil, and criminal jurisdiction [LHeb *sanhedhrīn gĕdhōlāh* great council]

**sanicle** /'sanikl/ *n* any of several widespread plants (genus *Sanicula*, esp *Sanicula europaea*) of the carrot family having fruits covered in hooked bristles and roots that were formerly used in medicine [ME, fr MF, fr ML *sanicula*, prob fr L *sanus* healthy]

**sanies** /'sayni‚eez/ *n* a thin sanious discharge from an ulcer, infected wound, etc [L]

**sanious** /'sayniəs/ *adj* consisting of a thin mixture of watery blood SERUM and pus with a slightly bloody tinge [L *saniosus*, fr *sanies*]

**sanitarian** /‚sani'teəriən/ *n, chiefly NAm* an expert on community sanitation; *esp* one employed by a public body

**sanitarium** /‚sani'teəriəm/ *n, pl* **sanitariums, sanitaria** /-riə/ *NAm* a sanatorium [NL, fr L *sanitat-*, *sanitas* health]

**sanitary** /'sanit(ə)ri/ *adj* **1** of or promoting health ⟨~ *measures*⟩ **2** free from filth, infection, or dangers to health [Fr *sanitaire*, fr L *sanitas*]

**sanitary belt** *n* a narrow belt which is worn to hold a SANITARY TOWEL in place

**sanitary napkin** *n*, *NAm* SANITARY TOWEL

**sanitary towel** *n* a disposable absorbent pad in a gauze covering, worn during menstruation or after childbirth to absorb the discharge from the womb

**sanitary ware** *n* ceramic plumbing fixtures (eg sinks or toilet bowls)

**sanitate** /'sanitayt/ *vt* to make sanitary, esp by providing with sanitary appliances or facilities [back-formation fr *sanitation*]

**sanitation** /,sani'taysh(ə)n/ *n* (the promotion of hygiene and prevention of disease by) the maintenance or improvement of sanitary conditions

**sanit·ize, -ise** /'sani,tiez/ *vt, chiefly NAm* **1** to make sanitary by cleaning, sterilizing, etc **2** to make more acceptable by removing offensive or undesirable features ⟨~ *a document*⟩ [L *sanitas* health] – **sanitizer** *n*, **sanitization** *n*

**sanitorium** /,sani'tawriəm/ *n, pl* **sanitoriums, sanitoria** /-riə/ *NAm* a sanatorium [by alter. (influenced by *sanitarium*)]

**sanity** /'sanəti/ *n* being sane; *esp* soundness or health of mind [ME *sanite*, fr L *sanit-, sanitas* health, sanity, fr *sanus* healthy, sane]

**San Jose scale** /,san hoh'zay/ *n* a SCALE INSECT (*Aspidiotus perniciosus*) that probably originated in Asia and that causes great damage to fruit trees in the USA [*San Jose*, city in California where it first appeared in the USA]

**sank** /sangk/ *past of* SINK

**Sankhya** /'sangkyə/ *n* an orthodox Hindu philosophy teaching salvation through knowledge of the distinction between matter and spirit [Skt *sāṁkyha*, lit., based on calculation]

**sannup** /'sanəp/ *n* a married male American Indian [Abnaki *senanbe*]

**sannyasi** /sun'yahsi/ *n* a Hindu beggar who has reached the last stage of earthly life [Hindi *sannyāsī*, fr Skt *sannyāsin*]

**sannyasin** /sun'yahsin/ *n* a sannyasi

**¹sans** /sanz/ *prep, archaic* without ⟨*my love to thee is sound,* ~ *crack or flaw* – Shak⟩ [ME *saun, sans,* fr MF *san, sans,* modif of L *sine* – more at SUNDER]

**²sans** *n, pl* **sans** SANS SERIF

**sansculotte** /,sanzkyoo'lot (*Fr* sãkylot)/ *n* **1** an extreme radical republican in France at the time of the Revolution **2a** a coarse or disreputable person **b** a radical or violent extremist in politics [Fr *sans-culotte*, lit., without breeches] – **sansculottic, sansculottish** *adj*, **sansculottism** *n*

**sansevieria** /,sansi'viəriə/ *n* any of various tropical chiefly Asian and African plants (genus *Sansevieria*) of the lily family that have slender sharp-edged variegated leaves and are often cultivated as house plants [NL, genus name, fr Raimondo di Sangro, Prince of *San Severo* †1774 It scholar]

**Sanskrit, sanscrit** /'sanskrit/ *n* **1** an ancient sacred INDIC language of India and of Hinduism **2** classical Sanskrit together with the older VEDIC and with Sanskritic [Skt *saṁskṛta*, lit., perfected, fr *sam* together + *karoti* he makes] – **Sanskrit** *adj*, **Sanskritist** *n*

**Sanskritic** /san'skritik/ *n* **1** INDIC **2** a group of INDIC languages (eg Pali, Hindi, and Punjabi) developed directly from Sanskrit – **Sanskritic** *adj*

**sans serif, sanserif** /,san 'serif/ *n* a letter or typeface with no SERIFS (decorative flourishes) [prob fr *sans* + modif of D *schreef* stroke – more at SERIF]

**Santa Claus** /'santə ,klawz, ,-- '-/ *also* **Santa** *n* FATHER CHRISTMAS [modif of D *Sinterklaas*, alter. of *Sint Nikolaas* Saint Nicholas, 4th-c bishop of Myra in Asia Minor and patron saint of children]

**Santa Gertrudis** /,santə gə'troohdis/ *n* (any of) a breed of cherry-red beef cattle developed in Texas from a Brahman-Shorthorn cross and valued for their hardiness in hot climates [*Santa Gertrudis*, section of the King Ranch in Kingsville, Texas]

**santir** /san'tiə/ *n* a Persian DULCIMER (stringed instrument) [Ar *sanṭīr, sanṭūr,* fr Gk *psaltērion* psaltery]

**santolina** /,santə'leenə, -'lienə/ *n* any of a genus (*Santolina*) of aromatic low-growing Mediterranean shrubs of the daisy family that have finely cut leaves and flower heads on long stalks [NL, genus name, alter. of L *santonica*]

**santonica** /san'tonikə/ *n* **1** an aromatic European wormwood plant (*Artemisia maritima*) **2** the dried unopened flower heads of a wormwood plant (*Artemisia cina*) containing santonin [NL, fr L (*herba*) *santonica* a plant (prob wormwood), fem of

*santonicus* of the Santoni, fr *Santoni,* a people of SW Gaul]

**santonin** /'santənin/ *n* a chemical compound, $C_{15}H_{18}O_3$, found in santonica plants and used formerly to treat infections with parasitic roundworms [ISV, fr NL *santonica*]

**santour** /san'tooə/ *n* a santir

**¹sap** /sap/ *n* **1a** the liquid in a plant; *specif* the watery solution containing dissolved sugars, mineral salts, etc that circulates through the conducting system of a plant **b(1)** a body liquid (eg blood) essential to life, health, or vigour **b(2)** vitality, vigour **2** *informal* a foolish or gullible person [ME, fr OE *sæp;* akin to OHG *saf* sap]

**²sap** *vt* **-pp-** to drain or deprive of sap

**³sap** *n* the extension of a trench from within the trench itself to a point beneath or near an enemy's fortifications [MF & OIt; MF *sappe* hoe, fr OIt *zappa*]

**⁴sap** *vb* **-pp-** *vi* to proceed by or dig a sap ~ *vt* **1** to subvert or destroy (as if) by undermining ⟨~ped *by floods, their houses fell* – John Dryden⟩ ⟨~ped *the morale of their troops*⟩ **2** to weaken or exhaust gradually ⟨*the heat and humidity* ~ped *his strength*⟩ **3** to operate against or pierce by a sap

**sapajou** /'sapəjooh/ *n* CAPUCHIN 3 (S American monkey) [Fr, fr Tupi]

**sapanwood** /'sapən,wood/ *n* SAPPANWOOD

**sapele** /sə'peeli/ *n* **1** any of several W African mahogany trees (genus *Entandrophragma*) with hard often lightweight cedar-scented wood **2** **sapele, sapele mahogany** the hard pinkish to deep reddish-brown often striped wood of a sapele, used esp for making furniture [native name in W Africa]

**saphead** /'sap,hed/ *n, informal* a stupid person; a sap – **sapheaded** *adj*

**saphenous** /sə'feenəs/ *adj, anatomy* of or being either of the two chief veins of the leg that lie just below the skin [*saphena* (saphenous vein), fr ME, fr ML, fr Ar *ṣāfin*]

**sapid** /'sapid/ *adj* **1** having flavour; *esp* having a strong agreeable flavour **2** *formal* agreeable to the mind; engaging [L *sapidus* tasty, fr *sapere* to taste – more at SAGE] – **sapidity** *n*

**sapiens** /'saypyənz/ *adj* of or being recent man (*Homo sapiens*) as distinguished from various extinct forms [NL (specific epithet of *Homo sapiens*), fr L, pp of *sapere* to be wise]

**sapient** /'saypyənt/ *adj, formal* possessing or expressing great wisdom or discernment [ME, fr MF, fr L *sapient-, sapiens,* fr prp of *sapere* to taste, be wise] – **sapience** *n*, **sapiently** *adv*

**sapless** /'saplis/ *adj* **1** having no sap; dry **2** lacking vitality; feeble, vapid – **saplessness** *n*

**sapling** /'sapling/ *n* **1** a young tree **2** a youth **3** a young greyhound

**sapodilla** /,sapə'dilə/ *n* **1** a tropical evergreen tree (*Achras zapota* of the family Sapotaceae, the sapodilla family) that has hard reddish wood, a milky juice that yields CHICLE (gummy substance used in chewing gum), and an edible fruit **2** **sapodilla, sapodilla plum** the fruit of the sapodilla, having a rough brownish skin and very sweet yellowish-brown pulp [Sp *zapotillo,* dim. of *zapote,* fr Nahuatl *tzapotl*]

**saponaceous** /,sapə'nayshəs/ *adj* **1** resembling or containing soap **2** *formal* marked by insincere flattery ⟨~ *condescension*⟩ [NL *saponaceus*, fr L *sapon-, sapo* soap, of Gmc origin; akin to OE *sāpe* soap] – **saponaceousness** *n*

**saponify** /sə'ponifie/ *vt* **1** to convert (eg fat) into (a) soap; *specif, chemistry* to break down (a fat) with alkali to form a soap and GLYCEROL **2** *chemistry* to break down (an ESTER) into the component acid and alcohol parts ~ *vi* to undergo saponifying [Fr *saponifier*, fr L *sapon-, sapo* soap] – **saponifier** *n*, **saponifiable** *adj*, **saponification** *n*

**saponin** /'sapənin/ *n* any of various GLUCOSIDES (chemical compounds derived from glucose) that occur in plants (eg soapwort), have the properties of detergents, and produce a soapy lather; *esp* a moisture-absorbing mixture of saponins used esp as a foaming agent and detergent [Fr *saponine*, fr L *sapon-, sapo* soap]

**saponite** /'sapəniet/ *n* a clay mineral that consists of a SILICATE of magnesium and aluminium chemically combined with water and that occurs in soft soapy formless masses in veins and cavities of rocks and minerals (eg SERPENTINE) [Sw *saponit*, fr L *sapon-, sapo* soap]

**sapor** /'saypaw, -pə/ *n* a property (eg bitterness) that affects the sense of taste; savour, flavour [ME, fr L – more at SAVOUR] – **saporous** *adj*

**sapota** /sə'pohtə/ *n* a sapodilla [modif of Sp *zapote*]

**sappanwood** *also* **sapanwood** /'sapən,wood/ *n* (the wood, from which a red dye is obtained, of) an E Indian tree (*Caes-*

*alpinia sappan*) of the pea family [Malay *sapang* heartwood of sappanwood + E *wood*]

**sapper** /'sapə/ *n* 1 a soldier specializing in battlefield construction (eg digging trenches and laying mines) 2 a soldier of the Royal Engineers; *specif* a private in the Royal Engineers [⁴*sap* + ²*-er*]

**sapphic** /'safik/ *adj* 1 *of poetic metre* (consisting of a 4-line stanza made up chiefly of units of one strong and one weak beat (TROCHEES) and units of one strong and two weak beats (DACTYLS) 2 lesbian [*Sappho fl ab* 600 BC Gk poetess & reputed homosexual]

**sapphics** /'safiks/ *n pl* a verse in sapphic stanzas

**sapphire** /'safie·ə/ *n* 1 any transparent or translucent variety of CORUNDUM (very hard mineral) of a colour other than red, that is used or is of the quality to be used as a gem; *esp* a highly valued transparent rich blue variety – compare RUBY 2 a deep purplish-blue colour [ME *safir*, fr OF, fr L *sapphirus*, fr Gk *sappheiros*, fr Heb *sappīr*, fr Skt *śanipriya*, lit., dear to the planet Saturn, fr *Sani* Saturn + *priya* dear] – **sapphire** *adj*

**sapphirine** /'safirien/ *adj* 1 made of sapphire 2 resembling a sapphire, esp in colour

**sapphism** /'safiz(ə)m/ *n* lesbianism [*Sappho* + *-ism*] – **sapphist** *n*

**sappy** /'sapi/ *adj* 1a containing much sap b resembling or consisting largely of SAPWOOD (soft outer wood of a tree) 2 *chiefly NAm informal* 2a foolishly sentimental; mawkish b lacking in good sense; silly – **sappiness**

**sapr-** /sapr-/, **sapro-** *comb form* 1 putrefaction ⟨*sapro*genic⟩ 2 dead or decaying organic matter ⟨*sapro*phyte⟩ [Gk, fr *sapros* rotten]

**saprobe** /'saprohb/ *n* a saprobic organism [ISV *sapr-* + Gk *bios* life – more at QUICK]

**saprobic** /sa'prohbik/ *adj* living on dead or decaying organic matter; saprophytic or saprozoic; *also* living in or being an environment rich in organic matter and relatively free from oxygen – **saprobically** *adv*

**saprogenic** /ˌsaproh'jenik, ˌsaprə-/ *adj* of, causing, or resulting from putrefaction or decay – **saprogenicity** *n*

**saprolite** /'saprəliet/ *n* disintegrated rock that lies in its original place – **saprolitic** *adj*

**sapropel** /'saprə,pel/ *n* a mud, sludge, or ooze rich in decaying organic matter (eg algae) that collects in swamps, below stagnant water, etc [ISV *sapr-* + Gk *pēlos* clay, mud]

**sapropelic** /ˌsaprə'pelik/ *adj* living in or formed from sapropel ⟨~ *coal*⟩

**saprophagous** /sa'profəgəs, sə-/ *adj, esp of an animal* feeding on decaying matter [NL *saprophagus*, fr *sapr-* + *-phagus* -phagous] – **sparophage** *n*

**saprophyte** /'saprəfiet/ *n* a saprophytic organism [ISV]

**saprophytic** /ˌsaproh'fitik, ˌsaprə-/ *adj* 1 *esp of a plant, bacterium, or fungus* living on or obtaining nourishment from dead or decaying plant and animal tissues 2 of or being nutrition in which food is obtained from dead or decaying organic matter – **saprophytically** *adv*

**saprozoic** /ˌsaprə'zoh·ik/ *adj* saprophytic – used of an animal – **saprozoite** *n*

**sapsago** /'sapsəgoh/ *n* a very hard green skim-milk Swiss cheese flavoured with the powdered leaves of an aromatic plant (*Trigonella coerulea*) of the pea family, and shaped in flattened cones [modif of Ger *schabziger*, fr *schaben* to scrape + Ger dial. *ziger* whey, whey cheese]

**sapsucker** /'sap,sukə/ *n* any of various N American woodpeckers (esp genus *Sphyrapicus*) that feed on the sap of trees

**sapwood** /'sap,wood/ *n* the younger softer outer portion of the wood of a tree trunk or branch, that lies below the bark and surrounds the central core of harder HEARTWOOD, consists of living tissue that conducts water, and is more porous, less durable, and usu lighter in colour than the heartwood

**saraband, sarabande** /'sarəband, ,--'-/ *n* 1 a stately court dance of the 17th and 18th centuries resembling the minuet 2 a musical composition or movement (eg in a Baroque suite) with three beats to the bar and the accent on the second beat [Fr *sarabande*, fr Sp *zarabanda*]

**Saracen** /'sarəs(ə)n/ *n* a member of a nomadic people of the deserts between Syria and Arabia; *broadly* a Muslim at the time of the Crusades [ME, fr LL *Saracenus*, fr LGk *Sarakēnos*] – **Saracen, Saracenic** *adj*

**Saran** /sə'ran/ *trademark* – used for a tough flexible plastic that softens when heated and can be formed into fibres, moulded articles, protective coatings, etc

**sarape** /sə'rahpi/ *n* SERAPE (woollen Mexican shawl)

**sarc-** /sahk-/, **sarco-** *comb form* 1 flesh ⟨*sarco*phagous⟩ 2 STRIATED MUSCLE ⟨*sarco*plasmic⟩ [Gk *sark-, sarko-*, fr *sark-, sarx*]

**sarcasm** /'sahkaz(ə)m/ *n* 1 a sharp and usu satirical or ironic remark designed to taunt or inflict pain ⟨*tired of his contemptuous* ~s⟩ 2 (the use of) caustic and often ironic language to express contempt or bitterness, esp towards an individual **synonyms** see WIT [Fr *sarcasme*, fr LL *sarcasmos*, fr Gk *sarkasmos*, fr *sarkazein* to tear flesh, bite the lips in rage, sneer, fr *sark-, sarx* flesh; akin to Av *thwarəs* to cut]

**sarcastic** /sah'kastik/ *adj* 1 containing or constituting sarcasm ⟨~ *criticism*⟩ 2 using or tending to use sarcasm; caustic ⟨*a* ~ *critic*⟩ [fr *sarcasm*, by analogy to *enthusiasm:enthusiastic*] – **sarcastically** *adv*

**synonyms** Sarcastic, ironic, satirical, caustic, and sardonic can all mean "able or trying to wound". Sarcastic implies the cruel and witty exposure of somebody's weaknesses ⟨*a horrid sarcastic demoniacal laughter, that almost sent the schoolmistress into fits* – W M Thackeray⟩. Such an exposure may also be ironic or ironical, "expressing the opposite of the intended literal meaning" ⟨*a man so excessively ugly that he went by the ironical appellation of "beauty"* – Herman Melville⟩; but the mockery suggested by ironic(al) is not necessarily very cruel. Satirical applies particularly to the witty written censure of vice and folly, using irony and sarcasm. Caustic emphasizes a bitterness which need not be witty ⟨*a bitter, caustic, and backbiting humour* – Sir Walter Scott⟩. Sardonic implies cynical disdain, which may be quite cheerful ⟨*came to the funeral, full of calm, sardonic glee* – Arnold Bennett⟩.

**sarcenet, sarsenet** /'sahsnit/ *n* a soft thin silk used for dresses, veilings, or trimmings [ME *sarcenet*, fr AF *sarzinett*, prob fr *Sarzin* Saracen, fr LL *Saracenus*]

**sarcocarp** /'sahkoh,kahp/ *n, botany* 1 a usu thickened and fleshy middle part (MESOCARP) of a fruit 2 a fleshy fruit [Fr *sarcocarpe*, fr *sarc-* + *-carpe* -carp]

¹**sarcoid** /'sahkoyd/ *adj* of or resembling flesh, esp in consistency; fleshy, spongy ⟨~ *tissues*⟩

²**sarcoid** *n* 1 any of various diseases characterized esp by the formation of swellings or lumps in the skin 2 a swelling characteristic of sarcoid or of sarcoidosis

**sarcoidosis** /ˌsahkoy'dohsis/ *n, pl* **sarcoidoses** /-seez/ a long-lasting disease of unknown cause that is characterized by the formation of lumps or swellings, esp in the LYMPH NODES, lungs, bones, and skin [NL]

**sarcolemma** /ˌsahkə'lemə/ *n* the thin transparent sheath enclosing a STRIATED MUSCLE fibre [NL, fr *sarc-* + Gk *lemma* husk – more at LEMMA] – **sarcolemmal** *adj*

**sarcoma** /sah'kohmə/ *n, pl* **sarcomas, sarcomata** /-mətə/ a usu cancerous tumour arising esp in muscle, ligaments, tendons, and similar binding and supporting tissue (CONNECTIVE TISSUE) [NL, fr Gk *sarkōmat-, sarkōma* fleshy growth, fr *sarkoun* to grow flesh, fr *sark-, sarx* flesh] – **sarcomatous** *adj*

**sarcomatosis** /sah,kohmə'tohsis/ *n, pl* **sarcomatoses** /-seez/ a disease characterized by the presence and spread of sarcomas [NL]

**sarcomere** /'sahkəmiə/ *n* any of the repeating structural units making up a FIBRIL (long threadlike element forming part of a fibre) of STRIATED MUSCLE – **sarcomeric** *adj*

**sarcophagous** /sah'kofəgəs, sahco'fajik/ *adj* flesh-eating, carnivorous [L *sarcophagus* flesh-eating, fr Gk *sarkophagos*] – **sarcophagy** *n*

**sarcophagus** /sah'kofəgəs/ *n, pl* **sarcophagi** /-gi, -gie/ *also* **sarcophaguses** a stone coffin; *esp* one bearing carved ornament or inscription [L *sarcophagus* (*lapis*) limestone used for coffins, fr Gk (*lithos*) *sarkophagos*, lit., flesh-eating stone, fr *sark-* *sarc-* + *phagein* to eat – more at BAKSHEESH]

**sarcoplasm** /'sahkoh,plaz(ə)m, 'sahkə-/ *n* the jellylike material (CYTOPLASM) surrounding the FIBRILS (long threadlike elements) of a STRIATED MUSCLE fibre [NL *sarcoplasma*, fr *sarc-* + *plasma*] – **sarcoplasmic** *adj*

**sarcoplasmic reticulum** /ˌsahkoh,plazmik ri'tikyooləm/ *n* the complex series of intermeshing membranes (ENDOPLASMIC RETICULUM) inside a STRIATED MUSCLE fibre

**sarcoptic mange** /sah'koptik/ *n* a skin disease (MANGE) caused by mites (genus *Sarcoptes*) burrowing in the skin, esp of the head and face; *esp* SCABIES when occurring in domestic animals [NL *Sarcoptes*, genus of mites, fr *sarc-* + Gk *koptein* to cut – more at CAPON]

**sarcosome** /'sahkə,sohm/ *n* a MITOCHONDRION (energy-producing body in a cell) of a STRIATED MUSCLE fibre [NL *sarcosoma*, fr *sarc-* + *-soma* -some] – **sarcosomal** *adj*

**sard** /sahd/ *n* a deep orange-red variety of CHALCEDONY (form of quartz) used as a gemstone [Fr *sarde*, fr L *sarda*]

**sardine** /sah'deen/ *n, pl* **sardines**, *esp collectively* **sardine 1** any of several small or immature soft-finned fishes of the herring family; *esp* the young of the European pilchard (*Sardinia pilchardus*) when of a size suitable for preserving for food **2** any of various small fishes (eg an anchovy) resembling the true sardines or similarly preserved for food [ME *sardeine*, fr MF *sardine*, fr L *sardina*]

**Sardinian** /sah'dinyən, -ni·ən/ *n* **1** a native or inhabitant of Sardinia **2** the ROMANCE language of Sardinia [*Sardinia*, island in the Mediterranean] – **Sardinian** *adj*

**sardius** /'sahdiəs/ *n* **1** (a) sard **2** a precious stone worn by the Jewish High Priest [LL, fr (*lapis*) *sardius* (stone) of Sardis, fr Gk *sardios* (*lithos*), fr *Sardeis* Sardis, ancient city in Asia Minor]

**sardonic** /sah'donik/ *adj* disdainfully or cynically humorous; derisively mocking ⟨*a ~ comment*⟩ ⟨*his ~ expression*⟩ **synonyms** see SARCASTIC [Fr *sardonique*, fr Gk *sardonios*, alter. (influenced by *Sardonios* Sardinian, referring to a Sardinian plant reputed to cause convulsive grimaces) of *sardanios*] – **sardonically** *adv*

**sardonyx** /'sahdəniks/ *n* an onyx having parallel bands of orange-red sard and milky-white CHALCEDONY (form of quartz) and used as a gemstone [ME *sardonix*, fr L *sardonyx*, fr Gk, prob fr *sardios* sard + *onyx* onyx, nail]

**sargasso** /sah'gasoh/ *n, pl* **sargassos** a large mass of floating vegetation, esp sargassums, in the sea [Pg *sargaço*]

**sargassum** /sah'gasəm/ *n* any of a genus (*Sargassum*) of brown seaweeds that have a branching THALLUS (plant body) with outgrowths variously differentiated as leafy segments, sporebearing structures, and small hollow floats or AIR BLADDERS that enable the seaweed to float on the surface of the water [NL, genus name, fr ISV *sargasso*]

**sarge** /sahj/ *n, informal* a sergeant [by shortening & alter.]

**sari** *also* **saree** /'sahri/ *n* a garment worn by Hindu women that consists of a length of lightweight cloth draped so that one end forms a long skirt and the other a head or shoulder covering [Hindi *sārī*, fr Skt *śāṭī*]

**sarin** /'sahrən, zah'reen/ *n* an extremely poisonous chemical warfare agent, $C_4H_{10}FO_2P$, that is a NERVE GAS causing respiratory failure, convulsions, coma, and death [Ger]

**sark** /sahk/ *n, dial chiefly Scot* a shirt [ME (Sc) *serk*, fr OE *serc*; akin to ON *serkr* shirt]

**sarking** /'sahking/ *n, Br* boards or felt fixed between rafters and roofing material (eg slates or tiles) [ME (Sc), fr *serken* to clothe in a shirt, sheathe, fr *serk* shirt]

**sarky** /'sahki/ *adj, chiefly Br informal* sarcastic [by shortening & alter.]

**sarod** *also* **sarode** /sə'rohd/ *n* a lute of N India [Hindi *sarod*, fr Per] – **sarodist** *n*

**sarong** /sə'rong, 'sahrong/ *n* **1** a loose skirt made of a long strip of cloth wrapped round the body and traditionally worn by men and women in Malaysia and the Pacific islands **2** cloth for sarongs [Malay *kain sarong* cloth sheath]

**saros cycle** /'sayros/ *n* a cycle of about 6585 days during which a particular sequence of eclipses occurs and after which the centres of the sun and moon return to the same relative positions [Gk *saros*, fr Assyrian-Babylonian *shāru* period of 3600 years]

**sarracenia** /ˌsarə'seenyə/ *n* any of an originally N American genus (*Sarracenia*) of plants of the PITCHER-PLANT family with large conspicuous flowers and large tubular or urn-shaped leaves adapted to catch and digest insects [NL, genus name, fr Michel *Sarrazin* †1734 Fr physician & naturalist]

**sarrusophone** /sə'roohzəfohn, -'ru-/ *n* an instrument of the oboe family that is made of metal and is used esp in military bands [*Sarrus*, 19th-c Fr bandmaster + *-o-* + *-phone*]

**sarsaparilla** /ˌsahs(ə)pə'rilə/ *n* **1a** any of various tropical American trailing or climbing plants (genus *Smilax*) of the lily family with prickly stems **b** the dried roots of a sarsaparilla or an extract of these used esp as a flavouring **2** *chiefly NAm* a sweetened fizzy drink flavoured with birch oil and SASSAFRAS (dried root bark) [Sp *zarzaparrilla*, fr *zarza* bush + *parrilla*, dim. of *parra* vine]

**sarsen** /'sahs(ə)n/ *n* a large mass of sandstone left after the erosion of a once continuous bed or layer [short for *sarsen stone*, prob alter. of *Saracen stone*, ie a pagan stone or monument]

**sarsenet** /'sahsnit/ *n* SARCENET (soft thin silk)

**sartorial** /sah'tawri·əl/ *adj, formal or humorous* with regard to clothing ⟨*~ elegance*⟩ – used esp with reference to men [L *sartor* tailor] – **sartorially** *adv*

**sartorius** /sah'tawri·əs/ *n, pl* **sartorii** /-ri·ee/ a long muscle that runs from the front of the thigh to the inside of the leg just below the knee and that assists in bending the knee and in rotating the leg to the cross-legged sitting position [NL, fr L *sartor* tailor, fr *sartus*, pp of *sarcire* to mend – more at EXORCISE; fr its being the muscle involved in adopting the cross-legged position of a tailor]

**Sarum** /'seərəm/ *adj* of or being the Roman Catholic rite as modified in Salisbury and used in England, Wales, and Ireland before the Reformation [ML *Sarum* Salisbury, prob by shortening & alter. fr *Sarisburia*]

**Sasanian** /sə'saynyən/ *adj or n* SASSANIAN (former ruling Persian dynasty)

**¹sash** /sash/ *n* a band of cloth worn round the waist or over one shoulder as a dress accessory or as the emblem of an honorary or military order [Ar *shāsh* muslin] – **sashed** *adj*

**²sash** *n, pl* **sash** *also* **sashes** the frame in which panes of glass are set in a window or door; *also* a window frame constructed so as to slide in vertical channels [prob modif of Fr *châssis* chassis (taken as pl)]

**¹sashay** /sa'shay/ *vi, NAm informal* **1** to walk or move casually or nonchalantly; saunter **2** to strut or move about ostentatiously **3** to proceed in a zigzag or sideways manner [alter. of *chassé*]

**²sashay** *n* a square-dance figure in which partners sidestep in a circle round each other with the man moving behind the woman

**sash cord** *n* a cord used to connect a SASH WEIGHT to a window sash

**sashimi** /'sushimi/ *n* a Japanese dish consisting of thinly sliced raw fish [Jap]

**sash weight** *n* either of two counterweights for balancing a window sash in a desired position

**sash window** *n* a window having two sashes that slide vertically in a frame, thus enabling the upper or lower part of the window to be opened

**sasin** /'sasin/ *n* BLACKBUCK (Indian antelope) [origin unknown]

**saskatoon** /ˌsaskə'toohn/ *n* a SERVICEBERRY shrub (*Amelanchier alnifolia*) of the N and W USA and Canada, with sweet edible usu purple berries [*Saskatoon*, city in SW Canada]

**Sasquatch** /'saskwach/ *n* a mysterious hairy manlike animal reported as existing in the mountain areas of W Canada [of Salishan origin]

**¹sass** /sas/ *n, NAm informal* impudent talk; backchat [back-formation fr *sassy*]

**²sass** *vt, NAm informal* to talk impudently or disrespectfully to

**sassafras** /'sasəfras/ *n* **1** a tall eastern N American tree (*Sassafras albidum*) of the laurel family with aromatic leaves, small clusters of yellow flowers, and dark blue berries **2** the dried aromatic root, esp the root bark, of the sassafras, used as a flavouring agent and as the source of a yellowish oil used for flavouring and in perfumery [Sp *sasafrás*]

**¹Sassanian, Sasanian** /sə'saynyən, -niən/ *adj* (having the characteristics) of the Sassanid dynasty of ancient Persia or its art or architecture

**²Sassanian, Sasanian** *n* a Sassanid

**Sassanid** /'sasənid/ *n* a member of a dynasty of Persian kings of the 3rd to 7th centuries AD [NL *Sassanidae* Sassanids, fr *Sassan*, founder of the dynasty] – **Sassanid** *adj*

**Sassenach** /'sasənakh/ *n, Scot & Irish chiefly derog* an English person [Ir Gael *Sasanach*, of Gmc origin; akin to OE *Seaxan* Saxons]

**sasswood** /'sas,wood/ *n* a W African tree (*Erythrophloeum guineense*) of the pea family with poisonous bark and hard strong insect-resistant wood [alter. of *sassywood*, fr *sassy* (prob of African origin; akin to Ewe *se³ se³wu³*, an African timber tree) + *wood*]

**sassy** /'sasi/ *adj, NAm informal* **1** impudent, saucy **2** vigorous, lively [alter. of *saucy*]

**sassy bark** *n* the bark of the sasswood tree formerly used as a poison in ORDEALS (primitive means of determining guilt or innocence)

**sat** /sat/ *past of* SIT

**Satan** /'sayt(ə)n/ *n* the adversary of God and lord of evil in Judaism and Christianity [ME, fr OE, fr LL, fr Gk, fr Heb *śāṭān* adversary, plotter]

**satang** /sa'tang, '--/ *n, pl* **satang, satangs** – see *baht* at MONEY table [Thai *satǎn*]

**satanic** /sə'tanik/ *adj* 1 (characteristic) of Satan or satanism ⟨~ *pride*⟩ ⟨~ *rites*⟩ 2 characterized by extreme cruelty or malevolence – **satanically** *adv*

**satanism** /'sayt(ə)niz(ə)m/ *n, often cap* 1 innate or calculated wickedness; diabolism 2 obsession with or attraction to evil; *specif* worship of Satan by the travesty of Christian ceremonies – **satanist** *n, often cap*

**satchel** /'sachəl/ *n* a usu stiff rectangular canvas and leather bag often with a shoulder strap; *esp* one carried by schoolchildren [ME *sachel*, fr MF, fr L *sacellus*, dim. of *saccus* bag – more at SACK] – **satchelful** *n*

¹**sate** /sayt, sat/ *archaic past of* SIT

²**sate** /sayt/ *vt* 1 to surfeit with something needed or desired; glut 2 to satisfy (eg a thirst) by indulging to the full *synonyms* see ²SATIATE [prob by shortening & alter. fr *satiate*]

**sateen** /sa'teen/ *n* a smooth durable shiny fabric resembling satin [alter. of *satin*]

**satellite** /'satl·iet/ *n* 1 an obsequious follower; a minion, sycophant 2a a heavenly body orbiting another of larger size b a man-made object or vehicle intended to orbit the earth, the moon, or another heavenly body 3 somebody or something attendant, subordinate, or dependent; *esp* a country politically and economically subject to another more powerful country 4 a town or suburb that is physically separate from an adjacent city but dependent on it (eg as a source of employment) [MF, fr L *satellit-*, *satelles* attendant] – **satellite** *adj*

**satiable** /'saysh(y)əbl/ *adj, formal* capable of being appeased or satisfied

¹**satiate** /'sayshiət, -ayt/ *adj, formal* filled to satiety; satiated

²**satiate** /'sayshiayt/ *vt* to satisfy (eg a need or desire or a person) to the point of excess [L *satiatus*, pp of *satiare*, fr *satis* enough – more at SAD] – **satiation** *n*

*synonyms* Satiate, sate, glut, gorge, surfeit, cloy, and pall can all mean "fill to excess". Satiate and sate once both implied merely complete satisfaction but now usually, especially sate, suggest overindulgence ⟨*so overwhelmed with information that our curiosity became sated*⟩. Glut and gorge can both mean either "fill" or "overfill", glut suggesting the sheer volume of what is ingested ⟨*leeches glutted with blood*⟩ and gorge suggesting a greed that is only abated at bursting point ⟨*gorge himself on eggs and bacon*⟩. Surfeit, and still more cloy, emphasizes the disgust or boredom that comes from excess, cloy adding the idea that what now disgusts was originally pleasant ⟨*Cordelia has been cloyed by her sisters' excessive protestations of affection* – Rebecca West⟩. Pall implies the loss of power to attract ⟨*seaside holidays began to pall*⟩ △ saturate

**satiety** /sə'tie·əti, 'sayshyəti/ *n, formal* 1 being fed or gratified to or beyond capacity; a surfeit, repletion 2 the aversion caused by overindulgence or sensual excess [MF *satieté*, fr L *satietat-*, *satietas*, fr *satis*]

¹**satin** /'satin/ *n* a fabric (eg of silk) in SATIN WEAVE with shiny face and dull back [ME, fr MF, prob fr Ar *zaytūnī*, fr *zaytūn*, ancient seaport in China]

²**satin** *adj* 1 made of or covered with satin ⟨~ *shoes*⟩ 2 satin, satiny suggestive of satin, esp in shiny appearance or smoothness to the touch ⟨*panels with an oiled* ~ *finish*⟩

**satin bird** *n* an Australian BOWERBIRD (*Ptilonorhynchus violaceus*) with glossy plumage that is violet-blue in the male and a light grey-green in the female

**satinet, satinette** /ˌsati'net/ *n* 1 a thin silk satin or imitation satin 2 a variation of SATIN WEAVE used in making satinet

**satin spar** *n* a soft fine fibrous variety of the calcium-containing minerals CALCITE or GYPSUM

**satin stitch** *n* a long embroidery stitch nearly alike on both sides and worked in straight parallel lines to block in a large area so closely as to resemble satin

**satin weave** *n* a weave in which the vertical threads (WARP 1a) predominate on the face to produce a smooth-faced fabric

**satinwood** /'satinˌwood/ *n* 1 an E Indian tree (*Chloroxylon swietenia*) of the mahogany family with shiny yellowish-brown wood; *also* any of various trees with similar wood 2 the wood of a satinwood used in furniture making, decorative inlay, marquetry, etc

**satire** /'satie·ə/ *n* 1 a literary work holding up human vices and follies to ridicule or scorn; *also* the genre of literature or drama constituted by such works 2 biting wit, irony, or sarcasm intended to expose and discredit foolishness or vice *synonyms* see SARCASTIC, WIT △ satyr [MF, fr L *satura*, *satira*, fr (*lanx*) *satura* full plate, medley, fr fem of *satur* sated; akin to L *satis* enough – more at SAD] – **satiric, satirical** *adj*, **satirically** *adv*

**satirist** /'satirist/ *n* somebody who satirizes; *esp* a writer of satires

**satir·ize, -ise** /'satiˌriez/ *vt* to censure or ridicule by means of satire ~ *vi* to utter or write satire

**satisfaction** /ˌsatis'faksh(ə)n/ *n* 1a the penance exacted by the Roman Catholic and Anglican churches as a punishment for a sin b reparation for sin and fulfilment of the demands of divine justice, achieved for mankind by the death of Christ 2a fulfilment of a need or want b being satisfied; contentment c a source or means of pleasure or fulfilment 3a compensation for a loss, insult, or injury; atonement, restitution b the discharge of a legal obligation or claim (eg by payment of a debt) c vindication of one's honour, esp through a duel ⟨*demand* ~⟩ 4 full assurance or certainty ⟨*proved to the* ~ *of the court*⟩ [ME, fr MF, fr LL *satisfaction-*, *satisfactio*, fr L, reparation, amends, fr *satisfactus*, pp of *satisfacere* to satisfy]

**satisfactory** /ˌsatis'fakt(ə)ri/ *adj* satisfying needs or requirements; adequate – **satisfactorily** *adv*, **satisfactoriness** *n*

**satisfy** /'satisˌfie/ *vt* 1a to carry out the terms of (eg a contract); discharge b to meet a financial obligation to 2 to make reparation to (an injured party) in law; indemnify 3a to make content; please ⟨*music that* satisfies *all ages*⟩ b to gratify to the full; appease ⟨satisfied *his longing to travel abroad*⟩ c to meet the requirements of ⟨~ *the examiners*⟩ 4a to convince ⟨satisfied *that he is innocent*⟩ b to put an end to; dispel ⟨~ *every objection*⟩ 5a to conform to (eg criteria); fulfil ⟨~ *examination requirements*⟩ b to make valid by fulfilling a condition ⟨*values that* ~ *an equation*⟩ ⟨~ *a hypothesis*⟩ ~ *vi* to be adequate; suffice; *also* to please ⟨*a taste that* satisfies⟩ [ME *satisfien*, fr MF *satisfier*, modif of L *satisfacere*, fr *satis* enough + *facere* to do, make – more at SAD, DO] – **satisfyingly** *adv*, **satisfiable** *adj*

*usage* Since **satisfied** and **happy** can mean "pleased", one should perhaps avoid using them to mean "convinced of something bad". The question ⟨*are you* satisfied/happy *that they are all dead?*⟩ suggests that we hope so.

**satori** /sə'tawri/ *n* a state of intuitive illumination sought in ZEN (Japanese) Buddhism [Jap]

**satrap** /'satrəp/ *n* 1 the governor of a province in ancient Persia 2 a subordinate ruler; *esp* one who is despotic [ME, fr L *satrapes*, fr Gk *satrapēs*, fr OPer *xshathrapāvan*, lit., protector of the dominion]

**satrapy** /'satrəpi/ *n* the territory or jurisdiction of a satrap

**satsuma** /sat'soohmə/ *n* (any of several cultivated mandarin trees that bear) a sweet seedless type of mandarin orange *synonyms* see TANGERINE [*Satsuma*, former province of Japan]

**saturable** /'sachoorəbl/ *adj* capable of saturation

**saturate** /'sachoorayt/ *vt* 1 to treat, provide, or fill with something to the point where no more can be absorbed, dissolved, or retained ⟨*water* ~d *with salt*⟩ 2a to fill completely with something that permeates or pervades ⟨*moonglow ...* ~s *an empty sky* – Henry Miller⟩ b to fill to capacity 3 to cause to combine chemically until there is no further tendency to combine △ satiate [L *saturatus*, pp of *saturare*, fr *satur* sated – more at SATIRE] – **saturant** *adj or n*, **saturator** *n*

**saturated** /'sachooraytid/ *also* **saturate** /'sachoorayt/ *adj* 1 full of moisture (eg water); thoroughly soaked 2a *of a solution* containing the maximum amount of dissolved material that can be present under normal conditions; not capable of absorbing or dissolving more of something b *of a vapour* containing the maximum amount of the gaseous form of a liquid c *of a chemical compound* unable or not tending to form products by chemical addition or by uniting directly with another compound; *esp* containing no DOUBLE BONDS or TRIPLE BONDS between carbon atoms and therefore not reacting to add other atoms or chemical groups to the molecule

**saturation** /ˌsatchoo'raysh(ə)n/ *n* 1 saturating or being saturated 2 the conversion of an UNSATURATED chemical compound to a saturated compound (eg by reaction with hydrogen) 3 a state of maximum impregnation: eg 3a the presence in a solution of the maximum amount of dissolved material b an atmospheric condition corresponding to the maximum amount of WATER VAPOUR that can be present in the atmosphere at a particular temperature c *physics* magnetization to the point beyond which a further increase in the intensity of the magnetizing force will produce no further magnetization 4 the property of a colour that represents its degree of freedom from dilution with white, grey, or black; the purity of a colour: 4a the degree of difference from the grey having the same lightness – used with reference to the colour of an object b the degree of difference from the colour of the hueless or neutral light-source of the same brightness – used with reference to the colour of a light source **5** the point at which a market is supplied with all the goods it will absorb **6** an overwhelming concentration of military forces or firepower ⟨~ *bombing raids*⟩

**Saturday** /'satəday, -di/ *n* the 7th day of the week; the day falling between Friday and Sunday [ME *saterday*, fr OE *sæterndæg;* akin to OFris *sāterdei;* both fr a prehistoric WGmc compound whose first component was borrowed fr L *Saturnus* Saturn and whose second is represented by OE *dæg* day] – **Saturdays** *adv*

**Saturn** /'satən, 'sa,tuhn/ *n* the planet sixth in order from the sun, that is noted for its system of rings composed of small particles that revolve in a plane about the planet [L *Saturnus,* fr *Saturnus* Saturn, god of agriculture]

**saturnalia** /,satə'naylyə/ *n, pl* **saturnalias** *also* **saturnalia 1** *taking sing or pl vb, cap* the festival of Saturn in ancient Rome beginning on December 17, observed as a time of general and unrestrained merry-making **2** an unrestrained often licentious celebration; an orgy [L, fr neut pl of *saturnalis* of the god Saturn, fr *Saturnus*] – **saturnalian** *adj*

**Saturnian** /sə'tuhnyən/ *adj* **1** of or influenced by the planet Saturn **2** *archaic* of the god Saturn or the golden age of his reign

**saturniid** /sə'tuhni·id/ *n* any of a large family (Saturniidae) of moths (e g the EMPEROR MOTH or the ATLAS MOTH) with stout hairy bodies and strong usu brightly coloured wings [deriv of NL *Saturnia,* genus of moths, fr L, daughter of the god Saturn] – **saturniid** *adj*

**saturnine** /'satə,nien/ *adj* **1** born under or influenced astrologically by the planet Saturn **2a** having a cold and sluggish temperament **b** having a gloomy or sullen disposition **3** *archaic* **3a** of the metal lead **b** of, being, or produced by LEAD POISONING [(1,2) ME, fr MF *saturnin,* fr (assumed) ML *saturninus,* fr L *Saturninus;* (3) arch. *saturn* lead, fr ME *saturne,* fr ML *saturnus,* fr L *Saturnus*] – **saturninely** *adv*

**saturnism** /'satəniz(ə)m/ *n, archaic* LEAD POISONING [arch. *saturn* lead] – **saturnic** *adj*

**satyagraha** /'sutyə,grah·hə, su'tyahgrə·hə/ *n* pressure for social and political reform through friendly resistance as practised by Mahatma Gandhi and his followers in India [Skt *satyāgraha,* lit., insistence on truth]

**satyr** /'satə/ *n* **1** *often cap* a minor woodland god of Greek mythology having certain characteristics of a horse or goat (e g horns and cloven hooves) and associated with Dionysian revelry **2** a lecherous man; *esp* one having satyriasis △ satire [ME, fr L *satyrus,* fr Gk *satyros*] – **satyric** *adj*

**satyriasis** /,satə'rie·əsis/ *n* excessive sexual desire in a male – compare NYMPHOMANIA [LL, fr Gk, fr *satyros*]

**satyrid** /sə'tie·ərid/ *n* any of a family (Satyridae) of usu brownish butterflies with pale-centred eyespots, that feed mainly on grasses as larvae and have one or more main wing veins swollen at the base [NL *Satyridae,* group name, deriv of Gk *satyros*] – **satyrid** *adj*

**satyr play** *n* a usu bawdy comic play of ancient Greece having a mythological theme and a chorus representing satyrs

¹**sauce** /saws/ *n* **1a** a liquid or soft preparation used as a relish, dressing, or accompaniment to food ⟨*white* ~⟩ ⟨*chocolate* ~⟩ **b** *NAm* stewed or tinned fruit eaten as a dessert **2** something that adds zest or piquancy **3** *informal* pert or impudent language or actions; cheek **4** *slang* intoxicating drink; booze [ME, fr MF, fr L *salsa,* fem of *salsus* salted, fr pp of *sallere* to salt, fr *sal* salt – more at SALT]

²**sauce** *vt* **1** to dress or prepare with a sauce or seasoning **2** to impart zest or piquancy to **3** *informal* to be rude or impudent to **4** *archaic* to make less harsh or more acceptable

**sauce boat** *n* a small esp china vessel with a handle and indentation for pouring that is used for holding sauce, gravy, etc at table

**saucebox** /-,boks/ *n, informal* a saucy impudent person

**saucepan** /'sawspən/ *n* a deep usu cylindrical cooking pan typically having a long handle and a lid and used on top of a cooker esp for boiling or braising vegetables and for cooking sauces, stews, etc

**saucer** /'sawsə/ *n* **1** a small usu circular shallow dish or plate with a central indentation in which a cup is set **2** something resembling a saucer in shape; *esp* FLYING SAUCER [ME, plate containing sauce, fr MF *saussier,* fr *sausse, sauce*] – **saucerlike** *adj*

**saucy** /'sawsi/ *adj* **1a** disrespectfully bold and impudent **b** engagingly forward and flippant; irrepressible **2** smart, trim ⟨*a* ~ *ship*⟩ – **saucily** *adv,* **sauciness** *n*

**sauerbraten** /'sowə,brahtən (*Ger* zaʊərbrɑːtən)/ *n* a German dish of spiced braised beef [Ger, fr *sauer* sour + *braten* roast meat]

**sauerkraut** /'sowə,krowt/ *n* finely cut cabbage fermented in a brine made from its juice with salt – compare COLESLAW [Ger, fr *sauer* sour + *kraut* cabbage]

**sauna** /'sawnə/ *n* **1** (the room or building used for) a Finnish steam bath in which the steam is provided by water thrown on hot stones **2** (a room or cabinet used for) a dry heat bath [Finnish]

**saunter** /'sawntə/ *vi* to walk about in an idle or casual manner; stroll [prob fr ME *santren* to muse] – **saunter** *n,* **saunterer** *n*

**Sauraseni** /,sowrə'sayni/ *n* a PRAKRIT language of India [Skt *Saurasenī*]

**saurian** /'sawri·ən/ *n* any of a group (Sauria) of reptiles including the lizards and in older classifications the crocodiles and various extinct forms (e g the dinosaurs and ICHTHYOSAURS) that resemble lizards [deriv of Gk *sauros* horse mackerel, lizard; akin to Gk *psauein* to touch, graze] – **saurian** *adj*

**saurischian** /saw'riskiən/ *n* any of an order (Saurischia) of dinosaurs that had a three-branched pelvis – compare ORNITHISCHIAN [deriv of Gk *sauros* lizard + L *ischium* hip-joint] – **saurischian** *adj*

**sauropod** /'sawrə,pod/ *n* any of a suborder (Sauropoda) of plant-eating dinosaurs with a long neck and tail, a small head, and 5-toed feet [NL *Sauropoda,* suborder of dinosaurs, fr Gk *sauros* lizard + *pod-, pous* foot] – **sauropod, sauropodous** *adj*

**saury** /'sawri/ *n* a slender long-jawed fish (*Scombresox saurus*) found in temperate parts of the Atlantic [NL *saurus* lizard, fr Gk *sauros*]

**sausage** /'sosij; *NAm* 'saw-/ *n* **1** a fresh, precooked, or dried cylindrical mass of seasoned minced meat (e g pork) or a meat substitute often mixed with a filler (e g bread crumbs) and a binding substance (e g dried whey) and usu enclosed by a casing of prepared animal intestine **2** something shaped like a sausage ⟨*rolled the towel into a* ~⟩ [ME *sausige,* fr ONF *saussiche,* fr LL *salsicia,* fr L *salsus* salted – more at SAUCE]

**sausage dog** *n, informal* a dachshund

**sausage machine** *n* **1** a machine that shapes and encases sausage meat and produces sausages in a linked string **2** something that produces articles or moulds ideas, characters, etc in complete uniformity ⟨*this school is a* ~⟩

**sausage roll** *n* a small pastry-encased roll or oblong of sausage meat

¹**sauté** /'sohtay, 'saw- (*Fr* sote)/ *n* a sautéed food or dish [Fr, pp of *sauter* to jump, fr L *saltare* – more at SALTATION] – **sauté** *adj*

²**sauté** *vt* **sautés; sautéing; sautéed, sautéd** /-tayd/ to fry (potatoes, vegetables, etc) in a small amount of fat

**Sauternes,** *NAm* **Sauterne** /soh'tuhn, '--/ *n* a usu sweet golden-coloured table wine made in the commune of Sauternes in the Bordeaux region of France; *also* a similar wine made elsewhere ⟨*Spanish* ~⟩

**sauve qui peut** /,sohv kee 'puh (*Fr* sov ki pφ)/ *n* a complete rout; a state of panic [Fr, save (himself) who can]

¹**savage** /'savij/ *adj* **1a** not domesticated or under human control; untamed ⟨~ *beasts*⟩ **b** lacking in social or moral restraints; fierce, barbarous **2** rugged, rough ⟨~ *scenery*⟩ **3** boorish, rude ⟨~ *bad manners*⟩ **4** lacking a developed culture; uncivilized [ME *sauvage,* fr MF, fr ML *salvaticus,* alter. of L *silvaticus* of the woods, wild, fr *silva* wood, forest] – **savagely** *adv,* **savageness, savagery** *n*

²**savage** *n* **1** somebody belonging to a primitive society **2** a brutal person **3** a rude or unmannerly person

³**savage** *vt* to attack or treat brutally; *esp* to maul ⟨*dogs that* ~ *small children*⟩

**savanna, savannah** /sə'vanə/ *n* a tropical or subtropical grassland with scattered trees and shrubs and drought-resistant undergrowth – compare PRAIRIE, PAMPAS, VELD [Sp *zavana,* fr Taino *zabana*]

**savant** /'sav(ə)nt/ *n* a learned person; *esp* one who has exceptional knowledge of a particular field (e g science or literature) [Fr, fr prp of *savoir* to know, fr L *sapere* to be wise – more at SAGE]

**savarin** /'sav(ə)rin (*Fr* savrɛ̃)/ (the mould for) a rich yeast-leavened cake baked in a ring mould and soaked with a liqueur-flavoured syrup [Fr, fr Anthelme Brillat-*Savarian* † 1826 Fr politician & gourmet]

**savate** /sə'vat/ *n* a form of boxing in which blows are delivered with either the hands or the feet [Fr, lit., old shoe]

¹**save** /sayv/ *vt* **1a** to deliver from sin **b** to rescue or deliver from danger or harm **c** to preserve or guard from injury, destruction, or loss **2a** to put aside as a store or reserve; accumulate **b** to put aside for a particular use ⟨~s *her best dishes for company and her old dresses for her daughter*⟩ **c** to keep from being spent, wasted, or lost ⟨~*£70 on a new car*⟩ ⟨~d *time by taking a short cut*⟩ **d** to economize in the use of; conserve, husband ⟨~ *petrol*⟩ ⟨~ *your strength*⟩ **3a** to make unnecessary; avoid, obviate ⟨*it* ~s *an hour's waiting*⟩ ⟨~s *me going into town*⟩ **b(1)** to prevent (a match) from being lost to an opponent **b(2)** to prevent an opponent from scoring or winning (eg a trick, goal, or point) or scoring with (a ball) **4** to maintain, preserve ⟨~ *appearances*⟩ ~ *vi* **1** to rescue or deliver somebody (eg from danger or evil) **2a** to put aside money – often + *up* **b** to be economical in use or expenditure **3** to make a save ⟨*the fullback* ~d *on the line*⟩ **antonyms** spend, consume [ME *saven*, fr OF *salver*, fr LL *salvare*, fr L *salvus* safe – more at SAFE] – **savable, saveable** *adj*, **saver** *n*

²**save** *n* an act of preventing an opponent from scoring or winning; *esp* an act of preventing the ball from going into the goal in soccer

³**save** *prep, chiefly formal* other than; but, except ⟨*no hope* ~ *one*⟩ [ME *sauf*, fr OF, fr *sauf*, adj, safe – more at SAFE]

⁴**save** *conj, formal* **1** were it not; only ⟨*couldn't have done it* ~ *for your help*⟩ ⟨*would have protested* ~ *that he was a friend*⟩ **2** but, except – used before a word often taken to be the subject of a clause ⟨*no one knows about it* ~ *she*⟩

'**save-,all** *n* something that prevents waste, loss, or damage (eg a device to hold a candle end in a candlestick and permit it to burn to the very end)

,**save-as-you-'earn** *n* a government saving scheme whereby a person undertakes to contribute a specified amount from his/her pay each week or month and receives at the end of a fixed period the savings plus interest

**saveloy** /'saviloy/ *n* a red precooked highly seasoned dry sausage [modif of Fr *cervelas*, deriv of L *cerebellum*, dim. of *cerebrum* brain]

**Savile Row** /,savl 'roh/ *adj* extremely well cut and tailored ⟨*a* ~ *suit*⟩ [*Savile Row* in London, location of fashionable tailors]

**savin** /'savin/ *n* **1** a low-growing spreading Eurasian juniper bush (*Juniperus sabina*) that has dark green leaves and small bluish-black berries and whose young shoots yield a poisonous oil formerly used medicinally; *also* this oil **2** RED CEDAR 1 (N American juniper tree) [ME, fr MF *savine*, fr L *sabina*]

¹**saving** /'sayving/ *n* **1** preservation from danger or destruction; deliverance **2** something that is saved ⟨*a* ~ *of 40 per cent*⟩ **3a** *pl* money put by over a period of time **b** **saving, savings** *pl* the excess of income over expenditures [gerund of *save*]

²**saving** *prep* **1** except, save **2** without disrespect to [prp of *save*]

³**saving** *conj* except, save

**saving grace** *n* a redeeming quality or feature

**savings account** *n* an account (eg in a bank) on which interest is usu paid and from which withdrawals can be made usu only by presentation of a passbook or by written authorization on a prescribed form – compare DEPOSIT ACCOUNT

**savings and loan association** *n, NAm* BUILDING SOCIETY

**savings bank** *n* a bank organized to receive SAVINGS ACCOUNTS only

**savings bond** *n* a nontransferable registered US bond issued in denominations of $25 to $1000

**savings certificate** *n* a certificate bought from a savings bank (eg the Post Office) stating that a certain usu small sum has been deposited by the person buying the certificate. Interest paid on such investments is usu free of tax.

**savings stamp** *n* a stamp which is bought (eg from the Post Office) and saved usu in a special book and which may be cashed when required or used in payment of a bill ⟨*buys* savings stamps *towards his television licence*⟩

**saviour,** *NAm chiefly* **savior** /'sayvyə/ *n* **1** one who brings salvation; *specif, cap* Jesus **2** one who saves somebody or something from danger or destruction [ME *saveour*, fr MF, fr LL *salvator*, fr *salvatus*, pp of *salvare* to save]

**savoir faire** /,savwah 'feə (*Fr* savwar fɛr)/ *n* capacity for

appropriate action; *esp* polished self-assurance in social behaviour [Fr *savoir-faire*, lit., knowing how to do]

**savory** /'sayv(ə)ri/ *n* any of several chiefly Mediterranean plants (genus *Satureia*, esp *Satureia hortensis* and *Satureia montana*) of the mint family that have white, lilac, or pink flowers and narrow aromatic leaves and are used as herbs in cooking [ME *saverey*, deriv of L *satureia*]

¹**savour,** *NAm chiefly* **savor** /'sayvə/ *n* **1** the characteristic taste or smell of something ⟨*the* ~ *of roast pork*⟩ **2** a particular flavour or smell **3** a (pleasantly stimulating) distinctive quality ⟨*felt that argument added* ~ *to conversation*⟩ **synonyms** see ²SMELL [ME, fr OF, fr L *sapor;* akin to L *sapere* to taste – more at SAGE]

²**savour,** *NAm chiefly* **savor** *vi* to have a specified smell or quality ⟨*arguments that* ~ *of cynicism*⟩ ~ *vt* **1a** to have experience of; taste **b** to taste or smell with pleasure; relish **c** to enjoy the apprehension or experience of, esp at length ⟨~ing *the pleasures of country life*⟩ **2** to delight in; enjoy

¹**savoury,** *NAm chiefly* **savory** /'sayv(ə)ri/ *adj* having savour: eg **a** piquantly pleasant to the mind ⟨*a* ~ *collection of essays*⟩ **b** morally wholesome; edifying – usu neg ⟨*his reputation was anything but* ~⟩ **c(1)** pleasing to the palate **c(2)** salty, spicy, meaty, etc, rather than sweet **antonyms** bland, acrid – **savouriness** *n*

²**savoury,** *NAm chiefly* **savory** *n* a dish of piquant or stimulating flavour served usu at the end of a main meal but sometimes as an appetizer

**Savoyard** /sə'voyahd (*Fr* savwajar)/ *n* a devotee, performer, or producer of the comic operas of W S Gilbert and Sir Arthur Sullivan [*Savoy* theatre in London, built for the presentation of Gilbert and Sullivan operas]

**savoy cabbage, savoy** /sə'voy; *often* 'savoy *when attrib*/ *n* a hardy cabbage with compact heads of wrinkled and curled leaves [trans of Fr *chou de Savoie* cabbage of Savoy, fr *Savoie* Savoy, region in SE France]

¹**savvy** /'savi/ *vb, slang* to know, understand [modif of Sp *sabe* he knows, fr *saber* to know, fr L *sapere* to taste; be wise – more at SAGE]

²**savvy** *n, slang* practical know-how; shrewd judgment ⟨*political* ~⟩

¹**saw** /saw/ *past of* SEE

²**saw** *n* a hand or power tool with a toothed part (eg a blade or disc) used to cut hard material (eg wood, metal, or bone) [ME *sawe*, fr OE *sagu;* akin to OHG *sega* saw, L *secare* to cut, *secula* sickle] – **sawlike** *adj*

³**saw** *vb* **sawed, sawn** /sawn/ *vt* **1** to cut with a saw **2** to make or shape by cutting with a saw **3** to cut through or sever as though with a saw ~ *vi* **1a** to use a saw **b** to cut (as if) with a saw **2** to undergo cutting with a saw ⟨*wood that* ~s *easily*⟩ **3** to make motions as though using a saw ⟨~ed *at the reins*⟩ – **sawer** *n*

⁴**saw** *n* a maxim, proverb ⟨*an old Scots* ~⟩ [ME *sawe*, fr OE *sagu* discourse; akin to OHG & ON *saga* tale, OE *secgan* to say – more at SAY]

**Sawan** /'sah·wən/ *n* – see MONTH table [Hindi *sāwan*, fr Skt *śrāvaṇa*]

**sawbill** /'saw,bil/ *n* any of various fish-eating ducks with slender serrated bills; *esp* MERGANSER

**sawbones** /'saw,bohnz/ *n, pl* **sawbones, sawboneses** *humorous* a doctor; *specif* a surgeon

**sawbuck** /'saw,buk/ *n, NAm slang* a 10-dollar bill [orig meaning 'sawhorse'; prob fr the resemblance of the Roman numeral X (10) to the ends of a sawhorse]

¹**sawder** /'sawdə/ *n, informal* flattery – in *soft sawder* [obs var of *solder*]

²**sawder** *vt, informal* to flatter

**sawdust** /'saw,dust/ *n* fine particles of wood produced in sawing

,**saw-'edged** *adj* having a toothed or jagged edge

,**sawed-'off** *adj, chiefly NAm* sawn-off

**sawfish** /'saw,fish/ *n* any of a family (Pristidae) of large elongated sharklike rays that have a long flattened serrated snout and live in warm shallow seas and in or near the mouths of rivers principally in tropical America and Africa

**sawfly** /'saw,flie/ *n* any of numerous insects (suborder Symphyta) related to the wasps, bees, and ants whose female usu has a sawlike egg-laying organ used to cut slits in leaves, stems, etc in which the eggs are laid, and whose larva typically resembles a plant-feeding caterpillar

**sawgrass** /'saw,grahs/ *n* any of various sedges (genus *Cladium*) having sharp serrations on the edges of the leaves

**sawhorse** /'saw‚haws/ *n* a rack on which wood is laid for sawing by hand; *esp* one with X-shaped ends

**sawmill** /'saw‚mil/ *n* a factory or machine that cuts wood

**sawney** /'sawni/ *n, informal* a simpleton [prob alter. of *zany*] – **sawney** *adj*

**‚sawn-'off** *adj* **1** having the end removed by sawing; *specif, of a shotgun* having the end of the barrel and sometimes the stock sawn off **2** *informal* short in stature

**'saw-‚off** *n, Can* an arrangement in which one concession is balanced against another; a trade-off

**'saw-‚pit** *n* the pit in which the lower sawyer stands while timber is being cut with a PIT SAW

**saw set** *n* an instrument used to set the teeth of a saw at an angle alternately to the right and left of the plane of the saw

**sawtooth** /'saw‚toohth/, **sawtoothed** /-‚toohtht/ *adj* (arranged or having parts arranged) like the teeth of a saw; serrated ⟨*a ~ roof*⟩

**sawyer** /'sawyə/ *n* somebody employed to saw timber

**¹sax** /saks/ *n* ZAX (slater's axe)

**²sax** *n* a saxophone

**Saxe blue** /saks/ *n* a light blue colour with a greenish tinge [Fr *Saxe* Saxony, region in Germany]

**saxhorn** /-‚hawn/ *n* any of a group of BRASS INSTRUMENTS ranging from soprano to bass and having a conical tube, an oval shape, a cup-shaped mouthpiece, and finger-operated valves to vary the pitch [(Antoine Joseph) Adolphe *Sax* †1894 Belgium maker of musical instruments + E *horn*]

**saxicolous** /‚sak'sikələs/, **saxicoline** /sak'sikəlien/ *adj* living or growing on or among rocks ⟨*~ lichens*⟩ [L *saxum* rock + *-cola* inhabitant; akin to L *colere* to inhabit – more at WHEEL]

**saxifrage** /'saksifrij, -‚frayj/ *n* any of a genus (*Saxifraga* of the family Saxifragaceae, the saxifrage family) of plants with usu small showy flowers and often tufted leaves, many of which are grown in rock gardens [ME, fr MF, fr LL *saxifraga*, fr L, fem of *saxifragus* breaking rocks, fr *saxum* rock + *frangere* to break; akin to OE *sæx* knife, *sagu* saw – more at SAW, BREAK]

**Saxon** /'saks(ə)n/ *n* **1a** a member of a Germanic people that invaded England together with the Angles and Jutes in the 5th century AD and merged with them to form the Anglo-Saxon people **b** an Englishman or Lowlander as distinguished from a Welshman, Irishman, or Highlander **2** a native or inhabitant of Saxony **3a** the GERMANIC language or dialect of any of the Saxon peoples **b** the GERMANIC element in the English language, esp as distinguished from the French and Latin [ME, fr LL *Saxones* Saxons, of Gmc origin; akin to OE *Seaxan* Saxons] – **Saxon** *adj*

**Saxonism** /'saksəniz(ə)m/ *n* a Saxon idiom in English

**saxony** /'saksəni/ *n, often cap* **1** a fine soft woollen fabric **2** a fine closely twisted knitting yarn [*Saxony*, region in Germany]

**saxophone** /'saksə‚fohn/ *n* any of a group of woodwind instruments that range from soprano to bass, have a conical metal tube and finger keys, and are used extensively in jazz music [Fr, fr Adolphe *Sax* + Fr *-phone*] – **saxophonic** *adj*, **saxophonist** *n*

**saxtuba** /‚saks'tyoohbə/ *n* a bass saxhorn [Antoine *Sax* + E *tuba*]

**¹say** /say/ *vb* **says** /sez/; **said** /sed/ *vt* **1a** to state in spoken words; declare ⟨*he ~s he's thirsty*⟩ **b** to form an opinion as to ⟨*can't ~ when I met him*⟩ **2a** to utter, pronounce ⟨*can't ~ her h's*⟩ ⟨*he* said *"Can you swim?"*⟩ **b** to recite, repeat ⟨said *his prayers*⟩ **3a** to indicate, show ⟨*the clock ~s half past 12*⟩ **b** to give expression to; communicate ⟨*a glance that* said *all that was necessary*⟩ ⟨*I* said *to myself "That's funny"*⟩ ⟨*I ~s press button A*⟩ **4** to allege – usu pass ⟨*the house is* said *to be 300 years old*⟩; compare SAID ~ *vi* **1** to express oneself; speak ⟨*start when I ~*⟩ ⟨*I'd rather not ~*⟩ **2** *NAm* I SAY – used interjectionally [ME *sayen*, fr OE *secgan*; akin to OHG *sagēn* to say, Gk en *nepein* to speak, tell] – **sayer** *n* – **I say** *chiefly Br* – used as an expression of surprise or to attract attention – not now in vogue – **not to say** and indeed; or perhaps even ⟨*impolite*, not to say *rude*⟩ – **say when** to tell somebody when to stop (e g when he/she is pouring a drink) – **that is to say 1** in other words; IN EFFECT **2** or at least ⟨*he's coming*, that is to say *he promised to*⟩ – **to say nothing of** without even considering; not to mention – see also **say** FAIRER

**²say** *n, pl* **says** /sayz/ **1** an expression of opinion – esp in **have one's say 2** a right or power to influence action or decisions ⟨*had no ~ in the matter*⟩; *esp* the authority to make final decisions

**³say** *adv* **1** at a rough estimate; about ⟨*the picture is worth, ~,*

*two thousand pounds*⟩ **2** FOR EXAMPLE ⟨*we could leave next week, ~ on Monday*⟩ [fr imper of ¹*say*]

**saying** /'saying/ *n* something said; *esp* a maxim, proverb

**'say-‚so** *n* **1a** someone's unsupported assertion; a bare assurance **b** an authoritative pronouncement ⟨*left the hospital on the ~ of his doctor*⟩ **2** the right of final decision; say

**sayyid** /'sie‧id/ **1** an Islamic chief or leader **2** lord, sir – used as a courtesy title for a Muslim of rank or lineage [Ar]

**'S-‚bend** *n* a doubly curved joint in a waste pipe designed to exclude odours, germs, etc from a building

**¹scab** /skab/ *n* **1** MANGE (contagious skin disease) or scabies of domestic animals; *esp* mange of sheep caused by a parasitic mite (*Psoroptes communis*) **2** a crust of dried hardened blood, watery blood SERUM, or pus covering a skin wound **3a** a contemptible person **b** a blackleg **4** any of various bacterial or esp fungus diseases of plants (e g fruit trees and cereals) characterized by roughened crusted spots on the leaves, fruits, stems, etc; *also* any of these spots [ME, of Scand origin; akin to OSw *skabbr* scab; akin to OE *sceabb* scab, L *scabies* mange, *scabere* to scratch, shave – more at SHAVE]

**²scab** *vi* **-bb-** **1** to become covered with a scab **2** to act as a scab

**¹scabbard** /'skabəd/ *n* a sheath for a sword, dagger, or bayonet [ME *scaubert*, fr AF *escaubers*, of Gmc origin]

**²scabbard** *vt* to put in a scabbard

**'scabbard-‚fish** *n* any of various widely distributed marine fishes (family Trichiuridae) that have a long narrow body and sharp pointed daggerlike teeth

**scabby** /'skabi/ *adj* **1a** covered with or full of scabs ⟨*~ skin*⟩ **b** diseased with scab ⟨*a ~ animal*⟩ ⟨*~ potatoes*⟩ **2** mean, contemptible ⟨*a ~ trick*⟩ **3** squalid, shabby ⟨*~ tenements*⟩

**scabies** /'skaybiz/ *n, pl* **scabies** a contagious skin disease caused by a parasitic mite (genus *Sarcoptes,* esp *Sarcoptes scabei*) that burrows in the skin, and characterized by itchy lesions and pus-filled patches covered by scabs; *specif* scabies occurring in human beings [L] – **scabietic** *adj*

**scabiosa** /‚skaybi'ohsə, ‚skabi-/ *n* a scabious [NL, genus name, fr ML, scabious]

**¹scabious** /'skaybi‧əs/ *n* any of a genus (*Scabiosa* of the family Dipsacaceae, the scabious family) of plants with dense heads of often blue, lilac, or violet flowers [ME *scabiose*, fr ML *scabiosa*, fr L, fem of *scabiosus*, adj; fr its supposed ability to cure scabies]

**²scabious** *adj* **1** scabby **2** of or resembling scabies ⟨*~ eruptions*⟩ [L *scabiosus*, fr *scabies*]

**scabrous** /'skaybrəs/ *adj* **1** rough to the touch; *esp* having a roughened surface covered with small raised patches, scales, points, etc ⟨*yellowed ~ skin*⟩ ⟨*a ~ leaf*⟩ **2** dealing with indecent or offensive themes; salacious **3** *formal* intractable, knotty ⟨*a ~ problem*⟩ **synonyms** see ¹ROUGH **antonyms** glabrous, smooth [L *scabr-, scaber* rough, scurfy; akin to L *scabies* mange – more at SCAB] – **scabrously** *adv*, **scabrousness** *n*

**¹scad** /skad/ *n, pl* **scad**, *esp for different types* **scads** any of several spiny-finned fishes (family *Carangidae*); *esp* HORSE MACKEREL [origin unknown]

**²scad** *n,* **scads** *n pl, chiefly NAm informal* a large number or quantity ⟨*~s of money*⟩ ⟨*hooked a ~ of little fish – Field & Stream*⟩ [prob alter. of E dial. *scald* a multitude]

**scaffold** /'skafohld, -f(ə)ld/ *n* **1a** a temporary or movable platform for workmen (e g bricklayers, painters, or miners) to stand or sit on when working at a height above the floor or ground **b** a platform on which a criminal is executed (e g by hanging or beheading) **c** a platform above ground or floor level **2** a supporting framework [ME, fr ONF *escafaut*, modif of (assumed) VL *catafalicum* – more at CATAFALQUE] – **scaffolder** *n*

**scaffolding** /'skafəlding/ *n* a system of scaffolds; *also* material (e g metal poles or boards) for scaffolds

**scag** /skag/ *n, slang* heroin [origin unknown]

**scagliola** /skal'yohlə/ *n* an imitation of ornamental marble consisting of finely ground GYPSUM mixed with glue [It, lit., little chip]

**scalable** /'skayləbl/ *adj* capable of being scaled

**¹scalar** /'skaylə/ *adj* **1** having a continuous series of steps; graduated ⟨*~ chain of authority*⟩ ⟨*~ cells*⟩ **2** *maths* **2a** capable of being represented by a point on a scale ⟨*a ~ quantity*⟩ **b** of a scalar or SCALAR PRODUCT ⟨*~ multiplication*⟩ [L *scalaris* of a ladder, fr *scalae* stairs, ladder – more at SCALE]

**²scalar** *n* **1** *maths* an element of the FIELD over which a VECTOR SPACE is constructed **2** a quantity (e g mass or time) that has magnitude but no direction – compare VECTOR

**scalare** /skə'leəri/ *n* a small S American spiny-finned fish (*Pterophyllum scalare*) with a narrow black and silver striped body, that is often kept in aquariums [NL, specific epithet, fr L, neut of *scalaris* of a ladder; fr the barred pattern on its body]

**scalariform** /skə'larifawm/ *adj, biology* resembling a ladder in having cross bars or markings like the rungs of a ladder ⟨∼ *cells in plants*⟩ [NL *scalariformis*, fr L *scalaris* + -*iformis* -iform] – **scalariformly** *adv*

**scalar product** *n, maths* a REAL NUMBER obtained by multiplying together the lengths of two VECTORS and the cosine of the angle between them

**scalawag** /'skaləwag/ *n, NAm* a scallywag

¹**scald** /skawld/ *vt* **1** to burn (as if) with hot liquid or steam ⟨*escaping steam from the burst pipe* ∼ed *those in the engine room*⟩ **2a** to subject to the action of boiling water or steam (eg in order to kill microorganisms) **b** to heat until just short of boiling ⟨∼ *milk*⟩ ∼ *vi* **1** to scald something **2** to become scalded [ME *scalden*, fr ONF *escalder*, fr LL *excaldare* to wash in warm water, fr L *ex-* + *calida, calda* warm water, fr fem of *calidus* warm – more at CAULDRON]

²**scald** *n* **1** an injury to the body, similar to a burn, caused by scalding **2** an act or process of scalding **3** a burning and browning of plant tissues resulting from heat sometimes combined with intense light; *also* a plant disease having similar effects

³**scald** *n* SKALD (Scandinavian bard)

**scalding** /'skawlding/ *adj* **1** causing (the sensation of) scalding or burning ⟨*a* ∼ *cup of coffee*⟩ **2** *of weather* scorchingly hot ⟨*they trudged on and on under the* ∼ *desert sun*⟩ **3** biting, scathing ⟨*a series of* ∼ *editorials*⟩

¹**scale** /skayl/ *n* **1** either pan or tray of a BALANCE (device used for weighing) **2** **scales** *pl, also* **scale** an instrument or machine for weighing; *esp* one consisting of a pivoting bar with a platform for weights at one end and a pan to hold the item to be weighed at the other [ME, bowl, scale of a balance, fr ON *skál;* akin to ON *skel* shell – more at SHELL] – **tip the scales 1** to register weight ⟨tips the scales *at 8 stone 4 pounds*⟩ **2** to shift the balance of power or influence ⟨*his greater experience* tipped the scales *in his favour*⟩

²**scale** *vt* to weigh on scales ∼ *vi* to have a specified weight on scales

³**scale** *n* **1a** a small flattened rigid plate forming part of the outer skin of a fish, reptile, etc **b** a small thin plate resembling a fish scale ⟨∼s *of mica*⟩ ⟨*the* ∼s *on a moth's wing*⟩ **2** a small thin dry flake of dead skin shed from the body, esp in certain skin diseases **3** a thin coating, layer, or incrustation: **3a(1)** a black scaly coating of oxide that forms on the surface of iron when heated and that must be removed before further processing can take place **a(2)** a similar coating forming on other metals when heated **b** a hard incrustation, usu rich in the chemical compound calcium sulphate, that is deposited on the inside of a kettle, hot water pipes, etc by the evaporation or constant passage of hard water **4** a modified leaf; *esp* one that protects a bud of a SEED PLANT before it opens **5a** any of the small overlapping usu metal pieces forming the outer surface of scale armour **b** SCALE ARMOUR **6a** SCALE INSECT **b** infestation with or disease caused by SCALE INSECTS [ME, fr MF *escale*, of Gmc origin; akin to OE *scealu* shell, husk – more at SHELL] – **scaled** *adj*, **scaleless** *adj*

⁴**scale** *vt* **1** to remove the scale or scales from (eg by scraping) ⟨∼ *a fish*⟩ **2** to remove in thin layers or scales ⟨∼ *paint from a wall*⟩ **3** to cover with scale ⟨*hard water* ∼s *a boiler*⟩ ∼ *vi* **1** to separate and come off in scales; flake **2** to shed scales ⟨*in this phase some patients may* ∼ *more markedly than others*⟩ **3** to become encrusted with scale – **scaler** *n*

⁵**scale** *n* **1** a series of rising or falling musical notes with a regular pattern of intervals between them **2** something graduated, esp when used as a measure or rule: eg **2a** a series of spaces marked by lines and used to register or record something (eg the height of mercury in a thermometer) **b** a graduated line on a map or chart indicating the length used to represent a larger unit of measure (eg 1 centimetre = 1 kilometre) **c** an instrument consisting of a strip (eg of wood, plastic, or metal) with one or more sets of graduated and numbered intervals for measuring or marking off distances or dimensions **3** a graduated system ⟨*a* ∼ *of taxation*⟩ ⟨*she seems to have slipped down the social* ∼⟩ **4** a proportion between two sets of dimensions (eg between those of a drawing and its original) ⟨*on model railways 1 to 64 is a common* ∼⟩ **5** a graded series

of tests or of performances used in rating a person's intelligence or achievement **6a** *obs* a ladder, staircase **b** *archaic* a means of ascent [ME, ladder, rung, graduated line, fr LL *scala* ladder, staircase, fr L *scalae,* pl, stairs, rungs, ladder; akin to L *scandere* to climb – more at SCAN] – **scale** *adj* – **to scale** according to the proportions of an established scale of measurement ⟨*floor plans drawn to scale*⟩

⁶**scale** *vt* **1** to climb up or reach (as if) by means of a ladder; surmount ⟨*the attackers had first to* ∼ *a high wall*⟩ **2a** *maths* to change the scale of – often + *up* or *down* **b** to arrange in a graduated series ⟨∼ *a test*⟩ **c(1)** to measure (as if) by a scale **c(2)** to measure or estimate the amount of (eg timber) **d** to pattern, make, regulate, set, or estimate according to some rate or standard ⟨*a production schedule* ∼d *to actual need*⟩ ⟨∼ *down imports*⟩ – often + *up* or *down* ∼ *vi* **1** to climb (as if) by a ladder **2** to rise in a graduated series **3** to measure **4** to change the scale of something – **scalable** *adj*

**scale armour** *n* armour made of small metallic scales attached to leather or cloth

**scale insect** *n* any of numerous small but very prolific insects (esp family Coccidae) that are TRUE BUGS and that have winged males, scalelike females attached to the infested plant, and young that suck the juices of plants

**scale leaf** *n* a modified usu small and scaly leaf (eg a bud scale or BRACT or the leaf of a cypress tree)

**scalelike** /'skayl,liek/ *adj* resembling a scale; *specif* reduced to a minute structure resembling a scale ⟨∼ *leaves*⟩

**scalene** /'skayleen/ *adj, of a triangle* having the three sides of unequal length [LL *scalenus,* fr Gk *skalēnos*, lit., uneven; akin to Gk *skolios* crooked – more at CYLINDER]

**scalepan** /-,pan/ *n* a pan of a scale for weighing

**scaler** /'skaylə/ *n* **1** one who or that which scales **2** an electronic device that operates an apparatus for making permanent records (eg of results of experiments), or that puts out a single pulse when it has received a predetermined number of input impulses

**scall** /skawl/ *n* scurf or a scabby disorder (eg of the scalp) [ME, fr ON *skalli* bald head]

**scallion** /'skalyən/ *n* **1** a leek **2** SPRING ONION; *also* a young onion with an undeveloped bulb **3** *chiefly NAm* a shallot [ME *scaloun* shallot, fr AF *scalun,* fr (assumed) VL *escalonia,* fr L *ascalonia (caepa)* onion of Ascalon, fr fem of *ascalonius* of Ascalon, fr *Ascalon-, Ascalo* Ascalon, seaport in S Palestine]

¹**scallop** /'skoləp/ *n* **1a** any of many marine INVERTEBRATE animals (family Pectinidae of the phylum Mollusca) that are related to the mussels and clams, have a shell consisting of two wavy-edged halves each with a fan-shaped pattern of ridges, and that swim by opening and closing the halves of the shell **b** the large muscle of a scallop used as food **2** one half of a scallop shell or a similarly shaped dish used for baking esp seafood **3** any of a continuous series of circle segments or angular projections forming a border (eg to a piece of material) [ME *scalop,* fr MF *escalope* shell, of Gmc origin; akin to MD *schelpe* shell]

²**scallop** *vt* **1** to bake in a scallop shell or shallow baking dish usu with a sauce and covered with breadcrumbs ⟨∼ed *potatoes*⟩ **2a** to shape, cut, or finish (eg an edge or border) in scallops **b** to form scallops in ∼ *vi* to gather or dredge for scallops

**scallywag** /'skali,wag/, *NAm chiefly* **scalawag** /'skaləwag/ *n* a rogue, rascal [origin unknown]

¹**scalp** /skalp/ *n* **1a** the part of the skin of the top and back of the human head usu covered with hair **b** the part of a mammal (eg a wolf or fox) corresponding to the human scalp **2a** a part of the human scalp with attached hair, cut or torn from an enemy as a token of victory, esp formerly by N American Indian warriors **b** a trophy of victory **3** *chiefly Scot* a projecting bare or rocky mound (eg on a beach) [ME, of Scand origin; akin to ON *skālpr* sheath; akin to MD *schelpe* shell]

²**scalp** *vt* **1** to remove the scalp of **2** *NAm informal* **2a** to buy and sell so as to make small quick profits ⟨∼ *stocks*⟩ ⟨∼ *grain*⟩ **b** to obtain cheaply in the hope of reselling at greatly increased prices ⟨∼ *theatre tickets*⟩ ∼ *vi* **1** to take scalps **2** to profit by slight rises and falls on the market – **scalper** *n*

**scalpel** /'skalpl/ *n* a small very sharp straight thin-bladed knife used esp for dissection or surgery [L *scalpellus, scalpellum,* dim. of *scalper, scalprum* chisel, knife, fr *scalpere* to carve – more at SHELF]

**scalp lock** *n* a long tuft of hair left on the crown of the shaved head of a warrior of some N American Indian tribes; *also* a similar hairstyle worn by some young people in the early 1980s ⟨*skinheads, punks, and people with dyed* scalp locks⟩

**scaly** /'skayli/ *adj* **1a** covered with, composed of, or rich in scale or scales **b** flaky; having a loose easily peeled surface **2** of animals covered with scales **3** infested with SCALE INSECTS ⟨~ *fruit*⟩ **4** *chiefly NAm* despicable, inferior – **scaliness** *n*

**scaly anteater** *n* a pangolin

**scammony** /'skaməni/ *n* a twining plant (*Convolvulus scammonia*) of the bindweed family found in Asia Minor whose large thick root yields a resin that is used medicinally as a laxative; *also* the root of scammony or a resin derived from it [ME *scamonie*, fr L *scammonia*, fr Gk *skammōnia*]

**¹scamp** /skamp/ *n* **1** a rascal, rogue **2** an impish or playful young person [obs *scamp* to roam about idly, prob fr or akin to *scamper*] – **scampish** *adj*

**²scamp** *vt* to perform in a hasty, careless, or haphazard manner ⟨*don't ~ work in order to catch up*⟩ [perh of Scand origin; akin to ON *skammr* short – more at SCANT]

**¹scamper** /'skampə/ *vi* to run about nimbly and playfully ⟨*the rabbits ~ed off when they heard the noise*⟩ [prob fr obs D *schampen* to flee, fr MF *escamper*, fr It *scampare*, fr (assumed) VL *excampare* to decamp, fr L *ex-* + *campus* field – more at CAMP]

**²scamper** *n* a playful dash or scurry

**scampi** /'skampi/ *n, pl* **scampi** a prawn; *specif* a large prawn often eaten fried in batter [It, pl of *scampo*]

**¹scan** /skan/ *vb* **-nn-** *vt* **1** to read or mark (a piece of text) so as to show METRICAL (having arranged and measured rhythm) structure **2a** to subject to critical examination **b** to examine all parts of in a systematic manner ⟨~ *the hills with binoculars*⟩ **c** to glance from point to point of often hastily, casually, or in search of a particular item ⟨~ *the small ads looking for a job*⟩ **3a** to examine successive small portions of (eg an object) with a sensing device (eg a PHOTOMETER or a beam of radiation) **b** to make a detailed examination of (part or all of the body) using any of a variety of sensing devices (eg ones using ULTRASONIC waves, rays of heat radiation, X rays, or rays from radioactive materials) **c** to examine (an object or region) using a radar scanner **d** to change (an image) into an electrical signal by moving an electron beam across it according to a predetermined pattern (eg for television transmission); *also* to reproduce (an image) from an electrical signal (eg on a television screen) **e** to examine (a section of MAGNETIC TAPE or other computer data source) for the presence of recorded data ~ *vi, of verse* to conform to a METRICAL pattern ⟨*lines that ~ boldly*⟩ [ME *scannen*, fr LL *scandere*, fr L, to climb; akin to Gk *skandalon* trap, stumbling block, offence, Skt *skandati* he leaps] – **scannable** *adj*

**²scan** *n* **1** an act or process of scanning **2** a radar display **3** a radar or television trace **4** a depiction (eg a photograph) of the distribution of a radioactive material in something (eg a bodily organ)

**¹scandal** /'skandl/ *n* **1a** discredit brought on religion by unseemly conduct in a religious person **b** conduct that causes or encourages a lapse of faith or of religious obedience in another **2** loss of reputation caused by an (alleged) breach of the accepted standards of moral or social behaviour; disgrace **3a** a circumstance or action that causes general offence or indignation or that disgraces those associated with it **b** a person who conspicuously causes scandal **4** malicious or damaging gossip ⟨*attack with ~ and abuse*⟩ **5** anger, indignation, or chagrin brought about by a gross infringement of accepted moral, social, or religious standards [LL *scandalum* stumbling block, offence, fr Gk *skandalon*]

**²scandal** *vt* **1** to bring into disrepute; defame **2** *obs* to disgrace

**scandal·ize, -ise** /'skandl,iez/ *vt* **1** to speak falsely or maliciously of **2** to offend the moral sense of; shock – **scandalizer** *n*, **scandalization** *n*

**scandalmonger** /-,mung·gə/ *n* a person who spreads scandal

**scandalous** /'skandələs/ *adj* **1** likely to damage a reputation; libellous ⟨~ *remarks*⟩ **2** offending accepted standards of social or moral behaviour; shocking – **scandalously** *adv*, **scandalousness** *n*

**scandent** /'skandənt/ *adj, of a plant* having a climbing mode of growth ⟨~ *stems*⟩ [L *scandent-, scandens*, prp of *scandere* to climb – more at SCAN]

**Scandian** /'skandiən/ *adj* **1** Scandinavian **2** of the languages of Scandinavia [L *Scandia*] – **Scandian** *n*

**Scandinavian** /,skandi'nayvyən, -vi·ən/ *n* **1** a native or inhabitant of Scandinavia **2** NORTH GERMANIC (subdivision of the GERMANIC branch of languages) – **Scandinavian** *adj*

**scandium** /'skandi·əm/ *n* a light silvery-white metallic chemical element found in small quantities in many ores of RARE-EARTH ELEMENTS and also in tin and tungsten ores [NL, fr L *Scandia*, ancient name of southern Scandinavian peninsula]

**scanner** /'skanə/ *n* something that scans: eg **a** a device that automatically monitors a system or process **b** a device for sensing recorded data **c** the rotating aerial of a radar set

**scansion** /'skansh(ə)n/ *n* **1** the analysis of verse to show its METRE (rhythmic pattern) **2** the way in which a particular piece of verse scans [LL *scansion-, scansio*, fr L, act of climbing, fr *scandere* to climb]

**¹scant** /skant/ *adj* **1a** barely sufficient; inadequate **b** lacking in quantity; meagre **2** having a small or insufficient supply *of* ⟨*he's fat, and ~ of breath* – Shak⟩ **3** *dial NAm* excessively sparing; parsimonious **4** *chiefly NAm* falling short of a specified quantity or duration ⟨*a ~ half hour*⟩ [ME, fr ON *skamt*, neut of *skammr* short; akin to Gk *koptein* to cut – more at CAPON] – **scantly** *adv*, **scantness** *n*

**²scant** *adv* scarcely, hardly

**³scant** *vt* **1** to restrict or withhold the supply of; stint ⟨~ *an allowance*⟩ **2** to pay scant attention to ⟨*a subject ~ed in the press*⟩ **3** *archaic* to make small or meagre; skimp

**scantling** /'skantling/ *n* **1a** the dimensions of timber and stone used in building **b** the dimensions of a frame or STRAKE (band of hull planking or plates) used in shipbuilding **2** a small piece of timber (eg an upright piece in the framework of a house) **3** *archaic* a small quantity or amount [alter. of ME *scantilon*, lit., mason's or carpenter's gauge, fr ONF *escantillon*]

**scanty** /'skanti/ *adj* **1** barely sufficient **2** not adequate in extent or amount [E dial. *scant* scanty supply, fr ME, fr ON *skamt*, fr neut of *skammr* short] – **scantily** *adv*, **scantiness** *n*

**¹scape** /skayp/ *vb, archaic* to escape [ME *scapen*, short for *escapen*]

**²scape** *n* **1** a leafless flower stalk arising directly from the root of a plant (eg in the dandelion) **2** the shaft of an antenna, feather, etc [L *scapus* shaft, stalk – more at SHAFT]

**-scape** /-,skayp/ *comb form* (→ *n*) view of (a specified type of scene); *also* pictorial representation of (a specified type of scene) ⟨*seascape*⟩ [fr *landscape*]

**¹scapegoat** /'skayp,goht/ *n* **1** a goat which had the guilt for the sins of the Jewish people ritually transferred to it and was then sent into the wilderness in the biblical ceremony for YOM KIPPUR (Jewish holiday of penitence) **2** somebody or something made to bear the blame for others' faults [¹*scape*; intended as trans of Heb *'azāzēl* (prob name of a demon), as if *'ēz 'ōzēl* goat that departs, Lev 16:8 (AV)]

**²scapegoat** *vt* to make a scapegoat of

**scapegrace** /-,grays/ *n* an incorrigible rascal [¹*scape*]

**¹scaphoid** /'skafoyd/ *adj, of a bone* NAVICULAR (shaped like a boat) [NL *scaphoides*, fr Gk *skaphoeidēs*, fr *skaphos* boat]

**²scaphoid** *n* a boat-shaped bone of the wrist or ankle; NAVICULAR

**scaphopod** /'skafə,pod/ *n* TOOTH SHELL (burrowing marine animal with a tapering tubular shell) [deriv of Gk *skaphos* boat + *pod-, pous* foot]

**scapolite** /'skapəliet/ *n* any of a group of rare minerals that are complex SILICATES of aluminium, calcium, and sodium, that occur as glassy prisms in calcium-rich METAMORPHIC rocks (eg marble and GNEISS), and that include some used as semiprecious stones [Fr, fr L *scapus* shaft + Fr *-o-* + *-lite*; fr the shape of its crystals]

**scapula** /'skapyoolə/ *n, pl* **scapulae** /-lie, -li/, **scapulas** either of a pair of large flat triangular bones lying one on each side of the upper part of the back – called also SHOULDER BLADE △ spatula [NL, fr L, shoulder blade, shoulder]

**¹scapular** /'skapyoolə/ *n* **1a** a long wide band of cloth with an opening for the head worn front and back over the shoulders as part of a monk's or nun's habit **b** a pair of small cloth squares joined by shoulder tapes and worn under the clothing on the chest and back as a symbol of religious devotion or sign of membership of certain lay religious associations **2a** a scapula **b** any of the feathers covering the base of a bird's wing [ME *scapulare*, fr LL, fr L *scapula* shoulder]

**²scapular** *adj* of the shoulder, the scapula, or scapular feathers [NL *scapularis*, fr *scapula*]

**¹scar** /skah/ *n* **1** an isolated or protruding rock **2** a steep rocky formation; a bare place on the side of a mountain [ME *skere*, fr ON *sker* reef; akin to ON *skera* to cut – more at SHEAR]

**²scar** *n* **1** a mark left (eg on the skin) by the healing of a wound, burn, etc **2** a mark left on a stem or branch at the place at which a fallen leaf, harvested fruit, or other plant part was attached **3a** a mark or indentation indicating damage or wear ⟨*the* ∼s *of bullets on the . . . church door* – Kay Boyle⟩ **b** a mark that spoils; a blemish ⟨*the gravel pits have left a* ∼ *on the landscape*⟩ **4** a lasting moral or emotional injury ⟨*one of his men had been killed . . . in a manner that left a* ∼ *upon his mind* – H G Wells⟩ [ME *escare, scar,* fr MF *escare* scab, fr LL *eschara,* fr Gk, hearth, scab] – **scarless** *adj*

³**scar** *vb* **-rr-** *vt* **1** to mark (as if) with a scar **2** to do lasting injury to ∼ *vi* **1** to form a scar **2** to become scarred

**scarab** /'skarəb/ *n* **1** a scarabaeus; *broadly* a scarabaeid beetle **2** a representation of a beetle made esp of stone or glazed earthenware and used in ancient Egypt as a TALISMAN (charm to bring good luck), an ornament, and a symbol of life after death [MF *scarabee,* fr L *scarabaeus*]

**scarabaeid** /,skarə'bee·id/ *n* any of a family (Scarabaeidae) of stout-bodied beetles with LAMELLATE antennae that include the DUNG BEETLES, the plant-eating CHAFERS, and the tropical Goliath and Hercules beetles [deriv of L *scarabaeus*] – **scarabaeid** *adj*

**scarabaeiform** /,skarə'bee·i,fawm/ *adj, of an insect larva* C-shaped with short true legs and a soft fleshy body – compare APODOUS, CAMPODEIFORM, ERUCIFORM [*scarabae*us + *-iform*]

**scarabaeus** /,skarə'bee·əs/ *n* **1** a large black or nearly black DUNG BEETLE (*Scarabaeus sacer*) **2** SCARAB 2 [L]

**scaramouch, scaramouche** /'skarəmoohch, -mowch/ *n* **1** *cap* a stock character in the COMMEDIA DELL'ARTE (Italian comedy of the 16th and 17th centuries) who is a portrayal of a Spanish don and is characterized by boastfulness and cowardice **2** *archaic* a cowardly buffoon [Fr *Scaramouche,* fr It *Scaramuccia*]

¹**scarce** /skeəs/ *adj* **1** being in short supply; not plentiful or abundant **2** few in number; rare **synonyms** see ²RARE [ME *scars,* fr ONF *escars,* fr (assumed) VL *excarpsus,* lit., plucked out, pp of L *excerpere* to pluck out – more at EXCERPT] – **scarceness** *n*

²**scarce** *adv, archaic* scarcely, hardly

**scarcely** /-li/ *adv* **1a** by a narrow margin; only just ⟨*had* ∼ *finished eating*⟩ **b** almost not ⟨∼ *ever wore this mantle* – Arnold Bennett⟩ **2a** certainly not ⟨*could* ∼ *interfere in a private dispute*⟩ **b** probably not ⟨*he could* ∼ *have been better qualified*⟩
*usage* see HARDLY

**scarcity** /'skeəsəti/ *n* the quality or state of being scarce; *esp* scarcity of essential provisions (e g food or fuel)

¹**scare** /skeə/ *vt* **1** to frighten suddenly; alarm **2** to drive by frightening – usu + *off* or *away* ⟨∼d *off the intruder*⟩ ∼ *vi* to become scared ⟨*doesn't* ∼ *easily*⟩ – see also **scare the** SHIT **out of** [ME *skerren,* fr ON *skirra,* fr *skjarr* shy, timid] – **scarer** *n*
**scare up** *vt, chiefly NAm* to produce hastily or with difficulty ⟨*we might be able to* scare up *a few more men for the party*⟩

²**scare** *n* **1** a sudden or uncalled-for fright **2** a widespread state of alarm or panic ⟨*a bomb* ∼⟩ – **scare** *adj*

**scarecrow** /-,kroh/ *n* **1a** an object usu suggesting a human figure that is set up to frighten birds (e g crows) away from crops **b** something that is intended to frighten but is really harmless **2** *informal* a skinny or ragged person

**scared** /skeəd/ *adj* thrown into or living in a state of fear, fright, or panic

**scaredy-cat** /'skeədi ,kat/ *n, informal* an easily frightened person [*scared* + *-y* + *cat*]

**scaremonger** /-,mung·gə/ *n* someone who (needlessly) raises or encourages alarms – **scaremongering** *n*

**scarey** /'skeəri/ *adj* scary

¹**scarf** /skahf/ *n, pl* **scarves** /skahvz/, **scarfs** **1** a strip, square, or triangular piece of cloth worn round the shoulders or neck or over the head usu for decoration, warmth, or protection **2a** a military or official sash which usu indicates rank **b** *archaic* TIPPET **3** (part of Anglican clergyman's clothing) [ONF *escarpe* sash, sling] – **scarfed** *adj*

²**scarf** *n, pl* **scarfs** **1** either of the CHAMFERED (cut at an angle) or cutaway ends of pieces of timber that fit together to form a SCARF JOINT **2** SCARF JOINT **3** a notch cut in a tree before felling so that the tree will fall in a particular direction [ME *skarf,* prob of Scand origin; akin to ON *skarfr* scarf; akin to OE *scieran* to cut – more at SHEAR] – **scarfed** *adj*

³**scarf, scarph** /skahf/ *vt* **1** to join with a SCARF JOINT **2** to form a scarf on

**scarf joint** *n* a method of joining two pieces of timber to form one continuous straight piece without any variation in width, in which the ends of the two pieces are CHAMFERED (cut at an angle), HALVED (with a piece half the width cut out), or notched to fit each other

**scarf ring** *n* an ornamental device usu in the shape of a double ring through which two ends of a scarf are drawn to hold it in place

**scarfskin** /-,skin/ *n* EPIDERMIS (outer layer of the skin); *esp* that forming the cuticle of a nail [¹*scarf*]

**scarification** /,skarifi'kaysh(ə)n, ,skeə-/ *n* **1** the act or process of scarifying **2** a mark or marks made by scarifying

**scarify** /'skarifie, 'skeə-/ *vt* **1** to make scratches or small cuts in (e g the skin) ⟨∼ *an area for vaccination*⟩ **2** to injure the feelings of (e g by harsh criticism) **3** to break up and loosen the surface of (e g a field or road) **4** to cut or soften the outside of (a hard seed) to speed up penetration of water and thus hasten germination [MF *scarifier,* fr LL *scarificare,* alter. of L *scarifare,* fr Gk *skariphasthai* to scratch an outline, sketch – more at SCRIBE] – **scarifier** *n,* **scarificator** *n*
*usage* This word has nothing to do with "scare".

**scarious** /'skeəri·əs/ *adj, biology* dry and membranous ⟨*a plant with* ∼ *leaves*⟩ [NL *scariosus*]

**scarlatina** /,skahlə'teenə/ *n* SCARLET FEVER [NL, fr ML *scarlata* scarlet] – **scarlatinal** *adj*

¹**scarlet** /'skahlət/ *n* a vivid red colour tinged with orange [ME *scarlat, scarlet,* fr OF or ML; OF *escarlate,* fr ML *scarlata,* fr Per *saqalāt,* a kind of rich cloth]

²**scarlet** *adj* **1** of the colour scarlet **2** glaringly offensive ⟨*his sins were* ∼*, but his books were read* – Hilaire Belloc⟩

**scarlet fever** *n* a contagious fever caused by a bacterium (*Streptococcus pyogenes*) that attacks the RED BLOOD CELLS and is characterized by inflammation of the nose, throat, and mouth, headache, sickness, and a red rash

**scarlet hat** *n* a cardinal's hat, often used as a symbol of rank

**scarlet letter** *n* a scarlet letter A formerly worn by a woman convicted of adultery [fr a practice in 17th-century New England, described in the novel *The Scarlet Letter* by Nathaniel Hawthorne †1864 US writer]

¹**scarlet pimpernel** *n* a common pimpernel (*Anagallis arvensis*) of the primrose family that has usu red but sometimes white or purplish flowers that close in cloudy weather

²**scarlet pimpernel** *n* a person who smuggles refugees across a border [*The Scarlet Pimpernel,* assumed name of the hero of novels by Baroness Orczy †1947 E writer]

**scarlet runner** *n* RUNNER 7

**scarlet woman** *n* **1** the Roman Catholic church – used by some extreme Protestant sects to express their dislike of the ritual and in their eyes corruption of the Roman Catholic church **2** *euph* a woman who is sexually promiscuous; *esp* a prostitute [fr the description of 'the great whore' dressed in scarlet in Rev 17]

¹**scarp** /skahp/ *n* **1** the inner side of a ditch below the PARAPET (wall, rampart, etc) of a fortification **2a** a line of cliffs produced by FAULTING (movement along cracks in the earth's crust) or erosion **b** a low steep slope along a beach caused by erosion by the action of waves [It *scarpa*]

²**scarp** *vt* to cut down vertically or to a steep slope ⟨∼ *a coast into rugged cliffs*⟩

**scarper** /'skahpə/ *vi, Br informal* to run away [prob partly fr It *scappare,* fr (assumed) VL *excappare* – more at ESCAPE; partly fr rhyming slang *Scapa [Flow]* go, fr *Scapa Flow,* port & naval base in the Orkneys]

**scarph** /skahf/ *vt* ³SCARF

**scar tissue** *n* the fibrous tissue that grows over a wound, burn, etc and forms a scar

**scary** *also* **scarey** /'skeəri/ *adj, informal* **1** causing fright; alarming ⟨*told us a* ∼ *story*⟩ **2** easily scared; timid

¹**scat** /skat/ *vi* **-tt-** *informal* **1** to depart rapidly **2** *NAm* to move swiftly [*scat,* interj used to drive away a cat]

²**scat** *n* an animal dropping; a piece of dung [Gk *skat-, skōr* excrement – more at SCAT-]

³**scat** *n* jazz singing using improvised nonsense syllables instead of words [perh imit] – **scat** *vi*

**scat-** /skat-/, **scato-** *comb form* dung, excrement ⟨scato*phagy*⟩ [Gk *skato-,* fr *skat-, skōr* excrement; akin to OE *scearn* dung, L mus*cerda* mouse dropping]

¹**scathe** /skaydh/ *n, archaic* harm, injury [ME *skathe,* fr ON *skathi;* akin to OE *sceatha* injury, Gk *askēthēs* unharmed] – **scatheless** *adj*

²**scathe** *vt* 1 to denounce vehemently 2 *poetic* to do harm to; *specif* to scorch, sear

**scathing** /'skaydhing/ *adj* bitterly severe; scornful ⟨*a* ∼ *condemnation*⟩ – **scathingly** *adv*

**scatology** /ska'toləji/ *n* 1 the biologically orientated study of excrement (e g for the purposes of scientific classification or determination of an animal's diet) 2 interest in or treatment of obscene matters esp in literature; *also* literature characterized by scatology – **scatological** *adj*

¹**scatter** /'skatə/ *vt* 1 to cause (a group or collection) to separate widely ⟨*a dog* ∼ing *a flock of sheep*⟩ 2a to distribute at irregular intervals ⟨∼s *his toy cars all over the house*⟩ b to distribute recklessly and at random ⟨∼s *money as if he were rich*⟩ 3 to sow (seed) by casting in all directions; strew 4a to reflect (e g a beam of light particles) irregularly and diffusely b to diffuse or disperse (a beam of radiation) 5 *archaic* to fling away heedlessly; squander ∼ *vi* to separate and go in various directions [ME *scateren*] – **scatterer** *n*, **scatteringly** *adv*

   **synonyms** Scatter, disperse, dissipate, and dispel all mean "cause to separate or vanish". Scatter implies the widespread, haphazard, and often rapid separation of a group ⟨scatter *a mob with tear gas*⟩. Disperse suggests a more complete breaking up, which may be of a mass rather than a group ⟨wind disperses *the clouds*⟩. Dissipate implies reduction to nothing, by squandering or evaporation ⟨*from the far-off wooded hills the haze . . . had not yet* dissipated – D H Lawrence⟩. Dispel emphasizes the idea of driving away rather than of separation into parts, and so is often used of abstractions ⟨dispel *a rumour*⟩.

²**scatter** *n* 1 the act of scattering 2 a small supply or number randomly distributed or strewn about ⟨*a* ∼ *of orange lights*⟩ 3 *statistics* the state or extent of being scattered: e g 3a DISPERSION b FREQUENCY DISTRIBUTION

**scatterbrain** /-ˌbrayn/ *n* somebody who is incapable of concentration – **scatterbrained** *adj*

**scatter cushion** *n* a small loose cushion usu used to increase the comfort of the sitter on sofas, armchairs, etc

**scatter diagram** *n* a two-dimensional graph consisting of points whose positions (COORDINATES) represent values of two VARIABLES under study

**scattergood** /'skatəˌgood/ *n* a wasteful person; a spendthrift

'**scatter-ˌgun** *n, chiefly NAm* a shotgun that discharges a large number of pellets

¹**scattering** /'skatəring/ *n* 1 an act or process in which something scatters or is scattered 2 something scattered; *esp* a small number or quantity interspersed here and there ⟨*a* ∼ *of visitors*⟩

²**scattering** *adj* 1 dispersing in various directions 2 found or placed far apart and at random 3 *NAm* divided among many or several candidates ⟨∼ *votes*⟩ – **scatteringly** *adv*

**scatter rug** *n* a small rug used, esp with others, in a room (e g to fill a vacant area of floor)

**scatty** /'skati/ *adj, Br* 1 apt to be forgetful 2 mildly eccentric; slightly odd ⟨*a thoroughly* ∼ *idea for making money*⟩ [prob fr *scatter*brain + -*y*]

**scaup** /skawp/ *also* **scaup-duck** *n, pl* **scaups**, *esp collectively* **scaup** any of several diving ducks (genus *Aythya*, esp *Aythya marila*) that are generally black with white markings and that dive for shellfish [perh alter. of *scalp* (bed of shellfish)]

**scavenge** /'skavinj/ *vt* 1a to remove (e g dirt or refuse) from an area b to feed on (carrion or refuse) 2a to remove (burned gases) from the cylinder of an INTERNAL-COMBUSTION ENGINE after a working stroke b to remove (e g an undesirable constituent) from a substance or region by chemical or physical means c to clean and purify (molten metal) by combining with or causing the combination of impurities to form compounds that can be easily removed 3 to salvage from discarded or refuse material; *also* to salvage usable material from ∼ *vi* 1 to work or act as a scavenger 2 to search for reusable material 3 to obtain food by scavenging ⟨*dogs* scavenging *on kitchen waste*⟩ [back-formation fr *scavenger*]

**scavenger** /'skavinjə/ *n* 1 one who or that which scavenges: e g 1a a refuse collector b a rag-and-bone man c a chemical used to remove or make harmless an undesirable substance 2 an animal or organism that feeds habitually on refuse or carrion [alter. of earlier *scavager* person who cleans streets, fr ME *skawager* official who collected a toll on goods sold by nonresident merchants (and was later responsible for keeping streets clean), fr *skawage* toll on goods sold by nonresident merchants, fr ONF *escauwage* inspection]

**scazon** /'skayzon/ *n* a line of poetry with a faltering rhythm, esp one consisting of two IAMBS (one weak and one strong syllable) and a TROCHEE (one strong and one weak syllable) or SPONDEE (two strong syllables) [L, fr Gk *skazōn*, lit., limping person or thing, fr prp of *skazein* to limp – more at SHANK]

**scena** /'shaynə/ *n* an elaborate solo vocal musical composition that consists of a RECITATIVE (narrative speechlike passage) usu followed by one or more ARIA (song) sections [It, lit., scene, fr L]

**scenario** /si'nahri·oh, -'neə-/ *n, pl* **scenarios** 1a a brief outline or synopsis of a dramatic work b an outline for the LIBRETTO (words) of an opera 2a SCREENPLAY (written form of a story prepared for film production) b SHOOTING SCRIPT (completely detailed film or television script set out for use during shooting) 3 (an account or synopsis of) a projected, planned, or anticipated course of action or events ⟨*on this* ∼ *unemployment could reach 5 million by 1990*⟩ 4 a background, scene ⟨*Oxford is not an obvious* ∼ *for dramatic confrontation – Isis*⟩ [It, fr L *scaenarium*, fr *scaena* stage]

   **usage** The pronunciation /si'nahri·oh/ is recommended for BBC broadcasters.

**scenarist** /si'nahrist, -'neə-/ *n* a writer of scenarios, esp for films

¹**scend** /send/ *vi* to rise or heave upward under the influence of a natural force (e g on a wave) [alter. (influenced by *ascend*) of *send*]

²**scend** *n* the lifting motion of a wave

**scene** /seen/ *n* 1 any of the smaller subdivisions of a dramatic work: e g 1a a division of an act presenting continuous action in one place b a single situation or unit of dialogue in a play or film ⟨*the* ∼ *where the wife discovers her husband in bed with the au pair*⟩ c an episode or sequence in a film or television programme 2a a stage setting b a real or imaginary vista suggesting a stage setting ⟨*a sylvan* ∼⟩ 3 the place of an occurrence or action; location ⟨∼ *of the crime*⟩ 4 a display of violent or unrestrained feeling ⟨*make a* ∼⟩ 5a a sphere of activity or interest ⟨*the drug* ∼⟩ ⟨*philosophy is not my* ∼⟩; *also* the people active in a particular sphere ⟨*the poets are very much a different* ∼ *from the novelists* – Margaret Drabble⟩ b *informal* something in which one is interested or with which one is involved or concerned ⟨*B movies may have their admirers, but they aren't my* ∼⟩ [MF, stage, fr L *scena, scaena* stage, scene, fr Gk *skēnē* temporary shelter, tent, building forming the background for a dramatic performance, stage; akin to Gk *skia* shadow – more at SHINE] – **behind the scenes** out of the public view; IN PRIVATE ⟨*a decision made* behind the scenes *by the civil servants of the Department*⟩

**scene dock** *n* a space near the stage in a theatre where scenery is stored

**scenery** /'seen(ə)ri/ *n* 1 the painted scenes or hangings and accessories used on a theatre stage 2 the visual aspect of landscape, esp when considered attractive

**sceneshifter** /-ˌshiftə/ *n* a worker who moves the scenery in a theatre

**scenic** /'seenik/ *also* **scenical** /-kl/ *adj* 1 of the stage, a stage setting, or stage representation 2a displaying fine natural scenery ⟨*a* ∼ *route*⟩ b of natural scenery 3 *of a painting, sculpture, tapestry, etc* depicting an action, event, or episode ⟨*a painting in which the* ∼ *element is subsidiary to the depiction of landscape*⟩ – **scenically** *adv*

**scenic railway** *n* a miniature railway (e g at a fun fair) with artificial scenery along the way

¹**scent** /sent/ *vt* 1a to perceive by the sense of smell b to get or have an inkling of ⟨∼ *trouble*⟩ 2 to infuse or fill with a usu pleasant smell ⟨∼ *a handkerchief*⟩ ∼ *vi* to use the nose in seeking or tracking prey ⟨*hounds* ∼ing *in the undergrowth*⟩ [ME *senten*, fr MF *sentir* to feel, smell, fr L *sentire* to perceive, feel – more at SENSE]

²**scent** *n* 1 an odour: e g 1a a smell left by an animal on a surface that it has passed over, by which the animal may be traced ⟨*hounds followed the fox's* ∼⟩ b a characteristic or particular smell; *esp* one that is agreeable ⟨*the* ∼ *of violets*⟩ 2a power of smelling; the sense of smell ⟨*a keen* ∼⟩ b power of detection; a nose ⟨*a* ∼ *for troublemakers*⟩ 3 a course of pursuit or discovery ⟨*throw one off the* ∼⟩ 4 a hint, suggestion ⟨*a* ∼ *of an impending argument*⟩ 5 PERFUME 2 6 a mixture prepared for use as a lure in hunting or fishing *synonyms* see ²SMELL – **scentless** *adj*

**scented** /'sentid/ *adj* having scent: e g a having the sense of smell b having a perfumed smell ⟨*a* ∼ *flower*⟩ c having or exhaling an odour ⟨*a* ∼ *handkerchief*⟩

**scepsis** /'skepsis/ *n* the doubting as a method in philosophy of anything which is not capable of vigorous formal proof; *broadly* a sceptical outlook or attitude [NL, fr Gk *skepsis* examination, doubt, sceptical philosophy, fr *skeptesthai*]

**sceptic** /'skeptik/ *n* **1** an adherent or advocate of the philosophical doctrine of scepticism **2** a person disposed to scepticism, esp regarding religion or religious principles **3** a person with a mistrustful attitude to life or other people △ **septic** [L or Gk; L *scepticus*, fr Gk *skeptikos*, fr *skeptikos* thoughtful, fr *skeptesthai* to look, consider – more at SPY]

**sceptical** /'skeptikl/ *adj* relating to, characteristic of, or marked by scepticism ⟨*a ~ listener*⟩

**scepticism** /'skepti,siz(ə)m/ *n* **1a** the belief or philosophical doctrine that certain knowledge, either generally or in a particular sphere, is unattainable **b** the use of scepsis as a method or principle in philosophy; the practice of doubting or suspending judgment on anything not capable of rigorous formal proof **2** doubt concerning basic religious principles (eg eternal life and divine guidance) **3** an attitude of doubt or mistrust either in general or towards a particular object *synonyms* see UNCERTAINTY

¹**sceptre**, *chiefly NAm* **scepter** /'septə/ *n* **1** a staff or baton borne by a ruler as a sign of royal authority **2** a royal or imperial authority; sovereignty [ME *sceptre*, fr OF *ceptre*, fr L *sceptrum*, fr Gk *skēptron* staff, sceptre – more at SHAFT]

²**sceptre**, *chiefly NAm* **scepter** *vt* to endow with the sceptre as a symbol of royal authority

**schadenfreude** /'shahdn,froydə (Ger ʃɑːdənfrɔɪdə)/ *n* enjoyment or satisfaction obtained from contemplation of the misfortunes of others [Ger, fr *schaden* damage, injury + *freude* joy]

**schappe** /'shapə/, **schappe silk** *n* fabric or yarn spun from silk waste; SPUN SILK [Ger dial. (Swiss) *schappe* raw silk waste]

¹**schedule** /'shedyool, -jəl; *also, esp NAm* 'skedyool, -jəl/ *n* **1** a statement of supplementary details appended to a legal or legislative document **2** a list, catalogue, or inventory ⟨*a ~ of the contents of the flat*⟩ **3** a timetable; *also* the times fixed in a timetable ⟨*trains that always run behind ~*⟩ **4** a plan of things to be done and the order in which to do them; a programme, proposal **5** a body of items to be dealt with; an agenda **6** *obs* a written document [ME *cedule*, fr MF, slip of paper, note, fr LL *schedula* slip of paper, dim. of L *scheda*, *scida* sheet of papyrus, fr (assumed) Gk *schidē*; akin to Gk *schizein* to split – more at SHED]

²**schedule** *vt* **1a** to place on a schedule **b** to make a schedule of ⟨*~d his income and debts*⟩ **2** to appoint or designate to occur at a fixed time ⟨*~d to be released in July*⟩ **3** *Br* to place on a list of buildings or historical remains protected by law – **scheduler** *n*

**scheelite** /'sheeliet/ *n* a white, yellowish, or brownish mineral that consists of calcium TUNGSTATE, CaWO₄, and that is an important source of tungsten and its compounds [Ger *scheelit*, fr Karl *Scheele* †1786 Sw chemist]

**schema** /'skeemə/ *n*, *pl* **schemata** /-mətə/ a diagrammatic representation; a plan, outline [Gk *schēmat-*, *schēma*]

¹**schematic** /ski'matik/ *adj* of a scheme or schema; diagrammatic [NL *schematicus*, fr Gk *schēmat-*, *schēma*] – **schematically** *adv*

²**schematic** *n* a schematic drawing or diagram

**schematism** /'skeemətiz(ə)m/ *n* the arrangement of parts in a pattern or according to a scheme; design; *also* a particular systematic arrangement

**schematize, -ise** /'skeemə,tiez/ *vt* **1** to form into a scheme or systematic arrangement **2** to express or depict schematically [Gk *schēmatizein*, fr *schēmat-*, *schēma*] – **schematization** *n*

¹**scheme** /skeem/ *n* **1** a graphic sketch or outline **2** a concise statement or table **3a** a plan or programme for a course of action; a project ⟨*a hydroelectric ~*⟩ **b** an organized system of financial investment, insurance, etc ⟨*a company pension ~*⟩ **4** a crafty or secret strategy; a plot **5** a systematic arrangement of parts or elements; a design ⟨*a colour ~*⟩ **6** *archaic* **6a** a mathematical or astronomical diagram **b** a representation of the astrological aspects of the planets at a particular time [L *schemat-*, *schema* arrangement, figure, fr Gk *schēmat-*, *schēma*, fr *echein* to have, hold, be in (such) a condition; akin to OE *sige* victory, Skt *sahate* he prevails]

²**scheme** *vt* to form a scheme for ⟨*~ an escape*⟩ *~vi* to make plans; *also* to plot, intrigue – **schemer** *n*

**scheming** /'skeeming/ *adj* given to forming schemes; *esp* shrewdly devious and intriguing

**schemozzle** /shi'mozl/ *n* a shemozzle

**scherzando** /skeət'sandoh/ *n, adv, or adj*, *pl* **scherzandi** /-di/, **scherzandos** (a musical composition to be played) in a sprightly or playful manner [It, fr verbal of *scherzare* to joke, of Gmc origin; akin to MHG *scherzen* to leap for joy, joke; akin to Gk *skairein* to gambol – more at CARDINAL]

**scherzo** /'skeətsoh/ *n, pl* **scherzi** /-tsi/, **scherzos** a sprightly instrumental musical composition or movement in quick, usu triple, time [It, lit., joke, fr *scherzare*]

**Schick test** /shik/ *n* a test of a person's susceptibility to diphtheria in which a diluted diphtheria TOXIN is injected into the skin causing the formation of an inflamed red patch in those who are at risk [Béla *Schick* †1967 US (Hungarian-born) paediatrician]

**Schiff's reagent** /shifs/ *n* a solution of FUCHSINE (bluish-red dye) decolorized by treatment with SULPHUR DIOXIDE that gives a useful test for the presence of ALDEHYDES (highly volatile organic chemical compounds) because they restore the colour of the dye – compare FEULGEN REACTION [Hugo *Schiff* †1915 Ger chemist]

**schiller** /'shilə/ *n* a bronzy iridescent lustre (eg of a mineral) [Ger]

**schilling** /'shiling/ *n* – see MONEY table [Ger, fr OHG *skilling*, a gold coin – more at SHILLING]

**schipperke** /'shipəki/ *n* (any of) a Belgian breed of small stocky usu black dogs with a foxlike head and erect triangular ears [Flem, dim. of *schipper* skipper; fr its use as a watchdog on boats]

**schism** /'siz(ə)m, 'skiz(ə)m/ *n* **1** separation into opposed factions **2a** formal division in or separation from a religious body **b** the offence of causing or encouraging schism [ME *scisme*, fr MF *cisme*, fr LL *schismat-*, *schisma*, fr Gk, cleft, division, fr *schizein* to split]

¹**schismatic** /siz'matik, skiz-/ *n* a person who creates or takes part in schism

²**schismatic** *also* **schismatical** /-kl/ *adj* **1** (having the character) of schism **2** guilty of schism – **schismatically** *adv*

**schismatist** /'sizmətist, 'skiz-/ *n* a schismatic

**schismatize, -ise** /'sizmətiez, 'skiz-/ *vi* to take part in schism; *esp* to create disunity (eg in the church) *~ vt* to cause schism in

**schist** /shist/ *n* a medium- to coarse-grained crystalline METAMORPHIC rock that can be split into thin layers [Fr *schiste*, fr L *schistos* (*lapis*), lit., stone that splits easily, fr Gk *schistos* that may be split, fr *schizein* to split]

**schistose** /'shistohs/ *also* **schistous** /'shistəs/ *adj* of schist; *esp* having the character or structure of a schist

**schistosome** /'shistə,sohm/ *n* any of a genus (*Schistosoma* of the class Trematoda) of elongated worms with the sexes separate, that parasitize the blood vessels of birds and mammals and that in human beings cause schistosomiasis; *broadly* a worm of the family (Schistosomatidae) that includes this genus – called also BILHARZIA [NL *Schistosoma*, genus name, fr Gk *schistos* + *sōma* body – more at SOMAT-] – **schistosome** *adj*, **schistosomal** *adj*

**schistosomiasis** /,shistəsoh'mie·əsis/ *n, pl* **schistosomiases** /-seez/ infestation with or disease caused by schistosomes; *specif* a severe endemic disease of human beings in Egypt, tropical Africa, and S America marked esp by blood loss and tissue damage – called also BILHARZIA, BILHARZIASIS [NL, fr *Schistosoma*]

**schiz-** /skits-/, **schizo-** *comb form* **1** split; cleft ⟨schizo*carp*⟩ **2** characterized by or involving splitting or division ⟨schizo*genesis*⟩ **3** schizophrenia ⟨schizo*thymia*⟩ [NL, fr Gk *schizo-*, fr *schizein* to split]

**schizo** /'skitsoh/ *n, pl* **schizos** *informal* a schizophrenic person – **schizo** *adj*

**schizocarp** /'skitsoh,kahp/ *n* a dry compound fruit (eg of the hollyhock or the geranium) that splits into several single-seeded parts when it is ripe [ISV]

**schizogony** /skit'sogəni/ *n* ASEXUAL REPRODUCTION by dividing many times into identical spores that is characteristic of SPOROZOANS (single-celled parasitic organisms) (eg the malaria parasite) [NL *schizogonia*, fr *schiz-* + L *-gonia* -gony] – **schizogonous, schizogonic** *adj*

**schizoid** /'skitsoyd/ *adj* **1** characterized by, resulting from, tending towards, or suggestive of schizophrenia **2** *informal* showing conflicting or contradictory attitudes ⟨*his review of the film seemed a bit ~, he seemed to feel guilty about having enjoyed it*⟩ [ISV] – **schizoid** *n*

**schizomycete** /ˌskitsohˈmieseet, -mieˈseet/ *n* a bacterium [deriv of Gk *schizo-* schiz-+ *mykēt-, mykēs* fungus – more at MYC-] – **schizomycetous** *adj*

**schizont** /ˈskitsont/ *n* a stage in the LIFE CYCLE of a SPOROZOAN (single-celled parasitic organism) that contains many nuclei and reproduces by schizogony [ISV *schiz-* + *-ont*]

**schizophrene** /ˈskitsəfreen/ *n* one affected with schizophrenia; a schizophrenic [Ger *schizophren*, fr *schizophrenie* schizophrenia]

**schizophrenia** /ˌskitsəˈfreenyə/ *n* any of a group of mental disorders characterized by loss of contact with reality, disintegration of personality expressed as disturbance of feeling, behaviour, thought, etc, and usu by delusions, hallucinations, etc [NL, fr Ger *schizophrenie*, fr *schiz-* + Gk *phrēn* mind] – **schizophrenic** *adj or n*, **schizophrenically** *adv*

**schizophyte** /ˈskitsohfiet/ *n* any of a group (*Schizophyta*) of living things that in some systems of classification includes all organisms that do not have a distinct nucleus (e g the bacteria and the BLUE-GREEN ALGAE) and in others is confined to the bacteria alone [deriv of Gk *schizo-* + *phyton* plant – more at PLANT] – **schizophytic** *adj*

**schizothymia** /ˌskitsohˈthiemyə/ *n* a tendency towards INTROVERSION (a turning away from external reality towards self-absorption) that, while remaining within the bounds of normality, somewhat resembles schizophrenia [NL, fr *schiz-* + *-thymia*] – **schizothymic** *adj*

**schlemiel, schlemihl** /shləˈmiəl/ *n, chiefly NAm informal or dial* an unlucky bungling person who is easily victimized [Yiddish *shlumiel*]

**schlepp** /shlep/ *vb, chiefly NAm informal or dial* to drag, haul [Yiddish *shleppen*, fr MHG *sleppen*, fr MLG *slēpen*]

**schlieren** /ˈshliərən/ *n pl* 1 small masses or streaks in IGNEOUS rock (rock formed by cooling and solidification of molten rock material) that differ in composition from the main body 2 regions of varying density and hence REFRACTIVE INDEX in a transparent medium, that are often caused by pressure or temperature differences or flaws and that appear as streaks on a photograph when a beam of light is passed through the medium [Ger, fr Ger dial., lit., ulcers] – **schlieric** *adj*

**schlock** /shlok/ *adj, chiefly NAm informal or dial* of low quality or value ⟨*churn out ~ TV series* – Clive James⟩ [Yiddish *shlak*, fr *shlak* curse, cheap merchandise, lit., blow, fr MHG *slag, slac*, fr OHG *slag*, fr *slahan* to strike – more at SLAY] – **schlock** *n*

**schm-** /shm-/ *comb form, chiefly NAm informal* – used as an expression of disbelief or contempt, or to dismiss an idea, by naming the object and then repeating the name with "schm-" added to the front or replacing the initial letter ⟨*newspapers*, schm*ewspapers – who needs them?*⟩ [fr the many Yiddish words, often of derogatory meaning (e g *shmok* fool, *shmatte* rag), beginning *shm-* or *schm-*]

**schmaltz, schmalz** /shmalts/ *n* (an artistic production, esp a piece of music, displaying) an excessively sentimental or florid atmosphere or tone [Yiddish *shmalts*, lit., rendered fat, fr MHG *smalz*; akin to OHG *smelzan* to melt – more at SMELT] – **schmaltzy** *adj*

**Schmidt** /shmit/ *adj* of or being an optical system (e g for a telescope or camera) that uses an OBJECTIVE (image-forming lens system) made up of a concave spherical mirror having in front of it a transparent plate to minimize SPHERICAL ABERRATION (distortion caused by the spherical shape of the mirror), which is used esp for astronomical observation and enables wide areas of sky to be photographed in a single exposure [Bernhard *Schmidt* †1935 Ger optical scientist]

**schmo, schmoe** /shmoh/ *n, pl* **schmoes** *chiefly NAm informal or dial* a stupid person; a jerk [prob modif of Yiddish *shmok*]

**schmuck** /shmuk/ *n, chiefly NAm informal or dial* a fool [Yiddish *shmok* penis, fool, fr Ger *schmuck* adornment]

**schnapps, schnaps** /shnaps/ *n, pl* **schnapps** a strong alcoholic drink; *esp* strong gin as originally made in the Netherlands [Ger *schnaps*, lit., dram of liquor, fr LG, fr *snappen* to snap]

**schnauzer** /ˈshnowzə, ˈshnowtsə/ *n* any of three breeds of dog originating in Germany that have a long head, small ears, heavy eyebrows, moustache and beard, and a wiry coat [Ger, fr *schnauze* snout – more at SNOUT]

**schnitzel** /ˈshnits(ə)l/ *n* a (veal) escalope [Ger, lit., shaving, chip, fr MHG, dim. of *sniz* slice; akin to OHG *snīdan* to cut, OE *snithan*, Czech *snět* bough]

**schnorkel** /ˈs(h)nawkl/ *vi or n* (to) snorkel

**schnorrer** /ˈshnawrə/ *n, chiefly NAm informal or dial* a beggar; *esp* a habitual sponger [Yiddish *shnorer*]

**schnozzle** /ˈshnozəl/ *n, chiefly NAm informal or dial* a nose [prob modif of Yiddish *shnoitsl*, dim. of *shnoits* snout, fr Ger *schnauze*]

**schola cantorum** /ˌskohlə kanˈtawrəm/ *n, pl* **scholae cantorum** /ˌskohlie ~/ 1 a singing school, esp for church choristers; *specif* the choir or choir school of a monastery or cathedral 2 an enclosure designed for a choir and located in the centre of the nave in early church buildings [ML, school of singers]

**scholar** /ˈskolə/ *n* 1 someone who attends a school or studies under a teacher; a pupil 2a someone who has done advanced study in a special field **b** a learned person 3 the holder of a scholarship *synonyms* see PUPIL [ME *scoler*, fr OE *scolere* & OF *escoler*, fr ML *scholaris*, fr LL, of a school, fr L *schola* school]

**scholarly** /-li/ *adj* characteristic of or suitable for learned persons; learned, academic ⟨~ *journals*⟩

**scholarship** /-ship/ *n* 1 a grant of money awarded (e g by a college or foundation) to a student of academic merit to pay for education, books, upkeep, etc while studying 2 the character, methods, or achievements of a scholar; learning 3 a fund of knowledge and learning ⟨*drawing on the ~ of the ancients*⟩ *synonyms* see KNOWLEDGE

**Scholarship level** *n, often cap L* an examination in any of many subjects that is the highest of the three levels of the GENERAL CERTIFICATE OF EDUCATION, is usu taken at about the age of 18, and is a partial qualification for university entrance; *also* a subject taken in this examination – called also S LEVEL

**¹scholastic** /skəˈlastik, sko-/ *adj* 1a *often cap* of Scholasticism ⟨~ *theology*⟩ ⟨~ *philosophy*⟩ **b** suggestive or characteristic of a scholastic, esp in empty or unnecessary subtlety or dryness; pedantic ⟨*turned out dull ~ reports*⟩ 2 of schools or scholars; *esp* of secondary school [ML & L; ML *scholasticus* of the schoolmen, fr L, of a school, fr Gk *scholastikos*, fr *scholazein* to keep a school, fr *scholē* school] – **scholastically** *adv*

**²scholastic** *n* 1a *cap* a follower or practitioner of Scholasticism **b** one who is fond of academic quibbling; a pedant 2 a student in a scholasticate

**scholasticate** /skəˈlastikayt/ *n* a school of the third level of general study for those preparing for membership in a Roman Catholic religious order [NL *scholasticatus*, fr *scholasticus* student in a scholasticate]

**scholasticism** /skəˈlasti,siz(ə)m/ *n* 1a *cap* a philosophical movement dominant in W Christian civilization from the 9th until the 17th century that combined religious dogma with the tradition of the writings of the CHURCH FATHERS (writers accepted by the church as authoritative witnesses to its teaching and practice), esp of St Augustine, and later with the philosophy of Aristotle **b** NEO-SCHOLASTICISM (contemporary movement aimed at reviving Scholasticism) 2 close or pedantic adherence to the traditional teachings or methods of a school or sect

**scholiast** /ˈskohli,ast/ *n* a maker of scholia; an annotator [MGk *scholiastēs*, fr *scholiazein* to write scholia on, fr Gk *scholion*] – **scholiastic** *adj*

**scholium** /ˈskolyəm/ *n, pl* **scholia** /-liə/, **scholiums** 1 a marginal annotation or comment (e g on the text of a classic by an early grammarian) 2 a remark or observation related but not essential to a demonstration or argument [NL, fr Gk *scholion*, fr dim. of *scholē* lecture]

**¹school** /skoohl/ *n* 1 an organization that provides instruction: e g 1a an institution for the teaching of children **b**(1) a group of scholars and teachers pursuing knowledge together that with similar groups constituted a medieval university **b**(2) any of the four faculties of a medieval university **b**(3) an institution for specialized higher education associated with or forming a part or faculty of a university ⟨*the London* School *of Economics*⟩ **c** an establishment offering specialized instruction ⟨*a ~ of beauty culture*⟩ ⟨*driving ~*s⟩ **d** *NAm* a college, university 2a(1) the process of teaching or learning esp at a school **a**(2) attendance at a school **a**(3) a session of a school ⟨*see you after ~*⟩ **b** a school building **c** *taking sing or pl vb* the pupils or students attending a school; *also* these plus the teachers 3 a source of knowledge ⟨*experience was his ~*⟩ 4a persons who adhere to the same doctrine or teacher (e g in philosophy or theology) ⟨*the Frankfurt ~*⟩ **b** a group of artists under a common stylistic influence **c** a body of persons with similar opinions ⟨*a ~ of thought*⟩ ⟨*a gardener of the old ~*⟩ **d** *informal* a group assembled for some (illegal) purpose (e g gambling) ⟨*a poker ~*⟩ 5 *pl, cap* the final honours examination for the Oxford BA [ME *scole*, fr OE *scōl*, fr L *schola*, fr Gk *scholē* leisure, discussion, lecture, school; akin to Gk *echein* to hold – more at SCHEME]

²**school** *vt* **1** to educate in an institution of learning **2a** to teach or drill in a specified knowledge or skill ⟨*well* ~ed *in languages*⟩ ⟨~ *a horse*⟩ **b** to discipline or habituate to something ⟨~ *oneself in patience*⟩ **synonyms** see TEACH

³**school** *n* a large number of fish or other aquatic animals of one kind swimming together [ME *scole,* fr MD *schole;* akin to OE *scolu* multitude, *scylian* to separate – more at SKILL]

⁴**school** *vi* to swim or feed in a school ⟨*porpoises are* ~ing⟩

**school age** *n* the age at which children are legally required to start attending school; *also* the period of life during which such attendance is required

**schoolbag** /'skoohl,bag/ *n* a bag for carrying schoolbooks and other articles required by a schoolchild

**school board** *n* an elected committee formerly in charge of local state schools

**schoolboy** /-,boy/ *n* a boy attending school ⟨*the whining* ~, *with his satchel and shining morning face* – Shak⟩ – **schoolboyish** *adj*

**school bus** *n* a vehicle used for transporting children to or from school or on activities connected with school

**School Certificate** *n* a British secondary-school examination that was the forerunner of the GENERAL CERTIFICATE OF EDUCATION

**schoolchild** /-,chield/ *n* a child attending school

**school council** *n* an elected body of schoolchildren who help to manage the affairs of their school

**schooldays** /'skoohl,dayz/ *n pl* the period of life when one attends school

**school edition** *n* an edition of a book issued esp for use in schools and usu simplified, condensed, or emended esp with glossaries or explanatory matter

**schoolfellow** /-,feloh/ *n* a schoolmate

**schoolgirl** /'skoohl,guhl/ *n* a girl attending school – **schoolgirlish** *adj*

**schoolhouse** /-,hows/ *n* a building used as a school; *esp* a country primary school

**schooling** /'skoohling/ *n* **1a** instruction in school **b** training or guidance gained from practical experience **2** the cost of instruction and maintenance at school **3** the training of an animal (e g a horse); *esp* the teaching and exercising of horse and rider in the formal techniques of horse riding

**schoolkid** /-,kid/ *n, informal* a schoolchild

**school-'leaver** *n, Br* a pupil who is about to leave or has recently left school

**schoolman** /'skoohlmən/ *n* **1** someone skilled in DISPUTATION (defence of a thesis by formal logic) **2** *cap* SCHOLASTIC 1a

**schoolmarm, schoolma'am** /-,mahm/ *n* **1a** a prim, old-fashioned, and fussy woman **b** *chiefly NAm* a prim or fussily correct person ⟨*the point of view of the* ~ (*for convenience's sake, the term is used bisexually) who . . . objects to all linguistic change* – Thomas Pyles⟩ **2** *chiefly NAm* a schoolmistress; *esp* a rural or small-town schoolmistress [*school* + *marm,* alter. of ma'am] – **schoolmarmish, schoolma'amish** *adj*

**schoolmaster** /-,mahstə/ *n* **1** *fem* **schoolmistress** a schoolteacher **2** one who or that which disciplines or directs

**schoolmate** /-,mayt/ *n* a companion at school

**school practice** *n* TEACHING PRACTICE (practical experience in a school as part of a schoolteacher's training)

**schoolroom** /-,roohm, -room/ *n* a room where a school is held or where children are taught

**schools** /skoohlz/ *adj, Br* of or intended for schools, esp primary schools ⟨*a* ~ *broadcast*⟩

**Schools Council** *n* the official British body that conducts inquiries into the activities of and subjects covered by schools

**schoolteacher** /-,teechə/ *n* a person who teaches in a school

**schooltime** /'skoohl,tiem/ *n* **1** the time for beginning a session of school, or during which school is held **2** schooldays

**school welfare officer** *n* someone employed by a state school system to investigate welfare concerns of pupils, esp continued absences

**schoolwork** /-,wuhk/ *n* lessons done in classes at school or assigned to be done at home

**schooner** /'skoohnə/ *n* **1** a fast sailing vessel with FORE-AND-AFT rig having two masts with a smaller sail on the foremast and with the mainmast nearly at the centre of the ship; *broadly* any of various larger fore-and-aft rigged sailing vessels with three to seven masts **2a(1)** a relatively tall narrow glass used esp for a large measure of a fortified wine

(e g sherry or port) **a(2)** the contents of or quantity contained in a schooner; *specif, Br* the capacity of a schooner used as a measure (e g for sherry) **b** *chiefly NAm & Austr* a large tall drinking glass, esp for beer **3** *NAm* PRAIRIE SCHOONER (covered wagon) [origin unknown]

**schorl** /shawl/ *n* a black TOURMALINE (mineral sometimes used as a gem) containing a high percentage of iron [Ger *schörl*] – **schorlaceous** *adj*

**schottische** /sho'teesh/ *n* **1** a dance with a two-beat rhythm resembling a slow polka, in which the dancers move round in a circle **2** music for the schottische [Ger, fr *schottisch* Scottish, fr *Schotte* Scot; akin to OE *Scottas* Scots]

**schtick** /shtik/ *n* SHTICK

¹**schuss** /shoos (*Ger* ʃʊs)/ *n* a straight high-speed ski run [Ger, lit., shot, fr OHG *scuz* – more at SHOT]

²**schuss** *vt* to make a schuss over ⟨~ *a slope*⟩ ~ *vi* to ski directly down a slope – **schusser** *n*

**schwa** /shwah/ *n* **1** an unstressed mid-central vowel that is the usual sound of the first and last vowels of *banana* **2** the symbol ə used for the schwa sound [Ger, fr Heb *shĕwā*]

**Schwann cell** /shvan/ *n* a long thin cell that forms part of the thin outer sheath (NEURILEMMA) of a NERVE FIBRE [Theodor *Schwann* †1882 Ger naturalist]

**schwarmerei** /'shvahmərie (*Ger* ʃwɛrmərai)/ *n* naive or sentimental over-enthusiasm [Ger *schwärmerei,* fr *schwärmen* to be enthusiastic, lit., to swarm]

**sciaenid** /sie'eenid/ *n* any of a family (Sciaenidae) of flesh-eating spiny-finned fishes that are found mainly in tropical or subtropical seas and that include many which are eaten as food [deriv of Gk *skiaina,* a kind of fish] – **sciaenid** *adj,* **sciaenoid** *adj or n*

**sciagram** /'sie-ə,gram/ *n* a figure formed by shading in the outline of a shadow [ISV *scia-* (fr Gk *skia* shadow) + *-gram* – more at SHINE]

**sciatic** /sie'atik/ *adj* **1** of or situated near the hip **2** of or caused by sciatica ⟨~ *pains*⟩ [MF *sciatique,* fr LL *sciaticus,* alter. of L *ischiadicus* of pain in the hip, fr Gk *ischiadikos,* fr *ischiad-, ischias* sciatica, fr *ischion* hip joint]

**sciatica** /sie'atikə/ *n* pain along the course of a SCIATIC NERVE (e g caused by displacement of a disc of cartilage between two bones in the spine), esp in the back of the thigh; *broadly* pain in the lower back, buttocks, hips, or adjacent parts [ME, fr ML, fr LL, fem of *sciaticus*]

**sciatic nerve** *n* either of the pair of nerves that arise in the pelvis and pass down through the buttocks and the back of the thigh

**science** /'sie-əns/ *n* **1a** a branch of systematized knowledge as an object of study ⟨*the* ~ *of theology*⟩ **b** something (e g a skill or technique) that may be studied or learned systematically ⟨*the* ~ *of boxing*⟩ **c** any of the NATURAL SCIENCES ⟨*students specializing in a* ~⟩ – sometimes taken to include mathematics **2a** coordinated knowledge of the operation of general laws, esp as obtained and tested through scientific method **b** scientific knowledge of the physical world and its phenomena; NATURAL SCIENCE **3** a system or method (purporting to be) based on scientific principles **4** *archaic* the possession of knowledge as distinguished from ignorance or misunderstanding – compare NESCIENCE **synonyms** see KNOWLEDGE [ME, fr MF, fr L *scientia,* fr *scient-, sciens* having knowledge, fr prp of *scire* to know; akin to L *scindere* to cut – more at SHED] – **blind somebody with science** to impress or overwhelm somebody with a display of technical knowledge

**science fiction** *n* fiction of a type originally set in the future and dealing principally with the impact of actual or imagined science upon society or individuals, but now including also works of literary fantasy

**sciential** /sie'ensh(ə)l/ *adj* **1** relating to or producing knowledge or science **2** endowed with knowledge

**scientific** /,sie-ən'tifik/ *adj* of or exhibiting the methods or principles of science [ML *scientificus* producing knowledge, fr L *scient-, sciens* + *-i-* + *-ficus* -fic] – **scientifically** *adv*

**scientific method** *n* principles and procedures employed in the pursuit of systematic knowledge and involving the recognition and formulation of a problem, the collection of data through observation and experiment, and the formulation and testing of HYPOTHESES (theories, suppositions, etc)

**scientific notation** *n* a system in which numbers are expressed as products consisting of a number between 1 and 10 and a power of 10 ⟨*14000 in* ~ *is 1.4 × 10⁴*⟩

**scientific socialism** *n* Marxism; *esp* that portion of Marx's teachings dealing with the laws of social change and the final inevitability of communism – no longer used technically

**scientism** /'sie·ən,tiz(ə)m/ *n* **1** methods and attitudes (held to be) typical of the natural scientist **2** an exaggerated trust in the ability or suitability of the methods of NATURAL SCIENCE to explain social or psychological phenomena or to solve pressing human problems

**scientist** /'sie·əntist/ *n* **1** someone learned in science, esp NATURAL SCIENCE; a scientific investigator **2** *cap* a believer of CHRISTIAN SCIENCE

**Scientology** /,sie·ən'toləji/ *trademark* – used for a religious and psychotherapeutic movement begun in 1952 by L Ron Hubbard, which rejects the idea of a supreme being, but believes in reincarnation and in a human being's ability to improve his/her own condition by developing his/her highest potential through a prescribed course of study and psychological means – **scientologist** *n, often cap*

**sci-fi** /'sie ,fie/ *adj or n* (of or being) SCIENCE FICTION

**scilicet** /'sieli,set/ *adv* namely; TO WIT – used to introduce a word (eg in clarification or reiteration) [ME, fr L, surely, to wit, fr *scire* to know + *licet* it is permitted, fr *licēre* to be permitted – more at LICENCE]

**scilla** /'silə/ *n* any of a genus (*Scilla*) of European plants of the lily family that grow from bulbs and bear usu clusters or spikes of blue, pink, or white bell-shaped flowers – called also SQUILL [NL, genus name, fr L, squill – more at SQUILL]

**scimitar** /'simitə, -tah/ *n* a sword, used chiefly by Arabs and Turks in former times, that has a curved blade which narrows towards the hilt [It *scimitarra*, perh fr Per *shimshīr*]

**scintigraphy** /sin'tigrəfi/ *n* a diagnostic technique in which a two-dimensional picture of a body part is obtained after the administration of a radioactive substance by detecting and measuring the emitted radiation [*scinti*llation + -*graphy*; fr the scintillation counter used to record radiation on the picture] – **scintigraphic** *adj*

**scintilla** /sin'tilə/ *n* an iota, trace ⟨*not a ~ of evidence*⟩ [L, spark, speck]

**scintillate** /'sinti,layt/ *vi* **1** to emit sparks **2** to emit quick flashes as if throwing off sparks; *also* to sparkle, twinkle ⟨*fixed stars that ~ in the sky*⟩ **3** to be brilliant or vivacious ⟨scintillating *witticisms*⟩ **synonyms** see ¹FLASH [L *scintillatus*, pp of *scintillare* to sparkle, fr *scintilla* spark] – **scintillant** *adj or n*, **scintillator** *n*

**scintillation** /,sinti'laysh(ə)n/ *n* **1** an act or instance of scintillating; *esp* the twinkling of a planet, star, etc **2a** a spark or flash emitted in scintillating **b** a flash of light produced when a PHOTON, ALPHA PARTICLE, or other form of radiation hits a substance (eg ZINC SULPHIDE) that is capable of phosphorescence **3** a dazzling outburst (eg of wit) **4** a flash of the eye (eg in anger or gaiety)

**scintillation counter** *n* a device that detects and registers scintillations and is thus used to measure the intensity of high-energy radiation or to detect ELEMENTARY PARTICLES

**sciolism** /'sie·əliz(ə)m/ *n* a superficial pretence of learning [LL *sciolus* smatterer, fr dim. of L *scius* knowing, fr *scire* to know – more at SCIENCE] – **sciolist** *n*, **sciolistic** *adj*

**scion** /'sie·ən/ *n* **1** a detached living portion of a plant joined to a stock in grafting and usu supplying parts above the ground to the resulting graft **2** a (male) descendant or offspring [ME, fr MF *cion*, of Gmc origin; akin to OHG *chīnan* to sprout, split open, OE *cīnan* to gape]

**scirocco** /shi'rokoh, si-/ *n* SIROCCO (wind of N Mediterranean coast)

**scirrhous** /'sirəs/ *adj* **1** of or being a scirrhus **2** hard or hardened (as if) with fibrous tissue

**scirrhus** /'sirəs/ *n, pl* **scirrhi** /-ri/ a hard slow-growing cancerous tumour, esp in the breast, consisting mostly of fibrous tissue [NL, fr Gk *skiros, skirrhos*, fr *skiros* hard]

**scissile** /'sisiel/ *adj* capable of being cut smoothly or split easily ⟨*a ~ peptide bond in a protein*⟩ [Fr, fr L *scissilis*, fr *scissus*, pp of *scindere* to split – more at SHED]

**scission** /'sizh(ə)n/ *n* **1** a division or split in a group or unity; a schism **2** an action or process of cutting, dividing, or splitting; *also* the state of being cut, divided, or split [Fr, fr LL *scission-, scissio*, fr L *scissus*, pp]

¹**scissor** /'sizə/ *n* a brand or type of scissors

²**scissor** *vt* to cut, cut up, cut out, or cut off (as if) with scissors ⟨*~ offending lengths of film*⟩

**scissors** /'sizəz/ *n pl* **1** a cutting instrument having two blades pivoted so that their cutting edges slide past each other **2** *taking*

*sing or pl vb* **2a** a gymnastic feat (eg on a horse or parallel bars) in which the leg movements suggest the opening and closing of scissors **b** SCISSORS HOLD **c** a style of high jumping in which the jump is approached at a diagonal angle, the body held upright, and the legs cross over in a scissors-like movement, passing at the highest point of the jump [ME *sisoures*, fr MF *cisoires*, fr LL *cisorium* cutting instrument, irreg fr L *caesus*, pp of *caedere* to cut – more at CONCISE]

**scissors hold** *n* a wrestling hold in which the legs are locked round the head or body of an opponent

**scissors kick** *n* a swimming kick in which the legs move from the hip and come together like scissor blades

**sciurine** /'sieyoorin, -rien/ *adj* of or belonging to a family (Sciuridae) of rodents that includes squirrels, marmots, etc [deriv of L *sciurus* squirrel – more at SQUIRREL] – **sciurine** *n*, **sciuroid** *adj*

**scler-** /sklə-/, **sclero-** *comb form* **1** hard ⟨*sclerite*⟩ ⟨*scleroblast*⟩ ⟨*scleroid*⟩ **2** sclera ⟨*scleritis*⟩ [NL, fr Gk *sklēr-, sklēro-*, fr *sklēros* – more at SKELETON]

**sclera** /'sklɪərə/ *n, pl* **scleras, sclerae** /-rie/ the dense fibrous opaque white outer coat enclosing the eyeball except the part covered by the CORNEA (transparent covering over the iris and the pupil) [NL, fr Gk *sklēros* hard] – **scleral** *adj*

**sclereid** /'sklɛri·id/ *n* a sclerenchymatous plant cell [*scler*enchyma + -*id*]

**sclerenchyma** /sklɪə'rengkimə/ *n, pl* **sclerenchymas, sclerenchymata** /-mətə/ a protective or supporting tissue in more evolutionarily advanced plants composed of cells with woody and often mineralized walls [NL, fr *scler*- + -*enchyma*] – **sclerenchymatous** *adj*

**sclerite** /'sklɪəriet/ *n* a plate or structure hardened with calcium or the horny substance CHITIN; *esp* such a plate forming the external covering that gives support to the soft tissues of insects, spiders, crabs, etc [ISV]

**scleroderma** /,sklɪəroh'duhmə/ *n, pl* **sclerodermas, sclerodermata** /-mətə/ a disease of the skin characterized by thickening and hardening of the lower tissue layers [NL, fr *scler*- + -*derma*]

**scleroid** /'sklɪəroyd/ *adj*, of an organism or a body part hard, hardened

**sclerometer** /sklɪə'romitə/ *n* an instrument for determining the relative hardnesses of materials [ISV]

**scleroprotein** /,sklɪəroh'prohteen/ *n* any of various fibrous proteins (eg the COLLAGENS found in ligaments, tendons, and cartilage and the KERATINS found in hair, horns, and nails) [ISV]

**sclerose** /'sklerohs, 'sklɪə-/ *vt* to cause sclerosis in; increase the fibrous content of *~ vi* to undergo sclerosis [back-formation fr *sclerosis*]

**sclerosis** /sklə'rohsis/ *n, pl* **scleroses** /-seez/ **1** abnormal hardening of tissue, esp from overgrowth of fibrous tissue or increase in tissue between organs; *also* a disease characterized by sclerosis **2** the natural hardening of plant cell walls usu by the formation of LIGNIN (woody substance) [ME *sclirosis*, fr ML, fr Gk *sklērōsis* hardening, fr *sklēroun* to harden, fr *sklēros* hard]

¹**sclerotic** /sklə'rotik/ *adj* **1** being or relating to the sclera **2** of or affected with sclerosis

²**sclerotic** *n* SCLERA (opaque white covering of the eyeball) [ML *sclerotica*, fr (assumed) Gk *sklērōtos*, verbal of Gk *sklēroun* to harden]

**sclerotin** /'sklɛrətin, sklə'rohtin/ *n* an insoluble protein found in the hard outer covering of insects, spiders, crabs, etc [(assumed) Gk *sklērōtos* + ISV -*in*]

**sclerotium** /sklə'rohshyəm/ *n, pl* **sclerotia** /-shyə, -tyə/ a compact mass of hardened fungal threads containing reserve food material that in some fungi becomes detached, remains dormant during the winter, and produces reproductive structures bearing spores in the spring to infect young plants [NL, fr (assumed) Gk *sklērōtos*] – **sclerotial** *adj*

**sclerotization** /,sklɛrətie'zaysh(ə)n/ *n* the quality or state of being sclerotized

**sclerotized** /'sklɛrətiezd/ *adj* hardened by substances other than CHITIN – used chiefly of the hard outer covering of an insect [*sclerotic* + -*ize* + -*ed*]

**sclerous** /'sklɪərəs/ *adj* hard, bony

¹**scoff** /skof/ *n* **1** an expression of scorn, derision, or contempt; a jeer **2** an object of scorn, mockery, or derision [ME *scof*, prob of Scand origin; akin to obs Dan *skof* jest; akin to OFris *skof* mockery]

²**scoff** *vi* to show contempt by derisive acts or language; mock – often + *at* ⟨~ *at conventional wisdom*⟩ – **scoffer** *n*

³**scoff** *vb, chiefly Br informal vi* to devour greedily ~ *vt* to eat hastily or without regard to manners [prob fr E dial. *scaff,* of unknown origin]

⁴**scoff** *n, informal* food [partly fr ³*scoff;* partly fr Afrik *skof* quarter of a day, meal, fr D *schoft*]

¹**scold** /skohld/ *n* 1 a person, esp a woman, who habitually nags or quarrels 2 a scolding [ME *scald, scold,* prob of Scand origin; akin to ON *skāld* poet, Icel *skālda* to make scurrilous verse]

²**scold** *vi* 1 to find fault noisily and at length 2 *obs* to quarrel noisily; brawl ~ *vt* to reprimand usu severely or angrily; reprove sharply – **scolder** *n*

synonyms Scold, upbraid, berate, nag, abuse, rail, and revile all mean "attack in words". Scold suggests sharp irritation, as when correcting a disobedient child. Upbraid implies a more formal and more or less justifiable anger, as of an official superior. Berate suggests a violent prolonged abusiveness ⟨berate *her husband for his drinking*⟩. Nag indicates persistent tormenting about supposed shortcomings, often combined with pressure to some sort of action. Abuse, rail, and revile can entail speaking malevolently about someone or something not present. Abuse suggests angry and intemperate language ⟨abuse *the government*⟩. Rail is strongly abusive and often also contemptuous ⟨went abroad to rail *at the insecurity and the poverty* – Edmund Wilson⟩. Revile is very strong, indicating ranting denunciation ⟨revile *them as traitors*⟩.

**scolding** /'skohlding/ *n* 1 the action of one who scolds 2 a harsh reproof

**scolecite** /'skolisiet, 'skoh-/ *n* a usu colourless or white mineral of the ZEOLITE group that is the water-containing form of calcium aluminium silicate, $CaAl_2Si_3O_{10}.3H_2O$, and occurs in radiating groups of crystals, in fibrous masses, and as slender prismatic crystals [Ger *skolezit,* fr Gk *skōlēk-, skōlēx* worm; fr the wormlike motion of some forms when heated]

**scolex** /'skohleks/ *n, pl* **scolices** /sko'leeseez/ the head of an adult or larval tapeworm usu bearing hooks and suckers with which it attaches itself to the tissues of the infected organism [NL *scolic-, scolex,* fr Gk *skōlēk-, skōlēx* worm; akin to Gk *skelos* leg – more at CYLINDER]

**scoliosis** /,skoli'ohsis/ *n, pl* **scolioses** /-seez/ a sideways curvature of the spine – compare KYPHOSIS, LORDOSIS [NL, fr Gk *skoliōsis* crookedness of a bodily part, fr *skolios* crooked – more at CYLINDER] – **scoliotic** *adj*

**scollop** /'skoləp/ *n* a scallop

**scombroid** /'skombroyd/ *n* any of a suborder (Scombroidea) of spiny-finned sea fishes (eg the mackerel) that are of great economic importance as food fishes [deriv of Gk *skombros* mackerel] – **scombroid** *adj*

¹**sconce** /skons/ *n* a bracket candlestick or group of candle-sticks; *also* an electric light fixture patterned on a candle sconce [ME, fr MF *esconse* screened lantern, fr OF, fr fem of *escons,* pp of *escondre* to hide, fr L *abscondere* – more at ABSCOND]

²**sconce** *n* a small freestanding defensive work (eg a fort or mound) [D *schans,* fr Ger *schanze*]

³**sconce** *vt, Br informal* to inflict the sconce on

⁴**sconce** *n, Br informal* a forfeit imposed for a social misdemeanour, formerly common at Oxford and Cambridge Universities, that involves consuming or supplying a quantity of drink (eg beer); *also* the mug used for this purpose [origin unknown]

**scone** /skohn; *or* skon/ *n* a small light cake made from a dough or batter containing little fat, lightened with a raising agent (eg baking powder), and baked in a hot oven or on a heated metal plate (GRIDDLE) [perh fr D *schoonbrood* fine white bread, fr *schoon* pure, clean + *brood* bread]

¹**scoop** /skoohp/ *n* 1a a large ladle for taking up or skimming liquids b a deep shovel for lifting and moving granular material (eg corn or sand) c a handled utensil of shovel shape or with a hemispherical bowl for spooning out soft food (eg ice cream) d a small spoon-shaped utensil for cutting or gouging (eg in surgical operations) 2a an act or the action of scooping b the amount held by a scoop ⟨a ~ *of sugar*⟩ 3a a hollowed-out place; a cavity b a part forming or surrounding an opening for channelling a fluid (eg air) into a desired path 4a (the successful securing of) material for publication or broadcast esp when obtained in competition with others ⟨brought off a ~ *in securing his memoirs*⟩ b the reporting of a news story ahead or to the exclusion of competitors [ME *scope,*

fr MD *schope;* akin to OHG *skepfen* to shape – more at SHAPE] – **scoopful** *n*

²**scoop** *vt* 1 to take out or up (as if) with a scoop 2 to empty by scooping 3 to make hollow; dig out 4 to report a news item in advance or to the exclusion of (a competitor) 5 *chiefly Br informal* to obtain by swift action or sudden good fortune ⟨~ *the lion's share of an aid programme*⟩ – **scooper** *n*

**scoot** /skooht/ *vb, informal vi* to go suddenly and swiftly; dart ~ *vt* to cause to move or depart hastily or abruptly – often + *out* [prob of Scand origin; akin to ON *skjōta* to shoot – more at SHOOT] – **scoot** *n*

**scooter** /'skoohtə/ *n* 1 a child's vehicle consisting of a narrow board with usu one wheel at each end and with a handlebar or an upright steering handle attached to the axle of the front wheel, which is propelled by pushing against the ground with one foot while standing on the board 2 MOTOR SCOOTER

¹**scope** /skohp/ *n* 1 space or opportunity for unhampered action, thought, or development ⟨no ~ *for developing this line of argument in this paper*⟩ 2a extent of treatment, activity, or influence ⟨the ~ *of an inquiry*⟩ b extent of understanding or perception ⟨a mind remarkable for its ~ – John Buchan⟩ [It *scopo* purpose, goal, fr Gk *skopos;* akin to Gk *skeptesthai* to watch, look at – more at SPY]

²**scope** *n* any of various devices for viewing: eg a a microscope b a telescope c OSCILLOSCOPE d a radarscope □ (*a&b*) not usu used technically [-*scope*]

-**scope** /-skohp/ *comb form* (→ *n*) instrument for viewing or observing ⟨microscope⟩ [NL -*scopium,* fr Gk -*skopion;* akin to Gk *skeptesthai*]

**scopolamine** /skoh'poləmeen, -min/ *n* HYOSCINE (sedative drug) [Ger *scopolamin,* fr NL *Scopolia,* genus of plants + Ger *amin* amine]

-**scopy** /-skəpi/ *comb form* (→ *n*) viewing; observation ⟨radioscopy⟩ [Gk -*skopia,* fr *skeptesthai*]

**scorbutic** /skaw'byoohtik/ *adj* of or resembling scurvy; *also* diseased with scurvy [NL *scorbuticus,* fr *scorbutus* scurvy, prob of Gmc origin; akin to OE *scurf*] – **scorbutically** *adv*

¹**scorch** /skawch/ *vt* 1 to burn so as to produce a change in colour and texture 2a to parch (as if) with intense heat b to criticize or deride harshly or bitterly 3 to devastate completely, esp before abandoning – used in *scorched earth,* of property, crops, etc of possible use to an enemy ~ *vi* 1 to become scorched 2 to travel at great and usu excessive speed [ME *scorcnen, scorchen,* prob of Scand origin; akin to ON *skorpna* to shrivel up – more at SHRIMP] – **scorchingly** *adv*

²**scorch** *n* 1 a mark resulting from scorching 2 a browning of plant tissues usu from disease or heat

**scorcher** /'skawchə/ *n* 1 one who or that which scorches 2 *informal* a very hot day

¹**score** /skaw/ *n, pl* **scores**, (*1a,b*) **scores**, **score** 1a twenty b a group of 20 things – used in combination with a CARDINAL NUMBER ⟨fivescore⟩ c *pl* an indefinite large number d a unit of weight, esp for pigs, equal to 20 or sometimes 21 pounds (9.1 or 9.5 kilograms) 2a a line (eg a scratch or incision) made (as if) with a sharp instrument b a mark or notch used for keeping an account or tally 3a an account or reckoning kept by marks or notches b an account of debts c an amount due 4 a grievance or injury kept in mind for requital; a grudge ⟨settle an old ~⟩ 5a a reason, ground ⟨complain on the ~ *of maltreatment*⟩ b a subject, topic ⟨have no doubts on that ~⟩ 6a the written or printed copy of the whole of a musical composition, often with each of the instrumental and vocal parts separately displayed one above the other b a musical composition; *specif* the music for a film or theatrical production c a complete description of a dance composition with the dancers' moves written in symbolic form 7a a number that expresses accomplishment (eg in a game or test) or quality (eg of a product) b an act (eg a goal, run, or try) in any of various games or contests that increases the score c(1) *slang* success; *esp* success in obtaining illicit drugs c(2) *slang* a single dose of an illicit drug; enough of an illicit drug for one's immediate needs 8 the stark inescapable facts of a situation ⟨knows the ~⟩ 9 *archaic* a mark used as a starting point in a race [ME *scor,* fr ON *skor* notch, tally, twenty; akin to OE *scieran* to cut – more at SHEAR] – **scoreless** *adj*

²**score** *vt* 1a to keep a record of (eg expenditure) (as if) by notches on a tally; reckon – often + *up* b to enter (a debt) in an account – usu + *to* or *against* c to cancel or strike out (eg record of a debt) with a line or notch – often + *out* 2 to mark with lines, grooves, scratches, or notches 3 to rebuke severely;

scold ⟨*the itch to ~ people off* – J C Powys⟩ **4a(1)** to gain (eg points) in a game or contest ⟨~d *eight runs*⟩ **a(2)** to have as a value in a game or contest; count ⟨*a try ~s four points*⟩ **b** to gain, win ⟨~d *a success with his latest novel*⟩ **5a** to write or arrange (music) for specific voice or instrumental parts or a combination of both **b** to compose or arrange (music) for an orchestra; orchestrate **c** to compose a musical score for (eg a film) **6** *NAm* to determine the worth of; grade ⟨~ *a test*⟩ ⟨~ *each candidate*⟩ **7** *slang* to obtain (illicit drugs) ⟨~ *marijuana*⟩ ~ *vi* **1a** to keep score in a game or contest **b** to make a score in a game or contest **2** to obtain a rating or grade ⟨*children who ~ high in intelligence tests*⟩ **3a** to gain or have an advantage or a success **b** *slang* **b(1)** to achieve sexual success **b(2)** to obtain illicit drugs – **scorer** *n* – **score off somebody** *Br* to get the better of somebody in a debate or argument – see also **score** POINTS **off**

**scoreboard** /-ˌbawd/ *n* a usu large board or device for publicly displaying the score of a game or match (eg at a stadium or sports ground)

**scorecard** /ˈskawˌkahd/ *n* a card for recording a score (eg of a game of golf)

**scorekeeper** /ˈskawˌkeepə/ *n* an official who records the score during a game or contest

'**score-ˌline** *n* the result of a sports match

**scoresheet** /ˈskawˌsheet/ *n* a sheet of paper for recording the scores of a game

**scoria** /ˈskawri·ə/ *n, pl* **scoriae** /-ri·ie/ **1** the refuse from the melting of metals or the purification of ores; slag **2** rough lava containing many cavities and resembling clinker [ME, fr L, fr Gk *skōria*, fr *skōr* excrement – more at SCAT-] – **scoriaceous** *adj*

**scorify** /ˈskawrifie/ *vt* to remove the nonmetallic elements from (an ore) by producing scoria; *esp* to analyse the composition of (a metal) by blending a portion of molten ore with lead and the mineral BORAX – **scorification** *n*

'**scorn** /skawn/ *n* **1** an emotion involving both anger and loathing; vigorous contempt **2** an expression of extreme contempt ⟨*poured ~ on the whole affair*⟩ **3** an object of extreme disdain, contempt, or derision [ME, fr OF *escarn*, of Gmc origin; akin to OHG *scern* jest; akin to Gk *skairein* to gambol – more at CARDINAL] – **scornful** *adj*, **scornfully** *adv*, **scornfulness** *n*

²**scorn** *vt* **1** to reject with outspoken or angry contempt ⟨~ed *all warnings of disaster*⟩ **2** to refuse out of scorn; disdain ⟨~ed *to reply to the charge*⟩ ~ *vi* to show disdain or derision; mock, scoff – **scorner** *n*

**scorpaenid** /skawˈpeenid/ *n* SCORPION FISH [deriv of Gk *skorpaina*, a kind of fish] – **scorpaenid** *adj*

**Scorpio** /ˈskawpioh/ *n* **1** SCORPIUS **2a** the 8th sign of the zodiac in astrology, held to govern the period October 23 – November 21 approx **b** somebody born under this sign [L, fr Gk *Skorpios*, lit., scorpion] – **Scorpian** *adj or n*

**scorpioid** /ˈskawpioyd/ *adj* curved at the end like a scorpion's tail ⟨*a ~ flower head*⟩ [Gk *skorpioeidēs* resembling a scorpion, fr *skorpios*]

**scorpion** /ˈskawpyən/ *n* **1a** any of an order (Scorpionida of the class Arachnida) of INVERTEBRATE animals that are related to the spiders and ticks and have an elongated body with a narrow segmented tail bearing a highly poisonous sting at the tip **b** *cap* Scorpio **2** a whip studded with metal spikes [ME, fr OF, fr L *scorpion-, scorpio*, fr Gk *skorpios*; akin to OE *scieran* to cut – more at SHEAR]

**scorpion fish** *n* any of several spiny-finned sea fishes (family Scorpaenidae); *esp* one with a venomous spine on the fin on its back

**scorpion fly** *n* any of a family (Panorpidae) of flesh-eating insects that have cylindrical bodies and the male genitalia enlarged into a swollen bulb; *broadly* any of an order (Mecoptera) of primitive flesh-eating insects

**Scorpius** /ˈskawpiəs/ *n* a large constellation of the ZODIAC (imaginary belt in the heavens) lying across the MILKY WAY between Libra and Sagittarius and represented as a scorpion

**scorzonera** /ˌskawzəˈniərə/ *n* a European plant (*Scorzonera hispanica*) of the daisy family with a black edible root similar to that of salsify; *also* the root of scorzonera – called also BLACK SALSIFY [NL, fr Sp *escorzonera*, fr Catal *escurçonera*, fr *escurçó* viper; fr its allegedly healing the bites of vipers]

**scot** /skot/ *n* money imposed or paid as a tax [ME, fr ON *skot* shot, contribution – more at SHOT]

**Scot** *n* **1** a member of a Gaelic people originally of N Ireland

that settled in Scotland about AD 500 **2** a native or inhabitant of Scotland **synonyms** see ¹SCOTTISH [ME *Scottes* Scots, fr OE *Scottas* Irishmen, Scots, fr LL *Scotus* Irishman]

**scot and lot** *n* a parish tax formerly levied on British subjects according to their ability to pay

¹**scotch** /skoch/ *vt* **1** to injure so as to temporarily disable **2a** to stamp out; crush ⟨~ *a rebellion*⟩ **b** to repudiate by showing not to be true ⟨~ *rumours*⟩ [ME *scocchen* to gash]

²**scotch** *n* a slight cut; a score

³**scotch** *n* a wedge or block placed behind a wheel to prevent rolling or slipping downhill [origin unknown]

⁴**scotch** *vt* **1** to block with a scotch ⟨~ed *the back wheels as a precaution*⟩ **2** to hinder, thwart ⟨~ *schemes for sponsorship*⟩

¹**Scotch** *adj* Scottish – often considered incorrect by natives of Scotland **synonyms** see ¹SCOTTISH [contr of *Scottish*]

²**Scotch** *n* **1** Scots **2** *taking pl vb* the people of Scotland **3** *often not cap* SCOTCH WHISKY

**Scotch blackface** *n* (any of) a hardy breed of long-woolled meat-producing sheep that have a dark-coloured face

**Scotch broth** *n* a thick soup made with beef or mutton, vegetables, and pearl barley

**Scotch egg** *n* a hard-boiled egg covered with sausage meat, coated with breadcrumbs, deep-fried, and usu eaten cold

**Scotch fir** *n* SCOTS PINE

**Scotch-ˈIrish** *adj* (characteristic) of the population of N Ireland that is descended from Scottish Protestant settlers; *also* (characteristic) of members of this group who emigrated to the USA before 1846 or of those descended from them

**Scotchman** /ˈskochmən/, *fem* **Scotchwoman** *n* a Scotsman **synonyms** see ¹SCOTTISH

**Scotch mist** *n* very fine light drizzle

**Scotch pine** *n, chiefly NAm* SCOTS PINE

**Scotch tape** *trademark, chiefly NAm* – used for any of various adhesive tapes

**Scotch terrier** *n* SCOTTISH TERRIER

**Scotch whisky** *n* whisky distilled in Scotland, esp from malted barley

**Scotch woodcock** *n* buttered toast spread with anchovy paste and scrambled egg

**scoter** /ˈskohtə/ *n, pl* **scoters**, *esp collectively* **scoter** any of several dark-coloured sea ducks (genus *Melanitta*) of N coasts of Europe and N America and also some larger inland waters during the breeding season [origin unknown]

**ˌscot-ˈfree** *adj* without incurring any penalty, payment, or injury ⟨*got away ~*⟩

**scotia** /ˈskohshə/ *n* a deep concave moulding used in the bases of columns, esp in classical architecture [L, fr Gk *skotia*, fr fem of *skotios* dark, shadowy, fr *skotos* darkness – more at SHADE]

**Scotic** /ˈskotik/ *adj* of the ancient Scots

**Scotland Yard** /ˈskotlənd/ *n taking sing or pl vb* the criminal investigation department of the London metropolitan police force [*Scotland Yard*, street in London formerly the headquarters of the metropolitan police]

**scotoma** /skəˈtohmə/ *n, pl* **scotomas**, **scotomata** /-mətə/ a blind or partly blind area in the field of vision [NL *scotomat-, scotoma*, fr ML, dimness of vision, fr Gk *skotōmat-, skotōma*, fr *skotoun* to darken, fr *skotos* darkness] – **scotomatous** *adj*

**scotopic** /skəˈtopik, -ˈtoh-/ *adj* of or being vision in dim light with dark-adapted eyes that is controlled by the RODS of the retina and is concerned esp with the differentiation of shapes – compare PHOTOPIC [NL *scotopia* scotopic vision, fr Gk *skotos* darkness + NL *-opia*] – **scotopia** *n*

¹**Scots** /skots/ *adj* Scottish – used esp of the people and language and in a legal context **synonyms** see ¹SCOTTISH [ME *Scottis*, alter. of *Scottish*]

²**Scots** *n* the English language of Scotland

**Scotsman** /ˈskotsmən/, *fem* **Scotswoman** *n* a Scottish person **synonyms** see ¹SCOTTISH

**Scots pine** *n* a pine (*Pinus sylvestris*) of N Europe and Asia with spreading rusty-red branches, blue-green short rigid twisted needles, and hard yellow wood that provides valuable timber – called also SCOTCH FIR, SCOTCH PINE

**Scotticism** /ˈskotiˌsiz(ə)m/ *n* a characteristic feature of Scottish English, esp as contrasted with standard English [LL *scotticus* of the ancient Scots, fr *Scotus* Scot]

**scottie** /ˈskoti/ *n, informal* **1** *cap* a Scotsman – often used as a nickname **2** SCOTTISH TERRIER

¹**Scottish** /ˈskotish/ *adj* (characteristic) of Scotland, its people, or their language [ME, fr *Scottes* Scotsmen] – **Scottishness** *n*

**synonyms** The people of Scotland today prefer to use **Scottish** in reference to their country ⟨*the* **Scottish** *universities*⟩ ⟨**Scottish** *scenery*⟩ ⟨*her* **Scottish** *blood*⟩ or **Scots** in particular contexts ⟨**Scots** *law*⟩ ⟨*a* **Scots** *engineer*⟩ ⟨*married a* **Scotsman**⟩ rather than **Scotch**, the older term which was once used both by themselves and by outsiders ⟨*I'm pure* **Scotch** ... *the correct term is* **Scottish**, *but that sounds so pompous* – Margaret, Duchess of Argyll⟩. **Scotch** is still correctly used of whisky. The noun **Scot** is now rare except in rhetorical use. **usage** see BRITISH

²**Scottish** *n* the Scots language

**Scottish Gaelic** /'gahlik, 'gaylik/ *n* the Gaelic language of Scotland

**Scottish terrier** *n* any of an old Scottish breed of terrier that has short legs, a large head with small erect ears and a powerful muzzle, a broad deep chest, and a very hard coat of usu black wiry hair – called also SCOTCH TERRIER, SCOTTIE

**scoundrel** /'skowndrəl/ *n* a wicked or dishonest fellow; a villain [origin unknown] – **scoundrel** *adj*, **scoundrelly** *adj*

¹**scour** /'skowə/ *vi* **1** to hurry about, esp with the aim of finding ~ *vt* **1** to move through or range over usu swiftly **2** to make a rapid but thorough search of ⟨~ed *the countryside in search of her*⟩ [ME *scuren*, prob of Scand origin; akin to Sw *skura* to rush] – **scourer** *n*

²**scour** *vt* **1a** to rub vigorously in order to cleanse ⟨~ *a saucepan*⟩ **b** to remove by rubbing, esp with rough or abrasive material **2** to clean out by purging; purge **3** to clear (eg a pipe or ditch) by removing dirt and debris **4** to clean and free from impurities (as if) by washing ⟨~ *wool*⟩ **5** to clear, excavate, or remove (as if) by a powerful current of water ~ *vi* **1** to undertake scouring **2** *esp of cattle* to suffer from diarrhoea or dysentery; purge **3** to become clean and bright by being rubbed ⟨*old pans that* ~ *nicely*⟩ [ME *scouren*, prob fr MD *schuren*, fr OF *escurer*, fr LL *excurare* to clean off, fr L *ex-* + *curare* to care for, cleanse, fr *cura* care]

³**scour** *n* **1** a place that is scoured (eg by running water) **2** scouring action ⟨*the* ~ *of a glacier*⟩ **3 scours** *taking sing or pl vb*, **scour** diarrhoea or dysentery, esp in cattle **4** scouring; *also* damage done by scouring action

¹**scourge** /skuhj/ *n* **1** a whip; *esp* one used to inflict pain or punishment **2a** a means of vengeance or criticism ⟨*the* ~ *of his sarcasm*⟩ **b** a cause of great or widespread affliction [ME, fr AF *escorge*, fr (assumed) OF *escorgier* to whip, fr OF *es-* ex- + L *corrigia* shoelace, thong]

²**scourge** *vt* **1** to whip severely; flog **2a** to punish severely **b** to subject to affliction; devastate ⟨*a region* ~d *by malaria*⟩ **c** to subject to scathing criticism or satire – **scourger** *n*

**scouring rush** *n* HORSETAIL (flowerless plant); *esp* one (*Equisetum hyemale*) with hard rough stems formerly used for scouring

**scourings** /'skowəringz/ *n pl*, **scouring** *n* **1** material removed by scouring or cleaning; refuse **2** the lowest rank of society

**scouse** /skows/ *n* LOBSCOUSE (sailor's stew)

**Scouse** *n, informal* **1** a native or inhabitant of Liverpool **2** the dialect of Liverpool [fr the popularity of *scouse* (lobscouse) in Merseyside] – **Scouse** *adj*

**Scouser** /'skowsə/ *n, informal* a Scouse

¹**scout** /skowt/ *vi* **1** to make an advance survey (eg to obtain military information); reconnoitre **2** to conduct a search ~ *vt* **1** to observe or explore in order to obtain information or evaluate ⟨~ *the hills for guerrillas*⟩ **2** to find by making a search – often + *out* or *up* [ME *scouten*, fr MF *escouter* to listen, fr L *auscultare*]

²**scout** *n* **1** the act or an instance of scouting; a reconnaissance **2a** one sent to obtain information; *esp* a soldier, ship, or aircraft sent out in war to reconnoitre **b** a watchman, lookout **c** TALENT SCOUT an Oxford University college servant – compare BEDMAKER **4** *often cap* a member of a worldwide movement of boys and young men that was founded with the aim of developing qualities of leadership, responsibility, and comradeship and that lays stress on outdoor activities (eg camping and tracking); *specif* a member of the intermediate section of the British Scout movement for boys aged from 11 to 15

³**scout** *vt* to reject scornfully, esp by ridiculing ⟨~ *a new theory*⟩ ~ *vi* to scoff [of Scand origin; akin to ON *skūti* taunt; akin to OE *scēotan* to shoot – more at SHOOT]

**scout car** *n* a fast armoured military reconnaissance vehicle

**scouter** /'skowtə/ *n* one who or that which scouts; *specif, often cap* an adult leader in the Scout movement

**scouting** /'skowting/ *n* **1** the activity of one who or that which scouts **2** *often cap* the activities or philosophy of the Scout movement

**scoutmaster** /-,mahstə/ *n* the adult leader of a troop of scouts – no longer used technically

**scow** /skow/ *n* a large flat-bottomed usu unpowered boat with broad square ends used chiefly for transporting bulk material (eg ore, sand, or refuse) [D *schouw;* akin to OHG *scalta* punt pole]

¹**scowl** /skowl/ *vi* **1** to draw down or wrinkle the brows in an expression of displeasure **2** to exhibit a gloomy or threatening aspect ⟨*the mountains* ~ed *down over the valley*⟩ ~ *vt* to express or utter with a scowl [ME *skoulen*, prob of Scand origin; akin to Dan *skule* to scowl] – **scowler** *n*

²**scowl** *n* a facial expression of annoyance or displeasure; an angry frown

¹**scrabble** /'skrabl/ *vb, informal vi* **1** to scrawl, scribble **2** to grope or scratch *about* usu to find something **3a** to scramble, clamber **b** to struggle frantically to gain possession – often + *for* ⟨*urchins* scrabbling *for leftovers*⟩ ~ *vt* **1** to scrape together hurriedly ⟨~ *up a quick supper*⟩ **2** to scribble [D *schrabbelen* to scratch] – **scrabbler** *n*

²**scrabble** *n, informal* **1** scribble, scrawl **2** a persistent scratching or clawing **3** a scramble

**Scrabble** *trademark* – used for a board game in which players try to form words from letters carrying different scoring values

¹**scrag** /skrag/ *n* **1** a thin or bony person or animal **2 scragend, scrag** the bony end nearest the head of a neck of mutton or veal [perh alter. of ²*crag*]

²**scrag** *vt* **-gg-** **1a** to execute by hanging or GARROTTING (strangling esp with an iron collar) **b** to wring the neck of **2a** to choke; throttle **b** *informal* to seize roughly by the neck; *also* to attack in anger **3** *Br slang* to seize and beat (someone)

**scraggly** /'skragli/ *adj, chiefly NAm* irregular; *also* ragged, unkempt ⟨*a* ~ *beard*⟩

**scraggy** /'skragi/ *adj* **1** rough, jagged ⟨~ *rocks*⟩ **2** lean and lanky in growth or build; scrawny

**scram** /skram/ *vi* **-mm-** *informal* to go away at once; PUSH OFF ⟨~ *kid, you're not wanted*⟩ [short for *scramble*]

¹**scramble** /'skrambl/ *vi* **1a** to move or climb (eg up a steep slope) using hands as well as feet, esp hastily ⟨*if they had not been able to* ~ *up the cliff they might have been drowned by the tide*⟩ **b** to move with haste, urgency, or panic ⟨*they all* ~d *into the back of the car*⟩ **2a** to compete eagerly or chaotically for possession of something ⟨~ *for front seats*⟩ **b** to get or gather something with difficulty or in irregular ways ⟨~ *for a living*⟩ **3a** to spread or grow irregularly; sprawl, straggle **b** *of a plant* to climb over a support **4** *esp of an aircraft or its crew* to take off quickly in response to an alert ~ *vt* **1** to collect by scrambling – usu + *up* or *together* ⟨~d *up a hasty supper*⟩ **2a** to toss or mix together; jumble **b** to prepare (eggs) in a pan by stirring during cooking **3** to cause or order (an aircraft) to scramble **4** to make (a message) unintelligible to those without the means to decode it; *esp* to do this by electronic means [perh alter. of ¹*scrabble*]

²**scramble** *n* **1** an act of scrambling; a scrambling movement or struggle **2** a disordered mess; a jumble **3** a rapid emergency takeoff of fighter aircraft **4** a motorcycle race over very rough ground; *esp* a MOTO-CROSS race

**scrambler** /'skramblə/ *n* one who or that which scrambles: eg **a** a motorcycle designed for scrambling **b** an electronic device that scrambles esp telephone or radio messages

**scrambling** /'skrambling/ *n* MOTO-CROSS (motorcycle racing over a tight rough course)

**scran** /skran/ *n, informal* food; *esp* leftover scraps or remains of food [origin unknown]

**scrannel** /'skranl/ *adj, archaic* harsh, unmelodious [E dial., thin, poor, prob of Scand origin; akin to Norw *skran* shrivelled]

¹**scrap** /skrap/ *n* **1** *pl* fragments of discarded or leftover food **2a** a small detached fragment; a bit ⟨*a* ~ *of paper*⟩ **b** an excerpt from something written or printed ⟨*read* ~s *of a letter*⟩ **c** the smallest piece ⟨*not a* ~ *of evidence*⟩ **3** *pl* the remains of animal fat after melting down; cracklings **4a** the residue from a manufacturing process **b** manufactured articles or parts, esp of metal, rejected or discarded and useful only for reprocessing [ME, fr ON *skrap* scraps; akin to ON *skrapa* to scrape]

²**scrap** *vt* **-pp-** **1** to convert into scrap ⟨~ *a battleship*⟩ **2** to abandon or get rid of because no longer useful or effective; discard ⟨~ *outworn methods*⟩ – **scrappage** *n*

³**scrap** *n, informal* a minor fight or dispute [origin unknown]

⁴**scrap** *vi* **-pp-** *informal* to quarrel, fight ⟨*always* ~ping *with his sister*⟩ – **scrapper** *n*

**scrapbook** /-,book/ *n* a blank book in which mementos (e g newspaper cuttings or postcards) may be pasted

¹**scrape** /skrayp/ *vt* **1a** to remove (clinging matter) from a surface by usu repeated strokes of an edged instrument **b** to make (a surface) smooth or clean with strokes of an edged or rough instrument **2a** to grate harshly over or against ⟨*the keel* ~d *the stony bottom*⟩ **b** to damage or injure by contact with a rough surface ⟨~d *his shins on the rocks*⟩ **c** to draw roughly or noisily over a surface ⟨*stop* scraping *your feet!*⟩ **3** to collect or procure (as if) by scraping – often + *up* or *together* ⟨~ *the price of a pint together by returning empty bottles*⟩ **4** to draw and fasten (hair) *back* from the face ~ *vi* **1** to move in sliding contact with a rough or abrasive surface **2** to accumulate esp money by small but difficult economies ⟨scraping *and saving to educate their children*⟩ **3** to draw back the foot along the ground in making a bow – chiefly in *bow and scrape* **4** to get by with difficulty or succeed by a narrow margin – often + *in* or *through* ⟨*the candidate* ~d *through with a majority of six*⟩ – see also **scrape the bottom of the** BARREL, BOW **and scrape** [ME *scrapen,* fr ON *skrapa;* akin to OE *scrapian* to scrape, L *scrobis* ditch, Gk *keirein* to cut – more at SHEAR] – **scraper** *n*

²**scrape** *n* **1a** an act, process, or result of scraping **b** the sound of scraping **2** *informal* **2a** a disagreeable predicament, esp as a result of foolish behaviour ⟨*got in a* ~ *at school*⟩ **b** a quarrel, fight ⟨*a political* ~⟩

**scraperboard** /'skraypə,bawd/ *n* a board having a blackened surface which can be scraped away to form a black-and-white design; *also* a design made on such a board

**scrap heap** *n* **1** a pile of discarded (metal) waste; a rubbish dump **2** *informal* a place for things, ideas, or people of no further use or value ⟨*workers thrown on to the* ~ *by redundancy*⟩ ⟨*an idea consigned to the* ~ *of history*⟩

**scrapie** /'skraypi/ *n* a progressive degenerative disease of the CENTRAL NERVOUS SYSTEM in sheep that is caused by a virus and is characterized by intense itching leading to the animal's scraping away large areas of its fleece on fences, posts, etc, muscular tremors, progressive weakening, and finally death [¹*scrape*]

**scrapings** /'skraypingz/ *n pl* things scraped off, up, or together ⟨*here are the* ~ *from the bottom of the barrel – the letters that did not make it the first time round – Listener*⟩

**scrap merchant** *n, Br* someone who deals in scrap metal

**scrapple** /'skrapl/ *n* a seasoned mixture of minced meat (e g pork) and meal set in a mould and served sliced and fried [dim. of ¹*scrap*]

¹**scrappy** /'skrapi/ *adj* **1** consisting of scraps ⟨*a* ~ *lunch on Mondays*⟩ **2** having no plan, method, or overall design ⟨*a* ~ *education*⟩ – **scrappiness** *n*

²**scrappy** *adj, informal* fond of quarrels or disputes; aggressive

**scrapyard** /-,yahd/ *n, chiefly Br* a yard where scrap (e g scrap metal) is collected, sorted, and sometimes processed

¹**scratch** /skrach/ *vt* **1** to scrape or dig with the claws or nails **2** to tear, mark, or cut the surface of with something sharp or jagged **3** to scrape or rub lightly (e g to relieve itching) **4** to scrape together ⟨~ *a precarious living – Punch*⟩ **5** to write or draw on a surface ⟨~ed *his initials on the desk*⟩ **6a** to cancel or erase (as if) by drawing a line through ⟨~ *that last remark from the minutes*⟩ ⟨*the fixture was* ~ed *because the other side couldn't raise a team*⟩ **b** to withdraw (an entry) from a competition **7** to scribble, scrawl **8** to scrape along a rough surface ⟨~ *a match*⟩ ~ *vi* **1** to use the claws or nails in digging, tearing, or wounding **2** to scrape or rub oneself lightly (e g to relieve itching) **3** to amass money or get a living by hard work and saving **4** to make a thin grating sound ⟨*this pen* ~es⟩ **5** to withdraw from a contest or engagement **6** to make a scratch in billiards or snooker [blend of E dial. *scrat* to scratch and obs E *cratch* to scratch] – **scratcher** *n*

²**scratch** *n* **1** a mark or injury produced by scratching; *also* a slight wound **2** a scrawl, scribble **3** the sound of scratching **4a** the starting line in a race for competitors not receiving a handicap **b** the most rudimentary beginning ⟨*build a school system from* ~⟩ **5** standard or satisfactory condition or performance ⟨*not up to* ~⟩ **6** a contestant whose name is withdrawn **7a** a shot in billiards or snooker that involves a penalty; *specif* a shot that pockets the CUE BALL **b** a shot that scores by chance; a fluke

³**scratch** *adj* **1** made or done by chance and not as intended ⟨*a* ~ *shot*⟩ **2** arranged or put together haphazardly or hastily ⟨*a* ~ *team*⟩ **3** being without handicap or allowance ⟨*a* ~ *gol-*

*fer*⟩ **4** *chiefly NAm* used for hasty or trial attempts (e g at writing essays) ⟨*a* ~ *pad*⟩

**scratch test** *n* a test for allergic sensitivity to certain substances made by lightly scratching an extract of an allergy-producing substance into the skin and observing the body's reaction. A positive reaction will take place within about 20 minutes.

**scratchy** /'skrachi/ *adj* **1** tending to scratch or irritate; prickly ⟨~ *undergrowth*⟩ ⟨~ *wool*⟩ **2** making a scratching noise ⟨*a* ~ *pen*⟩ **3** made (as if) with scratches; careless ⟨~ *drawing*⟩ ⟨~ *handwriting*⟩ **4** uneven in quality; haphazard **5** irritable, fractious – **scratchiness** *n*

**scrawl** /skrawl/ *vb* to write or draw awkwardly, hastily, or carelessly [origin unknown] – **scrawl** *n,* **scrawler** *n,* **scrawly** *adj*

**scrawny** /'skrawni/ *adj* exceptionally thin and bony; *also* stunted ⟨~ *cattle*⟩ ⟨~ *desert vegetation*⟩ **antonyms** fleshy, plump [origin unknown] – **scrawniness** *n*

**screak** /skreek/ *vi, NAm & dial Br* to make a harsh shrill noise; screech [of Scand origin; akin to ON *skrækja* to screak; akin to ME *scremen* to scream] – **screak** *n,* **screaky** *adj*

¹**scream** /skreem/ *vi* **1a(1)** to voice a sudden loud piercing cry, esp in alarm, terror, or pain **a(2)** to produce harsh high tones ⟨*chain saws* ~ing *in the forest*⟩ **b** to move with or make a shrill noise resembling a scream ⟨*the gale* ~ed *through the trees*⟩ **2a** to speak or write with violent or hysterical expressions ⟨*a* ~ing *headline*⟩ **b** to laugh uncontrollably or dementedly **3** to produce a vivid or startling effect ⟨*a* ~ing *red*⟩ ~ *vt* to utter (as if) with a scream or screams – see also **scream blue** MURDER [ME *scremen;* akin to OHG *scrīan* to scream]

²**scream** *n* **1** a loud shrill penetrating cry or noise; *esp* one caused by fear, pain, etc **2** *informal* one who or that which provokes screams of laughter ⟨*he's a* ~ *when he's had a drink or two*⟩

**synonyms Scream, shriek,** and **screech** all refer to a piercing cry. **Scream** is the most general word. A **shriek** is a shorter and sharper sound, more uncontrolled and inarticulate. A **screech** is raucous and rasping, almost inhuman, and the word is particularly used, to sound funny or uncanny, of noises made by old women or birds.

**screamer** /'skreemə/ *n* **1** any of several S American waterbirds (family Anhimidae) with large stout bills, spurred wings, and a loud raucous cry **2** a sensationally startling headline **3** *slang* EXCLAMATION MARK

**screamingly** /'skreemingli/ *adv* to an extreme degree ⟨~ *funny*⟩

**scree** /skree/ *n* **1** an accumulation of loose stones or rocky debris lying on a slope or at the base of a hill or cliff **2** a mountain slope covered with or consisting of scree [of Scand origin; akin to ON *skritha* landslide, fr *skrītha* to creep; akin to OHG *scrītan* to go]

¹**screech** /skreech/ *vi* **1** to utter a high shrill piercing cry; cry out, esp in terror or pain **2** to make a sound resembling a screech ⟨*the car* ~ed *to a halt*⟩ ~ *vt* to utter (as if) with a screech [alter. of earlier *scritch,* fr ME *scrichen;* akin to ON *skrækja* to screech] – **screecher** *n*

²**screech** *n* a high shrill sound or cry **synonyms** see ²SCREAM

**screech owl** *n* **1** any of various owls with a harsh shrill cry; *esp* BARN OWL **2** any of various American owls (genus *Otus*); *esp* a small N American owl (*Otus asio*) with tufts of lengthened feathers on the head resembling ears

**screed** /skreed/ *n* **1** an overlong, dull, and often complaining speech or piece of writing; a diatribe **2** a strip (e g a wooden lath) that is fixed to a surface, esp a wall, to act as a guide to or check on the thickness of a substance (e g plaster) that is being applied to it **3** a levelling device drawn over freshly poured concrete [ME *screde* fragment, fr OE *scrēade* – more at SHRED]

¹**screen** /skreen/ *n* **1a** a usu movable piece of furniture that gives protection from heat or draughts or is used as an ornament ⟨*a fire* ~⟩ **b** an often ornamental partition serving to protect or separate rather than support **2a** something that shelters, protects, or conceals ⟨*a* ~ *of light infantry*⟩ **b** something behind which secret usu illicit practices are hidden **c** a manoeuvre in various sports whereby an opponent is legally cut off from the play; *specif* the act of impeding a defensive player in basketball **3a** a sieve or plate of perforated material usu set in a frame and used to separate coarser from finer parts **b** a device that shields from interference (e g from electrical or magnetic fields) ⟨*an electric* ~⟩ ⟨*a magnetic* ~⟩ **c** a frame holding a usu metallic netting, used esp in a window or

door to exclude pests (eg insects) **4a** a plain or semitransparent surface on which images (eg optical images or X-ray images) are projected or reflected **b** the part of a television set, radar receiver, VDU, etc on which the visual image or picture is displayed **c** a glass plate ruled with crossing opaque lines through which an image is photographed in making a HALFTONE (etched plate used for printing) **5a** the film industry ⟨*a star of stage and* ~⟩ **b** the medium of television **6** *Br* a windscreen [ME *screne*, fr MF *escren*, fr MD *scherm;* akin to OHG *skirm* screen, L *corium* skin – more at CUIRASS]

²**screen** *vt* **1** to guard from injury, danger, or punishment ⟨*a conspiracy to* ~ *the bandits*⟩ **2a** to give shelter or protection to (as if) with a screen **b** to separate (as if) with a screen; *also* to block (an opponent) from making or having a view of a particular manoeuvre (eg in basketball) – often + *off* **c** to provide with a screen or screens (eg to keep out pests) **3a** to pass (eg coal, gravel, or ashes) through a screen to separate the fine part from the coarse; *also* to remove by a screen **b** to test or check systematically: **b(1)** in order to separate into different groups ⟨~ *visa applications*⟩ **b(2)** to find a suitable candidate ⟨~ing *the job applications*⟩ **b(3)** for the presence of disease ⟨*patients who are regularly* ~ed *for cancer*⟩ **b(4)** for the presence of weapons ⟨*passengers were* ~ed *as they boarded the aircraft*⟩ **4a** to project (eg a film) on a screen **b** to show or broadcast (a film or television programme) **c** to present in a film or on television – *vi* **1** to appear on a cinema or television screen ⟨*actors who* ~ *well*⟩ **2** to provide a screen in a game or sport – **screenable** *adj*, **screener** *n*

**screening** /'skreening/ *n* **1** *pl but taking sing or pl vb* material (eg waste or fine coal) separated out by passage through or retention on a screen **2** screens used to protect or separate **3** metal or plastic mesh (eg for window screens) **4** a showing of a film or television programme

**screenplay** /-,play/ *n* the script of a film, including description of characters, details of scenes and settings, dialogue, and stage directions

**screen printing** *n* SILK SCREEN (printing through silk or other material treated so as to make some areas impervious) – **screen-printed** *adj*

**screen test** *n* a short film sequence used to assess an actor's suitability for a film role – **screen-test** *vt*

**screenwriter** /-,rieta/ *n* a writer of screenplays

¹**screw** /skrooh/ *n* **1** a simple machine for raising weights or applying pressure in which the applied force acts along a spiral path about a cylinder while the resisting force acts along the axis of the cylinder **2a** **screw, woodscrew** a usu pointed tapering short metal rod with a raised thread along all or part of its length and a usu slotted head that may be driven into material (eg wood or chipboard) by rotating (eg with a screwdriver) **b** a screw-bolt that can be turned by a screwdriver **3a** something like a screw in form or function; a spiral **b** a turn of a screw; *also* a twist resembling such a turn ⟨*give a* ~ *to the stake*⟩ **4** SCREW PROPELLER **5** a thumbscrew used for torture **6** a backwards spin given to a billiard or snooker ball by striking it below the centre **7** *chiefly Br* a small twisted paper packet (eg of salt or tobacco) **8** *slang* someone who drives a hard bargain; *also* a skinflint **9** *slang* a prison warder; a gaoler **10** *vulg* **10a** an act of sexual intercourse **b** a partner in sexual intercourse – see also **have a screw** LOOSE [ME, fr MF *escroe* female screw, nut, fr ML *scrofa*, fr L, sow] – **screwlike** *adj*

²**screw** *vt* **1a(1)** to attach, fasten, or close by means of a screw ⟨*make sure the lid is* ~ed⟩ ⟨~ *a handle onto a door*⟩ **a(2)** to unite by means of a screw or a twisting motion ⟨~ *the two pieces together*⟩ **a(3)** to press tightly in a device (eg a vice) operated by a screw **a(4)** to operate, tighten, or adjust by means of a screw **b** to cause to rotate spirally about an axis **2a(1)** to twist out of shape; contort ⟨~ed *up his face*⟩ **a(2)** to tighten the muscles round and partially close (an eye) ⟨~ed *her eyes tight to read the small writing*⟩ **a(3)** to crush into irregular folds; crumple ⟨~ed *up the letter and threw it away*⟩ **b** to put a spiral groove or ridge in; thread **3** to increase the intensity, quantity, or effectiveness of ⟨~ *up one's courage*⟩ **4** to give backwards spin to (a billiard or snooker ball) **5** *slang* **5a** to make oppressive demands on ⟨~ed *him for every penny he'd got*⟩ **b** to extract by pressure or threat; extort – usu + *from* or *out of* **6** *slang* – used interjectionally as an expression of annoyance ⟨~ *the lot of you!*⟩ **7** *vulg* to have sexual intercourse with ~ *vi* **1a** to rotate like or as a screw ⟨*the nut* ~s *on here*⟩ **b** to become attached or secured (as if) by screwing –

usu + *on* or *up* ⟨*panels that* ~ *on*⟩ **2** to turn or move with a twisting or writhing motion **3** *vulg* to have sexual intercourse – see also **have one's** HEAD **screwed on** □ (*vt 2a&3*) usu + *up* – **screwer** *n*

**screw up** *vt* **1** to tighten, fasten, or lock (as if) by a screw **2** *informal* to cause to become anxious or neurotic **3** *slang* to bungle, botch **4** *vulg* to ruin; FUCK UP

¹**screwball** /'skrooh,bawl/ *n, chiefly NAm informal* a whimsical, eccentric, or mad person [orig sense, a pitch in baseball that spins and swerves unexpectedly]

²**screwball** *adj, chiefly NAm informal* crazily eccentric or whimsical; ludicrous

'**screw-,bolt** *n* a blunt-tipped metal rod or pin for fastening objects together that has a head at one end and a screw thread at the other for screwing into a threaded hole (eg on a nut)

**screwdriver** /-,drievə/ *n* a tool for turning screws; *esp* one that has a small blade set crosswise to and at the end of a shaft

**screwed** /skroohd/ *adj, informal* drunk

**screw eye** *n* a device with a pointed threaded shaft like a screw and a head in the form of a loop

**screw pine** *n* any of a genus (*Pandanus* of the family Pandanaceae) of tropical and subtropical shrubs with slender palmlike stems, often huge proplike roots that grow from above the ground and support the stem, and a few branches that bear crowns of swordlike leaves at their ends

**screw propeller** *n* a device consisting of a central hub with radiating twisted blades that is used to propel a vehicle (eg a ship or aeroplane)

**screw thread** *n* the projecting spiral rib (eg on a fitting or pipe) by which parts can be screwed together; *specif* the thread on a screw

**screw top** *n* **1** a cover designed to be twisted tightly onto the top of a container (eg a jar or bottle) **2** an opening designed for a screw top to twist onto – **screwtop** *adj*

**screwy** /'skrooh-i/ *adj, chiefly NAm informal* crazily absurd, eccentric, or unusual; *also* mad – **screwiness** *n*

**scribble** /'skribl/ *vt* to write hastily or carelessly without regard to legibility or niceties of style ⟨*I'll just* ~ *a note to say when I'll be back*⟩ ~ *vi* to make random or meaningless marks with a pen, pencil, etc ⟨*the baby's* ~d *all over the wedding photographs*⟩ [ME *scriblen*, fr ML *scribillare*, fr L *scribere* to write] – **scribble** *n*

**scribbler** /'skriblə/ *n* **1** someone who scribbles **2** a minor or worthless author

¹**scribe** /skrieb/ *n* **1** a member of a learned class of laymen in ancient Israel through to New Testament times who studied the Scriptures and served as copyists, editors, teachers, and jurists **2a** an official or public secretary or clerk **b** a person who copied manuscripts in ancient and medieval times **3** *chiefly humorous* an author; *specif* a journalist [ME, fr L *scriba* official writer, fr *scribere* to write; akin to Gk *skariphasthai* to scratch an outline, *keirein* to cut – more at SHEAR] – **scribal** *adj*

²**scribe** *vi* to work as a scribe; write

³**scribe** *vt* **1** to mark a line on by scoring with a pointed instrument **2** to make (eg a line) by cutting, scratching, or gouging [prob short for *describe*]

⁴**scribe** *n* a scriber

**scriber** /'skriebə/ *n* a sharp-pointed tool for making marks, esp for marking out material (eg metal) to be cut

**scrim** /skrim/ *n* a durable plain-woven usu cotton fabric for use in clothing, curtain lining, building, and industry [origin unknown]

¹**scrimmage** /'skrimij/ *n* **1a** a minor battle; a skirmish **b** a confused fight; a scuffle **2a** a scrum in rugby **b** the interplay between two AMERICAN FOOTBALL teams that begins with the passing back of the ball from the ground and continues until the ball is dead **c** practice play (eg in AMERICAN FOOTBALL) between a team's squads [alter. of ¹*skirmish*]

²**scrimmage** *vi* to take part in a scrimmage – **scrimmager** *n*

**scrimp** /skrimp/ *vt* **1** to be niggardly in providing for ⟨~s *his family*⟩ **2** to make too small, short, or scanty; be excessively sparing with ⟨~ *provisions*⟩ ~ *vi* to be frugal, ungenerous, or mean; skimp [perh of Scand origin; akin to Sw *skrympa* to shrink, ON *skorpna* to shrivel up – more at SHRIMP] – **scrimpy** *adj*

**scrimshank** /'skrim,shangk/ *vi, Br informal* to avoid duties or obligations; shirk [origin unknown] – **scrimshanker** *n*

¹**scrimshaw** /'skrimshaw/ *n* **1** any of various carved or engraved articles made esp by sailors, usu from ivory or whale-

bone **2 scrimshawed** work **3** the art, practice, or technique of producing scrimshaw [origin unknown]

**²scrimshaw** *vt* to carve or engrave into scrimshaw ∼ *vi* to produce scrimshaw

**¹scrip** /skrip/ *n, archaic* a small bag or wallet [ME *scrippe,* fr ML *scrippum* pilgrim's knapsack]

**²scrip** *n* **1** a brief writing (e g a certificate, list, or prescription) **2** a small piece; a scrap **3** any of various documents used as evidence that the holder or bearer is entitled to receive something (e g an allotment of land); *esp* a certificate entitling the holder to a particular number of shares, bonds, etc △ script [(1, 2) short for *script;* (3) prob short for *subscription receipt*]

**¹script** /skript/ *n* **1a** something written; a text **b** an original document **c(1)** a manuscript **c(2)** the written text of a stage play, film, or broadcast; *specif* the one used in production or performance **2a** printed lettering resembling handwriting **b** written characters; handwriting **c** the characters used in writing a particular language; an alphabet ⟨*Russian* ∼⟩ [L *scriptum* thing written, fr neut of *scriptus,* pp of *scribere* to write – more at SCRIBE]

**²script** *vt* to prepare a script for or from

**scriptorium** /skrip'tawriəm/ *n, pl* **scriptoria** /-riə/ a room set apart for scribes in a medieval monastery [ML, fr L *scriptus*]

**scriptural** /'skripchərəl/ *adj* of, contained in, or according to a sacred writing; *esp* biblical ⟨*a* ∼ *tradition*⟩ – **scripturally** *adv*

**scripture** /'skripchə/ *n* **1a(1) Scriptures** *pl,* **Scripture** the books of the Old and New Testaments or of either of them; the Bible **a(2)** *often cap* a passage from the Bible **b** the sacred writings of a religion or a body of writings held to be authoritative **2** something written ⟨*the primitive man's awe for any* ∼ – George Santayana⟩ [ME, fr LL *scriptura,* fr L, act or product of writing, fr *scriptus*]

**scriptwriter** /'skript,rietə/ *n* someone who writes scripts for films or for radio or television programmes

**scrivener** /'skrivn·ə/ *n* **1** NOTARY (public official who authorizes documents, administers oaths, etc) **2** a person who, in former times, received money for investment at interest and arranged loans on security; a broker **3** *archaic* a professional copyist or scribe [ME *scriveiner,* alter. of *scrivein,* fr MF *escrivein,* fr (assumed) VL *scriban-, scriba,* alter. of L *scriba* scribe]

**scrod** /skrod/ *n, NAm* a young fish (e g a cod or haddock); *esp* one split and boned for cooking [perh fr obs D *schrood* shred; akin to OE *scrēade* shred – more at SHRED]

**scrofula** /'skrofyoolə/ *n* tuberculosis of the LYMPH GLANDS, esp of the neck, producing swelling – not now used technically [ML, fr LL *scrofulae,* pl, swellings of the lymph glands of the neck, fr pl of *scrofula,* dim. of L *scrofa* breeding sow]

**scrofulous** /'skrofyooləs/ *adj* **1** of or affected with scrofula **2a** having a diseased appearance **b** morally corrupt

**scroll** /skrohl/ *n* **1a** a roll (e g of paper or parchment) used for a written document **b** a ribbon with rolled ends that often bears a heraldic motto **2a** something resembling a scroll in shape; *esp* a stylized ornamental design imitating the spiral curves of a loosely or partly rolled parchment scroll **b** the curved head of a stringed musical instrument of the violin family **3** *archaic* a roster, list [ME *scrowle,* alter. of *scrowe,* fr MF *escroue* scrap, scroll, of Gmc origin; akin to OE *scrēade* shred] – **scrolled** *adj,* **scrolly** *adj*

**scroll saw** *n* **1** a thin handsaw for cutting curves or irregular designs **2** FRETSAW (narrow-bladed saw used within a frame for cutting curved outlines)

**scrollwork** /'skrohl,wuhk/ *n* ornamentation in scroll-like patterns; *esp* elaborate designs in wood, often made with a scroll saw

**scrooge** /skroohj/ *n, often cap, informal* a miserly person [Ebenezer *Scrooge,* character in *A Christmas Carol,* story by Charles Dickens †1870 E writer]

**scrotum** /'skrohtəm/ *n, pl* **scrota** /-tə/, **scrotums** the external pouch of the genital organs of most male mammals, that contains the testes [L; akin to L *scrupus* sharp stone – more at SHRED] – **scrotal** *adj*

**scrouge** /skrowj/ *vb, chiefly dial* to crowd, press [alter. of E dial. *scruze* to squeeze, perh alter. of *squeeze*]

**¹scrounge** /skrownj/ *vb, informal vt* **1** to procure (as if) by foraging **2** to beg, wheedle ⟨*can I* ∼ *a cigarette off you?*⟩ ∼ *vi* **1** to forage, hunt *around* **2** to wheedle [alter. of E dial. *scrunge* to wander about idly] – **scrounger** *n*

**²scrounge** *n, informal* – **on the scrounge** attempting to obtain something by wheedling or cajoling

**¹scrub** /skrub/ *n* **1a** vegetation consisting chiefly of stunted trees or shrubs **b** an area covered with scrub **2a** a domestic animal of mixed or unknown parentage and usu inferior type; a mongrel **b** a small or insignificant person; a runt [ME, alter. of *schrobbe* shrub – more at SHRUB]

**²scrub** *vb* **-bb-** *vt* **1a(1)** to clean by hard rubbing, esp with a stiff brush **a(2)** to remove by scrubbing ⟨∼ *the soot off old tiles*⟩ **b** to subject to friction; rub ⟨∼ *yourself with a towel*⟩ **2** WASH 6c(2) (purify a gas by passing through a liquid) **3** *informal* to abolish, abandon ⟨*let's* ∼ *that idea*⟩ ∼ *vi* to use hard rubbing in cleaning [of LG or Scand origin; akin to MLG & MD *schrubben* to scrub, Sw *skrubba*] – **scrub** *n*

**scrubber** /'skrubə/ *n* **1** one who or that which scrubs; *esp* an apparatus for removing impurities (e g from gases) **2** *Br slang* **2a** a female prostitute; *also* a promiscuous girl or woman **b** a coarse or unattractive person, esp a woman

**scrubbing brush** /'skrubing/, *NAm* **scrub brush** *n* a brush with hard bristles used for heavy cleaning, esp washing floors

**scrubby** /'skrubi/ *adj* **1** inferior in size or quality; stunted ⟨∼ *cattle*⟩ **2** covered with or consisting of scrub **3** *informal* lacking distinction; trashy ⟨*a* ∼ *comedy*⟩ [¹*scrub*]

**scrubland** /'skrublənd/ *n* land covered with scrub

**scrub pine** *n* a pine of dwarf, straggly, or scrubby growth, usu caused by adverse environmental conditions; *specif* a pine tree unsuitable for use as timber because of inferior or defective growth

**scrubwoman** /'skrub,woom(ə)n/ *n, NAm* a charwoman

**¹scruff** /skruf/ *n* the back *of* the neck; *the* nape [alter. of earlier *scuff,* of unknown origin]

**²scruff** *n, informal* **1** an untidily dressed or grubby person **2** a coarse or disreputable person ⟨*young* ∼s *who stir up trouble*⟩ [E, dial. *scruff* dandruff, something worthless, alter. of *scurf*]

**scruffy** /'skrufi/ *adj* **1** seedy, disreputable, run-down ⟨*living in a really* ∼ *neighbourhood*⟩ **2** slovenly and untidy, esp in appearance ⟨*don't come wearing those* ∼ *jeans*⟩ – **scruffiness** *n*

**scrum** /skrum/ *n* **1** a method of resuming play in rugby (e g after an infringement) in which the forwards of each side crouch in a tight formation with locked arms and with the two front rows of each team meeting shoulder to shoulder with their heads interlocking, the ball is put into play between them, and each side pushes to try to keep the other from the ball and gain possession of it themselves **2** *chiefly humorous* a disorderly struggle; a jostle ⟨*the morning* ∼ *to board the bus*⟩ [short for *scrummage,* alter. of *scrimmage*]

**'scrum-,cap** *n* protective headgear sometimes worn by rugby forwards

**scrum down** *vi* to form a scrum

**,scrum-'half** *n* the player in rugby who puts the ball into the scrum; *also* the position of this player

**scrummage** /'skrumij/ *vi or n* (to take part in) a scrum – **scrummager** *n*

**scrump** /skrump/ *vb, Br informal* to pilfer (e g apples) from an orchard [perh alter. of *scrimp*]

**scrumptious** /'skrum(p)shəs/ *adj, esp of food* delightful, delicious ⟨*a* ∼*, creamy cheesecake – Woman*⟩ [prob alter. of *sumptuous*] – **scrumptiously** *adv,* **scrumptiousness** *n*

**scrumpy** /'skrumpi/ *n, Br* dry rough usu strong cider [E dial. *scrump* something shrivelled, shrivelled apple]

**¹scrunch** /skrunch/ *vt* **1** to crunch, crush **2** to crumple, wrinkle – often + *up* ⟨∼ *up a sheet of cardboard*⟩ **3** *chiefly NAm* to contract, hunch – often + *up* ⟨*sitting with his shoulders* ∼ed *up*⟩ ∼ *vi* **1** to move with or make a crunching sound ⟨*her boots* ∼ed *in the snow*⟩ **2** *chiefly NAm* to hunch up; crouch [alter. of ¹*crunch*]

**²scrunch** *n* a crunching sound

**¹scruple** /'skroohpl/ *n* **1** a unit of weight equal to 20 grains (1.296 grams) **2** *archaic* a minute part or quantity; an iota [ME *scriple,* fr L *scrupulus* a unit of weight, fr *scrupulus* small sharp stone]

**²scruple** *n* **1** a moral consideration that discourages one from doing something **2** the quality or state of being scrupulous ⟨*had a moment of* ∼⟩ **3** a rigorous scrupulous concern ⟨*a passion for honesty and a* ∼ *for concision – London*⟩ **synonyms** see QUALM [MF *scrupule,* fr L *scrupulus* small sharp stone, cause of mental discomfort, scruple, dim. of *scrupus* sharp stone – more at SHRED]

**³scruple** *vi* to hesitate or be reluctant on grounds of conscience ⟨*would not* ∼ *to defend a criminal*⟩

**scrupulosity** /,skroohpyoo'losəti/ *n* the quality of being scrupulous, esp to an excessive degree

**scrupulous** /'skroohpyoolǝs/ adj 1 possessing moral integrity; inclined to have scruples 2 painstakingly exact; meticulous ⟨working with ∼ care⟩ **synonyms** see CAREFUL **antonyms** unscrupulous, remiss [ME, fr L scrupulosus, fr scrupulus] – **scrupulously** adv, **scrupulousness** n

**scrutable** /'skroohtǝbl/ adj, formal capable of being deciphered; comprehensible [LL scrutabilis searchable, fr L scrutari to search, investigate, examine – more at SCRUTINY]

**scrutineer** /ˌskroohti'niǝ/ n 1 someone who examines or observes 2 Br someone who takes or counts votes at an election

**scrutin-ize, -ise** /'skroohtiˌniez/ vt to examine closely or painstakingly ∼ vi to make a scrutiny – **scrutinizer** n

**scrutiny** /'skroohtini/ n 1 a searching study, inquiry, or inspection; an examination 2 a searching or critical look 3 close watch; surveillance ⟨keep prisoners under ∼⟩ [L scrutinium, fr scrutari to search, examine, fr scruta trash]

**scry** /skrie/ vi to discover facts, predict events, etc by CRYSTAL GAZING [short for descry]

**scuba** /'skoohbǝ; also 'skyoohbǝ/ n an aqualung [self-contained underwater breathing apparatus]

**scuba diver** n an underwater swimmer using aqualung equipment – **scuba dive** vi

**¹scud** /skud/ vi -dd- 1 to move or run swiftly, esp as if swept along ⟨clouds ∼ding along⟩ 2 of a ship to run before a gale [prob of Scand origin; akin to Norw skudda to push; akin to L quatere to shake – more at QUASH]

**²scud** n 1 the action of scudding; a rush 2a loose vapoury clouds driven swiftly by the wind b(1) a slight sudden shower b(2) mist, rain, snow, or spray driven by the wind c a gust of wind

**scudo** /'skoohdoh/ n, pl scudi /-di/ 1 any of various monetary units first used in the 15th century and used in Italy until the 19th century 2 a gold or silver coin representing one scudo [It, lit., shield, fr L scutum shield]

**¹scuff** /skuf/ vi 1 to slouch along without lifting the feet; shuffle 2 to become scratched, chipped, or roughened by wear ⟨patent leather soon ∼s⟩ ∼ vt 1 to cuff 2 to drag or shuffle (the feet) along while walking or back and forth while standing 3 to scratch, chip, or abrade the surface of ⟨∼ed the teak veneer⟩ 4 chiefly NAm to poke at with the toe [prob of Scand origin; akin to Sw skuffa to push]

**²scuff** n 1a the act or an instance of scuffing b a blemish or injury caused by scuffing 2 chiefly NAm a noise (as if) of scuffing

**¹scuffle** /'skufl/ vi 1 to struggle confusedly and at close quarters ⟨demonstrators scuffling with police⟩ 2 to move or hurry about with a shuffling gait; scurry [prob of Scand origin; akin to Sw skuffa to push]

**²scuffle** n 1 a confused impromptu usu brief fight 2 a soft confused shuffling sound

**¹scull** /skul/ n 1a an oar worked to and fro over the stern of a boat as a means of propulsion b either of a pair of light oars pulled by a single rower who holds one in each hand 2 a narrow light racing boat propelled by one, two, or four people using sculls 3 sculls pl, scull a race between two or more sculls 4 an act, time, or distance of sculling △ skull [ME sculle]

**²scull** vb to propel (a boat) by a scull or sculls – **sculler** n

**scullery** /'skul(ǝ)ri/ n a room for menial kitchen work (e g washing dishes and utensils and preparing vegetables) [ME, department of household in charge of dishes, fr MF escuelerie, fr escuelle bowl, fr L scutella drinking bowl – more at SCUTTLE]

**scullion** /'skulyǝn/ n, archaic a kitchen servant [ME sculion, fr MF escouillon dishcloth, alter. of escouvillon, fr escouve broom, fr L scopa, lit., twig; akin to L scapus stalk – more at SHAFT]

**sculp** /skulp/ vb, informal to sculpture [L sculpere to carve]

**sculpin** /'skulpin/ n, pl sculpins, esp collectively sculpin any of a family (Cottidae) of spiny large-headed broad-mouthed usu scaleless fishes [origin unknown]

**sculpt** /skulpt/ vb to sculpture [Fr sculpter, alter. of obs sculper, fr L sculpere]

**sculptor** /'skulptǝ/, fem **sculptress** /-tris/ n someone who sculptures; esp an artist who produces works of sculpture [L, fr sculptus, pp of sculpere]

**sculptural** /'skulptyoorǝl/ adj 1 of sculpture 2 like sculpture; sculpturesque ⟨the ∼ forms of desert outcrops⟩ – **sculpturally** adv

**¹sculpture** /'skulpchǝ/ n 1a the action or art of creating three-dimensional works of art out of mouldable or hard materials by carving, modelling, casting, etc b(1) work produced by

sculpture b(2) a three-dimensional work of art (e g a statue) 2 (a pattern of) impressed or raised markings, esp on a plant or animal part [ME, fr L sculptura, fr sculptus, pp of sculpere to carve, alter. of scalpere – more at SHELF]

**²sculpture** vt 1a to form an image or representation of from solid material (e g wood or stone) b to form (e g wood or stone) into a three-dimensional work of art 2 to change (the form of the earth's surface) by natural processes (e g erosion and deposition) 3 to shape (as if) by carving or moulding ∼ vi to work as a sculptor

**sculpturesque** /ˌskulpchǝ'resk/ adj like or done in the manner of sculpture – **sculpturesquely** adv

**¹scum** /skum/ n 1a pollutants or impurities risen to or collected on the surface of a liquid, esp as a foul filmy covering b the skin of impurities that forms on the surface of molten metals; DROSS 2a refuse b slang b(1) taking pl vb the lowest class; the dregs ⟨the ∼ of the earth⟩ b(2) an utterly corrupt or despicable person [ME, fr MD schum; akin to OHG scūm foam] – **scummy** adj

**²scum** vi -mm- to become covered (as if) with scum

**¹scumble** /'skumbl/ vt 1a to make (e g colour or a painting) less brilliant by covering with a thin coat of opaque or semi-opaque colour b to apply (a colour) in this manner 2 to soften the lines or colours of (a drawing) by rubbing lightly [freq of ²scum]

**²scumble** n 1 the act or effect of scumbling 2 a material used for scumbling

**scungy** /'skunji/ adj, Austr informal scruffy, grotty [perh fr Sc scunge sly or vicious person]

**scunner** /'skunǝ/ n, chiefly Scot an unreasonable or extreme dislike or prejudice [ME (Sc) skunniren to be annoyed]

**scunnered** /'skunǝd/ adj, chiefly Scot extremely fed up or exasperated ⟨I'm fair ∼ of it!⟩

**¹scupper** /'skupǝ/ n 1 an opening cut in a ship's bulwarks for draining water from the deck 2 an opening in the wall of a building through which water can drain from a floor or flat roof [ME skopper]

**²scupper** vt, chiefly Br 1 to sink (one's own ship), esp deliberately 2 informal to wreck; PUT PAID TO ⟨∼ed our plans for a reunion⟩ [origin unknown; orig sense, to ambush; (1) perh alter. (influenced in sense by ¹scupper) of ³scuttle]

**scurf** /skuhf/ n 1 thin dry scales detached from the skin; specif dandruff 2 matter adhering to or peeling from a surface in the form of flakes or scales 3a a scaly deposit or covering on some plant parts; also a darkening and roughening of a plant surface b a plant disease characterized by scurf [ME, of Scand origin; akin to Icel skurfa scurf; akin to OHG scorf scurf, L carpere to pluck – more at HARVEST] – **scurfy** adj

**scurrile** /'skuriel, -rǝl/ adj, archaic scurrilous [MF, fr L scurrilis, fr scurra buffoon, jester]

**scurrility** /skǝ'riliti/ n 1 the quality or state of being scurrilous 2a scurrilous or abusive language b an offensively vulgar or abusive remark **synonyms** see ²ABUSE

**scurrilous** /'skurilǝs/ adj 1a using or given to coarse language b wicked and unscrupulous in behaviour ⟨∼ imposters who rob poor people⟩ 2 containing obscenities or coarse abuse ⟨a campaign filled with ∼ accusations and rebuttals⟩ [L scurrilis] – **scurrilously** adv, **scurrilousness** n

**scurry** /'skuri/ vi 1 to move briskly, esp with short hurried steps; scamper 2 to move back and forth in an agitated, confused, or nervous manner [short for hurry-scurry, redupl of hurry] – **scurry** n

**¹scurvy** /'skuhvi/ adj disgustingly mean or contemptible; despicable ⟨a ∼ trick⟩ [scurf + ¹-y] – **scurvily** adv, **scurviness** n

**²scurvy** n a DEFICIENCY DISEASE caused by a lack of vitamin C and marked by spongy gums, loosening of the teeth, and bleeding into the skin and MUCOUS MEMBRANES

**scurvy grass** n any of several European and N American plants (genus Cochlearia, esp Cochlearia officinalis) of the cabbage family with clusters of small usu white or mauve flowers and fleshy leaves that were formerly eaten to prevent scurvy

**scut** /skut/ n a short erect tail (e g of a hare) [origin unknown]

**scutage** /'skyoohtij/ n a tax levied on a tenant of a knight's estate in place of military service [ME, fr ML scutagium, fr L scutum shield]

**¹scutch** /skuch/ vt 1 to separate the woody fibre from (flax or hemp) by beating 2 to open (cotton fibre) by beating and form into a continuous sheet [(assumed) Fr escoucher to beat, fr (assumed) VL excuticare to beat out, fr L executere, fr ex- + quatere to shake, strike – more at QUASH]

²**scutch** n a scutcher

**scutcheon** /'skuchən/ n ESCUTCHEON (heraldic shield) [ME *scochon*, fr MF *escuchon*]

**scutcher** /'skuchə/ n something (e g an implement or machine) for scutching flax or cotton

**scute** /skyooht/ n an external usu bony or horny plate or large scale (e g on the belly of a snake or forming part of the protective cover of a crocodile, armadillo, etc) [NL *scutum*, fr L, shield – more at ESQUIRE]

**scutellate** /'skyoohtilət, -layt/, **scutellated** /-laytid/ adj 1 of or like a scutellum 2 having or covered with scutella

**scutellum** /skyooh'teləm/ n, pl **scutella** /-telə/ 1 any of several small shieldlike plant structures; *esp* a development of part of the COTYLEDON (leaf produced by a germinating seed) that separates the embryo from the ENDOSPERM (nutritive tissue) in the developing seed of some grasses 2 a hard plate or scale (e g on the foot of a bird or forming part of the top surface of an insect segment) [NL, dim. of L *scutum* shield] – **scutellar** adj

**scutter** /'skutə/ vi, *chiefly Br* to scurry, scamper [alter. of ⁴*scuttle*]

¹**scuttle** /'skutl/ n 1 a shallow open basket, used esp for carrying garden produce 2 a vessel that resembles a bucket and is used for storing, carrying, and dispensing coal indoors 3 *Br* the top part of a motor-car body in front of the two front doors, to which the windscreen and instrument panel are attached [ME *scutel*, fr L *scutella* drinking bowl, tray, dim. of *scutra* platter]

²**scuttle** n 1a a small opening or hatchway with a movable lid in the deck of a ship **b** a small opening in a ship's side fitted with a hinged glass window and metal lid that can be adjusted to admit light and air; a porthole **c** *NAm* a small covered hole in the roof or floor of a house 2 *NAm* a lid that closes a scuttle [ME *skottell*, prop fr OSp *escotilla*]

³**scuttle** vt 1 to sink (a ship) by making holes in the hull or opening SEACOCKS (valves in the hull below the water line) esp in order to avoid capture by an enemy 2 to destroy, wreck ⟨~ attempts to reach agreement⟩

⁴**scuttle** vi to scurry [prob blend of *scud* and *shuttle*]

⁵**scuttle** n 1 a quick shuffling pace 2 a short swift dash; *esp* a swift departure

**scuttlebutt** /-,but/ n 1 a cask on a ship's deck containing fresh water 2 *NAm informal* gossip [²*scuttle*]

**scutum** /'skyoohtəm/ n, pl **scuta** /-tə/ a plate made of bone, horn, etc; SCUTE [NL, fr L, shield – more at ESQUIRE]

**Scylla** /'silə/ n – **between Scylla and Charybdis** between two equally hazardous alternatives [*Scylla* (Gk *Skyllē*) a female sea monster, & *Charybdis*, a whirlpool, in Gk myth two hazards in the sea between Italy & Sicily]

**scyphistoma** /,sie'fistəmə/ n, pl **scyphistomae** /-mie/ *also* **scyphistomas** a sexually produced immature scyphozoan having a hollow cylindrical body that undergoes repeated constriction to form segments which successively split off and ultimately develop into free-swimming jellyfish (MEDUSAE) [NL, fr L *scyphus* cup + Gk *stoma* mouth]

**scyphozoan** /,siefə'zohən/ n any of a class (Scyphozoa of the phylum Coelenterata) of marine INVERTEBRATE animals comprising the jellyfishes that have an umbrella-shaped sexually reproducing body (MEDUSA) but lack a true POLYP stage (nonsexually reproducing stage) in their life cycle; a jellyfish [NL *Scyphozoa*, class name, fr L *scyphus* + NL *-zoa*] – **scyphozoan** adj

¹**scythe** /siedh/ n an implement used for cutting standing plants (e g grass), composed of a long curving blade fastened at an angle to a long handle [ME *sithe*, fr OE *sīthe*; akin to OE *sagu* saw – more at SAW]

²**scythe** vt to cut (as if) with a scythe

**Scythian** /'sidhi-ən/ n 1 a member of an ancient nomadic people inhabiting Scythia, a region north of the Black sea 2 the Iranian language of the Scythians [L *Scytha*, fr Gk *Skythēs*] – **Scythian** adj

**sea** /see/ n 1a sea, seas pl the great body of salty water that covers much of the earth; *broadly* the waters of the earth as distinguished from the land and air **b** a large more or less landlocked body of salt water ⟨*the Mediterranean* ~⟩ **c** an ocean **d** an inland body of water, esp if large or (somewhat) salt ⟨*the Caspian* ~⟩ **e** a small freshwater lake ⟨*the Sea of Galilee*⟩ 2a surface motion on a large body of water or its direction; *also* rough water; a heavy swell or wave **b** the disturbance of the ocean or other body of water due to the wind 3 something vast or overwhelming likened to the sea ⟨*a* ~ *of*

mud*⟩ ⟨a* ~ *of faces*⟩ 4 the seafaring life ⟨*to run away to* ~⟩ 5 ²MARE (dark area on the surface of the moon or Mars) [ME *see*, fr OE *sǣ*; akin to OS & OHG *sē* sea] – **sea** adj – **at sea 1** on the sea; *specif* on a sea voyage 2 unable to understand; lost, bewildered ⟨*he was all* at sea, *never having had to organize the household before*⟩ – **put (out) to sea** to start out on a journey by sea

**sea anchor** n a device, typically of canvas, towed to slow the drifting of a ship or seaplane and to keep it pointing into the wind

**sea anemone** n any of numerous usu brightly coloured marine INVERTEBRATE animals (order Actiniaria of the class Anthozoa) that are POLYPS having a hollow cylindrical body attached at one end (e g to rocks) and with a mouth at the other end surrounded by a cluster of tentacles equipped with stinging cells and superficially resembling a flower

'**sea-,bank** n a seawall

**sea bass** /bas/ n any of numerous chiefly marine fishes (family Serranidae), including many valued for food and sport, that are related to the GROUPERS but are usu smaller and more active, and that have an elongated body, a usu straight-edged or rounded tail, and a long fin on the back divided into two usu joined sections

**seabed** /'see,bed/ n the floor of the sea

**seabird** /-,buhd/ n a bird (e g a gull or albatross) frequenting the open sea

'**sea ,biscuit** n SHIP BISCUIT (hard bread or biscuit for use at sea)

**seaboard** /-,bawd/ n, *chiefly NAm* the land near a shore; *also* the seashore – **seaboard** adj

**seaboot** /'see,booht/ n a very high waterproof boot worn esp by sailors and fishermen

**seaborne** /-,bawn/ adj 1 conveyed on or over the sea ⟨*a* ~ *invasion*⟩ 2 dependent on overseas shipping ⟨~ *trade*⟩

**sea bream** n any of numerous marine spiny-finned food fishes (e g of the families Sparidae or Bramidae)

**sea breeze** n a cooling breeze blowing, usu during the day, inland from the sea

**sea butterfly** n any of a group (Pteropoda of the class Gastropoda, phylum Mollusca) of small marine INVERTEBRATE animals related to the snails and slugs that are either shell-less or have a delicate much reduced shell and that have the front lobes of the foot expanded into broad thin winglike organs with which they swim – called also PTEROPOD

**sea captain** n the master of a vessel, esp a merchant vessel

**sea change** n 1 a complete transformation 2 *archaic* a change brought about by the sea

**sea chest** n a sailor's storage chest for personal property

**sea coal** n 1 coal when conveyed by sea 2 *archaic* mineral coal as opposed to charcoal

**seacock** /'see,kok/ n a valve in the hull of a vessel through which water may be admitted (e g to ballast tanks)

**sea cow** n either of two aquatic plant-eating mammals: **a** DUGONG **b** MANATEE

**sea cucumber** n HOLOTHURIAN (sea animal with a long flexible muscular body); *esp* one whose body is cucumber-shaped

**sea devil** n, *NAm* MANTA RAY

**seadog** /-,dog/ n FOGBOW (arc or circle of light sometimes seen in fog)

**sea dog** n a veteran sailor

**seadrome** /'see,drohm/ n a usu floating aerodrome on water serving esp as an intermediate or emergency landing place

**sea duck** n a DIVING DUCK (e g a SCOTER or eider) that frequents the sea

**sea eagle** n any of various fish-eating eagles

'**sea-,ear** n ABALONE (shellfish with a flattened shell)

**sea elephant** n ELEPHANT SEAL

**sea fan** n any of various GORGONIAN corals (genus *Gorgonia* and related genera) with a horny branching fan-shaped or treelike skeleton

**seafarer** /-,feərə/ n a mariner [*sea* + ¹*fare* +²*-er*]

**seafaring** /-,feəring/ n travel by sea; *esp* the occupation of a sailor – **seafaring** adj

**sea feather** n any of various GORGONIAN corals with a feathery branching skeleton

**sea fire** n marine BIOLUMINESCENCE (light given off by living organisms)

**seafloor** /'see,flaw/ n the seabed

**sea fog** n a fog in a coastal area caused by the difference in land and sea temperatures

**seafood** /-,foohd/ *n* edible marine animals, esp fish, shellfish, and crabs, lobsters, etc

**seafront** /-,frunt/ *n* the part of a coastal town next to the sea

**seagirt** /-,guht/ *adj, poetic* surrounded by the sea ⟨*this ~ isle*⟩

**seagoing** /-,goh·ing/ *adj* of or designed for travel on the sea; seafaring

**sea gooseberry** *n* CTENOPHORE (sea animal resembling a jellyfish)

**sea green** *adj or n* (of) a bluish-green or yellow-green colour

**sea gull** *n* a gull; *esp* a gull with a marine habitat

**sea hare** *n* any of various large marine INVERTEBRATE animals (genus *Aplysia* of the phylum Mollusca) related to the snails and slugs that have an arched back, a much reduced internal shell but no external shell, and tentacles that project like ears

**sea holly** *n* a European coastal plant (*Eryngium maritimum*) of the carrot family with bluish spiny leaves and pale blue flowers

**sea horse** *n* **1** a mythical creature that is half horse and half fish **2** any of numerous small sea fishes (family Syngnathidae) that swim in an upright position and have a body covered in rings of bony plates, a head and upper body shaped like the head and neck of a horse, and a curled tail

**seakale** /-,kayl/ *n* **1** a European plant (*Crambe maritima*) of the cabbage family with a fleshy root and waxy bluish-green leaves sometimes used as a vegetable **2** *also* **seakale beet** CHARD (plant with large edible leaves and stalks)

**'sea-,keeping** *n* the ability of a ship to maintain normal operations in a rough sea

**sea king** *n* a medieval Norse pirate chief

**¹seal** /seel/ *n, pl* **seals,** *esp collectively* **seal 1** any of numerous flesh-eating aquatic mammals (families Phocidae and Otariidae) that breed on land, occur chiefly in cold regions, and have limbs modified into webbed flippers adapted primarily to swimming; *esp* FUR SEAL **2a** the skin of a FUR SEAL **b** SEALSKIN [ME *sele,* fr OE *seolh;* akin to OHG *selah* seal]

**²seal** *vi* to hunt seal

**³seal** *n* **1a** something that confirms, ratifies, or makes secure; a guarantee, assurance ⟨*a ~ of authenticity*⟩ **b(1)** an emblem or word impressed or stamped on a document as a mark of authenticity **b(2)** an article used to impress such a word or emblem (eg on wax or moist clay); *also* a disc, esp of wax, bearing such an impression **c** a usu ornamental adhesive stamp that may be used to close a letter or package **2a** a closure (eg a wax seal on a document) that must be broken in order to give access **b** a tight and effective closure (eg against the passage of gas or water) **3** a seal that is a symbol of authority or mark of office ⟨*the Keeper of the Seals*⟩ [ME *seel,* fr OF, fr L *sigillum,* fr dim. of *signum* sign, seal] – **under seal** with an authenticating seal attached – **set one's seal** to give approval and endorsement – + *on* or *to*

**⁴seal** *vt* **1** to confirm or make secure (as if) by a seal ⟨*~ed it with his approval*⟩ **2a** to set or affix an authenticating seal to; *also* to authenticate, ratify **b** to mark with a stamp or seal (eg as evidence of size, weight, capacity, or quality) **3a** to fasten (as if) with a seal, esp to prevent or discourage interference **b** to close or make secure against access, leakage, or passage by a fastening or coating; *esp* to make airtight ⟨*the jars must be ~ed if the jam is to keep*⟩ **c** to fix in position or close breaks in with a filling (eg of plaster) **4** to determine irrevocably ⟨*that answer ~ed our fate*⟩ – **sealable** *adj*

**seal off** *vt* to close securely, esp in order to prevent passage ⟨*troops* sealed off *the airport*⟩

**'sea-,lane** *n* an established sea route

**sealant** /'seelənt/ *n* a sealing agent ⟨*radiator ~*⟩

**sea lavender** *n* any of a genus (*Limonium*) of mostly coastal plants of the thrift family with bluish-purple flowers

**sea lawyer** *n* an argumentative contentious sailor; *broadly* any contentious or argumentative person

**sealed-beam** /seeld/ *adj* of or being an electric light (eg a car headlight) having a light-emitting filament, a prefocussed reflector, and often a lens contained in one sealed unit

**sea legs** *n pl* bodily adjustment to the motion of a ship, indicated esp by the ability to walk steadily and by freedom from seasickness

**sea leopard** *n* an antarctic seal (*Hydrurga leptonyx*) with a grey coat spotted with black

**¹sealer** /'seelə/ *n* **1** a coat (eg of SIZE) applied to prevent subsequent coats of paint, varnish, etc from sinking in **2** *chiefly NAm* an inspector of weights and measures [⁴*seal* + ²*-er*]

**²sealer** *n* a mariner or ship engaged in hunting seals [²*seal* + ²*-er*]

**sealery** /'seeləri, 'siə-/ *n* a seal fishery

**sea lettuce** *n* any of several seaweeds (esp genus *Ulva* of the family Ulvaceae) with edible green translucent fronds

**sea level** *n* the level of the surface of the sea, esp at its average position midway between high and low tide

**sea lily** *n* CRINOID (sea animal with feathery arms related to the starfish); *esp* one that remains permanently attached to the sea bottom by means of a stalk

**sealing wax** /'seeling/ *n* a hard material made up of resinous substances (eg shellac, rosin, and turpentine) that becomes soft when heated and is used for sealing things (eg letters or parcels)

**sea lion** *n* any of several large Pacific EARED SEALS (genera *Zalophus* and *Otaria*) that are capable of movement on land and are related to the FUR SEALS but lack their valuable coat

**sea loch** *n* a loch connecting to the sea

**'sea-,lord** *n, often cap* either of two members of the Admiralty Board of the Ministry of Defence who are also serving naval officers

**seal point** *n* a SIAMESE CAT with a cream or fawn-coloured body and dark greyish yellowish brown paws, tips of the ears, and other extremities – compare BLUE POINT [¹*seal;* fr its colour]

**seal ring** *n* a signet ring engraved with a seal

**sealskin** /,skin/, seal *n* **1** the skin of a FUR SEAL; *also* leather made from this **2** a garment (eg a jacket, coat, or cape) of sealskin – **sealskin** *adj*

**Sealyham terrier, Sealyham** /'seeli·əm/ *n* (any of) a Welsh breed of sturdy short-legged terriers with a long head, strong jaws, and a chiefly white coat [*Sealyham,* estate in Dyfed in Wales]

**¹seam** /seem/ *n* **1** a line of stitching joining two separate pieces of fabric (eg cloth or leather), esp along their edges **2** the space between adjacent planks or STRAKES (continuous planking or plates) of a ship **3a** a line, groove, or ridge formed at the meeting of two edges **b** a layer or bed of rock, coal, etc **c** a line left by a cut or wound; *also* a wrinkle [ME *seem,* fr OE *sēam;* akin to OE *sīwian* to sew – more at SEW] – **seamless** *adj,* **seamlike** *adj* – **burst at the seams** to be as full as someone or something can be; *esp* to be large to the point of discomfort ⟨*she ate so much pudding she was* bursting at the seams⟩

**²seam** *vt* **1** to join (as if) by sewing **2** to mark with a seam, furrow, or scar ~ *vi* **1** to become marked with lines suggesting seams **2** *of a bowled ball in cricket* to deviate from a straight line after bouncing on its seam

**seaman** /'seemən/ *n* **1** a sailor, mariner **2** – see MILITARY RANKS table

**seaman apprentice** *n* – see MILITARY RANKS table

**seamanlike** /'seem(ə)n,liek/, **seamanly** /-li/ *adj* characteristic of or befitting a competent seaman

**seaman recruit** *n* – see MILITARY RANKS table

**seamanship** /'seem(ə)nship/ *n* the art or skill of handling, working, and navigating a ship

**seamark** /-,mahk/ *n* **1** a line on a coast marking the limit of high tide **2** a conspicuous object serving as a guide for navigators

**seam bowling** *n* usu faster bowling in cricket in which the ball is made to bounce on its seam and thereby deviate from a straight line; *broadly* any fast bowling – compare SPIN BOWLING – **seam bowler** *n*

**seamer** /'seemə/ *n* one who or that which seams: eg **a** a seam bowler **b** a ball bowled by a seam bowler

**sea mew** *n* a gull

**sea mile** *n* NAUTICAL MILE

**seamount** /-,mownt/ *n* an underwater mountain rising from the ocean floor

**sea mouse** *n* a large marine worm (esp genus *Aphrodite* of the class Polychaeta) with a broad segmented body covered on the back with hairlike bristles

**seamster** /'seemstə/ *n* a person employed at sewing; *esp* a tailor [ME *semester, semster,* fr OE *sēamestre* seamstress, tailor, fr *sēam* seam]

**seamstress** /'seemstris/ *n* a woman whose occupation is sewing

**seamy** /'seemi/ *adj* **1** less reputable or attractive; unpleasant, sordid ⟨*the ~ side of the building trade*⟩ **2** *archaic* having the rough side of the seam showing – **seaminess** *n*

**séance** /'say·on(h)s/ *n* **1** a meeting for discussion; a session **2** a meeting at which spiritualists attempt to communicate with the dead [Fr, fr *seoir* to sit, fr L *sedēre* – more at SIT]

**sea otter** *n* a rare large marine otter (*Enhydra lutris*) of the N Pacific coasts that attains a maximum length of nearly 2 metres (6 feet) and feeds largely on shellfish

**sea pen** *n* any of numerous marine INVERTEBRATE animals (order Pennatulacea of the class Anthozoa) related to the corals, that form colonies having a fleshy featherlike form

**seapiece** /'see,pees/ *n* a seascape as depicted by an artist

**'sea-,pink** *n* a thrift (*Armeria maritima*) with dense pink or white rounded flower heads that grows esp on the seashore

**seaplane** /-,playn/ *n* an aeroplane designed to take off from and land on the water

**seaport** /-,pawt/ *n* a port, harbour, or town accessible to sea-going ships

**sea power** *n* 1 a nation that commands great naval strength 2 naval strength

**sea purse** *n* the horny EGG CASE of skates and of some sharks

**seaquake** /-,kwayk/ *n* an earthquake occurring at the seabed [*sea* + *-quake* (as in *earthquake*)]

**'sear** /siə/ *adj* SERE (withered)

**'sear** *vi, archaic* to become dried or withered ∼ *vt* 1 to make withered and dried up; parch 2a to burn, scorch, or injure (as if) with a sudden application of intense heat b to brown the surface of (meat) by frying quickly in hot fat 3 to mark (as if) with a branding iron ⟨*a sight which was* ∼ed *on my memory*⟩ 4 to make callous or insensitive ⟨*a* ∼ed *conscience*⟩ [ME *seren*, fr OE *sēarian* to become sere, fr *sēar* sere] – **searingly** *adv*

**'sear** *n* a mark or scar left by searing

**'sear** *n* the catch that holds the hammer of a gunlock at or halfway towards the firing position [prob fr MF *serre* grasp, fr *serrer* to press, grasp, fr LL *serare* to bolt, latch, fr L *sera* bar for fastening a door]

**'search** /suhch/ *vt* 1 to look through or over carefully or thoroughly in trying to find or discover something: eg **1a(1)** to examine in seeking something ⟨∼ed *the horizon*⟩ **a(2)** to read through carefully; check; *esp* to examine written records for information about ⟨∼ *land titles*⟩ **b(1)** to investigate or explore by probing concealed places or suspicious circumstances **b(2)** to examine (a person) for concealed articles (eg weapons or drugs) **c** to scrutinize as if to discover or penetrate intention or nature ⟨*first* ∼ *your feelings*⟩ 2 to uncover, find, or ascertain by investigation – usu + *out* ⟨∼ *out the relevant facts*⟩ 3 to cover (an area) with gunfire ∼ *vi* 1 to look or inquire carefully or thoroughly ⟨∼ed *for the papers*⟩ 2 to make painstaking investigation or examination ⟨∼ *into all matters*⟩ [ME *cerchen*, fr MF *cerchier* to go about, survey, search, fr LL *circare* to go about, fr L *circum* round about] – **searchable** *adj*, **searcher** *n* – **search me** – used to express ignorance of an answer ⟨*"where are my keys?"* *"Search me* – *I didn't see where you put them"*⟩

**'search** *n* 1 an act or process of searching; *esp* an organized act of searching; a hunt ⟨*the* ∼ *for the raiders continues*⟩ 2 an act of boarding and inspecting a ship on the high seas (eg by customs officials) by RIGHT OF SEARCH

**searching** /'suhching/ *adj* 1 making a careful or thorough search 2 piercing, penetrating ⟨*a* ∼ *gaze*⟩ ⟨*the* ∼ *wind*⟩ – **searchingly** *adv*

**searchless** /'suhchlis/ *adj, poetic* not decipherable; inscrutable

**searchlight** /-,liet/ *n* an apparatus for projecting a movable beam of light; *also* a beam of light projected by such an apparatus

**search party** /'suhch ,pahti/ *n* a group of people engaged in an organized search (eg for a missing person)

**search warrant** *n* a warrant granted by a judge or magistrate authorizing a search (eg of a house) for stolen goods or unlawful possessions

**sea room** *n* unobstructed room for a ship to manoeuvre at sea

**sea rover** *n, archaic* 1 a pirate 2 a pirate ship

**seascape** /-,skayp/ *n* a usu extensive view of the sea; *specif* an expanse of sea as depicted by an artist

**sea scorpion** *n* SCULPIN (spiny fish)

**sea scout** *n, often cap both Ss* a member of a Scout troop that specializes in sea and water activities

**sea serpent** *n* a large monster resembling a serpent, often reported to have been seen but never proved to exist

**seashell** /-,shel/ *n* the shell of a sea animal, esp a MOLLUSC (eg a whelk, limpet, clam, or oyster)

**seashore** /-'shaw/ *n* 1 land next to the sea 2 all the ground between the ordinary high-water and low-water marks

**seasick** /-,sik/ *adj* suffering from or suggestive of the MOTION SICKNESS associated with travelling by boat or hovercraft – **seasickness** *n*

**seaside** /-,sied/ *n* the district or land bordering the sea, esp as a holiday place

**sea slug** *n* a shell-less marine snail, slug, or related animal; *specif* NUDIBRANCH

**sea snail** *n* 1 a creeping marine snail (eg a whelk) with a spiral shell 2 any of numerous small slimy fishes (family Liparididae) that are scaleless and soft-bodied and have the PELVIC FINS (frontmost pair of fins on the underside of the body) modified to form a sucker

**sea snake** *n* 1 any of numerous poisonous aquatic snakes (family Hydrophidae) of the Pacific regions, with a tail shaped like an oar 2 SEA SERPENT

**'season** /'seez(ə)n/ *n* **1a** a period characterized by a specified circumstance or feature ⟨*a* ∼ *of religious revival*⟩ **b** a suitable or natural time or occasion ⟨*when my* ∼ *comes to sit on David's throne* – John Milton⟩ **c** an indefinite length of time; a while ⟨*sent home to her mother for a* ∼⟩ **2a** a period of the year characterized by or associated with a particular activity or phenomenon ⟨*hay fever* ∼⟩: eg **2a(1)** a period associated with some phase or activity of agriculture (eg growth or harvesting) **a(2)** a period marked by special activity in some field ⟨*the theatrical* ∼⟩ ⟨*the hunting* ∼⟩ **a(3)** a period in which an animal engages in some activity (eg migrating or mating) **a(4)** a period characterized by a particular kind of weather ⟨*a long rainy* ∼⟩ **b** any of the four quarters into which the year is commonly divided **c** the time of a major holiday; *specif, often cap* the Christmas season ⟨*send the* Season's *greetings*⟩ [ME, fr OF *saison*, fr L *sation-*, *satio* act of sowing, fr *satus*, pp of *serere* to sow – more at SOW] – **in season 1** at the right time ⟨*a word of advice given in* season⟩ 2 *of food* at the stage of greatest abundance and quality 3 *of game* legally available to be hunted or caught 4 *of a female animal* ready to receive a mate ⟨*the bitch is in* season⟩ – **out of season** not IN SEASON

**'season** *vt* **1a** to give (food) more flavour or zest by adding seasoning or savoury ingredients; *also* to add seasoning to **b** to make less harsh or unpleasant; temper ⟨*advice* ∼ed *with wit*⟩ **2a** to treat or expose (eg timber) over a period so as to prepare for use **b** to make fit or expert by experience ⟨*a* ∼ed *veteran*⟩ ∼ *vi* to become seasoned [ME *sesounen*, fr MF *assaisoner* to ripen, season, fr OF, fr *a-* (fr L *ad-*) + *saison* season] – **seasoner** *n*

**seasonable** /'seez(ə)nnəbl/ *adj* 1 occurring in good or proper time; opportune, timely ⟨∼ *advice*⟩ 2 suitable to the season or circumstances ⟨*a* ∼ *frost*⟩ – **seasonableness** *n*, **seasonably** *adv*

*usage* Not to be confused with **seasonal**. Frost is **seasonable** (= normal for the season) if it happens in January. Bird migration is **seasonal** (= happening at particular seasons). *antonym* unseasonable

**seasonal** /'seez(ə)nl/ *adj* 1 of or occurring at a particular season ⟨∼ *vegetables*⟩ ⟨∼ *storms*⟩ 2 determined by seasonal need or availability ⟨∼ *employment*⟩ ⟨∼ *industries*⟩ *antonym* perpetual – **seasonally** *adv*

**seasoning** /'seez(ə)ning/ *n* something that serves to season; *esp* an ingredient (eg salt, spices, herbs, or mustard) added to food primarily for flavouring

**season ticket** *n, Br* a ticket (eg to all of a football club's home games or for an unlimited number of journeys by public transport on the same route) valid during a specified time and usu sold at a reduced rate – compare COMMUTATION TICKET

**sea spider** /'see ,spiedə/ *n* any of various small marine INVERTEBRATE animals (class Pycnogonida of the phylum Arthropoda) that have usu four pairs of long slender legs and superficially resemble spiders

**sea squirt** *n* any of various TUNICATES (small primitive sea animals with a tough outer membrane) that are permanently attached to a surface (eg a rock) for all their adult lives; ASCIDIAN

**'seat** /seet/ *n* **1a** a special chair (eg a throne) of one in authority; *also* the status symbolized by it **b** a piece of furniture (eg a chair, stool, or bench) for sitting in or on **c** the particular part of something on which one rests in sitting ⟨*the* ∼ *of a chair*⟩ ⟨*trouser* ∼⟩; *also* the part of the body that bears the weight in sitting; the buttocks **d** a place for sitting ⟨*took his* ∼ *next to her*⟩ ⟨*a grassy* ∼⟩ **2a** a unit of seating accommodation ⟨*a* ∼ *for the game*⟩ **b** a right of sitting ⟨*lost his* ∼ *in the Commons*⟩ **c** membership of an exchange (eg a stock exchange) **3a** a place where something is established or practised; an abode ⟨*an ancient ~ of learning*⟩ **b** a place from which authority is exercised ⟨*the ~ of government*⟩ **c** a body part in which some function or condition is centred ⟨*the brain is the ~ of the mind*⟩ **d** a large country mansion ⟨*retired to his ~ in Wiltshire*⟩ **4** posture in or a way of sitting on horseback ⟨*she has a good ~*⟩ **5a** a part at or forming the base of something **b** a part (eg a socket) or surface on or in which another part or surface rests ⟨*a valve ~*⟩ [ME *sete*, fr ON *sæti;* akin to OE *sittan* to sit]

²**seat** *vt* **1a** to install in a position of authority ⟨*the year in which the king was ~ed*⟩ **b(1)** to cause to sit or assist in finding a seat ⟨*~ed her next to the door*⟩ **b(2)** to provide seats for ⟨*a theatre ~ing 1000 people*⟩ **c** to put (eg oneself) in a sitting position **2** to mend the seat of or provide a new seat for ⟨*~ a pair of trousers*⟩ ⟨*~ a cane chair*⟩ **3** to fit to or with a seat ⟨*~ a valve*⟩ *~ vi* **1** to fit correctly on a seat **2** *of a garment* to become baggy at the seat – **seater** *n*

**seat belt** *n* an arrangement of straps designed to secure a person in a seat (eg during the takeoff of an aeroplane or while travelling in a car)

**-seater** /-,seetə/ *comb form* (→ *n or adj*) (something) designed to seat (a specified number) ⟨*a 200-seater airliner*⟩

**seating** /'seeting/ *n* **1a** the act of providing with seats **b** the arrangement of seats (eg in a theatre) **2a** material for covering or upholstering seats **b** a base on or in which something rests ⟨*a valve ~*⟩

**sea trout** *n* **1** any of various trouts that as adults inhabit the sea but ascend rivers to spawn; *esp* a European and N African marine variety of the BROWN TROUT (*Salmo trutta*) that migrates to fresh water to spawn **2** any of various marine fishes resembling trouts – called also SALMON TROUT

**sea urchin** *n* any of various marine INVERTEBRATE animals (esp of the order Echinoida, class Echinoidea) related to the starfishes, that typically have a more or less spherical form and a thin brittle shell covered with movable spines

**seawall** /-'wawl/ *n* a wall or embankment to protect the shore from erosion by the sea or to act as a breakwater

¹**seaward** /'seewəd/ *n* the direction or side away from land and towards the open sea

²**seaward** *adj* **1** facing or directed towards the sea **2** coming in off the sea ⟨*a ~ wind*⟩

**seawards** /'seewədz/, **seaward** *adv* towards the sea

**seawater** /'see,wawtə/ *n* water in or from the sea

**seaway** /-,way/ *n* **1** a moderate or rough sea **2** a ship's progress **3** the sea as a route for travel; *also* an ocean traffic lane **4** a deep inland waterway that admits ocean shipping

**seaweed** /-,weed/ *n* **1** a plant growing in the sea; *specif* any of various marine algae, typically having thick slimy fronds **2** a mass or growth of seaweeds – **seaweedy** *adj*

**sea whip** /-,wip/ *n* any of various GORGONIAN corals that occur in a variety of bright colours and have a flexible little-branched skeleton

**seaworthy** /-,wuhdhi/ *adj* fit or safe for a sea voyage ⟨*a ~ ship*⟩ – **seaworthiness** *n*

**sea wrack** /-,rak/ *n* seaweed; *esp* seaweed cast ashore in masses

**seax** /saks/ *n* a heraldic sword resembling the scimitar but having a semicircular notch on the concave edge [ME *sexe* knife, short sword, fr OE *seax, sæx;* akin to ON *sax* knife, sword]

**sebaceous** /si'bayshəs/ *adj* of, secreting, or being sebum or other fatty material ⟨*a ~ secretion*⟩ ⟨*~ glands*⟩ [L *sebaceus* made of tallow, fr *sebum* tallow – more at SOAP]

**sebacic acid** /si'baysik/ *n* an acid, $HOOC(CH_2)_8COOH$, used esp in the manufacture of synthetic resins and rubbers [ISV, fr L *sebaceus*]

**seborrhoea** /,sebə'riə/ *n* abnormally increased secretion and discharge of sebum (eg on the scalp) [NL, fr L *sebum* + NL *-rrhoea*]

**sebum** /'seebəm/ *n* fatty matter secreted by sebaceous glands of the skin that acts as a lubricant for the hair and skin [L, tallow, grease]

¹**sec** /sek/ *n, Br informal* a second, moment ⟨*hang on a ~!*⟩

²**sec** *adj, of wine* not sweet; dry [Fr, lit., dry – more at SACK]

**secant** /'seekənt/ *n* **1** a straight line cutting a curve at two or more points – compare ³CHORD 2 **2a** a straight line drawn from the centre of a circle through one end of a circular arc to a tangent that meets the circle at the other end of the arc **b** the mathematical function that is the reciprocal of COSINE [NL *secant-, secans*, fr L, prp of *secare* to cut – more at SAW]

**secateurs** /,sekə'tuhz/ *n pl*, **secateur** *n, chiefly Br* pruning shears [Fr *sécateur*, fr L *secare* to cut]

¹**secco** /'sekoh/ *n* FRESCO SECCO (wall painting on dry plaster) [It, fr *secco* dry, fr L *siccus* – more at SACK]

²**secco** *adj or adv* **1** short and very STACCATO – used as a direction in music **2** *of a recitative* accompanied only by the instruments playing the continuing bass part (CONTINUO) [It, lit., dry]

**secede** /si'seed/ *vi* to withdraw formally from an organization or fellowship (eg a church, political party, or federation) [L *secedere*, fr *sed-, se-* apart (fr *sed, se* without) + *cedere* to go – more at IDIOT, CEDE] – **seceder** *n*

**secern** /si'suhn/ *vt, formal* to separate in the mind; distinguish, discriminate [L *secernere* to separate – more at SECRET]

**secession** /si'sesh(ə)n/ *n* an act of seceding [L *secession-, secessio*, fr *secessus*, pp of *secedere*]

**secessionism** /si'seshənizm/ *n* the doctrine or policy of seceding

**secessionist** /si'seshənist/ *n* a person who joins in a secession or maintains that secession is a right

**seclude** /si'kloohd/ *vt* **1** to remove or separate from human company or interference; isolate **2** to make hidden; SHUT OFF [ME *secluden* to keep away, fr L *secludere* to separate, seclude, fr *se-* apart + *claudere* to close – more at CLOSE]

**secluded** /si'kloohdid/ *adj* **1a** screened or hidden from view ⟨*a ~ garden*⟩ **b** rarely visited; remote ⟨*a ~ valley*⟩ **2** living in seclusion; solitary ⟨*~ monks*⟩ – **secludedly** *adv*, **secludedness** *n*

**seclusion** /si'kloohzh(ə)n/ *n* **1** secluding or being secluded ⟨*lived in deep ~*⟩ **2** a secluded or isolated place **synonyms** see SOLITUDE [ML *seclusion-, seclusio*, fr L *seclusus*, pp of *secludere*] – **seclusive** *adj*, **seclusively** *adv*, **seclusiveness** *n*

¹**second** /'sekənd/ *adj* **1a** next to the first in place or time ⟨*was ~ in line*⟩ **b(1)** next to the first in value, quality, or degree ⟨*selected him as ~ choice*⟩ **b(2)** inferior, subordinate ⟨*was ~ to none*⟩ **c** standing next below the top of a grade or rank in authority or importance ⟨*~ mate*⟩ **2** alternate, other ⟨*elects a mayor every ~ year*⟩ **3** resembling or suggesting a prototype; another ⟨*a ~ Napoleon*⟩ **4** being the forward gear or speed one higher than first in a motor vehicle **5** relating to or having a part typically subordinate to or lower in pitch than the first part in orchestral, choral, or other music ⟨*the ~ basses*⟩ – see also **play second** FIDDLE, **at second** HAND *usage* see FIRSTLY [ME, fr OF, fr L *secundus* second, following, favourable, fr *sequi* to follow – more at SUE] – **second, secondly** *adv*

²**second** *n* **1a** – see NUMBER table **b** one who or that which is next after the first in rank, position, authority, or precedence ⟨*the ~ in line*⟩ **2** one who aids, supports, or stands in for another; *esp* the assistant of a duellist or boxer **3a** a musical interval between one note and the note next to it in a DIATONIC scale (ordinary 8-note scale) **b** a note separated from another by this interval; *specif* the note following the first note (TONIC) of a scale; SUPERTONIC **c** the harmonic combination of two notes a second apart **4** *usu pl* an article of merchandise that is usu slightly flawed and does not meet the manufacturer's regular standard **5** the act or declaration by which a parliamentary motion is seconded **6a** a place next below the first in a competition, examination, or contest **b** *also* **second class** *often cap* the second level of honours degree from a British university **7** the second forward gear or speed of a motor vehicle **8** *pl, informal* a second helping of food

³**second** *n* **1a** a 60th part of a minute of time or of a minute of angular measurement **b** the basic SI unit of time, equal to the duration of 9 192 631 770 oscillations of the radiation corresponding to the transition between two specific ENERGY LEVELS of the caesium ISOTOPE $_{55}Cs^{133}$ **2** *chiefly informal* an instant of time; a moment ⟨*wait a ~ will you?*⟩ [ME *secunde*, fr ML *secunda*, fr L, fem of *secundus* second; fr its being the second sexagesimal division of a unit, as a minute is the first]

⁴**second** *vt* **1** to give support or encouragement to; assist ⟨*~ed his efforts at improvement*⟩ **2** to endorse (a motion or nomination) so that voting or debate may begin [L *secundare*, fr *secundus* second, favourable] – **seconder** *n*

⁵**second** /si'kond/ *vt, chiefly Br* to transfer (eg a teacher, businessman, or official) from a regularly assigned position for temporary duty with another organization [Fr *second*, n, second position (in the phrase *en second* in second position, subordinate), fr *second*, adj] – **secondment** *n*

¹**secondary** /'sekənd(ə)ri/ *adj* **1a** of second rank, importance, or value ⟨*~ streams*⟩ **b** of or being the second strongest degree

of stress in speech ⟨*the fourth syllable of* basketball team *carries ~ stress*⟩ **c** *of a Latin, Greek, or Sanskrit verb tense* expressing past time **2a** immediately derived from something original, primary, or basic; derivative **b** of (the circuit of) or being an electrical current that has been created (INDUCED) by a current in another circuit ⟨*a ~ coil*⟩ ⟨*~ voltage*⟩ **3** *chemistry* **3a** characterized by or resulting from the substitution of two atoms or chemical groups in a molecule by other atoms or groups **b(1)** being or containing a carbon atom united to two other carbon atoms ⟨*a ~ compound*⟩ **b(2)** being a chemical group attached to a secondary carbon atom **c** *of an amine* having the nitrogen atom attached to two carbon atoms and one hydrogen atom; containing the group NH **4a** not first in order of occurrence or development **b** of or produced by the activity of plant tissue (e g CAMBIUM or PHELLOGEN) capable of dividing to form new cells and tissues, other than that at a growing point; *esp* of or being SECONDARY THICKENING or a tissue, esp XYLEM (water-conducting tissue) or PHLOEM (food-conducting tissue) formed during secondary thickening **5a** of the second order or stage in a series or sequence **b** dependent on, consequent on, or caused by a previously existing condition or disease **c** of or being a manufacturing industry – compare PRIMARY, TERTIARY **d** of or being the second segment of the wing of a bird or the feathers of this segment **e** of a SECONDARY SCHOOL ⟨*~ education*⟩ – **secondarily** *adv*, **secondariness** *n*

²**secondary** *n* **1** someone who occupies a subordinate or auxiliary position; a deputy **2** a secondary electrical circuit or coil **3** any of the main feathers of the forearm of a bird

**secondary cell** *n* STORAGE CELL (battery or other device storing electric charge)

**secondary colour** *n* a colour formed by mixing two PRIMARY COLOURS

**secondary consumer** *n* a CARNIVORE (meat-eater) that eats HERBIVORES (plant-eating animals) – compare PRIMARY CONSUMER, TERTIARY CONSUMER

**secondary emission** *n* the emission of electrons from a surface as a result of bombardment of the surface by particles (e g electrons or IONS) from another source

**secondary growth** *n* SECONDARY THICKENING

**secondary modern, secondary modern school** *n* a British state school providing, esp before the introduction of comprehensive schools, a less academic type of education from the age of 11 usu to 16 for pupils not selected for grammar or technical schools

**secondary root** *n* any of the branches of the PRIMARY ROOT (main root) of a plant

**secondary school** *n* a school intermediate between primary school and higher education

**secondary sex characteristic** *also* **secondary sexual characteristic** *n* a physical or mental characteristic (e g the breasts of a female mammal or the courting plumage of a male bird) that appears in members of one sex at puberty or in the breeding season and is not directly concerned with reproduction

**secondary syphilis** *n* the second stage of syphilis that appears from two to six months after the initial infection, is marked esp by skin rash but also by lesions in organs and tissues, and that lasts from 3 to 12 weeks

**secondary technical school** *n* a British state school providing a technical type of education for selected children from the age of 11 to 16 or 18

**secondary thickening** *n* growth in the diameter of a plant stem or root resulting from the formation of extra supporting tissue and water- and food-conducting tissues (XYLEM and PHLOEM) by the activity of CAMBIUM

**second base** *n* the base that must be touched second by a batter in baseball when attempting a run; *also* the position of the player defending the area round this base – **second baseman** *n*

‚**second-'best** *adj* next after the best

**second best** *n* one who or that which comes after the best in quality or worth

**second blessing** *n* divine grace as a second gift of the Holy Spirit that follows an initial experience of conversion

**second childhood** *n* the period of life when one's mental faculties decline; dotage

¹‚**second-'class** *adj* **1** of a second class ⟨*a ~ honours degree*⟩ **2** inferior, mediocre; *also* socially, politically, or economically deprived ⟨*~ citizens*⟩

²**second-class** *adv* **1** in accommodation next below the best ⟨*travel ~*⟩ **2** by second-class mail ⟨*send the letters ~*⟩

**second class** *n* **1** the second and usu next to highest group in a classification **2** SECOND 6b (university degree) **3** a postal class that enables internal mail of the UK to be sent more cheaply and less swiftly than first-class mail

**Second Coming** *n* the return of Christ to judge the world on the last day

**second cousin** *n* a child of a FIRST COUSIN of either of one's parents

**second-degree burn** *n* a burn marked by pain, blistering, and superficial destruction of skin with accumulation of blood and watery fluid in the tissues beneath the burn – compare FIRST-DEGREE BURN, THIRD-DEGREE BURN

**Second Empire** *adj* (characteristic) of a style (e g of furniture) popular in mid-19th-century France and marked by heavy ornate modification of EMPIRE styles

**second estate** *n, often cap S&E* the second of the traditional political classes; *specif* the nobility

**second fiddle** *n* a secondary or subordinate role or function – in *play second fiddle*

**second growth** *n* forest trees that regenerate naturally after removal of the first growth by felling or by fire

‚**second-'guess** *vt, NAm* to reconsider with the benefit of hindsight – **second-guesser** *n*

¹**secondhand** /-'hand/ *adj* **1a** received from or through an intermediary ⟨*~ knowledge*⟩ **b** not original; derivative ⟨*~ ideas*⟩ **2a** acquired after being owned or used by another; not new ⟨*~ books*⟩ **b** dealing in secondhand goods ⟨*a ~ bookshop*⟩

²**secondhand** *adv* indirectly; AT SECOND HAND ⟨*heard the news ~*⟩

**second hand** *n* the hand marking seconds on the face of a watch or clock

‚**second-in-com'mand** *n* a person, esp a military officer, next in rank to a commander or director

**second lieutenant** *n* – see MILITARY RANKS table

**second man** *n, Br* a train driver's assistant

**second mortgage** *n* a mortgage incurred after a first mortgage, which has second claim for repayment

**second nature** *n* an action or ability that is habitual or instinctive, or has become so by much repetition ⟨*acting is ~ to her*⟩

**secondo** /se'kondoh/ *n, pl* **secondi** /-di/ the second part in a piece of music for more than one performer; *esp* the lower part (e g in a piano duet) [It, fr *secondo*, adj, second, fr L *secundus*]

**second person** *n* **1** a set of language forms (e g verb forms and pronouns) referring to the person or thing addressed in the utterance in which they occur **2** a linguistic form (e g *you*) belonging to such a set

‚**second-'rate** *adj* of inferior quality or value; mediocre – **second-rateness** *n*, **second-rater** *n*

**second reading** *n* **1** the stage in the British legislative process following the FIRST READING and usu providing for debate on the principal features of a bill before its submission to a committee for consideration of details **2** the stage in the US legislative process that occurs when a bill has been reported back after a committee has drawn up details and that provides an opportunity for full debate and amendment before a vote is taken

**second sight** *n* the ability to foresee future events; clairvoyance

**second-story man** *n, NAm* CAT BURGLAR

‚**second-'string** *adj, chiefly NAm* being a substitute as distinguished from a regular player (e g in a football team)

**second string** *n* a person, thing, or course of action planned as an alternative should a first choice fail [fr the reserve bowstring carried by an archer in case the first breaks]

**second thigh** *n* GASKIN (part of the hind leg of an animal, esp a horse)

**second thoughts** *n pl, NAm* **second thought** *n* a reconsideration or revised opinion of a previous decision ⟨*began to have ~*⟩

**second wind** /wind/ *n* a renewed amount of energy or endurance after a period of severe exertion – esp in *get one's second wind*

**secrecy** /'seekrəsi/ *n* **1** the habit or practice of keeping secrets or maintaining privacy or concealment **2** the condition of being hidden or concealed ⟨*complete ~ surrounded the conference*⟩ [alter. of earlier *secretie*, fr ME *secretee*, fr *secre* secret, fr MF *secré*, fr L *secretus*]

¹**secret** /'seekrit/ *adj* **1a** kept from knowledge or view; hidden

**b** marked by the practice of discretion; secretive **c** not acknowledged or declared ⟨*a ~ bride*⟩ **d** conducted in secret ⟨*a ~ trial*⟩ **2** retired, secluded ⟨*~ harbours*⟩ **3** revealed only to the initiated; known by only a small group of people ⟨*~ rites*⟩ **4** designed to escape observation or detection ⟨*a ~ panel*⟩ **5** containing information whose unauthorized disclosure could endanger national security – compare CONFIDENTIAL, RESTRICTED, TOP SECRET [ME, fr MF, fr L *secretus*, fr pp of *secernere* to separate, distinguish, fr *se-* apart + *cernere* to sift – more at SECEDE, CERTAIN] – **secretly** *adv*

**synonyms** Secret, covert, clandestine, surreptitious, furtive, stealthy, and underhand all mean "existing or done so as to escape attention". Secret is the most general word, and can apply to things and places ⟨**secret** *document*⟩ ⟨**secret** *passage*⟩. All the others essentially refer to behaviour. Covert stresses the idea of concealed or veiled action ⟨**covert** *yawns*⟩ ⟨**covert** *malice*⟩. Clandestine refers to something done in wary secrecy and often illegally ⟨**clandestine** *marriage*⟩ ⟨**clandestine** *publications*⟩. Surreptitious suggests something done secretly and with opportune cleverness ⟨*enjoying a* **surreptitious** *cigarette* – P G Wodehouse⟩. Furtive implies the slinking caution of someone anxious to escape notice ⟨*take a* **furtive** *shortcut across the garden*⟩, and stealthy adds to this the suggestion of slowly proceeding to do something sinister ⟨*the* **stealthy** *tread of the murderer*⟩. Underhand or underhanded stresses the dishonesty of secret action rather than the mere fact of its secrecy ⟨*stoop to* **underhand** *methods to gain his end*⟩.

**²secret** *n* **1a** something kept hidden or unexplained; a mystery **b** a fact concealed from others or shared confidentially with a few **c** a method or practice made known only to a privileged few ⟨*a trade ~*⟩ **2** a prayer traditionally said inaudibly by the officiating priest just before the first part (PREFACE) of the Mass **3** something taken to be the key to a desired end ⟨*the ~ of long life*⟩ – **in secret** in a private place or manner; secretly

**secret agent** *n* a spy

**secretagogue** /si'kreetəgog/ *n* a substance that stimulates secretion (e g of digestive juices by the stomach or pancreas) [*secretion* + *-agogue*]

**secretaire** /ˌsekrə'teə/ *n* WRITING DESK; *esp* one with a top section containing drawers, shelves, etc; ESCRITOIRE [Fr *secrétaire* escritoire, secretary (person), fr MF *secretaire* secretary (person), fr ML *secretarius*]

**secretariat** /ˌsekrə'teəri·ət/ *n* **1** the office of secretary **2** *taking sing or pl vb* a body of people engaged in secretarial duties; *specif* the clerical staff of an organization **3** the administrative department of a government organization [Fr *secrétariat*, fr ML *secretariatus*, fr *secretarius*]

**secretary** /'sekrətri; *also* -ˌteri/ *n* **1** someone employed to handle correspondence and manage routine work for a superior **2a** COMPANY SECRETARY **b** an officer of an organization (e g a club or society) responsible for its records and correspondence **3** an officer of state who superintends a government administrative department **4** a secretaire [ME *secretarie*, fr ML *secretarius*, confidential employee, secretary, fr L *secretum* secret, fr neut of *secretus*, pp] – **secretarial** *adj*, **secretaryship** *n*

**usage** The pronunciation /'sekrətri/ rather than /'sekətri/ or /'sek(r)əˌteri/ is recommended for BBC broadcasters.

**secretary bird** *n* a large long-legged African bird of prey (*Sagittarius serpentarius*) that feeds largely on reptiles [prob fr the resemblance of its crest to a bunch of quill pens stuck behind the ear]

**secretary-'general** *n, pl* **secretaries-general** a principal administrative officer (e g of the United Nations)

**secret ballot** *n* an official ballot that is marked in secret, usu at polling stations

**¹secrete** /si'kreet/ *vt* to form and give off (a secretion) [back-formation fr *secretion*]

**²secrete** *vt* to deposit or conceal in a hidden place; hide ⟨*~ opium about his person*⟩ [alter. of obs *secret*, fr **¹***secret*]

**secretin** /si'kreetin/ *n* a hormone produced by the SMALL INTESTINE that is secreted in response to the presence of acidic partly digested food and that stimulates secretion of PANCREATIC JUICE·by the pancreas and bile by the liver [*secretion* + *-in*]

**secretion** /si'kreesh(ə)n/ *n* **1a** the process carried out by a cell or gland of making and releasing some material that is either specialized for a particular function (e g saliva or a hormone) or is isolated for excretion from the body (e g urine) **b** a product of secretion formed by an animal or plant; *esp* one performing a specific useful function in the organism **2** the act of hiding something; concealment [(1) Fr *sécrétion*, fr L *secretion-*, *secretio* separation, fr *secretus*, pp of *secernere* to separate – more at SECRET; (2) **²***secrete*] – **secretionary** *adj*

**secretive** /'seekrətiv/ *adj* inclined to secrecy; not open or outgoing in speech or behaviour **synonyms** see SILENT **antonym** frank [back-formation fr *secretiveness*, part trans of Fr *secrétivité*] – **secretively** *adv*, **secretiveness** *n*

**secretor** /si'kreetə/ *n* a person of blood group A, B, or AB who secretes the particular chemical substances characteristic of these blood groups in body fluids (e g saliva)

**secretory** /si'kreetəri/ *adj* of or promoting secretion; *also* produced by secretion

**secret police** *n* a police organization operating largely in secrecy, esp for the political purposes of its government

**secret service** *n* a governmental agency concerned with national security and operating largely in secret; *esp, cap both Ss* a British government intelligence department attached to the Home Office – not usu used technically

**secret society** *n* a society (e g for the promotion of a common interest, esp moral or political) whose members make special oaths, use secret passwords and rites, and keep their activities secret from others

**sect** /sekt/ *n* **1a** a dissenting or breakaway religious body; *esp* one regarded as extreme or heretical **b** a group within a religion; a denomination **2a** a group that maintains strict allegiance to a doctrine or leader **b** (an often contentious group within) a party [ME *secte*, fr MF & LL & L; MF, group, sect, fr LL *secta* organized ecclesiastical body, fr L, way of life, class of persons, fr *sequi* to follow]

**¹-sect** /-sekt/ *comb form* (→ *adj*) cut; divided ⟨*pinnati*sect⟩ [L *sectus*, pp of *secare* to cut – more at SAW]

**²-sect** *comb form* (→ *vb*) cut; divide ⟨*bi*sect⟩ [L *sectus*]

**¹sectarian** /sek'teəri·ən/ *adj* **1** (characteristic) of or involving a sect or sectarian ⟨*~ violence in N Ireland*⟩ **2** limited in character or scope; parochial – **sectarianism** *n*, **sectarianize** *vb*

**²sectarian** *n* **1** an adherent of a sect; *esp* a fanatical one **2** a bigoted or narrow-minded person

**sectary** /'sektəri/ *n* a member of a sect

**sectile** /'sektiel/ *adj* capable of being smoothly severed by a knife [L *sectilis*, fr *sectus*] – **sectility** *n*

**¹section** /'seksh(ə)n/ *n* **1a** the action or an instance of cutting or separating by cutting; *esp* the action of dividing (e g tissues) surgically ⟨*caesarean ~*⟩ **b** a part removed or separated (as if) by cutting **2** a distinct part or portion of something written; *esp* a subdivision of a chapter **3a** a shape or area as it would appear if a solid form were cut through by one plane **b** the plane figure resulting from the cutting through of a solid form by one plane **4** a sign § commonly used in printing as a mark for the beginning of a section and as the fourth in the series of REFERENCE MARKS **5** a piece of land one square mile (about 2.6 square kilometres) in area forming one of the 36 subdivisions of a US township **6** a distinct part of a territorial or political area, community, or group of people **7** a part when considered in isolation ⟨*the northern ~ of the route*⟩ **8** *taking sing or pl vb* a subdivision of a platoon, troop, or battery that is the smallest tactical military unit **9** a very thin slice (e g of tissue) suitable for examination under a microscope **10a** BLOCK SECTION (section of railway track controlled by one set of signals) **b** a length of railway track under the care of a particular set of men **11** any of several component parts that may be separated and reassembled ⟨*a bookcase in ~s*⟩ **12** a division of an orchestra composed of one class of instruments ⟨*the percussion ~*⟩ **13** a printed sheet that is folded to form part (e g eight leaves) of a book **14** *chiefly NZ* a designated plot of land, esp for building [L *section-*, *sectio*, fr *sectus*]

**²section** *vt* **1** to cut or separate into sections **2** to represent in sections (e g by a drawing)

**sectional** /'seksh(ə)nl/ *adj* **1a** of a section **b** restricted to a particular group or locality ⟨*~ interests*⟩ **2** composed of or divided into sections ⟨*~ furniture*⟩ – **sectionalize** *vt*, **sectionally** *adv*

**sectionalism** /'seksh(ə)nlˌiz(ə)m/ *n* an excessive concern for the interests of a region or group

**Section Eight** *n* a discharge from the US Army on the grounds of unfitness for service (e g through undesirable character traits) [*Section VIII*, US Army Regulation 615-360, in force between 1922 & 1944]

**section gang** n, NAm a crew of railway workers employed to maintain a section of track

**section hand** n, NAm a worker belonging to a section gang

¹**sector** /'sektə/ n 1 a part of a circle bounded by two radii and the portion of the circumference between them – compare SEGMENT 2a **2a** a subdivision of a defensive military position **b** a portion of a military front or area of operation **3** a distinctive part (eg of an economy) ⟨the public ~⟩ [LL, fr L, cutter, fr sectus, pp of secare to cut – more at SAW]

²**sector** vt to divide into sectors

**sectorial** /sek'tawri·əl/ adj 1 of a sector 2 having the shape of a sector of a circle

¹**secular** /'sekyoolə/ adj **1a** of this world rather than the heavenly or spiritual; temporal ⟨~ concerns⟩ **b** not overtly or specifically religious ⟨~ music⟩ **c** not ecclesiastical or clerical ⟨~ landowners⟩ **2** not bound by monastic vows or rules; specif of or being clergy not belonging to a particular religious order or congregation ⟨a ~ priest⟩ **3a** taking place once in an age or century **b** surviving or recurring through ages or centuries synonyms see ²PROFANE antonyms religious, denominational [ME, fr OF seculer, fr LL saecularis, fr L, coming once in an age, fr saeculum breed, generation; akin to L serere to sow – more at SOW] – **secularity** n, **secularly** adv

²**secular** n, pl **seculars, secular 1** a secular clergyman (eg a parish priest) **2** a layman

**secularism** /'sekyoolə,riz(ə)m/ n disregard for or rejection of religious beliefs and practices – **secularist** n, **secularist, secularistic** adj

**secular·ize, -ise** /'sekyoolə,riez/ vt 1 to make secular 2 to transfer (eg property) from ecclesiastical to civil or lay use or possession 3 to convert to or imbue with secularism – **secularization** n, **secularizer** n

¹**secure** /si'kyooə/ adj **1a** calm in mind; serene **b** confident in opinion or hope; having no doubt **2a** free from danger **b** free from risk of loss ⟨~ employment⟩ **c** affording safety ⟨a ~ hideaway⟩ **d** firm, dependable ⟨~ foundation⟩ **3** assured, certain ⟨victory is ~⟩ **4** archaic overconfident antonyms precarious, insecure [L securus safe, secure, fr se without + cura care – more at IDIOT, CURE] – **securely** adv, **secureness** n

²**secure** vt **1a** to make safe from risk or danger; protect against intrusion or disturbance ⟨~ a supply line from enemy raids⟩ ⟨~ d the lid with a padlock⟩ **b** to guarantee against loss or denial ⟨a bill to ~ the rights of strikers⟩ **c** to guarantee payment to (a creditor) or of (an obligation) ⟨~ a note by a pledge of collateral⟩ **2** to make fast; shut tightly ⟨~ a door⟩ **3a** to obtain, esp as the result of effort ⟨~d a cabin for the voyage⟩ ⟨spared no effort to ~ his ends⟩ **b** to effect; BRING ABOUT ⟨~ the release of a prisoner⟩ **4** to release (naval personnel) from work or duty ~ vi 1 of naval personnel to stop work; go off duty **2** of a ship to berth; TIE UP synonyms see OBTAIN – **securer** n

**securement** /si'kyooəmənt/ n the act or process of securing

**security** /si'kyooərəti/ n **1** the quality or state of being secure: eg **1a** freedom from danger; safety **b** freedom from fear or anxiety **c** stability, dependability ⟨job ~⟩ **2a** something deposited or pledged to guarantee the fulfilment of an obligation **b** SURETY (person who undertakes to fulfil another's obligation) **3** an evidence of debt or of ownership (eg a stock certificate or bond) **4a** something that makes secure; protection **b(1)** measures taken to protect against esp espionage or sabotage **b(2)** taking sing or pl vb an organization or department whose task is to maintain security

**Security Council** n a permanent council of the United Nations having primary responsibility for the maintenance of peace and security

**security police** n police engaged primarily in protective measures against espionage

**sedan** /si'dan/ n, NAm & Austr a saloon car [sedan (sedan chair), perh deriv of L sella stool, seat, fr sedere to sit]

**sedan chair** n a portable often enclosed chair, esp of the 17th and 18th centuries, designed to seat one person and carried on poles by two people

¹**sedate** /si'dayt/ adj calm and even in temper or pace; tranquil, composed synonyms see SERIOUS antonym flighty [L sedatus, fr pp of sedare to calm; akin to sedēre to sit – more at SIT] – **sedately** adv, **sedateness** n

²**sedate** vt to dose with a sedative [back-formation fr sedative]

**sedation** /si'daysh(ə)n/ n the induction of a relaxed easy state, esp by the use of sedatives; also this state

¹**sedative** /'sedətiv/ adj tending to calm, moderate, or tranquillize nervousness or excitement

²**sedative** n something sedative; esp a sedative drug

**sedentary** /'sed(ə)ntri/ adj **1** esp of a bird not migratory; resident **2** doing or requiring much sitting ⟨a ~ occupation⟩ **3** of an animal permanently attached to a surface (eg a rock or the sea bottom) ⟨~ barnacles⟩ [MF sedentaire, fr L sedentarius, fr sedent-, sedens, prp of sedēre to sit]

**seder** /'saydə/ n, often cap a Jewish domestic or community service including a ceremonial dinner held on the first evening of the Passover and sometimes repeated on the second, in commemoration of the exodus from Egypt [Heb sēdher order]

**sedge** /sej/ n any of a family (Cyperaceae, the sedge family) of usu tufted grasslike marsh plants with long narrow leaves, usu solid triangular stems, and minute flowers in spikes; esp any of a widely distributed genus (Carex) of sedges [ME segge, fr OE secg; akin to MHG segge sedge, OE sagu saw – more at SAW] – **sedgy** adj

**sedge warbler** n a small European songbird (Acrocephalus schoenobaenus) of the warbler group that breeds in marshy places and has streaked brown upper parts, a reddish-brown rump, creamy underparts, and a pale stripe above the eye

**sedilia** /sə'dili·ə, si-/ n pl the usu three seats on the south side of a church near the altar, often in a recess in the wall, that are used by officiating clergy during intervals of a service [L, pl of sedile seat, fr sedēre]

¹**sediment** /'sedimənt/ n **1** the matter that settles to the bottom of a liquid **2** material from the earth's crust deposited by water, wind, or glaciers [MF, fr L sedimentum settling, fr sedēre to sit, sink down]

²**sediment** vt to deposit as sediment ~ vi 1 to settle to the bottom in a liquid **2** to deposit sediment

**sedimentary** /,sedi'ment(ə)ri/ adj **1** of, formed from, or containing sediment ⟨~ deposits⟩ **2** of a rock formed from fragments of rocks and minerals or the inorganic remains (eg shells and skeletons) of sea urchins, corals, etc that have been carried and deposited by water, wind, or ice and have then accumulated and hardened (eg by compression and cementing)

**sedimentation** /,sedimen'taysh(ə)n/ n the action or process of forming or depositing sediment; settling

**sedimentology** /,sedimen'toləji/ n a branch of geology that deals with sedimentary rocks and deposits – **sedimentologic, sedimentological** adj, **sedimentologically** adv, **sedimentologist** n

**sedition** /si'dish(ə)n/ n incitement to defy or rise up against lawful authority [ME, civil discord, tumult, fr MF, fr L sedition-, seditio, lit., separation, fr se- apart + ition-, itio act of going, fr itus, pp of ire to go – more at SECEDE, ISSUE] – **seditionary** adj

**seditious** /si'dishəs/ adj **1** tending to arouse or take part in sedition; guilty of sedition **2** of or constituting sedition – **seditiously** adv, **seditiousness** n

**seduce** /si'dyoohs/ vt **1** to incite to disobedience or disloyalty **2** to lead astray (eg from moral principles), esp by persuasion or false promises **3** to carry out the physical seduction of **4** to attract, coax ⟨foods that ~ a patient back to health⟩ synonyms see ²LURE [LL seducere, fr L, to lead away, fr se- apart + ducere to lead – more at TOW] – **seducer** n

**seduction** /si'duksh(ə)n/ n **1** the act of seducing to wrongdoing; specif the enticement or persuasion of a person, esp a female virgin, to sexual intercourse (eg by flattery and guile) **2** something that seduces; a temptation **3** something that attracts or allures ⟨the ~ of riches⟩ [MF, fr LL seduction-, seductio, fr L, act of leading aside, fr seductus, pp of seducere]

**seductive** /si'duktiv/ adj tending to seduce; having alluring or charming qualities ⟨a ~ woman⟩ ⟨a ~ spring morning⟩ – **seductively** adv, **seductiveness** n

**seductress** /si'duktris/ n a female seducer [obs seductor male seducer, fr LL, fr seductus, pp]

**sedulity** /si'dyoohliti/ n, formal painstaking activity or observance; diligence

**sedulous** /'sedyooləs/ adj, formal **1** involving or accomplished with steady perseverance ⟨~ craftsmanship⟩ **2** diligent in application or pursuit ⟨a ~ student⟩ synonyms see ¹BUSY [L sedulus, fr sedulo sincerely, diligently, fr se without + dolus guile – more at IDIOT, TALE] – **sedulously** adv, **sedulousness** n

**sedum** /'seedəm/ n any of a widely distributed genus (Sedum) of fleshy-leaved plants of the stonecrop family that includes the stonecrops [NL, genus name, fr L, houseleek]

¹**see** /see/ vb **saw** /saw/; **seen** /seen/ vt **1a** to perceive by the eye (looked for her but couldn't ~ her in the crowd) ⟨saw that she was in difficulties⟩ **b** to look at; inspect ⟨can I ~ your ticket

*please?*⟩ **2a** to have experience of; undergo ⟨~ *army service*⟩ ⟨*won't ~ 40 again*⟩ ⟨*a coat that has ~*n *better days*⟩ **b** to come to know; (try to) find out; ascertain ⟨~ *if you can mend it*⟩ **3a** to form a mental picture of; imagine, visualize ⟨*I can still ~ her as she was years ago*⟩ ⟨*I can't ~ him objecting*⟩ **b** to regard ⟨*could never ~ him as a thief*⟩ **4a** to perceive the meaning or importance of; understand ⟨~ *a joke*⟩ ⟨*I ~ what you mean*⟩ **b** to be aware of; recognize ⟨~ *the point*⟩ **5a** to observe, watch ⟨*want to ~ how he handles the problem*⟩ **b(1)** to read ⟨~ *page 17*⟩ **b(2)** to read of ⟨saw *it in the paper*⟩ **c** to attend as a spectator ⟨~ *a play*⟩ **d** to be a witness of ⟨~ *the New Year in*⟩ ⟨*can't ~ her neglected*⟩ **6** to ensure; make certain ⟨~ *that order is kept*⟩ **7a** to prefer to have ⟨*I'll ~ him hanged first*⟩ **b** to find acceptable or attractive ⟨*can't understand what he ~*s *in her*⟩ **8** *of a period of time* to be marked by ⟨*the fifth century* saw *the collapse of the Western Roman Empire*⟩ **9a** to call on; visit ⟨~ *the dentist*⟩ **b(1)** to keep company with, esp in courtship ⟨*had been ~*ing *each other for a year*⟩ **b(2)** to meet to a specified extent ⟨*haven't ~*n *much of her lately*⟩ **c** to grant an interview to; receive ⟨*the president will ~ you*⟩ **10** to accompany, escort ⟨~ *the girls home*⟩ **11** to meet (a bet) in poker or to equal the bet of (a player); call **12** to receive as payment or profit ⟨~ *less than £50 after tax deductions*⟩ ~ *vi* **1a** to give or pay attention ⟨~ *here!*⟩ **b** to look about ⟨*come to the window and ~*⟩ **2a** to have the power of sight **b** to perceive objects by sight ⟨*too dark to ~*⟩ **3** to grasp something mentally; have insight; understand ⟨~ *into the future*⟩ ⟨*it's Sunday, ~!*⟩ **4** to make investigation or inquiry; consider, deliberate ⟨*let me ~*⟩ [ME *seen*, fr OE *sēon*; akin to OHG *sehan* to see, OE *secgan* to say – more at SAY] – **see you** – used to express farewell – see also **see** EYE **to eye (with)/** THINGS**/one's** WAY **to**

**synonyms** See, behold, notice, remark, espy, descry, perceive, discern, survey, and view all mean "be visually aware of something". See is the most general word, and could replace any of the others insofar as they do not depend on the will, since see is involuntary. The somewhat literary behold often suggests awe and dignity ⟨**beheld** *the innumerable Persian host crossing the Hellespont* – George Grote⟩. Notice and the formal remark both imply that one's attention is captured by a visual impression, remark perhaps emphasizing the close observation of detail ⟨*a passerby would have* **remarked** *an elderly shopkeeper bent apparently on a day in the country* – John Buchan⟩. The rather formal espy and descry also indicate that the attention has been captured, adding the idea of acuteness of vision, enabling one to espy usually small or obscure things ⟨**espy** *a tiny flower in the crack*⟩ or to descry usually distant ones ⟨**descry** *the Crystal Palace on a clear day*⟩. Perceive and discern suggest that mental insight is applied to what is seen, discern particularly emphasizing fine discrimination ⟨**discern** *a subtle difference*⟩. Survey and view imply a purposive overall looking, survey suggesting something seen as a whole from a height ⟨**survey** *the landscape*⟩ and view often emphasizing inspection for a purpose ⟨**view** *a house before buying*⟩. Observe and contemplate suggest attention paid to something for some time, observe being used particularly for scientific study and contemplate for meditative gazing ⟨*he affected to be... *contemplating *the tip of his shining boot* – Edith Wharton⟩. **usage** The very common use of **you see** as a meaningless addition to speech is widely disliked.

**see about** *vt* **1** to deal with **2** to consider further ⟨*we'll see about that*⟩

**see off** *vt* **1a** to attend to or be present at the departure of ⟨*saw his parents* off *on holiday*⟩ **b** to dismiss **2** *informal* to avert, repel ⟨see *him* off *Rover!*⟩

**see out** *vt* **1** to escort (a visitor) to an exit ⟨*can you* see *yourselves* out?⟩ **2** to last until the end of ⟨*enough fuel to see the winter* out⟩

**see through** *vt* **1** to grasp the true nature of ⟨*saw through his deceptions*⟩ **2** to undergo or endure to the end ⟨*bravely saw the fight through*⟩ **3** to provide for, support, or satisfy the needs of, esp for a particular period ⟨*that overcoat should see me through the winter*⟩ ⟨*enough money to see us through the week*⟩

**see to** *vt* to attend to; care for

²**see** *n* **1** the area over which a bishop exercises authority **2** *archaic* a cathedral [ME *se*, fr OF, fr L *sedes* seat; akin to L *sedēre* to sit – more at SIT]

¹**seed** /seed/ *n, pl* **seeds**, *esp collectively* **seed 1a(1)** the grains or ripened OVULES (structures containing egg cells) of plants used for sowing **a(2)** the fertilized ripened OVULE of a FLOWERING PLANT containing an embryo together with its food reserves

and protective coat and normally capable of germination to produce a new plant; *broadly* a plant part (eg a spore, bulb, or corm) that can propagate **a(3)** a small dry seedlike fruit (eg a grain of a cereal grass) **b** an animal structure or product that can propagate: eg **b(1)** semen, sperm **b(2)** a small egg (eg of an insect) **b(3)** a young or larval form of an animal suitable for transplanting; *specif* a SEED OYSTER or related animal (eg a mussel) in this condition; SPAT **c** the condition or stage of bearing seed ⟨*in ~*⟩ **2** progeny ⟨*the ~ of Abraham*⟩ **3** a source of development or growth; a germ ⟨*sowed the ~*s *of discord*⟩ **4** something (eg a tiny particle or a bubble in glass) that resembles a seed in shape or size **5** a competitor who has been seeded in a tournament ⟨*the fifth ~ beat the top ~ in the final*⟩ [ME, fr OE *sǣd;* akin to OHG *sāt* seed, OE *sāwan* to sow – more at SOW] – **seed** *adj*, **seeded** *adj*, **seedlike** *adj* – **go/run to seed 1** to (start to) develop seed **2** to lose vigour, fitness, etc; decay

**usage** Seed in large quantities is a mass noun with no plural ⟨*a sack of grass* seed⟩. The plural **seeds** is used for small quantities ⟨*grow a few* seeds *in a saucer*⟩.

²**seed** *vi* **1** to sow seed **2** *of a plant* to produce or shed seed ~ *vt* **1a** to plant seeds in; sow ⟨~ *land to grass*⟩ **b** to provide with something that causes or stimulates growth or development ⟨*a nuclear reactor ~*ed *with plutonium*⟩ **c** to inoculate **d** to treat with solid particles to stimulate crystallization, condensation, etc; *esp* to treat (a cloud) in this way to produce rain, snow, etc **2** to place (seeds) in the ground for growth; sow **3** to extract the seeds from (eg raisins) **4a** to arrange (tournament players or teams) so that superior ones will not meet in early rounds **b** to rank (a contestant) relative to others in a tournament on the basis of previous record ⟨*the top-seeded tennis star*⟩

**seedbed** /-,bed/ *n* **1** (a bed of) usu fine soil prepared for planting seed **2** a place or source of growth or development ⟨*the ~ of revolution*⟩

**seedcake** /-,kayk/ *n* **1** a sweet cake containing aromatic seeds (eg caraway seeds) **2** OIL CAKE (residue after extracting oil from seeds)

**seed coat** *n* an outer protective covering of a seed

**seed corn** *n* **1** corn of good quality that is used for sowing **2** an invaluable resource for future development

**seedeater** /-,eetǝ/ *n* a bird (eg a finch) whose diet consists basically of seeds

**seeder** /'seedǝ/ *n* **1** an implement for planting or sowing seeds **2** a device for seeding fruit **3** one who or that which seeds clouds to produce rain, snow, etc

**seed fern** *n* any of an order (Cycadofilicales syn Pteridospermales) of extinct seed-bearing plants with fernlike foliage

**seed leaf** *n* COTYLEDON 2 (first leaf produced by a germinating seed)

**seedless** /'seedlǝs/ *adj* lacking seeds ⟨*a ~ orange*⟩

**seedling** /'seedling/ *n* **1** a plant grown from seed rather than from a cutting **2** a young plant: eg **2a** a very young tree smaller than a sapling **b** a nursery plant before permanent transplantation – **seedling** *adj*

**seed money** *n, NAm* money used for setting up a new enterprise

**seed oyster** *n* a young oyster, esp of a size for transferring to another bed to start a new colony

**seed pearl** *n* a very small and often imperfect pearl

**seed plant** *n* a plant (eg a flowering plant or conifer) that bears seeds; SPERMATOPHYTE

**seedpod** /'seed,pod/ *n* a pod (eg of a pea)

**seed potato** *n* a small potato tuber used for sowing

**seedsman** /'seedzmǝn/ *n* **1** someone who sows seeds **2** a dealer in seeds

**seed stock** *n* a supply (eg of seed) for planting; *broadly* a source of new individuals ⟨*leaving a ~ of trout in the streams*⟩

**seedtime** /-,tiem/ *n* the season of sowing

**seed vessel** *n* PERICARP (part of a fruit surrounding the seed)

**seedy** /'seedi/ *adj* **1a** containing or full of seeds ⟨*a ~ fruit*⟩ **b** *of glass* containing many tiny air bubbles **2** inferior in condition or quality: eg **2a** shabby, grubby ⟨*~ clothes*⟩ **b** somewhat disreputable; run-down ⟨*a ~ district*⟩ **c** *informal* slightly unwell; debilitated ⟨*felt ~ and went home early*⟩ – **seedily** *adv*, **seediness** *n*

**seeing** /'see·ing/ *conj* in view of the fact; since – often + *that* or, in nonstandard use, + *as how*

**seeing eye, seeing eye dog** *n* GUIDE DOG

**seek** /seek/ *vb* **sought** /sawt/ *vt* **1** to resort to; go to ⟨~ *the* *shade on a hot day*⟩ **2a** to go in search of; look for – often + *out* **b** to try to discover ⟨~ *a solution to the problem*⟩ **3** to ask for; request ⟨~s *advice*⟩ **4** to try to acquire or gain; pursue ⟨~ *fame*⟩ **5** to make an effort; attempt, aim – + infin ⟨~ *to cater for every taste*⟩ ~ *vi* **1** to make a search or inquiry **2a** to be sought ⟨*the connection between dress and war is not far to* ~ – Virginia Woolf⟩ **b** to be lacking ⟨*in critical judgment . . . they were sadly to* ~ – *TLS*⟩ [ME *seken*, fr OE *sēcan;* akin to OHG *suohhen* to seek, L *sagire* to perceive keenly, Gk *hēgeisthai* to lead] – **seeker** *n*

**seel** /seel/ *vt* **1** to close the eyes of (eg a hawk) by drawing threads through the eyelids **2** *archaic* to close up (the eyes) [alter. of ME *silen*, fr MF *siller*, fr ML *ciliare*, fr L *cilium* eyelid – more at SUPERCILIOUS]

**seem** /seem/ *vi* **1** to give the impression of being ⟨*he* ~s *unhappy*⟩ ⟨*she* ~s *a bore*⟩ **2** to appear to the observation or understanding ⟨*I* ~ *to have caught a cold*⟩ ⟨*it* ~s *he lost his passport*⟩ **3** to give evidence of existing ⟨*there* ~s *no reason*⟩ [ME *semen*, of Scand origin; akin to ON *sōma* to beseem, befit, *samr* same – more at SAME] – **would seem** to seem to one ⟨*it would seem to be raining*⟩

*usage* Some writers on usage dislike *can't* **seem** *to*. It can be replaced by **seem** *unable to* or merely by *can't* ⟨*he* **seems** *unable to lift it*⟩.

¹**seeming** /'seeming/ *n* outward appearance as distinguished from true character; semblance

²**seeming** *adj* apparent rather than real ⟨*wealth gave them a* ~ *security*⟩ **synonyms** see APPARENT

**seemingly** /'seemingli/ *adv* **1** so far as can be seen or judged; evidently **2** to outward appearance only

**seemly** /'seemli/ *adj* **1a** good-looking; handsome **b** pleasing to the eye; attractive **2** in accord with good taste or propriety; decorous **3** *archaic* suited to the occasion, purpose, or person; fit [ME *semely*, fr ON *sæmiligr*, fr *sæmr* becoming; akin to ON *sōma* to beseem] – **seemliness** *n*, **seemly** *adv*

¹**seep** /seep/ *vi* to pass slowly (as if) through fine pores or small openings; ooze ⟨*water* ~ed *in through a crack*⟩ [alter. of earlier *sipe*, fr ME *sipen*, fr OE *sipian;* akin to MLG *sipen* to seep]

²**seep** *n* **1** a spot where a fluid (eg water, oil, or gas) contained in the ground oozes slowly to the surface and often forms a pool **2** *NAm* a small spring – **seepy** *adj*

**seepage** /'seepij/ *n* **1** the process of seeping **2** a quantity of fluid that has seeped (eg through porous material)

¹**seer** /siə/, *fem* **seeress** /'siəris/ *n* **1** somebody who sees **2a** somebody who predicts future events; a prophet **b** a person credited with exceptional moral and spiritual insight **3** somebody who practises divination

²**seer** *n, pl* **seers, seer** any of various Indian units of weight; *esp* a unit equal to about 1 kilogram (about 2 pounds) [Hindi *ser*]

**seersucker** /'siə,sukə/ *n* a light fabric often used for summer dresses, shirts, etc, made of linen, cotton, or rayon and usu striped and slightly puckered [Hindi *śīrśaker*, fr Per *shīr-o-shakar*, lit., milk and sugar]

¹**seesaw** /'see,saw/ *n* **1** an alternating up-and-down or backwards-and-forwards movement; *also* anything (eg a process or movement) that alternates ⟨*a* ~ *of shame and defiance*⟩ **2a** a game in which two children or groups of children ride on opposite ends of a plank balanced in the middle so that one end goes up as the other goes down **b** the plank or apparatus so used [prob redupl of ³*saw*] – **seesaw** *adj*

²**seesaw** *vi* **1a** to move backwards and forwards or up and down **b** to play at seesaw **2a** to alternate **b** to vacillate ~ *vt* to cause to move with a seesaw motion

¹**seethe** /seedh/ *vt, archaic* to boil, stew ~ *vi* **1a** to be in a state of agitated usu confused movement ⟨*swarms of midges* ~d *everywhere*⟩ **b** to churn or foam as if boiling **2** to feel or express violent emotion ⟨*he* ~d *with rage*⟩ **3** *archaic* to boil [ME *sethen*, fr OE *sēothan;* akin to OHG *siodan* to seethe, Lith *siausti* to rage]

²**seethe** *n* a state of seething; (a) turmoil

**seething** /'seedhing/ *adj* **1** intensely hot; boiling ⟨*a* ~ *inferno*⟩ **2** constantly moving or active; agitated

'**see-,through** *adj* transparent

¹**segment** /'segmənt/ *n* **1a** a separated piece of something; a bit, fragment ⟨*chop the stalks into short* ~s⟩ **b** any of the constituent parts into which a thing is divided or marked off (as if) by natural boundaries ⟨*all* ~s *of the population agree*⟩ **c** any of the sections into which the body or a jointed structure of an animal is divided; *specif* any of the series of similar re-peating parts into which the body of an ANNELID worm (eg an earthworm) or of an insect, crab, centipede, or other ARTHROPOD is divided **2** *maths* a portion cut off from a geometrical figure by one or more points, lines, or planes: eg **2a** a part of a circular area bounded by a straight line connecting two points of that circle and the arc opposite to it – compare SECTOR 1 **b** a part of a sphere cut off by a plane or included between two parallel planes **c** the part of a line between two points **3** *linguistics* any of the series of units into which an utterance may be divided [L *segmentum*, fr *secare* to cut – more at SAW] – **segmentary** *adj*

²**segment** /seg'ment/ *vt* to separate or divide into segments

**segmental** /seg'mentl/ *adj* **1** (having the form) of a segment of a circle ⟨~ *arch*⟩ ⟨~ *pediment*⟩ **2** (composed) of or divided into segments; *esp* based on or arranged according to the division of a body or body part into a series of similar segments ⟨~ *ganglia*⟩ **3** resulting from segmentation; subsidiary – **segmentally** *adv*

**segmentation** /,segmən'taysh(ə)n, -men-/ *n* **1** the process of dividing into segments **2** the splitting of a single cell to form many cells (eg in a developing egg); CLEAVAGE **3** the condition of having a body or body part made up of similarly structured segments; METAMERISM

**segmentation cavity** *n* BLASTOCOEL (central cavity of an early stage of an embryo)

**segmented** /seg'mentid/ *adj* divided into or composed of similar segments or sections ⟨~ *worms*⟩

**segno** /'senyoh/ *n, pl* **segnos, segni** a notational sign; *specif* the sign that marks the beginning or end of a musical repeat [It, sign, fr L *signum*]

¹**segregate** /'segrigayt/ *vt* **1** to separate or set apart from others or from a main body; isolate **2** to cause or force separation of (eg dangerous criminals from the rest of society) or in (eg a community) ~ *vi* **1a** to withdraw **b** to separate off from a larger mass or body and gather in one place **2** to practise or enforce a policy of segregation **3** to undergo genetic segregation **synonyms** see ¹SEPARATE *antonym* integrate [L *segregatus*, pp of *segregare*, fr *se*- apart + *greg*-, *grex* herd – more at SECEDE, GREGARIOUS] – **segregative** *adj*

²**segregate** /'segrigət, -,gayt/ *n* somebody who or something that is in some respect segregated

**segregated** /'segri,gaytid/ *adj* **1a** set apart or separated from others of the same kind or group **b** divided in facilities or administered separately for members of different groups or races ⟨~ *education*⟩ **c** restricted to members of one group or one race by a policy of segregation ⟨~ *schools*⟩ **2** practising or maintaining segregation, esp of races ⟨~ *states*⟩

**segregation** /,segri'gaysh(ə)n/ *n* **1** segregating or being segregated **2a** the separation or isolation of a race, class, or ethnic group, esp by discriminatory means (eg enforcing residence in a restricted area, setting up barriers to social intercourse, or providing separate educational facilities) **b** the separation for special treatment or observation of individuals or items from a larger group ⟨*the* ~ *of political prisoners from common criminals*⟩ **3** the separation of the members of a pair of genes coding for the same inheritable characteristic (eg eye colour) and their distribution to different cells during MEIOSIS (splitting of a cell to form four new cells) in which the reproductive cells (eg sperm and eggs) are formed

**segregationist** /,segri'gayshənist/ *n* a person who believes in or practises segregation, esp of races – **segregationist** *adj*

¹**segue** /'saygway, 'seg-/ *vb imperative* **1** proceed to what follows without pause **2** perform the music that follows in the same way as that which has preceded it □ used as a direction in music [It, there follows, fr *seguire* to follow, fr L *sequi* – more at SUE]

²**segue** *vi* **segueing** to proceed without pause from one musical number or theme to another

³**segue** *n* a transition from one musical number to another

**seguidilla** /,segi'dilyə, -'deel-/ *n* (the music for) a Spanish dance in triple time with many regional variations [Sp, dim. of *seguida* sequence, fr *seguir* to follow, fr L *sequi*]

**seicento** /say'chentoh/ *n* the 17th century in Italy, esp with reference to its literature and art [It, lit., six hundred, fr *sei* six (fr L *sex*) + *cento* hundred – more at SIX, CINQUECENTO]

**seiche** /saysh/ *n* a periodic movement of the surface of a lake or landlocked sea that varies in length from a few minutes to several hours [Fr]

**Seidlitz powder** /'sedlits/ *n* a mild laxative consisting of one powder of SODIUM BICARBONATE and ROCHELLE SALT and another of TARTARIC ACID that are mixed in water and drunk while bubbling [*Seidlitz* (Sedlčany), village in Bohemia, Czechoslovakia; fr the similarity of its effect to that of the water of the village]

**seigneur** /say'nyuh, se'nyuh/ *n, often cap* a feudal lord [MF, fr ML *senior*, fr L, adj, elder – more at SENIOR]

**seigneurial** /say'nyuhriəl/ *adj* of or befitting a seigneur; manorial

**seigneury** /'saynyəri/ *n* **1** the territory under the government of a feudal lord **2** lordship, dominion; *specif* the power or authority of a feudal lord

**seignior** /'saynyə/ *n* a seigneur [ME *seignour*, fr MF *seigneur*]

**seigniorage, seignorage** /'saynyərij/ *n* a government revenue from the manufacture of coins, calculated as the difference between the FACE VALUE and the metal value and manufacturing costs of the coins; *also* a charge made by a mint for turning bullion brought to it into coin [ME *seigneurage*, fr MF, right of the lord (esp to coin money), fr *seigneur*]

**seigniory, seignory** /'saynyəri/ *n* (a) seigneury

**seignorial** /say'nyawriəl/ *adj* seigneurial

**¹seine** /sayn/ *n* a large net with weights on one edge and floats on the other that hangs vertically in the water and is used to enclose fish when its ends are pulled together or are drawn ashore [ME, fr OE *segne*; akin to OHG *segina* seine; both fr a prehistoric WGmc word borrowed fr L *sagena* seine, fr Gk *sagēnē*]

**²seine** *vi* to fish with or catch fish with a seine ~ *vt* to fish for or in with a seine – **seiner** *n*

**seisin** *also* **seizin** /'seezin/ *n, law* **1** the possession of land in feudal times by the person occupying and using it **2** the possession of a freehold estate in land [ME *seisine, sesin,* fr OF *saisine,* fr *saisir* to seize]

**seism** /'siez(ə)m/ *n* an earthquake [Gk *seismos* shock, earthquake, fr *seiein* to shake; akin to Skt *tveṣati* he is violently moved]

**seism-, seismo-** *comb form* earthquake; vibration ⟨*seismometer*⟩ [Gk, fr *seismos*]

**seismic** /'siezmik/, **seismal** /-ml/ *adj* **1** of, subject to, being, or caused by an earthquake or other vibration of the earth **2** of a vibration on a celestial body (eg the moon) comparable to a seismic event on earth – **seismicity** *n*

**seismogram** /'siezmə,gram/ *n* a record made by a seismograph [ISV]

**seismograph** /'siezmə,grahf, -,graf/ *n* an apparatus to measure and record earth tremors [ISV] – **seismographer** *n,* **seismography** *n,* **seismographic** *adj*

**seismology** /seiz'moləji/ *n* a science that deals with earthquakes and other vibrations of the earth [ISV] – **seismologist** *n,* **seismological** *adj*

**seismometer** /siez'momitə/ *n* a seismograph; *esp* one that measures the actual movements of the ground (eg on the earth or the moon) [ISV] – **seismometric** *adj,* **seismometry** *n*

**sei whale** /say/ *n* a common and widely distributed small white-spotted RORQUAL (*Balaenoptera borealis*) [part trans of Norw *seihval,* fr *sei* coalfish + *hval* whale; fr its habit of following the coalfish in search of food]

**seize** /seez/ *vt* **1a seise** /seez/ *also* **seize** *law* **1a(1)** to put (a person) in legal possession of property, esp land **a(2)** to vest ownership of a freehold estate in **b** *also* **seise** to put in possession of something ⟨*the biographer will be* ~d *of all pertinent papers*⟩ **2** to take possession of, esp by legal authority; confiscate ⟨*police* ~d *a large quantity of heroin*⟩ **3a** to take possession of by force; capture **b** to take prisoner; arrest **4a** to take hold of abruptly or eagerly ⟨~d *his arm and pulled him clear of the fire*⟩ **b** to understand clearly and entirely; comprehend **5a** *esp of a disease* to attack or overwhelm physically; afflict ⟨*suddenly* ~d *with an attack of lumbago*⟩ **b** to possess (the mind) completely or overwhelmingly; captivate ⟨~d *the imagination of thousands*⟩ **6** to bind or fasten together with a lashing of cord or twine ~ *vi* **1** to take or lay hold of something suddenly or forcibly – usu + *on* or *upon* ⟨~d *on her idea for a new TV series*⟩ **2** *esp of machine parts* (eg *brakes or pistons*) to become stuck to another moving part through excessive pressure, temperature, or friction – often + *up* [ME *saisen,* fr OF *saisir* to put in possession of, fr ML *sacire,* of Gmc origin; akin to OHG *sezzen* to set – more at SET] – **seizer** *n*

  **seize up** *vi, chiefly NAm informal* to become jammed, obstructed, or inoperative, esp because of undue strain ⟨*the engine seized up*⟩

**seizure** /'seezhə/ *n* **1a** seizing or being seized **b** the taking possession of somebody or something by legal process **2** a sudden attack (eg of disease)

**sejant** /'seej(ə)nt/ *adj, of a heraldic animal* sitting [modif of MF *seant,* prp of *seoir* to sit, fr L *sedēre* – more at SIT]

**sekt** /sekt/ *n, often cap* a German sparkling wine [Ger, modif of Fr *sec* dry – more at SACK]

**selachian** /si'laykiən/ *n* any of a group (Selachii) of fishes with cartilage skeletons, that is considered to include the sharks and dogfishes and sometimes the rays and skates [deriv of Gk *selachos* cartilaginous phosphorescent fish; akin to Gk *selas* brightness – more at SELEN-] – **selachian** *adj*

**seladang** /sə'lahdahng, -dang/ *n* GAUR (large wild ox) [Malay *sēladang*]

**selaginella** /,seləji'nelə/ *n* any of a genus (*Selaginella* of the family Selaginellaceae) of CLUB MOSSES (primitive plants) with branching stems, scalelike leaves, and spore-bearing leaves (SPOROPHYLLS) arranged in spikes or cones [NL, genus name, fr L *selagin-, selago,* a plant resembling the savin]

**selah** /'seelə/ *interj* – a term of uncertain meaning found in the Hebrew text of the Psalms and Habakkuk and carried over untranslated into some English versions [Heb *selāh*]

**¹seldom** /'seldəm/ *adv* in few instances; rarely, infrequently ⟨*very* ~⟩ ⟨~, *if ever*⟩ [ME, fr OE *seldan;* akin to OHG *seltan* seldom, L *sed, se* without – more at IDIOT]

  **usage** Seldom and **rarely** should not be followed by *ever* or *or ever* ⟨⚠ *he* **seldom** *ever writes to us*⟩. There can be no objection to *if ever* or *or never* here ⟨*he* **rarely** *or never went out*⟩.

**²seldom** *adj* rare, infrequent

**¹select** /si'lekt/ *adj* **1** picked out in preference to others **2a** of special value or quality; superior, choice **b** exclusively or fastidiously chosen, esp on the basis of social characteristics ⟨*a* ~ *membership*⟩ **3** judicious in choice; discriminating ⟨~ *appreciation*⟩ [L *selectus,* pp of *seligere* to select, fr *se-* apart (fr *sed, se* without) + *legere* to gather, select – more at LEGEND] – **selectness** *n*

**²select** *vt* to take according to preference from among a number; choose; PICK OUT ~ *vi* to make a selection or choice *synonyms* see ¹CHOICE – **selectable** *adj*

**select committee** *n taking sing or pl vb* a committee of a legislative body that is established to examine one particular matter and that is not permanent

**selectee** /si,lek'tee/ *n, NAm* a conscript

**selection** /si'leksh(ə)n/ *n* **1** selecting or being selected **2a** somebody who or something that is selected; a choice; *also* a collection of selected items **b** a range of things from which to choose **3** a natural or artificially imposed process that results or tends to result in the survival and propagation only of those organisms that have suitable attributes for their situation, with the result that the inherited traits of the survivors are perpetuated in successive generations – compare NATURAL SELECTION **4** the principle or practice of selecting pupils or students for differential education according to academic ability *synonyms* see ¹CHOICE

**selective** /si'lektiv/ *adj* **1** of or characterized by selection; selecting or tending to select ⟨*a* ~ *weed killer*⟩ **2** of or being an electronic circuit or apparatus having the ability to respond to a particular frequency or band of frequencies – **selectively** *adv,* **selectiveness** *n,* **selectivity** *n*

**selective service** *n, NAm* a system under which men are called up for military service

**selectman** /si'lektmən/ *n* a member of a board of officials elected in towns of all New England states except Rhode Island to serve as the chief administrative authority of the town

**selector** /si'lektə/ *n* somebody who or something that selects; *esp, Br* one who chooses the members of a sports team

**¹selen-, seleno-** *comb form* moon ⟨*selenium*⟩ ⟨*selenography*⟩ [L *selen-,* fr Gk *selēn-,* fr *selēnē;* akin to Gk *selas* brightness, L *sol* sun – more at SOLAR]

**²selen-, seleni-, seleno-** *comb form* selenium ⟨*seleniferous*⟩ ⟨*selenide*⟩ [Sw, fr NL *selenium*]

**selenate** /'selinayt/ *n* any of various chemical compounds (SALTS or ESTERS) formed by combination between SELENIC ACID and a metal atom, an alcohol, or another chemical group [Sw *selenat,* fr *selen* selenic]

**selenic** /si'leenik/ *adj* of or containing selenium, esp with a relatively high VALENCY [Sw *selen,* fr NL *selenium*]

**selenic acid** /si'leenik, -'lenik/ *n* a strong acid, $H_2SeO_4$, that in solution in water dissolves gold and platinum

**selenide** /'selinied/ *n* a compound of selenium with one other chemical element or group

**seleniferous** /ˌseliˈnif(ə)rəs/ *adj* containing or yielding selenium ⟨~ *vegetation*⟩ ⟨~ *soils*⟩ [ISV]

**selenious** /siˈleeniəs/ *adj* of or containing selenium, esp with a relatively low VALENCY [ISV]

**selenite** /ˈseliniet/ *n* a colourless transparent variety of GYPSUM (calcium mineral) occurring as distinct crystals or crystalline masses [L *selenites*, fr Gk *selēnitēs* (*lithos*), lit., stone of the moon, fr *selēnē;* fr the belief that it waxed and waned with the moon]

**selenium** /siˈleeni-əm/ *n* a nonmetallic solid chemical element that resembles sulphur in its reactions, is obtained chiefly as a by-product in copper refining, and occurs in various forms, of which a grey stable form varies in electrical conductivity under the influence of light and is used in electronic devices (e g SOLAR CELLS) [NL, fr Gk *selēnē* moon – more at SELEN-; named by analogy to *tellurium* (fr L *tellus* earth)]

**selenium cell** *n* a PHOTOELECTRIC CELL (device that generates or controls an electric current when exposed to light) containing an insulated strip of selenium and used in photographic light meters, burglar alarms, etc

**selenocentric** /siˌleenohˈsentrik/ *adj* of the centre of the moon; *also* seen from or involving the moon as a centre [ISV]

**selenography** /ˌseliˈnogrəfi/ *n* **1** the science dealing with the physical features of the moon **2** the physical geography of the moon – **selenographer** *n*, **selenographist** *n*, **selenographic** *adj*

**selenology** /ˌseliˈnoləji/ *n* a branch of astronomy that deals with the moon – **selenologist** *n*, **selenological** *adj*

¹**self** /self/ *pron, commercialese* myself, himself, herself ⟨*cheque payable to* ~⟩ [ME (intensive pron), fr OE; akin to OHG *selb*, intensive pron, L *sui* (reflexive pron) of oneself – more at SUICIDE]

²**self** *adj* **1a** *of a bird, animal, etc* self-coloured **b** identical throughout, esp in colour; uniform **2** *obs* identical, same

³**self** *n, pl* **selves** /selvz/ **1** the entire being of an individual; *esp* the union of elements (e g body, emotions, thoughts, and sensations) that constitute the individuality and identity of a person **2a** a person's individual character ⟨*his true* ~ *was revealed*⟩ **b** an aspect of a person's character ⟨*her better* ~⟩ **3** personal interest, advantage, or welfare ⟨*took no thought of* ~⟩

⁴**self** *vb* to induce or undergo self-pollination or self-fertilization (in)

**self-** *comb form* **1a** oneself; itself ⟨self-*supporting*⟩ **b** of oneself or itself ⟨self-*abasement*⟩ **c** by oneself or itself ⟨self-*propelled*⟩ ⟨self-*acting*⟩ ⟨self-*starting*⟩ **2a** to, with, for, or in oneself or itself ⟨self-*confident*⟩ ⟨self-*addressed*⟩ **b** of or in oneself or itself inherently ⟨self-*evident*⟩ ⟨self-*explanatory*⟩ [ME, fr OE, fr *self*]

**self-aˈbandonment** *n* **1** a surrender of selfish interests or desires **2** a lack of self-restraint – **self-abandoned** *adj*

**self-aˈbasement** *n* humiliation of oneself, esp in response to a sense of inferiority or guilt

**self-ˈabnegating** *adj* self-denying – **self-abnegation** *n*

**self-abˈsorbed** *adj* absorbed in one's own thoughts, activities, or welfare

**self-abˈsorption** *n* preoccupation with oneself

**self-aˈbuse** *n* **1** reproach of oneself **2** masturbation

**self-ˈacting** *adj* (capable of) acting of or by itself; automatic

**self-ˈactual-ize, -ise** *vi* to realize fully one's personal (e g intellectual) potential – **self-actualizer** *n*, **self-actualization** *n*

**self-adˈdressed** *adj* addressed for return to the sender ⟨*a* ~ *envelope*⟩

**self-adˈhesive** *adj* SELF-SEALING 2

**self-adˈjusting** *adj* adjusting by itself; *specif* returning automatically to a previous position

**self-afˈfected** *adj* conceited, self-loving

**self-agˈgrandizement** *n* the act or process of making oneself more influential or wealthy, esp by ruthless means – **self-aggrandizing** *adj*

**self-annihiˈlation** *n* annihilation of self-awareness (e g in mystical contemplation of God)

**self-apˈpointed** *adj* assuming an authority not ratified by others ⟨*a* ~ *guardian of public morals*⟩

**self-asˈsertion** *n* **1** the act of asserting oneself or one's own rights, claims, or opinions **2** the act of asserting one's superiority over others – **self-asserting** *adj*, **self-assertingly** *adv*, **self-assertive** *adj*, **self-assertively** *adv*, **self-assertiveness** *n*

**self-asˈsurance** *n* assurance of one's own powers and abilities; self-confidence – **self-assured** *adj*, **self-assuredly** *adv*, **self-assuredness** *n*

**self-aˈware** *adj* aware of one's own personality or individuality – **self-awareness** *n*

**self-beˈtrayal** *n* self-revelation

**self-ˈbinder** *n* a harvesting machine that cuts grain and binds it into bundles

**self-ˈcatering** *adj, chiefly Br, of holiday accommodation* provided with lodging and cooking facilities but not meals ⟨*a* ~ *holiday*⟩ ⟨~ *chalets*⟩

**self-ˈcentred** *adj* **1** independent of outside force or influence; self-sufficient **2** concerned excessively with one's own desires or needs; selfish – **self-centredly** *adv*, **self-centredness** *n*

**self-ˈcharging** *adj* able to charge itself ⟨*a* ~ *battery*⟩

**self-ˈclosing** *adj* closing or shutting automatically after being opened

**self-ˈcocking** *adj, of a firearm* cocked by the operation of some part of the mechanism ⟨~ *on closing the bolt*⟩

**self-colˈlected** *adj* self-possessed

**self-ˈcoloured** *adj* of a single colour ⟨*a* ~ *flower*⟩

**self-comˈmand** *n* self-control

**self-comˈpatible** *adj* capable of effective self-pollination that results in the production of seeds and fruits – compare SELF-INCOMPATIBLE – **self-compatibility** *n*

**self-comˈplacent** *adj* self-satisfied – **self-complacency** *n*, **self-complacently** *adv*

**self-comˈposed** *adj* having or showing mental or spiritual composure; calm – **self-composedly** *adv*, **self-composedness** *n*

**self-conˈceit** *n* an exaggerated opinion of one's own abilities or importance; vanity – **self-conceited** *adj*

**self-ˈconcept** *n* a self-image

**self-conˈcern** *n* undue concern for one's own welfare – **self-concerned** *adj*

**self-conˈfessed** *adj* openly acknowledged; avowed ⟨*a* ~ *debauchee*⟩

**self-ˈconfidence** *n* confidence in oneself and in one's powers and abilities – **self-confident** *adj*, **self-confidently** *adv*

**self-congratuˈlation** *n* a complacent acknowledgment of one's own superiority or good fortune – **self-congratulatory** *adj*

**self-ˈconscious** *adj* **1a** conscious of oneself as a possessor of mental states and originator of actions; aware of oneself as an individual **b** intensely aware of oneself; conscious ⟨*a rising and* ~ *social class*⟩; *also* expressing such awareness ⟨~ *art*⟩ **2** uncomfortably conscious of oneself as an object of notice; ill at ease – **self-consciously** *adv*, **self-consciousness** *n*

**self-conˈsistent** *adj* having each element logically consistent with the rest; internally consistent ⟨*a* ~ *set of proofs*⟩ – **self-consistency** *n*

**self-ˈconstituted** *adj* constituted by oneself or itself

**self-conˈtained** *adj* **1** complete in itself; independent ⟨*a* ~ *flat*⟩ ⟨*each episode of the series is* ~⟩ **2a** self-possessed **b**

formal and reserved in manner – **self-containedly** *adv,* **self-containedness** *n,* **self-containment** *n*

,**self-con'tent** *n* self-satisfaction – **self-contented** *adj,* **self-contentedly** *adv,* **self-contentedness, self-contentment** *n*

,**self-contra'diction** *n* 1 contradiction of oneself 2 a statement or proposition that contains two contradictory elements or ideas – **self-contradicting** *adj,* **self-contradictory** *adj*

,**self-con'trol** *n* restraint of one's own impulses or emotions – **self-controlled** *adj*

,**self-cor'recting** *adj* compensating for or correcting one's own errors or weaknesses

,**self-'critical** *adj* 1 unduly critical of oneself or itself 2 able to judge one's own motives or actions impartially – **self-criticism** *n*

,**self-de'ceit** *n* self-deception

,**self-de'ceiving** *adj* 1 practising self-deception ⟨*a ~ hypocrite*⟩ 2 serving to deceive oneself ⟨*~ excuses*⟩ – **self-deceived** *adj,* **self-deceiver** *n*

,**self-de'ception** *n* the act of deceiving oneself; the state of being deceived by oneself (e g about one's character or motives) – **self-deceptive** *adj*

,**self-de'feating** *adj* acting so as to defeat its own purpose

,**self-de'fence** *n* 1 the act of defending or justifying oneself 2 the legal right to defend oneself with reasonable force against (the threat of) violence – **self-defensive** *adj*

,**self-de'nial** *n* a restraint or limitation of one's desires or their gratification *synonyms* see ABSTINENCE

,**self-de'nying** *adj* showing self-denial – **self-denyingly** *adv*

,**self-'deprecating, self-deprecatory** *adj* given to self-depreciation *synonyms* see DEPRECATE – **self-deprecatingly** *adv*

,**self-depreci'ation** *n* disparagement or understatement of oneself

,**self-de'spair** *n* despair of oneself; hopelessness

,**self-de'struct** *vi,* chiefly *NAm* to destroy itself ⟨*the junta of Greek colonels ~ed in 1974 – Time*⟩ – compare DESTRUCT

,**self-de'struction** *n* destruction of oneself or itself; *esp* suicide – **self-destructive** *adj,* **self-destructiveness** *n*

,**self-determi'nation** *n* 1 free choice of one's own actions or states without outside influence 2 determination by the people of a particular place of their own political status – **self-determined** *adj,* **self-determining** *adj*

,**self-de'velopment** *n* development of one's own mind or capacities

,**self-de'votion** *n* devotion of oneself, esp in service or sacrifice ⟨*his ~ to science cost him his life*⟩ – **self-devoted, self-devoting** *adj,* **self-devotedly** *adv,* **self-devotedness** *n*

,**self-di'gestion** *n* decomposition or breakdown of plant or animal tissue by processes originating inside the organism; AUTOLYSIS

,**self-di'rected** *adj* directed by oneself; *specif* not guided or impelled by an outside influence ⟨*a ~ personality*⟩ – **self-directing** *adj,* **self-direction** *n*

,**self-'discipline** *n* control or training of oneself, usu for the sake of improvement – **self-disciplined** *adj*

,**self-dis'trust** *n* a lack of confidence in oneself; diffidence – **self-distrustful** *adj*

,**self-'doubt** *n* self-distrust – **self-doubting** *adj*

,**self-'dramatizing** *adj* seeing and presenting oneself as an important or dramatic figure – **self-dramatization** *n*

,**self-'drive** *adj,* chiefly *Br,* of a hired vehicle intended to be driven by the hirer; not chauffeur-driven – **self-driven** *adj*

,**self-ef'facement** *n* the act of making oneself inconspicuous, esp because of modesty; humility – **self-effacing** *adj,* **self-effacingly** *adv*

,**self-e'lected** *adj* self-appointed

,**self-em'ployed** *adj* earning income directly from one's own business, trade, or profession rather than as salary or wages from an employer – **self-employment** *n*

,**self-en'richment** *n* the act or process of increasing one's intellectual or spiritual resources

,**self-e'steem** *n* 1 a confidence and satisfaction in oneself; self-respect 2 self-conceit

,**self-'evident** *adj* requiring no proof; obvious – **self-evidence** *n,* **self-evidently** *adv*

,**self-exami'nation** *n* 1 the analysis of one's conduct, beliefs, or motives 2 inspection of one's own body parts (e g of one's breasts) in order to detect early signs of disease

,**self-ex'cited** *adj,* of an electrical generator using part of the current it produces to activate its current-producing mechanism

,**self-'executing** *adj,* of a law, contract, etc taking effect immediately without prior legislative procedures ⟨*a ~ treaty*⟩

,**self-ex'istent** *adj* existing independently of any cause or agency – **self-existence** *n*

,**self-ex'planatory** *adj* capable of being understood without explanation

,**self-ex'pression** *n* 1 the expression of one's own personality (e g through painting or poetry); the assertion of one's individual traits 2 the assertion of one's own character through uninhibited behaviour – **self-expressive** *adj*

,**self-'feed** *vt* **self-fed** to provide rations for (animals) in bulk so as to permit the selection by the animal of the required amount and type of food – compare HAND-FEED

,**self-'feeder** *n* a machine or device for automatically renewing a supply of material (e g fuel); *esp* one for feeding livestock that automatically supplies measured amounts of food

,**self-'fertile** *adj,* of a plant or animal capable of reproducing by self-fertilization; made fertile by means of its own pollen or sperm – compare SELF-STERILE – **self-fertility** *n*

,**self-fertil·i'zation, -isation** *n* fertilization of a plant or animal effected by union of egg cells with pollen or sperm from the same individual – compare CROSS-FERTILIZATION

,**self-flagel'lation** *n* extreme criticism of oneself

,**self-'flattery** *n* an exaggeration of one's good qualities and achievements which passes over one's weakness or mistakes – **self-flattering** *adj*

,**self-for'getful** *adj* having or showing no thought of self or selfish interests; unselfish – **self-forgetfully** *adv,* **self-forgetfulness** *n*

,**self-ful'filling** *adj* 1 marked by or achieving fulfilment of oneself or itself 2 happening as a result of having been asserted or assumed beforehand ⟨*a ~ prophecy*⟩ – **self-fulfilment** *n*

,**self-'generated** *adj* generated or originated from within oneself ⟨*~ humour*⟩

,**self-'giving** *adj* self-sacrificing, unselfish

,**self-glorifi'cation** *n* a feeling or expression of one's own superiority; the exaltation of oneself

,**self-'glorifying** *adj* boastful

,**self-'governing** *adj* having control over oneself or one's own affairs; *specif* having self-government; autonomous

,**self-'government** *n* 1 government under the control and direction of the people of a town, state, country, etc rather than by an outside authority; *broadly* control of one's own affairs – compare HOME RULE 2 *archaic* self-control – **self-governed** *adj*

,**self-gratifi'cation** *n* the act of satisfying one's desires

,**self-gratu'lation** *n* self-congratulation – **self-gratulatory** *adj*

,**self-'guided** *adj* 1 guided by an internal mechanism 2 undertaken without a guide ⟨*~ tour*⟩

,**self-'hardening** *adj* hardening by itself without chemical or

| | | | |
|---|---|---|---|
| **self-convicted** *adj* | **self-dependence** *n* | **self-emancipation** *n* | **self-exertion** *n* |
| **self-created** *adj* | **self-dependent** *adj* | **self-energizing** *adj* | **self-exile** *n* |
| **self-creation** *n* | **self-described** *adj* | **self-enforcing** *adj* | **self-exiled** *adj* |
| **self-cultivation** *n* | **self-description** *n* | **self-engrossed** *adj* | **self-expanding** *adj* |
| **self-culture** *n* | **self-descriptive** *adj* | **self-enhancement** *n* | **self-explaining** *adj* |
| **self-damning** *adj* | **self-destroyer** *n* | **self-enjoyment** *n* | **self-exploration** *n* |
| **self-debasement** *n* | **self-destroying** *adj* | **self-evaluation** *n* | **self-financed** *adj* |
| **self-dedication** *n* | **self-devouring** *adj* | **self-evolved** *adj* | **self-financing** *adj* |
| **self-degradation** *n* | **self-discovery** *n* | **self-exaltation** *n* | **self-focussing** *adj* |
| **self-deluded** *adj* | **self-dissatisfaction** *n* | **self-exalting** *adj* | **self-formed** *adj* |
| **self-delusion** *n* | **self-distributing** *adj* | **self-exaltingly** *adv* | **self-generating** *adj* |
| **self-denigrating** *adj* | **self-educated** *adj* | **self-exclusion** *n* | **self-given** *adj* |
| **self-denigration** *n* | **self-education** *n* | **self-exculpation** *n* | **self-glory** *n* |

physical treatment; *esp, of steel* hardening in air without needing to be cooled by immersion in oil or water

,self-'hatred *n* hatred of oneself; *specif* hatred redirected towards oneself in frustration or despair

,self-'heal *n* any of several plants sometimes held to possess healing properties; *specif* a small common violet-flowered creeping plant (*Prunella vulgaris*) of the mint family

,self-'help *n* the action or an instance of improving or helping oneself without dependence on others

selfhood /'selfhood/ *n* **1a** the state of existing as a unique individual **b** (the) personality **2** selfishness

,self-humili'ation *n* the act or an instance of humbling or abasing oneself

,self-i'dentity *n* **1** sameness of a thing with itself **2** a sense of one's own individuality – **self-identical** *adj*

,self-ig'nite *vi* to become ignited without flame or spark (e g under high compression and temperature as in a diesel engine) – **self-ignition** *n*

,self-'image *n* one's conception of oneself or of one's role

,self-immo'lation *n* a deliberate and willing sacrifice of oneself

,self-im'portance *n* **1** an exaggerated sense of one's own importance; self-conceit **2** arrogant or pompous behaviour – **self-important** *adj*, **self-importantly** *adv*

,self-im'posed *adj* imposed on one by oneself; voluntarily undertaken

,self-in'clusive *adj* enclosing itself; complete in itself ⟨a ~ system⟩

,self-incom'patible *adj* incapable of effective self-pollination – compare SELF-COMPATIBLE – **self-incompatibility** *n*

,self-incrimi'nation *n* incrimination of oneself; *specif* the supplying of information (e g evidence in a court) which would subject oneself to criminal prosecution – **self-incriminating** *adj*

,self-in'duced *adj* **1** induced by oneself or itself ⟨~ hysteria⟩ **2** produced by self-induction ⟨a ~ voltage⟩

,self-in'ductance *n* the degree to which an ELECTROMOTIVE FORCE (energy causing current to flow) is induced in an electric circuit by a variation of current in the same circuit; INDUCTANCE caused by self-induction

,self-in'duction *n* the INDUCTION of an ELECTROMOTIVE FORCE (energy causing current to flow) in an electric circuit by a varying current in the same circuit

,self-in'dulgence *n* excessive or unrestrained gratification of one's own appetites, desires, or whims – **self-indulgent** *adj*, **self-indulgently** *adv*

,self-'interest *n* **1** one's own interest or advantage ⟨~ requires that we be generous in foreign aid⟩ **2** a concern for one's own advantage and well-being ⟨acted out of ~ and fear⟩ – **self-interested** *adj*, **self-interestedness** *n*

,self-in'volved *adj* self-absorbed

selfish /'selfish/ *adj* **1** preoccupied with oneself; pursuing or caring for one's own advantage, pleasure, or well-being without regard for others **2** arising from concern with one's own welfare or advantage in disregard of others ⟨a ~ act⟩ [³self + -ish] – **selfishly** *adv*, **selfishness** *n*

,self-justifi'cation *n* the act or an instance of making excuses for oneself – **self-justificatory** *adj*

,self-'justifying *adj* **1** seeking to justify oneself, esp to avoid blame **2** automatically justifying its existence or occurrence ⟨~ extravagance⟩; *specif* automatically adjusting (JUSTIFYING) type to fill a full line ⟨a ~ typewriter⟩

,self-'knowledge *n* knowledge or understanding of one's own capabilities, character, feelings, or motives

selfless /'selflis/ *adj* having no concern for self; unselfish –

selflessly *adv*, **selflessness** *n*

,self-'limited, **self-limiting** *adj* limited by one's or its own nature; *specif, medicine* running a definite and limited course ⟨a ~ disease⟩

,self-'liquidating *adj* **1** of a commercial transaction in which goods are converted into cash in a short time **2** generating funds from its own operations to repay the investment made to create it ⟨a ~ housing project⟩

,self-'loader *n* a SEMIAUTOMATIC (automatically reloaded) firearm

,self-'loading *adj, of a firearm* semiautomatic

,self-'love *n* love of self: **a** conceit, narcissism **b** a concern for one's own happiness or advantage – **self-loving** *adj*

,self-'luminous *adj* emitting light from within itself

,self-'made *adj* **1** made such by one's own actions **2** raised from poverty or obscurity by one's own efforts ⟨a ~ man⟩

,self-'mastery *n* self-control

,self-'motivated *adj* driven by one's own internal impetus; self-starting

,self-'moved *adj* moved by inherent power without external agency or cause – **self-moving** *adj*

,self-'murder *n* suicide

,self-'operating *adj* self-acting

,self-o'pinion *n* **1** high or exaggerated opinion of oneself; self-conceit **2** stubborn insistence on one's views – **self-opinioned** *adj*

,self-o'pinionated *adj* **1** conceited **2** stubbornly holding to one's own opinion; opinionated – **self-opinionatedness** *n*

,self-organi'zation *n* organization of oneself or itself; *specif* the act or process of forming or joining a TRADE UNION

,self-'penned *adj* written or composed by oneself

,self-per'ception *n* a perception or appraisal of oneself; *esp* a self-image

,self-per'petuating *adj* capable of continuing or renewing oneself or itself indefinitely ⟨~ board of trustees⟩ – **self-perpetuation** *n*

,self-'pity *n* pity for oneself; *esp* a self-indulgent dwelling on one's own sorrows or misfortunes – **self-pitying** *adj*, **self-pityingly** *adv*

,self-'poised *adj* **1** balanced without support **2** possessing poise through self-command or self-discipline

,self-polli'nation *n* the transfer of pollen from the ANTHER (male pollen-producing structure) of a flower to the STIGMA (part of the female reproductive organ) of the same flower or sometimes to that of a genetically identical flower (e g of the same plant or CLONE) – compare CROSS-POLLINATION – **self-pollinate** *vb*

,self-'portrait *n* **1** a portrait of an artist done by him-/herself **2** a description of one's character or personality given by oneself

,self-pos'sessed *adj* having or showing self-possession; composed in mind or manner; calm – **self-possessedly** *adv*

,self-pos'session *n* control of one's emotions or behaviour, esp when under stress; PRESENCE OF MIND; composure

,self-preser'vation *n* **1** preservation of oneself or one's interests from destruction or harm **2** an instinctive tendency to act so as to safeguard one's own existence

,self-pro'claimed *adj* self-styled

,self-pro'pelled *adj* **1** **self-propelled, self-propelling** possessing the means for its own propulsion ⟨a ~ vehicle⟩ **2** mounted on a vehicle rather than towed ⟨a ~ artillery piece⟩

,self-pro'tection *n* protection of oneself; self-defence – **self-protective** *adj*

,self-purifi'cation *n* **1** purification by natural means ⟨~ of water⟩ **2** purification of oneself

| | | | |
|---|---|---|---|
| **self-hate** *n* | **self-instruction** *n* | **self-management** *n* | **self-originated** *adj* |
| **self-hating** *adj* | **self-instructional** *adj* | **self-mockery** *n* | **self-parodist** *n* |
| **self-healing** *adj or n* | **self-interpretation** *n* | **self-mocking** *adj or n* | **self-parody** *n* |
| **self-humbling** *adj* | **self-introductory** *adj* | **self-mortification** *n* | **self-pleasing** *adj* |
| **self-hypnosis** *n* | **self-isolation** *n* | **self-mutilating** *adj* | **self-powered** *adj* |
| **self-hypnotism** *n* | **self-judgment** *n* | **self-mutilation** *n* | **self-praise** *n* |
| **self-idolatry** *n* | **self-labelled** *adj* | **self-negating** *adj* | **self-preoccupation** *n* |
| **self-improvement** *n* | **self-limitation** *n* | **self-neglect** *n* | **self-preoccupied** *adj* |
| **self-infatuated** *adj* | **self-loathing** *n* | **self-observation** *n* | **self-preparation** *n* |
| **self-inflated** *adj* | **self-locking** *adj* | **self-obsessed** *adj* | **self-pride** *n* |
| **self-inflicted** *adj* | **self-lubricating** *adj* | **self-occupied** *adj* | **self-produced** *adj* |
| **self-initiated** *adj* | **self-maintaining** *adj* | **self-ordained** *adj* | **self-professed** *adj* |
| **self-instructed** *adj* | **self-maintenance** *n* | **self-oriented** *adj* | **self-promotion** *n* |

,self-'questioning *n* examination of one's own actions and motives – **self-questioning** *adj*

**self-raising flour** *n* a commercially prepared mixture of flour containing a raising agent

,self-'rating *n* the assessing of one's own rating with reference to a standard scale

,self-reali'zation *n* fulfilment by oneself of the possibilities inherent in one's nature

,self-reali'zationism *n* the ethical theory that the highest human good consists in fulfilling one's innate capacities

,self-re'cording *adj* making an automatic record 〈~ *instruments*〉

,self-re'gard *n* 1 concern or consideration for oneself or one's own interests 2 self-respect – **self-regarding** *adj*

,self-'registering *adj* registering automatically 〈*a ~ barometer*〉

,self-'regulating *adj* regulating itself; *esp* automatic 〈*a ~ mechanism*〉 – **self-regulative, self-regulatory** *adj*, **self-regulation** *n*

,self-re'liance *n* reliance upon one's own efforts and abilities; independence – **self-reliant** *adj*

,self-renunci'ation *n* renunciation of one's own desires or ambitions, esp for the sake of others

,self-'replicating *adj* reproducing itself autonomously 〈*DNA is a ~ molecule*〉 – **self-replication** *n*

,self-re'proach *n* the act of blaming or censuring oneself – **self-reproachful** *adj*, **self-reproachfully** *adv*, **self-reproaching** *adj*, **self-reproachingly** *adv*

,self-re'spect *n* a proper respect for one's human dignity – **self-respecting** *adj*

,self-re'straint *n* restraint imposed on oneself, esp on the expression of one's feelings

,self-re'vealing *adj* marked by self-revelation 〈*a ~ glance*〉

,self-reve'lation *n* disclosure of one's own thoughts or feelings, esp without deliberate intent

,self-'righteous *adj* assured of one's own righteousness, esp in contrast with the actions and beliefs of others; narrow-mindedly moralistic – **self-righteously** *adv*, **self-righteousness** *n*

,self-'righting *adj* capable of righting itself when capsized 〈*a ~ boat*〉

,self-'rule *n* SELF-GOVERNMENT 1 – **self-ruling** *adj*

,self-'sacrifice *n* sacrifice of oneself or one's well-being for the sake of an ideal or for the benefit of others – **self-sacrificing** *adj*, **self-sacrificingly** *adv*

**selfsame** /'self,saym/ *adj* precisely the same; identical 〈*he left the ~ day*〉 *synonyms* see ¹SAME *antonym* diverse – **selfsameness** *n*

,self-satis'faction *n* a smug satisfaction with oneself or one's position or achievements

,self-'satisfied *adj* feeling or showing self-satisfaction 〈*a ~ smile*〉 – **self-satisfying** *adj*

,self-'scrutiny *n* self-examination

,self-'sealing *adj* 1 capable of sealing itself (e g after puncture) 〈*a ~ fuel tank*〉 2 capable of being sealed by pressure without the addition of moisture or an adhesive 〈*~ envelopes*〉

,self-'searching *adj* self-questioning

,self-'seeker *n* somebody who is self-seeking

'self-,seeking *adj* seeking only to safeguard or further one's own interests; selfish – **self-seeking** *n*

,self-se'lection *n* 1 selection by oneself; *esp* selection of goods by retail customers from display racks or counters in a store 2 selection of oneself (e g for voluntary study of a subject) – **self-selected** *adj*

,self-'service *also chiefly NAm* **self-serve** *n* 1 the serving of oneself (e g in a cafeteria or supermarket) with things to be paid for at a cashier's desk, usu upon leaving 2 *informal* a shop or cafeteria where one serves oneself 〈*did you try the ~?*〉 – **self-service** *adj*

,self-'serving *adj* serving one's own interests, esp at the expense of honesty or the welfare of others

,self-'slain *adj, archaic* killed by one's own hand

,self-'slaughter *n, archaic* suicide

,self-'sow /soh/ *vi* **self-sown** /sohn/, **self-sowed** /sohd/ *of a plant* to grow from seeds spread naturally (e g by wind or water)

,self-'starter *n* 1 an electric motor used to start an INTERNAL-COMBUSTION ENGINE without a crank; *also* the switch that starts this motor 2 a person with initiative; *esp* one who is able to work without supervision – **self-starting** *adj*

,self-'sterile *adj, of a plant or animal* incapable of reproducing by self-fertilization; sterile to its own pollen or sperm – compare SELF-FERTILE – **self-sterility** *n*

,self-stimu'lation *n* stimulation of oneself as a result of one's own activity or behaviour 〈*electrical ~ of the brain in rats*〉 – **self-stimulatory** *adj*

,self-'styled *adj* called by oneself, esp without justification 〈*~ experts*〉

,self-sub'sistence *n* the quality or state of subsisting independently of any external cause – **self-subsistent** *adj*

,self-'sufficient *adj* 1 able to maintain oneself or itself without outside aid; capable of providing for one's own needs 〈*a community ~ in dairy products*〉 2 having esp unwarranted assurance of one's own ability or worth; haughty – **self-sufficiency** *n*

,self-suf'ficing *adj* self-sufficient – **self-sufficingly** *adv*, **self-sufficingness** *n*

,self-sup'porting *adj* 1 meeting one's needs by one's own labour or income 2 supporting itself or its own weight 〈*a ~ wall*〉 – **self-support** *n*, **self-supported** *adj*

,self-sur'render *n* surrender of the self; the yielding up (e g to a person or influence) of oneself or one's will

,self-su'staining *adj* 1 maintaining or able to maintain oneself by independent effort 2 maintaining or able to maintain itself once started 〈*a ~ nuclear reaction*〉

,self-'taught *adj* 1 having knowledge or skills acquired by one's own efforts 〈*a ~ musician*〉 2 learnt by oneself without formal instruction 〈*~ knowledge*〉

,self-'treatment *n* treatment of one's own disease, esp by drugs or medicine, without medical supervision or prescription

,self-'violence *n, euph* suicide

,self-'will *n* stubborn or wilful adherence to one's own desires or ideas; obstinacy – **self-willed** *adj*, **self-willedly** *adv*, **self-willedness** *n*

**self-winding** /,self'wiending/ *adj* not needing to be wound by hand 〈*a ~ watch*〉

**Seljuk** /sel'joohk/, **Seljukian** *adj* 1 (characteristic) of any of several Turkish dynasties ruling over a great part of western Asia in the 11th, 12th, and 13th centuries 2 (characteristic) of a Turkish people ruled over by a Seljuk dynasty [Turk *Selçuk*, name of the reputed ancestor of the dynasties] – **Seljuk, Seljukian** *n*

¹**sell** /sel/ *vb* **sold** /sohld/ *vt* 1 to deliver or give up in violation of duty, trust, or loyalty; betray – often + *out* **2a(1)** to give up (property) in exchange, esp for money **a(2)** to offer for sale 〈*~s insurance*〉 **b** to give up in return for something else, esp foolishly or dishonourably 〈*sold a heritage for the sake of profit*〉 **c** to exact a price for 〈*sold their lives dearly*〉 3 to hand over to the power of another 〈*sold his soul to the devil*〉 4 to dispose of or manage for selfish gain instead of in accordance with conscience, justice, or duty 〈*juries who sold their verdicts*〉 5 to make acceptable, believable, or desirable by persuasion 〈*~ an idea*〉 6 to cause or promote the sale of 〈*advertising ~s newspapers*〉 7 to achieve a sale of 〈*a book which*

| | | | |
|---|---|---|---|
| **self-propagating** *adj* | **self-renewing** *adj* | **self-restricted** *adj* | **self-trained** *adj* |
| **self-propulsion** *n* | **self-renouncing** *adj* | **self-rewarding** *adj* | **self-transformation** *n* |
| **self-punishing** *adj* | **self-repeating** *adj* | **self-ridicule** *n* | **self-trust** *n* |
| **self-punishment** *n* | **self-repellent** *adj* | **self-schooled** *adj* | **self-understanding** *n* |
| **self-raised** *adj* | **self-repose** *n* | **self-stick** *adj* | **self-validating** *adj* |
| **self-recognition** *n* | **self-repression** *n* | **self-sustained** *adj* | **self-vindicating** *adj* |
| **self-recrimination** *n* | **self-reproof** *n* | **self-therapy** *n* | **self-vindication** *n* |
| **self-reflecting** *adj* | **self-reproving** *adj* | **self-torment** *n* | **self-worship** *n* |
| **self-reflection** *n* | **self-reprovingly** *adv* | **self-tormenting** *adj* | **self-worshipper** *n* |
| **self-reformation** *n* | **self-resentment** *n* | **self-tormentor** *n* | **self-worth** *n* |
| **self-renewal** *n* | **self-restraining** *adj* | **self-torture** *n* | |

sold *a million copies*⟩ **8** *informal* to persuade to accept or enjoy something – usu + *on* ⟨~ *children on reading*⟩ **9** *informal* to deceive, cheat – usu pass ⟨*we've been sold!*⟩ ~ *vi* **1** to transfer something to another's ownership by sale **2** to achieve a sale; *also* to achieve satisfactory sales ⟨*hoped that the new line would* ~⟩ **3** to have a specified price – + *at* or *for* – see also **sell somebody a** PUP, **sell down the** RIVER [ME *sellen*, fr OE *sellan*; akin to OHG *sellen* to sell, ON *sala* sale, Gk *helein* to take] – **sellable** *adj*

**sell off** *vt* to dispose of completely by selling, esp at a reduced price

**sell out** *vt* **1** to dispose of completely by selling **2** to sell all the goods of (a debtor) in order to satisfy creditors ~ *vi* **1** SELL UP **2** to betray one's cause or associates – usu + *on*

**sell up** *vb, chiefly Br vt* to sell (e g one's house or business) in a conclusive or forced transaction ~ *vi* to sell one's property (e g an estate or business) ⟨*sold up and emigrated to Australia*⟩

²**sell** *n, informal* a deliberate deception; a hoax

**seller** /'selə/ *n* **1** somebody who offers for sale **2** a product offered for sale and selling well, to a specified extent, or in a specified manner ⟨*a million-copy* ~⟩ ⟨*a poor* ~⟩

**seller's market** *n* a market in which goods are scarce, buyers have a limited range of choice, and prices are high; *broadly* a market in which demand exceeds supply – compare BUYER'S MARKET

**selling plate** /'seling/ *n* a race in which the winning horse is auctioned

'**selling-**,**plater** /,playtə/ *n* **1** a horse that runs chiefly in SELLING PLATES **2** an inferior racehorse

**selling point** /'seling/ *n* an aspect or detail of something that is emphasized (e g in selling or promoting)

**selling race** *n* a race in which the winning horse must be put up for auction

**sellotape** /'selə,tayp/ *vt* to fix (as if) with Sellotape

**Sellotape** /'selətayp/ *trademark* – used for a usu transparent adhesive tape

'**sell-**,**out** *n* **1** the act or an instance of selling out **2** a performance, exhibition, or contest for which all tickets or seats are sold **3** somebody who sells out

**seltzer** /'seltsə/ *n* **1** a natural medicinal MINERAL WATER **2** an artificially prepared MINERAL WATER containing CARBON DIOXIDE [modif of Ger *selterser* (*wasser*) water of Selters, fr Nieder*selters*, village in SW Germany]

**selvage, selvedge** /'selvij/ *n* **1a** the edge on either side of a fabric, esp a woven fabric, so finished as to prevent unravelling; *specif* a narrow border often of different or heavier threads than the fabric and sometimes in a different weave **b** an edge (e g of fabric or wallpaper) meant to be cut off and discarded **2** an outer or peripheral part: e g **2a** a border, edge **b** the edge plate of a lock through which the bolt is projected [ME *selvage*, prob fr MFlem *selvegge, selvage*, fr *selv* self + *egge* edge; akin to OE *self* & to OE *ecg* edge – more at EDGE] – **selvaged, selvedged** *adj*

**selves** /selvz/ *pl of* SELF

**semanteme** /si'manteem/ *n* SEMEME (minimal element of meaning) [Fr *sémantème*, fr *sémantique* semantic + *-ème* -eme]

**semantic** /si'mantik/ *adj* **1** of meaning in language; *esp* drawing distinctions between connotations of words or symbols **2** of semantics [Gk *sēmantikos* significant, fr *sēmainein* to signify, mean, fr *sēma* sign, token; akin to Skt *dhyayati* he thinks] – **semantically** *adv*

**semantics** /sə'mantiks/ *n pl* **1** *taking sing vb* **1a** the branch of linguistics concerned with meaning **b(1)** SEMIOTICS (philosophical theory of signs and symbols) **b(2)** a branch of SEMIOTICS dealing with the relation between signs and the objects they refer to **2** *taking sing or pl vb* **2a** (the interpretation of) the meaning of a word, phrase, etc ⟨*there are real differences between the two things - it's not just a matter of* ~⟩ **b** the exploitation of implied and ambiguous meanings (e g in propaganda) – **semanticist** *n*

¹**semaphore** /'semə,faw/ *n* **1** an apparatus for conveying information by visual signals (e g by the position of one or more pivoted arms) **2** a system of visual signalling by two flags held one in each hand [Gk *sēma* sign, signal + ISV *-phore*]

²**semaphore** *vt* to convey (information) (as if) by semaphore ~ *vi* to send signals (as if) by semaphore

**semasiology** /si,maysi'oləji/ *n* SEMANTICS 1 [Ger *semasiologie*, fr Gk *sēmasia* meaning, fr *sēmainein* to mean] – **semasiologist** *n,* **semasiological** *adj*

**sematic** /si'matik/ *adj, of the conspicuous coloration of a*

poisonous or distasteful *animal* warning of danger and hence protective ⟨*the* ~ *coloration of the wasp*⟩ [Gk *sēmat-, sēma* sign]

**semblable** /'sembləbl/ *adj, archaic* **1** similar **2** apparent, seeming [ME, fr MF, fr OF, fr *sembler* to be like, seem] – **semblably** *adv*

**semblance** /'semblən s/ *n* **1** an outward and often deceptive appearance *of* ⟨*wrapped in a* ~ *of euphoria*⟩ **2** the slightest trace *of* ⟨*didn't have a* ~ *of a chance*⟩ [ME, fr MF, fr OF *sembler* to be like, seem – more at RESEMBLE]

**semé** /'semay/ *adj* covered or sprinkled with many small heraldic designs (e g flowers or stars) [MF, pp of *semer* to sow, fr L *seminare*, fr *semen*] – **semé** *n*

**semeiology** /,semi'oləji, ,seemi-/ *n* SEMIOLOGY (study of signs)

**sememe** /'semeem/ *n* a minimal language element expressing a single idea – called also SEMANTEME [*semantic* + *-eme*]

**semen** /'seemən/ *n* a liquid product of the male reproductive tract that consists of sperms suspended in secretions of accessory glands, is conveyed to the female reproductive tract during sexual intercourse, and is thick, sticky, and whitish in man [NL, fr L, seed; akin to OHG *sāmo* seed, L *serere* to sow – more at SOW]

**semester** /si'mestə/ *n* either of the two terms into which an academic year is divided, esp in America and Germany [Ger, fr L *semestris* half-yearly, fr *sex* six + *mensis* month – more at SIX, MOON] – **semestral, semestrial** *adj*

¹**semi** /'semi/ *n, pl* **semis** *Br informal* a semidetached house

²**semi** *n,* **semis** *n pl, informal* a semifinal match or round

**semi-** /semi-/ *prefix* **1a** precisely half of: **1a(1)** forming a bisection of ⟨*semiellipse*⟩ ⟨*semioval*⟩ **a(2)** being a usu vertically bisected form of (a specified architectural feature) ⟨*semiarch*⟩ ⟨*semidome*⟩ **b(1)** occurring halfway through (a specified period of time) ⟨*semiannual*⟩ ⟨*semicentenary*⟩ – compare BI- **b(2)** on one half or side only ⟨*semidetached*⟩ **2** to some extent; partly, incompletely ⟨*semicivilized*⟩ ⟨*semi-independent*⟩ ⟨*semidry*⟩ – compare DEMI-, HEMI- **3a** partial, incomplete ⟨*semiconsciousness*⟩ ⟨*semidarkness*⟩ **b** having some of the characteristics of ⟨*semiporcelain*⟩ ⟨*semimetal*⟩ **c** quasi ⟨*semigovernmental*⟩ ⟨*semimonastic*⟩ [ME, fr L; akin to OHG *sāmi-* half, Gk *hēmi-*]

**semiabstract** /,semi'abstrakt/ *adj* having subject matter that is easily recognizable although the form is stylized ⟨~ *art*⟩ – **semiabstraction** *n*

**semiannual** /-'anyoo(ə)l/ *adj* **1** occurring every six months or twice a year – compare BIANNUAL **2** lasting for half a year – **semiannually** *adv*

**semiaquatic** /,semiə'kwotik, -'kwat-/ *adj* growing equally well in water or near to water; *also* frequenting but not living wholly in water

**semiarid** /,semi'arid/ *adj* characterized by light rainfall; *specif* having from about 25 to about 50 millimetres (10 to 20 inches) of annual precipitation – **semiaridity** *n*

**semiautomatic** /-awtə'matik/ *adj* not fully automatic: e g **a** operated partly automatically and partly by hand **b** *of a firearm* using gas pressure or force of recoil and mechanical spring action to eject the empty cartridge case after the first shot and load the next cartridge from the magazine, but requiring release and another press of the trigger for each successive shot – **semiautomatic** *n,* **semiautomatically** *adv*

**semiautonomous** /,semi·aw'tonəməs/ *adj* largely self-governing within a larger political or organizational entity

**semibreve** /-,breev/ *n* a musical note with the time value of two MINIMS or four CROTCHETS

**semibreve rest** *n* a musical REST (indicating silence) of the same time value as a semibreve

**semicentenary** /-sen'teenəri, -'tenəri/ *n* a 50th anniversary or its celebration – **semicentenary** *adj*

**semicentennial** /-sen'teni·əl/ *n or adj, chiefly NAm* (a) semicentenary

**semicircle** /-,suhkl/ *n* **1** a half of a circle **2** an object or arrangement in the form of a half circle [L *semicirculus*, fr *semi-* + *circulus* circle] – **semicircular** *adj*

**semicircular canal** /,semi'suhkyoolə/ *n* any of the loop-shaped tubular parts of the INNER EAR that together constitute a SENSE ORGAN concerned with maintaining balance

**semicivilized** /,semi'siviliezd/ *adj* partly civilized

**semiclassical** /-'klasikl/ *adj* having some of the characteristics of the classical; *specif* of or being music considered intermediate between classical and popular

**semicolon** /-'kohlon/ *n* a punctuation mark ; used chiefly in a coordinating function between major sentence elements (e g between independent clauses of a compound sentence)

**semicolonial** /ˌsemikə'lohniəl/ *adj* **1** nominally independent but actually under foreign domination **2** dependent on foreign nations as suppliers of manufactured goods and as purchasers of raw materials – **semicolonialism** *n*

**semiconducting** /-kən'dukting/ *adj* (having the characteristics) of a semiconductor

**semiconductor** /-kən'duktə/ *n* a substance (eg silicon) whose electrical conductivity at room temperature is between that of a conductor and that of an insulator, and whose conductivity increases with a rise in temperature or the presence of certain impurities. Semiconductors are used extensively in transistors and many other electronic devices.

**semiconscious** /-'konshəs/ *adj* incompletely conscious; not fully aware or responsive – **semiconsciously** *adv*, **semiconsciousness** *n*

**semiconservative** /ˌsemikən'suhvətiv/ *adj* of or being RE-PLICATION (production of an exact copy) (eg of DNA) in which the original separates into parts, each of which is incorporated into a new whole and serves as a TEMPLATE (pattern for replication) for the formation of the missing parts – **semiconservatively** *adv*

**semicrystalline** /ˌsemi'kristəlien/ *adj* incompletely or imperfectly crystalline

**semicylindrical** /-si'lindrikl/ *adj* having the shape of a longitudinal half of a cylinder

**semidarkness** /-'dahknis/ *n* partial darkness; shade

**semideponent** /ˌsemidi'pohnənt/ *adj*, *of a verb* DEPONENT (passive in form but active in meaning) in perfect tenses only

**semidesert** /'semiˌdezət/ *n* an area that has some of the characteristics of a desert and is often located between a desert and grassland or woodland

**semidetached** /-di'tacht/ *adj* forming one of a pair of houses joined into one building by a common wall – **semidetached** *n*

**semidiameter** /-die'amitə/ *n* a radius; *specif* the apparent radius of a more or less spherical celestial body

**semidiurnal** /-die'uhnl/ *adj* **1** of, lasting, or accomplished in half a day **2** occurring twice a day **3** occurring approximately every twelve hours ⟨*the ~ tides*⟩

**semidivine** /ˌsemidi'vien/ *adj* more than mortal but not fully divine

**semidocumentary** /-dokyoo'ment(ə)ri/ *n* a film or television programme that incorporates factual material in presenting a fictional story – **semidocumentary** *adj*

**semidome** /'semiˌdohm/ *n* a half dome covering a semicircular structure or recess – **semidomed** *adj*

**semidomesticated** /ˌsemidə'mestikaytid/, **semidomestic** *adj* of or living in semidomestication

**semidomestication** /ˌsemidəˌmesti'kaysh(ə)n/ *n* a captive state (eg in a zoo) of a wild animal in which its living conditions, and often its breeding, are controlled by man

**semidominant** /ˌsemi'dominənt/ *adj* producing an intermediate PHENOTYPE (visible characteristics of an organism) in the HETEROZYGOUS (having two different versions of a gene coding for one inherited characteristic) condition ⟨*a ~ mutant gene*⟩

**semidouble** /ˌsemi'dubl/ *adj*, *of a plant flower* having more than the normal number of petals or RAY FLOWERS (strap-shaped flowers arranged round the edge) though retaining some pollen-bearing STAMENS (male reproductive organs) or some hermaphrodite DISC FLOWERS (small flowers arranged in a central circle) ⟨*a ~ daisy*⟩

**semidrying** /-'drie·ing/ *adj*, *of an oil* that dries imperfectly or slowly ⟨*cottonseed oil is ~*⟩

**semierect** /ˌsemi·i'rekt/ *adj* **1** incompletely upright in bodily posture ⟨*~ primates*⟩ **2** erect for half the length ⟨*~ stems*⟩

**¹semifinal** /-'fienl/ *adj* **1** next to the last in a knockout competition **2** of, participating in, or being a semifinal or semifinals

**²semifinal** /ˌ--'--, '--,--/ *n* **1** a match whose winner goes through to the final of a knockout tournament **2** *pl* a semifinal round – **semifinalist** *n*

**semifinished** /ˌsemi'finisht/ *adj* partially finished or processed; *esp*, *of steel* rolled from raw ingots into shapes (eg bars or plates) suitable for further processing

**semifitted** /-'fitid/ *adj*, *of clothes, esp a dress* not too closely shaped to the lines of the body

**semiflexible** /ˌsemi'fleksəbl/ *adj* **1** moderately but not fully flexible **2** *of a book cover* consisting of a heavy flexible board under the covering material

**semifluid** /-'flooh·id/ *adj* having the qualities of both a liquid and a solid; VISCOUS (thick and slow-flowing) ⟨*fluid and ~ lubricants*⟩ – **semifluid** *n*

**semiformal** /-'fawml/ *adj* being or suitable for an occasion of moderate formality ⟨*a ~ dinner*⟩ ⟨*~ gowns*⟩

**semifossil** /ˌsemi'fosl/ *adj* incompletely fossilized

**semigovernmental** /ˌsemiguvən'mentl, -guvə'mentl *the last pron is disliked by some speakers/ adj* having some governmental functions and powers

**ˌsemi-inde'pendent** *adj* partially independent; *specif* SEMI-AUTONOMOUS

**ˌsemi-indi'rect** *adj*, *of lighting* using a translucent reflector that transmits some primary light while reflecting most of it

**semilethal** /ˌsemi'leethəl/ *n* a mutation that in the HOMO-ZYGOUS (having identical versions of a gene coding for one inherited characteristic) condition produces more than 50 per cent mortality, but not complete mortality – **semilethal** *adj*

**semiliquid** /-'likwid/ *adj* semifluid – **semiliquid** *n*

**semiliterate** /ˌsemi'lit(ə)rət/ *adj* **1a** able to read and write on an elementary level **b** able to read, but unable to write **2** having limited knowledge or understanding

**semilunar** /-'loohnə/ *adj*, *anatomy* shaped like a crescent [NL *semilunaris*, fr L *semi-* + *lunaris* lunar]

**semilunar valve** *n* any of the crescent-shaped pocketlike flaps that occur in two sets of three to form the aortic valve or the pulmonary valve that prevent blood flowing backwards into the heart

**semilustrous** /ˌsemi'lustrəs/ *adj* slightly lustrous

**semimanufactures** /'semimanyooˌfakchəz/ *n pl* products (eg steel or newsprint) that are made from raw materials and that require further processing to become finished goods

**ˌsemi-'matt** *adj* having a slight lustre

**semimetal** /-'metl/ *n* a chemical element (eg arsenic) possessing some metallic properties but not capable of being shaped by pressure; METALLOID **2** – **semimetallic** *adj*

**semimicro** /ˌsemi'miekroh/ *adj* of or dealing with quantities intermediate between those treated as micro and macro ⟨*~ analysis for chlorine*⟩ ⟨*a ~ balance*⟩

**semimonastic** /ˌsemimə'nastik/ *adj* having some features characteristic of a monastic order

**semimonthly** /-'munthli/ *adj or adv* occurring twice a month – compare BIMONTHLY

**seminal** /'seminl/ *adj* **1** (consisting) of, storing, or conveying seed or semen **2** containing or contributing the seeds of future development; creative ⟨*a ~ book*⟩ ⟨*one of the most ~ of the great poets*⟩ [ME, fr MF, fr L *seminalis*, fr *semin-*, *semen* seed – more at SEMEN] – **seminally** *adv*

**seminal duct** *n* a tube or passage that serves, either mainly or exclusively, as a duct to carry sperm from the TESTIS (male SEX GLAND) and in man is made up of the small tubes of the EPIDIDYMIS, the VAS DEFERENS, and the EJACULATORY DUCT

**seminal fluid** *n* **1** semen **2** the part of the semen that is produced by various accessory glands; semen excepting the sperm

**seminal vesicle** *n* a pouch on either side of the male reproductive tract that is variously formed in different mammals, is connected with the SEMINAL DUCT, and serves for temporary storage of semen

**seminar** /'semiˌnah/ *n* **1** a group of students studying and doing research under a university teacher and meeting to exchange results **2a** an advanced or graduate class often featuring informality and discussion **b** a scheduled meeting of a seminar; *also* a room for such meetings **3** a meeting for exchanging and discussing information [Ger, fr L *seminarium* seminary]

**seminarian** /ˌsemi'neəri·ən/, **seminarist** /'seminərist/ *n* a student in a seminary, esp of the Roman Catholic church

**seminary** /'semin(ə)ri/ *n* **1a** an institution of secondary or higher education; *esp* an academy for young ladies in former times **b** an institution for the training of candidates for the priesthood, esp in the Roman Catholic church **2** *archaic* a place in which something originates and develops [ME, seedbed, nursery, seminary, fr L *seminarium*, fr *semin-*, *semen* seed]

**seminiferous** /ˌsemi'nif(ə)rəs, ˌsee-/ *adj* producing or bearing seed or semen [L *semin-*, *semen* seed + E *-iferous*]

**seminiferous tubule** *n* any of the coiled threadlike small tubes that make up the bulk of the TESTIS (male SEX GLAND) and have a lining from which the sperm are produced

**Seminole** /'seminohl/ *n*, *pl* **Seminoles**, *esp collectively* **Seminole** a member of an American Indian people of Florida [Creek *simaló-ni*, *simanó-li*, lit., wild, fr AmerSp *cimarrón* (cf MAROON)]

**seminomad** /ˌsemi'nohmad/ *n* a member of a people living usu in portable or temporary dwellings and practising seasonal migration, but having a base camp at which some crops are cultivated – **seminomadic** adj

**seminude** /,semi'noohd, -'nyoohd/ adj half naked – **seminudity** n

**semiofficial** /-ə'fish(ə)l/ adj having some official authority or standing ⟨a ~ statement⟩ – **semiofficially** adv

**semiology, semeiology** /,semi'oləji, ,seemi-/ n 1 the study of signs; esp semiotics 2 wordless language ⟨the ~ of music⟩ [Gk sēmeion sign] – **semiologist** n, **semiological** adj

**semiopaque** /,semioh'payk/ adj nearly opaque

**semiotics** /,semi'otiks, ,see-/ n taking sing vb a general philosophical theory of signs and symbols that deals esp with their function in both artificially constructed and natural languages and comprises the study of their formal or grammatical relationships (SYNTACTICS), their meaning (SEMANTICS), and their relationship (PRAGMATICS) to their users [Gk sēmeiōtikos observant of signs, fr sēmeiousthai to interpret signs, fr sēmeion sign; akin to Gk sēma sign – more at SEMANTIC] – **semiotic** also **semiotical** adj, **semiotician** n

**semipalmated** /,semipal'maytid/ adj, of a bird's foot having the front toes joined only part way down with a web ⟨the ~ feet of the plover⟩

**semiparasitic** /,semiparə'sitik/ adj of or being a parasitic organism: **a** that is not dependent on its HOST (organism harbouring a parasite) for all its nutriments **b** that has some freeliving stages in its LIFE CYCLE

**semipermanent** /-'puhmənənt/ adj 1 lasting or intended to last for a long time but not permanent 2 having the characteristics of something permanent but subject to change or review ⟨a ~ agreement⟩ – **semipermanently** adv

**semipermeable** /-'puhmi·əbl/ adj partially but not freely or wholly permeable; specif permeable to some usu small molecules but not to other usu larger particles ⟨a ~ membrane⟩ – **semipermeability** n

**semiplastic** /-'plastik; also -'plah-/ adj not fully plastic

**semipolitical** /,semipə'litikl/ adj of or involving some political features or activity

**semipostal** /'semi,pohstl/ n, chiefly NAm a postage stamp sold at a premium over its postal value, esp so that the additional proceeds can go to charity

**semiprecious** /-'preshəs/ adj, of a gemstone of less commercial value than a precious stone

**semipro** /-'proh/ adj or n, pl **semipros** informal (a) semiprofessional

**¹semiprofessional** /-prə'fesh(ə)nl/ adj 1 engaging in an activity for pay or gain but not as a full-time occupation ⟨a ~ dance band⟩ 2 engaged in by semiprofessional players – **semiprofessionally** adv

**²semiprofessional** n somebody who engages in an activity (eg a sport) semiprofessionally

**semipublic** /,semi'publik/ adj 1 having some features of a public institution; specif maintained as a public service by a private non-profitmaking organization 2 partly but not entirely public

**semiquantitative** /,semi'kwontitətiv, -taytiv/ adj constituting or involving less than quantitative precision – **semiquantitatively** adv

**semiquaver** /-,kwayvə/ n a musical note with the time value of half a quaver

**semiquaver rest** n a musical REST (indicating silence) of the same time value as a semiquaver

**semiretired** /,semiri'tie·əd/ adj working only part-time, esp because of age or ill health – **semiretirement** n

**semirigid** /-'rijid/ adj 1 rigid to some degree or in some parts 2 of an airship having a flexible cylindrical gas container with a stiffening structure (KEEL) attached underneath to carry the load

**semisedentary** /,semi'sedənt(ə)ri/ adj staying in one place during part of the year and nomadic otherwise ⟨~ tribes⟩

**semiskilled** /-'skild/ adj of, being, or requiring workers who have less training than skilled workers but more than unskilled workers

**semisoft** /-'soft/ adj moderately soft; specif firm but easily cut ⟨~ cheese⟩

**semisolid** /-'solid/ adj having the qualities of both a solid and a liquid; highly VISCOUS (thick and slow-flowing) – **semisolid** n

**semisweet** /,semi'sweet/ adj slightly sweetened ⟨~ chocolate⟩

**semisynthetic** /-sin'thetik/ adj 1 produced by chemical

alteration of a starting material that is natural ⟨~ penicillins⟩ 2 containing both chemically identified and complex natural ingredients

**Semite** /'seemiet/ n a member of any of a group of peoples of SW Asia, chiefly represented now by the Jews and Arabs, but in ancient times also by the BABYLONIANS, ASSYRIANS, ARAMAEANS, CANAANITES, and PHOENICIANS [Fr sémite, fr Sem Shem, eldest son of Noah, fr LL, fr Gk Sēm, fr Heb Shēm]

**semiterrestrial** /,semitə'restriəl/ adj 1 growing on boggy ground 2 frequenting but not living wholly on land

**¹Semitic** /si'mitik/ adj 1 (characteristic) of the Semites; specif Jewish 2 of a branch of the AFRO-ASIATIC language family that includes Hebrew, Aramaic, Arabic, and Ethiopic

**²Semitic** n any or all of the Semitic languages

**Semitics** /si'mitiks/ n taking sing vb the study of the language, literature, and history of Semitic peoples

**Semitism** /'semi,tiz(ə)m/ n 1 a characteristic feature of a Semitic language occurring in another language 2 policy favourable to Jews; predisposition in favour of Jews

**Semitist** /'semitist/, **Semiticist** /si'mitisist/ n a scholar of the Semitic languages, cultures, or histories

**semitone** /-,tohn/ n the smallest interval between two notes in common use in European classical music; the interval (eg E-F or B-C) between two adjacent keys on a keyboard instrument – **semitonal, semitonic** adj, **semitonally, semitonically** adv

**semitrailer** /-,traylə/ n 1 a trailer having rear wheels but supported by a towing tractor at the front 2 NAm & Austr an articulated lorry

**semitranslucent** /,semitrans'loohs(ə)nt, -trahns-/ adj partially translucent

**semitransparent** /,semitrans'parənt, -trahns-/ adj partially transparent

**semitropical** /-'tropikl/ also **semitropic** adj SUBTROPICAL (bordering the tropics)

**semivowel** /-,vowl/ n (a letter or other symbol representing) a speech sound (eg /y/ or /w/) intermediate between a vowel and a consonant

**semiweekly** /-'weekli/ adj or adv appearing or taking place twice a week – compare BIWEEKLY

**semiyearly** /,semi'yiəli, -'yuhli/ adj occurring twice a year; biannual

**semolina** /,semə'leenə/ n the purified hard parts of wheat grains, esp from HARD WHEAT (eg DURUM wheat), left after the grinding of flour, and used for pasta and in milk puddings [It semolino, dim. of semola bran, fr L simila fine wheat flour (cf SIMNEL CAKE)]

**sempervivum** /,sempə'veevəm, -'vievəm/ n any of a large genus (Sempervivum of the Orpine family) of African and Eurasian fleshy plants often grown in rock gardens [NL, fr L, neut of sempervivus ever-living, fr semper ever + vivus living – more at QUICK]

**sempiternal** /,sempi'tuhnl/ adj, chiefly poetic everlasting, eternal [ME, fr LL sempiternalis, fr L sempiternus, fr semper ever, always, fr sem- one, same (akin to ON samr same) + per through – more at SAME, FOR] – **sempiternity** n, **sempiternally** adv

**semplice** /'semplichi/ adj or adv in a simple unaffected manner – used as a direction in music [It, fr L simplic-, simplex – more at SIMPLE]

**sempre** /'sempri/ also **'sempray/** adv always – used in musical directions ⟨~ legato⟩ [It, fr L semper]

**sempstress** /'sem(p)stris/ n a seamstress [fem of sempster, var of seamster]

**¹sen** /sen/ n, pl **sen** – see yen at MONEY table [Jap]

**²sen** n, pl **sen** – see rupiah at MONEY table [Indonesian sén, prob fr E cent]

**³sen** n, pl **sen** – see dollar, riel at MONEY table [prob fr Indonesian sén]

**⁴sen** n, pl **sen** – see ringgit at MONEY table [Malay, prob fr E cent]

**senary** /'seen(ə)ri/ adj of, based on, or characterized by six; compounded of six things or six parts ⟨~ scale⟩ ⟨~ division⟩ [L senarius consisting of six, fr seni six each, fr sex six]

**senate** /'senit/ n 1 taking sing or pl vb an assembly or council usu possessing high deliberative and law-making functions: eg **1a** the supreme council of the ancient Roman republic and empire **b** the second and higher chamber in the two-chamber law-making bodies of some nations (eg the USA and Australia), states, or provinces 2 the hall or chamber in which a senate meets 3 taking sing or pl vb the governing body of some universities that is responsible for maintaining academic standards and regulations and is usu composed of the principal or representative members of the teaching staff, and sometimes also such members of the student body – compare COUNCIL 5 [ME *senat*, fr OF, fr L *senatus*, lit., council of elders, fr *sen-*, *senex* old, old man – more at SENIOR]

**senator** /'senətə/ *n* a member of a senate [ME *senatour*, fr OF *senateur*, fr L *senator*, fr *senatus*]

**senatorial** /ˌsenə'tawriəl/ *adj* of or befitting a senator or senate ⟨~ *office*⟩ ⟨~ *rank*⟩

**senatorial district** *n* a territorial division from which a senator is elected – compare CONGRESSIONAL DISTRICT

**senatorian** /ˌsenə'tawriən/ *adj* senatorial; *specif* of the ancient Roman senate

**senatorship** /'senətəship/ *n* the office or position of senator

**senatus** /sə'naytəs/ *n, pl* **senatus** a Scottish university senate [L, senate]

**senatus consultum** /siˌnahtəs kon'sooltəm/ *n, pl* **senatus consulta** /~ kon'sooltə/ a decree of the ancient Roman senate [L, decree of the senate]

¹**send** /send/ *vb* **sent** /sent/ *vt* **1** to cause to go: eg **1a** to drive or throw in a specified direction ⟨sent *the ball between the goalposts*⟩ **b** to deliver ⟨sent *a blow to his chin*⟩ **c** to propel violently ⟨sent *him sprawling*⟩ **d** to incite or compel to go ⟨*the crash* sent *them scuttling out of their houses*⟩ **2** of *God, fate, etc* to cause to happen or be ⟨~ *her victorious*⟩ **3** to dispatch to (someone) by a means of communication ⟨~ *her a telegram*⟩ **4a** to direct, order, or request to go ⟨~ *a gunboat*⟩ **b** to permit or enable to attend a specified course of study ⟨~ *a child to college*⟩ **c** to direct by advice or reference ⟨~ *him to the dictionary*⟩ **d** to cause or order to depart; dismiss **5** to cause to assume a specified state ⟨sent *him into a rage*⟩ **6** to cause to issue: eg **6a** to pour out; discharge ⟨clouds ~ing *forth rain*⟩ **b** to utter ⟨~ *forth a cry*⟩ **c** to emit ⟨sent *out waves of perfume*⟩ **d** to grow out (parts) in the course of development ⟨*a plant* ~ing *forth shoots*⟩ **7** to consign to a destination (eg death or a place of imprisonment) **8** to cause to be transmitted by an agent ⟨~ *flowers by telephone*⟩ **9** *informal* to delight, thrill ⟨*that music really* ~s *me*⟩ – no longer in vogue ~ *vi* **1a** to dispatch someone to convey a message or do an errand ⟨~ *out for coffee*⟩ **b** to dispatch a request or order ⟨*have to* ~ *to Germany for spares*⟩ **2** SCEND (rise up on a wave) **3** to transmit [ME *senden*, fr OE *sendan*; akin to OHG *sendan* to send, OE *sith* road, journey, OIr *sēt*] – **sender** *n* – **send packing** to dismiss roughly or in disgrace – see also SEND TO COVENTRY

**send down** *vt, Br* **1** to dismiss (a student) from a university for bad behaviour **2** *informal* to send (a criminal) to prison

**send for** *vt* to request by message to come; summon

**send in** *vt* **1** to cause to be delivered to an authority, group, or organization ⟨send in *a letter of complaint*⟩ **2** to assign with a view to tackling a crisis or difficulty ⟨send in *a receiver to deal with the bankruptcy*⟩

**send off** *vt* **1** to dispatch **2** to attend to the departure of – compare SEE OFF **3** *of a referee* to order (a player) to leave the playing area

**send on** *vt* **1** to dispatch (eg luggage) in advance **2** to forward (readdressed letters)

**send out** *vt* **1** to issue for circulation ⟨*had sent the invitation* out⟩ **2** to dispatch (eg an order) from a shop or place of storage

**send round** *vt* to circulate ⟨*a notice is being* sent *round*⟩

**send up** *vt* **1** *chiefly Br* to imitate or copy the style of for comic effect or to mock ⟨*observes life with some care before sending it* up – *TLS*⟩ **2** *chiefly NAm* SEND DOWN 2

²**send** *n* SCEND (lifting motion of wave)

**sendings** /'sendingz/ *n pl* things sent by post

'**send-ˌoff** *n* a usu enthusiastic demonstration of goodwill at the beginning of a venture (eg a trip)

'**send-ˌup** *n, chiefly Br* a satirical imitation, esp on stage or television; a parody

**sene** /'saynay/ *n* – see *tala* at MONEY table [Samoan, fr E *cent*]

**seneca** /'senikə/ *n* senega

**Seneca** /'senikə/ *n, pl* **Senecas**, *esp collectively* **Seneca** **1** a member of an American Indian people of western New York **2** the IROQUOIAN language of the Seneca people [D *Sennecaas*, pl, the Seneca, Oneida, Onondaga, and Cayuga people collectively, fr Mahican *A'sinnika* Oneida]

**senecio** /sə'nekioh, sə'neeshioh/ *n, pl* **senecios** any of a genus (*Senecio*) of widely distributed yellow-flowered plants of the daisy family including many common weeds (eg groundsel or

ragwort) [NL, genus name, fr L, old man, groundsel (fr its hoary pappus), fr *sen-*, *senic-*, *senex* old man]

**senectitude** /si'nekti,tyoohd/ *n, formal or humorous* old age [ML *senectitudo*, alter. of L *senectus* old age, fr *sen-*, *senic-*, *senex* old, old man – more at SENIOR]

**senega** /'senigə/ *n* the dried root of a N American MILKWORT (type of plant) (*Polygala senega*); *also* any of several extracts of senega used as an EXPECTORANT (medicine taken to clear congestion) [alter. of *Seneca*; fr its use by the Seneca as a remedy for snakebite]

**senesce** /si'nes/ *vi* to grow old; wither [L *senescere*, fr *sen-*, *senex* old]

**senescence** /si'nes(ə)ns/ *n* **1** the phase of plant growth from full maturity to death that is characterized by an accumulation of products of METABOLISM (life-supporting chemical processes), increase in respiratory rate, and a loss in dry weight in esp leaves and fruit **2** *formal* being or becoming old [*senescent* fr L *senescent-*, *senescens*, prp of *senescere*] – **senescent** *adj*

**seneschal** /'senish(ə)l/ *n* an agent or bailiff in charge of a lord's estate in medieval times [ME, fr MF, of Gmc origin; akin to Goth *sineigs* old, & to OHG *scalc* servant – more at SENIOR]

**sengi** /'seng·gi/ *n, pl* **sengi** – see *zaire* at MONEY table [native name in Zaire]

**senhor** /se'nyaw/ *n, pl* **senhors, senhores** /-rees, -reez/ **1** a Portuguese-speaking man **2** *often cap* – used as a title equivalent to *Mr* before the name of a Portuguese-speaking man or used without a name as a generalized term of direct address [Pg, fr ML *senior* superior, lord, fr L, adj, elder]

**senhora** /se'nyawrə/ *n* **1** a married Portuguese-speaking woman **2** *often cap* – used as a title equivalent to *Mrs* before the name of a married Portuguese-speaking woman (or, occasionally, an unmarried older woman) or used without a name as a generalized term of direct address [Pg, fem of *senhor*]

**senhorita** /ˌsenyə'reetə/ *n* **1** an unmarried Portuguese-speaking girl or woman **2** *often cap* – used of or to an unmarried Portuguese-speaking girl or woman as a title equivalent to *Miss* [Pg, fr dim. of *senhora*]

**senile** /'seeniel/ *adj* **1** (characteristic) of or showing old age ⟨~ *weakness*⟩; *esp* showing a loss of mental faculties associated with old age **2** approaching the end of a geological cycle of erosion [L *senilis*, fr *sen-*, *senex* old, old man] – **senilely** *adv*

**senility** /si'niləti/ *n* being senile; *specif* the physical and mental infirmity of old age

¹**senior** /'seenyə, 'seeni-ə/ *n* **1** a person who is older than another specified person ⟨*five years his* ~⟩ **2a** a person of higher standing or rank **b** *NAm* a student in the final year preceding graduation from a school of secondary or higher level [ME, fr L, fr *senior*, adj]

²**senior** *adj* **1** higher in standing or rank ⟨~ *officers*⟩ **2** *chiefly NAm* elder – used to distinguish a father with the same name as his son **3** *NAm* of seniors [ME, fr L, older, elder, compar of *sen-*, *senex* old; akin to Goth *sineigs* old, Gk *henos*]

**senior aircraftman** *n* – see MILITARY RANKS table

**senior chief petty officer** *n* – see MILITARY RANKS table

**senior citizen** *n, euph* a person beyond the usual age of retirement – used mainly in official documents ⟨*if you have a senior citizen's railcard, you get cheaper fares*⟩

**Senior Common Room** *n* **1** a common room for teachers, lecturers, etc **2** *taking sing or pl vb* the staff community in a college

**senior house officer** *n* the grade of British hospital doctor senior to HOUSEMAN that is held by a doctor in training; *also* a doctor holding this post

**seniority** /ˌseeni'orəti/ *n* **1** being senior **2** a privileged status attained by length of continuous service (eg in a company)

**senior master sergeant** *n* – see MILITARY RANKS table

**senior nursing officer** *n* one who is in charge of the nursing staff in a British hospital

**senior registrar** *n* the grade of British hospital doctor senior to REGISTRAR; *also* a doctor holding this post

**senior wrangler** *n* the winner of the highest mark in the examinations for a Cambridge mathematics degree

**seniti** /'seniti/ *n, pl* **seniti** /~/ – see *pa'anga* at MONEY table [Tongan, modif of E *cent*]

**senna** /'senə/ *n* **1** any of a genus (*Cassia*) of plants, shrubs, and trees of the pea family that are native to warm regions **2** the dried leaflets or pods of various sennas (esp *Cassia acutifolia* and *Cassia angustifolia*) used as a laxative [NL, fr Ar *sanā*]

**sennet** /'senit/ *n* a signal call on a trumpet or cornet for entrance or exit on the stage [prob alter. of *signet* (in obs sense, "signal")]

**sennight** *also* **se'nnight** /'seniet/ *n, archaic* a week [ME, fr OE *seofon nihta* seven nights]

**sennit** /'senit/ *n* **1** a braided cord or fabric (e g of plaited rope yarns) **2** a straw or grass braid for hats [perh fr Fr *coussinet*, dim. of *coussin* cushion; fr its use to protect cables from fraying]

**senor, señor** /se'nyaw/ *n, pl* **senors, señores** /-rays/ **1** a Spanish-speaking man **2** *often cap* – used as a title equivalent to *Mr* before the name of a Spanish-speaking man or used without a name as a generalized term of direct address [Sp *señor*, fr ML *senior* superior, lord, fr L, adj, elder]

**senora, señora** /se'nyawra/ *n* **1** a married Spanish-speaking woman **2** *often cap* – used as a title equivalent to *Mrs* before the name of a married Spanish-speaking woman (or, occasionally, an unmarried older woman) or used without a name as a generalized term of direct address [Sp *señora*, fem of *señor*]

**senorita, señorita** /,senyə'reetə/ *n* **1** an unmarried Spanish-speaking girl or woman **2** *often cap* – used of or to an unmarried Spanish-speaking girl or woman as a title equivalent to *Miss* [Sp *señorita*, fr dim. of *señora*]

¹**sensate** /'sensayt/ *adj* endowed with bodily senses ⟨*a ~ being*⟩ [LL *sensatus*, fr L *sensus* sense]

²**sensate** *adj* of or apprehended through the senses [ML *sensatus*, fr LL, endowed with sense] – **sensately** *adv*

**sensation** /sen'saysh(ə)n/ *n* **1a** a mental process (e g seeing, hearing, or smelling) resulting from stimulation of a SENSE ORGAN, often as distinguished from awareness of the process – compare PERCEPTION **b** a state of awareness of a usu specified kind resulting from internal bodily conditions or external factors; a feeling, sense ⟨*~s of fatigue and elation*⟩ **2a** a surge of intense interest or excitement ⟨*their elopement caused a ~*⟩ **b** a cause of excitement ⟨*the fire was the ~ of the season*⟩; *esp* one (e g a person) in some respect remarkable or outstanding [ML *sensation-, sensatio*, fr LL *sensatus* endowed with sense]

**sensational** /sen'saysh(ə)nl/ *adj* **1** of or concerned with sensation or the senses **2** arousing or tending to arouse (e g by lurid details) an immediate, intense, and usu superficial interest or emotional reaction **3** *informal* exceptionally or unexpectedly excellent or impressive ⟨*you look ~*⟩ – **sensationally** *adv*

**sensationalism** /sen'sayshənəliz(ə)m/ *n* **1** the use of sensational subject matter or style **2** a theory that limits experience as a source of knowledge to sensation or sense perceptions – **sensationalist** *n*, **sensationalistic** *adj*

¹**sense** /sens/ *n* **1** a meaning conveyed or intended; an import, signification; *esp* any of a range of meanings a word or phrase may bear, esp as isolated in a dictionary entry **2a** the faculty of perceiving the external world or internal bodily conditions by means of SENSE ORGANS – compare FEELING, HEARING, SIGHT, SMELL, TASTE, KINAESTHESIA **b** a specialized animal function or mechanism (e g sight, hearing, smell, taste, or touch) basically involving a stimulus and a SENSE ORGAN **3** *senses pl,* sense conscious awareness or rationality ⟨*when he came to his ~s he was shocked to hear what he had done*⟩ **4a** a particular ability to use the sense for a specified purpose ⟨*a good ~ of balance*⟩ **b** a definite but often vague awareness or impression ⟨*felt a ~ of insecurity*⟩ ⟨*a ~ of danger*⟩ **c** an awareness that motivates action or judgment ⟨*done out of a ~ of justice*⟩ **d** a capacity for discernment and appreciation ⟨*her ~ of humour*⟩ **5** the prevailing view; *the* consensus ⟨*the ~ of the meeting*⟩ **6a** an ability to put the mind to effective use; intelligence **b** agreement with sound judgment or practical intelligence ⟨*this decision makes ~*⟩ **7** *maths* either of two opposite directions of motion (e g of a point, line, or surface) [MF or L; MF *sens* sensation, feeling, mechanism of perception, meaning, fr L *sensus*, fr *sentire,* pp of *sentire* to perceive, feel; akin to OHG *sin* mind, sense, OE *sith* journey – more at SEND] – **talk sense** to voice rational, logical, or sensible thoughts

²**sense** *vt* **1a** to perceive by the senses **b** to be or become conscious of, esp without knowing how or why ⟨*~ danger*⟩ **2** to detect (e g a punched or printed symbol) automatically ⟨*the card reader ~s holes in punched cards*⟩ **3** *formal* to grasp, comprehend ⟨*~ the import of a remark*⟩

¹**sense-,datum** *n, pl* **sense-data** an immediate unanalysable experience (e g an afterimage) resulting from the stimulation of any of the senses – called also SENSUM

**senseless** /-lis/ *adj* deprived of, deficient in, or contrary to sense: e g **a** unconscious ⟨*knocked ~*⟩ **b** foolish, stupid ⟨*it was some ~ practical joke* – A Conan Doyle⟩ **c** meaningless,

purposeless ⟨*a ~ murder*⟩ – **senselessly** *adv*, **senselessness** *n*

**sense organ** *n* a specialized bodily structure that responds to a stimulus (e g heat or sound waves) by initiating waves of excitation in associated sensory NERVE FIBRES, which convey them to the central NERVOUS SYSTEM, where they are interpreted as corresponding sensations; a receptor

**sensibility** /,sensə'biləti/ *n* **1** ability to have sensations; sensitiveness ⟨*tactile ~*⟩ **2 sensibilities** *pl,* **sensibility** heightened susceptibility to feelings of pleasure or pain (e g in response to praise or blame) ⟨*a man of strong sensibilities*⟩ **3** the ability to discern and respond freely to something (e g emotion in another) **4** refined or exaggerated sensitiveness in feelings and tastes △ **sensibleness**

**sensible** /'sensəbl/ *adj* **1** having, containing, or indicative of good sense or sound reason; reasonable, judicious ⟨*~ men*⟩ ⟨*made a ~ answer*⟩ **2** *formal* capable of being felt or perceived: e g **2a** perceptible to the senses or to reason or understanding ⟨*felt a ~ chill*⟩ ⟨*his distress was ~ from his manner*⟩ **b** large enough to be observed or noticed; considerable ⟨*a ~ decrease*⟩ **c** accessible to sense perception ⟨*the ~ world*⟩ **3** *formal* capable of receiving sensory impressions ⟨*~ to pain*⟩ **4** *formal* **4a** apprehending through the mind or senses; aware, cognizant *of* ⟨*~ of my limitations*⟩ **b** conscious **5** *archaic* sensitive **synonyms** SEE PERCEPTIBLE *antonyms* foolish, absurd, fatuous, silly (for 1), insensible (for 3 & 4) [ME, fr MF, fr L *sensibilis*, fr *sensus*, pp] – **sensibleness** *n*, **sensibly** *adv*

**sensible horizon** *n* HORIZON 1b(1)

**sensillum** /sen'siləm/ *n, pl* **sensilla** /-lə/ a simple SENSE ORGAN, usu in the form of a spine, plate, rod, cone, or peg, that is composed of one or a few cells with a nerve connection [NL, dim. of ML *sensus* sense organ, fr L, sense]

¹**sensitive** /'sensətiv/ *adj* **1** SENSORY **2 2a** receptive to sense impressions **b** capable of being stimulated or activated by external agents (e g light, gravity, or contact) ⟨*a photographic emulsion ~ to red light*⟩ ⟨*~ protoplasm*⟩ **3** highly responsive or susceptible: e g **3a(1)** easily provoked or hurt emotionally **a(2)** finely aware of the attitudes and feelings of others; *also* finely aware of subtleties (e g of a work of art) **b** excessively or abnormally susceptible; hypersensitive ⟨*~ to egg protein*⟩ **c** readily fluctuating in price or demand ⟨*~ commodities*⟩ **d** capable of registering minute differences; delicate ⟨*~ scales*⟩ **e** readily affected or changed by external agents (e g light or chemical stimulation) **f** *of a radio receiving set* highly responsive to incoming waves **4** concerned with highly classified information ⟨*a ~ government document*⟩ **5** needing careful or tactful handling; delicate, tricky ⟨*a ~ issue*⟩ [ME, fr MF *sensitif*, fr ML *sensitivus*, irreg fr L *sensus*] – **sensitively** *adv*, **sensitiveness** *n*

²**sensitive** *n* a person having occult or psychic powers

**sensitive plant** *n* any of several MIMOSAS (esp *Mimosa pudica*) with leaves that fold or droop when touched; *broadly* any of various plants that move when touched

**sensitivity** /,sensə'tivəti/ *n* being sensitive: e g **a** the capacity of an organism or SENSE ORGAN to respond to stimulation; irritability **b** the quality or state of being hypersensitive **c** the degree to which a radio receiving set responds to incoming waves **d** the capacity of being easily hurt **e** acute awareness of **e(1)** the needs and emotions of others **e(2)** subtleties (e g of a work of art)

**sensit·ization, -isation** /,sensətie'zaysh(ə)n/ *n* **1** being sensitized, esp to an ANTIGEN (foreign substance that activates the production of disease-fighting antibodies) (e g penicillin) **2** sensitizing

**sensit·ize, -ise** /'sensətiez/ *vt* to make sensitive or hypersensitive ~ *vi* to become sensitive [*sensitive* + *-ize, -ise*] – **sensitizer** *n*

**sensitometry** /,sensi'tomitri/ *n* the scientific study of light-sensitive materials [ISV *sensitive* + *-o-* + *-metry*] – **sensitometer** *n*, **sensitometric** *adj*

**sensor** /'sensə, -saw/ *n* a device that responds to a physical stimulus (e g heat, light, sound, pressure, magnetism, or a particular motion) and transmits a resulting impulse (e g for measurement or operating a control); *also* SENSE ORGAN [L *sensus*, pp of *sentire* to perceive – more at SENSE]

**sensorimotor** /,sensəri'mohtə/ *adj* of or functioning in both sensory and MOTOR (conveying impulses from the CENTRAL NERVOUS SYSTEM to the muscles) aspects of bodily activity

**sensorineural** /,sensəri'nyooərəl/ *adj* of or involving the aspects of sense perception that involve transmission by nerves ⟨*~ hearing loss*⟩ [*sensory* + *neural*]

**sensorium** /sen'sawri·əm/ *n, pl* **sensoriums, sensoria** /-riə/ the parts of the brain or the mind concerned with the reception and interpretation of sensory stimuli; *broadly* the entire sensory apparatus [LL, sense organ, fr L *sensus* sense]

**sensory** /'sens(ə)ri/, **sensorial** /sen'sawriəl/ *adj* 1 of or concerned with sensation or the senses 2 *of a nerve fibre* conveying NERVE IMPULSES from the SENSE ORGANS to the NERVE CENTRES; AFFERENT – **sensorially** *adv*

**sensual** /'sensyoo·əl, -shoo-/ *adj* 1 sensory ⟨~ *perception*⟩ 2 of or consisting in the gratification of the senses (e g touch) or the indulgence of appetites, esp for sex or food and drink ⟨~ *pleasures*⟩ 3a devoted to or preoccupied with the senses or appetites, esp as opposed to moral, spiritual, or intellectual interests ⟨*the ~ woman*⟩ ⟨*the average ~ man*⟩ b voluptuous ⟨~ *curves of her body*⟩ c SENSUOUS 3 □ compare SENSUOUS [ME, fr LL *sensualis*, fr L *sensus* sense + *-alis* -al] – **sensualism** *n*, **sensualist** *n*, **sensuality** *n*, **sensualize** *vt*, **sensually** *adv*

**sensum** /'sensəm/ *n, pl* **sensa** /-sə/ SENSE-DATUM [ML, fr L, neut of *sensus*, pp of *sentire* to feel – more at SENSE]

**sensuous** /'sensyoo·əs, -shoo-əs/ *adj* 1 providing or characterized by gratification of the senses; appealing strongly to the senses ⟨*dancer's lithe and ~ movements*⟩ ⟨~ *feel of velvet*⟩ 2 suggesting or producing rich imagery or sense impressions ⟨~ *verse*⟩ ⟨*Rimski-Korsakov's ~ music for* Scheherazade⟩ 3 suggesting a temperament marked by strong physical desires ⟨*her full ~ lips*⟩ 4 *formal* of the senses or objects that can be perceived by the senses □ compare SENSUAL [L *sensus* sense + E *-ous*] – **sensuously** *adv*, **sensuousness, sensuosity** *n*

**Sensurround** /'sens(y)ə,rownd/ *trademark* – used for a sound-reproducing system developed for use in films, that employs low frequencies to heighten the spectators' sense of physical involvement with the action depicted on the screen

**sent** /sent/ *past of* SEND

¹**sentence** /'sentəns/ *n* 1a a decision of a court or judge; *specif* one formally pronounced by a court or judge and imposing a period of imprisonment or supervision or a fine b the punishment so imposed ⟨*serve a ~*⟩ 2 a grammatically self-contained speech unit consisting of a word, or a grammatically related group of words, that expresses an assertion, a question, a command, a wish, or an exclamation. It is usu shown in writing with a capital letter at the beginning of the first or only clause, and with appropriate punctuation at the end of the last or only clause. 3 PERIOD 1b (self-contained section of music) 4 PROPOSITION 2 (expression that can be described as true or false) 5 *archaic* a maxim, saying 6 *obs* an opinion; *esp* an authoritative or formal decision [ME, fr OF, fr L *sententia*, lit., feeling, opinion, fr (assumed) *sentent-, sentens*, irreg prp of *sentire* to feel – more at SENSE] – **sentential** *adj*, **sententially** *adv*

²**sentence** *vt* 1 to impose a judicial sentence on 2 to consign to a usu unpleasant fate ⟨*development that ~s rural industries to extinction*⟩

**sentence stress** *n, linguistics* the manner in which stresses are distributed on the syllables of words assembled into sentences

**sententia** /sen'tenshə/ *n usu pl, pl* **sententiae** /-shi·ie/ *formal* APHORISM (concise pithy saying) [L, lit., feeling, opinion – more at SENTENCE]

**sententious** /sen'tenshəs/ *adj* 1 terse, pithy 2 given to or full of 2a terse or pithy sayings b pompous moralizing [ME, fr L *sententiosus*, fr *sententia* sentence, maxim] – **sententiously** *adv*, **sententiousness** *n*

**senti** /'senti/ *n, pl* **senti** /~/ – see *shilingi* at MONEY table [Swahili, modif of E *cent*]

**sentience** /'sensh(ə)ns/ *n, formal* 1 a sentient quality or state 2 rudimentary feeling and perception, as distinguished from thought and the higher emotions

**sentient** /'sensh(ə)nt/ *adj, formal* 1 capable of perceiving through the senses; conscious 2 aware ⟨*he is ~ of the difficulties*⟩ 3 keenly sensitive in perception or feeling [L *sentient-, sentiens*, prp of *sentire* to perceive, feel] – **sentiently** *adv*

**sentiment** /'sentimənt/ *n* 1a an attitude, thought, or judgment prompted or coloured by feeling or emotion b a specific view or attitude; an opinion ⟨*held similar ~s on the matter*⟩ 2a feeling, emotion b sensitive feeling; refined sensibility, esp as expressed in a work of art c indulgently romantic or nostalgic feeling 3 the emotional significance of a communication as distinguished from its overt meaning *synonyms* see OPINION [Fr or ML; Fr, fr ML *sentimentum*, fr L *sentire*]

**sentimental** /,senti'mentl/ *adj* 1a of or characterized by sentiment b resulting from feeling rather than reason ⟨*kept the gift for its ~ value*⟩ 2 having an excess of superficial sentiment – **sentimentally** *adv*

**sentimentalism** /,senti'mentəliz(ə)m/ *n* 1 the tendency to favour or indulge in sentimentality 2 an excessively sentimental idea or its expression – **sentimentalist** *n*

**sentimentality** /,sentimen'taləti/ *n* 1 being sentimental, esp in an affected or indulgent manner 2 sentimentalism

**sentimental·ize, -ise** /,senti'mentəliez/ *vi* to indulge in sentiment – *vt* to make an object of usu superficial sentiment; romanticize ⟨*he has ~d Japan* – D J Enright⟩ – **sentimentalization** *n*

**sentimo** /sen'teemoh/ *n, pl* **sentimos** – see *peso* at MONEY table [Pilipino, fr Sp *céntimo*]

¹**sentinel** /'sentinl/ *n* one who or that which keeps guard; a sentry [MF *sentinelle*, fr OIt *sentinella*, fr *sentina* vigilance, fr *sentire* to perceive, fr L]

²**sentinel** *vt* -ll- (*NAm* -l-, -ll-) 1 to watch over as a sentinel 2 to provide with a sentinel 3 to post as a sentinel

**sentry** /'sentri/ *n* a guard, watch; *esp* a soldier standing guard at a gate, door, etc [perh fr obs *sentry* sanctuary, watch tower, alter. of ME *seintuarie* sanctuary]

**sentry box** *n* a shelter for a standing sentry

'**sentry-,go** *n* duty as a sentry [fr the phrase *sentry, go!*]

**senza** /'sentsah/ *prep* without – used in music directions ⟨~ *sordini*⟩ [It]

**sepal** /'sepl/ *n* any of the modified leaves that together form the CALYX and encircle the petals of a flower [NL *sepalum*, fr *sepa-* (fr Gk *skepē* covering) + *-lum* (as in *petalum* petal)]

**sepaloid** /'seepəloyd, 'sep-/ *adj* resembling or functioning as a sepal

**-sepalous** /-'sepələs/ *comb form* (→ *adj*) having (such or so many) sepals ⟨*gamosepalous*⟩ [*sepal* + *-ous*]

**separable** /,sep(ə)rəbl/ *adj* capable of being separated or distinguished – **separableness** *n*, **separably** *adv*, **separability** *n*

¹**separate** /'sepərayt/ *vt* 1a to set or keep apart; detach, divide, sever b to make a distinction between; distinguish ⟨~ *religion from magic*⟩ c to disperse in space or time; scatter ⟨*widely ~d hamlets*⟩ 2 to cause (a married couple) to cease living together as man and wife, esp by judicial decree 3 to isolate, segregate 4a to isolate from a mixture or compound ⟨~ *cream from milk*⟩ b to divide into constituent parts or types 5 *NAm* to sever contractual relations with (someone); discharge ⟨*was ~d from the army*⟩ 6 *archaic* to set aside for a special purpose ~ *vi* 1 to become divided or detached; draw or come apart 2a to sever an association; withdraw ⟨~ *from a federation*⟩ b to cease to live together as man and wife 3 to go in different directions 4 to become isolated from a mixture □ (*vt4*) often + *out* [ME *separaten*, fr L *separatus*, pp of *separare*, fr *se-* apart + *parare* to prepare, procure – more at SECEDE, PARE]

*synonyms* Separate, divide, part, divorce, sever, sunder, diverge, and segregate all mean "make or become disunited". Separate and divide can both mean "occupy a position between" ⟨*the Channel* separates/divides *England from France*⟩. Separate also implies a scattering of units ⟨*the war* separated *the family*⟩, while divide emphasizes either categorization into portions ⟨divide *the cake into three*⟩ or mutual antagonism ⟨*suspicion* divided *neighbour from neighbour*⟩. Part suggests the separation of one thing ⟨*cable* parted *under the strain*⟩ or of closely united elements ⟨*the two friends* parted *at the station*⟩. Divorce even more implies the separation of a very close union ⟨divorce *church from state*⟩. Sever and the somewhat figurative sunder both imply violent separation: sever by cutting ⟨sever *the head from the body*⟩ and sunder by tearing or wrenching. Diverge involves a drawing apart from a common point ⟨*dialects of the same language which have* diverged *widely*⟩. Segregate implies the isolation of a part, particularly of a social group, from a main body ⟨segregate *gifted children into special classes*⟩. antonyms combine, unite

²**separate** /'sep(ə)rət/ *adj* 1 set or kept apart; detached, separated 2a not shared with another; individual ⟨~ *rooms*⟩ b *often cap* estranged from a parent body ⟨~ *churches*⟩ 3a existing independently; autonomous b different in kind; distinct ⟨*six ~ ways of cooking an egg*⟩ c proper or belonging to each individually ⟨*their ~ achievements are so very different*⟩ *synonyms* see ¹SINGLE – **separately** *adv*, **separateness** *n*

³**separate** *n pl* 1 garments (e g skirts, shirts, and trousers) that are designed to be worn together, in different combinations, to form an interchangeable outfit 2 components of an audio or

video system (e g loudspeakers, amplifiers, or screens) that are bought separately rather than as part of a fully integrated unit (e g a MUSIC CENTRE)

**separation** /ˌsepəˈraysh(ə)n/ *n* **1** separating or being separated **2a** a point, line, or means of division **b** an intervening space; a gap, break **3a** cessation of cohabitation between husband and wife by mutual agreement or judicial decree **b** *NAm* termination of a contractual relationship (e g employment or military service)

**separationist** /ˌsepəˈrayshənist/ *n* a separatist

**separatism** /ˈseprəˌtiz(ə)m/ *n* a belief in, movement for, or state of separation (e g religious schism, political secession, or racial segregation)

**separatist** /-tist/ *n, often cap* somebody who favours separatism: e g **a** *cap* a member of a group of 16th- and 17th-century English Protestants preferring to separate from, rather than to reform, the Church of England **b** an advocate of independence or self-government for a part of a political unit (e g a nation) **c** an advocate of racial or cultural separation – **separatist** *adj, often cap*, **separatistic** *adj*

**separative** /ˈsep(ə)rətiv/ *adj* tending to separate or cause separation

**separator** /ˈsepəˌraytə/ *n* one who or that which separates; *specif* a device for separating liquids of different SPECIFIC GRAVITIES (e g cream from milk), or liquids from solids

**Sephardi** /siˈfahdi/ *n, pl* **Sephardim** /-dim/ a member or descendant of the non-Yiddish-speaking western branch of European Jews that settled in Spain and Portugal – compare ASHKENAZI [LHeb *sĕphāradhī*, fr *sĕphāradh* Spain, fr Heb, region where Jews were once exiled (Obad 1:20)] – **Sephardic** *adj*

**¹sepia** /ˈseepyə/ *n* **1a** the inky secretion of a cuttlefish **b** a brown melanin-containing pigment from the ink of cuttlefishes **2** a print or photograph of a brown colour resembling sepia **3** a rich dark brown colour [NL, genus comprising cuttlefish, fr L, cuttlefish, fr Gk *sēpia;* akin to Gk *sēpein* to make putrid, *sapros* rotten]

**²sepia** *adj* **1** of the colour sepia **2** made of or done in sepia ⟨~ *print*⟩

**sepiolite** /ˈseepiəliet/ *n* MEERSCHAUM **1** (claylike mineral) [Ger *sepiolith*, fr Gk *sēpion* cuttlebone (fr *sēpia*) + Ger *-lith* -lite]

**sepoy** /ˈseepoy/ *n* an Indian soldier employed by a European power, esp Britain [Pg *sipai*, fr Hindi *sipāhī*, fr Per, cavalryman]

**seppuku** /seˈpoohkooh/ *n* HARA-KIRI (type of suicide) [Jap]

**sepsis** /ˈsepsis/ *n, pl* **sepses** /-seez/ a condition caused by a poison resulting from the spread of bacteria or their products from a focus of infection; *esp* SEPTICAEMIA [NL, fr Gk *sēpsis* decay, fr *sēpein* to make rotten]

**sept** /sept/ *n* a branch of a family; *esp* a clan [prob alter. of *sect*]

**septal** /ˈseptl/ *adj* of a SEPTUM (dividing body membrane)

**septate** /ˈseptayt/ *adj* divided by or having a SEPTUM (dividing body membrane)

**September** /sepˈtembə, səp-/ *n* the 9th month of the year according to the GREGORIAN CALENDAR (standard Western calendar) – see MONTH table [ME *Septembre*, fr OF, fr L *September* (seventh month of the ancient Roman calendar), fr *septem* seven – more at SEVEN]

**septendecillion** /ˌsepˌtendiˈsilyən/ *n* – see NUMBER table [L *septendecim* seventeen (fr *septem* seven + *decem* ten) + E *-illion* (as in *million*) – more at TEN]

**septennial** /sepˈtenyəl/ *adj* **1** consisting of or lasting for seven years **2** occurring or performed every seven years [LL *septennium* period of seven years, fr L *septem* + *-ennium* (as in *biennium*)] – **septennially** *adv*

**septentrional** /sepˈtentriənl/ *adj, formal* northern [ME, fr L *septentrionalis*, fr *septentriones* the seven stars in Ursa Major or Ursa Minor, the northern regions, fr *septem* seven + *triones*, pl of *trio* plough-ox]

**septet** /sepˈtet/ *n* **1** a musical composition for seven instruments or voices **2** *taking sing or pl vb* a group or set of seven; *esp* a group of seven musicians performing together [Ger, fr L *septem*]

**septic** /ˈseptik/ *adj* **1** causing decomposition of animal or plant matter **2** (characteristic) of or involving sepsis △ sceptic [L *septicus*, fr Gk *sēptikos*, fr *sēpein* to make rotten – more at SEPIA ]

**septicaemia** /ˌseptiˈseemyə, -miˈə/ *n* invasion of the bloodstream by disease-causing microorganisms from a local seat of infection accompanied esp by chills, fever, and collapse – compare SEPSIS [NL, fr L *septicus* + NL *-aemia*]

**septicidal** /ˌseptiˈsiedl/ *adj, esp of a fruit* DEHISCENT (opening spontaneously, esp to release seeds) longitudinally at or along a septum [NL *septum* + L *-cidere* to cut, fr *caedere* – more at CONCISE]

**septic tank** *n* a tank in which the solid matter of continuously flowing sewage is disintegrated by bacteria

**septillion** /sepˈtilyən/ *n* – see NUMBER table [Fr, fr L *septem* + Fr *-illion* (as in *million*) – more at SEVEN]

**septrin** /ˈseptrin/ *trademark* – used for the antibacterial drug co-trimoxazole

**septuagenarian** /ˌsepchooˌəjiˈneəriˈən, ˌseptwə-/ *n* a person between 70 and 79 years old [LL *septuagenarius* 70 years old, fr L, of or containing 70, fr *septuageni* 70 each, fr *septuaginta*] – **septuagenarian** *adj*

**Septuagesima** /ˌsepchooəˈjesimə, ˌseptwə-/ *n* the third Sunday before Lent [ME, fr LL, fr L, fem of *septuagesimus* 70th, fr *septuaginta* seventy; fr its being the 70th day before Easter]

**Septuagint** /ˈsepchooəˌjint, ˈseptwə-/ *n* a pre-Christian Greek version of the Jewish Scriptures, arranged and edited by Jewish scholars and adopted by Greek-speaking Christians [LL *Septuaginta*, fr L, seventy, irreg fr *septem* seven + *-ginta* (akin to L v*iginti* twenty) – more at SEVEN, VIGESIMAL; fr the approximate number of its translators] – **Septuagintal** *adj*

**septum** /ˈseptəm/ *n, pl* **septa** /-tə/ a dividing wall or membrane, esp between bodily spaces or masses of soft tissue – compare DISSEPIMENT [NL, fr L *saeptum* enclosure, fence, wall, fr *saepire* to fence in, fr *saepes* fence, hedge; akin to Gk *haimasia* stone wall]

**sepulchral** /siˈpulkrəl/ *adj* **1** of the burial of the dead **2** suited to or suggestive of a tomb; funereal ⟨*a* ~ *whisper*⟩ – **sepulchrally** *adv*

**¹sepulchre,** *NAm chiefly* **sepulcher** /ˈsepəlkə/ *n* **1** a place of burial; a tomb **2** a receptacle for religious relics, esp in an altar [ME *sepulcre*, fr OF, fr L *sepulcrum, sepulchrum*, fr *sepelire* to bury; akin to Gk *hepein* to care for, Skt *sapati* he serves]

**²sepulchre,** *NAm chiefly* **sepulcher** *vt, archaic* to place or enclose in a sepulchre

**sepulture** /ˈsep(ə)lchə/ *n, formal* burial, interment [ME, fr OF, fr L *sepultura*, fr *sepultus*, pp of *sepelire*]

**sequacious** /siˈkwayshəs/ *adj, formal* **1** easily led; subservient **2** lacking in original thought **3** following in a smooth or logical sequence ⟨~ *music*⟩ ⟨~ *thoughts*⟩ [L *sequac-, sequax* inclined to follow, fr *sequi*] – **sequaciously** *adv*, **sequacity** *n*

**sequel** /ˈseekwəl/ *n* **1** a consequence, result **2a** subsequent development or course of events **b** the next instalment (e g of a speech or narrative); *esp* a play, film, or literary work continuing the course of a narrative begun in a preceding one – compare PREQUEL **3** a sequela ⟨*negative* ~s *of silicone injections – Cleo*⟩ [ME, fr MF *sequelle*, fr L *sequela*, fr *sequi* to follow – more at SUE]

**sequela** /siˈkweelə/ *n, pl* **sequelae** /-lie/ an aftereffect of disease, injury, or surgery [NL, fr L, sequel]

**¹sequence** /ˈseekwəns/ *n* **1** a hymn in irregular metre read or sung between the GRADUAL (verses read or sung from esp the Psalms) and a reading from the gospels in masses for special occasions (e g Easter) **2** a continuous or connected series: e g **2a** an extended series of poems united by theme ⟨*a sonnet* ~⟩ **b** RUN 3f (three consecutive playing cards) **c** a succession of repetitions of a melodic phrase or harmonic pattern, getting higher or lower – compare IMITATION 3, OSTINATO **d** a set of mathematical elements following the same order as the NATURAL NUMBERS **e(1)** a succession of related shots or scenes developing a single subject or phase of a film story **e(2)** an episode, esp in a film **3a** order of succession **b** the order of structural units (e g AMINO ACIDS in a protein or chemical bases in DNA or RNA) in a complex biological molecule **4** a subsequent but not resultant occurrence or course **5** a continuous progression **6** *chiefly NAm* a consequence, sequel [ME, fr ML *sequentia*, fr LL, sequel, lit., act of following, fr L *sequent-, sequens*, prp of *sequi*]

**²sequence** *vt* **1** to place in ordered sequence **2** to determine the order of the BASES in a molecule of DNA or RNA ⟨*each of the 22 transfer RNAs which had been* ~d *by that time – Nature*⟩

**sequence of tenses** *n* the dependence of the tense of a subordinate verb (e g *could* in "he said he could") on that of a main verb

**sequencer** /ˈseekwənsə/ *n* any of various devices for arranging things (e g informational items or the events in the launching of a rocket) into a sequence, or for separating things (e g AMINO ACIDS from protein) in a sequence

**sequent** /'seekwənt/ *adj, formal* **1** consecutive, succeeding **2** consequent, resultant [L *sequent-, sequens,* prp]

**sequential** /si'kwensh(ə)l/ *adj* **1** of or arranged in a sequence; serial ⟨~ *file systems*⟩ **2** following in sequence **3** of or based on a method of testing a statistical hypothesis using a sequence of samples, each of which determines the decision to accept or reject the hypothesis or to continue sampling – **sequentially** *adv*

**sequester** /si'kwestə/ *vt* **1a** to set apart; segregate **b** to seclude, withdraw ⟨~ *oneself from urban life*⟩ ⟨*a quiet* ~ed *spot*⟩ **2** to seize by sequestration **3** to hold (e g a metallic ion) in solution usu by inclusion in an appropriate complex [ME *sequestren,* fr MF *sequestrer,* fr LL *sequestrare* to surrender for safekeeping, set apart, fr L *sequester* agent, depositary, bailee; akin to L *sequi* to follow]

**sequestrate** /si'kwestrayt/ *vt* to sequester [LL *sequestratus,* pp of *sequestrare*]

**sequestration** /,seekwe'straysh(ə)n/ *n* **1** sequestering or being sequestered **2** judicial seizure of a person's (e g a debtor's) property until legal claims are met or an order of the court is complied with **3** the formation of a sequestrum

**sequestrum** /si'kwestrəm/ *n, pl* **sequestrums** *also* **sequestra** /-strə/ a fragment of dead bone detached from adjoining sound bone [NL, fr L, legal sequestration; akin to L *sequester* bailee]

**sequin** /'seekwin/ *n* **1** a former gold coin of Italy and Turkey **2** a very small disc of shining metal or plastic used for ornamentation, esp on clothing [Fr, fr It *zecchino,* fr *zecca* mint, fr Ar *sikkah* die, coin]

**sequined, sequinned** /'seekwind/ *adj* ornamented (as if) with sequins

**sequoia** /si'kwoyə/ *n* either of two huge coniferous Californian trees of the pine family that can reach a height of over 100 metres (about 300 feet): **a** BIG TREE **b** REDWOOD [NL, genus name, fr *Sequoya* (George Guess) †1843 AmerInd scholar]

**sera** /'siərə/ *pl of* SERUM (watery part of a body liquid)

**serac** /'seerak/ *n* a pinnacle, sharp ridge, or block of ice among the crevasses of a glacier [Fr *sérac,* lit., a kind of white cheese, fr ML *seracium* whey, fr L *serum* whey – more at SERUM]

**seraglio** /se'rahli·oh, -lyoh/ *n, pl* **seraglios 1** HAREM **1a** (house or area for women) **2** a palace of a sultan [It *serraglio* enclosure, seraglio; partly fr ML *serraculum* bar of a door, bolt, fr LL *serare* to bolt; partly fr Turk *saray* palace – more at SEAR]

**serai** /se'rie/ *n* CARAVANSERAI (large inn in Eastern countries) [Turk & Per; Turk *saray* mansion, palace, fr Per *sarāi* mansion, inn]

**seral** /'siərəl/ *adj* of or constituting an ecological sere

**serang** /sə'rang/ *n* the head of a ship's crew in India or the E Indies [Per *sarhang* commander, boatswain, fr *sar* chief + *hang* authority]

**serape** /sə'rahpi/ *n* an often brightly coloured woollen shawl worn over the shoulders, esp by Mexican men [MexSp *sarape*]

**seraph** /'seraf/ *n, pl* **seraphim** /-fim/, **seraphs 1** any of the 6-winged angels standing in the presence of God **2** *pl* the highest of the nine orders of angelic beings in the CELESTIAL HIERARCHY [LL *seraphim,* pl, fr Heb *śĕrāphīm*]

**seraphic** /sə'rafik/ *adj* of a seraph; *broadly* suggesting innocent blissfulness; serene ⟨*a* ~ *smile*⟩ – **seraphically** *adv*

**Serb** /suhb/ *n* **1** a native or inhabitant of Serbia **2** SERBIAN **2** [Serb *Srb*] – **Serb** *adj*

**Serbian** /'suhbiən/ *n* **1** SERB **1 2a** the Serbo-Croatian language as spoken in Serbia **b** a literary form of Serbo-Croatian using the CYRILLIC alphabet – compare CROATIAN [*Serbia,* former Balkan kingdom (now a republic of Yugoslavia)] – **Serbian** *adj*

**Serbo-Croatian** /,suhboh kroh'aysh(ə)n/ *n* **1** the SLAVONIC language of the Serbs and Croats. Its Serbian variety is written in the CYRILLIC alphabet and its CROATIAN in the Latin alphabet. **2** one whose native language is Serbo-Croatian – **Serbo-Croatian** *adj*

**¹sere, sear** /siə/ *adj, chiefly poetic* shrivelled, withered [ME, fr OE *sēar* dry; akin to OHG *sōrēn* to wither, Gk *hauos* dry]

**²sere** *n* a series of ecological communities that succeed one another in the biological development of an area [L *series* series]

**serein** /sə'rayn/ *n* a mist or fine rain falling from an apparently

cloudless sky [Fr, fr MF *serain* evening, nightfall, fr L *sero* late]

**¹serenade** /,serə'nayd/ *n* **1a** a complimentary vocal or instrumental performance; *esp* one given outdoors at night for a woman **b** a work so performed **2** an instrumental composition in several movements written for a small ensemble [Fr *sérénade,* fr It *serenata,* fr *sereno* clear, calm (of weather), fr L *serenus*]

**²serenade** *vt* to perform a serenade in honour of ~ *vi* to play a serenade – **serenader** *n*

**serenata** /,seri'nahtə/ *n* an 18th-century nonreligious dramatic choral work, usu composed in honour of an individual or event [It, serenade]

**serendipity** /,serən'dipəti/ *n* the faculty of making chance discoveries of pleasing or valuable things [fr its possession by the heroes of the Per fairy tale *The Three Princes of Serendip* (*Serendip,* ancient name for Sri Lanka, fr Ar *Sarandīb,* deriv of Skt *Siṃhalānāṃ Dvīpaḥ,* lit., island of the Sinhalese)] – **serendipitous** *adj*

**serene** /sə'reen/ *adj* **1** free of storms or adverse changes; clear, fine ⟨~ *skies*⟩ ⟨~ *weather*⟩ **2** marked by or suggesting a state of spiritual repose and tranquillity ⟨*a* ~ *smile*⟩ **3** august – used as part of a title ⟨*His* Serene *Highness*⟩ synonyms see ²CALM [L *serenus;* akin to OHG *serawēn* to become dry, Gk *xēros* dry] – **serenely** *adv,* **sereneness, serenity** *n*

**serf** /suhf/ *n* a member of a class of agricultural labourers in a FEUDAL society, bound in service to a lord, and esp transferred with the land they worked if its ownership changed hands △ surf [Fr, fr L *servus* slave, servant, serf – more at SERVE] – **serfage, serfdom** *n*

**serge** /suhj/ *n* a durable fabric with a pronounced diagonal rib on the front and the back △ surge [ME *sarge,* fr MF, fr (assumed) VL *sarica,* fr L *serica,* fem of *sericus* silken – more at SERICEOUS]

**sergeancy** /'sahjənsi/ *n* the function, office, or rank of a sergeant

**sergeant** /'sahj(ə)nt/ *n* **1** a police officer ranking in Britain between constable and inspector **2** *Br also* **serjeant** – see MILITARY RANKS table **3** SERJEANT-AT-LAW (barrister) [ME, servant, attendant, sergeant, fr OF *sergent, serjant,* fr L *servient-, serviens,* prp of *servire* to serve]

**sergeant aircrew** *n* – see MILITARY RANKS table

**sergeant-at-'arms** *n, pl* **sergeants-at-arms** *often cap S&A* SERJEANT-AT-ARMS (parliamentary official)

**sergeant first class** *n* – see MILITARY RANKS table

**sergeant major** *n, pl* **sergeant majors, sergeants major 1** – see MILITARY RANKS table **2a** WARRANT OFFICER in the British army or Royal Marines

**¹serial** /'siəri·əl/ *adj* **1** of or constituting a series, rank, or row ⟨~ *order*⟩ **2** appearing in successive instalments ⟨*a* ~ *story*⟩ **3** of or being music based on a series of notes in an arbitrary but fixed order without regard for traditional musical keys; *esp* TWELVE-TONE ⟨~ *technique*⟩ – **serially** *adv*

**²serial** *n* **1a** a work appearing (e g in a magazine or on television) in parts at intervals **b** a single part of a serial work; an instalment **2** a publication (e g a newspaper or journal) issued as one of a consecutively numbered and indefinitely continued series △ cereal – **serialist** *n*

**serialism** /'siəri·ə,liz(ə)m/ *n* serial music; *also* the theory or practice of composing serial music

**serial·ize, -ise** /'siəri·əliez/ *vt* to arrange or publish in serial form – **serialization** *n*

**serial number** *n* a number indicating position in a series and used as a means of identification

**¹seriate** /'siəri·ət/ *adj, formal* arranged in a series or an ordered sequence [(assumed) NL *seriatus,* fr L *series*] – **seriately** *adv*

**²seriate** /'siəriayt/ *vt, formal* to arrange in a series

**seriatim** /,siəri'atim, ,seri-, -'aytim/ *adv, formal* in a series; item by item [ML, fr L *series*]

**sericeous** /si'rishəs/ *adj, of a plant or animal part* finely hairy ⟨*a* ~ *leaf*⟩ [LL *sericeus* silken, fr L *sericum* silk garment, silk, fr neut of *sericus* silken, fr Gk *sērikos,* fr *Sēres,* a people of E Asia (prob the Chinese) producing silk in ancient times]

**sericin** /'serisin/ *n* a gelatinous protein that cements the two filaments of FIBROIN in a silk fibre [ISV, fr L *sericum* silk]

**sericulture** /'seri,kulchə/ *n* the production of raw silk by raising silkworms [L *sericum* silk + E *culture*] – **sericultural** *adj,* **sericulturist** *n*

**seriema** /,seri'emə, ,seri'eemə/ *n* either of two large long-legged S American birds (*Cariama cristata* and *Chunga burmeisteri*) that have a crested head, short wings, and limited powers of flight – also called CARIAMA [Tupi *çariama, seriema*, lit., crested]

**series** /'siəriz, -reez/ *n, pl* **series 1** a number of things or events of the same kind following one another in space or time ⟨*a concert* ∼⟩ ⟨*the hall opened into a* ∼ *of small rooms*⟩; *broadly* any group of systematically related items **2** a usu infinite mathematical sequence whose terms are to be added together **3a** the coins or currency of a particular country and period **b** a group of postage stamps of different denominations **4** a succession of volumes or issues published with related subjects or authors, similar format and price, or continuous numbering **5** a division of rock formations that is smaller than a SYSTEM, and comprises rocks deposited during a geological epoch **6** a group of chemical compounds related in composition and structure **7** an arrangement of the parts or elements in an electric circuit whereby the whole current passes through each part or element in turn – esp in *in series* ⟨*batteries arranged in series*⟩; compare PARALLEL 4b **8a** a number of games (e g of cricket) played between two teams ⟨*a 5-match* ∼ *between England and Australia*⟩ **b** three consecutive games in tenpin bowling [L, fr *serere* to join, link together; akin to Gk *eirein* to string together, *hormos* chain, necklace]

**series winding** *n* a winding of the coils in an electric motor or generator in which the ARMATURE (part in which an electric current is induced) coil and the FIELD-MAGNET coil are in series with the external circuit – **series-wound** *adj*

**serif** /'serif/ *n* any of the short lines stemming from, and at an angle to, the upper and lower ends of the strokes of a letter [prob fr D *schreef* stroke, line, fr MD, fr *schriven* to write, fr L *scribere* – more at SCRIBE] – **seriffed** *adj*

**serigraph** /'seri,grahf, -,graf/ *n* a print made by a SILK-SCREEN process [L *sericum* silk + Gk *graphein* to write, draw – more at CARVE ] – **serigrapher** *n*, **serigraphy** *n*

**serin** /'serin/ *n* a small European finch (*Serinus serinus*) related to the canary [Fr]

**serine** /'sereen, 'siə-, -rin/ *n* an AMINO ACID, HOCH₂CH(NH₂)COOH, that occurs as a structural part of many proteins [ISV *sericin* + *-ine*]

**seriocomic** /,siərioh'komik/ *adj* combining the serious with the comic ⟨*a* ∼ *novel*⟩ [*serious* + *-o-* + *comic*] – **seriocomically** *adv*

**serious** /'siəri·əs/ *adj* **1** grave or thoughtful in appearance or manner; sober **2a** requiring careful attention and application ⟨∼ *study*⟩ **b** of or about a weighty or important matter ⟨*a* ∼ *play*⟩ **3a** not jesting or deceiving; in earnest ⟨*you can't be* ∼*!*⟩ **b** deeply interested or committed ⟨∼ *fishermen*⟩ ⟨*get some* ∼ *drinking in*⟩ **4a** not easily answered or solved ⟨∼ *objections*⟩ **b** having important or dangerous consequences; critical ⟨*a* ∼ *injury*⟩ [ME *seryows*, fr MF or LL; MF *serieux*, fr LL *seriosus*, alter. of L *serius*] – **seriousness** *n*

synonyms **Serious, grave, solemn, sober, sedate, staid,** and **earnest** all mean "not light or frivolous". When they are used of people, **serious** implies diligence and a sense of responsibility ⟨**serious** *students*⟩. **Grave** suggests the dignity associated with weighty matters ⟨*councillors with* **grave** *faces*⟩. **Solemn** may indicate awesomeness and absence of levity ⟨**solemn** *mourners*⟩. **Sober** implies calm self-control ⟨**sober** *churchgoers*⟩. **Sedate** and **staid** emphasize habitual calmness and propriety, **staid** particularly suggesting prim self-restraint ⟨*the* **staid** *Roman citizen was repelled by the wild dances* – John Buchan⟩. **Earnest** indicates a steady intensity of purpose in doing something ⟨*was* **earnest** *in his endeavours to convert the natives*⟩. antonyms **light, flippant**

**seriously** /'siəriəsli/ *adv* **1** in a sincere manner; earnestly **2** to a serious extent; severely

**serious-'minded** *adj* having a serious outlook on life – **serious-mindedly** *adv*, **serious-mindedness** *n*

**serjeant** /'sahj(ə)nt/ *n* **1** serjeant, sergeant a serjeant-at-law **2** *Br* SERGEANT 2 – used in official lists

**serjeant-at-'arms, sergeant-at-arms** *n, pl* **serjeants-at-arms** *often cap S&A* an officer attending the Speaker or Lord Chancellor in the British parliament and having the right of arrest; *also* a similar officer in other law-making bodies

**serjeant-at-'law** *n, pl* **serjeants-at-law** *often cap S&L* a member of a former class of barristers of the highest rank

**sermon** /'suhmən/ *n* **1** a religious discourse delivered in public, usu by a clergyman, as a part of a liturgical service **2** a speech on conduct or duty; *esp* one that is unduly long or tedious [ME, fr OF, fr ML *sermon-, sermo*, fr L, speech, conversation, prob fr *serere* to link together – more at SERIES] – **sermonic** *adj*

**sermon·ize, -ise** /'suhmə,niez/ *vi* **1** to give moral advice in an officious or dogmatic manner **2** *chiefly derog* to deliver a sermon – **sermonizer** *n*

**Sermon on the Mount** *n* an ethical discourse of Jesus recorded in Matthew 5–7 and paralleled briefly in Luke 6:20–49

**sero-** *comb form* serum ⟨*serology*⟩ [L *serum*]

**serology** /si'roləji/ *n* a branch of medical science dealing with SERUMS (watery part of body liquids), esp BLOOD SERUM, and their reactions and properties [ISV] – **serologist** *n*, **serological** *adv*, **serologically** *adv*

**seropurulent** /,siəroh'pyooərələnt, ,seroh-/ *adj* consisting of a mixture of SERUM (watery part of a body liquid) and pus ⟨*a* ∼ *exudate*⟩

**serosa** /si'rohsə, -zə/ *n* a usu enclosing SEROUS MEMBRANE [NL, fr fem of *serosus* serous, fr L *serum*] – **serosal** *adj*

**serotinal** /si'rotinl/ *adj* of the latter and usu drier part of summer [L *serotinus* coming late]

**serotine** /'serotien/ *n* an insect-eating bat (*Vespertilio serotinus*) common in southern and central Europe [Fr *sérotine*, fr L *serotina*, fem of *serotinus*; fr its flying late in the evening]

**serotinous** /si'rotinəs/ *adj* **1** late; *esp* developing or flowering late in the season **2** *of a cone* lasting on the tree for several years [L *serotinus* coming late, fr *sero* late – more at SOIREE ]

**serotonin** /,serə'tohnin/ *n* a chemical compound (AMINE), $C_{10}H_{12}N_2O$, that is a powerful VASOCONSTRICTOR (substance causing constriction of blood vessels) and is found esp in the BLOOD SERUM and tissues of the gut of mammals – called also HYDROXYTRYPTAMINE [*sero-* + *tonic* + *-in*]

**serous** /'siərəs/ *adj* of, resembling, or producing SERUM (watery part of a body liquid); *esp* thin and watery ⟨*a* ∼ *exudate*⟩ [MF *sereux*, fr *serum*, fr L]

**serous membrane** /'siərəs/ *n* a thin membrane (e g the PERITONEUM lining the abdomen) with cells that secrete a serous fluid; *esp* a serosa

**serow** /'seroh/ *n* any of several GOAT ANTELOPES (genus *Capricornis*) of E Asia which are usu rather dark and heavily built and some of which have distinct manes [Lepcha *să-ro* long-haired Tibetan goat]

**serpent** /'suhpənt/ *n* **1** *chiefly poetic or dial* a snake **2** an old-fashioned bass woodwind instrument of serpentine form **3** *archaic* a foul or unpleasant creature that creeps, hisses, or stings **4** *archaic* the Devil **5** *archaic* a wily treacherous person [ME, fr MF, fr L *serpent-, serpens*, fr prp of *serpere* to creep; akin to Gk *herpein* to creep, Skt *sarpati* he creeps]

**¹serpentine** /'suhpən,tien/ *adj* **1** of or like a snake (e g in form or movement) **2** subtly tempting; wily, artful **3a** winding or turning one way and another **b** having a compound curve whose central curve is convex [ME, fr MF *serpentin*, fr LL *serpentinus*, fr L *serpent-, serpens*] – **serpentinely** *adv*

**²serpentine** *n* something that winds sinuously; *specif* a serpentine movement in DRESSAGE (test of accurate horsemanship)

**³serpentine** *n* a mineral consisting essentially of magnesium silicate, $Mg_3Si_2O_7.2H_2O$, having a dull green colour and often a mottled appearance [ME, fr ML *serpentina, serpentinum*, fr LL, fem & neut of *serpentinus* resembling a serpent]

**serpentinite** /'suhpəntie,niet/ *n* a rock that consists essentially of serpentine [ISV]

**serpiginous** /suh'pijinəs/ *adj* creeping, spreading; *esp* healing over in one portion while continuing to advance in another ⟨*a* ∼ *ulcer*⟩ [ML *serpigin-, serpigo* creeping skin disease, fr L *serpere* to creep] – **serpiginously** *adv*

**serranid** /'serənid/ *n* any of a large family (Serranidae) of flesh-eating spiny-finned marine fishes which have an oblong compressed body covered with toothed scales [deriv of L *serra* saw] – **serranid** *adj*, **serranoid** *adj or n*

**¹serrate** /se'rayt, sə-/ *vt* to mark or provide with serrations [LL *serratus*, pp of *serrare* to saw, fr L *serra*]

**²serrate** /'serət, -rayt/ *adj* notched or toothed at the edge; *specif, of a leaf* having marginal teeth pointing forwards or towards the tip [L *serratus*, fr *serra* saw]

**serration** /se'raysh(ə)n, sə-/ *n* **1** the condition of being serrate **2** a formation resembling the teeth of a saw **3** any of the teeth of a serrate margin

**serried** /'serid/ *adj* **1** crowded or pressed together; compact ⟨*the crowd collected in a* ∼ *mass* – W S Maugham⟩ **2** marked by ridges; serrated ⟨*the* ∼ *outline of the distant hills*⟩ [fr pp of arch. *serry* to press close, fr MF *serré*, pp of *serrer* to press, crowd, fr LL *serare* to bolt, latch, fr L *sera* lock, bolt; (2) alter. of *serrate*] – **serriedly** *adv*, **serriedness** *n*

**sertularian** /,suhtyoo'leəriən/ *n* any of a genus (*Sertularia* of the order Hydroida, class Hydrozoa) of delicate branching aquatic animals [NL *Sertularia*, genus name, fr L *sertula*, dim. of *serta* garland, clover-like plant, fr fem of *serius*, pp of *serere* to link together, entwine – more at SERIES] – **sertularian** *adj*

**serum** /'siərəm/ *n, pl* **serums, sera** /-rə/ **1** the watery portion of an animal fluid remaining after COAGULATION (curdling or clotting): **1a** BLOOD SERUM; *esp* immune blood serum that contains specific immune bodies (eg antibodies) **b** WHEY (watery part of milk) **c** a normal or diseased serous fluid (eg in a blister) **2** the watery part of a plant liquid [L, whey, serum; akin to Gk *oros* whey, serum, *hormē* onset, assault, Skt *sarati* it flows]

**serum albumin** *n* a crystallizable ALBUMIN (type of protein), or mixture of albumins, that normally constitutes more than half of the protein in BLOOD SERUM and serves to maintain the OSMOTIC PRESSURE (apparent pressure exerted by a liquid owing to the amount of substances dissolved in it) of the blood

**serum globulin** *n* a GLOBULIN (type of protein), or mixture of globulins, occurring in BLOOD SERUM and containing most of the ANTIBODIES (disease-fighting bodies) of the blood

**serum hepatitis** *n* an often fatal inflammation of the liver caused by a virus that is contracted esp by contact with an infected person's blood

**serval** /'suhv(ə)l/ *n* a long-legged African wildcat (*Felis capensis*) with large untufted ears and a tawny black-spotted coat [Fr, fr Pg *lobo cerval* lynx, fr ML *lupus cervalis*, lit., deer-like wolf]

**servant** /'suhv(ə)nt/ *n* one who or that which works for or is at the service of others (*the BBC is a ~ of the public*); *specif* somebody employed to perform personal or domestic duties for another – compare PUBLIC SERVANT [ME, fr OF, fr prp of *servir*]

**¹serve** /suhv/ *vi* **1a** to act as a servant **b** to do military or naval service **2** to assist the officiating priest at Mass **3a** to be of use; fulfil a specified purpose – often + *as* **b** to be favourable, opportune, or convenient (*told the story whenever occasion ~d*) **c** to prove reliable or trustworthy (*it was last year, if memory ~s*) **d** to hold a post or office; discharge a duty (*~ on a jury*) **4** to prove adequate or satisfactory; suffice (*dress that ~s for all occasions*) **5a** to act as a waiter **b** to distribute drinks or helpings of food **6** to attend to customers in a shop **7** to put the ball or shuttle in play in any of various games (eg tennis, volleyball, or badminton) ~ *vt* **1a** to act as a servant to **b** to give the service and respect due to (a superior) **c** to comply with the commands or demands of; gratify (*~d the will of lustful women*) **d** to give military or naval service to (*~d France in the last war*) **e** to perform the duties of (*~d his presidency*) **2** to assist the officiating priest at (Mass) **3a** to work through or perform (a term of service) (*~d his time as a mate*) **b** to undergo (a term of imprisonment) **4a** to wait on at table **b** to supply (food or drink) to guests or diners **5a(1)** to provide with something needed or desired (*three schools ~ the area*) **a(2)** to supply (something needed or desired) (*garages refused to ~ petrol*) **b** to attend to (a customer) in a shop **6** to prove adequate or satisfactory for; suffice (*a smile would ~ him for encouragement*) (*this sharp stone will ~ my purposes*) **7a** to bring to notice, deliver, or execute (eg a writ or summons) as required by law **b** to make legal service on (a person named in a writ or summons) **8** *of a male animal* to copulate with **9** to wind yarn or wire tightly round (a rope or stay) for protection **10** to act so as to help or benefit (*the citizen's duty to ~ society*) **11** to put (the ball or shuttlecock) in play (eg in tennis or badminton) **12** *formal* to treat or act towards in a specified way (*he ~d me ill*) **13** *archaic* to pay a lover's or suitor's court to (a lady) (*that gentle lady, whom I love and ~ – Edmund Spenser*) [ME *serven*, fr OF *servir*, fr L *servire* to be a slave, serve, fr *servus* slave, servant, perh of Etruscan origin]

**serve up** *vt, informal* to furnish or supply (something required or expected)

**²serve** *n* the act of putting the ball or shuttlecock in play in any of various games (eg volleyball, badminton, or tennis); *also* a turn to serve

**server** /'suhvə/ *n* **1** somebody who serves food or drink **2** the player who serves (eg in tennis) **3** something (eg a salver or tongs) used in serving food or drink **4** an assistant to the officiating priest at Mass

**servery** /'suhv(ə)ri/ *n* a room, counter, or hatch (eg in a pub) from which food is served

**¹service** /'suhvis/ *n* **1a** work or duty performed for someone (*on active ~*) **b** employment as a servant (*entered his ~*) **2a** the function performed by one who or that which serves (*these shoes have given me good ~*) **b** help, use, benefit (*be of ~ to them*) **c** contribution to the welfare of others **d** disposal for use or assistance (*I'm always at your ~*) **3a** a form followed in worship or in a religious ceremony (*the burial ~*) **b** a meeting for worship (*held evening ~s*) **c** a musical setting of the various elements of a church service (*Stanford's ~ in B flat*) **4** the act of serving: eg **4a** a helpful act; a favour (*did him a ~*) **b** **service, services** *pl* a piece of useful work that does not produce a tangible commodity (*charge for professional ~s*) **c** a serve **d** the usu routine repair and maintenance of a machine or motor vehicle (*the car is due for its 6000 mile ~*) **5** a set of articles for a particular use; *specif* a set of matching tableware for serving a specified meal, food, or drink (eg tea or coffee) (*a 24-piece dinner ~*) **6a** an administrative division (eg of a government or business) (*the consular ~*) **b** any of a nation's military forces (eg the army or navy) **7a** a facility supplying some public demand (*telephone ~*) (*bus ~*); *specif, pl* facilities (eg restaurants, toilets, and petrol stations) provided for the users of a motorway **b** a facility providing maintenance and repair (*television ~*) **c** a facility providing broadcast programmes (*East European Service*) **d** *pl* utilities (eg gas, water, sewage, or electricity) available or connected to a building **8** the act of bringing a legal writ, process, or summons to notice as prescribed by law **9** the act of copulating with a female animal **10** a specialized branch of a hospital medical staff (*obstetrical ~*) [ME, fr OF, fr L *servitium* condition of a slave, body of slaves, fr *servus* slave] – **break somebody's service** to win a tennis game in which one's opponent is the server

**²service** *adj* **1** of the armed services **2** used in serving or delivering (*tradesmen use the ~ entrance*) **3a** providing services (*the ~ industries*) **b** offering repair, maintenance, or incidental services

**³service** *vt* to perform services for: eg **a** to repair or provide maintenance for (*~ a vacuum cleaner*) **b** to meet interest payments on and provide for the eventual repayment of the capital of (eg government debt) **c** to perform any of the business functions auxiliary to production or distribution of (eg goods) **d** *of a male animal* SERVE 8 – **servicer** *n*

**synonyms** One **services** something (eg a machine or a debt) that needs periodical attention, and a bull may **service** a cow; but **service** cannot otherwise replace the more general verb **serve**.

**⁴service, service tree** *n* **1** an African and Eurasian tree (*Sorbus domestica*) of the rose family resembling the related MOUNTAIN ASHES but having larger flowers and larger edible fruit **2** WILD SERVICE TREE [ME *serves*, pl of *serve* serviceberry, service tree, fr OE *syrfe*, fr (assumed) VL *sorbea*, fr L *sorbus* service tree]

**serviceable** /'suhvisəbl/ *adj* **1** fit to use; suited for a purpose **2** wearing well in use; durable *synonyms* see USEFUL – **serviceability** *n*, **serviceableness** *n*, **serviceably** *adv*

**serviceberry** /'suhvisb(ə)ri/ *n* any of various N American trees and shrubs (genus *Amelanchier*) of the rose family sometimes cultivated for their showy white flowers or edible purple or red fruits

**service book** *n* a book containing forms of worship used in religious services

**service box** *n* the area in which a player stands while serving in various court games (eg squash)

**service cap** *n* a flat-topped visor cap worn as part of a military uniform – compare GARRISON CAP

**service car** *n, NZ* a bus used on long-distance journeys

**service ceiling** *n* the altitude at which, under standard air conditions, a particular aircraft can no longer rise at a rate greater than a particular designated comparatively small rate (eg 30 metres (100 feet) per minute) – compare ABSOLUTE CEILING

**service charge** *n* a proportion of a bill added on to the total bill to pay for service, usu instead of tips

**service court** *n* a part of the court into which the ball or shuttle must be served

**service flat** *n, Br* a flat for which the rent includes a charge for certain services (eg cleaning or the provision of food)

**service line** *n* a line marked on a court in various games parallel to the front wall (eg in handball) or to the net (eg in tennis) to mark a boundary which must not be overstepped in serving

**serviceman** /-mən/ *n* **1** *fem* **servicewoman** a member of the armed forces **2** *chiefly NAm* somebody employed to repair or maintain equipment

**service mark** *n* a mark or device used in the USA to identify a service (e g transport or insurance) offered to customers

**service module** *n* a spacecraft module that contains propellant tanks, FUEL CELLS, and the main rocket engine

**service road** *n* a road that often runs parallel to a major road and that provides local access

**service station** *n* a retail station for servicing motor vehicles, esp with oil and petrol

**service tree** *n* ⁴SERVICE

**serviette** /‚suhvi'et/ *n* a table napkin [Fr, fr MF, fr *servir* to serve]

> *usage* Some people dislike **serviette** as a genteelism, and prefer to say **napkin**.

**servile** /'suhviel/ *adj* **1** of or befitting a slave or a menial position ⟨*a ∼ task*⟩ **2** slavishly or unctuously submissive; abject, obsequious *antonym* authoritative [ME, fr L *servilis*, fr *servus* slave – more at SERVE] – **servilely** *adv*, **servileness, servility** *n*

**serving** /'suhving/ *n* a single portion of food or drink; a helping

**servitor** /'suhvitə/ *n, archaic or formal* a male servant [ME *servitour*, fr MF, fr LL *servitor*, fr L *servitus*, pp of *servire* to serve]

**servitude** /'suhvityoohd/ *n* **1** deprivation of fundamental human (e g moral or intellectual) liberties; bondage ⟨*live in ∼ to the state*⟩ ⟨*penal ∼*⟩ **2** a right in Roman and Scottish law by which something (e g a piece of land) owned by one person is subject to a specific use or enjoyment by another [ME, fr MF, fr L *servitudo* slavery, fr *servus* slave]

> *synonyms* **Servitude, bondage,** and **slavery** all mean "the state of subjection to a master". **Servitude** may mean only lack of liberty, but usually implies involuntary service to someone. The somewhat rhetorical **bondage** emphasizes the state of being "bound" to a laborious captivity ⟨*she had gone into* **bondage** *among the aristocracy as a governess* – Virginia Woolf⟩. **Slavery** is strictly the condition of being the human property of another person, who may or may not require one to work.

**servo** /'suhvoh/ *n, pl* **servos** **1** a servomotor **2** a servomechanism

**servomechanism** /'suhvoh‚mekəniz(ə)m/ *n* an automatic device for controlling large amounts of power by means of very small amounts of power and automatically correcting performance of a mechanism [*servo-* (as in *servomotor*) + *mechanism*]

**servomotor** /'suhvoh‚mohtə/ *n* a power-driven mechanism that supplements a primary control operated by a comparatively feeble force (e g in a servomechanism) [Fr *servomoteur*, fr L *servus* slave, servant + Fr *-o-* + *moteur* motor, fr L *motor* mover – more at MOTOR]

**-ses** /-seez/ *pl of* -SIS

**sesame** /'sesəmi/ *n* **1** an E Indian erect plant (*Sesamum indicum* of the family Pedaliaceae, the sesame family); *also* its small somewhat flat seeds used as a source of oil and as a flavouring agent **2** OPEN SESAME [alter. of earlier *sesam, sesama,* fr L *sesamum, sesama,* fr Gk *sēsamon, sēsamē,* of Sem origin; akin to Assyr *šamaššamu* sesame, Ar *simsim*]

**sesame oil** *n* a pale yellow bland semidrying fatty oil obtained from sesame seeds and used chiefly as an edible oil, in the preparation of various drugs, and in cosmetics and soaps

**sesamoid** /'sesəmoyd/ *adj or n* (of or being) a nodular mass of bone or cartilage in a tendon, esp at a joint or bony prominence [Gk *sēsamoeidēs,* lit., resembling sesame seed, fr *sēsamon*]

**Sesotho** /si'soohtoo/ *n* the BANTU language of the MOSOTHO people of Lesotho

**sesqui-** /seskwi-/ *comb form* **1** one and a half times ⟨*sesquicentennial*⟩ **2** containing three (specified atoms, chemical groups, or molecules) usu combined with two of a different type in the molecular structure ⟨*sesquihydrate*⟩ [L, one and a half, half again, lit., and a half, fr *semis* half (fr *semi-*) + *-que* (enclitic) and; akin to Gk *te* and, Skt *ca,* Goth *-h, -uh*]

**sesquicarbonate** /‚seskwi'kahbənayt/ *n* a chemical compound (SALT) that is neither a simple normal CARBONATE nor a simple BICARBONATE but often a combination of the two

**sesquicentenary** /‚seskwisen'teenəri, -'tenəri/ *n* a 150th anniversary or its celebration – **sesquicentenary** *adj*

**sesquicentennial** /-sen'teni‚əl/ *n or adj* (a) sesquicentenary

**sesquipedalian** /-pə'daylyən/ *adj, formal or humorous* **1** containing many syllables ⟨*∼ terms*⟩ **2** fond of or characterized

by the use of long words, esp to excess ⟨*a ∼ orator*⟩ ⟨*a ∼ style*⟩ [L *sesquipedalis,* lit., a foot and a half long, fr *sesqui-* + *ped-, pes* foot – more at FOOT]

**sessile** /'sesiel/ *adj* **1** attached directly by the base; not having a stalk ⟨*a ∼ leaf*⟩ **2** permanently attached or established; not free to move about ⟨*∼ polyps*⟩ [L *sessilis* of or fit for sitting, low, dwarf (of plants), fr *sessus,* pp] – **sessility** *n*

**sessile oak** *n* DURMAST

¹**session** /'sesh(ə)n/ *n* **1** a meeting or series of meetings of a body (e g a court or council) for the transaction of business; a sitting **2** the period between the first meeting of a legislative or judicial body and its final adjournment **3** the ruling body of a Presbyterian congregation, consisting of the pastor and the elders in active service **4** the period during the year or day in which a school conducts classes **5** a period devoted to a particular activity, esp by a group of people ⟨*a recording ∼*⟩ ⚠ cession [ME, fr MF, fr L *session-, sessio,* lit., act of sitting, fr *sessus,* pp of *sedēre* to sit – more at SIT]

²**session** *adj* employed at recording sessions, esp to provide backing ⟨*a ∼ guitarist*⟩

**sessional** /'sesh(ə)nl/ *adj* **1** of a session **2** *Austr* of a medical system in which a doctor works fixed periods or sessions – **sessionally** *adv*

**Sessions** /'sesh(ə)nz/ *n pl* **1** PETTY SESSIONS **2** QUARTER SESSIONS

**sesterce** /'sestuhs/ *n* an ancient Roman coin worth ¼ DENARIUS [L *sestertius,* fr *sestertius* two and a half times as great (fr its being equal originally to two and a half asses), fr *semis* half (fr *semi-*) + *tertius* third – more at THIRD]

**sestertium** /ses'tuhti‚əm/ *n, pl* **sestertia** a monetary unit in ancient Rome worth 1000 sesterces [L, fr gen pl of *sestertius* (in the phrase *milia sestertium* thousands of sesterces)]

**sestertius** /-ti-əs/ *n, pl* **sestertii** a sesterce

**sestet** /ses'tet/ *n* a stanza or poem of six lines; *specif* the last six lines of a PETRARCHAN SONNET – compare SEXTET [It *sestetto,* fr *sesto* sixth, fr L *sextus* – more at SEXT]

**sestina** /se'steenə/ *n* a lyrical poem form consisting of six, usu unrhymed, stanzas of six lines each and a three-line ENVOY. The six end words of the lines of the first stanza recur as end words of the following five stanzas in a successively rotating order, and as the middle and end words of the lines of the envoy. [It, fr *sesto* sixth]

¹**set** /set/ *vb* **-tt-; set,** (*vt* **26**) **setted** *vt* **1** to cause to sit; place in or on a seat **2a** to put (a fowl) on eggs to hatch them **b** to put (eggs) for hatching under a fowl or in an incubator **3** to place (oneself) in position to start running in a race **4a** to place with care or deliberate purpose and with relative stability ⟨*∼ a ladder against the wall*⟩ ⟨*∼ a stone on the grave*⟩ **b** PLANT 1a ⟨*∼ seedlings*⟩ **c**(1) to make (e g a trap) ready to catch prey **c**(2) to fix (a hook) firmly into the jaw of a fish **d** to put aside (e g dough) to rise **5** to direct with fixed attention ⟨*∼ your mind to it*⟩ **6** to cause to assume a specified condition ⟨*∼ the room to rights*⟩ ⟨*∼ the house on fire*⟩ ⟨*∼ my mind at rest*⟩ ⟨*slaves were ∼ free*⟩ **7a** to appoint or assign to an office or duty ⟨*∼ him over them as foreman*⟩ **b** to post, station ⟨*∼ sentries*⟩ **8a** to place in a specified relation or position ⟨*a dish to ∼ before a king*⟩ ⟨*∼ the door ajar*⟩ **b** to place in a specified setting ⟨*the story is ∼ in 17th-century Spain*⟩ **9a** to fix as a distinguishing sign ⟨*the years have ∼ their mark on him*⟩ **b** to affix **c** to apply ⟨*∼ pen to paper*⟩ ⟨*∼ a match to kindling*⟩ **10** to fix or decide on as a time, limit, or regulation; prescribe ⟨*∼ a wedding day*⟩ ⟨*∼ the rules for the game*⟩ **11a** to establish as the most extreme, esp the highest, level ⟨*∼ a new record*⟩ **b** to furnish as a pattern or leader ⟨*∼ an example*⟩ ⟨*∼ the pace*⟩ ⟨*∼ a fashion*⟩ **c** to allot as or compose for a task ⟨*∼ the children some homework*⟩ ⟨*∼ a crossword*⟩ **12a** to adjust (a device, esp a measuring device) to a desired position ⟨*∼ the alarm for 7:00*⟩ ⟨*∼ a thermostat at 70°*⟩; *also* to adjust (e g a clock) in conformity with a standard ⟨*∼ his watch by the radio*⟩ **b** to restore to normal position or connection when dislocated or fractured ⟨*∼ a broken bone*⟩; *also* REDUCE 6 ⟨*∼ a fracture*⟩ **c** to spread to the wind ⟨*∼ the sails*⟩ **13a** to put in order for use ⟨*∼ a place for a guest*⟩ **b** to provide music or instrumentation for (a text) **c** to make scenically ready for a performance ⟨*∼ the stage*⟩ **d**(1) to arrange (type) for printing ⟨*∼ type by hand*⟩ **d**(2) to put into type or its equivalent (e g on film) ⟨*∼ the first word in italic*⟩ **14a** to put a fine edge on by grinding or honing ⟨*∼ a razor*⟩ **b** to bend slightly the tooth points of (a saw) alternately in opposite directions **c** to sink (the head of a nail) below the surface **15** to fix in a desired position (e g by heating or stretching) **16** to fix (the hair) in a

desired style by waving, curling, or arranging usu while wet **17a** to adorn or surround with something affixed or infixed; stud, dot ⟨*clear sky* ~ *with stars*⟩ ⟨*river all* ~ *about with fever trees* – Rudyard Kipling⟩ **b** to fix (eg a precious stone) in a border of metal; place in a setting **18a** to place in a relative rank or category ⟨~ *duty before pleasure*⟩ **b** to fix at a specified amount ⟨~ *bail at £500*⟩ **c** to value, rate ⟨*his promises were* ~ *at naught*⟩ **d** to place as an estimate of worth ⟨~ *a high value on life*⟩ **19** to place in relation for comparison ⟨~ *him beside Michelangelo*⟩; *also* to offset ⟨~ *our gains against our losses*⟩ **20a** to direct to action ⟨~ *him to write a report*⟩ **b** to put into activity or motion ⟨~ *the clock going*⟩ ⟨*it* ~ *me wondering*⟩ **c** to incite to attack or antagonism ⟨*war* ~ s *brother against brother*⟩ **21a** to place by transporting ⟨*was* ~ *ashore on the island*⟩ **b** to put and fix in a direction ⟨~ *our faces towards home once more*⟩ **c** *of a dog* to point out the position of (game) by holding a fixed attitude **22** to defeat (an opponent or his/her contract) in bridge **23a** to fix firmly; give rigid form to ⟨~ *his jaw in determination*⟩ **b** to make (a dye or colour) permanent **24** to cause to become firm or solid ⟨~ *jelly by adding pectin*⟩ **25** to cause (eg fruit) to develop **26a** to divide (an age-group of pupils) into sets **b** to teach (a school subject) by dividing the pupils into sets ⟨*maths and science are* ~ ted⟩ ~ *vi* **1** *of a fowl* to cover and warm eggs to hatch them **2** to place oneself in position in preparation for an action (eg running) – *also* used as an interjection to command runners to put themselves into the starting position before a race **3** *of a plant part* to undergo development usu as a result of pollination **4** to pass below the horizon; go down ⟨*the sun* ~ s⟩ **5** to make an attack – + *on* or *upon* ⟨*the dog* ~ *on the trespassers*⟩ **6** to have a specified direction in motion; flow, tend ⟨*the wind was* ~ ting *south*⟩ **7** *of a dog* to indicate the position of game by crouching or pointing **8** to dance face to face with another in a SQUARE DANCE ⟨~ *to your partner and turn*⟩ **9a** to become solid or thickened by chemical or physical alteration ⟨*the cement* ~ s *rapidly*⟩ **b** *of a dye or colour* to become permanent **c** *of a broken bone* to become whole by knitting together **d** *of metal* to acquire a permanent twist or bend from strain **10** *chiefly dial* to sit [ME *setten*, fr OE *settan;* akin to OHG *sezzen* to set, OE *sittan* to sit]

**usage** The dialect use of **set (set)** instead of **sit (sat)** should be **avoided in formal writing** ⟨*the collar* sits (not △ sets) *awkwardly*⟩ ⟨*the food* sat (not △ set) *heavily on his stomach*⟩. The two verbs have a few senses in common, since one can **set** or **sit** a baby in its pram, and a hen **sits** or **sets** while her eggs are hatching. **Set** is chiefly transitive, though cement **sets** and so does the sun; **sit** is chiefly intransitive, though one **sits** a horse or an examination.

**set about** *vt* **1** to attack ⟨set about *the intruder with a rolling pin*⟩ **2** to begin to do ⟨*how to* set about *losing weight*⟩

**set apart** *vt* **1** to reserve for a particular purpose; save **2** to make noticeable or outstanding ⟨*his height* sets *him* apart⟩

**set back** *vt* **1** to prevent or hinder the progress of; impede, delay **2** *informal* to cost ⟨*a new suit* set *him* back *a full week's wages*⟩ – see also SETBACK

**set by** *vt* to put aside for future use; reserve

**set down** *vt* **1** to place at rest on a surface or on the ground; deposit **2** to cause or allow (a passenger) to alight from a vehicle **3** to land (an aircraft) on the ground or water **4a** to ordain, establish ⟨set down *fixed rules of conduct*⟩ **b** to put in writing **5a** to regard, consider ⟨set *him* down *as a liar*⟩ **b** to attribute, ascribe ⟨set *his success* down *to sheer perseverance*⟩

**set forth** *vt* **1** to publish **2** to give an account or statement of; explain ~ *vi* to start out on a journey

**set in** *vt* to insert; *esp* to stitch (a small part) within a large article ⟨set in *a sleeve of a dress*⟩ ~ *vi* **1** to become established ⟨*take medicine before sickness* sets in⟩ **2** to blow or flow towards shore ⟨*the wind was beginning to* set in⟩ – see also SET-IN

**set off** *vt* **1a** to put in relief; show up by contrast **b** to adorn, embellish **c** to make distinct or outstanding; enhance **2** to treat as a compensating item ⟨set off *the three totals against one another*⟩ **3a** to set in motion; cause to begin **b** to cause to explode – usu + *on* or *upon* ⟨*the dog* ~ *on the trespassers*⟩ **4** to measure off on a surface **5** *chiefly NAm* to compensate for; offset ⟨*more variety in the Lancashire weather to* set off *its most disagreeable phases – Geographical Journal*⟩ – see also SET-OFF ~ *vi* to start out on a course or a journey ⟨set off *for home*⟩

**set on** *vt* **1** to urge to attack or pursue ⟨set *his dog* on the

*intruders*⟩ **2** to incite to action; instigate ⟨set on *to rebellion by their leaders*⟩

**set out** *vt* **1** to state or describe at length; expound ⟨*a pamphlet* setting out *his ideas in full*⟩ **2a** to arrange and present graphically or systematically **b** to mark out (eg a design); lay out the plan of **c** to create or construct according to a plan or design ⟨set *gardens* out *on waste ground*⟩ **3** to begin with a definite purpose or goal; intend, undertake ⟨*you* set out *deliberately to annoy me*⟩ ~ *vi* to start out on a course, a journey, or a career – see also SET-OUT

**set to** *vi* **1** to make an eager or determined start on a job or activity **2** to begin fighting – see also SET-TO

**set up** *vt* **1a** to raise to and fix in a high or prominent position ⟨set *a flag* up⟩ **b** to put forward (eg a theory) for acceptance; propound **2a** to erect ⟨set up *a statue*⟩ **b** to assemble and prepare for use or operation ⟨set up *a printing press*⟩ **c** to put (a machine) in readiness or adjustment for a tooling operation **3a** to give voice to, esp loudly; raise ⟨set up *a din*⟩ **b** to create; BRING ABOUT ⟨*issues that* set up *personal tensions*⟩ **4** to place in a high office or powerful position ⟨set up *the general as dictator*⟩ **5** to raise the spirits of; elate, gratify **6a** to put forward as exemplary **b** to claim (oneself) to be a specified thing ⟨sets *herself* up *as an authority*⟩ **7a** to found, institute ⟨set up *a fund for orphans*⟩ **b** to install oneself in ⟨*decided to* set up *office in Liverpool*⟩ ⟨set up *house together*⟩ **8a** to provide with an independent livelihood ⟨set *her up in business*⟩ **b** to bring or restore to health or success ⟨*a drink will* set *you* up⟩ **c** to provide with what is necessary or useful – usu + *with* or *for* ⟨*we're well* set up *with logs for the winter*⟩ **9** to erect (a perpendicular or a figure) on a base in a drawing **10** to prepare detailed plans for ⟨set up *a bank robbery*⟩ **11** *informal* to pay for (drinks) **12** *Br & Austr slang* to act so as to cause to appear guilty; incriminate, frame ~ *vi* **1** to start business ⟨set up *as a house agent*⟩ ⟨setting up *in the wine trade*⟩ **2** to make pretensions ⟨setting up *for a wit*⟩ – see also SET-UP

**²set** *adj* **1** intent, determined ⟨~ *on going*⟩ **2** fixed by authority or binding decision; prescribed, specified ⟨~ *hours of study*⟩ **3** intentional, premeditated ⟨*did it of* ~ *purpose*⟩ **4a** reluctant to change; fixed by habit ⟨~ *in his ways*⟩ **b** conventional, stereotyped ⟨*her speech was full of* ~ *phrases*⟩ **5** immovable, rigid ⟨*a* ~ *frown*⟩ **6** dogged, persistent ⟨~ *defiance*⟩ **7** in readiness; prepared ⟨*all* ~ *for an early morning start*⟩ **8** *of a meal* consisting of a specific combination of dishes available at a fixed price **9** *Br* having a specified bodily form; built ⟨*a slimly* ~ *youth*⟩ [ME *sett*, fr pp of *setten* to set]

**³set** *n* **1a** the act or action of setting **b** the condition of being set **2a** mental inclination, tendency, or habit; bent ⟨*a* ~ *towards mathematics*⟩ **b** a state of predisposition to act in a certain way in response to an anticipated stimulus or situation ⟨*the influence of mental* ~ *on the effect experienced by users of marijuana*⟩ **3** *taking sing or pl vb* a number of things of the same kind that belong or are used together or that form a unit ⟨*a chess* ~⟩ ⟨*a dinner* ~⟩ ⟨*a* ~ *of rooms*⟩ ⟨*a* ~ *of Dickens*⟩ ⟨*a good* ~ *of teeth*⟩ **4** direction of flow ⟨*the* ~ *of the wind*⟩ **5** form or carriage of the body or of its parts ⟨*the graceful* ~ *of her head*⟩ **6** the manner of adjustment ⟨*the* ~ *of her hat*⟩ **7a** amount of deflection from a straight line; *specif* the degree to which the teeth of a saw have been set **b** the extent to which a ship may be forced off course by the tidal current **8** permanent change of form (eg of metal) due to repeated or excessive stress **9** the act or result of arranging the hair by curling or waving **10a** a young plant or rooted cutting ready for transplanting **b** a small bulb, corm, or (piece of) tuber used for propagation ⟨*onion* ~ s⟩ **11** the width of the body of a piece of type **12** an artificial setting for a scene of a theatrical or film production **13** a sett **14** a division of a tennis match won by the side that wins at least six games beating the opponent by two games or by winning a TIE BREAKER **15** *taking sing or pl vb* a clutch of eggs **16** the basic formation in a country-dance or SQUARE DANCE **17** a session of music (eg jazz or dance music), usu followed by an intermission; *also* the music played at one session **18** *taking sing or pl vb* a group of people associated by common interests ⟨*the smart* ~⟩ **19** a collection of mathematical elements (eg numbers or points) – called also CLASS **20** an apparatus of electronic components assembled so as to function as a unit ⟨*a radio* ~⟩ **21** a usu offensive formation in football **22** *taking sing or pl vb* a group of pupils of roughly equal ability who study a particular subject together but are differently grouped for other subjects – compare STREAM [ME, fr *setten* to set & *sett,* pp of *setten;* (3 & similar senses) partly fr MF *sette* religious group, sect, fr L *secta*]

**seta** /'seetə/ *n, pl* **setae** /-ti/ a slender usu rigid or bristly and springy organ or part of an animal or plant [NL, fr L *saeta, seta* bristle – more at SINEW] – **setal** *adj*

**setaceous** /si'tayshəs/ *adj* **1** having or covered with setae or bristles; bristly **2** resembling a seta or bristle – **setaceously** *adv*

**setback** /-,bak/ *n* **1** a checking of progress **2** a defeat, reverse **3** a placing of a building, or part of a building, behind the building line to allow ventilation and light to nearby areas

**set book** *n, Br* a text prescribed for an examination

**se tenant** /sə 'tenant (*Fr* sə tə'nã)/ *adj, of postage stamps* joined together as in the original sheet; *esp* so joined but differing in design, overprint, colour, or perforation [Fr, lit., holding one another]

¹**set-,in** *adj* cut separately and sewn in ⟨~ *sleeves*⟩

²**set-in** *n* an insert

**setline** /-,lien/ *n, NAm* a long heavy fishing line to which several hooks are attached in series

¹**set-,off** *n* **1** something that is set off against another thing: **1a** a decoration, adornment **b** a compensation, counterbalance **2** the discharge of a debt or claim by setting against it a separate sum owed by the creditor to the debtor; *also* this sum itself **3** unintentional transfer of ink (e g from a freshly printed sheet)

**setose** /'seetohs/ *adj, biology* having or covered with setae; setaceous, bristly [L *setosus, saetosus,* fr *seta, saeta* bristle]

¹**set-,out** *n* **1** an array, display **2** items set out; an arrangement **3** the beginning, outset

**set piece** *n* **1** a realistic piece of stage scenery standing by itself **2** a composition (e g in literature) executed in a conventional or ideal form, often with studied artistry and brilliant effect **3** an arrangement of fireworks that forms a pattern while burning **4** any of various moves in soccer or rugby (e g a corner kick or free kick) by which the ball is put back into play after a stoppage – **set-piece** *adj*

**set point** *n* a situation (e g in tennis) in which one player will win the set by winning the next point; *also* the point won

**setscrew** /-,skrooh/ *n* **1** a screw that clamps one part of a machine to another in a set position and prevents relative motion between the parts **2** a screw for regulating or setting an adjustment of part of a machine (e g a valve opening or the tension of a spring)

**set scrum** *n* a situation in Rugby Union football, after a minor infringement, in which the ball is inserted into the tunnel formed by the eight forwards of each team pushing against each other – compare MAUL 2, RUCK 3

**set square** *n, chiefly Br* a drawing instrument consisting of a thin flat triangle (e g of wood or plastic) with one angle of 90° and the other two of 45°, or one angle of 90°, one of 60°, and one of 30°, that is used to mark out or test angles

**sett, set** /set/ *n* **1** the burrow of a badger **2** a usu rectangular block of stone or wood formerly used for paving streets [³*set*]

**settee** /se'tee/ *n* a long often upholstered seat with a back and usu arms for seating more than one person; *broadly* a sofa *synonyms* see SOFA [alter. of *settle*]

**setter** /'setə/ *n* **1** one who or that which sets **2** a large gundog of a type that was formerly trained to crouch on finding game but is now expected to point; *specif* IRISH SETTER

**set theory** *n* a branch of mathematics or of SYMBOLIC LOGIC that deals with the nature and relations of sets – **set theoretic** *adj*

**setting** /'seting/ *n* **1** the manner, position, or direction in which something (e g a dial) is set **2** the metal frame in which a gem, decorative stone, etc is mounted; *also* the style of such a frame **3a** the background, surroundings **b** the time and place of the action of a literary, dramatic, or cinematic work **c** the scenery used in a theatrical or film production **4** the music composed for a text (e g a poem) **5** PLACE SETTING

**setting coat** *n* the finishing coat of plaster

¹**settle** /'setl/ *n* a wooden bench with arms, a high solid back, and an enclosed base which can be used as a chest *synonyms* see SOFA [ME, place for sitting, seat, chair, fr OE *setl;* akin to OHG *sezzal* seat, L *sella* seat, chair, saddle, OE *sittan* to sit]

²**settle** *vt* **1** to place firmly or comfortably ⟨~d *himself in an armchair*⟩ **2a** to establish in residence ⟨~ *refugees on farmland*⟩ **b** to furnish with inhabitants; colonize **3a** to cause to sink and become compacted ⟨*rain* ~d *the dust*⟩ **b** to clarify by causing the sediment to sink ⟨*put eggshells in the coffee to* ~ *it*⟩ **4a** to free from pain, discomfort, disorder, or disturbance ⟨*took a drink to* ~ *his nerves*⟩ **b** to make subdued or well-

behaved ⟨*one word from the referee* ~d *him*⟩ **5a** to fix or resolve conclusively ⟨~ *the question*⟩ **b** to establish or secure permanently ⟨~ *the order of royal succession*⟩ **6** to arrange in an orderly or suitable position **7a** to bestow legally for life on a person ⟨~d *her estate on her son*⟩ **b** to arrange for or make a final disposition of ⟨~d *her affairs*⟩ **8** *of a male animal* to make pregnant; cause to conceive ~ *vi* **1** to come to rest ⟨*a sparrow* ~d *on the windowsill*⟩ **2a** to sink gradually to the bottom; subside ⟨*let the dust* ~ *before applying paint*⟩ **b** to become clearer by depositing sediment or scum **c** to become compact by sinking **d** *of a building, the ground, etc* to sink slowly to a lower level; subside **3a** to become established in a specified place ⟨*a cold* ~d *in his chest*⟩ **b** to become fixed or permanent ⟨*his mood* ~d *into apathy*⟩ **c** to establish a residence or colony ⟨~d *in Canada for a few years*⟩ **4a** to become calm or orderly – often + *down* **b** to adopt an ordered or stable life-style – usu + *down* ⟨*marry and* ~ *down*⟩ **5a** to adjust differences or accounts – often + *with* or *up* **b** to end a legal dispute by the agreement of both parties, without court action ⟨~ *out of court*⟩ *antonyms* unsettle, disturb [ME *settlen* to seat, bring to rest, come to rest, fr OE *setlan,* fr *setl* seat]

**settle for** *vi* to be content with; accept

**settle in** *vi* to become comfortably established ⟨*children quickly* settle in *at a new school*⟩ ~ *vt* to assist in becoming comfortably established

**settlement** /-mənt/ *n* **1** the act or process of settling **2a** an act of bestowing or giving possession of property, title, etc (e g by deed or will) **b** the sum, estate, or income secured to a person by such a settlement **3a** a newly settled place or region **b** a small village; *esp* an isolated one **4** an organization providing various community services (e g educational, recreational, and cultural facilities) in an underprivileged area **5** an agreement resolving differences ⟨*reached a* ~ *on the strike*⟩

**settler** /'setlə/ *n* a person who settles something (e g a new region)

**settling** /'setling/ *n,* **settlings** *n pl* sediment, dregs

**settlor** /'setlə/ *n* a person who makes a legal settlement or creates a trust of property

¹**set-,to** *n, pl* **set-tos** *informal* a usu brief and vigorous conflict

¹**set-,up** *n* **1** the way in which something is set up: e g **1a** the preparation and adjustment of machines for an assigned task **b** the manner in which the elements or components of a machine or apparatus are arranged, designed, or assembled **2** an arrangement; *also* an organization **3** the final arrangement of the scenery and props for a scene of a theatrical or cinematic production **4** *chiefly NAm* carriage of the body; bearing **5** *NAm* glass, ice, and mixer served to patrons who supply their own alcohol **6** *chiefly NAm informal* a task or contest with a prearranged or artificially easy outcome

**seven** /'sev(ə)n/ *n* **1** – see NUMBER table **2** the seventh in a set or series ⟨*the* ~ *of diamonds*⟩ **3** something having seven parts or members or a denomination of seven **4** *pl but taking sing or pl vb* a rugby game played with teams of seven players each – see also at SIXES and sevens [ME, fr *seven,* adj, fr OE *seofon;* akin to OHG *sibun* seven, L *septem,* Gk *hepta*] – **seven** *adj or pron,* **sevenfold** *adj or adv*

**seven seas** *n pl* all the oceans of the world ⟨*a pirate who had sailed the* ~⟩

**seventeen** /,sev(ə)n'teen/ *n* – see NUMBER table [*seventeen,* adj, fr ME *seventene,* fr OE *seofontēne,* fr *seofon* seven + *tien* ten] – **seventeen** *adj or pron,* **seventeenth** *adj or n*

**seventh** /'sev(ə)nth/ *n* **1** – see NUMBER table **2a** a musical interval between one note and another seven notes away from it counting inclusively in a DIATONIC scale (ordinary 8-note scale) **b** a note seven notes away from another counting inclusively; *specif* the note seven notes away from the first note (TONIC) of a scale; LEADING NOTE **c** the harmonic combination of two notes a seventh apart – **seventh** *adj or adv*

**seventh chord** *n* a chord made up of a fundamental note with the notes three, five, and seven notes above it counting inclusively in a DIATONIC scale (ordinary 8-note scale)

¹**Seventh-,Day** *adj* advocating or observing Saturday as the Christian Sabbath ⟨~ *Adventists*⟩

**seventh heaven** *n, chiefly humorous* a state of supreme rapture or bliss ⟨*she was in the* ~ *with her new train set*⟩ [fr the seventh being the highest of the seven heavens of Muslim and cabalistic doctrine]

**seventy** /'sev(ə)nti/ *n* **1** – see NUMBER table **2** *pl* the numbers 70 to 79; *specif* a range of temperatures, ages, or dates within

a century characterized by those numbers – often + *the*
[*seventy,* adj, fr ME, fr OE *seofontig,* short for *hundseofontig,*
fr *hundseofontig,* n, group of 70, fr *hund* hundred + *seofon*
seven + *-tig* group of ten – more at HUNDRED, -TY] – **seventy**
*adj or pron,* **seventieth** *adj or n,* **seventyfold** *adj or adv*
**,seventy-'eight** *n* 1 – see NUMBER table 2 a gramophone
record that plays at 78 revolutions per minute – usu written 78
– **seventy-eight** *adj or pron*
**seven-year itch** *n* a feeling of marital discontent tending to
lead to infidelity, allegedly experienced after about seven years
of marriage
**sever** /'sevə/ *vt* 1 to put or keep apart; separate; *esp* to remove
(a major part or portion) (as if) by cutting 2 to break off;
terminate ⟨~ *economic links*⟩ ~ *vi* to become separated
*synonyms* see ¹SEPARATE [ME *severen,* fr MF *severer,* fr L
*separare* – more at SEPARATE] – **severance** *n*
**severable** /'sevərəbl/ *adj* capable of being severed; *esp* capable
of being divided into legally independent rights or obligations
– **severability** *n*
¹**several** /'sev(ə)rəl/ *adj* **1a** more than one; various ⟨*walls built
at ~ times*⟩ **b** more than two but fewer than many ⟨~
*hundred times*⟩ ⟨*moved ~ inches*⟩ 2 *formal* **2a** separate or distinct from one another; respective ⟨*the ~ members of the committee*⟩ ⟨*specialists in their ~ fields*⟩ **b(1)** individually owned
or controlled; exclusive – compare COMMON **b(2)** relating
separately to each individual involved ⟨*a ~ judgment*⟩ [ME,
separate, distinct, fr AF, fr ML *separalis,* fr L *separ* separate,
back-formation fr *separare* to separate]
²**several** *pron taking pl vb* an indefinite number more than two
and fewer than many ⟨~ *of the guests*⟩ – **severalfold** *adj or
adv*
**severally** /'sev(ə)rəli/ *adv, formal* each by itself, herself, or
himself; separately
**severalty** /-ti/ *n* 1 possession or ownership of property (e g
land) by a single person in his/her own right as opposed to
joint possession; sole or exclusive possession of an ascertained
share of property ⟨*tenants in ~*⟩ **2a** land owned in severalty **b**
the quality or state of being held in severalty 3 *formal* the
quality or state of being several or distinct [MF *severalte,* fr
AF *severalté,* fr *several*]
**severance pay** /'sevərəns/ *n* an allowance, usu based on length
of service, that is payable to an employee on termination of
employment
**severe** /si'viə/ *adj* **1a** strict in judgment or control **b** having a
stern expression or character; austere 2 rigorous in restraint,
punishment, or requirements; stringent ⟨~ *penalties*⟩ ⟨~
*legislation*⟩ 3 strongly critical or condemnatory; censorious
⟨*a ~ critic*⟩ 4 maintaining or requiring strict self-discipline ⟨*a
~ moralist*⟩ 5 sober or restrained in decoration or manner;
plain **6a** marked by harsh or extreme conditions ⟨~ *winters*⟩
**b** inflicting great pain or distress; grievous ⟨*a ~ wound*⟩ 7
requiring much effort; arduous ⟨*a ~ test*⟩ 8 of a serious or
considerable degree or extent; grave ⟨~ *depression*⟩ *antonyms*
tolerant, tender [MF or L; MF, fr L *severus*] – **severely** *adv,*
**severeness** *n,* **severity** *n*
**Seville orange** /se'vil, 'sevl/ *n* a reddish-orange fruit with a
bitter rind and sour flesh used esp for making marmalade; *also*
an orange tree (*Citrus aurantium*) that bears this fruit [*Seville,*
province & city in SW Spain]
**Sèvres** /'seəvrə/ *n* an often elaborately decorated fine porcelain
made at Sèvres near Paris
**sew** /soh/ *vb* **sewed** /sohd/; **sewn** /sohn/, **sewed** *vt* 1 to unite,
fasten, or attach by stitches made with a needle and thread 2
to close or enclose by sewing ⟨~ *the money in a bag*⟩ 3 to
make or mend by sewing ~ *vi* to practise or engage in sewing
[ME *sewen,* fr OE *siwian;* akin to OHG *siuwen* to sew, L *suere*]
– **sewer** *n*
**sew up** *vt* 1 to mend, close (e g a hole), or enclose by sewing
2 *chiefly informal* to bring to a successful or satisfactory conclusion ⟨*sew up pay negotiations*⟩ 3 *chiefly NAm informal*
to get exclusive use or control of
**sewage** /'s(y)ooh·ij, 's(y)oo·ij/ *n* waste matter carried off by
sewers [²*sewer* + *-age*]
¹**sewer** /'sooh·ə; *also* 'syooh·ə/ *n* a medieval household officer
often of high rank in charge of serving the dishes at table and
sometimes of seating and tasting [ME, fr AF *asseour,* lit.,
seater, fr OF *asseoir* to seat – more at ASSIZE]
²**sewer** *n* an artificial usu underground conduit to carry off
waste matter, esp excrement, from houses, schools, towns, etc
and surface water from roads and paved areas [ME, fr MF

*esseweur, seweur,* fr *essewer* to drain, fr (assumed) VL *ex-
aquare,* fr L *ex-* + *aqua* water – more at ISLAND]
**sewerage** /'s(y)ooərij/ *n* 1 sewage 2 the removal and disposal
of sewage and surface water by sewers 3 a system of sewers
**sewing** /'soh·ing/ *n* 1 the act, action, or work of someone or
something that sews 2 work that has been or is to be sewn
¹**sex** /seks/ *n* 1 either of two divisions of organisms distinguished respectively as male or female 2 the sum of the structural, functional, and behavioural characteristics of living
beings that are involved in the process of reproduction and
that distinguish males and females **3a** sexually motivated
phenomena or behaviour **b** sexual intercourse 4 genitalia [ME,
fr L *sexus*]
²**sex** *vt* 1 to identify the sex of ⟨~ *chicks*⟩ 2 *informal* to increase
the sexual appeal of – often + *up*
**sex-** /seks-/, **sexi-** *comb form* six ⟨*sexivalent*⟩ ⟨*sexpartite*⟩ [L
*sex* – more at SIX]
**sexagenarian** /,seksəji'neəri·ən/ *n* a person between 60 and 69
years old [L *sexagenarius* of or containing 60, 60 years old, fr
*sexageni* 60 each, fr *sexaginta* sixty, irreg fr *sex* six + *-ginta*
(akin to L vi*ginti* twenty) – more at SIX, VIGESIMAL] – **sexagenarian** *adj*
**Sexagesima** /,seksə'jesimə/ *n* the second Sunday before Lent
[LL, fr L, fem of *sexagesimus* sixtieth; fr its being approximately 60 days before Easter]
**sexagesimal** /-'jesiməl/ *adj* of or based on the number 60 [L
*sexagesimus* sixtieth, fr *sexaginta* sixty]
**sex appeal** *n* 1 sexual attractiveness 2 *chiefly NAm* potential
for popularity; general attractiveness
**sex cell** *n* GAMETE (sperm, egg, or other mature reproductive
cell); *also* a cell from which a gamete develops
**sex chromosome** *n* a CHROMOSOME (strand of gene-carrying
material) that is concerned directly with the inheritance of sex
and that governs the inheritance of various sex-linked and sex-
limited characteristics; *esp* either of a pair of chromosomes in
many organisms including humans, that, according to whether
they are identical or dissimilar, determines the sex of the
organism – compare X CHROMOSOME, Y CHROMOSOME
**sexdecillion** /,seksdi'silyən/ *n* – see NUMBER table [L *sedecim,
sexdecim* sixteen (fr *sex* six + *decem* ten) + E *-illion* (as in
*million*)]
**sexed** /sekst/ *adj* 1 having sex or sexual instincts, esp to a
specified degree ⟨*under ~*⟩ 2 having sex appeal, esp to a
specified degree ⟨*a highly ~ actor*⟩
**sex gland** *n* a testis, ovary, or other gland in which sperm,
eggs, etc are produced; GONAD
**sex hormone** *n* a hormone that affects the growth or function
of the reproductive organs or the development of SECONDARY
SEX CHARACTERISTICS (e g facial hair in men)
**sexi-** /seksi-/ – see SEX-
**sexism** /'sek,siz(ə)m/ *n* 1 a belief that sex determines intrinsic
worth, capacities, and role in society and that sexual differences
produce an inherent superiority of a particular sex, usu the
male 2 discrimination on the basis of sex; *esp* prejudice against
women on the part of men – **sexist** *adj or n*
**sex kitten** *n, informal* a woman who makes a display of her
sex appeal
**sexless** /-lis/ *adj* **1a** lacking sexuality or sexual intercourse ⟨~
*marriage*⟩ **b** devoid of sex characteristics; neuter 2 lacking
sex appeal – **sexlessly** *adv,* **sexlessness** *n*
'**sex-,limited** *adj* of or being (the inheritance of) a gene or
genetic characteristic whose effect is shown in only one sex
'**sex-,linkage** *n* the condition of being sex-linked; *also* the
transmission or genetic inheritance of sex-linked genes and
characteristics
'**sex-,linked** *adj* 1 *of a gene* located on a SEX CHROMOSOME 2 *of
an inheritable characteristic* (e g colour blindness) determined by
a sex-linked gene and therefore much commoner in one sex
than in the other
**sex object** *n* a person regarded exclusively as the means of
sexual satisfaction
**sexology** /sek'soləji/ *n* the study of sexual behaviour or of the
interaction of the sexes, esp among human beings
**sexploitation** /,seksploy'taysh(ə)n/ *n, informal or humorous*
the employment of sex for commercial gain, esp in films and
publications [blend of *sex* and *exploitation*]
**sexpot** /-,pot/ *n, humorous* SEX KITTEN
**sex shop** *n* a shop selling goods (e g pornographic magazines)
relating to sex and sexual practices
**sext** /sekst/ *n, often cap* the fourth of the CANONICAL HOURS,

originally fixed for 12 noon [ME *sexte*, fr LL *sexta*, fr L, sixth hour of the day, fr fem of *sextus* sixth, fr *sex* six]

**sextant** /'sekstənt/ *n* an instrument for measuring angles that is used, esp in navigation, to observe the altitudes of celestial bodies and so determine the observer's position on the earth's surface [NL *sextant-, sextans* sixth part of a circle, fr L, sixth part, fr *sextus* sixth]

**sextet** /sek'stet/ *n* 1 a musical composition for six instruments or voices 2 *taking sing or pl vb* a group or set of six, esp of six musicians performing together □ compare SESTET [alter. of *sestet*]

**sextillion** /ˌseks'tilyən/ *n* – see NUMBER table [Fr, irreg fr *sex-* + *-illion* (as in *million*)]

**sextodecimo** /ˌsekstoh'desi,moh/ *n, pl* **sextodecimos** SIX-TEENMO (size of paper) [L, abl of *sextus decimus* sixteenth, fr *sextus* sixth + *decimus* tenth – more at DECIMAL]

**sexton** /'sekstən/ *n* a church officer or employee who takes care of the church property and, at some churches, rings the bell for services and digs graves [ME *secresteyn, sexteyn*, fr MF *secrestain*, fr ML *sacristanus* – more at SACRISTAN]

**sexton beetle** *n* BURYING BEETLE (beetle that buries the carcasses of small animals)

**¹sextuple** /'sekstyoopl/ *adj* 1 having six units or members 2 six times as great or as many 3 marked by six beats per bar of music ⟨~ *time*⟩ [prob fr ML *sextuplus*, fr L *sextus* sixth + *-plus* multiplied by – more at DOUBLE] – **sextuple** *n*

**²sextuple** *vb* to make or become six times as much or as many

**sextuplet** /'sekstyooplit/ *n* 1 a combination of six of a kind 2 any of six offspring born at one birth 3 a group of six equal musical notes performed in the time ordinarily given to four of the same value

**sexual** /'seksyoo(ə)l, -sh(ə)l/ *adj* 1 of or associated with sex or the sexes ⟨~ *differentiation*⟩ ⟨~ *conflict*⟩ 2 having or involving sex or SEXUAL REPRODUCTION [LL *sexualis*, fr L *sexus* sex] – **sexually** *adv*

**sexual intercourse** *n* 1 heterosexual intercourse involving penetration of the vagina by the penis; coitus 2 intercourse involving genital contact between individuals other than penetration of the vagina by the penis

**sexuality** /ˌseksyoo'aliti/ *n* the quality or state of being sexual: eg a the condition of having a sex b sexual activity c the expression of sexual receptivity or interest

**sexual·ize, -ise** /'seksyoo(ə)liez, -shəliez/ *vt* to make sexual; endow with a sexual character or significance

**sexual relations** *n pl* sexual intercourse

**sexual reproduction** *n* reproduction involving the joining of a female GAMETE (eg an egg cell) with a male gamete (eg a sperm cell)

**sexy** /'seksi/ *adj, informal* sexually suggestive or stimulating; erotic – **sexily** *adv*, **sexiness** *n*

**Seyfert galaxy** /'seefət, 'siefət/ *n* any of a class of SPIRAL GALAXIES that have small compact very bright nuclei of variable light intensity, and whose emission of light and radio waves indicates the presence of hot gases in rapid motion [Carl K *Seyfert* †1960 US astronomer]

**¹sforzando** /sfawt'sandoh/ *adj or adv* with prominent stress or accent – used as a direction in music [It, verbal of *sforzare* to force]

**²sforzando** *n, pl* **sforzandos, sforzandi** /-di/ a sforzando note or chord

**sfumato** /sfooh'mahtoh/ *n* a technique in painting of delicately blending one tone into another so as to produce softened outlines [It, fr pp of *sfumare* to evaporate, fr *s-* (fr L *ex-*) + *fumare* to smoke, fr L]

**sgraffito** /sgra'feetoh/ *n, pl* **sgraffiti** /-ti/ decoration in which parts of a surface layer (eg of plaster or clay) are cut or scratched away in a pattern or design to expose a different coloured ground; *also* something decorated with sgraffito [It, fr pp of *sgraffire* to scratch, produce sgraffito]

**sh** /sh/ *interj* – used, often in prolonged or reduplicated form, to urge or command silence

**Sha'ban** /shə'bahn, shah-/ *n* – see MONTH table [Ar *sha'bān*]

**Shabbat** /sha'baht, 'shahbəs/ *n, pl* **Shabbatim** /shə'bahtim, shə'bawsəm/ the Jewish Sabbath [Heb *shabbāth*]

**shabby** /'shabi/ *adj* 1a threadbare or faded from wear ⟨*a ~ sofa*⟩ b dilapidated, run-down ⟨*a ~ district*⟩ 2 dressed in worn or grubby clothes; seedy ⟨*a ~ tramp*⟩ 3a wretched, despicable ⟨*nothing but a ~ villain*⟩ b shameful, unfair ⟨*what a ~ trick, driving off and leaving me to walk home!*⟩ c inferior in quality; slipshod ⟨*an argument full of ~ reasoning*⟩ [E dial.

*shab* scab, low fellow, fr ME, scab, fr OE *sceabb*] – **shabbily** *adv*, **shabbiness** *n*

**shabraque, shabrack** /'shabrak/ *n* a saddlecloth used esp by European light cavalry regiments in former times [Fr *schabraque*, fr Ger *schabracke*, fr Hung *csáprág*, fr Turk *çaprak*]

**Shabuoth** /shah'vooh·oth, -əs/ *n* a Jewish holiday observed on the sixth and seventh of SIVAN in commemoration of the revelation of the TEN COMMANDMENTS at Mt Sinai – called also SHEVUOTH [Heb *shābhū'ōth*, lit., weeks]

**shack** /shak/ *n* a small crudely built dwelling or shelter [perh back-formation fr E dial. *shackly* rickety; or perh fr MexSp *jacal* hut, fr Nahuatl *xacalli*]

**¹shackle** /'shakl/ *n* 1 something (eg a manacle or fetter) that confines the legs or arms 2 **shackles** *pl*, **shackle** something that restricts or prevents free action or expression 3 any of various devices for securing something; *esp* a U-shaped piece of metal with a pin or bolt to close the opening [ME *schakel*, fr OE *sceacul*; akin to ON *skökull* pole of a cart]

**²shackle** *vt* 1a to bind with shackles; fetter b to make fast with shackles 2 to deprive of freedom of thought or action by means of restrictions or handicaps; impede – **shackler** *n*

**shack up** *vi, informal* to take up residence with and have a sexual relationship with somebody; *also* to spend the night as a partner in sex – usu + *together* or *with*

**shad** /shad/ *n, pl* **shad**, *esp for different types* **shads** any of several soft-finned European and N American food fishes (genus *Alosa*) of the herring family that differ from the typical herrings in having a relatively deep body and in swimming up rivers from the sea to breed [(assumed) ME, fr OE *sceadd*; akin to L *scatēre* to bubble]

**shaddock** /'shadək/ *n* a very large thick-rinded usu pear-shaped citrus fruit that differs from the closely related grapefruit esp in having a loose rind and often coarse dry pulp; *also* the tree (*Citrus grandis*) that bears shaddocks [Captain *Shaddock*, 17th-c E seaman who brought seed of the tree from the E Indies to Barbados]

**¹shade** /shayd/ *n* 1a partial darkness caused by the interception of rays of light b relative obscurity or insignificance ⟨*places that put even the Cotswolds ... into the ~ – In Britain*⟩ 2a shelter (eg by foliage) from the direct heat and glare of the sun b a place so sheltered from the sun 3 a transitory or illusory appearance 4 *pl* 4a the shadows that gather as night falls b the netherworld, hades 5 a ghost 6 something that intercepts or diffuses light or heat: eg 6a a lampshade b *chiefly NAm* b(1) *pl, informal* sunglasses b(2) a window blind 7 the reproduction of the effect of shade in painting or drawing 8a a colour produced by a pigment or dye mixture having some black in it b a particular level of depth or brightness of a colour ⟨*a ~ of pink*⟩ 9 a minute difference or amount ⟨*the ~s of meaning in a poem*⟩ *synonyms* see ¹SHADOW [ME, fr OE *sceadu*; akin to OHG *scato* shadow, Gk *skotos* darkness] – **shadeless** *adj* – **a shade** to a small extent; somewhat ⟨*a shade too much salt*⟩

**²shade** *vt* 1a to shelter or screen by intercepting radiated light or heat b to cover with a shade 2 to darken or obscure (as if) with a shadow 3 to cast into the shade (eg by an exhibition of superiority); eclipse, obscure 4a to represent the effect of shade or shadow on b to add shading to c to colour so that the shades pass gradually from one to another 5 to change by gradual transition ~ *vi* to pass by slight changes or imperceptible degrees – usu + *into* or *off into* ⟨*the dark red ~*d *into black at the edge*⟩ – **shader** *n*

**'shade-,grown** *adj* grown in the shade; *specif* grown under cloth ⟨*~ tobacco*⟩

**shade tree** *n* a tree grown primarily to produce shade

**shading** /'shayding/ *n* the use of marking within outlines to suggest three-dimensionality, shadow, or degrees of light and dark in a picture or drawing

**shadoof** *also* **shaduf** /shə'doohf/ *n* a counterbalanced SWEEP (pole on a pivot) used since ancient times esp in Egypt for raising water (eg for irrigation) [Ar *shādūf*]

**¹shadow** /'shadoh/ *n* 1a partial darkness caused by an opaque body interposed so as to cut off rays from a light source ⟨*turned into the ~ of woods – John Buchan*⟩ b a dark area resembling shadow ⟨*~s under his eyes from fatigue*⟩ 2 a reflected image 3 shelter from danger or observation ⟨*under the ~ of the flag*⟩ 4a a faint representation or suggestion ⟨*~s of future difficulties*⟩ b a mere semblance or imitation of something ⟨*she wore herself to a ~ by studying too hard*⟩ 5 a dark figure cast upon a surface by a body intercepting light rays

⟨*the trees cast their* ∼s *on the wall*⟩ **6** a phantom **7** *pl* darkness **8** a shaded or darker portion of a picture **9** an attenuated form; a vestige ⟨*after his illness he was only a* ∼ *of his former self*⟩ **10a** an inseparable companion or follower **b** someone (eg a spy or detective) who shadows **11** a small degree or portion; a trace ⟨*without a* ∼ *of doubt*⟩ **12** a source of gloom or disquiet ⟨*his death cast a* ∼ *on the festivities*⟩ **13** pervasive and often disabling influence ⟨*governed under the* ∼ *of his predecessor*⟩ [ME *shadwe*, fr OE *sceaduw-, sceadu* shade, shadow] – **shadowless** *adj*, **shadowlike** *adj*

  *synonyms* You can *cast* a **shadow**, but not a **shade**, which has no particular shape.

²**shadow** *vt* **1** to cast a shadow over **2** to represent or prefigure obscurely or faintly – often + *forth* or *out* **3** to follow (a person) secretly; keep under surveillance **4** to shade **5** *archaic* to shelter, protect **6** *obs* to shelter from the sun ∼ *vi* **1** to pass gradually or by small degrees **2** to become overcast (as if) with shadows ⟨*his face* ∼ed *at the thought*⟩ – **shadower** *n*

³**shadow** *adj* **1a** identical with another in form but without the other's power or status ⟨*a* ∼ *government in exile*⟩ **b** of or being a group of leaders of a parliamentary opposition who constitute the probable membership of the cabinet when their party is returned to power and who act as opposition spokesmen on major issues ⟨∼ *cabinet*⟩ ⟨∼ *spokesman on employment*⟩ **2a** having an indistinct pattern ⟨∼ *plaid*⟩ **b** having darker sections of design ⟨∼ *lace*⟩ **3** shown by throwing the shadows of performers or puppets on a screen ⟨*a* ∼ *dance*⟩

'**shadow-,box** *vi* to box with an imaginary opponent, esp as a form of training – **shadow-boxing** *n*

**shadowgraph** /'shadoh,grahf, -,graf/ *n* a photographic image resembling a shadow

**shadowy** /'shadoh-i/ *adj* **1a** of the nature of or resembling a shadow; insubstantial **b** scarcely perceptible; indistinct **2** lying in or obscured by shadow ⟨*deep* ∼ *interiors*⟩ – **shadowily** *adv*, **shadowiness** *n*

**shady** /'shaydi/ *adj* **1** producing or affording shade ⟨*a* ∼ *tree*⟩ **2** sheltered from the direct heat or light of the sun ⟨*a* ∼ *spot*⟩ **3a** of questionable merit; uncertain, unreliable ⟨*a* ∼ *deal*⟩ **b** *informal* of doubtful integrity; disreputable ⟨*he's a* ∼ *character*⟩ – **shadily** *adv*, **shadiness** *n*

¹**shaft** /shahft/ *n* **1a(1)** the long handle of a spear or similar weapon **a(2)** a spear, lance **b** a pole; *specif* either of two long pieces of wood between which a horse is hitched to a vehicle **c(1)** an arrow; *esp* one for a longbow **c(2)** the body or stem of an arrow extending from the NOCK to the head **2** a sharply delineated beam of light shining from an opening **3** something suggestive of the shaft of a spear or arrow, esp in having a long slender cylindrical form: eg **3a** the trunk of a tree **b** the cylindrical pillar between the capital and the base of a column **c** the handle of a tool or implement (eg a hammer or golf club) **d** a usu cylindrical bar used to support rotating pieces or to transmit power or motion by rotation **e** the central stem of a feather **f** the relatively straight part of a long bone (eg the thigh bone) between the enlarged ends **g** a small architectural column (eg at each side of a doorway) **h** *NAm* a monument in the form of a column or obelisk **i** a man-made vertical or sloping passage of uniform and limited cross section, that leads underground to a mine, well, etc and is used esp for finding or mining ore, raising water, or ventilating underground workings (eg in a cave) **j** a vertical opening or passage through the floors of a building ⟨*a lift* ∼⟩ **4a** a projectile thrown like a spear or shot like an arrow **b** a scornful, satirical, or pithily critical remark; a barb **c** *NAm informal* harsh or unfair treatment – esp in *give the shaft, get the shaft* synonyms see ¹HAFT [ME, fr OE *sceaft*; akin to OHG *scaft* shaft, L *scapus* shaft, stalk, Gk *skēptron* staff, L *capo* capon – more at CAPON]

²**shaft** *vt* **1** to fit with a shaft **2** *NAm slang* to treat unfairly or harshly

**shafting** /'shahfting/ *n* shafts or material for shafts

¹**shag** /shag/ *n* **1a** an unkempt or uneven tangled mass or covering (eg of hair) **b** long coarse or matted fibre or nap **c** something (eg cloth or a carpet) of or containing shag or having a shag pile **2** a strong coarse tobacco cut into fine shreds **3** a European bird (*Phalacrocorax aristotelis*) that is distinguished from the closely related European cormorant by its smaller size and lack of white on its face [(assumed) ME *shagge*, fr OE *sceacga*; akin to ON *skegg* beard, OSlav *skokŭ* leap; (3) prob fr its shaggy crest]

²**shag** *vt* **-gg-** to make rough or shaggy

³**shag** *vb* **-gg-** **1** *vulg* to fuck, screw **2** *Br slang* to make utterly exhausted – usu + *out* [origin unknown]

⁴**shag** *n, vulg* an act of sexual intercourse; *esp* a sex orgy

**shagbark, shagbark hickory** /'shag,bahk/ *n* (the wood of) a N American hickory tree (*Carya ovata*) with sweet edible nuts and a grey shaggy loose outer bark that peels off in long strips

**shaggy** /'shagi/ *adj* **1a** covered with or consisting of long, coarse, or matted hair **b** *of a fabric* having a rough nap, texture, or surface **2** unkempt – **shaggily** *adv*, **shagginess** *n*

,**shaggy-'dog story** /'shagi/ *n* a protracted and inconsequential funny story whose humour lies in the pointlessness or irrelevance of the conclusion

**shagreen** /sha'green/ *n* **1** an untanned leather covered with small round granulations and usu dyed green **2** the rough skin, covered with small close-set knobbly lumps, of various sharks and rays [by folk etymology fr Fr *chagrin*, fr Turk *saǧrı*] – **shagreen** *adj*

**shah** /shah/ *n, often cap* a sovereign of Iran [Per *shāh* king – more at CHECK] – **shahdom** *n*

¹**shake** /shayk/ *vb* **shook** /shook/; **shaken** *vi* **1** to move to and fro with rapid usu irregular motion **2** to vibrate, esp from the impact of a blow or shock **3** to tremble as a result of physical or emotional disturbance **4** to be subject to instability; totter ⟨*"The Shaking of the Foundations"* – Paul Tillich⟩ **5** to move something briskly to and fro or up and down, esp in order to mix **6** to shake hands ⟨*if you've agreed then* ∼ *on it*⟩ **7** to trill ∼ *vt* **1** to brandish, wave, or flourish, esp in a threatening manner **2** to cause to move with a rapidly alternating motion **3** to cause to quake, quiver, or tremble **4** to cause to waver; weaken ⟨∼ *one's faith*⟩ **5** to put in a specified state by repeated quick jerky movements ⟨shook *himself free from the woman's grasp*⟩ **6** to dislodge or eject by quick jerky movements of the support or container ⟨shook *the dust from the cloth*⟩ **7** to clasp (the hand of another) in greeting or farewell or to convey goodwill or agreement **8** to agitate the feelings of; upset ⟨*the news* shook *him*⟩ **9** ³TRILL **10** *NAm informal* to get away from; GET RID OF ⟨∼ *a habit*⟩ – see also **shake a** LEG [ME *shaken*, fr OE *sceacan*; akin to ON *skaka* to shake, Skt *khajati* he agitates] – **shakable, shakeable** *adj*

  *synonyms* Shake, agitate, quake, convulse, rock, wobble, shiver, tremble, quiver, and shudder all mean "move to and fro more or less unsteadily". **Shake** is the most general, and often entails sharp unsettling violence ⟨*high wind* **shaking** *the nest to and fro*⟩. **Agitate** suggests a strong tossing ⟨*trees* **agitated** *by the storm*⟩. **Quake** and particularly **convulse** are even stronger, entailing violent irregular spasms ⟨*earthquake* **convulsed** *the island*⟩. **Rock** and **wobble** often imply a swinging that threatens collapse ⟨*bus* **rocked** *on the rough mountain road*⟩, with **wobble** particularly suggesting clumsy uncertainty ⟨*baby's head* **wobbled** *on my shoulder*⟩. **Shiver, tremble, quiver,** and **shudder** all suggest a quick slight vibration; **shiver** being chiefly associated with cold, **tremble** and to a lesser extent **quiver** often involving fear, and **shudder** implying a convulsive movement of aversion ⟨**shudder** *at the thought of such contamination*⟩. See ¹SWING

**shake down** *vi* **1** to make up and occupy an improvised bed **2a** to become comfortably established, esp in a new place or occupation **b** to settle (as if) by shaking ∼ *vt* **1** to give a shakedown test to **2** to settle the contents of (as if) by shaking ⟨shake down *a stove*⟩ **3** *chiefly NAm* to bring about a reduction of ⟨shake down *the number of immigrants*⟩ **4** *NAm informal* to obtain money from in a dishonest or illegal manner **5** *NAm informal* to make a thorough search of (a person); frisk – see also SHAKEDOWN

**shake off** *vt* to free oneself from ⟨shook off *a heavy cold*⟩ ⟨shook off *his gloom*⟩

**shake up** *vt* **1** to jar (as if) by a physical shock ⟨*the collision* shook up *both drivers*⟩ **2** *informal* to reorganize by extensive and often drastic measures – see also SHAKE-UP

²**shake** *n* **1** an act of shaking ⟨*indicated her disapproval with a* ∼ *of the head*⟩ **2** a blow or shock that upsets the balance or equilibrium of something **3** something produced by shaking: eg **3a** a fissure in timber usu separating and parallel to ANNUAL RINGS of growth **b** a fissure or crack in rock layers **4** a wavering, vibrating, or alternating motion caused by a blow or shock **5** TRILL **1a 6** a shingle split from a shortish piece of log **7** *chiefly NAm* MILK SHAKE **8** *pl, informal* a condition of uncontrollable trembling (eg from chill or fever); *specif* DELIRIUM TREMENS – usu + *the* **9** *informal* a moment ⟨*I'll be round in two* ∼s⟩ **10** *chiefly NAm informal* an earthquake – **no great shakes** *informal* of no great worth; not very good [prob orig referring to a shake of dice]

**shakedown** /'shayk,down/ *n* **1** a makeshift bed (eg one made up on the floor) **2** a testing under operating conditions of something new (e g a ship) to look for possible shortcomings **3** *NAm informal* an act or instance of shaking someone down; *esp* extortion **4** *NAm informal* a thorough search

**shakeout** /'shayk‚owt/ *n* **1a** a minor economic recession **b** a sharp break in a particular industry that usu follows overproduction or excessive competition and tends to force out weaker producers **2** a sharp lowering of prices; *esp* a sharp usu brief decline in a commodity or security market that drives weak or frightened speculators from the market **3** a shake-up

**shaker** /'shayka/ *n* **1** one who or that which shakes; *esp* a container or utensil used in shaking ⟨*cocktail* ~⟩ ⟨*flour* ~⟩ **2** *cap* a member of an American sect originating in England in 1747, practising celibacy and a self-denying communal life, and looking forward to the millennium [(2) fr a dance with shaking movements formerly performed as part of the sect's act of worship] – **Shaker** *adj*, **Shakerism** *n*

**¹Shakespearean, Shakespearian** *also* **Shaksperean, Shaksperian** /'shayk'spiarian/ *adj* of or having the characteristics of Shakespeare or his writings ⟨*a* ~ *breadth of vision*⟩

**²Shakespearean, Shakespearian** *also* **Shaksperean, Shaksperian** *n* an authority on or devotee of Shakespeare

**Shakespeareana, Shakespeariana** /‚shayk‚spiari'ahna/ *n taking pl vb* collected items by, about, or relating to Shakespeare

**Shakespearean sonnet** *n* a sonnet consisting of three 4-line units and a couplet with a rhyme scheme of *abab cdcd efef gg* – compare **Petrarchan sonnet**

**'shake-‚up** *n*, *informal* an act or instance of shaking up; *specif* an extensive and often drastic reorganization (e g of manpower in a company)

**shaking palsy** /'shayking/ *n* PARKINSON'S DISEASE – not now used technically

**shako** /'shahkoh, 'shakoh/ *n*, *pl* **shakos, shakoes** a stiff military hat with a high crown and plume [Fr, fr Hung *csákó*]

**Shakta** /'shukta/ *n or adj* (an adherent) of Shaktism [Skt *śākta*, fr *Sakti*]

**Shakti** /'shukti/ *n* the dynamic energy of a Hindu god personified as his female consort; *broadly* cosmic energy as conceived in Hindu thought [Skt *Sakti*]

**Shaktism** /'shuk‚tiz(a)m/ *n* a Hindu sect worshipping Shakti under various names (e g Kali or Durga) in a cult of devotion to the female principle, often with magical rites and orgies

**shaky** /'shayki/ *adj* **1** characterized by shakes ⟨~ *timber*⟩ **2a** lacking stability; precarious ⟨*a* ~ *coalition*⟩ **b** lacking in firmness (e g of beliefs or principles) **c** lacking in authority or reliability; questionable ⟨~ *allegiance*⟩ **3a** unsound in health; poorly **b** characterized by or affected with shaking **4** likely to give way or break down; rickety ⟨*a* ~ *chair*⟩ – **shakily** *adv*, **shakiness** *n*

**shale** /shayl/ *n* a dark fine-grained smooth rock that splits easily into thin parallel layers or flakes and is formed by the compression and consolidation of layers of clay deposited as sediment over a long period [ME, shell, scale, fr OE *scealu* – more at SHELL]

**shale oil** *n* a crude dark oil obtained from some types of shale by heating

**shall** /shal; *strong* shal/ *vb pres sing & pl* **shall**; *past* **should** /shad; *strong* shood/ *va* **1** – used to express a command or exhortation ⟨*you* ~ *go*⟩ or what is legally mandatory ⟨*it* ~ *be unlawful to carry firearms*⟩ **2a** – used to express what is inevitable or seems likely to happen in the future ⟨*we* ~ *have to be ready*⟩ ⟨*we* ~ *see*⟩ **b** – used in the question form to express simple futurity ⟨~ *you pay him?*⟩ ⟨*when* ~ *we expect you?*⟩ or with the force of an offer or suggestion ⟨~ *I open the window?*⟩ **3** – used to express determination ⟨*they* ~ *not pass*⟩ **4** *archaic* **4a** will have to; must **b** will be able to; can ~ *vi*, *archaic* to be about to go; *also* to have to go ⟨*he to England* ~ *along with you* – Shak⟩ [ME *shal* (1&3 sing. pres indic), fr OE *sceal*; akin to OHG *scal* (1&3 sing. pres indic) ought to, must, Lith *skola* debt]

*usage* In formal British English south of the Border, **shall** has traditionally been used to express the pure future in the first person ⟨*when shall we three meet again?* – Shak⟩ and to express commands and promises in the second and third persons ⟨*thou shalt not steal* – Book of Common Prayer⟩; while conversely **will** expresses commands and promises in the first person ⟨*give me my robe, for I will go* – Shak⟩ and the pure future in the second and third persons ⟨*England expects that every man will do his duty* – Horatio, Viscount Nelson⟩. Today, under the combined influence of Scottish, Irish, and American English, this distinction is dying out, with the result that **will, won't** commonly replace **shall, shan't**, or both **will** and **shall** are replaced by the neutral **'ll**, which means either. British English still uses **shall** *I* in questions ⟨*shall I open the window?* (= do you want me to)⟩ and a useful distinction can still be made between ⟨*shall you join us?* (= are you going to)⟩ and ⟨*will you join us?* (= please do)⟩.

**shalloon** /sha'loohn/ *n* a lightweight twilled fabric of wool or worsted used chiefly for the linings of coats and uniforms [*Châlons*-sur-Marne, town in NE France]

**shallop** /'shalap/ *n* a small open boat propelled by oars or sails and used chiefly in shallow waters [MF *chaloupe*]

**shallot** /sha'lot/ *n* a plant (*Allium ascalonicum*) of the lily family that resembles the related onion and produces small clustered bulbs; *also* its bulb used esp for pickling and in seasoning [modif of Fr *échalote*, deriv of (assumed) VL *escalonia* – more at SCALLION]

**¹shallow** /'shaloh/ *adj* **1** having little depth ⟨~ *water*⟩ **2** having little inward or backward extension ⟨*office buildings have taken the form of* ~ *slabs* – Lewis Mumford⟩ **3a** lacking in penetration ⟨~ *generalizations*⟩ **b** superficial in knowledge, thought, or feeling ⟨*a* ~ *demagogue*⟩ **4** displacing comparatively little air; weak ⟨~ *breathing*⟩ **5** not marked or accentuated ⟨*the plane went into a* ~ *dive*⟩ ⟨*a* ~ *curve*⟩ *synonyms* see SUPERFICIAL *antonym* deep [ME *schalowe*] – **shallowly** *adv*, **shallowness** *n*

**²shallow** *vb* to make or become shallow

**shallows** /'shalohz/ *n taking sing or pl vb*, **shallow** *n* a shallow place or area in a body of water

**shalom** /sha'lohm, sha'lom/ *interj* – used as a Jewish greeting and farewell △ slalom [Heb *shālōm* peace]

**shalom aleichem** /a'layk(h)am/ *interj* – used as a traditional Jewish greeting [Heb *shālōm 'alēkhem* peace unto you]

**shalt** /shalt/ *archaic pres 2 sing of* SHALL

**¹sham** /sham/ *n* **1** a trick intended to delude; a hoax **2** cheap falseness; hypocrisy ⟨*the* ~ . . . *of the empty pageant* – Oscar Wilde⟩ **3** a decorative piece of cloth made to simulate an article of personal or household linen (e g a pillowcase) and used in place of or over it **4** an imitation or counterfeit purporting to be genuine **5** a person who shams [perh fr E dial. *sham* shame, alter. of E *shame*]

**²sham** *vb* -mm- *vt* to act so as to counterfeit ⟨*I* ~ *med a headache to get away*⟩ ~ *vi* to create a deliberately false impression *synonyms* see ¹PRETEND

**³sham** *adj* **1** not genuine; imitation ⟨~ *pearls*⟩ **2** pretended, feigned ⟨*a* ~ *battle*⟩ ⟨~ *indignation*⟩

**shaman** /'shahman, 'shay-/ *n* a priest believed to exercise magic power (e g for healing and divination), esp through ecstatic trances [Russ or Tungus; Russ, fr Tungus *šaman*]

**shamanism** /'shahma‚niz(a)m, 'shay-/ *n* a religion of the URALALTAIC peoples of N Asia and Europe characterized by belief in an unseen world of gods, demons, and ancestral spirits responsive only to the shamans; *also* any similar religion – **shamanist** *n*, **shamanistic** *adj*

**shamateur** /'shamata, ‚shama'tuh/ *n*, *derog* a sports player who is officially classed as amateur but who takes payment [blend of *sham* and *amateur*] **shamateurism** *n*

**¹shamble** /'shambl/ *vi* to walk awkwardly with dragging feet; shuffle [arch. *shamble* bowed, malformed, prob fr *shamble* table for displaying meat for sale; prob fr a person's bowed legs resembling the trestles of a table]

**²shamble** *n* a shambling gait – **shambly** *adj*

**shambles** /'shamblz/ *n*, *pl* **shambles 1** a slaughterhouse **2a** a place of carnage **b** a scene or a state of great destruction ⟨*the place was left a* ~ *by hooligans*⟩ **c** a state of chaos or confusion; a mess **3** *archaic* a butcher's stall [pl of arch. *shamble* meat market, table for displaying meat for sale, fr ME *shamel*, fr OE *scamul* counter, stool, deriv of L *scamnum* bench, stool]

**shambolic** /sham'bolik/ *adj*, *Br informal* utterly chaotic or confused [irreg fr *shambles*]

**¹shame** /shaym/ *n* **1a** a painful emotion caused by consciousness of guilt, shortcomings, impropriety, or disgrace **b** susceptibility to such emotion ⟨*was not upset because he had no* ~⟩ **2** humiliating disgrace or disrepute; ignominy **3** something that brings regret or disgrace ⟨*it's a* ~ *you weren't there*⟩ *antonyms* glory, pride [ME, fr OE *scamu*; akin to OHG *scama* shame] – **put to shame** to disgrace by comparison ⟨*their garden puts ours to shame*⟩

**²shame** *vt* **1** to bring shame to; disgrace **2** to put to shame by outdoing **3** to fill with a sense of shame **4** to compel by causing to feel guilty ⟨~d *into confessing*⟩

³**shame** *interj* – used for expressing censure or reproach, esp on moral grounds

**shamefaced** /-'fayst/ *adj* **1** showing modesty; bashful **2** showing shame; ashamed [alter. of arch. *shamefast,* fr ME, fr OE *scamfæst,* fr *scamu* shame + *fæst* fixed, fast] – **shamefacedly** *adv,* **shamefacedness** *n*

**shameful** /-f(ə)l/ *adj* **1** bringing disrepute or ignominy; disgraceful **2** arousing the feeling of shame – **shamefully** *adv,* **shamefulness** *n*

**shameless** /-lis/ *adj* **1** devoid of shame; insensible to disgrace **2** showing lack of shame; disgraceful – **shamelessly** *adv,* **shamelessness** *n*

**shammer** /'shamə/ *n* somebody who shams

**shammy** /'shami/ *n* CHAMOIS 2 [by alter.]

¹**shampoo** /sham'pooh/ *vt* **shampoos; shampooing; shampooed 1a** to clean (e g the hair) with soap and water or with a special cleaning preparation **b** to wash the hair of **c** to clean the hair or surface of with shampoo ⟨~ *the carpet*⟩ **2** *archaic* to massage [Hindi *cāpo,* imper of *cāpnā* to press, shampoo] – **shampooer** *n,* **shampooist** *n*

²**shampoo** *n, pl* **shampoos 1** a washing of the hair, esp by a hairdresser **2** a soap, detergent, etc used for shampooing

**shamrock** /'sham,rok/ *n* any of several plants whose leaves have three leaflets and that are used as a floral emblem by the Irish: e g **a** a yellow-flowered clover (*Trifolium dubium*) **b** WOOD SORREL **c** WHITE CLOVER [IrGael *seamrōg*]

**Shan** /shahn/ *n, pl* **Shans,** *esp collectively* **Shan 1** a member of a group of MONGOLOID peoples of SE Asia **2** the Thai languages of the Shan

**shandrydan** /'shandri,dan/ *n* **1** a chaise with a hood **2** a rickety vehicle [origin unknown]

**shandy** /'shandi/ *n* a drink consisting of beer mixed with lemonade or GINGER BEER [short for *shandygaff,* of unknown origin]

**shanghai** /,shang'hie/ *vt* **shanghais; shanghaiing; shanghaied** /-'hied/ **1** to compel to join a ship's crew, esp by stupefying with drink or drugs – compare PRESS-GANG **2** to put into an awkward or unpleasant position by trickery [*Shanghai,* seaport in E China; fr the formerly widespread use of this method to secure sailors for voyages to the Orient] – **shanghaier** *n*

**Shangri-la** /,shang-gri 'lah/ *n* **1** a remote imaginary place where life approaches perfection **2** a place of idyllic seclusion [*Shangri-La,* imaginary land depicted in the novel *Lost Horizon* by James Hilton †1954 E novelist]

¹**shank** /shangk/ *n* **1a** the part of the leg between the knee and the ankle in human beings; *also* the corresponding part in various other VERTEBRATE animals **b** the leg **c** a cut of beef, veal, mutton, or lamb from the upper or the lower part of the leg **2** a straight narrow usu vital part of an object: e g **2a** the straight part of a nail or pin **b** a straight part of a plant; a stem, stalk **c** the part of an anchor between the ring and the crown **d** the part of a fishhook between the eye and the bend **e** the part of a key between the handle and the section (BIT) that acts on the lock **f** the section (TANG) of a knife, sword, etc that connects with the handle **g** the narrow part of the sole of a shoe beneath the instep **3** a part of an object by which it can be attached to something else: e g **3a(1)** a projection on the back of a solid button (e g a leather or metal button) **a(2)** a short stem of thread that holds a sewn button away from the cloth **b** the projecting part of a knob handle that contains the spindle socket **c** the end of a tool (e g a drill) that is gripped in a CHUCK **4** the rectangular solid base of a piece of printing type **5** *chiefly NAm* the early or late part of a period of time ⟨*the ~ of the evening*⟩ [ME *shanke,* fr OE *scanca;* akin to ON *skakkr* crooked, Gk *skazein* to limp] – **shanked** *adj*

²**shank** *vt* SOCKET 2

**shanks's mare** *n, chiefly NAm* SHANKS'S PONY

**shanks's pony** *n, chiefly humorous* one's own feet or legs considered as a means of transport ⟨*went home by ~*⟩ [*shanks,* pl of ¹*shank* (sense 1b)]

**shanny** /'shani/ *n* a small European BLENNY (type of fish) (*Blennius pholis*) that is olive green with irregular dark spots [origin unknown]

**shan't** /shahnt/ shall not

**shantung** /,shan'tung/ *n* a silk fabric in plain weave, with a slightly irregular surface due to the use of wild silk yarns [*Shandong* [*Shantung*], province in NE China]

¹**shanty** /'shanti/ *n* a small crudely built or dilapidated dwelling

or shelter, usu of wood; a shack [CanF *chantier,* fr Fr, gantry, fr L *cantherius* trellis]

²**shanty, shantey** *n* a song sung by sailors in rhythm with their work [modif of Fr *chanter* to sing – more at CHANT]

**shantyman** /'shanti,man/ *n* somebody who lives in a shanty

**shantytown** /-,town/ *n* a town or part of a town consisting mainly of shanties

¹**shape** /shayp/ *vt* **1** to form, create; *esp* to give a particular form or shape to ⟨~d *the clay into a cube*⟩ **2** to adapt in shape so as to fit neatly and closely ⟨*a dress* ~d *to her figure*⟩ **3a** to devise, plan ⟨*together* ~d *a dark conspiracy*⟩ **b** to embody in a specified form ⟨*shaping a folktale into an epic*⟩ **4a** to make fit or appropriate; adapt ⟨~ *a character for management*⟩ **b** to determine or direct the course of (e g a person's life) **c** to modify (behaviour) by rewarding responses that tend towards a desired result **5** *obs* to ordain, decree ~ *vi* **1** to happen; TAKE PLACE ⟨*if things* ~ *right*⟩ **2** to assume or approach a desired form or character – often + *up* [ME *shapen,* alter. of OE *scieppan;* akin to OHG *skepfen* to shape] – **shapable, shapeable** *adj,* **shaper** *n*

²**shape** *n* **1a** the visible or tangible form of a particular item or kind of item **b(1)** spatial form ⟨*all solids have*⟩ **b(2)** a circle, square, or other standard geometrical form **2** the contour of the body, esp of the trunk; the figure **3a** a phantom, apparition **b** an assumed appearance; a guise ⟨*the devil in the* ~ *of a serpent*⟩ **4a** definite form (e g in thought or words) ⟨*the plan slowly took* ~⟩ **b** a fit or ordered condition ⟨*got the car into* ~⟩ **5** a general structure or plan ⟨*the final* ~ *of society*⟩ **6** a form in which other things can be shaped; a mould ⟨*a* ~ *for moulding jellies*⟩ **7** the condition of a person or thing, esp at a particular time ⟨*in excellent* ~ *for his age*⟩ – **shaped** *adj* – **in shape** in an original, normal, or fit condition ⟨*exercises to keep in shape*⟩ – **lick into shape** to put into proper form or condition [fr the former belief that bear cubs were born shapeless and had to be licked into shape by their parents] – **take shape** to assume a definite or distinctive form

**shapeless** /-lis/ *adj* **1** having no definite shape **2a** deprived of usual or proper shape; misshapen ⟨*a* ~ *old hat*⟩ **b** lacking in elegance or grace of form ⟨*a* ~ *young girl*⟩ – **shapelessly** *adv,* **shapelessness** *n*

**shapely** /-li/ *adj* having a pleasing shape; well-proportioned – **shapeliness** *n*

**shapen** /'shaypən/ *adj, archaic* given or assuming a definite shape – usu in combination ⟨*an ill*-shapen *body*⟩ [archaic pp of *shape*]

**shard** /shahd/ *n* **1** *also* **sherd** a piece or fragment of something brittle (e g earthenware) **2** SHERD 2 (fragments of ancient pottery) [ME, fr OE *sceard;* akin to OE *scieran* to cut – more at SHEAR]

¹**share** /sheə/ *n* **1a** a portion belonging to, due to, or contributed by an individual **b** a full or fair portion ⟨*he's had his* ~ *of fun*⟩ **2a** the part allotted or belonging to any of a number owning property or interest together **b** any of the equal portions into which property or invested capital is divided; *specif* any of the equal interests or rights into which the entire capital stock of a company is divided, the ownership of which is regularly evidenced by one or more certificates **c** *pl, chiefly Br* the proprietorship element in a company, usu represented by transferable certificates [ME, fr OE *scearu* cutting, tonsure; akin to OE *scieran* to cut]

²**share** *vt* **1** to divide and distribute in shares; apportion – usu + *out* **2** to partake of, use, experience, or enjoy with others **3** to grant or give a share in ~ *vi* **1** to have a share or part – often + *in* **2** to apportion and take shares of something – usu + *out* or *with* – **shareable, sharable** *adj,* **sharer** *n*

` synonyms Share, participate, and partake all mean "have in common with others". Share is the most general, and can mean that one grants part of something to another ⟨share *your lunch with a friend*⟩ or merely that something is mutually possessed ⟨*diseases which man* shares *with animals* – *Time*⟩. Participate applies particularly to the taking part in a communal experience or enterprise ⟨participate *in the election*⟩. The rather formal partake implies the acquiring of part of something, particularly food, drink, or experience, and by extension means merely "consume" ⟨partake *of a glass of whisky*⟩.

³**share** *n* the blade of any of various farm implements; *esp* a ploughshare [ME *schare,* fr OE *scear;* akin to OHG *scaro* ploughshare, OE *scieran* to cut]

**share certificate** *n* a document showing ownership of one or more shares in a company

**sharecropper** /-,kropə/ *n, NAm* a tenant farmer, esp in the southern USA, who lives on credit provided by the landlord and receives an agreed share of the value of the crop – **share-crop** *vb*

**shareholder** /-,hohldə/ *n* someone or something (eg a person or company) that holds or owns a share in property

**sharemilking** /-,milking/ *n, NZ* the system of helping an owner of dairy cattle with milking in exchange for a share in the profits – **sharemilker** *n*

**'share-,out** *n* a distribution, apportionment

**'share-,pusher** *n, Br* a dealer who sells shares other than through the regular channels and often fraudulently

**sharif** /sha'reef/ *n* a descendant of the prophet Muhammad through his daughter Fatima; *broadly* someone of noble ancestry or political preeminence in a predominantly Islamic country △ sheriff [Ar *sharīf*, lit., illustrious] – **sharifian** *adj*

**'shark** /shahk/ *n* any of numerous mainly marine fishes of medium to large size that have a cartilage skeleton, a long tapering body, GILL SLITS at the sides and a mouth on the underside, and a tough usu dull grey skin. They are typically active predators and are sometimes dangerous to man. [origin unknown]

**²shark** *n* **1** a greedy unscrupulous person who exploits others by usury, extortion, or trickery **2** *NAm informal* somebody who excels greatly, esp in a specified field – compare WHALE [prob modif (influenced in form & meaning by **¹shark**) of Ger *schurke* scoundrel]

**³shark** *vb, archaic vt* to obtain by illicit means ~ *vi* to make a living by fraud or trickery

**sharkskin** /-,skin/ *n* **1** the hide of a shark; *also* leather made from this **2a** a smooth stiff durable fabric in twill or basket weave with small woven designs **b** a smooth crisp fabric with a dull finish made usu of rayon in basket weave

**¹sharp** /shahp/ *adj* **1** adapted to cutting or piercing: eg **1a** having a thin keen edge or fine point **b** bitingly cold; icy ⟨a ~ wind⟩ **c** composed of hard angular grains; gritty ⟨~ sand⟩ **2a** keen in intellect; quick-witted **b** keen in perception; acute ⟨~ sight⟩ **c** keen in attention; vigilant ⟨keep a ~ lookout⟩ **d** paying shrewd usu selfish attention to personal gain ⟨a ~ trader⟩ **3** keen in action or manner: eg **3a** full of activity or energy; vigorous ⟨a ~ trot⟩ **b** capable of acting or reacting strongly; *esp* caustic ⟨a ~ soap⟩ **4** severe, harsh: eg **4a** inclined to or marked by irritability or anger; fiery ⟨a ~ temper⟩ **b** causing intense usu sudden anguish ⟨a ~ pain⟩ **c** cutting in language or implication ⟨a ~ rebuke⟩ **5** affecting the senses or sense organs intensely: eg **5a(1)** pungent, tart, or acid, esp in flavour ⟨~ cheese⟩ **a(2)** acrid **b** having a shrill or piercing sound **c** issuing in a brilliant burst of light ⟨a ~ flash⟩ **6a** characterized by hard lines and angles ⟨~ features⟩ **b** involving an abrupt change in direction or one at an acute angle ⟨a ~ turn⟩ **c** clear in outline or detail; distinct ⟨a ~ image⟩ **d** conspicuously clear ⟨~ contrast⟩ **7** *of a musical note* **7a** raised by a SEMITONE (distance between adjacent notes on a piano) ⟨~⟩ **b** higher than the intended pitch – compare **¹FLAT 9 8** *informal* stylish, dressy [ME, fr OE *scearp*; akin to OE *scieran* to cut – more at SHEAR] – **sharply** *adv*, **sharpness** *n*

  *synonyms* **Sharp, keen,** and **acute** can all mean "showing alert competence". **Sharp** suggests quickness of perception and a certain clever and perhaps tricky resourcefulness. **Keen** implies skill in quick analysis ⟨**keen** debate⟩. **Acute** emphasizes discrimination and penetration ⟨as the **acute** reader will not have failed to note – Havelock Ellis⟩. *antonyms* **dull, blunt**

**²sharp** *adv* **1** in a sudden quick manner; sharply ⟨the car pulled up ~⟩ **2** exactly, punctually ⟨4 o'clock ~⟩ **3** above the proper musical pitch – compare **³FLAT 3**

  *usage* **Sharp** as an adverb is chiefly used in certain fixed phrases, and cannot replace **sharply**, the usual adverb ⟨speak **sharply** to him⟩ ⟨**sharply** contrasted colours⟩.

**³sharp** *n* **1** one who or that which is sharp: eg **1a** (a character on the musical stave indicating) a note one semitone higher than a specified note **b** a relatively long needle with a sharp point and a small rounded eye, for use in general sewing **c** *NAm* a real or self-styled expert **2** *chiefly NAm* a swindler, sharper

**sharpen** /'shahpən/ *vt* to make sharp or sharper ⟨~ a pencil⟩ ⟨~ a musical note⟩ – compare FLATTEN 2 ~ *vi* to grow or become sharp or sharper – **sharpener** *n*

**sharp end** *n* the active area or part of an industry or organization; FRONT LINE 2

**sharpening stone** /'shahpəning/ *n* a stone with which edge tools can be sharpened by rubbing; a whetstone

**sharper** /'shahpə/ *n* a cheat, swindler; *esp* a gambler who habitually cheats [**¹sharp + ²-er**]

**,sharp-'eyed** *adj* having keen sight; *also* keenly observant or penetrating

**sharpie, sharpy** /'shahpi/ *n, NAm informal* an exceptionally shrewd or cunning person; *esp* a sharper

**sharpish** /'shahpish/ *adv, Br informal* with haste; somewhat quickly ⟨we'd better move ~ to get some tea⟩

**,sharp-'nosed** *adj* **1** having a pointed nose or snout **2** having a keen sense of smell

**sharp practice** *n* dealing in which advantage is taken or sought unscrupulously

**,sharp-'set** *adj* **1** set at a sharp angle or so as to present a sharp edge **2** eager for food; very hungry – **sharp-setness** *n*

**sharpshooter** /-,shoohtə/ *n* a good marksman – **sharpshooting** *n*

**,sharp-'sighted** *adj* **1** having acute vision **2** mentally keen or alert; sharp-witted – **sharp-sightedly** *adv*, **sharp-sightedness** *n*

**,sharp-'tongued** *adj* cutting or sarcastic in speech; quick to rebuke

**,sharp-'witted** *adj* having or showing acute discernment or mental alertness

**shashlik** *also* **shashlick** /,shahsh'lik, 'shahslik/ *n* a kebab [Russ *shashlyk*, of Turkic origin]

**shat** /shat/ *past of* SHIT

**¹shatter** /'shatə/ *vt* **1a** to break into pieces (eg by a sudden blow) **b** to cause to break down; impair, disable ⟨his nerves were ~ed⟩ **2** to cause the disruption or annihilation of; wreck **3** *informal* to have a forceful or violent effect on the feelings of ⟨she was absolutely ~ed by the news⟩ **4** *informal* to cause to be utterly exhausted ⟨felt ~ed by the long train journey⟩ ~ *vi* **1** to break suddenly apart; disintegrate **2** to drop leaves, petals, fruit, etc ⟨the wheat ~ed in the fields⟩ [ME *schateren*] – **shatteringly** *adv*

**²shatter** *n* **1** *pl* fragments, shreds ⟨the broken vase lay in ~s⟩ **2** an act of shattering; the state of being shattered

**shatterproof** /'shatə,proohf/ *adj* made so as not to shatter ⟨~ glass⟩

**¹shave** /shayv/ *vb* **shaved, shaven** *vt* **1a** to remove in thin layers or shreds – often + *off* ⟨~ off a thin slice of cheese⟩ **b** to cut off thin layers or slices from ⟨~ a board with a plane⟩ **c** to cut or trim closely ⟨a closely ~d lawn⟩ **2a** to remove the hair from (a part of the body) by cutting close to the roots **b** to cut off (hair or beard) close to the skin **3** to come very close to or brush against in passing **4** *NAm* to discount (a note) at an exorbitant rate ~ *vi* to cut off hair or beard close to the skin [ME *shaven*, fr OE *scafan*; akin to L *scabere* to scratch, *capo* capon]

**²shave** *n* **1** a tool or machine for shaving **2** a thin slice; a shaving **3** an act or process of shaving **4** an act of narrowly missing or avoiding something (eg a source of danger or risk) ⟨that was a close ~!⟩

**shavehook** /-,hook/ *n* a tool for scraping that has a usu triangular blade set at right angles to a shaft

**shaveling** /'shayvling/ *n* **1** *chiefly derog* a tonsured clergyman; a priest **2** *archaic* a youth

**shaver** /'shayvə/ *n* **1** an implement or machine for shaving; *specif* an electric-powered razor **2** *informal* a boy, youngster **3** *archaic* a swindler

**shavetail** /-,tayl/ *n, NAm* a pack mule, esp when newly broken in [fr the practice of shaving the tails of newly broken mules to distinguish them from untrained ones]

**Shavian** /'shayvyən/ *n* an admirer or devotee of G B Shaw, his writings, or his social and political theories [*Shavius*, latinized form of George Bernard *Shaw* †1950 Br (Ir-born) playwright & socialist] – **Shavian** *adj*

**shaving** /'shayving/ *n* **1** the action of one who or that which shaves **2** *usu pl* something shaved off ⟨wood ~s⟩

**shaving brush** *n* a brush for applying soap to the face before shaving

**¹shaw** /shaw/ *n, archaic* a clump of bushes or small trees; a thicket [ME, fr OE *sceaga*; akin to ON *skegg* beard – more at SHAG]

**²shaw** *n, chiefly Br* the stalks and leaves of a cultivated crop (eg potatoes or turnips) [prob alter. of *show*]

**shawl** /shawl/ *n* a usu decorative square, oblong, or triangular piece of fabric that is worn to cover the head or shoulders [Per *shāl*]

**shawl collar** *n* a collar that is rolled back and follows a continuous line round the neck and down the front edges of a garment

**shawm** /shawm/ *n* an early double-reed woodwind instrument [ME *schalme*, fr MF *chalemie*, modif of LL *calamellus*, dim. of L *calamus* reed, fr Gk *kalamos* – more at HAULM]

**Shawnee** /shaw'nee/ *n*, *pl* **Shawnees**, *esp collectively* **Shawnee** 1 a member of an American Indian people originally of the central Ohio valley 2 the ALGONQUIAN language of the Shawnee people [back-formation fr obs *Shawnese*, fr Shawnee *Shaaw-anwaakī*]

**Shawwal** /shə'wahl/ *n* – see MONTH table [Ar *shawwāl*]

**shay** /shay/ *n* CHAISE 1 [back-formation fr *chaise*, taken as pl]

**¹she** /shi; *strong* shee/ *pron* 1 that female person or creature who is neither speaker nor hearer ⟨*~ is my mother*⟩ – compare HE, HER, IT, THEY 2 – used to refer to something regarded as feminine (eg by personification) ⟨*~ was a fine ship*⟩ [ME, prob alter. of *hye*, alter. of OE *hēo* she – more at HE]

**²she** /shee/ *n* a female person or animal ⟨*is the baby a he or a ~?*⟩ – often in combination ⟨*she-cat*⟩

**shea butter** /shiə/ *n* a pale solid fat obtained from the seeds of the SHEA TREE and used as a food and in making soap and candles

**sheaf** /sheef/ *n*, *pl* **sheaves** /sheevz/ 1 a quantity of plant material, esp the stalks and ears of a cereal grass (eg corn), bound together 2 a collection of items laid one against the other ⟨*a ~ of papers*⟩ [ME *sheef*, fr OE *scēaf*; akin to OHG *scoub* sheaf, Russ *chub* forelock] – **sheaflike** *adj*

**shea nut** /shiə/ *n* the seed of the SHEA TREE

**¹shear** /shiə/ *vb* **sheared, shorn** /shawn/ *vt* **1a** to cut off the hair from ⟨*with shorn scalp*⟩ **b** to cut or clip (hair, wool, a fleece, etc) from someone or something; *also* to cut something from ⟨*~ a lawn*⟩ **c** to cut (as if) with shears ⟨*~ a metal sheet in two*⟩ **2** to cut with something sharp **3** to deprive of something as if by cutting off – usu pass + *of* ⟨*has been shorn of his authority*⟩ **4a** to subject to a shear force; *esp* to deform, displace, or separate by subjecting to a shear force **b** to cause (eg a rock mass) to move along the plane of contact ~ *vi* **1** to cut through something (as if) with a sharp instrument; slice ⟨*gulls ~ed through the sky*⟩ **2** to become deformed, displaced, or separated under the action of a shear force ⟨*the bolt may ~ off*⟩ **3** *chiefly Scot* to reap crops with a sickle [ME *sheren*, fr OE *scieran* to ON *skera* to cut, L *curtus* shortened, Gk *keirein* to cut, shear] – **shearer** *n*

  *usage* The normal past participle is **shorn** for hair or wool, particularly when it is used as an adjective ⟨*a shorn lamb*⟩, and **sheared** for metal ⟨*the bolt has sheared off*⟩.

**²shear** *n* **1a shears** *pl*, *shear* **1a(1)** a cutting implement similar or identical to a pair of scissors but typically larger **a(2)** any of various cutting tools or machines operating by the action of opposed cutting edges of metal **b shears** *pl but taking sing or pl vb*, **shear** *also* **sheer** SHEERLEGS (hoisting apparatus) **2a** an action or force that causes or tends to cause parallel planes in a body to slide or become displaced with respect to one other in a direction parallel to their plane of contact **b** (the extent of) a deformation of a body or displacement of a body part caused by a shear force **3** *chiefly Br* the action or an instance of shearing – used in combination to indicate the approximate age of sheep in terms of shearings undergone ⟨*a sheep of two ~s*⟩

**shearlegs** /'shiə,legz/ *n* SHEERLEGS (hoisting apparatus)

**shearling** /-ling/ *n*, *chiefly Br* a sheep after its first shearing

**shear pin** *n* an easily replaceable pin inserted at a critical point in a machine and designed to break when subjected to excess stress

**shearwater** /-,wawtə/ *n* any of numerous seabirds (esp genus *Puffinus*) that are related to the petrels and albatrosses and usu skim close to the waves when flying

**sheatfish** /'sheet,fish/ *n* WELS (type of catfish) [alter. of *sheathfish*, fr *sheath* + *fish*]

**sheath** /sheeth/ *n*, *pl* **sheaths** /sheedhz/ 1 a case or cover for a blade (eg of a knife or sword) 2 a cover or case of a plant or animal body or body part: eg **2a** the tubular fold of skin into which the penis of many mammals is retracted **b(1)** the lower part of a leaf (eg of a grass) that encloses a stem **b(2)** a SPATHE (leaflike structure) that surrounds the flowers in some plants (eg the cuckoopint) 3 a cover or support that is applied like or resembles the sheath of a blade: eg **3a** SHEATHING 2 **b** a condom [ME *shethe*, fr OE *scēath*; akin to OHG *sceida* sheath, L *scindere* to cut – more at SHED]

**sheathbill** /'sheeth,bil/ *n* any of several white WADING BIRDS

(family Chionididae) of colder parts of the southern hemisphere that have a horny sheath over the base of the upper part of the bill

**sheath dress** *n* a woman's very closely fitting dress

**sheathe** *also* **sheath** /sheedh/ *vt* 1 to put into or provide with a sheath ⟨*~d her dagger*⟩ 2 to plunge or bury (eg a sword) in flesh 3 to withdraw (a claw) into a sheath 4 to encase or cover with something (eg thin boards or sheets of metal) that protects [ME *shethen*, fr *shethe* sheath] – **sheather** *n*

**sheathing** /'sheedhing/ *n* 1 the action of one who or that which sheathes something 2 material used to sheathe something: eg **2a** a covering of boards or of waterproof material on the outside wall of a frame house or on a timber roof **b** metal plates on a ship's hull

**sheath knife** *n* a knife that has a fixed blade and is designed to be carried in a sheath

**shea tree** /shiə/ *n* a tropical African tree (*Butyrospermum parkii*) of the sapodilla family with fatty nuts that yield SHEA BUTTER [Bambara *sí*]

**¹sheave** /sheev/ *n* a grooved wheel (eg in a pulley block) [ME *sheve*; akin to OE *scēath* sheath]

**²sheave** *vt* to gather and bind into a sheaf [fr *sheaf*, by analogy to *grief*:*grieve*]

**shebang** /shi'bang/ *n*, *chiefly NAm informal* an affair, business ⟨*she's head of the whole ~*⟩ [perh alter. of *shebeen*]

**Shebat** /she'vat/ *n* – see MONTH table [Heb *shēbhāt*]

**shebeen** /shi'been/ *n*, *chiefly Irish* an unlicensed or illegally operated drinking establishment [IrGael *síbín* bad ale]

**Shechinah, Shekinah** /she'kienə/ *n* the presence of God in the world as conceived in Jewish theology [Heb *shēkhīnāh*]

**¹shed** /shed/ *vb* **-dd-; shed** *vt* 1 to be incapable of holding or absorbing; repel ⟨*a duck's plumage ~s water*⟩ **2a** to cause (blood) to flow by wounding or slaying **b** to pour forth; let flow ⟨*~ tears*⟩ **c** to give off in a stream ⟨*fish ~ding their eggs in spawning*⟩ **d** to give off or out; cast ⟨*his book ~s some light on this subject*⟩ **3a(1)** to cast off (eg a natural body covering); moult **a(2)** to let fall (eg leaves) **a(3)** to eject (eg seed or spores) from a natural receptacle **b** to rid oneself of as superfluous or burdensome ⟨*researchers who ~ their colleagues*⟩ ~ *vi* 1 to become dispersed; scatter ⟨*grains that easily shatter and ~*⟩ 2 to cast off or lose a natural covering (eg hair) ⟨*the cat is shedding*⟩ [ME *sheden* to divide, separate, fr OE *scēadan*; akin to OHG *skeidan* to separate, L *scindere* to cut, split, Gk *schizein* to split]

**²shed** *n* 1 WATERSHED (ridge of land between drainage areas) 2 a passageway between the threads of the warp, through which the shuttle is passed in weaving

**³shed** *n* a small lightly built structure for shelter or storage; *esp* a single-storeyed building with one or more sides open [alter. of earlier *shadde*, prob fr ME *shade* shade]

**she'd** /shid; *strong* sheed/ she had; she would

**¹sheen** /sheen/ *adj*, *archaic* shining, resplendent [ME *shene* beautiful, shining, fr OE *scīene*; akin to OE *scēawian* to look – more at SHOW]

**²sheen** *vi*, *archaic* to be bright; shine

**³sheen** *n* **1a** a bright or shining quality or condition; brightness, lustre **b** a subdued shininess or glitter of a surface **c** a lustrous surface imparted to textiles through finishing processes or use of shiny yarns 2 a textile exhibiting notable sheen – **sheeny** *adj*

**sheeny** /'sheeni/ *n*, *derog* a Jew [origin unknown]

**sheep** /sheep/ *n*, *pl* **sheep** 1 any of numerous RUMINANT (cud-chewing) mammals (genus *Ovis*) related to the goats but stockier and lacking a beard in the male; *specif* one (*Ovis aries*) long bred and domesticated, esp for its flesh and coat of typically long curly wool 2 an inane or docile person; *esp* one easily influenced or led – see also WOLF in sheep's clothing [ME, fr OE *scēap*; akin to OHG *scāf* sheep]

**sheepcote** /-,kot, -,koht/ *n*, *chiefly Br* a sheepfold

**'sheep-,dip** *n* a liquid preparation of insecticides, disinfectants, etc into which sheep are plunged, esp to destroy parasites (eg lice and ticks) on them

**sheepdog** /-,dog/ *n* a dog used to tend, drive, or guard sheep; *esp* BORDER COLLIE

**sheepfold** /-,fohld/ *n* a pen or shelter for sheep

**sheepherder** /-,huhdə/ *n*, *NAm* a shepherd

**sheepish** /'sheepish/ *adj* 1 resembling a sheep in meekness, stupidity, or timidity 2 embarrassed by consciousness of a fault ⟨*a ~ look*⟩ – **sheepishly** *adv*, **sheepishness** *n*

**sheep ked** /ked/ *n* a wingless bloodsucking fly (*Melophagus* *ovinus*) that feeds chiefly on sheep, causing skin irritation and often infection

**sheepo** /'sheepoh/ *n, pl* **sheepos** *Austr & NZ* a person who puts sheep into the pens where shearing is done

**sheep's eyes** *n pl* wistful amorous glances ⟨making ∼ at her⟩

**sheep's fescue** /'feskyooh/ *n* a hardy European grass (*Festuca ovina*) with very thin leaves that is widely used for lawns [fr its use for sheep pasture]

**sheepshank** /-,shangk/ *n* 1 a knot for shortening a line 2 *Scot* something of no worth or importance

**sheepshearer** /'sheep,shiərə/ *n* someone who shears sheep

**sheepshearing** /-,shiəring/ *n* 1 the act of shearing sheep 2 the time or season for shearing sheep; *also* a festival held at this time

**sheepskin** /-,skin/ *n* 1 the skin of a sheep; *also* leather made from this 2 the skin of a sheep dressed with the wool on ⟨a ∼ coat⟩

**sheep's sorrel** *n* 1 a small sorrel (*Rumex acetosella*) with narrow leaves and reddish flowers

**sheep station** *n, Austr & NZ* a very large property for breeding sheep

**sheep tick** *n* 1 a bloodsucking tick (*Ixodes ricinus*) whose young cling to bushes and readily drop onto and attach themselves to passing animals (e g sheep and cattle) 2 SHEEP KED – compare ¹TICK 2

**sheep walk** *n, chiefly Br* a tract of land on which sheep are pastured

**sheepyard** /'sheep,yahd/ *n, Austr & NZ* a yard where sheep are kept

¹**sheer** /shiə/ *adj* 1 of very thin or transparent texture; diaphanous ⟨∼ tights⟩ 2a unqualified, utter ⟨∼ ignorance⟩ ⟨a ∼ waste of money⟩ b not mixed or mingled with anything else; pure, unadulterated ⟨won through by ∼ determination⟩ 3 marked by great and unbroken steepness; precipitous ⟨a ∼ cliff⟩ 4 *informal* strikingly reminiscent of ⟨the piece was ∼ Mozart⟩ 5 *obs* bright, shining [ME *schere* freed from guilt, prob alter. of *skere*, fr ON *skærr* pure; akin to OE *scīnan* to shine] – **sheerly** *adv*, **sheerness** *n*

²**sheer** *adv* 1 straight up or down without a break ⟨rugged cliffs rose ∼ out of the sea⟩ 2 *informal* altogether, completely ⟨his name went ∼ out of my head⟩

³**sheer** *vi* to deviate from a course; swerve ∼ *vt* to cause to sheer [perh alter. of ¹*shear*]

  **sheer off** *vi, chiefly Br* to depart or turn away abruptly, esp in order to evade

⁴**sheer** *n* 1 a turn, deviation, or change in a course (e g of a ship) 2 the angle which a ship takes to the cable when moored to a single anchor

⁵**sheer** *n* the curvature from front to rear of a ship's deck as observed when looking from the side [perh alter. of ²*shear*]

**sheerlegs, shearlegs** /-,legz/ *n taking sing or pl vb, pl* **sheerlegs, shearlegs** a hoisting apparatus consisting of two or more upright spars lashed together at their upper ends with tackle for lifting heavy loads (e g masts or guns) [²*shear* + *legs*]

**sheers** /shiəz/ *n taking sing or pl vb*, **sheer** *n* a sheerlegs

¹**sheet** /sheet/ *n* 1 a broad piece of cloth; *specif* a rectangle of cloth (e g of linen or cotton) used as an article of bed linen 2a(1) a usu rectangular piece of paper; *esp* one manufactured for printing a(2) a rectangular piece of heavy paper with a plant specimen mounted on it ⟨a herbarium of 100,000 ∼ s⟩ b *usu pl* a printed section for a book, esp before it has been folded, cut, or bound c a newspaper, periodical, or occasional publication ⟨a gossip ∼⟩ d the unseparated postage stamps printed by one impression of a plate on a single piece of paper; *also* a joined set (PANE) of stamps 3 a broad usu flat expanse ⟨a ∼ of ice⟩ 4 a suspended or moving expanse ⟨a ∼ of flame⟩ ⟨∼ s of rain⟩ 5a a piece of something that is thin in comparison to its length and breadth b a flat metal baking utensil 6 *maths* a surface or part of a surface (e g of a geometrical figure) on which it is possible to pass from any one point of it to any other without leaving the surface [ME *shete*, fr OE *scȳte*; akin to OE *scēotan* to shoot – more at SHOOT] – **sheetlike** *adj*

²**sheet** *vt* 1 to cover with a sheet; *esp* to shroud 2 to provide with sheets 3 to form into sheets ∼ *vi* to come down in sheets ⟨the rain ∼ed against the windows⟩ – **sheeter** *n*

³**sheet** *adj* rolled or spread out in a sheet ⟨∼ steel⟩

⁴**sheet** *n* 1 a rope that regulates the angle at which a sail is set in relation to the wind 2 *pl* the spaces at either end of an open boat not occupied by seats [ME *shete*, fr OE *scēata* lower

corner of a sail; akin to OE *scȳte* sheet] – **three sheets in/to the wind** drunk

**sheet anchor** *n* 1 a large strong anchor formerly carried in the middle of a ship for use in an emergency 2 a principal support or dependable thing or person, esp in danger; a mainstay [alter. (prob influenced by ⁴*sheet*) of earlier *shoot anchor*, fr ME *shute anker*]

**sheet bend** *n* a knot or hitch used for temporarily fastening a rope to a loop in another rope or through a hole

'**sheet-,fed** *adj* of or printed by a press that prints on paper in sheet form

**sheet glass** *n* glass made in large sheets directly from the furnace

**sheeting** /'sheeting/ *n* 1a material suitable for making into sheets b sheets 2 a lining (e g of wood or steel) used to support an embankment or the walls of an excavation

**sheet lightning** *n* lightning in diffused or sheet form due to reflection and diffusion by the clouds and sky

**sheet metal** *n* metal in the form of a thin sheet

**sheet music** *n* music printed on large unbound sheets of paper

**sheikh, sheik** /shayk, sheek/ *n* 1 an Arab chief 2 **sheik, sheikh** a romantically attractive or dashing man [Ar *shaykh*]

  **usage** The pronunciation /shayk/ is recommended for BBC broadcasters.

**sheikhdom, sheikdom** /'shaykd(ə)m, 'sheekd(ə)m/ *n* a region under the rule of a sheikh

**sheila, sheilah** /'sheelə/ *n, Austr, NZ, & SAfr informal* a young woman; a girl [alter. (influenced by the forename *Sheila*) of earlier *shaler*, of unknown origin]

**shekel** /'shekl/ *n* 1a any of various ancient units of weight; *esp* a Hebrew unit equal to about 16.3 grams (just over ¹/₂ ounce) b a monetary unit based on a shekel weight of gold or silver 2a a coin weighing one shekel b – see MONEY table 3 *pl, informal chiefly humorous* money [Heb *sheqel*]

**Shekinah** /she'kienə/ *n* SHECHINAH

**shelduck** /'shelduk/, *masc* **sheldrake** /'sheldrayk/ *n pl* **shelducks**, *esp collectively* **shelduck** any of various Eurasian ducks (genus *Tadorna*); *esp* a common mostly black, white, and chestnut duck (*Tadorna tadorna*) slightly larger than the mallard [*sheldrake* fr ME, fr *sheld-* (akin to MD *schillede* particoloured) + *drake*; *shelduck* fr *sheld*rake + *duck*]

**shelf** /shelf/ *n, pl* **shelves** /shelvz/ 1a a thin flat usu long and narrow piece of material (e g wood) fastened horizontally (e g on a wall) at a distance from the floor to hold objects ⟨book ∼⟩ b any of several similar pieces in a cupboard, bookcase, or similar structure c the contents of a shelf 2 something resembling a shelf in form, position, or function: e g 2a a usu partly submerged sandbank or ledge of rocks b a flat projecting layer of rock, ice, etc c the submerged border of a continent or island; CONTINENTAL SHELF [ME, prob fr OE *scylfe*; akin to L *scalpere, sculpere* to carve, OE *sciell* shell] – **shelfful** *n*, **shelflike** *adj* – **off the shelf** available from stock; not made to order – **on the shelf** 1 in a state of inactivity or uselessness 2 *of a single woman* considered unlikely to marry, esp because too old

**shelf ice** *n* an extensive ice sheet originating on land but continuing out to sea beyond the depths at which it rests on the sea bottom

'**shelf-,life** *n* the length of time for which a product (e g a tinned or packaged food) may be stored or displayed (e g on shelves in a shop) without serious deterioration

¹**shell** /shel/ *n* 1a a hard rigid often largely calcium-containing covering of an animal (e g an oyster, snail, crab, or turtle) b the hard or tough outer covering of an egg, esp a bird's egg 2 the covering or outside part of a fruit or seed, esp when hard or fibrous ⟨a nut ∼⟩ 3 shell material or shells ⟨an ornament made of ∼⟩ 4 something that resembles a shell: e g 4a a framework or exterior structure; *esp* the outer frame of a building whose interior is unfinished or has been destroyed (e g by fire) b an external case or outside covering ⟨the ∼ of a ship⟩ c a hollow form devoid of substance ⟨mere effigies and ∼ s of men – Thomas Carlyle⟩ d an edible case for holding a filling ⟨a pastry ∼⟩ e a reinforced concrete arched or domed roof that is used primarily over large unpartitioned areas 5 a cold and reserved attitude that conceals the presence or absence of feeling ⟨wish he'd come out of his ∼⟩ 6 a narrow light racing rowing boat propelled by one or more rowers 7 any of various spherical regions surrounding the nucleus of an atom at various distances from it and each occupied by a group of electrons

of approximately equal energy **8a** a projectile for cannon containing a charge that explodes in flight or on impact **b** a metal or paper case which holds the charge in cartridges, fireworks, etc **9** *NAm* a plain usu sleeveless blouse or jumper [ME, fr OE *sciell;* akin to OE *scealu* shell, ON *skel,* L *silex* pebble, flint, Gk *skallein* to hoe] – **shell** *adj,* **shelly** *adj*

²**shell** *vt* **1a** to take out of a natural enclosing or protective cover (eg a shell, husk, pod, or capsule) ⟨~ *peanuts*⟩ ⟨~ *prawns*⟩ **b** to separate the kernels of (eg an ear of maize, wheat, or oats) from the cob, ear, or husk **2** to fire shells at, upon, or into; bombard **3** to score heavily against (eg an opposing pitcher in baseball) ~ *vi* **1** to fall or scale off in thin pieces **2** to cast the shell or exterior covering; fall out of the pod or husk ⟨*nuts which* ~ *on falling from the tree*⟩ – **sheller** *n*

**shell out** *vb, informal* to pay (money)

**she'll** /shil; *strong* sheel/ she will; she shall

¹**shellac** /'shelak/ *n* **1** the purified form of a resin (LAC) produced by various insects, usu obtained as thin orange or yellow flakes and often bleached white **2** a preparation of lac dissolved usu in alcohol and used esp in making varnish and polish; *specif* FRENCH POLISH **3a** a material containing shellac formerly used for making gramophone records **b** an old 78-rpm gramophone record [¹*shell* + *lac;* trans of Fr *laque en écailles* lac in thin flakes]

²**shellac** *vt* **-ck-** **1** to treat, esp by coating, with shellac or a shellac varnish **2** *chiefly NAm informal* to defeat overwhelmingly

**shellacking** /'shelaking/ *n, chiefly NAm informal* a decisive defeat

**shellback** /'shel,bak/ *n* an old or veteran sailor

**shelled** /'sheld/ *adj* **1** having a shell, esp of a specified kind – often in combination ⟨*pink*-shelled⟩ ⟨*thick*-shelled⟩ **2a** having had the shell removed ⟨~ *oysters*⟩ ⟨~ *nuts*⟩ **b** removed from the pod or cob ⟨~ *peas*⟩

**shellfire** /'shel,fieə/ *n* the firing or shooting of shells

**shellfish** /-,fish/ *n, pl* **shellfish,** *esp for different types* **shellfishes** an aquatic INVERTEBRATE animal with a shell; *esp* an edible MOLLUSC (eg an oyster, mussel, whelk, or winkle) or CRUSTACEAN (eg a crab or prawn)

**shell game** *n, chiefly NAm* THIMBLERIG (swindling game) played esp with three walnut shells

**shell jacket** *n* a short tight military jacket worn buttoned up the front

**shell pink** *n or adj* (a) light yellowish-pink

**shellproof** /-,proohf/ *adj* constructed so as to resist attack by shells or bombs

**shell shock** *n* a mental disorder characterized by neurotic and often hysterical symptoms that occurs under conditions (eg wartime combat) that cause intense stress – **shell-shock** *vt*

**Shelta** /'sheltə/ *n* a secret jargon of Irish vagrants [origin unknown]

¹**shelter** /'sheltə/ *n* **1** something, esp a structure, that affords cover or protection ⟨*an air-raid* ~⟩ **2** the state of being covered and protected; refuge ⟨*took* ~⟩ [perh fr obs *sheltron* phalanx, fr ME *scheltrom,* fr OE *scieldtruma,* fr *scield* shield + *truma* troop] – **shelterless** *adj*

²**shelter** *vt* **1** to serve as a shelter for; protect ⟨*a thick hedge* ~*ed the orchard*⟩ **2** to keep concealed or protected ⟨~*ed her family in a mountain cave*⟩ ~ *vi* **1** to take shelter **2** to seek concealment – **shelterer** *n*

**shelterbelt** /'sheltə,belt/ *n* a barrier of trees and shrubs that protects something (eg crops) from wind and storm and lessens erosion

**shelty, sheltie** /'shelti/ *n* **1** SHETLAND PONY **2** SHETLAND SHEEPDOG [prob of Scand origin; akin to ON *Hjalti* Shetlander]

**shelve** /shelv/ *vt* **1** to provide with shelves **2** to place on a shelf **3a** to remove from active service; dismiss **b** to put off or aside ⟨~ *a project*⟩ ~ *vi* to slope, incline [fr *shelves,* pl of *shelf*] – **shelver** *n*

¹**shelving** /'shelving/ *n* **1a** the state of sloping **b** the degree of slope ⟨*a* ~ *of 20 degrees*⟩ **2** a sloping surface or place

²**shelving** *n* **1** material for constructing shelves **2** shelves

**Shema** /shə'mah/ *n* the Jewish confession of faith beginning "Hear, O Israel . . . " [Heb *shēma'* hear]

**Shemini Atzereth** /shə,meeni aht'serət, -'seroth/ *n* a Jewish festival following the seventh day of SUKKOTH (harvest festival) and marked by a special prayer for seasonal rain [Heb *shēmīnī 'ăṣereth,* fr Heb *shēmīnī* eighth + *'ăṣereth* assembly]

**Shemite** /'shemiet/ *n* a Semite [*Shem,* eldest son of Noah] – **Shemitic, Shemitish** *adj*

**shemozzle** /shi'mozl/ *n, informal* a source or scene of confusion or dispute; a to-do, mix-up [modif of Yiddish *shlimazel* bad luck, difficulty, misfortune, fr *shlim* bad, ill + *mazel* luck]

**shenanigan** /shi'nanigən/ *n, informal* **1** deliberate deception; trickery – compare HOCUS-POCUS **2** – **shenanigans** *pl,* **shenanigan** boisterous mischief; high jinks [origin unknown]

**Sheol** /'shee,ohl, ,-'-/ *n* the abode of the dead in early Hebrew thought [Heb *Shĕ'ōl*]

¹**shepherd** /'shepəd/ *n* **1** *fem* **shepherdess** /-des/ someone who tends sheep **2** a pastor [ME *sheepherde,* fr OE *scēaphyrde,* fr *scēap* sheep + *hierde* herdsman; akin to OE *heord* herd]

²**shepherd** *vt* **1** to tend as a shepherd **2** to guide, marshal, or conduct (people) like sheep ⟨~*ed the children onto the train*⟩

**shepherd dog** *n* a sheepdog

**shepherd's check** *n* a pattern of small even black-and-white checks; *also* a fabric woven in this pattern

**shepherd's pie** *n* a hot dish of minced meat, esp lamb, with a mashed potato topping – compare COTTAGE PIE

**shepherd's plaid** *n* SHEPHERD'S CHECK

**shepherd's purse** *n* a white-flowered plant (*Capsella bursa-pastoris*) of the cabbage family that has small flat heart-shaped pods and is a common weed

**sherard·ize, -ise** /'shcrədiez/ *vt* to coat (eg an article of iron or steel) with zinc by heating for several hours in an enclosed space with zinc dust at a temperature below the melting point of zinc [*Sherard* Cowper-Coles †1936 E inventor]

¹**Sheraton** /'sherət(ə)n/ *adj* of or being a style of furniture that originated in England around 1800 and is characterized by having straight lines and graceful proportions [Thomas *Sheraton* †1806 E furniture designer]

²**Sheraton** *n* a piece of furniture made by or in the style of Sheraton

**sherbet, sherbert** /'shuhbət/ *n* **1** an oriental cold drink of sweetened and diluted fruit juice **2** a water ice with egg white, gelatine, or sometimes milk added **3** a sweet powder that effervesces in liquid and is eaten dry or used to make fizzy drinks; *also* a drink made with sherbet [Turk & Per; Turk *şerbet,* fr Per *sharbat,* fr Ar *sharbah* drink, fr *shariba* to drink (cf SYRUP)]

**sherd** /shuhd, shahd/ *n* **1** SHARD **1** (brittle fragment) **2** *also* **shard** fragments of pottery vessels found on sites and in refuse deposits where pottery-making peoples have lived

**sherif** /she'reef/ *n* SHARIF (descendant of Muhammad)

**sheriff** /'sherif/ *n* **1a** the former representative of the Crown in each English shire who had wide judicial and executive powers **b** the chief judge of a county or district in Scotland **2** the honorary chief executive officer of the Crown in each English county who has mainly judicial and ceremonial duties **3** an elective officer in the USA responsible for law enforcement in each county [ME *shirreve,* fr OE *scīrgerēfa,* fr *scīr* shire + *gerēfa* reeve – more at REEVE] – **sheriffdom** *n*

**sheriff court** *n* the main inferior court in Scotland, dealing with both civil and criminal cases and having appeal to the HIGH COURT OF JUSTICIARY

**sherlock** /'shuh,lok/ *n, often cap* a person showing unusual powers of observation and deduction in solving any problem – often used ironically ⟨*all right* ~*, you tell us who turned the lights off*⟩ △ shylock [*Sherlock* Holmes, detective in stories by Sir Arthur Conan Doyle †1930 Sc writer]

**Sherpa** /'shuhpə/ *n* a member of a Tibetan people living on the high southern slopes of the Himalayas and skilled in mountain climbing

**sherry** /'sheri/ *n* a blended FORTIFIED WINE from southern Spain that varies in colour from very light to dark brown and has a distinctive nutty flavour; *also* a similar wine produced elsewhere ⟨*Cyprus* ~⟩ [alter. of earlier *sherris* (taken as pl), fr *Xeres* (now *Jerez*), city in SW Spain]

**she's** /shiz; *strong* sheez/ she is; she has

**Shetland** /'shetlənd/ *n* **1** a Shetland pony or sheepdog **2** *often not cap* **2a** a lightweight loosely twisted yarn of Shetland wool used for knitting and weaving **b** a fabric or a garment made from Shetland wool [*Shetland* islands off N Scotland]

**Shetland pony** *n* (any of) a breed of small stocky shaggy hardy ponies that originated in the Shetland islands

**Shetland sheepdog** *n* (any of) a breed of small dogs developed in the Shetland islands that resemble miniature collies and have a short dense undercoat and a profuse outer coat of long hair

**Shetland wool** *n* fine wool from sheep raised in the Shetland islands; *also* yarn spun from this

**sheugh** /shux/ *n, chiefly Scot* a ditch, trench [ME *sough* bog, gutter]

**sheva** /shə'vah/ *n* SCHWA (unstressed vowel)

**Shevuoth** /she'vooh·oth/ *n* SHABUOTH (Jewish holiday)

**shew** /show/ *vb, archaic Br* to show

**shewbread, showbread** /'shoh,bred/ *n* consecrated unleavened bread ritually placed by the Jewish priests of ancient Israel on a table in the sanctuary of the Tabernacle on the Sabbath [trans of Ger *schaubrot*]

**Shia** /'shee·ə/ *n* 1 *taking pl vb* the Muslims of the branch of Islam comprising sects deriving authority from Muhammad's cousin and son-in-law Ali and his appointed successors the Imams, and believing in the concealment and messianic return of the last recognized Imam – compare SUNNI 2 a member of the Shia [Ar *shī'ah* sect – more at SHIITE]

**shibboleth** /'shibə,leth/ *n* 1a a catchword, slogan b a use of language that distinguishes a group of people c a commonplace belief or saying ⟨*the ~ that crime does not pay*⟩ 2 a custom or usage regarded as a criterion for distinguishing members of one group [Heb *shibbōleth* stream; fr the use of this word as a test to distinguish Gileadites from Ephraimites, who pronounced it *sibbōleth* (Judges 12:6)]

**shickered** /'shikəd/ *adj, Austr & NZ informal* drunk [Yiddish *shiker*, fr Heb *shikkōr*, fr *shikhar* to be drunk]

**shiel** /sheel/ *n, chiefly Scot* a shieling

**¹shield** /sheeld/ *n* 1 a piece of armour (eg of wood, metal, or leather), carried in use on the arm or in the hand, that is used esp for warding off blows and can be variously sized or shaped 2 someone or something that protects or defends; a defence 3 a piece of material or a pad attached inside a garment (eg a dress) at the armpit to protect the garment from perspiration 4a a fixture designed to protect people from injury from moving parts of machinery or live electrical conductors b a structure (eg of concrete or lead) that acts as a physical barrier to radioactive particles 5 a defined area, the surface of which constitutes a heraldic field, on which heraldic arms are displayed; *esp* one that is wide at the top and rounds to a point at the bottom 6 an armoured screen protecting an otherwise exposed gun 7 a circular iron or steel framework that supports the ground ahead of the permanent lining in tunnel excavation 8 a structure (eg a CARAPACE, scale, or plate) forming (part of) the outer protective covering of some animals (eg a lobster or tortoise) 9 the mass of rock, dating from the PRECAMBRIAN (earliest geological era), that forms the central part of a continent 10 something resembling a shield: eg 10a a trophy awarded in recognition of achievement (eg in a sporting event) b a decorative or identifying emblem [ME *sheld*, fr OE *scield*; akin to OE *sciell* shell]

**²shield** *vt* 1a to protect (as if) with a shield; provide with a protective cover or shelter b to cut off from observation; hide ⟨*accomplices who ~ a pilferer from view*⟩ 2 *obs* to forbid
*synonyms* see DEFEND – **shielder** *n*

**shieldbug** /-,bug/ *n* any of various approx shield-shaped TRUE BUGS (superfamily Pentatomoidea), some of which have a very pungent unpleasant smell

**shieling** /'sheeling, -lən/ *n, dial Br* 1 a mountain hut used as a shelter by shepherds 2 a summer pasture in the mountains [ME (northern) *schele, shale*]

**shier** /'shie·ə/ *compar of* SHY

**shiest** /'shieist/ *superl of* SHY

**¹shift** /shift/ *vt* 1 to exchange for or replace by another; change ⟨*the traitor ~*ed *his allegiance*⟩ 2a to change the place, position, or direction of; move ⟨*I can't ~ the grand piano*⟩ b to make a change in (place) ⟨*unto Southampton do we ~ our scene* – Shak⟩ 3 to change (a sound) phonetically as a language evolves 4 *informal* to get rid of; DISPOSE OF ~ *vi* 1a to change place or position ⟨*~*ing *uneasily in his chair*⟩ b to change direction ⟨*the wind ~*ed⟩ c to depress the SHIFT KEY (eg on a typewriter) 2a to assume responsibility ⟨*had to ~ for herself*⟩ b to resort to expedients; GET BY 3 *of a sound* to become changed phonetically as a language evolves – see also **shift GEAR** 4 *NAm* to change gear in a motor vehicle [ME *shiften*, fr OE *sciftan* to divide, arrange; akin to OE *scēadan* to divide –more at SHED] – **shiftable** *adj*, **shifter** *n*

**²shift** *n* 1a a deceitful or underhand scheme or method; a subterfuge, dodge b *usu pl* an expedient tried in difficult circumstances ⟨*put to extraordinary ~*s *to keep the ship afloat*⟩ 2a a woman's slip or chemise b a woman's usu loosely fitting or semifitted dress 3a a change in direction ⟨*a ~ in the wind*⟩ b a change in emphasis, judgment, or attitude 4a *taking sing or pl vb* a group who work (eg in a factory) in alternation with other groups b a scheduled period of work or duty ⟨*on the night ~*⟩ 5 a change in place, position, or function: eg 5a a change in the position of the hand on a fingerboard (eg of a violin) b (the relative displacement of rock masses on opposite sides of) a fault or fault zone c a change in frequency and therefore in position of a line or band in a spectrum (eg of light) – compare DOPPLER EFFECT d a movement of BITS (smallest units of information) in a section of computer memory to the right or left a particular number of places as part of a computer operation (eg multiplication) 6 a removal from one person or position to another; a transfer 7 systematic sound change as a language evolves 8 a bid in bridge in a suit other than the suit one's partner has bid – compare JUMP 9 *NAm* the gear change in a motor vehicle – **get a shift on** *informal* to set to work energetically or faster than before – **make shift** to manage, contrive ⟨*we could* make shift *to live under a debauchee or a tyrant* – T B Macaulay⟩

**shift key** *n* a key on a keyboard (eg of a typewriter) that when held down permits a different set of characters, esp the capitals, to be printed

**shiftless** /-lis/ *adj* 1 lacking resourcefulness; inefficient 2 lacking ambition or motivation; lazy [²*shift* (in the arch. sense 'resourcefulness') + *-less*] – **shiftlessly** *adv*, **shiftlessness** *n*

**shifty** /-ti/ *adj* 1 full of expedients; resourceful 2 given to deception, evasion, or fraud; slippery 3 indicative of a fickle or devious nature ⟨*~ eyes*⟩ – **shiftily** *adv*, **shiftiness** *n*

**shigella** /shi'gelə/ *n, pl* **shigellae** /-li/ *also* **shigellas** any of a genus (*Shigella*) of bacteria that cause dysenteries in animals, esp human beings [NL, genus name, fr Kiyoshi *Shiga* †1957 Jap bacteriologist]

**Shih Tzu** /shee'tsooh/ *n* (any of) an old Chinese breed of small alert active dogs that have square short unwrinkled muzzles, short muscular legs, and massive amounts of long dense hair [Chin (Pek) *shī zi gǒu* [*shi¹ tzŭ³ kou³*] Pekingese dog, fr *shī* (*shi¹*) lion + *zĭ* (*tzŭ³*) son + *gǒu* (*kou³*) dog]

**Shii** /'sheeie/ *n or adj* (a) Shiite

**Shiism** /'sheeieiz(ə)m/ *n* Islam as taught by the Shia

**Shiite** /'sheeiet/ *n* a Shia Muslim [Ar *shiya'īy*, lit., partisan, fr *shī'ah* following, sect, fr *shā'a* to accompany] – **Shiite** *adj*

**¹shikar** /shi'kah/ *n, Ind* hunting [Hindi *shikār*, fr Per]

**²shikar** *vb* **-rr-** *Ind* to hunt

**shikari** /shi'kahri/ *n, pl* **shikaris** *Ind* a big-game hunter; *esp* a professional hunter or guide [Hindi *shikārī*, fr Per, fr *shikār* hunting]

**shiksa, shikse** /'shiksə/ *n, chiefly derog* a non-Jewish girl [Yiddish *shikse*, fem of *sheykets, sheygets* non-Jewish boy, fr Heb *shegeṣ* blemish, abomination]

**shilingi** /shi'ling·i/ *n, pl* **shilingi** /~/ – see MONEY table [Swahili, fr E *shilling*]

**shill** /shil/ *n, NAm* a person who poses (eg as a customer or gambler) so as to entice others [prob short for *shillaber*, of unknown origin] – **shill** *vi*

**shillelagh** *also* **shillalah** /shi'layli/ *n* an Irish cudgel [*Shillelagh*, town in SE Ireland famed for its oak trees]

**shilling** /'shiling/ *n* 1a a former money unit of the UK worth 12 old pence or £¹/₂₀ b a money unit equal to £¹/₂₀ of any of various other countries in or formerly in the Commonwealth 2 a coin representing one shilling 3 any of several early American coins 4 – see MONEY table [ME, fr OE *scilling*; akin to OHG *skilling*, a gold coin; both fr a prehistoric Gmc compound represented by OE *scield* shield and by OE *-ling*]

**Shilluk** /shi'loohk/ *n, pl* **Shilluks,** *esp collectively* **Shilluk** 1 a member of a Negro people of the Sudan dwelling mainly on the W bank of the White Nile 2 the NILOTIC language of the Shilluk people

**shilly-shally** /'shili ,shali/ *vi* 1 to show hesitation or lack of decisiveness 2 to dawdle [*shilly-shally*, adv, irreg redupl of *shall I*] – **shilly-shally** *n, adj, or adv*

**shilpit** /'shilpit/ *adj, Scot* starved or sickly in appearance [origin unknown]

**¹shim** /shim/ *n* a thin often tapered piece of material (eg wood, metal, or stone) used to fill in space between things (eg for support, levelling, or adjustment of fit) [origin unknown]

**²shim** *vt* **-mm-** to fill out or level up by the use of a shim or shims

**¹shimmer** /'shimə/ *vi* 1 to shine with a softly tremulous or wavering light; glimmer 2 to appear in a fluctuating wavy form

⟨*the* ~ing *heat from the pavement*⟩ *synonyms* see ¹FLASH [ME *schimeren,* fr OE *scimerian;* akin to OE *scīnan* to shine – more at SHINE]

²**shimmer** *n* **1** a light that shimmers; subdued sheen **2** a wavering and distortion of the visual image of a far object, usu resulting from heat-induced changes in the amount by which the atmosphere bends light rays – **shimmery** *adj*

¹**shimmy** /'shimi/ *n* **1** a chemise **2** a jazz dance characterized by a shaking of the body from the shoulders downwards **3** *NAm* an abnormal vibration, esp in the front wheels of a motor vehicle [(1) by alter; (2) short for *shimmy-shake &* *shimmy-shiver*]

²**shimmy** *vi* **1** to shake, quiver, or tremble (as if) in dancing a shimmy **2** *NAm, esp of car wheels* to vibrate abnormally

¹**shin** /shin/ *n* the front part of the leg of a VERTEBRATE animal below the knee; *also* a cut of meat from this part of the front leg of a 4-legged animal ⟨*a* ~ *of beef*⟩ [ME *shine,* fr OE *scinu;* akin to OHG *scina* shin, OE *scēadan* to divide – more at SHED]

²**shin** *vb* **-nn-** *vi* to climb by gripping with the hands or arms and the legs and hauling oneself up or lowering oneself down ⟨~ned *up the tree*⟩ ~ *vt* **1** to kick on the shins **2** to climb by shinning

³**shin** *n* the 22nd letter of the Hebrew alphabet [Heb *shīn*]

**Shin** /shin, sheen/ *n* a major Japanese Buddhist sect that emphasizes salvation by faith in exclusive worship of Amida Buddha [Jap, lit., belief, faith]

**Shina** /'sheenə/ *n* the DARD language of Gilgit in northern Kashmir

**shinbone** /-,bohn/ *n* TIBIA 1

**shindig** /'shindig/ *n, informal* **1** a usu boisterous social gathering **2** SHINDY 2 [prob alter. of *shindy*]

**shindy** /'shindi/ *n, pl* **shindys, shindies** *informal* **1** SHINDIG 1 **2** a quarrel, brawl [prob alter. of *shinny*]

¹**shine** /shien/ *vb* **shone** /shon/, (*vt* 2) **shined** *vi* **1** to emit light **2** to be bright with reflected light **3** to be outstanding or distinguished ⟨*she always* ~s *in mathematics*⟩ **4** to have a radiant or lively appearance ⟨*his face* shone *with enthusiasm*⟩ **5** to be conspicuously evident or clear ⟨*courage that* ~s *in adversity*⟩ ~ *vt* **1a** to cause to emit light **b** to direct the light of ⟨shone *her torch into the corner*⟩ **2** to make bright by polishing ⟨~d *his shoes*⟩ *synonyms* see ¹GLOW [ME *shinen,* fr OE *scīnan;* akin to OHG *skīnan* to shine, Gk *skia* shadow]

²**shine** *n* **1** brightness caused by the emission or reflection of light; lustre, sheen **2** brilliance, splendour ⟨*pageantry that has kept its* ~ *over the centuries*⟩ **3** fine weather; sunshine ⟨*come rain, come* ~⟩ **4a** a polish given to shoes **b** an act of polishing shoes **5** *chiefly NAm informal* a fancy, crush ⟨*took a* ~ *to her*⟩

**shiner** /'shienə/ *n, slang* BLACK EYE [¹*shine* + ²*-er*]

¹**shingle** /'shing·gl/ *n* **1** a small thin tile, esp of wood and often with one end thicker than the other, for laying in overlapping rows as a covering for the roof or sides of a building **2** a woman's haircut, popular in the 1920s, in which the hair is trimmed short and shaped in to the nape of the neck – called also ETON CROP **3** *NAm* a small signboard (e g of a doctor or lawyer) [ME *schingel,* prob deriv of L *scindula* wooden slat, alter. of *scandula*]

²**shingle** *vt* **1** to cover (as if) with shingles **2** to cut and shape (the hair) in the style of a shingle

³**shingle** *n* **1** coarse rounded pebbles, esp on the seashore, differing from ordinary gravel only in the larger size of the stones **2** a place (e g a beach) strewn with shingle [prob of Scand origin; akin to Norw *singel* coarse gravel] – **shingle, shingly** *adj*

**shingles** /'shing·glz/ *n taking sing vb* a disease that is caused by a virus and is characterized by inflammation of certain nerve endings resulting in often intense pain and skin lesions that follow the affected nerve pathways usu from the middle of the back round to the abdomen. The virus responsible is similar to, if not identical to, the virus causing chicken pox but more often affects adults than children. – called also HERPES ZOSTER [ME *schingles,* by folk etymology fr ML *cingulus,* fr L *cingulum* gird!c – more at CINGULUM]

**Shingon** /'shingon, 'sheen-/ *n* a secret Japanese Buddhist sect claiming the achievement of Buddhahood in this life through its prescribed rituals [Jap, lit., true word]

**shining** /'shiening/ *adj* **1** emitting or reflecting light; bright **2** radiant and often splendid in appearance; resplendent **3** possessing a distinguished quality; outstanding ⟨*a* ~ *example of bravery*⟩

¹**shinny** *also* **shinney** /'shini/ *n* shinty

²**shinny** *vi, NAm informal* SHIN 1 [alter. of ²*shin*]

**shinsplints** /'shin,splints/ *n taking sing vb, chiefly NAm* painful muscular swelling of the lower leg that is a common injury in athletes who regularly run on hard surfaces

**Shinto** /'shintoh/ *n* the native religion of Japan, consisting chiefly in devotion to the gods of natural forces (ANIMISM) and veneration of the Emperor as a descendant of the sun-goddess [Jap *shintō*] – **Shinto** *adj,* **Shintoism** *n,* **Shintoist** *n or adj,* **Shintoistic** *adj*

**shinty** /'shinti/ *n* a variation of HURLING (Irish form of hockey) played in Scotland [alter. of *shinny,* perh fr ¹*shin* + ¹*-y*]

**shiny** /'shieni/ *adj* **1** bright or glossy in appearance; lustrous, polished ⟨~ *new shoes*⟩ **2** *esp of material, clothes, etc* rubbed or worn to a smooth surface that reflects light – **shininess** *n*

¹**ship** /ship/ *n* **1a** a large seagoing vessel **b** a square-rigged sailing vessel having a BOWSPRIT and usu three masts and able to set TOPGALLANT sails on all three **2** a boat; *esp* one propelled by power or sail **3** *taking sing or pl vb* a ship's crew **4** an airship, aircraft, or spacecraft [ME, fr OE *scip;* akin to OHG *skif* ship, OE *scēadan* to divide – more at SHED] – **dress ship** to hoist national ensigns at all the masts of a ship as a mark of respect – **dress ship overall** to hoist a line of flags and pennants from the bow to the mastheads to the stern of a ship on special occasions – **when one's ship comes in** when one becomes rich or successful

²**ship** *vb* **-pp-** *vt* **1** to place or receive on board a ship for transport **2** to put in place for use ⟨~ *the tiller*⟩ **3** to take into a ship or boat ⟨~ *the gangplank*⟩ **4** to engage for service on a ship **5** *of a boat or ship* to take (e g water) over the side **6** *informal* to cause to be transported ⟨~ped *him off to boarding school*⟩ **7** *obs* to provide with a ship ~ *vi* **1** to embark on a ship **2** to go or travel by ship **3** to engage to serve on shipboard – **shippable** *adj*

**-ship** /-ship/ *suffix* (*n* → *n*) **1** state, condition, or quality of ⟨*friend*ship⟩ **2a** office, status, or profession of ⟨*professor*ship⟩ **b** period during which (a specified office or position) is held ⟨*during his dictator*ship⟩ **3** art or skill of ⟨*horseman*ship⟩ ⟨*scholar*ship⟩ **4** *taking sing or pl vb* whole group or body sharing (a specified class or state) ⟨*reader*ship⟩ ⟨*member*ship⟩ **5** one entitled to a (specified rank, title, or appellation) ⟨*his Lord*ship⟩ [ME, fr OE *-scipe;* akin to OHG *-scaft* -ship, OE *scieppan* to shape – more at SHAPE]

**ship biscuit** *n* SHIP'S BISCUIT

¹**shipboard** /-,bawd/ *n* – **on shipboard** on board a ship

²**shipboard** *adj* existing or taking place on board a ship ⟨*a* ~ *romance*⟩

**shipborne** /'ship,bawn/ *adj* transported or designed to be transported by ship ⟨~ *aircraft*⟩

**shipbuilder** /-,bildə/ *n* a person or company that designs or constructs ships – **shipbuilding** *n*

**ship canal** *n* a canal large enough to allow the passage of seagoing vessels

**ship fever** *n* typhus [fr its prevalence aboard crowded ships]

**shiplap** /'ship,lap/ *n* wooden covering, esp of a ship's hull, in which the boards are joined so that the edges of each board lap over the edges of adjacent boards to make a flush joint – **shiplap** *vb*

**shipload** /-,lohd/ *n* as much or as many as a ship will carry

**shipman** /'shipmən/ *n* **1** a shipmaster **2** *archaic* a seaman, sailor

**shipmaster** /'ship,mahstə/ *n* a ship's captain

**shipmate** /-,mayt/ *n* a fellow sailor

**shipment** /-mənt/ *n* **1** the act or process of shipping **2** the quantity of goods shipped ⟨*a* ~ *of oranges*⟩

**ship money** *n* a tax levied at various times in England until 1640, to provide ships for the national defence

**ship of the line** *n* a ship of war large enough to have a place in the line of battle

**shipowner** /-,ohnə/ *n* the owner of a ship or of a share in a ship

**shippen** *also* **shippon** /'shipən/ *n, dial* a cattle shed [ME *shepen, shipen,* fr OE *scypen, scipen, scepen* – more at SHOP]

**shipper** /'shipə/ *n* a person or company that ships goods by any form of conveyance

**shipping** /'shiping/ *n* **1a** ships ⟨~ *should avoid the area*⟩ **b** the body of ships in one place or belonging to one port or country ⟨*British merchant* ~⟩ **2** the act or business of a shipper

**shipping articles, ship's articles** *n pl* the terms of agreement between the captain of a ship and the seamen with respect to wages, length of time for which they are at sea, and related matters

**shipping clerk** *n* one who is employed in a shipping room to assemble, pack, and dispatch or receive goods

**ship rat** *n* a rat, esp the black rat (*Rattus rattus*), that infests ships

**ship-'rigged** *adj* square-rigged

**ship's biscuit, ship biscuit** *n, chiefly Br* a hard biscuit for eating on board ship

**shipshape** /-,shayp/ *adj* trim, tidy *synonyms* see ²NEAT [short for earlier *shipshapen*, fr *ship* + *shapen*, archaic pp of *shape*]

**ship's papers** *n pl* the documents relating to the ownership, nationality, and cargo of a ship

**shipway** /-,way/ *n* 1 the structure on which a ship is built and from which it is launched 2 SHIP CANAL

**shipworm** /-,wuhm/ *n* any of various elongated marine clams (esp family Teredinidae) that resemble worms, burrow in submerged wood, and damage wooden ships and wooden columns supporting a wharf

**¹shipwreck** /-,rek/ *n* 1 a wrecked ship or its remains 2 the destruction or loss of a ship 3 an irrevocable collapse or destruction ⟨*suffered the* ~ *of his fortune*⟩ [alter. (influenced by *wreck*) of earlier *shipwrack*, fr ME *schipwrak*, fr OE *scipwræc*, fr *scip* ship + *wræc* something driven by the sea – more at WRACK]

**²shipwreck** *vt* **1a** to cause to undergo shipwreck **b** to ruin **2** to destroy (a ship) by grounding or foundering □ *usu pass*

**shipwright** /-,riet/ *n* a carpenter skilled in ship construction and repair

**shipyard** /'shipyahd/ *n* a yard, place, or enclosure where ships are built or repaired

**shiralee** /,shirə'lee/ *n, Austr* SWAG 2a [origin unknown]

**shire** /shie·ə/ *n* **1a** an administrative subdivision; *specif* an English county, esp one with a name ending in *-shire* **b** *pl* the fox-hunting district of the English midlands, consisting chiefly of Leicestershire and Northamptonshire **2** (any of) a British breed of large heavy draught horses with a fringe of long hairs on the legs [ME, fr OE *scīr* office, shire; akin to OHG *scīra* care]

**shire town** *n* COUNTY TOWN

**shirk** /shuhk/ *vb* to evade (a responsibility, task, or duty) ⟨~ *one's obligations*⟩ [perh fr Ger *schurke* scoundrel (cf ²SHARK]) – **shirker** *n*

**Shirley poppy** /'shuhli/ *n* a variable garden poppy with bright single or double flowers in red, pink, blue, or white [*Shirley* vicarage, near Croydon in Surrey, where it was developed]

**shirr** /shuh/ *vt* **1** to draw (e g cloth) together in a shirring **2** *chiefly NAm* to bake (eggs removed from the shell) in a small dish until set [origin unknown]

**shirring** /'shuhring/ *n* a decorative gathering on blouses, dresses, etc made by drawing up the material along two or more parallel lines of stitching or by stitching in rows of elastic thread or an elastic webbing – compare RUCHE

**shirt** /shuht/ *n* a garment for the upper, esp male, body; *esp* one that opens the full length of the centre front and has sleeves and a collar [ME *shirte*, fr OE *scyrte*; akin to ON *skyrta* shirt, OE *scort* short (cf SKIRT)] – **put one's shirt on** *informal* to bet heavily on – see also KEEP **one's shirt on**

**shirtfront** /'shuht,frunt/ *n* the front of a shirt; *specif* one that is stiffened for evening wear

**shirting** /'shuhting/ *n* fabric suitable for shirts

**shirtless** /'shuhtlis/ *n* very poor; poverty-stricken

**'shirt-,sleeve** *also* **shirt-sleeves, shirt-sleeved** *adj* **1a** without a jacket ⟨*a* ~ *audience*⟩ **b** suitable for going without a jacket ⟨~ *weather*⟩ **2** marked by informality and directness ⟨~ *diplomacy*⟩

**'shirt-,sleeves** *n pl* – **in one's shirt-sleeves** not wearing a jacket

**shirttail** /'shuht,tayl/ *adj, NAm* only distantly related ⟨*a* ~ *cousin on her father's side*⟩

**shirtwaist** /-,wayst/ *n, NAm* a shirtwaister

**shirtwaister** /-,waystə/ *n, chiefly Br* a fitted dress that is fastened usu with buttons down the centre front to just below the waist or to the hem

**shirty** /'shuhti/ *adj, informal* bad tempered; fractious [fr the phrase *to get somebody's shirt out* to make somebody angry] – **shirtiness** *n*

**shish kebab** /,shish ki'bab/ *n* a kebab cooked on skewers [Arm *shish kabab*]

**¹shit** /shit/ *vb* **-tt-; shitted, shit, shat** /shat/ *vulg vi* to defecate ~ *vt* to defecate in ⟨~ *his pants*⟩ [alter. (influenced by ²*shit* and the past and pp forms) of earlier *shite*, fr ME *shiten*, fr OE *-scītan;* akin to MLG & MD *schiten* to defecate, OHG *scīzan*, ON *skīta* to defecate, OE *scēadan* to divide, separate – more at SHED]

**²shit** *n, vulg* **1** faeces – sometimes used interjectionally to express annoyance **2** an act of defecation **3a** nonsense, rubbish **b** a least amount or degree of care or consideration; ⟨*don't give a* ~ *what he says*⟩ **4** a despicable person ⟨*he's an absolute* ~⟩ **5** *slang* marijuana [fr (assumed) ME, fr OE *scite* (attested only in place names); akin to MD *schit, schitte* excrement, OE *scītan* to defecate] – **in the shit** *vulg* in trouble – **scare the shit out of** *vulg* to frighten, terrify – **when the shit hits the fan** *vulg* when real trouble begins

**shite** /shiet/ *vb or n, Br vulg* (to) shit

**shithead** /'shit·hed/ *n, slang* a marijuana addict

**shittah** /'shitə/ *n, pl* **shittahs, shittim** /-tim/ a tree of uncertain identity but prob an acacia (e g *Acacia seyal*) from the wood of which the Hebrew ark and tabernacle fittings were made [Heb *shiṭṭāh*]

**shittimwood** /'shitim,wood/ *also* **shittim** *n* the wood of the shittah tree [Heb *shiṭṭīm*, pl of *shiṭṭāh*]

**shitty** /'shiti/ *adj, vulg* nasty, unpleasant

**shivaree** /,shivə'ree/ *n, NAm* CHARIVARI (mock serenade) [by alter.] – **shivaree** *vt*

**¹shiver** /'shivə/ *n* any of the small pieces that result from the shattering of something brittle [ME; akin to OE *scēadan* to divide – more at SHED] – **shivery** *adj*

**²shiver** *vb* to break into many small fragments; shatter

**³shiver** *vi* to tremble, esp with cold or fever *synonyms* see ¹SHAKE [ME *shiveren*, alter. of *chiveren*]

**⁴shiver** *n* an instance of shivering; a tremor – **shivery** *adj*

**shivoo** /shie'vooh/ *n, Austr informal* a party, spree [prob fr E dial. *shebo, shevo, sheevo* tumult, disturbance]

**shmo** /shmoh/ *n* SCHMO (fool)

**¹shoal** /shohl/ *also* **shoaly** /-li/ *adj* shallow [alter. of ME *shold*, fr OE *sceald* – more at SKELETON]

**²shoal** *n* **1** a shallow **2** a sandbank or sandbar just below the surface of the sea or a river; *esp* one that is exposed at low tide

**³shoal** *vi* to become shallow or less deep ~ *vt* **1** to come to a shallow or less deep part of **2** to cause to become shallow or less deep

**⁴shoal** *n taking sing or pl vb* a large group; a crowd; *specif* a large group of fish moving as a body [(assumed) ME *shole*, fr OE *scolu* multitude – more at SCHOOL]

**⁵shoal** *vi* to gather in a shoal; throng

**¹shock** /shok/ *n* a pile of sheaves of grain or stalks of maize set up in a field with the butt ends down to dry [ME; akin to MHG *schoc* heap, OE *hēah* high – more at HIGH] – **shock** *vt*

**²shock** *n* **1** the impact or encounter of individuals or groups in combat **2** a violent shake or jar; concussion ⟨*an earthquake* ~⟩ **3a(1)** a disturbance in the balance or permanence of something (e g a system) **a(2)** a sudden or violent disturbance of thoughts or emotions ⟨*fresh* ~s *of wonder* – George Meredith⟩ **b** something that causes such disturbance ⟨*the news came as a terrible* ~⟩ **4** *medicine* a state of serious depression of most bodily functions associated with reduced blood volume and BLOOD PRESSURE and caused usu by severe injuries, bleeding, or burns **5** ELECTRIC SHOCK **6a** apoplexy **b** CORONARY THROMBOSIS (heart attack) [MF *choc*, fr *choquer* to strike against, fr OF *choquier*, prob of Gmc origin; akin to MD *schocken* to jolt]

**³shock** *vt* **1a** to cause to feel sudden surprise, terror, horror, or offence **b** to cause to undergo a physical or nervous shock **c** to cause (a person or animal) to experience an electric shock **2** to impel (as if) by a shock ⟨~ed *him into realizing his selfishness*⟩ ~ *vi, archaic* to meet with a shock; collide

**⁴shock** *adj, journalistic* surprising ⟨*vicar in* ~ *mercy dash*⟩

**⁵shock** *n* a thick bushy mass, usu of hair [perh fr ¹*shock*]

**⁶shock** *adj* bushy, shaggy – usu in combination ⟨*shock-headed*⟩

**shock absorber** *n* any of various devices for absorbing the energy of sudden impulses or shocks in machinery, structures, or vehicles

**shocker** /'shokə/ *n* **1** one who or that which shocks; *esp* something horrifying or offensive (e g a sensational novel or drama) **2** *informal* an incorrigible or naughty person (e g a child)

**shocking** /'shoking/ *adj* **1** giving cause for indignation or offence **2** *informal* very bad ⟨*had a* ~ *cold*⟩ ⟨~ *weather*⟩ – **shockingly** *adv*

**shocking pink** *adj or n* striking, vivid, bright, or intense pink

**shockproof** /-,proohf/ *adj* resistant to shock; constructed so as to absorb shock without damage ⟨*a* ~ *watch*⟩

**shock therapy** *n* a treatment (eg ELECTROCONVULSIVE THERAPY) for some serious mental disorders that involves artificially inducing a coma or convulsions

**shock treatment** *n* SHOCK THERAPY

**shock troops** *n pl* troops chosen for assault because of their high morale, training, and discipline

**shock wave** *n* 1 BLAST 5c 2 a compressional wave formed whenever the speed of a body (eg an aircraft) relative to a medium (eg the air) exceeds that at which the medium can transmit sound 3 a violent disturbance or reaction ⟨~s of rebellion⟩

**shod** /shod/ *adj* 1a wearing shoes, boots, etc b equipped with (a specified type of) tyres 2 furnished or equipped with a (metal) shoe – often in combination [ME, fr pp of *shoen* to shoe, fr OE *scōgan*, fr *scōh* shoe – more at SHOE]

¹**shoddy** /'shodi/ *n* 1a a wool of better quality and longer fibre length than MUNGO, reclaimed from materials that are not felted b a fabric, often of inferior quality, manufactured wholly or partly from reclaimed wool 2a an inferior but usu pretentious imitation b pretentious vulgarity (eg in art) [origin unknown]

²**shoddy** *adj* 1 made wholly or partly of shoddy 2a cheaply imitative; vulgarly pretentious b hastily or poorly done; inferior c shabby – **shoddily** *adv*, **shoddiness** *n*

¹**shoe** /shooh/ *n* 1a an outer covering for the human foot that does not extend above the ankle and has a thick or stiff sole and often an attached heel b a metal plate or rim for the hoof of an animal 2 something that protects or covers: eg 2a a metal tip attached to a pole or staff b the casing of a pneumatic tyre; *broadly* a tyre 3 a device that slows, stops, or controls the motion of an object; *esp* the part of a vehicle's braking system that presses on the brake drum 4 a device (eg a clip or track) on a camera that permits attachment of accessory items 5 a container for several packs of playing cards which allows the cards to be dispensed singly (eg in baccarat) 6 *NAm* the gear change in a motor vehicle [ME *shoo*, fr OE *scōh*; akin to OHG *scuoh* shoe, OE *hȳd* hide] – **fill somebody's shoes** to take over somebody's job, position, or responsibilities

²**shoe** *vt* **shoeing**; **shod** /shod/ *also* **shoed** /shoohd/ 1 to fit (eg a horse) with a shoe 2 to protect or reinforce with a usu metal shoe – **shoer** *n*

**shoebill** /'shooh,bil/ *n* a large storklike WADING BIRD (*Balaeniceps rex*) that has dark bluish-brown plumage, a large broad hooked beak, and lives in the papyrus swamps of the White Nile

**shoeblack** /'shooh,blak/ *n* a bootblack

**shoehorn** /-,hawn/ *n* a curved piece of horn, wood, or metal, with a handle, that is used to ease the heel into the back of a shoe

'**shoe-,horn** *vt* to force into a limited space ⟨*soon be* ~ing *passengers into the trains* – *The Guardian*⟩

**shoelace** /-,lays/ *n* a lace or string for fastening a shoe

**shoemaker** /-,maykə/ *n* one whose occupation is making or repairing shoes

¹**shoestring** /-,string/ *n* 1 a shoelace 2 a very small sum of money; an amount of capital (almost) inadequate to meet one's needs ⟨*start a business on a* ~⟩ [(2) fr shoestrings being a typical item sold by pedlars]

²**shoestring** *adj* operating on, accomplished with, or consisting of a small amount of money ⟨*a* ~ *budget*⟩

**shoetree** /'shooh,tree/ *n* a device of wood or plastic and metal inserted in a shoe to keep it in shape when not being worn

**shofar** /'shohfah, -fə/ *n*, *pl* **shofroth** /shoh'froht, -'frawt, -frohs/ a ram's-horn trumpet blown by the ancient Hebrews in battle and high religious observances and used in synagogues before and during ROSH HASHANAH and at the conclusion of YOM KIPPUR [Heb *shōphār*]

**shogun** /'shohgən/ *n* any of a line of military governors ruling Japan before the revolution of 1867–68 [Jap *shōgun* general] – **shogunate** *n*

**sholom** /shə'lom/ *interj* SHALOM (Hebrew greeting)

**shone** /shon/ *past of* SHINE

¹**shoo** /shooh/ *interj* – used in frightening away an animal, esp a domestic one [ME *schowe*]

²**shoo** *vt* to drive away (as if) by crying "Shoo!"

'**shoo-,in** *n*, *NAm informal* somebody (eg a contestant) who is a certain and easy winner

¹**shook** /shook/ *past* & *chiefly dial past part of* SHAKE

²**shook** *n* 1 a bundle of parts (eg of boxes) ready to be put together 2 ¹SHOCK (sheaves of corn set in a pile to dry) 3 *NAm* a set of wooden staves and end pieces for making a cask or barrel [origin unknown]

,**shook-'up** *adj*, *chiefly NAm informal* upset, shaken ⟨*was all* ~ *after his defeat*⟩ [*shook*, substandard pp of *shake*]

**shoon** /shoohn, shohn/ *chiefly dial pl of* SHOE

¹**shoot** /shooht/ *vb* **shot** /shot/ *vt* 1a to eject or impel or cause to be ejected or impelled by a sudden release of tension (eg of a bowstring or by a flick of a finger) ⟨~ *an arrow*⟩ ⟨~ *a marble*⟩ b to drive forth or cause to be driven forth b(1) by an explosion (eg of a powder charge in a firearm or of ignited fuel in a rocket) b(2) by a sudden release of gas or air ⟨~ *darts from a blowpipe*⟩ c to drive (eg a ball or puck) forth or away, esp towards a goal or hole, by striking or pushing with the arm, hand, or foot or with an implement d to throw or cast off or out, esp with force ⟨*the horse shot his rider out of the saddle*⟩ e(1) to utter (eg words or sounds) rapidly, suddenly, or violently ⟨~ing *staccato inquiries* – Angus Wilson⟩ e(2) to emit (eg light or flame) suddenly and rapidly e(3) to send forth with suddenness or intensity ⟨*shot a look of anger at him*⟩ f to discharge or empty (eg rubbish) from a container 2 to affect by shooting: eg 2a to strike and esp wound or kill with a missile, esp from a bow or gun b to remove or destroy by use of firearms ⟨*shot out the light*⟩; *also* to wreck, explode c to pursue with a firearm or bow for food or in sport ⟨~ *grouse*⟩ 3a to push or slide (eg the bolt of a door or lock) into or out of a fastening b to pass (a shuttle) through the warp threads in weaving c to thrust forwards; stick out ⟨*toads* ~ing *out their tongues*⟩ d to put forth in growing – usu + *out* or *forth* e to place, send, or bring into position abruptly 4a to engage in (a sport, game, or part of a game that involves shooting); play ⟨~ *pool*⟩ ⟨~ *a round of golf*⟩ b to score by shooting ⟨~ *a basket*⟩ 5 to hunt over with a gun or bow ⟨~ *a tract of woodland*⟩ 6a to cause to move suddenly or swiftly forward ⟨*shot the* car onto the highway⟩ b to send or carry quickly; dispatch ⟨~ *the letter on to me as soon as you receive it*⟩ 7 to variegate as if by applying colour in streaks, flecks, or patches – usu pass ⟨*hair shot with grey*⟩ 8 to pass swiftly by, over, or along ⟨~ing *rapids*⟩ 9 to plane (eg the edge of a board) straight or true 10a to detonate, ignite ⟨~ *a charge of dynamite*⟩ b to effect by blasting 11 to determine the altitude of 12 to take a picture or series of pictures or television images of; photograph, film; *also* to make (a film, videotape, etc) 13 *informal* to pass through (a road junction or traffic lights) without slowing down or stopping ⟨*he shot the lights*⟩ 14 *informal* to place or offer (a bet) on the result of casting dice ⟨~ 5⟩ 15 *slang* to take (a drug) by hypodermic needle ~ *vi* 1a to go or pass rapidly or violently ⟨*sparks* ~ing *up*⟩ ⟨*his feet shot out from under him*⟩ b to move ahead by superior speed, force, momentum, etc c to stream out suddenly; spurt ⟨*blood shot from the wound*⟩ d to dart (as if) in rays from a source of light e to dart with a piercing sensation ⟨*pain shot up his arm*⟩ 2a to cause a weapon or other device to discharge a missile b to use a firearm or bow, esp for sport (eg in hunting) 3 to propel a missile ⟨*guns that* ~ *many miles*⟩ 4 to protrude, project – often + *out* ⟨*a mountain-range* ~ing *out into the sea*⟩ 5a to grow or sprout (as if) by putting forth shoots b to develop, mature 6a to propel an object (eg a ball) in a particular way b to drive the ball or puck in hockey, football, etc towards a goal 7 to cast dice 8 to slide into or out of a fastening ⟨*a bolt that* ~s *in either direction*⟩ 9a to record (eg on cinefilm or videotape) a series of visual images; make a film or videotape b to operate a camera or set cameras in operation; film – see also **shoot one's** BOLT/CRAPS/a LINE/**one's** MOUTH off *synonyms* see HUNT [ME *sheten, shuten*, fr OE *scēotan*; akin to ON *skjōta* to shoot, Lith *skudrus* quick]

**shoot at**/**for** *vt* to aim at; strive for

**shoot down** *vt*, *informal* to say "no" firmly to (a person or proposal) ⟨*another idea shot down by the planning department*⟩

**shoot through** *vi*, *Austr* & *NZ* to leave; *specif* to make a hasty or pre-emptive departure ⟨*a well-known absconder, shooting through at the slightest opportunity* – *The Age* (*Melbourne*)⟩

**shoot up** *vi* 1 to grow or increase rapidly ⟨*when youngsters start to shoot up* – *Annabel*⟩ ⟨*house prices have shot up in recent months*⟩ 2 *slang* to inject a narcotic drug into a vein; mainline

²**shoot** *n* 1 a sending out of new growth or the growth sent out: eg 1a a stem or branch with its leaves, buds, etc, esp when not yet mature b an offshoot c a similar formation of

crystal **2a** an act of shooting (eg with a bow or firearm): **2a(1)** a shot **a(2)** the firing of a missile, esp by artillery **b(1)** a shooting trip or party **b(2)** (land over which is held) the right to shoot game **c(1)** a shooting match ⟨*skeet* ∼⟩ **c(2)** a round of shots in a shooting match **d(1)** the action of shooting with a camera **d(2)** a launching of a rocket device or a guided missile esp experimentally **3a** a motion or movement of rapid thrusting: eg **3a(1)** a sudden or rapid advance **a(2)** a rush of water down a steep descent **a(3)** THRUST 2b **a(4)** a falling of a detached mass of earth or ice **a(5)** *chiefly NAm* a momentary darting sensation; a twinge **b** a bar of rays; a beam ⟨*a* ∼ *of sunlight*⟩ **4** any of various inclined channels or troughs through which something (eg water, logs, or grain) is moved **5** an elongated usu vertical body of ore in a vein **6** *chiefly NAm* CHUTE 1,2 [(3a(2),4) perh by folk etymology fr Fr *chute* – more at CHUTE]

³**shoot** *interj* – used to express annoyance or surprise [euphemism see DIALECT [ME *shoppe,* fr OE *shit*]

**shooter** /'shoohtə/ *n* one who or that which shoots: eg **a** a person empowered to score goals in netball **b** a repeating pistol – usu in combination ⟨*six*-shooter⟩ **c** the player in the game of CRAPS who throws the dice, and against whom all the other players are betting, until he/she makes a losing shot and another player takes over

**shooting** /'shoohting/ *n, chiefly Br* **1** the right to shoot game in a designated area **2** the area designated for shooting game

**shooting brake** *n, Br* ESTATE CAR

**shooting gallery** *n* a usu covered range equipped with targets for practice with firearms

**shooting iron** *n, NAm slang* a firearm – no longer in vogue

**shooting match** *n, informal* an affair, matter – chiefly in *the whole shooting match*

**shooting script** *n* the final fully detailed version of a screenplay in which scenes are grouped in the order most convenient for shooting

**shooting star** *n* a meteor that burns up as it enters the atmosphere and that hence appears as a sudden brief streak of light in the night sky

**shooting stick** *n* a spiked walking stick with a handle that opens into a seat, used esp by spectators at sporting events

'**shoot-,out** *n* **1** a usu decisive battle fought with handguns or rifles **2** *informal* an often forceful difference of opinion; a confrontation

¹**shop** /shop/ *n* **1a** a building or room for the retail sale of merchandise **b** an establishment or office where business of a specified nature is carried on ⟨*hairdresser's* ∼⟩ ⟨*betting* ∼⟩ **2** a place where articles are manufactured, assembled, or repaired; *esp* a part of a factory where a particular manufacturing process takes place ⟨*the machine* ∼⟩ **3** a school laboratory equipped for instruction in manual arts; *also* manual arts as a school subject **4** the jargon or subject matter peculiar to an occupation or sphere of interest – chiefly in *talk shop* **synonyms** see DIALECT [ME *shoppe,* fr OE *sceoppa* booth; akin to OHG *scopf* shed, OE *scypen, scipen, scepen* cattle shed] – **all over the shop** dispersed over a large area – **set up shop** to establish one's business – **talk shop** to talk about one's job, esp outside working hours

²**shop** *vb* -**pp**- *vi* **1** to visit a shop or shops with intent to purchase goods **2** to make a search; hunt ⟨∼ *for winning designs*⟩ ∼ *vt* **1** *NAm* to examine the stock or offerings of ⟨∼ *the stores for Christmas gift ideas*⟩ **2** *Br informal* to inform against, esp to the police ⟨*the robber who changed sides and* ∼ped *his mates – Daily Mirror*⟩ – **shopper** *n*

**shop around** *vi* to investigate a market or situation in search of the best buy or alternative

³**shop** *adj* purchased from a shop rather than natural or homemade; manufactured, ready-made ⟨∼ *clothes*⟩ ⟨∼ *bread*⟩

**shop assistant** *n, Br* one employed to sell goods in a retail shop

**shopfloor** /,shop'flaw/ *n* the area in which machinery or workbenches are located in a factory or mill, esp considered as a place of work ⟨*problems on the* ∼⟩; *also, taking sing or pl vb* the workers in an establishment, esp union members, as distinct from the management ⟨*from* ∼ *to governmental level*⟩

**shopfront** /-,frunt/ *n* the front side of a shop or shop building facing the street

**shopkeeper** /-,keepə/ *n* a person who operates a retail shop

**shoplift** /-,lift/ *vb* to steal (goods on display) from a shop [back-formation fr *shoplifter*] – **shoplifter** *n,* **shoplifting** *n*

**shopping** /'shoping/ *n* goods (eg groceries or clothing) purchased on a shopping trip

**shopping centre** *n* a group of retail shops and service establishments of different types, often designed to serve a community or neighbourhood

**shopsoiled** /-,soyld/ *adj, chiefly Br* **1** deteriorated (eg soiled or faded) through excessive handling or display in a shop **2** no longer fresh or effective; jaded, worn-out ⟨*the* ∼ *slogans of fascism*⟩

**shop steward** *n, Br* a union member elected as a union representative of usu manual workers in one workplace

**shoptalk** /'shop,tawk/ *n, chiefly NAm* SHOP 4

**shopwalker** /-,wawkə/ *n, Br* a person employed in a large shop to oversee the shop assistants and aid customers

**shopwindow** /-'windoh/ *n* **1** a usu large display window in which a shop shows merchandise **2** SHOWCASE 2

**shopworn** /-,wawn/ *adj, chiefly NAm* shopsoiled

**shoran** /'shaw,ran/ *n* a system of short-range aircraft navigation in which radar signals are sent out and returned by two ground stations of known position [*short-range navigation*]

¹**shore** /shaw/ *n* **1** the land bordering the sea or another usu large body of water; *specif* the coast **2** land as distinguished from the sea ⟨*shipboard and* ∼ *duty*⟩ [ME, fr (assumed) OE *scor;* akin to OE *scieran* to cut – more at SHEAR]

²**shore** *vt* **1** to support with shores; prop **2** to give support to; brace, sustain – usu + *up* ⟨∼ *up farm prices*⟩ [ME *shoren;* akin to ON *skortha* to prop]

³**shore** *n* a prop for preventing sinking or sagging

**shorebird** /'shaw,buhd/ *n* any of a suborder (Charadrii) of WADING BIRDS (eg plovers, sandpipers, or snipes) that are common on seashores or inland mud flats – called also WADER

**shore crab** *n* any of various crabs living between the tidemarks; *esp* one (*Carcinus maenas*) found in many parts of the world

**shore leave** *n* time granted to members of a ship's crew to go ashore

**shoreline** /'shaw,lien/ *n* the line where a body of water and the shore meet; *also* the strip of land along this line

**shorewards** /-woodz/ *adv* towards the shore

**shoring** /'shawring/ *n* **1** the act of supporting (as if) with shores **2** a system or quantity of shores

**shorn** /shawn/ *past part of* SHEAR

¹**short** /shawt/ *adj* **1** having little or insufficient length or height **2a** not extended in time; brief ⟨*a* ∼ *vacation*⟩ **b** *of the memory* not retentive **c** expeditious, quick ⟨*made* ∼ *work of the problem*⟩ **d** seeming to pass quickly ⟨*made great progress in just a few* ∼ *years*⟩ **3a** *of a speech sound* having a relatively short duration **b** being the member of a pair of similarly spelt vowel sounds that is shorter in duration ⟨∼ *i* in sin⟩ **c** *of a syllable in verse* **c(1)** of relatively brief duration **c(2)** unstressed **4** limited in distance ⟨*a* ∼ *walk*⟩ **5a** not coming up to a measure or requirement ⟨*in* ∼ *supply*⟩ ⟨*a lot* ∼ *of ideal*⟩ **b** not reaching far enough ⟨*the throw was* ∼ *by five metres*⟩ **c** insufficiently supplied ⟨∼ *of cash*⟩ **6a** abrupt, curt **b** quickly provoked ⟨*a* ∼ *temper*⟩ **7** payable at an early date; short-term **8a** *of baked goods* crisp and easily broken owing to the presence of fat; crumbly ⟨∼ *pastry*⟩ **b** *of metal* brittle under certain conditions **9a** not lengthy or protracted; concise **b** made briefer; abbreviated ⟨*Sue is* ∼ *for Susan*⟩ **10a** not having goods or property that one has sold in anticipation of a fall in prices **b** of or being a sale of securities or commodities that the seller does not possess or has not contracted for at the time of the sale ⟨∼ *sale*⟩ **11a** of or occupying a fielding position in cricket near the batsman **b** *of a bowled ball in cricket* bouncing relatively far from the batsman ⟨*he played excellent shots off anything* ∼⟩ [ME, fr OE *scort;* akin to OHG *scurz* short, ON *skera* to cut – more at SHEAR] – **shortish** *adj,* **shortness** *n* – **nothing short of** nothing less than; something which is ⟨*the plan is* nothing short of *revolutionary*⟩ – see also **in short** ORDER, **in the short** RUN

²**short** *adv* **1** in a curt manner ⟨*tends to talk* ∼ *with people*⟩ **2** for or during a brief time ⟨*short-lasting*⟩ **3** in an abrupt manner; suddenly ⟨*the car stopped* ∼⟩ **4** at a point or degree before a specified or intended goal or limit ⟨*the shells fell* ∼⟩ ⟨*stopped* ∼ *of murder*⟩ **5** clean across ⟨*the axle was snapped* ∼⟩ **6** *of a financial deal* (as if) by a short sale *usage* see SHORTLY – **be taken/caught short** *Br* to feel a sudden embarrassing need to defecate or urinate – **cut short 1** to abbreviate **2** IN-

TERRUPT 1 – **run short** to become insufficient – **run short of** RUN OUT OF

**³short** *n* **1** the sum and substance; the upshot – *usu* + *the* ⟨*the ~ of it is, he's in disgrace*⟩ **2a** a short syllable or vowel **b** a short sound or signal (e g in Morse code) **3** *pl* a by-product of wheat milling that includes the germ, bran, and some flour **4** *pl* knee-length or less than knee-length trousers **5a** somebody who operates on the short side of the market **b** *pl* short-term bonds **6** SHORT CIRCUIT **7** a brief often documentary or educational film **8** *Br* a drink of spirits; *esp* such a drink as opposed to beer ⟨*is your girlfriend on ~s or will she have a pint?*⟩ **9** *usu pl, chiefly NAm* a deficiency – **for short** as an abbreviation – **in short** by way of summary; briefly – see also the LONG and the short of it

**⁴short** *vt* **1** to short-circuit **2** *NAm* to shortchange, cheat

**short account** *n* **1** the account of a short seller (e g in stock exchange dealings) **2** the total of open short sales in a given item of trade or in the stock market as a whole

**shortage** /'shawtij/ *n* a lack, deficit

**short back and sides** *n taking sing vb* a haircut for a man in which the hair round the ears and at the neck is cut very short or shaven ⟨*got a ~ before his job interview*⟩

**shortbread** /-ˌbred/ *n* a thick crumbly biscuit made from flour, sugar, and fat

**shortcake** /-ˌkayk/ *n* **1** shortbread **2** a thick short cake resembling biscuit that is usu sandwiched with a layer of fruit and cream and eaten as a dessert ⟨*strawberry ~*⟩

**shortchange** /-'chaynj/ *vt* **1** to give less than the correct amount of change to **2** *informal* to cheat – **shortchanger** *n*

**short-'circuit** *vt* **1** to apply a SHORT CIRCUIT to or cause a short circuit in (so as to render inoperative) **2** to bypass, circumvent

**short circuit** *n* a connection of comparatively low resistance accidentally or intentionally made between two points on a circuit between which the resistance is normally much greater

**shortcoming** /-ˌkuming/ *n usu pl* a deficiency, defect ⟨*felt his ~s made him unsuited to management*⟩

**short covering** *n* the buying in of property (e g securities) by a short seller to meet the requirements of a short sale

**shortcrust pastry** /-ˌkrust/ *n* a basic pastry used for pies, flans, and tarts and made with half as much fat as flour

**shortcut** /-ˌkut/ *n* **1** a route more direct than one normally taken **2** a procedure quicker and more direct than that customarily followed

**short-'cycle** *adj* of or being a short higher education course not leading to a degree

**'short-ˌday** *adj, of a plant* producing flowers on exposure to short periods of daylight – compare DAY-NEUTRAL, LONG-DAY

**short division** *n* arithmetic division in which the successive steps can be worked out mentally

**short-eared owl** *n* a very widely distributed brown owl (*Asio flammeus*) that has very short ear tufts and often hunts by day

**shorten** /'shawt(ə)n/ *vt* **1a** to reduce the length or duration of **b** to cause to seem shorter or shorter ⟨*~ed the long wait by telling stories*⟩ **2** to add fat to (e g pastry dough) in order to make tender and flaky **3** to reduce the area or amount of (sail that is set) *~ vi* to become short or shorter *antonyms* lengthen, elongate, extend – **shortener** *n*

**shortening** /'shawt(ə)n·ing/ *n* **1** the action or process of making or becoming short; *specif* the dropping of the end of a word so as to produce a shorter word **2** an edible fat (e g butter or lard) used to shorten pastry, biscuits, etc

**shortfall** /-ˌfawl/ *n* (the degree or amount of) a failure to achieve a goal or suffice for a need; a deficiency

**shorthand** /-ˌhand/ *n* **1a** a method of rapid writing that substitutes symbols and abbreviations for letters, words, or phrases **b** notes written in shorthand **2** a system or instance of rapid or abbreviated communication ⟨*verbal ~*⟩ – **shorthand** *adj*

**shorthanded** /-'handid/ *adj* short of the usual or requisite number of staff; undermanned

**shorthand typist** *n* somebody who takes shorthand notes, esp from dictation, and later transcribes them using a typewriter

**short head** *n* HEAD 13

**shorthorn** /-ˌhawn/ *n, often cap* (any of) a breed of red, roan, or white BEEF CATTLE originating in NE England and including good milk-producing strains – called also DURHAM

**short-horned grasshopper** *n* any of a family (Acrididae) of grasshoppers with short heavy antennae

**short hundredweight** *n* HUNDREDWEIGHT 2b

**shortie** /'shawti/ *n or adj, informal* (a) shorty

**shortleaf pine** /'shawtˌleef/ *n* a pine tree (*Pinus echinata*) of S USA that has short usu paired flexible needles and cinnamon-coloured bark; *also* the yellow wood of this pine

**shortlist** /'shawtˌlist/ *vt, Br* to place (e g a candidate) on a SHORT LIST

**short list** *n, Br* a list of selected candidates (e g for a job) from whom a final choice must be made

**ˌshort-'lived** *adj* not living or lasting long *antonym* agelong

**shortly** /-li/ *adv* **1a** in a few words; briefly **b** in an abrupt manner **2a** in a short time ⟨*we shall be there ~*⟩ **b** at a short interval ⟨*~ after sunset*⟩

*usage* The adverbs **shortly** and **short** can each mean "abruptly"; but since **shortly** can also mean "briefly" or "soon" one should be careful to avoid ambiguity, as ⟨*I'll speak shortly*⟩ has three meanings.

**'short-ˌrack** *vt* to restrict the movement of (a horse) by tying the head to a ring at eye level

**ˌshort-'range** *adj* **1** SHORT-TERM 1 **2** fit for or capable of travelling (only) short distances ⟨*a ~ missile*⟩

**short run** *n* a relatively brief period of time – chiefly in *in the short run* – **short-run** *adj*

**short shrift** *n* **1** a brief respite for confession before execution **2** abrupt or inconsiderate treatment

**short sight** *n* MYOPIA

**shortsighted** /-'sietid/ *adj* **1** nearsighted **2** lacking foresight – **shortsightedly** *adv*, **shortsightedness** *n*

**ˌshort-'spoken** *adj* curt

**ˌshort-'staffed** *adj* having fewer than the usual number of workers

**shortstop** /'shawtˌstop/ *n* (the player stationed at) the fielding position in baseball for defending the area between second and third base

**short story** *n* a piece of prose fiction, shorter than a novel, usu dealing with a few characters and often concentrating on the creation of mood rather than plot

**ˌshort-'tempered** *adj* having a quick temper

**ˌshort-'term** *adj* **1** involving or covering a relatively short period of time ⟨*~ plans*⟩ **2a** of or constituting a financial operation or obligation based on a brief term, esp one of less than a year **b** generated by assets held for less than six months

**short time** *n* reduced working hours because of a lack of work ⟨*men thrown on the dole or put on ~*⟩ – compare OVERTIME

**short title** *n* an abbreviated title, esp of an Act of Parliament

**short ton** /tun/ *n* a US unit of weight that is equal to 2000 pounds (approx 746·48 kilograms)

**ˌshort-'waisted** *adj* unusually short from the shoulders to the waist

**shortwave** /-ˌwayv/ *n* **1** shortwave, shortwaves *pl* a band of RADIO WAVES having wavelengths between about 120 metres and 20 metres and typically used for amateur transmissions or long-range broadcasting **2** a radio transmitter operating on shortwaves

**ˌshort-'winded** *adj* **1** affected with or characterized by shortness of breath **2** brief or concise in speaking or writing

**ˌshort-'woolled** *adj, esp of sheep* having short but fine wool

**shorty, shortie** /'shawti/ *n, informal* one who or that which is short; *esp* a short nightdress – **shorty** *adj*

**Shoshone, Shoshoni** /shə'shohni/ *n, pl* **Shoshones, Shoshonis** *also esp collectively* **Shoshone, Shoshoni** a member of any of a group of American Indian peoples originally ranging through California, Colorado, Idaho, Nevada, Utah, and Wyoming

**Shoshonean** /shə'shohniən/ *n* a language family of the UTO-AZTECAN group comprising the languages of most of the Uto-Aztecan peoples in the USA

**¹shot** /shot/ *n, pl* **shots**, (2a) **shot 1a** an action of shooting **b** a directed propelling of a missile; *specif* a directed discharge of a firearm **c** a stroke or throw in a game (e g tennis, billiards, or basketball); *also* a kick aimed at the goal in soccer **d** a blast **e** a hypodermic injection of a drug or vaccine ⟨*needed a ~ of morphine to deaden the pain*⟩ ⟨*has he had his tetanus ~*⟩ **2a(1)** something propelled by shooting; *esp* small lead or steel pellets forming a charge for a shotgun **a(2)** a single nonexplosive projectile for a gun or cannon **b(1)** a metal sphere that is thrown (PUT 1b(2)) for distance as an athletic field event **b(2)** this event **3** the distance that a missile is or can be projected; range, reach **4** one who shoots; *esp* a marksman **5** a pointed or telling remark **6a** a single photographic exposure; *esp* a snapshot **b** a single sequence of a film or a television programme taken by one camera without interruption **7** a charge of explosives **8** *informal* **8a** an attempt, try ⟨*had a ~ at mending the puncture*⟩ **b** a (wild) guess, conjecture **9** *informal* a charge due for payment (eg for a round of drinks) – chiefly in *pay one's shot* **10a** *informal* a small amount applied at one time; a dose ⟨*give the patient a ~ of oxygen*⟩ **b** *NAm informal* a single drink of spirits ⟨*barman! Give me a ~ of bourbon!*⟩ [ME, fr OE *scot;* akin to ON *skot* shot, OHG *scuz,* OE *scēotan* to shoot] – **like a shot** very rapidly – **shot in the arm** a stimulus, boost [*shot* 1e] – **shot in the dark** a wild guess – see also CALL **the shots**

²**shot** *adj* **1** *of a fabric* having colour effects which change with the light; iridescent ⟨*~ silk*⟩ **2** suffused or streaked with colour ⟨*hair ~ with grey*⟩ ⟨*~ enamel*⟩ **3** infused or permeated *with* a quality or element ⟨*~ through with wit*⟩ **4** *informal* utterly exhausted or ruined ⟨*his nerves are ~*⟩ – **be/get shot of** *chiefly Br informal* GET RID OF

³**shot** *interj* – used for expressing approval of a good stroke in a ball game (eg tennis or table tennis)

¹**shotgun** /-,gun/ *n* an often double-barrelled smoothbore shoulder weapon for firing quantities of shot at short ranges

²**shotgun** *adj* **1** of or using a shotgun **2** *informal* enforced ⟨*a ~ merger*⟩ **3** *chiefly NAm informal* covering a wide field with hit-or-miss effectiveness; indiscriminate ⟨*~ propaganda*⟩

**shotgun wedding** *n, informal* a wedding forced or required, esp because of the bride's pregnancy

**shot hole** *n* a drilled hole in which a charge of dynamite is exploded

**shot put** /poot/ *n* SHOT 2b(2) – **shot-putter** *n*, **shot putting** *n*

**shotten** /'shot(ə)n/ *adj, of a fish* having ejected the spawn and so of inferior food value ⟨*~ herring*⟩ [ME *shotyn,* fr pp of *shuten* to shoot]

**should** /shəd; *strong* shood/ *past of* SHALL **1** – used (eg in the main clause of a conditional sentence) to introduce a contingent fact, possibility, or presumption ⟨*I ~ be surprised if he wrote*⟩ ⟨*it's odd that you ~ mention that*⟩ **2a** ought to ⟨*you ~ brush your teeth after every meal*⟩ **b** need not – in *should worry* **3** – used in reported discourse to represent *shall* or *will* ⟨*she banged on the door and said we ~ be late – Punch*⟩ **4** will probably ⟨*with an early start, they ~ be here by noon*⟩ **5** – used to soften direct statement ⟨*I ~ have thought it was colder than that*⟩ ⟨*who ~ open the door but Fred*⟩ [ME *sholde,* fr OE *sceolde* owed, was obliged to; akin to OHG *scolta* owed, was obliged to]

*usage* When **should** and **would** are used in reported speech to represent the pure future, the distinction between them has traditionally been the same as that between **shall** and **will**: **should** for the first person ⟨*we said we* **should** *come*⟩ and **would** for the second and third; **would** and **'d** are today replacing **should** ⟨*we said we* **would/we'd** *come*⟩ just as **will** is replacing **shall**. In conditional sentences, **should** may be taken to mean "ought to", as in ⟨*I* **should** *help you if I had time*⟩ which has two meanings, and this ambiguity can be avoided by the use of **would** instead of **should**. In all their other senses, **should** and **would** are used with the first, second, and third persons alike, although where there is a choice between them **should** is the more formally correct for the first person ⟨*I* **should**/**I'd** *like to know*⟩. See SHALL, ¹OUGHT

¹**shoulder** /'shohldə/ *n* **1** the part of the human body formed of the bones, joints, and muscles by which the arm is connected with the trunk; *also* the corresponding part of other VERTEBRATE animals **2** *pl* **2a** the two shoulders and the upper part of the back ⟨*shrugged his ~s*⟩ **b** capacity for bearing a burden (eg of blame or responsibility) ⟨*placed the guilt squarely on his ~s*⟩ **3** a cut of meat including the upper joint of the foreleg and adjacent parts **4** the part of a garment at the wearer's shoulder **5** an area next to a higher, more prominent, or more important part: eg **5a(1)** the slope of a hill or mountain near the top **a(2)** a sideways protrusion of a hill or mountain **b** the flat top of the body of a piece of printing type from which the BEVEL rises **c** either edge of a road; *specif* that part of a road to the side of the surface on which vehicles travel; *a verge* **d** the part of a ring where the setting joins the band **6** a rounded or sloping part (eg of a stringed instrument or a bottle) where the neck joins the body **7** a period intermediate between high season and low season in terms of the cost of fares, accommodation, etc [ME *sholder,* fr OE *sculdor;* akin to OHG *scultra* shoulder, OE *sciell* shell – more at SHELL] – **shouldered** *adj* – **give somebody the cold shoulder** to ignore or snub somebody – **put one's shoulder to the wheel** to (begin to) work hard, esp in cooperation with others – **rub shoulders with** to associate

or come into contact with – **straight from the shoulder** without evasion; honestly – see also CHIP **on one's shoulder**

²**shoulder** *vt* **1** to push or thrust (as if) with the shoulder ⟨*~ed his way through the crowd*⟩ **2a** to place or carry on the shoulder ⟨*~ed his rucksack*⟩ **b** to assume the burden or responsibility of ⟨*~ the costs*⟩ *~ vi* to push with the shoulders aggressively; jostle

**shoulder bag** *n* a bag that has a strap attached at each side of sufficient length for the bag to be hung over the shoulder

**shoulder belt** *n* an anchored seat belt worn across the upper torso and over one shoulder for safety, esp in a moving motor car

**shoulder blade** *n* SCAPULA

**shoulder board** *n* either of a pair of broad pieces of stiffened cloth worn on the shoulders of a military uniform and carrying insignia

**shoulder flash** *n, chiefly Br* a bright cloth patch worn on (the shoulder of) a military uniform as an identifying mark

**shoulder girdle** *n* PECTORAL GIRDLE

'**shoulder-,in** *n* a movement in DRESSAGE (manoeuvres by a trained horse) with the forehead of the horse bent laterally away from the line of advance

**shoulder knot** *n* **1** an ornamental knot of ribbon or lace worn on the shoulder in the 17th and 18th centuries **2** a detachable ornament of braided wire cord worn on the shoulders of a ceremonial uniform by a commissioned officer

**shoulder mark** *n* SHOULDER BOARD

**shoulder strap** *n* a strap that passes across the shoulder and holds up an article or garment

**shoulder to shoulder** *adv* **1** adjacent **2** united

**shouldest** /shoodist/, **shouldst** /shoodst/ *archaic past 2 sing of* SHALL

**shouldn't** /'shoodnt/ should not

¹**shout** /showt/ *vi* **1** to utter a sudden loud cry **2** to speak excitedly; enthuse ⟨*her job was nothing to ~ about*⟩ **3** *Austr & NZ informal* to buy a round of drinks *~ vt* **1** to utter in a loud voice ⟨*Austr & NZ informal* **2a** to buy something, esp a drink, for (another person) ⟨*the cook went on ~ing Mr Clegg – Frank Sargeson*⟩ **b** to buy (something, esp a drink) for someone else ⟨*dropped in to see if you'd ~ an old friend a drink – The Sun (Melbourne)*⟩ [ME *shouten*] – **shouter** *n*

**shout down** *vt* to drown the words of (a speaker) by shouting

²**shout** *n* **1** a loud cry or call **2** *informal* ⁴ROUND 7

**shouting distance** /'showting/ *n, chiefly NAm* a short distance; easy reach – usu + *within* ⟨*lived within ~ of his cousins*⟩

**shove** /shuv/ *vt* **1** to push along with steady force **2** to push in a rough, careless, or hasty manner; thrust ⟨*~d the book into his coat pocket*⟩ *~ vi* **1** to force a way forwards ⟨*bargain hunters shoving up to the counter*⟩ **2** to move something by pushing ⟨*you pull and I'll ~*⟩ *synonyms* see ¹PUSH [ME *shoven,* fr OE *scūfan* to thrust away; akin to OHG *scioban* to push, OSlav *skubati* to tear] – **shove** *n,* **shover** *n*

**shove off** *vi, informal* to go away; leave ⟨*he's shoved off for home*⟩ – often imper ⟨*shove off, I'm busy!*⟩

,**shove-'halfpenny** *n* a game played on a special very smooth board in which players shove discs (eg coins) into marked scoring areas by aligning each disc's edge with the bottom edge of the board and striking it with the heel of the hand

¹**shovel** /'shuvl/ *n* **1a** a hand or mechanical implement consisting of a broad scoop or a hollowed out blade with a handle, used to lift and throw loose material **b** something like a shovel; *esp* a part of a digging or earth-moving machine **2** a shovelful [ME, fr OE *scofl;* akin to OHG *scūfla* shovel, OE *scūfan* to thrust away] – **shoveller** *n*

²**shovel** *vb* **-ll-** (*NAm* **-l-, -ll-**) *vt* **1** to shift with a shovel ⟨*~ snow from a path*⟩ **2** to dig or clear with a shovel **3** to throw or convey clumsily or in a mass as if with a shovel ⟨*~led his food into his mouth*⟩ *~ vi* to use a shovel

**shovelful** /-f(ə)l/ *n, pl* **shovelfuls** *also* **shovelsful** as much as a shovel will hold

**shovel hat** *n* a shallow-crowned hat with a wide brim curved up at the sides, worn esp formerly by some clergymen

**shovelhead** /'shuvl,hed/ *n* any of several fishes with heads resembling shovels; *esp* a shark (*Sphyrna tiburo*) that is smaller than the related hammerhead and has a narrower head

**shoveller** /'shuvl•ə, 'shuvlə/, *NAm chiefly* **shoveler** /'shuvələ/ *n* any of several DABBLING DUCKS (genus *Anas,* esp *Anas clypeata*) that have large and very broad beaks

**shovelman** /'shuvəlmən, -man/ *n* one who works with a shovel or a power shovel

¹**show** /shoh/ *vb* **shown** /shohn/, **showed** *vt* **1** to cause or permit to be seen; exhibit ⟨~ed *his painting to the judges*⟩ **2** to present as a public spectacle; perform **3** to reveal by one's condition, nature, or behaviour ⟨*was reluctant to* ~ *his feelings*⟩ **4** to demonstrate by one's achievements ⟨~ed *herself to be a fine pianist*⟩ **5a** to point out to somebody ⟨~ed *him where he lived*⟩ **b** to conduct, usher ⟨~ed *me to an aisle seat*⟩ **6** to accord, grant ⟨~ *respect to one's elders*⟩ **7a** to make evident; indicate ⟨*a letter that* ~ed *his true feelings*⟩ **b** to have as an attribute; manifest ⟨*trade figures* ~ed *a large deficit*⟩ ⟨*the patient is* ~ing *some improvement*⟩ **8** to allege, plead – used esp in law ⟨~ *cause*⟩ **9a** to establish or make clear by argument or reasoning ⟨~ *a plan to be faulty*⟩ **b** to inform, instruct ⟨~ed *me how to solve the problem*⟩ **10** to present (an animal) for judging in a show ~ *vi* **1** to be or come in view; be noticeable ⟨*anger* ~ed *in his face*⟩ ⟨*has a tear in his coat but it doesn't* ~⟩ **2** to appear in a specified way ⟨~ *to good advantage*⟩ **3** to be staged or presented ⟨*a film now* ~ing⟩ **4** *chiefly NAm* to put in an appearance ⟨*failed to* ~ *for the award*⟩ – compare SHOW UP; see also **show one's** FACE/**a clean pair of** HEELS [ME *shewen, showen,* fr OE *scēawian* to look, look at, see; akin to OHG *scouwōn* to look, look at, L *cavēre* to be on one's guard] – **shower** *n*

**synonyms Show, manifest, evidence, evince, demonstrate, display, exhibit, expose, parade,** and **flaunt** all mean "make apparent". **Show** is the most general, and can replace any of the others. **Manifest, evidence,** and the formal **evince** all imply that something is made perceptible, often involuntarily ⟨*dog* **evinced** *a desire to go out*⟩. **Manifest** often implies in addition making so obvious that no close attention is required, and **evidence** stresses the giving of good reason to believe ⟨*is a good businesswoman, as is* **evidenced** *by her success*⟩. **Demonstrate, display,** and **exhibit** may be involuntary ⟨*he* **exhibited** *no fear*⟩ ⟨*this remark* **demonstrates/displays** *his ignorance*⟩ or intentional, in which case **demonstrate** suggests orderly exposition and proof ⟨*he* **demonstrated** *the truth of his hypothesis*⟩, **exhibit** stresses the formal making prominent of something to attract attention, and **display** emphasizes the showing of something to best advantage ⟨**display** *new fabrics to the buyers*⟩. **Expose** often suggests the unmasking of something shameful that is brought out of concealment ⟨**expose** *the pretensions of a quack*⟩, while by contrast **parade** and **flaunt** imply boastful ostentation ⟨**parade** *his knowledge of Greek*⟩ and **flaunt** particularly emphasizes impudent mockery ⟨*the winners* **flaunting** *their victory*⟩.

**show off** *vt* to exhibit proudly ⟨*wanted to* show *his new car* off⟩ ~ *vi* to seek attention or admiration by conspicuous behaviour ⟨*boys* showing off *on their bicycles*⟩ – see also SHOW-OFF

**show over** *vt, chiefly Br* to take on a tour of inspection of ⟨*prospective buyers were* shown over *the new house*⟩

**show up** *vt* **1** to reveal the shortcomings of ⟨*showed her* up *by winning*⟩ **2** *informal* to embarrass ~ *vi* **1a** to be plainly evident; STAND OUT **b** to appear in a specified light or manner ⟨*showed* up *badly in the semifinals*⟩ **2** *informal* to arrive ⟨*showed* up *late for his own wedding*⟩

²**show** *n* **1** a display ⟨*a* ~ *of hands*⟩ – often in **on show** ⟨*all antiques on* ~ *are genuine*⟩ **2a** a false semblance; a pretence ⟨*he made a* ~ *of friendship*⟩ **b** a more or less true appearance of something; a sign ⟨*a* ~ *of reason*⟩ **c** an impressive display ⟨*a* ~ *of strength*⟩ **d** ostentation **3** something exhibited, esp for wonder or ridicule; a spectacle **4a** a large display or exhibition arranged to arouse interest or stimulate sales ⟨*the Boat* ~⟩ **b** a competitive exhibition of animals, plants, etc to demonstrate quality in breeding **5** a public presentation: e g **5a** a theatrical presentation **b** a radio or television programme **6** an indication of metal in a mine or of gas or oil in a well **7** a bloodstained vaginal discharge indicating the onset of labour **8** *informal* an enterprise, affair ⟨*he ran the whole* ~⟩ **9** *chiefly NAm informal* a chance ⟨*gave him a* ~ *in spite of his background*⟩ – **good/bad show** *Br informal* a good or bad state of affairs – often used interjectionally to express approval or disapproval; not now in vogue – **steal the show** to attract most attention; be the most popular – see also GIVE **the show away**

**show biz** /biz/ *n, informal* SHOW BUSINESS

**showboat** /'shoh,boht/ *n* a (paddle-wheel) river steamship containing a theatre and carrying a troupe of actors who present plays for riverside communities

**showbread** /-,bred/ *n* shewbread

**show business** *n* the arts, occupations, and businesses (e g the theatre, films, and television) that comprise the entertainment industry

¹**showcase** /'shoh,kays/ *n* **1** a case, box, or cabinet with a glass front or top used for displaying and protecting articles in a shop or museum **2** a setting or surround for exhibiting something to best advantage ⟨*this programme is a* ~ *for her talents*⟩ – **showcase** *adj*

²**showcase** *vt, NAm* to exhibit

**showdown** /-,down/ *n* **1** the placing of poker hands face up on the table to determine the winner of a round (POT) **2** the final settlement of a contested issue or the confrontation by which it is settled

¹**shower** /'showə/ *n* **1a** a fall of rain of short duration **b** a similar fall of sleet, hail, or snow **2** something like a rain shower ⟨*a* ~ *of tears*⟩ ⟨~s *of sparks from a bonfire*⟩ **3 shower, shower bath** an apparatus with a nozzle that provides a stream of water for spraying the body of a person standing upright; *also* an act of washing oneself using such an apparatus **4** *chiefly NAm* a (surprise) party (eg for a bride-to-be or expectant mother) given by friends who bring presents often of a particular kind **5** *taking sing or pl vb, Br slang* a motley or inferior collection of people [ME *shour,* fr OE *scūr;* akin to OHG *scūr* shower, L *caurus* northwest wind] – **showery** *adj*

²**shower** *vi* **1** to descend (as if) in a shower ⟨*letters* ~ed *on him in praise and protest*⟩ **2** to take a shower bath ~ *vt* **1a** to wet copiously (eg with water) in a spray, fine stream, or drops **b(1)** to cause to fall in a shower ⟨*factory chimneys* ~ed *soot on the district*⟩ **b(2)** to cause a shower to fall on ⟨*factory chimneys* ~ed *the neighbourhood with soot*⟩ **2** to bestow or present in abundance ⟨~ed *him with honours*⟩

**shower box** *n, NZ* a cubicle containing a shower

**showerproof** /-,proohf/ *adj, of a fabric or garment* treated so as to give protection from a slight wetting (e g a shower)

**shower tray** *n* a fixed waterproof plastic or tiled tray with drainage, used for standing in while taking a shower

**showgirl** /'shoh,guhl/ *n* CHORUS GIRL; *broadly* a female stage performer whose presence is purely decorative

**showing** /'shoh·ing/ *n* **1** an act of putting something on view; a display, exhibition **2** performance in competition ⟨*made a good* ~ *in the finals*⟩ **3a** a statement or presentation of a case **b** appearance, evidence ⟨*on present* ~ *this industry has little future*⟩

**showjumping** /-,jumping/ *n* the competitive riding of horses one at a time over a set course of obstacles in which the winner is judged according to ability and speed – **showjumper** *n*

**showman** /-mən/ *n* **1** somebody who presents a theatrical show; *also* the manager of a circus or fairground **2** a person with a flair for dramatically effective presentation – **showmanship** *n*

'**show-,off** *n* **1** the act of showing off **2** one who shows off; an exhibitionist

**showpiece** /-,pees/ *n* a prime or outstanding example used for exhibition – **showpiece** *adj*

**showplace** /-,plays/ *n* a place (eg a park or STATELY HOME) that is a beautiful or distinguished example of its kind

**showroom** /-,roohm/ *n* a room where (samples of) goods for sale are displayed

**showstopper** /'shoh,stopə/ *n* an act, song, or performer that wins applause so prolonged as to interrupt a performance

**show trial** *n* a trial conducted by a (usu totalitarian) state to make an impression at home or abroad

**showy** /'shoh·i/ *adj* **1** making an attractive show; striking ⟨~ *blossoms*⟩ **2** given to or marked by pretentious display; gaudy – **showily** *adv,* **showiness** *n*

**shrank** /shrangk/ *past of* SHRINK

**shrapnel** /'shrapnəl/ *n, pl* **shrapnel 1** a hollow projectile that contains bullets or pieces of metal and that is exploded by a bursting charge to produce a shower of fragments **2** bomb, mine, or shell fragments thrown out during explosion [Henry *Shrapnel* †1842 E artillery officer]

¹**shred** /shred/ *n* a narrow strip cut or torn off; *also* a fragment, scrap [ME *shrede,* fr OE *scrēade;* akin to OHG *scrōt* piece cut off, L *scrupus* sharp stone, OE *scieran* to cut – more at SHEAR] – **shreddy** *adj*

²**shred** *vb* **-dd-** *vt* **1** to cut or tear into shreds **2** *archaic* to cut off; prune ~ *vi* to come apart in or be reduced to shreds – **shredder** *n*

**shredded wheat** *n* cooked partially dried wheat that is

shredded and moulded into cakes or biscuits which are then baked and eaten usu as a breakfast cereal

**shrew** /shrooh/ *n* **1** shrew, shrewmouse any of numerous small chiefly nocturnal mouselike mammals (family Soricidae) related to the moles and distinguished by a long pointed snout, very small eyes, and velvety fur **2** an ill-tempered nagging woman; a scold [ME *shrewe* evil or scolding person, fr OE *scrēawa* shrewmouse]

**shrewd** /shroohd/ *adj* **1a** severe, hard ⟨*a ~ knock*⟩ **b** bitter, piercing ⟨*a ~ wind*⟩ **2a** marked by keen discernment and hardheaded practicality ⟨*~ common sense*⟩ **b** wily and artful ⟨*a ~ operator*⟩ **3** *archaic* mischievous, injurious **4** *obs* shrewish [ME *shrewed* wicked, mischievous, fr *shrewe* + *-ed*] – **shrewdly** *adv*, **shrewdness** *n*

**synonyms** Shrewd, astute, perspicacious, and sagacious all mean "showing sound practical judgment". Shrewd emphasizes hardheaded native common sense and often cunning ⟨shrewd reply⟩ ⟨shrewd business sense⟩. Astute adds to this the suggestion of worldly wisdom that is not easily misled ⟨an astute observer of the political scene⟩. Perspicacious may indicate unusual insight into the workings of the mysterious. The rather formal sagacious suggests a mature farsighted wisdom based on experience ⟨sagacious old statesman⟩. Compare INTELLIGENT

**shrewish** /'shrooh·ish/ *adj* ill-tempered; intractable – **shrewishly** *adv*, **shrewishness** *n*

**shri** /shree, sree/ *n* SRI (Indian title)

**¹shriek** /shreek/ *vi* **1** to utter or make a shrill piercing sound ⟨*~ with laughter*⟩ ⟨*jets ~ed overhead*⟩ **2** to cry out sharply in a high-pitched voice; screech ⟨*~ an alarm*⟩ **2** to express in a manner suggestive of a shriek ⟨*poems that ~ their message*⟩ [prob irreg fr ME *shriken* to shriek; akin to ME *scremen* to scream]

**²shriek** *n* a shrill usu wild or involuntary cry; *also* a similar sound ⟨*the ~ of chalk on the blackboard*⟩ **synonyms** see ²SCREAM

**shrieval** /'shreevl/ *adj* of a sheriff [obs *shrieve* sheriff, fr ME *shirreve* – more at SHERIFF]

**shrievalty** /'shreev(ə)lti/ *n, chiefly Br* **1** the (term of) office of a sheriff **2** the jurisdiction of a sheriff

**shrieve** /shreev/ *vb, archaic* to shrive

**shrift** /shrift/ *n, archaic* **1** the act of shriving; confession **2** a remission of sins pronounced by a priest in the sacrament of penance [ME, fr OE *scrift*, fr *scrīfan* to shrive – more at SHRIVE]

**shrike** /shriek/ *n* any of numerous usu largely grey or brownish songbirds (family Laniidae) that have strong notched hooked beaks, feed chiefly on insects and small animals, and often impale their prey on thorns or barbed wire – called also BUTCHER-BIRD [perh fr (assumed) ME *shrik*, fr OE *scrīc* thrush; akin to ME *shriken* to shriek]

**¹shrill** /shril/ *vi* to make a high-pitched piercing sound ⟨*alarm bells ~ed as the robbers raced away*⟩ ~ *vt* to scream [ME *shrillen*]

**²shrill** *adj* **1a** having, making, or being a sharp high-pitched tone or sound; piercing **b** accompanied by sharp high-pitched sounds or cries ⟨*~ gaiety*⟩ **2** having a vivid effect on the senses ⟨*~ light*⟩ **3** strident, intemperate ⟨*~ anger*⟩ – **shrill** *adv*, **shrillness** *n*, **shrilly** *adv*

**³shrill** *n* a shrill sound ⟨*the ~ of the ship's whistle*⟩

**¹shrimp** /shrimp/ *n, pl* **shrimps**, (*1*) **shrimps**, *esp collectively* **shrimp 1** any of numerous mostly small marine 10-legged INVERTEBRATE animals (suborder Natantia of the order Decapoda, class Crustacea) that have a semitransparent long slender flexible body, fanlike tail, long legs, and long whiplike antennae and that are commercially important as food; *also* a small INVERTEBRATE animal (e g an AMPHIPOD or a BRANCHIOPOD) resembling the true shrimps **2** *informal or humorous* a very small or puny person [ME *shrimpe*; akin to ON *skorpna* to shrivel up, L *curvus* curved – more at CROWN] – **shrimpy** *adj*

**²shrimp** *vi* to fish for or catch shrimps – usu used in *go shrimping* – **shrimper** *n*

**¹shrine** /shrien/ *n* **1a** a case, box, or receptacle; *esp* one in which sacred relics (e g the bones of a saint) are kept **b** a place in which devotion is paid to a saint or deity; a sanctuary **c** a niche containing a religious image **2** a receptacle (e g a tomb) for the dead; *esp* the tomb of one (e g a saint) considered holy or of hallowed memory **3** a place or object hallowed by its history or associations ⟨*Oxford is a ~ of learning*⟩ [ME, fr OE *scrīn*, fr L *scrinium* case, chest]

**²shrine** *vt* to enshrine

**¹shrink** /shringk/ *vb* **shrank** /shrangk/ *also* **shrunk** /shrungk/; **shrunk, shrunken** /'shrungkən/ *vi* **1** to draw back the body or part of it (e g from something painful or horrible); cower **2a** to contract to a smaller volume or extent (e g as a result of heat or moisture) **b** to become reduced in size **c** to lose substance or weight ⟨*beef ~s in cooking by losing water and fat*⟩ **d** to decline in value; dwindle ⟨*the ~ing pound*⟩ **3** to show reticence or reluctance (e g before a difficult or unpleasant duty); recoil ~ *vt* to cause to contract or shrink; *specif* to compact (cloth) by a treatment (e g washing, boiling, or steaming) that results in contraction [ME *shrinken*, fr OE *scrincan*; akin to MD *schrinken* to draw back, L *curvus* curved – more at CROWN] – **shrinkable** *adj*, **shrinker** *n*

**usage** The usual past participle is shrunk ⟨my socks have shrunk⟩ but shrunken is the adjectival form ⟨shrunken heads⟩. **synonyms** see ²CONTRACT, ¹RECOIL **antonyms** stretch, swell, expand

**²shrink** *n* **1** the act of shrinking **2** shrinkage **3** *humorous* a psychoanalyst; *also* a psychiatrist [(3) short for *headshrinker*]

**shrinkage** /'shringkij/ *n* **1** the act or process of shrinking **2** the loss in weight of carcasses during shipment and storage, esp if frozen, and in the process of preparing the meat for consumption **3** the degree of shrinking ⟨*suffered a ten per cent ~ in transit*⟩ **4** loss of merchandise from a shop by shoplifting

**shrinking violet** /'shringking/ *n, informal* a meek or very shy person

**'shrink-,wrap** *vt* -pp- to wrap (e g a book or meat) in tough clear plastic film that is then shrunk (e g by heating) to form a tightly fitting sealed package

**shrive** /shriev/ *vb* **shrived, shrove** /shrohv/; **shriven** /'shrivən/, **shrived** *archaic vt* **1** to administer the sacrament of penance to **2** to free from guilt ~ *vi* to confess one's sins, esp to a priest [ME *shriven*, fr OE *scrīfan* to shrive, prescribe; akin to OHG *scrīban* to write; both fr a prehistoric WGmc word borrowed fr L *scribere* to write – more at SCRIBE]

**shrivel** /'shrivl/ *vb* -ll- (*NAm* -l-, -ll-) *vi* **1** to contract into wrinkles, esp through loss of moisture **2** to become reduced to impotence or ineptitude ~ *vt* to cause to shrivel [perh of Scand origin; akin to Sw dial. *skryvla* to wrinkle]

**¹shroff** /shrof/ *n* a banker or money changer in the Far East; *esp* one who tests and evaluates coin [Hindi *ṣarrāf*, fr Ar]

**²shroff** *vt* to sort (coins) into good and bad pieces

**Shropshire** /'shropshiə, -shə/ *n* (any of) an English breed of dark-faced hornless sheep that are more popular in the USA than in the UK and are raised primarily for meat and secondarily for their fine dense wool [*Shropshire* (Salop), county in W England]

**¹shroud** /shrowd/ *n* **1a** a burial garment (e g a winding-sheet) **b** something like an enveloping garment ⟨*a ~ of smoke hung over the town*⟩ **2** something that covers and guards (e g a usu fibreglass guard that protects a spacecraft from the heat of launching) **3a** any of the ropes or wires forming part of the STANDING RIGGING and leading, usu in pairs, from a ship's mastheads to the sides of the ship to give lateral support to the masts **b** any of the cords that suspend the harness of a parachute from the canopy [ME, fr OE *scrūd*; akin to OE *scrēade* shred – more at SHRED]

**²shroud** *vt* **1a** to cut off from view; obscure ⟨*trees ~ed by a thick mist*⟩ **b** to veil under another appearance (e g by obscuring or disguising) ⟨*may be accused of ~ing their work in polysyllabic technical terms – British Book News*⟩ **2** to dress for burial **3** *archaic* to cover for protection or concealment ~ *vi, archaic* to take shelter

**'shroud-,laid** *adj, of a rope* having four strands and a core

**Shrovetide** /'shrohv,tied/ *n* the period, usu of three days, immediately before ASH WEDNESDAY [ME *schroftide*, fr *schrof-* (fr *shriven* to shrive) + *tide*]

**Shrove Tuesday** *n* the Tuesday before ASH WEDNESDAY; PANCAKE DAY [ME *schroftewesday*, fr *schrof-* (as in *schroftide*) + *tewesday* Tuesday]

**¹shrub** /shrub/ *n* a low-growing usu many-stemmed woody plant [ME *schrobbe*, fr OE *scrybb* brushwood; akin to Norw *skrubbebær* dwarf cornel] – **shrubby** *adj*

**²shrub** *n* a drink made of sweetened fruit juice and spirits, esp rum [Ar *sharāb* drink (cf SYRUP)]

**shrubbery** /'shrub(ə)ri/ *n* a planting or growth of shrubs

**shrug** /shrug/ *vb* -gg- to lift and contract (the shoulders), esp to express aloofness, aversion, doubt, or lack of knowledge ⟨*I asked if he knew the answer, but he ~ged*⟩ [ME *schruggen* to shiver, shrug] – **shrug** *n*

**shrug off** *vt* to brush aside; disregard, belittle ⟨shrugs off *the problem*⟩

**shrunk** /shrungk/ *past & past part of* SHRINK

**shrunken** /'shrungkən/ *past part of* SHRINK

**shtetl** *also* **shtetel** /'shtetl/ *n, pl* **shtetlach** /'shtetlahkh/ a small Jewish town or village formerly found in Eastern Europe [Yiddish, fr MHG *stetel,* dim. of *stat* place, town, city, fr OHG, place – more at STEAD]

**shtick** /shtik/ *n, chiefly NAm* an entertainment routine; a turn [Yiddish *shtik,* lit., piece, fr MHG *stücke,* fr OHG *stucki*]

**shubunkin** /shə'bungkin, shooh-/ *n* a goldfish that is mottled, esp with blue, and is often kept in aquaria [Jap]

¹**shuck** /shuk/ *n* 1 *chiefly NAm* a pod, husk (e g the outer covering of a nut or of maize) 2 *NAm* the shell of an oyster or clam 3 **shucks** *pl,* **shuck** *NAm* something of no value ⟨*not worth* ~s⟩ 4 *pl, informal* – used interjectionally to express disappointment or polite self-depreciation ⟨~s, *it was nothing*⟩ [origin unknown]

²**shuck** *vt, NAm* 1 to strip of shucks 2 to remove or dispose of like a shuck – often + *off* ⟨~ *off clothing*⟩ ⟨~ *off bad habits*⟩ – **shucker** *n*

**shudder** /'shudə/ *vi* 1 to tremble with a sudden brief convulsive movement (e g from shock, revulsion, or fear) 2 to quiver, vibrate *synonyms* see ¹SHAKE [ME *shoddren;* akin to OHG *skutten* to shake, Lith *kuteti* to shake up] – **shudder** *n*

¹**shuffle** /'shufl/ *vt* 1 to mix together in a confused mass; jumble 2 to put or thrust aside in an evasive or haphazard manner ⟨~d *the whole matter out of his mind*⟩ 3a to rearrange (e g playing cards, dominoes, or tiles) to produce a random order b to move about or back and forth, esp so as to create disorder or confusion; shift ⟨~ *funds among various accounts*⟩ 4a to move (the feet) by sliding clumsily along or back and forth without lifting b to perform (e g a dance) with a dragging sliding step ~ *vi* 1 to work into or out of adroitly; worm ⟨~d *out of the difficulty somehow*⟩ 2 to act or speak in a shifty or evasive manner 3a to move or walk by sliding or dragging the feet b to dance in a lazy nonchalant manner with scraping and tapping motions of the feet c to perform in a clumsy or half-hearted manner ⟨*allowed to* ~ *through his lessons* – George Eliot⟩ 4 to mix playing cards by shuffling [perh irreg fr ¹*shove*] – **shuffler** *n*

²**shuffle** *n* 1 an evasion of the issue; an equivocation 2a an act of shuffling (e g of cards) b a right or turn to shuffle ⟨*was reminded that it was his* ~⟩ 3 (a dance characterized by) a dragging sliding movement

**shuffleboard** /-,bawd/ *n* 1 a game in which players use long-handled cues to shove wooden discs into scoring areas of a diagram marked on a smooth surface 2 a diagram on which shuffleboard is played [alter. of obs *shove-board*]

**shufti** /'shufti/ *n, Br informal* a look, glance ⟨*have a* ~ *at the radar screen*⟩ [perh of Ar origin; akin to Ar dial. *shaufa* sight, view]

**shul** /shool/ *n* a synagogue [Yiddish, fr MHG *schuol,* lit., school]

**shun** /shun/ *vt* -**nn**- to avoid deliberately, esp habitually; eschew ⟨*actors who* ~ *publicity*⟩ [ME *shunnen,* fr OE *scunian*] – **shunner** *n*

¹**shunt** /shunt/ *vt* 1 to turn off to one side; *esp* to move (e g a train) from one track to another 2 to provide with or divert by means of an electrical shunt 3 to divert (blood) from one part of the body to another by means of a surgical shunt 4 *Br* to move (railway vehicles) to different positions on the same track within terminal areas ~ *vi* 1 to move into a sidetrack 2 to travel back and forth ⟨~ed *between the two towns*⟩ [ME *shunten* to flinch] – **shunter** *n*

²**shunt** *n* 1 a means or mechanism for turning or thrusting aside: e g 1a a conductor joining two points in an electrical circuit so as to form a parallel or alternative path through which a portion of the current may pass (e g for regulating the amount passing in the main circuit) b a surgical passage created between two blood vessels to divert blood from one part of the body to another c *chiefly Br* SIDING 1 2 *informal* a usu minor collision of motor vehicles ⟨*Front offside wing bent ... A recent* ~, *not even rusted.* – Len Deighton⟩

**shunting yard** /'shunting/ *n* MARSHALLING YARD

**shunt winding** *n* a winding in an electric motor so arranged as to divide the ARMATURE current and lead a portion of it round the field-magnet coils – **shunt-wound** *adj*

¹**shush** /sh, shush/ *n* 1 – used interjectionally to demand silence 2 *informal* peace and quiet; silence ⟨*quiet, please, children! Let's have a bit of* ~!⟩

²**shush** *vt, informal* to tell to be quiet, esp by saying "Shush!"

¹**shut** /shut/ *vb* -**tt**-; **shut** *vt* 1a to place in position to close an opening ⟨~ *the lid*⟩ b to prevent entrance to or exit from – often + *up* ⟨~ *up the cottage for the winter*⟩ 2 to confine (as if) by enclosure ⟨~ *him in the cupboard*⟩ 3 to fasten with a lock or bolt 4 to close by bringing enclosing or covering parts together ⟨~ *the eyes*⟩ 5 to cause to cease or suspend operation – often + *up* or *down* ⟨~ *up shop*⟩ ~ *vi* 1 to become closed ⟨*flowers that* ~ *at night*⟩ 2 to cease or suspend operation – often + *up* or *down;* see also **keep one's** MOUTH **shut** □ compare ¹CLOSE **antonym** open [ME *shutten,* fr OE *scyttan;* akin to OE *scēotan* to shoot – more at SHOOT]

**shut away** *vt* to remove or isolate from others ⟨*governments that* shut *dissidents* away⟩

**shut in** *vt* to confine, enclose ⟨shut *himself* in *for days on end*⟩

**shut off** *vt* 1a to cut off, stop ⟨shut *the water* off⟩ b to stop the operation of (e g a machine) ⟨shut *the motor* off⟩ 2 to isolate, separate – usu + *from* ⟨*a village* shut off *from the rest of the world*⟩ to cease operating; stop ⟨*the heater* shuts off *automatically*⟩ – see also SHUTOFF

**shut out** *vt* 1 to exclude 2 *chiefly NAm* to prevent (an opponent) from scoring in a game or contest

**shut up** *vt, informal* to cause (somebody) to be silent; *esp* to force (a speaker) to stop talking ⟨*I wish the chairman would* shut *him* up⟩ ~ *vi* to become silent; *esp* to stop talking ⟨shut up, *I can't concentrate!*⟩

²**shut** *n* the line of union at a welded joint

**shutdown** /-,down/ *n* the cessation or suspension of an activity (e g work in a mine or factory)

'**shut-,eye** *n, informal* sleep

¹'**shut-,in** *n or adj, chiefly NAm* (an invalid) confined (e g in hospital) by illness or incapacity

²**shut-in** *n* a narrow gorge-shaped part of an otherwise wide valley

**shutoff** /-,of/ *n* 1 something (e g a valve) that shuts off 2 *chiefly NAm* a stoppage, interruption

¹**shutter** /'shutə/ *n* 1 one who or that which shuts 2a a usu movable hinged outside wooden cover for a window, usu fitted as one of a pair b a usu movable cover or screen (e g over a door or as part of stage scenery) 3 a mechanical device that limits the passage of light; *esp* a camera attachment that exposes the film or plate by opening and closing an aperture 4 the movable slots in the box enclosing the swell organ part of a PIPE ORGAN, which are opened to increase the volume of sound – **shutterless** *adj* – **put up the shutters** to cease business, either at the end of a day's work or permanently

²**shutter** *vt* 1 to close with shutters 2 to provide with shutters

**shuttering** /'shut(ə)ring/ *n* a temporary mould placed to support concrete while setting

¹**shuttle** /'shutl/ *n* 1a a usu spindle-shaped device that holds a bobbin and is used in weaving for passing the crosswise thread (WEFT) between the lengthwise threads (WARP) b a spindle-shaped device holding the thread in tatting, knotting, or netting c a sliding thread holder that carries the lower thread in a sewing machine through a loop of the upper thread to make a stitch 2 a lightweight conical object with a rounded nose that is hit as the object of play in badminton and that consists of a feathered cork or moulded plastic imitation 3a (a route used in) a regular going back and forth over a specified and often short route by a vehicle (e g an aeroplane) ⟨*a London Glasgow* ~ *service*⟩ b a vehicle used in a shuttle; *specif* a reusable space vehicle [ME *shittle,* prob fr OE *scytel* bar, bolt; akin to ON *skutill* bolt, OE *scēotan* to shoot – more at SHOOT]

²**shuttle** *vb* 1 to (cause to) move or travel to and fro rapidly or frequently 2 to transport or be transported (as if) in or by a shuttle ⟨*crewmen were* ~d *to the shore in dinghies*⟩

¹**shuttlecock** /'shutl,kok/ *n* 1 SHUTTLE 2 2 a basis for contention; FOOTBALL 3 ⟨*the bill became a political* ~ *in Parliament*⟩

²**shuttlecock** *vt* to send or toss to and fro; bandy ⟨~ed *between the opinions of others* – Good Housekeeping⟩

**shuttle diplomacy** *n* diplomacy (e g peace negotiations) carried out by a top-level intermediary who travels frequently between the various countries concerned ⟨*Dr Kissinger's* ~ *in southern Africa*⟩

¹**shy** /shie/ *adj* **shier, shyer; shiest, shyest** 1 easily alarmed; timid 2 tending to avoid a person or thing; distrustful 3 wary of committing oneself; circumspect, reluctant – often + *of* ⟨~ *of disclosing his income*⟩; often in combination ⟨*camera*-shy⟩ 4 sensitively reserved or retiring; bashful; *also* expressive of such

a state or nature ⟨*spoke in a ~ voice*⟩ **5** *chiefly NAm informal* lacking, short ⟨*we're three points ~ of what we need to win*⟩ [ME *schey*, fr OE *scēoh*; akin to OHG *sciuhen* to frighten off, OSlav *ščuti* to chase] – **shyly** *adv*, **shyness** *n* – **fight shy of** to avoid facing or meeting

> **synonyms Shy, bashful, diffident, modest, coy,** and **demure** all mean "reluctant to obtrude oneself". **Shy** applies to a timid avoidance of contact with others, perhaps from lack of social experience ⟨*too shy to address the meeting*⟩. **Bashful** suggests a young person's awkwardness in company ⟨**bashful** *children afraid of the guests*⟩. **Diffident** emphasizes distrust of one's own powers ⟨*am* **diffident** *about advising you*⟩. **Modest** may imply absence of undue conceit. **Coy** applies particularly to affected shyness ⟨*lady was not* **coy,** *but made the first advances*⟩ and **demure** to affected modesty, with an added suggestion of sedate decorum. *antonyms* **brazen,** obtrusive

²**shy** *vi* **1** to start suddenly aside in fright or alarm; recoil **2** to move or dodge to evade a person or thing – *usu + away* and/or *from* ⟨*they shied away from buying the flat when they learnt the full price*⟩ – **shy** *n*

³**shy** *vb, informal vt* to throw (eg a stone) with a jerking movement; fling ~ *vi* to make a sudden throw [perh fr ¹*shy*]

⁴**shy** *n, informal* **1** the act of shying; a toss, throw **2** a verbal sally ⟨*took a few* shies *at the integrity of his opponent*⟩ **3** an experimental attempt; a try ⟨*made a few* shies *at roller-skating*⟩ **4** a stall (eg at a fairground) in which people throw balls at targets (eg coconuts) in order to knock them down

**shylock** /'shielok/ *n, informal* an extortionate moneylender; *broadly* any extortionate or mean person [*Shylock*, evil moneylender in Shakespeare's play *The Merchant of Venice*] – **shylock** *vi*

**shyster** /'shiestə/ *n, chiefly NAm* a person who is professionally unscrupulous, esp in the practice of law or politics; a pettifogger [prob fr *Scheuster* *fl*1840 US attorney frequently rebuked in a New York court for pettifoggery]

**si** /see/ *n, music* TE – used in French and Italian fixed-doh systems of SOLMIZATION to refer not to the 7th note of any scale, but to the note B in whatever scale or context it may occur [It]

**sial** /'sie·əl/ *n* the discontinuous outer layer of the earth's crust that is composed of relatively light rocks (eg granite), is rich in silica and aluminium, and is held to underlie the land masses of the continents – compare SIMA [ISV, fr *si*lica + *alu*mina] – **sialic** *adj*

**sialagogue** /sie'aləgog/ *n* a drug that promotes the flow of saliva [NL *sialagogus* promoting the flow of saliva, deriv of Gk *sialon* saliva + *agein* to drive, lead]

**sialic acid** /sie'alik/ *n* any of a group of AMINO sugars found esp as components of blood GLYCOPROTEINS and MUCOPROTEINS (complex substances containing protein and carbohydrate) [Gk *sialon* saliva]

**siamang** /'sie·əmang/ *n* a large black gibbon (*Hylobates syndactylus*) found in the forests of Sumatra and Malaysia that has an inflatable air sac under its chin by which it produces a resonant booming call, that has its 2nd and 3rd toes joined, and that feeds chiefly on fruit [Malay]

¹**Siamese** /,sie·ə'meez/ *adj* (characteristic) of Thailand, the Thais, or Thai [*Siam* (now Thailand), country in SE Asia]

²**Siamese** *n, pl* **Siamese 1** THAI 1 **2** THAI 2 **3** SIAMESE CAT

**Siamese cat** *n* (any of) a breed of slender blue-eyed short-haired domestic cats of oriental origin with pale fawn or grey body and darker ears, paws, tail, and face

**Siamese fighting fish** *n* a brightly coloured highly aggressive long-finned freshwater fish (*Betta splendens*) of Thailand and Malaysia that is a popular aquarium fish

**Siamese twin** *n* either of a pair of identical twins joined together typically at the front, back, or side of the head or along the trunk of the body [fr Chang †1874 and Eng †1874 congenitally united twins born in Siam]

¹**sib** /sib/ *adj* related by blood; akin [ME, fr OE *sibb*, fr *sibb* kinship; akin to OHG *sippa* kinship, family, L *suus* one's own – more at SUICIDE]

²**sib** *n* **1a** *taking pl vb* kindred, relatives **b** a blood relation; a kinsman or kinswoman **2** a brother or sister considered irrespective of sex; *broadly* any two or more individuals having a parent in common **3** *taking sing or pl vb* a group of people descended on one side from a real or supposed ancestor

¹**sibilant** /'sibilənt/ *adj* having, containing, or producing a hissing sound (eg /sh, zh, s, z/) ⟨*a ~ speech sound*⟩ ⟨*a ~ snake*⟩ [L *sibilant-, sibilans*, prp of *sibilare* to hiss, whistle, of imit origin] – **sibilance, sibilancy** *n*, **sibilantly** *adv*

²**sibilant** *n* a sibilant speech sound

**sibilate** /'sibilayt/ *vi* **1** to utter an initial sibilant; prefix an /s/-sound **2** *formal* to hiss ~ *vt* **1** to pronounce with a sibilant **2** *formal* to hiss [L *sibilatus*, pp of *sibilare*] – **sibilation** *n*

**sibling** /'sibling/ *n* SIB 2

**sibling species** *n* any of two or more species that are nearly indistinguishable in form and structure

**sibyl** /'sibil/ *n, often cap* any of several female prophets credited to widely separate parts of the ancient world (eg Babylonia, Egypt, Greece, and Italy); *broadly* any female prophet △ sylph [ME *sibile, sybylle*, fr MF & L; MF *sibile*, fr L *sibylla*, fr Gk] – **sibylic, sibyllic** *adj*, **sibylline** *adj*

**sic** *adv* intentionally so written – used after a printed word or passage to indicate that it is intended exactly as printed or that it exactly reproduces an original ⟨*said he seed* [~] *it all*⟩ [L, so, thus – more at SO]

**siccative** /'sikətiv/ *n* DRIER 2 (substance accelerating the drying of paints, inks, etc) [LL *siccativus* making dry, fr L *siccatus*, pp of *siccare* to dry, fr *siccus* dry – more at SACK]

**sice** /sies/ *n* a syce (Indian groom)

¹**sick** /sik/ *adj* **1a**(1) ill, ailing ⟨*a ~ child*⟩ **a**(2) of or intended for use in illness ⟨*~ pay*⟩ ⟨*a ~ bay*⟩ **b** likely to vomit; queasy, nauseated ⟨*felt ~ in the car*⟩ – often in combination ⟨*carsick*⟩ ⟨*airsick*⟩ **2** spiritually or morally enfeebled or corrupt ⟨*heal my soul diseased and ~* – John Wesley⟩ **3a** sickened by intense emotion (eg shame or fear) ⟨*~ with fear*⟩ ⟨*worried ~*⟩ **b** having a strong aversion because of surfeit; satiated ⟨*~ of flattery*⟩ **c** filled with disgust or chagrin ⟨*gossip that makes one ~*⟩ **d** distressed and longing for something that one has lost or been parted from ⟨*~ for one's home*⟩ – often in combination ⟨*homesick*⟩ **4a** mentally or emotionally disturbed; morbid ⟨*a ~ relationship with a destructive man* – *Cosmopolitan*⟩ **b** macabre, sadistic ⟨*~ jokes*⟩ **5** lacking vigour; sickly; eg **5a** declining or inactive after a period of speculative activity ⟨*grain futures were ~*⟩ **b** incapable of yielding a profitable crop, esp because of buildup of organisms causing disease – often in combination ⟨*clover-sick soils*⟩ **c** *informal* badly outclassed ⟨*looked ~ in the contest*⟩ *synonyms* see ¹ILL [ME *sek, sik*, fr OE *sēoc*; akin to OHG *sioh* sick, MIr *socht* depression] – **be sick** *chiefly Br* to vomit ⟨*was ~ on the rug*⟩ – **go sick** to stay away from work on the plea of sickness

²**sick** *n, Br informal* vomit ⟨*the room smelt of ~*⟩

³**sick** *vt, Br informal* to vomit – *usu + up*

**sick and tired** *adj, informal* thoroughly bored or sated; fed up ⟨*I'm* sick and tired *of you nattering*⟩

**sick bay** *n* a compartment or room (eg in an institution or ship) used as a dispensary and hospital; *broadly* a place for the care of the sick or injured

**sickbed** /-,bed/ *n* the bed upon which one lies ill

**sick call** *n* **1** a home visit paid by a cleric or a doctor to a sick parishioner or patient **2** *chiefly NAm* SICK PARADE

**sicken** /'sikən/ *vt* **1** to cause to feel ill or nauseated **2** to drive to the point of despair or loathing ~ *vi* **1** to become ill; show signs of illness ⟨*looked as if she was ~ing for a cold*⟩ **2** to be driven to despair or loathing – **sickener** *n*

**sickening** /'sikəning/ *adj* **1** causing sickness; nauseating ⟨*a ~ smell*⟩ **2** very horrible or repugnant ⟨*fell to the floor with a ~ thud*⟩ – **sickeningly** *adv*

**sicker** /'sikə/ *adj, chiefly Scot* secure, safe; *also* dependable [ME *siker*, fr OE *sicor*; akin to OHG *sichor* secure; both fr a prehistoric WGmc word borrowed fr L *securus* secure] – **sicker, sickerly** *adv*

**sick headache** *n, chiefly NAm* (a) migraine

**sickie** /'siki/ *n, chiefly Austr slang* a day's absence from work claimed as sick leave ⟨*South Australia's law enforcers are too fond of taking "~s"* – *Nation Review (Melbourne)*⟩

**sickish** /'sikish/ *adj* **1** somewhat nauseated; queasy **2** somewhat sickening **3** *archaic* somewhat ill; sickly – **sickishly** *adv*, **sickishness** *n*

¹**sickle** /'sikl/ *n* **1** an agricultural tool for reaping hay, grass, corn, etc, consisting of a curved metal blade with a short handle **2** a cutting mechanism (eg of a reaper, combine harvester, or mower) consisting of a bar with a series of cutting parts [ME *sikel*, fr OE *sicol*; akin to OHG *sichila* sickle; both fr a prehistoric WGmc word borrowed fr L *secula* sickle – more at SAW]

²**sickle** *adj, poetic* having the curve of a sickle blade ⟨*the ~ moon*⟩

³**sickle** *vt* to mow, reap, or cut with a sickle ~ *vi* to become crescent-shaped ⟨*the ability of red blood cells to ~*⟩

**sick leave** *n* **1** absence from work because of illness **2** the number of days per year for which an employer agrees to pay employees who are sick

**sickle cell** *n* an abnormal crescent-shaped RED BLOOD CELL that occurs in the blood of people affected with SICKLE-CELL ANAEMIA

**sickle-cell anaemia** *n* a hereditary anaemia occurring mainly in Negroes in which most of the RED BLOOD CELLS become sickle-shaped causing abdominal pain, jaundice, and recurrent short periods of fever and which results from HOMOZYGOSITY for a specific gene – compare SICKLE-CELL TRAIT

**sickle-cell trait** *n* a hereditary usu symptomless condition occurring mainly in Negroes in which some of the RED BLOOD CELLS tend to become sickle-shaped and which results from HETEROZYGOSITY for the gene that causes SICKLE-CELL ANAEMIA in HOMOZYGOUS people

**sickle feather** *n* any of the long curved tail feathers of a domestic cock

¹**sickly** /'sikli/ *adj* **1** somewhat unwell; *also* habitually ailing **2** produced by or associated with sickness ⟨*a ~ complexion*⟩ ⟨*a ~ appetite*⟩ **3** producing or tending to produce disease; unwholesome ⟨*a ~ climate*⟩ **4** suggesting sickness: **4a** languid, feeble ⟨*a ~ flame*⟩ ⟨*a ~ plant*⟩ **b** strained, uneasy ⟨*a ~ smile*⟩ **5a** tending to produce nausea ⟨*a ~ taste*⟩ **b** mawkish, saccharine ⟨*~ sentiment*⟩ – **sickliness** *n*, **sickly, sickily** *adv*

²**sickly** *vt, archaic* to make sick or sickly

**sickness** /-nis/ *n* **1a** ill health; illness **b** a disturbed, weakened, or unsound condition (e g of a nation or institution) **2** a specific disease **3** nausea, queasiness

**sick out** *n, NAm & WI* a strike in which all the employees at a particular workplace report sick simultaneously

**sick parade** *n* a usu daily (army) parade at which individuals report as sick to the medical officer; *also* the period of time during which sick parade is held

**sick pay** *n* salary or wages paid to an employee while on sick leave

**sickroom** /-,roohm, -,room/ *n* a room (e g in a school) set aside for sick people; *broadly* a room in which someone is confined by sickness

**sic passim** /,sik 'pasim/ *adv* so throughout – used of a word or idea to be found throughout a book or a writer's work [L]

**siddur** /'sidə, 'sidooə/ *n, pl* **siddurim** /si'dooərim/ a Jewish prayer book containing both Hebrew and Aramaic prayers used in the E European (ASHKENAZIC) daily liturgy [MHeb *siddūr*, lit., order, arrangement]

¹**side** /sied/ *n* **1a** the right or left part of the wall or trunk of the body ⟨*a pain in the ~*⟩ **b** the right or left half of the animal body or of a meat carcass ⟨*a ~ of beef*⟩ **c** one lengthways half of a hide **2** a location, region, or direction considered in relation to a centre or line of division ⟨*the south ~ of the city*⟩ ⟨*surrounded on all ~s*⟩ **3** a surface forming a border or face of an object **4** an outer portion of something considered as facing in a particular direction ⟨*the upper ~ of a sphere*⟩ **5** a slope of a hill, ridge, etc **6a** a boundary line of a geometrical figure ⟨*each ~ of a square*⟩ **b** *maths* FACE 4a(5) **c** either surface of a thin object ⟨*one ~ of a record*⟩ ⟨*the right ~ of the cloth*⟩ **7** neighbourhood, company ⟨*he never left her ~*⟩ **8** taking sing or pl vb a person or group in competition or dispute with another ⟨*which ~ are you in?*⟩ **9** the attitude or activity of a person or group in competition or dispute with another; part ⟨*took my ~ in the argument*⟩ **10** a line of descent traced through a parent ⟨*grandfather on his mother's ~*⟩ **11** an aspect or part of something viewed in contrast with some other aspect or part ⟨*the better ~ of his nature*⟩ **12** a position viewed as opposite to or contrasted with another ⟨*two ~s to every question*⟩ **13** the direction of a specified tendency – + *on the* ⟨*she was somewhat on the short ~*⟩ **14** *Br* sideways spin imparted to a billiard or snooker ball **15** *Br* a secondary-school department offering a particular curriculum ⟨*the Science ~*⟩ **16** *Br informal* a television channel ⟨*put the other ~ on*⟩ [ME, fr OE *sīde;* akin to OHG *sīta* side, OE *sīd* ample, wide, *sāwan* to sow – more at SOW] – **bit on the side** (a person with whom one has) occasional sexual intercourse, usu outside marriage – **get on the right side of** *informal* to win the favour of – **on the side 1** in addition to a principal occupation; *specif* as a dishonest or illegal secondary activity ⟨*he's really an accountant, but he does a bit of plumbing* on the side⟩ **2** *chiefly NAm* in addition to the main portion ⟨*jumboburger with fries and coleslaw* on the side⟩ – **split one's sides** to laugh heartily – see also get out of BED **on the wrong side**

²**side** *adj* **1a** of the side **b** situated on the side ⟨*~ window*⟩ **2a** directed towards or from the side ⟨*~ thrust*⟩ ⟨*~ wind*⟩ **b** made on the side, esp in secret ⟨*~ payment*⟩ **c** additional to the main part or portion ⟨*~ order of french fries*⟩ **d** incidental, subordinate ⟨*~ issue*⟩ ⟨*~ view*⟩

³**side** *vi* to take sides; join or form sides ⟨*~d with the rebels*⟩

⁴**side** *n, informal* a swaggering or assuming manner; arrogance ⟨*she's got no ~, that's one thing in her favour*⟩ [obs *side* proud, boastful, fr ME, wide, capacious, fr OE *sīd*]

**-side** *comb form* (*n → n*) district bordering (a river) ⟨*Tweed*-side⟩ ⟨*Thames*side⟩

**side arm** *n usu pl* a weapon (e g a sword, revolver, or bayonet) worn at the side or in the belt

**sideband** /-,band/ *n* a band of frequencies (e g of radio waves) on either side of and higher or lower than the frequency of a CARRIER (wave necessary for transmission of a signal) that is produced by MODULATION of the carrier and contains the information being transmitted

**sideboard** /-,bawd/ *n* **1** a usu flat-topped piece of dining-room furniture having cupboards and shelves for holding articles of table service (e g table linen, cutlery, etc) **2** *pl, Br* whiskers on the sides of the face that extend from the hairline to below the ears and are usu worn with an unbearded chin

**sidebone** /'sied,bohn/ *n* OSSIFICATION (turning to bone) of the cartilage in a horse's heel often causing lameness

**sideburns** /-,buhnz/ *n pl* SIDEBOARDS 2 [anagram of *burnsides*] – **sideburned** *adj*

**side by side** *adv* **1** beside one another ⟨*walked ~ down the aisle*⟩ **2** in the same place, time, or circumstance ⟨*lived peacefully ~ for many years*⟩ – **side-by-side** *adj*

**sidecar** /-,kah/ *n* a car attached to the side of a motorcycle or motor scooter for one or more passengers

**sided** /'siedid/ *adj* having sides, usu of a specified number or kind ⟨*one*-sided⟩ ⟨*glass*-sided⟩ – **sidedness** *n*

**side dish** *n* any of the foods accompanying and subordinate to the main dish of a course

**sidedress** /'sied,dres/, **sidedressing** *n* **1** fertilizers used to sidedress a crop **2** the act or process of side-dressing a crop

'**side-,dress** *vt* to place fertilizers on or in the soil near the roots of (a growing crop) often by means of a cultivator having a fertilizer-distributing attachment

**side drum** *n* SNARE DRUM

**side effect** *n* a secondary and usu adverse effect (e g of a drug) ⟨*forced to stop taking the drug because of the ~s*⟩

'**side-,glance** *n* a passing allusion; an indirect or cursory reference

**sidehill** /'sied,hil/ *n, NAm* a hillside – **sidehill** *adj*

**side horse** *n* POMMEL HORSE

**side issue** *n* an issue apart from the main point

**sidekick** /-,kik/ *n, chiefly NAm informal* one who is closely associated with another, esp as a subordinate

**sidelight** /-,liet/ *n* **1** incidental or additional information **2a** the red port light or the green starboard light carried by ships moving at night **b** a light at the side of a (motor) vehicle

¹**sideline** /'sied,lien/ *n* **1** a line at right angles to a goal line or end line and marking a side of a court or field of play (e g in tennis) **2a** a line of goods manufactured or esp sold in addition to one's principal line **b** a business or activity pursued in addition to a full-time occupation **3** **sidelines** *pl,* **sideline** the standpoint of people not immediately participating (e g in a sports competition) – chiefly in *on the sidelines* ⟨*his injury put him on the ~s for the rest of the season*⟩

²**sideline** *vt, chiefly NAm* to put (a player) out of action; put on the sidelines

¹**sidelong** /-,long/ *adv* **1** towards the side; obliquely **2** on the side ⟨*~ the plough beside the field-gate lay* – William Morris⟩ [alter. of *sideling*, fr ME *sidling*, fr ¹*side* + *-ling*]

²**sidelong** *adj* **1** inclining to one side; slanting **2a** directed to one side ⟨*~ glances*⟩ **b** indirect rather than straightforward

**sideman** /-,man/ *n* a member of a band or orchestra, esp a jazz or swing band, other than the leader or featured performer

,**side-'on** *adv* with one side facing in a given direction; *also* in profile

**sidepiece** /'sied,pees/ *n* a piece forming, contained in, or attached to the side of something ⟨*the ~ of a carriage*⟩

**sider-** /'siedə-/, **sidero-** *comb form* iron ⟨*siderolite*⟩ ⟨*siderosis*⟩ [MF, fr L, fr Gk *sidēr-, sidēro-,* fr *sidēros*]

**sidereal** /sie'diəri·əl/ *adj* of or expressed in relation to stars or constellations; astral [L *sidereus*, fr *sider-*, *sidus* star, constellation; akin to Lith *svidus* shining]

**sidereal day** *n* the period of a complete rotation of the earth upon its axis, measured with respect to a particular FIXED STAR; 23 hours, 56 minutes, 4.09 seconds of solar time

**sidereal hour** *n* the 24th part of a SIDEREAL DAY

**sidereal minute** *n* the 60th part of a SIDEREAL HOUR

**sidereal month** *n* the period of time in which the moon goes round the earth, measured with respect to a particular FIXED STAR; 27 days, 7 hours, 43 minutes, 11.5 seconds of solar time

**sidereal second** *n* the 60th part of a SIDEREAL MINUTE

**sidereal time** *n* 1 time based on the SIDEREAL DAY 2 the hour angle of the March equinox at a particular place

**sidereal year** *n* the period of time in which the earth goes once round the sun, measured with respect to a particular FIXED STAR; 365 days, 6 hours, 9 minutes, and 9.54 seconds of solar time

**¹siderite** /'siedəriet/ *n* a naturally occurring yellow or brown FERROUS carbonate, FeCO₃, that is a valuable iron ore [Ger *siderit*, fr Gk *sidēros* iron] – **sideritic** *adj*

**²siderite** *n* a meteorite consisting mainly of the metals iron and nickel – **sideritic** *adj*

**siderolite** /'siedəraliet/ *n* a meteorite containing similar amounts of metal (e g iron or nickel) and stone

**siderostat** /'siedəroh‚stat/ *n* an astronomical instrument similar to a COELOSTAT, for reflecting an observed object in a fixed direction [ISV, fr L *sider-*, *sidus* star + ISV *-stat*]

**¹sidesaddle** /'sied‚sadl/ *n* a saddle for women on which the rider, wearing a long skirt, sits with both legs on the same side of the horse

**²sidesaddle** *adv* (as if) on a sidesaddle

**sideshow** /-‚shoh/ *n* 1a a minor show offered in addition to a main exhibition (e g of a circus) b a fairground booth or counter offering a game of luck or skill (e g hoopla) 2 an incidental diversion

**sideslip** /'sied‚slip/ *vi* **-pp-** 1 *esp of a motor vehicle* to skid sideways 2 *of an aircraft* to make a sideways and downward manoeuvre – **sideslip** *n*

**sidesman** /'siedzmən/ *n* any of a group of people in an Anglican church who assist the churchwardens, esp in taking the collection at services

**sidespin** /'sied‚spin/ *n* rotary motion of a moving ball about a vertical axis (e g in tennis) [¹*side* + *spin*]

**sidesplitting** /'sied‚spliting/ *adj* causing raucous laughter

**sidestep** /'sied‚step/ *vb* **-pp-** *vi* 1 to step sideways or to one side 2 to evade an issue or decision – *vt* 1 to move quickly out of the way of; dodge (~ *a blow*) 2 to bypass, evade (*adept at* ~*ping awkward questions*)

**side step** *n* 1 a step aside (e g in boxing to avoid a punch) 2 a step taken sideways (e g when climbing on skis)

**side street** *n* a minor street branching off a main thoroughfare

**sidestroke** /'sied‚strohk/ *n* a swimming stroke that is performed while lying on one's side and in which the arms are usu swept backwards and downwards and the legs do a scissors kick

**¹sideswipe** /'sied‚swiep/ *vt*, *chiefly NAm* to strike with a glancing blow along the side (~*d a parked car*)

**²sideswipe** *n* 1 *chiefly NAm* an act or instance of sideswiping; a glancing blow 2 *informal* an incidental deprecatory remark, allusion, or reference

**side table** *n* a table designed to be placed against a wall or away from a main table

**¹sidetrack** /'sied‚trak/ *n* 1 an unimportant line of thinking that is followed instead of a more important one 2 *NAm* a railway siding

**²sidetrack** *vt* to divert from a course or purpose; distract

**sidewalk** /'sied‚wawk/ *n*, *NAm* a pavement

**sidewards** /'siedwoodz/, *NAm chiefly* **sideward** /-wood/ *adv* towards one side

**sideways** /'sied‚wayz/, *NAm also* **sideway** /-way/ *adv or adj* 1 to or from the side (*a* ~ *movement*); *also* ASKANCE 1 2 with one side forward (*turn it* ~) 3 to a position of equivalent rank (~ *recruiting in the army* – *The Economist*)

**'side-‚wheel** *adj*, *of an esp steam boat* having a PADDLE WHEEL on each side

**'side-‚wheeler** *n* a side-wheel steamer

**'side-‚whiskers** *n pl* whiskers on the side of the face usu worn long; *broadly* sideboards

**'side-‚wind** *n* an indirect influence or effect

**sidewinder** /'sied‚wiendə/ *n*, *chiefly NAm informal* a heavy swinging blow from the side

**sidewise** /'sied‚wiez/ *adv* sideways

**siding** /'sieding/ *n* 1 a short railway track connected with the main track 2 *NAm* material (e g boards or metal sheets) forming the exposed surface of the outside walls of wooden-framed buildings

**sidle** /'siedl/ *vi* 1 to move obliquely (*the ship* ~*d into her berth*) 2 to walk timidly, furtively, or hesitantly; edge along – usu + *up* ~ *vt* to cause to move or turn sideways (*the rider* ~*d his horse up to the fence*) [prob back-formation fr *sideling* (sideways) – more at SIDELONG] – **sidle** *n*

**¹siege** /seej/ *n* **1a** a military blockade of a city or fortified place to compel it to surrender; *also* the duration of or operations carried out in a siege **b** a prolonged assault (e g by illness or argument) **2** *obs* a seat reserved for a person of distinction; a throne [ME *sege*, fr OF, seat, blockade, fr (assumed) VL *sedicum*, fr *sedicare* to settle, fr L *sedēre* to sit – more at SIT ] – **lay siege to** 1 to besiege militarily (*laid siege to the town*) 2 to pursue diligently or persistently

**²siege** *vt* to besiege

**siege economy** *n* an economic system in which emphasis is laid on national self-sufficiency (e g by restricting imports)

**siemens** /'seemənz/ *n*, *pl* **siemens** the SI unit of electrical conductance equivalent to one amp per volt; the reciprocal of an OHM (unit of electrical resistance) [Werner von *Siemens* †1892 Ger electrical engineer]

**sienna** /si'enə/ *n* an earthy substance containing chemical compounds of iron and usu of manganese, that is brownish-yellow when raw and orange-red or reddish-brown when burnt and is used to colour paint, ink, etc [It *terra di Siena*, lit., Siena earth, fr *Siena*, *Sienna*, town in Italy]

**sierozem** /‚syerə'zhem, 'syerəzhəm/ *n* any of a group of light-coloured soils that are low in animal or plant matter and are found in semiarid and arid regions [Russ *serozem*, fr *seryĭ* grey + *zemlya* earth]

**sierra** /si'eərə/ *n* 1 a range of mountains, esp with a serrated or irregular outline 2 the area round a sierra [Sp, lit., saw, fr L *serra*]

**Sierra** – a communications code word for the letter *s*

**sierran** /si'eərən/ *adj* 1 of a sierra (~ *foothills*) 2 *cap* of the Sierra Nevada mountains in W USA

**siesta** /si'estə/ *n* an afternoon nap or rest [Sp, fr L *sexta* (*hora*) noon, lit., sixth hour – more at SEXT]

**sieva bean** /'seevə/ *n* any of several small-seeded beans closely related to and sometimes classed as LIMA BEANS; *also* the seed of a sieva bean [origin unknown]

**¹sieve** /siv/ *n* a device with a meshed or perforated bottom that will allow the passage of liquids or fine solids while retaining coarser material [ME *sive*, fr OE *sife*; akin to OHG *sib* sieve, Serb *sipiti* to drizzle]

**²sieve** *vt* to sift

**sieve cell** *n* an elongated tapering cell with a number of small perforated areas in its walls, that is concerned with conducting nutrient solutions of chemical compounds in the PHLOEM tissue of GYMNOSPERMS (e g conifers, cycads, and ginkgos) and lower VASCULAR PLANTS (e g ferns and horsetails)

**sieve plate** *n* a perforated wall or part of a wall at the end of any of the individual cells making up the SIEVE TUBE (plant vessel for conducting nutrient solutions)

**sieve tube** *n* a tube consisting of an end-to-end series of thin-walled living cells separated by SIEVE PLATES that is concerned chiefly with conducting nutrient solutions of chemical compounds in the PHLOEM tissue of flowering plants

**siffleur** /si'fluh, 'siflə/ *n* a performer or entertainer whose act consists of whistling (music) [Fr, fr *siffler* to whistle, deriv of L *sibilare* to hiss, whistle]

**sift** /sift/ *vt* **1a** to put through a sieve (~ *flour*) **b** to separate or separate out (as if) by passing through a sieve **2a** to study or examine so as to pick out the best or most valuable; screen (~ *the seedlings before transplanting*) **b** to study or investigate thoroughly; probe, scrutinize (*will* ~ *this matter to the utmost* – Sir Walter Scott) **3** to scatter (as if) with a sieve (~ *sugar on a cake*) to screen, select – usu + *through* (~ *through a pile of applications*) [ME *siften*, fr OE *siftan*; akin to OE *sife* sieve]

**sifter** /'siftə/ *n* one who or that which sifts; *specif* a castor

**sifting** /'sifting/ *n* 1 the act or process of sifting 2 *pl* sifted material, esp that which is separated out and rejected

**¹sigh** /sie/ *vi* 1 to take a long deep audible breath (e g in weariness or grief) 2 *esp of the wind* to make a sound like sighing

⟨*wind* ~ing *in the branches*⟩ **3** to grieve, yearn – usu + *for* ⟨~ing *for the days of his youth*⟩ ~ *vt* **1** to express by or with sighs **2** *archaic* to utter sighs over; mourn [ME *sihen*, alter. of *sichen*, fr OE *sīcan;* akin to MD ver*siken* to sigh] – **sigher** *n*

²**sigh** *n* **1** an act of sighing, esp when expressing an emotion or feeling (e g weariness or relief) **2** a sound of or resembling sighing ⟨~s *of the summer breeze*⟩

¹**sight** /siet/ *n* **1** something seen; *esp* a spectacle ⟨*the familiar ~ of the postman coming along the street*⟩ **2a** *pl* the things (e g impressive or historic buildings), esp in a particular place, regarded as worth seeing ⟨*spent a day in London seeing the* ~s⟩ **b** something ridiculous or displeasing in appearance ⟨*you must get some sleep, you look a* ~⟩ **3a** the process, power, or function of seeing; *specif* the one of the five basic physical senses by which light received by the eye is interpreted by the brain as a representation of the forms, brightness, and colour of the objects of the real world **b** mental or spiritual perception – compare SECOND SIGHT **c** manner of regarding; judgment, opinion ⟨*in her mother's* ~ *the marriage was a disaster*⟩ **4a** the act of looking at or beholding ⟨*fainted at the* ~ *of blood*⟩ **b** regard, perusal ⟨*this letter is for your* ~ *only*⟩ **c** a view, glimpse ⟨*got a* ~ *of the Queen*⟩ **d** an observation (e g by a navigator) to determine direction or position **5a** a perception of an object by the eye **b** the range of vision **6** presentation of a note or bill to the maker or draftee; demand ⟨*a draft payable on* ~⟩ **7a** a device for guiding the eye (e g in aiming a firearm or bomb) **b** a device with a small aperture through which objects are to be seen and by which their direction is ascertained **8** *informal* a great deal; a lot ⟨*got a* ~ *more working freelance*⟩ [ME, fr OE *gesiht* faculty or act of sight, thing seen; akin to OHG *gisiht* sight, OE *sēon* to see] – **at first sight** when viewed without proper investigation ⟨at first sight *the place seems very dull*⟩ – **at/on sight** as soon as presented to view ⟨*instructions were that the murderer should be shot* on sight⟩ – **heave in/into sight** to come into view – **keep sight of** BEAR IN MIND – **out of sight 1** beyond all expectation or reason ⟨*prices have risen* out of sight *during the past year*⟩ **2** *chiefly NAm informal* marvellous, wonderful – not now in vogue – **set one's sights (on)** to focus one's concentration or intentions (on) ⟨*should be more ambitious and not* set your sights *too low*⟩ – **sight for sore eyes** somebody or something whose appearance or arrival is an occasion for joy or relief

²**sight** *adj* **1** based on recognition or comprehension without previous study ⟨*a* ~ *translation*⟩ **2** payable on presentation

³**sight** *vt* **1** to get or catch sight of ⟨*several whales were* ~ed⟩ **2** to look at (as if) through a sight; *esp* to test for straightness **3** to aim (e g a weapon) by means of sights **4a** to equip (e g a gun) with sights **b** to adjust the sights of ~ *vi* to take aim (e g in shooting) – **sighting** *n*

**sight bill** *n* a bill payable on presentation; DEMAND NOTE

**sighted** /'sietid/ *adj* having sight, esp of a specified kind – often in combination ⟨*clear-*sighted⟩

**sightless** /'sietlis/ *adj* **1** lacking sight; blind **2** *poetic* invisible – **sightlessness** *n*

**sightline** /'siet,lien/ *n* a line of sight from a member of a theatre audience to some part of the stage; *specif* a line behind which an actor is not visible to (some portion of) the audience ⟨*the wide auditorium and narrow proscenium arch gave the theatre very poor* ~s⟩

**sightly** /'sietli/ *adj* **1** pleasing to the eye; attractive **2** *chiefly NAm* affording a fine view ⟨*homes in a* ~ *location*⟩ – **sightliness** *n*

¹**sight-,read** *vb* **sight-read** /red/ to read (e g a foreign language) or perform (music) without previous preparation or study to read at sight; *esp* to perform music at sight [back-formation fr *sight reader*] – **sight reader** *n*

**sight screen** *n* a large usu white movable screen placed on the boundary of a cricket field behind the bowler to improve the batsman's view of the ball

**sightsee** /'siet,see/ *vi* to make a tour of interesting or attractive sights [back-formation fr *sightseeing*, n] – **sightseer** *n*

**sightseeing** /'siet,seeing/ *n* touring interesting or attractive sights – often in *go sightseeing* ⟨*went on holiday* ~ *in Scotland*⟩ ⟨*a* ~ *trip*⟩

**sight unseen** *adv* without previous inspection or appraisal ⟨*bought the car* ~⟩

**sigil** /'sijil/ *n* a seal, signet [L *sigillum* – more at SEAL]

**siglum** /'siglǝm/ *n, pl* **sigla** /-lǝ/ an abbreviation (e g a special character) used in a manuscript, coin, or seal [LL, perh fr L *sigillum*, dim. of *signum* sign]

**sigma** /'sigmǝ/ *n* **1** the 18th letter of the Greek alphabet **2** *also* **sigma particle** an unstable ELEMENTARY PARTICLE (minute particle of matter) of the BARYON family existing in states having positive, negative, or neutral electrical charges with masses respectively 2328, 2343, and 2333 times the mass of an electron [Gk, of Sem origin; akin to Heb *sāmekh* samekh alphabet]

**sigmate** /'sigmit,'sig,mayt/ *n* having the shape or form of the Greek sigma or the letter S

**sigmoid** /'sigmoyd/ *also* **sigmoidal** /sig'moydl/ *adj* **1a** curved like the letter C **b** curved in two directions like the letter S **2** of or being the SIGMOID FLEXURE of the intestine [Gk *sigmoeidēs*, fr *sigma;* fr a common form of sigma shaped like the Roman letter C] – **sigmoidally** *adv*

**sigmoid colon** *n* SIGMOID FLEXURE

**sigmoid flexure** *n* the contracted and crooked part of the LARGE INTESTINE occurring at the end of the COLON immediately above the RECTUM

¹**sign** /sien/ *n* **1a** a motion or gesture by which a thought, command, or wish is made known **b** SIGNAL 1 **c** a meaningful unit of language (e g a word) **2** a mark with a conventional meaning, used to replace or supplement words **3** any of the 12 divisions of the zodiac **4a(1)** a character (e g a flat or sharp) used in musical notation **a(2)** SEGNO (musical repeat sign) **b** a character (e g ÷) indicating a mathematical operation; *also* either of two characters + and – that form part of the symbol of a number and characterize it as positive or negative **5 sign, signboard** a board or notice carrying advertising matter or giving warning, command, information or direction ⟨*her hobby was photographing unusual inn* ~s⟩ **6a** something material or external that stands for or signifies something spiritual ⟨*an outward and visible* ~ *of inward and spiritual grace* – *Book of Common Prayer*⟩ **b** something serving to indicate the presence or existence of something ⟨*saw no* ~ *of him anywhere*⟩ **c** a presage, portent ⟨~s *of an early spring*⟩ **d** objective evidence of plant or animal disease that usu causes no perceptible disability **7** a remarkable event indicating the will of a deity [ME *signe*, fr OF, fr L *signum* mark, token, sign, image, seal; prob akin to L *secare* to cut – more at SAW]

²**sign** *vt* **1a** to place a sign on **b** CROSS 2 **c** to indicate, represent, or express by a sign **2a** to put a signature to; ratify or attest by hand or seal ⟨*the prisoner* ~ed *a confession*⟩ **b** to assign formally – often + *over* ⟨~ed *over his property to his brother*⟩ **c(1)** to write down (one's name) **c(2)** to write as the name of (oneself) ⟨~ed *herself "George Eliot"*⟩ **3** to warn, order, or request by a sign ⟨~ed *him to enter*⟩ **4** to engage or hire by securing the signature of on a contract of employment ⟨~ed *a new striker from Arsenal*⟩ – often + *on* or *up* ~ *vi* **1** to write one's signature, esp in token of assent, responsibility, or obligation ⟨~ *here*⟩ **2** to make a sign or signal **3** to use SIGN LANGUAGE – see also **sign one's own** DEATH WARRANT/**the PLEDGE** [ME *signen*, fr MF *signer*, fr L *signare* to mark, sign, seal, fr *signum*] – **signer** *n*

**sign in** *vi* to record one's arrival by signing a register or punching a card ~ *vt* to record the arrival of (a person) or receipt of (an article) by signing ⟨*all deliveries must be* signed in *at the main gate*⟩

**sign off** *vi* **1** to announce the end of a message, programme, or broadcast and finish broadcasting; broadly to finish **2a** to end a letter (e g with a signature) **b** to end the receipt of medical treatment, unemployment benefit, etc by signing a document

**sign on** *vi* **1** to commit oneself to a job by signature or agreement; enlist ⟨signed on *as a member of the crew*⟩ **2** to announce the start of broadcasting **3** *Br* to register as unemployed, esp at an employment exchange

**sign out** *vi* to indicate one's departure by signing in a register ⟨signed out *of the hospital*⟩ ~ *vt* to record or approve the release or withdrawal of ⟨sign *books* out *of a library*⟩

**sign up** *vi* to join an organization or accept an obligation by signing a contract; *esp* to enlist in the armed services ~ *vt* to cause to sign a contract

¹**signal** /'signǝl/ *n* **1** an act, event, or watchword that has been agreed on as the occasion of concerted action ⟨*waited for the* ~ *to begin the attack*⟩ **2** something that occasions action ⟨*his scolding was a* ~ *for the little girl to start crying*⟩ **3** a conventional sign (e g a siren or flashing light) made to give warning or command ⟨*a* ~ *that warns of an air raid*⟩ **4a** an object used to transmit or convey information beyond the range of the human voice **b** the sound or image conveyed in telegraphy, telephony, radio, radar, or television **c** the varia-

tions of a physical quantity (eg pressure, current, or voltage) by which information may be transmitted in an electronic circuit or system: eg **c(1)** the wave that is used to MODULATE (vary the strength or frequency of) a CARRIER (wave carrying information to be transmitted) ⟨*the video* ~⟩ **c(2)** the wave produced by the modulation of a carrier by a signal ⟨*a radio* ~⟩ **5** *archaic* a token, indication [ME, fr MF, fr ML *signale*, fr LL, neut of *signalis* of a sign, fr L *signum*]

²**signal** *vb* **-ll-** (*NAm* **-l-, -ll-**) *vt* **1** to warn, order, or request by a signal ⟨~led *the fleet to turn back*⟩ **2a** to communicate by signals ⟨~led *their refusal*⟩ **b** to constitute a characteristic feature of (a meaningful linguistic form) ⟨*'s' at the end of cats* ~s *the plural*⟩ **3** to be a sign of; mark ⟨*his resignation* ~led *the end of a long career*⟩ ~ *vi* to make or send a signal – **signaller**, *NAm chiefly* **signaler** *n*

³**signal** *adj* **1** used in signalling ⟨*a* ~ *beacon*⟩ **2** *formal* distinguished from the ordinary; conspicuous ⟨*a* ~ *achievement*⟩ [modif of Fr *signalé*, pp of *signaler* to distinguish, fr OIt *segnalare* to signal, distinguish, fr *segnale* signal, fr ML *signale*]

**signalbox** /'signəl,boks/ *n, Br* a raised building above or beside a railway line from which signals and points are worked

**signal·ize, -ise** /'signəliez/ *vt* **1** *chiefly NAm* to point out carefully or distinctly; draw attention to **2** *formal* to make noteworthy; distinguish ⟨*a performance* ~d *by consummate artistry*⟩ [³*signal* + *-ize, -ise*] – **signalization** *n*

**signally** /'signəli/ *adv, formal* in a signal manner; remarkably ⟨*a* ~ *tactless decision*⟩

**signalman** /'signəlmən/ *n* a person employed to operate railway signals

**signatory** /'signət(ə)ri/ *n* a signer with another or others ⟨*signatories to a petition*⟩; *esp* a government bound with others by a signed convention or treaty [L *signatorius* of sealing, fr *signatus*, pp] – **signatory** *adj*

**signature** /'signəchə/ *n* **1a** the name of a person written with his/her own hand **b** the act of signing one's name **2** a letter or figure placed usu at the bottom of the first page on each sheet of printed pages (eg of a book) as a direction to the binder in gathering the sheets; *also* the sheet itself **3** *music* **3a** KEY SIGNATURE **b** TIME SIGNATURE **4** the part of a medical prescription in the USA which contains the directions to the patient **5** a distinguishing or identifying mark, feature, or quality ⟨*elegant leaps and highlifts became one of the* ~s *of the ballet company*⟩ [MF or ML; MF, fr ML *signatura*, fr L *signatus*, pp of *signare* to sign, seal]

**signature tune** *n* a melody, passage, or song used to identify a programme, entertainer, etc

**signboard** /'sien,bawd/ *n* SIGN 5

¹**signet** /'signit/ *n* **1** a personal seal used officially in the place of a signature **2** the impression made (as if) by a signet **3** a small seal with an inscribed figure (eg in a finger ring) [ME, fr MF, dim. of *signe* sign, seal]

²**signet** *vt* to stamp or authenticate with a signet

**signet ring** *n* a finger ring engraved with a signet, seal, or monogram

**significance** /sig'nifikəns/ *n* **1a** something conveyed as a meaning, often latently or indirectly **b** the quality of conveying or implying **2a** the quality of being important; consequence **b** the quality of being statistically significant *antonyms* insignificance, meaninglessness

**significance level** *n, statistics* LEVEL OF SIGNIFICANCE

**significancy** /sig'nifikənsi/ *n* significance

**significant** /sig'nifikənt/ *adj* **1** having meaning; *esp* expressive ⟨*the painter's task to pick out the* ~ *details* – Herbert Read⟩ **2** suggesting or containing a veiled or special meaning ⟨*perhaps her glance was* ~⟩ **3a** having or likely to have influence or effect; far-reaching, important ⟨*the budget brought no* ~ *changes*⟩ **b** probably caused by something other than chance ⟨*statistically* ~ *correlation between vitamin deficiency and disease*⟩ [L *significant-, significans*, prp of *significare* to signify] – **significantly** *adv*

**significant figures** *n pl* the specified number of digits in a number, that are considered to give correct or sufficient information on its accuracy, and are read from the first nonzero digit on the left to the last nonzero digit on the right, unless a final zero expresses greater accuracy

**signification** /,signifi'kaysh(ə)n/ *n* **1** signifying by symbolic means (eg signs) **2** the meaning that a term, symbol, or character normally conveys or is intended to convey

**significative** /sig'nifikətiv/ *adj* **1** indicative **2** significant, suggestive – **significatively** *adv*, **significativeness** *n*

**signify** /'signifie/ *vt* **1** to mean, denote **2** to show, esp by a conventional token (eg word, signal, or gesture) ~ *vi* to have significance; matter [ME *signifien*, fr OF *signifier*, fr L *significare* to indicate, mean, fr *signum* sign] – **signifiable** *adj*, **signifier** *n*

**signing** /'siening/ *n* **1** somebody who is signed (eg by a football club) ⟨*the club's newest recruit was a popular* ~ *with the fans*⟩ **2** (the use of) sign language for the deaf

**signiory** /'seenyəri/ *n* SEIGNEURY (feudal authority or the area in which it is exercised)

**sign language** *n* **1** a system of hand gestures used for communication (eg by the deaf) **2** unsystematic communication chiefly by gesture between people speaking different languages

**sign manual** *n, pl* **signs manual** a signature; *specif* the sovereign's signature on a grant or charter [¹*sign* + *manual*, adj]

'**sign-,off** *n* an act of signing off ⟨*the local radio station has a midnight* ~⟩

**sign of the cross** *n* a movement of the hand forming a cross, esp on forehead, shoulders, and chest, to profess Christian faith or invoke divine protection or blessing

'**sign-,on** *n* an act of signing on ⟨*the local radio station has a 6 am* ~⟩ ⟨*there are few jobs not requiring any sort of* ~⟩

**signor** /'seen,yaw, ,-'-/ *n, pl* **signors, signori** /-ri/ **1** an Italian man **2** *often cap* – used of or to an Italian man as a title equivalent to *Mr* [It *signore, signor*, fr ML *senior* superior, lord – more at SENOR]

**signora** /seen'yawrə/ *n, pl* **signoras, signore** /-ray/ **1** an Italian married woman **2** *often cap* – used as a title equivalent to *Mrs* before the name of a married Italian woman (or, occasionally, an unmarried older woman) or used without a name as a generalized term of direct address [It, fem of *signore, signor*]

**signore** /seen'yawray/ *n, pl* **signori** /-ri/ – used in speech but not in writing as a generalized term of direct address to an Italian man [It]

**signorina** /,seenyaw'reenə/ *n, pl* **signorinas, signorine** /-nay/ **1** an unmarried Italian girl or woman **2** *often cap* – used of or to an unmarried Italian girl or woman as a title equivalent to *Miss* [It, fr dim. of *signora*]

**signory, signiory** /'seenyəri/ *n* SEIGNEURY (feudal authority or the area in which it is exercised) [ME *signorie*, fr MF *seigneurie*]

¹**signpost** /'sien,pohst/ *n* a post (eg at a road junction) with signs on it to direct travellers

²**signpost** *vt* **1** to provide with signposts or guides **2** to indicate or mark, esp in an obvious or blatant manner

**sika deer** /'seekə/ *n* a small reddish brown deer (*Sika nippon*) introduced into Britain from Japan and now living wild in many areas [Jap *shika*]

**Sikh** /seek/ *n or adj* (an adherent) of an Indian religion incorporating Islamic and Hindu elements and marked by belief in one God, reincarnation, and predetermination of a person's life by his/her actions in a previous life and the rejection of caste and idol worship [Hindi, lit., disciple] – **Sikhism** *n*

**silage** /'sielij/ *n* fodder (eg grass, clover, or corn) converted, esp in a SILO (sealed storage container), into succulent feed for livestock through processes of bacterial fermentation [short for *ensilage*]

**silane** /'silayn, 'sie-/ *n* any of various chemical compounds of silicon and hydrogen that have the general formula $Si_nH_{2n+2}$, and correspond to members of the ALKANE series of chemical compounds composed of carbon and hydrogen [ISV *silicon* + *methane*]

**sild** /sild/ *n, pl* **silds**, *esp collectively* **sild** any of various young herring other than sprats that are canned in oil like sardines, esp in Norway [Norw]

¹**silence** /'sieləns/ *n* **1** forbearance from speech or noise; muteness – often interjectional **2** absence of sound or noise; stillness **3** failure to mention a particular thing ⟨*can't understand the government's* ~ *on such an important topic*⟩ **4a** oblivion, obscurity ⟨*promising writers who vanish into* ~⟩ **b** secrecy ⟨*broke the* ~ *surrounding the development of the new rocket*⟩ [ME, fr OF, fr L *silentium*, fr *silent-, silens*]

²**silence** *vt* **1** to put or reduce to silence; still **2a** to restrain from expression; suppress ⟨~ *fears*⟩ **b** to put to rest; quell ⟨~ *doubts by fine results*⟩ **3** to cause (hostile firing) to cease by return fire, bombing, etc

**silencer** /'sielənsə/ *n* **1** a silencing device for a pistol, rifle, etc **2** *chiefly Br* a device for deadening the noise of the exhaust gas release of an INTERNAL-COMBUSTION ENGINE

**silent** /'sielənt/ *adj* **1a** making no utterance; mute, speechless **b**

disinclined to speak; not talkative **2** free from sound or noise; still **3a** endured without utterance ⟨~ *grief*⟩ **b** conveyed by refraining from reaction or comment; tacit ⟨~ *assent*⟩ **4a** making no mention; uninformative ⟨*history is* ~ *about this man*⟩ **b** taking no active part in the conduct of a business ⟨~ *partner*⟩ **5** *of a letter* not pronounced (e g the *b* in *doubt*); MUTE 3 **6** *medicine* not exhibiting the usual signs or symptoms of presence ⟨*a* ~ *infection*⟩ ⟨*the tumour produced a* ~ *area on the scan*⟩ **7** without spoken dialogue ⟨*a* ~ *film*⟩ [L *silent-*, *silens*, fr prp of *silēre* to be silent; akin to Goth ana*silan* to subside, L *sinere* to let go, lay – more at SITE] – **silently** *adv*, **silentness** *n*

synonyms Silent, taciturn, reserved, reticent, tight-lipped, uncommunicative, secretive, and noncommittal can all mean "disinclined to speak". Silent and taciturn imply a habit of not volunteering speech, taciturn adding the idea of grudging unsociability ⟨taciturn *farmer drove us all the way in silence*⟩. Reserved, reticent, tight-lipped, uncommunicative, and secretive all imply deliberate restraint in speech. Reserved suggests a habitual cautious formality and unwillingness to be friendly. Reticent is not habitual, and suggests a particular reluctance to speak of one's own affairs. Tight-lipped implies a very rigid restraint ⟨tight-lipped *throughout her ordeal*⟩. Uncommunicative and secretive imply the deliberate withholding of information, with secretive emphasizing a devious concealment. Noncommittal implies that one does speak, but without making the desired clear statement. See ²QUIET antonyms talkative, forthcoming, garrulous

**silent butler** *n*, *NAm* a receptacle with hinged lid for collecting table crumbs and the contents of ashtrays

**silent majority** *n taking sing or pl vb* a majority, esp of a population, whose unexpressed (moderate) opinion is contrasted with that of a vociferous (radical) minority

**silent partner** *n*, *chiefly NAm* SLEEPING PARTNER

**silenus** /sie'leenəs/ *n*, *pl* **sileni** /-ni/ (a figure of) a minor woodland deity and companion of Dionysus in ancient Greek mythology with a horse's ears and tail [L, fr Gk *silēnos*, fr *Silēnos* foster father of Dionysus]

**silesia** /sie'leeshiə/ *n* **1** a soft sturdy lightweight cotton twill used esp for lining **2** *archaic* a linen cloth of Silesian origin [*Silesia*, former Prussian province]

¹**silhouette** /ˌsilooh'et/ *n* **1** a portrait in profile cut from dark material and mounted on a light background or one sketched in outline and filled in with black – compare ¹PROFILE 1 **2** the shape of a body as it appears against a lighter background ⟨*the* ~ *of an aircraft against the dawn sky*⟩ [Fr, fr Etienne de *Silhouette* †1767 Fr controller-general of finances; prob fr his petty economies]

²**silhouette** *vt* to represent by a silhouette; *also* to project on a background like a silhouette ⟨*the last moments of the film with the lovers* ~d *against the sunset*⟩

**silic-** /silik-/, **silico-** *comb form* silicon ⟨silicone⟩ [*silicon*]

**silica** /'silikə/ *n* a chemical compound containing silicon and oxygen, $SiO_2$, that occurs in crystalline, AMORPHOUS (without regular shape), and impure forms (e g in quartz, opal, and sand respectively) and that is used in the manufacture of glass [NL, fr L *silic-*, *silex* flint, quartz]

**silica gel** *n* granular silica resembling coarse white sand in appearance but possessing many fine pores and therefore extremely adsorbent

**silicate** /'silikət, -kayt/ *n* any of various chemical compounds (SALTS or ESTERS) formed by combination between SILICIC ACID and a metal atom, an alcohol, or other chemical group; *esp* any of numerous insoluble often complex metal salts that contain silicon and oxygen, constitute the largest class of minerals, and are used in building materials (e g cement, bricks, and glass) [*silicic (acid)*]

**siliceous, silicious** /si'lishəs/ *adj* of or containing silica or a silicate ⟨~ *limestone*⟩ [L *siliceus* of flint, fr *silic-*, *silex*]

**silici-** *comb form* silica ⟨silicify⟩ [NL *silica*]

**silicic** /si'lisik/ *adj* of or derived from silica or silicon [NL *silica* & NL *silicium* silicon (fr *silica*)]

**silicic acid** *n* any of various weakly acid substances obtained as gelatinous masses by treating silicates with acids

**silicicolous** /ˌsili'sikələs/ *adj* growing or thriving in siliceous soil ⟨~ *plants*⟩

**silicide** /'sili,sied/ *n* a chemical compound composed of silicon and another chemical element or a chemical group [ISV *silic-* + *-ide*]

**silicification** /si,lisifi'kaysh(ə)n/ *n* the action or process of silicifying; the state of being silicified

**silicified wood** /si'lisified/ *n* a translucent quartz (CHALCEDONY) in the form of petrified wood often preserving even microscopic details of the replaced wood

**silicify** /si'lisifie/ *vt* to convert into or impregnate with silica ~ *vi* to become silicified

**silicle** /'silikl/ *n* a silicula

**silicon** /'silikən/ *n* a nonmetallic chemical element with a VALENCY of four that occurs in combination with other elements as the most abundant element next to oxygen in the earth's crust, and is used esp in alloys △ silicone [NL *silica* + E *-on* (as in *carbon*)]

**silicon carbide** *n* a very hard dark chemical compound, SiC, of silicon and carbon that is used as an abrasive and as a heat-resisting material and in electrical resistors

**silicon chip** *n* CHIP 4

**silicon controlled rectifier** *n* THYRISTOR (electrical device for converting ALTERNATING CURRENT into DIRECT CURRENT)

**silicone** /'silikohn/ *n* any of various complex chainlike chemical compounds (POLYMERS) composed of repeated silicon-containing units, obtained as oils, greases, or plastics and used esp for water-resistant and heat-resistant lubricants, varnishes, binders, and electrical insulators, and in cosmetic surgery [*silic-* + *-one*]

**silicone rubber** *n* rubber made from various elastic silicone substances and noted for its retention of flexibility, resilience, and TENSILE STRENGTH over a wide temperature range

**silicosis** /ˌsili'kohsis/ *n* a condition of massive increase of fibrous tissue within the lungs marked by shortness of breath and caused by prolonged inhalation of silica dusts, esp by miners and masons – compare PNEUMOCONIOSIS [NL] – **silicotic** *adj or n*

**silicula** /si'likyoolə/ *n* a short broad siliqua characteristic of plants (e g SHEPHERD'S PURSE) of the cabbage family [NL, fr L, dim. of *siliqua*]

**silicule** /'sili'kyoohl/ *n* a silicula

**siliqua** /'silikwə, -lee-/ *n* a narrow elongated usu many-seeded capsule that is characteristic of plants of the cabbage family and separates when ripe into two or four segments to disperse the seeds [NL fr L, pod, husk; akin to L *silic-*, *silex* flint – more at SHELL]

**silique** /si'leek/ *n* a siliqua [Fr, fr NL *siliqua*]

¹**silk** /silk/ *n* **1** a fine continuous protein fibre produced, usu for cocoons, by various insect larvae; *esp* a lustrous tough elastic fibre produced by silkworms and used for textiles **2** thread, yarn, or fabric made from silk filaments **3a** a garment of silk **b** (a distinctive silk gown worn by) a King's or Queen's Counsel **c** *pl* the cap and shirt of a jockey made in the registered racing colour of his/her stable **4a** a silky material or filament (e g that produced by a spider to make a web) **b** the tuft of fine fibres (STYLES) at the tip of an ear of maize **5** a parachute [ME, fr OE *seolc*, prob of Baltic or Slav origin; akin to OPruss *silkas* silk, OSlav *shelkŭ*]

²**silk** *adj*, *of paint* matt with a slight sheen; ²EGGSHELL 2

**silk cotton** *n* the silky or cottony seed covering of various SILK-COTTON TREES; *esp* KAPOK

'**silk-,cotton tree** *n* any of various tropical trees of the baobab family with lobed leaves and large fruits with the seeds enveloped by silk cotton; *esp* CEIBA

**silken** /'silkən/ *adj* **1** made of silk **2** resembling silk, esp in softness or lustre **3a** clothed in silk ⟨~ *ankles*⟩ **b** luxurious

**silk gland** *n* a gland that produces a sticky fluid that is extruded in filaments and hardens into silk on exposure to air: e g **a** either of a pair of greatly enlarged and modified salivary glands of an insect larva (e g of the silkworm moth) that produce a compound filament from which a larval or pupal cover (e g a cocoon) is spun **b** any of two or more abdominal glands of a spider that open through specialized organs (SPINNERETS) and produce a filament used chiefly in the spinning of webs

**silk hat** *n* a hat with a tall cylindrical crown and a silk-plush finish worn by men as a dress hat

**silk moth** *n* the silkworm

**silk oak, silky oak** *n* any of various Australian timber trees (family Protaceae and esp genus *Grevillea*) with mottled wood used esp in cabinetmaking and veneering

**silk screen, silk-screen printing** *also* **silk-screen process** *n* a stencil process in which paint or ink is forced onto the material to be printed, through the meshes of a prepared silk or organdie screen which has the areas which are not to be printed blocked off with some impervious material – **silk-screen** *vt*

,**silk-'stocking** *adj* **1** aristocratic, well-to-do ⟨*a* ~ *district*⟩ **2** of the American FEDERALIST party

**silk stocking** n 1 an aristocratic or wealthy person 2 FEDER-ALIST 3 (member of a former major US political party)

**silkworm** /'silk,wuhm/ n a moth whose larva spins a large amount of strong silk in constructing its cocoon; esp an Asiatic moth (*Bombyx mori*) whose rough wrinkled hairless yellowish caterpillar produces the silk used commercially

**silky** /'silki/ adj **1a** resembling or consisting of silk; silken **b** suave, ingratiating ⟨a ~ voice⟩ **2** having or covered with fine soft hairs, down, or scales – **silkily** adv, **silkiness** n

**sill** /sil/ n **1** a horizontal piece (e g a timber) that forms the lowest member or one of the lowest members of a framework or supporting structure: e g **1a** the horizontal piece at the base of a window **b** the threshold of a door **2** a usu horizontal sheet of IGNEOUS (formed by the cooling and solidification of molten material) rock injected while in a molten state between layers of existing rock formations below the earth's surface **3** a submerged ridge at relatively shallow depth separating two deeper bodies of water [ME *sille*, fr OE *syll;* akin to OHG *swelli* beam, threshold, Gk *selis* crossbeam]

**sillabub** /'silə,bub/ n SYLLABUB (cream dessert flavoured with sherry, brandy, etc)

**sillimanite** /'siliməniet/ n a brown, greyish, or pale green mineral, $Al_2SiO_5$, that contains aluminium, silicon, and oxygen often occurring as fibrous or columnar crystals [Benjamin *Silliman* †1864 US geologist]

**¹silly** /'sili/ adj **1a** showing a lack of common sense or sound judgment ⟨a very ~ mistake⟩ **b** trifling, frivolous ⟨a ~ remark⟩ ⟨he's just being ~⟩ **2** stunned, dazed ⟨scared ~⟩ ⟨knocked me ~⟩ **3** of or occupying a fielding position in cricket in front of and dangerously near the batsman ⟨~ mid-off⟩ **4** chiefly Br – used as a generalized usu mild intensive ⟨howled my ~ eyes out – Annabel⟩ **5** archaic helpless, weak ⟨provided that you do no outrages on ~ women and poor passengers – Shak⟩ **6** archaic plain, unsophisticated ⟨the ~ herdman all astonnied stands n Earl of Surrey⟩ **7** archaic feebleminded [ME *sely, silly* happy, innocent, pitiable, feeble, fr (assumed) OE *sælig*, fr OE *sæl* happiness; akin to OHG *sālig* happy, L *solari* to console, Gk *hilaros* cheerful] – **sillily** adv, **silliness** n, **silly** adv

**²silly** n, informal a silly person – often used as a term of address

**silly-billy** /,-- '--, '-- ,--/ n, informal or humorous a silly or foolish person; an idiot – used esp by or to children [*Billy*, nickname for *William;* prob fr William IV †1837 King of England]

**silly season** n, journalistic a period when newspapers resort to trivial or frivolous matters through lack of important news

**silo** /'sieloh/ n, pl **silos 1** a trench, pit, or esp a tall cylinder (e g of wood or concrete) usu sealed to exclude air and used for making and storing silage **2** an underground structure for housing a GUIDED MISSILE [Sp, fr L *sirus*, fr Gk *siros* pit for storing corn]

**siloxane** /si'loksayn/ n any of various chemical compounds containing alternate silicon and oxygen atoms in either a linear or cyclic arrangement usu with one or two carbon-containing chemical groups attached to each silicon atom [*sil*icon + *ox*ygen + meth*ane*]

**¹silt** /silt/ n **1** a loose material that results from the weathering of rocks and consists of particles that are coarser than those of clay but finer than those of sand; also soil composed chiefly of this material – compare SAND, CLAY, LOAM **2** a deposit of sediment (e g by a river) [ME *cylte*, prob of Scand origin; akin to Dan *sylt* salt marsh; akin to OHG *sulza* salt marsh, OE *sealt* salt] – **silty** adj

**²silt** vb to make or become choked or obstructed with silt – often + up – **siltation** n

**siltstone** /'silt,stohn/ n a rock composed chiefly of hardened silt

**Silures** /'silyooreez/ n pl a people of ancient Britain chiefly occupying S Wales [L]

**Silurian** /sie'l(y)ooəri·ən/ adj **1** of the Silures or their dwelling-place **2** of or being a period of the PALAEOZOIC era of geological history between the ORDOVICIAN and DEVONIAN periods or the corresponding system of rocks marked by an abundance of marine INVERTEBRATE animals (e g corals) – **Silurian** n

**silva** /'silvə/ n SYLVA (forest trees of a particular region)

**silvan** /'silvən/ adj SYLVAN (characteristic of woods or forests)

**¹silver** /'silvə/ n **1** a white metallic chemical element that can be shaped, drawn out into wires, or hammered into sheets, is capable of a high degree of polish, and chiefly has a VALENCY of one in chemical compounds, and that has the highest thermal and electric conductivity of any substance **2** silver as a commodity ⟨the value of ~ has risen⟩ **3** coins made of silver or a mixture (ALLOY) of copper and nickel ⟨9 in notes and the rest in ~⟩ **4** articles, esp tableware (e g plates, dishes, and cutlery), made of or plated with silver; also similar articles, esp cutlery, made of other metals **5** a whitish grey colour **6** informal SILVER MEDAL ⟨won a ~ at the Olympic Games⟩ [ME, fr OE *seolfor;* akin to OHG *silbar* silver]

**²silver** adj **1** made of silver **2a** resembling silver, esp in having a white lustrous sheen **b** giving a soft, clear, ringing sound **c** eloquently persuasive ⟨a ~ tongue⟩ **3** consisting of or yielding silver ⟨~ ore⟩ **4** relating to or characteristic of silver **5** of, marking, or being a 25th anniversary ⟨~ wedding⟩

**³silver** vt **1a** to cover with silver (e g by ELECTROPLATING) **b** to coat with a substance (e g a metal) resembling silver ⟨~ a glass with an amalgam of tin and mercury⟩ **2** to impart a silvery lustre or whiteness to – **silverer** n

**silver birch** n a common Eurasian birch tree (*Betula pendula*) with slender silvery-white upper branches and a black grooved lower trunk

**silver bromide** n a chemical compound, $AgBr$, that darkens on exposure to light and is mush used as a light-sensitive coating in the preparation of emulsions for photographic materials

**silver chloride** n a chemical compound, $AgCl$, that darkens on exposure to light and is used esp for preparing antiseptic medications and in silver plating

**silver fir** n any of various fir trees (genus *Abies*, esp *Abies alba*) that have leaves that are white or silvery white underneath and that are commonly planted for ornament

**silverfish** /'silvə,fish/ n **1** any of various silvery fishes (e g a silversides) **2** any of various small wingless insects (order Thysanura); esp one (*Lepisma saccharina*) that is found in houses and sometimes causes damage by feeding on wallpaper, starched fabrics, etc

**silver foil** n **1** SILVER PAPER **2** tinfoil

**silver fox** n a genetically determined colour phase of the American RED FOX in which the fur is black with white tips; also the valuable fur or pelt from a fox in this colour phase

**silver glance** n ARGENTITE (valuable ore of silver)

**silver grey** adj or n light lustrous grey

**silver iodide** n a chemical compound, $AgI$, that darkens on exposure to light and is used esp in photography, in medicine as an antiseptic, and in artificial rainmaking

**silver lining** n **1** the edge of a cloud as it catches the sun **2** a consoling or hopeful aspect [(2) fr the proverb *every cloud has a silver lining*]

**silverly** /'silvəli/ adv with silvery appearance or sound

**silver maple** n a common N American maple tree (*Acer saccharinum*) with deeply lobed leaves that are light green on the upper surface and silvery white underneath; also the hard close-grained but brittle light brown wood of this tree

**silver medal** n a medal of silver awarded to somebody who comes second in competitions, esp in athletics – compare BRONZE MEDAL, GOLD MEDAL – **silver medallist** n

**silvern** /'silv(ə)n/ adj, archaic made of or resembling silver

**silver nitrate** n a caustic chemical compound, $AgNO_3$, that in contact with carbon-containing matter turns black and is used as a reagent in chemical analysis, in photography, and as an antiseptic

**silver paper** n paper with a coating or lamination resembling silver

**silver plate** n **1** a plating of silver **2** tableware and cutlery of silver or a silver-plated metal

**silver screen** n the film industry

**silverside** /'silvə,sied/ n, Br a cut of beef from the outer part of the top of the leg below the AITCHBONE (cut containing the hipbone), that is boned and often salted [fr its being considered the best cut]

**silversides** /'silvə,siedz/ n taking sing or pl vb any of various small fishes (family Atherinidae) with a silvery stripe along each side of the body

**silversmith** /'silvə,smith/ n somebody who makes articles of silver

**silver spoon** n wealth; esp inherited wealth – esp in born with a silver spoon in his mouth

**silver standard** n a monetary standard under which the currency unit is defined by a stated quantity of silver

**silver-'tongued** adj eloquent

**silverware** /'silvə,weə/ n articles of silver; SILVER PLATE 2

**silverweed** /'silvə,weed/ n any of various somewhat silvery plants; *esp* a plant (*Potentilla anserina*) of the rose family with 5-lobed leaves that are covered in a dense mat of silvery hairs on the underside

**silvery** /'silv(ə)ri/ *adj* **1** having a soft clear musical tone; resonant ⟨*a* ~ *voice*⟩ **2** having the lustre or whiteness of silver **3** containing or consisting of silver – **silveriness** *n*

**silver Y moth** *n* any of several moths (genus *Plusia*); *esp* a moth (*Plusia gamma*), the caterpillar of which removes the leaves of garden flowers (eg carnations) [fr the silvery Y-shaped marking on its forewings]

**silvicolous** /sil'vikələs/ *adj* living in woodlands [L *silvicola* inhabitant of a wood, fr *silva* wood + *colere* to inhabit – more at WHEEL]

**silvics** /'silviks/ *n taking sing vb* the study of the life history, characteristics, and ecology of forest trees [NL *silva* sylva] – **silvical** *adj*

**silviculture** /'silvi,kulchə/ *n* a branch of forestry dealing with the development and care of forests [Fr, fr L *silva, sylva* forest + *cultura* culture] – **silvicultural** *adj*, **silviculturist** *n*

**sima** /'siemə/ *n* the continuous lower layer of the earth's crust that is composed of relatively heavy rocks (eg basalt), is rich in silica and magnesium, and is held to underlie the oceans – compare SIAL [Ger, fr *silizium* silicon + *magnesium*] – **simatic** *adj*

**simazine** /'siməzeen/ *n* a selective herbicide, $C_7H_{12}ClN_5$, used to control grassy weeds among crop plants [*sim-* (prob alter. of *sym-* symmetrical, prefix used in names of organic compounds) + tri*azine*]

**Simchas Torah** /'simkahs/ *n* SIMHAT TORAH

**Simhat Torah** /'simkahs/ *n* a Jewish holiday observed on the 23rd (or in Israel the 22nd) of TISHRI (7th month of the Jewish ecclesiastical calendar) in celebration of the completion of the annual reading of the TORAH (Jewish scriptures equivalent to the first five books of the Bible) [Heb *śimḥath tōrāh* rejoicing of the Torah]

**simian** /'simi-ən/ *adj or n* (of or resembling) a monkey or ape [L *simia* ape, perh fr *simus* snub-nosed, fr Gk *simos*]

**similar** /'similə/ *adj* **1** marked by correspondence or resemblance, esp of a general kind ⟨~ *but not identical*⟩ **2** alike in one or more essential aspects ⟨*these two signatures are* ~⟩ **3** *maths* having equal angles, but sides of different length ⟨~ *triangles*⟩ – compare CONGRUENT 2 [Fr *similaire*, fr L *similis* like, similar – more at SAME] – **similarly** *adv*
  *usage* Similar should be used with *to*, and not with any other word ⟨△ *dressed in* similar *clothes as yours*⟩. **synonyms** see ¹SAME
  **antonym** different

**similarity** /simi'larəti/ *n* **1** the quality or state of being similar; resemblance **2** a comparable aspect; correspondence

**simile** /'simili/ *n* a FIGURE OF SPEECH explicitly comparing two unlike things (eg in *cheeks like roses*) – compare METAPHOR [L, comparison, fr neut of *similis*]

**similitude** /si'milityoohd/ *n, formal* **1a** a counterpart, double **b** a visible likeness; an image **2** an imaginative comparison; a simile **3** (an instance of) correspondence in kind or quality [ME, fr MF, resemblance, likeness, fr L *similitudo*, fr *similis*]

**simmer** /'simə/ *vi* **1a** *of a liquid* to bubble gently at or just below boiling **b** *of food* to cook in a simmering liquid **2a** to be on the point of developing or coming to fruition; ferment ⟨*ideas* ~*ing in the back of his mind*⟩ **b** to be agitated by suppressed emotion; seethe ⟨~ *with anger*⟩ ~ *vt* to cook (food) in a simmering liquid [alter. of E dial. *simper*, fr ME *simperen*, of imit origin]
  **simmer down** *vi* to become calm or less excited

**simnel cake** /'simnəl/ *n, Br* a rich fruit cake traditionally filled with a layer of almond paste and baked esp for mid-Lent and Easter [ME *simenel* bread or bun made of fine flour, fr OF, fr L *simila* fine wheat flour (cf SEMOLINA)]

**simoniac** /si'mohniak/ *n* somebody who practises simony [ME, fr MF or ML; MF *simoniaque*, fr ML *simoniacus*, fr LL *simonia* simony] – **simoniac, simoniacal** *adj*, **simoniacally** *adv*

**simonize** /'simə,niez/ *vt* to polish (as if) with wax [fr *Simoniz*, a trademark]

**simon-'pure** *adj* of untainted purity or integrity; *also* pretentiously or hypocritically pure [fr the phrase *the real Simon Pure* (the authentic person or thing), alluding to a character impersonated by another in the play *A Bold Stroke for a Wife* by Susanna Centlivre †1723 E dramatist]

**simony** /'siməni, 'sie-/ *n* the buying or selling of a church office or ecclesiastical preferment [LL *simonia*, fr *Simon* Magus 1st-c Samaritan sorcerer (Acts 8:9–24)]

**simoom** /si'moohm/ *n* a hot dry violent dust-laden wind from an Asian or African desert **synonyms** see ¹WIND [Ar *samūm*]

**simoon** /si'moohn/ *n* a simoom

**simp** /simp/ *n, chiefly NAm informal* a simpleton

**simpatico** /sim'pati,koh, -'pah-/ *adj, informal* congenial, likable [It *simpatico* & Sp *simpático*, deriv of L *sympathia* sympathy]

**¹simper** /'simpə/ *vi* to smile in a foolish self-conscious manner ~ *vt* to say with a simper ⟨~ed *her apologies*⟩ [perh of Scand origin; akin to Dan dial. *simper* affected, coy] – **simperer** *n*

**²simper** *n* a foolish self-conscious smile

**¹simple** /'simpl/ *adj* **1a** free from guile or vanity; innocent, unassuming **b** free from elaboration or showiness; unpretentious ⟨*wrote in a* ~ *style*⟩ **2** of humble birth or lowly position ⟨*a* ~ *farmer*⟩ **3a** lacking knowledge or experience; ignorant ⟨*a* ~ *amateur of the arts*⟩ **b** lacking intelligence; *esp* mentally retarded **c** lacking sophistication; naive **4a** sheer, unqualified ⟨*the* ~ *truth of the matter*⟩ **b** free of secondary complications ⟨*a* ~ *fracture*⟩ **c** *of a sentence* consisting of only one main clause and no subordinate clauses **d** *chemistry* composed essentially of one basic substance or element; fundamental **e** not made up of many like units ⟨*a* ~ *eye*⟩ – compare COMPOUND 1 **5** *music* free from ORNAMENTS (embellishing notes) ⟨~ *harmony*⟩ **6a** *botany* **6a(1)** not subdivided into branches or leaflets ⟨*a* ~ *leaf*⟩ **a(2)** consisting of a single CARPEL (female reproductive organ) **a(3)** *of a fruit* developing from a single ovary (female reproductive structure producing seeds) **b** *genetics* controlled by a single gene ⟨~ *inherited characters*⟩ **7** not limited or restricted; unconditional ⟨*a* ~ *obligation*⟩ **8** readily understood or performed; straightforward ⟨*a* ~ *task*⟩ ⟨*the adjustment was* ~ *to make*⟩ **9** *of a statistical hypothesis* specifying exact values for the stated statistical conditions **synonyms** see ¹NATURAL **usage** see SIMPLISTIC **antonyms** wise, complex [ME, fr OF, plain, uncomplicated, artless, fr L *simplus* (fr *sem-, sim-* one + *-plus* multiplied by) & *simplic-, simplex* (fr *sem-, sim-* + *-plic-, -plex* -fold), lit., single; akin to Gk *diplak-, diplax* double – more at SAME, DOUBLE] – **simpleness** *n*

**²simple** *n, archaic* **1a** a person of humble station ⟨*thought very little of anybody*, ~s *or gentry* – Virginia Woolf⟩ **b** a simpleton **2a** a medicinal plant **b** a vegetable drug having only one ingredient **3** a single component of a complex; *specif* an irreducible constituent

**simple closed curve** *n, maths* a closed plane curve (eg a circle or ellipse) that does not intersect itself

**simple equation** *n* LINEAR EQUATION (mathematical equation in which no variable is raised to a power higher than one)

**simple fraction** *n* a fraction having WHOLE NUMBERS for the figures above and below the line (NUMERATOR and DENOMINATOR) – compare COMPLEX FRACTION

**simple harmonic motion** *n* a vibratory motion (eg the swing of a pendulum) in which the acceleration is proportional and opposite in direction to the displacement of the body from an equilibrium position; the projection on a diameter of a point in uniform motion round a circle

**simple-'hearted** *n* having a sincere and unassuming nature; artless

**simple interest** *n* interest paid or calculated on only the original capital sum loaned

**simple machine** *n* any of various elementary mechanisms formerly considered as the elements of which all machines are composed and including the lever, the wheel and axle, the pulley, the inclined plane, the wedge, and the screw

**simpleminded** /,simpl'miendid/ *adj* devoid of subtlety; unsophisticated; *also* mentally retarded – **simplemindedly** *adv*, **simplemindedness** *n*

**simple sugar** *n* MONOSACCHARIDE (eg glucose or fructose)

**simpleton** /'simplt(ə)n/ *n* a person lacking common sense or intelligence [¹*simple* + *-ton* (as in surnames such as *Washington*)]

**simple vow** *n* a public vow taken by a member of a Roman Catholic religious order that allows him/her to retain his/her property and that while forbidding marriage, recognizes any marriage that may be entered into as valid under CANON LAW – compare SOLEMN VOW

**¹simplex** /'simpleks/ *adj* **1** simple, single **2** allowing telecommunication in only one direction at a time [L *simplic-, simplex* – more at SIMPLE]

**²simplex** *n* **1** *linguistics* a simple word **2** *maths* a spatial configuration of *n* dimensions determined by $n + 1$ points in a space of dimension equal to or greater than *n* ⟨*a triangle to-*

*gether with its interior determined by its three vertices is a two-dimensional* ~ *in the plane or any space of higher dimension*⟩ – **simplicial** *adj*, **simplicially** *adv*

**simpliciter** /sim'plisitə/ *adv* in or by itself; simply [L, fr *simplic-, simplex*]

**simplicity** /sim'plisəti/ *n* **1** the state or quality of being simple or uncompounded **2a** lack of subtlety or penetration; naivety **b** stupidity, silliness **3** freedom from affectation or guile; sincerity, straightforwardness **4a** directness of expression; clarity **b** restraint in ornamentation; austerity, plainness [ME *simplicite*, fr MF *simplicité*, fr L *simplicitat-, simplicitas*, fr *simplic-, simplex*]

**simplify** /'simplifie/ *vt* to make simple or simpler: eg **a** to reduce to basic essentials **b** to diminish in scope or complexity; streamline ⟨~ *a manufacturing process*⟩ **c** to make more intelligible; clarify ~ *vi* to become simple or simpler [Fr *simplifier*, fr ML *simplificare*, fr L *simplus* simple] – **simplifier** *n*, **simplification** *n*

**simplism** /'simpliz(ə)m/ *n* the act or an instance of oversimplifying; *esp* the reduction of a problem to a false simplicity by ignoring complications

**simplistic** /sim'plistik/ *adj* deliberately or affectedly uncomplicated; naive – **simplistically** *adv*
   **usage** Simplistic should not be confused with the often appreciative word **simple**. Compare ⟨*a nice* **simple** *explanation*⟩ ⟨*a stupid* **simplistic** *generalization*⟩.

**simply** /'simpli/ *adv* **1a** without ambiguity; clearly ⟨*a* ~ *worded reply*⟩ **b** without ornamentation or show; plainly ⟨~ *furnished*⟩ **c** without affectation or subterfuge; candidly **2a** solely, merely ⟨*eats* ~ *to keep alive*⟩ **b** without any question ⟨*the concert was* ~ *marvellous*⟩

**simply ordered** *adj, maths* PARTIALLY ORDERED

**simulacrum** /,simyoo'laykrəm/ *n, pl* **simulacra** /-krə/ *also* **simulacrums** *formal* **1** an image, representation ⟨*a reasonable* ~ *of reality* – Martin Mayer⟩ **2** an often superficial or misleading likeness of something; a semblance [L, fr *simulare*]

**simulate** /'simyoo,layt/ *vt* **1** to assume the outward qualities or appearance of, usu with the intent to deceive **2** to make a functioning model of (a system, device, or process) (eg using a computer) *synonyms* see DISSIMULATE, ¹PRETEND [L *simulatus*, pp of *simulare* to copy, represent, feign, fr *similis* like – more at SAME]

**simulation** /,simyoo'laysh(ə)n/ *n* **1** the act or process of simulating **2** an imitation; a counterfeit **3** the representation of the functioning of one system or process by means of the functioning of another; *esp* one that models a system or process in mathematical terms ⟨*a computer* ~ *of an industrial process*⟩

**simulator** /'simyoolaytə/ *n* one who or that which simulates; *esp* a device that simulates various conditions or the mechanisms involved in operating a system, in order to train operators or for the purposes of research

**simultaneous** /,siməl'taynyəs, -ni·əs/ *adj* **1** existing, occurring, or functioning at the same time; coincident in time **2** satisfied by the same values of the variables ⟨~ *equations*⟩ [(assumed) ML *simultaneus*, fr L *simul* at the same time – more at SAME] – **simultaneously** *adv*, **simultaneousness, simultaneity** *n*

**¹sin** /sin/ *n* **1a** an offence against moral or religious law **b** an action that is considered highly reprehensible ⟨*it's a* ~ *to waste food*⟩ **2** a state of estrangement or separation from God resulting from disobedience to his laws – compare ORIGINAL SIN [ME *sinne*, fr OE *synn*; akin to OHG *sunta* sin] – **sinless** *adj*, **sinlessly** *adv*, **sinlessness** *n* – **live in sin** to live together as man and wife without being married

**²sin** *vi* **-nn-** **1** to commit a sin **2** to commit an offence – often + *against* ⟨*writers who* ~ *against good taste*⟩ – **sinner** *n*

**³sin** *n* the 21st letter of the Hebrew alphabet [Heb *śin*]

**Sinanthropus** /si'nanthrəpəs/ *n* PEKING MAN (early type of human being) [NL, fr LL *Sinae*, pl, Chinese + Gk *anthrōpos* man – more at SINOLOGUE]

**sinapism** /'sinə,piz(ə)m/ *n* MUSTARD PLASTER (adhesive dressing containing powdered mustard) [LL *sinapismus*, deriv of Gk *sinapi* mustard]

**sin bin** *n* **1** *euph* a brothel **2** *informal* an enclosure occupied by a player (eg in ice hockey) who has been temporarily sent off

**¹since** /sins/ *adv* **1** continuously from then until now ⟨*has stayed there ever* ~⟩ **2** before now; ago ⟨*should have done it long* ~⟩ **3** between then and now; subsequently ⟨*has* ~ *become rich*⟩ □ + tenses formed with *to have* [ME *sins*, contr of *sithens*, fr *sithen*, fr OE *siththan*, fr *sith* than since that, fr *sith* since + *tham*, dat of *thæt* that; akin to OHG *sīd* since, L *serus* late, OE *sāwan* to sow]

**²since** *prep* in the period between (a specified past time) and now ⟨*haven't met* ~ *1973*⟩; from (a specified past time) until now ⟨*it's a long time* ~ *breakfast*⟩ – + present tenses and tenses formed with *to have*

**³since** *conj* **1** between now and the past time when ⟨*has held two jobs* ~ *he graduated*⟩; continuously from the past time when ⟨*ever* ~ *he was a child*⟩ **2** in view of the fact that; because ⟨~ *it was raining he wore a hat*⟩ ⟨*more interesting,* ~ *rarer*⟩ **3** *obs* when *usage* see AGO

**sincere** /sin'siə/ *adj* **1** free from deceit or hypocrisy; honest, genuine ⟨~ *interest*⟩ **2** marked by genuineness; authentic ⟨*the only* ~ *glimpse . . . of Dante* – J R Lowell⟩ **3** *archaic* free from adulteration; pure ⟨*a* ~ *doctrine*⟩ ⟨~ *wine*⟩ [MF, fr L *sincerus*] – **sincereness, sincerity** *n*
   *synonyms* Sincere, unfeigned, natural, unaffected, wholehearted, hearty, and heartfelt can all mean "genuine in feeling". Sincere emphasizes the absence of hypocrisy ⟨*the missionaries were prompted by a* **sincere** *desire for good* – Herman Melville⟩. Unfeigned stresses the absence of pretence ⟨*greeted them with* **unfeigned** *delight*⟩. Natural and unaffected imply that one shows one's true nature without artificiality, **unaffected** suggesting also lack of sophistication. Wholehearted and particularly **hearty** imply not only earnest feeling but its vigorous display, **hearty** suggesting robust exuberance ⟨*a* **hearty** *laugh*⟩. By contrast **heartfelt** emphasizes depth, rather than display, of feeling ⟨*our sympathy for you therefore is* **heartfelt**, *for we are sharing the same sufferings* – Winston Churchill⟩. *antonyms* insincere, hypocritical

**sincerely** /sin'siəli/ *adv* in a sincere manner – often in *yours sincerely* as an ending to a letter
   *usage* Yours sincerely ends a letter of medium formality that begins with the recipient's name: *Dear Mr Jones, Dear Ms Jackson,* etc. Compare ¹FAITHFUL

**sinciput** /'sinsiput/ *n, pl* **sinciputs, sincipita** /sin'sipitə/ **1** the forehead **2** the upper half of the skull [L *sincipit-, sinciput,* fr *semi-* + *caput* head – more at HEAD]

**sine** /sien/ *n* a fundamental and important mathematical function that for an angle is the ratio of the side opposite to the angle to the hypotenuse in a right-angled triangle and that can be expressed algebraically as

$$\sin x = x - \frac{x^3}{3!} + \frac{x^5}{5!} - \frac{x^7}{7!} + \cdots$$

– compare COSINE, TANGENT [ML *sinus*, fr L, curve]

**sinecure** /'sinikyooə, 'sie-/ *n* **1** an office or position that provides an income while requiring little or no work **2** *archaic* a church office providing an income but without responsibility for pastoral or spiritual matters △ cynosure [ML *sine cura* without cure of souls] – **sinecurism** *n*, **sinecurist** *n*

**sine curve** *n, maths* the continuous S-shaped graph of the equation *y* = *a*sin*bx* where *a* and *b* are constants

**sine die** /,sieni 'dee·ay, 'die·ee, ,sini/ *adv* without any future date being designated (eg for resumption); indefinitely ⟨*the meeting adjourned* ~⟩ [L, without day]

**sine qua non** /,sini kway 'non, kway 'nohn, ,sieni/ *n* an absolutely indispensable or essential thing [LL, without which not]

**¹sinew** /'sinyooh/ *n* **1** *anatomy* a tendon **2a** solid resilient strength ; vigour ⟨*intellectual and moral* ~ – G K Chalmers⟩ **b** **sinews** *pl*, **sinew** the chief means of support; a mainstay ⟨*the* ~*s of political stability*⟩ **3** *obs* a nerve [ME *sinewe*, fr OE *seono*; akin to OHG *senawa* sinew, L *saeta* bristle] – **sinewy** *adj*

**²sinew** *vt, poetic* to strengthen as if with sinews; sustain

**sine wave** /sien/ *n* an oscillation having a waveform in which the amount of vertical displacement at each point is proportional to the sine of the horizontal distance from a reference point; *also* SINE CURVE

**sinfonia** /,sinfə'nee·ə/ *n, pl* **sinfonie** /,sinfə'nee,ay/, **sinfonias** **1a** an orchestral composition used as an introduction to choral works (eg opera), esp in the 18th century; an overture **b** an instrumental interlude in baroque opera; RITORNELLO **2** a symphony [It, fr L *symphonia* symphony]

**sinfonia concertante** /,sinfə'nee·ə ,konsuh'tanti, ,koncheə'tahnti/ *n* a concerto for more than one solo instrument [It, lit., symphony in concerto style]

**sinfonietta** /sin,fohni'etə/ *n* **1** a short or lightly orchestrated symphony **2** a small symphony orchestra; *also* a small orchestra of strings only [It, dim. of *sinfonia*]

**sinful** /'sinf(ə)l/ *adj* tainted with, marked by, or full of sin; wicked *synonyms* see ¹BAD – **sinfully** *adv*, **sinfulness** *n*

**¹sing** /sing/ *vb* **sang** /sang/, **sung** /sung/; **sung** *vi* **1a** to produce musical sounds by means of the voice **b** to utter words in musical notes with changes in the tone, pitch, or loudness of the voice to convey meaning **c** to work or spend time as a singer ⟨~s *in the church choir*⟩ **2** to make a shrill whining or whistling sound ⟨*a kettle* ~ing *on the fire*⟩ **3** to relate or celebrate something in verse **4** to produce musical or melodious sounds **5** to buzz, ring ⟨*a punch that made his ears* ~⟩ **6** to make a loud clear utterance – usu + *out* ⟨~ *out in the darkness*⟩ **7** *slang* to give information or evidence ⟨sang *to a grand jury in return for a promise of leniency*⟩ ~ *vt* **1** to produce (musical sounds) by means of the voice; *esp* to utter (words, musical scales, etc) in musical notes **2a** to relate or celebrate in verse **b** to express vividly or enthusiastically ⟨~ *his praises*⟩ **3** to chant, intone ⟨~ *a requiem mass*⟩ **4** to bring to a specified state by singing ⟨~s *the child to sleep*⟩ [ME *singen,* fr OE *singan;* akin to OHG *singan* to sing, Gk *omphē* voice] – **sing-able** *adj,* **singer** *n*
**²sing** *n, informal* SINGSONG 2
**'sing-,along** *n, informal* SINGSONG 2
**¹singe** /sinj/ *vt* **singeing; singed** to burn superficially or slightly; scorch; *esp* to remove the hair, down, or nap from (eg fabric or plucked poultry), usu by passing rapidly over a flame [ME *sengen,* fr OE *sengan;* akin to OHG bi*sengan* to singe]
**²singe** *n* a superficial burn; a scorch
**singer** /'sing-ə/ *n* one who or that which sings ⟨*canaries are good* ~s⟩; *esp* a professional vocal musician
**Singer** /'sing-ə/ *trademark* – used for a domestic sewing machine
**Singhalese** /,sing-gə'leez/ *n or adj, pl* **Singhalese** (a) Sinhalese
**¹single** /'sing-gl/ *adj* **1a** not married **b** of the unmarried state **2** not accompanied by others; solitary, sole ⟨*the* ~ *survivor of the disaster*⟩ **3a(1)** consisting of or having only one part or feature ⟨*use double, not* ~ *thread*⟩ **a(2)** having one aspect as opposed to two or more; uniform ⟨*a* ~ *standard for men and women*⟩ **a(3)** consisting of only one in number ⟨*holds to a* ~ *ideal*⟩ **b** *of a plant or flower* having the normal number of petals or RAY FLOWERS (outermost strap-shaped flowers of daisylike plants) – compare DOUBLE **4a** consisting of a separate unique whole; individual ⟨*every* ~ *citizen*⟩ ⟨*food is our most important* ~ *need*⟩ **b** of, suitable for, or involving only one person ⟨*a* ~ *portion of chips*⟩ ⟨*a* ~ *room*⟩ **5a** honest, sincere ⟨*a* ~ *devotion*⟩ **b** steadfastly attentive ⟨*an eye* ~ *to the truth*⟩ **6** having no rival or comparison; singular ⟨~ *among his fellows*⟩ [ME, fr MF, fr L *singulus* one only; akin to L *sem-* one – more at SAME] – **singleness** *n*
*synonyms* Single, separate, individual, particular, sole, solitary, and unique all mean "one as distinguished from others". **Single** stresses the idea of not being accompanied or combined ⟨*a* **single** *currency system*⟩. **Separate** implies distinctness from others ⟨**separate** *dining rooms*⟩ and **individual** implies distinctness from a mass ⟨**individual** *Yorkshire puddings*⟩. **Particular** applies to a definite identifiable one ⟨*claims of the United States or any particular state* – US Constitution⟩. **Sole, solitary,** and **unique** can all mean "only" ⟨*his* **sole/solitary/unique** *failing*⟩. **Sole** often expresses exclusive possession ⟨**sole** *claim to the property*⟩. **Solitary** adds the idea of isolation ⟨*a* **solitary** *tree*⟩. **Unique** indicates the only one, which is unlike all others and stands alone ⟨*the manuscript of Beowulf is* **unique**⟩.
**²single** *n* **1a** a single thing or amount; *esp* a single measure of spirits **b** a (young) unmarried adult ⟨*a* ~s *club*⟩ **c** a gramophone record, esp of popular music, with a single short track on each side **2** a single run scored in cricket **3** a golf match between two players – compare SINGLES **4** a flower having the number of petals or RAY FLOWERS (outermost strap-shaped flowers of daisylike plants) typical of the species **5** single, single malt a high quality unblended Scottish malt whisky **6** *Br* a ticket bought for a trip to a place but not back again – compare RETURN 8
**³single** *vt, Br* to thin out (seedlings)
**single out** *vt* to select or distinguish from a number or group ⟨*was* singled out *for special treatment*⟩
**'single-,acting** *adj* acting or effective in one direction or way; *esp, of an engine* being a RECIPROCATING ENGINE (engine converting to-and-fro motion into circular motion) in which the working fluid (eg steam) acts on one side of the piston only
**'single-,action** *adj, of a firearm* requiring the hammer to be cocked before firing

**single bed** *n* a bed designed for one person to sleep in – **single-bedded** *adj*
**,single-'blind** *adj* of or being an experimental procedure designed to eliminate false results, in which the experimenters, but not the subjects, know the makeup of the test and control groups during the actual course of the experiments – compare DOUBLE-BLIND
**,single-'breasted** *adj* having a centre fastening with one row of buttons ⟨*a* ~ *coat*⟩ – compare DOUBLE-BREASTED
**,single-'chamber** *adj* having or consisting of one legislative chamber; unicameral
**single combat** *n* combat between two people
**single cream** *n* cream that is thinner and lighter than DOUBLE CREAM, contains 18 per cent butterfat, and is suitable for pouring – compare DOUBLE CREAM
**single cross** *n, genetics* a first-generation hybrid between two selected lines, usu of closely related individuals that have been interbred in order to fix certain desirable characteristics and eliminate certain unfavourable characteristics – compare DOUBLE CROSS
**,single-'decker** *n* something (eg a bus or cake) that has a single deck, level, or layer
**single entry** *n* a method of bookkeeping that recognizes only one side of a business transaction and usu consists only of a record of cash and personal accounts with debtors and creditors
**single file** *n* a line (eg of people) moving one behind the other – **single file** *adv*
**,single-'handed** *adj* **1** performed or achieved by one person or with one on a side ⟨*a* ~ *crossing of the Atlantic*⟩ **2** working or managing alone or unassisted by others **3** using or requiring the use of only one hand ⟨*hit a powerful* ~ *backhand shot*⟩ – **single-handedly** *adv,* **singlehandedness** *n*
**,single-'hearted** *adj* sincerely and unswervingly devoted (eg to a person or cause) – **single-heartedly** *adv,* **single-heartedness** *n*
**single honours** *n taking sing or pl vb* a university first-degree course in a single subject – compare COMBINED HONOURS, JOINT HONOURS
**,single-'minded** *adj* **1** having a single overriding purpose **2** *archaic* sincere, single-hearted – **single-mindedly** *adv,* **single-mindedness** *n*
**,single-'phase** *adj* of an electrical circuit energized by a single alternating voltage
**single reed** *n* a thin flat cane reed attached to the mouthpiece of a woodwind instrument of the clarinet family that vibrates to provide the instrument's sound
**singles** /'sing-glz/ *n taking sing vb, pl* **singles** a game (eg of tennis) with one player on each side
**,single-'space** *vt* to type (copy) leaving no blank lines between lines of text ~ *vi* to type on every line
**singlestick** /'sing-gl,stik/ *n* one-handed fighting or fencing with a wooden stick or sword; *also* the weapon used
**singlet** /'sing-glit/ *n* **1** a single line in a spectrum **2** *chiefly Br* a vest; *also* a similar garment worn by athletes [*single* + *-et* (as in *doublet*); (2) fr its having only one thickness of cloth]
**singleton** /'sing-glt(ə)n/ *n* **1** a card that is the only one of its suit in a dealt hand **2** an individual as opposed to a pair or group; *specif* an offspring born singly [¹*single* + *-ton* (as in *simpleton*)]
**,single-'track** *adj* **1** having only one track ⟨~ *railway*⟩ **2** absorbed in only one thing; one-track ⟨*a* ~ *approach to the problem*⟩
**singletree** /'sing-gl,tree/ *n, chiefly NAm* WHIFFLETREE (bar to which the straps of a horse's harness are fastened)
**singly** /'sing-gli/ *adv* **1** in isolation from others; individually **2** single-handed
**singsong** /'sing,song/ *n* **1** a manner of speaking characterized by a rise and fall in pitch or a monotonous rhythm of the voice **2** a session of group singing – **singsong, singsongy** *adj*
**singspiel** /'sing,shpeel (Ger 'zi-)/ *n* a usu comic dramatic musical work popular in Germany, esp in the latter part of the 18th century, consisting of spoken dialogue interspersed with popular or folk songs [Ger, fr *singen* to sing + *spiel* play]
**singular** /'sing-gyoolə/ *adj* **1a** of a separate person or thing; individual **b** *linguistics* of or being a word form (eg *I, house, cow, is*) denoting one person, thing, or instance **c** of a single instance or something considered by itself; not general ⟨*a* ~ *proposition in logic*⟩ **2** distinguished by superiority; exceptional ⟨*a man of* ~ *attainments*⟩ **3** set apart from everyday experience; extraordinary ⟨*on the way home we had a* ~ *adventure*⟩

**4** very unusual or strange; peculiar ⟨*the air had a ~ chill*⟩ ⟨*the ~ events leading up to the murder*⟩ **5** of or being esp a MATRIX (set of mathematical elements arranged in rows and columns) having a DETERMINANT equal to zero *synonyms* see STRANGE [ME *singuler*, fr MF, fr L *singularis*, fr *singulus* only one – more at SINGLE] – **singularly** *adv*, **singularize** *vt*
**singularity** /ˌsing-gyooˈlarəti/ *n* **1** something singular: eg **1a** a separate unit **b** an unusual or distinctive trait; a peculiarity **2** the quality or state of being singular **3** *maths* SINGULAR POINT **4** BLACK HOLE (hypothetical celestial body)
**singular point** *n* a point at which a mathematical function is undefined (eg by reason of division by zero or non-existence of a DERIVATIVE)
**Sinhalese** /ˌsinhəˈleez/, **Singhalese** /ˌsing-gəˈleez/ *n, pl* **Sinhalese, Singhalese 1** a member of a people that inhabit Sri Lanka and form a major part of its population **2** the INDIC (Indian branch of Indo-European) language of the Sinhalese [Skt *Siṁhala* Sri Lanka (Ceylon), island in the Indian Ocean] – **Sinhalese** *or* **Singhalese** *adj*
**sinister** /ˈsinistə/ *adj* **1** (darkly or insidiously) evil or productive of vice **2** of or situated on the left side or to the left of something, esp in heraldry – compare BEND SINISTER **3** threatening evil or ill fortune; ominous **4** *archaic* highly unfavourable; unlucky [ME *sinistre*, fr L *sinistr-*, *sinister* on the left side, unlucky, inauspicious] – **sinisterly** *adv*, **sinisterness** *n*
　　*synonyms* **Sinister, baleful, malign,** and **dire** all mean "threatening disaster". **Sinister** implies a lurking danger that shows itself only indirectly ⟨*a sinister figure robed in heavy black*⟩. **Baleful** and **malign** apply to the direct expression of ill will ⟨*baleful/malign glances*⟩ and **malign** and **dire** to what is in itself harmful ⟨*living in a malign environment*⟩. **Baleful** and **dire** apply also to prophecies of evil ⟨*proposals to substitute vaccination for eradication of the disease produced dire forecasts*⟩.
**sinistral** /ˈsinistrəl/ *adj* of or inclined to the left: eg **a** left-handed **b** *of a snail shell* having whorls turning from the right towards the left as viewed with the tip towards the observer – compare DEXTRAL **c** – **sinistrally** *adv*
**sinistrorse** /ˈsiniˌstraws, ˌ--ˈ-/ *adj* **1** *of a plant* twining spirally upwards round an axis from right to left – compare DEXTRORSE **2** SINISTRAL **b** [NL *sinistrorsus*, fr L, towards the left side, fr *sinistr-*, *sinister* + *versus*, pp of *vertere* to turn – more at WORTH]
**sinistrous** /ˈsinistrəs/ *adj, archaic* sinister
**Sinitic** /siˈnitik/ *adj* of the Chinese, their language, or their culture [LL *Sinae*, pl, Chinese + E *-itic* (as in *Semitic*) – more at SINOLOGUE]
**¹sink** /singk/ *vb* **sank** /sangk/, **sunk** /sungk/; **sunk** *vi* **1a**(1) to go down below a surface (eg of a liquid or soft substance); submerge **a**(2) to go to the bottom ⟨*the ship* sank *in heavy seas*⟩ **b** to become partly buried (eg in mud) ⟨sank *up to his ankles in the soft sand*⟩ **2a**(1) to fall or drop to a lower place or level ⟨sank *to her knees*⟩ ⟨*his voice* sank *to a whisper*⟩ **a**(2) to flow at a lower depth or level **b** to disappear from view ⟨*a red sun* ~ing *slowly in the west*⟩ **c** to take on a hollow appearance ⟨sunken *cheeks*⟩ **d** to subside gradually; settle ⟨*my cakes always* ~ *when they come out of the oven*⟩ **3** to become deeply absorbed ⟨sank *into a reverie*⟩ **4a** to go downwards in quality, state, or condition ⟨*~ into decay and eventual ruin* – Ivor Bulmer-Thomas⟩ ⟨sank *into apathy*⟩ **b** to grow less in amount or worth ⟨*profits* sank *to an all-time low*⟩ **5a** to become depressed ⟨*~ing spirits*⟩ **b** to deteriorate physically ⟨*the patient was* ~ing *fast and hadn't long to live*⟩ ~ *vt* **1a** to cause to sink ⟨*~ a battleship*⟩ **b** to force down, esp into the ground **c** to cause (something) to penetrate ⟨sank *the dagger into his chest*⟩ **2** to engage (oneself) completely in ⟨sank *himself in his work*⟩ **3a** to dig or bore (a well or shaft) in the earth; excavate **b** to form by cutting or excising ⟨*~ words in stone*⟩ **4** to overwhelm, defeat ⟨*if we don't reach the frontier by midnight we're* sunk⟩ **5** to lower in standing or reputation **6** to lower or soften (the voice) in speaking **7** to pay no heed to; ignore, suppress ⟨sank *their differences and signed the agreement*⟩ ⟨*wondered if she should* ~ *her dignity and give in*⟩ **8** to repay (eg a debt) **9** to invest ⟨sank *his savings in the business*⟩ **10** *chiefly Br* to drink down ⟨*~ a couple of pints of bitter*⟩ [ME *sinken*, fr OE *sincan*; akin to OHG *sinkan* to sink, Arm *ankanim* I fall] – **sinkable** *adj*
　　*usage* The usual past tense today is **sank** ⟨*they* sank *a frigate*⟩ and the past participle is **sunk** ⟨*the frigate has* sunk⟩. The related adjective **sunken** is used only before a noun, and is the usual choice where no human agency is involved ⟨sunken *cheeks*⟩.

**sink in** *vi* **1** to enter a solid through its surface ⟨*don't leave the ink to* sink in⟩ **2** to become understood ⟨*the lesson had* sunk in⟩
**²sink** *n* **1a** a pool or pit for the deposit of waste or sewage; a cesspool **b** a ditch or tunnel for carrying off sewage; a sewer **c** a basin, esp in a kitchen, connected to a drain and usu a water supply for washing **2** a place of vice or corruption **3** the lowest part of a mine shaft into which water drains; a sump **4a** a depression in the land surface where water collects; *esp* one having a saltwater lake with no outlet **b** a sinkhole **5** a body or process that acts as a storage device or disposal mechanism: eg **5a** HEAT SINK; *broadly* a device that collects or disperses energy (eg radiation) **b** a reactant with or absorber of a substance ⟨*soil is a ~ for carbon dioxide*⟩
**sinkage** /ˈsingkij/ *n* **1** the process or degree of sinking **2** a sunken area; a depression
**sinker** /ˈsingkə/ *n* **1** one who or that which sinks; *specif* a weight for sinking a fishing line, SEINE (large net that hangs vertically in the water), etc **2** *NAm informal* a doughnut – see also HOOK, **line, and sinker**
**sinkhole** /ˈsingk,hohl/ *n* **1** a hollow place or depression in which drainage collects **2** a hollow, esp in a limestone region, that communicates with an underground cavern or passage
**sinking fund** /ˈsingking/ *n, economics* a fund set up and added to by usu regular deposits for paying off the original capital sum of a debt
**sinless** /ˈsinlis/ *adj* free from sin; innocent – **sinlessly** *adv*, **sinlessness** *n*
**sinner** /ˈsinə/ *n* someone who sins; a wrongdoer; *broadly* a person, individual ⟨*so which of you miserable ~s is going to buy me another drink?*⟩
**Sino-** /sienoh-/ *comb form* **1** Chinese nation, people, or culture ⟨Sino*phile*⟩ **2** Chinese and ⟨Sino-*Tibetan*⟩ [Fr, fr LL *Sinae*]
**sinoatrial** /ˌsienohˈaytriəl/ *adj* of, involving, or being the SINOATRIAL NODE ⟨*~ block*⟩ [NL *sinus* + *atrium*]
**sinoatrial node** *n* a small mass of tissue that is embedded in the muscles of the upper righthand chamber of the heart of birds and mammals and that acts as a PACEMAKER by originating the impulses stimulating the heartbeat
**sinologue** /ˈsienəlog, ˈsinə-/ *n* a specialist in sinology; a sinologist [Fr, fr LL *Sinae*, pl, Chinese (fr Gk *Sinai*, fr Ar *Sīn* China) + Fr *-logue*]
**sinology** /sieˈnoləji, si-/ *n* the study of the Chinese and esp of their language, literature, history, and culture – **sinological** *adj*, **sinologist** *n*
**sinopia** /siˈnohpiə/ *n, pl* **sinopias, sinopie** /-piay/ a red to reddish-brown powdered colouring substance obtained from soil containing the red-coloured chemical compound FERRIC OXIDE, that was used in fresco painting in the 13th and 14th centuries [It, fr L *sinopis*, fr Gk *sinōpis*, fr *Sinōpē* Sinope, ancient seaport in Asia Minor]
**Sino-Tibetan** /ˌsienoh tiˈbet(ə)n/ *adj or n* (of or being) a language family comprising Tibeto-Burman and Chinese
**sinsyne** /sinˈsien/ *adv, chiefly Scot* since that time [ME (Sc) *sensyne*, fr *sen* since (contr of ME *sithen*) + *syne* since – more at SINCE, SYNE]
**¹sinter** /ˈsintə/ *n* a silicon- or calcium-containing deposit formed by the evaporation of (hot) spring water [Ger, fr OHG *sintar* slag – more at CINDER]
**²sinter** *vb* to make into or become a coherent mass by heating without melting – **sinterability** *n*
**sinuate** /ˈsinyoo,ayt/ *adj, of a leaf* having a wavy edge with strong indentations [L *sinuatus*, pp of *sinuare* to bend, fr *sinus* curve] – **sinuately** *adv*
**sinuatrial** /ˌsienyooˈaytriəl, ˌsinyoo-/ *adj* sinoatrial
**sinuosity** /ˌsinyooˈosəti/ *n* **1** the quality or state of being sinuous **2** something that is sinuous; a bend, curve
**sinuous** /ˈsinyoo·əs/ *adj* **1a** of or having a serpentine or wavy form; winding **b** lithe, supple ⟨*dancers with a ~ grace*⟩ **2** intricate, tortuous ⟨*~ argumentation*⟩ [L *sinuosus*, fr *sinus*] – **sinuously** *adv*, **sinuousness** *n*
**sinus** /ˈsienəs/ *n* a cavity, hollow: eg **a** a narrow passage by which pus is discharged from a deep abscess or boil **b**(1) any of several cavities in the substance of a bone of the skull that usu communicate with the nostrils and contain air **b**(2) a channel for blood returning to the heart (eg a BLOOD VESSEL) **b**(3) a widening in a body duct or tube (eg a BLOOD VESSEL) **c** a cleft or indentation between adjoining lobes (eg of a leaf) [NL, fr L, curve, fold, hollow]
**sinusitis** /ˌsienəˈsietis/ *n* inflammation of a sinus in the nose [NL]

**sinusoid** /'sienə,soyd/ *n* **1** *maths* SINE CURVE **2** a minute space or passage for blood in the tissues of an organ (e g the liver) [(1) ML *sinus* sine; (2) NL *sinus*] – **sinusoidal** *adj*, **sinusoidally** *adv*

**sinusoidal projection** /,sienə'soydl/ *n* an equal-area map projection capable of showing the entire surface of the earth with all parallels as evenly spaced straight lines, the central MERIDIAN (imaginary semicircle passing through both poles) as one half the length of the equator, and all other meridians as curved lines

**sinus venosus** /vi'nohsəs/ *n* an enlarged pouch that adjoins the heart, is formed by the union of the large SYSTEMIC veins, and is the passage through which blood from the veins enters the heart in fish, amphibians, and reptiles and in the embryos of birds and mammals [NL, venous sinus]

**Sion** /'sie·ən/ *n* Zion

**Siouan** /'sooh·ən/ *n* **1** a language family or group of central and eastern N America **2** a member of any of the peoples speaking Siouan languages – **Siouan** *adj*

**Sioux** /sooh/ *n, pl* **Sioux** /sooh, soohz/ **1** a N American Indian tribe; the Dakota **2** Siouan [Fr, short for *Nadowessioux*, fr Ojibwa *Nadoweisiw*]

**¹sip** /sip/ *vb* **-pp-** *vi* to take a sip of something, esp repeatedly ~ *vt* **1** to drink delicately or a little at a time **2** to take sips from [ME *sippen;* akin to LG *sippen* to sip] – **sipper** *n*

**²sip** *n* (a small quantity imbibed by) sipping

**¹siphon, syphon** /'siefən/ *n* **1a** a tube bent to form two vertical legs of unequal length by which a liquid can be transferred over the wall of a container to a lower level by using atmospheric pressure **b** a bottle for holding aerated water that is driven out through a tube by the pressure of the gas when a valve in the tube is opened **2** any of various tubular organs in animals, esp clams, mussels, oysters, etc, that are used for drawing in or ejecting fluids [Fr *siphon*, fr L *siphon-*, *sipho* tube, pipe, siphon, fr Gk *siphōn*]

**²siphon, syphon** *vt* to convey, draw off, or empty (as if) by a siphon ~ *vi* to pass or become conveyed (as if) by a siphon

**siphonophore** /'sie'fonəfaw, 'siefə-/ *n* any of an order (Siphonophora of the class Hydrozoa) of compound free-swimming or floating marine INVERTEBRATE animals related to jellyfish that are mostly delicate, transparent, and coloured and that are made up of a collection (COLONY) of specialized individuals [deriv of Gk *siphōn* + *pherein* to carry – more at BEAR]

**siphonostele** /'siefənə,steel/ *n* a cylindrical column of stem tissue (STELE) consisting of a central core of pith surrounded by vessels for transporting water and nutrients through the plant [Gk *siphōn* tube, siphon] – **siphonostely** *n*, **siphonostelic** *adj*

**sippet** /'sipit/ *n, chiefly Br* **1** a small usu triangular piece of dry toast or fried bread used esp for garnishing **2** a piece of food (e g bread) dipped in gravy, soup, etc [irreg fr *sop* + *-et*]

**sir** /sə/; *strong* suh/ *n* **1a** *cap* – used as a title before the Christian name of a knight or baronet and before the name of a man addressed as *Sir* ⟨*the proprietor was now a* ~ – Max Beerbohm⟩ **2a** – used without a name as a form of respectful or polite address to a man ⟨*can I help you,* ~?⟩ **b** *cap* – used with *Dear* as a conventional form of address at the beginning of a letter **3** *archaic* a man of rank or position [ME, fr *sire*]
*usage* One can say **sir** before a man's first name ⟨**Sir** *John*⟩ or before his whole name ⟨**Sir** *John Falstaff*⟩, but not before his surname alone ⟨⚠ **Sir** *Falstaff*⟩.

**sirdar** /'suh,dah, ,-'-/ *n* **1** somebody of high rank (e g a hereditary noble or military chief), esp in India **2** somebody holding a position of authority in India: eg **2a** a foreman **b** TENANT FARMER [Hindi *sardār*, fr Per]

**¹sire** /sie·ə/ *n* **1** the male parent of a (domestic) animal **2** *archaic* **2a** a father **b** a male ancestor **c** an originator, author ⟨*the* ~ *of an immortal strain* – P B Shelley⟩ **3** *archaic* a man of rank or authority; *esp* a lord – used as a title and form of address [ME, father, master, fr OF, fr L *senior* older – more at SENIOR]

**²sire** *vt* **1** to beget – esp with reference to a male domestic animal **2** to bring into being; originate

**siree** /sə'ree/ *n* sirree

**siren** /'sierən/ *n* **1** *often cap* any of a group of partly human female creatures in Greek mythology that lured mariners to destruction by their singing **2a** a woman who sings with bewitching sweetness **b** a dangerously alluring or seductive woman; a temptress **3a** an apparatus producing musical tones by the rapid interruption of a current of air, steam, etc by a perforated rotating disc **b** a usu electrically operated device for producing a penetrating warning sound ⟨*an ambulance* ~⟩ ⟨*air-raid* ~ s⟩ **4** any of a genus (*Siren*) of eel-shaped amphibians with small forelimbs but neither hind legs nor pelvis and with permanent external gills as well as lungs [ME, fr MF & L; MF *sereine*, fr LL *sirena*, fr L *siren*, fr Gk *seirēn*; (3) Fr *sirène*, fr MF *sereine*; (4) NL, genus name, fr L]

**sirenian** /sie'reenyən, -ni·ən/ *n* any of an order (Sirenia) of aquatic plant-eating mammals including the manatee and dugong [NL *Sirenia*, order name, fr L *siren*]

**siren suit** *n* a one-piece garment like a BOILER SUIT with usu a zip in the front from the crotch to the neck edge so that it can be easily put on and taken off [fr its being easy to put on when an air-raid siren sounded]

**sirloin** /'suh,loyn/ *n* a cut of beef from the upper part of the hind LOIN (lower back between the ribs and hips) just in front of the rump [alter. (prob influenced by supposed derivation fr "Sir Loin" – cf BARON) of earlier *surloin*, modif of MF *surlonge*, fr *sur* over (fr L *super*) + *loigne*, *longe* loin – more at OVER]

**sirocco** /si'rokoh/ *n, pl* **siroccos** **1a** a hot dust-laden wind from the Libyan deserts that blows onto the N Mediterranean coast chiefly in Italy, Malta, and Sicily **b** a warm moist oppressive southeasterly wind in the same regions **2** a hot or warm wind originating from a cyclone in an arid or heated region *synonyms* see WIND [It *scirocco*, *sirocco*, fr Ar *sharq* east]

**sirrah** *also* **sirra** /'sirə/ *n, obs* – used as a form of address implying inferiority in the person addressed [alter. of *sir*]

**sirree** *also* **siree** /sə'ree/ *n, NAm* sir – used for emphasis, usu after *yes* or *no* [by alter.]

**'sir-,reverence** *n, obs* – used as an expression of apology before a statement that might be taken as offensive [prob alter. (influenced by *sir*) of *save-reverence*, trans of ML *salva reverentia* saving (your) reverence]

**Sir Roger de Coverley** /di 'kuvəli/ *n* an English country-dance in which dancing partners face one another in two rows [alter. (influenced by *Sir Roger de Coverley*, fictitious country gentleman appearing in early 18th-c essays by Joseph Addison and Sir Richard Steele) of earlier *roger of coverly*, prob fr *Roger* (male forename) + *of* + *Coverly*, a place name (perh alter. of *Calverley* in Yorkshire or *Cowley* in Oxfordshire)]

**sirup** /'sirəp/ *n, NAm* (a) syrup – **sirupy** *adj*

**sirvente** /sə'vent/ **sirventes** /-teez/ *n, pl* **sirventes** /-teez/ a usu moral or religious song of the French Provençal troubadours satirizing social vices [Fr, fr Prov *sirventes*, lit., servant's song, fr *sirvent* servant, fr L *servient-*, *serviens*, prp of *servire* to serve]

**sis** /sis/ *n, chiefly NAm informal* sister – used esp in direct address

**-sis** /-sis/ *suffix* (→ *n*) *pl* **-ses** /-seez/ process or action of ⟨*peristalsis*⟩ [L, fr Gk, fem suffix of action]

**sisal** /'siesl/ *n* **1** a strong durable white fibre used esp for ropes and twine **2** a widely cultivated W Indian plant (*Agave sisalana*) of the amaryllis family whose leaves yield sisal; *also* any of several fibres similar to true sisal [MexSp, fr *Sisal*, port in Yucatán, Mexico]

**siskin** /'siskin/ *n* a small sharp-beaked chiefly greenish and yellowish finch (*Carduelis spinus*) of temperate Europe and Asia that is related to the goldfinch [Ger dial. *sisschen*, dim. of MHG *zīse* siskin, of Slav origin; akin to Czech *čížek* siskin]

**sissy** /'sissi/ *n or adj* (a) cissy

**¹sister** /'sistə/ *n* **1a** a female having the same parents as another **b** a female having only one parent in common with another; HALF SISTER **2** *often cap* **2a** a member of a women's religious order; *specif* (the title given to) a female fellow member of a Christian church **b** a Roman Catholic nun **3** a woman related to another by a common tie or interest (e g adherence to feminist principles) **4** *chiefly Br* a female nurse; *esp* one who is next in rank below a NURSING OFFICER and is in charge of a ward or a small department **5** *informal* a girl, woman – used esp in direct address [ME *suster*, *sister*, partly fr OE *sweostor* and partly fr ON *systir* sister; akin to L *soror* sister] – **sisterly** *adj*

**²sister** *adj* related (as if) by sisterhood; essentially similar ⟨~ *ships*⟩

**sisterhood** /'sistəhood/ *n* **1a** the state of being a sister **b** sisterly relationship **2** *taking sing or pl vb* a community or society of sisters; *specif* a society of women bound by religious vows **3** *the* women's movement ⟨*the* ~ *is powerful!*⟩

**'sister-in-,law** *n, pl* **sisters-in-law 1** the sister of one's husband or wife **2a** the wife of one's brother **b** the wife of one's husband's or wife's brother

**sister of mercy** *n* a nun engaged in educational or charitable work

**Sistine** /ˌsistien,ˈsisteen/ *adj* 1 of any of the popes named Sixtus 2 of the Sistine chapel in the Vatican [It *sistino,* fr NL *sixtinus,* fr *Sixtus,* name of five popes (including *Sixtus IV* †1484 builder of the Sistine Chapel)]

**sistrum** /ˈsistrəm/ *n, pl* **sistrums, sistra** /ˈsistrə/ an ancient percussion instrument, used esp in Egypt, and consisting of a thin metal frame with numerous metal rods or loops that jingle when shaken [ME, fr L, fr Gk *seistron,* fr *seiein* to shake – more at SEISM]

**Sisyphean, Sisyphian** /ˌsisiˈfee-ən/ *adj* both endless and fruitless ⟨*a ~ task*⟩ [*Sisyphus* (Gk *Sisyphos*), mythical king of Corinth condemned in Hades to roll uphill a heavy stone that constantly rolled down again]

**¹sit** /sit/ *vb* **-tt-; sat** *vi* **1a** to rest on the buttocks or haunches ⟨*~ in a chair*⟩ **b** to perch, roost **2** to occupy a place as a member of an official body ⟨*~ on the parish council*⟩ **3** to be in session for official business ⟨*lives in Chelsea when Parliament is ~*ting⟩ **4** to cover eggs for hatching; brood **5a** to take up a position for being painted or photographed **b** to act or serve as a model **6a** to lie or hang relative to a wearer ⟨*the collar ~s awkwardly*⟩ **b** to affect one (as if) with weight ⟨*the food sat heavily on his stomach*⟩ **7** to lie, rest ⟨*a kettle ~*ting *on the stove*⟩ **8** to be situated ⟨*the house ~s well back from the road*⟩ **9** to remain inactive or unused ⟨*the car just ~s in the garage all day*⟩ **10** to take an examination; be an examination candidate – usu + *for* ⟨*sat for an Oxford scholarship*⟩ **11** to baby-sit ~ *vt* **1** to cause to be seated; place on or in a seat **2** to sit on (eggs) **3** to keep one's seat on ⟨*he ~s a horse very well*⟩ **4** *Br* to take part in (an examination) as a candidate ⟨*is going to ~ ten O Levels this summer*⟩ – see also **sit on** the FENCE/**on one's HANDS**, **sitting** PRETTY, **sit** TIGHT *usage* see ¹SET [ME *sitten,* fr OE *sittan;* akin to OHG *sizzen* to sit, L *sedēre,* Gk *hezesthai* to sit, *hedra* seat]

**sit back** *vi* to relinquish one's efforts or responsibility ⟨*magistrates who sit back and accept police objections – Yorkshire Post*⟩

**sit down** *vb* to seat or become seated – see also SIT-DOWN

**sit in** *vi* to stage an occupation of one's place of work or study as a protest – see also SIT-IN

**sit in on** *vt* to participate in as a visitor or observer ⟨*sit in on a group discussion*⟩

**sit on** *vt* **1** to repress, squash **2** to delay action or decision concerning

**sit out** *vt* **1** to refrain from participating in, esp by remaining seated ⟨*sit the next dance out*⟩ **2** to remain until the end of or the departure of ⟨*sit the film out*⟩

**sit up** *vi* **1a** to rise from a reclining to a sitting position **b** to sit with the back straight **2** to show interest, alertness, or surprise ⟨*news that made him sit up*⟩ **3** to stay up after the usual time for going to bed ⟨*sat up to watch the late film*⟩

**²sit** *n* an act or period of sitting ⟨*had a long ~ at the station between trains*⟩

**sitar** /siˈtah/ *n* an Indian lute with a long neck and a varying number of strings [Hindi *sitār*] – **sitarist** *n*

**sitcom** /ˈsit,kom/ *n* SITUATION COMEDY [*situation comedy*]

**'sit-,down** *n* **1** sit-down, **sit-down strike** a strike by workers while continuing to occupy their place of employment as a protest and a means of forcing their employer to comply with their demands **2** *informal* a period of sitting ⟨*after our long walk we welcomed a cup of tea and a ~*⟩

**¹site** /siet/ *n* **1a** an area of ground that was, is, or will be occupied by a structure or set of structures (eg a building, town, or monument) ⟨*an archaeological ~*⟩ **b** an area of ground or scene of some specified activity ⟨*caravan ~*⟩ ⟨*battle ~*⟩ ⟨*building ~*⟩ **2** the place, scene, or point of something ⟨*the ~ of the wound*⟩ [ME, place, position, fr MF or L; MF, fr L *situs,* fr *situs,* pp of *sinere* to leave, place, lay; akin to L *serere* to sow – more at SOW]

**²site** *vt* to place on a site or in position; locate △ cite

**sith** /sith/ *adv, prep, or conj, archaic* since

**'sit-,in** *n* a continuous occupation of a building by a body of people as a protest and means towards forcing compliance with demands – compare WORK-IN

**Sitka spruce** /ˈsitkə/ *n* a tall spruce tree (*Picea sitchensis*) native to N America that has thin reddish-brown bark and flat needles [*Sitka,* town in Alaska]

**sitosterol** /sieˈtostə,rol/ *n* any of several STEROLS (fat-containing chemical compounds) that are widespread, esp in plant products (eg WHEAT GERM or SOYA-BEAN OIL), and are used as starting materials for the synthesis of STEROID drugs [Gk *sitos* grain + E *sterol*]

**sitter** /ˈsitə/ *n* **1** somebody that sits (eg as an artist's model) **2** a baby-sitter **3** *informal* an easy chance or opportunity, esp when missed: eg **3a** an easy shot at goal in soccer **b** an easy catch in cricket **c** SITTING DUCK

**¹sitting** /ˈsiting/ *n* **1** a single occasion of continuous sitting (eg for a portrait or meal) **2a** a brooding over eggs for hatching **b** a batch of eggs for incubation **3** a session ⟨*a Parliamentary ~*⟩

**²sitting** *adj* **1** that is sitting ⟨*a ~ hen*⟩ **2** in office or actual possession of a seat ⟨*the ~ member for Leeds East*⟩ **3a** used in or for sitting ⟨*a ~ position*⟩ **b** performed while sitting ⟨*a ~ shot*⟩ [(1,2) fr prp of ¹*sit;* (3) fr gerund of ¹*sit*]

**sitting duck** *n* an easy or defenceless target for attack, criticism, or exploitation

**sitting room** *n* a room, esp in a private house, used for recreation and relaxation

**synonyms** Some people prefer to use **sitting room** or **living room** for the room where one relaxes in one's home, rather than **lounge**, which they regard as a genteelism in this sense. **Lounge** is the usual word for a room in a public place where one can sit comfortably ⟨*hotel* **lounge**⟩ ⟨*airport departure* **lounge**⟩. **Living room** may be preferred to **sitting room** where the only other rooms are kitchen, bathroom, and bedrooms. **Drawing room** is either a rather formal word for **sitting room** or suggestive of a larger and grander room.

**sitting target** *n* SITTING DUCK

**sitting tenant** *n, Br* a tenant who is at the present time in occupation (eg of a house or flat)

**sitting trot** *n* a trot in which the rider does not rise from the saddle

**¹situate** /ˈsityoo,ayt, ˈsichoo-, -ət/ *adj, formal* having a site; located [ML *situatus,* pp of *situare* to place, fr L *situs*]

**²situate** /ˈsityoo,ayt, ˈsichoo-/ *vt* to place in a site, situation, or category; locate

**situated** /ˈsityoo,aytid, ˈsichoo-/ *adj* **1** located **2** supplied to the specified extent with money or possessions ⟨*comfortably ~*⟩ **3** being in the specified situation ⟨*rather awkwardly ~*⟩

**situation** /ˌsityooˈaysh(ə)n, ˌsichoo-/ *n* **1a** the way in which something is placed in relation to its surroundings **b** a locality ⟨*a house in a windswept ~*⟩ **2** position in life; status **3** position with respect to conditions and circumstances ⟨*the military ~ remains obscure*⟩ **4a** the circumstances at a particular moment; *esp* a critical or problematic state of affairs ⟨*the ~ called for swift action*⟩ **b** a particular (complicated) state of affairs at a stage in the action of a narrative or drama **5** *formal* a position of employment; a post ⟨*found a ~ as a gardener*⟩ **6** *archaic* a condition; *esp* state of health – **situational** *adj,* **situationally** *adv*

**usage** The excessive use of both **situation** and **position** in the sense "state of affairs" ⟨*in a face-to-face* **situation**⟩ ⟨*the* **position** *in regard to exports*⟩ is widely disliked as a cliché. **synonyms** see ¹STATE

**situation comedy** *n* a radio or television comedy series that involves the same basic cast of characters in a succession of connected or unconnected episodes – called also SITCOM

**'sit-,up** *n* **1** the movement of raising the upper body into a sitting position from a position lying flat on the back, without bending the legs **2** *pl* a series of situps performed as an exercise to improve physical fitness

**situs** /ˈsietəs/ *n* the place where something exists or originates; *specif* the place where something (eg a right) is held to be located in law [L – more at SITE]

**sitz bath** /sits, zits/ *n* a tub in which one baths in a sitting posture; *also* a bath so taken, esp therapeutically [part trans of Ger *sitzbad,* fr *sitz* act of sitting + *bad* bath]

**SI unit** *n* any of an internationally agreed system of units used widely in science and technology, that is based on the metre-kilogram-second system, has the metre, kilogram, second, ampere, kelvin, mole, and candela as its basic units, and uses standard prefixes (eg micro-, kilo-, and mega-) to indicate multiples or fractions of 10 [Fr *Système International d'Unités* international system of units]

**Sivan** /seeˈvahn/ *n* – see MONTH table [Heb *Sīwān*]

**six** /siks/ *n* **1** – see NUMBER table **2** the sixth in a set or series ⟨*the ~ of spades*⟩ **3** something having six parts or members or a denomination of six: eg **3a** an ice-hockey team **b** a 6-cylinder engine or motor car **c** a shot in cricket that crosses the boundary before it bounces and so scores six runs – compare BOUNDARY, FOUR **d** the smallest unit in the organization of a cub-scout or brownie-guide pack **4** *taking pl vb, cap the* Common Market countries prior to 1973 [ME, fr *six*, adj, fr OE *six, siex*; akin to OHG *sehs* six, L *sex*, Gk *hex*] – **six** *adj or pron,* **sixfold** *adj or adv* – **at sixes and sevens** in disorder; confused [orig a phrase used in dicing] – **for six** so as to be totally wrecked or defeated ⟨*trade balance went* for six – *The Economist*⟩ [*six* 3c] – **six of the best** *Br* a severe beating, usu consisting of six strokes with a cane

**sixer** /'siksə/ *n* the leader of a cub-scout or brownie-guide six

**'six-,gun** *n* a 6-chambered revolver

**sixmo** /'siksmoh/ *n, pl* **sixmos** the size of a piece of paper cut six from a sheet of standard size; *also* a book, a page, or paper of this size

**'six-,pack** *n* (a container for) 6 bottles or cans sold as a single item

**sixpence** /,siks'pəns/ *n* a small coin worth six old pence

**sixpenny** /'sikspəni/ *adj* costing or worth sixpence

**'six-,shooter** *n* a six-gun

**sixteen** /,sik'steen/ *n* – see NUMBER table [ME *sixtene*, fr OE *sixtȳne*, adj, fr *six* + *tīen* ten] – **sixteen** *adj or pron,* **sixteenth** *adj or n*

**sixteenmo** /,sik'steenmoh/ *n, pl* **sixteenmos 1** the size of a piece of paper cut 16 from a sheet of standard size; *also* a book, a page, or paper of this size **2** a book format in which a folded sheet forms eight leaves; *also* a book in this format

**sixteens** /'sik'steenz/ *n* a book format in which a folded sheet forms 16 leaves

**sixteenth note** /siks'teenth/ *n, NAm* a semiquaver

**sixteenth rest** *n, NAm* a musical REST (indicating silence) of the same time value as a semiquaver

**sixth** /siksth/ *n* **1** – see NUMBER table **2** *music* **2a** a musical interval between one note and another six notes away from it counting inclusively in a DIATONIC scale (ordinary 8-note scale) **b** a note six notes away from another counting inclusively; *specif* the note six notes away from the first note (TONIC) of a scale; SUBMEDIANT **c** the harmonic combination of two notes a sixth apart – **sixth** *adj or adv,* **sixthly** *adv*

usage The pronunciation /siks/ should be avoided in careful speech.

**sixth form** *n taking sing or pl vb* the highest section of a British secondary school that is usu entered at about age 16 after taking Ordinary level – **sixth-former** *n*

**sixth form college** *n* a British state school for pupils beyond age 16

**sixth sense** *n* a keen intuitive power viewed as analogous to the five physical senses ⟨*some ~ told him that danger was near*⟩

**Sixtine** /'siksteen/ *adj* sistine

**sixty** /'siksti/ *n* **1** – see NUMBER table **2** *pl* the numbers 60-69; *specif* a range of temperatures, ages, or dates in a century characterized by those numbers [ME, fr *sixty*, adj, fr OE *siextig*, n, group of sixty, fr *siex* six + *-tig* [1]-ty] – **sixtieth** *adj or n,* **sixty** *adj or pron,* **sixtyfold** *adj or adv*

**,sixty-'fourth note** *n, NAm* a hemidemisemiquaver

**,sixty-'fourth rest** *n, NAm* a musical REST (indicating silence) of the same time value as a hemidemisemiquaver

**,sixty-'nine** *n* SOIXANTE-NEUF

**sizable, sizeable** /'siezəbl/ *adj* fairly large; considerable – **sizableness** *n,* **sizably** *adv*

**sizar, sizer** /'siezə/ *n* a poor student (eg at Cambridge) who paid lower fees and originally acted as a servant to other students in return [*sizar* alter. of *sizer*, fr [1]*size* (in arch. sense, "allowance of food and drink, esp to a university student")]

**'size** /siez/ *n* **1a** physical magnitude, extent, or bulk; relative or proportionate dimensions **b** relative amount or number **c** bigness ⟨*you should have seen the ~ of him*⟩ **2** any of a series of graduated measures, esp of manufactured articles (eg of clothing), conventionally identified by numbers or letters ⟨*a ~ 7 hat*⟩ **3** actual state of affairs ⟨*that's about the ~ of it*⟩ [ME *sise* assize, regulation, fixed standard of food and drink, magnitude, fr MF, fr OF, short for *assise* – more at ASSIZE] – **cut somebody down to size** to reduce somebody's pride or standing, esp by making him/her appear foolish – **try something on/out for size** to test for appropriateness or applicability

**²size** *vt* **1** to make in a particular size ⟨*systems ~d to fit anyone's living room*⟩ **2** to arrange or grade according to size or bulk

**size up** *vi* to conform to requirements or specification ~ *vt* **1** to form an opinion of **2** to estimate the size of

**³size** *n* any of various thick gluey materials (eg preparations

of glue, flour, varnish, or resins) used for filling the pores in surfaces (eg of paper, textiles, leather, or plaster) or for applying colour or metal leaf (eg to book edges or covers) [ME *sise*, prob fr MF, setting, fixing, fr OF, settlement, assize]

**⁴size** *vt* to coat, stiffen, or glaze (as if) with size

**⁵size** *adj* SIZED **1** – usu in combination ⟨*a bite-size biscuit*⟩

**sizeable** /'siezəbl/ *adj* sizable

**sized** /siezd/ *adj* **1** having a specified size or bulk – usu in combination ⟨*a medium-sized house*⟩ **2** arranged or graded according to size

**sizer** /'siezə/ *n* SIZAR (college servant)

**sizing** /'siezing/ *n* ³SIZE

**sizzle** /'sizl/ *vi* **1** to hiss and spit (as if) while frying **2** to be very hot **3** to seethe with deep anger or resentment ~ *vt* to cause to sizzle [perh freq of *siss* (to hiss), fr ME *sissen*, of imit origin] – **sizzle** *n,* **sizzler** *n*

**sizzling** /'sizling, 'sizl·ing/ *adj* **1** very hot **2** full of zest or pungency; racy ⟨*a jester of ~ personality* – Richard Buckle⟩

**sjambok** /'shambok/ *vt or n* -kk- *SAfr* (to beat with) a heavy leather whip, esp of rhinoceros or hippopotamus hide ⟨*. . . left home after her husband ~ked their pregnant daughter* – *Rand Daily Mail*⟩ [Afrik *sambok, sjambok*, fr Malay *cambok* large whip, fr Hindi *cābuk*]

**ska** /skah/ *n* popular music of W Indian origin that was the forerunner of REGGAE [Jamaican E, of imit origin]

**skag** /skag/ *n, nautical* SKEG (small fin)

**skail** /skayl/ *vb, Scot* to disperse, scatter [ME *skailen, scalen,* prob of Scand origin; akin to ON *skilja* to separate, divide]

**skald, scald** /skawld, skold/ *n* a composer and reciter of heroic poetry in ancient Scandinavia; *broadly* a bard [ON *skāld* – more at SCOLD] – **skaldic** *adj*

**skat** /skat/ *n* **1** a 3-handed card game played with 32 cards in which players bid for the privilege of attempting any of several contracts **2** an extra hand of two cards in skat that may be used by the winner of the bid [Ger, modif of It *scarto* discard, fr *scartare* to discard, fr *s-* (fr L *ex-*) + *carta* card]

**¹skate** /skayt/ *n, pl* **skate,** *esp for different types* **skates** any of numerous ray fishes (eg of the genus *Raja*) having large flat PECTORAL FINS and a short tail, many of which are important food fishes [ME *scate*, fr ON *skata*]

**²skate** *n* **1a** ROLLER SKATE **b** ICE SKATE **2** a period of skating [modif of D *schaats* stilt, skate, fr (assumed) ONF *escache* stilt; akin to OF *eschace* stilt] – **get/put one's skates on** *informal* to hurry up

**³skate** *vi* **1a** to move along on skates by gliding the feet forwards alternately **b** to perform specific movements on skates, as in FIGURE SKATING **2** to glide or slide over a surface ~ *vt* to go along (a place or distance) or perform (an action) by skating ⟨*~d the length of the rink*⟩ – see also **skate on thin** ICE

**skate over/round** *vt* to avoid dealing with (problems, dangerous issues, etc); GLOSS OVER

**skate through** *vt* to achieve easy success in

**skateboard** /'skayt,bawd/ *n* a narrow board about 60 centimetres (2 feet) long mounted on roller-skate wheels and ridden, usu standing up, for sport – **skateboarder** *n,* **skateboarding** *n*

**skater** /'skaytə/ *n* **1** one who skates **2** POND SKATER (type of insect)

**skating** /'skayting/ *n* the act, art, or sport of gliding on skates

**skating rink** *n* RINK 1b

**skatole** *also* **skatol** /'skatohl/ *n* a foul-smelling compound, $C_9H_9N$, found in the intestines and faeces, in the musky substance produced by CIVET CATS, and in several plants, or made synthetically, and used in perfumes as a fixative [ISV, fr Gk *skat-, skōr* excrement – more at SCAT-]

**skean, skene** /skeen/ *n* **1** a Gaelic dagger; DIRK **2** SKEAN DHU [IrGael *scian* & ScGael *sgian*]

**skean dhu** /skeen 'dhooh/ *n* a dagger worn by Scottish Highlanders in full dress [ScGael *sgian dubh*, lit., black dagger]

**skedaddle** /ski'dadl/ *vi, informal* to run away; *specif* to scatter – often imper [origin unknown] – **skedaddle** *n,* **skedaddler** *n*

**skeet** /skeet/, **skeet shooting** *n* clay-pigeon shooting in which targets are hurled across the shooting range from traps on either side to simulate the flight of birds [modif of ON *skjōta* to shoot – more at SHOOT]

**¹skeeter** /'skeetə/ *n, chiefly Austr & NAm* a mosquito [by shortening & alter.]

**²skeeter** *n* a skeet shooter

**skeg** /skeg/ *n* **1** a small fin fixed to the rear end of a yacht's keel 2 a fin situated on the bottom of a surfboard at the back that is used for steering and to give stability □ **called also** SKAG [D *scheg;* akin to OSlav *skokŭ* leap – more at SHAG]

**skeigh** /skeekh/ *adj, chiefly Scot, esp of a horse or woman* proudly spirited; skittish [perh of Scand origin; akin to Sw *skygg* shy; akin to OE *scēoh* shy – more at SHY]

**skein** /skayn/ *n* **1** a loosely coiled length of yarn or thread; HANK 1 **2** something suggesting the twists or coils of a skein; a tangle ⟨*unravel the* ∼ *of evidence*⟩ **3** a flock of wildfowl (e g geese or ducks) in flight [ME *skeyne,* fr MF *escaigne*]

**skeletal** /'skelitl/ *adj* of, forming, attached to, or resembling a skeleton – **skeletally** *adv*

**¹skeleton** /'skelitn/ *n* **1a** a supportive or protective usu rigid structure or framework of an organism; *esp* the bony or more or less cartilaginous framework supporting the soft tissues and protecting the internal organs of a VERTEBRATE animal (e g a fish or mammal) **b** a set of real or replica bones of a human being or animal joined together in their correct positions, esp for medical study **2** something reduced to its bare essentials; an outline **3** an extremely thin person or animal **4a** a basic structural framework **b** the straight or branched chain or ring of atoms that forms the basic structure of a carbon-containing molecule [NL, fr Gk, neut of *skeletos* dried up; akin to Gk *skellein* to dry up, *sklēros* hard, OE *sceald* shallow] – **skeletonic** *adj* – **skeleton in the cupboard,** *NAm* **skeleton in the closet** a secret cause of shame, esp in a family

**²skeleton** *adj* reduced to the bare essentials; minimal ⟨*ran a* ∼ *service during the strike*⟩

**skeleton·ize, -ise** /'skelitəniez/ *vt* to produce in or reduce to skeleton form ⟨∼ *a leaf*⟩ ⟨∼ *a news story*⟩

**skeleton·izer, -iser** /'skelitəniezə/ *n* any of various larvae of butterflies or moths that eat the PARENCHYMA (soft plant tissue) of leaves reducing them to a skeleton of veins

**skeleton key** *n* a key, esp one with most or all of the serrations absent, that is able to open many simple locks

**skeleton shrimp** *n* any of various slender marine shrimplike animals (*Caprella* and related genera of the order Amphipoda, class Crustacea) that are found on seaweed and branching plantlike organisms (e g HYDROIDS and BRYOZOANS)

**skellum** /'skeləm/ *n, chiefly Scot* a scamp, rascal [D *schelm,* fr LG; akin to OHG *skelmo* person deserving death]

**skelp** /skelp/ *vt* **skelped** *also* **skelpit** /'skelpit/ *chiefly Scot* to slap, spank [ME *skelpen,* prob of imit origin] – **skelp** *n*

**skelter** /'skeltə/ *vi* to scurry [fr *-skelter* (in *helter-skelter*)]

**skep** /skep/ *n* **1** a farm basket used esp in mucking out stables **2** a beehive; *esp* a domed hive made of twisted straw [ME *skeppe* basket, basketful, fr OE *sceppe,* fr ON *skeppa* bushel; akin to OE *scieppan* to form, create – more at SHAPE]

**skepsis** /'skepsis/ *n, chiefly NAm* SCEPSIS (philosophical doubt)

**skeptic** /'skeptik/ *n, chiefly NAm* a sceptic – **skeptical** *adj,* **skeptically** *adv*

**skepticism** /'skeptisiz(ə)m/ *n, chiefly NAm* scepticism

**skerry** /'skeri/ *n, chiefly Scot* a rocky island; a reef [of Scand origin; akin to ON *sker* skerry & to ON *ey* island; akin to L *aqua* water – more at SCAR, ISLAND]

**¹sketch** /skech/ *n* **1a** a rough drawing representing the chief features of an object or scene and often made as a preliminary study **b** a tentative draft (e g for a literary work) **2** a brief description or outline ⟨*gave a* ∼ *of his personality*⟩ **3a** a short informal literary composition that is intentionally slight in treatment and discursive in style **b** a short evocative musical composition, usu for piano **c** a short theatrical piece having a single scene; *esp* a comic variety act [D *schets,* or It *schizzo,* fr *schizzare* to splash]

**²sketch** *vt* to make a sketch, rough draft, or outline of ∼ *vi* to draw or paint a sketch, esp of a landscape – **sketcher** *n*

**sketchblock** /'skech,blok/ *n* a sketchbook

**sketchbook** /'skech,book/ *n* a book consisting of usu detachable leaves of paper used for sketches

**sketchy** /'skechi/ *adj* **1** of the nature of a sketch; roughly outlined **2** lacking completeness, clarity, or substance; superficial, scanty – **sketchily** *adv,* **sketchiness** *n*

**¹skew** /skyooh/ *vi* **1** to take an oblique course; twist, swerve **2** *archaic* to look askance ∼ *vt* **1** to make skew **2a** to distort, bias **b** to cause to deviate from a true value, EXPECTED VALUE, or symmetrical form ⟨∼ed *statistical data*⟩ [ME *skewen* to escape, skew, fr ONF *escuer* to shun, of Gmc origin; akin to OHG *sciuhen* to frighten off – more at SHY]

**²skew** *adj* **1** set, placed, or running obliquely; slanting **2** *esp of*

*a statistical distribution* more developed on one side or in one direction than another; not symmetrical

**³skew** *n* **1** obliqueness, slant ⟨*sleeves rolled up and tie on the* ∼⟩ **2** a deviation from a straight line or symmetrical curve

**skewback** /'skyooh,bak/ *n* a stone or course of masonry with an inclined face against which either end of a segmental arch abuts

**skewbald** /'skyooh,bawld/ *n or adj* (an animal, esp a horse) marked with spots and patches of white and usu brown [*skewed* (skewbald; fr ME, prob fr *skew, skewe* cloud, sky) + *bald* 3]

**skew curve** *n* a curve in three-dimensional space that does not lie in a single plane

**¹skewer** /'skyooh·ə/ *n* **1** a long pin of wood or metal used chiefly to hold a piece of meat together while roasting or to hold small pieces of food for grilling (e g for a kebab) **2** something resembling a meat skewer in form or function [prob alter. of E dial. *skiver,* of unknown origin]

**²skewer** *vt* to fasten or pierce (as if) with a skewer

**skewness** /'skyoohnis/ *n* lack of straightness or symmetry; distortion; *esp* the condition or degree of asymmetry in a FREQUENCY DISTRIBUTION

**skew-'whiff** /'wif/ *adv or adj, Br informal* not straight; askew [*¹skew* + *²whiff*]

**¹ski** /skee/ *n, pl* **skis** **1a** either of a pair of long narrow strips of wood, metal, or plastic, curving upwards in front, attached to the feet for gliding over snow **b** WATER SKI **2** a runner shaped like a ski (e g the special landing gear of an aircraft for landing on snow or ice) [Norw, fr ON *skīth* stick of wood, ski; akin to OHG *skīt* stick of wood, OE *scēadan* to divide – more at SHED]

**²ski** *vb* **skiing** /'skee·ing/; **skied** /skeed/ to glide (over) on skis as a way of travelling on snow or as a recreation or sport – **skiable** *adj,* **skier** *n*

**skibob** /'skee,bob/ *n* a bicycle-like vehicle with two short skis in place of wheels that is used for gliding downhill over snow by a rider wearing miniature skis for balance [*¹ski* + *bob* (as in *bobsleigh*)] – **skibobber** *n,* **skibobbing** *n*

**ski boot** *n* a rigid padded boot extending just above the ankle that is securely fastened to the foot and is locked into position on the ski by a set of fastenings

**¹skid** /skid/ *n* **1** a plank or log used to support, lift, or move a structure or heavy object **2** a wooden fender hung over a ship's side to protect it when handling cargo **3** a usu iron shoe attached to a chain and placed under a wheel to act as a braking device on a hill **4** skidding, esp of a vehicle or wheels; a slide ⟨*got into a nasty* ∼ *on the corner*⟩ **5** a runner used as part of the landing gear of an aircraft or helicopter **6** *pl, informal* a road to defeat or downfall – in *hit the skids, on the skids* [perh of Scand origin; akin to ON *skīth* stick of wood]

**²skid** *vb* **-dd-** *vt* **1** to apply a brake or skid to **2** *chiefly NAm* to haul along, slide, hoist, or store on skids ∼ *vi* **1** *of a vehicle, wheels, or driver* **1a** to slide forwards without (the wheels) turning, as when brakes are applied suddenly **b** to fail to grip the road surface; *specif* to slip sideways out of control, as on a slippery road **2** *of an aircraft* to move sideways away from the centre of curvature when turning **3** to slide, slip ⟨*spectacles that had* ∼ded *down his nose* – *Punch*⟩

**skiddoo, skidoo** /ski'dooh/ *vi, chiefly NAm informal* to go away; leave – often imper [prob alter. of *skedaddle*]

**skiddy** /'skidi/ *adj* likely to skid or cause skidding ⟨*a wet* ∼ *road*⟩

**'skid-,lid** *n, Br informal* CRASH HELMET

**skidpan** /'skid,pan/ *n, chiefly Br* a prepared slippery road surface on which vehicle drivers may practise the control of skids

**skid road** *n, NAm* **1** a road along which logs are hauled **2** a district of a town frequented by lumberjacks

**skid row** /roh/ *n, chiefly NAm informal* a district frequented by down-and-outs, vagrants, and alcoholics [alter. of *skid road*]

**skiff** /skif/ *n* a small light boat [MF or OIt; MF *esquif,* fr OIt *schifo,* of Gmc origin; akin to OE *scip* ship]

**skiffle** /'skifl/ *n* a style of popular music of the late 1950s played by a group on guitars accompanied by improvised or nonstandard instruments (e g washboards or JEW'S HARPS) [perh imit]

**skijoring** /skee'jawring/ *n* a winter sport in which a person wearing skis is drawn over snow or ice by a horse or vehicle [modif of Norw *skikjøring,* fr *ski* + *kjøring* driving] – **skijorer** *n*

**ski jump** *n* (a jump made by a skier, esp from) a high ramp overhanging a slope, specially prepared for competitive jumping – **ski jump** *vi*

**skilful,** *NAm chiefly* **skillful** /'skilf(ə)l/ *adj* **1** possessing or displaying skill; expert **2** requiring skill ⟨*a ∼ task*⟩ *synonyms* see PROFICIENT *antonyms* unskilful, awkward – **skilfully** *adv,* **skilfullness** *n*

**ski lift** *n* a power-driven conveyor consisting usu of a series of bars or seats suspended from a continuous overhead moving cable and used for transporting skiers or sightseers up and down a long slope or mountainside – called also SKI TOW

¹**skill** /skil/ *n* **1a** special ability in a particular field, esp acquired by learning and practice; proficiency **b** manual dexterity ⟨*knitted with remarkable ∼*⟩ **2** a task, technique, trade, etc requiring skill **3** *obs* a cause, reason [ME *skil,* fr ON, distinction, knowledge; akin to OE *scylian* to separate, *sciell* shell – more at SHELL] – **skill-less, skilless** *adj*

²**skill** *vi, archaic* to make a difference; matter [ME *skilen,* fr ON *skilja* to separate, divide]

**skilled** /skild/ *adj* **1** having acquired mastery of or proficiency in something (eg a technique or trade) **2** of, being, or requiring workers with skill and training in a particular occupation, craft, or trade – compare UNSKILLED, SEMISKILLED *synonyms* see PROFICIENT

**skillet** /'skilit/ *n* **1** *chiefly Br* a small saucepan usu having three or four legs and used for cooking on the hearth **2** *chiefly NAm* FRYING PAN [ME *skelet,* perh fr MF *escuelete* small platter, dim. of *escuele* platter, deriv of L *scutella*]

**skilling** /'skiling/ *n* a small copper coin of low value formerly in use in Scandinavia [Sw, Norw, & Dan, fr ON *skillingr,* a gold coin; akin to OE *scilling* shilling]

**skillion** /'skilyən/ *n, Austr* a lean-to [alter. of E dial. *skeeling, skilling* outhouse, lean-to, fr ME *skelyng*]

**skilly** /'skili/ *n* a thin gruel or broth, often used formerly in prisons and workhouses [by shortening & alter. fr *skilligalee,* of unknown origin]

¹**skim** /skim/ *vb* **-mm-** *vt* **1a** to clear (a liquid) of floating matter ⟨*∼ boiling syrup*⟩ **b** to remove (eg film or scum) from the surface of a liquid **c** to remove cream from by skimming **d(1)** to remove the best or most accessible part from **d(2)** to remove (the choicest part or members) from something; cream **2a** to pass swiftly or lightly over **b** to read, study, or examine cursorily and rapidly; *specif* to glance through (eg a book) for the chief ideas or the plot **3** to throw in a gliding path; *specif* to throw so as to ricochet along the surface of water **4** to cover (as if) with a film, scum, or layer ⟨*the standing water was ∼*med *with ice* – William Faulkner⟩ *∼ vi* **1a** to pass lightly or hastily; glide or skip along or just above a surface **b** to give a cursory glance or consideration – often + *through* **2** to become coated with a thin layer of film or scum **3** to put on a finishing coat of plaster [ME *skimmen,* prob alter. of *scumen* to remove from, fr *scum*]

²**skim** *n* **1** a thin layer, coating, or film **2** the act of skimming **3** something skimmed; *specif* skimmed milk

³**skim** *adj* having the cream removed by skimming ⟨*∼ milk*⟩

¹**skimble-skamble** /,skimbl 'skambl/ *adj, archaic* senseless, rambling [*scamble* to stumble along]

²**skimble-,skamble** *n, archaic* nonsense

**skimmer** /'skimə/ *n* **1** something used for skimming; *specif* a flat perforated scoop or spoon **2** any of several long-winged sea birds (genus *Rhynchops*) related to the terns that feed by flying with the elongated lower part of the beak immersed in the sea

**Skimmer** *trademark* – used for a plastic disc used in throwing games

**skimming** /'skiming/ *n,* **skimmings** *n pl* that which is skimmed from a liquid

¹**skimp** /skimp/ *adj* scanty, meagre [perh alter. of *scrimp*]

²**skimp** *vt* to give insufficient or barely sufficient attention or effort to or money for *∼ vi* to be very sparing or parsimonious; scrimp

**skimpy** /'skimpi/ *adj* inadequate, scanty ⟨*a ∼ meal*⟩ – **skimpily** *adv,* **skimpiness** *n*

¹**skin** /skin/ *n* **1a(1)** the external covering of an animal (eg a fur-bearing mammal or a bird) separated from the body usu with its hair or feathers; a pelt **a(2)** a specimen of a VERTEBRATE animal (eg in a museum); *esp* an unmounted specimen **2a** the pelt of an animal, esp prepared for use as leather or fur ⟨*it took 40 ∼s to make the coat*⟩ – compare ⁴HIDE **b** something made of animal skin: eg **b(1)** a sheet of parchment or VELLUM **b(2)** a container for wine or water **3a** the external limiting layer

of an animal body, esp when forming a tough but flexible cover relatively impermeable from outside while intact **b** any of various outer or surface layers (eg a rind, husk, or film) ⟨*a sausage ∼*⟩ ⟨*onion ∼*⟩ **4** the life or welfare of a person; neck – esp in *save one's skin* **5** a sheathing or casing forming the outside surface of a structure (eg a ship or aircraft) **6** a film on the surface of a liquid, usu formed on cooling **7** a person's colour or complexion [ME, fr ON *skinn;* akin to OE *scinn* skin, MHG *schint* fruit peel, W *ysgythru* to cut] – **skinless** *adj* – **by the skin of one's teeth** by a very narrow margin [fr Job's complaint that illness had left him only 'with the skin of my teeth' (Job 19:20)] – **get under somebody's skin** to irritate, provoke, or interest somebody intensely – **jump out of one's skin** to start or move suddenly through fear – **no skin off somebody's nose** no disadvantage to somebody – **under the skin** beneath apparent or surface differences; at heart

²**skin** *vb* **-nn-** *vt* **1** to cover (as if) with a skin ⟨*a wooden frame ∼*ned *with rubber*⟩ – often + *over* **2a** to strip of skin; flay ⟨*∼ a carcass*⟩ **b** to remove (the outer covering) from (something); strip, peel ⟨*∼ an onion*⟩ ⟨*∼ the insulation from the wire*⟩ **c** to cut, graze, or damage the surface of ⟨*fell and ∼*ned *his knee*⟩ **3** *chiefly NAm* to censure, castigate **4** *informal* to strip of money or property; fleece *∼ vi* to become covered (as if) with (new) skin – usu + *over* ⟨*the wound had ∼*ned *over within a week*⟩ – see also **keep one's skinned**

,**skin-'deep** *adj* **1** as deep as the skin **2** shallow, superficial ⟨*beauty is only ∼*⟩ – **skin-deep** *adv*

**skin diving** *n* the activity or sport of swimming under water with a face mask, flippers, and sometimes an aqualung – **skin diver** *n*

**skin effect** *n* an effect characteristic of the distribution of an electrical current in a conductor at high frequencies by virtue of which most of the current passes through the surface of the conductor rather than in its interior

**skin flick** *n, informal* a film characterized by nudity and explicit sex *synonyms* see CINEMA

**skinflint** /'skin,flint/ *n* a mean person; a miser [²*skin* + *flint*]

**skin food** *n* any of various cosmetic preparations for improving the condition of the skin

**skinful** /'skin,f(ə)l/ *n, informal* a large amount, esp of alcoholic drink

**skin game** *n, NAm* a swindling game or trick [²*skin* 4]

**skin graft** *n* a piece of skin that is surgically removed from one area to replace skin in a defective or damaged area (eg one that has been burned) – **skin grafting** *n*

**skinhead** /'skin,hed/ *n* a person with close-shaven hair; *esp* a youth following a trend current in Britain esp in the early 1970s, characterized by this hairstyle, working clothes, and an aggressive manner

**skink** /skingk/ *n* any of a family (Scincidae) of mostly small lizards that have small scales and are common in tropical Africa and Asia [L *scincus,* fr Gk *skinkos*]

**skinned** /skind/ *adj* **1** having skin, esp of a specified kind – usu in combination ⟨*dark-*skinned⟩ **2** stripped of skin

**skinner** /'skinə/ *n* **1** one who deals in skins, pelts, or hides **2** one who removes skins or processes them

**Skinner box** *n* a laboratory apparatus in which an animal is caged for experiments in conditioning and which typically contains a lever that must be pressed by the animal to gain reward or avoid punishment [B F *Skinner b*1904 US psychologist]

**skinny** /'skini/ *adj* **1** of or like skin **2** very thin; lean, emaciated *antonyms* plump, fleshy – **skinniness** *n*

'**skinny-,dipping** /'skini/ *n, chiefly NAm informal* swimming in the nude – **skinny-dipper** *n*

'**skin-,popping** *n, slang* injection of a narcotic drug under the skin rather than into a vein

**skint** /skint/ *adj, Br informal* penniless, broke [alter. of *skinned,* pp of ²*skin*]

**skin test** *n* a test performed on the skin and used in detecting allergies or immunity to disease

**skintight** /,skin'tiet/ *adj, of clothes* extremely closely fitted to the body ⟨*∼ jeans*⟩

¹**skip** /skip/ *vb* **-pp-** *vi* **1a** to move about with light leaps and bounds; gambol **b** to move forwards with springing steps, esp hopping on alternate feet **2** to swing a rope round the body over the head and under the feet, jumping over it each time **3a** to bounce across a surface; ricochet **b** to flit *about* unmethodically **4** to leave hurriedly or secretly; abscond – usu + *off* or *out* ⟨*∼*ped *out without paying his bill*⟩ **5a** to pass over

or omit an interval, section, or step ⟨the story ~s to the present day⟩ **b** MISFIRE 1 **c** NAm to omit a grade in school in advancing to the next ~ vt **1a** to pass over without observing or mentioning; omit ⟨you can ~ the formalities⟩ **b** to leave out (a step in a progression or series) **2** to cause to ricochet across a surface; skim ⟨~ a stone over a pond⟩ **3** to fail to attend; miss ⟨decided to ~ church that Sunday⟩ **4** chiefly NAm informal to depart from quickly and secretly ⟨~ped town⟩ [ME skippen, perh of Scand origin; akin to Sw dial. skopa to hop]

²**skip** n **1a** a light bounding step or gait **b** a jump or period of jumping over a skipping-rope **2** an act of omission (eg in reading) **3** a college servant at Trinity College, Dublin – compare BEDMAKER [(3) short for skip-kennel (footman, lackey), fr ¹skip + kennel (gutter), deriv of L canalis pipe, channel – more at CANAL]

³**skip** n **1a** a bucket or cage for carrying men and materials (eg in mining or quarrying) **b** SKEP 1 (basket) **2** a large open metal container for waste material, esp builders' rubble [alter. of skep]

⁴**skip** n **1** the captain of a side in some games (eg curling or bowls) **2** a skipper [short for ²skipper]

⁵**skip** vt -pp- to act as skipper of

**skip distance** n the minimum distance between a transmitter and a receiver at which radio waves reflected from the IONOSPHERE (upper region of earth's atmosphere) can be received

**skipjack** /'skip,jak/ n, pl **skipjacks**, (1) **skipjacks**, esp collectively **skipjack 1** any of various fishes that jump above or play at the surface of the water **2** CLICK BEETLE [¹skip + ¹jack; (2) fr its habit of suddenly springing into the air]

¹**skipper** /'skipə/ n **1** one who or that which skips **2** any of numerous small stout-bodied butterflies (superfamily Hesperioidea) that differ from the typical butterflies in the arrangement of veins in the wings and the form of the antennae

²**skipper** n **1** the master of a ship; esp the master of a fishing, small trading, or pleasure boat **2** chiefly informal **2a** the captain or first pilot of an aircraft **b** Br a leader (eg the captain of a sports team) **3** Br informal PAL 2 [ME, fr MD schipper, fr schip ship; akin to OE scip ship – more at SHIP]

³**skipper** vt to act as skipper of (eg a boat)

¹**skipping-,rope** /'skiping/ n a rope with two handles used for skipping, esp as an exercise or children's game

**skip-,tracer** n, chiefly NAm a person employed to trace people who disappear without paying bills

**skirl** /skuhl/ vi or n (to emit) the high shrill tone or music characteristic of the bagpipe [ME (Sc) skrillen, skirlen, of Scand origin; akin to OSw skrælla to rattle; akin to OE scrallettan to sound loudly]

¹**skirmish** /'skuhmish/ n **1** a minor or irregular military engagement, usu between small outlying detachments **2** a brief preliminary conflict; broadly any minor or petty dispute [ME skyrmissh, alter. of skarmish, fr MF escarmouche, fr OIt scaramuccia, of Gmc origin; akin to OHG skirmen to defend]

²**skirmish** vi **1** to engage in a skirmish – often + with **2** to search about (eg for supplies); scout around – **skirmisher** n

¹**skirr** /skuh/ vi to move rapidly, esp with a whirring or grating sound ⟨birds ~ed off from the bushes – D H Lawrence⟩ ~ vt to pass rapidly over, esp in search of something; scour ⟨~ the country round – Shak⟩ [perh alter. of ¹scour]

²**skirr** n a whirr, roar [prob imit]

¹**skirt** /skuht/ n **1a(1)** a free-hanging part of a garment extending from the waist down **a(2)** a garment worn by women and girls that hangs from and fits closely round the waist **b** either of two usu leather flaps on a saddle covering the straps on which the stirrups are hung **c** a flexible wall containing the air cushion of a hovercraft – called also APRON **d** the lower branches of a tree when near the ground **2** skirts pl, **skirt** the borders or outer edge of an area or group; the margin **3** a part or attachment serving as a rim, border, or edging **4** Br a cut of beef from the flank, usu lean but membranous **5** slang women considered as sexual objects ⟨an avid ~ chaser⟩ – chiefly in bit of skirt [ME, fr ON skyrta shirt, kirtle – more at SHIRT] – **skirted** adj

²**skirt** vt **1** to extend along or form the border or edge of; border **2a** to go or pass round; specif to go round or keep away from in order to avoid danger or discovery **b** to avoid through fear of difficulty or dispute; evade ⟨~ed the important issues⟩ ~ vi to be, lie, or move along an edge, border, or margin ⟨~ round the coast⟩ – **skirter** n

**skirting** /'skuhting/ n **1** a border, edging **2** fabric suitable for skirts **3 skirting board, skirting** Br a board, often with

decorative moulding, that is fixed to the base of a wall and that covers the joint of the wall and floor

**ski run** /skee/ n a slope or trail for skiing

**skit** /skit/ n a satirical or humorous story or sketch ⟨did a ~ on Queen Victoria⟩ – compare LAMPOON [origin unknown]

¹**skite** /skiet/ vi, Scot to slide obliquely; skip [prob of Scand origin; akin to ON skjōta to shoot]

²**skite** vi, Austr & NZ informal to brag, boast [prob fr E dial. skite to defaecate, fr ME skyten, fr ON skīta]

**ski tow** n SKI LIFT

**skitter** /'skitə/ vi **1** to glide or skip lightly or swiftly **2** to skim along a surface **3** to twitch a fishing lure or baited hook through or along the surface of water ~ vt to cause to skitter [prob freq of ¹skite] – **skitter** n

**skittish** /'skitish/ adj **1a** lively or frisky in behaviour **b** unpredictable, capricious **2** easily frightened; restive ⟨a ~ horse⟩ **3** coy, bashful [ME] – **skittishly** adv, **skittishness** n

**skittle** /'skitl/ n **1** pl but taking sing vb a bowling game played by rolling a wooden ball or disc at a standing group of nine pins in order to knock over as many of them as possible **2** any of the pins used in skittles [perh. of Scand origin; akin to ON skutill bolt – more at SHUTTLE]

**skittle out** vt to dismiss (a batting side in cricket) for a low score, usu in rapid succession

**skive** /skiev/ vt **1** to cut off (eg leather or rubber) in thin layers or pieces; pare **2** Br informal to evade (work, duty, etc), Br informal ~ vi to evade one's work or duty, esp out of laziness; shirk – often + off [of Scand origin; akin to ON skīfa to slice] – **skive** n

**skiver** /'skievə/ n **1** a thin soft leather made from a split sheepskin **2** a person or tool that skives something (eg leather) **3** Br informal one who skives; a shirker

¹**skivvy** /'skivi/ n, Br derog a female domestic servant who performs menial tasks [origin unknown]

²**skivvy** vi to act as a skivvy

**skoal** /skohl/ interj – used as a drinking toast [Dan skaal, lit., cup; akin to ON skāl bowl – more at SCALE]

**skolly** /'skoli/ n, chiefly SAfr a young non-white thug [Afrik, prob fr D schoelje rogue, rascal]

**skua** /'skyooh-ə/ n any of several large dark-coloured seabirds (family Stercorariidae) of northern and southern seas that are strong fliers and that tend to harass weaker birds until they drop or disgorge the fish they have caught – compare GREAT SKUA [NL, fr Faeroese skūgvur; akin to ON skūfr tassel, skua, OE scēaf sheaf – more at SHEAF]

**skulduggery, skullduggery** /skul'dugəri/ n devious trickery; esp underhand or unscrupulous behaviour [alter. of earlier sculduddery (gross or lewd conduct), of unknown origin]

¹**skulk** /skulk/ vi **1** to move in a stealthy or furtive manner; slink **2** to hide or conceal oneself, esp out of cowardice or for a sinister purpose; lurk **3** chiefly Br to malinger, shirk [ME skulken, of Scand origin; akin to Dan skulke to shirk, play truant] – **skulker** n

²**skulk** n one who skulks

**skull** /skul/ n **1** the skeleton of the head of a VERTEBRATE animal forming a bony or cartilaginous case that encloses and protects the brain and chief SENSE ORGANS and supports the jaws **2** derog the seat of understanding or intelligence; the brain ⟨get that fact into your thick ~!⟩ [ME skulle, of Scand origin; akin to Sw skulle skull] – **skulled** adj

**skull and crossbones** /'kros,bohnz/ n, pl **skulls and crossbones** a representation of a human skull over two crossed thigh bones, usu used as a warning of danger to life and formerly on pirate flags

**skullcap** /'skul,kap/ n **1** a closely fitting cap; esp a light brimless cap fitting over the crown of the head, as sometimes worn by Jewish men and certain priests – compare YARMULKE **2** any of various plants (genus Scutellaria) of the mint family having a helmet-shaped CALYX (circle of leaflike structures supporting the flower) **3** CALVARIA (upper portion of skull)

¹**skunk** /skungk/ n, pl **skunks**, (1a) **skunks**, esp collectively **skunk 1a** any of various common omnivorous black and white American mammals (esp genus Mephitis) that are related to the weasels and have a pair of anal glands from which a foul-smelling secretion is ejected **b** the fur of a skunk **2** informal a thoroughly obnoxious person [of Algonquian origin; akin to Abnaki segakw skunk]

²**skunk** vt, NAm informal to defeat (an opponent) outright, esp without allowing to score

¹**sky** /skie/ n, **skies** n pl **1** the earth's atmosphere and space

beyond as seen from the earth; the firmament, heavens **2** HEAVEN 2 **3a** the appearance of the sky with regard to weather conditions ⟨*a clear* ∼⟩ **b** the climate ⟨*temperate English skies* – G G Coulton⟩ **4** the highest degree ⟨*praised him to the skies*⟩ – see also PIE **in the sky** [ME, cloud, sky, fr ON *skȳ* cloud; akin to OE *scēo* cloud, L *cutis* skin – more at HIDE]

²**sky** *vt* **skied, skyed 1** to hang (e g a painting) high on a wall **2** *chiefly Br* to throw or hit (e g a ball) high in the air; *specif* to hit (a cricket ball) high in the air, esp in such a way as to give a catch

**sky blue** *adj or n* (of) the light blue colour of the sky on a clear day

**skyborne** /'skie,bawn/ *adj* airborne ⟨∼ *troops*⟩

**skycap** /'skie,kap/ *n, NAm* one employed to carry hand luggage at an airport – compare REDCAP [¹*sky* + *-cap* (as in *redcap*)]

**skydiving** /'skie,dieving/ *n* the sport of jumping from an aircraft at a moderate altitude (e g 1800 metres or 6000 feet) and executing various body manoeuvres before pulling the rip cord of a parachute – **sky diver** *n*

**Skye terrier** /skie/ *n* (any of) a Scottish breed of long-haired terriers with a long head, a long low body, and short straight legs [*Skye,* island of the Inner Hebrides in NW Scotland]

**skyey** /'skie·i/ *adj* of or like the sky; ethereal

¹**sky-'high** *adv* **1a** high into the air **b** to a high level or degree ⟨*prices rose* ∼⟩ **2** in an enthusiastic manner **3** to bits; apart – in *blow something sky-high*

²**sky-high** *adj, esp of prices* very high

**skyjack** /'skie,jak/ *vt* to hijack (an aircraft in flight) [*sky* + hi*jack*] – **skyjacker** *n*

¹**skylark** /'skie,lahk/ *n* a common largely brown African and Eurasian lark (*Alauda arvensis*) noted for its song, esp as uttered in vertical flight or while hovering

²**skylark** *vi* to act in a high-spirited or mischievous manner; frolic [¹*sky* + ²*lark;* orig sense, to frolic in the rigging of a ship] – **skylarker** *n*

**skylight** /'skie,liet/ *n* **1** the diffused and reflected light of the sky **2** an opening in a roof or ceiling that is usu filled with glass and is designed to admit daylight

**skyline** /'skie,lien/ *n* **1** the apparent juncture of earth and sky; the horizon **2** an outline (e g of buildings or a mountain range) against the background of the sky

**sky pilot** *n, slang* a clergyman; *specif* a military chaplain

¹**skyrocket** /'skie,rokit/ *n* ²ROCKET 1a

²**skyrocket** *vi* to shoot up suddenly and steeply ⟨*shares in copper are* ∼ing⟩ ∼ *vt* to send up steeply and suddenly

**skysail** /'skie,sayl, -sl/ *n* a sail set above the ROYAL sail (sail near the top) on a mast

**skyscape** /'skie,skayp/ *n* an expanse of sky, esp as depicted by an artist ⟨*the drama of quickly changing* ∼s – *In Britain*⟩

**skyscraper** /'skie,skraypə/ *n* a very tall building; *esp* one containing offices

**skywards** /'skiewədz/ *adv* towards the sky; upwards – **skyward** *adj*

**sky wave** *n* a radio wave that is propagated by reflection from the IONOSPHERE (upper region of earth's atmosphere)

**skyway** /'skie,way/ *n* a route used by aircraft; AIR LANE

**skywriting** /'skie,rieting/ *n* the formation of writing in the sky by means of a visible substance (e g smoke) emitted from an aircraft; *also* the writing so formed

¹**slab** /slab/ *n* **1** a large flat rectangular usu thick piece of stone, concrete, or other hard material **2** a thick flat piece or slice (e g of cake or bread) **3** the rough outside piece cut from a log when squaring it **4** *Br informal* a mortuary table ⟨*laid out on the* ∼⟩ [ME *slabbe*]

²**slab** *vt* **-bb-** **1** to divide or form into or lay with slabs **2** to remove a slab from (a log)

³**slab** *adj, archaic* thick, viscous [prob of Scand origin; akin to obs Dan *slab* slippery]

'**slab-,sided** *adj, chiefly NAm* having flat sides

¹**slack** /slak/ *adj* **1** insufficiently prompt, diligent, or careful; negligent, lax **2** characterized by slowness, indolence, or lack of activity; sluggish ⟨*a* ∼ *pace*⟩ ⟨*a* ∼ *market*⟩ ⟨*the tide was* ∼⟩ **3a** not tense or tight ⟨*a* ∼ *rope*⟩ **b** lacking in usual or normal firmness and steadiness; relaxed ⟨∼ *muscles*⟩ ⟨∼ *supervision*⟩ [ME *slak,* fr OE *sleac;* akin to OHG *slah* slack, L *laxus* slack, loose, *languēre* to languish, Gk *lēgein* to stop] – **slackly** *adv,* **slackness** *n*

²**slack** *vt* **1** to be sluggish or negligent in performing or doing **2** to slacken, loosen **3** SLAKE 2 ∼ *vi* **1** to be or become slack; slacken ⟨*our enthusiasm* ∼ed *off*⟩ **2** *informal* to be lazy or not work properly ⟨*caught* ∼ing⟩

*synonyms* One **slacks** or **slakes** lime or one's thirst, but only **slack,** not **slake,** can mean "lessen", "loosen", or "shirk".

³**slack** *n* **1** cessation in movement or flow; *specif* SLACK WATER **2a** a part of something (e g a sail or a rope) that hangs loose without tension **b** an extra or loosely attached part or group – esp in *take up the slack* **3** *pl* trousers, esp for casual wear **4** a lull or decrease in activity; *also* a dull season or period

⁴**slack** *n* coal in very small particles [ME *sleck*]

**slacken** /'slakən/ *vt* **1** to make less active, rapid, or intense ⟨∼ *speed at a crossroads*⟩ **2** to make slack (e g by lessening tension or firmness) ⟨∼ *sail*⟩ ∼ *vi* **1** to become slack or negligent ⟨*determined not to* ∼ *as a correspondent* – Jane Austen⟩ **2** to become less active, rapid, or intense ▢ often + *off* **antonyms** quicken, tighten

**slacker** /'slakə/ *n* a person who shirks work or obligation

**slacksuit** /'slak,soot/ *n, chiefly NAm* a casual outfit of slacks and matching top

**slack tide** *n* SLACK WATER

**slack water** *n* the period at the turn of the tide when there is little or no horizontal motion of tidal water

**slag** /slag/ *n* **1** the waste material from smelting metal ores; cinder **2** the rough cindery lava from a volcano **3** *Br* coalmining waste (e g shale, coal dust, etc) **4** *Br slang* a dirty slovenly woman, esp with loose morals [MLG *slagge*]

**slagheap** /'slag,heep/ *n, Br* a high mound of waste material (e g from coal mining)

**slag wool** *n* ROCK WOOL (insulating substance)

**slain** /slayn/ *past part of* SLAY

**slake** /slayk/ *vt* **1** to satisfy, quench ⟨∼ *your thirst*⟩ **2** to cause (e g lime) to heat and crumble by treatment with water; hydrate **3** *archaic* to lessen the force of; moderate ∼ *vi* **1** to become slaked; crumble ⟨*lime may* ∼ *spontaneously in moist air*⟩ **2** *archaic* to die down; abate **synonyms** see ²SLACK [ME *slaken* to abate, allay, loosen, fr OE *slacian* to slacken, fr *sleac* slack]

**slaked lime** /slaykt/ *n* LIME 2b

**slalom** /'slahləm/ *n* a skiing race against time on a zigzag or wavy course between upright obstacles (e g flags); *also* any similar race in other sports (e g canoeing) △ shalom [Norw, lit., sloping track]

¹**slam** /slam/ *n* **1** GRAND SLAM (winning of all tricks in bridge) **2** LITTLE SLAM (winning of all tricks but one in bridge) [origin unknown]

²**slam** *n* **1** a banging noise; *esp* one made by slamming a door **2** an act of slamming [prob of Scand origin; akin to Icel *slæma* to slam]

³**slam** *vb* **-mm-** *vt* **1** to strike or beat vigorously; knock ⟨∼med *the ball into the back of the net*⟩ **2** to shut forcibly and noisily; bang **3a** to throw or slap down on or against something with a noisy impact ⟨∼med *his fist on the table*⟩ **b** to force into sudden and violent action ⟨∼ *on the brakes*⟩ **4** *informal* to criticize harshly ∼ *vi* **1** to make a banging noise, esp in closing ⟨*the door* ∼med *to behind him*⟩ **2** *informal* to move violently or angrily ⟨*he* ∼med *out of his office*⟩

¹**slam-'bang** *adj, informal* **1** excessively loud or violent ⟨*a* ∼ *clatter*⟩ **2** *chiefly NAm* all-out ⟨*made a* ∼ *effort to win*⟩

²**slam-bang** *adv, informal* **1** with a slamming noise **2** *NAm* recklessly, carelessly

**slammer** /'slamə/ *n, slang* a prison [³*slam* + ²*-er*]

¹**slander** /'slahndə/ *n* **1** the utterance of false charges or misrepresentations which damage another's reputation, esp as a legal offence **2** a false and defamatory oral statement about a person ▢ compare LIBEL [ME *sclaundre, slaundre,* fr OF *esclandre,* fr LL *scandalum* stumbling block, offence – more at SCANDAL] – **slanderous** *adj,* **slanderously** *adv,* **slanderousness** *n*

²**slander** *vt* to utter slander against; defame **synonyms** see ²MALIGN – **slanderer** *n*

¹**slang** /slang/ *n* **1** language peculiar to a particular group, profession, etc; jargon **2** informal vocabulary that is composed typically of new words and meanings, extravagant picturesque figures of speech, impolite or vulgar references, etc, and that belongs rather to familiar conversation than to the written language **synonyms** see DIALECT [origin unknown] – **slang** *adj,* **slangy** *adj,* **slangily** *adv,* **slanginess** *n*

²**slang** *vb* to abuse with or use harsh or coarse language ⟨*the two drivers are* ∼ing *each other* – *Punch*⟩

**slanging match** /'slang·ing/ *n, chiefly Br informal* a usu futile exchange of abuse between two or more opposed parties

¹**slant** /slahnt/ *vi* **1** to turn or incline from the horizontal or vertical or a correct level; slope **2** to take a diagonal course,

direction, or path ~ *vt* **1** to give an oblique or sloping direction to **2** to interpret or present in accord with a particular interest; bias ⟨*stories* ~ed *towards youth*⟩; *specif* to distort maliciously or dishonestly [ME *slenten* to fall obliquely, of Scand origin; akin to Sw *slinta* to slide; akin to OE *slīdan* to slide] – **slantingly** *adv*

²**slant** *n* **1** a slanting direction, line, or plane; a slope ⟨*placed the mirror at a* ~ ⟩ **2a** something that slants **b** SOLIDUS **2** (punctuation mark) **3a** a particular or personal point of view, attitude, or opinion **b** an unfair bias or distortion (e g in a piece of writing) **4** *chiefly NAm informal* a brief look; a glance ⟨*take a* ~ *at him*⟩ – **slant** *adj*, **slantways** *adv*, **slantwise** *adv or adj*

**slant height** *n, maths* **1** the length of a line from the edge of the base to the point of a circular-based cone **2** the height of a side of a pyramid whose triangular sides are equal

¹**slap** /slap/ *n* **1** a quick sharp blow, esp with the open hand **2** a noise that suggests a slap; *esp* a noise resulting from slackness between parts of a machine [LG *slapp*, of imit origin] – **slap in the face** a rebuff, insult – **slap on the back** an expression of congratulations

²**slap** *vt* **-pp-** **1** to strike sharply (as if) with the open hand **2** to put, place, or throw with careless haste or force ⟨~ *paint on a wall*⟩

**slap down** *vt, informal* **1** to restrain or quash the initiative of rudely or forcefully **2** to censure, reprimand

³**slap** *adv, informal* directly, smack ⟨*landed* ~ *on top of a holly bush*⟩ [prob fr LG *slapp*, fr *slapp*, n]

**slap and tickle** *n, Br informal* playful lovemaking

,**slap-'bang** *adv, informal* **1** in a highly abrupt or forceful manner **2** precisely ⟨~ *in the middle*⟩

**slapdash** /'slap,dash/ *adj* haphazard, slipshod, careless

**slaphappy** /'slap,hapi/ *adj, informal* **1** punch-drunk **2** irresponsibly casual or carefree ⟨*the* ~ *state of our democracies* – Alistair Cooke⟩

**slapjack** /'slap,jak/ *n* **1** a US card game in which each player tries to be the fastest to slap his/her hand on any jack that appears face up **2** *NAm* a pancake; *specif* one cooked on a griddle

**slap shot** *n* a shot in ice hockey made with a swinging stroke

**slapstick** /'slap,stik/ *n* **1** a device made of two flat pieces of wood fastened at one end so as to make a loud noise when used by an actor to strike a person **2** comedy stressing farce and horseplay; knockabout comedy – **slapstick** *adj*

'**slap-,up** *adj, chiefly Br informal* marked by lavish consumption or luxury ⟨*a* ~ *Christmas nosh* – Sunday Mirror⟩ [³*slap*]

¹**slash** /slash/ *vt* **1a** to cut with violent usu random sweeping strokes **b** to make (one's way) by or as if by cutting down obstacles **2** to lash ⟨~ *him with bridle reins* – Sir Walter Scott⟩ **3** to cut slits in (e g a garment) so as to reveal an underlying fabric or colour **4** to criticize cuttingly **5** to reduce drastically; cut ⟨*prices* ~ed⟩ ~ *vi* **1** to cut or lash about recklessly or brutally (as if) with an edged blade **2** *of rain* to fall fast and obliquely; drive **synonyms** see ²TEAR [ME *slaschen*, prob fr MF *eslachier* to break]

²**slash** *n* **1** the act of slashing; *also* a long cut or stroke made (as if) by slashing **2** an ornamental slit in a garment **3** SOLIDUS **2** (punctuation mark) **4** *chiefly Br slang* an act of urinating

³**slash** *n, NAm* a low swampy area often overgrown with brush [prob alter. of *plash* (marshy pool), fr ME *plasche*, fr OE *plæsc*]

,**slash-and-'burn** *adj* characterized or developed by GIRDLING (cutting of bark), felling, and burning shrubs or trees to make land available, usu temporarily, for arable crops

**slasher** /'slashə/ *n* one who or that which slashes; *specif* BILLHOOK (cutting tool)

**slashing** /'slashing/ *adj* **1** incisively satirical or critical **2** driving, pelting ⟨*journeyed through* ~ *rain*⟩ **3** vivid, brilliant ⟨*a* ~ *juxtaposition of reds and greens*⟩ – **slashingly** *adv*

**slash pine** *n* a pine (*Pinus elliottii*) that is native to the SE USA and is an important source of turpentine and timber [³*slash*]

¹**slat** /slat/ *n* **1** a thin narrow flat strip, esp of wood or metal: e g **1a** a lath **b** a shutter of a louvre (e g a VENETIAN BLIND) **c** a stave **d** any of the thin flat members in the back of a LADDER-BACK chair **2** ¹SLOT **2** (hole through an aircraft's wing to improve airflow) [ME, slate, fr MF *esclat* splinter, fr OF, fr *esclater* to burst, splinter] – **slat, slatted** *adj*

²**slat** *vb* **-tt-** *chiefly NEng vt* to strike or throw vigorously ~ *vi* to flap noisily ⟨*the sails were* ~ting *in the gale*⟩ [prob of Scand origin; akin to ON *sletta* to slap, throw]

¹**slate** /slayt/ *n* **1** a piece of construction material (e g layered rock) used for roofing **2** a dense fine-grained METAMORPHIC (altered by heat and pressure) rock produced by the compression of various sediments (e g clay or shale) and easily split into smooth thin layers **3** a tablet of material, esp slate, used for writing on **4** a dark bluish or greenish grey colour **5** *NAm* a list of candidates for nomination or election [ME, fr MF *esclat* splinter] – **slate** *adj*, **slatelike** *adj* – **on the slate** on credit

²**slate** *vt* **1** to cover with slates or a slatelike substance ⟨~ *a roof*⟩ **2** *chiefly NAm* to register, schedule, or designate for action or appointment

³**slate** *vt, chiefly Br informal* to criticize or censure severely [prob alter. of ²*slat*]

**slater** /'slaytə/ *n* **1** one who slates roofs **2a** a wood-louse **b** any of various marine animals related to the woodlice [(2) ¹*slate* + ²*-er*; fr its colour]

¹**slather** /'slahdhə/ *n*, **slathers** *n pl, chiefly NAm informal* a great quantity ⟨~s *of luck*⟩ [origin unknown]

²**slather** *vt, NAm informal* **1** to spread thickly or lavishly **2** to squander

**slating** /'slayting/ *n* **1** the work of a slater **2** material used for slating; slates

**slattern** /'slatən/ *n* an untidy slovenly woman; a slut **synonyms** see SLUT [prob fr Ger *schlottern* to hang loosely, slouch; akin to D *slodderen* to hang loosely, *slodder* slut]

**slatternly** /'slatənli/ *adj* **1a** untidy and dirty through persistent neglect; slovenly **b** careless, disorderly **2** characteristic of a slut – **slatterniness** *n*

**slaty** /,slayti/ *adj* of, containing, or resembling slate; *esp* grey like slate

¹**slaughter** /'slawtə/ *n* **1** the act of killing; *specif* the butchering of livestock for market **2** the killing of great numbers of human beings (e g in battle); carnage, massacre [ME, of Scand origin; akin to ON *slātra* to slaughter; akin to OE *sleaht* slaughter, *slēan* to slay – more at SLAY] – **slaughterous** *adj*

²**slaughter** *vt* **1** to kill (animals) for food; butcher **2a** to kill in a bloody or violent manner; slay **b** to kill in large numbers; massacre **3** *informal* to beat (opposing players) outright – **slaughterer** *n*

**slaughterhouse** /'slawtə,hows/ *n* an establishment where animals are butchered

**slaughterman** /'slawtəmən/ *n* one who works in a slaughterhouse

**Slav** /slahv/ *n* a person who speaks a SLAVONIC language as his/her native tongue [ME *Sclav*, fr ML *Sclavus*, fr LGk *Sklabos*, fr *Sklabēnoi* Slavs, of Slav origin; akin to OSlav *Slověne*, a Slavonic people in N Greece] – **Slav** *adj*

¹**slave** /slayv/ *n* **1** a person held in servitude as the property of another; a bondman **2** a person who is helplessly dominated by a specified thing or person ⟨*a* ~ *to drink*⟩ **3** a mechanical device (e g the typewriter unit of a computer) that is directly controlled by and often copies the actions of another **4** a drudge ⟨*women who are merely kitchen* ~s⟩ [ME *sclave*, fr OF or ML; OF *esclave*, fr ML *sclavus*, fr *Sclavus* Slav; fr the enslavement in the early Middle Ages of many Slavonic peoples of central Europe] – **slave** *adj*

²**slave** *vt* **1** to make directly responsive to another mechanism **2** *archaic* to enslave ~ *vi* **1** to work like a slave; toil – often + *away* **2** to traffic in slaves

**slave driver** *n* **1** an overseer of slaves **2** a harsh taskmaster

**slaveholder** /'slayv,hohldə/ *n* an owner of slaves – **slaveholding** *adj or n*

¹**slaver** /'slavə/ *vi* to drool, slobber [ME *slaveren*, of Scand origin; akin to ON *slafra* to slaver; akin to MD *slabben* to slaver, L *labi* to slip – more at SLEEP]

²**slaver** /'slavə/ *n* saliva dribbling from the mouth

³**slaver** /'slayvə/ *n* a person or ship engaged in the SLAVE TRADE

**slavery** /'slayv(ə)ri/ *n* **1** drudgery, toil **2a** the state of being a slave; enforced servitude **b** the practice of owning slaves **synonyms** see SERVITUDE

**slave state** *n* a state of the USA in which Negro slavery was legal until the American Civil War

**slave trade** *n* traffic in slaves; *esp* the transportation of Negroes to America for profit prior to the American Civil War

**slavey** /'slayvi/ *n, informal* a hard-working domestic servant; a drudge

**Slavic** /'slahvik, 'slavik/ *adj or n* Slavonic

**Slavicist** /ˌslavisist, 'slah-/, **Slavist** /'slahvist/ n a specialist in the Slavonic languages or literatures

**slavish** /'slayvish/ adj 1 (characteristic) of a slave; esp abjectly servile 2 obsequiously imitative; devoid of originality 3 archaic despicable, base – **slavishly** adv, **slavishness** n

**slavocracy** /slay'vokrəsi/ n a powerful faction of slaveholders and advocates of slavery in the South before the American Civil War

**¹Slavonian** /slə'vohnyən, -ni-ən/ n SLOVENE 1b (native of Slovenia) [Slavonia, region in SE Europe, fr ML Sclavonia, Slavonia land of the Slavs, fr Sclavus Slav]

**²Slavonian** adj 1 SLOVENE (of Slovenia) 2 archaic Slavonic

**¹Slavonic** /slə'vonik/ adj (characteristic) of the Slavs or their languages [NL slavonicus, fr ML Sclavonia, Slavonia]

**²Slavonic** n 1 a branch of the INDO-EUROPEAN language family containing Byelorussian, Bulgarian, Czech, Polish, Serbo-Croatian, Slovene, Russian, and Ukrainian 2 OLD CHURCH SLAVONIC (ancient Slavonic language)

**slavophil** /'slahvəfil, 'slavə-/, **slavophile** /-fiel/ n, often cap a foreign admirer of the Slavs; an advocate of Slavonic, specif Russian, culture

**slaw** /slaw/ n, chiefly NAm coleslaw

**¹slay** /slay/ **slew** /slooh/; **slain** /slayn/ 1 poetic or journalistic to kill violently or with great bloodshed; slaughter 2 informal to affect overpoweringly (e g with awe or delight); overwhelm *synonyms* see ¹KILL [ME slen, fr OE slēan to strike, slay; akin to OHG slahan to strike, MIr slacain I beat] – **slayer** n

**²slay** n SLEY (weaving implement)

**sleave** /sleev/ n, archaic SKEIN (loosely wound yarn) ⟨sleep that knits up the ravelled ~ of care – Shak⟩ [obs sleave to divide (silk) into filaments, fr (assumed) ME sleven, fr OE -slæfan to cut – more at SLIVER]

**sleave silk** n, obs rough (FLOSS) silk that is easily separated into filaments for embroidery

**sleazy** /'sleezi/ adj squalid and disreputable [origin unknown] – **sleazily** adv, **sleaziness** n

**¹sled** /sled/ n, chiefly NAm ²SLEDGE [ME sledde, fr MD; akin to OE slīdan to slide]

**²sled** vb **-dd-** chiefly NAm to sledge – **sledder** n

**sledding** /'sleding/ n, NAm GOING 3 ⟨the job was hard ~⟩

**¹sledge** /slej/ n a sledgehammer [ME slegge, fr OE slecg; akin to ON sleggja sledgehammer, OE slēan to strike – more at SLAY]

**²sledge** n 1 a vehicle with runners that is used for transporting esp goods over snow or ice and is often pulled by dogs 2 Br a toboggan [D dial. sleedse; akin to MD sledde sled]
> *synonyms* **Sledge, sled,** and **sleigh** all mean "vehicle moving on runners over snow". **Sledge** is the commonest word in British English both for the small downhill toboggan and for the larger vehicle that is pulled on the level. In American English the small downhill one is usually called a **sled**, and the larger one a **sled** or, particularly when horse-drawn, a **sleigh**.

**³sledge** vb, chiefly Br vi to travel or play on a sledge ⟨go sledging as soon as the snow is deep enough⟩ ~ vt to transport on a sledge

**sledge dog** n a dog trained to draw a sledge, esp in the Arctic regions

**¹sledgehammer** /'slej,hamə/ n a large heavy hammer that is wielded with both hands [¹sledge] – **sledgehammer** vb

**²sledgehammer** adj clumsy, heavy-handed ⟨a ~ package of spending cuts⟩

**¹sleek** /sleek/ vt to slick [ME sleken, alter. of sliken]

**²sleek** adj 1a smooth and glossy as if polished ⟨~ dark hair⟩ b looking healthy and well-groomed ⟨~ cattle grazing⟩ 2 excessively or artfully suave; ingratiating 3 elegant, stylish [alter. of ²slick] – **sleeken** vt, **sleekly** adv, **sleekness** n

**sleekit** /'sleekit/ adj, chiefly Scot crafty, sly [Sc, fr pp of ¹sleek]

**¹sleep** /sleep/ n 1 the natural periodic suspension of consciousness that is essential for the physical and mental well-being of higher animals 2 a state resembling sleep: e g 2a torpor b death c the state of an animal during hibernation ⟨the bear's winter ~⟩ 3 a period spent sleeping ⟨need a good long ~⟩ 4 informal dried mucus that sometimes collects in the eye corners when sleeping [ME slepe, fr OE slǣp; akin to OHG slāf sleep, L labi to slip, slide] – **sleeplike** adj – **go to sleep** 1 to fall asleep 2 of a part of the body to lose sensation; become numb ⟨my foot has gone to sleep⟩

**²sleep** vb **slept** /slept/ vi 1 to rest in a state of sleep 2 to be in a state (e g of quiescence or death) resembling sleep ⟨the seeds of a later art can ~ – Peter Levi⟩ 3 to spend a specified period in sleep ⟨~ the night with us⟩ 4 informal to have sexual relations – + with or together ~ vt 1 to provide sleeping accommodation for ⟨the boat ~s six⟩ 2 poetic to be slumbering in ⟨slept the sleep of the dead⟩

**sleep around** vi, informal to be sexually promiscuous

**sleep in** vi 1 LIVE IN 2 to sleep late, either intentionally or accidentally

**sleep off** vt to sleep until the effects of (usu excessive drinking or eating) have passed ⟨sleep it off⟩

**sleep on** vt to postpone (a decision), esp overnight ⟨sleep on it and let me know tomorrow⟩

**sleep out** vi 1 to sleep out of doors 2 LIVE OUT

**sleeper** /'sleepə/ n 1 one who or that which sleeps 2a a horizontal beam of timber, stone, or steel on or near the ground to support a superstructure b chiefly Br any of the timber, concrete, or steel transverse supports to which railway rails are fixed 3 a railway passenger carriage divided into compartments having berths for sleeping 4 a small gold ring worn in the ear lobe to keep the hole open after the ear has been pierced 5 chiefly NAm informal someone or something unpromising or unnoticed that suddenly attains prominence or value

**sleeping bag** n 1 a bag of warm material for sleeping in, esp when sleeping out or camping 2 a sleeping garment for babies resembling a loose bag with arms

**sleeping car** /'sleeping/ n SLEEPER 3

**sleeping partner** n a partner who takes no active part in the running of a firm's business

**sleeping pill** n a drug, esp a BARBITURATE, that is taken in tablet or capsule form to induce sleep

**sleeping policeman** n a hump in a road designed to slow vehicles to a low speed

**sleeping sickness** n 1 a serious disease that is prevalent in much of tropical Africa, is marked by fever, protracted lethargy, tremors, and loss of weight, is caused by either of two TRYPANOSOMES (single-celled parasites) (Trypanosoma gambiense and Trypanosoma rhodesiense), and is transmitted by TSETSE FLIES – called also TRYPANOSOMIASIS 2 any of various viral infections that cause brain inflammation, lethargy, and sleepiness

**sleepless** /'sleeplis/ adj 1 not able to sleep; insomniac 2 affording no sleep ⟨a ~ night⟩ 3 unceasingly active – **sleeplessly** adv, **sleeplessness** n

**sleepout** /'sleep,owt/ n, Austr a part of a verandah that is enclosed by glass or lightweight partitions and can be used as an extra bedroom

**sleepwalker** /'sleep,wawkə/ n SOMNAMBULIST – **sleepwalk** vi

**sleepy** /'sleepi/ adj 1a ready to fall asleep; drowsy b (characteristic) of sleep 2 lacking alertness; sluggish, lethargic 3 sleep-inducing; soporific 4 having little activity; tranquil ⟨a ~ little village⟩ 5 beginning to rot ⟨pears can go ~ ... in the middle – The Times⟩ – **sleepily** adv, **sleepiness** n

**sleepyhead** /'sleepi,hed/ n a sleepy person – usu said to a child

**¹sleet** /sleet/ n 1 partly frozen rain, or snow and rain falling together 2 chiefly NAm a thin coating of ice; a glaze [ME slete; akin to MHG slōz hailstone, ME sloor mud – more at SLUR] – **sleety** adj

**²sleet** vi to send down sleet ⟨it's ~ing⟩

**sleeve** /sleev/ n 1 a part of a garment covering an arm or upper arm 2 something like a sleeve in shape or use; esp a tubular machine part designed to fit over another part 3 a paper or often highly distinctive cardboard covering that protects a gramophone record when not in use [ME sleve, fr OE slīefe; akin to OE slēfan to slip (clothes) on, slūpan to slip, OHG sliofan, L lubricus slippery] – **sleeved** adj, **sleeveless** adj – **have up one's sleeve** to have in reserve ⟨he had some new ideas up his sleeve⟩ – see also ACE **up one's sleeve**

**sleeving** /'sleeving/ n the covering of an insulated electric cable

**¹sleigh** /slay/ n a usu horse-drawn vehicle for carrying esp passengers over snow and ice and resembling an open carriage on runners – compare ²SLEDGE [D slee, alter. of slede; akin to MD sledde sled]

**²sleigh** vi to drive or travel in a sleigh

**sleigh bell** n any of various bells commonly attached to (the harness of a horse drawing) a sleigh: e g a a small hollow spherical bell with a loose pellet inside b a hemispherical bell with an attached clapper

**sleight** /sliet/ n, archaic 1 deceitful craftiness; also a stratagem 2 dexterity, skill [ME, fr ON *slægth*, fr *slægr* sly – more at SLY]

**sleight of hand** *n* 1 manual skill or dexterity (as if) in conjuring or juggling 2 clever deception

**slender** /'slendə/ *adj* **1a** spare in build; *esp* gracefully slim **b** small or narrow in circumference or width in proportion to length or height **c** excessively thin; tenuous, flimsy ⟨*held by a ~ thread*⟩ **2** limited or inadequate in amount; meagre ⟨*a man of ~ means*⟩ [ME *sclendre, slendre*] – **slenderly** *adv*, **slenderness** *n*

**slender·ize, -ise** /'slendəriez/ *vb*, *chiefly NAm informal* to make or become slender

**slender loris** *n* a slim-bodied LORIS (small mammal) (*Loris gracilis*) of S India and Ceylon

¹**sleuth** /slooth/ *n*, *informal* a detective, investigator [short for *sleuthhound*]

²**sleuth** *vb*, *informal vi* to act as a detective ~ *vt* to track, trace

**sleuthhound** /'slooth,hownd/ *n* **1** a hound that tracks by scent; *specif* a bloodhound **2** *informal* a detective [ME, fr *sleuth* track of an animal or person (fr ON *slōth*) + *hound*]

**S level** /es/ *n*, *often cap L* SCHOLARSHIP LEVEL (top level of GCE)

¹**slew** /sloo/ *past of* SLAY

²**slew** *n*, *NAm* a marshy pool or inlet [var of *slough*]

³**slew** *vb* 1 to turn, twist, or swing about a fixed point that is usu the axis **2** to (cause to) skid ⟨*~ a car round a corner*⟩ [origin unknown]

⁴**slew** *n* 1 position or inclination after slewing 2 a slewing movement

⁵**slew** *n*, *NAm informal* a large number or quantity [IrGael *sluagh*]

**slewed** /sloohd/ *adj*, *chiefly Br informal* drunk

**sley, slay** /slay/ *n* a movable frame that carries the comblike device (REED 5) in a loom [ME *sleye*, fr OE *slege*, lit., act of beating, stroke; akin to OHG *slag* blow, OE *slēan* to strike, slay]

¹**slice** /slies/ *n* **1a** a thin broad flat piece cut from a larger whole ⟨*a ~ of ham*⟩ **b** a wedge-shaped piece (e g of pie or cake) **2** a spatula used for spreading paint or printer's ink **3** a utensil (e g a FISH SLICE) with a broad blade used for lifting, turning, or serving food **4** a flight of a ball that deviates from a straight course in the direction of the dominant hand of the player propelling it; *also* a ball following such a course – compare HOOK **5a** a portion, share ⟨*a ~ of the profits*⟩ **b** a part or section detached from a larger whole ⟨*a sizable ~ of the public – Punch*⟩ [ME, fr MF *esclice* splinter, fr OF, fr *esclicier* to splinter, of Gmc origin; akin to OHG *slīzan* to tear apart – more at SLIT]

²**slice** *vt* 1 to cut through (as if) with a knife ⟨*~ a melon in two*⟩ **2** to cut into slices or sections ⟨*~d bread*⟩ **3** to hit (a ball) so that a slice results ~ *vi* 1 to slice something 2 to cut or pass *through* or *into* like a knife – **sliceable** *adj*, **slicer** *n*

**slice-of-'life** *adj* of or marked by the accurate transcription (e g into drama) of a segment of real life [fr the n phrase *slice of life*, trans of Fr *tranche de vie*]

¹**slick** /slik/ *vt* to make sleek or smooth ~ *vi*, *NAm informal* to spruce – usu + *up* [ME *sliken*; akin to OHG *slīhhan* to glide, Gk *leios* smooth]

²**slick** *adj* **1a** superficially plausible; glib, smooth **b** cleverly and effectively executed; polished ⟨*a ~ performance*⟩ **c** deft, skilful ⟨*~ goal-keeping*⟩ **2** of a tyre having no tread **3** *chiefly NAm* having a glassy surface; smooth, slippery – **slick** *adv*, **slickly** *adv*, **slickness** *n*

³**slick** *n* **1a** something having a smooth or slippery surface **b** a film of oil covering a patch of water, as spilled from an oil tanker **2** an implement for producing an even or polished surface **3** a car tyre made without a tread for maximum grip on the road (e g in motor racing) **4** *NAm* GLOSSY MAGAZINE

**slickenside** /'slikənsied/ *n* a flat often grooved surface produced on rock by the movement of one surface over another surface in close contact under pressure (e g in faulting) [E dial. *slicken* smooth (alter. of E ²*slick*) + E *side*] – **slickensided** *adj*

**slicker** /'slikə/ *n*, *NAm* **1** an oilskin; *broadly* a raincoat **2** *informal* **2a** an artful crook; a swindler **b** a city dweller, esp of natty appearance or sophisticated mannerisms [(1) ²*slick;* (2) *slick* (to defraud cleverly), fr ²*slick*]

¹**slide** /slied/ *vb* **slid** /slid/ *vi* **1a** to move in continuous contact with a smooth surface **b** to glide over snow or ice **2** to slip or fall by loss of grip or footing **3a** to pass quietly and un-

obtrusively; steal ⟨*the fox* slid *through the meadow*⟩ **b** to move smoothly and easily ⟨slid *into place*⟩ **4** to pass by smooth or imperceptible gradations ⟨*the economy* slid *from recession to depression*⟩ ~ *vt* 1 to cause to glide or slip 2 to place or introduce unobtrusively or stealthily ⟨slid *the bill into his hand*⟩ [ME *sliden*, fr OE *slīdan;* akin to MHG *slīten* to slide, Gk *leios* smooth – more at LIME] – **let slide** to allow (e g a situation) to deteriorate by taking no action

²**slide** *n* **1a** an act or instance of sliding **b(1)** a downward course; a fall ⟨*~ in living standards*⟩ **b(2)** PORTAMENTO (slide from one musical note to another) **2** a sliding part or mechanism: e g **2a** a U-shaped section of tube in the trombone that is pushed out and in to produce notes of different pitch **b(1)** a moving piece of a mechanism that is guided by a part along which it slides **b(2)** a guiding surface or channel (e g a feeding mechanism) along which something slides **3** a descent of a mass of earth, rock, or snow down a hill or mountainside – often in combination ⟨*land*slide⟩ **4a** a track or slope suitable for sliding or tobogganing **b** a chute with a slippery surface (e g in a children's playground) **5a** a flat piece of glass on which an object is mounted for examination under a microscope **b** a photographic transparency on a small plate or film suitably mounted for projection ⟨*holiday* ~s⟩ **6** *Br* a hair-slide

**slide fastener** *n*, *NAm* ZIP 3

**slide rule** *n* a calculating instrument consisting in its simple form of a ruler with a central slide, both of which are graduated in such a way that the addition of lengths corresponds to the multiplication of numbers

**slide valve** *n* a valve that opens and closes a passageway by sliding over a hole

**slideway** /'slied,way/ *n* a part (e g of a machine) along which something slides

**sliding door** /'slieding/ *n* a door that slides sideways along a track rather than opening from hinges

**sliding scale** *n* a flexible scale (e g of wages, tariffs, or subsidies) that is geared to some other variable factor (e g cost-of-living index or price changes) so that levels of one can be set according to levels of the other

**sliding seat** *n* a seat in a racing rowing boat that slides forwards and backwards with the rower's movements so as to add the rower's leg power to the rowing stroke

¹**slight** /sliet/ *adj* **1a** having a slim or frail build **b** lacking strength or bulk; flimsy **2a** unimportant, trivial ⟨*the damage was ~*⟩ **b** not serious or involving risk; minor ⟨*caught a ~ chill*⟩ **c** small in degree or amount; scanty, meagre ⟨*~ knowledge of the language*⟩ [ME, smooth, slight, prob fr MD *slicht;* akin to OHG *slīhhan* to glide – more at SLICK] – **slightly** *adv*, **slightness** *n* – **in the slightest** at all; a bit ⟨*I don't mind* in the slightest⟩

²**slight** *vt* 1 to treat as slight or unimportant; make light of ⟨*~ed my efforts at reform*⟩ **2** to treat with disdain or pointed indifference; snub **3** *NAm* to perform or attend to carelessly or inadequately

³**slight** *n* 1 an act of slighting 2 a humiliating affront; a snub

**slighting** /'slieting/ *adj* characterized by disregard or disrespect; disparaging ⟨*a ~ remark*⟩ – **slightingly** *adv*

**slily** /'slieli/ *adv* slyly

¹**slim** /slim/ *adj* **-mm-** **1a** of small or narrow circumference or width, esp in proportion to length or height **b** slender in build; not chubby; trim **2** scanty, slight ⟨*a ~ chance of success*⟩ *antonym* chubby (of people) [D, bad, inferior, fr MD *slimp* crooked, bad; akin to MHG *slimp* awry] – **slimly** *adv*, **slimness** *n*

²**slim** **-mm-** *vt* to cause to be or appear more slender ⟨*a style that ~s the waist*⟩ ~ *vi* to (try to) become thinner (e g by dieting and exercise)

**slim down** *vt* to reduce in number or extent ⟨*a slimmed down organization*⟩

¹**slime** /sliem/ *n* 1 soft wet mud 2 a thick runny slippery substance usu regarded as unpleasant or offensive ⟨*a pond covered in green ~*⟩ **3** mucus or a mucuslike substance secreted by various animals (e g slugs and catfishes) [ME, fr OE *slīm;* akin to OHG *slīmen* to smooth, L *lima* file – more at LIME]

²**slime** *vt* to smear or cover with slime

**slime mould** *n* MYXOMYCETE (any of a group of simple organisms usu classified as fungi)

**slimline** /'slim,lien/ *adj* 1 SLIM 1a 2 making one look slim ⟨*a ~ tracksuit*⟩ **3** of or being a slender fluorescent tube used in lamps and lighting

**slimmer** /'slimə/ *n* a person who is trying to lose weight (e g by dieting and exercise)

**slimming** /'sliming/ *adj* giving an effect of slenderness ⟨*a dress with a ~ hipline*⟩

**slimpsy** /'slimpsi/ *adj, NAm* slimsy [blend of *limp* and *slimsy*]

**slimsy** /'slimzi/ *adj, NAm* flimsy, frail [blend of *slim* and *flimsy*]

**slimy** /'sliemi/ *adj* **1** of or like slime; VISCOUS and slippery; *also* covered with or yielding slime **2** *informal* vile, offensive **3** *chiefly Br informal* characterized by obsequious flattery; offensively ingratiating – **slimily** *adv*, **sliminess** *n*

¹**sling** /sling/ *vt* **slung** /slung/ **1** to cast with a careless and usu sweeping or swirling motion; fling ⟨slung *the coat over her shoulder*⟩ **2** to throw (eg a stone) with a sling **3** *Br informal* to remove or expel unceremoniously ⟨*was* slung *out of the team for misconduct*⟩ **synonyms** see ¹THROW [ME *slingen*, prob fr ON *slyngva* to hurl; akin to OE & OHG *slingan* to creep, twist, Lith *slinkti*] – **slinger** *n*

**sling off** *vi, chiefly Austr informal* to jeer *at* or *about*; mock

²**sling** *n* an act of slinging or hurling a stone or other missile

³**sling** *n* **1** a simple weapon for throwing stones that usu consists of a short strap that is looped round the missile, whirled round, and then released at one end **2a** a usu looped line used to hoist, lower, or carry something **b** a device (eg a rope net) for enclosing material to be hoisted by a tackle or crane **3a** a usu three-cornered piece of cloth suspended from the neck to support an injured arm or hand **b** a device similar to a sling for carrying a baby [ME, perh fr MLG *slinge;* akin to OHG *slinga* sling, *slingan* to creep, twist]

⁴**sling** *vt* **slung** /slung/ to place in a sling for hoisting or lowering

⁵**sling** *n* an alcoholic drink served hot or iced and usu made of whisky, brandy, or esp gin with plain or carbonated water, sugar, and sometimes BITTERS ⟨*gin ~*⟩ ⟨*rum ~*⟩ [origin unknown]

**slingback** /'sling,bak/ *n* a backless shoe that is attached at the heel by a strap passing round the back of the ankle

**slingshot** /'sling,shot/ *n, NAm* a catapult

¹**slink** /slingk/ *vb* **slunk** /slungk/ *also* **slinked** *vi* **1** to go or move stealthily or furtively (eg in fear or shame); steal **2** to move in a sinuous provocative manner ~ *vt, esp of a domestic animal* to give premature birth to [ME *slinken*, fr OE *slincan* to creep; akin to OE *slingan* to creep, twist]

²**slink** *n* the prematurely born young (eg a calf) of an animal; *also* the flesh or skin of such young

³**slink** *adj* born prematurely or abortively ⟨*a ~ calf*⟩

**slinky** /'slingki/ *adj* **1** characterized by slinking; stealthily quiet ⟨*~ movements*⟩ **2** sleek and sinuous in movement or outline; *esp* following the lines of the body in a sensual flowing manner ⟨*a ~ catsuit*⟩ – **slinkily** *adv*, **slinkiness** *n*

¹**slip** /slip/ *vb* **-pp-** *vi* **1a** to move with a smooth sliding motion **b** to move or pass quietly, quickly, and unobtrusively ⟨*~ped out of the meeting early*⟩ ⟨*the years ~ped by*⟩ **2a** to escape (eg from memory or consciousness) **b** to be uttered inadvertently ⟨*the words just ~ped out*⟩ **3a** to slide out of place or away from a support or one's grasp **b** to lose one's balance (eg by sliding on or down a slippery surface); skid ⟨*~ on the stairs*⟩ **4** to get speedily *into* or *out of* clothing ⟨*~ped into his coat*⟩ **5** to make a mistake; blunder – often + *up* **6** to fall off from a standard or accustomed level by degrees; decline, lapse ⟨*her work has ~ped a bit lately*⟩ **7** SIDESLIP **8** *of a clutch* to fail to engage properly ~ *vt* **1** to cause to move easily and smoothly; slide **2a** to escape or free oneself from ⟨*the dog ~ped his collar*⟩ **b** to escape from (one's memory or notice) ⟨*I had intended keeping the appointment but it ~ped my mind*⟩ **3** to cast, shed ⟨*the snake ~ped its skin*⟩ **4** to put *on* or take *off* (a garment) quickly and casually ⟨*~ your coat off*⟩ **5a** to let loose from a restraining leash or grasp **b** to cause to slip open; release, undo ⟨*~ a lock*⟩ **c** to let go of **d** to detach rather than bring aboard (an anchor or anchor cable), esp when leaving an anchorage in haste **6** to insert, place, or pass quietly or secretly ⟨*~ped a pound note into her hand*⟩ **7** *of an animal* to abort **8** to dislocate (a bone) – compare SLIPPED DISC **9** to transfer (a stitch) from one needle to another without knitting it **10** to keep in partial engagement by resting a foot continuously on the pedal ⟨*~ the clutch*⟩ **11** to avoid (a punch) by moving the body or head quickly to one side [ME *slippen,* fr MD or MLG; akin to Gk *olibros* slippery, *leios* smooth – more at LIME] – **let slip 1** LET FALL **2** to fail to take ⟨let slip *a chance*⟩ – see also **slip through one's** FINGERS

²**slip** *n* **1** a sloping ramp extending out into the water to serve as a place for landing, repairing, or building ships; a slipway **2a** a mistake in judgment, policy, or procedure; a blunder **b** an

inadvertent and trivial mistake or error ⟨*a ~ of the tongue*⟩ **3** a lead (eg for a dog) made so that it can be quickly released **4a** the act or an instance of slipping ⟨*a ~ on the ice*⟩; *also* a sudden mishap ⟨*many a ~ between the cup and the lip*⟩ **b** (a movement producing) a small geological fault **c** a fall from some level or standard; a decline ⟨*a ~ in share prices*⟩ **5** a women's undergarment hanging from the shoulders or the waist **6** a case into which something is slipped; *specif* a pillowcase **7a** retrograde movement of a belt on a pulley **b** the amount of leakage past the piston of a pump or the impellers of a blower **8** a disposition or tendency to slip easily **9** the action or an instance of sideslipping **10** any of several fielding positions in cricket that are close to the batsman and just to the right of the wicketkeeper for a right-handed batsman ⟨*caught at ~*⟩ ⟨*caught in the ~*s⟩; *also* a fieldsman occupying any of these positions **11** any of the ends of the cords or tapes to which book sections are sewn and which are attached to the covers in binding – **give somebody the slip** to escape from or elude somebody

³**slip** *n* **1** a small shoot or twig cut for planting or grafting; SCION **2a** a long thin strip (eg of wood or glass) **b** a small piece of paper; *specif* a printed form **3** a young and slim person ⟨*a mere ~ of a girl*⟩ **4** *NAm* a long seat or narrow pew [ME *slippe,* prob fr MD or MLG, split, slit, flap]

⁴**slip** *vt* **-pp-** to take cuttings from (a plant); divide into slips ⟨*~ a geranium*⟩

⁵**slip** *n* a semifluid mixture of clay and water used by potters (eg for coating or decorating wares) [ME *slyp* slime, fr OE *slypa* slime, paste; akin to OE *slūpan* to slip – more at SLEEVE]

**slip carriage** *n* a railway carriage that can be detached without stopping the train

**slipcase** /'slip,kays/ *n* a protective container with one open end for one or more books

**slip coach** *n* SLIP CARRIAGE

**slipcover** /'slip,kuvə/ *n, NAm* **1** LOOSE-COVER **2** a book cover; DUST JACKET

**slipform** /'slip,fawm/ *vt* to construct with the use of a SLIP FORM

**slip form** *n* a mould for concrete that is moved slowly as the concrete is placed during construction (eg of a building or pavement)

**slipknot** /'slip,not/ *n* **1** RUNNING KNOT (knot that slips along the rope) **2** a knot that can be untied by pulling

**slip-off slope** *n* the gentle slope of a river bed and bank on the inside of a meander curve

'**slip-,on** *n* a shoe or garment without fastenings that can be easily slipped on or off – **slip-on** *adj*

**slippage** /'slipij/ *n* **1** (the amount or extent of) slipping **2** a loss in transmission of power; *also* the difference between theoretical and actual output (eg of power)

**slipped disc** /slipt/ *n* a protrusion of one of the cartilage discs between spinal vertebrae causing pressure on spinal nerves and usu resulting in intense pain in the lower back or hip

¹**slipper** /'slipə/ *n* a light soft shoe that is worn around the house, esp with nightwear [ME, fr *slippen* to slip]

²**slipper** *vt* to beat with a slipper, esp as a child's punishment

**slipper bath** *n* **1** a bath that is covered over at the end at which the feet and legs go **2** *pl* public baths

**slipper limpet** *n* a limpet (genus *Crepidula*) that is a serious pest of oyster beds

**slipper satin** *n* a heavy lustrous high-quality satin

**slippery** /'slip(ə)ri/ *adj* **1a** causing or tending to cause something to slide or fall, esp by being icy, greasy, wet, or polished ⟨*~ roads*⟩ **b** tending to slip from the grasp ⟨*~ eel*⟩ **2** not firmly fixed; unstable ⟨*a ~ situation*⟩ **3** not to be trusted; shifty [alter. of ME *slipper,* fr OE *slipor;* akin to MLG *slipper* slippery, *slippen* to slip] – **slipperiness** *n*

**slippy** /'slipi/ *adj, informal* SLIPPERY

**slip ring** *n* a conducting metal ring that makes sliding contact with the BRUSHES to take or deliver current (eg in a dynamo or motor) [²*slip*]

**slip road** *n, Br* a short one-way road providing access to or exit from a major road, esp a motorway

'**slip-,sheet** *vt* to insert SLIP SHEETS between (newly printed sheets)

**slip sheet** *n* a sheet of paper placed between newly printed sheets to prevent unwanted transfer of ink [¹*slip*]

**slipshod** /'slip,shod/ *adj* **1** careless, slovenly ⟨*~ reasoning*⟩ **2** *archaic* wearing very loose or worn shoes; down-at-heel [¹*slip* + *shod*]

**slipslop** /'slip,slop/ *n, archaic* **1** sloppy food or drink **2** inane or shallow talk or writing; twaddle [redupl of ²*slop*] – **slip-slop** *adj*

**slip stitch** *n* **1** a concealed stitch for sewing folded edges (eg hems) made by alternately running the needle inside the fold and picking up a thread or two from the body of the article **2** an unworked stitch; *specif* a knitting stitch that is transferred from one needle to another without working it – **slipstitch** *vt*

¹**slipstream** /'slip,streem/ *n* **1** a stream of gas or liquid (eg air or water) driven backwards by a revolving propeller **2** an area of reduced air pressure and forward suction immediately behind a rapidly moving vehicle **3** something that sweeps one along in its course ⟨*people who service the jet set and ride in its ~ – Woman's Own*⟩

²**slipstream** *vi* to drive or ride in a slipstream and so gain the advantage of reduced air resistance (eg in a bicycle race)

'**slip-,up** *n* a mistake, oversight

**slipway** /'slip,way/ *n* ²SLIP 1; *esp* one on which ships are built

¹**slit** /slit/ *vt* **-tt-; slit 1** to make a slit in **2** to cut or tear into long narrow strips *synonyms* see ²TEAR [ME *slitten;* akin to MHG *slitzen* to slit, OHG *slīzan* to tear apart, OE *sciell* shell – more at SHELL] – **slitter** *n*

²**slit** *n* a long narrow cut or opening – **slit** *adj,* **slitless** *adj*

**slither** /'slidhə/ *vi* **1** to slide unsteadily, esp (as if) on a slippery surface **2** to slip or slide like a snake – *vt* to cause to slide [ME *slideren,* fr OE *slidrian,* freq of *slīdan* to slide] – **slithery** *adj*

**slit pocket** *n* a pocket suspended on the wrong side of a garment from a finished slit on the right side that serves as its opening

**slit trench** *n* a narrow trench, esp for shelter in battle from bomb and shell fragments

¹**sliver** /'slivə/ *n* **1** a small slender usu sharp piece cut or torn off; a splinter ⟨*a ~ of glass*⟩ **2** an untwisted strand or rope of textile fibre produced by a combing machine [ME *slivere,* fr *sliven* to slice off, fr OE *-slīfan;* akin to OE *-slǣfan* to cut]

²**sliver** *vt* to cut or break into slivers – *~ vi* to become split into slivers; splinter

**slivovitz** /'slivəvits, 'slee-, -vich/ *n* a dry usu colourless plum brandy made esp in the Balkan countries [Serbo-Croatian *šljivovica,* fr *šljiva, sliva* plum; akin to Russ *sliva* plum – more at LIVID]

**slob** /slob/ *n, informal* a slovenly or uncouth person [Ir *slab* mud] – **slobbish** *adj*

¹**slobber** /'slobə/ *vi* **1** to let saliva dribble from the mouth; drool **2** to give vent to emotion effusively and esp oversentimentally – often + *over – vt* to smear (as if) with food or saliva dribbling from the mouth ⟨*the baby ~ed his bib*⟩ [ME *sloberen;* akin to LG *slubberen* to sip, Lith *lūpa* lip] – **slobberer** *n*

²**slobber** *n* **1** saliva drooled from the mouth **2** drivelling or oversentimental language or conduct – **slobbery** *adj*

**slob ice** *n, Can* heavy sludgy usu sea ice that is packed into a dense mass

**sloe** /sloh/ *n* (the small blue-black spherical sour fruit of) the blackthorn [ME *slo,* fr OE *slāh* – more at LIVID]

,**sloe-'eyed** *adj* **1** having soft dark bluish or purplish black eyes **2** having slanted eyes

**sloe gin** *n* a reddish liqueur consisting of gin in which sloes and sugar have been steeped

¹**slog** /slog/ *vb* **-gg-** *vt* **1** to hit (eg a cricket ball or an opponent in boxing) hard and often wildly; slug **2** to plod (one's way) perseveringly, esp in the face of difficulty – *vi* **1** to walk or travel slowly and laboriously; plod ⟨*~ged through the snow*⟩ **2** to work laboriously **3** to strike a hard and often wild blow [origin unknown] – **slogger** *n*

²**slog** *n* **1** persistent hard work ⟨*a hard ~ teaching the child to read*⟩ **2** an arduous march or tramp **3** a hard and often wild hit

**slogan** /'slohgən/ *n* **1** a war cry or rallying cry formerly used by a Scottish clan **2** a phrase used repeatedly to express and esp make public a particular view, position, or aim **3** a brief catchy phrase used in advertising or promotion [alter. of earlier *slogorn,* fr ScGael *sluagh-ghairm* army cry] – **sloganeer** *n*

**slogan·ize, -ise** /'slohgəniez/ *vt* to express as a slogan – **sloganizer** *n*

**sloid, sloyd** /sloyd (*Swedish* sljd)/ a Swedish system of manual training involving woodwork [Sw *slöjd* skill, skilled labour; akin to ON *slǣgth* cunning – more at SLEIGHT]

**sloop** /sloohp/ *n* a single-masted sailing vessel with a FORE-AND-AFT mainsail suspended from the mast along its front edge and the headsail set on the FORESTAY (stay running from the head of the mast to the bow of the ship to support the mast) [D *sloep*]

**sloop of war** *n* a small warship carrying guns on one deck only

**sloot** /slooht/ *n, SAfr* a small watercourse or irrigation channel [Afrik, fr D, ditch, fr MD]

¹**slop** /slop/ *n* **1** a loose smock or overall **2** *pl* articles (eg clothing) sold to sailors from a SLOP CHEST [ME *sloppe,* prob fr MD *slop;* akin to OE ofer*slop* surplice, overall]

²**slop** *n* **1** liquid mud; slush **2 slops** *pl,* **slop** thin tasteless drink or liquid food **3** liquid spilt or splashed **4 slops** *pl,* **slop 4a** food waste or a thin gruel fed to animals **b** liquid household refuse (eg dirty water or urine) **5** mawkish sentiment in speech or writing; gush [ME *sloppe,* prob fr OE *-sloppe* dung; akin to OE *slyppe, slypa* slime, paste – more at ⁵SLIP]

³**slop** *vb* **-pp-** *vt* **1a** to cause (a liquid) to spill over the side of a container **b** to splash or spill liquid on **2** to dish out messily ⟨*~ soup into a bowl*⟩ **3** to eat or drink greedily or noisily; gobble **4** to feed slop to ⟨*~ the pigs*⟩ *~ vi* **1** to tramp through mud or slush **2a** to become spilled or splashed **b** to exceed a boundary or limit; spill *over* **3** to show mawkish sentiment; gush – usu + *over* **4** to slouch, flop ⟨*to ~ on to a traffic bollard – Punch*⟩ ⟨*~ping around the house in a dressing gown*⟩

**slop out** *vi, of a prisoner* to empty slops from a chamber pot

**slop basin** *n, Br* a bowl for receiving the dregs left in tea or coffee cups at table

**slop bowl** *n, Br* SLOP BASIN

**slop chest** *n* a store of clothing and personal articles (eg tobacco) carried on merchant ships for issue to the crew and usu charged against their wages [¹*slop*]

¹**slope** /slohp/ *vi* **1** to take an oblique course **2** to lie at a slant; incline – *vt* to cause to incline or place at a slant – see also **slope** ARMS [ME *slope* obliquely] – **sloper** *n*

**slope off** *vi, informal* to go away, esp furtively or to avoid work; sneak off

²**slope** *n* **1** ground that forms a natural or artificial incline: eg **1a** *usu pl* the side of a mountain or hill **b** the part of a continent draining to a particular ocean **2** an inclined surface **3** upward or downward inclination or (degree of) slant; gradient **4** *maths* **4a** the TANGENT of the angle made by a straight line with the x-axis **b** the slope of a straight line touching a curve at a point

**slop pail** *n* a pail for household slops; *esp* one for receiving bedroom slops (eg used washing water or the contents of a chamber pot)

**sloppy** /'slopi/ *adj* **1a** wet so as to splash or spatter; slushy ⟨*a ~ racetrack*⟩ ⟨*a ~ kiss*⟩ **b** wet or smeared (as if) with something slopped over **c** disagreeably wet; watery ⟨*~ porridge*⟩ **2** slovenly, careless ⟨*she's a ~ dresser*⟩ ⟨*did ~ work*⟩ **3** disagreeably effusive or oversentimental **4** *of a garment* loose and usu casual ⟨*a ~ sweater*⟩ – **sloppily** *adv,* **sloppiness** *n*

**sloppy joe** /joh/ *n* a large baggy jumper [*Joe,* nickname for *Joseph*]

**slopwork** /'slop,wuhk/ *n* **1** the manufacture of cheap ready-made clothing **2** hasty slovenly work – **slopworker** *n*

¹**slosh** /slosh/ *n* **1** slush **2** the slap or splash of liquid **3** *chiefly Br informal* a heavy blow; a bash ⟨*gave him a ~ on the head*⟩ [prob blend of *slop* and *slush*] – **sloshy** *adj*

²**slosh** *vi* **1** to flounder or splash through water, mud, or slush **2** to flow with a splashing motion ⟨*water ~ed all round him*⟩ *~ vt* **1** to splash (something) about in liquid **2a** to splash (a liquid) about, on, or into something **b** to pour or apply clumsily and hastily ⟨*~ed the paint onto the wall*⟩ **3** to make wet by splashing **4** *chiefly Br informal* a hit, beat ⟨*~ed him on the head with a bucket*⟩

**sloshed** /slosht/ *adj, informal* drunk

¹**slot** /slot/ *n* **1** a narrow opening or slit (eg for inserting a coin) **2** a passage through the wing of an aircraft or missile for improving airflow over the wing so as to increase lift and delay stalling of the wing – called also SLAT **3** a place or position in an organization, series, or schedule [ME, the hollow of the breastbone, fr MF *esclot,* of unknown origin]

²**slot** *vb* **-tt-** *vt* **1** to cut a slot in **2** to place in or assign to a slot – often + *in* or *into* ⟨*~ted some reading in as he waited*⟩ **3** to insert neatly ⟨*ran round the goalkeeper and ~ted the ball in*⟩ *~ vi* to fit in a slot or by means of slots ⟨*a do-it-yourself bookcase that ~s together in seconds*⟩ ⟨*it ~s in neatly between the larger and smaller versions*⟩

**³slot** *n, pl* **slot** the track of an animal (eg a deer) [MF *esclot* hoofprint, track, prob of Scand origin; akin to ON *slōth* track (cf SLEUTHHOUND)]

**sloth** /slohth/ *n* **1** disinclination to action or work; indolence **2** any of several slow-moving tree-dwelling mammals that inhabit tropical forests of S and Central America, hang face upwards from the branches, and feed on leaves, shoots, and fruits *synonyms* see LETHARGY [ME *slouthe*, fr *slow*] – **slothful** *adj*, **slothfully** *adv*, **slothfulness** *n*

**sloth bear** *n* a common bear (*Melursus labiatus*) of India and Sri Lanka with a long snout

**slot machine** *n* **1** a machine (eg for selling refreshments) whose operation is begun by dropping a coin or token into a slot – compare VENDING MACHINE **2** *chiefly NAm* FRUIT MACHINE

**slot seam** *n* CHANNEL SEAM

**¹slouch** /slowch/ *n* **1** a gait or posture characterized by ungainly stooping of the head and shoulders or excessive relaxation of body muscles **2** *informal* a lazy, incompetent, or awkward person – usu neg ⟨*no ~ at football*⟩ [origin unknown]

**²slouch** *vi* **1** to walk with or assume a slouch ⟨*~ed behind the wheel*⟩ **2** to hang down limply; droop ~ *vt* to cause to droop ⟨*~ a hat over the eyes*⟩ – **sloucher** *n*

**slouch hat** *n* a soft usu felt hat with a wide flexible brim

**¹slough** /slow/ *n* **1a** a place of deep mud or mire **b** a swamp, bog **2** a state of hopeless dejection or moral degradation ⟨*a ~ of self-pity*⟩ **3** *chiefly NAm* a marshy inlet or backwater [ME *slogh*, fr OE *slōh*; akin to MHG *slouche* ditch] – **sloughy** *adj*

**²slough** *also* **sluff** *n* /sluf/ **1** the cast-off skin of a snake **2** a mass of dead tissue separating from an ulcer **3** something that may be shed or cast off ⟨*when shall this ~ of sense be cast* – A E Housman⟩ [ME *slughe*; akin to MHG *slūch* snakeskin, Lith *šliaužti* to crawl]

**³slough** *also* **sluff** /sluf/ *vi* **1a** to become shed or cast off **b** to cast off a skin **c** to separate in the form of dead tissue from living tissue **2** to crumble slowly and fall away ⟨*the ~ing of surface rock*⟩ ~ *vt* **1** to cast off (eg a skin or shell) **2a** to get rid of or discard as irksome or objectionable – usu + *off* **b** to dispose of (a losing card in bridge) by discarding

**slough of despond** /slow/ *n* a state of extreme despondency [fr the *Slough of Despond*, deep bog into which the hero Christian falls in the allegory *Pilgrim's Progress* by John Bunyan †1688 E preacher & writer]

**Slovak** /'slohvak/ *n* **1** a member of a SLAVONIC people of E Czechoslovakia **2** the SLAVONIC language of the Slovaks [Slovak *Slovák*, lit., Slav] – **Slovak** *adj*, **Slovakian** *adj or n*

**sloven** /'sluvn/ *n* one habitually negligent of neatness or cleanliness, esp in personal appearance *synonyms* see SLUT [ME *sloveyn* rascal, perh fr Flem *sloovin* woman of low character]

**Slovene** /'slohveen/ *n* **1a** a member of a SLAVONIC people living in Yugoslavia **b** a native or inhabitant of Slovenia **2** the SLAVONIC language of the Slovenes [Ger, fr Slovene *Sloven*] – **Slovene** *adj*, **Slovenian** *adj or n*

**slovenly** /'sluvnli, 'slo-/ *adj* **1** untidy, esp in personal appearance or habits **2** slipshod, careless ⟨*~ in thought*⟩ – **slovenliness** *n*, **slovenly** *adv*

**¹slow** /sloh/ *adj* **1a** lacking in intelligence; dull ⟨*a ~ student*⟩ **b** naturally inert or sluggish ⟨*a ~ imagination*⟩ **2a** lacking in readiness, promptness, or willingness ⟨*a shop with ~ service*⟩ **b** not quickly aroused or excited ⟨*was ~ to anger*⟩ **3a** flowing or proceeding with little speed or at less than usual speed ⟨*traffic was ~*⟩ **b** exhibiting or marked by reduced speed ⟨*he moved with ~ deliberation*⟩ **c**(1) low, feeble ⟨*~ fire*⟩ **c**(2) of an oven set at a low temperature **4** requiring a long time; gradual ⟨*a ~ convalescence*⟩ **5a** having qualities that hinder or prohibit rapid progress or action ⟨*a ~ road*⟩ **b** tending to cause something (eg a ball) to bounce or run slowly ⟨*a ~ putting green*⟩ **6** registering a time earlier than the correct one ⟨*his clock is ~*⟩ **7a** lacking in liveliness or variety; boring **b** marked by reduced sales or patronage ⟨*business was ~*⟩ **8** of or being slow esp spin bowling *synonyms* see STUPID [ME, fr OE *slāw*; akin to OHG *slēo* dull, Skt *srēvayati* he causes to fail] – **slowish** *adj*, **slowly** *adv*, **slowness** *n*

**²slow** *adv* in a slow manner; slowly

*usage* The use of **slow** as an adverb has been established in English since the 16th century ⟨*how slow this old Moon wanes* – Shak⟩, but is today considered less formal than **slowly**. **Slow** is particularly used with verbs of motion, and in certain set expressions such as

**go-slow**, but both alternatives are usually possible ⟨*drive slow/ slowly*⟩ ⟨*you should speak slower/more slowly*⟩.

**³slow** *vb* to make or become slow or slower ⟨*~ a car*⟩ ⟨*production of new cars ~ed*⟩

**slowcoach** /'sloh,kohch/ *n* someone who thinks or acts slowly

**slowdown** /'sloh,down/ *n* a slowing down ⟨*a business ~*⟩

**slow-'footed** *adj* moving at a very slow pace; plodding ⟨*a ~ novel*⟩ – **slow-footedness** *n*

**slow learner** *n* a child who is behind others in educational attainment

**slow loris** /'loris/ *n* a stocky relatively heavy-limbed LORIS (nocturnal tree-living animal) (*Nycticebus coucang*) of India and the E Indies

**slow match** *n* a match or fuse made so as to burn slowly and evenly, and used for firing (eg of blasting charges)

**slow motion** *n* a technique in filming which allows an action to be shown as if it is taking place unnaturally slowly, and usu involves increasing the number of frames exposed in a given time and then projecting the film at the standard speed – **slow-motion** *adj*

**slow neutron** *n* a neutron with low KINETIC ENERGY (energy of motion)

**slowpoke** /-,pohk/ *n, chiefly NAm* a slowcoach

**slow-'witted** *adj* slow in perception and understanding; mentally dull

**slowworm** /'sloh,wuhm/ *n* a legless European lizard (*Anguis fragilis*) with a grey-brown snakelike body, popularly believed to be blind [alter. (influenced by ¹*slow*) of ME *sloworm*, fr OE *slāwyrm*, fr *slā-* (akin to Sw *slå* earthworm) + *wyrm* worm]

**sloyd** /sloyd/ *n* SLOID (training in the use of tools)

**¹slub** /slub/ *n* a small thickened section in a yarn or thread [origin unknown] – **slub** *adj*

**²slub** *vt* -**bb**- to draw out and twist (eg slivers of wool) slightly in preparation for spinning [back-formation fr *slubbing*]

**³slub** *n* slubbing

**slubbing** /'slubing/ *n* ROVING (twisted roll or strand of fibres) [origin unknown]

**sludge** /sluj/ *n* **1** mud, mire; *esp* a muddy deposit (eg on a riverbed); ooze **2** a slimy or slushy mass, deposit, or sediment: eg **2a** precipitated solid matter produced by water and sewage treatment processes **b** muddy sediment in a steam boiler **c** a precipitate or settling (eg a mixture of impurities and acid) from a MINERAL OIL **3** new sea ice forming in thin detached crystals [prob alter. of *slush*] – **sludgy** *adj*

**¹slue** /slooh/ *n, NAm* SLOUGH (swamp or creek)

**²slue** *vb, chiefly NAm* ³SLEW (to turn or twist about)

**³slue** *n, chiefly NAm* ⁴SLEW (result of turning or twisting)

**sluff** /sluf/ *vb or n* ²·³SLOUGH

**¹slug** /slug/ *n* **1** a sluggard **2** any of numerous slimy elongated chiefly ground-living INVERTEBRATE animals (family Limacidae of the class Gastropoda, phylum Mollusca) related to the snails that are found in most parts of the world where there is a reasonable supply of moisture and have no shell or only a much reduced one [ME *slugge*, of Scand origin; akin to Norw dial. *slugga* to walk sluggishly; akin to ME *sloor* mud – more at SLUR]

**²slug** *n* **1** a lump, disc, or cylinder of material (eg plastic or metal): eg **1a**(1) a musket ball **a**(2) *informal* a bullet **b** a piece of metal roughly shaped for subsequent processing **c** *NAm* a disc for insertion in a slot machine; *esp* one used illegally instead of a coin **2a** a strip of metal used in printing that is thicker than a LEAD (strip used to separate lines of type) **b** a line of type cast as one piece **3** the unit of mass in the FOOT-POUND-SECOND system that will acquire an acceleration of one foot per second per second when acted upon by a force of one pound; 32.174 pounds (about 14.6 kilograms) **4** *chiefly NAm informal* a quantity of spirits that can be swallowed at a single gulp; a swig [prob fr ¹*slug*]

**³slug** *n, informal* **1** a heavy blow, esp with the fist **2** *Austr* a sharp rise in price [prop var of ²*slog*]

**⁴slug** *vt* -**gg**- *informal* **1** to hit hard (as if) with the fist or a bat **2** *Austr* to overcharge

**slugabed** /'slugəbed/ *n* a person who stays in bed out of laziness; *broadly* a sluggard

**sluggard** /'slugəd/ *n* a habitually lazy person or animal [ME *sluggart, slogart*, fr *slugge* slug + *-art, -ard*] – **sluggard** *adj*, **sluggardly** *adj*

**slugger** /'slugə/ *n* one who or that which strikes hard or with heavy blows: eg **a** a hard-hitting batter in baseball **b** a boxer who punches hard but has usu little defensive skill

**sluggish** /'slugish/ *adj* **1** averse to activity or exertion; lazy; *also* torpid **2** slow to respond (e g to stimulation or treatment) ⟨*a ~ engine*⟩ **3a** markedly slow in movement, flow, or growth **b** economically inactive or slow ⟨*a ~ market*⟩ *synonyms* see LETHARGY [ME, fr *slugge* slug] – **sluggishly** *adv*, **sluggishness** *n*

¹**sluice** /sloohs/ *n* **1a** an artificial passage for water (e g in a millstream) fitted with a valve or gate for stopping or regulating flow **b** a body of water pent up behind a floodgate **2** a dock gate; a floodgate **3a** a stream flowing through a floodgate **b** a channel to drain or carry off surplus water **4** a long inclined trough usu on the ground (e g for washing gold-bearing earth or for floating logs) [alter. of ME *scluse*, fr MF *escluse*, fr LL *exclusa*, fr L, fem of *exclusus*, pp of *excludere* to exclude]

²**sluice** *vt* **1** to draw off by or through a sluice **2a** to wash with or in water running (as if) through or from a sluice ⟨*trying to ~ his face without wetting his cuffs* – Richard Llewellyn⟩ **b** to drench with a sudden vigorous flow; flush **3** to transport (e g logs) in a sluice **4** *informal* to swish or swill (liquid, esp water) on or *around* ⟨*sluicing the wine around your mouth and between the teeth*⟩ ~ *vi* to pour (as if) from a sluice

**sluice gate** *n* a small gate for emptying the chamber of a canal lock or regulating the amount of water passing through a channel

**sluiceway** /'sloohs,way/ *n* an artificial channel into which water is let by a sluice

**sluit** /slooht/ *n, SAfr* SLOOT (irrigation or drainage ditch) [Afrik, alter. of *sloot*]

¹**slum** /slum/ *n* **1 slums** *pl*, **slum** an area, esp in a city, marked by overcrowding, run-down housing, and poverty **2** a squalid or disagreeable place to live (e g a street or house) [origin unknown]

²**slum** *vi* **-mm- 1** to live in squalor or on very slender means – often + *it* **2** to visit a place on a much lower social level, esp out of curiosity or for amusement; *also* to take on the characteristics of a lower social class – **slummer** *n*

¹**slumber** /'slumbə/ *vi* **1** to sleep, esp lightly; doze **2a** to be in a torpid or slothful state **b** to lie dormant or latent ⟨*a ~*ing *volcano*⟩ [ME *slumberen*, freq of *slumen* to doze, prob fr *slume* slumber, fr OE *slūma*; akin to Lith *slugti* to diminish – more at SLUR] – **slumberer** *n*

²**slumber** *n* **1a slumber**, **slumbers** *pl* sleep **b** a light sleep **2** lethargy, torpor

**slumberous**, **slumbrous** /'slumb(ə)rəs/ *adj* **1** heavy with sleep; sleepy ⟨*~ eyelids*⟩ **2** inducing sleep; soporific **3** marked by or suggestive of a state of sleep or lethargy; drowsy ⟨*a ~ peace pervaded every province* – Pearl Buck⟩

**slumbery** /'slumb(ə)ri/ *adj, archaic* slumberous

**slummy** /'slumi/ *adj* of or suggestive of a slum ⟨*a ~ little pub near the cattle market*⟩

¹**slump** /slump/ *vi* **1a** to fall or sink abruptly ⟨*morale ~ed with news of the defeat*⟩ **b** to drop down suddenly and heavily; collapse ⟨*~ed to the floor*⟩ **2** to have or take on a slack or drooping posture or carriage; slouch **3** to go into a slump ⟨*sales ~ed*⟩ [prob of Scand origin; akin to Norw *slumpa* to fall; akin to L *labi* to slide – more at SLEEP]

²**slump** *n* **1** a marked or sustained decline, esp in economic activity or prices **2** a period of unsuccessful play by a team or individual

**slung** /slung/ *past of* SLING

**slunk** /slungk/ *past of* SLINK

¹**slur** /sluh/ *vb* **-rr-** *vi* **1** to pass *over* without due mention, consideration, or emphasis ⟨*~red over certain facts*⟩ **2** to utter or pronounce words unclearly by running together and omission of sounds **3** to drag, shuffle ~ *vt* **1** to perform (successive notes of different pitch) in a smooth or connected manner **2a** to run together, omit parts of, or pronounce unclearly (words, sounds, etc) **b** to utter in a slurred manner [prob fr LG *slurrn* to shuffle; akin to ME *sloor* mud]

²**slur** *n* **1a** (a curved line connecting) notes to be sung to the same syllable or performed without a break **b** the combination of two or more slurred notes **2** a slurring manner of speech

³**slur** *vb* **-rr-** *vt* **1** to cast aspersions on; disparage **2** to make indistinct; obscure ~ *vi, of a sheet being printed* to slip so as to cause a slur [E dial. *slur* thin mud, fr ME *sloor*; akin to MHG *slier* mud, Lith *slugti* to diminish]

⁴**slur** *n* **1a** an insulting or disparaging remark; a slight **b** a shaming or degrading effect; a blot, stigma **2** a blurred spot on a printed sheet, esp as caused by movement of the FORME (type, blocks, etc) during the impression; *broadly* a smudge

**slurp** /sluhp/ *vb* to eat or drink noisily or with a sucking sound [D *slurpen;* akin to MLG *slorpen* to slurp] – **slurp** *n*

**slurry** /'sluri/ *n* a watery mixture of insoluble matter (e g mud, lime, or manure) [ME *slory*]

¹**slush** /slush/ *n* **1** a watery, semiliquid substance; *esp* partly melted snow **2a** liquid mud; mire **b** GROUT (substance for filling cracks esp in masonry) made from PORTLAND CEMENT, sand, and water **3** waste grease and fat from cooking – used esp by seamen **4** worthless and usu oversentimental material (e g literature) [perh of Scand origin; akin to Norw *slusk* slush] – **slushy** *adj*

²**slush** *vt* **1** to splash or coat with slush **2** to wash by drenching with water ~ *vi* **1** to splash in or through slush **2** to fill in (e g joints) with slush or grout

**slush fund** *n, chiefly NAm* a fund for bribing (public) officials or carrying on corrupting propaganda

**slut** /slut/ *n* **1** a dirty slovenly woman **2** an immoral woman; *esp* a prostitute **3** a female dog; a bitch [ME *slutte*] – **sluttish** *adj*, **sluttishly** *adv*, **sluttishness** *n*

*synonyms* Only a woman can be a **slut** or **sluttish**, a **slattern** or **slatternly**. A **slut** is even dirtier than a **slattern**. Men as well as women can be **slovens** or **slovenly**.

**sly** /slie/ *adj* **slier** *also* **slyer**; **sliest** *also* **slyest** /'slie·ist/ **1a** clever in concealing one's ends or intentions; furtive ⟨*the ~ fox*⟩ **b** lacking in integrity and candour; crafty ⟨*a ~ scheme*⟩ **2** lightly mischievous; roguish ⟨*gave me a ~ glance*⟩ **3** *chiefly dial* wise or clever in practical affairs [ME *sli*, fr ON *slægr*; akin to OE *slēan* to strike – more at SLAY] – **slyly** *adv*, **slyness** *n* – **on the sly** in a manner intended to avoid notice; secretly

*synonyms* Sly, cunning, foxy, crafty, wily, artful, tricky, and guileful all mean "using devious means to one's ends". Sly implies skilful concealment often combined with an amusing mischievousness. Cunning suggests the effective use of sometimes limited intelligence in overreaching or circumventing, and perhaps some deficiency of moral principle ⟨*he's always slipping out at night. They're cunning as the devil, these naturals* – Dorothy Sayers⟩. Foxy suggests a certain practised wariness ⟨*concealed his business interests with foxy secretiveness*⟩. Crafty and wily emphasize subtlety and fertility in the inventing of stratagems ⟨*a wily old diplomat*⟩. Artful often connotes no more than a sophisticated indirectness of dealing ⟨*an artful approach to the problem*⟩. All the foregoing words might be used with some admiration, but tricky and guileful are decidedly censorious, tricky suggesting unscrupulous shiftiness rather than skill, and guileful perhaps actual treachery.

**slyboots** /'slie,boohts/ *n pl but taking sing vb* a sly tricky person; *esp* one who is cunning or mischievous in an engaging way

'**sly-,grog** *n, Austr & NZ* drink sold illicitly

**slype** /sliep/ *n* a narrow passage; *specif* one between the TRANSEPT (cross-part of a church between the nave and the choir) and CHAPTER HOUSE or DEANERY in an English cathedral or abbey [prob fr Flem *slijpe* place for slipping in and out]

**S-M** /,es'em/ *n* SADOMASOCHISM (sexual pleasure from giving or receiving pain)

¹**smack** /smak/ *n* **1** a characteristic taste or flavour; *also* a slight hint of taste or quality ⟨*his work has a curious ~ of the vulgar about it*⟩ **2** a small quantity [ME, fr OE *smæc;* akin to OHG *smac* taste, Lith *smaguriauti* to nibble]

²**smack** *vt* **1** to open (the lips) with a sudden sharp sound, esp in anticipation or enjoyment of food or drink **2** to kiss loudly and heartily **3a** to slap smartly, esp in punishment ⟨*~ his ugly face*⟩ **b** to strike with the sound of a smack ~ *vi* to make or give a smack [akin to MD *smacken* to strike]

³**smack** *n* **1** a quick sharp noise made by smacking the lips **2** a loud kiss **3** a sharp blow, esp from something flat; a slap

⁴**smack** *adv, informal* squarely and sharply; directly ⟨*drove ~ into the car parked opposite*⟩

⁵**smack** *n* a small inshore fishing vessel [D *smak* or LG *smack*]

⁶**smack** *n, slang* heroin [perh fr Yiddish *shmek* sniff, whiff, pinch (of snuff)]

**smacker** /'smakə/ *n* **1** one who or that which smacks; *esp* a loud kiss **2** *Br slang* a pound sterling; *also, NAm* a dollar

**smacking** /'smaking/ *adj* brisk, lively ⟨*a ~ breeze*⟩

**smack of** *vt* **1** to have a taste or flavour of **2** to have a trace or suggestion of ⟨*a proposal that smacks of treason*⟩ [¹*smack*]

¹**small** /smawl/ *adj* **1a** having relatively little size or slight dimensions **b** immature, young ⟨*~ children*⟩ **2a** lower-case **b** not having a capital letter denoting a title and thus showing a reference to a general sense of a word rather than to a group

(eg a political party or artistic movement) using the same word with a capital letter as its name ⟨*my philosophy . . . is a liberal one, with a ~ "l"* – Reg Prentice⟩ **3a** minor in influence, power, or rank ⟨*only has a ~ say in the matter*⟩ **b** operating on a limited scale ⟨*a ~ farmer*⟩ **4a** lacking in strength ⟨*a ~ voice*⟩ **b** weak, diluted **5a** little in measurable aspect (eg quantity, amount, or value) **b** made up of few individuals or units ⟨*a ~ audience*⟩ **6a** of little consequence; trivial, unimportant ⟨*a ~ matter*⟩ **b** humble, modest ⟨*a ~ beginning*⟩ **c** limited in degree ⟨*paid ~ heed to his warning*⟩ ⟨*of no ~ importance*⟩ **7a** mean, petty ⟨*a harsh ~ man*⟩ **b** reduced to a humiliating position [ME *smal*, fr OE *smæl*; akin to OHG *smal* small, L *malus* bad] – **smallish** *adj*, **smallness** *n*

**synonyms** Small, little, tiny, wee, diminutive, minute, minuscule, microscopic, miniature, and petite all mean "below the average size". Small and little are the most general, and could replace any of the others, although little often carries an added suggestion of affection ⟨*her poor little hands*⟩ or of pettiness ⟨*silly little bureaucrats*⟩. Tiny and wee mean "very small" with the same suggestion of affection ⟨*a tiny baby*⟩, and wee having also a dialectal flavour. Even smaller, and in roughly descending scale of size, are diminutive, minute, minuscule, and microscopic, with minuscule sometimes adding the idea of pettiness ⟨*a minuscule salary*⟩ and microscopic the idea of fine precision. Miniature refers to things scaled down from the normal size ⟨*miniature railway*⟩. Petite applies specifically to a pleasingly small woman ⟨*petite actress*⟩. antonym large

²**small** *adv* **1** in or into small pieces **2** without force or loudness; faintly, timidly ⟨*speak as ~ as you will* – Shak⟩ **3** in a small manner or size ⟨*write ~*⟩
³**small** *n* **1** a part smaller and esp narrower than the remainder ⟨*the ~ of the back*⟩ **2** *pl* **2a** small-sized goods **b** *Br informal* small articles of underwear – used with reference to laundry ⟨*soaking his wife's ~s* – Punch⟩
**small ad** /ad/ *n*, *Br* a classified advertisement
**small arm** *n usu pl* a firearm fired while held in the hands
**small beer** *n* **1** weak or inferior beer **2** *informal* people or matters of little importance
'**small-,bore** *adj* being or involving a firearm of a relatively small calibre, esp 5.6 millimetres (0.22 inch) – compare FULL-BORE
**small calorie** *n* CALORIE 1a (unit of heat)
**small capital** *n* a letter having the form of but smaller than a capital letter (eg in THESE WORDS)
**small change** *n* **1** coins, esp of low value **2** something trifling or commonplace
**small-claims court** *n* a special court intended to simplify and speed up the process of handling small claims on debts
**small fry** *n* young or insignificant people, animals, or things – **small-fry** *adj*
**smallgoods** /'smawl,goodz/ *n*, *Austr* meat (eg bacon, sausages, or ham) sold in a form partially or completely prepared for eating
**smallholding** /'smawl,hohlding/ *n*, *chiefly Br* a small farm – **smallholder** *n*
**small hours** *n pl* the hours immediately following midnight
**small intestine** *n* the part of the intestine that lies between the stomach and COLON, consists of DUODENUM, JEJUNUM, and ILEUM, secretes digestive juices and ENZYMES, and is the chief site of the absorption of digested foodstuffs
,**small-'minded** *adj* **1** having narrow interests or outlook ⟨*a ~ man*⟩ **2** typical of a small-minded person; marked by pettiness, narrowness, or meanness ⟨*~ conduct*⟩ – **smallmindedly** *adv*, **small-mindedness** *n*
**small potatoes** *n pl but taking sing or pl vb*, **small potato** *n*, *informal* a person or matter of little importance
**smallpox** /'smawl,poks/ *n* an acute infectious, formerly often fatal, virus disease characterized by fever and a rash on the skin followed by the appearance of PUSTULES (blisters containing pus) that dry up and form scabs, eventually leaving permanent scars
**small print** *n* something made deliberately obscure; *specif* a part of a document (eg a contract) that is usu in small type and often confusingly worded and that specifies restrictions and conditions making the document less attractive than it might at first have seemed
'**small-,scale** *adj* small in scope or extent; *esp* small in operation ⟨*a ~ undertaking*⟩
**small screen** *n* television – usu + the
**small slam** *n* LITTLE SLAM (winning of tricks in bridge)

**small stuff** *n* small rope used on board ship (eg SPUN YARN or MARLINE) usu identified by the number of threads it contains
**smallsword** /'smawl,sawd/ *n* a light tapering sword for thrusting used chiefly in duelling and fencing
**small talk** *n* light or casual conversation; chitchat
'**small-,time** *adj* insignificant in operation and status; petty ⟨*~ hoodlums*⟩ – **small-timer** *n*
**small white** *n* a small white butterfly (*Pieris rapae*), common in many parts of the world, the pale green caterpillar of which is a serious pest on vegetable crops (eg cabbage, cauliflower, and mustard) – compare CABBAGE WHITE
**smalt** /smawlt, smolt/ *n* a deep blue pigment used esp as a colouring for glass and pottery and made from a mixture of chemical compounds including SILICA, POTASH, and OXIDE of cobalt [MF, fr OIt *smalto*, of Gmc origin; akin to OHG *smelzan* to melt – more at SMELT]
**smaltite** /'smawl,tiet/ *n* a bluish white or grey mineral with a metallic lustre that is essentially an ARSENIDE of cobalt and nickel [alter. of *smaltine*, fr Fr, fr *smalt*]
**smalto** /'smawltoh/ *n*, *pl* **smalti** /-ti/ coloured glass or enamel used in mosaic work; *also* a piece of such glass or enamel [It, smalt, smalto]
**smaragd** /'smaragd/ *n* a green gem; *esp* an emerald [ME *smaragde*, fr L *smaragdus*] – **smaragdine** *adj*
**smaragdite** /'smarag,diet/ *n* a green mineral of the AMPHIBOLE group [Fr, fr L *smaragdus* emerald – more at EMERALD]
**smarm** /smahm/ *vb*, *informal vt* **1** to make (one's way) by obsequiousness or fawning ⟨*~ing his way into the upper reaches of a society* – TLS⟩ **2** to smear or plaster – often + on or down ⟨*~ on a thick layer of makeup*⟩ ⟨*hair ~ed down with grease*⟩ ~ *vi* to seek favour by a servile or insinuating behaviour; fawn [origin unknown]
**smarmy** /'smahmi/ *adj* revealing or marked by oily flattery or smugness; unctuous ⟨*a tone of ~ self-satisfaction* – New Yorker⟩
'**smart** /smaht/ *vi* **1** to cause or be the cause or seat of a sharp pain; *also* to feel or have such a pain **2** to feel or endure distress, remorse, or embarrassment ⟨*~ing from a rebuke*⟩ **3** to pay a heavy or stinging penalty ⟨*would have to ~ for this foolishness*⟩ [ME *smerten*, fr OE *smeortan*; akin to OHG *smerzan* to pain, L *mordēre* to bite, Gk *marainein* to waste away]
²**smart** *adj* **1** making one smart; causing a sharp stinging ⟨*gave him a ~ blow with the ruler*⟩ **2** marked by often sudden forceful activity or vigorous strength ⟨*a ~ tug on the reins*⟩ **3** brisk, spirited ⟨*walking at a ~ pace*⟩ **4a** mentally alert; bright **b** shrewd ⟨*a ~ investment*⟩ **5a** witty, clever **b** impertinently witty or facetious ⟨*was sacked for being ~ with his boss*⟩ **6a** neat, trim **b** stylish or elegant in dress or appearance ⟨*she's a ~ dresser*⟩ ⟨*a ~ new coat of paint*⟩ **c** characteristic of or frequented by fashionable society ⟨*a ~ restaurant*⟩ **d** of or being the most modern technology; *specif*, of a missile or bomb containing a device that guides it to its target – **smartly** *adv*, **smartness** *n*
³**smart** *adv* in a smart manner; smartly
⁴**smart** *n* **1** a smarting pain; *esp* a stinging local pain **2** acute grief or remorse ⟨*was not the sort to get over ~s* – Sir Winston Churchill⟩
**smart alec, smart aleck** /'alik/ *n*, *derog* an obnoxiously conceited or arrogant person with pretensions to knowledge or cleverness [*Alec*, nickname for *Alexander*] – **smart-alecky**, **smart-aleck** *adj*
'**smart-,ass** /ahs/ *n or adj*, *slang* SMART ALEC
**smart bomb** *n* a bomb that can be guided (eg by a laser beam) to its target
**smarten** /'smaht(ə)n/ *vt* to make smart or smarter; *esp* to spruce ~ *vi* to smarten oneself □ usu + up
**smartish** /'smahtish/ *adj*, *Br informal* in a rapid manner; quickly ⟨*better get dressed ~*⟩
**smart money** *n* (money ventured by) someone having inside information or much experience [²*smart* (cf earlier *smart money* compensation for injuries, fr ⁴*smart*)]
**smart set** *n* ultrafashionable society – usu + the
**smarty-pants** /'smahti ,pants/ *n*, *pl* **smarty-pants** *informal* SMART ALEC
'**smash** /smash/ *vt* **1** to break in pieces by violence; shatter **2a** to drive, throw, or hit violently, esp causing breaking or shattering; crash **b(1)** to hit (eg a tennis ball) with a smash **b(2)** to hit (eg a ball) with a forceful stroke ⟨*~ed the ball through the covers*⟩ **3** to destroy utterly; wreck – often + up

~ *vi* **1** to crash *into;* collide ⟨~ed *into a tree*⟩ **2** to become wrecked **3** to go to pieces suddenly under collision or pressure **4** to carry out a smash (eg in tennis) [perh blend of *smack* and *mash*]

²**smash** *n* **1a(1)** a smashing blow, attack, or collision ⟨*a five-car* ~⟩ **a(2)** the result of smashing; *esp* a wreck due to collision **b** a hard overhand downward stroke (eg in tennis or badminton) **2** the condition of being smashed or shattered **3a** the action or sound of smashing; crash **b** utter collapse; ruin; *esp* bankruptcy **4** *informal* a smash hit

³**smash** *adv* with a resounding crash

**smash-and-'grab** *n or adj, chiefly Br* (a robbery) committed by smashing a shop window and snatching the goods on display

**smashed** /smasht/ *adj, informal* extremely drunk

**smasher** /'smashə/ *n* **1** one who or that which smashes or crushes ⟨*a* ~ *of a blow*⟩ **2** *chiefly Br informal* **2a** something that is very fine or impressive ⟨*a* ~ *of a moustache*⟩ **b** an extremely attractive person ⟨*looked a real* ~ *in her uniform* – *Daily Mirror*⟩

**smash hit** *n, informal* an outstanding success ⟨*his latest play is a* ~⟩

**smashing** /'smashing/ *adj* extremely good; excellent ⟨*a* ~ *film*⟩ – **smashingly** *adv*

**'smash-,up** *n* **1** a complete collapse **2** a violent collision of motor vehicles

**smatter** /'smatə/ *n* a smattering

**smattering** /'smat(ə)ring/ *n* **1** limited or superficial knowledge ⟨*a* ~ *of French*⟩ **2** a small scattered number or amount ⟨*a* ~ *of spectators*⟩ [fr gerund of *smatter* (to spatter, speak with superficial knowledge, dabble in), fr ME *smateren*]

**smaze** /smayz/ *n, NAm* a combination of haze and smoke similar to but less damp than smog [*smoke* + *haze*]

¹**smear** /smiə/ *n* **1** a mark or blemish made (as if) by smearing a substance **2** material smeared on a surface (eg of a microscopic slide for examination); *also* a preparation made by smearing material on a surface ⟨*a cervical* ~⟩ **3** a usu unsubstantiated charge or accusation ⟨*took the article as a personal* ~⟩ [ME *smere* grease, ointment, fr OE *smeoru;* akin to OHG *smero* grease, Gk *smyris* emery, *myron* ointment]

²**smear** *vt* **1a** to spread with something sticky, greasy, or viscous **b** to spread esp thickly over a surface **2a** to stain or dirty (as if) by smearing **b** to sully, besmirch; *specif* to blacken the reputation of **3** to obliterate, obscure, or blur (as if) by smearing ~ *vi* to become smeared ⟨*don't touch the paint or it will* ~⟩ – **smearer** *n,* **smeary** *adj*

**smear campaign** *n* an organized attempt (eg through newspapers or television) to blacken the reputation of a person or group

**smear word** *n* a slanderous or defamatory word or phrase

**smectic** /'smektik/ *adj* of or being a type of LIQUID CRYSTAL (liquid having properties of a crystalline solid) characterized by the arrangement of the molecules in layers with the longest axes of the molecules perpendicular to the plane of the layers – compare CHOLESTERIC, NEMATIC [L *smecticus* cleansing, having the properties of soap, fr Gk *smēktikos,* fr *smēchein* to clean]

**smeddum** /'smedəm/ *n, Scot* mettle, steadfastness [(assumed) ME, powder, dust, fr OE *smedma*]

**smegma** /'smegmə/ *n* the secretion of a SEBACEOUS (producing fatty substances) gland; *specif* the cheesy fatty matter that collects between the end of the penis (GLANS PENIS) and the foreskin of a man or round the clitoris and LABIA MINORA (parts of the external genital organs) of a woman [NL, fr L, detergent, soap, fr Gk *smēgma,* fr *smēchein* to wash off, clean]

¹**smell** /smel/ *vb* **smelled, smelt** /smelt/ *vt* **1** to perceive the odour or scent of through stimuli affecting the OLFACTORY NERVES **2** to detect or become aware of as if by the sense of smell ⟨smelt *trouble coming and left by a side entrance*⟩ ~ *vi* **1** to use the sense of smell **2a(1)** to have a usu specified odour or scent ⟨*sweet*-smelling *violets*⟩ ⟨*these clothes* ~ *damp*⟩ **a(2)** to have a characteristic aura or atmosphere; be suggestive ⟨*reports of survivors seemed to* ~ *of truth*⟩ **a(3)** to have a specified import when smelt; seem ⟨*the paper* ~s *peculiar*⟩ **b(1)** to have an offensive odour; stink **b(2)** to appear evil, dishonest, or corrupt ⟨*from a moral standpoint, his political views* ~⟩ – see also **smell a** RAT [ME *smellen;* akin to MD *smölen* to scorch, Russ *smalit'*] – **smeller** *n*

**usage 1 Smelled** and **smelt** are equally common in British English, but **smelled** is the commoner American form. **2** When **smell** means

"have a specified smell" it is followed by an adjective ⟨smell *funny*⟩ or by a phrase ⟨smell *of onions*⟩. When **smell** means "stink" it may be followed by an adverb ⟨*the room* smells *horribly*⟩. This is because an adverb always describes the degree or way of smelling rather than what is smelt ⟨smelt *extraordinarily nice*⟩ ⟨smells *deliciously of roses*⟩.

**smell out** *vt* **1** to detect or discover (as if) by smelling ⟨*the dog* smelt out *the criminal*⟩ **2** to fill with an esp offensive smell ⟨*the cigarettes* smelt out *the room*⟩

²**smell** *n* **1a** the process, function, or power of smelling **b** the one of the five basic physical senses by which the qualities of gaseous or readily vaporized substances in contact with certain sensitive areas in the nose are interpreted by the brain as characteristic odours **2** the property of a thing that affects the olfactory SENSE ORGANS; odour **3** a pervading quality; an aura ⟨*the* ~ *of affluence, of power* – Harry Hervey⟩ **4** an act or instance of smelling

**synonyms Smell, odour, scent, fragrance, perfume, savour, aroma, bouquet, stench,** and **stink** all mean "quality perceptible to the nose". **Smell** and the more formal **odour** are the most general, and could replace any of the others. **Scent, fragrance,** and **perfume** are neutral or agreeable. **Scent** carries over, from its association of the trail left by an animal, the idea of a distinctive and delicate physical emanation ⟨the **scent** *of her hair*⟩. **Fragrance** and **perfume** are particularly associated with flowers, **fragrance** being usually lighter ⟨the **fragrance** *of primroses*⟩ and **perfume** more penetrating ⟨the *heady* **perfume** *of tropical frangipani*⟩. **Savour, aroma,** and **bouquet** are agreeable, **savour** combining the pleasures of smell and taste ⟨the **savour** *of roasting meat*⟩, **aroma** being pungent and spicy ⟨the **aroma** *of a log fire*⟩, and **bouquet** being chiefly the smell of wine. **Stench** and **stink** are strong offensive smells, often of decay ⟨the **stink** *of rotten fish*⟩.

**smelling salts** /'smeling/ *n pl but taking sing or pl vb* a usu scented preparation of AMMONIUM CARBONATE and AMMONIA WATER (eg SAL VOLATILE) sniffed as a stimulant to relieve faintness

**smelly** /'smeli/ *adj* having a smell; *esp* having an unpleasant smell

¹**smelt** /smelt/ *n, pl* **smelts,** *esp collectively* **smelt** any of various small fishes (family Osmeridae, esp genus *Osmerus*) that closely resemble the trouts in general structure, live along coasts and ascend rivers to spawn or are landlocked in inland waters, and have delicate oily flesh with a distinctive smell and taste [ME, fr OE; akin to Norw *smelte* whiting]

²**smelt** *vt* **1** to melt (eg ore) often with an accompanying chemical change, esp to separate the metal **2** to separate (metal) by smelting; to refine, reduce [D or LG *smelten;* akin to OHG *smelzan* to melt, OE *meltan*]

**smelter** /'smeltə/ *n* one who or that which smelts: eg **a** a worker who smelts ore **b** an owner or operator of a smeltery **c smelter, smeltery** an establishment for smelting

**smew** /smyooh/ *n* a MERGANSER (type of duck) (*Mergus albellus*) of N Europe and Asia, the male of which is mostly white with black patches round the eyes [akin to MHG *smiehe* smew]

**smidgen, smidgeon, smidgin** /'smijin/ *n, chiefly NAm* a small amount; a bit [alter. of *smitch,* prob fr E dial. var of *smutch*]

**smilax** /'smielaks/ *n* **1** SARSAPARILLA **1a** (tropical American plant) **2** a tender climbing vinelike plant (*Asparagus asparagoides*) that has glossy bright green leaves and is often grown for ornament [L, bindweed, yew, fr Gk]

¹**smile** /smiel/ *vi* **1** to have or assume a smile **2a** to look or regard with amusement or scorn ⟨~d *at his own weakness*⟩ **b** to bestow approval ⟨*Heaven seemed to* ~ *on her labours*⟩ **c** to appear pleasant or agreeable ⟨*a green and* smiling *landscape*⟩ ~ *vt* **1** to affect with or by smiling ⟨~d *away his embarrassment*⟩ **2** to utter or express with a smile **3** to move the facial muscle so as to produce (a smile) [ME *smilen;* akin to OE *smerian* to laugh, L *mirari* to wonder, Skt *smayate* he smiles] – **smiler** *n,* **smiley** *adj,* **smilingly** *adv*

²**smile** *n* **1** a change of facial expression in which the corners of the mouth curve slightly upwards and which expresses esp amusement, pleasure, approval, or sometimes scorn **2** a pleasant or encouraging appearance – **smileless** *adj*

**smirch** /smuhch/ *vt* **1** to make dirty, stained, or discoloured, esp by smearing **2** to bring discredit or disgrace on ⟨~ed *his reputation*⟩ – **smirch** *n*

**smirk** /smuhk/ *vi* to smile in a fatuous or affected manner; simper [ME *smirken,* fr OE *smearcian* to smile; akin to OE *smerian* to laugh] – **smirk** *n,* **smirkingly** *adv*

**smite** /smiet/ *vb* **smote** /smoht/; **smitten** /'smit(ə)n/, **smote** *vt* 1 to strike sharply or heavily, esp with (an implement held in) the hand 2a to kill, severely injure, or damage by smiting b to attack or afflict suddenly and injuriously ⟨smitten *by disease*⟩ 3 to cause to strike ⟨smote *his hand against his side*⟩ 4a to affect as if by a sharp or sudden blow ⟨smitten *with grief*⟩ b to cause a sudden and strong attraction ⟨smitten *by her beauty*⟩ ~ *vi* 1 to deliver a blow (as if) with the hand or something held 2 to beat down or come forcibly *on* or *upon* [ME *smiten*, fr OE *smītan* to pollute, smear; akin to OHG bismīzan to defile] – **smiter** *n*

**smith** /smith/ *n* 1 a worker in metals; *specif* a blacksmith 2 a maker – often in combination ⟨gunsmith⟩ ⟨songsmith⟩ [ME, fr OE; akin to OHG *smid* smith, Gk *smilē* wood-carving knife]

**smithereens** /ˌsmidhə'reenz, '--,-/ *n pl* fragments, bits ⟨*the house was blown to* ~ *by the explosion*⟩ [IrGael *smidirīn*, dim. of *smiodar* fragment]

**smithery** /'smith(ə)ri/ *n* 1 the work, art, or trade of a smith 2 a smithy

**smithsonite** /'smithsə,niet/ *n* a usu white or nearly white mineral, $ZnCO_3$, that is mined as a source of zinc [James *Smithson* †1829 Br chemist]

**smithy** /'smidhi/ *n* the workshop of a smith

**¹smock** /smok/ *n* 1 a light loose garment resembling a SMOCK FROCK, esp in being gathered into a yoke; *also* smock frock 2 *archaic* a woman's undergarment; *esp* a chemise [ME *smok*, fr OE *smoc*; akin to OHG *smocco* adornment]

**²smock** *vt* to ornament (eg a garment) with smocking

**smock frock** *n* an outer garment worn chiefly by farm labourers, esp in the 18th and 19th centuries, and resembling a long loose shirt gathered into a yoke

**smocking** /'smoking/ *n* a decorative embroidery or SHIRRING made by gathering cloth in regularly spaced round or diamond-shaped tucks held in place with ornamental stitching

**smog** /smog/ *n* a fog made heavier and darker by smoke and chemical fumes [blend of *smoke* and *fog*] – **smogless** *adj*

**smoggy** /'smogi/ *adj* characterized by or abounding in smog

**¹smoke** /smohk/ *n* 1a the gaseous products of burning carbon-containing materials, made visible by the presence of small particles of carbon b a suspension of particles in a gas 2 a mass or column of smoke 3 fumes or vapour resembling smoke 4 something of little substance, permanence, or value 5 something that obscures 6 an act or spell of smoking plant material, esp tobacco 7 *informal* something (eg a cigarette) that is smoked 8 *Br informal* a large town or city; *esp* London – + *the* ⟨*I'll come and see you next time I visit the* ~⟩; used by people from rural areas [ME, fr OE *smoca;* akin to MHG *smouch* smoke, Gk *smychein* to smoulder] – **smokeless** *adj*, **smokelike** *adj* – **to go up in smoke** to come to nothing; disappear ⟨*all his plans* went up in smoke⟩

**²smoke** *vi* 1a to emit smoke b to discharge smoke excessively or faultily ⟨*cheap candles that* ~ *and gutter*⟩ 2 to inhale and exhale the fumes of burning plant material, esp tobacco; *esp* to smoke tobacco habitually ~ *vt* 1a to fumigate b to drive out or away by smoke ⟨~ *a fox from its den*⟩ c to stupefy or exterminate (eg bees or wasps) by smoke 2 to colour or darken (as if) with smoke ⟨~d *glasses*⟩ 3 to cure (eg meat or fish) by exposure to smoke traditionally from green wood, turf, or peat 4 to inhale and exhale the smoke of (eg cigarettes) 5 *archaic* to suspect 6 *archaic* to ridicule – **smokable** *adj*

**smoke out** *vt* 1 to drive out or away by smoke 2 to bring to public view or knowledge

**smokehouse** /'smohk,hows/ *n* a building where meat or fish is cured in a dense wood smoke

**smokejack** /'smohk,jak/ *n* a device for turning a spit that is driven by rising gases in a chimney

**smokeless** /'smohkləs/ *adj* 1 producing little or no smoke ⟨~ *fuel*⟩ 2 having little or no smoke; *specif* in which no smoke is allowed ⟨*a* ~ *zone*⟩

**smokeless powder** *n* any of a class of substances used as propelling agents for explosives that produce comparatively little smoke on explosion

**smoke-oh** /'smohk,oh/ *n, Austr & NZ informal* SMOKO (rest period)

**smoke pipe** *n* a usu thin metal pipe that connects a source of smoke to a chimney

**smokeproof** /'smohk,proohf/ *adj* impermeable to smoke

**smoker** /'smohkə/ *n* 1 one who regularly or habitually smokes tobacco 2 a railway carriage or compartment in which smoking is allowed 3 an informal gathering for men only

**smoke screen** *n* 1 a screen of smoke to hinder enemy observation of a military force, area, or activity 2 something designed to conceal, confuse, or deceive

**smokestack** /'smohk,stak/ *n* a chimney or funnel through which smoke and gases are discharged; *specif* one on a ship or locomotive

**smoke tree** *n* either of two small shrubby trees (genus *Cotinus*) of the sumach family often grown for their large clusters of minute feathery flowers that look like a cloud of smoke: a one (*Cotinus coggygria*) of S Europe and Asia b one (*Cotinus americanus*) of S USA

**smoking jacket** /'smohking/ *n* a man's loosely fitting jacket formerly worn while smoking

**smoking room** *n* a room (eg in a club or hotel) set aside for smokers

**'smoking-,room** *adj* marked by indecency or impropriety; smutty ⟨~ *jokes*⟩

**smoko** /'smohkoh/ *n, Austr & NZ informal* a short rest period; TEA BREAK [¹*smoke* 6 + *o, oh*, interj]

**¹smoky** *also* **smokey** /'smohki/ *adj* 1 emitting smoke, esp in large quantities ⟨*a* ~ *fire*⟩ 2a having the characteristics or appearance of smoke b suggestive of smoke, esp in flavour, smell, or colour 3a filled with smoke b made black or grimy by smoke – **smokily** *adv*, **smokiness** *n*

**²smoky** *n* a small haddock that is gutted and smoked whole until the skin becomes brown and the flesh is cooked

**smoky quartz** *n* CAIRNGORM (type of mineral)

**smoky topaz** *n* CAIRNGORM (type of mineral)

**smolder** /'smohldə/ *vi or n, NAm* (to) smoulder

**smolt** /smohlt/ *n* a young salmon or sea trout that is about two years old and that is at the stage of development when it takes on the silvery colour of the adult [ME (Sc)]

**¹smooch** /smoohch/ *vi, informal* 1 to kiss, pet 2 *Br* to dance slowly, holding one's partner in a close embrace; ⟨~ing *with her boyfriend*⟩ [alter. of E dial. *smouch* to kiss, prob of imit origin]

**²smooch** *n, informal* an act of smooching

**¹smooth** /smoohdh/ *adj* 1a having a continuous even surface b free from hair or hairlike projections c *of liquid* of an even consistency; free from lumps d giving no resistance to sliding; frictionless 2 free from difficulties or obstructions ⟨*the* ~ *course of his life*⟩ 3 even and uninterrupted in movement or flow 4 excessively and often artfully suave; ingratiating ⟨*a* ~ *salesman*⟩ 5a equable, composed ⟨*a* ~ *disposition*⟩ b urbane, courteous 6 not sharp or acid; bland ⟨*a* ~ *sherry*⟩ **synonyms** see ³LEVEL, SUAVE **antonym** rough [ME *smothe*, fr OE *smōth;* akin to OS *smōthi* smooth] – **smooth** *adv*, **smoothly** *adv*, **smoothness** *n*

**²smooth** *vt* 1 to make smooth 2 to free from what is harsh or disagreeable ⟨~ed *out his style*⟩ 3 to dispel or alleviate (eg enmity, perplexity, or an awkward situation) – often + *away* or *over* 4 to free from obstruction or difficulty 5a to press flat – often + *out* b to remove expression from (one's face); compose 6 to cause to lie evenly and in order – often + *down* ⟨~ed *down his hair*⟩ 7 to free (eg a graph or data) from irregularities by ignoring random variations ~ *vi* to become smooth – **smoother** *n*

**³smooth** *n* 1 a smooth or agreeable side or aspect ⟨*take the rough with the* ~⟩ 2 an act of smoothing 3 a smooth part; *specif* the side of a sports racket on which the binding round the top and bottom string is smooth and continuous ⟨*call rough or* ~⟩ – see also **take the** ROUGH **with the smooth**

**smoothbore** /'smoohdh,baw/ *adj, of a firearm* having a smooth-surfaced bore; not RIFLED – **smoothbore** *n*

**smooth breathing** *n* a mark ' used in Greek over some initial vowels to show pronunciation without an h-sound (lack of ASPIRATION) – compare ROUGH BREATHING

**smoothen** /'smoohdh(ə)n/ *vb* to make or become smooth

**,smooth-'faced** *adj* clean-shaven

**smooth hound** *n* any of various dogfishes (genus *Mustelus*) [fr the absence of a spine in front of the dorsal fin]

**smoothie, smoothy** /'smoohdhi/ *n, informal* 1 a person with polished manners 2 a person who behaves with suave self-assurance; *esp* a man with an ingratiating manner towards women

**smoothing iron** *n, archaic* IRON 2c (implement for pressing clothes, linen, etc)

**smooth muscle** *n* muscle tissue that lacks cross bandings, that is made up of elongated spindle-shaped cells having a central nucleus, and is found in VERTEBRATE animals in abdominal structures (eg the stomach and bladder) as thin sheets performing involuntary functions and in all or most of the musculature of INVERTEBRATE animals other than ARTHROPODS (insects, spiders, crabs, etc) – compare STRIATED MUSCLE

**smooth snake** *n* any of several European nonpoisonous snakes (genus *Coronella*, esp *Coronella austriaca*) that are reddish brown in colour and have smooth scales

**'smooth-,tongued** *adj* ingratiating and persuasive in speech

**smorgasbord** /'smawgəs,bawd, 'smuh-/ *n* a luncheon or supper buffet offering a variety of foods and dishes (eg HORS D'OEUVRES, hot and cold meats, smoked and pickled fish, cheeses, salads, and relishes) [Sw *smörgåsbord*, fr *smörgås* open sandwich + *bord* table]

**smorrebrod** /'smorəbrod (*Danish* 'smœrə,brœd)/ *n* a small savoury OPEN SANDWICH, served esp in Denmark [Dan *smjorrebjod*, fr *smjor* butter + *bjod* bread]

**smote** /smoht/ *past of* SMITE

**'smother** /'smudhə/ *n* 1 thick stifling smoke 2 a dense cloud of gas or particles (eg dust) floating in the air 3 a confused mass of things [ME, alter. of *smorther*, fr *smoren* to smother, fr OE *smorian* to suffocate; akin to MD *smoren* to suffocate] – **smothery** *adj*

**'smother** *vt* 1 to overcome or kill with smoke or fumes 2a to kill by depriving of air **b** to overcome or discomfort (as if) through lack of air **c** to suppress (a fire) by excluding oxygen 3a to cause (a fire) to smoulder **b** to suppress expression or knowledge of; conceal ⟨~ *a yawn*⟩ ⟨~ed *his rage*⟩ **c** to prevent the growth or development of ⟨~ *a child with too much care*⟩ **d** to cover thickly; blanket ⟨*snow* ~ed *the trees and hedgerows*⟩ **e** to overwhelm ⟨*aunts who always* ~ed *him with kisses*⟩ 4 to cook in a covered pan or pot with little liquid over low heat – *vi* to become smothered

**'smoulder,** *NAm chiefly* **smolder** /'smohldə/ *n* 1 dense sluggish smoke 2 a smouldering fire [ME *smolder*; akin to ME *smellen* to smell]

**'smoulder,** *NAm chiefly* **smolder** *vi* 1 to burn feebly with little flame and often with much smoke 2 to exist in a state of suppressed ferment ⟨*workers* ~ing *with revolutionary thoughts*⟩ ⟨*resentment* ~ed *in her*⟩ 3 to reveal suppressed anger, hate, or jealousy ⟨*eyes* ~ing *with hate*⟩

**'smudge** /smuj/ *vt* 1 to soil (as if) with a smudge 2a to rub, daub, or wipe in a smeary manner **b** to make indistinct; blur ⟨*couldn't read the* ~d *address*⟩ 3 *NAm* to disinfect or protect by means of smoke – *vi* 1 to make a smudge 2 to become smudged [ME *smogen*]

**'smudge** *n* 1a a blurry spot or streak **b** a stain of disgrace; a blot **c** an indistinct mass; a blur ⟨*the house became just a* ~ *on the horizon*⟩ 2 *NAm* a smouldering mass producing dense smoke placed outdoors on the windward side (eg of a crop) for protection (eg from frost or insects) – **smudgily** *adv*, **smudginess** *n*, **smudgy** *adj*

**smug** /smug/ *adj* **-gg-** highly self-satisfied and complacent ⟨*a* ~ *smile*⟩ ⟨~ *self-righteous moralists*⟩ [prob modif of LG *smuck* neat, fr MLG, fr *smucken* to dress] – **smugness** *n*, **smugly** *adv*

**smuggle** /'smugl/ *vt* 1 to import or export secretly contrary to the law, esp without paying customs and excise duties 2 to convey or introduce surreptitiously ⟨~d *his notes into the examination*⟩ – *vi* to import or export something in violation of customs laws [LG *smuggeln* & D *smokkelen*] – **smuggler** *n*

**'smut** /smut/ *vb* **-tt-** *vt* 1 to stain or taint with smut 2 to affect (a crop or plant) with smut – *vi* to become affected by smut ⟨*treated grain will not* ~⟩ [prob alter. of earlier *smot* to stain, fr ME *smotten*; akin to MHG *smutzen* to stain]

**'smut** *n* 1 matter that soils or blackens; *specif* a particle of soot 2 any of various destructive diseases, esp of cereal grasses, caused by parasitic fungi (order Ustilaginales) and marked by transformation of the affected plant organs into dark masses of spores; *also* a fungus causing a smut 3 obscene language or matter

**smutch** /smuch/ *n* a dark or injurious stain; a smudge [prob irreg fr 'smudge] – **smutch** *vt*, **smutchy** *adj*

**smutty** /'smuti/ *adj* 1 soiled or tainted with smut; *esp* affected with smut fungus 2 shabbily obscene or indecent 3 resembling smut in appearance; sooty – **smuttily** *adv*, **smuttiness** *n*

**'snack** /snak/ *vi, chiefly NAm* to eat a snack [ME *snaken* to bite, prob fr MD *snacken* to snap at, bite]

**'snack** *n* a light meal; food eaten between regular meals – **snack** *adj*

**snack bar** *n* a place where snacks are served usu at a counter

**snackette** /,snak'et/ *n, WI* SNACK BAR

**'snaffle** /'snafl/ *n* a simple usu jointed bit for a bridle [origin unknown]

**'snaffle** *vt, informal* to take possession of, esp by crafty or devious means; pinch [origin unknown]

**'snafu** /sna'fooh/ *adj, chiefly NAm informal* snarled up; awry ⟨*situation normal all fucked up* (or *fouled up*)⟩

**'snafu** *vt or n, chiefly NAm informal* (to bring into a state of) total confusion or commotion

**'snag** /snag/ *n* 1a a stub or stump remaining after a branch has been chopped or torn off **b** a tree or branch embedded in a lake or stream bed and constituting a hazard to navigation 2a a rough, sharp, or jagged projecting part **b** any of the secondary branches of an antler 3 a concealed or unexpected difficulty or obstacle ⟨*the* ~ *is, there's no train on Sundays*⟩ 4 an irregular tear or flaw made (as if) by catching on a snag ⟨*a* ~ *in her stocking*⟩ [of Scand origin; akin to ON *snagi* clothes peg] – **snaggy** *adj*

**'snag** *vb* **-gg-** *vt* 1 to catch (as if) on a snag ⟨~ged *her tights on the barbed wire*⟩ 2 to clear (eg a river) of snags 3 *chiefly NAm* to halt or impede as if by catching on a snag 4 *chiefly NAm* to catch or obtain by quick action ⟨~ged *a taxi*⟩ – *vi* to become snagged

**snail** /snayl/ *n* 1 any of a class (Gastropoda of the phylum Mollusca) of INVERTEBRATE animals that live on land or in freshwater and have a soft body enclosed by an external spiral shell; *esp* one (*Helix aspersa*) found commonly in gardens 2 a slow-moving or sluggish person or thing [ME, fr OE *snægl;* akin to OHG *snecko* snail, *snahhan* to creep, Lith *snåke* snail] – **snaillike** *adj*

**snail-paced** /payst/ *adj* moving very slowly

**snail's pace** /'snaylz/ *n* a very slow rate of progress

**'snake** /snayk/ *n* 1 any of numerous limbless scaly reptiles (suborder Serpentes or Ophidia) with a long tapering body and with salivary glands often modified to produce venom which is injected through grooved or tubular fangs 2 a sly treacherous person 3 something long, slender, and flexible; *specif* a long flexible rod or cable, usu of steel, that is used to clear blocked pipes 4 a system in which the values of the currencies of countries in the COMMON MARKET are allowed to vary against each other within narrow limits [ME, fr OE *snaca;* akin to OE *snægl* snail] – **snakelike** *adj*

**'snake** *vt* 1 to wind (eg one's way) in the manner of a snake 2 *NAm* to move (eg logs) by dragging – *vi* to crawl, move, or extend silently, secretly, or windingly

**snakebird** /'snayk,buhd/ *n* DARTER (water bird) [fr its snakelike neck]

**snakebite** /'snayk,biet/ *n* the bite of a snake, esp a venomous snake

**snake charmer** *n* an entertainer, esp of Asia, who exhibits the power to control venomous snakes supposedly by magic, usu using music and rhythmical movements

**snake dance** *n* a ceremonial dance in which snakes or their images are handled, invoked, or symbolically imitated – **snake-dance** *vi*

**snake fly** *n* any of a family (Raphidiidae) of completely ground-living net-winged insects that have a long thin PRO-THORAX (body section next to the head) that resembles a neck

**snake in the grass** *n* a secretly treacherous friend or associate

**snakeroot** /'snayk,rooht/ *n* any of numerous plants which have roots sometimes believed to cure snakebites; *also* the root of such a plant

**snakes and ladders** *n pl but taking sing vb* a board game in which players move counters along numbered squares on a chequered board to the throw of a. dice, and may move upwards and forwards along pictures of ladders and be forced downwards and backwards along pictures of snakes

**'snake's-,head** *n* a European plant (*Fritillaria meleagris*) of the lily family that grows in damp meadowland and has a usu single purple-and-white checked bell-shaped flower on a slender drooping stem

**snakeskin** /'snayk,skin/ *n* (leather made from) the skin of a snake

**snakeweed** /'snayk,weed/ *n* any of several plants associated with snakes (eg in appearance, habitat, or use in treatment of snakebite)

**snaky** /'snayki/ *adj* 1 of, formed of, or entwined with snakes ⟨*the Gorgon with* ~ *hair* – Joseph Addison⟩ 2 serpentine, snakelike ⟨*the* ~ *arms of an octopus*⟩ 3 slyly venomous or treacherous ⟨*oiliness and* ~ *insinuation* – Thomas De Quincey⟩ **4** abounding in snakes – **snakily** *adv*

**¹snap** /snap/ *vb* **-pp-** *vi* **1a** to make a sudden closing of the jaws; seize something sharply with the mouth ⟨*fish* ~ping *at the bait*⟩ **b** to grasp or snatch at something eagerly ⟨~ *at any chance*⟩ **2** to utter sharp biting words; give an irritable or testy retort ⟨~ped *at his pupil when she apologized for being late*⟩ **3a** to break suddenly with a sharp cracking sound ⟨*the twig* ~ped⟩ **b** to give way suddenly under strain ⟨*her patience finally* ~ped⟩ **4a** to make a sharp or cracking sound **b** to close or fit in place with an abrupt movement or sharp sound ⟨*the catch* ~ped *shut*⟩ ~ *vt* **1** to seize (as if) with a snap of the jaws ⟨~ped *the food right out of his hand*⟩ **2** to take possession or advantage of suddenly or eagerly – usu + *up* ⟨*shoppers* ~ping *up bargains*⟩ ⟨~ped *up his offer*⟩ **3** to utter curtly or abruptly ⟨~ped *out an answer without hesitation*⟩ **4** to cause to break or give way suddenly, esp with a sharp cracking sound ⟨~ped *the end off the twig*⟩ **5a** to cause to make a snapping sound ⟨~ *a whip*⟩ ⟨~ped *her fingers*⟩ **b** to put into or remove from a particular position by a sudden movement or with a sharp sound ⟨~ *the lid shut*⟩ **6a** to take photographically ⟨~ *a picture*⟩ **b** to take a snapshot of; photograph [D or LG *snappen;* akin to MHG *snappen* to snap] – **snap out of it** to free oneself from something (eg a mood or habit) by an effort of will

   **snap back** *vi* to make a quick or vigorous recovery ⟨snapped back *after his appendicitis*⟩

**²snap** *n* **1** an abrupt closing (eg of the mouth in biting or of scissors in cutting) **2a** an act or instance of seizing abruptly; a sudden snatching or biting at something **b** a short rapid movement ⟨*lithe* ~s *of its tail*⟩ **c** a sudden sharp breaking of something slender, thin, or brittle **3a** a sound made by snapping ⟨*shut the book with a* ~⟩ **b** a brief sharp and usu curt speech or retort **4** a sudden spell of harsh weather ⟨*a cold* ~⟩ **5** a catch or fastening that closes or locks with a click ⟨*the* ~ *of a bracelet*⟩ **6** a thin brittle biscuit ⟨*ginger* ~⟩ **7** a snapshot **8a** physical, intellectual, or spiritual vigour; energy, resilience **b** a pungent pleasing quality ⟨*a story with plenty of* ~⟩ **9** a card game in which each player tries to be the first to shout "snap" when two cards of identical value are laid successively **10** *dial N Eng* **10a** a small meal or snack; *esp* elevenses **b** food; *esp* food taken by a workman (eg a miner) to eat at work (eg for lunch) **11** *chiefly NAm* something that is easy and presents no problems; a cinch ⟨*the history course was a* ~⟩

**³snap** *adv* with (the sound of) a snap ⟨*the rope went* ~ *under the strain*⟩

**⁴snap** *adj* **1** performed suddenly, unexpectedly, or without deliberation ⟨*a* ~ *general election*⟩ ⟨*a* ~ *judgment*⟩ **2** shutting or fastening with a click or by means of a device that snaps ⟨*a* ~ *lock*⟩ **3** *NAm* very easy or simple ⟨*a* ~ *course*⟩

**⁵snap** *interj, Br* – used to draw attention to an identity or similarity ⟨~*! You're reading the same book as me*⟩

**snap bean** *n, NAm* GREEN BEAN

**'snap-,brim** *n* a usu felt hat with a brim turned up at the back and down in front and with a dented crown

**snapdragon** /'snap,drag(ə)n/ *n* ANTIRRHINUM; *esp* a garden plant (*Antirrhinum majus*) [fr the fancied resemblance of the flowers to the face of a dragon]

**snap fastener** *n, NAm* a press-stud

**'snap-,on** *adj* designed to snap into position and fit tightly ⟨~ *cuffs*⟩

**snapper** /'snapə/ *n, pl* **snappers,** (*2a,b*) **snappers,** *esp collectively* **snapper 1a** one who or that which snaps **b**(1) SNAPPING TURTLE **b**(2) CLICK BEETLE **2a** any of numerous active carnivorous fishes (family Lutjanidae) of warm seas important as food and often as sport fishes **b** any of several immature fishes (eg the young of the bluefish) that resemble a snapper

**snapping turtle** /'snaping/ *n* a large American freshwater turtle (*Chelydra serpentina*) that has powerful jaws

**snappish** /'snapish/ *adj* **1a** given to curt irritable speech **b** arising from annoyance or irritability; testy ⟨*a* ~ *reply*⟩ **2** inclined to snap or bite ⟨*a* ~ *dog*⟩ – **snappishly** *adv*, **snappishness** *n*

**snappy** /'snapi/ *adj* **1** snappish **2a** quickly or hurriedly made or performed **b** full of zest or animation ⟨~ *repartee*⟩ **c** stylish, smart ⟨*a* ~ *dresser*⟩ – **snappily** *adv*, **snappiness** *n* – **make it/look snappy** to be quick; hurry up – usu *imper*

**snap roll** *n* a manoeuvre in which an aircraft is made, by quick movement of the controls, to complete a full sideways roll while maintaining an approximately level line of flight

**snapshot** /'snap,shot/ *n* a photograph, usu with personal associations, made with a hand-held camera ⟨*the* ~s *of my sister's wedding*⟩

**snap shot** *n* a quick shot (eg with a rifle) made without deliberately taking aim

**¹snare** /sneə/ *n* **1a** a trap often consisting of a noose for catching birds or small animals **b** something by which one is entangled, trapped, or deceived **2** any of the catgut strings or metal spirals placed over the skin at one end of a SNARE DRUM to produce a rattling sound **3** a surgical instrument consisting usu of a wire loop constricted by a mechanism in the handle and used for removing tissue masses (eg tonsils) [ME, fr OE *sneare,* fr ON *snara;* akin to Gk *narkē* numbness, OHG *snuor* cord – more at NARROW]

**²snare** *vt* **1a** to capture (as if) by use of a snare **b** to win or procure by artful or skilful manoeuvres ⟨~ *a top job*⟩ **2** to entangle or hold as if in a snare ⟨*any object that* ~d *his eye*⟩ **synonyms** see ¹CATCH – **snarer** *n*

**snare drum** *n* a small double-headed drum with one or more snares stretched across its lower head – called also SIDE DRUM

**¹snarl** /snahl/ *n* **1** a tangle, esp of hair or thread; a knot **2** a confused or complicated situation; *esp* a snarl-up [ME *snarle* snare, prob dim. of *snare*] – **snarly** *adj*

**²snarl** *vt* **1** to cause to become knotted and intertwined; tangle **2** to make excessively confused or complicated ~ *vi* to become snarled □ (*2 vt; vi*) often + *up* – **snarler** *n*

**³snarl** *vi* **1** to growl with bared teeth **2** to speak in a vicious or bad-tempered manner ~ *vt* to utter or express with a snarl or by snarling [freq of obs *snar* to growl, prob of imit origin] – **snarl** *n*, **snarler** *n*

**'snarl-,up** *n* a state of confused immobility ⟨*a traffic* ~⟩

**¹snatch** /snach/ *vi* to attempt to seize something suddenly – often + *at* ⟨~ *at a rope*⟩ ~ *vt* **1** to take or grasp abruptly or hastily ⟨~ *a quick glance*⟩ **2** to seize or grab suddenly and usu forcibly, wrongfully, or with difficulty [ME *snacchen* to give a sudden snap, seize; akin to MD *snacken* to snap at] – **snatcher** *n*

**²snatch** *n* **1** a snatching at or of something **2a** a brief period of time or activity ⟨*caught* ~es *of sleep*⟩ **b** something fragmentary or hurried ⟨*caught a brief* ~ *of their conversation*⟩ **3** a lift in weight-lifting in which the weight is raised from the floor directly to an overhead position usu with a lunge or squat under the weight – compare CLEAN 2, JERK 3, PRESS **4** *informal* a robbery **5** *chiefly NAm vulg* the female genitals

**snatch block** *n* a BLOCK (system of pulleys) that can be opened on one side to receive a rope

**snatch squad** *n, Br* a squad of police or soldiers trained to force their way into the middle of a mass of rioters or demonstrators and arrest and bring out ringleaders

**snatchy** /'snachi/ *adj* marked by breaks in continuity; spasmodic, irregular

**snazzy** /'snazi/ *adj, informal* stylishly or flashily attractive ⟨*what a* ~ *tie!*⟩ [perh blend of *snappy* and *jazzy*]

**¹sneak** /sneek/ *vb* **sneaked** *NAm also* **snuck** /snuk/ *vi* **1** to go stealthily or furtively; slink ⟨*boys* ~ing *over the orchard wall*⟩ **2** to behave in a furtive or servile manner **3** *Br informal* to tell tales ⟨*pupils never* ~ *on their classmates*⟩ ~ *vt* to put, bring, or take in a furtive or artful manner ⟨~ *a smoke behind the toolshed*⟩ [akin to OE *snīcan* to sneak along, OHG *snahhan* to creep – more at SNAIL]

   **sneak up on** *vt* to approach or act on stealthily

**²sneak** *n* **1** a person who acts in a stealthy, furtive, or shifty manner **2** the act or an instance of sneaking **3** *Br informal* a person, esp a schoolchild, who tells tales against others – **sneaky** *adj*

**³sneak** *adj* occurring without warning; surprise ⟨*a* ~ *attack*⟩

**sneaker** /'sneekə/ *n* **1** someone who sneaks **2** *chiefly NAm* a plimsoll – **sneakered** *adj*

**sneaking** /'sneeking/ *adj* **1** characteristic of a sneak; furtive, underhand **2** mean, contemptible **3a** not openly expressed or acknowledged ⟨*a* ~ *desire for publicity*⟩ **b** instinctively felt but unverified ⟨*a* ~ *suspicion*⟩ – **sneakingly** *adv*

**sneak preview** *n* a special advance showing of a film usu announced but not named

**sneak thief** *n* a thief who steals without using violence or forcibly breaking into buildings

**sneck** /snek/ *n, dial Br* a latch [ME *snekke*]

**¹sneer** /sniə/ *vi* **1** to smile or laugh with a curl of the lips to express scorn or contempt **2** to speak or write in a scornfully jeering manner ~ *vt* to utter with a sneer [prob akin to MHG *snerren* to chatter, gossip – more at SNORE] – **sneerer** *n*, **sneeringly** *adv*

**²sneer** *n* the act of sneering; a sneering expression or remark

**¹sneeze** /sneez/ *vi* to make a sudden violent involuntary audible expiration of breath, esp as a result of irritation to the nose and nasal passages (eg by inhaling dust or smoke) or sometimes to the eyes (eg by bright light) [ME *snesen*, alter. of *fnesen*, fr OE *fnēosan*; akin to MHG *pfnūsen* to snort, sneeze, Gk *pnein* to breathe] – **sneezer** *n*, **sneezy** *adj*
  **sneeze at** *vt* to make light of

**²sneeze** *n* an act or fact of sneezing

**sneezewort** /'sneez,wuht/ *n* a strong-scented Eurasian plant (*Achillea ptarmica*) of the daisy family that is found in damp and shady places and has clusters of small white flowers, and the powdered dried leaves of which induce sneezing

**snell** /snel/ *adj, chiefly Scot* keen, piercing ⟨*a ~ wind smote us – Scotsman*⟩ [ME, quick, severe, vigorous, fr OE, quick; akin to OHG *snel* bold, agile]

**snelskrif** /'snel,skrif/ *n* a system of shorthand for the Afrikaans language ⟨*practical experience in shorthand*/Snelskrif *and Typing – The Argus* (*Cape Town*)⟩ [Afrik, fr D *snelschrift* shorthand, fr *snel* quick + *schrift* writing]

**¹snick** /snik/ *vt* 1 to cut slightly; nick 2 to edge a ball in cricket [prob fr obs *snick or snee* to engage in cut-and-thrust fighting – more at SNICKERSNEE]

**²snick** *n* 1 a small cut; a nick 2 an act or instance of edging a ball in cricket

**snicker** /'snikə/ *vi or n* (to) snigger [imit] – **snickerer** *n*, **snickery** *adj*

**snickersnee, snick-a-snee, snick-or-snee** /,snikə'snee, '--,-/ *n* a large knife; *esp* one used as a weapon [obs *snick or snee* to engage in cut-and-thrust fighting, alter. of earlier *steake or snye*, fr D *steken of snijden* to thrust or cut]

**snicket** /'snikit/ *n, N Eng* a narrow pathway bordered by bushes or hedges [E dial. *snicket* something small or insignificant]

**snide** /snied/ *adj* 1 counterfeit, bogus ⟨*you must not print ~ money – The Listener*⟩ 2 slyly disparaging; insinuating ⟨*~ remarks*⟩ 3 *chiefly NAm* mean, low ⟨*a ~ trick*⟩ [origin unknown] – **snidely** *adv*, **snideness** *n*

**¹sniff** /snif/ *vi* 1 to draw air audibly up the nose, esp for smelling or clearing the nose and nasal passages ⟨*~ed at the flowers*⟩ ⟨*don't ~, use a handkerchief*⟩ 2 to show or express disdain or scorn *at* ⟨*not to be ~ed at*⟩ ~ *vt* 1 to smell or take by inhalation through the nose 2 to utter in a haughty manner 3 to detect or become aware of (as if) by smelling ⟨*~ out trouble*⟩ [ME *sniffen*, of imit origin]

**²sniff** *n* 1 an act or sound of sniffing 2 a quantity that is sniffed ⟨*a good ~ of sea air*⟩

**sniffer** /'snifə/ *n, informal* one who or that which sniffs: eg a someone who takes drugs illicitly by sniffing – compare GLUE-SNIFFING b someone who habitually sniffs instead of blowing his/her nose

**sniffish** /'snifish/ *adj* sniffy – **sniffishly** *adv*, **sniffishness** *n*

**¹sniffle** /'snifl/ *vi* 1 to sniff repeatedly; snuffle 2 to speak (as if) with sniffling [freq of *sniff*] – **sniffler** *n*

**²sniffle** *n* 1 an act or sound of sniffling 2 **sniffles** *pl*, **sniffle** a cold marked by discharge from the nose

**sniffy** /'snifi/ *adj, informal* having or expressing a haughty attitude; disdainful, supercilious – **sniffily** *adv*, **sniffiness** *n*

**snifter** /'sniftə/ *n, informal* 1 a small drink of spirits 2 *NAm* BALLOON GLASS (large goblet usu used for brandy) [E dial., sniff, snort, fr ME *snifteren* to sniff, snort]

**snig** /snig/ *vt* **-gg-** *Austr & NZ* to drag (logs) without using a sledge [origin unknown]

**¹snigger** /'snigə/ *vi* to laugh in a partly suppressed often derisive manner [alter. of *snicker*] – **sniggerer** *n*

**²snigger** *n* an act or sound of sniggering

**sniggle** /'snigl/ *vi* to fish for eels by lowering a baited hook into a place where they may be hiding ~ *vt* to catch (an eel) by sniggling [E dial. *snig* small eel, fr ME *snygge*]

**¹snip** /snip/ *n* **1a** a small piece that is snipped off; *also* a fragment, bit b a cut or notch made by snipping c an act or sound of snipping 2 a small white or light mark (eg between a horse's nostrils) 3 *pl but taking sing or pl vb* shears used esp for cutting sheet metal by hand 4 *Br* a bargain ⟨*something of a ~ at this price – Good Housekeeping*⟩ 5 *NAm* a presumptuous or impertinent person; *esp* a pert girl 6 *Br informal* something easy to do; a cinch [fr or akin to D & LG *snip*]

**²snip** *vb* **-pp-** *vt* to cut or cut off (as if) with shears or scissors,

esp with short rapid strokes ~ *vi* to make a short quick cut (as if) with shears or scissors – **snipper** *n*

**¹snipe** /sniep/ *n, pl* **snipes**, *esp collectively* **snipe** any of various birds (suborder Charadrii) that usu have long slender straight beaks; *esp* any of several game birds (*Gallinago* and related genera, esp *Gallinago gallinago*) that occur esp in marshy areas and resemble the related woodcocks [ME, of Scand origin; akin to ON *snípa* snipe; akin to OHG *snepfa* snipe]

**²snipe** *vi* 1 to hunt or shoot snipe **2a** to shoot *at* exposed individuals of an enemy's forces, esp when not in action and usu from in hiding at long range b to shoot or shoot at by sniping c to aim a snide or obliquely critical attack *at* – **sniper** *n*

**snippet** /'snipit/ *n* a small part, piece, or item; *esp* a fragment of writing or conversation [¹*snip* + *-et* ]

**snippety** /'snipəti/ *adj* 1 made up of snippets 2 snippy – **snippetiness** *n*

**snippy** /'snipi/ *adj* 1 unduly brief; scrappy 2 *chiefly NAm* brusque, curt [²*snip*]

**snit** /snit/ *n, NAm, Austr, & NZ informal* a bad or sulky mood ⟨*he's been in a terrible ~ all week*⟩ [origin unknown]

**¹snitch** /snich/ *vb, informal vi* to turn informer; squeal ~ *vt* to pilfer, pinch *synonyms* see ROB [prob fr slang *snitch* blow on the nose, nose, informer; vt prob influenced by ¹*snatch*] – **snitcher** *n*

**²snitch** *n, informal* a (petty) theft

**¹snivel** /'snivl/ *vi* **-ll-** (*NAm* **-l-, -ll-**) 1 to have a runny nose 2 to sniff mucus up the nose audibly; snuffle 3 to cry or whine with snuffling 4 to speak or act in a whining, snuffling, tearful, or weakly emotional manner [ME *snivelen*, fr (assumed) OE *snyflan*; akin to D *snuffelen* to snuffle, *snuffen* to sniff, Gk *nan* to flow – more at NOURISH] – **sniveller** *n*

**²snivel** *n* an act or instance of snivelling

**¹snob** /snob/ *n* 1 someone who blatantly attempts to cultivate or imitate those he/she admires as social superiors **2a** one who tends to rebuff, patronize, or avoid those he/she regards as inferior b one who has an air of smug superiority in matters of knowledge or taste ⟨*a cultural ~*⟩ 3 *archaic* a cobbler [arch. *snob* member of the lower classes, vulgar or ostentatious person, fr E dial., shoemaker] – **snobbism** *n*, **snobby** *adj*

**²snob** *adj, informal* designed or suitable for snobs ⟨*~ schools such as Eton*⟩

**snobbery** /'snob(ə)ri/ *n* the quality or an instance of snobbishness

**snobbish** /'snobish/ *adj* being, characteristic of, or befitting a snob – **snobbishly** *adv*, **snobbishness** *n*

**SNOBOL** /'snohbol/ *n* a high-level computer language for handling strings of symbols [*String Oriented Symbolic Language*]

**Sno-Cat** /'snoh ,kat/ *trademark* – used for a tracklaying vehicle designed for travel on snow

**snoek** /snoohk/ *n* any of several vigorous active marine fishes: eg a BARRACOUTA b BARRACUDA [Afrik, fr D, pike]

**snog** /snog/ *vi* **-gg-** *Br slang* to kiss and cuddle [perh alter. of ²*snug*] – **snog** *n*

**¹snood** /snoohd/ *n* 1 a net or fabric bag pinned or tied on at the back of a woman's head for holding the hair 2 *Scot* a ribbon or band for a woman's hair [(assumed) ME, fr OE *snōd*; akin to OIr *snáth* thread, OE *nǣdl* needle]

**²snood** *vt* to wear (the hair) in a snood

**snook** /snoohk/ *n* a gesture of derision made by putting the thumb to the nose and spreading the fingers out [origin unknown] – **cock a snook/cock snooks at somebody** to express one's contempt for somebody by means of insolent gestures or behaviour

**¹snooker** /'snoohkə/ *n* 1 a game played on a billiard table in which players hit a white ball (CUE BALL) with a cue in order to pocket 15 red balls and 6 variously coloured balls 2 a position of the balls in the game of snooker in which a direct shot would lose points [prob fr earlier slang *snooker* new military cadet (the game being devised by army officers in India in the 1870s)]

**²snooker** *vt* 1 to prevent (an opponent) from making a direct shot in the game of snooker by playing the CUE BALL so that another ball rests between it and any ball the opponent may legitimately play 2 *informal* to present an obstacle to; thwart – **snookered** *adj*

**¹snoop** /snoohp/ *vi* to look or pry in a sneaking or interfering manner [D *snoepen* to buy or eat on the sly; akin to D *snappen* to snap] – **snooper** *n*

**²snoop** *n* 1 someone who snoops 2 the act or an instance of snooping

**snoot** /snooht/ *n* **1** *NAm* a grimace expressing contempt **2** *informal* **2a** a snout **b** a nose [ME *snute* snout]

**snooty** /'snoohti/ *adj, informal* **1** haughty, disdainful **2** characterized by snobbish attitudes ⟨*a ~ neighbourhood*⟩ – **snootily** *adv*, **snootiness** *n*

¹**snooze** /snoohz/ *vi, informal* to take a nap; doze [origin unknown] – **snoozer** *n*

²**snooze** *n, informal* a nap

¹**snore** /snaw/ *vi* to breathe during sleep with a rough hoarse noise due to vibration of the SOFT PALATE ~ *vt* to spend (time) in sleeping – + *away* ⟨*he ~d away the best part of the afternoon and only woke up when it started to rain*⟩ [ME *snoren*; akin to MLG *snorren* to drone, MHG *snerren* to chatter] – **snorer** *n*

²**snore** *n* **1** an act of snoring **2** (a noise similar to) the noise of snoring

¹**snorkel** /'snawkl/ *n* **1** a tube housing air intake and exhaust pipes that can be extended above the surface of the water from a submerged submarine **2** any of various devices resembling a snorkel in function; *specif* a J-shaped tube allowing a SKIN DIVER to breathe while face down in the water [Ger *schnorchel*]

²**snorkel** *vi* **snorkeled; snorkeling** /-kl·ing/ to operate or swim submerged with only a snorkel above water – **snorkeler** *n*

¹**snort** /snawt/ *vi* **1a** to force air violently through the nose with a harsh explosive sound **b** to express scorn, anger, indignation, or surprise by a snort **2** to emit explosive sounds resembling snorts **3** *informal* to inhale a drug ~ *vt* **1** to utter with or express by a snort ⟨*~ed his contempt*⟩ **2** to expel or emit (as if) with snorts **3** *informal* to inhale (a drug) ⟨*~ coke*⟩ – compare DROP 10 [ME *snorten*, prob of imit origin]

²**snort** *n* **1** an act or sound of snorting **2** *informal* a small drink usu of spirits; a snifter

**snorter** /'snawta/ *n* **1** one who or that which snorts **2** *informal* something that is extremely powerful, difficult, or impressive

**snot** /snot/ *n* **1** mucus from the nose **2** *slang* a snotty person [ME, fr OE *gesnot;* akin to OHG *snuzza* nasal mucus, Gk *nan* to flow – more at NOURISH]

**snotty** /'snoti/ *adj* **1** *informal* foul with mucus from the nose ⟨*a ~ child*⟩ **2** *slang* arrogantly or snobbishly unpleasant **3** *slang* contemptible but cheeky

¹**snout** /snowt/ *n* **1a(1)** a long projecting nose (eg of a pig) **a(2)** a forward extension of the head of various animals (eg a weevil); ROSTRUM (beaklike part of an animal) **b** the human nose, esp when large or grotesque **2** something resembling an animal's snout in position, function, or shape (eg a nozzle) **3** *slang* tobacco [ME *snute;* akin to Ger *schnauze* snout] – **snouted** *adj*, **snoutish** *adj*, **snouty** *adj*

²**snout** *vi, informal* to root, grub

¹**snow** /snoh/ *n* **1a** water falling in the form of white flakes consisting of small ice crystals formed directly from the water vapour in the atmosphere at a temperature of less than 0°C (32°F) **b(1)** a descent or shower of snow crystals **b(2)** fallen snow crystals ⟨*the ~ lay thick on the ground*⟩ **2** something resembling snow: eg **2a** a dessert made of stiffly beaten egg whites, sugar, and fruit pulp ⟨*apple ~*⟩ **b** any of various congealed or crystallized substances resembling snow in appearance **c** small transient light or dark spots on a television or radar screen, usu caused by weakness or absence of a signal **d** *slang* **d(1)** cocaine crystals **d(2)** heroin in powdered form [ME, fr OE *snāw;* akin to OHG *snēo* snow, L *niv-, nix*, Gk *nipha* (acc)] – **snowless** *adj*

²**snow** *vi* to send down snow ⟨*it's ~ing*⟩ ~ *vt* **1** to cause to fall like or as snow **2** to cover, shut in, block, or isolate (as if) with snow – usu in passive + *in* or *up* ⟨*found themselves ~ed in after the blizzard*⟩ **3** to whiten like snow ⟨*his hair was ~ed by age*⟩ **4** *chiefly NAm* to deceive, persuade, or charm glibly

**snow under** *vt* **1** to overwhelm, esp with more than can be handled or absorbed ⟨*snowed under with applications for the job*⟩ **2** *NAm* to defeat by a large margin ⟨*snowed under by 4000 votes for his opponent*⟩

³**snow** *n* a sailing vessel that is basically a BRIG (two-masted square-rigged sailing ship) with an additional small mast for a TRYSAIL (fore-and-aft sail) immediately behind the others [modif of D *snauw*, prob fr LG *snau*]

¹**snowball** /'snoh,bawl/ *n* **1** a round mass of snow pressed or rolled together, esp for throwing **2** any of several cultivated shrubs (genus *Viburnum*) of the honeysuckle family with clusters of white flowers **3** a dance in which one couple start to

dance, but when the music stops they separate and each chooses a different partner, and so on usu until everyone in the room is dancing **4** a cocktail drink made of advocaat with lemonade

²**snowball** *vt* **1** to throw snowballs at **2** to cause to increase, expand, or multiply at a rapidly accelerating rate ~ *vi* **1** to throw snowballs **2** to increase, expand, or multiply at a rapidly accelerating rate

**snowbank** /'snohbangk/ *n* a mound or slope of snow

**snowberry** /'snohb(ə)ri/ *n* any of several white-berried shrubs (esp genus *Symphoricarpos*) of the honeysuckle family; *esp* a low-growing originally N American shrub (*Symphoricarpos rivularis*) with pink flowers in small clusters that is commonly planted in gardens

'**snow-,blind, snow-blinded** *adj* affected with SNOW BLINDNESS

**snow blindness** *n* inflammation and painful sensitiveness to light caused by exposure of the eyes to ultraviolet rays reflected from snow or ice

**snowblink** /'snoh,blingk/ *n* a white glare in the sky over a snowfield

**snowbound** /'snoh,bownd/ *adj* confined or surrounded by snow

**snow-broth** /'snoh,broth/ *n* newly melted snow, esp when mixed with stream water

**snow bunting** /'bunting/ *n* a Eurasian and N American BUNTING (finchlike bird) (*Plectrophenax nivalis*) that breeds in the arctic regions and is a winter visitor to Europe

**snowcap** /'snoh,kap/ *n* a covering cap of snow (eg on a mountain top) – **snowcapped** *adj*

**snowdrift** /'snoh,drift/ *n* a bank of drifted snow

**snowdrop** /'snoh,drop/ *n* a European plant (*Galanthus nivalis*) of the daffodil family that grows from a bulb and bears nodding white flowers that appear in very early spring, often while the snow is on the ground

**snowfall** /'snoh,fawl/ *n* a fall of snow; *specif* the amount of snow that falls in a single shower or in a given period

**snow fence** *n* a usu slatted fence placed across the path of prevailing winds to protect (eg a building, road, or railway track) from drifting snow

**snowfield** /'snoh,feeld/ *n* a broad level expanse of snow; *esp* a permanent mass of snow (eg at the head of a glacier)

**snowflake** /'snoh,flayk/ *n* a flake or crystal of snow

**snow goose** *n* a large white goose (*Anser caerulescens*) with black-tipped wings that breeds chiefly in N America

'**snow-,house** *n, chiefly Can* an igloo

,**snow-in-'summer** *n* a white-flowered creeping European plant (*Cerastium tomentosum*) of the pink family commonly grown in rock gardens

**snow job** *n, chiefly NAm* an involved attempt to persuade or deceive by overwhelming with information or flattery [²*snow* 4]

**snow leopard** *n* a showily marked big cat (*Felis uncia*) of upland central Asia with long heavy fur that is greyish white irregularly blotched with brownish black in summer, and almost pure white in winter

**snow line** *n* the level (eg height above sea level or line of latitude) beyond which land is permanently covered in snow

**snowmaker** /'snoh,maykə/ *n* a device for making snow artificially – **snowmaking** *adj*

**snowman** /'snoh,man/ *n* snow shaped, esp by children, to resemble a human figure

**snowmobile** /'snohmə,beel/ *n* any of various motor-powered vehicles for travel on snow or ice [¹*snow* + auto*mobile*] – **snowmobiler** *n*

**snowpack** /'snoh,pak/ *n* a seasonal accumulation of slow-melting packed snow

¹**snowplough** /'snoh,plow/ *n* **1** any of various vehicles or devices used for clearing away snow **2** a turn in skiing with the skis in the snow ploughing position

²**snowplough** *vi* to force the heels of one's skis outwards, keeping the tips together, in order to descend slowly, slow down, or stop

**snowscape** /'snoh,skayp/ *n* a snow-covered landscape

**snowshoe** /'snoh,shooh/ *n* a light oval wooden frame strung with thongs and strengthened by two crosspieces that is attached to the foot to enable a person to walk on soft snow without sinking

**snowslide** /'snoh,slied/ *n* a snowslip

**snowslip** /'snoh,slip/ *n* a usu light avalanche of snow

**snowstorm** /'snoh,stawm/ *n* **1** a storm of or with snow **2** something that resembles a snowstorm

**snow tyre** *n* a motor-vehicle tyre with a tread designed to give added grip on snow or ice

**snow-'white** *adj* spotlessly white

**snowy** /'snoh·i/ *adj* **1a** composed of (melted) snow **b** characterized by or covered with snow **2a** whitened (as if) by snow ⟨*ground ~ with fallen blossom*⟩ **b** snow-white – **snowily** *adv*, **snowiness** *n*

**snowy owl** *n* a very large white round-headed arctic owl (*Nyctea scandiaca*) that migrates south into Europe and N America in the winter

**¹snub** /snub/ *vt* **-bb-** **1** to check or interrupt with sharp words; rebuke **2** to check (eg a rope) suddenly while running out, esp by winding around a fixed object (eg a post); *also* to bring (eg a boat) to a halt by snubbing a line **3** to treat with contempt, esp by deliberately ignoring **4** *NAm* to stub out (eg a cigarette) [ME *snubben*, of Scand origin; akin to ON *snubba* to scold; akin to Icel *sneypa* to scold]

**²snub** *n* **1** an act or an instance of snubbing; *esp* a slight **2** a snub nose

**³snub, snubbed** /snubd/ *adj* short and stubby ⟨*a ~ nose*⟩ [fr ¹*snub* in the arch. sense 'to shorten, cut off the end of'] – **snubness** *n*

**snubber** /'snubə/ *n* **1** one who or that which snubs **2** *NAm* SHOCK ABSORBER

**snubby** /'snubi/ *adj* **1** snub **2** snub-nosed – **snubbiness** *n*

**snub-nosed** /nohzd/ *adj* **1** having a short and slightly turned-up nose **2** having a very short barrel ⟨*a ~ revolver*⟩

**snuck** /snuk/ *NAm past of* SNEAK – nonstandard

**¹snuff** /snuf/ *n* the charred part of a candlewick [ME *snoffe*]

**²snuff** *vt* **1** to trim the snuff of (a candle) by pinching or by the use of snuffers **2a** to extinguish (a flame) by the use of a snuffer or snuffers **b** to make extinct; put an end to – usu + *out* ⟨*an accident that ~ed out a life*⟩ – **snuff it** *informal* to die

**³snuff** *vt* **1** to draw forcibly through or into the nostrils **2** to scent, smell **3** *of an animal* to sniff at in order to examine ~ *vi* **1** to inhale through the nose noisily and forcibly; *also* to sniff or smell inquiringly **2** to take snuff [akin to D *snuffen* to sniff, snuff – more at SNIVEL]

**⁴snuff** *n* the act of snuffing; a sniff

**⁵snuff** *n* a preparation of powdered often scented tobacco that is usu inhaled through the nostrils and sometimes chewed [D *snuf*, short for *snuftabak*, fr *snuffen* to snuff + *tabak* tobacco]

**snuffbox** /'snuf,boks/ *n* a small often ornate box for holding snuff, usu carried about the person

**¹snuffer** /'snufə/ *n* **1** *pl* an implement somewhat like a pair of scissors for trimming the wick of a candle or for extinguishing it **2** an implement for extinguishing candles that consists of a small hollow cone attached to a handle

**²snuffer** *n* one who or that which snuffs or sniffs; *also* someone who takes snuff

**¹snuffle** /'snufl/ *vi* **1** to sniff usu audibly and repeatedly **2** to draw air through an obstructed nose with a sniffing sound **3** to speak in nasal or whining tones ~ *vt* to utter with much snuffling [akin to D *snuffelen* to snuffle – more at SNIVEL] – **snuffler** *n*

**²snuffle** *n* **1** the act or sound of snuffling **2** a nasal twang **3** **snuffles** *pl*, **snuffle** a cold in the nose; sniffles

**¹snuffy** /'snufi/ *adj* **1** quick to become annoyed or take offence; huffy **2** supercilious, disdainful [³*snuff* + ¹-*y*]

**²snuffy** *adj* **1** resembling snuff **2** addicted to the use of snuff **3** soiled with snuff [⁵*snuff* + ¹-*y*]

**¹snug** /snug/ *adj* **-gg-** **1a** *of a ship* trim and seaworthy **b** fitting closely and comfortably ⟨*a ~ coat*⟩ **2a** enjoying or giving warm secure shelter and opportunity for modest ease and contentment **b** marked by relaxation and informality ⟨*a ~ evening among friends*⟩ **3** giving a degree of comfort and ease ⟨*a ~ income*⟩ **4** offering safe concealment ⟨*a ~ hideout*⟩ *synonyms* see COMFORTABLE [perh of Scand origin; akin to Sw *snygg* tidy; akin to ON *snöggr* shorn, bald, L *novacula* razor] – **snug** *adv*, **snugly** *adv*, **snugness** *n*

**²snug** *vb* **-gg-** *vi* to snuggle ~ *vt* **1** to hug or wrap round closely ⟨*a belt that ~s the waist*⟩ **2** to make snug ⟨*~ the place for winter*⟩

**³snug** *n*, *Br* a small private room or compartment in a pub; *also* a snuggery [short for *snuggery*]

**snuggery** /'snug(ə)ri/ *n*, *chiefly Br* a snug cosy place; *esp* a small room ⟨*a warm little ~ under the eaves*⟩

**snuggle** /'snugl/ *vb*, *informal vi* to curl up comfortably or cosily; nestle ~ *vt* to draw close, esp for comfort or in affection ⟨*the dog ~d his muzzle under his master's arm*⟩ [freq of ²*snug*]

**¹so** /soh; *also* (*occasional weak form*) sə/ *adv* **1a** in this way; thus ⟨*as it ~ happens*⟩ ⟨*while she was ~ employed*⟩ – often used as a substitute for a preceding word or word group ⟨*do you really think ~?*⟩ ⟨*became chairman and remained ~*⟩ ⟨*are you ready? If ~, let's go*⟩ ⟨*why ~?*⟩; compare EVEN SO, JUST SO, QUITE SO **b** in the same way; *also* ⟨*worked hard and ~ did she*⟩ – used after *as* to introduce a parallel ⟨*as the French drink wine, ~ the English like their beer*⟩ **2a** in such a way – used, esp before *as* or *that*, to introduce a result ⟨*the book is ~ written that a child could understand it*⟩ or to introduce the idea of purpose ⟨*hid ~ as not to get caught*⟩ **b** to such an extreme degree ⟨*had never been ~ happy*⟩ ⟨*left her because he loved her ~*⟩ ⟨*never seen ~ beautiful a child*⟩ – used before *as* to introduce a comparison, esp in the negative ⟨*not ~ fast as mine*⟩, or, esp before *as* or *that*, to introduce a result ⟨*~ clearly guilty as to leave no doubt*⟩ ⟨*~ fast that I can't keep up*⟩ ⟨*was ~ tired I went to bed*⟩; compare SO LONG AS **c** to a definite but unspecified extent or degree ⟨*can only do ~ much in a day*⟩ – compare SO MANY, SO MUCH **d(1)** most certainly; indeed ⟨*I hope to win and ~ I shall*⟩ **d(2)** *chiefly dial & NAm* – used, esp by children, to counter a negative charge ⟨*you did ~!*⟩ ⟨*I can ~ do it*⟩ **e** very ⟨*haven't been feeling ~ well lately*⟩ ⟨*I'm ~ glad you could come!*⟩ **3a** then, subsequently ⟨*and ~ home and to bed*⟩ **b** therefore, consequently ⟨*the witness is biased and ~ unreliable*⟩ ⟨*were tired and ~ went to bed*⟩ **c** as a concomitant – after *as* ⟨*as the wind increased, ~ the sea grew rougher*⟩ *usage* see ⁴AS [ME, fr OE *swā*; akin to OHG *sō* so, L *sic* so, thus, *si* if, Gk *hōs* so, thus, L *suus* one's own – more at SUICIDE] – **or so** – used to indicate an approximation or conjecture ⟨*I've known him 20 years or so*⟩; compare AND SO ON, AND SO FORTH – **so far as** to the extent or degree that – **so that** – used to introduce a subordinate clause expressing purpose

**²so** /soh/ *conj* **1a** with the result that ⟨*her diction is good, ~ every word is clear*⟩ **b** THAT 2a(1); IN ORDER THAT ⟨*be quiet ~ he can sleep*⟩ **2a** for that reason; therefore ⟨*don't want to go, ~ I won't*⟩ **b(1)** – used as an introductory particle ⟨*~ here we are*⟩ often to belittle a point under discussion ⟨*~ what?*⟩ **b(2)** – used interjectionally to indicate awareness of a discovery ⟨*~, that's who did it*⟩ or surprised dissent **3** *archaic* provided that *usage* In formal writing, the idea of "purpose" is better expressed by **so that** ⟨*be quiet so that he can sleep*⟩ or by **so as to** ⟨*be quiet so as to let him sleep*⟩ rather than by **so** alone; but **so** alone may correctly mean "with the result that".

**³so** /soh/ *adj* **1** conforming with actual facts; true ⟨*said things that were not ~*⟩ **2** disposed in a definite order ⟨*his books are always exactly ~*⟩ – compare JUST SO

**⁴so** /soh/ *n*, *music* SOH

**¹soak** /sohk/ *vi* **1** to lie immersed in liquid (eg water), esp so as to become saturated or softened ⟨*put the clothes to ~*⟩ **2a** to enter or pass through something (as if) by pores or small openings; permeate **b** to become fully felt or appreciated – usu + *in* or *into* **3** *informal* to drink alcohol excessively ~ *vt* **1** to permeate so as to wet, soften, or fill thoroughly **2a** to place in a surrounding element, esp liquid, to wet or penetrate thoroughly **b** to immerse the mind and feelings of; engross ⟨*~ yourself in art history*⟩ **3** to extract (as if) by steeping ⟨*~ the dirt out*⟩ **4a** to draw in (as if) by absorption ⟨*~ed up the sunshine*⟩ **b** *informal* to intoxicate (oneself) with alcohol **5** *informal* **5a** to charge an excessive amount of money; levy too much money from ⟨*~ed the taxpayers*⟩ **b** *chiefly NAm* to punish severely [ME *soken*, fr OE *socian*; akin to OE *sūcan* to suck] – **soakage** *n*, **soaker** *n*

**²soak** *n* **1a** soaking or being soaked **b** that (eg liquid) in which something is soaked **2** *informal* **2a** a drunkard **b** a drinking bout

**soakaway** /'sohkə,way/ *n*, *Br* a hole dug in the ground and filled with gravel or rubble into which rain or waste water flows and naturally drains away

**soaker** /'sohkə/ *n* a thin piece of lead placed between slates or tiles, esp at junctions of the roof with walls or at the meeting of two slopes of a roof, in order to improve waterproofing

**'so-and-,so** *n*, *pl* **so-and-sos, so-and-so's** **1** an unnamed or unspecified person or thing ⟨*Miss So-and-so*⟩ **2** *euph* a disliked or unpleasant person ⟨*the cheeky ~!*⟩

**¹soap** /sohp/ *n* **1** a substance used for cleansing and EMUL-SIFYING (stabilizing oil-and-water mixtures) that lathers when rubbed in water and consists essentially of chemical compounds (SALTS) formed by the combination between sodium or potassium and FATTY ACIDS **2** a chemical compound (SALT) formed by the combination between a FATTY ACID and a metal [ME *sope*, fr OE *sāpe;* akin to OHG *seifa* soap, L *sebum* tallow] – **soapless** *adj*

²**soap** *vt* **1** to rub soap over or into **2** *informal* to flatter – often + *up*

**soapbark** /'sohp,bahk/ *n* a Chilean tree (*Quillaja saponaria*) of the rose family with shining leaves and white flowers; *also* its bark that is rich in a lather-producing substance (SAPONIN) and is used as a substitute for soap and to EMULSIFY oils

**soapberry** /'sohpb(ə)ri, -,beri/ *n* any of a genus (*Sapindus* of the family Sapindaceae) of chiefly tropical woody plants; *also* the fruit of a soapberry (esp *Sapindus saponaria*) that contains a lather-producing substance (SAPONIN) and is used as a substitute for soap

**soapbox** /'sohp,boks/ *n* an improvised platform used by a self-appointed or informal orator – **soapbox** *adj*

**soapmaking** /'sohp,mayking/ *n* the act, process, or occupation of making soap

**soap opera** *n* a serialized radio or television drama in which ordinary domestic situations are given melodramatic or sentimental treatment [fr its formerly being often sponsored in the USA by soap manufacturers]

**soapstone** /'sohp,stohn/ *n* a soft greyish green or brown stone that has a soapy feel and is mainly composed of the minerals TALC, CHLORITE, and often some MAGNETITE

**soapsuds** /'sohp,sudz/ *n pl* SUDS 1

**soapwort** /'sohp,wuht/ *n* a European plant (*Saponaria officinalis*) of the pink family that has clusters of pink or white flowers and leaves which yield a detergent when bruised

**soapy** /'sohpi/ *adj* **1** covered with soap; lathered **2** containing or combined with soap or SAPONIN (soaplike substance produced by certain plants) **3a** resembling or having the qualities of soap; *esp* being smooth and slippery **b** suave, ingratiating – **soapily** *adv,* **soapiness** *n*

¹**soar** /saw/ *vi* **1a** to fly high in the air **b(1)** to sail or hover in the air, often at a great height; glide **b(2)** *of a glider* to fly using THERMALS (upward currents of hot air) to maintain or gain height **2** to rise upwards in position or status ⟨*a* ~ing *reputation*⟩ **3** to rise rapidly or to a very high level ⟨*temperatures* ~ed *into the upper thirties*⟩ **4** to be of majestic or imposing height or stature; tower ⟨*snow-covered mountains* ~ed *above us*⟩ [ME *soren,* fr MF *essorer* to air, soar, fr (assumed) VL *exaurare* to air, fr L *ex-* + *aura* air – more at AURA] – **soarer** *n*

²**soar** *n* **1** the range, distance, or height attained in soaring **2** the act of soaring; upward flight

**soaring** /'sawring/ *n* the act or process of soaring; *specif* the act or sport of flying a heavier-than-air craft without power by using rising air currents (THERMALS)

¹**sob** /sob/ *vb* **-bb-** *vi* **1** to cry or weep with convulsive catching of the breath **2** to make a sound like that of a sob or sobbing ~ *vt* **1** to bring (e g oneself) to a specified state by sobbing ⟨~*bed himself to sleep*⟩ **2** to express or utter with sobs ⟨~*bed out her grief*⟩ [ME *sobben*]

²**sob** *n* **1** an act or sound of sobbing **2** a sound like that of a sob

**SOB** /,es,oh'bee/ *n, slang* SON OF A BITCH; bastard [*son of a bitch*]

¹**sober** /'sohbə/ *adj* **1a** sparing in the use of food and drink; abstemious **b** not addicted to intoxicating drink **c** not drunk **2** gravely or earnestly thoughtful **3** calmly self-controlled; sedate **4** subdued in tone or colour **5** showing no excessive or extreme qualities of emotion, conjecture, or prejudice: e g **5a** well balanced; realistic ⟨*a* ~ *estimate*⟩ ⟨*the* ~ *truth*⟩ **b** sane, rational *synonyms* see SERIOUS *antonyms* drunk, merry, excited [ME *sobre,* fr MF, fr L *sobrius;* akin to L *ebrius* drunk] – **soberly** *adv,* **soberness** *n*

²**sober** *vb* to make or become sober – usu + *up*

**sobersided** /,sohbə'siedid/ *adj, informal* excessively earnest or serious-minded

**sobersides** /'sohbə,siedz/ *n, pl* **sobersides** *informal* a sober-sided person

**sobriety** /sə'brie·əti/ *n, formal* the quality or state of being sober *synonyms* see ABSTINENCE [ME *sobrietie,* fr MF *sobrieté,* fr L *sobrietat-, sobrietas,* fr *sobrius* sober]

**sobriquet** /'sohbri,kay/ *n* a nickname [Fr, fr MF *soubriquet* tap under the chin, nickname]

**sob story** *n, informal* a sentimental story or account intended chiefly to elicit pity or sympathy ⟨*a long non-stop* ~ *about his misfortunes* – *Evening Argus* (*Brighton*)⟩

**sob stuff** *n, informal* material designed to have a sentimental or strongly emotional appeal ⟨*last night's film was real* ~⟩

**socage, soccage** /'sokij/ *n* feudal tenure of land usu in return for agricultural service fixed in amount and kind, or payment of money rent, and not burdened with any duty to perform military service for the feudal overlord [ME, fr *soc* soke] – **socager** *n*

'**so-,called** *adj* **1** commonly named; popularly so termed ⟨*involved in* ~ *campus politics*⟩ **2** falsely or improperly so named ⟨*deceived by his* ~ *friend*⟩

**soccer** /'sokə/ *n* a football game that is played with a round ball between teams of 11 players each, that features the kicking, dribbling, and heading of the ball, and in which use of the hands and arms is prohibited except to the goalkeepers [by shortening & alter. fr *association* (*football*)]

¹**sociable** /'sohshəbl/ *adj* **1** *of an animal* inclined by nature to companionship with others of the same species; social, gregarious **2a** inclined to seek or enjoy companionship; affable, companionable **b** conducive to friendliness or cordial social relations ⟨*spent a* ~ *evening at the club*⟩ [MF or L; MF, fr L *sociabilis,* fr *sociare* to join, associate, fr *socius* companion] – **sociableness** *n,* **sociably** *adv,* **sociability** *n*

²**sociable** *n, NAm*

¹**social** /'sohsh(ə)l/ *adj* **1** involving allies or confederates ⟨*the* Social *War between the Athenians and their allies*⟩ **2a** sociable **b** of or promoting warm companionship or friendly relations ⟨*a* ~ *club*⟩ ⟨*a full* ~ *life*⟩ **c** designed for social activities ⟨*a sports hall with large* ~ *area*⟩ **3a** tending to form cooperative relationships with one's fellows; gregarious ⟨*man is a* ~ *being*⟩ **b** living and breeding in more or less organized communities ⟨~ *insects*⟩ **c** *of a plant species* tending to grow thickly in patches or clumps so as to take over the area in which it is growing **4** of human society, the interactions between individuals and between groups, or the welfare of people as members of society ⟨~ *institutions*⟩ **5a** of or based on status or prestige in a particular society ⟨*a member of his* ~ *set*⟩ **b** (characteristic) of the upper classes ⟨*writes a column of* ~ *gossip*⟩ [L *socialis,* fr *socius* companion, ally, associate; akin to L *sequi* to follow – more at SUE]

²**social** *n* a social gathering usu connected with a church or club

**social class** *n* CLASS 1 (ranking in society)

**social climber** *n* one who strives to gain a higher social position or acceptance in fashionable society – **social climbing** *n*

**social compact** *n* SOCIAL CONTRACT

**social contract** *n* **1** an actual or supposed agreement among individuals forming an organized society or between (part of) the community and the governing power that defines and limits the rights and duties of each **2** an unwritten agreement between the government and the TUC whereby trade unions regulate wage demands in return for beneficial concessions in the government's programme [trans of Fr *contrat social* (orig used by Jean Jacques *Rousseau* †1778 Fr philosopher)]

**social democracy** *n* **1** a political movement advocating a gradual and peaceful transition from capitalism to socialism by democratic means **2** *cap* the principles and policies of a Social Democratic party

**social democrat** *n* **1** an adherent or advocate of political social democracy **2** *cap* a member or supporter of a Social Democratic party

**social democratic** *adj* of or being a political party that advocates the principles and policies of political social democracy: e g **a** *cap* of or being a political party of the UK formed on March 26th 1981 and associated with the creation of an open, classless, and more equal society **b** *cap* of or being a political party of the Federal Republic of Germany founded in 1875 that aims for democratic socialism through a gradual reform within the parliamentary system

**social disease** *n* **1** VENEREAL DISEASE **2** a disease (e g tuberculosis) whose incidence is directly related to social and economic factors

**social engineering** *n* the planning of society and desirable social change by the management of people in accordance with their place and function in society; applied SOCIAL SCIENCE – **social engineer** *n*

**socialism** /'sohsh(ə)l,iz(ə)m/ *n* **1** an economic and political theory advocating collective or state ownership and administration of the means of production and distribution of goods **2a** the practical application of the theory of socialism in society; *broadly* a system of society or group living in which there is no private property **b** a system or condition of society in which the means of production, distribution, and exchange are owned and administered by the state for the benefit of all **3** a stage of society in Marxist theory between capitalism and communism that differs from capitalism by having the means of production under collective control and differs from communism in distributing goods and benefits in accordance with the usefulness of the work an individual performs

**¹socialist** /-ist/ *n* **1** someone who advocates or practises socialism **2** *cap* a member of a socialist party or political group

**²socialist** *adj* **1** of or promoting socialism ⟨*a ~ state*⟩ ⟨*~ tendencies*⟩ **2** *cap* of or constituting a political party advocating socialism

**socialistic** /-'istik/ *adj* of or tending towards socialism – **socialistically** *adv*

**socialist realism** *n, often cap S&R* **1** a Marxist theory of the role and function of the arts in an evolving socialist state that evaluates artistic production according to the contribution it makes to the development of social consciousness and the extent to which it reaffirms the social goals to which the society is advancing; *also* the theory that holds that such criteria are the only valid ones for evaluating any work of art **2** crudely propagandistic art produced in communist countries exulting the dignity of labour, the wisdom of the leadership, etc – **social realist** *n*

**socialite** /'sohsh(ə)liet/ *n* a socially active or prominent person

**sociality** /ˌsohshi'aləti/ *n* **1a** the quality or state of being sociable **b** an instance of being sociable **2** the tendency to associate in or form social groups

**social·ization, -isation** /ˌsohshəlie'zaysh(ə)n/ *n* the process or result of socializing; *specif* the learning process beginning at infancy by which an individual acquires the values, rules, skills, and attitudes relevant to his/her participation in society – compare ACCULTURATION

**social·ize, -ise** /'sohsh(ə)l‚iez/ *vt* **1** to make social; *esp* to fit or train for life in society **2** to constitute on a socialist basis ⟨*~ industry*⟩ **3** to adapt to social needs or uses ⟨*~ science*⟩ ~ *vi* to act in a sociable manner ⟨*~ with his students*⟩ – **socialization** *n,* **socializer** *n*

**socialized medicine** *n, NAm* medical and hospital services provided for the members of a class or population that is administered by an organized group (eg a state agency) and paid for by taxation, endowments, etc

**socially** /'sohshəli/ *adv* **1** in a social manner **2** with respect to society **3** by or through society

**social-minded** *adj* socially conscious or responsible

**social science** *n* **1** the scientific study of the institutions and functioning of human society and the relationships between members of society **2** a subject (eg economics or political science) dealing with a particular aspect of human society – **social scientist** *n*

**social secretary** *n* someone who handles the social arrangements of a person or group

**social security** *n* **1** the state provision (eg through retirement pensions and sickness and unemployment benefits) for the economic security and social welfare of the individual and his family **2** SUPPLEMENTARY BENEFIT (allowance paid during unemployment)

**social service** *n* activity or assistance designed to promote social welfare; *esp, pl* the organized services (eg education, health, and housing) provided by the state

**social studies** *n pl* studies relating to social relationships and the functioning of society

**social work** *n* (the methods or activities of) any of various professional agencies or services practically involved with the investigation and alleviation of the problems of the economically underprivileged, socially maladjusted, handicapped, etc – **social worker** *n*

**societal** /sə'sie·ətl/ *adj* of society; social ⟨*~ forces*⟩ – **societally** *adv*

**¹society** /sə'sie·əti/ *n* **1** companionship or association with others; friendly or intimate fellowship; company **2** a voluntary association of individuals for common ends; *esp* an organized group working together or periodically meeting because of common interests, beliefs, or profession **3a(1)** the human race considered in terms of its complex structure of social institutions and organization and its mode of life **a(2)** an enduring

and cooperating social group whose members have developed organized patterns of relationships through interaction with one another ⟨*the role of cattle in the lives of the pastoralist societies of SE Africa*⟩ **b** a community, nation, or broad grouping of people having common traditions, institutions, and collective activities and interests ⟨*the spread of literacy in European ~ in the 18th century*⟩ **4a** a section of a community characterized by particular aims or standards of living or conduct; a social circle or a group of social circles clearly identifiable as such ⟨*move in polite ~*⟩ ⟨*literary ~*⟩ **b** a part of a community whose wealth permits considerable leisure and that regards itself as the arbiter of fashion and manners ⟨*a famous ~ hostess*⟩ **5a(1)** a natural group of plants usu of a single species or habit within an ASSOCIATION (unit of an ecological community) **a(2)** ASSOCIATION 6 **b** the offspring of a pair of insects living and working as a social unit (eg a hive of bees); *broadly* a closely integrated group of organisms [MF *societé,* fr L *societat-, societas,* fr *socius* companion – more at SOCIAL]

**²society** *adj* (characteristic) of fashionable society ⟨*a ~ wedding*⟩

**Socinian** /soh'sini·ən/ *n* a follower of a 16th- and 17th-century theological movement that denied the divinity of Christ and thus the notion of the Trinity, but in other respects regarded the Bible as authoritative [NL *socinianus,* fr Faustus *Socinus* (Fausto Sozzini) †1604 It theologian] – **Socinian** *adj,* **Socinianism** *n*

**socio-** /ˌsohs(h)ioh-/ *comb form* **1** society ⟨*sociography*⟩ **2** social ⟨*sociolinguistic*⟩; social and ⟨*sociopolitical*⟩ [Fr, fr L *socius* companion]

**sociobiology** /ˌsohs(h)iohbie'oləji/ *n* the scientific study of animal behaviour from the point of view that all behaviour has evolved by NATURAL SELECTION – **sociobiologist** *n,* **sociobiological** *adj,* **sociobiologically** *adv*

**sociocultural** /ˌsohs(h)ioh'kulchərəl/ *adj* of or involving a combination of social and cultural factors – **socioculturally** *adv*

**socioeconomic** /ˌsohs(h)ioh‚eekə'nomik, ‚ekə-/ *adj* of or involving a combination of social and economic factors

**sociogram** /'sohs(h)iə‚gram/ *n* a diagrammatic representation of the social relations (ie ties of friendship or kinship) among members of a social group; *also* the plotted results of a sociometric study

**sociolinguistic** /ˌsohs(h)iohling'gwistik/ *adj* **1** of the social aspects of language **2** of sociolinguistics – **sociolinguistically** *adv*

**sociolinguistics** /-ling'gwistiks/ *n pl but taking sing vb* the study of linguistic behaviour as determined by social or cultural factors – **sociolinguist** *n*

**sociology** /ˌsohs(h)i'oləji/ *n* **1** the science of society, social institutions, and social relationships; *specif* the systematic study of the development, structure, interaction, and collective behaviour of organized groups of human beings **2** the scientific analysis of a usu specified social institution, activity, or form as a functioning whole and as it relates to the rest of society ⟨*the ~ of disarmament*⟩ **3** SYNECOLOGY (ecology of communities) [Fr *sociologie,* fr *socio-* + *-logie* -logy] – **sociologist** *n,* **sociological** *also* **sociologic** *adj*

**sociometry** /ˌsohs(h)i'omətri/ *n* the study and measurement of social relationships (eg friendships) in a usu small group of people [ISV] – **sociometric** *adj*

**sociopolitical** /ˌsohs(h)iohpə'litikl/ *adj* of or involving a combination of social and political factors

**socioreligious** /ˌsohs(h)iohri'lijəs/ *adj* involving a combination of social and religious factors

**¹sock** /sok/ *n pl* **socks** (*NAm also* **sox**) **1** a knitted or woven covering for the foot usu extending above the ankle and sometimes to the knee **2** a shoe worn by actors in Greek and Roman comedy **3** a usu white band of colour extending from a horse's hoof to the first ankle joint (FETLOCK) **4** *archaic* a low shoe or slipper [ME *socke,* fr OE *socc,* fr L *soccus*] – **pull one's socks up/pull up one's socks** to make an effort to show greater application or improve one's performance – **put a sock in it** *Br slang* to be quiet; stop talking or making a noise – often *imper*

**²sock** *vt, informal* to hit, strike, or apply forcefully [prob of Scand origin; akin to ON *sökkva* to cause to sink; akin to OE *sincan* to sink] – **sock it to somebody** *chiefly NAm informal* to impress or astound somebody by doing something very well or vigorously – not now in vogue

**³sock** *n, informal* a vigorous or forceful blow; a punch ⟨*gave him a ~ on the chin*⟩

**sockdolager, sockdologer** /sok'dolǝjǝ/ *n, chiefly NAm informal* **1** something that settles a matter; a decisive blow or assertion **2** something remarkable ⟨*a ~ of a snowstorm*⟩ [prob based on ²*sock* + -*logy* + ²-*er*]

¹**socket** /'sokit/ *n* **1** an opening or hollow that forms a holder for something: eg **1a** any of various bony hollows in the body into which some other part normally fits ⟨*the eye ~*⟩ **b** a device in an electrical circuit into which a plug, bulb, etc can be fitted **2** a short tube that is shaped at one end to fit over a nut or bolt-head and that has a square hole at the other end to receive the driving shaft of a suitable handle [ME *soket*, fr AF, dim. of OF *soc* ploughshare, of Celt origin; akin to MIr *soc* ploughshare, lit., snout of a hog; akin to OE *sugu* sow – more at SOW] – **socketry** *n*

²**socket** *vt* **1** to provide with or place in a socket **2** *Br* to hit (a golf ball) with the extreme heel of the club causing a sharp movement to the right in flight

**sockeye** /'sok,ie/ *n* a small but commercially important salmon of the Pacific Ocean (*Oncorhynchus nerka*) that ascends rivers of the N USA and Canada to spawn in spring [by folk etymology fr Salish dial. *suk-kegh*]

**socking** /'soking/ *adv, chiefly Br informal* very, extremely – usu + *great* ⟨*so they get . . .this ~ great gun-dog* – *Observer Magazine*⟩

**socle** /'sokl/ *n* a projecting usu moulded part at the base of a wall or column [Fr, fr It *zoccolo* sock, socle, fr L *socculus,* dim. of *soccus* sock]

¹**Socratic** /so'kratik/ *adj* of Socrates, his followers, or his philosophical method of casting doubt on received opinions and questioning others to show that they have no real grounds for their beliefs or to demonstrate that they have an inborn knowledge of truths or ideas of which they are ignorant [*Socrates* †399 BC Gk philosopher] – **Socratically** *adv*

²**Socratic** *n* a follower of Socrates

**Socratic irony** *n* a pretence of ignorance in order to entice another into exposing his/her pretensions of knowledge through skilful questioning

¹**sod** /sod/ *n* **1** TURF 1a(2); *also* the grass-covered surface of the ground **2** *informal* one's native land ⟨*back to the old ~*⟩ [ME, fr MD or MLG *sode;* akin to OFris *sātha* sod]

²**sod** *n, chiefly Br informal* **1** a male homosexual; a bugger **2** an objectionable person, esp male **3** a fellow ⟨*he's not a bad little ~ taken by and large* – Noel Coward⟩ [short for *sodomite*]

³**sod** *vt* -**dd**- *Br slang* to damn – usu used in the imperative as an oath ⟨*~ you!*⟩

**sod off** *vi, Br slang* to go away; depart – usu in imperative

**soda** /'sohdǝ/ *n* **1a** any of several chemical compounds containing sodium: eg **1a(1)** SODIUM CARBONATE **a(2)** SODIUM BICARBONATE **a(3)** SODIUM HYDROXIDE **b** sodium – used in combination ⟨*~ alum*⟩ **2a** SODA WATER **2 b** *chiefly NAm* a sweet drink consisting of SODA WATER, flavouring, and often ICE CREAM [It, barilla plant (formerly burned as a source of sodium carbonate), soda, fr (assumed) ML, barilla plant]

**soda ash** *n* commercial SODIUM CARBONATE in a form that does not contain water

**soda biscuit** *n* a biscuit made with sour milk or buttermilk and raised with SODIUM BICARBONATE

**soda bread** *n* a bread raised with SODIUM BICARBONATE and CREAM OF TARTAR

**soda fountain** *n* **1** *chiefly NAm* an apparatus with delivery tube and taps for drawing soda water **2** *NAm* a counter where sodas, sundaes, and ice cream are prepared and served

**soda lime** *n* a mixture of the chemical compounds SODIUM HYDROXIDE and CALCIUM HYDROXIDE used esp to absorb moisture and gases

**sodalist** /'sohdl,ist/ *n* a member of a sodality

**sodalite** /'sohdǝ,liet/ *n* a transparent to translucent mineral that consists of a sodium aluminium silicate with some chlorine, $Na_4Al_3Si_3O_{12}Cl$, has a glassy or greasy lustre, and is found in various IGNEOUS rocks [*soda* + -*lite*]

**sodality** /soh'dalǝti/ *n* **1** a brotherhood, community **2** an organized society or fellowship; *specif* a devotional or charitable association of lay Roman Catholics [L *sodalitat-, sodalitas* comradeship, club, fr *sodalis* comrade – more at ETHICAL]

**soda nitre** *n* the naturally occurring form of SODIUM NITRATE

**soda water** *n* **1** a weak solution of SODIUM BICARBONATE with some acid added to cause fizziness (EFFERVESCENCE) **2** a drink consisting of water containing CARBON DIOXIDE under pressure causing it to fizz when poured into a glass

¹**sodden** /'sod(ǝ)n/ *adj* **1a** dull or expressionless, esp from

habitual drunkenness ⟨*his ~ features*⟩ **b** torpid, unimaginative ⟨*~ minds*⟩ **2a** full of moisture or water; saturated ⟨*the ~ ground*⟩ **b** heavy, damp, or doughy because of imperfect cooking ⟨*~ bread*⟩ *synonyms* see ¹WET [ME *soden*, fr pp of *sethen* to seethe] – **soddenly** *adv,* **soddenness** *n*

²**sodden** *vb* to make or become sodden

**sodding** /'soding/ *adj or adv, Br slang* – used as a meaningless intensive

**sodium** /'sohdi·ǝm, 'sohdyǝm/ *n* a silver white chemical element of the ALKALI METAL group that is soft, waxy, and easily worked, occurs abundantly in nature in combination with other chemical compounds, and is very active chemically [NL, fr E *soda*]

**sodium benzoate** *n* a chemical compound, $C_6H_5COONa$, used chiefly as a food preservative

**sodium bicarbonate** *n* a white weakly alkaline chemical compound, $NaHCO_3$, used esp in BAKING POWDERS, FIRE EXTINGUISHERS, and medicine to neutralize stomach acidity

**sodium carbonate** *n* a chemical compound, $Na_2CO_3$, used esp in making soaps and chemicals, in water softening, in cleaning and bleaching, and in photography: eg **a** a strongly alkaline chemical compound that readily absorbs moisture **b** WASHING SODA

**sodium chlorate** *n* a chemical compound, $NaClO_3$, used esp as a bleach, a weed killer, and in the manufacture of dyes

**sodium chloride** *n* a chemical compound, $NaCl$, used esp as a seasoning for food

**sodium cromoglycate** /,krohmoh'gliekayt/ *n* a synthetic drug, $C_{23}H_{14}Na_2O_{11}$, used in the preventative treatment of allergic reactions, esp asthma and HAY FEVER – compare INTAL [*cromoglycate* fr *cromoglycic acid,* fr *chrom-* + *glyc-* + -*ic*]

**sodium cyanide** *n* a white poisonous chemical compound, $NaCN$, used in extracting gold and silver from ores, in fumigating, and in treating steel

**sodium dichromate** *n* a red chemical compound, $Na_2Cr_2O_7$, used esp in tanning leather, in cleaning metals, and as an OXIDIZING AGENT in the manufacture of dyes

**sodium fluoride** *n* a poisonous chemical compound, $NaF$, that is used in very small quantities in the FLUORIDATION of water to prevent tooth decay, in metallurgy, as a FLUX (substance used to assist fusion of metals), and as a pesticide

**sodium fluoroacetate** *n* a poisonous chemical compound, $CH_2FCOONa$, used esp in rat poison

**sodium hydroxide** *n* a white brittle strongly caustic solid chemical compound, $NaOH$, that is used esp in making soap, rayon, and paper

**sodium hypochlorite** *n* an unstable chemical compound, $NaOCl$, produced usu in a water-based solution and used as a bleach and disinfectant

**sodium hyposulphite** *n* SODIUM THIOSULPHATE

**sodium metasilicate** /,metǝ'silikayt/ *n* a corrosive chemical compound, $Na_2SiO_3$, used esp as a detergent or as a substitute for PHOSPHATES in the manufacture of detergents

**sodium nitrate** *n* a chemical compound, $NaNO_3$, found in crude form in Chile, and used as a fertilizer and OXIDIZING AGENT in and curing meat

**sodium nitrite** *n* a chemical compound, $NaNO_2$, used esp in dye manufacture and as a meat preservative

**sodium pump** *n* the process by which sodium ions are actively transported across a cell membrane; *esp* the process by which the appropriate internal and external concentrations of sodium and potassium ions are maintained in a nerve fibre, and which involves the ACTIVE TRANSPORT of sodium ions outwards and the inward movement of potassium ions

**sodium salicylate** *n* a chemical compound, $OHC_6H_4CO_2Na$, that is used chiefly as a painkiller, for reducing fever, and in the treatment of rheumatism

**sodium sulphate** *n* a bitter chemical compound, $Na_2SO_4$, used esp in detergents, in the manufacture of wood pulp and rayon, in dyeing and finishing textiles, and in its form containing water as a laxative – compare GLAUBER'S SALT

**sodium thiosulphate** /,thie·oh'sulfayt/ *n* a chemical compound, $Na_2S_2O_3$, used esp as a photographic fixing agent and as a REDUCING AGENT or as a bleach

**sodium tripolyphosphate** /,trie,poli'fosfayt/ *n* a chemical compound, $Na_5O_{10}P_3$, that is a major component of many detergents and is also used as a meat preservative

**sodium-vapour lamp, sodium lamp** *n* a DISCHARGE LAMP in which the electrical discharge takes place through sodium vapour causing a characteristic yellow-orange light and which is used esp for street lighting

**Sodom** /'sodəm/ n a place notorious for vice and depravity – compare GOMORRAH [*Sodom,* city in ancient Palestine destroyed by God for its wickedness (Gen 18:20, 21; 19:24–28)]

**sodomite** /'sodəmiet/ n someone who practises sodomy

**sodomy** /'sodəmi/ n a copulationlike sexual act other than normal intercourse between a man and a woman: eg **a** the penetration of the penis into the mouth or esp the anus of another, esp another male **b** BESTIALITY 2 (sexual relations between a human being and an animal) [ME, fr OF *sodomie,* fr LL *Sodoma* Sodom; fr the homosexual desires of the men of the city (Gen 19:1–11)]

**sod's law** n, *often cap, slang* the tendency for things to go wrong; fate ⟨*one set of points . . .has stopped the show. The engineers and scientists say it is* Sod's Law – *The Guardian*⟩ [²*sod*]

**soever** /soh'evə/ adv **1** *poetic* to any possible or known extent – used after an adjective preceded by *how* ⟨*how fair ~ she may be*⟩ or a superlative preceded by *the* ⟨*the most selfish ~ in this world*⟩ **2** *formal* of any or every kind; at all – used after a noun modified esp by *any, no,* or *what* ⟨*he gives no information ~*⟩

**sofa** /'sohfə/ n a long padded seat with a back and two arms or raised ends that typically seats two to four people [Ar *ṣuffah* long bench]

*synonyms* A **sofa, settee, settle, davenport, chesterfield, couch, chaise longue,** and **ottoman** are all pieces of furniture that more than one person can sit on. A **sofa** has a back and two arms. A **settee** need not have arms, and is generally less upholstered than a sofa. A **settle** is a more primitive benchlike affair, with wooden arms and a high wooden back. **Davenport** is an American word for a large sofa (it also means a writing desk). A **chesterfield** is a tightly padded usually leather sofa, with upright armrests often the same height as the back. **Couch** is another word for sofa, but a **couch** may also have one raised head-end and be meant for reclining on. One also reclines on a **chaise longue,** which has a head-end and one armrest. An **ottoman** is an upholstered box, and has no arms and usually no back.

**soffit** /'sofit/ n the underside of a part of a building (eg of an overhang or staircase); *esp* the INTRADOS (interior curve) of an arch [Fr *soffite,* fr It *soffitto,* fr (assumed) VL *suffictus,* pp of L *suffigere* to fasten underneath – more at SUFFIX]

¹**soft** /soft/ adj **1a** pleasing or agreeable to the senses; bringing ease, comfort, or quiet ⟨*the ~ influences of home*⟩ **b** having a bland or mellow rather than a sharp or acid taste **c(1)** not bright or glaring; subdued ⟨*a ~ glow*⟩ **c(2)** having or producing relatively little photographic contrast ⟨*a ~ photographic print*⟩; *also* having a slight intentional blurring ⟨*a photograph in ~ focus*⟩ **d** quiet in pitch or volume; not harsh or strident **e** *of the eyes* having a liquid or gentle appearance **f** smooth or delicate in texture; not rough or irritating to the touch ⟨*~ cashmere*⟩ ⟨*~ fur*⟩ **g(1)** balmy or mild in weather or temperature **g(2)** falling or blowing with slight force or impact; not violent ⟨*~ breezes*⟩ **2a** demanding little effort; easy ⟨*a ~ job*⟩ **b** dealing with ideas, opinions, etc rather than facts and figures; inexact ⟨*the ~ sciences*⟩ **3a** *of c and g* pronounced /s/ and /j/ respectively (eg in *acid* and *age*) – not used technically **b** *of a consonant sound* VOICED (uttered with vibration of the vocal chords) **c(1)** *of a consonant sound* (eg in *Russian*) articulated with or followed by /y/; PALATAL **c(2)** *of a vowel sound* (eg in *Russian*) preceded by /y/ **4** having a rounded or gently curved outline ⟨*~ hills against the horizon*⟩ **5** marked by a kindness, lenience, or moderation: eg **5a(1)** not being or involving harsh or onerous terms; easy ⟨*took the ~ option*⟩ **a(2)** based on negotiation and conciliation rather than on a show of power or on threats ⟨*took a ~ line towards the enemy*⟩ **b** tending to ingratiate or disarm; engaging, conciliatory ⟨*a ~ answer turns away wrath* – Prov 15:1 (RSV)⟩ **c(1)** marked by restraint; mild, low-keyed ⟨*bookshops selling ~ porn*⟩ **c(2)** *of a drug* not of the most addictive or harmful kind ⟨*marijuana is regarded as a ~ drug*⟩ **6a** easily affected with tender emotions; impressionable **b** readily influenced, swayed, or imposed upon; compliant **c(1)** lacking firmness or strength of character; feeble, unmanly **c(2)** marked by a gradually declining trend; not firm ⟨*wool prices are increasingly ~*⟩ **d** amorously attracted, esp secretly – + *on* ⟨*has been ~ on her for years*⟩ **7a** made weak or lacking energy as the result of ease or luxury **b** mentally deficient; feebleminded **8a** yielding to physical pressure ⟨*a ~ mattress*⟩ ⟨*~ ground*⟩ **b** of a consistency that may be shaped, moulded, spread, or easily cut ⟨*~ dough*⟩ ⟨*~*

*cheese*⟩ **c** easily magnetized and demagnetized **d** relatively lacking in hardness ⟨*~ iron*⟩ ⟨*~ wood*⟩ **9** deficient in or free from substances (eg chemical compounds containing calcium and magnesium) that prevent lathering of soap ⟨*~ water*⟩ **10** having relatively low energy ⟨*~ X rays*⟩ **11** occurring at such a speed and under such circumstances as to avoid or prevent damage on impact ⟨*~ landing of a spacecraft on the moon*⟩ **12** not protected against enemy attack; vulnerable ⟨*a ~ above-ground launching site*⟩ [ME, fr OE *sōfte,* alter. of *sēfte;* akin to OHG *semfti* soft] – **softish** adj, **softly** adv, **softness** n

²**soft** n a soft object, material, or part ⟨*the ~ of the thumb*⟩

³**soft** adv in a soft or gentle manner; softly

*usage* Soft as an adverb is now chiefly used in literary contexts ⟨*how* soft *the poplars sigh* – A E Housman⟩ and cannot replace softly, the usual adverb ⟨*whistle* softly⟩.

**softball** /'soft,bawl/ n a game similar to baseball played on a smaller field with a larger and softer ball

**soft-'boil** n to boil (an egg in its shell) to the point at which the white solidifies but the yolk remains unset [back-formation fr *soft-boiled*]

**softbound** /'soft,bownd/ adj soft-cover

**soft breathing** n SMOOTH BREATHING (mark to show that certain vowels are not aspirated)

**soft-'centred** n, *of a sweet, esp a chocolate* having a soft substance (eg cream or jelly) in the centre

**soft chancre** n CHANCROID (ulceration of the genital organs)

**soft coal** n BITUMINOUS COAL

**'soft-,core** adj mildly titillating; *specif* containing pictures of female sexual organs but excluding depiction of male sexual organs and highly explicit pictures or descriptions of (perverse) sexual acts – compare HARD-CORE

**'soft-'cover** adj bound in flexible covers; not bound in hard covers; *specif* paperback ⟨*~ books*⟩

**soft drink** n any of several sweetened and flavoured nonalcoholic drinks that are often based on SODA WATER and often served chilled

**soften** /'sof(ə)n/ vt **1** to make soft or softer **2a** to weaken the military resistance or the morale of, esp by harassment (eg preliminary bombardment) **b** to impair the strength or resistance of ⟨*~ him up with compliments*⟩ ~ vi to become soft or softer □ (2) often + *up* – **softener** n

**'soft-,finned** adj, *of a fish* having fins in which the membrane is supported entirely or mostly by soft or jointed flexible rays – compare SPINY-FINNED

**soft fruit** n, *chiefly Br* edible fruit (eg strawberries, raspberries, and blackcurrants) that is small, stoneless, and grows on low bushes

**soft furnishings** n pl, *chiefly Br* articles (eg curtains or chair covers) that tend to increase the comfort, utility, or appearance of a room or piece of furniture; *also* the materials used to make these

**soft goods** n pl textiles and textile products (eg clothing)

**soft hail** n GRAUPEL (granular snow)

**softhead** /'soft,hed/ n a silly or feebleminded person

**softheaded** /,soft'hedid/ adj **1** foolish, stupid **2** impractical, visionary – **softheadedly** adv, **softheadedness** n

**softhearted** /,soft'hahtid/ adj kind, compassionate – **softheartedly** adv, **softheartedness** n

**softie** /'softi/ n a softy

**,soft-'land** vb to (cause to) make a soft landing on a celestial body (eg the moon) [back-formation fr *soft landing*] – **soft-lander** n

**soft option** n an easy alternative ⟨*took the ~ and withdrew the troops*⟩

**soft palate** n the fold at the back of the HARD PALATE (roof of the mouth) that partially separates the mouth and throat (PHARYNX)

**soft paste, soft-paste porcelain** n a type of translucent pottery made from a mixture of refined clay and ground glass fired at a low temperature – compare HARD PASTE

**soft pedal** n a foot pedal on a piano that changes the tone by, in the case of a GRAND PIANO, causing the hammers to strike only two of three strings to each key, or, in the case of an UPRIGHT PIANO, either moving the hammers nearer to the strings or placing felt between the hammers and the strings – compare UNA CORDA

**,soft-'pedal** vb -ll- (*NAm* -l-, -ll-) vt **1** to use the SOFT PEDAL in playing **2** to minimize the effect or importance of, esp by talking cleverly or evasively; PLAY DOWN ⟨*~ the issue of arms sales*⟩ ~ vi to play something down

**soft roe** *n* ROE 1b (sperm of a fish)

**soft rot** *n* a mushy, watery, or slimy decay of plants or their parts caused by bacteria or fungi

**soft scale** *n* a translucent yellow to brown SCALE INSECT (*Coccus hesperidum*) found on garden plants and in greenhouses

**soft sell** *n* the use of suggestion or gentle persuasion in selling rather than aggressive pressure – compare HARD SELL

**'soft-,shell, soft-shelled** /'soft,sheld/ *adj* having a soft or fragile shell, esp as a result of recent moulting

**soft-shelled turtle** *n* any of numerous aquatic turtles (family Trionychidae) that have sharp claws and jaws and a flat shell covered with soft leathery skin instead of with horny plates

**'soft-,shoe** *adj* of or being tap dancing done in soft-soled shoes without metal taps

**soft soap** *n* 1 a semifluid soap 2 *informal* flattery

**,soft-'soap** *vt, informal* to persuade or mollify with flattery or smooth words – **soft-soaper** *n*

**,soft-'spoken** *adj* having a mild or gentle voice; *also* suave

**soft spot** *n* a sentimental weakness ⟨*has a ~ for him*⟩

**soft touch** *n, informal* someone who is easily imposed on or taken advantage of

**software** /'soft,weə/ *n* 1 the entire set of programs, procedures, and related documentation associated with a system, esp a computer system; *specif* computer programs 2 something used or associated with and usu contrasted with hardware; *esp* instructional materials for use with audiovisual equipment

**soft wheat** *n* a wheat with soft kernels high in starch but usu low in GLUTEN (type of protein)

**'softwood** /'soft,wood/ *n* 1 the wood of a coniferous tree (e g pine) including both soft and hard parts 2 a tree that yields softwood

**'softwood** *adj* 1 having or made of softwood 2 consisting of immature still pliable tissue ⟨*~ cuttings for propagating plants*⟩

**,soft-'wooded** *adj* 1 having soft wood that is easy to work or finish 2 SOFTWOOD 1

**softy, softie** /'softi/ *n, informal* 1 an excessively sentimental or susceptible person 2 a feeble, effeminate, or foolish person

**Sogdian** /'sogdiən/ *n* 1 a native or inhabitant of Sogdiana, central Asia 2 an Iranian language of the Sogdians [L *Sogdiani*, pl, fr pl of *sogdianus* adj, Sogdian, fr OPers *Sughuda* Sogdiana] – **Sogdian** *adj*

**soggy** /'sogi/ *adj* 1 saturated or heavy with water or moisture: e g 1a waterlogged, soaked ⟨*a ~ lawn*⟩ b SODDEN 2b 2 heavily dull; lacking vigour ⟨*~ prose*⟩ [E dial. *sog* to soak, of unknown origin] – **soggily** *adv*, **sogginess** *n*

**soh, so** /soh/ *n* the 5th note in the SOL-FA method of representing the musical scale [ME *sol*, fr ML – more at GAMUT]

**soi-disant** /,swah 'deezonh/ *adj* self-styled, so-called ⟨*a ~ artist*⟩ [Fr, lit., saying oneself]

**soigné** /'swahnyay, -'-/, *fem* **soignée** /~/ *adj* 1 elegantly maintained; modish ⟨*a ~ restaurant*⟩ 2 well-groomed, sleek [Fr, fr pp of *soigner* to take care of, fr ML *soniare*]

**'soil** /soyl/ *vt* 1 to defile morally; corrupt ⟨*~ed his mind with evil knowledge*⟩ 2 to stain or make unclean, esp superficially; dirty ⟨*~ a rug*⟩ 3 to blacken or tarnish (e g a person's reputation) by word or deed ~ *vi* to become soiled or dirty [ME *soilen*, fr OF *soiller* to wallow, soil, fr *soil* pigsty, prob fr L *suile*, fr *sus* pig – more at SOW]

**'soil** *n* 1 stain, defilement 2 something that spoils or pollutes: e g 2a refuse b sewage c dung, excrement

**'soil** *n* 1 firm land; earth 2a loose material composed of weathered rock and usu decayed vegetation and animal matter that covers large parts of the land surface of the earth or another planet; *also* the upper layer of such material that may be dug or ploughed and in which plants grow b a layer of soil with a characteristic PROFILE (series of layers or zones) that is developed from a certain type of parent material (e g rock) under climatic and vegetational conditions 3 country, land ⟨*his native ~*⟩ 4 *the* agricultural life or calling 5 a medium in which something takes hold and develops [ME, fr AF, fr L *solium* seat; prob akin to L *sedēre* to sit – more at SIT] – **soily** *adj*

**'soil** *vt* to feed (livestock) in the barn or an enclosure with fresh grass or green food; *also* to purge (livestock) by feeding on green food [origin unknown]

**soilage** /'soylij/ *n* green crops cut for feeding confined animals

**soilborne** /'soyl,bawn/ *adj* transmitted by or in soil ⟨*~ fungi*⟩

**soil conservation** *n* management of soil so as to obtain the greatest yields while improving and protecting the soil

**soilless** /-lis/ *adj* carried on without soil ⟨*~ agriculture*⟩

**soil pipe** *n* a pipe for carrying off wastes from toilets

**soil science** *n* the scientific study of soils

**soil series** *n* a category in the classification of soils comprising soils with similar characteristics developed from similar parent materials under comparable climatic and vegetational conditions

**soilure** /'soylyə/ *n, formal* a stain

**soiree, soirée** /'swahray/ *n* a party or reception held in the evening [Fr *soirée* evening period, evening party, fr MF, fr *soir* evening, fr L *sero* at a late hour, fr *serus* late – more at SINCE]

**soixante-neuf** /,swasont 'nuhf/ *n* mutual CUNNILINGUS (stimulation of the female sex organs by the lips and tongue) and FELLATIO (stimulation of the penis by the mouth); mutual fellatio; mutual cunnilingus [Fr, lit., sixty-nine]

**'sojourn** /'sojən, 'su, -juhn/ *n* a temporary stay ⟨*a ~ in the country*⟩ [ME *sojorn*, fr OF, fr *sojorner*]

**'sojourn** *vi, formal* to stay as a temporary resident ⟨*~ed for a month at a resort*⟩ **synonyms** see 'STAY [ME *sojornen*, fr OF *sojorner*, fr (assumed) VL *subdiurnare*, fr L *sub* under, during + LL *diurnum* day – more at SUB-, JOURNEY] – **sojourner** *n*

**soke** /sohk/ *n* 1 the right in Anglo-Saxon and early English law to hold a local court of justice and receive certain fees and fines 2 the district included in a soke jurisdiction ⟨*the Soke of Peterborough*⟩ [ME *soc, soke*, fr ML *soca*, fr OE *sōcn* inquiry, jurisdiction; akin to OE *sēcan* to seek]

**sokeman** /'sohkmən/ *n* a man who is under the soke of another; a tenant by SOCAGE (feudal tenure of land by non-military service)

**'sol** /sol/ *n, music* SOH

**'sol** /sohl/ *n* a former French coin worth 12 DENIERS; *also* a corresponding monetary unit [ME, fr MF – more at SOU]

**'sol** /sohl/ *n, pl* **soles** /'sohlays/ – see MONEY table [AmerSp, fr Sp, sun, fr L]

**'sol** /sol/ *n* a COLLOIDAL solution composed of solid particles dispersed in a liquid medium [-*sol* (as in *hydrosol*), fr *solution*]

**Sol** /sol/ *n* the sun [ME, fr L]

**sola** /'sohlə/ *pl of* SOLUM (soil layer)

**'solace** /'soləs/ *n* 1 relief from or comfort in grief or anxiety 2 a source of relief or consolation [ME *solas*, fr OF, fr L *solacium*, fr *solari* to console – more at SILLY]

**'solace** *vt* 1 to give solace to; console ⟨*~d himself with dreams of fame*⟩ 2 to alleviate, relieve ⟨*~ grief*⟩ – **solacement** *n*, **solacer** *n*

**solanaceous** /,solə'nayshəs/ *adj* of the potato family (Solanaceae) of FLOWERING PLANTS [NL *Solanaceae*, family name, fr *Solanum*]

**solan goose** /'sohlən/ *n* GANNET (type of large seabird) [ME *soland*, fr ON *sūla* pillar, gannet + *önd* duck; akin to OE *sȳl* pillar and to OHG *anut* duck, L *anas*]

**solanin** /'solənin/ *n* solanine

**solanine** /'solənin, -neen/ *n* a bitter poisonous chemical compound (ALKALOID), $C_{45}H_{73}NO_{15}$, present in several plants of the potato family, esp in tomatoes and green potatoes [Fr *solanine*, fr L *solanum* nightshade]

**solanum** /soh'laynəm/ *n* any of a genus (*Solanum*) of nonwoody plants, shrubs, or trees (e g BLACK NIGHTSHADE and aubergine) of the potato family that have often prickly-veined leaves and a fruit that is a berry [NL, genus name, fr L, nightshade]

**'solar** /'sohlə/ *adj* 1 of or derived from the sun, esp as affecting the earth 2 measured by the earth's course in relation to the sun ⟨*~ time*⟩ ⟨*~ year*⟩; *also* relating to or reckoned by solar time 3 produced or operated by the action of the sun's light or heat; *also* using the sun's rays ⟨*~ energy*⟩ [ME, fr L *solaris*, fr *sol* sun; akin to OE & ON *sōl* sun, Gk *hēlios*]

**'solar** *n* an upper room in a medieval house [ME, fr OE; akin to MD *solre* loft, flat roof, OHG *solāri* loft; all fr a prehistoric WGmc word borrowed fr L *solarium* part of a house exposed to the sun]

**solar battery** *n* an electrical apparatus consisting of one or more SOLAR CELLS

**solar cell** *n* a device (e g a PHOTOVOLTAIC cell or a THERMOPILE) that is able to convert the energy of sunlight into electrical energy and is used as a power source

**solar constant** *n, astronomy* the quantity of radiant solar heat received perpendicularly to a given area of the earth's surface during a given time, after allowing for atmospheric absorption, that has an average value of about 1390 watts per square metre

**solar day** *n* the time taken by the earth to make one complete revolution on its axis; the interval between two crossings of the MERIDIAN (imaginary circle passing through both poles) by the sun

**solar flare** *n* a sudden temporary outburst of energy from a small area of the sun's surface

**solar house** *n* a house equipped with glass areas, SOLAR PANELS, etc and so planned as to utilize the sun's rays extensively in heating

**solarium** /sə'leəri-əm/ *n, pl* **solaria** /sə'leəri-ə/ *also* **solariums** a room exposed to the sun and used esp for treatment of illness by exposure to warmth and light and for relaxation [L, fr *sol*]

**solar·ization, -isation** /,sohlərie'zaysh(ə)n/ *n* 1 an act or process of solarizing 2 a reversal or partial reversal of the tones of a photographic image in order to bring out detail, highlight parts, etc, that is obtained by intense or continued exposure

**solar·ize, -ise** /'sohləriez/ *vt* 1 to expose to sunlight; *specif* to affect by the action of the sun's rays 2 to subject (photographic materials) to solarization

**solar panel** *n* 1 a large number of SOLAR CELLS grouped together (e g in a spacecraft) 2 a device that heats water by using solar energy

**solar plexus** /'pleksəs/ *n* 1 an interlacing network (PLEXUS) of nerves in the abdomen that is situated behind the stomach and in front of the AORTA (main artery) and from which nerve fibres are distributed to the liver, intestines, bladder, etc 2 the pit of the stomach [fr the radiating nerve fibres, likened to the sun's rays]

**solar system** *n* the sun together with the planets and other celestial bodies that are held by its attraction and revolve round it

**solar wind** /wind/ *n* the continuous flow of electrically charged particles from the sun's surface into and through interplanetary space

**solar year** *n* the exact time taken by the earth to move round the sun; about 365¼ SOLAR DAYS

**solate** /'solayt/ *vi* to change to a SOL (solution comprising particles dispersed in a liquid) – **solation** *n*

**solatium** /sə'laysh(i)əm/ *n, pl* **solatia** /-sh(i)ə/ 1 a compensation (e g money) given as solace for suffering, loss, or hurt feelings 2 HONORARIUM (payment for services where no price is fixed) [LL *solacium, solatium*, fr L, solace]

**sold** /sohld/ *past of* SELL

**soldan** /'sohldən, 'soldən/ *n, archaic* a sultan; *esp* the sultan of Egypt [ME, fr MF, fr Ar *sulṭān*]

**¹solder** /'sohldə, 'soldə/ *n* 1 a metal or metallic alloy used when melted to join metallic surfaces; *esp* an alloy of lead and tin so used 2 something that unites or cements [ME *soudure*, fr MF, fr *souder* to solder, fr L *solidare* to make solid, fr *solidus* solid]

**²solder** *vt* 1 to unite or make whole by solder – compare WELD 1a 2 to bring into or restore to firm union ⟨*a friendship* ~ed *by common interests*⟩ ~ *vi* 1 to use solder 2 to become united or repaired (as if) by solder – **solderer** *n*, **solderability** *n*

**soldering iron** /'sohld(ə)ring, 'sol-/ *n* a device with a pointed or wedge-shaped end that is usu electrically heated and that is used to melt material that is to be soldered

**¹soldier** /'sohljə/ *n* 1a someone engaged in military service, esp in the army b an enlisted man or woman c a skilled warrior 2a any of a specialized form (CASTE) of wingless sterile termites usu differing from workers in having a larger sized head and body and long jaws b any of a type of worker ants distinguished by an exceptionally large head and jaws 3 something straight, upright, or in ranks (e g a brick placed on end) [ME *soudier*, fr OF, fr *soulde* pay, fr LL *solidus* gold coin – more at SOLIDUS] – **soldierly** *adj or adv*, **soldiership** *n* – **come/play the old soldier** 1 to claim to have wisdom and maturity gained from long experience 2 to claim illness or disability, esp in order to avoid one's responsibilities

**²soldier** *vi* 1a to serve as a soldier b to behave in a soldierly manner ⟨*have to really* ~ *in such a crack unit*⟩ c to press doggedly forward – usu + *on* ⟨~ed *on without a windscreen*⟩ 2 *informal* to make a pretence of working while really idling

**soldier beetle** *n* any of various brightly coloured soft-bodied beetles (family Cantharidae); *esp* a reddish-coloured carnivorous beetle (*Rhagonycha fulva*)

**soldiering** /'sohljəring/ *n* the life, service, or practice of someone who soldiers

**soldier of fortune** *n* someone who seeks an adventurous, esp military, life wherever chance allows

**soldiery** /'sohljəri/ *n* 1a *taking sing or pl vb* a body of soldiers b a set of soldiers of a specified sort ⟨*a drunken* ~⟩ 2 the profession or technique of soldiering

**soldo** /'soldoh/ *n, pl* **soldi** /-dee/ a former Italian coin worth five CENTESIMI [It, fr LL *solidus* gold coin]

**,sold-'out** *adj* 1 having all available tickets or places sold, esp in advance 2 having sold the entire stock of a particular product ⟨*wanted petrol but the garage was* ~⟩

**¹sole** /sohl/ *n* 1a the undersurface of a foot b the part of a garment or article of footwear on which the sole rests 2 the usu flat bottom or lower part of something or the base on which something rests [ME, fr MF, fr L *solea* sandal; akin to L *solum* base, ground, soil] – **soled** *adj*

**²sole** *vt* to provide with a sole ⟨~ *a shoe*⟩

**³sole** *n, pl* **soles**, *esp collectively* **sole** any of several flatfishes (family Soleidae) that have small mouths, small or rudimentary fins, and small eyes placed close together, including some valued as superior food fishes; *also* any of various flatfishes of other families that are used as food [ME, fr MF, fr L *solea* sandal, a flatfish]

**⁴sole** *adj* 1 *esp of a woman* not married – used chiefly in law 2 being the only one ⟨*she was her mother's* ~ *confidante*⟩ 3 functioning independently and without assistance or interference ⟨*let conscience be the* ~ *judge*⟩ 4 belonging or relating exclusively to one individual or group ⟨~ *rights of publication*⟩ 5 *archaic* solitary, lonely ⟨*sitting* ~ *by the hearth*⟩ **synonyms** see ¹SINGLE [ME, alone, fr MF *seul*, fr L *solus*] – **soleness** *n*

**solecism** /'soli,siz(ə)m/ *n* 1 a minor blunder in speech or writing 2 a deviation from what is proper or normal; *esp* a breach of etiquette or decorum △ solipsism [L *soloecismus*, fr Gk *soloikismos*, fr *soloikos* speaking incorrectly, lit., inhabitant of Soloi, fr *Soloi*, city in ancient Cilicia in Asia Minor where a substandard form of Attic was spoken] – **solecistic** *adj*

**solely** /'sohl(l)i/ *adv* 1 without another; singly ⟨*was* ~ *responsible*⟩ 2 to the exclusion of all else ⟨*done* ~ *for money*⟩

**solemn** /'soləm/ *adj* 1a marked by the invocation of a religious sanction b performed or uttered so as to be rendered legally binding ⟨*a* ~ *oath*⟩ 2 marked by the observance of established form or ceremony; *specif* celebrated with full religious rites and ceremony 3a conveying a deep sense of reverence or exaltation; sublime ⟨*was stirred by the* ~ *music*⟩ b marked by seriousness and sobriety c sombre, gloomy ⟨*a suit of* ~ *black*⟩ **synonyms** see SERIOUS [ME *solemne*, fr MF, fr L *sollemnis, solemnis* ceremonial, formal, solemn] – **solemnify** *vt*, **solemnly** *adv*, **solemnness** *n*

**solemnity** /sə'lemnəti/ *n* 1 formal or ceremonious observance of an occasion or event ⟨*welcomed the ambassador with fitting* ~⟩ 2 a solemn event or occasion 3 a solemn character or state ⟨*the* ~ *of his words*⟩

**solemn·ize, -ise** /'soləmniez/ *vt* 1 to observe or honour with solemnity 2 to perform with pomp or ceremony; *esp* to celebrate (a marriage) with religious rites 3 to make solemn; dignify – **solemnization** *n*

**solemn mass** *n* HIGH MASS (Mass in which certain parts are sung)

**solemn vow** *n* an absolute and irrevocable vow taken in public by a member of a Roman Catholic order which prevents the individual from owning personal property or from making a marriage that can be recognized by the church – compare SIMPLE VOW

**solenette** /,sohli'net/ *n* a small European sole (*Solea lutea*) [irreg fr ³*sole* + *-ette*]

**solenoid** /'solənoyd, 'soh-/ *n* a coil of wire commonly in the form of a long cylinder that, when carrying a current, produces a magnetic field and draws in a movable usu iron rod and is used for converting electrical energy into mechanical energy (e g in switches) [Fr *solénoïde*, fr Gk *sōlēnoeidēs* pipe-shaped, fr Gk *sōlēn* pipe – more at SYRINGE] – **solenoidal** *adj*

**sole piece** *n* a timber or girder laid on the ground beneath a SHORE (supporting prop) in order to receive and distribute the load of the object being supported [¹*sole*]

**soleplate** /'sohl,playt/ *n* 1 the lower plate of a wall built around a frame on which the bases of the upright parts (STUDS) of the frame stand 2 the undersurface of an iron used for pressing cloth or clothing

**solera** /soh'leərə/ *n* a group of barrels used in the production of Spanish sherry and Madeira for the gradual blending of young and mature wines; *also* the system of sherry and Madeira production using soleras [Sp, traverse beam, stone base, lees of wine, fr *suelo* ground, lees, fr L *solum* ground, base]

**sol-fa** /'sol ,fah/ *n* 1 the syllables *doh, ray, me*, etc used in singing the notes of the scale 2 SOLMIZATION (use of syllables to denote musical notes); *also* a singing exercise using syllables to denote musical notes **3** TONIC SOL-FA (system of solmization)

**solfatara** /,solfə'tahrə/ *n* a volcanic area or vent that yields only hot vapours and sulphur-containing gases [It, fr *solfo* sulphur, fr L *sulfur*]

**solfège** /sol'fezh/ *n* **1** the application of the SOL-FA syllables to a musical scale or to a melody **2** a singing exercise, esp using sol-fa syllables; *also* practice in sight-reading vocal music using the sol-fa syllables [Fr, fr It *solfeggio*]

**solfeggio** /sol'feji·oh/ *n* solfège △ arpeggio [It, fr *sol-fa*]

**soli** /'sohli/ *pl of* SOLO

**solicit** /sə'lisit/ *vt* **1** to make a formal or earnest appeal to; entreat; *esp* to approach with a request or plea **2** to urge strongly or insist on (eg one's cause) **3a** to attempt to lure or entice, esp into evil **b** to accost publicly with an offer of sex, esp as or in the manner of a prostitute **4** to try to obtain by usu urgent requests or pleas ⟨~ *military aid*⟩ **5** *formal* to require; CALL FOR ⟨*the situation* ~s *the closest attention*⟩ ~ *vi* **1** to make entreaty; importune **2** to accost someone with an offer of sex, esp as or in the manner of a prostitute [ME *soliciten* to disturb, take charge of, fr MF *solliciter*, fr L *sollicitare* to disturb, fr *sollicitus* anxious, fr *sollus* whole (fr Oscan; akin to Gk *holos* whole) + *citus*, pp of *ciēre* to move] – **solicitant** *n*, **solicitation** *n*

**solicitor** /sə'lisitə/ *n* **1** someone who solicits **2** a qualified lawyer who advises clients on all legal matters, represents them in the lower courts, and prepares cases for barristers to try in higher courts **3** the chief law officer of a US municipality, county, or government department – **solicitorship** *n*

**solicitor general** *n*, *pl* **solicitors general 1** *often cap S&G* a law officer of the Crown ranking after the ATTORNEY GENERAL (chief law officer) in England **2** a federally appointed assistant to the US ATTORNEY GENERAL; *also* the chief law officer in certain states

**solicitous** /sə'lisitəs/ *adj* **1** full of concern or anxiety; apprehensive ⟨~ *about the future*⟩ **2** full of desire; eager ⟨~ *of approval*⟩ ⟨~ *to amuse*⟩ **3** meticulously careful ⟨~ *in matters of dress*⟩ **4** arising from or expressing solicitude ⟨a ~ *inquiry about his health*⟩ [L *sollicitus*] – **solicitously** *adv*, **solicitousness** *n*

**solicitude** /sə'lisityoohd/ *n* **1** the state of being solicitous; concern, anxiety; *also* excessive care or attention **2 solicitudes** *pl*, **solicitude** a cause of care or concern *synonyms* see ¹CARE *antonym* negligence

**¹solid** /'solid/ *adj* **1a** without an internal cavity; not hollow ⟨a ~ *ball of rubber*⟩ **b(1)** set in type or printed with minimum spacing between lines; *esp* set without LEADS (metal strips placed between lines of type to regulate spacing) **b(2)** joined without a hyphen ⟨a ~ *compound*⟩ **c** not interrupted by an opening or division ⟨a ~ *wall*⟩ **2** having, involving, or dealing with three dimensions or with solids **3a** of uniformly close and coherent texture; not loose or spongy; compact **b** neither liquid nor gas; retaining shape without needing external support (eg a container) **4** of good substantial quality or kind ⟨~ *comfort*⟩: eg **4a** sound, convincing ⟨~ *reasons*⟩ **b** well constructed from durable materials ⟨~ *furniture*⟩ **5a** having no break or interruption ⟨*waited three* ~ *hours*⟩ **b** unanimous ⟨*had the* ~ *support of his party*⟩ **6a** financially secure **b** earnest or serious in character or intent ⟨*sent the President a* ~ *memorandum – The Economist*⟩ **7** of a single substance or character: eg **7a** entirely of one metal or containing the minimum of alloy necessary to add hardness ⟨~ *gold*⟩ **b** of uniform colour or tone **8** *chiefly NAm informal* being in staunch or intimate association ⟨~ *with his boss*⟩ *antonyms* hollow, liquid [ME *solide*, fr MF, fr L *solidus*; akin to Gk *holos* whole – more at SAFE] – **solidly** *adv*, **solidness** *n*, **solidify** *vb*, **solidification** *n*, **solidity** *n*

**²solid** *adv* in a solid manner ⟨*the grease had set* ~⟩; *also* unanimously

**³solid** *n* **1** a geometric figure (eg a cube or sphere) having three dimensions **2a** a substance that does not flow perceptibly under moderate stress **b solids** *pl*, **solid** the part of a solution or suspension that when freed from solvent or suspending medium has the qualities of a solid ⟨*milk* ~s⟩ **3** something that is solid: eg **3a** a solid colour **b** a compound word whose members are joined together without a hyphen

**solid angle** *n* a three-dimensional spread of directions from a point (eg from the vertex of a cone or at the intersection of 3 planes), that is usu measured in STERADIANS

**solidarity** /,soli'darəti/ *n* unity (eg of a group or class) that produces or is based on community of interests, objectives, and standards *synonyms* see UNITY [Fr *solidarité*, fr *solidaire* characterized by solidarity, fr L *solidum* whole sum, fr neut of *solidus* solid]

**solid geometry** *n* a branch of geometry that deals with three-dimensional figures

**solid of revolution** *n* a surface or solid shape that can be described exactly by a plane figure revolving about an axis

**,solid-'state** *adj* **1** relating to the properties, structure, or reactivity of solid material; *esp* relating to the arrangement or behaviour of ions, molecules, nucleons, electrons, and holes in the crystals of a substance (eg a SEMICONDUCTOR) or to the effect of crystal imperfections on the properties of a solid substance ⟨~ *physics*⟩ **2** using the electric, magnetic, or PHOTIC (involving light) properties of solid materials; not using THERMIONIC VALVES (devices producing a flow of electrons from a heated conductor) ⟨a ~ *stereo system*⟩

**solidus** /'solidəs/ *n*, *pl* **solidi** /-die, -di/ **1** an ancient Roman gold coin introduced by Constantine and used until the fall of the Byzantine Empire **2** a punctuation mark / used esp to denote "or" (eg in *and/or*), "and or" (eg in *straggler/deserter*), "per" (eg in *feet/second*), or "cum" (eg in *restaurant/bar*) or to separate shillings and pence (eg in *2/6* and *7/-*), the terms of a fraction, or esp numbers in a list – called also OBLIQUE, SLASH, VIRGULE **3** a curve, usu on a graph showing the relationship between temperature and the composition of a mixture (eg of a substance when melting or solidifying), below which only the solid phase can exist – compare LIQUIDUS [(1) ME, fr LL, fr L, solid; (2) ML, shilling, fr LL (3) L, solid]

**solifluction** /,soli'fluksh(ə)n/ *n* the slow creeping of saturated fragmentary material, (eg soil) down a slope that usu occurs in regions of permanent frost [L *solum* soil + -*i*- + *fluction-*, *fluctio* act of flowing, fr *fluctus*, pp of *fluere* to flow – more at FLUID]

**soliloquy** /sə'liləkwi/ *n* **1** the act of talking to oneself **2** a dramatic monologue that gives the illusion of being a series of unspoken reflections [LL *soliloquium*, fr L *solus* alone + *loqui* to speak] – **soliloquize** *vi*, **soliloquist** *n*

**solipsism** /'solip,siz(ə)m/ *n* a theory holding that only the self can be shown to exist and that the external world is merely an idea or construction devised by the self △ solecism [L *solus* alone + *ipse* self] – **solipsist** *n*, **solipsistic** *adj*

**solitaire** /'soli,tea, ,--'-/ *n* **1** a single gem (eg a diamond) set alone **2** a game played by one person in which a number of objects (eg pegs or balls) are removed from a cross-shaped pattern by jumping one over its neighbour, which is then removed, and so on, with the aim of having only one piece left **3** *chiefly NAm* PATIENCE 2 (card game for one person) [Fr, fr *solitaire*, adj, solitary, fr L *solitarius*]

**¹solitary** /'solit(ə)ri/ *adj* **1a** being, living, or going alone or without companions **b** dispirited by isolation ⟨*left* ~ *by his wife's death*⟩ **2** unfrequented, remote ⟨*lived in a* ~ *place*⟩ **3** taken, passed, or performed without companions ⟨a ~ *weekend*⟩ **4** being the only one; sole ⟨*the* ~ *example*⟩ **5a** occurring singly and not as part of a group or cluster ⟨~ *flowers*⟩ **b** not gregarious, colonial, social, or compound ⟨~ *bees*⟩ *synonyms* see ¹SINGLE [ME, fr L *solitarius*, fr *solitas* solitude, fr *solus* alone] – **solitariness** *n*, **solitarily** *adv*

**²solitary** *n* **1** someone who habitually seeks solitude; a recluse **2** *informal* SOLITARY CONFINEMENT

**solitary confinement** *n* the state of being confined in isolation, esp as a punishment for a prisoner

**solitude** /'solityoohd/ *n* **1** the quality or state of being alone or remote from society; seclusion **2** a lonely place (eg a desert) [ME, fr MF, fr L *solitudin-*, *solitudo*, fr *solus*]

*synonyms* Solitude, **isolation**, **seclusion**, and **retirement** all mean "state of being alone". **Solitude** implies only the absence of other people, as in a desert or wilderness. **Isolation** suggests that the person or group concerned has been stranded, quarantined, or otherwise cut off from others. **Seclusion** also suggests being kept apart from others, but more by way of enclosure or concealment where one may yet be accessible ⟨*in the* seclusion *of her bedroom*⟩. **Retirement** implies a voluntary withdrawal into privacy.

**solleret** /,solə'ret/ *n* a flexible steel shoe forming part of a medieval suit of armour [Fr, fr MF, dim. of OF *soller* shoe, deriv of L *sub*- + *talus* ankle]

**solmization** /,solmie'zaysh(ə)n/ *n* the act, practice, or system of using syllables to denote musical notes or the degrees of a musical scale [Fr *solmisation*, fr *solmiser* to sol-fa, fr *sol* + *mi* + *-iser* -ize]

**¹solo** /'sohloh/ *n, pl* **solos 1a** a musical composition for a single voice or instrument with or without accompaniment **b** the part of a work for an accompanied soloist (eg a concerto) in which the soloist performs alone **2** a performance by only one person **3** a flight by one person alone in an aircraft; *esp* a person's first solo flight **4** any of various card games in which a player elects to play without a partner against the other players [It, fr *solo* alone, fr L *solus*] – **soloist** *n*

**²solo** *adv* without a companion; alone ⟨*fly* ~ ⟩

**³solo** *adj* **1** being done or performed alone; unaccompanied ⟨~ *flight*⟩ ⟨*piece for* ~ *piano*⟩ **2** being a single parent ⟨*housekeeper to care for* ~ *father* – *New Zealand Herald (Auckland)*⟩

**⁴solo** *vi* **soloed; soloing** to perform by oneself; *esp* to fly solo in an aircraft

**Solomon's seal** /'soləmənz/ *n* **1** an emblem consisting of two interlaced triangles forming a 6-pointed star and formerly used as an AMULET (charm to guard against evil), esp against fever **2** any of a genus (*Polygonatum*) of plants of the lily family with drooping usu greenish-white bell-shaped flowers, long smooth fleshy leaves, and gnarled underground stems (RHIZOMES) [*Solomon* (Heb *Shĕlōmōh*), 10th-c BC king of Israel; (2) prob fr the fancied resemblance to the emblem of scars on the rhizome]

**solonchak** /,solən'chak/ *n* any of a group of usu pale soils that contain large amounts of soluble chemical compounds (SALTS) and are found esp in poorly drained arid or semiarid areas [Russ, salt marsh]

**solonetz** *also* **solonets** /,solə'netz/ *n* any of a group of dark-coloured hard soils that have an underlying CLAYPAN (impenetrable layer of clay) and are found esp in arid and semiarid areas [Russ *solonets* salt extracted from the earth] – **solonetzic** *adj*

**so long** *interj, informal* – used to express farewell [prob by folk etymology fr Gael *slán*, lit., health, security, fr OIr *slān;* prob akin to L *salvus* safe – more at SAFE]

**solo whist** *n* a version of the card game whist, played by four players, in which the player who makes the highest bid to make, or sometimes not to make, tricks attempts to do so against all the other players or in a one-game alliance with a volunteer partner against the other two players

**solstice** /'solstis/ *n* **1** one of the two points on the ECLIPTIC (apparent path travelled by the sun) at which the distance from the CELESTIAL EQUATOR is greatest and which is reached by the sun each year about June 22nd and December 22nd **2** the time of the sun's passing a solstice which occurs in the northern hemisphere on June 22nd and on December 22nd which are hence the longest and shortest days of the year respectively [ME, fr OF, fr L *solstitium*, fr *sol* sun + *status*, pp of *sistere* to come to a stop, cause to stand; akin to L *stare* to stand – more at SOLAR, STAND]

**solstitial** /sol'stish(ə)l/ *adj* **1** (characteristic) of a solstice, esp the summer solstice **2** happening or appearing at or associated with a solstice [L *solstitialis*, fr *solstitium*]

**solubility** /,solyoo'bilǝti/ *n* **1** the quality or state of being soluble **2** the amount of a substance that will dissolve in a given amount of another substance

**solubil·ize, -ise** /'solyoobi,liez/ *vt* to make soluble or increase the solubility of – **solubilization** *n*

**soluble** /'solyoobl/ *adj* **1a** capable of being dissolved (as if) in a liquid **b** capable of being made into an EMULSION (creamy oil-and-water mixture) ⟨*a* ~ *oil*⟩ **2** capable of being solved or explained ⟨~ *questions*⟩ [ME, fr MF, capable of being loosened or dissolved, fr LL *solubilis*, fr L *solvere* to loosen, dissolve – more at SOLVE] – **solubleness** *n*, **solubly** *adv*

**soluble glass** *n* WATER GLASS 2 (syrupy substance used for protective coatings)

**solum** /'sohləm/ *n, pl* **sola** /-lə/, **solums** the layer of soil lying above the parent material from which it was formed and altered (eg by weathering and plant growth) that includes the two uppermost soil zones (A- and B-HORIZONS) [NL, fr L, ground, soil]

**solus** /'sohloos/ *adv or adj* alone – often used in stage directions [L]

**solute** /so'lyooht/ *n* a dissolved substance [L *solutus*, pp]

**solution** /sə'loohsh(ə)n/ *n* **1a** an action or process of solving a problem **b** an answer to a problem; an explanation; *specif* a set of values of the variables that satisfies a mathematical equation **2a** an act or the process by which a solid, liquid, or

gaseous substance is uniformly mixed with a liquid or sometimes a gas or solid **b** a typically liquid uniform mixture formed by this process **c** the condition of being dissolved **d** a liquid containing a dissolved substance **3** a bringing or coming to an end; a discharge ⟨*the* ~ *of a debt*⟩ [ME, fr MF, fr L *solution-, solutio*, fr *solutus*, pp of *solvere* to loosen, solve]

**solution set** *n* the set of all the values that satisfy a mathematical equation

**Solutrean, Solutrian** /,solyoo'tree·ən, sə'lyoohtri·ən/ *adj* of an Upper PALAEOLITHIC culture characterized by leaf-shaped finely flaked stone implements [*Solutré*, village in France where remains of the period were found]

**solvable** /'solvəbl/ *adj* capable of solution or of being solved, resolved, or explained – **solvability** *n*

**¹solvate** /'solvayt/ *n* a complex ION (electrically charged atom) formed by the chemical or physical combination of a solute ion or molecule with a solvent molecule; *also* a substance (eg a HYDRATE) containing such ions [*solvent* + *-ate*]

**²solvate** *vt* to convert into a solvate ~ *vi* to become or behave as a solvate – **solvation** *n*

**Solvay process** /'solvay/ *n* an industrial process for making SODIUM CARBONATE from COMMON SALT by passing carbon dioxide into ammonia-containing brine resulting in the formation of SODIUM BICARBONATE which is then heated strongly to produce the carbonate [Ernest *Solvay* †1922 Belgian chemist]

**solve** /solv/ *vt* **1** to find a solution for ⟨~ *a problem*⟩ **2** to pay (eg a debt) in full ~ *vi* to solve something ⟨*substitute the known values of the constants and* ~ *for* x⟩ [ME *solven* to loosen, fr L *solvere* to loosen, solve, dissolve, fr *sed-, se-* apart + *luere* to release – more at SECEDE, LOSE] – **solver** *n*

**¹solvent** /'solvənt/ *adj* **1** able to pay all legal debts; *also* having money in hand **2** having the power to dissolve; causing solution ⟨~ *fluids*⟩ ⟨~ *action of water*⟩ [L *solvent-, solvens*, prp of *solvere* to dissolve, pay] – **solvency** *n*, **solvently** *adv*

**²solvent** *n* **1** a usu liquid substance capable of dissolving or dispersing one or more other substances **2** something that provides a solution or explanation ⟨*no* ~ *for industrial stagnation*⟩ **3** something that eliminates or lessens the effect of something, esp something unwanted ⟨*ridicule is the* ~ *of prejudice*⟩ – **solventless** *adj*

**solvolysis** /sol'voləsis/ *n* a chemical reaction (eg HYDROLYSIS) of a solvent and solute that results in the formation of new compounds [NL, fr E *solv*ent + *-o-* + NL *-lysis*] – **solvolytic** *adj*

**¹soma** /'sohmə/ *n* an intoxicating plant juice used in ancient India as an offering to the gods and as a drink of immortality by worshippers in VEDIC ritual and itself worshipped as a Vedic god [Skt; akin to Avestan *haoma*, a Zoroastrian ritual drink, Gk *hyein* to rain – more at SUCK]

**²soma** *n* **1** all of an organism except the GERM CELLS (reproductive cells) **2** the body of an organism [NL *somat-, soma*, fr Gk *sōmat-, sōma* body]

**Somali** /sə'mahli, soh-/ *n, pl* **Somalis**, *esp collectively* **Somali** a member, or the language, of a people of Somaliland apparently of mixed Mediterranean and Negroid stock

**so many** *adj* **1** a certain number of ⟨*read* ~ *chapters each night*⟩ **2** – used as an intensive before plurals ⟨*behaved like* ~ *animals*⟩

**somat-, somato-** *comb form* soma; somatic cell ⟨*somatopleure*⟩ [NL, fr Gk *sōmat-, sōmato-*, fr *sōmat-, sōma* body; akin to L *tumēre* to swell – more at THUMB]

**somatic** /soh'matik, sə-/ *adj* **1** of or affecting the body or its cells, esp as distinguished from the GERM CELLS (reproductive cells) or the mind **2** of the wall of the body; PARIETAL [Gk *sōmatikos*, fr *sōmat-, sōma*] – **somatically** *adv*

**somatic cell** *n* any of the cells of the body of a plant or animal that compose its tissues, organs, and parts other than the GERM CELLS (reproductive cells)

**somatogenic** /,sohmatə'jenik/ *adj* originating in, affecting, or acting through the body

**somatology** /,sohmə'toləji/ *n* a branch of physical anthropology primarily concerned with the study of the evolution, variation, and classification of the physical characteristics of mankind through measurement and observation [NL *somatologia*, fr *somat-* + *-logia* -logy] – **somatological** *adj*

**somatoplasm** /'soh'matə,plaz(ə)m/ *n* **1** the substance that makes up the essential material (PROTOPLASM) of SOMATIC CELLS **2** SOMATIC CELLS as distinguished from GERM CELLS (reproductive cells) – **somatoplastic** *adj*

**somatopleure** /'sohmətə,plooə, -,pluh/ *n* a layer of cells in the developing embryo of a VERTEBRATE animal that gives rise to the body wall and consists of parts of the MESODERM and the ECTODERM (embryonic tissue layers) [NL *somatopleura*, fr *somat-* + Gk *pleura* side] – **somatopleuric** *adj*

**somatosensory** /soh,matə'sensəri/ *adj* of or being sensory activity having its origin elsewhere than in the special SENSE ORGANS (e g eyes and ears) and conveying information about the state of the body proper and its immediate environment

**somatotrophic hormone** /soh,matə'trohfik/ *n* GROWTH HORMONE 1 [*somat-* + *-trophic*]

**somatotrophin** /soh,matə'trohfin/, **somatotropin** /-'trohpin/ *n* GROWTH HORMONE 1 [*somatotrophic, somatotropic* + *-in*]

**somatotype** /soh'matə,tiep/ *n* body type; physique – **somatotypic** *adj*, **somatotypically** *adv*

**sombre**, *NAm chiefly* **somber** /'sombə/ *adj* **1** so shaded as to be dark and gloomy ⟨narrow ~ *passages*⟩ **2a** of a serious bearing; grave **b** of a dismal or depressing character; melancholy ⟨~ *thoughts*⟩ **3** dull or dark coloured [Fr *sombre*, prob deriv of L *sub-* + *umbra* shade, shadow] – **sombrely** *adv*, **sombreness** *n*

**sombrero** /som'breəroh/ *n, pl* **sombreros** a high-crowned hat of felt or straw with a very wide brim, usu turned up at the edge, worn esp in Mexico [Sp, fr *sombra* shade]

**sombrous** /'sombrəs/ *adj, archaic* sombre [Fr *sombre*]

**1some** /sum; *senses 1c and 1d* səm; *strong* sum/ *adj* **1a** being an unknown, undetermined, or unspecified unit or thing ⟨~ *person knocked*⟩ ⟨~ *film or other*⟩ **b** being an unspecified member of a group or part of a class ⟨~ *gems are hard*⟩ ⟨~ *red wine is quite sweet*⟩ **c** being an appreciable number, part, or amount of ⟨fire continued for ~ *hours*⟩ ⟨have ~ *consideration for others*⟩ **2** being of an unspecified amount or number ⟨give me ~ *water*⟩ – used as an indefinite plural of A ⟨have ~ *apples*⟩ **3** *informal* **3a** important, striking ⟨that was ~ *party*⟩ **b** no kind of ⟨~ *friend you are!*⟩ **4** at least one – used in logic to indicate that not all members of a certain class are also members of another class ⟨~ *swans are black*⟩, or as a natural language gloss for the EXISTENTIAL QUANTIFIER ⟨there is ~ *x such that both x is a King of France and x is bald*⟩ *usage* see SOMEONE [ME *som*, adj & pron, fr OE *sum;* akin to OHG *sum* some, Gk *hamē* somehow, *homos* same – more at SAME]

**2some** /sum/ *pron, pl* **some 1** some part, quantity, or number but not all ⟨~ *of my friends*⟩ **2** *chiefly NAm* an indefinite additional amount ⟨ran a mile and then ~⟩

**3some** /sum/ *adv* **1** ABOUT 3a ⟨~ *80 houses*⟩ **2** somewhat – used in Br English *some more* and more widely in NAm ⟨felt ~ *better*⟩ – **some little** a fair amount of – **some few** quite a number of

**1-some** /-s(ə)m/ *suffix* (→ *adj*) characterized by a (specified) thing, quality, state, or action ⟨awesome⟩ ⟨burdensome⟩ ⟨cuddlesome⟩ [ME *-som*, fr OE *-sum;* akin to OHG *-sam* -some, OE *sum* some]

**2-some** *suffix* (→ *n*) group of (so many) members and esp persons ⟨foursome⟩ [ME (northern) *-sum*, fr ME *sum*, pron, one, some]

**3-some** /-,sohm/ *comb form* (→ *n*) **1** intracellular particle ⟨lysosome⟩ **2** chromosome ⟨monosome⟩ [NL *-somat-, -soma,* fr Gk *sōmat-, sōma* – more at SOMAT-]

**1somebody** /'sumbədi/ *pron* some indefinite or unspecified person; someone ⟨~ *will come in*⟩
*usage* Since **somebody** and **someone** are used with a singular verb, it seems logical that they should be followed by a singular pronoun ⟨somebody has lost his umbrella⟩ and this singular construction should be preferred for formal writing. The plural pronoun ⟨somebody has lost their umbrella⟩ is often used today, however, to avoid using either *he* for both sexes or the awkward *he or she*. See ELSE

**2somebody** *n* a person of position or importance

**somedeal** /'sum,deel/ *adv, archaic* somewhat

**somehow** /'sum,how/ *adv* **1a** by some means not known or designated **b** no matter how ⟨got to get across ~⟩ **2** for some mysterious reason

**someone** /'sumwən, -,wun/ *pron* somebody
*usage* Compare ⟨marry someone (= somebody) *from Sheffield*⟩ ⟨choose some one (= some single) *subject to study*⟩; see SOMEBODY

**someplace** /'sum,plays/ *adv, chiefly NAm* somewhere

**somersault** /'sumə,sawlt/ *n* a leaping or rolling movement, performed either in the air or on the ground, in which a person turns forwards or backwards in a complete revolution bringing the feet over the head and finally landing on the feet [MF

**sombresaut** leap, deriv of L *super* over + *saltus* leap, fr *saltus*, pp of *salire* to jump – more at OVER, SALLY] – **somersault** *vi*

**somerset** /'sumə,set/ *vi or n* (to) somersault [by alter.]

**1something** /'sumthing/ *pron* **1a** some indeterminate or unspecified thing ⟨~ *hot to drink*⟩ ⟨look for ~ *cheaper*⟩ – used to replace forgotten matter or to express vagueness ⟨in nineteen-fifty-something⟩ ⟨she's supposed to be liberated or ~⟩ ⟨he's ~ or other in the Foreign Office⟩ **b** some part; a certain amount ⟨seen ~ of her work⟩ **2a** a person or thing of consequence ⟨make ~ of one's life⟩ ⟨their daughter is quite ~⟩ ⟨hopes to get ~ for nothing⟩ **b** some truth or value ⟨there's ~ in what you say⟩ – **something of a** a fairly notable example or instance of something specified ⟨he's something of a story-teller⟩

**2something** *adv* **1** in some degree; somewhat ⟨~ *over £5*⟩ ⟨shaped ~ like a funnel⟩ – also used to suggest approximation ⟨~ like 1,000 people⟩ **2** *informal* to an extreme degree ⟨swears ~ awful⟩

**something else** *pron, informal* one who or that which makes others pall in comparison ⟨her apple strudels were ~⟩

**1sometime** /'sum,tiem/ *adv* **1** at some unspecified future time ⟨I'll do it ~⟩ **2** at some point of time in a specified period ⟨~ last night⟩ ⟨~ next week⟩ **3** *archaic* in the past; formerly **4** *archaic* occasionally; NOW AND AGAIN

**2sometime** *adj* having been formerly; LATE 2b ⟨the ~ chairman⟩

**1sometimes** /'sum,tiemz/ *adv* at intervals; occasionally; NOW AND AGAIN

**2sometimes** *adj, archaic* sometime, former

**someway** /'sum,way/ *also* **someways** *adv, chiefly NAm* somehow

**1somewhat** /'sumwot/ *pron* something ⟨was ~ of an error⟩

**2somewhat** *adv* to some degree; slightly

**somewhen** /'sum,wen/ *adv* sometime

**1somewhere** /'sum,weə/ *adv* **1** in, at, or to some unknown or unspecified place ⟨makes reference to it ~⟩ **2** to a place or state symbolizing positive accomplishment or progress ⟨at last we're getting ~⟩ **3** in the vicinity of; approximately ⟨~ about nine o'clock⟩

**2somewhere** *n* an undetermined or unnamed place

**somewhither** /'sum,widhə/ *adv, archaic* to some place; somewhere

**-somic** /-sohmik/ *comb form* (→ *adj*) having (so many) times the haploid number of one of the chromosomes ⟨trisomic⟩ – compare -PLOID [ISV *3-some* + *-ic*] – **-somy** *comb form* (→ *n*)

**somite** /'sohmiet/ *n* any of the longitudinal series of segments into which the body of many INVERTEBRATE animals (e g earthworms and centipedes) and the embryos of VERTEBRATE animals is divided [ISV, fr Gk *sōma* body – more at SOMAT-] – **somitic** *adj*

**sommelier** /,sumə'lyay/ *n, pl* **sommeliers** /~/ a waiter in a restaurant in charge of wines and their service [Fr, fr MF, court official charged with transportation of supplies, pack animal driver, fr OProv *saumalier* pack animal driver, fr *sauma* pack animal, load of a pack animal, fr LL *sagma* packsaddle, fr Gk]

**somnambulant** /som'nambyool(ə)nt/ *adj* (addicted to) walking while asleep

**somnambulist** /som'nambyoolist/ *n* someone who walks in his/her sleep [NL *somnambulus*, fr L *somnus* sleep + *ambulare* to walk] – **somnambulism** *n*, **somnambulate** *vi*, **somnambulistic** *adj*, **somnambulistically** *adv*

**somnifacient** /,somni'fayshənt/ *adj, esp of a drug* sleep-inducing; HYPNOTIC 1 [L *somnus* sleep + E *-facient*] – **somnifacient** *n*

**somniferous** /som'nifərəs/ *adj* sleep-inducing; soporific [L *somnifer*, fr *somnus* + *-fer* -ferous] – **somniferously** *adv*

**somnolent** /'somnələnt/ *adj* **1** tending to induce sleep ⟨a ~ sermon⟩ **2** inclined to or heavy with sleep; drowsy [ME *somnolent*, fr MF, fr L *somnolentus*, fr *somnus* sleep; akin to OE *swefn* sleep, Gk *hypnos*] – **somnolence** *n*, **somnolently** *adv*

**1so much** *adv* to the degree indicated or suggested ⟨if they lose their way, ~ the better for us⟩

**2so much** *adj* **1** a certain amount of ⟨can spend only ~ time on it⟩ **2** – used as an intensive before MASS NOUNS (nouns denoting concepts or extended substances) ⟨sounded like ~ nonsense⟩

**3so much** *pron* **1** something (e g an amount or price) unspecified or undetermined ⟨charge ~ a mile⟩ **2** all that can or need be said or done ⟨~ for the history of the case⟩

**so much as** *adv* even ⟨can't ~ remember his name now⟩

**son** /sun/ n **1a** a human male having the relation of child to parent; *broadly* any male offspring **b** a male adopted child **c** *often pl* a male descendant **2** *cap* the second person of the Trinity; Christ **3a** a person closely associated with or deriving from a specified background, place, etc ⟨a ~ of the welfare state⟩ **b** something considered as a son ⟨a theatre missile that can be seen as a ~ of the big ICBMs of the 1970s⟩ **4** – used as an informal form of address, esp by a man to a boy or by an older to a younger man [ME *sone*, fr OE *sunu*; akin to OHG *sun* son, Gk *hyios*]

**sonance** /'sohnəns/ n, *archaic* sound [L *sonare* to sound + E *-ance*]

**sonant** /'sohnənt/ adj **1** of a speech sound VOICED (uttered with a vibration of the vocal chords) **2** of a consonant sound SYLLABIC (constituting a syllable or the main part of a syllable) [L *sonant-, sonans*, prp of *sonare* to sound – more at SOUND] – **sonant** n

**sonar** /'sohnə/ n an apparatus that detects the presence and location of a submerged object (eg a submarine) by means of sonic and supersonic waves reflected back to it from the object [*sound navigation ranging*]

**sonata** /sə'nahtə/ n an instrumental musical composition typically for one or two instruments and of three or four movements in contrasting forms and different but usu related keys [It, fr *sonare* to sound, fr L]

**sonata form** n a musical form that is used esp for the first movement of a sonata, symphony, concerto, etc, and consists basically of an EXPOSITION, a DEVELOPMENT, and a RECAPITULATION in which usu two themes are introduced, developed, and then repeated – called also FIRST MOVEMENT FORM

**sonatina** /ˌsonə'teenə/ n a short, often simplified, sonata [It, dim. of *sonata*]

**sonde** /sond/ n any of various devices for testing physical conditions (eg at high altitudes or inside the body); *esp* RADIOSONDE [Fr, lit., sounding line – more at SOUND]

**sone** /sohn/ n a subjective unit of loudness for an average listener equal to the loudness of a 1000-cycle sound that has an intensity 40 decibels above the listener's own threshold of hearing [ISV, fr L *sonus* sound – more at SOUND ]

**son et lumière** /ˌson ay looh'myeə (Fr sɔ̃ ɛ lymjɛr)/ n an entertainment presented at night at a historical site (eg a cathedral or STATELY HOME) that uses lighting effects and recorded sound to narrate its history [Fr, lit., sound and light]

**song** /song/ n **1** the act, art, or product of singing **2** poetry ⟨famous in ~ and story⟩ **3** a short musical composition of words and music **4** a melody for a lyric poem or ballad **5** a vehement reaction; SONG AND DANCE **6** a very small sum ⟨sold for a ~⟩ [ME, fr OE *sang*; akin to OE *singan* to sing] – **songful** adj, **songfully** adv, **songfulness** n

**song and dance** n, *informal* **1** *chiefly Br* a fuss, commotion ⟨it's nothing to make a ~ about⟩ **2** *NAm* an involved explanation designed to confuse or mislead

**songbird** /-ˌbuhd/ n **1** a bird that utters a succession of musical tones **2** a PASSERINE bird

**songbook** /'songˌbook/ n a collection of songs; *specif* a book containing vocal music (eg hymns)

**song cycle** n a group of related songs designed to form a musical entity

**songfest** /'songˌfest/ n SINGSONG 2 (group-singing session)

**Song of Solomon** /'soləmən/ n – see BIBLE table [*Solomon* (fr LL, fr Heb *Shlōmōn*), 10th-c BC King of Israel]

**Song of Songs** n – see BIBLE table [trans of Heb *shir hash-shīrīm*]

**songsmith** /'songˌsmith/ n a composer of songs

**song sparrow** n a common N American sparrow (*Melospiza melodia*) that is brownish above and white below and that is noted for its melodious song

**songster** /'songstə/, *fem* **songstress** /-stris/ n a skilled singer

**song thrush** n a common African and Eurasian thrush (*Turdus philomelos*) that has a brown back and wings and a pale breast with small dark spots

**songwriter** /'songˌrietə/ n a person who composes words or music for songs, esp popular songs – **songwriting** n

**sonic** /'sonik/ adj **1** of a wave or vibration having a frequency within the audibility range of the human ear **2** using, produced by, or relating to sound waves ⟨~ altimeter⟩ **3** of or being the speed of sound in air at sea level equal to about 340 metres per second (741 miles per hour) [L *sonus* sound – more at SOUND] – **sonically** adv

**sonicate** /'soniˌkayt/ vt to disrupt (eg bacteria) by treatment with high-frequency sound waves [*sonic* + *-ate*] – **sonicator** n, **sonication** n

**sonic bang** n SONIC BOOM

**sonic barrier** n SOUND BARRIER

**sonic boom** n a sound resembling an explosion produced when a SHOCK WAVE formed at the nose of an aircraft travelling at supersonic speed reaches the ground

**'son-in-ˌlaw** n, pl **sons-in-law** the husband of one's daughter

**sonless** /'sunlis/ adj not possessing or never having had a son

**sonly** /'sunli/ adj befitting a son; filial

**sonnet** /'sonit/ n a fixed verse form of Italian origin consisting of fourteen lines, typically of ten syllables each, rhyming according to any of various schemes; *also* a poem in this pattern – compare ENGLISH SONNET, ITALIAN SONNET [It *sonetto*, fr OProv *sonet* little song, fr *son* sound, song, fr L *sonus* sound]

**sonneteer** /ˌsoni'tiə/ n a composer of sonnets, esp without high standards

**sonny** /'suni/ n, *informal* a young boy – usu used in address [*son* + ⁴*-y*]

**sonobuoy** /'sohnohˌboy/ n a buoy equipped for detecting underwater sounds and transmitting them by radio [L *sonus* sound + E *-o-* + *buoy*]

**son of a bitch** n, pl **sons of bitches** *informal* BASTARD 3

**son of a gun** n, pl **sons of guns** *informal* a man who wins the approval of his associates, esp by showing manly, daring, or humorous qualities – used esp by a man of a close friend

**son of God** n, pl **sons of God 1** *often cap S* a superhuman or divine being (eg an angel) **2** *cap S* MESSIAH 1 **3** a person established in the love of God by divine promise

**son of man** /man/ n, pl **sons of men 1** *usu pl* a human being **2** *often cap S&M* **2a** God's messiah destined to preside over the final judgment of mankind **b** Christ

**sonority** /sə'norəti/ n **1** the quality or state of being sonorous; resonance **2** a sonorous tone or speech

**sonorous** /'sonərəs, 'soh-; *also* sə'nawrəs/ adj **1** giving out sound (eg when struck) **2** pleasantly rich or loud in sound **3** imposing or impressive in effect or style ⟨made a ~ speech to the assembly⟩ **4** having a high or a specified degree of sonority ⟨~ sounds like /ah/ and /aw/⟩ (L *sonorus*; akin to L *sonus* sound] – **sonorously** adv, **sonorousness** n

*usage* The pronunciation /sə'nawrəs/ is recommended for BBC broadcasters.

**sonship** /'sunship/ n the relationship of son to father

**sonsy, sonsie** /'sunzi/ adj, *chiefly Scot* buxom, comely [Sc *sons* health]

**sool** /soohl, sool/ vt, *Austr & NZ* to incite, urge on ⟨grandfather would have ~ed the blacks on to exact their justice – Arthur Upfield⟩ [E dial. *sowl, sole, sool* to pull by the ears]

**'soon** /soohn/ adv **1** before long; without undue time lapse ⟨~ after sunrise⟩ **2a** in a prompt manner; speedily ⟨as ~ as possible⟩ ⟨the ~er the better⟩ – compare AS SOON AS **b** with ease; readily ⟨burglars can ~ open locks – Daily Mirror⟩ **3** in agreement with one's preference; willingly – in comparisons ⟨I'd ~er walk than drive⟩ ⟨I'd just as ~ not⟩ **4** *archaic* before the usual time **5** *obs* immediately [ME *soone*, fr OE *sōna*; akin to OHG *sān* immediately] – **as/soon as** immediately after or as – **no sooner ... than** immediately after or as ⟨no sooner had I sat down than the phone rang again⟩

*usage* The construction *no sooner ... when* ⟨I had no sooner arrived when the phone rang⟩ should be avoided in formal writing.

**²soon** adj advanced in time; early ⟨the ~est date that can be arranged – The Times⟩

**sooner or later** /'soohnə/ adv at some uncertain future time; eventually

**'soot** /soot/ n a fine black powder that consists chiefly of carbon and is formed by burning or separated from fuel during burning [ME, fr OE *sōt*; akin to OIr *sūide* soot, OE *sittan* to sit]

**²soot** vt to coat or cover with soot ⟨the stone was ~ed – Edna O'Brien⟩

**'sooth** /soohth/ adj, *archaic* **1** true, real **2** soft, sweet [ME, fr OE *sōth*; akin to OHG *sand* true, Gk *eteos*, L *esse* to be] – **soothy** adv

**²sooth** n, *archaic* a truth, fact

**soothe** /soohdh/ vt **1** to please (as if) by attention or concern; placate ⟨~ an angry crowd with promises⟩ **2** to relieve, alleviate **3** to bring comfort, consolation, or reassurance to ~ vi to bring peace, ease, or composure *synonyms* see RELIEVE [ME *sothen* to prove the truth, fr OE *sōthian*, fr *sōth* true] – **soother** *n*, **soothingly** *adv*

**soothsay** /'soohth,say/ *vi* to practise soothsaying – **soothsayer** *n*

**soothsaying** /'soohth,saying/ *n* the act of predicting the future [²*sooth* + *saying*]

**sooty** /'sooti/ *adj* **1a** of or producing soot ⟨∼ *fires*⟩ **b** dirtied with soot **2** of the colour of soot – **sootily** *adv*, **sootiness** *n*

**sooty mould** *n* a dark growth of the rootlike filaments of fungus, growing in the sugary deposit (HONEYDEW) left by insects on plants; *also* a fungus producing such growth

¹**sop** /sop/ *n* **1** SIPPET **2** (food dipped in liquid) **2** something offered as a concession, appeasement, or bribe [ME *soppe*, fr OE *sopp*; akin to OE *sūpan* to swallow – more at SUP]

²**sop** *vt* **-pp-** **1a** to soak or dip (as if) in liquid ⟨∼ *bread in gravy*⟩ **b** to wet thoroughly; drench **2** to mop up (e g water) so as to leave a dry surface **3** to give a bribe or conciliatory offering to

**sophism** /'sofiz(ə)m/ *n* **1** an argument apparently correct but actually false; *esp* such an argument used to deceive **2** SOPHISTRY 1

**sophist** /'sofist/ *n* **1** *cap* any of various ancient Greek teachers of RHETORIC (the art of persuasive speaking or writing), philosophy, and the art of successful living noted for their subtle and often SPECIOUS (having a false look of truth) reasoning **2** a philosopher, thinker **3** a faultfinding or false reasoner [L *sophista*, fr Gk *sophistēs*, lit., expert, wise man, fr *sophizesthai* to become wise, deceive, fr *sophos* clever, wise]

**sophistic** /sə'fistik/, **sophistical** /-kl/ *adj* **1** of sophistry or the ancient Sophists ⟨∼ *rhetoric*⟩ ⟨∼ *subtleties*⟩ **2** having a false look of truth; possible but false ⟨∼ *reasoning*⟩ – **sophistically** *adv*

¹**sophisticate** /sə'fistikayt/ *vt* **1** to alter so as to deceive; *esp* to adulterate **2** to deprive of genuineness or natural simplicity; *esp* to deprive of naivety and make worldly-wise **3** to make elaborate or complex ⟨∼ *the mechanism of a watch*⟩ [ME *sophisticaten*, fr ML *sophisticatus*, pp of *sophisticare*, fr L *sophisticus* sophistic, fr Gk *sophistikos*, fr *sophistēs* sophist]

²**sophisticate** /sə'fistikət, -kayt/ *n* a sophisticated person

**sophisticated** /sə'fisti,kaytid/ *adj* **1** not in a natural, pure, or original state; adulterated ⟨*a* ∼ *oil*⟩ **2** deprived of inborn or original simplicity: e g **2a** highly complicated or developed; complex ⟨∼ *electronic devices*⟩ **b** worldly-wise, knowing ⟨*a* ∼ *adolescent*⟩ **c** intellectually subtle or refined ⟨*a* ∼ *novel*⟩ ⟨*a* ∼ *columnist*⟩ [ML *sophisticatus*] – **sophisticatedly** *adv*

**sophistication** /sə,fisti'kaysh(ə)n/ *n* **1** sophism, equivocation **2** the process of making impure or weak; adulteration **3** the process or result of becoming cultured, knowledgeable, or worldly-wise; *esp* cultivation, urbanity **4** the process or result of becoming more complex, developed, or subtle; *also* an instance of this

**sophistry** /'sofistri/ *n* **1** seemingly true but falsely subtle reasoning or argumentation **2** SOPHISM 1

**sophomore** /'sofə,maw/ *n*, *NAm* a student in his/her second year at college or secondary school [prob fr Gk *sophos* wise + *mōros* foolish – more at MORON] – **sophomoric** *adj*

**Sophonias** /,sofə'nie-əs, ,soohfə-/ *n* – see BIBLE table [LL, Zephaniah]

**sophy** /'sohfy/ *n*, *archaic* a sovereign of Persia in former times [Per *Safi*]

**-sophy** /-səfi/ *comb form* (→ *n*) knowledge; wisdom; science ⟨*anthroposophy*⟩ [ME *-sophie*, fr OF, fr L *-sophia*, fr Gk, fr *sophia* wisdom, fr *sophos* wise]

**sopor** /'sohpə/ *n* deep or lethargic sleep that is usu caused by disease [L; akin to L *somnus* sleep – more at SOMNOLENT]

**soporiferous** /,sopə'rifərəs/ *adj* soporific [L *soporifer*, fr *sopor* + *-fer* -ferous] – **soporiferousness** *n*

¹**soporific** /,sopə'rifik/ *adj* **1a** causing or tending to cause sleep **b** tending to reduce awareness or alertness **2** of or marked by sleepiness or lethargy

²**soporific** *n* something that induces sleep; a hypnotic

¹**sopping** /'soping/ *adj* wet through; soaking [fr prp of ²*sop*]

²**sopping** *adv* to an extreme degree of wetness ⟨∼ *wet*⟩

**soppy** /'sopi/ *adj* **1a** soaked through; saturated ⟨*a* ∼ *lawn*⟩ **b** very wet ⟨∼ *weather*⟩ **2** *informal* weakly sentimental; mawkish ⟨*you get so* ∼ *about couples* – Iris Murdoch⟩ **3** *chiefly Br informal* silly, inane [¹*sop* + ¹*-y*] – **soppily** *adv*, **soppiness** *n*

**sopranino** /,soprə'neenoh/ *n*, *pl* **sopraninos** a musical instrument (e g a recorder or saxophone) higher in pitch than the soprano [It, dim. of *soprano*]

¹**soprano** /sə'prahnoh/ *n*, *pl* **sopranos** **1** the highest part in 4-part (vocal) harmony **2** the highest singing voice of women, boys, or CASTRATI (male singers castrated in boyhood); *also* a person having this voice **3** a member of a family of instruments having the highest range [It, adj & n, fr *sopra* above, fr L *supra* – more at SUPRA-]

²**soprano** *adj* relating to or having the range or part of a soprano

**sora** /'sawrə/ *n* a small short-billed N American RAIL (type of wading bird) (*Porzana carolina*) common in marshes [origin unknown]

¹**sorb** /sawb/ *n* any of several African and Eurasian trees of the rose family; *esp* ⁴SERVICE [Fr *sorbe* fruit of the service tree, fr L *sorbum*]

²**sorb** *vt* to take up and hold by either ADSORPTION (uptake in a layer on the surface) or absorption [back-formation fr *absorb* & *adsorb*] – **sorbable** *adj*, **sorbability** *n*, **sorbtion** *n*

**Sorb** *n* **1** WEND (member of a Slavic people of E Germany) **2** the language of the Wends [Ger *Sorbe*, fr Sorbian *Serb*] – **Sorbian** *adj or n*

**sorbate** /'saw,bayt/ *n* a sorbed substance

**sorbent** /'sawbənt/ *n* a substance that sorbs [L *sorbent-, sorbens*, prp of *sorbēre* to suck up – more at ABSORB]

**sorbet** /'sawbit/ *n* WATER ICE; *also* SHERBET 2 [MF, a fruit drink, fr OIt *sorbetto*, fr Turk *şerbet* – more at SHERBET]

**sorbic acid** /'sawbik/ *n* an acid, $CH_3CH:CHCH:CHCOOH$, obtained from the unripe fruits of the MOUNTAIN ASH or man-made and used as a fungicide and food preservative [¹*sorb*]

**sorcerer** /'saws(ə)rə/, *fem* **sorceress** /-ris/ *n* a person who practises sorcery; a wizard

**sorcerous** /'saws(ə)rəs/ *adj* of sorcery; magical

**sorcery** /'saws(ə)ri/ *n* the art and practice of using magical power, esp with the aid of evil spirits [ME *sorcerie*, fr OF, fr *sorcier* sorcerer, fr (assumed) VL *sortiarius*, fr L *sort-, sors* chance, lot]

**sordid** /'sawdid/ *adj* **1a** dirty, filthy ⟨∼ *animals*⟩ **b** wretched, squalid ⟨*a* ∼ *little bed-sit*⟩ **2** marked by baseness or crudity; vile ⟨∼ *motives*⟩ **3** meanly greedy; niggardly **4** of a dull or muddy colour *synonyms* see ¹DIRTY, ¹MEAN [L *sordidus*, fr *sordes* dirt – more at SWART] – **sordidly** *adv*, **sordidness** *n*

**sordino** /saw'deenoh/ *n*, *pl* **sordini** /-ni/ ²MUTE 3 (device to reduce or soften the tone of a musical instrument) ⟨*a passage played con* sordini⟩ [It, fr *sordo* silent, fr L *surdus* – more at SURD]

¹**sore** /saw/ *adj* **1a** causing pain or distress **b** painfully sensitive; tender ⟨∼ *muscles*⟩ **c** hurt or inflamed so as to be or seem painful ⟨∼ *runny eyes*⟩ ⟨*a dog limping on a* ∼ *leg*⟩ **2a** causing difficulty, aggravation, anxiety, or distress ⟨*overtime is a* ∼ *point with him*⟩ **b** severe ⟨*in* ∼ *straits*⟩ **3** aggrieved, touchy **4** *chiefly NAm* angry, vexed – see also SIGHT **for sore eyes** [ME *sor*, fr OE *sār*; akin to OHG *sēr* sore, L *saevus* fierce] – **soreness** *n*

²**sore** *n* **1** a localized sore spot on the body; *esp* one (e g an ulcer) with the tissues broken or grazed and usu with infection **2** a source of pain or vexation; an affliction

³**sore** *adv*, *archaic* sorely

**sorehead** /'saw,hed/ *n*, *NAm informal* a person easily angered or disgruntled – **soreheaded** *adj*

**sorely** /'sawli/ *adv* **1** in a sore manner; painfully, grievously **2** much, extremely ⟨∼ *needed changes*⟩

**sorghum** /'sawgəm/ *n* **1** any of an economically important genus (*Sorghum*) of African and Eurasian tropical grasses similar to maize in habit but with the seed-bearing spikes in pairs on a hairy stalk; *esp* any of several cultivated plants (e g sorgo) derived from a common species of sorghum (*Sorghum vulgare*) **2** the syrup from the juice of a sorgo that resembles cane syrup [NL, genus name, fr It *sorgo*]

**sorgo** /'sawgoh/ *n* a sorghum cultivated primarily for the sweet juice in its stems from which sugar and syrup are made, but also used for fodder and silage [It]

**soricine** /'sori,sien/ *adj* resembling a shrew ⟨∼ *bats*⟩ [L *soricinus*, fr *soric-, sorex* shrew; akin to L *susurrus* hum – more at SWARM]

**sororal** /'sorərəl/ *adj* (characteristic) of a sister; sisterly [L *soror* sister – more at SISTER]

**sororate** /'sorə,rayt/ *n* the marriage of one man with two or more sisters, usu one after the other and after the first has died or proved to be barren [L *soror* sister]

**sorority** /sə'roriti/ *n* a club of girls or women esp at an American college; a female fraternity [ML *sororitas* sisterhood, fr L *soror* sister]

**¹sorrel** /'sorəl/ *n* **1** a sorrel-coloured animal; *esp* a sorrel-coloured horse **2** a brownish-orange to light brown colour [ME *sorelle*, fr MF *sorel*, n & adj, fr *sor* reddish-brown, prob of Gmc origin]

**²sorrel** *n* **1** a dock plant **2** WOOD SORREL [ME *sorel*, fr MF *surele*, fr OF, fr *sur* sour, of Gmc origin; akin to OHG *sūr* sour – more at SOUR]

**¹sorrow** /'soroh/ *n* **1** deep distress and regret (e g over the loss of something precious) **2** a cause of grief or sadness **3** the outward expression of grief or sadness *synonyms* see GRIEF *antonym* joy [ME *sorow*, fr OE *sorg;* akin to OHG *sorga* sorrow, OSlav *sraga* sickness]

**²sorrow** *vi* to feel or express sorrow – **sorrower** *n*

**sorrowful** /-f(ə)l/ *adj* **1** full of or marked by sorrow **2** expressing or inducing sorrow ⟨*a ~ tale*⟩ – **sorrowfully** *adv,* **sorrowfulness** *n*

**sorry** /'sori/ *adj* **1** feeling regret, penitence, or pity ⟨*felt ~ for the poor wretch*⟩ ⟨*I'm ~ I forgot your birthday*⟩ **2** inspiring sorrow, pity, scorn, or ridicule ⟨*looked a ~ sight in his torn clothes*⟩ [alter. (influenced by *sorrow*) of ME *sary, sory,* fr OE *sārig,* fr *sār* sore] – **sorrily** *adv,* **sorriness** *n*

**¹sort** /'sawt/ *n* **1a** a group constituted on the basis of any common characteristic; a class, kind **b** an instance of a kind ⟨*a ~ of herbal medicine*⟩ **2** a nature, disposition ⟨*people of an evil ~*⟩ **3a** a letter or character that is one element of a FOUNT (set of type of a single size and style) **b** a character or piece of type that is not part of a regular fount **4** *informal* a person, individual ⟨*he's not a bad ~*⟩ **5** *archaic* manner of being or acting; way, manner ⟨*every reader had in some ~ to be a student* – G M Trevelyan⟩ *usage* see ¹KIND *synonyms* see ¹TYPE [ME, fr MF *sorte,* prob fr ML *sort-, sors,* fr L, chance, lot] – **after a sort** in a rough or haphazard way – **of sorts, of a sort** of an inconsequential or mediocre quality ⟨*a poet of sorts*⟩ – **out of sorts 1** somewhat ill **2** grouchy, irritable – **sort of** *informal* KIND OF ⟨*sort of seven to half past* – SEU S⟩

**²sort** *vt* **1a** to put in a rank or particular place according to kind, class, or quality ⟨*~ the good apples from the bad*⟩ – often + *through* **b** to arrange in an orderly manner; put in order – usu + *out* ⟨*~ out papers on a desk*⟩ **2** *chiefly Scot* to put in working order; mend ⟨*~ a vacuum cleaner*⟩ – **sortable** *adj,* **sorter** *n*

**sort out** *vt* **1** to clarify or resolve, esp by thoughtful consideration ⟨*sorting out his problems*⟩ **2** to separate from a mass or group ⟨*sort out the important papers and throw the rest away*⟩ **3** to make (e g a person) less confused or unsettled ⟨*hoped the doctor would sort him out*⟩ **4** *chiefly Br informal* to take vengeance on, esp by violent means ⟨*"I'll sort you out, you . . .bastards" – Daily Mirror*⟩ – see also SORT-OUT

**sort with** *vt, formal* to correspond to; agree with

**sortie** /'sawti/ *n* **1** a sudden emergence of troops from a defensive position against the enemy **2** a single mission or attack by one aircraft **3** a brief trip, esp to a hostile or unfamiliar place [Fr, fr MF, fr *sortir* to escape] – **sortie** *vi*

**sortilege** /'sawtilij/ *n* **1** DIVINATION (fortune-telling) by drawing lots **2** sorcery [ME, fr ML *sortilegium,* fr L *sortilegus* foretelling, fr *sort-, sors* lot + *-i-* + *legere* to gather – more at LEGEND]

**sortition** /saw'tish(ə)n/ *n* the act or an instance of casting lots [L *sortition-, sortitio,* fr *sortitus,* pp of *sortiri* to cast or draw lots, fr *sort-, sors* lot]

**'sort-,out** *n, chiefly Br informal* an act of tidying up ⟨*I'll have a ~ of my desk and see if I can find the letter*⟩

**sorus** /'sawrəs/ *n, pl* **sori** /-ri/ a cluster of reproductive bodies of a fungus, fern, alga, or other lower plant: e g **a** any of the dots on the underside of some fertile fern leaves (FRONDS) consisting of a cluster of spore-producing capsules or bodies (SPORANGIA) **b** (a body containing) a mass of spores in some parasitic fungi, that burst through the outer skin (EPIDERMIS) of the plant on which the fungus is a parasite **c** a group of ANTHERIDIA (organs in which mature male reproductive cells are produced) on the body (FROND) of a seaweed [NL, fr Gk *sōros* heap; akin to L *tumēre* to swell – more at THUMB]

**SOS** /,es oh 'es/ *n* **1** an internationally recognized signal of distress which is rendered in Morse code as ▪▪▪ ▬▬▬ ▪▪▪ **2** a call or request for help or rescue [letters chosen purely for being simple to transmit and recognize in Morse code]

**¹so-so** /'soh ,soh/ *adv* moderately well; tolerably, passably

**²so-so** *adj* neither very good nor very bad; middling

**¹sostenuto** /,sostə'nyoohtoh, -'nooh-/ *adj or adv* sustained to

or beyond the full value of the note – used as a direction in music [It, fr pp of *sostenere* to sustain, fr L *sustinēre*]

**²sostenuto** *n, pl* **sostenutos** a sostenuto movement or passage

**sot** /sot/ *n* a drunkard [ME, fool, fr OE *sott*]

**soteriology** /soh,tiəri'oləji/ *n* theology dealing with salvation, esp as effected by Jesus [Gk *sōtērion* salvation, fr *sōtēr* saviour, fr *sōzein* to save; akin to Gk *sōma* body – more at SOMAT-] – **soteriological** *adj*

**Sothic cycle** /'sothik, 'soh-/ *n* a cycle of 1460 SOTHIC YEARS

**Sothic year** *n* an ancient Egyptian year of 365¼ days [Gk *Sōthis* the star Sirius]

**Sotho** /'soohtoo, 'sohtoh/ *n, pl* **Sothos,** *esp collectively* **Sotho 1** a group of closely related languages of the BANTU group of southern African languages; *esp* SESOTHO (language of Lesotho) **2** a member of the Bantu-speaking people of Lesotho in southern Africa

**sottish** /'sotish/ *adj* resembling a sot; drunken; *also* dull, stupid – **sottishly** *adv,* **sottishness** *n*

**sotto voce** /,sotoh 'vohchi/ *adv or adj* **1** under the breath; in an undertone; *also* in a private manner **2** at a very low volume – used as a direction in music [It *sottovoce,* lit., under the voice]

**sou** /sooh/ *n, pl* **sous 1** any of various former French coins of low value: e g **1a** ²SOL **b** a 5-centime piece of the period before 1914 **2** the smallest amount of money ⟨*hadn't a ~ to his name*⟩ [Fr, fr OF *sol,* fr LL *solidus* gold coin – more at SOLIDUS]

**soubise** /sooh'beez/ *n* a sauce, esp WHITE SAUCE, containing onion [Fr, fr Charles de Rohan, Prince de *Soubise* †1787 Fr nobleman]

**soubrette** /sooh'bret/ *n* **1** (an actress who plays) a coquettish maid or frivolous young woman in comedies **2** a soprano who sings supporting roles in comic opera [Fr, fr Prov *soubreto,* fem of *soubret* coy, fr *soubra* to surmount, exceed, fr L *superare* – more at INSUPERABLE]

**soubriquet** /'soohbri,kay/ *n* SOBRIQUET (nickname)

**souchong** /sooh'chong, -'shong/ *n* a large-leaved BLACK TEA, esp from China [Chin (Pek) *xiǎo zhǒng (hsiao³ chung³),* lit., small sort]

**¹soufflé** /'soohflay/ *n* a light fluffy dish made with egg yolks and stiffly beaten egg whites: **a** a sweet or savoury hot dish in which the egg is incorporated into a thick sauce and the mixture baked **b** a usu sweet uncooked dish made by whisking up eggs, cream, sugar, usu fruit juice, and gelatine, and leaving the mixture to set [Fr, fr *soufflé,* pp of *souffler* to blow, puff up, fr L *sufflare,* fr *sub-* + *flare* to blow – more at BLOW]

**²soufflé, souffléed** /'soohflayd/ *adj* puffed or made light by or in cooking

**sough** /sow/ *vi* to make a sighing or rushing sound like that of wind in the trees [ME *swoughen,* fr OE *swōgan;* akin to Goth *gaswogjan* to groan, Lith *svagėti* to sound] – **sough** *n*

**sought** /sawt/ *past of* SEEK

**'sought-,after** *adj* greatly desired or courted ⟨*the world's most ~ concert entertainers* – *Saturday Review*⟩

**souk** /soohk/ *n* an often covered market in a Muslim country [Ar *sūq* market]

**¹soul** /sohl/ *n* **1** the immaterial essence or animating principle of life or of an individual life, sometimes attributed to things ordinarily regarded as inanimate (e g the stars) **2** the spiritual principle embodied in human beings and all rational and spiritual beings, and often held to be immortal **3** all that constitutes a person's self **4a** an active or essential part ⟨*minorities are the very ~ of democracy*⟩ **b** a moving spirit; a leader ⟨*the ~ of the rebellion*⟩ **5a** the moral and emotional nature of human beings in contrast to their mind or intellect **b** a quality that stimulates the mind or emotions **c** spiritual vitality; fervour **6** a person ⟨*she's a kind old ~*⟩ **7** exemplification, personification ⟨*he is the ~ of integrity*⟩ **8a** a strong positive feeling esp of intense sensitivity and emotional fervour conveyed esp by black American performers **b** NEGRITUDE (pride in the African heritage) **c** soul, soul music music that originated in black American GOSPEL singing (singing of popular religious songs), is closely related to RHYTHM AND BLUES (style of pop music), and is characterized by intensity of feeling and earthiness **d** soul brother, soul male black – used esp by other blacks [ME *soule,* fr OE *sāwol;* akin to OHG *sēula* soul] – **souled** *adj*

**²soul** *adj* **1** (characteristic) of black Americans or their culture **2** designed for or controlled by black Americans ⟨*~ radio stations*⟩

**soul food** *n* food (eg chitterlings and ham hocks) traditionally eaten by southern US blacks

**soulful** /-f(ə)l/ *adj* full of or expressing feeling, esp intense or excessive feeling ⟨*a* ~ *song*⟩ – **soulfully** *adv,* **soulfulness** *n*

**soul kiss** *n* FRENCH KISS

**soulless** /-lis/ *adj* **1** having no soul or no warmth or greatness of feeling **2** bleak, uninviting ⟨*a bare,* ~ *room – Annabel*⟩ – **soullessly** *adv,* **soullessness** *n*

**soul mate** *n* either of two people, esp of opposite sex, intimately associated with one another; *esp* a lover

**'soul-,searching** *n* scrutiny of one's mind and conscience, esp with regard to aims and motives

**¹sound** /sownd/ *adj* **1a** free from injury or disease; healthy **b** free from flaw, defect, or decay ⟨~ *timber*⟩ **2** solid, firm; *also* stable **3a** free from error, fallacy, or misapprehension ⟨~ *reasoning*⟩ **b** showing or grounded in thorough knowledge and experience ⟨~ *scholarship*⟩ **c** legally valid ⟨*a* ~ *title*⟩ **d** logically valid and based on true premises **e** conforming to accepted views; orthodox **4a** deep and undisturbed ⟨*a* ~ *sleep*⟩ **b** thorough, severe ⟨*a* ~ *whipping*⟩ **5** showing integrity and good judgment *synonyms* see VALID *antonyms* unsound, fallacious [ME, fr OE *gesund;* akin to OHG *gisunt* healthy] – **soundly** *adv,* **soundness** *n*

**²sound** *adv* fully, thoroughly ⟨~ *asleep*⟩
   *usage* The adverbs **sound** and **soundly** can each mean "thoroughly", but **sound** is used almost entirely with *sleep* and *asleep* ⟨*you'll sleep the sounder for it*⟩ and cannot replace **soundly,** the usual adverb ⟨*scolded them* **soundly**⟩.

**³sound** *n* **1a** the effect resulting from stimulation of the specialized cells and groups of cells that receive auditory stimuli; the sensation perceived by the sense of hearing **b** a particular auditory impression or quality; a noise, tone ⟨*the* ~ *of children laughing*⟩ **c** energy that is produced by a vibrating body, is transmitted by longitudinal waves of pressure that travel outwards from the source through a medium (eg air), and is the objective cause of hearing **2** a speech sound ⟨*a peculiar r-sound*⟩ ⟨*-cher of "teacher" and* -ture *of "creature" have the same* ~⟩ **3a** meaningless noise ⟨*full of* ~ *and fury, signifying nothing* – Shak⟩ **b** the impression conveyed (eg by a report) ⟨*he's having a rough time by the* ~ *of it*⟩ **4** hearing distance; earshot **5a** recorded sounds (eg on records or film soundtracks) **b** radio broadcasting as opposed to television **c** that part of television equipment that processes sound signals **6** a characteristic musical style ⟨*the big band* ~⟩ ⟨*the Liverpool* ~ *of the 1960s*⟩ **7** *archaic* fame, tidings [ME *soun,* fr OF *son,* fr L *sonus;* akin to OE *swinn* melody, L *sonare* to sound, Skt *svanati* it sounds]

**⁴sound** *vi* **1a** to make a sound **b** to resound **c** to give a summons by sound ⟨*the bugle* ~s *to battle*⟩ **2** to have a specified import when heard; seem ⟨*his story* ~s *incredible*⟩ ~ *vt* **1a** to cause to emit sound ⟨~ *a trumpet*⟩ **b** to give out (a sound) ⟨~ *an A*⟩ **2** to put into words; voice **3a** to make known; proclaim ⟨~ *his praises far and wide*⟩ **b** to order, signal, or indicate by a sound ⟨~ *the alarm*⟩ ⟨~s *the hour*⟩ **4** esp *medicine* to examine or test the condition of by causing to emit sounds (eg by tapping) ⟨~ *the lungs*⟩ – **soundable** *adj*
   *usage* **Sound** is followed by an adjective when it means "seem when heard" ⟨*you* **sound** *disappointed*⟩ ⟨*that* **sounds** *all right*⟩. It should not correctly be followed by an infinitive verb ⟨⚠ *he* **sounds** *to be furious*⟩.

**sound off** *vi, informal* **1** to voice opinions freely and vigorously **2** *chiefly NAm* to speak loudly

**⁵sound** *n* **1a** a long broad inlet of the sea, generally parallel to the coast **b** a long passage of water connecting two larger bodies of water or separating a mainland and an island **2** the AIR BLADDER (air-filled pouch controlling buoyancy) of a fish [ME, fr OE *sund* swimming, sea & ON *sund* swimming, strait; akin to OE *swimman* to swim]

**⁶sound** *vt* **1** to measure the depth of; fathom ⟨~ *a well*⟩ **2** to try to find out the views or intentions of; probe – often + *out* ⟨~ *him out about the new proposals*⟩ **3** to explore or examine (a body cavity) with a sound ~ *vi* **1a** to ascertain the depth of water, esp with a SOUNDING LINE **b** to look into or investigate the possibility ⟨*sent commissioners . . . to* ~ *for peace* – Thomas Jefferson⟩ **2** *of a fish or whale* to dive down suddenly [ME *sounden,* fr MF *sonder,* fr *sonde* sounding line, prob of Gmc origin; akin to OE *sundline* sounding line, *sund* sea]

**⁷sound** *n* **1** SOUNDING LINE **2** *medicine* an elongated instrument for examining body cavities (eg the bladder) [Fr *sonde,* fr MF]

**sound barrier** *n* a sudden large increase in aerodynamic DRAG (resisting forces) that occurs as an aircraft nears the speed of sound

**soundboard** /'sownd,bawd/ *n* **1** a thin resonant board (eg the BELLY of a violin) so placed in a musical instrument as to reinforce its sound by SYMPATHETIC vibration (vibration caused in one body by vibrations in another) **2** SOUNDING BOARD 1a

**sound bow** /boh/ *n* the thick part of a bell against which the clapper strikes

**sound box** *n* **1** a device in an early form of gramophone, containing a thin flexible disc (DIAPHRAGM) that is attached to a needle and that vibrates to reproduce sounds from the undulations of the groove on a record or cylinder **2** the hollow resonating chamber in the body of a musical instrument (eg a violin)

**sound effect** *n usu pl* a sound, other than speech or music, used to create an effect in a play, radio programme, film, etc; *esp* an artificially produced sound which imitates an effect (eg the shaking of a metal sheet to sound like thunder)

**sounder** /'sowndə/ *n* one who or that which sounds; *specif* a device for taking soundings

**sound hole** *n* an opening in the soundboard of a musical instrument for increasing resonance

**¹sounding** /'sownding/ *n* **1a** the measuring of a depth of water, esp using a SOUNDING LINE **b** the depth so ascertained **c** *pl* a place or part of a body of water where a SOUNDING LINE will reach the bottom **2** measurement of atmospheric conditions at various altitudes **3** soundings *pl,* **sounding** a probe, test, or sampling of opinion or intention [⁶*sound*]

**²sounding** *adj* **1a** sonorous, resounding **b** making a usu specified sound or impression – usu in combination ⟨*clear-*sounding⟩ ⟨*odd-*sounding⟩ **2a** pompous, inflated **b** imposing ⟨*drop a* ~ *name*⟩ [⁴*sound*] – **soundingly** *adv*

**sounding board** *n* **1a** a structure behind or over a pulpit, rostrum, or platform to direct sound forwards **b** a device or agency that helps spread opinions or ideas **c** someone whose reaction serves as a test for new ideas **2** SOUNDBOARD 1

**sounding line** *n* a line or wire weighted at one end for measuring depths

**sounding rocket** *n* a rocket used to obtain information about atmospheric conditions at various altitudes

**¹soundless** /'sowndlis/ *adj* incapable of being sounded; unfathomable [⁶*sound*]

**²soundless** *adj* making no sound; silent [³*sound*] – **soundlessly** *adv*

**sound pollution** *n* NOISE POLLUTION

**sound post** *n* a post in an instrument of the viol or violin family set nearly under the BRIDGE for support and for transmitting sound vibrations to the back

**¹soundproof** /-,proohf/ *adj* impervious to sound ⟨~ *glass*⟩

**²soundproof** *vt* to insulate so as to make soundproof

**sound shift** *n* SHIFT 7 (sound changes during the history of a language)

**soundtrack** /'sownd,trak/ *n* **1** the band near the edge of a film that carries the sound recording; *also* the sound thus carried **2** the recorded music from a film

**soup** /soohp/ *n* **1** a liquid food typically having a meat, fish, or vegetable stock as a base and often thickened and containing pieces of solid food **2** something having or suggesting the consistency of soup: eg **2a** a heavy fog **b** a solution or liquid containing particles in suspension, that contains all the basic chemical molecules needed for life; *esp* PRIMORDIAL SOUP **c** *slang* nitroglycerine **3** *informal* an awkward or embarrassing predicament ⟨*he's really in the* ~ *over that business last night*⟩ [Fr *soupe* sop, soup, of Gmc origin; akin to ON *soppa* soup, OE *sopp* sop]

**soupçon** /'sooh(p)son, -sonh (*Fr* susɔ̃)/ *n* a little bit; a trace, dash [Fr, lit., suspicion, fr (assumed) VL *suspection-, suspectio,* fr L *suspectus,* pp of *suspicere* to suspect – more at SUSPECT]

**soup kitchen** *n* an establishment giving out minimum food requirements (eg soup and bread) to the needy

**soupspoon** /'soohp,spoohn/ *n* a spoon usu having a rounded bowl and used for eating soup

**soup up** *vt* **1** to increase the power or liveliness of ⟨soup up *an engine*⟩ **2** *informal* to make more attractive, interesting, etc [prob fr E slang *soup* drug injected into a racehorse to improve its performance]

**soupy** /'soohpi/ *adj* **1** having the consistency of soup **2** *informal* sentimental, mawkish

**¹sour** /sowə/ *adj* **1** being or inducing the one of the four basic taste sensations that is produced chiefly by acids ⟨~ *pickles*⟩

– compare BITTER, SALT, SWEET **2a(1)** having the acid taste or smell (as if) of fermentation; turned ⟨~ *milk*⟩ **a(2)** relating to fermentation **b** smelling or tasting of decay; rancid, rotten ⟨~ *breath*⟩ **c(1)** wrong, awry ⟨*a project gone* ~⟩ **c(2)** disenchanted, embittered ⟨*went* ~ *on Marxism*⟩ **3a** unpleasant, distasteful ⟨*a* ~ *job like washing dishes*⟩ **b** morose, bitter **c** not up to the usual, expected, or standard quality or pitch **4** *esp of soil* excessively acidic **5** *esp of petroleum products* containing foul-smelling sulphur compounds [ME, fr OE *sūr;* akin to OHG *sūr* sour, Lith *suras* salty] – **sourish** *adj*, **sourly** *adv*, **sourness** *n*

²**sour** *n* **1a** something sour **b** the primary taste sensation produced by something sour **2** *chiefly NAm* a cocktail made with a usu specified spirit, lemon or lime juice, sugar, and sometimes soda water ⟨*a whisky* ~⟩

³**sour** *vb* to make or become sour

**source** /saws/ *n* **1** the point of origin of a stream of water **2a** a generative force; a cause **b(1)** a means of supply ⟨*a secret* ~ *of wealth*⟩ **b(2)** a person, publication, etc that supplies information, esp at firsthand **c(1)** a place of origin; a beginning **c(2)** one who or that which initiates; an author, inspiration **c(3)** something (e g a computer program) that constitutes a starting point or base for subsequent development or transformation into another form **3** *archaic* a spring, fountain **synonyms** see ORIGIN [ME *sours*, fr MF *sors, sourse*, fr OF, fr pp of *sourdre* to rise, spring forth, fr L *surgere* – more at SURGE] – **sourceless** *adj*

**source book** *n* a fundamental document or record (e g of history, literature, art, or religion) upon which subsequent writings, beliefs, or practices are based; *also* a compilation of such documents

**source language** *n* a language that is to be translated into another language – compare TARGET LANGUAGE

**sour cherry** *n* a small Eurasian tree (*Prunus cerasus*) of the rose family widely grown for its bright red to almost black soft-fleshed acid fruits; *also* the fruit of this tree – compare SWEET CHERRY, MORELLO

**sour cream, soured cream** *n* cream which has been deliberately made sour by the addition of LACTIC ACID-forming bacteria, for use in cooking, salads, etc

**sourdough** /'sowə₋doh/ *n* **1** bread dough in which the yeast is still active, that is reserved from one baking for use as a leaven in the next **2** *NAm* a veteran inhabitant, esp an old-time prospector, of Alaska or northwestern Canada [(2) fr the use of sourdough for making bread in prospectors' camps]

**sour grapes** *n pl* disparagement of something achieved or owned by another that has proved unattainable by oneself [fr Aesop's fable of the fox who, finding himself unable to reach some grapes, claimed that they were sour anyway]

**sour gum** *n* BLACK GUM (tree of E USA)

**sour mash** *n, chiefly NAm* grain MASH (crushed grain steeped in hot water) for brewing or distilling that has been added to a base of previously fermented mash in order to obtain greater acidity

**sour orange** *n* (the bitter fruit of) a citrus tree (*Citrus aurantium*) that is used esp as a rootstock in grafting other citrus trees

**sourpuss** /-₋poos/ *n, informal* a habitually gloomy or bitter person [²*puss*]

**soursop** /'sowə₋sop/ *n* a tropical American tree (*Annona muricata*) of the custard-apple family that produces a large spiny green-skinned fruit with a slightly acid edible pulp; *also* the fruit of this tree – compare SWEETSOP

**sousaphone** /'soohzə₋fohn/ *n* a large BRASS INSTRUMENT of low range that is designed to encircle the player and rest on the left shoulder and is used primarily in American marching bands [John Philip *Sousa* †1932 US bandmaster & composer]

**sous chef** /'sooh ₋shef/ *n* an assistant cook in a restaurant or hotel [Fr]

¹**souse** /sows/ *vt* **1** to pickle ⟨~d *herring*⟩ **2a** to plunge in liquid; immerse **b** to drench, saturate **3** *informal* to make drunk; intoxicate ~ *vi* to become immersed or drenched [ME *sousen*, fr MF *souz, souce* pickling solution, of Gmc origin; akin to OHG *sulza* brine, OE *sealt* salt]

²**souse** *n* **1** an act of sousing; a wetting ⟨*gave him a* ~ *with a hosepipe*⟩ **2** PICKLE 1a (brine or vinegar in which foods are preserved) **3** *chiefly NAm* something pickled; *esp* seasoned and chopped pork trimmings, fish, or shellfish **4** *informal* **4a** a drunkard **b** a drinking spree; a binge

³**souse** *vi, archaic* to swoop down; plunge [obs *souse* swooping

of a hawk, fr ME *souce* start of a bird's flight, alter. of *sours*, fr MF *sourse*, fr *sourdre* to rise]

**soutache** /sooh'tash/ *n* a narrow braid with a herringbone pattern, used as trimming [Fr, fr Hung *sujtás*]

**soutane** /sooh'tan/ *n* a cassock [Fr, fr It *sottana*, lit., undergarment, fr fem of *sottano* being underneath, fr ML *subtanus*, fr L *subtus* underneath; akin to L *sub* under – more at UP]

**souter** /'soohtə/ *n, chiefly Scot & NEng* a shoemaker [ME, fr OE *sūtere*, fr L *sutor*, fr *sutus*, pp of *suere* to sew – more at SEW]

**souterrain** /'soohtə₋rayn/ *n* a prehistoric underground stone-built passage or chamber, commonly associated with stone forts in Ireland and Scotland [Fr, fr *sous* under + *terrain* ground]

¹**south** /sowth; *also* sowdh (*in names*) *before words beginning with a vowel*/ *adv* to, towards, or in the south **synonyms** see ¹NORTH [ME, fr OE *sūth;* akin to OHG *sund-* south, OE *sunne* sun]

²**south** *adj* **1** situated towards or at the south ⟨*the* ~ *entrance*⟩ **2** coming from the south ⟨*a* ~ *wind*⟩

³**south** *n* **1** the direction of the SOUTH POLE of the earth; *also* the compass point that corresponds to this direction and is directly opposite to north **2** *often cap* regions or countries lying to the south of a specified or implied point of orientation; *also, taking sing or pl vb* the inhabitants of these regions: e g **2a** the part of England lying south of an imaginary line between the Severn and the Wash **b** the part of the USA lying south of Pennsylvania and the Ohio river and east of the Mississippi; *esp* the states of Alabama, Arkansas, Florida, Georgia, N Carolina, S Carolina, Texas, Virginia, Tennessee, Louisiana, and Mississippi whose attempt to break away from union with the North precipitated the American Civil War **3** the right side of a church looking towards the altar from the NAVE (main body of a church) **4** *often cap* **4a** the one of the four positions at 90-degree intervals that lies to the south or at the bottom of a conventional diagram **b** a person (e g a bridge player) occupying the South in the course of a specified activity; *specif* the DECLARER (player who first bid the trump suit for the partnership that made the highest bid) in bridge ☐ (*2*) usu + *the*

**South African** *n* a native or inhabitant of the Republic of South Africa – **South African** *adj*

**South African Dutch** *n pl* the AFRIKAANS-speaking people of South Africa

**southbound** /'sowth₋bownd/ *adj* travelling, heading, or leading south ⟨*roadworks on the* ~ *carriageway*⟩

**south by east** *adj, adv, or n* (from, towards, or in the direction of) the compass point that is one point east of due south; 168° 45′ clockwise from north

**south by west** *adj, adv, or n* (from, towards, or in the direction of) the compass point that is one point west of due south; 191° 15′ clockwise from north

**South Caucasian** *n* a language family of the S Caucasus that includes GEORGIAN – **South Caucasian** *adj*

**Southdown** /'sowth₋down/ *n* (any of) an English breed of small hornless meat-producing sheep with medium-length wool [*South Downs*, hills in SE England]

¹**southeast** /-'eest/ *adv* to, towards, or in the southeast ⟨*heading* ~⟩

²**southeast** *n* **1** the compass point midway between south and east; *also* the general direction to which this corresponds **2** *often cap* the regions or countries lying to the southeast of a specified or implied point of orientation; *esp, Br* the southeast of England, esp the London area – **southeastward** *adj or n*, **southeastwards** *adv*

³**southeast** *adj* **1** coming from the southeast ⟨*a* ~ *wind*⟩ **2** situated towards or at the southeast ⟨*the* ~ *corner*⟩

**southeast by east** *adj, adv, or n* (from, towards, or in the direction of) the compass point that is one point east of southeast; 123° 45′ clockwise from north

**southeast by south** *n* (from, towards, or in the direction of) the compass point that is one point south of southeast; 146° 15′ clockwise from north

¹**southeasterly** /-'eestəli/ *adj or adv* situated towards, belonging to, or coming from the southeast; southeast [²*southeast* + *-erly* (as in *easterly*)]

²**southeasterly, southeaster** *n* a strong wind from the southeast

**southeastern** /-'eestən/ *adj* **1** *often cap* (characteristic) of a region conventionally designated Southeast **2** southeast [²*southeast* + *-ern* (as in *eastern*)] – **southeasternmost** *adj*

**Southeasterner** /ˌsowth'eestənə/ n a native or inhabitant of a southeastern region

¹**southerly** /'sudhəli/ adj or adv situated towards, belonging to, or coming from the south; south ⟨the ~ shore of the lake⟩ [³south + -erly (as in easterly)]

²**southerly**, NAm also **souther** n a wind from the south

**southerly buster** n, Austr a strong to gale force south wind of New South Wales

¹**southern** /'sudhən/ adj 1a cap (characteristic) of a region conventionally designated South b of or constituting a southern dialect 2a lying or directed towards the south b coming from the south ⟨a ~ breeze⟩ 3 south of the CELESTIAL EQUATOR synonyms see ¹NORTH [ME southern, southren, fr OE sütherne; akin to OHG sundrōni southern, OE süth south] – **southernly** adj, **southernmost** adj, **southernness** n

²**southern** n, often cap the dialect of English spoken in the SE seaboard and Gulf states of the USA roughly from Virginia as far east as Houston, Texas

**Southern English** n 1 RECEIVED PRONUNCIATION (standard pronunciation of southern British English) 2 chiefly NAm southern

**Southerner** /'sudhənə/ n a native or inhabitant of the South

**Southernism** /'sudhə‚niz(ə)m/ n an expression or pronunciation characteristic of the S USA

**southern lights** n pl AURORA AUSTRALIS

**southernwood** /-‚wood/ n a shrubby fragrant European plant (Artemisia abrotanum) of the daisy family, that is closely related to wormwood, has bitter foliage, and is widely grown in gardens

**southing** /'sowdhing, -thing/ n 1 distance due south in latitude from the preceding point of measurement 2 southerly progress

**southland** /'sowthland/ n, often cap, poetic land in the south; the south of a country

**southpaw** /-‚paw/ n a left-hander; specif a boxer who leads with the right hand and guards with the left – **southpaw** adj

**south pole** n 1a often cap S&P the southernmost point of the earth's axis of rotation; also the corresponding point of a celestial body (eg a planet) other than the earth b the southernmost point on the CELESTIAL SPHERE (imaginary sphere surrounding earth) about which the stars, planets, etc seem to revolve 2 the southward-pointing pole of a magnet

**Southron** /'sudhrən/ n 1 chiefly Scot an Englishman 2 chiefly S US an American Southerner [southron, adj (southern), fr ME (Sc), alter. of southren]

‚**south-south'east** /ˌ- -'-; esp tech ‚sow sow'eest/ adj, adv, or n (from, towards, or in the direction of) the compass point that is midway between south and southeast; 157° 30′ clockwise from north

‚**south-south'west** /ˌ- -'-; esp tech ‚sow sow'est/ adj, adv, or n (from, towards, or in the direction of) the compass point that is midway between south and southwest; 202° 30′ clockwise from north

¹**southward** /'sowthwəd; naut 'sudhəd/ adj moving or extending southwards

²**southward** n the southward direction or part; the south ⟨a marvellous view to the ~⟩

**southwards** /'sowthwədz; naut 'sudhədz/ adv towards the south

¹**southwest** /ˌsowth'west; esp tech ‚sow'west/ adv to, towards, or in the southwest ⟨lies 20 miles ~ of Paris⟩

²**southwest** n 1 the compass point midway between south and west; also the general direction to which this corresponds 2 often cap the regions or countries lying to the southwest of a specified or implied point of orientation; esp, the southwest of England, esp Somerset, Devon, and Cornwall – **southwestward** adj or n, **southwestwards** adv

³**southwest** adj 1 coming from the southwest ⟨a ~ wind⟩ 2 situated towards or at the southwest ⟨the ~ corner⟩

**southwest by south** adj, adv, or n (from, towards, or in the direction of) the compass point that is one point south of southwest; 213° 45′ clockwise from north

**southwest by west** adj, adv, or n (from, towards, or in the direction of) the compass point that is one point west of southwest; 236° 15′ clockwise from north

¹**southwesterly** /-li/ adj or adv situated towards, belonging to, or coming from the southwest; southwest [²southwest + -erly (as in westerly)]

²**southwesterly, southwester** n a strong wind from the southwest

**southwestern** /-'westən/ adj 1 often cap (characteristic) of a

region conventionally designated Southwest 2 southwest [²southwest + -ern (as in western)] – **southwesternmost** adj

**Southwesterner** /sowth'westənə/ n a native or inhabitant of a southwestern region

¹**souvenir** /ˌsoohvə'niə/ n something that serves as a reminder (eg of a place or past event); a memento [Fr, lit., act of remembering, fr MF, fr (se) souvenir to remember, fr L subvenire to come up, come to mind – more at SUBVENTION] – **souvenir** adj

²**souvenir** vt, informal to steal as a souvenir; pilfer

**sou'wester** /ˌsow'westə/ n 1 a southwesterly 2a a long usu oilskin waterproof coat worn esp at sea during stormy weather b a waterproof hat with a wide slanting brim longer at the back than in front

¹**sovereign** /'sovrin/ n 1a one possessing sovereignty b one who or that which exercises supreme authority within a limited sphere; a chief c an acknowledged leader ⟨the rose, ~ among flowers⟩ 2 a former British gold coin worth one pound [ME soverain, fr OF, fr soverain, adj]

²**sovereign** adj 1a supreme in power or authority ⟨~ ruler⟩ b unlimited in extent; absolute ⟨~ power⟩ c enjoying political autonomy; independent ⟨a ~ state⟩ 2a of outstanding excellence or importance ⟨their ~ sense of humour – Sir Winston Churchill⟩ ⟨liberty is a ~ conception⟩ b having generalized healing powers ⟨a ~ remedy⟩ c of an unqualified nature; utmost ⟨~ contempt⟩ 3 relating to, characteristic of, or befitting a sovereign [ME soverain, fr MF, fr OF, fr (assumed) VL superanus, fr L super over, above – more at OVER] – **sovereignly** adv

**sovereignty** /'sovrənty/ n 1a supreme power, esp over a politically organized body b freedom from external influence or control; autonomy c controlling influence 2 one who or that which is sovereign; esp an autonomous state [ME soverainte, fr MF soveraineté, fr OF, fr soverain]

**soviet** /'sohvyət, -yet, 'so-/ n 1 an elected governmental or administrative council in a Communist country, esp the USSR; also a meeting of such a council 2 pl, cap the people, esp the political and military leaders, of the USSR [Russ sovet] – **soviet** adj, often cap, **sovietism** n, often cap
usage The pronunciations /'sohvyet/ or /'sohvyət/ but not /'sov-/ are recommended for BBC broadcasters. See RUSSIAN

**soviet·ize, -ise** /'sohvyətiez/ vt, often cap 1 to bring under Soviet control 2 to force into conformity with Soviet cultural patterns or government policies – **sovietization** n, often cap

**sovkhoz** /ˌsuf'khoz, sof'koz/ n, pl **sovkhozy** /-zi/, **sovkhozes** a state-owned farm of the USSR paying wages to the workers [Russ, short for sovetskoe khozyaistvo soviet farm]

**sovran** /'sovrən/ n or adj, poetic (a) sovereign [by alter. (influenced by It sovrano, adj, fr OF soverain)] – **sovranty** n

¹**sow** /sow/ n 1 an adult female pig; also the adult female of various other animals (eg the grizzly bear) 2a a channel that conducts molten metal, esp iron, to moulds b a mass of metal solidified in such a mould [ME sowe, fr OE sugu; akin to OE & OHG sū sow, L sus pig, swine, hog, Gk hys]

²**sow** /soh/ vb **sown** /sohn/, **sowed** vi to plant seed for growth, esp by scattering ~ vt 1a to scatter (eg seed) upon the earth for growth; broadly to plant b to strew (as if) with seed c to introduce into a selected environment; implant 2 to cause the growth of; foment ⟨~ suspicion⟩ 3 to disperse, disseminate – see also **sow one's wild** OATS △ sew [ME sowen, fr OE sāwan; akin to OHG sāwen to sow, L serere] – **sower** n

**sowbelly** /'sow‚beli/ n fat salted pork or bacon

**sow bug** /sow/ n, chiefly NAm a wood-louse

**sow thistle** /sow/ n any of a genus (Sonchus, esp Sonchus oleraceus) of plants of the daisy family that have fleshy stems, milky juice, prickly leaves, and yellow flowerheads and that are common in Europe, esp as weeds

**soy** /soy/ n 1 soy, soy sauce an oriental brown liquid sauce made by pickling fermented SOYA BEANS in brine 2 soybean also soy SOYA BEAN [Jap shōyu, fr Chin (Cant) shī-yaū, lit., soya-bean oil]

**soya** /'soyə/ n soy [D soja, fr Jap shōyu]

**soya bean** n (the edible seed, rich in oil and protein, of) an Asian plant (Glycine max) of the pea family widely grown for its seeds and for forage and soil improvement

**soya-bean oil** n a pale yellow oil that is obtained from SOYA BEANS and is used chiefly as a cooking oil and in the manufacture of paints, varnishes, linoleum, printing ink, and soap

**sozzled** /'soz(ə)ld/ adj, chiefly Br slang & humorous drunk [fr pp of sozzle (to splash, souse, intoxicate)]

**spa** /spah/ *n* **1** a usu fashionable resort with mineral springs **2** a spring of MINERAL WATER (water naturally containing mineral salts) [*Spa*, watering place in E Belgium]

**¹space** /spays/ *n* **1** a period of time; *also* its duration **2a** a limited extent in one, two, or three dimensions: e g **2a**(1) distance **a**(2) area **a**(3) volume **b** an amount of room set apart or available ⟨*parking* ∼⟩ ⟨*floor* ∼⟩ **3** any of the degrees between or above or below the lines of a musical stave **4a** the limitless three-dimensional extent in which objects and events occur and have relative position and direction **b** physical space independent of what occupies it **5** the region beyond the earth's atmosphere or beyond the SOLAR SYSTEM **6a** a blank area on a page (e g separating words or lines) **b** a piece of type less than the height necessary to make an impression; *esp* one narrower than the letter *n* **c** the distance moved by a typewriter carriage in typing one character **7** a set of mathematical entities (e g the theoretical positions occupied by all the points on a straight line) that obey a set of AXIOMS (predetermined rules agreed to be true) ⟨*Euclidean* ∼⟩ **8** a brief interval during which a telegraph key is not causing electrical contact to be made **9** LINAGE 1 (number of lines of printed or written matter) **10** a seat, berth, or standing room on a public vehicle [ME, fr OF *espace*, fr L *spatium* area, room, interval of space or time – more at SPEED]

**²space** *vt* to place at intervals or arrange with space between – often + *out* ∼ *vi* to leave one or more blank spaces (e g in a line of typing) – **spacer** *n*

**'space-,age** *adj* suggestive of the technology of the SPACE AGE; ultra-modern, futuristic

**space age** *n* the era in which the exploration of space and space travel has become possible

**spaceband** /'spays,band/ *n* a device on a LINECASTER (machine that casts type in lines) that provides variable but even spacing between words in a JUSTIFIED line (line set to be the same length as the others)

**space bar** *n* the horizontal bar below the lowest row of keys on a typewriter, that is pressed to make a space

**space charge** *n* an electric charge caused by a collection of charged particles (e g electrons) that is distributed throughout a three-dimensional region (e g the region round the source of electrons in a THERMIONIC VALVE)

**spacecraft** /-,krahft/ *n, pl* **spacecraft** a manned or unmanned device that is designed to orbit the earth or to travel beyond the earth's atmosphere

**,spaced-'out, spaced** *adj, informal* excited or stupefied (as if) by a narcotic drug

**spaceflight** /-,fliet/ *n* (a) flight beyond the earth's atmosphere

**space heating** *n* the heating of spaces, esp for human comfort, by any means (e g solid fuel, electricity, or oil) with the heater either within the space or external to it – **space heater** *n*

**space lattice, lattice** *n* the geometrical arrangement of the atoms, ions, etc in a crystal

**spaceless** /'spayslis/ *adj* **1** having no limits; boundless **2** occupying no space

**spaceman** /-,man/, *fem* **spacewoman** *n* **1** someone who travels outside the earth's atmosphere **2** a visitor to earth from outer space

**space mark** *n* the mark ⧣ indicating that there should be a space, esp in printed matter

**space medicine** *n* a branch of medicine that deals with the physiological and biological effects on the human body of flight beyond the earth's atmosphere

**space platform** *n* SPACE STATION

**spaceport** /'spays,pawt/ *n* an installation for testing and launching spacecraft

**spacer** /'spaysə/ *n* a part of a gene that alternates with regions carrying information that codes for the production of a protein or NUCLEIC ACID, but itself does not carry coding information

**spaceship** /-,ship/ *n* a manned spacecraft

**space shuttle** *n* a vehicle that is designed to serve as a reusable transport between the earth and an orbiting SPACE STATION

**space station** *n* a manned artificial satellite designed for a fixed orbit about the earth and to serve as a base (e g for scientific observation)

**space suit** *n* **1** a suit equipped with life supporting provisions to make life in space possible for its wearer **2** G SUIT (suit designed to counteract the effects of acceleration)

**'space-,time, space-time continuum** *n* **1** a reference system of one temporal and three spatial dimensions by which any physical object or event can be located **2** (the properties characteristic of) the whole or a portion of physical reality described by a four-dimensional space-time system

**space walk** *n* a trip outside a spacecraft made by an astronaut in space – **space walk** *vi*, **spacewalker** *n*, **spacewalking** *n*

**spacewards** /'spayswədz/ *adv* towards space

**space warp** *n* a hypothetical discontinuity in space that enables one to travel easily to distant stars and galaxies

**spacey** /'spaysi/ *adj, informal* of or in a spaced-out state ⟨*music with a* ∼ *effect*⟩

**spacial** /'spayshəl/ *adj* SPATIAL (of space)

**spacing** /'spaysing/ *n* **1a** the act of providing with spaces or placing at intervals **b** an arrangement in space ⟨*alter the* ∼ *of the chairs*⟩ **2** the distance between any two objects in a usu regularly arranged series

**spacious** /'spayshəs/ *adj* **1** containing ample space; roomy ⟨*a* ∼ *residence*⟩ **2a** broad or vast in area ⟨*a country of* ∼ *plains*⟩ **b** large in scale or space; expansive ⟨*a more* ∼ *and stimulating existence than the farm could offer* – H L Mencken⟩ [ME, fr MF *spacieux*, fr L *spatiosus*, fr *spatium* space, room] – **spaciously** *adv*, **spaciousness** *n*

**¹spade** /spayd/ *n* **1** a digging implement that typically has a flat usu rectangular blade on a long handle and can be pushed into the ground with the foot **2** a spade-shaped instrument [ME, fr OE *spadu;* akin to Gk *spathē* blade of a sword or oar, OHG *spān* chip of wood – more at SPOON] – **spadeful** *n* – **call a spade a spade 1** to call a thing by its right name however coarse **2** to speak frankly and bluntly

**²spade** *vt* to dig up, excavate, or shape (as if) with a spade ∼ *vi* to work with a spade – **spader** *n*

**³spade** *n* **1a** a black spearhead-shaped figure marked on a playing card; *also* a card marked with one or more of these figures **b** *pl but taking sing or pl vb* the suit comprising cards identified by this figure **2** *often cap, derog* a black [It *spada* or Sp *espada* broad sword (used as a mark on playing cards); both fr L *spatha*, fr Gk *spathē* blade]

**spade beard** *n* **1** an oblong beard with square ends **2** a beard rounded off at the top and pointed at the bottom – **spade-bearded** *adj*

**spadework** /-,wuhk/ *n* **1** work done with a spade **2** the hard plain preparatory work in an undertaking

**spadille** /spə'dil, spə'diəl/ *n* the highest trump in various card games (e g OMBRE) [Fr, fr Sp *espadilla*, dim. of *espada* broad sword, spade (in cards)]

**spadix** /'spaydiks/ *n, pl* **spadices** /-diseez/ a spike of tiny tightly packed flowers (e g in a cuckoopint or similar plant of the arum family) borne on a fleshy or succulent stem and usu enclosed by a leaflike sheath (SPATHE) [NL *spadic-, spadix*, fr L, frond torn from a palm tree, fr Gk *spadik-, spadix*, fr *span* to draw, pull – more at SPAN]

**spae** /spay/ *vt* **spaed; spaeing** *chiefly Scot* to foretell, prophesy [ME *span*, fr ON *spā;* akin to OHG *spehōn* to watch, spy – more at SPY]

**spaghetti** /spə'geti/ *n* pasta in the form of thin usu solid strings smaller in diameter than macaroni [It, fr pl of *spaghetto*, dim. of *spago* cord, string]

**spahi** /'spah,(h)ee/ *n, pl* **spahis 1** any of a former corps of irregular Turkish cavalry **2** any of a former corps of Algerian native cavalry in the French Army [MF, fr Turk *sipahi*, fr Per *sipāhī* cavalryman]

**spake** /spayk/ *archaic past of* SPEAK

**¹spall** /spawl/ *n* a small splinter or chip, esp of stone [ME *spalle*]

**²spall** *vt* to break up (e g stone) into fragments (as if) by chipping with a hammer ∼ *vi* **1** to break off fragments; chip **2** to undergo spallation – **spallable** *adj*

**spallation** /spə'laysh(ə)n/ *n* a nuclear reaction in which the bombardment of an atomic nucleus with high-energy particles or PHOTONS (particles of RADIANT ENERGY) results in the ejection of protons, neutrons, etc from the nucleus [²*spall* + *-ation*]

**spalpeen** /spal'pi·n, '--/ *n, chiefly Irish* a rascal [IrGael *spailpīn* labourer, rascal]

**Spam** /spam/ *trademark* – used for a tinned pork LUNCHEON MEAT

**¹span** /span/ *archaic past of* SPIN

**²span** *n* **1** the distance from the end of the thumb to the end of the little finger of a spread hand; *also* a former English unit of length equal to 9 inches (about 0.23 metre) **2** an extent, distance, stretch, or spread between two limits: e g **2a**

a limited stretch (eg of time); *esp* an individual's lifetime **b** the full reach or extent ⟨*the remarkable ~ of his memory*⟩ **c** the distance or extent between ABUTMENTS or supports (eg of a bridge); *also* a part of a bridge between supports **d** the distance from wing tip to wing tip of an aircraft; a wingspan [ME, fr OE *spann;* akin to OHG *spanna* span, MD *spannen* to stretch, hitch up, L *pendere* to weigh, Gk *span* to draw, pull]

³**span** *vt* **-nn- 1a** to measure (as if) by the hand with fingers and thumb extended **b** to measure **2a** to extend across ⟨*his career ~*ned *four decades*⟩ **b** to form an arch over ⟨*a small bridge ~*ned *the pond*⟩ **c** to place or construct a span over **3** *of a set of mathematical elements* to be capable of forming by a suitable combination (LINEAR COMBINATION) of its elements, any element of ⟨*a given mathematical set*⟩ ⟨*a set of vectors that ~*s *a vector space*⟩

⁴**span** *n taking sing or pl vb, chiefly NAm & SAfr* a pair of animals (eg oxen) usu matched in appearance and action and driven together [D, fr MD, fr *spannen* to hitch up]

**spandrel, spandril** /'spandrəl/ *n* the space between the right or left exterior curve of an arch and an enclosing right angle [ME *spandrell,* fr AF *spaundre,* fr OF *espandre* to spread out – more at SPAWN]

¹**spangle** /'spang·gl/ *n* **1** a sequin **2** a small glittering object or particle ⟨*gold ~*s *of dew* – Edith Sitwell⟩ [ME *spangel,* dim. of *spang* shiny ornament, prob of Scand origin; akin to ON *spöng* spangle; akin to OE *spang* buckle, MD *spannen* to stretch]

²**spangle** *vt* to set or sprinkle (as if) with spangles ~ *vi* to glitter as if covered with spangles; sparkle

**Spaniard** /'spanyəd/ *n* a native or inhabitant of Spain [ME *Spaignard,* fr MF *Espaignart,* fr *Espaigne* Spain, fr L *Hispania*]

**spaniel** /'spanyəl/ *n* **1** (a member of) any of several breeds of small or medium-sized mostly short-legged dogs usu having long wavy hair which forms feathery tufts behind the legs and beneath the tail, and large drooping ears **2** a fawning servile person [ME *spaniell,* fr MF *espaignol,* lit., Spaniard, fr (assumed) VL *Hispaniolus,* fr L *Hispania* Spain]

**Spanish** /'spanish/ *n* **1** the official language of Spain and of the countries colonized by Spaniards, that is one of the ROMANCE group of languages developed from Latin **2** *taking pl vb* the people of Spain [*Spanish,* adj, fr ME *Spainish,* fr *Spain*] – **Spanish** *adj*

**Spanish American** *n* **1** a native or inhabitant of any of the countries of S and Central America in which Spanish is the national language **2** a native or inhabitant of the USA whose native language is Spanish and whose culture is of Spanish origin – **Spanish-American** *adj*

**Spanish bayonet** *n* any of several YUCCAS (treelike tropical plants of the lily family); *esp* one (*Yucca aloifolia*) with a short trunk, white blossom, and rigid leaves ending in spines

**Spanish chestnut** *n* (the sweet edible nut of) a large widely cultivated chestnut tree (*Castanea sativa*)

**Spanish fly** *n* **1** a large green BLISTER BEETLE (*Lytta vesicatoria*) of S Europe **2** CANTHARIS 2 (preparation of dried Spanish fly or other beetles used formerly as an aphrodisiac)

**Spanish guitar** *n* a guitar of the classical (ACOUSTIC) type, esp as distinct from an electric guitar

**Spanish moss** *n* an EPIPHYTIC plant (plant that grows, but is not parasitic, on other plants) (*Tillandsia usneoides*) of the pineapple family that hangs in long tufts of greyish-green strands from the branches of trees in the S USA and the W Indies

**Spanish omelette** *n* an omelette containing cooked chopped vegetables (eg potato, green pepper, onion, and tomato) and usu not folded in half

**Spanish onion** *n* a large mild-flavoured onion

**Spanish paprika** *n* PIMIENTO (type of red SWEET PEPPER)

¹**spank** /spangk/ *vt* to strike, esp on the buttocks, (as if) with the open hand [imit] – **spank** *n*

²**spank** *vi* to move quickly, smartly, or spiritedly ⟨*~*ing *along in his new car*⟩ [back-formation fr *spanking*]

**spanker** /'spangkə/ *n* a FORE-AND-AFT sail (sail set lengthwise) on the mast nearest the stern of a SQUARE-RIGGED ship (one with sails set at right angles to its length) [origin unknown]

¹**spanking** /'spangking/ *adj* **1** remarkable of its kind; striking **2** fresh and vigorous; brisk ⟨*rode off at a ~ pace*⟩ [origin unknown] – **spankingly** *adv*

²**spanking** *adv* completely and impressively ⟨*a ~ clean floor*⟩ ⟨*a ~ new car*⟩

**spanner** /'spanə/ *n* a tool with an end suitably shaped to grip a mechanical part that is to be held or turned; *also, chiefly Br* such a tool with two ends suitable for holding or turning nuts or bolts with nut-shaped heads [Ger, instrument for winding the spring in a wheel-lock gun, fr *spannen* to stretch; akin to MD *spannen* to stretch – more at SPAN] – **(put/throw) a spanner in the works** *informal* (to cause) an obstruction or hindrance (eġ to a plan or operation)

¹**spar** /spah/ *n* **1** a stout pole **2a** a stout rounded pole (eg a mast, boom, gaff, or yard) used to support or control a sail **b**(1) any of the main lengthwise supporting parts of the wing of an aircraft that carry the ribs **b**(2) LONGERON (lengthwise supporting part of an aircraft fuselage) [ME *sparre;* akin to OE *spere* spear]

²**spar** *vi* **-rr- 1** to strike or fight with feet or spurs in the manner of a gamecock **2a** to box; *esp* to gesture without landing a blow, so as to draw one's opponent or create an opening **b** to engage in a practice or exhibition bout of boxing **c** FENCE 2 (play at a cricket ball and miss) **3** to skirmish, wrangle ⟨*politicians who prolong debates by ~*ring⟩ [prob alter. of ²*spur*]

³**spar** *n* a sparring match or session

⁴**spar** *n* any of various transparent to translucent usu lustrous nonmetallic minerals (eg FLUORSPAR) that typically split into flakes or layers along definite planes [LG; akin to OE *spærstān* gypsum, *spæren* of plaster]

¹**spare** /speə/ *vt* **1** to refrain from destroying, punishing, or harming **2** to refrain from using ⟨*~ the rod and spoil the child*⟩ **3** to relieve of the necessity of doing or undergoing something ⟨*~ yourself the trouble*⟩ **4** to refrain from; avoid ⟨*~*d *no expense*⟩ **5** to use or dispense frugally – chiefly neg ⟨*don't ~ the butter*⟩ **6a** to give up as surplus to requirements ⟨*do you have any cash to ~?*⟩ **b** to have left over, unused, or unoccupied ⟨*time to ~*⟩ ⟨*can you ~ a room?*⟩ ~ *vi* **1** to be frugal ⟨*some will spend and some will ~* – Robert Burns⟩ **2** to refrain from doing harm; be lenient [ME *sparen,* fr OE *sparian;* akin to OHG *sparōn* to spare, OE *spær,* adj, spare] – **spareable** *adj,* **sparer** *n*

²**spare** *adj* **1** not in use; *esp* reserved for use in emergency ⟨*a ~ tyre*⟩ **2a** in excess of what is required; surplus **b** not taken up with work or duties; free ⟨*~ time*⟩ **3** sparing, concise ⟨*a ~ prose style*⟩ **4** healthily lean; wiry **5** *informal* not abundant; meagre **6** *Br informal* extremely angry or distraught ⟨*I nearly went ~ with anxiety* – Practical Gardening⟩ **antonyms** corpulent (for sense 4), profuse (for sense 5) [ME, fr OE *spær;* akin to OSlav *sporǔ* abundant, OE *spēd* prosperity – more at SPEED] – **sparely** *adv,* **spareness** *n*

³**spare** *n* **1** a spare or duplicate item or part; *specif* a spare part for a motor vehicle **2** the knocking down of all 10 pins with the two balls of a frame in TENPIN BOWLING; *also* the score thus made

**spare part** *n* a replacement for a component that may cease or has ceased to function ⟨*went to the garage for spare parts*⟩ ⟨*spare-part surgery*⟩

**sparerib** /-'rib/ *n usu pl* a pork rib with most of the surrounding meat removed for use as bacon [by folk etymology fr LG *ribbesper* pickled pork ribs roasted on a spit, fr MLG, fr *ribbe* rib + *sper* spear, spit]

**spare tyre** *n, informal* a roll of excess body fat round or just above the waist

**sparge** /spahj/ *vt* to moisten or rinse by sprinkling; spray – used esp in brewing [prob fr MF *espargier,* fr L *spargere* to scatter] – **sparge** *n,* **sparger** *n*

**sparing** /'speəring/ *adj* **1** not wasteful; frugal ⟨*we must be ~ with the butter*⟩ **2** meagre, scant ⟨*the map is ~ of information*⟩ – **sparingly** *adv*

**synonyms Sparing, economical, frugal,** and **thrifty** all mean "careful in using resources". **Sparing** and **economical** can apply to the use of anything ⟨**sparing/economical** *in his use of words*⟩. **Sparing** emphasizes general restraint, and **economical** stresses the skilful use of things to their best advantage ⟨*an* **economical** *housewife*⟩. **Frugal** implies temperate simplicity and the avoidance of luxury. **Thrifty** often suggests diligence in earning money as well as frugality in using it ⟨**thrifty** *hardworking farmers*⟩. Compare STINGY **antonyms** lavish, prodigal

¹**spark** /spahk/ *n* **1a** a small hot fiery particle thrown out from a burning substance or remaining when burning has nearly finished ⟨*~*s *from a fire*⟩ **b** a hot glowing particle struck from a larger mass and usu caused by friction between hard surfaces ⟨*~*s *flying from under a hammer*⟩ **2a** a sudden short-lasting discharge of electrical energy through a gas (eg air)

separating two electrical conductors or electrically charged bodies. A spark, seen as a bright flash of light, occurs when a difference in the voltage between the conductors or bodies causes the insulating properties of the gas to break down, resulting in a brief flow of electric current. **b** the spark produced by a SPARKING PLUG **3** a sparkle, flash **4** something that sets off or stimulates an event, development, etc ⟨*provided the ~ that helped the team to rally*⟩ **5** a trace, esp one which may develop; a germ ⟨*still retains a ~ of decency*⟩ **6** *pl but taking sing vb, informal* **6a** a radio operator on a ship **b** an electrician [ME *sparke,* fr OE *spearca;* akin to MD *sparke* spark, L *spargere* to scatter, Gk *spargan* to swell]

**²spark** *vi* **1a** to give off sparks **b** to flash or fall like sparks **2** to produce sparks; *specif* to have the electric ignition working ~ *vt* **1** to cause to be suddenly active; prompt, precipitate – usu + *off* ⟨*the question* ~ed *off a lively discussion*⟩ **2** to stir to activity; incite ⟨*a player can* ~ *his team to victory*⟩ – **sparker** *n*

**³spark** *n* **1** a foppish young man; a gallant **2** a lover, beau **3** a lively and usu witty person – chiefly in *bright spark* [perh of Scand origin; akin to ON *sparkr* sprightly; (3) prob influenced by ¹*spark*] – **sparkish** *adj*

**⁴spark** *vb, chiefly NAm* to woo, court – **sparker** *n*

**spark chamber** *n* a device used to detect radiation or investigate the path of a high-energy particle, that consists of a parallel series of electrically charged metal plates, wires, etc separated by a chemically inert gas (e g neon). A particle passing between the plates alters the electrical insulation properties of the gas, temporarily allowing the flow of electricity that is seen as a series of sparks that follow the path of the particle.

**spark coil** *n* an INDUCTION COIL (device for obtaining intermittent pulses of high voltage electricity) for producing the spark that ignites the fuel in a car engine or other petrol engine

**spark gap** *n* a usu air-filled space between two electrical conductors (e g in a SPARKING PLUG) in which electric sparks occur

**sparking plug** /'spahking/ *n, Br* a part that fits into the cylinder head of an INTERNAL-COMBUSTION ENGINE (e g of a car) and produces the electric spark which ignites the air-fuel mixture

**¹sparkle** /'spahkl/ *vi* **1a** to give off sparks **b** to give off or reflect glittering points of light; scintillate **2** to effervesce ⟨*wine that* ~s⟩ **3** to show brilliance, animation, or liveliness ⟨*the dialogue* ~s *with wit*⟩ ⟨*eyes sparkling with anger*⟩ ~ *vt* to cause to glitter or shine *synonyms see* ¹FLASH [ME *sparklen,* freq of *sparken* to spark]

**²sparkle** *n* **1** a little spark; a scintillation **2** the quality or state of sparkling **3a** vivacity, gaiety **b** the quality or state of being effervescent ⟨*a wine full of* ~⟩ [ME, dim. of *sparke*]

**sparkler** /'spahklə/ *n* one who or that which sparkles: e g **a** a hand-held firework that throws off brilliant sparks on burning **b** *informal* a (cut and polished) diamond

**sparkling wine** /'spahkling/ *n* an effervescent red or esp white table wine

**spark plug** *n, chiefly NAm* **1** SPARKING PLUG **2** one who initiates or stimulates an undertaking – **sparkplug** *vt*

**spark transmitter** *n* an obsolete type of radio transmitter that uses the electrical energy discharged by a CAPACITOR (device for storing electrical charge) through a SPARK GAP as a source of RADIO WAVES

**sparky** /'spahki/ *adj, informal* lively, vivacious – **sparkily** *adv*

**sparling** /'spahling/ *n, pl* **sparlings,** *esp collectively* **sparling** a European SMELT (small food fish resembling a trout) (*Osmerus eperlanus*) [ME *sperling,* fr MF *esperling,* fr MD *spierlinc,* fr *spier* shoot, blade of grass]

**sparring partner** /'spahring/ *n* a boxer's companion for practice in sparring during training; *broadly* a habitual opponent (e g in friendly argument)

**sparrow** /'sparoh/ *n* any of several small dull-coloured songbirds (genus *Passer* of the family Ploceidae) related to the finches; *esp* HOUSE SPARROW [ME *sparow,* fr OE *spearwa;* akin to OHG *sparo* sparrow, Gk *psar* starling]

**sparrowgrass** /-ˌgrahs/ *n, chiefly dial* asparagus [by folk etymology fr *asparagus*]

**sparrow hawk** *n* a small Eurasian and N African hawk (*Accipiter nisus*) with a long tail and short rounded wings that preys on smaller birds

**sparse** /spahs/ *adj* of few and scattered parts; *esp* not thickly grown or settled [L *sparsus* spread out, fr pp of *spargere* to scatter – more at SPARK] – **sparsely** *adv,* **sparseness** *n,* **sparsity** *n*

**¹Spartan** /'spaht(ə)n/ *n* **1** a native or inhabitant of ancient Sparta **2** a person of great courage and endurance [ME, fr L *Spartanus,* adj & n, fr *Sparta,* city in ancient Greece] – **Spartanism** *n*

**²Spartan** *adj* **1** of Sparta in ancient Greece **2a** marked by rigorous self-discipline or self-denial ⟨*a* ~ *athlete*⟩ **b** marked by austere simplicity or frugality ⟨*a* ~ *lunch*⟩ **c** having or showing courage and endurance; not daunted by pain, hardship, or danger

**spasm** /'spaz(ə)m/ *n* **1** (an) involuntary and abnormal contraction of a muscle or of the muscular wall of a hollow organ **2** a sudden violent and brief effort or emotion ⟨~s *of helpless mirth – Punch*⟩ [ME *spasme,* fr MF, fr L *spasmus,* fr Gk *spasmos,* fr *span* to draw, pull – more at SPAN]

**spasmodic** /spaz'modik/ *adj* **1a** relating to, being, or affected or characterized by muscular spasms **b** resembling a spasm, esp in sudden violence ⟨*a* ~ *jerk*⟩ **2** acting or proceeding in fits and starts; intermittent ⟨~ *attempts at studying*⟩ **3** subject to emotional outbursts; excitable *synonyms see* PERIODIC *antonym* constant [NL *spasmodicus,* fr Gk *spasmōdēs,* fr *spasmos*] – **spasmodical** *adj,* **spasmodically** *adv*

**spasmolytic** /ˌspazmə'litik/ *adj* tending or having the power to relieve muscular spasms or convulsions [ISV *spasmo-* (fr Gk *spasmos* spasm) + *-lytic* (fr Gk *lytikos* able to loose) – more at LYTIC] – **spasmolytic** *n,* **spasmolytically** *adv*

**¹spastic** /'spastik/ *adj* **1** of or characterized by muscular spasms ⟨*a* ~ *colon*⟩ **2** being a spastic ⟨*a* ~ *child*⟩ **3** spasmodic ⟨*a* ~ *influx of data*⟩ **4** *slang* ineffectual, incompetent [L *spasticus,* fr Gk *spastikos* drawing in, fr *span* to draw, pull] – **spastically** *adv,* **spasticity** *n*

**²spastic** *n* **1** someone who is suffering from SPASTIC PARALYSIS or a condition, esp CEREBRAL PALSY, involving paralysis and muscular incoordination from birth **2** *derog* a clumsy or ineffectual person

**spastic paralysis** *n* paralysis with involuntary contraction or uncontrolled movements of the affected muscles – compare CEREBRAL PALSY

**¹spat** /spat/ *past of* SPIT

**²spat** *n, pl* **spats,** *esp collectively* **spat** a young BIVALVE (animal having a shell composed of two hinged halves), esp an oyster [origin unknown]

**³spat** *n* **1** a cloth or leather gaiter covering the instep and ankle **2** a streamlined covering for an aircraft wheel [short for *spatterdash* (legging), fr ¹*spatter* + ¹*dash*]

**⁴spat** *n* **1** *NAm* a light splash ⟨*a* ~ *of rain*⟩ **2** *chiefly dial* a slap, smack **3** *informal* a brief petty quarrel or outburst *synonyms see* ²QUARREL [prob imit]

**⁵spat** *vi* **-tt-** *NAm* **1** to quarrel pettily or briefly **2** to strike with a sound like that of rain falling in large drops

**¹spatchcock** /'spachˌkok/ *n* a fowl that is dressed, split open, and cooked by frying or grilling immediately after its slaughter [prob alter. of *spitchcock*]

**²spatchcock** *vt* **1** to cook (a fowl or small game bird) by splitting along the backbone and frying or grilling **2** to insert or put together (written material) in a forced or incongruous way

**spate** /spayt/ *n* **1** flood ⟨*a river in full* ~⟩ **2a** *taking sing or pl vb* a large number or amount, esp occurring in a short space of time ⟨*the recent* ~ *of fire bombs – The Guardian*⟩ **b** a sudden or strong outburst; a rush ⟨*a* ~ *of anger*⟩ [ME]

**spathe** /spaydh/ *n* a large sheathing leaflike structure (BRACT) or pair of bracts enclosing the flower head of a plant, esp a SPADIX (spike of tiny tightly packed flowers) on the same stem ⟨*the* ~ *of cuckoopint*⟩ [NL *spatha,* fr L, broad sword – more at SPADE]

**spathic** /'spathik/ *adj, of a mineral or ore* resembling the mineral SPAR; *esp* splitting easily or tending to split into flakes or thin layers [Ger *spath, spat* spar; akin to OHG *spān* chip – more at SPOON]

**spathulate** /'spathyoolət/ *adj, esp of a plant part* spatulate ⟨~ *petals of a flower*⟩ [LL *spathula, spatula* spatula]

**spatial, spacial** /'spaysh(ə)l/ *adj* relating to, occupying, occurring in, or having the character of space [L *spatium* space – more at SPEED] – **spatially** *adv,* **spatiality** *n*

**spatiotemporal** /ˌspayshioh'temp(ə)rəl/ *adj* **1** having both spatial and temporal qualities **2** of space-time [L *spatium* + *tempor-, tempus* time – more at TEMPORAL] – **spatiotemporally** *adv*

**spätlese** /'shpaytˌlayzə/ (Ger ʃpɛːtleːzə)/ *n, often cap* a German and Austrian white TABLE WINE made from late-gathered and therefore riper grapes [Ger, fr *spät* late + *lese* harvest, vintage]

**¹spatter** /'spatə/ *vt* **1** to splash or sprinkle (as if) with drops of liquid; *also* to soil in this way ⟨*his coat was ~ed with mud*⟩ **2** to scatter (as if) by splashing or sprinkling ⟨*~ water*⟩ **3** to injure by aspersion; defame ⟨*~ his good reputation*⟩ *~ vi* to spurt out in scattered drops ⟨*blood ~ing everywhere*⟩ [akin to Flem *spetteren* to spatter]

**²spatter** *n* **1a** the act or process of spattering **b** the sound of spattering **2** a drop or splash spattered on something, or a spot or stain due to spattering

**spatula** /'spatyoolə, -chələ/ *n* any of various implements typically having a flat thin dull-edged blade and used esp for spreading or mixing soft substances (e g food or paint), scooping something (e g powdered chemicals), or lifting △ scapula [LL, spoon, spatula, dim. of L *spatha* spoon, sword – more at ³SPADE]

**spatulate** /'spatyoolat, -chə-/ *adj* shaped like a spatula ⟨*~ spines of a caterpillar*⟩; *esp, of a leaf* having a broad rounded tip and a narrow base

**spavin** /'spavin/ *n* a swelling; *esp* a bony enlargement or soft swelling of a horse's HOCK (leg joint equivalent to the ankle) associated with strain [ME *spavayne*, fr MF *espavain*] – **spavined** *adj*

**¹spawn** /spawn/ *vt* **1a** *of an aquatic animal* to produce or deposit (eggs) **b** to induce (fish) to spawn **c** to plant with mushroom spawn **2** to bring forth, esp abundantly; generate *~ vi* **1** to deposit spawn **2** to produce young, esp in large numbers [ME *spawnen*, fr AF *espaundre*, fr OF *espandre* to spread out, expand, fr L *expandere*] – **spawner** *n*

**²spawn** *n* **1** the mass of eggs of an aquatic animal (e g a frog, fish, or oyster) that lays many small eggs together **2** *taking sing or pl vb* offspring, product; *esp* numerous offspring **3** MYCELIUM (rootlike network of filaments making up most of the body of a fungus); *esp* mycelium prepared for propagating mushrooms

**spay** /spay/ *vt* to remove the ovaries of (a female animal) [ME *spayen*, fr MF *espeer* to cut with a sword, fr OF, fr *espee* sword, fr L *spatha* sword – more at SPADE]

**speak** /speek/ *vb* **spoke** /spohk/; **spoken** /'spohkən/ *vi* **1a** to utter words or articulate sounds with the ordinary voice; talk **b(1)** to give voice to thoughts or opinions ⟨*why don't you ~ for yourself?* – H W Longfellow⟩ **b(2)** to exchange remarks with someone, esp in greeting ⟨*she saw me but she didn't ~*⟩ **b(3)** to be on speaking terms ⟨*still were not ~ing after the dispute*⟩ **c(1)** to address a group ⟨*the professor spoke on his latest discoveries*⟩ **c(2)** to address one's remarks ⟨*I shall ~ to that point shortly*⟩ **2a** to express thoughts or feelings in writing ⟨*diaries that ~ of his desire for fame*⟩ **b** to express oneself **c** to act as spokesman *for* ⟨*spoke for the whole group*⟩ **3a** to express thoughts or feelings by other than verbal means ⟨*actions ~ louder than words*⟩ **b** to make a communication; convey meaning or significance ⟨*nature ~s to us ... through our senses* – Susanne K Langer⟩ **4** to make a claim *for*; reserve ⟨*several of the new houses are already spoken for*⟩ **5** to make a characteristic or natural sound ⟨*all at once the thunder spoke* – George Meredith⟩ **6** to be indicative or suggestive ⟨*his battered shoes spoke of a long journey*⟩ *~ vt* **1a** to utter with the speaking voice; pronounce **b** to express with the voice; declare ⟨*free to ~ their minds*⟩ **2** to make known in writing **3** to (be able to) use in oral communication ⟨*~s Spanish*⟩ **4** to convey by other than verbal means; reveal ⟨*his eager smile... spoke devotion* – Hugh Walpole⟩ [ME *speken*, fr OE *sprecan, specan*; akin to OHG *sprehhan* to speak, Gk *spharageisthai* to crackle] – **speakable** *adj* – **so to speak** – used as an apologetic qualification for an imprecise, unusual, ambiguous, or unclear phrase ⟨*this bus service has gone downhill*, so to speak⟩ – **to speak of** worthy of mention or notice – usu neg ⟨*no talent to speak of*⟩ – see also **speak the same** LANGUAGE, **in a** MANNER **of speaking**

*synonyms* Speak, talk, discourse, converse, chat, gossip, and chatter all mean "express thoughts by pronouncing words". Speak and talk, the most general, are partly interchangeable, but speak rather than talk suggests either a less continuous flow ⟨*scarcely spoke when we met*⟩ or, like discourse, a formal address to a group ⟨*spoke at the meeting*⟩ ⟨*discoursed on nuclear physics*⟩. Talk, converse, chat, and gossip imply a conversation between people. Converse suggests a serious discussion; chat and gossip suggest familiar talk about trifles, with gossip implying in addition the ex-change of behind-the-scenes information. Chatter implies fast, incessant, and perhaps irritating monologue or dialogue about very little.

**speak out** *vi* **1** to speak loudly enough to be heard **2** to speak boldly; express an opinion frankly ⟨*spoke out on the issues*⟩

**speak up** *vi* **1** to speak more loudly – often imper **2** to express an opinion freely ⟨*speak up for truth and justice* – Clive Bell⟩

**speakeasy** /'speek,eezi/ *n* a place where alcoholic drinks were illegally sold during PROHIBITION in the USA in the 1920s and 30s [fr the need to *speak easy* (softly) in ordering illicit goods]

**speaker** /'speekə/ *n* **1a** someone who speaks; *specif* one who speaks a specified language ⟨*an Italian-speaker*⟩ **b** someone who makes a public speech **c** someone who acts as a spokesman **2** the presiding officer of a debating or lawmaking assembly (e g the HOUSE OF COMMONS) **3** a loudspeaker

**speakership** 'speekəship/ *n* the position of speaker, esp of a lawmaking body

**speaking** /'speeking/ *adj* **1a** capable of speech; *also* able to speak a specified language ⟨*French-speaking*⟩ **b** containing chiefly native speakers of a specified language – usu in combination ⟨*English-speaking countries*⟩ **2** highly significant or expressive; eloquent **3** being a close or vivid representation ⟨*a ~ portrait of her daughter*⟩

**speaking tube** *n* a pipe through which conversation may be conducted (e g between different parts of a building)

**¹spear** /spiə/ *n* **1** a thrusting or throwing weapon with long shaft and sharp head or blade used esp by hunters or foot soldiers **2** a sharp-pointed instrument with barbs used in spearing fish **3** a spearman [ME *spere*, fr OE; akin to OHG *sper* spear, L *sparus*]

**²spear** *adj* paternal, male ⟨*the ~ side of the family*⟩ – compare DISTAFF [¹*spear*]

**³spear** *vt* to pierce, strike, or take hold of (as if) with a spear ⟨*~ salmon*⟩ ⟨*~ed a sausage from the dish*⟩ – **spearer** *n*

**⁴spear** *n* a usu young blade, shoot, or sprout (e g of asparagus or grass) [alter. of ¹*spire*]

**⁵spear** *vi, of a plant* to thrust a spear upwards

**spearfish** /-,fish/ *n, pl* **spearfish, spearfishes** any of several large powerful sea fishes (genus *Tetrapturus*) related to the MARLINS and SAILFISHES

**speargun** /'spiə,gun/ *n* a device used for firing a spear in underwater fishing

**¹spearhead** /-,hed/ *n* **1** the sharp-pointed head of a spear **2** a leading element or force in a development or course of action ⟨*the ~ of propaganda is the slogan*⟩

**²spearhead** *vt* to serve as leader or leading force of

**spearman** /-,man/ *n* someone armed with a spear

**spearmint** /-,mint/ *n* a common European plant (*Mentha spicata*) of the mint family that has spikes of pink or lilac flowers and strong-smelling leaves from which an aromatic oil, used as a flavouring, is obtained

**spearwort** /'spiə,wuht/ *n* any of several Eurasian plants (esp *Ranunculus flammula* and *Ranunculus lingua*) of the buttercup family, that grow esp in wet and marshy places and have yellow flowers and spear-shaped leaves

**spec** /spek/ *n, chiefly Br informal* a speculation ⟨*one company worth trying as a ... ~* – The Economist⟩ – **on spec** *Br informal* as a risk or speculation; in the hope of finding or obtaining something desired ⟨*the play may be sold out, but it would be worth going to the theatre* on spec⟩

**¹special** /'spesh(ə)l/ *adj* **1** distinguished from others of the same category, esp because in some way superior **2** held in particular esteem ⟨*a ~ friend*⟩ **3** of or constituting a (biological) species; SPECIFIC **4** **4** other than or in addition to the usual ⟨*a ~ day of thanksgiving*⟩ ⟨*a ~ edition of a newspaper*⟩ **5** designed or undertaken for a particular end, occasion, or need ⟨*devised a ~ method of restoring paintings*⟩ [ME, fr OF or L; OF *especial*, fr L *specialis* individual, particular, fr *species* species] – **specially** *adv*, **specialness** *n*

*usage* Although special(ly) and especial(ly) are interchangeable in almost all contexts, some careful writers recognize a distinction between special(ly) meaning "for a particular purpose" ⟨*a special train*⟩ ⟨*specially chosen for the job*⟩ and especial(ly) meaning "more than others" ⟨*an especial friend*⟩ ⟨*not especially clever*⟩.

**²special** *n* **1** something that is not part of a regular series **2** one who or that which is reserved or produced for a special use, occasion, or treatment ⟨*caught the commuter ~ to work*⟩ **3** *Br* SPECIAL CONSTABLE; *esp* B SPECIAL

**Special Branch** *n taking sing or pl vb, Br* a police department concerned with political security

**special constable** *n, Br* a person employed as a policeman when extra assistance is needed (e g in times of emergency)

**special deposit** *n* a percentage of the total deposits of all banks that is required to be deposited with the Bank of England, thus restricting the availability of credit

**special drawing right** *n* a right to buy additional foreign currency from the International Monetary Fund

**special effect** *n usu pl* an unusual visual or acoustic effect; *esp* one simulated by artificial means (e g photographic techniques) to create an illusion of reality in a film or television programme ⟨King Kong *was noted for its* ~s⟩

**specialism** /'spesh(ə)l,iz(ə)m/ *n* **1** specialization in an occupation or branch of knowledge **2** a field of specialization; a speciality

**specialist** /'spesh(ə)list/ *n* **1a** someone who devotes him-/herself to a special occupation or branch of knowledge **b** a medical practitioner limiting his/her practice to a specific medical area ⟨*a child* ~⟩ ⟨*an ear, nose, and throat* ~⟩ **2** – see MILITARY RANKS table – **specialist, specialistic** *adj*

**speciality** /,speshi'aləti/ *n* **1** a distinctive mark or quality; *also* the state of having such a mark or quality **2** a special object or class of objects; *esp* a product of a special kind or of special excellence ⟨*bread pudding was mother's* ~⟩ **3a** a special aptitude or skill **b** a particular occupation or branch of knowledge – **speciality** *adj*

**special·ization, -isation** /,speshəliez'aysh(ə)n/; *also* -liz-/ *n* **1** a making or becoming specialized **2a** structural adaptation of a plant or animal part to a particular function, or of an organism for life in a particular environment **b** a plant or animal part or an organism adapted by specialization

**special·ize, -ise** /'spesh(ə)liez/ *vt* **1** to specify in detail; particularize **2** to apply or direct to a specific end or use ⟨~d *his study*⟩ ~ *vi* **1** to concentrate one's efforts in a special or limited activity or field **2** to undergo biological specialization; *esp* to change so as to adapt to a particular mode of life or environment (e g in the course of evolution)

**special·ized, -ised** /'speshəliezd/ *adj* intended or fitted for a specific purpose or occupation ⟨~ *personnel*⟩

**special licence** *n* a British form of marriage licence permitting marriage without the publication of banns or at a time and place other than those normally prescribed by law

**special pleading** *n* **1** the allegation of special or new matter in a legal action to offset the effect of matter pleaded by the opposite side, as distinguished from a direct denial of the matter pleaded **2** argument that ignores the damaging or unfavourable aspects of a case

**special school** *n* a school for mentally or physically handicapped children

**special theory of relativity** *n, physics* RELATIVITY 3a

**specialty** /'spesh(ə)lti/ *n* **1** a legal agreement embodied in a formally sealed document **2** *chiefly NAm* a speciality [ME *specialte*, fr MF *especialté*, fr LL *specialitat-, specialitas*, fr L *specialis* special]

**special verdict** *n* a verdict in a court of law in which the jury merely sets out the facts as proved and leaves the court to decide legal guilt or innocence

**speciation** /,speeshi'aysh(ə)n/ *n* the evolutionary development of new biological species; the process, involving physical separation of some organisms from a main interbreeding group, by which a new species is formed – **speciational** *adj*, **speciate** *vi*

**specie** /'speeshi/ *n* money in coin [L *in specie* in kind] – **in specie** in the same or similar form or kind ⟨*ready to return insult* in specie⟩; *also* in coin

**¹species** /'speeshiz; *also* speesiz *the last pron is disliked by some speakers*/ *n, pl* **species** **1a** a class of individuals having common attributes and designated by a common name; *specif* a logical division of a GENUS or more comprehensive class **b(1)** a category in the biological classification of living things that ranks immediately below a GENUS, comprises related organisms or populations potentially capable of interbreeding, and is designated by a two-name form (e g *Homo sapiens*) that consists of the name of a genus followed by a distinguishing Latin or latinized uncapitalized noun or adjective **b(2)** an individual or kind belonging to a biological species **c** a particular kind of atomic nucleus, atom, molecule, or ion **2** the consecrated bread and wine of the ROMAN CATHOLIC or EASTERN ORTHODOX communion **3** *chiefly derog* a kind, sort ⟨*a dangerous* ~ *of crim-*

*inal*⟩ **synonyms** see ¹TYPE [L, appearance, kind, species, fr *specere* to look, look at – more at SPY]

**²species** *adj* belonging to a biological species as distinct from a horticultural variety ⟨*a* ~ *rose*⟩

**¹specific** /spə'sifik/ *adj* **1a** constituting or falling into a specifiable category **b** being or relating to those properties of something that allow it to be assigned to a particular category ⟨*the* ~ *qualities of a drug*⟩ ⟨*a* ~ *distinction between vice and virtue*⟩ **2a** confined to a particular individual, group, or circumstance ⟨*a disease* ~ *to horses*⟩ **b** having a specific rather than a general influence (e g on a body part, disease, or chemical reaction) ⟨*antibodies* ~ *for the smallpox virus*⟩ **3** free from ambiguity; explicit, particular ⟨~ *instructions*⟩ **4** of or constituting a species, esp a biological species ⟨*distinctive* ~ *characters*⟩ **5a** *physics* being any of various arbitrary physical constants; *esp* one relating an expression of quantity to unit mass, volume, or area ⟨~ *gravity*⟩ **b** imposed at a fixed rate per unit (e g of weight or count) ⟨~ *import duties*⟩ – compare AD VALOREM [LL *specificus*, fr L *species*] – **specifically** *adv*

**²specific** *n* **1a** something specially adapted to a purpose or use **b** a drug or remedy having a specific remedial effect on a disease **2** a characteristic quality or trait **3** *pl, chiefly NAm* **3a** particulars ⟨*haggling over the legal and financial* ~s – *Time*⟩ **b** SPECIFICATIONS 2a

**specification** /,spesifi'kaysh(ə)n/ *n* **1** the act or process of specifying **2a** **specifications** *pl,* specification a detailed precise description of something (e g a building or car), esp in the form of a plan or proposal **b** a written description of an invention for which a patent is sought

**specific character** *n* a characteristic distinguishing one biological species from another or from every other species of the same genus

**specific epithet** *n* TRIVIAL NAME (Latin name denoting the species of an animal, plant, etc)

**specific gravity** *n* RELATIVE DENSITY (measure of the density of a substance compared with that of a standard) when the standard substance is pure water – not now used technically in chemistry and physics

**specific heat** *n* the heat, usu measured in joules, required to raise the temperature of a unit mass (e g 1 kilogram) of a substance by unit temperature (e g 1° kelvin)

**specific impulse** *n* the forward force (THRUST) produced per unit rate of consumption of propellant fuel that is a measure of the efficiency of a rocket engine

**specificity** /,spesi'fisəti/ *n* the quality, condition, or property of being specific: e g **a** the condition of affecting, acting on, or being restricted to a particular individual or group of organisms ⟨*host* ~ *of a parasite*⟩ **b** the property of a chemical catalyst of participating in or altering the rate of only one or a few chemical reactions; *also* the property of an ENZYME of speeding up the reactions of only one or a few substances

**specific performance** *n* a remedy in the legal system of EQUITY (protection of rights) that requires performance of a contract strictly or substantially according to its terms, and is ordered where compensatory damages would be inadequate

**specify** /'spesifie/ *vt* **1** to name or state explicitly or in detail **2** to include as an item in a specification ⟨~ *oak flooring*⟩ [ME *specifien*, fr OF *specifier*, fr LL *specificare*, fr *specificus*] – **specifiable** *adj*, **specifier** *n*

**specimen** /'spesimin/ *n* **1a** an item or part typical of a group or whole; a sample **b** a sample of urine, blood, tissue, etc taken for medical examination **2a** a distinct individual within a particular category **b** *chiefly derog* a person, individual *synonyms* see EXAMPLE [L, fr *specere* to look at, look]

**speciosity** /,speeshi'osəti; *also* ,speesi- *the last pron is disliked by some speakers*/ *n, formal* the quality or state of being specious; speciousness

**specious** /'speesh(y)əs/ *adj* **1** having deceptive attraction or fascination **2** superficially sound or genuine but actually false or wrong ⟨~ *reasoning*⟩ **3** *obs* showy △ spacious [ME, beautiful, attractive, fr L *speciosus* beautiful, plausible, fr *species*] – **speciously** *adv*, **speciousness** *n*

**¹speck** /spek/ *n* **1** a small spot or blemish, esp from stain or decay **2a** a small particle ⟨*a* ~ *of sawdust*⟩ **b** something of insignificant size ⟨*the car became a* ~ *on the horizon*⟩ [ME *specke*, fr OE *specca*]

**²speck** *vt* to mark with specks

**¹speckle** /'spekl/ *n* a little speck (e g of colour) [ME; akin to OE *specca*]

²**speckle** *vt* **1** to mark with speckles ⟨*the* ∼d *eggs of a thrush*⟩ **2** to be distributed in or on like speckles

¹**specs** /speks/ *n pl, informal* GLASSES 2b(2) [contr of *spectacles*]

²**specs** *n pl* specifications

**spectacle** /'spektəkl/ *n* **1a** something exhibited as unusual, noteworthy, or entertaining; *esp* a striking or dramatic public display or show **b** an object of scorn or ridicule, esp owing to odd appearance or behaviour ⟨*made a* ∼ *of herself*⟩ **2** *pl* GLASSES 2b(2) [ME, fr MF, fr L *spectaculum*, fr *spectare* to watch, fr *spectus*, pp of *specere* to look, look at – more at SPY]

**spectacled** /'spektəkəld/ *adj* **1** having or wearing glasses **2** having markings suggesting a pair of glasses ⟨*the* ∼ *salamander*⟩

¹**spectacular** /spek'takyoolə/ *adj* of or constituting a spectacle; sensational ⟨*a* ∼ *display of fireworks*⟩ [L *spectaculum*] – **spectacularly** *adv*

²**spectacular** *n* something (e g a stage show) that is spectacular

**spectate** /spek'tayt, '-,-/ *vi* to be present as a spectator (e g at a sports event) [back-formation fr *spectator*]

**spectator** /spek'taytə/ *n* **1** someone who attends an event or activity in order to watch **2** someone who looks on without participating; an onlooker ⟨*rescuers were hampered by* ∼s⟩ [L, fr *spectatus*, pp of *spectare* to watch] – **spectator** *adj*

**spectator sport** *n* a sport which attracts many spectators

**spectra** /'spektrə/ *pl of* SPECTRUM

**spectral** /'spektral/ *adj* **1** of or suggesting a spectre; ghostly **2** of or made by a SPECTRUM (array of the separated components of a wave, esp of light) – **spectrally** *adv*, **spectralness** *n*, **spectrality** *n*

**spectral classification** *n* the classification of stars according to their characteristic spectral lines or bands into ten primary classes each having ten subdivisions

**spectre**, *NAm chiefly* **specter** /'spektə/ *n* **1** a visible ghost **2** something that haunts or perturbs the mind; a phantasm ⟨*the* ∼ *of hunger*⟩ – compare OGRE 2 [Fr *spectre*, fr L *spectrum* apparition, fr *specere* to look, look at – more at SPY]

**spectro-** *comb form* spectrum ⟨spectro*scope*⟩ [NL *spectrum*]

**spectrogram** /'spektrə,gram/ *n* a photograph or diagram of a spectrum (e g of light from a star) [ISV]

**spectrograph** /-,grahf, -,graf/ *n* an instrument (e g a spectroscope) for dispersing radiation (e g light or sound waves) into a spectrum and photographing or mapping the spectrum [ISV] – **spectrographic** *adj*, **spectrographically** *adv*, **spectrography** *n*

**spectroheliogram** /,spektroh'heelyə,gram/ *n* a photograph of the sun made by filtering out or otherwise removing all but one wavelength of the sun's light and showing its bright regions (FACULAE) and cloudy PROMINENCES

**spectroheliograph** /-'heelyə,grahf, -,graf/ *n* an apparatus for making spectroheliograms [ISV] – **spectroheliography** *n*

**spectrohelioscope** /-'heelyə,skohp/ *n* **1** a spectroheliograph **2** an instrument similar to a spectroheliograph used for visual as distinguished from photographic observations [ISV]

**spectrometer** /spek'tromitə/ *n* **1** an instrument used in determining the REFRACTIVE INDEX of a substance **2** a spectroscope – compare MASS SPECTROMETER [ISV] – **spectrometry** *n*, **spectrometric** *adj*

**spectrophotometer** /,spektrohfoh'tomitə/ *n* an instrument for measuring the relative intensities of the ultraviolet, infrared, or visible light in different parts of a spectrum, or the amount of light of a particular wavelength that is absorbed by a chemical sample [ISV] – **spectrophotometry** *n*, **spectrophotometric, spectrophotometrical** *adj*, **spectrophotometrically** *adv*

**spectroscope** /'spektrə,skohp/ *n* an instrument for producing, observing, and analysing a spectrum [ISV] – **spectroscopic, spectroscopical** *adj*, **spectroscopically** *adv*, **spectroscopist** *n*

**spectroscopy** /spek'troskəpi/ *n* **1** the branch of physics that deals with the theory and interpretation of interactions between matter and radiation (e g X rays or light) **2** the production and analysis of spectra using a spectroscope

**spectrum** /'spektrəm/ *n, pl* **spectra** /-trə/, **spectrums 1** an array of the components of an emission (e g of atomic particles) or wave (e g of light) separated and arranged in the order of some varying characteristic (e g wavelength, mass, or energy): e g **1a** a series of images formed when a beam of a particular type of ELECTROMAGNETIC RADIATION (e g X rays, ultraviolet radiation, or RADIO WAVES) is dispersed and then brought to a focus so that the components of the beam are arranged in the order of their wavelengths; *specif, also* **visible spectrum** the series of colours ranging from red, having the longest wavelength, to violet, with the shortest wavelength, that is produced when a beam of WHITE LIGHT (light containing all the visible light wavelengths) is dispersed (e g by a prism) **b** ELECTROMAGNETIC SPECTRUM (the entire range of frequencies or wavelengths of all ELECTROMAGNETIC RADIATION, from GAMMA RAYS to RADIO WAVES) **c** the range of frequencies of sound waves – compare ELECTROMAGNETIC SPECTRUM **2** an interrelated sequence or range ⟨*a wide* ∼ *of interests*⟩ [NL, fr L, apparition – more at SPECTRE]

**specular** /'spekyoolə/ *adj* **1** (having the qualities) of a mirror **2** conducted with the aid of a medical speculum [L *specularis*, fr *speculum* mirror] – **specularly** *adv*, **specularity** *n*

**speculate** /'spekyoolayt/ *vi* **1a** to meditate *on* or ponder *about* a subject; reflect **b** to consider something casually and usu inconclusively ⟨*we may* ∼ *about strangers*⟩ **2** to make an investment or engage in a commercial transaction that involves a business risk in hope of gain; *esp* to buy or sell in expectation of profiting from market fluctuations [L *speculatus*, pp of *speculari* to observe, spy out, watch for, fr *specula* watchtower, fr *specere* to look, look at] – **speculator** *n*

**speculation** /,spekyoo'laysh(ə)n/ *n* the practice or an act of speculation; *esp* (engagement in) one or more transactions that involve business risk in hopes of obtaining commensurate gain

**speculative** /'spekyoolətiv/ *adj* **1** involving, based on, or constituting intellectual speculation; *also* theoretical rather than demonstrable ⟨∼ *knowledge*⟩ **2** marked by questioning curiosity ⟨*students with* ∼ *minds*⟩

**speculum** /'spekyooləm/ *n, pl* **specula** /-lə/ *also* **speculums 1** an instrument inserted into a body passage for medical inspection or treatment **2a** an ancient mirror, usu of bronze or silver **b** a reflector in an optical instrument **3** a patch of colour on the SECONDARY feathers (feathers of the section of the wing nearest the body) of many birds, esp ducks [L, mirror, fr *specere*]

**speech** /speech/ *n* **1a** the communication or expression of thoughts in spoken words **b** the exchange of spoken words; conversation **2a** something that is spoken; an utterance **b** a public discourse; an address **3a** a language, dialect **b** an individual manner of speaking **4** the power of expressing or communicating thoughts by speaking *synonyms* see LANGUAGE [ME *speche*, fr OE *sprǣc, spǣc*; akin to OE *sprecan* to speak – more at SPEAK]

**speech community** *n taking sing or pl vb* a group of people sharing characteristic patterns of vocabulary, grammar, and/or pronunciation

**speech day** *n* an annual ceremonial day at a British school when parents attend, speeches are made, and prizes are presented

**speech form** *n* LINGUISTIC FORM (e g a word or sentence)

**speechify** /'speechifie/ *vi* to make a speech; declaim, esp pompously

**speechless** /-lis/ *adj* **1a** unable to speak; dumb **b** deprived of speech (e g through horror or amazement) **2** refraining from speech; silent **3** incapable of being expressed in words ⟨*a shape of* ∼ *beauty* – P B Shelley⟩ – **speechlessly** *adv*, **speechlessness** *n*

¹**speed** /speed/ *n* **1a** the act or state of moving swiftly; swiftness **b** rate of motion; *specif* the magnitude of a VELOCITY (rate of change of position with time) irrespective of direction **c** power of motion; impetus **2** rate of performance or execution ⟨*tried to increase his reading* ∼⟩ **3a** the sensitivity to light of a photographic film, plate, or paper expressed numerically **b** the power of a lens or optical system (e g in a camera) to admit more or less light ⟨*a high-*speed *lens*⟩ **c** the duration of a photographic exposure **4** *chiefly NAm* a gear in motor vehicles **5** *slang* (any of several stimulant amphetamine drugs chemically related to) METHAMPHETAMINE **6** *archaic* good fortune; success [ME *spede* success, prosperity, swiftness, fr OE *spēd;* akin to OHG *spuot* prosperity, speed, L *spes* hope, *spatium* space] – **at speed 1** while moving fast **2** in a short time

²**speed** *vb* **sped** /sped/, **speeded** *vi* **1a** to make haste ⟨*sped to her bedside*⟩ **b** to travel at excessive or illegal speed ⟨*drivers who are fined for* ∼ing⟩ **2** *archaic* **2a** to meet with success or prosperity **b** to fare; GET ALONG ⟨*I should like to know how you* ∼ – Charles Dickens⟩ ∼ *vt* **1a** to cause to move quickly; hasten **b** to attend to the departure of ⟨∼ *the parting guest*⟩ **2** to discharge; SEND OUT ⟨∼ *an arrow*⟩ **3** *archaic* **3a** to cause or

help to succeed or prosper **b** to promote the success or development of – **speeder** *n*, **speedster** *n*

   *usage* The past tense and past participle **sped** are not used in motoring contexts, or in **speed up** (*we've* **speeded** (not △ **sped**) **up** *the process*).

**speed up** *vb* to (cause to) move, work, or take place faster; accelerate

**speedball** /-ˌbawl/ *n, slang* cocaine mixed with heroin, morphine, or an amphetamine drug, and usu taken by injection

**speedboat** /'speedˌboht/ *n* a fast motorboat

**speed freak** *n, slang* someone who habitually misuses stimulant amphetamine drugs, esp METHAMPHETAMINE

**speed limit** *n* the maximum speed permitted by law in a given area or under specified circumstances

**speedo** /'speedoh/ *n, Br informal* a speedometer

**speedometer** /spee'domitə, spi-/ *n* **1** an instrument for indicating speed; TACHOMETER (instrument measuring speed of rotation) **2** an instrument for indicating the distance travelled as well as the speed of travel; *also* ODOMETER (distance-measuring instrument)

**'speed-ˌreading** *n* a method of reading rapidly by skimming – **speed-read** *vt*

**speed trap** *n* (an operation carried out on) a stretch of road along which police officers are stationed and often concealed, or devices (e g radar) are placed, in order to catch vehicles exceeding the SPEED LIMIT

**'speed-ˌup** *n* an acceleration

**speedway** /-ˌway/ *n* **1** a usu oval racecourse for motorcycles **2** the sport of racing motorcycles usu belonging to professional teams on closed cinder or dirt tracks **3** *NAm* a public road on which fast driving is allowed; *specif* a motorway

**speedwell** /-ˌwel/ *n* any of a genus (*Veronica*) of plants of the foxglove family that mostly have slender stems and small blue or whitish flowers

**Speedwriting** *trademark* – used for a shorthand writing system which uses combinations of the letters of the alphabet instead of symbols

**speedy** /'speedi/ *adj* swift, quick **synonyms** see ¹FAST **antonym** dilatory – **speedily** *adv*, **speediness** *n*

**speer, speir** /spiə/ *vb, chiefly Scot* to ask, enquire [ME (Sc) *speren*, fr OE *spyrian* to follow a track, seek after; akin to OE *spor* spoor]

**speiss** /spies/ *n* a mixture of impure metallic arsenic-containing chemical compounds that forms when certain ores (e g of lead) are smelted [Ger *speise*, lit., food, fr (assumed) VL *spesa*, fr LL *expensa* expense]

**speleology** /ˌspeeli'oləji/ *n* the scientific study or exploration of caves [L *speleum* cave (fr Gk *spēlaion*) + ISV *-o-* + *-logy*] – **speleologist** *n*, **speleological** *adj*

**¹spell** /spel/ *n* **1a** a spoken word or form of words held to have magic power; an incantation **b** a state of enchantment **2** a compelling influence or attraction ⟨*wrote under the* ~ *of Marxist dogma*⟩ [ME, talk, tale, fr OE; akin to OHG *spel* talk, tale, Gk *apeilē* boast]

**²spell** *vb* **spelt** /spelt/, *NAm chiefly* **spelled** /spelt, speld/ *vt* **1a** to name, write, or print the letters of in order or in a specified manner ⟨spelt *my name wrong*⟩ **b** *of letters* to form (a word) ⟨*c-a-t* ~ s *cat*⟩ **2** *chiefly journalistic* to amount to; mean ⟨*crop failure would* ~ *stark famine for the whole region*⟩ ~ *vi* **1** to form words with letters **2** to write words correctly ⟨*graduates who still can't* ~⟩ [ME *spellen*, fr OF *espeller*, of Gmc origin; akin to OE *spell* talk]

   *usage* **Spelt** is the commoner inflection in British English, but **spelled** is the commoner American form.

**spell out** *vt* **1** to read slowly and haltingly **2** to come to understand; discern ⟨*tried in vain to* spell out *his meaning*⟩ **3** to explain clearly and in detail ⟨*compelled to* spell out *the embarrassing truth*⟩

**³spell** *vb* **spelled** /speld/ *vt* **1** to give a brief rest to **2** *chiefly NAm* to relieve for a time; stand in for ⟨*the two guards* ~ed *each other*⟩ ~ *vi, chiefly Austr* to rest from work or activity for a time [ME *spelen*, fr OE *spelian;* akin to OE *spala* substitute]

**⁴spell** *n* **1** a period spent in a job or occupation ⟨*did a* ~ *in catering*⟩ **2a** a short or indefinite period ⟨*waited a* ~ *before advancing*⟩ **b** a stretch of a specified type of weather ⟨*beware of cold* ~s *in April*⟩ **3** a period of illness, depression, or other abnormal physical or mental state ⟨*having one of her bad* ~s⟩; *also* a sudden brief attack or fit of dizziness, shivering, coughing, etc **4** *chiefly Austr* a period of rest from work, activity, or use **5** *archaic* a shift of workers

**⁵spell** *n, N Eng* a small splinter, esp of wood [prob alter. of ME *speld* spark, splinter, fr OE; akin to OHG *spaltan* to split]

**spellbind** /'spelˌbiend/ *vt* **spellbound** /-ˌbownd/ to bind or hold (as if) by a spell or charm; bewitch [back-formation fr *spellbound*]

**spellbinder** /-ˌbiendə/ *n* a speaker of compelling eloquence

**spellbound** /-ˌbownd/ *adj* held (as if) by a spell ⟨*a* ~ *audience*⟩

**spelldown** /'spelˌdown/ *n, NAm* SPELLING BEE

**speller** /'spelə/ *n* **1** someone who spells words **2** a book with exercises for teaching spelling

**spelling** /'speling/ *n* **1** the forming of words from letters according to accepted usage; orthography **2** the sequence of letters that make up a particular word

**spelling bee** *n* a spelling competition

**spelling pronunciation** *n* an artificial pronunciation of a word (e g of *forehead* as /'fawhed/ rather than /'forid/) based on the spelling

**¹spelt** /spelt/ *n* a primitive wheat (*Triticum spelta*) with light red grains borne in pairs, that was formerly widely cultivated [ME, fr OE, fr LL *spelta*, of Gmc origin; akin to MHG *spelte* split piece of wood, OHG *spaltan* to split – more at SPILL]

**²spelt** *chiefly Br past of* ²SPELL

**spelter** /'speltə/ *n* zinc; *esp* zinc containing impurities and cast in slabs for commercial use [prob modif of MD *speauter*]

**speltz** /spelts/ *n* spelt [Ger *spelz*, fr OHG *spelza*, fr LL *spelta*]

**spelunker** /spi'lungkə/ *n, NAm* someone who makes a hobby of exploring and studying caves [L *spelunca* cave, fr Gk *spēlynx;* akin to Gk *spēlaion* cave] – **spelunking** *n*

**spence** /spens/ *n, archaic* a pantry [ME, fr MF *despense*, fr ML *dispensa*, fr L, fem of *dispensus*, pp of *dispendere* to weigh out – more at DISPENSE]

**spencer** /'spensə/ *n* a short waist-length jacket [George John, 2nd Earl *Spencer* †1834 E politician]

**Spencerian** /spen'siəriən/ *adj* of Herbert Spencer or Spencerianism [Herbert *Spencer* †1903 E philosopher]

**Spencerianism** /spen'siərianiz(ə)m/ *n* the philosophy of Herbert Spencer based on a conception of the mechanically determined evolution of the cosmos from relative simplicity to relative complexity

**spend** /spend/ *vb* **spent** /spent/ *vt* **1** to use up or pay out; expend ⟨~ *£90 on a new suit*⟩ **2a** to wear out; exhaust ⟨*the storm gradually* spent *itself*⟩ **b** to consume wastefully; squander ⟨*the forests are not ours to* ~⟩ **3** to cause or permit to elapse; pass ⟨spent *the summer at the beach*⟩ **4** to give up; sacrifice ~ *vi* **1** to pay out resources, esp money **2** to become expended or consumed – see also **spend** a PENNY [ME *spenden*, fr OE & OF; OE *spendan*, fr L *expendere* to expend; OF *despendre*, fr L *dispendere* to weigh out – more at DISPENSE] – **spendable** *adj*, **spender** *n*

**spending money** /'spending/ *n* POCKET MONEY

**spendthrift** /-ˌthrift/ *n* one who spends carelessly or wastefully – **spendthrift** *adj*

**Spenglerian** /speng'gliəriən/ *adj* of the theory of world history developed by Oswald Spengler which holds that all major cultures undergo similar cyclical developments from birth to maturity to decay [Oswald *Spengler* †1936 Ger philosopher] – **Spenglerian** *n*

**Spenserian sonnet** /spen'siəriən/ *n* a sonnet consisting of three interlocked groups of four lines (QUATRAINS) and a two-line group (COUPLET) with a rhyme scheme *abab bcbc cdcd ee* [Edmund *Spenser* †1599 E poet]

**Spenserian stanza** *n* a division of a poem (STANZA) consisting of eight lines of five IAMBS each and an ALEXANDRINE (line of 12 syllables), rhyming in the pattern *ababbcbcc*

**spent** /spent/ *adj* **1a** used up; consumed **b** exhausted of active or useful components or qualities ⟨~ *grain*⟩ ⟨~ *matches*⟩ **2** drained of energy; exhausted ⟨~ *after his nightlong vigil*⟩ **3** exhausted of spawn or sperm ⟨*a* ~ *salmon*⟩ [ME, fr pp of *spenden* to spend]

**sperm** /spuhm/ *n, pl* **sperms**, *esp collectively* **sperm 1a** the male fertilizing liquid; semen **b** a male GAMETE (mature reproductive cell); *specif* a spermatozoon **2** a product (e g spermaceti or oil) of the SPERM WHALE [ME, fr MF *esperme*, fr LL *spermat-, sperma*, fr Gk, lit., seed; akin to Gk *speirein* to sow – more at SPROUT]

**sperm-** /spuhm-/, **spermo-**, **sperma-**, **spermi-** *comb form* seed; germ; sperm ⟨sperma*theca*⟩ ⟨spermi*cidal*⟩ [Gk *sperm-, spermo-*, fr *sperma*]

**spermaceti** /ˌspuhmə'seeti, -'seti/ *n* a waxy solid obtained from the oil of whales, esp SPERM WHALES, and used in ointments, cosmetics, and candles [ME *sperma cete,* fr ML *sperma ceti* whale sperm]

**spermagonium** /ˌspuhmə'gohniəm/ *n, pl* **spermagonia** /-niə/ a flask-shaped or flattened capsule in which spermatia are produced in some fungi and lichens [NL, fr *sperm-* + Gk *gonos* procreation – more at ARCHEGONIUM]

**spermary** /'spuhməri/ *n* an organ (eg a testis) in which male reproductive cells are developed [NL *spermarium,* fr Gk *sperma*]

**spermat-** /spuhmat-/, **spermato-** *comb form* sperm- ⟨spermati*d*⟩ ⟨spermato*cyte*⟩ [MF, fr LL, fr Gk, fr *spermat-, sperma*]

**spermatheca** /ˌspuhmə'theekə/ *n* a sac for sperm storage in the female reproductive tract of many INVERTEBRATE animals [NL, fr *sperm-* + *theca*] – **spermathecal** *adj*

**spermatic** /spuh'matik/ *adj* relating to, resembling, carrying, or full of sperm ⟨∼ *duct*⟩

**spermatic cord** *n* a cord that suspends the testis within the scrotum and contains the VAS DEFERENS (sperm-carrying duct) and vessels and nerves of the testis

**spermatid** /'spuhmətid/ *n* any of the cells that are formed by division of the secondary spermatocytes and that differentiate into spermatozoa

**spermatium** /spuh'maytiˌəm, -shiˌəm/ *n, pl* **spermatia** /-tiə, -shiə/ a cell that functions or is held to function as a male GAMETE (reproductive cell) in some lower plants (eg fungi and algae) and is incapable of movement [NL, fr Gk *spermation,* dim. of *spermat-, sperma*] – **spermatial** *adj*

**spermatocide** /'spuhmətəsied, spuh'matəsied/ *n* a spermicide – **spermatocidal** *adj*

**spermatocyte** /'spuhmətəsiet, spuh'matəsiet/ *n* a cell giving rise to SPERM CELLS; *esp* a cell of the last generation or next to the last generation preceding the spermatozoae

**spermatogenesis** /ˌspuhmətə'jenəsis, ˌspuhˌmatə'jenəsis/ *n* the process of male GAMETE (reproductive cell) formation including CELL DIVISION by MEIOSIS and transformation of the four resulting spermatids into spermatozoa [NL] – **spermatogenic, spermatogenetic** *adj*

**spermatogonium** /ˌspuhmətə'gohnyəm, -niˌəm/ *n, pl* **spermatogonia** /-nyə, -niˌə/ a male GERM CELL that divides to produce the reproductive cells [NL, fr *spermat-* + Gk *gonos* procreation – more at ARCHEGONIUM] – **spermatogonial** *adj*

**spermatophore** /spuh'matəˌfaw, 'spuhmətohˌfaw/ *n* a capsule, packet, or mass enclosing spermatozoa extruded by the male and conveyed to the female in the insemination of various INVERTEBRATE animals (eg the spider) [ISV]

**spermatophyte** /spuh'matəˌfiet, 'spuhmətəˌfiet/ *n* any of a group (Spermatophyta) of higher plants that produce seeds, including the conifers and FLOWERING PLANTS [deriv of NL *spermat-* + Gk *phyton* plant – more at PHYT-] – **spermatophytic** *adj*

**spermatozoid** /ˌspuhmətə'zohˌid/ *n* a male GAMETE (reproductive cell) of lower plants (eg algae) that is capable of movement and is usu produced in an ANTHERIDIUM [ISV, fr NL *spermatozoa*]

**spermatozoon** /-'zohˌən/ *n, pl* **spermatozoa** /-'zohˌə/ 1 a male GAMETE (reproductive cell) of an animal, having a rounded or elongated head and a long tail-like FLAGELLUM (whiplike structure) used for movement 2 a spermatozoid [NL, fr *spermat-* + *-zoon*] – **spermatozoal** *adj*

**sperm cell** *n* a male GAMETE (reproductive cell); a cell (GERM CELL) that gives rise to male gametes

**spermi-** /spuhmi-/ – see SPERM-

**spermicide** /'spuhmisied/ *n* a substance that kills sperm, esp as a contraceptive – called also SPERMATOCIDE – **spermicidal** *adj*

**spermidine** /'spuhmideen, -din/ *n* an ALIPHATIC (composed of straight or branching chains of carbon atoms) chemical compound, $C_7H_{19}N_3$, that is an AMINE and is found esp in semen [*sperm-* + *-idine*]

**spermiogenesis** /ˌspuhmiˌoh'jenəsis/ *n* 1 transformation of a SPERMATID into a spermatozoon 2 SPERMATOGENESIS (formation of sperm) [NL, fr *spermium* spermatozoon + *-o-* + L *genesis*]

**sperm nucleus** *n* either of the two nuclei that derive from the GENERATIVE NUCLEUS of a POLLEN GRAIN and function in the fertilization of a SEED PLANT

**spermo-** – see SPERM-

**sperm oil** *n* a pale yellow oil obtained from the SPERM WHALE

**sperm whale** *n* a large TOOTHED WHALE (*Physeter macroce-*

*phalus*), esp of tropical and subtropical seas, that has a vast blunt head in the front part of which is a cavity containing a mixture of SPERMACETI (white waxy substance) and oil [short for *spermaceti whale*]

**-spermy** /-spuhmi/ *comb form* (→ *n*) state of exhibiting or resulting from (a specified type of) fertilization ⟨*agamo*spermy⟩ [Gk *sperma* seed, sperm]

**sperrylite** /'speriliet/ *n* a mineral, $PtAs_2$, consisting of a platinum ARSENIDE that occurs in grains and minute crystals of a bluish-white colour [Francis L *Sperry,* 19th-c Can chemist + E *-lite*]

**spessartine** /'spesəteen/ *n* spessartite

**spessartite** /'spesətiet/ *n* a GARNET (type of mineral) that contains manganese and aluminium and varies from pale yellow to deep orange in colour [Fr, fr *Spessart* mountain range in S Germany]

**¹spew** /spyooh/ *vb* 1 to vomit 2 to pour out in great quantity or force; gush ⟨*pornography* ∼ing *from the presses*⟩ ⟨*a volcano* ∼ing *ash and lava*⟩ [ME *spewen,* fr OE *spīwan;* akin to OHG *spīwan* to spit, L *spuere,* Gk *ptyein*] – **spewer** *n*

**²spew** *n* 1 vomit 2 material that gushes or is ejected from a source

**sphagnum** /'sfagnəm, 'spagnəm/ *n* 1 any of an order (Sphagnales, containing the single genus *Sphagnum*) of atypical mosses that grow only in wet acid areas (eg bogs), where their remains become compacted with other plant debris to form peat 2 a mass of sphagnum plants [NL, genus name, fr L *sphagnos,* a moss, fr Gk]

**sphalerite** /'sfaləriet/ *n* a widely distributed ore of zinc composed essentially of ZINC SULPHIDE, ZnS [Ger *sphalerit,* fr Gk *sphaleros* deceitful, fr *sphallein* to cause to fall – more at SPILL; fr its often being mistaken for galena]

**sphene** /sfeen/ *n* a black or brown mineral, $CaTiSiO_5$, that is a silicate of calcium and titanium and often contains varying amounts of other chemical elements (eg manganese and iron) – called also TITANITE [Fr *sphène,* fr Gk *sphēn* wedge – more at SPOON; fr the shape of its crystals]

**sphenodon** /'sfeenədon, 'sfenə-/ *n* TUATARA (lizardlike reptile) [NL, deriv of Gk *sphēn* wedge + *odōn* tooth – more at TOOTH] – **sphenodont** *adj*

**sphenoid** /'sfenoyd/ *n or adj* (a bone at the base of the skull) shaped like a wedge [NL *sphenoides* wedge-shaped, fr Gk *sphēnoeidēs,* fr *sphēn* wedge] – **sphenoidal** *adj*

**spher-** /sfiər-/, **sfer-**, **sphero-** *also* **sphaer-**, **sphaero-** *comb form* sphere ⟨spher*ule*⟩ ⟨sphero*meter*⟩ [L *sphaer-,* fr Gk *sphair-, sphairo-,* fr *sphaira* sphere]

**spheral** /'sfiərəl/ *adj* 1 spherical 2 symmetrical, harmonious

**¹sphere** /sfiə/ *n* 1a any of the revolving spherical transparent shells in which, according to ancient astronomy, the stars, sun, planets, and moon are set b a globe depicting such a sphere; *broadly* a globe 2a a globular body; a ball b a planet or star c (a volume or solid enclosed by) a surface consisting of all points at a given distance in space from a point constituting its centre 3 natural, normal, or proper place; *esp* social position or class 4 a field of action, existence, or influence ⟨*out of my* ∼⟩ 5 *poetic* the apparent surface of the heavens of which half forms the dome of the visible sky [ME *spere* globe, celestial sphere, fr MF *espere,* fr L *sphaera,* fr Gk *sphaira,* lit., ball]

**²sphere** *vt* 1 to place or enclose in a sphere 2 to form into a sphere

**sphere of influence** *n* a territorial area within which the political influence or the interests of one nation are dominant

**spherical** /'sferikl/ *also* **spheric** *adj* 1 having the form of a sphere or of any of its segments 2 relating to or dealing with a sphere or its properties; *specif* of or being geometry which takes the surface of a sphere as analogous to the plane, and arcs of GREAT CIRCLES (circles having the same centre as the sphere) as analogous to straight lines ⟨∼ *triangle*⟩ ⟨∼ *trigonometry*⟩ – **spherically** *adv*, **sphericity** *n*

**spherical aberration** *n* ABERRATION (failure to produce a true or clear image) in an optical system that is caused by the spherical form of a lens or mirror

**spherical angle** *n* the angle between two intersecting arcs of GREAT CIRCLES (circles having the same centre as the sphere) of a sphere measured by the angle formed by the tangents to the arcs at the point of intersection

**spherical coordinate** *n* a point that defines a position in space; any of three COORDINATES that are used to locate a point in space and that comprise the radius of the sphere on which the point lies, the angle formed by the point, the centre of the sphere, and a given axis of the sphere, and the angle between the plane of the first angle and a given reference plane through the axis of the sphere

**spherics** /'sferiks/ *n taking sing or pl vb* ATMOSPHERICS

**spheroid** /'sfiəroyd/ *n* a mathematical figure resembling a sphere – **spheroidal** *adj*, **spheroidally** *adv*

**spherometer** /ˌsfiə'romitə/ *n* an instrument for measuring the curvature of a surface [ISV]

**spheroplast** /'sferəplahst, 'sfiərə-/ *n* a modified bacterium that is characterized by partial loss of the cell wall and by increased sensitivity to the concentration of substances dissolved in the medium in which it occurs and that can result from various nutritional or environmental factors or be induced artificially by digesting the bacterial wall with the enzyme LYSOZYME

**spherule** /'sfiər(y)oohl, 'sfe-/ *n* a little sphere or globule [LL *sphaerula*, dim. of L *sphaera* sphere]

**spherulite** /'sfiər(y)oo,liet, 'sfe-/ *n* a usu spherical crystalline body of radiating crystal fibres often found in glasslike volcanic rocks (e g obsidian) – **spherulitic** *adj*

**sphery** /'sfiari/ *adj, poetic* 1 celestial 2 round, spherical

**sphincter** /'sfingktə/ *n* a muscular ring surrounding and able to contract or close a bodily opening (e g of the bladder or anus) [LL, fr Gk *sphinktēr*, lit., band, fr *sphingein* to bind tight] – **sphincteral** *adj*

**sphingid** /'sfinjid/ *n* a hawkmoth [deriv of Gk *sphing-, sphinx* sphinx]

**sphingosine** /'sfing·gəsin, -seen/ *n* a chemical compound, $C_{18}H_{33}(OH)_2NH_2$, that is an ALCOHOL with atoms arranged in a long chain structure and is found esp in nervous tissue and cell membranes [Gk *sphingos* (gen of *sphinx*) + E *-ine;* fr riddles it posed to its first investigators]

**sphinx** /sfinks/ *n, pl* **sphinxes, sphinges** /-jeez/ 1 an enigmatic or mysterious person 2 an ancient Egyptian image in the form of a recumbent lion having the head of a human, ram, or hawk 3 a hawkmoth [ME *Spynx* female monster in Gk mythology who killed everyone who failed to solve a riddle she asked, fr L *Sphinx*, fr Gk; akin to Gk *sphinktēr* sphincter]

**sphygmograph** /'sfigmə,grahf, -,graf/ *n* an instrument that records graphically the movements or character of the pulse in the arteries [Gk *sphygmos* pulse + ISV *-graph*] – **sphygmographic** *adj*, **sphygmography** *n*

**sphygmomanometer** /ˌsfigməmə'nomitə/ *n* an instrument for measuring blood pressure, esp the blood pressure in the arteries [Gk *sphygmos* pulse + ISV *manometer*] – **sphygmomanometric** *adj*, **sphygmomanometrically** *adv*, **sphygmomanometry** *n*

**spic, spick** /spik/ *n, NAm derog* SPIK (Spanish American person)

**spica** /'spiekə/ *n, pl* **spicae** /'spiekie, 'spiesee/, **spicas** a figure-of-eight bandage used to immobilize a limb, esp at a joint [L, spike of grain – more at SPIKE]

**spicate** /'spiekayt/ *adj* pointed, spiked; *specif* arranged in the form of a spike ⟨*a* ∼ *inflorescence*⟩ [L *spicatus,* pp of *spicare* to arrange in the shape of heads of grain, fr *spica*]

**spiccato** /spi'kahtoh/ *n or adj, pl* **spiccatos** (a technique, performance, or passage) played using the bow so that it rebounds from the string – used as a direction in music for stringed instruments [It, pp of *spiccare* to detach, pick off]

**¹spice** /spies/ *n, pl* **spices,** (4) **spice 1a** any of various aromatic vegetable products (e g pepper, ginger, or nutmeg) used to season or flavour foods **b** such products collectively **2** something that adds zest or relish ⟨*variety's the very* ∼ *of life* – William Cowper⟩ **3** a pungent or aromatic smell **4** *N Eng dial* a sweet **5** *archaic* a small quantity or amount; a dash [ME, fr OF *espice,* fr LL *species* spices, fr L, species]

**²spice** *vt* **1** to season with spice **2** to add zest or relish to ⟨*cynicism* ∼d *with wit*⟩

**spicebush** /-ˌboosh/ *n* an aromatic N American shrub (*Lindera benzoin*) of the laurel family that bears dense clusters of small yellow flowers followed by red or yellow berries

**spice cake** *n, N Eng dial* a rich fruit cake

**spicery** /'spies(ə)ri/ *n* **1** spices **2** a spicy quality, flavour, or fragrance **3** *archaic* a place where spices are stored

**spick-and-span, spic-and-span** /ˌspik ənd 'span/ *adj* spotlessly clean and tidy; spruce [short for *spick-and-span-new,* fr obs *spick* spike + *and* + *span-new* (brand-new), fr ME, part trans of ON *spānnȳr,* fr *spānn* chip of wood + *nȳr* new]

**spicula** /'spiekyoolə/ *n, pl* **spiculae** /-lie/ a spicule, prickle [NL, fr ML, arrowhead, alter. of L *spiculum,* dim. of *spica* spike of grain] – **spicular** *adj*

**spiculate** /'spikyoolət, -layt/ *adj* covered with or having spicules – **spiculation** *n*

**spicule** /'spikyoohl, 'spie-/ *n* **1** a minute slender pointed usu hard body; *esp* any of the minute calcium- or silicon-containing bodies that together support the tissue of various INVERTEBRATE animals (e g a sponge) **2** a jet of relatively cool gas rising through the lower atmosphere of the sun [NL *spicula* & L *spiculum*] – **spiculiferous** *adj*

**spiculum** /'spikyooləm/ *n, pl* **spicula** /-lə/ an organ having the form of a spicule; *broadly* SPICULE 1 [L, small sharp organ, arrowhead]

**spicy** /'spiesi/ *adj* **1a** having the quality, flavour, or fragrance of spice **b** strongly seasoned with spices; piquant **2** lively, spirited ⟨*a* ∼ *temper*⟩ **3** somewhat scandalous or racy ⟨∼ *gossip*⟩ – **spicily** *adv,* **spiciness** *n*

**spider** /'spiedə/ *n* **1** any of an order (Araneida of the class Arachnida) of INVERTEBRATE animals related to the scorpions, ticks, and mites, having a body with two main divisions, four pairs of legs, and two or more pairs of abdominal organs (SPINNERETS) for spinning threads of silk used in making cocoons for their eggs, nests for themselves, or webs for entangling their prey **2** any of various devices consisting of a frame or skeleton with radiating arms or spokes **3** a support (REST 6) for a snooker cue that is raised on legs to enable the player to hit the ball from above when other balls are in the way **4** *NAm* a cast-iron frying pan originally made with short legs on feet to stand among coals on the hearth [ME, alter. of *spithre;* akin to OE *spinnan* to spin]

**spider beetle** *n* any of a family (Ptinidae) of beetles, the larvae of which are pests of stored produce

**spider crab** *n* any of numerous crabs (esp family Majidae) with extremely long legs and nearly triangular bodies

**spiderman** /'spiedə,man/ *n, chiefly Br* a person who works at great height, esp in erecting steel structures of buildings

**spider mite** *n* RED SPIDER

**spider monkey** *n* any of a genus (*Ateles*) of monkeys of N and S America with long slender limbs, a rudimentary or absent thumb, and a very long prehensile tail

**spider's web** *n* the silken web spun by most spiders and used as a resting place and a trap for small prey; *esp* the geometrically patterned web spun by garden spiders

**spiderweb** /-ˌweb/ *n, NAm* SPIDER'S WEB

**spiderwort** /-ˌwuht/ *n* TRADESCANTIA (type of plant) [fr its spidery leaves]

**spidery** /'spied(ə)ri/ *adj* **1a** resembling a spider in form or manner; *specif* long, thin, and sharply angular like the legs of a spider ⟨∼ *handwriting*⟩ **b** resembling a spider's web; *esp* composed of fine threads or lines in a weblike arrangement ⟨∼ *lace*⟩ **2** infested with spiders

**spiegeleisen** /'shpeegə,liez(ə)n, 'spee-/ *n* PIG IRON (crude iron) that contains 15 to 30 per cent manganese and 4.5 to 6.5 per cent carbon [Ger, fr *spiegel* mirror + *eisen* iron]

**¹spiel** /s(h)peel/ *vb, chiefly NAm informal vi* to talk volubly or extravagantly; spout ∼ *vt* to tell or describe glibly and at length – usu + *off* [Ger *spielen* to play, fr OHG *spilōn;* akin to OE *spilian* to revel] – **spieler** *n*

**²spiel** *n, informal* a glib line of talk, usu designed to influence or persuade; patter

**spier** /'spie·ə/ *n* a spy

**spiffing** /'spifing/ *adj, chiefly Br informal* extremely good; excellent ⟨*auntie is a* ∼ *cook*⟩ – no longer in vogue [E dial. *spiff* smart, well-dressed]

**spiffy** /'spifi/ *adj, chiefly NAm informal* smart, spruce [E dial. *spiff*]

**spifflicate, spifflicate** /'spiflikayt/ *vt, Br chiefly humorous* to defeat or destroy utterly; flatten [origin unknown]

**spigot** /'spigət/ *n* **1** a small plug used to stop up the vent of a cask; a bung **2** the part of a tap, esp on a barrel, which controls the flow **3** a plain end of a piece of piping or guttering that fits into a socket on an adjoining piece; *broadly* a projecting part **4** *NAm* ¹TAP 1b [ME, prob deriv of L *spica* spike of grain]

**spik, spic, spick** /spik/ *n, NAm derog* a Spanish-speaking (Latin) American [alter. of *spig,* short for *spigotty,* prob fr the broken E phrase *no speaka de English* ('I don't speak English'), supposed to be much used by Spanish Americans]

**¹spike** /spiek/ *n* **1** a very large nail **2** a pointed usu metal object or projection: e g **2a** any of a row of pointed iron projections on the top of a wall or fence **b** an upright metal rod on which rejected copy is impaled in a newspaper office **c** any of several metal projections set in the sole and heel of a running shoe to improve grip **3** something resembling a spike: e g **3a** a young mackerel not over 15 centimetres (6 inches) long **b** an unbranched antler of a young deer **4** the act or an instance of spiking in volleyball **5a** a pointed element in a graph or tracing **b** an unusually high and sharply defined maximum (e g on a graph) **6** *pl* TRACK SHOES **7** ACTION POTENTIAL (voltage pulse in a stimulated nerve) **8** *slang* HYPODERMIC NEEDLE [ME, prob fr MD; akin to L *spina* thorn – more at SPINE]

**²spike** *vt* **1** to fasten, attach, or provide with spikes ⟨~ *the soles of climbing boots*⟩ **2** to disable (a cannon loaded at the discharging end) temporarily by driving a spike into the hole through which the charge is ignited **3** to pierce with or impale on a spike; *specif* to reject (newspaper copy) (as if) by impaling on the spike **4a** to add spirits to (a nonalcoholic drink) **b** to add something highly reactive (e g a radioactive tracer) to **5** to drive (a volleyball) from a front-line position sharply downwards into an opponent's court **6** *chiefly NAm* to suppress or thwart completely ⟨~d *the rumour*⟩ – **spiker** *n*

**³spike** *n* **1** an ear of grain **2** an elongated plant INFLORESCENCE (arrangement of flowers on the stem) similar to a RACEME but having the flowers stalkless on the main stem [ME *spik* head of grain, fr L *spica*; akin to L *spina* thorn]

**spiked** /spiekt/ *adj* **1** having an INFLORESCENCE (arrangement of flowers on the stem) that is a spike **2** having a sharp projecting point

**spikelet** /'spieklit/ *n* a small or secondary spike; *specif* any of the small spikes that make up the compound INFLORESCENCE (arrangement of flowers on the stem) of a grass or sedge

**spikenard** /'spieknahd/ *n* (a fragrant ancient ointment believed to have been derived from) an E Indian aromatic plant (*Nardostachys jatamansi*) of the valerian family [ME, fr MF or ML; MF *spicanarde*, fr ML *spica nardi*, lit., spike of nard]

**spike-tooth harrow** *n* a HARROW (implement for breaking up the soil) with straight teeth set in horizontal bars

**spiky** /'spieki/ *adj* **1** having a sharp projecting point or points **2** caustic, aggressive ⟨*a* ~ *retort*⟩

**¹spile** /spiel/ *n* **1** SPIGOT 1 (plug) **2** *NAm* a spout inserted in a tree (e g a SUGAR MAPLE) to draw off sap [prob fr D *spijl* stake; akin to L *spina* thorn – more at SPINE]

**²spile** *vt* to supply with a spile

**spilite** /'spieliet, -leet/ *n* a greenish-grey rock with a composition similar to BASALT that usu occurs in PILLOW LAVAS between beds of marine sediments [Fr, fr Gk *spilos* spot, stain]

**¹spill** /spil/ *vb* **spilt** /spilt/, *NAm chiefly* **spilled** /spilt, spild/ *vt* **1** to cause (blood) to be shed ⟨*soldiers eager to* ~ *their enemies' blood*⟩ **2** to cause or allow (usu liquid) to fall, flow, or run out of a container so as to be lost or wasted, esp accidentally ⟨*spilt his tea all over the table*⟩ **3a** to empty, discharge ⟨*the train spilt its passengers onto the platform*⟩ **b** to empty (a sail) of wind **4** to throw off or out ⟨*a horse* ~ed *him*⟩ **5** *informal* to let out; divulge, disclose ⟨~ *a secret*⟩ ~ *vi* **1a** to flow or fall out, over, or off and become wasted, scattered, or lost **b** to cause or allow something to spill ⟨*don't* ~ *your soup!*⟩ **2** to spread profusely or beyond limits ⟨*crowds spilt into the streets*⟩ **3** to fall from one's place (e g on a horse) – see also **spill the beans**, **cry over spilt** MILK [ME *spillen*, fr OE *spillan* to kill, destroy, squander; akin to OHG *spaltan* to split, L *spolia* spoils, Gk *sphallein* to cause to fall] – **spillable** *adj*, **spillage** *n*, **spiller** *n*

**usage Spilt** is the commoner inflection in British English, but **spilled** is the commoner American form. **Spilt** is the usual British adjectival form ⟨**spilt** *milk*⟩.

**spill over** *vi* to overflow (e g into an adjacent or related area)

**²spill** *n* **1** the act or an instance of spilling; *esp* a fall from a horse or vehicle **2** a quantity spilt; spillage **3** spillway, spill a channel for surplus water to run over or round an obstruction (e g a dam)

**³spill** *n* a splinter or slender piece; *esp* a thin twist of paper or sliver of wood used for lighting a fire [ME *spille*]

**spillikin** /'spilikin/ *n* **1** any of the pieces used in the game of spillikins **2** *pl but taking sing vb* a game in which a set of thin rods or straws is allowed to fall in a heap, from which each player in turn tries to remove them one at a time without disturbing the rest [prob fr obs D *spelleken* small peg]

**spillover** /'spil,ohvə/ *n* **1** the act or an instance of spilling over **2** a quantity that spills over

**spilosite** /'spielə,siet/ *n* a spotted rock or slate produced by the METAMORPHISM (alteration by heat and pressure) of clay

slate by contact with MAGMA (~ molten rock in the earth) [Ger *spilosit*, fr Gk *spilos* spot]

**spilth** /spilth/ *n, archaic* **1** the act or an instance of spilling **2** something spilt

**¹spin** /spin/ *vb* **-nn-**; **spun** /spun/ *vi* **1** to draw out and twist fibre into yarn or thread **2** *esp of a spider or insect* to form a thread by extruding a sticky rapidly hardening liquid **3a** to revolve rapidly; whirl **b** *of wheels* to revolve rapidly without gripping (e g in mud or wet grass) **c** to have the sensation of spinning; reel ⟨*my head is* ~ning⟩ **4** to move swiftly, esp on wheels or in a vehicle **5** to fish with a SPINNING lure **6a** *of an aircraft* to fall in a spin **b** to plunge helplessly and out of control ~ *vt* **1a** to draw out and twist into yarns or threads **b** to produce (yarn or thread) by drawing out and twisting a fibrous material **2** to form (e g a web or cocoon) by spinning **3** to compose and tell (a usu long involved tale) ⟨*a retired clown* ~ning *yarns about circus life*⟩ **4a** to cause to revolve rapidly ⟨~ *a top*⟩ **b** to project (a ball) so as to revolve in the air and deviate from a straight line on bouncing **5** to shape into threadlike form in manufacture; *also* to manufacture by a whirling process **6** to spin-dry – see also **spin a** YARN [ME *spinnen*, fr OE *spinnan*; akin to OHG *spinnan* to spin, L *sponte* voluntarily, Gk *span* to draw – more at SPAN]

**spin out** *vt* **1** to cause to last longer, esp by thrift ⟨spinning out *their meagre rations*⟩ **2** to extend, prolong ⟨spin out *a repair job*⟩ **3** to dismiss (a batsman in cricket) by SPIN BOWLING

**²spin** *n* **1a** the act or an instance of spinning or twirling **b** the whirling motion imparted (e g to a cricket ball) by spinning **2a** an aerial manoeuvre or flight condition in which the aircraft rotates about its vertical and longitudinal axis while plunging steeply downwards, its wings being in a state of complete or partial stall **b** a plunging descent or downward spiral **3** (a measure of) the property of an ELEMENTARY PARTICLE (minute particle of matter) that corresponds to intrinsic ANGULAR MOMENTUM (quantity of rotational motion), that can be thought of as rotation of the particle about an axis through its centre, and that is mainly responsible for magnetic properties ⟨*an electron has a* ~ *of* $+\frac{1}{2}$ *and* $-\frac{1}{2}$⟩ **4** *informal* a short excursion, esp by motor vehicle ⟨*go for a* ~ *in the Rolls*⟩ **5** *informal* a state of mental confusion; a panic ⟨*in a* ~⟩ – compare FLAT SPIN – **spinless** *adj*

**spina bifida** /,spienə 'bifidə/ *n* a congenital condition in which there is a defect in the formation of the spine allowing the MENINGES (membranes surrounding the SPINAL CORD) to protrude and usu associated with disorder of the nerves supplying the lower part of the body [NL, cleft spine]

**spinach** /'spinij, -nich/ *n* **1** a plant (*Spinacia oleracea*) of the goosefoot family cultivated for its edible leaves; *also* the leaves of spinach eaten as a vegetable **2** *NAm informal* something unwanted or irrelevant [MF *espinache, espinage*, fr OSp *espinaca*, fr Ar *isfānākh*, fr Per]

**spinach beet** *n* CHARD (beet with dark green leaves often cooked as a vegetable)

**¹spinal** /'spienl/ *adj* **1** of or situated near the backbone **2a** of or affecting the SPINAL CORD ⟨~ *reflexes*⟩ **b** having the SPINAL CORD functionally isolated (e g by cutting it surgically) from the brain ⟨*experiments on* ~ *animals*⟩ **3** of or resembling a spine – **spinally** *adv*

**²spinal** *n* a spinal anaesthetic

**spinal canal** *n* NEURAL CANAL (canal that contains the SPINAL CORD)

**spinal column** *n* the AXIAL SKELETON of the trunk and tail of a VERTEBRATE animal consisting of a jointed series of vertebrae and protecting the SPINAL CORD; the backbone

**spinal cord** *n* the cord of nervous tissue that extends from the brain lengthwise along the back in the SPINAL CANAL, gives off the SPINAL NERVES, carries impulses to and from the brain, and serves as a centre for initiating and coordinating many reflex actions

**spinal ganglion** *n* a GANGLION (small mass of nerve tissue) on the DORSAL ROOT of each SPINAL NERVE that is one of a series of ganglia containing CELL BODIES of SENSORY (transmitting impulses to the brain) nerves

**spinal nerve** *n* any of the paired nerves that arise from the SPINAL CORD of a VERTEBRATE animal, supply muscles of the trunk and limbs, connect with the nerves of the SYMPATHETIC NERVOUS SYSTEM, and normally form 31 pairs in human beings

**spin bowling** *n* slow bowling in which a cricket ball is made to spin by the bowler and so deviate from a straight line as it bounces – compare SEAM BOWLING – **spin bowler** *n*

**¹spindle** /'spindl/ *n* **1a** a rounded stick with tapered ends used to form and twist the yarn in hand spinning **b** the long slender pin by which the thread is twisted in a SPINNING WHEEL **c** any of various rods or pins holding a bobbin in a textile machine (eg a spinning frame) **d** the pin in the shuttle of a loom **e** the bar or shaft, usu of square section, that carries the knobs and actuates the latch or bolt of a lock **2** something shaped like a spindle: eg **2a** a spindle-shaped figure seen in microscopic sections of dividing cells along which the CHROMOSOMES (strands of gene-carrying material) are distributed **b** MUSCLE SPINDLE (organ in muscle that is sensitive to stretch) **3a** a turned often decorative piece of wood (eg a table leg) **b** NEWEL (principal post in a staircase) **c** a pin or axis that revolves or on which something turns [ME *spindel*, fr OE *spinel*; akin to OE *spinnan* to spin

**²spindle** *vi* **1** to shoot or grow into a long slender stalk **2** to grow to stalk or stem rather than to flower or fruit – **spindler** *n*

**spindle cell** *n* a cell that tapers towards each end; *esp* a slender cell containing a nucleus that is concerned with blood clotting in nonmammalian VERTEBRATE animals and is equivalent to the BLOOD PLATELET of mammals

**'spindle-,legged** *adj* having long spindly legs

**'spindle-,shanked** *adj, informal* spindle-legged

**spindle tree, spindle** *n* any of a genus (*Euonymus* of the family Celastraceae, the spindle tree family) of often evergreen shrubs, small trees, or climbing plants typically having red fruits and hard wood formerly used for spindle making; *esp* a European shrub or small tree (*Euonymus europaeus*)

**spindling** /'spindling/ *adj* spindly

**spindly** /'spindli/ *adj* **1** having an unnaturally tall or slender appearance suggestive of physical weakness ⟨~ *legs*⟩ **2** frail or flimsy in appearance or structure

**spindrift** /'spindrift/ *n* spray blown from waves during a gale at sea [alter. of Sc *speendrift*, fr *speen* to drive before a strong wind + E *drift*]

**,spin-'dry, spin** *vt* to remove water from (wet laundry) by placing in a rapidly rotating perforated drum – **spin-drier** *n*

**spine** /spien/ *n* **1a** SPINAL COLUMN (backbone) **b** something resembling a SPINAL COLUMN or constituting a central axis or chief support **c** the bound edge of a book, usu lettered with the title and author's name **2** a stiff pointed plant part; *esp* one that is a modified leaf or leaf part **3** a sharp rigid projecting part on an animal: eg **3a** a spicule **b** a stiff unsegmented bony structure (RAY) supporting the fin of a fish **c** a pointed prominence on a bone [ME, thorn, spinal column, fr L *spina*; akin to Latvian *spina* twig] – **spined** *adj*

**'spine-,chilling** *adj* terrifying in a sinister way ⟨a ~ *tale of phantoms and black magic*⟩ ⟨the ~ *consequences of a nuclear war*⟩ – **spine-chiller** *n*

**'spine-,freezing** *adj* spine-chilling

**spinel** /spi'nel/ *n* **1** a hard crystalline mineral, $MgAl_2O_4$, consisting of an oxide of magnesium and aluminium that varies from colourless to ruby-red or black and is used as a gem **2** any of a group of minerals that are essentially oxides of magnesium, ferrous iron, zinc, or manganese and occur mostly in METAMORPHIC (altered by heat and pressure) rocks [It *spinella*, dim. of *spina* thorn, fr L]

**spineless** /'spienlis/ *adj* **1** free from spines, thorns, or prickles **2a** having no spinal column; INVERTEBRATE **b** lacking strength of character – **spinelessly** *adv*, **spinelessness** *n*

**spinet** /'spinit, spi'net/ *n* **1** a usu small harpsichord having the strings at an angle to the keyboard **2** SQUARE PIANO – not used technically **3** *NAm* **3a** a small low UPRIGHT PIANO **b** a small electronic organ [It *spinetta*, prob fr Giovanni *Spinetti* fl 1503, its reputed inventor]

**spin fishing** *n* spinning

**spinifex** /'spienifeks/ *n* **1** any of several grasses (genus *Spinifex*) that are common on the sea shores of Australia and SE Asia and have spiny seeds **2** any of several coarse Australian grasses (genus *Triodia*) with spiny leaves [NL, genus name, fr L *spina* + *facere* to make – more at DO]

**spinnaker** /'spinəkə/ *n* a large triangular sail set forward of a yacht's mast on a long light pole and used when sailing in the same direction as the wind [perh alter. of *Sphinx*, name of the yacht that first used this type of sail]

**spinner** /'spinə/ *n* **1** one who or that which spins **2** a fisherman's LURE (artificial bait) that revolves when drawn through the water **3** a usu conical FAIRING (smooth part for reducing

drag) fitted to an aeroplane propeller hub **4** a farm machine with rotary blades that is used in harvesting esp potatoes **5a** a bowler of SPIN BOWLING **b** a ball delivered by such a bowler

**spinneret** /,spinə'ret/ *n* **1** an organ (eg of a spider or caterpillar) for producing threads of silk from the secretion of silk glands **2** *also* **spinnerette** a small metal plate, thimble, or cap with fine holes through which a chemical solution (eg of cellulose) is forced in the spinning of man-made filaments (eg nylon) [*spinner* + *-et*]

**spinney** /'spini/ *n, Br* a small wood with undergrowth; a copse [MF *espinaye* thorny thicket, fr *espine* thorn, fr L *spina*]

**spinning** /'spining/ *n* a method of fishing in which a LURE (artificial bait) is cast by use of a light flexible rod, a spinning reel, and a light line

**spinning frame** /'spining/ *n* a machine that draws, twists, and winds yarn

**spinning jenny** /'jeni/ *n* an early multiple-spindle machine for spinning wool or cotton [*Jenny*, nickname for *Jane*]

**spinning wheel** *n* a small domestic machine for spinning yarn or thread by means of a spindle driven by a hand- or foot-operated wheel

**'spin-,off** *n* **1** a secondary or derived product or effect; a by-product ⟨*household products that are* ~s *of space research*⟩; *also* a further development, offshoot, or ramification of an idea, product, policy, etc ⟨a ~ *from a successful TV series*⟩ ⟨~s *into many trades and industries resulting from investment in one*⟩ **2** *chiefly NAm* the distribution by a business to its shareholders of particular assets, esp the shares of a subsidiary company – **spin-off** *adj*, **spin off** *vt*

**spinor** /'spinə, -naw/ *n* a quantity resembling a VECTOR whose components are COMPLEX NUMBERS in a two-dimensional or four-dimensional space and which is used esp in the mathematical description of spinning particles (eg electrons) and in the theory of relativity [ISV *spin* + *-or* (as in *vector*)]

**spinose** /'spienohs, -nohz/ *adj* SPINY **1** ⟨a *fly with black* ~ *legs*⟩ – **spinosely** *adv*, **spinosity** *n*

**spinous** /'spienəs/ *adj* SPINY **1,3** ⟨~ *appendages*⟩ ⟨a ~ *larva*⟩

**Spinozism** /spi'nohziz(ə)m/ *n* the doctrine of Spinoza that reality consists of one substance with an infinite number of attributes, of which only thought and spatial EXTENSION (size) can be apprehended by the human mind [Baruch *Spinoza* † 1677 D philosopher] – **Spinozist** *n*, **Spinozistic** *adj*

**spinster** /'spinstə/ *n* **1** a woman who has never been married **2** a woman who is past the usual age for marrying or seems unlikely to marry **3** *archaic* a person, esp a woman, whose occupation is to spin [ME *spinnestere*, fr *spinnen* to spin + *-estere* -ster] – **spinsterhood** *n*, **spinsterish** *adj*

**spinthariscope** /spin'thariskohp/ *n* an instrument that consists of a fluorescent screen and a magnifying lens system for visual detection of ALPHA PARTICLES (nuclear particles with positive electric charge) [Gk *spintharis* spark + E *-scope*]

**spin the bottle** *n* **1** SPIN THE PLATE when played with a bottle **2** a kissing game in which one's partner is the one a bottle points to when it stops spinning

**spin the plate** *n* a game in which something round (eg a plate) is spun on edge and the name of a player is called, upon which the named player must catch the spinning object before it falls or pay a forfeit

**spinule** /'spienyoohl/ *n* a minute spine [L *spinula*, dim. of *spina* thorn – more at SPINE] – **spinulose** *adj*

**spiny** /'spieni/ *adj* **1** covered or armed with spines; *broadly* bearing spines, prickles, or thorns **2** full of difficulties, obstacles, or annoyances; thorny ⟨~ *problems*⟩ **3** slender and pointed like a spine – **spininess** *n*

**spiny anteater** *n* ECHIDNA (type of Australasian animal)

**'spiny-,finned** *adj, of a fish* having fins supported with one or more stiff unbranched bony spines (RAYS) – compare SOFT-FINNED

**spiny-headed worm** *n* any of a small phylum (Acanthocephala) of unsegmented parasitic worms that have a PROBOSCIS (tubular structure projecting from the head) bearing hooks by which attachment is made to the intestinal wall of the host

**spiny lobster** *n* any of several edible INVERTEBRATE animals (family Palinuridae of the class Crustacea) distinguished from the true lobster by the simple unenlarged first pair of legs and the spiny shell – called also CRAYFISH

**spir-** /spie·ə-/, **spiri-, spiro-** *comb form* coil; twist ⟨spir*ula*⟩ ⟨spiro*chaete*⟩ [LL *spir-*, fr L *spira* coil – more at ³SPIRE]

**spiracle** /'spierəkl, 'spirəkl/ *n* **1** a breathing hole: eg **1a** the blowhole of a whale **b** an external opening of the tubes of the respiratory system of a spider, beetle, centipede or other ground-living ARTHROPOD, that in an insect is usu one of a series of small openings located along each side of the THORAX (central body region) and abdomen **2** *formal* a hole or shaft that lets air into a confined space; a vent [L *spiraculum*, fr *spirare* to breathe – more at SPIRIT] – **spiracular** *adj*

**spiraea,** *NAm* **spirea** /spie'riə/ *n* **1** any of a genus (*Spiraea*) of plants or shrubs of the rose family having small white or pink flowers in dense clusters and commonly grown in gardens **2** any of several garden plants resembling the true spiraeas; *esp* any of various shrubs (genus *Astilbe*) of the saxifrage family [NL, genus name, fr L, a type of shrub, fr Gk *speiraia*, prob fr *speira* ³spire]

**¹spiral** /'spie·ərəl/ *adj* **1a** winding round and round a centre in ever increasing or decreasing circles; shaped like a plane spiral **b** winding round while moving up or down a central axis; HELICAL ⟨~ *staircase*⟩ **2** advancing to higher levels through a series of cyclical movements ⟨*a* ~ *theory of social development*⟩ [ML *spiralis*, fr L *spira* coil] – **spirally** *adv*

**²spiral** *n* **1a** the path of a point in a plane moving round a central point while continuously receding from or approaching it **b** a three-dimensional curve (eg a HELIX) with one or more turns about an axis **2** a single turn or coil in a spiral object **3a** something having a spiral form **b** a spiral flight **4** a continuously expanding and accelerating increase or decrease ⟨*wage* ~*s*⟩

**³spiral** *vb* **-ll-** (*NAm* **-l-,** **-ll-**) *vi* **1** to go in a spiral course **2** to increase uncontrollably ⟨~*ling costs*⟩ ~ *vt* to cause to take a spiral course or shape

**spiral binding** *n* a book or notebook binding in which a continuous spiral wire or plastic strip is passed through holes along one edge – **spiral-bound** *adj*

**spiral galaxy** *n* a galaxy consisting of a central nucleus or bar-shaped structure from which usu two spiral arms extend

**spiralism** /'spierəliz(ə)m/ *n* combined upward mobility in career, residence, and social status

**spiral nebula** *n* SPIRAL GALAXY

**spiral of Archimedes** /ˌahki'meediz/ *n* a plane curve that is generated by a point moving away from or towards a fixed point at a constant rate while it rotates about the fixed point at a constant rate, and that has the equation $\rho = a\,\theta$ in POLAR COORDINATES [*Archimedes* †212 BC Gk mathematician]

**spirant** /'spie·ərənt/ *n* FRICATIVE (consonant sound /f/, /th/, etc) [ISV, fr L *spirant-, spirans*, prp of *spirare* to breathe – more at SPIRIT] – **spirant** *adj*

**¹spire** /spie·ə/ *n* **1** a slender tapering blade or stalk (eg of grass) **2** the upper tapering part of something (eg a tree or antler); a pinnacle **3** a tapering roof or other construction surmounting a tower – compare STEEPLE [ME, fr OE *spīr;* akin to MD *spier* blade of grass, L *spina* thorn – more at SPINE] – **spired, spiry** *adj*

**²spire** *vi* to taper up to a point like a spire

**³spire** *n* **1** a spiral, coil **2** the inner or upper part of a spiral snail, whelk, or other GASTROPOD shell consisting of all the whorls except the one in contact with the body [L *spira* coil, fr Gk *speira;* akin to Gk *sparton* rope, esparto, Lith *springti* to choke in swallowing] – **spired** *adj*

**⁴spire** *vi* to rise (as if) in a spiral

**spirea** /spie'riə/ *n, NAm* SPIRAEA (type of plant)

**spiri-** – see SPIR-

**spirillum** /spi'riləm/ *n, pl* **spirilla** /-lə/ any of a genus (*Spirillum*) of long curved bacteria having a FLAGELLUM (whiplike structure used for movement); *broadly* a spiral filamentous bacterium (eg a SPIROCHAETE) [NL, genus name, fr dim. of L *spira* coil]

**¹spirit** /'spirit/ *n* **1** the animating or vital force of living organisms **2** a supernatural being or essence: eg **2a** *cap* HOLY SPIRIT **b** SOUL 2 **c** a being that is bodiless but can become visible; *specif* a ghost **d** a malevolent being that enters and possesses a person **3** **spirits** *pl,* temper or state of mind, esp when lively or excited ⟨*in high* ~*s*⟩ **4** the immaterial intelligent or conscious part of a person **5** the motivating principle or attitude influencing or characterizing something ⟨*undertaken in a* ~ *of fun*⟩ **6** liveliness, energy, or courage in a person or his/her actions ⟨*she showed great* ~ *during her imprisonment*⟩ **7** a person of a specified kind or character ⟨*a kindred* ~⟩ **8** enthusiastic loyalty ⟨*team* ~⟩ **9a** DISTILLATE 1: eg **9a(1)** **spirits** *pl,* **spirit** distilled liquor of high alcoholic content (eg gin, whisky, and rum) **a(2)** **spirits** *pl,* **spirit** any of various readily vaporizing liquids obtained by distillation or breakdown

(CRACKING) of petroleum, wood, etc **a(3)** ETHANOL **b** a usu readily vaporizing solvent (eg an alcohol, ESTER, or HYDROCARBON) **c** **spirit, spirits** *pl but taking sing or pl vb* an alcoholic solution of a readily vaporizing substance ⟨~ *of camphor*⟩ **10a** prevailing characteristic or feeling ⟨~ *of the age*⟩ **b** the true meaning of something (eg a rule or instruction) in contrast to its verbal expression ⟨~ *of the law*⟩ [ME, fr OF or L; OF, fr L *spiritus*, lit., breath; akin to L *spirare* to blow, breathe, ON *fisa* to break wind] – **spiritless** *adj* – **in spirits** in a cheerful or lively frame of mind – **out of spirits** in a gloomy or depressed frame of mind

**²spirit** *vt* **1** to infuse with spirit; *esp* to animate, inspire ⟨*hope and apprehension of feasibleness* ~*s all industry* – John Goodman⟩ – often + *up* **2** to carry off, esp secretly or mysteriously – usu + *away* ⟨*was* ~*ed away to a mountain hideout*⟩

**spirited** /'spiritid/ *adj* **1** full of energy, animation, or courage ⟨*a* ~ *discussion*⟩ **2** having a specified frame of mind – often in combination ⟨*low-spirited*⟩ – **spiritedly** *adv,* **spiritedness** *n*

**spirit gum** *n* a solution (eg of GUM ARABIC in ether) used esp for attaching false hair to the skin

**spiritism** /'spiriˌtiz(ə)m/ *n* SPIRITUALISM 2a – **spiritist** *n,* **spiritistic** *adj*

**spirit lamp** *n* a lamp in which a vaporizing liquid fuel (eg METHYLATED SPIRITS) is burnt

**spirit level** *n* a device that uses the position of a bubble in a curved transparent tube of liquid to indicate whether a surface is level

**spirit of hartshorn** /'hahts,hawn/ *n,* **spirits of hartshorn** *taking sing or pl vb* AMMONIA WATER

**spiritoso** /ˌspiri'tohsoh/ *adj* animated – used as a direction in music [It, fr *spirito* spirit, fr L *spiritus*]

**spiritous** /'spiritəs/ *adj* **1** spirituous **2** *archaic* pure, refined

**spirit rapping** *n* communication by rapping on a table, held to be made by the spirits of the dead – **spirit rapper** *n*

**spirits of salt** *n taking sing or pl vb, archaic* HYDROCHLORIC ACID

**spirits of wine** *n taking sing or pl vb, archaic* purified spirit; ETHANOL

**¹spiritual** /'spirichooəl/ *adj* **1** of or consisting of the spirit as opposed to the body ⟨*man's* ~ *needs*⟩ **2a** of sacred matters ⟨~ *songs*⟩ **b** ecclesiastical rather than lay or temporal ⟨*lords* ~⟩ ⟨~ *authority*⟩ **3** concerned with religious values **4** based on or related by closeness of spirit ⟨*our* ~ *home*⟩ ⟨*his* ~ *heir*⟩ **5** of supernatural beings or phenomena [ME, fr MF & LL; MF *spirituel*, fr LL *spiritualis*, fr L, of breathing, of wind, fr *spiritus*] – **spiritually** *adv,* **spiritualness** *n*

**²spiritual** *n* a usu emotional religious song of a kind developed esp among blacks in the southern USA

**spiritualism** /'spirichooə,liz(ə)m/ *n* **1** the doctrine that spirit is the ultimate reality **2a** *also* **spiritism** a belief that spirits of the dead communicate with the living, esp through a medium or at a séance **b** the doctrines and practices of those holding this belief **c** *cap* a movement comprising religious organizations emphasizing spiritualism – **spiritualist** *n, often cap,* **spiritualistic** *adj*

**spirituality** /ˌspirichoo'aləti/ *n* **1** sensitivity or attachment to religious values ⟨*a man of deep* ~⟩ **2** practice of personal devotion and prayer ⟨*a study of Byzantine* ~⟩ **3** being spiritual **4** *usu pl, archaic* something that in ecclesiastical law belongs to the church or to a cleric as such **5** *taking sing or pl vb, archaic* the clergy as a whole

**spiritual·ize, -ise** /'spirichooəliez/ *vt* **1** to make spiritual; elevate to a spiritual plane ⟨*illness and solitude did much to* ~ *his mind*⟩ **2** to give a spiritual meaning to or understand in a spiritual sense – **spiritualization** *n*

**spiritualty** /'spirichooəlti/ *n, archaic* SPIRITUALITY 4, 5

**spirituel** /'spirichoo,el/, *fem* **spirituelle** /~/ *adj* having or marked by a refined and esp sprightly or witty nature [Fr, lit., spiritual]

**spirituous** /'spirichooəs/ *adj* containing or impregnated with alcohol obtained by distillation ⟨~ *liquors*⟩

**spiritus asper** /ˌspiritəs 'aspə/ *n* ROUGH BREATHING (sign in Greek language) [LL]

**spiritus lenis** /ˌspiritəs 'leenis/ *n* SMOOTH BREATHING (sign in Greek language) [LL]

**¹spiro-** – see SPIR-

**²spiro-** *comb form* breathing ⟨*spirograph*⟩ [ISV, fr L *spirare* to breathe – more at SPIRIT]

**spirochaetal,** *NAm* **spirochetal** /ˌspie·əroh'keetl/ *adj* caused by spirochaetes

**spirochaete**, *NAm* **spirochete** /'spie-ərohkeet/ *n* any of an order (Spirochaetales) of slender spirally undulating bacteria including those causing syphilis and RELAPSING FEVER [NL *Spirochaeta*, genus of bacteria, fr L *spira* coil + Gk *chaitē* long hair]

**spirograph** /'spie-ərə,grahf, -,graf/ *n* an instrument for recording movements made in breathing [ISV] – **spirographic** *adj*, **spirography** *n*

**spirogyra** /,spie-ərə'jie-ərə/ *n* any of a genus (*Spirogyra*) of freshwater GREEN ALGAE whose cells contain spiral chlorophyll bands [NL, genus name, fr Gk *speira* coil + *gyros* ring, circle – more at SPIRE, COWER]

**spirometer** /spie-ə'romitə/ *n* an instrument for measuring the air entering and leaving the lungs [ISV] – **spirometry** *n*, **spirometric** *adj*

**spirt** /spuht/ *n or vb* [2,3]SPURT

**spirula** /'spieroolə/ *n* any of a genus (*Spirula* of the class Cephalopoda, phylum Mollusca) of small INVERTEBRATE animals related to the squids and octopuses, having a many-chambered shell in a flat spiral [NL, genus name, fr dim. of L *spira* coil]

**[1]spit** /spit/ *n* **1** a slender pointed rod for holding meat over a source of heat (e g an open fire) **2** an elongated often hooked strip of sand or shingle extending from the coast [ME, fr OE *spitu;* akin to L *spina* thorn, spine]

**[2]spit** *vt* **-tt-** to fix (as if) on a spit; impale

**[3]spit** *vb* **-tt-; spat** /spat/, **spit** *vt* **1** to eject from the mouth **2a** to express (hostile or malicious feelings) (as if) by spitting ⟨spat *his contempt*⟩ **b** to utter vehemently or with a spitting sound ⟨spat *out his words*⟩ **3** to emit as if by spitting ⟨*the guns* spat *fire*⟩ **4** to set alight ⟨~ *a fuse*⟩ ~ *vi* **1a** to eject saliva as an expression of aversion or contempt – usu + *at* or on **b** to eject saliva from the mouth; expectorate **2** to rain very lightly – chiefly in *spit with rain* **3** to sputter ⟨*sausages* ~ting *in the pan*⟩ **4** *of a cat* to make a characteristic rasping noise to show hostility ⟨~ting *and arching her back as the dog approached*⟩ [ME *spitten*, fr OE *spittan*, of imit origin] – **spit it out** to say what is on one's mind without further delay – usu imper

*usage* **Spat** is the commoner past in British English, but **spat** and **spit** are equally common American forms.

**[4]spit** *n* **1a(1)** spittle, saliva **a(2)** the act or an instance of spitting **b** a frothy secretion exuded by some insects, esp FROGHOPPERS **2** perfect likeness – often in *spit and image* ⟨*he's the very* ~ *and image of his father*⟩

**[5]spit** *n, chiefly Br* **1** (a layer of earth) the depth of the blade of a spade **2** a spadeful of earth [D, fr MD; akin to MD *spitten* to dig]

**spit and polish** *n* extreme attention to cleanliness, orderliness, smartness of appearance, and ceremonial, esp at the expense of operational efficiency [fr the practice of polishing objects such as shoes by spitting on them and then rubbing them with a cloth]

**spitchcock** /'spich,kok/ *n* an eel that is split and grilled or fried – compare SPATCHCOCK [origin unknown] – **spitchcock** *vt*

**[1]spite** /spiet/ *n* **1** petty ill will, malice, or vindictiveness **2** an instance of spite; grudge ⟨*a* ~ *against the clergy*⟩ **synonyms** see VINDICTIVE [ME, short for *despite*] – **spiteful** *adj*, **spitefully** *adv* – **in spite of** REGARDLESS OF; IN DEFIANCE OF

**[2]spite** *vt* **1** to treat vindictively (e g by thwarting or humiliating) **2** to annoy or offend out of spite

**spitfire** /'spit,fie-ə/ *n* a quick-tempered or volatile person

**spitting cobra** /'spiting/ *n* either of two venomous African snakes that eject their venom towards the victim without striking: e g **a** a cobra (*Naja nigricollis*) **b** RINGHALS

**spitting image** *n* exact likeness; [4]SPIT 2 [alter. of *spit and image*]

**spittle** /'spitl/ *n* **1** saliva **2** [4]SPIT 1b [ME *spetil*, fr OE *spætl;* akin to OE *spittan* to spit]

**spittlebug** /-,bug/ *n* FROGHOPPER

**spittle insect** *n* FROGHOPPER

**spittoon** /spi'toohn/ *n* a receptacle for spit, usu placed on the floor in pubs and other public places – called also CUSPIDOR [[4]*spit* + *-oon* (as in *balloon*)]

**spitz** /spits/ *n* any of several stocky heavy-coated dogs of northern origin that have pointed muzzles and ears [Ger, fr *spitz* pointed; fr the shape of its ears and muzzle]

**spiv** /spiv/ *n, Br informal* a slick fellow who has no regular employment and lives by sharp practice or petty fraud; *specif* a small-time BLACK MARKETEER at the end of World War II [alter. of E dial. *spiff* flashy dresser, fr *spiff* dandified] – **spivvy** *adj*, **spivvery** *n*

**splanchnic** /'splangknik/ *adj* of the internal organs; VISCERAL [NL *splanchnicus*, fr Gk *splanchnikos*, fr *splanchna* entrails; akin to Gk *splēn* spleen]

**splanchnology** /splangk'noləji/ *n* a branch of anatomy concerned with the VISCERA (internal organs) [NL *splanchnologia*, fr Gk *splanchna* entrails]

**[1]splash** /splash/ *vi* **1a** to move about vigorously in a liquid, esp striking the surface, causing it to fly up and spatter ⟨~ed *about in the bath*⟩ **b** to move through or into a liquid and cause it to spatter ⟨~ *through a flooded meadow*⟩ **2a(1)** to become spattered about ⟨*milk* ~ed *all over the floor*⟩ **a(2)** to spread or scatter in the manner of splashed liquid ⟨*sunlight* ~ed *over the lawn*⟩ **b** to flow, fall, or strike with a splashing sound ⟨*a brook* ~ing *over rocks*⟩ ~ *vt* **1a(1)** to dash a liquid or semiliquid substance on or against **a(2)** to soil or stain with splashed liquid **b** to mark or overlay with patches of contrasting colour **c** to display prominently; *specif* to print (an item) in a conspicuous position in a newspaper or magazine ⟨*the affair was* ~ed *all over the local papers* – *Woman's Journal*⟩ **2a** to cause (a liquid or semiliquid substance) to spatter about, esp with force **b** to scatter in the manner of a splashed liquid ⟨*sunset* ~ed *its colours across the sky*⟩ **3** *chiefly Br* to spend money liberally; splurge – usu + *out* ⟨~ed *out on a new dinner service*⟩ **3** *chiefly Br* to spend (money) liberally or ostentatiously – usu + *about* or *around* [alter. of *plash*]

**[2]splash** *n* **1a(1)** splashed liquid or semiliquid substance **a(2)** a spot or daub (as if) from splashed liquid ⟨*a mud* ~ *on the wing*⟩ **b** a usu vivid patch of colour or of something coloured ⟨~es *of yellow tulips*⟩ **c** a small but usu significant amount; a dash ⟨*a* ~ *of soda in my whisky*⟩ **2** the action or sound of splashing **3a** a vivid impression created esp by ostentatious activity or showy appearance; a sensation **b** ostentatious display; *specif* a conspicuous featuring of an item in a newspaper or magazine – **splashy** *adj*

**splashback** /-,bak/ *n* a panel or screen (e g behind a washbasin or cooker) to protect the wall from splashes

**splashboard** /'splash,bawd/ *n* a plank used to close a sluice or spillway of a dam

**splashdown** /-,down/ *n* the landing of a spacecraft in the ocean; *also* the time scheduled for this – **splash down** *vi*

**[1]splat** /splat/ *n* a single flat often ornamental piece of wood forming the centre of a chair back [obs *splat* to spread flat, fr ME *splatten* to split open]

**[2]splat** *n* a splattering or slapping sound, as of the noise of the impact when something falls and is flattened [imit] – **splat** *adv*

**[3]splat** *vb* **-tt-** to (cause to) make a splat ⟨*the tomato* ~ted *against the wall*⟩

**splatter** /'splatə/ *vb* to (cause to) scatter or fall (as if) in heavy drops ⟨*rain* ~ed *against the windscreen*⟩ [prob blend of *splash* and *spatter*] – **splatter** *n*

**[1]splay** /splay/ *vt* **1** to spread out **2** to make (e g the sides of an opening) wider at one end than the other ~ *vi* **1** to become splayed **2** to slope, slant [ME *splayen*, short for *displayen* – more at DISPLAY]

**[2]splay** *n* **1** a slope or BEVEL, esp of the sides of a door or window **2** a spread, expansion

**[3]splay** *adj* turned outwards ⟨~ *knees*⟩

**splayfoot** /-,foot/ *n* a foot abnormally flattened and spread out – **splayfoot, splayfooted** *adj*

**spleen** /spleen/ *n* **1** a highly VASCULAR (containing blood vessels) ductless organ near the stomach or intestine of most VERTEBRATE animals that is concerned with final destruction of BLOOD CELLS, storage of blood, and production of LYMPHOCYTES (white blood cells) **2** a mixture of ill will and bad temper **3** *archaic* melancholy **4** *obs* the source of emotions or passions [ME *splen*, fr MF or L; MF *esplen*, fr L *splen*, fr Gk *splēn;* akin to L *lien* spleen] – **spleeny, spleenful** *adj*

**spleenwort** /-,wuht/ *n* any of a genus (*Asplenium*) of ferns having spore clusters borne obliquely on the upper side of a leaf vein [fr the former belief in its power to cure disorders of the spleen]

**splen-, spleno-** *comb form* spleen ⟨splen*ectomy*⟩ ⟨spleno*megaly*⟩ [L, fr Gk *splēn-, splēno-*, fr *splēn*]

**splendent** /'splendənt/ *adj, archaic* **1** shining, gleaming ⟨~ *lustre*⟩ **2** illustrious, brilliant ⟨~ *genius*⟩ [ME, fr LL *splendent-, splendens*, fr L, prp of *splendēre* to shine]

**splendid** /'splendid/ *adj* **1** possessing or displaying splendour:

e g **1a** shining, brilliant **b** magnificent, sumptuous, grand ⟨*the banquet was a ∼ affair*⟩ **2** illustrious, distinguished **3** of the best or most enjoyable kind; excellent ⟨∼ *motives*⟩ ⟨*a ∼ picnic*⟩ [L *splendidus*, fr *splendēre* to shine; akin to Gk *splēdos* ashes, Skt *sphuliṅga* spark] – **splendidly** *adv*, **splendidness** *n*

**splendiferous** /splen'dif(ə)rəs/ *adj, informal* splendid ⟨*his ∼ eruption of eloquence – TLS*⟩ [*splendour* + -*i*- + -*ferous*] – **splendiferously** *adv*, **splendiferousness** *n*

**splendour**, *NAm chiefly* **splendor** /'splendə/ *n* **1** great brightness or lustre; brilliance **2** grandeur, pomp **3** something splendid [ME *splendure*, fr AF *splendur*, fr L *splendor*, fr *splendēre* to shine] – **splendorous** *also* **splendrous** *adj*

**splenectomy** /spli'nektəmi/ *n* surgical removal of the spleen [ISV] – **splenectomized** *adj*

**splenetic** /spli'netik/ *adj* **1** marked by bad temper, animosity, or spite ⟨*an ailing ∼ old man*⟩ **2** *archaic* given to melancholy [LL *spleneticus*, fr L *splen* spleen] – **splenetic** *n*, **splenetically** *adv*

**splenic** /'spleenik, 'splenik/ *adj* of or located in the spleen ⟨∼ *blood flow*⟩ [L *splenicus*, fr Gk *splēnikos*, fr *splēn* spleen]

**splenius** /'spleenyəs/ *n*, *pl* **splenii** /-ni·i/ a flat oblique muscle of each side of the back of the neck [NL, fr L *splenium* plaster, compress, fr Gk *splēnion*, fr *splēn*]

**splenomegaly** /ˌspleenoh'megəli/ *n* enlargement of the spleen [ISV *splen-* + Gk *megal-*, *megas* large – more at MUCH]

**¹splice** /splies/ *vt* **1a** to join (e g two ropes) by interweaving the strands **b** to join (e g film, magnetic tape, wire, or timber) by overlapping the ends, binding with adhesive tape, soldering, etc **c** to attach, insert ⟨*revised the book and ∼*d *in some photographs*⟩ **2** *Br informal* to marry. – usu passive ⟨*met in June and got ∼*d *in July*⟩ [obs D *splissen*; akin to MD *splitten* to split] – **splicer** *n*

**²splice** *n* **1** a joining or joint made by splicing **2** the wedge-shaped end of a cricket-bat handle that is inserted into the blade

**spline** /splien/ *n* **1** a thin wood or metal strip used in building construction **2** a piece, ridge, or groove that prevents a shaft from turning freely in a surrounding tubular part but usu allows lengthways motion [origin unknown] – **splined** *adj*

**¹splint** /splint/ *n* **1** a thin flexible strip of wood suitable for interweaving (e g into baskets) **2** a rigid support for immobilizing an injured body part (e g a broken arm) **3** a bony enlargement on the upper part of the CANNON BONE of a horse, usu on the inside of the leg [ME, fr MLG *splinte, splente*; akin to OHG *spaltan* to split – more at SPILL]

**²splint** *vt* **1** to support and immobilize (e g a broken bone) with a splint **2** to brace (as if) with splints

**splint bone** *n* either of the two slender rudimentary bones on either side of the CANNON BONE in the limbs of horses and related animals

**¹splinter** /'splintə/ *n* **1** a sharp thin piece, esp of wood or glass, split or broken off lengthways ⟨*a ∼ in one's finger*⟩ **2 splinter group, splinter** a small group or faction broken away from a parent body [ME, fr MD; akin to MLG *splinte* splint] – **splintery** *adj*

**²splinter** *vt* **1** to split or tear into long thin pieces; shatter **2** to split into fragments, parts, or factions ∼ *vi* to become splintered

**¹split** /split/ -**tt**-; **split** *vt* **1** to divide lengthways, usu along a grain or seam or by layers; *broadly* to divide, separate ⟨*the river ∼*s *the town in two*⟩ **2a(1)** to tear or rend apart; burst **a(2)** to subject (an atom or atomic nucleus) to artificial disintegration, esp by FISSION **b** to affect as if by shattering or tearing apart ⟨*a roar that ∼ the air*⟩ **3** to divide into parts or portions: e g **3a** to divide between people; share ⟨∼ *a bottle of wine at dinner*⟩ **b** to divide into opposing factions, parties, or groups ⟨*the bill ∼ the opposition*⟩ **c(1)** to divide or break down (a chemical compound) into constituents ⟨∼ *a fat into glycerol and fatty acids*⟩ **c(2)** to remove by such separation ⟨∼ *off carbon dioxide*⟩ **d** to divide (shares) by issuing a larger number to existing shareholders, usu without increase in total PAR VALUE (value printed on the share certificates) **e** *NAm* to mark (a ballot) or cast (a vote) so as to vote for candidates of different parties **4** to separate (constituent parts) by putting something in between ⟨∼ *an infinitive*⟩ ∼ *vi* **1a** to become split lengthways or into layers **b** to break apart; burst, rupture **2a** to become divided up or separated off ⟨∼ *into factions*⟩ **b** to sever relations or connections – often + *up* ⟨∼ *up after six months' marriage*⟩ **c** *informal* to leave, esp hurriedly or abruptly **3** *informal* to share something (e g loot or profits) with others – often + *with* **4** *informal* to let out a secret; act as an informer

– often + *on* ⟨*on the point of ∼*ting *on the gang* – Dorothy Sayers⟩ **5** *informal, of the head* to be affected by severe headache – see also **split the** DIFFERENCE/HAIRS/**one's** SIDES synonyms see ²TEAR [D *splitten*, fr MD; akin to OHG *spaltan* to split – more at SPILL] – **splitter** *n*

**²split** *n* **1a** a narrow break made (as if) by splitting; a tear, crack **b** an arrangement of pins left standing after the first bowl in TENPIN BOWLING with space for pins between them so that it is very difficult to knock them all down with the second bowl **2** a piece or section split off **3** a division into divergent or antagonistic groups or elements; a breach ⟨*a ∼ in party ranks*⟩ **4a** splitting **b** *pl but taking sing vb* the act of lowering oneself to the floor or leaping into the air with the legs spread (e g one to each side) and extended to form a straight line at right angles to the trunk **5** a wine bottle holding a quarter of the usual amount; *also* a small bottle of mineral water, tonic water, etc **6** a sweet dish composed of sliced fruit, esp banana, ice cream, syrup, and often nuts and whipped cream

**³split** *adj* **1** divided, fractured, or torn **2** prepared for use by splitting ⟨∼ *bamboo*⟩ ⟨∼ *hides*⟩

**split decision** *n* a decision as to the result of a boxing match reflecting a division of opinion among the referee and judges

**split end** *n usu pl* the end of a human hair that has split into two or more strands

**split infinitive** *n* an infinitive with another word, usu an adverb, between *to* and the verb (e g in "to really start") – see "Ten Vexed Points"

**split-'level** *adj* **1** divided so that the floor level of rooms in one part is approximately midway between the levels of two successive storeys in an adjoining part ⟨*a ∼ house*⟩ **2** *of a cooker* having the oven and heating rings separated into different units – **split-level** *n*

**split pea** *n* a dried pea split in half for use in soups, PEASE PUDDING, etc

**split personality** *n* a personality structure composed of two or more internally consistent groups of behaviour tendencies and attitudes, each acting more or less independently of the other

**split pin** *n* a strip of metal folded double that can be used as a fastener by inserting it through a hole and then bending back the ends; COTTER PIN

**split ring** *n* a metal ring (e g a key ring) formed from a double coil of wire in such a way that things may be attached to it or removed from it

**split screen** *n* an effect in which two juxtaposed images are displayed simultaneously on a film or television screen

**split second** *n* a fractional part of a second; a flash – **split-second** *adj*

**split shift** *n* a shift of working hours divided into two or more working periods at times (e g mornings and evenings) separated by more than normal periods of time off

**split ticket** *n*, *NAm* a ballot cast by a voter who votes for candidates of more than one party – compare STRAIGHT TICKET

**split tin** *n*, *Br* a long loaf with the crust divided lengthways down the middle

**splitting** /'spliting/ *adj, of a headache* acutely painful

**splodge** /sploj/ *vt or n, Br informal* (to make) a large irregular blot (on); blotch [prob alter. of *splotch*] – **splodgy** *adj*

**splosh** /splosh/ *vb or n, informal* (to make or move with) a loud splash ⟨∼*ing the water around in his bath*⟩ [alter. of *splash*]

**splotch** /sploch/ *vt or n, chiefly NAm informal* (to) splodge [perh blend of *spot* and *blotch*] – **splotchy** *adj*

**¹splurge** /spluhj/ *n, informal* **1** an ostentatious effort or display **2** an extravagant spending spree [perh blend of *splash* and *surge*]

**²splurge** *vb, informal vi* **1** to make a splurge **2** to spend money extravagantly – often + *on* ⟨∼ *on a slap-up meal*⟩ ∼ *vt* to spend extravagantly or ostentatiously

**splutter** /'splutə/ *vi* **1** to make a noise as if spitting: e g **1a** to spit out bits of food, saliva, etc noisily, as when choking in surprise or laughing **b** to eject small fragments or splashes with a crackling or popping sound ⟨*a fire ∼*ing *in the grate*⟩ **2** to speak hastily and confusedly; sputter ∼ *vt* to utter hastily and confusedly [prob alter. of *sputter*] – **splutter** *n*, **splutterer** *n*, **spluttery** *adj*

**Spode** /spohd/ *n* ceramic ware (e g BONE CHINA or fine porcelain) made at the works established by Josiah Spode at Stoke [Josiah *Spode* †1827 E potter]

**spodumene** /'spodyoomeen/ *n* a white to yellowish, purplish, or emerald-green PYROXENE mineral, LiAlSi₂O₆, that is a lithium aluminium silicate and occurs in crystals often of great size [Fr *spodumène* or Ger *spodumen*, fr Gk *spodoumenos*, prp of *spodousthai* to be burnt to ashes, fr *spodos* ashes]

¹**spoil** /spoyl/ *n* **1 spoils** *pl*, **spoil 1a** plunder taken from an enemy in war or a victim in robbery; loot **b** something gained by special effort or skill **c** *chiefly NAm* public offices made the property of a victorious party **2** earth and rock excavated or dredged **3** an object damaged or flawed in the making [ME *spoile*, fr MF *espoille*, fr L *spolia*, pl of *spolium* – more at SPILL]

²**spoil** *vb* **spoilt** /spoylt/, **spoiled** /spoylt, spoyld/ *vt* **1a** to damage seriously; ruin ⟨*heavy rain* ~t *the crops*⟩ **b** to impair the enjoyment of; mar ⟨*a quarrel* ~t *the celebration*⟩ **c** to fill in (eg a voting paper) wrongly so as to render invalid ⟨~t *papers*⟩ **2a** to impair the character of by overindulgence ⟨~ *an only child*⟩ **b** to treat indulgently; pamper ⟨~ *your guests with fresh lobster*⟩ **c** to cause to be dissatisfied with something inferior – usu + *for* ⟨*the meals at this hotel will* ~ *us for canteen food*⟩ **3** *archaic* **3a** to despoil, strip **b** to pillage, rob ~ *vi* **1** to become unfit for use or consumption, usu as a result of decay ⟨*fruit soon* ~s *in warm weather*⟩ **2** to have an eager desire *for* – esp in *spoiling for a fight* **3** *archaic* to practise pillage and robbery [ME *spoilen*, fr MF *espoillier*, fr L *spoliare* to strip, plunder, rob, fr *spolium*] – **spoilable** *adj*

> **usage** Spoilt and spoiled are equally common in British English, but **spoiled** is the commoner American form. **Spoilt** is the usual British adjective ⟨*a spoilt child*⟩. **synonyms** see INJURE

**spoilage** /'spoylij/ *n* **1** spoiling or being spoiled **2** something spoiled or wasted **3** loss by being spoiled

**spoiler** /'spoylə/ *n* **1** one who or that which spoils **2** a long narrow plate along the upper surface of an aircraft wing that may be raised for reducing lift and increasing drag **3** an air deflector at the front or rear of the body of a car, esp a racing car, to reduce the tendency to lift off the road at high speeds

**spoilsman** /'spoylzmən/ *n*, *chiefly NAm* one who serves a political party for a share of the spoils; *also* one who sanctions such practice

**spoilsport** /-,spawt/ *n*, *informal* one who spoils the fun of others

**spoils system** *n*, *chiefly NAm* a practice of regarding public offices and their financial rewards as plunder to be distributed to members of the victorious party

¹**spoke** /spohk/ *past & archaic past part of* SPEAK

²**spoke** *n* **1a** any of the small radiating bars inserted in the hub of a wheel to support the rim **b** something resembling the spoke of a wheel **2** a rung of a ladder **3** any of the projecting handles of a ship's wheel [ME, fr OE *spāca*; akin to MD *spike* spike] – **put a spoke in somebody's wheel** to frustrate or thwart somebody's plans – **put one's spoke in** to interfere

³**spoke** *vt* to provide with spokes

**spoken** /'spohkən/ *adj* **1a** delivered by word of mouth; oral ⟨*a* ~ *request*⟩ **b** used in speaking or conversation; uttered ⟨*the* ~ *word*⟩ **2** characterized by speaking in a specified manner – usu in combination ⟨*soft*-spoken⟩ ⟨*plain*spoken⟩ [fr pp of *speak*]

'**spoken-,for** *adj* reserved, taken; *specif* engaged to be married

**spokeshave** /-,shayv/ *n* a plane having a blade set between two handles and used for shaping curved surfaces [²*spoke* + *shave*]

**spokesman** /'spohksmən/, *fem* **spokeswoman** *n* one who speaks on behalf of another or others [prob irreg fr *spoke*, obs pp of *speak*]

**spokesperson** /-,puhs(ə)n/ *n* a spokesman or spokeswoman

**spoliate** /'spohli·ayt/ *vt* to despoil, plunder [L *spoliatus*, pp]

**spoliation** /,spohli'aysh(ə)n/ *n* **1a** the act of plundering **b** the state of being plundered, esp in war **2a** the act of damaging or injuring, esp irreparably ⟨*the* ~ *of a magnificent piece of scenery* – *Scots Magazine*⟩ **b** the changing or mutilation of a legal document in order to render it invalid [ME, fr L *spoliation-, spoliatio*, fr *spoliatus*, pp of *spoliare* to plunder – more at SPOIL] – **spoliator** *n*, **spoliatory** *adj*

**spondee** /'spondee/ *n* a unit (FOOT 4) of poetic metre consisting of two long or stressed syllables [ME *sponde*, fr MF or L; MF *spondee*, fr L *spondeus*, fr Gk *spondeios*, fr *spondeios* of a libation, fr *spondē* libation – more at SPOUSE; fr its use in music accompanying libations] – **spondaic** *adj or n*

**spondulicks** /spon'dyoohliks/ *n pl*, *informal chiefly humorous* money ⟨*you certainly made the* ~ *fly* – Joyce Cary⟩ [perh fr

Gk *spondylikos*, adj, fr *spondylos* species of shell sometimes used as currency]

**spondylitis** /,spondi'lietəs/ *n* inflammation of the spinal vertebrae [NL, fr Gk *sphondylos, spondylos* vertebra, lit., whorl; akin to Gk *sphadazein* to jerk, *sphendonē* sling]

¹**sponge** /spunj, spunzh/ *n* **1** any of a phylum (Porifera) of aquatic lower INVERTEBRATE animals that are colonies composed of two layers of cells supported by mineral fibres (SPICULES) and organized to form a network of interconnecting chambers, and that as adults remain permanently attached to rocks, sand, etc **2a** an elastic porous mass of interlacing horny fibres that forms the internal skeleton of various sponges and is able when wetted to absorb water **b** a piece of sponge (eg for bathing or cleaning) **c** a porous rubber or cellulose product used similarly to a sponge **d** a sponging ⟨*give my back a* ~⟩ **3** a pad (eg of folded gauze) used in surgery and medicine (eg to remove discharge or apply medication) **4** one who lives on others; a sponger **5a** raised dough (eg for yeast bread) **b** a SPONGE CAKE or sweet steamed pudding made from a sponge-cake mixture or of a spongy texture **c** a metal (eg platinum) in the form of a porous solid composed of fine particles **d** the egg mass of a crab – see also THROW **in the sponge** [ME, fr OE, fr L *spongia*, fr Gk]

²**sponge** *vt* **1** to cleanse, wipe, or moisten (as if) with a sponge – often + *down* or *off* **2** to erase or destroy (as if) with a sponge – often + *out* ⟨*whole paragraphs had been* ~d *out*⟩ **3** to obtain by sponging on another ⟨~ *the price of a pint*⟩ **4** to soak *up* with or in the manner of a sponge ~ *vi* **1** to obtain assistance, esp financial, by exploiting natural generosity or organized welfare facilities – often + *on* or *off* **2** to dive or dredge for sponges – esp in *go sponging* – **spongeable** *adj*

**sponge bag** *n*, *Br* a waterproof bag for holding toiletries

**sponge cake** *n* a light sweet cake made with (approximately) equal quantities of sugar, flour, and eggs but no fat

**sponge cloth** *n* any of various soft porous fabrics, esp in a loose honeycomb weave

**sponge finger** *n* a thin crisp piece of sugar-coated sponge, used esp in trifles

**sponger** /'spunjə/ *n* one who or that which sponges; *specif* one who lives off others, esp by exploiting natural generosity

**sponge rubber** *n* cellular rubber resembling a natural sponge in structure and used for cushions, vibration dampeners, etc

**spongin** /'spunjin/ *n* a protein that is the chief constituent of flexible supporting fibres in sponge skeletons [Ger, fr L *spongia* sponge]

**spongy** /'spunji/ *adj* **1** resembling a sponge, esp in being soft, porous, absorbent, and compressible **2a** lacking in strength and solidity; soft ⟨~ *wood*⟩ **b** in the form of a metallic sponge ⟨~ *iron*⟩ **3** moist and soft like a sponge full of water; soggy ⟨*a* ~ *moor*⟩ – **sponginess** *n*

**sponson** /'spuns(ə)n/ *n* **1a** a projection from the side of a ship or tank enabling a gun to fire forwards **b** an air chamber along the side of a canoe to increase stability and buoyancy **2** a light air-filled structure protruding from the hull of a seaplane to steady it on water [prob by shortening & alter. fr *expansion*]

¹**sponsor** /'sponsə/ *n* **1** a person who presents a candidate for baptism or confirmation and undertakes responsibility for his/her religious education or spiritual welfare; a godparent **2** one who assumes responsibility for some other person or thing **3** a person or organization that pays for a project or activity: eg **3a** one that pays (part of) the cost of a cultural or sporting event **b** a person who contributes towards a charity by giving money for a participant's efforts in an organized fund-raising event (eg a sponsored walk) **c** *chiefly NAm* one that pays the cost of a radio or television programme, usu in return for limited advertising time during its course [LL, fr L, guarantor, surety, fr *sponsus*, pp of *spondēre* to promise – more at SPOUSE] – **sponsorship** *n*, **sponsorial** *adj*

²**sponsor** *vt* to be or stand as sponsor for

**spontaneous** /spon'taynyəs, -ni·əs/ *adj* **1** proceeding from natural feeling or innate tendency without external constraint ⟨*a* ~ *expression of gratitude*⟩ **2** springing from a sudden impulse; unpremeditated ⟨*a* ~ *offer of help*⟩ **3** controlled and directed internally; self-acting ⟨~ *movement characteristic of living things*⟩ **4** produced without being planted or without human labour; indigenous **5** developing without apparent external influence, force, cause, or treatment ⟨~ *recovery from a severe illness*⟩ **6** not contrived or manipulated; natural [LL *spontaneus*, fr L *sponte* of one's free will, voluntarily – more at SPIN] – **spontaneously** *adv*, **spontaneousness, spontaneity** *n*

*synonyms* Spontaneous, impulsive, automatic, mechanical, involuntary, and instinctive can all mean "done without forethought". Spontaneous and impulsive emphasize the absence of external constraint: spontaneous suggesting action prompted by feeling ⟨*spontaneous laughter*⟩ and impulsive suggesting impetuous and perhaps unreasonable behaviour ⟨*impulsive spending on luxuries*⟩. Automatic, mechanical, and involuntary by contrast emphasize the absence of choice: automatic suggesting a prompt invariable response that may be the result of training, and mechanical adding to that the idea of "perfunctory" or "routine". Involuntary may entail the presence of external constraint ⟨*involuntary unemployment*⟩. Instinctive applies to behaviour that is not dictated by reason, but natural to a member of one's species ⟨*instinctive fear of drowning*⟩. See [1]VOLUNTARY *antonyms* studied, deliberate *usage* The pronunciation of **spontaneity** as /ˌspontə'nayəti/ is recommended for BBC broadcasters.

**spontaneous combustion** *n* self-ignition of combustible material through chemical action (e g OXIDATION) of its constituents

**spontaneous generation** *n* ABIOGENESIS (development of living organisms from inanimate matter)

**spontoon** /spon'toohn/ *n* a short pike formerly carried by subordinate officers of infantry [Fr *sponton*, fr It *spuntone*, fr *punta* sharp point, fr (assumed) VL *puncta* – more at POINT]

[1]**spoof** /spoohf/ *vt, informal* 1 to deceive, hoax 2 to make good-natured fun of; lampoon ⟨*a comedy that* ∼s *travelling salesmen*⟩ [*Spoof*, a hoaxing game invented by Arthur Roberts †1933 E comedian]

[2]**spoof** *n, informal* 1 a hoax, deception 2 a light, humorous, but usu telling parody – compare CARICATURE – **spoof** *adj*

[1]**spook** /spoohk/ *n, informal* a ghost, spectre [D; akin to MLG *spōk* ghost] – **spookish** *adj*

[2]**spook** *vb, chiefly NAm informal vt* 1 HAUNT 3 2 to make frightened or frantic; scare; *esp* to startle into violent activity (e g stampeding) ⟨∼ed *the herd of horses*⟩ ∼ *vi* to become frightened

**spooky** /'spoohki/ *adj, informal* 1 causing irrational fear, esp because suggestive of supernatural presences; eerie 2 *NAm, of an animal* easily frightened *synonyms* see [2]WEIRD

[1]**spool** /spoohl/ *n* 1 a cylindrical device which has a rim or ridge at each end and a hole, usu through the middle, for a pin or spindle and on which thread, wire, tape, etc is wound 2 material or the amount of material wound on a spool 3 *chiefly NAm* a reel for cotton, thread, etc [ME *spole*, fr MF or MD; MF *espole*, fr MD *spoele*; akin to OHG *spuola* spool]

[2]**spool** *vb* to wind (on a spool)

[1]**spoon** /spoohn/ *n* 1a an eating, cooking, or serving implement consisting of a small shallow round or oval bowl with a handle b a spoonful 2 something curved like the bowl of a spoon (e g a usu metal or shell fishing lure) 3 a wooden-headed golf club having a slightly shorter shaft and giving more lift than a BRASSIE – no longer in vogue [ME, fr OE *spōn* splinter, chip; akin to OHG *spān* splinter, chip, Gk *sphēn* wedge]

[2]**spoon** *vt* 1 to take up and usu transfer in a spoon ⟨*sat placidly* ∼ing *up yogurt – Time*⟩ 2 to propel (a ball) weakly upwards ∼ *vi* 1 to spoon a ball 2 to indulge in caressing, kissing, and amorous talk – no longer in vogue [(*vi* 2) fr [1]*spoon* in the arch. senses "simpleton, doting lover"]

**spoonbill** /-ˌbil/ *n* any of several wading birds (family Plataleidae) that are related to the ibises and have the beak greatly expanded and flattened at the tip

'**spoon-ˌbilled** *adj* having the bill or snout expanded and flattened at the end

**spoon bread** *n, chiefly S & Mid US* soft bread made of maize mixed with milk, eggs, and fat and served with a spoon

**spoondrift** /'spoohnˌdrift/ *n* SPINDRIFT (sea spray) [alter. of Sc *speendrift* – more at SPINDRIFT]

**spoonerism** /'spoohnəˌriz(ə)m/ *n* a transposition of usu initial sounds of two or more words (e g in *tons of soil* for *sons of toil*) [William *Spooner* †1930 E clergyman & scholar]

'**spoon-ˌfeed** *vt* 1 to feed by means of a spoon 2a to present (e g information or entertainment) in an easily assimilable form that precludes independent thought or critical judgment ⟨∼ *political theory to students*⟩ b to present information to in this manner

**spoonful** /-f(ə)l/ *n, pl* **spoonfuls** *also* **spoonsful** as much as a spoon will hold; *specif* a teaspoonful ⟨*how many* ∼s *do you take in tea?*⟩

**spoony, spooney** /'spoohni/ *adj, informal* 1 silly, foolish; *esp* excessively sentimental 2 sentimentally in love; besotted – no longer in vogue [E slang *spoon* simpleton] – **spoony** *n*

[1]**spoor** /spooə, spaw/ *n* a track, trail, or droppings, esp of a wild animal *synonyms* see [1]TRACE [Afrik, fr MD; akin to OE *spor* footprint, spoor, *spurnan* to kick – more at SPURN]

[2]**spoor** *vb* to track (an animal) by a spoor

**spor-, spori-, sporo-** *comb form* seed; spore ⟨spor*angium*⟩ ⟨spor*icidal*⟩ [NL *spora*]

**sporadic** /spə'radik, spaw-/ *adj* occurring occasionally, intermittently, or in scattered instances *synonyms* see PERIODIC [ML *sporadicus*, fr Gk *sporadikos*, fr *sporadēn* here and there, fr *sporad-, sporas* scattered; akin to Gk *speirein* to sow] – **sporadically** *adv*

**sporadic E layer** *n* a layer of IONIZATION (area containing free electrically charged particles) occurring irregularly within the E REGION of the IONOSPHERE (upper part of the earth's atmosphere)

**sporangiophore** /spə'ranji-əˌfaw/ *n* a stalklike structure bearing sporangia

**sporangium** /spə'ranji-əm/ *n, pl* **sporangia** /-jiə/ a case or cell within which usu asexual spores are produced [NL, fr *spor-* + Gk *angeion* vessel – more at ANGI-] – **sporangial** *adj*

[1]**spore** /spaw/ *n* a primitive usu single-celled resistant reproductive body produced by plants, PROTOZOANS (single-celled microorganisms), and some INVERTEBRATE animals and capable of development into a new individual either directly or after fusion with another spore [NL *spora* seed, spore, fr Gk, act of sowing, seed, fr *speirein* to sow – more at SPROUT] – **spored** *adj*

[2]**spore** *vi* to produce or reproduce by spores

**spore case** *n* a case containing spores; a sporangium

**spore fruit** *n* a specialized structure that produces spores; FRUITING BODY

**sporicide** /'spawrisied/ *n* something that kills spores or inhibits their growth – **sporicidal** *adj*

**sporiferous** /spaw'rifərəs/ *adj* bearing or producing spores

**sporocarp** /'spawrohˌkahp, 'sporə-/ *n* a structure (e g in RED ALGAE, fungi, or mosses) in or on which spores are produced [ISV *spor-* + Gk *karpos* fruit – more at HARVEST]

**sporocyst** /'spawrohsist, -rə-/ *n* a nondividing cell (e g in MYXOMYCETES and algae) that may give rise to asexual spores [ISV] – **sporocystic** *adj*

**sporogenesis** /-'jenəsis/ *n* 1 reproduction by spores 2 spore formation [NL]

**sporogenous** /spə'rojinəs/, **sporogenic** /ˌspawrə'jenik, ˌsporə-/ *adj* of, involving, or reproducing by sporogenesis

**sporogonium** /ˌspawrə'gohniəm, ˌsporə-/ *n, pl* **sporogonia** /-niə/ the sporophyte of a moss or LIVERWORT (simple plant) consisting typically of a stalk bearing a capsule in which spores are produced and remaining permanently attached to the plant body [NL, fr *spor-* + *-gonium* (as in *archegonium*)]

**sporogony** /spaw'rogəni, -'rojəni, spo-/ *n* reproduction by spores; *specif* spore formation in a sporozoan by development of a cyst and subsequent division of a ZYGOTE (reproductive cell formed after fertilization) [ISV] – **sporogonous, sporogonic** *adj*

**sporophore** /'spawrəfaw, 'sporə-/ *n* the part (e g a SPORE FRUIT of a fungus or the placenta of a SEED PLANT) of a sporophyte that develops spores [ISV]

**sporophyll** /'spawrəfil, 'sporə-/ *n* a spore-bearing and usu greatly modified leaf (e g of a fern) [ISV]

**sporophyte** /'spawrəˌfiet/ *n* (a member of) the generation of a plant exhibiting ALTERNATION OF GENERATIONS that develops from the fertilized GAMETES (reproductive cells), bears the asexual spores from which the GAMETOPHYTES (gamete-producing generation) will develop, and in all higher plants (e g conifers and FLOWERING PLANTS) forms the visible body of the plant [ISV] – **sporophytic** *adj*

**sporopollenin** /ˌspawrə'polənin, ˌsporə-/ *n* a relatively chemically inert POLYMER (complex chemical compound composed of a chain of repeating subunits) that makes up the outer layer of pollen grains and spores of higher plants [ISV *spor-* + *pollen* + *-in*]

**sporotrichosis** /ˌspawrətri'kohsis, ˌsporə-, spəˌrotri'kohsis/ *n* infection with or a disease caused by fungi (genus *Sporotrichum*) that is characterized by nodules and abscesses and that occurs esp in human beings and horses [NL, fr *Sporotrichum*, genus name, fr *spor-* + Gk *trich-, thrix* hair]

**-sporous** /-sp(ə)rəs/ *comb form* (→ *adj*) having (such or so many) spores ⟨*homo*sporous⟩ [NL *spora* spore] – **-spory** *comb form* (→ *n*)

**sporozoan** /ˌspawrə'zoh·ən/ *n* any of a large class (Sporozoa) of strictly parasitic PROTOZOANS (single-celled microorganisms) that have a complicated life cycle usu involving both asexual and sexual generations, often in different hosts, and include important disease-causing agents (e g malaria parasites) [NL *Sporozoa*, class name, fr *spor-* + *-zoa*] – **sporozoan** *adj*

**sporozoite** /ˌspawrə'zoh·iet/ *n* an infective form of some sporozoans that is a product of sporogony and initiates an asexual cycle in the new host [NL *Sporozoa* + ISV *-ite*]

**sporran** /'sporən/ *n* a pouch of animal skin with the hair or fur on that is worn in front of the kilt with traditional Highland dress [ScGael *sporan* purse]

¹**sport** /spawt/ *vt* 1 to exhibit for all to see; SHOW OFF ⟨∼ *a new hat*⟩ 2 to put forth as a sport or bud variation ∼ *vi* 1 to play about happily; frolic ⟨*lambs* ∼ing *in the meadow*⟩ 2a to mock, jest **b** to dally, trifle *with* 3 to deviate or vary abruptly from type (e g by bud variation); mutate [ME *sporten* to divert, disport, short for *disporten;* (*vt* 2 & *vi* 3) ²*sport* 5]

²**sport** *n* 1a a source of diversion or recreation; a pastime **b(1)** a usu outdoor activity or game requiring physical skill and having a set of rules or code of practice, that is engaged in either individually or as one of a team for exercise or recreation or as a profession **b(2)** such activities collectively ⟨*do you like* ∼?⟩ 2a fun, jest ⟨*only made the remark in* ∼⟩ **b** mockery, derision ⟨*then make* ∼ *at me* – Shak⟩ 3a something tossed or driven about like a plaything ⟨*was made the* ∼ *of fate*⟩ **b** a laughingstock 4a a person whose conduct is appropriate to a sportsman, esp in being a good loser **b** a fair generous-minded likable person ⟨*be a* ∼!⟩ 5 an individual exhibiting a sudden deviation from type beyond the normal limits of individual variation, usu as a result of mutation 6 *chiefly NAm* SPORTSMAN 1 7 *chiefly NAm* a playboy 8 *Austr & NZ* – used as a form of familiar address, chiefly to men 9 *archaic* sexual play

**sporting** /'spawting/ *adj* 1a concerned with, used for, or suitable for sport **b** fond of or taking part in sports ⟨∼ *nations*⟩ **c** marked by or calling for sportsmanship; sportsmanlike **d** involving such risk as a sports competitor might take or encounter ⟨*a* ∼ *chance*⟩ 2 *chiefly NAm* of or for sports that involve betting or gambling – **sportingly** *adv*

**sportive** /'spawtiv/ *adj* 1 frolicsome, playful 2 of sports – **sportively** *adv*, **sportiveness** *n*

**sports** /spawts/, *NAm chiefly* **sport** *adj* 1 of or suitable for sports ⟨∼ *equipment*⟩ 2 styled in a manner suitable for casual or informal wear ⟨∼ *coat*⟩

**sports car**, *NAm also* **sport car** *n* a low usu 2-seater and often open-topped car designed for quick response, easy manoeuvrability, and high-speed driving

**sports day** *n*, **sports** *n pl* an annual event held by many British schools involving athletic competitions

**sports jacket** *n* a man's jacket, esp of tweed or checked fabric, that is for informal wear

**sportsman** /-mən/ *n* 1 *fem* **sportswoman** a person who engages in sports (e g either team games or hunting and fishing) 2 a person who is fair, generous, a good loser, and a gracious winner – **sportsmanlike**, **sportsmanly** *adj*, **sportsmanship** *n*

**sportswriter** /'spawts,rietə/ *n* one who writes about sports, esp for a newspaper

**sporty** /'spawti/ *adj, informal* 1 fond of or appropriate to sport 2a fun-loving, rakish, or dissipated; fast ⟨*ran around with a very* ∼ *crowd*⟩ **b** flashy, showy ⟨∼ *clothes*⟩ 3 suggestive of or capable of giving good sport ⟨*the car had a very* ∼ *feel*⟩ – **sportily** *adv*, **sportiness** *n*

**sporulation** /ˌspor(y)oo'laysh(ə)n/ *n* the formation of spores; *esp* division into many small spores (e g after development of a cyst) [ISV, fr NL *sporula*, dim. of *spora* spore] – **sporulate** *vi*, **sporulative** *adj*

¹**spot** /spot/ *n* 1 a blemish on character or reputation; a stain ⟨*the only* ∼ *on the family name*⟩ 2a a small usu round area different (eg in colour or texture) from the surrounding surface **b(1)** an area marred or marked (e g by dirt) **b(2)** a small rounded surface patch of diseased or decayed tissue ⟨*the* ∼s *that appear in measles*⟩ ⟨*rust* ∼s *on a leaf*⟩; *also* a pimple **c** a conventionalized design used on playing cards to distinguish suits and indicate values – called also PIP 3 a particular place or area ⟨*a nice* ∼ *for a picnic*⟩ 4a a particular position (e g in an organization or hierarchy) ⟨*a good* ∼ *as the director's secretary*⟩ **b(1)** a place on an entertainment programme; a slot **b(2)** a brief space between broadcast television or radio pro-

grammes used for an announcement or advertising 5 SPOTLIGHT 1a 6 *chiefly NAm* an object having a specified number of spots or a specified numeral on its surface ⟨*played the three-*spot *into the corner pocket*⟩ 7 *informal* a usu difficult or embarrassing position; a fix 8 *chiefly Br informal* a small amount; a bit ⟨*had a* ∼ *of bother with the car*⟩ [ME; akin to MD *spotte* stain, speck, ON *spotti* small piece] – **on the spot** 1 immediately; AT ONCE ⟨*do it* on the spot⟩ 2 at the place of action ⟨*we had no doctor* on the spot⟩ 3 in an awkward or difficult situation ⟨*his subordinate's mistake put him* on the spot⟩ 4 in one place; without travelling away ⟨*running* on the spot⟩

²**spot** *vb* **-tt-** *vt* 1 to sully the character or reputation of; disgrace 2 to mark or mar (as if) with spots 3a to single out; identify; *also* to identify in advance ⟨∼ *the winners*⟩ **b** to detect, notice ⟨∼ *a mistake*⟩ **c** to watch for and record the sighting of ⟨∼ *rare species of duck*⟩ **d(1)** to locate accurately ⟨∼ *an enemy position*⟩ **d(2)** to cause to strike accurately ⟨∼ *the battery's fire*⟩ 4a to lie at intervals in or on; stud – usu pass ⟨*hillsides* ∼ted *with cornfields*⟩ **b** to scatter in various places – usu pass ⟨*salesmen are* ∼ted *throughout the country*⟩ 5 to fix (as if) in the beam of a spotlight 6 *chiefly NAm* to schedule in a particular spot or at a particular time 7 *NAm* to remove a spot from ∼ *vi* 1 to become stained or discoloured in spots 2 to cause a spot; leave a stain ⟨*thought gin didn't* ∼⟩ 3 to act as a spotter; *esp* to locate targets 4 *chiefly Br* to fall lightly in scattered drops ⟨*it's* ∼ting *with rain again*⟩ – **spottable** *adj*

³**spot** *adj* 1a on the spot or in or for a particular spot ⟨∼ *coverage of the news*⟩ **b** available for immediate delivery after sale ⟨∼ *commodities*⟩ **c(1)** paid out immediately after sale ⟨∼ *cash*⟩ **c(2)** involving immediate cash payment ⟨*a* ∼ *sale*⟩ **d** broadcast between scheduled programmes ⟨∼ *announcements*⟩ 2 given on the spot or restricted to a few random places or instances ⟨*a* ∼ *check*⟩ ⟨∼ *prizes*⟩; *also* selected at random or as a sample

'**spot-,check** *vb* to sample or investigate on the spot and usu at random

**spot kick** *n, informal* a soccer PENALTY KICK

**spotless** /-lis/ *adj* 1 free from dirt or stains; immaculate ⟨∼ *kitchens*⟩ 2 pure, unblemished ⟨∼ *reputation*⟩ – **spotlessly** *adv*, **spotlessness** *n*

¹**spotlight** /-,liet/ *n* 1a a projected spot of light used for brilliant illumination of a person or object on a stage **b** full public attention ⟨*held the political* ∼⟩ 2a a light designed to project a narrow intense beam on a small area; *also* the beam projected by a spotlight **b** something that illuminates brightly or elucidates

²**spotlight** *vt* **spotlighted**, **spotlit** 1 to illuminate with a spotlight 2 to draw particular attention to ⟨*an article* ∼ing *the difficulties of school leavers*⟩

,**spot-'on** *adj, Br informal* absolutely correct; exactly right – **spot-on** *adv*

**spot pass** *n* a basketball pass made to a predetermined spot on the court rather than directly to a player

**spot price** *n* the price of a commodity or security when bought for immediate delivery

**spotted** /'spotid/ *adj* 1 marked with spots ⟨∼ *hyena*⟩ 2 sullied, tarnished 3 characterized by the appearance of spots

**spotted dick** /dik/ *n, Br* a steamed or boiled sweet suet pudding containing currants [*Dick*, nickname for *Richard*]

**spotted dog** *n, Br* SPOTTED DICK

**spotted fever** *n* any of various spot-producing fevers (e g typhus)

**spotted flycatcher** *n* an African and Eurasian FLYCATCHER (type of insect-eating bird) (*Muscicapa striata*) that has a grey-brown back, a spotted crown, and streaked whitish breast

**spotter** /'spotə/ *n* 1 one who or that which makes or applies a spot (e g for identification) 2 one who keeps watch or observes; *esp* a person who watches for and notes down vehicles (e g aircraft or trains)

**spotty** /'spoti/ *adj* 1a marked with spots; spotted **b** suffering from acne; *broadly* characteristically adolescent 2 lacking evenness or regularity, esp in quality ⟨∼ *attendance*⟩ – **spottily** *adv*, **spottiness** *n*

**spousals** /'spowzəlz/ *n pl*, **spousal** *n*, *archaic* the wedding ceremony; nuptials [ME *spousaille*, fr MF *espousailles*, fr L *sponsalia*, fr *sponsus* betrothed] – **spousal** *adj*

¹**spouse** /spows/ *n* a married person; a husband or wife [ME, fr OF *espous* (masc) & *espouse* (fem), fr L *sponsus* betrothed man, groom & *sponsa* betrothed woman, bride, fr *sponsus*, pp

of *spondēre* to promise, betroth; akin to Gk *spendein* to make a libation, promise, *spondē* libation (pl, treaty)]

²**spouse** *vt, archaic* to marry

¹**spout** /spowt/ *vt* 1 to eject (eg liquid) in a copious stream ⟨*wells* ~ing *oil*⟩ 2 to speak or utter in a strident, pompous, or hackneyed manner; declaim ⟨~ *party slogans*⟩ ~ *vi* 1 to issue with force or in a jet; spurt 2 to eject material, esp liquid, in a jet 3 *informal* to declaim [ME *spouten;* akin to MD *spoiten* to spout, OE *spīwan* to spew] – **spouter** *n*

²**spout** *n* 1 a pipe or conductor through which a liquid is discharged or conveyed in a stream: eg 1a a pipe for carrying rainwater from a roof b a projecting tube or lip to enable liquid to be poured from a teapot, kettle, etc 2 a discharge or jet of liquid (as if) from a pipe; *esp* a waterspout 3 *archaic* a pawnshop; *also* a lift or chute in a pawnshop leading to a storeroom – **spouted** *adj* – **up the spout** 1 *informal* beyond hope of improvement; ruined 2 *slang* pregnant [orig sense, pawned]

**sprachgefühl** /'shprahkgə,foohl/ (*Ger* ʃprɑːxgəfyːl)/ *n* sensibility to the established usage of a language [Ger, fr *sprache* language + *gefühl* feeling]

¹**sprag** /sprag/ *n* a pointed stake or steel bar for locking the wheel of a stationary vehicle [perh of Scand origin; akin to Sw dial. *spragge* branch]

²**sprag** *n* a young cod [origin unknown]

¹**sprain** /sprayn/ *n* 1 a sudden or violent twist or wrench of a joint with stretching or tearing of ligaments 2 a sprained condition [origin unknown]

   **synonyms** In common parlance, **sprain** applies particularly to ankles and wrists. It is more serious than a **strain**, which usually entails the stretching but not tearing of a muscle or tendon rather than a ligament.

²**sprain** *vt* to subject to sprain

**sprang** /sprang/ *past of* SPRING

**sprat** /sprat/ *n* 1 a small European herring (*Clupea sprattus*) closely related to the common herring 2 a small or young herring; *also* the young of a similar fish (eg an anchovy) [alter. of ME *sprot*, fr OE *sprott*]

¹**sprawl** /sprawl/ *vi* 1 to clamber awkwardly; scramble ⟨*two men* ~ed *out of the upturned car*⟩ 2 to lie or sit with arms and legs spread out carelessly or ungracefully ⟨*reading* ~ed *across a chair*⟩ 3 to spread or develop irregularly ⟨*a town that* ~s *across the countryside*⟩ ~ *vt* to cause (eg one's limbs) to spread out [ME *sprawlen*, fr OE *sprēawlian*]

²**sprawl** *n* 1 a sprawling position 2 an irregular spreading mass or group ⟨*a* ~ *of buildings*⟩

¹**spray** /spray/ *n* 1 a usu flowering branch or shoot of a plant 2 a small decorative arrangement of flowers and leaves (eg on a dress) 3 something (eg a jewelled pin) resembling a spray [ME]

²**spray** *n* 1 fine droplets of water blown or falling through the air ⟨*the* ~ *from the waterfall*⟩ **2a** a jet of vapour or finely divided liquid b a device (eg an atomizer) by which liquid is discharged or applied in a spray **c(1)** an application of a spray ⟨*give the roses a* ~⟩ **c(2)** a substance (eg paint or insecticide) so applied 3 something (eg a number of small flying objects) resembling a spray ⟨*a* ~ *of shotgun pellets*⟩ [obs *spray* to sprinkle, fr MD *sprayen;* akin to Gk *speirein* to scatter – more at SPROUT]

³**spray** *vt* 1 to discharge, disperse, or apply as a spray ⟨~ *paint on the wall*⟩ 2 to direct a spray on ⟨~ *the wall with paint*⟩ ⟨~ed *the room with a machine gun – Daily Mirror*⟩ ~ *vi* 1 to take the form of a spray 2 to disperse or apply a spray – **sprayer** *n*

**spray gun** *n* a device for applying a substance (eg paint or insecticide) in the form of a spray

¹**spread** /spred/ *vb* **spread** *vt* **1a** to open or extend over a larger area ⟨~ *her legs*⟩ – often + *out* ⟨~ *out the map*⟩ ⟨~ *out one's handwriting*⟩ b to stretch out; extend ⟨~ *its wings for flight*⟩ c to form (the lips) into a long narrow slit (eg when pronouncing the vowel /ee/) **2a** to distribute over an area ⟨~ *manure*⟩ b to distribute over a period or among a group ⟨~ *the work over a few weeks*⟩ c to apply as a layer or covering ⟨~ *butter on bread*⟩ ⟨~ *a tablecloth*⟩; *also* to cover or overlay with something ⟨~ *bread with butter*⟩ d to prepare for dining; set ⟨~ *the table*⟩ **3a** to make widely known or felt ⟨~ *the news*⟩ b to extend the range or incidence of ⟨~ *a disease*⟩ c to diffuse, emit ⟨*flowers* ~ing *their fragrance*⟩ 4 to force apart ⟨*the locomotive* ~ *the rails*⟩ ~ *vi* **1a** to become dispersed, distributed, or scattered ⟨*a race that* ~ *across the globe*⟩ b to become widely known or felt ⟨*panic* ~ *rapidly*⟩ **2a** to cover a

greater area; expand ⟨*a shadow* ~ *across his face*⟩ b to extend over a specified period of time 3 to be forced apart (eg from pressure or weight) – see also SPREAD ONE'S WINGS [ME *spreden*, fr OE *sprǣdan;* akin to OHG *spreiten* to spread, OE *-sprūtan* to sprout – more at SPROUT] – **spreadable** *adj*, **spreadability** *n*

²**spread** *n* **1a** (the extent of) spreading; expansion b an extent of time; a stretch 2 something spread out: eg **2a** a surface area; an expanse ⟨*a* ~ *of land*⟩ **b(1)** a prominent display in a newspaper or periodical **b(2)** (the matter occupying) two facing pages (eg of a newspaper), usu with printed matter running across the fold c a wide obstacle for a horse to jump d *dial NAm* a ranch 3 something spread on or over a surface: eg **3a** a food product suitable for spreading (eg on bread or biscuits) ⟨*cheese* ~⟩ b a sumptuous meal; a feast c a cloth cover; *esp* a bedspread 4 the distance between two points; a gap, span

¹**spread-,eagle** *vi* 1 to perform a SPREAD EAGLE (eg in skating) 2 to stand or lie with arms and legs stretched out wide; sprawl ~ *vt* 1 to stretch out into the position of a spread eagle ⟨~d *him on a log*⟩ 2 to spread across; straddle 3 to defeat utterly; rout

²**spread-eagle** *adj, NAm* marked by bombastic and esp American patriotism; chauvinistic ⟨~ *oratory*⟩ [fr the spread eagle on the Great Seal of the USA]

**spread eagle** *n* 1 a representation of an eagle with wings raised and legs extended 2 something resembling or suggestive of a spread eagle; *specif* a skating movement executed with the skates heel to heel in a straight line

**spreader** /'spredə/ *n* 1 a machine for scattering material (eg manure) over an area 2 WETTING AGENT (substance used to aid absorption of a liquid by a solid)

**spreading factor** *n* HYALURONIDASE (enzyme that facilitates the passage of liquids through tissues)

**spreadsheet** *n* a software system in which large groups of numerical data can be displayed on a VDU in a set format (eg in rows and columns) and rapid automatic calculations can be made

**sprechgesang** /'shprekgə,zang (*Ger* ʃpreçgəzaŋ)/ *n, often cap* singing in which notes are unsustained, as in speech [Ger, lit., speaking song]

**spree** /spree/ *n* a bout of unrestrained indulgence in an activity ⟨*went on a shopping* ~⟩; *esp* a binge [perh alter. of Sc *spreath* cattle raid, foray, fr ScGael *spreidh* cattle, fr L *praeda* booty – more at PREY]

¹**sprig** /sprig/ *n* 1 a small shoot or twig 2 an ornament in the form of a sprig 3 a small headless nail 4 *chiefly derog* a young offspring; *specif* a youth [ME *sprigge*]

²**sprig** *vt* **-gg-** 1 to drive sprigs into 2 to decorate with a representation of plant sprigs

**sprightly** /'spritli/ *adj* marked by a buoyant vitality and liveliness; spirited ⟨*a* ~ *75 year old*⟩ **synonyms** see NIMBLE **antonym** languid [obs *spright* sprite, alter. of *sprite*] – **sprightliness** *n*, **sprightly** *adv*

¹**spring** /spring/ *vb* **sprang** /sprang/, **sprung** /sprung/; **sprung** *vi* **1a(1)** to move suddenly (as if) by jumping; dart, bound **a(2)** to be resilient or elastic; *also* to move by elastic force ⟨*the lid* sprang *shut*⟩ b to become warped ⟨*the boards* sprang *as the wood dried*⟩ 2 to issue suddenly and copiously; pour out ⟨*the tears* sprang *from her eyes*⟩ **3a** to grow as a plant b to issue by birth or descent – usu + *from* c to come into being; arise – usu + *from* ⟨*the project* ~s *from earlier research*⟩ 4 to rise up suddenly; appear ⟨*blood* sprang *to his cheeks*⟩ ⟨*factories* ~ing *up all over*⟩ 5 to extend in height; rise ⟨*the tower* ~s *to 90 metres*⟩ ~ *vt* 1 to cause to spring 2 to split, crack ⟨*wind* sprang *the mast*⟩ **3a** to cause to operate suddenly ⟨~ *a trap*⟩ b to bring into a specified state by pressing or bending ⟨~ *a bar into place*⟩ c to bend by force 4 to leap over 5 to produce or disclose suddenly or unexpectedly; surprise someone with – usu + *on* ⟨~ *a surprise on them*⟩ 6 to make lame; strain 7 *informal* to release or cause to be released from prison [ME *springen*, fr OE *springan;* akin to OHG *springan* to jump, Gk *sperchesthai* to hasten]

**spring up** *vi* to begin to blow ⟨*a breeze quickly* sprang *up*⟩

²**spring** *adj, of a cereal crop* sown in the spring and harvested in the same year as sown – compare WINTER

³**spring** *n* **1a** a source of supply; *esp* a source of water issuing from the ground b **springs** *pl*, **spring** a place where water with specific properties (eg medicinal) rises naturally to the ground surface c an ultimate source or motivating force, esp of thought or action ⟨*the inner* ~s *of being*⟩ **2a** the season of new growth between winter and summer which in the N hemisphere is usu taken to comprise the months of March, April, and May; *also* the period

extending from the March EQUINOX (time when day and night are of equal length) to the June SOLSTICE (longest day of the year) **b** SPRINGTIME 3 **3** a mechanical part (eg of bent or coiled metal) that recovers its original shape when released after deformation **4** the springing back to normal position of a mechanical part when tension is released **5a** the act or an instance of leaping up or forward; a bound **b(1)** capacity for springing; resilience, springiness ⟨*no* ~ *left in the mattress*⟩ **b(2)** bounce, energy ⟨*a man with* ~ *in his step*⟩ **6 spring, springing** the point or plane at which an arch or vault curve rises from its support – **springless** *adj*, **springlike** *adj*

⁴**spring** *vt* **sprung** /sprung/ to equip with springs or elasticity ⟨*a sprung mattress*⟩

**springal** /'spring·əl/ *n* a springald

**springald** /'spring·əld/ *n, archaic* a young man; a stripling [prob fr ME, a kind of catapult, fr MF *espringale*]

**spring balance** *n* BALANCE 1b (weighing device)

**Spring Bank Holiday** *n* SPRING HOLIDAY

**springboard** /-ˌbawd/ *n* **1a** a flexible diving board secured at one end that a diver jumps off to gain extra height **b** a board used similarly to gain height for certain gymnastic events **2** something that provides an initial stimulation or impetus ⟨*a* ~ *for further economic effort*⟩

**springbok** /'springbok/ *n, pl* **springboks**, (*1*) **springboks,** *esp collectively* **springbok 1** a swift and graceful southern African gazelle (*Antidorcas euchore*) noted for its habit of springing lightly and suddenly into the air **2** *often cap* a sportsman or sportswoman representing S Africa, esp at rugby or cricket, in an international match or tour abroad [Afrik, fr *spring* to jump + *bok* male goat]

**spring chicken** *n* **1** *chiefly NAm* a young chicken, usu of about 1.5 kilograms (3 pounds), that is suitable for cooking **2** *chiefly humorous* a young person – usu neg ⟨*she's no* ~⟩

ˌ**spring-'clean** *vb* **1** to give a complete and thorough cleaning to (eg a house or furnishings) **2** to put into a proper or more satisfactory order ⟨~ *a government department*⟩ ~ *vi* to be occupied in spring-cleaning [back-formation fr *spring-cleaning*, fr ³*spring* 2] – **spring-clean, spring-cleaning** *n*

**springe** /sprinj, sprinzh/ *n* a snare for catching small mammals or birds [ME *sprenge, springe;* akin to OE *springan* to spring]

**springer** /'spring·ə/ *n* **1** the first stone of an arch where its curvature begins **2** one who or that which springs; *esp* SPRINGER SPANIEL

**springer spaniel** *n* a large spaniel, usu having a wavy silky coat, that is used chiefly for finding and flushing out small game

**spring fever** *n* a feeling of restlessness or arousal often associated with the onset of spring

**springform pan** /'spring,fawm/ *n* a loose-bottomed round metal cooking tin or mould that has an upright rim fastened in shape by a clamp, which when released causes the rim to spring open allowing the prepared food (eg a cheesecake) to be easily removed [fr the spring by which the rim is attached to the bottom]

**spring green** *n usu pl* a young green cabbage that is picked before the heart has fully developed

**springhead** /'spring,hed/ *n* a fountainhead

**Spring Holiday, Spring Bank Holiday** *n* the last Monday in May observed as a public holiday in England, Wales, and N Ireland, replacing the former Whitsuntide holiday

**springing** /'spring·ing/ *n* SPRING 6

**springing line** *n* the line connecting the two opposite points at which the curve of an arch or vault begins

ˌ**spring-'loaded** *adj* loaded or secured by means of spring tension or compression ⟨*a* ~ *bolt*⟩

**spring onion** *n* an onion (*Allium fistulosum*) with a small mild-flavoured thin-skinned bulb and long shoots that is chiefly eaten raw in salads – called also SALAD ONION, SCALLION

**spring roll** *n* a thin rolled fried pancake of dough or batter stuffed with a savoury mixture, typically consisting of quickly fried crunchy vegetables (eg bean sprouts) and shredded meats

**springtail** /-ˌtayl/ *n* any of an order (Collembola) of small primitive wingless insects common in soil and leaf litter that have a small forked springlike organ at the end of the abdomen with which they leap – called also COLLEMBOLAN

**springtide** /'spring,tied/ *n* springtime

**spring tide** *n* a tide of greater-than-average range occurring at or round the times of new and full moon

**springtime** /-ˌtiem/ *n* **1** the season of spring **2** youth **3 springtime, spring** an early or flourishing stage of development

**spring tine** *n* SPRING TOOTH

**spring tooth** *n* a springy usu flat and curved tooth (eg on a cultivator)

**spring wagon** *n, NAm* a light four-wheeled sprung wagon drawn by one or two horses

**springwood** /'spring,wood/ *n* the softer more porous portion of an ANNUAL RING of wood that develops early in the growing season – compare SUMMERWOOD

**springy** /'spring·i/ *adj* **1** full of springs of water ⟨*treacherous* ~ *country*⟩ **2** having an elastic or bouncy quality; resilient ⟨*walked with a* ~ *step*⟩ – **springily** *adv*, **springiness** *n*

¹**sprinkle** /'springkl/ *vt* **1** to scatter in fine drops or particles **2a** to occur at (random) intervals on; dot – often pass ⟨*meadows* ~d *with flowers*⟩ **b** to distribute at intervals (as if) by scattering **c** to wet lightly ~ *vi* **1** to scatter a liquid in fine drops **2** to rain lightly in scattered drops [ME *sprenklen, sprinclen;* akin to MHG *spreckel, sprenkel* spot, OE *spearca* spark]

²**sprinkle** *n* **1** an instance of sprinkling; *specif* a light fall of rain **2** a sprinkling

**sprinkler** /'springklə/ *n* a device for spraying a liquid, esp water: eg **a** a fire-extinguishing sprinkler system **b** an apparatus for watering a lawn

**sprinklered** /'springkləd/ *adj* having an automatic sprinkler system

**sprinkler system** *n* a heat-activated system for protecting a building against fire by means of overhead pipes which convey water or some other liquid to outlets

**sprinkling** /'springkling/ *n* a small quantity or number, esp falling in scattered drops or particles or distributed randomly

¹**sprint** /sprint/ *vi* to run or ride a bicycle at top speed, esp for a short distance [of Scand origin; akin to Sw dial. *sprinta* to jump, hop; akin to OHG *sprinzan* to jump up, Gk *spyrthizein*] – **sprinter** *n*

²**sprint** *n* **1** (an instance of) sprinting **2a** a short fast race: eg **2a(1)** a foot race of up to 400 metres (440 yards) run at top speed **a(2)** a bicycle race of up to about 1500 metres (1650 yards) **b** a burst of speed, esp at the end of a race

**sprit** /sprit/ *n* a spar that crosses a four-cornered sail fixed lengthways to the ship, diagonally to support the peak [ME *spret, sprit,* fr OE *sprēot* pole, spear; akin to OE -*sprūtan* to sprout]

**sprite** /spriet/ *n* **1** a (playful graceful) fairy ⟨*water* ~⟩ **2** an elfin person [ME *sprit,* fr OF *esprit,* fr L *spiritus* spirit]

**spritsail** /'sprits(ə)l, -ˌsayl/ *n* a sail extended by a sprit

**spritzig** /'shpritsig (*Ger* ʃprɪtsɪç)/ *adj, of wine* fizzy, sparkling [Ger, fr *spritzen* to squirt, splash]

**sprocket** /'sprokit/ *n* **1** a tooth or projection on the rim of a wheel, shaped so as to engage the links of a chain **2** *also* **sprocket wheel** a wheel or cylinder having sprockets (eg to engage a bicycle chain or for pulling film through a projector) [origin unknown]

**sprog** /sprog/ *n, Br slang* a child, youngster [origin unknown]

¹**sprout** /sprowt/ *vi* **1** to grow, spring up, or come forth as (if) a sprout **2** to send out sprouts or new growth ⟨*potatoes kept too warm will* ~ *prematurely*⟩ ~ *vt* to send forth or up; cause to develop; grow ⟨*the town* ~ed *factory chimneys*⟩ [ME *sprouten,* fr OE -*sprūtan;* akin to OHG *spriozan* to sprout, Gk *speirein* to scatter, sow]

²**sprout** *n* **1a** a (young) shoot (eg from a seed or root) **b** BRUSSELS SPROUT **2** something (eg a young offspring) compared to a sprout

**sprouting broccoli** /'sprowting/ *n* BROCCOLI 2

¹**spruce** /sproohs/ *n* any of a genus (*Picea*) of evergreen trees (eg Norway spruce and Sitka spruce) of the pine family with a cone-shaped head of dense needle-like leaves and soft light wood grown for timber, ornament, and the christmas trade; *also* any of several similar coniferous trees (eg Douglas fir) [obs *Spruce* Prussia, fr ME, alter. of *Pruce,* fr OF]

²**spruce** *adj* neat or smart in dress or appearance; trim ⟨*his* ~ *black coat and his bowler hat* – W S Maugham⟩ *synonyms* see ²NEAT [perh fr obs *Spruce leather* leather imported from Prussia] – **sprucely** *adv*, **spruceness** *n*

³**spruce** *vt* to make spruce ~ *vi* to make oneself spruce – usu + *up*

**spruce beer** *n* an alcoholic drink flavoured with spruce; *esp* one made from spruce twigs and leaves boiled with molasses or sugar and fermented with yeast

**spruce pine** *n* a large American pine (*Pinus glabra*) with light, soft, or weak wood; *also* any of several similar pines

**sprucer** /'sproohsə/ *n, Br slang* somebody who lies or deceives, esp for comic effect; a trickster [origin unknown] – **spruce** *vb*

**¹sprue** /sprooh/ *n* a long-lasting usu tropical disease of the stomach and intestines, marked esp by diarrhoea, loss of weight and energy, and vitamin-deficiency symptoms [D *spruw;* akin to MLG *sprüwe,* a kind of tumour]

**²sprue** *n* (a waste piece formed in) the hole through which molten metal or plastic is poured or forced into a mould [origin unknown]

**spruik** /'sprooh·ik/ *vi, Austr slang* to address a public meetings, harangue [origin unknown] – **spruiker** *n*

**spruit** /sprayt/ *n, SAfr* a small watercourse that is usu dry except in the rainy season [Afrik, sprout, small stream, fr MD *sprute,* fr *spruten* to sprout]

**sprung** /sprung/ *past and past part of* SPRING – used esp of a mattress with springs

**sprung rhythm** *n* a poetic rhythm, used esp by Gerard Manley Hopkins, designed to approximate the natural rhythm of speech and characterized by irregular FEET, each usu containing a single accented syllable and a number of unstressed syllables

**spry** /sprie/ *adj* **sprier, spryer; spriest, spryest** vigorously active; lively, nimble ⟨*75 years old and still* ~ *as a kitten*⟩ *synonyms* see NIMBLE *antonyms* torpid, doddering (of the old) [perh of Scand origin; akin to Sw dial. *sprygg* spry] – **spryly** *adv,* **spryness** *n*

**¹spud** /spud/ *n* **1** a small narrow spade **2** *informal* a potato [ME *spudde* dagger]

**²spud** *vb* **-dd-** *vt* **1** to dig up or remove with a spud – often + *up* **2** to begin to drill (an oil well) ~ *vi* **1** to use a spud **2** to begin to drill an oil well

**'spud-,bashing** *n, Br informal* the peeling of potatoes, esp when done as a punishment in a military camp

**spume** /spyoohm/ *vi or n* (to) froth, foam ⟨*shore ... ruffed with sea* ~ – Han Suyin⟩ [ME, fr MF, fr L *spuma* – more at FOAM] – **spumous** *adj,* **spumy** *adj,* **spumescent** *adj*

**spun** /spun/ *past of* SPIN

**spun glass** *n* **1** fibreglass **2** blown glass that has slender threads of glass incorporated in it

**spunk** /spungk/ *n* **1** (any of various fungi used to make) tinder **2** *informal* spirit, pluck **3** *Br vulg* semen [ScGael *spong* sponge, tinder, fr L *spongia* sponge]

**spun rayon** *n* a yarn or fabric made from short fibres (STAPLES) of rayon

**spun silk** *n* a yarn or fabric made from silk waste that has been boiled to remove the gum

**spun sugar** *n* **1** sugar boiled until it forms long threads on cooling, gathered up and shaped, and used to decorate cold desserts **2** *chiefly NAm* CANDY FLOSS

**spun yarn** *n* **1** a textile yarn spun from short-stranded fibres **2** a small rope or cord formed of two or more rope yarns loosely twisted together and used for SEIZINGS (rope fastenings), esp on board ship

**¹spur** /spuh/ *n* **1a** a pointed or wheel-shaped metal device secured to the heel of a rider's boot and pressed or moved against a horse's flank to urge it on **b** *pl* recognition and reward for achievement ⟨*won his academic* ~s⟩ **2** a goad to action; a stimulus, incentive ⟨*my background was a definite* ~ *to achievement – Woman's Journal*⟩ **3** something projecting like or suggesting a spur: e g **3a** a projecting root or branch of a tree **b(1)** a stiff sharp spine (e g on the wings or legs of a bird or insect); *esp* one on a cock's leg **b(2)** a metal spike fitted to a fighting cock's leg **c** a hollow tubular projection of a plant flower head (e g in larkspur, columbine, and some orchids) **4** a ridge that extends sideways from a mountain (range) **5** a short piece of road or railway connecting with a major route (e g a motorway) [ME *spure,* fr OE *spura;* akin to OE *spurnan* to kick –more at SPURN; (1b) fr the acquisition of spurs by a person achieving knighthood] – **on the spur of the moment** suddenly; ON IMPULSE

**²spur** *vb* **-rr-** *vt* **1** to urge (a horse) on with spurs **2** to incite to usu faster action or greater effort; stimulate – usu + *on* **3** to put spurs on ~ *vi* to urge a horse on; ride hard ⟨~ *into the fray*⟩

**spurge** /spuhj/ *n* any of various mostly shrubby plants (esp genus *Euphorbia* of the family Euphorbiaceae, the spurge family) with a bitter milky juice used formerly as a laxative, very small simple flowers, and showy BRACTS (small leaflike structures) [ME, fr MF, purge, spurge, fr *espurgier* to purge, fr L *expurgare* – more at EXPURGATE]

**spur gear** *n* a GEAR WHEEL with teeth parallel to its axis, used to transmit power between parallel shafts

**spurge laurel** *n* a low Eurasian evergreen shrub (*Daphne laureola* of the family Thymelaeaceae) with smooth oblong leaves and small greenish stalked flowers growing along a central main stem

**spurious** /'spyooəri·əs/ *adj* **1** of illegitimate birth; bastard **2** having a superficial usu deceptive resemblance or correspondence; false ⟨~ *fruit*⟩ ⟨~ *labour pains*⟩ **3a** of deliberately falsified or mistakenly attributed origin; forged **b** of a deceitful nature or quality ⟨*a completely* ~ *witness*⟩ **4** based on mistaken ideas ⟨*it would be* ~ *to claim special privileges*⟩ [LL & L; LL *spurius* false, fr L, of illegitimate birth, fr *spurius,* n, bastard] – **spuriously** *adv,* **spuriousness** *n*

**spurn** /spuhn/ *vi* **1** *archaic* to show scorn or contempt – usu + *at* ⟨~ *at danger*⟩ **2** *obs* to kick ~ *vt* **1** to thrust against or away with the foot **2** to reject with disdain or contempt; scorn ⟨~ *a lover*⟩ [ME *spurnen,* fr OE *spurnan;* akin to OHG *spurnan* to kick, L *spernere* to despise, Gk *spairein* to quiver] – **spurn** *n,* **spurner** *n*

**,spur-of-the-'moment** *adj* occurring or undertaken suddenly and without premeditation ⟨*a* ~ *decision*⟩

**spurred** /spuhd/ *adj* **1** wearing spurs **2** *esp of a plant* having one or more spurs ⟨*a* ~ *flower*⟩

**spurrey, spurry** /'spuri/ *n, pl* **spurreys, spurries** any of several small sprawling usu white-flowered plants (genera *Spergula* and *Spergularia*) of the pink family growing near the sea and invading crops; *esp* CORN SPURREY [D *spurrie,* fr ML *spergula*]

**spurrier** /'spuhri·ə/ *n* somebody who makes spurs

**¹spurt** /spuht/ *vi or n* (to make) a sudden brief burst of increased effort, activity, or speed [origin unknown]

**²spurt** *vi* to gush out in a jet; spout ⟨*blood* ~ed *from a severed artery*⟩ to expel in a stream or jet; squirt [perh akin to MHG *spürzen* to spit, OE *-sprūtan* to sprout – more at SPROUT]

**³spurt** *n* a sudden forceful gush; a jet

**spurtle** /'spuhtl/ *n, chiefly Scot* a wooden stick for stirring porridge [origin unknown]

**spur wheel** *n* SPUR GEAR

**sputnik** /'sputnik, 'spootnik/ *n* SATELLITE 2b – used chiefly with reference to Soviet satellites [Russ, lit., travelling companion, fr *s, so* with + *put'* path + *-nik,* agentive suffix]

**¹sputter** /'sputə/ *vt* **1** to eject from the mouth with spitting or explosive sounds **2** to utter hastily or explosively in confusion, anger, or excitement; splutter **3** to dislodge (atoms) from the surface of a material by collision with high energy particles, esp by use of a DISCHARGE TUBE; *also* to deposit (a metallic film) by such a process ~ *vi* **1** to spit or squirt particles of food or saliva noisily from the mouth **2** to speak explosively or incoherently **3** to make explosive popping sounds [akin to D *sputteren* to sputter, OE *-sprūtan* to sprout] – **sputterer** *n*

**²sputter** *n* **1** confused and excited speech **2** (the sound of) sputtering

**sputum** /'spyoohtəm/ *n, pl* **sputa** /-tə/ *medicine* material spat out from the mouth made up of saliva and other discharges from the windpipe and other respiratory passages; *esp* such material used in the diagnosis of tuberculosis, bronchitis, etc [L, fr neut of *sputus,* pp of *spuere* to spit – more at SPEW]

**¹spy** /spie/ *vt* **1** to keep under secret surveillance, usu for hostile purposes – often + *out* ⟨~ *out the land*⟩ **2** to catch sight of; see ⟨spied *him lurking in the bushes*⟩ **3** to search or look for intently – usu + *out* ⟨~ *out a means of escape*⟩ ~ *vi* **1** to observe or search for something; look **2** to watch secretly; act as a spy – often + *on* [ME *spien,* fr OF *espier,* of Gmc origin; akin to OHG *spehōn* to spy; akin to L *specere* to look, look at, *species* appearance, species, Gk *skeptesthai* & *skopein* to watch, look at, consider]

**²spy** *n* **1a** one who or that which keeps secret watch on somebody or something **b** a person who attempts to gain information in one country, company, etc and communicate it to another usu hostile one **2** an act of spying

**spyglass** /'spiehglahs/ *n* a small telescope

**spymaster** /'spie,mahstə/ *n* somebody in charge of a secret state espionage organization

**squab** /skwob/ *n, pl* **squabs, (1) squabs,** *esp collectively* **squab 1** a fledgling bird; *specif* a fledgling pigeon about four weeks old **2** a short fat person **3a** a sofa, ottoman **b** a stuffed cushion for a chair, sofa seat, or car seat [prob of Scand origin; akin to Sw dial. *skvabb* anything soft and thick] – **squab** *adj*

**squabble** /'skwobl/ *vi or n* (to engage in) a noisy or heated quarrel, esp over trifles *synonyms* see ²QUARREL [prob of Scand origin; akin to Sw dial. *skvabbel* dispute] – **squabbler** *n*

**squab pie** *n* **1** a pigeon pie **2** a mutton or pork pie containing onion and apple

**squacco** /'skwakoh/ *n, pl* **squaccos** a small shortnecked crested heron (*Ardeola ralloides*) of S Europe, Asia, and Africa [It dial. *squacco*]

¹**squad** /skwod/ *n taking sing or pl vb* **1** a group of no more than 12 soldiers assembled for a purpose ⟨*a drill* ∼⟩ **2** a small group working as a team (eg a team of players) ⟨*a special police* ∼⟩ ⟨*the England* ∼⟩ [MF *esquade*, fr OSp & OIt; OSp *escuadra* & OIt *squadra*, derivs of (assumed) VL *exquadrare* to make square – more at SQUARE]

²**squad** *vt* **-dd-** to arrange in squads

**squad car** *n, chiefly NAm* a police car having radio communication with headquarters – called also CRUISER, PROWL CAR

**squaddy** /'skwodi/ *n, chiefly Br informal* a member of an army squad; *esp* a private [alter. (influenced by *squad*) of *swaddy*, fr *swad* (soldier), prob fr obs *swad* bumpkin, lout]

**squadron** /'skwodrən/ *n taking sing or pl vb* a unit of military organization: **a** a unit of cavalry or of an armoured regiment, usu consisting of three or more troops **b** a variable naval unit consisting of a number of warships on a particular operation ⟨*the south Atlantic* ∼⟩ **c** a unit of an air force consisting usu of between 10 and 18 aircraft [It *squadrone*, aug of *squadra* squad]

**squadron leader** *n* – see MILITARY RANKS table

**squalene** /'skwayleen/ *n* a chemical compound, $C_{30}H_{50}$, that is widely distributed in nature (eg in seeds and esp in shark-liver oils) and is an important intermediate in the reaction to produce STEROLS (eg cholesterol) [ISV, fr NL *squalus*, genus name of sharks]

**squalid** /'skwolid/ *adj* **1** filthy and degraded from neglect or poverty ⟨∼ *ramshackle tenements*⟩ **2** SORDID 2 *synonyms* see ¹DIRTY [L *squalidus* – more at SQUALOR] – **squalidly** *adv*, **squalidness** *n*

¹**squall** /skwawl/ *vi* to cry out raucously; scream ∼ *vt* to utter in a squalling voice [of Scand origin; akin to ON *skval* useless chatter] – **squall** *n*, **squaller** *n*

²**squall** *n* **1** a sudden violent wind, often with rain or snow **2** a short-lived commotion ⟨*a minor domestic* ∼⟩ [prob of Scand origin; akin to Sw *skval* rushing water] – **squally** *adj*

**squalor** /'skwolə/ *n* the quality or state of being squalid [L; akin to L *squalidus* squalid, *squama* scale]

**squam-, squamo-** *comb form* scale; squama ⟨squam*ous*⟩ [NL, fr L *squama*]

**squama** /'skwaymə, 'skwahmə/ *n, pl* **squamae** /-mi/ (a structure resembling) a scale [L]

**squamate** /'skwaymayt/ *adj* scaly ⟨∼ *reptiles*⟩

**squamation** /skwə'maysh(ə)n/ *n* **1** the state of being scaly **2** the arrangement of scales on an animal

**squamosal** /skwə'mohsl/ *adj* **1** squamous **2** of or being a thin platelike bone of the skull of many VERTEBRATE animals corresponding to the squamous portion of the bone covering the temple (TEMPORAL BONE) in man

**squamose** /'skwaymohs, 'skwah-/ *adj* squamous

**squamous** /'skwaymos, 'skwahmos/ *adj* **1a** covered with or consisting of scales; scaly **b** *biology* of or being an EPITHELIUM (tissue covering an external surface or lining a body cavity) that consists at least in its outer layers of small flat scalelike cells **2** of or being the front upper portion of the compound bone covering the temple (TEMPORAL BONE) in various mammals (eg man) [L *squamosus*, fr *squama* scale] – **squamously** *adv*, **squamousness** *n*

**squamous cell** *n, biology* a cell of or derived from squamous EPITHELIUM (tissue covering an external surface or lining a body cavity)

**squamulose** /'skwaymyoolohs/ *adj* having small scales [L *squamula*, dim. of *squama*]

**squander** /'skwondə/ *vt* **1** to disperse, scatter **2** to spend extravagantly, foolishly, or wastefully; dissipate ⟨∼ed *his earnings on drink*⟩ [origin unknown] – **squander** *n*, **squanderer** *n*

¹**square** /skweə/ *n* **1** a usu T-shaped or L-shaped instrument used to draw, measure, or test RIGHT ANGLES; *also* SET SQUARE **2** a rectangle with all four sides equal **3** something shaped like a square: eg **3a** a square headscarf **b** an area of ground for a particular purpose (eg military drill) **c** an arrangement of letters, numbers, etc in a square – compare MAGIC SQUARE **4** any of the quadrilateral spaces marked out on a board or diagram used for playing games **5** the number obtained when a number is multiplied by itself **6** an open space in a town, city, etc

formed at the meeting of two or more streets, and often laid out with grass and trees **7** a solid object or piece approximating to a cube or having a square as its principal face **8** an unopened cotton flower with its enclosing BRACTS (small leaflike structures) **9** *informal* somebody who is excessively conventional or conservative in tastes or outlook – no longer in vogue [ME, fr MF *esquarre*, fr (assumed) VL *exquadra*, fr *exquadrare* to square, fr L *ex-* + *quadrare* to square – more at QUADRATE] – **on the square 1** at right angles **2** in a fair open manner; honestly – **out of square** not an exact right angle

²**square** *adj* **1a** having four equal sides and four RIGHT ANGLES **b** forming a RIGHT ANGLE ⟨*a* ∼ *corner*⟩ **2a** approximating to a cube ⟨*a* ∼ *cabinet*⟩ **b** of a shape or build suggesting strength and solidity; broad in relation to length or height ⟨∼ *shoulders*⟩ **c** square in cross section ⟨∼ *tower*⟩ **3a** *of a unit of length* denoting an area equal to that of a square whose edges are of the specified length ⟨*a* ∼ *mile*⟩ ⟨*six* ∼ *feet*⟩ **b** being of a specified length in each of two equal dimensions meeting at a right angle ⟨*10 metres* ∼⟩ **4a** exactly adjusted, arranged, or aligned; neat and orderly **b** fair, honest, or straightforward ⟨∼ *in all his dealings*⟩ **c** leaving no balance; settled ⟨*the accounts are all* ∼⟩ **d** even, tied ⟨*after four games they were* ∼⟩ **e** blunt, unequivocal ⟨*a* ∼ *refusal*⟩ **5** set at right angles with the mast and keel – used of the spars of a square-rigged ship **6** of, occupying, or passing through a fielding position at right angles to the line between the wickets and level with the batsman's wicket ⟨∼ *cover*⟩ **7** *informal* excessively conservative; dully conventional – no longer in vogue – **squarely** *adv*, **squareness** *n*, **squarish** *adj*

³**square** *vt* **1a** to make square or rectangular ⟨∼ *a building stone*⟩ **b** to test for deviation from a RIGHT ANGLE, straight line, or plane surface **2** to set approximately at RIGHT ANGLES or so as to present a rectangular outline ⟨∼d *his shoulders*⟩ **3a** to multiply (a number) by itself; raise to the second power **b** to find a square equal in area to ⟨∼ *a circle*⟩ **4** to regulate or adjust in accord with a standard or principle ⟨∼ *our actions by the opinions of others* – John Milton⟩ **5a** to balance, settle ⟨∼ *an account*⟩ **b** to even the score of (a contest) **6** to mark off into squares or rectangles **7a** to bring into agreement; reconcile ⟨∼ *theory with practice*⟩ **b** *informal* to bribe ∼ *vi* **1** to match or agree precisely – usu + *with* **2** to settle matters; *esp* to pay the bill – often + *up*

**square away** *vi* to set the spars of a square-rigged ship at right angles to the mast and keel so as to sail before the wind ∼ *vt, NAm informal* to put in order or in readiness

**square up** *vt* **1** to prepare oneself to meet a (challenge) ⟨squared up to *the situation*⟩ **2** to take a fighting stance towards (an opponent)

⁴**square** *adv* **1** in a straightforward or honest manner ⟨told him ∼⟩ **2a** so as to face or be face to face ⟨*the house stood* ∼ *to the road*⟩ **b** at RIGHT ANGLES **3** DIRECTLY 1 ⟨*hit a nail* ∼ *on the head*⟩ **4** in a resolute manner ⟨*looked him* ∼ *in the eye*⟩

'**square-ˌbashing** *n, chiefly Br informal* military drill, esp marching, on a barrack square

**square bracket** *n* either of a pair of punctuation marks [ ] used in writing and printing to enclose matter or in mathematics and logic to show that a complex expression should be treated as a single unit – called also BRACE

**square dance** *n* a formation dance (eg a quadrille) for four couples who form a hollow square and respond to the commands of a caller – **square dancer** *n*, **square dancing** *n*

**square deal** *n* an honest and fair arrangement or transaction ⟨*got a* ∼ *on that trade-in*⟩

**squarehead** /'skweə,hed/ *n, chiefly NAm derog* a German, Dutch, or Scandinavian person, esp an immigrant

**square leg** *n* a fielding position in cricket between a third of the way and halfway to the boundary on the LEG SIDE of the pitch, situated in line with the batsman's wicket; *also* the fieldsman occupying this position

**square matrix** *n* a mathematical MATRIX (arrangement of numbers or other mathematical elements) with an equal number of rows and columns

**square meal** *n* a satisfying meal

**square measure** *n* a system of units for measuring area

**square one** *n* the starting point ⟨*our plan failed, so we were back to* ∼⟩ [prob fr some game like ludo played on a board with numbered squares]

**square piano** *n* an early piano that has an oblong case and that is horizontally strung

**squarer** /'skweərə/ *n* somebody who squares; *esp* a workman who squares timber or stone

**square rig** *n* a sailing-ship rig in which the principal sails are SQUARE SAILS – **square-rigged** *adj*, **square-rigger** *n*

**square root** *n* a number which when multiplied by itself is a given number ⟨*the ~ of 9 is ±3*⟩

**square sail** *n* a 4-sided sail that is set across a ship in a side-to-side direction and held open by a horizontal rod (YARD) that is suspended at its centre from a mast

**square shooter** *n*, *NAm informal* a just or honest person

**square-'shouldered** *adj* having shoulders that present a rectangular outline – compare ROUND-SHOULDERED

**square wave** *n*, *physics* the rectangular WAVEFORM (graphical representation of a wave) of a quantity that varies periodically and abruptly from one to the other of two uniform values

**squarrose** /'skwarohs, 'skworohs/ *adj*, *of a plant or animal (part)* having a rough, hairy, or scaly surface [L *squarrosus* scurfy, scabby]

**¹squash** /skwosh/ *vt* **1a** to press or beat into a pulp or a flat mass; crush **b** to apply pressure to by pushing or squeezing ⟨*got ~ed on the crowded platform*⟩ **2** to reduce to silence or inactivity; PUT DOWN ⟨*~ a revolt*⟩ ⟨*~ed him with a cutting remark*⟩ ~ *vi* **1** to flatten out under pressure or impact **2** to squeeze, press ⟨*we ~ed into the front row of spectators*⟩ [MF *esquasser*, fr (assumed) VL *exquassare*, fr L *ex-* + *quassare* to shake – more at QUASH] – **squasher** *n*

**²squash** *n* **1** the impact caused by the fall of a heavy soft body; *also* the soft dull sound of such an impact ⟨*fruit fell to the gravel with a ~*⟩ **2** a crushed mass; *esp* a mass of people crowded into a restricted space **3** *also* **squash rackets** an indoor game played usu by two people in a 4-walled court with light long-handled rackets and a small rubber ball that can be played off any wall **4** *Br* a SOFT DRINK made from sweetened and often concentrated citrus fruit juice, usu drunk diluted ⟨*orange ~*⟩ **5** *obs* something soft and easily crushed; *specif* an unripe pod of peas [(3) fr the soft squashy ball]

**³squash** *adv* with a squash or a squashing sound

**⁴squash** *n*, *pl* **squashes**, **squash** any of various fruits of plants (genus *Cucurbita*) of the marrow family usually cultivated as vegetables and for livestock feed; *also* an esp climbing plant that bears squashes [by shortening & alter. fr earlier *isquoutersquash*, fr Natick & Narraganset *askútasquash*]

**squashy** /'skwoshi/ *adj* soft ⟨*~ melons*⟩ ⟨*~ ground*⟩ ⟨*a ~ cushion*⟩ – **squashily** *adv*, **squashiness** *n*

**¹squat** /skwot/ *vb* **-tt-** *vi* **1** to cause (oneself) to crouch or sit on the ground **2** to occupy as a squatter ~ *vi* **1** to crouch close to the ground as if to escape detection; cower ⟨*a ~ting hare*⟩ **2** to assume or maintain a position in which the body is supported on the feet and the knees are bent so that the haunches rest on or near the heels **3** to occupy property as a squatter [ME *squatten*, fr MF *esquatir*, fr *es-* ex- (fr L *ex-*) + *quatir* to press, fr (assumed) VL *coactire* to press together, fr L *coactus*, pp of *cogere* to drive together – more at COGENT]

**²squat** *n* **1a** the act of squatting **b** the posture of somebody or something that squats **2** *informal* an empty building occupied by or available to squatters

**³squat** *adj* **-tt-** **1** with the heels drawn up under the haunches **2a** low to the ground ⟨*~ red-brick bungalows*⟩ **b** disproportionately short and thick ⟨*a ~ red neck*⟩ – **squatly** *adv*, **squatness** *n*

**squatter** /'skwotə/ *n* **1** one who squats: e g **1a** somebody who occupies usu otherwise empty property without right of ownership or payment of rent **b** somebody who settles on public land under government regulation with the purpose of acquiring legal possession **2** *Austr* somebody who owns large tracts of grazing land

**squatty** /'skwoti/ *adj*, *chiefly NAm* dumpy, thickset

**squaw** /skwaw/ *n* **1** a N American Indian (married) woman **2** *chiefly NAm derog* a woman, wife [of Algonquian origin; akin to Natick *squáas* woman]

**squawk** /skwawk/ *vi or n* **1** (to utter) a harsh abrupt scream (like that) characteristic of certain birds (eg parrots) **2** (to make) a loud or vehement protest [prob blend of *squall* and *squeak*] – **squawker** *n*

**squaw man** *n* a white man married to a N American Indian woman and usu living as one of her tribe

**¹squeak** /skweek/ *vi* **1** to utter or make a squeak **2** to pass, succeed, or win by a narrow margin – esp + *by* or *through* **3** *informal* SQUEAL 2a ~ *vt* to utter (words) in a shrill piping tone [ME *squeken*, prob of imit origin]

**²squeak** *n* **1** a short shrill cry or noise **2** *informal* an escape –

chiefly in *a narrow squeak* – **squeaky** *adj*

**squeaker** /'skweekə/ *n* **1** one who or that which squeaks **2** a young unfledged pigeon

**¹squeal** /skweel/ *vi* **1** to utter or make a squeal **2** *informal* **2a** to turn informer ⟨*bribed to ~ on his boss*⟩ **b** to complain, protest ~ *vt* to utter or express (as if) with a squeal [ME *squelen*, prob of imit origin] – **squealer** *n*

**²squeal** *n* a shrill sharp cry or noise

**squeamish** /'skweemish/ *adj* **1a** easily nauseated; queasy **b** affected with nausea; nauseated **2a** excessively fastidious or scrupulous in manners, conduct, or convictions **b** easily shocked or offended; prudish [ME *squaymisch*, modif of AF *escoymous*] – **squeamishly** *adv*, **squeamishness** *n*

**¹squeegee** /'skweejee/ *n* a blade of leather or rubber set on a handle and used for spreading, pushing, or wiping liquid material on, across, or esp off a surface (e g a window); *also* a smaller similar device or a small rubber roller with handle used by a photographer or lithographer, esp for squeezing water out of wet prints [prob imit]

**²squeegee** *vt* **squeegeed**; **squeegeeing** to smooth, wipe, or treat with a squeegee

**¹squeeze** /skweez/ *vt* **1a** to apply physical pressure to esp opposite sides of; compress ⟨*he ~d her hand reassuringly*⟩ **b** to extract or discharge under pressure ⟨*~ juice from a lemon*⟩ **c** to force or thrust (as if) by compression; cram ⟨*~ clothes into a suitcase*⟩ **2a(1)** to obtain by force or extortion ⟨*dictators who ~ money from the poor*⟩ **a(2)** to deprive by extortion ⟨*~ the peasants*⟩ **b** to cause economic hardship to ⟨*a firm ~d by rising costs*⟩ **c** to reduce (profits) **3** to crowd into a limited area, time span, or schedule ⟨*small houses ~d between railway and canal*⟩ ⟨*we'll ~ you in at three o'clock*⟩ **4** to force (another player) to discard a card to his/her disadvantage, esp in bridge ~ *vi* **1** to exert pressure; *also* to practise extortion or oppression **2** to force one's way ⟨*~ through a door*⟩ **3** to pass, win, or survive narrowly ⟨*managed to ~ through the month on sick pay*⟩ [alter. of obs *quease*, fr ME *queysen*, fr OE *cwȳsan*; akin to Icel *kveisa* stomach cramps] – **squeezable** *adj*, **squeezability** *n*, **squeezer** *n*

**²squeeze** *n* **1a** an act or instance of squeezing; a compression **b** a handshake; *also* an embrace **2a** a quantity squeezed out from something ⟨*a ~ of lemon*⟩ **b** *informal* a condition of being crowded together; a crush ⟨*it was a tight ~ with six in the car*⟩ **3a** financial pressure caused by restricting credit, used esp by a government to reduce price inflation **b** *informal* pressure brought to bear on somebody – chiefly in *put the squeeze on* **4** a forced act of discarding a card in bridge

**'squeeze-,box** *n*, *informal* an accordion

**squeezy bottle** /'skweezi/ *n* a bottle of flexible plastic that must be pressed to dispense its contents

**squegging** /'skweging/ *n* a type of OSCILLATION (flow of electric current that periodically changes direction) in an electronic system in which the oscillations build up to a maximum and then fall to zero [*squeg* (to oscillate irregularly), based on squeeze and *wedge*]

**¹squelch** /skwelch/ *n* **1** a sound (like that) of soft wet matter under suction ⟨*the ~ of mud*⟩ **2** *informal* an act of suppressing; *esp* a retort that silences an opponent [imit] – **squelchy** *adj*

**²squelch** *vt* **1** to fall or stamp on so as to crush **2a** to suppress completely; quell, squash **b** to silence ~ *vi* **1** to emit a sucking sound like that of an object being withdrawn from mud **2** to splash noisily in or through water, slush, or mud ⟨*~ through a miry farm gateway* – Adrian Bell⟩ – **squelcher** *n*, **squelchy** *adj*

**¹squib** /skwib/ *n* **1a** a small cylindrical firework that fizzes and ends with a bang **b** a faulty firework which fizzles out; *also* something resembling this **2** a small electric or explosive device used to ignite a charge; *also* a similar device used to fire an igniter in a rocket **3** a short witty or satirical speech or piece of writing [origin unknown]

**²squib** *vb* **-bb-** *vi* **1** to speak, write, or publish squibs **2** to fire a squib ~ *vt* **1a** to utter in an offhand manner **b** to produce squibs against; lampoon **2** to shoot off; fire

**¹squid** /skwid/ *n*, *pl* **squids**, *esp collectively* **squid** any of numerous soft-bodied marine INVERTEBRATE animals (esp of the genera *Loligo* and *Ommastrephes* of the class Cephalopoda, phylum Mollusca) that have a long tapered body, a large head, ten suckered tentacles, and usu a slender internal shell-like support [origin unknown]

**²squid** *vi* **-dd-** to fish with or for squid

**squidgy** /'skwiji/ *adj*, *chiefly Br informal* soft and clammy ⟨*a ~ lump of dough*⟩ [imit]

**squiffy** /'skwifi/ *adj, informal* slightly drunk; tipsy [origin unknown]

**squiggle** /'skwigl/ *vi or n, informal* (to form) a short wavy twist or line, esp in handwriting or drawing [blend of *squirm* and *wriggle*] – **squiggly** *adj*

**squill** /skwil/ *n* **1a** a Mediterranean plant (*Urginea maritima*) of the lily family, having clusters of small white flowers **b** the dried sliced bulb of squill used esp as a medicine to ease coughing **2** SCILLA (plant of the lily family) **3** a squilla [ME, fr L *squilla, scilla* sea onion, fr Gk *skilla*]

**squilla** /'skwilə/ *n, pl* **squillas, squillae** /'skwili/, **squills** any of various shrimplike INVERTEBRATE animals (esp genus *Squilla* of the class Crustacea) that burrow in mud or beneath stones in shallow water along the seashore [NL, genus name, fr L, squill, prawn]

**squinch** /skwinch/ *n* an arch, lintel, etc placed across the internal corner of a square structure to support something octagonal or circular (e g a dome) – compare PENDENTIVE [alter. of earlier *scunch* back part of the side of an opening, short for *scuncheon, sconcheon,* fr ME *sconcheon,* fr MF *escochon,* fr *coing* wedge, corner]

**¹squinny** /'skwini/ *vi* to squint, peer ⟨~ing *short-sightedly* – *The Guardian*⟩ [prob fr obs *squin* obliquely, fr ME *skuin*]

**²squinny** *n* SQUINT 1 – **squinny** *adj*

**¹squint** /skwint/ *adj* **1** *of an eye* looking or tending to look obliquely or askance (e g with envy or disdain) **2** *of the eyes* having a squint; crossed [short for *asquint,* adv, obliquely, fr ME, of unknown origin]

**²squint** *vi* **1a** to have an indirect bearing, reference, or aim **b** to deviate from a true line **2a** to look in a squint-eyed manner **b** to be cross-eyed **c** to look or peer with eyes partly closed (e g from the effect of sunlight) ~ *vt* to cause (an eye) to squint – **squinter** *n,* **squintingly** *adv*

**³squint** *n* **1** (a visual disorder marked by) the inability to direct both eyes to the same object because of imbalance of the muscles of the eyeball **2** an instance of squinting **3** HAGIOSCOPE (opening in a church wall giving a view of the altar) **4** *informal* a glance, look – chiefly in *have/take a squint at* – **squinty** *adj*

**squint-'eyed** *adj* **1** having eyes that squint, esp inwards **2** looking askance (e g in envy)

**¹squire** /skwie·ə/ *n* **1** a shield-bearer or armour-bearer of a knight **2a** a male attendant, esp on an important personage **b** a man who devotedly accompanies a lady; a gallant **3a** a member of the British gentry ranking below a knight and above a gentleman **b** an owner of a country estate; *esp* the principal landowner in a village or district **4** *Br informal* PAL **2** [ME *squier,* fr OF *esquier* – more at ESQUIRE] – **squirish** *adj*

**²squire** *vt* to attend on or escort (a woman)

**squirearchy, squirarchy** /'skwie·ə,rahki/ *n taking sing or pl vb* **1** the gentry or landed-proprietor class **2** government by a landed gentry – **squirearchical** *adj*

**squireen** /skwi'reen/ *n* a petty landowner, esp in Ireland [*squire* + *-een,* dim. suffix, fr IrGael *-ín*]

**squirm** /skwuhm/ *vi* **1** to twist about like a worm; wriggle **2** to feel or show acute discomfort at something embarrassing, shameful, or unpleasant [perh imit] **squirm** *n,* **squirmer** *n,* **squirmy** *adj*

**¹squirrel** /'skwirəl/ *n, pl* **squirrels,** *esp collectively* **squirrel 1** any of various African, Eurasian, and N American small to medium-sized tree-dwelling rodents (family Sciuridae) that have a long bushy tail and strong hind legs and that feed on nuts and seeds **2** the reddish-brown or grey fur of a squirrel [ME *squirel,* fr MF *esquireul,* fr (assumed) VL *scuriolus,* dim. of *scurius,* alter. of L *sciurus,* fr Gk *skiouros,* fr *skia* shadow + *oura* tail; akin to OHG *ars* buttocks, OIr *err* tail – more at SHINE]

**²squirrel** *vt* **-ll-** (*NAm* **-l-,** **-ll-**) to hoard – often + *away* [fr the squirrel's habit of storing up nuts and seeds for winter use]

**squirrel cage** *n* **1** (a type of induction motor having) a ROTOR with cylindrically arranged metal bars **2** a way of life, task, etc that is repetitive, purposeless, and inescapable [fr the toy treadmill often provided in the cage of a squirrel or other small animal]

**squirrel gun** *n* SQUIRREL RIFLE

**squirrel monkey** *n* a small soft-haired S American monkey (*Saimiri sciureus*) that has a long tail and is coloured chiefly yellowish grey with a white face and black nose

**squirrel rifle** *n* a small-bore rifle [fr its being suitable only for shooting small game]

**squirrel-tail grass** *n* a grass (*Hordeum marinum*) growing on European saltmarshes and having a bushy flowerhead

**¹squirt** /skwuht/ *vi* to issue in a sudden forceful stream from a narrow opening; spurt ~ *vt* **1** to cause to squirt **2** to direct a thin jet (e g of water) at ⟨~ed *his sister with a water pistol*⟩ [ME *squirten;* akin to LG *swirtjen* to squirt] – **squirter** *n*

**²squirt** *n* **1a** an instrument (e g a syringe) for squirting a liquid **b** a small rapid stream of liquid; a jet **2** *informal* **2a** a young person; *esp* an impudent one ⟨*the little* ~*'s pinched my slippers*⟩ **b** a small or insignificant person

**squirting cucumber** /'skwuhting/ *n* a chiefly Mediterranean hairy plant (*Ecballium elaterium*) of the marrow family with an oblong fruit that bursts from its stalk when ripe and forcibly ejects the seeds

**squish** /skwish/ *vb, informal* to squash to make or move with a slight squelching or sucking sound [alter. of *squash*] – **squish** *n*

**squishy** /'skwishi/ *adj, informal* soft, yielding, and damp – **squishiness** *n*

**squit** /skwit/ *n, Br informal* a petty or insignificant person [perh fr E dial. *squit* to squirt]

**sri** /s(h)ree/ *n* – used as a conventional title of respect when addressing or speaking of an Indian male [Skt *śrī,* lit., majesty, holiness; akin to Gk *kreiōn* ruler, master]

**Sri Lankan** /sri 'langkən/ *n or adj* (a native or inhabitant) of Sri Lanka, an island republic of S Asia

**SS** /,es 'es/ *n taking sing or pl vb* a paramilitary unit of Nazis created to serve as bodyguard to Hitler and later expanded to take charge of intelligence, central security, policing action, and extermination of undesirables [Ger, abbr for *Schutzstaffel* elite guard]

**¹-st** /-ist/ *suffix* (*adj or adv* → *adj or adv*) – used to form the superlative degree of adjectives and adverbs of one syllable, and of some adjectives and adverbs of two or more syllables, that end in *e* ⟨*surest*⟩ ⟨*completest*⟩; compare ¹-EST

**²-st** *suffix* – used to form the archaic second person singular of English verbs (with *thou*) that end in *e* ⟨*diest*⟩ ⟨*comest*⟩; compare ²-EST

**³-st** *suffix* – used after the figure 1 to indicate the ordinal number *first* ⟨*1st*⟩ ⟨*91st*⟩

**¹stab** /stab/ *n* **1** a wound produced by a pointed weapon **2a** a thrust (as if) with a pointed weapon **b(1)** a sharp spasm of pain **b(2)** a pang of intense emotion ⟨*felt a* ~ *of remorse*⟩ **3** *informal* an attempt, try ⟨*have a* ~ *at cookery*⟩ [ME *stabbe*] – **stab in the back** a treacherous action or statement

**²stab** *vb* **-bb-** *vt* **1** to wound or pierce by the thrust of a pointed weapon **2** to thrust, jab ⟨~ *a fork into a sausage*⟩ ⟨~*bed his finger at the page*⟩ to thrust at somebody or something (as if) with a pointed weapon – **stabber** *n*

**¹stabile** /'staybiel/ *adj* **1** stationary, stable **2** resistant to chemical change; stable [L *stabilis* – more at STABLE] – **stabilate** *n*

**²stabile** *n* an abstract sculpture or construction similar in appearance to a mobile but stationary

**stability** /stə'biləti/ *n* **1** the quality, state, or degree of being stable: e g **1a** the strength to stand firm or endure; steadiness **b** *physics* the property of a body that causes it to return to its original condition after being disturbed **c** *chemistry* resistance to chemical change or to physical disintegration **d** *meteorology* the condition of an air mass which has no upward movement **2** residence for life in one monastery ⟨*monks taking a vow of* ~⟩

**stabil·ize, -ise** /'staybl,iez/ *vt* **1** to make stable or firm **2** to hold steady: e g **2a** to maintain the stability of (e g an aircraft) by means of a stabilizer **b** to limit fluctuations of (e g prices) **c** to establish a minimum price for ~ *vi* to become stable, firm, or steadfast – **stabilization** *n*

**stabil·izer, -iser** /'staybl,iezə/ *n* something that stabilizes something: e g **a** a substance added to an unstable substance (e g an explosive or plastic) or to a system (e g an emulsion) to prevent or retard an unwanted alteration of chemical or physical state **b** a GYROSCOPE (heavy wheel spinning inside a frame) device to keep ships steady in a rough sea **c** either of a pair of brackets carrying small wheels that can be fitted on each side of the rear wheel of a bicycle to stabilize a novice cyclist **d** *chiefly NAm* the horizontal tailplane of an aircraft

**¹stable** /'staybl/ *n* **1** **stables** *pl,* **stable** a building in which domestic animals, esp horses, are sheltered and fed; *esp* such a building having stalls or compartments **2** *taking sing or pl vb* **2a** the racehorses or racing cars owned by one person or organization **b** a group of athletes (e g boxers) or performers under one management **c** a group, collection ⟨*a tycoon who owns a*

~ *of newspapers*⟩ [ME, fr OF *estable,* fr L *stabulum,* fr *stare* to stand – more at STAND] – **stableman** *n*

²**stable** *vt* to put or keep in a stable ~ *vi* to live (as if) in a stable

³**stable** *adj* **1a** securely established; fixed, solid ⟨~ *land*⟩ ⟨*a* ~ *community*⟩ **b** not subject to change or fluctuation; unvarying ⟨*a* ~ *population*⟩ ⟨*a* ~ *currency*⟩ **c** permanent, enduring ⟨*dictatorship always appears* ~ – *Christian Science Monitor*⟩ **2** not subject to feelings of mental or emotional insecurity; sane, well-adjusted ⟨*a* ~ *personality*⟩ **3a(1)** placed or constructed so as to resist forces tending to cause (change of) motion **a(2)** *physics* designed so as to develop forces that restore the original condition when disturbed from a condition of equilibrium or steady motion **b(1)** able to resist alteration in chemical, physical, or biological properties ⟨~ *emulsions*⟩ **b(2)** *of an atomic nucleus, elementary particle, etc* not spontaneously radioactive ⟨*a* ~ *isotope*⟩ [ME, fr OF *estable,* fr L *stabilis,* fr *stare* to stand] – **stableness** *n,* **stably** *adv*

**stable door** *n* a door divided horizontally so that the lower or upper part can be shut separately

**stable fly** *n* a two-winged fly (*Stomoxys calcitrans*) that bites and sucks blood, is abundant about stables, and often enters houses esp in autumn

**stable lad** *n* a groom in a racing stable

**stablemate** /'staybl,mayt/ *n* a horse stabled with another; *also* somebody or something having the same origin, work place, etc as another

**stable rubber** *n* a towel for rubbing down horses and wiping stable equipment

**stabling** /'staybling/ *n* (a building providing) indoor accommodation for animals

**stablish** /'stablish/ *vb, archaic* to establish [by shortening] – **stablishment** *n, archaic*

**staccato** /stə'kahtoh/ *adj* **1** *music* **1a** cut short or separated in performing; disconnected ⟨~ *notes*⟩ **b** marked by short clear-cut playing or singing of notes or chords ⟨*a* ~ *style*⟩ **2** abrupt, disjointed ⟨*recited the poem in a* ~ *voice*⟩ [It, fr pp of *staccare* to detach, deriv of OF *destachier* – more at DETACH] – **staccato** *adv,* **staccato** *n*

**staccato mark** *n* a pointed vertical stroke or a dot placed over or under a musical note to be performed staccato

¹**stack** /stak/ *n* **1** a large usu cone-shaped pile (eg of hay or straw) left standing in the field for storage **2** an (orderly) pile or heap **3** a British unit of measure, esp for firewood, that is equal to 108 cubic feet (about 3.06 cubic metres) **4a** CHIMNEY STACK **b** a smokestack **c** a pillar-shaped rocky islet near a cliffy shore that has been detached from the mainland by wave erosion **5** a pyramid of three rifles interlocked **6** **stacks** *pl,* **stack** a structure of shelves for compact storage of books **7** a pile of chips sold to or won by a poker player **8** a store of data (eg in a computer) from which the most recently stored item must be the first retrieved **9** a group of loudspeakers for a public-address sound system **10** a number of aircraft waiting to land at an airport **11** **stacks** *pl,* **stack** *informal* a large quantity or number ⟨~ s *of money*⟩ [ME *stak,* fr ON *stakkr;* akin to OE *staca* stake]

²**stack** *vt* **1** to arrange in a stack; pile **2** to arrange secretly for cheating ⟨*the cards were* ~ed⟩ – often + *against* **3** to assign (an aircraft) to a particular altitude and position within a group of aircraft circling before landing ~ *vi* to form a stack – **stacker** *n*

**stack up** *vi, NAm* **1** to add up, total **2** to measure up, compare – usu + *against*

**stacked** /stakt/ *adj, chiefly NAm slang, of a woman* shapely and having large breasts

**stacte** /'staktee/ *n* a sweet spice used by the ancient Jews in preparing incense [L, fr Gk *staktē,* fr fem of *staktos* oozing out in drops, fr *stazein* to drip – more at STAGNATE]

**staddle** /'stadl/ *n* **1** a base or framework, esp of stone, for a stack of hay or straw **2** a supporting framework [ME *stathel* base, support, fr OE *stathol;* akin to OE *stede* place – more at STEAD]

**stade** /stayd/ *n* STADIUM 1 [MF *estade,* fr L *stadium*]

**stadia** /'staydi·ə/ *n, pl* **stadias** a surveying method for determination of distances and differences of height by means of a telescopic instrument having two horizontal lines through which the marks on a graduated staff are observed; *also* the instrument or staff used [It, prob fr L, pl of *stadium*]

**stadium** /'staydi·əm/ *n, pl* **stadiums** *also* **stadia** /'staydi·ə/ **1** any of various ancient Greek units of length, usu of about 185

metres (about 202 yards) **2a** a course for footraces in ancient Greece, originally one stadium in length **b** a tiered structure with seats for spectators surrounding an ancient Greek running track **c** a sports ground surrounded by a large usu unroofed building with tiers of seats for spectators **3** a stage in a life history; *esp* the period between successive moults in the development of an insect **4** a stage or period in the development of a disease [ME, fr L, fr Gk *stadion,* alter. of *spadion,* fr *span* to pull – more at SPAN]

**stadtholder** /'stat,hohldə/ *n* **1** a viceroy in a province of the Netherlands **2** a chief executive officer of the United Provinces of the Netherlands [part trans of D *stadhouder,* fr *stad* place + *houder* holder] – **stadtholderate** *n,* **stadtholdership** *n*

¹**staff** /stahf/ *n, pl* **staffs, staves,** (5&6) **staffs 1a** a long stick carried in the hand for support in walking or as a weapon **b** a supporting rod: eg **b(1)** a crosspiece in a ladder or chair; a rung **b(2)** a flagstaff **b(3)** *archaic* SHAFT 1a **c** a club, cudgel **2a** a crosier **b** a rod carried as a symbol of office or authority **3** *music* STAVE 4 **4** any of various graduated sticks or rules used for measuring; a rod **5** *taking sing or pl vb* **5a** the body of people in charge of the internal operations of an institution, business, etc **b** a group of officers appointed to assist a commanding officer **c** the personnel who assist a superior (eg a director) in carrying out an assigned task **d** the body of teachers at a school or university **6** a member of a staff [ME *staf,* fr OE *stæf;* akin to OHG *stab* staff, *stampfōn* to stamp – more at STAMP] – **staff** *adj*

²**staff** *vt* **1** to supply with a staff or with workers **2** to serve as a staff member of

³**staff** *n* a building material having a PLASTER OF PARIS base and used in exterior wall coverings of temporary buildings [prob fr Ger *staffieren* to trim, decorate]

**staff association** *n* an organization of employees within a single firm; *esp* one having some of the functions of a trade union but dominated by the employer

**staffer** /'stahfə/ *n, chiefly NAm* a member of a staff (eg of a newspaper)

**staff nurse** *n, Br* a qualified nurse in the staff of a hospital who is next in rank below a sister

**staff officer** *n* a commissioned officer assigned to a military commander's staff

**staff of life** *n* a sustaining part of a diet – used esp with reference to bread

**staff sergeant** *n* – see MILITARY RANKS table

¹**stag** /stag/ *n, pl* **stags,** (1) **stags,** *esp collectively* **stag 1** an adult male red deer; *broadly* the male of any of various deer (esp genus *Cervus*) **2** a male animal castrated after maturity – compare STEER 1 **3** a young adult male domestic fowl **4** *Br* a person who buys newly issued shares in the hope of selling them to make a quick profit [ME *stagge,* fr OE *stagga;* akin to ON *andarsteggi* drake, OE *stingan* to sting]

²**stag** *vi* **-gg-** to attend a dance or party without a woman companion

³**stag** *adj* **1** of or intended for men only ⟨*a* ~ *night*⟩ ⟨*a* ~ *party*⟩ **2** pornographic – **stag** *adv*

**stag beetle** *n* any of numerous mostly large beetles (esp *Lucanus carvus* of the family Lucanidae) having males with long and often branched mouthparts suggesting the antlers of a stag

¹**stage** /stayj/ *n* **1a** any of a series of positions or stations one above the other; a step **b** the height of the surface of a river above an arbitrary zero point **2a(1)** a raised platform **a(2)** the area of a theatre where the acting takes place including the wings and storage space **a(3)** *the* acting profession; *also the* theatre as an occupation or activity **b** a centre of attention or scene of action **3a** a scaffold for workmen **b** the small platform of a microscope on which an object is placed for examination **4a** a place of rest formerly provided for those travelling by stagecoach; a station **b** the distance between two stopping places on a road **c** a stagecoach **5a** a period or step in a progress, activity, or development; *esp* any of the distinguishable periods of growth and development of a plant or animal ⟨*the larval* ~ *of an insect*⟩ **b** a living organism passing through a (specified) stage ⟨*the tadpole is the larval* ~ *of a frog*⟩ **c** any of the divisions (eg one day's riding or driving between predetermined points) of a race or rally that is spread over several days **6** a connected group of components in an electrical circuit that performs some well-defined function (eg amplification) and that forms part of a larger electrical circuit **7** a propulsion unit of a rocket with its own fuel and container **8** *chiefly Br* a

bus stop from which or to which fares are calculated; FARE STAGE [ME, fr OF *estage,* fr (assumed) VL *staticum,* fr L *stare* to stand – more at STAND] – **on the stage** in or with the acting profession ⟨*don't put your daughter* on the stage, *Mrs Worthington* – Noel Coward⟩ – **set the stage for** to provide the necessary basis or preparation for ⟨*this trend will* set the stage for *higher earnings*⟩

²**stage** *vt* 1 to produce (eg a play) on a stage 2 to produce and organize for public view ⟨~d *the event to get maximum publicity*⟩ 3 to set (a play, film, etc) in a specified historical period or place ⟨*it was* ~d *in Venice in the time of Casanova*⟩

**stagecoach** /'stayj,kohch/ *n* a horse-drawn passenger and mail coach that formerly ran on a regular schedule between established stops

**stagecraft** /'stayj,krahft/ *n* the effective management of theatrical devices or techniques

**stage direction** *n* a description (eg of a character or setting) or direction (eg to indicate sound effects, movement or positioning of actors, or lighting) provided in the text of a play

**stage door** *n* the entrance to a theatre that is used by those who work there

**stage fright** *n* nervousness felt at appearing before an audience

**stagehand** /'stayj,hand/ *n* a theatre worker who handles scenery, props, or lights

**stage left** *adv* on or to the left of an actor facing the audience

'**stage-,manage** *vt* to arrange or direct, esp from behind the scenes, so as to achieve a desired result ⟨*he* ~d *her dramatic disclosure so as to obtain the maximum publicity*⟩ [back-formation fr *stage manager*] – **stage management** *n*

**stage manager** *n* one who is in charge of the stage and related matters before and during a performance

**stage name** *n* the name used professionally by an actor

**stager** /'stayjə/ *n* an experienced person; a veteran – chiefly in *old stager*

**stage right** *adv* on or to the right of an actor facing the audience

**stage set** *n* scenery and props arranged for a particular scene in a play

**stagestruck** /'stayj,struk/ *adj* fascinated by the stage; *esp* having an ardent desire to become an actor

**stage whisper** *n* 1 a loud whisper by an actor that can be heard by the audience but is supposed for dramatic effect to be inaudible to others on stage 2 a deliberately audible whisper

**stagey** /'stayji/ *adj* stagy

**stagflation** /stag'flaysh(ə)n/ *n* a state of affairs in which inflation in the economy is accompanied by a constant or falling level of total production [blend of *stagnation* and *inflation*]

**staggard** /'stagəd/ *n* a male red deer in the fourth year of life [ME, fr *stagge* stag + -*ard*]

'**stagger** /'stagə/ *vi* 1a to reel from side to side; totter b to move on unsteadily 2 to rock violently; shake ⟨*the ship* ~ed⟩ 3 to waver in purpose or action; hesitate ~ *vt* 1 to dumbfound, astonish 2 to arrange in any of various alternations or overlappings of position or time ⟨~ *work shifts*⟩ ⟨~ *teeth on a cutter*⟩ 3 to adjust (eg the wings of a biplane) so that the foremost edge of one wing projects beyond the foremost edge of another wing [alter. of earlier *stacker,* fr ME *stakeren,* fr ON *stakra,* freq of *staka* to push; akin to OE *staca* stake] – **staggerer** *n*

²**stagger** *n* 1 *pl but taking sing or pl vb* an abnormal condition of domestic mammals, esp horses, and birds associated with damage to the brain and spinal cord and marked by lack of muscle coordination and a reeling unsteady gait 2 a reeling or unsteady walk or stance 3 the amount by which the foremost edge of an upper wing of a biplane is advanced over that of a lower

**staggering** /'stag(ə)ring/ *adj* astonishing, overwhelming – **staggeringly** *adv*

**staggy** /'stagi/ *adj, of a female or castrated male domestic animal* having the appearance of a mature male ['*stag* + '-*y*]

**staging** /'stayjing/ *n* 1 a scaffolding or other temporary platform 2 the business of running or driving stagecoaches; *also* journeying in stagecoaches 3 the putting of a play on the stage 4 the assembling of troops or military supplies in a particular place 5 the disengaging and discarding of a burned-out rocket unit from a space vehicle during flight

**staging area** *n* an area in which troops are assembled and prepared before a new operation or mission

**Stagirite** /'stajiriet/ *n* a native or inhabitant of Stagira ⟨*Aristotle the* ~⟩ [Gk *Stagirītēs,* fr *Stagira,* city in ancient Macedonia]

**stagnant** /'stagnont/ *adj* 1a not flowing in a current or stream; motionless ⟨~ *water*⟩ b stale ⟨*long disuse had made the air* ~ *and foul* – Bram Stoker⟩ 2 dull, inactive – **stagnancy** *n,* **stagnantly** *adv*

**stagnate** /stag'nayt/ *vi* to become or remain stagnant [L *stagnatus,* pp of *stagnare,* fr *stagnum* body of standing water; akin to Gk *stazein* to drip] – **stagnation** *n*

**stagnicolous** /stag'nikələs/ *adj* living in stagnant water, swamps, etc

**stag party** *n* an all-male party; *esp* one held by a bridegroom on the eve of his wedding

**stagy, stagey** /'stayji/ *adj* of the stage; theatrical; *esp* marked by showy pretence or artificiality ⟨*a* ~ *production*⟩ – **stagily** *adv,* **staginess** *n*

'**staid** /stayd/ *adj* sedate and often primly self-restrained; sober, grave **synonyms** see SERIOUS [fr pp of ³*stay*] – **staidly** *adv,* **staidness** *n*

²**staid** *archaic past of* STAY

'**stain** /stayn/ *vt* 1 to discolour, soil 2 to suffuse with colour 3a to taint with guilt, vice, or corruption b to bring dishonour to 4 to colour (eg wood, glass, cloth, or a biological specimen) by processes or dyes affecting (eg chemically) the material itself ~ *vi* 1 to become stained 2 to cause staining [ME *steynen;* partly fr MF *desteindre* to discolour, fr OF, fr *des-* dis- + *teindre* to dye, fr L *tingere* to wet, dye; partly fr or akin to ON *steina* to paint] – **stainable** *adj*

²**stain** *n* 1a a soiled or discoloured spot b a natural spot or patch of different colour 2 a moral taint; a stigma 3a a preparation (eg of dye or pigment) used in staining; *esp* one capable of penetrating the pores of wood b a dye or mixture of dyes used in microscopy to make minute and transparent structures visible, to differentiate tissue elements, or to produce specific chemical reactions

**stainability** /,staynə'biləti/ *n* the capacity of cells and cell parts to stain specifically and consistently with particular dyes and stains

**stained glass** /staynd/ *n* glass coloured or stained for use in (church) windows, esp by having metallic oxides fused into it, by having pigments burnt into it, or by being encased in coloured glass

**stainer** /'staynə/ *n* a pigment added to a paint to modify its colour

**stainless** /'staynlis/ *adj* 1 free from stain or stigma 2 (made from materials) resistant to stain, specif to rust – **stainlessly** *adv*

**stainless steel** *n* an alloy of iron with chromium and sometimes nickel or manganese that is highly resistant to rusting and ordinary corrosion

**stair** /steə/ *n* 1 **stairs** *pl,* **stair** a series of (flights of) steps for passing from one level to another ⟨*a narrow winding* ~⟩ ⟨*she stood at the top of the* ~s⟩ 2 a single step of a stairway [ME *steir,* fr OE *stæger;* akin to OE & OHG *stīgan* to rise, Gk *steichein* to walk] – **below stairs** (in) servants' quarters

**staircase** /'steə,kays/ *n* 1 the structure or part of a building containing a stairway 2 a flight of stairs; *also* such a flight with the supporting framework, casing, and banister

'**stair-,rod** *n* a rod (eg of metal) that holds a stair carpet in place in the angle between two steps

**stairway** /'steə,way/ *n* one or more flights of stairs, usu with intermediate landings

**stairwell** /'steə,wel/ *n* a vertical shaft in which stairs are located

**staithe** /staydh/ *n, Br* a structure on a wharf from which coal may be loaded; *broadly* a wharf [ME *stathe,* of Scand origin; akin to ON *stöth* landing place, wharf]

'**stake** /stayk/ *n* 1 a pointed piece of material (eg wood) used for driving into the ground as a marker or support 2a a post to which a person was formerly bound for execution by burning b execution by burning at a stake – + *the* ⟨*she'd go to the* ~ *for her convictions*⟩ 3a something, esp money, that is staked for gain or loss b **stakes** *pl,* **stake** the prize in a contest, esp a horse race c an interest or share in an undertaking (eg a commercial venture) 4 *pl but taking sing or pl vb, often cap* a horse race in which all the horses are evenly matched (eg in age and weight carried) – chiefly in names of races 5 a group of wards forming an administrative district in the Mormon Church [ME, fr OE *staca;* akin to MLG *stake* stake, L *tignum* beam] – **at** stake at issue; in jeopardy – **pull (up) stakes** to leave; MOVE OUT

**²stake** *vt* **1a** to mark the limits of (as if) by stakes – often + *off* or *out* **b** to lay claim to (a territory) (as if) by staking – often + *off* or *out* **2** to tether to a stake **3** to bet, hazard **4** to fasten up or support (e g plants) with stakes **5** *chiefly NAm* to back financially ⟨*I'll ~ you to a Chinese takeaway*⟩ – see also **stake a/one's CLAIM (to)**

**stake out** *vt, chiefly NAm* **1** to assign (e g a policeman) to an area, usu to conduct a surveillance **2** to conduct or maintain surveillance – see also STAKEOUT

**stakeholder** /'stayk,hohldə/ *n* a person entrusted with the stakes of bettors

**stakeout** /'stayk,owt/ *n, chiefly NAm* a surveillance maintained by the police of an area or a person suspected of a criminal activity

**stake race** *n* a horse race in which each horse carries a weight that takes into account its previous wins rather than its current form

**stakey** /'stayki/ *adj, Can informal* sufficiently provided with money

**Stakhanovite** /sta'kanə,viet/ *n* a Soviet industrial worker awarded incentives in the form of recognition and special privileges for output exceeding production norms [Alexei G *Stakhanov* †1977 Russ miner] – **Stakhanovism** *n*

**stalactite** /'stalək,tiet/ *n* a deposit of CALCIUM CARBONATE (chalky mineral) resembling an icicle hanging from the roof or sides of a cavern [NL *stalactites*, fr Gk *stalaktos* dripping, fr *stalassein* to let drip – more at STALE] – **stalactitic** *adj*

**stalag** /'stahlag/ *n* a German prison camp for noncommissioned officers and lower ranks [Ger, short for *stammlager* base camp, fr *stamm* base + *lager* camp]

**stalagmite** /'staləgmiet/ *n* a deposit of CALCIUM CARBONATE (chalky mineral) like an inverted stalactite formed on the floor of a cave by the constant drip of water [NL *stalagmites*, fr Gk *stalagma* drop or *stalagmos* dripping; akin to Gk *stalassein* to let drip] – **stalagmitic** *adj*

**¹stale** /stayl/ *adj* **1a** *esp of food or gaseous drinks* tasteless, flat, dry, or hard from age **b** *of air* musty, foul **2** tedious from familiarity ⟨*a ~ joke*⟩ **3** impaired in legal force or effect through lack of timely action ⟨*a ~ affidavit*⟩ ⟨*a ~ debt*⟩ **4** impaired in vigour or effectiveness, esp from overexertion or overpreparation [ME, aged (of ale); akin to MD *stel* stale] – **stalely** *adv*, **staleness** *n*

**²stale** *vb* to make or become stale

**³stale** *n* the urine of a domestic animal (e g a horse) [ME; akin to MLG *stal* horse urine, Gk *stalassein* to let drip]

**⁴stale** *vi, esp of a camel or a horse* to urinate

**stalemate** /'stayl,mayt/ *n* **1** a drawn position in chess in which only the king can move and although not in check can move only into check **2** a drawn contest; deadlock; *also* the state of being stalemated [obs *stale* stalemate, fr ME, fr AF *estale*, lit., fixed position, fr OF *estal* place, position] – **stalemate** *vt*

**Stalinism** /'stahli,niz(ə)m, 'sta-/ *n* the political, economic, and social principles and policies associated with Stalin; *esp* the theory and practice of communism developed by Stalin from Marxism-Leninism and characterized esp by the theory of socialism in one country, as opposed to that of permanent revolution, by rigid centralized authoritarianism, by widespread use of terror, and often by emphasis on Russian nationalism [Joseph *Stalin* †1953 Russ political leader] – **Stalinist** *n or adj*, **Stalinize** *vt*, **Stalinoid** *n or adj*

**¹stalk** /stawk/ *vi* **1** to pursue or approach quarry or prey stealthily **2** to walk stiffly or haughtily ~ *vt* **1** to hunt or approach by stalking ⟨*~ deer*⟩ **2a** to go through (an area) in search of prey or quarry ⟨*~ the woods for deer*⟩ **b** to go through or permeate in a threatening or ghostly manner ⟨*hunger ~ed Europe*⟩ [ME *stalken*, fr OE *bestealcian*; akin to OE *stealc* lofty, *stelan* to steal – more at STEAL] – **stalker** *n*

**²stalk** *n* **1** the stalking of quarry or prey **2** a stiff or haughty walk

**³stalk** *n* **1a** the main stem of a nonwoody plant often with its attached parts (e g leaves) **b** STEM 1b **2** a slender upright object; *also* a supporting or connecting (animal) part (e g a peduncle) ⟨*the ~ of a crinoid*⟩ [ME *stalke*; akin to OE *stealc* lofty] – **stalked** *adj*, **stalkless** *adj*, **stalky** *adj*

**'stalk-,eyed** *adj, esp of a crab, shrimp, or related animal* having the eyes raised on stalks

**stalking-horse** /'stawking/ *n* **1** (a figure like) a horse, behind which a hunter hides while stalking game **2** something used to

mask a purpose; a pretext **3** *chiefly NAm* a candidate put forward to divide the opposition or to conceal someone's real candidacy

**¹stall** /stawl/ *n* **1** any of usu several compartments for domestic animals in a stable or barn **2a** a seat in the chancel of a church with back and sides wholly or partly enclosed with wooden panels **b** a church pew **3a** a booth, kiosk, stand, or counter at which articles are displayed or offered for sale **b** SIDESHOW 1b **4** a protective sheath for an injured finger or toe **5** a small compartment ⟨*a shower ~*⟩ **6** *Br* **6a** a seat on the main floor of an auditorium (e g in a theatre); *esp* one near the front **b** *pl* the people sitting in the stalls [ME, fr OE *steall*; akin to OHG *stal* place, stall, L *locus* (OL *stlocus*) place, Gk *stellein* to set up, place, send]

**²stall** *vt* **1** to put or keep in a stall **2a** to bring to a standstill; block **b** to cause (e g a car engine) to stop, usu inadvertently **c** to cause (an aircraft or aerofoil) to go into a stall ~ *vi* **1** to come to a standstill; *esp, of an engine* to stop suddenly because of an inadequate fuel supply or engine failure **2** to experience a stall in flying

**³stall** *n* the condition of an aerofoil or aircraft when the airflow is so obstructed (e g from moving forwards too slowly) that lift is lost

**⁴stall** *vi* to play for time; delay ~ *vt* to hold off, divert, or delay, esp by evasion or deception [obs *stall*, n, lure, decoy, alter. of *stale*, fr ME, fr AF *estale*] – **stall** *n*

**stallage** /'stawlij/ *n* a charge for the use of or right to erect a stall (e g in a market)

**'stall-,feed** *vt* **stall-fed** /-,fed/ to feed in a stall, esp so as to fatten ⟨*~ an ox*⟩

**stallholder** /'stawl,hohldə/ *n* one who runs a market stall

**stalling angle** /'stawling/ *n, aerospace* CRITICAL ANGLE

**stallion** /'stalyən/ *n* an uncastrated male horse; *esp* one kept for breeding; *also* a male animal (e g a dog or a sheep) kept primarily as a stud [ME *stalion*, fr MF *estalon*, of Gmc origin; akin to OHG *stal* stall]

**¹stalwart** /'stawlwət/ *adj* **1** marked by outstanding strength and vigour of body, mind, or spirit ⟨*~ common sense*⟩ **2** dependable, staunch ⟨*a ~ ally*⟩ **synonyms** see STRONG [ME, alter. of *stalworth*, fr OE *stǣlwierthe* serviceable, prob fr *stǣl* place + *wierthe* worth, worthy] – **stalwartly** *adv*, **stalwartness** *n*

**²stalwart** *n* a stalwart person; *specif* a staunch supporter

**stamen** /'staymən/ *n, pl* **stamens** *also* **stamina** /'sta(y)minə/ the organ of a flower that produces the male GAMETE (reproductive cell) in the form of pollen, and consists of an ANTHER (pollen-producing part) supported by a stalklike FILAMENT [L, warp, thread; akin to Gk *stēmōn* thread, *histanai* to cause to stand – more at STAND]

**stamin-** /stamin-/, **stamini-** *comb form* stamen ⟨stamin*ody*⟩ ⟨stamin*iferous*⟩ ⟨stamin*al*⟩ [L *stamin-*, *stamen*]

**stamina** /'staminə/ *n* endurance; STAYING POWER [L, pl of *stamen* warp, thread of life spun by the Fates]

**staminal** /'sta(y)minl/ *adj* (consisting) of a stamen

**staminate** /'staminət, -nayt/ *adj* **1** having or producing stamens **2** MALE 1a(2)

**staminode** /'stayminohd/ *n* an abortive or sterile stamen [NL *staminodium*, fr *stamin-* + *-odium* thing resembling, fr Gk *-ōdēs* like]

**staminodium** /,staymi'nohdi-əm/ *n, pl* **staminodia** /-diə/ a staminode

**staminody** /'sta(y)minədi/ *n* the transformation of floral organs (e g petals) into stamens [*stamin-* + Gk *-ōdēs* like]

**stammer** /'stamə/ *vb* to speak or utter with involuntary stops and repetitions – compare STUTTER [ME *stameren*, fr OE *stamerian*; akin to OHG *stamalōn* to stammer, Lith *stumti* to push] – **stammer** *n*, **stammerer** *n*

**¹stamp** /stamp/ *vt* **1** to pound or crush (e g ore) with a pestle or a heavy instrument **2a** to strike or beat forcibly with the bottom of the foot **b** to bring down (the foot) forcibly **3a** to impress, imprint ⟨*~ "paid" on the bill*⟩ ⟨*an image ~ed on his memory*⟩ **b** to attach a (postage) stamp to **4** to cut out, bend, or form with a stamp or DIE (moulding device) **5a** to provide with a distinctive character ⟨*~ed with an air of worldly wisdom*⟩ **b** CHARACTERIZE 2 ~ *vi* **1** POUND 1,2a **2** to strike or thrust the foot forcibly or noisily downwards [ME *stampen*; akin to OHG *stampfōn* to stamp, L *temnere* to despise, Gk *stembein* to shake up]

**stamp out** *vt* to eradicate, destroy ⟨stamp out *crime*⟩

**²stamp** *n* **1** a device or instrument for stamping **2** the impression or mark made by stamping or imprinting **3a** a distinctive character, indication, or mark ⟨*a martinet of the old* ∼⟩ **b** a lasting imprint ⟨*the* ∼ *of time on his features*⟩ **4** the act of stamping **5** a printed or stamped piece of paper that for some restricted purpose is used as a token of credit or occasionally of debit: eg **5a** POSTAGE STAMP **b** REVENUE STAMP **c** TRADING STAMP

**'stamp-col,lecting** *n* PHILATELY – **stamp collector** *n*

**stamp duty** *n* a tax collected by means of a stamp purchased and affixed (eg to a legal document)

**¹stampede** /stam'peed/ *n* **1** a wild headlong rush or flight of frightened animals **2** a sudden mass movement of people at a common impulse [AmerSp *estampida*, fr Sp, crash, fr *estampar* to stamp, of Gmc origin; akin to OHG *stampfōn* to stamp]

**²stampede** *vt* **1** to cause to run away in headlong panic ⟨*the noise* ∼d *the herd*⟩ **2** to cause (a group of people) to act on mass impulse ∼ *vi* **1** to flee headlong in panic **2** to act on mass impulse – **stampeder** *n*

**stamper** /'stampə/ *n* one who or that which stamps: eg **a** somebody who performs an industrial stamping operation **b** any of various stamping machines

**stamping ground** /'stamping/ *n* a favourite or habitual haunt

**stamp mill, stamping mill** *n* a mill in which ore is crushed with stamps; *also* a machine for stamping ore

**stamp tax** *n* STAMP DUTY

**stance** /stahns, stans/ *n* **1a** a way of standing or being placed; a posture **b** an intellectual or emotional attitude ⟨*took an anti-union* ∼⟩ **2** the position of body or feet from which a sportsman (eg a batsman or golfer) plays **3** *chiefly Scot* a bus stop [MF *estance* position, posture, stay, fr (assumed) VL *stantia*, fr L *stant-, stans*, prp of *stare* to stand]

**¹stanch, staunch** /stawnch, stahnch/ *vt* **1** to check or stop the flow of ⟨∼ed *her tears*⟩; *also* to stop the flow of blood from (a wound) **2a** to stop or check the course of ⟨*trying to* ∼ *the crime wave*⟩ **b** to make watertight; stop up **3** *archaic* to allay, extinguish [ME *staunchen*, fr MF *estancher*, fr (assumed) VL *stanticare*, fr L *stant-, stans*, prp] – **stancher** *n*

**²stanch** *adj* ²STAUNCH

**¹stanchion** /'stahnsh(ə)n/ *n* **1** an upright bar, post, or strut (eg for supporting a roof) **2** a device that fits loosely round a cow's neck and limits forward and backward motion (eg in a stall) [ME *stanchon*, fr MF *estanchon*, fr OF, aug of *estance* stay, prop]

**²stanchion** *vt* **1a** to provide with stanchions **b** to support or brace (as if) with a stanchion **2** to secure (eg a cow) by a stanchion

**¹stand** /stand/ *vb* **stood** *vi* **1a** to support oneself on the feet in an erect position **b** to be a specified height when fully erect ⟨∼s *six feet two*⟩ **c** to rise to or maintain an erect position ⟨*his hair stood on end*⟩ **2a** to take up or maintain a specified position or posture ⟨∼ *aside*⟩ **b** to maintain one's position ⟨∼ *firm*⟩ **3** to be in a specified state or situation ⟨∼s *accused*⟩ **4** to hold a course at sea; sail in a specified direction ⟨∼ing *into harbour*⟩ **5a** to have or maintain a relative position (as if) in a graded scale ⟨∼s *first in his class*⟩ **b** to be in a position to gain or lose because of an action taken or a commitment made ⟨∼s *to make quite a profit*⟩ **6a** to rest or remain upright on a base or lower end ⟨*a clock* stood *on the mantelpiece*⟩ **b** to occupy a place or location ⟨*the house* ∼s *on a hill*⟩ **7** to remain stationary or inactive ⟨*the car* stood *in the garage for a week*⟩ **8** to gather slowly and remain ⟨*tears* ∼ing *in her eyes*⟩ **9a** to exist in a definite (written or printed) form ⟨*copy a passage exactly as it* ∼s⟩ ⟨*that is how the situation* ∼s *at present*⟩ **b** to remain valid or efficacious ⟨*the order given last week still* ∼s⟩ **10** *of a male animal, esp a stallion* to be available as a stud **11** *chiefly Br* to be a candidate in an election **12** *obs* to hesitate ⟨∼ *not upon the order of your going* – Shak⟩ ∼ *vt* **1a** to endure or undergo ⟨∼ *trial*⟩ ⟨*this book will* ∼ *the test of time*⟩ **b** to tolerate, bear; PUT UP WITH ⟨∼ *pain*⟩ ⟨*can't* ∼ *his boss*⟩ **c** to benefit from; do with ⟨*looks as if he could* ∼ *a good sleep*⟩ **2** to remain firm in the face of ⟨∼ *a siege*⟩ **3a** to perform the duty of ⟨∼ *guard*⟩ **b** to participate in (a military formation) **4** to cause to stand; set upright ⟨∼ *it in the window*⟩ **5** *informal* to pay the cost of (a treat); pay for ⟨*I'll* ∼ *you a dinner*⟩ – see also **stand a** CHANCE/**on** CERE-MONY/**on** one's own (two) FEET (at FOOT/**one's** GROUND, **not have a** LEG **to stand on, it stands to** REASON, **stand one**

in good STEAD, **stand** TREAT *synonyms* see ²BEAR [ME *standen*, fr OE *standan*; akin to OHG *stantan, stān* to stand, L *stare*, Gk *histanai* to cause to stand, set, *histasthai* to stand, be standing] – **stander** *n*

**stand by** *vi* **1** to be present but remain aloof or inactive ⟨*calmly* stood by *and watched those trying to help*⟩ **2** to wait in a state of readiness ⟨stand by *for action*⟩ ∼ *vt* to remain loyal or faithful to ⟨stood by *the agreement*⟩ – see also STANDBY

**stand down** *vi* **1** to leave the witness box **2** *chiefly Br* to relinquish (one's candidature for) an office or position ⟨stood down *in favour of a better candidate*⟩ ⟨stood down *as Lord Mayor*⟩ **3** *chiefly Br, of a soldier* to go off duty ∼ *vt, chiefly Br* to send (soldiers) off duty; *broadly* to dismiss (workers); LAY OFF 1

**stand for** *vt* **1** to be a symbol for; represent **2** to put up with; permit

**stand in** *vi* to act as a stand-in

**stand off** *vi* **1** to stay at a distance in social contact; be standoffish **2** to sail or remain away from the shore **3** *of a horse* to take off early for a jump ∼ *vt* **1** to keep from advancing; repel **2** *Br* LAY OFF 1 – see also STANDOFF

**stand on** *vt* **1** to depend upon **2** to insist on ⟨*she* stands on *her principles*⟩

**stand out** *vi* **1a** to appear (as if) in relief; project **b** to be prominent or conspicuous **2** to steer away from shore **3** to be stubborn in resolution or resistance – often + *against* ⟨*they* stood out *against the school closure*⟩ – see also STANDOUT

**stand to** *vi* to take up a position of readiness (eg for action or inspection) ⟨*ordered the men to* stand to⟩

**stand up** *vi* **1** to rise to or maintain a standing or upright position **2** to remain sound and intact under stress, attack, or close scrutiny ⟨*does his argument* stand up⟩ **3** *of a wicket keeper* to take up a fielding position immediately behind the stumps ∼ *vt, informal* to fail to keep an appointment with ⟨*he* stood *her up twice in one week*⟩ – see also STAND-UP

**stand up for** *vt* to defend against attack or criticism

**stand up to** *vt* **1** *of a wicket keeper* **1a** to take up a fielding position immediately behind (the wicket) **b** to take up a position behind the wicket to field (bowling or a bowler) **2** to withstand efficiently or unimpaired ⟨*a car which can* stand up *to rough handling*⟩ **3** to face boldly

**²stand** *n* **1** an act, position, or place of standing ⟨*took up a* ∼ *near the exit*⟩ **2a** a standstill; *also* a halt for defence or resistance **b(1)** a usu defensive effort of some length or success ⟨*a united* ∼ *against the plans for the new motorway*⟩ **b(2)** an instance or occurrence of two batsmen being in together in cricket, esp one that lasts a long time or in which many runs are scored ⟨*a good* ∼ *for the fourth wicket*⟩; *also* the runs scored during such a stand ⟨*a* ∼ *of over 100*⟩ **c(1)** a stop made by a touring theatre company, rock group, etc to give a performance – compare ONE-NIGHT STAND **c(2)** a town where such a stop is made **3** a strongly or aggressively held position, esp on a debatable issue ⟨*do you take a* ∼ *on women's liberation?*⟩ **4a** stands *pl*, **stand** a structure of tiered seats for spectators of a sport or spectacle **b** *pl* the occupants of such seats **c** a raised platform serving as a point of vantage or display (eg for a speaker or exhibit) **5a** a small usu temporary and usu open-air stall where goods are sold or displayed for sale ⟨*a hot dog* ∼⟩ **b** a usu temporary structure erected (eg at an exhibition) to display or demonstrate wares **6** a place where a passenger vehicle awaits hire ⟨*a taxi* ∼⟩ **7** a frame on or in which something may be placed for support ⟨*an umbrella* ∼⟩ **8** a group of plants or esp trees growing in a continuous area ⟨*a fine* ∼ *of horse chestnut*⟩ **9** *NAm the* witness-box

**¹standard** /'standəd/ *n* **1** a conspicuous object (eg a banner) formerly carried at the top of a pole and used to mark a rallying point, esp in battle, or to serve as an emblem **2a** a long narrow tapering flag that is personal to an individual or corporation and bears heraldic insignia **b** the personal flag of a member of a royal family or of a head of state **c** a distinctive flag carried by cavalry or armoured regiments **d** a banner **3a** something established by authority, custom, or general consent as a model or example; a criterion **b** a (prescribed) degree of quality or worth **c** *pl* moral integrity; principles **4** something set up and established by authority as a rule for the measure of quantity, weight, extent, value, or quality **5a** the fineness and legally fixed weight of the metal used in coins **b** the commodity (eg gold) that is agreed to be the basis of value in a monetary system **6** a stanchion, support **7a** a shrub or soft-stemmed plant grown with an erect main stalk so that it forms or resembles a tree ⟨*a ~ rose*⟩ **b** a fruit tree grafted on a stock that does not induce dwarfing **8a** the large irregular upper petal of a flower of a pea, bean, clover, etc **b** any of the three inner usu erect and incurved petals of an iris **9** something standard: e g **9a** a musical composition, esp a popular song, that has become a part of the established repertoire **b** a model of a car supplied without optional extras **10** a school class or level in English elementary schools before 1944 [ME, fr MF *estandard* rallying point, standard, of Gmc origin; akin to OE *standan* to stand and to OE *ord* point – more at ODD]

²**standard** *adj* **1a** being or conforming to a standard, esp as established by law or custom ⟨*~ weight*⟩ **b(1)** sound and usable but not of top quality **b(2)** of or being the smallest size of a range of marketed products ⟨*available in ~, family, super, and mega packs*⟩ **2a** regularly and widely used, available, or supplied ⟨*a ~ socket*⟩ **b** well established and very familiar ⟨*the ~ weekend television programmes*⟩ **3** having recognized and permanent value ⟨*a ~ reference work*⟩ **4** *of language* uniform and well established by usage in the speech and writing of educated people and widely recognized as acceptable ⟨*~ pronunciation*⟩ ⟨Standard *English*⟩

'**standard-,bearer** *n* **1** one who carries a standard or banner **2** the leader of an organization, movement, or party

**standardbred** /'standǝd,bred/ *n, often cap, NAm* any of an American breed of light trotting and pacing horses bred for speed and noted for endurance

**standard deviation** *n* an important measure used in statistics to describe the extent to which values of a VARIABLE are scattered about their MEAN (average); the SQUARE ROOT of the average of the squares of the differences of each value from the mean

**standard error** *n* a measure used in statistics equal to the STANDARD DEVIATION of a set of values divided by the SQUARE ROOT of the total number of values

**standard gauge** *n* a railway gauge of 1.435 metres ($56\frac{1}{2}$ inches), used on most railways – **standard-guage** *adj*

**standard·ize, -ise** /'standǝ,diez/ *vt* **1** to compare with a standard **2** to bring into conformity with a standard – **standardization** *n*

**standard lamp** *n* a movable domestic lamp with a tall support that stands on the floor

**standard of living** *n* **1** the necessities, comforts, and luxuries enjoyed or aspired to by an individual or group – compare COST OF LIVING **2** a level of welfare or subsistence maintained by an individual, group, or community and shown esp by the level of consumption of necessities, comforts, and luxuries

**standard operating procedure** *n* established or prescribed methods of assembly, manufacture, etc to be followed routinely for the performance of specific operations or in specific situations – called also STANDING OPERATING PROCEDURE

**standard score** *n* an individual test score (e g in an examination) expressed as the deviation from the average score of the group in units of STANDARD DEVIATION

**standard scratch score** *n, Br* a score for a particular golf course depending on its total length and equal to that of a SCRATCH player (player without a handicap)

**standard time** *n* the officially established time, with reference to GREENWICH MEAN TIME, of a region or country

**standaway** /'standǝ,way/ *adj, of (part of) a garment* standing out from the body ⟨*a ~ neckline*⟩

'**standby** /'stand,bie/ *n, pl* **standbys** **1a** somebody or something to be relied upon, esp in emergencies **b** a favourite or reliable choice or resource **2** somebody or something held in reserve ready for use; a substitute – **on standby** ready or available for immediate action or use

²**standby** *adj* **1** held near at hand and ready for use ⟨*~ equipment*⟩ **2** relating to the act or condition of standing by ⟨*~ duty*⟩ ⟨*~ allowances*⟩

**standee** /stan'dee/ *n, NAm* somebody who occupies standing room

'**stand-,in** *n* **1** somebody who is employed to occupy an actor's place while lights or cameras are prepared, or who takes the actor's place in scenes of danger **2** SUBSTITUTE 1

'**standing** /'standing/ *adj* **1** used or designed for standing in ⟨*~ places*⟩ **2** not yet cut or harvested ⟨*~ timber*⟩ ⟨*~ grain*⟩ **3a** not being used or operated ⟨*a ~ engine*⟩ **b** not flowing; stagnant ⟨*~ water*⟩ **4a** remaining at the same level, degree, or amount for an indeterminate period ⟨*a ~ offer*⟩ **b** continuing in existence or use indefinitely ⟨*a ~ disgrace to the*

*country*⟩ **5** established by law or custom ⟨*a ~ joke*⟩ **6** done from a standing position ⟨*a ~ jump*⟩ ⟨*a ~ ovation*⟩ [(1) fr gerund of '*stand*; (2-6) fr prp of '*stand*]

²**standing** *n* **1** a place to stand in; a location **2a** length of service or experience, esp as determining rank, pay, or privilege **b** position, status, or condition in relation to a society, group, or profession; *esp* good reputation ⟨*his ~ in the Labour party*⟩ **c** position relative to a standard of achievement or to achievements of competitors **3** maintenance of position or condition; duration ⟨*a custom of long ~*⟩

**standing army** *n* a permanent army of paid soldiers

**standing committee** *n* a permanent committee appointed, esp by a legislative body (e g Parliament), to consider a particular subject

**standing crop** *n* the total amount or number of living things (e g the fish in a pond or organisms in their environment) in a particular place at any given time

**standing martingale** /'mahtin,gayl/ *n* a device for checking the upward movement of a horse's head, that consists of a strap fastened to the girth, passing between the forelegs, supported by a neck strap, and connected to the noseband

**standing operating procedure** *n* STANDARD OPERATING PROCEDURE

**standing order** *n* **1** *usu pl* a rule governing the procedure of an organization (e g a legislative body), which endures until specifically changed or cancelled ⟨*will a member please call for a suspension of* standing orders?⟩ **2** an instruction (e g to a banker or newsagent) in force until specifically changed

**standing rigging** *n* permanent rigging (e g stays and shrouds) used primarily to secure the masts and fixed spars of a vessel or to support radio, radar, and other equipment carried aloft

**standing room** *n* space for standing; *esp* accommodation available for spectators or passengers after all seats are filled

**standing stone** *n* MENHIR (prehistoric stone monument)

**standing wave** *n, physics* a pattern of vibration of a body or physical system formed when two waves (e g sound waves) vibrating at the same FREQUENCY travel in opposite directions through the system (e g along a wire) and oppose each other's motion so that the AMPLITUDE of the combined wave varies from place to place, is constantly zero at fixed points, and has fixed maximum values at other points

'**standoff** /'stand,of/ *adj* **1a** that can be released by an aircraft a long way from a target ⟨*a ~ missile*⟩ **b** suitable for attack by a stand-off weapon **c** able to operate a stand-off weapon **2** *NAm* standoffish **3** *NAm* used for holding something at a distance from a surface ⟨*a ~ insulator*⟩

²**standoff** *n, NAm* **1** a counterbalancing effect **2** a tie, deadlock ⟨*the two teams played to a ~*⟩

'**stand-,off, stand-off half** *n* the player in rugby positioned between the scrum-half and the three-quarter backs; *also* the position itself

**standoffish** /,stand'ofish/ *adj* somewhat cold and reserved – **standoffishly** *adv,* **standoffishness** *n*

**standout** /'stan,dowt/ *n, NAm* one who or that which is prominent or conspicuous, esp because of excellence

**standover** /'stan,dohvǝ/ *adj or n, Austr* (of or being) a criminal who uses or threatens physical violence ⟨*nearly killed by a ~ gang for £30 – The Age (Melbourne)*⟩

**standpipe** /'stand-,piep/ *n* **1** a high vertical pipe or reservoir that is used to secure a uniform pressure in a water-supply system **2** a pipe connected to a water main and fitted with a tap that is used for outdoor water supply (e g for watering gardens)

**standpoint** /'stand,poynt/ *n* a position from which objects or principles are viewed and according to which they are compared and judged ⟨*look at it from my ~*⟩

**standstill** /'stand,stil/ *n* a state where motion or progress is absent; a stop

'**stand-,up** *adj* **1a** erect, upright **b** stiffened to stay upright without folding over ⟨*a ~ collar*⟩ **2** performed in or requiring a standing position ⟨*a ~ meal*⟩ **3** (having an act) consisting of jokes usu performed solo, and standing before an audience without props or scenery ⟨*a ~ comic*⟩

**stane** /stayn/ *n, Scot* a stone

**Stanford-Binet test** /,stanfǝd bi'nay/ *n* an intelligence test prepared at Stanford University as a revision of the BINET-SIMON SCALE [*Stanford* University, California, USA]

'**stang** /stang/ *vt, chiefly Scot* to sting [ME *stangen*, fr ON *stanga* to prick; akin to ON *stinga* to sting]

²**stang** *n* SATANG (Thai coin) [Thai]

**stanhope** /'stanəp/ *n* a light carriage with two or four wheels [Fitzroy *Stanhope*, †1864 Br clergyman]

**staniel** /'stanyəl/ *n* a kestrel [ME *stanyel*, fr OE *stāngella*, fr *stān* stone + *gellan* to yell]

**Stanislavski method** /ˌstanis'lavski/ *n* METHOD 3 (technique of acting) [Konstantin *Stanislavski* †1938 Russ actor]

¹**stank** /stangk/ *past of* STINK

²**stank** *n, Br* 1 a small dam; a weir 2 *dial* 2a a pond, pool **b** a ditch containing water [ME, pond, fr OF *estanc*]

**stannary** /'stanəri/ *n,* **stannaries** *n pl* a region containing tin-works [ML *stannaria* tin mine, fr LL *stannum* tin]

**stannic** /'stanik/ *adj* of or containing tin, esp when having a VALENCY of four [Fr *stannique*, fr LL *stannum* tin, fr L, an alloy of silver and lead, prob of Celt origin; akin to Cornish *stēn* tin] – **stanniferous** *adj*

**stannic sulphide** *n* an insoluble solid chemical compound that is a SULPHIDE of tin, $SnS_2$, that is usu in the form of gold powder or crystals, and is used in gold paint – called also MOSAIC GOLD

**stannite** /'staniet/ *n* a steel-grey or iron-black mineral that is a SULPHIDE of copper, iron, and tin, $Cu_2FeSnS_4$, has a metallic lustre, and is used as a source of tin [LL *stannum* tin]

**stannous** /'stanəs/ *adj* of or containing tin, esp when having a VALENCY of two [ISV, fr LL *stannum*]

**stanza** /'stanzə/ *n* a division of a poem consisting of a series of lines arranged together in a usu recurring pattern of metre and rhyme [It, stay, abode, room, stanza, fr (assumed) VL *stantia* stay – more at STANCE] – **stanzaic** *adj*

**stapedectomy** /ˌstapə'dektəmi/ *n* an operation performed to relieve some types of deafness whereby the stapes bone is surgically removed and replaced by an artificial structure (e g using stainless steel wire) [ISV, fr NL *staped-, stapes*] – **stapedectomized** *adj*

**stapedial** /stə'peedi‧əl/ *adj* of or located near the stapes

**stapes** /'staypeez/ *n, pl* **stapes, stapedes** /'staypi‚deez/ the innermost of the chain of three small bones in the ear of a mammal [NL *staped-, stapes*, fr ML, stirrup, alter. of LL *stapia*, prob of Gmc origin]

**staph** /staf/ *n* a staphylococcus – **staph** *adj*

**staphylinid** /ˌstafi'lienid/ *n* any of a family (Staphylinidae) of often predatory beetles that have a long body and very short wing covers beneath which the wings are folded crossways – called also ROVE BEETLE [NL *Staphylinidae*, family name, deriv of Gk *staphylē* bunch of grapes] – **staphylinid** *adj*

**staphylococcus** /ˌstafiloh'kokəs/ *n, pl* **staphylococci** /-kie/ any of various spherical bacteria (esp genus *Staphylococcus*) that occur singly, in pairs or fours, or in irregular clusters, are unable to move independently, and that include parasites of the skin and membranes lining the nose, mouth, etc that cause boils and infections of wounds, esp in hospitals [NL, genus name, fr Gk *staphylē* bunch of grapes (akin to OE *stæf* staff) + NL *coccus*] – **staphylococcal** *adj,* **staphylococcic** *adj*

¹**staple** /'staypl/ *n* 1 a U-shaped metal loop, both ends of which are driven into a surface to hold the hook, hasp, or bolt of a lock, secure a rope, or fix a wire in place 2 a small piece of wire with ends bent at right angles which can be driven through thin layers of material, esp paper, and clinched to hold the layers together [ME *stapel* post, staple, fr OE *stapol* post; akin to MD *stapel* step, heap, place of trade, OE *steppan* to step]

²**staple** *vt* to provide with or secure by staples

³**staple** *n* 1 a town appointed, usu by royal authority in the Middle Ages, to be the centre for merchants involved in the sale or export of commodities in bulk 2 a place of supply; a source 3 a chief commodity or product of a place 4a a commodity for which the demand is constant **b** something having widespread and constant use or appeal **c** the sustaining or principal element; the substance 5 RAW MATERIAL 6a a textile fibre (e g wool or rayon) of relatively short length that when spun and twisted forms a yarn rather than a continuous strand (FILAMENT) **b** the length of a piece of such textile fibre as a distinguishing characteristic of the raw material [ME, fr MD *stapel* place of trade]

⁴**staple** *adj* 1 used, needed, or enjoyed constantly, usu by many individuals 2 produced regularly or in large quantities ⟨~ *crops such as wheat and rice*⟩ 3 principal, chief

¹**stapler** /'stayplə/ *n* a merchant dealing in staple goods or in staple fibre

²**stapler** *n* a small usu hand-operated device for inserting wire staples

¹**star** /stah/ *n* **1a** any natural luminous body visible in the sky,

esp at night **b** any of millions of self-luminous celestial bodies of great mass, heat, and light, fuelled by nuclear fusion reactions **2a** *usu pl* **2a(1)** a planet or a configuration of the planets that is held in astrology to influence a person's destiny, character, etc **a(2)** an astrological forecast; a horoscope **b** a waxing or waning fortune or fame ⟨*her* ~ *was rising*⟩ **3a** a stylized figure with five or more points that represents a star **b** an often star-shaped ornament or medal worn as a badge of honour, authority, or rank or as the insignia of an order **c** an asterisk **d** a stylized star used singly or as one of a group to place something in a scale of relative excellence ⟨*awarded the hotel four* ~s⟩ – compare FIVE-STAR, FOUR-STAR, ONE-STAR, THREE-STAR, TWO-STAR **e** a white starlike spot on a horse's forehead **4a** the principal member of a theatrical or operatic company who usu plays the chief roles **b** a highly publicized entertainer **c** an outstandingly talented performer ⟨*a* ~ *of the running track*⟩ **d** a person who stands out among his/her fellows ⟨*she's the* ~ *of the Lower Sixth*⟩ [ME *sterre*, fr OE *steorra;* akin to OHG *sterno* star, L *stella*, Gk *astēr, astron*] – **starless** *adj,* **starlike** *adj*

²**star** *vb* **-rr-** *vt* 1 to sprinkle or adorn (as if) with stars **2a** to mark with a star as being the foremost **b** to mark with an asterisk 3 to advertise or display prominently; feature ⟨*the film* ~s *a famous stage personality*⟩ ~ *vi* 1 to play the most prominent or important role in a production ⟨*now* ~*ring in a West-End musical*⟩ 2 to perform outstandingly

³**star** *adj* 1 of, being, or appropriate to a star ⟨*received* ~ *treatment*⟩ 2 of outstanding excellence; preeminent ⟨*a* ~ *athlete*⟩

**star apple** *n* a tropical American tree (*Chrysophyllum cainito*) of the sapodilla family grown for ornament or fruit; *also* its apple-shaped greenish edible fruit which when cut reveals a star-shaped seed pattern

¹**starboard** /'stahbəd/ *adj or n* (of or at) the right side of a ship or aircraft when facing forwards – compare PORT [ME *sterbord*, fr OE *stēorbord*, fr *stēor-* steering oar + *bord* ship's side – more at STEER, BOARD]

²**starboard** *vt* to turn or put (a helm or rudder) to the right

¹**starch** /stahch/ *vt* to stiffen (as if) with starch [ME *sterchen*, prob fr (assumed) OE *stercan* to stiffen; akin to OE *stearc* stiff – more at STARK]

²**starch** *n* 1 a white odourless tasteless complex carbohydrate, $(C_6H_{10}O_5)_n$, that is the chief storage form of carbohydrate in plants, is present in many foodstuffs (e g potatoes and rice), and is used also in adhesives, in laundering, and in pharmacy and medicine 2 a stiff formal manner; formality – **starcher** *n*

**Star Chamber** *n* a court of the Privy Council in England that was abolished in 1641, had primarily criminal jurisdiction, and was noted for its arbitrary and oppressive procedures; *broadly, often not cap* any oppressive court or tribunal – ¹**star-ˌchamber** *adj*

**starchy** /'stahchi/ *adj* 1 containing, consisting of, or resembling starch ⟨~ *food*⟩ 2 formal, stiff – **starchily** *adv,* **starchiness** *n*

¹**star-ˌcrossed** *adj* not favoured by the stars; ill-fated ⟨*a pair of* ~ *lovers take their life* – Shak⟩

**stardom** /'stahdəm/ *n* 1 the status or position of a celebrity or star ⟨*the actress quickly reached* ~⟩ 2 the body of professional stars

**stardust** /'stah‚dust/ *n, journalistic* a feeling or impression of romance or magic

¹**stare** /steə/ *vi* 1 to look fixedly, often with wide-open eyes 2 to stand out conspicuously ⟨*the error* ~d *from the page*⟩ 3 *esp of an animal's coat* to appear rough and lustreless because of illness; *also* to bristle with aggression, fear, etc ~ *vt* to bring to a specified state by staring ⟨~d *him into submission*⟩ – see also **stare one/somebody in the** FACE **synonyms** see ¹GAZE [ME *staren*, fr OE *starian;* akin to OHG *starēn* to stare, L *strenuus* strenuous, Gk *stereos* solid, Lith *starinti* to stiffen] – **starer** *n*

**stare out** *vt* to cause to look away by staring into the eyes

²**stare** *n* a staring look ⟨*a blank* ~⟩

**starets** /'stahr(y)əts/ *n, pl* **startsy** /'stahtsi/ a spiritual director or religious teacher in the Orthodox Church; *specif* a spiritual adviser who is not necessarily a priest and who is turned to by monks or laymen for spiritual guidance [Russ, lit., old man, fr *staryĭ* old]

**star facet** *n* any of the eight small triangular surfaces surrounding the flat top of a BRILLIANT (carved gemstone or diamond)

**starfish** /'stah‚fish/ *n* any of a class (Asteroidea of the phylum

Echinodermata) of marine INVERTEBRATE animals that have a body consisting of a central disc surrounded by usu five equally spaced arms and that feed largely on oysters, clams, etc

**starflower** /'stah‚flowə/ n any of various plants having starlike flowers; esp STAR-OF-BETHLEHEM

**stargaze** /'stah‚gayz/ vi 1 to gaze at stars 2 to gaze raptly, contemplatively, or absentmindedly; esp to daydream [back-formation fr *stargazer*]

**stargazer** /'stah‚gayzə/ n 1 any of several marine spiny-finned fishes (family Uranoscopidae) with the eyes on top of the head 2 chiefly humorous one who gazes at the stars: eg 2a an astrologer b an astronomer

**star grass** n any of various plants of the daffodil family having long grasslike leaves and yellow star-shaped flowers, found in temperate and tropical regions

¹**stark** /stahk/ adj 1a rigid (as if) in death b rigidly conforming (eg to a pattern or doctrine); absolute ⟨~ discipline⟩ 2 sheer, utter ⟨~ nonsense⟩ 3a barren, desolate b(1) having few or no ornaments; bare ⟨a ~ white room⟩ b(2) harsh, blunt ⟨the ~ realities of death⟩ 4 sharply delineated ⟨a ~ outline⟩ 5 archaic strong, robust [ME, stiff, strong, fr OE stearc; akin to OHG starc strong, Lith starinti to stiffen – more at STARE] – **starkly** adv, **starkness** n

²**stark** adv to an absolute or complete degree; wholly ⟨~ naked⟩ ⟨~ raving mad⟩

**starkers** /'stahkəz/ adv or adj, Br slang stark naked – used predicatively ⟨lying ~ on the sand⟩ [stark + -ers (as in crackers)]

**starlet** /'stahlit/ n a young film actress being coached and publicized for starring roles

**starlight** /'stah‚liet/ n the light of the stars

**starling** /'stahling/ n any of a family (Sturnidae, esp genus *Sturnus*) of usu dark social birds; esp a dark brown or, in summer, glossy greenish-black speckled European bird (*Sturnus vulgaris*) naturalized in the USA, S Canada, Australia, and New Zealand, that is often a pest [ME, fr OE stærlinc, fr stær starling + -ling, -linc -ling; akin to OHG stara starling, L sturnus]

**starlit** /'stah‚lit/ adj lit by the stars

**star-of-Bethlehem** /'bethlihem/ n any of a genus (Ornithogalum) of plants of the lily family with narrow grasslike leaves and white star-shaped flowers; esp a European one (Ornithogalum umbellatum) with greenish flowers – called also STAR-FLOWER

**star of Bethlehem** n a star which according to Mt 2:1–11 guided the Wise Men to the infant Jesus

**Star of David** /'dayvid/ n a 6-pointed star made from two superimposed triangles that is a symbol of Judaism and the State of Israel [David † ab973 BC king of Judah & Israel]

**starry** /'stahri/ adj 1a adorned or studded with stars b (consisting) of the stars; stellar c shining like stars; sparkling d having parts arranged like the rays of a star; stellate 2 (seemingly) as high as the stars ⟨~ speculations⟩ 3 starry-eyed

‚**starry-'eyed** adj regarding an object or a prospect in an unrealistically favourable light; specif given to dreamy, impracticable, or overoptimistic thinking

**Stars and Stripes** n taking sing vb the flag of the USA, having 13 alternately red and white horizontal stripes and a blue rectangle in the top left-hand corner with white stars representing the states

**star sapphire** n a sapphire that when cut with a CONVEX (curving outwards) surface and polished reflects light to give a star-like pattern

**star shell** n 1 a shell that on bursting releases a brilliant light and is used for illumination and signalling 2 a shell with an illuminating projectile

'**star-‚spangled** adj studded with stars

**star stone** n any precious stone showing a starlike pattern when cut and polished; esp STAR SAPPHIRE

'**star-‚studded** adj full of or covered with stars ⟨a ~ cast⟩ ⟨a ~ uniform⟩

**star system** n the practice of casting famous performers in film and theatrical roles, esp in order to exploit their popular appeal

¹**start** /staht/ vi 1a to move suddenly and violently; spring ⟨~ed angrily to his feet⟩ b to react with a sudden brief involuntary movement ⟨~ed when a shot rang out⟩ 2a to issue with sudden force ⟨blood ~ing from the wound⟩ b to come into being, activity, or operation ⟨when does the film ~?⟩ 3 to (seem to) protrude ⟨his eyes ~ing from their sockets⟩ 4 to

become loosened or forced out of place ⟨one of the planks has ~ed⟩ 5a to begin a course or journey ⟨~ed towards the door⟩ ⟨~ed out at dawn⟩ b to range from a specified initial point ⟨holiday prices ~ from around £80⟩ 6 to begin an activity or undertaking; esp to begin work 7 to be a participant at the start of a sporting contest ~ vt 1 to cause to leave a place of concealment; flush ⟨~ a rabbit⟩ 2 to bring up for consideration or discussion 3 to bring into being ⟨~ a rumour⟩ 4 to cause to become loosened or displaced 5 to begin the use or employment of ⟨~ a fresh loaf of bread⟩ 6a to cause to move, act, operate, or do something specified ⟨~ the motor⟩ ⟨the noise ~ed the baby crying⟩ b to act as starter of (eg a race) c to cause to enter or begin a game, contest, or business activity ⟨only had £500 to ~ him⟩; broadly to put in a starting position d to care for during early stages 7 to perform or undergo the first stages or actions of; begin ⟨~ed studying music at the age of five⟩ 8 archaic to startle, alarm **synonyms** see BEGIN **antonym** stop [ME sterten; akin to MHG sterzen to stand up stiffly, move quickly, Lith starinti to stiffen – more at STARE] – **start something** informal to cause trouble – **to start with** 1 at the beginning; initially 2 taking the first point to be considered – see also **start the** BALL **rolling**

²**start** n 1a a sudden involuntary bodily movement or reaction (eg from surprise or alarm) b a brief and sudden action or movement c a sudden capricious impulse or outburst 2 a beginning of movement, activity, or development 3a a lead or handicap conceded at the start of a race or competition b an advantage, lead; HEAD START ⟨gained a three days' ~ on the police⟩ ⟨his background gave him a good ~ in politics⟩ 4 a place of beginning – see also in FITS and starts

**starter** /'stahtə/ n 1 somebody who initiates or sets going: eg 1a somebody who gives the signal to start a race b somebody who dispatches vehicles 2a somebody who is in the starting line-up of a race or competition b somebody who begins to engage in an activity or process 3 one who or that which causes something to begin operating: eg 3a a self-starter b material containing microorganisms (eg yeasts) used to induce fermentation (eg in milk or beer) c a chemical compound used to start a chemical reaction 4a something that is the beginning of a process, activity, or series b starters pl, starter chiefly Br informal the first course of a meal – compare APPETIZER – **for starters** chiefly Br informal in the first place; as a beginning – **under starter's orders** committed to begin a course of action; specif in position to start a race

**star thistle** n 1 a spiny Eurasian plant (Centaurea calcitrapa) of the daisy family that has purple flowers and is a widely naturalized weed 2 any of various often spiny KNAPWEEDS (thistlelike plants)

**starting block** /'stahting/ n a device that consists of two blocks mounted on either side of an adjustable frame that is usu fixed to the ground and that provides a runner with a rigid surface against which to brace his/her feet at the start of a race

**starting gate** n 1 a mechanically operated barrier used as a starting device for races (eg horse races) 2 a barrier that when knocked aside by a competitor (eg a skier) starts an electronic timing device

**starting grid** n GRID 3 (lines indicating the starting positions of cars on a racetrack)

**starting handle** n, Br a crank used to start an internal-combustion engine

**starting stalls** n pl a line of stalls or traps in which horses or dogs are enclosed at the beginning of a race and from which they are released simultaneously by the opening of mechanical barriers at the front of each stall

**startle** /'stahtl/ vi to move or jump suddenly (eg in surprise or alarm) ⟨the horse ~s easily⟩ ~ vt to frighten or surprise suddenly and usu not seriously; cause to make a sudden movement, esp from surprise or alarm [ME stertlen, freq of sterten to start] – **startlingly** adv

**star turn** n, chiefly Br the major skit or number in a variety show; broadly the most widely publicized person or item in a group

**starvation** /stah'vaysh(ə)n/ n starving or being starved

**starvation wages** n wages insufficient to provide the ordinary necessities of life

**starve** /stahv/ vi 1a to die from lack of food b to suffer or feel extreme hunger ⟨starving children of the Third World⟩ 2 to suffer or perish from deprivation ⟨~d for affection⟩ 3 archaic or dial 3a to die of cold b to suffer greatly from cold ~ vt 1a to kill with lack of food **b** to deprive of food ⟨starving *herself in an attempt to lose weight*⟩ **c** to cause to capitulate (as if) by depriving of food ⟨~d *them into submission*⟩ **2** to cause to suffer from not having the specified thing ⟨*children* ~d *of affection*⟩ ⟨*the engine was* ~d *of petrol and wouldn't start*⟩ **3** *archaic or dial* to kill with cold [ME *sterven* to die, fr OE *steorfan;* akin to OHG *sterban* to die, Lith *starinti* to stiffen – more at STARE]

¹**starveling** /'stahvling/ *n* a person or animal that is thin (as if) from lack of food

²**starveling** *adj* **1** starving ⟨*a* ~ *child*⟩ **2** insufficient, meagre

¹**stash** /stash/ *vt* to store in a usu secret place for future use – often + *away* [origin unknown]

²**stash** *n, chiefly NAm* **1** a hiding place; a cache **2** something stored or hidden away

**stasis** /'staysis/ *n, pl* **stases** /-seez/ **1** a slowing or stoppage of the normal flow of body fluids: eg **1a** slowing of the current of circulating blood **b** reduced movement of material through the intestines, causing constipation **2** a state of static balance or equilibrium; stagnation [NL, fr Gk, act or condition of standing, stopping, fr *histasthai* to stand – more at STAND]

**-stasis** /-'staysis/ *comb form* (→ *n*), *pl* **-stases** /-seez/ **1** stoppage; slowing down; inhibition ⟨*haemo*stasis⟩ ⟨*bacterio*stasis⟩ **2** stable state ⟨*homoeo*stasis⟩ [NL, fr Gk *stasis* standing, stopping]

**-stat** /-stat/ *comb form* (→ *n*) **1** agent or device for regulating ⟨*thermo*stat⟩ ⟨*rheo*stat⟩ **2** instrument for reflecting (something specified) constantly in one direction ⟨*helio*stat⟩ **3** agent causing inhibition of growth of (something specified) without destruction ⟨*bacterio*stat⟩ [NL *-stata*, fr Gk *-statēs* one who or that which stops or steadies, fr *histanai* to cause to stand – more at STAND]

**statant** /'stayt(ə)nt/ *adj, of a heraldic animal* standing in profile with all feet on the ground [L *status*, pp of *stare* to stand + E *-ant*]

¹**state** /stayt/ *n* **1a** a mode or condition of being ⟨*a* ~ *of readiness*⟩ **b(1)** a specified condition of mind or temperament ⟨*in a highly nervous* ~⟩ **b(2)** a condition of abnormal tension or excitement ⟨*don't get in a* ~ *about it*⟩ **2a** a condition or stage in the physical being of something ⟨*insects in the larval* ~⟩ ⟨*the gaseous* ~ *of water*⟩ **b** any of various conditions characterized by definite quantities (eg of energy, ANGULAR MOMENTUM, or MAGNETIC MOMENT) in which an atomic system may exist **3a** social position; *esp* high rank **b(1)** elaborate or luxurious style of living **b(2)** formal dignity; pomp – usu + *in* **4a** *taking sing or pl vb* a body of people constituting a special class in a society, esp in former times; ESTATE 1 **b** *pl* the members or representatives of the ESTATES assembled in a legislative body **5a** *taking sing or pl vb* a politically organized body of people usu occupying a definite territory; *esp* one that is sovereign **b** the political organization of such a body of people **6** the operations or concerns of the central government of a country ⟨*matters of* ~⟩ **7** *often cap* a constituent unit of a nation having a federal government ⟨*the United* States *of America*⟩ [ME *stat*, fr OF & L; OF *estat*, fr L *status*, fr *status*, pp of *stare* to stand – more at STAND] – **lie in state** *of a deceased person, esp a head of state* to be placed on public view before burial so that people may pay their respects – see also **turn** State's EVIDENCE

*synonyms* State, condition, situation, and status can all mean "circumstances under which somebody or something exists". **State** and **condition** imply a particular form in which something exists, usually at a particular time or place ⟨remained in a weakened **state**/**condition** for months⟩. **Condition** often implies the effect of outside influences upon health, appearance, or usefulness ⟨roads in bad **condition**⟩. **Situation** often applies to a critical or problematical set of circumstances ⟨an unfortunate **situation** has developed⟩. **Status** applies particularly to position in a hierarchy ⟨his **status** as executive assistant gave him access to confidential reports⟩.

²**state** *vt* **1** to set, esp by regulation or authority; specify **2a** to express the particulars of, esp in words; report **b** to declare, announce ⟨~d *his intentions*⟩ – **statable, stateable** *adj*

**State attorney, State's attorney** *n* an officer appointed to represent a state in legal proceedings in the USA; PROSECUTING ATTORNEY

**state bank** *n* a commercial bank in America established by state charter and not required to be a member of the Federal Reserve System

**state capitalism** *n* an economic system in which capitalism is modified by a varying degree of state ownership and control

**state church** *n, often cap S&C* an officially recognized national church

**statecraft** /-,krahft/ *n* the art of conducting state affairs

**stated** /'staytid/ *adj* **1** fixed, regular ⟨*the president shall, at* ~ *times, receive . . . a compensation – US Constitution*⟩ **2** set down explicitly; declared – **statedly** *adv*

**State Enrolled Nurse** *n* a nurse who has successfully followed a two-year course in practical nursing in Britain

**statehood** /'stayt-hood/ *n* the condition of being a state ⟨*Israel's emergence to* ~⟩; *esp* the condition or status of a state of the USA

**statehouse** /-,hows/ *n* the building which houses the law-making body of a state of the USA

**stateless** /-lis/ *adj* having no nationality ⟨*a* ~ *person*⟩ – **statelessness** *n*

**stately** /-li/ *adj* **1** marked by lofty or imposing dignity ⟨*a* ~ *old lady*⟩ ⟨~ *language*⟩ **2** impressive in size or proportions *synonyms* see ¹GRAND – **stateliness** *n,* **stately** *adv*

**stately home** *n, Br* a large country residence, usu of historical or architectural interest and open to the public

**statement** /'staytmənt/ *n* **1** the act or process of stating or presenting orally or on paper **2** something stated: eg **2a** a report of facts or opinions ⟨*went down to the police station to make a* ~⟩ **b** a single declaration or remark; an assertion **3** *philosophy* PROPOSITION 2 **4** the presentation of a theme in a musical composition **5** a summary of a financial account ⟨*received a bank* ~ *every month*⟩ **6** an outward expression of thought, feeling, etc made without words ⟨*painted the room bright blue to make a* ~⟩ **7** the smallest meaningful self-contained unit of text in a computer program

**state of emergency** *n* EMERGENCY 4

,**state-of-the-'art** *adj* using well-known or current available technology so as to avoid a long development time ⟨*a* ~ *aircraft design*⟩

**state of the art** *n* the level of development (eg of a device, process, technique, or science) reached at a particular time

**state prison** *n* a prison maintained by a state of the USA for the imprisonment of people convicted of serious crimes

**stater** /'staytə/ *n* any of various ancient gold or silver coins of the Greek city-states [ME, fr LL, fr Gk *statēr*, lit., a unit of weight, fr *histanai* to cause to stand, weigh – more at STAND]

**State Registered Nurse** *n* a fully qualified nurse in Britain

**stateroom** /-,roohm, -room/ *n* **1** a large room in a palace or similar building, for use on ceremonial occasions **2a** a private cabin in a ship; *esp* a large and comfortable cabin used by an officer or first-class passenger **b** *NAm* a private room in a railway carriage with one or more berths and a toilet

**States** /stayts/ *n taking sing or pl vb* the USA ⟨*back from the* ~⟩

**state school** *n* a British school that is publicly financed and that provides compulsory free education – not used by educationalists

**state's evidence** *n, often cap S* **1** a person who gives evidence for the prosecution in US state or federal criminal proceedings **2** evidence given for the prosecution in US criminal proceedings; *specif* such evidence given by an accomplice in a crime against the other people charged with that crime – compare KING'S EVIDENCE, QUEEN'S EVIDENCE

**States General** *n pl* **1** the assembly of the three orders of clergy, nobility, and THIRD ESTATE (bourgeoisie) in France before the Revolution **2** the legislature of the Netherlands from the 15th century to 1796

**stateside** /-,sied/ *adj or adv, NAm* of, in, or to the USA [(*United*) *States* + *side*]

**statesman** /'staytsmən/, *fem* **stateswoman** *n* **1** somebody versed in the principles or art of government; *esp* somebody actively engaged in conducting the business of a government or in shaping its policies **2** one who exercises political leadership wisely and without narrow partisanship – **statesmanlike** *adj,* **statesmanly** *adj,* **statesmanship** *n*

**state socialism** *n* an economic system with limited socialist characteristics introduced gradually by political action

**states' righter** *n* one who advocates strict interpretation of the US constitutional guarantee of states' rights

**states' rights** *n pl, often cap S&R* all rights not vested by the US Constitution in the federal government nor forbidden by it to the separate states

**state trial** *n* a trial for offences against the state

**state trooper** *n* a state policeman in the USA

**state university** *n* a university maintained and administered by one of the states of the USA as part of the state public educational system

**¹static** /'statik/ *also* **statical** /-kl/ *adj* **1** exerting force by reason of weight alone without motion ⟨~ *load*⟩ ⟨~ *pressure*⟩ **2** of or concerned with bodies at rest or forces in equilibrium **3** characterized by a lack of movement, animation, progression, or change ⟨*a ~ population*⟩ **4** standing or fixed in one place; stationary ⟨*brilliant indoor ~ presentations*⟩ **5** of or producing stationary charges of electricity; electrostatic **6** of or caused by radio static **7** *of a computer memory* using devices that will preserve the stored information indefinitely without the need for any periodic attention or adjustment – compare DYNAMIC [NL *staticus*, fr Gk *statikos* causing to stand, skilled in weighing, fr *histanai* to cause to stand, weigh – more at STAND] – **statically** *adv*

**²static** *n* (the electrical disturbances causing) unwanted signals in a radio or television system; *specif* atmospherics [short for *static electricity*]

**-static** *comb form* (→ *adj*) **1** causing slowing of; inhibiting ⟨*bacterio*static⟩ **2** maintaining in a steady state; regulating ⟨*thermo*static⟩ ⟨*homoeo*static⟩

**statice** /'statisi/ *n* SEA LAVENDER [NL, genus of coastal plants, fr L, an astringent plant, fr Gk *statikē*, fr fem of *statikos* causing to stand, astringent]

**static line** *n* a cord attaching a parachute pack to an aircraft to open the parachute after the person jumping is clear of the craft

**statics** /'statiks/ *n taking sing or pl vb* a branch of mechanics dealing with the relations of forces that produce equilibrium among solid bodies

**static tube** *n* an open-ended tube used to measure the static pressure in a stream of liquid or gas

**¹station** /'staysh(ə)n/ *n* **1a** the place or position in which something or someone stands or is assigned to stand or remain **b** the point from which a measurement is made in surveying **2** a stopping place; *esp* (the buildings at) a regular or major stopping place for trains, buses, etc that allows passengers to board the transport **3** any of the STATIONS OF THE CROSS **4a** a post or sphere of duty or occupation **b** a post or area to which a military or naval force is assigned; *also, taking sing or pl vb* the officers or society at a station **c** a stock farm or ranch of Australia or New Zealand **5** standing, rank ⟨*a woman of high ~*⟩ **6** a place for specialized observation and study of scientific phenomena ⟨*a marine biology ~*⟩ **7a** a place established to provide a public service ⟨*petrol ~*⟩ ⟨*power ~*⟩ ⟨*polling ~*⟩ **b** POLICE STATION **c** FIRE STATION **8a** (the equipment in) an establishment equipped for radio or television transmission or reception **b** a radio or television channel [ME *stacioun*, fr MF *station*, fr L *station-, statio*, fr *status*, pp of *stare* to stand – more at STAND]

**²station** *vt* to assign to or set in a station or position; post

**stational mass** /'staysh(ə)nl/ *n* **1** a mass formerly celebrated by the pope at designated churches in Rome on appointed holy days **2** a mass celebrated during Lent by a Roman Catholic bishop at a church in each deanery of his diocese

**stationary** /'staysh(ə)n(ə)ri/ *adj* **1a** having a fixed position; immobile **b** GEOSTATIONARY ⟨*a ~ satellite hovering over the city*⟩ **2** unchanging in condition △ stationery

**stationary front** *n* the boundary between two air masses neither of which is replacing the other

**stationary wave** *n* STANDING WAVE (pattern of vibration formed by the combination of two waves)

**stationer** /'staysh(ə)nə/ *n* **1** one who deals in stationery **2** *archaic* **2a** a bookseller **b** a publisher [ME *staciouner*, fr ML *stationarius* tradesman, bookseller, fr *station-, statio* shop, fr L, station]

**stationery** /'staysh(ə)n(ə)ri/ *n* materials (e g paper, pens, and ink) for writing or typing; *specif* paper and envelopes for letter writing △ stationary

**station house** *n, NAm* POLICE STATION

**stationmaster** /-,mahstə/ *n* an official in charge of a railway station

**stations of the cross** *n pl, often cap S&C* **1** a series of usu 14 images or pictures, esp in a church, that represent the stages of Christ's suffering and death **2** an act of devotion involving meditation before the stations of the cross

**station wagon** *n, chiefly NAm* ESTATE CAR

**statism** /'stay,tiz(ə)m/ *n* concentration of economic controls and planning in the hands of the state – **statist** *n or adj*

**statistic** /stə'tistik/ *n* a single term or quantity in or computed

from a collection of statistics; *specif* (a function used to obtain) a numerical value (e g the STANDARD DEVIATION or mean) used in describing and analysing statistics [back-formation fr *statistics*]

**statistical** /stə'tistikl/ *adj* of or employing the principles of statistics – **statistically** *adv*

**statistical mechanics** *n taking sing vb* a branch of mechanics dealing with the calculation of properties of matter (e g pressure) by the application of the principles of statistics to the mechanics of a system consisting of a large number of parts having motions that differ by small steps over a large range

**statistician** /,stati'stish(ə)n/ *n* **1** one who compiles statistics **2** a specialist in the principles and methods of statistics

**statistics** /stə'tistiks/ *n pl* **1** *taking sing vb* a branch of mathematics dealing with the collection, analysis, interpretation, and presentation of masses of numerical data **2** *taking pl vb* a collection of quantitative data [Ger *statistik* study of political facts and figures, fr NL *statisticus* of politics, fr L *status* state]

**stative** /,staytiv/ *adj, of a verb* expressing a bodily or mental state as opposed to an action or event

**stato-** *comb form* equilibrium ⟨*stato*lith⟩ [ISV, fr Gk *statos* stationary, fr *histasthai* to stand – more at STAND]

**statoblast** /'statoh,blahst/ *n* **1** a bud in a freshwater BRYOZOAN (INVERTEBRATE animal living in branching colonies) that is enclosed during the winter and develops into a new individual in spring **2** GEMMULE **b** (reproductive bud of a sponge) [ISV *stato-* + *-blast*]

**statocyst** /'statoh,sist/ *n* an organ of balance occurring esp in INVERTEBRATE animals and consisting usu of a liquid-filled sac in which are suspended chalky particles [ISV]

**statolatry** /stay'tolətri/ *n* advocacy of a highly centralized and all-powerful national government [¹*state* + *-o-* + *-latry*]

**statolith** /'statoh-lith/ *n* **1** any of the chalky particles in a statocyst **2** any of various solid bodies (e g starch grains) in the CYTOPLASM (jellylike material) of plant cells that may be responsible by changes in their position for changes in orientation of a part or organ [ISV]

**stator** /'staytə/ *n* a stationary part in a machine in or about which a rotor revolves [NL, fr L, one who stands, fr *status*, pp of *stare* to stand – more at STAND]

**statoscope** /'statəskohp/ *n* an instrument for indicating small changes in the altitude of an aircraft [ISV]

**¹statuary** /'statyooəri/ *n* statues collectively

**²statuary** *adj* of or suitable for statues ⟨*~ marble*⟩

**statue** /'statyooh, -chooh/ *n* a three-dimensional representation usu of a person, animal, or mythical being that is carved (e g in stone or wood), or cast (e g in bronze or plaster), or modelled in some plastic material (e g clay) [ME, fr MF, fr L *statua*, fr *statuere* to set up – more at STATUTE]

**statuesque** /,statyoo'esk/ *adj* resembling a statue, esp in massive dignity, shapeliness, or formal beauty – **statuesquely** *adv*, **statuesqueness** *n*

**statuette** /,statyoo'et/ *n* a small statue

**stature** /'stachə/ *n* **1** natural height (e g of a person) in an upright position **2** quality or status gained by growth, development, or achievement [ME, fr OF, fr L *statura*, fr *status*, pp of *stare* to stand]

**status** /'staytəs, 'statəs/ *n* **1** the condition of a person or thing in the eyes of the law ⟨*special tax ~*⟩ **2a** position or rank in relation to others ⟨*the ~ of a father*⟩ **b(1)** relative rank in a hierarchy of prestige or esp in a hierarchically arranged social structure **b(2)** high social position; prestige ⟨*a man of ~ in the community*⟩ **3** state of affairs; a situation *usage* The pronunciation /'staytəs/ is recommended for BBC broadcasters. *synonyms* see ¹STATE [L – more at STATE]

**status quo** /kwoh/ *n* the existing state of affairs ⟨*seeks to preserve the ~*⟩ [L, state in which]

**status symbol** *n* a possession serving to show high social status or wealth

**statutable** /'statyootəbl/ *adj* made, regulated, or imposed by or in conformity to statute; statutory ⟨*~ tonnage*⟩ – **statutably** *adv*

**statute** /'statyooht/ *n* **1** (an official document recording) a law passed by a legislative body and formally placed on record **2** an act of a corporation or of its founder intended as a permanent rule, usu for the conduct of its internal affairs ⟨*university ~s*⟩ **3** a subsidiary addition to an international agreement (e g a treaty); *esp* one that establishes an agency and regulates its scope or authority [ME, fr OF *statut*, fr LL *statutum* law, regulation, fr L, neut of *statutus*, pp of *statuere* to set up, station, fr *status* position, condition, state]

**statute book** *n* the whole body of laws passed by the legislative body of a state, whether or not published as a whole

**statute law** *n* the body of written law established by a legislative body

**statute mile** *n* MILE 1b

**statute of limitations** *n* a statute stipulating certain time limits after which rights cannot be enforced by legal action

**statutory** /'statyoot(ə)ri/ *adj* 1 of statutes 2 enacted, created, prescribed, or regulated by statute ⟨*a* ~ *age limit*⟩ – **statutorily** *adv*

**statutory instrument** *n* an official document recording an order, rule, or regulation that has been made by a minister exercising his/her delegated legislative powers and that has been approved by parliament but that does not constitute a statute or Act of Parliament

**statutory rape** *n, NAm* sexual intercourse with a female who is below the statutory age of consent

¹**staunch** /stawnch/ *vt* to stanch

²**staunch** *adj* **1a** watertight, sound **b** strongly built; substantial **2** steadfast in loyalty or principle [ME, fr MF *estanche*, fem of *estanc*, fr OF, fr *estancher* to stanch] – **staunchly** *adv*, **staunchness** *n*

**staurolite** /'stawrəliet/ *n* a yellowish-brown to black mineral, $(Fe,Mg)_2Al_9Si_4O_{23}(OH)$, that is an iron aluminium silicate and often occurs in crystals twinned so as to resemble a cross [Fr, fr Gk *stauros* cross + Fr *-lite* – more at STEER] – **staurolitic** *adj*

¹**stave** /stayv/ *n* **1** ¹STAFF 1,2 (stick or rod); *esp* a rung of a chair or ladder **2** any of the narrow strips of wood or narrow iron plates placed edge to edge to form the sides, covering, or lining of a vessel or structure (eg a barrel or the hull of a ship) **3** a stanza of a poem **4** a set of usu five horizontal spaced lines on and between which music is written [back-formation fr *staves*]

²**stave** *vb* **staved, stove** /stohv/ *vt* **1** to break in the staves of **2** to smash a hole in ⟨~ *in a boat*⟩; *also* to crush or break inwards ⟨staved *in several ribs*⟩ – usu + *in* **3** to fit (a ladder, chair, etc) with staves ~ *vi, of a boat or ship* to become stove in

   **stave off** *vt* to ward or fend off, esp temporarily ⟨*a small snack to* stave off *hunger*⟩

**staves** /stayvz/ *pl of* STAFF

**stavesacre** /'stayvz,aykə/ *n* a Eurasian LARKSPUR (type of plant) (*Delphinium staphisagria*); *also* its poisonous seeds that have an EMETIC (causing vomiting) and laxative action [by folk etymology fr ME *staphisagre*, fr ML *staphis agria*, fr Gk, lit., wild raisin]

¹**stay** /stay/ *n* a strong rope, now usu of wire, used to support a ship's mast or similar tall structure (eg a flagstaff); a guy rope [ME, fr OE *stæg;* akin to ON *stag* stay, OE *stēle* steel] – **in stays** *of a sailing vessel* in the process of going about from one tack to another

²**stay** *vt* **1** to support (eg a chimney) (as if) with stays **2** to incline (a mast) forward by the stays **3** to put (a ship) onto another tack ~ *vi, of a ship* to change to another tack

³**stay** *vb* **stayed** *also* **staid** *vi* **1** to continue in a place or condition; remain ⟨~ *here*⟩ ⟨~ed *awake*⟩ **2** to reside temporarily, esp as a guest ⟨*her mother-in-law came to* ~⟩ ⟨*would prefer to* ~ *at a hotel*⟩ **3a** to keep even in a contest or rivalry ⟨~ *with the leaders*⟩ **b** *of a racehorse* to run well over long distances **4** *chiefly Scot & Ind* to have one's home; live ⟨~s *in a flat in Glasgow*⟩ **5** *archaic* **5a** to stop going forward; pause ⟨~, *stand apart, I know not which is which* – Shak⟩ **b** to stop doing something; cease ~ *vt* **1** to last out (eg a race) ⟨*unable to* ~ *the course*⟩ **2** to remain during ⟨~ed *the whole time*⟩ **3** to stop or delay the proceeding, advance, or cause of; halt ⟨~ *an execution*⟩ **4** to quiet the hunger of temporarily **5** *archaic* to wait for; await ⟨*I will not* ~ *thy questions* – Shak⟩ – see also **stay** PUT [ME *stayen*, fr MF *ester* to stand, stay, fr L *stare* – more at STAND]

   **synonyms** Stay, sojourn, remain, wait, abide, tarry, and linger all mean "continue to be in a place". **Stay** is the most general, but may imply residence as a guest ⟨stay *in a hotel*⟩. **Sojourn** is a formal word for a temporary stay ⟨sojourn *for a while in France*⟩. **Remain** often suggests staying behind after others have left. **Wait** entails expectation. **Abide** emphasizes long patient waiting or duration ⟨*a book whose influences will* abide⟩. **Tarry** and **linger** both suggest a departure delayed after the proper time, **linger** particularly emphasizing the reluctance to leave ⟨lingered *to admire the fre-*

*scoes*⟩. **usage** Careful writers prefer to use **stay**, rather than **stop**, for the meaning "lodge temporarily" ⟨*we're* staying/stopping *with friends*⟩ and to confine **stop** to a shorter break in a journey ⟨stop *somewhere for dinner*⟩.

⁴**stay** *n* **1a** the action of halting; the state of being stopped **b** a stopping or suspension of procedure by judicial or executive order ⟨*a* ~ *of execution*⟩ **2** a temporary residence in a place ⟨*a brief* ~ *in hospital*⟩ **3** *NAm* capacity for endurance

⁵**stay** *n* **1** one who or that which serves as a prop; a support **2a** a thin strip of metal, plastic, bone, etc used to stiffen corsets **b** *pl* a corset stiffened with bones **3** a small piece of tape or cloth sewn to a garment to reinforce a point of strain (eg under a bound buttonhole) or to prevent stretching (eg at a waistline) [MF *estaie*, of Gmc origin; akin to OHG *stān* to stand – more at STAND]

⁶**stay** *vt* **1** to provide physical or moral support for; sustain **2a** to reinforce or prevent stretching of with a stay **b** to secure or sew with a STAY STITCH

'**stay-at-,home** *n or adj* (somebody) preferring to remain in his/her own home, locality, or country

**stayer** /'stayə/ *n* somebody who or something that stays: eg **a** a persistent or determined person **b** a racehorse that habitually stays the course

**staying power** /'staying/ *n* capacity for endurance; stamina

**staysail** /'stay,sayl; *naut* -səl/ *n* a sail hoisted on a stay; *esp* a triangular sail between two masts

**stay stitch** *n* a line of stitches sewn round an edge (eg a neckline) before making up a garment in order to prevent the cloth from stretching

¹**stead** /sted/ *n, obs* a locality, place [ME *stede*, fr OE; akin to OHG *stat* place, *stān* to stand] – **in somebody's stead** in somebody's place; instead of somebody ⟨*acted* in his brother's stead⟩ – **stand one in good stead** to be of advantage or service to one ⟨*took careful notes which later* stood her in good stead⟩

²**stead** *vt, archaic* to be of advantage to; help

**steadfast** /'sted,fahst, -fəst/ *adj* **1a** firmly fixed; steady, immovable ⟨*a* ~ *gaze*⟩ **b** not subject to change **2** firm in belief, determination, or adherence; loyal, unwavering – **steadfastly** *adv*, **steadfastness** *n*

**steading** /'steding/ *n* a small farm [ME *steding*, fr *stede* place, farm]

¹**steady** /'stedi/ *adj* **1a** firm in position; not shaking, rocking, etc **b** direct or sure in movement; unfaltering ⟨*a* ~ *hand*⟩ **2** showing or continuing with little variation or fluctuation; stable, uniform ⟨*a* ~ *breeze*⟩ ⟨~ *prices*⟩ **3a** not easily moved or upset; calm ⟨~ *nerves*⟩ **b** constant in feeling, principle, or purpose; dependable **c** not given to dissipation; sober [¹*stead* + ¹*-y*] – **steadily** *adv*, **steadiness** *n*

   **synonyms** Steady, constant, even, equable, and uniform all mean "not varying or changing". **Steady** and **constant** applied to human character imply dependable steadfastness, **steady** emphasizing sober self-control and **constant** stressing loyalty. An **even** or **equable** character is one of natural calmness, with less emphasis on strength of purpose, **equable** stressing unruffled tranquillity. **Uniform** applies to things rather than people, and involves a sameness which may come from conformity to a rule or pattern ⟨*bushes clipped to a* uniform *height*⟩. When applied to processes and levels, **steady** and **even** imply unvarying persistence ⟨a steady/an even *pace*⟩ and **constant** often suggests something continually recurring ⟨constant *banging*⟩, while **equable** implies a lack of extremes ⟨*a more* equable *winter climate in France* – Osbert Sitwell⟩. **antonyms** unsteady, nervous, jumpy

²**steady** *vb* to make, keep, or become steady – **steadier** *n*

³**steady** *adv* **1** in a steady manner; steadily **2** on the course set – used as a direction to the helmsman of a ship – **go steady** *informal* to have a long-term relationship (*with* a boyfriend or girlfriend)

⁴**steady** *n, informal* a boyfriend or girlfriend with whom one has a long-term relationship

**steady state** *n* a dynamically balanced state or condition of a system or process that tends to remain when once achieved

**steady state theory** *n* a theory in cosmology: the universe has always existed and has always been expanding, with matter being created continuously – compare BIG BANG THEORY

**steak** /stayk/ *n* **1a** a tender slice of meat cut from a fleshy part (eg the rump) of a carcass and suitable for grilling or frying ⟨*gammon* ~s⟩; *esp* a slice of beef ⟨*rump* ~⟩ **b** a poorer-quality less tender beef cut usu from the neck and shoulder and suitable for braising or stewing ⟨~ *and kidney pie*⟩ **c** a cross-sectional slice from between the centre and tail of a large fish

– compare CUTLET 2 minced beef prepared for cooking or for serving in the manner of a steak [ME *steke*, fr ON *steik;* akin to ON *steikja* to roast on a stake, *stik* stick, stake – more at STICK]

**steak tartare** *n* raw minced steak mixed with raw egg, onions, and seasonings

¹**steal** /steel/ *vb* **stole** /stohl/; **stolen** /'stohlən/ *vi* **1** to take dishonestly the property of another ⟨*taught the children it was wrong to* ∼⟩ **2** to come or go secretly, unobtrusively, gradually, or unexpectedly ⟨stole *up on him and startled him*⟩ ∼ *vt* **1a** to take without permission, esp secretly or by force and with intent to keep or make use of wrongfully ⟨stole *a bicycle*⟩ ⟨stole *my idea for a novel*⟩ **b** to appropriate entirely to oneself or beyond one's proper or equal share ⟨∼ *the show*⟩ **2** to accomplish, obtain, or convey in a secretive, unobserved, or furtive manner ⟨∼ *a visit*⟩ ⟨stole *a glance at him*⟩ **3** to seize, gain, or win by trickery or skill ⟨*a football player adept at* ∼*ing the ball*⟩ – see also **steal a** MARCH **on/upon, steal the** SHOW/**somebody's** THUNDER *synonyms* see ROB [ME *stelen,* fr OE *stelan;* akin to OHG *stelan* to steal] – **stealer** *n*

²**steal** *n, NAm informal* BARGAIN 2b ⟨*it's a* ∼ *at that price*⟩

**stealth** /stelth/ *n* **1** the act or action of proceeding furtively, secretly, or unobtrusively **2** the state of being furtive or unobtrusive [ME *stelthe,* lit., theft; akin to OE *stelan* to steal]

**stealthy** /'stelthi/ *adj* **1** cautious and secret in action or character **2** intended to escape observation; furtive *synonyms* see ¹SECRET – **stealthily** *adv,* **stealthiness** *n*

¹**steam** /steem/ *n* **1** a vapour given off by a heated substance **2a** the vapour into which water is converted when heated to its boiling point **b** the mist formed by the condensation of water vapour when cooled **3a** energy or power generated (as if) by steam under pressure ⟨*full* ∼ *ahead*⟩ **b** driving force; power, effort ⟨*got there under his own* ∼⟩ ⟨*ran out of* ∼ *before they completed the task*⟩ **4** a railway system powered by steam ⟨*the age of* ∼⟩ [ME *stem,* fr OE *stēam;* akin to D *stoom* steam] – **let off steam** to release pent-up energy, emotional tension, etc ⟨*needed to* let off steam *after exams*⟩

²**steam** *vi* **1** to rise or pass off as vapour **2** to give off steam or vapour **3a** to move or travel (as if) by steam power (eg in a steamship) **b** to proceed quickly **4** to become cooked by steam **5** to be angry; boil ⟨∼*ing over the insult she had received*⟩ **6** to become covered *up* or *over* with steam or condensation ⟨*his glasses* ∼ed *up*⟩ ∼ *vt* **1** to give out as fumes; exhale **2** to apply steam to; *esp* to expose to the action of steam (eg for softening or cooking) ⟨∼ed *the stamp off the envelope*⟩ ⟨*a* ∼ed *pudding*⟩

³**steam** *adj, Br humorous* antiquated, traditional ⟨*learn a language by* ∼ *methods*⟩

**steamboat** /-,boht/ *n* a boat propelled by steam power; *esp* one designed for river or coastal traffic

**steam boiler** *n* a boiler for producing steam

**steam chest** *n* the chamber from which steam is distributed to a cylinder of a STEAM ENGINE

**steamed-up** *adj, informal* excited, angry

**steam engine** *n* a stationary or locomotive engine driven or worked by steam; *esp* a RECIPROCATING ENGINE (engine in which to-and-fro motion is converted into circular motion) having a piston driven in a closed cylinder by steam

**steamer** /'steemə/ *n* **1** a device in which articles are steamed; *esp* a vessel in which food is cooked by steam **2a** a ship propelled by steam **b** an engine, machine, or vehicle operated or propelled by steam

**steam iron** *n* an electric iron with a compartment holding water that is converted to steam by the iron's heat and emitted through the flat surface onto the fabric being pressed

**steam radio** *n, Br humorous* radio considered as antiquated in comparison with television

¹**steamroller** /-,rohlə/ *n* **1** a steam-driven machine equipped with wide heavy rollers for compacting road surfaces during road-making; *broadly* ROAD ROLLER **2** a crushing force, esp when ruthlessly applied to overcome opposition

²**steamroller** *also* **steamroll** *vt* **1** to crush or consolidate with a steamroller **2a** to overwhelm by greatly superior force ⟨∼ *the opposition*⟩ **b** to force to a specified state or condition by the use of overwhelming pressure ⟨∼ed *the bill through Parliament*⟩ ∼ *vi* to move or proceed with irresistible force

**steamship** /-,ship/ *n* STEAMER 2a

**steam turbine** *n* a turbine driven by the pressure of steam discharged at high velocity against the turbine blades

**steamy** /'steemi/ *adj* **1** consisting of, characterized by, or full

of steam **2** *informal* erotic ⟨*a* ∼ *love scene*⟩ – **steamily** *adv,* **steaminess** *n*

**steapsin** /sti'apsin/ *n* the LIPASE (enzyme that promotes the breakdown of fats) in the digestive juice produced by the pancreas [Gk *stear* fat + E *-psin* (as in *pepsin*)]

**stearate** /'stiərayt/ *n* any of various chemical compounds (SALTS or ESTERS) formed by combination between STEARIC ACID and a metal atom, an alcohol, or another chemical group

**stearic** /'stiərik, sti'arik/ *adj* **1** of, obtained from, or resembling stearin or tallow **2** of STEARIC ACID ⟨∼ *esters*⟩ [Fr *stéarique,* fr Gk *stear* fat]

**stearic acid** *n* a FATTY ACID, $CH_3(CH_2)_{16}COOH$, that is obtained from hard fat (eg tallow) and whose chemical compounds are used in the manufacture of soap and candles; *also* a commercial mixture of stearic and PALMITIC ACIDS

**stearin** /'stiərin/ *n* **1** an ESTER (chemical compound) formed by combination between GLYCEROL and STEARIC ACID **2** the solid portion of a fat **3** stearine [Fr *stéarine,* fr Gk *stear* fat]

**stearine** /'stiərin/ *n* commercial STEARIC ACID

**steat-** /stee-ət-/, **steato-** *comb form* fat ⟨steato*lysis*⟩ [Gk, fr *steat-, stear* – more at STONE]

**steatite** /'stee-ətiet/ *n* **1** SOAPSTONE (soft greyish green or brown stone with a soapy texture) **2** an electrically insulating porcelain composed largely of steatite [L *steatitis,* a precious stone, fr Gk, fr *steat-*] – **steatitic** *adj*

**steatolysis** /,stee-ə'toləsis/ *n* the breakdown of neutral fats into GLYCEROL and free FATTY ACIDS [NL]

**steatopygia** /,stee-ətoh'piji-ə/ *n* a substantial development of fat on the buttocks, esp of females, that is common among the Hottentots and some black peoples [NL, fr *steat-* + Gk *pygē* rump, buttocks; akin to Latvian *pauga* cushion, Gk *physan* to blow – more at FOG] – **steatopygic, steatopygous** *adj*

**steatorrhoea** /,stee-ətə'riə/ *n* an excess of fat in the faeces [NL, fr *steat-* + *-rrhoea*]

**stedfast** /'sted,fahst/ *adj* steadfast

**steed** /steed/ *n, chiefly poetic* a horse; *esp* a spirited horse for state or war [ME *stede,* fr OE *stēda* stallion; akin to OE *stōd* stud – more at STUD]

¹**steel** /steel/ *n* **1** commercial iron that is essentially an alloy containing carbon in any amount up to about 1.7 per cent, is MALLEABLE (easily worked) under suitable conditions, and is distinguished from CAST IRON by its malleability and lower carbon content **2** an instrument or implement (characteristically) of steel: eg **2a** a tool (eg a ridged rod with a handle) for sharpening knives **b** a piece of steel for striking sparks from flint **c** a strip of steel used for stiffening a garment, esp a corset; ⁵STAY 2a **d** *poetic* a thrusting or cutting weapon **3** a quality (eg of mind or spirit) that suggests steel, esp in strength or hardness ⟨*nerves of* ∼⟩ **4** the steel manufacturing industry [ME *stele,* fr OE *stýle, stēle;* akin to OHG *stahal* steel, Skt *stakati* he resists]

²**steel** *vt* **1** to overlay, point, or edge with steel **2a** to make unfeeling; harden ⟨∼ed *himself against her entreaties*⟩ **b** to fill with resolution or determination ⟨∼ed *herself to tell them the news*⟩

³**steel** *adj* **1** made of steel **2** of the production of steel **3** resembling steel

**steel band** *n* taking *sing or pl vb* a band, developed originally in Trinidad, that plays tuned percussion instruments cut out of oil drums – **steelbandsman** *n*

**steel blue** *n* **1** a dark greyish-blue colour **2** any of the blue colours assumed by steel at various temperatures in tempering – **steel blue** *adj*

**steel engraving** *n* **1** the art or process of engraving on steel **2** an impression taken from an engraved steel plate

**steel grey** *adj or n* (of) a dark bluish-grey

**steel guitar** *n* a usu electric instrument with steel strings that are plucked while being pressed with a movable steel bar; HAWAIIAN GUITAR

**steelhead** /'stiəl,hed, 'steel-/ *n* a large N American RAINBOW TROUT

**steel wool** *n* an abrasive material composed of long fine loosely compacted steel fibres and used esp for scouring and burnishing

**steelworks** /-,wuhks/ *n* taking *sing or pl vb,* *pl* **steelworks** an establishment where steel is made – **steelworker** *n*

**steely** /'steeli/ *adj* **1** made of steel **2** resembling steel (eg in hardness, strength, or colour) ⟨∼ *determination*⟩ ⟨*a* ∼ *gaze*⟩ – **steeliness** *n*

**steelyard** /-,yahd/ *n* a balance in which an object to be weighed is suspended from the shorter arm of a lever and the weight determined by moving a counterbalance along a graduated scale on the longer arm until equilibrium is attained [prob fr [3]*steel* + *yard* (in the obs sense "rod")]

**steenbok** /'steen,bok/, **steinbok** /~, 'stien,bok/ *n* any of a genus (*Raphicerus*) of small antelopes of the plains of S and E Africa [Afrik *steenbok;* akin to OE *stānbucca* ibex; both fr a prehistoric WGmc compound whose elements are represented respectively by OE *stān* stone and OE *bucca* buck]

[1]**steep** /steep/ *adj* **1** making a large angle with the plane of the horizon; almost vertical ⟨*a ~ rock face*⟩ ⟨*the stairs were very ~*⟩ **2** being or characterized by a rapid and severe decline or increase ⟨*a ~ drop in living standards*⟩ **3** *informal* difficult to accept, comply with, or carry out; excessive [ME *stepe,* fr OE *stēap* high, steep, deep; akin to MHG *stief* steep, ON *staup* lump, knoll, cup] – **steepen** *vb,* **steepish** *adj,* **steeply** *adv,* **steepness** *n*

[2]**steep** *n* a steep place; a precipice

[3]**steep** *vt* **1** to soak in a liquid at a temperature under the boiling point (eg for softening, bleaching, or extracting an essence) **2** to cover with or plunge into a liquid (eg in bathing, rinsing, or soaking) **3** to imbue with or subject thoroughly to (some strong or pervading influence) ⟨*~ed in history*⟩ *~ vi* to undergo the process of soaking in a liquid ⟨*left the shirt to ~ overnight*⟩ [ME *stepen;* akin to Sw *stöpa* to steep] – **steeper** *n*

[4]**steep** *n* **1** the state or process of being steeped **2** (a tank holding) a liquid in which something is steeped

**steeple** /'steepl/ *n* a spire on top of a church tower; *broadly* a spire and the tower that supports it [ME *stepel,* fr OE *stēpel* tower; akin to OE *stēap* steep]

**steeplechase** /-,chays/ *n* **1a** a horse race across country **b** a horse race over jumps; *specif* a race between qualified horses under National Hunt rules, over a course longer than 2 miles (about 3.2 kilometres) containing brush fences higher than 4 feet 6 inches (about 1.4 metres) – compare FLAT 6, HURDLE 2c **2** a middle-distance running race over obstacles; *specif* such a race of 3000 metres (about 3280 yards) in which the runners have to clear 28 hurdles and 7 water jumps [fr the orig use of church steeples as landmarks to guide the riders] – **steeplechase** *vi,* **steeplechaser** *n,* **steeplechasing** *n*

**steeplejack** /-,jak/ *n* one who climbs tall structures (eg chimneys, towers, or steeples) to paint, repair, or demolish them

[1]**steer** /stia/ *n* **1** a male bovine animal castrated before sexual maturity – compare STAG 2 **2** an ox less than four years old [ME, fr OE *stēor* young ox; akin to OHG *stior* young ox, Skt *sthavira, sthūra* stout, thick, broad]

[2]**steer** *vt* **1** to direct the course of; *esp* to guide (eg a ship) by mechanical means (eg a rudder) ⟨*~ed the ship into the harbour*⟩ ⟨*~ed the visitors into the living room*⟩ ⟨*~ed the conversation away from dangerous topics*⟩ **2** to set and hold to (a course) *~ vi* **1** to direct the course (eg of a ship or motor vehicle) ⟨*~ed carefully into the parking space*⟩ **2** to pursue a course ⟨*~ed for home*⟩ **3** to be subject to guidance or direction ⟨*a car that ~s well*⟩ – see also steer CLEAR [ME *steren,* fr OE *stīeran;* akin to OE *stēor*- steering oar, Gk *stauros* stake, cross, *stylos* pillar, Skt *sthavira, sthūra* stout, thick, L *stare* to stand – more at STAND] – **steerable** *adj,* **steerer** *n*

[3]**steer** *n, NAm* a hint as to procedure; a tip ⟨*angry after getting a bum ~*⟩

**steerage** /'stiərij/ *n* **1** the act or practice of steering; *broadly* direction **2** a large section without cabins in a passenger ship for passengers paying the lowest fares [(2) fr its orig being located near the rudder]

**steerage-,way** *n* a rate of motion sufficient to make a ship or boat respond to movements of the rudder

**steering column** /'stiəring/ *n* the column that encloses the connections between the STEERING WHEEL and the STEERING GEAR of a vehicle (eg a car)

**steering committee** *n taking sing or pl vb* a managing or directing committee; *specif* a committee that determines the order in which business will be taken up in Parliament

**steering gear** *n* a mechanism by which something is steered

**steering wheel** *n* a handwheel by means of which one steers a motor vehicle, ship, etc

**steersman** /'stiazmən/ *n* a helmsman

[1]**steeve** /steev/ *vt* to stow (cargo) in a ship's hold [ME *steven,* prob fr Sp *estibar* or Pg *estivar* to pack tightly, fr L *stipare* to press together (cf STEVEDORE)]

[2]**steeve** *n* a long spar used in stowing cargo

**stegosaur** /'stegə,saw/ *n* any of a suborder (Stegosauria) of dinosaurs with strongly developed bony armour along the back [NL *Stegosauria,* group name, fr *Stegosaurus,* genus name]

**stegosaurus** /,stegə'sawrəs/ *n* any of a genus (*Stegosaurus*) of large stegosaurs of the late JURASSIC and early CRETACEOUS geological periods [NL, genus name, fr Gk *stegos* roof + *sauros* lizard]

**stein** /s(h)tien/ *n* a usu earthenware beer mug often with a hinged lid; *also* the quantity that a stein holds [Ger *steingut* stoneware or *steinkrug* stone jug, fr *stein* stone + *gut* goods or *krug* jug]

**steinbok** /'steenbok, 'stienbok/ *n* STEENBOK (type of antelope)

**stela** /'stiələ, 'stee-/ *n, pl* **stelae** /-lie/ a stele [NL, fr L, fr Gk *stēlē;* akin to Gk *stellein* to set up – more at STALL]

**stele** /'steeli, steel/ *n* **1** a usu carved or inscribed stone slab or pillar used esp as a gravestone **2** the usu cylindrical central region of food- and water-conducting tissue in the stem of a plant [NL, fr Gk *stēlē*] – **stelar** *adj*

**stellar** /'stelə/ *adj* **1a** of the stars **b** composed of stars **2** principal, leading ⟨*a ~ role*⟩ [LL *stellaris,* fr L *stella* star – more at STAR]

**stellate** /'stelət, -layt/ *also* **stellated** /-laytid/ *adj* resembling a star, esp in shape ⟨*a ~ leaf*⟩ ⟨*a ~ cell*⟩ [L *stellatus,* fr *stella* star]

**stelliform** /'steli,fawm/ *adj* shaped like a star ⟨*a starfish is a ~ echinoderm*⟩ [NL *stelliformis,* fr L *stella* + *-iformis* -iform]

**stellular** /'stelyoolə/ *adj* **1** having the shape of a star **2** marked with stars

[1]**stem** /stem/ *n* **1a** the main trunk of a plant; *specif* a primary plant stalk that develops buds and shoots instead of roots **b** a plant part (eg a branch or leafstalk) that supports another (eg a leaf or fruit) **c** a bunch of bananas **2** the bow or prow of a vessel; *specif* the principal part of the frame at the bow to which the sides are fixed – compare STERN **3** a line of ancestry; a stock; *esp* a fundamental line from which others have arisen **4** the part of a word that has unchanged spelling, to which different endings may be added to indicate case, gender, number, tense, etc **5** something that resembles a plant stem: eg **5a** a main usu vertical stroke of a letter or musical note **b** the tubular part of a tobacco pipe projecting from the bowl, through which smoke is drawn **c** the often slender and cylindrical upright support between the base and bowl of a wineglass **d** a shaft of a watch used for winding [ME, fr OE *stefn, stemn* stem of a plant or ship; OE *stefn* akin to OE *stæf* staff; OE *stemn* akin to OE *standan* to stand] – **stemless** *adj* – **from stem to stern** from end to end; thoroughly

[2]**stem** *vt* **-mm-** **1** to make headway against (eg an adverse tide, current, or wind) **2** to check or go counter to (something adverse) [[1]*stem* 2] – **stemmer** *n*

[3]**stem** *vb* **-mm-** *vi* to originate – usu + *from ~ vt* **1** to remove the stem from **2** to make stems for (eg artificial flowers) [[1]*stem* 1] – **stemmer** *n*

[4]**stem** *vb* **-mm-** *vt* **1a** to stop or dam up (eg a river) **b** to stop or check (as if) by damming; *esp* to stanch ⟨*~ a flow of blood*⟩ **2** to turn (skis) in stemming *~ vi* to retard oneself by forcing the heel of one or both skis outwards from the line of progress [ME *stemmen* to dam up, fr ON *stemma;* akin to OE *stamerian* to stammer]

[5]**stem** *n* an act or instance of stemming on skis

**stem cell** *n* an unspecialized cell (eg in bone marrow) that gives rise to differentiated cells (eg blood cells)

**stem christie** /'kristi/ *n, often cap C* a turn in skiing in which the back end of one ski is forced outwards from the line of progress and the other ski is then brought parallel to it

**stemma** /'stemə/ *n, pl* **stemmata** /-mətə/ *also* **stemmas** **1** a simple eye present in some insects **2** a scroll (eg among the ancient Romans) containing a genealogical list **3** a tree showing the relationships of the manuscripts of a literary work [L, wreath, pedigree (fr the wreaths placed on ancestral images), fr Gk, wreath, fr *stephein* to crown, wreathe]

**stemmed** /stemd/ *adj* having a usu specified kind of stem – usu in combination ⟨*long-stemmed roses*⟩

**stemmy** /'stemi/ *adj* having many or excessively long stems, esp in relation to the amount of foliage

**stem rust** *n* **1** a RUST (disease caused by a fungus) attacking the stem of a plant; *esp* a destructive disease, esp of wheat, caused by a rust fungus (*Puccinia graminis*) which produces reddish-brown or black lesions **2** the fungus causing stem rust

**stem turn** *n* a skiing turn executed by stemming the outside ski

**stemware** /'stem,weə/ *n, NAm* glass drinking vessels mounted on a stem

**Sten** /sten/, **Sten gun** *n* a lightweight 9-millimetre British submachine gun [Major *S*heppard, 20th-c E army officer + Mr *T*urpin, 20th-c E civil servant + *Eng*land]

**sten-** /sten-/, **steno-** *comb form* narrow; little ⟨steno*bathic*⟩ ⟨steno*grapher*⟩ [Gk, fr *stenos* narrow]

**stench** /stench/ *n* a stink **synonyms** see ²SMELL [ME, fr OE *stenc;* akin to OE *stincan* to stink] – **stenchy** *adj*

¹**stencil** /'stens(ə)l/ *n* 1 an impervious material (eg a sheet of paper or metal) perforated with lettering or a design through which a substance (eg ink, paint, or metallic powder) is forced onto a surface to be printed 2 something (eg a pattern, design, or print) that is produced by means of a stencil 3 a printing process that uses a stencil 4 **stencil, stencil paper** a sheet of strong tissue paper impregnated or coated (eg with paraffin or wax) for use esp in typing a stencil [ME *stanselen* to ornament with sparkling colours, fr MF *estanceler, fr estancele* spark, fr (assumed) VL *stincilla, fr* L *scintilla*]

²**stencil** *vt* -ll- *(NAm* -l-, -ll-) 1 to produce by stencil 2 to mark or paint with a stencil – **stenciller** *n*

**steno** /'stenoh/ *n, pl* **stenos** *NAm informal* 1 a stenographer 2 stenography

**stenobathic** /,stenə'bathik/ *adj, of an aquatic organism* able to live only within narrow limits of depth [*sten-* + Gk *bathos* depth – more at BATH-]

**stenographer** /ste'nogrəfə/ *n* SHORTHAND TYPIST

**stenography** /ste'nogrəfi/ *n* the art or process of writing in shorthand and the subsequent transcription of shorthand notes; *also* written shorthand notes – **stenographic** *adj,* **stenographically** *adv*

**stenohaline** /,stenoh'hayleen, -lien/ *adj* unable to withstand wide variation in the amount of salt present in the surrounding water [ISV *sten-* + Gk *halinos* of salt, fr *hals* salt – more at SALT]

**stenophagous** /stə'nofəgəs/ *adj* eating few kinds of foods ⟨~ *insects*⟩ [ISV]

**stenosed** /stə'nohzd, 'nohst/ *adj* affected with stenosis

**stenosis** /sti'nohsis/ *n, pl* **stenoses** /-seez/ a narrowing or constriction of the diameter of a body passage or opening [NL, fr Gk *stenōsis* act of narrowing, fr *stenoun* to narrow, fr *stenos* narrow] – **stenotic** *adj*

**stenotherm** /'stenəthuhm/ *n* an organism unable to survive wide variation in temperature [back-formation fr *stenothermal,* fr *sten-* + Gk *thermē* heat] – **stenothermy** *n,* **stenothermal** *adj*

**stenotopic** /,steno'topik/ *adj, of a living organism* having a narrow range of adaptability to changes in environmental conditions [*sten-* + Gk *topos* place – more at TOPIC]

**stenotype** /'stenətiep/ *trademark* – used for a small machine rather like a typewriter, used to record speech in a phonetic shorthand – **stenotype** *vt,* **stenotypist** *n,* **stenotypy** *n*

**stenter** /'stentə/ *n* TENTER (frame for drying and stretching cloth) [*stent* (to stretch out), fr ME *stenten,* by shortening & alter. fr *extenden* to extend]

**stentor** /'stentaw/ *n* 1 a person with a loud voice 2 any of a widely distributed genus (*Stentor*) of PROTOZOANS (single-celled organisms) that bear CILIA (hairlike projections) and have a trumpet-shaped body attached to a surface by the smaller end with the mouth at the larger end [*Stentor,* mythical Greek herald noted for his loud voice, fr L, fr Gk *Stentōr*]

**stentorian** /sten'tawri·ən/ *adj, esp of a voice* extremely loud

¹**step** /step/ *n* 1 a rest for the foot in ascending or descending: eg 1a a single tread and riser on a stairway; a stair **b** a ladder rung **c** *pl* a series of steps, usu outside, and often made of stone ⟨*went down the* ~s *to the harbour*⟩ ⟨*took a photograph of them on the* ~s *of the church*⟩ **d** *pl* a stepladder 2a(1) an advance or movement made by raising the foot and bringing it down elsewhere **a(2)** a combination of foot or foot and body movements constituting a unit or a repeated pattern ⟨*a dance* ~⟩ **a(3)** manner of walking; stride ⟨*walked with a spring in his* ~⟩ **b** FOOTPRINT 1 **c** the sound of a footstep ⟨*heard his* ~s *in the hall*⟩ **3a** the space passed over in one step **b** a short distance ⟨*just a* ~ *from the beach*⟩ **c** the height of one stair 4 *pl* a course, way ⟨*directed his* ~s *towards the river*⟩ **5a** a degree, grade, or rank in a scale **b** a stage in a process ⟨*was guided through every* ~ *of her career*⟩ 6 a socket on a ship designed to receive an upright spar; *esp* a block supporting the base of a mast 7 **step, steps** *pl* an action, proceeding, or measure often

occurring as one in a series ⟨*marriage is a serious* ~⟩ ⟨*is taking* ~s *to improve the situation*⟩ 8 a part resembling a step and usu occurring in a series (eg in a piece of machinery) 9 *chiefly NAm* a musical interval of a SECOND (interval between one note and the one above or below it in the DIATONIC scale) [ME, fr OE *stæpe;* akin to OHG *stapfo* step, *stampfōn* to stamp] – **steplike** *adj,* **stepped** *adj* – **break/keep step** (to cease) to march, walk, dance, etc in step – **in step** 1 with each foot moving to the same time as the corresponding foot of others, or in time to music 2 in harmony or agreement ⟨*keep in step with fashion*⟩ – **out of step** not IN STEP – **step by step** gradually – **watch one's step** to behave or proceed with caution

²**step** *vb* **-pp-** *vi* 1a to move by raising the foot and bringing it down elsewhere or by moving each foot in succession ⟨~ *ped off the pavement*⟩ ⟨~*ped over a log*⟩ **b** to dance 2a to move, esp a short distance, on foot ⟨~ *this way, please*⟩ ⟨~*ped down the road to visit his sister*⟩ **b** to be on one's way; leave – often + *along* **c** to move briskly ⟨*kept us* ~*ping*⟩ 3 to press down on something with the foot; tread ⟨~ *on the brake*⟩ ⟨~*ped on a rusty nail*⟩ 4 to come as if at a single step ⟨~*ped into a good job*⟩ 5 *obs* to advance, proceed ~ *vt* 1 to take by moving the feet in succession ⟨~ *three paces*⟩ 2 to go through the steps of; perform ⟨~ *a minuet*⟩ 3 to make (a spar or mast) erect by fixing the lower end in a socket (STEP 6) 4 to measure by steps usu + *off* or *out* ⟨~ *out 50 yards*⟩ **5a** to provide with steps **b** to make steps in ⟨~ *a key*⟩ 6 to construct or arrange (as if) in steps ⟨*craggy peaks with terraces* ~*ped up the sides – Time*⟩ – **step on it/the gas** *informal* to increase one's speed; hurry up – see also **step out of** LINE

**step down** *vt* to lower the voltage of (an electric current) by means of a transformer ~ *vi* to retire, resign ⟨*stepped down as chairman of the board – Current Biog*⟩ – see also STEP-DOWN

**step in** *vi* 1 to make a brief informal visit 2 to intervene in an affair or dispute – see also STEP-IN

**step into** *vt* to attain or adopt with ease ⟨*stepped into a fortune*⟩

**step out** *vi* 1 to leave or go outside, usu for a short distance and for a short time ⟨*stepped out for a smoke*⟩ 2 to go or march at a vigorous or increased pace 3 *chiefly NAm* to lead an active social life

**step up** *vt* 1 to increase the voltage of (an electric current) by means of a transformer 2 to increase, augment, or advance by one or more steps ⟨*step up production*⟩ ~ *vi* 1 to come forward ⟨*step up to the front*⟩ 2 to undergo an increase ⟨*business is stepping up*⟩ see also STEP-UP

**step-** *comb form* related by virtue of a remarriage and not by blood ⟨*step*parent⟩ ⟨*step*sister⟩ [ME, fr OE *stēop-;* akin to OHG *stiof-* step-, *stiufen* to bereave]

**stepbrother** /-,brudhə/ *n* a son of one's stepparent by a former marriage

,**step-by-'step** *adj* marked by successive degrees usu of limited extent; gradual – **step-by-step** *adv*

**stepchild** /-,chield/ *n, pl* **stepchildren** /-,childrən/ a child of one's husband or wife by a former marriage

**step dance** *n* a dance in which steps are emphasized rather than gesture or posture

**stepdaughter** /-,dawtə/ *n* a daughter of one's husband or wife by a former marriage

'**step-,down** *adj or n* (of or being) an electrical device for reducing a high voltage to a lower voltage

**stepfather** /-,fahdhə/ *n* the husband of one's mother by a subsequent marriage

**stephanite** /'stefəniet/ *n* a mineral, $Ag_5SbS_4$, that consists of a SULPHIDE of silver and antimony [Ger *stephanit,* fr Archduke *Stephan* of Austria †1867]

**stephanotis** /,stefə'nohtis/ *n* any of a genus (*Stephanotis*) of tropical woody climbing plants of the milkweed family that are found in Malaysia and Madagascar and have fragrant white flowers [NL, genus name, fr Gk *stephanōtis* fit for a crown, fr *stephanos* crown, fr *stephein* to crown]

'**step-,in** *adj, of a garment* put on by being stepped into

**stepladder** /-,ladə/ *n* a portable set of steps with a hinged frame for steadying

**stepmother** /-,mudhə/ *n* the wife of one's father by a subsequent marriage

**stepparent** /-,peərənt/ *n* the husband or wife of one's mother or father by a subsequent marriage

**steppe** /step/ *n* 1 any of the vast usu level and treeless plains in SE Europe or Asia 2 arid land found usu in regions of extreme temperature range and with sandy wind-blown soil [Russ *step*]

'stepping-,stone *n* 1 a stone on which to step (e g in crossing a stream) 2 a means of progress or advancement

step rocket *n* a multistage rocket whose sections are fired successively

stepsister /-,sistə/ *n* a daughter of one's stepparent by a former marriage

stepson /-,sun/ *n* a son of one's husband or wife by a former marriage

'step-,up *adj or n* (of or being) an electrical device for increasing a low voltage to a higher voltage

stepwise /-wiez/ *adj* 1 marked by or proceeding in steps 2 *chiefly NAm* moving by STEPS to adjacent musical notes

-ster /-stə/ *comb form* (→ *n*) 1 somebody who or something that does, handles, or operates ⟨*tap*ster⟩ ⟨*team*ster⟩ 2 somebody who or something that makes or uses ⟨*song*ster⟩ ⟨*pun*ster⟩ 3 somebody who or something that is associated with or participates in ⟨*game*ster⟩ ⟨*gang*ster⟩ 4 somebody who or something that is ⟨*young*ster⟩ [ME, fr OE -*estre* female agent; akin to MD -*ster*]

steradian /stə'raydyən/ *n* a unit of measure of SOLID ANGLES that is equal to the solid angle which with its point in the centre of a sphere cuts off an area of the surface of the sphere numerically equal to the square of the radius of the sphere [*stere*- + *radian*]

stercoraceous /,stuhkə'rayshəs/ *n* 1 of, being, or containing dung 2 foul, revolting [L *stercor*-, *stercus* dung]

stere /stiə/ *n* a metric unit of volume equal to one cubic metre (about 1.3 cubic yards) [Fr *stère*, fr Gk *stereos* solid]

stere- /steri-, stiəri-/, stereo- *comb form* 1 solid; solid body ⟨*stereo*taxis⟩ ⟨*stereo*metry⟩ 2a stereoscope ⟨*stereo*psis⟩ ⟨*stereo*graphy⟩ b having, involving, or dealing with three dimensions of space ⟨*stereo*chemistry⟩ [NL, fr Gk, fr *stereos* solid – more at STARE]

¹stereo /'sterioh, 'stiərioh/ *n, pl* stereos 1 STEREOTYPE 1 (plate for printing) 2a a stereoscopic method, system, or effect b a stereoscopic photograph 3a stereophonic reproduction ⟨*a concert broadcast in* ∼⟩ b a stereophonic sound system ⟨*lounged in his room listening to his new* ∼⟩ [(2) short for *stereoscopy*; (3) short for *stereophonic*]

²stereo *adj* 1 STEREOSCOPIC 2 STEREOPHONIC

stereobate /-,bayt/ *n* a solid structure of masonry used as a foundation [Fr or L; Fr *stéréobate*, fr L *stereobates* foundation, fr Gk *stereobatēs*, fr *stere*- + *bainein* to step, go – more at COME]

stereochemistry /-'kemistri/ *n* (a branch of chemistry that deals with) the spatial arrangement of atoms and groups within the molecules of a substance and its relation to the properties of the substance [ISV] – stereochemical *adj*, stereochemically *adv*

stereogram /'sterioh,gram, 'stiə-/ *n* 1 a diagram or picture representing objects in such a way as to give an impression of solidity or relief 2 a stereograph 3 *Br* a stereo radiogram [ISV]

stereograph /'sterioh,grahf, 'stiə-, -,graf/ *n* a pair of stereoscopic pictures of the same object taken from slightly different points of view, or a single picture composed of two superimposed stereoscopic images, that gives a three-dimensional effect when viewed with a stereoscope or special glasses [ISV] – stereograph *vt*

stereography /,steri'ogrəfi, ,stiəri-/ *n* 1 the art, process, or technique of drawing solid bodies on a flat surface 2 stereoscopic photography – stereographic *adj*, stereographically *adv*

stereoisomer /sterioh'iesəmə, stiəri-/ *n* any of a group of related forms (ISOMERS) of a molecule in which atoms are linked in the same order but differ in their spatial arrangement [ISV] – stereoisomeric *adj*, stereoisomerism *n*

stereometric /,steriə'metrik, ,stiə-/ *adj* having or representing a simple readily measurable solid form [NL *stereometricus*, fr Gk *stereometrikos*, fr *stereometria* measurement of solids, fr *stere*- + -*metria* -metry] – stereometry *n*

stereomicroscope /,sterioh'miekrəskohp, stiə-/ *n* a microscope having a set of lenses for each eye to make an object appear in three dimensions – stereomicroscopic *adj*, stereomicroscopically *adv*

stereophonic /,steri-ə'fonik, ,stiəri-, -rioh-/ *adj* 1 of, giving, or constituting the effect of sounds coming from spatially distinguishable sources 2 of or being a system for sound reproduction in which the sound is split into and reproduced by two different channels to give spatial effect [ISV *stere*- + *phonic*] – stereophonically *adv*, stereophony *n*

stereophotography /,sterioh-fə'togrəfi, stiə-/ *n* stereoscopic photography [ISV] – stereophotographic *adj*

stereopsis /,steri'opsis, stiə-/ *n* stereoscopic vision [NL, fr *stere*- + Gk *opsis* vision – more at OPTIC]

stereopticon /steri'optikon, stiə-/ *n* a double slide projector arranged so that one view dissolves into another [NL, fr *stere*- + Gk *optikon*, neut of *optikos* optic]

stereoregular /,sterioh'regyoolə, stiə-/ *adj* of or involving regularity in the STEREOCHEMISTRY (arrangement in space of the atoms of a molecule) in a structure that is a POLYMER (complex chemical substance composed of a linked series of repeating units) – stereoregularity *n*

stereoscope /'steri-ə,skohp, 'stiəri-ə-/ *n* an optical instrument with two eyepieces through which the observer views two pictures taken from points of view a little way apart, to get the effect of a single three-dimensional picture

stereoscopic /,steriə'skopik, stiə-/ *adj* 1 of a stereoscope 2 of or characterized by the seeing of objects in three dimensions ⟨∼ *vision*⟩ – stereoscopically *adv*

stereoscopy /,steri'oskəpi, ,stiəri-/ *n* 1 a science that deals with stereoscopic effects and methods 2 the seeing of objects in three dimensions [ISV]

stereospecific /,sterioh-spə'sifik, stiə-/ *adj* being, produced by, or involved in a process that depends on the specific spatial arrangement (STEREOCHEMISTRY) of the atoms of a substance ⟨*many enzymes act as* ∼ *catalysts in biological reactions*⟩ ⟨∼ *plastics*⟩ – stereospecifically *adv*, stereospecificity *n*

stereotaxic /,sterioh'taksik, stiə-/ *adj* of or being a technique or apparatus used in research or surgery of the nervous system for directing the tip of a delicate instrument (e g a needle or an electrode) in three planes into a predetermined area of the brain [NL *stereotaxis* stereotaxic technique (fr *stere*- + *taxis*) + E -*ic*] – stereotaxically *adv*

stereotropism /,steri'otrəpiz(ə)m, ,stiə-/ *n* THIGMOTROPISM (directional growth of a plant influenced by contact with a solid object) [ISV]

¹stereotype /'steri-ə,tiep, 'stiəri-/ *n* 1 a printing plate made by making a cast, usu in TYPE METAL, from a mould of a printing surface; *also* the process by which such a plate is made 2 somebody or something that conforms to a fixed or general pattern; *esp* a standardized, usu oversimplified, mental picture or attitude that is held in common by members of a group ⟨*he is the* ∼ *of the small businessman*⟩ [Fr *stéréotype*, fr *stéré*- stere- + *type*] – stereotypical *also* stereotypic *adj*

²stereotype *vt* 1a to make a stereotype from b to print from a stereotype 2a to repeat without variation; make hackneyed b to develop a mental stereotype of – stereotyper *n*

stereotyped /'steriə,tiept, 'stiə-/ *adj* lacking originality or individuality

stereotypy /'steriə,tiepi, 'stiə-/ *n* 1 the making of stereotype printing plates 2 frequent almost mechanical repetition (e g in schizophrenia) of the same posture, movement, or form of speech

steric /'stiərik, 'sterik/ *adj* of or involving the arrangement of atoms in space; spatial [ISV *stere*- + -*ic*] – sterically *adv*

sterigma /stə'rigmə/ *n, pl* sterigmata /-mətə/ *also* sterigmas any of the slender stalks at the top of the BASIDIUM (specialized cell) of some fungi from the tips of which the spores (BASIDIOSPORES) are produced; *broadly* a stalk or filament that bears CONIDIA (asexual spores) or SPERMATIA (male reproductive cells) [NL, fr Gk *stērigma* support, fr *stērizein* to prop]

sterilant /'sterilənt/ *n* something that sterilizes

sterile /'steriel/ *adj* 1a failing to produce or incapable of producing offspring ⟨*a* ∼ *hybrid*⟩ b failing to bear or incapable of producing fruit or spores c incapable of germinating ⟨∼ *seeds*⟩ d *of a flower* incapable of producing or failing to produce seed 2a unproductive of vegetation ⟨*a* ∼ *arid region*⟩ b deficient in ideas or originality c free from living organisms, esp microorganisms 3 bringing no rewards or results; not productive ⟨*the* ∼ *search for jobs*⟩ [L *sterilis*; akin to Goth *stairo* sterile, Gk *steira*] – sterilely *adv*, sterility *n*

synonyms Sterile, infertile, barren, unfruitful, and impotent all mean "unable to produce offspring or fruit". Sterile and infertile imply inability to procreate because of some deficiency; but sterile, rather than infertile, also means "uncreative" ⟨*a* sterile *author*⟩. Barren and unfruitful emphasize the lack of issue, and particularly childlessness in a human; but barren also means "unrewarding" ⟨barren *speculations*⟩ and unfruitful more specifically implies lack of expected result ⟨unfruitful *negotiations*⟩. Impotent refers particularly to a man's inability to copulate, but also means "powerless" ⟨impotent *fury*⟩. **antonym** fertile

**steril·ize, -ise** /'steriliez/ *vt* to make sterile: e g **a(1)** to deprive of the power of reproducing **a(2)** to make incapable of germination **b** to make powerless, useless, or unproductive **c** to free from living microorganisms ⟨ ~ d *milk*⟩ – **sterilizable** *adj*, **sterilizer** *n*, **sterilization** *n*

**sterlet** /'stuhlit/ *n* a small sturgeon (*Acipenser ruthenus*) that is found in the Caspian sea and its rivers and is a source of caviar [Russ *sterlyad'*]

**¹sterling** /'stuhling/ *n* **1** British money **2** (articles of) sterling silver [ME, silver penny, prob fr (assumed) OE *steorling* coin with a star on it, fr OE *steorra* star]

**²sterling** *adj* **1a** of or calculated in terms of British sterling **b** payable in sterling **2a** *of silver* having a fixed standard of purity; *specif* 92.5 per cent pure **b** made of sterling silver **3** conforming to the highest standard ⟨ ~ *character*⟩

**sterling area** *n* a group of countries whose currencies are tied to British sterling

**¹stern** /stuhn/ *adj* **1a** hard or severe in nature or manner; austere **b** expressive of severe displeasure; harsh ⟨*a* ~ *reprimand*⟩ ⟨*a* ~ *glance*⟩ **2** forbidding or gloomy in appearance **3** inexorable, relentless ⟨ ~ *necessity*⟩ **4** firm, unyielding ⟨*a* ~ *resolve*⟩ [ME *sterne*, fr OE *styrne*; akin to OE *starian* to stare] – **sternly** *adv*, **sternness** *n*

**²stern** *n* **1** the rear end of a ship or boat – compare STEM **2** a back or rear part; the last or latter part [ME, rudder, prob fr Scand origin; akin to ON *stjörn* act of steering; akin to OE *stīeran* to steer – more at STEER]

**sternal** /'stuhnl/ *adj* of the sternum

**stern chase** *n* a chase in which a pursuing ship follows in the path of another [²*stern*]

**stern chaser** *n* a cannon mounted in the stern of a sailing ship for firing at a pursuing vessel

**sternforemost** /stuhn'fawmohst, -məst/ *adv* with the stern in advance; backwards

**sternite** /'stuhniet/ *n* the part or shield on the underside of a segment of an insect, spider, crab, or other ARTHROPOD; *esp* the horny plate that forms the underside of a segment of the abdomen or occasionally the THORAX (central body part) of an insect [ISV, fr Gk *sternon* chest]

**sternmost** /'stuhn,mohst/ *adj* farthest astern

**sternocostal** /,stuhnoh'kostl/ *adj* of or situated between the sternum and ribs [NL *sternum* + E *-o-* + *costal*]

**sternpost** /-,pohst/ *n* the principal supporting structure at the stern of a ship, extending from the keel to the deck

**sternsheets** /'stuhn,sheets/ *n pl* the space in the stern of an open boat not occupied by the THWARTS (benches for the rowers)

**sternum** /'stuhnəm/ *n, pl* **sternums, sterna** /-nə/ a compound bone or cartilage connecting the ribs or the shoulder girdle or both; the breastbone [NL, fr Gk *sternon* chest, breastbone; akin to OHG *stirna* forehead, L *sternere* to spread out – more at STREW]

**sternutation** /,stuhnyoo'taysh(ə)n/ *n* the act, fact, or noise of sneezing – used technically [L *sternutation-, sternutatio*, fr *sternutatus*, pp of *sternutare* to sneeze, fr *sternutus*, pp of *sternuere* to sneeze; akin to Gk *ptarnysthai* to sneeze] – **sternutatory** *adj*

**sternutator** /'stuhnyoo,taytə/ *n* a substance (e g an irritant gas) that induces sneezing and often tears and vomiting

**sternwards** /'stuhnwədz/ *adv* aft, astern

**sternway** /'stuhn,way/ *n* backward movement of a ship

**¹stern-,wheeler** *n* a steamer with a PADDLE WHEEL at the stern

**steroid** /'steroyd, 'stiə-/ *n* any of numerous chemical compounds containing the ring of carbon atoms characteristic of the sterols and including the sterols and various hormones (e g testosterone) and GLYCOSIDES (e g digitalis), which have important physiological effects [ISV *sterol* + *-oid*] – **steroid, steroidal** *adj*

**steroidogenesis** /stə,roydoh'jenəsis, ,stiəroydoh-/ *n* synthesis of steroids [NL]

**steroidogenic** /,stə,roydoh'jenik, ,stiəroydoh-/ *adj* of or involved in steroidogenesis ⟨ ~ *cells*⟩ ⟨ ~ *response of ovarian tissue*⟩

**sterol** /'sterol/ *n* any of various solid CYCLIC (containing a ring of carbon atoms) alcohols (e g cholesterol) widely distributed in animal and plant fats [ISV, fr *-sterol* (as in *cholesterol*)]

**stertor** /'stuhtə/ *n* the act or fact of producing a snoring sound; laboured breathing or snoring [NL, fr L *stertere* to snore; akin to L *sternuere* to sneeze]

**stertorous** /'stuhtərəs/ *adj* characterized by a harsh snoring or gasping sound – **stertorously** *adv*

**stet** /stet/ *vt* **-tt-** to order the retention of (a word or passage previously ordered to be deleted or omitted from a manuscript or printer's proof) by marking with the word *stet* [L, let it stand, fr *stare* to stand – more at STAND]

**stethoscope** /'stethə,skohp/ *n* an instrument used to detect and study sounds produced in the body [Fr *stéthoscope*, fr Gk *stēthos* chest + Fr *-scope*] – **stethoscopic** *adj*, **stethoscopically** *adv*

**stetson** /'stets(ə)n/ *n* a broad-brimmed high-crowned felt hat [John *Stetson* †1906 US hatmaker]

**¹stevedore** /'steevədaw/ *n* a docker [Sp *estibador*, fr *estibar* to pack, fr L *stipare* to press together – more at STIFF]

**²stevedore** *vt* to handle (cargo) as a stevedore; *also* to load or unload the cargo of (a ship) in port ~ *vi* to work as a stevedore

**Stevengraph** /'steevən,grahf, -,graf/, **Stevensgraph** /steevənz-/ *n* a woven silk picture [Thomas *Stevens* †1888 E weaver]

**¹stew** /styooh/ *n* **1a** a savoury dish usu of meat or fish and vegetables stewed and served in the same liquid **b** a mixture composed of many usu unrelated parts **2** *informal* a state of excitement, worry, or confusion ⟨*got in a* ~ *over his exams*⟩ **b** a difficult situation; a fix, mess ⟨*we're in a real* ~⟩ **3** *usu pl, archaic* a brothel **4** *archaic* a public hot baths **5** *obs* a utensil used for boiling [ME *stu* cauldron, heated room, brothel, fr MF *estuve*, fr (assumed) VL *extufa* – more at STOVE]

**²stew** *vi* **1** to become cooked by stewing **2** *of tea* to become strong and bitter as a result of infusing for too long **3** *informal* to swelter, esp from confinement in a hot or stuffy atmosphere **4** *informal* to become agitated or worried; fret ~ *vt* **1** to cook (e g meat or fruit) slowly by boiling gently or simmering in liquid ⟨ ~ *ed apple*⟩ **2** to allow (tea) to become strong and bitter by infusing for too long

**¹steward** /'styooh-əd/ *n* **1** one who administers property or financial affairs; *esp* one employed in a large household or estate to manage domestic concerns (e g the supervision of servants, collection of rents, and keeping of accounts); a manager **2** SHOP STEWARD **3a** *fem* **stewardess** /'styooh-ədis, ,styooh-ə'des/ an employee on a ship, aircraft, coach, or train who attends to the needs of passengers and serves food **b** one who supervises the provision and distribution of food and drink in a club, college, hotel, etc **4** an official who actively organizes, supervises, or officiates at an esp public event (e g a race meeting) [ME, fr OE *stīweard*, fr *stī* hall, sty + *weard* ward]

**²steward** *vt* to act as a steward for; manage ~ *vi* to perform the duties of a steward

**stewardship** /'styooh-ədship/ *n* **1** the office, duties, and obligations of a steward **2** the individual's responsibility to manage his/her life and property with proper regard to the rights of others

**stewed** /styoohd/ *adj, informal* drunk

**sthenic** /'sthenik/ *adj* **1** *esp of a disease* marked by excessive vitality or nervous energy **2** having a short, broad, and powerful build; pyknic, endomorphic [NL *sthenicus*, fr Gk *sthenos* strength]

**stibine** /'stibien/ *n* a colourless poisonous inflammable gas, $SbH_3$, formerly used as a fumigating agent [ISV, fr L *stibium* antimony]

**stibnite** /'stibniet/ *n* a mineral consisting of antimony TRISULPHIDE, $Sb_2S_3$, that occurs in lead-grey crystals of metallic lustre and is the chief source of antimony [alter. of obs *stibine* stibnite, fr Fr, fr L *stibium* antimony, fr Gk *stibi*, fr Egypt *sṭm*]

**stichomythia** /,stikoh'mithiə/ *also* **stichomythy** /sti'komithi/ *n* a form of dialogue (e g in classical Greek drama) in which two speakers utter alternate lines [Gk *stichomythia*, fr *stichomythein* to speak dialogue in alternate lines, fr *stichos* line, verse + *mythos* speech, myth – more at HEMISTICH] – **stichomythic** *adj*

**¹stick** /stik/ *n* **1** a woody piece or part of a tree or shrub: e g **1a** a usu dead twig or slender branch cut or broken from a tree or shrub **b** a cut or broken branch or piece of wood gathered esp for fuel or construction material **2a** a long slender piece of wood: e g **2a(1)** a club or staff used as a weapon **a(2)** WALKING STICK **a(3)** a mast or spar on a ship **b(1)** an implement used for striking or propelling an object (e g a ball or puck) in a game (e g hockey) **b(2)** *pl* the raising of a player's stick above the shoulder in a game of hockey **c** something (e g the threat of force) used to force compliance **d** *the* cane used as a punishment; *also* a caning or beating ⟨*if you don't behave,*

*I'll give you the* ~〉 **e** a baton symbolizing an office or dignity; a rod **3** any of various implements resembling a stick in shape, origin, or use: eg **3a(1)** COMPOSING STICK (tray in which type is placed in typesetting) **a(2)** a joystick; CONTROL COLUMN (lever in an aircraft which controls the direction of movement) **a(3)** GEAR LEVER **b** a stickful of type **4** something prepared (eg by cutting, moulding, or rolling) in a relatively long and slender often cylindrical form 〈*a* ~ *of toffee*〉 〈*a* ~ *of dynamite*〉 **5** a stick-shaped plant stalk (eg of celery or rhubarb) **6a** a number of bombs arranged for release from a plane at intervals across a target **b** a number of parachutists dropping together **7** *informal* **7a** a person of a specified type 〈*a decent old* ~ - Robert Graves〉 **b** a dull, stiff, or spiritless person **8** *pl, informal* a rural district considered as remote or backward – + *the* 〈*lives out in the* ~s〉 **9** *informal* a piece of furniture **10** *Br informal* hostile comment or activity 〈*gave the Local Authority plenty of* ~〉 **11** *slang* JOINT 4 (marijuana cigarette) – see also **get the wrong END of the stick** [ME *stik,* fr OE *sticca;* akin to ON *stik* stick, OE *stician* to stick]

²**stick** *vt* **sticked 1** to provide a stick as a support for (eg a plant); stake **2** to set (type) in a composing stick; compose

³**stick** *vb* **stuck** /stuk/ *vt* **1a** to pierce with something pointed; stab **b** to kill by piercing 〈~ *a pig*〉 **2** to push or thrust so as or as if to pierce **3a** to fasten in position (as if) by piercing 〈stuck *a pistol in his belt*〉 **b** IMPALE 1 **c** to push, thrust 〈stuck *his head out of the window*〉 **4** to cover or adorn (as if) by sticking things on 〈*walls* stuck *with posters*〉 **5** to attach (as if) by causing to adhere to a surface 〈~ *a stamp on the envelope*〉 **6** to halt the movement or action of **7** *informal* to baffle, stump 〈*got* stuck *doing his maths homework*〉 **8** *informal* to put or set in a specified place or position 〈~ *your coat over there*〉 **9** *informal* to saddle with something disadvantageous or disagreeable 〈*why do I always get* stuck *with the gardening?*〉 **10** *informal* to refrain from granting, giving, or allowing (something indignantly rejected by the speaker); stuff, keep 〈*you can* ~ *the job for all I care!*〉 **11** *chiefly Br informal* to bear, stand 〈*can't* ~ *his voice*〉 ~ *vi* **1** to hold to something firmly (as if) by adhesion: **1a** to become fixed in place by means of a pointed end **b** to become fast (as if) by miring or by gluing or plastering 〈stuck *in the mud*〉 **2a** to remain in a place, situation, or environment 〈*don't want to* ~ *in this job for the rest of my life*〉 **b** to hold fast or adhere resolutely; cling 〈~ *to the truth*〉 **c** to remain effective 〈*the charge will not* ~〉 **d** to keep close in a chase or competition 〈~ *with the leaders*〉 **3** to become blocked, wedged, or jammed 〈*I can't get this drawer open – it keeps* ~ing〉 **4a** to hesitate, scruple 〈*would* ~ *at nothing to get what they wanted*〉 **b** to be unable to proceed **c** to decline another card from the dealer in pontoon – compare TWIST 5 **5** to project, protrude – often + *out* or *up* [ME *stikken,* fr OE *stician;* akin to OHG *sticken* to prick, L *instigare* to urge on, goad, Gk *stizein* to tattoo] – **get stuck in/into** to become engaged in (an activity) esp enthusiastically or determinedly – **stuck on** *informal* infatuated with 〈*he's really* stuck *on her*〉

**stick around** *vi, informal* to stay or wait about; linger

**stick by** *vt* to continue to support

**stick out** *vi* **1a** to jut out; project **b** to be prominent or conspicuous – often in *stick out a mile, stick out like a sore thumb* **2** to be persistent (eg in a demand or an opinion) – usu + *for* ~ *vt* to endure to the end – often in *stick it out*

**stick up** *vi* to stand upright or on end; protrude ~ *vt, slang* to rob at gunpoint – see also STICKUP

**stick up for** *vt* to speak or act in defence of; support

⁴**stick** *n, informal* adhesive quality or substance

**sticker** /'stikə/ *n* **1** somebody who or something that pierces with a point **2a** somebody who or something that sticks or causes sticking **b** a slip of paper with a gummed back that, when moistened, sticks to a surface **3** somebody who is determined and persevering, esp in the face of difficulty

**stick figure** *n* a stylized drawing of a human being or sometimes an animal showing the head as a circle and all other parts as straight lines

**stickful** /'stikf(ə)l/ *n* as much set type as fills a COMPOSING STICK

**sticking plaster** /'stiking/ *n* an adhesive plaster, esp for covering superficial wounds

**sticking point** *n* an item resulting or likely to result in an impasse

**stick insect** *n* any of various usu wingless insects (esp family Phasmatidae) with a long thin body resembling a stick

'**stick-in-the-,mud** *n* one who dislikes and avoids change; *esp* an old fogey

**stickit** /'stikit/ *adj, Scot* **1** unfinished **2** having failed, esp in an intended profession [Sc, fr pp of E ³*stick*]

**stickjaw** /'stikjaw/ *n* a substance (eg toffee, chewing gum, or thick treacly pudding) of a sweet and sticky nature that is difficult to chew

**stickleback** /'stikl,bak/ *n* any of numerous small scaleless fishes (family Gasterosteidae) that have two or more spines on the back in front of the dorsal fin [ME *stykylbak,* fr OE *sticel* goad (akin to OE *stician* to stick) + ME *bak* back]

**stickler** /'stiklə/ *n* **1** one who insists on exactness or completeness in the observance of something 〈*a* ~ *for obedience*〉 **2** something that baffles or puzzles; a poser [*stickle* (to act as umpire, contend, scruple), fr ME *stightlen* to arrange, strive, freq of *stighten* to arrange, fr OE *stihtan;* akin to ON *stētta* to support, establish]

**stickman** /'stikman/ *n, chiefly NAm* a player, usu of specified competence, in any of various games played with a stick; *esp* a lacrosse player

**stick shift** *n, NAm* a manually operated gear change

**sticktight flea** /'stiktiet/ *n* a tropical flea (*Echidnophaga gallinicea*) that is a destructive parasite on poultry in the S USA; *also* any of various related fleas (family Pulicidae)

**stickup** /'stik,up/ *n, slang* a robbery at gunpoint; a holdup

**stickwork** /'stik,wuhk/ *n* the use (eg in hockey, ice hockey, or lacrosse) of one's stick in offensive and defensive techniques

**sticky** /'stiki/ *adj* **1a** adhesive 〈~ *tape*〉 **b(1)** viscous, gluey **b(2)** coated with a sticky substance 〈~ *hands*〉 **2** humid, muggy; *also* clammy 〈*a hot and* ~ *day*〉 **3a** disagreeable, unpleasant 〈*came to a* ~ *end*〉 **b** awkward, stiff 〈*after a* ~ *beginning became good friends*〉 **c** difficult, problematic 〈*a rather* ~ *question*〉 – **stickily** *adv,* **stickiness** *n*

**stickybeak** /'stiki,beek/ *n, Austr & NZ informal* an inquisitive person – **stickybeak** *vi*

**sticky wicket** *n* **1** a cricket pitch drying after rain and therefore difficult to bat on **2** *informal* a difficult or precarious situation – often in *on a sticky wicket*

¹**stiff** /stif/ *adj* **1a** not easily bent; rigid 〈~ *paper*〉 **b** lacking in suppleness and often painful 〈~ *muscles*〉 **c** of a mechanism impeded in movement 〈*this lock is very* ~〉 **2a** firm, unyielding **b** marked by reserve or decorum; formal **c** lacking in ease or grace; stilted, wooden **3** hard fought 〈*a* ~ *match*〉 **4a** exerting great force; forceful 〈*a* ~ *breeze*〉 **b** potent 〈*a* ~ *drink*〉 **5** of a dense or glutinous consistency; thick 〈*a* ~ *paste*〉 **6a** harsh, severe 〈*given a* ~ *sentence for his part in the crime*〉 **b** arduous 〈*a* ~ *climb*〉 **7** of a ship not easily heeled over by an external force (eg the wind) **8** expensive, steep 〈*paid a* ~ *price*〉 **9** *chiefly NAm slang* drunk – see also **(keep a) stiff upper LIP** [ME *stif,* fr OE *stif;* akin to MD *stijf* stiff, L *stipare* to press together, Gk *steibein* to tread on] – **stiffen** *vb,* **stiffener** *n,* **stiffening** *n,* **stiffish** *adj,* **stiffly** *adv,* **stiffness** *n*

**synonyms** Stiff, rigid, inflexible, inelastic, taut, and tense mean "literally or figuratively difficult to bend". Stiff is the most general, but is used more than the others for stilted formality of behaviour 〈*a stiff smile*〉. Rigid and inflexible apply to what cannot be bent without damage 〈*the rigid wings of a plane*〉, inflexible emphasizing lack of pliability and incapacity for change 〈*an inflexible rule*〉. Inelastic stresses rather that something cannot be stretched 〈*an inelastic schedule*〉. Taut and tense, by contrast, imply a stiffness caused by being stretched tightly, taut perhaps suggesting mere keyed-up alertness 〈*taut nerves*〉 and tense a strain that is actually debilitating. **antonyms** relaxed, supple

²**stiff** *adv* **1** in a stiff manner; stiffly 〈*stood up straight and* ~ - R L Stevenson〉 **2** to an extreme degree; intensely, seriously 〈*worried* ~〉 〈*bored* ~〉 〈*frozen* ~〉

³**stiff** *n, slang* a corpse

,**stiff-'necked** *adj* haughty, stubborn **synonyms** see OBSTINATE

**stiff upper lip** *n* the ability to face misfortune impassively or without appearing perturbed

¹**stifle** /'stiefl/ *n* the joint next above the HOCK in the hind leg of a 4-legged animal (eg a horse) corresponding to the knee in humans [ME]

²**stifle** *vt* **1a** to overcome or kill by depriving of oxygen; suffocate, smother **b** to muffle 〈~ *noises*〉 **2a** to cut off (eg the voice or breath) 〈~d *a scream*〉 **b** to prevent the development or expression of; check, suppress 〈~ *his anger*〉 〈~ *a revolt*〉 ~ *vi* to become suffocated (as if) by lack of oxygen [alter. of ME *stuflen,* prob modif of MF *estouffer*] – **stiflingly** *adv*

**stigma** /'stigmə/ *n, pl* **stigmata** /stig'mahtə, 'stigmətə/, **stig-**

**mas,** (2a) **stigmata 1a** a mark of shame or discredit ⟨*the ~ of bankruptcy*⟩ **b** an identifying mark or characteristic; *specif* a specific diagnostic sign of a disease **2a** *pl, Christianity* marks resembling the wounds of the crucified Christ, believed to be impressed on the bodies of certain saintly people as a mark of God's favour ⟨*St Francis of Assisi received the ~*ta⟩ **b** PETECHIA (tiny discoloured spot on the skin) **3** a small spot, scar, or opening on a plant or animal: eg **3a** a coloured spot on the wing of a butterfly or moth **b** the thickened edge of the wing of an ant, bee, etc **c** the eyespot of some single-celled organisms **4** the portion of the female part (CARPEL) of a flower which receives the POLLEN GRAINS and on which they germinate **5** *archaic* a scar left by a hot iron; a brand [L *stigmat-, stigma* mark, brand, fr Gk, fr *stizein* to tattoo – more at STICK] – **stigmal** *adj*

**stigmasterol** /stig'mastərol/ *n* a chemical compound (STEROL), $C_{29}H_{48}O$, obtained esp from the oils of Calabar beans and soya beans [NL Physo*stigma* (genus including the Calabar bean) + ISV *sterol*]

¹**stigmatic** /stig'matik/ *adj* **1** having or conveying a social stigma **2** of supernatural stigmata **3** *esp of a bundle of light rays* intersecting at a single point; ANASTIGMATIC – **stigmatically** *adv*

²**stigmatic, stigmatist** /'stigmətist, stig'mahtist/ *n, Christianity* a person marked with stigmata

**stigmatism** /'stigmətiz(ə)m/ *n* the condition of an optical system (eg a lens) in which rays of light from a single point converge in a single focal point – compare ASTIGMATISM [L *stigmat-, stigma* mark]

**stigmat·ize, -ise** /'stigmətiez/ *vt* **1** to describe or identify in disparaging terms ⟨*a stigmatizing label*⟩ **2** *Christianity* to mark with stigmata – **stigmatization** *n*

**stilbene** /'stilbeen/ *n* a chemical compound, $C_6H_5CH=CHC_6H_5$, that is a HYDROCARBON and is used as a PHOSPHOR (substance that emits light) and in making dyes [ISV, fr Gk *stilbein* to glitter]

**stilbite** /'stilbiet/ *n* a ZEOLITE mineral, $NaCa_2Al_5Si_{13}O_{36}.14H_2O$, consisting of a silicate of aluminum, calcium, and sodium and often occurring in sheaflike aggregations of crystals [Fr, fr Gk *stilbein* to glitter]

**stilboestrol,** *NAm* **stilbestrol** /stil'beestrəl/ *n* a synthetic chemical compound, $(HOC_6H_4C(C_2H_5):)_2$, similar to the hormone OESTROGEN [*stilbene* + *oestrus* + *-ol*]

¹**stile** /stiel/ *n* **1** a step or set of steps for passing over a fence or wall **2** a turnstile △ style [ME, fr OE *stigel;* akin to OE *stǣger* stair – more at STAIR]

²**stile** *n* any of the vertical parts in a frame or panel (eg a door frame) into which the horizontal parts are fitted [prob fr D *stijl* post]

**stiletto** /sti'letoh/ *n, pl* **stilettos, stilettoes 1** a small rodlike dagger with a slender blade **2** a pointed instrument for piercing holes (eg for eyelets) in leather, cloth, etc **3** *Br* an extremely narrow tapering high heel on a woman's shoe; *also* a shoe with a stiletto heel [It, dim. of *stilo* stylus, dagger, fr L *stilus* stylus – more at STYLE]

¹**still** /stil/ *adj* **1a** devoid of or abstaining from motion ⟨*~ water*⟩ ⟨*sit ~*⟩ **b** having no effervescence; not carbonated ⟨*~ orange*⟩ **c** of, being, or designed for taking a static photograph as contrasted with a moving picture **d** engaged in taking still photographs ⟨*a ~ photographer*⟩ **2a** uttering no sound; quiet **b** low in sound; subdued, muted **3a** calm, tranquil **b** free from noise or turbulence *synonyms* see ²QUIET [ME *stille,* fr OE; akin to OHG *stilli* still, OE *steall* stall] – **stillness** *n*

²**still** *vb, chiefly poetic* **vt 1a** to allay, calm ⟨*~ed her fears*⟩ **b** to put an end to; settle **2** to cause the sound or motion of to cease; quiet ~ *vi* to become motionless or silent

³**still** *adv* **1** as before; even at this or that time ⟨*drink it while it's ~ hot*⟩ ⟨*was he ~ there? No, he'd already left*⟩ ⟨*has he read yet? No, he ~ can't*⟩ **2** in spite of that; nevertheless ⟨*even experts ~ make mistakes*⟩ ⟨*very unpleasant; ~, we can't help it*⟩ **3a** EVEN 2b ⟨*a ~ more difficult problem*⟩ **b** YET 1a **4** *archaic* always, continually

⁴**still** *n* **1** a still photograph; *specif* a photograph of actors or a scene from a film reproduced for publicity or documentary purposes **2** *chiefly poetic* quiet, silence ⟨*in the ~ of the night*⟩

⁵**still** *vb* to distil [ME *stillen,* short for *distillen* to distil]

⁶**still** *n* **1** a distillery **2** an apparatus used in distillation, esp of spirits, comprising either the chamber in which the vaporization is carried out or the entire equipment

**stillage** /'stilij/ *n* a stand or frame on which articles are kept off the floor (eg while drying or awaiting packing) [modif of D *stellage* scaffolding, fr MD, fr *stellen* to place]

**stillbirth** /'stil,buhth/ *n* the birth of a dead infant

**stillborn** /'stil,bawn/ *adj* **1** dead at birth **2** failing from the start; abortive – **stillborn** *n*

**still hunt** *n* a quiet pursuing, esp of game – **still-hunt** *vb*

**still life** *n, pl* **still lifes 1** a picture showing an arrangement of inanimate objects (eg fruit or flowers) **2** the artistic genre consisting of pictures of inanimate objects

**stillman** /'stilmən/ *n* **1** one who owns or operates a still **2** one who tends distillation equipment (eg in an oil refinery)

¹**stilly** /'stil·li/ *adv* in a calm manner; quietly [¹*still* + *-ly*]

²**stilly** /'stili/ *adj, poetic* still, quiet ⟨*oft in the ~ night ere slumber's dreams have bound me* – Thomas Moore⟩ [⁴*still* + *-y*]

**stilt** /stilt/ *n, pl* **stilts,** (2) **stilts,** *esp collectively* **stilt 1a** either of two poles each with a rest or strap for the foot that enable the user to walk at a distance above the ground **b** any of a set of piles or posts that support a building above ground or water level **2** any of various notably long-legged 3-toed wading birds (genera *Himantopus* and *Cladorhynchus*) that are related to the avocets, frequent inland ponds and marshes, and nest in small colonies [ME *stilte* crutch, handle of a plough, stilt; akin to OHG *stelza* stilt, OE *steall* position, stall – more at STALL]

**stilted** /'stiltid/ *adj* **1** *of an arch* having a curve commencing at a point higher than the level of the support (IMPOST) **2** lacking in spontaneity or restricted by convention; formal, stiff ⟨*painted in a curiously flat and ~ way*⟩ ⟨*~ conversation*⟩ – **stiltedly** *adv,* **stiltedness** *n*

**Stilton** /'stilt(ə)n/ *n* a cream-enriched white cheese that has a wrinkled rind and is often blue-veined [*Stilton,* village in Cambridgeshire in England, where the cheese (made in Leicestershire) was orig sold]

**stimulant** /'stimyoolənt/ *n* **1** something (eg a drug) that produces a temporary increase of the functional activity or efficiency of an organism or any of its parts – compare DEPRESSANT **2** a stimulus, incentive – **stimulant** *adj*

*synonyms* Both a **stimulant** and a **stimulus** stimulate, but in general use drinks and drugs are **stimulants,** whereas an abstract incentive is usually a **stimulus** ⟨*the approach of Christmas acted as a stimulus to finish the job*⟩.

**stimulate** /'stimyoo,layt/ *vt* **1** to excite to growth or to (greater) activity; animate ⟨*reading ~s the mind*⟩ ⟨*she was ~d to greater efforts*⟩ **2a** to function as a physiological stimulus to ⟨*light ~s some plants*⟩ **b** to arouse or affect by the action of a stimulant (eg a drug) ~ *vi* to act as a stimulant or stimulus [L *stimulatus,* pp of *stimulare,* fr *stimulus* goad; akin to L *stilus* stake, stylus – more at STYLE] – **stimulator** *n,* **stimulation** *n,* **stimulative** *adj,* **stimulatory** *adj*

**stimulus** /'stimyooləs/ *n, pl* **stimuli** /-li, -lie/ something that rouses or incites to activity: eg **a** an incentive **b** STIMULANT 1 **c** something (eg an environmental change) that directly influences the activity of living organisms (eg by exciting a sensory organ or evoking muscular contraction or glandular secretion) [L]

¹**sting** /sting/ *vb* **stung** /stung/ *vt* **1a** to give an irritating or poisonous wound to, esp with a sting ⟨*stung by a bee*⟩ **b** to affect with sharp quick pain ⟨*hail stung their faces*⟩ **2** to cause to suffer acute mental pain ⟨*stung with remorse*⟩; *also* to incite or goad thus ⟨*her taunts stung him into action*⟩ **3** *informal* to overcharge, cheat ⟨*stung by a street trader*⟩ ~ *vi* **1** to use a sting; have stings ⟨*nettles ~*⟩ **2** to feel a sharp burning pain; smart ⟨*my eyes are ~ing from the smoke*⟩ [ME *stingen,* fr OE *stingan;* akin to ON *stinga* to sting, Gk *stachys* spike of grain, *stochos* target, aim] – **stingingly** *adv*

²**sting** *n* **1a** the act of stinging; *specif* the thrust of a sting into the flesh **b** a wound or pain caused (as if) by stinging **2** a sharp organ (eg of a bee, scorpion, or stingray) of offence and defence usu connected with a poison gland or otherwise adapted to wound by piercing and injecting a poisonous secretion **3** a stinging element, force, or quality ⟨*a joke with a ~ in the tail*⟩ – **stingless** *adj*

**stinger** /'sting·ə/ *n* **1** somebody who or something that stings **2** STING 2 **3** a sharp blow or remark **4** a cocktail of white CRÈME DE MENTHE and brandy

**stinging hair** /'sting·ing/ *n* a glandular hair (eg of a nettle) whose base secretes a stinging liquid

**stinging nettle** *n* NETTLE 1

**stingo** /'sting·goh/ *n, chiefly Br* a strong beer [irreg fr ²*sting*]

**stingray** /-,ray/ *n* any of numerous rays (eg of the family Dasyatidae) with one or more large sharp barbed spines on the back near the base of the whiplike tail capable of inflicting severe wounds

**stingy** /'stinji/ *adj, informal* **1** mean or ungenerous in giving or spending **2** meanly scanty or small [E dial., sharp, peevish, prob fr (assumed) E dial. *stinge*, n, sting; akin to OE *stingan* to sting] – **stingily** *adv*, **stinginess** *n*

synonyms Stingy, mean, niggardly, parsimonious, penny-pinching, tight, tightfisted, closefisted, and miserly can all mean "unwilling to share". Stingy, mean, and niggardly refer to a notable lack of liberality in giving and scantiness in what is given; mean emphasizes a contemptible lack of generosity and niggardly the grudging of any contribution to other people's welfare. Parsimonious and penny-pinching imply an extreme frugality, which penny-pinching carries so far as to suggest foolish little economies. Tight, and particularly tightfisted and closefisted, refer to an extreme reluctance to part with money, to which miserly adds a more positive idea of greedy hoarding. antonym generous. Compare SPARING

**¹stink** /stingk/ *vi* **stank** /stangk/, **stunk** /stungk/; **stunk** **1** to give off a strong offensive smell **2** *informal* to be offensive **3** *informal* to possess something to an offensive degree – usu + with ⟨*he* ~s *with money*⟩ **4** *informal* to be extremely bad in quality; *also* to be in bad repute ⟨*your plan* ~s⟩ ⟨*his name* ~s⟩ [ME *stinken*, fr OE *stincan*; akin to OHG *stinkan* to emit a smell] – **stinky** *adj*

**stink out** *vi* **1** to cause to stink or be filled with a stench ⟨*the leaking gas* stank *the house* out⟩ **2** to drive out (as if) by subjecting to an offensive or suffocating smell

**²stink** *n* **1** a strong offensive smell; a stench **2** *informal* an esp public outcry against something undesirable; *broadly* a fuss, trouble ⟨*raised a* ~ *over the plans for the new airport*⟩ **3** *pl but taking sing vb*, *Br slang* chemistry as a school subject *synonyms* see ²SMELL

'**stink-,bomb** *n, Br* a small capsule which emits a foul smell when broken

**stinkbug** /'stingk,bug/ *n* SHIELDBUG (type of insect)

**stinker** /'stingkə/ *n* **1** any of several large PETRELS (types of seabird) that have an offensive smell **2** *informal* somebody who or something that stinks: *eg* **2a** an offensive or contemptible person **b** something of very poor quality **3** *informal* something extremely difficult or unpleasant ⟨*the examination was a real* ~⟩

**stinkhorn** /-,hawn/ *n* a foul-smelling fungus (order Phallales, esp *Phallus impudicus*)

**¹stinking** /'stingking/ *adj* **1** strong and offensive to the sense of smell **2** *informal* severe and unpleasant ⟨*a* ~ *cold*⟩ **3** *slang* offensively drunk – **stinkingly** *adv*

**²stinking** *adv, informal* to an offensive degree ⟨~ *rich*⟩

**stinking mayweed** /'may,weed/ *n* a foul-smelling Eurasian plant (*Anthemis cotula*) of the daisy family, having white strap-shaped flowers surrounding a centre of yellow DISC FLOWERS [*mayweed* fr *may-* (fr ME *maythe*, a plant of the daisy family, fr OE *mægtha*) + *weed*]

**stinking smut** *n* ²BUNT (disease of wheat)

**stinkpot** /'stingk,pot/ *n* **1** an earthen jar filled with materials that give off an offensive and suffocating smell, formerly sometimes thrown onto the deck of an enemy ship **2** *informal* STINKER 2

**stinkweed** /-,weed/ *n* any of various foul-smelling plants

**stinkwood** /-,wood/ *n* **1** any of several trees with a wood of unpleasant odour; *esp* a southern African tree (*Ocotea bullata*) of the laurel family yielding a valued cabinet wood **2** the wood of a stinkwood

**¹stint** /stint/ *vt* **1** to restrict to a small share or allowance; be frugal with **2** *archaic* to put an end to; stop ~ *vi* **1** to be sparing or frugal **2** *archaic* to stop, desist [ME *stinten*, fr OE *styntan* to blunt, dull; akin to ON *stuttr* scant, L *tundere* to beat, OE *stocc* stock] – **stinter** *n*

**²stint** *n* **1** restraint, limitation ⟨*expended their resources without* ~⟩ **2** a definite quantity or period of work or activity assigned ⟨*done my* ~ *for today*⟩ ⟨*did a 2-year* ~ *in the army*⟩ *synonyms* see ¹TASK

**³stint** *n, pl* **stints,** *esp collectively* **stint** any of several small SANDPIPERS (types of bird) [ME *stynte*]

**stipe** /stiep/ *n* a usu short plant stalk: *eg* **a** the stem supporting the cap of a fungus **b** a part that connects the HOLDFAST (organ of attachment) and BLADE (leaflike portion) of an algal frond **c** the stalk of a fern frond **d** an elongation of the RECEPTACLE (enlarged portion of the stem supporting the flower) beneath the OVARY (seed-producing structure) of some FLOWERING PLANTS [NL *stipes*, fr L, tree trunk; akin to L *stipare* to press together – more at STIFF] – **stiped** *adj*

**stipend** /'stiepend/ *n* a fixed sum of money paid periodically (eg to a clergyman) as a salary or to meet expenses [alter. of ME *stipendy*, fr L *stipendium*, fr *stip-*, *stips* gift + *pendere* to weigh, pay – more at PENDANT]

**¹stipendiary** /stie'pendyəri, sti-/ *adj* **1** receiving a stipend; paid ⟨*a* ~ *curate*⟩ **2** of a stipend

**²stipendiary** *n* somebody who receives a stipend

**stipendiary magistrate** *n* a legally qualified paid magistrate

**stipes** /'stiepeez/ *n, pl* **stipites** /'stipi,teez/ PEDUNCLE (stalklike structure); *esp* the second lower segment of a MAXILLA (specialized mouthpart) of an insect, shrimp, lobster, or related animal [NL *stipit-*, *stipes*, fr L, tree trunk] – **stipitate** *adj*

**¹stipple** /'stipl/ *vt* **1a** to paint, engrave, or draw with small short touches or dots that together produce an even or softly graded shadow **b** to apply (eg paint) by repeated small touches **2** to speckle, fleck **3** *building* to roughen (a clay or other surface) with metal brushes [D *stippelen* to spot, dot; akin to L *stipare* to press together] – **stippler** *n*

**²stipple** *n* (the effect produced by) a method of painting using small points, larger dots, or longer strokes to represent degrees of light and shade

**stipular** /'stipyoolə/ *adj* of, resembling, or provided with stipules ⟨~ *glands*⟩

**¹stipulate** /'stipyoolayt/ *vt* **1** to specify as a condition or requirement of an agreement or offer ⟨~ *quality and quantity*⟩ **2** to give a guarantee of in making an agreement [L *stipulatus*, pp of *stipulari* to demand some term in an agreement] – **stipulator** *n*

**stipulate for** *vt* to demand as an express term in an agreement ⟨*we stipulated for marble*⟩

**²stipulate** /'stipyoolət/ *adj* having stipules

**stipulation** /,stipyoo'laysh(ə)n/ *n* something stipulated; *esp* a condition, requirement, or item specified in a legal document – **stipulatory** *adj*

**stipule** /'stipyoohl/ *n* either of a pair of small leaflike or membranous projections developed at the base of the leaf or leaf-stalk in many plants (eg roses) [NL *stipula*, fr L, stalk; akin to L *stipes* tree trunk] – **stipuled** *adj*

**¹stir** /stuh/ *vb* **-rr-** *vt* **1a** to cause a slight movement or change of position of ⟨*the breeze* ~*red the leaves*⟩ **b** to disturb the quiet of; agitate **2a** to move (a liquid or semiliquid), esp by a continued circular movement with a spoon or other device, in order to blend the ingredients ⟨*I can't* ~ *my coffee without spilling it*⟩ **b** to mix (as if) by stirring ⟨~ *pigment into paint*⟩ **3** to bestir, exert ⟨*unable to* ~ *himself to wash the car*⟩ **4a** to rouse to activity; produce strong feelings in ⟨*the news* ~*red him to action*⟩ **b** to provoke – often + *up* ⟨~ *up trouble*⟩ ~ *vi* **1a** to make a slight movement **b** to begin to move (eg in waking) **2** to (begin to) be active or busy **3** to pass an implement through a substance with a circular movement **4** to be able to be stirred ⟨*will the cream* ~, *or is it too thick?*⟩ – see also **stir one's** STUMPS [ME *stiren*, fr OE *styrian*; akin to MHG *stürn* to incite]

**²stir** *n* **1a** a state of disturbance, agitation, or brisk activity **b** widespread notice and discussion; an impression ⟨*caused quite a* ~ *in the neighbourhood*⟩ **2** a slight movement **3** a stirring movement

**³stir** *n, slang* (a) prison [perh modif of Romany *stariben, sturraben*]

**stirabout** /'stuhrə,bowt/ *n* a porridge of Irish origin consisting of oatmeal or maize boiled in water or milk and stirred

'**stir-,crazy** *adj, slang* insane or mentally disturbed (as if) as a result of long imprisonment

'**stir-,frying** *n* a Chinese method of preparing food in which small pieces of food are stirred together while being rapidly fried in hot oil – **stir-fry** *vt*

**stirk** /stuhk/ *n, Br* a young bull or cow, esp between one and two years old [ME, fr OE *stirc*; akin to L *sterilis* sterile]

**Stirling's formula** /'stuhlingz/ *n, maths* a formula, $\sqrt{2\pi n}\ n^n e^{-n}$ that gives the approximate value of the FACTORIAL of a very large number *n* [James *Stirling* †1770 Sc mathematician]

**stirps** /stuhps/ *n, pl* **stirpes** /'stuhpeez/ **1** a branch of a family or the person from whom it is descended **2** a category in the biological classification of living things: *eg* **2a** a group of animals equivalent to a superfamily **b** a race or subspecies of plants with characteristics retained by cultivation [L, lit., stem, stock – more at TORPID]

**stirrer** /'stuhrə/ *n* **1** one who or that which stirs **2** *slang* somebody (accused of) stirring up contention; a troublemaker

**stirring** /'stuhring/ *adj* rousing, inspiring

**stirrup** /'stirəp/ *n* **1** stirrup, stirrup iron either of a pair of D-shaped metal frames or hoops in which a rider's foot is placed, that are attached by a strap to a saddle, and are used to assist mounting and as a support while riding **2** a piece of metal, wood, etc resembling a stirrup (e g a support or clamp in carpentry and machinery) [ME *stirop*, fr OE *stigrāp;* akin to OHG *stegareif* stirrup; both fr a prehistoric NGmc-WGmc compound whose first element is akin to OHG *stīgan* to go up and whose second element is represented by OE *rāp* rope – more at STAIR]

**stirrup cup** *n* a farewell drink, usu alcoholic; *specif* one taken on horseback before a hunt

**stirrup leather** *n* the strap suspending a stirrup

**stirrup pump** *n* a portable hand pump held in position by a foot bracket and used esp in fire fighting

¹**stitch** /stich/ *n* **1** a local sharp and sudden pain, esp in the side, often caused by running or exercise **2a** a single in-and-out movement of a threaded needle in sewing, embroidering, or the closure of wounds **b** a portion of thread left in the material after one stitch **3a** a single loop of thread or yarn round a knitting needle, crochet hook, etc **b** such a loop after being worked to form one of a series of links in a fabric **4** a series of stitches that are formed in a particular manner or constitute a complete step or design **5** a method of stitching **6** *informal* the least scrap, esp of clothing – usu neg ⟨*without a ~ on*⟩ [ME *stiche*, fr OE *stice* prick, stitch in the side; akin to OE *stician* to stick] – **in stitches** in a state of uncontrollable laughter

²**stitch** *vt* **1a** to fasten, join, or close (as if) with stitches; sew **b** to work on or decorate (as if) with stitches **2** to unite by means of staples to make stitches; sew

**stitchery** /'stichəri/ *n* needlework; *esp* creative and decorative embroidery, patchwork, etc

**stitchwort** /'stich‚wuht/ *n* any of several chickweeds (genus *Stellaria*) that have small white flowers [fr its former use to relieve pains in the side]

**stithy** /'stidhi/ *n, archaic* a smithy [ME, fr ON *stethi;* akin to OE *stede* place – more at STEAD]

**stoat** /stoht/ *n, pl* **stoats,** *esp collectively* **stoat** a European weasel (*Mustela erminea*) with a long black-tipped tail [ME *stote*]

**stoccado** /stə'kahdoh/ *n, pl* **stoccados** *archaic* a thrust with a rapier [OIt *stoccata*, fr *stocco* point of a sword, fr MF *estoc*, of Gmc origin]

**stochastic** /stoh'kastik/ *adj, maths & statistics* of or being statistically random sequential processes in which the probabilities at each step depend on the outcomes of previous steps ⟨*~ models*⟩; *broadly* random [Gk *stochastikos* skilful in aiming, fr *stochazesthai* to aim at, guess at, fr *stochos* target, aim, guess – more at STING] – **stochastically** *adv*

¹**stock** /stok/ *n* **1** a supporting framework or structure: e g **1a** *pl* the frame or timbers holding a ship during construction **b** *pl* a device consisting of a wooden frame with holes in which the feet or feet and hands can be locked, in which petty criminals were formerly held for public punishment **c(1)** the part (e g of wood, metal, or plastic) to which the barrel and firing mechanism of a gun (e g a rifle or pistol) are attached **c(2)** the butt of an implement (e g a whip or fishing rod) **c(3)** BRACE 3 **d(1)** a long beam on a field gun forming the third support point in firing **d(2)** the beam of a plough to which handles, cutting blades, and MOULDBOARD are secured **2a** the main stem of a plant; a trunk **b(1)** a plant (part) united with a branch or shoot (SCION) in grafting and supplying mostly underground parts to a graft **b(2)** a plant from which cuttings are taken **3** the crosspiece of an anchor **4a** the original (e g a person, race, or language) from which others derive; a source **b(1)** *taking sing or pl vb* the descendants of one individual; a family, lineage **b(2)** a colony of individual usu single-celled organisms **c** ³RACE 2, 3a **d(1)** a group of languages related more closely than those of a PHYLUM **d(2)** FAMILY 4b – used esp with reference to American languages ⟨*in the Southeast also were . . . outliers of the Siouan ~. This family occupied. . .* – H A Gleason⟩ **5a(1)** the equipment, materials, or supplies of an establishment **a(2)** *taking sing or pl vb* livestock **b** a store or supply accumulated (e g of raw materials or finished goods) **6a** a debt or fund due (e g from a government) for money loaned at interest; *also, Br* capital or a debt or fund which continues to bear interest even though the original sum is not usually redeemable **b(1)** shares **b(2)** a portion of the shares of one or more companies **b(3)**

**stock certificate, stock** *NAm* SHARE CERTIFICATE **7** any of a genus (*Matthiola*) of plants or shrubs of the cabbage family grown for their sweet-scented flowers **8** a wide band or scarf worn round the neck in the 18th century and esp by some clergymen or as part of formal hunting costume today **9a** the liquid in which meat, fish, or vegetables have been simmered that is used as a basis for soup, gravy, or sauce **b** raw material from which something is made **c** the portion of a pack of cards not distributed to the players at the beginning of a game **10a(1)** an estimate or appraisal of something ⟨*take ~ of the situation*⟩ **a(2)** the estimation in which somebody or something is held ⟨*his ~ with the electorate remains high* – Newsweek⟩ **b** confidence or faith placed in someone or something ⟨*put little ~ in his testimony*⟩ **11** STOCK CAR [ME *stok*, fr OE *stocc* tree-trunk, stump, block of wood; akin to OHG *stoc* stick, MIr *tūag* bow] – **in stock** in the shop and ready for delivery or purchase; ON HAND – **out of stock** having no more on hand; SOLD OUT – **on the stocks** in preparation but unfinished ⟨*a new play* on the stocks⟩ [*stock* 1a]

²**stock** *vt* **1** to fit to or with a stock **2** to provide with (a) stock; supply ⟨*~ a stream with trout*⟩ **3** to procure or keep a stock of ⟨*we don't ~ that brand*⟩ ~ *vi* **1** *of a plant* to send out new shoots **2** to take in a stock – often + up ⟨*~ up on tinned food*⟩

³**stock** *adj* **1a** kept in stock regularly ⟨*clearance sale of ~ goods*⟩ **b** regularly and widely available or supplied ⟨*dresses in all the ~ sizes*⟩ **2a** kept for breeding purposes; brood ⟨*a ~ mare*⟩ **b** devoted to the breeding and rearing of livestock ⟨*a ~ farm*⟩ **c** used or intended for livestock ⟨*a ~ train*⟩ **3** of a JOINT-STOCK COMPANY (company of individuals holding shares) **4** *chiefly derog* commonly used or brought forward; standard ⟨*the ~ answer*⟩

¹**stockade** /sto'kayd/ *n* **1** a line of stout posts set vertically to form a defence **2a** an enclosure or pen made with posts and stakes **b** an enclosure in which prisoners are kept [Sp *estacada*, fr *estaca* stake, of Gmc origin; akin to OE *staca* stake]

²**stockade** *vt* to fortify or surround with a stockade

**stockbreeder** /'stok‚breedə/ *n* one who is engaged in the breeding and care of livestock – **stockbreeding** *n*

**stockbroker** /'stok‚brohkə/ *n* somebody who earns a living by buying and selling stocks and shares on behalf of others – **stockbroking, stockbrokerage** *n*

**stockbroker belt** *n, Br informal* a suburb of a large town or city containing large detached houses inhabited chiefly by wealthy commuters

**stockcar** /'stok‚kah/ *n, NAm* a covered latticed railway wagon for livestock

**stock car** *n* a car having the (strengthened) body of an ordinary assembly-line model which is used in racing and often destroyed in collision

**stock company** *n, NAm* **1** JOINT-STOCK COMPANY **2** a repertory company

**stock dove** *n* a Eurasian dove (*Columba oenas*) that is smaller and darker than a woodpigeon [ME *stokdove*, fr *stok* tree-trunk + *dove* dove; prob fr its nesting in hollow trees]

**stock exchange** *n* (a building occupied by) an association of professional stockbrokers and other dealers organized to provide an auction market among themselves for the purchase and sale of stocks and shares

**stockfish** /'stok‚fish/ *n* cod, haddock, hake, etc dried in the open air without salt [ME *stokfish*, fr MD *stocvisch*, fr *stoc* stick + *visch* fish]

**stockholder** /'stok‚hohldə/ *n* an owner of stock; a shareholder

**stock horse** *n* a horse used or bred for herding, esp on Australian sheep or cattle stations

**stockinet, stockinette** /‚stoki'net/ *n* a soft elastic usu cotton fabric used esp for bandages [alter. of earlier *stocking net*]

**stocking** /'stoking/ *n* **1a** a usu knitted closely fitting often nylon covering for the foot and leg **b** a sock **2** something resembling a stocking; *esp* a band of white colour extending up to a horse's knee or hock [²*stock* (in the obs sense "to cover with a stocking") + *-ing*] – **stockinged** *adj*

**stocking frame** *n* a knitting machine

**stocking mask** *n* a stocking worn over the head and face by a criminal for disguise

**stocking stitch** *n* a knitting stitch made by alternately knitting and PURLING rows of stitches to form a fabric with an even surface and uniform pattern

**stock-in-'trade** *n* **1** the equipment necessary to or used in a trade or business **2** something that resembles the standard equipment of a tradesman or business ⟨*the tact and charm that are the ~ of a successful society society hostess*⟩

**stockist** /'stokist/ *n, Br* somebody (eg a retailer) who stocks goods, esp of a particular kind or brand

**stockjobber** /'stok,jobə/ *n* **1** a stock exchange member who deals only with brokers or other jobbers **2** *chiefly NAm derog* a stockbroker – **stockjobbing** *n*

**stockkeeper** /'stok,keepə/ *n* **1** one (eg a herdsman or shepherd) who has charge or care of livestock **2** *NAm* STOREKEEPER 1

**stockman** /'stokmən/ *n* somebody who owns or works with livestock (eg cattle or sheep)

**stock market** *n* STOCK EXCHANGE; *also* transactions on it

¹**stockpile** /'stok,piel/ *n* an accumulated store: eg **a** a reserve supply of something essential accumulated within a country for use during a shortage **b** a store of something inadvertently accumulated ⟨*~s of unsold cars*⟩

²**stockpile** *vt* **1** to place or store in or on a stockpile **2** to accumulate a stockpile of – **stockpiler** *n*

**stockpot** /'stok,pot/ *n* **1** a pot in which soup stock is prepared or kept **2** the contents of a stockpot; *esp* a stock or soup made from a variety of meats and vegetables

**stockproof** /'stok,proohf/ *adj* proof against livestock ⟨*a ~ fence*⟩

**stockroom** /'stok,roohm, -room/ *n* a storage place for supplies or goods used in a business

**stock saddle** *n* a deep-seated saddle with a high pommel and broad skirts used originally by American cattlemen

**stock-'still** *adj* completely motionless ⟨*stood ~*⟩

**stocktaking** /'stok,tayking/ *n* **1** the checking or taking of an inventory of goods or supplies on hand (eg in a shop) **2** the estimation of a situation at a given moment (eg by considering past progress and resources)

**stockwhip** /'stok,wip/ *n, chiefly Austr & NZ* a long leather whip with a heavy handle, used for driving stock

**stocky** /'stoki/ *adj* short, sturdy, and relatively thick in build – **stockily** *adv*, **stockiness** *n*

**stockyard** /'stok,yahd/ *n* a yard in which cattle, sheep, pigs, or horses are kept temporarily for slaughter, market, or shipping

¹**stodge** /stoj/ *vt, informal* to stuff full, esp with food [origin unknown]

²**stodge** *n* **1** thick filling, esp starchy, food (eg porridge) **2** *informal* turgid and unimaginative writing

**stodgy** /'stoji/ *adj* **1** *of food* heavy and filling **2** *informal* **2a** dull, boring ⟨*a ~ novel*⟩ **b** drab **c** dowdy – **stodgily** *adv*, **stodginess** *n*

**stoep** /stoohp/ *n, SAfr* a raised veranda or open porch ⟨*a front ~, lounge, dining-room – Cape Times (Cape Town)*⟩ [Afrik, fr MD – more at STOOP]

**stogie, stogy** /'stohji/ *n* **1** *NAm* a stout coarse shoe **2** *chiefly NAm* a cheap roughly made slender cylindrical cigar; *broadly* a cigar [*Conestoga*, town in Pennsylvania, USA]

¹**stoic** /'stoh·ik/ *n* **1** *cap* a member of an ancient Greek or Roman school of philosophy founded by Zeno, equating happiness with knowledge and holding that wisdom consists in self-mastery and submission to natural law **2** somebody who is or claims to be indifferent to pleasure or pain; a self-controlled person [ME, fr L *stoicus*, fr Gk *stōīkos*, lit., of the portico, fr *Stoa* (*Poikilē*) the Painted Portico, portico at Athens where the philosopher Zeno taught]

²**stoic, stoical** *adj* **1** *cap* (characteristic) of the Stoics or their doctrines ⟨*Stoic logic*⟩ **2** not affected by or showing passion or feeling; *esp* firmly restraining response to pain or distress ⟨*a ~ indifference to cold*⟩ – **stoically** *adv*

    *usage* Stoic and stoical are often used interchangeably, but some people like to confine **stoical** to the general sense "brave" and to use only **stoic** for the sense connected with the Stoics. Compare ⟨*the* **Stoic** *virtues*⟩ ⟨*a* **stoical** *explorer*⟩.

**stoichiometry** /,stoyki'omətri/ *n* **1** a branch of chemistry that deals with the application of the laws of definite proportions and of the conservation of matter and energy to chemical activity **2** (the determination of) the quantitative relationship between two or more substances, esp in processes involving chemical or physical change [Gk *stoicheion* element + E *-metry*] – **stoichiometric** *adj*, **stoichiometrically** *adv*

**stoicism** /'stoh·i,siz(ə)m/ *n* **1** *cap* the philosophy of the Stoics **2a** indifference to pleasure or pain; impassiveness **b** repression of emotion

**stoke** /stohk/ *vt* to supply (eg a fire) with fuel; *also* to poke or

stir up (eg a fire) ~ *vi* to supply a furnace, fire, etc with fuel; *also* to poke or tend a furnace, fire, etc [D *stoken*; akin to MD *stuken* to push]

**stoke up** *vb* **1** to supply (a furnace, fire, etc) with fuel; tend (a furnace or fire) **2** to feed or eat abundantly ⟨*she stoked herself* up *on baked beans*⟩

**stokehold** /'stohk,hohld/ *n* a compartment containing a steamship's boilers and furnaces

**stokehole** /'stohk,hohl/ *n* **1** a hole through which a furnace is stoked **2** the space in which stokers work when tending a ship's furnaces

**stoker** /'stohkə/ *n* somebody employed to tend a furnace and supply it with fuel; *specif* somebody who tends a ship's steam boiler

¹**stole** /stohl/ *past of* STEAL

²**stole** *n* **1** a church vestment consisting of a long usu silk band traditionally worn by bishops and priests over both shoulders and hanging down in front, and by deacons over the left shoulder **2** a long wide strip of material worn like a shawl by women, esp with evening dress [ME, fr OE, fr L *stola* long robe, fr Gk *stolē* equipment, robe, fr *stellein* to set up, make ready – more at STALL]

**stolen** /'stohlən/ *past part of* STEAL

**stolid** /'stolid/ *adj* difficult to arouse emotionally or mentally; unemotional △ solid [L *stolidus* dull, stupid; akin to OHG *stal* place – more at STALL] – **stolidly** *adv*, **stolidity** *n*

**stollen** /'s(h)tohlən (Ger ʃtɔlən)/ *n, pl* **stollen, stollens** a sweet yeast bread of German origin containing fruit and nuts [Ger, fr OHG *stollo* post, support]

**stolon** /'stohlon/ *n* **1a** a horizontal branch from the base of a plant (eg a strawberry) that produces new plants; a runner **b** a creeping threadlike part of a fungus (eg of bread mould) produced on the surface of the substance on which it is growing and connecting a group of CONIDIOPHORES (spore-producing structures) **2** an extension of the body wall of a lower INVERTEBRATE animal (eg a colonial BRYOZOAN) that develops buds giving rise to new individuals which usu remain united by the stolon [NL *stolon-, stolo*, fr L, branch, sucker; akin to Arm *steln* branch, OHG *stal* place] – **stolonate** *adj*

**stoloniferous** /,stohlə'nifərəs/ *adj* bearing or developing stolons – **stoloniferously** *adv*

**stom-, stomo-** *comb form* stomat- ⟨*stomodaeum*⟩ [Gk & NL *stoma*]

**stoma** /'stohmə/ *n, pl* **stomata** /'stohmətə, stoh'mahtə/ *also* **stomas** **1** any of various small simple body openings, esp in a lower animal (eg a sponge) **2** any of the minute openings in the EPIDERMIS (outer protective surface) of a plant organ (eg a leaf) through which oxygen and CARBON DIOXIDE are exchanged; *also* the opening with its associated cellular structures **3** an artificial permanent opening, esp in the abdominal wall, made in a surgical procedure [NL, fr Gk *stomat-, stoma* mouth]

¹**stomach** /'stumək/ *n* **1a** a saclike organ formed by a widening of the digestive tract of a VERTEBRATE animal, that is between the OESOPHAGUS and the DUODENUM, and in which the first stages of digestion occur **b** a cavity in an INVERTEBRATE animal that corresponds to a stomach **c** the part of the body that contains the stomach; the belly, abdomen ⟨*hands folded across his ~*⟩ **2a** desire for food; hunger; appetite **b** inclination, desire – usu neg ⟨*had no ~ for an argument*⟩ [ME *stomak*, fr MF *estomac*, fr L *stomachus* gullet, oesophagus, stomach, fr Gk *stomachos*, fr *stoma* mouth; akin to MBret *staffu* mouth, Avestan *staman-*] – **on an empty stomach** not having eaten anything ⟨*it's unwise to drink* on an empty stomach⟩ – **turn somebody's stomach 1** to disgust somebody completely ⟨*that sort of conduct* turns my stomach⟩ **2** to sicken or nauseate somebody ⟨*the foul smell* turned his stomach⟩

²**stomach** *vt* **1** to find palatable or digestible ⟨*can't ~ rich food*⟩ **2** to bear without protest or resentment; brook ⟨*couldn't ~ her attitude*⟩ □ usu neg

**stomachache** /'stumək,ayk/ *n* pain in (the region of) the stomach

**stomacher** /'stuməkə/ *n* a separate panel of richly embroidered or jewelled fabric ending in a point at or below the waist and worn on the centre front of a bodice by both men and women in the 15th and 16th centuries

**stomachic** /stə'makik/ *adj* **1** of the stomach ⟨*~ vessels*⟩ **2** stimulating the function of the stomach; improving digestion – **stomachic** *n*, **stomachically** *adv*

**stomach poison** *n* any of various chemical substances used as pesticides that are applied to the surface of the food plant and are effective against pests that chew the surface tissues

**stomach pump** *n* a suction pump with a flexible tube for removing liquids from the stomach or injecting liquids into it

**stomachy** /'stuməki/ *adj* having a large stomach

**stomal** /'stohməl/ *adj* stomatal

**stomat-** /stohmət-/, **stomato-** *comb form* mouth; stoma ⟨stomat*itis*⟩ ⟨stomato*logy*⟩ [NL, fr Gk, fr *stomat-*, *stoma*]

**stomatal** /'stohmətl, 'sto-/ *adj* of or constituting a STOMA (small opening) ⟨~ *behaviour of bean plants*⟩

**stomatitis** /,stohmə'tietis/ *n, pl* **stomatitides** /,stohmə'titədeez, -'tietə-/, **stomatitises** any of numerous inflammatory diseases of the mouth [NL]

**stomatology** /,stohmə'toləji/ *n* a branch of medicine dealing with the mouth and its disorders [ISV] – **stomatologist** *n*, **stomatological** *also* **stomatologic** *adj*

**stomatopod** /'stohmətə,pod, 'sto-/ *n* MANTIS SHRIMP [NL *Stomatopoda*, order name, deriv of Gk *stomat-* + *pod-*, *pous* foot] – **stomatopod** *adj*

**stomo-** – see STOM-

**stomodaeum, stomodeum** /,stohmə'dee·əm, ,stomə-/ *n, pl* **stomodaea** /-'dee·ə/ *also* **stomodaeums, stomodea** *also* **stomodeums** the front or upper part of the digestive tract that is lined with ECTODERM (outer embryonic tissue layer) [NL, fr *stom-* + Gk *hodaion*, neut of *hodaios* being on the way, fr *hodos* way – more at CEDE] – **stomodaeal, stomodeal** *adj*

**¹stomp** /stomp/ *vb, informal* to stamp [by alter.]

**²stomp** *n* a jazz dance originating in the southern States of the US in about 1900 and characterized by heavy stamping; *also* the jazz music for this dance

**¹stone** /stohn/ *n, pl* **stones**, (3) **stone** *also* **stones 1** a piece of hard compacted earthy or mineral matter: **1a(1)** such a piece of indeterminate size or shape; *esp* one smaller than a boulder **a(2)** rock **b** a piece of rock for a specified function: e g **b(1)** a building or paving block **b(2)** a precious stone; a gem **b(3)** a grindstone **b(4)** a sharpening stone; a whetstone **b(5)** a smooth flat usu metal surface on which a printing FORME is made up from type or blocks **b(6)** a surface on which a lithographic drawing, text, or design is drawn **c** CALCULUS 1a (mass of mineral particles in an organ or duct) **2** something resembling a small stone: e g **2a** the hard central portion of a fruit (e g a peach) **b** a hard stony seed (e g of a date) **3** any of various units of weight; *esp* an imperial unit equal to 14 pounds (about 6.35 kilograms) **4a** a heavy round flat-bottomed stone with a goosenecked handle used in the game of curling **b** a round playing piece used in various games (e g backgammon or go) [ME, fr OE *stān;* akin to OHG *stein* stone, Gk *stear* hard fat] – **leave no stone unturned** to make every possible effort to find or obtain something

**²stone** *vt* **1** to hurl stones at; *esp* to kill by pelting with stones **2** to face, pave, or fortify with stones **3** to remove the stones or seeds of (a fruit) ⟨~d *raisins*⟩ **4** to rub, scour, or polish with or on a stone – **stoner** *n*

**³stone** *adj* **1** (made) of stone **2** of a greyish-beige colour

**Stone Age** *n* the first known period of prehistoric human culture, characterized by the use of stone tools and weapons, and conventionally divided into PALAEOLITHIC, MESOLITHIC, and NEOLITHIC

**stone axe** *n* an axe with blunt edges used for cutting stone

**¹stone-,blind** *adj* totally blind – **stone-blindness** *n*

**stone boiling** *n* a primitive method of heating liquid by plunging hot stones into it

**stone canal** *n* a tube in many starfish, SEA URCHINS, and related animals that contains chalky deposits and leads from the ring of the water-circulatory system surrounding the mouth to the opening (MADREPORITE) on the opposite surface of the animal

**stone cell** *n* a more or less spherical SCLEREID (plant cell with thickened woody walls) ⟨~s *give the gritty texture of pears*⟩

**stonechat** /'stohn,chat/ *n* (any of various birds related to) a common small Eurasian bird (*Saxicola torquata*) of the thrush family, the male of which has a black head and chestnut underparts [¹*stone* + ²*chat* 3; prob fr its cry sounding like the clinking of pebbles]

**stone circle** *n* a circle of upright monoliths of prehistoric, mostly BRONZE AGE, origin found only in the British Isles and having a presumed ritual function

**,stone-'cold** *adj* completely cold; lacking warmth

**stonecrop** /'stohn,krop/ *n* any of several plants (genus *Sedum* of the family Crassulaceae, the stonecrop family) with usu fleshy leaves that grow esp on rocks and walls; *esp* an evergreen creeping one (*Sedum acre*) with pungent leaves and yellow star-shaped flowers

**stone curlew** *n* a large wading bird (*Burhinus oedicnemus*) with large yellow eyes and yellow legs that is widely distributed in Eurasia, Africa, and tropical America; *also* a related bird (*Burhinus magnirostris*) of Australia

**stonecutter** /'stohn,kutə/ *n* a person or machine that cuts, carves, or dresses stone – **stonecutting** *n*

**stoned** /stohnd/ *adj, informal* **1** drunk **2** under the influence of a drug (e g marijuana) taken esp for pleasure; high [fr pp of ²*stone* (in the sense "to make numb or insensible")]

**,stone-'dead** *adj* completely lifeless

**,stone-'deaf** *adj* totally deaf – **stone-deafness** *n*

**stonefish** /'stohn,fish/ *n* any of several small spiny venomous SCORPION FISHES (esp genus *Synanceja*) common among coral reefs of the tropical Indian and Pacific oceans

**stonefly** /'stohn,flie/ *n* any of an order (Plecoptera) of insects that have aquatic carnivorous larvae with gills, and an adult that is used by anglers for bait – called also PLECOPTERAN [fr the larvae being found under stones in streams]

**stone fruit** *n* DRUPE (fruit containing a central stone)

**'stone-,ground** *adj, of flour* ground with millstones

**stone lily** *n* a fossil CRINOID (primitive marine animal related to the starfish)

**stone marten** *n* BEECH MARTEN (mammal related to the weasel)

**stonemason** /'stohn,mays(ə)n/ *n* MASON 1 – **stonemasonry** *n*

**stone parsley** *n* a European and Mediterranean plant (*Sison amomum*) of the carrot family having clusters of white flowers and fragrant seeds

**stone pine** *n* a Mediterranean pine tree with a flat spreading top and edible seeds

**stone saw** *n* a saw without teeth used for cutting stone

**stone's throw** *n* a short distance

**stonewall** /'stohn,wawl/ *vi, chiefly Br* **1** to bat excessively defensively and cautiously in cricket; *broadly* to behave obstructively or defensively, esp in discussion or argument **2** to obstruct or delay parliamentary debate – **stonewaller** *n*

**stone wall** *n* a wall-like resistance or obstruction (e g in policies or public affairs)

**stoneware** /'stohn,weə/ *n* hard opaque ceramic ware (e g jasperware) that is fired at a high temperature, has a glassy surface, and is nonporous – compare EARTHENWARE – **stoneware** *adj*

**stonework** /'stohn,wuhk/ *n* **1** a structure or part built of stone; masonry **2** the shaping, preparation, or setting of stone – **stoneworker** *n*

**stonewort** /'stohn,wuht/ *n* any of a family (Characeae) of freshwater GREEN ALGAE often encrusted with chalky deposits

**stonkered** /'stongkəd/ *adj, Austr & NZ* tired, beaten [perh fr Sc *stunkard, stonkerd* sulky, sullen]

**stony** *also* **stoney** /'stohni/ *adj* **1** containing many stones or having the nature of stone; rocky **2a** insensitive to pity or human feeling; obdurate **b** showing no movement or reaction; dumb, expressionless ⟨*a ~ glance*⟩ **3** *Br informal* stony-broke – **stonily** *adv*, **stoniness** *n*

**,stony-'broke** *adj, Br informal* completely without funds; broke

**stonyhearted** /,stohni'hahtid/ *adj* unfeeling, cruel – **stony-heartedness** *n*

**stood** /stood/ *past of* STAND

**¹stooge** /stoohj/ *n* **1** somebody who usu speaks the feed lines in a comedy duo **2** *informal* somebody who plays a subordinate or compliant role to another ⟨*the Mayor's ~*⟩ **3** *chiefly NAm informal* a nark; STOOL PIGEON [origin unknown]

**²stooge** *vi, informal* **1** to act as a stooge – usu + *for* **2** to move, esp fly, aimlessly to and fro or at leisure – usu + *around* or *about*

**stook** /stook/ *n, chiefly Br* ¹SHOCK (group of sheaves of grain) [ME *stowke, stouk;* akin to OE *stocc* tree-trunk, stump – more at STOCK] – **stook** *vb*

**¹stool** /stoohl/ *n* **1a** a seat usu without back or arms, supported by three or four legs or by a central pedestal **b** a low bench or portable support for the feet or for kneeling on; a footstool **2** a discharge of faecal matter **3a** a stump or group of stumps of a tree, esp when producing suckers **b** a plant crown from which shoots grow out **c** a shoot or growth from a stool **4a** a seating for a mullion or jamb on a windowsill **b** *chiefly NAm* a windowsill **5** *archaic* a toilet seat [ME, fr OE *stōl;* akin to OHG *stuol* chair, OSlav *stolǔ* seat, throne, OE *standan* to stand] – **fall between two stools** to be unable to decide between two alternatives and so to be unable to profit from either

²**stool** *vi* to throw out shoots from a stump or crown

**stoolball** /'stoohl,bawl/ *n* a game resembling cricket that is played chiefly in S England, esp by women, and that is characterized by underarm bowling

**stoolie** /'stoohli/ *n, NAm informal* a nark; STOOL PIGEON

**stool pigeon** *n* **1** a tethered pigeon used as a decoy to entice others within a net **2** a person acting as a decoy; *esp, chiefly NAm* a nark [prob fr the early practice of fastening the decoy bird to a stool]

¹**stoop** /stoohp/ *vi* **1a** to bend the body forwards and downwards, sometimes simultaneously bending the knees **b** to stand or walk with a temporary or habitual forward inclination of the head, body, or shoulders **2a** to condescend ⟨*the gods* ~ *to intervene in the affairs of men*⟩ **b** to lower oneself morally ⟨~ed *to spying*⟩ **3** *of a bird* to fly or dive down swiftly, usu to attack prey; swoop ~ *vt* to bend (a part of the body) forwards and downwards [ME *stoupen,* fr OE *stūpian;* akin to OE *stēap* steep, deep – more at STEEP]

²**stoop** *n* **1a** an act of bending the body forwards **b** a temporary or habitual forward bend of the back and shoulders **2** the descent of a bird (e g a peregrine falcon), esp on its prey

³**stoop** *n, chiefly NAm* a porch, platform, entrance stairway, or small veranda at a house door [D *stoep;* akin to OE *stæpe* step – more at STEP]

¹**stop** /stop/ *vb* **-pp-** *vt* **1a** to close by filling or obstructing **b** to hinder or prevent the passage of ⟨~ *the flow of blood*⟩ **2a** to close up or block off (an opening); plug **b** to make impassable; choke, obstruct **c** to cover over or fill in (a hole or crevice); *specif* to fill (a hole in a tooth) with amalgam or other filling **3** to restrain, prevent **4a** to cause to cease; check, suppress **b** to discontinue ⟨~ *running*⟩ **5a** to deduct or withhold (a sum due) ⟨~ped *his wages*⟩ **b** to instruct one's bank not to honour or pay ⟨~ *a cheque*⟩ **6a** to arrest the progress or motion of; cause to halt ⟨~ped *the car*⟩ **b** to parry (a sword stroke) **c** to beat in a boxing match by a knockout; *broadly* to defeat ⟨~ped *him in the first round*⟩ **d** to pinch out the growing tip of (a plant) **7** to change the pitch of (e g a violin string) by pressing with the finger or (e g a wind instrument) by closing one or more finger holes or (e g a brass instrument) by putting the hand or a mute into the bell **8** to hold a high card and enough protecting cards in bridge to be able to block (an opponent's scoring run) **9** *informal* to get in the way of, esp so as to be wounded or killed ⟨~ped *a bullet*⟩ ~ *vi* **1a** to cease activity or operation **b** to come to an end, esp suddenly; close, finish **2a** to cease to move on; halt **b** to pause, hesitate **3** to break one's journey; stay – often + *off* ⟨~ped *off at Lisbon*⟩ **4** to become choked; clog **5a** *chiefly Br* to remain ⟨~ *at home*⟩ **b** *chiefly NAm* to make a brief call; DROP 6 – usu + *by usage* see ³STAY [ME *stoppen,* fr OE *-stoppian;* akin to OHG *stopfōn* to stop, stuff; both fr a prehistoric WGmc word borrowed fr (assumed) VL *stuppare* to stop with tow, fr L *stuppa* tow, fr Gk *styppē*] – **stoppable** *adj*

**stop down** *vt* to reduce the effective opening of (a lens) by means of a DIAPHRAGM (adjustable light-controlling disc)

²**stop** *n* **1** a cessation, end ⟨*soon put a* ~ *to that*⟩ **2a(1)** (a switch or handle operating) a graduated set of organ pipes of similar design and tone quality **a(2)** a corresponding set of vibrators or reeds of a reed organ **a(3)** a set of JACKS (fork-shaped devices) on a harpsichord **b** a means of regulating the pitch of a musical instrument **3a** something that impedes, obstructs, or brings to a halt; an impediment, obstacle **b** the circular opening (APERTURE) of an optical system (e g a camera lens); *also* a marking of a series (e g of f-numbers) on a camera for indicating settings of the DIAPHRAGM (adjustable light-controlling disc) **c** STOPPER **2 4** a device for arresting or limiting motion **5** stopping or being stopped **6a** a halt in a journey; a stay ⟨*made a brief* ~ *to refuel*⟩ **b** a stopping place ⟨*a bus* ~⟩ **7** a consonant in the articulation of which there is a stage (e g in the /p/ of *apt* or the /g/ of *tiger*) when the breath passage is completely closed – compare CONTINUANT **8** a hollow in the face of an animal, esp of a dog or cat, at the junction of forehead and face **9** – used in telegrams and cables to indicate a full stop **10** *chiefly Br* any of several punctuation marks; *specif* FULL STOP – **pull out all the stops** to make every effort to achieve an effect or action [*stop* 2a(1)]

³**stop** *adj* serving or designed to stop ⟨~ *line*⟩ ⟨~ *signal*⟩

‚**stop-and-'go** *adj* of or involving frequent stops ⟨~ *driving*⟩

**stop bath** *n* an acid bath used to check photographic development of a negative or print

**stopcock** /'stop,kok/ *n* a valve for stopping or regulating flow (e g of liquid through a pipe)

¹**stope** /stohp/ *n* a usu steplike underground excavation formed as ore is removed [prob fr LG *stope,* lit., step; akin to OE *stæpe* step – more at STEP]

²**stope** *vi* to mine by means of a stope ~ *vt* to extract (ore) from a stope – **stoper** *n*

**stopgap** /'stop,gap/ *n* something that serves as a temporary expedient; a makeshift

‚**stop-'go** *adj, Br* characterized by periods of alternating (economic) activity and inactivity ⟨*the government has adopted a deliberate* ~ *policy to try to curb inflation while retaining full employment*⟩

**stoplight** /'stop,liet/ *n* **1** TRAFFIC LIGHT **2** *chiefly NAm* a brake-light

'**stop-‚off** *n* a stopover

**stopover** /'stop,ohvə/ *n* a stop at an intermediate point in a journey

**stoppage** /'stopij/ *n* **1** stopping or being stopped **2a** a strike ⟨*an all-out* ~ *by railwaymen*⟩ **b** a usu spontaneous form of strike that is often quickly settled **3** *Br* a deduction from pay

**stop payment** *n* a depositor's order to a bank to refuse to honour a specified cheque drawn by him/her

**stopped end** *n, Br* a finished square end of a wall

¹**stopper** /'stopə/ *n* **1** somebody who or something that brings to a halt or causes to stop operating or functioning; a check; *esp* a playing card that will stop the run of a suit **2** somebody who or something that closes, shuts, or fills up; *specif* something (e g a bung or cork) used to plug an opening

²**stopper** *vt* to close or secure (as if) with a stopper

¹**stopping** /'stoping/ *adj, of a train* that stops at all intermediate stations

²**stopping** *n* material for filling in cracks and gaps **a** in wood **b** in a tooth

'**stop-‚press** *n* (space reserved for) late news inserted in a special column of a newspaper after printing has begun – **stop-press** *adj*

**stop valve** *n* a valve closing a pipe to prevent the passage of liquid or gas

**stopwatch** /'stop,woch/ *n* a watch having a hand that can be started and stopped at will for exact timing (e g of a race)

**stopwork** /'stop,wuhk/ *n, Austr & NZ* STRIKE 3

**storage** /'stawrij/ *n* **1a** (a) space for storing **b** the memory of a computer **2a** storing or being stored; *specif* the safekeeping of goods in a depository (e g a warehouse) **b** the price charged for keeping goods in a storehouse **3** the production, by means of electric energy, of chemical reactions that when allowed to reverse themselves generate electricity again without serious loss

**storage battery** *n* STORAGE CELL

**storage cell** *n* a cell or connected group of cells that converts chemical energy into electrical energy by reversible chemical reactions and that may be recharged by passing a current through it in the direction opposite to that of its discharge; an accumulator

**storage radiator** *n, Br* an electric device that is used for storing heat when electricity is cheaply available (e g at night) and for radiating heat when electricity is expensive (e g in the daytime)

**storax** /'stawraks/ *n* **1a** a fragrant BALSAM (oily substance) obtained from the bark of an Asiatic tree (*Liquidambar orientalis*) of the witch-hazel family and used esp in perfumery **b** a similar BALSAM from the SWEET GUM **2** any of a genus (*Styrax* of the family Styracaceae) of trees or shrubs with usu hairy leaves and flowers in drooping clusters, which yield BENZOIN (fragrant oily substance) [ME, fr LL, alter. of L *styrax,* fr Gk]

¹**store** /staw/ *vt* **1** to furnish, supply; *esp* to provide with a store for the future ⟨~ *a ship with provisions*⟩ **2** to collect as a reserve supply; accumulate ⟨~ *vegetables for winter use*⟩ – often + *up* or *away* **3** to place or leave in a location (e g a warehouse, library, or computer memory) for preservation or later use or disposal **4** to provide storage room for; hold ⟨*boxes for storing the surplus*⟩ ~ *vi* to be able to be stored successfully ⟨*perishable food that won't* ~⟩ [ME *storen,* fr OF *estorer* to construct, restore, store, fr L *instaurare* to renew, restore, fr *in-* + *-staurare* (akin to Gk *stauros* stake) – more at STEER] – **storable** *adj*

²**store** n **1a** something that is stored or kept for future use **b** pl articles (e g of food) accumulated for some specific object and drawn upon as needed; stock, supplies ⟨military ~s⟩ **c** something accumulated **d** a source from which things may be drawn as needed; a reserve fund **e** items (e g bombs or fuel tanks) carried externally on a combat aircraft **2** storage – usu + in ⟨furniture kept in ~⟩ **3** a large quantity, supply, or number; an abundance **4** a storehouse, warehouse **5a** a large shop usu selling a variety of goods; DEPARTMENT STORE **b** chiefly NAm SHOP 1 **6** chiefly Br STORAGE 1b **7** Br a young meat animal suitable for fattening – **in store** about to happen; imminent ⟨there's a surprise in store for you⟩ – **set store** to consider valuable, trustworthy, or worthwhile, esp to the specified degree – + by or on ⟨don't set much store by his advice⟩

³**store** adj **1** of, kept in, or used for a store **2** NAm purchased from a shop; manufactured, ready-made ⟨~ clothes⟩ ⟨~ bread⟩

'**store-,bought** adj, NAm STORE 2

¹**storefront** /'staw,frunt/ n, NAm a shopfront

²**storefront** adj, NAm occupying a room or suite of rooms at ground level and immediately behind a shopfront in a building facing directly onto the street ⟨a ~ school⟩

**storehouse** /'staw,hows/ n **1** a building for storing goods (e g provisions); a warehouse **2** an abundant supply or source; a repository

**storekeeper** /'staw,keepə/ n **1** somebody who keeps and records stock (e g in a warehouse); somebody who keeps an inventory of goods on hand, shipped, or received **2** NAm a shopkeeper – **storekeeping** n

**storeman** /'stawmən/ n, Br somebody who is employed to organize and handle stored goods or parts, esp in industry

**storeroom** /-roohm, -room/ n a room or space for the storing of goods or supplies

**storeship** /'staw,ship/ n a ship used to carry supplies

**storey,** NAm chiefly **story** /'stawri/ n **1** a set of rooms on one floor level of a building **2** a horizontal division of a building's exterior not necessarily corresponding exactly with the storeys within **3** any of several distinctive layers of vegetation within a structured community (e g a forest) ⟨the trees occupy the top ~⟩ usage see ¹FLOOR [ME storie, fr ML historia picture, storey, fr L, history, tale; prob fr pictures adorning the windows of medieval buildings]

**storeyed,** NAm chiefly **storied** /'stawrid/ adj having a specified number of storeys ⟨a 2-storeyed house⟩

**storiated** /'stawri,aytid/ adj ornamented with elaborate designs [ML historiatus, pp of historiare to tell a story in pictures, fr LL, to relate, fr L historia]

**storied** /'stawrid/ adj celebrated in story or history

**stork** /stawk/ n any of various large African and Eurasian wading birds (family Ciconiidae) that have long stout beaks and very long legs, and are related to the ibises and herons [ME, fr OE storc; akin to OHG storah stork, OE stearc stiff – more at STARK]

**storksbill** /'stawks,bil/ n any of several plants (genus Erodium) of the geranium family with elongated beaked fruits and small star-shaped pink flowers

¹**storm** /stawm/ n **1a** a violent disturbance of the weather marked by high winds and usu by rain, snow, hail, sleet, or thunder and lightning **b** a heavy fall of rain, snow, or hail **c(1)** wind having a speed of 103 to 117 kilometres per hour (about 64 to 72 miles per hour) **c(2)** WHOLE GALE **d** a serious disturbance of any element of nature **2** a disturbed or agitated state; a sudden or violent commotion **3** a paroxysm, crisis **4** a violent shower of objects (e g missiles) **5** a tumultuous outburst ⟨a ~ of abuse⟩ **6** a violent assault on a defended position synonyms see ¹WIND [ME, fr OE; akin to OHG sturm storm, OE styrian to stir] – **by storm** (as if) by using a bold frontal attack ⟨took the meeting by storm⟩ – **storm in a teacup** a great disturbance or scandal over something insignificant

²**storm** vi **1a** of wind to blow with violence **b** to rain, hail, snow, or sleet ⟨it was ~ing in the mountains⟩ **2** to move in a sudden assault or attack ⟨~ed ashore at zero hour⟩ **3** to be in or to exhibit a violent passion; rage ⟨~ing at the unusual delay⟩ **4** to rush about or move impetuously, violently, or angrily ⟨the mob ~ed through the streets⟩ ~ vt to attack or take (e g a fortified place) by storm synonyms see ¹ATTACK

**stormbound** /'stawm,bownd/ adj confined or delayed by a storm or its effects

**storm cone** n, Br a usu tarred canvas cone hoisted in any of several positions (e g point uppermost) or combinations to give warning of the direction of an impending storm

**storm door** n, NAm an additional door placed outside an ordinary outside door for protection against severe weather

**storm lantern** n, chiefly Br HURRICANE LAMP

**storm petrel** n any of various small PETRELS (types of bird); esp a small sooty black white-marked petrel (Hydrobates pelagius) frequenting the N Atlantic and Mediterranean

**storm sash** n a storm window

**storm trooper** n **1** a member of a Nazi party militia notorious for violence and brutality **2** a member of a force of shock troops

**stormwater** /'stawm,wawtə/ n surface water produced by heavy rain ⟨a ~ drainage system⟩

**storm window** n an extra window placed outside an ordinary window as a protection against severe weather

**stormy** /'stawmi/ adj **1** of, characterized by, or indicative of a storm ⟨a ~ day⟩ ⟨a ~ autumn⟩ **2** marked by turmoil or fury ⟨a ~ life⟩ ⟨a ~ conference⟩ – **stormily** adv, **storminess** n

**stormy petrel** n **1** STORM PETREL **2** somebody who is fond of strife

¹**story** /'stawri/ n **1a** an account of incidents or events **b** a statement of the facts of a situation in question ⟨according to their ~⟩ **c** an anecdote; esp an amusing one **2a** a fictional narrative shorter than a novel; specif SHORT STORY **b** the plot of a literary or dramatic work **3** a widely circulated rumour **4** a lie, falsehood – used chiefly to or by children **5** a legend, romance **6** a news article or broadcast [ME storie, fr OF estorie, fr L historia – more at HISTORY]

²**story** n, chiefly NAm a storey

**storybook** /'stawri,book/ adj, journalistic fairy-tale ⟨a ~ romance⟩

**story line** n STORY 2b

**storyteller** /'stawri,telə/ n **1** somebody who tells anecdotes **2** a reciter of tales, esp to children **3** a liar, fibber **4** one who writes stories

**stoss** /stos (Ger ʃto:s)/ adj facing towards the direction from which a glacier flows or once flowed ⟨the ~ slope of a hill⟩ [Ger stoss-, fr stossen to push; akin to L tundere to beat – more at STINT]

**stot** /stoht/ vb -tt- Scot to (cause to) bounce or rebound [origin unknown]

**stotinka** /sto'tingkə, stoh-/ n, pl **stotinki** /-ki/ – see lev at MONEY table [Bulgarian]

**stoup** /stoohp/ n **1** a large drinking mug or glass; also the contents of a stoup **2** a usu stone basin at the entrance of a church for holy water [ME stowp, prob of Scand origin; akin to ON staup cup – more at STEEP]

¹**stour** /stooə, stowə/ adj, chiefly Scot stern, harsh [ME stor violent, severe, numerous, strong, fr OE stōr violent; akin to OHG stuori large, OE standan to stand]

²**stour** n, chiefly Scot (a cloud of) dust [ME, conflict, tumult, flying dust, fr OF estor conflict, of Gmc origin; akin to OHG storm storm]

¹**stoush** /stowsh/ vt, Austr to beat, thrash [perh fr E dial. stashie, stash uproar, quarrel]

²**stoush** n, Austr a fight, quarrel

¹**stout** /stowt/ adj **1a** brave, bold ⟨~ knights⟩ **b** firm, resolute ⟨~ resistance⟩ **2** physically or materially strong: **2a** sturdy, vigorous **b** staunch, enduring **c** solid, substantial **3** forceful ⟨a ~ attack⟩; also violent ⟨a ~ blow⟩ **4** chiefly euph corpulent, fat synonyms see STRONG [ME, fr OF estout, of Gmc origin; akin to OHG stolz proud] – **stoutish** adj, **stoutly** adv, **stoutness** n

²**stout** n a heavy-bodied beer that is darker and sweeter than porter, is made with roasted malt and a relatively high percentage of hops, and usu has a thick foaming head

**stouthearted** /,stowt'hahtid/ adj having a stout heart or spirit; courageous – **stoutheartedly** adv, **stoutheartedness** n

¹**stove** /stohv/ n **1** an enclosed appliance that burns fuel or uses electricity to provide heat chiefly for domestic purposes, esp space heating, water heating, cooking, or a combination of these **2** chiefly Br a hothouse, esp for the cultivation of tropical exotic plants; broadly a greenhouse **3** chiefly Br a cooker [ME, steam room, fr MD or MLG, heated room, steam room; akin to OHG stuba heated room, steam room; both fr a prehistoric WGmc-NGmc word borrowed fr (assumed) VL extufa, deriv of L ex- + Gk typhein to smoke – more at DEAF]

²**stove** past of STAVE

'**stove-,in** adj, informal smashed inwards ⟨to repair his car's ~ wing⟩

**stovepipe** /'stohv,piep/ *n* **1** a piping of large diameter, usu of sheet metal, used as a stove chimney or to connect a stove with a flue **2** a tall narrow top hat worn in Victorian times

**stover** /'stohvə/ *n, chiefly dial Eng* fodder [ME, modif of AF *estovers* necessary supplies, fr OF *estoveir* to be necessary, fr L *est opus* there is need]

**stow** /stoh/ *vt* **1** to put away; store **2a** to pack away in an orderly fashion in an enclosed space **b** to fill (eg a ship's hold) with cargo; load **3** *informal* to cram in (eg food) – usu + *away* ⟨~ed *away a huge dinner*⟩ **4** *slang* to stop, desist – esp in *stow it* [ME *stowen* to place, fr *stowe* place, fr OE *stōw*; akin to OFris *stō* place, Gk *stylos* pillar – more at STEER]

**stow away** *vi* to hide oneself aboard a vehicle, esp a ship, as a means of travelling without payment or escaping from a place undetected

**stowage** /'stoh·ij/ *n* **1a** an act or process of stowing **b** goods in storage or to be stowed **2a** storage capacity **b** a place for storage **3** the state of being stored

**¹stowaway** /'stoh·ə,way/ *n* a person who stows away in a ship, plane, or other vehicle

**²stowaway** *adj* designed to be dismantled or folded for storage ⟨~ *tables*⟩

**STP** *n* a synthetic hallucination-producing drug, $C_{12}H_{19}NO_2$, chemically related to the stimulant drugs MESCALINE and AMPHETAMINE [fr *STP*, a trademark for a petrol additive]

**strabismus** /strə'bizməs/ *n* SQUINT 1 [NL, fr Gk *strabismos* condition of squinting, fr *strabizein* to squint, fr *strabos* squint-eyed; akin to Gk *strephein* to twist – more at STROPHE] – **strabismic** *adj*

**¹straddle** /'stradl/ *vi* **1** to stand or esp sit with the legs wide apart **2** to buy in one market and sell short in another ~ *vt* **1** to stand, sit, or be astride ⟨~ *a horse*⟩ **2** to be noncommittal or vacillate with regard to ⟨~ *an issue*⟩ **3** to be on land on each side of ⟨*the village* ~s *the frontier*⟩ **4** to bracket (a target) with missiles (eg shells or bombs) [irreg fr *stride*] – **straddler** *n*

**²straddle** *n* **1** a financial contract or option giving the holder the double privilege of selling securities to or buying securities from the maker of the contract **2** the state of being LONG (holding securities) in one market and SHORT (selling securities not possessed) in another

**strafe** /strahf, strayf/ *vt* to rake (eg ground troops) with fire at close range, esp with machine-gun fire from low-flying aircraft [Ger *Gott strafe England* God punish England, slogan of the Germans in World War I] – **strafe** *n*, **strafer** *n*

**¹straggle** /'stragl/ *vi* **1** to lag behind or stray away from the main body of something, esp from a line of march **2** to move or spread untidily away from the main body of something ⟨*straggling branches*⟩ [ME *straglen*] – **straggler** *n*

**²straggle** *n* a straggling group (eg of people or objects) ⟨*a little* ~ *of mourners* – Elizabeth Bowen⟩

**straggly** /'stragli/ *adj* loosely spread out or scattered irregularly ⟨*a* ~ *beard*⟩

**¹straight** /strayt/ *adj* **1a** free from curves, bends, angles, or irregularities ⟨~ *hair*⟩ ⟨*a* ~ *timber*⟩ ⟨*a* ~ *stream*⟩ **b** *maths* generated by a point moving continuously in the same direction and that can be expressed by a LINEAR EQUATION ⟨*a* ~ *line*⟩ ⟨*the* ~ *segment of a curve*⟩ **c** of, occupying, or passing through a fielding position in cricket in front of the batsman and near the line between the wickets or its extension behind the bowler ⟨*a* ~ *drive*⟩ **2** direct, uninterrupted: eg **2a** holding to a direct or proper course or method ⟨*a* ~ *thinker*⟩ **b** candid, frank ⟨*gave me a* ~ *answer*⟩ ⟨~ *talking*⟩ **c** coming directly from a trustworthy source ⟨*a* ~ *tip on the horses*⟩ **d** consecutive ⟨*six* ~ *wins*⟩ **e** of an internal-combustion engine having the cylinders arranged in a single straight line ⟨*a* ~ *eight-cylinder engine*⟩ **f** upright, vertical ⟨*the picture isn't quite* ~⟩ **3a** honest, fair ⟨~ *dealing*⟩ **b** properly ordered or arranged (eg with regard to finance) ⟨*be* ~ *after the end of the month*⟩ ⟨*set us* ~ *on that issue*⟩ **c** correct ⟨*get the facts* ~⟩ **d** *esp of an alcoholic drink* free from extraneous elements; unmixed ⟨~ *gin*⟩ **e** *esp of a theatrical production* not deviating from the general norm or prescribed pattern ⟨*preferred acting in* ~ *dramas to musicals or comedies*⟩ **f(1)** conventional in appearance, habits, opinions, etc; *also* SQUARE **7 f(2)** not using or under the influence of drugs **4** being the only form of remuneration ⟨*a salesman on* ~ *commission*⟩ **5** *of a horse* having the hind legs following in the track of the forelegs **6a** *chiefly NAm* marked by no exceptions or deviations in support of a principle or party ⟨*a* ~ *ballot*⟩ **b** *chiefly NAm* having a fixed price for each regardless of the number sold ⟨*cigars 20*

*cents* ~⟩ **7** *informal* heterosexual – usu contrasted with *gay* [ME *streght, straight*, fr pp of *strecchen* to stretch] – **straightish** *adj*, **straightly** *adv*, **straightness** *n*

**²straight** *adv* **1** in a straight manner **2** without delay or hesitation; immediately ⟨~ *after breakfast*⟩ – **go straight** to leave a life of crime; live honestly – see also **straight from the shoulder**

**³straight** *n* **1** something straight: eg **1a** a straight line or arrangement **b** a straight part of a racecourse; *esp* HOME STRAIGHT **2** a poker hand containing five cards in sequence but not of the same suit **3** *informal* **3a** a conventional person **b** a heterosexual

**straight and narrow** *n the* way of life that is morally and legally irreproachable [prob alter. of *strait and narrow*; fr Christ's words in Mt 7:14 (AV), "strait is the gate and narrow is the way which leadeth unto life"]

**straight angle** *n, maths* the angle which is made by a straight line and which equals 180°

**¹straightaway** /,straytə'way/ *adv* without hesitation or delay; immediately

**²straightaway** *adj, NAm* proceeding in a straight line; continuous in direction

**³straightaway** *n, NAm* a straight course: eg **a** STRAIGHT 2 **b** a straight and unimpeded stretch of road or way

**straightbred** /'strayt,bred/ *adj* produced from a single breed, strain, or type ⟨*a* ~ *Angus heifer*⟩ – compare CROSSBRED – **straightbred** *n*

**straight chain** *n, chemistry* an OPEN CHAIN of esp carbon atoms in the structure of a molecule to which no side chains are attached

**straightedge** /'strayt,ej/ *n* a bar or piece of material (eg of wood or plastic) with a straight edge for testing straight lines and surfaces or drawing straight lines

**straighten** /'strayt(ə)n/ *vb* to make or become straight – usu + *up* or *out* – **straightener** *n*

**straight face** *n* a face giving no evidence of emotion, esp amusement ⟨*keep a* ~⟩ – **straight-faced** *adj*, **straight-facedly** *adv*

**straight fight** *n* a contest, esp an election contest, between two candidates only

**straight flush** *n* a poker hand containing five cards of the same suit in sequence

**straightforward** /strayt'faw·wəd/ *adj* **1** free from evasiveness or ambiguity; direct, candid ⟨*a* ~ *account*⟩ **2** presenting no hidden difficulties ⟨*a perfectly* ~ *problem*⟩ **3** clear-cut, precise – **straightforwardly** *adv*, **straightforwardness** *n*

**straightjacket** /'strayt,jakit/ *n* a straitjacket

**straightlaced** /,strayt'layst/ *adj, chiefly NAm* straitlaced

**'straight-,line** *adj* spread uniformly or spreading accumulation or payments uniformly, esp in equal parts, over a given term ⟨~ *amortization*⟩ ⟨~ *depreciation*⟩

**straight off** *adv, informal* immediately; AT ONCE

**,straight-'out** *adj, NAm* **1** forthright, blunt ⟨*gave him a* ~ *answer*⟩ **2** outright, thoroughgoing ⟨*a* ~ *Democrat*⟩

**straight razor** *n* CUTTHROAT 2

**straight ticket** *n, NAm* a ballot cast for all the candidates of one party – compare SPLIT TICKET

**straight up** *adv, Br informal* truly, honestly – used esp in asking or replying to a question ⟨*"This car's worth a good £500." "Straight up?" "Straight up."*⟩

**straightway** /'strayt,way/ *adv, archaic* immediately, forthwith ⟨~ *the clouds began to part*⟩

**¹strain** /strayn/ *n* **1a** a lineage, ancestry **b** a group of plants, animals, microorganisms, etc having presumed common ancestry, with clear-cut physiological but usu not morphological distinctions ⟨*a high-yielding* ~ *of winter wheat*⟩; *broadly* a specified group (eg a race, line, or ecotype) at a level lower than a species **c** kind, sort ⟨*discussions of a lofty* ~⟩ **2a** inherited but not dominant character, quality, or disposition ⟨*a* ~ *of madness in the family*⟩ **b** a trace, streak ⟨*a* ~ *of fanaticism*⟩ **3a** a tune, air **b** strains *pl, strain* a passage of verbal or musical expression ⟨*the* ~s *of a Strauss waltz*⟩ **4** the tone or manner of an utterance or of a course of action or conduct ⟨*he continued in the same* ~⟩ [ME *streen* offspring, lineage, fr OE *strēon* gain, acquisition; akin to OHG *gistriuni* gain, L *struere* to heap up – more at STRUCTURE]

**²strain** *vt* **1a** to draw tight; cause to clasp firmly ⟨~ *the bandage over the wound*⟩ **b** to stretch to maximum extension and tautness ⟨~ *a canvas over a frame*⟩ **2a** to exert (eg oneself) to the utmost ⟨*he* ~ed *every sinew to no avail*⟩ **b** to injure by overuse, misuse, or excessive pressure ⟨~ed *a muscle*⟩ **c** to cause a change of form or size in (a body) by application of external force **3** to squeeze or clasp tightly: e g **3a** to hug **b** to compress painfully; constrict **4a** to cause to pass through a strainer; filter **b** to remove by straining ⟨~ *lumps out of the gravy*⟩ **5** to stretch beyond a proper limit ⟨*that story* ~s *my credulity*⟩ **6** *obs* to squeeze out; extort ~ *vi* **1a** to make violent efforts; strive ⟨*has to* ~ *to reach the high notes*⟩ **b** to suffer a strain, wrench, or distortion ⟨*ships* ~ing *at their anchors*⟩ **c** to contract the muscles forcefully in attempting to eject something (e g faeces) from the body **2** to pass (as if) through a strainer ⟨*the liquid* ~s *readily*⟩ **3** to show great resistance; resist strongly **4** to show signs of strain; continue with considerable difficulty or effort ⟨~ing *under the pressure of work*⟩ [ME *strainen*, fr MF *estraindre*, fr L *stringere* to bind or draw tight, press together; akin to Gk *strang-*, *stranx* drop squeezed out, *strangalē* halter]

³**strain** *n* straining or being strained: e g **a** (a force, influence, or factor causing) excessive physical or mental tension ⟨*her responsibilities were a constant* ~⟩ **b** excessive or difficult exertion or labour **c** bodily injury from excessive tension, effort, or use; *esp* one resulting from a wrench or twist and involving undue stretching of muscles or ligaments ⟨*back* ~⟩ **d** deformation of a material body subjected to stress; *also* the amount of such deformation usu equal to the change in a dimension (e g length or volume) divided by the original dimension *synonyms* see ¹SPRAIN

**strained** /straynd/ *adj* **1** done or produced with excessive effort **2** subjected to considerable tension ⟨~ *relations*⟩

**strainer** /'straynə/ *n* something that strains: e g **a** a device (e g a sieve or filter) to retain solid pieces while a liquid passes through ⟨*tea* ~⟩ **b** any of various devices for stretching or tightening something

**strain gauge** *n* EXTENSOMETER (instrument for measuring deformation)

**straining beam** /'strayning/ *n* a short piece of timber in a triangular roof structure used to hold the ends of struts or rafters in place

**strainometer** /stray'nomitə/ *n* EXTENSOMETER (instrument for measuring deformation)

¹**strait** /strayt/ *adj, archaic* narrow ⚠ straight [ME, fr OF *estreit*, fr L *strictus* strait, strict, fr pp of *stringere* to bind or draw tight] – **straitly** *adv*, **straitness** *n*

²**strait** *n* **1** strait, straits *taking sing or pl vb* a narrow passageway connecting two large bodies of water **2** **straits** *pl*, **strait** a situation of perplexity or distress ⟨*in dire* ~s⟩

**straiten** /'strayt(ə)n/ *vt* **1** to subject to severely restricting difficulties, esp of a financial kind – often in *straitened circumstances* **2** *archaic* to restrict in range or scope

**straitjacket, straightjacket** /'strayt,jakit/ *n* **1** a cover or outer garment of strong material (e g canvas) with very long sleeves, used to bind the body, esp the arms, closely in restraining a violent prisoner or patient **2** something that restricts or confines like a straitjacket – **straitjacket** *vt*

**straitlaced**, *NAm also* **straightlaced** /,strayt'layst/ *adj* excessively strict in manners or morals – **straitlacedly** *adv*, **straitlacedness** *n*

**Straits dollar** /strayts/ *n* a dollar formerly issued by British Malaya and used in much of S and E Asia and the E Indies [*Straits* Settlements, former British crown colony in SE Asia]

**strake** /strayk/ *n* **1** (the width of) a continuous band of hull planking or plates running from stem to stern on the side of a ship **2** a segment of an iron tyre [ME; akin to OE *streccan* to stretch – more at STRETCH]

**stramonium** /strə'mohnyəm, -niəm/ *n* **1** THORN APPLE 2 **2** the dried leaves of a DATURA (type of poisonous plant) used in medicine, esp in the treatment of asthma [NL, of unknown origin]

¹**strand** /strand/ *n* the land bordering a body of water; a shore, beach [ME, fr OE; akin to ON *strönd* strand, L *sternere* to spread out – more at STREW]

²**strand** *vt* **1** to run, drive, or cause to drift onto a shore; run aground ⟨*left our boats* ~ed – William Beebe⟩ **2** to leave in a strange or an unfavourable place, esp without funds or means to depart ~ *vi* to become stranded

³**strand** *n* **1a** any of the fibres, threads, strings, or wires twisted, plaited, or laid parallel before further twisting or plaiting into yarn, thread, rope, cable, or cordage **b** something (e g a molecular chain) resembling a strand **2** an elongated or twisted and plaited body resembling a rope ⟨*a* ~ *of pearls*⟩ **3** any of

the elements interwoven in a complex whole ⟨*pick up the* ~s *of married life*⟩ ⟨*follow the* ~s *of the story*⟩ [ME *strond*]

⁴**strand** *vt* **1** to break a strand of (a rope) accidentally **2** to form (e g a rope) from strands

**stranded** /'strandid/ *adj* having a strand or strands, esp of a specified kind or number – usu in combination ⟨*the double-stranded molecule of DNA*⟩ – **strandedness** *n*

**strange** /straynj/ *adj* **1** not native to or naturally belonging in a place; of external origin, kind, or character **2a** not known, heard, or seen before; new, unfamiliar **b** exciting wonder or surprise; extraordinary, odd **3** lacking experience or acquaintance; unaccustomed, unversed ⟨*she was* ~ *to their ways*⟩ **4** *archaic* (characteristic) of another country; foreign [ME, fr OF *estrange*, fr L *extraneus*, lit., external, fr *extra* outside – more at EXTRA-] – **strangely** *adv*

*synonyms* Strange, peculiar, singular, unique, unparalleled, odd, queer, eccentric, quaint, and outlandish all mean "different from what is usual or expected". Strange, the most general, applies to whatever commands attention by its unfamiliarity. Peculiar and singular add to this the idea of being different from others, peculiar applying particularly to what is puzzling ⟨*died in* peculiar *circumstances*⟩ and singular sometimes coming close to unique. Unique may mean "very unusual" but may also, like unparalleled, refer to what has no equal or counterpart ⟨*tropical blossoms of quite* unique *and almost monstrous beauty* – G K Chesterton⟩. Odd, queer, and eccentric refer particularly to departure from the norm or from convention; odd often stressing whimsical fantasy ⟨*the* oddest *sense of being herself invisible* – Virginia Woolf⟩, queer often applying to what is slightly reprehensible, and eccentric applying particularly to unconventional behaviour. Quaint describes what is pleasingly odd, usually in an old-fashioned way ⟨*a* quaint *figure in doublet and hose*⟩, while outlandish refers to what is not only odd but also barbaric or uncouth ⟨*an* outlandish *way of cooking rice*⟩. *antonym* familiar

**strangeness** /'straynjnis/ *n, physics* the QUANTUM property that explains the unexpectedly long lifetime possessed by certain ELEMENTARY PARTICLES (minute particles of matter) (e g kaons)

**strange particle** *n, physics* a short-lived unstable ELEMENTARY PARTICLE (minute particle of matter) (e g a kaon or a sigma) that is created in high-energy particle collisions and has a strangeness QUANTUM NUMBER different from zero

**stranger** /'straynjə/ *n* **1a** a foreigner, alien **b** a person in the house of another as a guest, visitor, or intruder **c** somebody who is unknown or with whom one is unacquainted **d** somebody who does not belong to or is kept from the activities of a group **e** *law* somebody not party to an act, contract, or title; somebody who interferes without right **2** somebody ignorant of or unacquainted with someone or something ⟨*a* ~ *to books*⟩ [ME, fr MF *estrangier* foreign, foreigner, fr *estrange*]

**strangle** /'strangl/ *vt* **1a** to choke to death by compressing the throat with something (e g a hand or rope); throttle **b** to obstruct seriously or fatally the normal breathing of ⟨*the bone wedged in his throat and* ~d *him*⟩ **c** to stifle **2** to suppress or hinder the rise, expression, or growth of ~ *vi* **1** to become strangled **2** to die (as if) from interference with breathing [ME *stranglen*, fr MF *estrangler*, fr L *strangulare*, fr Gk *strangalan*, fr *strangalē* halter – more at STRAIN] – **strangler** *n*

**stranglehold** /'strang·gl,hohld/ *n* **1** an illegal wrestling hold by which one's opponent is choked **2** a force or influence that prevents free movement or expression

**strangles** /'stranglz/ *n taking sing or pl vb* a contagious feverish disease of horses caused by a bacterium (*Streptococcus equi*) and marked by nasal discharge, inflammation, and abscesses between the jawbones [pl of obs *strangle* act of strangling]

**strangulate** /'strang·gyoo,layt/ *vt* **1** to strangle **2** to constrict or compress (a blood vessel, loop of intestine, etc) in a way that interrupts the ability to act as a passage ⟨*a* ~d *hernia*⟩ ~ *vi* to become strangulated [L *strangulatus*, pp of *strangulare*] – **strangulation** *n*

**strangury** /'strangyoori/ *n, medicine* slow and painful urination [ME, fr L *stranguria*, fr Gk *strangouria*, fr *strang-*, *stranx* drop squeezed out + *ourein* to urinate, fr *ouron* urine – more at STRAIN, URINE]

¹**strap** /strap/ *n* **1** a band, plate, or loop of metal for binding objects together or for clamping an object in position **2a** a narrow usu flat strip or thong of a flexible material, esp leather, used for securing, holding together, or wrapping **b** something made of a strap forming a loop ⟨*a watch* ~⟩ **c** a leather or rubber loop hanging from the roof of a bus or train to aid

standing passengers **3** a shoe fastened with a usu buckled strap **4** SHOULDER STRAP **5** a strapline **6** a strip of leather used for flogging, esp formerly in schools; *also* punishment by this means – + *the* ⟨*gave him the* ∼⟩ [alter. of *strop*, fr ME, band or loop of leather or rope, fr OE, thong for securing an oar; akin to MHG *strupfe* strap; all fr a prehistoric WGmc word borrowed fr L *struppus* band, strap, fr Gk *strophos* twisted band; akin to Gk *strephein* to twist – more at STROPHE]

²**strap** *vt* -**pp**- **1a(1)** to secure with or attach by means of a strap **a(2)** to support (eg a sprained joint) with overlapping strips of adhesive plaster **b** to bind, constrict **2** to beat or punish with a strap **3** to rub down (a horse); groom

**straphanger** /'strap,hang·ə/ *n, informal* a standing passenger in a tram, bus, or (underground) train who holds a hanging leather or rubber loop for support – **straphang** *vi*

**strap hinge** *n* a door or gate hinge with a long flap

**strapless** /'straplis/ *adj* having no strap; *specif* made or worn without shoulder straps, leaving the shoulders bare ⟨*a* ∼ *evening dress*⟩

**strapline** /'strap,lien/ *n* a subsidiary headline in a newspaper or magazine

**strappado** /stra'pahdoh, -'pay-/ *n, pl* **strappadoes, strappados** (an instrument used to inflict) a former punishment or torture consisting of hoisting the victim by a rope and letting him/her fall almost to the ground [modif of It *strappata*, lit., sharp pull, fr *strappare* to pull sharply]

**strapped** /strapt/ *adj, NAm slang* having no money; broke

¹**strapping** /'straping/ *adj* big, strong, and sturdy in build

²**strapping** *n* (material used in) the application of adhesive plaster in overlapping strips (eg round a sprained ankle) to reduce motion or to hold surgical dressings in place

**strapwork** /'strap,wuhk/ *n* decoration resembling plaited straps

**strass** /stras/ *n* PASTE **3** (glass for artificial gems) [Fr *stras*, *strass*]

¹**strata** /'strahtə/ *pl of* STRATUM

²**strata** *n, pl* **stratas** a stratum ⟨*this* ∼ *of society*⟩ – disapproved of by some speakers

    ***usage*** Although **strata** is a plural, it is often used instead of senses 2b & 3 of **stratum** as an aggregate singular noun ⟨*this* **strata** *of society*⟩; but this usage, and the plural form ⟨*these* **stratas**⟩, are widely disliked.

**stratagem** /'stratəjəm/ *n* **1** an artifice or trick in war for deceiving and outwitting the enemy **2** a cleverly contrived trick or scheme for gaining an end; a ruse [It *stratagemma*, fr L *strategema*, fr Gk *stratēgēma*, fr *stratēgein* to be a general, manoeuvre, fr *stratēgos* general, fr *stratos* army (akin to L *status*, pp of *sternere* to spread out) + *agein* to lead – more at STRATUM, AGENT]

**strategic** /strə'teejik/, **strategical** /-kl/ *adj* **1** of, marked by, or important to strategy ⟨*a* ∼ *retreat*⟩ – compare TACTICAL **2a** required for the conduct of war ⟨∼ *materials*⟩ **b** of great importance within an integrated whole or to a planned effect ⟨*emphasized* ∼ *points*⟩ **3** designed or trained to strike an enemy at the sources of its military, economic, or political power ⟨*a* ∼ *bomber*⟩ – **strategically** *adv*

**strategist** /'stratijist/ *n* somebody skilled in strategy

**strategy** /'stratiji/ *n* **1a(1)** the science and art of employing all the resources of a nation or group of nations to carry out agreed policies in peace or war **a(2)** the science and art of military command exercised to meet the enemy in combat under advantageous conditions – compare TACTICS **b** a variety of or instance of the use of strategy **2a** a careful plan or method **b** the art of devising or employing plans towards achieving a goal [Gk *stratēgia* generalship, fr *stratēgos* general]

**strath** /strath/ *n* a flat wide river valley or the low-lying grassland along it, esp in Scotland [ScGael *srath*]

**strathspey** /,strath'spay/ *n* (the music for) a Scottish dance that is similar to but slower than a reel and is marked by gliding steps [*Strath Spey*, district in NE Scotland]

**strati-** /strati-/ *comb form* stratum ⟨*stratiform*⟩ [NL *stratum*]

**straticulate** /stra'tikyoolət, -,layt/ *adj, esp of rocks* having thin parallel strata [(assumed) NL *straticulum*, dim. of *stratum*]

**stratification** /,stratifi'kaysh(ə)n/ *n* **1** stratifying or being stratified **2** a stratified formation, esp of rock

**stratificational grammar** *n* a grammar based on the theory that language consists of a series of strata ordered in ranks and linked together by rules

**stratiform** /'strati,fawm/ *adj, esp of a rock* having a stratified formation

**stratify** /'stratifie/ *vt* **1** to form, deposit, or arrange in strata **2** to store (seeds) in layers alternating with moisture-holding material (eg earth or peat) ∼ *vi* to become arranged in strata [NL *stratificare*, fr *stratum* + L *-ificare* -ify]

**stratigraphy** /strə'tigrəfi/ *n* **1** the arrangement of rock strata **2** geology that deals with the origin, composition, distribution, and succession of strata [ISV] – **stratigraphic** *adj*, **stratigraphically** *adv*

**strato-** *comb form* stratus and ⟨*stratocumulus*⟩ [NL *stratus*]

**stratocracy** /strə'tokrəsi/ *n* a military government [Gk *stratos* army – more at STRATAGEM]

**stratocumulus** /,strahtoh'kyoohmyooləs, ,straytoh-/ *n, meteorology* stratified CUMULUS (type of cloud formation) consisting of large balls or rolls of dark cloud which often cover the whole sky esp in winter [NL]

**stratosphere** /'stratə,sfiə/ *n* **1** the upper part of the atmosphere which is above approximately 11 kilometres (about 7 miles) depending on latitude, season, and weather and in which temperature changes little with changing height and clouds of water are rare – compare IONOSPHERE, TROPOSPHERE **2** a very high or the highest region on a graded scale ⟨*the* ∼ *of English society – New Yorker*⟩ [Fr *stratosphère*, fr NL *stratum* + *-o-* + Fr *sphère* sphere, fr L *sphaera*] – **stratospheric** *adj*

**stratum** /'strahtəm, 'straytəm/ *n, pl* **strata** /-tə/ **1** an approximately horizontal layer or series of layers of any uniform material: eg **1a** a sheetlike mass of SEDIMENTARY rock or earth of one kind lying between layers of other kinds **b** a layer of the sea or atmosphere **c** *biology* a layer of tissue or cells ⟨*deep* ∼ *of the skin*⟩ **d** a layer in which archaeological material (eg artefacts, skeletons, and dwelling remains) is found on excavation **2a** a part of a historical or sociological series representing a period or a stage of development **b** a level of society consisting of people of the same or similar class or status, esp with regard to education or culture **3** a subgroup within a larger population that is being statistically sampled *usage* see STRATA [NL, fr L, spread, bed, fr neut of *stratus*, pp of *sternere* to spread out – more at STREW] – **stratal** *adj*

**stratus** /'strahtəs, 'straytəs/ *n, pl* **strati** /-ti/ a massive broad uniformly thick low cloud formation about 600 metres to 2100 metres (about 2000 to 7000 feet) above the earth [NL, fr L, pp of *sternere*]

¹**straw** /straw/ *n* **1a** stalks of grain after threshing; *broadly* dry stalky plant residue used like grain straw (eg for bedding, packing, or thatching) **b** a natural or artificial heavy fibre used for weaving, plaiting, or braiding **2** a dry coarse stem, esp of a cereal grass **3a** something of small value or significance ⟨*she doesn't care a* ∼⟩ **b** something too insubstantial to provide support or help in a desperate situation ⟨*clutching at* ∼s⟩ **4a** something (eg a hat) made of straw **b** a tube (eg of waxed paper, plastic, or glass) for sucking up a drink **5** a pale yellow colour [ME, fr OE *strēaw*; akin to OHG *strō* straw, OE *strewian* to strew] – **strawy** *adj* – **straw in the wind** a slight hint of an approaching event or trend

²**straw** *adj* **1** made of straw ⟨*a* ∼ *rug*⟩ **2** of or used for straw ⟨*a* ∼ *barn*⟩ **3** of the colour of straw ⟨∼ *hair*⟩ **4** of little or no value; worthless

³**straw** *vt* **1** to cover (as if) with straw **2** to provide with straw

**strawberry** /'strawb(ə)ri/ *n* **1** a juicy edible usu red fruit that is technically an enlarged pulpy RECEPTACLE (enlarged tip of stem from which flower parts arise) bearing numerous small seeds; *also* any of several white-flowered creeping plants (genus *Fragaria*) of the rose family that bear strawberries **2** a pinkish-red colour [prob fr the strawy appearance of the seeds on the surface] – **strawberry** *adj*

**strawberry blonde** *n* (a woman with hair of) a reddish-blonde colour – **strawberry blonde** *adj*

**strawberry mark** *n* a usu red raised birthmark composed of small blood vessels

**strawberry roan** *n* a horse with a light red ground colour intermingled with white hairs

**strawberry tree** *n* a European evergreen tree (*Arbutus unedo*) of the heather family with clustered white flowers and fruits like strawberries

**strawboard** /'straw,bawd/ *n* coarse cardboard made of straw pulp and used usu for boxes and book covers

**straw poll** *n* an assessment of the relative strength of opposing parties, usu made by taking an unofficial vote (eg at a casual gathering) [prob fr the phrase *straw in the wind*]

**straw vote** *n, NAm* STRAW POLL

**¹stray** /stray/ *vi* to leave a proper place or course; wander: e g **a** to become separated from a flock or companions **b** to roam about without fixed direction or purpose **c** to become distracted from an argument or chain of thought ⟨~ed *from the point*⟩ **d** to wander accidentally from a fixed or chosen route; deviate **e** to err, sin [ME *straien*, fr MF *estraier*, fr (assumed) VL *extragare*, fr L *extra-* outside + *vagari* to wander – more at EXTRA-, VAGARY] – **strayer** *n*

**²stray** *n* **1a** a domestic animal wandering at large or lost **b** a person, animal, or thing that strays **2** *usu pl* STATIC (electrical disturbance in radio or television receivers) [ME, fr OF *estraié*, pp of *estraier*]

**³stray** *adj* **1** having strayed; wandering, lost ⟨*a* ~ *cow*⟩ **2** occurring at random or sporadically ⟨*a few* ~ *hairs*⟩ **3** not serving any useful purpose; unwanted ⟨~ *light*⟩

**¹streak** /streek/ *n* **1** a line or band of a different colour or texture from the background; a stripe **2a** the colour of the fine powder of a mineral obtained by scratching or rubbing it against a hard white surface, and constituting an important distinguishing characteristic **b** *microbiology* a sample containing microorganisms (e g bacteria) implanted in a line on a solid culture medium (e g agar jelly) for growth **c** any of several virus diseases of plants (e g the potato, tomato, or raspberry) resembling MOSAIC (disease characterized by mottling of leaves) but usu producing at least some linear markings **3a** an inherent quality; *esp* one which is only occasionally manifested ⟨*had a mean* ~ *in him*⟩ **b** a consecutive series ⟨*was on a winning* ~⟩ **4** a sudden flash (of lightning) **5** *informal* a run through a public place by a naked person for the purpose of shocking or amusing [ME *streke*, fr OE *strica*; akin to OHG *strich* line, L *striga* row – more at STRIKE]

**²streak** *vt* to make streaks on or in ⟨*tears* ~ing *her face*⟩ ~ *vi* **1** to move swiftly; rush ⟨*a jet* ~ing *across the sky*⟩ **2** *informal* to run naked through a public place

**streaked** /streekt/ *adj* marked with stripes or smeary lines

**streaker** /ˈstreekə/ *n, informal* a person who runs naked through a public place in order to shock or amuse

**streaky** /ˈstreeki/ *adj* **1** marked with streaks **2** *of meat, esp bacon* having lines of fat and lean **3** varying in quality or effectiveness; unreliable **4** *of a shot in cricket* hit off the edge of the bat – **streakiness** *n*

**¹stream** /streem/ *n* **1a** a body of running water narrower than a river; *broadly* any body of running water (e g a river or brook) flowing in a channel on the earth **b** a body of flowing liquid or gas **2a** a steady succession (e g of words or events) ⟨*kept up an endless* ~ *of chatter*⟩ **b** a constantly renewed supply ⟨*a steady* ~ *of applicants*⟩ **c** a continuous moving procession ⟨*a* ~ *of traffic*⟩ **3** an unbroken flow (e g of gas or particles of matter) **4a** a prevailing attitude or direction of opinion - esp in go *against/with the stream* **b** a dominant influence or line of development ⟨*backwaters in the* ~ *of history*⟩ **5** *Br* any of several groups in a school to which pupils of the same age-group are assigned according to their general academic ability ⟨*the A* ~⟩ – compare SET [ME *streme*, fr OE *strēam*; akin to OHG *stroum* stream, Gk *rhein* to flow, Skt *sarati* it flows – more at SERUM] – **on stream** in or into production ⟨*more oil fields are soon due to come* on stream⟩ – see also SWIM **against the stream**

**²stream** *vi* **1a** to flow (as if) in a stream **b** to extend in a beam or trail ⟨*light* ~s *from the window*⟩ ⟨*a meteor* ~ed *through the sky*⟩ **2** to run profusely with liquid ⟨*her eyes were* ~ing *from the onions*⟩ ⟨*walls* ~ing *with condensation*⟩ **3** to trail out at full length ⟨*her hair* ~ing *back as she ran*⟩ **4** to pour in large numbers in the same direction ⟨*came* ~ing *out of the house*⟩ **5** *Br* to practise the division of pupils into streams ~ *vt* **1** to emit freely or in a stream ⟨*his eyes* ~ed *tears*⟩ **2** *Br* to divide (a school or an age-group of pupils) into streams

**streambed** /ˈstreem.bed/ *n* the channel (formerly) occupied by a stream

**streamer** /ˈstreemə/ *n* **1a** a long narrow flag that streams in the wind; *esp* a pennant **b** a long narrow strip resembling or suggesting a banner floating in the wind; *esp* a party decoration of coloured paper **c** BANNER 2 (headline) **2a** a long extension of the sun's CORONA (surrounding circle of light) visible only during a total solar eclipse **b** *pl* AURORA BOREALIS

**¹streamline** /ˈstreem.lien/ *n* **1** *physics* the path of a particle of a liquid or gas relative to a solid body past which the liquid or gas is moving in smooth flow without turbulence **2a** a contour given to a body (e g a car or plane) so as to minimize resistance to motion through air, water, etc **b** a smooth or flowing line designed as if for decreasing air resistance

**²streamline** *vt* **1** to design or construct with a streamline **2** to bring up to date; modernize **3** to make (e g a business or manufacturing process) simpler or more efficient; *esp* to integrate more effectively

**streamlined** /ˈstreem.liend/ *adj* **1a** shaped to reduce resistance to motion through a liquid or gas (e g air) **b** stripped of nonessentials; compact **c** effectively integrated; organized **2** having flowing lines **3** brought up to date; modernized **4** OF STREAMLINE FLOW

**streamline flow** *n* an uninterrupted flow (e g of air) past a solid body in which the direction at every point remains unchanged with the passage of time

**stream of consciousness** *n* **1** individual conscious experience considered as a series of processes or experiences continuously moving forward in time **2** INTERIOR MONOLOGUE

**¹street** /street/ *n* **1a** a thoroughfare, esp in a city, town, or village, that is wider than an alley or lane and that usu has buildings on either side and includes pavements **b** the part of a street reserved for vehicles **c** a thoroughfare together with the buildings on each side ⟨*lives in a fashionable* ~⟩ **2** *taking sing or pl vb* the people occupying buildings in a street ⟨*the whole* ~ *knew about the accident*⟩ **3** *cap* a district (e g Fleet Street or Wall Street) identified with a particular profession [ME *strete*, fr OE *strēt*; akin to OHG *strāza* street; both fr a prehistoric WGmc word borrowed fr LL *strata* paved road, fr L, fem of *stratus*, pp of *sternere* to spread out – more at STREW] – **on the street** homeless, vagrant – **on the streets** earning a living as a prostitute – **up/down somebody's street** suited to one's abilities or tastes ⟨*hang gliding is right* up my street⟩

*usage* Sherlock Holmes lived *in Baker* **Street**, but it would be *on Baker* **Street** in American English. *synonyms* see ROAD

**²street** *adj* **1a** adjoining or giving access to a street ⟨*the* ~ *door*⟩ **b** carried on or taking place in the street ⟨~ *fighting*⟩ ⟨~ *trading*⟩ **c** living or working on the streets ⟨*a* ~ *peddler*⟩ **d** located in, used for, or serving as a guide to the streets ⟨*a* ~ *map*⟩ **2** caused by a STREET VIRUS ⟨~ *distemper*⟩

**street arab** *n, often cap A* ARAB 2a

**streetcar** /ˈstreet.kah/ *n, NAm* a tram

**streetlight** /ˈstreet.liet/ *n* any of a series of lights spaced at intervals on posts along a public street or highway

**streets** /streets/ *adv, chiefly Br* FAR AND AWAY ⟨~ *ahead of the other girls*⟩

**street theatre** *n* drama dealing with contemporary social and political issues and often performed out of doors

**street virus** *n* a virulent or natural virus (e g that causing rabies) as distinct from one that has been weakened and made less harmful in a laboratory

**streetwalker** /ˈstreet.wawkə/ *n* a female prostitute; *esp* one who solicits in the streets – compare CALL GIRL – **streetwalking** *n*

**streetwise** *adj* familiar with the life of city streets, esp with its disreputable or criminal underworld; *broadly* resourceful at surviving and prospering in modern urban conditions

**strength** /streng(k)th/ *n* **1** the quality or state of being strong; capacity for exertion or endurance **2** capacity to resist force; solidity, toughness **3** capacity to resist attack; impregnability **4a** legal, logical, or moral force ⟨*the* ~ *of evidence*⟩ **b** a strong quality or inherent asset ⟨*the* ~s *and the weaknesses of the book are evident*⟩ **5a** degree of potency of effect or of concentration **b** intensity of light, colour, sound, or smell **c** vigour of expression **6** force as measured in members ⟨*an army at full* ~⟩ **7** one regarded as embodying or affording force or firmness; a support **8** firmness of, or a rising tendency in, prices ⟨*stock markets were displaying remarkable drive and* ~ – *Financial Times*⟩ **9** a basis – chiefly in *on the strength of* [ME *strengthe*, fr OE *strengthu*; akin to OHG *strengi* strong – more at STRONG] – **strengthless** *adj* – **from strength to strength** with continuing success and progress

*usage* The pronunciation /strength/ rather than /strenth/ is recommended for BBC broadcasters.

**strengthen** /ˈstrength(ə)n, ˈstrengkth(ə)n/ *vb* to make or become stronger – **strengthener** *n*

**strenuous** /ˈstrenyooəs/ *adj* **1** vigorously active; energetic ⟨*a* ~ *imagination*⟩ **2** marked by or requiring effort or stamina; arduous *synonyms* see LIVELY [L *strenuus* – more at STARE] – **strenuously** *adv*, **strenuousness** *n*, **strenuosity** *n*

**strep** /strep/ *n, informal* a streptococcus

**strep throat** *n, informal* an inflamed sore throat caused by a streptococcal infection

**strepto-** *comb form* twisted; twisted chain ⟨strepto*coccus*⟩

[NL, fr Gk, fr *streptos* twisted, fr *strephein* to twist – more at STROPHE]

**streptobacillus** /ˌstreptoh-bəˌsiləs/ *n* any of various nonmoving BACILLI (rod-shaped bacteria) in which the individual cells are joined in a chain [NL]

**streptococcus** /ˌstreptəˈkokəs/ *n, pl* **streptococci** /-ˈkoki, -ˈkoksi/ any of a genus (*Streptococcus*) of nonmoving chiefly parasitic bacteria that divide only in one plane, occur in pairs or chains but not in packets, and include many that cause diseases of human beings and domestic animals; *broadly* a COCCUS (spherical bacterium) occurring in chains [NL, genus name, fr *strepto-* + *coccus*] – **streptococcal, streptococcic** *adj*

**streptokinase** /ˌstreptohˈkienayz, -nays/ *n* an ENZYME produced by some streptococci that is active in promoting the breakdown of blood clots

**streptolysin** /ˌstreptəˈliesin/ *n* a poisonous substance produced by streptococci that is able to break down BLOOD CELLS

**streptomyces** /ˌstreptəˈmieseez/ *n, pl* **streptomyces** any of a genus (*Streptomyces*) of mostly soil bacteria including some that form antibiotics (eg streptomycin) as products of their METABOLISM (life-supporting chemical processes) [NL, fr *strepto-* + Gk *mykēs* fungus]

**streptomycete** /ˌstreptəˈmieseet, ˌ---ˈ-/ *n* any of a family (Streptomycetaceae) of rod-shaped bacteria (eg a streptomyces) that grow in the form of a branching network of filaments and are typically SAPROPHYTES (organisms feeding on dead and decaying plant and animal matter) in the soil but include a few parasites of plants and animals [NL *Streptomycet-, Streptomyces,* genus name]

**streptomycin** /ˌstreptəˈmiesin/ *n* an antibiotic, $C_{21}H_{39}H_7O_{12}$, obtained from a soil bacterium (*Streptomyces griseus*) that is active against many bacteria and is used esp in the treatment of bacterial infections (eg tuberculosis) in humans

**streptothricin** /ˌstreptəˈthriesin, -ˈthrisin/ *n* an antibiotic that is obtained from a bacterium (*Streptomyces lavendulae*) and is used in the treatment of diseases (eg hepatitis) [NL *Streptothric-, Streptothrix,* genus of bacteria, fr *strepto-* + *-thrix* having hairlike filaments, fr Gk *trich-, thrix* hair]

**¹stress** /stres/ *n* **1** constraining force or influence: eg **1a** the force per unit area producing or tending to produce deformation of a body; *also* the state of a body under such stress **b** (a physical, chemical, or emotional factor that causes) bodily or mental tension that may be a factor in disease causation ⟨*suffering from* ∼⟩ **c** strain, pressure **2** emphasis, weight ⟨*lay* ∼ *on a point*⟩ **3a** intensity of utterance given to a speech sound, syllable, or word so as to produce relative loudness **b** relative force or prominence given to a syllable in verse **c** a syllable having relative force or prominence **d** musical accent [ME *stresse* stress, distress, fr *destresse* – more at DISTRESS] – **stressful** *adj,* **stressfully** *adv*

**²stress** *vt* **1** to subject to phonetic stress; accent **2** to subject to physical or mental stress **3** to lay stress on; emphasize

**stressless** /ˈstreslis/ *adj* having no stress; *specif* having no accent ⟨*a* ∼ *syllable*⟩ – **stresslessness** *n*

**stress mark** *n* a mark used before, after, or over a written syllable to show that this syllable is to be stressed when spoken

**stressor** /ˈstresə, ˈstresaw/ *n* a stimulus that causes stress

**'stress-ˌverse** *n* verse whose rhythm is produced by recurrence of stresses without regard to number of syllables or to any fixed distribution of unstressed elements

**¹stretch** /strech/ *vt* **1** to extend (eg one's limbs or body) in a reclining position – often + *out* ⟨∼ed *himself out on the carpet*⟩ **2** to hold out; extend – often + *out* ⟨∼ed *out his arm*⟩ **3** to extend to full length ⟨∼ed *her neck to see what was going on*⟩ **4** to extend (oneself or one's limbs), esp so as to relieve muscular stiffness ⟨*opened his eyes and* ∼ed *himself luxuriously*⟩ **5** to pull taut ⟨*canvas was* ∼ed *on a frame*⟩ **6a** to enlarge or distend, esp by force ⟨∼ *a shoe*⟩ **b** to expand or extend as if by physical force ⟨∼ *one's mind with a good book*⟩ **c** to strain ⟨∼ed *his already thin patience*⟩ **7** to cause to reach or continue (eg from one point to another or across a space) ⟨∼ *a wire between two posts*⟩ **8a** to enlarge or extend beyond natural or proper limits ⟨*the rules can be* ∼ed *this once*⟩ **b** to expand (eg by improvisation) to fulfil a larger function ⟨∼ing *his pay packet*⟩ **9** *informal* to fell (as if) with a blow – often + *out* ⟨∼ed *him out on the carpet*⟩ ∼ *vi* **1a** to extend in space; reach, spread ⟨*broad plains* ∼ing *to the sea*⟩ **b** to extend over a period of time **2** to become extended without breaking **3a** to

extend one's body or limbs ⟨*awoke and* ∼ed *luxuriously*⟩ **b** to lie down at full length – see also **stretch a** POINT [ME *strecchen,* fr OE *streccan;* akin to OHG *strecchan* to stretch, OE *starian* to stare] – **stretchable** *adj,* **stretchy** *adj,* **stretchability** *n*

**²stretch** *n* **1a** an exercise of the understanding, the imagination, etc beyond ordinary or normal limits ⟨*impossible by any* ∼ *of the imagination*⟩ **b** an extension of the scope or application of something **2** the extent to which something may be stretched ⟨*at full* ∼⟩ **3** stretching or being stretched **4a** a continuous expanse or length ⟨*a* ∼ *of woods*⟩ **b** a continuous period of time ⟨*can write for eight hours at a* ∼⟩ **5a** STRAIGHT 1b **b** a final stage **6** the capacity for being stretched; elasticity **7** *informal* a short walk to relieve fatigue **8** *informal* a period of imprisonment ⟨*a nine-year* ∼⟩

**³stretch** *adj* capable of being stretched (eg to fit various shapes and sizes); elastic ⟨∼ *fabric*⟩

**stretcher** /ˈstrechə/ *n* **1** somebody who or something that stretches; *esp* a mechanism for stretching or expanding something **2a** a brick or stone laid with its length parallel to the face of the wall – compare HEADER **b** a timber or rod used, esp when horizontal, as a tie in a structural framework (eg for building) **c** a wooden frame over which a canvas for painting is stretched and fastened **3** a device, consisting of a sheet of canvas or other fabric stretched between two poles, for carrying a sick, injured, or dead person; *broadly* any easily movable lightweight carrier for such a purpose **4** a rod or bar extending between two legs of a chair or table **5** a board in a rowing boat that serves as a rest for a rower's feet

**'stretcher-ˌbearer** *n* somebody who carries one end of a stretcher

**stretchmarks** /ˈstrechˌmahks/ *n pl* marks left on the abdomen after pregnancy

**'stretch-ˌout** *n, NAm* an economizing measure that spreads a limited quantity over a larger field than was originally intended

**stretch receptor** *n* MUSCLE SPINDLE (type of sensory structure in muscle)

**stretto** /ˈstretoh/ *also* **stretta** /ˈstretə/ *n, pl* **stretti** /-ti/, **strettos** **1a** the overlapping of answer with subject in a musical FUGUE **b** the part of a fugue characterized by this overlapping **2** a concluding musical passage performed in a quicker tempo [It, fr *stretto* (masc) & *stretta* (fem) narrow, close, fr L *strictus*]

**strew** /strooh/ *vt* **strewed, strewn** /stroohn/ **1** to spread by scattering ⟨*war left refugees* strewn *over half the continent*⟩ **2** to cover (as if) with something scattered ⟨∼ing *the roads with litter*⟩ **3** to become dispersed over as if scattered [ME *strewen, strowen,* fr OE *strewian, strēowian;* akin to OHG *strewen* to strew, L *sternere* to spread out, Gk *stornynai*]

**strewth** /stroohth/ *interj, chiefly Br* struth

**stria** /ˈstrie-ə/ *n, pl* **striae** /ˈstrieˌie/ **1** a minute groove or channel on the surface of a rock, crystal, etc, or on the skin **2** a narrow line, groove, ridge, or band (eg of colour), esp when one of a parallel series [L, furrow, channel – more at STRIKE]

**striate** /ˈstrieˌayt/ *vt* to mark with striae

**striated** /ˈstrieˌaytid/, **striate** /ˈstrie-ət/ *adj* **1** marked with striae **2** of or being striated muscle

**striated muscle** *n* muscle tissue that is marked by alternate light and dark cross striations, is made up of elongated fibres containing several nuclei, and is found in the VOLUNTARY MUSCLES clothing the skeleton of VERTEBRATE animals and in all or most of the musculature of insects, spiders, crabs, and other ARTHROPODS – compare CARDIAC MUSCLE, SMOOTH MUSCLE

**striation** /strieˈaysh(ə)n/ *n* **1a** striated **b** an arrangement of striae **2** a stria **3** any of the alternate light and dark cross bands of a striated muscle fibre

**stricken** /ˈstrikən/ *adj* **1** hit or wounded (as if) by a missile **2** afflicted or overwhelmed (as if) by disease, misfortune, or sorrow **3** made incapable or unfit; incapacitated [fr pp of *strike*]

**¹strickle** /ˈstrikl/ *n* **1** an instrument for levelling off measures of grain **2** a tool for sharpening scythes **3** a foundry tool for smoothing the surface of a filled core or mould [ME *strikell;* akin to OE *strīcan* to stroke – more at STRIKE]

**²strickle** *vt* to smooth or form with a strickle

**strict** /strikt/ *adj* **1a** stringent in requirement or control ⟨*under* ∼ *orders*⟩ **b** severe in discipline ⟨*a* ∼ *teacher*⟩ **2a** inflexibly maintained or adhered to; complete ⟨∼ *secrecy*⟩ **b** rigorously conforming to rules or standards ⟨*a* ∼ *teetotaller*⟩ **3** narrowly construed; restricted ⟨*on a* ∼ *interpretation of the Act*⟩ **4** exact, precise ⟨*in the* ~ *sense of the word*⟩ [L *strictus*, fr pp of *stringere* to bind tight – more at STRAIN] – **strictly** *adv*, **strictness** *n*

**stricture** /'strikchə/ *n* **1** an abnormal narrowing of a body passage; *also* the narrowed part **2 strictures** *pl*, **stricture 2a** something that closely restrains or limits; a restriction ⟨*moral* ~s⟩ **b** an adverse criticism; a censure [ME, fr LL *strictura*, fr L *strictus*, pp of *stringere* to bind tight]

¹**stride** /stried/ *vb* **strode** /strohd/; **stridden** /'stridən/ *vi* **1** to walk (as if) with long steps **2** to take a very long step ~ *vt* **1** to bestride, straddle **2** to move over or along (as if) with long steps ⟨*the captain* ~s *the deck*⟩ [ME *striden*, fr OE *strīdan*; akin to MLG *striden* to straddle, OE *starian* to stare] – **strider** *n*

²**stride** *n* **1** a long step **2** an act of striding **3 strides** *pl*, **stride** an advance ⟨*the housing programme has made great* ~s⟩ **4a** a movement (e g of a horse) completed when the feet regain the initial relative positions; *also* the distance covered in a stride **b** the most effective natural pace **c** a state of maximum competence or capability ⟨*get into one's* ~⟩ **5** a striding gait ⟨*her loose-limbed* ~⟩ **6** *pl*, *Austr informal* trousers – **take in one's stride** to confront or deal with without becoming flustered or upset ⟨*took the dangers in her stride*⟩

**strident** /'stried(ə)nt/ *adj* characterized by harsh, insistent, and discordant sound ⟨*a* ~ *voice*⟩; loud or obtrusive ⟨~ *slogans*⟩ **synonyms** see VOCIFEROUS [L *strident-*, *stridens*, prp of *stridere*, *stridēre* to make a harsh noise; akin to Gk & L *strix* owl] – **stridence** *n*, **stridency** *n*, **stridently** *adv*

**stride piano** *n* an early style of jazz piano playing in which the right hand plays the melody while the left hand alternates between a single note and a chord played an octave or more higher [fr the repeated strides taken by the left hand]

**stridor** /'striedaw/ *n*, *medicine* a harsh vibrating sound heard during breathing out when the air passages are obstructed [L, squeak, hiss, shriek, fr *stridere*, *stridēre*]

**stridulate** /'stridyoolayt/ *vi*, *esp of a cricket, grasshopper, etc* to make a shrill creaking noise by rubbing together special body structures [back-formation fr *stridulation*, fr Fr, fr L *stridulus* shrill, squeaky] – **stridulation** *n*, **stridulatory** *adj*

**stridulous** /'stridyooləs/ *adj*, formed characterized by a shrill creaking sound [L *stridulus*, fr *stridere*, *stridēre*] – **stridulously** *adv*

**strife** /strief/ *n* bitter sometimes violent conflict or dissension ⟨*political* ~⟩ [ME *strif*, fr OF *estrif*, prob fr *estriver* to contend – more at STRIVE] – **strifeless** *adj*

**strigil** /'strijil/ *n* an instrument used by ancient Greeks and Romans for scraping moisture, esp sweat, off the skin after bathing or exercising [L *strigilis*; akin to L *stringere* to touch lightly – more at STRIKE]

**strigose** /'striegohs/ *adj*, *biology* **1** having bristles or scales lying against a surface ⟨*a* ~ *leaf*⟩ **2** marked with fine grooves; STRIATED ⟨*the* ~ *wing cases of a beetle*⟩ [NL *strigosus*, fr *striga* bristle, fr L, furrow]

¹**strike** /striek/ *vb* **struck** *also* **stricken** /'strikən/ *vi* **1** to take a course; go ⟨*struck off through the brush*⟩ **2a** to aim a blow **b** to make a military attack; *also* to fight **c** to collide forcefully **3a** *of the time* to be indicated by a clock, bell, or chime ⟨*six had just* struck⟩ **b** to make known the time by sounding ⟨*the clock* struck⟩ **4** *of a fish* to seize bait or a lure **5a** *of a plant cutting* to take root **b** *of a seed* to germinate **6** to stop work in order to force an employer to comply with demands ~ *vt* **1a** to strike at; hit **b** to make an attack on **c** to inflict (a blow) **2a** to haul down (a flag) **b** to dismantle (e g a stage set) **c** to take down the tents of (a camp) **3** to afflict suddenly ⟨*stricken by a heart attack*⟩ **4a** to engage in (a battle); fight **b** to make a military attack on **5** to delete, cancel ⟨~ *a name from a list*⟩ **6a** to send down or out ⟨*trees* struck *roots deep into the soil*⟩ **b** to penetrate painfully ⟨*the news* struck *him to the heart*⟩ **7** to indicate by sounding ⟨*the clock* struck *seven*⟩ **8a** *of light* to fall on **b** *of a sound* to become audible to **9** to cause suddenly to become ⟨struck *him dead*⟩ **10** to produce (e g coins or medals) by stamping with a die or punch **11a** to produce (fire) by striking **b** to cause (a match) to light **12a** to make a mental impact on ⟨*they were* struck *by its speed*⟩ ⟨*how does that* ~ *you?*⟩ **b** to occur suddenly to **13** to make and ratify (a bargain) **14** to play or produce (as if) by playing a musical instrument ⟨struck *a series of chords on the piano*⟩ ⟨struck *a gloomy note*⟩ **15a** to hook (a fish) by a sharp pull on the line **b** *of a fish* to snatch at (bait) **16** to arrive at (a balance) by computation **17** to find; COME ACROSS ⟨~ *oil*⟩ **18**

to assume (a pose) **19a** to place (a plant cutting) in a medium for growth and rooting **b** to propagate (a plant) in this manner **20** to cause (an arc) to form (e g between electrodes of an ARC LAMP) **21** *of an insect* to lay eggs on or in **22** *NAm* to engage in a strike against (an employer) – see also **strike a** CHORD [ME *striken*, fr OE *strīcan* to stroke, go; akin to OHG *strīhhan* to stroke, L *stringere* to touch lightly, *striga*, *stria* furrow]

**usage** The past participle form **stricken** is now used almost entirely as an adjective meaning "afflicted". **synonyms** see ¹MOVE

**strike down** *vt* **1** to afflict suddenly; lay low ⟨struck down *by malaria*⟩ **2** to cause to die suddenly ⟨*a young poet* struck down *in his prime*⟩

**strike off** *vt* **1** to sever with a stroke **2** to delete the name of (e g a doctor or solicitor) from a register of practitioners because of misconduct or malpractice, *of a horse* to begin cantering

**strike out** *vt* **1** to delete **2** *of a baseball pitcher* to retire (a batter) by a strikeout ~ *vi* **1** to set out vigorously ⟨struck out *towards the coast*⟩ **2** to make an out in baseball by a strikeout **3** to finish one's turn in tenpin bowling with consecutive strikes; *specif* to bowl three strikes in the last frame

**strike up** *vi* **1** to begin to sing or play or to be sung or played ⟨*a march* struck up *and the parade began*⟩ ~ *vt* **1** to cause to begin singing or playing ⟨strike up *the band*⟩ **2** to cause to begin ⟨strike up *a conversation*⟩

²**strike** *n* **1** STRICKLE (type of tool for flattening or levelling) **2** an act of striking **3** a work stoppage by a body of workers, made as a protest or to force an employer to comply with demands **4** the direction of a horizontal line formed at the intersection of an upward-sloping geological STRATUM (layer of rock) and a horizontal plane **5** a pull on a line by a fish in striking **6** a success in hitting or finding something; *esp* a discovery of a valuable mineral deposit ⟨*a lucky oil* ~⟩ **7** a pitched ball in baseball that is either missed by the batter or hit outside the foul lines and that counts against him/her **8** the knocking down of all ten pins with the first bowl in a frame in tenpin bowling **9** the opportunity to receive the bowling in cricket by virtue of being the batsman at the wicket towards which the bowling is being directed ⟨*Boycott kept the* ~ *for five successive overs*⟩ **10** the establishment of roots and plant growth **11** infestation of the skin (e g of sheep) with fly maggots ⟨*blowfly* ~⟩ **12a** a military attack; *esp* an air attack on a single target **b** *taking sing or pl vb* a group of aircraft taking part in such an attack

**strikebound** /'striek,bownd/ *adj* subjected to a strike

**strikebreaker** /'striek,braykə/ *n* somebody hired to replace a striking worker – compare BLACKLEG, SCAB

**strikebreaking** /'striek,brayking/ *n* action designed to break up a strike

**strike fault** *n* a geological fault which runs parallel to the strike of associated strata

**strikeover** /'striek,ohvə/ *n* the striking of a typewriter character on a spot occupied by another character

**strike pay** *n* an allowance obtained from members' subscriptions and paid by a trade union to its members on strike

**striker** /'striekə/ *n* one who or that which strikes: eg **a** a player in any of several games who strikes (e g a soccer player whose main duty is to score goals) **b** a worker on strike

**striking** /'strieking/ *adj* attracting attention or notice, esp through unusual or conspicuous qualities ⟨*a woman of* ~ *beauty*⟩ – **strikingly** *adv*

**Strine** /strien/ *n*, *sometimes not cap* Australian English, esp when represented in writing in a humorous form ⟨*"Emma Chisit?" is* ~ *for "How much is it?"*⟩ [supposed Australian pronunciation of *Australian*]

¹**string** /string/ *n* **1** a narrow cord used to bind, fasten, or tie **2** a plant fibre (e g a leaf vein) **3a** the gut or wire cord of a musical instrument **b(1)** *usu pl* a stringed instrument of an orchestra **b(2)** *pl* the players of such instruments **4** *taking sing or pl vb* **4a** a group of objects threaded on a string ⟨*a* ~ *of beads*⟩ **b(1)** a series of things arranged (as if) in a line ⟨*a* ~ *of cars*⟩ **b(2)** a sequence of like items (e g numbers or words) **c** a group of business properties or concerns under one ownership and usu scattered geographically ⟨*a* ~ *of shops*⟩ **d** the animals, esp horses, belonging to or used by one person **5** somebody who is selected (e g for a sports team) as a choice of the specified rank; *also*, *taking sing or pl vb* a group of players so selected – often in combination ⟨*usually plays for the first* ~⟩ ⟨*a second*-string *player*⟩ **6** *taking sing or pl vb* a succession,

sequence ⟨*a* ~ *of successes*⟩ **7a** either of the inclined sides of a stair supporting the treads and risers **b** STRING COURSE **8** the action of LAGGING (deciding who begins by rolling the CUE BALL) in billiards, the player who has the first shot in the frame being the one whose ball rebounds nearer to the end from which it was rolled **9** *pl* conditions or obligations attached to something ⟨*no* ~s *attached*⟩ **10** *archaic* a cord (e g a tendon or ligament) of an animal body – see also PULL **strings** [ME, fr OE *streng;* akin to L *stringere* to bind tight – more at STRAIN] – **stringed** *adj,* **stringless** *adj*

²**string** *vb* **strung** /strung/ *vt* **1** to equip with strings **2a** to thread (as if) on a string **b** to thread with objects **c** to tie, hang, or fasten with string **3** to remove the strings of ⟨~ *beans*⟩ **4a** to extend or stretch like a string ⟨~ *wires from tree to tree*⟩ **b** to set out in a line or series ~ *vi* **1** to move, progress, or lie in a string **2** to form into strings
  **string along** *vb, informal* **1** to accompany someone, esp rather reluctantly ⟨string along *with the crowd*⟩ **2** to agree; GO ALONG **1** to keep dangling or waiting **2** to deceive, fool ⟨string him along *with false promises*⟩ □ (*vi*) usu + *with*
  **string out** *vb, slang* to (cause to) be addicted to or affected by drugs
  **string up** *vt* to hang; *specif* to kill by hanging ⟨*they* strung him up *from the nearest tree*⟩

³**string** *adj* made with wide meshes and usu of string ⟨~ *vest*⟩ ⟨~ *bag*⟩
**string bass** /bays/ *n* DOUBLE BASS
**string bean** *n, chiefly NAm* a FRENCH BEAN or RUNNER BEAN the pods of which are cooked usu sliced, and which have stringy fibres between the sides of the pods
**string course** *n* a horizontal ornamental band (e g of bricks) on the outside of a building
**stringed instrument** *n* a musical instrument (e g a violin or harp) sounded by drawing a bow across, striking, or plucking tense strings
**stringendo** /strin'jendoh/ *adv* with quickening of speed (e g to a climax) – used as a direction in music [It, verbal of *stringere* to press, fr L, to bind tight]
**stringent** /'strinj(ə)nt/ *adj* **1** rigorous or strict, esp with regard to rules or standards **2** marked by money scarcity and credit strictness [L *stringent-, stringens,* prp of *stringere* to bind tight] – **stringency** *n,* **stringently** *adv*
**stringer** /'string·ə/ *n* **1** one who or that which strings **2** a narrow vein or irregular strand of mineral crossing a rock mass of different material **3a** a long horizontal timber used to connect uprights in a structure or to support a floor **b** STRING 7a **c** a tie in a triangular wooden roof support **4** a longitudinal structural part (e g in an aircraft fuselage or wing or ship's hull) to reinforce the skin **5** a usu provincial or overseas correspondent who works for a publication or news agency on a part-time basis; *broadly* a correspondent **6** somebody or something estimated to be of specified worth – usu in combination ⟨*first*-stringer⟩ ⟨*second*-stringer⟩
**stringhalt** /'string,hawlt/ *n* lameness in the hind legs of a horse caused by muscular spasms [¹*string* 10 + ¹*halt*] – **stringhalted** *adj*
**stringing** /'string·ing/ *n* the gut, silk, or nylon with which a racket is strung
**string orchestra** *n taking sing or pl vb* an orchestra consisting usu of violins, violas, cellos, and DOUBLE BASSES
**stringpiece** /'string,pees/ *n* the heavy squared timber lying along the top of the piles forming a dock front or timber pier
'**string-,pulling** *n, informal* using one's (secret) influence to attain an end – **string-puller** *n*
**string quartet** *n* **1** *taking sing or pl vb* a group of four performers on stringed instruments, usu including two violins, a viola, and a cello **2** a composition for string quartet
**string tie** *n* a narrow tie, often worn in a bow or with a ring fastening
**stringy** /'string·i/ *adj* **1a** containing, consisting of, or resembling fibrous material or string ⟨~ *hair*⟩ **b** lean and sinewy in build; wiry **2** capable of being drawn out to form a string (e g of a sticky substance) – **stringiness** *n*
**stringybark** /'string·i,bahk/ *n* (the thick fibrous bark of) any of several Australian eucalyptus trees
¹**strip** /strip/ *vb* **-pp-** *vt* **1a** to remove clothing, covering, or surface material from **b** to deprive *of* possessions, privileges, rank, or functions **2a** to remove superficial or inessential material from ⟨*a prose style* ~ped *to the bone*⟩ **b** to remove furniture, equipment, or accessories from ⟨~ *a ship for*

*action*⟩ **3** to remove (wallpaper, paint, etc) from a surface **4** to make bare or clear (e g by cutting or grazing) **5** to finish a milking of (a cow or goat) by pressing the last available milk from the teats **6a** to remove cured leaves from the stalks of (tobacco) **b** to remove the midrib from (tobacco leaves) **7** to tear or damage the thread or teeth of (e g a screw or cog) **8** to separate (components) from a mixture or solution by boiling, evaporation, etc **9** to press eggs or male reproductive secretion out of (a fish) ~ *vi* **1a** to take off clothes; undress **b** to perform a striptease **2** to come off in sheets or scales; peel [ME *strippen,* fr OE *-strīpan;* akin to OHG *stroufen* to strip] – **strippable** *adj*
**strip in** *vt* to insert (typeset material and photographs) into a prepared space in a sheet from which a printing plate can be made
²**strip** *n* **1a** a long narrow piece of material **b** a long narrow area of land or water **2** LANDING STRIP **3** STRIP CARTOON **4** a tobacco leaf that has had the midrib removed **5** *Br* clothes worn by a sports team ⟨*Arsenal's* ~ *of red and white*⟩ [perh fr MLG *strippe* strap] – **tear somebody off a strip** *informal* to reprimand somebody severely
**strip cartoon** *n* a series of drawings (e g in a magazine) in narrative sequence – called also COMIC STRIP
**strip club** *n, Br* a club which features striptease artists
'**strip-,cropping** *n* the growing of a cultivated crop (e g maize) in alternate strips with a turf-forming crop (e g hay) to minimize land erosion – **strip-crop** *vb*
¹**stripe** /striep/ *n* a blow with a rod or lash [ME; akin to MD *stripe*]
²**stripe** *n* **1a** a line or long narrow band differing in colour or texture from the adjoining parts **b(1)** a textile design consisting of lines or bands against a plain background **b(2)** a fabric with a striped design **2** a narrow strip of braid or embroidery, usu in the form of a bar, arc, or V shape, that is worn usu on the sleeve of a military uniform to indicate rank or length of service **3** *chiefly NAm* a distinct variety or sort; a type ⟨*men of the same political* ~⟩ **4** a narrow white mark down a horse's face from eyes to nose [prob fr MD; akin to OE *strica* streak – more at STREAK] – **striped** *adj,* **stripeless** *adj*
³**stripe** *vt* to make stripes on
**stripey** /'striepi/ *adj* stripy
**strip farming** *n* **1** the growing of crops in separate strips of land allotted to individual farmers in such a way that good and bad land may be fairly distributed, esp in the Middle Ages in Europe, and in underdeveloped countries today **2** stripcropping
**striping** /'strieping/ *n* **1** marking with stripes **2a** the stripes marked or painted on something **b** a design of stripes
**strip light** *n* FLUORESCENT LAMP
**strip lighting** *n* lighting provided by one or more STRIP LIGHTS
**stripling** /'stripling/ *n* an adolescent boy [ME, prob fr *stripe* strip + -*ling*]
**strip mine** *n, chiefly NAm* a mine that is worked by excavation on the surface without underground tunnelling – **strip-mine** *vt,* **strip miner** *n*
**stripper** /'stripə/ *n* a person, substance, or machine that strips: e g **a** somebody who performs a striptease **b** a machine that separates a desired part of an agricultural crop **c** a tool or solvent for removing something, esp paint, from surfaces
**strip poker** *n* a poker game in which a player pays his/her losses by removing articles of clothing
**stript** /stript/ *archaic past of* STRIP
**striptease** /,strip'teez/ *n* an act or entertainment in which a performer, esp a woman, undresses gradually in view of the audience – **stripteaser** *n*
**stripy, stripey** /'striepi/ *adj* marked by stripes or streaks
**strive** /striev/ *vi* **strove** /strohv/ *also* **strived; striven** /'striv(ə)n/ **1** to struggle in opposition; contend **2** to try hard; endeavour [ME *striven,* fr OF *estriver,* of Gmc origin; akin to MHG *streben* to endeavour, OE *strīdan* to stride] – **striver** *n*
**strobe** /strohb/ *n* **1** a stroboscope **2** a device that uses a flashtube for high-speed illumination (e g in a stroboscope or in photography) [by shortening & alter.]
**strobe lighting** *n* flashing intermittent lights (e g at a disco) produced by a stroboscope
**strobila** /'strohbilə, strə'bielə/ *n, pl* **strobilae** /-li, -lay/ a linear series of similar animal structures: e g **a** the chain of segments forming the body of a tapeworm **b** the chain of individuals produced by repeated transverse division of a jellyfish larva

[NL, fr Gk *strobilē* plug of lint shaped like a pinecone, fr *strobilos* pinecone] – **strobilar** *adj*

**strobilation** /ˌstrohbi'laysh(ə)n/ *n* growth (eg of a tapeworm) or asexual reproduction (eg of a jellyfish) by the formation of strobilae [NL *strobila*]

**strobile** /'strohbiel/ *n* STROBILUS 1

**strobil·ization, -isation** /ˌstrohbilie'zaysh(ə)n/ *n* strobilation

**strobilus** /stroh'bieləs/ *n, pl* **strobili** /-li/ 1 a collection of spore-producing parts resembling a cone (eg in the CLUB MOSSES and horsetails) 2 CONE 1a (reproductive part of pines and related plants) [NL, fr LL, pinecone, fr Gk *strobilos* twisted object, top, pinecone, fr *strobos* action of whirling – more at STROPHE]

**stroboscope** /'strohbəˌskohp/ *n* an instrument for observing and measuring motion, esp rotation or vibration, by allowing intermittent viewing of the moving object, so that the motion appears slowed or stopped: eg **a** a revolving disc with holes round the edge through which something is viewed **b** a lamp that illuminates a moving object by flashing intermittently at varying frequencies **c** something (eg a cardboard disc) with regularly spaced marks to be viewed under intermittent light that is used to set up the speed of the turntable of a record player [Gk *strobos* whirling + ISV *-scope*]

**stroboscopic** /ˌstrohbə'skopik/ *adj* of or using a stroboscope or strobe – **stroboscopically** *adv*

**strode** /strohd/ *past of* STRIDE

**stroganoff** /'strogənof/ *n, often cap* a rich dish of strips of meat (eg beef) cooked in a sour-cream sauce [Count Paul *Stroganoff*, 19th-c Russ diplomat]

**¹stroke** /strohk/ *vt* to pass the hand over gently in one direction; *also* to caress [ME *stroken*, fr OE *strācian;* akin to OHG *strīhhan* to stroke – more at STRIKE] – **stroker** *n*

**²stroke** *n* 1 the act of striking; *esp* a blow with a weapon or implement 2 a single unbroken movement; *esp* one that is repeated 3 a striking of the ball in a game (eg cricket or tennis); *specif* any of several (attempted) strikings of a golf ball, the total number of which constitute the score in a game ⟨went round in 62 ~s⟩ 4a a (sudden) action by which something is done, produced, or achieved ⟨~ of lightning⟩ ⟨a ~ of genius⟩ **b** an unexpected occurrence ⟨~ of luck⟩ 5 sudden reduction or loss of consciousness, sensation, and voluntary motion caused by rupture or obstruction (eg by a blood clot) of an artery of the brain 6a any of a series of propelling beats or movements against a resisting medium (eg air or water) ⟨a ~ of the oar⟩; *also* the technique used in such a movement, esp in swimming or rowing ⟨what ~ does she swim?⟩ ⟨rowed a fast ~⟩ **b** an oarsman who sits at the back of a racing rowing boat, esp one with eight or four rowers, and sets the pace for the rest of the crew 7a a vigorous or energetic effort – usu neg ⟨never does a ~⟩ **b** a delicate or clever touch in a story, description, or construction 8 a heartbeat 9 (the distance of) the movement in either direction of a mechanical part (eg a PISTON ROD) 10 the sound of a striking clock ⟨at the ~ of twelve⟩ 11 an act of stroking or caressing 12a a mark or dash made by a single movement of a pen, brush, etc – often in combination ⟨a brushstroke⟩ **b** any of the lines of an alphabetic character 13 *Br* SOLIDUS (oblique mark) [ME; akin to OE *strīcan* to stroke – more at STRIKE] – **at a stroke** by a single action – **off one's stroke** (performing) below one's capability because of difficult circumstances

**³stroke** *vt* **1a** to mark with a short line ⟨~ *the* t's⟩ **b** to cancel by drawing a line through ⟨~d *out his name*⟩ 2 to set the stroke for (a rowing crew) or for the crew of (a rowing boat) 3 to hit; *esp* to hit (a ball) with a controlled swinging blow ~ *vi* to row at a specified number of strokes a minute

**stroke play** *n* a golf competition scored by total number of strokes – compare MATCH PLAY

**stroll** /strohl/ *vi* to walk in a leisurely or idle manner; ramble ~ *vt* to walk at leisure along or about [prob fr Ger dial. *strollen*] – **stroll** *n*

**stroller** /'strohlə/ *n* 1 STROLLING PLAYER 2 *NAm* a pushchair

**strolling** /'strohling/ *adj* going from place to place, esp in search of work ⟨~ *musicians*⟩

**strolling player** *n* a travelling actor

**stroma** /'strohmə/ *n, pl* **stromata** /'strohmətə/ **1a** the supporting framework of an animal organ, usu consisting of CONNECTIVE TISSUE (supporting and packing tissue) **b** the spongy framework of some cells (eg a RED BLOOD CELL) 2a a compact mass of fungus threads producing a spore-producing body **b** the colourless material in a CHLOROPLAST (specialized plant cell

part) in which chlorophyll-containing layers are embedded [NL *stromat-, stroma,* fr L, bed covering, fr Gk *strōmat-, strōma,* fr *stornynai* to spread out – more at STREW] – **stromal, stromatal** *adj,* **stromatic** *adj*

**stromatolite** /stroh'matəliet/ *n* a rock formed from LAYERS of fossilized BLUE-GREEN ALGAE [L *stromat-, stroma* bed covering + E *-o-* + *-lite*] – **stromatolitic** *adj*

**strong** /strong/ *adj* 1 having or marked by great physical power; robust 2 having moral or intellectual power 3 having great resources (eg of wealth or talent) ⟨a ~ economy⟩ ⟨a film with a ~ cast⟩ 4 of a specified number ⟨an army ten thousand ~⟩ 5a striking or superior of its kind ⟨a ~ resemblance⟩ **b** effective or efficient, esp in a specified area ⟨~ on logic⟩ 6 forceful, cogent ⟨~ evidence⟩ 7 not mild or weak; extreme, intense: eg 7a rich in some active agent (eg a flavour or extract) ⟨~ beer⟩ ⟨~ tea⟩ **b** of a colour intense, pure **c** of an acid or base forming electrically charged atoms or groups of atoms freely, in solution **d** magnifying by REFRACTING (changing the direction of light) greatly ⟨a ~ lens⟩ 8 moving with vigour or force ⟨a ~ wind⟩ 9 ardent, zealous ⟨a ~ supporter⟩ 10a not easily injured; solid **b** not easily subdued or taken ⟨a ~ fort⟩ 11 well established; firm ⟨~ beliefs⟩ 12 not easily upset or nauseated ⟨a ~ stomach⟩ 13 having an offensive or intense smell or flavour; rank 14 *esp of flour* containing a high proportion of GLUTEN (protein substance giving dough its elastic properties) and suitable for use in making bread and pasta 15 tending to steady or higher prices ⟨a ~ market⟩ 16 of or being a verb or verb conjugation that forms the past tense and past participle by internal vowel change rather than by adding to the end of the word (eg *strive, strove, striven* or *drink, drank, drunk*) – compare WEAK 7 17 of a syllable pronounced with some degree of stress and with full vowel quality ⟨/ov/ is the ~ form of of⟩ [ME, fr OE *strang;* akin to OHG *strengi* strong, L *stringere* to bind tight – more at STRAIN] – **strong** *adv,* **strongish** *adj,* **strongly** *adv* – **come it strong** *slang* to exaggerate ⟨to say I hate her would be coming it a bit strong⟩

**synonyms** Strong, stout, sturdy, tough, stalwart, and tenacious can all mean "able to resist or endure". **Strong** is the most general, and could often replace the others. **Stout, sturdy,** and **tough** imply a resistance derived from solidity; **stout** emphasizes substantial construction ⟨stout *ropes*⟩ or undaunted resolution ⟨stout *hearts*⟩, **sturdy** suggests rugged health ⟨sturdy *yeomanry*⟩, and **tough** implies flexible strength ⟨tough *meat*⟩ or hardiness ⟨a tough *old salt*⟩. **Stalwart** and **tenacious** suggest staunch persistence, **stalwart** often implying a dependable loyalty ⟨stalwart *Conservatives*⟩ and **tenacious** a stubborn holding on despite discouragement ⟨tenacious *dieters*⟩. **antonym** Weak **usage** Strong as an adverb is chiefly used in certain fixed phrases ⟨still going strong⟩, and cannot replace **strongly,** the usual adverb ⟨strongly disagree⟩.

**strongarm** /'strongˌahm/ *adj* using or involving bullying methods or undue force ⟨~ tactics⟩

**'strong-ˌarm** *vt, NAm* 1 to use force on; assault 2 to rob by force

**strongbox** /'strongˌboks/ *n* a strongly made chest or case for money or valuables

**strong breeze** *n* wind having a speed of 39 to 49 kilometres per hour (about 25 to 31 miles per hour); a wind of force six on the Beaufort scale **synonyms** see ¹WIND

**strong drink** *n* intoxicating liquor

**strong force** *n* STRONG INTERACTION

**strong gale** *n* wind having a speed of 75 to 88 kilometres per hour (about 47 to 54 miles per hour); a gale of force nine on the Beaufort scale **synonyms** see ¹WIND

**stronghold** /'strongˌhohld/ *n* 1 a fortified place 2a a place of security, refuge, or survival ⟨one of the last ~s of the Gaelic language⟩ **b** a place dominated by a specified group or marked by a specified characteristic ⟨a Tory ~⟩

**strong interaction** *n, physics* a fundamental interaction between ELEMENTARY PARTICLES that is more powerful than any other known force and is responsible for the forces that bind protons and neutrons in atomic nuclei and for particle creation processes that occur in collisions between high-energy particles – compare WEAK INTERACTION

**strong language** *n* forcible and esp abusive language; swearing

**strong man** *n* 1 a man (eg in a circus) who performs feats of muscular strength 2 *informal* an autocratic leader of an organization or state

**ˌstrong-'minded** *adj* having a vigorous mind; *esp* marked by firmness and independence of thought and judgment – **strong-mindedly** *adv*, **strong-mindedness** *n*

**strongpoint** /'strong,poynt/ *n* **1** a small fortified defensive position **2** HARDPOINT (strengthened point on aircraft wing)

**strong point** *n* something in which one excels; one's forte

**strong room** *n* a room for money or valuables that is specially constructed to be fireproof and burglarproof

**strong suit** *n* **1** the suit in a hand, esp at bridge or whist, containing playing cards of the highest value **2** STRONG POINT

**strongyle** /'stronjil/ *n* any of various roundworms (family Strongylidae of the phylum Nematoda) related to the hookworms and mostly parasitic in the digestive system and body tissues of the horse [deriv of Gk *strongylos* round, compact; akin to L *stringere* to bind tight – more at STRAIN]

**strongylosis** /,stronji'lohsis/ *n* infestation with or disease caused by strongyles [NL]

**strontia** /'strontyə/ *n* a white solid chemical compound that is an oxide of strontium, SrO, resembling lime and BARYTA [NL, fr obs E *strontian*, fr *Strontian*, village in Scotland where it was discovered]

**strontianite** /'strontyə,niet/ *n* a mineral consisting of strontium carbonate, $SrCO_3$, and occurring in various forms and colours

**strontium** /'strontyəm/ *n* a soft easily worked metallic chemical element, that has a VALENCY of two, belongs to the ALKALINE-EARTH group, occurs naturally only in chemical compounds, and that is used esp in colour TV tubes, in crimson fireworks, and in the production of some FERRITES (magnetic chemical compounds) [NL, fr *strontia*] – **strontic** *adj*

**strontium 90** *n* a heavy radioactive ISOTOPE (one of several forms of an atom that contain the same number of protons) of strontium having a total of 90 protons and neutrons in the nucleus, that is present in the fallout from nuclear explosions, and that is dangerous because like calcium it can be deposited in the bones of human beings and animals

¹**strop** /strop/ *n* a strap; *specif* a leather band for sharpening a cutthroat razor [ME – more at STRAP]

²**strop** *vt* **-pp-** to sharpen (e g a razor) on a strop

**strophanthin** /stroh'fanthin/ *n* any of several poisonous (mixtures of) GLYCOSIDES (chemical compounds containing sugars) that are obtained from African plants (genera *Strophanthus* and *Acocanthera*) of the periwinkle family, contain OUABAIN as their main active component, and are used as heart stimulants [ISV, fr NL *Strophanthus*, genus of tropical plants, fr Gk *strophos* twisted band + *anthos* flower]

**strophe** /'strohfi/ *n* **1a** a turning movement made by the classical Greek chorus from one side to the other of the orchestra **b** the part of a Greek choral ode sung during this movement of the chorus **2a** a rhythmic system composed of two or more lines repeated as a unit within a poem; *esp* such a unit recurring in a series **b** a verse of a poem; STANZA [Gk *strophē*, lit., act of turning, fr *strephein* to turn, twist; akin to Gk *strobos* action of whirling]

**strophic** /'strofik, 'stroh-/ *adj* **1** of, containing, or consisting of strophes **2** using the same music for successive verses of a song – compare THROUGH-COMPOSED

**strophoid** /'strofoyd, 'stroh-/ *n* a plane curve that is generated by a point whose distance from the y-axis along a variable straight line which always passes through a fixed point is equal to the y-intercept and that has the equation $r = a(\sec\theta - \sin\theta\tan\theta)$ [Fr *strophoïde*, fr Gk *strophos* twisted band (fr *strephein* to twist) + -*oïde* -oid]

**stroppy** /'stropi/ *adj, Br informal* quarrelsome, obstreperous [perh by shortening & alter. fr *obstreperous*]

**strove** /strohv/ *past & chiefly dial past part* of STRIVE

**struck** /struk/ *past* of STRIKE

**structural** /'strukch(ə)rəl/ *adj* **1a** of or affecting structure ⟨~ *stability*⟩ **b** used in or suitable for building structures ⟨~ *clay*⟩ ⟨~ *steel*⟩ **c** involved in or caused by structure, esp of the economy ⟨~ *unemployment*⟩ **2** of the physical makeup of a plant or animal body **3** of or resulting from the effects of folding or faulting of the earth's crust; TECTONIC **4** concerned with or relating to structure rather than history or comparison ⟨~ *linguistics*⟩ – **structurally** *adv*

**structural engineering** *n* a branch of CIVIL ENGINEERING that deals with the design and building of large structures (e g dams or bridges)

**structural formula** *n* a detailed chemical formula of a substance showing the arrangement within its molecule of atoms and of the bonds between them

**structural gene** *n* a gene that codes for the sequence of AMINO ACIDS making up a protein molecule (e g an ENZYME) by means of a specific MESSENGER RNA (biochemical compound acting as template for protein formation) – compare REGULATOR GENE

**structuralism** /'strukch(ə)rə,liz(ə)m/ *n* **1** a branch of linguistics concerned with language structure **2** a method or approach used in anthropology, literary criticism, linguistics, etc associated esp with Claude Lévi-Strauss, that seeks to analyse data in terms of the significance of underlying relationships and patterns of organization, often expressed in a logical symbolism – **structuralist** *n or adj*

**structural isomerism** *n* ISOMERISM (different arrangement of the same group of atoms to give separate chemical compounds) in which atoms are joined in a different order

**structural·ize, -ise** /'strukchərəliez/ *vt* to organize or incorporate into a structure – **structuralization** *n*

¹**structure** /'strukchə/ *n* **1a** something (e g a building) that is constructed **b** something arranged in a definite pattern of organization ⟨*a rigid class* ~⟩ **2** manner of construction; makeup ⟨*Gothic in* ~⟩ **3a** the arrangement of particles or parts in a substance or body ⟨*soil* ~⟩ ⟨*molecular* ~⟩ **b** arrangement or interrelation of elements ⟨*economic* ~⟩ [ME, act of building, fr L *structura*, fr *structus*, pp of *struere* to heap up, build; akin to L *sternere* to spread out – more at STREW]

²**structure** *vt* to form into a structure

**structureless** /'strukchəlis/ *adj* lacking structure; *esp* without living cells ⟨*a* ~ *membrane*⟩ – **structurelessness** *n*

**strudel** /'stroohdl/ *n* a German pastry made from a thin sheet of dough rolled up with filling and baked ⟨*apple* ~⟩ [Ger, lit., whirlpool]

¹**struggle** /'strugl/ *vi* **1** to make violent strenuous efforts against opposition **2** to proceed with difficulty or with great effort ⟨*struggling to maintain his composure*⟩ [ME *struglen*] – **struggler** *n*

²**struggle** *n* **1** a violent effort or exertion; a determined attempt in adverse circumstances **2** a hard-fought contest

**struggle for existence** *n* the competition (e g for food, space, or light) among members of a natural population that tends to eliminate less efficient individuals and thereby increases the chance of desirable inheritable characteristics being passed on from the more efficient survivors – not used technically; compare NATURAL SELECTION

¹**strum** /strum/ *vb* **-mm-** *vt* **1a** to brush the fingers lightly over the strings of (a musical instrument) in playing ⟨~ *a guitar*⟩; *also* to thrum **b** to play (music) on a guitar ⟨~ *a tune*⟩ **2** to cause to sound vibrantly ⟨*winds* ~*ming the telegraph wires*⟩ ~ *vi* **1** to strum a stringed instrument **2** to sound vibrantly [imit] – **strummer** *n*

²**strum** *n* an act, instance, or sound of strumming

**struma** /'stroohmə/ *n, pl* **strumae** /-mie/, **strumas** **1** GOITRE (swelling of the thyroid) **2** a swelling at the base of the spore-containing part of many mosses **3** *archaic* SCROFULA (tuberculosis of glands esp in the throat) [(1,3) L – more at STRUT; (2) NL, fr L] – **strumose** *adj*

**strumpet** /'strumpit/ *n, archaic* a female prostitute [ME]

**strung** /strung/ *past of* STRING

**strung out** *adj, NAm slang* **1** excited by or addicted to a drug ⟨*junkies* ~ *on heroin*⟩ **2** physically wasted or distressed (as if) from long-term drug addiction

**strung-'up** *adj, Br informal* highly nervous; tense

¹**strut** /strut/ *vi* **-tt-** **1** to walk with a proud or erect gait **2** to walk with a pompous and affected air; swagger [ME *strouten* to swell, protrude stiffly, bluster, fr OE *strūtian* to exert oneself; akin to L *struma* goitre, OE *starian* to stare] – **strutter** *n*

²**strut** *n* **1** a structural piece designed to resist pressure in the direction of its length **2** a pompous step or walk

³**strut** *vt* **-tt-** to provide, stiffen, support, or hold apart (as if) with a strut

**struth, strewth** /stroohth/ *interj, chiefly Br* – used to express surprise, alarm, or annoyance [short for *God's truth*]

**struthious** /'stroohthyəs/ *adj* of or like the ostriches; RATITE (having a flat breastbone with no attached flight muscles) [LL *struthio* ostrich, irreg fr Gk *strouthos*]

**strychnine** /'strikneen/ *n* a bitter poisonous chemical compound, $C_{21}H_{22}N_2O_2$, that is obtained from the seeds of NUX VOMICA and related plants (genus *Strychnos*) and that is used as a poison (e g for rodents) and medicinally in small amounts as a stimulant to the CENTRAL NERVOUS SYSTEM [Fr, fr NL *Strychnos*, genus name, fr L, nightshade, fr Gk]

**strychninism** /'strikneeniz(ə)m, -niniz(ə)m/ *n* chronic strychnine poisoning

**Stuart** /'styoo-ət/ *adj* of or supporting the Scottish royal house that ruled Scotland from 1371 to 1603 and Britain from 1603 to 1649 and from 1660 to 1714 [Robert *Stewart* (Robert II of Scotland) †1390] – **Stuart** *n*

¹**stub** /stub/ *n* **1a** STUMP **2 b** a short piece remaining on a stem or trunk where a branch has been lost **2** something made or worn to a short or blunt shape **3** a short blunt part left after a larger part has been broken off or used up; a butt ⟨*pencil* ∼⟩ ⟨*cigarette* ∼⟩ **4** something cut short or stunted **5a** a small part of a page (eg of a chequebook) attached to the spine as a record of the contents of the part torn away **b** the part of a ticket returned to the user after inspection [ME *stubb,* fr OE *stybb;* akin to Gk *stypos* stem, *typtein* to beat – more at TYPE]

²**stub** *vt* **-bb- 1a** to grub up by the roots **b** to clear (land) by uprooting stumps **c** to hew or cut down (a tree) close to the ground **2** to extinguish (eg a cigarette) by crushing – usu + *out* **3** to strike (one's foot or toe) against an object

**stub axle** *n* a short axle bearing one wheel (eg one of the front wheels of a car)

**stubble** /'stubl/ *n* **1** the stalky remnants of plants, esp cereal grasses, which remain in the soil after harvest **2** a rough surface or growth resembling stubble; *esp* a short growth of beard [ME *stuble,* fr OF *estuble,* fr L *stupula* stalk, straw, alter. of *stipula* – more at STIPULE] – **stubble, stubbly** *adj*

**stubborn** /'stubən/ *adj* **1a(1)** unreasonably or perversely unyielding; mulish **a(2)** justifiably unyielding; resolute **b** suggestive or typical of a strong stubborn nature ⟨*a* ∼ *jaw*⟩ **2** performed or carried on in an unyielding, obstinate, or persistent manner ⟨∼ *strife*⟩ **3** difficult to handle, manage, or treat; refractory, intractable ⟨*a* ∼ *cold*⟩ *synonyms* see OBSTINATE *antonym* docile [ME *stuborn*] – **stubbornly** *adv,* **stubbornness** *n*

¹**stubby** /'stubi/ *adj* resembling a stub; short and thick ⟨∼ *fingers*⟩

²**stubby** *n, Austr* a small beer bottle

¹**stucco** /'stukoh/ *n, pl* **stuccos, stuccoes 1a** a material usu made of cement, sand, and a small percentage of lime and applied in a soft state to form a hard covering for outside walls; rendering **b** a fine plaster used in classical architecture for FRESCOES (paintings on plaster) or mouldings and in later (eg Regency) styles used to imitate stone; *broadly* any smooth rendering for interiors and exteriors **2** stucco, stuccowork work done in stucco [It, of Gmc origin; akin to OHG *stucki* piece, crust, OE *stocc* stock]

²**stucco** *vt* to coat or decorate with stucco

**stuck** /stuk/ *past of* STICK

'**stuck-in-the-,mud** *adj* (characteristic) of or being a stick-in-the-mud

,**stuck-'up** *adj, informal* superciliously self-important or conceited

¹**stud** /stud/ *n* **1a** *taking sing or pl vb* a group of animals, esp horses, kept primarily for breeding **b** a place (eg a farm) where a stud is kept **2** a studhorse; *broadly* a male animal kept for breeding **3** *vulg* a sexually active man; *specif* one considered to have an unusually active sex life [ME *stod,* fr OE *stōd;* akin to OE *standan* to stand]

²**stud** *n* **1** any of the smaller upright posts in the framework of a building to which panelling or laths are fastened; SCANTLING **2a** a boss, rivet, or nail with a large head used (eg on a shield or belt) for ornament or protection **b** a solid button with a shank or eye on the back inserted through an eyelet in a garment as a fastener or ornament ⟨*collar* ∼⟩ **3a** any of various pieces (eg a rod or pin) projecting from a machine and serving chiefly as a support or axis **b** a cleat ⟨*football boots with* ∼s⟩; *esp* a metal cleat inserted in a horseshoe or snow tyre to increase grip **c** a length of rod with a screw thread at each end, used to join mechanical parts together **4** *NAm* the height from floor to ceiling [ME *stode,* fr OE *studu;* akin to OE *stōw* place – more at STOW]

³**stud** *vt* **-dd- 1** to provide (eg a building or wall) with studs **2** to decorate, cover, or protect with studs **3** to set (a place or thing) thickly with a number of prominent objects ⟨*sky* ∼ded *with stars*⟩

**studbook** /'stud,book/ *n* an official record (eg in a book) of the pedigree of purebred horses, dogs, etc

**studding** /'studing/ *n* **1** material (eg timber) for building studs **2** building studs, esp as part of a wall

**studding sail** /'studing/ *n* an additional light sail set at the side of a SQUARE SAIL in light winds [origin unknown]

**student** /'styood(ə)nt/ *n* **1** a scholar, learner; *esp* one who attends a college or university **2** an attentive and systematic observer ⟨*a* ∼ *of human nature*⟩ *synonyms* see PUPIL [ME, fr L *student-, studens,* fr prp of *studēre* to study – more at STUDY]

**student body** *n taking sing or pl vb* the total number of students at an educational institution

**student government** *n* the organization and management of student life, activities, or discipline by various student organizations in a school or college

**student grant** *n* STUDENTSHIP 2

**studentship** /'styoohd(ə)nt,ship/ *n* **1** the state of being a student **2** *Br* a grant for university study

**student's t distribution** *n, often cap S, statistics* T DISTRIBUTION (statistical function) [*Student,* pen name of W S Gossett †1937 Br statistician]

**student teacher** *n* a student who is engaged in teaching practice

**student teaching** *n* TEACHING PRACTICE

**student union** *n* **1** (a building housing) an organization that is attached to a college or university (eg Oxford or Cambridge) and is devoted to student activities **2** a union which is run by the students of an educational institution, which is usu affiliated to a national union, and which organizes and funds recreational activities; *also* the building in which the union offices are housed

**student village** *n* a group of separate houses or flats provided for the students at some universities

**studhorse** /'stud,haws/ *n* a stallion kept esp for breeding

**studied** /'studid/ *adj* **1** knowledgeable, learned **2** carefully considered or prepared; thoughtful **3** produced or marked by conscious design or premeditation ⟨∼ *indifference*⟩ – **studiedly** *adv,* **studiedness** *n*

**studio** /'styoohdi-oh/ *n, pl* **studios 1a** the workroom of a painter, sculptor, or photographer **b** a place for the study of an art (eg dancing, singing, or acting) **2** a place where films are made; *also, taking sing or pl vb* a film production company, including its premises and employees ⟨*a famous Hollywood* ∼ *closed down*⟩ **3** a room equipped for the production of radio or television programmes [It, lit., study, fr L *studium*]

**studio couch** *n* an upholstered usu backless couch that can be converted into a double bed, often by sliding from underneath it the frame of a single bed – compare BEDSETTEE

**studio flat** *n* a small flat consisting typically of a main room, kitchen, and bathroom

**studious** /'styoohdi-əs/ *adj* **1a** of or concerned with study **b** given to study **2a** diligent or serious in intent ⟨*made a* ∼ *effort*⟩ **b** marked by or suggesting purposefulness or diligence ⟨*a* ∼ *expression on his face*⟩ **c** STUDIED **3** – **studiously** *adv,* **studiousness** *n*

**stud poker** *n* a form of poker in which each player's first card is dealt face down and the next four face up, with a round of betting taking place after each of the last four rounds of dealing

**studwork** /'stud,wuhk/ *n* work supported, strengthened, held together, or ornamented by studs

¹**study** /'studi/ *n* **1** a state of deep thought or contemplation; a reverie – esp *in a brown study* **2a** the application of the mind to the acquisition of knowledge ⟨*years of* ∼⟩ **b** such application in a particular field or to a specified subject ⟨*the* ∼ *of Latin*⟩ **c** careful or extended consideration ⟨*the proposal is under* ∼⟩ **d(1)** a careful examination or analysis of a phenomenon, development, or question **d(2)** a paper in which such a study is published **3** a building or room devoted to study **4** consciously reasoned effort; purpose, intent **5a** a branch or department of learning; a subject **b** the activity or work of a student ⟨*returning to her* studies *after the vacation*⟩ **c** something attracting close attention or examination **6a** an artistic work intended as a preliminary outline or an experimental interpretation of specific features or characteristics **b** a literary work composed as an experimental or esp as an exploratory analysis of a particular subject **7** a musical composition for technical practice; ÉTUDE [ME *studie,* fr OF *estudie,* fr L *studium* mental application, eagerness, devotion, study, fr *studēre* to concentrate on, favour, study]

²**study** *vi* **1** to engage in study **2** to undertake formal study of a subject ∼ *vt* **1** to read in detail, esp with the intention of learning ⟨*actor* ∼ing *his part*⟩ **2** to engage in the study of ⟨∼ *biology*⟩ ⟨∼ *medicine*⟩ **3** to consider attentively or in detail ⟨studied *the timetable*⟩ **4** *formal* to endeavour, try – + infin ⟨*I shall* ∼ *to improve*⟩ – **studier** *n*

**study group** *n taking sing or pl vb* a group of people who meet regularly for informal discussion of the subject they are studying

**¹stuff** /stuf/ *n* **1** materials not specified but usu identifiable from the context: e g **1a** possessions, PERSONAL PROPERTY ⟨*can I leave my ~ here?*⟩ **b** materials, supplies, or equipment used in various activities ⟨*the plumber brought his ~*⟩ **c** matter of a particular kind ⟨*sold tons of the ~*⟩ **d** something (e g a drug or food) consumed by human beings ⟨*he used to drink but is now off the ~*⟩; *esp, slang* an addictive drug **e** a group or scattering of miscellaneous objects or articles ⟨*pick that ~ up off the floor*⟩ **2** material to be manufactured, worked, or used in construction **3** a finished textile suitable for clothing; *esp* wool or worsted material **4** an unspecified material substance ⟨*volcanic rock is curious ~*⟩ **5** the essence or basic quality of a usu abstract thing ⟨*the ~ of greatness*⟩ **6** *NAm* spin imparted to a thrown or hit ball to make it curve or change course **7** *informal* subject matter ⟨*a teacher who knows his ~*⟩ **8** *informal* worthless ideas, opinion, or writing; rubbish ⟨*don't give me any of that ~*⟩ [ME, fr MF *estoffe,* fr OF, fr *estoffer* to equip, stock, prob fr MHG *stopfen* to stop up, stuff, fr OHG *stopfōn* – more at STOP] – **do one's stuff** to perform to the top of one's capabilities – often imper ⟨*get out there and* do your stuff!⟩

**²stuff** *vt* **1a** to fill by packing things in; cram ⟨*~ed his pockets with sweets*⟩ **b** to gorge (oneself) with food ⟨*~ed himself with turkey*⟩ **c** to fill or line (e g meat or vegetables) with a stuffing **d** to fill (e g a cushion) with a soft material or padding **e** to fill the skin of (an animal) for mounting **f** to stop up (a hole) by packing in material; plug **2** to fill by intellectual effort – usu + *with* ⟨*~ing their heads with facts*⟩ **3** to choke or block *up* (the nasal passages) **4a** to force into a limited space; thrust ⟨*~ed a lot of clothing into a laundry bag*⟩ **b** to put (e g a ball or puck) into a target of play, esp a goal, forcefully from close range **5** *Br vulg, of a male* to have sexual intercourse with – **get stuffed!** *Br vulg* – used as a forceful expression of disagreement or anger

**stuffed shirt** *n, informal* a smug, conceited, and usu pompous person with an inflexibly conservative or reactionary attitude

**stuffer** /'stufə/ *n* **1** one who or that which stuffs **2** an enclosure (e g a leaflet) inserted in an envelope in addition to a bill, statement, or notice **3** a series of extra threads or yarns running lengthways in a fabric to add weight and bulk and to form a backing, esp for carpets

**stuffing** /'stufing/ *n* material used to stuff; *esp* a seasoned mixture used to stuff food (e g meat, vegetables, or eggs) – **knock the stuffing out of somebody 1** to beat somebody severely **2** to cause somebody to lose vigour or vitality; debilitate

**stuffing box** *n* a device that prevents leakage along a moving part (e g a PISTON ROD) passing through a hole in a vessel (e g a cylinder) containing steam, water, or oil, and that consists of a chamber of compressible material arranged round the moving part and between it and the hole

**stuffy** /'stufi/ *adj* **1** ill-natured, ill-humoured **2a** badly ventilated; close **b** stuffed up ⟨*a ~ nose*⟩ **3** lacking in vitality or interest; stodgy, dull **4** narrowly inflexible in standards of conduct; prim, straitlaced – **stuffily** *adv,* **stuffiness** *n*

**stultify** /'stultifie/ *vt* **1** *law* to allege or prove to be of unsound mind and hence not responsible **2a** to cause to appear or be stupid, foolish, or ridiculous **b** to make futile or useless, esp through enfeebling or repressive influence ⟨*centralization* stultifies *local initiative*⟩ [LL *stultificare* to make foolish, fr L *stultus* foolish; akin to L *stolidus* stolid] – **stultification** *n*

**¹stumble** /'stumbl/ *vi* **1a** to lapse into sin or wrongdoing **b** to make an error; blunder **2** to trip in walking or running **3a** to walk unsteadily or clumsily – + *along* ⟨*stumbling along the lane*⟩ **b** to speak or act in a hesitant or faltering manner – ⟨*~d through his speech*⟩ **4a** to come unexpectedly or by chance – + *upon, on,* or *across* ⟨*~ on the truth*⟩ **b** to fall or move carelessly – usu + *into* [ME *stumblen,* prob fr Scand origin; akin to Norw dial. *stumle* to stumble; akin to OE *stamerian* to stammer] – **stumbler** *n,* **stumblingly** *adv*

**²stumble** *n* an act or instance of stumbling

**stumbling block** /'stumbling/ *n* **1** an obstacle to belief or understanding **2** an obstacle to progress

**stumer** /'styoohmə/ *n, Br slang* a sham, fraud: e g **a** a worthless or forged cheque **b** a counterfeit coin or currency note [origin unknown]

**¹stump** /stump/ *n* **1a** the part of an arm, leg, etc remaining

attached to the body trunk after the rest is removed **b** a body part that is small, nonfunctional, or underdeveloped compared with that of an ancestor or closely related organism **2** the part of a plant, esp a tree, remaining in the ground attached to the root after the stem is cut **3** a remaining part; a stub **4a** any of the three upright wooden rods that together with the BAILS (small wooden pegs) form the wicket in cricket **b** *pl but taking sing or pl vb, chiefly Austr* the close of play in a cricket match **5** (a sound of) a heavy tread; footsteps **6** *chiefly NAm* a place or occasion for political public speaking [ME *stumpe;* akin to OHG *stumpf* stump, ME *stampen* to stamp] – **draw stumps** to finish a day's play in cricket – **stir one's stumps** *informal* to begin to move or awaken – often imper [*stumps* in the humorous sense "legs"]

**²stump** *vt* **1** to reduce to a stump; trim **2** *of a wicketkeeper in cricket* to dismiss (a batsman who is outside the POPPING CREASE (restricting line) but not attempting to run) by breaking the wicket with the ball before it has touched another fieldsman **3** to baffle, bewilder **4** to walk over or along heavily or clumsily **5** *NAm* to travel over (a region) making political speeches or supporting a cause ~ *vi* **1** to walk heavily or noisily **2** *NAm* to go about making political speeches or supporting a cause

**stump up** *vb, Br informal* to pay (what is due) in full, esp unwillingly

**³stump** *vt or n* (to treat with) a short thick roll of leather, felt, or paper usu pointed at both ends and used to soften or blur lines drawn in crayon, pencil, charcoal, pastel, or chalk [n Fr or Flem; Fr *estompe,* fr Flem *stomp,* lit., stub, fr MD; akin to OHG *stumpf* stump; vb fr n]

**stumper** /'stumpə/ *n, informal* **1** a wicketkeeper **2** a puzzling question; a teaser

**stumpy** /'stumpi/ *adj* short and thick; stubby

**stun** /stun/ *vt* **-nn-** **1** to make senseless, numb, or dizzy (as if) by a blow; daze **2** to overcome, esp with astonishment or disbelief; astonish [ME *stunen,* modif of OF *estoner* – more at ASTONISH]

**stung** /stung/ *past of* STING

**stunk** /stunk/ *past of* STINK

**stunner** /'stunə/ *n* **1** one who or that which stuns **2** *informal* an unusually beautiful or attractive person or thing

**stunning** /'stuning/ *adj, informal* strikingly beautiful or attractive – **stunningly** *adv*

**stunsail, stuns'l** /'stuns(ə)l/ *n* STUDDING SAIL [by contr]

**¹stunt** /stunt/ *vt* to hinder or arrest the growth or development of; dwarf [E dial. *stunt* stubborn, stunted, abrupt, prob of Scand origin; akin to ON *stuttr* scant – more at STINT] – **stuntedness** *n*

**²stunt** *n* **1** a check in growth **2** something (e g an animal) that is stunted **3** a plant disease in which dwarfing occurs

**³stunt** *n* an unusual or difficult feat performed chiefly to gain attention or publicity [prob alter. of *stump* (challenge)]

**⁴stunt** *vi* to perform stunts

**stunt man,** *fem* **stunt woman** *n* a person hired to perform dangerous or spectacular feats; *esp* one who performs such feats as a stand-in for an actor in a film or a television programme

**stupa** /'stoohpə/ *n* a Buddhist shrine in the form of an earthen or brick mound usu containing sacred relics [Skt *stūpa*]

**stupe** /styoohp/ *n* a hot wet often medicated cloth applied externally (e g to stimulate the circulation) [ME, fr L *stuppa* coarse part of flax, tow, fr Gk *styppē*]

**stupefaction** /,st(y)oohpi'faksh(ə)n/ *n* stupefying or being stupefied [NL *stupefaction-, stupefactio,* fr L *stupefactus,* pp of *stupefacere*]

**stupefy** /'st(y)oohpifie/ *vt* **1** to make stupid, groggy, or insensible **2** to astonish [MF *stupefier,* modif of L *stupefacere,* fr *stupēre* to be astonished + *facere* to make, do – more at DO]

**stupendous** /styooh'pendəs/ *adj* **1** causing astonishment or wonder; awesome, marvellous **2** of astonishing size or greatness; tremendous [L *stupendus,* gerundive of *stupēre*] – **stupendously** *adv,* **stupendousness** *n*

**¹stupid** /'styoohpid/ *adj* **1** slow-witted, obtuse **2** dulled in feeling or sensation; torpid ⟨*still ~ from the sedative*⟩ **3** marked by or resulting from mental dullness; senseless **4a** lacking interest or point **b** *informal* annoying, exasperating ⟨*this ~ torch won't work*⟩ [MF *stupide,* fr L *stupidus,* fr *stupēre* to be benumbed, be astonished; akin to Gk *typtein* to beat – more at TYPE] – **stupidly** *adv,* **stupidness, stupidity** *n*

*synonyms* **Stupid, dumb, dull, slow, dense, obtuse,** and **crass** can all mean "unable to grasp ideas". **Stupid** and the rather informal **dumb** suggest merely a temporary or permanent lack of understanding ⟨**stupid** *of me to forget*⟩ ⟨*too* **dumb** *to know the difference*⟩. **Dull** and **slow** emphasize intellectual sluggishness and lack of liveliness ⟨*a dull pupil*⟩. **Dense** suggests imperviousness to ideas. **Obtuse** may imply a lack of delicate feelings ⟨*too* **obtuse** *to take the hint*⟩. **Crass** applies particularly to a fatheaded lack of discrimination ⟨**crass** *incompetence*⟩. **antonyms** intelligent, bright, quick, clever

²**stupid** *n, informal* a stupid person – often used as a term of address

**stupor** /'styoohpə/ *n* 1 a condition characterized by great lessening or suspension of sense or feeling ⟨*a drunken* ∼⟩ 2 a state of extreme apathy or sluggishness often resulting from stress or shock; a daze [ME, fr L, fr *stupēre*] – **stuporous** *adj* **synonyms** Both **stupor** and **torpor** mean a sluggish state, but **stupor** is largely mental, and is typically caused by drugs or shock, while **torpor** is a physical condition, as of an animal in hibernation.

**sturdy** /'stuhdi/ *adj* 1a soundly and strongly built or constituted; stout b hardy c sound in design or execution; substantial 2a having physical strength or vigour; robust b firm, resolute ⟨*put up a* ∼ *defence of her argument*⟩ **synonyms** see STRONG [ME, fierce, brave, stubborn, fr OF *estourdi* stunned, fr pp of *estourdir* to stun, fr (assumed) VL *exturdire* to be dizzy as a thrush that is drunk from eating grapes, fr L *ex- + turdus* thrush – more at THRUSH] – **sturdily** *adv*, **sturdiness** *n*

**sturgeon** /'stuhj(ə)n/ *n* any of various usu large elongated edible fishes (e g of the genus *Acipenser*) that are widely distributed in the temperate areas of the N hemisphere, whose roe is made into caviar, and from which ISINGLASS (type of gelatin) is prepared [ME, fr OF *estourjon*, of Gmc origin; akin to OE *styria* sturgeon]

**Sturm und Drang** /ˌstuhm ənt 'drang, ˌshtooəm (*Ger* ʃtʊrm ʊnt draŋ)/ *n* 1 a late 18th-century German literary movement characterized by highly emotional works containing rousing action that often deal with the individual's revolt against society 2 turmoil [Ger, fr *Sturm und Drang* (*Storm and Stress*), drama by Friedrich von Klinger †1831 Ger writer]

¹**stutter** /'stutə/ *vi* 1 to speak with involuntary hesitation or disruption of speech (e g by spasmodic repetition or prolongation of vocal sounds) 2 to move or act in a halting or spasmodic manner ⟨*the old car* ∼s *uphill*⟩ ∼ *vt* to say, speak, or sound (as if) with a stutter □ compare STAMMER [freq of E dial. *stut* to stutter, fr ME *stutten;* akin to D *stotteren* to stutter, L *tundere* to beat – more at STINT] – **stutterer** *n*

²**stutter** *n* 1 an act or instance of stuttering 2 a speech disorder involving stuttering accompanied by fear and anxiety

¹**sty** /stie/ *n, pl* **sties** *also* **styes** 1 a pigsty 2 a filthy dwelling ⟨*her house was a perfect* ∼⟩ [ME, fr OE *stig;* akin to ON *-stī* sty]

²**sty, stye** /stie/ *n, pl* **sties, styes** an inflamed swelling of the SEBACEOUS (secreting oily lubricant substances) gland at the edge of an eyelid [short for obs *styan*, fr (assumed) ME, alter. of OE *stīgend*, fr *stīgan* to go up, rise – more at STAIR]

**stygian** /'stiji·ən/ *adj, often cap, formal* 1 extremely dark 2 gloomy or forbidding in appearance ⟨*the* ∼ *expression on her heavy features*⟩ [L *stygius*, fr Gk *stygios*, fr *Styg-, Styx* Styx, mythical river of the underworld]

¹**styl-** /stiel-/, **stylo-** *comb form* pillar ⟨*stylolite*⟩ [L, fr Gk, fr *stylos* – more at STEER]

²**styl-, styli-, stylo-** *comb form* style; styloid structure ⟨*stylate*⟩ ⟨*styliferous*⟩ ⟨*stylographic*⟩ [L *stilus* stake, stalk – more at STYLE]

**stylar** /'stielə/ *adj* 1 of or being an elongated part 2 of the style of a plant OVARY (seed-producing structure) [¹*style*]

**-stylar** /-'stielə, -'stielah/ *comb form* (→ *adj*) having (such or so many) pillars ⟨*amphistylar*⟩ [Gk *stylos* pillar]

¹**style** /stiel/ *n* 1a a stylus for writing b an extension of a plant OVARY (seed-producing organ) bearing a STIGMA (pollen-receiving structure) at its tip c a slender elongated part (e g a bristle) on an animal 2a a manner of expression in language, esp when characteristic of an individual, period, school, or nation ⟨*a classic* ∼⟩ b a manner or tone assumed in conversation c the custom or plan followed (e g in a publication or by a publishing house) in spelling, capitalization, punctuation, and printing arrangement and display 3 a mode of address; a title 4a(1) a manner of behaving or performing, esp as sanctioned by some standard a(2) a distinctive or characteristic manner b a fashionable or luxurious mode of life ⟨*lived in* ∼⟩ c excellence, skill, distinction, or grace in performance,

manner, social behaviour, or appearance d *informal* the typical way of life or mode of action of an individual; an individual's attitudes and their consistent expression ⟨*stealing's not my* ∼⟩ [ME *stile, style*, fr L *stilus* stake, stylus, style of writing; akin to OE *stician* to stick] – **styleless** *adj*, **stylelessness** *n*

²**style** *vt* 1 to call by an identifying term; name ⟨∼ d *themselves socialists*⟩ 2a to cause to conform to a customary style (e g for publication) ⟨*took hours to* ∼ *the manuscript*⟩ b to make (e g clothing or furniture) according to a particular fashion ⟨*dresses specially* ∼d *for the summer season*⟩ – **styler** *n*

³**style** *n* a stile

¹**-style** /-stiel/ *comb form* (→ *adj*) resembling ⟨*leather*-style *briefcase*⟩

²**-style** *comb form* (→ *adv*) in the style or manner of ⟨*seated on the floor Indian*-style⟩

**stylebook** /'stiel,book/ *n* a book explaining, describing, or illustrating a particular style (e g of writing or printing)

**stylet** /'stielit/ *n* 1a a slender surgical probe b a thin wire inserted into a CATHETER (tube for passing liquid to or from body parts) to maintain rigidity, or into a hollow needle to keep it clear of obstruction c a pointed instrument (e g for engraving) 2 a relatively rigid elongated part (e g a piercing mouthpart) of an animal 3 STILETTO 1 [Fr, fr MF *stilet* stiletto, fr OIt *stiletto*]

**styli-** – see ²STYL-

**styliform** /'stieli,fawm/ *adj* resembling a style; bristle-shaped ⟨*an insect's* ∼ *copulatory organ*⟩ [NL *stiliformis*, fr L *stilus + -formis* -form]

**stylish** /'stielish/ *adj* having style; *specif* fashionably elegant – **stylishly** *adv*, **stylishness** *n*

**stylist** /'stielist/ *n* 1 an expert in or model of style; *esp* a writer who cultivates a fine literary style 2 one who develops, designs, or advises on styles; *specif* a hairdresser

**stylistic** /stie'listik/ *adj* of esp literary or artistic style – **stylistically** *adv*

**stylistics** /stie'listiks/ *n taking sing or pl vb* 1 a branch of literary study concerned with the analysis of various elements of style (e g metaphor and diction) 2 the study of the devices in a language that produce expressive value

**stylite** /'stieliet/ *n* any of several early Christian hermits living on the tops of pillars [LGk *stylitēs*, fr Gk *stylos* pillar – more at STEER] – **stylitic** *adj*

**styl·ize, -ise** /'stieliez/ *vt* to make (e g a work of art) conform to a conventional style; *specif* to represent or design according to a stylistic pattern for aesthetic effect rather than according to nature ⟨*a* ∼d *pattern of roses and acanthus*⟩ – **stylization** *n*

**stylo-** – see ¹,²STYL-

**stylobate** /'stielə,bayt/ *n* a continuous flat step or pavement on which a row of architectural columns is placed [L *stylobates*, fr Gk *stylobatēs*, fr *stylos* pillar + *bainein* to walk, go – more at COME]

**stylograph** /'stielə,grahf, -,graf/ *n* a fountain pen that has a fine point fitted with a needle which by pressure of the point on a surface is pushed back to release the flow of ink

**stylographic** /ˌstielə'grafik/ *adj* 1 of stylography 2 of or being a stylograph

**stylography** /stie'lografi/ *n* the method or art of writing or drawing lines with a stylus or similar instrument

**styloid** /'stieloyd/ *adj* styliform – used esp of slender pointed skeletal body parts (e g on the longer bone of the forearm)

**stylolite** /'stielə,liet/ *n* a small column of rock (e g limestone) with lengthways grooves, that occurs naturally in a mass of the same material [ISV ¹*styl- + -lite*]

**stylopodium** /ˌstielə'pohdiəm/ *n, pl* **stylopodia** /-diə/ a disc-shaped or conical expansion at the base of the STYLE (part of reproductive structure) in plants of the carrot family [NL, fr ²*styl-* + Gk *podion* small foot, base – more at PEW]

**-stylous** /-stieləs/ *comb form* (→ *adj*), *of a plant* having (such or so many) STYLES (parts of reproductive organs) in the floral structure ⟨*monostylous*⟩

**stylus** /'stieləs/ *n, pl* **styli** /-li/, **styluses** an instrument for writing, marking, incising, or following a groove: e g a an instrument used by the ancient Egyptians and other peoples for writing on clay or waxed tablets b a hard-pointed pen-shaped instrument for marking on stencils used in a reproducing machine c a tiny piece of material (e g diamond or fibre) with a rounded tip used in a gramophone to follow the groove on a record; a needle [modif of L *stilus* stake, stylus – more at STYLE]

**¹stymie** *also* **stymy** /'stiemi/ *n* a condition on a golf putting green where the path of a ball to the hole is blocked by another player's ball [perh fr Sc *stymie* person with poor eyesight]

**²stymie** *also* **stymy** *vt* **stymieing** *also* **stymying** **1** to block (an opponent) at golf by interposing one's own ball before the hole **2** *informal* to present an obstacle to; thwart ⟨*our plan was* ~d *by bad weather*⟩

**¹styptic** /'stiptik/ *adj* tending to contract or bind; astringent; *esp* tending to check bleeding [ME *stiptik*, fr L *stypticus*, fr Gk *styptikos*, fr *styphein* to contract]

**²styptic** *n* a styptic drug

**styptic pencil** *n* a cylindrical stick of a medicated styptic substance used esp in shaving to stop the bleeding from small cuts

**styrax** /'stie·əraks, 'stieraks/ *n* STORAX (bark and sweet resin from Asiatic tree) [L, fr Gk]

**styrene** /'stie·əreen, 'stiereen/ *n* a colourless liquid chemical compound, $C_6H_5CH=CH_2$, containing double chemical bonds, and used chiefly in making synthetic rubber, resins, and plastics – compare POLYSTYRENE [ISV, fr L *styrax*]

**suable** /'s(y)ooh·əbl/ *adj* liable to be sued in court – **suably** *adv*, **suability** *n*

**suasion** /'swayzh(ə)n/ *n*, *formal* the act of influencing or persuading [ME, fr L *suasion-*, *suasio*, fr *suasus*, pp of *suadēre* to urge, persuade; akin to L *suavis*] – **suasive** *adj*, **suasively** *adv*, **suasiveness** *n*

**suave** /swahv/ *adj* **1** smoothly though often superficially affable and polite **2** smooth or blandly elegant in quality ⟨*a* ~ *performance*⟩ [MF, pleasant, sweet, fr L *suavis* – more at SWEET] – **suavely** *adv*, **suaveness** *n*, **suavity** *n*

   **synonyms Suave, smooth, urbane, bland, diplomatic,** and **politic** can all mean "ingratiatingly tactful and polite". **Suave** and **smooth** imply sophisticated polish and the avoidance of social friction ⟨**suave** *apologies*⟩, sometimes with the suggestion of insincerity ⟨*a* **smooth** *young salesman*⟩. **Urbane** suggests a confident courtesy based on wide social experience. **Bland** stresses lack of irritation, and placid affability ⟨*a* **bland** *old cleric*⟩. **Diplomatic** and **politic** apply particularly to tactful behaviour, with **politic** emphasizing the shrewd handling of others for one's own ends. *antonyms* bluff, gauche

**¹sub** /sub/ *n*, *informal* a substitute

**²sub** *vi* **-bb-** *informal* to act as a substitute

**³sub** *n* a subeditor

**⁴sub** *vt* **-bb-** to subedit

**⁵sub** *n*, *Br informal* a small loan; *esp* an advance on future earnings [short for *subsistence*] – **sub** *vt*

**⁶sub** *n*, *Br informal* a subscription, dues ⟨*pay my* ~ *to the Labour Party*⟩

**⁷sub** *n*, *informal* a submarine

**⁸sub** *n* a photographic SUBSTRATUM (thin coating of gelatine) [short for *substratum*]

**⁹sub** *vt* **-bb-** to apply a SUBSTRATUM (e g a coating of gelatine) to (e g a photographic film)

**¹⁰sub** *vt* **-bb-** to subcontract

**sub-** /sub-/ *prefix* **1** under; beneath; below ⟨*subsoil*⟩ ⟨*submarine*⟩ ⟨*subabdominal*⟩ **2a** subordinate; secondary; next in rank below ⟨*subeditor*⟩ **b** subordinate portion of; subdivision of ⟨*subcommittee*⟩ ⟨*subspecies*⟩ ⟨*subculture*⟩ **c** repeated or further instance of (a specified action or process) ⟨*subcontract*⟩ ⟨*sublet*⟩ **3a** bearing an incomplete, partial, or inferior resemblance to; approximately ⟨*subdominant*⟩ ⟨*subovate*⟩ ⟨*subVictorian*⟩ ⟨*subliterature*⟩ **b** of a chemical compound containing less than the usual or normal amount of (a specified element or chemical group) in its molecular structure ⟨*suboxide*⟩ **4a** almost; nearly ⟨*suberect*⟩ **b** adjacent to; bordering on ⟨*subarctic*⟩ [ME, fr L, under, from below, up, near, fr *sub* under, close to – more at UP]

**subacid** /sub'asid/ *adj* **1** moderately acid ⟨~ *fruit juices*⟩ **2** rather tart ⟨~ *comments*⟩ [L *subacidus*, fr *sub-* + *acidus* acid] – **subacidly** *adv*, **subacidness** *n*, **subacidity** *n*

**subacute** /,subə'kyooht/ *adj* moderately acute ⟨*a* ~ *angle*⟩ ⟨*a* ~ *flower petal*⟩ ⟨~ *inflammation*⟩ – **subacutely** *adv*

**subadult** /,sub'adult; *also* ,subə'dult/ *n* an individual (e g an insect) that has passed through the juvenile period but not yet attained typical adult characteristics – **subadult** *adj*

**subaerial** /sub'eəriəl/ *adj* situated, formed, or occurring on or near the surface of the earth ⟨~ *erosion*⟩ ⟨~ *roots*⟩ – **subaerially** *adv*

**subahdar, subadar** /'soohbə,dah/ *n* the chief Indian officer of an Indian company in the former British Indian army [Per *ṣūb-adār* governor of a province]

**subalpine** /,sub'alpien/ *adj* **1** of the lower slopes of the Alps **2** *cap* of or growing on high upland slopes below the treeline

**¹subaltern** /'subəlt(ə)n/ *adj* low in rank or status; subordinate [LL *subalternus*, fr L *sub-* + *alternus* alternate, fr *alter* other (of two) – more at ALTER]

**²subaltern** *n* somebody holding a subordinate position; *specif*, *Br* a commissioned officer in the Army ranking below captain

**subalternate** /,subawl'tuhnət/ *n*, *philosophy* a PARTICULAR proposition that may be inferred from a general one (UNIVERSAL)

**subalternation** /,subawltə'naysh(ə)n/ *n*, *philosophy* the relation of a subalternate to a UNIVERSAL (logical proposition applying to a whole category of things)

**subantarctic** /,suban'tahktik/ *adj* (characteristic) of or being a region just outside the ANTARCTIC CIRCLE – compare SUBARCTIC

**subapical** /sub'aypikl/ *adj* situated below or near an APEX (top) – **subapically** *adv*

**subapostolic** /,sub,apə'stolik/ *adj* of the age immediately following that of the Apostles

**,sub-'aqua** /,sub 'akwə/ *adj* of underwater recreations or sports (e g SKIN DIVING with an aqualung) [L *sub aqua* under water]

**subaquatic** /,subə'kwotik, -ə'kwatik/ *adj* **1** of a plant living in wet areas round the edges of ponds, streams, etc **2** of life, conditions, or pursuits under water [ISV]

**subaqueous** /,sub'akwiəs, -'aykwiəs/ *adj* existing, formed, or taking place in or under water ⟨*a precipitate formed in the* ~ *layer in the test tube*⟩

**subarctic** /,sub'ahktik/ *adj* (characteristic) of or being a region immediately outside the ARCTIC CIRCLE – compare SUBANTARCTIC – **subarctic** *n*

**subassembly** /'subə,sembli/ *n* an assembled unit (e g a machine component) designed to be incorporated with other units in a finished product

**subatmospheric** /,subatmə'sferik/ *adj* less or lower than that of the atmosphere ⟨~ *temperatures*⟩

**subatomic** /,subə'tomik/ *adj* of or being particles or processes occurring within an atom or particles smaller than an atom

**subaudible** /,sub'awdəbl/ *adj*, *of a sound* having a frequency or intensity below the limit of hearing

**subaudition** /,subaw'dish(ə)n/ *n*, *formal* **1** the act of understanding or supplying something implied but not expressed **2** something that is understood or supplied by implication in comprehending a text [LL *subaudition-*, *subauditio*, fr *subauditus*, pp of *subaudire* to understand, fr L *sub-* + *audire* to hear – more at AUDIBLE]

**subaverage** /sub'av(ə)rij/ *adj* of a lower level or quality than a norm ⟨~ *intelligence*⟩ ⟨~ *education*⟩

**subbase** /'sub,bays/ *n* an underlying support (e g a pedestal foot or skirting) placed below what is normally considered a base; *esp* crushed stone or other easily drained filling used under a roadbed

**subbasement** /'sub,baysmənt/ *n* a basement below the true basement of a building

**subbing** /'subing/ *n* SUBSTRATUM e (thin coating of gelatine on a film)

**subcabinet** /'sub,kab(ə)nit/ *adj* of or being a high administrative position in the US government that ranks below the cabinet level

**subcalibre** /,sub'kalibə/ *adj*, *of ammunition* of smaller calibre than the barrel used for firing

**subcelestial** /,subsi'lestiəl/ *adj*, *formal* situated beneath the heavens; *specif* worldly

**subcellular** /,sub'selyoolə/ *adj* (occurring) within living cells ⟨~ *processes*⟩; *also* derived from the artificial disruption of cells ⟨~ *particles*⟩

**subchloride** /,sub'klawried/ *n* **1** a compound of chlorine and another chemical element containing a relatively small proportion of chlorine **2** a BASIC chloride [ISV]

**subclass** /'sub,klahs/ *n* a division of a class: e g **a** a category in the biological classification of living things ranking immediately below a class **b** a subset

**subclavian** /,sub'klayviən/ *adj* (of or being an artery, nerve, etc) situated under the collarbone [NL *subclavius*, fr *sub-* + *clavicula* clavicle] – **subclavian** *n*

**subclimax** /,sub'kliemaks/ *n* an ecological stage or community that immediately precedes a CLIMAX (stable ecological state); *esp* one held in relative stability by fire or through the influence of soil or biological factors

**subclinical** /,sub'klinikl/ *adj* having symptoms that are so slight, esp because the condition has not developed sufficiently, that they are not detectable by the usual clinical tests ⟨*a ~ infection*⟩ – **subclinically** *adv*

**subcommittee** /'sʌbkə,miti/ *n taking sing or pl vb* a subdivision of a committee usu organized for a specific purpose

**subcompact** /,sʌb'kɒmpakt/ *n, NAm* a small motor car

¹**subconscious** /,sʌb'kɒnʃəs/ *adj* **1** *psychology* existing in the mind but not admitted to consciousness ⟨*his ~ motive*⟩ **2** imperfectly or incompletely conscious ⟨*a ~ state*⟩ □ compare UNCONSCIOUS – **subconsciously** *adv*, **subconsciousness** *n*

²**subconscious** *n, psychology* the mental activities below the threshold of consciousness

**subcontinent** /,sʌb'kɒntinənt/ *n* **1** a landmass (eg Greenland) of great size but smaller than any of the generally recognized continents **2** a vast subdivision of a continent; *specif, often cap* the Indian subcontinent – **subcontinental** *adj*

¹**subcontract** /,sʌbkən'trakt/ *vt* **1** to engage another person, company, etc (THIRD PARTY) to perform under a subcontract all or part of (work included in an original contract) **2** to undertake (work) under a subcontract ~ *vi* to let out or undertake work under a subcontract

²**subcontract** /,sʌb'kɒntrakt/ *n* a contract between a party to an original contract and another person, company, etc (THIRD PARTY); *esp* one to provide all or a specified part of the work or materials required in the original contract

**subcontractor** /'sʌbkən,traktə/ *n* a person or company contracting to perform part or all of another's contract

**subcontrariety** /,sʌbkɒntrə'rieəti/ *n, philosophy* the relation existing between subcontrary propositions in logic

**subcontrary** /,sʌb'kɒntrəri/ *n, philosophy* either of a pair of propositions in logic so related to each other that while both may be true both cannot be false – **subcontrary** *adj*

**subcool** /,sʌb'koohl/ *vt* SUPERCOOL (cool below freezing point)

**subcortex** /,sʌb'kawteks/ *n* the parts of the brain immediately beneath the CEREBRAL CORTEX (area of brain controlling higher-thought ability) [NL]

**subcortical** /,sʌb'kawtikl/ *adj* of, involving, or being groups of NERVE CELLS below the CEREBRAL CORTEX (area of brain controlling higher-thought ability) ⟨*~ lesions*⟩

**subcritical** /,sʌb'kritikl/ *adj* **1** *of a material capable of nuclear fission* of insufficient size to sustain a CHAIN REACTION (reaction which promotes continuing similar reaction) ⟨*a ~ mass of fissile material*⟩ **2** designed for use with material (eg uranium) capable of nuclear fission of subcritical mass ⟨*a ~ reactor*⟩

**subcrustal** /,sʌb'krʌstl/ *adj* situated or occurring below a crust, esp the crust of the earth

**subculture** /'sʌb,kʌlchə, ,-'--/ *n* **1a** a CULTURE (living cells, tissues, etc maintained in artificially prepared media) (eg of bacteria) grown from another culture **b** an act or instance of producing a subculture **2** (an ethnic, regional or economic group having) a shared pattern of behaviour, beliefs, attitudes, and values within a society and distinguishable from the overall culture of that society – **subcultural** *adj*, **subculture** *vb*

**subcutaneous** /,sʌbkyooh'taynyəs, -niəs/ *adj* situated, living, used, or made under the skin ⟨*~ parasites*⟩ ⟨*~ fat*⟩ [LL *subcutaneus*, fr L *sub-* + *cutis* skin – more at HIDE] – **subcutaneously** *adv*

**subdeacon** /,sʌb'deekən/ *n* a cleric ranking below a deacon: eg **a** a cleric in the former lowest of the ROMAN CATHOLIC major orders **b** a cleric in minor orders in an Eastern church **c** a minister performing various duties (eg reading the Epistle) in a high mass of the ROMAN CATHOLIC church [ME *subdecon*, fr LL *subdiaconus*, fr L *sub-* + LL *diaconus* deacon]

**subdean** /sʌb'deen/ *n* an administrative assistant to a university dean

**subdiaconate** /,sʌbdie'akənit, -nayt/ *n* the office or rank of a subdeacon

**subdivide** /,sʌbdi'vied, '--,-/ *vt* **1** to divide the parts of into more parts **2** to divide into several parts; *esp* to divide (a tract of land) into building plots ~ *vi* to separate or become separated into subdivisions [ME *subdividen*, fr LL *subdividere*, fr L *sub-* + *dividere* to divide] – **subdividable** *adj*, **subdivider** *n*, **subdivision** *n*

**subdominant** /,sʌb'dɒminənt/ *n* **1** something dominant to an inferior or partial degree (eg an ecologically important form of life subordinate in influence to the forms dominant in a community) **2** the fourth note of a DIATONIC scale (ordinary 8-note musical scale) – called also FOURTH – **subdominance** *n*, **subdominant** *adj*

**subdue** /səb'dyooh/ *vt* **1** to conquer and bring into subjection; vanquish **2** to bring under control, esp by an exertion of the will; curb ⟨*~d her foolish fears*⟩ **3** to bring under cultivation **4** to reduce the intensity or degree of (eg sound or colour) [ME *sodewen*, *subduen* (influenced in form and meaning by L *subdere* to subject), fr MF *soduire* to seduce (influenced in meaning by L *seducere* to seduce), fr L *subducere* to withdraw, fr *sub-* up + *ducere* to lead] – **subduer** *n*

**subdued** /səb'dyoohd/ *adj* **1** brought under control (as if) by military conquest **2** reduced or lacking in force, intensity, or strength ⟨*~ colours*⟩ – **subduedly** *adv*

**subedit** /'sʌb,edit/ *vt* **1** to act as subeditor of **2** *chiefly Br* to edit (eg newspaper copy) in preparation for printing; COPY-EDIT [back-formation fr *subeditor*]

**subeditor** /,sʌb'editə/ *n* **1** an assistant editor **2** *chiefly Br* somebody who edits copy for printing; COPY EDITOR – **subeditorial** *adj*

**subentry** /'sʌb,entri/ *n* an entry (eg in a catalogue or an account) made under a more general entry

**subepidermal** /,sʌbepi'duhml/ *adj* situated beneath or constituting the innermost part of the EPIDERMIS (thin outer layer of the skin)

**suber** /'soohbə, 'syoohbə/ *n* corky plant tissue (PHELLEM) [NL, fr L, cork tree, cork]

**suberect** /,sʌbi'rekt/ *adj* standing or growing in a nearly erect position ⟨*a ~ shrub*⟩

**suberin** /'syoohbərin/ *n* a complex fatty or waxy substance that is the basis of cork [Fr *subérine*, fr L *suber* cork]

**suber·ization, -isation** /,syoohbərie'zaysh(ə)n/ *n* conversion of plant cell walls into corky tissue by impregnation with suberin – **suberized** *adj*

**subfamily** /'sʌb,faməli/ *n* **1** a category in the biological classification of living things ranking immediately below a FAMILY **2** *taking sing or pl vb* a major subgroup of languages within a language family; *specif* one including more than one branch ⟨*the Indo-Iranian ~ of Indo-European*⟩ [ISV]

**subfield** /'sʌb,feeld, -,fiəld/ *n* a subset of a mathematical FIELD that is itself a field

**subfix** /'sʌb,fiks/ *n* a sign, letter, or character written below or below and beside another [*sub-* + *-fix* (as in *prefix*)]

**subfreezing** /,sʌb'freezing/ *adj* lower than is required to produce freezing ⟨*~ temperature*⟩; *also* marked by a subfreezing temperature ⟨*~ weather*⟩

¹**subfusc** /'sʌb,fusk/ *adj* drab, dusky ⟨*a grey, impoverished, ~ community*⟩ [L *subfuscus* brownish, dusky, fr *sub-* + *fuscus* dark brown – more at DUSK]

²**subfusc** *n* formal academic dress for members of a university, esp Oxford University

**subgenus** /'sʌb,jeenəs/ *n* a category in the biological classification of living things ranking below a genus and above a species [NL]

**subglacial** /,sʌb'glays(h)yəl/ *adj* of the bottom of a glacier or the area immediately underlying a glacier – **subglacially** *adv*

**subgrade** /'sʌb,grayd/ *n* a surface of earth or rock levelled off to receive a foundation (eg of a road)

**subgroup** /'sʌb,groohp/ *n* **1** *taking sing or pl vb* a subordinate group whose members usu share some common distinguishing quality **2** a subset of a mathematical GROUP that is itself a group

**subhead** /'sʌb,hed/, **subheading** /-,heding/ *n* **1** a heading of a subdivision (eg in a document) **2** a subordinate caption, title, or headline (eg in a newspaper)

**subhuman** /,sʌb'hyoohmən/ *adj* less than human: eg **a** failing to attain the level (eg of morality or intelligence) associated with or expected of normal human beings ⟨*~ behaviour*⟩ **b** unsuitable to or unfit for human beings ⟨*~ living conditions*⟩ **c** of a group of animals lower than human beings ⟨*the ~ primates*⟩

**subimago** /,sʌbi'maygoh/ *adj* the winged form of a mayfly that occurs between the NYMPH (larval form) and the IMAGO (adult form) [NL]

**subinterval** /'sʌb,intəv(ə)l/ *n* **1** a difference (INTERVAL) in musical pitch that is a subdivision of a larger or major interval **2** *maths* an INTERVAL (set of numbers between two given numbers) that is a subdivision of a larger interval

**subirrigate** /,sʌb'irigayt/ *vt* to water from beneath (eg by the periodic rise of underground water); *also* to irrigate below the surface (eg by a system of underground porous pipes) – **subirrigation** *n*

**subito** /'soohbitoh/ *adv* immediately, suddenly – used as a direction in music [It, fr L, suddenly, fr *subitus* sudden – more at SUDDEN]

**subjacent** /ˌsub'jays(ə)nt/ *adj, formal* **1** situated under or below; *also* situated lower though not directly below ⟨*hills and ~ valleys*⟩ **2** forming a basis; underlying ⟨*~ causes*⟩ [L *subjacent-, subjacens*, prp of *subjacēre* to lie under, fr *sub-* + *jacēre* to lie – more at ADJACENT] – **subjacency** *n*, **subjacently** *adv*

**¹subject** /'subjikt/ *n* **1** somebody who is placed under authority or control: eg **1a** a vassal **b(1)** somebody subject to a ruler (eg a monarch) and governed by his/her law **b(2)** somebody who lives in the territory of, enjoys the protection of, and owes allegiance to a sovereign power or state ⟨*a British ~*⟩ **2** *philosophy* **2a** something to which a quality, attribute, or relation may be attributed **b** a material or essential substance (SUBSTRATUM) **c** the entity (eg the mind or ego) that sustains or assumes the form of thought or consciousness; the self **3a** a department of knowledge or learning; the content of one course or of one part of an examination ⟨*take three ~s at A level*⟩ **b(1)** somebody or something that is acted upon ⟨*the helpless ~ of his cruelty*⟩ **b(2)** an individual whose reactions are studied **b(3)** *medicine* a dead body for anatomical study and dissection **c(1)** something concerning which something is said or done ⟨*a ~ of dispute*⟩ **c(2)** something represented or indicated in a work of art **d(1)** the part (TERM) of a logical proposition about which something is affirmed or denied; *also* that which is denoted by this term **d(2)** *linguistics* the word or phrase about which something is stated in a sentence or clause ⟨*in "paper is white", "paper" is the ~*⟩ **e** *music* the principal melodic phrase on which a musical composition or movement is based [ME, fr MF, fr L *subjectus* one under authority & *subjectum* subject of a proposition, fr masc & neut of *subjectus*, pp of *subicere* to subject, lit., to throw under, fr *sub-* + *jacere* to throw – more at JET] – **subjectless** *adj*

synonyms **Subject, object, topic,** and **theme** can all mean "that to which one's attention is directed". **Subject** and **object** are sometimes interchangeable ⟨*a* **subject**/*an* **object** *of study*⟩, but **subject** emphasizes that a thing is represented or treated of ⟨*the* **subject** *of a portrait*⟩ while **object** implies that a thing is directly examined ⟨*an* **object** *of ridicule*⟩. A **topic** is often one subsection or aspect of a **subject**. A **theme** is a general **subject**, or basic unifying idea ⟨*the title Persuasion states the* **theme** *of the novel*⟩.

**²subject** *adj* **1** owing obedience or allegiance to the power or dominion of another ⟨*~ nations*⟩ **2a** suffering a particular liability or exposure ⟨*~ to temptation*⟩ **b** having a tendency or inclination; prone ⟨*~ to colds*⟩ **3** dependent or conditional on something, esp for final validity ⟨*the plan is ~ to approval*⟩ □ usu + *to* – **subject to** depending on; conditionally upon ⟨subject to *your approval, I propose to operate*⟩

**³subject** /səb'jekt/ *vt* **1** to bring under control, dominion, or influence **2** to make liable; expose ⟨*pomposity ~s one to ridicule*⟩ **3** to cause to undergo something ⟨*~ someone to cross-examination*⟩ □ usu + *to* – **subjection** *n*

**¹subjective** /səb'jektiv/ *adj* **1** of or being a grammatical subject; *esp* NOMINATIVE (marking the subject of a verb) **2a(1)** relating to, arising from, or determined by the mind or self ⟨*~ reality*⟩ **a(2)** characteristic of or belonging to reality as seen or sensed by the thinking observer rather than as independent of the observer **b** relating to or being experience or knowledge as conditioned by personal mental characteristics or states **3a** peculiar to a particular individual; personal ⟨*~ judgments*⟩ **b** arising from conditions within the brain or sense organs and not directly caused by external stimuli ⟨*~ sensations*⟩ **c** arising out of or identified by means of one's awareness of one's own states and processes ⟨*a ~ symptom of disease*⟩ **d** lacking in reality or substance; illusory – **subjectively** *adv*, **subjectiveness** *n*, **subjectivize** *vt*, **subjectivity** *n*

**²subjective** *n* something that is subjective; *also* NOMINATIVE (grammatical case used for subject)

**subjective complement** *n* a grammatical complement (eg "sick" *in "he had fallen sick"*) referring to the subject of a linking verb

**subjectivism** /səb'jekti‚viz(ə)m/ *n, philosophy* **1a** a theory that limits knowledge to conscious states and elements **b** a theory that stresses the subjective elements in experience **2** a doctrine that individual feelings or reactions form the basis of moral or aesthetic judgments – **subjectivist** *n*, **subjectivistic** *adj*

**subject matter** *n* material presented for consideration in discussion, thought, or study

**subject teacher** *n* a teacher of one subject to various school forms – compare FORM TEACHER

**subjoin** /ˌsub'joyn/ *vt, formal* to annex, append ⟨*~ed a statement of expenses to his report*⟩ [MF *subjoindre*, fr L *subjungere* to join beneath, add, fr *sub-* + *jungere* to join – more at YOKE]

**sub judice** /ˌsub 'joohdisi/ *adv* before a judge or court; under judicial consideration; *esp* not yet judicially decided and therefore unable to be discussed or reported [L]

**subjugate** /'subjoogayt/ *vt* to conquer and hold in subjection [ME *subjugaten*, fr L *subjugatus*, pp of *subjugare*, lit., to bring under the yoke, fr *sub-* + *jugum* yoke – more at YOKE] – **subjugator** *n*, **subjugation** *n*

**subjunction** /səb'jungksh(ə)n/ *n, formal* **1** subjoining or being subjoined **2** something subjoined

**¹subjunctive** /səb'jungktiv/ *adj* of or being the grammatical MOOD (eg that of "were" in *"I wish I were in Philadelphia"*) that represents an act or state not as fact but as dependent or possible or viewed emotionally (eg with doubt or desire) [LL *subjunctivus*, fr L *subjunctus*, pp of *subjungere* to join beneath, subordinate]

**²subjunctive** *n* (a verb form expressing) the subjunctive mood

**subkingdom** /'sub‚kingd(ə)m/ *n* a category in the biological classification of living things ranking immediately below a KINGDOM

**sublate** /sə'blayt/ *vt, chiefly philosophy* **1** to negate, deny **2** to cancel, eliminate [L *sublatus* (pp of *tollere* to take away, lift up), fr *sub-* up + *latus*, pp of *ferre* to carry – more at SUB-, TOLERATE, BEAR] – **sublation** *n*

**¹sublease** /'sub‚lees/ *n* a lease by a tenant of the whole or part of leased premises to a subtenant for a shorter term than his/her own, and under which he/she retains some right or interest under the original lease

**²sublease** /‚sub'lees/ *vt* to make or obtain a sublease of

**¹sublet** /‚sub'let/ *vi* -tt-; **sublet 1a** to lease or rent all or part of (a leased or rented property) to another person **b** to lease or rent all or part of (a leased or rented property) from the original lessee or tenant **2** to subcontract *vt* to lease or rent (part of) a leased or rented property

**²sublet** /'sub‚let/ *n* property, esp housing, obtained by or available for subletting

**sublethal** /‚sub'leeth(ə)l/ *adj* (slightly) less than lethal ⟨*~ mutation*⟩ ⟨*~ pollution*⟩ – **sublethally** *adv*

**sublieutenant** /‚sublef'tenənt; *Royal Navy* -lə'tenənt; *NAm* -looh'tenənt/ *n* – see MILITARY RANKS table

**sublimate** /'sublimayt/ *vt* **1** SUBLIME 1 **2** *psychology* to divert the expression of (an instinctual, esp sexual, desire or impulse) from a primitive form to one that is considered more socially or culturally acceptable [ML *sublimatus*, pp of *sublimare*] – **sublimation** *n*

**¹sublime** /sə'bliem/ *vt* **1** to cause to pass from the solid to the vapour state without passing through the liquid state (and again condense to solid form) **2a(1)** to elevate or exalt, esp in dignity or honour **a(2)** to render finer (eg in purity or excellence) **b** to convert (something inferior) into something of higher worth *~ vi* to pass directly from the solid to the vapour state [ME *sublimen*, fr MF *sublimer*, fr ML *sublimare* to refine, sublime, fr L, to elevate, fr *sublimis*] – **sublimable** *adj*, **sublimer** *n*

**²sublime** *adj* **1** lofty, grand, or exalted in thought, expression, or manner **2** of outstanding spiritual, intellectual, or moral worth **3** tending to inspire awe, usu because of elevated quality (eg of beauty, nobility, or grandeur) [L *sublimis*, lit., to or in a high position, fr *sub* under, up to + *limen* threshold, lintel – more at UP, LIMB] – **sublimely** *adv*, **sublimeness** *n*

**subliminal** /‚sub'liminl/ *adj* **1** *of a stimulus* inadequate to produce a conscious sensation or perception – compare SUPRALIMINAL **2** existing, functioning, or having effects below the threshold of consciousness ⟨*the ~ mind*⟩ ⟨*~ advertising*⟩ [*sub-* + L *limin-, limen* threshold] – **subliminally** *adv*

**sublimity** /sə'bliməti/ *n* being sublime; *also* something sublime or exalted

**sublingual** /‚sub'ling-gwəl/ *adj* situated, occurring, or administered under the tongue [NL *sublingualis*, fr L *sub-* + *lingua* tongue – more at TONGUE] – **sublingually** *adv*

**¹sublittoral** /‚sub'litorəl/ *adj* **1** situated, occurring, or growing between the high and low watermarks **2** constituting the sublittoral

**²sublittoral** *n* **1** the region in the sea between the lowest point exposed by a very low tide and the edge of the CONTINENTAL SHELF **2** the region in a lake between the limit of rooted plant growth and the depth at which the lake consists of distinct layers of different temperatures

**sublunary** /ˌsub'loohnəri/ *also* **sublunar** /-'loohnə/ *adj, poetic* **1** situated beneath the moon; terrestrial **2** mundane ⟨*dull ~ lovers – John Donne*⟩ [modif of LL *sublunaris*, fr L *sub-* + *luna* moon – more at LUNAR]

**subluxation** /ˌsubluk'saysh(ə)n/ *n, medicine* partial dislocation (eg of one of the bones in a joint) [*sub-* + *luxation*]

**submachine gun** /ˌsubmə'sheen/ *n* an automatic or semiautomatic portable rapid-firing firearm of limited range that uses pistol-type ammunition

**submandibular** /ˌsubman'dibyoolə/ *adj* submaxillary

**submarginal** /sub'mahjinl/ *adj* **1** next to a margin or a marginal part or structure ⟨*~ spots on an insect wing*⟩ **2** falling below a minimum necessary for some purpose (eg economic exploitation) ⟨*~ hill farms*⟩ ⟨*~ economic conditions*⟩ – **submarginally** *adv*

**¹submarine** /ˌsubmə'reen/ *adj* being, acting, or growing under water, esp in the sea ⟨*~ plants*⟩

**²submarine** /'submə,reen, ˌ--'-/ *n* **1** a vessel designed for undersea operations; *esp* a submarine warship that is armed chiefly with torpedoes or missiles and uses electric, diesel, or nuclear propulsion **2** *chiefly NAm* a large sandwich made from a long roll split and generously filled (eg with cold meats, cheese, onion, lettuce, and tomato)

**submariner** /'submə,reenə, sub'marinə/ *n* a crewman of a submarine

**submaxilla** /ˌsub'maksilə, -mak'silə/ *n, pl* **submaxillae** /-lie/ *also* **submaxillas** the lower jaw or lower of two upper jawbones; *specif* a human jawbone [NL]

**¹submaxillary** /ˌsubmak'siləri/ *adj* **1** of or situated below the lower jaw **2** of, being, or associated with either of a pair of submaxillary salivary glands

**²submaxillary** *n* a submaxillary part (eg an artery or bone)

**submaximal** /ˌsub'maksiml/ *adj* of, being, or producing a physiological response lower than the maximum obtainable

**submediant** /ˌsub'meedi·ənt/ *n* the sixth note of a DIATONIC scale (ordinary 8-note musical scale), represented in sol-fa by *lah* – called also SIXTH

**submerge** /səb'muhj/ *vt* **1** to put under water **2** to cover (as if) with water; inundate ⟨*~d the town*⟩ **3** to make obscure or subordinate; obliterate ⟨*personal lives ~d by professional responsibilities*⟩ *~ vi* to go under water [L *submergere*, fr *sub-* + *mergere* to plunge – more at MERGE] – **submergence** *n*, **submergible** *adj*

**submerged** /səb'muhjd/ *adj* **1** covered with water **2** SUBMERSED b **3** sunk in poverty and misery **4** cryptic, hidden ⟨*a ~ gene effect*⟩

**submerse** /səb'muhs/ *vt* to submerge [L *submersus*, pp of *submergere*] – **submersion** *n*

**submersed** /səb'muhst/ *adj* submerged: eg **a** covered with water **b** (adapted for) growing under water ⟨*~ plants*⟩

**¹submersible** /səb'muhsəbl/ *adj* capable of going under water

**²submersible** *n* something submersible; *esp* a vessel used for deep-sea exploration and maintenance work that is either navigable or attached to a surface ship by cable

**submicroscopic** /ˌsubmiekrə'skopik/ *adj* **1** too small to be seen in an ordinary microscope **2** of or dealing with the very minute ⟨*the ~ world*⟩ [ISV] – **submicroscopically** *adv*

**subminiature** /ˌsub'minəchə/ *adj* very small – used esp of electronic components that are smaller than those designated *miniature* [ISV]

**submission** /səb'mish(ə)n/ *n* **1a** an act of submitting something for consideration, inspection, comment, etc **b** *law* an agreement to submit a dispute to legal arbitration; *also* the document setting out the agreement **2** the condition of being submissive, humble, or compliant **3a** an act of submitting to the authority or control of another **b** a forced surrender in wrestling *synonyms* see ²SURRENDER [ME, fr MF, fr L *submission-, submissio* act of lowering, fr *submissus*, pp of *submittere*] – **submissible** *adj*

**submissive** /səb'misiv/ *adj* willing to submit to others – **submissively** *adv*, **submissiveness** *n*

**submit** /səb'mit/ *vb* **-tt-** *vt* **1a** to yield or surrender to the authority or will of another **b** to subject to a process, condition, or practice **2a** to send or commit to another (eg for decision or judgment) ⟨*~ a question to the courts*⟩ **b** to make available; offer ⟨*~ a bid on a contract*⟩ ⟨*~ a report*⟩ **c** to put forward as an opinion; suggest ⟨*we ~ that the charge is not proved*⟩ *~ vi* **1a** to yield or surrender oneself to the authority or will of another **b** to permit oneself to be subjected to something ⟨*had to ~ to surgery*⟩ **2** to defer to the opinion or authority of

another □ (*except 2b & 2c*) usu + *to synonyms* see ¹YIELD [ME *submitten*, fr L *submittere* to lower, submit, fr *sub-* + *mittere* to send] – **submittal** *n*

**submitochondrial** /ˌsubmietoh'kondriəl/ *adj* (composed) of particles obtained by ULTRACENTRIFUGATION (high-speed spinning in a device for separating particles of different sizes) of MITOCHONDRIA (energy-producing bodies in a cell) ⟨*~ fraction*⟩

**submontane** /ˌsub'montayn/ *adj* situated at the foot or near the base of a mountain [LL *submontanus* lying under a mountain, fr L *sub-* + *mont-, mons* mountain – more at MOUNT]

**submucosa** /ˌsubmyooh'kohzə/ *n, anatomy* a supporting layer of loose CONNECTIVE TISSUE directly under a MUCOUS MEMBRANE (tissue lining body cavities and passages) [NL] – **submucosal** *adj*, **submucosally** *adv*

**submucous** /ˌsub'myoohkəs, ˌ-,--/ *adj or n, anatomy* (of) submucosa

**submultiple** /ˌsub'multipl/ *n* a number that can divide another number exactly, without a remainder; a factor ⟨*8 is a ~ of 72*⟩

**subnormal** /ˌsub'nawməl/ *adj* **1** lower or smaller than normal **2** having less of something, esp intelligence, than is normal; *specif* having an INTELLIGENCE QUOTIENT of less than 70 *synonyms* see ABNORMAL [ISV] – **subnormally** *adv*, **subnormality** *n*

**subnuclear** /ˌsub'nyoohkliə/ *adj* below the level of organization of the nucleus of a living cell ⟨*~ particles*⟩

**suboceanic** /ˌsubohshi'anik/ *adj* situated, taking place, or formed under water, esp beneath the sea or its bottom ⟨*~ oil resources*⟩

**suboptimal** /ˌsub'optiml/ *adj* suboptimum

**suboptimum** /ˌsub'optiməm/ *adj* less than optimum

**suborbital** /ˌsub'awbitl/ *adj* **1** situated beneath the eyesocket **2** being or involving less than one complete orbit (eg of the earth or moon) ⟨*a spacecraft's ~ flight*⟩; *also* intended for suborbital flight ⟨*a ~ rocket*⟩

**suborder** /'sub,awdə/ *n* a division of an order; *esp* a category in the biological classification of living things ranking immediately below an ORDER

**¹subordinate** /sə'bawdinət/ *adj* **1** placed in or occupying a lower class or rank; inferior **2** subject to or controlled by authority **3a** *of a clause* functioning as a noun, adjective, or adverb in a complex sentence ⟨*the ~ clause "when he heard" in "he laughed when he heard"*⟩ **b** *of a conjunction* grammatically subordinating ⟨*the ~ conjunction "because" in "they climbed it because it was there"*⟩ [ME *subordinat*, fr ML *subordinatus*, pp of *subordinare* to subordinate, fr L *sub-* + *ordinare* to order – more at ORDAIN] – **subordinate** *n*, **subordinately** *adv*, **subordinateness** *n*

**²subordinate** /sə'bawdinayt/ *vt* **1** to place in a lower order or class **2** to make subject or subservient; subdue – **subordinative** *adj*, **subordination** *n*

**suborn** /sə'bawn/ *vt* to induce (someone) to commit perjury or another illegal act [MF *suborner*, fr L *subornare*, fr *sub-* secretly + *ornare* to furnish, equip – more at ORNATE] – **suborner** *n*

**subovate** /ˌsub'ohvayt, ˌ-,--/ *adj* approximately egg-shaped

**suboxide** /ˌsub'oksied/ *n* an OXIDE (compound of oxygen with one other chemical element or group) containing a relatively small proportion of oxygen [ISV]

**subparallel** /ˌsub'parəlel/ *adj* nearly parallel; not quite parallel

**subphylum** /ˌsub'fieləm/ *n* a division of a PHYLUM; *esp* a category in the biological classification of living things ranking immediately below a phylum [NL]

**subplot** /'sub,plot/ *n* a subordinate plot in fiction or drama

**¹subpoena** /sə(b)'peenə/ *n* a writ commanding a person to appear in court in order to give evidence or produce documents [ME *suppena*, fr L *sub poena* under penalty (the first words of the writ)]

**²subpoena** *vt* **subpoenaing**; **subpoenaed** /-,peenəd/ to serve or summon with a subpoena

**subpolar** /ˌsub'pohlə/ *adj* (characteristic) of or being a region just outside a POLAR CIRCLE: **a** subantarctic **b** subarctic

**subpopulation** /'sub,popyoo,laysh(ə)n/ *n* an identifiable subdivision of a population

**sub-'postmaster**, *fem* **sub-postmistress** *n* somebody who has charge of a SUB-POST OFFICE and is an agent rather than an employee of the POST OFFICE

**sub-post office** *n* a POST OFFICE in the UK that is not wholly Government-owned and that offers a somewhat smaller range of services than a main post office

**subpotent** /ˌsubˈpoht(ə)nt/ *adj, of a drug or other preparation* less than effective – **subpotency** *n*

**subprogram** /ˈsubˌprohgram, -grəm/ *n* a semi-independent portion of a program (eg for a computer)

**subregion** /ˈsubˌreej(ə)n/ *n, ecology* a subdivision of a region; *esp* any of the primary divisions of a region with regard to the biological distribution of plants and animals [ISV] – **subregional** *adj*

**subring** /ˈsubˌring/ *n* a subset of a mathematical RING which is itself a ring

**subrogate** /ˈsubrəgayt/ *vt, formal* to put in the place of another; substitute [L *subrogatus*, pp of *subrogare, surrogare* – more at SURROGATE]

**subrogation** /ˌsubrəˈgaysh(ə)n/ *n* the substitution of one person for another as a creditor so that the new creditor succeeds to the former's rights

**sub rosa** /ˌsub ˈrohzə/ *adv* in strict confidence; secretly [NL, lit., under the rose; prob fr an old custom of hanging a rose over the council table to indicate that all present were sworn to secrecy]

**subroutine** /ˈsubroohˌteen/ *n* a subordinate routine; *esp* a sequence of computer instructions for performing a specified task that can be used repeatedly in a program or in different programs [ISV]

¹**subsample** /ˈsubˌsahmpl/ *vt* to draw statistical samples from a previously selected group or population); sample a sample of

²**subsample** *n* a sample or specimen obtained by subsampling

**subscribe** /səbˈskrieb/ *vt* **1** to write (one's name) underneath; sign **2a** to sign with one's own hand in token of consent or obligation **b** to give a written pledge to contribute; *also* to give in accordance with such a pledge ⟨~ *s large sums to charity*⟩ ~ *vi* **1** to sign one's name to a document **2a** to give consent or approval to something written by signing ⟨*found him unwilling to* ~ *to the agreement*⟩ **b** to give money (eg to charity) **c** to pay regularly in order to receive a publication or service; *also* to receive a periodical or service regularly on order **d** to agree to buy and pay for shares, esp of a new issue ⟨~ *d for 1000 shares*⟩ **3** to feel favourably disposed; agree ⟨*I* ~ *to your sentiments*⟩ □ (*2a, 2b, 2c, 3 vi*) usu + *to* [ME *subscriben*, fr L *subscribere*, lit., to write beneath, fr *sub-* + *scribere* to write – more at SCRIBE]

**subscriber** /səbˈskriebə/ *n* **1** somebody who subscribes **2** the owner of a telephone who pays rental and call charges

**subscriber trunk dialling** *n* the system by which a telephone user can dial direct to any telephone within the system without being connected by an operator

**subscript** /ˈsubˌskript/ *n* a distinguishing symbol or letter written immediately below or below and to the right or left of another character [L *subscriptus*, pp of *subscribere*] – **subscript** *adj*

**subscription** /səbˈskripsh(ə)n/ *n* **1a** the acceptance (eg of religious articles of faith) attested by the signing of one's name **b** the act of signing one's name (eg in witnessing a document) **2** something that is subscribed: eg **2a** *formal* an autograph signature **b** a sum subscribed **c(1)** a purchase by prepayment for a certain number of issues (eg of a periodical) **c(2)** an application to purchase shares of a new issue **d** a method of offering or presenting a series of public performances, esp in the USA ⟨*a* ~ *concert*⟩ **e** *Br* membership fees paid regularly [ME *subscripcioun* signature, fr L *subscription-, subscriptio*, fr *subscriptus*, pp of *subscribere*]

**subscription library** *n* a LENDING LIBRARY to which borrowers pay a membership fee either instead of or in addition to a charge for each book borrowed

**subsection** /ˈsubˌseksh(ə)n/ *n* **1** a subdivision of a section **2** a subordinate part or branch

**subsellium** /ˌsubˈseliəm/ *n* MISERICORD (hinged choir seat) [L, low seat, fr *sub-* + *sella* seat, chair]

¹**subsequence** /ˈsubsikwəns/ *n, formal* being subsequent; *also* a subsequent event

²**subsequence** /ˌsubˈseekwəns/ *n* a mathematical SEQUENCE (ordered set of numbers, symbols, etc, corresponding to ordinary numbers) that is part of another sequence

**subsequent** /ˈsubsikwənt/ *adj* following in time or order; succeeding [ME, fr L *subsequent-, subsequens*, prp of *subsequi* to follow closely, fr *sub-* near + *sequi* to follow – more at SUB-, SUE] – **subsequent** *n*, **subsequently** *adv*, **subsequentness** *n*

*usage* Things happen **subsequent(ly)** *to* other things ⟨*a discussion* **subsequent** *to the lecture*⟩. **synonyms** see CONSEQUENT

**subsere** /ˈsubˌsiə/ *n* a secondary SUCCESSION (sequence of

ecological changes in the development of a plant community) arising after a CLIMAX (stable ecological state) community has been interrupted (eg by fire) [*sub-* + ²*sere*]

**subserve** /səbˈsuhv/ *vt, formal* to serve as a means of promoting (eg a purpose or action) [L *subservire* to serve, be subservient, fr *sub-* + *servire* to serve]

**subservience** /səbˈsuhviˌəns/, **subserviency** /-si/ *n* **1** a subservient or subordinate place or function **2** obsequious servility

**subservient** /səbˈsuhviˌənt/ *adj* **1** useful in an inferior capacity; subordinate **2** serving as a means to promote some purpose **3** obsequiously submissive; servile [L *subservient-, subserviens*, prp of *subservire*] – **subserviently** *adv*

**subset** /ˈsubˌset/ *n* a set that is included within a larger set; *esp* a mathematical SET each of whose elements is also an element of a given set

**subshrub** /ˈsubˌshrub/ *n* **1** a usu low-growing bushy shrub having woody stems and branches with nonwoody tips that die back annually **2** UNDERSHRUB (low-growing shrub) – **subshrubby** *adj*

**subside** /səbˈsied/ *vi* **1** to sink or fall to the bottom; settle **2a** *of water* to sink to a low or lower level; *esp* to return to a normal level **b** *of ground* to cave in; collapse **3** to let oneself settle down; sink ⟨~ *d into a chair*⟩ **4** to become quiet; lessen ⟨*as the fever* ~ *s*⟩ ⟨*his anger* ~ *d*⟩ [L *subsidere*, fr *sub-* + *sidere* to sit down, sink; akin to L *sedēre* to sit – more at SIT] – **subsidence** *n*

*usage* The pronunciation of **subsidence** as /səbˈsied(ə)ns/ rather than /ˈsubsid(ə)ns/ is recommended for BBC broadcasters.

¹**subsidiary** /səbˈsidyəri, -ˈsij(ə)ri/ *adj* **1** serving to help or supplement; auxiliary ⟨~ *details*⟩ **2** of secondary importance; *specif* TRIBUTARY **3** ⟨*a* ~ *stream*⟩ [L *subsidiarius*, fr *subsidium* reserve troops] – **subsidiarily** *adv*

²**subsidiary** *n* one who or that which is subsidiary; *esp* a company wholly controlled by another – compare HOLDING COMPANY, INVESTMENT COMPANY

**subsid-ize, -ise** /ˈsubsiˌdiez/ *vt* to provide with a subsidy: eg **a** to purchase the assistance of by payment of a subsidy **b** to aid or promote (eg a private enterprise) with public money ⟨~ *a shipping line*⟩ – **subsidization** *n*, **subsidizer** *n*

**subsidy** /ˈsubsidi/ *n* a grant or gift of money: eg **a** a sum of money formerly granted by Parliament to the crown and raised by special taxation **b** money granted by one state to another, often in return for some assistance **c** a grant by a government to a person or organization (eg a company or cultural body) to assist an enterprise considered advantageous to the public △ subsidence [ME, fr L *subsidium* reserve troops, support, assistance, fr *sub-* near + *sedēre* to sit]

**subsist** /səbˈsist/ *vi* **1a** to have existence; be **b** to persist, continue **2** to have the bare necessities of life; be kept alive ⟨*to* ~ *on a pension*⟩ **3** *philosophy* **3a** to hold true **b** to be logically conceivable as the subject of true statements [LL *subsistere* to exist, fr L, to come to a halt, remain, fr *sub-* + *sistere* to come to a stand; akin to L *stare* to stand – more at STAND]

**subsistence** /səbˈsist(ə)ns/ *n* **1a(1)** real being; existence ⟨*an abstraction without real* ~⟩ **a(2)** the condition of remaining in existence; continuation, persistence **a(3)** inherence, inseparability ⟨~ *of a quality in a body*⟩ **b** *philosophy* something by which an individual is what it is **c** *philosophy* the character possessed by whatever is logically conceivable **2** the means of subsisting: eg **2a** the minimum (eg of food and shelter) necessary to support life **b** a source or means of obtaining the bare necessities of life [ME, fr LL *subsistentia*, fr *subsistent-, subsistens*, prp of *subsistere*] – **subsistent** *adj*

**subsistence farming** *n* **1** (a system of) farming that provides all or almost all the goods required by the farm household, usu without any significant surplus for sale **2** (a system of) farming that produces a minimum and often inadequate return to the farmer

**subsistence level** *n* a standard of living just sufficient to provide the basic necessities of life

¹**subsoil** /ˈsubˌsoyl/ *n* the layer of weathered material that underlies the surface soil

²**subsoil** *vt* to turn, break, or stir the subsoil of – **subsoiler** *n*

**subsolar point** /ˌsubˈsohlə/ *n* the point on the earth's surface at which the sun is vertically overhead

**subsonic** /ˌsubˈsonik/ *adj* **1** of or being a speed less than that of sound in air **2** (capable of) moving at, or using air currents moving at, a speed less than that of sound **3** INFRASONIC 1 [ISV] – **subsonically** *adv*

**subspace** /ˈsubˌspays/ *n, mathematics* a subset of a space; *esp* one that has the properties (e g those of a VECTOR SPACE) of the including space

**sub specie aeternitatis** /,sub ,speki·ay ietuhni'tahtis, ,speeshi/ *adv* seen in its essential or universal form or nature [NL, lit., under the aspect of eternity]

**subspecies** /'sub,speeshiz/ *n* a subdivision of a species: e g **a** a category in the biological classification of living things that ranks immediately below a species and designates a distinguishable and geographically isolated group whose members interbreed successfully with those of other subspecies of the same species **b** a named subdivision (e g a race or variety) of a classified species [NL] – **subspecific** *adj*

**substage** /'sub,stayj/ *n* an attachment to a microscope by means of which accessories (e g mirrors, DIAPHRAGMS, or CONDENSERS) are held in place beneath the stage platform of the instrument

**substance** /'substəns/ *n* **1a** essential nature; essence **b** a fundamental or characteristic part or quality ⟨*debated matters of ~ rather than procedure*⟩ **c** correspondence with reality ⟨*the allegations were without ~*⟩ **2** *philosophy* ultimate reality that underlies all outward manifestations and change **3a** (a) physical material from which something is made or which has a separate existence ⟨*an oily ~*⟩ **b** matter of particular or definite chemical constitution **4** material possessions; property ⟨*a man of ~*⟩ [ME, fr OF, fr L *substantia*, fr *substant-*, *substans*, prp of *substare* to stand under, fr *sub-* + *stare* to stand – more at STAND] – **substanceless** *adj* – **in substance** with respect to essentials; fundamentally

**substance P** *n* a PEPTIDE (chain of AMINO ACIDS smaller than a protein) that is present esp in the digestive system and PITUITARY GLAND and that causes reduction in blood pressure and contraction of muscle (e g that in the walls of the intestines and blood vessels) not under voluntary control [*Powder*]

**substandard** /,sub'standəd/ *adj* deviating from or falling short of a standard or norm: e g **a** of a quality lower than that prescribed (e g by law) **b** conforming to a pattern of language in widespread use but not accepted as correct by the prestige group in a community – compare NONSTANDARD **c** constituting a greater than normal risk to an insurer

**substantial** /səb'stansh(ə)l/ *adj* **1a** consisting of or relating to substance **b** not imaginary or illusory; real, true **c** important, essential **2** ample to satisfy and nourish; full ⟨*a ~ meal*⟩ **3a** well-to-do, prosperous **b** considerable in quantity; significantly large ⟨*earned a ~ wage*⟩ **4** firmly constructed; sturdy **5** being largely but not wholly the specified thing ⟨*a ~ lie*⟩ – **substantial** *n*, **substantialize** *vb*, **substantially** *adv*, **substantialness** *n*, **substantiality** *n*

**substantiate** /səb'stanshi·ayt/ *vt* to establish (e g a statement, claim, or charge) by proof or evidence; verify *synonyms* see CONFIRM – **substantiation** *n*, **substantiative** *adj*

¹**substantive** /'substəntiv/ *n* a noun; *broadly* a word or phrase functioning grammatically as a noun [ME *substantif*, fr MF, fr *substantif*, adj, having or expressing substance, fr LL *substantivus*] – **substantival** *adj*, **substantivize** *vt*

²**substantive** /'substəntiv, səb'stantiv (*usu* səb'stantiv *when applied to position, rank, etc*)/ *adj* **1** being a totally independent entity; not inferred or derived **2a** real rather than apparent; firm; *also* enduring, permanent **b** belonging to the substance of a thing; essential **c** indicating or expressing existence ⟨*the ~ verb is the verb* to be⟩ **d** *of a dye* requiring or involving no fixative ⟨*a ~ dyeing process*⟩ **3a** relating to or functioning as a noun ⟨*a ~ phrase*⟩ **b** *philosophy* relating to or functioning as a noun in logic **4** creating and defining rights and duties ⟨*~ law*⟩ **5** permanent and definite rather than temporary or acting ⟨*~ rank of colonel*⟩ [ME, fr LL *substantivus* having substance, fr L *substantia* substance] – **substantively** *adv*, **substantiveness** *n*

**substation** /'sub,staysh(ə)n/ *n* a subsidiary POWER STATION in which (the voltage of an) electric current is transformed for use

**substituent** /sub'stityoo-ənt/ *n* an atom or chemical group that replaces another atom or chemical group in a molecule [L *substituent-*, *substituens*, prp of *substituere*] – **substituent** *adj*

¹**substitute** /'substityooht/ *n* **1** one who or that which takes the place of another **2** a word that replaces another word, phrase, or clause in a context [ME, fr L *substitutus*, pp of *substituere* to put in place of, fr *sub-* + *statuere* to set up, place – more at STATUTE] – **substitute** *adj*

²**substitute** *vt* **1a** to put in the place of another; exchange ⟨*~ 4 for x in the equation* $x^3 - 3x^2 + 10 = 6$⟩ **b** to introduce (an atom or chemical group) as a substituent; *also* to alter (e g a

chemical compound) by introduction of a substituent ⟨*a ~*d benzene ring⟩ **2** to take the place of; replace; *also* to introduce a substitute for ⟨*~*d *their centre forward in the second half*⟩ *~ vi* to serve as a substitute – **substitutable** *adj*

*usage* Correctly, when saccharine is used instead of sugar, saccharine is **substituted** *for* sugar or **replaces** sugar, and sugar is **replaced** *by* or *with* saccharine. Substitute is now increasingly used instead of **replace** ⟨**substitute** *sugar by/with/in place of saccharine*⟩, particularly in scientific and technical contexts ⟨*X is* **substituted** *by Y in surface structure*⟩, but it is clearer to preserve the distinction.

**substitution** /,substi'tyoohsh(ə)n/ *n* **1** the substituting of one person or thing (e g a mathematical quantity) for another **2** something that functions as a substitute – **substitutional** *adj*, **substitutionally** *adv*, **substitutionary** *adj*

**substitutive** /'substi,tyoohtiv/ *adj* serving or suitable as a substitute; of or involving substitution – **substitutively** *adv*

**substrate** /'substrayt/ *n* **1** a substratum **2** the base on which an organism lives ⟨*limpets live on a rocky ~*⟩ **3** a substance acted upon chemically (e g by an ENZYME) [ML *substratum*]

**substratum** /,sub'strahtəm, -'straytəm/ *n*, *pl* **substrata** /-tə/ an underlying support; a foundation: e g **a** *philosophy* matter that is considered as the enduring basis of all the qualities or phenomena (e g colour) that can be perceived by the senses **b** the material of which something is made and from which it derives its special qualities; *also* a basis ⟨*his argument has a ~ of truth*⟩ **c** a layer beneath the surface soil; *specif* the subsoil **d** SUBSTRATE 2 **e** a thin coating (e g of hardened gelatine) applied to the support of a photographic film or plate to bind the sensitive emulsion to it [ML, fr L, neut of *substratus*, pp of *substernere* to spread under, fr *sub-* + *sternere* to spread – more at STREW]

**substructure** /'sub,strukchə/ *n* a foundation, groundwork – **substructural** *adj*

**subsume** /səb'syoohm/ *vt* to classify within a larger category or under a general principle [NL *subsumere*, fr L *sub-* + *sumere* to take up – more at CONSUME]

**subsumption** /səb'sumpshən/ *n* **1** MINOR PREMISE (proposition containing the subject of the conclusion of a formal argument) **2** *formal* subsuming or being subsumed; *also* something subsumed [NL *subsumption-*, *subsumptio*, fr *subsumptus*, pp of *subsumere*]

**subsurface** /sub'suhfis/ *n* earth material (e g rock) near but not exposed at the surface of the ground – **subsurface** *adj*

**subsystem** /sub'sistəm/ *n* a secondary or subordinate system

**subteenage** /sub'tee,nayj/ *adj* of, intended for, or being children below the age of adolescence

**subtemperate** /sub'tempərət/ *adj* less than typically temperate ⟨*a ~ climate*⟩; *also* of the colder parts of the TEMPERATE ZONES (areas typified by mild moderate weather)

**subtenant** /'sub,tenənt/ *n* a person who rents from a tenant – **subtenancy** *n*

**subtend** /səb'tend/ *vt* **1** to denote the end points of the lines that diverge to make (an angle) or the end points of (an arc of a circle), and hence to define the arc or angle itself ⟨*an arc ~*ed *by a chord*⟩ ⟨*an angle ~*ed *by an arc*⟩ **2** *of a plant part* to occupy an adjacent and usu lower position to and often so as to embrace or enclose ⟨*a bract that ~*s *a flower*⟩ **3** *formal* to underlie so as to include [L *subtendere*, lit., to stretch beneath, fr *sub-* + *tendere* to stretch – more at THIN]

**subterfuge** /'subtə,fyoohj/ *n* **1** deception by craft or scheming in order to conceal, escape, or evade ⟨*employing ~ to get her own way*⟩ **2** a deceptive device or scheme [LL *subterfugium*, fr L *subterfugere* to escape, evade, fr *subter-* secretly (fr *subter* underneath; akin to L *sub* under) + *fugere* to flee – more at UP, FUGITIVE]

**subterminal** /,sub'tuhminl/ *adj* situated or occurring near but not precisely at an end ⟨*a ~ band of colour on the tail feathers*⟩ [*sub-* + *terminal*]

**subterranean** /,subtə'raynyən, -ni·ən/, **subterraneous** /-nyəs, -niəs/ *adj* **1** being, lying, or operating under the surface of the earth **2** existing or working out of sight or in secret; hidden [L *subterraneus*, fr *sub* under + *terra* earth – more at UP, TERRACE] – **subterraneanly** *adv*

**subthreshold** /sub'thresh-ohld/ *adj* not sufficient to produce a specified response ⟨*~ dosage*⟩ ⟨*a ~ stimulus*⟩

**subtile** /'sut(ə)l/ *adj*, *archaic* subtle [ME, fr L *subtilis*] – **subtilely** *adv*, **subtileness** *n*

**subtil·ize, -ise** /'suti,liez/ *vt* to make subtle *~ vi* to act or think subtly – **subtilization** *n*

**subtilty** /'sutəlti/ *n, archaic* subtlety

**¹subtitle** /'sub,tietl/ *n* **1** a secondary or explanatory title **2a** a printed fragment of dialogue or narrative inserted between the scenes in a silent film **b** a printed translation of the dialogue of a foreign film or television programme that appears at the bottom of the screen; *also* a printed part of the words spoken in the same language (eg for the benefit of the deaf)

**²subtitle** *vt* to give a subtitle to; prepare subtitles for

**subtle** /'sutl/ *adj* **1a** delicate, elusive ⟨*a ~ fragrance*⟩ **b** difficult to understand or distinguish; obscure ⟨*~ differences in sound*⟩ **2a** perceptive, refined ⟨*the artist's ~ awareness of colour values*⟩ **b** having or showing keen insight and ability to penetrate deeply and thoroughly ⟨*a ~ scholar*⟩ **3a** highly skilful; expert ⟨*~ workmanship*⟩ **b** cunningly made or contrived; ingenious **4** artful, crafty **5** operating unnoticeably ⟨*~ poisons*⟩ [ME *sutil, sotil*, fr OF *soutil*, fr L *subtilis*, lit., finely woven, fr *sub-* + *tela* web; akin to L *texere* to weave – more at TECHNICAL] – **subtleness** *n*, **subtly** *adv*

**subtlety** /'sutl·ti/ *n* **1** the quality or state of being subtle: eg **1a** the quality of being delicate or elusive **b** acuteness of mind **2** something subtle; *esp* a fine distinction [ME *sutilte*, fr OF *sutilté*, fr L *subtilitat-, subtilitas*, fr *subtilis*]

**subtopic** /'sub,topik/ *n* a secondary topic; any of the subdivisions into which a topic may be divided

**¹subtotal** /,sub'tohtl/ *adj* somewhat less than complete; nearly total – **subtotally** *adv*

**²subtotal** *n* the sum of part of a series of figures, or total of one of a group of columns of figures forming one large column

**³subtotal** *vb* to work out a subtotal (for)

**subtract** /səb'trakt/ *vt* to take away by subtraction ⟨*~ 5 from 9*⟩ *~ vi* to perform a subtraction [L *subtractus*, pp of *subtrahere* to draw from beneath, withdraw, fr *sub-* + *trahere* to draw – more at DRAW] – **subtracter** *n*

**subtraction** /səb'traksh(ə)n/ *n* an act, process, or instance of removing something from a whole: eg **a** the withdrawing or withholding from someone of a legal right to which he/she is entitled **b** the operation of finding for two given numbers a third number which when added to the second yields the first

**subtractive** /səb'traktiv/ *adj* **1** tending to subtract **2** constituting or involving subtraction

**subtrahend** /,subtrə'hend/ *n* a number that is to be subtracted from another [L *subtrahendus*, gerundive of *subtrahere*]

**subtropical** /,sub'tropikl/ *also* **subtropic** *adj* of or being the geographical regions bordering on the tropical zone [ISV]

**subtropics** /,sub'tropiks/ *n pl* subtropical regions

**subtype** /'sub,tiep/ *n* a subdivision of a type

**subulate** /'syoohbyoolət, -,layt/ *adj* elongated and tapering to a fine point ⟨*a ~ leaf*⟩ [NL *subulatus*, fr L *subula* awl; akin to OHG *siula* awl, L *suere* to sew – more at SEW]

**subumbrella** /'subəm,brelə/ *n* the concave undersurface of a jellyfish

**subunit** /'sub,yoohnit/ *n* a unit that forms an individually distinct part of a more comprehensive unit ⟨*~s of a protein*⟩

**suburb** /'subuhb/ *n* **1a** an outlying part of a city or large town **b** a smaller community adjacent to or within commuting distance of a city or large town **2** *pl* the residential area on the outskirts of a city or large town [ME, fr L *suburbium*, fr *sub-* near + *urbs* city]

**suburban** /sə'buhbən/ *adj* **1** of or situated, happening, or living in a suburb **2a** characteristic of suburbs **b** limited and unadventurous in outlook; uninteresting, dull

**suburbanism** /sə'buhbəniz(ə)m/ *n* the characteristic way of life of suburban dwellers

**suburbanite** /sə'buhbə,niet/, **suburban** *n* someone who lives in the suburbs

**suburban·ization, -isation** /sə'buhbənie'zaysh(ə)n/ *n* **1** the quality or state of being suburbanized **2** the act of suburbanizing

**suburban·ize, -ise** /sə'buhbə,niez/ *vt* to make suburban; give a suburban character to

**suburbia** /sə'buhbyə/ *n* **1** the suburbs of a city **2** suburbanites as a distinctive social element

**subvariety** /'subvə,rie·əti/ *n* a subdivision of a variety

**subvention** /səb'vensh(ə)n/ *n* the provision of assistance or financial support: eg **a** an endowment **b** a subsidy [LL *subvention-, subventio* assistance, fr L *subventus*, pp of *subvenire* to come up, come to the rescue, fr *sub-* up + *venire* to come – more at SUB-, COME] – **subventionary** *adj*

**subversion** /səb'vuhsh(ə)n/ *n* subverting or being subverted; *esp* a systematic attempt to overthrow or undermine a government or political system by people working secretly within the country involved [ME, fr MF, fr LL *subversion-, subversio*, fr L *subversus*, pp of *subvertere*] – **subversionary** *adj*, **subversive** *adj or n*, **subversively** *adv*, **subversiveness** *n*

**subvert** /səb'vuht/ *vt* **1** to overthrow or undermine the powers or influence of (eg an established government or authority) **2** to pervert or corrupt by undermining the morals, allegiance, or faith of [ME *subverten*, fr MF *subvertir*, fr L *subvertere*, lit., to turn from beneath, fr *sub-* + *vertere* to turn – more at WORTH] – **subverter** *n*

**subviral** /sub'vie·ərəl/ *adj* relating to, being, or caused by a piece or a structural part (eg a protein) of a virus ⟨*~ infection*⟩

**subvocal** /sub'vohkl/ *adj* characterized by the occurrence in the mind of words in speech order with or without inaudible movements of the speech organs – **subvocally** *adv*

**subway** /'sub,way/ *n* an underground way: eg **a** a passage under a street (eg for pedestrians, power cables, or water or gas mains) **b** *chiefly NAm* an underground railway

**sub-'zero** *adj* being below zero, esp in temperature; *also* marked by or intended for sub-zero temperature

**succeed** /sək'seed/ *vi* **1a** to come next after another in possession of something; *specif* to inherit sovereignty, rank, or title ⟨*to ~ to the throne*⟩ **b** to follow after another in order **2a** to have a favourable result; turn out well ⟨*the arrangement seemed to ~*⟩ **b** to attain a desired object or end ⟨*to ~ in ousting one's rivals*⟩ *~ vt* **1** to follow in sequence, esp immediately **2** to come after as heir or successor [ME *succeden*, fr L *succedere* to go up, follow after, succeed, fr *sub-* near + *cedere* to go – more at SUB-, CEDE] – **succeeder** *n*

*usage* One succeeds *in* doing something, not ⚠ *to* do something.

**succès de scandale** /sook,say də skon'dahl (*Fr* syksɛ də skǎdal)/ *n* something (eg a work of art) that wins popularity or notoriety because of its scandalous nature rather than its merits; *also* the reception given to such a piece [Fr, lit., success of scandal]

**succès d'estime** /sook,say de'steem (*Fr* syksɛ dɛstim)/ *n* something (eg a work of art) that wins critical respect but not popular success; *also* the reception given to such a piece [Fr, lit., success of esteem]

**succès fou** /sook,say 'fooh (*Fr* syksɛ fu)/ *n* an extraordinary success [Fr, lit., mad success]

**success** /sək'ses/ *n* **1a** degree or measure of succeeding ⟨*met with poor ~*⟩ **b** a favourable outcome of an undertaking; *specif* the attainment of wealth or fame **2** one who or that which achieves success [L *successus*, fr *successus*, pp of *succedere*]

**successful** /-f(ə)l/ *adj* **1** resulting in success **2** gaining or having gained success – **successfully** *adv*, **successfulness** *n*

**succession** /sək'sesh(ə)n/ *n* **1a** the order in which, or the conditions under which, one person after another succeeds to a property, title, throne, etc **b** the right of a person or line to succeed **c** the line having such a right **2a** the act or process of following in order; a sequence **b(1)** the act or process of one person's taking the place of another in the enjoyment of or liability for his/her rights or duties or both **b(2)** the act or process of a person's becoming beneficially entitled to a deceased person's property, property interest, or title **c** the continuance of corporate structure and organization ⟨*a corporation which has unlimited ~*⟩ **d** the sequence of changes in the composition of an ecological community as the available competing organisms, esp the plants, respond to and modify the environment until a relatively stable state (CLIMAX) is reached ⟨*the highlights of the ~ were the weed, grass, and forest communities*⟩ **3** *taking sing or pl vb* a number of people or things that follow each other in sequence ⟨*a ~ of wet days was/were responsible for the delay*⟩ [ME, fr MF or L; MF, fr L *succession-, successio*, fr *successus*, pp] – **successional** *adj*, **successionally** *adv*

**succession state** *n* any of a number of states that succeed a former state in sovereignty over a certain territory

**successive** /sək'sesiv/ *adj* **1** following in succession or in order according to a series; following each other without interruption **2** produced in succession **synonyms** see CONSECUTIVE – **successively** *adv*, **successiveness** *n*

**successor** /sək'sesə/ *n* one who or that which follows another; *esp* a person who succeeds to a throne, title, estate, office, etc [ME *successour*, fr OF, fr L *successor*, fr *successus*, pp]

**successor state** *n* SUCCESSION STATE

**success story** *n* an account of a person's progress from obscurity or poverty to fame or wealth; *also* such a progress

**succinate** /'suksi,nayt/ *n* any of various chemical compounds (SALTS or ESTERS) formed by combination between SUCCINIC ACID and a metal atom, an alcohol, or another chemical group

**succinct** /sək'singkt/ *adj* clearly expressed in few words; concise *synonyms* see CONCISE *antonyms* diffuse, discursive [ME, girdled, fr L *succinctus* girded up, concise, fr pp of *succingere* to gird from below, tuck up, fr *sub-* + *cingere* to gird – more at CINCTURE] – **succinctly** *adv*, **succinctness** *n*

**succinic acid** /sək'sinik/ *n* an acid, $HOOC(CH_2)_2COOH$, found widely in nature and active in energy-yielding chemical reactions in organisms [Fr *succinique*, fr L *succinum* amber; fr its occurrence in amber]

**succinic dehydrogenase** /,deehie'drojənayz/ *n* an iron-containing ENZYME that promotes the removal of water from SUCCINIC ACID to give FUMARIC ACID, and often the reverse reaction, in life-supporting chemical processes esp in animal tissues, bacteria, and yeast

**succinyl** /'suksinil/ *n* either of two chemical groups of SUCCINIC ACID: **a** a chemical group $OC(CH_2)_2CO$, which has a VALENCY of two **b** a chemical group $HOOC(CH_2)_2CO$, which has a valency of one [ISV]

**succinylcholine** /'suksinil,kohleen/ *n* SUXAMETHONIUM (synthetic drug used to relax muscles) [*succinyl* + *choline*]

**succory** /'suk(ə)ri/ *n* CHICORY (plant used in salad) [alter. of ME *cicoree*]

**succotash** /'sukətash/ *n* a dish of beans and green maize cooked together [of Algonquian origin; akin to Narraganset *msəkwataš* succotash]

**¹succour**, *NAm chiefly* **succor** /'sukə/ *n* **1** relief; *also* aid, help **2** something that gives relief [ME *succur*, fr earlier *sucurs* (taken as pl), fr OF *sucors*, fr ML *succursus*, fr L, pp of *succurrere* to run up, run to help, fr *sub-* up + *currere* to run – more at CAR]

**²succour**, *NAm chiefly* **succor** *vt* to go to the aid of (someone in want or distress); relieve *synonyms* see ¹HELP

**succuba** /'sukyoobə/ *n, pl* **succubae** /-,bie, -,bi/ a succubus [LL, prostitute]

**succubus** /'sukyoobəs/ *n, pl* **succubi** /-,bi, -,bie/ a demon assuming female form to have sexual intercourse with men in their sleep – compare INCUBUS [ME, fr ML, alter. of LL *succuba* prostitute, fr L *succubare* to lie under, fr *sub-* + *cubare* to lie, recline – more at HIP]

**succulence** /'sukyoolans/ *n* **1** the state of being succulent **2** succulent feed ⟨*wild game subsisting on* ~⟩

**¹succulent** /'sukyoolənt/ *adj* **1a** full of juice; juicy **b** appetizing because of juiciness; toothsome **2** *of a plant* having juicy fleshy tissues [L *suculentus*, fr *sucus, succus* juice, sap; akin to L *sugere* to suck – more at SUCK] – **succulently** *adv*

**²succulent** *n* a succulent plant (eg a cactus)

**succumb** /sə'kum/ *vi* **1** to yield or give in *to* superior strength or force, or overpowering appeal or desire **2** to be brought to an end by the effect of destructive or disruptive forces; die *synonyms* see ¹YIELD [Fr & L; Fr *succomber*, fr L *succumbere*, fr *sub-* + *-cumbere* to lie down; akin to L *cubare* to lie]

**¹such** /such; *also* (*occasional weak form*) səch/ *adj or adv* **1a** of a kind, quality, or extent ⟨~ *a paper as* The Times⟩ ⟨~ *food as they can eat*⟩ ⟨*his habits are* ~ *that we rarely meet*⟩ – used before *as* to introduce an example or comparison ⟨*tears* ~ *as angels weep* – John Milton⟩ ⟨*behaviour* ~ *as hers*⟩ ⟨~ *trees as oak or pine*⟩ **b** of the same sort ⟨*other* ~ *clinics throughout the country*⟩ ⟨*deeply moved by* ~ *acts of kindness*⟩ ⟨*there's no* ~ *place*⟩ **2** of so extreme a degree or extraordinary a nature ⟨*never heard* ~ *a hubbub*⟩ ⟨~ *tall buildings*⟩ ⟨*ever* ~ *a lot of people*⟩ ⟨*in* ~ *a hurry*⟩ ⟨*his excitement was* ~ *that he shouted*⟩ ⟨*how can you bother me at* ~ *a time*⟩ ⟨*no wonder you're tired after* ~ *a marathon*⟩ ⟨*we've had* ~ *fun!*⟩ ⟨*it wasn't* ~ *an ordeal, really*⟩ – used before *as* to suggest that a name is unmerited ⟨*we forced down the soup*, ~ *as it was*⟩ [ME, fr OE *swilc;* akin to OHG *sulīh* such; both fr a prehistoric Gmc compound whose constituents are represented by OE *swā* so & by OE *gelīc* like – more at SO, LIKE]

**usage 1** When *such* introduces an example or comparison, it should be followed by *as* and not by any other word ⟨*such cases of hardship as* (not △ *that* or *which*) *I see in my profession*⟩. **Such** *that* introduces a result ⟨*made* **such** *a noise that we had to close the windows*⟩. **2 Such** as means "of a kind like" and cannot replace **as** to mean "in the way that". In ⟨*to change our out-of-date, unfair rating system* **such** *as Liberals have been suggesting*⟩ it is the

change, and not the system, that the Liberals have been suggesting, so **such** should be omitted here.

**²such** *pron, pl* **such** **1** *pl* such people; those ⟨~ *of the girls as came*⟩ ⟨~ *as wish to leave may do so*⟩ **2** that thing, fact, or action ⟨~ *was the result*⟩ **3** *pl* similar people or things ⟨*tin and glass and* ~⟩ – **as such** intrinsically considered; in him /herself, itself, or themselves ⟨*the gift was worth little* as such⟩

**such and such** *adj* not named or specified ⟨*said he went to* ~ *a place*⟩

**¹suchlike** /-,liek/ *adj* of like kind; similar

**²suchlike** *pron, pl* **suchlike** one of the same sort; a similar person or thing

**¹suck** /suk/ *vt* **1a** to draw (eg liquid) into the mouth by a force of suction produced by movements of the lips and tongue ⟨~ed *milk from his mother's breast*⟩ **b** to draw something (eg liquid) from or consume by such movements ⟨~ *an orange*⟩ ⟨~ *a sweet*⟩ **c** to take into the mouth as if sucking out a liquid ⟨~ed *his burned finger*⟩ **2a** to draw (as if) by suction ⟨*plants* ~ing *moisture from the soil*⟩ **b** to draw by irresistible force ⟨~ed *into the conspiracy*⟩ ~ *vi* **1** to draw something in (as if) by exerting suction; *esp* to draw milk from a breast or udder with the mouth **2** to make a sound or motion associated with or caused by suction ⟨*his pipe* ~ed *wetly*⟩ [ME *souken*, fr OE *sūcan;* akin to OHG *sūgan* to suck, L *sugere*, Gk *hyein* to rain]

**suck off** *vt, vulg* to stimulate to orgasm with the mouth or tongue

**suck up** *vi* to act in an obsequious manner *to* ⟨*sucking up to the director in the hope of getting a good part*⟩

**²suck** *n* **1** the act of sucking **2** a sucking movement or force

**¹sucker** /'sukə/ *n* **1a** a human infant or young animal that sucks at a breast or udder; a suckling; *esp* a young pig **b** a device for creating or regulating suction (eg a piston or valve in a pump) **c(1)** a device made of a flexible airtight material (eg rubber) that can cling to a surface by suction **c(2)** a pipe or tube through which something is drawn by suction **d(1)** an organ in various animals for clinging or holding **d(2)** a mouth (eg of a leech) adapted for sucking or clinging **2** a shoot from the roots or lower part of the stem of a plant **3** any of numerous freshwater fishes (family Catostomidae) closely related to the carps but distinguished from them by having thick soft lips **4** a lollipop **5** JUMPING PLANT LOUSE **6** *informal* **6a** a person easily cheated or deceived **b** a person irresistibly attracted by a specified type of object ⟨*a* ~ *for chocolate*⟩

**²sucker** *vt* to remove suckers from (a plant) ⟨~ *tobacco*⟩ ~ *vi, of a plant* to send out suckers

**sucking** /'suking/ *adj* not yet weaned; *broadly* very young

**sucking louse** *n* any of an order (Anoplura) of wingless insects comprising the true lice with mouthparts adapted to sucking body fluids

**suckle** /'sukl/ *vt* **1a** to give milk to from the breast or udder ⟨*a mother* suckling *her child*⟩ **b** to nurture; BRING UP 1 ⟨*a pagan* ~d *in a creed outworn* – William Wordsworth⟩ **2** to suck milk from the breast or udder of ⟨*lambs* suckling *the ewes*⟩ [prob back-formation fr *suckling*]

**suckler** /'suklə/ *n* a suckling

**suckling** /'sukling/ *n* a young unweaned animal [¹*suck* + ¹*-ling*]

**sucrase** /'soohkrayz, 'syoohrayz/ *n* INVERTASE (an ENZYME that aids the digestion of sugar) [ISV, fr Fr *sucre* sugar – more at SUGAR]

**sucre** /'soohkray/ *n* – see MONEY table [Sp, fr Antonio José de *Sucre* †1830 S American liberator]

**sucrose** /'s(y)oohkrohs, -krohz/ *n* a sugar, $C_{12}H_{22}O_{11}$, that occurs naturally in most land plants and is the sugar obtained from sugarcane or SUGAR BEET [ISV, fr Fr *sucre* sugar]

**suction** /'suksh(ə)n/ *n* **1** the act or process of sucking **2a** the act or process of exerting a force on a solid, liquid, or gaseous body by means of reduced air pressure over part of its surface **b** the force so exerted **3** a device (eg a pipe) used in a machine that operates by suction [LL *suction-, suctio*, fr L *suctus*, pp of *sugere* to suck – more at SUCK] – **suctional** *adj*

**suction pump** *n* a pump in which the liquid to be raised is drawn into the partial vacuum left in a vessel (eg a cylinder) when a valved piston is drawn out

**suction stop** *n* CLICK 1b (speech sound)

**suctorial** /suk'tawri-əl/ *adj* adapted for sucking; *esp* serving to draw up liquid or to cling by suction ⟨*a* ~ *mouth*⟩ [NL *suctorius*, fr L *suctus*, pp]

**suctorian** /suk'tawriən/ *n* any of a class (Suctoria) of complex

PROTOZOANS (single-celled organisms) which in early development move by means of small hairlike structures (CILIA), but which in maturity remain fixed to a surface, lack the power of movement, and feed through specialized sucking tentacles [NL *Suctoria*, group name, fr neut pl of *suctorius* suctorial]

**Sudanic** /sooh'danik/ *n* the African languages which belong to neither the BANTU nor HAMITIC groups, and are spoken in a belt extending from Senegal to S Sudan [the *Sudan*, region in N Africa] – **Sudanic** *adj*

**sudd** /sud/ *n* floating vegetable matter that forms obstructive masses in the upper White Nile [Ar, lit., obstruction]

**sudden** /'sud(ə)n/ *adj* **1a** happening or coming unexpectedly ⟨*a ~ shower*⟩ **b** changing in character all at once ⟨*a gradual slope broken by the ~ descent to the beach*⟩ **2** marked by or showing abruptness or haste [ME *sodain*, fr MF, fr L *subitaneus*, fr *subitus* sudden, fr pp of *subire* to come up, fr *sub*- up + *ire* to go – more at SUB-, ISSUE] – **suddenly** *adv*, **suddenness** *n*

**sudden death** *n* **1** unexpected death or death occurring within minutes from any cause other than violence ⟨sudden death *from a heart attack*⟩ **2** an extra period of play to break a tie (eg in golf) that ends the moment one side or player gains the lead

**sudoriferous** /ˌsoohdə'rif(ə)rəs, ˌsyooh-/ *adj* producing or carrying sweat ⟨~ *glands*⟩ ⟨*a ~ duct*⟩ [LL *sudorifer*, fr L *sudor* sweat + -*ifer* -iferous – more at SWEAT]

**sudorific** /ˌs(y)oohdə'rifik/ *adj* DIAPHORETIC (able to increase secretion of sweat) [NL *sudorificus*, fr L *sudor*] – **sudorific** *n*

**Sudra** /'s(y)oohdrə/ *n* a Hindu of the lowest caste traditionally restricted to ritually unclean and menial occupations [Skt *śūdra*] – **Sudra** *adj*

**suds** /sudz/ *n taking sing or pl vb* **1** soapy water; *also* the lather or froth on such water **2** *chiefly NAm* (the bubbles on the surface of) beer [prob fr MD *sudse* marsh; akin to OE *sēothan* to seethe – more at SEETHE] – **sudsless** *adj*

**sudsy** /'sudzi/ *adj* full of suds; frothy, foamy

**sue** /s(y)ooh/ *vt* **1a** to bring a legal action against **b** to carry (a legal action) through to decision **2** to appeal to (a court) ~ *vi* **1** to make a request or application; plead – usu + *for* or *to* ⟨*to ~ for peace*⟩ **2** to take legal proceedings in court [ME *suen* to follow, make legal claim to, bring legal action against, fr OF *suivre*, fr (assumed) VL *sequere*, fr L *sequi* to follow, come or go after; akin to Gk *hepesthai* to follow] – **suer** *n*

**¹suede, suède** /swayd/ *n* **1** leather with a rough surface produced by rubbing to make a nap of short fibres **2** a fabric finished with a rough surface to resemble suede [Fr *(gants de) Suède* Swedish (gloves)]

**²suede** *vt* to give a suede finish or nap to (a fabric or leather) ~ *vi* to give cloth or leather a suede finish

**suet** /'s(y)ooh·it/ *n* the hard fat about the kidneys and loins in beef and mutton that yields TALLOW (fat used in soap, candles, etc) and that is used in cooking [ME *sewet*, fr (assumed) AF, dim. of AF *sue*, fr L *sebum* tallow, suet – more at SOAP]

**suffer** /'sufə/ *vt* **1a** to submit to or be forced to endure ⟨~ *martyrdom*⟩ **b** to feel keenly; labour under ⟨~ *thirst*⟩ **2** to undergo, experience **3** to put up with, esp as inevitable or unavoidable **4** *archaic*, permit ⟨*the eagle* ~s *little birds to sing* – Shak⟩ ~ *vi* **1** to endure death, pain, or distress **2** to sustain loss or damage **3** to be handicapped or at a disadvantage [ME *suffren*, fr OF *souffrir*, fr (assumed) VL *sufferire*, fr L *sufferre*, fr *sub*- up + *ferre* to bear – more at SUB-, BEAR] – **sufferable** *adj*, **sufferableness** *n*, **sufferably** *adv*, **sufferer** *n*

　　*usage* One **suffers** *from* a disease or disability ⟨she **suffers** *from* varicose veins⟩, but **suffer** *with* is often used where actual pain is involved ⟨*been* **suffering** *a lot with her bad leg*⟩. **synonyms** see ²BEAR

**sufferance** /'suf(ə)rəns/ *n* **1** permission or tolerance implied by a lack of interference or objection ⟨*he was only there on ~*⟩ **2** capacity to withstand; endurance

**suffering** /'suf(ə)ring/ *n* the state or experience of one who or that which suffers

**suffice** /sə'fies/ *vi* to meet or satisfy a need; be sufficient ⟨*a brief note will ~*⟩ – often + an impersonal *it* ⟨*~ it to say that they are dedicated*⟩ ~ *vt* to be enough for [ME *sufficen*, fr MF *suffis*-, stem of *suffire*, fr L *sufficere*, lit., to put under, fr *sub*- + *facere* to make, do – more at DO] – **sufficer** *n*

**sufficiency** /sə'fish(ə)nsi/ *n* **1** sufficient means to meet one's needs; *also* a modest but adequate scale of living **2** the quality or state of being sufficient; adequacy

**sufficient** /sə'fish(ə)nt/ *adj* **1** enough to meet the needs of a situation or a proposed end ⟨*~ provisions for a month*⟩ **2** being a SUFFICIENT CONDITION [ME, fr L *sufficient*-, *sufficiens*, fr prp of *sufficere*] – **sufficiently** *adv*

　　*synonyms* Sufficient, enough, adequate, and ample all mean "fulfilling a requirement". Sufficient is more formal than enough, but their meaning is similar. Enough is often placed after a noun ⟨money enough⟩ and may be used ironically to mean "too much" ⟨I've had enough *of your excuses!*⟩. Adequate is particularly used of standard or ability, and often means "barely enough" ⟨his French *is* adequate *but not brilliant*⟩. Ample, by contrast, implies an abundance ⟨an ample income⟩. *antonym* insufficient.

**sufficient condition** *n* **1** a proposition in logic or mathematics whose truth assures the truth of another proposition – compare NECESSARY CONDITION **2** a state of affairs whose existence assures the existence of another state of affairs

**¹suffix** /'sufiks/ *n* an AFFIX (eg -*ness* in "happiness") appearing at the end of a word or phrase – compare INFIX, PREFIX [NL *suffixum*, fr L, neut of *suffixus*, pp of *suffigere* to fasten underneath, fr *sub*- + *figere* to fasten – more at DYKE] – **suffixal** *adj*

**²suffix** *vt* to attach as a suffix – **suffixation** *n*

**suffocate** /'sufəˌkayt/ *vt* **1a** to stop the respiration of (eg by strangling or asphyxiation) **b** to deprive of oxygen **c** to make uncomfortable (as if) by want of cool fresh air **2** to impede or stop the development of ~ *vi* to become suffocated: **a** to die from being unable to breathe **b** to be uncomfortable (as if) through lack of air [L *suffocatus*, pp of *suffocare* to choke, stifle, fr *sub*- + *fauces* throat] – **suffocatingly** *adv*, **suffocative** *adj*, **suffocation** *n*

**Suffolk** /'sufək/ *n* **1** (any of) an English breed of black-faced hornless sheep kept for meat **2 Suffolk, Suffolk punch** (any of) an English breed of chestnut-coloured draught horses [*Suffolk*, county in E England; (2) E dial. *punch* short stocky person or animal, prob short for *Punchinello*]

**¹suffragan** /'sufrəgən/ *also* -jən/ *n* **1** a bishop of a diocese (eg in the ROMAN CATHOLIC church and the CHURCH OF ENGLAND) subordinate to a METROPOLITAN (bishop of a province) **2** a bishop assisting a bishop of a diocese in the CHURCH OF ENGLAND and not having the right of succession [ME, fr MF, fr ML *suffraganeus*, fr *suffragium* support, prayer]

　　*usage* The pronunciation /'sufrəgən/ is recommended for BBC broadcasters.

**²suffragan** *adj* **1** of or being a suffragan **2** subordinate to the authority of a METROPOLITAN (bishop of a province) or archbishop

**suffrage** /'sufrij/ *n* **1** a short prayer of intercession, usu in a series **2** a vote given in favour of a question or in the choice of a person for an office **3** the right of voting; franchise; *also* the exercise of such right [(1) ME, fr MF, fr ML *suffragium*, fr L, vote, political support; (2-3) L *suffragium*]

**suffragette** /ˌsufrə'jet/ *n* a woman who advocates suffrage for her sex; *esp* a woman using militant methods to press for female suffrage in Britain at the beginning of the 20th century

**suffragist** /'sufrəjist/ *n* someone who advocates extension of suffrage, esp to women

**suffuse** /sə'fyoohz/ *vt* to spread over or through in the manner of fluid or light; flush, permeate ⟨*a blush ~d her cheeks*⟩ [L *suffusus*, pp of *suffundere*, lit., to pour beneath, fr *sub*- + *fundere* to pour – more at FOUND] – **suffusion** *n*, **suffusive** *adj*

**Sufi** /'soohfi/ *n* a Muslim mystic [Ar *ṣūfiy*, lit., (man) of wool; prob fr his woollen garments] – **Sufi** *adj*, **Sufism** *n*, **Sufic** *adj*

**¹sugar** /'shoogə/ *n* **1a** a sweet substance that consists wholly or essentially of SUCROSE, is colourless or white when pure, tending to brown when less refined, is usu obtained commercially from sugarcane or sugar beet, and is nutritionally important as a source of CARBOHYDRATE and as a sweetener and preservative of other foods **b** any of various water-soluble chemical compounds that vary widely in sweetness and comprise a group of simple carbohydrates (OLIGOSACCHARIDES) including sucrose **2** a unit (eg a spoonful, cube, or lump) of sugar ⟨*one ~ or two?*⟩ **3** ³DEAR 1b (term of endearment) [ME *sucre*, fr MF, fr ML *zuccarum*, fr OIt *zucchero*, fr Ar *sukkar*, fr Per *shakar*, fr Skt *śarkarā*; akin to Skt *śarkara* pebble]

**²sugar** *vt* **1** to make palatable or attractive; sweeten **2** to sprinkle or mix with sugar ~ *vi* **1** to form or be converted into sugar **2** to become granular; granulate

**sugar beet** *n* a white-rooted beet grown for the sugar in its roots

**sugarcane** /'shoogəˌkayn/ *n* a stout tall grass (*Saccharum offi-*

*cinarum*) that is widely grown in warm regions as a source of sugar

**,sugar-'coated** *adj* **1** covered with a hard coat of sugar **2** made superficially attractive

**sugar daddy** *n, informal* a usu elderly man who provides luxuries for a young woman in return for sex and/or companionship

**sugarloaf** /'shoogə,lohf/ *n* a moulded cone of refined sugar – **sugar-loaf** *adj*

**sugar maple** *n* a maple with a sweet sap; *specif* one (*Acer saccharum*) of NE America with hard close-grained wood much used for fine furniture and sap that is the chief source of MAPLE SYRUP and MAPLE SUGAR

**sugar of lead** *n* LEAD ACETATE (poisonous chemical compound)

**sugarplum** /'shoogə,plum/ *n* a small round sweet usu of flavoured and coloured boiled sugar

**sugary** /'shoog(ə)ri/ *adj* **1** containing, resembling, or tasting of sugar **2a** exaggeratedly and usu insincerely sweet; honeyed 〈*his ~ deprecating voice* – D H Lawrence〉 **b** cloyingly sweet; sentimental

**suggest** /sə'jest/ *vt* **1a** to mention or imply as a possibility; intimate 〈*~ed that he might bring his family*〉 **b** to propose as desirable or fitting 〈*~ a stroll*〉 **c** to put forward for consideration 〈*~ a solution to a problem*〉 **2a** to call to mind by thought or association **b** to serve as a motive or inspiration for 〈*a play ~ed by a historic incident*〉 [L *suggestus*, pp of *suggerere* to put under, furnish, suggest, fr *sub-* + *gerere* to carry] – **suggester** *n*

**synonyms** Suggest, imply, hint, intimate, and insinuate can all mean "convey an idea indirectly". **Suggest** and **imply** are often used without a human subject, referring to a process which arouses a train of thought in the listener or observer. **Imply** is often used when something is conveyed as well as what is said explicitly, and may indicate a more logical connection than **suggest**. Hint, intimate, and insinuate involve the covert expression of meaning: hint may refer to the use of rather pointed clues 〈hinted *broadly that she would like an invitation*〉; intimate has associations of veiled delicacy rather than blunt forthrightness 〈intimated *shyly that she was pregnant*〉; insinuate applies to the sly underhand expression of something usually discreditable 〈insinuated *that he had been fiddling his taxes*〉. **usage** Suggest is correctly used either with or without *that* 〈*I* suggested (*that*) *he should leave*〉.

**suggestible** /sə'jestəbl/ *adj* easily influenced by suggestion – **suggestibility** *n*

**suggestion** /sə'jesch(ə)n/ *n* **1a** the act or process of suggesting **b** something suggested **2a** the process by which one thought leads to another, esp through association of ideas **b** the act or process of impressing something (eg an idea, attitude, or desired action) on the mind of another **3** a slight indication; a trace 〈*a ~ of a smile*〉

**suggestive** /sə'jestiv/ *adj* **1a** giving a suggestion; indicative 〈*~ of a past era*〉 **b** full of suggestions; mentally stimulating **c** stirring mental associations; evocative **2** suggesting something improper or indecent; risqué – **suggestively** *adv*, **suggestiveness** *n*

**suicidal** /,s(y)ooh·i'siedl/ *adj* **1** involving or of the nature of suicide **2** marked by an impulse to commit suicide **3a** dangerous, esp to life **b** destructive to one's own interests – **suicidally** *adv*

**¹suicide** /'s(y)ooh·i,sied/ *n* **1a** the act or an instance of taking one's own life intentionally **b** ruin of one's own interests 〈*political ~*〉 **2** someone who commits or attempts suicide [L *sui* of oneself (akin to OE & OHG *sīn* his, L *suus* one's own, Skt *sva* oneself, one's own) + E *-cide*] – **suicide** *vb*

**²suicide** *adj* likely to bring about death or disaster; extremely dangerous 〈*a ~ decision*〉

**sui generis** /,sooh·i 'jenəris/ *adj, formal* constituting a class alone; unique, peculiar [L, of its own kind]

**sui juris** /'jooəris/ *adj* having full legal rights or capacity [L, of one's own right]

**suint** /'soohint, swint/ *n* dried sweat of sheep deposited in the wool and rich in potassium-containing chemical compounds [Fr, fr MF, fr *suer* to sweat, fr L *sudare* – more at SWEAT]

**¹suit** /s(y)ooht/ *n* **1** an action or process in a court for the recovery of a right or claim **2** an act or instance of suing or seeking by entreaty; an appeal; *specif* courtship 〈*she seemed deaf to his ~*〉 **3** a group of things forming a unit or collection; a set: eg **3a** a complete set of armour **b** a complete set of sails –compare SUITE 2 **4a** an outer costume of two or more matching pieces that are designed to be worn together

**b** a costume to be worn for a specified purpose or under particular conditions **5a** all the playing cards in a pack bearing the same symbol (ie hearts, clubs, diamonds, or spades) **b** all the dominoes in a set bearing the same number **c** all the cards or counters in a particular suit held by one player 〈*a 5-card ~*〉 **d** the suit led 〈*follow ~*〉 [ME *siute* act of following, retinue, sequence, set, fr OF, act of following, retinue, fr (assumed) VL *sequita*, fr fem of *sequitus*, pp of *sequere* to follow – more at SUE] – **follow suit 1** to play a card of the same suit as the card led **2** to follow an example set

**²suit** *vi* **1** to be in accordance; agree – usu + *with* 〈*the position ~s with his abilities*〉 **2** to be appropriate or satisfactory 〈*these prices don't ~*〉 **3** to put on specially required clothing (eg a uniform or protective garb) – usu + *up* ~ *vt* **1** to accommodate, adapt 〈*~ the action to the word*〉 **2a** to be good for the health or well-being of; agree with 〈*rich food doesn't ~ me*〉 **b** to be becoming to; look right with 〈*a lipstick that ~ed her colouring*〉 **3** to meet the needs or wishes of; please 〈*~s me fine*〉

**suitable** /'s(y)oohtəbl/ *adj* **1** meeting the requirements of a use, purpose, or situation **2** satisfying conditions for social acceptability; proper **synonyms** see ³FIT **antonyms** unsuitable, unbecoming – **suitability** *n*, **suitableness** *n*, **suitably** *adv*

**suitcase** /-,kays/ *n* a rectangular usu rigid case, with a hinged lid and a handle, for carrying articles (eg clothes)

**suite** /sweet/ *n* **1** *taking sing or pl vb* a retinue; *esp* the personal staff accompanying an official on business **2** a group of things forming a unit or collection; a set: eg **2a** a group of rooms occupied as a unit **b(1)** a 17th- and 18th-century form of music for an instrumental ensemble consisting of a series of dances in the same key or related keys **b(2)** a modern instrumental composition in several movements of differing character **b(3)** an orchestral concert arrangement in suite form of material drawn from a longer work (eg a ballet) **c** a set of matching furniture (eg a settee and two armchairs) for a room 〈*a 3-piece ~*〉 – compare SUIT 3 [Fr, alter. of OF *siute* – more at SUIT]

**suiting** /'s(y)oohting/ *n* fabric suitable for suits

**suitor** /'s(y)oohtə/ *n* one who courts a woman or seeks to marry her [ME, follower, pleader, fr AF, fr L *secutor* follower, fr *secutus*, pp of *sequi* to follow – more at SUE]

**sukiyaki** /,soohki'yaki, -'yahki/ *n* a Japanese dish consisting of thin slices of meat, soya-bean curd, and vegetables cooked in soy sauce, sake, and sugar [Jap]

**sukkah** /'sookə, 'sookah/ *n* a booth or shelter with a roof of branches and leaves that is used esp for meals during Sukkoth [Heb *sukkāh*]

**Sukkoth** /'sukoht, 'sukohth (*Hebrew* su:'kɔt)/ *n* a Jewish harvest festival beginning on the 15th of TISHRI (7th month of the Jewish year) and commemorating the temporary shelters used by the Jews during their wandering in the wilderness [Heb *sukkōth*, pl of *sukkāh*]

**sulcate** /'sulkayt/ *adj, of a plant or animal part* scored with furrows running lengthways 〈*a ~ seedpod*〉 [L *sulcatus*, pp of *sulcare* to furrow, fr *sulcus* furrow]

**sulcus** /'sulkəs/ *n, pl* **sulci** /'sulsie/ a furrow, groove; *esp* a shallow furrow on the surface of the brain separating adjacent ridges (CONVOLUTIONS) [L; akin to OE *sulh* plough, Gk *holkos* furrow, *helkein* to pull]

**sulf-, sulfo-** *comb form, chiefly NAm* sulph-

**sulfur** /'sulfə/ *n, chiefly NAm* sulphur

**¹sulk** /sulk/ *vi* to be moodily silent [back-formation fr *sulky*]

**²sulk** *n* **1 sulks** *pl*, **sulk** the state of one who is sulking 〈*had a case of the ~s*〉 **2** a sulky mood or spell 〈*in a ~*〉

**¹sulky** /'sulki/ *adj* characterized by sulking or given to spells of sulking [prob alter. of obs *sulke* sluggish] – **sulkily** *adv*, **sulkiness** *n*

**²sulky** *n* a light 2-wheeled 1-horse vehicle for one person used esp in trotting races [prob fr ¹*sulky*; fr its holding a solitary person]

**sullage** /'sulij/ *n* **1** refuse, sewage **2** mud deposited by flowing water; silt [prob fr MF *soiller, souiller* to soil – more at SOIL]

**sullen** /'sulən/ *adj* **1a** persistently and silently gloomy or resentful; ill-humoured and unsociable **b** suggesting a sullen state; lowering 〈*~ sky*〉 **2** dismal, gloomy **3** moving sluggishly [ME *solain* sullen, solitary, prob fr (assumed) MF, fr L *solus* alone] – **sullenly** *adv*, **sullenness** *n*

**sully** /'suli/ *vt* to spoil the purity of; tarnish, defile 〈*no scandal sullied his reputation*〉 [prob fr MF *soiller* to soil]

**sulph-, sulpho-** *comb form* sulphur; containing sulphur in the molecular structure ⟨sulpho*chloride*⟩ ⟨sulph*anilamide*⟩ [modif (influenced by *sulphur*) of Fr *sulf-, sulfo-*, fr L *sulfur* sulphur]

**sulphadiazine** /ˌsulfə'die-ə,zeen/ *n* a sulpha drug, $C_{10}H_{10}N_4O_2S$, that is used esp in the treatment of MENINGITIS (inflammation of membrane surrounding the brain and SPINAL CORD) [*sulpha* + *diazine*]

**sulpha drug** /'sulfə/ *n* any of various synthetic antibacterial drugs that are sulphonamides, closely related chemically to sulphanilamide, and that act by interfering with the body functions of bacteria, thereby rendering them more susceptible to the body's defence mechanisms [*sulpha*nilamide]

**sulphamethoxazole** /ˌsulfəmi'thoksəzohl/ *n* a SULPHA DRUG, $C_{10}H_{11}N_3O_3S$, used esp as a component of CO-TRIMOXAZOLE (a mixture of antibacterial drugs) [*sulpha* + *meth-* + *ox-* + *azole*]

**sulphanilamide** /ˌsulfə'niləmied/ *n* a sulphonamide, $H_2NC_2H_4$ $SO_2NH_2$, that is the chemical compound to which most of the sulpha drugs are related [ISV *sulph-* + *anil*ine + *amide*]

**sulphatase** /'sulfə,tayz/ *n* any of various ENZYMES that speed up the breakdown of sulphur-containing ESTERS into acids and alcohols, and that are found in animal tissues and in microorganisms [ISV *sulphate* + *-ase* ]

**¹sulphate** /'sulfayt/ *n* **1** any of various chemical compounds (SALTS or ESTERS) formed by combination between SULPHURIC ACID and a metal atom, an alcohol, or another chemical group **2** an ANION (negatively charged group of atoms), $SO_4$, characteristic of SULPHURIC ACID and the sulphates, having a VALENCY of two [modif of Fr *sulfate*, fr L *sulfur*]

**²sulphate** *vt* **1** to treat or combine with SULPHURIC ACID or a sulphate **2** to convert into a sulphate **3** to form a deposit of a whitish scale of sulphate of lead on (the plates of a STORAGE BATTERY) ∼ *vi* to become sulphated

**sulphhydryl** /sulf'hiedril/ *n* a highly reactive chemical group, SH, that is characteristic of MERCAPTANS (compounds similar to alcohols and PHENOLS) and that is present in many biologically active compounds (e g various proteins, COENZYMES, and inhibitors of ENZYMES) [ISV *sulph-* + *hydr-* + *-yl*]

**sulphide** /'sulfied/ *n* **1** any of various chemical compounds (SALTS or ESTERS) formed by combination between HYDROGEN SULPHIDE and a metal atom, an alcohol, or another chemical group **2** a chemical compound, containing two atoms per molecule, that is formed by reaction of sulphur usu with a chemical element with a greater tendency to release electrons than itself [ISV]

**sulphinyl** /'sulfənil/ *n* the chemical group SO, that has a VALENCY of two [*sulphin*ic acid ($RSO_2H$)+ -*yl*]

**sulphite** /'sulfiet/ *n* **1** any of various compounds (SALTS or ESTERS) formed by combination between SULPHUROUS ACID and a metal atom, an alcohol, or other chemical group **2** an ANION (negatively charged group of atoms), $SO_3$, characteristic of SULPHUROUS ACID and the sulphites, having a VALENCY of two [modif of Fr *sulfite*, alter. of *sulfate* sulphate]

**sulpho-** – see SULPH-

**sulphon-** /sulfon-/ *comb form* sulphonic ⟨sulphon*amide*⟩

**sulphonamide** /sul'fonəmied/ *n* an AMIDE (e g SULPHANILAMIDE) of a SULPHONIC ACID; *also* SULPHA DRUG

**¹sulphonate** /'sulfənayt/ *n* any of various chemical compounds (SALTS or ESTERS) formed by combination between SULPHONIC ACID and a metal atom, an alcohol, or other chemical group

**²sulphonate** *vt* to introduce the sulphonic chemical group into; *broadly* to treat (an organic chemical substance) with SULPHURIC ACID

**sulphone** /'sulfohn/ *n* any of various compounds containing the sulphonyl chemical group with two chemical bonds between its sulphur atom and usu a carbon atom [ISV *sulph-* + *-one*]

**sulphonic** /sul'fonik, -'fohnik/ *adj* of, being, or derived from the acid chemical group, $SO_3H$, which has a VALENCY of one [ISV *sulphone* + *-ic*]

**sulphonic acid** *n* any of numerous acids that contain the sulphonic chemical group and that may be prepared from SULPHURIC ACID by replacement of a HYDROXYL chemical group by either an inorganic ANION (negatively charged atom or group of atoms) or an organic chemical group with a VALENCY of one

**sulphonium** /'sulfohniəm/ *n* a chemical group or CATION (positively charged group of atoms), $SH_3$, with a VALENCY of one [NL, fr *sulph-* + amm*onium*]

**sulphonyl** /'sulfənil, -niel/ *n* a chemical group, $SO_2$, that has a VALENCY of two [ISV *sulphon-* + *-yl*]

**sulphonylurea** /ˌsulfənilyoo(ə)'ree-ə, -'yooəri·ə, -niel-/ *n* any of several synthetic compounds (e g the drugs TOLBUTAMIDE and CHLORPROPAMIDE) related to the sulphonamides and given by mouth to lower the concentration of glucose in the blood in the treatment of DIABETES MELLITUS [NL, fr ISV *sulphonyl* + NL *urea*]

**sulphoxide** /sul'foksied/ *n* any of a class of organic chemical compounds characterized by a SULPHINYL group with two chemical bonds between its sulphur atom and carbon atom [ISV]

**¹sulphur,** *chiefly NAm* **sulfur** /'sulfə/ *n* **1** a nonmetallic chemical element that occurs either free or combined esp in SULPHIDES and SULPHATES, is a constituent of proteins, exists in several different (ALLOTROPIC) forms including yellow crystals, resembles oxygen chemically but is less active and more acidic, and is used esp in the chemical and paper industries, in rubber VULCANIZATION (treatment to add strength, elasticity, etc), and in medicine for treating skin diseases **2** a pale greenish-yellow colour [ME *soufre, sulphur*, fr OF & L; ME *soufre* fr OF, fr L *sulfur, sulpur, sulphur;* ME *sulphur* fr L]

**²sulphur, sulphurate** /-ayt/ *vt* to treat with sulphur or a chemical compound containing sulphur – **sulphuration** *n*

**sulphur bottom whale** *n* BLUE WHALE [fr the yellowish splotches on its belly]

**sulphur dioxide** *n* a heavy pungent toxic gas, $SO_2$, that is easily condensed to a colourless liquid, that is used industrially esp in making sulphuric acid, in bleaching, and as a food preservative, and that is a major air pollutant esp in industrial areas

**sulphureous** /sul'fyooəriəs/ *adj* sulphurous [L *sulphureus*, fr *sulphur*]

**¹sulphuret** /'sulfyoorət/ *n* SULPHIDE [NL *sulphuretum*, fr L *sulphur*]

**²sulphuret** /'sulfyooret/ *vt* **-tt-** (*NAm* **-t-, -tt-**) to combine or impregnate with sulphur

**sulphuric** /sul'fyooərik/ *adj* of or containing sulphur, esp with a relatively high VALENCY ⟨∼ *esters*⟩ [modif of Fr *sulfurique*, fr L *sulfur*]

**sulphuric acid** *n* a heavy corrosive oily strong acid, $H_2SO_4$, that has a VALENCY of two, is colourless when pure, and is used extensively in industry, as a dehydrating agent, and as an OXIDIZING AGENT

**sulphur·ize, -ise** /'sulfəriez/ *vt* to sulphur

**sulphurous** /'sulf(ə)rəs, sul'fyooərəs/ *adj* **1a** resembling or coming out of sulphur, esp burning sulphur **b** of or containing sulphur, esp with a relatively low VALENCY ⟨∼ *esters*⟩ **2a** of or dealing with the fire of hell; infernal **b** scathing, virulent ⟨∼ *denunciations*⟩ **c** profane, blasphemous ⟨∼ *language*⟩ [L *sulphurosus*, fr *sulphur*]

**sulphurous acid** /sul'fyooərəs/ *n* a weak chemically unstable acid, $H_2SO_3$, that has a VALENCY of two, is known only in solution and through its salts, and is used for bleaching and as a REDUCING AGENT

**sulphuryl** /'sulfəril/ *n* SULPHONYL – used esp in names of inorganic chemical compounds [ISV *sulphur* + *-yl*]

**sultan** /'sult(ə)n/ *n* a sovereign of a Muslim state [MF, fr Ar *sulṭān*]

**sultana** /səl'tahnə/ *n* **1** a female member of a sultan's family; *esp* a sultan's wife **2a** a pale yellow seedless grape grown for wine-making and used dried in cakes, puddings, etc **b** a dried sultana [It, fem of *sultano* sultan, fr Ar *sulṭān*]

**sultanate** /'sultənət/ *n* **1** the office, dignity, or power of a sultan **2** a state or country governed by a sultan

**sultry** /'sultri/ *adj* **1a** very hot and humid; sweltering ⟨*a* ∼ *day*⟩ **b** burning hot; torrid **2a** hot with passion or anger **b** (capable of) exciting strong sexual desire ⟨∼ *glances*⟩ [obs *sulter* to swelter, alter. of *swelter*] – **sultrily** *adv*, **sultriness** *n*

**Sulu** /'soohlooh/ *n, pl* **Sulus,** *esp collectively* **Sulu** a member of a Muslim Malay people of the SW Philippines [Malay *Suluk*]

**¹sum** /sum/ *n* **1** an indefinite or specified amount of money ⟨*a small* ∼⟩ ⟨*the* ∼ *of 15*⟩ **2** the whole amount; the aggregate **3a** a brief but comprehensive summary of the chief points of an argument or exposition; a summation **b** the gist ⟨*the* ∼ *and substance of an argument*⟩ **4a(1)** *the* result of adding numbers ⟨*the* ∼ *of 5 and 7 is 12*⟩ **a(2)** the mathematical limit of the sum of the first *n* terms of an infinite series as *n* increases indefinitely **b** *chiefly informal* numbers to be added; *broadly* a problem in arithmetic **c** *maths* UNION **2d** (set of all elements contained in two or more sets) [ME *summe*, fr OF, fr L *summa*, fr fem of *summus* highest; akin to L *super* over – more at OVER] – **summable** *adj*, **summability** *n* – **in sum** in short; briefly

²**sum** *vt* **-mm-** to calculate the sum of: **a** to add **b** to count

**sum up** *vt* **1** to be the sum of; bring to a total ⟨*10 victories* summed up *his record*⟩ **2** to state succinctly; summarize ⟨sum up *the evidence presented*⟩ **3** to consider and form or express a judgment on ∼ *vi* to present a summary or summing-up – see also SUMMING-UP

**sumach,** *NAm chiefly* **sumac** /'s(h)oohmak/ *n* **1** any of a genus (*Rhus* of the family Anacardiaceae, the sumach family) of trees, shrubs, and woody climbing plants (eg poison ivy) that have feathery leaves that turn to brilliant colours in the autumn, loose clusters of red or whitish berries, and in some cases foliage poisonous to the touch **2** a material used in tanning and dyeing that consists of dried powdered leaves and flowers of various sumachs [ME *sumac*, fr MF, fr Ar *summāq*]

**Sumerian** /sooh'miəri·ən, -'meəri·ən/ *n* **1** a native or inhabitant of Sumer **2** the language of the Sumerians that has no known relationship with any other language [*Sumer*, region in ancient Babylonia] – **Sumerian** *adj*

**summa** /'soomah/ *n*, *pl* **summae** /-mee/ a comprehensive treatise; *esp* one by a SCHOLASTIC philosopher (an adherent to a medieval Christian philosophical movement) [ML, fr L, sum]

**summand** /'sumand, su'mand/ *n* a term in a summation; an addend [ML *summandus*, gerund of *summare* to sum, fr L *summa*]

**summar·ize, -ise** /'suməriez/ *vt* to express as or reduce to a summary ∼ *vi* to make a summary – **summarization** *n*, **summarizer** *n*

¹**summary** /'suməri/ *adj* **1** concise but comprehensive ⟨*a ∼ report*⟩ **2a** done quickly without delay or formality ⟨*a ∼ dismissal*⟩ **b** of or using a summary proceeding ⟨*a ∼ trial*⟩; *specif* tried or triable in a magistrate's court ⟨*a ∼ offence*⟩ **synonyms** see CONCISE **antonyms** verbose, circumstantial [ME, fr ML *summarius*, fr L *summa* sum] – **summarily** *adv*

²**summary** *n* a brief account covering the main points of something – compare ABRIDGEMENT

**summat** /'sumət/ *pron*, *dial NEng* something [alter. of ¹*somewhat*]

**summate** /su'mayt/ *vt* to add together; SUM UP [back-formation fr *summation*]

**summation** /su'maysh(ə)n/ *n* **1** the act or process of forming a sum; addition **2** a sum, total **3** cumulative action or effect; *esp* the process by which a sequence of stimuli that are individually inadequate to produce a response are cumulatively able to induce a nerve impulse **4** the act or an instance of summing up an argument – **summational** *adj*

¹**summer** /'sumə/ *n* **1** the season between spring and autumn which in the N hemisphere is usu taken to comprise the months of June, July, and August; *also* the period extending from the June SOLSTICE (longest day of the year) to the September EQUINOX (time when day and night are of equal length) **2** the warmer half of the year **3** a period of maturity or full potential ⟨*still in the ∼ of one's life*⟩ ⟨*high ∼ of English literature*⟩ **4** *chiefly poetic* a year ⟨*a girl of seventeen ∼*s⟩ [ME *sumer*, fr OE *sumor*; akin to OHG & ON *sumer* summer, Skt *samā* year, season]

²**summer** *vi* to pass the summer ∼ *vt* to keep or carry through the summer; *esp* to provide (eg cattle or sheep) with pasture during the summer

³**summer** *n* a large horizontal beam or stone used esp in building: eg **a** the lintel of a door or window or the beam across the top of a fireplace; BRESSUMER **b** a block of stone forming the cap of a pier (eg to support a lintel or arch) **c** **summer, summertree** a large girder supporting floor timbers [ME, packhorse, beam, fr MF *somier*, fr (assumed) VL *sagmarius*, fr LL *sagma* packsaddle, fr Gk]

**summer cypress** *n* a densely branched Eurasian plant (*Kochia scoparia*) of the goosefoot family grown for its foliage that turns red in autumn – called also BURNING BUSH

**summerhouse** /-,hows/ *n* a small building in a garden or park designed to provide a shady place in summer

**summer pudding** *n* a cold dessert consisting of SOFT FRUITS (eg raspberries and blackcurrants) encased by a basin-shaped mould of white bread

**summer savory** *n* a European herb (*Satureia hortensis*) of the mint family used in cookery

**summer school** *n* a course of teaching that is held during the summer vacation esp on university premises and is usu for groups who do not otherwise study together

**summer solstice** *n* the SOLSTICE that occurs in June in the N hemisphere or in December in the S hemisphere – compare WINTER SOLSTICE

**summertime** /-,tiem/ *n* the summer season or a period like summer

**Summer Time** *n* BRITISH SUMMER TIME

**summerwood** /'sumə,wood/ *n* the harder less porous portion of the ring of wood added each year to a plant's trunk or stem that develops late in the growing season – compare SPRINGWOOD

**summery** /'sum(ə)ri/ *adj* **1** of, resembling, or fit for summer **2** warm, friendly ⟨*a ∼ smile*⟩

**summing-'up** /'suming/ *n* **1** a concluding summary (eg to a talk) **2** a survey of the evidence in a case given by a judge to the jury before it considers its verdict

**summit** /'sumit/ *n* **1** a top, apex; *esp* the highest point; a peak **2** the topmost level attainable ⟨*the ∼ of human fame*⟩ **3a** the highest level of officials; *esp* (the diplomatic representatives of) heads of government **b** a conference of highest-level officials (eg heads of government) [ME *somete*, fr MF, fr OF, dim. of *sum* top, fr L *summum*, neut of *summus* highest – more at SUM]

**synonyms** Summit, peak, pinnacle, apex, climax, culmination, zenith, and acme all mean, literally or figuratively, "the highest point attainable". A mountain top is a **summit** or, if pointed, a **peak**; a rock so pointed as to resemble a church spire is a **pinnacle**; an **apex** is also the pointed tip of anything. All these words can be used figuratively ⟨*the* **summit** *of his career*⟩ ⟨*the* **pinnacles** *of human achievement*⟩. Climax, culmination, and zenith all apply to the highest point of intensity in a process, **zenith** particularly suggesting that there will be a subsequent descent ⟨*had passed the* **zenith** *of her fame*⟩. **Acme** is used chiefly for the supreme degree of something abstract ⟨*reached the* **acme** *of perfection*⟩. **antonyms** bottom, base

**summon** /'sumən/ *vt* **1** to issue a call to come together; convene; convoke **2** to command to appear in court by means of a summons **3** to call upon for specified action ⟨*∼ them to be in readiness*⟩ **4** to call upon to come; send for ⟨*∼ a doctor*⟩ **5** to call into being or action; *esp* to draw out of oneself with an effort – often + *up* ⟨*∼-ed up his courage for the battle*⟩ [ME *somonen*, fr OF *somondre*, fr (assumed) VL *summonere*, alter. of L *summonēre* to remind secretly, fr *sub-* secretly + *monēre* to warn – more at SUB-, MIND] – **summoner** *n*

¹**summons** /'sumənz/ *n* **1** the act of summoning; *esp* a call by authority to appear at a place named or to attend to a duty **2** a warning or notification to appear in court; *esp* a written notification to be served on a person warning him to appear in court on a specified day to answer a charge or claim **3** something (eg a call) that summons [ME *somouns*, fr OF *somonse*, fr pp of *somondre*]

²**summons** *vt* SUMMON 2

**summum bonum** /'soomoom ,boonoom/ *n*, *formal* the supreme good from which all others are derived [L]

**summum genus** /'genəs, 'gaynəs, 'jeenəs/ *n*, *pl* **summa genera** /'jenərə/ a logical GENUS (group marked by common characteristics) that cannot be categorized under any higher genus [NL, lit., highest genus]

**sumo** /'s(y)oohmoh/ *n* a Japanese form of wrestling in which a contestant loses if he is forced out of the contest area or if any part of his body apart from the soles of his feet touches the ground [Jap *sumō*]

**sump** /sump/ *n* **1** a pit or reservoir serving as a drain or receptacle for liquids: eg **1a** a cesspit **b** a pit at the lowest point in a circulating or drainage system (eg the oil-circulating system of an INTERNAL-COMBUSTION ENGINE) **c** *chiefly Br* the lower section of the crankshaft housing used as a lubricating oil reservoir in an INTERNAL-COMBUSTION ENGINE **2** the part of a mine shaft which is lowest and into which water drains **3** *Br* CRANKCASE (housing for a crankshaft in a car, pump, etc) [(1,3) ME *sompe* swamp; (2) Ger *sumpf*, lit., marsh, fr MHG – more at SWAMP]

**sumpter** /'sumptə/ *n*, *archaic* a pack animal [short for *sumpter horse*, fr ME *sumpter* driver of a packhorse, fr MF *sometier*, fr (assumed) VL *sagmatarius*, fr LL *sagmat-*, *sagma* packsaddle, fr Gk]

**sumptuary** /'sumptyoori/ *adj* **1** designed to regulate personal expenditures and esp to prevent extravagance and luxury ⟨*of a splendour ... beyond what was allowed by the ∼ regulations of the colony* – Nathaniel Hawthorne⟩ **2** designed to regulate habits on moral or religious grounds [L *sumptuarius*, fr *sumptus* expense, fr *sumptus,* pp of *sumere* to take, spend – more at CONSUME]

**sumptuary law** *n* law limiting private expenditure esp on luxuries in the interest of the State

**sumptuous** /'sum(p)choo·əs, -tyoo-/ *adj* lavishly rich, costly, luxurious, or magnificent ⟨~ *banquets*⟩ [MF *sumptueux,* fr L *sumptuosus,* fr *sumptus* expense] – **sumptuously** *adv,* **sumptuousness** *n*

**sum total** *n* 1 a total arrived at through the counting of sums 2 total result; totality

¹**sun** /sun/ *n* **1a** the star nearest to and round which the earth and other planets revolve, and which is situated at some distance from the centre of the galaxy **b** a self-luminous celestial body; a star; *esp* one round which planets revolve **2** the heat or light radiated from the sun **3** one resembling the sun, usu in brilliance **4** glory, splendour [ME *sunne,* fr OE; akin to OHG *sunna* sun, L *sol* – more at SOLAR] – **catch the sun** to become suntanned or sunburnt – **under the sun** in the world; ON EARTH ⟨he was the last person under the sun *I wanted to see*⟩ – see also a PLACE in the sun, a TOUCH of the sun

²**sun** *vb* **-nn-** *vt* to expose (as if) to the rays of the sun ~ *vi* to sun oneself

,**sun-and-'planet** *adj, of gears* arranged so that one cogwheel moves round a larger cogwheel

**sunbake** /'sun,bayk/ *vi or n, Austr* (to) sunbathe

**sunbaked** /-,baykt/ *adj* baked or dried by exposure to sunshine

**sunbath** /'sun,bahth/ *n* a sunbathe

¹**sunbathe** /'sun,baydh/ *n* a period of sunbathing

²**sunbathe** *vi* to expose the body to sunlight or a sunlamp, esp while lying or sitting

**sunbeam** /-,beem/ *n* a ray of light from the sun

**sun bear** *n* a small black bear (*Helarctos malayanus*) of SE Asian forests that lives on honey and insects [fr the yellow patch on its chest]

**Sunbelt** /'sun,belt/ *n* the S USA from Virginia to S California
'**sun-,belt** *n* an area with a warm sunny climate; *esp* one in which people prefer to live and work so as to be able to enjoy superior recreational opportunities ⟨a *rethinking of traditional values, with the 'good life' of the* ~ *taking precedence over the 'rat race' of the industrial cities* – Geographical Magazine⟩ – **sun-belt** *adj*

**sunbird** /-,buhd/ *n* any of numerous small brilliantly coloured songbirds (family Nectariniidae) of tropical Asia and Africa, that resemble hummingbirds

**sunblind** /-,bliend/ *n, chiefly Br* a shade on a window (eg a VENETIAN BLIND or awning) that gives protection from the sun's rays

**sunbonnet** /-,bonit/ *n* a bonnet with a wide brim framing the face and usu having a ruffle at the back to protect the neck from the sun

**sunbow** /-,boh/ *n* an arch resembling a rainbow made by the sun shining through vapour or mist

¹**sunburn** /-,buhn/ *vb* **sunburned, sunburnt** *vt* to burn, discolour, or tan by exposure to the sun ~ *vi* to become sunburnt [back-formation fr *sunburned,* fr *sun* + *burned*]

²**sunburn** *n* inflammation of the skin caused by overexposure to sunlight

**sunburst** /-buhst/ *n* an ornament or jewelled brooch representing a sun surrounded by rays

**sundae** /'sunday/ *n* an ice cream served with a topping (eg of crushed fruit, syrups, nuts, or whipped cream) [prob alter. of *Sunday*]

**sun dance** *n* an American Indian religious ceremony consisting of dancing, symbolic rites, and often self-torture performed in honour of the sun

¹**Sunday** /'sunday, -di/ *n* **1** the 1st day of the week; the day falling between Saturday and Monday, observed by Christians as a day of rest and worship **2** a newspaper published on Sundays ⟨solemn *discussion in the posh* ~s – Leslie Sellers⟩ [ME, fr OE *sunnandæg;* akin to OHG *sunnūntag* Sunday; both fr a prehistoric WGmc-NGmc compound whose components are represented by OE *sunne* & by OE *dæg* day] – **Sundays** *adv*

²**Sunday** *adj* **1** of or associated with Sunday **2** *chiefly derog* amateur ⟨~ *painters*⟩ ⟨~ *drivers*⟩

³**Sunday** *vi* to spend Sunday ⟨was ~ing *in the country*⟩

**Sunday best** *n taking sing or pl vb, informal* one's best clothes

,**Sunday-go-to-'meeting** *adj, chiefly NAm informal* appropriate for Sunday churchgoing ⟨her new ~ *dress*⟩

**Sunday punch** *n, chiefly NAm informal* a powerful or devastating blow; *esp* a knockout punch

**Sunday school** *n* a school for religious education, esp of children, that is held on Sunday usu by a church; *also* its teachers and pupils

**sun deck** *n* **1** the upper deck on a passenger ship **2** *chiefly NAm* a roof or terrace used for sunbathing

**sunder** /'sundə/ *vt, formal* to break apart or in two; sever finally and completely or with violence *synonyms* see ¹SEPARATE *antonym* link [ME *sunderen,* fr OE *gesundrian, syndrian;* akin to OHG *suntarōn* to sunder, L *sine* without]

**sundew** /'sun,dyooh/ *n* any of a genus (*Drosera* of the family Droseraceae, the sundew family) of bog plants that attract and trap insects by means of glistening hairs on the leaves and that digest them by a juice produced by the leaves

**sundial** /-,die·əl/ *n* an instrument to show the time of day by the shadow of a GNOMON (pointer) on a graduated plate or cylindrical surface

**sun disc** *n* an ancient Near Eastern symbol consisting of a disc with stylized wings emblematic of a sun-god (eg Ra in Egypt)

**sun dog** *n* **1** PARHELION (bright spot on a luminous circle parallel to the horizon) **2** a small nearly round halo on the PARHELIC CIRCLE (luminous circle parallel to the horizon at the altitude of the sun)

**sundown** /-,down/ *n* SUNSET 2

**sundowner** /'sun,downə/ *n* **1** *chiefly Br* a drink taken at sundown; the first drink of an evening **2** *Austr* a hobo, tramp [(2) fr his habit of arriving at sundown, too late to do any work, at a place where he hopes to obtain food and lodging]

**sundrenched** /-,drencht/ *adj* exposed to much hot sunshine ⟨the ~ *shores of the Caribbean*⟩

¹**sundry** /'sundri/ *adj* miscellaneous, various ⟨~ *articles*⟩ [ME, different for each, fr OE *syndrig;* akin to OHG *suntarīg* sundry, OE *syndrian* to sunder, L *sine* without]

²**sundry** *pron taking pl vb* an indeterminate number ⟨recommended *by all and* ~⟩

³**sundry** *n* **1** *pl* miscellaneous small articles, details, or items **2** *Austr* EXTRA 1d (run in cricket not scored from the bat)

**sunfast** /'sun,fahst/ *adj* resistant to fading by sunlight ⟨~ *dyes*⟩

**sunfish** /-,fish/ *n* **1** a large marine fish (*Mola mola*) that has a bony skeleton, long pointed fins on its back, and a nearly oval body, and that reaches a length of 3 metres (about 10 feet) and a weight of 2 tonnes (about 2 tons)

**sunflower** /-,flowə/ *n* any of a genus (*Helianthus*) of tall singlestemmed plants of the daisy family with a single large flower head having yellow strap shaped flowers and edible seeds that yield an edible oil and are often used as animal feed

**sung** /sung/ *past of* SING

**Sung** /soong/ *n* a Chinese dynasty dated from AD 960 to 1280 that was overthrown by the Mongols under Kublai Khan and was noted for achievements in philosophy, literature, and art, including the development of printing from movable type

**sunglasses** /-,glahsiz/ *n pl* glasses to protect the eyes from the sun

**sung mass** *n* a mass in which prescribed parts are sung by the priest and congregation

'**sun-,god,** *fem* **sun-goddess** *n* a deity that represents or personifies the sun in various religions

**sunk** /sungk/ *past of* SINK

**sunken** /'sungkən/ *adj* **1** submerged; *esp* lying at the bottom of a body of water **2a** hollow, recessed ⟨~ *cheeks*⟩ **b** lying or constructed below the surrounding or normal level ⟨a ~ *garden*⟩ *synonyms* see ¹SINK [fr obs pp of *sink*]

**sunk fence** *n* a ditch with a RETAINING WALL used to divide lands without defacing a landscape – called also HA-HA

**sunlamp** /'sun,lamp/ *n* an electric lamp designed to emit light radiation of wavelengths from ULTRAVIOLET TO INFRARED and used esp for tanning the skin and for therapy

**sunless** /'sun,lis/ *adj* lacking sunshine; dark, cheerless

**sunlight** /-,liet/ *n* the light of the sun; sunshine

**sunlit** /-,lit/ *adj* lighted (as if) by the sun

**sun lounge** *n, Br* a room with large windows positioned so as to admit as much sunshine as possible

**sunlounger** /'sun,lownjə/ *n* a folding portable bed, usu made from canvas on a metal frame and sometimes padded, used for sunbathing, as a garden seat, etc

**sunn** /sun/, **sunn hemp** *n* an E Indian plant (*Crotalaria juncea*) of the pea family with slender branches and yellow flowers; *also* a valuable fibre derived from its bark that resembles hemp and that is lighter and stronger than jute [Hindi *san,* fr Skt *śaṇa*]

**sunna** /'soonə, 'sunə/ *n, often cap* the body of Islamic custom and practice based on Muhammad's words and deeds [Ar *sunnah*]

**Sunni** /'sooni/ *n* 1 the Muslims of the branch of Islam that adheres to the orthodox tradition and acknowledges the first four CALIPHS (religious leaders) as rightful successors of Muhammad – compare SHIA 2 a Sunnite [Ar *sunnīy*, fr *sunnah*] – **Sunni** *adj*

**Sunnism** /'soo,niz(ə)m/ *n* Islam as taught by the Sunni

**Sunnite** /'sooniet/ *n* a Sunni Muslim

**sunny** /'suni/ *adj* 1 marked by brilliant sunlight; full of sunshine ⟨*a ∼ day*⟩ 2 cheerful, optimistic ⟨*a ∼ disposition*⟩ 3 exposed to, brightened, or warmed by the sun ⟨*the ∼ side of the house*⟩ – **sunnily** *adv*, **sunniness** *n*

**'sunny-,side up** *adj, of an egg* fried on one side only so that the yolk is uppermost

**sun parlour** *n, chiefly NAm* SUN LOUNGE

**sunray pleats** /'sunray/ *n* a series of very narrow overlapping KNIFE PLEATS (single pleats in the same direction) that are usu produced in fabric commercially

**sunrise** /-,riez/ *n* 1 the apparent rising of the sun above the horizon; *also* the atmospheric effects accompanying this 2 the time when the topmost part of the sun appears above the horizon as a result of the rotation of the earth

**sunroof** /-,roohf/ *n* a motorcar roof having an openable panel

**sunscreen** /'sun,skreen/ *n* a screen to protect against sun; *esp* a substance used in suntan preparations to protect the skin from excessive ultraviolet radiation – **sunscreening** *adj*

**sunseeker** /'sun,seekə/ *n* a person who travels to an area of warmth and sun, esp in winter

**sunset** /'sunsit, -,set/ *n* 1 the apparent descent of the sun below the horizon; *also* the atmospheric effects accompanying this 2 the time when the topmost part of the sun disappears below the horizon as a result of the rotation of the earth 3 a period of decline; *esp* old age

**sunshade** /-,shayd/ *n* something used as a protection from the sun's rays: e g a a parasol b an awning

**sunshine** /-,shien/ *n* 1a the sun's light or direct rays b the warmth and light given by the sun's rays c a spot or surface on which the sun's light shines 2 something (e g a condition or influence) that, or someone who, radiates warmth, cheer, or happiness – **sunshiny** *adj*

**sunspot** /-,spot/ *n* a transient marking on the visible surface of the sun, that is relatively cooler than its surroundings and consequently appears black

**sunstroke** /-,strohk/ *n* HEATSTROKE (high-temperature sweatless condition) caused by prolonged direct exposure to the sun

**sunstruck** /'sunstruk/ *adj* affected by sunstroke

**sunsuit** /'sunsooht, -syooht/ *n* an outfit (e g of halter-neck top and shorts) worn usu for sunbathing and leisure

**suntan** /-,tan/ *n* a browning of the skin caused by the formation of pigment after exposure to the sun

**suntrap** /-,trap/ *n* a sheltered place that receives a large amount of sunshine

**sunup** /-,up/ *n, informal* sunrise

**sunward** /'sunwəd/ *adj* facing the sun

**sunwards** /'sunwədz/, **sunward** *adv* towards the sun

**sunwise** /-,wiez/ *adv* clockwise

**Suomi** /'sooh·əmi/ *n* 1 *taking pl vb* the Finnish people 2 the Finnish language [Finn]

**'sup** /sup/ *vb* **-pp-** *chiefly dial* **vt** to drink (liquid) in small mouthfuls [ME *suppen*, fr OE *sūpan, suppan*; akin to OHG *sūfan* to drink, sip, OE *sūcan* to suck – more at SUCK]

**²sup** *n, chiefly dial* a mouthful, esp of liquid or broth; a sip; *also* a small quantity of liquid ⟨*a ∼ of tea*⟩

**³sup** *vi* **-pp-** 1 to eat the evening meal 2 to make one's supper – + *on* or *off* ⟨*∼ on roast beef*⟩ [ME *soupen, suppen*, fr OF *souper*, fr *soupe* sop, soup – more at SOUP]

**'super** /'s(y)oohpə/ *n* 1 a removable upper storey of a beehive 2 a SUPERFINE (high quality) grade or extra large size 3 *informal* **3a** SUPERNUMERARY (extra person); *esp* a supernumerary actor **b** a superintendent, supervisor; *esp* a police superintendent [(1) short for earlier *superhive*; (2,3) by shortening]

**²super** *adj* 1 SUPERFINE (extremely fine in size or texture, or high quality) 2 *informal* **2a** of great value, excellence, or superiority; superb ⟨*is a ∼ cook*⟩ **b** – used as a general term of approval ⟨*a ∼ time*⟩ ⟨*it was just ∼*⟩ [short for *superfine*]

**super-** /s(y)oohpə-/ *prefix* **1a(1)** higher in quantity, quality, or degree than; more than ⟨*superhuman*⟩ **a(2)** in addition; extra

⟨*supertax*⟩ **b(1)** exceeding or so as to exceed a norm ⟨*superheat*⟩ ⟨*supersaturate*⟩ **b(2)** to an excessive degree ⟨*supersubtle*⟩ ⟨*supersensitive*⟩ **c** surpassing all or most others of its kind (e g in size or power) ⟨*supertanker*⟩ **2a** situated or placed above, on, or at the top of ⟨*superlunary*⟩ ⟨*superscript*⟩ **b** next above or higher ⟨*supertonic*⟩ ⟨*superoctave*⟩ **3** having (the specified atom or group of atoms) present in an unusually large proportion ⟨*superphosphate*⟩ **4** constituting a wider category of ⟨*superfamily*⟩ **5** superior in status, title, or position ⟨*superpower*⟩ [L, over, above, in addition, fr *super* over, above, on top of – more at OVER]

**superable** /'s(y)oohpərəb(ə)l, -prəb(ə)l/ *adj* capable of being overcome or conquered [L *superabilis*, fr *superare* to surmount – more at INSUPERABLE] – **superableness** *n*, **superably** *adv*

**superabound** /,s(y)oohpərə'bownd/ *vi, formal* to be very or excessively abundant [ME *superabounden*, fr LL *superabundare*, fr L *super-* + *abundare* to abound]

**superabundant** /,s(y)oohpərə'bund(ə)nt/ *adj* more than ample; excessive [ME, fr LL *superabundant-, superabundans*, fr prp of *superabundare*] – **superabundance** *n*, **superabundantly** *adv*

**superadd** /-'ad/ *vt, formal* to add over and above something [ME *superadden*, fr L *superaddere*, fr *super-* + *addere* to add] – **superaddition** *n*

**superannuable** /-'anyoo-əbl/ *adj* offering or affording a pension on retirement ⟨*a ∼ post*⟩ [*superannu*ation + *-able*]

**superannuate** /-'anyooayt/ *vt* 1 to make or declare obsolete or out-of-date 2 to retire on a pension, esp because of age or infirmity ∼ *vi* to become antiquated [back-formation fr *superannuated*] – **superannuation** *n*

**superannuated** /,s(y)oohpə'ranyoo,aytid/ *adj* incapacitated or disqualified for work, use, or continuance by advanced age: e g **a** obsolete **b** retired on a pension [ML *superannuatus*, pp of *superannuari* to be too old, fr L *super-* + *annus* year – more at ANNUAL]

**superb** /s(y)ooh'puhb/ *adj* marked to the highest degree by grandeur, excellence, brilliance, or competence [L *superbus* proud, grand, fr *super* above + *-bus* (akin to OE *bēon* to be) – more at OVER, BE] – **superbly** *adv*, **superbness** *n*

**superblock** /'s(y)oohpə,blok/ *n, NAm* an extensive commercial or residential area barred to through traffic and provided with pedestrian paths

**'supercalender** /,s(y)oohpə'kalində/ *n* a stack of highly polished rollers used to give a very smooth finish to paper

**²supercalender** *vt* to process (paper) in a supercalender

**supercargo** /-,kahgoh/ *n* an officer on a merchant ship in charge of the commercial concerns of the voyage [Sp *sobrecargo*, fr *sobre-* over (fr L *super-*) + *cargo*]

**supercharge** /'s(y)oohpə,chahj/ *vt* 1 to charge greatly or excessively (e g with energy or tension) ⟨*∼d rhetoric*⟩ 2 to supply a charge to (e g an engine) at a pressure higher than that of the surrounding atmosphere 3 PRESSURIZE 1 (maintain normal atmospheric pressure at high altitude)

**supercharger** /'s(y)oohpə,chahjə/ *n* a device (e g a compressor) for supplying air or fuel to an INTERNAL-COMBUSTION ENGINE at a higher-than-normal pressure

**superciliary** /,s(y)oohpə'siliəri/ *adj* of or adjoining the eyebrow; SUPRAORBITAL (above the eye) [NL *superciliaris*, fr L *supercilium*] – **superciliary** *n*

**supercilious** /-'sili·əs/ *adj* coolly and disdainfully haughty *synonyms* see PROUD △ superficial [L *superciliosus*, fr *supercilium* eyebrow, haughtiness, fr *super-* + *-cilium* (akin to *celare* to hide) – more at HELL] – **superciliously** *adv*, **superciliousness** *n*

**superclass** /'s(y)oohpə,klahs/ *n* a category in the biological classification of living things ranking between a PHYLUM or division and a CLASS

**supercoil** /'s(y)oohpə,koyl/ *n* a molecule (e g of NUCLEOPROTEIN) in the form of a complex coil – **supercoiled** *adj*

**superconducting** /,s(y)oohpəkən'dukting/ *adj* exhibiting superconductivity

**superconductive** /,s(y)oohpəkən'duktiv/ *adj* superconducting

**superconductivity** /-,konduk'tivəti/ *n* a complete disappearance of resistance to the passage of an electric current in various metals and alloys at temperatures near ABSOLUTE ZERO (hypothetical temperature at which there is complete absence of heat) – **superconductor** *n*

**supercool** /-'koohl/ *vt* to cool (a liquid) below its freezing point without solidification or crystallization ~ *vi* to become supercooled

**supercritical** /-'kritikl/ *adj, of an aircraft aerofoil, esp a wing* moving slower than sound while the surrounding air moves relatively faster than sound and therefore offering increased lift and speed

**,super-'duper** /'doohpə/ *adj, informal* of exceedingly great value or superiority; extra super ⟨*a* ~ *racing bike*⟩ [redupl of *super*]

**superego** /-,eegoh, -,egoh/ *n* the one of the three divisions of the mind in psychoanalytic theory that is only partly conscious, is developed mainly from the child/parent relationship, reflects social rules, and functions as a conscience to reward and punish – compare EGO, ID [*super-* + *ego*]

**superelevate** /,s(y)oohpə'elivayt/ *vt* ²BANK 1c (to build up a slope on a curve in a road, railway, etc)

**superelevation** /-,eli'vaysh(ə)n/ *n* **1** the vertical difference between the heights of inner and outer edges of a banked road, railway rails, etc **2** additional elevation

**supereminent** /,s(y)oohpə'eminənt/ *adj* extremely high, distinguished, or conspicuous [LL *supereminent-, supereminens*, fr L, prp of *supereminēre* to stand out above, fr *super-* + *eminēre* to stand out – more at EMINENT] – **supereminence** *n*, **supereminently** *adv*

**supererogation** /,s(y)oohpə,erə'gaysh(ə)n/ *n, formal* the act of performing more than is required by duty, obligation, or need [ML *supererogation-, supererogatio*, fr *supererogatus*, pp of *supererogare* to perform beyond the call of duty, fr LL, to expend in addition, fr L *super-* + *erogare* to expend public funds after asking the consent of the people, fr *e-* + *rogare* to ask – more at RIGHT]

**supererogatory** /-i'rogət(ə)ri/ *adj, formal* **1** observed or performed to an extent beyond that asked for or required **2** superfluous, nonessential

**superfamily** /'s(y)oohpə,faməli/ *n* a category in the biological classification of living things ranking next above a FAMILY; *also* a corresponding category in the classification of languages

**super featherweight** *n* JUNIOR LIGHTWEIGHT (boxer)

**superfecundation** /,s(y)oohpə,feekən'daysh(ə)n/ *n* **1** successive fertilization of two or more egg cells produced at the same time, as a result of separate instances of sexual intercourse, esp with different males **2** fertilization at one time of an unusually large number of egg cells for the species

**superficial** /-'fish(ə)l/ *adj* **1a(1)** of a surface **a(2)** lying on, not penetrating below, or affecting only the surface ⟨~ *wounds*⟩ **b** *of a unit of measure* square ⟨*a* ~ *metre*⟩ **2a** concerned only with the obvious or apparent; shallow **b** lying on the surface; external **c** apparent rather than real ⟨*the* ~ *charm of a glib intellectual*⟩ [ME, fr LL *superficialis*, fr L *superficies* surface] – **superficially** *adv*, **superficialness** *n*

  *synonyms* Superficial, shallow, cursory, and uncritical can all mean "lacking in depth and thoroughness". Superficial and shallow apply to a failure to penetrate beyond the obvious ⟨*a superficial explanation*⟩, shallow often adding the suggestion that this failure comes from an inherent lack of emotional or intellectual depth ⟨*a shallow character*⟩. Cursory applies to actions not done thoroughly because of too much haste ⟨*a cursory inspection*⟩, and uncritical describes judgments made without proper analysis ⟨*an uncritical estimate*⟩. *antonyms* deep, profound, thorough △ supercilious

**superficial fascia** *n* the thin layer of loose fatty CONNECTIVE TISSUE underlying the skin and binding it to the parts beneath

**superficiality** /,s(y)oohpə,fishi'aləti/ *n* **1** the quality or state of being superficial **2** something superficial

**superficies** /-'fisheez/ *n, pl* **superficies** *formal* **1** a surface **2** the external aspects or appearance of a thing [L, surface, fr *super-* + *facies* face, aspect – more at FACE]

**superfine** /-,fien/ *adj* **1** excessively refined or delicate **2** of extremely fine size or texture ⟨~ *toothbrush bristles*⟩ ⟨~ *sugar*⟩ **3** *esp of merchandise* of high quality or grade

**superfluid** /,s(y)oohpə'floohid/ *n* a liquid (eg helium below about -271°C) that flows with negligible internal friction and carries heat extremely readily – **superfluidity** *n*

**superfluity** /-'flooh·əti/ *n* **1** excess, oversupply **2** something unnecessary or superfluous [ME *superfluitee*, fr MF *superfluité*, fr LL *superfluitat-, superfluitas*, fr L *superfluus*]

**superfluous** /s(y)ooh'puhfloo·əs/ *adj* exceeding what is sufficient or necessary; extra ⟨~ *words*⟩ [ME, fr L *superfluus*, lit., running over, fr *superfluere* to overflow, fr *super-* + *fluere* to flow – more at FLUID]

**superfoetation,** *chiefly NAm* **superfetation** /,s(y)oohpəfee'taysh(ə)n/ *n* successive fertilization of two or more egg cells produced at separate times, resulting in the presence of embryos of different ages in the same uterus [ML *superfetation-, superfetatio*, fr L *superfetatus*, pp of *superfetare* to conceive while already pregnant, fr *super-* + *fetus* act of bearing young, offspring]

**supergalaxy** /'s(y)oohpə,galəksi/ *n* a large cluster of galaxies

**¹supergene** /'s(y)oohpə,jeen/ *n* a group of linked genes occurring together on a segment of a CHROMOSOME (strand of gene-carrying material) and acting and inherited as a unit [*super-* + *gene*]

**²supergene** *adj, esp of an ore deposit* deposited or enriched by downward-moving solutions of minerals [*super-* + *gene* (as in *hypogene*)]

**supergiant** /-,jie·ənt/ *n* a star of very great brightness, enormous size, and low density

**supergrass** /'s(y)oohpə,grahs/ *n, journalistic* someone who gives information to the police about major or celebrated criminal activities ⟨*British Steel Corporation's attempt to turn journalists into* ~*es via their High Court action – Time Out*⟩

**¹superheat** /,s(y)oohpə'heet/ *vt* **1a** to heat (a liquid) above the boiling point without conversion into vapour **b** to heat (a vapour not in contact with its own liquid) so as to cause to remain free from suspended liquid droplets ⟨~*ed steam*⟩ **2** to overheat ⟨~*ed protest*⟩ – **superheater** *n*

**²superheat** /'s(y)oohpə,heet/ *n* the extra heat given in superheating, at a given pressure, a vapour that contains the maximum amount of gaseous molecules possible at that pressure and that is not in contact with its own liquid; *also* the corresponding rise of temperature of the vapour

**¹superheterodyne** /-'hetərə,dien/ *adj* of or using a form of radio or television reception in which the RADIO FREQUENCY signal is combined with a wave of a frequency such that the result is a signal superimposed on a CARRIER wave of intermediate frequency

**²superheterodyne** *n* a superheterodyne radio receiver

**superhigh frequency** /'s(y)oohpə,hie/ *n* a radio frequency in the range between 300 and 30000 megahertz

**superhighway** /-,hieway/ *n, NAm* a motorway

**superhuman** /-'hyoohmən/ *adj* **1** being above the human; divine ⟨~ *beings*⟩ **2** exceeding normal human power, size, or capability; herculean ⟨*a* ~ *effort*⟩ – **superhumanly** *adv*, **superhumanness** *n*, **superhumanity** *n*

**superimpose** /-im'pohz/ *vt* to place or lay over or above something ⟨*to* ~ *speech on recorded music*⟩ – **superimposable** *adj*, **superimposition** *n*

**superincumbent** /-in'kumbənt/ *adj* lying or resting and usu exerting pressure on something else [L *superincumbent-, superincumbens*, prp of *superincumbere* to lie on top of, fr *super-* + *incumbere* to lie down on – more at INCUMBENT] – **superincumbently** *adv*

**superinduce** /,s(y)oohpə'injoohs/ *vt* to introduce as an addition over or above something already existing [L *superinducere*, fr *super-* + *inducere* to lead in – more at INDUCE] – **superinduction** *n*

**superinfect** /,s(y)oohpəin'fekt/ *vt* to cause or produce superinfection in

**superinfection** /,s(y)oohpəin'feksh(ə)n/ *n* reinfection or a second infection with the same type of parasite (eg a bacterium, fungus, or virus)

**superintend** /,s(y)oohpərin'tend/ *vt* **1** to be in charge of; direct **2** to direct the carrying out of (eg a job of work) [LL *superintendere*, fr L *super-* + *intendere* to attend, direct attention to – more at INTEND]

**superintendence** /-in'tend(ə)ns/ *n* the act or function of superintending or directing; supervision

**superintendency** /-in'tend(ə)nsi/ *n* **1** the office, post, or jurisdiction of a superintendent **2** superintendence

**superintendent** /-in'tend(ə)nt/ *n* **1** someone who supervises or manages something, esp a place, operation, or instruction **2** a police officer of high rank (eg ranking next above an inspector in the British police) [ML *superintendent-, superintendens*, fr LL, prp of *superintendere*] – **superintendent** *adj*

**¹superior** /s(y)ooh'piəri·ə/ *adj* **1** situated higher up; upper **2** of higher rank, quality, or importance **3** courageously or serenely indifferent or unyielding (eg to something painful or disheartening) **4a** greater in quantity or numbers ⟨*escaped by* ~ *speed*⟩ **b** excellent of its kind; better ⟨*her* ~ *memory*⟩ **5** relating to or being a SUPERSCRIPT (letter or symbol printed immediately or diagonally above another) **6a** *of an animal structure* situated above or in front of another part, esp a corresponding part ⟨*a ~ artery*⟩ **b** *of a plant part* situated above or near the top of another part: eg **b(1)** *of a calyx* attached to and apparently arising from the OVARY (seed-bearing organ) **b(2)** *of an ovary* free from a surrounding flower part (eg the calyx) **7** more comprehensive ⟨*a genus is ~ to a species*⟩ **8** *of a planet* orbiting further from the sun than the earth is **9** affecting or assuming an air of superiority; supercilious [ME, fr MF *superieur*, fr L *superior*, compar of *superus* upper, fr *super* over, above – more at OVER] – **superiority** *n*

*usage* Things are **superior** *to*, not *than*, other things ⟨△ *a man of greatly* **superior** *abilities than mine*⟩. Compare INFERIOR

²**superior** *n* **1** someone who is above another in rank, station, or office; *esp* the head of a religious house or order **2** one who or that which surpasses another in quality or merit **3** SUPERSCRIPT (letter or symbol printed immediately or diagonally above another)

**superior conjunction** *n* a CONJUNCTION (apparent meeting or passing of two celestial bodies) in which a lesser or secondary celestial body passes farther from the observer than the primary body round which it revolves ⟨*~ of Saturn*⟩

**superior court** *n* a court whose decisions have the power to settle points of law; *esp* the HIGH COURT or COURT OF APPEAL in England and Wales

**superior general** *n*, *pl* **superiors general** the superior of a religious order or congregation

**superiority complex** *n* an exaggeratedly high opinion of oneself – compare MEGALOMANIA **2**

**superiorly** /s(y)ooh'pieri·əli/ *adv* **1** in or to a higher position or direction **2** in a higher or better manner or degree; *also* in a haughty or condescending manner

**superior vena cava** *n* the branch of the VENA CAVA (main vein) of a VERTEBRATE animal that brings blood back from the head and front part of the body to the heart – called also PRECAVA

**superjacent** /ˌs(y)oohpə'jays(ə)nt/ *adj*, *formal* lying above or on something; overlying ⟨*~ rocks*⟩ [L *superjacent-, superjacens*, prp of *superjacēre* to lie over or upon, fr *super-* + *jacēre* to lie; akin to L *jacere* to throw – more at JET]

**superjet** /'s(y)oohpəˌjet/ *n* a supersonic jet airplane

¹**superlative** /s(y)ooh'puhlətiv/ *adj* **1** of or constituting the form of an adjective or adverb (eg *slowest*) expressing an extreme or unsurpassed level or extent **2** surpassing all others; supreme [ME *superlatif*, fr MF, fr LL *superlativus*, fr L *superlatus* (pp of *superferre* to carry over, raise high), fr *super-* + *latus*, pp of *ferre* to carry – more at TOLERATE, BEAR] – **superlatively** *adv*, **superlativeness** *n*

²**superlative** *n* **1** the superlative degree or form (eg of an adjective or adverb) in a language **2** the superlative or utmost degree of something; the acme **3** an exaggerated expression, esp of praise

**superlunary** /ˌs(y)oohpə'loohnəri/ *also* **superlunar** *adj* beyond the moon; celestial [L *super-* + *luna* moon – more at LUNAR]

**superman** /-man/ *n* **1** a superior type of man that according to the 19th-century German philosopher Nietzsche has learnt to renounce fleeting pleasures and attain fulfilment and dominance through the use of creative power **2** *informal* a person of extraordinary or superhuman power or achievements [trans of Ger *übermensch*]

**supermarket** /-ˌmahkit/ *n* a usu large self-service retail shop selling food and household merchandise – compare HYPERMARKET **2** a large shop selling an exceptionally wide variety of goods of a specified type ⟨*a furniture ~*⟩

**supernal** /s(y)ooh'puhn(ə)l/ *adj*, *formal* **1** belonging to or coming from a celestial realm; heavenly **2** located in or belonging to the sky [ME, fr MF, fr L *supernus*, fr *super* over, above – more at OVER] – **supernally** *adv*

**supernatant** /-'nayt(ə)nt/ *adj* **1** floating on the surface **2** *of a liquid* lying above settled solid material [L *supernatant-, supernatans*, prp of *supernatare* to float, fr *super-* + *natare* to swim – more at NATANT] –**supernatant** *n*

**supernatural** /-'nach(ə)rəl/ *adj* **1** of an order of existence beyond the visible observable universe; *esp* of God or a god, demigod, spirit, or devil **2a** departing from what is usual or normal, esp so as to appear to transcend the laws of nature **b** attributed to an invisible agent (eg a ghost or spirit) [ML *supernaturalis*, fr L *super-* + *natura* nature] – **supernatural** *n*, **supernaturally** *adv*, **supernaturalness** *n*

**supernaturalism** /ˌs(y)oohpə'nachərəˌliz(ə)m/ *n* **1** the quality

or state of being supernatural **2** belief in a supernatural power and order of existence – **supernaturalistic** *adj*

**supernormal** /-'nawml/ *adj* **1** exceeding the normal or average **2** being beyond normal human powers; paranormal *synonyms* see ABNORMAL – **supernormally** *adv*, **supernormality** *n*

**supernova** /-'nohvə/ *n*, *pl* **supernovae** /'nohvie, -vi/ *also* **supernovas** a type of NOVA (star which can suddenly increase its light output) in which the brightness may reach 100 million times that of the sun

¹**supernumerary** /-'nyoohm(ə)rəri/ *adj* **1** exceeding the usual, stated, required, or prescribed number ⟨*a ~ tooth*⟩ **2** not listed among the regular components of a group, esp a military organization [LL *supernumerarius*, fr L *super-* + *numerus* number – more at NIMBLE]

²**supernumerary** *n* **1** a supernumerary person or thing: eg **1a** a person employed not for regular service but for use in case of need **b** a person serving no apparent function **2** an actor employed to play a nonspeaking part in a play or film; an extra

**superorder** /'s(y)oohpəˌawdə/ *n* a category in the biological classification of living things between an ORDER and a CLASS or a SUBCLASS

**superordinate** /-'awdinət/ *adj* superior in rank, class, or status [*super-* + *-ordinate* (as in *subordinate*)]

**superorganism** /ˌs(y)oohpə'awgəniz(ə)m/ *n* an organized society (eg of a social insect) that functions as an organic whole – **superorganic** *adj*

**superovulation** /-ˌovyoo'laysh(ə)n/ *n* production or discharge of excessive numbers of egg cells at one time – **superovulate** *vi*

**superparasitism** /ˌs(y)oohpə'parəsieˌtiz(ə)m/ *n* infestation of a host by more than one parasitic individual usu of one kind – used esp of parasitic insects

**superphosphate** /-'fosfayt/ *n* **1** an acid PHOSPHATE **2** a soluble mixture of PHOSPHATES used as fertilizer and made from insoluble inorganic phosphates by treatment with SULPHURIC ACID

**superphysical** /ˌs(y)oohpə'fizik(ə)l/ *adj* being above or beyond the physical world or explanation on physical principles

**superpose** /ˌs(y)oohpə'pohz/ *vt* **1** to lay (eg a geometric figure) upon another so as to make all like parts coincide **2** *formal* to place or lay over or above; superimpose [Fr *superposer*, back-formation fr *superposition*, fr LL *superposition-, superpositio*, fr L *superpositus*, pp of *superponere* to superpose, fr *super-* + *ponere* to place – more at POSITION] – **superposable** *adj*, **superposition** *n*

**superposed variety** *n* a language or dialect that is used by a group of speakers and is not their mother tongue

**superpower** /-ˌpowə/ *n* an extremely powerful nation; *specif* any of a very few dominant states in a period when most of the world is divided politically into these states and lesser states under their influence and/or control

**supersaturated** /ˌs(y)oohpə'sachooraytid/ *adj* **1** *of a solution* containing more dissolved substance than a SATURATED solution **2** *of a vapour* containing more molecules than a SATURATED vapour – **supersaturation** *n*

**superscribe** /-'skrieb/ *vt* **1** to write or engrave on the top or outside **2** to write something (eg a name or address) on the outside or cover of; address [L *superscribere*, fr *super-* + *scribere* to write – more at SCRIBE]

**superscript** /-ˌskript/ *n* a distinguishing symbol or letter written immediately above, or above and to the right or left of, another character [L *superscriptus*, pp of *superscribere*] – **superscript** *adj*

**superscription** /-'skripsh(ə)n/ *n* **1** the act of superscribing **2** something written or engraved on the surface of, outside, or above something else; an inscription; *also* an address [ME, fr MF, fr LL *superscription-, superscriptio*, fr L *superscriptus*]

**supersede** /-'seed/ *vt* **1a** to cause to be set aside **b** to force out of use as inferior **2** to take the place, position, or office of ⟨*to ~ someone as treasurer*⟩ ⟨*buses ~d trams*⟩ **3** to displace in favour of another; supplant, replace ⟨*to ~ a written test by an oral*⟩ [MF *superseder* to refrain from, fr L *supersedēre* to be superior to, refrain from, fr *super-* + *sedēre* to sit – more at SIT] – **superseder** *n*, **supersedure** *n*

**supersensible** /ˌs(y)oohpə'sensib(ə)l/ *adj* being above or beyond that which is apparent to the senses

**supersensitive** /ˌs(y)oohpə'sensitiv/ *adj* **1** HYPERSENSITIVE (abnormally sensitive to a drug or other agent) **2** specially treated to increase sensitivity ⟨*a ~ photographic emulsion*⟩ – **supersensitiveness** *n*, **supersensitivity** *n*

**supersensory** /ˌs(y)oohpəˈsensəri/ adj supersensible

**supersession** /ˌs(y)oohpəˈsesh(ə)n/ n, formal superseding or being superseded [ML supersession-, supersessio, fr L supersessus, pp of supersedēre] – **supersessive** adj

¹**supersonic** /ˌs(y)oohpəˈsonik/ adj 1 of a wave or vibration having a frequency above the upper threshold of human hearing of about 20000 hertz – compare SONIC 1 2 using or produced by supersonic waves or vibrations 3 of or being speeds greater than the speed of sound in air – compare SONIC 3 4 moving, capable of moving, or using air currents moving at supersonic speed 5 of supersonic aircraft or missiles ⟨the ∼ age⟩ [L super- + sonus sound – more at SOUND] – **supersonically** adv

²**supersonic** n a supersonic wave or frequency

**supersonics** /ˌs(y)oohpəˈsoniks/ n taking sing vb 1 ULTRASONICS 2 the industry involved in the manufacture of supersonic aircraft

**superstar** /ˈs(y)oohpəˌstah/ n a star (eg in sport, cinema, or pop music) who is considered extremely talented, has exceptionally great public appeal, and can usu command a high salary

**superstition** /-ˈstish(ə)n/ n 1a a belief or practice resulting from ignorance, fear of the unknown, trust in magic or chance, or misunderstanding of cause and effect b an irrational abject attitude of mind towards the supernatural, nature, or God, resulting from superstition 2 a belief maintained despite evidence to the contrary [ME supersticion, fr MF, fr L superstition-, superstitio, fr superstit-, superstes standing over (as witness, victor, or survivor), fr super- + stare to stand – more at STAND] – **superstitious** adj, **superstitiously** adv

**superstore** /-ˌstaw/ n a very large supermarket, usu selling food and drinks, household goods, clothing, electrical goods, etc and often situated on the outskirts of a town; HYPERMARKET 2

**superstratum** /ˈs(y)oohpəˌstrahtəm/ n an overlying stratum or layer

**superstructure** /-ˌstrukchə/ n 1 a structure built as a vertical extension of something else: eg 1a the part of a building above the ground b the structural part of a ship above the main deck c the sleepers, rails, and fastenings of a railway track as distinct from the ballast they are laid on 2 an entity, concept, or complex based on a more fundamental one; specif social institutions (eg law or politics) that are in Marxist theory built on the economic base – **superstructural** adj

**supersubtle** /ˌs(y)oohpəˈsutl/ adj extremely or excessively subtle – **supersubtlety** n

**supertanker** /-ˌtangkə/ n a very large tanker vessel

**supertax** /-ˌtaks/ n a tax paid in addition to normal tax by people with high incomes; esp SURTAX

**supertonic** /-ˈtonik/ n the second note of a DIATONIC scale (ordinary 8-note musical scale), represented in sol-fa by ray – called also SECOND

**supervene** /-ˈveen/ vi, chiefly formal to happen unexpectedly; esp to happen in a way that interrupts some process or planned course of action [L supervenire, fr super- + venire to come – more at COME] – **supervention** n

**supervenient** /ˌs(y)oohpəˈveenyənt/ adj, formal coming or occurring as something additional, extraneous, or unexpected [L supervenient-, superveniens, prp of supervenire] – **supervenience** n

**supervise** /ˈs(y)oohpəˌviez/ vt to superintend, oversee [ML supervisus, pp of supervidēre, fr L super- + vidēre to see – more at WIT]

**supervision** /-ˈvizh(ə)n/ n the action, process, or occupation of supervising; esp a critical watching and directing (eg of activities or a course of action)

**supervisor** /ˈs(y)oohpəviezə/ n someone who supervises; esp, NAm an administrative officer in charge of a business, local government, or school unit or operation – **supervisory** adj

**supinate** /ˈs(y)oohpiˌnayt/ vb to (cause to) assume a position of supination [L supinatus, pp of supinare to lay on the back, fr supinus supine]

**supination** /ˌs(y)oohpiˈnaysh(ə)n/ n 1 rotation of the forearm and hand so that the palm faces forwards or upwards and the two bones of the forearm (RADIUS and ULNA) lie parallel to each other; also a corresponding movement of the foot – compare PRONATION 2 the position resulting from supination

**supinator** /ˈs(y)oohpiˌnaytə/ n a muscle that produces the motion of supination [NL, fr L supinatus, pp]

¹**supine** /ˈs(y)oohˌpien, ˌ-ˈ-/ adj 1a lying on the back or with

the face upwards b in a position of supination 2 exhibiting indolent or apathetic inertia or passivity; esp mentally or morally slack **synonyms** see INACTIVE **usage** see PRONE [L supinus; akin to L sub under, up to – more at UP] – **supinely** adv, **supineness** n

²**supine** n 1 a noun form in Latin derived from the stem of the PAST PARTICIPLE of a verb (eg dictu in "mirabile dictu") 2 an English infinitive with to [ME supyn, fr LL supinum, fr L, neut of supinus, adj]

**supper** /ˈsupə/ n 1 a usu light evening meal served when dinner is taken at midday or as the last meal of the day; also the food prepared for a supper 2 a social affair featuring a supper; esp an evening social, often for raising funds ⟨a church ∼⟩ [ME, fr OF souper, fr souper to sup – more at SUP]

**supplant** /səˈplahnt/ vt 1 to take the place of (another), esp by force or treachery 2a to wipe out and supply a substitute ⟨efforts to ∼ the vernacular⟩ b to take the place of and serve as a substitute, esp by reason of superior excellence or power [ME supplanten, fr MF supplanter, fr L supplantare to overthrow by tripping up, fr sub- + planta sole of the foot – more at PLACE] – **supplantation** n, **supplanter** n

**supple** /ˈsupl/ adj 1a compliant, often to the point of submissiveness b readily adaptable or responsive to new situations 2a capable of being bent or folded without creases, cracks, or breaks; pliant ⟨∼ leather⟩ b able to perform bending or twisting movements with ease and grace; lithe ⟨∼ legs of a dancer⟩ c easy and fluent without stiffness or awkwardness ⟨a ∼ voice⟩ **synonyms** see ¹PLASTIC **antonym** stiff [ME souple, fr OF, fr L supplic-, supplex submissive, suppliant, lit., bending under, fr sub- + plic- (akin to plicare to fold) – more at PLY] – **supplely, supply** adv, **suppleness** n

¹**supplement** /ˈsuplimənt/ n 1 something that completes, remedies a deficiency, or makes an addition ⟨dietary ∼s⟩ 2a a part added to or issued as a continuation of a book or periodical to correct errors or make additions b a treatise published in a series by a learned journal 3a an angle that when added to a given angle gives a total of 180° b a part of a circle (ARC) that when added to a given arc forms a semicircle **synonyms** see ¹COMPLEMENT [ME, fr L supplementum, fr supplēre to fill up, complete – more at SUPPLY]

²**supplement** /ˈsupliment/ vt to add a supplement to ⟨∼s his income by doing odd jobs⟩ – **supplementer** n, **supplementation** n

**supplemental** /ˌsupliˈmentl/ adj serving to supplement – **supplemental** n

**supplementary** /ˌsupliˈment(ə)ri/ adj 1 added as a supplement; additional ⟨a ∼ power source⟩ 2 of an angle or arc being either of a pair whose sum is 180°

**supplementary benefit** n, Br money paid by the state for the economic welfare of people (eg the old or unemployed) with insufficient income to live on; esp SOCIAL SECURITY benefit paid to those who do not qualify for UNEMPLOYMENT BENEFIT

**supplementary unit** n a dimensionless unit of measurement (eg a RADIAN) required in addition to the basic units of a system to derive other units

**suppletion** /səˈpleesh(ə)n/ n the occurrence of a word form as a member of the set of inflections of another totally different form (eg went as the past tense of go, or better as the comparative form of good) [ML suppletion-, suppletio act of supplementing, fr L suppletus, pp of supplēre] – **suppletive** adj

**suppletory** /ˈsuplit(ə)ri/ adj, formal supplying deficiencies; supplementary [L suppletus, pp]

**suppliance** /ˈsuplie-əns/ n entreaty, supplication

¹**suppliant** /ˈsupliənt/ n someone who supplicates [ME, fr MF, fr prp of supplier to supplicate, fr L supplicare]

²**suppliant** adj 1 humbly imploring; entreating ⟨a ∼ sinner who seeks forgiveness⟩ 2 expressing supplication ⟨∼ arms upraised⟩ – **suppliantly** adv

**supplicant** /ˈsuplikənt/ n or adj (a) suppliant – **supplicantly** adv

**supplicate** /ˈsuplikayt/ vi to beg humbly; esp to pray to God ∼ vt to ask humbly and earnestly of or for **synonyms** see BEG [ME supplicaten, fr L supplicatus, pp of supplicare, fr supplic-, supplex suppliant – more at SUPPLE] – **supplication** n

**supplicatory** /ˈsuplikətəri/ adj expressing supplication; suppliant ⟨a ∼ prayer⟩

¹**supply** /səˈplie/ vt 1a to provide for; satisfy ⟨supplies a longfelt need⟩ b to provide, furnish ⟨∼ food to the navy⟩ ⟨supplied him with the details⟩ c to substitute for another in; specif to serve as a supply in (a church or pulpit) ∼ vi to serve as a

supply or substitute [ME *supplien*, fr MF *soupleier*, fr L *supplēre* to fill up, supplement, supply, fr *sub-* up + *plēre* to fill – more at SUB-, FULL] – **supplier** *n*

²**supply** *n* **1** a clergyman temporarily taking the place of another who is absent **2a** the quantity or amount (eg of a commodity) needed or available ⟨*a fresh ~ of beef*⟩ ⟨*beer was in short ~ in that hot weather* – Nevil Shute⟩ **b supplies** *pl*, **supply** provisions, stores **3** the act or process of filling a want or need ⟨*the ~ of raw materials to industry*⟩ **4** the quantities of goods and services offered for sale at specified prices at some period of time – compare DEMAND 2b **5 supply teacher, supply** a teacher who is on call to fill temporary vacancies in British schools when regular teachers are absent

³**supply** *adj* of or for the raising of government revenue ⟨*a ~ bill*⟩

¹**support** /sə'pawt/ *vt* **1** to endure bravely or quietly; bear, tolerate ⟨*could not ~ such rude behaviour*⟩ **2a(1)** to promote the interests or cause of ⟨*actively ~s free speech*⟩ **a(2)** to uphold or defend as valid or right; advocate ⟨*~ed the judge's decision*⟩ **a(3)** to argue or vote for ⟨*~s the Labour Party*⟩ **a(4)** to be an enthusiastic or loyal follower of ⟨*~s West Ham*⟩ **b(1)** to assist, help **b(2)** to act with (a principal actor) **b(3)** to bid in bridge so as to show support for **c** to provide with substantiation; corroborate ⟨*~ an alibi*⟩ **3a** to pay the costs of; maintain **b** to provide a basis for the existence or subsistence of ⟨*one acre can ~ one person*⟩ **4a** to hold up or serve as a foundation or prop for ⟨*steel girders ~ the building*⟩ **b** to maintain (a price) at a desired level by purchases or loans; *also* to maintain the price of by purchases or loans **5** to keep from fainting, yielding, or losing courage; comfort ⟨*~ed by her indomitable courage*⟩ **6** to keep (something) going ⟨*oxygen ~s combustion*⟩ [ME *supporten*, fr MF *supporter*, fr LL *supportare*, fr L, to carry, fr *sub-* + *portare* to carry – more at FARE]

*synonyms* **Support, sustain, maintain, uphold, advocate, back,** and **champion** all mean "favour actively against opposition". **Support** is the most general. **Sustain** and **maintain** entail the continued support, perhaps financial, of something already in existence, **sustain** additionally implying relief to the spirits ⟨**sustained** *by his religious faith*⟩ and **maintain** often implying perseverance in an opinion or practice ⟨**maintain** *their native customs*⟩. **Uphold** also applies to what is already in existence, but with a stronger sense of facing opposition ⟨**uphold** *their morale*⟩. **Advocate** applies to what does not yet exist ⟨**advocate** *that changes should be made*⟩. **Back** and **champion** suggest defence or assistance for people or causes that need it, **back** particularly suggesting heartening encouragement ⟨**back** *you up at the interview*⟩ and **champion** implying a militant defence or advocacy ⟨**championed** *women's rights*⟩.

²**support** *n* **1** supporting or being supported **2** one who or that which supports; *esp* maintenance, sustenance ⟨*without visible means of ~*⟩ **3** taking sing or pl vb a body of supporters

**supportable** /sə'pawtəbl/ *adj* capable of being supported – **supportability, supportableness** *n*, **supportably** *adv*

**supporter** /sə'pawtə/ *n* one who or that which supports or acts as a support: eg **a** an adherent or advocate ⟨*a Manchester United ~*⟩ **b** either of two figures (eg of men or animals) placed one on each side of a heraldic shield as if holding or guarding it

**supporting** /sə'pawting/ *adj* **1** that supports ⟨*a ~ wall*⟩ ⟨*full ~ cast*⟩ **2** of or being a film other than the main feature on a cinema programme

**supportive** /sə'pawtiv/ *adj* providing or intended to provide support ⟨*~ evidence for the charge*⟩; *esp* sustaining morale ⟨*the Prime Minister needs a ~ husband*⟩

**support level** *n* a price level on a declining market at which a security resists further decline owing to increased attractiveness to traders and investors

**supposable** /sə'pohzəbl/ *adj* capable of being supposed; conceivable – **supposably** *adv*

**suppose** /sə'pohz/ *vt* **1a** to lay down tentatively as a hypothesis, assumption, or proposal ⟨*~ a fire broke out*⟩ ⟨*~ we wait a bit*⟩ **b(1)** to hold as an opinion; believe ⟨*they ~d they were early*⟩ **b(2)** to think probable or in keeping with the facts ⟨*seems reasonable to ~ that he would profit*⟩ **b(3)** to conjecture, think ⟨*when do you ~ he'll arrive?*⟩ **2** to conceive, imagine **3** to require as a condition; presuppose ⟨*these plans ~ the timetable to be accurate*⟩ [ME *supposen*, fr MF *supposer*, fr ML *supponere* (perf indic *supposui*), fr L, to put under, substitute, fr *sub-* + *ponere* to put – more at POSITION]

*usage* Both **suppose** and **supposing** can initiate a proposal ⟨**suppose/supposing** *we wait a bit*⟩ or introduce an imaginary situation

⟨**suppose/supposing** *they saw you*⟩ but **supposing** is also used like **if** ⟨*even* **supposing** *they're late, we can always sit in the bar*⟩. *synonyms* see ²CONJECTURE *antonyms* know, prove

**supposed** /sə'pohzd/ *adj* **1a** held as an opinion; believed; *also* mistakenly believed; imagined ⟨*the sight which makes ~ terror true* – Shak⟩ **b** considered probable or certain; expected ⟨*~ profits*⟩ **c** understood ⟨*you will be ~ to refer to my grandaunt* – G B Shaw⟩ **2a** pretended ⟨*twelve hours are ~ to elapse between Acts I and II* – Sir Arthur Sullivan⟩ **b** alleged ⟨*incriminating things they may be ~ to have said*⟩ **3a** devised for the specified purpose; intended ⟨*pills that are ~ to kill pain*⟩ **b** made or fashioned by design ⟨*what's that button ~ to do*⟩ **4a** required by authority ⟨*soldiers are ~ to obey their commanding officers*⟩ **b** allowed, permitted – usu neg ⟨*was not ~ to have visitors*⟩ **c** expected because of moral, social, or other obligation ⟨*parents are ~ to keep small children off the road*⟩ □ (*except 1a,b*) chiefly in *be supposed to* – **supposedly** *adv*

**supposing** /sə'pohzing/ *conj* by way of hypothesis ⟨*~ they saw you*⟩ *usage* see SUPPOSE

**supposition** /ˌsupə'zish(ə)n/ *n* **1** something that is supposed; a hypothesis **2** the act of supposing [ME, fr LL *supposition-, suppositio*, fr L, act of placing beneath, fr *suppositus*, pp of *supponere*] – **suppositional** *adv*, **suppositionally** *adv*

**suppositious** /ˈsupəˌzishəs/ *adj, formal* supposititious [by contr]

**supposititious** /səˌpozi'tishəs/ *adj, formal* **1a** fraudulently substituted; spurious **b** *of a child* **b(1)** falsely presented as a genuine heir **b(2)** illegitimate **2** of the nature of or based on a supposition; hypothetical ⟨*whether the anticipation be mine or that of a ~ observer* – Victor Lowe⟩ [L *suppositicius*, fr *suppositus*, pp of *supponere* to substitute; (2) influenced in meaning by *supposition*] – **supposititiously** *adv*, **supposititiousness** *n*

**suppositive** /sə'pozitiv/ *adj, formal* characterized by, involving, or implying supposition – **suppositively** *adv*

**suppository** /sə'pozət(ə)ri/ *n* a cone or cylinder of solid usu medicated material for insertion into a body passage or cavity (eg the rectum or vagina), where it melts and releases the active substances [ML *suppositorium*, fr LL, neut of *suppositorius* placed beneath, fr L *suppositus*, pp of *supponere* to put under]

**suppress** /sə'pres/ *vt* **1** to put down by authority or force; subdue **2** to keep from public knowledge: eg **2a** to keep secret **b** to stop or prohibit the publication or revelation of **3a** to exclude (eg a thought or feeling) from consciousness, esp deliberately – compare REPRESS 2b **b** to keep from giving vent to; check ⟨*~ed his impulse to laugh*⟩ **4a** to arrest; HOLD BACK ⟨*~ a cough*⟩ ⟨*~ a haemorrhage*⟩ **b** to inhibit the growth or development of; stunt **5** to inhibit (eg a gene) from expressing genetic characteristics [ME *suppressen*, fr L *suppressus*, pp of *supprimere*, fr *sub-* + *premere* to press – more at PRESS ] – **suppressible** *adj*, **suppressibility**, *n* **suppression** *n*

*synonyms* One can **suppress** or **repress** a riot, or a laugh. **Suppress** implies the total abolishing of something, while **repress** may entail merely curbing without abolishing it. One can **suppress**, but not **repress**, knowledge or information.

**suppressant** /sə'pres(ə)nt/ *n* something (eg a drug) that tends to suppress rather than eliminate something undesirable

**suppressive** /sə'presiv/ *adj* tending or serving to suppress – **suppressiveness** *n*

**suppressor** /sə'presə/ *n* **1** one who or that which suppresses; *esp* a gene that suppresses the expression of another NONALLELIC (not coding for the same characteristic) gene when both are present **2** an electrical component (eg a CAPACITOR or RESISTOR) added to a circuit to suppress OSCILLATIONS (regular alterations of electrical current) that would otherwise cause radio interference

**suppurate** /'supyoo,rayt/ *vi* to form or discharge pus [L *suppuratus*, pp of *suppurare*, fr *sub-* + *pur-, pus* pus – more at FOUL] – **suppurative** *adj*, **suppuration** *n*

**supra** /'s(y)oohprə, -prah/ *adv* earlier in this writing; above [L]

**supra-** /s(y)oohprə-/ *prefix* **1** SUPER- 2a ⟨*supraorbital*⟩ **2** transcending; above ⟨*supranational*⟩ [L, fr *supra* above, beyond, earlier; akin to L *super* over – more at OVER]

**supraliminal** /ˌs(y)oohprə'limin(ə)l/ *adj* intense enough to be consciously perceived; *esp* sufficient to produce a response or sensation ⟨*a ~ stimulus*⟩ – compare SUBLIMINAL [*supra-* + L *limin-, limen* threshold – more at LIMB] – **supraliminally** *adv*

**supramolecular** /ˌs(y)oohprəmə'lekyoolə/ *adj* more complex than a molecule; *also* composed of many molecules

**supranational** /ˌs(y)oohprə'nash(ə)nl/ *adj* transcending national boundaries, authority, or interests ⟨*a* ~ *authority*⟩ ⟨*taking a* ~ *view of economic problems*⟩ – **supranationalism** *n*, **supranationalist** *n*, **supranationality** *n*

**supraorbital** /s(y)oohprə'awbitl/ *adj* situated or occurring above the eye socket [NL *supraorbitalis*, fr L *supra-* + ML *orbita* eye socket]

**supraordinate** /ˌs(y)oohprə'awdinət/ *adj* higher up in an ordered hierarchy (e g of grammatical components); superordinate [*supra-* + *-ordinate* (as in *subordinate*)]

¹**suprarenal** /s(y)oohprə'reenl/ *adj* situated above or in front of the kidneys; ADRENAL [NL *suprarenalis*, fr L *supra-* + *renes* kidneys]

²**suprarenal** *n* a suprarenal part; *esp* ADRENAL GLAND (adrenalin-producing gland)

**suprarenal gland** *n* ADRENAL GLAND (adrenalin-producing gland)

**suprasegmental** /ˌs(y)oohprəseg'ment(ə)l/ *adj* of or being a linguistic feature (e g stress or pitch) that occurs concurrently with sounds (PHONEMES) in making up a meaningful utterance [*supra-* + *segment* + *-al*]

**supravital** /ˌs(y)oohprə'viet(ə)l/ *adj* of or constituting the biological staining of living tissues or cells surviving after removal from a living body by dyes that can penetrate living substance and induce more or less rapid degenerative changes – compare INTRAVITAM 2 [ISV] – **supravitally** *adv*

**supremacist** /s(y)ooh'premasist/ *n* an advocate or adherent of group supremacy; *esp* WHITE SUPREMACIST (believer in superiority of white races over black)

**supremacy** /s(y)ooh'premasi/ *n* the quality or state of being supreme; *also* supreme authority or power [*supreme* + *-acy* (as in *primacy*)]

**suprematism** /s(y)ooh'premətiz(ə)m/ *n*, *often cap* an art movement dating from about 1913 that was characterized by abstract works using simple geometrical shapes and was essentially an extreme form of CUBISM [Fr *suprématie* supremacy] – **suprematist** *n* or *adj*

**supreme** /s(y)ooh'preem/ *adj* 1 highest in rank or authority ⟨*the* ~ *commander*⟩ 2 highest in degree or quality ⟨ ~ *endurance and bravery in battle*⟩ [L *supremus*, superl of *superus* upper – more at SUPERIOR] – **supremely** *adv*, **supremeness** *n*

**Supreme Being** *n* GOD 1; *specif* the superior deity of the GNOSTICS (adherents of a pre- and early-Christian cult) – compare DEMIURGE

**Supreme Court** *n* 1 the highest judicial tribunal in a nation or state 2 a court in England and Wales formed by the amalgamation of several SUPERIOR COURTS and consisting of the HIGH COURT, COURT OF APPEAL, and CROWN COURT

**Supreme Soviet** *n* the highest legislative body of the Soviet Union consisting of two chambers, one of which represents the overall population and the other the constituent republics

**supremo** /s(y)ooh'preemoh/ *n, pl* **supremos** *chiefly Br informal* 1 a ruler, leader, or director with unlimited powers ⟨*England's soccer* ~⟩ 2 an administrator with particular responsibility for a specified matter ⟨*appointed a water* ~ *to cope with the drought*⟩ [Sp & It, fr *supremo* supreme, fr L *supremus*]

**supremum** /s(y)ooh'preeməm/ *n, maths* the least number greater than or equal to all members of a given set of numbers – called also LEAST UPPER BOUND; compare INFIMUM [L, neut of *supremus*]

**sur-** /suh-, sə-/ *prefix* above; over; beyond ⟨sur*tax*⟩ ⟨sur*real*⟩ ⟨sur*face*⟩ [ME, fr OF, fr L *super-*]

**sura** /'soorə/ *n* a chapter of the KORAN (Muslim holy book) [Ar *sūrah*, lit., row]

**surah** /'soorə/ *n* a soft TWILLED fabric (fabric woven with an appearance of diagonal lines) of silk or rayon [prob alter of *surat* (a type of cotton), fr *Surat*, city in W India]

**surbase** /ˌsuh,bays/ *n* a moulding just above the base of a wall, pedestal, or podium

¹**surbased** /'suh,bayst/ *adj* having a rise of less than half the span ⟨*a* ~ *arch*⟩ [Fr *surbaissé*, fr pp of *surbaisser* to lower, flatten, fr *sur-* + *baisser* to lower, fr *bas* low]

²**surbased** *adj* having a surbase [*surbase* + *-ed*]

¹**surcease** /suh,sees/ *vb, formal vi* to desist from action; *also* to come to an end to and to put an end to; discontinue [ME *sursesen*, *surcesen*, fr MF *sursis*, pp of *surseoir*, fr L *supersedēre* – more at SUPERSEDE]

²**surcease** *n, formal* a cessation; *esp* a temporary respite or end

¹**surcharge** /'suh,chahj/ *vt* 1a to overcharge b to subject to an additional charge c to show an omission in (an account) for which credit ought to have been given 2 to fill or load to excess ⟨*an atmosphere that was* ~d *with war hysteria*⟩ 3a to mark a new value or a surcharge on (a stamp) b to overprint ⟨ ~ *a bank note*⟩ 4 *Br* to overstock [ME *surchargen*, fr MF *surchargier*, fr *sur-* + *chargier* to charge]

²**surcharge** *n* 1a an additional tax or cost b an extra fare ⟨*a sleeping car* ~⟩ c an instance of surcharging an account 2 surcharging or being surcharged 3a(1) an overprint on a stamp; *esp* one that alters the value a(2) a stamp bearing a printed surcharge b an overprint on a currency note 4 earth behind and higher than the top of a RETAINING WALL (wall to hold back earth, loose rock, etc)

**surcingle** /'suh,sing-gl/ *n* 1 a belt, band, or girth passing round the body of a horse, usu to bind a saddle, rug, or pack fast to the horse's back 2 *archaic* the girdle, cord, or sash of a clergyman's cassock [ME *sursengle*, fr MF *surcengle*, fr *sur-* + *cengle* girdle, fr L *cingulum* – more at CINGULUM]

**surcoat** /'suh,koht/ *n* an outer coat or cloak; *specif* a loose tunic worn over armour [ME *surcote*, fr MF, fr *sur-* + *cote* coat]

¹**surd** /suhd/ *adj, of a speech sound* uttered without vibration of the vocal chords; VOICELESS [L *surdus* deaf, silent, stupid; akin to L *susurrus* hum – more at SWARM]

²**surd** *n* 1 an IRRATIONAL root (e g √2); *also* an algebraic expression containing IRRATIONAL NUMBERS or COMPLEX NUMBERS ⟨2 + 5*i is a* ~⟩ 2 a surd speech sound

¹**sure** /shooə, shaw/ *adj* 1 firmly established; secure ⟨*a* ~ *hold*⟩ 2 reliable, trustworthy ⟨*a* ~ *friend*⟩ 3 marked by or given to feelings of confident certainty ⟨*he was* ~ *he was right*⟩ ⟨*you're always so* ~⟩ 4 admitting of no doubt; certain, indisputable ⟨*spoke from* ~ *knowledge*⟩ 5a bound to happen; inevitable, destined ⟨ ~ *disaster*⟩ b incapable of failing; bound ⟨*he is* ~ *to win*⟩ [ME, fr MF *sur*, fr L *securus* secure] – **sureness** *n* – **for sure** (as) a certainty – **sure enough** as one might confidently expect ⟨*we laid the trap and* sure enough *he fell into it*⟩ – **to be sure** it must be acknowledged; admittedly

**synonyms** Sure, certain, positive, confident, assured, and cocksure all mean "having no doubt". Sure and surely are often interchangeable with certain and certainly, but in British English certain(ly) is preferred where one really knows the truth. Compare ⟨surely (= I believe) *you must be tired?*⟩ ⟨*yes, I* certainly (NAm surely, sure) *am tired!*⟩. Positive suggests a firm conviction of one's rightness, to which confident sometimes adds the idea of a perhaps excessive conviction based on faith. Assured suggests that one has been freed of all doubt. Cocksure always implies presumptuous vanity ⟨*that arrogant and* cocksure *materialist* – Aldous Huxley⟩. **usage** Some people dislike the pronunciation /shaw/. **antonyms** unsure, diffident

²**sure** *adv, chiefly NAm informal* surely, certainly ⟨*I* ~ *am tired*⟩ – often used in giving an affirmative reply ⟨ ~, *I'll be there*⟩

**usage** Sure is used as an adverb in **sure enough**, and in the phrase **as sure as** ⟨as sure as *I'm standing here*⟩; it cannot replace surely in the meanings "safely" or "confidently".

**sure enough** *adv* as one might confidently expect ⟨*we laid the trap and* ~ *he fell into it*⟩

**surefire** /-'fie-ə/ *adj, informal* certain to succeed ⟨*a* ~ *recipe*⟩

**surefooted** /-'footid/ *adj* not liable to stumble, fall, or err – **surefootedly** *adv*, **surefootedness** *n*

**surely** /-li/ *adv* 1 in a sure manner: 1a without danger; safely ⟨*driving slowly but* ~⟩ b(1) with assurance; confidently ⟨*handled poetic forms* ~ *and imaginatively*⟩ b(2) without doubt; certainly ⟨*they will* ~ *be heard from soon*⟩ b(3) (as if) inevitably ⟨*slowly but* ~ *the great ship went down*⟩ 2 it is to be believed, hoped, or expected that ⟨ ~ *you like beer*⟩ **synonyms** see ¹SURE *usage* see ²SURE

**surety** /'shooəriti/ *n* 1a a formal engagement (e g a pledge) given for the fulfilment of an undertaking; a guarantee b ground of confidence or security 2 a person who assumes legal liability for the debt, default, or failure in duty (e g appearance in court) of another 3 *formal* the state of being certain or confident [ME *surte*, fr MF *surté*, fr L *securitat-*, *securitas* security, fr *securus* secure] – **suretyship** *n*

¹**surf** /suhf/ *n* 1 the swell of the sea that breaks on the shore or on sandbanks, reefs, etc 2 the foam, splash, and sound of breaking waves △ serf [origin unknown]

²**surf** *vi* to engage in surfing; ride the surf – **surfer** *n*

**surfable** /ˌsuhfəbl/ *adj, esp of a wave or beach* suitable for surfing

¹**surface** /'suhfis/ *n* 1 the exterior or upper boundary or layer

of an object or body **2** a plane or curved two-dimensional LOCUS of points (eg the boundary of a three-dimensional region) ⟨*plane* ~⟩ ⟨~ *of a sphere*⟩ **3a** the external or superficial aspect of something ⟨*look beneath the* ~⟩ **b** an external part or layer ⟨*sand down the damaged* ~⟩ **4** a complete AEROFOIL (part of an aircraft designed to produce lift) used for sustaining flight, for control, or to increase stability [Fr, fr *sur-* + *face*] – **on the surface** to all outward appearances; superficially

²**surface** *vt* **1** to give a surface to: eg **1a** to make smooth; plane **b** to apply the surface layer to ⟨~ *a road*⟩ **2** to bring (eg a submarine) to the surface ~ *vi* **1** to work on or at the surface **2** to come to the surface ⟨*waiting for the scandal to* ~⟩ **3** *informal* to wake up; *also* GET UP 1a ⟨*he never* ~s *before ten*⟩ – **surfacer** *n*

³**surface** *adj* **1a** of, located on, or designed for use at the surface of something **b** situated or employed on the surface of the earth ⟨~ *transport*⟩ ⟨*miners and* ~ *workers*⟩ **2** appearing on the surface only; lacking depth; superficial ⟨~ *realism*⟩

,**surface-'active** *adj* altering the properties at a surface, esp lowering the SURFACE TENSION (eg of water) ⟨*soaps and wetting agents are typical* ~ *substances*⟩

**surface harden** *vt* FACE-HARDEN (harden the surface of, esp steel)

**surface mail** *n* mail sent by any means other than airmail

**surface structure** *n, linguistics* a formal representation of the form of a sentence as it is actually spoken or written; *also* the structure which such a representation specifies – compare DEEP STRUCTURE

**surface tension** *n* a property of liquids that produces an effect such that their surfaces act as if they were elastic skins under tension, that tends to minimize their surface areas, and that is due to unbalanced intermolecular forces

**surface-to-air missile** *n* a usu guided missile launched from the ground against a target in the air

**surfacing** /'suhfising/ *n* material forming or used to form a surface

**surfactant** /suh'fakt(ə)nt/ *n* a surface-active substance (eg a detergent) [*surf*ace-*act*ive + *-ant*] – **surfactant** *adj*

**surfboard** /'suhf,bawd/ *n* a usu long narrow buoyant board (eg of lightweight wood or fibreglass-covered foam) used in surfing – **surfboard** *vi*, **surfboarder** *n*

**surfboat** /-,boht/ *n* a boat for use in heavy surf

¹**surfeit** /'suhfit/ *n* **1** an overabundant supply; an excess **2** an intemperate or immoderate indulgence in something (eg food or drink) **3** disgust caused by excess [ME *surfait*, fr MF, fr *surfaire* to overdo, fr *sur-* + *faire* to do, fr L *facere* – more at DO]

²**surfeit** *vt* to feed, supply, or give to excess; cloy, satiate *synonyms* see ²SATIATE – **surfeiter** *n*

**surficial** /suh'fish(ə)l/ *adj* of a surface [*surf*ace + *-icial* (as in *superficial*)]

**surfie** /'suhfi/ *n, Austr informal* someone whose way of life is centred round surfing

**surfing** /'suhfing/ *n* the activity or sport of riding towards the shore on the front part of a wave, esp while standing or lying on a surfboard

**Surform** /'suhfawm/ *trademark* – used for a wood-shaping tool that has a blade pierced by many sharp-edged holes

¹**surge** /suhj/ *vi* **1** to rise and fall actively; toss ⟨*a ship surging in heavy seas*⟩ **2** to rise and move in waves or billows; swell **3** *of a rope* to loosen round a WINDLASS, capstan, or other winding device **4** *of an electrical current or voltage* to rise suddenly to an excessive or abnormal value **5** to move with a surge or in surges ⟨*felt the blood* surging *to her cheeks*⟩ ~ *vt* to allow (eg a rope) to surge ⟨~ *a hawser to prevent its parting*⟩ [MF *sourge-*, stem of *sourdre* to rise, surge, fr L *surgere* to go straight up, rise, fr *sub-* up + *regere* to lead straight – more at SUB-, RIGHT]

²**surge** *n* **1** the motion of swelling, rolling, or sweeping forwards like that of a wave or series of waves ⟨*a* ~ *of interest*⟩ **2a** a large wave or billow; a swell **b** a series of swells or large billows; *also* the resulting rise of water level **3** a short-lived sudden rise of current in an electrical circuit △ serge

**surgeon** /'suhj(ə)n/ *n* a medical specialist who practises surgery [ME *surgien*, fr AF, fr OF *cirurgien*, fr *cirurgie* surgery]

**surgeon fish** *n* any of various tropical fishes (family Acanthuridae) that have one or more sharp movable spines near the base of the tail [fr the spines resembling a surgeon's instruments]

**surgeon general** *n, pl* **surgeons general** the chief medical officer of a branch of the US armed services or of a US public health service

**surgeon's knot** *n* any of several knots used in tying surgical thread stitches; *esp* a REEF KNOT with a double turn in the first loop

**surgery** /'suhj(ə)ri/ *n* **1** the branch of medicine that deals with diseases and conditions requiring or suited to operative or manual procedures **2** a room or area where surgery is performed **3a** the work done by a surgeon **b** an operation ⟨*is undergoing* ~⟩ **4** *Br* (the hours of opening of) a place where a doctor or dentist gives advice and treatment **5** *Br* a session at which a member of a profession (eg a lawyer) or esp an elected representative (eg an MP) is available for usu informal consultation (eg by constituents) ⟨*the Conservative ran very good* surgeries – *The Times*⟩ [ME *surgerie*, fr OF *cirurgie, surgerie*, fr L *chirurgia*, fr Gk *cheirourgia*, fr *cheirourgos* surgeon, fr *cheirourgos* working with the hand, fr *cheir* hand + *ergon* work – more at CHIR-, WORK]

**surgical** /'suhjikl/ *adj* **1a** of surgeons or surgery ⟨~ *skills*⟩ **b** used in or in connection with surgery ⟨*a* ~ *stocking*⟩ **2** following or resulting from surgery [*surgeon* + *-ical*] – **surgically** *adv*

**surgical spirit** *n, Br* a mixture of METHYLATED SPIRITS with a small quantity of OIL OF WINTERGREEN and CASTOR OIL, used esp as a skin disinfectant

**suricate** /'syooərikayt/ *n* MEERKAT (S African animal related to a mongoose) [Fr *surikate*, prob fr a native name in S Africa]

**surjection** /suh'jekshən/ *n* a mathematical mapping for which every element of a set is corresponded to by the elements of another set [Fr, fr *sur* over, on, onto + *-jection* (as in *projection*)]

**surjective** /suh'jektiv/ *adj* being a mathematical surjection

**surly** /'suhli/ *adj* **1** irritably sullen and churlish in mood or manner **2** menacing or threatening in appearance ⟨~ *weather*⟩ [alter. of *sirly* lordly, imperious, fr ME, fr *sir*] – **surlily** *adv*, **surliness** *n*

¹**surmise** /suh'miez/ *vt* to imagine or infer on slight grounds; guess ⟨*he* ~d *that it was true*⟩ *synonyms* see ²CONJECTURE *antonym* ascertain [ME *surmisen* to accuse, fr MF *surmis*, pp of *surmetre*, fr L *supermittere* to throw on, fr *super-* + *mittere* to send] – **surmiser** *n*

²**surmise** /suh'miez, 'suhmiez/ *n, formal* a thought or idea based on scanty evidence; a conjecture

**surmount** /suh'mownt/ *vt* **1** to rise above; overcome, conquer ⟨~ *an obstacle*⟩ **2** to get to the top of; climb **3** to stand or lie at the top of [ME *surmounten*, fr MF *surmonter*, fr *sur-* + *monter* to mount] – **surmountable** *adj*

¹**surname** /'suh,naym/ *n* the name shared in common by members of a family [ME, fr *sur-* + *name*]

²**surname** *vt* to give a surname to

**surpass** /suh'pahs/ *vt* **1** to become better, greater, or stronger than; exceed **2** to go beyond; overstep **3** to transcend the reach, capacity, or powers of ⟨*her beauty* ~es *description*⟩ [MF *surpasser*, fr *sur-* + *passer* to pass] – **surpassable** *adj*

**surpassing** /suh'pahsing/ *adj* greatly exceeding others; of a very high degree – **surpassingly** *adv*

**surplice** /'suhplis/ *n* a loose white ecclesiastical outer garment, usu of knee length, with large open sleeves [ME *surplis*, fr OF *surpliz*, fr ML *superpellicium*, fr *super-* + *pellicium* coat of skins, fr L, neut of *pellicius* made of skins, fr *pellis* skin – more at FELL; fr its being orig worn over fur garments]

**surplus** /'suhpləs/ *n* **1a** the amount that remains over and above what is used or needed **b** an excess of income over expenditure **2** the excess of a company's net worth over the value of its capital stock [ME, fr MF, fr ML *superplus*, fr L *super-* + *plus* more – more at PLUS] – **surplus** *adj*

**surplusage** /'suhpləsij/ *n* **1** SURPLUS 1a **2** excessive or nonessential matter

**surplus value** *n* the difference in Marxist theory between the value of work done or of commodities produced by employees and the wages paid by the employer

**surprint** /,suh,print/ *vt or n* (to) overprint

¹**surprise** /sə'priez/ *n* **1** an act of taking unawares **2** something that surprises **3** the state of being surprised; astonishment [ME, fr MF, fr fem of *surpris*, pp of *surprendre* to take over, surprise, fr *sur-* + *prendre* to take – more at PRIZE]

²**surprise** *vt* **1** to attack unexpectedly; *also* to capture by an unexpected attack **2a** to take unawares ⟨*to* ~ *someone in the*

act⟩ **b** to detect or bring out by taking unawares ⟨*to* ~ *a secret out of someone*⟩ **3** to strike with wonder or amazement, esp because unexpected or extraordinary – **surpriser** *n*
　　**synonyms** Surprise, astonish, amaze, astound, flabbergast, and dumbfound all mean "impress forcibly through unexpectedness". The other words are all stronger than surprise, and are here arranged approximately in ascending order of strength. Astonish and even more amaze imply being momentarily dazed or speechless. Astound, the informal flabbergast, and dumbfound suggest actual shock at being confronted with something almost incredible. **usage** One is surprised (= taken unawares) *by* ⟨*they were surprised by her husband*⟩; one is surprised (= amazed) *at* or *that* ⟨*I'm* surprised *at you!*⟩ ⟨*we were* surprised *that they answered*⟩.

**surprising** /sə'priezing/ *adj* of a nature that causes surprise – **surprisingly** *adv*

**surra** /'sooərə/ *n* a severe disease of domestic animals that is caused by a PROTOZOAN (single-celled organism) (*Trypanosoma evansi*), is transmitted by biting insects, and is characterized by fever and internal bleeding [Marathi *sūra* wheezing sound]

**surreal** /sə'riəl/ *adj* **1** having a strange dreamlike irrational quality or atmosphere **2** SURREALISTIC 1 [back-formation fr *surrealism*]

**surrealism** /sə'riə,liz(ə)m/ *n, often cap* a movement in art and literature dating from about 1919 reflecting the influence of psychoanalysis and seeking to use the incongruous images formed by the unconscious to transcend reality as perceived by the conscious mind; *also* surrealistic practices or atmosphere [Fr *surréalisme*, fr *sur-* + *réalisme* realism] – **surrealist** *n or adj*

**surrealistic** /sə,riə'listik/ *adj* **1** of surrealism **2** SURREAL 1 ⟨*the* ~ *quality of Chinese politics* – *Newsweek*⟩ – **surrealistically** *adv*

**surrebutter** /,suhri'butə/ *n* the reply made by the plaintiff in the fourth round of PLEADING (allegations and counter-allegations in a legal action) to the defendant's REBUTTER (answer to the surrejoinder) [*sur-* + *rebutter*]

**surrejoinder** /,suhri'joyndə/ *n* the reply made by the plaintiff in the third round of PLEADING (allegations and counter-allegations in a legal action) to the defendant's REJOINDER [*sur-* + *rejoinder*]

¹**surrender** /sə'rendə/ *vt* **1a** to yield (something) to the power, control, or possession of another, esp under compulsion ⟨~ed *the fort*⟩ ⟨~ *one's passport*⟩ **b** to give up completely or agree to forgo, esp in favour of another **2a** to give (oneself) up into the power of another, esp as a prisoner **b** to give (oneself) over to something (eg an influence or course of action) ~ *vi* to give oneself up into the power of another; yield [ME *surrenderen*, fr MF *surrendre*, fr *sur-* + *rendre* to give back, yield – more at RENDER]

²**surrender** *n* **1** the action or an instance of surrendering oneself or something **2** the voluntary cancellation of an insurance policy by the party insured, in return for a payment
　　**synonyms** Surrender, submission, and capitulation all mean "the act of yielding to another". Surrender is the most general, implying a compulsory or voluntary yielding to somebody's power or possession. Submission emphasizes rather the idea of subordinating oneself to somebody's authority. Capitulation is surrender usually by acquiescence and on prearranged conditions.

**surreptitious** /,surəp'tishəs/ *adj* **1** done, made, or acquired by stealth; clandestine **2** acting or doing something clandestinely; stealthy **synonyms** see ¹SECRET [ME, fr L *surrepticius*, fr *surreptus*, pp of *surripere* to snatch secretly, fr *sub-* + *rapere* to seize – more at RAPID] – **surreptitiously** *adv*, **surreptitiousness** *n*

**surrey** /'suri/ *n, NAm* a 4-wheeled 2-seat horse-drawn pleasure carriage [*Surrey*, county in SE England]

¹**surrogate** /'surəgayt/ *vt, formal* to put in the place of another; substitute [L *surrogatus*, pp of *surrogare* to choose in place of another, substitute, fr *sub-* + *rogare* to ask – more at RIGHT]

²**surrogate** /'surəgət/ *n* **1a** a person appointed to act in place of another; a deputy; *specif, chiefly Br* a clergyman appointed to act for a bishop in granting marriage licences **b** a local judicial officer in some states of the USA (eg New York) who has jurisdiction over the validation of wills, the settlement of estates, and the appointment and supervision of guardians **2** one who or that which serves as a substitute ⟨*a* ~ *wife*⟩

**surrogation** /,surə'gaysh(ə)n/ *n* the use of surrogates (eg condensed versions of documents) in place of longer items (eg the documents themselves) in an information retrieval system

¹**surround** /sə'rownd/ *vt* **1a(1)** to enclose on all sides; envelop

⟨*was* ~ed *by a crowd of people* – Jonathan Swift⟩ **a(2)** to enclose so as to cut off communication or retreat **b** to form the entourage of ⟨*flatterers who* ~ *the king*⟩ **c** to be part of the environment of ⟨~ed *by luxury*⟩ **d** to extend round the margin or edge of; encircle ⟨*a wall* ~s *the old city*⟩ **2** to cause to be encompassed, encircled, or enclosed by something ⟨*he* ~ed *himself with able advisers*⟩ [ME *surrounden* to overflow, fr MF *suronder*, fr LL *superundare*, fr L *super-* + *unda* wave – more at WATER; influenced in meaning by ⁶*round*]

²**surround** *n* something (eg border or edging) that surrounds

**surroundings** /sə'rowndingz/ *n pl* the circumstances, conditions, or objects by which one is surrounded; one's environment

**surround sound** *n* sound reproduction that aims to give the effect of sounds coming from spatially distinguishable sources

**surroyal** /suh'royəl/ *n* any of the branches (TINES) of an antler above the third branch (ROYAL ANTLER) of a large deer, that are usu attained at the age of four years [ME *surryal*, fr *sur-* + *royal* royal antler]

**sursum corda** /'suhsəm,kawdə/ *n, often cap S&C* a short verse or sentence (VERSICLE) said or sung before the introductory section (PREFACE) of a communion service that invites the congregation to give thanks [LL, (lift) up (your) hearts; fr its opening words]

**surtax** /'suhtaks/ *n* a graduated INCOME TAX formerly imposed in the UK in addition to the normal income tax if one's net income exceeded a fixed amount – called also SUPERTAX

**surtout** /'suhtooh/ *n* a man's long closely fitting overcoat, worn esp in the late 19th century [Fr, fr *sur* over (fr L *super*) + *tout* all, fr L *totus* whole]

**surveillance** /suh'vayləns, sə-; *also* -'vayəns/ *n* close watch kept over someone or something (eg by a detective); *also* supervision [Fr, fr *surveiller* to watch over, fr *sur-* + *veiller* to watch, fr L *vigilare*, fr *vigil* watchful – more at VIGIL] – **surveil** *vt*, **surveillant** *n*
　　**usage** The pronunciation /suh'vayləns/ is recommended for BBC broadcasters.

¹**survey** /suh'vay, '--/ *vt* **1a** to examine as to condition, situation, or value; appraise **b** to make a survey of **2** to determine and delineate the form, extent, and position of (eg a tract of land) by taking linear and angular measurements and by applying the principles of geometry and trigonometry **3** to view or consider comprehensively **4** to inspect, scrutinize ⟨*he* ~ed *us in a lordly way* – Alan Harrington⟩ ~ *vi* to make a survey **synonyms** see ¹SEE [ME *surveyen*, fr MF *surveeir* to look over, fr *sur-* + *veeir* to see – more at VIEW]

²**survey** /'suhvay/ *n* surveying or being surveyed; *also* something surveyed

**surveying** /suh'vaying/ *n* **1a** the occupation or art of carrying out surveys **b** the act of carrying out a survey **2** a branch of applied mathematics that deals with the determination of the area of any portion of the earth's surface, the lengths and directions of the bounding lines, and the contour of the surface, and with accurately delineating the whole on paper

**surveyor** /sə'vay·ə/ *n* one who or that which surveys; *esp* someone whose occupation is surveying land

**surveyor's level** *n* an instrument for measuring the relative heights of land, consisting of a telescope and a SPIRIT LEVEL mounted on a tripod and revolving about a vertical axis

**survival** /sə'vievl/ *n* **1a** the action or process of living or continuing longer than another person or thing **b** the continuation of life or existence ⟨*problems of* ~ *in arctic conditions*⟩ **2** one who or that which survives, esp after others of its kind have disappeared

**survival of the fittest** *n* NATURAL SELECTION (evolutionary process whereby only individuals most suited to the environment survive)

**survival value** *n* usefulness in the struggle for existence

**survive** /sə'viev/ *vi* to remain alive or in existence; live on ⟨*managed to* ~ *on bread and water*⟩ ~ *vt* **1** to remain alive or in being after the death or passing away of ⟨*his son* ~d *him*⟩ ⟨~d *its usefulness*⟩ **2** to continue to exist or live after ⟨~d *the earthquake*⟩ [ME *surviven*, fr MF *survivre* to outlive, fr L *supervivere*, fr *super-* + *vivere* to live – more at QUICK] – **survivable** *adj*, **survivability** *n*, **survivor** *n*

**sus** /sus/ *n, slang* suspicion of loitering with intent to commit a crime ⟨~ *laws*⟩ ⟨*arrested on* ~⟩ [short for *suspicion*]

**susceptance** *n* the part of the ADMITTANCE or an electrical circuit that is related to the CAPACITANCE or INDUCTANCE of the circuit [*susceptibility* + -*ance*]

**susceptibility** /sə‚septə'biləti/ *n* **1** being susceptible; *esp* lack of ability to resist some outside agent (e g a disease-causing agent or a drug); sensitivity **2a** a susceptible temperament or constitution **b** *pl* feelings, sensibilities **3a** the ratio of the amount of magnetization in a substance to the force magnetizing it **b** the ratio of the amount of separation (POLARIZATION) of positive and negative electric charge occurring in a substance to the strength of the applied ELECTRIC FIELD

**susceptible** /sə'septəbl/ *adj* **1** capable of submitting to an action, process, or operation – often + *of* or *to* ⟨*a theory* ∼ *of proof*⟩ **2** open, subject, or unresistant to some stimulus, influence, or agency **3** easily moved or emotionally affected; impressionable, responsive – often + *to* [LL *susceptibilis*, fr L *susceptus*, pp of *suscipere* to take up, admit, fr *sub-*, *sus-* up + *capere* to take – more at SUB-, HEAVE] – **susceptibleness** *n*, **susceptibly** *adv*

**susceptive** /sə'septiv/ *adj* **1** receptive **2** susceptible – **susceptiveness** *n*, **susceptivity** *n*

**suslik** /'suslik/ *n* any of several rather large short-tailed gregarious burrowing rodents (genus *Citellus*) of E Europe or N Asia [Russ]

**¹suspect** /'suspekt/ *adj* (deserving to be) regarded with suspicion; suspected [ME, fr MF, fr L *suspectus*, fr pp of *suspicere*]

**²suspect** *n* someone who is suspected; *esp* one suspected of a crime

**³suspect** /sə'spekt/ *vt* **1** to have doubts of; distrust **2** to imagine (someone) to be guilty or answerable without conclusive proof ⟨∼ *him of giving false information*⟩ **3** to imagine to exist or be true, likely, or probable ⟨*we* ∼ed *trouble*⟩ ⟨*I* ∼ *that he is correct*⟩ [ME *suspecten*, fr L *suspectare*, fr *suspectus*, pp of *suspicere* to look up at, admire, distrust, fr *sub-*, *sus-* up, secretly + *specere* to look at – more at SUB-, SPY]

**suspend** /sə'spend/ *vt* **1** to debar temporarily from a privilege, office, membership, or employment ⟨∼ *a worker on full pay*⟩ **2a** to cause to stop temporarily ⟨∼ *the bus service*⟩ **b** to set aside or make temporarily inoperative ⟨∼ *the rules*⟩ **3** to defer till later on particular conditions ⟨∼ *sentence*⟩ **4** to hold in an undetermined or undecided state awaiting fuller information ⟨∼ *judgment*⟩ **5a** to hang; *esp* to hang so as to be free on all sides except at the point of support ⟨∼ *a ball by a thread*⟩ **b** to keep from falling or sinking by some invisible support (e g buoyancy) ⟨*dust* ∼ed *in the air*⟩ **6** to hold (a musical note) over into the following chord ∼ *vi* **1** to cease temporarily from operation **2** to stop payment or fail to meet obligations **3** to hang [ME *suspenden*, fr OF *suspendre* to hang up, interrupt, fr L *suspendere*, fr *sub-*, *sus-* up + *pendere* to cause to hang, weigh – more at PENDANT]

**suspended animation** /sə'spendid/ *n* temporary suspension of the vital body functions (e g in people nearly drowned)

**suspender** /sə'spendə/ *n* **1** one who or that which suspends **2** a device by which something may be suspended: e g **2a** *Br* an elasticated band with a fastening device for holding up a sock **b** *Br* any of the fastening devices on a SUSPENDER BELT or corset that holds up a woman's stockings **c suspenders** *pl*, **suspender** *NAm* BRACES 4c

**suspender belt** *n*, *Br* a garment consisting of two pairs of short straps hanging from a belt or girdle to which are attached fastening devices for holding up a woman's stockings

**suspense** /sə'spens/ *n* **1** the state of being suspended; suspension **2a** mental uncertainty; anxiety **b** pleasant excitement as to a decision or outcome ⟨*a novel of* ∼⟩ **3** the state or character of being undecided or doubtful [ME, fr MF, fr *suspendre*] – **suspenseful** *adj*

**suspension** /sə'spensh(ə)n/ *n* **1** suspending or being suspended: e g **1a** temporary removal from office or privileges **b** temporary withholding (e g of belief or decision) **c** temporary abolishing of a law or rule **d(1)** the holding over of one or more notes of a chord into the following chord, producing a momentary discord; *specif* such a dissonance in which the note or notes suspended are then moved downwards to create concord – compare RETARDATION **d(2)** the note held over in a suspension **e** stoppage of payment of business obligations through insolvency or financial failure – used esp with reference to a business or bank **f** a device in speaking or writing whereby the principal idea is deferred to the end of a sentence or longer unit **2a** hanging or being hung **b(1)** the state of a substance when it exists as particles with but undissolved in a liquid, gas, or solid **b(2)** a substance in this state **b(3)** a system consisting of a solid dispersed in a solid, liquid, or gas, usu in

particles of larger than COLLOIDAL size – compare EMULSION **3a** a device by which something (e g a MAGNETIC NEEDLE in a compass) is suspended **b** the system of devices (e g springs) supporting the upper part of a vehicle on the axles **c** the act, process, or manner in which the pendulum or BALANCE WHEEL of a timepiece is suspended [LL *suspension-*, *suspensio*, fr L *suspensus*, pp of *suspendere*]

**suspension bridge** *n* a bridge that has its roadway suspended from two or more cables usu passing over towers and securely anchored at the ends

**suspension points** *n pl*, *chiefly NAm* a set of usu three spaced full stops used to indicate an omission from a text

**suspensive** /sə'spensiv/ *adj* **1** stopping temporarily; suspending **2** characterized by suspense, suspended judgment, or indecisiveness **3** characterized by suspension – **suspensively** *adv*

**suspensoid** /sə'spensoyd/ *n* a SOL (mixture of substances not forming a true solution) composed of a liquid containing solid particles that are LYOPHOBIC (not readily dispersed) – compare EMULSOID [ISV *suspens*ion + coll*oid*] – **suspensoidal** *adj*

**suspensor** /sə‚spensə/ *n* **1** a suspensory **2** a group of cells in a plant that serves to push the developing embryo into the nutritive tissue (ENDOSPERM) [NL, fr *suspensus*, pp]

**¹suspensory** /sə'spens(ə)ri/ *adj* **1** held in suspension; *also* fitted or serving to suspend **2** SUSPENSIVE l

**²suspensory** *n* something (e g a ligament or muscle) that suspends or holds up something (e g an organ)

**suspensory ligament** *n* a ligament or membrane supporting an organ or part: e g **a** a ringlike fibrous membrane connecting the lens of the eye to the wall of the eyeball and holding the former in position **b** the sickle-shaped ligament of the liver

**suspicion** /sə'spish(ə)n/ *n* **1a** the act or an instance of suspecting something wrong without proof or on slight evidence; mistrust **b** a state of mental uneasiness and uncertainty; doubt **2** a slight touch or trace ⟨*just a* ∼ *of garlic*⟩ **synonyms** see UNCERTAINTY [ME, fr L *suspicion-*, *suspicio*, fr *suspicere* to suspect – more at SUSPECT]

**suspicious** /sə'spishəs/ *adj* **1** tending to arouse suspicion; questionable ⟨∼ *circumstances*⟩ **2** tending to suspect; distrustful ⟨∼ *of strangers*⟩ **3** expressing or indicative of suspicion ⟨*a* ∼ *glance*⟩ – **suspiciously** *adv*, **suspiciousness** *n*

**suspire** /sə'spie·ə/ *vi*, *formal* to draw a long deep breath; sigh [ME *suspiren*, fr L *suspirare*, fr *sub-* + *spirare* to breathe – more at SPIRIT] – **suspiration** *n*

**suss** /sus/ *vt*, *Br slang* to uncover the truth about ⟨*soon* ∼ed *that he was lying*⟩ – often + *out* ⟨*she's got him well* ∼ed *out*⟩ [by shortening & alter. fr *suspect*]

   **suss out** *vt*, *Br slang* to investigate, reconnoitre ⟨*sussed him out and found he was lying*⟩ ⟨*sussed out the area to find the good pubs*⟩

**Sussex spaniel** /'susiks/ *n* (any of) a British breed of short-legged short-necked long-bodied spaniels with a flat or slightly wavy golden coat [*Sussex*, county in SE England]

**sustain** /sə'stayn/ *vt* **1** to give support or relief to **2** to supply with sustenance; nourish ⟨*plant life* ∼s *the living world*⟩ **3** to cause to continue; prolong; KEEP UP ⟨∼ *a conversation*⟩ **4** to support the weight of; prop; *also* to carry, withstand ⟨*beams can't* ∼ *the weight of the roof*⟩ **5** to buoy up the spirits of; keep from flagging ⟨*hope* ∼ed *them*⟩ **6a** to bear up under; endure **b** to suffer, undergo ⟨∼ed *heavy losses*⟩ ⟨∼ed *a broken leg*⟩ **7** to allow or admit as valid ⟨*the court* ∼ed *the motion*⟩ **8** to support by adequate proof; confirm ⟨*testimony that* ∼s *our contention*⟩ **9** to act the part of (a character) ⟨*able to* ∼ *general roles*⟩ [ME *sustenen*, fr OF *sustenir*, fr L *sustinēre* to hold up, sustain, fr *sub-*, *sus-* up + *tenēre* to hold – more at SUB-, THIN] – **sustainable** *adj*, **sustainer** *n*

   *usage* Some people dislike the use of **sustain** to mean merely "suffer" ⟨**sustain** *injuries*⟩ without any sense of "endure bravely" as in ⟨**sustain** *a siege*⟩. **synonyms** see ¹SUPPORT

**sustaining** /sə'stayning/ *adj* serving to sustain someone or something ⟨*a* ∼ *meal*⟩

**sustenance** /'sustinəns/ *n* **1a** a means of support, maintenance, or subsistence; a living **b** food, provisions; *also* nourishment **2** sustaining or being sustained **3** something that gives support, endurance, or strength [ME, fr MF, fr *sustenir*]

**sustentation** /‚susten'taysh(ə)n/ *n*, *formal* sustaining or being sustained; *esp* maintenance, upkeep [ME, fr MF, fr L *sustentation-*, *sustentatio* act of holding up, fr *sustentatus*, pp of *sust-*

*entare* to hold up, fr *sustentus*, pp of *sustinēre*] – **sustentative** *adj*

**Susu** /'soohsooh/ *n, pl* **Susus**, *esp collectively* **Susu 1** a member of a W African people of Mali, Guinea, and the area along the northern border of Sierra Leone **2** the language of the Susu people

**susurration** /ˌsyoohsə'raysh(ə)n/ *n, formal* a whispering or rustling sound; a murmur [ME, fr LL *susurration-, susurratio*, fr L *susurratus*, pp of *susurrare* to whisper, fr *susurrus* whisper, hum – more at *swarm*]

**sutler** /'sutlə/ *n* a supplier of provisions to an army in former times, often established in a shop on an army post [obs D *soeteler*, fr LG *suteler* sloppy worker, camp cook; akin to OE be*sūtian* to dirty, Gk *hyein* to rain – more at SUCK]

**sutra** /'soohtrə/ *n* **1** a Hindu, esp VEDIC, sacred saying or writing; *also* a collection of these sayings or writings **2** a discourse of the Buddha [Skt *sūtra* thread, string of precepts, sutra; akin to L *suere* to sew – more at SEW]

**suttee** /ˌsu'tee, '-,-/ *n* the act or custom of a Hindu widow willingly being burnt to death on the funeral pile of her husband as an indication of her devotion to him; *also* a woman cremated in this way [Skt *satī* wife who performs suttee, lit., good woman, fr fem of *sat* true, good; akin to OE *sōth* true – more at SOOTH]

**¹suture** /'soohchə/ *n* **1a** a strand or fibre of catgut, silk, etc used to sew parts of the living body **b** a stitch made with a suture **c** the act or process of sewing with sutures **2a** a uniting of parts **b** the seam or seamlike line along which two things or parts are sewn or united **3a** the joining line in an immovable joint (eg between the bones of the skull); *also* such a joint **b** a furrow at the junction of adjacent bodily parts; *esp* a line along which a fruit, seedpod, etc will split to release the seed [MF & L; MF, fr L *sutura* seam, suture, fr *sutus*, pp of *suere* to sew – more at SEW] – **sutural** *adj*, **suturally** *adv*

**²suture** *vt* to unite, close, or secure with sutures ⟨~ *a wound*⟩

**suxamethonium** /ˌsuksəme'thohnium/ *n* a synthetic drug containing the chemical group $[(CH_3)_3N(CH_2)_2\ O_2CH_2C]_2{}^{2+}$, that blocks the action of ACETYLCHOLINE (substance transmitting nerve impulses) on VOLUNTARY MUSCLE and that is injected into the blood stream to relax muscles in surgery [*suxa-* (alter. of *succinic*) + *meth-* + *-onium*]

**suzerain** /'soohz(ə)rayn/ *n* **1** a superior feudal lord to whom fidelity is due; an overlord **2** a dominant state controlling the foreign relations of a subordinate state but allowing it sovereign authority in its internal affairs [Fr, fr (assumed) MF *suserain*, fr MF *sus* up (fr L *sursum*, fr *sub-* up + *versum* -wards, fr neut of *versus*, pp of *vertere* to turn) + *-erain* (as in *soverain* sovereign)]

**suzerainty** /'soohzərənti/ *n* the authority of a suzerain; overlordship [Fr *suzeraineté*, fr MF *susereneté*, fr (assumed) MF *suserain*]

**Suzuki method** /sə'zoohki/ *trademark* – used for a method of teaching esp young children to play stringed instruments (eg the violin)

**svarabhakti** /ˌsfurə'bukti/ *n* the insertion of a vowel sound between /r/ or /l/ and a consonant (eg when pronouncing *film* as /filəm/) [Skt, lit., part of a vowel, fr *svara* sound, vowel + *bhakti* portion, part]

**svedberg** /'sfedbuhg, sved-/ *also* **svedberg unit** *n* a unit of time amounting to $10^{-13}$ seconds that is used in measuring the speed of sediment formation when a solution containing a solid (eg a protein) suspended as fine particles is spun in an ULTRACENTRIFUGE (device that can spin at very high speeds). The speed of sedimentation is used to calculate the MOLECULAR WEIGHT of the protein or other suspended substance. [The *Svedberg* †1971 Sw chemist]

**svelte** /sfelt, svelt/ *adj* **1** elegantly and lithely slender **2** sophisticated, suave [Fr, fr It *svelto*, fr pp of *svellere* to pluck out, modif of L *evellere*, fr *e-* + *vellere* to pluck – more at VULNERABLE] – **sveltely** *adv*, **svelteness** *n*

**Svengali** /sfen'gahli, sven-/ *n* someone who attempts, usu with sinister motives, to mould another to his will [*Svengali*, sinister hypnotist in the novel *Trilby* by George Du Maurier †1896 E artist & writer]

**¹swab, swob** /swob/ *n* **1a** a mop **b(1)** a wad of absorbent material usu wound round one end of a small stick and used for applying medication or for removing material from an area **b(2)** a specimen taken with a swab **c** a sponge attached to a long rod and used to clean the bore of a firearm **2** *informal* a useless or contemptible person [prob fr obs D *swabbe*; akin to LG *swabber* mop]

**²swab, swob** *vt* **-bb-** **1** to clean (eg a floor or wound) (as if) with a swab **2** to apply medication to (as if) with a swab ⟨~ *bed the wound with a medicated pad*⟩ – **swabber** *n*

**swaddle** /'swodl/ *vt* **1** to wrap (an infant) in SWADDLING CLOTHES **2** to swathe, envelop [ME *swadelen, swathelen*, prob alter. of *swedelen, swethelen*, fr *swethel* swaddling band, fr OE; akin to OE *swathian* to swathe]

**swaddling bands** /'swodling/ *n pl* SWADDLING CLOTHES

**swaddling clothes** *n pl* **1** narrow strips of cloth wrapped round an infant to restrict movement **2** limitations or restrictions imposed on the immature or inexperienced

**¹swag** /swag/ *vb* **-gg-** *vi* to hang heavily; sag ~ *vt* to hang (eg tapestries or curtains) in heavy folds [prob of Scand origin; akin to ON *sveggja* to cause to sway; akin to OHG *swingan* to swing]

**²swag** *n* **1a** something (eg a moulded decoration) hanging in a curve between two points; a festoon **b** a suspended cluster (eg of flowers) hanging in such a way **c** an arrangement of fabric hanging in a heavy curve or fold **2** *chiefly Austr* **2a** a pack or roll of personal belongings **b** *informal* a large amount ⟨*collected a ~ of prizes – Australian Women's Weekly*⟩ **3** *informal* goods acquired, esp by unlawful means; loot, spoils

**¹swage** /swayj/ *n* a tool used by workers in metals for shaping their work by holding it on the work, or the work on it, and striking with a hammer [ME, ornamental border, fr MF *souage*]

**²swage** *vt* to shape (as if) by means of a swage

**swage block** *n* a perforated cast-iron or steel block with a variety of grooved sides that is used in shaping metal (eg into bolts)

**¹swagger** /'swagə/ *vi* to behave in an arrogant or pompous manner; *esp* to walk with an air of overbearing self-confidence or self-satisfaction [prob fr ¹*swag* + *-er* (as in *chatter*)] – **swaggerer** *n*, **swaggeringly** *adv*

**²swagger** *n* **1** an act or instance of swaggering **2a** arrogant or conceitedly self-assured behaviour **b** ostentatious display or bravado

**³swagger** *n, NZ* a swagman

**swagger stick** *n* a short light usu leather-covered stick carried esp by army officers

**swaggie** /'swagi/ *n, Austr & NZ* a swagman

**swagman** /'swag,man/ *n, chiefly Austr* a tramp; *esp* one who carries a swag and travels through the Australian bush

**Swahili** /swah'heeli/ *n, pl* **Swahilis**, *esp collectively* **Swahili 1** a member of a BANTU-speaking people of Zanzibar and the adjacent coast **2** a BANTU language used in trade and government over much of E Africa and in the Congo region [Ar *sawāhil*, pl of *sāhil* coast]

**swain** /swayn/ *n, chiefly poetic* **1** a peasant; *specif* a shepherd **2** a male admirer or suitor [ME *swein* boy, servant, fr ON *sveinn*; akin to OE *swān* swain, L *suus* one's own – more at SUICIDE] – **swainish** *adj*, **swainishness** *n*

**swale** /swayl/ *n* a low-lying or depressed and often wet stretch of land [ME, shade, prob of Scand origin; akin to ON *svalr* cool; akin to OE *swelan* to burn – more at SWELTER]

**¹swallow** /'swoloh/ *n* any of numerous small long-winged migratory songbirds (family Hirundinidae, the swallow family) that are noted for their graceful flight, that have a short beak and usu a forked tail, occur in all parts of the world except New Zealand and polar regions, and that feed on insects caught on the wing; *esp* a common variety (*Hirundo rustica*) of Africa and Eurasia that has a deeply forked tail, dark upperparts, chiefly white underparts, and a chestnut throat [ME *swalowe*, fr OE *swealwe*; akin to OHG *swalawa* swallow, Russ *soloveĭ* nightingale]

**²swallow** *vt* **1** to take through the mouth and OESOPHAGUS into the stomach **2** to envelop or take in as if by swallowing; absorb – often + *up* ⟨~ *ed up by the shadows*⟩ **3** to accept without question, protest, or resentment ⟨~ *an insult*⟩ ⟨*a hard story to ~*⟩ **4** to retract; TAKE BACK ⟨*had to ~ his words*⟩ **5** to refrain from expressing or showing; repress ⟨~ *ed his anger*⟩ **6** to utter (eg words) indistinctly ~ *vi* **1** to receive something into the body through the mouth and OESOPHAGUS **2** to perform the action characteristic of swallowing something, esp under emotional stress ⟨~ *ed hard before jumping*⟩ [ME *swalowen*, fr OE *swelgan*; akin to OHG *swelgan* to swallow] – **swallowable** *adj*, **swallower** *n*

**³swallow** *n* **1** the passage connecting the mouth to the stomach **2** a capacity for swallowing **3a** an act of swallowing **b** an amount that can be swallowed at one time **4** an opening in a

BLOCK (case containing a pulley or pulleys) on a ship between the SHEAVE (grooved wheel) and frame through which the rope passes

**swallow dive** *n, Br* a forward dive executed with the head back, back arched, and arms spread sideways and then brought together above the head to form a straight line with the body as the diver enters the water hands first [¹*swallow*]

**swallow hole** *n, chiefly Br* SINK HOLE 2 (depression in rock) [³*swallow*]

**swallowtail** /-,tayl/ *n* 1 a deeply forked and tapering tail (eg of a swallow) 2 a tailcoat 3 any of various large butterflies (esp genus *Papilio*) with the hind wing lengthened into a structure resembling a tail – **swallow-tailed** *adj*

**swallowwort** /-,wuht/ *n* 1 CELANDINE 1 (plant of the poppy family) 2 any of several plants of the milkweed family used to induce vomiting, to activate the bowels, and to increase excretion of urine [fr the shape of the pods resembling a swallow with outspread wings]

**swam** /swam/ *past of* SWIM

**swami** /'swahmi/ *n, pl* **swamies, swamis** 1 a Hindu ascetic or religious teacher; *specif* a senior member of a religious order – used as a title 2 one who resembles or emulates a swami; a pundit, seer [Hindi *svāmī*, fr Skt *svāmin* owner, lord, fr *sva* one's own – more at SUICIDE]

¹**swamp** /swomp/ *n* (an area of) wet spongy land saturated and sometimes partially or intermittently covered with water; (a) marsh [alter. of ME *sompe*, fr MD *somp* morass; akin to MHG *sumpf* marsh, Gk *somphos* spongy] – **swamp** *adj*

²**swamp** *vt* 1 to fill (as if) with water; inundate, submerge 2 to overwhelm by an excess of work, difficulties, etc ~ *vi* to become submerged

**swamp buggy** *n, NAm* a vehicle used to negotiate swampy terrain: eg **a** an amphibious tractor **b** a flat-bottomed boat driven by an aeroplane propeller

**swampland** /'swomp,land/ *n* swamp

**swampy** /'swompi/ *adj* consisting of or resembling swamp; marshy – **swampiness** *n*

¹**swan** /swon/ *n* 1 any of various heavy-bodied long-necked mostly pure white aquatic birds (family Anatidae) that are related to but larger than the geese, walk awkwardly, fly strongly, and are graceful swimmers 2 one who or that which suggests or resembles a swan, esp in gracefulness 3 *cap* the constellation CYGNUS [ME, fr OE; akin to MHG *swan*, L *sonus* sound – more at SOUND]

²**swan** *vi* **-nn-** *informal* to wander or travel aimlessly, usu for pleasure ⟨went ~ning *round Europe*⟩

³**swan** *n, informal* an act of or time spent swanning

**swan dive** *n, NAm* SWALLOW DIVE (dive executed with the arms spread)

**swanherd** /-,huhd/ *n* someone who tends swans

¹**swank** /swangk/ *vi, informal* to swagger; SHOW OFF [perh fr MHG *swanken* to sway; akin to MD *swanc* supple]

²**swank** *n, informal* 1 arrogance or ostentation of dress or manner; pretentiousness, swagger 2 a person who swanks

**swanky** /'swangki/ *adj, informal* 1 characterized by showy display; ostentatious ⟨*a* ~ *car*⟩ 2 fashionably elegant; smart ⟨*a* ~ *restaurant*⟩

**swan mussel** *n* a common European freshwater mussel (*Anodonta cygnea*)

**swan neck** *n* an S-shaped curve in an object (eg a pipe or tube)

**swannery** /'swon(ə)ri/ *n* a place where swans are bred or kept

**swansdown** /'swonz,down/ *n* 1 the soft downy feathers of the swan, used esp as trimming on articles of dress 2 a heavy cotton flannel that has a thick NAP (velvetlike surface of raised threads) on the face

**swanskin** /'swon,skin/ *n* 1 the skin of a swan with the down or feathers on it 2 fabric resembling flannel and having a soft NAP (velvetlike surface of raised threads) or surface

**swan song** *n* 1 a song of great sweetness said to be sung by a dying swan 2 *informal* a farewell appearance or final act or pronouncement

**swan-upping** /-'uping/ *n* the annual inspection and marking of royal swans on the River Thames [*upping* fr gerund of ³*up* (in the sense "to drive up and catch")]

¹**swap, swop** /swop/ *vb* **-pp-** *vt* to give in exchange; barter ⟨~ *my penknife for your football*⟩ ~ *vi* to make an exchange – sometimes + *over* ⟨~ *over to a metric system*⟩ [ME *swappen* to strike, of imit origin; fr the practice of striking hands in closing a business deal] – **swapper** *n*

²**swap, swop** *n* 1 the act or process of exchanging one thing for another 2 something exchanged for another

**swap shop** *n* a place where, or an organization in which, secondhand items (eg clothes or games) are exchanged

**swaraj** /swə'rahj/ *n* Indian national or local self-government [Skt *svarāj* self-ruling, fr *sva* one's self + *rājya* rule – more at SUICIDE, RAJ] – **swarajist** *n*

**sward** /swawd/ *n* 1 the grassy surface of land; turf 2 a piece of ground covered with short grass [ME, fr OE *sweard, swearth* skin, rind; akin to MHG *swart* skin, hide, L o*perire* to cover – more at WEIR] – **swarded** *adj*

**swarf** /swahf, swawf/ *n* material (eg metallic particles and abrasive fragments) removed by a cutting or grinding tool [of Scand origin; akin to ON *svarf* file dust; akin to OE *sweorfan* to file away – more at SWERVE]

¹**swarm** /swawm/ *n* 1a(1) a great number of honeybees emigrating from a hive with a queen to start a new colony elsewhere **a**(2) a colony of honeybees settled in a hive **b** an aggregation of free-floating or free-swimming single-celled organisms – usu used with reference to ZOOSPORES 2a *taking sing or pl vb* a large number of animate or inanimate things massed together and usu in motion; a throng ⟨~s *of sightseers*⟩ **b** a number of similar geological features or phenomena close together in space or time ⟨*an earthquake* ~⟩ [ME, fr OE *swearm;* akin to OHG *swaram* swarm, & prob to L *susurrus* hum]

²**swarm** *vi* 1a to form and depart from a hive in a swarm **b** to escape in a swarm (eg of swarm spores from a SPORANGIUM) 2 to move or assemble in a crowd; throng 3 to contain a swarm; teem – usu + *with* ⟨*streets* ~ing *with cars*⟩ ~ *vt* to fill with a swarm; throng – **swarmer** *n*

³**swarm** *vi* to climb; *specif* to climb with the hands and feet; shin – usu + *up* ⟨~ *up a pole*⟩ to climb, mount; *specif* to shin [origin unknown]

**swarm spore** *n* any of various minute mobile sexual or asexual spores; *esp* ZOOSPORE

**swart** /swawt/ *adj, archaic* swarthy [ME, fr OE *sweart;* akin to OHG *swarz* black, L *sordes* dirt] – **swartness** *n*

**swarthy** /'swawdhi/ *adj* of a dark colour, complexion, or cast ⟨~ *skin*⟩ [alter. of obs *swarty*, fr *swart*] – **swarthiness** *n*

**Swartkrans man** /,sfaht,kruns/, **Swartkrans ape-man** *n* a prehistoric man (*Homo erectus capensis*) with jaws and teeth resembling those of modern man [*Swartkrans*, region in S Africa]

¹**swash** /swosh/ *n* 1a a body of splashing water **b** a narrow channel of water lying within a sandbank or between a sandbank and the shore 2 a dashing of water against or on something [prob imit]

²**swash** *vi* to move with a splashing sound ~ *vt* to cause to splash

³**swash** *adj, of a typographical letter* having strokes ending in an extended flourish (obs *swash* slanting, of unknown origin)

**swashbuckler** /-,buklə/ *n* 1 a swaggering adventurer or daredevil 2 a novel or drama dealing with a swashbuckler [²*swash* + *buckler* (orig suggesting "one who clashes his sword on a shield")]

**swashbuckling** /-,bukling/ *adj* characteristic of or behaving like a swashbuckler

**swastika** /'swostikə/ *n* an ancient symbol or ornament in the form of a GREEK CROSS (cross with arms of equal length) with the ends of the arms extended at right angles all in the same rotary direction; *esp* this symbol with arms extended clockwise as the emblem of the Nazi party and Third Reich [Skt *svastika*, fr *svasti* welfare, fr *su-* well + *asti* he is; fr its being regarded as a good luck symbol]

¹**swat** /swot/ *vt* **-tt-** to hit with a sharp slapping blow; *esp* to kill (an insect) with such a blow [E dial., to squat, alter. of E *squat*]

²**swat** *n* 1 a quick and crushing blow 2 a swatter 3 a long hit in baseball; *esp* HOME RUN (hit enabling the batter to make a complete circuit)

³**swat** *vi* **-tt-** to swot – **swat** *n*

**swatch** /swoch/ *n* a sample piece (eg of fabric); *also* a collection of samples [origin unknown]

**swath** /swawth/ *n* 1a the whole sweep of a scythe or machine in mowing **b** a row of cut grain or grass left by a scythe or mowing machine 2 a long broad strip 3 a stroke (as if) of a scythe 4 a space cleared as if by a scythe ⟨*cutting a* ~ *through all the intricate arguments*⟩ [ME, fr OE *swæth* footstep, trace; akin to MHG *swade* swath]

¹**swathe** /swaydh/ *vt* 1 to bind or wrap (as if) with a bandage 2 to envelop ⟨~d *in mist*⟩ [ME *swathen*, fr OE *swathian;* akin

to ON *svatha* to swathe, Lith *svaigti* to become dizzy] – **swather** *n*

**²swathe** *n* **1** a band used in swathing **2** something that envelops

**³swathe** *n* a swath

**swathing bands** /'swawthing, 'swaydhing/ *n pl* SWADDLING CLOTHES (narrow strips of cloth wrapped round an infant)

**swatter** /'swotə/ *n* one who or that which swats; *specif* a flyswatter

**¹sway** /sway/ *vi* **1a(1)** to swing slowly and rhythmically back and forth from a base or pivot **a(2)** to go while swaying ⟨~ed *unsteadily downstairs*⟩ **b** to move gently from an upright to a leaning position **2** to fluctuate or alternate between one attitude or opinion and another ~ *vt* **1a** to cause to swing, rock, or oscillate **b** to cause to bend downwards to one side **2a** to exert a guiding or controlling influence on ⟨*too much* ~ed *by ambition*⟩ **b** to change the opinions of, esp by the eloquence or force of argument ⟨~ *a hostile crowd*⟩ **3** to hoist in place ⟨~ *up a mast*⟩ **4** *archaic* to govern, rule **synonyms** see ¹MOVE, ¹SWING [alter. of earlier *swey* to fall, swoon, fr ME *sweyen,* prob of Scand origin; akin to ON *sveigja* to sway; akin to OE *swathian* to swathe] – **swayer** *n*

**²sway** *n* **1** swaying or being swayed; an oscillating, fluctuating, or sweeping motion **2a** a controlling influence or power; dominance ⟨*the Church held* ~⟩ **b** authority, rule

**swayback** /-,bak/ *n* **1** an abnormal sagging of the back, esp in horses **2** a sagging back – **swaybacked** *adj*

**Swazi** /'swahzi/ *n, pl* **Swazis**, *esp collectively* **Swazi 1** a member of a BANTU-speaking people of Swaziland in southern Africa **2** a BANTU language of the Swazi people

**¹swear** /sweə/ *vb* **swore** /swaw/; **sworn** /swawn/ *vt* **1** to utter or take (an oath) solemnly **2a** to assert as true or promise under oath ⟨*a sworn affidavit*⟩ **b** to assert or promise emphatically or earnestly ⟨*he swore he didn't know the man*⟩ ⟨*she swore not to be late*⟩ **3a** to put to an oath; administer an oath to **b** to bind by an oath ⟨*swore him to secrecy*⟩ **4** to bring into a specified state by swearing ⟨*swore his life away*⟩ ~ *vi* **1** to take an oath **2** to use profane or obscene language; curse [ME *sweren,* fr OE *swerian;* akin to OHG *swerien* to swear, Russ *svara* quarrel] – **swearer** *n*

**swear by** *vt* to place great confidence in

**swear in** *vt* to introduce into office, a witness-box, etc by administration of an oath

**swear off** *vt* to vow to abstain from ⟨swear off *smoking*⟩

**swear out** *vt, NAm* to procure (a warrant for arrest) by making a sworn accusation

**swear to** *vt* to have a positive conviction of ⟨*couldn't* swear to *his being the same man*⟩

**²swear** *n* an act or instance of using swearwords

**swearword** /'sweə,wuhd/ *n* a profane or obscene oath or word

**¹sweat** /swet/ *vb* **sweated**, *NAm chiefly* **sweat** *vi* **1a** to excrete moisture in visible quantities through the openings of the SWEAT GLANDS; perspire **b** to exert oneself so as to cause perspiration; work hard **2a** to emit or exude moisture ⟨*cheese* ~s *in ripening*⟩ **b** to gather surface moisture in beads as a result of condensation ⟨*stones* ~ *at night*⟩ **c(1)** *esp of tobacco* to ferment **c(2)** to putrefy **3** to undergo anxiety or mental or emotional tension – often + *on* ⟨~ing *on the result of the exam*⟩ **4** to become exuded through pores or a porous surface; ooze ~ *vt* **1** to (seem to) emit from pores; exude **2** to produce by hard work or drudgery ⟨~ing *out one book after another*⟩ **3** to get rid of or lose (as if) by sweating or being sweated ⟨~ *off weight*⟩ ⟨~ *out a fever*⟩ **4** to make wet with perspiration **5a** to cause (eg a patient) to sweat **b** to drive hard; overwork **c** to exact work from at low wages and under unfair or unhealthy conditions **6** to cause to exude or lose moisture: eg **6a** to subject (eg tobacco leaves) to fermentation **b** to cook (eg vegetables) gently in melted fat until the juices run out **7** to remove particles of metal from (a coin) by abrasion **8a** to melt (eg solder) by heating so as to cause a flow, esp between surfaces to join them; *also* to join by such means ⟨~ *a pipe joint*⟩ **b** to heat so as to extract a constituent that will melt easily ⟨~ *bismuth ore*⟩ **c** to apply heat to; steam **9** *NAm informal* to extract something valuable from by unfair or dishonest means; fleece – see also **sweat** BLOOD [ME *sweten,* fr OE *swǣtan,* fr *swāt* sweat; akin to OHG *sweiz* sweat, Gk *hidrōs,* L *sudor* sweat, *sudare* to sweat]

**sweat out** *vt, informal* to endure or wait through the course of

**²sweat** *n* **1** the fluid excreted from the SWEAT GLANDS of the skin; perspiration **2** moisture issuing from or gathering in drops on a surface **3a** the condition of one sweating or sweated **b** a spell of sweating **4** *informal* hard work; drudgery **5** *informal* a state of anxiety or impatience – compare COLD SWEAT, OLD SWEAT – **sweatless** *adj* – **no sweat** *informal* it's no trouble; it's easily done ⟨*I'll wash up,* no sweat!⟩

**sweatband** /-,band/ *n* a band of material worn round the head or wrist or inserted in a hat or cap to absorb sweat

**sweatbox** /'swet,boks/ *n* **1** a device for sweating something (eg hides in tanning or dried figs) **2** a place in which someone is made to sweat; *esp* a narrow box in which a prisoner is placed for punishment

**sweated** /'swetid/ *adj* of, subjected to, or produced under a system involving low wages and unfair or unhealthy conditions ⟨~ *labour*⟩ ⟨~ *goods*⟩

**sweater** /'swetə/ *n* **1** one who or that which sweats or causes sweating **2** ²JUMPER 1

**sweat gland** *n* a simple gland of the skin that secretes perspiration, in humans is widely distributed in nearly all parts of the skin, and that consists typically of a coiled tube in the fatty layer beneath the skin connected by a duct to a minute pore on the surface of the skin

**sweating sickness** /'sweting/ *n* an epidemic fever characterized by profuse sweating and usu early mortality that appeared in Britain in the 15th and 16th centuries

**sweatlet** /'swetlit/ *n* a band of towelling worn round the wrist, esp in tennis, to absorb perspiration

**sweat shirt** *n* a loose collarless pullover of heavy cotton JERSEY

**sweatshop** /'swet,shop/ *n* a place of work in which workers are employed for long hours at low wages and under unhealthy conditions

**sweaty** /'sweti/ *adj* **1** covered with or smelling of sweat **2** causing sweat ⟨*a* ~ *day*⟩ ⟨~ *work*⟩ – **sweatily** *adv*, **sweatiness** *n*

**swede** /sweed/ *n* **1** *cap* a native or inhabitant of Sweden **2** a large type of turnip (*Brassica napobrassica*) of the cabbage family, with edible yellow flesh [(1) LG or obs D; (2) fr its having been introduced into Scotland from Sweden]

**Swedenborgian** /,sweed(ə)n'bawjiən/ *adj* of the teachings of Emanuel Swedenborg, or the Church of the New Jerusalem based on his teachings [Emanuel *Swedenborg* †1772 Sw scientist & theologian] – **Swedenborgian** *n*, **Swedenborgianism** *n*

**Swedish** /'sweedish/ *n* **1** the language spoken in Sweden and in part of Finland, which belongs to the NORTH GERMANIC group of languages **2** *taking pl vb* the people of Sweden – **Swedish** *adj*

**Swedish massage** *n* massage with SWEDISH MOVEMENTS

**Swedish movements** *n pl* a system of active and passive exercise of muscles and joints

**¹sweep** /sweep/ *vb* **swept** /swept/ *vt* **1a** to remove from a surface (as if) with a broom or brush ⟨swept *the crumbs from the table*⟩ **b** to destroy completely; WIPE OUT – usu + *away* **c** to remove or take with a single continuous forceful action ⟨swept *the books off the desk*⟩ **d** to drive or carry along with irresistible force ⟨*a wave of protest that* swept *the opposition into office*⟩ **2a** to clean (as if) with a broom or brush **b** to clear by repeated and forcible action **c** to move across, through, or along swiftly, violently, or overwhelmingly ⟨*fire* swept *the business quarter*⟩ ⟨*a new craze* ~ing *the country*⟩ **d** to win an overwhelming victory in ⟨~ *the polls*⟩ **3** to move lightly over with a swift continuous movement ⟨*his fingers* swept *the keyboard*⟩ **4** to trace or describe the path or extent of (eg a line, circle, or angle) **5** to cover the entire range of ⟨*his eyes* swept *the horizon*⟩ **6a** to play a sweep in cricket at (a ball) or at the bowling of (a bowler) **b** to row (a boat) using sweeps ~ *vi* **1a** to clean a surface (as if) with a broom **b** to move swiftly, forcefully, or devastatingly ⟨*the wind* swept *through the treetops*⟩ **2** to go with stately or sweeping movements ⟨*his formidable wife* swept *past him to greet us* – Maurice Cranston⟩ **3** to move or extend in a wide curve or range ⟨*the hills* ~ *down to the sea*⟩ **4** to play a sweep in cricket – see also **sweep the** BOARD, **sweep something under the** CARPET, **sweep somebody off his/her** FEET (at FOOT) [ME *swepen; akin to OE swāpan* to sweep – more at SWOOP]

**²sweep** *n* **1** something that sweeps or works with a sweeping motion: eg **1a** a long pole or timber pivoted on a tall post and used to raise and lower a bucket in a well **b** a triangular cultivator blade that cuts off weeds under the soil surface **c** a windmill sail **d** a long oar **2a** an instance of sweeping; *specif* a clearing out or away (as if) with a broom **b** the removal from the table in one play in the card game CASSINO of all the cards by pairing or combining **3** a military reconnaissance or attack ranging over a particular area **4a** a movement of great range and force ⟨*the great ~ of the industrial revolution*⟩ **b** a curving or circular course or line **c** the extent of a sweeping movement; scope **d** a broad extent ⟨*unbroken ~ of woodland*⟩ **5** CHIMNEY SWEEP **6** a sweepstake **7** deviation from parallelism or perpendicularity with respect to a reference line ⟨*~ of an airplane wing*⟩; *esp* a sweepback **8** an attacking stroke in cricket played on bended knee with a horizontal bat designed to send the ball behind the batsman on the LEG SIDE and usu played against slower bowlers

**sweepback** /-ˌbak/ *n* the backward slant of an aircraft wing in which the outer portion of the wing is behind the inner portion

**sweeper** /'sweepə/ *n* **1** one who or that which sweeps **2** a defensive player in soccer who plays behind the backs as a last line of defence before the goalkeeper

¹**sweeping** /'sweeping/ *n* **1** the act or action of one who or that which sweeps ⟨*gave the room a good ~*⟩ **2** *pl* refuse, rubbish, etc collected by sweeping

²**sweeping** *adj* **1a** moving or extending in a wide curve or over a wide area **b** having a curving line or form **2a** extensive ⟨*~ reforms*⟩ **b** marked by wholesale and indiscriminate inclusion ⟨*~ generalities*⟩ – **sweepingly** *adv*, **sweepingness** *n*

¹**sweep-ˌnet** *n* a large fishing net which is dragged through the water

**sweep-second hand** *n* a hand marking seconds on a watch or clock mounted with the other hands and read on the same dial

**sweepstake** /-ˌstayk/ *n*, **sweepstakes** *n taking sing vb, pl* **sweepstakes 1a** a race or contest in which the entire prize is awarded to the winner **b** a contest, competition **2** any of various lotteries [ME *swepestake* one who wins all the stakes in a game, fr *swepen* to sweep + *stake*]

¹**sweet** /sweet/ *adj* **1a(1)** pleasing to the taste **a(2)** being or inducing a taste similar to that of sugar that is one of the four basic taste sensations – compare BITTER, SALT, SOUR **b(1)** *of a beverage* containing a sweetening ingredient; not dry **b(2)** *of wine* retaining a portion of natural sugar **2a** pleasing to the mind or feelings; agreeable – often used as a generalized term of approval **b** marked by gentle good humour or kindliness **c** fragrant **d** delicately pleasing to the ear or eye **e** saccharine, cloying **3** much loved; dear **4a** not sour, rancid, decaying, or stale; wholesome ⟨*~ milk*⟩ **b** not salt or salted; fresh ⟨*~ butter*⟩ **c** *of land* free from excessive acidity **d** free from noxious gases and smells **e** free from excess of acid, sulphur, or other corrosive chemical compounds [ME *swete*, fr OE *swēte*; akin to OHG *suozi* sweet, L *suavis*, Gk *hēdys*] – **sweetish** *adj*, **sweetly** *adv*, **sweetness** *n* – **sweet on** in love with

²**sweet** *adv* in a sweet manner ⟨*how ~ the music sounded*⟩

³**sweet** *n* **1** something that is sweet to the taste: eg **1a** *Br* a dessert **b** *Br* a toffee, truffle, or other small piece of confectionery prepared with (flavoured or filled) chocolate or sugar; *esp* one made chiefly of (boiled and crystallized) sugar **2** a sweet taste sensation **3** a darling, sweetheart

**sweet alyssum** *n* a European plant (*Lobularia maritima*) of the cabbage family having clusters of small fragrant usu white flowers

ˌ**sweet-and-'sour** *adj* seasoned with a sauce containing sugar and vinegar or lemon juice ⟨*~ pork*⟩

**sweet basil** *n* a common herb (*Ocimum basilicum*) of the mint family that has white flowers tinged with purple and leaves that are used as a seasoning

**sweet bay** *n* ³BAY 1a

**sweet birch** *n* a common birch (*Betula lenta*) of E USA that has hard dark-coloured wood and scaly brown bark containing an oil that readily vaporizes

**sweetbread** /-ˌbred/ *n* either of two glands (THYMUS or PANCREAS) of a young animal (eg a calf or lamb) used for food

**sweetbrier** /-ˌbrie·ə/ *n* a Eurasian wild rose (esp *Rosa rubiginosa*) with stout prickles, white to deep rosy pink single flowers, and fragrant leaves

**sweet cherry** *n* a cultivated white-flowered Eurasian cherry (*Prunus avium*) of the rose family that is widely grown for its large sweet-flavoured fruits; *also* its fruit

**sweet chestnut** *n* SPANISH CHESTNUT (chestnut with edible nuts)

**sweet cicely** /'sisəli/ *n* a European plant (*Myrrhis odorata*) of the carrot family that has a strong aniseed smell and that is sometimes used as a herb [*cicely* by folk etymology by *seseli* (a genus of plants), fr NL, fr L *seselis*, fr Gk]

**sweet clover** *n* MELILOT (yellow-flowered plant)

**sweet corn** *n* a maize (esp *Zea mays saccharata*) with kernels that contain a high percentage of sugar; *also* the milky kernels of young tender ears of sweet corn used as a vegetable

**sweeten** /'sweet(ə)n/ *vt* **1** to make (more) sweet **2** to soften the mood or attitude of **3** to make less painful or trying **4** to free from a harmful or undesirable quality or substance; *esp* to remove chemical compounds of sulphur from ⟨*~ natural gas*⟩ **5** to make more valuable or attractive; *esp* to increase (a pot not won on the previous deal in a card game) by adding stakes before another deal ~ *vi* to become sweet – **sweetener** *n*

**sweetening** /'sweet(ə)ning/ *n* something that sweetens

**sweet FA** *n, Br euph* nothing at all

**sweet fanny adams** *n, often cap F&A, Br euph* nothing at all [Br naval slang *Fanny Adams* tinned meat, stew, fr *Fanny Adams* †1867 E girl who was murdered and dismembered; prob used here as euphemistic expansion of *sweet FA*]

**sweet flag** *n* a marsh plant (*Acorus calamus*) of the arum family with long leaves and an aromatic root

**sweet gum** *n* **1** a N American tree (*Liquidambar styraciflua*) of the witch-hazel family with corky branches and hard wood **2** the HEARTWOOD (older harder nonliving wood in a tree trunk) of the sweet gum or the reddish-brown timber prepared from it

**sweetheart** /-ˌhaht/ *n* a darling, lover

**sweetie** /'sweeti/ *n, Br informal* **1** SWEET 1b (sweetmeat) **2** SWEET 3 (darling); *also* SWEETIE PIE 2

**sweetie pie** *n, informal* **1** a sweetheart – used as a term of address **2** a pleasing or attractive person

**sweeting** /'sweeting/ *n* **1** a sweet apple **2** *archaic* a sweetheart

**sweet itch** *n* an irritable skin condition of horses caused by various allergies, esp to spring grass

**sweetmeal** /'sweetmiəl, -meel/ *adj* containing sugar and wholemeal flour ⟨*~ biscuits*⟩

**sweetmeat** /-ˌmeet/ *n* a crystallized fruit, sugar-coated nut, or other sweet or delicacy rich in sugar; *esp, formal* SWEET 1b

**sweetness and light** /'sweetnis/ *n* amiability, congeniality

**sweet pea** *n* a garden plant (*Lathyrus odoratus*) of the pea family having slender climbing stems and large fragrant flowers; *also* its flower

**sweet pepper** *n* a large mild thick-skinned CAPSICUM fruit; *also* a pepper plant bearing this fruit

**sweet potato** *n* a tropical climbing plant (*Ipomoea batatas*) of the bindweed family that has purplish flowers; *also* its large thick sweet and nutritious root that is cooked and eaten as a vegetable

**sweetsop** /'sweetˌsop/ *n* a tropical American evergreen tree (*Annona squamosa*) of the custard-apple family that produces a fruit with a thick green skin and sweet edible pulp; *also* the fruit of this tree – compare SOURSOP

**sweet spot** *n* the central part on the strung face of a sports racket, from which the ball may be hit with greatest impact

**sweet talk** *n, chiefly NAm informal* flattery

ˈ**sweet-ˌtalk** *vb, chiefly NAm informal vt* to blandish, coax ~ *vi* to use flattery

**sweet tooth** *n* a craving or fondness for sweet food – **sweet-toothed** *adj*

**sweet vernal grass** *n* a slender fragrant Eurasian grass (*Anthoxanthum odoratum*)

**sweet william** *n, often cap W* a widely cultivated Eurasian plant (*Dianthus barbatus*) of the pink family with clusters of small white to deep red or purple flowers often showily mottled or striped [fr the name *William*]

¹**swell** /swel/ *vb* **swelled**; **swollen** /'swohlən/, **swelled** *vi* **1a** to expand (eg in size, volume, or numbers) gradually beyond a normal or original limit ⟨*the population ~ed*⟩ **b** to be distended or puffed up ⟨*her ankle has* swollen *up badly*⟩ **c** to form a bulge or rounded protuberance; curve outwards or upwards **2** to become filled with pride and arrogance **3** to become charged with emotion ⟨*her heart ~ed with grief*⟩ ~ *vt* **1** to affect with a powerful or expansive emotion **2** to increase the size, number, or intensity of [ME *swellen*, fr OE *swellan*; akin to OHG *swellan* to swell]

*usage* The past participle is **swollen** when the implication is of harmful excess ⟨*her* **swollen** *ankle*⟩ ⟨*the river was* **swollen** *by the flood water from the mountains*⟩ and **swelled** for more neutral in-

crease ⟨*our numbers were* **swelled** *by the arrival of the Yorkshire contingent*⟩. **Swelled** is used adjectivally only in **swelled head**.
*synonyms* see EXPAND *antonym* shrink

²**swell** *n* **1a** the condition of being swollen **b** a rounded protuberance or bulge **2** a long often massive surge of water, often continuing beyond or after its cause (e g a gale) **3a** the act or process of swelling **b** a gradual increase and decrease of the loudness of a musical sound **c(1)** a device used in an organ for controlling loudness; *esp* SWELL BOX **c(2)** **swell organ, swell** the second most important division of an organ, in which the pipes are enclosed in a SWELL BOX; *also* the keyboard (MANUAL 3) controlling this division – compare GREAT ORGAN **4** *informal* **4a** a person dressed in the height of fashion **b** a person of high social position

³**swell** *adj, informal* **1a** stylish **b** socially prominent **2** *chiefly NAm* excellent – used as a generalized term of enthusiasm

**swell box** *n* a chamber in an organ containing a set of pipes and having shutters that open or shut to regulate the volume of sound

'**swell-,butted** *adj, of a tree* greatly enlarged at the base

**swelled head** *n* an exaggerated opinion of oneself – **swelled-headed** *adj*, **swelled-headedness** *n*

**swelling** /'sweling/ *n* **1** something that is swollen; *specif* an abnormal body protuberance or localized enlargement **2** the condition of being swollen

'**swelter** /'sweltə/ *vi* to suffer, sweat, or be faint from heat [ME *sweltren*, freq of *swelten* to die, be overcome by heat, fr OE *sweltan* to die; akin to OHG *swelzan* to burn up]

²**swelter** *n* **1** a state of oppressive heat **2** an excited or overwrought state of mind; a sweat ⟨*in a* ~⟩

**sweltering** /'swelt(ə)ring/ *adj* oppressively hot – **swelteringly** *adv*

'**swept-,back** /swept/ *adj* possessing SWEEPBACK (backward slant of an aircraft wing)

'**swept-,wing** *adj, of an aircraft* having swept-back wings

**swerve** /swuhv/ *vi* to turn aside abruptly from a straight line or course; deviate ~ *vt* to cause to turn aside or deviate [ME *swerven*, fr OE *sweorfan* to wipe, file away; akin to OHG *swerban* to wipe off, Gk *syrein* to drag] – **swerve** *n*

'**swift** /swift/ *adj* **1** (capable of) moving with great speed ⟨*a* ~ *horse*⟩ ⟨*a* ~ *gallop*⟩ **2** occurring suddenly or within a very short time ⟨*a* ~ *visit to the shops*⟩ **3** quick to respond; ready ⟨*a* ~ *temper*⟩ ~ *to act*⟩ *synonyms* see 'FAST *antonym* sluggish [ME, fr OE; akin to OE *swifan* to revolve – more at SWIVEL] – **swiftly** *adv*, **swiftness** *n*

²**swift** *adv* swiftly ⟨swift-*flowing*⟩

³**swift** *n* **1** any of several lizards (esp of the genus *Sceloporus*) that run swiftly **2a** a reel for winding yarn or thread **b** any of the large cylinders that carry forward the material in a CARDING machine (machine for combing fibres before spinning); *also* a comparable cylinder in another machine **3** any of numerous darkly coloured birds (family Apodidae, esp *Apus apus*) that are noted for their fast darting flight in pursuit of insects, spend most of their lives on the wing, and that are related to the hummingbirds and nightjars although superficially much resembling swallows

'**swig** /swig/ *n, informal* a quantity drunk in one swallow [origin unknown]

²**swig** *vb* -**gg**- *informal vt* to drink in long draughts ⟨~ *cider*⟩ ~ *vi* to take a swig; drink – **swigger** *n*

'**swill** /swil/ *vt* **1** to wash, drench; *esp* to wash by flushing with water – often + *out* or *down* **2** to drink greedily ⟨~ *beer*⟩ **3** to feed (e g a pig) with swill ~ *vi* to drink or eat freely, greedily, or to excess [ME *swilen*, fr OE *swillan*] – **swiller** *n*

²**swill** *n* **1a** a semiliquid food for animals (e g pigs) composed of edible refuse mixed with water or skimmed or sour milk **b** rubbish, waste **2** something suggestive of slop or rubbish; refuse **3** a swig

'**swim** /swim/ *vb* -**mm**-; **swam**; **swum** *vi* **1** to propel oneself in water by bodily movements (e g of the limbs, fins, or tail) **2** to move with a motion like that of swimming; glide ⟨*a cloud* swam *slowly across the moon*⟩ **3a** to float on a liquid; not sink ⟨*oil* ~s *on water*⟩ **b** to surmount difficulties; not go under ⟨*sink or* ~, *live or die, survive or perish* – Daniel Webster⟩ **4** to become immersed (as if) in or flooded (as if) with a liquid ⟨*liver* ~*ming in gravy*⟩ ⟨*his heart* swam *with joy*⟩ **5** to have a floating or dizzy effect or sensation ~ *vt* **1a** to cross by swimming ⟨~ *a stream*⟩ **b** to use (a stroke) in swimming **2** to cause to swim or float [ME *swimmen*, fr OE *swimman;* akin to OHG *swimman* to swim] – **swimmer** *n* – **swim against the tide/stream** to

move counter to or work against the prevailing or popular trend

²**swim** *n* **1** a smooth gliding motion **2** an act or period of swimming ⟨*went for an early morning* ~⟩ **3a** an area frequented by fish **b** the main current of activity ⟨*be in the* ~⟩

**swim bladder** *n* the AIR BLADDER of a fish that serves as an accessory buoyancy mechanism

**swimmable** /'swiməbl/ *adj* capable of being swum

**swimmeret** /'swiməret/ *n* any of a series of small unspecialized limbs under the abdomen of many lobsters, shrimps, and related CRUSTACEANS, that are used in some cases (e g by crabs) for swimming but usu for carrying eggs

'**swimming** /'swiming/ *n* the act, art, or competitive sport of one who or that which swims or dives

²**swimming** *adj* **1** that swims ⟨*a* ~ *bird*⟩ **2** adapted to or used in or for swimming ⟨~ *trunks*⟩ [(1) fr prp of '*swim;* (2) fr gerund of '*swim*]

**swimming bath** *n*, **swimming baths** *n taking sing or pl vb, pl* **swimming baths** *Br* a usu indoor SWIMMING POOL

**swimming cap** *n* a waterproof cap that fits closely round the head and is used by swimmers to contain the hair and usu to keep it dry

**swimming costume** *n, chiefly Br* a closely fitting usu woman's garment for swimming

**swimmingly** /-li/ *adv, informal* very well; splendidly ⟨*everything went* ~⟩

**swimming pool** *n* an artificial pool made for people to swim in

**swimmy** /'swimi/ *adj* **1** verging on, causing, or affected by dizziness or giddiness **2** *of vision* blurred, unsteady – **swimmily** *adv*, **swimminess** *n*

**swimsuit** /-,s(y)ooht/ *n* SWIMMING COSTUME

'**swindle** /'swindl/ *vi* to obtain money or property by fraud or deceit ~ *vt* to take money or property from by fraud or deceit [back-formation fr *swindler*, fr Ger *schwindler* giddy person, fr *schwindeln* to be dizzy, fr OHG *swintilōn*, freq of *swintan* to diminish, vanish; akin to OE *swindan* to vanish] – **swindler** *n*

²**swindle** *n* an act or instance of swindling; a fraud

**swine** /swien/ *n, pl (1)* **swine**, *(2&3)* **swines**, **swine 1** a pig – used chiefly technically or in literature **2** *informal* a contemptible person **3** *informal* something unpleasant ⟨*a* ~ *of a job*⟩ [ME, fr OE *swīn;* akin to OHG *swīn* swine, L *sus* – more at SOW]

**swine fever** *n* a highly infectious often fatal virus disease of pigs characterized by fever, loss of appetite, and diarrhoea

**swineherd** /-,huhd/ *n* someone who tends pigs

**swine vesicular disease** *n* a virus disease of pigs characterized by blistering on the feet, legs, snout, and tongue

'**swing** /swing/ *vb* **swung** /swung/ *vt* **1a** to cause to move vigorously through a wide curve or circle ⟨~ *an axe*⟩ **b** to cause to sway to and fro **c(1)** to cause to pivot or rotate **c(2)** to cause to face or move in another direction ⟨~ *the car into a side road*⟩ **d** to make (a delivery of a cricket ball) swing **2** to suspend so as to allow to sway or turn ⟨~ *a hammock between trees*⟩ **3** to move from one point to another by suspension ⟨*huge cranes that* ~ *cargo up over the ship's side and into the hold*⟩ **4** to play or sing (e g a melody) in the style of swing music **5** *informal* **5a(1)** to influence decisively ⟨~ *a lot of votes*⟩ **a(2)** to bring round by influence **b** to succeed in doing, making, or having; manage; BRING ABOUT ⟨*wasn't able to* ~ *that trip to Vienna*⟩ ~ *vi* **1a** to move freely to and fro, esp when hanging from an overhead support **b** *of a bowled ball in cricket* to deviate from a straight path while travelling through the air before reaching the batsman **2a** to die by hanging ⟨*I'll see you* ~ *for this*⟩ **b** to hang freely from a support **3** to move in or describe a circle or arc: **3a** to turn (as if) on a hinge or pivot ⟨*she swung* on *her heel*⟩ **b** to turn in place **c** to convey oneself by grasping a fixed support ⟨~ *aboard the train*⟩ **4a** to have a steady pulsing rhythm **b** to play or sing with a lively compelling rhythm; *specif* to play swing music **5** to shift or fluctuate from one condition, form, position, or object of attention or favour to another ⟨~ *between optimism and pessimism*⟩ **6a** to move along rhythmically ⟨~ing *down the street*⟩ **b** to start up in a smooth vigorous manner ⟨*ready to* ~ *into action*⟩ **7** to hit or aim at something with a sweeping arm movement – often + *out* **8a** *informal* to be lively and up-to-date **b** *slang* to engage freely in sex; *specif* to engage in wifeswapping – see also **swing the** LEAD [ME *swingen* to beat, fling, hurl, rush, fr OE *swingan* to beat, fling oneself, rush; akin to OHG *swingan* to fling, rush] – **swingable** *adj*, **swingably** *adv* synonyms **Swing, sway, oscillate, vibrate, undulate, fluctuate,** and **waver** all mean "move to and fro or up and down more or less rhythmically". **Swing** suggests the free vigorous movement, through an arc, of something that is often hung from above ⟨**swing** *an axe*⟩ ⟨**swing** *a hammock*⟩. **Sway** implies a slower swinging, often of something light, flexible, and upright ⟨*bamboos* **swaying** *in the gentle wind*⟩. **Oscillate** and **vibrate** both imply very regular movement, **oscillate** suggesting the rapid swinging of a pendulum and **vibrate** the even faster but less pronounced throbbing of a string on a musical instrument. **Undulate** and **fluctuate** both refer particularly to up-and-down movement or appearance, **undulate** being regular and wavelike ⟨*undulating landscape*⟩ and **fluctuate** being irregular and applied chiefly to abstractions ⟨*fluctuating prices*⟩. **Waver** is also irregular, and suggests an unsteady faltering ⟨*wavering column of smoke*⟩. See ¹SHAKE

²**swing** *n* 1 an act or instance of swinging; a swinging movement: eg **1a(1)** a stroke or blow delivered with a sweeping arm movement ⟨*a batsman with a powerful* ~⟩ **a(2)** a sweeping or rhythmic movement of the body or a body part **a(3)** a dance figure in which two dancers revolve with joined arms or hands **a(4)** jazz dancing in moderate tempo with a lilting rhythm **b(1)** the regular movement of a freely suspended object (eg a pendulum) to and fro along an arc **b(2)** back and forward sweep ⟨*the* ~ *of the tides*⟩ **c(1)** steady pulsing rhythm (eg in poetry or music) **c(2)** a steady vigorous movement characterizing an activity or creative work **d(1)** a trend towards a high or low point in a fluctuating cycle (eg of business activity) **d(2)** a shift from one condition, form, position, or object of attention or favour to another ⟨*a* ~ *of 10% to the Liberals*⟩ **2a** liberty of action; free scope **b** the driving power of something swung or hurled **3** the progression of an activity, process, or phase of existence ⟨*the work is in full* ~⟩ ⟨*getting into the* ~ *of things*⟩ **4** the arc or range through which something swings **5** something that swings freely from or on a support; *esp* a suspended seat on which one may swing to and fro **6** a curving course or outline **7** jazz played usu by a large dance band and characterized by a steady lively rhythm, simple harmony, and a basic melody often submerged in improvisation – **swing** *adj*

**swingalong** /'swingǝlong/ *adj, informal* lacking sedateness or depth; lightweight, frivolous

**swingbridge** /'swing,brij/ *n* a bridge that has (part of) its roadway able to be swung aside to allow passage (eg for ships)

**swing door** *n* a door that can be pushed open from either side and that swings closed when released

**swingeing, swinging** /'swinjing/ *adj, chiefly Br* very great in force, degree, or size; severe ⟨~ *cuts in public expenditure*⟩ [fr prp of *swinge* (to beat, scourge), fr ME *swengen* to shake, fr OE *swengan;* akin to OE *swingan* to beat]

**swinger** /,swingǝ/ *n* one who or that which swings: eg **a** a bowled ball in cricket that swings in a usu specified direction – usu in combination ⟨*an away-*swinger⟩ **b** *informal* a lively and up-to-date person **c** *slang* one who engages freely in sex, esp in wife-swapping

**swinging** /'swing·ing/ *adj, informal* lively and up-to-date [fr prp of ¹*swing*]

¹**swingle** /'swing·gl/ *n* a wooden instrument like a large knife that is used for beating and cleaning flax [ME *swingel*, fr MD *swinghel;* akin to OE *swingan* to beat]

²**swingle** *vt* to clean (flax) by beating with a swingle

**swinglebar** /'swing·gl,bah/ *n* a swingletree

**swingletree** /'swing·gl,tree/ *n* the pivoted swinging bar to which the side straps (traces) of a harness are attached and by which a vehicle or implement (eg a plough) is drawn – called also WHIFFLETREE [¹*swingle* + *tree*]

**swingometer** /,swing'omitǝ/ *n, informal* a device for representing statistical movements, esp in the electoral support of a political party, by means of an adjustable pointer attached to a dial [²*swing* + *-o-* + ²*-meter*]

**swings and roundabouts** *n pl* a situation where a loss made on one transaction is offset by a gain on another

,**swing-'wing** *adj* of or being an aircraft having movable wings giving the best angles of backward slant (SWEEPBACK) for both low and high speeds

**swinish** /'swienish/ *adj* of, suggesting, or characteristic of swine; beastly – **swinishly** *adv*, **swinishness** *n*

¹**swink** /swingk/ *vi, archaic* to toil, slave [ME *swinken*, fr OE *swincan;* akin to OHG *swingan* to rush – more at SWING]

²**swink** *n, archaic* labour, drudgery

¹**swipe** /swiep/ *n, informal* a strong sweeping blow [prob alter. of *sweep*]

²**swipe** *vb, informal* *vi* to strike or hit out *at* with a sweeping motion ~ *vt* 1 to strike or wipe with a sweeping motion 2 to steal, pilfer *synonyms* see ROB

**swipes** /swieps/ *n pl, Br slang* weak, inferior, or spoiled beer [origin unknown]

¹**swirl** /swuhl/ *n* **1a** a whirling mass or motion; an eddy **b** a whirling confusion ⟨*a* ~ *of events*⟩ **2** a twisting shape, mark, or pattern **3** an act or instance of swirling **4** *chiefly Br* an amusement ride consisting of freely pivoted cars on a revolving frame [ME (Sc), prob of imit origin] – **swirly** *adj*

²**swirl** *vi* 1 to move in eddies or whirls **2** to have a twist or convolution ~ *vt* to cause to swirl – **swirlingly** *adv*

¹**swish** /swish/ *vi* to move with the sound of a swish ⟨*windscreen wipers* ~ing⟩ ~ *vt* to move with a swish ⟨*the horse* ~ed *its tail*⟩ [imit] – **swisher** *n*, **swishingly** *adv*

²**swish** *n* **1a** a sharp hissing sound (eg of a whip cutting the air) **b** a light sweeping or brushing sound (eg of someone walking in a full silk skirt) **2** a swishing movement – **swishy** *adj*

³**swish** *adj, informal* smart, fashionable [origin unknown]

¹**Swiss** /swis/ *n, pl* **Swiss** 1 a native or inhabitant of Switzerland **2** *often not cap* any of various fine sheer fabrics of cotton originally made in Switzerland [MF *Suisse*, fr MHG *Swīzer*, fr *Swīz* Switzerland, country in central Europe]

²**Swiss** *adj* (characteristic) of Switzerland or the Swiss

**Swiss chard** *n* CHARD (plant with edible leaves and stalks)

**Swiss roll** *n* a cake consisting of a thin sheet of SPONGE CAKE spread with jam, cream, or other filling and rolled up

¹**switch** /swich/ *n* 1 a slender flexible twig, whip, or rod ⟨*a riding* ~⟩ **2** an act or instance of switching: eg **2a** a blow with a switch **b** a shift from one to another **3** a tuft of long hairs at the end of the tail of an animal (eg a cow) **4** a device for making, breaking, or changing the connections in an electrical circuit **5** a tress of hair that is attached to a person's own hair for some hairstyles **6** *NAm* **6a** railway points **b** a railway siding [perh fr MD *swijch* twig]

²**switch** *vt* 1 to strike or beat (as if) with a switch **2** to whisk, lash ⟨*a cat* ~ing *his tail*⟩ **3** to make a shift in or exchange of ⟨~ *the talk to another subject*⟩ ⟨~ *places*⟩ **4a** to shift to another electrical circuit by means of a switch **b** to operate an electrical switch so as to turn (eg a light) *off* or *on* **5** *chiefly NAm* to turn from one railway track to another; shunt ~ *vi* 1 to lash from side to side **2** to make a shift or exchange – **switchable** *adj*, **switcher** *n*

**switchback** /-,bak/ *n* 1 a zigzag road or railway in a mountainous region; *esp* an arrangement of zigzag railway tracks for surmounting the grade of a steep hill **2a** a road with alternating ascents and descents **b** *chiefly Br* any of various amusement rides; *esp* ROLLER COASTER

**switchblade** /-,blayd/ *n, NAm* a flick-knife

**switchboard** /-,bawd/ *n* an apparatus consisting of a panel or frame on which are mounted insulated switching, measuring, controlling, and protective devices which can be connected to a number of circuits; *specif* an arrangement for the manual switching of telephone calls

,**switched-'on** *adj, informal* alive to experience; responsive, alert; *also* swinging

**switchgear** /-,giǝ/ *n* equipment used for the switching of esp large electrical currents

**switchman** /-mǝn/ *n, NAm* someone who works a switch (eg on a railway); a pointsman

**switchover** /-,ohvǝ/ *n* a conversion to a different system or method

**switch selling** *n* the practice of interesting a buyer by advertising a low-priced product and then trying to sell him/her a more expensive one

**switchyard** /-,yahd/ *n* 1 a usu enclosed area for the switching facilities of a POWER STATION **2** *NAm* MARSHALLING YARD (place where trains are stored, shunted, etc)

**Switzer** /'switsǝ/ *n, archaic* a Swiss [MHG *Swīzer*]

¹**swivel** /'swivl/ *n* a device joining two parts so that the moving part can pivot freely [ME; akin to OE *swīfan* to revolve, ON *sveigja* to sway – more at SWAY]

²**swivel** *vb* **-ll-** (*NAm* **-l-, -ll-**) to swing or turn (as if) on a swivel ⟨~led *his eyes in various directions*⟩ ⟨*the stool* ~led *and I fell off*⟩

**swivel chair** *n* a chair that swivels on its base

**swivel gun** *n* a gun mounted on a swivel so that it can be swung from side to side

**‚swivel-'hipped** *adj* moving with or characterized by movement with a twisting motion of the hips

**swivel pin** *n* any of the pins on which a front wheel of a motor vehicle rotates for steering when there is INDEPENDENT SUSPENSION

**swiz, swizz** /swiz/ *n, pl* **-zz-** *Br informal* **1** something that does not live up to one's hopes or expectations; a disappointment **2** a fraud, swindle [prob short for *swizzle*]

**¹swizzle** /'swizl/ *n, Br informal* a swiz [prob alter. of *swindle*]

**²swizzle** *vt* to mix or stir (as if) with a SWIZZLE STICK [*swizzle* (alcoholic cocktail), of unknown origin] – **swizzler** *n*

**swizzle stick** /'swizl/ *n* a thin rod used to stir mixed drinks, esp to release some of the bubbles from sparkling drinks

**swob** /swob/ *vt or n* **-bb-** (to) swab

**swollen** /'swohlən/ *past part of* SWELL

**swollen head** *n* an exaggerated opinion of oneself; self-conceit

**¹swoon** /swoohn/ *vi* **1** to faint **2** to become enraptured ⟨~ing *with joy*⟩ [ME *swounen*] – **swooner** *n*, **swooningly** *adv*

**²swoon** *n* **1** a partial or total loss of consciousness; a faint **2** a state of bewilderment or ecstasy; a daze, rapture ⟨*a floating ~ of . . . erotic longing* – William Faulkner⟩

**¹swoop** /swoohp/ *vi* to move abruptly with a sweep; *specif* to make a sudden attack or raid – often + *down* ⟨*the eagle ~ed down on its prey*⟩ ~ *vt* to carry off abruptly; sweep, snatch ⟨~ed *her off the swing into his arms* – Helen Howe⟩ [alter. of ME *swopen* to sweep, fr OE *swāpan*; akin to ON *svatha* to swathe – more at SWATHE] – **swooper** *n*

**²swoop** *n* an act or instance of swooping ⟨*arrested in a drug-squad ~*⟩ – **at one fell swoop** all at once; *also* with a single concentrated effort

**swoosh** /swoosh, swoohsh/ *vi or n* (to make or move with) a rushing sound ⟨*a car ~ed by*⟩ [imit]

**swop** /swop/ *vb or n* **-pp-** (to) swap

**sword** /sawd/ *n* **1a** a cutting or thrusting weapon with a long usu sharp-pointed and sharp-edged blade, sometimes used as a symbol of honour or authority **b** death caused (as if) by being cut down with a sword – usu + *the* **2** the use of force (eg in war) ⟨*the pen is mightier than the ~* Edward Bulwer-Lytton⟩ **3** coercive power ⟨*the ~ of Justice*⟩ **4** something (eg the beak of a swordfish) that resembles a sword [ME, fr OE *sweord*; akin to OHG *swert* sword, Av *xvara* wound] – **swordlike** *adj* – **cross swords 1** to fight **2** to disagree strongly; argue *with* – **put to the sword** to kill (esp a prisoner) with a sword

**sword cane** *n* a swordstick

**sword dance** *n* **1** a ceremonial folk dance performed by men in a circle who brandish swords **2** a dance performed over or round swords; *esp* a Scottish-Highland solo dance usu performed in the angles formed by two swords crossed on the ground – **sword dancer** *n*

**swordfish** /-,fish/ *n* a very large oceanic food fish (*Xiphias gladius*) that has a long swordlike beak formed by the bones of the upper jaw

**sword grass** *n* any of various grasses or sedges having leaves with a sharp or toothed edge

**sword knot** *n* an ornamental cord or tassel tied to the hilt of a sword

**sword of Damocles** /'daməkleez/ *n, often cap S* an impending disaster [fr the legend of the sword suspended by a single hair over the head of Damocles, a courtier of ancient Syracuse, as a reminder of the insecurity of a tyrant's happiness]

**swordplay** /-,play/ *n* the art, skill, or practice of wielding a sword, esp in fencing – **swordplayer** *n*

**swordsman** /'sawdzmən/ *n* **1** someone skilled in swordplay; *esp* a sabre fencer **2** a soldier armed with a sword

**swordsmanship** /-ship/ *n* swordplay

**swordstick** /'sawd,stik/ *n* a stick, esp a walking stick, in which a sword blade is concealed

**'sword-‚swallower** *n* a performer (eg at a circus) who causes or allows sword-blades to pass down his/her throat

**swordtail** /-,tayl/ *n* a small brightly marked Central American TOPMINNOW (type of fish) (*Xiphophorus helleri*) often kept in tropical aquariums and bred in many colours

**swore** /swaw/ *past of* SWEAR

**sworn** /swawn/ *past part of* SWEAR

**¹swot** /swot/ *n, Br derog* a student who studies excessively, usu to the exclusion of leisure activities [alter. of *sweat*]

**²swot** *vb* **-tt-** *Br informal vi* to study hard ⟨~ *for an exam*⟩ – often + *up* ⟨~ *up on my French*⟩ ~ *vt* to study (a subject) intensively – usu + *up* ⟨~ting *his history up*⟩

**swum** /swum/ *past part of* SWIM

**swung** /swung/ *past of* SWING

**swung dash** *n* a character ~ used in printing esp to conserve space by representing part or all of a previously spelt-out word

**sybarite** /'sibəriet/ *n, often cap* one who likes to indulge in sensual pleasures [fr the notorious luxury of the people of the ancient city of Sybaris in Italy] – **sybaritic** *adj*, **sybaritically** *adv*, **sybaritism** *n*

**sycamine** /'sikəmien/ *n* a mulberry [L *sycaminus*, fr Gk *syka-minos*, of Sem origin; akin to Heb *shiqmāh* mulberry tree, sycamore]

**sycamore** /'sikə,maw/ *n* **1** a tree (*Ficus sycomorus*) of the Middle East that is the sycamore of Scripture, is grown as a SHADE TREE, and has sweet edible fruit similar to the common fig **2** a Eurasian maple (*Acer pseudoplatanus*) that is widely planted as a SHADE TREE **3** *NAm* a plane tree; *esp* a very large spreading tree (*Platanus occidentalis*) of E and central N America [ME *sicamour*, fr MF *sicamor*, fr L *sycomorus*, fr Gk *sykomoros*, prob modif of a Sem word akin to Heb *shiqmāh* sycamore]

**syce, sice** /sies/ *n* a groom, esp in India [Hindi *sā'is*, fr Ar]

**sycee** /sie'see/ *n* silver money formerly used in China and made in the form of ingots measured by weight and usu stamped [Chin (Cant) *sai sz*, lit., fine silk]

**syconium** /sie'kohnyəm, -ni-əm/ *n, pl* **syconia** /-nyə, -ni-ə/ a fleshy fruit (eg a fig) in which the seeds are borne within an enlarged succulent concave or hollow receptacle [NL, fr Gk *sykon* fig + NL *-ium*]

**sycophancy** /'sikə,fansi/ *n* ingratiating and servile flattery; *also* the character or behaviour of a sycophant

**sycophant** /'sikə,fant/ *n* a self-seeking flatterer; a toady [L *sycophanta* informer, swindler, sycophant, fr Gk *sykophantēs* informer, fr *sykon* fig + *phainein* to show] – **sycophant, sycophantic** *adj*

**sycosis** /sie'kohsis/ *n* a long-lasting inflammatory disorder of the HAIR FOLLICLES (tubular sheaths which enclose hair roots) esp of the chin, marked by raised spots, pustules, and rounded scabby lumps [NL, fr Gk *sykōsis*, fr *sykon* fig]

**Sydneysider** /'sidni,siedə/ *n, Austr* a person from Sydney

**syenite** /'sie·i,niet/ *n* a coarse-grained IGNEOUS (formed by the slow cooling and solidification of molten material) rock that is composed chiefly of the mineral FELDSPAR [L *Syenites* (*lapis*) stone of Syene, fr *Syene*, ancient city in Egypt] – **syenitic** *adj*

**syli** /'sili/ *n* – see MONEY table [Susu, lit., elephant]

**syllabarium** /'siləbəriəm/ *n, pl* **syllabaria** a syllabary [NL]

**syllabary** /'siləbəri/ *n* a table or list of syllables; *specif* a set of written characters each one of which represents a syllable [NL *syllabarium*, fr L *syllaba* syllable]

**¹syllabic** /si'labik/ *adj* **1** of or denoting syllables ⟨~ *stress*⟩ **2** constituting (the nucleus of) a syllable; *esp* not accompanied in the same syllable by a vowel sound ⟨/n/ *is* ~ *in* rotten *but not in* running⟩ **3** enunciated with distinct separation of syllables **4** of or constituting a type of verse distinguished primarily by count of syllables rather than by rhythmical arrangement according to accents or duration [LL *syllabicus*, fr Gk *syllabikos*, fr *syllabē* syllable] – **syllabically** *adv*

**²syllabic** *n* a syllabic character or sound

**syllabicate** /si'labi,kayt/ *vt* to syllabify – **syllabication** *n*

**syllabicity** /silab'isəti/ *n* the state of being or the power of forming a syllable

**syllabify** /si'labifie/ *vt* to form or divide into syllables [L *syllaba* syllable] – **syllabification** *n*

**syllab·ize, -ise** /'siləbiez/ *vt* to syllabify [ML *syllabizare*, fr Gk *syllabizien*, fr *syllabē* syllable]

**¹syllable** /'siləbl/ *n* **1** an uninterruptible unit of spoken language that consists of one vowel sound or of a syllabic consonant alone or of either with one or more consonant sounds preceding or following **2** one or more letters roughly corresponding to a syllable of spoken language **3** the smallest conceivable expression or unit of something; a jot ⟨*not a ~ of truth in it*⟩ [ME, fr MF *sillabe*, fr L *syllaba*, fr Gk *syllabē*, fr *syllambanein* to gather together, fr *syn-* + *lambanein* to take] –more at LATCH

**²syllable** *vt* to give a number or arrangement of syllables to (a word or verse)

**syllabub** /'siləbub/ *n* a cold dessert consisting of sweetened cream or milk thickened usu by curdling with an acidic liquid (eg wine, cider, or fruit juice) or sometimes by whipping or adding gelatine [origin unknown]

**syllabus** /'siləbəs/ *n, pl* **syllabi, syllabuses** a summary of a course of study or of examination requirements [LL, alter. of L *sillybus* label for a book, fr Gk *sillybos*]

**syllepsis** /si'lepsis/ *n, pl* **syllepses** /-seez/ **1** the use of a word to cover more than one function by modifying or governing syntactically two or sometimes more words with only one of which it formally agrees (eg *knows* in "neither he nor I knows") **2** the use of a word in the same grammatical relation to two adjacent words but in different senses (eg *departed* in "departed in tears and a taxi") *synonyms* see ZEUGMA [L, fr Gk *syllēpsis*, fr *syllambanein* to gather together] – **sylleptic** *adj*

**syllogism** /'silə.jiz(ə)m/ *n* **1** a pattern of deductive reasoning consisting of two given or assumed propositions (MAJOR PREMISE and MINOR PREMISE) and a conclusion (eg "all men are mortal; Socrates is a man; therefore Socrates is mortal") **2** deductive reasoning [ME *silogisme*, fr MF, fr L *syllogismus*, fr Gk *syllogismos*, fr *syllogizesthai* to syllogize, fr *syn-* + *logizesthai* to calculate, fr *logos* reckoning, word – more at LEGEND] – **syllogistic** *adj*, **syllogistically** *adv*

**syllog·ize, -ise** /'silə.jiez/ *vi* to reason by means of syllogisms ~ *vt* to put (eg facts or an argument) into syllogistic form [ME *sylogysen*, fr LL *syllogizare*, fr Gk *syllogizesthai*]

**sylph** /silf/ *n* a slender graceful woman or girl – compare NYMPH △ sibyl [NL *sylphus* imaginary being inhabiting the air, prob carried by Paracelsus (cf GNOME)] – **sylphlike** *adj*

**sylva, silva** /'silvə/ *n* the forest trees of a region or country – compare FAUNA, FLORA [NL, fr L, forest, grove]

**sylvan, silvan** /'silvən/ *adj, chiefly poetic* **1a** living or located in the woods or forest **b** (characteristic) of the woods or forest **2a** made, shaped, or formed of woods or trees ⟨~ *vegetation*⟩ **b** abounding in woods, groves, or trees; wooded [ML *silvanus*, *sylvanus*, fr L *silva, sylva* forest, grove]

**sylvanite** /'silvə.niet/ *n* a mineral, $(Au,Ag)Te_2$, that contains the chemical elements gold, silver, and tellurium and often occurs in crystals resembling written characters [Fr *sylvanite*, fr NL *sylvanium* tellurium, fr *Transylvania*, region in Romania]

**sylvatic** /sil'vatik/ *adj* **1** SYLVAN 1a ⟨~ *rodents*⟩ **2** occurring in or affecting wild animals ⟨~ *diseases*⟩ [L *silvaticus* of the woods, wild, fr *silva* forest (cf SAVAGE)]

**sylvine** /'silveen/ *n* a mineral that is a natural POTASSIUM CHLORIDE, KCl, and occurs in colourless cubes or crystalline masses

**sylvite** /'silviet/ *n* sylvine [Fr, *sylvine*, fr NL *sal digestivus Sylvii* digestive salt of Sylvius, fr *Sylvius* latinized name of Jacques Dubois †1555 Fr physician]

**sym-** – see SYN-

**symbiont** /'simbi.ont/ *n* an organism living in symbiosis; *esp* the smaller member of a symbiotic pair [deriv of Gk *symbiount-*, *symbiōn*, prp of *symbioun* to live together] – **symbiontic** *adj*

**symbiosis** /.simbi'ohsis, -bie-/ *n, pl* **symbioses** /-seez/ **1** the living together of two dissimilar organisms in more or less intimate association or close union **2** the intimate living together of two dissimilar organisms in a mutually beneficial relationship [NL, fr Ger *symbiose*, fr Gk *symbiōsis* state of living together, fr *symbioun* to live together, fr *symbios* living together, fr *sym-* + *bios* life – more at QUICK] – **symbiotic** *adj*, **symbiotically** *adv*

**symbiote** /'simbi.oht, -bie-/ *n* a symbiont [Fr, fr Gk *symbiōtēs* companion, fr *symbioun* to live together]

**symbol** /'simbl/ *n* **1** something that stands for or suggests something else by reason of relationship, association, convention, or accidental resemblance; *esp* a visible sign of something invisible ⟨*the lion is a* ~ *of courage*⟩ **2** an arbitrary or conventional sign used in writing or printing to represent operations, quantities, elements, relations, or qualities in a particular field (eg chemistry or music) **3** a consciously perceived object or act that in psychoanalytic theory represents an object or process of the unconscious mind ⟨*phallic* ~s⟩ △ cymbal [L *symbolum* token, sign, symbol, fr Gk *symbolon*, lit., token of identity verified by comparing its other half, fr *symballein* to throw together, compare, fr *syn-* + *ballein* to throw – more at DEVIL]

**symbolic, symbolical** /sim'bolik/ *adj* **1** of or constituting a symbol **2a** using or exhibiting a symbol ⟨*a* ~ *author*⟩ **b** consisting of or proceeding by means of symbols ⟨~ *language*⟩ **3** characterized by symbolism ⟨*a* ~ *dance*⟩ – **symbolically** *adv*

**symbolic logic** *n* a method of developing and representing logical principles by means of a formalized system of symbols

**symbolism** /'simbə.liz(ə)m/ *n* **1a** the art or practice of representing things by symbols or giving things a symbolic meaning **b** the use of conventional or traditional signs in the representation of divine beings and spirits **2** a system of symbols **3** the literary and artistic mode of expression of the symbolists

**symbolist** /'simbəlist/ *n* **1** someone who uses symbols or symbolism **2** any of a group of writers and artists in France from about 1880 who in reaction against realism concerned themselves esp with the METAPHYSICAL (supernatural) and mysterious and sought to express ideas and emotions with the greatest possible precision by the use of symbolic language, images, etc – **symbolist** *adj*

**symbolistic** /.simbə'listik/ *adj* of or pertaining to symbolism

**symbol·ize, -ise** /'simbə.liez/ *vt* **1** to serve as a symbol of **2** to represent, express, or identify by a symbol – **symbolization** *n*, **symbolizer** *n*

**symbology** /sim'boləji/ *n* **1** the art of expression by symbols **2** the study or interpretation of symbols **3** SYMBOLISM 2 [*symbol* + *-logy*]

**symmetallism** /si'metə.liz(ə)m/ *n* a system of coinage in which the unit of currency consists of a particular weight of an alloy of two or more metals (eg gold and silver) [*syn-* + *-metallism* (as in *bimetallism*)]

**symmetric** /si'metrik/ *adj* **1** of or being a (mathematical) relation (eg 'is not equal to' or 'has the same parents as') such that if $x * y$ then $y * x$, where $*$ denotes the relation **2** symmetrical

**symmetrical** /si'metrikl/ *adj* **1** having, involving, or exhibiting symmetry **2** having corresponding points whose connecting lines are bisected by a given point or perpendicularly bisected by a given line or plane ⟨~ *curves*⟩ **3a** capable of division by a longitudinal plane into similar halves ⟨~ *plant parts*⟩ **b** *of a flower* having the same number of members in each WHORL (circular arrangement of like flower parts) of FLORAL LEAVES (eg petals or sepals) **4** affecting corresponding parts simultaneously and similarly ⟨*a* ~ *rash*⟩ **5** *of a chemical compound* having symmetry in the molecular structure; *esp* being a derivative with groups substituted symmetrically in the molecule – **symmetrically** *adv*, **symmetricalness** *n*

**symmetric difference** *n* the set of points belonging to one or other of two mathematical sets but not to both of them

**symmetric matrix** *n* a matrix that is equal to its own TRANSPOSE (matrix having the rows and columns interchanged)

**symmetr·ize, -ise** /'simi.triez/ *vt* to make symmetrical – **symmetrization**

**symmetry** /'simitri/ *n* **1** balanced proportions; *also* beauty of form arising from balanced proportions **2** the property of being symmetrical; *esp* correspondence in size, shape, and relative position of parts on opposite sides of a dividing line, centre, or other axis – compare BILATERAL SYMMETRY, RADIAL SYMMETRY **3** a rigid motion (eg rotation about an axis) of a geometric figure that determines a BIJECTIVE mapping onto itself **4** the property possessed by a physical phenomenon whereby it remains unaffected by certain changes (eg of orientation in space, of the sign of the electric charge, or of the direction of time flow) [L *symmetria*, fr Gk, fr *symmetros* symmetrical, fr *syn-* + *metron* measure – more at MEASURE]

¹**sympathetic** /.simpə'thetik/ *adj* **1** existing or operating through an affinity, interdependence, or mutual association **2a** not discordant or antagonistic **b** appropriate to one's mood, inclinations, or disposition **3** given to, marked by, or arising from sympathy, compassion, friendliness, and sensitivity to others' emotions ⟨*a* ~ *gesture*⟩ **4** favourably inclined; approving ⟨*not* ~ *to the idea*⟩ **5a** of or relating to the SYMPATHETIC NERVOUS SYSTEM **b** mediated by or acting on the sympathetic nerves **6** relating to musical sounds produced by SYMPATHETIC VIBRATION or to strings sounded by sympathetic vibration *synonyms* see ²KIND *antonym* unsympathetic [NL *sympatheticus*, fr L *sympathia* sympathy] – **sympathetically** *adv*

²**sympathetic** *n* a sympathetic structure; *esp* SYMPATHETIC NERVOUS SYSTEM

**sympathetic nervous system** *n* the part of the AUTONOMIC NERVOUS SYSTEM that contains NERVE FIBRES that transmit impulses by producing ADRENALIN or NORADRENALIN and tends to depress secretion (eg of digestive juices in the gut), decrease the tension and elasticity of SMOOTH MUSCLE, and cause the contraction of blood vessels – compare PARASYMPATHETIC NERVOUS SYSTEM

**sympathetic strike** *n* SYMPATHY STRIKE

**sympathetic vibration** *n* a vibration produced in one body by the vibrations of exactly the same frequency in a neighbouring body

**sympathin** /'simpəthin/ *n* a substance (e g ADRENALIN or NORADRENALIN) that is secreted by sympathetic nerve endings and acts as a chemical transmitter of impulses [ISV, fr ²*sympathetic*]

**sympath·ize, -ise** /'simpəthiez/ *vi* **1** to react or respond in sympathy **2** to share in suffering or grief; commiserate – often + *with* ⟨~ *with a friend in trouble*⟩; *also* to express such sympathy **3** to be in sympathy intellectually – often + *with* ⟨~ *with a proposal*⟩ – **sympathizer** *n*

**sympatholytic** /ˌsimpəthoh'litik/ *adj* tending to oppose the physiological results of sympathetic nervous activity or of drugs that produce this activity [ISV *sympath*etic + *-o-* + *-lytic*] – **sympatholytic** *n*

**sympathomimetic** /ˌsimpəthohmi'metik/ *adj* simulating sympathetic nervous action in physiological effect ⟨~ *drugs*⟩ [ISV *sympath*etic + *-o-* + *mimetic*] – **sympathomimetic** *n*

**sympathy** /'simpəthi/ *n* **1a** an affinity, association, or relationship between people or things in which each is simultaneously affected in a similar way **b** unity or harmony in action or effect **2a** inclination to think or feel alike; emotional or intellectual accord **b** sympathies *pl*, sympathy feeling of loyalty; tendency to give favour or support ⟨*Tory* sympathies⟩ **3a** the act or capacity of entering into or sharing the feelings or interests of another **b** the feeling or mental state brought about by such sensitivity ⟨*have* ~ *for the poor*⟩ [L *sympathia*, fr Gk *sympatheia*, fr *sympathēs* having common feelings, sympathetic, fr *syn-* + *pathos* feelings, emotion, experience – more at PATHOS]

*usage* One *has* or *feels* sympathy *for* another, which stresses the idea of compassion, or one is *in* sympathy *with* another, which suggests shared feelings. *synonyms* see EMPATHY

**sympathy strike** *n* a strike in which the strikers have no direct grievance against their own employer but attempt to support or aid usu another group of workers on strike

**sympatric** /sim'patrik/ *adj* occurring in the same area; *specif* occupying the same range without loss of identity from interbreeding – compare ALLOPATRIC [*syn-* + Gk *patra* fatherland, fr *patēr* father – more at FATHER] – **sympatrically** *adv*, **sympatry** *n*

**sympetalous** /sim'petələs/ *adj* GAMOPETALOUS (having united petals) – **sympetaly** *n*

**symphonic** /sim'fonik/ *adj* **1** (having the form or character) of a symphony ⟨~ *music*⟩ **2** suggestive of a symphony, esp in form, interweaving of themes, or harmonious arrangement ⟨*a* ~ *drama*⟩ – **symphonically** *adv*

**symphonic poem** *n* an extended orchestral composition, usu freer in form than a symphony, that illustrates a theme or tells a story – called also TONE POEM

**symphonious** /sim'fohniəs/ *adj, formal* agreeing, esp in sound; harmonious – **symphoniously** *adv*

**symphonist** /'simfənist/ *n* **1** a composer of symphonies **2** a member of a symphony orchestra

**symphony** /'simfəni/ *n* **1a** RITORNELLO 1 (recurrent instrumental passage in a vocal work) **b** SINFONIA 1a (orchestral composition played as an introduction to choral works) **c**(1) a usu long and complex composition for SYMPHONY ORCHESTRA, traditionally in three or four movements of contrasting styles and keys, usu with one in SONATA FORM, but more variable in recent times **c**(2) a composition of similar proportions (e g for organ) **2** something that in its harmonious complexity or variety suggests a symphonic composition ⟨*the room was a* ~ *in blue*⟩ **3** chiefly NAm **3a** SYMPHONY ORCHESTRA **b** NAm a SYMPHONY ORCHESTRA concert [ME *symphonie*, fr OF, fr L *symphonia*, fr Gk *symphōnia*, fr *symphōnos* agreeing in sound, fr *syn-* + *phōnē* voice, sound – more at BAN]

**symphony orchestra** *n* a large orchestra usu consisting of string, woodwind, brass, and percussion instruments that plays symphonic works

**symphyseal** /simfə'zee·əl/ *also* **symphysial** /sim'fizi·əl/ *adj* of or constituting a symphysis

**symphysis** /'simfisis/ *n, pl* **symphyses** /-seez/ **1** a joining in the central plane of two similar bones on opposite sides of the body ⟨*pubic* ~⟩ **2** a largely or completely immovable joint between bones; *esp* one with the surfaces connected by pads of fibrous cartilage without a joint membrane [NL, fr Gk, state of growing together, fr *symphyesthai* to grow together, fr *syn-* + *phyein* to make grow, bring forth – more at BE]

**sympodial** /sim'pohdi·əl/ *adj* having or involving the formation of an apparent main AXIS (stem) from successive secondary axes ⟨~ *branching of a cymose inflorescence*⟩ [NL *sympodium* apparent main axis formed from secondary axes, fr Gk *syn-* + *podion* base – more at -PODIUM] – **sympodially** *adv*

**symposium** /sim'pohzyəm, -zi·əm/ *n, pl* **symposia**, /-zyə, -z·ə/ **symposiums 1** a convivial party (e g after a banquet in ancient Greece) with music and conversation **2a** a formal meeting at which several specialists deliver short addresses on a topic or on related topics – compare COLLOQUIUM **b** a collection of opinions on a subject; *esp* one published by a periodical **3** *formal* a discussion [L, fr Gk *symposion*, fr *sympinein* to drink together, fr *syn-* + *pinein* to drink – more at POTABLE]

**symptom** /'simptəm/ *n* **1a** subjective evidence or indication of disease or physical disturbance; *broadly* something that indicates the presence of bodily disorder **b** a reaction of a plant to a PATHOGEN (disease-causing agent) **2** something that indicates the existence of something else [LL *symptomat-*, *symptoma*, fr Gk *symptōmat-*, *symptōma* happening, attribute, symptom, fr *sympiptein* to happen, fr *syn-* + *piptein* to fall – more at FEATHER] – **symptomless** *adj*

**symptomatic** /ˌsimptə'matik/ *adj* **1a** being a symptom of a disease **b** having the characteristics of a specified disease but arising from another cause ⟨~ *epilepsy after a brain injury*⟩ **2** concerned with, affecting, or acting on symptoms ⟨~ *treatment for influenza*⟩ **3** characteristic, indicative ⟨*his behaviour was* ~ *of his character*⟩ – **symptomatically** *adv*

**symptomatology** /ˌsimptəmə'toləji/ *n* **1** a branch of medical science concerned with the symptoms of diseases **2** the symptoms characteristic of a disease – **symptomatological, symptomatologic** *adj*, **symptomatologically** *adv*

**syn-, sym-** *prefix* **1** with; along with; together ⟨*sympathy*⟩ ⟨*synthesis*⟩ **2** at the same time ⟨*synaesthesia*⟩ □ usu *sym-* before *p, b,* and *m* [ME, fr OF, fr L, fr Gk, fr *syn* with, together with]

**synaeresis** /si'niorisis/ *n* **1** SYNIZESIS (contraction of two syllables into one) **2** SYNERESIS 2 (separation of a liquid from a gel)

**synaesthesia** /ˌsinees'theez(h)yə/ *n* a sensation in one part of the body accompanying or brought about by a stimulus in a different part; *esp* a subjective sensation or image of a sense (e g of colour) other than the one (e g of sound) being stimulated [NL, fr *syn-* + *-aesthesia* (as in *anaesthesia*)] – **synaesthetic** *adj*

**synagogue, synagog** /'sinəgog/ *n* **1** a Jewish congregation **2** the house of worship and communal centre of a Jewish congregation [ME *synagoge*, fr OF, fr LL *synagoga*, fr Gk *synagōgē* assembly, synagogue, fr *synagein* to bring together, fr *syn-* + *agein* to lead – more at AGENT] – **synagogal** *adj*

**synaloepha, synalepha** /ˌsinə'leefə/ *n* the reduction of two adjacent vowels to one syllable (e g in *th' army* for *the army*) [NL, fr Gk *synaloiphē*, fr *synaleiphein* to clog up, coalesce, unite two syllables into one, fr *syn-* + *aleiphein* to anoint]

**¹synapse** /'sienaps/ *n* the point (between two nerve cells) across which a nerve impulse is transmitted [NL *synapsis*, fr Gk, juncture, fr *synaptein* to fasten together, fr *syn-* + *haptein* to fasten] – **synaptic** *adj*

**²synapse** *vi* to form a synapse or come together in synapsis

**synapsis** /si'napsis/ *n, pl* **synapses** the coming together of corresponding CHROMOSOMES (strands of gene-carrying material in a cell) resulting in their ultimate association and the formation of cross-shaped areas of contact (CHIASMATA) that is characteristic of the first phase of MEIOSIS (cell division producing the sex cells) and is probably the mechanism for genetic CROSSING-OVER (interchange of genes or segments of chromosomes) [NL, fr Gk, juncture] – **synaptic** *adj*, **synaptically** *adv*

**synarthrosis** /ˌsinah'throhsis/ *n, pl* **synarthroses** /-seez/ an immovable joint in which the bones are united by intervening fibrous CONNECTIVE TISSUES [Gk *synarthrōsis*, fr *syn-* + *arthrōsis* jointing – more at ARTHROSIS]

**¹sync** *also* **synch** /singk/ *n, informal* synchronization ⟨*the film was running out of* ~⟩ – **sync** *adj*

**²sync** *also* **synch** *vt, informal* to match the film and soundtrack of so that they run exactly in synchronization – often + *up*

**syncarpous** /sin'kahpəs/ *adj, of a flower, fruit, etc* having the CARPELS (female reproductive organs) united in a compound OVARY (structure containing the seeds) – **syncarpy** *n*

**synchro-** *comb form* synchronized; synchronous ⟨*synchroflash*⟩ ⟨*synchromesh*⟩

**synchrocyclotron** /ˌsingkroh'sieklə,tron/ *n* a modified CYCLO-

TRON (device for producing a beam of high-energy particles) that achieves greater energies for the electrically charged particles by compensating for the variation in mass that the particles experience with increasing velocity

**synchroflash** /'singkroh,flash/ *adj* using or produced with a mechanism for synchronizing the firing or peak brilliance of a flashgun with the opening of a camera shutter

**synchromesh** /'singkrə,mesh/ *adj* designed to synchronize the speeds of the different moving parts involved in a gear change so that it can be effected smoothly – **synchromesh** *n*

**synchronic** /sing'kronik/ *also* **synchronical** /-kl/ *adj* **1** synchronous **2** of or dealing with phenomena, esp of language, at one point in time and ignoring previous historical developments – compare DIACHRONIC – **synchronically** *adv*

**synchronism** /'singkrə,niz(ə)m/ *n* **1** the quality or state of being synchronous; simultaneousness **2** chronological arrangement of historical events and personages so as to indicate coincidence or coexistence; *also* a table showing such concurrences – **synchronistic** *adj*

**synchron-ize, -ise** /'singkrə,niez/ *vi* to happen at the same time ~ *vt* **1** to represent or arrange (events) to indicate coincidence or coexistence **2** to make synchronous in operation ⟨~ *watches*⟩ **3** to make (sound) exactly simultaneous with the action in a film or a television programme – **synchronization** *n*, **synchronizer** *n*

**synchronized swimming** /'singkrə,niezd/ *n* exhibition or competitive swimming in which the movements of one or more swimmers are synchronized with a musical accompaniment so as to form changing patterns

**synchronous** /'singkrənəs/ *adj* **1** happening, existing, or arising at precisely the same time **2a** going on or operating together at exactly the same rate **b** recurring together **3** involving or indicating synchronism **4a** having the same PERIOD (time taken to complete one cycle or one repeating event); *also* having the same period and PHASE **b** *of an orbit* GEOSTATIONARY (at a distance from the earth such that a satellite appears fixed) [LL *synchronos*, fr Gk, fr *syn-* + *chronos* time] – **synchronously** *adv*, **synchronousness** *n*

**synchronous motor** *n* an electric motor having a speed strictly proportional to the frequency of the operating current

**synchrony** /'singkrəni/ *n* synchronistic occurrence, arrangement, or treatment

**synchrotron** /'singkrətron/ *n* **1** an apparatus for imparting very high speeds to electrically charged particles by means of a combination of a high-frequency ELECTRIC FIELD and a low-frequency MAGNETIC FIELD **2** SYNCHROTRON RADIATION

**synchrotron radiation** *n* electromagnetic radiation emitted by high-energy charged particles (eg electrons) when they are accelerated by a MAGNETIC FIELD in a region of the universe (eg in a nebula) [fr its having been first observed in a synchrotron]

**synclinal** /,sing'klienl/ *adj* **1** inclined down from opposite directions so as to meet **2** having or relating to a folded rock structure in which the sides dip toward a common line or plane [Gk *syn-* + *klinein* to lean – more at LEAN]

**syncline** /'singklien/ *n* a trough or inverted arch of STRATIFIED (layered) rock in which the beds dip towards each other from either side – compare ANTICLINE [back-formation fr *synclinal*]

**syncopate** /'singkə,payt/ *vt* **1** to shorten or produce by syncope ⟨~ *suppose to* s'pose⟩ **2** to modify or affect (musical rhythm) by syncopation – **syncopator** *n*

**syncopation** /,singkə'paysh(ə)n/ *n* **1** a temporary displacement of the regular rhythmic accent in music, caused typically by stressing the weak beat **2** a syncopated rhythm, passage, or dance step – **syncopative** *adj*

**syncope** /'singkəpi/ *n* **1** temporary loss of consciousness; fainting **2** the dropping of one or more sounds or letters in the body of a word (eg in *fo'c'sle* for *forecastle*) [LL, fr Gk *synkopē*, lit., cutting short, fr *synkoptein* to cut short, fr *syn-* + *koptein* to cut – more at CAPON] – **syncopal** *adj*

**syncretic** /sing'kretik/ *adj* characterized or brought about by syncretism; syncretistic

**syncretism** /'singkri,tiz(ə)m/ *n* **1** the combination of different forms of (religious) belief or practice **2** illogical or inconsistent compromise in religion or philosophy **3** the fusion of two or more originally different inflectional forms of words (eg the use of *was* for 2 sing. and pl subjects as well as for 1 and 3 sing. in nonstandard English) [NL *syncretismus*, fr Gk *synkrētismos* federation of Cretan cities, fr *syn-* + *Krēt-, Krēs* Cretan] – **syncretist** *n or adj*, **syncretistic** *adj*

**syncret·ize, -ise** /'singkri,tiez/ *vt* to attempt to unify or reconcile (eg principles or sects) ~ *vi* to become unified or reconciled

**syncytium** /sin'siti·əm/ *n*, *pl* **syncytia** /-tiə/ a mass of living material containing many nuclei resulting from fusion of several cells (eg in the body of a SLIME MOULD) or repeated division of nuclei without accompanying CELL DIVISION and formation of cell walls; *also* an organism consisting of such a structure [NL, fr *syn-* + *cyt-*] – **syncytial** *adj*

**syndactyly** /sin'daktili/, **syndactylism** /-,liz(ə)m/ *n* a union of two or more digits that is normal in many birds (eg kingfishers) and in some lower mammals (eg the kangaroos) and occurs in human beings as an inherited abnormality marked by webbing of two or more fingers or toes [NL *syndactylia*, fr *syn-* + Gk *daktylos* finger]

**syndesmosis** /,sindes'mohsis/ *n*, *pl* **syndesmoses** /-seez/ a joint in which the touching surfaces of the bones are rough and are bound together by a ligament [NL, fr Gk *syndesmos* fastening, ligament, fr *syndein* to bind together, fr *syn-* + *dein* to bind] – **syndesmotic** *adj*

**syndetic** /sin'detik/, **syndetical** /-kl/ *adj* using conjunctions to join clauses; *also* connected by means of a conjunction ⟨~ *clauses*⟩ [Gk *syndetikos*, fr *syndein* to bind together] – **syndetically** *adv*

**syndic** /'sindik/ *n* an agent chosen or accredited to represent and transact business for a university or corporation [Fr, fr LL *syndicus* representative of a corporation, fr Gk *syndikos* assistant at law, advocate, representative of a state, fr *syn-* + *dikē* judgment, case at law – more at DICTION]

**syndical** /'sindikl/ *adj* **1** of a syndic or a committee that assumes the powers of a syndic **2** of syndicalism

**syndicalism** /'sindikl,iz(ə)m/ *n* **1** a revolutionary doctrine according to which workers should seize control of the economy and the government by direct means (eg a general strike) **2** a system of economic organization in which industries are owned and managed by the workers **3** a theory of government based on functional rather than territorial representation [Fr *syndicalisme*, fr *chambre syndicale* trade union] – **syndicalist** *adj or n*

¹**syndicate** /'sindikət/ *n* **1a** the office or jurisdiction of a syndic **b** *taking sing or pl vb* a council or body of syndics **2** *taking sing or pl vb* a group of people or concerns who combine to carry out a particular transaction (eg buying or renting property) or to promote some common interest **3** a business concern that acquires and sells materials for publication in a number of newspapers or periodicals simultaneously **4** *taking sing or pl vb*, *chiefly NAm* a loose association of racketeers in control of organized crime [Fr *syndicat*, fr *syndic*]

²**syndicate** /'sindi,kayt/ *vt* **1** to form into to or manage as a syndicate **2** to sell (eg a cartoon) to a syndicate or for publication in many newspapers or periodicals at once ~ *vi* to unite to form a syndicate – **syndicator** *n*, **syndication** *n*

**syndrome** /'sindrohm/ *n* **1** a group of signs and symptoms that occur together and characterize a particular (medical) abnormality **2** a set of concurrent emotions, actions, etc that usu form an identifiable pattern [NL, fr Gk *syndromē* combination, syndrome, fr *syn-* + *dramein* to run – more at DROMEDARY]

¹**syne** /sien; *often* zien/ *adv*, *chiefly Scot* since then; ago [ME (northern), prob fr ON *sīthan*; akin to OE *siththan* since – more at SINCE]

²**syne** *conj or prep*, *Scot* since

**synecdoche** /si'nekdəki/ *n* a FIGURE OF SPEECH by which a part is used to mean the whole (eg *fifty sail* for *fifty ships*), the whole to mean a part (eg in "Leeds defeated Stoke"), the species to mean the genus, the genus to mean the species, or the name of the material to mean the thing made (eg *boards* for *stage*) [L, fr Gk *synekdochē*, fr *syn-* + *ekdochē* sense, interpretation, fr *ekdechesthai* to receive, understand, fr *ex* from + *dechesthai* to receive; akin to Gk *dokein* to seem good – more at EX-, DECENT] – **synecdochic**, **synecdochical** *adj*, **synecdochically** *adv*

**synecology** /,sini'koləji/ *n* a branch of ecology that deals with the structure, development, and distribution of ecological communities [Ger *synökologie*, fr *syn* + *ökologie* ecology] – **synecologic**, **synecological** *adj*, **synecologically** *adv*

**syneresis**, **synaeresis** /si'niərisis/ *n* **1** SYNIZESIS (contraction of two syllables into one) **2** the separation of liquid from a gel caused by contraction [LL *synaeresis*, fr Gk *synairesis*, fr *synairein* to contract, fr *syn-* + *hairein* to take]

**synergic** /si'nuhjik/ *adj* working together; cooperating ⟨~ *muscles*⟩ – **synergically** *adv*

**synergism** /'sinə,jiz(ə)m, si'nuh-/ *n* a cooperative action between two or more agencies (eg drugs or muscles) whose combined effect is greater than the sum of their separate effects [NL *synergismus*, fr Gk *synergos* working together, fr *syn-* + *ergon* work – more at WORK]

**synergist** /'sinəjist, 'sinuh-/ *n* something (eg a chemical or muscle) that enhances the effectiveness of an active agent; *broadly* either member of a synergistic pair

**synergistic** /,sinə'jistik, si,nuh-/ *adj* **1** having the capacity to act in synergism ⟨~ *drugs*⟩ **2** of or resembling synergism ⟨*a* ~ *reaction*⟩ ⟨*a* ~ *effect*⟩ – **synergistically** *adv*

**synergy** /'sinəji, si'nuhji/ *n* combined action or operation (eg of muscles); *specif* synergism [NL *synergia*, fr Gk *synergos* working together]

**synesis** /'sinisis/ *n, pl* **syneses** a grammatical construction in which agreement or reference is according to sense rather than strict syntax (eg *anyone* in the singular and *them* in the plural in "if anyone calls, tell them I am out") [NL, fr Gk, understanding, sense, fr *synienai* to bring together, understand, fr *syn-* + *hienai* to send – more at JET]

**syngamy** /'sing·gəmi/ *n* sexual reproduction by union of GAMETES (reproductive cells) [ISV *syn-* + *-gamy*]

**syngeneic** /,sinjə'nayik, -'nee·ik/ *adj* genetically too similar to provoke a reaction by ANTIGENS (substances that stimulate the production of antibodies) ⟨~ *grafts within an inbred strain*⟩ [Gk *syngeneia* kinship (fr *syn-* + *genos* kind, kin) + E *-ic* – more at KIN]

**syngenesis** /sin'jenəsis/ *n* sexual reproduction; *specif* derivation of the ZYGOTE (cell formed after fertilization) from both paternal and maternal substances [NL, fr *syn* + *genesis*]

**syngenetic** /sinjə'netik/ *adj* of or formed by syngenesis – compare EPIGENETIC

**synizesis** /,sin'zeesis/ *n* contraction of two syllables into one by uniting two adjacent vowels that do not form a DIPHTHONG (eg in pronouncing the *-ee-* of *eleemosynary* as /i/ rather than /i·i/) [LL, fr Gk *synizēsis*, fr *synizein* to sit down together, collapse, blend, fr *syn-* + *hizein* to sit down; akin to L *sidere* to sit down – more at SUBSIDE]

**synkaryon** /sin'kari,on/ *n* a cell nucleus formed by the fusion of two previously existing nuclei [NL, fr Gk *syn-* + *karyon* nut – more at CAREEN]

**synod** /'sinəd, 'sinod/ *n* **1** a formal meeting to decide ecclesiastical matters **2** a church governing or advisory council: eg **2a** the governing assembly of an Anglican PROVINCE (division under an archbishop), diocese, or deanery **b** a Presbyterian governing body ranking between the PRESBYTERY (ruling body) and the general assembly **c** a regional or national organization of Lutheran congregations **3** the ecclesiastical district governed by a synod [LL *synodus*, fr LGk *synodos*, fr Gk, meeting, assembly, fr *syn-* + *hodos* way, journey – more at CEDE] – **synodal** *adj*

**synodical** /si'nodikl/ *adj* **1** synodical, synodic of a synod **2** synodic, synodical of CONJUNCTION (apparent meeting or passing of two stars, planets, or satellites); *esp* relating to the period between two successive CONJUNCTIONS of the same celestial bodies

**synodic month** *n* LUNAR MONTH (period between new moons)

**synoecete** /si'neeseet/ *n* an insect that lives in the nest of a colony of ants or termites and is tolerated with indifference by its hosts [Gk *synoiketes* fellow lodger, fr *synoikein* to live together, fr syn- + *oikos* house]

**synoecious** /si'neeshəs/ *adj* having male or female parts on the same flower [*syn-* + *-oecious* (as in *dioecious*)]

**synoekete** /si'neekeet/ *n* a synoecete

**synonym** /'sinənim/ *n* **1** any of two or more words or expressions of the same language that have the same or nearly the same meaning in some or all senses ⟨*the* ~s *tight and* drunk *or* full stop *and* period⟩ – compare HOMONYM **2** a symbolic or figurative name (eg *Elysium* for "a happy place") [ME *sinonyme*, fr L *synonymum*, fr Gk *synōnymon*, fr neut of *synōnymos* synonymous, fr *syn-* + *onyma* name – more at NAME] – **synonymic, synonymical** *adj*, **synonymity** *n*

**synonymist** /'sinənimist/ *n* someone who lists, studies, or distinguishes synonyms

**synonym·ize, -ise** /si'noni,miez/ *vt* **1a** to give or analyse the synonyms of (a word) **b** to provide (eg a dictionary) with synonymies **2** to demonstrate (a scientific name) to be a synonym

**synonymous** /si'nonimas/ *adj* having the character of a synonym; *also* alike in meaning or significance – **synonymously** *adv*

**synonymy** /si'nonimi/ *n* **1a** the study or distinguishing of synonyms **b** a list or collection of synonyms **2** being synonymous

**synopsis** /si'nopsis/ *n, pl* **synopses** /-seez/ **1** a condensed statement or outline (eg of a narrative or treatise); an abstract **2** the abbreviated CONJUGATION of a verb in one person (eg the first person singular of all tenses) only **3** a book containing the first three Gospels of the New Testament printed in parallel columns [LL, fr Gk, lit., comprehensive view, fr *synopsesthai* to be going to see together, fr *syn-* + *opsesthai* to be going to see – more at OPTIC]

**synops·ize, -ise** /si'nopsiez/ *vt* to make a synopsis of (eg a novel)

**synoptic** /si'noptik/ *also* **synoptical** /-kl/ *adj* **1** giving a general view of a whole **2** characterized by comprehensiveness or breadth of view **3a** presenting texts or data in parallel columns for comparison **b** *often cap* of or being the first three Gospels of the New Testament **4** relating to or displaying conditions (eg atmospheric or weather conditions) as they exist simultaneously over a broad area [Gk *synoptikos*, fr *synopsesthai*] – **synoptically** *adv*

**synovia** /si'nohvi·ə, sie-/ *n* a transparent sticky thick lubricating liquid secreted by a membrane of a joint, tendon sheath, etc [NL, prob coined by Paracelsus (cf GNOME)]

**synovial** /si'nohviəl, sie-/ *adj* of, being, or secreting synovia

**synovitis** /,sienə'vietəs/ *n* inflammation of a synovial membrane [NL]

**synsepalous** /sin'sepələs/ *adj, of a flower* GAMOSEPALOUS (having united sepals)

**syntactic** /sin'taktik/, **syntactical** /-kl/ *adj* of or conforming to the rules of syntax or syntactics [NL *syntacticus*, fr Gk *syntaktikos* arranging together, fr *syntassein* to arrange] – **syntactically** *adv*

**syntactics** /sin'taktiks/ *n taking sing or pl vb* a branch of SEMIOTICS (theory of signs and symbols) dealing with the formal relations between signs or expressions in abstraction from what they signify

**syntagm** /'sin,tag(ə)m/ *n* a syntactic sequence of linguistic forms; a linguistic construction [NL *syntagma* collection of statements, fr Gk, fr *syntassein*] – **syntagmatic** *adj*

**syntax** /'sintaks/ *n* **1a** the way in which words are put together to form phrases, clauses, or sentences **b** the part of grammar dealing with this **2** syntactics, esp as dealing with the formal properties of language *synonyms* see GRAMMAR [Fr or LL; Fr *syntaxe*, fr LL *syntaxis*, fr Gk, fr *syntassein* to arrange together, fr *syn-* + *tassein* to arrange – more at TACTICS]

**synthesis** /'sinthəsis/ *n, pl* **syntheses** /-seez/ **1a** the composition or combination of parts or elements so as to form a whole – compare ANALYSIS **b** the production of a substance by the union of chemical elements, groups, or simpler compounds or by the breaking down of a complex compound into simpler forms **c** the act or process of combining often diverse conceptions into a coherent whole; *also* the complex so formed **2** *philosophy* **2a** deductive reasoning **b** the combination of THESIS (proposition to be proved) and ANTITHESIS (contrast of ideas) in the third stage of a DIALECTICAL process (process of intellectual investigation by discussion and reasoning) [Gk, fr *syntithenai* to put together, fr *syn-* + *tithenai* to put, place – more at DO] – **synthesist** *n*

**synthes·ize, -ise** /'sinthi,siez/ *vt* **1** to combine or produce by synthesis **2** to make a synthesis of ~ *vi* to make a synthesis

**synthes·izer, -iser** /'sinthə,siezə/ *n* **1** one who or that which synthesizes ⟨*he is an expert* ~ *of diverse views*⟩ **2** an electronic apparatus that produces a wide variety of sounds, can be altered in many ways (eg to mimic musical instruments), and is usu played by means of a keyboard

**synthetase** /'sinthi,tayz/ *n* LIGASE (enzyme that speeds up the linking together of two molecules) [*synthetic* + *-ase*]

¹**synthetic** /sin'thetik/ *also* **synthetical** /-kl/ *adj* **1** *philosophy* relating to or involving synthesis; not analytic ⟨*the* ~ *aspects of philosophy*⟩ **2** *philosophy* **2a** asserting of a subject a PREDICATE (proposition that is affirmed or denied in logic) that is not part of the meaning of that subject **b** EMPIRICAL (originating from experience or observation) **3** *linguistics* characterized by the addition of inflections (eg the English possessive *-'s*) rather than by the use of separate words (eg the preposition *of*) to show a word's function in a sentence ⟨~ *languages such*

*as Latin*⟩ **4a** produced artificially; man-made ⟨~ *dyes*⟩ ⟨~ *drugs*⟩ ⟨~ *silk*⟩ **b** sham, bogus; *also* insincere *synonyms* see ARTIFICIAL [Gk *synthetikos* of composition, component, fr *syntithenai* to put together] – **synthetically** *adv*

²**synthetic** *n* something resulting from synthesis rather than occurring naturally; *esp* a product (eg a drug or plastic) of chemical synthesis

**synthetic resin** *n* RESIN 2a (man-made resin chiefly used in plastics)

**synthetic rubber** *n* RUBBER 2b (man-made rubberlike substance)

**syphil-, syphilo-** *comb form* syphilis ⟨syphilo*logy*⟩ ⟨syphiloma⟩ [NL, fr *syphilis*]

**syphilis** /'sifəlis/ *n* a long-lasting contagious disease that is usu VENEREAL (sexually transmitted) and often CONGENITAL (acquired before birth), is caused by a SPIROCHAETE (spiral bacterium) (*Treponema pallidum*), and is characterized by a clinical course in three stages continued over many years – compare PRIMARY SYPHILIS, SECONDARY SYPHILIS, TERTIARY, SYPHILIS [NL, fr *Syphilus*, hero of the poem *Syphilis sive Morbus Gallicus·*(*Syphilis or the French disease*) by Girolamo Fracastoro †1553 It physician & poet] – **syphilitic** *adj or n*

**syphilology** /ˌsifi'loləji/ *n* a branch of medicine that deals with syphilis – **syphilologist** *n*

**syphon** /'siefən/ *vb or n* (to) siphon

**Syriac** /'siriak/ *n* **1** an eastern dialect of ARAMAIC (language of SW Asia widely spoken in former times) used as a literary and liturgical language by several eastern Christian churches **2** ARAMAIC spoken by Christian communities [L *syriacus* of Syria, fr Gk *syriakos*, fr *Syria*, ancient country in Asia] – **Syriac** *adj*

**syringa** /sə'ring·gə/ *n* **1** MOCK ORANGE (shrub with fragrant white flowers) **2** lilac [(1) NL, fr Gk *syring-, syrinx* pipe, tube; fr its stems being used to make pipe-stems; (2) NL, genus name, fr Gk *syring-, syrinx*]

¹**syringe** /sə'rinj/ *n* a device used to inject gases or liquids into or withdraw them from something (eg the body or its cavities): eg **a** a device that consists of a nozzle of varying length and a compressible rubber bulb and is used for injection or flushing out **b** an instrument (eg for the injection of medicine or the withdrawal of body liquids) that consists of a hollow barrel fitted with a plunger and a hollow needle **c** a gravity device consisting of a reservoir fitted with a long rubber tube ending with a changeable nozzle that is used for flushing out the vagina or bowels [ME *syring*, fr ML *syringa*, fr LL, injection, fr Gk *syring-, syrinx* panpipe, tube; akin to Gk *sōlēn* pipe, Skt *tūṇava* flute]

²**syringe** *vt* to flush out or spray (as if) with a syringe

**syringomyelia** /sə,ring·gohmie'eeliə/ *n* a long-lasting progressive disease of the SPINAL CORD associated with muscle wasting, spasticity, and reduction in sensitivity to pain and heat [NL, fr Gk *syring-, syrinx* tube, channel + *myelos* marrow, spinal cord] – **syringomyelic** *adj*

**syrinx** /'siringks/ *n, pl* **syringes** /si'rinjeez/, **syrinxes** **1** a panpipe **2** the vocal organ of birds that is a special modification of the lower part of the windpipe [(1) Gk; (2) NL, fr Gk]

**syrphid** /'suhfid/ *n* a hoverfly [NL *Syrphidae*, group name, fr *Syrphus*, type genus]

**syrphus fly** /'suhfəs/ *n* a hoverfly [NL *Syrphus*, genus of flies, fr Gk *syrphos* gnat]

**syrup** /'sirəp/ *n* **1a** a thick sticky solution of sugar and water, often flavoured, or mixed with medicinal substances **b** the concentrated juice of a fruit or plant (eg the SUGAR MAPLE); *esp* the concentrated raw sugar juice obtained from crushed sugarcane after evaporation and before crystallization in sugar manufacture **2** cloying sweetness or sentimentality [ME *sirup*, fr MF *sirop*, fr ML *syrupus*, fr Ar *sharāb* drink, wine, syrup, fr *shariba* to drink (cf SHERBET)] – **syrupy** *adj*

**systaltic** /si'staltik, si'stawltik/ *adj* marked by regular contraction and dilation; pulsating [Gk *systaltos*, (assumed) verbal of *systellein* to contract – more at SYSTOLE]

**system** /'sistəm/ *n* **1** a regularly interacting or interdependent group of items forming a unified whole ⟨*a number* ~⟩: eg **1a(1)** a group of interacting bodies under the influence of

related forces ⟨*a gravitational* ~⟩ **a(2)** an assemblage of substances that is in or tends to equilibrium ⟨*a thermodynamic* ~⟩ **b(1)** a group of body organs that together perform one or more usu specified functions ⟨*the digestive* ~⟩ **b(2)** the body considered as a functional unit ⟨*overeating is bad for the* ~⟩ **c** a group of related natural objects or forces ⟨*a river* ~⟩ **d** a group of devices or an organization forming a network, esp for distributing something or serving a common purpose ⟨*a telephone* ~⟩ ⟨*a heating* ~⟩ ⟨*a road* ~⟩ ⟨*a data processing* ~⟩ **e** a major division of rocks usu larger than a SERIES and including all formed during a geological period or era **f** a form of social, economic, or political organization ⟨*the capitalist* ~⟩ **2** an organized set of doctrines, ideas, or principles, usu intended to explain the arrangement or working of a systematic whole ⟨*the Newtonian* ~ *of mechanics*⟩ **3a** an arrangement or established procedure ⟨*the touch* ~ *of typing*⟩ **b** a manner of classifying, symbolizing, or formalizing ⟨*a taxonomic* ~⟩ ⟨*the decimal* ~⟩ **4** harmonious arrangement or pattern; order ⟨*bring* ~ *out of confusion* – Ellen Glasgow⟩ **5** an organized society or social situation regarded as stultifying; ESTABLISHMENT 2 – + *the* ⟨*can't beat the* ~⟩ [LL *systemat-, systema*, fr Gk *systēmat-, systēma*, fr *synistanai* to combine, fr *syn-* + *histanai* to cause to stand – more at STAND] – **systemless** *adj*

**systematic** /ˌsistə'matik/ *also* **systematical** /-kl/ *adj* **1** relating to or consisting of a system ⟨~ *thought*⟩ **2** presented or formulated as a system; systematized **3a** methodical in procedure or plan ⟨~ *investigation*⟩ ⟨*a* ~ *scholar*⟩ **b** marked by thoroughness and regularity ⟨~ *efforts*⟩ **4** of or concerned with classification; *specif* TAXONOMIC (concerning classification of plants and animals) [LL *systematicus*, fr Gk *systēmatikos*, fr *systēmat-, systēma* system] – **systematically** *adv*, **systematicness** *n*

**systematic error** *n, maths* a statistical error that is not determined by chance but by an effect (BIAS) that distorts the information in a definite direction

**systematics** /ˌsistə'matiks/ *n taking sing vb* **1** the science of classification **2a** a system of classification **b** the classification and study of living things with regard to their natural relationships; TAXONOMY

**systematism** /'sistimə,tiz(ə)m/ *n* the practice of forming intellectual systems

**systematist** /'sistəmətist, si'stemətist, si'stee-/ *n* **1** a maker or follower of a system **2** a specialist in TAXONOMY (classification of plants and animals) and evolution; TAXONOMIST

**systemat·ize, -ise** /'sistəmətiez/ *vt* to arrange in accord with a definite plan or scheme; order systematically ⟨*the need to* ~ *his work*⟩ – **systematization** *n*, **systematizer** *n*

¹**systemic** /si'steemic, si'stemik/ *adj* of or common to a system: eg **a** affecting the body generally **b** acting through the body systems after absorption or ingestion by making the organism, esp a plant, toxic to a pest (eg a mite or insect) ⟨~ *insecticides*⟩ – **systemically** *adv*

²**systemic** *n* a systemic pesticide

**systemic circulation** *n* the part of the blood circulation concerned with the distribution of blood to the tissues through the AORTA (main artery) rather than to the lungs through the PULMONARY ARTERY

**system·ize, -ise** /'sistəmiez/ *vt* to systematize – **systemization** *n*

**systems analysis** *n* the analysis of an activity (eg a procedure, a business, or a physiological function) typically by mathematical means in order to define its goals or purposes and to discover ways of accomplishing them most efficiently

**systems analyst** *n* a specialist in SYSTEMS ANALYSIS

**systole** /'sistəli/ *n* a rhythmically recurrent contraction; *esp* the contraction of the heart by which the blood is forced onwards and the circulation kept up – compare DIASTOLE [Gk *systolē*, fr *systellein* to contract, fr *syn-* + *stellein* to send – more at STALL] – **systolic** *adj*

**syzygy** /'siziji/ *n* a configuration in which three celestial bodies (eg the sun, moon, and earth during a solar or lunar eclipse) lie in a (nearly) straight line [LL *syzygia* conjunction, fr Gk, fr *syzygos* yoked together, fr *syn-* + *zygon* yoke – more at YOKE] – **syzgial** *adj*

# T

**t, T** /tee/ *n, pl* **t's, ts, T's, Ts 1a** the 20th letter of the English alphabet **b** a graphic representation of or device for reproducing the letter **t c** a speech counterpart of printed or written *t* **2** one designated *t*, esp as the 20th in order or class **3** something shaped like the letter T – **to a T, to a tee** to perfection; exactly [short for *to a tittle*]

**t'** /t/ *definite article, NEng dial* the

**'t** /t/ *pron, archaic or poetic* it ⟨'*twill suffice*⟩

**ta** /tah/ *n, Br informal* thanks [baby talk]

**Taal** /tahl/ *n* the Afrikaans language [Afrik, fr D, language; akin to OE *talu* talk – more at TALE]

**¹tab** /tab/ *n* **1a** a short projecting device (e g a flap or loop): e g **1a(1)** a small hand grip **a(2)** a usu labelled projection from a card used as an aid in filing **b** an appendage, extension: e g **b(1)** any of a series of small pendants forming a decorative border or edge of a garment **b(2)** a narrow curtain used esp for masking offstage space **c** a small auxiliary AEROFOIL (winglike part) hinged to one of the main movable controlling surfaces of an aircraft (e g a TRAILING EDGE) to help stabilize the aircraft in flight **2** TABULATOR **b** (device on a typewriter for arranging words, numbers, etc in columns) **3** *pl* TABLEAU CURTAIN **4** *Br* ¹TAG 2 (binding on the end of a shoelace) **5** *chiefly NAm* a creditor's statement; a bill, cheque ⟨*the company will pick up the* ∼⟩ [perh akin to *tug;* (2,3) by shortening; (5) partly short for *table*] – **keep tabs/a tab on** to keep under close surveillance; watch ⟨*the police are* keeping tabs on *him*⟩

**²tab** *vt* **-bb-** **1** to provide or ornament with tabs **2** TABULATE (arrange in columns) **3** *NAm* to single out; designate

**tabanid** /'tabənid/ *n* a horsefly [deriv of L *tabanus* horsefly]

**tabard** /'tabəd/ *n* a short loose-fitting sleeveless or short-sleeved coat or cape: e g **a** a tunic with a knight's coat of arms on it, worn over his armour **b** a herald's official cape or coat with his lord's coat of arms on it **c** a straight-hanging sleeveless overgarment; *esp* one having slits at the sides for part or all of its length and worn by women and girls [ME, fr OF *tabart*]

**tabaret** /'tabərit/ *n* a hard-wearing upholstery fabric with alternate satin and PLAIN-WEAVE stripes [prob alter. of *tabby*]

**Tabasco** /tə'baskoh/ *trademark* – used for a hot spicy sauce made from peppers

**¹tabby** /'tabi/ *n* **1** a PLAIN-WEAVE fabric **2a** a domestic cat with a usu brownish, grey, or yellow coat striped and mottled with darker shades **b** a female domestic cat **3** *archaic* a plain silk TAFFETA fabric, esp with an irregular wavy (MOIRÉ) finish [Fr *tabis*, fr ML *attabi*, fr Ar '*attābī*, fr Al-'*Attābiya*, quarter in Baghdad where the silk fabric was manufactured]

**²tabby** *adj* striped and mottled with darker colour; brindled ⟨*a* ∼ *cat*⟩

**tabernacle** /'tabə,nakl/ *n* **1** *often cap* a tent sanctuary used by the Israelites during the Exodus **2** a receptacle for the consecrated bread and wine used at Communion; *esp* an ornamental locked box fixed to the middle of the altar and used for storing unused consecrated bread **3** a house of worship; *specif* a large building or tent used for evangelistic services **4** a support in which a mast is set and pivoted so that it can be lowered (e g to negotiate a bridge) [ME, fr OF, fr LL *tabernaculum*, fr L, tent, dim. of *taberna* hut – more at TAVERN] – **tabernacular** *adj*

**tabes** /'taybeez/ *n, pl* **tabes** wasting accompanying a long-lasting disease [L – more at THAW] – **tabetic** *adj or n*

**tabes dorsalis** /daw'sahlis/ *n* LOCOMOTOR ATAXIA (disease of the nervous system) [NL, dorsal tabes]

**tabinet** /'tabinet/ *n* a fabric of silk and wool that resembles POPLIN and is usu given an irregular wavy finish (MOIRÉ) [prob alter. of *tabby*]

**tabla** /'tahblə/ *n* a pair of small different-sized hand drums used esp in Indian classical music [Hindi *ṭabla*, fr Ar *ṭabla*]

**tablature** /'tabləchə/ *n* a notation for a musical instrument indicating the string, FRET (ridge on the fingerboard of a stringed

instrument), keys, or fingering to be used instead of the note to be sounded [MF, fr ML *tabulatus* tablet, fr L *tabula*]

**¹table** /'taybl/ *n* **1** TABLET **1a** (slab for inscribing) **2a** *pl* backgammon **b** either of the two leaves of a backgammon board or either half of a leaf **3a** a piece of furniture consisting of a smooth flat slab (e g of wood) fixed on legs **b(1)** the food served at a meal; fare ⟨*keeps a good* ∼⟩ **b(2)** an act or instance of assembling to eat; a meal ⟨*sit down to* ∼⟩ ⟨*father mentioned the matter at* ∼⟩ **c(1)** a group of people assembled (as if) at a table ⟨*a famous poker* ∼, *which challenged all comers* – Harvey Fergusson⟩ **c(2)** a legislative or negotiating session ⟨*bring the warring nations to the peace* ∼⟩ **4a** a systematic arrangement of data, usu in rows and columns, for ready reference **b** a systematically arranged list of figures, information, etc ⟨*a* ∼ *of contents*⟩ **5a** the upper flat surface of a precious stone **b(1)** **table, tableland** a broad area elevated on all sides; a plateau **b(2)** a horizontal STRATUM (layer of rock) **6** something that resembles a table, esp in having a flat level surface [ME, fr OE *tabule* & OF *table;* both fr L *tabula* board, tablet, list] – **on the table** *chiefly Br* under or put forward for discussion ⟨*so far the management have put nothing on the* table⟩ – **turn the tables** to cause a complete reversal of circumstances [fr players of chess, draughts, etc reversing the board (table) so that their positions are reversed] – see also **lay/put one's CARDS on the table**

**²table** *adj* suitable for a table or for use at table ⟨∼ *manners*⟩

**³table** *vt* **1** to enter in a table **2a** *Br* to place on the agenda for discussion **b** *NAm* to remove (a parliamentary motion) from consideration indefinitely

**tableau** /'tabloh/ *n, pl* **tableaux** *also* **tableaus** /'tabloh, 'tablohz/ **1** a graphic description or representation; a picture ⟨*winsome* ∼x *of old-fashioned literary days* – J D Hart⟩ **2** a striking or artistic grouping **3** a depiction of a scene, usu presented on a stage by silent and motionless costumed participants [Fr, fr MF *tablel* dim. of *table;* (3) short for *tableau vivant*, fr Fr, lit., living picture]

**tableau curtain** *n* a stage curtain that opens in the centre and has its sections drawn upwards and outwards to produce a draped effect

**tablecloth** /-,kloth/ *n* an often decorative cloth spread over a dining table before the places are set, often to protect the surface of the table

**table d'hôte** /,tahblə 'doht/ *n* a meal, often of several prearranged courses, served to all guests at a stated hour and fixed price – compare À LA CARTE [Fr, lit., host's table]

**tableful** /'tayblful/ *n* as much or as many as a table can hold or accommodate

**table linen** *n* linen (e g tablecloths and napkins) for the table

**tablemat** /-,mat/ *n* a small often decorative mat placed under a hot dish to protect the surface of a table from heat

**table salt** *n* fine grained free-flowing salt suitable for use at the table and in cooking; refined SODIUM CHLORIDE treated with small quantities of chemical compounds (e g magnesium silicate or calcium phosphate) to prevent caking

**tablespoon** /-,spoohn/ *n* **1** a large spoon used for serving **2** a tablespoonful

**tablespoonful** /-,spoohnf(ə)l/ *n, pl* **tablespoonfuls** *also* **tablespoonsful** **1** as much as a tablespoon will hold **2** a unit of measure used esp in cookery and equal to about 14.2 cubic centimetres (4 fluid drachms)

**tablet** /'tablit/ *n* **1a** a flat slab or plaque suitable for, or bearing an inscription **b** a thin slab or any of a set of portable inflexible sheets used for writing on **c** a pad of writing paper **2a** a compressed or moulded block of a solid material ⟨*a* ∼ *of soap*⟩ **b** a small mass of medicinal material (e g in the shape of a disc); *also* a capsule of medicinal material [ME *tablett*, fr MF *tablete*, dim. of *table*]

**table talk** *n* informal conversation (as if) at a dining table; *esp*

**tab** 1526

the social talk of a celebrity recorded for publication

**table tennis** *n* a game resembling lawn tennis that is played on a tabletop with bats and a small hollow plastic ball

**tableware** /-ˌweə/ *n* utensils (e g glasses, dishes, plates, and cutlery) for table use

**table wine** *n* an unfortified wine usu served with food

¹**tabloid** /'tabloyd/ *adj* **1** compressed or condensed into small scope ⟨~ *criticism*⟩ **2** (characteristic) of tabloids ⟨~ *journalism*⟩ [fr *Tabloid*, a trademark for a concentrated form of drugs and chemicals]

²**tabloid** *n* a newspaper of which two pages make up one printing plate and which contains news in condensed form and much photographic matter – compare BROADSHEET

¹**taboo** *also* **tabu** /təˈbooh/ *adj* **1a** too sacred or evil to be touched, named, or used ⟨*the person of the tribal chief is* ~⟩ **b** set apart as unclean or accursed **2** placed under a general prohibition; *esp* forbidden on grounds of morality, tradition, or social usage ⟨~ *words*⟩ [Tongan *tabu*]

²**taboo** *also* **tabu** *n, pl* **taboos** *also* **tabus** **1** a prohibition against touching, saying, or doing something for fear of immediate harm from a supernatural force **2** a prohibition imposed by social custom or as a protective measure **3** belief in or observance of taboos

³**taboo** *also* **tabu** *vt* **taboos** *also* **tabus**; **tabooing** *also* **tabuing**; **tabooed** *also* **tabued 1** to set apart as taboo, esp by marking with a ritualistic symbol **2** to avoid or ban as taboo

**tabor** *also* **tabour** /'taybə/ *n* a small drum with one head of soft calfskin used to accompany a pipe or FIFE (small flute) played by the same person [ME, fr OF, perh modif of Per *tabīr* drum (cf TAMBOUR)]

**tabouret,** *NAm chiefly* **taboret** /'tabərit/ *n* a cylindrical seat or stool without arms or back [Fr *tabouret*, lit., small drum, fr MF, dim. of *tabor, tabour*]

**tabular** /'tabyoolə/ *adj* **1a** having a broad flat surface **b** having two parallel flat surfaces; laminar ⟨~ *crystals*⟩ **2a** of or arranged in a table; *specif* set up in rows and columns **b** computed by means of a table [L *tabularis* of boards, fr *tabula* board, tablet] – **tabularly** *adv*

**tabula rasa** /ˌtabyoolə 'rahsə/ *n, pl* **tabulae rasae** /ˌtabyooli 'rahsi/ the mind conceived of as blank or empty before receiving outside impressions [L, smoothed or erased tablet]

**tabulate** /'tabyoolayt/ *vt* to arrange in tabular form [L *tabula* tablet] – **tabulation** *n*

**tabulator** /'tabyooˌlaytə/ *n* one who or that which tabulates: e g **a** a business machine that sorts and selects information from marked or perforated cards **b** an attachment to a typewriter that moves the carriage or the printing head along a set distance and is used for arranging data in columns

**tacamahac** /'takəməˌhak/ *n* **1** any of several aromatic GUM RESINS used in ointments and for incense **2** BALSAM POPLAR (N American SHADE TREE) [Sp *tacamahaca*, fr Nahuatl *tecamaca*]

**tace** /tas, tays/ *n* TASSE (plates forming the skirt of a suit of armour)

**tacet** /'tayset/ *interj* – used as a direction in music to indicate that a particular instrument is not to play during a movement or long section [L, (it) is silent, fr *tacēre* to be silent – more at TACIT]

**tacheometer** /ˌtakiˈomitə/ *n* TACHYMETER [Fr *tachéomètre*, irreg fr Gk *tachys* swift + Fr *-mètre* -meter]

**tachinid** /'takinid/ *n* any of a family (Tachinidae) of bristly usu greyish or black flies whose parasitic larvae are often important in the biological control of insect pests [NL *Tachinidae*, group name, fr *Tachina*, type genus, fr Gk *tachinos* swift, fr *tachos* speed] – **tachinid** *adj*

**tachism** /'tashiz(ə)m/ *n, often cap* ACTION PAINTING (painting using techniques of throwing, smearing, etc) [Fr *tachisme*, fr *tache* stain, spot, blob, fr MF *teche, tache*, of Gmc origin; akin to OS *tēkan* sign – more at TOKEN ] – **tachist** *also* **tachiste** *adj or n*

**tachistoscope** /təˈkistəˌskohp/ *n* an apparatus for briefly exposing visual images that is used in the study of usu human learning, attention, and perception [Gk *tachistos* (superl of *tachys* swift) + ISV *-scope*] – **tachistoscopic** *adj*, **tachistoscopically** *adv*

**tacho** /'takoh/ *n, pl* **tachos** *informal* a tachometer

**tachograph** /'takəˌgrahf, -ˌgraf/ *n* a device for automatically recording the speed and time of travel of a vehicle, esp a lorry [Gk *tachos* speed + E *-graph*]

**tachometer** /taˈkomitə/ *n* a device for indicating speed of rotation (e g of a vehicle engine) [Gk *tachos* speed + E *-meter*]

**tachy-** /taki-/ *comb form* rapid; accelerated ⟨*tachy*cardia⟩

⟨*tachy*graphy⟩ [Gk, fr *tachys* swift]

**tachycardia** /ˌtakiˈkahdi-ə/ *n* relatively rapid heart action, whether normal (e g after exercise) or indicative of disease – compare BRADYCARDIA [NL]

**tachygraphy** /taˈkigrəfi/ *n* **1** the art or practice of rapid writing; *esp* the shorthand of the ancient Greeks and Romans **2** the abbreviated form of writing Greek and Latin used in manuscripts of the Middle Ages [Gk *tachygraphos* shorthand writer, fr *tachy-* + *graphein* to write – more at CARVE] – **tachygraphic** *also* **tachygraphical** *adj*

**tachylyte** *also* **tachylite** /'takiˌlayt/ *n* a black glassy IGNEOUS (formed by the slow cooling and solidification of molten rock) rock having the same composition as BASALT [Ger *tachylyt*, fr Gk *tachy-* + *lyein* to dissolve – more at LOSE]

**tachymeter** /taˈkimitə/ *n* **1** a surveying instrument for determining quickly the distances, directions, and height of distant objects **2** a speed indicator □ called also TACHEOMETER [ISV *tachy-* + *-meter*]

**tacit** /'tasit/ *adj* **1** implied, understood, or indicated but not actually expressed ⟨~ *consent*⟩ **2a** arising without explicit contract or agreement **b** arising by operation of law ⟨~ *mortgage*⟩ [Fr or L; Fr *tacite*, fr L *tacitus* silent, fr pp of *tacēre* to be silent; akin to OHG *dagēn* to be silent] – **tacitly** *adv*, **tacitness** *n*

**taciturn** /'tasiˌtuhn/ *adj* not communicative or talkative by nature **synonyms** see SILENT **antonym** garrulous [Fr or L; F *taciturne*, fr L *taciturnus*, fr *tacitus*] – **taciturnity** *n*

¹**tack** /tak/ *n* **1** a small short sharp-pointed nail usu with a broad flat head **2** the lower forward corner of a FORE-AND-AFT sail (sail set lengthways) **3a** the direction of a sailing vessel with respect to the direction of the wind ⟨*starboard* ~, *with the wind to starboard*⟩ **b** the run of a sailing vessel on one tack **c** a change of course from one tack to another when CLOSE-HAULED (having the sails set for sailing as nearly into the wind as possible) **d** a zigzag movement on land **e** a course or method of action; *esp* one sharply divergent from that previously followed **4** a long loose straight stitch usu used to hold two or more layers of fabric together temporarily **5** a sticky or adhesive quality or condition **6** SADDLERY 2 (saddles, stirrups, harnesses, etc) [ME *tak* something that attaches; akin to MD *tac* sharp point]

²**tack** *vt* **1** to fasten or attach (e g a carpet) with tacks **2a** to join in a slight or hasty manner **b** to sew with long loose stitches in order to join or hold in place temporarily prior to fine or machine sewing **3a** to add as a supplement – often + *on* ⟨~ *a postscript on a letter*⟩ **b** to add (a rider) to a parliamentary bill **4** to change the course of (a sailing vessel with sails set to sail as nearly into the wind as possible) from one tack to the other by turning the bow through the wind ~ *vi* **1a** to tack a sailing vessel **b** *of a sailing vessel* to be tacked **2a** to follow a zigzag course **b** to change one's policy or attitude abruptly – **tacker** *n*

  **tack up** *vt* to saddle and bridle (a horse)

³**tack** *n, informal* food, provisions [origin unknown]

¹**tackle** /'takl/ *n* **1** a set of the equipment used in a particular activity; gear ⟨*fishing* ~⟩ **2a** a ship's rigging **b** an assemblage of ropes and pulleys arranged to gain mechanical advantage for hoisting and pulling **3** the act or an instance of tackling [ME *takel*; akin to MD *takel* ship's rigging]

²**tackle** *vt* **1** to attach or secure (as if) with tackle; harness – often + *up* **2a** to take hold of or grapple with; seize; *esp* to attempt to stop or subdue by so doing ⟨*warned the public not to* ~ *the intruders*⟩ **b(1)** to take or attempt to take the ball from (an opposing player) in hockey, soccer, lacrosse, etc **b(2)** to seize and pull down or stop (an opposing player with the ball) in rugby or AMERICAN FOOTBALL **3** to set about dealing with ⟨~ *the problem*⟩ ~ *vi* to tackle an opposing player – **tackler** *n*

**tackling** /'takling/ *n* gear, tackle

**'tack-ˌroom** *n* a room where saddles, harness, etc are kept

¹**tacky** /'taki/ *adj* somewhat sticky to the touch ⟨~ *varnish*⟩ [²*tack*] – **tackiness** *n*

²**tacky** *adj, NAm slang* shabby, seedy [*tacky* (an inferior horse or person), of unknown origin] – **tackily** *adv*, **tackiness** *n*

**tact** /takt/ *n* **1** sensitive mental or aesthetic perception ⟨*converted the novel into a play with remarkable skill and* ~⟩ **2** a keen sense of what to do or say in order to maintain good relations with others or avoid giving offence [Fr, sense of touch, fr L *tactus*, fr *tactus*, pp of *tangere* to touch – more at TANGENT]

**tactful** /'taktf(ə)l/ *adj* having or showing tact – **tactfully** *adv*, **tactfulness** *n*

¹**tactic** /'taktik/ *adj* **1** of or showing biological TAXIS (reflex

movement in response to light, temperature, etc) **2** *formal* of arrangement or order [NL *tacticus*, fr Gk *taktikos* – more at TACTICS]

**²tactic** *n* **1** a method of employing forces in combat **2** a device for accomplishing an end [NL *tactica*, fr Gk *taktikē*, fr fem of *taktikos*]

**tactical** /'taktikl/ *adj* **1** of combat tactics: eg **1a** involving operations of local importance or brief duration **b** of or designed for air attack in close support of friendly ground forces **2a** of tactics: eg **2a(1)** of small-scale actions serving a larger purpose **a(2)** made or carried out with only a limited or immediate end in view **b** characterized by adroit planning or manoeuvring to accomplish a purpose – **tactically** *adv*

**tactician** /tak'tish(ə)n/ *n* a person skilled in tactics

**tactics** /'taktiks/ *n taking sing or pl vb* **1a** the science and art of disposing and manoeuvring forces in combat – compare STRATEGY **b** the art or skill of employing available means to accomplish an end **2** a system or mode of procedure [NL *tactica*, pl, fr Gk *taktika*, fr neut pl of *taktikos* of order, of tactics, fit for arranging, fr *tassein* to arrange, place in battle formation; akin to Lith pa*togus* comfortable]

**tactile** /'taktiel/ *adj* **1** perceptible by touch; tangible **2** of or relating to the sense of touch [Fr or L; Fr, fr L *tactilis*, fr *tactus*, pp of *tangere* to touch – more at TANGENT] – **tactilely** *adv*

**tactile corpuscle** *n* an END ORGAN (sensory structure at the end of a nerve) of touch

**tactility** /tak'tiləti/ *n* **1** the capability of being felt or touched **2** responsiveness to stimulation of the sense of touch

**taction** /'takshən/ *n* touch, contact – used technically [L *taction-, tactio*, fr *tactus*, pp]

**tactless** /'taktlis/ *adj* marked by lack of tact – **tactlessly** *adv*, **tactlessness** *n*

**tactual** /'takchooəl, -chəl/ *adj* TACTILE 2 [L *tactus* sense of touch – more at TACT] – **tactually** *adv*

**tad** *n, chiefly NAm informal* a small boy; a lad [prob fr E dial. *tad* toad, fr ME *tode*]

**tadpole** /'tad,pohl/ *n* a larva of an amphibian; *specif* a frog or toad larva that has a rounded body with a long tail bordered by fins and external gills soon replaced by internal gills and that undergoes a METAMORPHOSIS (change in structure and way of life) to the adult [ME *taddepol*, fr *tode* toad + *polle* head – more at POLL]

**taedium vitae** /'teediəm 'veetay, 'vietee/ *n, formal* weariness or loathing of life [L]

**tael** /tayl/ *n* **1** any of various units of weight of E Asia; *esp* LIANG (old Chinese unit of weight) **2** any of various Chinese units of value based on the value of a tael weight of silver [Pg, fr Malay *tahil*]

**taenia, NAm also tenia** /'teenyə, -ni·ə/ *n, pl* **taeniae, taenias, NAm also teniae, tenias** **1** a band of nerve tissue or muscle **2** any of numerous tapeworms (genus *Taenia*) [L, fr Gk *tainia;* akin to Gk *teinein* to stretch – more at THIN]

**taeniacide** /'teeniə,sied/ *n* a substance that destroys tapeworms

**taeniasis** /tee'nie·əsis/ *n* infestation with or disease caused by tapeworms [NL, fr L *taenia* tapeworm]

**taffeta** /'tafitə/ *n* a crisp PLAIN-WOVEN lustrous fabric of various fibres used esp for women's clothing [ME, fr MF *taffetas*, fr OIt *taffetta*, fr Turk *tafta*, fr Per *tāftah* woven]

**taffrail** /'taf,rayl, 'tafrəl/ *n* a rail round the stern of a ship [alter. (influenced by ¹*rail*) of earlier *tafferel* (carved) panel, upper flat part of a ship's stern (often adorned with carvings), fr D *tafereel*, fr MD, picture, fr OF *tablel* – more at TABLEAU]

**taffy** /'tafi/ *n, NAm* a toffee, usu of molasses or brown sugar, that is pulled until porous and light-coloured [origin unknown]

**Taffy** /'tafi/ *n, Br chiefly derog* a Welshman [modif of W *Dafydd* David, a common Welsh forename]

**tafia** /'tafiə/ *n* a W Indian rum made esp from distilled sugarcane juice [Fr, fr W Indian Creole, alter. of *ratafia*]

**¹tag** /tag/ *n* **1** a loose hanging piece of torn cloth; a tatter **2** a rigid binding on an end of a shoelace **3** a piece of hanging or attached material; *specif* a flap or loop on a garment by which to hang it up, or that carries information (eg washing instructions) **4a** a trite quotation used for superficial effect **b** a recurrent or characteristic verbal expression **c** tag, tag line a final speech or line (eg in a play or joke); *esp* one that serves to clarify a point or create a dramatic effect **5a** a cardboard, plastic, or metal marker used for identification or classification **b** a descriptive or identifying word or phrase accompanying or replacing a name **6** a small piece of bright material (eg tinsel) round the shank of the hook at the end of the body of an

artificial fishing fly [ME *tagge*, prob of Scand origin; akin to Sw *tagg* barb]

**²tag** *vb* **-gg-** *vt* **1** to provide or mark (as if) with a tag: eg **1a** to supply with an identifying marker ⟨~ged *every item in his shop*⟩ **b** to provide with a name or with a word or phrase accompanying or replacing a name; label, brand ⟨had him ~ged *as a chauvinist from the start*⟩ **2** to attach as an addition; append – often + *on* **3** LABEL 2 (distinguish a chemical compound or substance by making it radioactive) **4** *chiefly NAm* to follow closely and persistently ~ *vi* to keep close ⟨~ging *behind*⟩

**³tag** *n* a game in which one player chases others and tries to make one of them "it" by touching him/her [origin unknown]

**⁴tag** *vt* **-gg-** **1** to touch (as if) in a game of tag **2** to touch the hand of (one's partner) in TAG WRESTLING

**Tagalog** /tə'gahlog/ *n, pl* **Tagalogs**, *esp collectively* **Tagalog 1** a member of a people of central Luzon in the Philippines **2** a language of the Tagalog people which belongs to the AUSTRONESIAN family of languages

**tag day** *n, NAm* FLAG DAY

**tag end** *n* the last part ⟨the ~ *of the day*⟩

**tagetes** /'tajitəs/ *n, pl* **tagetes** MARIGOLD 2 [NL, genus name, prob fr *Tages*, ancient Etruscan god]

**tagliatelle** /,talyə'teli/ *n* pasta made with egg and shaped in narrow ribbons [It, pl of *tagliatella*, deriv of *tagliare* to cut, fr LL *taliare* – more at TAILOR]

**tagmeme** /'tagmeem/ *n* a functional linguistic element consisting of a slot or niche in a sentence that can be occupied by any item of the appropriate class – used in the linguistic analysis proposed by the US linguist Kenneth Pike [Gk *tagma* arrangement, order, row + E *-eme*]

**tag wrestling** *n* a form of wrestling involving two teams of two wrestlers, only one of whom is in the ring at one time and may ask his partner to replace him by touching his hand

**tahina** /tah'heenə/ *n* tahini

**tahini** /tah'heeni/ *n* a thick oily paste made from sesame seeds [Ar *ṭaḥīna*]

**Tahitian** /tah'heesh(ə)n/ *n* **1** a native or inhabitant of Tahiti **2** the language of the Tahitians which belongs to the POLYNESIAN group of the AUSTRONESIAN family of languages [*Tahiti*, island in the S Pacific] – **Tahitian** *adj*

**tahr** /tah/ *n* THAR (Himalayan goat)

**tahsil** /tə'seel/ *n* a district administration or tax subdivision in India [Hindi *taḥṣīl*, fr Ar, collection of revenue]

**tahsildar** /tah'seeldah/ *n* a collector of taxes in India [Hindi *taḥṣīldar*]

**Tai** /tie/ *n, pl* **Tai** a member of a widespread group of peoples in SE Asia associated ethnically with valley paddy-rice culture

**taiaha** /'tie·əhah/ *n* a Maori hand weapon made of hardwood that has a long shaft with one bladed and one pointed end, and that is sometimes held as a ceremonial accompaniment to public speaking [Maori]

**taiga** /'tiegə/ *n* moist coniferous forest that borders the arctic, begins where the TUNDRA (region where the subsoil is permanently frozen) ends, and is dominated by spruces and firs [Russ *taïga*]

**¹tail** /tayl/ *n* **1** (an extension or prolongation of) the rear end of the body of an animal **2** something (eg the luminous train of a comet) resembling an animal's tail in shape or position **3** *pl* **3a** COAT TAILS **b** a tailcoat; *broadly* formal evening dress for men including a tailcoat and a white bow tie **4** the back, last, lower, or inferior part of something **5** **tails** *pl, also* **tail** the reverse of a coin ⟨~s, *you lose*⟩ – compare HEAD **6** *taking sing or pl vb* the group of relatively inexpert batsmen who bat towards the end of a side's innings **7** the bottom edge or margin of a printed page **8** the rear part of an aircraft consisting of horizontal and vertical stabilizing surfaces with attached control surfaces **9** *informal* a person (eg a detective) who follows or keeps watch on someone ⟨put a ~ on him this evening⟩ **10** *informal* the trail of a fugitive ⟨had the police on his ~⟩ **11** *chiefly NAm slang* the buttocks **12** *Br vulg* women considered as sexual objects ⟨a nice bit of ~⟩ [ME, fr OE *tægel*; akin to OHG *zagal* tail, OIr *dúal* lock of hair] – **tailed** *adj*, **tailless** *adj*, **tail-like** *adj* – **turn tail** to flee; RUN AWAY – see also **not make** HEAD **or tail of**

**²tail** *vt* **1** to connect at an end, or end to end **2a** to remove the tail of (an animal); dock **b** to remove the stalk of (eg a gooseberry) – compare ²TOP 1b **3a** to make or provide with a tail **b** to follow or be drawn behind like a tail **4** to fasten an end of (a tile, brick, or timber) into a wall or other support **5** *informal* to follow in order to keep a watch on ~ *vi* **1** to form or move in a straggling line **2** to grow progressively smaller, fainter, or more scattered; abate – usu + *off* or *away* ⟨*productivity* ~ed *off*⟩ **3** to be fastened by the end – used of a timber, tile, or brick built into a support **4** to follow closely; tag

³**tail** *adj* limited as to TENURE (right or term of holding something); ENTAILED [ME *taille*, fr AF *taylé*, fr OF *taillié*, pp of *taillier* to cut, limit – more at TAILOR]

⁴**tail** *n* ENTAIL 1a (restriction of inheritance to direct descendants) – often in *in tail*

**tailback** /-,bak/ *n* a long queue of motor vehicles, esp when caused by an obstruction that blocks the road

**tailboard** /-,bawd/ *n* a hinged or removable board or gate at the rear of a vehicle

**tailbone** /'tayl,bohn/ *n* **1** a VERTEBRA (bone of the spine) forming the tail **2** COCCYX (end of the spine in humans and apes)

**tailcoat** /-,koht/ *n* a coat with tails; *esp* a man's formal evening coat with two long tapering skirts at the back – **tailcoated** *adj*

**tail covert** *n* any of the COVERTS (feathers covering the bases of quills) of a bird's tail feathers

**tail end** *n* **1** the back end; the rear ⟨*at the* ~ *of the queue*⟩ **2** the concluding period ⟨*the* ~ *of the session*⟩ **3** *informal* the rump, buttocks

**tailender** /-,endə/ *n* a relatively inexpert batsman who bats towards the end of a side's innings

**tail fin** *n* the hindmost fin of a fish

¹**tailgate** /-,gayt/ *n, chiefly NAm* a tailboard

²**tailgate** *vi, chiefly NAm* to drive dangerously close behind another vehicle – **tailgater** *n*

**tailing** /'tayling/ *n* **1 tailings** *pl*, **tailing** residue separated in the preparation of various products (eg grain or ores) **2** the part of a projecting stone or brick inserted in a wall

**taille** /tie (*Fr* 'ta:j)/ *n* a tax formerly levied by a French king or lord on his subjects or on lands held from him [Fr, fr OF, fr *taillier* to cut, tax]

**taillight** /'tayl,liet/ *n* a usu red warning light mounted at the rear of a vehicle

¹**tailor** /'taylə/ *n* someone whose occupation is making or altering garments, esp men's outer garments; *specif* someone who sews outer garments by hand [ME *taillour*, fr OF *tailleur*, fr *taillier* to cut, fr LL *taliare*, fr L *talea* twig, cutting; akin to Gk *tēlis* fenugreek]

²**tailor** *vi* to do the work of a tailor ~ *vt* **1a** to make or fashion as the work of a tailor; *specif* to cut and stitch (a garment) so as to hang and fit well **b** to make or adapt to suit a special need or purpose ⟨*plays* ~ed *for young audiences*⟩ **2** to provide or fit with clothes **3** to style with trim straight lines and finished handwork

**tailorbird** /'taylə,buhd/ *n* any of numerous Asiatic, E Indian, and African warblers (family Sylviidae) that stitch leaves together to support and hide their nests

**tailored** /'tayləd/ *adj* **1** made by a tailor **2** fashioned or fitted to resemble a tailor's work; *specif* cut so as to fit the figure well **3a** having the look of one fitted by a good tailor ⟨*a slim, smartly* ~ *man*⟩ **b** appearing well cared for ⟨~ *lawns*⟩

**tailoring** /'tayləring/ *n* **1a** the business or occupation of a tailor **b** the work or workmanship of a tailor **2** the making or adapting of something to suit a particular purpose

,**tailor-'made** *adj* **1a** made by a tailor or with a tailor's care and style **b** made-to-measure **c** appearing like one turned out by a good tailor **2** made or fitted for a particular, usu specified, use or purpose

**tailor's chalk** *n* a usu thin flat piece of compressed FRENCH CHALK used by tailors and sewers to make temporary marks on cloth (eg to mark seams or darts)

**tailor's tack** *n* a very loose tacking stitch usu made through a paper pattern and one or more layers of fabric which are then cut apart to leave thread markings giving details of the pattern in each layer

**tailpiece** /-,pees/ *n* **1** a piece added at the end; an appendage **2** a triangular piece from which the strings of a stringed instrument are stretched to the pegs **3** a short beam or rafter with one end fastened (TAILED) in a wall and the other end supported by a beam (HEADER) across an opening **4** an ornament placed below the text of a page (eg at the end of a chapter)

**tailpipe** /-,piep/ *n* the part of a jet engine that carries the exhaust gases rearwards and discharges them through an opening

**tailplane** /-,playn/ *n* the horizontal stabilizing surfaces of an aircraft's tail

**tailrace** /'tayl,rays/ *n* **1** the stream of a MILLRACE (channel in which water flows to and from a watermill) beyond the mill-

wheel **2** a channel in which TAILINGS (residues separated from ore) are floated off

**tailspin** /-,spin/ *n* **1** SPIN 2a (aerial manoeuvre) **2** a mental or emotional collapse; loss of capacity to cope or react **3** a sharp financial depression ⟨*may tip the economy into a* ~ – *Newsweek*⟩

**tailstock** /-,stok/ *n* an adjustable part of a LATHE (machine for turning objects to be worked) that holds the fixed spindle

**tail to the wall** *n* RENVERS (equestrian movement)

**tailwater** /'tayl,wawtə/ *n* excess surface water draining from esp a field under cultivation

**tail wind** *n* a wind having the same general direction as the course of an aircraft or ship

**Taino** /'tienoh/ *n, pl* **Tainos**, *esp collectively* **Taino 1** a member of an extinct ARAWAKAN people (group of S American Indian people) of the Greater Antilles and the Bahamas **2** the language of the Taino people [Sp]

¹**taint** /taynt/ *vt* **1** to touch or affect slightly with something bad ⟨*people* ~ed *with prejudice*⟩ **2** to affect with putrefaction; spoil **3** to contaminate morally; corrupt ⟨*scholarship* ~ed *by envy*⟩ ~ *vi* **1** to become affected with putrefaction; spoil **2** *obs* to become weak **synonyms** see CONTAMINATE [ME *tainten* to colour & *taynten* to convict, prove guilty; ME *tainten*, fr AF *teinter*, fr MF *teint*, pp of *teindre*, fr L *tingere*; ME *taynten*, fr MF *ataint*, pp of *ataindre* – more at TINGE, ATTAIN]

²**taint** *n* a contaminating mark or influence ⟨*free from every* ~ *but that of vice* – William Cowper⟩ – **taintless** *adj*

**taipan** /'tiepan/ *n* an exceedingly venomous snake (*Oxyuranus scutellatus*) of N Australia and the Pacific islands [native name in Australia]

**Taiping** /tie'ping/ *n* a supporter of or participant in a rebellion (1848–65) against the Manchu dynasty in China [Chin (Pek) *tai bing* (*t'ai*⁴ *ping*²) peaceful]

**taj** /tahj/ *n* a tall conical hat worn in Muslim countries [Ar *taj*, fr Per, crown, crest, cap]

**Tajik** /'tahjik, tah'jeek/ *n* a member of a people of Iranian blood and speech who resemble Europeans and are dispersed among the populations of Afghanistan and Turkestan

**Tajiki** /'tahjiki, tah'jeeki/ *n* the Iranian language of the Tajik people

**taka** /'tahkə, 'tahkah/ *n* – see MONEY table [Bengali *ṭākā* rupee, taka, fr Skt *ṭaṅka*, a stamped coin]

**takahe** /'tahkə,hee/ *n* a rare flightless New Zealand bird (*Notornis mantelli*) related to the RAILS [Maori]

¹**take** /tayk/ *vb* **took** /took/; **taken** /'taykən/ *vt* **1** to get into one's hands or into one's possession, power, or control; appropriate: eg **1a** to seize or capture physically ⟨*enemy forces have* ~n *the airport*⟩ ⟨*took 1500 prisoners*⟩ ⟨*children* ~n *by tigers*⟩ **b** to get possession of (eg fish or game) by killing or capturing **c(1)** to move against (an opponent's piece in chess) and remove from play; capture **c(2)** to win in a card game ⟨*able to* ~ *twelve tricks with that hand*⟩ **d** to acquire as property by sovereign right ⟨~n *by the state*⟩ **e(1)** to catch (a batted or bowled ball) in basketball or cricket ⟨~ *it on the fly*⟩ ⟨*well* ~n *by the wicketkeeper*⟩ **e(2)** to cause a batting side in cricket to lose (a wicket) **2** to grasp, grip ⟨*took her arm and led her across the road*⟩ **3a** to catch or attack through the effect of a sudden force or influence ⟨~n *ill*⟩ ⟨~n *with the giggles*⟩ **b** to catch or come upon in a specified situation or action ⟨~n *in adultery*⟩ ⟨*his death took us by surprise*⟩ **c** to strike or hit in or on a specified part ⟨*the blow took him on the chin*⟩ **d** to gain the approval of; captivate, delight ⟨*was quite* ~n *with her at their first meeting*⟩ ⟨*whichever* ~s *your fancy*⟩ **4a** to receive into one's body, esp through the mouth ⟨~ *poison*⟩ ⟨~ *a glass of water*⟩ ⟨*do you* ~ *sugar?*⟩ **b** to expose oneself to (eg sun or air) for pleasure or physical benefit **c** to partake of (a meal) ⟨~s *dinner about seven*⟩ **5a** to bring into or receive in a particular human relationship or connection ⟨*reduced to* taking *lodgers*⟩ ⟨*it's time he* took *a wife*⟩ ⟨*Miss Jones* ~s *us for French*⟩ **b** to copulate with (a passive partner) **6a** to acquire, borrow, or use without authority or right **b(1)** to obtain or receive for regular use (eg by lease, contract, or subscription) ⟨~ *a cottage for the summer*⟩ ⟨~s *The Sun*⟩ **b(2)** to buy ⟨*the salesman persuaded him to* ~ *the estate car*⟩ **7a** to assume ⟨~ *shape*⟩ ⟨*took the name of Phillips*⟩ ⟨*gods often* took *the form of a human being*⟩ **b** to perform or conduct as a duty or task ⟨~ *Evensong*⟩ ⟨*a teacher* taking *prep*⟩ **c** to commit oneself to ⟨~ *a vow*⟩ ⟨*a decision*⟩ ⟨*his mother* took *his side*⟩ **d** to involve oneself in ⟨~ *no notice*⟩ ⟨~ *pity on him*⟩ ⟨~ *the trouble to learn Chinese*⟩ **e** to adopt or advance

as a point of view or defence ⟨~ *a more lenient view*⟩ ⟨*a point well* ~n⟩ – often used imperatively to introduce an example ⟨~ *Shakespeare, now*⟩ **f** to claim as rightfully one's own; assume ⟨~ *the credit*⟩ ⟨~ *the liberty of refusing*⟩ **8** to secure by competition ⟨took *third place*⟩ **9** to pick out; choose ⟨~ *any card*⟩ **10** to adopt, choose, or avail oneself of for use ⟨~ *a chance*⟩ ⟨~ *stronger measures*⟩: eg **10a** to have recourse to as an instrument for doing something ⟨~ *a scythe to the weeds*⟩ **b** to use as a means of transport or progression ⟨~ *a plane to Paris*⟩ ⟨~ *the third turning on the right*⟩ **c(1)** to have recourse to for safety or refuge ⟨~ *shelter*⟩ **c(2)** to proceed to occupy or hold ⟨~ *a seat*⟩ ⟨~ *office*⟩ ⟨~ *possession*⟩ **d(1)** to consume (eg space or time) completely; USE UP ⟨~s *a long time to dry*⟩ **d(2)** to make use of; accept ⟨~s *size nine*⟩ ⟨*the camera* ~s *35mm film*⟩ **d(3)** to need, require ⟨*it* ~s *some believing*⟩ ⟨*transitive verbs* ~ *an object*⟩ ⟨*it* ~s *an Italian to make a good pizza*⟩ – compare WHAT IT TAKES **11a** to derive, draw ⟨~s *its title from the name of the hero*⟩ **b(1)** to obtain or ascertain as the result of a special procedure ⟨~ *his temperature*⟩ ⟨~ *a census*⟩ **b(2)** to get or record in writing; WRITE DOWN ⟨~ *notes*⟩ **b(3)** to get or record by photography ⟨~ *some slides*⟩ ⟨~ *the children in their party clothes*⟩ **b(4)** to get by transference from one surface to another ⟨~ *fingerprints*⟩ **12** to receive or accept, whether willingly or reluctantly ⟨~ *a bribe*⟩ ⟨~ *a bet*⟩ ⟨~ *a risk*⟩: eg **12a** to receive when bestowed or tendered ⟨~ *a degree*⟩ ⟨~ *the salute*⟩ **b(1)** to submit to; endure, undergo ⟨took *a fearful mauling*⟩ – often with *it* ⟨*can't* ~ *it any longer*⟩ **b(2)** to support, withstand ⟨*won't* ~ *my weight*⟩ ⟨*I can* ~ *a lot of Mozart*⟩ **c(1)** to accept as true; believe ⟨took *his word for it*⟩ ⟨~ *it from me*⟩ **c(2)** to follow ⟨~ *my advice*⟩ **c(3)** to accept with the mind in a specified way ⟨~ *things as they come*⟩ ⟨~ *the news calmly*⟩ **d** to indulge in and enjoy ⟨~ *one's ease*⟩ ⟨~ *a holiday*⟩ **e** to receive or accept in payment, compensation, or reparation ⟨*they won't* ~ *dollars*⟩ **13a(1)** to let in; admit ⟨*the boat was taking water fast*⟩ **a(2)** to accommodate ⟨*the suitcase wouldn't* ~ *another thing*⟩ **b** to be affected or seized injuriously by (eg a disease); contract ⟨~ *cold*⟩ **14a** to apprehend, understand ⟨*slow to* ~ *his meaning*⟩ **b** to consider; LOOK UPON ⟨~ *it as settled*⟩ ⟨took *the report at face value*⟩ **c** to feel, experience ⟨~ *pleasure*⟩ ⟨~ *offence*⟩ ⟨~ *a fancy to her*⟩ **15a** to lead, carry, or remove with one to another place ⟨*this bus will* ~ *you into town*⟩ ⟨~ *him a cup of tea*⟩ **b** to require or cause to go ⟨*his ability will* ~ *him to the top*⟩ **16a** to obtain by removing ⟨~ *eggs from a nest*⟩ **b** to subtract ⟨~ *two from four*⟩ **17** to undertake and make, do, or perform ⟨~ *a walk*⟩ ⟨~ *aim*⟩ ⟨~ *legal action*⟩ ⟨~ *one's revenge*⟩ **18a** to deal with ⟨~ *the comments one at a time*⟩ **b** to consider or view in a specified relation ⟨~n *together, the details were significant*⟩ **c** to apply oneself to the study of or undergo examination in ⟨~ *music lessons*⟩ ⟨~ *six subjects at O level*⟩ **d** to apply oneself to passing or surmounting ⟨took *the corner on two wheels*⟩ **19** to cheat, swindle ⟨*was* ~n *for £5000 by a con man*⟩ **20** euph to remove by death ⟨*was* ~n *in his prime*⟩ ~ *vi* **1** to obtain possession: eg **1a** to capture **b** to receive property as one's own in law ⟨~ *under a will*⟩ **c** *of a fish* to receive a lure or bait **2** to lay hold; catch, hold **3** to establish the natural or intended effect: eg **3a** to establish a take ⟨*90 per cent of the grafts* ~⟩ ⟨*did your vaccination* ~?⟩ **b** to begin to grow; strike root ⟨*have the cuttings* ~n *yet?*⟩ **c** to act, work ⟨*hoped the lesson he taught would* ~⟩ ⟨*dry fuel* ~s *readily*⟩ ⟨*glue that* ~s *well on cloth*⟩ **d** to prove attractive; win popular favour **4a** to be seized or attacked as specified; become ⟨took *ill*⟩ **b** to be capable of being moved in a specified way; come ⟨*it* ~s *to pieces for cleaning*⟩ **c** to admit of being photographed **5** *NAm* to go; SET OUT ⟨~ *after a bag snatcher*⟩ **6** *chiefly dial* – used as an intensifier or redundantly with *and* and a complementary verb ⟨took *and ducked her in the pond*⟩ **synonyms** see BRING [ME *taken*, fr OE *tacan*, fr ON *taka;* akin to MD *taken* to take] – **take for granted 1** to assume as true, real, or expected **2** to value too lightly – **take it out of 1** TAKE IT OUT ON **2** to fatigue, exhaust ⟨*this work certainly* takes it out of *you*⟩ – **take it out on** to vent anger, frustration, or vexation on – **take somebody out of him-/herself** to provide somebody with needful diversion – **take the biscuit/cake** to be the best or worst example or instance of something [fr the cake formerly offered as prize in various contests] – **what it takes** the qualities or resources needed for success or for attainment of a goal

**take after** *vt* **1** to take as an example; follow **2** to resemble (an older relative) in appearance, character, or aptitudes

**take apart** *vt* **1** to disassemble, dismantle **2** to analyse or dissect, esp in order to discover or reveal a weakness, flaw, or fallacy **3** to treat roughly or harshly; tear into

**take back** *vt* to make a retraction of; withdraw

**take down** *vt* **1** to pull to pieces; *esp* to disassemble ⟨take *a rifle* down⟩ **2** to lower the spirit or vanity of; humble **3a** to write down **b** to record by mechanical means **4** to lower without removing ⟨took down *his trousers*⟩ ~ *vi* to be capable of being taken to pieces – see also TAKEDOWN

**take for** *vt* to suppose to be; *esp* to suppose mistakenly to be ⟨*do you* take *me* for *an idiot?*⟩

**take in** *vt* **1** to draw into a smaller compass ⟨take in *the slack of a line*⟩: **1a** to furl (eg a sail or flag) **b** to make (a garment) smaller (eg by altering the positions of the seams or making tucks) – compare LET OUT **2a** to receive as a guest or lodger **b** to give shelter to **c** to take into custody; *esp* to take to a police station as a prisoner or for questioning **3** to receive (work) into one's house to be done for pay ⟨take in *washing*⟩ **4** to encompass within its limits **5** to include in an itinerary ⟨*the holiday* took in *Venice*⟩ **6** to receive into the mind; perceive, understand **7** *informal* to deceive, trick – see also TAKE-IN

**take off** *vt* **1** to remove ⟨take *your shoes* off⟩ **2a** to release ⟨take *the brake* off⟩ **b** to discontinue, withdraw ⟨took off *the morning train*⟩ **c** to take or allow as a discount; deduct ⟨took *10 per cent* off⟩ **3** to take or spend (a period of time) as a holiday or rest or in a way that constitutes a departure from one's regular activity ⟨took *two weeks* off *in August*⟩ **4a** to copy from an original; reproduce **b** to make a likeness of; portray **c** to mimic ⟨*mannerisms that his critics delighted in* taking off⟩ **5** *euph* to take the life of ⟨taken off *by pneumonia*⟩ ~ *vi* **1** to start off or away; SET OUT; depart ⟨took off *without delay*⟩ **2a** to branch off (eg from a main stream or stem) **b** to have a point of origin – usu + *from* **c** to begin a leap or spring **d** to leave the surface; begin flight – see also TAKEOFF

**take on** *vt* **1a** to begin to perform or deal with; undertake ⟨took on *new responsibilities*⟩ **b** to contend with as an opponent ⟨took on *the neighbourhood bully*⟩ **2** to engage, hire **3** to assume or acquire (eg an appearance or quality) (as if) as one's own ⟨*the city square* takes on *a festive air*⟩ ~ *vi* **1** to become fashionable ⟨*the style didn't* take on *from the start*⟩ **2** *informal* to show one's feelings, esp of grief or anger, in a demonstrative way ⟨*they cried and* took on *something terrible*⟩ – Bob Hope⟩

**take out** *vt* **1a(1)** to extract ⟨took *the appendix* out⟩ **a(2)** to exclude, omit **b** to find release for; vent – usu + *on* ⟨*don't* take *your resentment* out *on me!*⟩ **c** to eliminate, destroy ⟨took out *the installations by bombing*⟩ **2** to escort or accompany (eg a member of the opposite sex) in public **3a** to obtain from the proper authority ⟨take out *a warrant*⟩ **b** to acquire (insurance) by making the necessary payment **4** to make a higher bid than (a bridge partner) in a different suit – see also TAKEOUT

**take over** *vt* to assume control or possession of or responsibility for ⟨*military leaders* took over *the government*⟩ ~ *vi* **1** to assume control or possession **2** to become dominant – see also TAKEOVER

**take to** *vt* **1** to take in hand; take care of **2** to betake oneself to ⟨take to *the woods*⟩ **3** to apply or devote oneself to (eg a practice, habit, or occupation) ⟨take to *begging*⟩ **4** to adapt oneself to; respond to ⟨takes to *water like a duck*⟩ **5** to conceive a liking for

**take up** *vt* **1a** to lift; pick up **b** to remove by lifting or pulling up ⟨*the council's* taking *the old tramlines* up⟩ **2a** to assume ⟨take up *a hostile attitude*⟩ **b** to receive internally or on the surface and hold ⟨*plants* take up *nutrients*⟩ **3** to enter upon (eg a business, activity, or subject of study) ⟨took up *Greek*⟩ ⟨*when did he* take up *drinking so much?*⟩ **4a** to proceed to deal with ⟨take up *one problem at a time*⟩ **b** to raise (a matter) for consideration ⟨took *her case* up with a lawyer⟩ **5** to establish oneself in ⟨took up *residence in town*⟩ **6** to occupy (eg space, time, or attention) entirely or exclusively; fill up ⟨*outside activities* took up *too much of his time*⟩ **7** to make tighter or shorter (eg by adjustment of parts or by pulling extension up or in) **8** to respond favourably to a bet, challenge, or proposal of – often + *on* ⟨*I'll* take *you* up *on that*⟩ **9** to begin again or take over from another ⟨*your turn to* take up *the tale* – John Buchan⟩ ~ *vi* to make a beginning where another has left off; resume – see also TAKE-UP

**take up with** *vt* to begin an association with; consort with

²**take** *n* **1** an act or the action of taking (eg by seizing, accepting, or otherwise coming into possession): eg **1a(1)** the action

of killing, capturing, or catching something (eg game or fish) ⟨*a good ~ by the wicketkeeper*⟩ **a(2)** the act or an instance of seizing bait **b** the uninterrupted recording, filming, or televising of something (eg a gramophone record or film sequence) **2** something taken: **2a** the amount of money received (eg from a business venture, sale, or admission charge); the proceeds, takings **b** a share, cut ⟨*wanted a bigger ~*⟩ **c** the number or quantity (eg of animals, fish, or pelts) taken at one time; a catch, haul **d** the recording or scene produced by one take **3a** a local or general bodily reaction indicative of successful vaccination (eg against smallpox) **b** a successful union (eg of a stem graft) **4** a section of copy (eg for a newspaper) given to a COMPOSITOR for typesetting

**takeaway** /'taykə,way/ *n, Br* **1** a meal that is taken away from its place of sale rather than eaten on the premises ⟨*a Chinese ~ for supper*⟩ **2** a shop that sells takeaways ⟨*a meal from the Chinese ~*⟩

**takedown** /'tayk,down/ *adj* constructed so as to be readily taken apart ⟨*a ~ rifle*⟩

**take-home pay** *n* the part of gross salary or wages remaining after deductions (eg for income tax)

**'take-,in** *n* an act of taking in, esp by deceiving

**takeoff** /-,of/ *n* **1** an imitation, esp in the way of caricature **2a** an act of leaving or a rise from a surface (eg in making a jump, dive, or flight or in the launching of a rocket) **b** a starting point; a point at which one takes off

**takeout** /'tayk,owt/ *n* **1** the action or an act of taking out; *esp* a bid made in bridge that takes a partner out of a bid, DOUBLE, or REDOUBLE (bids that increase the value of tricks won and lost) **2** *NAm* a takeaway

**takeout double** *n* a DOUBLE (bid that increases the value of tricks won and lost) made in bridge to convey information to one's partner and to invite a bid from him/her – compare PENALTY DOUBLE

**takeover** /-,ohvə/ *n* the action or an act of taking over; *esp* an act of gaining control of a business company by buying a majority of the shares – **take-over** *adj*

**taker** /'taykə/ *n* one who or that which takes; *esp* one who accepts a gift or bet

**'take-,up** *n* **1** the action of taking up (eg by gathering, contraction, absorption, or adjustment) **2** any of various devices for tightening or drawing in something (eg slack or lost motion)

**takin** /'tahkeen/ *n* a large heavily built cud-chewing mammal (*Budorcas taxicolor*) of Tibet related to the goats [Mishmi]

**'taking** /'tayking/ *n* **1** seizure **2a** *pl* receipts, esp of money **b** a take of fish or animals **3** *chiefly Scot* an unhappy state; a plight **4** *archaic* a state of violent agitation and distress

**'taking** *adj* attractive, captivating

**'tala** /'tahlə/ *n* any of the ancient traditional rhythmic patterns of Indian music – compare RAGA [Skt *tāla*, lit., hand-clapping]

**'tala** *n* – see MONEY table [Samoan, modif of E *dollar*]

**talapoin** /'talə,poyn/ *n* a small GUENON monkey (*Cercopithecus talapoin*) of W Africa [Fr, lit., Buddhist monk, fr Pg *talapão*, fr Mon *tala par lord*]

**talc** /talk/ *n* **1** a soft mineral that consists of a silicate of magnesium, $Mg_3Si_4O_{10}(OH)_2$, is usu whitish, greenish, or greyish with a soapy feel, and occurs as masses of flakes, granules, or fibres **2** TALCUM POWDER [MF *talc* mica, fr ML *talk*, fr Ar *ṭalq*] – **talcose** *adj*

**talcum powder** /'talkəm/ *n* **1** powdered talc **2** a powder for toilet use consisting of perfumed talc or talc and a mild antiseptic [ML *talcum* mica, alter. of earlier *talk*]

**tale** /tayl/ *n* **1a** a series of events or facts told or presented; an account **b(1)** a report of a private or confidential matter ⟨*dead men tell no ~s*⟩ **b(2)** a malicious report or piece of gossip **2a** a usu fictitious narrative; a story **b** an intentionally untrue statement; a falsehood ⟨*always preferred the ~ to the truth* – Sir Winston Churchill⟩ **3** *formal* a count, tally ⟨*the short ~ of English dead* – L G Pine⟩ [ME, fr OE *talu;* akin to ON *tala* talk, & prob to L *dolus* guile, deceit, Gk *dolos*]

**talebearer** /-,beərə/ *n* a telltale, gossip – **talebearing** *adj or n*

**talent** /'talənt/ *n* **1a** any of several ancient units of weight (eg a unit of Palestine and Syria equal to 3000 shekels or a Greek unit equal to 6000 drachmas) **b** a monetary unit equal to the value of a talent of gold or silver **2a** a special often creative or artistic aptitude **b** the natural abilities of a person; *esp* a person's general intelligence or mental power **3** a person of talent in a field or activity; *also, taking sing or pl vb* a group of people of such talent **4** *taking sing or pl vb, slang* sexually attractive people ⟨*sat eyeing the local ~*⟩ **5** *archaic* a character-

istic feature, aptitude, or disposition of a person or animal [ME, fr OE *talente*, fr L *talenta*, pl of *talentum* unit of weight or money, fr Gk *talanton;* akin to L *tollere* to lift up – more at TOLERATE; (2–5) fr the parable of the talents in Mt 25:14–30] – **talented** *adj*, **talentless** *adj*

**talent scout** *n* a person engaged in discovering and recruiting people with talent in a specialized field or activity

**talent show** *n* a show consisting of a series of individual performances by amateurs who may be selected for training or professional engagements if talented

**'talent-,spot** *vi, informal* to look for people with talent in a specialized field or activity – **talent-spotter** *n*

**taler** /'tahlə/ *n* any of numerous silver coins issued by various German states from the 15th to the 19th centuries [Ger – more at DOLLAR]

**talesman** /'tayleezmən/ *n* a person added to a jury, usu from among bystanders, to make up a deficiency in the available number of jurors [ME *tales* talesmen, fr ML *tales de circumstantibus* such (persons) of the bystanders; fr the wording of the writ summoning them]

**'tale-,teller** *n* **1** someone who tells tales or stories **2** a telltale – **tale-telling** *adj or n*

**talipes** /'talipeez/ *n* clubfoot – used technically [NL, fr L *talus* ankle + *pes* foot – more at FOOT]

**talipot** /'talipot/ *n* a tall showy fan-leaved palm (*Corypha umbraculifera*) of Ceylon, the Philippines, and S India bearing a crown of huge leaves that are used as umbrellas and fans, and are cut into strips for writing paper [Bengali *tālipōt* palm leaf]

**talisman** /'talizmən/ *n, pl* **talismans 1** an object bearing an engraved sign or character believed to act as a charm to avert evil and bring good fortune **2** something believed to produce magical or miraculous effects [Fr *talisman* or Sp *talismán* or It *talismano,* fr Ar *ṭilsam,* fr MGk *telesma,* fr Gk, consecration, fr *telein* to initiate into the mysteries, complete, fr *telos* end – more at WHEEL] – **talismanic** *adj,* **talismanically** *adv*

**'talk** /tawk/ *vt* **1** to express in speech; utter ⟨*~ nonsense*⟩ **2** to make the subject of conversation or discourse; discuss ⟨*~ business*⟩ **3** to bring to a specified state by talking; *esp* to persuade by talking ⟨*~ed them into agreeing*⟩ ⟨*couldn't ~ him out of it*⟩ **4** to use (a language) for conversing or communicating; speak ~ *vi* **1a** to express or exchange ideas by means of spoken words **b** to convey information or communicate in any way (eg with signs or sounds) ⟨*can make a trumpet ~*⟩ **c** to have discussions; confer ⟨*~ with the enemy*⟩ **2a** to use speech; speak **b** to imitate human speech ⟨*his budgie can ~*⟩ **3a** to speak idly; chatter **b** to gossip ⟨*you know how people ~*⟩ **c** to reveal secret or confidential information ⟨*you'll never make me ~*⟩ **4** to give a talk; lecture *synonyms* see SPEAK [ME *talken;* akin to OE *talu* tale] – **talker** *n* – **you can/can't talk** you are just as bad yourself ⟨*you say I'm untidy* – you can talk *with your room in such a mess!*⟩ – see also **talk through one's** HAT, **talk the hind** LEG **off a donkey, talk** NINETEEN **to the dozen, talk** SENSE/SHOP/TURKEY

**talk back** *vi* to answer inpertinently

**talk down** *vt* **1** to defeat or silence by argument or by loud talking **2** to help (eg a pilot or aircraft) to land in bad visibility by radioing instructions from the ground ~ *vi* to speak in a condescending or oversimplified fashion

**talk out** *vt* **1** to clarify or settle by discussion ⟨*tried to talk out their differences*⟩ **2** to prevent (a bill) from being passed by a legislative assembly by continuing discussion beyond the allotted time

**talk over** *vt* to review or consider in conversation; discuss

**talk round** *vt* to persuade by talking

**'talk** *n* **1** a verbal exchange of thoughts or opinions; a conversation **2** pointless or fruitless discussion or speech ⟨*it's just a lot of ~*⟩ **3** **talks** *pl,* **talk** a formal discussion, negotiation, or exchange of views; a conference **4a** mention, report **b** rumour, gossip **5** the topic of interested comment, conversation, or gossip ⟨*the ~ of the town*⟩ **6** an often informal address or lecture **7** communicative sounds or signs resembling or functioning as talk ⟨*bird ~*⟩ ⟨*baby ~*⟩

**talkative** /'tawkətiv/ *adj* given to talking – **talkatively** *adv,* **talkativeness** *n*

*synonyms* **Talkative, chatty, glib, loquacious, garrulous, voluble,** and **effusive** all mean "given to talking". **Talkative** is the most neutral word, suggesting merely a disposition to enjoy conversation ⟨*his wife was considerably younger . . . and* **talkative** *where he was monosyllabic* – Dorothy Sayers⟩. The more informal **chatty** implies a taste for light familiar talk. **Glib** suggests superficial or dishonest ease in speech ⟨made a lot of **glib** excuses⟩; both **chatty** and **glib** can be used of writing in their respective veins ⟨a **chatty** magazine article about cats⟩ ⟨turn out one **glib** book after another⟩. **Loquacious** is a formal word for fluent and usually excessive talkativeness. **Garrulous** stresses rambling and often tedious talkativeness ⟨a garrulous old man⟩. **Voluble** implies a very fluent uncheckable torrent of speech. **Effusive** entails emotional gushing ⟨became **effusive** over the beautiful baby⟩. antonyms silent, laconic, taciturn

**talkie** /'tawki/ n a film with a synchronized sound track synonyms see CINEMA [talk + movie]

**'talk-,in** n, informal a usu informal gathering for discussion and exchange of ideas; esp one in which one or more major speakers starts the discussion with a talk

**talking book** /'tawking/ n a gramophone record or tape recording of someone reading a book or magazine aloud, produced for the benefit of the blind

**talking head** n usu pl, chiefly derog someone talking directly to the audience on television (e g reading the news, being interviewed, or giving an opinion) without any illustrative material (e g film or photographs) being used to enlarge on the subject matter ⟨The talking heads, even the nice looking ones, add little to my sense of knowledge – The Listener⟩

**talking picture** /'tawking/ n a talkie

**talking point** n a subject of conversation or argument

**talking shop** n, informal a place or institution (e g a parliament) where matters are discussed, often with no useful outcome

**'talking-,to** n a reprimand, scolding ⟨gave the boys a firm ~⟩

**talk show** n CHAT SHOW

**tall** /tawl/ adj 1a high in stature; of above average height ⟨a ~ man⟩ ⟨~ trees⟩ b of a specified height ⟨five feet ~⟩ 2a long from bottom to top ⟨a ~ book⟩ b of a plant of a higher growing variety or species 3a large or formidable in amount, extent, or degree ⟨a ~ order to fill⟩ b pompous, high-flown ⟨~ talk about the vast mysteries of life – W A White⟩ c highly exaggerated; incredible, improbable ⟨a ~ story⟩ d difficult, demanding ⟨a ~ order⟩ synonyms see ¹HIGH [ME, ready, handsome, brave, prob fr OE getæl quick, ready; akin to OHG gizal quick, OE talu tale] – **tall** adv, **tallish** adj, **tallness** n – **walk tall** to bear oneself proudly; feel very confident

**tallage** /'talij/ n 1 a tax levied in the Middle Ages on royal towns and CROWN LANDS 2 a tax levied by a lord on his tenants [ME taillage, tallage, fr OF taillage, fr taillier to cut, limit, tax – more at TAILOR]

**tallboy** /'tawl,boy/ n 1 a tall chest of drawers supported on a low legged base 2 a double chest of drawers, usu with the upper section slightly smaller than the lower [tall + boy]

**tallith** /'talith, 'tahlith, -lis/ n, pl **tallithim** /,tahlə'seem,-'teem, -'theem/,**taleysim** /tə'laysim/ a shawl with fringed corners, traditionally worn over the head or shoulders by Jewish men during morning prayers [Heb ṭallīth cover, cloak]

**'tallow** /'taloh/ n, a white nearly tasteless fatty solid that is obtained by melting down the fat of cattle and sheep, and is used chiefly in soap, candles, and lubricants [ME talgh, talow; akin to MD talch tallow] – **tallowy** adj

**²tallow** vt to grease or smear with tallow

**'tally** /'tali/ n 1 a device for visibly recording or accounting esp business transactions: e g 1a a wooden rod notched with marks representing numbers and split lengthwise through the notches so that each of two parties may have a record of a transaction and of the amount due or paid b any of various bookkeeping forms or sheets c a mechanical counter held in the hand and operated with a button or lever 2a a recorded reckoning or account (e g of items or charges) ⟨keep a daily ~ of accidents⟩ b a record of the score (e g in a game) 3 a part or person that corresponds to an opposite or companion object or member; a counterpart [ME talye, fr ML talea, tallia, fr L talea twig, cutting – more at TAILOR]

**²tally** vt 1a to mark (as if) on a tally; tabulate b to list or check off (e g a cargo) by items c to register (e g a score) in a contest 2 to make a count of; reckon 3 to cause to correspond ~ vi 1a to make a tally (as if) by tabulating b to register a point in a contest; score 2 to correspond, match ⟨their stories ~⟩

**tally-ho** /,tali 'hoh/ n a call of a huntsman at the sight of a fox [prob fr Fr taïaut, a cry used to urge hounds in deer-hunting]

**tallyman** /'talimən/ n 1 someone who tallies, checks, or keeps an account or record (e g of receipt of goods) 2 Br someone who sells goods on credit; also a person who calls at regular intervals to collect payments for goods on hire purchase

**Talmud** /'talmood, 'tahl-/ n the authoritative writings of Jewish tradition comprising the MISHNAH and GEMARA [LHeb talmūdh,

lit., instruction] – **talmudic** also **talmudical** adj, often cap, **talmudism** n, often cap

**Talmudist** /'talmoodist, 'tahl-/ n a specialist in talmudic studies

**talon** /'talən/ n 1 the claw of an animal, esp a bird of prey 2a a part or object shaped like or suggestive of a claw b the shoulder of the bolt of a lock on which the key acts to shoot the bolt 3a cards laid aside in a pile in the game of patience b STOCK 9c (cards not dealt out at the beginning of a game) [ME, fr MF, heel, spur, fr (assumed) VL talon-, talo, fr L talus ankle, anklebone] – **taloned** adj

**'talus** /'taylas/ n 1 a slope formed esp by an accumulation of rock debris 2 rock debris at the base of a cliff [Fr, fr L talutium slope indicating presence of gold under the soil]

**²talus** n, pl **tali** /-li/ 1 a square-shaped bone of humans which joins with the lower leg bones (TIBIA and FIBULA) to form the ankle joint and bears the weight of the body; the anklebone; broadly the equivalent bone (ASTRAGALUS) of an animal other than a human 2 the entire ankle joint [NL, fr L]

**tamale** /tə'mahli/ n a Mexican dish of minced meat seasoned usu with chilli, rolled in maize flour, wrapped in maize husks, and steamed [MexSp tamales, pl of tamal, fr Nahuatl tamalli]

**tamandua** /,tamən'dooə, tə'mandoo·ə/ n a tree-dwelling anteater (Tamandua tetradactyla) of central and S America [Pg tamanduá, fr Tupi]

**tamara** /'tamərə/ n a mixture of spices (e g cloves and cinnamon) used esp in Indian dishes [origin unknown]

**tamarack** /'tamərak/ n 1 any of several American larches; esp a larch (Larix laricina) of the N USA, Canada, and Alaska 2 the wood of a tamarack [origin unknown]

**tamarau** /'tamə,row/ n a small dark sturdily built buffalo (Bubalus mindorensis) native to Mindoro in the Philippines [Tagalog tamaráw]

**tamarin** /'tamərin/ n any of numerous small S American marmosets (genus Leontocebus) with silky fur and a long tail [Fr, fr Galibi]

**tamarind** /'tamərind/ n a tropical tree (Tamarindus indica) of the pea family with hard yellow wood, PINNATE (having leaflets arranged in pairs on either side of the stalk) leaves and yellow flowers streaked with red; also its fruit, which has an acid pulp used for preserves or in a cooling laxative drink [Sp & Pg tamarindo, fr Ar tamr hindī, lit., Indian date]

**tamarisk** /'tamərisk/ n any of a genus (Tamarix of the family Tamaricaceae, the tamarisk family) of chiefly tropical shrubs and trees having tiny narrow leaves and masses of minute pink or white flowers; esp one (Tamarix gallica) that is native in the Mediterranean region [ME tamarisc, fr LL tamariscus, fr L tamaric-, tamarix]

**tambala** /tahm'bahlə/ n, pl **tambala, tambalas** – see kwacha at MONEY table [native name in Malawi, lit., cockerel]

**'tambour** /'tambooə/ n 1 a drum 2a an embroidery frame consisting of a set of two interlocking hoops between which cloth is stretched before stitching b embroidery made on a tambour frame 3 a rolling top or front (e g of a rolltop desk) consisting of narrow strips of wood glued on canvas [Fr, fr Ar ṭanbūr, modif of Per tabīr]

**²tambour** vb to embroider (e g cloth) using a tambour – **tambourer** n

**tamboura, tambura** /tam'booərə/ n an Asian musical instrument with a long neck and four strings, used to produce a drone accompaniment to singing or other instruments [Per ṭambūra]

**tambourine** /,tambə'reen/ n a small drum; esp a shallow oneheaded drum with loose metallic discs at the sides that is held in the hand and played by shaking, striking with the hand, or rubbing with the thumb [MF tambourin, dim. of tambour]

**'tame** /taym/ adj 1 changed from a state of native wildness, esp so as to be trainable and useful to humans; domesticated ⟨~ animals⟩ 2 made docile and submissive; subdued 3 lacking spirit, zest, or interest; insipid ⟨a ~ campaign⟩ antonyms fierce, wild [ME, fr OE tam; akin to OHG zam tame, L domare to tame, Gk damnanai] – **tamely** adv, **tameness** n

**²tame** vt 1a to make tame; domesticate b to subject to cultivation 2 to deprive of spirit; humble, subdue ⟨the once revolutionary . . . party, long since ~d – TLS⟩ 3 to soften; TONE DOWN ⟨~d the language in the play⟩ ~ vi to become tame – **tamable, tameable** adj, **tamer** n

**Tamil** /'tamil/ n 1 a DRAVIDIAN language of S India and of Sri Lanka 2 a Tamil-speaking person

**tamis** /'tami, 'tamis/ n, pl **tamises** a cloth sieve [Fr]

**Tammany** /'taməni/ adj, chiefly NAm of or constituting a

group or organization exercising or seeking municipal political power by methods often associated with corruption and autocratic control [*Tammany Hall*, headquarters of the Tammany Society, political organization in New York City which controlled and plundered the city in 1865–71] – **Tammanyism** *n*

**Tammuz** /'tamoohz,-ooz/ *n* – see MONTH table [Heb *Tammūz*]

**¹tammy** /'tami/ *vt* to strain (e g a sauce or soup) through a fine-mesh cloth (e g of wool or muslin) [*tammy* (cloth sieve), prob alter. of *tamis*]

**²tammy** *n* a tam-o'-shanter [by shortening & alter.]

**tam-o'-shanter** /ˌtam ə 'shantə/ *n* a woollen cap of Scottish origin with a tight headband, a wide flat circular crown, and usu a pom-pom in the centre [*Tam o' Shanter*, hero of the poem of that name by Robert Burns †1796 Sc poet]

**¹tamp** /tamp/ *vt* **1** to fill up (a drill hole above a blasting charge) with material (e g clay) to confine the force of the explosion **2** to drive in or down by a succession of light or medium blows ⟨~ *wet concrete*⟩ – often + *down* [prob backformation fr obs *tampion, tampin* plug, fr ME, fr MF *tapon, tampon*, fr (assumed) OF *taper* to plug, of Gmc origin; akin to OE *tæppa* tap] – **tamper** *n*

**²tamp** *n* a tool for tamping

**tamper** /'tampə/ *vi* **1** to carry on underhand or improper negotiations (e g by bribery) **2a** to interfere so as to cause weakening or change for the worse **b** to interfere without permission ⟨*the car lock had been* ~ed *with*⟩ **c** to try foolish or dangerous experiments □ usu + *with* [prob fr MF *temprer* to temper, mix, meddle – more at TEMPER] – **tamperer** *n*, **tamperproof** *adj*

**tampion** /'tampi·ən/ *n* a wooden plug or a metal or canvas cover for keeping dampness and dust out of the muzzle of a gun when not in use [obs *tampion, tampin* plug – more at TAMP]

**¹tampon** /'tampon/ *n* a plug (e g of cotton) introduced into a cavity (e g the vagina) usu to absorb secretions, stop bleeding, etc [Fr, lit., plug – more at TAMP]

**²tampon** *vt* to plug with a tampon

**tam-tam** /'tam ˌtam/ *n* **1** a tom-tom **2** a gong; *esp* any of a tuned set in a SE Asian flute, string, and percussion orchestra (GAMELAN orchestra) [Hindi *ṭamṭam*]

**Tamworth** /'tamwəth/ *n* (any of) a breed of large long-bodied red pigs that are used chiefly for bacon [*Tamworth*, town in Staffordshire, England]

**¹tan** /tan/ *vb* **-nn-** *vt* **1a** to convert (hide) into leather by treatment with an infusion of tannin-rich bark or other substance causing a similar effect **b** to convert (protein) to leather or a similar substance **2** to make (skin) tan, esp by exposure to the sun **3** *informal* to thrash, whip ~ *vi* to get or become tanned – see also **tan somebody's** HIDE [ME *tannen*, fr MF *tanner*, fr ML *tannare*, fr *tanum, tannum* tanbark, prob fr Celt origin] – **tanner** *n*

**²tan** *n* **1** a tanning material or its active agent (e g tannin) **2** a brown colour imparted to the skin by exposure to the sun or wind **3** a light yellowish-brown colour [Fr, tanbark, fr OF, fr ML *tanum*] – **tannish** *adj*

**³tan** *adj* **1** of or used for tan or tanning **2** of the colour of tan

**Tanach** /*Hebrew* ta'nax/ *n* the Jewish scriptures, which have three sections: the LAW, PROPHETS, and HAGIOGRAPHA [MHeb *tnk*, abbr of Heb *tōrāh, nĕbhī'īm, kĕthūbhīm* Pentateuch, Prophets, Hagiographa]

**tanager** /'tanəjə/ *n* any of numerous chiefly woodland American birds (family Thraupidae) of which the males are brightly coloured [NL *tanagra*, fr Pg *tangará*, fr Tupi]

**tanbark** /'tanˌbahk/ *n* a bark rich in tannin bruised or cut into small pieces and used in tanning

**¹tandem** /'tandəm/ *n* **1a** a 2-seat carriage drawn by horses harnessed one before the other; *also* a team so harnessed **b** a bicycle or tricycle having two or more seats one behind the other **2** a group of two or more arranged one behind the other or used or acting in conjunction [L, at last, at length (taken to mean "lengthwise"), fr *tam* so; akin to OE *thæt* that] – **in tandem 1** in a tandem arrangement **2** in partnership or conjunction

**²tandem** *adv* one after or behind another ⟨*ride* ~⟩

**³tandem** *adj* **1** consisting of things or having parts arranged one behind the other ⟨*a* ~ *pushchair*⟩ **2** working in conjunction with each other

**tandoor** /'tanˌdaw,-ˌdooh/ *n, pl* **tandoors, tandoori** a tall urn-shaped Indian clay oven typically fired by charcoal [Hindi *tāndur*, fr Ar *tannūr*, fr Aram *tannūra*, fr Akkadian *tinūru*]

**tandoori** /tan'dawri/ *n* food (e g a chicken) usu marinated in yoghurt, spices, etc and cooked in a tandoor, usu on a long

spit; *also* a N Indian method of cooking using a tandoor [Hindi *tānduri*, fr *tāndur* oven]

**¹tang** /tang/ *n* **1** a projecting shank or tongue (e g on a knife, file, or sword) that connects with and is enclosed by a handle **2a** a sharp distinctive often lingering flavour **b** a pungent smell **c** something having the effect of a tang (e g in stimulation of the senses) ⟨*treated murder as a joke with a* ~ *to it* – Graham Greene⟩ **3a** a faint suggestion; a trace **b** a distinguishing characteristic that sets apart or gives a special individuality [ME, of Scand origin; akin to ON *tangi* point of land, tang] – **tanged** *adj*

**²tang** *vt* to provide with a tang

**³tang** *n* any of various large coarse seaweeds (esp genus *Fucus*) [of Scand origin; akin to Dan & Norw *tang* seaweed]

**⁴tang** *vb* to clang, ring [imit]

**⁵tang** *n* a sharp twanging sound

**Tang** *n* a Chinese dynasty dated from AD 618 to 907 and marked by wide contacts with other cultures and by the development of printing and the flourishing of poetry and art – compare MING [Chin (Pek) *táng* (*t'ang²*)]

**tangelo** /'tanjiloh/ *n, pl* **tangelos** a cross between a tangerine or mandarin orange tree and a grapefruit or other closely related tree (e g a SHADDOCK); *also* its fruit [blend of *tangerine* and *pomelo*]

**tangency** /'tanjənsi/ *n* the quality or state of being tangent (e g at a point of a curve)

**¹tangent** /'tanjənt/ *adj* **1** being a tangent or TANGENT PLANE ⟨*straight line* ~ *to a curve*⟩ **2a** having a common tangent at a point ⟨~ *curves*⟩ **b** having a common tangent plane at a point ⟨~ *surfaces*⟩ [L *tangent-, tangens*, prp of *tangere* to touch; akin to OE *thaccian* to touch gently, stroke]

**²tangent** *n* **1** a fundamental and important mathematical function that for an angle is the ratio of the side opposite the angle to the side adjacent to the angle in a right-angled triangle and that hence can be expressed by $\tan x = \sin x/\cos x$ – compare COSINE, SINE **2** tangent, tangent line **2a** a straight line that touches a curve at one point only **b** a straight line that is the limiting position of a SECANT (straight line cutting a curve at two or more points) of a curve through a fixed point and variable point on the curve as the variable point approaches the fixed point – used technically **3** an abrupt change of course; a digression ⟨*the speaker went off on a* ~⟩ **4** an upright flat-ended metal pin at the inner end of the key of a CLAVICHORD (pianolike instrument) that strikes the string to produce the note **5** a straight section between curves on a road or railway [NL *tangent-, tangens*, fr *linea tangens* tangent line]

**tangential** /tan'jensh(ə)l/ *adj* **1** (of the nature) of a tangent **2** acting along or lying in a tangent ⟨~ *forces*⟩ **3a** divergent, digressive **b** touching lightly; incidental, peripheral ⟨~ *comment*⟩ – **tangentially** *adv*

**tangent plane** *n* a plane that touches a curved surface at only one point

**tangerine** /tanjə'reen/ *n* **1a** any of various mandarin oranges that have deep orange to almost scarlet skin and pulp and are widely cultivated in warm regions; *broadly* MANDARIN **3b b** a tree producing tangerines **2** a strong reddish-orange colour [Fr *Tanger* Tangier, city & port in Morocco]

> *synonyms* The **tangerine** is one kind of **mandarin**; another kind is the **satsuma**, which is seedless. The almost seedless **clementine** is a hybrid of the **tangerine** and the orange.

**tangi** /'tangˈgi/ *n* a period of ceremonial mourning that according to Maori custom precedes burial of the deceased; *also* the feast held at the ceremony [Maori]

**¹tangible** /'tanjəbl/ *adj* **1a** capable of being perceived, esp by the sense of touch **b** substantially real; material **2** capable of being precisely understood by the mind **3** capable of being assessed at an actual or approximate value ⟨~ *assets*⟩ *synonyms* SEE PERCEPTIBLE **antonym** intangible [LL *tangibilis*, fr L *tangere* to touch] – **tangibly** *adv*, **tangibility** *n*

**²tangible** *n* something tangible; *esp* a tangible asset

**¹tangle** /'tangˈgl/ *vt* **1** to involve so as to be trapped, hampered, obstructed, or embarrassed ⟨~d *in a hopeless controversy*⟩ **2** to bring together or intertwine in intricate and disordered confusion – often + *up* ~ *vi* **1** to become tangled **2** *informal* to engage in conflict or argument – usu + *with* **synonyms** see ¹COMPLEX [ME *tangilen*, prob fr Scand origin; akin to Sw dial. *taggla* to tangle]

**²tangle** *n* **1** a tangled twisted mass (e g of branches) confusedly interwoven **2a** a complicated or confused state or condition **b** a state of perplexity or complete bewilderment **3** *informal* a dispute, quarrel

**tangly** /'tang·gli/ *adj* full of tangles or knots; intricate, disordered

¹**tango** /'tang·goh/ *n, pl* **tangos** a ballroom dance of Latin-American origin with four beats to the bar and a basic pattern of step-step-step-step-pause, and characterized by long pauses and stylized body positions; *also* the music for this dance [AmerSp]

²**tango** *vi* **tangos; tangoing; tangoed** to dance the tango

**Tango** – a communications code word for the letter *t*

**tangram** /'tang·grəm, -,gram/ *n* a Chinese puzzle made by cutting a square into five triangles, a square, and a parallelogram which are capable of being recombined in many different figures [perh fr Chin (Pek) *táng* (*t'ang²*) Chinese + E -*gram*]

**tangy** /'tangi/ *adj* having or suggestive of a tang

¹**tank** /tangk/ *n* **1** a usu large receptacle for holding, transporting, or storing liquids or gas **2** an enclosed heavily armed and armoured combat vehicle that moves on caterpillar tracks **3a** *dial* a pond, pool **b** *Ind* a pool built as a water supply [Pg *tanque* pond, alter. of *estanque*, fr *estancar* to stanch, fr (assumed) VL *stanticare* – more at STANCH] – **tankful** *n*

²**tank** *vt* to place, store, or treat in a tank

**tanka** /'tangkə/ *n* an unrhymed Japanese verse form of five lines containing 5, 7, 5, 7, and 7 syllables respectively; *also* a poem in this form – compare HAIKU [Jap]

**tankage** /'tangkij/ *n* **1a** the capacity or contents of a tank **b** all the tanks required for a purpose **2** dried animal residues usu freed from the fat and gelatine and used as fertilizer and feedstuff **3a** the act or process of putting or storing in tanks **b** fees charged for storage in tanks

**tankard** /'tangkəd/ *n* **1** a tall one-handled drinking vessel; *esp* a silver or pewter mug with a lid **2** the quantity that a tankard holds [ME]

**tank destroyer** *n* an armoured fighting vehicle designed for engaging enemy armoured vehicles

,**tanked-'up, tanked** *adj, Br informal* drunk

**tank engine** *n* a steam locomotive that carries its own water and coal and does not have a separate vehicle (TENDER) for carrying them

**tanker** /'tangkə/ *n* a ship, aircraft, or road or rail vehicle designed to carry fluid, esp liquid, in bulk: eg **a** a ship designed to carry oil **b** an aircraft used for transporting fuel and usu capable of refuelling other aircraft in flight – **tankerful** *n*

**tank farm** *n* an area with tanks for storage of oil

**tank top** *n* a sleeveless usu knitted upper garment with a U-shaped neckline and no fastenings that is usu worn over another garment (eg a shirt or jumper) [earlier *tank suit* one-piece swimming costume, fr ¹*tank* (in the sense "swimming pool")]

**tank wagon** *n* a railway wagon for carrying liquids

**tannage** /'tanij/ *n* the act, process, or result of tanning

**tannate** /'tanayt/ *n* a compound of a tannin [Fr, fr *tannin*]

**tanner** /'tanə/ *n, Br informal* a coin worth six old pence [origin unknown]

**tannery** /'tanəri/ *n* a place where tanning is carried on

**tannic** /'tanik/ *adj* of, resembling, or derived from tan or a tannin [Fr *tannique*, fr *tannin*]

**tannic acid** *n* TANNIN 1

**tannin** /'tanin/ *n* **1** any of various soluble astringent complex substances of plant origin (eg bark) used esp in tanning, dyeing, and the making of ink **2** a substance that has a tanning effect [Fr, fr *tanner* to tan]

**tanning** /'taning/ *n* **1** the process by which a skin is tanned to produce leather **2** a browning of the skin by exposure to sun **3** a natural darkening and hardening of the CUTICLE (outer skin layer) of an insect immediately after moulting **4** *informal* a beating, thrashing

**tannoy** /'tanoy/ *vb* to broadcast over a Tannoy

**Tannoy** /'tanoy/ *trademark* – used for an apparatus that is used to broadcast to a large number of people, esp throughout a large building

**tan oak** *n* an evergreen oak (*Lithocarpus densiflora*) native to NW America that yields bark rich in tannin and differs from the typical oaks esp in having erect catkins

**Tanoan** /'tanohən/ *n* a language family of New Mexico belonging to the Aztec-Tanoan PHYLUM (large group) and related to the Uto-Aztecan phylum [*Tano*, a group of former Indian peoples in New Mexico] – **Tanoan** *adj*

**tansy** /'tanzi/ *n* an aromatic plant (*Chrysanthemum vulgare*) of the daisy family that has finely divided leaves and large clusters of yellow buttonlike flowers and is a common weed; *broadly*

any of various plants (genus *Chrysanthemum*) of the daisy family [ME *tanesey*, fr OF *tanesie*, fr ML *athanasia*, fr Gk, immortality, fr *athanatos* immortal, fr *a-* + *thanatos* death; prob fr its long-lasting flowers]

**tantalate** /'tantə,layt/ *n* any of various chemical compounds (SALTS) formed by combination between tantalic acid and a metal atom or another chemical group

**tantalic** /tan'talik/ *adj* of or derived from tantalum; *esp* being one of the weak acids derived from the chemical compound that is the PENTOXIDE of tantalum and known chiefly in tantalates

**tantalite** /'tantə,liet/ *n* a heavy dark lustrous mineral, (Fe, Mn) $Ta_2O_6$, consisting essentially of iron and tantalum oxide [Sw *tantalit*, fr NL *tantalum*]

**tantal·ize, -ise** /'tantəliez/ *vt* to tease or torment (as if) by presenting something desirable to the view but continually keeping it out of reach ~ *vi* to cause one to be tantalized [*Tantalus*, mythical king of Phrygia condemned in Hades to stand up to his chin in water that receded whenever he stooped to drink and under branches of fruit that receded whenever he tried to grasp them, fr L, fr Gk *Tantalos*] – **tantalizer** *n*

**tantal·izing, -ising** /'tantəliezing/ *adj* possessing a quality that arouses or stimulates desire or interest; *also* mockingly or teasingly out of reach – **tantalizingly** *adv*

**tantalum** /'tantələm/ *n* a hard grey-white acid-resisting metallic chemical element of the VANADIUM family found combined in rare minerals (eg tantalite and COLUMBITE) [NL, fr L *Tantalus*; fr its inability to absorb acid]

**tantalus** /'tantələs/ *n* a locked container for holding bottles or decanters of wine, spirits, etc in which the contents are visible but not obtainable without a key [fr *Tantalus*]

**tantamount** /'tantə,mownt/ *adj* equivalent in value, significance, or effect ⟨~ *to a declaration of war*⟩ [obs *tantamount*, n, equivalent, fr AF *tant amunter* to amount to as much]

**tantara** /'tantərə, tan'tahrə/ *n* the blare of a trumpet or horn [L *taratantara*, of imit origin]

**tantivy** /tan'tivi/ *n* a tantara [prob imit]

**tantra** /'tantrə, 'tuntrə/ *n, often cap* **1** any of a body of later Hindu and Buddhist scriptures marked by mysticism and magic **2** the doctrine and cult deriving from the tantras and including esp the worship of the Hindu god Shakti [Skt, lit., warp, fr *tanoti* he stretches, weaves; akin to Gk *teinein* to stretch – more at THIN] – **tantric** *adj, often cap*, **Tantrism** *n*, **Tantrist** *n*

**tantrum** /'tantrəm/ *n* a fit of childish bad temper [origin unknown]

**tanyard** /'tanyahd/ *n* the section or part of a tannery that houses tanning vats

**tanzanite** /'tanzə,niet/ *n* a mineral that is a deep blue variety of ZOISITE and is used as a gemstone [*Tanzania*, country in E Africa]

**Tao** /tow/ *n* **1** the principle of creative harmony which Taoists believe orders the universe **2** *often not cap* the path of virtuous conduct according to the teachings of the Chinese philosopher Confucius [Chin (Pek) *daò* (*tao⁴*), lit., way]

**Taoiseach** /'theeshəkh/ *n* the prime minister of the Republic of Ireland [IrGael, lit., leader]

**Taoism** /'towiz(ə)m/ *n* a Chinese mystical philosophy traditionally founded by Lao-tzu in the 6th century BC that teaches action in conformity with nature rather than striving against it; *also* a religion developed from this philosophy together with folk and Buddhist religion and concerned with obtaining long life and good fortune often by magical means [*Tao* + -*ism*] – **Taoist** *adj or n*, **Taoistic** *adj*

**Taos** /tows/ *n* a language of the TANOAN family

¹**tap** /tap/ *n* **1a** a plug for a hole, esp in a barrel **b** a device consisting of a spout and valve attached to a pipe, bowl, etc to control the flow of a fluid **2** the procedure of removing liquid (eg from a body cavity) ⟨*a pleural* ~⟩ **3** a tool for forming an internal screw thread **4** an intermediate point in an electric circuit where a connection may be made **5** the action or an instance of wiretapping [ME *tappe*, fr OE *tæppa*; akin to OHG *zapho* tap] – **on tap 1** *of beer* ON DRAUGHT **2** readily available

²**tap** *vt* -**pp**- **1** to let out or cause to flow by piercing or by drawing a plug from the containing vessel ⟨~ *wine from a cask*⟩ **2a** to pierce so as to let out or draw off a liquid ⟨~ *maple trees*⟩ **b** to draw from or on ⟨~ *new sources of revenue*⟩: eg **b(1)** to connect an electronic listening device to (a telegraph or telephone wire) in order to acquire information illegally or secretly **b(2)** to connect in (an electrical circuit) to another

circuit **3** to form an internal screw thread in by means of a tap **4** to connect (a street gas or water main) with a local supply **5** *informal* to get money from as a loan or gift – **tapper** *n*

³**tap** *vb* **-pp-** *vt* **1** to strike lightly, esp with a slight sound **2** to give a light blow with ⟨~ *a pencil on the table*⟩ **3** to produce or bring about by repeated light blows ⟨~ped *out a letter on the typewriter*⟩ ~ *vi* **1** to strike a light audible blow; rap **2** to perform a TAP DANCE [ME *tappen*, fr MF *taper* to strike with the flat of the hand, of Gmc origin; akin to MHG *tāpe* paw, blow dealt with the paw] – **tapper** *n*

⁴**tap** *n* **1a** a light usu audible blow; *also* its sound **b** any of several usu rapid drumbeats on a SNARE DRUM **2** a small plate for the sole or heel of a shoe made from hard material (e g metal)

¹**tapa** /'tahpə/ *n* **1** the bark of the PAPER MULBERRY tree **2** a coarse cloth made in the Pacific islands from the pounded bark of the PAPER MULBERRY, breadfruit, and other plants and usu decorated with geometric patterns [Marquesan & Tahitian]

²**tapa** *n usu pl* a snack or appetizer, esp as eaten in Spanish-speaking countries [Sp, fr *tapar* to stop up, cover]

**tap dance** *n* a STEP DANCE tapped out audibly by means of shoes with hard soles or soles and heels to which taps have been added – **tap-dance** *vi*, **tap dancer** *n*, **tap dancing** *n*

¹**tape** /tayp/ *n* **1** a narrow band of woven fabric **2** the string stretched chest-high above the finishing line of a running race **3a** a narrow flexible strip or band; *esp* MAGNETIC TAPE **b** a narrow roll of paper on which a teleprinter prints **5** **tape measure, tape** a narrow strip (e g of cloth or steel) marked off in units (e g inches or centimetres) for measuring [ME, fr OE *tæppe*]

²**tape** *vt* **1** to fasten, tie, bind, cover, or support with tape **2** to measure with a tape measure **3** to record on tape, esp MAGNETIC TAPE ⟨~ *an interview*⟩ ~ *vi* to record something on tape, esp MAGNETIC TAPE – **have somebody/something taped** *informal* to fully understand or have learnt how to deal with somebody or something

**tape deck** *n* a mechanism or self-contained unit that causes MAGNETIC TAPE to move past the heads of a magnetic recording device in order to generate electrical signals or make a recording

**tape grass** *n* a submerged aquatic plant (*Vallisneria spiralis* of the family Vallisneriaceae) with long ribbonlike leaves

**tape machine** *n* a telegraphic receiving instrument that automatically prints out information (e g share prices) on paper tape

¹**taper** /'taypə/ *n* **1a** a slender candle **b** a long waxed wick used esp for lighting candles, lamps, pipes, or fires **c** a feeble light **2a** a tapering form or figure **b** gradual diminution of thickness, diameter, or width in an elongated object **c** a gradual decrease [ME, fr OE *tapor, taper*]

²**taper** *vi* **1** to become gradually smaller in thickness, diameter, or width towards one end **2** to diminish gradually ⟨*his voice* ~ed *off*⟩ ~ *vt* to cause to taper □ often + *off*

'**tape-re,cord** /ri,kawd/ *vt* to make a tape recording of [back-formation fr *tape recording*]

**tape recorder** *n* a device for recording signals, esp sounds, on MAGNETIC TAPE and for subsequently reproducing them; *esp* such a device that includes an amplifier and loudspeaker

**taperer** /'taypərə/ *n* a person who bears a taper in a religious procession

**tapestry** /'tapəstri/ *n* **1** a heavy handwoven textile used for hangings, curtains, and upholstery and characterized by complicated pictorial designs **2** a machine-made imitation of tapestry used chiefly for upholstery **3** embroidery on canvas resembling woven tapestry **4** something resembling tapestry (e g in complexity or richness of design) [ME *tapistry*, modif of MF *tapisserie*, fr *tapisser* to carpet, cover with tapestry, fr OF *tapis* carpet, fr Gk *tapēs* rug, carpet] – **tapestried** *adj*

**tapestry carpet** *n* a carpet in which the designs are printed in colours on the threads before the fabric is woven

**tapetum** /tə'peetəm/ *n*, *pl* **tapeta** /-tə/ **1** a layer of nourishing cells that envelops the spore-producing tissue in the SPORANGIUM (walled structure containing spores) of higher plants **2** any of various membranous layers or areas, esp of the CHOROID COAT (layer outside the retina) and retina of the eye [NL, fr L *tapete* carpet, tapestry, fr. Gk *tapēt-, tapēs* rug, carpet]

**tapeworm** /'tayp,wuhm/ *n* any of numerous parasitic CESTODE worms (e g of the genus *Taenia*) that have a usu long body composed of a chain of segments in which eggs develop, a head bearing suckers and often hooks for attachment, and that when

adult infect the intestine of humans or other VERTEBRATE animals [fr its shape]

**taphole** /'tap,hohl/ *n* a hole for a tap; *specif* a hole at or near the bottom of a furnace or ladle through which molten metal, slag, etc can be tapped

**tapioca** /,tapi'ohkə/ *n* **1** a usu granular preparation of CASSAVA (tropical plant) starch used esp in puddings and as a thickening in liquid food; *also* a dish (e g a MILK PUDDING) containing tapioca **2** **tapioca, tapioca plant** a CASSAVA plant [Sp & Pg, fr Tupi *typyóca*]

**tapiolite** /'tapiəliet/ *n* a mineral, FeTa₂O₂, that consists of an oxide of iron and tantalum and resembles TANTALITE [Sw *tapiolit*, fr *Tapio*, Finnish god of forests]

**tapir** /'taypə/ *n*, *pl* **tapirs**, *esp collectively* **tapir** any of several large chiefly nocturnal hoofed mammals (family Tapiridae) found in tropical America, Malaya, and Sumatra that have long snouts and are related to the horses and rhinoceroses [Tupi *tapiíra*]

**tapis** /'tapee, 'tapi (*Fr* tapi)/ *n*, *obs* tapestry or similar material used for hangings and floor and table coverings [MF – more at TAPESTRY]

**tappet** /'tapit/ *n* a lever or projection moved by some other piece (e g a CAM) intended to tap or touch something else to cause a particular motion (e g in the gear that operates valves in certain types of engine) [³*tap* + *-et*]

**tappit hen** /'tapit/ *n*, *Scot* a drinking vessel with a knob on the lid [Sc, lit., crested hen, fr *tappit*, alter. of E *topped*]

**taproom** /'tap,roohm, -room/ *n* a bar; *specif* a room (e g in a tavern) where alcoholic drinks, esp beer, are kept on tap

**taproot** /-,rooht/ *n* a main root that grows vertically downwards and gives off small side roots [¹*tap*]

**taps** /taps/ *n taking sing or pl vb*, *chiefly NAm* the last bugle call at night blown as a signal that lights are to be put out; *also* a similar call blown at military funerals and memorial services [prob alter. of earlier *taptoo* tattoo – more at TATTOO]

**tapster** /'tapstə/ *n* someone employed to serve drinks in a bar

**tapu** /'tahpooh, -'-/ *n or adj*, *pl* **tapus** *NZ* (a) taboo [Maori]

¹**tar** /tah/ *n* **1a** a dark brown or black usu strong-smelling thick liquid obtained by DESTRUCTIVE DISTILLATION (decomposition by heat) of organic material (e g wood, coal, or peat) **b** a substance in some respects resembling tar; *esp* a residue present in smoke from burning tobacco that contains combustion by-products (e g resins, acids, and ESSENTIAL OILS) **2** *informal* a sailor [ME *terr, tarr*, fr OE *teoru*; akin to OE *trēow* tree – more at TREE; (2) short for *tarpaulin*]

²**tar** *vt* **-rr-** to smear or cover (as if) with tar or TARMACADAM ⟨~red *roads*⟩ – **tar and feather** to smear (a person) with tar and cover with feathers as a punishment or humiliation

**Taracahitian** /,tarəkə'heesh(ə)n/ *adj* of or constituting a language family of the UTO-AZTECAN group (PHYLUM) [*Tarahumara* (a Mexican people) + *Cahita* (a Mexican people)]

**taradiddle, tarradiddle** /'tarə,did(ə)l/ *n*, *informal* **1** a minor falsehood **2** pretentious nonsense [origin unknown]

**taramasalata, taramosalata** /,tarəməsə'lahtə/ *n* a pinkish paste made from the roe of GREY MULLET or smoked cod, seasoned with garlic and lemon juice, and served as an appetizer [NGk *taramosalata*, fr *taramas* preserved roe + *salata* salad]

**tarantass** /,tahrən'tas/ *n* a low 4-wheeled Russian carriage [Russ *tarantas*]

**tarantella** /,tarən'telə/ *n* **1** a vivacious folk dance of southern Italy with two strong beats to the bar, each followed by two weaker beats **2** music suitable for the tarantella and usu alternating between major and minor keys [It, fr *Taranto*, city in S Italy]

**tarantism** /'tarən,tiz(ə)m/ *n* a nervous disease causing dancelike body movements, which occurred in 15th- to 17th-century Italy and was popularly attributed to the bite of the tarantula [NL *tarantismus*, fr *Taranto*]

**tarantula** /tə'ranchoolə/ *n*, *pl* **tarantulas** *also* **tarantulae** /-li/ **1** a European WOLF SPIDER (*Lycosa tarentula*) formerly held to be the cause of tarantism **2** any of various large hairy spiders (family Theraphosidae) that are typically rather sluggish and though capable of biting sharply are not significantly poisonous to humans [ML, fr OIt *tarantola*, fr *Taranto*]

**tarboosh** *also* **tarbush** /tah'boohsh/ *n* a usu red roughly cylindrical brimless hat similar to the fez worn esp by Muslim men [Ar *ṭarbūsh*]

**tardigrade** /'tahdi,grayd/ *n or adj* (any) of a division (Tardigrada of the phylum Arthropoda) of microscopic INVERT-

EBRATE animals that have a flattened body with four pairs of clawed legs and that live usu in water or damp moss [deriv of L *tardigradus* slow-moving, fr *tardus* slow + *gradi* to step, go – more at GRADE]

**tardy** /'tahdi/ *adj* **1** moving or progressing slowly; sluggish **2** delayed beyond the expected or proper time; late [alter. of earlier *tardif*, fr MF, fr (assumed) VL *tardivus*, fr L *tardus*] – **tardily** *adv*, **tardiness** *n*

synonyms Tardy, dilatory, late, behindhand, and overdue all mean "after the right time". Tardy applies to people's failure to be in time, either from unpunctuality or through unavoidable delay ⟨**tardy** arrivals at the theatre disturbing the rest of the audience⟩. Dilatory definitely implies that the failure to be in time is due to people's inertia or indifference ⟨though **dilatory** in undertaking business, he was quick in its execution – Jane Austen⟩. Late focuses on the fact of not being in time, and need not imply blame ⟨a **late** spring⟩ ⟨train was **late**⟩. Behindhand refers to the inability to keep pace ⟨**behindhand** with my work⟩. Overdue emphasizes the idea that something ought to have happened by now ⟨her baby is **overdue**⟩. The degree to which something is late, behindhand, or overdue can be specified ⟨ten minutes **late**⟩ ⟨a week **behindhand**⟩ ⟨long **overdue**⟩. antonyms prompt, punctual

**¹tare** /teə/ *n* **1a** the seed of a VETCH (plant of the pea family) **b** any of several VETCHES (esp *Vicia sativa* and *Vicia hirsuta*) **2** *pl* a weed found in grainfields which is usu held to be DARNEL – used in the Bible [ME]

**²tare** *n* **1a** the weight of the wrapping material or container in which goods are packed **b** a deduction from the total weight of a substance and its container made in allowance for the weight of the container **2** the weight of an unloaded goods vehicle **3** a counterweight; *esp* an empty vessel similar to a container used to counterbalance change in weight of the container due to conditions (of temperature, moisture, etc) [ME, fr MF, fr OIt *tara*, fr Ar *ṭarḥa*, lit., that which is removed]

**³tare** *vt* to weigh in order to calculate the tare

**targe** /tahj/ *n, archaic* a light shield [ME, fr OF]

**¹target** /'tahgit/ *n* **1** a small round shield **2a** an object to fire at in practice or competition; *esp* one consisting of a series of concentric circles marked esp on a paper or wooden surface, with a bull's-eye at the centre **b** something (eg an aircraft, ship, or installation) fired at or attacked **3a** an object of ridicule, criticism, etc **b** something to be affected by an action or development **c** a goal to be achieved **4** a sliding sight on a surveyor's LEVELLING STAFF **5a** the surface, usu of platinum or tungsten, on which the stream of CATHODE RAYS (electrons projected at high speed) in an X-ray tube is focussed and from which the X rays are emitted **b** a body, surface, or material bombarded with nuclear particles or electrons [ME, fr MF *targette*, dim. of *targe* light shield, of Gmc origin; akin to ON *targa* shield]

**²target** *vt* **1** to make a target of; *esp* to set as a goal **2** to aim at a target – often + *on* ⟨missiles have been ∼ed *on Moscow*⟩

usage Although **target** is often used today to mean a "goal", our sense of its earlier meaning as an object to fire at makes it odd to speak of *reaching, achieving, raising*, or *exceeding* a **target**, of being *short* of it, or of its being *within sight*.

**target date** *n* the date set for an event or for the completion of a project, goal, or quota

**target language** *n* **1** a language into which another language is to be translated – compare SOURCE LANGUAGE **2** a language which is to be learnt

**target practice** *n* the act of shooting at a target to improve one's aim

**Targum** /'tahgəm/ *n* an ARAMAIC (old language of the Middle East) translation or paraphrase of a portion of the OLD TESTAMENT [LHeb *targŭm*, fr Aram, translation]

**¹tariff** /'tarif/ *n* **1a** a schedule of duties imposed by a government on imported, or in some countries exported, goods **b** a duty or rate of duty imposed in such a schedule **2** (a schedule of) the rates or charges of a business or public service (eg an electricity board) **3** *chiefly Br* a menu [It *tariffa*, fr Ar *ta'rīf* notification]

**²tariff** *vt* to make a tariff on; value according to a tariff

**tarlatan** /'tahlətən/ *n* a thin usu stiffened cotton fabric in open PLAIN WEAVE (with alternately interlacing threads) [Fr *tarlatane*]

**¹tarmac** /'tahmak/ *n* **1** tarmacadam **2** a runway or road surfaced with tarmac

**²tarmac** *vt* **-ck-** to apply tarmac to

**tarmacadam** /ˌtahmə'kadəm/ *n* **1** a surface (eg of a road or

runway) constructed by spraying or pouring a tar binder over layers of crushed stone and then rolling – compare MACADAM **2** a mixture of tar and materials such as sand, gravel, etc used for surfacing roads

**tarn** /tahn/ *n* a small steep-banked mountain lake or pool [ME *tarne*, of Scand origin; akin to ON *tjörn* small lake; akin to OE *teran* to tear]

**tarnation** /tah'naysh(ə)n/ *n, chiefly NAm euph* damnation [alter. (influenced by *tarnal*, alter. of *eternal*) of *darnation*, alter. of *damnation*]

**¹tarnish** /'tahnish/ *vt* **1** to dull or destroy the lustre of (as if) by air, dust, or dirt; soil, stain **2a** to detract from the good quality of ⟨his fine dreams now slightly ∼ed⟩ **b** to bring disgrace on; sully ∼ *vi* to become tarnished [MF *terniss-*, stem of *ternir* to dull] – **tarnishable** *adj*

**²tarnish** *n* something that tarnishes; *esp* a film of chemically altered material on the surface of a metal (eg silver)

**tarnished plant bug** *n* a common and widespread destructive bug (*Lygus rugulipennis*) that causes decline and disfigurement of plants by sucking sap from buds, leaves, and fruits

**taro** /'tahroh/ *n, pl* **taros** a plant (*Colocasia esculenta*) of the arum family grown throughout the tropics for its edible starchy thick fleshy underground stems and in temperate regions for ornament; *also* its underground stems [Tahitian & Maori]

**tarok** /'tarok/ *n* an old card game popular in central Europe and played with a pack containing 40, 52, or 56 cards equivalent to modern playing cards plus the 22 tarots [It *tarocchi* tarots]

**tarot** /'taroh/ *n* any of a set of 22 pictorial playing cards used for fortune-telling and serving as trumps in tarok [MF, fr It *tarocchi* (pl)]

**tarpan** /'tahpan/ *n* an extinct wild brown horse (*Equus caballus gomelini*) of Central Asia [Russ]

**tarpaulin** /tah'pawlin/ *n* material (eg waterproofed canvas) used for protecting objects or ground exposed to the elements; *also* a piece of such material [earlier *tarpauling, tarpawling*, prob fr ¹*tar* + ¹*pall* + *-ing*]

**tarpon** /'tahpən/ *n, pl* **tarpons**, *esp collectively* **tarpon** a large silvery elongated sea fish (*Tarpon atlanticus*) that is common off the coast of Florida [origin unknown]

**tarradiddle** /'tarəˌdid(ə)l/ *n* TARADIDDLE

**tarragon** /'tarəgən/ *n* a European plant (*Artemisia dracunculus*) of the daisy family grown for its pungent aromatic leaves which are used as a flavouring (eg in making chicken dishes and vinegar); *also* its leaves [MF *targon*, fr ML *tarchon*, fr Ar *ṭarkhūn*]

**Tarragona** /ˌ(Spanish tarra'yona)/ a sweet fortified wine made in Catalonia in Spain [Sp, fr *Tarragona*, Spain]

**tarrah** /tə'rah/ *interj, Br informal* goodbye, ta-ta [origin unknown]

**tarriance** /'tari(ə)ns/ *n, formal* the act or an instance of tarrying

**¹tarry** /'tari/ *vi* **1a** to delay or be slow in acting or doing **b** to linger in expectation; wait **2** to stay in or at a place *synonyms* see ³STAY [ME *tarien*]

**²tarry** /'tahri/ *adj* of, like, or covered with tar

**¹tarsal** /'tahs(ə)l/ *adj* **1** of the tarsus **2** being or relating to plates of dense CONNECTIVE TISSUE that stiffen the eyelids

**²tarsal** *n* a tarsal part (eg a bone or cartilage)

**tarseal** /'tahseel/ *n, NZ* TARMAC – **tarsealed** *adj*

**tarsia** /'tahsi·ə/ *n* INTARSIA (mosaic, usu of wood) [It, fr Ar *tarsī*]

**tarsier** /'tahsi·ə/ *n* any of several small nocturnal tree-dwelling E Indian mammals (genus *Tarsius*) related to the lemurs [Fr, fr *tarse* tarsus, fr NL *tarsus*; fr its very long tarsal bones]

**tarsometatarsus** /ˌtahsohˌmetə'tahsis/ *n* the large compound bone of the tarsus of a bird; *also* the segment of the limb it supports [NL, fr *tarsus* + *-o-* + *metatarsus*]

**tarsus** /'tahsəs/ *n, pl* **tarsi** /-sie/ **1** the part of the foot of a VERTEBRATE animal between the METATARSUS and the leg; the ankle; *also* the small bones that support this part of the limb **2** the tarsometatarsus **3** the part of the limb of an insect, spider, crab, or related animal that is furthest from the body **4** the tarsal plate of the eyelid [NL, fr Gk *tarsos* wickerwork mat, flat of the foot, ankle, edge of the eyelid; akin to Gk *tersesthai* to become dry – more at THIRST]

**¹tart** /taht/ *adj* **1** agreeably sharp or acid to the taste **2** marked by a biting, acrimonious, or cutting quality ⟨a ∼ reply⟩ [ME, fr OE *teart* sharp, severe; akin to MHG *traz* spite] – **tartish** *adj*, **tartishly** *adv*, **tartly** *adv*, **tartness** *n*

²**tart** *n* **1** a pastry shell or shallow pie containing a usu sweet filling (e g jam, custard, or fruit) **2** *informal* a female prostitute; *broadly* a girl or woman who is or who appears (e g by the clothes she wears) to be of immoral character [ME *tarte*, fr MF; (2) prob partly short for *sweetheart*]

**tartan** /'taht(ə)n/ *n* **1** a textile design of Scottish origin consisting of checks of varying width and colour, usu patterned to designate a particular clan **2** a fabric, specif a TWILLED (woven with an appearance of diagonal lines) woollen fabric, with tartan design **3** a garment made of tartan [prob fr MF *tiretaine* linsey-woolsey]

**tartan Tory** *n, derog* a Scottish Conservative

¹**tartar** /'tahtə/ *n* **1** a substance consisting essentially of CREAM OF TARTAR that is derived from the juice of grapes and deposited in wine casks together with yeast and other suspended material as a pale or dark reddish crust or sediment; *esp* a recrystallized product yielding CREAM OF TARTAR when further purified **2** an incrustation on the teeth consisting of salivary secretion, food residue, and various calcium-containing chemical compounds – compare PLAQUE [ME, fr ML *tartarum*]

²**tartar** *n* **1** *cap, NAm chiefly* **Tatar 1a** a member of a group of peoples found mainly in the Tartar Republic of the USSR, the N Caucasus, Crimea, and parts of Siberia **b** the language of the Tartars, which belongs to the TURKIC subfamily of languages **2** *often cap, informal* **2a** a person of irritable or violent temper **b** a person who is unexpectedly formidable **c** a rigorously exacting person ⟨*a ~ when it comes to punctuality*⟩ [ME *Tartre*, fr MF *Tartare*, deriv of Per *Tātār*, of Turkic origin] – **Tartar** *adj*, **Tartarian** *adj*

**Tartarean** /tah'teəriən,-'tari-/ *adj* of or like Tartarus, a section of the abode of the dead in Greek mythology that was reserved for punishment of the worst offenders; infernal [L *tartareus*, fr Gk *tartareios*, fr *Tartaros* Tartarus]

**tartar emetic** *n* a complex tartrate containing the chemical elements antimony and potassium, $2[K.SbO.C_4H_4O_6].H_2O$, that is used in dyeing as a MORDANT (substance that combines with and fixes a dye) and in medicine esp in the treatment of SCHISTOSOMIASIS (tropical disease caused by parasitic worms)

**tartaric acid** /tah'tarik/ *n* a strong acid, $HOOCCH(OH)CH(OH)COOH$, of plant origin that occurs in four different structural forms, is usu obtained from tartar, and is used esp in food and medicines, in photography, and in making various chemical compounds (e g SALTS and ESTERS)

**tartar sauce, tartare sauce** /'tahtə/ *n* mayonnaise with chopped pickles, olives, capers, and parsley added [Fr *sauce tartare*]

**tartlet** /'tahtlit/ *n* a small tart

**tartrate** /'tahtrayt/ *n* any of various chemical compounds (SALTS or ESTERS) formed by combination between TARTARIC ACID and a metal atom, an alcohol, or another chemical group [ISV, fr Fr *tartre* tartar, fr ML *tartarum*]

**tart up** *vt, chiefly Br informal* to dress up, esp with cheap or gaudy ornaments and decorations ⟨*tarted up pubs and restaurants for the spenders* – Arnold Ehrlich⟩

**tarty** /'tahti/ *adj, informal* of or like a prostitute or tarted-up woman – **tartiness** *n*

**Tarzan** /'tahz(ə)n, 'tahzan/ *n* a well-built, agile, and very strong man [*Tarzan*, hero of adventure stories by Edgar Rice Burroughs †1950 US writer]

**tash** /tash/ *n, Br informal* a moustache [by shortening & alter.]

¹**task** /tahsk/ *n* **1** a usu assigned piece of work, often to be finished within a certain time **2** something hard or unpleasant that has to be done; a chore **3** a duty, function [ME *taske*, fr ONF *tasque*, fr ML *tasca* tax or service imposed by a feudal superior, fr *taxare* to tax] – **take/call/bring somebody to task** to subject somebody to adverse criticism; reprimand somebody

*synonyms* Task, assignment, duty, job, chore, and stint all mean "piece of work to be done". A **task** is typically more or less brief and burdensome, and is either imposed by authority ⟨*read the book as a school holiday* **task**⟩ or undertaken voluntarily ⟨*set himself the* **task** *of weeding the border*⟩. An **assignment** is a definite piece of work imposed by authority ⟨*the reporter's* **assignment** *was to interview the minister*⟩. **Duty** usually suggests what one must or should do because of one's occupation or position ⟨*it's not one of a waitress's* **duties** *to wash the glasses*⟩. **Job** is a general word which can mean one's paid employment, but in this context it particularly means a task assigned and undertaken at a stated rate ⟨*building the bridge was a bigger* **job** *than the firm expected*⟩. A **chore**

is a small recurrent piece of work ⟨*do the morning* **chores** *on the farm*⟩ or a tedious one ⟨*all that photocopying will be rather a* **chore**⟩. A **stint** is a measured or timed amount of work ⟨*ten pages is my daily* **stint**⟩.

²**task** *vt* **1** to assign a task to **2** to burden with great labour; subject to severe exertion ⟨*~s his mind with petty details*⟩ **3** *obs* to impose a tax on

**task force** *n* a temporary grouping, usu of armed forces, under one leader for the purpose of accomplishing a definite objective

**taskmaster** /-,mahstə/, *fem* **taskmistress** /-,mistris/ *n* one who assigns tasks, esp with specified severity ⟨*a hard ~*⟩

**Tasmanian devil** /taz'maynyən, -ni-ən/ *n* a powerful bearlike flesh-eating burrowing Tasmanian marsupial mammal (*Sarcophilus harrisi*) that is about the size of a badger and has a black coat marked with white on the chest [*Tasmania*, island off SE Australia]

**Tasmanian wolf** *n* a flesh-eating marsupial mammal (*Thylacinus cynocephalus*) that somewhat resembles a dog and was formerly common in Australia but is now limited to the remoter parts of Tasmania – called also THYLACINE

**tasse** /tas/ *n* any of a series of overlapping metal plates in a suit of armour that form a short skirt over the body below the waist [perh fr MF *tasse* purse, pouch]

¹**tassel** /'tasl/ *n* **1** a dangling ornament (e g for a curtain, bedspread, or end of a belt) consisting of a bunch of cords or threads, usu of even length, fastened at one end **2** something resembling a tassel; *esp* the end male flower of some plants, esp maize [ME, clasp, tassel, fr OF, prob fr (assumed) VL *tassellus*, fr L *taxillus* small die; akin to L *talus* anklebone, die]

²**tassel** *vb* **-ll-** (*NAm* **-l-, -ll-**) *vt* to decorate with tassels ~ *vi* to form tassel flowers

¹**taste** /tayst/ *vt* **1** to experience, undergo ⟨*has ~d the frustration of defeat*⟩ **2** to test the flavour of by taking a little into the mouth **3** to eat or drink, esp in small quantities ⟨*the first food he has ~d in two days*⟩ **4** to perceive or recognize (as if) by the sense of taste ⟨*could ~ the salt on his lips*⟩ ⟨*her confidence grew after she ~d success*⟩ ~ *vi* **1** to test the flavour of something by taking a small part into the mouth **2a** to have a specified flavour ⟨*the milk ~s sour*⟩ – often + *of* ⟨*this drink ~s of aniseed*⟩ **b** to have a specified import when tasted; seem ⟨*the stew ~s peculiar*⟩ **3** *formal* to have perception, experience, or enjoyment; partake – often + *of* ⟨*~ of the fruits of your labour*⟩ [ME *tasten* to touch, test, taste, fr OF *taster*, fr (assumed) VL *taxitare*, freq of L *taxare* to touch – more at TAX]

*usage* When **taste** means "seem when tasted" it is followed by an adjective ⟨**taste** *salty*⟩ or by a phrase ⟨**taste** *of turpentine*⟩. An adverb used with **taste** describes the way of testing a flavour ⟨*she* **tasted** *it cautiously*⟩.

²**taste** *n* **1a** the act of tasting **b** a small amount tasted **c** a small amount; a bit; *esp* a sample of experience ⟨*her first ~ of success*⟩ **2** the one of the five basic physical senses by which the qualities of dissolved substances in contact with TASTE BUDS on the tongue are interpreted by the brain as one or a combination of the four basic taste sensations: sweet, bitter, sour, or salt **3** the quality of a dissolved substance as perceived by the sense of taste **4a** a sensation produced by the stimulation of the sense of taste typically combined with those of touch and smell; a flavour **b** the distinctive quality of an experience ⟨*his attempt to cheat left a bad ~ in my mouth*⟩ **5** individual preference; inclination **6** critical judgment, discernment, or appreciation **7** *obs* a test

**taste bud** *n* any of the small SENSE ORGANS, chiefly on the surface of the tongue, that receive and transmit the sensation of taste

**tasteful** /-f(ə)l/ *adj* having, showing or conforming to good taste – **tastefully** *adv*, **tastefulness** *n*

**tasteless** /-lis/ *adj* **1a** having no taste; insipid ⟨*~ vegetables*⟩ **b** arousing no interest; dull **2** not having or showing good taste – **tastelessly** *adv*, **tastelessness** *n*

**taster** /'taystə/ *n* **1** one who or that which tastes; *esp* someone who tests something (e g tea) for quality by tasting **2** a device for tasting or sampling; *esp* a tastevin

**tastevin** /'tayst,vanh/ *n* a shallow metal cup used in testing wine [Fr *tâte-vin, taste-vin*, fr MF *taste vin* drunkard, cup for testing wine, fr *taster* to test, taste + *vin* wine, fr L *vinum*]

**tasty** /'taysti/ *adj* **1** having a marked and appetizing flavour **2** strikingly attractive or interesting ⟨*stopped to listen to a ~ bit of gossip*⟩ – **tastily** *adv*, **tastiness** *n*

**¹tat** /tat/ *vb* **-tt-** *vi* to work at tatting ~ *vt* to make by tatting [back-formation fr *tatting*]

**²tat** *n, Br informal* low quality material or matter [back-formation fr *tatty*]

**ta-ta** /'tah ˌtah/ *interj, chiefly Br informal* – used to express farewell [baby talk]

**tatami** /ta'tahmi/ *n, pl* **tatami, tatamis** a straw mat of a standard size used as a floor covering in a Japanese home [Jap]

**Tatar** /'tahtə/ *n* ²TARTAR 1

**tater** /'taytə/ *n, dial* a potato [by shortening & alter.]

**tatie** /'tayti/ *n, dial* a potato [by shortening & alter.]

**tatter** /'tatə/ *n* 1 a part torn and left hanging; a shred 2 *pl* tattered clothing; rags [ME, of Scand origin; akin to ON *tǫturr* tatter; akin to OHG *zotta* matted hair, tuft] – **in tatters 1** torn in pieces; ragged 2 in disarray; useless

**tatterdemalion** /ˌtatədi'maly(ə)n, -'mal-/ *n* a person dressed in ragged clothing; a ragamuffin [*tatter* + *-demalion,* of unknown origin]

**tattered** /'tatəd/ *adj* 1 wearing ragged clothes ⟨*a* ~ *barefoot boy*⟩ 2 torn into shreds; ragged 3 dilapidated

**tattersall** /'tatəˌsawl/ *n* 1 a pattern of coloured lines forming squares of solid background 2 a fabric woven or printed in a tattersall pattern [fr the pattern of the horse-blankets orig used at *Tattersall's* horse market in London]

**tattie, tatty** /'tati/ *n, dial* a potato [by shortening & alter.]

**tatting** /'tating/ *n* 1 a delicate thread lace formed usu by making loops and knots using a single cotton thread and a small shuttle 2 the act, process, or art of making tatting [origin unknown]

**¹tattle** /'tatl/ *vb* **tattling** *vi* 1 to talk idly; chatter, gossip 2 to disclose secrets by gossiping ~ *vt* to utter or disclose in gossip or chatter [MD *tatelen;* akin to ME *tateren* to tattle] – **tattler** *n*

**²tattle** *n* idle talk; chatter, gossip

**tattletale** /'tatlˌtayl/ *n, chiefly NAm* a tattler, telltale

**¹tattoo** /ta'tooh/ *n, pl* **tattoos 1a** an evening drum or bugle call sounded as notice to troops to return to quarters **b** an outdoor military exercise given by troops as a usu evening entertainment 2 a rapid rhythmic beating or rapping [alter. of earlier *taptoo,* fr D *taptoe,* fr the phrase *tap toe!* taps shut!]

**²tattoo** *vb* **tattoos; tattooing; tattooed** *vt* to beat or rap rhythmically on; drum on ~ *vi* to give a series of rhythmic taps

**³tattoo** *n, pl* **tattoos 1** the act or practice of tattooing the skin 2 an indelible mark or figure fixed on the body by the insertion of pigment under the skin [Tahitian *tatau*]

**⁴tattoo** *vt* **tattoos; tattooing; tattooed 1** to mark or colour (the skin) with tattoos 2 to mark the skin with (a tattoo) ⟨~ed *a flag on his chest*⟩ – **tattooer, tattooist** *n*

**¹tatty** /'tati/ *adj, informal* rather worn or frayed; shabby, dilapidated [perh akin to OE *tætteca* rag, ON *tǫturr* tatter – more at TATTER]

**²tatty** *n, dial* a potato [by shortening & alter.]

**tau** /taw, tow/ *n* the 19th letter of the Greek alphabet [Gk, of Sem origin; akin to Heb *tāw* taw]

**tau cross** *n* a T-shaped cross, sometimes having expanded ends and foot

**taught** /tawt/ *past of* TEACH

**¹taunt** /tawnt/ *vt* to reproach or challenge in a mocking or insulting manner; jeer at **synonyms** see ²RIDICULE [perh fr MF *tenter* to try, tempt – more at TEMPT] – **taunter** *n,* **tauntingly** *adv*

**²taunt** *n* a sarcastic challenge or insult

**taupe** /tohp/ *adj or n* (of) a brownish-grey colour [n Fr, lit., mole, fr L *talpa; adj* fr *n*]

**¹taurine** /'tawreen, -rin/ *adj* of or like a bull [L *taurinus,* fr *taurus* bull; akin to Gk *tauros* bull, MIr *tarb*]

**²taurine** *n* a chemical compound, $NH_2CH_2CH_2SO_3H$, that is an AMINO ACID of neutral reaction found in the juices of muscle, esp in INVERTEBRATE animals, and is produced by the breakdown of taurocholic acid [ISV, fr L *taurus* bull; fr its having been discovered in ox bile]

**taurocholic** /ˌtawroh'kohlik/ *adj* of or being an acid, $(HO)_3C_{23}H_{36}CONHCH_2CH_2SO_3H$, that is DELIQUESCENT (absorbs moisture from the air), and occurs in the form of its sodium SALT in the bile of man, the ox, and various carnivores [L *taurus* + ISV *-o-* + *cholic* (acid)]

**Taurus** /'tawrəs/ *n* 1 a constellation of the ZODIAC (imaginary belt in the heavens) lying between Aries and Gemini, close to Orion, and represented as a bull **2a** the 2nd sign of the zodiac in astrology, held to govern the period April 21- May 22 approx **b** somebody born under this sign [ME, fr L, lit., bull] – **Taurean** *adj* or *n*

**¹taut** /tawt/ *adj* **1a** having no give or slack; tightly drawn; tensely stretched **b** showing anxiety; tense 2 kept in proper order or condition ⟨*a* ~ *ship*⟩ **synonyms** see ¹STIFF *antonym* slack △ taught [ME *tought*] – **tautly** *adv,* **tautness** *n*

**²taut** *vt, Scot* to mat, tangle [origin unknown]

**taut-, tauto-** *comb form* same ⟨*tautomerism*⟩ ⟨*tautonym*⟩ [LL, fr Gk, fr *tauto* the same, contr of *to auto*]

**tauten** /'tawt(ə)n/ *vb* to make or become taut

**tautog** /'tawtog/ *n* an edible fish (*Tautoga onitis*) of the WRASSE family found along the Atlantic coast of the USA [Narraganset *tautauog,* pl]

**tautological** /ˌtawtə'lojikl/ *adj* tautologous – **tautologically** *adv*

**tautologous** /taw'toləgəs *also* -jes/ *adj* 1 involving or containing rhetorical tautology; redundant 2 true by virtue of its logical form, analytic [Gk *tautologos,* fr *taut-* + *legein* to say –more at LEGEND] – **tautologously** *adv*

**tautology** /taw'toləji/ *also* **tautologism** /-jiz(ə)m/ *n* 1 needless repetition of an idea, statement, or word (eg in "He sat alone by himself"); *also* an instance of this 2 a logically tautologous statement (eg "Her statement is either true or false") [LL *tautologia,* fr Gk, fr *tautologos*]

**tautomer** /'tawtəmə/ *n* any of the forms of a tautomeric compound [ISV, fr *tautomeric*]

**tautomeric** /ˌtawtə'merik/ *adj* of or marked by tautomerism [ISV]

**tautomerism** /taw'toməriz(ə)m/ *n* ISOMERISM (relationship between chemical compounds having the same composition but differing in structure and chemical properties) in which the related forms (ISOMERS) change into one another with great ease so that they ordinarily exist together in equilibrium

**tavern** /'tavən/ *n* an establishment where alcoholic drinks are sold to be drunk on the premises; *also* an inn [ME *taverne,* fr OF, fr L *taberna,* lit., shed, hut, shop, fr *trabs* beam]

**taverner** /'tavənə/ *n* someone who keeps a tavern

**¹taw** /taw/ *vt* to prepare (skins), usu by a dry process (eg with ALUM or salt) [ME *tawen* to prepare for use, fr OE *tawian;* akin to L *bonus* good]

**²taw** *n* the line from which players shoot at marbles [origin unknown]

**³taw** *vi* to shoot or propel a marble

**⁴taw** *n* the 23rd and last letter of the Hebrew alphabet [Heb *tāw,* lit., mark, cross]

**¹tawdry** /'tawdri/ *n, formal* cheap showy finery [obs *tawdry lace* necklace, alter. of *St Audrey's lace,* fr *St Audrey* (Etheldreda) †679 queen of Northumbria; fr its being orig sold at a fair commemorating St Audrey]

**²tawdry** *adj* cheap and tastelessly showy in appearance and quality – **tawdrily** *adv,* **tawdriness** *n*

**tawny** /'tawni/ *adj* 1 of a warm sandy colour like that of well-tanned skin ⟨*the lion's* ~ *coat*⟩ 2 *of port* having a golden-brown colour as a result of several years' maturation in barrel [ME, fr MF *tanné,* pp of *tanner* to tan] – **tawny** *n,* **tawniness** *n*

**tawny owl** *n* a common brown European owl (*Strix aluco*)

**tawpie** /'tawpi/ *n, chiefly Scot* a foolish or awkward young person [of Scand origin; akin to Norw *tåpe* simpleton]

**tawse** /tawz/ *also* **taws** *n, chiefly Scot* a leather strap slit into strips at the end, used esp for beating children; *also the* punishment of being beaten with a tawse ⟨*gave him three of the* ~⟩ [prob fr pl of obs *taw* (tawed leather)]

**¹tax** /taks/ *vt* 1 to assess or determine judicially the amount of (costs in a court action) 2 to levy a tax on 3 to charge, accuse; *also* to censure ⟨~ed *him with neglect of his duty*⟩ 4 to make onerous and rigorous demands on ⟨*the job* ~ed *his strength*⟩ [ME *taxen* to estimate, assess, tax, fr MF *taxer,* fr ML *taxare,* fr L, to feel, estimate, censure, freq of *tangere* to touch – more at TANGENT] – **taxable** *adj,* **taxability** *n,* **taxer** *n*

**²tax** *n* 1 a charge, usu of money, imposed by a government on people or property, esp to raise revenue 2 a heavy charge or demand

**synonyms** Tax, duty, rates, excise, customs, toll, and dues are all words for obligatory payments to an authority. Tax was formerly levied directly on people, and duty on goods and transactions; but there is no longer any distinction in Britain between the two, and tax is the more general word. We speak of *value-added* tax as well as of *income* **tax**. **Rates** are the taxes charged by a British local authority, and assessed on the value of property. **Excise** is strictly speaking the internal tax on goods such as Scotch whisky produced within the country, and **customs** are strictly speaking the taxes on goods such as French brandy imported from outside, though the two are sometimes loosely confused. The most familiar use of **toll** is for the charge on using a bridge or a road (eg some foreign motorways). **Dues** may be paid to any authority ⟨*harbour* **dues**⟩ including a private body such as a club or trade union.

**tax-, taxo-** *also* **taxi-** *comb form* arrangement ⟨tax*eme*⟩ ⟨taxi*dermy*⟩ [Gk *taxi-*, fr *taxis*]

**taxa** /'taksə/ *pl of* TAXON (biological group or division)

**taxation** /tak'saysh(ə)n/ *n* **1** the action of taxing; *esp* the imposition of taxes **2** revenue obtained from taxes **3** the amount assessed as a tax

**tax avoidance** *n* the legal avoiding of paying taxes, by minimizing activities that make one liable for tax or by claiming for properly allowable deductions from income before tax – compare TAX-DEDUCTIBLE, TAX EVASION

**tax-de'ductible** *adj* that may legally be deducted from one's income or capital before tax is assessed on them ⟨~ *expenses*⟩

**taxeme** /'takseem/ *n* a linguistic feature (eg a difference in pronunciation or word order) that differentiates one utterance from another otherwise identical utterance, and so shows their difference in meaning [*tax-* + *-eme*] – **taxemic** *adj*

**tax evasion** *n* deliberate failure to pay taxes, usu by falsely reporting taxable income or property – compare TAX AVOIDANCE

**tax-ex'empt** *adj, NAm* tax-free

**tax exile** *n* a person who lives abroad in order to avoid paying high taxes in his/her home country

**tax-'free** *adj* exempted from tax

**tax haven** *n* a country with a relatively low level of taxation, esp on incomes, and where people with high incomes live in order to avoid high taxation in their home country

¹**taxi** /'taksi/ *n, pl* **taxis** *also* **taxies** a taxicab; *also* a similarly operated boat or aircraft

²**taxi** *vb* **taxis, taxies; taxiing, taxying; taxied** *vi* **1** to ride in a taxicab **2a** *of an aircraft* to go at low speed along the surface of the ground or water **b** to operate an aircraft on the ground under its own power ~ *vt* **1** to transport by taxi **2** to cause (an aircraft) to taxi

**taxi-** – see TAX-

**taxicab** /-,kab/ *n* a car that can be hired, together with its driver, to carry passengers for a fare usu calculated by the distance travelled [*taxi*meter *cab*]

**taxi dancer** *n* someone employed (eg in a dance hall) to dance with patrons who pay for each dance

**taxidermy** /'taksi,duhmi/ *n* the art of preparing, stuffing, and mounting the skins of animals [deriv of Gk *taxis* arrangement + *derma* skin] – **taxidermist** *adj*, **taxidermic** *n*

**taximan** /'taksimən/ *n, chiefly Br* a taxi driver

**taximeter** /'taksi,meetə/ *n* an instrument for use in a hired vehicle (eg a taxicab) for automatically calculating and showing the fare due [Fr *taximètre*, modif of Ger *taxameter*, fr ML *taxa* tax, charge (fr *taxare* to tax) + Ger *-meter*]

**taxing** /'taksing/ *adj* onerous, wearing ⟨a ~ *operatic role*⟩ – **taxingly** *adv*

**taxi rank** *n* a place where taxicabs park, usu to wait for customers

**taxis** /'taksis/ *n, pl* **taxes** /-seez/ **1** the manual restoration of a displaced body part; *specif* manual pressure used to reduce a hernia **2a** reflex movement by a freely moving and usu simple organism (eg a bacterium) in response to a directional source of stimulation (eg a light or a temperature or chemical gradient) **b** a reflex movement involving a taxis ☐ (2) compare TROPISM [Gk, arrangement, order, fr *tassein* to arrange – more at TACTICS]

**-taxis** /-taksis/ *comb form* (→ *n*), *pl* **-taxes** /-takseez/ **1** arrangement; order ⟨*homo*taxis⟩ ⟨*para*taxis⟩ **2** orientation or movement towards or in relation to (a specified force or agent) ⟨*chemo*taxis⟩ [NL, fr Gk, fr *taxis*] – **-tactic** *comb form* (→ *adj*)

**taxiway** /'taksi,way/ *n* a usu paved strip for taxiing (eg from the terminal to a runway) at an airport

**taxman** /'taks,man/ *n* **1** an official who collects taxes **2** *Br informal the* INLAND REVENUE personified

**taxo-** – see TAX-

**taxon** /'takson/ *n, pl* **taxa** *also* **taxons 1** a taxonomic group or entity **2** the name applied to a taxonomic group in a formal system of standardized names [NL, back-formation fr ISV *taxonomy*]

**taxonomy** /tak'sonəmi/ *n* **1** the study of the general principles of scientific classification; SYSTEMATICS **2** classification; *specif* orderly classification of plants and animals according to their presumed natural relationships [Fr *taxonomie*, fr *tax-* + *-nomie* -nomy] – **taxonomic** *adj*, **taxonomically** *adv*, **taxonomist** *n*

**taxpayer** /-,payə/ *n* someone who pays or is liable for a tax

**taxpaying** /-,paying/ *adj* of or subject to the paying of a tax

**tax return** *n* a formal statement made to the INLAND REVENUE of one's income and allowable deductions for tax purposes

**-taxy** /-taksi/ *comb form* (→ *n*) -taxis [Gk *-taxia*, fr *tassein* to arrange]

**Taylor's series, Taylor series** *n, maths* a POWER SERIES that gives the expansion of a function *f* (*x*) in the NEIGHBOURHOOD of a point *a* provided that all DERIVATIVES exist and the series CONVERGES [Brook *Taylor* †1731 E mathematician]

**tazza** /'tatsə/ *n* a shallow cup or vase on a pedestal [It, cup, fr Ar *tassah*, fr Per *tast*]

**TB** *n* tuberculosis [abbr for *tubercle bacillus*]

¹**T-,bar** *n* **1** a metal bar or beam having a cross-section of the form of the letter T **2** a mechanical device in the shape of a T: eg **2a** a T-shaped wrench (eg for removing and replacing SPARKING PLUGS) **b** a T-shaped bar on a SKI LIFT by which skiers are pulled up a slope

²**T-bar** *adj* having or being a pair of straps that fasten a shoe so that one lies along the length of the upper foot and one circles the ankle to form the shape of a T

**'T-,bone, T-bone steak** *n* a thick steak from the thin end of a beef sirloin containing a T-shaped bone and a small piece of fillet

**TCP** *trademark* – used for a water-based solution of certain chemical compounds that is used as an antiseptic

**t distribution** *n* a PROBABILITY DENSITY FUNCTION that is used esp in testing whether a statistical sample is likely to have come from a larger sample of known statistical properties

**te, ti** /tee/ *n* the 7th note in the scale in the SOL-FA method of representing the musical scale [alter. of *si*]

**tea** /tee/ *n* **1a** a shrub (*Camellia sinensis*) of the camellia family cultivated esp in tropical and subtropical Asia **b** the leaves, leaf buds, and parts of the stem of the tea plant prepared and cured for the market, classed according to method of manufacture (eg GREEN TEA, BLACK TEA, or OOLONG), and graded according to leaf size (eg ORANGE PEKOE, PEKOE, or SOUCHONG) **2a** an aromatic beverage prepared from tea leaves by steeping in boiling water **b** *pl* cups of tea ⟨*two* ~s *please*⟩ **3** any of various plants somewhat resembling tea in appearance or properties; *also* an INFUSION (solution formed by soaking in hot water) of their leaves used medicinally or as a beverage ⟨*camomile* ~⟩ **4a** refreshments, usu including tea with sandwiches, cakes, or biscuits, served in the late afternoon **b** a light late-afternoon or early-evening meal that is usu less substantial than the midday meal; *also* the food prepared for a tea – compare HIGH TEA **5** *slang* cannabis; *specif* marijuana [Chin (Amoy) *te* (*t'e*)]

**tea bag** *n* a cloth or filter paper bag holding enough tea for an individual serving when infused with boiling water

**tea ball** *n* a perforated metal ball-shaped container that holds tea leaves and is used in brewing tea, esp in a cup

**tea boy** *n, Br* a person, esp a young man, whose job is to make tea for the other employees (eg in an office or factory)

**tea bread** *n* any of various light often sweet breads or plain cakes usu raised (eg with BAKING POWDER) and served esp at HIGH TEA

**tea break** *n, Br* a short pause during the working day, usu in the middle of the morning or afternoon, for refreshment (eg tea or coffee)

**tea cake** *n* a flat round yeast-raised bread bun that is often sweet, contains currants, and is usu eaten toasted with butter

**teach** /teech/ *vb* **taught** /tawt/; **teaching** *vt* **1a** to cause to know a subject ⟨*would rather* ~ *older than younger children*⟩ **b** to cause to know how ⟨*is* ~ing *me to drive*⟩ **c** to accustom to some action or attitude ⟨~ *students to think for themselves*⟩ **d** to make to know the disagreeable consequences of some action ⟨*I'll* ~ *you to come home late*⟩ **2** to guide the studies of **3** to impart the knowledge of ⟨~ *algebra*⟩ ⟨*can't* ~ *an old dog new tricks*⟩ **4a** to instruct by precept, example, or experience **b** to seek to make known and accepted ⟨*experience* ~es *us our limitations*⟩ ~ *vi* to provide instruction; act as a teacher [ME *techen* to show, instruct, fr OE *tǣcan*; akin to OE *tācn* sign – more at TOKEN] *synonyms* Teach, instruct, train, discipline, school, drill, tutor, coach, and educate all mean "cause to gain knowledge or skill". Teach is the most general word, which could replace any of the others. Instruct implies methodical, formal, and perhaps authoritarian teaching in a specific area ⟨**instruct** *them in safety procedures*⟩. Train resembles **instruct** but entails a longer procedure ⟨*a trained anaesthetist*⟩. Discipline and school both involve subjection to control, often one's own, and may concern behaviour rather than knowledge ⟨**discipline/school** *oneself to eat less*⟩ with school carrying a further suggestion of arduous indoctrination. One can train or school animals ⟨**train** *performing seals*⟩ ⟨**school** *a horse*⟩. Drill suggests the repetition and practice of a routine ⟨**drill** *them till they can say it backwards*⟩. Tutor and coach both apply to individual and perhaps unofficial teaching ⟨**tutor/coach** *her own son in the evenings*⟩, but coach is also used of nonacademic training ⟨**coach** *the swimming team*⟩. Educate implies all-round development of a learner's capacities, involving experience as well as formal instruction ⟨**educate** *oneself by travel and reading*⟩.

**teachable** /'teechəbl/ *adj* 1 capable of being taught 2 apt and willing to learn – **teachability, teachableness** *n*, **teachably** *adv*

**teacher** /'teechə/ *n* one who or that which teaches; *esp* someone whose occupation is to instruct

**teachers' centre** *n*, an official establishment providing educational services and resources and in-service training for the teachers of an area in Britain

**teachers college** *n*, *NAm* COLLEGE OF EDUCATION

**teacher's pet** *n* someone who ingratiates him-/herself with an authority, esp a teacher

**teachers' training college** *n* COLLEGE OF EDUCATION – not now used technically

**tea chest** *n* a large square chest used for exporting tea ⟨*stored his books in tea chests*⟩

**'teach-,in** *n* 1 an extended meeting for lectures, debates, and discussions, esp on a topical and often controversial issue 2 *informal* a usu informal gathering for developing the participants' knowledge, esp by discussion and the exchange of ideas ⟨*Portugal is having to hold its emergency political ~ on the edge of the precipice* – Richard Kershaw⟩

**'teaching** /'teeching/ *n* 1 the act, practice, or profession of imparting knowledge 2 something taught; *esp* a doctrine ⟨*the ~s of Confucius*⟩

**²teaching** *adj* who teaches ⟨*a ~ doctor*⟩ 2 used in or for teaching; of teaching [(1) fr prp of *teach-;* (2) fr gerund of *teach*]

**teaching aid** *n* a device (e g a record player, map, or picture) used by a teacher to reinforce or supplement classroom instruction

**teaching hospital** *n* a hospital that is affiliated with a medical school and provides medical students with the opportunity of gaining practical experience under supervision

**teaching machine** *n* any of various mechanical devices for presenting a programme of instructional material

**teaching practice** *n* practical teaching in a school undertaken by a trainee teacher

**tea cloth** *n* 1 a small cloth for a table or trolley on which tea is to be served 2 TEA TOWEL

**teacup** /'tee,kup/ *n* a small cup with a capacity usu less than 8 FLUID OUNCES (about 0.23 litre) used for hot beverages, esp tea 2 the quantity contained in a teacup; the capacity of a teacup – see also STORM in a teacup – **teacupful** *n*

**tea dance** *n* a dance held in the late afternoon

**tea garden** *n* 1 a public garden where tea and light refreshments are served 2 a tea plantation

**tea gown** *n* a semiformal gown formerly worn esp for afternoon entertaining at home

**teahouse** /'tee,hows/ *n* a restaurant, esp in China or Japan, where tea and light refreshments are served

**teak** /teek/ *n* 1 a tall E Indian timber tree (*Tectona grandis*) of the family Verbenaceae, the teak family) 2 **teak, teakwood** the hard yellowish-brown wood of the teak, used esp for furniture and shipbuilding [Pg *teca*, fr Malayalam *tēkka*]

**teal** /teel/ *n*, *pl* **teals**, *esp collectively* **teal** any of several small DABBLING DUCKS (genus *Anas*) of Africa, Eurasia, and America; *esp* a Eurasian teal (*Anas crecca*), the male of which has a distinctive green and chestnut head [ME *tele;* akin to MD *teling* teal]

**tea lady** *n*, *chiefly Br* a woman who makes and/or serves tea, coffee, etc (e g in a factory or office)

**tea leaf** *n* 1 *usu pl* a fragment of a leaf of the tea plant, esp after infusion or soaking 2 *Br slang* a thief [(2) rhyming slang]

**'team** /teem/ *n* 1a a group of two or more draught animals harnessed to the same vehicle or implement; *also* these with their harness and attached vehicle b a draught animal, often with harness and vehicle c a drawn vehicle (e g a wagon) 2 a group of animals: e g 2a a brood, esp of young pigs or ducks b a matched group of animals for exhibition 3 *taking sing or pl vb* a number of people associated together in work or activity: e g 3a a group on one side (e g in a sporting contest or a debate) b a crew, gang [ME *teme*, fr OE *tēam* offspring, lineage, group of draught animals; akin to OE *tēon* to draw, pull – more at TOW]

**²team** *vt* 1 to yoke or join in a team 2 to combine so as to form a harmonizing arrangement ⟨*~ the shoes with the dress*⟩ 3 *chiefly NAm* to convey or haul with a team of animals ~ *vi* 1 to come together (as if) in a team – usu + *up* ⟨*let's ~ up with them for a night out*⟩ 2 to form a harmonizing combination – usu + *up* 3 *chiefly NAm* to drive a team (e g of draught animals) or a lorry

**³team** *adj* of or performed by a team ⟨*a ~ effort*⟩

**team handball** *n* a game developed from soccer that is played indoors between two teams of seven players, each of whose aim is to put the ball into a goal by throwing, catching, and dribbling it with the hands

**teammate** /'teem,mayt/ *n* a fellow member of a team

**team play** *n* cooperative effort ⟨*need for ~ in wartime*⟩

**team spirit** *n* willingness to act in a cooperative manner as part of a team

**teamster** /'teemstə/ *n* 1 someone who drives a team of animals 2 *NAm* a lorry driver

**team teaching** *n* a system whereby a group of teachers with various qualifications undertake jointly a programme of work with a large group of pupils

**teamwork** /-,wuhk/ *n* work done by several associates with each doing a part but all putting the efficiency of the whole before personal prominence

**teapot** /'tee,pot/ *n* a pot with a lid, spout, and handle in which tea is brewed and served

**teapoy** /'tee,poy/ *n* 1 a 3-legged ornamental stand or table 2 a table containing one or more receptacles for holding tea [Hindi *tipai*]

**'tear** /tiə/ *n* 1a a drop of clear salty liquid secreted by the LACHRYMAL gland (tear gland situated above the eye), diffused between the eye and eyelids to lubricate the parts, and often shed as a result of emotion, esp grief b a secretion of profuse tears that overflow the eyelids and dampen the face 2 *pl* an act of weeping or grieving ⟨*broke into ~s*⟩ 3 a transparent drop of liquid or hardened liquid matter (e g resin) [ME, fr OE *tæhher, tēar;* akin to OHG *zahar* tear, L *dacruma, lacrima*, Gk *dakry*] – in tears crying; weeping

**²tear** /teə/ *vb* tore /taw/; torn /tawn/ *vt* 1a to separate parts of or pull apart by tearing; rend b to wound by tearing; lacerate ⟨*~ the skin*⟩ 2 to divide, disrupt, or distress by the effect of contrary forces ⟨*a mind torn with doubts*⟩ ⟨*she was torn between going and staying*⟩ 3 to remove by force; wrench ⟨*~ a cover off a box*⟩ 4 to make or effect (as if) by tearing ⟨*~ a hole in the paper*⟩ ~ *vi* 1 to separate on being pulled; rend ⟨*this cloth ~s easily*⟩ 2 to move or act with violence, haste, or force ⟨*went ~ing down the street*⟩ – see also tear one's HAIR (out), tear somebody off a STRIP [ME *teren*, fr OE *teran;* akin to OHG *zeran* to] – **tearer** *n*

*synonyms* Tear, rip, rend, split, cleave, slit, and slash all mean "separate forcibly". Tear and rip may both involve merely pulling. Tear implies a crude ragged process, leaving irregular edges ⟨**tear** *a newspaper in half*⟩ ⟨*citizen* **torn** *to pieces by the mob*⟩. Rip is often less crude and more purposeful than **tear**, though rapid, and usually involves tearing along a seam or grain so as to leave straight edges ⟨**rip** *a sleeve out of a jacket*⟩. The somewhat rhetorical rend suggests great violence ⟨*clouds* **rent** *by sudden flashes of lightning*⟩. Split, cleave, slit, and slash suggest the use of some tool or weapon. One splits hard things along a grain, and usually for their entire length ⟨**split** *logs for firewood*⟩. Cleave suggests less precision than **split**, and implies the violent separation, with a sharp tool or weapon, of something hard ⟨*struck the final blow,* **cleaving** *the archbishop's skull* – E V Lucas⟩. One usually slits something soft with something sharp, producing a long narrow cut often methodically and dexterously made ⟨*surgeon* **slit** *the abdominal wall*⟩. Slash implies a swinging, violent, imprecise cut with a sharp blade ⟨*his face was* **slashed** *with duelling scars*⟩.

**tear at** *vt* to cause distress or pain to ⟨*it* tore at *my heart to see her go*⟩

**tear away** *vt* to remove (oneself or another) reluctantly ⟨*he could hardly* tear *himself* away *from the book*⟩

**tear down** *vt* to pull down, esp violently; demolish

**tear into** *vt* to attack physically or verbally or without restraint or caution

**tear off** *vt* to compose rapidly ⟨tore off *two letters before dinner*⟩

**tear up** *vt* 1 to tear into pieces 2 to cancel or annul, usu unilaterally ⟨tore up *the treaty*⟩

³**tear** /teə/ *n* 1a damage from being torn – chiefly in WEAR AND TEAR b a hole or flaw made by tearing 2 *NAm informal* a spree ⟨*go on a* ∼⟩

**tearaway** /'teərə,way/ *n, chiefly Br informal* an unruly and reckless young person

**teardrop** /'tiə,drop/ *n* 1 ¹TEAR 1a 2 something shaped like a dropping tear; *specif* ¹DROP 2a (pendant on a piece of jewellery)

**tearful** /-f(ə)l/ *adj* 1 flowing with or accompanied by tears ⟨∼ *entreaties*⟩ 2 causing tears 3 inclined or about to cry ⟨*was feeling a bit* ∼⟩ – **tearfully** *adv*, **tearfulness** *n*

**teargas** /'tiə,gas/ *vt* **-ss-** to use TEAR GAS on

**tear gas** /tiə/ *n* a solid, liquid, or gaseous substance that on dispersion in the air blinds the eyes with tears and is used chiefly in dispelling crowds

**tearing** /'teəring/ *adj* 1 causing continued or repeated pain or distress 2 *informal* violent, precipitate ⟨*in a* ∼ *hurry*⟩

**tearjerker** /'tiə,juhkə/ *n, informal* an excessively sentimental story, play, film, etc designed to provoke tears – **tear-jerking** *adj*

**tearless** /'tiəlis/ *adj* shedding no tears; free from tears – **tearlessly** *adv*, **tearlessness** *n*

**tear-off** /teə/ *n* part of a piece of paper intended to be removed by tearing, usu along a marked or perforated line

**tearoom** /'tee,roohm/ *n* a restaurant where light refreshments are served

**tea rose** *n* any of numerous hybrid garden roses descended chiefly from a Chinese rose (*Rosa odorata*) with abundant large usu tea-scented blossoms

**tear sheet** /teə/ *n* a sheet torn from a publication, usu to prove insertion of an advertisement to an advertiser

**tearstain** /'tiə,stayn/ *n* a spot or streak left by tears – **tearstained** *adj*

**teary** /'tiəri/ *adj* 1 wet or stained with tears 2 causing tears; sentimental ⟨*a* ∼ *story*⟩ – **tearily** *adv*

¹**tease** /teez/ *vt* 1a to disentangle and straighten by combing ⟨∼ *wool*⟩ b to teasel 2 to tear in pieces; *esp* to shred (a tissue or specimen) for microscopic examination 3a to disturb or annoy by persistent irritating or provoking b to attempt to provoke to anger, resentment, or confusion; goad c to persuade to acquiesce, esp by persistent small efforts; coax; *also* to obtain by repeated coaxing ⟨∼d *the money out of her father*⟩ 4 *chiefly NAm* to backcomb (the hair) – *vi* to tease someone or something [ME *tesen*, fr OE *tǣsan;* akin to OHG *zeisan* to tease] – **teasingly** *adv*

²**tease** *n* 1 teasing or being teased 2 someone who derives pleasure from teasing

¹**teasel, teazel, teazle** /'teezl/ *n* 1a a tall African and Eurasian prickly plant (*Dipsacus fullonum*) of the scabious family with flower heads that are covered with stiff hooked BRACTS (small leaflike parts) and are used when dried to raise the surface of woollen cloth; *also* a flower head of teasel b any of various plants (genus *Dipsacus*) related to the true teasel 2 a wire substitute for the flower head of the teasel, used in teaselling [ME *tesel*, fr OE *tǣsel;* akin to OE *tǣsan* to tease]

²**teasel** *vt* **-ll-** (*NAm* **-l-**, **-ll-**) to brush (cloth) with teasels so as to raise the surface

**teaser** /'teezə/ *n* 1 a perplexing difficult problem 2 TEASE 2

**tea set** *n* a matching set of usu china utensils (eg teapot, jug, cups and saucers, and plates) needed for serving tea

**tea shop** *n, chiefly Br* a tearoom

**Teasmade** /'teezmayd/ *trademark* – used for an electrical appliance that can be set to make a pot of tea at a specified time and that sounds an alarm when the tea is ready

**teaspoon** /'tee,spoohn/ *n* 1 a small spoon used esp for eating soft foods and stirring beverages 2 a teaspoonful

**teaspoonful** /-f(ə)l/ *n, pl* **teaspoonfuls** *also* **teaspoonsful** 1 as much as a teaspoon can hold 2 a unit of measure equal to ¹⁄₃ tablespoonful (about 4.73 cubic centimetres)

**teat** /teet/ *n* 1a the protuberance through which milk is drawn from an udder or breast; a nipple b a rubber mouthpiece with one or more holes in it, attached to the top of a baby's feeding bottle 2 a small projection (eg on a mechanical part) [ME *tete*, fr OF, of Gmc origin; akin to OE *tit* teat, MHG *zitze*] – **teated** *adj*

**teatime** /'tee,tiem/ *n* the customary time for tea; late afternoon or early evening

**tea towel** *n* a cloth for drying the dishes

**tea tray** *n* a tray on which a tea service is carried

**tea-tree** *n* any of various shrubs or trees of the myrtle family, the leaves of which can be used as a substitute for tea; *esp* MANUKA

**tea trolley** *n, chiefly Br* a small trolley used in serving tea or light refreshments

**tea wagon** *n, chiefly NAm* TEA TROLLEY

**toazel, teazle** /'teezl/ *n* a teasel

**Tebet** /'tayvəs (*Hebrew* te'vet)/ *n* – see MONTH table [Heb *Ṭēbhēth*]

**tec** /tek/ *n, informal* a detective [by shortening]

**tech** /tek/ *n, Br informal* a TECHNICAL SCHOOL or TECHNICAL COLLEGE

**technetium** /tek'neesh(y)əm/ *n* a metallic chemical element produced artificially (eg from uranium) [NL, fr Gk *technētos* artificial, fr *technasthai* to devise by art, fr *technē* art]

**technical** /'teknikl/ *adj* 1a having special and usu practical knowledge, esp of a mechanical or scientific subject b marked by or characteristic of specialization 2 of a particular subject; *esp* of a practical subject organized on scientific principles 3 marked by a strict legal interpretation or rigid application of the rules ⟨*had* ∼ *responsibility for all his subordinates*⟩ 4 of technique 5 of or produced by ordinary commercial processes without being subjected to special purification 6 resulting chiefly from internal market factors rather than external influences ⟨∼ *reaction of the stock market*⟩ [Gk *technikos* of art, skilful, fr *technē* art, craft, skill; akin to Gk *tektōn* builder, carpenter, L *texere* to weave, OHG *dahs* badger] – **technicalness** *n*

**technical college** *n* any of a number of British regional institutions offering full-time and part-time courses in various subjects but with a bias towards skills and trades and at a less advanced level than a polytechnic

**technical foul** *n* a foul (eg in basketball) that involves no physical contact with an opponent and that is usu incurred by unsportsmanlike conduct – compare PERSONAL FOUL

**technicality** /,tekni'kaləti/ *n* 1 the quality or state of being technical 2 something technical: eg 2a a detail meaningful only to a specialist b a detail arising from a strict or literal interpretation of a rule or law ⟨*convicted on a* ∼⟩

**technical knockout** /'nok,owt/ *n* the termination of a boxing match when a boxer is unable or is declared by the referee to be unable (eg because of injuries) to continue the fight

**technically** /'teknikli/ *adv* 1 in a technical manner 2 according to a strict interpretation ⟨∼ *that was a foul*⟩

**technical school** *n* a SECONDARY SCHOOL providing education with a technical or commercial bias for children selected usu by examination and from the age of 11 to 16 or 18

**technical sergeant** *n* – see MILITARY RANKS table

**technical studies** *n taking sing or pl vb* a subject taught in SECONDARY SCHOOLS that aims at developing manual skill and familiarity with tools and machines

**technician** /tek'nish(ə)n/ *n* 1 a specialist in the technical details of a subject or occupation ⟨*a medical* ∼⟩ 2 one who has acquired the technique of an area of specialization (eg an art) ⟨*a superb* ∼ *and an artist of ingenuity*⟩

**Technicolor** /'tekni,kulə/ *trademark* – used for a process of colour photography in the cinema in which the three PRIMARY COLOURS are recorded on separate films and then combined in a single print

¹**technicolour** /'tekni,kulə/ *n* 1 vivid and often garish colour 2 artificial or showy brilliance ⟨*the* ∼ *of sexual glamour*⟩

²**technicolour, technicoloured** /-,kuləd/ *adj* displaying bright, artificial, or tasteless colours ⟨*Texan tourists in their* ∼ *suits*⟩

**technics** /'tekniks/ *n taking sing or pl vb* TECHNOLOGY 1

**technique** /tek'neek/ *n* 1 the manner in which technical details are treated (eg by a writer) or basic physical movements are used (eg by a dancer or athlete); *also* ability to treat such details or use such movements ⟨*good piano* ∼⟩ 2a a body of technical methods (eg in a craft or in scientific research) b a method of accomplishing a desired aim [Fr, fr *technique* technical, fr Gk *technikos*]

**techno-** *comb form* **1** art; craft ⟨techno*graphy*⟩ **2** technical; technological ⟨techno*cracy*⟩ [Gk, fr *technē*]

**technocracy** /tek'nokrəsi/ *n, chiefly derog* government by technicians; *specif* organization and management of society and industrial resources by technical experts

**technocrat** /'teknəkrat/ *n, chiefly derog* **1** an advocate of technocracy **2** a member of a technocratic government

**technocratic** /,teknə'kratik/ *adj* of or like a technocrat or a technocracy

**technological** /,teknə'lojik(ə)l/ *adj* **1** of or characterized by technology ⟨~ *advances*⟩ **2** resulting from improvements in technical processes that increase productivity of machines and eliminate manual operations or operations done by older machines ⟨~ *unemployment*⟩ – **technologically** *adv*

**technological university** *n* COLLEGE OF ADVANCED TECHNOLOGY

**technologist** /tek'noləjist/ *n* a specialist in technology

**technology** /tek'noləji/ *n* **1** (the theory and practice of) applied science **2** the totality of the means and knowledge used to provide objects necessary for human sustenance and comfort [Gk *technologia* systematic treatment of an art, fr *techno-* + *-logia* -logy]

**technopolis** /tek'nopəlis/ *n* **1** a society dominated by and dependent upon technology **2** a place which is a centre for industries and businesses manufacturing and dealing in high-technology equipment – **technopolitan** *adj*

**technostructure** /'teknoh,strukchə/ *n* the network of professionally skilled managers (eg scientists, engineers, and administrators) that increasingly tends to control the economy

**techy** /'techi/ *adj* tetchy

**tectonic** /tek'tonik/ *adj* of tectonics: eg **a** architectural **b** of the deformation of the earth's crust, the forces involved in or producing such deformation, and the resulting forms [LL *tectonicus*, fr Gk *tektonikos* of a builder, fr *tektōn* builder – more at TECHNICAL] – **tectonically** *adv*

**tectonics** /tek'toniks/ *n taking sing or pl vb* **1** the science or art of construction (eg of a building) **2** geological structural features **3a** a branch of geology concerned with structure, esp FOLDING and FAULTING of the earth's crust **b** *also* **tectonism** DIASTROPHISM (process that produces continents, ocean basins, mountains, etc)

**tectum** /'tekt(ə)m/ *n, pl* **tecta** /-tə/ a bodily structure resembling or serving as a roof; *esp* the back part of the MIDBRAIN [NL, fr L, roof, dwelling, fr neut of *tectus*, pp of *tegere* to cover – more at THATCH] – **tectal** *adj*

**ted** /ted/ *vt* **-dd-** to turn over and spread (eg new-mown grass) for drying [(assumed) ME *tedden*; akin to OHG *zetten* to spread, Gk *daiesthai* to divide, distribute – more at TIDE]

**Ted** *n, informal* a teddy boy

**tedder** /'tedə/ *n* one who or that which teds; *specif* a machine for turning over and spreading hay to hasten drying and curing

**teddy** /'tedi/ *n* a teddy bear – used esp by or to children

**teddy bear** *n* a soft stuffed toy bear [*Teddy*, nickname of Theodore Roosevelt †1919 26th US president; fr a cartoon depicting the president sparing the life of a bear cub while hunting]

**teddy boy** *n* any of a group of youths or young men in Britain in the mid-1950s, who wore long greased swept-back hair, tight trousers, and long Edwardian jackets and were associated with unruly behaviour; *also* a male dressing in this manner subsequently [*Teddy*, nickname for Edward, ie King Edward VII †1910]

**Te Deum** /,tay 'dayəm, ,tee 'dee-/ *n, pl* **Te Deums** a Christian hymn of praise to God usu sung as part of the service of MORNING PRAYER [ME, fr LL *te deum laudamus* thee, God, we praise; fr the opening words of the hymn]

**tedious** /'teedi·əs/ *adj* tiresome because of length or dullness; boring ⟨a ~ *public ceremony*⟩ [ME, fr LL *taediosus*, fr L *taedium*] – **tediously** *adv*, **tediousness** *n*

**tedium** /'teedi·əm/ *n* tediousness; *also* boredom [L *taedium* disgust, irksomeness, fr *taedēre* to disgust, weary]

**¹tee** /tee/ *n* **1** something shaped like a capital T **2** a mark aimed at in various games (eg curling) [ME] – **to a tee** TO A T

**²tee** *n* **1** a peg or a small mound used to raise a golf ball for striking at the beginning of play on a hole **2** the area from which a golf ball is struck at the beginning of play on a hole [back-formation fr obs *teaz* (taken as pl); perh akin to Icel *tjá* to show, mark]

**³tee** *vt* to place (a ball) on a tee – often + *up*

**tee off** *vi* **1** to drive a golf ball from a tee **2** to begin, start

**¹tee-hee** /,tee 'hee/ *interj* – used to express amusement or derision [ME *te he*, of imit origin]

**²tee-hee** *vi* to laugh in a silly manner; giggle

**¹teem** /teem/ *vt, obs* to bring forth; give birth to ~ *vi* **1** to become filled to overflowing; abound – often + *with* ⟨*lakes that* ~ *with fish*⟩ **2** to be present in large quantity ⟨*fish* ~ *in the river*⟩ **3** *obs* to become pregnant; conceive △ team [ME *temen*, fr OE *tīman*, *tāman*; akin to OE *tēam* offspring – more at TEAM] – **teemingly** *adv*, **teemingness** *n*

**²teem** *vt* to pour ⟨~ *molten metal into a mould*⟩ ~ *vi, Br* to rain hard; pour ⟨~ *usu* + *down* or in *teem with rain* [ME *temen*, fr ON *tœma*; akin to OE *tōm* empty]

**teen** /teen/ *adj, informal* teenage

**teenage** /'teenayj/, **teenaged** *adj* of or being people in their teens *synonyms* see ¹YOUNG

**teenager** /'teenayjə/ *n* a person in his/her teens

**teens** /teenz/ *n pl* the numbers 13 to 19 inclusive; *specif* the years 13 to 19 in a lifetime or century [-*teen* (as in *thirteen*, *fourteen*, etc)]

**teensy** /'teenzi, 'teensi/, **teensy-weensy** /,teenzi 'weenzi, ,teensi 'weensi/ *adj, informal* tiny [baby-talk alter. of *teeny*, *teeny-weeny*]

**teentsy** /'teentsi/, **teentsy-weentsy** /,teentsi 'weentsi/ *adj, informal* teensy

**teeny** /'teeni/ *adj, informal* tiny [by alter. (influenced by *weeny*)]

**teenybopper** /'teeni ,bopə/ *n, informal* **1** a person in his or her early teens **2** a young teenager, esp a girl, who zealously follows the latest fashionable trends, esp in clothes and pop music [*teen* + *-y* + *bopper*] – **teeny-bopperish** *adj*

**teeny-weeny** *also* **teenie-weenie** /,teeni 'weeni/ *adj, informal* tiny

**teepee** /'tee,pee/ *n* TEPEE (N American Indian tent)

**tee shirt** *n* a T-shirt

**¹teeter** /'teetə/ *vi* **1** to move unsteadily; wobble, waver ⟨a *passive person who* ~s *between conformity and revolt*⟩ **2** *chiefly NAm* to seesaw [ME *titeren* to totter, reel; akin to OHG *zittarōn* to shiver, Gk *dramein* to run]

**²teeter** *n, chiefly NAm* a seesaw

**teeterboard** /'teetə,bawd/ *n* a board placed on a raised support in such a way that a person standing on one end of the board is thrown into the air if another person jumps on the opposite end

**teeth** /teeth/ *pl of* TOOTH

**teethe** /teedh/ *vi* to cut one's teeth, esp one's first or MILK TEETH; grow teeth

**teething problems** *n* TEETHING TROUBLES

**teething ring** /'teedhing/ *n* a usu rubber or plastic ring for a teething baby to bite on

**teething troubles** *n pl* usu temporary problems occurring with new machinery or during the initial stages of an activity or enterprise

**teetotal** /tee'tohtl/ *adj* of or practising teetotalism [*total* + *total (abstinence)*] – **teetotally** *adv*

**teetotalism** /tee'tohtliz(ə)m/ *n* the principle or practice of complete abstinence from alcoholic drinks – **teetotalist** *n*

**teetotaller**, *NAm chiefly* **teetotaler** /tee'tohtl·ə/ *n* someone who practises or advocates teetotalism

**teetotum** /,tee'tohtəm/ *n* a small top usu inscribed with letters and used in games of put-and-take; *broadly* any small top spun with the fingers [¹*tee* + L *totum* all, fr neut of *totus* whole; fr the letter *T* inscribed on one side as an abbr of *totum* (take) all]

**teff** /tef/, **teff grass** *n* an economically important African cereal grass (*Eragrostis abyssinica*) that is grown for its grain which yields a white flour and as a forage and hay crop [Amharic *tēf*]

**Teflon** /'teflon/ *trademark* – used for POLYTETRA-FLUOROETHYLENE (tough plastic with nonstick properties)

**teg** /teg/ *n, chiefly Br* a sheep in its second year [origin unknown]

**tegmen** /'tegmən/ *n, pl* **tegmina** /'tegmənə/ a protective layer or covering; INTEGUMENT: eg **a** either of the leathery front wings of a grasshopper, cricket, cockroach, etc that cover and protect the hind wings – compare ELYTRON **b** the thin inner coat of a seed **c** the thin plate of bone covering the MIDDLE EAR [NL *tegmin-*, *tegmen*, fr L, covering, fr *tegere* to cover – more at THATCH]

**tegmental** /teg'mentl/ *adj* of or associated with a tegmen or a tegmentum

**tegmentum** /teg'mentəm/ *n, pl* **tegmenta** /-'mentə/ a covering, tegmen; *esp* an outer covering (eg a protective scale or layer of scales of a bud) [NL, fr L *tegumentum, tegmentum* covering, fr *tegere*]

**tegument** /'tegyoomənt/ *n, biology* INTEGUMENT (enclosing protective layer or covering) [ME, fr L *tegumentum*] – **tegumental, tegumentary** *adj*

**tektite** /'tektiet/ *n* a usu small rounded stony mass with a glassy appearance, that is green to black in colour and is probably of meteoritic origin [ISV, fr Gk *tēktos* molten, fr *tēkein* to melt – more at THAW] – **tektitic** *adj*

**tel-, telo-** *comb form* end 〈telo*phase*〉 [ISV, fr Gk *telos* – more at WHEEL]

**telaesthesia**, *NAm chiefly* **telesthesia** /ˌteləs'theezyə, -zh(y)ə/ *n* the receiving of an impression of an object at a distance without the use of the SENSE ORGANS (eg the eyes or ears) [NL, fr *tele-* + *aesthesia*]

**telangiectasia** /telˌanjiˌek'tayzyə, tiˌlanji-, -zh(y)ə/, **telangiectasis** /-'ektəsis/ *n, pl* **telangiectasias, telangiectases** /-seez/ an abnormal dilation of blood capillaries and ARTERIOLES (tiny end branches of arteries) that often forms an ANGIOMA (tumour made up of blood vessels) [NL, fr *tel-* + *angi-* + *ectasia, ectasis* dilation, fr Gk *ektasis* extension, fr *ekteinein* to stretch out, fr *ex-* + *teinein* to stretch – more at THIN] – **telangiectatic** *adj*

**tele** /'teli/ *n, informal* a telly

**tele-, tel-** *comb form* **1** distant; at a distance; over a distance 〈tele*gram*〉 〈telo*pathy*〉 **2a** telegraph 〈tele*printer*〉 **b** television 〈tele*cast*〉 [NL, fr Gk *tēle-, tēl-*, fr *tēle* far off – more at PALAE-]

**telecamera** /'teliˌkam(ə)rə/ *n* a television camera

**telecast** /'telikahst/ *vt* to televise [*tele-* + broad*cast*] – **telecast** *n*, **telecaster** *n*

**telecine** /'teliˌsini/ *n, chiefly Br* the conversion of filmed material into signals suitable for television broadcasting; *also* the broadcasting of such material [*tele-* + *cine*matograph]

**telecommunication** /ˌtelikəˌmyoohni'kaysh(ə)n/ *n* **1** communication over a distance (eg by telegraph) **2 telecommunications** *pl*, **telecommunication** a science that deals with telecommunication [ISV]

**teledu** /'telədooh/ *n* a small short-tailed flesh-eating mammal (*Mydaus meliceps*) of the mountains of Java and Sumatra that is related to the skunk, resembles the badger, and secretes an offensive-smelling liquid [Malay *tĕledu*]

**telefacsimile** /ˌtelifak'siməli/ *n* a system of transmitting and reproducing fixed graphic material (eg printing) by means of signals transmitted over telephone lines

**telegony** /ti'legəni/ *n* the supposed carrying over of the influence of a sire to the offspring resulting from subsequent matings of the dam with other males [ISV *tele-* + *-gony*]

**¹telegram** /'teligram/ *n* a message sent by telegraph and delivered as a written or typed note [*tele-* + *-gram*]

**²telegram** *vb* **-mm-** to telegraph

**¹telegraph** /'teligrahf, -graf/ *n* **1** an apparatus or system for communication at a distance by coded signals; *esp* such an apparatus or system that is based upon the making and breaking of an electric circuit **2** a telegram [Fr *télégraphe*, fr *télé-* tele- (fr Gk *tēle*) + *-graphe* -graph]

**²telegraph** *vt* **1a** to send or communicate (as if) by telegraph **b** to send a telegram to **c** to send by means of a telegraphic order 〈~ *flowers to a sick friend*〉 **2** to make known by signs, esp unknowingly and in advance 〈~ *a punch*〉 – **telegrapher** *n*, **telegraphist** *n*

**telegraphese** /ˌteligrah'feez, -gra-/ *n* terse and abbreviated language characteristic of telegrams, esp when considered to be humorously or excessively compressed

**telegraphic** /ˌteli'grafik/ *adj* **1** of the telegraph **2** concise, terse 〈*with* ~ *economy of words* – F S Mitchell〉 – **telegraphically** *adv*

**telegraphic address** *n* a word or set of words serving as an abbreviated direction for the delivery of telegrams to a person or organization

**telegraphy** /tə'legrəfi/ *n* the use or operation of a telegraphic apparatus or system

**telekinesis** /ˌteliki'neesis/ *n* PSYCHOKINESIS (movement of physical objects by the power of the mind) carried out at an appreciable distance [NL, fr Gk *tēle-* + *kinēsis* motion, fr *kinein* to move] – **telekinetic** *adj*, **telekinetically** *adv*

**telemark** /'telimahk/ *n, often cap* a turn in skiing in which the outside ski is advanced considerably ahead of the other ski and then turned inwards at a steadily widening angle until the turn is completed [Norw, fr *Telemark*, region in S Norway]

**¹telemeter** /tə'lemitə/ *n* **1** an instrument for measuring the distance of an object from an observer **2** an electrical apparatus for measuring a quantity (eg pressure, speed, or temperature) and transmitting the result (eg by radio) to a distant place at which it is indicated or recorded [ISV *tele-* + *-meter*]

**²telemeter** *vb* to obtain and transmit (eg the measurement of a quantity) by telemeter – **telemetry** *n*, **telemetric** *adj*, **telemetrically** *adv*

**telencephalon** /ˌtelən'sefəlon/ *n* the upper or front subdivision of the FOREBRAIN (uppermost or frontmost of the major divisions of the brain), comprising the CEREBRUM (largest approx hemispherical part of the brain) and associated structures [NL, fr *tel-* + *encephalon*] – **telencephalic** *adj*

**teleology** /ˌteli'oləji, ˌtee-/ *n* **1** (a doctrine) explaining phenomena (eg evolution) by reference to goals or purposes **2** the character attributed to nature or natural processes of being directed towards an end or designed according to a purpose [NL *teleologia*, fr Gk *tele-, telos* end, purpose + *-logia* -logy – more at WHEEL] – **teleologist** *n*, **teleological** *also* **teleologic** *adj*

**teleost** /'teliˌost, 'tee-/ *n* BONY FISH [deriv of Gk *teleios* complete, perfect (fr *telos* end) + *osteon* bone – more at OSSEOUS] – **teleost** *adj*, **teleostean** *adj or n*

**telepathy** /tə'lepəthi/ *n* communication directly from one mind to another without the use of the known senses [*tele-* + *-pathy*] – **telepathic** *adj*, **telepathically** *adv*, **telepathist** *n*

**¹telephone** /'telifohn/ *n* **1** a device for reproducing sounds at a distance; *specif* one for converting sounds into electrical impulses for transmission usu by wire to a particular receiver **2** the system of communications that uses telephones 〈*get in touch by* ~〉 [*tele-* + *-phone*]

**²telephone** *vi* to make a telephone call ~ *vt* **1** to send by telephone 〈~ *a message*〉 **2** to (attempt to) speak to by telephone 〈*when I* ~d *him there was no reply*〉 – **telephoner** *n*, **telephonic** *adj*

**telephone booth** *n, chiefly NAm* TELEPHONE BOX

**telephone box** *n, Br* a small booth containing a public telephone

**telephone directory** *n* a book giving the telephone numbers of subscribers

**telephone number** *n* a number assigned to a telephone and used to call that telephone

**telephone receiver** *n* a device (eg in a telephone) for converting electric impulses or varying current into sound

**telephonic** /ˌteli'fonik/ *adj* **1** conveying sound to a distance **2** of or conveyed by telephone – **telephonically** *adv*

**telephonist** /tə'lefənist/ *n, Br* a telephone switchboard operator

**telephony** /tə'lefəni/ *n* the use or operation of an apparatus for transmission of sounds between widely separated points with or without connecting wires

**¹telephoto** /'teliˌfohtoh/ *adj* **1** telephotographic 〈*a* ~ *effect*〉 **2** being a camera lens system used in conjunction with lenses of longer than normal FOCAL LENGTH and designed to give a close-up, usu large, image of a distant object

**²telephoto** *n, pl* **telephotos 1** a telephoto lens **2** a photograph taken with a camera having a telephoto lens

**telephotography** /ˌtelifə'togrəfi/ *n* the photography of distant objects (eg by a camera provided with a telephoto lens) [ISV] – **telephotographic** *adj*

**teleplay** /'teliˌplay/ *n* a play written specially for production on television

**teleprinter** /'teliˌprintə/ *n* a machine that has a typewriter keyboard for transmitting telegraphic or electrical signals (eg via a telephone line) to another similar machine or to a computer, and that can be activated by telegraphic signals or signals from a computer to produce typewritten copy

**teleprocessing** /ˌteli'prohsesing/ *n* computer processing via remote terminals

**TelePrompTer** /'teliˌpromptə/ *trademark* – used for a device for unrolling a magnified script in front of a speaker on television – compare AUTOCUE

**teleran** /'teləˌran/ *n* a system of navigation in which the results of a scan by ground-based radar are televised to the pilot of an aircraft so that he/she can see the positions of all aircraft in the vicinity [*tele*vision-*ra*dar *n*avigation]

**telerecord** /'teliriˌkawd/ *vt, Br* to record (a television programme) for later broadcast by conversion to a film rather than by videotaping – **telerecording** n

**¹telescope** /'teliskohp/ n **1** a usu tubular optical instrument for viewing distant objects by collecting and focussing light rays using a lens or mirror and magnifying the image so formed – compare REFLECTOR, REFRACTOR **2** any of various tubular optical instruments for magnifying small or distant objects **3** RADIO TELESCOPE [NL *telescopium*, fr Gk *tēleskopos* farseeing, fr *tēle-* tele- + *skopos* watcher; akin to Gk *skopein* to look – more at SPY]

**²telescope** vi **1** to slide or pass one within another like the cylindrical sections of a hand telescope **2** to force a way into or enter another lengthways as the result of collision **3** to become condensed or shortened ~ vt **1** to cause to telescope **2** to condense, shorten

**telescopic** /,teli'skopik/ adj **1a** of or performed with a telescope **b** suitable for seeing or magnifying distant objects **2** seen or discoverable only by means of a telescope ⟨~ *stars*⟩ **3** able to make out objects at a distance ⟨~ *eyes*⟩ **4** having parts that telescope ⟨a ~ *umbrella*⟩ – **telescopically** adv

**telesthesia** /,teləs'theezyə, -zh(y)ə/ n, NAm TELAESTHESIA (perception of distant object without use of the eyes, ears, etc) – **telesthetic** adj

**teletext** /'teli,tekst/ n a system of broadcasting material (e g news, weather forecasts, or journals) by printed text which can be received on a modified television set

**telethon** /'teli,thon/ n a long television programme, usu involving guest celebrities and designed to raise money for charity ⟨*the* Telethon, *a television marathon combining the lure of a variety special . . . and the audience-access pull of the phone-in* – *The Guardian*⟩ [tele- + -thon (as in *marathon*)]

**Teletype** /'teli,tiep/ trademark – used for a teleprinter

**Teletypesetter** /,teli'tiep,setə/ trademark – used for a telegraphic apparatus for the automatic operation of a keyboard typesetting machine

**teletypewriter** /,teli'tiep,rietə/ n, chiefly NAm a teleprinter

**teleutosorus** /ti,loohtə'sawrəs/ n a telium [NL, fr Gk *teleutē* end + NL *sorus*]

**teleutospore** /tə'loohtə,spaw/ n a teliospore [Gk *teleutē* end (akin to Gk *telos* end) + ISV *spore*]

**teleview** /'teli,vyooh/ vi to observe or watch by means of a television receiver – **televiewer** n

**televise** /'televiez/ vb to broadcast (an event or film) by television [back-formation fr *television*]

**television** /'televizh(ə)n, --'--/ n **1** an electronic system of transmitting changing visual images together with sound along a wire or through space to a distant receiver, by converting the images and sounds into electrical signals that are subsequently reconverted **2** a television receiving set **3a(1)** the television broadcasting industry **a(2)** a television broadcasting organization or station ⟨*Tyne-Tees* Television⟩ **b** the medium of television communication [Fr *télévision*, fr *télé-* tele- (fr Gk *tēle-*) + *vision*] – **televisionally** adv, **televisionary** adj

**televisual** /,teli'vizhyooəl/ adj, chiefly Br of or suitable for broadcast by television

**telex** /'teleks/ n **1** a communications service involving teleprinters connected by telephone wire, satellite, etc through automatic exchanges **2** a message transmitted or received by teletex [*teleprinter* + *exchange*] – **telex** vt

**telic** /'telik/ adj, formal tending towards a definite end [Gk *telikos* final, fr *telos* end – more at WHEEL] – **telically** adv

**teliospore** /'teelio,spaw/ n a thick-walled spore that is the final stage in the LIFE CYCLE of a RUST fungus, and that remains dormant during the winter and germinates in spring to produce the structure on which the next generation of spores are borne [Gk *teleios* complete (fr *telos* end) + E *spore*] – **teliosporic** adj

**telium** /'teeliəm/ n, pl **telia** /'teeliə/ a small distinct body containing a mass of teliospores on the plant on which a RUST fungus is parasitic [NL, fr Gk *teleios* complete] – **telial** adj

**¹tell** /tel/ vb **told** /tohld/ vt **1** to count, enumerate ⟨*all told there were 27 present*⟩ **2a** to relate in detail; narrate ⟨~ *me a story*⟩ **b** to give utterance to; say **3a** to make known; divulge, reveal **b** to express in words ⟨*she never told her love* – *Shak*⟩ **4a** to report to; inform **b** to assure emphatically ⟨*he did not do it, I* ~ *you*⟩ **5** to order, direct ⟨*told her to wait*⟩ **6** to ascertain by observing; find out, recognize ⟨*can never* ~ *whether he's lying or not*⟩ ~ vi **1** to give an account **2** to make a positive assertion; decide definitely ⟨*who can* ~?⟩ ⟨*you can never* ~ *for certain*⟩ **3** to act as an informer – often with on ⟨*his sister told on him, though he tried to stop her*⟩ **4** to take effect; have a

marked effect – often + on ⟨*the worry began to* ~ *on her nerves*⟩ **5** to serve as evidence or indication ⟨*will* ~ *against you in court*⟩ **synonyms** see ¹REVEAL [ME *tellen*, fr OE *tellan;* akin to OHG *zellen* to count, tell, OE *talu* tale]

**tell off** vt **1** to number and set apart; esp to assign to a special duty ⟨*told off a detail and put them to digging a trench*⟩ **2** to reprimand, scold, ⟨*told her off for talking in class*⟩ – see also TELLING-OFF

**²tell** n a mound formed by the accumulated debris (e g the mudbrick walls of collapsed buildings) of successive ancient settlements in the Middle East [Ar *tall* hill, mound]

**teller** /'telə/ n **1** someone who relates or communicates ⟨a ~ *of stories*⟩ **2** someone who reckons or counts: e g **2a** a person appointed to count votes **b** a member of a bank's staff concerned with the direct handling of money received or paid out

**telling** /'teling/ adj carrying great weight and producing a marked effect; impressive, effective ⟨*the most* ~ *evidence against him*⟩ **synonyms** see VALID – **tellingly** adv

**,telling-'off** n a harsh or severe reprimand; a scolding

**telltale** /'tel,tayl/ n **1** someone who spreads gossip, scandal, or rumours; a gossip; esp an informer **2** a device for indicating or recording something: e g **2a** a device for keeping a check on employees; esp TIME CLOCK **b** a device that shows the position of a vessel's rudder **c** a small piece of ribbon used to indicate wind direction or airflow on a sailing vessel **d** TIN **4** (resonant patch on the wall of a squash court) **e** NAm LOADING GAUGE (railway warning device) – **telltale** adj

**tellur-, telluro-** comb form **1** earth ⟨tellur*ian*⟩ **2** tellurium ⟨tellur*ide*⟩ [L *tellur-, tellus* earth, ground]

**¹tellurian** /tə'lyooəriən, -'looə-/ adj (characteristic) of the earth

**²tellurian** n, formal an inhabitant of the earth

**telluric** /tə'l(y)ooərik/ adj **1** of or containing tellurium, esp with a relatively high VALENCY **2** of the earth; terrestrial **3** being or relating to a usu natural electric current flowing on or just beneath the earth's surface

**telluride** /'telyooried/ n a compound of tellurium with one other chemical element or group [ISV]

**tellurite** /'telyooriet/ n a mineral, $TeO_2$, that consists of tellurium dioxide and occurs sparingly in tufts of white or yellowish crystals

**tellurium** /tə'l(y)ooəri·əm/ n a semimetallic chemical element related to sulphur, that occurs in a silvery white lustrous brittle crystalline form, in a dark noncrystalline form, or combined with metals, and that is used esp in alloys [NL, fr L *tellur-, tellus* earth]

**tellurometer** /,telyoo'romitə/ n a device that measures distance by means of RADIO WAVES

**tellurous** /'telyooərəs/ adj of or containing tellurium, esp with a relatively low VALENCY [ISV]

**telly, tele** /'teli/ n, chiefly Br informal (a) television [by shortening & alter.]

**telo-** – see TEL-

**telocentric** /,telə'sentrik/ adj, of a CHROMOSOME (*strand of gene-carrying material*) having the form of a straight rod owing to the terminal position of the CENTROMERE [ISV *tel-* + *centromere* + *-ic*] – **telocentric** n

**telolecithal** /,telələ'siethl/ adj, of an egg having a large amount of yolk concentrated at one end – compare HOMOLECITHAL, MEGALECITHAL [*tel-* + Gk *lekithos* yolk]

**telomere** /'teləmiə/ n either of the ends of a CHROMOSOME (strand of gene-carrying material) [ISV *tel-* + *-mere*]

**telophase** /,teləfayz, 'tee-/ n **1** the final stage of MITOSIS (splitting of a cell and its contents into two new cells), that is characterized by the appearance of two new nuclei each with the same number of CHROMOSOMES (strands of gene-carrying material) as the original cell, and that is subsequently followed by the division of the original cell into two cells **2** either of two stages in MEIOSIS (splitting of a cell and its contents, ultimately to form four new cells) that mark the ends of the first and second divisions of a cell, and in which respectively two and four new cells or cell nuclei are produced, each having half the number of chromosomes of the original cell [ISV]

**telos** /'telos, 'tee-/ n, pl **teloi** /-oy/ an ultimate end or goal [Gk – more at WHEEL]

**telpher** /'telfə/ n a container or light passenger car suspended from and running on aerial cables and working by electricity [irreg fr Gk *tēle-* tele- + *pherein* to bear – more at BEAR]

**telson** /'telsən/ n the last segment of the body of a scorpion, some insects, etc or of a segmented worm (e g an earthworm);

*esp* that of a crab, lobster, shrimp, or other CRUSTACEAN, that forms the middle lobe of the tail [NL, fr Gk, end of a ploughed field; prob akin to Gk *telos* end]

**Telugu** /'teləgooh/ *n, pl collectively* **Telugu 1** a member of the largest group of people of Andhra Pradesh in India **2** the language of the Telugu people, which belongs to the DRAVIDIAN family of languages

**temblor** /'temblə, -blaw/ *n, NAm* an earthquake ⚠ **trembler** [Sp, lit., trembling, fr *temblar* to tremble, fr ML *tremulare* – more at TREMBLE]

**temenos** /'temənos/ *n, pl* **temene** /-ni/ a temple courtyard or sacred precinct in ancient Greece [Gk, fr *temnein* to cut, separate – more at TOME]

**temerarious** /,temə'reəriəs/ *adj, formal* marked by temerity; rashly or presumptuously daring [L *temerarius*, fr *temere* rashly] – **temerariously** *adv*, **temerariousness** *n*

**temerity** /tə'merəti/ *n* unreasonable or foolhardy contempt of danger or opposition; rashness, recklessness **antonym** caution ⚠ timidity [ME *temeryte*, fr L *temeritas*, fr *temere* at random, rashly, lit., in the dark; akin to OHG *demar* darkness, L *tenebrae*, Skt *tamas*]

**Temne** /'temnee/ *n, pl* **Temnes**, *esp collectively* **Temne** a member, or the language, of a people of Sierra Leone in W Africa

**¹temp** /temp/ *n, informal* a temporary employee; *esp* someone (eg a typist or secretary) employed to work in an office for a limited period of time – **temp** *adv or adj*

**²temp** *vi, informal* to work as a temp

**¹temper** /'tempə/ *vt* **1** to moderate (something harsh) *with* the addition of something less severe ⟨~ *justice with mercy*⟩ **2** to appease, mollify ⟨~ed *and reconciled them both* – Richard Steele⟩ **3** to bring to a suitable state, esp by mixing in or adding a usu liquid ingredient: eg **3a** to mix (clay) with water or a modifier (eg GROG) and knead to a uniform texture **b** to mix oil with (pigment) in making paint ready for use **4a** to toughen or bring (esp steel) to the right degree of hardness by reheating, esp at a lower temperature than the previous heating or after cooling by immersion in oil, water, etc **b** to ANNEAL or toughen (glass) by a process of gradually heating and cooling **5** to make stronger and more resilient through hardship; toughen ⟨*troops* ~ed *in battle*⟩ **6** to adjust the pitch of (a note, chord, or instrument) to esp EQUAL TEMPERAMENT ~ *vi* to produce satisfactory temper (eg in a metal) [ME *temperen*, fr OE & OF; OE *temprian* & OF *temprer*, fr L *temperare* to moderate, mix, temper; prob akin to L *tempor-, tempus* time – more at TEMPORAL] – **temperable** *adj*, **temperer** *n*

**²temper** *n* **1a** characteristic tone; trend, tendency ⟨*the* ~ *of the times*⟩ **b** high quality of mind or spirit; courage, mettle **2** the state of a substance with respect to certain desired qualities (eg hardness, elasticity, or workability); *esp* the degree of hardness or resiliency given to steel by tempering **3a** a characteristic cast of mind or state of feeling; a disposition **b** calmness of mind; composure, equanimity ⟨*don't lose your* ~*!*⟩ **c** a state of feeling or frame of mind at a particular time ⟨*in a bad* ~⟩ **d(1)** heat of mind or emotion; proneness to anger ⟨*a display of* ~⟩ **d(2)** an angry or irritated state of feeling or frame of mind ⟨*kicked a policeman because he was in a* ~ – *Punch*⟩ **4** *archaic* **4a** a suitable proportion or balance of qualities a middle state between extremes; a mean, medium ⟨*virtue is ... a just* ~ *between propensities* – T B Macaulay⟩ **b** character, quality ⟨*the* ~ *of the land*⟩

**tempera** /'tempərə/ *n* a method of painting in which the pigment is mixed with a fairly thick liquid substance (eg egg yolk or glue) instead of oil; *also* a painting done in tempera [It *tempera*, lit., temper, fr *temperare* to temper, fr L]

**temperament** /'temprəmənt/ *n* **1a** a person's peculiar or distinguishing mental or physical character determined by which of the HUMOURS of medieval physiology was dominant in his/her make-up **b** characteristic disposition or frame of mind as expressed by an individual's mental or emotional responses ⟨*he is of a nervous* ~⟩ **c** extremely high or excessive sensitiveness or irritability **2** the modification of the musical intervals of the pure scale to produce a set of 12 fixed notes to the octave which enables a keyboard instrument to play in more than one key – compare EQUAL TEMPERAMENT **3** *archaic* the act or process of tempering or modifying; adjustment, compromise **4** *obs* the constitution of a substance, body, or organism with respect to the mixture or balance of its elements, qualities, or parts; make-up [ME, fr L *temperamentum*, fr *temperare* to mix, temper]

**temperamental** /,temprə'mentl/ *adj* **1** of or arising from temperament; constitutional ⟨~ *peculiarities*⟩ **2a** marked by ex-

cessive sensitivity and impulsive changes of mood ⟨*a* ~ *opera singer*⟩ **b** unpredictable in behaviour or performance – **temperamentally** *adv*

**temperance** /'tempərəns/ *n* **1** moderation in action, thought, or feeling; restraint **2** habitual moderation in the indulgence of the appetites; *specif* moderation in the use of or abstinence from intoxicating drink **synonyms** see ABSTINENCE [ME, fr L *temperantia*, fr *temperant-, temperans*, prp of *temperare* to moderate, be moderate]

**temperance hotel** *n* a hotel where alcohol is not supplied

**temperate** /'tempərət/ *adj* **1** marked by moderation: eg **1a** keeping or held within limits; not extreme or excessive ⟨*a* ~ *climate*⟩ **b** moderate in indulgence of appetite or desire **c** moderate in the consumption of alcoholic drink **d** marked by an absence or avoidance of extravagance, violence, or extreme partisanship; restrained **2a** having a moderate or mild climate ⟨~ *regions*⟩ **b** found in or associated with a temperate climate ⟨~ *insects*⟩ **3** of or being a BACTERIOPHAGE (virus parasitic in and typically destructive to bacteria) that exists in a form that rarely causes the disintegration of the bacterium carrying it [ME *temperat*, fr L *temperatus*, fr pp of *temperare*] – **temperately** *adv*, **temperateness** *n*

**temperate zone** *n, often cap T&Z* either of the two areas or regions between a POLAR CIRCLE and a tropic – compare FRIGID ZONE, TORRID ZONE

**temperature** /'temprəchə/ *n* **1** TEMPERAMENT 1B **2a** degree of hotness or coldness as measured on an arbitrary scale (eg a mercury thermometer graduated in degrees Celsius) **b** the degree of heat that is natural to the body of a living being **c** an abnormally high body heat **d** relative state of emotional warmth ⟨*aware of a change in the* ~ *of our friendship* – Christopher Isherwood⟩ [L *temperatura* mixture, moderation, fr *temperatus*, pp of *temperare*]

**temperature gradient** *n* the rate of change of temperature with displacement in a given direction (eg with increase of height)

**tempered** /'tempəd/ *adj* **1a** having the elements mixed in satisfying proportions; temperate **b** qualified, lessened, or diluted by the mixture or influence of an additional ingredient; moderated ⟨*a pale gleam of* ~ *sunlight fell through the leaves* – W H Hudson †1922⟩ **2** treated by tempering **3** having a specified temper ⟨*short-tempered*⟩ **4** *of a musical interval, intonation, or scale* conforming to temperament, esp EQUAL TEMPERAMENT

**tempersome** /'tempəs(ə)m/ *adj* quick-tempered

**¹tempest** /'tempist/ *n* **1** a violent storm, esp when accompanied by rain, hail, or snow **2** a tumult, uproar [ME, fr OF *tempeste*, fr (assumed) VL *tempesta*, alter. of L *tempestas* season, weather, storm, fr *tempus* time – more at TEMPORAL]

**²tempest** *vt* to raise a tempest in or round; disturb violently

**tempestuous** /tem'peschoo-əs/ *adj* of or resembling a tempest; turbulent, stormy ⟨~ *weather*⟩ ⟨*a* ~ *debate*⟩ [LL *tempestuosus*, fr OL *tempestus* season, weather, storm, fr *tempus*] – **tempestuously** *adv*, **tempestuousness** *n*

**Templar** /'templə/ *n* **1** a knight of a religious military order established in the early 12th century in Jerusalem for the protection of pilgrims and the Holy Sepulchre **2** a lawyer with chambers in the Inner or Middle Temple in London [ME *templer*, fr OF *templier*, fr ML *templarius*, fr L *templum* temple]

**template** /'templayt/, **templet** /'templit/ *n* **1** a short piece or block placed horizontally in a wall under a beam to distribute its weight or pressure (eg over a door) **2a(1)** a gauge, pattern, or mould (eg a thin plate or board) used as a guide to the form of a piece being made **a(2)** a molecule (eg of RNA or DNA) that carries information that codes or acts as a pattern for the structure of another molecule (eg a protein) **b** OVERLAY **d** (transparent sheet to be superimposed over another sheet) [prob fr Fr *templet*, dim. of *temple* temple of a loom]

**¹temple** /'templ/ *n* **1** a building designed for religious purposes: eg **1a** a building dedicated to the worship of a deity among any of various ancient civilizations (eg the Egyptians, the Greeks, and the Romans) and present-day non-Christian religions (eg Hinduism and Buddhism) **b** *often cap* any of three successive national sanctuaries in ancient Jerusalem **c** *chiefly NAm* a synagogue of REFORM JUDAISM or Conservative Judaism **2** a place devoted to a specified purpose ⟨*a* ~ *to music*⟩ **3** *NAm* a local lodge of any of various fraternal orders; *also* the building housing it [ME, fr OE & OF; OE *tempel* & OF *temple*, fr L *templum* space marked out for observation of auguries, temple; prob akin to L *tempus* time] – **templed** *adj*

²**temple** *n* **1** the flattened area on each side of the forehead of some mammals (eg human beings) **2** *NAm* either of the side supports of a pair of glasses jointed to the BOWS (parts of frame holding lenses) and passing on each side of the head [ME, fr MF, fr (assumed) VL *tempula*, alter. of L *tempora* (pl) temples; prob akin to L *tempor-, tempus* time]

³**temple** *n* a device in a loom for keeping the cloth stretched [ME *tempylle*, fr MF *temple*, prob fr L *templum* ¹temple, plank in a roof]

**tempo** /'tempoh/ *n, pl* **tempi** /'tempi/, **tempos 1** the speed of a musical piece or passage indicated by any of a series of directions (eg largo, presto, or allegro) and often by an exact metronome marking **2** rate of motion or activity; pace **3** a turn to move in chess in relation to the number of moves required to gain an objective [It, lit., time, fr L *tempus*]

¹**temporal** /'temp(ə)rəl/ *adj* **1a** of time as opposed to eternity or space; *esp* transitory, temporary **b** of earthly life **c** of lay or secular concerns **2** of grammatical tense or a distinction of time ⟨when *is a* ∼ *conjunction*⟩ *synonyms* see ²PROFANE *antonym* spiritual △ temporary [ME, fr L *temporalis*, fr *tempor-, tempus* time; akin to Lith *tempti* to stretch, & prob to L *tendere* to stretch – more at THIN] – **temporally** *adv*

²**temporal** *adj* of the temple or the equivalent part of the side of the skull [MF, fr LL *temporalis*, fr L *tempora* temples]

**temporal bone** *n* a large bone of the side and base of the human skull, that is composed of four fused parts and encloses the MIDDLE EAR

**temporality** /ˌtempə'raləti/ *n* **1a** civil or political as distinguished from spiritual or ecclesiastical power or authority **b** **temporalities** *pl*, **temporality** an ecclesiastical property or revenue **2** the quality or state of being temporal

**temporal·ize, -ise** /'temp(ə)rəˌliez/ *vt* to secularize

**temporal lobe** *n* a large lobe at the side of each CEREBRAL HEMISPHERE (rounded part forming half of the largest and top or frontmost part of the brain) that is in front of the OCCIPITAL LOBE and below the PARIETAL LOBE and contains a sensory area associated with hearing and speech

**temporarily** /'temprərəli, ˌtempə'rerəli USE *the last pron is disliked by some speakers*/ *adv* during a limited time

¹**temporary** /'tempɾəri; *also* 'tempəˌreri USE *the last pron is disliked by some speakers*/ *adj* lasting for a limited time *synonyms* see ¹TRANSIENT [L *temporarius*, fr *tempor-, tempus* time] – **temporariness** *n*

²**temporary** *n* a temp

**tempor·ize, -ise** /'tempəriez/ *vi* **1** to act to suit the time or occasion; yield to current or dominant opinion **2** to draw out discussions or negotiations so as to gain time △ extemporize [MF *temporiser*, fr ML *temporizare* to pass the time, fr L *tempor-, tempus* time] – **temporization** *n*, **temporizer** *n*

**tempt** /tempt/ *vt* **1** to entice, esp to evil, by promise of pleasure or gain ⟨∼ed *by the devil*⟩ **2** to try presumptuously; risk the disfavour of ⟨*shouldn't* ∼ *fate*⟩ **3a** to induce to do something **b** to cause to be strongly inclined ⟨*he was* ∼ed *to call it quits*⟩ **c** to appeal to; entice ⟨*the idea* ∼*s me*⟩ **4** *obs* to make trial of; test *synonyms* see ²LURE [ME *tempten*, fr OF *tempter, tenter*, fr L *temptare, tentare* to feel, try, tempt; akin to L *tendere* to stretch – more at THIN] – **temptable** *adj*

**temptation** /temp'taysh(ə)n/ *n* **1** tempting or being tempted, esp to evil; enticement **2** something tempting; a cause or occasion of enticement

**tempter** /'temptə/ *n* **1** *fem* **temptress** someone who tempts or entices **2** something tempting ⟨*the smoked salmon is a real* ∼ *but I think I'll have the avocado soup*⟩

**tempting** /'tempting/ *adj* having an appeal; enticing ⟨*a* ∼ *offer*⟩ – **temptingly** *adv*

**tempura** /tem'pooərə, 'tempərə/ *n* a Japanese dish of seafood or vegetables dipped in batter and fried [Jap *tenpura*]

**ten** /ten/ *n* **1** – see NUMBER table **2** the 10th in a set or series ⟨*the* ∼ *of diamonds*⟩ **3** something having 10 parts or members, or a denomination of 10 **4** *pl* the number occupying the position two to the left of the decimal point in the Arabic notation; *also, pl* this position **5** a note, bill, or coin worth ten units of currency (eg a 10-pound note or 10-pence piece) [ME, fr OE *tīene*, fr *tīen*, adj, ten; akin to OHG *zehan* ten, L *decem*, Gk *deka*] – **ten** *adj or pron*, **tenth** *adj, adv, or n*

**tenable** /'tenəbl/ *adj* capable of being held, maintained, or defended; defensible, reasonable [Fr, fr OF, fr *tenir* to hold, fr L *tenēre* – more at THIN ] – **tenableness** *n*, **tenably** *adv*, **tenability** *n*

**tenace** /'tenays/ *n* a combination of two cards (eg ace and

queen) of the same suit in one hand with one ranking two degrees below the other [modif of Sp *tenaza*, lit., forceps, prob fr L *tenacia*, neut pl of *tenax* holding fast]

**tenacious** /tə'nayshəs/ *adj* **1a** not easily pulled apart; cohesive, tough ⟨*a* ∼ *metal*⟩ **b** tending to adhere or cling, esp to another substance; sticky ⟨∼ *burs*⟩ ⟨∼ *clay*⟩ **2a** persistent in maintaining or adhering to something valued as habitual ⟨*a man very* ∼ *of his rights*⟩ **b** retentive ⟨*a* ∼ *memory*⟩ *synonyms* see STRONG [L *tenac-, tenax* holding fast, fr *tenēre* to hold] – **tenaciously** *adv*, **tenaciousness** *n*

**tenacity** /tə'nasəti/ *n* the quality or state of being tenacious

**tenaculum** /tə'nakyooləm/ *n, pl* **tenacula** /-lə/, **tenaculums** a slender sharp-pointed hook attached to a handle and used mainly in surgery for seizing and holding parts (eg arteries) [NL, fr LL, instrument for holding, fr L *tenēre* to hold]

**tenancy** /'tenənsi/ *n* **1** a holding of an estate under a title of ownership **2** temporary occupancy (eg of land or a house) under a lease or rental agreement; *also* the period of such occupancy

¹**tenant** /'tenənt/ *n* **1a** a person who holds or possesses real estate or sometimes personal property (eg an annuity) by any kind of right **b** a person who has the occupation or temporary possession of lands or tenements of another; *specif* a person who rents or leases a house or flat from a landlord **2** an occupant, dweller [ME, fr MF, fr prp of *tenir* to hold] – **tenantless** *adj*

²**tenant** *vt* to hold or occupy as a tenant; inhabit – **tenantable** *adj*

**tenant farmer** *n* a farmer who rents the land he/she works from another

**tenantry** /'tenəntri/ *n taking sing or pl vb* tenants collectively; *esp* the body of tenants on an estate

**tench** /tench/ *n, pl* **tenches**, *esp collectively* **tench** a Eurasian freshwater fish (*Tinca tinca*) related to the carp, that has a thick greenish or blackish skin and is noted for its ability to survive outside water [ME, fr MF *tenche*, fr LL *tinca*]

**Ten Commandments** *n pl* the ethical commandments of the Jewish and Christian religions given according to biblical accounts, by God to Moses on Mount Sinai and recorded in Ex 20:1–17

¹**tend** /tend/ *vi* **1** to pay attention; apply oneself – usu + *to* ⟨∼ *to your own affairs*⟩ **2** to act as an attendant; serve **3** *obs* to await ∼ *vt* **1a** to apply oneself to the care of; minister to ⟨*to* ∼ *the soldier's wounds*⟩ **b** to have or take charge of as a caretaker or overseer ⟨∼*s the sheep*⟩ **c** to cultivate, foster ⟨*to* ∼ *the crops*⟩ **d** to manage the operations of; mind ⟨∼ *the fire*⟩ **2** *nautical* to stand by (eg a rope) to prevent FOULING (tangling or becoming obstructed) [ME *tenden*, short for *attenden* to attend]

> ***usage*** The use of **tend** *to* for **attend** *to*, as in sense 1, should be avoided in formal writing. Acceptable alternatives are ⟨*the nurse* **tends** *the sick*/**attends** *to the sick*⟩ ⟨*the lady-in-waiting* **attends** *the queen*⟩.

²**tend** *vi* **1** to move, direct, or develop one's course in a specified direction **2** to show an inclination or tendency; conduce – + *to, towards*, or *to* and an infin [ME *tenden*, fr MF *tendre* to stretch, fr L *tendere* – more at THIN]

**tendency** /'tendənsi/ *n* **1a** a direction or approach towards a place, object, effect, or limit ⟨*that* ∼ *in art which is called abstract*⟩ **b** a proneness to a particular kind of thought or action ⟨*an instinctive* ∼ *towards temperance*⟩ **2** the purposeful trend of something written or said **3** a radical group that seeks to increase its influence and further its policies usu towards a specified end by working within a political party – compare GINGER GROUP [ML *tendentia*, fr L *tendent-, tendens*, prp of *tendere* to tend]

> *synonyms* **Tendency, inclination, trend, current, drift,** and **tenor** all mean "direction of action or thought". A **tendency** may amount to an impelling force ⟨*the whole* **tendency** *of evolution is towards a diminishing birthrate* – Havelock Ellis⟩, and may apply to an individual ⟨*has a* **tendency** *to be absentminded*⟩. **Inclination** usually refers to an individual thing or person ⟨*clutch has an* **inclination** *to slip*⟩ and often involves liking ⟨*a strong* **inclination** *towards study*⟩. A **trend** is usually a widespread movement or fashion ⟨*follow the prevailing* **trend** *towards smaller cars*⟩ or may suggest the general direction maintained by an irregular course ⟨*the long-term* **trend** *of the market is upwards*⟩. **Current**, by extension from the idea of swiftly moving water, suggests a clearly defined and perhaps irresistible widespread movement ⟨*a strong* **current** *of public opinion*⟩. By contrast **drift** implies being rather aimlessly

carried by external forces ⟨the drift *away from organized Christianity*⟩, but it can also mean "underlying obscure purport" ⟨*I see the whole* **drift** *of your argument* – Oliver Goldsmith⟩. **Tenor** also means a "purport", but a clearer one ⟨*his answer was bellicose in* **tenor**⟩, and it also suggests a continuous usually unvarying course ⟨*earth and sun preserve the even* **tenor** *of their ways*⟩.

**tendentious** *also* **tendencious** /ten'denshəs/ *adj* showing a tendency to favour a particular point of view; biased – **tendentiously** *adv*, **tendentiousness** *n*

¹**tender** /'tendə/ *adj* **1a** having a soft or yielding texture; easily broken, cut, or damaged **b** easily chewed; succulent ⟨~ *breasts of chicken in a cream sauce*⟩ **2a** physically weak; not able to endure hardship **b** immature, young ⟨*children of* ~ *years*⟩ **3** marked by, responding to, or expressing the softer emotions; fond, loving ⟨*a* ~ *lover*⟩ **4a** showing care; considerate, solicitous ⟨~ *regard*⟩ **b** highly susceptible to impressions or emotions; impressionable ⟨*a* ~ *conscience*⟩ **5a** appropriate or conducive to a delicate or sensitive constitution or character; gentle, mild ⟨~ *breeding*⟩ ⟨~ *irony*⟩ **b** delicate or soft in quality or tone ⟨*never before heard anyone make the piano sound so* ~⟩ **6a** sensitive to touch ⟨~ *skin*⟩ **b** sensitive to injury or insult; touchy ⟨~ *pride*⟩ **c** demanding careful and sensitive handling; ticklish ⟨*a* ~ *situation*⟩ **d** *of a ship* inclined to heel over easily under sail *synonyms* see LOVING [ME, fr OF *tendre*, fr L *tener* soft, young] – **tenderly** *adv*, **tenderness** *n*

²**tender** *vb* to make or become tender; soften, weaken

³**tender** *n* one who or that which tends: e g **a(1)** a ship used to attend other ships (e g to supply provisions) **a(2)** a boat or small steamer for communication between shore and a larger ship **a(3)** a warship that provides logistic support **b** a vehicle attached to a locomotive for carrying a supply of fuel and water **c** **tender, fire tender** an auxiliary fire fighting truck; *esp* one carrying hose and special equipment

⁴**tender** *vt* **1** to make a tender of **2** to present for acceptance; proffer ⟨~ed *his resignation*⟩ ~ *vi* to make a bid ⟨*six firms at least are expected to* ~ *for the contract*⟩ – **tenderer** *n*

⁵**tender** *n* **1** an unconditional offer of money or service towards paying off a debt or obligation made to avoid a penalty for nonpayment or nonperformance **2** an offer or proposal made for acceptance: e g **2a** a formal offer or bid, esp one in writing, for a contract (e g to carry out work or supply goods) **b** a public expression of willingness to buy not less than a specified number of shares at a fixed price from shareholders, usu in an attempt to gain control of the issuing company **3** **tender, legal tender** something that may be offered in payment; *specif* money [MF *tendre* to stretch, stretch out, offer – more at TEND]

**tenderfoot** /'tendə,foot/ *n*, *pl* **tenderfeet** /-,feet/ *also* **tenderfoots 1** an inexperienced beginner; a novice ⟨*a political* ~⟩ **2** *chiefly NAm* a newcomer in a comparatively rough or newly settled region; *esp* one not hardened to frontier or outdoor life

**tenderhearted** /,tendə'hahtid/ *adj* easily moved to love, pity, or sorrow; compassionate, impressionable – **tenderheartedly** *adv*, **tenderheartedness** *n*

**tender·ize, -ise** /'tendəriez/ *vt* to make (meat or meat products) tender by applying a process (e g beating) or substance (e g an ENZYME) that breaks down fibrous tissue – **tenderizer** *n*, **tenderization** *n*

**tenderloin** /'tendə,loyn/ *n* **1** a strip of tender meat consisting of a large internal muscle of the loin; *specif* a pork or beef fillet **2** *NAm* a district of a city noted for vice and corruption [(2) fr its offering a luxurious diet to a corrupt policeman]

,**tender-'minded** *adj* idealistic, optimistic, and dogmatic; *esp* reluctant to allow facts to undermine cherished assumptions

**tenderometer** /,tendə'romitə/ *n* a device for determining the maturity and tenderness of samples of food (e g fruits and vegetables)

**tendinous** /'tendinəs/ *adj* **1** of or resembling a tendon **2** consisting of tendons; sinewy ⟨~ *tissue*⟩ [NL *tendinosus*, fr *tendin-*, *tendo* tendon, alter. of ML *tendon-*, *tendo*]

**tendon** /'tendən/ *n* a tough inelastic cord or band of dense strong white fibrous CONNECTIVE TISSUE that connects a muscle with some other part (e g a bone) and transmits the force exerted by the muscle [ML *tendon-*, *tendo*, fr L *tendere* to stretch – more at THIN]

**tendresse** /ton'dres (*Fr* tãdrɛs)/ *n*, *formal* fondness ⟨*affected a certain* ~ *for the fashions of her youth*⟩ [Fr, fr MF, fr *tendre* tender]

**tendril** /'tendril/ *n* a slender spirally twisted sensitive plant organ consisting of a modified leaf, stem, etc, that serves to attach a climbing plant to its support [perh modif of MF *tend-*

*ron*, alter. of *tendon*, lit., tendon, fr ML *tendon-*, *tendo*] – **tendriled, tendrilled** *adj*, **tendrilous** *adj*

¹**-tene** /-teen/ *comb form* (→ *adj*) having (such or so many) chromosomal filaments ⟨*polytene*⟩ ⟨*pachytene*⟩ [L *taenia* ribbon, band – more at TAENIA]

²**-tene** *comb form* (→ *n*) stage of the first division of meiosis characterized by (such) chromosomal filaments ⟨*diplotene*⟩ ⟨*pachytene*⟩

**Tenebrae** /'tenəbray/ *n taking sing or pl vb* the service of MATINS and LAUDS for the last three days of Holy Week commemorating the sufferings and death of Christ [ML, fr L, darkness – more at TEMERITY]

**tenebrific** /,tenə'brifik/ *adj*, *formal* causing gloom or darkness [L *tenebrae* darkness]

**tenebrionid** /tə'nebriənid, tenə'brie-ənid/ *n* any of a family (Tenebrionidae) of firm-bodied mostly dark-coloured plant-eating beetles that often have much reduced and non functional hind wings, and whose larvae are usu hard cylindrical worms (e g the mealworm) [NL *Tenebrionidae*, group name, fr *Tenebrion-*, *Tenebrio*, type genus, fr L, one who works in darkness, fr *tenebrae* darkness] – **tenebrionid** *adj*

**tenebrous** /'tenəbrəs/ *adj*, *formal* **1** shut off from the light; dark, murky **2** hard to understand; obscure **3** causing gloom [ME, fr MF *tenebreus*, fr L *tenebrosus*, fr *tenebrae* darkness]

**tenement** /'tenəmənt/ *n* **1** land or any of various forms of INCORPOREAL (non-material) property treated like land that is held by one person from another; a holding **2a** a large building divided into flats; *esp* one meeting minimum standards and typically found in the poorer parts of a large city **b** a flat in a tenement [ME, fr MF, fr ML *tenementum*, fr L *tenēre* to hold – more at THIN]

**tenementary** /,tenə'ment(ə)ri/ *adj*, *formal* consisting of tenements

**tenesmus** /tə'nezməs/ *n* an uncomfortable but ineffectual urge to defecate or urinate [L, fr Gk *teinesmos*, fr *teinein* to stretch, strain – more at THIN]

**tenet** /'tenət/ *n* a principle, belief, or doctrine generally held to be true; *esp* one held in common by members of an organization, group, movement, or profession [L, he holds, fr *tenēre* to hold]

**tenfold** /'ten,fohld/ *adj* **1** having 10 units or members **2** being 10 times as great or as many – **tenfold** *adv*

**ten-gallon hat** *n* COWBOY HAT [fr its great size]

**tenia** /'teenyə/ *n*, *pl* **teniae** /'teeni,ie/, **tenias** *NAm* TAENIA

**ten minute rule** *n* a rule under which a Member of Parliament may introduce a PRIVATE MEMBER'S BILL by making a brief speech

**tenner** /'tenə/ *n*, *Br informal* a 10-pound note; *also* the sum of 10 pounds

**tennis** /'tenis/ *n* **1** REAL TENNIS **2** **tennis, lawn tennis** a usu outdoor singles or doubles game that is played with rackets and a light elastic ball on a flat court divided by a low net [ME *tenetz*, *tenys*, prob fr AF *tenetz* take, receive (as called by the server to his opponent), imper of *tenir* to hold, take]

**tennis elbow** *n* inflammation and pain of the elbow, usu resulting from excessive twisting movements of the hand

¹**tenon** /'tenən/ *n* a projecting part of a piece of material (e g wood) that inserts into a MORTISE (hole or slot) to make a joint [ME, fr OF, fr *tenir* to hold – more at TENABLE]

²**tenon** *vt* **1** to unite by a tenon **2** to cut or fit for insertion in a MORTISE (hole or slot forming part of a joint)

**tenon saw** *n* a woodworking saw that has a short usu rectangular blade, reinforced along the upper non-cutting edge by an extra strip of metal, and that is used for making straight cuts (e g for forming tenons)

¹**tenor** /'tenə/ *n* **1** the course of thought or implied line of argument of something spoken or written; purport, drift **2a** the melodic line usu forming the CANTUS FIRMUS (theme) in medieval music **b** the next to the lowest part in 4-part harmony **c** the highest natural adult male singing voice; *also* a person having this voice **d** a member of a family of instruments having a range immediately below that of the alto **3** a continuance in a course, movement, or activity ⟨*nothing disturbed the quiet even* ~ *of those Oxford summer days*⟩ **4** the average amount of metal or mineral in an ore *synonyms* see TENDENCY [ME, fr OF, fr L *tenor* uninterrupted course, fr *tenēre* to hold – more at THIN]

²**tenor** *adj* (having the range or part) of a tenor

**tenor clef** *n* a C CLEF designating a note written on the next to top line of the stave as MIDDLE C

**tenorite** /'tenəriet/ n a black mineral consisting of copper oxide, CuO, that occurs in the form of minute scales or earthy masses [It, fr M *Tenore* †1861 It botanist]

**tenosynovitis** /,tenoh,sinoh'vietəs, ,teenoh-/ n inflammation of the sheath covering a tendon [NL, fr Gk *tenōn* tendon (akin to Gk *teinein* to stretch) + NL *synovitis* – more at THIN]

**tenpin** /'ten,pin/ n 1 a bottle-shaped pin used in TENPIN BOWLING 2 *pl but taking sing vb*, NAm TENPIN BOWLING

**tenpin bowling** n an indoor bowling game using 10 pins and a large ball with two finger holes and a thumb hole, in which each player is allowed to bowl two balls in each of 10 rounds (FRAMES)

**tenrec** /'ten,rek/ n any of numerous small often spiny insect-eating mammals (family Tenrecidae) of Madagascar [Fr, fr Malagasy *tàndraka*]

¹**tense** /tens/ n 1 a distinction of form in a verb to specify the time or duration of the action or state it denotes 2 a set of modifications (INFLECTIONS) to the basic forms of a verb that express distinctions of time; *also* a member of such a set [ME *tens* time, tense, fr MF, fr L *tempus* – more at TEMPORAL]

²**tense** adj 1 stretched tight; made taut or rigid 2a feeling or showing nervous tension **b** marked by strain or suspense 3 *of a speech sound* (e g the vowel /ee/ in contrast with the vowel /i/) pronounced with the muscles in a relatively tense state – compare LAX *synonyms* see ¹STIFF *antonyms* relaxed, expansive [L *tensus*, fr pp of *tendere* to stretch – more at THIN] – **tensely** adv, **tenseness** n

³**tense** vb to make or become tense – often + up

**tensile** /'tensiel/ adj 1 capable of tension or of being stretched or drawn out; *broadly* DUCTILE 2 of or involving tension – **tensility** n

**tensile strength** n a measure of the ability of a material (e g a metal) to withstand tension or a pulling force, equal to the greatest stress it can bear along its length without breaking

**tensimeter** /ten'simitə/ n an instrument for measuring differences of VAPOUR PRESSURE [*tension* + *-meter*]

**tensiometer** /,tensi'omitə/ n 1 a device for measuring tension (e g of a fabric, yarn, or structural material) 2 a device for measuring TENSILE STRENGTH 3 an instrument for measuring the moisture content of soil 4 an instrument for measuring the SURFACE TENSION (force between molecules on the surface) of liquids [*tension* + *-meter*] – **tensiometric** adj, **tensiometry** n

¹**tension** /'tenshən/ n 1a the act or action of stretching or the condition or degree of being stretched to stiffness; tautness **b** the condition of being taut or rigid ⟨*muscular* ~⟩ 2a either of two forces that pull in opposite directions and cause or tend to cause extension of a material, body, or structure **b** the pressure exerted by a gas; *esp* PARTIAL PRESSURE (pressure exerted by a component of a mixture of gases) 3a mental or emotional unrest or unease often accompanied by an inability to relax, increased heart rate, etc; stress **b** a state of latent hostility or opposition between individuals or groups ⟨*the post-war period of East-West* ~ *known as the Cold War*⟩ **c** a balance maintained in an artistic work between opposing forces or elements 4 voltage or electrical potential, esp of a specified kind ⟨*high* ~⟩ 5 a device to produce a desired tension (e g in a loom or sewing machine) [MF or L; MF, fr L *tension-*, *tensio*, fr *tensus*, pp] – **tensional** adj, **tensionless** adj

²**tension** vt to subject to tension; *esp* to tighten to a desired or appropriate degree – **tensioner** n

**tensity** /'tensəti/ n being tense; tenseness

**tensive** /'tensiv/ adj of or causing tension

**tensometer** /ten'somitə/ n a tensiometer

**tensor** /'tensə, -,saw/ n 1 a muscle that stretches a body part 2 *maths & physics* a generalized VECTOR with more than two components each of which is a FUNCTION of the COORDINATES (numbers which indicate the exact position of the vector) of an arbitrary point in space of an appropriate number of dimensions [NL, fr L *tensus*, pp]

¹**tent** /tent/ n 1 a collapsible shelter (e g of canvas) held up by poles and used (e g by campers) as a temporary building 2 something that resembles a tent or that serves as a shelter; *esp* a canopy or enclosure placed over the head and shoulders of a patient to retain vapours or oxygen during medical treatment [ME *tente*, fr OF, fr L *tenta*, fem of *tentus*, pp of *tendere* to stretch – more at THIN] – **tentless** adj

²**tent** vi to live in a tent ~ vt 1 to cover (as if) with a tent 2 to house in tents

³**tent** vt, *chiefly Scot* to attend to [ME *tenten*, fr *tent* attention, short for *attent*, fr OF *attente*, fr *attendre* to attend]

**tentacle** /'tentəkl/ n 1 any of various elongated flexible sometimes branching structures borne by animals (e g a jellyfish or octopus) chiefly on the head or round the mouth, and used for feeling, grasping, etc 2a something that functions like a tentacle in grasping or feeling out **b** a sensitive hair on a plant, esp an insect-eating plant (e g the sundew) [NL *tentaculum*, fr L *tentare* to feel, touch, try – more at TEMPT] – **tentacled** adj

**tentacular** /ten'takyoolə/ adj 1 of or resembling tentacles 2 having tentacles [NL *tentaculum* tentacle]

**tentage** /'tentij/ n a collection of tents; tent equipment

**tentative** /'tentətiv/ adj 1 not fully worked out or developed ⟨~ *plans*⟩ 2 hesitant, uncertain ⟨*a* ~ *smile*⟩ [ML *tentativus*, fr L *tentatus*, pp of *tentare* to feel, try] – **tentative** n, **tentatively** adv, **tentativeness** n

**tented** /'tentid/ adj 1 covered with a tent or tents 2 shaped like a tent 3 consisting of tents

**tenter** /'tentə/ n 1 a frame or endless track with hooks or clips along two sides that is used for drying and stretching cloth 2 *archaic* a tenterhook [ME *teyntur, tentowre*, prob modif of ML *tentura*, fr L *tentus*, pp of *tendere* to stretch]

**tenterhook** /'tentə,hook/ n a sharp hooked nail used esp for fastening cloth on a tenter – **on tenterhooks** in a state of uneasiness or suspense

**tenth-'rate** /tenth/ adj of the lowest character or quality

**tentorium** /ten'tawriəm, -'toh-/ n the internal skeleton, composed of CHITIN, of an insect's head [NL, fr L, tent, fr *tentus*, pp]

**tentpegging** /'tent,peging/ n an event in horse riding sports or competitions in which the rider uses a lance to try to pick up a tent peg fixed in the ground while at full gallop

**tent stitch** n a short diagonal stitch used in embroidery and canvas work to form a solid background of even lines of parallel stitches

**tenuis** /'tenyoois/ n, pl **tenues** /-eez/ a speech sound that is an unaspirated voiceless STOP (sound produced by a complete blockage of the air stream) [ML, fr L, thin, slight]

**tenuity** /tə'nyooh·əti/ n, *formal* 1 lack of substance or strength 2 lack of thickness; slenderness, thinness 3 lack of density; rarefied quality or state [L *tenuitas*, fr *tenuis* thin, tenuous]

**tenuous** /'tenyoo·əs/ adj 1 not dense in consistency; rarefied ⟨*a* ~ *fluid*⟩ 2 not thick; slender ⟨*a* ~ *rope*⟩ 3 having little substance or strength; flimsy, weak ⟨~ *influences*⟩ ⟨*a* ~ *hold on reality*⟩ [L *tenuis* thin, slight, tenuous – more at THIN] – **tenuously** adv, **tenuousness** n

**tenure** /'tenyə/ n 1a the act, right, manner, or term of holding something (e g a landed property, a position, or an office) **b** *chiefly NAm* freedom from summary dismissal esp from a teaching post 2 *formal* a grasp, hold [ME, fr OF *teneüre, tenure*, fr ML *tenitura*, fr (assumed) VL *tenitura*, fr *tenēre* to hold – more at THIN] – **tenurial** adj, **tenurially** adv

**tenured** /'tenyəd/ adj, *chiefly NAm* having or offering tenure ⟨*a* ~ *post*⟩

**tenuto** /te'nyoohtoh/ adv or adj in a manner so as to hold a note or chord to its full value – used as a direction in music [It, fr pp of *tenere* to hold, fr L *tenēre*]

**teocalli** /,teeoh'kali/ n an ancient temple of Mexico or Central America usu built upon the flat summit of a pyramid-like mound; *also* the mound itself [Nahuatl, fr *teotl* god + *calli* house]

**teonanacatl** /,tayoh,nunə'kutl/ n any of several N and S American mushrooms (*Psilocybe* and related genera of the family Agaricaceae) that are sources of hallucinogenic drugs – compare SACRED MUSHROOM [Nahuatl, fr *teotl* god + *nanacatl* mushroom]

**teosinte** /,tee·oh'sinti/ n a tall grass (*Euchlaena mexicana*) of Mexico and Central America that resembles and is closely related to maize and is grown esp for fodder [MexSp, fr Nahuatl *teocentli*, fr *teotl* god + *centli* ear of corn]

**tepa** /'teepə/ n a chemical compound, $C_6H_{12}N_3OP$, that is used esp to produce sterility in insects, in finishing and flame-proofing textiles, and in the treatment of some forms of cancer [*tri-* + *ethylene* + *phosphor-* + *amide*]

**tepee** /'tee,pee/ n a N American Indian conical tent usu consisting of skins and used esp by the tribes of the Great Plains region [Dakota *tipi*, fr *ti* to dwell + *pi* to use for]

**tephigram** /'tefigram/ n a chart showing vertical variations of atmospheric conditions [*T*, symbol for temperature + *phi*, name of former symbol for entropy + *-gram*]

**tephra** /'tefrə/ n, *chiefly NAm* solid material (e g volcanic ash and cinders) ejected during the eruption of a volcano [NL, fr Gk, ashes]

**tepid** /'tepid/ *adj* **1** moderately warm; lukewarm ⟨*a* ~ *bath*⟩ **2** being without enthusiasm or conviction ⟨*a* ~ *interest*⟩ [L *tepidus*, fr *tepēre* to be moderately warm; akin to Skt *tapati* it gives out heat, OIr *tess* heat] – **tepidly** *adv*, **tepidness** *n*, **tepidity** *n*

**tepidarium** /ˌtepiˈdeəriəm, -ˈdah-/ *n*, *pl* **tepidaria** /-riə/ the chamber of a Roman bathhouse containing the warm bath – compare CALIDARIUM, FRIGIDARIUM, LACONICUM [L, fr *tepidus* tepid]

**TEPP** *n* a corrosive liquid phosphorus-containing organic chemical compound, $(C_2H_5)_4$ $P_2O_7$, that acts as a nerve poison by inhibiting the action of CHOLINESTERASE, and is used esp as an insecticide (e g in the control of aphids) [*tetraethyl pyrophosphate*]

**tequila** /təˈkeelə/ *n* **1** a Mexican agave (*Agave tequilana*) much cultivated as a source of MESCAL (alcoholic spirit) **2** a Mexican spirit made by redistilling MESCAL [Sp, fr *Tequila*, district of Mexico]

**ter-** *comb form* three times; threefold; three ⟨ter*centenary*⟩ [L, fr *ter;* akin to Gk & Skt *tris* three times, L *tres* three – more at THREE]

**tera-** *comb form* billion $(10^{12})$ ⟨tera*ton*⟩ ⟨tera*hertz*⟩ [ISV, fr Gk *teras* monster]

**terai** /təˈrie/ *n* a wide-brimmed felt sun hat worn esp in subtropical regions [*Tarai*, region in NE India]

**teraph** /'teraf/ *n*, *pl* **teraphim** /'terəfim/ a small household god or image of any of various ancient Semitic peoples [Heb *tĕrāphīm* (pl in form but sing. in meaning)]

**terat-, terato** *comb form* monster; monstrosity ⟨terat*ology*⟩ [Gk, fr *terat-, teras* marvel, monster; akin to Lith *keras* enchantment]

**teratogen** /təˈratəjən/ *n* something that causes developmental malformations in foetuses – **teratogenic** *adj*, **teratogenicity** *n*

**teratogenesis** /ˌterətəˈjenəsis/ *n* the production of developmental malformations in foetuses [NL, fr *terat-* + *genesis*]

**teratological** /ˌterətəˈlojikl/ *also* **teratologic** *adj* **1** abnormal in growth or structure **2** of teratology

**teratology** /ˌterəˈtolǝji/ *n* the study of malformations or serious deviations from the normal type in foetuses [ISV *terat-* + *-logy*] – **teratologist** *n*

**teratoma** /ˌterəˈtohmə/ *n* a tumour made up of a mixture of several types of tissue (e g bone, fat, tooth, and muscle) of different origin [NL, fr *terat-* + *-oma*] – **teratomatous** *adj*

**terbium** /'tuhbi-əm/ *n* a metallic chemical element of the RARE-EARTH group, usu having a VALENCY of three [NL, fr *Ytterby*, town in Sweden]

**terce** /tuhs/ *n*, *often cap* the third of the CANONICAL HOURS (time appointed for worship) of the Roman Catholic church that was originally fixed for 9 am [ME, third, terce – more at TIERCE]

**tercel** /'tuhsl/ *n* a male of any of various hawks (e g the peregrine falcon), esp when used in falconry [ME, fr MF, fr (assumed) VL *tertiolus*, fr dim. of L *tertius* third; perh fr the belief that the third egg of a clutch produced a male bird]

**tercentenary** /ˌtuhsenˈteenəri, -ˈtenəri/ *n* a 300th anniversary or its celebration – **tercentenary** *adj*

**tercentennial** /ˌtuhsenˈteni-əl/ *n*, *chiefly NAm* a tercentenary – **tercentennial** *adj*

**tercet** /'tuhsit/ *n* a unit or group of three lines of verse: **a** any of the 3-line STANZAS (sections) in TERZA RIMA (verse form with interlaced rhyme scheme) **b** either of the two groups of three lines forming the SESTET (last six lines) in an ITALIAN SONNET (sonnet with two sections in its rhyme pattern) [It *terzetto*, fr dim. of *terzo* third, fr L *tertius* – more at THIRD]

**terebene** /'terəbeen/ *n* a mixture of TERPENES (chemical compounds occurring in natural plant oils) obtained from OIL OF TURPENTINE and used in medicine as an antiseptic and expectorant [Fr *térébène*, fr *térébinthe* terebinth]

**terebinth** /'terəbinth/ *n* a small European tree (*Pistacia terebinthus*) of the sumach family that yields turpentine [ME *terebynt*, fr MF *terebinthe*, fr L *terebinthus* – more at TURPENTINE]

**terebinthine** /ˌterəˈbinthien/ *adj* (consisting of) or resembling turpentine [L *terebinthinus* of the terebinth]

**terebra** /'terəbrə/ *n*, *pl* **terebras, terebrae** /-ˌbri, -ˌbrie/ an OVIPOSITOR (egg-laying structure in female insects), esp of a HYMENOPTEROUS insect (e g a bee, wasp, or sawfly) that is modified for boring or sawing into plant tissues in order to deposit eggs or for stinging [NL, fr L, boring instrument, fr *terere* to rub, grind – more at THROW] – **terebrant** *adj*

**teredo** /təˈraydoh/ *n*, *pl* **teredos, teredines** /teˈredineez/ SHIPWORM (wormlike marine clam) [L *teredin-, teredo,* fr Gk *terēdōn;* akin to Gk *tetrainein* to bore – more at THROW]

**terephthalate** /ˌterəfˈthalayt/ *n* any of various chemical compounds (SALTS or ESTERS) formed by combination between TEREPHTHALIC ACID and a metal atom, an alcohol, or another chemical group; *esp* one that is a major starting material for polyester fibres and coatings

**terephthalic acid** /ˌterəfˈthalik/ *n* an organic chemical acid, $C_6H_4(COOH)_2$, used chiefly in the synthesis of polyester fibres and fabrics [ISV *terebene* + *phthalic acid*]

**terete** /təˈreet/ *adj*, *of a plant or animal part* approximately cylindrical with a smooth surface ⟨*a* ~ *seedpod*⟩ [L *teret-, teres* rounded, smooth; akin to L *terere* to rub]

**tergite** /'tuhgiet/ *n* the plate forming the back or upper surface of a segment of an insect, spider, crab, etc [ISV *terg-* (fr L *tergum* back) + *-ite*]

**tergiversate** /'tuhjivəˌsayt, -giv-/ *vi, formal* **1** to become a renegade **2** to act evasively or equivocally [L *tergiversatus*, pp of *tergiversari* to turn one's back, evade, fr *tergum* back + *versare* to turn, fr *versus,* pp of *vertere* to turn – more at WORTH] – **tergiversation** *n*, **tergiversationary** *adj*, **tergiversator** *n*

**tergum** /'tuhgəm/ *n*, *pl* **terga** /'tuhgə/ the back or upper part or surface of a segment of the body of an insect, spider, crab, etc [NL, fr L, back] – **tergal** *adj*

¹**term** /tuhm/ *n* **1a** an end, termination; *also* a point in time assigned for something (e g payment) **b** the time at which a pregnancy of normal length ends ⟨*had her baby at full* ~⟩ **2a** a limited or definite extent of time; *esp* the time for which something lasts; duration ⟨*lost circulation in the short* ~*, but in the long* ~ *. . .*⟩ ⟨*medium*-term *credit*⟩ **b** the whole period for which an estate is granted; *also* the estate or interest held for a term **c** any one of the periods of the year during which the courts are in session **3a** any of the three periods of instruction into which an academic year is divided **b** termtime **4** *maths* **4a** an expression connected with another by a plus or minus sign **b** an expression that forms part of a fraction or proportion or of a series or sequence **5** a concept, word, or phrase appearing as subject or PREDICATE (what is stated of the subject) in a logical proposition **6a** a word or expression with a precise meaning; *esp* one that is peculiar to a science, art, profession, or subject ⟨*legal* ~s⟩ **b** *pl* diction of a specified kind ⟨*spoke in flattering* ~s⟩ **7** *pl* provisions that are stated or offered for acceptance and that determine the nature and scope of an agreement; conditions ⟨~s *of sale*⟩ ⟨~s *of a treaty*⟩ **8** *pl* **8a** mutual relationship ⟨*on good* ~s *with him*⟩ **b** agreement, concord ⟨*come to* ~s⟩ **9** a square PEDESTAL (support of a column) with a bust at the top (e g of the Roman god Terminus) used as an ornament in classical architecture [ME *terme* boundary, end, fr OF, fr L *terminus;* akin to Gk *termōn* boundary, end, Skt *tarati* he crosses over – more at THROUGH] – **in terms of** in relation to; concerning

²**term** *vt* to apply a term to; call, name ⟨*wouldn't* ~ *it difficult*⟩

¹**termagant** /'tuhməgənt/ *n* **1** *cap* a violent stock character in early English drama (esp MIRACLE PLAYS) representing an imaginary Islamic deity **2** an overbearing or nagging woman; a shrew [ME]

²**termagant** *adj* overbearing, shrewish ⟨*life . . . wrecked by a* ~ *mother* – *Newsweek*⟩ – **termagantly** *adv*

**terminable** /'tuhminəbl/ *adj* capable of being terminated △ terminal [ME, fr *terminen* to terminate, fr OF *terminer*, fr L *terminare*] – **terminableness** *n*, **terminably** *adv*

¹**terminal** /'tuhminl/ *adj* **1a** of or being an end, extremity, boundary, or terminus ⟨*a* ~ *pillar*⟩ **b** growing at the end of a branch or stem ⟨*a* ~ *bud*⟩ **2a** of or occurring in a term or each term ⟨~ *payments*⟩ **b** occurring at or causing the end of life ⟨~ *cancer*⟩ **3a** occurring at or constituting the end of a period or series; concluding ⟨*the* ~ *moments of life*⟩ **b** not intended as preparation for further academic work ⟨*a* ~ *curriculum*⟩ △ terminable **antonym** initial [L *terminalis*, fr *terminus*] – **terminally** *adv*

²**terminal** *n* **1** a part that forms the end; an extremity, termination **2** an ornamental detail (e g a carving) at the end of something **3** a device attached to the end of a wire or cable or to an electrical apparatus (e g a battery) for making an electrical connection and completing an electrical circuit **4a** the place where one embarks on a plane, boat, or coach, or where one disembarks at the end of a journey; *also* AIR TERMINAL **b** *NAm*

a freight or passenger station that is central to a considerable area or serves as a junction at any point with other lines **5** a device (e g a VDU) through which a user can communicate with a computer *synonyms* see TERMINUS

**terminate** /'tuhminayt/ *vt* **1a** to bring to an end; close ⟨~ a *marriage by divorce*⟩ **b** to form the conclusion of ⟨*review questions* ~ *each chapter*⟩ **c** to discontinue the employment of ⟨*workers* ~d *because of falling demand*⟩ **2** to serve as an ending, limit, or boundary of ⟨*the corridor was* ~d *with glass doors*⟩ ~ *vi* **1** to extend only to a limit (e g a point or line); *esp* to reach a terminus ⟨*this train* ~s *at Glasgow*⟩ **2** to come to an end in time; cease to be – often + *in* or *with* ⟨*the coalition* ~d *with the election*⟩ **3** to form an ending, outcome, or result – often + *in* or *with* ⟨*the match* ~d *with the champion winning*⟩ *synonyms* see ¹CLOSE [L *terminatus*, pp of *terminare*, fr *terminus*]

**termination** /,tuhmi'naysh(ə)n/ *n* **1** the place or point at which something terminates: e g **1a** an end in time or existence; a conclusion ⟨*the* ~ *of life*⟩ **b** a limit in space or extent; a bound **c** the last part of a word; *esp* a suffix **2** the act of terminating **3** an outcome, result – **terminational** *adj*

**terminative** /'tuhmi,naytiv/ *adj* tending or serving to terminate; ending – **terminatively** *adv*

**terminator** /'tuhmi,naytə/ *n* **1** one who or that which terminates **2** the dividing line between the illuminated and the unilluminated part of the moon or other celestial body

**terminology** /,tuhmi'noləji/ *n* **1** the technical or special terms used in a business, art, science, or special subject; *also* the study of such terms **2** the establishing of standard translations for specialist terms in various areas (e g aeronautics), esp for use within international organizations [ML *terminus* term, expression (fr L, boundary, limit) + E -*o*- + -*logy*] – **terminological** *adj*, **terminologically** *adv*

**term insurance** *n* insurance for a specified period; *specif*, *chiefly Br* LIFE INSURANCE for a specified period under which payment is made only if the insured person dies within that period

**terminus** /'tuhminəs/ *n, pl* **termini** /-nie/, **terminuses 1** a finishing point; the end **2** a post or stone marking a boundary **3** the end of a transport line or travel route; *also* the station, town, or city at such a place **4** an extreme point or element; a tip ⟨*the* ~ *of a glacier*⟩ [L, boundary, end – more at TERM]

*synonyms* The British speak of an *air* or *bus* **terminal** and of a *railway* **terminus**, but the Americans use **terminus** and **terminal** interchangeably. *antonym* starting point

**terminus ad quem** /ad 'kwem/ *n* **1** a goal, object, or course of action; a destination, purpose **2** a final limiting point in time [NL, lit., limit to which]

**terminus a quo** /ah 'kwoh/ *n* **1** a point of origin **2** the first of two limiting points in time [NL, lit., limit from which]

**termitarium** /,tuhmi'teəri-əm, -mie-/ *n, pl* **termitaria** /-riə/ a termites' nest [NL]

**termite** /'tuh,miet/ *n* any of numerous pale-coloured soft-bodied insects (order Isoptera) that live in colonies consisting of winged sexual forms, wingless sterile workers, and usu soldiers that defend the colony. Most species feed on wood, often causing considerable damage to trees, buildings, etc. [NL *Termit-*, *Termes*, genus of termites, fr LL, a worm that eats wood, alter. of L *tarmit-*, *tarmes*; akin to Gk *tetrainein* to bore – more at THROW]

**termless** /'tuhmlis/ *adj* **1** having no term or end; boundless, unending **2** unconditioned, unconditional

**termly** /'tuhmli/ *adj* **1** happening each term ⟨*a* ~ *concert*⟩ **2** that occurs or falls due each term ⟨*increase* ~ *subscriptions*⟩ – **termly** *adv*

**term of years** *n* an estate or interest in land having a fixed and certain duration; a lease

**terms of reference** *n pl* the precise area within which someone or something (e g a committee) is empowered to act, make recommendations, etc ⟨*by making recommendations about policing, the enquiry into the causes of the riot went beyond its* ~⟩

**terms of trade** *n pl* the ratio of an index of export prices to the index of import prices

**termtime** /'tuhm,tiem/ *n* the period of an academic or legal term

**tern** /tuhn/ *n* any of numerous water birds (*Sterna* and related genera of the family Laridae) that are smaller and slenderer in body and bill than the related gulls and have narrower wings, often forked tails, a black cap, and a white body △ turn [of Scand origin; akin to Dan *terne* tern]

**ternary** /'tuhnəri/ *adj* **1a** of, arranged in, or proceeding by threes **b** having three elements, parts, or divisions; threefold; *specif* having three such parts with the first and third sections the same and a contrasting second section **c** ternate **2** of, being, or belonging to a system of numbers that has three as its base ⟨*a* ~ *logarithm*⟩ **3** of or containing three different chemical elements, atoms, or groups ⟨*sulphuric acid is a* ~ *acid*⟩ **4** third in order or rank [ME, fr L *ternarius*, fr *terni* three each; akin to L *tres* three – more at THREE]

**ternate** /'tuhnayt/ *adj, botany* **1** arranged in threes **2** made up of three leaflets or subdivisions ⟨*a* ~ *leaf*⟩ [NL *ternatus*, fr ML, pp of *ternare* to treble, fr L *terni* three each] – **ternately** *adv*

**terne** /tuhn/ *n* **1** an alloy of lead and tin typically in a ratio of four to one that is used as a coating in producing terneplate **2** **terneplate**, **terne** sheet iron or steel coated with terne [prob fr Fr *terne* dull, fr MF, fr *ternir* to tarnish]

**terotechnology** /,terohtek'noləji/ *n* a branch of technology that deals with the efficient installation, operation, and maintenance of equipment [Gk *tērein* to watch over + E -*o*- + *technology*]

**terpene** /'tuh,peen/ *n* any of a class of chemical compounds, $(C_5H_8)_n$, found esp in naturally occurring plant products (e g ESSENTIAL OILS, resins, and balsams); *esp* any of various chemical compounds, $C_{10}H_{16}$, that are present in essential oils (e g from conifers) and are used esp as solvents [ISV *terp-* (fr Ger *terpentin* turpentine, fr ML *terbentina*) + -*ene* – more at TURPENTINE] – **terpeneless** *adj*, **terpenic** *adj*, **terpenoid** *adj or n*

**terpineol** /tuh'pini,ol/ *n* any of three forms of a fragrant, often lilac-smelling, chemical alcohol, $C_{10}H_{17}OH$, that have the same composition but different arrangements of the atoms, occur in pine oil or other ESSENTIAL OILS present in plants, and are used in the manufacture of perfumes and soaps [ISV *terpine* $(C_{10}H_{18}(OH)_2)$ + -*ol*]

**terpsichorean** /,tuhpsikə'ree-ən, ,tuhpsi'kawri-ən/ *adj* of dancing [*Terpsichore* (Gk *Terpsichorē*), the muse of dancing and choral song]

**terra alba** /,terə 'albə/ *n* any of several white mineral substances: e g **a** finely ground GYPSUM used as a pigment **b** KAOLIN [NL, lit., white earth]

**¹terrace** /'teris/ *n* **1a** a colonnaded porch or promenade **b** a flat roof or open platform ⟨*a* ~ *overlooking the sea*⟩ **c** a relatively level paved or planted area adjoining a building **2a** a raised embankment with a level top **b** a horizontal or gently sloping ridge cut, usu as one of a series, into a hillside used for farming, in order to conserve moisture, prevent erosion, etc ⟨*the vines are grown on* ~s⟩ **3** a level usu narrow and steep-fronted area bordering a river, lake, or sea; *also* a similar undersea feature **4a** a row of houses or flats on raised ground or a sloping site **b** a row of houses joined into one building by common walls **c** a street [MF, pile of earth, platform, terrace, fr OProv *terrassa*, fr *terra* earth, fr L, earth, land; akin to L *torrēre* to parch – more at THIRST]

**²terrace** *vt* **1** to make into a terrace **2** to provide (e g a building) with a terrace

**terraced** /'terist/ *adj* being any of a continuous row of dwellings connected by common sidewalls ⟨~ *houses*⟩

**terracotta** /,terə'kotə/ *n* **1** an unglazed usu brownish-red fired clay used esp for statuettes and vases and as a building material (e g for roofing tiles) **2** a brownish-orange colour [It *terra cotta*, lit., baked earth] – **terracotta** *adj*

**terra firma** /'fuhmə/ *n* dry land; solid ground [NL, lit., solid land]

**terrain** /tə'rayn/ *n* **1** (the physical features of) a tract or area of land or ground **2** an environment, milieu; *specif* a field of activity or knowledge [Fr, land, ground, fr L *terrenum*, fr neut of *terrenus* of earth, fr *terra* earth]

**terra incognita** /,terə inkog'neetə, in'kognitə/ *n, pl* **terrae incognitae** /,teri inkog'neeti, in'kogniti/ unknown territory; an unexplored country or field of knowledge [L]

**terrane** /tə'rayn/ *n* the area or surface over which a particular rock or group of rocks is prevalent [alter. of *terrain*]

**terrapin** /'terəpin/ *n* any of various small freshwater reptiles (family Testudinidae) that resemble the closely related tortoises but are adapted for swimming; *esp* a N American terrapin (*Chrysemys picta*) with a flat green shell and red streak near the ear that is commonly kept as a pet [of Algonquian origin; akin to Delaware *torope* turtle]

**terraqueous** /te'raykwiəs, tə, -'rak-/ *adj* consisting of land and water [L *terra* land + E *aqueous*]

**terrarium** /tə'reəri·əm/ *n, pl* **terraria** /-riə/, **terrariums** an enclosure or closed container for rearing terrestrial animals or growing plants [NL, fr L *terra* + *-arium* (as in *aquarium*)]

**terrazzo** /te'rahtsoh/ *n* mosaic flooring consisting of small pieces of marble or granite set in concrete and given a high polish [It, lit., terrace, perh fr OProv *terrassa*]

¹**terrene** /te'reen, tə-/ *adj, formal* mundane, earthly [ME, fr L *terrenus* of earth, fr *terra* earth]

²**terrene** *n, formal* a land area; earth, terrain

**terreplein** /'teə,playn/ *n* the level space behind a parapet of a rampart where guns are mounted [MF, fr OIt *terrapieno*, fr ML *terraplenum*, fr *terra plenus* filled with earth]

**terrestrial** /tə'restri·əl/ *adj* **1a** of the earth or its inhabitants ⟨~ *magnetism*⟩ **b** mundane in scope or character; prosaic **2a** of land as distinct from air or water ⟨~ *transport*⟩ **b**(1) *of a plant or animal* living or growing on land or in the soil **b**(2) of terrestrial organisms ⟨~ *habits*⟩ **3** belonging to the class of planets that are like the earth (eg in density and composition) *antonym* celestial [ME, fr L *terrestris*, fr *terra* earth – more at TERRACE] – **terrestrial** *n*, **terrestrially** *adv*

**terret** /'terit/ *n* either of the rings on the top of a driving saddle through which the reins pass [ME *teret*, alter. of *toret*, fr MF, fr OF, dim. of *tour* circuit, ring – more at TURN]

**terrible** /'terəbl/ *adj* **1a** exciting extreme alarm or intense fear; terrifying **b** formidable in nature; awesome ⟨*a* ~ *responsibility*⟩ **c** requiring great effort or fortitude ⟨*a* ~ *order*⟩; *also* severe intense ⟨*a* ~ *winter*⟩ **2** extreme, great ⟨*a* ~ *amount of trouble arranging all this*⟩ **3** notably unattractive or objectionable; obnoxious ⟨*a* ~ *smell*⟩ **4** of very poor quality; awful ⟨*a* ~ *performance*⟩ [ME, fr MF, fr L *terribilis*, fr *terrēre* to frighten – more at TERROR] – **terribleness** *n*

**terribly** /'terəbli/ *adv, informal* very ⟨~ *lucky*⟩

**terricolous** /te'rikələs, tə-/ *adj* living on or in the ground or soil [L *terricola* inhabitant of the earth, fr *terra* earth + *colere* to inhabit – more at WHEEL]

**terrier** /'teri·ə/ *n* (a member of) any of various breeds of usu small dogs originally used by hunters to dig for small animals and drive them out from their underground burrows or shelters **2** *usu cap, Br* a member of a TERRITORIAL ARMY [Fr (*chien*) *terrier*, lit., earth dog, fr *terrier* of earth, fr ML *terrarius*, fr L *terra* earth; (2) by shortening & alter. fr *territorial*]

**terrific** /tə'rifik/ *adj* **1** exciting or fit to excite fear or awe **2** extraordinarily great or intense ⟨~ *speed*⟩ **3** unusually fine; magnificent [L *terrificus*, fr *terrēre* to frighten] – **terrifically** *adv*

**terrify** /'terifie/ *vt* **1** to fill with terror or apprehension **2a** to drive or impel by menacing; scare – often + *into* ⟨terrified *him into leaving*⟩ **b** to deter, intimidate ⟨*so complicated it would* ~ *the ordinary reader*⟩ [L *terrificare*, fr *terrificus*]

**terrifying** /'terifie·ing/ *adj* **1** causing terror or apprehension **2** of a formidable nature – **terrifyingly** *adv*

**terrigenous** /tə'rijənəs/ *adj* being or relating to sediment on the sea floor derived directly from the erosion of the surface of the land [L *terrigena* earthborn, fr *terra* earth + *gignere* to beget – more at KIN]

**terrine** /tə'reen/ *n* **1** an earthenware baking or cooking dish **2** a food, esp pâté, cooked and served or sold in a terrine [Fr – more at TUREEN]

¹**territorial** /,teri'tawri·əl/ *adj* **1a** of territory ⟨~ *government*⟩; *esp* of private property or land ⟨~ *disputes*⟩ **b** of or being a semi-independent territory ⟨gave the islands ~ *status*⟩ **2a** of or restricted to a particular area or district; local **b** exhibiting territoriality ⟨~ *birds*⟩ – **territorially** *adv*

²**territorial** *n* a member of a territorial army, esp the Territorial Army and Volunteer Reserve

**territorial army** *n* a voluntary force organized by locality to provide a trained army reserve that can be mobilized in an emergency

**Territorial Army and Volunteer Reserve** *n* the present-day British territorial army

**territoriality** /,teri,tawri'aləti/ *n* **1** territorial status **2a** persistent attachment to a specific territory **b** the pattern of behaviour associated with the defence by an animal of its territory

**territorial·ize, -ise** /,teri'tawriəliez/ *vt* to organize on a territorial basis – **territorialization** *n*

**territorial waters** *n pl* the waters, including inland waters, within which a nation or state exercises control or sovereignty

**territory** /'terit(ə)ri/ *n* **1a** a geographical area belonging to or under the jurisdiction of a government **b** an administrative subdivision of a country **c** a part of the USA not included within any state but organized with a separate legislature **d** a geographical area (eg a colonial possession) dependent on an external government but having some degree of independence **2a** an indeterminate geographical area **b** a field of knowledge or interest **c** a geographical area having a specified characteristic ⟨*in Rolls Royce* ~ – *Annabel*⟩ ⟨*Labour* ~⟩ **3a** an assigned area; *esp* one in which a representative, agent, or distributor operates **b** an area, often including a nesting site or den and an extent sufficient for food requirements, that is occupied and defended by an animal or group of animals [ME, fr L *territorium*, lit., land round a town, prob fr *terra* land + *-torium* (as in *praetorium*) – more at TERRACE]

**terror** /'terə/ *n* **1** a state of intense fear **2a** one who or that which inspires fear; a scourge **b** a frightening aspect ⟨*the* ~s *of invasion*⟩ **c** a cause of anxiety; a worry **3** *often cap* REIGN OF TERROR (period of government-organized repressive violence) **4** violence (eg the planting of bombs) committed by groups in order to intimidate a population or government into granting their demands ⟨*insurrection and revolutionary* ~⟩ **5** *informal* an appalling person or thing; *esp* a brat *synonyms* see ¹FEAR [ME, fr MF *terreur*, fr L *terror*, fr *terrēre* to frighten; akin to Gk *trein* to be afraid, flee, *tremein* to tremble – more at TREMBLE] – **terrorless** *adj*

**terrorism** /'terə,riz(ə)m/ *n* the systematic use of terror, esp as a means of coercion – **terrorist** *adj or n*, **terroristic** *adj*

**terror·ize, -ise** /'terə,riez/ *vt* **1** to fill with terror or anxiety **2** to coerce by threat or violence – often + *into* or *out of* – **terrorization** *n*

**'terror-,stricken** *adj* overcome with an uncontrollable terror

**'terror-,struck** *adj* terror-stricken

**terry** /'teri/ *n* an absorbent fabric (eg towelling) with uncut loops on both faces [perh modif of Fr *tiré*, pp of *tirer* to draw – more at TIRADE] – **terry** *adj*

**terse** /tuhs/ *adj* without superfluity; concise; *also* brusque, curt ⟨*a* ~ *reply*⟩ *synonyms* see CONCISE *antonym* verbose [L *tersus* clean, neat, fr pp of *tergēre* to wipe off; akin to Gk *trōgein* to gnaw, L *terere* to rub – more at THROW] – **tersely** *adv*, **terseness** *n*

**tertian** /'tuhsh(ə)n/ *adj* of or being attacks of a fever, esp malaria, that recur at approx 48-hour intervals [ME *tercian*, fr L *tertianus*, lit., of the third, fr *tertius* third – more at THIRD] – **tertian** *n*

¹**tertiary** /'tuhshəri/ *n* **1** a person belonging to a monastic THIRD ORDER; *esp* one living in secular society **2** *cap* the Tertiary period or system of rocks

²**tertiary** *adj* **1a** of third rank, importance, or value **b** of higher education **c** of or being a service industry – company PRIMARY, SECONDARY **d** of or being the third strongest degree of stress in speech ⟨*the third syllable of* basketball team *carries* ~ *stress*⟩ **2** *cap* of or being the first geological period of the CAINOZOIC era (present-day era), marked by the formation of high mountains (eg the Alps, Caucasus, and Himalayas) and the dominance of mammals on land; *also* of or being the system of rocks formed in this era **3** *chemistry* **3a** characterized by or resulting from the replacement of three atoms or chemical groups in a molecule by other atoms or groups ⟨*a* ~ *salt is formed from an acid by replacing three hydrogen atoms by metal atoms*⟩ **b**(1) being or containing a carbon atom united to three other carbon atoms ⟨*a* ~ *compound*⟩ **b**(2) being a chemical group attached to a tertiary carbon atom **c** *of an amine* having the nitrogen atom attached to three carbon atoms **4** occurring in or being a third stage [L *tertiarius* of or containing a third, fr *tertius* third]

**tertiary colour** *n* a colour produced by mixing two or more SECONDARY COLOURS

**tertiary consumer** *n* a CARNIVORE (meat-eating animal) that eats other carnivores – compare PRIMARY CONSUMER, SECONDARY CONSUMER

**tertiary education** *n* HIGHER EDUCATION

**tertiary syphilis** *n* the third stage of syphilis that develops after the disappearance of the symptoms of SECONDARY SYPHILIS, and is marked by ulcers and tumours of the skin and commonly by disorders (eg LOCOMOTOR ATAXIA) of the nervous system and of the heart and blood vessels

**tertium quid** /,tuhshi·əm 'kwid, ,tuhti·əm/ *n* **1** a middle course or an intermediate element ⟨*a* ~ *linking mind and matter*⟩ **2** a third party of ambiguous status ⟨*there was a* *man and his wife and a ~* – Rudyard Kipling⟩ [LL, lit., third something]

**tervalent** /tuh'vaylənt/ *adj, chemistry* having a VALENCY of three; TRIVALENT

**Terylene** /'terəleen, -lin/ *trademark* – used for a synthetic polyester textile fibre *synonyms* see NYLON

**terza rima** /,tuhtsə 'reemə/ *n* a verse form consisting of TERCETS (groups of three lines) usu in lines of five IAMBS each with an interlaced rhyme scheme (eg *aba, bcb, cdc*) [It, lit., third rhyme]

**tesla** /'teslə/ *n* the SI unit of MAGNETIC FLUX DENSITY (strength of the magnetic forces acting at a point in a MAGNETIC FIELD), equal to 1 weber per square metre [Nikola *Tesla* †1943 US (Austrian-born) electrician & inventor]

**tessellate** /'tesəlayt/ *vt* to form into or decorate with mosaic [LL *tessellatus,* pp of *tessellare* to pave with tesserae, fr L *tessella,* dim. of *tessera*]

**tessellated** /'tesə,laytid/ *adj, biology* having a chequered appearance ⟨~ *epithelium*⟩

**tessellation** /,tesə'laysh(ə)n/ *n* 1 tessellating or being tessellated 2 a tessellated pattern; a mosaic

**tessera** /'tesərə/ *n, pl* **tesserae** /-ri/ 1 a small tablet (eg of wood, bone, or ivory) used by the ancient Romans as a ticket, tally, voucher, or means of identification 2 a small piece (eg of marble, glass, or tile) used in mosaic [L, prob deriv of Gk *tessares* four – more at FOUR; fr its having four corners]

**tesseract** /'tesə,rakt/ *n* the four-dimensional equivalent of a cube [Gk *tessares* four + *aktis* ray – more at ACTIN-]

**tessitura** /,tesə't(y)ooərə/ *n* the part of the register or range in which most of the notes of a melody or voice part lie or in which a voice or instrument naturally sounds its best [It, lit., texture, fr L *textura*]

**¹test** /test/ *n* **1a** a critical examination, observation, or evaluation; a trial; *specif* the procedure of submitting a statement to such conditions or operations as will lead to its proof or disproof or to its acceptance or rejection ⟨*a ~ of a statistical hypothesis*⟩ **b** a basis for evaluation; a criterion **c** an ordeal or oath required as proof of conformity with a set of beliefs ⟨*no religious ~ is required for the franchise*⟩ ⟨*the* Test *Act of 1673 required all servants of the Crown to receive the sacraments of the Church of England*⟩ **2a** a means of testing: eg **2a(1)** a chemical or physical procedure or reaction, or a chemical REAGENT used to identify or test for the presence of a substance or constituent ⟨*iodine ~ for the presence of starch*⟩ **a(2)** something (eg a series of questions or exercises) for measuring the knowledge, intelligence, ability, etc of an individual or group **b** a positive result in such a test **3** TEST MATCH **4** a result or value determined by testing ⟨*a fishing line of 20 pounds ~*⟩ **5** *chiefly Br* CUPEL (small cup used in determining the amount or purity of a precious metal) [ME, vessel in which metals were tested, cupel, fr MF, fr L *testum* earthen vessel; akin to L *testa* earthen pot, shell, *texere* to weave – more at TECHNICAL]

**²test** *vt* **1** to put to the test; try ⟨~s *my patience*⟩ ⟨*wet roads that ~ a car's tyres*⟩ **2** to require a doctrinal oath of ~ *vi* to apply a test as a means of analysis or diagnosis – usu + *for* ⟨~ *for mechanical aptitude*⟩ – **testable** *adj,* **testability** *n*

**³test** *n* a hard or firm outer covering (eg a shell) of an INVERTEBRATE animal (eg a SEA URCHIN) [L *testa* shell]

**testa** /'testə/ *n, pl* **testae** /'testi/ the hard protective outer coat of a seed [NL, fr L, shell]

**testacean** /te'staysh(ə)n/ *n* any of an order (Testacea) of single-celled animals related to the amoeba, that have an external shell [deriv of L *testaceus* having a shell] – **testacean** *adj*

**testaceous** /te'stayshəs/ *adj* **1a** having or protected by a shell or shell-like outer covering ⟨*a ~ protozoan*⟩ **b** consisting of shell-like or calcium-containing material ⟨*stone of ~ composition*⟩ **2** of a light brick or terracotta colour [L *testaceus,* fr *testa* shell, earthen pot, brick]

**testacy** /'testəsi/ *n* the state of being testate

**testament** /'testəmənt/ *n* **1** *cap* either of the two main divisions of the Bible **2a** a tangible proof or tribute **b** an expression of conviction; a credo **3** an act or instrument by which a person states how his/her property is to be disposed of after death; *esp* a will **4** *archaic* a covenant between God and man □ compare TESTIMONY [ME, fr LL & L; LL *testamentum* covenant with God, holy scripture, fr L, last will, fr *testari* to be a witness, call to witness, make a will, fr *testis* witness; akin to L *tres* three & to L *stare* to stand; fr the witness's standing by as a third party in a litigation ] – **testamentary** *adj*

**testate** /'testayt/ *adj* having made a valid will ⟨*he died ~*⟩ [ME, fr L *testatus,* pp of *testari* to make a will]

**testator** /te'staytə/, *fem* **testatrix** /te'staytriks/ *n* a person who leaves a will or testament in force at his/her death [ME *testatour,* fr AF, fr LL *testator,* fr L *testatus,* pp]

**test ban** *n* a ban on the atmospheric testing of nuclear weapons mutually agreed to by countries possessing such weapons

**'test-,bed** *n* a piece of equipment for testing a component before it is installed in its final position

**test card** *n* a geometric pattern or fixed picture broadcast by a television transmitting station to help in the testing or adjustment of receivers

**test case** *n* a representative legal case the outcome of which is likely to serve as a precedent

**testcross** /'test,kros/ *n* a genetic cross between an animal or plant whose genetic make-up with respect to a particular inheritable characteristic (eg coat or petal colour) is to be determined and a corresponding individual that is HOMOZYGOUS (has a pair of identical genes) for and therefore shows the RECESSIVE version of the characteristic (version suppressed unless both members of the controlling gene pair are identical). If all the offspring resulting from the cross show the same version of the characteristic as that shown by the test individual, the latter is known to be pure-breeding; if some offspring show the recessive version, the test individual is a hybrid. – **testcross** *vt*

**'test-,drive** *vt* **-drove; -driven** to drive (a motor vehicle) before buying in order to discover its limitations or assess its positive features

**tested** /'testid/ *adj* subjected to or qualified through testing – often in combination ⟨*time*-tested *principles*⟩

**¹tester** /'testə/ *n* the canopy over a bed, pulpit, or altar [ME, fr MF *testiere* headpiece, head covering, fr *teste* head, fr LL *testa* skull, fr L, shell – more at TEST]

**²tester** *n* TESTON (old European coin) [modif of MF *testart,* fr *teston*]

**³tester** *n* one who or that which tests

**'test-,fire** *vt* to subject to a firing test ⟨~ *a gun*⟩

**'test-,fly** *vt* **-flew; -flown** to subject to a flight test ⟨~ *an experimental plane*⟩

**testicle** /'testikl/ *n* a testis of a mammal, usu together with its associated structures (eg the scrotum) [ME *testicule,* fr L *testiculus,* dim. of *testis*] – **testicular** *adj*

**testifier** /'testifie-ə/ *n* someone who testifies; a witness

**testify** /'testifie/ *vi* **1a** to make a statement based on personal knowledge or belief; bear witness **b** to serve as evidence or proof **2** to express a personal conviction **3** to make a solemn declaration under oath for the purpose of establishing a fact (eg in a court) ~ *vt* **1a** to bear witness to; attest **b** to serve as evidence of; prove **2** to make known (a personal conviction) **3** to declare under oath (eg before a court or tribunal) [ME *testifien,* fr L *testificari,* fr *testis* witness]

**¹testimonial** /,testi'mohnyəl, -ni-əl/ *adj* **1** of or constituting testimony **2** expressive of appreciation, gratitude, or esteem ⟨*a ~ dinner*⟩ ⟨*Arsenal staged a ~ match for their longest-serving player*⟩

**²testimonial** *n* **1** a written statement of a person's character, abilities, qualifications, etc; a letter of recommendation **2** an expression of appreciation, gratitude, or esteem (eg in the form of a gift or money); a tribute **3** a testimonial match – compare BENEFIT

**testimony** /'testiməni/ *n* **1** a passage of Scripture cited in an argument as evidence, proof, etc **2a** firsthand authentication of a fact; witness ⟨*the ~ of the great scientist confirmed the theory*⟩ **b** an outward sign ⟨*is ~ of his abilities*⟩ **c** a statement made by a witness under oath (eg in a court) **3** a public profession of religious experience □ compare TESTAMENT [ME, fr L, evidence, witness, fr *testis* witness – more at TESTAMENT]

**testing** /'testing/ *adj* requiring maximum effort or ability ⟨*a most difficult and ~ problem* – Ernest Bevin⟩

**testis** /'testis/ *n, pl* **testes** /'testeez/ a male reproductive gland that produces sperms [L, prob fr *testis* witness (fr its being evidence of virility)]

**test match, test** *n* any of a series of international sports matches, esp cricket matches

**teston** /'testən/, **testoon** /te'stoohn/ *n* any of several former European coins; *esp* a shilling of Henry VIII decreasing in value to ninepence and then to sixpence in Shakespeare's time [MF, fr OIt *testone,* aug of *testa* head, fr LL, skull – more at TESTER]

**testosterone** /te'stostərohn/ *n* a male STEROID hormone, $C_{19}H_{28}O_2$, that is produced by the testes or made synthetically and is responsible for inducing and maintaining male SECOND-

ARY SEX CHARACTERISTICS (e g the beard of a man) [*testis* + *-o-* + *sterol* + *-one*]

**test pilot** *n* a pilot who specializes in putting new or experimental aircraft through manoeuvres designed to test them (e g for strength) by flying them in abnormal conditions or subjecting them to extraordinary stress

'**test-,tube** *adj* **1** developed or produced as a result of scientific research, esp in the laboratory **2** *of a baby,* conceived by ARTIFICIAL INSEMINATION, esp outside the mother's body

**test tube** *n* a cylindrical tube of thin glass that is open at one end and is used in chemistry, biology, etc

**testudo** /te'styoohdoh/ *n, pl* **testudos** an overhead cover of overlapping shields or a movable roofed shelter used by the ancient Romans to protect an attacking force [L *testudin-, testudo,* lit., tortoise, tortoise shell; akin to L *testa* shell – more at TEST]

**testy** /'testi/ *adj* impatient, ill-humoured ⟨~ *remarks*⟩ [ME *testif* impetuous, fr AF, headstrong, fr OF *teste* head – more at TESTER] – **testily** *adv,* **testiness** *n*

**Tet** /tet/ *n* the Vietnamese New Year observed for three days beginning at the first new moon after January 20 [Vietnamese *têt*]

**tetanal** /'tet(ə)nəl/ *adj* of or derived from tetanus

'**tetanic** /te'tanik/ *adj* of, being, or tending to produce tetanus or tetany – **tetanically** *adv*

**tetan·ize, -ise** /'tetəniez/ *vt* to induce tetanus or prolonged contraction in ⟨~ *a muscle*⟩ – **tetanization** *n*

**tetanus** /'tet(ə)nəs/ *n* **1a** a severe short-lasting infectious disease that is characterized by prolonged involuntary contraction and rigidity of muscles usu under voluntary control, esp those of the jaw, and that is caused by a TOXIN (poison) released by a bacterium which has entered the body usu through a wound **b** the bacterium (*Clostridium tetani*) that causes tetanus **2** prolonged contraction of a muscle resulting from rapidly repeated nerve impulses [ME, fr L, fr Gk *tetanos,* fr *tetanos* stretched, rigid; akin to Gk *teinein* to stretch – more at THIN]

**tetany** /'tet(ə)ni/ *n* a condition in which muscles and the nerves supplying them become abnormally responsive to stimuli, that is marked by involuntary prolonged muscular contraction and is associated usu with a deficiency of calcium in the blood resulting from insufficient secretion of hormones from the PARATHYROID GLANDS [ISV, fr L *tetanus*]

**tetartohedral** /te,tahtə'heedrəl/ *adj, of a crystal* having a quarter of the surfaces required by complete symmetry – compare HEMIHEDRAL, HOLOHEDRAL [Gk *tetartos* fourth; akin to Gk *tettares* four – more at FOUR] – **tetartohedrally** *adv*

**tetchy** /'techi/ *adj* irritably or peevishly sensitive; touchy [perh fr obs *tetch* habit, bad habit, fr ME *tecche, tache,* fr MF *teche, tache* stain, spot, of Gmc origin] – **tetchily** *adv,* **tetchiness** *n*

'**tête-à-tête** /,tet ah 'tet (*Fr* tɛt a tɛt)/ *adv or adj* (in) private [Fr, lit., head to head]

²**tête-à-tête** *n* **1** a private conversation between two people **2** a seat (e g a sofa) designed for two people to sit facing each other – compare DOS-À-DOS

**tête-bêche, tete-beche** /besh/ *adj or adv* of a pair of stamps inverted in relation to one another either intentionally or through a printing error [Fr, fr *tête* head + *-bêche,* alter. of MF *bechevet* head against foot]

**teth** /tes, tet, teth/ *n* the 9th letter of the Hebrew alphabet [Heb *ṭeth*]

'**tether** /'tedhə/ *n* **1** something (e g a rope or chain) by which an animal is fastened so that it can browse only within a set area **2** the limit of one's strength or resources; scope – chiefly in *the end of one's tether* [ME *tethir,* prob of Scand origin; akin to ON *tjōthr* tether; akin to OHG *zeotar* pole of a wagon]

²**tether** *vt* to fasten or restrain (as if) by a tether

**tetra** /'tetrə/ *n* any of numerous small brightly coloured S American fishes (family Characidae) often bred in tropical aquariums [by shortening fr NL *Tetragonopterus,* former genus name, fr LL *tetragonum* quadrangle + Gk *pteron* wing – more at TETRAGONAL, FEATHER]

**tetra-, tetr-** *comb form* **1** four; having four; having four parts ⟨tetr*atomic*⟩ ⟨tetra*gon*⟩ **2** containing four (specified atoms or chemical groups) in the molecular structure ⟨tetrabasic⟩ ⟨tetracid⟩ [ME, fr L, fr Gk; akin to Gk *tettares* four – more at FOUR]

**tetrabasic** /,tetrə'baysik/ *adj* **1** *of an acid* having four hydrogen atoms capable of reacting as acids in each molecule **2** *of a chemical compound* containing four atoms of a metal with a

VALENCY of one, or their equivalent **3** *of a chemical* BASE TETRACID 1 [ISV] – **tetrabasicity** *n*

**tetrachloride** /,tetrə'klawried/ *n* a chloride containing four atoms of chlorine

**tetrachord** /'tetrə,kawd/ *n* a series of four musical notes in order with an interval of four notes of the DIATONIC scale (ordinary 8-note scale) between the first and last, the intervals between the individual notes being tone, tone, semitone [Gk *tetrachordon,* fr neut of *tetrachordos* of four strings, fr *tetra-* + *chordē* string – more at YARN]

¹**tetracid** /te'trasid/, **tetracidic** /tetrə'sidik/ *adj* **1** *esp of a chemical* BASE having four HYDROXYL groups capable of reacting as bases in each molecule **2** *of an acid* TETRABASIC 1

²**tetracid** *n* an acid having four acid hydrogen atoms

**tetracycline** /,tetrə'siekleen/ *n* any of several BROAD-SPECTRUM (effective against a wide range of microorganisms) antibiotics closely related in structure; *specif* one, $C_{22}H_{24}N_2O_8$, obtained esp from a soil bacterium (*Streptomyces viridifaciens*) [ISV *tetracyc*lic + *-ine*]

**tetrad** /'tetrad/ *n* a group or arrangement of four: e g **a** an element, atom, or chemical group with a VALENCY of four **b** a group of four cells arranged usu in the form of a tetrahedron and produced by the successive divisions of a mother cell ⟨*a ~ of spores*⟩ **c** a group of four CHROMATIDS that are produced by the longitudinal splitting of each of two paired CHROMOSOMES (strands of gene-carrying material in the nucleus of a cell) and become visible during the early stages of the first phase (PROPHASE) of MEIOSIS (CELL DIVISION resulting in four new cells) [Gk *tetrad-, tetras,* fr *tetra-*] – **tetradic** *adj*

**tetradrachm** /'tetrədram/ *n* an ancient Greek silver coin worth four drachmas [Gk *tetradrachmon,* fr *tetra-* + *drachmē* drachma]

**tetradymite** /te'tradəmiet/ *n* a pale steel-grey mineral, $Bi_2Te_2S$, consisting of a TELLURIDE and sulphide of bismuth having a metallic lustre [LGk *tetradymos* fourfold, fr Gk *tetra-* + *-dymos* (as in *didymos* double); fr its occurrence in compound twin crystals]

**tetradynamous** /,tetrə'dienəməs/ *adj* having six STAMENS, (male reproductive organs of a plant) four of which are longer than the others ⟨~ *plants of the mustard family*⟩ [ISV *tetra-* + Gk *dynamis* power – more at DYNAMIC]

**tetraethyl** /,tetrə'ethil, -'eethiel/ *adj* containing four ETHYL groups in the molecule [ISV]

**tetraethyl lead** *n* an oily poisonous liquid, $Pb(C_2H_5)_4$, used as a petrol additive to prevent KNOCKING (sharp metallic noises caused by faulty ignition) in INTERNAL-COMBUSTION ENGINES

**tetrafluoride** /,tetrə'flooəried/ *n* a FLUORIDE containing four atoms of fluorine

**tetrafluoroethylene** /,tetrə,flooəroh'ethəleen/ *n* a colourless gas, $C_2F_4$, that is POLYMERIZED (chemically combined with itself) in the production of POLYTETRAFLUOROETHYLENE (plastic used for coating metals, providing non-stick surfaces, etc)

**tetragonal** /te'tragənl/ *adj* (characteristic) of the TETRAGONAL SYSTEM [LL *tetragonalis* having four angles and four sides, fr *tetragonum* quadrangle, fr Gk *tetragōnon,* fr *tetra-* + *gōnia* angle – more at -GON] – **tetragonally** *adv*

**tetragonal system** *n* a crystal system characterized by three axes at right angles of which only the two side axes are equal

**tetragrammaton** /,tetrə'graməton/ *n* the four Hebrew letters that in the Roman alphabet are represented by YHWH or JHVH and form a biblical proper name of God – compare YAHWEH [ME, fr Gk, fr neut of *tetragrammatos* having four letters, fr *tetra-* + *grammat-, gramma* letter – more at GRAM]

**tetrahedral** /,tetrə'heedrəl/ *adj* **1** relating to, forming, or having the form of a tetrahedron **2** having four faces ⟨~ *angle*⟩ – **tetrahedrally** *adv*

**tetrahedrite** /tetrə'heedriet/ *n* a grey mineral, $(Cu,Fe)_{12}Sb_4S_{13}$, that chiefly consists of a sulphide of copper, iron, and antimony, often contains other chemical elements (e g silver), occurs in tetrahedral crystals and also in massive form, and is often a valuable source of silver [Ger *tetraëdrit,* fr LGk *tetraedros* having four faces]

**tetrahedron** /tetrə'heedrən/ *n, pl* **tetrahedrons, tetrahedra** /-drə/ a POLYHEDRON (solid 3-dimensional geometrical figure) of four faces [NL, fr LGk *tetraedron,* neut of *tetraedros* having four faces, fr Gk *tetra-* + *hedra* seat, face – more at SIT]

**tetrahydrate** /,tetrə'hiedrət, -'hiedrayt/ *n* a chemical compound combined with four molecules of water – **tetrahydrated** *adj*

**tetrahydrocannabinol** /ˌtetrəˌhiedrəkə'nabinol/ *n* a hallucination-inducing drug, $C_{21}H_{30}O_2$, that is the main active constituent of marijuana [*tetrahydro-* (combined with four atoms of hydrogen) + *cannabin* (cannabis resin) + *-ol*]

**tetrahydrofuran** /ˌtetrəˌhiedrə'fyooəran/ *n* an inflammable liquid , $C_4H_8O$, that is derived from FURAN and used as a solvent and as an intermediate in the production of nylon [*tetrahydro-* + *furan*]

**tetrahydroxy** /ˌtetrəhie'droksi/ *adj* containing four HYDROXYL groups in the molecule [*tetra-* + *hydroxyl*]

**tetrahymena** /ˌtetrə'hiemənə/ *n* any of a genus (*Tetrahymena*) of PROTOZOANS (minute single-celled organisms) that have CILIA (small hairlike structures) used esp for movement [NL, genus name, fr *tetra-* + Gk *hymēn* membrane]

**tetralogy** /te'traləji/ *n* a series of four connected works (eg operas or novels) [Gk *tetralogia* series of four dramas, fr *tetra-* + *-logia* -logy]

**tetramer** /'tetrəmə/ *n* a POLYMER (complex chemical substance) formed from the chemical combination of four identical sub units [*tetra-* + poly*mer*] – **tetrameric** *adj*

**tetramerous** /te'tramərəs/ *adj* having or characterized by the presence of four parts or of parts arranged in sets or multiples of four ⟨~ *flowers*⟩ [NL *tetramerus*, fr Gk *tetramerēs*, fr *tetra-* + *meros* part – more at MERIT]

**tetrameter** /te'tramitə/ *n* a line of verse consisting either of four measures of two units (FEET) of metre, or of four metrical feet (as in "Oh, who is it hath done this deed") [Gk *tetrametron*, fr neut of *tetrametros* having four measures, fr *tetra-* + *metron* measure – more at MEASURE]

**tetramethyl** /ˌtetrə'methəl, -'meethiel/ *adj* containing four METHYL groups in the molecule [ISV]

**tetramethyl lead** *n* a readily vaporizing poisonous liquid, $Pb(CH_3)_4$, used to prevent KNOCKING (sharp metallic noises caused by faulty ignition) in INTERNAL-COMBUSTION ENGINES

**¹tetraploid** /'tetrəˌployd/ *adj* having four times the basic (HAPLOID) number of CHROMOSOMES (strands of gene-carrying material) ⟨*a ~ cell*⟩ [ISV] – **tetraploidy** *n*

**²tetraploid** *n* a single cell, individual, or generation that is tetraploid

**tetrapod** /'tetrəˌpod/ *n* a VERTEBRATE animal (eg a frog, bird, or cat) with two pairs of limbs [NL *tetrapodus*, fr Gk *tetrapod-*, *tetrapous* four-footed, fr *tetra-* + *pod-*, *pous* foot – more at FOOT]

**tetrapyrrole** /ˌtetrə'piˌrohl/ *n* either of two chemical groups consisting of four PYRROLE (type of chemical compound with a circular arrangement of atoms) rings joined either in a straight chain or in a ring (eg in chlorophyll)

**tetrarch** /'tetrahk/ *n* **1** a governor of a quarter of a province **2** a subordinate prince [ME, fr L *tetrarcha*, fr Gk *tetrarchēs*, fr *tetra-* + *-archēs* -arch] – **tetrarchic** *adj*

**tetrarchy** /'tetrahki/ *n* government by four people ruling jointly

**tetraspore** /'tetrəˌspaw/ *n* any of the group of usu four asexual spores developed by MEIOSIS (type of CELL DIVISION) in certain algae [ISV] – **tetrasporic** *adj*

**tetrasyllable** /ˌtetrə'siləbl/ *n* a word of four syllables – **tetrasyllabic** *adj*

**tetratomic** /ˌtetrə'tomik/ *adj* **1** consisting of four atoms; having four atoms in the molecule **2** having four replaceable atoms or chemical groups [ISV]

**¹tetravalent** /ˌtetrə'vaylənt/ *adj* **1** having a VALENCY of four **2** genetics QUADRIVALENT **2** [ISV]

**²tetravalent** *n, genetics* QUADRIVALENT

**tetrazolium** /ˌtetrə'zohliəm/ *n* a chemical group or ion, $CH_3N_4$, that has a VALENCY of one and is similar in structure to ammonium; *also* any of several of its derivatives used to test for chemical activity in living cells [NL, fr ISV *tetrazole* $(CH_2N_4)$ + NL *-ium* (as in *ammonium*)]

**tetrode** /'tetrohd/ *n* a THERMIONIC VALVE (electronic device for directing a flow of electricity) that has four ELECTRODES (structures conducting electricity into or out of a device) which are a CATHODE, an ANODE, and two GRIDS [*tetra-* + *-ode*]

**tetrodotoxin** /teˌtrohdə'toksin/ *n* a poisonous chemical compound, $C_{11}H_{17}N_3O_8$, that has been obtained from a Japanese globefish and a newt and that acts by blocking the conduction of nerve impulses [ISV *tetrodo-* (fr NL *Tetrodon*, genus of tropical marine fishes) + *toxin*]

**tetroxide** /te'troksied/ *n* an OXIDE containing four atoms of oxygen [ISV]

**tetryl** /'tetril/ *n* a pale yellow explosive, $C_6H_2N(NO_2)CH_3$, used esp as a detonator [ISV *tetra-* + *-yl*]

**tetter** /'tetə/ *n* any of various skin diseases (eg ringworm, eczema, and HERPES) that produce spots, pimples, blisters, etc – not used technically [ME *teter*, fr OE; akin to OE *teran* to tear]

**Teuton** /'tyoohton/ *n* **1** a member of an ancient probably Germanic or Celtic people who probably lived in Jutland **2** a German [L *Teutoni*, pl]

**¹Teutonic** /tyooh'tonik/ *adj* (characteristic) of the Teutons – **Teutonically** *adv*

**²Teutonic** *n* Germanic

**Teutonism** /'tyoohtəˌniz(ə)m/ *n* GERMANISM (feature of German appearing in another language)

**Teutonist** /'tyoohtənist/ *n* GERMANIST (specialist in German)

**teuton·ize, -ise** /'tyoohtəniez/ *vt, often cap* to Germanize

**tex** /teks/ *n* a unit of weight that is a measure of the fineness of textile yarns and is equal to the weight in grams of one kilometre of the yarn – compare DENIER [Fr, fr *textile* textile]

**Texas citrus mite** /'teksəs/ *n* a RED SPIDER MITE (*Eutetrarychus banksi*) that damages the leaves of citrus trees [*Texas*, state in SW USA]

**Texas fever** *n* a RED-WATER FEVER of cattle in the USA that is caused by a PROTOZOAN (minute single-celled organism) and is transmitted by a tick (*Boophilus annulatus*)

**text** /tekst/ *n* **1a**(1) the original written or printed words and form of a literary work **a**(2) an edited or emended copy of an original work **b** a work containing such text **c** the words of a message ⟨*the ~ of a small ad*⟩ **2a** the main body of printed or written matter on a page **b** the principal part of a book exclusive of titles, introductions, etc and material at the end (eg appendices and index) **c** the printed score of a musical composition **3a**(1) a verse or passage of Scripture chosen esp for the subject of a sermon or for authoritative support (eg for a doctrine) **a**(2) a passage from an authoritative source providing an introduction or basis (eg for a speech) **b** a source of information or authority **4** a textbook **5a** a type suitable for printing running text **b** BLACK LETTER (heavy angular lettering as used in early printing) **6** a theme, topic **7** the words of something (eg a poem) set to music [ME, fr MF *texte*, fr ML *textus*, fr L, texture, context, fr *textus*, pp of *texere* to weave – more at TECHNICAL]

**¹textbook** /'tekstˌbook/ *n* a book used in the study of a subject; *specif* a standard authoritative one containing a presentation of the principles of a subject and used by students

**²textbook** *adj* conforming to the principle or descriptions in textbooks: eg **a** ideal ⟨*tried hard to be a ~ Mum*⟩ **b** typical ⟨*a ~ case*⟩

**text hand** *n* a style of large handwriting, esp as used in manuscripts

**textile** /'tekstiel/ *n* **1** cloth; *esp* a woven or knitted cloth **2** a fibre, filament, or yarn used in making cloth **3** a wearer of clothes – used by naturists [L, fr neut of *textilis* woven, fr *textus*, pp of *texere* to weave]

**textual** /'tekstyooəl, 'tekschooəl/ *adj* of or based on a text △ textural [ME, fr ML *textus* text] – **textually** *adv*

**textual criticism** *n* **1** the study of a literary work that aims to establish the original text **2** a critical study of literature emphasizing a close reading and analysis of the text

**textualist** /'tekstyooəlist, 'tekstchooəlist/ *n* a close student of the text of the Bible

**textuary** /'tekstyooəri, 'tekstchooəri/ *adj* textual

**¹texture** /'tekschə/ *n* **1a** something composed of closely interwoven elements; *specif* a woven cloth **b** the structure formed by the threads of a fabric ⟨*the open ~ of mesh*⟩ **2** identifying quality; character ⟨*the ~ of American culture*⟩ **3a** the size or organization of the constituent particles of a body or substance ⟨*a soil that is coarse in ~*⟩ **b** the visual or tactile surface characteristics and appearance of something, esp fabric ⟨*the ~ of an oil painting*⟩ ⟨*the roughish ~ of tweed*⟩ **4a** the distinctive or identifying part or quality ⟨*the rich ~ of his prose*⟩ **b** a pattern of musical sound created by notes or lines played or sung together [L *textura*, fr *textus*, pp of *texere* to weave – more at TECHNICAL] – **textural** *adj*, **texturally** *adv*, **textured** *adj*

**²texture** *vt* to give a particular texture to

**textured vegetable protein** *n* a vegetable substance that is used as a meat substitute and is made from high protein beans, esp soya beans, that are mixed to a paste, bulked by forcing through an oven at high pressure or by weaving fibres spun from the paste, and flavoured

**textus receptus** /ˌtekstəs riˈseptəs/ n the traditionally accepted text of a literary work (eg the Greek New Testament) [NL, lit., received text]

**'T-,group** n an ENCOUNTER GROUP that seeks to improve the communicative effectiveness of its members by involving them in the analysis of the roles they habitually adopt in their transactions with other people [Sensitivity Training group]

**1-th** /-th/, **-eth** /-ith/ suffix (→ adj) – used in forming ordinal numbers ⟨hundredth⟩ ⟨fortieth⟩ [ME -the, -te, fr OE -tha, -ta; akin to OHG -do -th, L -tus, Gk -tos, Skt -tha]

**2-th, -eth** suffix (→ n) – used in forming fractions ⟨a fortieth⟩ ⟨two hundredths of an inch⟩

**3-th** suffix (→ n) 1 act or process of ⟨growth⟩ ⟨birth⟩ 2 state or condition of ⟨dearth⟩ ⟨filth⟩ ⟨warmth⟩ [ME, fr OE; akin to OHG -ida, suffix forming abstract nouns, L -ta, Gk -tē, Skt -tā]

**1Thai** /tie/ n 1 a native or inhabitant of Thailand 2 the official language of Thailand 3 a group of languages including Thai, believed by some to belong to the SINO-TIBETAN language family

**2Thai** adj (characteristic) of Thailand, the Thais, or Thai

**thalamencephalon** /ˌthaləmenˈsefəlon/ n DIENCEPHALON (part of the forebrain) [NL, fr thalamus + encephalon]

**thalamic** /θəˈlamik/ adj of or involving the thalamus – **thalamically** adv

**thalamus** /ˈthaləməs/ n, pl **thalami** /-mie/ the largest subdivision of the DIENCEPHALON (part of the forebrain) forming a coordinating centre through which different nerve impulses are directed to appropriate parts of the CORTEX (outer area) of the brain [NL, fr Gk thalamos inner chamber]

**thalassaemia** /ˌthaləˈseemyə, -miˌə/ n a hereditary ANAEMIA (type of blood disease) common esp in Mediterranean regions that is characterized by deficient haemoglobin and by the presence of abnormally small RED BLOOD CELLS [NL, fr Gk thalassa sea + NL -aemia]

**thalassic** /θəˈlasik/ adj 1 of deep seas or the depths of the sea ⟨~ fishes with luminous organs⟩ 2 of or situated or developed about inland seas ⟨~ civilizations of the Aegean⟩ [Fr thalassique, fr Gk thalassa sea]

**thaler** /ˈtahlə/ n TALER (former German coin)

**thalidomide** /θəˈlidəmied/ adj or n (of or affected by) a sedative and hypnotic drug, $C_{13}H_{10}N_2O_4$, that was found to cause malformation of infants born to mothers using it during pregnancy ⟨~ children⟩ [phthalic acid + -id- (fr imide) + -o- + imide]

**thall-, thallo-** comb form 1a young shoot ⟨thallium⟩ b thallus ⟨thalloid⟩ 2 thallium ⟨thallic⟩ [NL, fr Gk, fr thallos – more at THALLUS]

**thallic** /ˈthalik/ adj of or containing thallium, esp with a VALENCY of three

**thallium** /ˈthaliˌəm/ n a sparsely but widely distributed poisonous metallic chemical element that resembles lead in physical properties and is used chiefly in the form of chemical compounds in PHOTOELECTRIC CELLS (devices converting light into an electric current) or as a pesticide [NL, deriv of Gk thallos green shoot; fr the bright green line in its spectrum]

**thalloid** /ˈthaloyd/ adj of, resembling, or consisting of a thallus

**thallophyte** /ˈthaləfiet/ n any of a primary group (Thallophyta) of living things in some systems of classification comprising plants with a plant body that is typically a thallus and including the algae, fungi, and lichens [deriv of Gk thallos + phyton plant – more at PHYT-] – **thallophytic** adj

**thallous** /ˈthaləs/ adj of or containing thallium with a VALENCY of one

**thallus** /ˈthaləs/ n, pl **thalli** /ˈthalie, -li/, **thalluses** a plant body (eg of an alga) that lacks differentiation into distinct parts (eg stem, leaves, and roots) and does not grow from an end point [NL, fr Gk thallos green shoot, fr thallein to sprout; akin to Alb dal I come forth]

**1than** /dhən; strong dhan/ conj 1a – used with comparatives to indicate the second member or the one taken as the point of departure in a comparison ⟨older ~ I am⟩ ⟨easier said ~ done⟩ b – used to indicate difference of kind, manner, or degree, esp with some adjectives and adverbs expressing diversity ⟨anywhere else ~ at home⟩ ⟨would starve rather ~ beg⟩ 2 to – usu only after prefer, preferable, and preferably 3 other than; but ⟨no alternative ~ to sack him⟩ 4 when – esp after scarcely and hardly 5 chiefly NAm from – usu only after

different, differently △ then [ME than, then then, than – more at THEN]

**2than** prep in comparison with ⟨older ~ me⟩ ⟨less ~ £1000⟩ *usage* 1 Since **than** is a conjunction as well as a preposition, **than** I/he/she/we/they are preferable, in formal writing, to **than** me/him/her/us/them ⟨she was more distinguished **than** he⟩. See DIFFERENT, HARDLY. 2 The construction ⟨he's as fat or fatter **than** Jane⟩ is widely disliked. It is better to say ⟨he's as fat as or fatter **than** Jane⟩ or ⟨he's as fat as Jane, or fatter⟩.

**Thanatos** /ˈthanətos/ n an instinctual desire for death that in Freudian theory is one of two primal instincts – compare EROS [Gk, death; akin to Skt adhvanit it vanished, L fumus smoke]

**thane** /thayn/ n 1 also **thegn** a free retainer of an Anglo-Saxon lord; esp one resembling a feudal baron by holding lands of and performing military service for the king 2 a Scottish feudal lord [ME theyn, fr OE thegn; akin to OHG thegan thane, Gk tiktein to bear, beget] – **thaneship** n

**thank** /thangk/ vt 1 to express gratitude to ⟨~ed her for the present – used in thank you, usu without a subject, to express gratitude politely ⟨~ you for the loan⟩; used in such phrases as thank God, thank heaven, usu without a subject to express gratitude or more often only the speaker's or writer's pleasure or satisfaction in something ⟨~ God he's safe⟩ 2 to hold responsible; blame ⟨had only himself to ~ for his loss⟩ [ME thanken, fr OE thancian; akin to OE thanc gratitude – more at THANKS] – **thanker** n

**thankful** /ˈthangkf(ə)l/ adj 1 conscious of benefit received; grateful ⟨for what we are about to receive make us truly ~⟩ 2 feeling or expressing thanks ⟨a ~ look in its eyes⟩ 3 well pleased; glad ⟨he was ~ that the room was dark⟩ – **thankfulness** n

**thankfully** /ˈthangkf(ə)li/ adv 1 in a thankful way 2 it is a matter for relief that ⟨but ~ things have changed – Honey⟩ *usage* The increasingly common use of **thankfully** to mean "it is a matter for relief that" is widely disliked both in Britain and in the USA. If one uses it, it is important to ensure that there is no ambiguity, since ⟨**thankfully**, she closed the door⟩ has two meanings; but it is sometimes a usefully impersonal word, since its user is not obliged to state who is experiencing the "relief".

**thankless** /ˈthangklis/ adj 1 not expressing or feeling gratitude; ungrateful ⟨~ children⟩ 2 not likely to obtain thanks; unappreciated ⟨a ~ task⟩; also unprofitable, futile ⟨a ~ job trying to grow tomatoes out of doors in England⟩ – **thanklessly** adv, **thanklessness** n

**thanks** /thangks/ n pl 1 kindly or grateful thoughts; gratitude ⟨express my ~⟩ 2 an expression of gratitude ⟨received with ~ the sum of £50⟩ – often in an utterance containing no verb and serving as a courteous and somewhat informal expression of gratitude ⟨many ~⟩ [pl of ME thank, fr OE thanc thought, gratitude; akin to OHG dank gratitude, L tongēre to know]

**thanksgiving** /thangksˈgiving, '---/ n 1 the act of giving thanks; expression of gratefulness, esp to God 2 a prayer expressing gratitude b cap THANKSGIVING DAY

**Thanksgiving Day** n a day appointed for giving thanks for divine goodness: eg a the fourth Thursday in November observed as a public holiday in the USA b the second Monday in October observed as a public holiday in Canada

**thankworthy** /ˈthangkˌwuhdhi/ adj worthy of thanks or gratitude; meritorious

**'thank-,you** n a polite expression of one's gratitude [fr the phrase (I) thank you used in expressing gratitude]

**thar** /thah/, **tahr** /tah/ n a Himalayan beardless wild goat (Hemitragus jemlaicus) [Nepali thār]

**1that** /dhat/ pron, pl those /dhohz/ 1a the thing or idea just mentioned ⟨after ~ he went to bed⟩ ⟨mouldy, ~ – News Of The World⟩ b a relatively distant person or thing introduced for observation or discussion ⟨~ is my father over there⟩ ⟨who is ~?⟩ ⟨those are chestnuts and these are elms⟩ c the thing or state of affairs there ⟨look at ~!⟩ – sometimes used disparagingly of a person d the kind or thing specified as follows ⟨the purest water is ~ produced by distillation⟩ ⟨the truth is ~ which is true⟩ ⟨cost is less than ~ of silk⟩ ⟨those ripe enough to eat⟩ e what is understood from the context ⟨take ~!⟩ ⟨how's ~?⟩ ⟨if you let boys do "~" they wouldn't respect you – Spare Rib⟩ 2 one of such a group; such ⟨~'s life⟩ 3 – used to indicate emphatic repetition of an idea previously expressed ⟨he was helpful, and ~ on an unusual degree⟩ ⟨is he capable? He is ~⟩ 4 pl the people; such ⟨those who think 5 dial Br he, she, it ⟨~ twirled ~'s tail – Akenfield⟩ *usage* see 1THIS [ME, fr OE thæt, neut demonstrative pron & definite article; akin to OHG *daz*, neut demonstrative pron & definite article, Gk *to*, L is*tud* neut demonstrative pron] – **be that as it may** regardless of that; IN ANY CASE – **that's a** THERE'S A – **that's that** that concludes the matter – compare ALL THAT, AND THAT, AT THAT, HOW'S THAT, LIKE THAT, THAT IS TO SAY

²**that** *adj, pl* **those 1** being the person, thing, or idea specified, mentioned, or understood ⟨*early ~ morning*⟩ ⟨*~ cake we bought*⟩ **2** the farther away or less immediately under observation ⟨*this chair or ~ one*⟩

³**that** /dhət; *strong* dhat/ *conj* **1a(1)** – used to introduce a noun clause as subject, object, or complement of a verb ⟨*said ~ he was afraid*⟩, a noun clause anticipated by *it* ⟨*it is unlikely ~ he'll be in*⟩, or a noun clause as complement to a noun or adjective ⟨*we are certain ~ it's true*⟩ ⟨*the certainty ~ it's true*⟩ ⟨*the fact ~ you're here*⟩ **a(2)** – used to introduce a clause modifying an adverb or adverbial expression ⟨*will go anywhere ~ he's invited*⟩ **b** – used to introduce an emotional exclamation ⟨*~ it should come to this!*⟩ or to express a wish ⟨*oh, ~ he would come!*⟩ **2a(1)** – used to introduce a subordinate clause expressing (1) purpose ⟨*cutting down expenses ~ her son might inherit an unencumbered estate* – W B Yeats⟩, (2) reason ⟨*rejoice ~ you are lightened of a load* – Robert Browning⟩, or (3) result ⟨*walked so fast ~ we couldn't keep up*⟩ **3** – used as a meaningless addition to a subordinating conjunction ⟨*if ~ thy bent of love be honourable* – Shak⟩

*usage* **1** When introductory **that** can be omitted it is usually shorter and neater to omit it, especially before short clauses ⟨*I'm glad* (**that**) *I came*⟩ ⟨*take anything* (**that**) *you want*⟩. The choice of whether or not to omit **that** often depends upon the relative formality of an introducing verb. Compare ⟨*he said he'd come*⟩ ⟨*he asserted* **that** *he would come*⟩ ⟨*I suppose you're right*⟩ ⟨*I assume* **that** *you are right*⟩ ⟨*she believes it's true*⟩ ⟨*she holds* **that** *it is true*⟩. One should not omit **that** where confusion may result. If **that** is omitted in ⟨*she said* (**that**) *before they left I should pay their bill*⟩ it is not clear whether her words were "Pay their bill" or "Pay it before they leave". **2** It is a common mistake to introduce an extra **that** when another clause has intervened ⟨*it seems* **that**, *if we are to finish in time,* (△) *that* *we shall have to work over the weekend*⟩.

⁴**that** /dhət; *strong* dhat/ *pron* **1** – used to introduce a usu restrictive relative clause in reference to a person, thing, or group as subject ⟨*nothing ~ matters*⟩ ⟨*it was George ~ told me*⟩ or as object of a verb or of a following preposition ⟨*the house ~ Jack built*⟩ ⟨*the hotel ~ we stayed in*⟩; compare WHO, WHICH, WHOM **2a** at, in, on, by, with, for, or to which ⟨*the reason ~ he came*⟩ ⟨*the way ~ he spoke*⟩ ⟨*the time ~ he arrived*⟩ **b** according to what; to the extent of what – used after a negative ⟨*has never been here ~ I know of*⟩ **3a** *archaic* that which **b** *obs* the person who – **that** was that had the specified former or maiden name ⟨*Miss Jones* that was⟩

*usage* Although **that** is somewhat less formal than **who**, it is perfectly correct to use it of people as well as things, and is often useful when one refers to both ⟨*the children and parcels* **that** *filled the car*⟩. **That** cannot be used after a preposition ⟨*the women with* **whom** (not △ **that**) *I work*⟩ ⟨*the room in* **which** (not △ **that**) *he sleeps*⟩. **That** can introduce restrictive relative clauses only, while **who** and **which** can introduce either restrictive or nonrestrictive ones. Compare ⟨*I broke the finger* **that/which** *I type with*⟩ ⟨*I broke my finger,* **which** (not △ **that**) *was very tiresome*⟩. See ²WHICH

⁵**that** /dhat/ *adv* **1** to the extent indicated or understood ⟨*a nail about ~ long*⟩ ⟨*she's ~ much older*⟩ **2** very, extremely – usu + neg ⟨*not really ~ expensive*⟩; compare ALL THAT **3** *dial Br* to such an extreme degree ⟨*I'm ~ hungry I could eat a horse*⟩ *usage* see ³THIS

**thataway** /'dhatə,way/ *adv, informal* in that direction or manner

¹**thatch** /thach/ *vt* to cover (as if) with thatch [ME *thecchen*, fr OE *theccan* to cover; akin to OHG *decchen* to cover, L *tegere*, Gk *stegein* to cover, *stegos* roof, Skt *sthagati* he covers] – **thatcher** *n*

²**thatch** *n* **1a** plant material (e g straw) used as a sheltering cover, esp of a house **b** a sheltering cover (e g a house roof) made of such material **2** *chiefly humorous* the hair of one's head; *broadly* anything resembling the thatch of a house

**thaumaturgist** /'thawmə,tuhjist/ *n* a performer of miracles; *esp* a magician

**thaumaturgy** /'thawmə,tuhji/ *n* the performance of miracles; *specif* magic [Gk *thaumatourgia*, fr *thaumatourgos* working miracles, fr *thaumat-, thauma* miracle + *ergon* work – more at THEATRE, WORK] – **thaumaturgic** *adj*

¹**thaw** /thaw/ *vt* to cause to thaw – often + *out* ~ *vi* **1a** to go from a frozen to a liquid state; melt **b** to become free of the effect (e g stiffness, numbness, or hardness) of cold as a result of exposure to warmth – often + *out* **2** to be warm enough to melt ice and snow – + *it* in reference to the weather **3** to become less hostile ⟨*relations with E Germany have ~ed*⟩ **4** to become less aloof, cold, or reserved [ME *thawen*, fr OE *thawian*; akin to OHG *douwen* to thaw, Gk *tēkein* to melt, L *tabes* wasting disease]

²**thaw** *n* **1** the action, fact, or process of thawing ⟨*the ~ in relations with W Europe*⟩ **2** a period of weather warm enough to thaw ice

**THC** *n* TETRAHYDROCANNABINOL (active constituent of marijuana) [tetrahydrocannabinol]

¹**the** /*before consonants* dhə; *strong and before vowels* dhee/ *definite article* **1a** – used before nouns when the referent has been previously specified by context or circumstance ⟨*put ~ cat out*⟩ ⟨*ordered bread and cheese, but didn't eat ~ cheese*⟩ **b** – indicating that a following noun is unique or universally recognized ⟨*~ Pope*⟩ ⟨*~ Lord*⟩ ⟨*~ sun*⟩ ⟨*~ night*⟩ ⟨*~ south*⟩ ⟨*~ future*⟩ **c** – used before a noun denoting time to indicate the present or the period under consideration ⟨*book of ~ month*⟩ **d** – used before certain proper names (e g of ships, rivers, mountain ranges, or well-known buildings) ⟨*~ Mayflower*⟩ ⟨*~ Rhine*⟩ ⟨*~ Alhambra*⟩ ⟨*~ Alps*⟩ **e** – used before the name of a familiar appurtenance of daily life to indicate a service at hand ⟨*talked on ~ telephone*⟩ ⟨*turned off ~ gas*⟩ **f** – used before the names of certain diseases or conditions ⟨*~ rheumatism*⟩ ⟨*~ jitters*⟩ **g** – used before the names of parts of the body or of the clothing instead of a possessive adjective ⟨*inflammation of ~ bladder*⟩ ⟨*took him by ~ sleeve*⟩ **h** – used before the name of a branch of human endeavour or proficiency ⟨*study ~ law*⟩ ⟨*play ~ piano*⟩; not usu used before the names of sports **i** – indicating an occupation or pursuit symbolically associated with a following noun ⟨*~ pulpit*⟩ ⟨*~ bottle*⟩ **j** – designating one of a class as the best or most worth singling out ⟨*this is ~ life*⟩ ⟨*you can't be ~ Elvis Presley!*⟩ **k** – used before the name of a Scottish clan to denote its chief ⟨*~ McTavish*⟩ **l** – used in prepositional phrases to indicate that the following noun serves as a basis for computation ⟨*sold by ~ dozen*⟩ **m** – used before the pl form of a number that is a multiple of 10 to denote a particular decade of a century or of a person's life ⟨*life in ~ twenties*⟩ **2a** which or who is – limiting the application of a modified noun to what is specified ⟨*~ right answer*⟩ ⟨*~ Kings Road*⟩ ⟨*Peter ~ Great*⟩ **b** – used before a noun to limit its application to that specified by what follows ⟨*~ poet Wordsworth*⟩ ⟨*~ University of London*⟩ ⟨*~ days of our youth*⟩ ⟨*~ man on my right*⟩ ⟨*didn't have ~ time to write*⟩ **3** – used before a singular noun to indicate generic use ⟨*~ dog is a mammal*⟩ ⟨*a history of ~ novel*⟩ **4a** that which is ⟨*nothing but ~ best*⟩ ⟨*an essay in ~ sublime*⟩ **b** those who are ⟨*~ élite*⟩ ⟨*~ British*⟩ ⟨*~ dead*⟩ **c** he or she who is ⟨*~ accused stands before you*⟩ **5** – used after *how, what, where, who,* and *why* to introduce various expletives ⟨*who ~ devil are you?*⟩ [ME, fr OE *thē*, masc demonstrative pron & definite article, alter. (influenced by oblique cases – e g *thæs,* gen – & neut, *thæt*) of *sē;* akin to Gk *ho,* masc demonstrative pron & definite article – more at THAT]

*usage* **1** The strong pronunciation /dhee/, before consonants as well as vowels, has always been common in conversational speech when the speaker pauses to select the following noun, but its introduction into more formal speaking (e g by broadcasters) as if in imitation of conversational style is widely disliked. In any case, **the** is always pronounced /dhee/ in contexts such as that in sense **1j** ⟨*you can't be* **the** *Elvis Presley!*⟩ **2** The journalist's omission of **the** before people's occupations ⟨*violinist Yehudi Menuhin*⟩ is disliked by some people, who prefer ⟨*Yehudi Menuhin,* **the** *violinist*⟩. **3 The** should be capitalized if it is the first word of a title ⟨**The** *Times*⟩.

²**the** *adv* **1** than before; than otherwise – with comparatives ⟨*none ~ wiser for attending*⟩ ⟨*so much ~ worse*⟩ **2a** to what extent ⟨*~ sooner the better*⟩ **b** to that extent ⟨*the sooner ~ better*⟩ **3** beyond all others – with superlatives ⟨*likes this ~ best*⟩ ⟨*with ~ greatest difficulty*⟩ [ME, fr OE *thȳ* by that, instrumental of *thæt* that]

³**the** *prep* PER 1 [¹*the*]

**the-, theo-** *comb form* god; God ⟨*theism*⟩ ⟨*theocentric*⟩ [ME *theo-,* fr L, fr Gk *the-, theo-,* fr *theos*]

¹**theatre,** *NAm chiefly* **theater** /'thiatə/ *n* **1a** an outdoor structure for dramatic performances or spectacles in ancient Greece

and Rome **b** a building for dramatic performances; *also* a cinema **2a** a place where the land rises by steps or gradations ⟨*a woody ~ of stateliest view* – John Milton⟩ **b** a room with rising tiers of seats (e g for lectures or surgical demonstrations) **3** a place of enactment of significant events or action ⟨*the ~ of public life*⟩ ⟨*the ~ of war*⟩ **4a** dramatic literature or performance **b** dramatic effectiveness ⟨*the effect is pure ~*⟩ **5** *the* theatrical world **6** *Br* OPERATING THEATRE [ME *theatre*, fr MF, fr L *theatrum*, fr GK *theatron*, fr *theasthai* to view, fr *thea* act of seeing; akin to GK *thauma* miracle]

²**theatre** *adj* of a theatre; *specif, of nuclear war or weapons* confined to or appropriate to a limited sphere of operations; not on an intercontinental scale

**theatregoer** /'thiəta,goh·ə/ *n* someone who frequently goes to the theatre – **theatregoing** *n*

,**theatre-in-the-'round** *n* performance of a drama on a stage surrounded by an audience; *also* a theatre arranged for this

**theatre of the absurd** *n* theatre that seeks to represent by bizarre or fantastic means the absurdity of human existence in a meaningless universe

**theatrical** /thi'atrikl/ *adj* **1** of the theatre or the presentation of plays ⟨*a ~ costume*⟩ **2** marked by pretence or artificiality of emotion **3** marked by extravagant display or exhibitionism; HISTRIONIC ⟨*a ~ gesture*⟩ – **theatricalism** *n*, **theatrically** *adv*, **theatricality** *n*

**theatrical·ize, -ise** /thi'atrikəliez/ *vt* **1** to adapt to the theatre; dramatize **2** to display in a showy or extravagant fashion – **theatricalization** *n*

**theatricals** /thi'atrikəlz/ *n pl* **1a** the performance of plays ⟨*amateur ~*⟩ **b** theatrical technique **2** showy or extravagant gestures

**thebe** /'tebay/ *n* – see *pula* at MONEY table [of Bantu origin]

**theca** /'theekə/ *n, pl* **thecae** /'thee,see, -,kee/ **1** an urn-shaped spore-containing upper part of the CAPSULE (box-like structure) of a moss **2** an enveloping sheath or case of an animal or animal part [NL, fr Gk *thēkē* case – more at TICK] – **thecal, thecate** *adj*

-**thecium** /-'thees(h)iəm/ *comb form* (→ *n*), *pl* -**thecia** /-'s(h)iə/ small usu botanical structure that contains ⟨*endothecium*⟩ [NL, fr Gk *thēkion*, dim. of *thēkē* case – more at TICK]

¹**thecodont** /'theekədont/ *adj* having the teeth inserted in sockets [ISV *thec-* (fr NL *theca*) + *-odont*]

²**thecodont** *n* a thecodont animal; *esp* any of an order (Thecodontia) of thecodont reptiles of the TRIASSIC period believed to be ancestral to the dinosaurs, birds, and crocodiles

**thee** /dhee/ *pron, archaic or dial* **1a** objective case of THOU – used with cap when addressing God **b** thou – used by Quakers, esp among themselves, in contexts where the subjective form would be expected ⟨*is ~ ready?*⟩ **2** thyself [ME, fr OE *thē*, acc & dat of *thū* – more at THOU]

**theft** /theft/ *n* **1** the act of stealing; *specif* dishonest appropriation of property with the intention of permanently depriving the rightful owner of it **2** *obs* something stolen [ME *thiefthe*, fr OE *thīefth*; akin to OE *thēof* thief]

**thegn** /thayn/ *n* THANE 1 (Anglo-Saxon landholder) [OE – more at THANE]

**theine** /'thee·in/ *n* caffeine [NL *theina*, fr *thea* tea, fr Chin (Amoy) *te* (*t'e*)]

**their** /dhə; *strong* dheə/ *adj* **1** of them or themselves, esp as possessors ⟨*~ furniture*⟩, agents ⟨*~ verses*⟩, or objects of an action ⟨*~ being seen*⟩ **2** his or her; his, her, its ⟨*anyone in ~ senses* – W H Auden⟩ □ used attributively [ME, fr *their*, pron, fr ON *theirra*, gen pl demonstrative & personal pron; akin to OE *thæt* that]

   *usage* The spelling of **theirs** meaning "the one belonging to them" as △ **their's** is a common confusion ⟨*the house became* **theirs** (not △ **their's**)⟩. See THEY. △ there, they're

**theirs** /dheəz/ *pron, pl* **theirs** **1** that which or the one who belongs to them – used without a following noun as a pronoun equivalent in meaning to the adjective *their*; compare phrases at ²MINE **2** his or hers; his, hers ⟨*I will do my part if everybody else will do ~*⟩ *usage* see THEY △ there's

**theism** /'thee,iz(ə)m/ *n* belief in the existence of a god or gods; *specif* belief in the existence of one God viewed as the creative source of man and the world, who transcends yet is immanent in the world – **theist** *n or adj*, **theistic** *adj*, **theistical** *adj*, **theistically** *adv*

   *synonyms* **Theism** can mean merely "belief in God". When it is contrasted with **deism** it means "belief, based on revelation as well

as on reason, in a God who rules the universe as well as having created it".

-**theism** /-thi,iz(ə)m/ *comb form* (→ *n*) belief in (such) a god or (such or so many) gods ⟨*monotheism*⟩ [MF -*théisme*, fr Gk *theos* god] – **-theist** *comb form* (→ *n*)

¹**them** /dhəm; *strong* dhem/ *pron, objective case of* THEY – compare phrases at ¹ME [ME; partly fr *tham*, fr OE *thæm, thām*, dat pl demonstrative pron & definite article; partly fr *theim*, fr ON, dat pl demonstrative & personal pronoun]

   *usage* As they, than they are preferable in formal writing to as them, than them. See ⁴AS, ²THAN, ME, THEY

²**them** /dhem/ *adj, nonstandard* those ⟨*~ blokes*⟩

,**them-and-'us** *adj* characterized by tension or resentment between those who exert authority and those over whom it is exerted

**thematic** /thi'matik/ *adj* **1a** of the STEM (part that remains unchanged) of a word **b** *of a vowel* being the last part of a word stem before an inflectional ending **c** *of a verb form* containing a thematic vowel **2** of or constituting a theme [Gk *thematikos*, fr *themat-, thema* theme] – **thematically** *adv*

**theme** /theem/ *n* **1** a subject of artistic representation or a topic of discourse **2** STEM 4 (part of a word that remains unchanged) **3** a melodic subject of a musical composition or movement **4** *NAm* a written exercise; a composition ⟨*a research ~*⟩ *synonyms* see ¹SUBJECT [ME *teme, theme*, fr OF & L; OF *teme*, fr L *thema*, fr Gk, lit., something laid down, fr *tithenai* to place – more at DO]

**theme park** *n, chiefly NAm* an amusement park in which the structures and settings are all based on a specific theme (e g space travel)

**theme song** *n* **1** a melody that occurs more than once in a musical play or in a film and characterizes the production or one of its characters **2** SIGNATURE TUNE

**themselves** /dhəm'selvz/ *pron taking pl vb* **1a** those identical people, creatures, or things that are they – used reflexively ⟨*nations that govern ~*⟩, for emphasis ⟨*the team ~ were delighted*⟩, or in absolute constructions ⟨*~ busy, they disliked idleness in others*⟩; compare ONESELF **b** himself or herself; himself, herself ⟨*hoped nobody would hurt ~*⟩ **2** their normal selves ⟨*soon be ~ again*⟩

¹**then** /dhen/ *adv* **1** at that time **2a** soon after that; next in order of time ⟨*walked to the door, ~ turned*⟩ **b** following next after in a series ⟨*first came the clowns, ~ came the elephants*⟩ **c** in addition, besides ⟨*~ there is the interest to be paid*⟩ **3a** in that case ⟨*~ why did you go?*⟩ ⟨*take it, ~, if you want it so much*⟩ **b** as may be inferred ⟨*your mind is made up, ~?*⟩ **c** accordingly, so – indicating causal connection in a discourse ⟨*our hero, ~, was greatly relieved*⟩ **d** as a necessary consequence ⟨*if the angles are equal, ~ the complements are equal*⟩ **e** – used to emphasize a contradiction ⟨*no she's not, ~!*⟩ **f** – used after *but* to offset a preceding statement ⟨*he lost the race, but ~ he never expected to win*⟩ △ than [ME *than, then* then, than, fr OE *thonne, thænne*; akin to OHG *denne* then, than, OE *thæt* that] – **then and there** on the spot; immediately ⟨*wanted the money* then and there⟩

²**then** *n* that time ⟨*since ~, he's been more cautious*⟩

³**then** *adj* existing or acting at that time ⟨*the ~ Secretary of State*⟩

**thenar** /'theenah, -nə/ *n* **1** the ball of the thumb **2** the palm of the hand; *also* the sole of the foot [NL, fr Gk – more at DEN] – **thenar** *adj*

**thence** /dhens/ *adv, chiefly formal* **1** from there ⟨*fly to London and ~ to Paris*⟩ – sometimes + *from* ⟨*depart from ~*⟩ **2** from that preceding fact or premise ⟨*it ~ transpired*⟩ **3** *archaic* from that time; thenceforth [ME *thannes*, fr *thanne* from that place, fr OE *thanon*; akin to OHG *thanan* from that place, OE *thænne* then – more at THEN]

**thenceforth** /,dhens'fawth/ *adv* from that time or point on

**thenceforward** /,dhens'faw·wood/ *adv* thenceforth

**theo-** – see THE-

**theobromine** /,thee·ə'brohmeen/ *n* an ALKALOID drug, $C_7H_8N_4O_2$, that is closely related to caffeine, occurs esp in cacao beans and tea, and is used esp as a DIURETIC (substance that increases the flow of urine) and heart stimulant [NL *Theobroma*, genus of trees (including the cacao tree), fr *the-* + Gk *brōma* food, fr *bibrōskein* to devour – more at VORACIOUS]

**theocentric** /,thiə'sentrik/ *adj* having God as the central interest and ultimate concern ⟨*a ~ culture*⟩ – **theocentricity** *n*, **theocentrism** *n*

**theocracy** /thi'okrəsi/ *n* government of a state by immediate divine guidance or by officials who are regarded as divinely guided; *also* a state under such government [Gk *theokratia,* fr *the-* + *-kratia* -cracy]

**theocrat** /'thee-ə,krat/ *n* 1 a person who rules in or lives under a theocratic form of government 2 a person who favours a theocratic form of government

**theocratic** /,thee-ə'kratik/ *also* **theocratical** /-kl/ *adj* of or being a theocracy – **theocratically** *adv*

**theodicy** /thi'odəsi/ *n* defence of God's goodness and omnipotence against arguments derived from existence of evil [modif of Fr *théodicée,* fr Gk *theos* god + *dikē* judgment, right – more at DICTION]

**theodolite** /thi'od(ə)l,iet/ *n* a surveyor's instrument for measuring horizontal and vertical angles [NL *theodelitus,* of unknown origin] – **theodolitic** *adj*

**theogony** /thi'ogəni/ *n* an account of the origin and genealogy of the gods [Gk *theogonia,* fr *the-* + *-gonia* -gony] – **theogonic** *adj*

**theologian** /,thee-ə'lohjən/ *n* a specialist in theology

**theological** /,thee-ə'lojikl/ *also* **theologic** *adj* 1 of theology 2 preparing for a religious vocation ⟨*a* ~ *student*⟩ – **theologically** *adv*

**theological college** *n* a college with a religious curriculum, esp for the training of candidates for the clergy

**theological virtue** *n* any of the three spiritual graces faith, hope, and charity which, according to medieval theology, draw the soul to God

**theolog·ize, -ise** /thi'olejiez/ *vi* to theorize theologically ~ *vt* to make theological; give a religious significance to – **theologizer** *n*

**theologue, theolog** /'thee-ə,log/ *n, informal* a theologian or theological student [L *theologus* theologian, fr Gk *theologos,* fr *the-* + *legein* to speak – more at LEGEND]

**theology** /thi'oləji/ *n* 1 the study of God and his relation to the world, esp by analysis of the origins and teachings of an organized religious community (eg the Christian church) 2a a theological theory or system ⟨*Thomist* ~⟩ ⟨*a* ~ *of atonement*⟩ b a distinctive body of theological opinion ⟨*Catholic* ~⟩ [ME *theologie,* fr L *theologia,* fr Gk, fr *the-* + *-logia* -logy]

**theonomous** /thi'onəmes/ *adj* governed by God; subject to God's authority [*the-* + *-nomous* (as in *autonomous*)] – **theonomously** *adv*

**theonomy** /thi'onəmi/ *n* the state of being theonomous; government by God [Ger *theonomie,* fr *theo-* the- (fr L) + *-nomie* -nomy]

**theophany** /thi'ofəni/ *n* a visible manifestation of God or a god [ML *theophania,* fr LGk *theophaneia,* fr Gk *the-* + *-phaneia* (as in *epiphaneia* appearance) – more at EPIPHANY] – **theophanic** *adj*

**theophylline** /thi'ofilin/ *n* an ALKALOID drug, $C_7H_8N_4O_2$, obtained from tea leaves or made synthetically that is closely related to THEOBROMINE and has similar properties and uses in medicine [ISV *theo-* (fr NL *thea* tea) + *phyll-* + *-ine* – more at THEINE]

**theorbo** /thi'awboh/ *n, pl* **theorbos** a 17th-century musical instrument like a large lute but having an extra upper set of pegs carrying long bass strings [modif of It *tiorba, tearba*]

**theorem** /'thiərəm, 'thee-ərəm/ *n* 1 a formula, proposition, or statement in mathematics or logic deduced or to be deduced from other more basic formulae or propositions 2 an idea accepted or proposed as a demonstrable truth, often as a part of a general theory; a proposition ⟨*the* ~ *that the best defence is offence*⟩ [LL *theorema,* fr Gk *theorēma,* fr *theorein* to look at, fr *theōros* spectator, fr *thea* act of seeing – more at THEATRE] – **theorematic** *adj*

**theoretical** /thiə'retikl, ,thee-ə-/ *also* **theoretic** *adj* 1a relating to or having the character of theory; abstract b confined to theory or speculation; speculative ⟨~ *mechanics*⟩ 2 given to or skilled in theorizing ⟨*a brilliant* ~ *physicist*⟩ 3 existing only in theory; hypothetical ⟨*gave as an example a* ~ *situation*⟩ [LL *theoreticus,* fr Gk *theorētikos,* fr *theorein* to look at] – **theoretically** *adv*

**theoretician** /,thiərə'tish(ə)n, ,thee-ə-/ *n* a person who specializes in the theoretical aspects of a subject

**theorist** /'thiərist, 'thee-ə-/ *n* a theoretician

**theor·ization, -isation** /,thiərie'zaysh(ə)n, ,thee-ə-/ *n* an act or product of theorizing

**theor·ize, -ise** /'thiə,riez, 'thee-ə-/ *vi* to form a theory; speculate – **theorizer** *n*

**theory** /'thiəri, 'thee-ə-/ *n* 1a a belief, policy, or procedure proposed or followed as the basis of action ⟨*her method is based on the* ~ *that all children want to learn*⟩ b an ideal or supposed set of facts, principles, or circumstances – often in *in theory* ⟨*in* ~, *we have always advocated freedom for all, but in practice . . .* ⟩ 2 the general or abstract principles of a subject ⟨*music* ~⟩ 3 a plausible or scientifically acceptable principle or body of principles offered to explain a phenomenon ⟨*wave* ~ *of light*⟩ 4a a hypothesis assumed for the sake of argument or investigation b an unproved assumption; a conjecture c a body of theorems presenting a concise systematic view of a subject ⟨~ *of equations*⟩ 5 abstract thought; speculation [LL *theoria,* fr Gk *theōria,* fr *theōrein* to look at]

**theory of games** *n* the analysis of a situation (eg in business or military strategy) in which opposing interests given specific information are allowed a choice of moves with the object of maximizing their wins and minimizing their losses – called also GAME THEORY

**theory of numbers** *n* NUMBER THEORY (study of the properties of the integers)

**theosophist** /thi'osəfist/ *n* 1 an adherent of theosophy 2 *cap* a member of a theosophical society

**theosophy** /thi'osəfi/ *n* 1 teaching about God and the world that stresses the validity of mystical insight 2 *often cap* the teachings of a modern movement originating in the USA in 1875 and following chiefly Buddhist and Hindu theories, esp of evolution and reincarnation [ML *theosophia,* fr LGk, fr Gk *the-* + *sophia* wisdom – more at -SOPHY] – **theosophical** *adj,* **theosophically** *adv*

**therapeusis** /,therə'pyoohsis/ *n taking sing or pl vb* therapeutics [NL, fr Gk, treatment, fr *therapeuein* to treat]

**therapeutic** /therə'pyoohtik/ *adj* of the treatment of disease or disorders by remedial agents or methods; medicinal ⟨~ *diets*⟩ [Gk *therapeutikos,* fr *therapeuein* to attend, treat, fr *theraps* attendant] – **therapeutically** *adv*

**therapeutic index** *n* a measure of the effectiveness of a drug that indicates how good the drug is at producing the desired effects without causing harmful side effects; the ratio of the largest dose producing no toxic side effects in half the subjects tested, to the smallest dose routinely producing the desired therapeutic effect in half the subjects tested

**therapeutics** /,therə'pyoohtiks/ *n taking sing or pl vb* a branch of medical science dealing with the application of remedies to diseases

**therapeutist** /,therə'pyoohtist/ *n* someone skilled in therapeutics

**therapist** /'therəpist/ *n* someone who specializes in therapy; *esp* a person trained in methods of treatment and rehabilitation other than the use of drugs or surgery ⟨*a speech* ~⟩

**therapsid** /thə'rapsid/ *n* any of an order (Therapsida) of reptiles of the PERMIAN and TRIASSIC periods that are believed to be ancestral to the mammals [NL *Therapsida,* group name, perh fr Gk *theraps* attendant] – **therapsid** *adj*

**therapy** /'therəpi/ *n* therapeutic treatment of bodily, mental, or social disorders [NL *therapia,* fr Gk *therapeia,* fr *therapeuein* to attend, treat]

**Theravada** /,therə'vaydə/ *n* a conservative branch of Buddhism comprising sects chiefly in Sri Lanka, Burma, Thailand, Laos, and Cambodia and adhering to the original Pali scriptures alone and to the nontheistic ideal of NIRVANA (ultimate state of bliss) for a limited select number – compare MAHAYANA [Pali *theravāda,* lit., doctrine of the elders]

¹**there** /dheə/ *adv* 1 in or at that place ⟨*stand over* ~⟩ – often used to draw attention or to replace a name ⟨~ *goes John*⟩ ⟨*hello* ~!⟩ 2 thither ⟨*went* ~ *after church*⟩ 3a now ⟨~ *goes the hooter*⟩ b at or in that point or particular ⟨~ *is where I disagree with you*⟩ 4 – used interjectionally to express satisfaction, approval, encouragement, or defiance ⟨~, *it's finished*⟩ ⟨*won't go, so* ~⟩ ⟨~, ~, *don't cry*⟩ △ their, they're [ME, fr OE *thær;* akin to OHG *dār* there, OE *thæt* that] – **put it there** – used as an invitation to shake hands – **there and back** for a round trip ⟨*costs £1 there and back*⟩ – **there and then** THEN AND THERE – **there it is** such is the unfortunate fact – **there's a** – used when urging a course of action ⟨*don't sulk there's a dear!*⟩ – **there you are 1** HERE YOU ARE **2** I told you so

²**there** *pron* – used to introduce a sentence or clause expressing the idea of existence ⟨*what is* ~ *to eat?* There *seem to be only eggs*⟩ ⟨~ *shall come a time*⟩; compare IT

*usage* Before a plural it should correctly be **there** *are,* although there *is* has been used before plurals by great writers ⟨**there's** *pansies, that's for thoughts* – Shak⟩ and is common in spoken English today ⟨**there's** *two experts in the studio*⟩. A problem arises when **there** introduces a list of items of which the first is singular ⟨**there** *is/are Mary and the children to consider*⟩. Here *are* is correct, but may be felt to sound odd before the singular *Mary*.

³**there** *n* that place or point

⁴**there** *adj* **1** – used for emphasis, esp after a demonstrative ⟨*those men* ~ *can tell you*⟩ ⟨*ask my daughter* ~⟩ **2** *substandard* – used for emphasis between *that* or *those* and the following noun ⟨*that* ~ *cow*⟩

**thereabouts** /ˌdheərə'bowts/ *NAm also* **thereabout** /ˌdheərə'bowt/ *adv* **1** in that vicinity **2** near that time, number, degree, or quantity ⟨*a boy of 18 or* ~⟩

**thereafter** /dheə'rahftə/ *adv, chiefly formal* **1** after that **2** *archaic* according to that; accordingly

**thereat** /dheə'rat/ *adv, formal* **1** at that place **2** at that occurrence

**thereby** /dheə'bie/ *adv* **1a** by that means **b** as a result of which ⟨~ *lost his chance to win*⟩ **2** in which connection ⟨~ *hangs a tale* – Shak⟩

**there'd** /dheəd/ there had; there would

**therefor** /ˌdheə'faw/ *adv, formal* for or in return for that ⟨*ordered a change and gave his reasons* ~⟩

**therefore** /'-,-; *also* ,-'-/ *adv* **1** for that reason; to that end ⟨*we must go. I will* ~ *call a taxi*⟩ **2** by virtue of that; consequently ⟨*was tired and* ~ *irritable*⟩ **3** on that ground; as this proves ⟨*I think,* ~ *I exist*⟩ [ME, fr *there* + *fore* for]

**therefrom** /dheə'from/ *adv, formal* from that or it

**therein** /dheə'rin/ *adv, formal* in that; *esp* in that respect ⟨~ *lies the problem*⟩

**thereinafter** /ˌdheərin'ahftə/ *adv, formal* in the following part of that matter (e g writing, document, or speech)

**thereinto** /dheə'rintooh/ *adv, archaic* into that or it

**there'll** /dheəl/ there will; there shall

**thereof** /dheə'rov/ *adv, formal* **1** of that or it **2** therefrom

**thereon** /dheə'ron/ *adv, chiefly formal* **1** on or onto that or it ⟨*a text with a commentary* ~⟩ **2** *archaic* thereupon

**thereto** /dheə'tooh/ *adv, formal* **1** to that matter or document ⟨*conditions attaching* ~⟩ **2** TO BOOT; IN ADDITION

**theretofore** /ˌdheətə'faw, -tooh-/ *adv, formal* up to that time ⟨*a* ~ *unknown author*⟩

**thereunder** /dheə'rundə/ *adv, formal* under that or it ⟨*the heading and the items listed* ~⟩

**thereupon** /ˌdheərə'pon/ *adv, chiefly formal* **1** on that matter ⟨*if all are agreed* ~⟩ **2** therefore, consequently **3** immediately after that

**therewith** /dheə'widh/ *adv, formal* **1** with that or it ⟨*a letter enclosed* ~⟩ **2** *archaic* thereupon, forthwith

**therewithal** /'dheəwidh,awl/ *adv, formal* **1** therewith **2** *archaic* besides

**theriaca** /thi'rie·əkə/, **theriac** /'thiəriak/ *n* a mixture of many drugs and honey, formerly believed to·be an antidote to poison [NL *theriaca*, fr L, antidote against poison – more at TREACLE] – **theriacal** *adj*

**theriomorphic** /ˌthiərioh'mawfik/ *adj* having an animal form ⟨~ *gods*⟩ [Gk *thēriomorphos*, fr *thērion* beast + *morphē* form – more at TREACLE]

**therm** /thuhm/ *n* any of several units of quantity of heat; *esp* a unit equal to 100 000 British thermal units (about 105 506 megajoules) [Gk *thermē* heat; akin to Gk *thermos* hot – more at WARM]

**therm-** /thuhm-/, **thermo-** *comb form* **1** heat ⟨*thermion*⟩ ⟨*thermostat*⟩ **2** thermoelectric ⟨*thermopile*⟩ [Gk, fr *thermē*]

**-therm** /-thuhm/ *comb form* (→ *n*) animal having (such) a body temperature ⟨*ectotherm*⟩ [Gk *thermē* heat]

**thermae** /'thuhmee/ *n pl* a public bathing establishment, esp in ancient Greece or Rome [L, fr Gk *thermai*, fr pl of *thermē* heat]

¹**thermal** /'thuhml/ *adj* **1** of or marked by the presence of HOT SPRINGS ⟨~ *waters*⟩ **2** of or caused by heat ⟨~ *stress*⟩ ⟨~ *insulation*⟩ **3** designed (e g with insulating air spaces) to prevent the dissipation of body heat ⟨~ *underwear*⟩ [Gk *thermē* heat] – **thermally** *adv*

²**thermal** *n* a rising body of warm air

**thermal barrier** *n* a limit to increase in aircraft or rocket speeds imposed by aerodynamic heating

**thermal neutron** *n* a neutron in thermal equilibrium with its surroundings

**thermal pollution** *n* the discharge of heated liquid (e g water) into natural waters at a temperature detrimental to the existing living organisms

**thermal spring** *n* HOT SPRING

**thermic** /'thuhmik/ *adj* THERMAL 2 ⟨~ *energy*⟩ – **thermically** *adv*

**Thermidor** /'thuhmi,daw/ *n* the 11th month of the French Revolutionary calendar, corresponding to 20 July – 17th August [Fr, fr Gk *thermē* heat + *dōron* gift]

**thermion** /'thuhm,i·ən, -on/ *n* an electrically charged particle, specif an electron, emitted by an INCANDESCENT (giving off light when heated) substance [ISV *therm-* + *ion*]

**thermionic** /ˌthuhmi'onik/ *adj* **1** of the emission of thermions **2** of or being a device (eg a valve) that uses thermionic electrons as charge carriers

**thermionic valve** *n* an electronic device (ELECTRON TUBE) in which a regulated flow of electrons is produced by thermionic emission from a heated CATHODE (conducting structure with a negative electric charge) that is esp used for controlling the flow of current in an electric circuit

**thermistor** /'thuh,mistə/ *n* a RESISTOR (device in an electrical circuit that resists the flow of current) made of a SEMICONDUCTOR (substance that conducts electricity to a limited extent) whose resistance varies significantly and in a known manner with the temperature [*therm*al res*istor*]

**Thermit** /'thuhmiet, -mət/ *trademark* – used for thermite

**thermite** /'thuhmiet/ *n* a mixture of aluminium powder and IRON OXIDE that when ignited produces a great deal of heat and is used in welding and in incendiary bombs [*therm-* + *-ite*]

**thermochemistry** /ˌthuhmoh'kemistri/ *n* a branch of chemistry that deals with the interrelation of heat with chemical reaction or physical change of state – **thermochemical** *adj*, **thermochemist** *n*

**thermocline** /'thuhmə,klien/ *n* a layer of water in a lake, sea, etc that separates an upper warmer lighter oxygen-rich zone from a lower colder heavier oxygen-poor zone; *specif* a layer in which temperature declines at least 1° Celsius with each metre increase in depth

**thermocoagulation** /ˌthuhmohkoh,agyoo'laysh(ə)n/ *n* surgical joining together of tissue by the application of heat

**thermocouple** /'thuhmə,kupl, -moh-/ *n* a THERMOELECTRIC COUPLE used to measure temperature differences

**thermoduric** /ˌthuhmoh'dyooərik/ *adj, of a microorganism* able to survive high temperatures; *specif* able to survive pasteurization [*therm-* + L *durare* to last – more at DURING]

**thermodynamic** /ˌthuhmoh-die'namik, -di-/, **thermodynamical** /-kl/ *adj* **1** of thermodynamics **2** being or relating to a system of atoms, molecules, COLLOIDAL particles, or larger bodies considered as an isolated group in the study of thermodynamic processes – **thermodynamically** *adv*

**thermodynamics** /ˌthuhmoh·die'namiks, -di-/ *n taking sing or pl vb* **1** physics that deals with the mechanical action of, or relations between, heat and other forms of energy **2** thermodynamic processes and phenomena – **thermodynamicist** *n*

**thermoelectric** /ˌthuhmoh·i'lektrik/ *adj* of or dependent on phenomena that involve relationships between the temperature and the electrical properties of a metal or of two metals in contact

**thermoelectric couple** *n* a union of two conductors (e g bars or wires of dissimilar metals joined at their ends) for producing a thermoelectric current

**thermoelectricity** /ˌthuhmoh·ilek'trisəti, -,elek-/ *n* electricity produced by the direct action of heat (e g by the unequal heating of a circuit composed of two dissimilar metals)

**thermoelement** /ˌthuhmoh'eləmənt/ *n* a device for measuring small currents, consisting of a wire heating element and a thermocouple in electrical contact with it [*thermo*couple + *element*]

**thermoform** /'thuhmə,fawm/ *vt* to give a final shape to (e g a plastic) with the aid of heat and usu pressure – **thermoformable** *adj*

**thermogram** /'thuhmə,gram/ *n* **1** the record made by a thermograph **2** a photographic record made by thermography

**thermograph** /'thuhmə,grahf, -graf/ *n* **1** a self-registering thermometer **2** a thermogram **3** the apparatus used in thermography [ISV]

**thermography** /thuh'mogrəfi/ *n* **1** a process of writing or printing involving heat; *esp* a process in which a printed design is dusted with powder that becomes rigid when heated, and is then heated to produce a glossy raised surface **2** a technique for detecting and measuring variations in the heat emitted by various regions of the body and transforming them into visible signals that can be recorded photographically (eg for the detection of tumours); *also* a similar technique used elsewhere (eg on engines) – **thermographic** *adj*, **thermographically** *adv*

**thermohaline** /ˌthuhmoh'haylien, -leen/ *adj* involving or dependent upon the combined effect of temperature and salt concentration on the density of water ⟨*a trans-equatorial ~ circulation in the E Pacific*⟩ [*therm-* + Gk *hal-, hals* salt – more at SALT]

**thermojunction** /ˌthuhmoh'junksh(ə)n/ *n* a junction of two dissimilar conductors used to produce a thermoelectric current

**thermolabile** /ˌthuhmoh'laybiel/ *adj* unstable when heated; *specif* subject to loss of characteristic properties on being heated to or above 55°Celsius ⟨*many enzymes are ~*⟩ [ISV *therm-* + *labile*] – **thermolability** *n*

**thermoluminescence** /ˌthuhmohloohmi'nes(ə)ns/ *n* LUMINESCENCE (emission of light or radiation) by certain substances when gently heated after they have been previously exposed to some other radiation. It is used as a method of dating archaeological finds, esp pottery. [ISV] – **thermoluminescent** *adj*

**thermolysis** /thuh'molǝsis/ *n* the dissipation of heat from the living body [NL] – **thermolytic** *adj*

**thermometer** /thǝ'momitǝ/ *n* an instrument for determining temperature consisting typically of a glass bulb attached to a fine tube of glass with a numbered scale and containing a liquid (eg mercury or coloured alcohol) that is sealed in and rises and falls with changes of temperature [Fr *thermomètre*, fr Gk *thermē* heat + Fr *-o-* +*-mètre* -meter – more at THERM] – **thermometric** *adj*, **thermometrically** *adv*

**thermometry** /thǝ'momǝtri/ *n* the measurement of temperature [ISV]

**thermonuclear** /ˌthuhmoh'nyoohkli·ǝ/ *adj* **1** of the transformations in the nucleus of atoms of low ATOMIC WEIGHT (eg hydrogen) that require a very high temperature (eg in the HYDROGEN BOMB or in the sun) ⟨*~ reaction*⟩ ⟨*~ weapon*⟩ **2** of or using a thermonuclear bomb ⟨*~ war*⟩ ⟨*~ attack*⟩ [ISV]

**thermoperiodism** /ˌthuhmoh'piǝri·ǝ,diz(ǝ)m/ *n* the sum of the responses of an organism, esp a plant, to appropriately fluctuating temperatures

**thermophile** /'thuhmǝ,fiel/ *n* a living organism thriving at relatively high temperatures – **thermophilic** *also* **thermophile, thermophilous** *adj*

**thermopile** /'thuhmǝ,piel/ *n* an apparatus that consists of a number of THERMOELECTRIC COUPLES combined so as to multiply the effect and is used for generating electric currents or for determining intensities of radiation [*therm-* + ³*pile*]

**thermoplastic** /ˌthuhmǝ'plastik/ *adj* capable of softening or melting when heated and of hardening again when cooled ⟨*~ synthetic resins*⟩ – compare THERMOSETTING – **thermoplastic** *n*, **thermoplasticity** *n*

**thermoreceptor** /'thuhmoh·ri,septǝ/ *n* a SENSE ORGAN that is stimulated by heat or cold

**thermoregulate** /ˌthuhmoh'regyoo,layt/ *vi* to maintain something (eg a living body) at a particular desired temperature ⟨*unable to ~ physiologically . . . most lizards ~ behaviourally –* Nature⟩

**thermoregulation** /ˌthuhmohregyoo'laysh(ǝ)n/ *n* the maintenance or regulation of temperature; *specif* the natural maintenance of the living body at a constant temperature [ISV]

**thermoregulator** /ˌthuhmoh'regyoo,laytǝ/ *n* a device (eg a thermostat) for the regulation of temperature [ISV]

**thermoregulatory** /ˌthuhmoh'regyoolǝt(ǝ)ri/ *adj* tending to maintain a body at a particular temperature whatever the temperature of its immediate surroundings

**thermoremanent** /ˌthuhmoh'remǝnǝnt/ *adj* being or relating to residual magnetism (REMANENCE) (eg in a rock cooled from a molten state or in a baked clay object containing magnetic minerals) that indicates the strength and direction of the earth's magnetic field at a former time – **thermoremanence** *n*

**thermos** /'thuhmos, -mǝs/ *adj or n* (of or like) a THERMOS FLASK ⟨*~ jug*⟩

**Thermos** *trademark* – used for a THERMOS FLASK

**thermoscope** /'thuhmǝ,skohp/ *n* an instrument for indicating changes of temperature by accompanying changes in volume (eg of a gas) [NL *thermoscopium*, fr *therm-* + *-scopium* -scope]

**thermoset** /'thuhmoh,set/ *n* a thermosetting resin or plastic

**thermosetting** /'thuhmoh,seting/ *adj* capable of becoming permanently rigid when heated or cured ⟨*a ~ resin*⟩ – compare THERMOPLASTIC

**Thermos flask** *n, often not cap T* a cylindrical container with a vacuum between an inner and an outer wall used to keep material, esp beverages, either hot or cold for considerable periods (eg when carried on a picnic)

**thermosphere** /'thuhmǝ,sfiǝ/ *n* the part of the earth's atmosphere that begins at about 80 kilometres (about 50 miles) above the earth's surface, extends to outer space, and is characterized by steadily increasing temperature with height – called also CHEMOSPHERE [ISV] – **thermospheric** *adj*

**thermostable** /ˌthuhmoh'staybl/ *adj* stable when heated; *specif* retaining characteristic properties on being moderately heated ⟨*a ~ bacterial proteinase*⟩ – **thermostability** *n*

¹**thermostat** /'thuhmǝ,stat/ *n* an automatic device for regulating temperature (eg by controlling the supply of gas or electricity to a heating apparatus); *also* a similar device for actuating fire alarms or for controlling automatic sprinklers – **thermostatic** *adj*, **thermostatically** *adv*

²**thermostat** *vt* **tt-** (*NAm* **-t-, -tt-**) to provide with or control by a thermostat

**thermotactic** /ˌthuhmǝ'taktik/ *adj* of or showing thermotaxis

**thermotaxis** /ˌthuhmǝ'taksis/ *n* **1** a TAXIS (movement of an organism in response to a stimulus) in which a TEMPERATURE GRADIENT constitutes the directive factor **2** the regulation of body temperature [NL, fr *therm-* + *-taxis*]

**thermotropism** /thuh'motrǝ,piz(ǝ)m/ *n* a TROPISM (curving growth movement of an organism in response to a stimulus) in which a TEMPERATURE GRADIENT determines the orientation [ISV] – **thermotropic** *adj*

**-thermy** /-,thuhmi/ *comb form* (→ *n*) **1** state of having (such) a body temperature ⟨*poikilothermy*⟩ **2** generation of heat ⟨*diathermy*⟩ [NL *-thermia*, fr Gk *thermē* heat – more at THERM]

**thesaurus** /thi'sawrǝs, 'thesǝrǝs/ *n, pl* **thesauri** /-rie, -ri/, **thesauruses** **1** a book of words or of information about a particular field or set of concepts; *esp* a book of words grouped according to their meaning **2** a list of subject headings or index terms, usu with a cross-reference system for use in the organization of a collection of documents for reference and retrieval [NL, fr L, treasure, collection, fr Gk *thēsauros*] – **thesaural** *adj*

**these** /dheez/ *pl of* THIS

**thesis** /'theesis/ *n, pl* **theses** /-,seez/ **1a** a proposition that a person (eg a candidate for academic honours) advances and offers to maintain by argument **b** a proposition to be proved or one advanced without proof; a hypothesis **2** the first stage of a reasoned argument presenting the case – compare SYNTHESIS **3** a dissertation embodying results of original research; *specif* one submitted for a doctorate in Britain or a master's degree in America – compare TREATISE **4a** the unstressed part of a metrical FOOT (eg "To", "or", in *"To be or not to be"*) **b** the accented part of a musical bar; a downbeat – compare ARSIS [L, fr Gk, lit., act of laying down, fr *tithenai* to put, lay down – more at DO; (4) LL, lowering of the voice, fr Gk, downbeat, more important part of foot, lit., act of laying down]

¹**thespian** /'thespi·ǝn/ *adj, often cap* relating to the drama; dramatic [*Thespis fl*534 BC Gk poet, reputed founder of Gk drama]

²**thespian** *n, chiefly formal or humorous* an actor

**Thessalonians** /ˌthesǝ'lohnyǝnz, -ni·ǝnz/ *n taking sing vb* – see BIBLE table [*Thessalonica*, ancient city in N Greece]

**theta** /'theetǝ, 'thaytǝ/ *n* the 8th letter of the Greek alphabet [Gk *thēta*, of Sem origin; akin to Heb *ṭēth* teth]

**theurgist** /'thee,uhjist/ *n* someone who practises theurgy; a magician

**theurgy** /'thee,uhji/ *n* **1** the art or technique of evoking the aid of a god or beneficent supernatural power **2** the intervention of a supernatural force in human affairs; *also* the effects produced by such an intervention [LL *theurgia*, fr LGk *theourgia*, fr *theourgos* miracle worker, fr Gk *the-* + *ergon* work – more at WORK] – **theurgic, theurgical** *adj*

**thew** /thyooh/ *n* **1** *usu pl* muscle, sinew ⟨*by the . . . sheer hard labour of our ~*s *we struggled on –* J R Fethney⟩ **2a** muscular power or development **b** strength, vitality ⟨*the naked ~ and sinew of the English language –* G M Hopkins⟩ [ME, personal quality, virtue, fr OE *thēaw;* akin to OHG *kathau* discipline]

**they** /dhay/ *pron taking pl vb* **1a** those people, creatures, or things ⟨*~ got married*⟩ ⟨*~ taste better with sugar*⟩; *also, chiefly Br* that group ⟨*ask the committee whether ~ approve*⟩ **b** HE/SHE ⟨*if anyone knows, ~ will tell you*⟩ **2a** PEOPLE 1 ⟨*~*

*say we'll have a hard winter*⟩ **b** the authorities ⟨~ *took my licence away*⟩ [ME, fr ON *their*, masc pl demonstrative & personal pron; akin to OE *thæt* that]

   **usage** The plural forms **they, them, their,** and **theirs** have long been used, and are often used today, to avoid using either *he, him,* etc for both sexes or the awkward *he or she, him or her* ⟨*nobody prevents you, do* they? – W M Thackeray⟩ ⟨*anyone in* their *senses* – W H Auden⟩; but the singular construction should be preferred for formal writing.

**they'd** /dhayd/ they had; they would

**they'll** /dhayl/ they will; they shall

**they're** /dhea/ they are ⚠ their, there

**they've** /dhayv/ they have

**thi-** /thie-/, **thio-** *comb form* containing sulphur in the molecular structure ⟨thio*phosphate*⟩ ⟨thi*amine*⟩ [ISV, fr Gk *thei-, theio-* fr *theion* sulphur]

**thiabendazole** /,thie·ə'bendə,zohl/ *n* a drug, $C_{10}H_7N_3S$, used in the control of parasitic roundworms and in the treatment of fungal infections [*thiazole* + *benz-* + *imide* + *azole*]

**thiaminase** /'thie'ami,nayz, -,nays/ *n* an ENZYME that promotes the breakdown of thiamine [ISV]

**thiamine** *also* **thiamin** /'thie·əmin/ *n* a water-soluble vitamin, $C_{12}H_{17}ON_4SCl.H_2O$, of the VITAMIN B COMPLEX that is widely distributed in plant and animal tissues, esp in pork and cereal grains, is essential for the normal breakdown of carbohydrates to yield energy, and whose lack results in inflammation of the nerves and disorders of nerve function – called also VITAMIN $B_1$ [*thiamine* alter. of *thiamin*, fr *thi-* + *-amin* (as in *vitamin*)]

**thiazide** /'thie·ə,zied/ *n* any of several synthetic drugs with similar molecular structures used as DIURETICS (substances that increase the flow of urine), esp in the treatment of high blood pressure and OEDEMA (excessive accumulation of liquid in the body) [*thia-* + *diazine* + *dioxide*]

**thiazine** /'thie·ə,zeen/ *n* any of various compounds that are characterized by a ring structure composed of four carbon atoms, one sulphur atom, and one nitrogen atom and include some important dyes and tranquillizers [ISV *thi-* + *azine*]

**thiazole** /'thie·ə,zohl/ *n* **1** a colourless liquid, $C_3H_3NS$, consisting of atoms arranged in a five-membered ring and having a smell like PYRIDINE **2** any of various thiazole derivatives including some used in the treatment of inflammation and others important as chemical ACCELERATORS (substances that speed up reactions) [ISV]

**¹thick** /thik/ *adj* **1a** having relatively great depth or extent between opposite surfaces ⟨*a* ~ *plank*⟩ **b** having comparatively large diameter in relation to its length ⟨*a* ~ *rod*⟩ **c** heavily built; thickset **2a** close-packed with units or individuals; dense ⟨*the air was* ~ *with snow*⟩ ⟨*a* ~ *forest*⟩ **b** great in number; numerous **c** having a glutinous or semifluid consistency; viscous ⟨~ *syrup*⟩ ⟨~ *soup*⟩ **d** sultry, stuffy **e** foggy, misty ⟨~ *weather*⟩ **f** impenetrable to the eye; profound ⟨~ *darkness*⟩ **3** measuring in thickness ⟨*a wall several inches* ~⟩ **4a** imperfectly articulated; indistinct ⟨~ *speech*⟩ **b** plainly apparent; pronounced, marked ⟨*a* ~ *French accent*⟩ **c** producing inarticulate speech ⟨*a* ~ *tongue*⟩ **5** sluggish, dull ⟨*my head feels* ~ *after too much alcohol*⟩ **6** *informal* obtuse, stupid **7** *informal* associated on close terms; intimate ⟨*was quite* ~ *with his boss*⟩ **8** *informal* unreasonable, unfair ⟨*called it a bit* ~ *to be fired without warning*⟩ – see also **get/give a thick EAR** [ME *thikke*, fr OE *thicce*; akin to OHG *dicki* thick, OIr *tiug*] – **thick** *adv*, **thickish** *adj*, – **thickly** *adv*

**²thick** *n* **1** the most crowded or active part ⟨*in the* ~ *of the battle*⟩ **2** the part of greatest thickness ⟨*the* ~ *of the thumb*⟩ – **through thick and thin** throughout every difficulty and obstacle

**thicken** /'thikən/ *vt* **1** to make thick, compact, dense, or viscous ⟨~ *gravy with flour*⟩ **2** to increase the depth or diameter of **3** to make inarticulate; blur ⟨*alcohol* ~ed *his speech*⟩ ~ *vi* **1a** to become dense ⟨*the mist* ~ed⟩ **b** to become concentrated in numbers, mass, or frequency ⟨*the crowd* ~ed⟩ **2** to grow blurred or obscure **3** to grow broader or bulkier **4** to grow more complicated or intense ⟨*the plot* ~s⟩ – **thickener** *n*

**thickening** /'thikəning/ *n* **1** the act of making or becoming thick **2** something used to thicken (e g flour to thicken gravy) **3** a thickened part or place

**thicket** /'thikit/ *n* **1** a dense growth of shrubbery or small trees **2** something resembling a thicket in density or impenetrability; a tangle ⟨*minds, existing in a* ~ *of practicalities and contingencies* –Richard Todd⟩ [(assumed) ME *thikket*, fr OE *thiccet*, fr *thicce* thick] – **thickety** *adj*

**thickhead** /'thik,hed/ *n, informal* a slow-witted or stupid person; a blockhead – **thick-headed** *adj*

**thickness** /'thiknis/ *n* **1** the quality or state of being thick **2** the smallest of the three dimensions of a solid object **3** the thick part of something **4** a layer, ply ⟨*a single* ~ *of canvas*⟩

**thickset** /thik'set/ *adj* **1** closely placed; *also* growing thickly ⟨*a* ~ *wood*⟩ **2** heavily built; burly

**thick-'skinned** *adj* **1** having a thick skin **2** callous, insensitive

**thick-'witted** *adj* dull, stupid

**thief** /theef/ *n, pl* **thieves** /theevz/ a person who steals, esp stealthily and without violence; *also* one who commits theft or larceny [ME *theef*, fr OE *thēof*; akin to OHG *diob* thief, Lith *tupėti* to crouch]

**thieve** /theev/ *vb* to steal, rob [fr *thief*, by analogy to *grief: -grieve*]

**thievery** /'theev(ə)ri/ *n* (a) theft

**thievish** /'theevish/ *adj* **1** given to stealing **2** (characteristic) of a thief – **thievishly** *adv*, **thievishness** *n*

**thigh** /thie/ *n* **1a** the segment of the hind limb nearest the body of a VERTEBRATE animal that extends from the hip to the knee and is supported by a single large bone **b** the segment of the leg immediately below the thigh in an animal (e g a bird or horse) in which the true thigh is obscured **c** the FEMUR of an insect **2** something resembling or covering a thigh [ME, fr OE *thēoh*; akin to OHG *dioh* thigh, L *tumēre* to swell – more at THUMB] – **thighed** *adj*

**thighbone** /'thie,bohn/ *n* FEMUR

**thigmotaxis** /,thigmə'taksis/ *n* a TAXIS (movement of an organism in response to a stimulus) in which contact, esp with a solid body, is the directive factor [NL, fr Gk *thigma* touch (fr *thinganein* to touch) + NL *-taxis*]

**thigmotropism** /,thigmoh'trohpiz(ə)m, thig'motrəpiz(ə)m/ *n* a TROPISM (curving growth movement of an organism in response to a stimulus) in which contact, esp with a solid or a rigid surface, is the orienting factor [Gk *thigma* touch + ISV *-o-* + *-tropism*]

**thill** /thil/ *n* a shaft of a vehicle [ME *thille*, perh fr OE, plank; akin to OHG *dili* plank, L *tellus* earth]

**thimble** /'thimbl/ *n* **1** a pitted metal or plastic cap or cover worn on the finger to push the needle in sewing **2a** a grooved ring of thin metal that fits into a spliced loop of rope to protect it from chafing **b** a movable ring, tube, or lining in a hole [ME *thymbyl*, prob alter. of OE *thȳmel* thumbstall, fr *thūma* thumb]

**thimbleful** /'thimbl·f(ə)l/ *n* as much as a thimble will hold; *broadly* a very small quantity

**thimblerig** /'thimbl,rig/ *n* **1** a swindling trick in which a small ball or pea is quickly shifted from under one to another of three small cups to fool the spectator guessing its location **2** someone who manipulates the cups in thimblerig; a thimblerigger [*thimble* + *⁴rig*] **thimblerig** *vi*, **thimblerigger** *n*

**¹thin** /thin/ *adj* **-nn-** **1a** having little depth or extent between opposite surfaces ⟨*a* ~ *book*⟩ **b** measuring little in cross section or diameter ⟨~ *rope*⟩ **2** not dense or closely-packed ⟨~ *hair*⟩ **3** without much flesh; lean, spare **4a** more rarefied than normal ⟨~ *air*⟩ **b** having less than the usual number; scanty ⟨~ *attendance*⟩ **c** few in number; scarce ⟨*a* ~ *crowd*⟩ ⟨*the army were* ~ *on the ground*⟩ **d** with few bids or offerings ⟨*a* ~ *market*⟩ **5a** lacking substance or strength ⟨~ *broth*⟩ ⟨*a* ~ *plot*⟩ **b** *of a soil* poor, infertile **6** flimsy, unconvincing ⟨*a* ~ *disguise*⟩ **7** somewhat feeble and lacking in resonance ⟨*a* ~ *voice*⟩ **8** lacking in intensity or brilliance ⟨~ *colour*⟩ **9** lacking sufficient photographic density or contrast **10** *informal* disappointingly poor or hard ⟨*had a* ~ *time of it*⟩ **antonym** thick [ME *thinne*, fr OE *thynne*; akin to OHG *dunni* thin, L *tenuis* thin, *tenēre* to hold, *tendere* to stretch, Gk *teinein*] – **thinly** *adv*, **thinness** *n*, **thinnish** *adj* – **wear thin 1** to become weak and ready to give way ⟨*his patience was* wearing thin⟩ **2** to become trite, unconvincing, or out-of-date ⟨*that argument* is wearing *a bit* thin⟩ – see also **skate on thin ICE, through THICK and thin**

**²thin** *adv* **-nn-** in a thin manner; thinly – esp in combination ⟨thin-*clad*⟩

**³thin** *vt* to make thin or thinner: **a** to reduce in thickness or depth; attenuate **b** to reduce in strength or density **c** to reduce in number or bulk ~ *vi* **1** to become thin or thinner **2** to diminish in strength, density, or number

**¹thine** /dhien/ *adj, archaic* thy – used esp before a word beginning with a vowel or *h* [ME *thin*, fr OE *thīn*]

**²thine** *pron, pl* **thine** *archaic or dial* that which belongs to thee

– used without a following noun as a pronoun equivalent in meaning to the adjective *thy;* used with cap when addressing God; still surviving in the speech of Quakers, esp among themselves [ME *thin,* fr OE *thīn,* fr *thīn* thy – more at THY]

**thin film** *n* a very thin layer of a substance (eg a metal) that is used to coat the surface of other solids, esp in electronic devices

**thing** /thing/ *n* **1a** a matter, affair, concern ⟨*we must settle this* ∼⟩ ⟨∼*s are not improving*⟩ **b** event, circumstance ⟨*that shooting was a terrible* ∼⟩ **2a(1)** a deed, act, achievement ⟨*do great* ∼*s*⟩ **a(2)** an activity, action ⟨*abusive moralising . . . is about the least productive* ∼ *to do* – *Nation Review (Melbourne)*⟩ **b** a product of work or activity ⟨*likes to make* ∼*s with her hands*⟩ **c** the aim of effort or activity ⟨*the* ∼ *is to get well*⟩ **d** something necessary or desirable ⟨*I've got just the* ∼ *for you*⟩ **3a** a separate and distinct object of thought (eg a quality, fact, or idea) **b** *philosophy* the concrete entity as distinguished from its appearances; the thing-in-itself **c** an inanimate object as distinguished from a living being **d** *pl* imaginary objects or entities; visual or auditory hallucinations ⟨*see* ∼*s*⟩ ⟨*hear* ∼*s*⟩ **4a** *pl* possessions, effects ⟨*pack your* ∼*s*⟩ **b** *law* an item of property **c** an article of clothing ⟨*not a* ∼ *to wear*⟩ **d** *pl* equipment or utensils, esp for a particular purpose ⟨*bring the tea* ∼*s*⟩ **5** an object or entity not precisely designated or capable of being designated ⟨*what's that* ∼ *you're holding?*⟩ ⟨*omelettes and* ∼*s* – *Annabel*⟩ **6a** a detail, point ⟨*checks every little* ∼⟩ **b** a material or substance of a specified kind ⟨*avoid starchy* ∼*s*⟩ **7a** a spoken or written observation or point ⟨*there are some good* ∼*s in her essay*⟩ **b** an idea, notion ⟨*says the first* ∼ *he thinks of*⟩ ⟨*for one* ∼ *. . .* ⟩ ⟨*a female bookie might not be a bad* ∼ – *Woman's Journal*⟩ **c** a piece of news or information ⟨*couldn't get a* ∼ *out of him*⟩ **8** an individual, creature ⟨*not a living* ∼ *in sight*⟩ ⟨*poor* ∼*!*⟩ **9** *the* proper or fashionable way of behaving, talking, or dressing ⟨*it's the latest* ∼⟩ **10** *informal* **10a** a preoccupation (eg a mild obsession or phobia) of a specified type ⟨*has a* ∼ *about driving*⟩ ⟨*working through her own teenage-rebellion* ∼ – *Annabel*⟩ – compare COMPLEX 2b **b** an intimate relationship; *esp* LOVE AFFAIR ⟨*had a* ∼ *going with her boss*⟩ **c** something (eg an activity) that offers special interest and satisfaction to the individual ⟨*letting students do their own* ∼ – *Newsweek*⟩ [ME, fr OE, thing, assembly; akin to OHG *ding* thing, assembly, Goth *theihs* time] – **of all things** – used to show surprise ⟨*wants a xylophone* of all things⟩ – **see things** to hallucinate

**Thing** *n* a legislative or deliberative assembly in a Scandinavian country [ON & Icel; Icel, assembly, parliament, fr ON]

**thingamabob** /'thing-əmə,bob/ *n, informal* a thingamajig [alter. of earlier *thingum,* fr *thing* + arbitrary suffix]

**thingamajig, thingumajig** /'thing-əmə,jig/ *n, informal* something or someone that is hard to classify, or whose name is unknown or forgotten [alter. of earlier *thingum*]

**thingie** /'thing-i/ *n, chiefly Br informal* a thingamajig ⟨*those pyramid-shaped* ∼*s* – *Punch*⟩ ⟨*old* ∼ *who lives down the road*⟩

**,thing-in-it'self, thing in itself** *n, pl* **things-in-themselves, things in themselves** *philosophy* the aspect of an object that remains after all its properties that are perceived by the senses are taken away; an object apprehended by thought or intuition rather than by experience [trans of Ger *ding an sich*]

**thingness** /'thing-nis/ *n* the quality or state of objective existence or reality

**thingummy** /'thing-əmi/ *n, informal* a thingamajig [alter. of earlier *thingum*]

¹**think** /thingk/ *vb* **thought** /thawt/ *vt* **1** to form or have in the mind **2** to have as an intention ⟨*thought to return early*⟩ **3a** to have as an opinion ⟨∼ *it's so*⟩ **b** to regard as; consider ⟨∼ *the rule unfair*⟩ **4a** to reflect on; ponder – often + *over* ⟨∼ *the matter over*⟩ **b** to determine by reflecting – often + *out* ⟨∼ *it out for yourself*⟩ **5** to call to mind; remember ⟨*I didn't* ∼ *to ask his name*⟩ **6** to devise by thinking usu + *up* ⟨*thought up a plan to escape*⟩ **7** to have as an expectation; anticipate ⟨*we didn't* ∼ *we'd have any trouble*⟩ **8** to have one's mind full of ⟨*talks and* ∼*s business*⟩ **9** to subject to the processes of logical thought – usu + *out* or *through* ⟨∼ *things out*⟩ ∼ *vi* **1a** to use the powers of judgment, conception, or inference; reason **b** to have in mind or call to mind a thought or idea – + *of* **2** to have the mind engaged in reflection; meditate – usu + *of* or *about* **3** to hold a view or opinion; regard – usu + *of* ⟨∼*s of himself as a poet*⟩ **4** to have consideration – usu + *of* ⟨*a man must* ∼ *first of his family*⟩ **5** to expect, suspect ⟨*better than he* ∼*s possible*⟩ [ME *thenken,* fr OE *thencan;* akin to OHG *denken* to think, L *tongēre* to know – more at THANK] – **thinkable** *adj,*

**thinker** *n* – **think better of** to decide on reflection to abandon (a plan) – **think much of** to have a high opinion of ⟨*didn't think much of the new car*⟩ – see also **have on one's thinking** CAP, **think on one's** FEET (at FOOT)

²**think** *n, informal* an act of thinking ⟨*have a* ∼ *about it*⟩ ⟨*if he thinks he can fool me, he's got another* ∼ *coming*⟩

¹**thinking** /'thingking/ *n* **1** the action of using one's mind to produce thoughts **2** opinion, judgment; *esp* opinion that is characteristic (eg of a period, group, or individual) ⟨*the current* ∼ *on immigration*⟩

²**thinking** *adj* marked by use of the intellect; rational, reflective ⟨∼ *viewers will form their own opinion*⟩ – **thinkingly** *adv,* **thinkingness** *n*

**think piece** *n* a news article consisting chiefly of background material and personal opinion and analysis

**think tank** *n taking sing or pl vb* an organization or group of people formed as a consultative body to evolve new ideas and offer expert advice on problems, often at a national level

**thin-layer chromatography** *n* CHROMATOGRAPHY (method of separating a mixture of dissolved substances) in which a thin layer (eg of siliceous fibres) is used as the absorbent separating medium – **thin-layer chromatographic** *adj*

**thinner** /'thinə/ *n* one who or that which thins: eg **a** a volatile liquid (eg turpentine) used esp to thin paint **b** a person or machine that pulls out superfluous plants to improve a crop

**,thin-'skinned** *adj* **1** having a thin skin or rind **2** unduly susceptible to criticism or insult; touchy

**thio-** – see THI-

**thio acid** /'thie-oh/ *n* an acid in which oxygen is partly or wholly replaced by sulphur [ISV, fr *thi-*]

**thiocarbamide** /,thie-oh'kahbə,mied/ *n* THIOUREA (type of chemical compound) [ISV]

**thiocyanate** /,thie-oh'sie-ə,nayt/ *n* any of various chemical compounds (SALTS OF ESTERS) formed by combination between thiocyanic acid and a metal atom, an alcohol, or another chemical group [ISV]

**thiocyanic** /,thie-ohsie'anik/ *adj* of or being a colourless strong-smelling unstable liquid acid, HSCN [ISV]

**thioguanine** /,thie-oh'gwahneen/ *n* a synthetic anticancer drug, $C_5H_5N_5S$, that is used similarly to MERCAPTOPURINE in the treatment of leukaemia

**Thiokol** /'thie-ə,kol, -,kohl/ *trademark* – used for polysulphide rubbers

**thiol** /'thie,ol, -,ohl/ *n* **1** MERCAPTAN (type of sulphur-containing chemical compound) **2** the chemical group SH, characteristic of MERCAPTANS [ISV *thi-* + ¹*-ol*] – **thiolic** *adj*

**thion-** *comb form* sulphur ⟨thion*ic*⟩ [ISV, fr Gk *theion*]

**thionate** /'thie-ə,nayt/ *n* any of various chemical compounds (SALTS OF ESTERS) formed by combination between a THIONIC ACID and a metal atom, an alcohol, or another chemical group [ISV]

**thionic** /thie'onik/ *adj* relating to or containing sulphur [ISV]

**thionic acid** *n* **1** any of various unstable acids of the general formula $H_2S_xO_6$ **2** a THIO ACID in which sulphur is linked to another atom by a DOUBLE BOND

**thiopental** /,thie-oh'pental/ *n, NAm* thiopentone [*thio-* + *pento*barbital]

**thiopentone** /,thie-oh'pentohn/ *n* a BARBITURATE drug, $C_{11}H_{17}NaO_2S$, used esp intravenously in the initiation of general anaesthesia and in psychotherapy [*thio* + *pento*barbitone]

**thiophen** /'thie-oh,fen/ *n* thiophene

**thiophene** /'thie-oh,feen/ *n* a liquid, $C_4H_4S$, from COAL TAR that resembles BENZENE, and is used in the manufacture of dyes, resins, etc, and as a solvent [ISV *thi-* + *phene* benzene – more at PHEN-]

**thiophosphate** /,thie-oh'fosfayt/ *n* any of various chemical compounds (SALTS OF ESTERS) formed by combination between a THIOPHOSPHORIC ACID and a metal atom, an alcohol, or other chemical group [ISV]

**thiophosphoric acid** /,thie-ohfos'forik/ *n* an acid derived from a PHOSPHORIC ACID by replacement of one or more atoms of oxygen with sulphur

**thiosulphate** /,thie-oh'sulfayt/ *n* any of various chemical compounds (SALTS OF ESTERS) formed by combination between THIOSULPHURIC ACID and a metal atom, an alcohol, or other chemical group [ISV]

**thiosulphuric acid** /,thie-ohsul'fyooərik/ *n* an unstable acid, $H_2S_2O_3$, derived from SULPHURIC ACID by replacement of one oxygen atom by sulphur and known only in solution or in chemical compounds (SALTS and ESTERS)

**thiotepa** /ˌthie-ə'teepə/ n a chemical compound, $C_6H_{12}N_3PS$, similar to TEPA that is used esp as an anticancer drug in the treatment of tumours [*thi-* + *tepa*]

**thiouracil** /ˌthie-oh'yooərəsil/ n a synthetic chemical compound, $C_4H_4N_2OS$, that depresses the function of the thyroid gland [ISV *thi-* + *uracil*]

**thiourea** /ˌthie-ohyoo(ə)'ree-ə, -'yooəri-ə/ n a bitter chemical compound, $NH_2CSNH_2$, resembling and similar in function to UREA that is used esp as a photographic and chemical reagent; *also* a derivative of this chemical compound [NL, fr *thi-* + *urea*]

**thiram** /'thieram/ n a chemical compound, $C_6H_{12}N_2S_4$, used esp as a fungicide and seed disinfectant [prob alter. of *thiuram* (the chemical group $NH_2CS$)]

**¹third** /thuhd/ adj **1a** next after the second in place or time ⟨*the* ~ *man in line*⟩ **b** ranking next to the second of a grade or degree in authority or precedence ⟨~ *mate*⟩ **c** being the forward gear or speed one higher than second in a motor vehicle **2a** being any of three equal parts into which something is divisible **b** being the last in each group of three in a series ⟨*take out every* ~ *card*⟩ *usage* see FIRSTLY [ME *thridde, thirde,* fr OE *thridda, thirdda;* akin to L *tertius* third, Gk *tritos, treis* three – more at THREE] – **third, thirdly** adv

**²third** n **1a** – see NUMBER table **b** one who or that which is next after second in rank, position, authority, or precedence ⟨*the* ~ *in line*⟩ **c third, third class** *often cap* the third and usu lowest level of British honours degree **2** any of three equal parts of something **3a** a musical interval between one note and another three notes away from it counting inclusively in a DIATONIC scale (ordinary 8-note scale) **b** a note three notes away from another counting inclusively; *specif* the note three notes away from the first note (TONIC) of a scale; MEDIANT **c** the harmonic combination of two notes a third apart **4** THIRD BASE **5** the third forward gear or speed of a motor vehicle

**third base** n the base that must be touched third by a batter in baseball who is attempting a run; *also* the position of the player defending the area round this base

**ˌthird-'class** adj of a class, rank, or grade next below the second – **third-class** adv

**third class** n **1** the third and usu next below second group in a classification **2** the least expensive class of accommodation (e g on a passenger ship) **3** THIRD 1c

**third degree** n the subjection of a prisoner to mental or physical torture in order to obtain a confession or information ⟨*gave him the* ~⟩

**third-degree burn** n a burn characterized by destruction of the skin and possibly the underlying tissues, by loss of liquid, and sometimes by shock – compare FIRST-DEGREE BURN, SECOND-DEGREE BURN

**third dimension** n thickness, depth; *also* a dimension that adds the effect of solidity to a two-dimensional system – **third-dimensional** adj

**third estate** n, *often cap T&E* the third of the traditional political orders; *specif* the Commons

**thirdhand** /ˌthuhd'hand/ adj **1** received from a second intermediary ⟨~ *information*⟩ **2** acquired after being used by two previous owners – **thirdhand** adv

**third home** n the position of the third most forward player in lacrosse; *also* the player occupying this position

**third man** n **1** a fielding position in cricket lying near the boundary on the OFF SIDE behind the slips; *also* the fieldsman occupying this position **2** the position of the third defender from the goalkeeper in lacrosse; *also* the player occupying this position

**third order** n, *often cap T&O* an organization composed of lay people who are under a religious rule and directed by a religious order but usu live in secular society

**ˌthird-'party** adj of a third party; *specif* of insurance covering loss or damage sustained by a person other than the insured

**third party** n **1** a person other than the principals ⟨*a* ~ *to a divorce proceeding*⟩ **2** a major political party operating over a limited period of time in addition to two other major parties in a state normally characterized by a two-party system **b** a political party whose electoral strength is so small as to prevent its gaining control of a government except in rare and exceptional circumstances

**third person** n **1** a set of language forms (e g verb forms and pronouns) referring neither to the speaker or writer of the utterance in which they occur nor to the one to whom that utterance is addressed **2** a language form (e g *she* and *is*) belonging to such a set

**third rail** n CONDUCTOR RAIL (electrified rail on a railway)

**ˌthird-'rate** adj third in quality or value; *broadly* of extremely poor quality – **third-rater** n

**third reading** n the final stage of the consideration of a legislative bill before a vote on its final disposition

**third sex** n homosexuals

**ˌthird-'stream** adj of or being music that incorporates elements of classical music and jazz

**third ventricle** n the middle unpaired VENTRICLE (inner cavity) of the brain bounded by parts of the TELENCEPHALON and DIENCEPHALON

**third world** n *taking sing or pl vb, often cap T&W* **1** a group of nations, esp in Africa and Asia, that are not aligned with either the communist or the capitalist blocs **2** all the underdeveloped nations of the world

**¹thirl** /thuhl/ n, *dial* a hole, perforation, opening [ME, fr OE *thyrel,* fr *thurh* through – more at THROUGH]

**²thirl** vt *dial Br* **1** to pierce, perforate **2** to thrill

**¹thirst** /thuhst/ n **1a** a sensation of dryness in the mouth and throat associated with a desire for liquids; *also* the bodily condition (e g of dehydration) that induces this sensation **b** a desire or need to drink **2** an ardent desire; a craving, longing [ME, fr OE *thurst;* akin to OHG *durst* thirst, L *torrēre* to dry, parch, Gk *tersesthai* to become dry]

**²thirst** vi **1** to feel thirsty; suffer thirst **2** to crave eagerly – **thirster** n

**thirstily** /'thuhstili/ adv with or on account of thirst

**thirsty** /'thuhsti/ adj **1a** feeling thirst **b** deficient in moisture; parched ⟨~ *land*⟩ **c** highly absorbent ⟨~ *towels*⟩ **2** having a strong desire; avid ⟨~ *for knowledge*⟩ – **thirstiness** n

**thirteen** /thuh'teen/ n – see NUMBER table [ME *thrittene,* fr *thrittene,* adj, fr OE *thrēotīne,* fr *thrīe, thrēo* three + *tīen* ten – more at TEN] – **thirteen** adj or pron, **thirteenth** adj or n

**thirty** /'thuhti/ n **1** – see NUMBER table **2** pl the numbers 30 to 39; *specif* the range of temperatures, ages, or dates in a century characterized by these numbers **3** a sign of completion; the end – usu written 30 ⟨*wrote* ~ *on the last page of his story*⟩ [ME *thritty,* fr *thritty,* adj, fr OE *thrītig,* fr *thrītig* group of 30, fr *thrīe* three + *-tig* group of ten – more at -TY] – **thirtieth** adj or n, **thirty** adj or pron, **thirtyfold** adj or adv

**ˌthirty-'eight** n **1** – see NUMBER table **2** a 0.38 inch (9.65 millimetres) calibre pistol – usu written .38 – **thirty-eight** adj or pron

**thirty-second note** n, *NAm* a demisemiquaver

**thirty-second rest** n, *NAm* a musical REST (indicating silence) with the same time value as a demisemiquaver

**ˌthirty-'twomo** /'toohmoh/ n, pl **thirty-twomos** the size of a piece of paper cut 32 from a sheet; *also* a book, a page, or paper of this size

**¹this** /dhis/ pron, pl **these** /theez/ **1a** the thing or idea that has just been mentioned ⟨*who told you* ~?⟩ **b** what is to be shown or stated ⟨*do it like* ~⟩ ⟨*I can only say* ~: *he wasn't here yesterday*⟩ **c** this time or place ⟨*expected to return before* ~⟩ **2a** a nearby person or thing introduced for observation or discussion ⟨~ *is my father*⟩ ⟨~ *is iron and that is tin*⟩ ⟨*hello!* ~ *is Anne Fry speaking*⟩ **b** the thing or state of affairs here ⟨*please carry* ~⟩ ⟨*what's all* ~?⟩ [ME, pron & adj, fr OE *thes* (masc), *this* (neut); akin to OHG *dese* this; akin to OE *thæt* that]

*usage* This conventionally refers to what is about to be stated ⟨*listen to this!*⟩ and to what is near ⟨*hold this*⟩. In addition, both **this** and **that** can refer to something previously mentioned, with **this** perhaps giving a greater effect of immediacy. Whichever is used, it is important that the thing, concept, or state of affairs referred to should be clearly identified. In ⟨*the children will perform their own musical version of Cinderella. This was decided on last term*⟩ it is not clear whether **this** refers to Cinderella, to the musical version, or to the idea of performing it.

**²this** adj, pl **these 1a** being the person, thing, or idea that is present or near in time or thought ⟨*early* ~ *morning*⟩ ⟨*who's* ~ *Mrs Fogg anyway?*⟩ **b** the nearer at hand or more immediately under observation ⟨~ *country*⟩ ⟨~ *chair or that one*⟩ **c** constituting the immediate past or future period ⟨*have lived here* ~ *ten years*⟩ **d** constituting what is to be shown or stated ⟨*have you heard* ~ *one?*⟩ **2** a certain ⟨*there was* ~ *Irishman . . .*⟩

**³this** adv **1** to this extent ⟨*known her since she was* ~ *high*⟩ **2** to this extreme degree – usu neg ⟨*didn't expect to wait* ~ *long*⟩

*usage* Some people dislike the use of **this** and **that** to mean "so extremely", and prefer to say ⟨*I didn't expect to wait as long as* **this**⟩ or ⟨*not really as expensive as* **all that**⟩.

**thistle** /'thisl/ *n* any of various prickly plants (esp genera *Carduus, Cirsium,* and *Onopordum*) of the daisy family with often showy heads of mostly tubular flowers; *also* any of various other prickly plants [ME *thistel,* fr OE; akin to OHG *distill* thistle] – **thistly** *adj*

**thistledown** /'thisl,down/ *n* the fluffy hairs from the ripe flower head of a thistle

**thistle funnel** *n* a funnel tube usu of glass with a bulging top and flaring mouth

¹**thither** /'dhidhə/ *adv, chiefly formal* to or towards that place – compare HITHER AND THITHER [ME, fr OE *thider;* akin to ON *thathra* there, OE *thæt* that]

²**thither** *adj* FAR 3

**thitherto** /,thithə'tooh, '--,-/ *adv* until that time

**thitherward** /'thithəwood/ *also* **thitherwards** *adv* towards that place; thither

**thixotropy** /thik'sotrəpi/ *n* the property of various GELS (semisolid jellylike mixtures, e g paints) of becoming liquid when disturbed (e g by shaking) – compare DILATANCY [ISV *thixo-* (fr Gk *thixis* act of touching, fr *thinganein* to touch) + *-tropy*] – **thixotropic** *adj*

**thlid** /thlid/ *n, Br slang* a stupid or incompetent person – used by children [*thalido*mide]

**tho** /dhoh/ *adv or conj, chiefly informal or poetic* though

¹**thole** /thohl/ *vb, dial* to endure [ME *tholen,* fr OE *tholian* – more at TOLERATE]

²**thole** *n* 1 a peg, pin 2 **thole, tholepin** /'thohl,pin/ either of a pair of wooden pegs serving as rowlocks in a boat [ME *tholle,* fr OE *thol;* akin to Gk *tylos* knob, callus, L *tumēre* to swell – more at THUMB]

**tholeiite** /'t(h)ohlə,iet/ *n* a BASALT (type of rock) that is rich in aluminium and low in potassium, typically underlies the depths of the sea, and is probably derived from the MANTLE (inner portion of the earth below the crust) [Ger *tholeiit,* fr *Tholey,* village in W Germany] – **tholeiitic** *adj*

**Thomism** /'toh,miz(ə)m/ *n* the system of the SCHOLASTIC philosopher and theologian St Thomas Aquinas [St *Thomas Aquinas* †1274 It theologian] – **Thomist** *n or adj,* **Thomistic** *adj*

**Thompson submachine gun** /'tom(p)sən/ *n* a submachine gun with a calibre of 0.45 inches (11.43 millimetres), a magazine or drum feed, a grip like that of a pistol, and a BUTTSTOCK [John T *Thompson* †1940 US army officer]

**thong** /thong/ *n* a narrow strip, esp of leather or hide [ME, fr OE *thwong;* akin to *thvengr* thong] – **thonged** *adj*

**thoracic** /thaw'rasik, thə-/ *adj* of, located within, or involving the thorax – **thoracically** *adv*

**thoracic duct** *n* the main trunk of the system of LYMPH (body fluid bathing the tissues) vessels that lies along the front of the SPINAL COLUMN, opens into the left SUBCLAVIAN vein, and carries lymph back to the bloodstream from esp the abdomen and lower limbs

**thoracotomy** /,thawrə'kotəmi/ *n* surgical cutting of the chest wall [L *thorac-, thorax* + ISV *-tomy*]

**thorax** /'thaw,raks/ *n, pl* **thoraxes, thoraces** /'thawrə,seez/ 1 the part of the body of a mammal between the neck and the abdomen; *also* its cavity in which the heart and lungs lie 2 the middle division of the body of an insect between the head and the abdomen; *also* the corresponding part of a CRUSTACEAN (e g a shrimp or lobster) or ARACHNID (e g a spider or scorpion) [ME, fr L *thorac-, thorax* breastplate, chest, fr Gk *thōrak-, thōrax*]

**thoria** /'thawri·ə, 'thoh-/ *n* a powdery white chemical compound, $ThO_2$, consisting of thorium oxide that is used esp as a CATALYST and in heat-resisting ceramic material and optical glass [NL, fr *thorium* + -a]

**thorianite** /'thawriə,niet, 'thoh-/ *n* a strongly radioactive mineral, $ThO_2$, that consists essentially of thorium oxide and often some RARE-EARTH ELEMENTS [irreg fr *thoria*]

**thoric** /'thawrik, 'thoh-/ *adj* of or containing thorium

**thorite** /'thawriet, 'thoh-/ *n* a radioactive mineral, $ThSiO_4$, that is brown to black or sometimes orange-yellow in colour, consists of thorium silicate, and resembles ZIRCON [Sw *thorit,* fr NL *thorium*]

**thorium** /'thawri·əm, 'thoh-/ *n* a radioactive metallic chemical element with a VALENCY of four that occurs combined in minerals and is usu associated with RARE EARTHS [NL, fr ON *Thōrr* Thor, Norse god of thunder, weather, & crops]

**thorn** /thawn/ *n* 1 a woody plant bearing sharp prickles or spines; *esp* any of a genus (*Crataegus*) of the rose family 2a a sharp rigid part on a plant; *specif* a short hard sharp-pointed leafless branch **b** any of various sharp spiny structures on an animal 3 something or someone that causes distress or irritation ⟨*he has been a* ~ *in my flesh for years*⟩ 4a the runic letter þ used in Old English and Middle English for either of the sounds of Modern English *th* (e g in *thin, then*) – compare ETH **b** the phonetic symbol ð representing the sound *th* in *then* [ME, fr OE; akin to OHG *dorn* thorn, Skt *trṇa* grass, blade of grass] – **thorned** *adj,* **thornless** *adj,* **thornlike** *adj*

**thorn apple** *n* 1 a haw 2 a tall very poisonous coarse plant (*Datura stramonium*) of the potato family with large white or violet trumpet-shaped flowers followed by spherical prickly fruits – called also STRAMONIUM

**thornback** /'thawn,bak/ *n* 1 **thornback, thornback ray** any of various fishes related to the rays that have spines on the back 2 a large European SPIDER CRAB (*Maja squinado*)

**thornbush** /'thawn,boosh/ *n* 1 any of various spiny or thorny shrubs or small trees 2 a low growth of thorny shrubs, esp in dry tropical regions

**thorny** /'thawni/ *adj* 1 full of or covered in thorns 2 full of difficulties or controversial points; ticklish ⟨*a* ~ *problem*⟩ – **thorniness** *n*

**thoron** /'thawron/ *n* a gaseous radioactive ISOTOPE (one of several forms of an atom that contain the same number of protons) of the chemical element radon that has a HALF-LIFE (time required for half the atoms in a quantity of radioactive substance to disintegrate) of about 55 seconds [NL, fr *thorium*]

¹**thorough** /'thurə/ *prep or adv, archaic* through [ME *thorow,* fr OE *thurh, thuruh*]

²**thorough** *adj* 1 carried through to completion; exhaustive ⟨*a* ~ *search*⟩ 2a marked by full detail ⟨*a* ~ *description*⟩ **b** careful about detail; painstaking ⟨*a* ~ *scholar*⟩ **c** complete in all respects; total ⟨~ *pleasure*⟩ **d** being fully and without qualification as specified ⟨*a* ~ *rogue*⟩ – **thoroughly** *adv,* **thoroughness** *n*

**thoroughbass** /-,bays/ *n* CONTINUO (bass part underlying the main musical theme)

¹**thoroughbred** /-,bred/ *adj* 1 thoroughly trained or skilled ⟨*after a lifetime's military service he was a* ~ *soldier*⟩ 2 bred from the best blood through a long line; purebred ⟨~ *dogs*⟩ 3a *cap* of or being a member of the Thoroughbred breed of horses **b** having the characteristics associated with good breeding or pedigree; *specif* elegant, aristocratic

²**thoroughbred** *n* 1 *cap* (any of) an English breed of light speedy horses kept chiefly for racing that originated from crosses between English mares of uncertain ancestry and Arabian stallions, in the early 18th century 2 a purebred or pedigree animal 3 somebody or something having the characteristics associated with good breeding or pedigree

**thoroughfare** /-,feə/ *n* 1 a way or place for passage: e g 1a a public way (e g a road, street, or path) open at both ends; *esp* a main road **b** a waterway (e g a strait or river) used for travel or shipping 2 passage, transit ⟨*no* ~⟩

**thoroughgoing** /-,goh·ing/ *adj* 1 extremely thorough or zealous 2 absolute, utter ⟨*a* ~ *nuisance*⟩

¹**thorough-,paced** *adj* 1a *of a horse* trained and able to perform well at all paces **b** thoroughly trained, accomplished 2 thoroughgoing

**thoroughpin** /'thurə,pin/ *n* a swelling just above the HOCK (joint in upper part of the hind leg) of a horse on both sides of the leg and slightly in front of the hamstring tendon that is often associated with lameness

**thorp, thorpe** /thawp/ *n, archaic* a village, hamlet [ME, fr OE; akin to OHG *dorf* village, L *trabs* beam, roof]

**those** /dhohz/ *pl of* ¹·²THAT [ME, fr *those* these, fr OE *thās,* pl of *thes* this – more at THIS]

¹**thou** /dhow/ *pron* the one being addressed; you – now chiefly dialect but sometimes used when addressing God in prayer and by Quakers as the universal form of address to one person; compare THEE, THINE, THY, YE, YOU [ME, fr OE *thū;* akin to OHG *dū* thou, L *tu,* Gk *sy*]

²**thou** /thow/ *vt* to address as *thou* ~ *vi* to use *thou* in address

³**thou** /thow/ *n, pl* **thou, thous** 1 *informal* a thousand – used esp with reference to monetary units (e g pounds or dollars) 2 a unit of length equal to $1/1000$ inch (about 0.0254 millimetre) [short for *thousand*]

¹**though** *also* **tho** /dhoh/ *adv* however, nevertheless ⟨*it's hard work. I enjoy it,* ~⟩ [ME, adv & conj, of Scand origin; akin to ON *thō* nevertheless; akin to OE *thēah* nevertheless, OHG *doh*]

*synonyms* Though is somewhat less formal than **although**. Though, but not **although**, can be used like *however* in the middle or at the end of a sentence ⟨*my legs are longer* **though** *to run away* – Shak⟩ and in the phrase **as though**.

²**though** *also* **tho** *conj* **1** in spite of the fact that; while ⟨~ *it's hard work, I enjoy it*⟩ **2** in spite of the possibility that; EVEN IF ⟨~ *the whole world turn to coal* – George Herbert⟩ **3** and yet; but ⟨*it works*, ~ *not as well as we hoped*⟩

¹**thought** /thawt/ *past of* THINK

²**thought** *n* **1a** the action or process of thinking; reflection ⟨*lost in* ~⟩ **b** serious consideration; regard ⟨*gave no* ~ *to the danger*⟩ **2a** reasoning or conceptual power **b** the power to imagine **3** something that is thought: e g **3a** an individual act or product of thinking ⟨*I've just had a* ~⟩ **b** a developed intention or plan ⟨*he had no* ~ *of leaving home*⟩ **c** something (e g an opinion or belief) in the mind ⟨*he spoke his* ~s *freely*⟩ **d** the intellectual product or the organized views and principles of a period, place, group, or individual ⟨*19th-century* ~⟩ **4** hope, expectation ⟨*gave up all* ~ *of winning*⟩ **5** a slight amount; a bit – in the adverbial phrase *a thought* ⟨*slapped him a* ~ *too heartily on the back* – Noel Coward⟩ *synonyms see* IDEA [ME, fr OE *thōht*; akin to OE *thencan* to think – more at THINK]

**thoughtful** /-f(ə)l/ *adj* **1a** absorbed in thought; meditative, pensive **b** characterized by careful reasoned thinking ⟨*a* ~ *analysis of the problem*⟩ **2** showing concern for others; considerate *antonym* thoughtless – **thoughtfully** *adv*, **thoughtfulness** *n*

**thoughtless** /-lis/ *adj* **1** lacking forethought; careless, rash **2** lacking concern for others; inconsiderate **3** devoid of the capacity for thought; insensate ⟨*the* ~ *forces of nature* – Bertrand Russell⟩ – **thoughtlessly** *adv*, **thoughtlessness** *n*

,**thought-'out** *adj* arrived at or produced by careful or deliberate consideration ⟨*her playing of the sonata seemed well* ~ *but an element of sparkle and spontaneity was lacking*⟩

**thousand** /'thowz(ə)nd/ *n, pl* **thousands, thousand 1** – see NUMBER table **2** the number occupying the position four to the left of the decimal point in the Arabic notation; *also, pl* this position **3** *usu pl* an indefinitely large number ⟨~s *of ants*⟩ [ME, fr OE *thūsend;* akin to OHG *dūsunt* thousand; both fr a prehistoric Gmc compound whose constituents are akin to Russ *tysyacha* thousand, Skt *tavas* strong, L *tumēre* to swell, & to OE *hund* hundred – more at THUMB] – **thousand** *adj*, **thousandth** *adj or n*

**Thousand Island dressing** *n* a usu pink mayonnaise-based salad dressing flavoured with tomatoes, green peppers, pimientos, etc [prob fr *Thousand Islands*, islands in the St Lawrence river between USA and Canada]

**Thracian** /'thraysh(y)ən/ *n* **1** a native or inhabitant of Thrace **2** the extinct language of the ancient Thracians, belonging to the INDO-EUROPEAN family of languages [L *Thracius*, adj, fr Gk ancient *Thraikios*, fr *Thraikē* Thrace, region & ancient country in SE Europe] – **Thracian** *adj*

¹**thrall** /thrawl/ *n* **1a** a slave, bondman **b** a person in a state of total dependence (e g on a person, habit, or drug) **2a** thrall, thralldom, *NAm chiefly* **thralldom** the state of being a thrall; slavery **b** a state of complete absorption or enslavement ⟨*her beauty held him in* ~⟩ [ME *thral*, fr OE *thrǣl*, fr ON *thrǣll*] – **thrall** *adj*

²**thrall** *vt, archaic* to enslave

¹**thrash** /thrash/ *vt* **1** THRESH **1** (separate the seeds from) **2a** to beat soundly (as if) with a stick or whip; flog **b** to defeat heavily or decisively ⟨~ed *the visiting team*⟩ **3** to swing, beat, or strike wildly or violently ⟨~ing *his arms*⟩ **4** to sail (a ship) to windward ~ *vi* **1** THRESH **1** (separate the seeds from the husks of grain) **2** to deal repeated blows (as if) with a stick or whip **3** to move or stir about violently; toss about – usu + *around* or *about* ⟨~ *around in bed with a fever*⟩ [alter. of *thresh*] – **thrasher** *n*, **thrashing** *n*

**thrash out** *vt* to discuss (e g a problem) exhaustively in order to find a solution; *also* to arrive at (e g a decision) in this way

²**thrash** *n* **1** an act of thrashing or thrashing about; *esp* wild and badly co-ordinated attempts to swim **2** *informal* a wild party, esp with wild music and dancing

**thrasher** /'thrashə/ *n* any of numerous brown long-tailed American songbirds (family Mimidae) [prob alter. of *thrush*]

**thrasonical** /thrə'sonikl/ *adj, formal* bragging, boastful [L *Thrason-, Thraso* Thraso, boastful soldier in the comedy *Eunuchus* by Terence †159 BC Roman dramatist] – **thrasoni-cally** *adv*

**thrave** /thrayv/ *n, Scot & N Eng dial* two stooks of corn, each consisting of twelve sheaves [ME, fr OE *threfe*, of Scand origin; akin to ON *threfi* thrave]

**thrawn** /thrawn/ *adj, chiefly Scot* lacking in pleasing or attractive qualities: e g **a** perverse, recalcitrant **b** crooked, misshapen [ME (Sc) *thrawin*, fr pp of ME *thrawen* to cause to twist, fr OE *thrāwan*] – **thrawnly** *adv*

¹**thread** /thred/ *n* **1a** a filament, group of filaments twisted together, or continuous strand formed by spinning and twisting together short textile fibres **b** a piece of thread **2a** any of various natural filaments ⟨*the* ~s *of a spider web*⟩ **b** something (e g a thin stream of liquid or a streak of light) resembling a thread in length and narrowness **c** a thin vein of mineral ore or narrow seam of coal **d** a projecting spiral ridge (e g on a bolt or pipe) by which parts can be screwed together **3** something continuous or drawn out: e g **3a** a train of thought ⟨*I've lost the* ~ *of this argument*⟩ **b** a pervasive recurring element ⟨*a* ~ *of melancholy marked all his writing*⟩ [ME *thred*, fr OE *thrǣd;* akin to OHG *drāt* wire, OE *thrāwan* to cause to twist or turn – more at THROW] – **threadiness** *n*, **threadless** *adj*, **threadlike** *adj* – **hang by a thread** to be in a very dangerous or precarious state ⟨*her life* hung by a thread⟩

²**thread** *vt* **1a** to pass a thread through the eye of (a needle) **b** to arrange a thread, yarn, etc in position for use in (a machine) **2a(1)** to pass something through the entire length of ⟨~ *a pipe with wire*⟩ **a(2)** to pass (e g a tape or film) into or through something ⟨~ed *elastic into the waistband*⟩ **a(3)** to load (a camera or projector) with film – often + *up* **b** to make (one's way) cautiously through or between ⟨~ed *her way through the crowd*⟩ **3** to string together (as if) on a thread ⟨~ *beads*⟩ **4** to intermingle or pervade (as if) with threads ⟨*dark hair* ~ed *with silver*⟩ ⟨*the novel was* ~ed *with despair*⟩ **5** to form a SCREW THREAD on or in ~ *vi* **1** to make one's way *through* **2** of boiling syrup to form a thread when poured from a spoon – **threader** *n*

**threadbare** /'thred,beə/ *adj* **1** having the nap worn off so that the thread shows; worn **2** shabby, poor **3** hackneyed ⟨~ *phrases*⟩ – **threadbareness** *n*

**thread mark** *n* a fine line of silk fibre put into a bank note to prevent forgery

**threadworm** /-,wuhm/ *n* PINWORM (small parasitic worm)

**thready** /'thredi/ *adj* **1a** of threadlike appearance or substance; fibrous ⟨*a* ~ *bark*⟩ **b** tending to form strands; viscid, stringy – used esp of a liquid **2** lacking in strength or vigour; thin, slight ⟨*a* ~ *voice*⟩ ⟨*a* ~ *pulse*⟩ – **threadiness** *n*

¹**threat** /thret/ *n* **1** an indication of something usu unpleasant to come ⟨*the air held a* ~ *of rain*⟩ **2** an expression of intention to inflict punishment, injury, or damage **3** somebody or something that is a source of imminent danger or harm; MENACE **2a** ⟨*the arms race is a* ~ *to world peace*⟩ ⟨*that troublemaker is a* ~ *to the smooth running of the company*⟩ [ME *thret* coercion, threat, fr OE *thrēat* coercion; akin to MHG *drōz* annoyance, L *trudere* to push, thrust]

²**threat** *vb, archaic* to threaten

**threaten** /'thret(ə)n/ *vt* **1** to utter threats against ⟨*he* ~ed *his employees with the sack*⟩ **2a** to give ominous signs of ⟨*the clouds* ~ *rain*⟩ **b** to be a source of harm or danger to; menace ⟨*famine* ~s *the city*⟩ **3** to announce as intended or possible; express as a threat ⟨*the workers* ~ed *a strike*⟩ ⟨*the king* ~ed *death to all traitors*⟩ ~ *vi* **1** to utter threats **2** to appear menacing ⟨*the sky* ~ed⟩ – **threatener** *n*, **threateningly** *adv*

*synonyms* Threaten, intimidate, and menace all mean "show intention to harm". Threaten and intimidate can both imply an attempt to influence somebody by promising punishment ⟨*another form of lying, which is extremely bad for the young, is to* threaten *punishments you do not mean to inflict* – Bertrand Russell⟩, and intimidate adds the idea of compelling submission by a display of superiority ⟨*was* intimidated *by his imposing presence into signing the document*⟩. Menace emphasizes the dire character of the danger ⟨*the devastating weapons which are at present being developed may* menace *every part of the world* – Clement Attlee⟩.

**three** /three/ *n* **1** – see NUMBER table **2** the third in a set or series ⟨*the* ~ *of hearts*⟩ **3** something having three parts or members or a denomination of three – see also **three** SHEETS **in the wind** [ME, fr *three*, adj, fr OE *thrīe* (masc), *thrēo* (fem & neut); akin to OHG *drī* three, L *tres*, Gk *treis*] – **three** *adj or pron*, **threefold** *adj or adv*

'**three-,ball** *adj* a golf match in which three players compete against one another with each using his/her own ball

**three-card monte** *n* a card game in which players bet on which of three face-down cards is which

**three-card trick** *n* a card game in which players place bets on which of three cards lying face downwards is the queen

**three-,colour** *adj* of or being a printing or photographic process in which three primary colours are used in combination to reproduce all the colours required

¹**three-'D, 3-D** *n* (an image or picture produced in) the three-dimensional form [*D*, abbr of *dimensional*]

²**three-D, 3-D** *adj* THREE-DIMENSIONAL 1, 2

**three-day event** *n* an equestrian contest involving DRESSAGE, CROSS-COUNTRY, and SHOWJUMPING and continuing over three days

,**three-'decker** /'dekə/ *n* **1** something with three tiers, layers, etc; *esp* a sandwich made with three slices of bread and two fillings **2** a book, esp a novel, in three volumes

,**three-di'mensional** *adj* **1** having three dimensions **2** giving the illusion of depth or varying distances – used of an image or a pictorial representation, esp when this illusion is enhanced by STEREOSCOPIC means **3** describing or being described in great depth; *esp* lifelike ⟨*a story with* ~ *characters*⟩ – **three-dimensionality** *n*

,**three-'handed** *adj* played by three players ⟨~ *bridge*⟩

**Three Hours** *n* a service of devotion between noon and three o'clock on GOOD FRIDAY

**three-legged race** *n* a race between pairs in which one contestant's right leg is tied to his/her partner's left leg

**three-line whip** *n* an instruction from a UK political party to its Members of Parliament that they must attend a debate and vote in the specified way on pain of being disciplined – compare FREE VOTE, TWO-LINE WHIP [fr the triple underlining of words on the written instruction]

,**three-'master** *n* a ship having three masts

**three of a kind** *n* three cards of the same rank in one hand

,**three-o-'three, 303** *n* a 0-303 inch calibre rifle

**threepence** /'threpəns, 'thrupəns/ *n* **1** the sum of three pence **2** a small twelve-sided British coin in use until early 1971 and worth three old pence

¹**threepenny** /'threp(ə)ni, 'threp-, 'thrip-, 'thrup-/ *adj* costing or worth threepence

²**threepenny, threepenny bit** *n* THREEPENCE 2

,**three-'phase** *adj* of or operating by means of a combination of three electrical circuits having alternating voltages that differ in phase by one third of a cycle

,**three-'piece** *adj* consisting of or made in three (matching) pieces ⟨*a* ~ *suit*⟩ – **three-piece** *n*

**three-point landing** *n* an aircraft landing in which the main wheels of the undercarriage touch the ground simultaneously with the tail wheel, SKID (runner), or nose wheel

**three-point turn** *n, Br* a usu three-stage manoeuvre for turning a vehicle to face the opposite direction in a confined space

**threequarter** /three'kwawtə/, **threequarter back** *n* (the position of) a player in rugby positioned between the HALFBACKS and the FULLBACK

**three-'quarter, three-quarters** *adj* **1** being or consisting of three fourths of the whole or standard size, length, amount, etc **2** *esp of a view of a rectangular object* including one side and one end ⟨*a* ~ *view of a vehicle*⟩ – **three-quarters** *adv*

**three-'quarter-bound** *adj, of a book* bound like a half-bound book but having the material on the spine extended to cover about one third of the boards – **three-quarter binding** *n*

**three-'quarters** *n taking sing or pl vb* a part or collection consisting of (roughly) three fourths of some larger whole or group ⟨*cut off* ~ *of the new growth to leave a stem about a foot long*⟩ ⟨~ *of the new class is girls*⟩

**three-ring circus** *n, chiefly NAm* **1** a circus with simultaneous performances in three rings **2** something confusing, engrossing, or spectacular

**three R's** *n pl the* fundamentals taught in primary school; *esp* reading, writing, and arithmetic [fr the facetious phrase *reading, 'riting, and 'rithmetic*]

**threescore** /-'skaw/ *n or adj* sixty

**threesome** /-s(ə)m/ *n* **1** a group of three people or things; a trio **2** a golf match in which one person plays his ball against two others using the same ball and playing each stroke alternately

**three-spined stickleback** *n* a stickleback (*Gasterosteus aculeatus*) found in fresh and salt waters that usu has three spines on its back

,**three-'star** *adj* of the third rank in a system for grading ex-

cellence applied to esp hotels, in which the highest standard is usu represented by the fifth rank ⟨~ *accommodation*⟩

,**three-'tier** *adj* of or being a school system whereby pupils pass through three successive schools (e g at ages 5, 8, and 12) rather than only two (e g at ages 5 and 11)

**three-toed sloth** *n* a sloth (*Bradypus tridactylus*) that has three toes on each foot – called also AI; compare TWO-TOED SLOTH

,**three-'valued** *adj* possessing three truth-values instead of the customary two of truth and falsehood ⟨~ *logic*⟩

,**three-'wheeler** *n* a vehicle, esp a small car, with three wheels

**thremmatology** /,thremə'toləji/ *n* the science of breeding domesticated animals and plants [Gk *thremmat-, thremma* nursling (akin to Gk *trephein* to nourish) + E -o- + -*logy* – more at ATROPHY]

**threnode** /'threnohd, 'three-/ *n* a threnody – **threnodist** *n*, **threnodic** *adj*

**threnody** /'threnədi, 'three-/ *n* a song of lamentation esp for the dead; an elegy [Gk *thrēnōidia*, fr *thrēnos* dirge (akin to Skt *dhraqti* it sounds) + *aeidein* to sing – more at ODE]

**threonine** /'three-əneen, -nin/ *n* an ESSENTIAL AMINO ACID, $CH_3CH(OH)CH(NH_2)CO_2H$, that is required by the body for normal development and health and forms part of many proteins [prob fr *threonic acid* $(C_4H_8O_5)$]

**thresh** /thresh/ *vt* **1** to separate the seeds of (a harvested plant, esp corn) from the husks and straw by beating, usu mechanically; *also* to separate (seed) in this way **2** to strike repeatedly ~ *vi* **1** to thresh grain **2** THRASH 2,3 [ME *threshen*, fr OE *threscan*; akin to OHG *dreskan* to thresh, L *terere* to rub – more at THROW]

**thresh out** *vt* THRASH OUT

**thresher** /'threshə/ *n* **1** somebody who or something that threshes; *specif* THRESHING MACHINE **2** a large shark (*Alopias vulpinus*) that is found in many parts of the world, and that has a very long curved upper part to its tail with which it is said to thresh the water to round up the fish on which it feeds

**threshing machine** /'threshing/ *n* a machine for threshing grain crops

**threshold** /'thresh,hohld, 'thresh·ohld/ *n* **1** the plank, stone, or piece of timber that lies under a door **2a** the doorway or entrance to a building **b** the point of entering or beginning ⟨*on the* ~ *of a new career*⟩ **3a** the level or strength of a stimulus which begins to produce a physiological or psychological effect ⟨*the* ~ *of consciousness*⟩ **b** a level, point, or value above which something is true or will occur **4** a level of price rises beyond which an addition to earnings is payable [ME *threshhold*, fr OE *threscwald*; akin to ON *threskjöldr* threshold, OE *threscan* to thresh]

**threw** /throoh/ *past of* THROW

**thrice** /thries/ *adv* **1** three times **2a** in a threefold manner or degree **b** to a high degree – usu in combination ⟨*thrice-blessed*⟩ [ME *thrie, thries*, fr OE *thriga*; akin to OFris *thria* three times, OE *thrīe* three]

**thrift** /thrift/ *n* **1** careful management, esp of money **2** any of a genus (*Armeria* of the family Plumbaginaceae, the thrift family) of tufted plants; *esp* a sea-pink **3** *chiefly Scot* gainful occupation **4** *archaic or NAm* healthy and vigorous growth (e g of a plant or animal) *synonyms* see SPARING [ME, fr ON, prosperity, fr *thrīfask* to thrive] – **thriftless** *adj*, **thrifty** *adj*, **thriftily** *adv*, **thriftiness** *n*

**thrill** /thril/ *vt* **1a** to cause to experience a sudden feeling of excitement **b** to cause to have a shivering or tingling sensation **2** *archaic* to cause to vibrate or tremble perceptibly ~ *vi* **1** to experience a sudden tremor of excitement or emotion ⟨*he* ~*ed to the sound of the music*⟩ **2** *archaic* to tingle, throb **3** *archaic* to tremble, vibrate [ME *thirlen, thrillen* to pierce, fr OE *thyrlian*, fr *thyrel* hole, fr *thurh* through – more at THROUGH ] – **thrill** *n*, **thrillingly** *adv*

**thriller** /'thrilə/ *n* somebody who or something that thrills; *esp* a work of fiction or drama characterized by a high degree of intrigue, adventure, or suspense

**thrips** /thrips/ *n, pl* **thrips** any of an order (Thysanoptera) of small to minute sucking insects, most of which feed on and damage plants [L, woodworm, fr Gk]

**thrive** /thriev/ *vi* **throve** /throhv/, **thrived; thriven** /'thriv(ə)n/ *also* **thrived 1** to grow vigorously; flourish **2** to gain in wealth or possessions; prosper [ME *thriven*, fr ON *thrīfask*, prob reflexive of *thrīfa* to grasp] – **thriver** *n*

**thro** /throoh/ *prep, chiefly informal or poetic* through

**throat** /throht/ *n* **1a** the front part of the neck **b** the passages through the neck from the mouth to the stomach and lungs **2** something resembling the throat, esp in being a narrow or constricted part or passageway: e g **2a** the opening of a tube-shaped organ, esp of a plant **b** the part of a tennis racket between the head and the handle **3** the upper forward corner of a four-cornered FORE-AND-AFT sail (sail set lengthwise) **4** the curved part of an anchor's arm where it joins the shank **5** *informal* a sore throat ⟨*Sundays ... she went to church, unless she had a* ~ – Patrick White⟩ [ME *throte*, fr OE; akin to OHG *drozza* throat, ON *throti* swelling] – **ram something down somebody's throat** to force somebody to accept or listen to something, esp by constant repetition

**throated** /'throhtid/ *adj* having a throat of a usu specified kind – usu in combination ⟨*white*-throated⟩

**throat lash** *n* a strap of a bridle or halter passing under a horse's throat

**throatlatch** /'throht,lach/ *n* THROAT LASH

'**throat-,mike** *n* a small, often concealed, microphone usu worn round the neck that picks up a speaker's words from the vibrations in his/her throat and is not spoken into directly

**throaty** /'throhti/ *adj* uttered or produced from low in the throat; hoarse, guttural ⟨*a* ~ *voice*⟩ – **throatily** *adv*, **throatiness** *n*

'**throb** /throb/ *vi* **-bb-** **1** to pulsate or pound with unusual force or rapidity **2** to beat or vibrate rhythmically **3** to feel or display strong emotion; quiver [ME *throbben*, prob of imit origin] – **throbber** *n*

²**throb** *n* a beat, pulse

**throes** /throhz/ *n pl* **1** pangs, spasms ⟨*death* ~⟩ ⟨~ *of childbirth*⟩ **2** hard or painful struggle ⟨*in the* ~ *of revolutionary change*⟩ [ME *thrawe, throwe, thrahe*, fr OE *thrag* time]

**thromb-** /thromb-/, **thrombo-** *comb form* blood clot; clotting of blood ⟨*thromb*osis⟩ ⟨*thrombo*plastic⟩ [Gk *thrombos* clot]

**thrombin** /'thrombin/ *n* an ENZYME that is formed from PROTHROMBIN and that assists in the clotting of blood by speeding up the rate of conversion of the protein FIBRINOGEN, dissolved in blood, to insoluble strands of FIBRIN [ISV]

**thrombocyte** /'thrombəsiet/ *n* **1** BLOOD PLATELET (particle in the blood that assists in clotting; *esp* one containing a nucleus that is present in VERTEBRATE animals other than mammals **2** a cell of an INVERTEBRATE animal with the function of blood clotting similar to BLOOD PLATELETS [ISV] – **thrombocytic** *adj*

**thrombocytopenia** /,thromboh·sietə'peenyə/ *n* a condition, characteristic of some diseases, in which the number of BLOOD PLATELETS circulating in the blood is abnormally low [NL, fr ISV *thrombocyte* + *-o-* + NL *-penia* deficiency of, fr Gk *penia* poverty, lack] – **thrombocytopenic** *adj*

**thromboembolism** /,thromboh'embaliz(ə)m/ *n* the blocking of a blood vessel by a piece of blood clot that has formed elsewhere in the body and broken away from its site of formation – **thromboembolic** *adj*

**thrombokinase** /,thromboh'kienayz/ *n* thromboplastin [ISV]

**thrombophlebitis** /,thromboh·fli'bietəs/ *n* inflammation of a vein associated with blood clots

**thromboplastic** /,thromboh'plastik; *also* -'plah-/ *adj* initiating or accelerating the clotting of blood [ISV *thromb-* + *-plastic*] – **thromboplastically** *adv*

**thromboplastin** /,thromboh'plastin/ *n* a complex ENZYME found esp in BLOOD PLATELETS that functions in the clotting of blood [ISV, fr *thromboplastic*]

**thrombosis** /throm'bohsis/ *n, pl* **thromboses** /-seez/ **1** the formation or presence of a blood clot within a blood vessel during life **2** CORONARY THROMBOSIS [NL, fr Gk *thrombōsis* clotting, deriv of *thrombos* clot] – **thrombotic** *adj*

**thrombus** /'thrombəs/ *n, pl* **thrombi** /-bi/ a clot of blood formed within a blood vessel and remaining attached to its place of origin – compare EMBOLUS [NL, fr Gk *thrombos* clot]

'**throne** /throhn/ *n* **1** the chair of state of a sovereign or bishop **2** royal power and dignity; sovereignty **3** *pl* the third of the nine orders of angelic beings in the CELESTIAL HIERARCHY ranking immediately below CHERUBIM and above DOMINATIONS [ME *trone, throne*, fr OF *trone*, fr L *thronus*, fr Gk *thronos* – more at FIRM]

²**throne** *vt* **1** to seat on a throne **2** to invest with royal rank or power

**throne room** *n* a room used by a sovereign for formal audiences

'**throng** /throng/ *n taking sing or pl vb* **1** a multitude of assembled people, esp when crowded together **2a** a large

number; a host **b** pressure ⟨*this* ~ *of business* – S R Crockett⟩ [ME *thrang, throng*, fr OE *thrang, gethrang*; akin to OE *thringan* to press, crowd, OHG *dringan*, Lith *trenkti* to jolt]

²**throng** *vt* **1** to crowd upon (esp a person) **2** to crowd into; pack, fill ⟨*shoppers* ~ing *the streets*⟩ ~ *vi* to crowd together in great numbers

**throstle** /'throsl/ *n* **1** *archaic or poetic* SONG THRUSH **2** a frame for spinning cotton, wool, etc [ME, fr OE – more at THRUSH; (2) fr the singing noise it produces]

'**throttle** /'throtl/ *vt* **1a(1)** to compress the throat of; choke **a(2)** to kill by throttling **b** to prevent or check expression or activity of; suppress **2a** to decrease the flow of (eg steam or fuel to an engine) by means of a valve **b** to regulate, esp reduce the speed of (eg an engine or vehicle), by such means – usu + *back* or *down* **c** to vary the thrust of (a rocket engine) during flight [ME *throtlen*, fr *throte* throat] – **throttler** *n*

²**throttle** *n* **1a** THROAT 1a **b** TRACHEA 1 (windpipe in humans and other higher animals) **2a** a valve for regulating the supply of a gas or liquid (eg fuel) to an engine **b** the lever or pedal controlling this valve **c** speed – chiefly in *(at) full throttle* [(1) perh alter. (influenced by '*throttle*) of E dial. *thropple* throat, fr ME *throppill*; (2) fr '*throttle*]

'**through** /throoh/ *prep* **1a(1)** into at one side or point and out at the other ⟨*drove a nail* ~ *the board*⟩ ⟨*a path* ~ *the woods*⟩ ⟨*a road* ~ *the desert*⟩ **a(2)** BY WAY OF 2 ⟨*left* ~ *the door*⟩ ⟨*look* ~ *a telescope*⟩ **a(3)** past ⟨*drove* ~ *a red light*⟩ ⟨*saw* ~ *the deception*⟩ **b** – used to indicate passage into and out of a treatment, handling, or process ⟨*flashed* ~ *my mind*⟩ ⟨*the matter has already passed* ~ *his hands*⟩ **2** – used to indicate means, agency, or intermediacy: e g **2a** by means of; by the agency of **b** by the fault of; BECAUSE OF ⟨*failed* ~ *ignorance*⟩ **c** by common descent from or relationship with ⟨*related* ~ *their grandfather*⟩ **3a** over the whole surface or extent of ⟨*homes scattered* ~ *the valley*⟩ **b** – used to indicate movement within a large expanse ⟨*flew* ~ *the air*⟩ **c** among or between the parts or single members of ⟨*monkeys swing* ~ *the trees*⟩ ⟨*search* ~ *my papers*⟩ **d** – used to indicate exposure to a usu specified set of conditions ⟨*put her* ~ *hell*⟩ **4a** – used to indicate a period of time: e g **4a(1)** during the entire period of ⟨*all* ~ *her life*⟩ **a(2)** till the end of ⟨*the tower stood* ~ *the earthquake*⟩ **a(3)** *chiefly NAm* up till and including ⟨*Monday* ~ *Friday*⟩ **b** against and in spite of (a noise) ⟨*heard his voice* ~ *the howling of the storm*⟩ **5a** – used to indicate completion, exhaustion, or accomplishment ⟨*got* ~ *the book*⟩ ⟨*went* ~ *a fortune in a year*⟩ **b** – used to indicate acceptance or approval, esp by an official body ⟨*got the bill* ~ *Parliament*⟩ [ME *thurh, thruh, through*, fr OE *thurh*; akin to OHG *durh* through, L *trans* across, beyond, Skt *tarati* he crosses over]

²**through** *adv* **1** from one end or side to the other ⟨*squeezed* ~⟩ **2a** all the way from beginning to end ⟨*read the letter* ~⟩ ⟨*train goes right* ~ *to London*⟩ – compare GO THROUGH **b** to a favourable or successful conclusion ⟨*see it* ~⟩ ⟨*I failed the exam, but he got* ~⟩ **c** *chiefly Br* in or into connection by telephone ⟨*put me* ~ *to him*⟩ **3** to the core; completely ⟨*wet* ~⟩ **4** into the open; out ⟨*break* ~⟩

³**through** *adj* **1a** extending from one surface to the other ⟨*a* ~ *beam*⟩ **b** admitting free or continuous passage; direct ⟨*a* ~ *road*⟩ **2a** allowing a continuous journey from point of origin to destination without change, transshipment, or further payment ⟨*a* ~ *train*⟩ ⟨*a* ~ *ticket*⟩ **b** starting at and destined for points outside a local zone ⟨~ *traffic*⟩ **3a** arrived at completion or accomplishment ⟨*he is* ~ *with the job*⟩ **b** washed-up, finished ⟨*you're* ~ – *that was your last chance*⟩ **c** having no further dealings ⟨*I'm* ~ *with women*⟩

**through and through** *adv* in every way; thoroughly, completely

'**through-com,posed** *adj, of a song* having new music provided for each stanza – compare STROPHIC [trans of Ger *durchkomponiert*]

**throughly** /'throohli/ *adv, archaic* in a thorough manner

'**throughout** /-'owt/ *adv* **1** in or to every part; everywhere ⟨*of one colour* ~⟩ **2** during the whole time or action; from beginning to end ⟨*remained loyal* ~⟩

²**throughout** *prep* **1** in or to every part of; THROUGH 3a ⟨*cities* ~ *Europe*⟩ **2** during the entire period of; THROUGH 4a(1) ⟨*troubled him* ~ *his life*⟩

**throughput** /-,poot/ *n* the amount of material handled or processed (eg by a computer) in a given time ⟨*that new software will increase the* ~ *dramatically*⟩

**throve** /throhv/ *past of* THRIVE

**¹throw** /throh/ *vb* **threw** /throoh/; **thrown** /throhn/ *vt* **1a** to propel through the air by a forward motion of the hand and arm **b** to propel, cast, or hurl through the air in some other manner, esp by mechanical means ⟨*siege catapults capable of throwing huge rocks at city walls*⟩ **2a** to cause to fall ⟨*threw his opponent*⟩ **b** to cause to fall off; unseat ⟨*the horse threw its rider*⟩ **3a** to move suddenly and with force; fling abruptly ⟨*threw himself down on the sofa*⟩ ⟨*threw her head back and laughed*⟩ **b** to hurl violently; dash ⟨*the ship was ~n against the rocks*⟩ **4a(1)** to put in a specified position or condition, esp suddenly or forcefully ⟨*the news threw him into confusion*⟩ **a(2)** to put *on* or *off* hastily or carelessly ⟨*threw on a coat*⟩ **b** to exert; BRING TO BEAR ⟨*threw all his weight behind the proposal*⟩ **c** to build, construct ⟨*threw a pontoon bridge over the river*⟩ **5** to shape by hand on a potter's wheel **6** to deliver (a punch) **7** to twist two or more filaments of (eg silk) into a thread or yarn **8** to make a cast of (dice or a specified number on dice) **9** to abandon; GIVE UP ⟨*threw caution to the winds*⟩ **10** to send forth; cast, direct ⟨*the setting sun threw long shadows*⟩ ⟨*he threw me a glance*⟩ **11** to make (oneself) dependent; commit (oneself) for help, support, or protection ⟨*threw himself on the mercy of the court*⟩ **12** of a female animal to give birth to ⟨*threw large litters*⟩ **13** to move (a lever) so as to connect or disconnect parts of a mechanism, esp a clutch or switch; *also* to make or break (a connection) with a lever **14** to project (the voice) **a** so that it appears to come from somewhere other than its true source **b** so that it is clearly audible over a wide area **15** *informal* **15a** to get the better of; disconcert ⟨*the problem didn't ~ her*⟩ **b** THROW OFF 4 ⟨*the dancers were completely ~n by the change in tempo*⟩ **16** *informal* to make a display of (a usu violent emotional state) ⟨*he threw a fit when he heard the price*⟩ **17** *chiefly NAm informal* to lose (as if) intentionally ⟨*threw the game by constantly double-faulting in the final set*⟩ **18** *informal* to give by way of entertainment ⟨*~ a party*⟩ *~ vi* to cast, hurl [ME *thrawen, throwen* to cause to twist, throw, fr OE *thrāwan* to cause to twist or turn; akin to OHG *drāen* to turn, L *terere* to rub, Gk *tetrainein* to bore, pierce] – **thrower** *n* – **throw in the sponge/towel** to abandon a struggle or contest; acknowledge defeat [fr a boxer's seconds throwing a sponge or towel into the ring as a sign of defeat] – see also **throw a** FIT, **throw the** BOOK **at, throw somebody in at the deep** END, **throw a** SPANNER **in the works, throw one's** WEIGHT **about, throw to the** WINDS

*synonyms* Throw, cast, toss, sling, chuck, fling, pitch, hurl, and heave can all mean "propel swiftly through the air". Throw is the most general word, which can replace any of the others. The now somewhat literary **cast**, once synonymous with **throw**, has been replaced by it except in certain specialized contexts ⟨cast *a net*⟩ ⟨cast *doubts*⟩. Toss, sling, and the informal chuck all suggest careless, nonchalant, and perhaps aimless throwing. Toss applies particularly to the upward throwing of light objects, with little force ⟨toss *hay*⟩. Sling implies a quick sweeping and swirling motion, which may be quite forceful ⟨sling *an inkwell at a fellow student*⟩. Chuck suggests a short jerky arm action, and is often used for the discarding of objects ⟨chuck *it in the dustbin*⟩. Fling entails force and recklessness, and also often carries the idea of violent discarding brought about by emotion ⟨*he loathed his own beauty, and,* flinging *the mirror on the floor, crushed it into silver splinters beneath his heel* – Oscar Wilde⟩. Pitch has specialized senses in sport, and carries over from that the idea of purposive throwing ⟨pitch *grenades at their legs*⟩. Hurl implies very violent throwing ⟨*was* hurled *against the wall by the blast*⟩. Heave applies to very heavy objects, which can be thrown at all only with strain and effort ⟨heave *the sack over the wall*⟩.

**throw away** *vt* **1** to get rid of as worthless or unnecessary; discard **2a** to use in a foolish or wasteful manner; squander **b** to fail to take advantage of; waste **3** to make (eg a line in a play) unemphatic by casual delivery

**throw back** *vt* **1** to delay the progress or advance of; check **2** to cause to rely; make dependent – + *on* or *upon*; usu pass ⟨*when outside help failed, he was* thrown back *on his own resources*⟩ **3** to reflect ⟨*the cliffs* throw back *an echo*⟩ *~ vi,* of an organism to revert to an earlier type or phase – see also THROWBACK

**throw in** *vt* **1** to add as a gratuity or supplement ⟨*buy three packets and I'll* throw in *a fourth one free*⟩ **2** to introduce or interject in the course of something; contribute ⟨threw in *a casual remark*⟩ **3** to cause (eg gears) to mesh; *also* to engage (a mechanism) ⟨throw in *the clutch*⟩ *~ vi* to enter into association or partnership *with* ⟨*agrees to* throw in with *a crooked*

*ex-cop – Newsweek*⟩ – see also THROW-IN

**throw off** *vt* **1a** to cast off, often in an abrupt or vigorous manner; abandon ⟨threw off *all restraint*⟩ ⟨threw off *her cold*⟩ **b** to escape from ⟨*soon* threw off *her pursuers*⟩ **c** to divert, distract ⟨*dogs* thrown off *by a false scent*⟩ **2** to emit; GIVE OFF ⟨*stacks* throwing off *plumes of smoke*⟩ **3** to produce or execute in an offhand manner ⟨*a review* thrown off *in an odd half hour*⟩ **4** to cause to deviate or err ⟨*the constant noise really* threw me off⟩ *~ vi* to begin hunting with a pack of hounds

**throw out** *vt* **1a** to remove from or force to leave a place, position, job, etc, usu in a sudden or unexpected manner; expel **b** THROW AWAY 1 (discard) **2a** to give expression to; utter ⟨threw out *a remark that utterly foxed him*⟩ **b** to suggest tentatively **3** to refuse to accept or consider; reject ⟨*the assembly* threw out *the proposed legislation*⟩ **4** to give forth from within; emit ⟨*the fire* threw out *heat*⟩ **5** to cause to extend from a main body ⟨throw out *a screen of cavalry*⟩ ⟨*rebuilt the house,* throwing out *a new wing to the west*⟩ **6** to confuse, disconcert ⟨*the question quite* threw *him* out⟩ **7** to disengage ⟨throw out *the clutch*⟩

**throw over** *vt* to forsake despite ties of affection or duty; abandon ⟨threw me over *for another woman*⟩

**throw together** *vt* **1** KNOCK TOGETHER ⟨threw together *a delicious curry in no time*⟩ **2** to bring into association ⟨*fate* threw us together⟩

**throw up** *vt* **1** to raise quickly ⟨threw up *his hands in horror*⟩ **2** to quit; GIVE UP 3b ⟨*the urge . . . to* throw up *all intellectual work* – Norman Mailer⟩ **3** to build hurriedly ⟨*new houses* thrown up *almost overnight*⟩ **4** to produce; BRING FORTH ⟨*science . . . will continue to* throw up *discoveries which threaten society – TLS*⟩ **5** to mention repeatedly by way of reproach *~ vi, informal* to vomit

**²throw** *n* **1a** an act of throwing **b** (the number thrown with) a cast of dice **c** a method or instance of throwing an opponent in wrestling or judo **2** the distance over which something may be thrown ⟨*lived only a stone's ~ from school*⟩ **3** the amount of displacement upwards or downwards of a rock or layer of the earth that is produced by a geological fault **4a** the extent of movement of a pivoted structure or device that moves backwards and forwards (eg a CAM or CRANK) **b** the distance moved in such motion **5** *NAm* a light cover (eg for a bed) **6** *informal* a chance, try

**¹throwaway** /-ə,way/ *n* **1** a line of dialogue (eg in a play) made to sound unimportant by casual delivery **2** *chiefly NAm* a free handbill or circular

**²throwaway** *adj* **1** designed to be discarded after use; disposable ⟨*~ containers*⟩ **2** written or spoken (eg in a play) with deliberate casualness ⟨*a ~ remark*⟩

**throwback** /-,bak/ *n* **1** reversion of (part of) an organism to an earlier type or phase; ATAVISM **2** an instance or product of throwback

**'throw-,in** *n* a throw made from the touchline in soccer to put the ball back in play after it has gone over the touchline

**throwster** /'throhstə/ *n* somebody who throws silk or synthetic filaments

**'throw-,weight** *n* the amount of explosive carried by a nuclear missile

**thru** /throoh/ *prep, adv, or adj, NAm* through

**¹thrum** /thrum/ *n* **1** (any of) a fringe of warp threads left on a loom after the cloth has been removed **2** **thrum, thrums** *pl* a tuft or short piece of rope yarn used in thrumming canvas [ME, fr OE *-thrum* (in *tungethrum* ligament of the tongue); akin to OHG *drum* fragment, L *terminus* boundary, end – more at TERM] – **thrum** *adj*

**²thrum** *vt* **-mm-** **1** to furnish with thrums; fringe **2** to insert short pieces of rope yarn or spun yarn in (a piece of canvas) to make a rough surface or a mat which can be wrapped about rigging to prevent chafing

**³thrum** *vb* **-mm-** *vi* **1** to play or pluck a stringed instrument idly; strum **2** to drum or tap idly **3** to sound with a monotonous hum *~ vt* **1** to play (eg a stringed instrument) in an idle or relaxed manner **2** to recite tiresomely or monotonously [imit]

**¹thrush** /thrush/ *n* any of numerous small or medium-sized songbirds (family Turdidae) which are mostly of a plain esp brown colour often with spotted underparts, and many of which are excellent singers: eg **a** SONG THRUSH **b** MISTLE THRUSH [ME *thrusche,* fr OE *thrysce;* akin to OE *throstle* thrush, OHG *droscala,* L *turdus*]

**²thrush** *n* **1** a disease that is caused by the growth of a fungus

(*Candida albicans*) on MUCOUS MEMBRANES (membranes lining body surfaces in contact with the exterior), esp in the mouth of infants or in the vagina, producing intense irritation and a whitish patchy appearance **2** a disorder of the feet in various animals, esp horses, characterized by the production of foul-smelling pus [prob of Scand origin; akin to Dan & Norw *trōske* thrush]

**¹thrust** /thrust/ *vb* **thrust** *vt* **1** to push or drive with force; shove **2** to cause to enter or pierce something (as if) by pushing ⟨~ *a dagger into her heart*⟩ **3** to push forth; extend ⟨~ *out roots*⟩ **4** to stab, pierce **5** to put (eg an unwilling person) forcibly into a course of action or position ⟨*was ~ into power*⟩ **6** to press, force, or impose the acceptance of *on* or *upon* somebody ⟨~ *new responsibilities upon him*⟩ ~ *vi* **1a** to force an entrance or passage – often + *into* or *through* **b** to push forward or upwards **2** to make a thrust, stab, or lunge (as if) with a pointed weapon ⟨~ *at her with a knife*⟩ *synonyms* see ¹PUSH [ME *thrusten, thristen,* fr ON *thrȳsta*]

**²thrust** *n* **1a** a forceful forward or upward push or lunge; *specif* a swift forward stroke with a pointed weapon **b**(1) a verbal attack **b**(2) a military attack **2a** a strong continued pressure **b** the sideways force of one part of a structure against another part (eg between stones in an arch) **c**(1) the force exerted through a propeller shaft to give forward motion **c**(2) the forward-directed reaction force produced by a high-speed jet of fluid discharged rearwards from a nozzle (eg in a jet engine) **d** a nearly horizontal geological fault **3** a movement (eg by a group of people) in a specified direction **4** salient or essential meaning ⟨*the ~ of her argument was that all war was evil*⟩ **5** *informal* drive, dynamism – **thrustful** *adj*

**thruster** *also* **thrustor** /'thrustə/ *n* somebody who or something that thrusts: eg **a** a rocket engine used esp to control the altitude of a spacecraft **b** *slang* a huntsman/-woman who rides too close to the hounds

**thrust fault** *n* a FAULT (fracture in the earth's crust) caused by compression in which the upper older layers of rock are thrust over the lower younger ones at a very low angle

**thrusting** /'thrusting/ *adj* aggressive, pushy

**thrust stage** *n* a stage that extends out into the auditorium of a theatre

**¹thud** /thud/ *vb* **-dd-** to (cause to) move or strike so as to make a thud [prob fr ME *thudden* to thrust, fr OE *thyddan*]

**²thud** *n* **1** ⁵BLOW 1 **2** a dull heavy sound; a thump

**thug** /thug/ *n* **1** *often cap* a member of a former religious sect in India given to robbery and murder **2** a rough, aggressive person; *esp* a violent criminal [Hindi *ṭhag,* lit, thief, fr Skt *sthaga* rogue, fr. *sthagati* he covers, conceals – more at THATCH] – **thuggery** *n*

**thuggee** /thu'gee/ *n* murder and robbery as practised by the Thugs of India [Hindi *ṭhagī* robbery, fr *ṭhag*]

**thulium** /'thyoohli•əm/ *n* a metallic chemical element with a VALENCY of three belonging to the RARE-EARTH group [NL, fr L *Thule* Thule, land at the northernmost point of the world, fr Gk *Thoulē*]

**¹thumb** /thum/ *n* **1** the short thick digit of the human hand that is next to the forefinger, has two bones, and can be placed face to face with any of the other digits; *also* the corresponding digit in lower animals **2** the part of a glove or mitten that covers the thumb **3** *architecture* a convex moulding; an ovolo [ME *thoume, thoumbe,* fr OE *thūma;* akin to OHG *thūmo* thumb, L *tumēre* to swell, Gk *sōs* safe, whole] – **under somebody's/the thumb** under somebody's control – see also **be/feel all** FINGERS **and thumbs**

**²thumb** *vt* **1a** to leaf through (pages) with the thumb **b** to soil or wear (as if) by repeated thumbing ⟨*a badly ~ed book*⟩ **2** to request or obtain (a lift) in a passing vehicle by signalling with the thumb ~ *vi* **1** to turn over pages ⟨~ *through a book*⟩ **2** to travel by thumbing lifts; hitchhike ⟨~ed *across the country*⟩

**thumb index** *n* a series of notches cut in the unbound edge of a book for ease of reference – **thumb-index** *vt*

**¹thumbnail** /'thum,nayl/ *n* the nail of the thumb

**²thumbnail** *adj* brief, concise ⟨*a ~ sketch*⟩

**thumb piano** *n* MBIRA (African musical instrument)

**thumbprint** /-,print/ *n* an impression made by the thumb; *esp* one used for identification purposes

**thumbscrew** /-,skrooh/ *n* **1** a screw having a flat-sided or ridged head so that it may be turned by the thumb and forefinger **2** an instrument of torture for crushing the thumb by means of a screw

**thumbs-'down** *n, informal* rejection, disapproval – usu + *the* ⟨*gave it the ~*⟩

**thumbstall** /-,stawl/ *n* a protective covering or sheath for the thumb

**thumbs-'up** *n, informal* approval, affirmation – usu + *the* ⟨*gave it the ~*⟩

**thumbtack** /-,tak/ *n, NAm* DRAWING PIN

**¹thump** /thump/ *vt* **1** to strike or beat (as if) with something thick or heavy so as to cause a dull sound; pound **2** to thrash; BEAT 1a **3** to produce (a tune, song, etc) mechanically or in a mechanical manner – usu + *out* ⟨~ed *out a tune on the piano*⟩ ~ *vi* **1** to inflict a thump or thumps **2** to produce a thumping sound; pound ⟨*his heart ~ed*⟩ [imit] – **thumper** *n*

**²thump** *n* (the sound of) a blow or knock (as if) with something blunt or heavy

**³thump** *adv* with a thump

**¹thumping** /'thumping/ *adj, Br informal* impressively large, great, or excellent ⟨*a ~ majority*⟩ [fr prp of ¹*thump*]

**²thumping** *adv, Br informal* VERY 1 – chiefly in *thumping great* and *thumping good*

**¹thunder** /'thundə/ *n* **1** the loud explosive or rumbling sound that follows a flash of lightning and is caused by sudden expansion of the air in the path of the electrical discharge **2a** a loud utterance or threat **b** anger, wrath ⟨*you'll risk his ~ if you're late*⟩ **3** a loud reverberating noise ⟨*the ~ of big guns*⟩ [ME *thoner, thunder,* fr OE *thunor;* akin to OHG *thonar* thunder, L *tonare* to thunder] – **steal somebody's thunder** to anticipate or preempt somebody's words or actions, thus lessening or destroying their effect

**²thunder** *vi* **1a** to give forth thunder – usu used impersonally ⟨*it ~ed*⟩ **b** to make a sound that resembles thunder; *also* to move fast making such a sound ⟨*horses ~ed down the road*⟩ **2** to roar, shout ~ *vt* to utter in a loud and usu threatening tone; roar – **thunderer** *n*

**thunderbird** /'thundə,buhd/ *n* a mythical bird believed by some N American Indians to cause lightning and thunder

**thunderbolt** /-,bohlt/ *n* **1a** a single discharge of lightning with the accompanying thunder **b** an imaginary bolt or missile cast to earth in a flash of lightning and held in Greek, Roman, and other mythologies to signify the wrath of a god or gods **2a** something that resembles lightning in suddenness, effectiveness, or destructive power **b** a vehement threat or censure

**thunderbox** /'thundə,boks/ *n, informal or humorous* a toilet

**thunderclap** /-,klap/ *n* **1** a single loud crash of thunder **2** something sharp, loud, or sudden like a clap of thunder

**thundercloud** /-,klowd/ *n* a cloud charged with electricity and producing thunder and lightning

**thunderhead** /-,hed/ *n* a rounded mass of CUMULONIMBUS cloud often appearing before a thunderstorm

**¹thundering** /'thundəring/ *adj, Br* very great, remarkable, or unusual ⟨*a ~ bore*⟩ [fr prp of ²*thunder*] – **thunderingly** *adv*

**²thundering** *adv, Br informal* VERY 1 – chiefly in *thundering good* and *thundering great*

**thunder lizard** *n* BRONTOSAUR (large dinosaur) [trans of NL *brontosaurus*]

**thunderous** /'thundərəs/ *adj* producing thunder; *also* making or accompanied by a noise like thunder ⟨~ *applause*⟩ – **thunderously** *adv*

**thunderpeal** /'thundəpiəl, -peel/ *n* a thunderclap

**thundershower** /'thundə,showə/ *n* a shower accompanied by lightning and thunder

**thunderstone** /'thundə,stohn/ *n* any of various stones (eg a meteorite or long narrow rock) which probably gave rise to the former belief in missiles sent from the sky in thunderbolts

**thunderstorm** /-,stawm/ *n* a storm accompanied by lightning and thunder

**thunderstruck** /-,struk/ *adj* astonished, dumbfounded

**thundery** /'thund(ə)ri/ *adj* producing or giving a warning of thunder ⟨*a ~ sky*⟩

**thurible** /'thyooərəbl/ *n* CENSER (vessel for burning incense) [ME *turrible,* fr MF *thurible,* fr L *thuribulum,* fr *thur-, thus* incense, fr Gk *thyos* incense, sacrifice, fr *thyein* to sacrifice – more at THYME]

**thurifer** /'thyooərifə/ *n* a person who carries a CENSER (vessel for burning incense) in a service of worship [NL, fr L *thurifer,* adj, incense-bearing, fr *thur-, thus* incense + *-ifer* -iferous]

**Thuringian** /thyoo'rinji•ən/ *n or adj* (a member) of an ancient Germanic people whose kingdom was overthrown by the Franks in the 6th century AD [L *Thuringi,* n pl]

**thurl** /thuhl/ *n* the hip joint in cattle [perh fr E dial., gaunt]

**Thursday** /'thuhzday, -di/ *n* the day of the week following Wednesday [ME, fr OE *thursdæg*, fr ON *thōrsdagr;* akin to OE *thunresdæg* Thursday, OHG *Donares tag;* all fr a prehistoric NGmc-WGmc compound whose components are represented by OHG *Donar*, Gmc god of the sky (fr *thonar, donar* thunder) & by OHG *tag* day – more at THUNDER, DAY] – **Thursdays** *adv*

**thus** /dhus/ *adv, chiefly formal* **1** in the manner indicated; in this way **2** to this degree or extent; so ⟨~ *far*⟩ **3** because of this preceding fact or premise; consequently **4** as an example [ME, fr OE; akin to MD *dus* thus, OE *thæt*, neut demonstrative pron – more at THAT]

**¹thwack** /thwak/ *vt* to strike (as if) with something flat or heavy; whack [imit]

**²thwack** *n* a sharp blow; a whack

**³thwack** *adv* with a thwack

**¹thwart** /thwawt/ *adv, obs* ATHWART (obliquely across) [ME *thwert*, fr ON *thvert*, fr neut of *thverr* transverse, oblique; akin to OHG *dwerah* transverse, oblique, L *torquēre* to twist – more at TORTURE]

**²thwart** *adj, archaic* situated or placed across something else; transverse – **thwartly** *adv*

**³thwart** *vt* **1** to run counter to; oppose, contravene **2** to defeat the hopes or aspirations of; frustrate – **thwarter** *n*

**⁴thwart** *n* a seat extending across a boat

**thy** /dhie/ *adj* of thee or thyself – now chiefly dialect but sometimes used in ecclesiastical or literary language and by Quakers among themselves [ME *thin, thy*, fr OE *thīn*, gen of *thū* thou – more at THOU]

**Thyestean** /'thie'estiən, ‚thie·e'stee·ən/ *adj* of the eating of human flesh; cannibal [*Thyestes*, character in Gk myth who unwittingly ate the flesh of his children]

**thylacine** /'thielə‚sien/ *n* TASMANIAN WOLF (doglike marsupial mammal) [NL *Thylacinus*, genus of marsupials, fr Gk *thylakos* sack, pouch]

**thylakoid** /'thielə‚koyd/ *n* any of a group of membranes of protein and LIPID in plant CHLOROPLASTS (specialized cell parts containing chlorophyll) where the light-involving chemical reactions of photosynthesis take place [ISV *thylak-* (fr Gk *thylakos* sack) + *-oid*]

**thyme** /tiem/ *n* any of a genus (*Thymus*) of plants of the mint family with small pungent aromatic leaves; *esp* a garden plant (*Thymus vulgaris*) used in cooking as a seasoning and formerly in medicine [ME, fr MF *thym*, fr L *thymum*, fr Gk *thymon*, fr *thyein* to make a burnt offering, sacrifice; akin to L *fumus* smoke – more at FUME]

**thymectomy** /'thie'mektəmi/ *n* surgical removal of the thymus – **thymectomize** *vt*

**-thymia** /-'thiemyə, -mi·ə/ *comb form* (→ *n*) state of mental health ⟨*schiz*othymia⟩ [NL, fr Gk, fr *thymos* mind – more at FUME]

**thymidine** /'thiemədeen/ *n* a chemical compound (NUCLEOSIDE), $C_{10}H_{14}N_2O_5$, that forms part of DNA and contains thymine attached to the sugar DEOXYRIBOSE [*thym*ine + *-idine*]

**thymine** /'thiemeen/ *n* a chemical compound, $C_5H_6N_2O_2$, that is a PYRIMIDINE and is one of the four BASES whose order in the molecular chain of DNA codes genetic information – compare ADENINE, CYTOSINE, GUANINE, URACIL [Ger *thymin*, fr NL *thymus*]

**thymocyte** /'thiemə‚siet/ *n* a cell of the thymus; *specif* a thymic LYMPHOCYTE [ISV]

**thymol** /'thie‚mol/ *n* a PHENOL, $C_6H_3(OH)(CH_3)(CH(CH_3)_2)$, that has antiseptic properties, is found esp in thyme oil or made synthetically, and is used chiefly as a fungicide and preservative [ISV, fr L *thymum* thyme]

**thymus** /'thieməs/ *n* a gland in the lower neck region of most VERTEBRATE animals that functions esp in the development of the body's immune system and in humans tends to waste away after sexual maturity △ thyroid [NL, fr Gk *thymos* warty excrescence, thymus] – **thymic** *adj*

**thyr-, thyro-** *comb form* thyroid ⟨*thyro*toxicosis⟩ ⟨*thyro*xine⟩

**thyratron** /'thierətron/ *n* a gas-filled electronic device (THERMIONIC VALVE) that has three electrodes, one of which, the GRID, controls only the start of a continuous current, thus giving the tube a trigger effect that can be used as a switching mechanism in electrical circuits [fr *Thyratron*, a trademark]

**thyristor** /'thie'ristə/ *n* an electronic device consisting essentially of a SEMICONDUCTOR (solid substance that conducts electricity to a limited extent), that is similar to the thyratron, and that is mainly used as a controlling mechanism in electrical circuits (e g as a switch or RECTIFIER) – called also SILICON CONTROLLED RECTIFIER [*thyr*atron + trans*istor*]

**thyrocalcitonin** /‚thieroh‚kalsi'tohnin/ *n* CALCITONIN (hormone from the thyroid gland)

**thyroglobulin** /‚thieroh'globyoolin/ *n* an iodine-containing protein of the thyroid gland that is the form in which hormones of the thyroid are stored [ISV]

**¹thyroid** /'thieroyd/ *also* **thyroidal** /thie'roydl/ *adj* **1** of or being (an artery, nerve, etc associated with) **a** the thyroid gland **b** the chief cartilage of the LARYNX (organ of vocalization) **2** suggestive of a disordered thyroid ⟨*a* ~ *personality*⟩ [NL *thyroides*, fr Gk *thyreoeidēs* shield-shaped, fr *thyreos* shield shaped like a door, fr *thyra* door – more at DOOR]

**²thyroid** *n* **1** thyroid, thyroid gland a large ENDOCRINE GLAND that lies at the base of the neck and produces hormones (e g thyroxine) that increase the rate of chemical reactions in the body and influence growth and development **2** a preparation of mammalian thyroid gland containing thyroid hormones used in treating conditions in which the thyroid gland produces insufficient quantities of hormones △ thymus

**thyroidectomy** /‚thieroy'dektəmi/ *n* surgical removal of thyroid gland tissue – **thyroidectomized** *adj*

**thyroiditis** /‚thieroy'dietəs/ *n* inflammation of the thyroid gland [NL]

**thyroid-stimulating hormone** *n* a hormone secreted by the front lobe of the PITUITARY GLAND that regulates the formation and secretion of thyroid hormones

**thyrotoxicosis** /‚thieroh‚toksi'kohsis/ *n* HYPERTHYROIDISM (overactivity of the thyroid gland) [NL]

**thyrotrophic** /‚thieroh'trohfik/, **thyrotropic** /-'tropik/ *adj* exerting or characterized by a direct influence on the secreting activity of the thyroid gland ⟨~ *functions*⟩

**thyrotrophin** /‚thieroh'trohfin/, **thyrotropin** /-'trohpin/ *n* THYROID-STIMULATING HORMONE [*thyrotroph*ic, *thyrotrop*ic + *-in*]

**thyrotropic hormone** /‚thierə'tropik, -'trohpik/ *n* THYROID-STIMULATING HORMONE

**thyroxine** /thie'rokseen, -sin/, **thyroxin** /-sin/ *n* an iodine-containing AMINO ACID, $C_{15}H_{11}I_4NO_4$, that is the major hormone produced by the thyroid gland, and that is made synthetically or obtained from animal thyroid glands to treat conditions in which the thyroid gland produces insufficient quantities of hormones [ISV *thyr-* + *ox-* + *-ine, -in*]

**thyrse** /thuhs/ *n* THYRSUS 2 [NL *thyrsus*, fr L, thyrsus]

**thyrsus** /'thuhsəs/ *n, pl* **thyrsi** /-si/ **1** a staff surmounted by a pine cone or by a bunch of vine or ivy leaves with grapes or berries that was carried by Bacchus and his followers **2** a flower cluster (e g in the lilac and horse chestnut) with a long main stem bearing short branches which in turn bear the flowers [(1) L, fr Gk *thyrsos;* (2) NL, fr L]

**thysanopteran** /‚thiesə'noptərən/ *n* THRIPS (type of small insect) [deriv of Gk *thysanos* tassel + *pteron* wing – more at FEATHER] – **thysanopteran** *adj*

**thysanuran** /‚thisə'nyooərən/ *n* BRISTLETAIL (type of wingless insect) [deriv of Gk *thysanos* tassel + *oura* tail – more at SQUIRREL] – **thysanuran** *adj*

**thyself** /dhie'self/ *pron* that identical person that is thou; yourself – now chiefly dialect but sometimes used in ecclesiastical or literary language and by Quakers among themselves

**ti** *n, music* TE (seventh note of the musical scale in SOL-FA) [alter. of *si*]

**tiara** /ti'ahrə/ *n* **1** a tall headdress formerly worn by Persians and differing in style according to the wearer's status **2** a 3-tiered crown bearing an orb and cross that is worn by the pope **3** a decorative usu jewelled band or semicircle worn on the head by women on formal occasions [L, royal Persian headdress, fr Gk]

**Tibetan** /ti'bet(ə)n/ *n* **1a** a member of the Mongoloid people of Tibet modified in the west and south by intermixture with Indian peoples and in the east with Chinese **b** a native or inhabitant of Tibet **2** the Tibeto-Burman language of the Tibetans [*Tibet*, country in central Asia] – **Tibetan** *adj*

**Tibeto-Burman** /ti‚betoh 'buhmən/ *n* a language family of Asia considered by some to be part of the Sino-Tibetan family – **Tibeto-Burman** *adj*

**tibia** /'tibi·ə/ *n, pl* **tibiae** /'tibi·ie/ *also* **tibias 1** the inner and usu larger of the two bones of the hind limb of a VERTEBRATE animal between the knee and ankle – called also SHINBONE; compare FIBULA **2** the fourth joint of the leg of an insect between the femur and tarsus [L] – **tibial** *adj*

**tibiofibula** /ˌtibioh'fibyoolə/ *n* a bone of the hind limb, esp in frogs and toads, that is formed by fusion of the tibia and FIBULA [NL]

**tic** /tik/ *n* **1** (a) local and habitual spasmodic motion of particular muscles, esp of the face; twitching **2** a persistent trait of character or behaviour ⟨*"you know" is a verbal* ∼ *of many inexperienced speakers*⟩ [Fr]

**tical** /ti'kahl, 'tikl/ *n, pl* **ticals, tical** BAHT (monetary unit of Thailand) [Thai, fr Malay *tikal,* a monetary unit]

**tic douloureux** /ˌtik, doohlə'ruh (*Fr* tik dulurø)/ *n* TRIGEMINAL NEURALGIA (intense pain caused by a facial nerve) [Fr, painful twitch]

¹**tick** /tik/ *n* **1** any of numerous bloodsucking INVERTEBRATE animals related to the spiders and scorpions that form a superfamily (Ixodoidea of the order Acarina, class Arachnida), are larger than the related mites, and that feed on warm-blooded animals, often transmitting infectious diseases **2** any of various usu wingless parasitic insects (e g the sheep ked) **3** an irritating or contemptible person – formerly common among schoolchildren [ME *tyke, teke;* akin to MHG *zeche* tick, Arm *tiz*]

²**tick** *n* **1** a light rhythmic audible tap or beat; *also* a series of such sounds ⟨*the* ∼ *of the clock*⟩ **2** a small spot or mark typically √; *esp* one used to mark something as correct, to draw attention to something, to check an item on a list, or to represent a point on a scale – compare CROSS 5 **3** *chiefly Br informal* a moment, second ⟨*I'll be with you in a* ∼⟩ [ME *tek;* akin to MHG *zic* light push]

³**tick** *vi* **1** to make the sound of a tick or a series of ticks **2** to function or behave characteristically ⟨*I'd like to know what makes him* ∼⟩ ∼ *vt* **1** to mark with a written tick ⟨∼*ed each item on the list*⟩ – often + *off* **2** to mark or count (as if) by ticks ⟨*a meter* ∼*ing off the cab fare*⟩

  **tick off** *vt, informal* to scold, rebuke ⟨*his father* ticked *him* off *for his impudence*⟩

  **tick over** *vi* **1** *of an engine* to be turned on and running but with the transmission disengaged so that motion is impossible **2** to continue to operate smoothly but quietly or at a minimum level ⟨*the firm is still* ticking over *but profits will be well down on last year*⟩

⁴**tick** *n* **1** a strong coarse fabric case of a mattress, pillow, or bolster **2** TICKING (linen or cotton fabric) [ME *tike,* prob fr MD; akin to OHG *ziahha* tick; both fr a prehistoric WGmc word borrowed fr L *theca* cover, fr Gk *thēkē* case; akin to Gk *tithenai* to place – more at DO]

⁵**tick** *n, Br informal* credit, trust; *also* a credit account – chiefly in *on* tick [short for ¹*ticket*]

**tickbird** /-ˌbuhd/ *n* OXPECKER (type of African bird)

'**tick-ˌborne** *adj* capable of being transmitted by the bites of ticks ⟨*a* ∼ *disease*⟩

**ticked** /tikt/ *adj, of an animal's coat, bird's plumage, etc* having one or more small areas of hair, plumage, etc of a different colour from the main body; *also* having hairs or feathers of one colour tipped with another colour

**ticker** /'tikə/ *n* something that ticks or produces a ticking sound: e g **a** a watch **b** *NAm* TAPE MACHINE (machine that prints out information on paper tape) **c** *informal* HEART 1A

**ticker tape** *n* paper tape on which a TAPE MACHINE prints out information

¹**ticket** /'tikit/ *n* **1a** a document that serves as a certificate, licence, or permit; *esp* a mariner's or pilot's certificate **b** a tag, label **2** a usu printed card or slip of paper entitling its holder to the use of certain services (e g a library) or showing that a fare, admission fee, etc has been paid **3** *Br* a certificate of discharge from the armed forces ⟨*get one's* ∼⟩ **4** *chiefly NAm* a list of candidates for nomination or election; *also* PLATFORM 1 **5** *informal* an official notification issued to somebody who has violated a traffic regulation ⟨*was caught doing over 60 down the High Street, but talked her way out of being given a* ∼⟩ **6** *informal* the correct, proper, or desirable thing ⟨*hot sweet tea is just the* ∼ – *Len Deighton*⟩ [obs Fr *etiquet* (now *étiquette*) notice attached to something, fr MF *estiquet,* fr *estiquier* to attach, fr MD *steken* to stick; akin to OHG *sticken* to prick – more at STICK]

²**ticket** *vt* **1** to attach a ticket to; label **2** to set aside for a particular purpose; designate **3** *NAm* to furnish or serve with a ticket ⟨∼*ed for illegal parking*⟩

**ticket agent** *n* **1** one who sells tickets for travel by train, boat, aircraft, or bus, usu on behalf of the companies that run these services **2** somebody whose business is selling tickets on behalf of people or organizations (e g theatres)

**ticket office** *n* BOOKING OFFICE

ˌ**ticket-of-'leave** *n, pl* **tickets-of-leave** a licence or permit formerly granted in Britain and the Commonwealth allowing a convict who had served part of his sentence to be released on certain conditions

**tick fever** *n* any of various diseases transmitted by the bites of ticks

¹**ticking** /'tiking/ *n* a strong linen or cotton often striped fabric that is used esp as a covering for mattresses or pillows [⁴*tick*]

²**ticking** *n* ticked marking (e g on a bird or mammal or on individual hairs) [²*tick*]

¹**tickle** /'tikl/ *vi* to have or cause a tingling or prickling sensation ⟨*my back* ∼*s*⟩ ∼ *vt* **1a** to excite or stir up agreeably; please **b** to provoke to laughter or merriment; amuse ⟨*were* ∼*d by the clown's antics*⟩ **2** to touch (e g a body part) lightly and repeatedly so as to excite the surface nerves and cause uneasiness, laughter, or spasmodic movements [ME *tikelen;* akin to OE *tinclian* to tickle]

²**tickle** *n* **1** a tickling sensation **2** the act of tickling

³**tickle** *n, Can* a narrow strip of water (e g a strait or a narrow entrance to a harbour) between two stretches of land [perh fr E dial. *stickle* rapids, shallow water]

**tickler** /'tiklə/ *n* **1** somebody who or something that tickles **2** *chiefly Br informal* a difficult or delicate problem or situation **3** *NAm* a device for jogging the memory; *specif* a file that is arranged to bring matters to timely attention

**ticklish** /'tiklish/ *adj* **1** sensitive to tickling **2** easily upset; touchy ⟨∼ *about his baldness*⟩ **3** requiring delicate handling; critical ⟨*a* ∼ *subject*⟩ – **ticklishly** *adv,* **ticklishness** *n*

**ticktacktoe** *also* ˌ**tic-tac-'toe** /ˌtiktak'toh/ *n, NAm* NOUGHTS AND CROSSES [*tic-tac-toe* (former game in which players with eyes shut brought a pencil down on a slate marked with numbers and scored the number hit)]

**ticktock** /'tik,tok, ,-'-/ *n* the rhythmic ticking sound of a clock [imit]

**ticky-tacky** /'tiki ,taki/ *n, NAm* sleazy or shoddy material [prob redupl of ²*tacky*]

**tic tac, tick tack** /'tik ,tak/ *n* **1** *Br* a secret system of hand signals used by bookmakers at a race meeting to give one another information about the state of betting **2** *NAm* ticktock [imit]

**tic tac man** /'tik ,tak ,man/ *n, Br* a bookmaker's assistant who signals changing odds at a race meeting using TIC TAC

**tidal** /'tiedl/ *adj* **1a** of, caused by, or having tides ⟨∼ *cycles*⟩ ⟨∼ *erosion*⟩ **b** periodically rising and falling or flowing and ebbing ⟨∼ *waters*⟩ **2** dependent (e g as to the time of arrival or departure) upon the state of the tide ⟨*a* ∼ *steamer*⟩ – **tidally** *adv*

**tidal volume** *n* the volume of air taken in and expelled in one inhalation and exhalation of a person at rest

**tidal wave** *n* **1a** TSUNAMI (high wave following earthquake, eruption, etc) **b** an unusual rise of water alongshore due to strong winds **2a** an unexpected, intense, and often widespread reaction (e g a sweeping majority vote or an overwhelming impulse) **b** an overwhelming quantity or influx ⟨*a great* ∼ *of books* – Benny Green⟩

**tidbit** /'tid,bit/ *n, NAm* a titbit

**tiddledywink** /'tidli,wingk/ *n* a tiddlywink

**tiddledywinks** /'tidli,wingks/ *n taking sing vb* tiddlywinks [prob fr E dial. *tiddly* little]

**tiddler** /'tidlə/ *n, Br* somebody or something small in comparison to others of the same kind; *esp* a minnow, stickleback, or other small fish [prob fr *tiddly* + ²*-er*]

**tiddly** /'tidli/ *adj, Br informal* **1** very small ⟨*a* ∼ *bit of food*⟩ **2** slightly drunk [prob alter. of *little*]

**tiddlywink** /'tidli,wingk/ *n* a small flat disc or counter (similar to one) used in the game of tiddlywinks [prob fr *tiddly*]

**tiddlywinks** /'tidli,wingks/ *n taking sing vb* a game whose object is to flick small discs from a flat surface into a small container with a larger disc

**tiddy oggy** /'tidi/ *n* OGGY (Cornish pasty) [*tiddy* (prob alter. of *tatie*) + *oggy,* of unknown origin]

¹**tide** /tied/ *n* **1a(1)** (a current of water resulting from) the periodic rise and fall of the surface of a body of water, esp the sea, that occurs usu twice a day and is caused by the gravitational attraction of the sun and moon **a(2)** a periodic movement in the earth's crust caused by the same forces that produce ocean tides **a(3)** a tidal distortion on one planet, moon, etc caused by the gravitational attraction of another **a(4)** one of the tidal movements of the atmosphere resembling those of the ocean

but produced by daily temperature changes **b** the level or position of water on a shore with respect to the tide; *also* the water at its highest level **2** something that fluctuates like the tides of the sea ⟨*the ~ of public opinion*⟩ **3** *chiefly poetic* **3a** a flowing stream; a current **b** *chiefly pl* the waters of the ocean **4a** a space of time; a period – now used only in combination ⟨*noontide*⟩ **b** *archaic* a fit or opportune time; an opportunity **c** (the season of) an ecclesiastical anniversary or festival – now used only in combination ⟨*Eastertide*⟩ – see also SWIM **against the tide** [ME, time, fr OE *tīd;* akin to OHG *zīt* time, Gk *daiesthai* to divide] – **tideless** *adj*

²**tide** *vi* **1** to flow in or like a tide; surge **2** to drift with the tide, esp in navigating a ship into or out of an anchorage, harbour, or river

   **tide over** *vt* to enable to live through or cope with, esp by providing with money, food, etc ⟨*gave me £10 to tide me over the weekend*⟩

**tideland** /'tied‚land, -lənd/ *n,* **tidelands** *n pl, chiefly NAm* land in the zone between low and high water marks

**tidemark** /-‚mahk/ *n* **1a** a high-water or sometimes low-water mark left by tidal water or a flood **b** a mark placed to indicate this point **2** the point which something has reached or below which it has receded ⟨*the ~ of the enemy advance*⟩ **3** *informal* a mark left on a bath that shows the level reached by the water; *also* a mark left on the body showing the limit of washing

**tide table** *n* a table that indicates the height of the tide at one place at different times of day throughout the year

**tidewaiter** /-‚waytə/ *n* a customs inspector formerly working on the docks or aboard ships

**tidewater** /-‚wawtə/ *n* **1a** water overflowing land at flood tide **b** *chiefly NAm* water (e g rivers and streams) affected by the ebb and flow of the tide **2** *NAm* low-lying coastal land

**tideway** /-‚way/ *n* (a current in) a channel in which the tide runs

**tidings** /'tiedingz/ *n pl* news, information ⟨*good ~ of great joy*⟩ [ME *tiding* event, piece of news, fr OE *tīdung,* fr *tīdan* to happen – more at BETIDE]

¹**tidy** /'tiedi/ *adj* **1a** neat and orderly in appearance or habits; well ordered and cared for **b** methodical, precise ⟨*a ~ mind*⟩ **2** *informal* large, substantial ⟨*a ~ profit*⟩ *synonyms* see ²NEAT *antonyms* untidy, disorderly [ME, timely, in good condition, fr *tide* time] – **tidily** *adv,* **tidiness** *n*

²**tidy** *vt* to put in order; make neat or tidy ~ *vi* to make things tidy □ often + *up* – **tidier** *n*

³**tidy** *n* **1a** a receptacle for odds and ends (e g sewing materials) **b sink tidy, tidy** a small often triangular receptacle, usu with drainage holes, for wet kitchen waste (e g potato peelings) **2** *chiefly NAm* a usu decorative (e g embroidered) cover used to protect the back, arms, or headrest of a chair or sofa from wear or dirt – compare ANTIMACASSAR

¹**tie** /tie/ *n* **1a** a line, ribbon, or cord used for fastening, uniting, or drawing something together **b** a rod, beam, etc holding two pieces of a structure together **2** something that serves as a connecting link: e g **2a** a moral or legal obligation to somebody or something that restricts freedom of action **b** a bond of kinship or affection **3** a curved line that joins two musical notes of the same pitch to denote a single sustained note with the time value of the two **4a** a match or game between two teams, players, etc in a championship or other knockout contest ⟨*a cup ~*⟩ **b** (a contest that ends in) a draw or dead heat **5** a narrow length of material designed to be worn, esp by men, round the neck under the collar of a shirt and tied in a knot in the front **6** *NAm* SLEEPER (piece of stone, metal, etc supporting railway track) [ME *teg, tye,* fr OE *tēag;* akin to ON *taug* rope, OE *tēon* to pull – more at TOW] – **tieless** *adj*

²**tie** *vb* **tying, tieing** *vt* **1a** to fasten, attach, or close by knotting **b** to form a knot or bow in ⟨*~ your scarf*⟩ **c** to make by tying constituent elements ⟨*~d a wreath*⟩ ⟨*~ a fishing fly*⟩ **d** to make a bond or connection **2a** to unite in marriage **b** to unite (musical notes) by a tie **c** to join (power systems) electrically **3** to restrain from independence or freedom of action or choice; constrain (as if) by authority or obligation – often + *down* ⟨*family responsibilities have always ~d her down*⟩ **4a** to even (the score) in a game or contest **b** to make an equal score in (a game) ~ *vi* **1** to make a tie; esp to make or have an equal score ⟨*they ~d for first place*⟩ – see also **have one's** HANDS **tied, tie oneself/somebody up in** KNOTS, **tie the** KNOT – **tier** *n*

   **tie in** *vt* to bring into connection *with;* coordinate ⟨*the illustrations were cleverly tied in with the text*⟩ ~ *vi* to be closely connected; *esp* to correspond ⟨*that ties in with what I know already*⟩ – see also TIE-IN

**tie up** *vt* **1** to attach, fasten, or bind securely; *also* to wrap up and fasten **2** to connect closely; link **3a** to place or invest in such a manner as to make unavailable for other purposes ⟨*his money was tied up in stocks*⟩ **b** to subject (e g property or a bequest) to legal conditions preventing sale or misuse **4a** to keep busy ⟨*was tied up in conference all day*⟩ **b** to make use of, esp to the exclusion of others **5** *chiefly NAm* to restrain from operation or progress ⟨*traffic was tied up for miles*⟩ ~ *vi* **1** to dock ⟨*the ferry ties up at the far quay*⟩ **2** to have a definite relationship; correspond ⟨*this ties up with what you were told before*⟩ – see also TIE-UP

‚**tie-and-'dye** *n* TIE-DYEING (method of dyeing textiles)

'**tie-‚beam** *n* a beam that acts as a tie; *esp* a beam connecting the lower ends of opposite principal rafters to prevent them from spreading apart

**tie break, tie breaker** *n* a contest or game used to select a winner from among contestants with tied scores; *esp* a means of establishing the winner of a set in tennis which has gone to six games all, consisting of a game played for the best of twelve points, or, if the score remains equal, until one player is two points ahead of the other

**tie clip** *n* a pin or clasp used to hold a tie in place

**tied cottage** /tied/ *n, chiefly Br* a cottage or house owned by an employer (e g a farmer) and reserved for occupancy by an employee

**tied house** *n* a public house in Britain that is bound to sell only the products of the brewery that owns it or rents it out – compare FREE HOUSE

'**tie-‚dye** *n* tie-dyeing

‚**tie-'dyeing** *n* a method of producing patterns in textiles by tying portions of the fabric or yarn so that they will not absorb the dye – **tie-dyed** *adj*

'**tie-‚in** *n* **1** something that ties in, relates, or connects **2** a book, record, or other material produced to coincide with the screening, broadcast, or performance of the work (e g a film or television production) which it has inspired or from which it is adapted

**tiemannite** /'teemaniet/ *n* a dark grey mineral that consists of the chemical compound mercuric selenide, HgSe [Ger *tiemannit,* fr W *Tiemann,* 19th-c Ger scientist who discovered it]

**tiepin** /-‚pin/ *n* a decorative pin used to hold the ends of a tie in place

¹**tier** /tiə/ *n* **1** a row, rank, or layer of articles; *esp* any of two or more rows or ranks arranged one above another ⟨*a three-tier wedding cake*⟩ **2** any of a series of levels or gradations (e g in an administration) ⟨*the top ~ of local government*⟩ [MF *tire* order, rank – more at ATTIRE]

²**tier** *vt* to place or arrange in tiers ~ *vi* to rise in tiers

¹**tierce** /tiəs, tuhs/ *n* TERCE (third of the daily services of Christian, esp Roman Catholic, worship)

²**tierce** *n* **1** any of various formerly used units of liquid capacity equal to ¹/₃ pipe (about 159 litres) **2** a sequence of three playing cards of the same suit **3** *obs* THIRD **1** [ME *terce, tierce,* third part, fr MF, fr fem of *terz,* adj, third, fr L *tertius* – more at THIRD]

**tiercel** /'tiəsl/ *n* TERCEL (male hawk)

**tiered** /tiəd/ *adj* having a usu specified number of tiers – usu in combination

'**tie-‚rod** *n* a rod (e g of steel) usu acting in tension, that is used to connect or hold in place two parts (e g in a vehicle)

**tie silk** *n* a silk fabric of firm resilient pliable texture used for ties and for blouses and accessories

'**tie-‚up** *n* **1** a connection, association ⟨*a political ~ with gangsters*⟩ **2** *chiefly NAm* a suspension or delay of an action, activity, or process; *specif* a traffic jam

**tiff** /tif/ *vi or n* (to have) a petty quarrel *synonyms* see ²QUARREL [origin unknown]

**tiffany** /'tifəni/ *n* a sheer silk gauze formerly used for clothing and trimmings [prob fr obs Fr *tiphanie* Epiphany, fr LL *theophania,* fr LGk, deriv of Gk *theos* god + *phainein* to show]

**tiffin** /'tifin/ *n* a meal or snack taken at midday or in the middle of the morning – used esp by British people living in India during British rule [prob alter. of *tiffing,* gerund of obs *tiff* to drink, eat between meals]

**tiger** /'tiegə/, *fem* **tigress** /'tiegris /tiegə/ *n, pl* **tigers,** (1) **tigers,** *esp collectively* **tiger 1a** a very large Asiatic flesh-eating big cat (*Panthera tigris*) having a tawny coat striped crossways with black **b** a domestic cat with a striped coat pattern **2** a fierce and often cruel or bloodthirsty person or quality **3** *Br archaic* a groom dressed in livery; *esp* a young boy working as a groom

[ME *tigre,* fr OE *tiger* & OF *tigre,* both fr L *tigris,* fr Gk, of Iranian origin; akin to Av *tighra-* pointed; akin to Gk *stizein* to tattoo – more at STICK] – **tigerish** *adj,* **tigerishly** *adv,* **tigerishness** *n,* **tigerlike** *adj*

**tiger beetle** *n* any of numerous active flesh-eating beetles (family Cicindelidae) having larvae that tunnel in the soil

**tiger cat** *n* **1** any of various medium-sized wildcats (eg the SERVAL or OCELOT) with striped or otherwise variegated coats **2** a striped or sometimes blotched tabby cat

**tiger lily** *n* an Asiatic lily (*Lilium tigrinum*) commonly grown for its drooping orange-coloured flowers densely spotted with black; *also* any of various lilies with similar flowers

**tiger moth** *n* any of a family (Arctiidae) of stout-bodied moths usu with broad striped or spotted wings

**tiger salamander** *n* a widely distributed N American salamander (*Ambystoma tigrinum*) that is brown or black above with vertical yellowish blotches on the sides that often run together underneath

**'tiger's-,eye** *also* **tigereye** *n* a usu yellowish-brown gemstone that is used esp in jewellery and is a form of the mineral CROCIDOLITE impregnated with silica

**tiger shark** *n* a large grey or brown stout-bodied shark (*Galeocerdo cuvieri* or *Galeocerdo arcticus*) that is dangerous to man and is found in most parts of the world, esp in warm seas

**tiger snake** *n* any of several venomous Australian snakes (genus *Notechis*), usu having dark stripes on the back; *esp* one (*Notechis scutatus*) with brown and yellow markings and an often fatal bite

**'tight** /tiet/ *adj* **1** so close or solid in structure as to prevent passage (eg of a liquid or gas); impervious ⟨*a ~ roof*⟩ – often in combination ⟨*an airtight compartment*⟩ **2a** fixed very firmly in place ⟨*loosen a ~ jar cover*⟩ **b** firmly stretched, drawn, or set ⟨*a ~ drumhead*⟩ ⟨*a ~ knot*⟩ **c** fitting usu too closely (eg for comfort) ⟨*~ shoes*⟩ **3** set close together ⟨*a ~ defensive formation in football*⟩ **4** forming a small usu acute angle ⟨*the aeroplane made a ~ turn in the air*⟩ **5** difficult to get through or out of; difficult ⟨*in a ~ situation*⟩ ⟨*a ~ spot*⟩ **6** well ordered or controlled ⟨*ran a ~ ship*⟩ **7** evenly contested; close ⟨*a ~ match*⟩ **8** packed, compressed or condensed to (near) the limit ⟨*a ~ bale*⟩ ⟨*a ~ literary style*⟩ ⟨*~ schedule*⟩ **9** closely spaced ⟨*a ~ line of print*⟩ **10a** difficult to obtain; scarce; *specif, of money* difficult to borrow, esp because of high demand or interest rates **b** *of a market* marked by scarcity **11** playing in unison ⟨*his three week old band was surprisingly ~ – The Age (Melbourne)*⟩ **12** *of timber* sound and free of flaws **13** *informal* stingy, miserly **14** *informal* drunk **synonyms** see STINGY **antonym** loose [ME, alter. of *thight,* of Scand origin; akin to ON *thēttr* tight; akin to MHG *dīhte* thick, Skt *tanakti* it causes to coagulate] – **tightly** *adv,* **tightness** *n* – **sit tight** to maintain one's position

**²tight** *adv* **1** fast, tightly ⟨*the door was shut ~*⟩ **2** in a sound manner; soundly, well ⟨*sleep ~*⟩

*usage* The adverbs **tight** and **tightly** can each mean "firm, fast" ⟨*the door was shut* **tight/tightly**⟩ but only **tightly** is used before a past participle ⟨*their hands were* **tightly** *clasped*⟩ and only **tight** in the phrase *sleep* **tight**.

**tighten** /'tiet(ə)n/ *vb* to make or become tight or tighter

**tighten up** *vb* to make or become more firm or severe – usu + *on* ⟨*the government is tightening up on tax dodgers*⟩

**tightfisted** /-'fistid/ *adj, informal* reluctant to part with money; TIGHT 13 **synonyms** see STINGY

**,tight-'lipped** *adj* **1** having the lips compressed (eg in determination or anger) **2** reluctant to speak; taciturn **synonyms** see SILENT

**tightrope** /-,rohp/ *n* **1** a rope or wire stretched taut high above the ground for acrobats to perform on **2** a dangerously precarious situation

**tights** /tiets/ *n pl, chiefly Br* a one-piece skintight garment covering the legs and usu also the feet and reaching to the waist

**tightwad** /'tiet,wod/ *n, chiefly NAm slang* a mean or miserly person

**tightwire** /'tiet,wie·ə/ *n* a tightrope made of wire

**tigon** /'tiegən/ *n* a hybrid offspring produced by a mating between a male tiger and a lioness [*tiger* + *lion*]

**Tigré** /'teegray/ *n* a Semitic language of NE Ethiopia

**tigress** /'tiegris/ *n* **1** a female tiger **2** an aggressive or passionate woman

**Tigrinya** /ti'greenyə/ *n* a Semitic language of N Ethiopia

**tike** /tiek/ *n* TYKE

**tiki** /'teeki/ *n* a Polynesian, esp Maori, image of an ancestor, either large and made of wood, or small and made of greenstone, often in the form of a pendant [Maori & Marquesan, fr *Tiki,* first man or creator of first man]

**til** /til, teel/ *n* SESAME (plant producing small edible seeds) [Hindi, fr Skt *tila*]

**tilapia** /ti'lapiə, -'laypiə/ *n* any of a genus (*Tilapia* of the family Cichlidae) of African freshwater fishes used as food [NL, genus name]

**tilbury** /'tilbəri/ *n* a light 2-wheeled horse-drawn carriage [*Tilbury,* 19th-c E coach builder]

**tilde** /'tildə/ *n* **1** a mark ˜ placed esp over the letter *n* (eg in Spanish *señor*) to denote the sound /ny/ or over vowels (eg in Portuguese *irmã*) to indicate nasality **2** the mark ~ (SWUNG DASH); *esp* one used in logic and mathematics to indicate esp negation or approximation [Sp, fr ML *titulus* tittle]

**¹tile** /tiel/ *n* **1** a thin slab of fired clay, stone, or concrete shaped according to use: eg **1a** a flat or curved slab for use on roofs **b** a flat and often ornamented slab for floors, walls, or surrounds **c** a tube-shaped or semicircular and open slab for constructing drains **2** a thin piece of resilient material (eg cork, linoleum, or rubber) used esp for covering floors or walls **3** (a surface of) tiles **4** a square or rectangular piece of wood, plastic, bone, or other material usu bearing special markings or figures, and used in playing certain games (eg mah-jong or scrabble) **5** *informal* a hat; *esp* SILK HAT [ME, fr OE *tigele;* akin to ON *tigl* tile; both fr a prehistoric WGmc-NGmc word borrowed fr L *tegula;* akin to L *tegere* to cover – more at THATCH] – **on the tiles** *informal* enjoying oneself socially, esp in an intemperate or wild manner ⟨*looks terrible this morning after a night out* on the tiles⟩ [fr the nocturnal prowling of cats on roofs]

**²tile** *vt* **1** to cover with tiles **2** to install drainage tiles in – **tiler** *n,* **tiling** *n*

**tilestone** /'tiel,stohn/ *n* stone suitable for use for roofing tiles

**¹till** /til, tl/ *prep* **1** until **2** *chiefly Scot* to *usage* see ¹UNTIL [ME, fr OE *til;* akin to ON *til* to, till, OE *til* good]

**²till** *conj* until

**³till** /til/ *vt* to work (eg land) by ploughing, sowing, and raising crops; cultivate [ME *tilien, tillen,* fr OE *tilian;* akin to OE *til* good, suitable, OHG *zil* goal] – **tillable** *adj,* **tiller** *n*

**⁴till** *n* **1a** a receptacle (eg a drawer or tray) in which money is kept in a shop or bank **b** CASH REGISTER **2** the money contained in a till [AF *tylle*]

**⁵till** *n* glacial drift consisting of clay, sand, gravel, and boulders intermingled rather than deposited in distinct layers [origin unknown]

**tillage** *n* **1** the operation of tilling land **2** cultivated land

**¹tiller** /'tilə/ *n* a lever used to steer a boat by moving the rudder from side to side [ME *tiler* stock of a crossbow, fr MF *telier,* lit., beam of a loom, fr ML *telarium,* fr L *tela* web – more at TOIL]

**²tiller** *n* a sprout, stalk; *esp* one growing from the base of a plant [(assumed) ME, fr OE *telgor, telgra* twig, shoot; akin to OHG *zelga* twig, Gk *daidalos* ingeniously formed – more at CONDOLE]

**³tiller** *vi, of a plant* to put forth tillers

**¹tilt** /tilt/ *vt* **1** to cause to slope ⟨*don't ~ the boat*⟩ **2a** to point or thrust (as if) in a tilt ⟨*~ a lance*⟩ **b** to charge against in a tilt ⟨*~ an adversary*⟩ ~ *vi* **1** to move or shift so as to lean or incline; slant **2** to engage in a combat with lances; joust [ME *tulten, tilten;* akin to Sw *tulta* to waddle] – **tiltable** *adj,* **tilter** *n*

**tilt at** *vt* **1** to aim or charge at with a lance **2** to make a verbal or written attack on – see also **tilt at** WINDMILLS

**²tilt** *n* **1a** a contest on horseback in which two combatants charging with lances or similar weapons try to unhorse each other; *also* an exercise or contest in which a mounted person charges at a mark **b** a thrust or charge with a lance or similar weapon **2a** a written or verbal attack – + *at* ⟨*produced a ~ at my critics*⟩ **b** a dispute, altercation ⟨*had a ~ with her boss*⟩ **c** speed, pace – chiefly in (*at*) *full tilt* **3a** the act of tilting; the state or position of being tilted **b** a sloping surface – **tilt** *adj*

**³tilt** *n* a usu canvas awning or canopy, esp for a wagon, boat, lorry or stall [ME *teld, telte* tent, canopy, fr OE *teld;* akin to OHG *zelt* tent]

**⁴tilt** *vt* to cover or provide with a tilt

**tilth** /tilth, tildh/ *n* **1** TILLAGE **2** the state of being tilled; *also* the condition of tilled land ⟨*land in good ~*⟩ **3** the state of aggregation of a soil produced by cultivation [ME, fr OE, fr *tilian* to till]

**tiltyard** /'tilt,yahd/ *n* a yard or place for tilting contests

**timbal** /'timbl/ *n, archaic* a kettledrum [Fr *timbale*, fr MF, alter. of *tamballe*, modif of OSp *atabal*, fr Ar *aṭ-ṭabl* the drum

**timbale** /'timbayl/ *n* 1 a creamy mixture of meat, fish, or vegetables baked in a cup-shaped mould; *also* the mould in which it is baked 2 a small pastry shell filled with a cooked timbale mixture [Fr, lit., kettledrum]

¹**timber** /'timbə/ *n* 1a growing trees or their wood b – used interjectionally to warn of a falling tree 2 wood that is suitable and has been dressed for carpentry, woodwork, or building 3a a large squared or dressed piece of wood ready for use or forming part of a structure b RIB 2a(1) (piece of wood forming part of a ship's frame) [ME, fr OE, building, wood; akin to OHG *zimbar* wood, room, L *domus* house, Gk *demein* to build] – **timber** *adj*, **timberman** *n*

²**timber** *vt* to frame, cover, or support with timbers

**timbered** /'timbəd/ *adj* 1 having walls framed by exposed timbers 2 covered with growing trees; wooded

**timber hitch** *n* a knot used to secure a line to a log or spar

**timbering** /'timb(ə)ring/ *n* (a set or arrangement of) timbers

**timberland** /'timbə,land/ *n, chiefly NAm* land covered with trees grown esp for commercial reasons

**timberline** /-,lien/ *n* TREE LINE (upper limit of tree growth)

**timber wolf** *n* a wolf (*Canis lupus lycaon*) formerly common over much of NE America

**timberwork** /'timbə,wuhk/ *n* a construction made of timber

**timbre** /'tambə, 'timbə, 'tahmbə/ (*Fr* tɛ̃:br) *also* **timber** /'timbə/ *n* the quality given to a sound by its overtones: e g a the resonance by which the ear recognizes and identifies a voiced speech sound b the quality of tone distinctive of a particular singing voice or musical instrument [Fr, fr MF, bell struck by a hammer, fr OF, drum, fr MGk *tymbanon* kettledrum, fr Gk *tympanon* – more at TYMPANUM]

**timbrel** /'timbrəl/ *n* a tambourine or small hand drum [dim. of obs *timbre* tambourine, fr ME, fr OF, drum]

¹**time** /tiem/ *n* 1a the measured or measurable period during which an action, process, or condition exists or continues; duration b a continuum in which events succeed one another from past through present to future ⟨*stand the test of* ~⟩ c free hours, days, etc; leisure ⟨*never have* ~ *to go out*⟩ 2a the point or period when something occurs; occasion ⟨*at the* ~ *of writing*⟩ b the period required for or taken up by the completion of an action ⟨*the winner's* ~ *was under four minutes*⟩ ⟨*our travelling* ~ *was about six hours*⟩ 3a a moment or period set aside or suitable for an activity or event ⟨*now is the* ~⟩ ⟨*a* ~ *for celebration*⟩ b an appointed, fixed, or customary moment or hour for something to happen, begin, or end ⟨*arrived ahead of* ~⟩; *esp, Br* closing time in a public house as fixed by law ⟨*hurry up please, it's* ~ – T S Eliot⟩ c a finite but unspecified interval ⟨*were happy enough for a* ~⟩ **4a time, times** *pl* a historical period; an age ⟨*modern* ~s⟩ ⟨*in the* ~ *of Elizabeth I*⟩ b a division of geological chronology c **times** *pl*, **time** conditions or circumstances prevalent during a period ⟨~s *are hard*⟩ ⟨*move with the* ~s⟩ d the present time ⟨*issues of the* ~⟩ e the expected moment of giving birth or dying ⟨*her* ~ *is near*⟩ f the end or course of a future period ⟨*only* ~ *will tell*⟩ ⟨*will happen in* ~⟩ 5a lifetime; *specif* the most successful period of one's life ⟨*was a great dancer in her* ~⟩ b a period of apprenticeship c a term of military service d *informal* a prison sentence ⟨*doing* ~ *for arson*⟩ 6 a season ⟨*very hot for this* ~ *of year*⟩ 7a a tempo b the grouping of the beats of music; a rhythm, metre 8a a moment, hour, day, or year as measured or indicated by a clock or calendar ⟨*what* ~ *is it?*⟩ b any of various systems (e g sidereal or solar) of reckoning time ⟨*Greenwich mean* ~⟩ 9a any of a series of recurring instances or repeated actions ⟨*you've been told many* ~s⟩ b *pl* b(1) multiplied instances ⟨*five* ~s *greater*⟩ b(2) equal fractional parts of which a specified number equal a comparatively greater quantity ⟨*seven* ~s *smaller*⟩ ⟨*three* ~s *closer*⟩ 10 an occasion or interval having a specified quality ⟨*a good* ~⟩ 11a the hours or days occupied by one's work ⟨*make up* ~⟩ b an hourly rate of pay ⟨*on double* ~⟩ 12 the end of the playing time of (a section of) a game – often used as an interjection [ME, fr OE *tīma*; akin to ON *tími* time, OE *tīd* – more at TIDE] – **against time** as fast as possible in order to finish within a limited period ⟨*racing against time to finish her work*⟩ – **ahead of time** earlier than necessary or expected – **ahead of one's time** having ideas too original or progressive for one's own day – **all in good time** when the occasion is right; IN DUE COURSE – **at times** at intervals; occasionally – **be high time** to be immediately necessary ⟨*it* is high time *you bought a new coat*⟩ – **behind the times** old-fashioned – **bide one's time** to wait until the appropriate time comes to initiate action or to proceed – **for the time being** for the present – **from time to time** at irregular intervals – **have no time for** to be unable or reluctant to spend time on; be unable to tolerate – **in good time** 1 at the right time 2 with time to spare; early – **in no time (at all)** very soon ⟨*will be here in no time*⟩ – **in time** 1 sufficiently early ⟨*arrived* in time *to catch the train*⟩ 2 eventually ⟨in time *he realized the error of his ways*⟩ 3 in correct tempo ⟨*learn to play* in time⟩ – **mark time** 1 to keep the time of a marching step by moving the feet alternately without advancing 2 to function listlessly or unproductively while waiting to progress or advance – **on time** at the appointed time – **pass the time of day** to exchange greetings or pleasantries (*with*) – **play for time** to act in a way that delays an action, event, etc until a time more favourable to oneself – **take one's time** to do something at a comfortable or leisurely pace – **time and (time) again** frequently, repeatedly – **time out of mind** a time longer ago than anyone can recall; TIME IMMEMORIAL 2 – see also **in the** NICK **of time**

**synonyms** If one arrives **in time** one may be early, but if one arrives **on time** one is neither early nor late.

²**time** *vt* 1 to arrange or set the time of; schedule ⟨*his departure is* ~d *for 4 o'clock*⟩ 2 to regulate the moment, speed, or duration of, esp to achieve the desired or maximum effect ⟨~d *his entrance well*⟩ ⟨~d *the exposure for one second*⟩ 3 to cause to keep time with something ⟨~d *her steps to the music*⟩ 4 to determine or record the time, duration, or speed of ⟨~ *a journey*⟩ ~ *vi* to keep or beat time ⟨*beat, happy stars,* timing *with things below* – Alfred Tennyson⟩

³**time** *adj* 1 of or recording time 2 (able to be) timed to function at a specific moment ⟨*a* ~ *bomb*⟩ ⟨*a* ~ *switch*⟩ 3a payable on a specified future day or a certain length of time after presentation for acceptance ⟨~ *loan*⟩ b based on payment by instalment or hire purchase ⟨*a* ~ *sale*⟩

**time and a half** *n* payment of a worker (e g for overtime) at one and a half times the regular wage rate

**time and motion** *adj* of or concerned with studying the efficiency of working methods, esp in industry

**time capsule** *n* a container holding historical records or objects representative of current culture that is deposited (e g in the foundations of a building) for preservation until discovery by those alive in some future age

**time card** *n* a card used with a TIME CLOCK to record an employee's starting and finishing times each day or on each job

**time chart** *n* 1 a chart showing the standard times in various parts of the world with reference to a specified time at a specified place 2 a table listing important events for successive years within a particular historical period

**time clock** *n* a clock that stamps an employee's starting and finishing times on a TIME CARD

'**time-con,suming** *adj* using or taking up a great deal of or too much time ⟨~ *chores*⟩ ⟨~ *tactics*⟩

**time deposit** *n* a bank deposit from which money may be withdrawn after advance notice to the bank has been given or a specified period of time has elapsed – compare DEMAND DEPOSIT

**time dilation** *n* a slowing of time observed when a body moves at a speed approaching that of light relative to the observer as predicted by the theory of RELATIVITY

**time exposure** *n* (a photograph taken by) exposure of a photographic film for a relatively long time, usu more than one second

'**time-,honoured** *adj* respected because of age or long usage ⟨~ *traditions*⟩

**time immemorial** /imi'mawri·əl/ *n* 1 *law* time before the keeping of officially recognized legal records, which according to English law is prior to the beginning of Richard I's reign in 1189 2 time so long past as to be beyond living memory or historical record

**timekeeper** /-,keepə/ *n* 1 a timepiece; *also* a clock that keeps time in a specified way ⟨*that old watch of your grandfather's is a good* ~⟩ 2 somebody or something that records time or times (e g the amount worked by employees) 3 an official who records the times of athletic events, the length of time a match has been in progress, etc – **timekeeping** *n*

**time killer** *n* something that passes the time; a diversion

**time lag** *n* an interval of time between two related phenomena (e g a cause and its effect)

'time-,lapse *adj* of or constituting a method of cinema photography in which a slow action (eg the opening of a flower bud) is filmed in successive stages so as to appear speeded up on the screen

timeless /-lis/ *adj* 1a unending, eternal b not restricted to a particular time or date ⟨*the ~ themes of love, solitude, joy, and nature – Writer*⟩ 2 not affected by time; ageless – **timelessly** *adv*, **timelessness** *n*

time limit *n* a fixed period within which something must be done

¹timely /'tiemli/ *adv* 1 in time; opportunely 2 *archaic* early, soon

²timely *adj* occurring at an appropriate time; opportune ⟨*a ~ intervention*⟩ – **timeliness** *n*

timeous /'tiemos/ *adj*, *chiefly Scot* timely – **timeously** *adv*

,time-'out *n*, *chiefly NAm* a brief suspension of activity; a break; *esp* a suspension of play in any of several sports (eg basketball)

timepiece /-,pees/ *n* a device (eg a clock or watch) to measure or show progress of time; *esp* one that does not chime

time policy *n* a marine insurance policy covering property for a specified period – compare VOYAGE POLICY

timer /'tiemə/ *n* somebody who or something that times: eg a a timepiece; *esp* a stopwatch for timing races b TIMEKEEPER c a device in the ignition system of an INTERNAL-COMBUSTION ENGINE that causes the spark to be produced in the cylinder at the correct time d a device (eg a clock or hourglass) that can be set to give an indication (eg a sound) when an interval of time has passed or that starts or stops a device at predetermined times

time reversal *n* a formal operation in mathematical physics that reverses the order in which a sequence of events occurs

times /tiemz/ *prep* multiplied by ⟨*two ~ two is four*⟩
**usage** The expression **times** *greater* ⟨*production is six* **times** *greater than in 1980*⟩ is misleading, since one could not say △ *once greater*. A clearer way to express the idea is ⟨*production is six* **times** *as great as in 1980*⟩.

timesaving /'tiem,sayving/ *adj* serving to shorten the amount of time necessary for a process, activity, etc – **time-saver** *n*

time scale *n* 1 the amount of time allotted for the completion of something ⟨*the ~ for the talks was of years rather than months*⟩ 2 a specified system of measuring time viewed esp in terms of the size of its typical units ⟨*on the ~ of modern cosmology – TLS*⟩

timeserver /-,suhvə/ *n* a person who fits his/her behaviour and ideas to the prevailing opinions of the time or of his/her superiors; a temporizer ⟨*a spineless ~ conniving at his bosses' activities*⟩

'time-,sharing *n* 1 simultaneous access to a computer by many users 2 a scheme whereby a number of people rent or buy a flat, villa, or other holiday accommodation jointly, thus being entitled to a fixed period in the accommodation each year, the length of which depends on the amount of money paid

time sheet *n* 1 a sheet for recording an employee's starting and finishing times each day or on each job 2 a sheet for summarizing hours worked by each worker during a pay period

time signature *n* a sign placed on a musical stave being usu a fraction (eg $\frac{3}{4}$ or $\frac{12}{8}$) whose lower figure indicates the kind of note taken as the time unit for the beat (eg four for a crotchet or eight for a quaver) and whose upper figure indicates the number of beats per bar

times sign *n* MULTIPLICATION SIGN

time switch *n* an electrical switch that operates automatically at a set time

¹timetable /'tiem,taybl/ *n* 1 a table of departure and arrival times of trains, buses, aeroplanes, or other forms of transport 2 a schedule showing a planned order or sequence of events; *specif* a schedule showing the times of classes (eg in a school or university)

²timetable *vt* to include or provide for in a timetable ⟨*not able to ~ the meeting for next week*⟩

time trial *n* a race against the clock, esp in bicycle racing, in which competitors are successively timed over a set distance or in which distance travelled is measured for a set time – **time trialing** *n*, **time trialist** *n*

time warp *n* an imaginary distortion of time in which the usual rules governing its progression do not apply; *broadly* a

period (eg of one's life) during which nothing seems to change or progress

timework /'tiem,wuhk/ *n* work paid for at a standard rate for the hour or the day – compare PIECEWORK – **timeworker** *n*

timeworn /-,wawn/ *adj* 1 worn or impaired by time ⟨*~ mansions*⟩ 2 age-old, ancient ⟨*~ procedures*⟩

time zone *n* a geographical region within which the same STANDARD TIME is used

timid /'timid/ *adj* lacking in courage, boldness, or self-confidence ⟨*a ~ person*⟩ ⟨*a ~ policy*⟩ [L *timidus*, fr *timēre* to fear] – **timidly** *adv*, **timidity** *n*, **timidness** *n*
**synonyms** Timid, timorous, nervous, and apprehensive all mean "lacking in confidence". Timid stresses lack of venturesomeness and the tendency to cling to what is safe ⟨*a timid person would rather remain miserable than do anything unusual* – Bertrand Russell⟩. Timorous suggests the shrinking hesitation of someone dominated by actual fear ⟨*spoke ... in a timorous tone, as though silence had been enjoined* – Arnold Bennett⟩. Nervous adds an element of agitation ⟨*a nervous titter*⟩ and, like apprehensive, implies unease about the future ⟨*nervous/apprehensive of what might happen*⟩.

timing /'tieming/ *n* selection of the precise moment for beginning or doing something for maximum effect

timocracy /tie'mokrəsi/ *n* government in which a the possession of a certain amount of property is necessary for office b love of honour is the ruling principle [MF *tymocracie*, fr ML *timocratia*, fr Gk *timokratia*, fr *timē* price, value, honour + *-kratia* -cracy – more at PAIN] – **timocratic, timocratical** *adj*

timorous /'tim(ə)rəs/ *adj* of a timid disposition; fearful; *also* marked by timidity ⟨*a ~ voice*⟩ [ME, fr MF *timoureus*, fr ML *timorosus*, fr L *timor* fear, fr *timēre* to fear] – **timorously** *adv*, **timorousness** *n*

timothy /'timəthi/, **timothy grass** *n* a European grass (*Phleum pratense*) that has long cylindrical spikes and is widely grown for hay [prob fr *Timothy* Hanson, 18th-c US farmer said to have introduced it from New England to the southern states of the USA]

Timothy *n* – see BIBLE table [*Timothy* (L *Timotheus*, fr Gk *Timotheos*), disciple of the apostle Paul]

timpani, timpany /'timpəni/ *n taking sing or pl vb* a set of two or three kettledrums played by one performer (eg in an orchestra) [It, pl of *timpano* kettledrum, fr L *tympanum* drum – more at TYMPANUM] – **timpanist** *n*

timps /timps/ *n pl*, *informal* timpani

¹tin /tin/ *n* 1 a soft faintly bluish white lustrous low-melting metallic chemical element that is soft and easily worked at ordinary temperatures and is used as a protective coating, in tinfoil, and in soft solders and alloys 2 a box, can, pan, vessel, or sheet made of tinplate: eg 2a a hermetically sealed tinplate container for preserving foods b any of various usu tinplate or aluminium containers of different shapes and sizes in which food is cooked, esp in an oven ⟨*roasting ~*⟩ ⟨*loaf ~*⟩ 3 the contents of or quantity contained in a tin 4 a strip of resonant metal below the board on the front wall of a squash court, above which all balls must be hit – see also **put the tin** LID **on** [ME, fr OE; akin to OHG *zin* tin] – **tinful** *n*

²tin *vt* **-nn-** 1 to cover or plate with tin or a tin alloy 2 *chiefly Br* to pack or preserve in tins; can

tinamou /'tinəmooh/ *n* any of a family (Tinamidae) of S American game birds [Fr, fr Galibi *tinamu*]

tincal /'tingkl/ *n* crude naturally-occurring BORAX (white mineral) [Malay *tingkal*]

tin can *n* a can made of tinplate; *broadly* TIN 2A

¹tinct /tingkt/ *adj*, *poetic* coloured, tinged [L *tinctus*, pp]

²tinct *n*, *archaic or poetic* a tint, tinge

tinctorial /tingk'tawri·əl/ *adj* of colours, dyeing, or staining; *also* imparting colour [L *tinctorius*, fr *tinctus*, pp] – **tinctorially** *adv*

¹tincture /'ting(k)chə/ *n* 1a a substance that colours, dyes, or stains b a colour, tint 2a a characteristic quality; a cast b a slight trace; a shade 3 a heraldic metal, colour, or fur 4 a solution of a medicinal substance in alcohol use ⟨*~ of iodine*⟩ 5 *informal* (a drink of) an alcoholic beverage, esp spirits [ME, fr L *tinctura* act of dyeing, fr *tinctus*, pp of *tingere* to tinge]

²tincture *vt* 1 to tint or stain with a colour; tinge 2 to imbue, impregnate ⟨*writing ~d with wit and wisdom*⟩

tinder /'tində/ *n* a dry highly inflammable substance of any type for lighting fires ⟨*bracken is tinder-dry after the drought*⟩ [ME, fr OE *tynder*; akin to OHG *zuntra* tinder, OE *tendan* to kindle] – **tindery** *adj*

**tinderbox** /-,boks/ *n* **1a** a metal box formerly used for holding tinder and usu a flint and steel for striking a spark **b** a highly inflammable object or place ⟨*the forest was a ~ after the drought*⟩ **2** a potentially very unstable place, situation, or person ⟨*prior to World War 1, the Balkans were the ~ of Europe*⟩

**tine, tyne** /tien/ *n* **1** a prong (e g of a fork) **2** a pointed branch of an antler [ME *tind,* fr OE; akin to OHG *zint* point, tine] – **tined** *adj*

**tinea** /'tini·ə/ *n* any of several fungal diseases of the skin; *esp* RINGWORM [ME, fr ML, fr L, worm, moth] – **tineal** *adj*

**tineid** /'tini·id/ *n* any of several usu small moths (family Tineidae), including various CLOTHES MOTHS [deriv of L *tinea* worm, moth]

**tin fish** *n, slang* a torpedo

**tinfoil** /,tin'foyl, '-,-/ *n* **1** a thin metal sheeting of tin, aluminium, or a tin alloy **2** SILVER PAPER

**ting** /ting/ *n* a high-pitched sound like that made by a light tap on a crystal goblet [*ting,* vb, fr ME *tingen,* of imit origin] – **ting** *vb*

**¹tinge** /tinj/ *vt* **tingeing, tinging 1** to colour with a slight shade or tint **2** to impart a slight smell, taste, or other quality to ⟨*happiness ~d with regret*⟩ [ME *tingen,* fr L *tingere* to dip, moisten, tinge; akin to OHG *dunkōn* to dip, Gk *tengein* to moisten]

**²tinge** *n* **1** a slight staining or suffusing colour **2** a slight modifying quality; a trace △ **twinge**

**tin glaze** *n* an opaque ceramic glaze containing tin oxide – **tin glaze** *vt*

**tingle** /'ting·gl/ *vi or n* (to feel or cause) a stinging, prickling, or thrilling sensation [vb ME *tinglen,* alter. of *tinklen* to tinkle, tingle; n fr vb] – **tinglingly** *adv,* **tingly** *adj*

**tin god** *n, informal* **1** a pompous and overbearing person; *esp* one who occupies a position of minor importance **2** one who or that which is the object of misplaced esteem or veneration

**tin hat** *n, informal* a present-day military metal helmet

**tinhorn** /'tin,hawn/ *n, NAm* a person (e g a gambler) who pretends to have money, ability, or influence

**¹tinker** /'tingkə/ *n* **1a** a usu itinerant mender of household utensils, esp in former times **b** an unskilful mender; a botcher **2** an act of tinkering **3** *chiefly Scot & Irish* a gipsy **4** *Br informal* a mischievous child [ME *tinkere*]

**²tinker** *vi* to repair, adjust, or work with something in an unskilled or experimental manner – usu + *at* or *with* ~ *vt* to repair, adjust, or experiment with – **tinkerer** *n*

**tinker's cuss** *n, Br slang* a least amount or degree of care or consideration – chiefly in *not give a tinker's cuss* ⟨*I wouldn't give a ~ for his opinion*⟩ [prob fr the tinkers' reputation for swearing]

**tinker's damn, tinker's dam** *n, NAm slang* TINKER'S CUSS

**¹tinkle** /'tingkl/ *vi* to make (a sound suggestive of) a tinkle ~ *vt* **1** to sound or make known (the time) by a tinkle **2** to cause to (make a) tinkle [ME *tinklen,* freq of *tinken* to tinkle, of imit origin] – **tinkly** *adj*

**²tinkle** *n* **1** a series of short light ringing or clinking sounds **2** *Br informal* a telephone call; ⁴RING 6b – esp in *give someone a tinkle* **3** *euph* an act of urinating ⟨*excuse me while I go for a ~*⟩

**tinman** /'tinmən/ *n* a tinsmith

**tinned** /tind/ *adj, chiefly Br* sealed in a tin for preservation ⟨*~ fruit*⟩

**tinner** /'tinə/ *n* **1** a tin miner **2** a tinsmith

**tinnitus** /ti'nietəs/ *n, medicine* a sensation of noise (e g a ringing or roaring) that has no external cause and usu results from disturbances of centres of the brain concerned with hearing [L, ringing, tinnitus, fr *tinnitus,* pp of *tinnire* to ring, of imit origin

**tinny** /'tini/ *adj* **1** of or containing tin **2a** having the taste, smell, or appearance of tin **b** not solid or durable; shoddy, cheap ⟨*a ~ car*⟩ **3** having a thin metallic sound ⟨*a ~ voice*⟩ – **tinnily** *adv,* **tinniness** *n*

**Tin Pan Alley** *n* a district that is a centre for composers and publishers of popular music; *also, taking sing or pl vb* the body of such composers and publishers

**tinplate** /-'playt/ *n* thin sheet iron or steel coated with tin

**tin-'plate** *vt* to plate or coat (e g a metal sheet) with tin

**tin-,pot** *adj, informal* paltry, inferior ⟨*a ~ little organization*⟩ ⟨*~ dictators*⟩

**¹tinsel** /'tins(ə)l/ *n* **1** metal, paper, or plastic used in the form of threads, strips, or sheets to produce a glittering and sparkling effect (e g in fabrics or decorations) **2** something superficial,

showy, or glamorous but of little real worth ⟨*the ~ of stardom*⟩ [MF *estincelle, estancele, etincelle* spark, glitter, spangle – more at STENCIL]

**²tinsel, tinselly** *adj* **1** made of or covered with tinsel **2** cheaply gaudy; tawdry

**³tinsel** *vt* **-ll-** (*NAm* **-l-, -ll-**) **1** to interweave or adorn (as if) with tinsel **2** to give a superficial brightness to

**tinsmith** /'tin,smith/ *n* a person who makes or repairs things of sheet metal (e g tinplate)

**tinstone** /'tin,stohn/ *n* CASSITERITE (brownish-black mineral from which tin is obtained)

**¹tint** /tint/ *n* **1a** a usu slight or pale coloration; a hue **b** any of several variations of a colour; *esp* one produced by adding white – compare SHADE **2** a shaded effect in engraving produced by fine parallel lines close together **3** a panel of light colour serving as background, esp for printing on [alter. of earlier *tinct,* fr L *tinctus* act of dyeing, fr *tinctus,* pp of *tingere* to tinge] – **tinter** *n*

**²tint** *vt* to apply a tint to; colour

**tintack** /'tin,tak/ *n, chiefly Br* a short broad-headed nail coated with tin

**tintinnabulary** /,tinti'nabyooləri/ *adj, formal* of or characterized by bells or their sounds [L *tintinnabulum* bell]

**tintinnabulation** /,tinti,nabyoo'laysh(ə)n/ *n, formal* **1** the ringing of bells **2** a jingling or tinkling sound as if of bells [L *tintinnabulum* bell, fr *tintinnare* to ring, jingle, of imit origin]

**Tintometer** /tin'tomitə/ *trademark* – used for a type of COLORIMETER (instrument for determining the intensity of colour)

**tintype** /'tin,tiep/ *n* FERROTYPE (positive photograph taken, esp formerly, on a thin iron or tin plate)

**tinware** /'tin,weə/ *n* articles, esp those for domestic use, made of tinplate

**tinwork** /'tin,wuhk/ *n* **1** articles made of tin **2** *pl but taking sing or pl vb* an establishment where tin is worked (e g by smelting or rolling)

**tiny** /'tieni/ *adj* very small or diminutive; minute *synonyms* see ¹SMALL [alter. of ME *tine,* of unknown origin] – **tinily** *adv,* **tininess** *n*

**¹tip** /tip/ *n* **1** the usu pointed end of something **2** a small piece or part serving as an end, cap, or point ⟨*a filter ~ cigarette*⟩ **3** a category of FLUE-CURED tobacco consisting of the two or three leaves pulled from the top of the plant stalk **4** GRASS TIP (light horseshoe) [ME; akin to MHG *zipf* tip, OE *tæppa* tap – more at TAP] – **tipped** *adj* – **on the tip of one's tongue 1** about to be uttered ⟨*it was on the tip of my tongue to tell him what I thought*⟩ **2** just eluding recall – **the tip of the iceberg** the small visible or evident part of a state of affairs or problem which is in fact much larger ⟨*the number of crimes reported is just the tip of the iceberg*⟩ [fr the small proportion of an iceberg which is visible above water]

**²tip** *vt* **-pp- 1a** to supply with a tip **b** to cover or adorn the tip of **2** to attach (an insert) in a book – often + *in*

**³tip** *vb* **-pp-** *vt* **1** to overturn, upset – usu + *over* or *up* **2a** to tilt **b** to raise and tilt forward in salute ⟨*~ped his hat*⟩ **3** *Br* **3a** to deposit by tilting; dump ⟨*the lorry ~ped its contents*⟩ **b** to transfer by tilting ⟨*~ in some of the cooking juices* – Jane Grigson⟩ ~ *vi* **1** to topple **2** to lean, slant – see also **tip the SCALES** [ME *tippen*]

**⁴tip** *n* **1** the act or an instance of tipping **2** a place for tipping something (e g rubbish or coal); a dump **3** *Br informal* a disgustingly untidy or shabby place

**⁵tip** *n* a light touch or blow [ME *tippe;* akin to LG *tippen* to tap]

**⁶tip** *vt* **-pp-** to strike lightly; tap

**⁷tip** *vb or n* **-pp-** *vt* (to give or present with) a sum of money in appreciation of a service performed ⟨*~ped the waiter a pound*⟩ [prob fr ⁶*tip*]

**⁸tip** *n* **1** a piece of useful or expert information **2** a piece of inside information which, acted on, may bring financial gain (e g by betting or investment) [prob fr ⁷*tip*]

**⁹tip** *vt* **-pp-** to mention as a prospective winner, success, or profitable investment ⟨*gilts are being ~ped in the forecasts*⟩

**tip off** *vt* to give a warning or a piece of confidential information or advice about or to ⟨*the police were tipped off about the raid*⟩ – see also TIP-OFF

**tip and run** *n* a form of cricket in which the batsman must attempt a run if he/she hits the ball

**tipcart** /'tip,kaht/ *n* a cart whose body can be tipped on the frame to empty its contents

**tipcat** /'tip,kat/ n (the peg used in) a game in which one player lightly strikes a tapered wooden peg with a bat and as it flies up strikes it again to drive it as far away as possible while fielders try to recover it [⁶*tip*]

**tipi** /'teepee/ n TEPEE (American Indian conical tent)

**'tip-,off** n a tip given usu as a warning

**tipper** /'tipə/ n 1 one who or that which tips 2 a lorry, trailer, etc whose body can be tipped on its chassis to empty the contents

**tippet** /'tipit/ n 1 a long hanging end of cloth attached to a sleeve, cap, or hood, esp in the 16th century 2 a shoulder cape of fur or cloth, often with hanging ends, worn by women 3 a long black scarf worn over the SURPLICE (white robe) by Anglican clergymen while conducting a service [ME *tipet*, prob fr *tip, tippe* ¹tip]

**¹tipple** /'tipl/ vb, informal vt to drink (alcoholic beverages), esp continuously in small amounts ~ vi to drink alcoholic beverages, esp by habit or to excess [back-formation fr obs *tippler* seller of drink, fr ME *tipler, tipeler*] – **tippler** n

**²tipple** n, informal an alcoholic drink, esp spirits; esp one habitually taken ⟨*what's your ~?*⟩

**³tipple** n, NAm a place where or an apparatus by which goods trucks (e g for coal) are loaded or emptied [E dial. *tipple* to tip over, freq of E *tip*]

**tippy** /'tipi/ adj liable to tip; unstable ⟨*a ~ boat*⟩

**tipstaff** /'tip,stahf/ n, pl **tipstaves** /-,stayvz/ an officer in certain lawcourts [obs *tipstaff* staff tipped with metal & carried by certain officials]

**tipster** /'tipstə/ n a person who gives or sells tips, esp for gambling or speculation

**tipstock** /'tip,stok/ n the detachable or movable forepart of the STOCK (support to which the barrel is attached) of a gun that forms a hold usu for the left hand [¹*tip*]

**tipsy** /'tipsi/ adj, informal 1 unsteady, staggering, or foolish from the effects of alcoholic drink; fuddled 2 askew ⟨*a ~ angle*⟩ [³*tip* + *-sy* (as in *tricksy*)] – **tipsily** adv, **tipsiness** n

**¹tiptoe** /-,toh/ n the tip of a toe; also the ends of the toes ⟨*walk on ~*⟩

**²tiptoe** adv (as if) on tiptoe

**³tiptoe** adj 1 standing or walking (as if) on tiptoe 2 cautious, stealthy

**⁴tiptoe** vi **tiptoeing** 1 to stand, walk, or raise oneself on tiptoe 2 to walk silently or stealthily as if on tiptoe

**¹'tip-,top** n the highest point or degree

**²tip-top** adj, informal excellent, first-rate ⟨*in ~ condition*⟩ – **tip-top** adv

**tipulid** /'tipyoolid/ n CRANE FLY (daddy longlegs) [deriv of L *tipula, tippula*, a water insect]

**tirade** /tie'rayd/ n a long vehement speech or denunciation [Fr, shot, tirade, fr MF, fr OIt *tirata*, fr *tirare* to draw, shoot; akin to Sp & Pg *tirar* to draw, shoot, OF *tirer*]

**¹tire** /tie-ə/ vi to become tired ~ vt 1 to fatigue 2 to wear out the patience of; bore [ME *tyren*, fr OE *tēorian, tȳrian*]

**²tire** n 1 a woman's headband or hair ornament 2 obs attire [ME, short for *attire*]

**³tire** vt 1 to adorn (the hair) with an ornament 2 obs to attire

**⁴tire** n, chiefly NAm a tyre

**tired** /tie-əd/ adj 1 weary, fatigued 2 exasperated; FED UP ⟨*~ of listening to your complaints*⟩ 3a trite, hackneyed ⟨*the same old ~ themes*⟩ b lacking freshness ⟨*a ~ skin*⟩ ⟨*~, overcooked asparagus*⟩ – **tiredly** adv, **tiredness** n

**tireless** /'tie-əlis/ adj indefatigable, untiring – **tirelessly** adv, **tirelessness** n

**tiresome** /'tie-əsəm/ adj wearisome, tedious – **tiresomely** adv, **tiresomeness** n

**tire store** n, Can a shop selling general hardware goods and accessories for cars

**tirewoman** /'tie-ə,woomən/ n, archaic a lady's maid [²*tire*]

**'tiring-,house** n a section of an Elizabethan theatre reserved for the actors and used esp for dressing and preparing for stage entrances [³*tire*]

**'tiring-,room** n, archaic a dressing room, esp in a theatre [³*tire*]

**tiro** /'tie,roh/ n, pl **tiros** TYRO (beginner)

**tisane** /ti'zahn/ n an infusion (e g of dried herbs) used as a beverage or for medicinal effects [ME, fr MF, fr L *ptisana*, fr Gk *ptisanē*, lit., crushed barley]

**Tishah-b'Ab** /ti,shah bə'ab/ n a Jewish holiday observed with fasting on the 9th of the month of Ab in memory of the destruction of the temples at Jerusalem [Heb *tish'āh bĕ Abh* ninth in Ab]

**Tishri** /'tish'ree/ n – see MONTH table [Heb *tishrī*]

**tissue** /'tishooh; also 'tisyooh/ n 1a a fine gauzy often nearly transparent fabric b a mesh, web ⟨*a ~ of lies*⟩ 2 a paper handkerchief 3 a collection of cells, usu of a similar type or with one type predominating, together with the substance between them, that form any of the materials of which a plant or animal body is composed and that usu perform a particular function ⟨*nerve ~*⟩ ⟨*muscular ~*⟩ [ME *tissu*, a rich fabric, fr OF, fr pp of *tistre* to weave, fr L *texere* – more at TECHNICAL] – **tissuey** adj

**tissue culture** n the process or technique of growing fragments of body tissue in a sterile artificial nourishing medium outside the organism; also a product of such a process

**tissue fluid** n the liquid filling the spaces between and bathing the cells of body tissues, that filters from the blood and ultimately drains into the LYMPHATIC system or diffuses back into the blood, and that provides the medium by which oxygen and nutrients pass into the tissues and CARBON DIOXIDE and waste products are removed

**tissue paper** n a very thin soft paper used esp for protecting something (e g by covering or wrapping)

**¹tit** /tit/ n 1 a teat or nipple 2 slang a woman's breast 3 slang an unpleasant person [ME, fr OE – more at TEAT]

**²tit, titmouse** n any of various small plump extremely active insect-eating songbirds (family Paridae, esp genus *Parus*) that have a short stubby beak, are often long-tailed, and mostly nest in holes in trees; broadly any of various similar small plump birds [ME *titmose*, fr (assumed) ME *tit* any small object or creature + ME *mose* titmouse, fr OE *māse*; akin to OHG *meisa* titmouse]

**titan** /'tiet(ə)n/, fem **titaness** /'tietənis, ,tietə'nes/ n somebody or something very large or strong; also somebody notable for outstanding achievement [Gk *Titan* one of a family of mythical giants once ruling the earth]

**titan-, titano-** comb form titanium ⟨*titanate*⟩ [NL *titanium*]

**titanate** /'tietənayt/ n any of various chemical compounds of TITANIUM DIOXIDE with an oxide of another metal

**tit and bum** adj, derog, of a magazine or newspaper featuring titillating pictures of naked women

**titania** /tie'taynə/ n TITANIUM DIOXIDE

**¹titanic** /tie'tanik/ adj colossal, gigantic ⟨*a ~ struggle*⟩ [Gk *titanikos* of the Titans] – **titanically** adv

**²titanic** /ti'tanik, tie-/ adj of or containing titanium, esp with a VALENCY of four [NL *titanium*]

**titaniferous** /,tietə'nifərəs/ adj of, containing, or yielding titanium ⟨*~ minerals*⟩

**titanism** /'tietəniz(ə)m/ n, often cap revolt against social or artistic conventions [fr the revolt of the mythical Titans against their father Uranus]

**titanite** /'tietəniet/ n SPHENE (titanium-containing mineral) [Ger *titanit*, fr NL *titanium*]

**titanium** /ti'taynyəm, tie-, -niəm/ n a silvery-grey metallic chemical element that is widely distributed in the earth's crust, occurs in the minerals ILMENITE and RUTILE, is strong, lightweight, and resistant to corrosion, and is used esp in alloys (e g steel) [NL, fr Gk *Titan*]

**titanium dioxide** n an oxide, $TiO_2$, of titanium that occurs naturally as the mineral RUTILE and is used in the form of a pure white powder as a pigment in paints, lacquers, etc

**titanium white** n (a brilliant white nontoxic pigment consisting chiefly of) TITANIUM DIOXIDE

**titanous** /'ti'tanəs, tie-/ adj of or containing titanium, esp with a VALENCY of three [ISV]

**titbit** /'tit,bit/ n 1 a choice morsel of food 2 a choice or pleasing piece (e g of news) [perh fr *tit-* (as in *titmouse*) + *bit*]

**titchy** /'tichi/ adj, chiefly Br informal small, scant ⟨*a ~ bit of food*⟩ [*tich, titch* (small person or thing), fr *Little Tich*, stagename of Harry Ralph †1928 dwarfish E comedian]

**titer** /'tietə, 'teetə/ n, NAm TITRE

**titfer** /'titfə/ n, Br slang a hat [rhyming slang *tit for (tat)*]

**tit for tat** /tat/ n an equivalent given in retaliation (e g for an injury) [prob alter. of earlier *tip for tap*, fr ⁵*tip* + *for* + ⁴*tap*]

**tithable** /'tiedhəbl/ adj subject or liable to payment of tithes

**¹tithe** /tiedh/ vt 1 to pay or give a tenth part of, esp for the support of the church 2 to levy a tithe on ~ vi to give a tenth of one's income as a tithe [ME *tithen*, fr OE *teogothian*, fr *teogotha* tenth] – **tither** n

**²tithe** n 1 a tax or contribution of a tenth part of something (e g income) for the support of a religious establishment; esp such a tax formerly due in an English parish to support the parish church **2** a tenth; *broadly* a small part [ME, fr OE *teo-gotha* tenth; akin to MLG *tegede* tenth; both fr a prehistoric WGmc derivative of the word represented by OE *tīen* ten – more at TEN]

**tithing** /'tiedhing/ *n* a former small administrative division of England apparently originally consisting of ten men with their families [ME, fr OE *tēothung*, fr *teogothian, tēothian* to tithe, take one tenth]

**titi** /'tee,tee/ *n, pl* **titis** any of various small S American monkeys (genus *Callicebus*) with long soft fur [Sp *titi*, fr Aymara *titi*, lit., little cat]

**titian** /'tish(ə)n/ *adj, often cap, esp of hair* reddish-brown [*Titian* (Tiziano Vecelli) †1576 It painter who often painted hair of this colour]

**titillate** /'titi,layt/ *vt* to excite pleasurably; arouse by stimulation [L *titillatus*, pp of *titillare* to tickle, stimulate sensually] – **titillation** *n*, **titillative** *adj*

**titivate, tittivate** /'titivayt/ *vb* to smarten up (oneself or another person or thing) [perh fr *¹tidy* + *-vate* (as in *renovate*)] – **titivation** *n*

**¹title** /'tietl/ *n* **1** (a document giving proof of) legal ownership ⟨*contesting his ~ to his grandfather's estate*⟩ **2a** something that justifies or substantiates a claim **b** an alleged or recognized right **3a** a descriptive or general heading (e g of a chapter in a book) **b** the heading of a legal document or statute **c** a TITLE PAGE and the printed matter on it **d** *pl* written material introduced into a film or television programme to represent credits, dialogue, or fragments of narrative **4** the distinguishing name of a work of art (e g a book, picture, or musical composition) **5** a descriptive name **6** a division of a legal document; *esp* one larger than a section or article **7** a literary work, as distinguished from a particular copy ⟨*published 25 ~s last year*⟩ **8** designation as champion ⟨*the world heavyweight ~*⟩ **9** a hereditary or acquired appellation given to a person or family as a mark of rank, office, or attainment [ME, fr OF, fr L *titulus* inscription, title]

**²title** *vt* **1** to provide a title for **2** to call by a title

**³title** *adj* of a title: e g **a** having the same name as the title of a production ⟨*played the ~ role in* Hamlet⟩ **b** having the same title as, or providing the title for, the collection or production of which it forms a part ⟨*the ~ story*⟩ ⟨*the ~ song*⟩ **c** of or being for a championship ⟨*a ~ match*⟩ **d** of or used with the titles which introduce a film or television programme ⟨*~ music*⟩

**titled** /'tietəld/ *adj* having a title, esp of nobility

**title deed** *n* a document constituting the evidence of a person's legal ownership

**titleholder** /'tietl,hohldə/ *n* a person who holds a title; *specif* a champion in a sporting competition

**title page** *n* a page of a book giving the title and usu also the author, publisher, and publication details

**titling** /'tietling/ *n* a set (²FOUNT) of type with capital letters but no small letters [fr its former common use on title pages]

**titmouse** /'tit,mows/ *n, pl* **titmice** /-,mies/ ²TIT (small bird)

**Titoism** /'teetoh,iz(ə)m/ *n* the policies associated with Tito; *specif* nationalist policies followed by a communist state independently of and often in opposition to the USSR [*Tito* (Josip Broz) †1980 President of Yugoslavia] – **Titoist** *n or adj*

**titrate** /'tietrayt/ *vb* to subject to or perform titration [*titre* + *-ate*] – **titratable** *adj*, **titrator** *n*

**titration** /tie'traysh(ə)n/ *n* a method or the process of determining the strength of a solution or the concentration of a substance in solution, by finding the smallest volume of a liquid of known concentration that is needed to bring about a complete reaction with a known volume of the test solution

**titre, *NAm chiefly* titer** /'tietə, 'teetə/ *n* **1** the strength of a solution or the concentration of a substance in solution as determined by titration **2** the smallest volume of a liquid needed to bring about a complete reaction in a titration [Fr *titre* title, proportion of gold or silver in a coin, fr OF *title* inscription, title]

**titrimetric** /,tietri'metrik/ *adj* employing or determined by titration [titration + *-i-* + *-metric*] – **titrimetrically** *adv*

**,tit-tat-'toe** *n, NAm* NOUGHTS AND CROSSES [var of *ticktack-toe*]

**titter** /'titə/ *vi* to laugh in a nervous, affected, or partly suppressed manner; giggle or snigger, esp girlishly [imit] – **titter** *n*

**tittie, titty** /'titi/ *n, chiefly Scot* a sister [prob baby-talk alter. of *sister*]

**tittivate** /'titivayt/ *vb* to titivate

**tittle** /'titl/ *n* **1** a point or small sign used as a DIACRITICAL (showing a different sound or value) mark in writing or printing **2** a very small amount [ME *titel*, fr ML *titulus*, fr L, title]

**'tittle-,tattle** /'tatl/ *vi or n* (to) gossip, prattle [redupl of *tattle*]

**¹tittup** /'titəp/ *n* a lively or spirited movement; a prance, caper [imit of the sound of a horse's hooves]

**²tittup** *vi* **-pp-** (*NAm* **-pp-, -p-**) to move in a lively prancing manner

**titty** /'titi/ *n, informal* ¹TIT 1,2 (nipple, breast)

**¹titular** /'tityoolə/ *adj* **1** in title only; nominal ⟨*the ~ head of a political party*⟩ **2** bearing a title; titled **3** of or constituting a title ⟨*the ~ hero of the play*⟩ [L *titulus* title] – **titularly** *adv*

**²titular** *n* a person holding a title

**Titus** /'tietəs/ *n* – see BIBLE table [*Titus* (fr LL, fr Gk *Titos*), disciple of the apostle Paul]

**tizz** /tiz/ *n, chiefly Br informal* a tizzy

**tizzwazz** /'tizwoz/ *n, Br informal* a tizzy [prob irreg redupl of *tizz*]

**tizzy** /'tizi/ *n, informal* a highly excited and confused state of mind [origin unknown]

**T junction, T-junction** *n* a junction formed by one road joining another at right angles

**Tlingit** /'tling·git/ *n, pl* **Tlingits,** *esp collectively* **Tlingit** a member or the language of a group of American Indian peoples of the islands and coast of S Alaska

**tmesis** /tə'meesis/ *n* separation of parts of a grammatical compound by another word or words (e g in *every-bloody-where*) [LL, fr Gk *tmēsis* act of cutting, fr *temnein* to cut – more at TOME]

**TNT** *n* TRINITROTOLUENE (high explosive) [*trinitrotoluene*]

**¹to** /tə; *strong and before vowels* tooh/ *prep* **1** – used to indicate a terminal point or destination: e g **1a** a place where a physical movement or an action or condition suggestive of movement ends ⟨*drive ~ the city*⟩ ⟨*threw the ball ~ me*⟩ ⟨*invited them ~ lunch*⟩ ⟨*went back ~ his original idea*⟩ **b** a direction ⟨*the road ~ London*⟩ ⟨*a mile ~ the south*⟩ ⟨*turned his back ~ the door*⟩ ⟨*tell her ~ her face*⟩ ⟨*a tendency ~ silliness*⟩ **c** a terminal point in measuring or reckoning or in a statement of extent or limits ⟨*10 miles ~ the nearest town*⟩ ⟨*cost from £5 ~ £10*⟩ ⟨*from 60 ~ 80 people*⟩ ⟨*moderate ~ cool temperatures*⟩ ⟨*stripped ~ the waist*⟩ ⟨*wet ~ the skin*⟩ ⟨*loyal ~ a man*⟩ ⟨*not ~ my knowledge*⟩ ⟨*add salt ~ taste*⟩ ⟨*did it ~ perfection*⟩ ⟨*doesn't know ~ this day*⟩ **d** a point in time before which a period is reckoned ⟨*five minutes ~ five*⟩ ⟨*from Monday ~ Friday*⟩ ⟨*how long ~ dinner?*⟩ **e** a point of contact or proximity ⟨*pinned it ~ my coat*⟩ ⟨*applied polish ~ the table*⟩ ⟨*danced cheek ~ cheek*⟩ **f** a purpose, intention, tendency, result, or end ⟨*came ~ our aid*⟩ ⟨*drink ~ his health*⟩ ⟨*a temple ~ Mars*⟩ ⟨*sang him ~ sleep*⟩ ⟨*sentenced ~ death*⟩ ⟨*beaten ~ death*⟩ ⟨*broken ~ pieces*⟩ ⟨*took her ~ wife*⟩ ⟨*go ~ seed*⟩ ⟨*lights changed ~ green*⟩ ⟨*held them ~ ransom*⟩ ⟨*something ~ your advantage*⟩ ⟨*all ~ no purpose*⟩ ⟨*much ~ my surprise*⟩ ⟨*learned ~ his cost*⟩ **g** the one to or for which something exists or is done or directed ⟨*kind ~ animals*⟩ ⟨*my letter ~ John*⟩ ⟨*it seems ~ me*⟩ ⟨*attitude ~ friends*⟩ ⟨*refers ~ the traditions*⟩ ⟨*spoke ~ his father*⟩ ⟨*known ~ the police*⟩ ⟨*gave a pound ~ the man*⟩ ⟨*he's an asset ~ the department*⟩ ⟨*that's one up ~ her*⟩ ⟨*what's that ~ him?*⟩ **2** – used **a** to indicate addition, attachment, connection, belonging, or possession ⟨*add 17 ~ 20*⟩ ⟨*the key ~ the door*⟩ ⟨*the title ~ the property*⟩ ⟨*secretary ~ a doctor*⟩ ⟨*a room ~ herself*⟩ ⟨*not a penny ~ my name*⟩ **b** to indicate accompaniment or response ⟨*danced ~ live music*⟩ ⟨*rose ~ the occasion*⟩ **3** – used to indicate relationship or conformity: e g **3a** relative position ⟨*perpendicular ~ the floor*⟩ ⟨*next door ~ me*⟩ **b** proportion or composition ⟨*400 ~ the box*⟩ ⟨*100 pence ~ the £*⟩ ⟨*30 miles ~ the gallon*⟩ ⟨*won by 17 points ~ 11*⟩ **c** correspondence to a standard ⟨*inferior ~ his earlier works*⟩ ⟨*second ~ none*⟩ ⟨*compared him ~ a god*⟩ ⟨*true ~ type*⟩ ⟨*different ~ mine*⟩ ⟨*drawn ~ scale*⟩ ⟨*trains ran ~ time*⟩ **4a** – used to indicate that the following verb is an infinitive ⟨*wants ~ go*⟩ ⟨*got work ~ do*⟩ ⟨*too fat ~ dance*⟩; now often used with an intervening adverb ⟨*~ really understand*⟩ in spite of the disapproval of many; often used by itself at the end of a clause in place of an infinitive suggested by the preceding context ⟨*knows more than he seems ~*⟩; see "Ten Vexed Points" **b** for the purpose of ⟨*did it ~ annoy her*⟩ △ **too, two** [ME, fr OE *tō*; akin to OHG *zuo* to, L *donec* as long as, until] – **to oneself** for one's exclusive use or knowledge

**²to** /tooh/ *adv* **1a** – used to indicate direction towards ⟨*you've put it wrong end* ∼⟩; compare TO AND FRO **b** as nearly as possible against the main force of the wind ⟨*the ship hove* ∼⟩ **2** *of a door or window* into contact, esp with the frame ⟨*the door slammed* ∼⟩ **3** – used to indicate application or attention; compare FALL TO, TURN TO **4** back into consciousness or awareness ⟨*brings her* ∼ *with smelling salts*⟩ **5** AT HAND ⟨*saw her close* ∼⟩ – **to and fro** from one place to another; backwards ⟨*going* to and fro *between home and office*⟩ ⟨*the rope swung* to and fro⟩

**toad** /tohd/ *n* **1** any of numerous tailless leaping amphibians (esp family Bufonidae) that differ from the related frogs in living more on land and in having a shorter squatter body with weaker hind limbs and a rough, dry, and warty skin; *esp* a common European toad (*Bufo bufo*) **2** a loathsome and contemptible person or thing [ME *tode*, fr OE *tāde, tādige*]

**toadeater** /'tohd₁eetə/ *n*, *archaic* a toady

**toadfish** /'tohd₁fish/ *n* any of various American marine fishes (family Batrachoididae) with a large thick head and wide mouth

**toadflax** /'tohd₁flaks/ *n* (any of numerous plants similar or related to) a common Eurasian plant (*Linaria vulgaris*) of the foxglove family that has showy yellow and orange flowers shaped like those of the snapdragon

**toadies** /'tohdiz/ *n pl but taking sing verb* ²TOAD-IN-THE-HOLE

**¹toad-in-the-'hole** *n* a dish of sausages baked in a thick Yorkshire-pudding batter

**²₁toad-in-the-'hole** *n* a game in which the 2–4 players throw usu brass discs at a target which is a small hole in the top of a wooden box

**toadstone** /'tohd₁stohn/ *n* an object (e g a stone) supposed to have been formed in the body of a toad and formerly worn as a charm or antidote to poison

**toadstool** /-₁stoohl/ *n* a fungus with an umbrella-shaped PILEUS (spore-producing body); *specif* a poisonous or inedible one as distinguished from an edible mushroom [ME *todestool, tadestool*, fr *tode, tade* toad + *stool*]

**¹toady** /'tohdi/ *n* somebody who flatters in the hope of gaining favours [by shortening & alter. fr *toadeater* (orig a mountebank's assistant who ate or pretended to eat allegedly poisonous toads to prove the value of his master's antidote)]

**²toady** *vi* to behave as a toady; be obsequious ⟨*toadied to his superiors*⟩ – **toadyism** *n*

**₁to-and-'fro** *n or adj* (activity involving alternating movement) forwards and backwards ⟨*the busy* ∼ *of the holiday shoppers*⟩ ⟨∼ *motion*⟩

**¹toast** /tohst/ *vt* **1** to make (e g a slice of bread) crisp, hot, and brown by heat **2** to warm thoroughly (e g at a fire) ∼ *vi* to become toasted; *esp* to become thoroughly warm [ME *tosten*, fr MF *toster*, fr LL *tostare* to roast, fr L *tostus*, pp of *torrēre* to dry, parch – more at THIRST]

**²toast** *n* **1** sliced bread browned on both sides by heat **2a** someone or something in whose honour people drink ⟨*the* ∼ *is: "The Queen"*⟩ **b** a person highly popular or admired in esp the specified place ⟨*she's the* ∼ *of London*⟩ **3** a proposal to drink or an act of drinking in honour of somebody or something [(2) fr the use of pieces of spiced toast to flavour drinks]

**³toast** *vt* to drink to as a toast

**toaster** /'tohstə/ *n* one who or that which toasts; *specif* an electrical appliance for toasting bread

**toasting fork** /'tohsting/ *n* a long-handled fork on which bread is held for toasting in front of or over a fire

**toastmaster** /-₁mahstə/, *fem* **toastmistress** *n* a person who presides at a banquet, proposes toasts, and introduces afterdinner speakers

**tobacco** /tə'bakoh/ *n*, *pl* **tobaccos** **1** any of a genus (*Nicotiana*) of chiefly American plants of the potato family with large rather sticky leaves and tubular flowers; *esp* a tall erect S American plant (*Nicotiana tabacum*) cultivated for its leaves **2** the leaves of cultivated tobacco prepared for use in smoking or chewing or as snuff; *also* cigars, cigarettes, or other manufactured products of tobacco **3** the smoking of tobacco as a habit ⟨*has sworn off* ∼⟩ [Sp *tabaco*, prob fr Taino, roll of tobacco leaves smoked by the Indians of the Antilles at the time of Columbus]

**tobacco mosaic** *n* any of several MOSAIC diseases (virus diseases characterized by mottling of the leaves) of tobacco and related plants

**tobacconist** /tə'bakənist/ *n*, *chiefly Br* a seller of tobacco, cigarettes, etc, esp in a shop [irreg fr *tobacco* + *-ist*]

**to-'be** *adj* that is to be; future – usu used after a noun; often in combination ⟨*a bride-to-be*⟩

**tober** /'tohbə/ *n*, *dial Br* a fairground with its rides and sideshows [Br slang *tober* road, fr Shelta *tobar*]

**Tobias** /tə'bie-əs, toh-/ *n* – see BIBLE table [*Tobias* (fr Gk), Jewish hero]

**Tobit** /'tohbit/ *n* – see BIBLE table [*Tobit* (Gk *Tōbit*), father of Tobias]

**¹toboggan** /tə'bogən/ *n* a long light sledge usu curved up at the front and used esp for gliding downhill over snow or ice [CanF *tobogan*, of Algonquian origin; akin to Micmac *tobâgun* sledge made of skin]

**²toboggan** *vi* **1** to ride on a toboggan **2** *NAm* to decline suddenly and sharply (e g in value) – **tobogganer, tobogganist** *n*

**toby** /'tohbi/, **toby jug** *n* a small jug or mug generally used for beer and usu shaped like a stout man with a three-cornered hat [*Toby*, nickname for *Tobias*]

**toccata** /tə'kahtə/ *n* a musical composition, usu for organ or harpsichord, written in a free almost improvisatory style and characterized by passages of rapidly played notes ⟨*Bach's* ∼ *and fugue in D minor*⟩ [It, fr *toccare* to touch, fr (assumed) VL – more at TOUCH]

**Toc H** /'tok ₁aych/ *n* a society of Christians for fellowship and charitable work, founded in Ypres in 1915 by Rev P T B Clayton [*toc* (signallers' former code word for the letter *t*) + *h*, initials of *Talbot House*, name of a club from which the society developed]

**Tocharian, Tokharian** /to'kahri-ən/ *n* **1** a member of a people of supposed European origin inhabiting central Asia during the first thousand years AD **2** an extinct INDO-EUROPEAN language of central Asia [L *Tochari* (pl), fr Gk *Tocharoi*] – **Tocharian** *adj*

**Tocharian A** *n* the eastern dialect of Tocharian

**Tocharian B** *n* the western dialect of Tocharian

**tocher** /'tokhə/ *n*, *chiefly Scot* a dowry [ScGael *tochar*]

**tocopherol** /to'kofə₁rol/ *n* any of several fat-soluble oily chemical compounds that are vitamins of the VITAMIN E group having the actions or functions associated with vitamin E to varying degrees [ISV, deriv of Gk *tokos* childbirth, offspring + *pherein* to carry, bear – more at BEAR]

**tocsin** /'toksin/ *n* **1** an alarm bell rung as a warning **2** a warning signal △ toxin [MF *toquassen*, fr OProv *tocasenh*, fr *tocar* to touch, ring a bell (fr assumed VL *toccare*) + *senh* bell (fr ML *signum*, fr LL, ringing of a bell, fr L, mark, sign) – more at TOUCH, SIGN]

**¹tod** /tod/ *n*, *chiefly Scot & N Eng* a fox [ME]

**²tod** *n* **1** any of various units of weight for wool; *esp* a unit equal to 28 pounds (about 12.7 kilograms) **2** *Br* a bushy clump (e g of ivy) [ME *todd, todde*; prob akin to OHG *zotta* tuft of hair]

**³tod** *n*, *Br* [rhyming slang *Tod (Sloan)* own, alone, prob fr James Forman (*Tod*) *Sloan* †1933 US jockey] – **on one's tod** *informal* alone

**today** /tə'day/ *adv or n* **1** (on) this day **2** (at) the present time or age ⟨*the youth of* ∼⟩ [adv ME, fr OE *tōdæge, tōdæg*, fr *tō* to, at + *dæge*, dat of *dæg* day; n fr adv]

**toddle** /todl/ *vi* **1** to walk haltingly as a young child does **2a** to stroll, saunter **b** *Br informal* to depart ⟨*I'll just* ∼ *off home*⟩ [origin unknown] – **toddle** *n*

**toddler** /'todlə/ *n* a young child who has just become able to walk

**toddy** /'todi/ *n* **1** the sap of various chiefly E Indian palm trees **2** a usu hot drink consisting of spirits mixed with water, sugar, and spices [Hindi *tārī* juice of the palmyra palm, fr *tār* palmyra palm, fr Skt *tāla*]

**to-'do** *n*, *pl* **to-dos** *informal* (a) bustle, fuss **synonyms** see ¹FUSS

**tody** /'tohdi/ *n* any of several tiny insect-eating W Indian birds (genus *Todus*) that are closely related to the kingfisher and have bright green and red plumage and relatively long flattish beaks [modif of Fr *todier*, fr L *todus*, a small bird]

**¹toe** /toh/ *n* **1a(1)** any of the digits at the end of a VERTEBRATE animal's foot **a(2)** the front part of a foot or hoof **b** the front of something worn on the foot ⟨*the* ∼ *of a boot*⟩ **2a** a part like a toe in its position or form ⟨*the* ∼ *of Italy*⟩ **b** the lowest part (e g of an embankment, dam, or cliff) – see also TREAD **on somebody's toes** [ME *to*, fr OE *tā*; akin to OHG *zēha* toe, L *digitus* finger, toe]

**²toe** *vb* **toeing** *vt* **1** to provide with a toe; *esp* to renew the toe of ⟨~ *a shoe*⟩ **2** to touch, reach, or drive with the toe ⟨~ *a football*⟩ **3** to drive (eg a nail) obliquely; *also* to fasten with nails or rods so driven ~ *vi, chiefly NAm* to stand, walk, or be placed so that the toes point in a specified direction ⟨~ *in*⟩ – see also **toe the** LINE

**toea** /'toh·ə/ *n, pl* **toea** – see *kina* at MONEY table [native name in Papua New Guinea]

**toe and heel** *n* HEEL AND TOE (simultaneous operating of brake and accelerator)

**toe cap** *n* a piece of material (eg leather or steel) attached to the toe of a shoe or boot to reinforce or decorate it

**toe clip** *n* a device fitted to a bicycle or tricycle pedal to keep the foot in place

**toe crack** *n* a SAND CRACK in the front of a horse's hoof

**toed** /tohd/ *adj* **1** having a toe or toes, esp of a specified kind or number – usu in combination ⟨*five*-toed⟩ ⟨*round*-toed *shoes*⟩ **2** driven obliquely or secured by oblique nailing ⟨*a ~ nail*⟩

**toe dance** *n* a dance performed on the tips of the toes – **toe-dance** *vi*, **toe dancer** *n*, **toe dancing** *n*

**toehold** /-ˌhohld/ *n* **1a** a hold or place of support for the toes (eg in climbing) **b** a slight footing ⟨*the firm had a ~ in the export market*⟩ **2** a wrestling hold in which the aggressor bends or twists his/her opponent's foot

**'toe-ˌin** *n* adjustment of the front wheels of a motor vehicle so that they are closer together at the front than at the back

**toenail** /'toh·nayl/ *n* the nail of a toe

**toff** /tof/ *n, chiefly Br informal* an upper-class usu well-dressed person – no longer in vogue [prob alter. of arch. *tuft* titled undergraduate at Oxford and Cambridge (fr the gold tassel or "tuft" on his cap)]

**toffee** *also* **toffy** /'tofi/ *n* a sweet with a texture ranging from chewy to brittle, made by boiling sugar, water, butter, etc [alter. of *taffy*]

**'toffee-ˌapple** *n* a toffee-covered apple on a stick

**'toffee-ˌnosed** *adj, Br informal* stuck-up

**toft** /toft/ *n, Br* an entire holding comprising a homestead and additional land [ME, fr OE, homestead, fr ON *topt*]

**tofu** /'tohfooh/ *n* BEAN CURD [Jap *tōfu*]

**tog** /tog/ *vt* **-gg-** *informal* to dress smartly – usu + *up* or *out* ⟨*all ~ged up in her best clothes*⟩ [*togs*]

**toga** /'tohgə/ *n* a loose outer garment worn in public by citizens of ancient Rome [L; akin to L *tegere* to cover – more at THATCH] – **togaed** *adj*

**toga virilis** /ˌtohgə vi'rilis/ *n, pl* **togae viriles** /ˌtohgie vi'rilayz/ the white toga of manhood assumed by boys of ancient Rome at the age of 15 [L, men's toga]

**together** /tə'gedhə/ *adv* **1a** in or into one place, mass, collection, or group ⟨*the men get ~ every Thursday for poker*⟩ **b** in joint agreement or cooperation; as a group ⟨*students and staff ~ presented the petition*⟩ **2a** in or into contact (eg connection, collision, or union) ⟨*mix these ingredients ~*⟩ ⟨*tie the ends ~*⟩ **b** in or into association, relationship, or harmony ⟨*colours that go well ~*⟩ ⟨*went to school ~*⟩ ⟨*the soloist and the orchestra weren't quite ~*⟩ **3a** at one time; simultaneously ⟨*everything happened ~*⟩ **b** in succession; without intermission ⟨*was depressed for days ~*⟩ **4** of a *single unit* in or into an integrated whole ⟨*pull yourself ~*⟩ **5a** to or with each other ⟨*eyes too close ~*⟩ – used as an intensive after certain verbs ⟨*join ~*⟩ ⟨*add ~*⟩ ⟨*confer ~*⟩ **b** considered as a unit; collectively ⟨*these arguments taken ~ make a convincing case*⟩ **usage** see WITH [ME *togedere*, fr OE *togædere*, fr *tō* to + *gædere* together; akin to MHG *gater* together, OE *gaderian* to gather] – **together with** with the addition of

**togetherness** /-nis/ *n* the feeling of belonging together

**toggery** /'togəri/ *n, informal* clothing [*togs* + *-ery*]

**'toggle** /'tog(ə)l/ *n* **1** a piece or device for holding or securing; *esp* a crosspiece attached to the end of or to a loop in a chain, rope, line, etc, usu to prevent slipping, to serve as a fastening, or as a grip for tightening **2** (a device having) a TOGGLE JOINT [origin unknown]

**'toggle** *vt* to provide or fasten (as if) with a toggle

**toggle joint** *n* a device consisting of two bars hinged together in such a way that when a force that tends to straighten the device is applied to the hinged joint, usu by means of a screw, force is also exerted along the bars and on parts next to or fixed to their ends

**toggle switch** *n* an electric switch that opens or closes a circuit by means of a projecting lever

**togs** /togz/ *n pl, informal* clothes ⟨*working ~*⟩ [pl of slang *tog* coat, short for obs cant *togeman, togman*]

**tohunga** /'tawhung·ə/ *n, NZ* a Maori priest or performer of sacred rites; a sage; MEDICINE MAN [Maori]

**'toil** /toyl/ *n* long strenuous fatiguing labour **synonyms** see [1]WORK **antonym** leisure [ME *toile*, fr AF *toyl*, fr OF *toeil* battle, confusion, fr *toeillier*] – **toilful, toilsome** *adj*

**'toil** *vi* **1** to work hard and long **2** to proceed with laborious effort ⟨~ing *wearily up the hill*⟩ [ME *toilen* to argue, struggle, fr AF *toiller*, fr OF *toeillier* to stir, disturb, dispute, fr L *tudiculare* to crush, grind, fr *tudicula* machine for crushing olives, dim. of *tudes* hammer; akin to L *tundere* to beat – more at STINT] – **toiler** *n*

**toile** /twul, twahl/ *n* **1** any of many plain or simple fabrics; *esp* linen **2** a pattern of a garment in cheap cloth for making copies from [Fr, cloth, linen]

**toile de Jouy** /ˌtwul də 'zhwee/ *n* an 18th-century French scenic pattern usu printed on cotton, linen, or silk in one colour on a light background; *broadly* any printed fabric of this sort [Fr, lit., cloth of Jouy, fr *Jouy*-en-Josar, town in N France]

**toilet** /'toylit/ *n* **1a** a fixture or arrangement for receiving and disposing of faeces and urine **b** a room, compartment, or building containing a toilet and sometimes a washbasin **2** cleansing in preparation for or in association with a medical or surgical procedure **3** *formal* the act or process of dressing oneself, arranging one's hair and facial appearance, etc **4** *formal* formal or fashionable (style of) dress **5** *archaic* DRESSING TABLE [MF *toilette* cloth put over the shoulders while dressing the hair or shaving, dim. of *toile* cloth]

**toilet paper** *n* a thin usu absorbent paper for cleaning oneself after defecating or urinating

**toilet powder** *n* a fine powder, usu with soothing or antiseptic ingredients, for sprinkling or rubbing over the skin (eg after bathing)

**toiletry** /'toylitri/ *n usu pl* an article or preparation (eg toothpaste, shaving cream, or cologne) used in washing, grooming oneself, etc

**toilet soap** *n* a mild soap that is often perfumed and coloured

**toilette** /toy'let, twah'let/ *n* TOILET 3,4 [Fr, fr MF]

**toilet training** *n* the process of training a child to control bladder and bowel movements and to use the toilet – **toilet train** *vt*

**toilet water** *n* (a) perfumed liquid containing a high percentage of alcohol for use in or after a bath or as a skin freshener or light perfume

**toils** /toylz/ *n pl* something by or with which one is held fast or is inextricably involved; a snare, trap ⟨*caught in the ~ of the law*⟩ [MF *toile* cloth, net, fr L *tela* web, fr *texere* to weave, construct – more at TECHNICAL]

**toilworn** /'toyl,wawn/ *adj* showing the effects of or worn out with toil ⟨~ *hands*⟩

**to-ing and fro-ing** /ˌtooh·ing ənd 'froh·ing/ *n, pl* **to-ings and fro-ings** (an instance of) bustling unproductive activity

**Tokay** /'tohkay, toh'kie/ *n* a usu sweet usu dark gold wine made near Tokaj in Hungary

**toke** /tohk/ *n, slang* a puff on a marijuana cigarette [origin unknown]

**'token** /'tohkən/ *n* **1** an outward sign or expression (eg of an emotion) ⟨*his tears were ~s of his grief*⟩ **2a** a characteristic mark or feature; a symbol, emblem ⟨*a white flag is a ~ of surrender*⟩ **b** an instance of a word or other linguistic form ⟨*the letter l is a type, of which there are two ~s in* sell⟩ – compare TYPE 3b **3a** a souvenir, keepsake **b** a small part representing the whole; an indication ⟨*this is only a ~ of what he hopes to accomplish*⟩ **c** something given or shown as a guarantee (eg of authority, right, or identity) **4** a coinlike piece issued **4a** as money by anyone other than a government ⟨*a Co-op ~*⟩ **b** for use in place of money (eg for a bus fare) **5** something (eg a card bearing a receipt) which can be used in payment or exchange for purchasing specified goods to a stated value ⟨*a gift ~*⟩ ⟨*a book ~*⟩ [ME, fr OE *tācen, tācn* sign, token; akin to OHG *zeihhan* sign, Gk *deiknynai* to show – more at DICTION] – **by the same token** furthermore and for the same reason

**'token** *adj* **1** done or given as a token, esp in partial fulfilment of an obligation or engagement ⟨*a ~ payment*⟩ **2** done or given merely for show; minimal, perfunctory ⟨~ *resistance*⟩

**tokenism** /'tohkə,niz(ə)m/ *n* the making of only a token effort; *esp* the policy or practice of integrating esp races or the sexes to only the minimum necessary to show that integration has taken place

**token money** *n* **1** money of regular government issue (e g paper currency or coins) having a greater face value than intrinsic value **2** a medium of exchange consisting of privately issued tokens

**Tokharian** /toh'kahrien/ *n* TOCHARIAN (member and language of an Asian people) – **Tokharian** *adj*

**tol-, tolu-** *comb form* toluene ⟨toluic⟩ [ISV, fr *tolu*]

**tola** /'tohlə/ *n* a unit of weight in India equal to about 11.66 grams (0.4114 ounce) [Hindi *tolā*, fr Skt *tulā* weight; akin to L *tollere* to lift up]

**tolbooth** /'tol,boohth, 'tohl-/ *n, Scot* **1** TOWN HALL **2** a jail, prison [ME *tolbothe, tollbothe* tollbooth, town hall, jail]

**tolbutamide** /tol'byoohtəmied/ *n* a drug, $H_3CC_6H_4SO_2NHCONH(CH_2)_3CH_3$, that lowers the amount of sugar in the blood and is given orally in the treatment of DIABETES MELLITUS [*tol-* + *buty*ric + *amide*]

**told** /tohld/ *past of* TELL – **all told** with everything taken into account; IN ALL

**Toledo** /to'laydoh/ *n, pl* **Toledos** a finely TEMPERED (heat-strengthened) sword or sword blade [*Toledo*, town in Spain]

**tolerable** /'tol(ə)rəbl/ *adj* **1** capable of being borne or endured ⟨~ *pain*⟩ **2** moderately good or agreeable; passable ⟨*a* ~ *singing voice*⟩ – **tolerably** *adv*, **tolerability** *n*

**tolerance** /'tolərəns/ *n* **1** the capacity to endure pain or hardship; fortitude, stamina **2a** the ability to withstand or adapt physiologically to the effects of a drug, a potentially harmful physiological stimulus (e g extreme heat or cold), etc without exhibiting the usual unfavourable responses ⟨*an addict's increasing* ~ *for a drug*⟩ **b** the relative capacity of a living organism or type of organism to survive, grow, or thrive in environmental conditions (e g an acidic soil or shade) unfavourable for most organisms **3a** indulgence for beliefs or practices differing from one's own **b** the act of allowing something; toleration **4** an allowable deviation from a standard dimension, weight, etc

**tolerant** /'tolərənt/ *adj* **1** inclined to tolerate; *esp* marked by forbearance or endurance **2** exhibiting tolerance (e g to a drug or an environmental condition) – **tolerantly** *adv*

**tolerate** /'tolərayt/ *vt* **1** to withstand or resist the action of (e g a drug) without grave or lasting injury **2** to allow to be or be done without prohibition, hindrance, or contradiction *synonyms* see ²BEAR [L *toleratus*, pp of *tolerare* to endure, put up with; akin to OE *tholian* to bear, L *tollere* to lift up, *latus* carried (suppletive pp. of *ferre*), Gk *tlēnai* to bear] – **tolerator** *n*, **tolerative** *adj*

**toleration** /tolə'raysh(ə)n/ *n* **1** the act or practice of tolerating **2** a government policy of allowing forms of religious belief not officially established in a country

**tolidine** /'tolideen/ *n* a chemical compound, $C_{14}H_{16}N_2$, used esp in the manufacture of dyes [ISV *tol-* + *-idine*]

¹**toll** /tol, tohl/ *n* **1** a fee paid for some right or privilege (e g of passing over a highway or bridge) or for services rendered (e g transport or the grinding of corn) **2** a grievous or ruinous price; *esp* cost in life or health ⟨*fever had taken a heavy* ~ *of her*⟩ ⟨*the death* ~ *was over 400*⟩ *synonyms* see ²TAX [ME, fr OE; akin to ON *tollr* toll; both fr a prehistoric WGmc-NGmc word borrowed fr (assumed) VL *tolonium*, alter. of LL *telonium* customshouse, fr Gk *tolōnion*, fr *telōnēs* collector of tolls, fr *telos* tax, toll; akin to Gk *tlēnai* to bear]

²**toll** /tohl/ *vt* **1** to sound (a bell) by pulling the rope **2** to signal, announce, or summon (as if) by means of a tolled bell ⟨*the clock* ~ed *each hour*⟩ ~ *vi* to sound with slow measured strokes [ME *tollen*, perh fr *tollen* to entice]

³**toll** /tohl/ *n* the sound of a tolling bell

**tollbooth** /'tolboohth, 'tohl-/ *n* a booth (e g on a bridge) where tolls are paid [ME *tolbothe, tollbothe* tollbooth, town hall, jail, fr *tol, toll* toll + *bothe* booth]

**toll bridge** /tol, tohl/ *n* a bridge at which a toll is charged for crossing

**toll call** *n, NAm* a long-distance telephone call at charges above a local rate

**tollgate** /'tol,gayt, tohl-/ *n* a barrier across a road or bridge to prevent passage until a toll is paid

**tollhouse** /'tol,hows, 'tohl-/ *n* a house or booth where tolls are paid

**tollie, tolly** /'toli/ *n, SAfr* a castrated calf [Afrik, fr Zulu *iThole* calf]

**tollman** /'tolmən, 'tohl-/ *n* a collector of tolls

**tollroad** /'tol,rohd, 'tohl-/ *n* a road maintained by collected tolls

**Toltec** /'toltek/ *n* a member of an American Indian people of central and S Mexico [Sp *tolteca*, of AmerInd origin] – **Toltecan** *adj*

**tolu** /to'looh/ *n* BALSAM OF TOLU (fragrant substance obtained from a tropical American tree) [Sp *tolú*, fr Santiago de *Tolú*, town in Colombia]

**tolu-** – see TOL-

**toluate** /'tolyooayt/ *n* any of various chemical compounds (SALTS or ESTERS) formed by combination between toluic acid and a metal atom, an alcohol, or another chemical group [ISV]

**toluene** /'tolyoo,een/ *n* a toxic inflammable liquid chemical compound, $C_6H_5CH_3$, that is used esp as a solvent and in the synthesis of organic chemical compounds [ISV]

**toluic** /to'looh-ik/ *adj* of or being a chemical acid, $CH_3C_6H_4COOH$, derived from toluene [ISV]

**toluidine** /to'lyooh-ideen/ *n* a chemical compound, $CH_3C_6H_4NH_2$, derived from toluene that is used in the manufacture of dyes and whose inhalation or absorption through the skin causes cancer of the bladder [ISV *tol-* + *-idine*]

**toluidine blue** *n* a chemical dye that is used to colour samples of tissues, cells, etc for study under the microscope and in medicine to treat bleeding

**toluol** /'tolyoo,ol/ *n* toluene, esp of commercial grade

**tolyl** /'tolil/ *adj or n* (being or containing) the chemical group, $CH_3C_6H_4$, having a VALENCY of one and derived from toluene [ISV]

**tom** /tom/ *n* the male of various animals; *esp* a tomcat [*Tom*, nickname for *Thomas*]

¹**tomahawk** /'tomə,hawk/ *n* a light axe used by N American Indians as a throwing or hand weapon [*tomahack* (in some Algonquian language of Virginia)]

²**tomahawk** *vt* to cut, strike, or kill with a tomahawk

**tomalley** /'tomali/ *n* the liver of the lobster, considered as a delicacy [of Cariban origin; akin to Galibi *tumali* sauce of lobster livers]

**tomato** /tə'mahtoh/ *n, pl* **tomatoes** **1** any of a genus (*Lycopersicon*) of S American plants of the potato family; *esp* one (*Lycopersicon esculentum*) widely cultivated for its edible fruit **2** the usu large rounded red, yellow, or green pulpy fruit of a tomato eaten as a vegetable [alter. of earlier *tomate*, fr Sp, fr Nahuatl *tomatl*]

¹**tomb** /toohm/ *n* **1a** an excavation in which a corpse is buried; a grave **b** a chamber or vault for the dead, built either above or below ground and usu serving as a memorial **2** a monument to a dead person, usu housing his/her remains; *also* CENOTAPH (memorial to the dead) **3** *the* state of being dead ⟨*came back from the* ~⟩ **4** *informal* a building or structure like a tomb; *esp* a large gloomy building [ME *tombe*, fr AF *tumbe*, fr LL *tumba* burial mound, fr Gk *tymbos*; akin to L *tumēre* to be swollen – more at THUMB] – **tombless** *adj*

²**tomb** *vt* to bury, entomb

**tombac** /'tombak/ *n* a yellow-coloured copper and zinc alloy, sometimes containing tin or arsenic, that is used esp for making cheap jewellery [Fr, fr D *tombak*, fr Malay *těmbaga* copper]

**tombola** /tom'bohlə/ *n* a lottery in which people buy numbered tickets from a revolving drum and are entitled to claim any prize on display that bears the same number as any ticket they hold [It, fr *tombolare* to tumble, fr *tombare* to fall, fr (assumed) VL *tumbare*, of imit origin]

**tombolo** /'tombəloh/ *n, pl* **tombolos** a sand or gravel ridge connecting an island with the mainland or another island [It, fr L *tumulus* mound]

**tomboy** /'tom,boy/ *n* a girl who behaves in a manner conventionally thought of as typical of a boy – **tomboyish** *adj*, **tomboyishness** *n*

**tombstone** /'toohm,stohn/ *n* a gravestone

**tomcat** /'tom,kat/ *n* a male cat

**tomcod** /'tom,kod/ *n* any of several CROAKERS (types of fish) of the Pacific coast

**Tom Collins** /,tom 'kolinz/ *n* a tall iced drink consisting of a gin base with lime, lemon juice, or soda and sugar [fr the name *Tom Collins*]

**Tom, Dick, and Harry** /,tom ,dik ənd 'hari/ *n* people taken at random – often + *every* ⟨*not every* ~ *can join this club*⟩

**tome** /tohm/ *n* **1** a (large scholarly) book **2** *archaic* a volume forming part of a larger work [MF or L; MF, fr L *tomus*, fr Gk *tomos* section, roll of papyrus, volume, fr *temnein* to cut; akin to L *tondēre* to shear, Gk *tendein* to gnaw]

**-tome** /-'tohm/ *comb form* (→ *n*) **1** tomological part or segment ⟨*myotome*⟩ **2** cutting instrument ⟨*microtome*⟩ [Gk *tomos* section]

**tome au raisin** /ˌtohm oh re'zanh (*Fr* tom o rɛzɛ̃)/ *n, often cap T&R* a white cheese covered with a rind of dried black grape pips and skins [Fr, Savoy cheese with grape]

**tomentose** /'tohməntohs/ *adj* covered with densely matted hairs ⟨*a ~ leaf*⟩ [NL *tomentosus*, fr *tomentum*]

**tomentum** /tə'mentəm/ *n, pl* **tomenta** /-tə/ **1** a covering of densely matted woolly hairs on a leaf, stem, etc **2** the network of minute blood vessels on the inner surface of the PIA MATER (innermost of the membranes covering the brain) [NL, fr L, cushion stuffing; akin to L *tumēre* to be swollen – more at THUMB]

**tomfool** /ˌtom'foohl/ *n* an extremely foolish or stupid person

**tomfoolery** /ˌtom'foohləri/ *n* foolish trifling; nonsense

**Tommy** /'tomi/, **Tommy Atkins** /'atkinz/ *n, informal* a British private soldier – no longer in vogue [*Thomas Atkins*, name used as model in official army forms]

**tommy bar** /'tomi/ *n, Br* a bar that can be inserted at right angles into a BOX SPANNER in order to turn it [*Tommy*, nickname for *Thomas*]

**tommy gun** *n, informal* THOMPSON SUBMACHINE GUN [by shortening & alter.]

**tommyrot** /'tomiˌrot/ *n, informal* utter foolishness or nonsense [E dial. *tommy* fool + E *rot*]

**tomogram** /'tohməgram/ *n* an X-ray photograph made by tomography

**tomography** /tə'mogrəfi/ *n* a technique used (eg in medical diagnosis) to obtain X-ray photographs in which the shadows of structures in front of and behind the section under scrutiny do not show [Gk *tomos* section + ISV *-graphy* – more at TOME]

**tomorrow** /tə'moroh/ *adv or n* **1** (on) the day after today **2** (in) the future ⟨*the world of ~*⟩ [ME *to morgen*, fr OE *tō morgen*, fr *tō* + *morgen* morrow, morning – more at MORN]

**tompion** /'tompi·ən/ *n* TAMPION (plug or cover for gun muzzle)

**Tom Thumb** *n* a dwarf type, race, or individual [*Tom Thumb*, legendary E dwarf]

**tomtit** /'tomˌtit/ *n* any of various small active birds; *esp* BLUE TIT [prob short for *tomtitmouse*, fr the name *Tom* + *titmouse*]

**¹tom-ˌtom** /tom/ *n* **1** a usu long and narrow small-headed drum commonly beaten with the hands **2** a monotonous beating or rhythmic sound [Hindi *ṭamṭam*]

**-tomy** /-təmi/ *comb form* incision; cutting ⟨*laparotomy*⟩ [NL *-tomia*, fr Gk, fr *-tomos* that cuts, fr *temnein* to cut – more at TOME]

**¹ton** /tun/ *n, pl* (*1&2*) **tons, ton,** (*3&5*) **tons 1** any of various units of weight: **1a** LONG TON **b** SHORT TON **c** TONNE **2a** REGISTER TON (unit for a ship's internal capacity) **b** a unit approximately equal to the volume of one LONG TON of seawater, used in reckoning the displacement of ships, and equal to 0.991 cubic metre (35 cubic feet) **c** FREIGHT TON (unit of cargo volume) **3 tons** *pl, ton informal* a great quantity ⟨*has ~s of money*⟩ **4** *informal* a great weight ⟨*this bag weighs a ~*⟩ **5** *informal* **5a** a speed of 100 miles per hour ⟨*caught by the police doing a ~ on my motorbike*⟩ **b** a score of 100 (eg in cricket) △ tun [ME *tunne* unit of weight or capacity – more at TUN]

**²ton** /tohn, tonh (*Fr* tɔ̃)/ *n* **1** the prevailing fashion **2** the quality or state of being fashionable [Fr, lit., tone, fr L *tonus*]

**tonal** /'tohn(ə)l/ *adj* **1** of tone or tonality **2** having tonality – **tonally** *adv*

**tonality** /toh'naləti/ *n* **1** tonal quality **2** the organization of all the notes and chords of a piece of music in relation to a keynote (TONIC 2) **3** the arrangement or interrelation of the colours or shades of a picture

**tondo** /'tondoh/ *n, pl* **tondi** /-di/ **1** a circular painting **2** a sculptured medallion [It, fr *tondo* round, short for *rotondo*, fr L *rotundus* – more at ROUND]

**¹tone** /tohn/ *n* **1 tone, tones** *pl* a vocal or musical sound; *esp* one of a specified quality ⟨*spoke in low ~s*⟩ ⟨*masculine ~s*⟩ **2a** a sound of a definite frequency with relatively weak overtones ⟨*wait till you hear the ~, then dial*⟩ **b** WHOLE TONE (distance between two musical notes) **3 tone, tones** *pl* an accent or inflection of the voice expressive of a mood or emotion ⟨*replied in a surly ~*⟩ **4** the pitch of a word, often used (eg in Chinese) to express differences of meaning **5** a particular pitch constituting an element in the intonation of a phrase or sentence ⟨*high ~*⟩ ⟨*low-rising ~*⟩ **6** style or manner of expression in speaking or writing ⟨*seemed wise to adopt a conciliatory ~*⟩

⟨*don't take that ~ with me*⟩ **7a** colour quality or value; a tint, shade **b** the colour that appreciably modifies a colour or white or black ⟨*grey walls of greenish ~*⟩ **8** the general effect of light, shade, and colour in a picture **9a** the state of a living body or of one of its organs or tissues of being physiologically healthy, functioning normally, and having the normal degree of tension or firmness and responsiveness to stimuli **b** the condition of slight tension normal to living animal tissue; *specif* muscular TONUS **10a** prevailing character, quality, or trend (eg of morals) ⟨*lowered the ~ of the discussion*⟩ **b** distinction, style **11** *chiefly NAm* a musical note [ME, fr L *tonus* tension, tone, fr Gk *tonos*, lit., act of stretching; akin to Gk *teinein* to stretch – more at THIN]

**²tone** *vt* **1** to impart tone to ⟨*medicine to ~ up the system*⟩ **2** to soften in colour, appearance, or sound; mellow **3** to change the normal silver image of (eg a photographic print) into a coloured image ~ *vi* **1** to assume a pleasing colour quality or tint **2** to blend or harmonize in colour – usu + *in*

**tone down** *vt* to reduce in intensity, violence, or force; moderate ⟨*he was told to* tone down *his views*⟩

**tone arm** *n* the movable arm of a record player or deck that carries the PICKUP (part containing the needle) and enables the needle to follow the groove

**tone control** *n* a means or device for controlling the relative amplification of different frequencies (eg bass and treble) so as to achieve more balanced sound reception

**toned** /tohnd/ *adj* **1** having (a specified) tone; characterized or distinguished by a tone – often in combination ⟨*shrill*-toned⟩ **2** *of paper* having a slight tint

**ˌtone-'deaf** *adj* unable to detect differences in musical pitch – **tone deafness** *n*

**tone group** *n* TONE UNIT

**tone language** *n* a language (eg Chinese or Bantu) in which variations in pitch (TONE 4) distinguish words of different meaning

**toneless** /'tohnlis/ *adj* lacking in tone or expression – **tonelessly** *adv*, **tonelessness** *n*

**toneme** /'tohneem/ *n* a linguistic element in a TONE LANGUAGE that can be distinguished from another otherwise identical element by its pitch (TONE 4), and that therefore serves to differentiate words or word parts [¹*tone* + *-eme*] – **tonemic** *adj*

**tone poem** *n* SYMPHONIC POEM (piece of orchestral music usu telling a story) – **tone poet** *n*

**toner** /'tohnə/ *n* one who or that which tones or is a source of tones: eg **a** a pure organic pigment **b** a solution used to impart colour to a silver photographic image **c** a substance used to develop a XEROGRAPHIC (dry-photocopied) image **d** a cosmetic preparation used on the hair to soften harsh colours or add shades

**ˌtone-ˌrow** /roh/ *n* the 12 CHROMATIC (including sharpened or flattened) notes of the OCTAVE placed in a chosen fixed order that form the basis of the material of a TWELVE-TONE musical composition – called also NOTE-ROW

**tonetic** /toh'netik/ *adj* of linguistic tones, TONE LANGUAGES, or intonation ⟨*~ notation*⟩ – **tonetically** *adv*

**tonetics** /tə'netiks, toh-/ *n taking sing vb* the use or study of linguistic tones

**tone unit** *n* a unit of speech consisting of a strongly stressed syllable (NUCLEUS 3) with or without other stressed and unstressed syllables

**tong** *n* a Chinese secret society or fraternal organization formerly notorious for gang warfare [Chin (Cant) *tong* (*t'ong*) hall, meeting place]

**tonga** /'tong·gə/ *n* a light 2-wheeled one-horse vehicle for two or four people in common use in India [Hindi *tāṅgā*]

**Tongan** /'tong·gən/ *n or adj* (an inhabitant, or the POLYNESIAN language) of the Tonga islands

**tongs** /tongz/ *n pl* any of various grasping devices consisting of two pieces joined at one end by a pivot or hinged like scissors [ME *tonges*, pl of *tonge*, fr OE *tang*; akin to OHG *zanga* tongs, Gk *daknein* to bite]

**¹tongue** /tung/ *n* **1a** a fleshy muscular movable organ attached to the floor of the mouth in most VERTEBRATE animals, that bears small glands and sensory structures that receive stimuli, and that functions esp in tasting and swallowing food and in human beings as a speech organ **b** a part in various INVERTEBRATE animals that is analogous to the tongue of VERTEBRATE animals **2** the tongue of an animal (eg an ox or sheep) used as food **3** the power of communication through speech **4a** a (spoken) language **b** manner or quality of utterance ⟨*a* *sharp* ~⟩ **c** *pl* ecstatic usu unintelligible utterance, esp in Christian worship ⟨*speak in* ~s⟩ ⟨*the gift of* ~s⟩ **d** the cry (as if) of a hound pursuing or in sight of game – esp in *give tongue* **5** a long narrow strip of land projecting into a body of water **6** something like an animal's tongue (eg in being elongated and fastened at one end only): eg **6a** a movable pin in a buckle **b** a piece of metal suspended inside a bell so as to strike against the sides as the bell is swung; a clapper **c** the pole of a (horse-drawn) vehicle **d** the flap under the lacing or buckle on the front of a shoe or boot **7a** the rib on one edge of a board that fits into a corresponding groove in an edge of another board to make a flush joint **b** FEATHER 4 (projecting part) **8** a tapering cone – in *tongue of flame/fire synonyms* see LANGUAGE [ME *tunge*, fr OE; akin to OHG *zunga* tongue, L *lingua*] – **tonguelike** *adj* – **with one's tongue in one's cheek** in a tongue-in-cheek manner – see also on the TIP of one's tongue

²**tongue** *vt* **1** to touch or lick (as if) with the tongue **2a** to cut a tongue on ⟨~ *a board*⟩ **b** to join (eg boards) by means of a TONGUE AND GROOVE **3** to articulate (notes) by tonguing **4** *archaic* to scold ~ *vi* **1** to project in a tongue **2** to articulate notes on a wind instrument by interrupting the stream of wind with the action of the tongue

**tongue and groove** *n* a joint made by a projecting rib (TONGUE 7a) on one edge of a board fitting into a corresponding groove on the edge of another board – **tongued and grooved** *adj*

**tongued** /tungd/ *adj* having a tongue of a specified kind – often in combination ⟨*sharp*-tongued⟩

**tongue-in-ʹcheek** *adj* characterized by irony or whimsical exaggeration – **tongue in cheek** *adv*

ʹ**tongue-ˌlashing** *n* a scolding, rebuke

**tongueless** /-lis/ *adj* **1** having no tongue **2** lacking power of speech; mute, silent

¹ʹ**tongue-ˌtie** *vt* to deprive of speech or the power of distinct articulation [back-formation fr *tongue-tied*]

²**tongue-tie** *n* a condition of limited mobility of the tongue due to the shortness of its FRAENUM (supporting membrane)

ʹ**tongue-ˌtied** *adj* **1** affected with tongue-tie **2** unable to speak freely (eg because of shyness)

**tongue twister** *n* a word or phrase difficult to say because of several similar consonant sounds (eg *"she sells seashells on the seashore"*)

**tonguing** /ʹtung·ing/ *n* use of the tongue in articulating notes on a wind instrument

**-tonia** /-tohnyə/ *comb form* (→ *n*) condition or degree of physiological or muscular tonus ⟨*myotonia*⟩ [NL, fr *tonus*]

¹**tonic** /ʹtonik/ *adj* **1a(1)** characterized by muscular TONUS ⟨~ *contraction of muscles*⟩ **a(2)** marked by prolonged muscular contraction ⟨~ *convulsions*⟩ **b** of, characterized by, or producing normal body tone **2** increasing or restoring physical or mental tone **3** of or based on the first note of a scale ⟨~ *harmony*⟩ **4** *of a syllable* bearing a principal stress or accent **5** of speech tones or TONE LANGUAGES [Gk *tonikos*, fr *tonos* tension, tone] – **tonically** *adv*

²**tonic** *n* **1a** something, esp a medicine, that increases body tone **b** something that invigorates, refreshes, or stimulates ⟨*a day in the country was a* ~ *for him*⟩ **c** a liquid cosmetic preparation for toning or cleansing the scalp, hair, face, etc **d** a carbonated mineral water flavoured with a small amount of quinine, lemon, and lime **2** the first note of a DIATONIC scale (ordinary 8-note musical scale) represented in sol-fa by *doh*; a keynote **3** a sound made with vibration of the VOCAL CORDS **4** an instance of TONIC ACCENT

**tonic accent** *n* the phonetic stress of a spoken syllable relative to others

**tonicity** /tohʹnisəti/ *n* **1** the property of possessing tone; *esp* healthy vigour of body or mind **2** muscular tone; TONUS

**tonic sol-fa** *n* a system of notation commonly used for sight-singing that represents the notes of the musical scale by syllables, esp *doh, ray, me, fah, soh, lah, te,* or, in written or printed music, by the first letters of these syllables

**tonight** /təʹniet/ *adv or n* (on) this night or the night following today ⟨*will do it* ~⟩ ⟨*on* ~*'s news*⟩ [adv ME *to night, to niht,* fr OE *tō niht,* fr *tō* to, at + *niht* night; n fr adv]

**tonka bean** /ʹtongkə/ *n* the seed of any of several trees (genus *Dipteryx*) of the pea family, that contains COUMARIN (substance with a smell of new-mown hay) and is used in perfumes and as a flavouring (eg in snuff and tobacco); *also* a tree bearing tonka beans [prob fr Tupi *tonka*]

**tonky** /ʹtongki/ *adj, NZ informal* socially pretentious; snobbish [perh blend of *tony* and *swanky*]

**tonnage** /ʹtunij/ *n* **1** a duty formerly levied on every cask of wine imported into England **2a** a duty or tax on vessels based on cargo capacity **b** a duty on goods per ton transported **3** ships in terms of the total number of tons registered or carried or of their carrying capacity ⟨*British merchant* ~⟩ **4a** the carrying capacity of a merchant ship in units of 100 cubic feet (about 2.83 cubic metres) **b** the volume or weight of water displaced by a warship **5** total weight in tons shipped, carried, or produced [(1) ME, fr OF *tonne* tun – more at TUNNEL; (2–5) ¹*ton* + *-age*]

**tonne, ton** /tun/ *n* a metric unit of weight equal to 1000 kilograms (2205 pounds) [Fr, fr *tonne* tun, fr OF – more at TUNNEL]

**tonneau** /ʹtonoh/ *n, pl* **tonneaus, tonneaux** /-nohz/ **1** the (rear) seating compartment of a car **2** a unit of capacity equal to 900 litres (about 200 gallons) used esp for wine [Fr, lit., tun, fr OF *tonel* – more at TUNNEL]

**tonner** /ʹtunə/ *n* an object (eg a ship) having a specified tonnage – in combination ⟨*a thousand-tonner*⟩

**tonometer** /tohʹnomitə/ *n* **1** an instrument or device (eg a TUNING FORK) for determining the exact pitch of tones **2** any of various instruments for measuring pressure (eg in the eyeball, or of the blood or a gas) [Gk *tonos* tone + E *-meter*] – **tonometry** *n*, **tonometric** *adj*

**tonoplast** /ʹtohnəplast, ʹto-/ *n* the membrane surrounding a gas or liquid-filled cavity (VACUOLE) in the CYTOPLASM (jellylike material outside the nucleus) of a plant cell [ISV *tono-* (fr Gk *tonos* tension) + *-plast* – more at TONE]

**tons** /tunz/ *adv, informal* very much ⟨*worked* ~ *better after a couple of pints*⟩

**tonsil** /ʹtons(ə)l/ *n* **1** either of a pair of prominent oval masses of spongy LYMPHOID tissue that lie one on each side of the throat at the back of the mouth **2** any of various small rounded masses of lymphoid tissue that are similar to tonsils [L *tonsillae*, pl, tonsils] – **tonsillar** *adj*

**tonsill-** /ʹtonsil-/, **tonsillo-** *comb form* tonsil ⟨tonsill*ectomy*⟩ ⟨tonsillo*tomy*⟩ [L *tonsillae*]

**tonsillectomy** /ˌtonsiʹlektəmi/ *n* the surgical removal of the tonsils

**tonsillitis** /ˌtonsiʹlietəs/ *n* inflammation of the tonsils [NL]

**tonsorial** /tonʹsawri·əl/ *adj, chiefly humorous* of a barber or his work [L *tonsorius*, fr *tonsus*, pp]

¹**tonsure** /ʹtonshə/ *n* **1** the Roman Catholic or Eastern rite of admission to the priesthood or a monastic order by the shaving of the whole or a part of the head **2** the shaven patch on a monk's or other cleric's head [ME, fr ML *tonsura*, fr L, act of shearing, fr *tonsus*, pp of *tondēre* to shear – more at TOME]

²**tonsure** *vt* to shave the head of; *esp* to confer the tonsure on

**tontine** /ʹtonteen, -ʹ-/ *n* a financial arrangement whereby a group of participants share various advantages on such terms that on the death or default of any member, his/her advantages are distributed among the remaining members until one member remains or an agreed period has elapsed; *also* the share or right of each individual [Fr, fr Lorenzo *Tonti* †1695 It banker]

ʹ**ton-ˌup** *adj, Br informal* of or being somebody who has achieved a score, speed, etc of 100 ⟨*darts* ~ *boys are in a record-breaking mood – The Sun*⟩ ⟨*the local motorcycle* ~ *boys*⟩

**tonus** /ʹtohnəs/ *n* TONE 9; *specif* a state of partial contraction or slight tension characteristic of normal muscle [NL, fr L, tension, tone]

**tony** /ʹtohni/ *adj, chiefly NAm* marked by an aristocratic or fashionable manner or style ⟨~ *private schools*⟩ [¹*tone* + ¹*-y*]

**Tony** *n, pl* **Tonys** a medallion awarded annually by a US professional organization for notable achievement in the theatre [*Tony,* nickname of Antoinette Perry †1946 US actress & producer]

**too** /tooh/ *adv* **1** also; IN ADDITION ⟨*sell the house and furniture* ~⟩ **2a** to a regrettable degree; excessively ⟨~ *large a house for us*⟩ ⟨*this time he has gone* ~ *far*⟩ **b** to a higher degree than meets a standard ⟨~ *pretty for words*⟩ **c** very ⟨*was only* ~ *pleased*⟩ ⟨*house was none* ~ *clean*⟩ **3** *chiefly NAm* indeed, so – used to counter a negative charge ⟨*"I didn't do it." "You did* ~*."*⟩ [ME, fr OE *tō* to, too – more at TO]

**usage** Too needs to be supplemented by another adverb before most past participles ⟨**too** *greatly admired*⟩ ⟨**too** *closely guarded*⟩ ⟨*not* **too** *far removed from bribery*⟩; but some past participles which have come to be treated as ordinary adjectives can take **too** alone ⟨**too** *tired/bewildered/limited*⟩. In marginal cases it is safer to insert another adverb for formal writing ⟨**too** (*much*) *surprised/amused/ interested/disgusted/distressed*⟩. △ **to**, **two**

**toodle-oo** /'toohdl ˌooh/ *interj* – used to express farewell; no longer in vogue

'**toodle-ˌpip** *interj* – used to express farewell; no longer in vogue

**took** /took/ *past of* TAKE

¹**tool** /toohl/ *n* **1a** an implement that is used, esp by hand, to carry out work of a mechanical nature (e g cutting, levering, or digging) – not usu used with reference to kitchen utensils or cutlery **b** (the cutting or shaping part in) a MACHINE TOOL **2a** something (e g an instrument or apparatus) used in performing an operation or necessary in the practice of a vocation or profession ⟨*books are the ∼s of a scholar's trade*⟩ **b** something that serves as a means to accomplishing an end **3** somebody who is used or manipulated by another; PUPPET 2 **4** *vulg* a penis [ME, fr OE *tōl;* akin to OE *tawian* to prepare for use – more at TAW] – **down tools** *chiefly Br* to stop working; *esp* to strike

*synonyms* **Tool**, **machine**, **implement**, **instrument**, **appliance**, **utensil**, **device**, and **gadget** all mean "piece of equipment for doing work". A **tool** is typically small and hand-held, performs a physical task (e g cutting, scraping, banging, or moulding), and can be powered: a hammer is a **tool** but so is an electric drill. A **machine** is typically larger and more elaborate than a **tool**, consisting of several parts that transmit forces, and need not be powered or perform a physical task: a crane is a **machine**, but so are a lawn mower and a cash register. An **implement** is usually a simple tool, particularly one used for agriculture: a rake or a spade is an **implement**. An **instrument** is either a delicate tool for skilled precision work, or a measuring device: a scalpel and a thermometer are **instruments**. An appliance is usually an item of domestic or office equipment powered from the mains: a vacuum cleaner and a liquidizer are **appliances**. A **utensil** is portable, and is usually in practice a domestic container: a saucepan is a **utensil**. A **device** is usually a piece of mechanical equipment ingeniously contrived for a stated purpose ⟨*an improved steering* **device**⟩. A **gadget** is a small often novel and electronic device that may form part of a piece of machinery ⟨*fire engine covered with* **gadgets**⟩.

²**tool** *vt* **1** to work, shape, or finish with a tool; *esp* to letter or ornament (e g leather) by means of hand tools **2** to equip (e g a plant or industry) with tools, machines, and instruments for production – often + *up* ∼ *vi* **1** to get tooled up for production – usu + *up* ⟨∼*ing up for the new models – Ethyl News*⟩ **2** *informal* to drive, ride ⟨∼*ed around the neighbourhood in a small car*⟩

³**tool** *n* a design (e g on the binding of a book) made by tooling

**toolbox** /-ˌboks/ *n* a box for (a workman's) tools

**toolholder** /-ˌhohldə/ *n* a device for holding a tool in a machine (e g a lathe)

**toolmaker** /-ˌmaykə/ *n* a skilled worker who makes, repairs, maintains, and calibrates the tools and instruments of a MACHINE SHOP – **toolmaking** *n*

**toolroom** /-ˌroohm, -room/ *n* a room where tools are kept; *esp* a room in a MACHINE SHOP in which tools are made, stored, and issued for use by workmen

**toolshed** /-ˌshed/ *n* a shed for storing (garden) tools

**tool steel** *n* any of several hard steels containing between 0.9 and 1.4 per cent carbon that are suitable for use in tools for cutting metal

**toom** /toohm/ *adj, chiefly Scot* empty [ME, fr OE *tōm* – more at TEEM]

**toon** /toohn/ *n* an E Indian and Australian tree (*Cedrela toona*) of the mahogany family with fragrant dark red wood and flowers from which a dye is obtained; *also* the wood of this tree [Hindi *tūn*, fr Skt *tunna*]

¹**toot** /tooht/ *vi* **1** to produce a short blast or similar sound ⟨*the horn* ∼*ed*⟩ **2** to cause an instrument to toot ⟨∼*ed as he rounded the corner*⟩ ∼ *vt* to cause to produce a short blast ⟨∼ *a whistle*⟩ [prob imit] – **tooter** *n*

²**toot** *n* a short blast (as if) on a horn, trumpet, whistle, etc

¹**tooth** /toohth/ *n, pl* **teeth** /teeth/ **1a** any of the hard bony structures that are borne on the jaws or other bones of the mouth of VERTEBRATE animals, and that serve esp for the seizing and tearing, biting, chewing, or grinding of food and as weapons **b** any of various usu hard and sharp projecting structures about the mouth or mouthlike part of an INVERTEBRATE animal **2** a taste, liking ⟨*a sweet* ∼⟩ **3** a projection

like the tooth of an animal in shape, arrangement, or action ⟨*a saw* ∼⟩: e g **3a** any of the regular projections on the rim of a cogwheel **b** a small sharp-pointed projection on the margin of a leaf, petal, etc **4** *pl* effective means of enforcement [ME, fr OE *tōth;* akin to OHG *zand* tooth, L *dent-, dens,* Gk *odont-, odous*] – **toothlike** *adj,* **toothless** *adj* – **get one's teeth into** to deal with enthusiastically or vigorously; become absorbed in – **in the teeth of 1** in direct opposition to ⟨*rule had been imposed by conquest* in the teeth of *obstinate resistance* – A J Toynbee⟩ **2** in or into direct contact or collision with ⟨*sail* in the teeth of *a hurricane – Current Biog*⟩ – **lie in/through one's (back) teeth** to lie shamelessly and unrestrainedly – **long in the tooth** *informal* old [fr the apparent lengthening of the teeth (really the recession of the gums) in old age] – **set one's teeth** to summon up one's courage in the face of something distasteful or frightening – **set somebody's teeth on edge** to cause somebody great irritation or discomfort – see also FLY **in the teeth of, by the** SKIN **of one's teeth**

²**tooth** *vt* **1** to provide with teeth, esp by cutting notches ⟨∼ *a saw*⟩ **2** to roughen the surface of ⟨∼ *a cement floor to prevent slipping*⟩ ∼ *vi, esp of cogwheels* to interlock

**toothache** /-ˌayk/ *n* pain in or round a tooth

**tooth and nail** *adv* with every available means; ALL OUT ⟨*fight* ∼⟩

**toothbrush** /-ˌbrush/ *n* a brush for cleaning the teeth

**toothbrushing** /'toohth,brushing/ *n* the action of using a toothbrush to clean teeth

**toothcomb** /-ˌkohm/ *n, Br* a comb with fine teeth

**toothed** /toohtht/ *adj* having teeth, esp of a specified kind or number – often in combination ⟨*buck*toothed⟩ ⟨*sharp-* toothed⟩

**toothed whale** *n* any of a suborder (Odontoceti) of whales with numerous simple conical teeth, including the dolphins, SPERM WHALE, porpoises, and KILLER WHALE – compare WHALEBONE WHALE

**toothing** /'toohdhing, 'toohthing/ *n* alternately projecting horizontal layers of stone left at the end of a brick wall to provide for a later continuation

**toothpaste** /-ˌpayst/ *n* a paste for cleaning the teeth

**toothpick** /-ˌpik/ *n* a pointed instrument (e g a small tapering piece of wood) used for removing food particles lodged between the teeth

**tooth powder** *n* a powder for cleaning the teeth

**tooth shell** *n* any of a class (Scaphopoda of the phylum Mollusca) of marine INVERTEBRATE animals with a tapering tubular shell; *also* this shell – called also SCAPHOPOD

**toothsome** /'toohths(ə)m/ *adj* **1** delicious ⟨*crisp* ∼ *fried chicken*⟩ **2** (sexually) attractive – **toothsomely** *adv,* **toothsomeness** *n*

**toothwort** /-ˌwuht/ *n* **1** a European plant (*Lathraea squamaria*) of the broomrape family that lives as a parasite on the roots of hazels, poplars, elms, etc and has white to pinkish flower spikes and stems, and an underground plant stem (ROOTSTOCK) covered with tooth-shaped scales **2** any of various N American and Eurasian plants (genus *Dentaria*) of the cabbage family with scaly rootstocks, including several cultivated for their showy typically white, pink, or pale purple flowers

**toothy** /'toohthi/ *adj* having or showing numerous, large, or prominent teeth ⟨∼ *grin*⟩ – **toothily** *adv*

**tootle** /'toohtl/ *vi* **1** to toot gently or continuously **2** *informal* to drive or move along in a leisurely manner [freq of ¹*toot*] – **tootle** *n,* **tootler** *n*

**tootsie** /'tootsi/ *n, informal* dear, sweetheart [origin unknown]

**tootsy** *also* **tootsie** /'tootsi/ *n* a foot – used chiefly to children [baby-talk alter. of *foot*]

¹**top** /top/ *n* **1a(1)** the highest point, level, or part of something; the summit, crown **a(2)** the (top of) the head – esp in *top to toe* **a(3)** the head of a plant, esp one with edible roots ⟨*beet* ∼s⟩ **a(4)** a garment worn on the upper body **b(1)** the highest or uppermost region or part **b(2)** the upper end, edge, or surface **2** a fitted or attached part serving as an upper piece, lid, or covering **3a** a platform surrounding the head of a lower mast that serves to spread the topmast rigging, strengthen the mast, and provide a standing place for people aloft **b** a comparable part on a ship without masts **4** *the* highest degree or pitch conceivable or attained; *the* acme, pinnacle **5** the part that is nearest in space or time to the source or beginning **6** (somebody or something in) the highest position (e g in rank or achievement) ⟨∼ *of the class*⟩ **7** TOP SPIN (forward spin) ⟨*put*

*a bit of* ~ *on the ball*⟩ **8 top, top gear** *Br* the transmission gear of a motor vehicle giving the highest ratio of propeller-shaft to engine-shaft speed and hence the highest speed of travel [ME, fr OE; akin to OHG *zopf* tip, tuft of hair] – **topped** *adj* – **blow one's top** to become furious; lose one's temper – **go over the top 1** to climb out of a trench in order to engage in battle **2** *chiefly Br* to act wildly or unrestrainedly – **off the top of one's head** in an impromptu manner ⟨*can't give you the figures* off the top of my head⟩ – **on top of 1a** in control of ⟨*keep* on top of *my job*⟩ **b** informed about **2** in sudden and unexpected proximity to ⟨*the situation was* on top of *me before I knew it*⟩ **3** in addition to ⟨on top of *everything else he managed to break his arm*⟩ – **on top of the world** in high spirits; in a state of exhilaration and well-being – **over the top** exaggerated; *esp* excessively dramatic

²**top** *vb* **-pp-** *vt* **1a** to cut the top off **b** to shorten or remove the top of (a plant); *also* to remove the stalk or CALYX (ring of leaflike parts round bud or flower) of (eg a gooseberry or strawberry) – compare TAIL 2b **c** to remove the most volatile parts from (eg crude petroleum) **2a** to cover with a top or on the top; provide, form, or serve as a top for **b** to supply with a decorative or protective finish or final touch – often + *off* **c** to complete the basic structure of (eg a high-rise building) by putting on a cap or uppermost section – usu + *out* or *off* ⟨*the new tower block was* ~ed *off yesterday*⟩ **3a** to be or become higher than; overtop ⟨~s *the previous record*⟩ **b** to be superior to; excel, surpass ⟨~s *everything of its kind in print*⟩ **c** to gain ascendancy over **4a** to rise to, reach, or be at the top of **b** to go over the top of; clear, surmount **5** to strike (a ball) above the centre, thereby imparting forward spin (TOP SPIN) ~ *vi* to reach a summit or crest – usu + *off* or *out* ⟨*the business-investment boom* ... *has* ~ped *out* – Newsweek⟩

**top up** *vt* **1** to make up to the full quantity, capacity, or amount; replenish ⟨*keeping stocks* topped up⟩ **2** to increase (a money sum set aside for a specific purpose) ⟨*the individual may* top up *the company car scheme rate by up to 15 per cent*⟩ **3** to replenish the drink of ⟨*can I* top *you* up?⟩

³**top** *adj* **1** of or at the top; uppermost **2** foremost, leading ⟨*one of the world's* ~ *journalists*⟩ **3** of the highest quality, amount, or degree ⟨~ *value*⟩ ⟨~ *form*⟩

⁴**top** *n* a child's toy that is usu pear-shaped or conical and has a tapering point on which it is made to spin [ME, fr OE]

**top-** /ˈtop-/, *comb form* place; locality ⟨*topology*⟩ ⟨*toponymy*⟩ [ME, fr LL, fr Gk, fr *topos* – more at TOPIC]

**topaz** /ˈtohpaz/ *n* **1** a hard mineral used as a gem, that consists of a SILICATE of aluminium containing fluorine, $Al_2SiO_4(F,OH)_2$, and occurs usu in translucent or transparent crystals that are colourless or various shades of yellow, blue, brown, or reddish-pink **2a** a yellow sapphire **b** a yellow quartz **3** either of two large brilliantly coloured S American hummingbirds (*Topaza pella* and *Topaza pyra*) [ME *topace*, fr OF, fr L *topazus*, fr Gk *topazos*]

**top billing** *n* **1** the position at the top of a theatrical bill, usu featuring the star's name **2** prominent emphasis, featuring, or advertising

**top boot** *n* a high boot, often with light-coloured leather bands round the upper part

**top brass** *n taking sing or pl vb* BRASS HATS (officials of high rank)

**top-ˈcat** *adj* first-class

**top-ˈclass** *adj* first-class

**topcoat** /-ˌkoht/ *n* **1** a (lightweight) overcoat **2** a final coat of paint

**topcross** /ˈtopˌkros/ *n* a cross between a superior or purebred male and inferior female stock in order to improve the average quality of the progeny; *also* an animal or plant resulting from such a cross

**top dog** *n, informal* a person in a position of authority, esp through victory in a hard-fought competition

**top drawer** *n* the highest level, esp of society – esp in *out of the top drawer* – **top-drawer** *adj*

ˈ**top-ˌdress** *vt* to scatter fertilizer over (land) without working it in – **topdressing** *n*

¹**tope** /tohp/ *vi* to drink alcoholic drink to excess [obs *tope*, interj used to wish good health before drinking, prob fr Fr, lit., (I) agree, accept a bet]

²**tope** *n* a small shark (*Galeorhinus galeus*) with a liver very rich in VITAMIN A [origin unknown]

³**tope** *n* STUPA (Buddhist shrine) [Hindi *top*, perh fr Skt *stūpa*]

**topee, topi** /ˈtohpi/ *n* a lightweight helmet-shaped hat made of pith or cork and worn esp in the tropics [Hindi *ṭopī*]

**toper** /ˈtohpə/ *n* a person who drinks alcoholic beverages, esp to excess

**top-ˈflight** *adj* of the highest grade or quality; best

¹**topgallant** /ˌtopˈgalənt, təˈgalənt/ *adj* of or being a part next above the TOPMAST (mast above the lowest mast) ⟨~ *sails*⟩ ⟨*the* ~ *mast*⟩ [¹*top* + ²*gallant*]

²**topgallant** *n* **1** a topgallant mast or sail **2** *archaic* the topmost point; the summit ⟨*the high* ~ *of my joy* – Shak⟩

**top gear** *n, Br* **1** TOP 8 (highest vehicle gear) **2** a state of intense or maximum activity

ˈ**top-ˌhamper** *n* the gear and fittings (eg spars and rigging) above a ship's upper deck

**top hat** *n* a man's tall-crowned hat that is usu made of silk or, esp formerly, of (imitation) beaver fur and is now used only for formal wear

ˌ**top-ˈheavy** *adj* **1** having the top part too heavy for or disproportionate to the lower part **2** capitalized beyond what is prudent ⟨~ *scheme*⟩

**Tophet** /ˈtohfet/ *n* a place or state of misery; hell [ME, shrine south of ancient Jerusalem where human sacrifices were performed (Jer 7:31), Gehenna, fr Heb *tōpheth*]

ˌ**top-ˈhole** *adj, chiefly Br informal* excellent, first-class – not now in vogue

**tophus** /ˈtohfəs/ *n, pl* **tophi** /-fī/ a hard chalky mass consisting of URATES, that is deposited in tissues (eg the cartilage round a joint), esp in gout [L, tufa]

**topi** /ˈtohpi/ *n* a topee

**topiary** /ˈtohpyəri/ *adj or n* (of or being) the practice or art of training, cutting, and trimming trees or shrubs into odd or ornamental shapes; *also* (characterized by) such work [L *topiarius* of ornamental gardening, fr *topia* ornamental gardening, irreg fr Gk *topos* place]

**topic** /ˈtopik/ *n* **1a** a heading in an outlined argument or exposition **b** the subject of (a section) of a discourse; THEME 1 **2** a subject for discussion or consideration *synonyms* see ¹SUBJECT [L *Topica* Topics (work by Aristotle), fr Gk *Topika*, fr *topika*, neut pl of *topikos* of a place, of a commonplace, fr *topos* place, commonplace; akin to OE *thafian* to agree]

**topical** /ˈtopikl/ *adj* **1a** of a place **b** designed for application to a small area of the body surface ⟨*a* ~ *remedy*⟩ **2a** of or arranged by topics ⟨*set down in* ~ *form*⟩ **b** referring to the topics of the day; of current interest – **topically** *adv*, **topicality** *n*

**topic sentence** *n* a sentence that states the main thought of a paragraph or of a larger unit of discourse

**topknot** /-ˌnot/ *n* **1** an ornament (eg of ribbons) worn as a headdress or as part of a hairstyle **2** a crest of feathers or a tuft or bun of hair on the top of the head

**topless** /ˈtoplis/ *adj* **1** having no top **2a** nude above the waist; *esp* having the breasts exposed **b** featuring topless waitresses or entertainers **3** *archaic* so high as to reach up beyond sight ⟨*and burnt the* ~ *towers of Ilium* – Christopher Marlowe⟩

ˌ**top-ˈlevel** *adj* very high or highest in level of authority, importance, or quality ⟨~ *management*⟩

ˌ**top-ˈline** *adj* top-level

**toplofty** /ˈtopˌlofti/ *adj, chiefly NAm* haughty, condescending – **toploftily** *adv*

**topmast** /ˈtopˌmahst/ *n* a mast that is next above the lowest mast

**topminnow** /ˈtopˌminoh/ *n* **1** any of a family (Poeciliidae) of numerous small VIVIPAROUS (giving birth to live young) fishes that feed on or near the surface of a body of water **2** KILLIFISH 1 (small egg-producing fish)

**topmost** /ˈtopmohst/ *adj* highest of all; uppermost

ˌ**top-ˈnotch** *adj, informal* of the highest quality; first-rate – **topnotcher** *n*

**topo-** – see TOP-

**topocentric** /ˌtopəˈsentrik, ˌtoh-/ *adj* relating to, measured from, or as if observed from a particular point on the earth's surface; having or relating to such a point as origin ⟨~ *co-ordinates*⟩ – compare GEOCENTRIC [*top-* + *-centric*]

**topograph** /ˈtopəgrahf, ˈtoh-, -graf/ *n* a detailed photograph of the surface of an object [back-formation fr *topography*]

**topographer** /təˈpogrəfə/ *n* one skilled in topography

**topographical** /ˌtopəˈgrafikl/ *adj* **1 topographical, topographic** of or concerned with topography ⟨*a* ~ *engineer*⟩ **2** of or concerned with the artistic representation of a particular locality ⟨*a* ~ *poem*⟩ ⟨~ *painting*⟩ – **topographically** *adv*

**topography** /tə'pogrəfi/ *n* **1a** the art or practice of making maps or charts of a region **b** topographical surveying **2a** the configuration of a land surface, including its relief and the position of its natural and man-made features **b** the physical or natural features of an object or entity and their structural relationships [ME *topographie* detailed description of a place, fr LL *topographia*, fr Gk, fr *topographein* to describe a place, fr *topos* place + *graphein* to write – more at CARVE]

**topological space** /ˌtopə'lojikl/ *n* a mathematical set with a collection of subsets forming a topology

**topology** /tə'poləji/ *n* **1** topographical study of a particular place; *specif* the history of a region as indicated by its topography **2a** a branch of mathematics that deals with geometric properties which are unaltered by elastic deformation (eg stretching or twisting) **b** a collection of subsets of a mathematical set which includes the empty set and the set itself and which is closed under unions and finite intersections **c** a configuration ⟨∼ *of a molecule*⟩ ⟨∼ *of a magnetic field*⟩ [ISV *top-* + *-logy*] – **topologist** *n*, **topological** *adj*, **topologically** *adv*

**toponym** /'topəˌnim, 'toh-/ *n* a place-name [ISV, back-formation fr *toponymy*]

**toponymic** /ˌtopə'nimik/, **toponymical** /-kl/ *adj* of toponyms or toponymy

**toponymy** /to'ponəmi, 'toh-/ *n* the study of the place-names of a region [ISV, fr *top-* + Gk *onyma, onoma* name – more at NAME]

**topos** /'topos/ *n, pl* **topoi** /-poy/ a standard rhetorical theme or topic; a commonplace [Gk, short for *koinos topos*, lit., common place – more at TOPIC]

**topper** /'topə/ *n* **1** one who or that which tops **2** TOP HAT **3** *informal* something (eg a joke) that caps everything preceding **4** *Br informal* a very agreeable person

¹**topping** /'toping/ *n* **1** something that forms a top: eg **1a** a garnish or edible decoration (eg a sauce, breadcrumbs, or whipped cream) placed on top of a food **b** a finishing layer of mortar on concrete **2** the action of one who or that which tops **3** something removed by topping

²**topping** *adj* **1** highest in rank or eminence **2** *chiefly Br* excellent – no longer in vogue

**topple** /'topl/ *vi* **1** to fall (as if) from being top-heavy **2** to be or seem unsteady; totter ∼ *vt* **1** to cause to topple **2** to overthrow [freq of ²*top*]

**tops** /tops/ *adj, informal* topmost in quality, ability, popularity, or eminence – used predicatively; often + *the* ⟨is ∼ *in his field*⟩ [pl of ¹*top*]

**topsail** /'topˌsayl, 'topsl/ *also* **tops'l** /'topsl/ *n* **1** the sail next above the lowest sail on a mast in a SQUARE-RIGGED ship **2** the sail set above and sometimes on the GAFF (sail support) in a FORE-AND-AFT rigged ship

**top secret** *adj* **1** demanding the greatest secrecy, usu for reasons of national security **2** containing information whose unauthorized disclosure could result in exceptionally grave danger to the nation – compare CONFIDENTIAL, RESTRICTED, SECRET

¹**topside** /'topˌsied/ *n* **1** *pl* the sides of a ship above the waterline **2** the upper portion of the IONOSPHERE (upper part of the earth's atmosphere) **3** a lean boneless cut of beef from the inner part of a ROUND (meat from above back leg)

²**topside** *adv or adj* **1** on deck **2** to or on the top or surface

**topsoil** /'topˌsoyl/ *n* surface soil, usu including the ORGANIC (containing matter derived from plants and animals) layer in which plants have most of their roots and which is turned over in ploughing

**top spin, top** *n* a rotary motion imparted to a ball (eg in tennis) that causes it to rotate forwards in the direction of its travel – compare BACKSPIN [¹*top*]

**topstitch** /'topˌstich/ *vt* to make a line of stitching on the outside of (a garment) close to a seam or finished edge – **topstitching** *n*

¹**topsy-turvy** /ˌtopsi 'tuhvi/ *adj or adv* **1** UPSIDE DOWN **2** in utter confusion or disorder [prob based on *tops* (pl of ¹*top*) + obs *terve* to turn upside down, fr ME *terven*] – **topsy-turviness** *n*, **topsy-turvily** *adv*, **topsy-turvydom** *n*

²**topsy-turvy** *n* the quality or state of being topsy-turvy; topsy-turviness

**topwork** /'topˌwuhk/ *vt* to graft branches or shoots of another variety of plant on the main stems of (eg fruit trees), usu to obtain more desirable fruit

**toque** /tohk/ *n* a woman's small soft brimless hat made in any

of various closely fitting shapes [MF, soft hat with a narrow brim worn esp in the 16th c, fr OSp *toca* headdress]

**tor** /taw/ *n* a high rock or pile of rocks, esp on top of a hill; *also* a high craggy hill – often used in place-names, esp of Devon, Cornwall, and the Peak District [ME, fr OE *torr*, prob of Celt órigin]

**Torah** /'tawrə/ *n* **1** *the* PENTATEUCH (first five books of the Old Testament); *broadly* the body of law and doctrine contained in Jewish Scripture and other sacred Jewish literature and oral tradition **2** a leather or parchment scroll of the Pentateuch used in a synagogue for religious services [Heb *tōrāh* law, instruction]

**torbernite** /'tawbəniet/ *n* a green radioactive mineral consisting of a phosphate of uranium and copper [Ger *torbernit*, fr *Torbern* Bergman †1784 Sw chemist]

**torch** /tawch/ *n* **1** a burning stick of wood containing RESIN or piece of twisted tallow-soaked fibre, used to give light and usu carried in the hand; FLAMBEAU **2** something (eg wisdom or knowledge) that gives enlightenment or guidance **3** a gas-burning instrument providing a hot flame esp for welding; a blowpipe **4** *Br* a small portable electric lamp powered by batteries [ME *torche*, fr OF, bundle of twisted straw or tow, torch, fr (assumed) VL *torca*; akin to L *torquēre* to twist – more at TORTURE] – **carry a torch for** to be in love with, esp without reciprocation; cherish a longing or devotion for ⟨*she still* carries a torch for *him even though their engagement is broken*⟩

**torchbearer** /-ˌbeərə/ *n* **1** one who carries a torch **2** someone in the forefront of a campaign or movement

**torchlight** /'tawchˌliet/ *n* light given by torches

**torchon** /'tawshən/ (*Fr* tɔrʃɔ̃) /*n* a coarse bobbin or machine-made lace made with fan-shaped designs forming a scalloped edge [Fr, duster, fr OF, bundle of twisted straw, fr *torche*]

**torch song** *n* a popular sentimental song of unrequited love

**tore** /taw/ *past of* TEAR

**toreador** /'toriˌəˌdaw/ *n* a torero [Sp, fr *toreado*, pp of *torear* to fight bulls, fr *toro* bull, fr L *taurus* – more at TAURINE]

**torero** /to'reəroh/ *n, pl* **toreros** a matador, bullfighter [Sp, fr LL *taurarius*, fr L *taurus* bull]

**toreutics** /tə'roohtiks/ *n taking sing vb* the art or process of working in metal, esp by embossing or indenting (CHASING) [Gk *toreutikos* of working in metal, fr *toreuein* to bore through, chase, fr *toreus* boring tool; akin to Gk *tetrainein* to bore – more at THROW] – **toreutic** *adj*

**tori** /'tawrie/ *pl of* TORUS

**torii** /'tawriˌee/ *n, pl* **torii** a Japanese gateway of light construction commonly built at the approach to a shrine associated with SHINTO (Japanese religion) [Jap]

¹**torment** /'tawment/ *n* **1** the infliction of torture (eg by the rack or wheel) **2** extreme pain or anguish of body or mind; agony **3** a source of vexation or pain [ME, fr OF, fr L *tormentum* torture, fr *torquēre* to twist – more at TORTURE]

²**torment** /taw'ment/ *vt* to cause severe usu persistent distress of body or mind to; harass, plague ⟨∼ed *by doubt*⟩

**tormentil** /'tawməntil/ *n* a common yellow-flowered Eurasian plant (*Potentilla erecta*) of the rose family with a root used in tanning and dyeing [ME *turmentill*, fr ML *tormentilla*, fr L *tormentum* torment; fr its use in allaying pain]

**tormentor** *also* **tormenter** /taw'mentə/ *n* **1** one who or that which torments **2** a fixed curtain or flat on each side of a theatre stage that prevents the audience from seeing into the wings **3** a covered screen used in a cinema studio to prevent echo during filming

**torn** /tawn/ *past part of* TEAR

**tornadic** /taw'nadik/ *adj* of or constituting a tornado

**tornado** /taw'naydoh/ *n, pl* **tornadoes, tornados** **1** a squall accompanying a thunderstorm in Africa **2** a violent or destructive whirlwind, usu progressing in a narrow path over the land and accompanied by a funnel-shaped cloud **3a** a very (destructively) active person or thing **b** an eruption of firing, booing, etc **4** *archaic* a tropical thunderstorm **synonyms** see WHIRLWIND [modif (influenced by Sp *tornado*, pp of *tornar* to turn) of Sp *tronada* thunderstorm, fr *tronar* to thunder, fr L *tonare* – more at THUNDER]

**toroid** /'tawroyd/ *n* a doughnut-shaped figure; *specif* a surface or solid generated by a plane closed curve (eg an ellipse or circle) rotated about a line that lies in the same plane as the curve but does not intersect it [NL *torus* + E *-oid*]

**toroidal** /taw'roydl/ *adj* of or shaped like a toroid; ring-shaped ⟨*a* ∼ *resistance coil*⟩ – **toroidally** *adv*

**¹torpedo** /taw'peedoh/ *n, pl* **torpedoes 1** ELECTRIC RAY (fish able to generate electricity) **2** a self-propelling cigar-shaped underwater explosive projectile used by submarines, aircraft, etc for attacking (e g ships) **3** *NAm* **3a** a charge of explosive enclosed in a container or case **b** a small firework that explodes when thrown against a hard object [L, lit., stiffness, numbness, fr *torpēre* to be stiff or numb; fr the paralysing effect of the electric ray's sting]

**²torpedo** *vt* **torpedoing; torpedoed 1** to hit or destroy (e g a ship) by torpedo **2** *informal* to destroy or nullify completely; wreck ⟨~ *a plan*⟩

**torpedo boat** *n* a boat designed for firing torpedoes; *specif* a small very fast lightly armoured warship armed primarily with torpedoes

**torpedo-boat destroyer** *n* a large, swift, and powerfully armed torpedo boat originally intended principally for the destruction of torpedo boats but later developed into the destroyer

**torpedo bomber** *n* a military aeroplane designed to carry torpedoes

**torpid** /'tawpid/ *adj* **1a** having temporarily lost the power of movement or feeling (e g in hibernation); dormant, numb **b** sluggish in functioning or acting ⟨*a ~ frog*⟩ ⟨*a ~ mind*⟩ **2** lacking in energy or vigour; apathetic, dull [L *torpidus*, fr *torpēre* to be stiff or numb; akin to L *stirps* trunk, stock, lineage, OE *starian* to stare – more at STARE] – **torpidly** *adv*, **torpidity** *n*

**torpor** /'tawpə/ *n* **1a** a state of mental and physical inactivity with partial or total insensibility; dormancy **b** extreme sluggishness of action or function **2** apathy, dullness *synonyms* see STUPOR [L, fr *torpēre*]

**¹torque** /tawk/ *n* a twisted usu metal collar or neck chain worn by the ancient Gauls, Germans, and Britons [Fr, fr L *torques*, fr *torquēre* to twist – more at TORTURE]

**²torque** *n* **1** a force that produces or tends to produce rotation or torsion ⟨*a car engine delivers ~ to the drive shaft*⟩; *also* a measure of the effectiveness of such a force that consists of the strength of the force multiplied by the perpendicular distance from the line of action of the force to the axis of rotation **2** a turning or twisting force [L *torquēre* to twist]

**torque converter** *n* a device for transmitting and amplifying torque, esp by hydraulic means

**torr** /taw/ *n, pl* **torr** a unit of pressure equal to 133.32 pascals (¹/₇₆₀ of a standard atmosphere) [Evangelista *Torricelli* †1647 It mathematician & physicist]

**torrent** /'torənt/ *n* **1** a violent stream of a liquid (e g water or lava) **2** a raging flood, downpour, etc ⟨~ s *of rain*⟩ **3** a tumultuous outpouring; a rush ⟨*a ~ of emotion poured from his lips*⟩ [Fr, fr L *torrent-, torrens*, fr *torrent-, torrens* burning, seething, rushing, fr prp of *torrēre* to parch, burn – more at THIRST]

**torrential** /tə'rensh(ə)l/ *adj* **1a** having the character of a torrent ⟨~ *rains*⟩ **b** resulting from the action of rapid streams ⟨~ *gravel*⟩ **2** resembling a torrent in violence or rapidity of flow – **torrentially** *adv*

**torrid** /'torid/ *adj* **1a** parched with heat, esp of the sun; hot ⟨~ *sands*⟩ **b** giving off intense heat; scorching **2** ardent, passionate ⟨~ *love letters*⟩ **3** very uncomfortable or unpleasant ⟨*batsmen had a ~ time against the fast bowlers*⟩ [L *torridus*, fr *torrēre*] – **torridly** *adv*, **torridness** *n*, **torridity** *n*

**torrid zone** *n* the belt of the earth between the tropics over which the sun is vertical at some period of the year – compare FRIGID ZONE, TEMPERATE ZONE

**torsion** /'tawsh(ə)n/ *n* **1** the act or process of twisting or turning something, esp by forces exerted on one end while the other is fixed or twisted in the opposite direction **2** the state of being twisted **3** the equal and opposite torque that an elastic solid exerts by reason of being under torsion **4** the twisting of a body organ on its own axis [LL *torsus*, pp of L *torquēre* to twist] – **torsional** *adj*, **torsionally** *adv*

**torsion balance** *n* an instrument used to measure minute forces (e g magnetic attraction and repulsion) by the torsion of a wire or filament

**torsk** /tawsk/ *n* a large edible marine fish (*Brosme brosme*) related to the cod [of Scand origin; akin to Norw, Sw, & Dan *torsk* cod]

**torso** /'tawsoh/ *n, pl* **torsos, torsi** /-si/ **1** the trunk of a sculptured, painted, or drawn representation of a human body; *esp* the trunk of a statue without the head and limbs **2** something (e g a piece of writing) that is mutilated or left unfinished **3** the human trunk [It, lit., stalk, fr L *thyrsus* stalk, thyrsus]

**tort** /tawt/ *n* a wrongful act, other than breach of contract, for which a civil action for damages can be brought [ME, fr MF, fr ML *tortum*, fr L, neut of *tortus* twisted, fr pp of *torquēre* to twist]

**torte** /'tawtə (*Ger* tortə)/ *n, pl* **torten** /'tawtən (*Ger* tortən)/, **tortes** a gateau; *esp* a round flat one topped with fruit, chocolate, etc [Ger, prob fr It *torta*, fr LL, round loaf of bread]

**tortfeasor** /'tawt,feezə/ *n* one who commits a tort [Fr *tort-faiseur*, fr MF, fr *tort* + *faiseur* doer, fr *fais-*, stem of *faire* to make, do, fr L *facere*]

**torticollis** /,tawti'kolis/ *n* a permanent twisting of the neck resulting in an abnormal carriage of the head [NL, fr L *tortus* twisted + *-i-* + *collum* neck – more at COLLAR]

**tortilla** /taw'teeyə/ *n* a round thin cake of unleavened maize bread, usu eaten hot with a topping or filling of minced meat or cheese [AmerSp, dim. of Sp *torta* cake, fr LL, round loaf of bread]

**tortious** /'tawchəs/ *adj* implying or involving a tort – **tortiously** *adv*

**tortoise** /'tawtəs, 'taw,toys/ *n* **1** any of several land reptiles (family Testudinidae, of the order Chelonia) with a toothless horny beak and a bony shell which encloses the trunk and into which the head, limbs, and tail may be withdrawn; *esp* a tortoise (*Testudo graeca*) commonly kept as a pet **2** somebody or something slow or laggard [ME *tortu, tortuce*, fr MF *tortue* – more at TURTLE]

**tortoise beetle** *n* any of a family (Chrysomelidae) of small tortoise-shaped beetles with larvae that feed on leaves

**¹tortoiseshell** /'tawtəs,shel/ *n* **1** the mottled horny substance of the shell of some marine turtles used in inlaying and in making various ornamental articles **2** any of several butterflies (family Nymphalidae) with striking orange, yellow, brown, and black coloration; *esp* a small tortoiseshell (*Aglais urticae*)

**²tortoiseshell** *adj* made of or resembling tortoiseshell, esp in having mottled black, brown, and yellow colouring ⟨~ *cat*⟩

**tortoni** /taw'tohni/ *n* ICE CREAM made with thick cream and often containing minced almonds, chopped maraschino cherries, and rum as flavouring [prob fr *Tortoni*, 19th-c It restaurateur in Paris]

**tortricid** /'tawtrisid/ *n* any of a family (Tortricidae) of small stout-bodied moths many of whose larvae live in nests formed by rolling up plant leaves or feed in fruits [NL *Tortricidae*, group name, fr *Tortric-, Tortrix*] – **tortricid** *adj*

**tortrix** /'tawtriks/ *n* a tortricid moth [NL *Tortric-, Tortrix*, genus of moths, fr L *tortus*, pp of *torquēre* to twist; fr the habit of twisting or rolling leaves]

**tortuosity** /,tawtyoo'osəti/ *n* **1** the quality or state of being tortuous **2** something winding or twisted; a bend

**tortuous** /'tawtyoo-əs/ *adj* **1** marked by repeated twists, bends, or turns; winding **2a** marked by devious or indirect tactics **b** circuitous, involved *usage* see TORTUROUS [ME, fr MF *tortueux*, fr L *tortuosus*, fr *tortus* twist, fr *tortus*, pp of *torquēre*] – **tortuously** *adv*, **tortuousness** *n*

**¹torture** /'tawchə/ *n* **1** the infliction of intense pain (e g from burning, crushing, or wounding) as a means of punishment, coercion, or sadistic gratification **2** (something causing) anguish of body or mind [Fr, fr LL *tortura*, fr L *tortus*, pp of *torquēre* to twist; akin to OHG *drāhsil* turner, Gk *atraktos* spindle]

**²torture** *vt* **1** to subject to torture **2** to cause intense suffering to; torment **3** to twist or wrench out of shape; *also* to pervert (e g the meaning of a word) – **torturer** *n*

**torturous** /'tawchərəs/ *adj* **1** of or involving torture ⟨*several ~ hours looking at his holiday snaps*⟩ **2** complicated, twisted ⟨*followed a ~ route*⟩ – **torturously** *adv*

*usage* It is probably clearer to restrict **torturous** to the "torture" sense, and to express the idea of "twisted" by the related adjective **tortuous**.

**torula** /'toryoolə, 'tawrələ, 'tawyələ/ *n, pl* **torulae** /-lie/ *also* **torulas** any of various fungi, esp yeasts, that lack sexual spores and do not produce alcoholic fermentations [NL, fr L *torus* protuberance]

**torus** /'tawrəs/ *n, pl* **tori** /-ri/ **1** a smooth rounded anatomical protuberance **2** a large moulding that curves outwards and is used in the bases of columns, esp in classical architecture **3a** RECEPTACLE 2b (enlarged upper portion of stem bearing flower parts) **b** a thickening on a membrane closing a PIT (depression in a cell wall) in some wood cells (e g those of cone-bearing trees) that may control water movement by blocking the pit opening **4** a ring-shaped surface or solid (eg that of a tyre inner tube) generated by a circle rotated about an axis in its plane that does not intersect the circle; *broadly* TOROID [NL, fr L, protuberance, bulge, convex moulding]

**Tory** /'tawri/ *n* **1** an Irish papist or royalist outlaw chiefly of the 17th century **2a** a member or supporter of a major British political group of the 18th and early 19th centuries favouring at first the Stuarts and later royal authority and the established church and seeking to preserve the traditional political structure and defeat parliamentary reform – compare WHIG **b** CONSERVATIVE 1b **3** an American upholding the cause of the crown against the supporters of colonial independence during the American Revolution **4** *often not cap* an extreme conservative, esp in political and economic principles [IrGael *tōraidhe* pursuer, robber, fr MIr *tōir* pursuit] – **Tory** *adj*, **Toryism** *n, often not cap*

**Tory Democracy** *n* a political philosophy advocating preservation of established institutions and traditional principles combined with political democracy and a social and economic programme designed to benefit the common man

**tosh** /tosh/ *n, informal* sheer nonsense; bosh, twaddle [origin unknown]

**¹toss** /tos/ *vt* **1a** to fling or heave repeatedly about, to and fro, or up and down ⟨*a ship* ~ed *by waves*⟩ **b** to exchange (words) argumentatively; BANDY **2 c** to mix lightly with a tossing motion; *esp* to mix lightly until well coated with a dressing ⟨~ *a salad*⟩ **2a** to throw with a quick, light, or careless motion ⟨~ *a ball around*⟩ **b** to throw up in the air ⟨~ed *by a bull*⟩ **c(1)** to flip (a coin) to decide an issue according to which face lands uppermost **3** to fling or lift with a sudden jerking motion ⟨~es *her head angrily*⟩ **c(2)** to toss a coin to decide an issue with ⟨*I'll* ~ *you for who goes first*⟩ ~ *vi* **1** to move restlessly or turbulently; *esp* to twist and turn repeatedly ⟨~ed *sleeplessly all night*⟩ **2** to move with a quick or spirited gesture; flounce **3** to decide an issue by flipping a coin ⟨*let's* ~ *for it*⟩ – often + *up* **synonyms** see ¹THROW [prob of Scand origin; akin to Sw dial. *tossa* to spread, scatter] – **tosser** *n*

**toss off** *vt* **1** to accomplish, provide, or dispose of readily or easily ⟨toss off *a few verses*⟩ **2** to consume quickly; *esp* to drink in a single draught ⟨tossed off *his glass*⟩ ~ *vi, Br informal* to masturbate

**²toss** *n* **1a** the state or fact of being tossed **b** a fall, esp from a horse – chiefly in *take a toss* **2** an act or instance of tossing: eg **2a** an abrupt tilting or upward fling **b** an act or instance of deciding by chance, esp by tossing a coin **c** a throw, pitch **3** *Br* a least amount or degree of care or consideration ⟨*I wouldn't give a* ~ *for what they say*⟩

**tossing the caber** *n* a Scottish sport in which the competitors attempt to throw a roughly trimmed tree trunk (CABER) as far as possible

**tosspot** /'tos,pot/ *n* a drunkard, sot

**'toss-,up** *n* **1** TOSS 2b **2** *informal* an even chance or choice

**tot** /tot/ *n* **1** a small child; a toddler **2** a small amount or allowance of alcoholic drink ⟨*a* ~ *of rum*⟩ [origin unknown]

**¹total** /'tohtl/ *adj* **1** comprising or constituting a whole; entire ⟨*the* ~ *amount*⟩ **2** complete, utter ⟨*a* ~ *success*⟩ **3** concentrating all available personnel and resources on a single objective ⟨~ *war*⟩ [ME, fr MF, fr ML *totalis*, fr L *totus* whole, entire] – **totally** *adv*

**²total** *n* **1** a product of addition; a sum **2** an entire quantity; an amount

**³total** *vt* **-ll-** (*NAm* **-l-, -ll-**) **1** to add up; compute **2** to make a total of; amount to

**total eclipse** *n* an eclipse in which one celestial body is completely obscured by the shadow or body of another

**total internal reflection** *n* the reflection of a light ray passing through one medium (eg glass) towards another less dense medium (eg air) such that if the ray meets the common surface (INTERFACE) of the media at an angle greater than a certain angle (CRITICAL ANGLE) it will be reflected back into the denser medium and will not pass through into the second

**totalism** /'tohtəliz(ə)m/ *n* totalitarianism – **totalistic** *adj*

**totalitarian** /,toh,tali'teəriən/ *adj* **1** of, advocating, or characteristic of centralized control by an authority with absolute power; authoritarian, dictatorial; *also* despotic **2** of or constituting a political regime based on subordination of the individual to the state and strict control over all aspects of the life and productive capacity of the nation **3** exercising autocratic powers [*total* + *-itarian* (as in *authoritarian*)] – **totalitarian** *n*, **totalitarianism** *n*, **totalitarianize** *vt*

**totality** /toh'taləti/ *n* **1** an entire amount; a sum, whole **2a** the quality or state of being total; wholeness **b** a period during which one body (eg the sun) is completely obscured by another (eg the moon) or by the shadow of another during an eclipse

**total-izator, -isator** /'tohtəl-ie,zaytə/ *n* a PARI-MUTUEL machine

**total-ize, -ise** /'tohtəliez/ *vt* **1** to add up; total **2** to express as a whole; summarize

**total-izer, -iser** /'tohtəliezə/ *n* something that totalizes: eg **a** a totalizator **b** a device (eg a meter) that records a remaining total (eg of fuel)

**totally ordered** *adj* having every pair of elements (eg of a mathematical set) PARTIALLY ORDERED and connected by a relation such that either $x * y$ or $y * x$ where * denotes the relation ⟨*the numbers 1,2,3,4, . . . are* ~⟩

**total utility** *n* the degree of utility of an economic good (eg an article or service) considered as a whole

**totara** /'tohtərə/ *n* a coniferous New Zealand tree (*Podocarpus totara* of the family Podocarpacea) similar to the RIMU; *also* the hard reddish wood of a totara [Maori]

**¹tote** /toht/ *vt, informal* **1** to carry by hand or on the person; lug ⟨~ *a gun*⟩ **2** to transport, convey [origin unknown]

**²tote** *n* **1** a burden, load **2** TOTE BAG

**³tote** *n* a totalizator [by shortening & alter.]

**tote bag, tote** *n* a large bag, esp one without fastenings, for carrying articles (eg shopping or personal possessions)

**totem** /'tohtəm/ *n* **1** a natural object (eg an animal or plant) serving as the emblem of a family or clan and often as a reminder of its ancestry; *also* a usu carved or painted representation of such an object **2** something that serves as an emblem or revered symbol [Ojibwa *ototeman* his totem]

**totemic** /toh'temik/ *adj* **1** of or characteristic of a totem or totemism ⟨*a* ~ *animal*⟩ **2** based on or practising totemism ⟨~ *clan structure*⟩ – **totemically** *adv*

**totemism** /'tohtə,miz(ə)m/ *n* **1** belief in kinship with or a mystical relationship between a group or an individual and a totem **2** a system of social organization based on totemic affiliations

**totemist** /'tohtəmist/ *n* **1** an adherent of totemism **2** a specialist in totemism

**totemistic** /,tohtə'mistik/ *adj* of totemists or totemism; totemic

**totem pole** *n* **1** a pole carved and painted with a series of totemic symbols representing family lineage and often mythical or historical incidents and erected before the houses of Indian tribes of the northwest coast of N America **2** an order of rank; a hierarchy

**tother, t'other** /'tudhə/ *pron or adj, chiefly dial* the other [ME *tother*, alter. (by incorrect division of *thet other* the other, fr *thet* the – fr OE *thæt* – + *other*) of *other* – more at THAT]

**totipotency** /toh'tipətənsi/ *n* ability to generate or regenerate a whole organism from a part

**totipotent** /toh'tipətənt/ *adj, of a cell or tissue* capable of developing into a complete organism or differentiating into any type of cell or tissue ⟨~ *blastomeres*⟩ ⟨*some tadpole cells are* ~⟩ [L *totus* whole, entire + E *potent*]

**¹totter** /'totə/ *vi* **1a** to tremble or rock as if about to fall; sway **b** to become unstable; threaten to collapse ⟨*a* ~ing *regime*⟩ **2** to move unsteadily; stagger, wobble [ME *toteren*] – **totteringly** *adv*

**²totter** *n* an unsteady gait; a wobble – **tottery** *adj*

**totting** /'toting/ *n, Br* the occupation of scavenging refuse for salable goods, esp illicitly [arch. *tot* bone, something salvaged from refuse, of unknown origin] – **totter** *n*

**,totting-'up** *n, Br informal* a former legal procedure whereby a person who had accumulated a certain number of convictions for traffic offences was disqualified from driving

**tot up** *vb, informal vt* to add together; total ⟨tot up *the score*⟩ ~ *vi* to increase by additions; mount ⟨*the money soon* tots up⟩ [*tot* (to add up), short for ³*total*]

**Touareg** /'twah,reg/ *n* TUAREG (member of African nomadic people)

**toucan** /'tooh,kan/ *n* any of a family (Ramphastidae) of fruit-eating birds of tropical America, with brilliant colouring and a very large but light and thin-walled beak [Fr, fr Pg *tucano*, fr Tupi]

**¹touch** /tuch/ *vt* **1** to bring a bodily part into contact with, esp so as to perceive through the sense of feeling; handle or feel gently, usu with the intent to understand or appreciate ⟨*loved to* ~ *the soft silk*⟩ **2** to strike or push lightly, esp with the hand or foot or an implement **3** to lay hands upon (somebody afflicted with the disease SCROFULA) with intent to heal – compare KING'S EVIL **4** to perform (a melody) by playing or singing **5a** to take into the hands or mouth – usu neg ⟨*never* ~es *alcohol*⟩ **b** to put hands upon in any way or degree ⟨*don't* ~ *anything before the police come*⟩; *esp* to commit violence against ⟨*swears he never* ~ed *the child*⟩ **6** to concern oneself with **7** to cause to be briefly in contact with something ⟨~ed *his spurs to his horse*⟩ ⟨~ *a match to the wick*⟩ **8a(1)** to meet without overlapping or penetrating; adjoin **a(2)** to get to; reach ⟨*the speedometer needle* ~ed *80*⟩ **b** to be TANGENT to **9** to affect the interest of; concern **10a** to leave a mark or impression on ⟨*few reagents will* ~ *gold*⟩ **b** to harm slightly (as if) by contact; taint, blemish ⟨*fruit* ~ed *by frost*⟩ ⟨*a horse* ~ed *in the wind*⟩ **c** to give a delicate tint, line, or expression to ⟨*a smile* ~ed *her lips*⟩ **11** to draw or delineate with light strokes **12a** to hurt the feelings of, wound ⟨~ed *him on a sensitive issue*⟩ **b** to move to sympathetic feeling ⟨~ed *by the loyalty of his friends*⟩ **13** *informal* to rival in quality or value ⟨*nothing can* ~ *that cloth for durability*⟩ **14** *informal* to induce to give or lend ⟨~ed *him for ten quid*⟩ ~ *vi* **1a** to feel something with a body part (e g the hand or foot) **b** to lay hands on a person to cure disease (e g scrofula) **2** to be in contact **3** to come close; verge ⟨*his actions* ~ *on treason*⟩ **4** to have a bearing; relate – + *on* or *upon* **5a** to make a brief or incidental stop on shore during a trip by water ⟨~ed *at several ports*⟩ **b** to treat a topic in a brief or casual manner – + *on* or *upon* ⟨~ed *upon many points*⟩ – see also **touch the right** CHORD, **touch** WOOD **synonyms** see ¹MOVE [ME *touchen,* fr OF *tuchier,* fr (assumed) VL *toccare* to knock, strike a bell, touch, of imit origin] – **touchable** *adj,* **toucher** *n* – **touch and go** highly uncertain or precarious ⟨*a touch and go situation*⟩

**touch down** *vt* to place (the ball in rugby) by hand on the ground, either on or over an opponent's goal line in scoring a try or behind one's own goal line as a defensive measure ~ *vi* to reach the ground; land – see also TOUCHDOWN

**touch off** *vt* **1** to describe or characterize with precision **2a** to cause to explode (as if) by touching with a naked flame **b** to release or initiate with sudden intensity ⟨*the charges touched off a storm of protest* – R A Billington⟩

**touch up** *vt* **1** to improve or perfect by small additional strokes or alterations; make good the minor and usu visible defects of **2** to stimulate (as if) by a flick of a whip **3** *informal* to fondle or caress sexually, esp in a furtive or unwelcome manner; touch with a view to arousing sexually – see also TOUCH-UP

²**touch** *n* **1** a light stroke, tap, or push **2** the act or fact of touching **3** the sense of feeling, esp as exercised deliberately with the hands, feet, or lips **4** mental or moral sensitivity, responsiveness, or tact ⟨*has a wonderful* ~ *in dealing with children*⟩ **5** a specified sensation produced by touching something; a feel ⟨*felt the soft* ~ *of her hand*⟩ **6** the testing of gold or silver on a TOUCHSTONE **7** something slight of its kind: e g **7a** a light attack ⟨*a* ~ *of fever*⟩ **b** a small amount; a trace, dash ⟨*a* ~ *of spring in the air*⟩ **c** a bit, little – chiefly in the adverbial phrase *a touch* ⟨*aimed a* ~ *too low and missed*⟩ **8a** a manner or method of touching or striking esp the keys of a keyboard instrument **b** the relative resistance to pressure of the keys of a keyboard (e g of a piano or typewriter) ⟨*piano with a stiff* ~⟩ **9** a set of CHANGES in bell ringing that is shorter than a PEAL **10** an effective and appropriate detail; *esp* one used in creating or improving an artistic composition ⟨*applies the finishing* ~es *to his story*⟩ **11** a distinctive or characteristic manner, trait, or quality ⟨*the* ~ *of a master*⟩ ⟨*a woman's* ~⟩ ⟨*service with a personal* ~⟩ **12** the state or fact of being in contact or communication ⟨*lost* ~ *with her cousin*⟩ ⟨*out of* ~ *with modern times*⟩ **13** the area outside the touchlines in soccer, hockey, etc, or outside and including the touchlines in rugby ⟨*kicked the ball into* ~⟩ **14** *slang* **14a** an act of soliciting or receiving a gift or loan of money **b** a person who can be easily induced to part with money – chiefly in *a soft touch* and *an easy touch* **15** *archaic* the playing of an instrument (e g a lute or piano) with the fingers; *also* musical notes or strains so produced – **a touch of the sun 1** slight sunstroke **2** mental weakness or aberration

**touchdown** /-ˌdown/ *n* **1** the act of touching down a football **2** the act or moment of touching down (e g of an aeroplane or spacecraft)

**touché** /tooh'shay/ (*Fr* tuʃe)/ *interj* – used to acknowledge a hit in fencing or the success of an argument, accusation, or witty

point [Fr, fr pp of *toucher* to touch, fr OF *tuchier*]

**touched** /tucht/ *adj* **1** emotionally moved (e g with gratitude) **2** *informal* slightly unbalanced mentally

**touchhole** /-ˌhohl/ *n* the hole in early cannons or firearms through which the charge was ignited

¹**touching** /'tuching/ *prep, formal* in reference to; concerning

²**touching** *adj* capable of arousing tenderness or compassion – **touchingly** *adv*

**touch judge** *n* a rugby linesman

**touch kick** *n* a kick in rugby that sends or attempts to send the ball over the touchline

**touchline** /-ˌlien/ *n* either of the lines that bound the sides of the field of play in rugby, soccer, etc

**touchmark** /-ˌmahk/ *n* an identifying maker's mark impressed on pewter

'**touch-me-ˌnot** *n* a Eurasian balsam plant (*Impatiens noli-tangere*) with spotted bright yellow flowers and seedpods that, when ripe, burst open on being touched

**touchpaper** /-ˌpaypə/ *n* paper impregnated with a substance (e g POTASSIUM NITRATE) so as to burn slowly and used esp for the ignition of fireworks

**touchstone** /-ˌstohn/ *n* **1** a black silicon-containing stone related to flint and formerly used to test the purity of gold and silver by the streak left on the stone when rubbed by the metal **2** a test or criterion for determining the quality or genuineness of something

**touch system** *n* a method of typewriting that assigns a particular finger to each key and makes it possible to type without looking at the keyboard

'**touch-ˌtype** *vi* to type by the TOUCH SYSTEM

'**touch-ˌup** *n* an act or instance of touching up ⟨*paint needs a* ~⟩; *esp, informal* an unwelcome or furtive sexual advance

**touchwood** /-ˌwood/ *n* wood so decayed as to be dry, crumbly, and useful for tinder

**touchy** /'tuchi/ *adj* **1** ready to take offence on slight provocation **2a** *of a body part* acutely sensitive or irritable **b** *of a chemical compound* highly explosive or inflammable **3** calling for tact, care, or caution in treatment ⟨*sexism was a* ~ *subject with his wife*⟩ – **touchily** *adv,* **touchiness** *n*

¹**tough** /tuf/ *adj* **1a** strong and flexible; not brittle or liable to cut, break, or tear easily **b** not easily chewed **2** characterized by severity or uncompromising determination ⟨*a* ~ *and inflexible foreign policy* – New Statesman⟩ ⟨*a* ~ *customer to deal with*⟩ **3** capable of enduring great hardship or exertion; hardy **4** very hard to influence; stubborn **5** extremely difficult or testing ⟨*a* ~ *question to answer*⟩ **6** stubbornly fought ⟨*a* ~ *contest*⟩ **7** unruly, rowdy **8** aggressive or threatening in behaviour **9** without softness or sentimentality **10** *informal* unfortunate, unpleasant ⟨~ *luck*⟩ – see also **tough** LUCK **synonyms** see STRONG **antonym** fragile [ME, fr OE *tōh;* akin to OHG *zāhi* tough] – **toughly** *adv,* **toughness** *n*

²**tough** *n* a tough person; *esp* somebody aggressively violent

³**tough** *adv* in a tough manner ⟨*talk* ~⟩

**toughen** /'tuf(ə)n/ *vb* to make or become tough

**toughie** *also* **toughy** /'tufi/ *n* somebody or something tough: e g **a** a rough rowdy person **b** a difficult problem

**ˌtough-ˈminded** *adj* realistic or unsentimental in disposition or outlook – **tough-mindedness** *n*

**toupee** /'tooh,pay/ *n* **1** a curl or lock of hair made into a topknot on a PERIWIG (wig common from 17th to 19th centuries) or natural hairstyle **2** a wig or hairpiece worn to cover a bald spot [Fr *toupet* forelock, fr OF, dim. of *top, toup,* of Gmc origin; akin to OHG *zopf* tuft of hair – more at TOP]

¹**tour** /tooə/ *n* **1** a period during which an individual or unit is engaged on a specific duty or stationed in one place ⟨*his regiment served a* ~ *of duty in Northern Ireland*⟩ **2a** a journey for business, pleasure, or education in which one returns to the starting point **b** a visit or outing (e g to a historic site or factory) for pleasure or instruction; an excursion ⟨*a guided* ~ *of the castle*⟩ **c** a series of professional engagements involving travel from place to place ⟨*a theatrical company on* ~⟩ **d** a bicycle race of several day-long stages – usu in the names of specific races ⟨*Tour of Britain*⟩ **3** TURN 1b (dance movement) [ME, fr MF, fr OF *tourn, tour* lathe, circuit, turn – more at TURN]

²**tour** *vi* to make a tour ~ *vt* **1** to make a tour of **2** to present (e g a theatrical production or concert) on a tour

**touraco** /'tooərə,koh/ *n, pl* **touracos** any of a family (Musophagidae) of African birds that are related to the cuckoos and have a long tail, a short stout often coloured beak, and red wing feathers [native name in western Africa]

**tourbillion** /tooə'bilyən/ *n* **1** a whirlwind **2** a vortex, esp of a whirlwind or whirlpool **3** a firework with a spiral flight [MF *tourbillon*, fr L *turbin-*, *turbo* – more at TURBINE]

**tourbillon** /'tooəbeeyonh (*Fr* turbijɔ̃)/ *n* a tourbillion

**tour de force** /ˌtooə də 'faws (*Fr* tuːr də fɔrs)/ *n, pl* **tours de force** /~/ a feat of strength, skill, or ingenuity [Fr]

**tour en l'air** /ˌtooər on 'leə (*Fr* tur ɑ̃ lɛr)/ a ballet turn in the air [Fr]

**tourer** /'tooərə/ *n* **1** TOURING CAR **2** a bicycle for touring

**touring car** 'tooəring/ *n* a motor car suitable for distance driving: eg **a** a vintage motor car with two seats, usu four doors, and a folding top **b** a motor car like a sports car but having good provision for luggage

**tourism** /'tooəˌriz(ə)m/ *n* **1** the practice of travelling for recreation **2** the organizing of tours for commercial purposes **3a** the promotion or encouragement of touring, esp at governmental level **b** the provision of services (eg accommodation) to cater for tourists

**tourist** /'tooərist/ *n* **1** somebody who makes a tour for recreation or culture **2** a member of a sports team that is visiting or has been chosen to visit another country in order to play usu international matches – **tourist** *adj*

**tourist class** *n* the lowest class of passenger accommodation (eg on a ship)

**touristic** /tooə'ristik/ *adj* of a tour, tourism, or tourists – **touristically** *adv*

**touristy** /'tooəristi/ *adj, chiefly derog* frequented by or appealing to tourists

**tourmaline** /'tooəməˌleen/ *n* a mineral, $(Na,Ca)(Li,Mg,Fe,Al)(Al,Fe)_6B_3Si_6O_{27}(O,OH,F)_4$, of variable colour that consists of a complex silicate and that is cut for use as a gem when transparent [Sinhalese *toramalli* carnelian]

**tournament** /'tooənəmənt, 'taw-/ *n* **1a** a medieval contest between two parties of mounted knights armed with usu blunted lances or swords **b** a series of sports for knights occurring at one time and place **2** a series of games or contests for a championship ⟨*the most prestigious tennis ~ is Wimbledon*⟩ [ME *tornement*, fr OF *torneiement*, fr *torneier* to tourney]

**tournedos** /'tooənəˌdoh/ *n, pl* **tournedos** a small steak cut from the centre of a beef fillet and usu larded, tied, and held in shape with a skewer during cooking [Fr, fr *tourner* to turn (fr OF) + *dos* back, fr L *dorsum* – more at TURN]

**¹tourney** /'tooəni, 'tawni/ *vi* to take part in a tournament, esp in the Middle Ages [ME *tourneyen*, fr MF *torneier*, fr OF, fr *torn*, *tourn* lathe, circuit]

**²tourney** *n* a tournament, esp in the Middle Ages

**tourniquet** /'tooəniˌkay, 'taw-/ *n* a device (eg a bandage twisted tight with a stick) for applying pressure to check bleeding or blood flow [Fr, turnstile, tourniquet, fr *tourner* to turn, fr OF – more at TURN]

**¹tousle** /'towzl/ *vt* to dishevel, rumple [ME *touselen*, freq of *-tousen* to pull roughly; akin to OHG *zirzūsōn* to pull to pieces]

**²tousle** *n* a tangled mass (eg of hair)

**¹tout** /towt/ *vi* **1** to solicit for customers **2a** *chiefly Br* to spy on racehorses in training in order to gain information for betting purposes **b** *Nam* to give a tip or solicit bets on a racehorse ~ *vt* **1** to spy on; watch **2a** to solicit or peddle importunately **b** *Br* to sell (tickets in great demand) at exploitative prices **3a** *Br* to spy out information about (eg a racing stable or horse) **b** *NAm* to give a tip or solicit bets on (a racehorse) [ME *tuten* to peer; akin to OE *tōtian* to stick out, Norw *tyte*]

**²tout, touter** *n* one who touts: eg **a** one who solicits custom, usu importunately **b** *Br* one who offers tickets for a sold-out entertainment (eg a concert or football match) at vastly inflated prices **c** *chiefly Br* one who spies out racing information for betting purposes **d** *chiefly NAm* one who gives tips or solicits bets on a racehorse

**³tout** *vt* to praise or publicize loudly or extravagantly ⟨~ed *as the ... most elaborate suburban shopping development – Wall Street Journal*⟩ [alter. of ¹*toot*]

**tout court** /ˌtooh 'kooə (*Fr* tu kur)/ *adv* without addition; simply ⟨*just call him Edinburgh ~*⟩ [Fr, fr *tout* all, quite + *court* short]

**tovarich, tovarish** /tə'vahrish (*Russ* tavariʃtʃ)/ *n* a comrade [Russ *tovarishch*]

**¹tow** /toh/ *vt* to draw or pull along behind, esp by a rope or chain; haul **synonyms** see ¹PULL [ME *towen*, fr OE *togian;* akin to OE *tēon* to draw, pull, OHG *ziohan* to draw, pull, L *ducere* to draw, lead]

**²tow** *n* **1** a rope or chain for towing **2** towing or being towed **3** something towed (eg a boat or car) **4** SKI LIFT – **in tow 1** in the state of being towed ⟨*a break-down lorry with a car in tow*⟩ **2a** under guidance or protection ⟨*taken in tow by a friendly neighbour*⟩ **b** in the position of a dependent or devoted follower or admirer ⟨*a young man passed with a good-looking girl in tow*⟩

**³tow** *n* **1** short or broken fibre (eg of flax or hemp) that is used esp for yarn, twine, or stuffing **2** a loose essentially untwisted strand of wool or man-made textile filaments [ME, fr OE *tow-* spinning; akin to ON *tō* tuft of wool for spinning, OE *tawian* to prepare for use – more at TAW]

**⁴tow** *n, chiefly Scot* (a) rope [ME (Sc), prob fr OE *toh-* (in *tohlīne* towline); akin to OE *togian* to tow]

**towage** /'toh·ij/ *n* **1** the act of towing **2** the price paid for towing

**toward** /tə'wawd/ *adj* **1** happening at the moment; afoot **2** propitious, favouring ⟨*a ~ breeze*⟩ **3** *archaic* coming soon; imminent **4** *obs* quick to learn; apt [ME, fr OE *tōweard* facing, imminent, fr *tō*, prep, to + *-weard* -ward]

**towardly** /'toh·ədli/ *adj, archaic* **1** favourable, propitious **2** developing favourably; promising **3** pleasant, affable – **towardliness** *n*, **towardly** *adv*

**¹towards** /tə'wawdz/, *NAm also* **toward** *prep* **1** moving or situated in the direction of ⟨*driving ~ town*⟩ ⟨*a cottage somewhere up ~ the lake*⟩ **2a** along a course leading to ⟨*a long stride ~ disarmament*⟩ **b** in relation to ⟨*an attitude ~ life*⟩ **3** turned in the direction of ⟨*his back was ~ me*⟩ **4** not long before ⟨*~ the end of the afternoon*⟩ **5a** in the way of assistance in ⟨*did all she could ~ increasing his confidence*⟩ **b** for the partial financing of ⟨*saving ~ a holiday*⟩ ⟨*will put it ~ a record*⟩ [ME *towardes*, fr OE *toweardes*, alter. of *tōweard*, adj]

**²towards** *adj* TOWARD 1,3

**¹towel** /'towəl/ *n* **1** an absorbent cloth or paper for wiping or drying something (eg crockery or the body) after washing **2** SANITARY TOWEL – see also THROW in **the towel** [ME *towaille*, fr OF *toaille*, of Gmc origin; akin to OHG *dwahila* towel; akin to OHG *dwahan* to wash, OPruss *twaxtan* bath cloth]

**²towel** *vb* -ll- (*NAm* -l-, -ll-) *vt* to rub or dry (eg the body) with a towel ~ *vi* to use a towel

**towelling**, *NAm chiefly* **toweling** /'towəling/ *n* a cotton or linen fabric, usu with a raised nap, often used for making towels

**¹tower** /'towə/ *n* **1** a building or structure typically higher than its diameter and high relative to its surroundings that may stand apart (eg a CAMPANILE) or be attached (eg a church belfry) to a larger structure and that may be fully walled in or of skeleton framework (eg an observation or transmission tower) **2** a citadel, fortress **3 tower block, tower** a tall multistorey building, usu containing flats or offices – compare SKYSCRAPER [ME *tour*, *tor*, fr OE *torr* & OF *tor*, *tur*, both fr L *turris*, fr Gk *tyrsis*] – **towered** *adj*, **towerlike** *adj*

**²tower** *vi* to reach or rise to a great height

**tower crane** *n* a crane pivoted at the top of a steel latticework tower, usu used in the erection of multi-storey buildings

**tower house** *n* a medieval fortified castle (eg in Scotland)

**towering** /'towəring/ *adj* **1** impressively high or great; imposing ⟨*~ pines*⟩ **2** reaching a high point of intensity; overwhelming ⟨*a ~ rage*⟩ **3** going beyond proper bounds; excessive ⟨*~ ambitions*⟩ – **toweringly** *adv*

**tower of strength** *n* one who can be relied on as a source of sympathy and support

**towhead** /'toh,hed/ *n* (somebody with) a head of hair resembling tow, esp in being flaxen or tousled – **towheaded** *adj*

**towline** /'toh,lien/ *n* a towrope

**towmond** /'tohmond/ *n, Scot* a twelvemonth, year [ME *towlmonyth*, fr OE *twelf mōnath*, fr *twelf* twelve + *mōnath* month]

**town** /town/ *n* **1a** a compactly settled area as distinguished from surrounding rural territory; *esp* one larger than a village but smaller than a city **b** a large densely populated urban area; a city **2** a neighbouring city, capital city, or metropolis ⟨*travels into ~ daily*⟩ **3** the business centre of a large town or city **4** the city or urban life as contrasted with the country or rural life **5** the townspeople ⟨*it was the talk of the ~*⟩ **6** *dial Br* a hamlet [ME, fr OE *tūn* enclosure, village, town; akin to OHG *zūn* enclosure, OIr *dūn* fortress] – **town** *adj* – **go to town 1** to work or act rapidly or efficiently **2** to indulge oneself ostentatiously ⟨*the papers went to town on the hidden life of Leroy – Sunday Times*⟩ – **on the town** in usu carefree pursuit of entertainment or amusement (eg city nightlife)

**town clerk** *n* **1** the chief official of a British town who until 1974 was appointed to administer municipal affairs and to act as secretary to the town council **2** a public officer in the USA charged with recording the official proceedings and statistics of a town

**town crier** /'krie·ə/ *n* a town officer who makes public proclamations

**townee, towny** /'towni, tow'nee/ *n, informal* a townsman, esp as distinguished from a country dweller or from a member of the academic community in a university town

**town hall** *n* the chief administrative building of a town

**town house** *n* **1** the city residence of one having a country seat or a chief residence elsewhere ⟨*stayed at their ~ during the social season*⟩ **2** an urban terrace house of three or more storeys, often having one storey as a garage

**town manager** *n* an official employed by an elected council to direct the administration of a town government

**town planning** *n* the study of the function of the various components of the urban environment and the planning of their arrangement and interrelationship for best results – **town planner** *n*

**townscape** /'town,skayp/ *n* the overall visual aspect of a town

**townsfolk** /'townz,fohk/ *n pl* townspeople

**township** /'township/ *n* **1** an ancient unit of administration in England identical in area with or being a division of a parish **2** any of various territorial and administrative units in the USA **3** an urban area inhabited by nonwhite citizens in S Africa **4** *Austr* a small town or settlement

**townsman** /'townzmən/ *n* **1** a native or resident of a town or city **2** a fellow citizen of a town

**townspeople** /-,peepl/ *n pl* the inhabitants of a town or city

**towny** /'towni/ *n* a townee

**towpath** /'toh,pahth/ *n* a path (eg along a canal) for use in towing boats

**towrope** /'toh,rohp/ *n* a line used in towing a boat, car, etc

**tox-** /toks-/, **toxi-, toxo-** *comb form* poison ⟨tox*aemia*⟩ [LL, fr L *toxicum* poison]

**toxaemia** /tok'seemyə, -mi·ə/ *n* **1** an abnormal condition associated with the presence of toxic substances in the blood **2** PRE-ECLAMPSIA (toxic condition occurring in pregnancy) [NL, fr *tox-* + *-aemia*]

**toxaphene** /'toksəfeen/ *n* a chlorine-containing insecticide, $C_{10}H_{10}Cl_8$, derived from CAMPHENE [fr *Toxaphene*, a trademark]

**toxic** /'toksik/ *adj* **1** of or caused by a poison or toxin **2** affected by a poison or toxin **3** poisonous [LL *toxicus*, fr L *toxicum* poison, fr Gk *toxikon* arrow poison, fr neut of *toxikos* of a bow, fr *toxon* bow, arrow] – **toxicity** *n*

**toxic-** /toksik-/, **toxico-** *comb form* tox- ⟨*toxicology*⟩ ⟨*toxicosis*⟩ [NL, fr L *toxicum*]

**¹toxicant** /'toksikənt/ *n* a toxic substance; *esp* one for insect control that kills rather than repels [ML *toxicant-, toxicans,* prp of *toxicare* to poison, fr L *toxicum*]

**²toxicant** *adj* poisonous

**toxicogenic** /,toksikə'jenik/ *adj* toxigenic

**toxicological** /,toksikə'lojikl/, **toxicologic** *adj* of toxicology or toxins – **toxicologically** *adv*

**toxicology** /,toksi'koləji/ *n* a branch of biology that deals with poisons and their effects and with medical, industrial, legal, or other problems arising from them – **toxicologist** *n*

**toxicosis** /,toksi'kohsis/ *n, pl* **toxicoses** /-seez/ a disorder caused by the action of a poison or toxin [NL]

**toxic shock syndrome** *n* a disease of esp young women that may be caused by toxins produced by certain bacteria and that has been linked with the use of tampons during menstruation

**toxigenic** /,toksi'jenik/ *adj* producing toxin ⟨*~ bacteria and fungi*⟩ – **toxigenicity** *n*

**toxin** /'toksin/ *n* an often extremely poisonous protein that is produced by a living organism (eg a bacterium), esp in the body of a host, and that typically stimulates the body to produce substances (ANTIBODIES) that counteract its action △ tocsin [ISV *tox-* + *-in*]

**toxin-ˈantitoxin** *n* a mixture of toxin and ANTITOXIN (substance combining with and counteracting a toxin) used esp formerly in immunizing against a disease (eg diphtheria) for which they are specific

**toxo-** – see TOX-

**toxoid** /'toksoyd/ *n* a toxin of a disease-causing organism treated so as to destroy its toxicity but leave it capable of inducing the formation of ANTIBODIES on injection [ISV *tox-* + *-oid*]

**toxophilite** /tok'sofiliet/ *n, formal* a lover of or expert at archery [Gk *toxon* bow, arrow + *philos* dear, loving] – **toxophilite** *adj,* **toxophily** *n*

**toxoplasma** /,toksə'plazmə/ *n* any of a genus (*Toxoplasma*) of parasitic PROTOZOANS (single-celled animals) that are related to the SPOROZOANS and are typically serious disease-producers in VERTEBRATE animals including humans [NL, genus name] – **toxoplasmic** *adj*

**toxoplasmosis** /,toksohplaz'mohsis/ *n, pl* **toxoplasmoses** /-seez/ a disease, affecting human beings, other mammals, and birds, that is caused by toxoplasmas invading the tissues and is often accompanied by damage to the CENTRAL NERVOUS SYSTEM, esp of infants [NL]

**¹toy** /toy/ *n* **1a** something (eg a preoccupation) that is paltry or trifling **b** a trinket, bauble **2a** something for a child to play with **b** something designed for amusement or diversion rather than for practical use ⟨*an executive ~*⟩ **3** something diminutive; *esp* a diminutive animal (eg of a small breed or variety) **4** something that can be toyed with **5** *Scot* a headdress of linen or wool hanging down over the shoulders and formerly worn by old women of the lower classes [ME *toye* amorous activity] – **toylike** *adj*

**²toy** *vi* **1** to engage in flirtation **2** to act or deal with something lightly or without purpose or conviction **3** to amuse oneself as if with a toy; play ⊡ usu + *with* – **toyer** *n*

**³toy** *adj* **1** designed or made for use as a toy ⟨*a ~ stove*⟩ **2** toylike, esp in being small

**toy dog** *n* a breed or variety of dog (eg poodle) that is very much smaller than the standard

**TPN** *n* NADP (substance assisting enzymes in biochemical reactions) [*triphosphopyridine nucleotide*]

**trabeated** /'traybiaytid/ *also* **trabeate** /-ət, -ayt/ *adj* designed or constructed with vertical posts and horizontal beams [L *trabes* beam] – **trabeation** *n*

**trabecula** /trə'bekyoolə/ *n, pl* **trabeculae** /-lie/ *also* **trabeculas** **1** a small bar, rod, bundle of fibres, or dividing membrane in the framework of a body organ or part **2** a fold, ridge, or bar projecting into or extending from a plant part [NL, fr L, little beam, dim. of *trabs, trabes* beam – more at THORP] – **trabecular** *adj,* **trabeculate** *adj*

**¹trace** /trays/ *n* **1** a mark or line left by something that has passed; *also* a footprint **2** a sign or evidence of some past thing; a vestige; *specif* ENGRAM (physical change in brain involved in creating a memory) **3** something traced or drawn; *esp* the graphic record made by a SEISMOGRAPH (apparatus measuring earth vibrations) or other recording instrument **4a** the intersection of a line or plane with a plane **b** (the path taken by) the spot that moves across the screen of a CATHODE-RAY TUBE (instrument that produces images by projecting electrons onto a fluorescent screen) **5** a minute and often barely detectable amount or indication ⟨*a ~ of a smile*⟩; *esp* an amount of a chemical constituent not quantitatively determined because of minuteness ⟨*the product contained a ~ of impurity*⟩ **6** *maths* the sum of the elements of the PRINCIPAL DIAGONAL of a MATRIX [ME, fr MF, fr *tracier* to trace]

*synonyms* Trace, **track, trail, spoor,** and **vestige** all mean "perceptible sign left behind". **Trace** is the most general word, applying to any mark, line, or slight indication ⟨**traces** *of Greek influence in Indian art*⟩. A **track** or **trail** is usually a series of marks left by something that has passed, **track** applying particularly to a wheeled vehicle and **trail** implying that the marks are to be followed. **Spoor** is a hunter's word, referring particularly to the evidence, including droppings and broken branches, that a wild animal has passed. A **vestige** is a remaining sign of something that no longer exists ⟨**vestiges** *of beauty in her aging face*⟩, or a small remaining bit.

**²trace** *vt* **1a** to delineate, sketch **b** to write (eg letters or figures) painstakingly **c** to copy (eg a drawing) by following the lines or letters as seen through a semitransparent superimposed sheet **d** to impress or imprint (eg a design or pattern) with a tracer **e** to record a tracing of, usu in the form of a curved, wavy, or broken line ⟨*~ the heart action*⟩ **f** to adorn with ornamental lines (eg architectural tracery) **2a** to follow the trail of **b** to follow back or study in detail or step by step ⟨*~ the history of the labour movement*⟩ **c** to discover signs, evidence, or remains of **3** *archaic* to travel over; traverse *~ vi* **1** to make one's way; *esp* to follow a track or trail **2** to be traceable historically [ME *tracen,* fr MF *tracier,* fr (assumed) VL *tractiare* to drag, draw, fr L *tractus,* pp of *trahere* to pull, draw – more at DRAW] – **traceable** *adj*, **traceableness** *n*, **traceably** *adv*, **traceability** *n*

³**trace** *n* either of two straps, chains, or lines of a harness for attaching a horse to a vehicle [ME *trais*, pl, traces, fr MF, pl of *trait* pull, draught, trace – more at TRAIT] – **kick over the traces** to cast off restraint, authority, or control

**trace clip** *n* a manner of clipping a horse's coat so as to leave long hair on the lower legs and on the back above the traces – **trace-clip** *vt*

**trace element** *n* a chemical element present in minute quantities; *esp* one essential to a living organism for its proper growth and development

**tracer** /'traysə/ *n* **1** one who or that which traces or searches out; *esp* a person who traces missing persons or property and esp goods lost in transit **2** a person (eg a draughtsman) or device (eg a stylus) that traces designs, patterns, or markings **3** ammunition containing chemicals that mark the flight of projectiles by burning to leave a trail of smoke or fire **4** a substance, esp one containing radioactive atoms, used to trace the course of a chemical or biological process

**tracery** /'traysəri/ *n* **1** ornamental stone openwork in architecture, esp in the head of a Gothic window **2** a decorative interlacing of lines (eg in a frost pattern or insect's wing) suggestive of Gothic tracery – **traceried** *adj*

**trache-, tracheo-** *comb form* **1** trachea ⟨trache*itis*⟩ ⟨tracheotomy⟩ **2** tracheal and ⟨tracheobronchial⟩ [NL, fr ML *trachea*]

**trachea** /trə'kee·ə/ *n, pl* **tracheae** /-kee·i/ *also* **tracheas** **1** the main trunk of the system of tubes by which air passes to and from the lungs in VERTEBRATE animals; the windpipe **2** VESSEL 3b (conducting tube in a plant); *also* any of its component cells **3** any of the small air-conveying tubes forming the respiratory system of most insects and many other related animals [ME, fr ML, fr LL *trachia*, fr Gk *tracheia* (*artēria*) rough (artery), fr fem of *trachys* rough; akin to Gk *thrassein* to trouble – more at DARK] – **tracheal** *adj*

**tracheary** /trə'kee·əri, 'traykiəri/ *adj* of, made up of, or being plant tracheae

**tracheate** /trə'kee·ət, 'traykiayt/ *also* **tracheated** /'traykiaytid/ *adj* having tracheae as breathing organs

**tracheid** /'trayki·id/ *n* a long tubular cell of plant tissue (XYLEM) that functions in water-conduction and support and has tapering closed ends and thickened woody walls [ISV *trache-* + *-id*] – **tracheidal** *adj*

**tracheitis** /ˌtrakiˈietəs/ *n* inflammation of the trachea [NL]

**tracheobronchial** /ˌtrakiohˈbrongkiəl/ *adj* relating to both trachea and bronchi ⟨~ *lesions*⟩

**tracheole** /'traykiohl/ *n* any of the minute delicate endings of a branched trachea of an insect [NL *tracheola*, dim. of *trachea*] – **tracheolar** *adj*

**tracheophyte** /'traykiəfiet, trə'kee·əfiet/ *n* any of a division (Tracheophyta) of plants in some systems of classification that comprises those forms (eg ferns and FLOWERING PLANTS) with a VASCULAR system which contains tracheids or tracheary elements [NL *Tracheophyta*, fr *trache-* + Gk *phyton* plant – more at PHYT-]

**tracheotomy** /ˌtrakiˈotəmi/ *n* the surgical operation of cutting into the trachea, esp through the skin, usu to relieve suffocation by inhaled matter

**trachoma** /trə'kohmə/ *n* a long-lasting contagious eye disease that is marked by small inflamed granules on the surface of the CONJUNCTIVA (membrane lining the eye and eyelids), is caused by a minute organism (*Chlamydia trachomatis*), and commonly causes blindness if left untreated [NL, fr Gk *trachōma*, fr *trachys* rough] – **trachomatous** *adj*

**trachyte** /'trakiet, 'tray-/ *n* a usu light-coloured volcanic rock consisting chiefly of the mineral FELDSPAR containing potassium [Fr, fr Gk *trachys* rough]

**trachytic** /trə'kitik/ *adj* of a texture of IGNEOUS rocks in which lath-shaped crystals of the mineral FELDSPAR are in almost parallel lines

**tracing** /'traysing/ *n* **1** the act of one who or that which traces **2** something that is traced: eg **2a** a copy (eg of a design or map) made on a superimposed semitransparent sheet **b** a graphic record made by an instrument that monitors some movement ⟨a seismographic ~ *that registers earth vibrations*⟩ **c** (a map of) the ground plan of a military installation

**tracing paper** *n* a semitransparent paper for tracing drawings

¹**track** /trak/ *n* **1a** detectable evidence (eg a line of footprints or a wheel rut) that something has passed **b** a path beaten (as

if) by feet; a trial **c** a made path or road **d** a specially laid-out course, esp for racing **e** the parallel rails of a railway **f(1)** any of a series of parallel elongated regions on a MAGNETIC TAPE on which a recording is made **f(2)** a more or less independent sequence of recording (eg a single song) visible as a distinct band on a gramophone record **g** ASSEMBLY LINE ⟨the ~s producing the Mini saloon⟩ **2** a recent or fossil footprint ⟨the huge ~ of a dinosaur⟩ **3a** the course along which something moves ⟨the ~ of a bullet⟩ **b** the projection on the earth's surface of the path along which something (eg a missile or an aircraft) has flown **4** the condition of being aware of a fact or development ⟨keep ~ of the costs⟩ ⟨lose ~ of the time⟩ **5a** the width of a wheeled vehicle from wheel to wheel, usu from the outside of the rims **b** either of two continuous usu metal belts on which a tracklaying vehicle travels **6** a rail or length of railing along which something, esp a curtain, moves or is pulled *synonyms* see ¹TRACE [ME *trak*, fr MF *trac*, perh of Gmc origin; akin to MD *tracken*, *trecken* to pull, haul – more at TREK] – **trackless** *adj* – **cover one's tracks** to conceal evidence of one's past actions in order to elude pursuit or investigation – **in one's tracks** where one stands or is at the moment; ON THE SPOT ⟨was stopped in his tracks⟩ – **make tracks** to set off; leave – **make tracks for** to go towards – **on the inside track** *chiefly NAm* possessing extensive (secret) knowledge ⟨he wouldn't make a good candidate – he's not on the inside track⟩

²**track** *vt* **1** to follow the tracks or traces of; trail **2** to observe or plot the course of (eg a spacecraft or missile) instrumentally **3** to pass over; traverse ⟨~ *a desert*⟩ **4a** to make tracks upon **b** *NAm* to carry on the feet and deposit ⟨~ *mud into the house*⟩ ~ *vi* **1a** of a gramophone needle to follow the groove of a record **b** of a pair of wheels to fit a track or rails **c** of a rear wheel of a vehicle to follow accurately the corresponding fore wheel on a straight track **d** of a horse to move with the hind feet accurately following the forefeet **2a** to move a film or television camera towards, beside, or away from a subject while shooting a scene **b** of a camera to undergo tracking – compare ⁴PAN, DOLLY **3** *NAm* to leave tracks (eg on a floor) – **tracker** *n*

**track down** *vt* to search for until found ⟨track *a criminal down*⟩ ⟨track down *their new telephone number*⟩

**trackage** /'trakij/ *n, NAm* **1** lines of railway track **2** a right to use the tracks of another railway line; RUNNING POWERS

**track chargeman** *n, Br* a worker employed to maintain a section of railway track

**tracked** /trakt/ *adj* **1** tracklaying **2** moving along a rail ⟨a ~ air-cushion vehicle⟩

**tracker action** /'trakə/ *n* a completely mechanical action in a musical organ

**track event** *n* an athletic event that is a race – compare FIELD EVENT

¹**tracklaying** /'trakˌlaying/ *n* the laying of tracks on a railway line – **tracklayer** *n*

²**tracklaying** *adj* of or being a vehicle that travels on two or more continuous usu metal belts

**trackless trolley** /'traklis/ *n, NAm* a trolleybus

**track record** *n* a record of past achievements (eg in public office)

**track shoe** *n* a lightweight usu leather shoe with metal spikes protruding from the sole, used by runners

**track suit** *n* a warm loose-fitting suit consisting of trousers and a jacket that is worn by athletes when training or waiting to compete

¹**tract** /trakt/ *n, often cap* verses of Scripture (eg from the Psalms) used at some Roman Catholic masses, esp during penitential seasons [ME *tracte*, fr ML *tractus*, fr L, action of drawing, extension; fr its being sung without a break by one voice]

²**tract** *n* a short practical treatise; *esp* a pamphlet of political or religious propaganda [ME, modif of L *tractatus* tractate]

³**tract** *n* **1** a region or area of land of indefinite extent **2** a system of body parts or organs that collectively serve some often specified purpose ⟨the digestive ~⟩; *esp* a bundle of NERVE FIBRES having a common origin, termination, and function **3** *archaic* extent or lapse of time [L *tractus* action of drawing, extension, fr *tractus*, pp of *trahere* to pull, draw – more at DRAW]

**tractable** /'traktəbl/ *adj* **1** easily led, taught, or controlled; docile ⟨a ~ horse⟩ **2** easily handled or wrought; malleable *synonyms* see OBEDIENT *antonyms* intractable, unruly [L *tractabilis*, fr *tractare* to handle, treat] – **tractableness** *n*, **tractably** *adv*, **tractability** *n*

**Tractarianism** /trak'teəri‧ə‚niz(ə)m/ *n* a system of High Church principles set forth in a series of tracts at Oxford (1833–41); the doctrines of the early OXFORD MOVEMENT – **Tractarian** *n or adj*

**tractate** /'traktayt/ *n* a treatise, dissertation [L *tractatus*, fr *tractatus*, pp of *tractare* to draw out, handle, treat – more at TREAT]

**traction** /'traksh(ə)n/ *n* 1 the act of pulling or the state of being pulled; *also* the force exerted in pulling 2 the drawing of a vehicle by power that causes motion; *also* the power employed 3a the adhesive friction of a body on a surface on which it moves ⟨*the ~ of a wheel on a rail*⟩ b a pulling force exerted on a part of the skeleton (eg in treating a fracture) by means of a special device ⟨*a ~ splint*⟩; *also* a state of tension created by such a pulling force ⟨*a leg in ~*⟩ [ML *traction-*, *tractio*, fr L *tractus*, pp] – **tractional** *adj*, **tractive** *adj*

**traction engine** *n* a large steam- or diesel-powered vehicle used to draw other vehicles or equipment over roads or fields and sometimes to provide power (eg for sawing or ploughing)

**¹tractor** /'traktə/ *n* 1 TRACTION ENGINE 2a a 4-wheeled or tracklaying rider-controlled vehicle used esp for pulling or using farm machinery b a truck with a short frame and consisting only of a driver's cab, that is used to haul a large trailer or trailers 3 an aircraft engine with the propeller mounted in front; *also* an aircraft having such an engine [NL, implement that pulls, fr L *tractus*, pp]

**²tractor** *adj* pulling or pulled through the air with force exerted from the front ⟨*a ~ monoplane is pulled by its propeller*⟩ – compare PUSHER

**¹trad** /trad/ *adj, chiefly Br informal* traditional

**²trad** *n* traditional jazz

**¹trade** /trayd/ *n* 1 a customary course of action; a practice ⟨*thy sin's not accidental, but a ~ –* Shak⟩ 2a the business or work in which one engages regularly; an occupation b an occupation requiring manual or mechanical skill; a craft c commerce as opposed to the liberal professions or landed property; *also* the social group deriving its income from commerce 3a the business of buying and selling or bartering commodities b BUSINESS 2d, MARKET 3b ⟨*when ~ was brisk*⟩ ⟨*novelties for the tourist ~*⟩ 4 taking sing or pl vb 4a a firm's customers; a clientele b *the* people or group of firms engaged in a particular business or industry ⟨*offer limited to members of the ~*⟩; *also* a branch of such business ⟨*the shoe ~*⟩ 5 usu pl TRADE WIND 6 chiefly NAm a transaction; *also* an exchange of property usu without the involvement of money 7 *archaic* a track or trail left by a man or animal; TREAD 1 8 *obs* dealings between persons or groups ⟨*have you any further ~ with us –* Shak⟩ [ME, course, way, track, fr MLG; akin to OHG *trata* track, course, OE *tredan* to tread]

**²trade** *vt* 1 to give in exchange for another commodity; barter; *also* to make an exchange of ⟨*~d secrets*⟩ 2 to engage in frequent buying and selling of ⟨eg shares or commodities) usu in search of quick profits ~ *vi* 1 to engage in the exchange, purchase, or sale of goods 2 to give one thing in exchange for another 3 *NAm* to make one's purchases; shop ⟨*~s at his store*⟩ 4 *obs* to have dealings; negotiate – **tradable** *also* **tradeable** *adj*

**trade down** *vi* to trade in something (eg a motor car) for something less expensive or valuable of its kind – compare TRADE UP

**trade in** *vt* to give as payment or part payment for a purchase or bill ⟨trade *an old car* in *for a new one*⟩ – see also TRADE-IN

**trade on** *vt* to take often unscrupulous advantage of; exploit ⟨*they* traded on *his good nature*⟩

**trade up** *vi* to trade in something (eg a motor car) for something more expensive or valuable of its kind – compare TRADE DOWN

**³trade** *adj* 1 of or used in trade ⟨*a ~ agreement*⟩ 2 intended for or limited to people in a business or industry ⟨*a ~ publication*⟩ ⟨*~ discount*⟩ 3 trade, trades, of, composed of, or representing the trades or trade unions ⟨*a ~ committee*⟩ 4 of or associated with a trade wind ⟨*the ~ belts*⟩

**trade book** *n* 1 a book intended for general readership 2 TRADE EDITION

**trade cycle** *n* the regularly recurrent fluctuation in the level of economic activity

**trade edition** *n* an edition of a book in a standard format intended for general distribution

**trade gap** *n* the value by which a country's imports exceed its exports

**'trade-‚in** *n* 1 an item of merchandise (eg a car or refrigerator) that is traded in 2 an act or instance of trading in

**trade language** *n* a mongrel language (eg a LINGUA FRANCA or pidgin) used esp in commercial communication

**¹trademark** /'trayd‚mahk/ *n* 1 a name or distinctive symbol or device attached to goods produced by a particular firm or individual and legally reserved to the exclusive use of the owner of the mark as maker or seller 2 a distinguishing characteristic or feature firmly associated with a person or thing; a hallmark

**²trademark** *vt* to secure trademark rights for; register the trademark of

**trade name** *n* 1a the name used for an article by the trade that deals in or with it b a name that is given by a manufacturer or seller to an article or service to distinguish it as produced or sold by him/her and that may be used and protected as a trademark 2 the name under which a concern does business

**'trade-‚off** *n* 1 a balancing of factors all of which are not attainable at the same time 2 a giving up of one thing in return for another

**trade price** *n* the price at which goods are sold to members in the same trade or by a manufacturer or wholesaler to a retailer

**trader** /'traydə/ *n* 1 one whose business is trading: eg 1a a retail or wholesale dealer; a merchant b a person who buys and sells (eg securities) on the US Stock Exchange for his/her own account in search of short-term profits 2 a ship engaged in trade

**trade route** *n* a land or sea route followed by traders; *esp* a sea-lane ordinarily used by merchant ships

**trades** /traydz/ *adj* TRADE 3

**tradescantia** /‚tradə'skanshə, ‚trayde'skanshi‧ə/ *n* any of a genus (*Tradescantia* of the family Commelinaceae) of plants with short-lived usu blue or violet flowers that are commonly grown as houseplants [NL, genus name, fr John *Tradescant* † 1638 E traveller & gardener]

**tradesman** /'traydzmən/ *n* 1a a shopkeeper b one who makes deliveries of regularly ordered household goods (eg food or coal) to private houses ⟨*the* tradesman's *entrance*⟩ 2 a workman in a skilled trade; a craftsman

**trade union** *also* **trades union** *n taking sing or pl vb* an organization of workers formed for the purpose of advancing its members' interests with respect to wages, benefits, and working conditions – **trade unionism** *n*, **trade unionist** *n*

**trade wind** *n* a wind blowing almost continually towards the equator from the northeast in the belt between the northern HORSE LATITUDES and the DOLDRUMS and from the southeast in the belt between the southern horse latitudes and the doldrums [obs *trade* in a regular course or direction, fr ¹*trade* (in the sense "course")]

**trading estate** /'trayding/ *n* INDUSTRIAL ESTATE

**trading post** *n* 1 a station of a trader or trading company established in a sparsely settled region where trade, esp in products of local origin (eg furs), is carried on 2 a trading station on the floor of a stock exchange

**trading profit** *n* profit coming from economic activity rather than from an increase in the value of assets – compare CAPITAL PROFIT

**trading stamp** *n* a printed stamp of a certain value given by a retailer to a customer, to be accumulated and exchanged for goods or cash

**tradition** /trə'dish(ə)n/ *n* 1 the handing down of information, beliefs, and customs by word of mouth or by example from one generation to another 2a an inherited pattern of thought or action (eg a religious practice or a social custom) b a convention or set of conventions associated with or representative of an individual, group, or period ⟨*the title poem represents a complete break with nineteenth-century ~ –* F R Leavis⟩ 3 cultural continuity in social attitudes and institutions [ME *tradicioun*, fr MF & L; MF *tradition*, fr L *tradition-*, *traditio* action of handing over, tradition – more at TREASON] – **traditionless** *adj*

**traditional** /trə'dish(ə)nl/ *adj* 1 of or handed down by tradition 2 of or being a style of jazz originally played in New Orleans in the early 1900s – **traditionally** *adv*, **traditionalize** *vt*

**traditionalism** /-iz(ə)m/ *n* 1 the doctrines or practices of those who follow or accept tradition 2 the beliefs of those opposed to modernism, liberalism, or radicalism (eg in religious matters) – **traditionalist** *n or adj*, **traditionalistic** *adj*

**traditionary** /trə'dishən(ə)ri/ *adj* traditional

**traduce** /trə'dyoohs/ *vt, formal* **1** to (attempt to) damage the reputation or standing of, esp by misrepresentation; defame **2** to violate, betray ⟨~ *a principle of law*⟩ *synonyms* see ²MALIGN [L *traducere* to lead across, transfer, lead (prisoners) in a procession, expose to scorn, fr *tra-, trans-* trans- + *ducere* to lead – more at TOW] – **traducement** *n*, **traducer** *n*

¹**traffic** /'trafik/ *n* **1a** import and export trade **b** the business of bartering or buying and selling **c** illegal or disreputable commercial activity ⟨*the drug* ~⟩ **2** exchange ⟨*a lively* ~ *in ideas* – F L Allen⟩ **3** goods, wares **4a** the movement (e g of vehicles or pedestrians) through an area or along a route **b** the vehicles, pedestrians, ships, or aircraft moving along a route **c** the information or signals transmitted over a communications system messages **5a** the passengers or cargo carried by a transport system **b** the business of transporting passengers or freight **6** *formal* communication or dealings between individuals or groups [MF *trafique*, fr OIt *traffico*, fr *trafficare* to trade]

²**traffic** *vb* **-ck-** *vi* to carry on traffic ~ *vt* **1** to travel over ⟨*heavily* ~ked *highways*⟩ **2** to trade, barter – **trafficker** *n*

**trafficator** /'trafi,kaytə/ *n Br* INDICATOR 1c; *esp* a hinged retractable illuminated arm on the side of a motor vehicle [blend of *traffic* and *indicator*]

**traffic circle** *n, NAm* ROUNDABOUT 2

**traffic cone** *n* a conical marker used on a road or highway (e g for indicating roadworks)

**traffic court** *n*, a minor court for petty prosecutions of traffic offences

**traffic engineering** *n* engineering dealing with the design of streets and control of traffic – **traffic engineer** *n*

**traffic island** *n* a paved or planted island in a road, designed to guide the flow of traffic and provide refuge for pedestrians

**traffic light** *n*, **traffic lights** *n pl* an automatically operated signal of coloured lights for controlling traffic, esp at junctions or roadworks

**traffic manager** *n* a supervisor of the traffic functions of a commercial or industrial organization

**traffic signal** *n* a signal (e g TRAFFIC LIGHTS) for controlling traffic

**traffic warden** *n* a British public employee who enforces car-parking regulations and helps in maintaining the traffic flow in urban areas

**tragacanth** /'tragəkanth/ *n* **1** a gum obtained from various Asiatic or E European plants (genus *Astragalus*, esp *Astragalus gummifer*) of the pea family, that swells in water, and is used in manufacturing (e g of books) and in pharmacy **2** a plant yielding tragacanth [MF *tragacanthe*, fr L *tragacantha*, fr Gk *tragakantha*, fr *tragos* goat + *akantha* thorn – more at ACANTH-]

**tragedian** /trə'jeedi-ən/ *n* **1** a writer of tragedies **2** *fem* **tragedienne** /trə,jeedi·'en/ an actor who plays tragic roles [*tragedian* fr ME *tragedien*, fr MF, fr *tragedie*; *tragedienne* fr Fr *tragedienne*, fr MF, fem of *tragedien*]

**tragedy** /'trajədi/ *n* **1a** a serious drama typically describing a conflict between the main character and a superior force (e g destiny) and having a disastrous conclusion evoking pity or terror – compare COMEDY 1 **b** the literary genre of tragic dramas **c** a tragic work of literature **2a** a disastrous often fatal event; a calamity **b** misfortune **3** tragic quality or element [ME *tragedie*, fr MF, fr L *tragoedia*, fr Gk *tragōidia*, prob fr *tragos* goat (akin to Gk *trōgein* to gnaw) + *aeidein* to sing – more at TERSE, ODE]

*usage* Some people dislike the use of **tragedy** for an event, such as a defeat on the football field, that involves neither death nor lasting misery.

**tragic** /'trajik/ *also* **tragical** /-kl/ *adj* **1** of, marked by, or expressive of tragedy ⟨*the* ~ *significance of the atomic bomb* – H S Truman⟩ **2** of, appropriate to, dealing with, or treated in tragedy ⟨*the* ~ *hero*⟩ **3a** deplorable, lamentable ⟨*a* ~ *waste of young talent*⟩ **b** marked by a sense of tragedy [L *tragicus*, fr Gk *tragikos*, irreg fr *tragōidia* tragedy] – **tragically** *adv*

*usage* **Tragic** is the commoner form. If **tragical** is used at all today, it is chiefly in the sense of "gloomy". Compare ⟨*in a* **tragical/tragic** *mood*⟩ ⟨*his* **tragic** *death*⟩.

**tragic flaw** *n* a flaw in the character of the hero of a tragedy that brings about his downfall

**tragic irony** *n* DRAMATIC IRONY

**tragicomedy** /,traji'komədi/ *n* a literary work, esp a drama, in which tragic and comic elements are mixed in a usu ironic way; *also* a situation or event of mixed comic and tragic

character [MF *tragicomedie*, fr OIt *tragicomedia*, fr OSp, fr L *tragicomoedia*, fr *tragicus* + *comoedia* comedy] – **tragicomic** *also* **tragicomical** *adj*

**tragopan** /'tragəpan/ *n* any of several brilliantly coloured Asiatic pheasants (genus *Tragopan*) [NL, genus name, fr L, an Ethiopian bird, fr Gk, fr *tragos* goat + *Pan* Pan, god of woods & shepherds]

**tragus** /'traygəs/ *n, pl* **tragi** /'trayji, -jie, -gi/ the prominence in front of the external opening of the ear [NL, fr Gk *tragos*, a part of the ear, lit., goat]

¹**trail** /trayl/ *vi* **1a** to hang down so as to sweep the ground ⟨*his coat* ~ed *in the dust*⟩ **b** to extend over a surface in a loose or straggling manner ⟨*a vine that* ~s *over the ground*⟩ **c** *of a plant, branch, etc* to grow to such a length as to droop over towards the ground ⟨~ing *branches of a weeping willow*⟩ **2a** to walk or proceed draggingly, heavily, or wearily; plod, trudge – usu + *along* **b** to lag behind; do poorly in relation to others **3** to move, flow, or extend slowly in thin streams ⟨*smoke* ~ing *from chimneys*⟩ **4a** to extend in an erratic course or line; straggle **b** to dwindle ⟨*voice* ~ing *off*⟩ **5** to follow a trail; track game ~ *vt* **1a** to drag loosely along a surface; allow to sweep the ground **b** to haul, tow **2a** to drag (e g a limb or the body) heavily or wearily **b** to carry or bring along as an addition, burden, or encumbrance **c** to draw along in one's wake ⟨~ing *clouds of glory do we come* – William Wordsworth⟩ **3a** to follow upon the scent or trace of; track **b** to follow behind, esp in the footsteps of **c** to lag behind (e g a competitor) [ME *trailen*, fr MF *trailler* to tow, fr (assumed) VL *tragulare*, fr L *tragula* sledge, dragnet]

²**trail** *n* **1** the part of a gun carriage that rests on the ground when the gun is UNLIMBERED (detached and ready for action) **2a** something that follows or moves along as if being drawn behind; a train ⟨*a* ~ *of admirers*⟩ **b(1)** the streak of light produced by a meteor **b(2)** a continuous line produced photographically by permitting the image of a celestial body (e g a star) to move over the plate **c** a chain of consequences; an aftermath ⟨*left a* ~ *of broken hearts behind her*⟩ **3a** a trace or mark left by one who or that which has passed; scent, track ⟨*a* ~ *of blood*⟩ ⟨*on the* ~ *of the killer*⟩ **b(1)** a track made by passage, esp through a wilderness **b(2)** a marked path through a forest or mountainous region **c** a course followed or to be followed ⟨*hit the campaign* ~⟩ *synonyms* see ¹TRACE – **trail-less** *adj*

**trailblazer** /-,blayzə/ *n* **1** one who marks a track to guide others; a pathfinder **2** PIONEER 2 ⟨*a* ~ *in astrophysics*⟩ – **trailblazing** *adj*

**trailer** /'traylə/ *n* **1** somebody who or something that trails **2** a trailing plant **3** a wheeled vehicle designed to be towed (e g by a lorry or car); *specif, NAm* CARAVAN 2b **4** a set of short excerpts from a film shown in advance for publicity purposes – **trailer** *vb*

**trailer truck** *n, NAm* an articulated lorry

**trailing edge** /'trayling/ *n* the rearmost edge of a moving object, esp of an AEROFOIL (surface providing lift to an aircraft)

¹**train** /trayn/ *n* **1** a part of a gown that trails behind the wearer **2a** a retinue, suite **b** a moving file of people, vehicles, or animals **3** the vehicles, men, and sometimes animals that accompany an army with baggage, supplies, ammunition, or siege artillery **4a** order or arrangement designed to lead to some result – chiefly in *in train* **b** a connected series of ideas, actions, or events ⟨*a* ~ *of thought*⟩ **c** accompanying or ensuing circumstances; aftermath ⟨*in the* ~ *of peace came industry* – T B Macaulay⟩ **5** a line of gunpowder laid to lead fire to a charge **6** a series of connected moving mechanical parts (e g gears) that transmit and modify motion **7** a connected line of railway carriages or wagons, with or without a locomotive **8** a series of parts or elements forming a coordinated system, esp for carrying on a process (e g of manufacture) automatically [ME, fr MF, fr OF, fr *trainer* to draw, drag] – **trainful** *n*

²**train** *vt* **1** to trail, drag **2** to direct the growth of (a plant), usu by bending, pruning, and tying **3a** to form by instruction, discipline, or drill **b** to teach so as to make fit, qualified, or proficient **4** to prepare (e g by exercise) for a test of skill **5** to aim at an object or objective; direct ⟨~ed *his rifle on the target*⟩ ~ *vi* **1** to undergo training **2** to go by train *synonyms* see TEACH [ME *trainen*, fr MF *trainer*, fr OF, fr (assumed) VL *traginare*; akin to L *trahere* to draw – more at DRAW] – **trainable** *adj*, **trainability** *n*

**trainband** /'trayn,band/ *n taking sing or pl vb* a 17th- or 18th-century militia company in England or America [alter. of *trained band*]

**trainbearer** /-ˌbeərə/ *n* an attendant who holds up the train of a robe or gown (eg on a ceremonial occasion)

**trainee** /ˌtrayˈnee/ *n* one who is being trained for a job – **traineeship** *n*

**trainer** /ˈtraynə/ *n* 1 someone who or something that trains: eg **1a** an aircraft or piece of equipment for training the crew of an aircraft **b** a person who trains the members of an athletic team (eg footballers) **c** a person who trains and prepares horses for racing 2 a plimsoll or similar sports shoe worn esp for running, jogging, etc

**training** /ˈtrayning/ *n* 1 the bringing of a person or animal to a desired degree of proficiency in some activity or skill ⟨*apprentice's undergoing* ~⟩ 2 the condition of being trained, esp for a test or contest ⟨*an athlete out of* ~⟩

**training college** *n, Br* a school offering specialized instruction ⟨*a* ~ *for traffic wardens*⟩

**trainload** /ˈtraynˌlohd/ *n* the full goods or passenger capacity of a railway train

**trainman** /ˈtraynmən/ *n* a member of a train crew

**train oil** *n* oil from a marine animal, esp a whale, that is used in the manufacture of margarine and cooking fats, in paints and varnishes, and in the treatment and dressing of leather [obs *train*, fr ME *trane*, fr MD *trane* or MLG *trān*]

**trainsick** /ˈtraynˌsik/ *adj* affected with MOTION SICKNESS induced by travelling by train – **train sickness** *n*

**traipse** /trayps/ *vi, informal* to walk or trudge about, often to little purpose [origin unknown] – **traipse** *n*

**trait** /trayt, tray/ *n* a distinguishing (personal) quality or characteristic; a peculiarity [MF, lit., act of drawing, fr L *tractus* – more at TRACT]
  *usage* The pronunciation /tray/ is recommended for BBC broadcasters. *synonyms* see ¹QUALITY

**traitor** /ˈtraytə/, *fem* **traitress** /ˈtraytris/, **traitoress** /ˈtraytəris/ *n* **1a** one who betrays another's trust **b** one who betrays an obligation or duty ⟨*a* ~ *to his class*⟩ 2 a person who commits treason *synonyms* see TREASON [ME *traitre*, fr OF, fr L *traditor*, fr *traditus*, pp of *tradere* to hand over, deliver, betray, fr *trans-*, *tra-* trans- + *dare* to give – more at DATE]

**traitorous** /ˈtrayt(ə)rəs/ *adj* 1 guilty or capable of treason 2 constituting treason ⟨~ *activities*⟩ – **traitorously** *adv*

**trajectory** /trəˈjektəri/ *n* 1 the curve that a planet, projectile, etc follows under the influence of certain forces, esp gravity 2 a path, progression, or line of development like a physical trajectory [NL *trajectoria*, fr fem of *trajectorius* of passing, fr L *trajectus*, pp of *traicere* to cause to cross, cross, fr *trans-*, *tra-* trans-+*jacere* to throw – more at JET]

**¹tram** /tram/ *n* a silk yarn consisting of two or more filaments twisted together [Fr *trame*, fr L *trama* warp]

**²tram** *n* 1 any of various vehicles: eg **1a** a boxlike wagon running on rails (eg in a mine) **b** *chiefly Br* a passenger vehicle running on rails and typically operating on urban streets 2 *pl* a tramline, tramway [E dial., shaft of a wheelbarrow, prob fr LG *traam*, lit., beam]

**³tram** *vb* **-mm-** to convey or be conveyed in a tram

**tramcar** /-ˌkah/ *n* 1 TRAM 1a 2 *chiefly Br* TRAM 1b

**tramline** /-ˌlien/ *n, Br* **1a** a track on which trams run **b** a company owning and operating trams; a tramway 2 *pl* either of the two pairs of sidelines on a tennis court that mark off the area used in doubles play; *also* the area between a pair of sidelines

**¹trammel** /ˈtraml/ *n* 1 a net for catching birds or fish; *esp* one having three layers with the middle one finer-meshed and slack and the two outer layers stretched and of coarse mesh so that fish attempting to pass in either direction carry some of the fine net through the coarse net and are thus trapped 2 a shackle used for making a horse amble 3 **trammels** *pl*, **trammel** something that impedes freedom of action; a restraint ⟨*the* ~s *of convention*⟩ **4a** an instrument for drawing ellipses **b** **trammels** *pl*, **trammel** a compass for drawing large circles that consists of a beam with two sliding parts **c** any of various gauges used for aligning or adjusting machine parts 5 *NAm* an adjustable hook for pots over a fireplace [ME *tramayle*, fr MF *tremail*, fr LL *tremaculum*, fr L *tres* three + *macula* mesh, spot – more at THREE]

**²trammel** *vt* **-ll-** (*NAm* **-l-**, **-ll-**) 1 to catch or hold (as if) in a net; enmesh 2 to prevent or impede the free play of; confine

**¹tramontane** /trəˈmontayn/ *adj* 1 transalpine 2 lying on or coming from the other side of a mountain range [It *tramontano*, fr L *transmontanus*, fr *trans-* + *mont-*, *mons* mountain – more at MOUNT]

**²tramontane** *n* one dwelling in a tramontane region; *broadly* a foreigner, barbarian

**¹tramp** /tramp/ *vi* 1 to walk or tread, esp heavily **2a** to travel about on foot **b** to journey as a tramp ~ *vt* 1 to tread on forcibly and repeatedly; trample 2 to travel or wander through on foot ⟨~ *the streets all day long*⟩ [ME *trampen*; akin to MLG *trampen* to stamp, OE *treppan* to tread – more at TRAP] – **tramper** *n*

**²tramp** *n* 1 a wandering vagrant who travels on foot from place to place and survives by taking the occasional job or by begging or stealing money and food 2 a usu long and tiring walk 3 the heavy rhythmic sound made by the tread of feet on a surface (eg a road or floor) 4 an iron plate to protect the sole of a shoe 5 **tramp, tramp steamer** a merchant vessel that does not work a regular route but carries general cargo to any port as required 6 *chiefly NAm* a promiscuous woman; *specif* a prostitute
  *usage* British speakers should remember that, to an American, **tramp** is likely to mean "promiscuous woman". Americans call a "vagrant" a **bum** or **hobo**.

**trample** /ˈtrampl/ *vi* 1 to tread heavily so as to bruise, crush, or injure ⟨*don't* ~ *on the flower beds*⟩ 2 to inflict injury with ruthlessness or contempt – usu + *on*, *over*, or *upon* ⟨*trampling on the rights of others*⟩ ~ *vt* to press down, crush, or injure (as if) by treading; stamp [ME *tramplen*, freq of *trampen* to tramp] – **trample** *n*, **trampler** *n*

**trampoline** /ˌtrampəˈleen, '---/ *n* a resilient sheet or web, usu of nylon, supported by springs in a metal frame and used as a springboard for acrobatic tricks, landing after pole-vaulting, etc [Sp *trampolin*, fr It *trampolino*, of Gmc origin; akin to MLG *trampen* to stamp] – **trampoliner**, **trampolinist** *n*

**trampolining** /ˌtrampəˈleening/ *n* the sport of jumping and tumbling on a trampoline

**tramroad** /ˈtramˌrohd/ *n* a track for hauling trams in a mine

**tramway** /-ˌway/ *n* 1 a tramroad in a mine 2 *Br* a system of tracks (eg laid in the surface of urban streets) for trams 3 *Br* a company owning and operating trams

**¹trance** /trahns/ *n* 1 a state of semiconsciousness or unconsciousness with reduced or absent sensitivity to external stimulation; a daze, stupor 2 a usu self-induced state of altered consciousness or ecstasy in which religious or mystical visions may be experienced 3 a state of profound abstraction or absorption [ME, fr MF *transe*, fr *transir* to pass away, swoon, fr L *transire* to pass, pass away – more at TRANSIENT] – **trancelike** *adj*

**²trance** *vt, poetic* to entrance, enrapture

**tranche** /trahnch/ (*Fr* trãʃ) *n* a block of shares usu supplementary to an already existing issue [Fr, lit., slice, fr OF, fr *trenchier*, *trancher* to cut]

**tranny, trannie** /ˈtrani/ *n, chiefly Br informal* TRANSISTOR RADIO [*transistor* + ⁴*-y*]

**tranquil** /ˈtrangkwil/ *adj* **1a** free from mental agitation ⟨~ *faith*⟩ **b** free from disturbance or commotion ⟨*a* ~ *scene*⟩ 2 unvarying in aspect; steady, stable ⟨*a* ~ *gaze*⟩ *synonyms* see ²CALM *antonym* troubled [L *tranquillus*] – **tranquilly** *adv*, **tranquilness**, **tranquillity** *n*

**tranquill·ize, -ise,** *NAm chiefly* **tranquilize** /ˈtrangkwiliez/ *vt* to make tranquil or calm; pacify; *esp* to relieve of mental tension and anxiety by drugs ~ *vi* 1 to become tranquil; relax 2 to make one tranquil

**tranquill·izer, -iser,** *NAm chiefly* **tranquilizer** /ˈtrangkwiliezə/ *n* 1 one who or that which tranquillizes 2 a drug (eg DIAZEPAM) used to tranquillize

**trans** /tranz/ *adj* characterized by having identical atoms or chemical groups on opposite sides of a chemical DOUBLE BOND in a molecule – usu printed in italic; often in combination ⟨*trans-dichlorethylene*⟩; compare CIS- [*trans-*]

**trans-** /tranz, trahnz/ *prefix* 1 on or to the other side of; across; beyond ⟨*transatlantic*⟩ ⟨*transcontinental*⟩ 2 beyond (a specified chemical element) in the PERIODIC TABLE ⟨*transuranic*⟩ 3 through ⟨*transcutaneous*⟩ ⟨*trans-sonic*⟩ 4 so or such as to change or transfer ⟨*transliterate*⟩ ⟨*translocation*⟩ ⟨*transship*⟩ [L *trans-*, *tra-* across, beyond, through, so as to change, fr *trans* across, beyond – more at THROUGH]

**transact** /tranˈzakt/ *vi* to carry on business to perform; CARRY OUT 1; *esp* to conduct ⟨*business to be* ~ed *by experts*⟩ [L *transactus*, pp of *transigere* to drive through, complete, transact, fr *trans-* + *agere* to drive, do – more at AGENT] – **transactor** *n*

**transactinide** /tranz'aktinied/ *adj* of or being actual or hypothetical chemical elements with ATOMIC WEIGHTS higher than those of the ACTINIDES ⟨~ *chemistry*⟩

**transaction** /tran'zaksh(ə)n, trahn-/ *n* **1** transacting **2a** something transacted; *esp* a business deal **b** *pl* the (published) record of the meeting of a society or association – **transactional** *adj*

**transalpine** /tran'zalpien, trahn-/ *adj* situated on the north side of the Alps ⟨Transalpine *Gaul*⟩ – compare CISALPINE [L *transalpinus*, fr *trans-* + *Alpes* the Alps]

**transaminase** /tranz'aminayz, -nays, trahn-/ *n* an ENZYME promoting transamination

**transamination** /tranz,ami'naysh(ə)n, trahn-/ *n* a reversible biochemical reaction that involves OXIDATION and REDUCTION and in which an AMINO group is transferred from a particular acid to another [*trans-* + *amin-* + *-ation*]

**transatlantic** /,tranzət'lantik, ,trahn-/ *adj* **1a** crossing or extending across the Atlantic ocean ⟨*a* ~ *cable*⟩ **b** of or involving crossing the Atlantic ocean ⟨~ *air fares*⟩ **2** situated beyond the Atlantic ocean **3** (characteristic) of people or places situated beyond the Atlantic ocean; *specif*, *chiefly Br* American ⟨*a* ~ *accent*⟩

**transceiver** /tran'seevə, trahn-/ *n* a combined radio transmitter and receiver that uses many of the same components for both transmission and reception [*transmitter* + *receiver*]

**transcend** /tran'send, trahn-/ *vt* **1a** to rise above or go beyond the limits of **b** to be prior to, or extend beyond and above (the universe or material existence) **2** to surpass, excel ⟨~ed *him in reputation*⟩ ~ *vi* to rise above or extend notably beyond ordinary limits [L *transcendere* to climb across, transcend, fr *trans-* + *scandere* to climb – more at SCAN]

**transcendence** /tran'send(ə)ns; *also* trahn-/ **transcendency** /tran'sendənsi; *also* trahn-/ *n* the quality or state of being transcendent

**transcendent** /tran'send(ə)nt; *also* trahn-/ *adj* **1a** exceeding usual limits; surpassing **b** beyond the limits of ordinary experience **c** beyond the limits of possible experience and knowledge – used in the philosophy of Kant **2** transcending the universe or material existence – compare IMMANENT [L *transcendent-, transcendens*, prp of *transcendere*] – **transcendently** *adv*
**synonyms** In general use **transcendent** is preferred for the meaning "surpassing" ⟨*a pianist of* **transcendent** *genius*⟩ and **transcendental** for "visionary" ⟨*a* **transcendental** *world of concepts* – C K Ogden & I A Richards⟩.

**transcendental** /,transen'dentl; *also* trahn-/ *adj* **1a** of or employing the basic categories (eg space and time) presupposed by knowledge and experience ⟨*a* ~ *proof*⟩ **b** transcending direct experience but not rational knowledge – used in the philosophy of Kant **2** TRANSCENDENT **1a 3a** being or relating to a TRANSCENDENTAL NUMBER **b** being, involving, or representing a function (eg sin*x*, log*x*, or e*x*) that cannot be expressed by a finite number of algebraic operations ⟨~ *curves*⟩ **4a** TRANSCENDENT **1b b** supernatural **c** abstruse, abstract **d** of transcendentalism – **transcendentally** *adv*

**transcendentalism** /-,iz(ə)m/ *n* **1** a philosophy that emphasizes the basic categories of knowledge and experience, or that asserts fundamental reality to be transcendent **2** a philosophy that asserts the primacy of the spiritual over the material **3** a transcendental outlook or attitude; *esp* visionary idealism – **transcendentalist** *adj or n*

**transcendental meditation** *n* a method, derived from Hinduism, of relaxing and refreshing oneself by silently repeating a mystical formula (MANTRA)

**transcendental number** *n* a number (eg e or π) that cannot be the root of an algebraic equation with rational coefficients – compare ALGEBRAIC NUMBER

**transcontinental** /,tranz,konti'nentl, trahnz-/ *adj* crossing or extending across a continent ⟨*a* ~ *railway*⟩

**transcribe** /tran'skrieb; *also* trahn-/ *vt* **1a** to make a written copy or version of (eg something written or printed) **b** to write in a different medium; transliterate ⟨~ *a word in phonetics*⟩ ⟨~ *shorthand*⟩ **c** to make a written version of (speech or a recording) **d** to record; WRITE DOWN ⟨~ *the witness's statement*⟩ **2a** to transfer (data) from one recording form to another **b** to record (eg on MAGNETIC TAPE) for broadcast at a later time; prerecord **3** to make a musical transcription of **4** to broadcast a sound recording of **5** to cause (eg DNA) to undergo genetic transcription [L *transcribere*, fr *trans-* + *scribere* to write – more at SCRIBE] – **transcribable** *adj*, **transcriber** *n*

**transcript** /'transkript, 'trahn-/ *n* **1a** a written, printed, or typed copy; *esp* a usu typewritten copy of dictated or recorded material or shorthand notes **b** an official or legal and often published copy ⟨*a court reporter's* ~⟩; *esp*, *chiefly NAm* an official copy of a student's educational record **2** a representation (eg of experience) in an art form **3** a length of NUCLEIC ACID (eg messenger RNA) produced by transcription [ME, fr ML *transcriptum*, fr L, neut of *transcriptus*, pp of *transcribere*]

**transcription** /tran'skripsh(ə)n, trahn-/ *n* **1** transcribing **2** a copy, transcript: eg **2a** an often free arrangement of a musical composition for some instrument or voice other than the original **b** a sound recording suitable for broadcasting and thus usu of high quality; *also* the programme broadcast from such a recording **3** the naturally occurring process of constructing a molecule of NUCLEIC ACID (eg messenger RNA) using a DNA molecule as a TEMPLATE (structure from which a replica can be made) with resulting transfer of genetic information to the newly formed molecule – compare TRANSLATION **2** – **transcriptional** *adj*, **transcriptionally** *adv*

**transcutaneous** /,tranzkyooh'tayniəs, trahnz-/ *adj* passing or entering through the skin ⟨~ *infection*⟩ ⟨~ *inoculation*⟩

**transduce** /tranz'dyoohs, trahnz-/ *vt* **1** to convert (eg energy or a message) into another form ⟨*essentially sense organs* ~ *physical energy into a nervous signal*⟩ **2** to bring about the transfer of (eg a gene) from one microorganism to another by means of infection with a virus, esp one that destroys bacteria [L *transducere* to lead across, transfer, fr *trans-* + *ducere* to lead – more at TOW]

**transducer** /tranz'dyoohsə, trahnz-/ *n* a device that transfers energy from one system to another; *esp* one that converts nonelectrical energy into electrical energy or vice versa ⟨*a microphone is an electroacoustic* ~⟩

**transduction** /tranz'duksh(ə)n, trahnz-/ *n* the action or process of transducing [L *transductus*, pp of *transducere*] – **transductional** *adj*

**¹transect** /tran'sekt/ *vt* to cut transversely [*trans-* + *-sect*] – **transection** *n*

**²transect** /'transekt, 'trahn-/ *n* a sample area (eg of vegetation), usu in the form of a long continuous strip, that is used to study the composition of plant species, animal populations, etc

**transept** /'transept/ *n* the part of a cross-shaped church that crosses at right angles to the east end of the central space (NAVE); *specif* either of the projecting ends of a transept ⟨*the south* ~⟩ [NL *transeptum*, fr L *trans-* + *septum, saeptum* enclosure, wall – more at SEPTUM] – **transeptal** *adj*

**transexual** /tran'seksyooəl, -sh(ə)l/ *n or adj* (a) transsexual

**¹transfer** /trans'fuh, trahns-/ *vb* **-rr-** *vt* **1a** to carry or take from one person, place, or situation to another; transport **b** to move or send to another location ⟨~red *his business to the capital*⟩; *specif* to move (a professional soccer player) to another football club **c** to cause to pass from one person or thing to another; transmit ⟨*power is* ~red *from the engine to the wheels*⟩ **d** to transform, change **2** to make over the possession or control of; convey ⟨~red *the title to his son*⟩ **3** to copy (eg a design) from one surface to another by contact ~ *vi* **1** to move to a different place, region, or situation; *esp* to withdraw from one educational institution to enrol at another **2** to change from one vehicle or transport system to another [ME *transferren*, fr L *transferre*, fr *trans-* + *ferre* to carry – more at BEAR] – **transferable, transferrable** *adj*, **transferability** *n*, **transferral** *n*, **transferrer** *n*

**²transfer** /'transfuh, 'trahns-/ *n* **1** conveyance of right, title, or interest in property from one person to another **2a** an act, process, or instance of transferring **b** TRANSFERENCE **2 c** the application of responses learned in one situation to similar situations **3** one who or that which transfers or is transferred; *esp* a graphic image transferred by contact from one surface (eg specially prepared paper) to another **4** a place where a transfer is made (eg from trains to ferries or where one form of power is changed to another) **5** *NAm* a ticket entitling a passenger on a public conveyance to continue a journey on another route

**transferable vote** /trans'fuhrəbl/ *n* a vote which in balloting by PROPORTIONAL REPRESENTATION may be transferred to a candidate other than the one marked as first choice

**transferase** /'transfərayz, -rays, 'trahns-/ *n* any ENZYME that promotes the transfer of a chemical group from one molecule to another

**transferee** /ˌtransfəˈree, ˌtrahns-/ *n* **1** a person to whom a property is transferred **2** one who is transferred

**transference** /ˈtransf(ə)rəns, transˈfuhrəns, trahns-/ *n* **1** an act, process, or instance of transferring **2** the redirection of feelings and desires, esp those unconsciously retained from childhood, towards a new object (e g towards a psychoanalyst conducting therapy) – **transferential** *adj*

**transfer fee** *n* the fee paid by one professional soccer club to another for the transfer of a player

**transfer list** *n* a list kept by a professional soccer club of players who are available for transfer – **transfer-list** *vt*

**transferor** /transˈfuhrə, trahns-/ *n* – a person who transfers a title, right, or property

**transfer paper** /ˈtransfuh, ˈtrahns-/ *n* a paper with a special coating for transferring a design or imprint to another surface by heat, pressure, or moisture

**transferrin** /transˈfuhrin, trahns-/ *n* a protein in blood that is capable of combining with electrically charged atoms of iron and transporting iron in the body [*trans-* + L *ferrum* iron]

**transfer RNA** *n* any of several relatively small RNAs, each of which transfers a particular AMINO ACID to a growing chain of amino acids at the place in a cell where proteins are formed – called also TRNA; compare MESSENGER RNA

**transfiguration** /ˌtransˌfigəˈraysh(ə)n, ˌtrahns-/ *n* **1a** a change in form or appearance; a metamorphosis **b** an exalting, glorifying, or spiritual change **2** *cap* the transfiguration of Christ on a mountaintop with three disciples looking on; *also* August 6 observed as a church festival commemorating this

**transfigure** /transˈfigə, trahns-/ *vt* to give a new and typically exalted or spiritual appearance to; transform outwardly and usu for the better [ME *transfiguren*, fr L *transfigurare*, fr *trans-* + *figurare* to shape, fashion, fr *figura* figure]

**transfinite** /transˈfieniet, trahns-/ *adj* **1** going beyond or surpassing any finite number, group, or magnitude – no longer used technically in mathematics **2** of or being a number that can be shown to be greater than or equal to the number of positive integers ⟨*the number of real numbers is a* ~ *quantity*⟩ [Ger *transfinit*, fr *trans-* (fr L) + *finit* finite, fr L *finitus*]

**transfix** /transˈfiks, trahns-/ *vt* **1** to pierce through (as if) with a pointed weapon; impale **2** to fix or hold motionless (as if) by piercing ⟨~ed *by horror*⟩ [L *transfixus*, pp of *transfigere*, fr *trans-* + *figere* to fasten, pierce – more at DYKE] – **transfixion** *n*

¹**transform** /transˈfawm, trahns-/ *vt* **1a** to change radically in composition or structure; metamorphose ⟨*desert* ~ed *into green fields*⟩ **b** to change the outward form or appearance of; alter ⟨*science has* ~ed *the world*⟩ **c** to change in character or condition; convert **2** to subject to mathematical transformation **3** to change (an electric current) in potential (e g from high voltage to low) or in type (e g from ALTERNATING CURRENT to DIRECT CURRENT) **4** *genetics* to cause (a cell) to undergo transformation ~ *vi* to become transformed; change [ME *transformen*, fr L *transformare*, fr *trans-* + *formare* to form, fr *forma* form] – **transformable** *adj*, **transformative** *adj*

²**transform** /ˈtransfawm, ˈtrahns-/ *n* **1** a mathematical element or term obtained from another by transformation **2** TRANSFORMATION **2 3** a linguistic structure (e g a sentence) producible by means of a transformation ⟨*"the duckling is killed by the farmer" is a* ~ *of "the farmer kills the duckling"*⟩

**transformant** /transˈfawmənt, trahns-/ *n* a cell from a transformed plant or animal cell culture

**transformation** /ˌtransfawˈmaysh(ə)n, ˌtrahns-/ *n* **1** transforming or being transformed **2** *maths* **2a(1)** the operation of changing (e g by rotation or MAPPING) one configuration or expression into another in accordance with a mathematical rule; *esp* a change of VARIABLES or coordinates **a(2)** the formula used for a transformation **b** FUNCTION 5a **3a** any of an ordered set of rules that convert the supposed underlying structures of a language into actual sentences **b** TRANSFORM 3 **4a** genetic modification of a cell, esp a bacterium, by introduction of DNA from a genetically different source **b** modification of plant or animal cell culture (e g by a cancer-producing virus) resulting in unlimited cell growth and division – **transformational** *adj*

**transformational grammar** /-nl/ *n* a grammar that explains equivalences and relations between sentences by the use of transformations to generate an infinite number of actual sentences from a finite set of supposed underlying structures

**transformationalist** /ˌtransfəˈmaysh(ə)nl·ist, ˌtrahns-/ *n* an adherent of TRANSFORMATIONAL GRAMMAR

**transformation scene** *n* a theatrical setting (e g in panto-mime) that changes, usu spectacularly, in sight of the audience

**transformer** /transˈfawmə, trahns-/ *n* one who or that which transforms; *specif* an electrical device for changing the voltage of an ALTERNATING CURRENT that consists of two coils (the primary and secondary WINDINGS) of wire wound round a common iron core so that when a current is passed through the primary coil, current is obtained in the secondary coil through electromagnetic INDUCTION. If the number of turns of wire in the secondary winding is greater than that in the primary, the voltage is increased (STEPPED UP), if less, the voltage is decreased (STEPPED DOWN).

**transfuse** /transˈfyoohz, trahns-/ *vt* **1a** to transmit, instil ⟨~s *his enthusiasm to others*⟩ **b** to diffuse into or through; permeate ⟨*sunlight* ~s *the bay*⟩ **2a** to transfer (e g blood) into a vein or artery **b** to subject (someone) to transfusion [ME *transfusen*, fr L *transfusus*, pp of *transfundere* to transfer by pouring, fr *trans-* + *fundere* to pour – more at FOUND] – **transfusible**, **transfusable** *adj*

**transfusion** /transˈfyoohzh(ə)n, trahns-/ *n* an act, process, or instance of transfusing; *esp* the act or process of transfusing liquid, esp blood, into a vein or artery – **transfusional** *adj*

**transgress** /transˈgres, trahns-/ *vt* **1** to go beyond limits set or prescribed by; violate ⟨~ *the divine law*⟩ **2** to pass beyond or go over (a limit or boundary) ~ *vi* **1** to violate a command or law; sin **2** to go beyond a boundary or limit [Fr *transgresser*, fr L *transgressus*, pp of *transgredi* to step beyond or across, fr *trans-* + *gradi* to step – more at GRADE] – **transgressive** *adj*, **transgressor** *n*

**transgression** /transˈgresh(ə)n, trahns-/ *n* an act, process, or instance of transgressing: e g **a** infringement or violation of a law, command, or duty **b** the spread of the sea over land areas and the consequent deposit of new sediments on older and different rocks

**tranship** /tranzˈship, trahnz-/ *vb* to transship

**transhumance** /transˈhyoohməns, trahns-/ *n* seasonal movement of livestock, esp sheep, between mountain and lowland pastures, usu under the care of herders [Fr, fr *transhumer* to practise transhumance, fr Sp *trashumar*, fr *tras-* trans- (fr L *trans-*) + L *humus* earth – more at HUMBLE] – **transhumant** *adj or n*

¹**transient** /ˈtranzi·ənt/ *adj* **1a** passing quickly away; transitory, short-lived **b** making only a brief stay ⟨*a* ~ *summer bird*⟩ **2** *philosophy* affecting something or producing results beyond itself [L *transeunt-, transiens*, prp of *transire* to go across, pass, fr *trans-* + *ire* to go] – **transience, transiency** *n*, **transiently** *adv*

*synonyms* Transient, transitory, evanescent, ephemeral, fleeting, fugitive, momentary, temporary, and provisional all mean "lasting only a short time". Transient refers to what passes by quickly ⟨**transient** *guests at a hotel*⟩. Transitory may stress the inevitability of change ⟨*the* **transitory** *pleasures of this life*⟩. Evanescent emphasizes the early fading of something too airy and insubstantial to last ⟨**evanescent** *sunset glow*⟩. Ephemeral often applies to what is of interest or value for only a short time ⟨**ephemeral** *fashions*⟩. Fleeting, on the other hand, may refer to something desirable that flies past too quickly ⟨*caught a* **fleeting** *glimpse*⟩. Fugitive emphasizes this idea, adding the suggestion of something trying to escape ⟨**fugitive** *hours of happiness*⟩. Momentary describes that which lasts only a moment ⟨*a* **momentary** *lapse of memory*⟩. Temporary things are usually meant to last only for a short time ⟨*a* **temporary** *wooden structure*⟩. Provisional emphasizes this idea, adding that of being provided to meet a present need ⟨*set up a* **provisional** *government until they can hold proper elections*⟩. *antonyms* perpetual, permanent

²**transient** *n* **1** a transient guest, visitor, or worker **2a** a temporary fluctuation of electrical current that occurs in a circuit because of a sudden change of voltage or load **b** a transient current or voltage

**transilluminate** /ˌtranziˈl(y)oohminayt, ˌtrahnz-/ *vt* to cause light to pass through; *esp* to pass light through (a body part) for medical examination – **transillumination** *n*, **transilluminator** *n*

**transistor** /tranˈzistə, trahn-/ *n* **1** any of several electronic SEMICONDUCTOR devices that have usu three electrodes and are used to control, generate, and amplify electrical signals **2 transistor radio, transistor** a radio using transistorized circuitry; *broadly* a small portable radio [¹*transfer* + *resistor*; fr its transferring an electrical signal across a resistor]

**transistor·ize, -ise** /tranˈzistoriez, trahn-/ *vt* to construct (a device) using transistors – **transistorization** *n*

**¹transit** /'transit, -zit/ *n* **1a** an act, process, or instance of passing or conveying through or over; passage ⟨*goods lost in* ~⟩ **b** a change, transition **2a** passage of a celestial body (eg a planet) over the MERIDIAN (imaginary circle passing through both poles) of a place or through the field of a telescope **b** passage of a smaller body (eg Venus) across the disc of a larger (eg the sun) **3** a surveyor's instrument for measuring horizontal and vertical angles with a telescope mounted so that it can be reversed **4** *NAm* conveyance of people or things from one place to another; transport [L *transitus*, fr *transitus*, pp of *transire* to go across, pass]

**²transit** *vi* to make a transit ~ *vt* **1a** to pass over or through; traverse **b** to cause to pass over or through; convey **2** to pass across (a MERIDIAN, a celestial body, or the field of view of a telescope) **3** to turn (a telescope) over about the horizontal transverse axis so that eyepiece and object are reversed

**transit instrument** *n* **1** a telescope for observing the time of transit of a celestial body over the MERIDIAN (imaginary circle passing through both poles) of a place **2** TRANSIT 3

**transition** /tran'zish(ə)n, trahn-/ *n* **1a** passage from one state, stage, or place to another; change ⟨*an age of* ~⟩ **b** a movement, development, or evolution from one form, stage, or style to another ⟨*a* ~ ... *from the inorganic to the organic* – W R Inge⟩ **2a** a change from one musical key to another **b** a musical passage leading from one section of a piece to another **3** an abrupt change in ENERGY LEVEL (eg of an atomic nucleus or a molecule) that is usu accompanied by loss or gain of a single QUANTUM of energy **4** a genetic mutation in RNA or DNA that results from the substitution of one PURINE compound for the other or of one PYRIMIDINE compound for the other [L *transition-, transitio*, fr *transitus*, pp of *transire*] – **transitional** *adj*, **transitionally** *adv*

**transition metal** *n* any of various metallic chemical elements (eg chromium, iron, and platinum) that have VALENCY electrons in two SHELLS instead of only one and form a wide variety of often coloured ION complexes (groups of atoms having an electrical charge)

**transitive** /'transitiv, 'trahn-, -zitiv/ *adj* **1** having or containing a DIRECT OBJECT ⟨*a* ~ *verb*⟩ ⟨*a* ~ *construction*⟩ **2** of or being a (mathematical) relation (eg 'is greater than' or 'is the ancestor of') such that if *x* * *y* and *y* * *z*, then *x* * *z* where * denotes the relation **3** of or characterized by transition [LL *transitivus*, fr L *transitus*, pp of *transire*] – **transitive** *n*, **transitively** *adv*, **transitiveness, transitivity** *n*

**transitory** /'transit(ə)ri, 'trahn-, -zi-/ *adj* **1** tending to pass away **2** of brief duration; temporary *synonyms* see ¹TRANSIENT **antonym** enduring [ME *transitorie*, fr MF *transitoire*, fr LL *transitorius*, fr L, of or allowing passage, fr *transitus*, pp of *transire*] – **transitorily** *adv*, **transitoriness** *n*

**translate** /trans'layt, trahns-/ *vt* **1a** to bear, remove, or change from one place or condition to another; transfer, transform ⟨*a country boy* ~ d *to the city*⟩ ⟨~ *ideas into action*⟩ **b** to convey to heaven or to an eternal condition, esp while alive **c** to transfer (a bishop) from one bishopric to another **2a** to turn into another language **b** to turn from one set of symbols into another **c** to express in different or more comprehensible terms; explain, interpret **3** to subject to mathematical translation **4** to subject (genetic information, esp MESSENGER RNA) to translation **5** *archaic* to fill with delight; enrapture ~ *vi* **1** to practise translation or make a translation; *also* to be capable of or adaptable to translation ⟨*a word that doesn't* ~ *easily*⟩ **2** to undergo a translation [L *translatus* (pp of *transferre* to transfer, translate), fr *trans-* + *latus*, pp of *ferre* to carry – more at TOLERATE, BEAR] – **translatable** *adj*, **translatability** *n*, **translator** *n*

**translation** /trans'laysh(ə)n, trahns-/ *n* **1** the act or process or an instance of translating: eg **1a** the act of rendering from one language into another; *also* a version thus produced **b** a change to a different condition, place, substance or form **c(1)** a transformation of mathematical coordinates in which the new axes are parallel to the old ones **c(2)** uniform motion of a body in a straight line, usu parallel to one of its sides or axes **2** the process of forming a protein molecule inside a living cell from information contained usu in MESSENGER RNA – compare TRANSCRIPTION 3 – **translational** *adj*

**translative** /trans'laytiv, trahns-/ *adj* of or producing translation between languages or systems

**translatory** /trans'laytəri, trahns-/ *adj* of or involving uniform motion in one direction

**transliterate** /tranz'litərayt, trahns-, trans-, trahns-/ *vt* to represent or spell in the characters of another alphabet △ translate [*trans-* + L *littera, litera* letter] – **transliteration** *n*

**translocation** /ˌtranzloh'kaysh(ə)n, ˌtrahnz-/ *n* a change of position: eg **a** the conduction of soluble material from one part of a plant to another **b** the exchange of parts between dissimilar CHROMOSOMES (strands of gene-carrying material) **c** the movement of a RIBOSOME (cell structure carrying out protein synthesis) relative to a strand of MESSENGER RNA that is the mechanism by which each successive segment of genetic information carried on the messenger RNA is made available for translation into the corresponding AMINO ACID – **translocate** *vb*

**translucent** /tranz'loohs(ə)nt, trahnz-/ *adj* permitting the passage of light: eg **a** clear, transparent ⟨*glass and other* ~ *materials*⟩ **b** transmitting and diffusing light so that objects beyond cannot be seen clearly ⟨*a* ~ *window of frosted glass*⟩ ⟨~ *porcelain*⟩ [L *translucent-, translucens*, prp of *translucēre* to shine through, fr *trans-* + *lucēre* to shine – more at LIGHT] – **translucence, translucency** *n*, **translucently** *adv*

**transmarine** /ˌtranzmə'reen/ *adj* being, coming from, or extending across the sea; overseas ⟨*a* ~ *people*⟩ [L *transmarinus*, fr *trans-* + *mare* sea – more at MARINE]

**transmigrate** /ˌtranzmie'grayt, ˌtrahnz-/ *vi* **1** *of a soul* to pass at death from one body or being to another **2** to migrate ~ *vt* to cause to transmigrate [L *transmigratus*, pp of *transmigrare* to migrate to another place, fr *trans-* + *migrare* to migrate] – **transmigrator** *n*, **transmigration** *n*, **transmigratory** *adj*

**transmissible** /trans'misəbl, trahns-/ *adj* capable of being transmitted

**transmission** /trans'mish(ə)n, trahns-, tranz-, trahnz-/ *n* **1** the act or process or an instance of transmitting ⟨~ *of a nerve impulse across a synapse*⟩ **2** the passage of RADIO WAVES between transmitting and receiving stations; *also* the act or process of transmitting by radio or television **3** an assembly of parts including the clutch, speed-changing gears, and the PROPELLER SHAFT by which the power is transmitted from a motor vehicle engine to an axle; *also* an assembly transmitting moving power on a bicycle **4** something (eg a message or television programme) that is transmitted [L *transmission-, transmissio*, fr *transmissus*, pp of *transmittere* to transmit] – **transmissive** *adj*, **transmissivity** *n*

**transmit** /trans'mit, trahns-, tranz-, trahnz-/ *vb* **-tt-** *vt* **1a** to send or transfer from one person or place to another **b** to cause or allow to spread: eg **b(1)** to convey (as if) by inheritance or heredity; HAND DOWN **b(2)** to pass on (infection) **2a(1)** to cause (eg light) to pass or be conveyed through a medium **a(2)** to allow the passage of; conduct ⟨*glass* ~ s *light*⟩ **b** to send out (a signal) either by RADIO WAVES or over a wire ~ *vi* to send out a signal either by RADIO WAVES or over a wire [ME *transmitten*, fr L *transmittere*, fr *trans-* + *mittere* to send] – **transmittable** *adj*, **transmittal** *n*

**transmittance** /trans'mit(ə)ns, trahns-/ *n* **1** transmission **2** a measure of the ability of a body or substance to transmit ELECTROMAGNETIC RADIATION (eg light)

**transmitter** /trans'mitə, trahns-/ *n* one who or that which transmits: eg **a** the portion of a telephonic or telegraphic instrument which sends the signals **b** a radio or television transmitting station or set **c** NEUROTRANSMITTER (substance that transmits nerve impulses)

**transmogrify** /tranz'mogrifie/ *vt, chiefly humorous* to transform, often with grotesque or humorous effect [perh alter. of *transmigrate*] – **transmogrification** *n*

**transmontane** /ˌtranzmon'tayn, trahns-/ *adj* TRAMONTANE (beyond mountains) [L *transmontanus*]

**transmutation** /ˌtranzmyoo(h)'taysh(ə)n, ˌtrahnz-/ *n* transmuting or being transmuted: eg **a** the conversion of base metals (eg iron and copper) into gold or silver **b** the conversion of one chemical element or NUCLIDE (type of atom) into another, either naturally or artificially – **transmutative** *adj*

**transmute** /tranz'myooht, trahnz-/ *vt* **1** to change in form, substance, or characteristics **2** to subject (eg an element) to transmutation ~ *vi* to undergo transmutation [ME *transmuten*, fr L *transmutare*, fr *trans-* + *mutare* to change – more at MISS] – **transmutable** *adj*, **transmutability** *n*

**transnational** /tranz'nash(ə)nl, trahnz-/ *adj* extending or going beyond national boundaries

**transoceanic** /ˌtranzohshi'anik, ˌtrahnz-/ *adj* **1** situated beyond the ocean **2** crossing or extending across the ocean ⟨*a* ~ *telephone cable*⟩

**transom** /'transəm/ *n* **1** a crosswise piece in a structure: eg **1a**

a lintel **b** a horizontal crossbar in a window, over a door, or between a door and a window above it **c** the horizontal bar or member of a cross or gallows **d** any of several crosswise timbers or beams secured to the sternpost of a boat; *also* the planking forming the stern of a square-ended boat **2** *chiefly NAm* a window above a door or other window, built on and commonly hinged to a transom; a fanlight [ME *traunsom*, prob fr L *transtrum*, fr *trans* across – more at THROUGH] – **transomed** *adj*

**transonic** *also* **transsonic** /tran'sonik/ *adj* **1** of or being a speed near the speed of sound in air – compare SUBSONIC, SUPERSONIC **2** moving, capable of moving, or using air currents moving at a transonic speed [*trans-* + *-sonic* (as in *supersonic*)]

**transpacific** /ˌtranzpə'sifik, ˌtrahnz-/ *adj* **1a** crossing or extending across the Pacific ocean ⟨∼ *airlines*⟩ **b** relating to or involving the crossing of the Pacific ocean ⟨∼ *air fares*⟩ **2** situated beyond the Pacific ocean

**transparency** /tran'sparənsi, trahn-/ *n* **1** *also* **transparence** the quality or state of being transparent **2** something transparent: eg **2a** a picture or design on glass, thin cloth, paper, or film designed to be viewed by light shining through it from behind or by projection; *esp* SLIDE 5b **b** a framework covered with thin cloth or paper bearing a device for public display (eg for advertisement) and lit from within

**transparent** /tran'sparənt, trahn-, -'speərənt/ *adj* **1a(1)** having the property of transmitting light without appreciable scattering, so that bodies lying beyond are entirely visible – compare TRANSLUCENT **b a(2)** able to be penetrated by a specified form of radiation (eg X rays or ultraviolet rays) **b** fine or sheer enough to be seen through ⟨∼ *nylon blouse*⟩ **2a** free from pretence or deceit; frank ⟨∼ *sincerity*⟩ **b** easily detected or seen through; obvious ⟨*a* ∼ *lie*⟩ **c** readily understood; clear ⟨*the meaning of this word is* ∼⟩ [ME, fr ML *transparent-, transparens*, prp of *transparēre* to show through, fr L *trans-* + *parēre* to show oneself – more at APPEAR] – **transparently** *adv*, **transparentness** *n*

**transpicuous** /tran'spikyooəs, trahn-/ *adj, formal* clearly seen through or understood [NL *transpicuus*, fr L *transpicere* to look through, fr *trans-* + *specere* to look, see – more at SPY]

**transpierce** /trans'piəs, trahn-/ *vt, chiefly poetic* to pierce through; penetrate [MF *transpercer*, fr OF, fr *trans-* (fr L) + *percer* to pierce]

**transpiration** /ˌtranspə'raysh(ə)n, trahn-/ *n* the act or process or an instance of transpiring; *esp* the passage of water vapour from plant cells to the atmosphere mainly through pores (STOMATA) in the surfaces of leaves

**transpire** /tran'spie·ə, trahn-/ *vt* to pass off or give passage to (a gas or liquid) through pores or openings; *esp* to excrete (eg water) in the form of a vapour through a skin or other living membrane ∼ *vi* **1** to give off a vapour; *specif* to give off or exude water vapour, esp from the surfaces of leaves **2** to pass in the form of a vapour from a living body **3** to become known; come to light **4** to occur; TAKE PLACE [MF *transpirer*, fr L *trans-* + *spirare* to breathe – more at SPIRIT]

*usage* Transpire has been used for almost 200 years to mean "occur", and by some distinguished writers ⟨*few changes – hardly any – have transpired among his ship's company* – Charles Dickens⟩ but some people still feel that its meaning should be confined to its technical senses and to "become known". In a sentence such as ⟨*I wonder what will* **transpire** *at the meeting*⟩ it is not clear which meaning is intended. *synonyms* see HAPPEN

**transplacental** /ˌtransplə'sentl, trahns-/ *adj* passing through or occurring by way of the placenta ⟨∼ *immunization of the foetus*⟩ [ISV] – **transplacentally** *adv*

**¹transplant** /trans'plahnt, trahns-/ *vt* **1** to lift and reset (a plant) in another soil or place **2** to remove from one place and settle or introduce elsewhere; transport **3** to transfer (an organ or tissue) from one part or individual to another ∼ *vi* to be capable of being transplanted ⟨*some shrubs do not* ∼ *well*⟩ [ME *transplaunten*, fr LL *transplantare*, fr L *trans-* + *plantare* to plant] – **transplantable** *adj*, **transplanter** *n*, **transplantability** *n*, **transplantation** *n*

**²transplant** /'trans,plahnt, 'trahns-/ *n* **1** the act or process of transplanting ⟨*doing a heart* ∼⟩ **2** something transplanted

**transpolar** /tranz'pohlə, trahnz-/ *adj* crossing or extending across either of the polar regions

**transponder** /tran'spondə, trahn-/ *n* a radio or radar set that responds to a designated signal by emitting a radio signal of its own [*transmitter* + *responder*]

**transpontine** /tranz'pontien, trahnz-/ *adj* situated on the farther side of a bridge; *specif, Br* situated on the south side of the Thames [*trans-* + L *pont-, pons* bridge – more at FIND]

**¹transport** /tran'spawt, trahn-/ *vt* **1** to transfer or convey from one place to another **2** to carry away with strong and often intensely pleasurable emotion **3** to send (a convict) to a penal colony overseas – compare BANISH *synonyms* see ¹CARRY [ME *transporten*, fr MF or L; MF *transporter*, fr L *transportare*, fr *trans-* + *portare* to carry – more at FARE] – **transportable** *adj*, **transportability** *n*

**²transport** /'transpawt, 'trahn-/ *n* **1** an act or process of transporting **2** **transports** *pl*, transport strong and often intensely pleasurable emotion ⟨∼*s of joy*⟩ **3a** a ship or aircraft for carrying soldiers or military equipment **b** a vehicle (eg a lorry or aeroplane) used to transport people or goods **c** means of conveyance or travel from one place to another ⟨*hospitals arranging* ∼ *for outpatients*⟩ **d** a system of public conveyance of passengers or goods **4** a transported convict **5** a mechanism for moving a tape, esp a MAGNETIC TAPE, or disk past a sensing or recording head

*synonyms* British English has traditionally used **transport** for the sense of "conveying" ⟨*Ministry of* **Transport**⟩ and for a means of conveyance, for both of which Americans use **transportation** ⟨*we can provide* **transportation**⟩. British and Americans alike use **transports** for "joy" and **transportation** for the transporting of convicts.

**transportation** /ˌtranspaw'taysh(ə)n, trahn-/ *n* **1** transporting or being transported **2** banishment to a penal colony **3** *NAm* **3a** TRANSPORT 3c **b** TRANSPORT 3d – **transportational** *adj*

**transport café** *n, Br* a roadside cafeteria that serves inexpensive meals and caters mainly for long-distance lorry drivers

**transporter** /tran'spawtə, trahn-/ *n* one who or that which transports; *esp* a vehicle for transporting large or heavy loads ⟨*a tank* ∼⟩ ⟨*a car* ∼⟩

**transporter bridge** *n* a bridge that carries vehicles over a waterway on a suspended movable platform

**transport manager** *n* a supervisor of the transport of a commercial or industrial organization

**¹transpose** /tran'spohz, trahn-/ *vt* **1** to change in form or nature; transform **2** to render into another language, style, or manner of expression; translate **3** to transfer from one place or period to another **4** to change the relative position or normal order of ⟨∼ *letters to change the spelling*⟩ **5** to write or perform (music) in a different key **6** to bring (a term) from one side of an algebraic equation to the other with change of sign ∼ *vi* to transpose music [ME *transposen*, fr MF *transposer*, fr L *transponere* (perf indic *transposui*) to change the position of, fr *trans-* + *ponere* to put, place – more at POSITION] – **transposable** *adj*

**²transpose** /'transpohz, 'trahn-/ *n* a mathematical MATRIX formed by interchanging the rows of a given matrix with its corresponding columns

**transposing instrument** /trans'pohzing, trahns-/ *n* a musical instrument (eg a trumpet or saxophone) that sounds notes at a fixed interval higher or lower than those written

**transposition** /ˌtranspə'zish(ə)n, ˌtrahnz-/ *n* **1** transposing or being transposed **2a** the transfer of a term of an algebraic equation from one side to the other with a change of sign **b** a mathematical permutation that is the interchange of two elements [ML *transposition-, transpositio*, fr L *transpositus*, pp of *transponere* to transpose] – **transpositional** *adj*

**transsexual, transexual** /tranz'seksyoo(ə)l, -sh(ə)l, trahnz-/ *n* **1** a person physically of one sex with an urge to belong to or resemble the opposite sex **2** a person having the characteristics or nature of both sexes – **transsexual** *adj*, **transsexualism** *n*, **transsexuality** *n*

**transship, tranship** /tranz'ship, trahnz-/ *vb* to transfer from one ship or vehicle to another for further transportation – **transshipment** *n*

**trans-'sonic** *adj* TRANSONIC (nearly supersonic)

**transtasman** /ˌtranz'tazmən, ˌtrahnz-/ *adj, NZ chiefly journalistic* **1** situated beyond the Tasman sea; *specif* AUSTRALIAN 1 **2** extending between or involving New Zealand and Australia ⟨∼ *trade*⟩

**transthoracic** /ˌtranztha'rasik, trahnz-/ *adj* done or made by way of the THORACIC (chest) cavity – **transthoracically** *adv*

**transubstantiate** /ˌtranz·səb'stanshiayt, ˌtrahnz-, -'stahn-/ *vt* **1** to change into another substance; transmute **2** to bring about transubstantiation in (the bread and wine used at Communion)

~ *vi* to undergo transubstantiation [ML *transubstantiatus,* pp of *transubstantiare,* fr L *trans + substantia* substance]

**transubstantiation** /ˌtranz·səbstanshiˈaysh(ə)n, ˌtrahnz-, -stahnshi-/ *n* **1** transubstantiating or being transubstantiated **2** the miraculous change by which, according to Roman Catholic and EASTERN ORTHODOX dogma, the bread and wine used at Communion become the body and blood of Christ when they are consecrated, although their appearance remains unchanged – compare CONSUBSTANTIATION

**transudate** /ˈtrans(y)oodayt, trahns-/ *n* a transuded substance

**transudation** /ˌtrans(y)ooˈdaysh(ə)n, ˌtrahns-/ *n* **1** transuding or being transuded **2** a transudate

**transude** /transˈyoohd, trahn-/ *vi* to pass through a membrane or permeable substance ~ *vt* to permit passage of [NL *transudare,* fr L *trans- + sudare* to sweat – more at SWEAT]

**transuranic** /ˌtranzyooˈranik, ˌtrahn-/ *n* any of the chemical elements (e g plutonium) with a greater number of protons in the nucleus than uranium – **transuranic** *adj*

**transvalue** /tranzˈvalyooh, trahnz-/ *vt* to revalue, esp on a basis that rejects accepted standards of value – **transvaluation** *n*

**¹transversal** /tranzˈvuhsl, trahnz-/ *adj* transverse ⟨~ *lines*⟩

**²transversal** *n* a line that crosses a system of lines

**¹transverse** /tranzˈvuhs, trahnz-, ˈ--/ *adj* **1** lying or being across; set crosswise **2** made at right angles to the straight line dividing the body or an organ symmetrically along its length ⟨*a ~ section*⟩ [L *transversus,* fr pp of *transvertere* to turn or extend across, fr *trans- + vertere* to turn – more at WORTH] – **transversely** *adv*

**²transverse** *n* something (e g a piece, section, or part) that is transverse

**transverse process** *n* a bony projection on the side of a vertebra

**transverse wave** *n* a wave (e g a wave on a string or a light wave) in which the vibrating element moves at right angles to the direction of advance of the wave – compare LONGITUDINAL WAVE

**transvestism** /tranzˈvestiz(ə)m, trahnz-/ *n* the adoption of the dress and often the behaviour of the opposite sex, esp to obtain sexual satisfaction [Ger *transvestismus,* fr L *trans- + vestire* to clothe – more at VEST] – **transvestite** *adj or n,* **transvestist** *n*

**¹trap** /trap/ *n* **1** a device for catching animals; *esp* one that holds by springing shut suddenly **2a** something designed to catch a person unawares; *also* PITFALL **2 b** a situation from which it is difficult or impossible to escape ⟨*caught in a poverty* ~⟩; *also* a plan designed to trick a person into such a situation ⟨*police laid a ~ for the criminal*⟩ **c trapdoor, trap** a lifting or sliding door covering an opening in a roof, ceiling, floor, etc **3a** a device for hurling CLAY PIGEONS into the air **b** a device from which a greyhound is released at the start of a race **4** a light usu one-horse carriage with springs **5** any of various devices for preventing passage of something, often while allowing other matter to proceed; *esp* a device for drains or sewers consisting of a bend or partitioned chamber in which the liquid forms a seal to prevent the passage of sewer gas **6** *pl* a group of percussion instruments (e g a BASS DRUM, SNARE DRUMS, and cymbals) used esp in a dance or jazz band **7** *chiefly NAm* a golf bunker **8** *slang* the mouth [ME, fr OE *treppe* & OF *trape* (of Gmc origin); akin to MD *trappe* trap, stair, OE *treppan* to tread, Skt *dravati* he runs]

**²trap** *vb* -pp- *vt* **1a** to catch or take (as if) in a trap **b** to place in a restricted position; confine ⟨~ *ped in the burning wreck*⟩ **2** to provide or set (a place) with traps **3** to stop, retain ⟨*these mountains ~ the rain*⟩ **4** to stop and control (the ball) in soccer, hockey, etc ~ *vi* to engage in trapping animals (e g for furs) *synonyms* see ¹CATCH – **trapper** *n*

**³trap** *vt* -pp- to adorn (as if) with trappings ⟨*a swaggering magenta cloak,* ~ped *with tassels* – Frederic Raphael⟩ [ME *trappen,* fr *trappe* cloth, modif of MF *drap* – more at DRAB]

**⁴trap, ˈtrapˌrock** *n* any of various dark-coloured fine-grained IGNEOUS rocks (e g BASALT or AMYGDALOID) used esp in road making [Sw *trapp,* fr *trappa* stair, fr MLG *trappe;* akin to MD *trappe* stair]

**trap-door spider** *n* any of various often large burrowing spiders (esp family Ctenizidae) that construct a tubular silk-lined underground nest topped with a hinged lid

**trapeze** /trəˈpeez/ *n* a gymnastic or acrobatic apparatus consisting of a short horizontal bar suspended by two parallel ropes [Fr *trapèze,* fr NL *trapezium*] – **trapezist** *n*

**trapezium** /trəˈpeezi·əm/ *n, pl* **trapeziums, trapezia** /-ziə/ **1** a

bone in the wrist at the base of the thumb **2a** *Br* a 4-sided figure having only two sides parallel **b** *chiefly NAm* TRAPEZOID **2a** [NL (orig in sense 2b), fr Gk *trapezion,* lit., small table, dim. of *trapeza* table, fr *tra-* four (akin to *tettares* four) + *peza* foot; akin to Gk *pod-, pous* foot – more at FOUR, FOOT]

**trapezius** /trəˈpeezi·əs/ *n* either of two large flat triangular muscles, one on each side of the upper part of the back, that serve chiefly to raise and rotate the shoulder blades [NL, fr *trapezium;* fr the pair on the back forming together the figure of a trapezium]

**trapezohedron** /trəˌpeezohˈheedrən/ *n, pl* **trapezohedrons, trapezohedra** /-drə/ a crystalline form whose faces are trapeziums [NL, fr *trapezium + -o- + -hedron*]

**trapezoid** /ˈtrapiˌzoyd, trəˈpeezoyd/ *n* **1** a bone in the wrist at the base of the forefinger **2a** *Br* a 4-sided figure having no two sides parallel **b** *chiefly NAm* TRAPEZIUM 2a [NL *trapezoïdes,* fr Gk *trapezoeidēs* trapezium-shaped, fr *trapeza* table] – **trapezoidal** *adj*

**¹trapnest** /ˈtrapˌnest/ *n* a nest equipped with a hinged door designed to trap and confine a hen so that individual egg laying may be determined

**²trapnest** *vt* to determine the number of eggs laid by (an individual hen) using a trapnest

**trappings** /ˈtrapingz/ *n pl* **1** (ornamental) coverings and harness for a horse **2** outward decoration or dress; ornamental equipment; *also* outward signs and accessories ⟨*all the ~ of power with none of the substance*⟩ [ME, fr gerund of *trappen* to adorn, fr *trappe* cloth]

**Trappist** /ˈtrapist/ *n* a monk of a reformed branch of the Cistercian Order noted for its austere rules and vow of silence [Fr *trappiste,* fr La *Trappe,* monastery in Normandy in France where the order was established in 1664] – **Trappist** *adj*

**trappy** /ˈtrapi/ *adj, chiefly informal* like a trap; tricky

**traprock** /ˈtrapˌrok/ *n* ⁴TRAP (type of fine-grained rock)

**traps** /traps/ *n pl, chiefly informal* personal belongings; luggage [ME *trappe* cloth – more at TRAP]

**trapshooting** /ˈtrapˌshoohting/ *n* shooting at CLAY PIGEONS hurled into the air from a trap so as to imitate the angles of flight of birds – **trapshooter** *n*

**¹trash** /trash/ *n* **1** something of little or no value: e g **1a** *chiefly NAm* junk, rubbish **b**(1) empty talk; nonsense **b**(2) inferior or worthless literary or artistic work **2** something in a crumbled or broken condition or mass; *esp* debris from pruning or processing plant material **3** *informal* a worthless person; *also, taking sing or pl vb* such people as a group [of Scand origin; akin to Norw *trask* trash; akin to OE *teran* to tear] – **trashery** *n*

**²trash** *vt* **1a** to free from trash or refuse; *specif* to strip outer leaves from (young sugarcane) **b** to reject as worthless **2** to destroy wilfully or maliciously; vandalize

**trash can** *n, NAm* a dustbin

**trash farming** *n, NAm* a method of cultivation in dry areas (e g in N America) in which the soil is loosened by methods that leave plant debris (e g stubble) on or near the surface to restrict erosion of the soil by the wind and to enrich the soil

**trashman** /ˈtrashˌman/ *n, NAm* a dustman

**trashy** /ˈtrashi/ *adj* of inferior quality or worth; rubbishy ⟨*a ~ novel*⟩ – **trashiness** *n*

**trass** /tras/ *n* a light-coloured rock, formed from fine volcanic debris and sometimes ground for use in making a hydraulic cement [D, fr Fr *terrasse* pile of earth, terrace, fr MF – more at TERRACE]

**trattoria** /ˌtratəˈree·ə/ *n, pl* **trattorias, trattorie** /-ˈree·ay/ an Italian restaurant [It, fr *trattore* innkeeper, restaurateur, fr Fr *traiteur,* fr *traiter* to treat, entertain, fr OF *traitier* – more at TREAT]

**trauma** /ˈtrawmə; *also* ˈtrowmə/ *n, pl* **traumas, traumata** /-mətə/ **1a** an injury (e g a wound) to living tissue caused by an outside agent ⟨*surgical* ~⟩ **b** a disordered mental or behavioural state resulting from mental or emotional stress or shock **2** *medicine & psychology* an agent, force, or mechanism that causes trauma [Gk *traumat-, trauma* wound]

**traumatic** /trawˈmatik; *also* trow-/ *adj* of or caused by trauma; *broadly* deeply shocking or disturbing – **traumatically** *adv*

**traumatism** /ˈtrawməˌtiz(ə)m; *also* ˈtrow-/ *n* the development or occurrence of trauma; *also* trauma

**traumat·ize, -ise** /ˈtrawmətiez; *also* ˈtrow-/ *vt* to inflict a trauma on – **traumatization** *n*

**trautonium** /trowˈtohniəm/ *n* an early electronic musical instrument that is played by touching a steel wire onto a steel bar [Friedrich *Trautwein* *fl* 1930 Ger acoustician + *-onium* (as in *euphonium*)]

**¹travail** /'travayl, trə'vayl/ *n* **1a** physical or mental exertion, esp of a painful or laborious nature; toil **b** agony, torment **2** *archaic* the pains of childbirth; labour *synonyms* see ¹WORK [ME, fr OF, fr *travaillier* to torture, toil, fr (assumed) VL *tripaliare* to torture, fr *tripalium* instrument of torture, fr L *tripalis* having three stakes, fr *tri-* + *palus* stake – more at POLE]

**²travail** *vi* **1** *formal* to labour hard; toil **2** *archaic* to suffer the pains of childbirth [ME *travailen*, fr OF *travaillier*]

**¹travel** /'travl/ *vb* **-ll-** (*NAm* **-l-**, **-ll-**) *vi* **1a** to go (as if) on a trip or tour; journey **b** to go as if by travelling; pass ⟨*the news* ~led *fast*⟩ ⟨*my mind* ~led *back to our last meeting*⟩ **c** to go from place to place as a SALES REPRESENTATIVE ⟨~s *in cosmetics*⟩ **2a** to move or be transmitted from one place to another ⟨*goods* ~ling *by plane*⟩ ⟨*the sound* ~led *in the still air*⟩ ⟨*wine* ~s *badly*⟩ **b** *esp of machinery* to move along a specified direction or path ⟨*the stylus* ~s *in a groove*⟩ **3** to walk or run more than one pace with a basketball, in violation of the rules **4** *informal* to move at high speed ⟨*a car that can really* ~⟩ ~ *vt* **1a** to journey through or over ⟨~ *the world*⟩ **b** to follow (a course or path) as if by travelling **2** to traverse (a specified distance) **3** to cover (a place or region) as a SALES REPRESENTATIVE **4** to cause to travel ⟨~led *the horse from one racecourse to another*⟩ [ME *travailen* to travail, journey, fr OF *travaillier* to travail]

**²travel** *n* **1a** the act of travelling; passage **b** *usu pl* a journey, esp to a distant or unfamiliar place ⟨*set off on his* ~⟩ **2a** movement, progression ⟨*the* ~ *of satellites round the earth*⟩ **b** the motion of a piece of machinery; *esp* alternate forward and backward motion

**travel agency** *n* an agency that gives information on and arranges travel

**travel agent** *n* a person engaged in selling and arranging personal transportation, tours, or trips for travellers

**travel bureau** *n* TRAVEL AGENCY

**travelled**, *NAm chiefly* **traveled** /'travəld/ *adj* **1** experienced in travel ⟨*a widely* ~ *journalist*⟩ **2** used by travellers ⟨*a well-travelled route*⟩ □ usu in combination

**traveller**, *NAm chiefly* **traveler** /'travlə, 'travl-ə/ *n* **1** one who or that which travels: e g **1a** one who goes on a trip or journey **b** SALES REPRESENTATIVE **c** *dial Br* a gipsy **2** *nautical* a metal ring which slides along a rope, spar, or rod; *also* the bar to which this ring is attached **3** any of various devices for handling something that is being moved sideways

**traveller's cheque** *n* a cheque for a fixed amount that is purchased from a bank, TRAVEL AGENCY, etc and that may be exchanged abroad for foreign currency

**traveller's joy** *also* **travellers' joy** *n* a wild white-flowered clematis (*Clematis vitalba*) of Europe and N Africa that has whitish-grey feathery flower-parts – called also OLD-MAN'S BEARD

**traveller's tree** *also* **travellers' tree** *n* a tropical or subtropical tree (*Ravenala madagascariensis* of the family Strelitziaceae) having leaf stalks that contain a clear watery drinkable sap

**travelling**, *NAm chiefly* **traveling** /'travəling/ *adj* **1** that travels ⟨*a* ~ *opera company*⟩ ⟨*a* ~ *executive*⟩ **2** carried by, used by, or accompanying a traveller ⟨*a* ~ *alarm clock*⟩ ⟨*a* ~ *companion*⟩ [(1) fr prp of ¹*travel*; (2) fr gerund of ¹*travel*]

**travelling bag** *n* a bag carried by hand and designed to hold a traveller's clothing and personal articles

**travelling fellowship** *n* a fellowship whose terms permit or direct the holder to travel for study or research

**travelling rug** *n* a warm rug for wrapping round esp the lower part of the body when travelling in a vehicle

**travelling salesman** *n* SALES REPRESENTATIVE

**travelogue**, *NAm also* **travelog** /'travə,log/ *n* **1** a talk or lecture on travel, usu illustrated by a film or slides **2** a narrated documentary film about travel [*travel* + *-logue*]

**travel sickness** *n* MOTION SICKNESS

**travers** /'travəz/ *n*, *pl* **travers** a movement in DRESSAGE in which the horse's haunches are bent to the side towards the line of advance – compare RENVERS [Fr, sideways movement]

**¹traverse** /'travuhs, -'-/ *n* **1** something that crosses or lies across **2** a formal denial of a matter of fact alleged by the opposite party in a legal pleading **3** a transverse gallery in a large building (e g a church) **4** a route or way across or over: e g **4a** a curving or zigzag way up a steep slope **b** the course followed in traversing **5** the act or an instance of traversing;

crossing **6a** a sideways movement (e g of the sliding part containing the cutter on a lathe); *also* a device for imparting such movement **b** the sideways movement of a gun about a pivot or on a carriage to change direction of fire **7** a travers **8** a survey consisting of a series of measured lines whose bearings are known [ME *travers*, fr MF *traverse*, fr *traverser* to cross, fr LL *transversare*, fr L *transversus*, pp of *transvertere* – more at TRANSVERSE]

**²traverse** /trə'vuhs, 'travuhs/ *vt* **1a** to go against or act in opposition to; obstruct, thwart **b** to deny (e g an allegation of fact or an indictment) formally in law **2** to pass or travel across, over, or through ⟨~ *a terrain*⟩ ⟨*light rays* traversing *a crystal*⟩ **3** to work through (a subject) carefully; examine **4** to lie or extend across; cross ⟨*the bridge* ~s *a brook*⟩ **5a** to move to and fro over or along **b** to ascend, descend, or cross (a slope or gap) at an angle **c** to move (a gun) to right or left on a pivot **6** to make or carry out a traverse survey of ~ *vi* **1** to move back and forth or from side to side **2** to climb or ski across rather than straight up or down a hill **3** to make a traverse survey – **traversable** *adj*, **traverser** *n*

**³traverse** /'travuhs, -'-/ *adj* lying across; transverse

**travertine** /'travətin/ *n* a mineral consisting of a limestone that has no clear crystalline form, is usu layered, and is formed as a deposit from spring waters or esp from hot springs [Fr *travertin*, deriv of L *Tiburtinus* of Tibur, fr *Tibur*, region in ancient Italy]

**¹travesty** /'travəsti/ *n* **1** a crude or grotesque literary or artistic imitation, usu ridiculously incongruous in style, treatment, or subject matter **2** a debased, distorted, or grossly inferior imitation ⟨*a* ~ *of justice*⟩ □ compare CARICATURE [obs *travesty* disguised, parodied, fr Fr *travesti*, pp of *travestir* to disguise, fr It *travestire*, fr *tra-* across (fr L *trans-*) + *vestire* to dress, fr L, fr *vestis* garment – more at WEAR]

**²travesty** *vt* to make a travesty of; parody, caricature

**travois** /trə'voy/ *n*, *pl* **travois** /trə'voyz/ *also* **travoises** a primitive vehicle used by N American Indians of the Great Plains region consisting of two trailing poles serving as shafts for a dog or horse and bearing a platform or net for the load [CanF, alter. of Fr *travail* shaft of a vehicle, fr MF, fr (assumed) VL *tripalium* instrument of torture]

**¹trawl** /trawl/ *vi* **1** to fish with a trawl **2** TROLL 2 (fish by drawing a line through the water) ~ *vt* **1** to catch (fish) with a trawl **2** to fish (an area) with a trawl [prob fr obs D *tragelen*, fr MD, fr *tragel* dragnet, prob fr L *tragula*]

**²trawl** *n* **1** a large conical net dragged along the sea bottom to catch fish or other marine life **2** *NAm* SETLINE (long heavy fishing line)

**trawler** /'trawlə/ *n* **1** a person who fishes by trawling **2** a boat used in trawling

**trawlerman** /'trawləmən/ *n* a fisherman who uses a trawl or mans a trawler

**tray** /tray/ *n* **1** an open receptacle with a flat bottom and a low rim for holding, carrying, or exhibiting articles **2** a usu metal or plastic container for holding correspondence [ME, fr OE *trīg, trēg;* akin to OE *trēow* tree – more at TREE] – **trayful** *n*

**treacherous** /'trech(ə)rəs/ *adj* **1** characterized by treachery; perfidious, disloyal **2a** of uncertain reliability; untrustworthy **b** providing insecure footing or support ⟨*a* ~ *surface of black ice*⟩ **c** marked by hidden dangers or hazards ⟨*the* ~ *waters round the coast*⟩ *synonyms* see TREASON – **treacherously** *adv*, **treacherousness** *n*

**treachery** /'trech(ə)ri/ *n* **1** violation of allegiance; betrayal of trust **2** an act of betrayal or treason *synonyms* see TREASON [ME *trecherie*, fr OF, fr *trechier, trichier* to deceive (cf TRICK)]

**treacle** /'treekl/ *n* **1** a medicinal compound formerly in wide use as an antidote against poison **2** something (e g a tone of voice) heavily sweet and cloying **3** *chiefly Br* **3a** any of the edible grades of molasses that have a high sugar content and are obtained in the early stages of sugar refining **b** GOLDEN SYRUP [ME *triacle*, fr MF, fr L *theriaca*, fr Gk *thēriakē* antidote against a poisonous bite, fr fem of *thēriakos* of a wild animal, fr *thērion* wild animal, dim. of *thēr* wild animal – more at FIERCE] – **treacly** *adj*

**¹tread** /tred/ *vb* **trod** /trod/ *also* **treaded; trodden** /'trod(ə)n/, **trod** *vt* **1a** to step or walk on or over **b** to walk along; follow ⟨~ing *the long road home*⟩ **2a** to beat or press with the feet; trample **b** to subdue or repress as if by trampling; crush **3** *of a male bird* to copulate with **4a** to form by treading; beat ⟨~ *a path*⟩ **b** to execute by stepping or dancing ⟨~ *a measure*⟩ ~ *vi* **1** to move on foot; walk **2a** to set foot **b** to put one's foot;

step ⟨trod *on a stone*⟩ **3** *of a male bird* to copulate [ME *treden,* fr OE *tredan;* akin to OHG *tretan* to tread] – **treader** *n* – **tread on somebody's toes/corns** to give offence to or hurt somebody's feelings, esp by encroaching on his/her rights – see also **tread** WATER

²**tread** *n* **1** a mark (eg a footprint or the imprint of a tyre) made (as if) by treading **2a** the action of treading; *also* an act of treading; a step **b** the sound or manner of stepping or treading ⟨*the heavy* ~ *of feet*⟩ **3** an injury caused to a horse's foot by overreaching or by another horse **4a** the part of a sole that touches the ground; *also* the pattern on the bottom of a sole **b(1)** the part of a wheel or tyre that makes contact with a road or rail **b(2)** the pattern of ridges or grooves made or cut in the face of a tyre **5** (the width of) the upper horizontal part of a step – compare RISER – **treadless** *adj*

¹**treadle** /'tredl/ *n* a lever pressed by the foot to drive a machine (eg a sewing machine) [ME *tredel* step of a stair, fr OE, fr *tredan* to tread]

²**treadle** *vi* to operate a treadle ~ *vt* to operate (a machine) by a treadle

**treadmill** /'tred,mil/ *n* **1a** a mill, used formerly to employ or punish prisoners, worked by people treading on steps inside a wide wheel with a horizontal axis **b** a mill worked by an animal treading an endless belt **2** a wearisome or monotonous routine

**treason** /'treez(ə)n/ *n* **1** the betrayal of a trust; treachery **2** the offence of violating the allegiance owed to a sovereign or government [ME *tresoun,* fr OF *traison,* fr ML *tradition-, tradi- tio,* fr L, act of handing over, fr *traditus,* pp of *tradere* to hand over, betray – more at TRAITOR] – **treasonable, treasonous** *adj,* **treasonably** *adv*

> **synonyms** The legal term for the offence against one's government is **treason,** and such an offence is **treasonable** or **treasonous.** A **traitor** is a person who either commits this offence or in a wider sense betrays a trust, and such betrayal is **treachery,** or is **traitorous** or **treacherous. Treacherousness** is associated with being **treacher- ous** in the sense "unreliable" ⟨*the* **treacherousness** *of the ice*⟩.

¹**treasure** /'trezhə/ *n* **1a** wealth (eg money, jewels, or preci- ous metals) accumulated or hoarded ⟨*buried* ~⟩ **b** wealth of any kind or in any form; riches **2** something of great worth or value; *also* someone who is highly valued or prized [ME *tresor,* fr OF, fr L *thesaurus,* fr Gk *thēsauros*]

²**treasure** *vt* **1** to collect and store up (something of value) for future use; hoard **2** to hold or preserve as precious; cherish, prize ⟨~d *those memories*⟩ – **treasurable** *adj*

¹**treasure-,house** *n* **1** a building where treasure is kept **2** a place or source where many valuable things can be found ⟨*that book is a real* ~ *of new information*⟩

**treasure hunt** *n* **1** a search for something of real or imagined value **2** a game in which each player or team tries, with the help of clues, to be first to find whatever has been hidden

**treasurer** /'trezh(ə)rə/ *n* a person appointed to take charge of the receipt, care, and expenditure of the funds of an organiza- tion – **treasurership** *n*

**treasure trove** /trohv/ *n* **1** treasure that anyone finds; *specif* gold or silver in the form of money, plate, or bullion which is found hidden and whose ownership is not known **2** a valuable or productive discovery or source [AF *tresor trové,* lit., found treasure]

**treasury** /'trezh(ə)ri/ *n* **1a** a place in which stores of wealth are kept **b** the place where collected funds, esp public revenues, are deposited, kept, and issued **c** funds kept in such a deposi- tory **2** *often cap* (a building which houses) a government de- partment in charge of finances, esp the collection, management, and expenditure of public revenues **3** a source or collection of treasures ⟨*a* ~ *of poems*⟩ **4** *obs* treasure

**Treasury bench** *n, often cap B* the first row of seats on the right of the speaker in the HOUSE OF COMMONS, that is used by senior government ministers

**treasury bill** *n* a BILL OF EXCHANGE issued by the treasury in return for money lent to the government

**treasury note** *n* a currency note issued by a governmental treasury; *esp* **a** one that was issued by the US Treasury in pay- ment for silver bullion purchased under the Sherman Silver Purchase Act of 1890 **b** one that was issued by the Treasury between 1914 and 1928 in denominations of £1 and 10 shillings and was legal tender – compare BANK NOTE

¹**treat** /treet/ *vi* **1** to pay another's expenses (eg for a meal or drink), esp as a compliment, as an expression of regard or friendship, or as a bribe ⟨*candidates must not* ~ *at parliamen- tary elections*⟩ **2** *formal* to discuss terms *with* someone;

negotiate ⟨~*ing with the enemy*⟩ ⟨~ *for peace*⟩ **3** *formal* to deal with a matter, esp in writing – usu + *of* ⟨*a book* ~*ing of conservation*⟩ ~ *vt* **1a** to deal with in speech or writing; ex- pound **b** to present or represent artistically **c** to deal with; handle ⟨*food is plentiful and* ~*ed with imagination* – Cecil Beaton⟩ **2a** to behave oneself towards; use ⟨~ *a horse cruelly*⟩ **b** to regard and deal with in a specified manner – usu + *as* ⟨~*ed it as a serious matter*⟩ **3a** to provide with free food, drink, or entertainment – usu + *to* ⟨*let me* ~ *you to a pint*⟩ **b** to provide with enjoyment or gratification – usu + *to* ⟨~*ed herself to a new coat*⟩ **4** to care for or deal with medically or surgically ⟨~ *a disease*⟩ ⟨~*ing a patient for pneumonia*⟩ **5** to act on with some agent, esp so as to improve or alter ⟨~ *a metal with acid*⟩ – see also **treat like** DIRT [ME *treten,* fr OF *traitier,* fr L *tractare* to handle, deal with, fr *tractus,* pp of *trahere* to draw – more at DRAW] – **treatable** *adj,* **treatability** *n,* **treater** *n*

²**treat** *n* **1** an entertainment given free of charge to those invited **2** a source of pleasure or amusement; *esp* an unexpected one ⟨*the cold beer on a hot day was a* ~⟩ – **a treat** *Br informal* very well, successfully, or pleasurably ⟨*the speech went down a treat*⟩ ⟨*the work's coming on a treat*⟩

**treatise** /'treetiz/ *n* **1** a formal written exposition of a subject ⟨*a* ~ *on higher education*⟩ – compare THESIS, DISSERTATION **2** *obs* a story, tale [ME *tretis,* fr AF *tretiz,* fr OF *traitier* to treat]

**treatment** /'treetmənt/ *n* **1a** the act or manner or an instance of treating someone or something; handling, usage **b** the tech- niques or actions customarily applied in a particular situation ⟨*the new author got the full* ~ *of cocktail parties and press interviews*⟩ **2a** a substance or technique used in treating; *esp* a therapy, course of drugs, etc prescribed to treat an illness or other medical condition **b** an experimental condition, proce- dure, etc that can be applied in a controlled manner and whose effect can be compared with other standardized treatments

**treaty** /'treeti/ *n* **1** the action of treating, esp of negotiating – chiefly in *in treaty* **2a** an agreement or arrangement made by negotiation: **2a(1)** PRIVATE TREATY **a(2)** a contract in writing between two or more political authorities (eg states or sover- eigns) formally signed by duly authorized representatives **b** a document in which such a contract is set down [ME *tretee,* fr MF *traité,* fr ML *tractatus,* fr L, handling, treatment, fr *trac- tatus,* pp of *tractare* to treat]

**treaty port** *n* any of numerous ports and inland cities in China, Japan, and Korea formerly open by treaty to foreign commerce

¹**treble** /'trebl/ *n* **1a** the highest part in written, sung, or played music; soprano; *also* a singer, esp a young boy, who performs this part **b** a member of a family of musical instruments having the highest range **c** a high-pitched or shrill voice, tone, or sound **d** the upper half of the whole range of pitches that a voice, instrument, etc can produce – compare BASS **e** the higher portion of the audio frequency range considered esp in relation to its electronic reproduction **2** something treble in construc- tion, uses, amount, number, or value: eg **2a** the middle narrow ring on a dart board, counting treble the stated score; *also* a throw in darts that lands there **b** *Br* a bet involving three selections in different events (eg horse races) such that, if the first selection is successful, the stake and winnings are bet on the second, and so on [ME, perh fr MF, trio, fr *treble,* adj]

> **synonyms Treble** and **triple** can both be used as noun, verb, and adjective, and are largely interchangeable in meaning. **Triple** is com- moner for something in three parts ⟨*a* **triple** *fence*⟩. In music they are sharply distinguished, since **treble** refers to pitch and **triple** to rhythm.

²**treble** *adj* **1a** having three parts or uses; threefold **b** being three times as great in number or as much in amount **2a** relat- ing to or having the range or part of a treble **b** high-pitched, shrill [ME, fr MF, fr L *triplus* – more at TRIPLE] – **trebly** *adv*

³**treble** *vb* to increase to three times the size, amount, or number

**treble chance** *n* a football pool in which winning depends chiefly on forecasting drawn matches; *broadly* FOOTBALL POOLS ⟨*won a fortune with eight draws on the* ~⟩

**treble clef** *n* **1** a symbol on a musical stave that designates a note written on the next to bottom line of the stave as the G above MIDDLE C **2** the musical stave that has a treble clef and on which the treble part of a musical composition is written □ called also G CLEF; compare BASS CLEF

**trebuchet** /'trebyooshet/ *n* a medieval military device for hurling missiles with great force [ME *trebochet,* fr MF *trebu- chet,* fr OF, fr *trebucher* to overthrow, stumble]

**trebucket** /'treebukit/ n a trebuchet

**trecento** /tray'chentoh/ n the 14th century, esp in Italian literature and art [It, lit., three hundred, fr L *tres* three + *centum* hundred – more at THREE, HUNDRED]

**tredecillion** /ˌtreedi'silyən/ n – see NUMBER table [L *tredecim* thirteen (fr *tres* three + *decem* ten) + E *-illion* (as in *million*) – more at THREE, TEN]

¹**tree** /tree/ n **1a** a tall woody plant having a single usu long and erect main stem, generally with few or no branches on its lower part **b** a shrub or herbaceous plant having the form of a tree ⟨*rose* ~s⟩ ⟨*a banana* ~⟩ **2** a piece of wood (eg a post or pole), usu adapted to a particular use **3a** SADDLETREE (frame of a saddle) **b** a device for inserting in a boot or shoe to preserve its shape when not being worn **4** something resembling a tree in form: eg **4a** *also* **tree diagram** a diagram or graph that branches usu from a single stem without forming loops or polygons ⟨*genealogical* ~⟩ **b** a much-branched system of channels, esp in an animal or plant body ⟨*the vascular* ~⟩ **5** *archaic* **5a** *the* cross on which Jesus was crucified **b** *the* gallows [ME, fr OE *trēow;* akin to ON *trē* tree, Gk *drys*, Skt *dāru* wood] – **treeless** *adj*, **treelike** *adj* – **bark up the wrong tree** to take useless action; act misguidedly – see also **not see the** WOOD **for the trees**

²**tree** vt **1** to drive to or up a tree ⟨~d *by a bull*⟩ ⟨*dogs* ~ing *game*⟩ **2** to put into a position of extreme disadvantage; corner; *esp* to bring to bay

**treecreeper** /-ˌkreepə/ n any of several small birds that have slender curved bills and are usu seen climbing up tree trunks; *esp* either of two European treecreepers (*Certhia familiaris* or *Certhia brachydactyla*) that are brown streaked with buff above and greyish-white below

**treed** /treed/ *adj* planted or grown with trees; wooded

**tree farm** n an area of forest land managed to ensure continuous commercial production of timber

**tree fern** n any of various ferns (chiefly of families Cyatheaceae and Marattiaceae) having a woody stem and resembling a tree

**tree frog** n any of numerous tailless tree-dwelling amphibians (esp family Hylidae)

**tree kangaroo** n any of several tree-dwelling wallabies (genus *Dendrolagus*) of Australia and New Guinea

**tree line** n the upper limit of tree growth in mountains or high latitudes – called also TIMBERLINE

**treen** /'tree·ən/ n small domestic articles, esp tableware, made of wood [ME *treen* wooden, fr OE *trēowen*, fr *trēow* tree, wood]

**treenail** *also* **trenail** /'tree.nayl, 'trenl/ n a wooden peg made usu of dry compressed timber so as to swell in its hole when moistened

**tree of heaven** n an ornamental Asiatic tree (*Ailanthus altissima*) with smooth bark, large leaves, and small greenish flowers [trans of Amboinese *ai lanto*]

**tree peony** n a shrubby Chinese peony (*Paeonia suffruticosa*) that has large showy flowers and is the source of many horticultural varieties

**tree pipit** n a small Eurasian bird (*Anthus trivialis*) that closely resembles the MEADOW PIPIT but has a slightly plumper form and yellowish breast

**tree shrew** n any of a family (Tupaiidae) of tree-dwelling insect-eating small mammals sometimes classified as true INSECTIVORES and sometimes as primitive ancestors of the PRIMATES

**tree sparrow** n a Eurasian sparrow (*Passer montanus*) the male and female of which have a similar appearance and are characterized by a black spot behind the eye and a chestnut crown

**tree surgeon** n a specialist in TREE SURGERY

**tree surgery** n treatment of diseased trees, esp for control of decay; *broadly* practices (eg pruning) forming part of the professional care of trees grown for ornament or to provide shade

**tree toad** n TREE FROG

**treetop** /-ˌtop/ n **1** the topmost part of a tree **2** *pl* the height or line marked by the tops of a group of trees

**tree wallaby** n TREE KANGAROO

**trefoil** /'trefoyl, 'tree-/ n **1a** (a) clover; *broadly* any of several plants of the pea family that have leaves made up of three leaflets **b** a leaf consisting of three leaflets **2** a stylized figure or ornament in the form of a leaf or flower with three lobes [ME, fr MF *trefeuil*, fr L *trifolium*, fr *tri-* + *folium* leaf]

**trehala** /tri'hahlə/ n a sweet edible substance constituting the

cocoon of an Asiatic beetle (genus *Larinus*) [Fr *tréhala*, fr Turk *tıgala*, fr Per *tīghāl*]

**trehalase** /'treehəlayz/ n an ENZYME that accelerates the breakdown of trehalose and is found in yeasts and moulds [ISV *trehalose* + *-ase*]

**trehalose** /'treehəlohs, -lohz/ n a sugar (DISACCHARIDE), $C_{12}H_{22}O_{11}$, stored instead of starch by many fungi and found in the blood of many insects [ISV *trehala* + *-ose*]

¹**trek** /trek/ n **1** a journey; *esp* a long or arduous one **2** *chiefly SAfr* **2a** a journey by ox wagon; *also* a stage of such a journey **b** an organized migration by a group of settlers [Afrik, fr MD *treck* pull, haul, fr *trecken*]

²**trek** vb **-kk-** vi **1** to travel; *esp* to make a long or arduous trip ⟨*had to* ~ *right across town*⟩ **2** to go PONY TREKKING **3** *chiefly SAfr* **3a** to travel by ox wagon **b** to migrate by ox wagon ~ *vt, chiefly SAfr* to draw, pull [Afrik, fr MD *trecken* to pull, haul, migrate; akin to OHG *trechan* to pull] – **trekker** n

¹**trellis** /'trelis/ n **1** a frame of latticework used as a screen or as a support for climbing plants **2** an arrangement resembling a lattice ⟨*a* ~ *of interlacing streams*⟩ [ME *trelis*, fr MF *treliz* fabric of coarse weave, trellis, fr (assumed) VL *trilicius* woven with triple thread, fr L *trilic-, trilix*, fr *tri-* + *licium* thread]

²**trellis** vt **1** to provide with a trellis; *esp* to train (eg a vine) on a trellis **2** to cross or interlace on or through; interweave

**trelliswork** /-ˌwuhk/ n latticework

**trematode** /'tremə.tohd, 'tree-/ n any of a class (Trematoda) of parasitic flatworms including the flukes [deriv of Gk *trēmatōdēs* pierced with holes, fr *trēmat-, trēma* hole, fr *tetrainein* to bore – more at THROW] – **trematode** *adj*

¹**tremble** /'trembl/ vi **1** to shake involuntarily (eg with fear or cold); shiver **2** to be affected (as if) by a quivering or vibratory motion ⟨*the building* ~d *from the blast*⟩ ⟨*his voice* ~d *with emotion*⟩ **3** to be affected with fear or apprehension ⟨~ *for the safety of another*⟩ ~ vt to cause to tremble **synonyms** see ¹SHAKE [ME *tremblen*, fr MF *trembler*, fr ML *tremulare*, fr L *tremulus* trembling, fr *tremere* to tremble; akin to Gk *tremein* to tremble] – **trembler** n, **trembly** *adj*

²**tremble** n **1** an act or instance of trembling: eg **1a** a fit or spell of involuntary shaking or quivering **b** a tremor or series of tremors **2** *pl but taking sing vb* a severe disorder of livestock, esp cattle, caused by eating some poisonous plants and characterized by muscular tremors, weakness, and constipation

**tremendous** /trə'mendəs/ *adj* **1** such as to arouse awe or fear **2** of extraordinary size, degree, or excellence [L *tremendus*, fr gerundive of *tremere* to tremble] – **tremendously** *adv*, **tremendousness** n

**tremie** /'tremi/ n a large funnel for laying concrete under water [Fr *trémie* hopper, fr L *trimodia* vessel holding three pecks, fr *modius* peck]

**tremolant** /'tremələnt/ *adj* ¹TREMULANT **2** [It *tremolante*] – **tremolant** n

**tremolite** /'tremə.liet/ n a white or grey mineral, $Ca_2Mg_5Si_8O_{22}(OH)_2$, of the AMPHIBOLE group that is a calcium magnesium silicate [Fr *trémolite*, fr *Tremola*, valley in Switzerland] – **tremolitic** *adj*

**tremolo** /'treməloh/ n, *pl* **tremolos** **1a** the rapid repetition of a musical note or of alternating notes to produce a tremulous effect **b** a perceptible rapid variation of pitch in the voice, esp in singing; vibrato **2** a mechanical device in an organ for causing a tremulous effect [It, fr *tremolo* tremulous, fr L *tremulus*]

**tremor** /'tremə/ n **1** a trembling or shaking, usu from physical weakness, emotional stress, or disease **2** a quivering or vibratory motion; *esp* a distinct small movement of the earth before or after a major earthquake **3** a thrill, quiver ⟨*experienced a sudden* ~ *of fear*⟩ [ME *tremour*, fr MF, fr L *tremor*, fr *tremere* to tremble]

¹**tremulant** /'tremyoolənt/ *adj* **1** tremulous, trembling **2** marked by tremolo [ML *tremulant-, tremulans*, prp of *tremulare* – more at TREMBLE]

²**tremulant** n a device in a musical instrument to impart a vibration causing a tremulant sound [Ger, fr It *tremolante*, fr *tremolante* tremulous, fr ML *tremulant-, tremulans*]

**tremulous** /'tremyooləs/ *adj* **1** characterized by or affected with trembling or tremors **2** affected with timidity; uncertain, wavering **3** resulting from or indicating a tremulous state; shaky ⟨~ *handwriting*⟩ ⟨~ *voice*⟩ [L *tremulus* – more at TREMBLE] – **tremulously** *adv*, **tremulousness** n

**trenail** /'tree.nayl, 'trenl/ n TREENAIL (wooden peg)

¹**trench** /trench/ n **1** a deep narrow excavation in the ground

(e g for the laying of underground pipes); *esp* one used for military defence, often with the excavated earth banked up in front for protection **2** a long, narrow, and usu steep-sided depression in the ocean floor – compare TROUGH [ME *trenche* track cut through a wood, fr MF, act of cutting, fr *trenchier* to cut, prob modif of L *truncare* to cut off – more at TRUNCATE]

²**trench** *vt* **1** to make a cut in; carve **2a** to protect (as if) with a trench **b** to dig a trench in (e g for drainage); ditch **c** to dig or plough deeply; *esp* to turn over (soil) two or more times the depth of a spade ~ *vi* **1a** to encroach, entrench ⟨~ing *on other domains which were more vital* – Sir Winston Churchill⟩ **b** to come close; verge **2** to dig a trench □ (*vi 1*) usu + *on* or *upon* – **trencher** *n*

**trenchant** /'trenchənt/ *adj* **1** keen, sharp **2** vigorously effective and articulate ⟨*a* ~ *analysis*⟩; *also* caustic ⟨~ *remarks*⟩ **3a** incisive, penetrating **b** clear-cut, distinct ⟨*the* ~ *divisions between right and wrong* – Edith Wharton⟩ [ME, fr MF, prp of *trenchier* to cut] – **trenchancy** *n,* **trenchantly** *adv*

**trench coat** *n* **1** a waterproof overcoat with a removable lining, designed for wear in trenches **2** a double-breasted raincoat with deep pockets, a belt, and epaulettes

**trencher** /'trenchə/ *n* a wooden platter for serving food [ME, fr MF *trencheoir,* fr *trenchier* to cut]

**trencherman** /'trenchəmən/ *n* a hearty eater

**trench fever** *n* an infectious disease marked by fever and pain in muscles, bones, and joints, that is caused by a microorganism (*Rickettsia quintana*) transmitted by the BODY LOUSE [fr its prevalence among soldiers serving in the trenches during World War I]

**trench foot** *n* a painful disorder of the foot resembling frostbite and resulting from exposure to cold and wet

**trench knife** *n* a knife with a strong double-edged blade about 20 centimetres (8 inches) long, suited for use in hand-to-hand fighting

**trench mouth** *n* **1** VINCENT'S ANGINA (bacterial disease of the tonsils) **2** VINCENT'S INFECTION (bacterial infection of the mouth, throat, etc)

**trench warfare** *n* warfare conducted from a relatively permanent system of trenches

¹**trend** /trend/ *vi* **1a** to extend in a specified direction ⟨*mountain ranges* ~ing *north and south*⟩ **b** to veer in a specified direction; bend ⟨*coastline that* ~s *westwards*⟩ **2a** to show a general tendency; incline ⟨*prices* ~ing *upwards*⟩ **b** to deviate, shift ⟨*opinions* ~ing *towards conservatism*⟩ [ME *trenden* to turn, revolve, fr OE *trendan;* akin to MHG *trendel* disc, spinning top, OE *teran* to tear – more at TEAR]

²**trend** *n* **1** a line of general direction ⟨*the* ~ *of the coast turned towards the west*⟩ **2a** a prevailing tendency or inclination ⟨*contemporary* ~s *in education*⟩ **b** a general movement; a swing ⟨*the* ~ *towards suburban living*⟩ **c** a current style or taste; a vogue ⟨*new fashion* ~s⟩ **3** the general movement in the course of time of a statistically detectable change; *also* a statistical curve reflecting such a change *synonyms* see TENDENCY

**trendsetter** /-,setə/ *n* a person who starts new trends, esp in fashion – **trendsetting** *n or adj*

¹**trendy** /'trendi/ *adj* very fashionable; up-to-date ⟨*he's a* ~ *dresser* – Sunday Mirror⟩; *also* characterized by unthinking adherence to the latest fashions or progressive ideas ⟨*his concern for good composition . . . prevents the up-to-date from dwindling into the merely* ~ – The Listener⟩ – **trendily** *adv,* **trendiness** *n,* **trendyism** *n*

²**trendy, trendie** *n, chiefly derog* a trendy person ⟨*wine bars . . . catering for young trendies* – Sunday Times⟩ ⟨*Harvard academic trendies* – Canadian Dimension⟩

¹**trepan** /tri'pan/ *n* **1** a primitive type of trephine **2** a heavy tool used in boring mine shafts [ME *trepane,* fr ML *trepanum,* fr Gk *trypanon* auger, fr *trypan* to bore, fr *trypa* hole; akin to Gk *tetrainein* to pierce – more at THROW]

²**trepan** *vt* -**nn**- **1** to use a trephine on (the skull) **2** to remove a disc or cylindrical core from (metal) with a MACHINE TOOL – **trepanation** *n*

³**trepan** *n, archaic* a snare, lure [origin unknown]

⁴**trepan** *vt* -**nn**- *archaic* to entrap, lure

**trepang** /tri'pang/ *n* any of several large SEA CUCUMBERS (esp genera *Actinopyga* and *Holothuria*) that are used, esp in Chinese cooking, for making soup – called also BÊCHE-DE-MER [Malay *tĕripang*]

**trephination** /,trefi'naysh(ə)n/ *n* an act or instance of perforating the skull with a surgical instrument

¹**trephine** /tri'feen/ *n* a surgical instrument for cutting out circular sections, esp of bone or the cornea of the eye [alter. of earlier *trefine, trafine,* fr L *tres fines* three ends, fr *tres* three + *fines,* pl of *finis* end – more at THREE]

²**trephine** *vt* to operate on or extract with a trephine

**trepidation** /,trepi'daysh(ə)n/ *n* **1** nervous agitation; apprehension, alarm **2** *archaic* a quivering, tremor *synonyms* see ¹FEAR [L *trepidation-, trepidatio,* fr *trepidatus,* pp of *trepidare* to tremble, fr *trepidus* agitated; akin to OE *thrafian* to urge, push, Gk *trapein* to press grapes]

**treponema** /,trepə'neemə/ *n, pl* **treponemata** /-'nemətə/, **treponemas** any of a genus (*Treponema*) of spirally coiled bacteria (SPIROCHAETES) that are parasites on warm-blooded creatures (e g human beings) and include organisms causing the diseases syphilis and yaws [NL *Treponemat-, Treponema,* genus name, deriv of Gk *trepein* to turn + *nēma* thread, fr *nēn* to spin – more at TROPE, NEEDLE] – **treponemal, treponematous** *adj*

**treponematosis** /,trepəneemə'tohsis, -nemə-/ *n, pl* **treponematoses** /-seez/ infection with or disease caused by treponemata [NL]

**treponeme** /'trepəneem/ *n* a treponema

¹**trespass** /'trespəs/ *n* **1a** a violation of moral or social ethics; a transgression; *esp* a sin **b** an unwarranted infringement **2a** an unlawful act against the person, property, or rights of another; *esp* wrongful entry on another's land **b** the action for damages done by such an act [ME *trespas,* fr OF, crossing, trespass, fr *trespasser* to go across]

²**trespass** *vi* **1a** to err, sin **b** to make an unwarranted or uninvited intrusion ⟨~ *on a busy executive's time*⟩ **2** to commit a trespass; *esp* to enter someone's property unlawfully [ME *trespassen,* fr MF *trespasser,* fr OF, lit., to go· across, fr *tres* across (fr L *trans*) + *passer* to pass – more at THROUGH, PASS] – **trespasser** *n*

**tress** /tres/ *n* **1** a plait of hair; a braid **2** *usu pl* a long lock of hair; *esp, pl* the long unbound hair of a woman [ME *tresse,* fr OF *trece*]

**tressed** /trest/ *adj* **1** having tresses – usu in combination ⟨*golden*-tressed⟩ **2** *obs* braided, plaited

**tressure** /'treshə, 'tresyooə/ *n* a narrow band within a heraldic shield, usu ornamented with stylized representations of lines (FLEURS-DE-LIS) [ME *tressour,* lit., band for the hair, fr MF *tressure,* fr *tresser* to plait]

**trestle** *also* **tressel** /'tresl/ *n* **1** a supporting framework (e g for a table) consisting typically of a horizontal bar held at each end by two divergent pairs of legs **2** a braced framework of timbers, piles, or girders for carrying a road or railway over a depression [ME *trestel,* fr MF, modif of (assumed) VL *transtellum,* fr L *transtillum,* dim. of *transtrum* traverse beam, transom – more at TRANSOM]

**trestle table** *n* a table consisting of a board or boards supported on trestles

**trestletree** /-,tree/ *n* either of a pair of short timber crosspieces fixed at the front and back of a ship's lower mast to support an upper mast

**trestlework** /'tresl,wuhk/ *n* a system of connected trestles supporting a structure (e g a bridge)

**trevally** /trə'vali/ *n* any of several marine spiny-finned Australian fishes (genus *Caranx*) that are eaten as food [origin unknown]

**trews** /troohz/ *n pl* **1** trousers; *specif* tartan trousers **2** tartan trousers, esp cut on the cross, worn with a PLAID (piece of tartan worn over the shoulder) in Highland dress [ScGael *triubhas*]

**trey** /tray/ *n* **1** the side of a dice or domino that has three spots **2** a playing card numbered three or having three main pips [ME *treye, treis,* fr MF *treie, treis,* fr L *tres* thrée]

**tri-** /trie-/ *comb form* **1** three ⟨*tripartite*⟩; having three elements or parts ⟨*trigraph*⟩ **2** into three ⟨*trisect*⟩ **3a** thrice ⟨*triweekly*⟩ **b** every third ⟨*trimonthly*⟩ [ME, fr L (fr *tri-, tres*) & Gk (fr *tri-, treis*) – more at THREE]

**triable** /'trie·əbl/ *adj* liable or subject to examination or trial in a court of law ⟨*a case* ~ *without a jury*⟩ – **triableness** *n*

**triac** /'trie·ak/ *n* a SEMICONDUCTOR device that acts as a high-speed electronic switch for ALTERNATING CURRENT power supplies [*tri-* (fr its having three layers) + -*ac*]

**triacetate** /trie'asitayt/ *n* **1** a chemical compound (ACETATE) containing three acetate groups in the molecular structure **2** a man-made textile fibre consisting of a triacetate of cellulose [ISV]

¹**triacid** /trie'asid/, **triacidic** /,trie·ə'sidik/ *adj* **1** *esp of a chemical*

*base* having three HYDROXYL groups capable of reacting as bases in each molecule **2** *of an acid* TRIBASIC 1 [ISV]

²**triacid** *n* an acid (eg PHOSPHORIC ACID) having three acid hydrogen atoms

**triad** /'trie,ad/ *n* **1** a union or group of three, esp three closely related or associated people, beings, or things; a trinity **2** a chord of three notes in a major or minor DIATONIC scale (ordinary 8-note scale), made up of a fundamental note with its THIRD and FIFTH that constitutes the HARMONIC basis of tonal music – called also COMMON CHORD **3** *often cap* any of various Chinese SECRET SOCIETIES, esp engaging in drug trafficking [L *triad-, trias*, fr Gk, fr *treis* three] – **triadic** *adj*, **triadically** *adv*

**triage** /tree'ahzh, '-,-/ *n* the sorting of and allocation of treatment to patients, esp battle and disaster victims, according to a system of priorities based on urgency [Fr, sorting, sifting, fr *trier* to sort, fr OF – more at TRY]

¹**trial** /trie·əl/ *n* **1a** the action or process of trying or putting to the test **b** a preliminary contest or match (eg to evaluate the comparative skills of players) **2** the formal examination and determination by a competent tribunal of the matter at issue in a civil or criminal case **3** a test of faith, patience, or stamina by suffering or temptation; *broadly* a source of vexation or annoyance **4a** an experiment to test quality, value, or usefulness ⟨*plant varieties undergoing field* ~s⟩ **b** *statistics* an instance of an experiment ⟨*what is the probability of getting* k *successes in* n ~s⟩ **5** an attempt, effort **6 trials** *pl*, **trial** a sporting contest for individual competition: eg **6a** a competition of vehicle-handling skills (eg in cars or on motorcycles), usu over rough ground **b** a competition in which a working animal's skills are tested ⟨*a sheepdog* ~⟩ **c** EVENT 3b (horseriding competition) [AF, fr *trier* to try]

²**trial** *adj* **1** of or used in a trial **2** made or done as a test or experiment ⟨*a* ~ *marriage*⟩ **3** used or tried out in a test or experiment

³**trial** *adj, of grammatical* NUMBER (*singular, plural, etc*) denoting reference to three ⟨*some Polynesian languages have* ~ *pronouns, so that there are different words for "us two" and "us three"*⟩ – compare DUAL [*tri-* + *-al*] – **trial** *n*

**trial and error** *n* a process of trying out a number of methods and discarding the least successful in order to find the best way to achieve a desired result; *also* a process of trying various methods at random until one of them works

**trial balance** *n* a statement of the debit and credit balances of accounts in a double-entry ledger at a given date, prepared primarily to test their equality

**trial balloon** *n* a project or scheme tentatively announced in order to test public opinion [orig referring to a balloon sent up to test air currents and wind speed]

**trial court** *n* the court before which issues of fact and law are first determined, as distinguished from a COURT OF APPEAL

**trialist** *also* **triallist** /'trie·əlist/ *n* one who takes part in a sports trial (eg in motorcycling or cricket)

**trial lawyer** *n, NAm* a lawyer engaged chiefly in cases before TRIAL COURTS

**trial run** *n* an exercise to test the performance of something (eg a vehicle or vessel); *also* EXPERIMENT 1

**triamcinolone** /,trie·am'sinəlohn/ *n* a synthetic STEROID drug, $C_{21}H_{27}FO_6$, that is a GLUCOCORTICOID used esp to counteract inflammation and to treat skin disorders [*tri-* + *amyl* + *cin*ene (a terpene) + *prednis*olone]

**triangle** /'trie,ang·gl/ *n* **1** a one-dimensional figure of three sides and three angles **2** a percussion instrument consisting of a steel rod bent into the form of a triangle open at one angle and sounded by striking with a small metal rod **3** TRIAD 1 – compare ETERNAL TRIANGLE **4** *NAm* SET SQUARE (instrument for marking or testing angles) [ME, fr L *triangulum*, fr neut of *triangulus* triangular, fr *tri-* + *angulus* angle]

**triangular** /trie'ang·gyoolə/ *adj* **1a** (having the form) of a triangle ⟨*a* ~ *plot of land*⟩ **b** having a triangular base or principal surface ⟨*a* ~ *table*⟩ ⟨*a* ~ *pyramid*⟩ **2a** between or involving a group of three usu closely related elements, things, or people ⟨*a* ~ *love affair*⟩ ⟨*a* ~ *contest*⟩ **b** *of a military group* based primarily on three units ⟨~ *division*⟩ [LL *triangularis*, fr L *triangulum*] – **triangularly** *adv*, **triangularity** *n*

**triangulate** /trie'ang·gyoolayt/ *vt* **1a** to divide into triangles **b** to give triangular form to **2** to survey, map, or determine by triangulation

**triangulation** /,trie,ang·gyoo'laysh(ə)n/ *n* the measurement of the elements necessary to determine the network of triangles

into which any part of the earth's surface is divided in surveying; *broadly* any trigonometric operation for finding a position or location by means of bearings from two fixed points a known distance apart

**triarchy** /'trie,ahki/ *n* **1** government by three people **2** a country under three rulers [Gk *triarchia*, fr *tri-* + *-archia* -archy]

**Triassic** /trie'asik/ *adj* of or being the earliest period of the MESOZOIC era or the corresponding system of rocks [ISV, fr L *trias* triad; fr the three subdivisions of the European Triassic] – **Triassic** *n*

**triatic stay** /trie'atik/ *n* a strong (wire) rope running horizontally between the tops of a ship's foremast and mainmast to help support the masts [origin unknown]

**triatomic** /,trie·ə'tomik/ *adj, chemistry* **1** having three atoms in the molecule ⟨*ozone is* ~ *oxygen*⟩ **2** having three replaceable atoms or chemical groups [ISV]

**triaxial** /trie'aksi·əl/ *adj* having or involving three axes [ISV] – **triaxiality** *n*

**triazine** /'trie·əzeen, -zin, trie'azeen, -zin/ *n* any of three chemical compounds, $C_3H_3N_3$, containing a ring composed of three carbon and three nitrogen atoms; *also* any of various derivatives of these, including several used as weedkillers [ISV *tri-* + *azine*]

**tribade** /'tribəd/ *n* the partner who takes the male role in tribadism; *broadly* a female homosexual [Fr, fr L *tribad-, tribas*, fr Gk, fr *tribein* to rub]

**tribadism** /'tribədiz(ə)m/ *n* sexual intercourse between women involving genital contact analogous to heterosexual intercourse – **tribadic** *adj*

**tribal** /'triebl/ *adj* (characteristic) of a tribe ⟨~ *customs*⟩ – **tribally** *adv*

**tribalism** /'triebl,iz(ə)m/ *n* **1** tribal consciousness and loyalty; *esp* exaltation of the tribe above other groups **2** strong loyalty or attachment to a group – **tribalistic** *adj*

**tribasic** /trie'baysik/ *adj* **1** *of an acid* having three hydrogen atoms capable of reacting as acids in each molecule **2** *of a chemical compound* containing three atoms of a metal having a VALENCY of one, or their equivalent **3** *of a chemical* BASE TRIACID 1

**tribe** /trieb/ *n* **1a** *taking sing or pl vb* a social group comprising numerous families, clans, or generations together with slaves, dependants, or adopted strangers **b** a political division of the Roman people, originally representing any of the three primitive tribes of ancient Rome **c** PHYLE (political subdivision of the ancient Athenians) **d** *taking sing or pl vb* a politically autonomous group that adheres to the same leaders, culture, and customs and is territorially defined **2** *taking sing or pl vb, chiefly derog* a group of people having a common character, occupation, or interest ⟨*attempts to portray the whole* ~ *of parliamentarians as either stupid or vicious – The Listener*⟩ **3a** a category in the biological classification of living things ranking above a genus and below a family; *also* a natural group irrespective of taxonomic rank ⟨*the cat* ~⟩ **b** a group of closely related animals or strains within a breed **4** *chiefly humorous* a group of things having common characteristics or properties ⟨*the cheese* ~⟩ ⟨*the pizza* ~ – Elizabeth David⟩ [ME, fr L *tribus*, a division of the Roman people, tribe]

**tribesman** /'triebzmən/, *fem* **tribeswoman** /-,woomən/ *n* a member of a tribe

**tribo-** /trieboh-/ *comb form* friction ⟨tribo*luminescence*⟩ [Fr, fr Gk *tribein* to rub; akin to L *terere* to rub – more at THROW]

**triboelectricity** /,triebohi,lek'trisəti, -,eelek-/ *n* a charge of electricity generated by friction (eg by rubbing glass with silk) – **triboelectric** *adj*

**tribology** /trie'boləji/ *n, Br* a branch of science that deals with the design, friction, wear, and lubrication of interacting surfaces in relative motion (eg in bearings or gears) [*tribo-* + *-logy*] – **tribologist** *n*, **tribological** *adj*

**triboluminescence** /,triebohloohmi'nes(ə)ns/ *n* emission of light (eg when sugar crystals are crushed) due to friction [ISV] – **triboluminescent** *adj*

**tribophysics** /,trieboh'fiziks/ *n taking sing or pl vb* the physics of friction

**tribrach** /'triebrak, 'tribrak/ *n* a unit of poetic metre (FOOT) consisting of three short syllables [L *tribrachys*, fr Gk, having three short syllables, fr *tri-* + *brachys* short – more at BRIEF] – **tribrachic** *adj*

**tribromide** /'triebroh,mied/ *n* a compound of a chemical element or group with three atoms of bromine

**tribulation** /ˌtribyoo'laysh(ə)n/ *n* distress or suffering resulting from oppression or persecution; *also* a trying or distressing experience [ME *tribulacion*, fr OF, fr LL *tribulation-, tribulatio*, fr L *tribulatus*, pp of *tribulare* to press, oppress, fr *tribulum* board used in threshing, fr *terere* to rub]

**tribunal** /trie'byoohnl/ *n* 1 a court or forum of justice; *specif* a board appointed to decide disputes of a specified kind ⟨*rent* ∼⟩ 2 something that judges or determines ⟨*the* ∼ *of public opinion*⟩ 3 *archaic* the seat of (one acting as) a judge [L, platform for magistrates, fr *tribunus* tribune]

**¹tribune** /'tribyoohn/ *n* 1 an official of ancient Rome elected by and from the common people to protect them from arbitrary action by the magistrates 2 an unofficial defender of the rights of the individual [ME, fr L *tribunus*, fr *tribus* tribe] – **tribuneship** *n*, **tribunate** *n*

**²tribune** *n* a dais or platform from which a meeting or assembly is addressed [Fr, fr It *tribuna*, fr L *tribunal*]

**Tribune group** *n* the group of left-wing Labour Members of Parliament

**Tribunite** /'tribyoohniet/ *n* a member or supporter of the TRIBUNE GROUP

**¹tributary** /'tribyoot(ə)ri/ *adj* 1 paying tribute to another to acknowledge submission, to obtain protection, or to purchase peace; subject 2 paid or owed as tribute 3 providing with material or supplies; contributory

**²tributary** *n* 1 a ruler or state that pays tribute to a conqueror 2 a stream feeding a larger stream or a lake

**tribute** /'tribyooht/ *n* 1a a payment by one ruler or nation to another in acknowledgment of submission or as the price of protection; *also* the tax levied for such a payment b an exorbitant charge levied by a person or group having the power of coercion 2a something (eg a gift or formal declaration) given or spoken as a testimonial of respect, gratitude, or affection ⟨*a floral* ∼⟩ ⟨*paying* ∼ *to his secretary for her help*⟩ b evidence of the worth or effectiveness of something specified – chiefly in *a tribute to* ⟨*the vote was a* ∼ *to their good sense*⟩ [ME *tribut*, fr L *tributum*, fr neut of *tributus*, pp of *tribuere* to allot, bestow, grant, pay, fr *tribus* tribe]

**tricarboxylic** /ˌtrie,kahbok'silik/ *adj*, *of a chemical compound* containing three CARBOXYL groups in the molecular structure

**tricarboxylic acid cycle** *n* KREBS CYCLE (energy-producing process in the tissues of living organisms)

**tricarpellate** /trie'kahpəlayt, -lət/, **tricarpellary** /-l(ə)ri/ *adj*, *botany* having or made up of three usu fused CARPELS (female reproductive organs in FLOWERING PLANTS)

**¹trice** /tries/ *vt* to haul up or in and lash or secure (eg a sail) – usu + *up* [ME *trisen, tricen* to pull, trice, fr MD *trisen* to hoist]

**²trice** *n* a brief space of time; an instant – chiefly in *in a trice* [ME *trise*, lit., pull, fr *trisen*]

**Tricel** /'triesel/ *trademark* – used for a silky crease-resistant man-made fibre

**triceps** /'trie,seps/ *n, pl* **tricepses** /-seez/ *also* **triceps** a muscle with three points of attachment; *esp* the large muscle along the back of the upper arm that acts to straighten the arm at the elbow [NL *tricipit-, triceps*, fr L, three-headed, fr *tri-* + *capit-, caput* head – more at HEAD]

**triceratops** /trie'serə,tops/ *n* any of a genus (*Triceratops*) of large plant-eating dinosaurs of the CRETACEOUS period, with three horns, a bony hood or crest on the neck, and hoofed toes [NL, genus name, fr *tri-* + *cerat-* + Gk *ōps* face – more at EYE]

**-trices** /-triseez/ *pl of* -TRIX

**trich-** /trik-/, **tricho-** *comb form* hair; filament ⟨trich*iasis*⟩ [NL, fr Gk, fr *trich-, thrix* hair; akin to MIr gairb*driuch* bristle]

**trichiasis** /tri'kie-əsis/ *n* a growing inwards of the hair round an opening; *esp* an ingrowing of the eyelashes which leads to irritation of the membrane (CONJUNCTIVA) lining the inner surface of the eyelid and covering the eyeball [LL, fr Gk, fr *trich-* + *-iasis*]

**trichina** /tri'kienə/ *n, pl* **trichinae** /-nie/ *also* **trichinas** 1 a small slender NEMATODE worm (*Trichinella spiralis*) whose larvae live as parasites in the muscles of flesh-eating mammals (eg human beings and pigs) 2 trichinosis [NL, fr Gk *trichinos* of hair, fr *trich-, thrix* hair] – **trichinal** *adj*

**trichin·ized, -ised** /'trikəniezd/ *adj* infested with trichinae ⟨∼ *pork*⟩

**trichinosis** /ˌtrikə'nohsis/ *n* infestation with or disease caused by trichinae and marked esp by muscular pain, fever, and OEDEMA (swelling of tissues) [NL]

**trichinous** /'trikinəs, tri'kienəs/ *adj* 1 infested with trichinae ⟨∼ *meat*⟩ 2 of or involving trichinae or trichinosis ⟨∼ *infection*⟩ [ISV]

**trichite** /'trikiet/ *n* a minute needlelike crystal or structure in a plant or animal [Ger *trichit*, fr Gk *trich-, thrix* hair]

**trichlorfon** /trie'klawfon/ *n* a chemical compound, $C_4H_8Cl_3O_4P$, that is used to kill insects and parasitic worms [*tri-* + *chlor-* + *-fon* (irreg fr *phosphonate*, a salt derived from phosphine)]

**trichloride** /ˌtrie'klawried/ *n* a compound of a chemical element or group with three atoms of chlorine [ISV]

**trichloroacetic acid** /trie,klawroh-ə'seetik, -ə'setik/ *n* a corrosive pungent-smelling acid, $CCl_3COOH$, that is used esp in biochemical investigations to precipitate protein and in medicine as a caustic and astringent [ISV]

**trichocyst** /'trikə,sist/ *n* any of the minute lassoing or stinging organs on the body of PROTOZOANS (single-celled animals), esp many CILIATES, that consist of a small sac containing a long thin thread that can be ejected – **trichocystic** *adj*

**trichoid** /'trikoyd/ *adj* resembling a hair; capillary [Gk *trichoeidēs*, fr *trich-, thrix* hair]

**trichology** /tri'koləji/ *n* the study and treatment of disorders of hair growth, specif baldness [ISV *trich-* + *-logy*] – **trichologist** *n*

**trichome** /'trie,kohm, 'tri-/ *n* a threadlike outgrowth; *esp* hair structure on the surface tissue of a plant [Ger *trichom*, fr Gk *trichōma* growth of hair, fr *trichoun* to cover with hair, fr *trich-, thrix* hair] – **trichomic** *adj*

**trichomonad** /ˌtrikə'mohnad/ *n* any of a genus (*Trichomonas*) of single-celled animals (PROTOZOANS) that have FLAGELLA (whiplike appendages) with which they move and are parasitic, chiefly in the reproductive and urinary tracts of many animals, including humans [NL *Trichomonad-, Trichomonas*, genus name, fr *trich-* + LL *monad, monas* monad] – **trichomonad, trichomonadal, trichomonal** *adj*

**trichomoniasis** /ˌtrikəmə'nie-əsis/ *n, pl* **trichomoniases** /-seez/ infection with or disease caused by trichomonads: eg a a usu sexually transmitted infection of the human genital tract, esp the vagina and male urethra, characterized by a persistent discharge and caused by a trichomonad (*Trichomonas vaginalis*) b a VENEREAL DISEASE of domestic cattle, marked by abortion and sterility c any of several intestinal diseases of various birds (eg turkeys and pigeons) [NL, fr *Trichomonas* + *-iasis*]

**trichopteran** /tri'koptərən/ *n* any of an order (Trichoptera) of insects consisting of the CADDIS FLIES [deriv of Gk *trich-, thrix* hair + *pteron* wing – more at FEATHER] – **trichopteran** *adj*

**trichotomy** /tri'kotəmi/ *n* division into three parts, elements, or classes [deriv of Gk *trichotomein* to cut into three parts, fr *tricha* threefold + *temnein* to cut] – **trichotomous** *adj*

**-trichous** /-trikəs/ *comb form* (→ *adj*) having (such) hair ⟨*peritrichous*⟩ [Gk *-trichos*, fr *trich-, thrix* hair – more at TRICH-]

**trichromatic** /ˌtriekroh'matik/ *adj* 1 (consisting) of three colours ⟨∼ *light*⟩ 2a of or being the theory that human colour vision involves three types of sensory receptors in the retina of the eye b characterized by trichromatism ⟨∼ *vision*⟩ [*tri-* + *chromatic*]

**trichromatism** /ˌtrie'krohmə,tiz(ə)m/ *n* 1 the quality or state of being trichromatic; the use of three colours (eg in photography) 2 vision in which all the PRIMARY COLOURS are perceived, though not necessarily with equal ease

**trichuriasis** /ˌtrikyoo'rie-əsis/ *n, pl* **trichuriases** /-seez/ infestation with or disease caused by WHIPWORMS (genus *Trichuris*) [NL, fr *Trichuris*, genus of worms, fr *trich-* + Gk *oura* tail]

**¹trick** /trik/ *n* 1a a crafty practice or stratagem meant to deceive or defraud b a mischievous act; a prank ⟨*played a harmless* ∼ *on me*⟩ c a deceptive, dexterous, or ingenious feat designed to puzzle or amuse ⟨*a conjuring* ∼⟩ ⟨*a dog that does* ∼s⟩ 2a a habitual peculiarity of behaviour or manner; a mannerism ⟨*had a* ∼ *of stammering slightly*⟩ b a deceptive appearance, esp when caused by art or sleight of hand; OPTICAL ILLUSION ⟨*a mere* ∼ *of the light*⟩ 3a a quick or effective way of getting a result; a knack b a technical device or contrivance (eg of an art or craft) ⟨*the* ∼s *of stage technique*⟩ ⟨∼s *of the trade*⟩ 4 the cards played in one round of a card game, often used as a scoring unit 5 a turn of duty at the helm of a ship 6 *NAm slang* a professional engagement of a prostitute; *also* a prostitute's client [ME *trik*, fr ONF *trique*, fr *trikier* to deceive, cheat, alter. of OF *trichier* (cf TREACHERY)] – **do the trick** to produce the desired result ⟨*another coat of paint should* do the *trick*⟩ – **how's tricks?** *informal* how are you?

**²trick** *adj* **1a** of or involving tricks or trickery ⟨~ *photography*⟩ ⟨*a* ~ *question*⟩ **b** skilled in or using tricks ⟨*a* ~ *cyclist*⟩ **c** being an imitation intended for humorous deception ⟨*a* ~ *spider*⟩ **2** *NAm* injured or crippled; **⁴GAME** ⟨*a* ~ *knee*⟩ **3** *archaic or dial* TRIG

**³trick** *vt* **1** to deceive by cunning or artifice; cheat – often + *into* or *out of* **2** to dress or embellish fancifully or showily; ornament – usu + *out* or *up* ⟨~ed *out in a gaudy uniform*⟩ – **tricker** *n*

**trick cyclist** *n, Br humorous* a psychiatrist [quasi-anagram]

**trickery** /'trikəri/ *n* the use of crafty underhand ingenuity to deceive or cheat

**¹trickle** /'trikl/ *vi* **1a** to flow or fall in drops ⟨*tears* ~d *down her cheeks*⟩ **b** to flow in a thin slow stream ⟨*water* trickling *down the walls*⟩ **2a** to move or go one by one or gradually ⟨*the audience* ~d *out of the hall*⟩ **b** to dissipate slowly ⟨*time* ~s *away*⟩ [ME *triklen*]

**²trickle** *n* a thin slow stream or movement

**trickle charger** *n* an apparatus for charging a rechargeable battery (ACCUMULATOR) at a steady slow rate

**trick or treat** *n* a children's Halloween custom of asking for treats (eg confectionery) from door to door under threat of playing tricks on householders who refuse – **trick-or-treat** *vi*

**trickster** /'trikstə/ *n* one who tricks: eg **a** a dishonest person who defrauds others by trickery **b** a person (eg a stage magician) skilled in the performance of tricks

**tricksy** /'triksi/ *adj* **1** full of tricks; mischievous, playful **2** difficult to follow or make out; intricate, complicated; *also* excessively elaborate **3** ostentatiously new and ingenious; gimmicky **4** *archaic* smartly attired; spruce **5** *archaic* having the craftiness of a trickster [*tricks* (pl of *trick*) + ¹-*y*] – **tricksiness** *n*

**tricktrack** /'trik,trak/ *n* TRICTRAC (form of backgammon)

**tricky** /'triki/ *adj* **1** inclined to or marked by trickery; sly **2** containing hidden or not easily recognized difficulties or hazards; ticklish ⟨*a* ~ *path through the swamp*⟩ **3** requiring skill, adroitness, or caution (eg in doing or handling) ⟨~ *gadgets*⟩; *also* ingenious ⟨*a* ~ *rhythm*⟩ **synonyms** see SLY – **trickily** *adv*, **trickiness** *n*

**triclad** /'trieklad/ *n* any of an order (Tricladida) of TURBELLARIAN flatworms (eg a PLANARIAN) that have the intestine divided into three main branches [NL *Tricladida*, group name, fr *tri-* + Gk *klados* branch – more at GLADIATOR] – **triclad** *adj*

**triclinic** /trie'klinik/ *adj, esp of a crystal* having three unequal axes intersecting at oblique angles [ISV *tri-* + -*clinic*]

**triclinium** /trie'klini·əm/ *n, pl* **triclinia** /-niə/ **1** a couch used by ancient Romans for reclining at meals, extending round three sides of a table, and usu divided into three parts **2** a dining room furnished with a triclinium [L, fr Gk *triklinion*, fr *tri-* + *klinein* to lean, recline – more at LEAN]

**tricolette** /,trikə'let/ *n* a usu silk or rayon knitted fabric used esp for women's clothing [*tricot* + -*lette* (as in *flannelette*)]

**¹tricolour** /'trie,kulə, 'trikələ/ *n* a flag of three colours ⟨*the French* ~⟩ [Fr *tricolore*, fr *tricolore* three-coloured, fr LL *tricolor*, fr L *tri-* + *color* colour]

**²tricolour** /'trie,kulə/ *adj* **1a** tricolour, tricoloured having or using three colours **b** *of a dog* having a coat of black, tan, and white **2** (characteristic) of a tricolour or a nation whose flag is a tricolour; *esp* French [Fr *tricolore*]

**tricorn** /'trie,kawn/ *adj* having three horns or corners [L *tricornis*]

**tricorne, tricorn** /'trie,kawn/ *n* COCKED HAT 1 [Fr *tricorne*, fr *tricorne* three-cornered, fr L *tricornis*, fr *tri-* + *cornu* horn – more at HORN]

**tricornered** /'tri,kawnəd/ *adj* having three corners

**tricot** /'trikoh (Fr triko)/ *n* **1** a plain knitted fabric of nylon, wool, rayon, silk, or cotton that has a close inelastic knit and is used esp in clothing (eg underwear) **2** a fine-ribbed clothing fabric of wool or wool and cotton [Fr, fr *tricoter* to knit]

**tricotine** /,trikə'teen, tree-/ *n* a sturdy fabric woven of tightly twisted yarns in a double twill [Fr, fr *tricot*]

**trictrac** *also* **tricktrack** /'trik,trak/ *n* an old form of backgammon played with pegs [Fr, of imit origin; fr the sound made by the pegs]

**tricuspid** /trie'kuspid/ *adj* having three cusps ⟨*a* ~ *molar*⟩ [L *tricuspid-, tricuspis*, fr *tri-* + *cuspid-, cuspis* point] – **tricuspid** *n*

**tricuspid valve** *n* RIGHT ATRIOVENTRICULAR VALVE (valve preventing backflow of blood in the heart)

**¹tricycle** /'triesikl/ *n* **1** a 3-wheeled pedal-driven vehicle **2** a 3-wheeled motor-driven light vehicle for a disabled driver [Fr (orig a 3-wheeled horse-drawn coach), fr *tri-* + Gk *kyklos* wheel – more at WHEEL]

**²tricycle** *vi* to ride or drive a tricycle – **tricyclist** *n*

**tricyclic** /trie'sieklik/ *adj, of a chemical compound* having a molecular structure containing three usu fused rings; *specif* belonging to a series of synthetic widely used chemically related drugs used to treat depression (eg IMIPRAMINE and AMITRIPTYLINE) [*tri-* + *cyclic*] – **tricyclic** *n*

**¹trident** /'tried(ə)nt/ *n* **1** a 3-pronged spear serving in classical mythology as the attribute of a sea god **2** a 3-pronged spear used by ancient Roman gladiators **3** a 3-pronged fish spear [L *trident-, tridens*, fr *trident-, tridens* having three teeth, fr *tri-* + *dent-, dens* tooth – more at TOOTH]

**²trident** *adj* having three prongs or points [L *trident-, tridens*]

**Tridentine** /tri'dentien/ *adj* of a Roman Catholic council held in Trento from 1545 to 1563; *esp* promulgated by or based on the deliberations of this council ⟨*the* ~ *mass*⟩ [NL *Tridentinus*, fr L *Tridentum* Trento (Trent), town in NE Italy]

**tridimensional** /,triedi'menshənl/ *adj* of or concerned with three dimensions ⟨~ *space*⟩ [ISV] – **tridimensionality** *n*

**triduum** /'tridyooəm, 'trie-/ *n* a period of three days of prayer, usu preceding a Roman Catholic festival [L, period of three days, fr *tri-* + -*duum* (akin to *dies* day) – more at DEITY]

**tried** /tried/ *adj* **1** found to be good, faithful, or trustworthy through experience or testing ⟨*a* ~ *recipe*⟩ **2** subjected to trials or severe provocation – often in combination ⟨*a sorely*-tried *father*⟩ [ME, fr pp of *trien* to try, test]

**triennial** /trie'enyəl, -ni·əl/ *adj* **1** consisting of or lasting for three years **2** occurring every three years – **triennial** *n*, **triennially** *adv*

**triennium** /trie'enyəm, -ni·əm/ *n, pl* **trienniums, triennia** /-niə/ a period of three years [L, fr *tri-* + *annus* year – more at ANNUAL]

**trier** /'trie·ə/ *n* **1** somebody who tries, makes an effort, or perseveres **2** an implement (eg a tapered hollow tube) used in obtaining samples of bulk material, esp foodstuffs, for examination and testing

**trierarch** /'trie·ərahk/ *n* **1** the commander of a TRIREME (ancient warship) **2** a citizen of ancient Athens who was required jointly or individually to fit out a TRIREME for the public service [L *trierarchus*, fr Gk *triērarchos*, fr *triērēs* trireme (fr *tri-* + -*ērēs* – akin to L *rēmus* oar) + -*archos* -arch – more at ROW]

**trierarchy** /'trie·ərahki/ *n* the ancient Athenian system whereby individual citizens jointly or individually furnished and maintained TRIREMES (warships) as part of their civic duty

**triethyl** /trie'eethil/ *adj, of a chemical compound* containing three ETHYL groups in the molecule [ISV]

**triffid** /'trifid/ *n* **1** any of a race of large fictional plants capable of locomotion and of attacking humans **2** *informal* a plant resembling a triffid in size, rapid growth, or fearsome appearance [*The Day of the Triffids*, novel by John Wyndham †1969 E writer]

**trifid** /'triefid/ *adj* deeply and narrowly cleft into three teeth, parts, or points ⟨*a* ~ *petal*⟩ [L *trifidus* split into three, fr *tri-* + *findere* to split – more at BITE]

**¹trifle** /'triefl/ *n* **1** something of little value or importance; *esp* an insignificant amount (eg of money) **2** a pewter of moderate hardness, used esp for small utensils **3** *chiefly Br* a dessert typically consisting of sponge cake spread with jam or jelly, sprinkled with crumbled macaroons, soaked in wine (eg sherry), and topped with custard and whipped cream [ME *trufle, trifle*, fr OF *trufe, trufle* mockery] – **a trifle** to some small degree; slightly ⟨a trifle *annoyed at the delay*⟩

**²trifle** *vi* **1a** to talk in a jesting or mocking manner or with intent to delude or mislead ⟨*I fear he did but* ~ *and meant to wreck thee* – Shak⟩ **b** to act heedlessly or frivolously; play – often + *with* ⟨*not a man to be* ~d *with*⟩ **2** to handle something idly; toy ~ *vt* to spend or waste in trifling or on trifles ⟨trifling *his time away*⟩ [ME *truflen, triflen*, fr OF *trufer, trufler* to mock, trick] – **trifler** *n*

**trifling** /'triefling/ *adj* lacking in significance or solid worth: eg **a** frivolous ⟨~ *talk*⟩ **b** trivial, insignificant ⟨*a* ~ *gift*⟩

**trifluralin** /trie'flooərəlin/ *n* a substance, $C_{13}H_{16}F_3N_3O_4$, used to kill weeds [*tri-* + *fluor-* + *aniline*]

**¹trifocal** /trie'fohkl/ *adj* having three FOCAL LENGTHS

**²trifocal** *n* **1** a trifocal glass or lens **2** *pl* glasses having lenses with three parts to correct for near, middle-distance, and distant vision

**trifoliate** /trie'fohli·ət, -ayt/ *adj* **1** having leaves with three leaflets ⟨*a* ~ *plant*⟩ **2** *of a leaf* having three leaflets

**trifoliate orange** *n* a hardy Chinese orange tree (*Poncirus trifoliata*) with trifoliate leaves and inedible fruit that is grown for ornament and esp as a stock for budding other oranges

**trifoliolate** /trie'fohliə‚layt/ *adj* TRIFOLIATE 2 [ISV]

**trifolium** /trie'fohliəm/ *n* any of a genus (*Trifolium*) of plants of the pea family that includes WHITE CLOVER and RED CLOVER [NL, genus name, fr L, trefoil – more at TREFOIL]

**triforium** /‚trie'fawri·əm/ *n, pl* **triforia** /-riə/ a gallery forming an upper storey to the aisle of a church and typically an arcaded storey above the arches of the NAVE (central part) and below the CLERESTORY [ML]

**triform** /'trie‚fawm/ *adj* having a triple form or nature [L *triformis*, fr *tri-* + *forma* form]

**trifurcate** /'triefuhkət, -kayt/ *adj* having three branches or forks [L *trifurcus*, fr *tri-* + *furca* fork] – **trifurcate** *vi*, **trifurcation** *n*

**¹trig** /trig/ *adj, archaic or dial* **1** stylishly or jauntily trim **2** *chiefly Br* firm, vigorous [ME, trusty, nimble, of Scand origin; akin to ON *tryggr* faithful; akin to OE *trēowe* faithful – more at TRUE]

**²trig** *vt* **-gg-** *dial chiefly Br* to put in order; tidy – usu + *up*

**³trig** *vt* **-gg-** *chiefly dial* to restrain from moving or shifting: eg **a** to stop or slow the motion of (a wheel), usu with a block **b** to support with props or wedges [perh of Scand origin; akin to ON *tryggja* to make firm, *tryggr* faithful]

**⁴trig** *n, chiefly dial* a stone or block used as a support in trigging

**⁵trig** *n, informal* TRIGONOMETRY (study of triangles)

**trigeminal** /,trie'jeminl/ *adj or n* (of) the TRIGEMINAL NERVE [NL *trigeminus* trigeminal nerve, fr L, threefold, fr *tri-* + *geminus* twin; fr its dividing into three branches]

**trigeminal nerve** *n* either of the 5th pair of CRANIAL NERVES that pass from the lower surface of the brain through the skull to supply the muscles of the jaws and the skin of the face and scalp

**trigeminal neuralgia** *n* intense spasms of pain involving one or more branches of the TRIGEMINAL NERVE – called also TIC DOULOUREUX

**¹trigger** /'trigə/ *n* **1** a piece (eg a lever) that can be moved to release a catch or spring; *esp* the tongue of metal in a firearm which when pressed releases the mechanism and fires the gun **2a** a stimulus that initiates a physiological or pathological process ⟨*the sight or smell of food may be a* ~ *for salivation*⟩ **b** a stimulus that initiates a reaction or signal in an electronic apparatus [alter. of earlier *tricker*, fr D *trekker*, fr MD *trecker* something that pulls, fr *trecken* to pull – more at TREK] – **trigger** *adj*, **triggered** *adj*

**²trigger** *vt* **1a** to release or activate by means of a trigger; *esp* to fire by pulling a mechanical trigger ⟨~ *a rifle*⟩ **b** to cause the explosion of ⟨~ *a missile with a proximity fuse*⟩ **2** to initiate, bring about, or set off as if by pulling a trigger – often + *off* ⟨*an indiscreet remark that* ~ed *off a fight*⟩ ~ *vi* to release a mechanical trigger

**triggerfish** /'trigə‚fish/ *n* any of numerous deep-bodied BONY FISHES (*Balistes* and related genera) of warm seas that have two or three stout erectile spines on the first fin on the back

**'trigger-‚happy** *adj* **1** irresponsible in the use of firearms; *esp* inclined to shoot before clearly identifying the target or when it is out of range **2a** inclined to be irresponsible in matters that might precipitate war; *broadly* aggressively belligerent **b** too prompt in one's response

**triglyceride** /trie'glisəried/ *n* an ESTER (chemical compound) that is formed by the combination of one molecule of the alcohol GLYCEROL and three organic acid molecules [ISV]

**triglyph** /'trie‚glif/ *n* a projecting rectangular tablet with three vertical grooves, used on an ornamental band (FRIEZE) in DORIC architecture – compare METOPE [L *triglyphus*, fr Gk *triglyphos*, fr *tri-* + *glyphein* to carve – more at CLEAVE] – **triglyphic, triglyphical** *adj*

**trigon** /'triegon/ *n* **1** TRIANGLE 1 **2** TRINE 2 (astrological position of two planets 120° apart) **3** an ancient triangular harp [L *trigonum*, fr Gk *trigōnon*, fr neut of *trigōnos* triangular, fr *tri-* + *gōnia* angle – more at -GON]

**trigonal** /'trigənl/ *adj* **1** triangular **2** of or being the division of the HEXAGONAL crystal system, or the forms belonging to it, characterized by a vertical axis of threefold symmetry – **trigonally** *adv*

**trigonometric function** /‚trigənə'metrik/ *n* **1** a function (specif the SINE, COSINE, TANGENT, COTANGENT, SECANT, or COSECANT) of an arc or angle most simply expressed in terms of the ratios of pairs of sides of a right-angled triangle **2** the inverse (eg the arc sine) of a trigonometric function

**trigonometry** /‚trigə'nomətri/ *n* the study of the properties of triangles and TRIGONOMETRIC FUNCTIONS and of their applications [NL *trigonometria*, fr Gk *trigōnon* triangle + *-metria* -metry] – **trigonometric** *also* **trigonometrical** *adj*, **trigonometrically** *adv*

**trigonous** /'trigənəs/ *adj* triangular in cross section ⟨*a* ~ *seed*⟩ [L *trigonus* triangular, fr Gk *trigōnos*]

**trigraph** /'trie‚grahf, -‚graf/ *n* **1** three letters spelling a single speech sound (eg *eau* in *beau*) **2** a cluster of three successive letters ⟨*the letters* are a high frequency ~ ⟩ – **trigraphic** *adj*

**trihedral** /trie'heedrəl/ *adj* **1** having three faces ⟨~ *angle*⟩ **2** of a trihedral angle – **trihedral** *n*

**trihybrid** /trie'hiebrid/ *n* an individual organism or strain of organisms that is HETEROZYGOUS (having two different versions of one gene) for three different genetic characteristics

**trihydroxy** /triehie'droksi/ *adj, of a chemical compound* containing three HYDROXYL groups in the molecule [ISV *tri-* + *hydroxyl*]

**triiodothyronine** /trie·ie‚ohdoh'thierəneen/ *n* an iodine-containing AMINO ACID, $C_{15}H_{12}I_3NO_4$, that is the principal hormone secreted by the THYROID GLAND, is formed naturally from THYROXINE by loss of one iodine atom per molecule, and is used esp in the treatment of conditions in which the thyroid gland produces insufficient quantities of hormones [*tri-* + *iod-* + *thyronine* (an amino acid from which thyroxine is derived)]

**trijet** /'triejet/ *adj* powered by three jet engines ⟨*a* ~ *aircraft*⟩ – **trijet** *n*

**trike** /triek/ *n, informal* a tricycle [by shortening & alter.]

**trilateral** /‚trie'lat(ə)rəl/ *adj* having three sides ⟨*a triangle is* ~⟩ [L *trilaterus*, fr *tri-* + *later-, latus* side] – **trilaterally** *adv*, **trilaterality** *n*

**trilby** /'trilbi/, **trilby hat** *n, chiefly Br* a soft felt hat with an indented crown [fr such a hat having been worn in the original stage version of *Trilby*, novel by George Du Maurier †1896 E artist & writer]

**trilinear** /‚trie'lini·ə/ *adj* of or involving three lines

**trilingual** /‚trie'ling·gwəl/ *adj* of, containing, or expressed in three languages; *also* using or able to use three languages, esp with the fluency of a native speaker – **trilingually** *adv*

**¹triliteral** /‚trie'lit(ə)rəl/ *adj* consisting of three letters, esp three consonants ⟨~ *roots in Semitic languages*⟩ [*tri-* + L *litera* letter] – **triliteralism** *n*

**²triliteral** *n* a triliteral root or word

**trilithon** /trie'lithon, '---/ *n* an ancient stone structure consisting of two large upright stones with a third resting across the top, as seen in the central feature of Stonehenge [NL, fr Gk, neut of *trilithos* of three stones, fr *tri-* + *lithos* stone]

**¹trill** /tril/ *vb, archaic or dial vi* **1** to twirl, revolve **2** to flow in a small stream or in drops; trickle ~ *vt* to cause (eg a liquid) to trill [ME *trillen*, prob of Scand origin; akin to Sw *trilla* to roll; akin to MD *trillen* to vibrate]

**²trill** *n* **1a** the rapid alternation of two musical notes that are two semitones apart – called also SHAKE **b** a rapid repetition of the same note, esp on a percussion instrument **2** a sound resembling a musical trill; a warble **3a** the rapid vibration of one speech organ against another (eg of the tip of the tongue against the ridge of flesh behind the front teeth, or of the fleshy fingerlike projection at the back of the mouth against the back of the tongue) **b** a speech sound, esp a consonant, made by a trill [It *trillo*, fr *trillare* to trill, prob fr D *trillen* to vibrate; akin to MD *trappe* step, trap]

**³trill** *vt* to utter as or with a trill ⟨~ *the* r⟩ ~ *vi* to play or sing with a trill; quaver – **triller** *n*

**trillion** /'trilyən/ *n* **1a** *Br* a million million millions ($10^{18}$) **b** *chiefly NAm* a million millions ($10^{12}$) **2** trillion, trillions *pl, informal* an indefinitely large number; a zillion ☐ (1) see NUMBER table [Fr, fr *tri-* + *-illion* (as in *million*)] – **trillion** *adj*, **trillionth** *adj or n*

**trilobed** /'trielohbd/, **trilobate**, /trie'lohbayt, '---/ *adj* having three lobes ⟨*a* ~ *leaf*⟩ – **trilobation** *n*

**trilobite** /'trielə‚biet/ *n* any of a group (Trilobita of the phylum Arthropoda) of extinct marine INVERTEBRATE animals of the PALAEOZOIC era that had the segments of the body divided into three lobes by furrows on the back [deriv of Gk *trilobos* three-lobed, fr *tri-* + *lobos* lobe]

**trilocular** /trie'lokyoolǝ/ *adj* having three cells or cavities ⟨*plants with* ~ *ovaries*⟩ [ISV]

**trilogy** /'trilǝji/ *n* **1** a group of three closely related literary or sometimes musical works **2** a group of three related things, topics, or sayings; a triad □ compare TRIO [Gk *trilogia* group of three related tragedies, fr *tri-* + *-logia* -logy]

¹**trim** /trim/ *vb* **-mm-** *vt* **1** to embellish (eg clothes) with ribbons, lace, or ornaments; adorn **2a** to make trim and neat, esp by cutting or clipping ⟨~ *a hedge*⟩ **b** to free of excess or superfluous matter (as if) by cutting ⟨~ *a tree*⟩ ⟨~ *a budget*⟩ **c** to remove (as if) by cutting ⟨~ med *thousands from the running costs of the department*⟩ **3a(1)** to adjust the balance and position in the water of (eg a ship) by arrangement of ballast, cargo, or passengers **a(2)** to adjust (eg an aircraft or submarine) for horizontal movement or for motion upwards or downwards **b** to adjust (eg cargo or a sail) to a desired position **4** *informal* **4a** to defeat resoundingly, esp at a gambling game **b** to cheat, swindle **5** *informal* to administer a beating to; thrash – no longer in vogue ~ *vi* **1a** to maintain a neutral attitude towards opposing parties or to favour each equally **b** to change one's views or position for reasons of expediency **2** to assume or cause a boat to assume a desired position in the water ⟨*a boat that* ~s *badly*⟩ [(assumed) ME *trimmen* to prepare, put in order, fr OE *trymian, trymman* to strengthen, arrange, fr *trum* strong, firm; akin to Skt *dāru* wood – more at TREE]

²**trim** *adj* **-mm-** **1** appearing neat or in good order; compact or clean-cut in outline or structure ⟨~ *houses*⟩ ⟨*a* ~ *figure*⟩ **2** *archaic* suitably adjusted, equipped, or prepared for service or use *synonyms* see ²NEAT *antonyms* tousled, unkempt – **trimly** *adv*, **trimness** *n*

³**trim** *n* **1** the readiness or fitness of a person or thing for action or use; *esp* physical fitness ⟨*at fifty he's still in* ~⟩ **2a** one's clothing or appearance **b** material used for decoration or trimming **c** the visible woodwork in the finish of a building, esp round openings **d** the decorative accessories of a motor vehicle **3a** the position of a ship or boat, esp with reference to the horizontal; *also* the difference between the depth in water of a vessel at the front and that at the back **b** the relation between the plane of a sail and the direction of the vessel **c** the inclination of an aircraft or spacecraft in flight with reference to a fixed point (eg the horizon), esp with the controls in some neutral position **4** something that is trimmed off or cut out **5** an act of trimming (eg by cutting or clipping) **6** *chiefly NAm* WINDOW DRESSING

**trimaran** /'triemǝˌran/ *n* a sailing vessel used for cruising or racing that has three hulls side by side [*tri-* + *-maran* (as in *catamaran*)]

**trimer** /'triemǝ/ *n* a large chemical molecule composed of three small identical molecules [ISV *tri-* + *-mer* (as in *polymer*)] – **trimeric** *adj*

**trimerous** /'trimǝrǝs/ *adj, of a flower* having the parts in threes – often written *3-merous* [NL *trimerus,* fr Gk *tri-* + *meros* part – more at MERIT]

**trimester** /tri'mestǝ, trie-/ *n* a period of (about) three months; *specif* any of the three periods of about three months into which human pregnancy may be divided ⟨*an abortion in the first* ~⟩ [Fr *trimestre,* fr L *trimestris* of three months, fr *tri-* + *mensis* month – more at MOON] – **trimestral** *also* **trimestrial** *adj*

**trimeter** /'trimitǝ/ *n* a line of verse consisting either of three measures of two units of metre (FEET), or of three metrical feet ⟨*the hymn opens with two* ~s: *Teach me, my God and King, In all things Thee to see*⟩ [L *trimetrus,* fr Gk *trimetros* having three measures, fr *tri-* + *metron* measure – more at MEASURE]

**trimethoprim** /trie'methǝprim/ *n* a synthetic drug, $C_{14}H_{18}N_4O_3$, used in the treatment of bacterial infections and malaria and esp as a component of the drug CO-TRIMOXAZOLE that is used to treat respiratory and urinary infections [*tri-* + *meth-* + *pyrimidine*]

**trimmed joist** /trimd/ *n* a beam or rafter fastened into a wall at one end and supported by a trimmer at the other

**trimmer** /'trimǝ/ *n* **1a** one who or that which trims articles; *esp* one who stows coal or freight on a ship so as to distribute the weight properly **b** an instrument or machine for trimming **c** an element (eg a capacitor) in an electrical circuit used to tune the circuit to a desired frequency **2** a short beam or rafter fitted at one side of an opening to support the free ends of

floor joists or rafters **3** a person who modifies his/her policy, position, or opinions out of expediency

**trimming** /'triming/ *n* **1** *pl* pieces cut off in trimming something; scraps **2** *usu pl* **2a** a decorative accessory or additional item (eg on the border of a garment) that serves to finish or complete ⟨~s *for a hat*⟩ **b** an additional garnish or accompaniment to a main item ⟨*turkey and all the* ~s⟩ **3** the operation of framing an opening (eg for a stairwell or chimney) in a floor or ceiling

**trimming joist** *n* a full length transverse beam or rafter that forms one side of an opening and receives one end of a trimmer

**trimonthly** /trie'munthli/ *adj* occurring every three months

**trimorph** /'trieˌmawf/ *n* any of the three crystalline forms of a trimorphic substance [ISV, back-formation fr *trimorphous*]

**trimorphic** /trie'mawfik/, **trimorphous** /-fǝs/ *adj* occurring in or having three distinct forms [Gk *trimorphos* having three forms, fr *tri-* + *-morphos* -morphous] – **trimorphism** *n*

**trimotor** /'trieˌmohtǝ/ *n* an aeroplane powered by three engines

**trim size** *n* the actual size (eg of a book page) after excess material in production has been cut off

**Trimurti** /tri'mooǝti/ *n* the triad of Hindu gods comprising Brahma, Vishnu, and Siva [Skt *-trimūrti,* fr *trimūrti* having three forms, fr *tri-* + *mūrti* body, form]

**trinary** /'trienǝri/ *adj* TERNARY (of or based on 3) [LL *trinarius,* fr L *trini* three each]

¹**trindle** /'trindl/ *n, dial Eng* a circular object; *specif* the wheel of a wheelbarrow [ME *trindel,* fr OE *trendel, tryndel* circle, ring – more at TRUNDLE]

²**trindle** *vi, dial* to roll, trundle

¹**trine** /trien/ *adj* **1** triple, threefold **2** of or being an astrological trine [ME, fr MF *trin,* fr L *trinus,* back-formation fr *trini* three each; akin to L *tres* three – more at THREE]

²**trine** *n* **1** a group of three; a triad **2** the respective astrological position (ASPECT 1a) of two celestial bodies 120 degrees apart – **trinal** *adj*

**Trinitarian** /trini'teǝri-ǝn/ *n* **1** a member of a religious teaching and nursing order for men (the Order of the Holy Trinity) founded in France in 1198 by John of Matha and Philip of Valois **2** an adherent of the doctrine of the Trinity – **Trinitarian** *adj*, **Trinitarianism** *n*

**trinitrophenol** /ˌtrieˌnietroh'feenol/ *n* PICRIC ACID (toxic acid used in explosives) [ISV *tri-* + *nitr-* + *phenol*]

**trinitrotoluene** /ˌtrieˌnietroh'tolyooˌeen/ *n* an inflammable derivative, $C_6H_2(CH_3)(NO_2)_3$, of the chemical TOLUENE used as an explosive and in chemical synthesis – called also TNT [ISV *tri-* + *nitr-* + *toluene*]

**Trinity** /'trinǝti/ *n* **1** the unity of Father, Son, and HOLY SPIRIT as three persons in one Godhead according to Christian theology **2** *not cap* a group of three closely related people or things **3** the Sunday after Whitsunday observed as a festival in honour of the Trinity [ME *trinite,* fr OF *trinité,* fr LL *trinitat-, trinitas* state of being threefold, fr L *trinus* threefold]

**Trinity House** *n* a British organization that licenses maritime pilots and maintains navigational markers (eg buoys and lighthouses)

**Trinity term** *n* the university term beginning after Easter

**Trinitytide** /'trinǝtiˌtied/ *n* the season of the church year between Trinity Sunday and Advent

**trinket** /'tringkit/ *n* a small trifling article; *esp* an ornament or piece of (cheap) jewellery [perh fr ME *trenket* small knife, fr ONF *trenquet,* fr *trenquer* to cut] – **trinketry** *n*

**trinket set** *n* a matching set of china or glass ornaments for a dressing table, consisting of a tray with several small (lidded) containers for trinkets, hairpins, etc, and often a branched ring stand and a pair of candlesticks

¹**trinomial** /trie'nohmyǝl, -miǝl/ *n* **1** a POLYNOMIAL (mathematical expression) of three terms **2** a biological name for an organism consisting of three terms of which the first designates the genus, the second the species, and the third the subspecies or variety – compare BINOMIAL [*tri-* + *-nomial* (as in *binomial*)]

²**trinomial** *adj* consisting of three mathematical terms

**trinucleotide** /ˌtrie'nyoohkli-ǝˌtied/ *n* any of a class of compounds consisting of three chemically linked NUCLEOTIDES; CODON

**trio** /'tree-oh/ *n, pl* **trios** **1a** a musical composition for three players or singers **b** the middle section of a MINUET or SCHERZO movement (eg in a symphony), of a march, or of various dance forms **2** *taking sing or pl vb* the performers of a musical or dance trio **3** *taking sing or pl vb* a group or set of three [Fr, fr It, fr *tri-* (fr L)]

**triode** /'trie,ohd/ *n* a 3-electrode THERMIONIC VALVE having a cathode, an anode, and a control grid [*tri-* + *-ode*]

**triolet** /'trie·əlit, 'tree-/ *n* a poem or stanza of eight lines in which the first line is repeated as the fourth and seventh and the second line as the eighth, with a rhyme scheme of *ABaAabAB* [Fr, prob dim. of It *trio*]

**triose** /'trie·ohz, -ohs/ *n* either of two sugars, $C_3H_6O_3$, that will not break down into simpler sugars and that contain three carbon atoms [ISV *tri-* + *-ose*]

**trioxide** /trie'oksied/ *n* an OXIDE containing three atoms of oxygen [ISV]

**¹trip** /trip/ *vb* **-pp-** *vi* **1a** to dance, skip, or walk with light quick steps **b** to proceed smoothly, lightly, and easily; flow ⟨*words that ~ off the tongue*⟩ **2** to catch the foot against something so as to stumble **3** to make a mistake or false step (e g in morality or accuracy) **4** to stumble or falter in speaking **5** *of a tooth of the escapement wheel of a watch* to run past the locking lever (PALLET) of an escapement without previously locking **6** to become operative or activated, esp by the release of a catch **7** *informal* to make a journey **8** *slang* to get high on a psychedelic drug (e g LSD); TURN ON – often + *out ~ vt* **1a** to cause to stumble **b** to cause to fail **2** to detect in a fault or blunder; CATCH OUT – usu + *up* **3** to raise (an anchor) from the bottom so as to hang free **4a** to pull (the spar supporting a sail) into a perpendicular position for lowering **b** to hoist (a topmast) far enough to enable the supporting bar (FID) to be withdrawn preparatory to housing or lowering **5** to release or operate (a device or mechanism), esp by releasing a catch or producing an electrical signal **6** *archaic* to perform (e g a dance) lightly or nimbly – still used in the humorous phrase *trip the light fantastic* □ (*vi 2, 3, & 4; vt 2*) often + *up* [ME *trippen*, fr MF *triper*, of Gmc origin; akin to OE *treppan* to tread – more at TRAP]

**²trip** *n* **1a** a voyage, journey, or excursion **b** a single round or tour (e g on a business errand) **2** an error, mistake **3** a quick light step **4** a faltering step caused by stumbling **5** (the activating of) a catch or other device for tripping a mechanism **6** *slang* an intense visionary experience undergone by someone who has taken a psychedelic drug (e g LSD); *broadly* any highly charged emotional experience ⟨*his divorce was a really bad ~*⟩ **7** *slang* an obsessive, self-indulgent, self-serving, or absorbing course of action or frame of mind; a kick ⟨*on a nostalgia ~*⟩ ⟨*power ~s – Nation Review (Melbourne)*⟩ **8** *slang* a sphere of activity; a scene; *also* a life-style ⟨*gave up the whole super-star ~*⟩

**tripack** /'trie,pak/ *n* a combination of three superimposed films or emulsions, each sensitive to a different PRIMARY COLOUR, for simultaneous exposure in one camera [*tri-* + *pack*]

**tripartite** /trie'pahtiet/ *adj* **1** divided into or composed of three (corresponding) parts **2** made between or involving three parties ⟨*a ~ treaty*⟩ [ME, fr L *tripartitus*, fr *tri-* + *partitus* divided – more at PARTITE] – **tripartitely** *adv*, **tripartition** *n*

**tripartite system** *n* a division of secondary education into GRAMMAR SCHOOLS, TECHNICAL SCHOOLS, and SECONDARY MODERN schools

**tripe** /triep/ *n* **1** the stomach tissue of an ox, cow, etc for use as food **2** *informal* something inferior, worthless, or offensive; rubbish [ME, fr OF] – **tripey** *adj*

**'trip-,hammer** *n* a massive hammer raised by machinery and then released to drop on work below

**triphenylmethane** /trie,feeniel'meethayn, -'feniel-/ *n* a chemical compound, $CH(C_6H_5)_3$, from which many dyes are made [ISV]

**¹triphibian** /trie'fibiən/ *n* a triphibian aircraft [*tri-* + *-phibian* (as in *amphibian*)]

**²triphibian** *adj* **1** designed or equipped to operate from a solid surface (e g of land or ice) or from water as well as in the air; amphibian ⟨*a ~ aircraft*⟩ **2** triphibious ⟨*a ~ military operation*⟩

**triphibious** /trie'fibi·əs/ *adj* employing or involving land, naval, and air forces and often including airborne troops in coordinated attack ⟨*~ operations*⟩ [*tri-* + *-phibious* (as in *amphibious*)]

**triphosphate** /trie'fosfayt/ *n* a chemical compound (SALT or ESTER) containing three phosphate groups

**triphosphopyridine nucleotide** /trie,fosfoh'pirədeen/ *n* NADP (chemical substance involved in many metabolic processes in living organisms)

**triphthong** /'trifthong, 'trip-/ *n* **1** a gliding vowel sound (e g /ie·ə/ in *fire*) that is one syllable in length but composed of three elements **2** TRIGRAPH (three letters spelling one sound) [*tri-* + *-phthong* (as in *diphthong*)] – **triphthongal** *adj*

**tripinnate** /trie'pinayt/ *adj, of a compound leaf* having branches of PINNATE leaflets (being arranged in pairs, one on each side of a stalk) that branch pinnately from a stalk that is itself pinnately branched from the main stem of the leaf – **tripinnately** *adv*

**tripitaka** /tripi'tahkə/ *n, often cap* the collection of books written in the sacred language PALI that make up the THERA-VADA Buddhist scriptures [Pali *tripiṭaka*, lit., three baskets, fr *tri* three + *piṭaka* basket]

**triplane** /'trie,playn/ *n* an aeroplane with three main pairs of wings arranged one above the other

**¹triple** /'tripl/ *vb* to make or become three times as great or as many *synonyms* see ¹TREBLE [ME *triplen*, fr LL *triplare*, fr L *triplus*, adj]

**²triple** *n* **1** a triple sum, quantity, or number **2** a combination, group, or series of three [ME, fr L *triplus*, adj]

**³triple** *adj* **1** having three units or members **2** three times as great or as many **3** three times repeated; treble **4** marked by three beats per bar of music ⟨*~ metre*⟩ **5a** having units of three components ⟨*the lively metre of "Hickory dickory dock" which starts with two ~ feet*⟩ **b** *of rhyme* involving correspondence of three syllables (e g in *unfortunate-importunate*) [MF or L; MF, fr L *triplus*, fr *tri-* + *-plus* multiplied by – more at DOUBLE] – **triply** *adv*

**triple bond** *n* a chemical bond consisting of three shared pairs of electrons between two atoms in a molecule

**triple counterpoint** *n* 3-part musical COUNTERPOINT (interweaving of parts) so written that any part may be played above or below any other

**triple crown** *n, often cap T&C* a title representing the winning of all three of a set of important sporting events

**triple jump** *n* an athletic field event consisting of a jump for distance that is made from a running start and combines a hop, a step, and a jump in succession

**triple point** *n* the condition of temperature and pressure under which the gaseous, liquid, and solid phases of a substance can exist in equilibrium

**triple-'space** *vt* to type (copy) leaving two blank lines between lines of text ~ *vi* to type on every third line

**triplet** /'triplit/ *n* **1** a unit of three lines of verse, esp when rhyming together **2a** a combination, set, or group of three **b** a group of three minute particles of matter (e g positive, negative, and neutral PIONS) with different electrical charge states but otherwise similar properties **c** any of the three states that a particle having one unit of the smallest amount of spin possible according to the QUANTUM THEORY may be in **3** any of three children or animals born at one birth **4** a group of three musical notes performed in the time of two of the same value [²*triple* + *-et* (as in *doublet*)]

**triplet code** *n* GENETIC CODE (the sequence of BASES in DNA determining the AMINO ACID sequence in proteins)

**triple-'tongue** *vi* to articulate groups of three notes in fast tempo on a wind instrument by using a combination of the tongue positions for *t* and *k* (e g *t, k, t*) for the notes of each successive group

**¹triplex** /'tripleks/ *adj* threefold, triple [L, fr *tri-* + *-plex* -fold – more at SIMPLE]

**²triplex** *n, NAm* a dwelling consisting of three separate apartments or of rooms on three floors ⟨*convert the building into eight ~es for resale – Globe and Mail (Toronto)*⟩

**Triplex** /'tripleks/ *trademark* – used for a patented form of laminated SAFETY GLASS

**¹triplicate** /'triplikət/ *adj* **1** consisting of or existing in three corresponding or identical parts or examples ⟨*~ invoices*⟩ **2** being the third of three things exactly alike ⟨*file the ~ copy*⟩ [ME, fr L *triplicatus*, pp of *triplicare* to triple, fr *triplic-*, *triplex* threefold]

**²triplicate** /'triplikayt/ *vt* **1** to make triple **2** to prepare in triplicate – **triplication** *n*

**³triplicate** /'triplikət/ *n* **1** any of three things exactly alike; *specif* any of three identical copies **2** three copies all alike – + *in* ⟨*typed in ~*⟩

**triplicity** /tri'plisəti, trie-/ *n* **1** any of the four groups of three symmetrically placed signs into which the signs of the zodiac are divided **2** the quality or state of being triple [ME *triplicite*, fr LL *triplicitas* condition of being threefold, fr L *triplic-*, *triplex* triple]

**triplite** /'tripliet/ n a dark brown crystalline mineral that consists of PHOSPHATES of the chemical elements manganese, iron, magnesium, and calcium [Ger *triplit*, fr L *triplus* triple; fr its splitting in three directions]

**triploblastic** /,triploh'blastik/ adj having three primary GERM LAYERS (differentiated layers of cells) [L *triplus* + E -o- + -*blastic*]

**triploid** /'triployd/ adj having or being three times the basic (HAPLOID) number of CHROMOSOMES (strands of gene-carrying material) [ISV, fr L *triplus* triple] – **triploid** n, **triploidy** n

**tripod** /'trie,pod/ n 1 an ancient Greek altar resting on three legs 2 a stool, table, or vessel (e g a cauldron) with three legs 3 a three-legged stand (e g for a camera) [L *tripod-, tripus*, fr Gk *tripod-, tripous*, fr *tripod-, tripous* three-footed, fr *tri-* + *pod-, pous* foot – more at FOOT] – **tripodal** adj

**tripoli** /'tripəli/ n a porous easily crumbled rock that consists of silica and is a natural abrasive [Fr, fr *Tripoli*, region in N Africa]

**tripos** /'triepos/ n either part of the honours examination for the Cambridge BA [modif of L *tripus* tripod; fr the three-legged stool formerly occupied by a graduate appointed to dispute satirically with candidates at the degree ceremonies]

**tripper** /'tripə/ n 1 a device (e g for operating a railway signal) that is activated by the release of a catch 2 *chiefly Br* one who goes on an outing or pleasure trip, esp one lasting only one day ⟨a coachload of day ∼s⟩

**trippery** /'tripəri/ adj, *chiefly Br derog* frequented by or appealing to trippers ⟨Blackpool is a rather ∼ resort⟩

**trippingly** /'tripingli/ adv nimbly; *also* fluently ⟨speak the speech . . . ∼ on the tongue – Shak⟩

**triptane** /'triptayn/ n a liquid chemical compound, $C_7H_{16}$, that has properties that reduce knocking in INTERNAL-COMBUSTION ENGINES and is used esp in aviation fuels to increase their power [irreg fr *tri-* + *butane*]

**triptych** /'trip,tik/ n 1 an ancient Roman writing tablet made of three waxed leaves hinged together 2 a picture or carving on three panels side by side; *esp* an altarpiece consisting of a central panel hinged to two flanking panels half its width that fold over it [Gk *triptychos* having three folds, fr *tri-* + *ptychē* fold]

**trip wire** n a concealed wire placed near the ground that is used, esp in military operations, to trip up an intruder or to actuate an explosive or warning device when pulled

**triquetrous** /trie'kweetrəs, 'kwet-/ adj TRIGONOUS (triangular in cross section) [L *triquetrus* three-cornered, fr *tri-*]

**triradiate** /trie'raydiət, -ayt/ adj having three radiating branches

**trireme** /'trie,reem/ n a galley with three banks of oars [L *triremis*, fr *tri-* + *remus* oar – more at ROW]

**tris-** prefix thrice; tripled – esp in complex chemical expressions [Gk *tris* – more at TER-]

**trisaccharide** /trie'sakəried/ n a sugar that yields on complete breakdown three sugar molecules that cannot be broken down into simpler sugars [ISV]

**trisect** /trie'sekt, '--/ vt to divide into three; *specif* to divide (an angle or line segment) into three equal parts [*tri-* + ²-*sect*] – **trisector** n, **trisection** n

**trishaw** /'trie,shaw/ n a passenger vehicle consisting of a tricycle with a rickshaw body over the rear wheels, most commonly seen in Oriental countries [*tricycle* + *rickshaw*]

**triskele** /'triskeel, trie-/ n a triskelion [Gk *triskelēs*]

**triskelion** /tris'kelyn, trie-, -on/ n a figure or symbol composed of three usu curved or bent branches radiating from a centre ⟨the ∼ of the Isle of Man⟩ [NL, fr Gk *triskelēs* three-legged, fr *tri-* + *skelos* leg]

**trismus** /'trizməs/ n spasm of the muscles involved in chewing; lockjaw [NL, fr Gk *trismos* gnashing (of teeth), fr *trizein* to squeak, gnash; akin to L *stridēre* to creak – more at STRIDENT]

**trisoctahedron** /,trisoktə'heedrən/ n a solid (e g a crystal) having 24 triangular faces of identical size and shape based on the edges of a regular octahedron, three for each of the octahedron's faces [*tris-* + *octahedron*]

**trisodium** /trie'sohdiəm/ adj containing three atoms of the chemical element sodium in the molecule

**trisomic** /trie'sohmik/ adj having an extra CHROMOSOME (strand of gene-carrying material) that is identical to the chromosomes of an existing pair in a cell [*tri-* + -*somic*] – **trisomic**, **trisome** n, **trisomy** n

**¹triste** /treest/ adj, *archaic* sad, melancholy ⟨he looked rather

∼, like his mother, a woman of little spirit – Rose Macaulay⟩ [ME, fr MF, fr L *tristis*]

**²triste** n a sad love song of Latin America ⟨strumming on a guitar and singing ∼s . . . from morning to night – Joseph Conrad⟩ [Sp, fr *triste* sad, fr L *tristis*]

**tristearin** /trie'stiərin/ n the crystallizable TRIGLYCERIDE, $(C_{17}H_{35}COO)_3C_3H_5$, of STEARIC ACID that is a solid fat found esp in lard and other natural fats [ISV *tri-* + *stearin*]

**trisubstituted** /trie'substityoohtid/ adj, *chemistry* having three substituent atoms or groups in the molecule

**trisulphide** /trie'sulfied/ n a compound of a chemical element or chemical group with three atoms of sulphur

**trisyllabic** /triesi'labik/ adj having three syllables ⟨a ∼ word⟩ [L *trisyllabus*, fr Gk *trisyllabos*, fr *tri-* + *syllabē* syllable] – **trisyllabically** adv

**trisyllable** /'trie,siləbl/ n a word of three syllables

**trite** /triet/ adj hackneyed from much use; stale, commonplace [L *tritus*, fr pp of *terere* to rub, wear away – more at THROW] – **tritely** adv, **triteness** n

**tritheism** /'triethi,iz(ə)m/ n the doctrine that the Father, Son, and HOLY SPIRIT are three distinct Gods [*tri-* + -*theism*] – **tritheist** n or adj, **tritheistic**, **tritheistical** adj

**tritiated** /'trishiaytid, 'triti-/ adj, *of a molecule* containing tritium in place of hydrogen atoms, esp as a radioactive label

**triticale** /,tritə'kayli/ n a cereal grass that is a hybrid between wheat and rye and has a high yield and rich protein content [NL, blend of *Triticum*, genus of wheat + *Secale*, genus of rye]

**tritium** /'trishi-əm, 'triti-əm/ n a radioactive ISOTOPE of hydrogen with atoms of three times the mass of ordinary light hydrogen atoms [NL, fr Gk *tritos* third – more at THIRD]

**¹triton** /'triet(ə)n/ n 1 any of various large marine INVERTEBRATE animals (esp family Cymatiidae of the class Gastropoda, phylum Mollusca) related to the snails and whelks, with a heavy elongated conical shell; *also* this shell 2 any of various aquatic salamanders; a newt [NL, genus name, fr L *Triton*, mythical demigod of the sea, fr Gk *Triton*]

**²triton** n the nucleus of a tritium atom [*tritium* + -*on*]

**tritone** /'trie,tohn/ n a difference (INTERVAL 1c) in pitch of three WHOLE TONES between musical notes [Gk *tritonon*, fr *tri-* + *tonos* tone]

**¹triturate** /'trityoorayt/ vt, *chemistry* 1 to crush, grind 2 to reduce to a fine powder by rubbing or grinding [LL *trituratus*, pp of *triturare* to thresh, fr L *tritura* act of rubbing, threshing, fr *tritus*, pp of *terere* to rub – more at THROW] – **triturator** n, **triturable** adj, **trituration** n

**²triturate** /'trityoorət/ n, *chemistry* a triturated substance

**¹triumph** /'trie,um(p)f/ n 1 a ceremony with which a general was greeted when returning to ancient Rome having won a decisive victory over a foreign enemy – compare OVATION 2 the joy or exultation of victory or success 3 a notable success, victory, or achievement *synonyms* see VICTORY [ME *triumphe*, fr MF, fr L *triumphus*] – **triumphal** adj

**²triumph** vi 1a of an ancient Roman general to receive the honour of a triumph b to celebrate victory or success boastfully or exultantly 2 to obtain victory – often + *over* ⟨∼ed over her illness to make a successful career⟩

**triumphalism** /trie'umfəliz(ə)m/ n a religious attitude emphasizing success and defeat of evil

**triumphant** /trie'um(p)fənt/ adj 1 victorious, conquering 2 rejoicing in or celebrating victory – **triumphantly** adv
*synonyms* A notable achievement is triumphant ⟨her triumphant success⟩ and so are the people who rejoice in such a success ⟨the triumphant team⟩ ⟨grinned triumphantly at me⟩. The celebration of a military victory is triumphal ⟨a triumphal procession⟩ ⟨the Arc de Triomphe in Paris is a triumphal arch⟩.

**triumvir** /trie'umvə, -viə/ n, pl **triumvirs** also **triumviri** /-vəri/ a member of a commission or ruling body of three [L, back-formation fr *triumviri*, pl, commission of three men, fr *trium virum* of three men] – **triumviral** adj

**triumvirate** /trie'umvirət/ n 1 the office or government of triumvirs 2 *taking sing or pl vb* 2a a body of triumvirs b a group or association of three

**triune** /'trie,yoohn/ adj, *often cap* three in one; *esp* of or being the Trinity ⟨the ∼ God⟩ [L *tri-* + *unus* one – more at ONE]

**¹trivalent** /trie'vaylənt, 'trivələnt/ adj 1 having a VALENCY of three 2 of or being a trivalent [ISV]

**²trivalent** n a group of three CHROMOSOMES (strands of gene-carrying material temporarily held together during the first stage of MEIOSIS (division of a cell into four new cells)

**trivet** /'trivit/ *n* **1** a three-legged usu iron stand for holding cooking vessels over or by a fire; *also* a bracket that hooks onto a grate for this purpose **2** a (metal) stand with three feet for holding a hot dish at table [ME *trevet*, fr OE *trefet*, prob modif of LL *triped-, tripes*, fr L, three-footed, fr *tri-* + *ped-, pes* foot – more at FOOT]

**trivia** /'trivi·ə/ *n taking sing or pl vb* unimportant matters or details; trifles [NL, fr pl of L *trivium* crossroads; influenced in meaning by E *trivial* & L *trivialis*]

**trivial** /'trivi·əl/ *adj* **1** commonplace, ordinary **2a** of little worth or importance; insignificant **b** of or being the mathematically simplest case; *specif* characterized by having all variables equal to zero ⟨*a ~ solution to an equation*⟩ [L *trivialis* found everywhere, commonplace, fr *trivium* crossroads, fr *tri-* + *via* way – more at VIA ] – **trivially** *adv*, **trivialness** *n*, **trivialize** *vt*, **trivialization** *n*, **triviality** *n*

**trivial name** *n* **1** the second part of a 2-word Latin name of an animal, plant, etc, that follows the genus name and denotes the species – called also SPECIFIC EPITHET **2** a common or vernacular name of an organism or chemical

**trivium** /'trivi·əm/ *n, pl* **trivia** /-viə/ a group of studies consisting of grammar, rhetoric, and logic and forming the lower division of the seven LIBERAL ARTS in medieval universities – compare QUADRIVIUM [ML, fr L, meeting of three ways, crossroads]

**triweekly** /ˌtrie'weekli/ *adj or adv* **1** (occurring or appearing) three times a week **2** (occurring or appearing) every three weeks

**-trix** /-triks/ *suffix* (→ *n*) *pl* **-trices** /-triseez, -trieseez/, **-trixes -trixes** **1** female ⟨*avia*trix⟩ ⟨*execu*trix⟩ **2** geometric line, point, or surface ⟨*direc*trix⟩ [ME, fr L, fem of *-tor*, suffix denoting an agent, fr *-tus*, pp ending + *-or*]

**tRNA** /ˌtee ahr en 'ay/ *n* TRANSFER RNA

**trocar** *also* **trochar** /'trohkah/ *n* a sharp-pointed instrument used esp to insert a fine tube into a body cavity as a drainage outlet [Fr *trocart*, fr *trois* three (fr L *tres*) + *carre* side of a sword blade, fr *carrer* to make square, fr L *quadrare* – more at THREE, QUADRATE]

**trochal** /'trohkl/ *adj* resembling a wheel ⟨*the ~ disc at the front end of the bodies of certain plankton*⟩ [Gk *trochos* wheel]

**trochanter** /tro'kantə/ *n* **1** a rough prominence at the upper part of the thighbone of many VERTEBRATE animals **2** the second segment of an insect's leg counting from the body [Gk *trochantēr*; akin to Gk *trechein* to run] – **trochanteral, trochanteric** *adj*

**troche** /trohsh/ *n* a usu circular soothing medicinal tablet or lozenge that is kept in the mouth until dissolved [alter. of earlier *trochisk*, fr LL *trochiscus*, fr Gk *trochiskos*, fr dim. of *trochos* wheel]

**trochee** /'troh‚kee/ *n* a unit of poetic metre (FOOT 4) consisting of one long or stressed syllable followed by one short or unstressed syllable (e g in *apple*) – compare IAMB [Fr *trochée*, fr L *trochaeus*, fr Gk *trochaios*, fr *trochaios* running, fr *trochē* run, course, fr *trechein* to run; akin to Gk *trochos* wheel, OIr *droch*] – **trochaic** *adj or n*

**trochilus** /'trokiləs/ *n, pl* **trochili** /-li/ CROCODILE BIRD (African plover) [NL, fr Gk *trochilos*; akin to Gk *trechein* to run]

**trochlea** /'trokli·ə/ *n, pl* **trochleas, trochleae** /-li·ie/ an anatomical structure resembling a pulley; *esp* a surface of a bone over which a tendon passes [NL, fr L, block of pulleys, fr Gk *trochileia*, akin to Gk *trechein* to run]

**trochlear** /'trokli·ə/ *adj* **1** of or being a trochlea **2** of or being a TROCHLEAR NERVE

**trochlear nerve, trochlear** *n* either of the 4th pair of CRANIAL NERVES that conduct impulses from the base of the brain to some of the eye muscles causing them to move

**trochoid** /'trohkoyd/ *n* the curve generated by a point on the radius of a circle or the radius extended as the circle rolls on a fixed straight line [Gk *trochoeidēs* like a wheel, fr *trochos* wheel] – **trochoidal** *adj*

**trochophore** /'trokə‚faw/ *n* a free-swimming larva, esp of marine segmented worms (e g the ragworm), that propels itself through the water by means of CILIA (short hairlike projections) [deriv of Gk *trochos* wheel + *pherein* to carry – more at BEAR]

**trockenbeerenauslese** /'trokənbeərənˌowslayzə (*Ger* trɔkənberːənaʊsleːzə)/ *n, often cap* a German and Austrian sweet golden-coloured wine made only from individually selected very ripe grapes that have been attacked by a special mould and have shrivelled to a raisinlike state [Ger, fr *trocken* dry + *beerenauslese*]

**trod** /trod/ *past of* TREAD

**trodden** /'trod(ə)n/ *past part of* TREAD

**troglodyte** /'troglədiet/ *n* **1** CAVEMAN 1 **2** a person resembling a troglodyte, esp in being solitary or unsocial or in having primitive or outmoded ideas **3** an ape (e g chimpanzee or gorilla) [L *troglodytae*, pl, fr Gk *trōglodytai*, fr *trōglē* hole, cave (akin to Gk *trōgein* to gnaw) + *dyein* to enter] – **troglodytic** *adj*

**trogon** /'trohgon/ *n* any of a family (Trogonidae) of tropical birds (e g the QUETZAL) with brilliant lustrous plumage [NL, genus name, fr Gk *trōgōn*, prp of *trōgein* to gnaw]

**troika** /'troykə/ *n* **1** (a Russian vehicle drawn by) three horses abreast **2** *taking sing or pl vb* a group of three; *esp* an administrative or ruling body of three people ⟨*replaced by a ~ of three coequal secretaries-general – Newsweek*⟩ [Russ *troĭka*, fr *troe* three; akin to OE *thrīe* three]

**troilite** /'troh‚iliet, 'troy-/ *n* a mineral, FeS, that is widely but sparsely distributed (e g on earth, in meteorites, and in lunar soil samples) [Ger *troilit*, fr Dominico *Troili*, 18th-c It scientist]

**Trojan** /'trohj(ə)n/ *n* **1** a native or inhabitant of Troy **2** one who shows qualities (e g pluck or endurance) attributed to the defenders of ancient Troy – chiefly in *work like a Trojan* [ME, fr L *trojanus* of Troy, fr *Troia, Troja* Troy, ancient city in Asia Minor, fr Gk *Troīa*] – **Trojan** *adj*

**Trojan horse** *n* someone or something intended to undermine or subvert from within [fr the legend of a large hollow wooden horse filled with Greek soldiers and brought within the walls of Troy by a trick so that the city could be captured]

**¹troll** /trohl, trol/ *vt* **1** to sing loudly **2** to fish for or in with a hook and line drawn through the water behind a moving boat ~ *vi* **1** to fish, esp by drawing a hook through the water **2** to sing or play an instrument in a jovial manner **3** *informal* to move about; stroll, saunter ⟨*travel writers ... ~ing around from free hotel to free hotel – The Bookseller*⟩ [ME *trollen* to move about, roll] – **troller** *n*

**²troll** *n* (a line with) a lure and hook used in trolling

**³troll** *n* a dwarf or giant of Germanic folklore inhabiting caves or hills [Norw *troll* & Dan *trold*, fr ON *troll* giant, demon; akin to MHG *trolle* monster, OE *treppan* to tread – more at TRAP]

**¹trolley** *also* **trolly** /'troli/ *n* **1** a device (e g a grooved wheel or skid) attached to a sprung pole on the roof of an electric vehicle that collects current from an overhead electric wire for powering the vehicle – compare PANTOGRAPH 2 **2** any of several types of wheeled vehicle or carriage running on or sprung onto an overhead rail or track; *esp* a trolleybus **3** *chiefly Br* a hand-propelled vehicle not operating on a rail or track: e g **3a** a shelved stand mounted on castors and used for conveying something (e g food or books) ⟨*a tea ~*⟩ ⟨*Scrumptious Sweet* Trolley – *Express & Star (Wolverhampton)*⟩ **b** a basket on wheels that is pulled or pushed by hand and used for carrying goods (e g purchases in a supermarket) **c** a hospital stretcher mounted on four or more castors ⟨*pushing ~ cases – Punch*⟩ **d(1)** a small wheeled luggage carrier for passengers' use at stations, airports, etc **d(2)** a large cage or platform mounted on wheels that is used for luggage or freight by porters **4** *Br* a small 4-wheeled wagon that runs on rails (e g in mines or factories) **5** **trolley car, trolley** *NAm* TRAM 1b [E dial. *trolley, troll* cart, truck, prob fr *¹troll*]

**²trolley, trolly** *vt* to convey by a trolley ~ *vi* to ride on a trolley

**trolleybus** /'troli‚bus/ *n* an electrically propelled bus running on a road and drawing power from two overhead wires via a trolley

**trollop** /'troləp/ *n* **1** a slovenly woman; a slattern **2** an immoral woman; a prostitute [prob irreg fr Ger dial. *trolle*, fr MHG *trulle* prostitute – more at TRULL] – **trollopy** *adj*

**trombidiasis** /ˌtrombi'die·əsis/ *n* infestation with CHIGGERS (blood-sucking mite larvae) [NL, fr *Trombidium*, genus of mites]

**trombone** /trom'bohn/ *n* a BRASS INSTRUMENT consisting of a long cylindrical metal tube with two turns and having a movable slide for varying the pitch and a usual range lower than that of the trumpet [It, aug of *tromba* trumpet, of Gmc origin; akin to OHG *trumba, trumpa* trumpet] – **trombonist** *n*

**trommel** /'troməl/ *n* a usu cylindrical or conical revolving screen used esp for screening or sizing rock, ore, or coal [Ger, drum, fr MHG *trummel*, dim. of *trumme* drum – more at DRUM]

**trompe l'oeil** /ˌtromp 'luh·i (*Fr* trɔ̃p lœːj)/ *n* **1** a style of painting in which objects are depicted with three-dimensional reality; *also* the use of a similar technique in interior decorating **2** a trompe l'oeil painting or effect [*Fr trompe-l'oeil*, lit., deceive the eye]

**tron** /tron/ *n, chiefly Scot* a marketplace; *also* a weighing machine used at a marketplace [AF *trone* weighing machine, fr OF, fr L *trutina* scales, fr Gk *trytanē*]

**-tron** /-tron/ *suffix* (→ *n*) **1** vacuum tube ⟨*magne*tron⟩ **2** device for the manipulation of subatomic particles ⟨*cyclo*tron⟩ [Gk, suffix denoting an instrument; akin to OE *-thor*, suffix denoting an instrument, L *-trum*]

**trona** /'trohnə/ *n* a grey-white or yellowish-white crystalline SODIUM CARBONATE mineral, $Na_2CO_3NaHCO_3 2H_2O$, that typically occurs as a deposit from SALT LAKES [Sw prob fr Ar *naṭrūn* natron]

**trone** /trohn/ *n, chiefly Scot* a tron

**¹troop** /troohp/ *n* **1** *taking sing or pl vb* **1a(1)** a subdivision of a cavalry or tank regiment corresponding to an infantry platoon **a(2)** an artillery unit smaller than a BATTERY **b** a collection of people or things **c** a unit of scouts under a leader **d** a herd, flock ⟨*answers to the animal group game: ... ~ of kangaroos* – *National Geographic World*⟩ ⟨*there will be ~*s *of finches and linnets up here* – Richard Jefferies⟩ **2** *pl* soldiers ⟨*send the ~*s *in*⟩ **3** troops *pl*, **troop** *taking sing or pl vb* a large number ⟨*~*s *of friends* – Shak⟩ □ compare ¹TROUPE [MF *trope, troupe* company, herd, of Gmc origin; akin to OE *thorp, throp* village – more at THORP]

**²troop** *vi* **1** to move in a group, esp in a way that suggests regimentation ⟨*everyone ~*ed *into the meeting*⟩ **2** to move in large numbers ⟨*the children and their friends ~*ed *in and out all day*⟩ **3** *archaic* to consort, associate – usu + *with* ⟨*a snowy dove ~*ing *with the crows* – Shak⟩; see also **troop the** COLOUR

**troop carrier** *n* a transport aeroplane used to carry troops

**trooper** /'troohpə/ *n* **1a** a cavalry soldier; *esp* a private in a cavalry or tank regiment **b** the horse of a cavalry soldier **2** *chiefly NAm & Austr* a mounted policeman □ compare TROUPER

**troopship** /'troohp,ship/ *n* a ship for carrying troops

**troostite** /'troohstiet/ *n* a variety of WILLEMITE (mineral consisting of zinc silicate) occurring in large reddish crystals in which the chemical element zinc is partly replaced by the element manganese [Gerard *Troost* †1850 US geologist]

**trop-** /trop-, trohp-/, **tropo-** *comb form* **1** turn; turning; change ⟨*tropo*sphere⟩ **2** tropism ⟨*trop*ic⟩ [ISV, fr Gk *tropos*]

**trope** /trohp/ *n* **1** a figurative use of a word or expression; FIGURE OF SPEECH **2** a phrase or verse added in medieval times to the sung parts of the Mass [L *tropus*, fr Gk *tropos* turn, way, manner, style, fr *trepein* to turn; akin to L *trepit* he turns]

**troph-** /trof-/, **tropho-** *comb form* nutritive ⟨*tropho*plasm⟩ [Fr, fr Gk, fr *trophē* nourishment]

**trophallaxis** /ˌtrofə'laksis/ *n* exchange of food (e g from special glands) between different species of organism or between adults and larvae of the same species; *also* the association of organisms, esp insects living in organized communities, on the basis of such behaviour [NL, fr *troph-* + Gk *allaxis* exchange, fr *allassein* to change, exchange, fr *allos* other – more at ELSE]

**trophic** /'trofik, 'trohfik/ *adj* **1** of nutrition or growth ⟨*~ disorders of muscle*⟩ **2** of a hormone influencing the activity of a gland [Fr *trophique*, fr Gk *trophikos*, fr *trophē* nourishment, fr *trephein* to nourish – more at ATROPHY] – **trophically** *adv*

**-trophic** /-'trohfik, -'trofik/ *comb form* (→ *adj*) **1a** of or characterized by (a specified mode of feeding) ⟨*zoo*trophic⟩ **b** requiring or utilizing (such) a kind of nutrient ⟨*poly*trophic⟩ **2** acting on or stimulating (something specified) ⟨*cortico*trophic⟩ ⟨*gonado*trophic⟩ [NL *-trophia* -trophy, fr Gk, fr *-trophos* nourishing, fr *trephein*] – **-trophism, -trophy** *comb form* (→ *n*)

**trophic level** *n* a stratum in an ecological FOOD WEB occupied by a group of organisms that eat similar food ⟨*all carnivores occupy the same ~ in an ecosystem*⟩

**-trophin** /-trohfin/ *comb form* (→ *n*) substance acting on or stimulating (something specified) ⟨*gonado*trophin⟩ ⟨*luteo*trophin⟩

**trophoblast** /'trofə,blast, 'troh-/ *n* a layer of cells that forms the outside of the early embryo of many placental mammals and functions in attaching the embryo to the wall of the uterus and in supplying it with nutrients [ISV] – **trophoblastic** *adj*

**trophozoite** /ˌtrofə'zoh·iet/ *n* a mature form in the LIFE CYCLE of some SPOROZOANS (parasitic single-celled microorganisms)

that divides asexually many times to produce the next stage in the life cycle

**trophy** /'trohfi/ *n* **1a** a memorial of an ancient Greek or Roman victory raised on the field of battle, or in the case of a naval victory on the nearest land **b** a representation of such a memorial (e g on a medal); *also* an architectural ornament representing a group of military weapons **2** something gained or awarded in victory or conquest, esp when preserved or mounted as a memorial ⟨*he had the cricket ball mounted as a ~*⟩; *also, often cap* a competition played for such a trophy ⟨*the NatWest Bank* Trophy⟩ [MF *trophee*, fr L *tropaeum, trophaeum*, fr Gk *tropaion*, fr neut of *tropaios* of a turning, of a rout, fr *tropē* turn, rout, fr *trepein* to turn – more at TROPE]

**¹tropic** /'tropik/ *n* **1** either of the two small circles of the CELESTIAL SPHERE (imaginary sphere containing the stars) on each side of and parallel to the equator at a distance of $23\frac{1}{2}$ degrees, which the sun reaches at its greatest distance north or south of the equator on the summer and winter solstices **2a** either of the two parallel lines of latitude on earth corresponding to the celestial tropics – compare TROPIC OF CANCER, TROPIC OF CAPRICORN **b** *pl, often cap* the region lying between these lines of latitude [ME *tropik*, fr L *tropicus* of the solstice, fr Gk *tropikos*, fr *tropē* turn]

**²tropic** /'trohpik/ *adj* **1** (characteristic) of (a) tropism **2** *of a hormone* influencing the activity of a specified gland [*trop-* + *-ic*]

**-tropic** /-'trohpik/ *comb form* (→ *adj*) **1** -tropic, -tropous /-trəpəs/ turning, changing, or tending to turn or change in (a specified manner) or in response to (a specified stimulus) ⟨*geo*tropic⟩ **2** -TROPHIC **2** [Fr *-tropique*, fr Gk *-tropos*, fr *trepein* to turn] – **-tropism, -tropy** *comb form* (→ *n*)

**tropical** /'tropikl/ *adj* **1** *also* **tropic** of, occurring in, or characteristic of the tropics; *esp, of weather* very hot and usu humid **2** *of a sign of the zodiac* beginning at either of the tropics **3** metaphorical, figurative [(3) L *tropicus*, fr Gk *tropikos*, fr *tropos* trope] – **tropically** *adv*

**tropic bird** /'tropik/ *n* any of several web-footed birds (genus *Phaëthon*) that are related to the gannets and are found chiefly in tropical seas, often far from land

**tropic of Cancer** /ˌtropik əv 'kansə/ *n* the line of latitude that is $23\frac{1}{2}$ degrees north of the equator and is the northernmost latitude reached by the overhead sun [fr the sign of the zodiac at a corresponding latitude on the celestial sphere]

**tropic of Capricorn** /ˌtropik əv 'kapri,kawn/ *n* the line of latitude that is $23\frac{1}{2}$ degrees south of the equator and is the southernmost latitude reached by the overhead sun

**-tropin** /-trohpin/ *comb form* (→ *n*) -trophin

**tropism** /'trohpiz(ə)m/ *n* **1** (an) involuntary orientation by (a part of) an organism, esp a plant, in which it grows, by turning or curving, in response to a source of stimulation (e g light) – compare TAXIS **2 2** an innate tendency to react in a definite manner to stimuli [ISV *-tropism*, deriv of Gk *tropos* turn] – **tropistic** *adj*

**tropo-** – see TROP-

**tropocollagen** /ˌtropə'koləjən, ˌtrohpə-/ *n* a soluble substance whose elongated asymmetrical molecules are the fundamental building units of COLLAGEN fibres that occur in bones and the loose fibrous supporting tissue of VERTEBRATE animals

**tropological** /ˌtropə'lojikl/ *also* **tropologic** *adj* **1** characterized or varied by FIGURES OF SPEECH; figurative **2** of or involving tropology; *also* moral – **tropologically** *adv*

**tropology** /tro'poləji/ *n* **1** the figurative use of words **2** a way of interpreting the Bible as moral teaching conveyed through metaphor [LL *tropologia*, fr LGk, fr Gk *tropos* trope + *-logia* -logy]

**tropomyosin** /ˌtropə'mie·əsin, ˌtrohp-/ *n* a rod-shaped protein of muscle that aids muscle contraction

**tropopause** /'tropə,pawz/ *n* the region at the top of the troposphere; *also* a comparable layer of a celestial body [ISV *troposphere* + *pause*]

**tropophilous** /tro'pofiləs/ *adj* physiologically adjusted to or thriving in an environment that undergoes marked periodic changes, esp in temperature, moisture, or light ⟨*monsoon forest ... is ~ in character, usually less lofty than the rain forest* – P W Richards⟩

**tropophyte** /'tropəfiet/ *n* a tropophilous plant – **tropophytic** *adj*

**troposphere** /'tropə,sfiə/ *n* the part of the atmosphere which is below the STRATOSPHERE, which extends outwards about 11 to 16 kilometres (about 7 to 10 miles) from the earth's surface, and in which generally temperature decreases rapidly with altitude and clouds form [ISV] – **tropospheric** *adj*

**-tropous** /-trəpəs/ *comb form* (→ *adj*) -TROPIC 1 〈*ana*tropous〉 [Gk *-tropos*]

**troppo** /'tropoh/ *adj, Austr informal* mentally deranged by the heat of the tropics; mad [¹*tropic-* + *-o*]

¹**trot** /trot/ *n* **1a** a moderately fast pace of a horse or other 4-legged animal in which the legs move in diagonal pairs – compare CANTER, GALLOP, RUN, WALK **b** a ride on horseback 〈*she joined the other riders in a ~ before breakfast*〉 **2** (an instance of moving at) a brisk pace 〈*a ~ round the shops*〉 〈*he came up at a ~ when they waved*〉 **3** *NAm informal* CRIB 7a (surreptitiously used translation) **4** *pl but taking sing or pl vb, humorous* diarrhoea – usu + *the* [ME, fr MF, fr *troter* to trot, of Gmc origin; akin to OHG *trottōn* to tread, OE *tredan*] – **on the trot** *informal* in succession

²**trot** *vb* **-tt-** *vi* **1** to ride, drive, or proceed at a trot **2** to proceed briskly; hurry 〈*I must ~ down to the shops before they close*〉 **~** *vt* **1** to cause to go at a trot **2** to traverse at a trot **3** *NZ* to go out with; court 〈*in those days he hadn't started to ~ the sheila he eventually married* – Frank Sargeson〉

**trot out** *vt* **1** to produce or bring forward (as if) for display or scrutiny **2** to produce or utter in a trite or predictable manner 〈*he trotted out all the old clichés*〉

³**trot** *n, chiefly derog* an old woman [ME *trate, tratte*]

⁴**trot** *n* a trotline; *also* any of the short lines with hooks that are attached to it at intervals

**Trot** *n, chiefly derog* a Trotskyite; *broadly* an extreme left-winger

**troth** /trohth/ *n, archaic* one's pledged word; *also* betrothal – chiefly in *plight one's troth* [ME *trouth* fidelity, fr OE *trēowth* – more at TRUTH]

**trotline** /'trot,lien/ *n* SETLINE (long fishing line with several hooks); *esp* a comparatively short one used near shore or along streams [prob fr ²*trot*]

**Trotskyism** /'trotski,iz(ə)m/ *n* the political, economic, and social principles advocated by Trotsky; *esp* adherence to the concept of permanent worldwide revolution as opposed to socialism in one country [Leon *Trotsky* †1940 Russ Communist leader] – **Trotskyist, Trotskyite** *n or adj*

**trotter** /'trotə/ *n* **1** an animal or person that trots; *specif* a horse trained for trotting races **2** the foot of an animal, esp a pig, used as food

**trotting** /'troting/ *n* the sport of racing horses moving at a fast trot and pulling 2-wheeled vehicles carrying the driver

**trotting pole** *n* a low bar for a horse to jump at a trot

**troubadour** /'troohbədaw, -dooə/ *n* any of a class of lyric poets and poet-musicians, chiefly in S France and N Italy from the 11th to the end of the 13th century, whose major theme was courtly love – compare TROUVÈRE [Fr, fr OProv *trobador*, fr *trobar* to compose, prob fr (assumed) VL *tropare*, fr L *tropus* trope]

¹**trouble** /'trubl/ *vt* **1a** to agitate mentally or spiritually; worry 〈*her long absence ~d him*〉 **b** to produce physical disorder in; afflict 〈*~d with deafness*〉 **c** to put to exertion or inconvenience 〈*could I ~ you to close the door?*〉 **2** to make (eg the surface of water) turbulent; ruffle 〈*the wind ~d the sea*〉 **~** *vi* **1** to become mentally agitated; worry 〈*refused to ~ over trifles*〉 **2** to make an effort; be at pains 〈*do not ~ to come*〉 – see also **pour** OIL **on troubled waters, fish in troubled** WATERS [ME *troublen*, fr OF *tourbler, troubler*, fr (assumed) VL *turbulare*, alter. of L *turbidare*, fr *turbidus* turbid, troubled] – **troubler** *n*, **troublingly** *adv*

²**trouble** *n* **1a** being troubled **b** an instance of distress, annoyance, or disturbance **2** a cause of disturbance, annoyance, or distress: eg **2a** **troubles** *pl*, **trouble** public unrest or demonstrations of dissatisfaction 〈*labour ~s*〉 **b** effort made; exertion 〈*went to some ~ to learn the language*〉 **c(1)** a disease, ailment, or condition of physical distress 〈*heart ~*〉 **c(2)** a malfunction 〈*engine ~*〉 〈*been having ~ with the plumbing*〉 **d** pregnancy outside marriage – chiefly in *in/into trouble* **e** a personal characteristic that is a handicap or a source of distress 〈*his greatest ~ was his gullibility*〉 **3** a problem, snag 〈*that's the ~ with these newfangled ideas*〉

**trouble and strife** *n, Br slang* a wife [rhyming slang]

**troublemaker** /'trubl,maykə/ *n* one who causes trouble, esp by making others discontented

**troubleshooter** /'trubl,shoohtə/ *n* **1** one who specializes or is expert in identifying the causes of and resolving disputes (eg

in business or politics) **2** *chiefly NAm* a skilled workman employed to locate faults and make repairs in machinery and technical equipment – **troubleshooting** *n*

**troublesome** /'trubls(ə)m/ *adj* **1** giving trouble or anxiety; annoying, burdensome 〈*a ~ cough*〉 〈*a ~ neighbour*〉 **2** full of trouble; agitated, turbulent 〈*~ times*〉 – **troublesomely** *adv*, **troublesomeness** *n*

**trouble spot** *n* a place where trouble (eg political unrest) occurs or is likely to occur

**troublous** /'trubləs/ *adj, archaic or formal* TROUBLESOME 2 – **troublously** *adv*, **troublousness** *n*

**trou-de-loup** /,trooh də 'looh (*Fr* tru də lu)/ *n usu pl, pl* **trous-de-loup** /~/ a sloping pit with a pointed stake in the middle that forms one of a group constructed as obstacles to the movements of an enemy [Fr, lit., wolf's hole]

**trough** /trof/ *n* **1a** a long shallow receptacle for the drinking water or feed of domestic animals 〈*a pig ~*〉 〈*few horse ~s are left in the streets now*〉 **b** a long narrow container used for domestic or industrial purposes 〈*a plant ~ in the sitting room*〉 **2a** a drain or channel for water; *esp* a gutter along the eaves of a building **b** a long narrow or shallow trench (eg between waves, ridges, etc; *esp* a long but shallow depression in the bed of the sea **3a** the (region round the) lowest point of a regularly recurring cycle of a varying quantity (eg a SINE WAVE) **b** an elongated area of low atmospheric pressure **c** a low point (in a trade cycle) [ME, fr OE *trog*; akin to OE *trēow* tree, wood – more at TREE]

**trounce** /trowns/ *vt* **1** to thrash or punish severely **2** to defeat decisively 〈*~d a top-class field of sprinters* – Cape Times〉 [origin unknown]

¹**troupe** /troohp/ *n taking sing or pl vb* a company, troop; *esp* a group of theatrical performers – compare ¹TROOP [Fr, fr MF – more at TROOP]

²**troupe** *vi* to travel in a troupe; *also* to perform as a member of a theatrical troupe 〈*a time when Helen Keller earned her living by trouping up and down the land in vaudeville* – Saturday Review〉 **~** *vt* to present (theatrical performances) in various places when travelling as a troupe 〈*they ~d their plays to camps in the area* – Theatre Arts〉

**trouper** /'troohpə/ *n* **1** a member of a troupe; *esp* a veteran actor **2** a loyal or dependable person – compare TROOPER

**troupial** /'troohpiəl/ *n* any of a family (Icteridae) of birds including the American blackbirds, grackles, and orioles; *specif* any of the large showy orioles (eg *Icterus icterus*) of Central and S America [Fr *troupiale*, fr *troupe*; fr its living in flocks]

**trousers** /'trowzəz/ *n pl* a 2-legged outer garment extending from the waist to the ankle or sometimes only to the knee [alter. of earlier *trouse*, fr ScGael *triubhas*] – **trouser** *adj* – **wear the trousers,** *NAm* **wear the pants** to have the controlling authority in a household

**trouser suit** *n, chiefly Br* a woman's suit consisting of a jacket and trousers

**trousseau** /'troohsoh/ *n, pl* **trousseaux, trousseaus** /-sohz/ the personal outfit of a bride including clothes, accessories, and sometimes household linen [Fr, fr OF, dim. of *trousse* bundle, fr *trousser* to truss]

**trout** /trowt/ *n, pl* **trouts, (***I***) trout,** *esp for different types* **trouts 1** any of various food and sport fishes (family Salmonidae), mostly smaller than the related salmons and restricted to cool clear fresh waters; *esp* any of various fishes (genus *Salmo*) some of which ascend rivers from the sea to breed – compare RAINBOW TROUT **2** *slang* an ugly unpleasant old woman [ME, fr OE *trūht*, fr LL *trocta, tructa*, a fish with sharp teeth, fr Gk *trōktēs*, lit., gnawer, fr *trōgein* to gnaw – more at TERSE]

**trouvaille** /trooh'vie (*Fr* truva:j)/ *n* a chance or unexpected find; *also* an interesting or original idea 〈*no instantly memorable ~s* – The Guardian〉 [Fr, fr OF *trover, trouver* to compose, find]

**trouvère** /trooh'veə (*Fr* truvɛ:r)/ *n* any of a class of poets writing narrative verse in N France from the 11th to the 14th centuries – compare TROUBADOUR [Fr, fr OF *troveor, troverre*, fr *trover* to compose, find, fr (assumed) VL *tropare* – more at TROUBADOUR]

**trove** /trohv/ *n* TREASURE TROVE

**trover** /'trohvə/ *n* a COMMON LAW action to recover the value of goods wrongfully taken or kept by another [MF *trover* to find]

**trow** /troh/ *vb, archaic* to think, believe [ME *trowen*, fr OE *trēowan*; akin to OE *trēowe* faithful, true – more at TRUE]

¹**trowel** /'trowəl/ *n* any of various smooth-bladed hand tools

used to apply, spread, shape, or smooth loose or soft material; *also* a scoop-shaped or flat-bladed garden tool for taking up and setting small plants [ME *truel*, fr MF *truelle*, fr LL *truella*, fr L *trulla*, dim. of *trua* ladle; akin to L *turbare* to disturb – more at TURBID]

²**trowel** *vt* -ll- (*NAm* -l-, -ll-) to smooth, mix, or apply (as if) with a trowel

**troy** /troy/ *adj* expressed in TROY WEIGHT [ME *troye*, fr *Troyes*, city in NE France]

**troy weight** *n* the series of units of weight based on the pound of 12 ounces and the ounce of 20 pennyweights or 480 grains

**truancy** /'trooh·ənsi/ *n* the action or an act of playing truant

¹**truant** /'trooh·ənt/ *n* one who shirks duty; *esp* one who stays away from school without permission [ME, vagabond, idler, fr OF, vagrant, of Celt origin; akin to ScGael *truaghan* wretch] – **truant** *adj* – **play truant** to truant

²**truant** *vi* to stay away from school without permission

**truanting** /'trooh·ənting/ *n* absenteeism from school

**truant officer** *n*, *NAm* SCHOOL WELFARE OFFICER

**truce** /troohs/ *n* 1 a (temporary) suspension of fighting, esp of considerable duration, by agreement of opposing forces; a cease-fire 2 an interval of rest or relief, esp from a disagreeable or painful state or action [ME *trewes*, pl of *trewe* agreement, fr OE *trēow* fidelity; akin to OE *trēowe* faithful – more at TRUE]

¹**truck** /truk/ *vb* to barter [ME *trukken*, fr OF *troquer*]

²**truck** *n* 1 (commodities suitable for) barter 2 *NAm* vegetables grown on a TRUCK FARM – **have no truck with** to refuse to have anything to do with

³**truck** *n* 1 a small wheel; *specif* a small strong wheel for a gun carriage on board a sailing ship 2 a small wooden cap at the top of a flagstaff or masthead, usu having holes for the ropes used for hoisting a flag or signal 3a a usu 4- or 6-wheeled vehicle for moving heavy loads; a lorry **b** a usu 2- or 4-wheeled cart for carrying heavy articles (eg luggage at railway stations) 4 BOGIE 3 (frame carrying train wheels) 5 *Br* an open railway goods wagon 6 *NAm* TROLLEY 3a [prob fr L *trochus* iron hoop, fr Gk *trochos* wheel – more at TROCHEE]

⁴**truck** *vt* to load or transport on a truck ~ *vi* 1 to transport goods by truck 2 *NAm* to be employed as a lorry driver 3 *informal* to walk or proceed, esp doggedly; plod, trudge

**truckage** /'trukij/ *n*, *NAm* transportation by truck; *also* the charge for this

¹**trucker** /'trukə/ *n*, *NAm* MARKET GARDENER [¹*truck* + ²-*er*]

²**trucker, truckman** /'trukmən/ *n*, *chiefly NAm* 1 one whose business is transporting goods by lorry 2 a lorry driver [⁴*truck* + ²-*er*]

**truck farm** *n*, *NAm* a farm devoted to the production of vegetables for the market; MARKET GARDEN [¹*truck*] – **truck farmer** *n*

**truckie** /'truki/ *n*, *Austr & NZ* TRUCKER 2

**trucking** /'truking/ *n*, *chiefly NAm* the process or business of transporting goods by lorry; road haulage

**truckle** /'trukl/ *vi* to act in a subservient or obsequious manner; submit – usu + *to* [fr the lower position of the truckle bed] – **truckler** *n*

**truckle bed** *n* a low bed, usu on castors that can be slid under a higher bed – called also TRUNDLE BED [ME *trookel*, *trocle* pulley, castor, fr L *trochlea* block of pulleys – more at TROCHLEA]

**truckload** /'truk,lohd/ *n* a load that fills a truck

**truckmaster** /'truk,mahstə/ *n*, *archaic* an officer in charge of trade with N American Indians, esp among the early settlers [²*truck*]

**truck system** *n* the once prevalent system of paying wages in goods instead of cash [²*truck*]

**truculent** /'trukyoolənt/ *adj* 1 scathingly harsh; cruel, savage ⟨*authors resented the critic's ~ articles in the press*⟩ 2 aggressively self-assertive; belligerent [L *truculentus*, fr *truc-*, *trux* fierce] – **truculence, truculency** *n*, **truculently** *adv*

¹**trudge** /truj/ *vb* to walk or march steadily and usu laboriously (along or over) ⟨~d *through deep snow*⟩ ⟨~d *the weary road home*⟩ [origin unknown] – **trudger** *n*

²**trudge** *n* a long tiring walk

**trudgen stroke** /'trujən/ *n* a swimming stroke executed on the front consisting of the alternating overarm movements of the crawl stroke and a SCISSORS KICK [John *Trudgen*, 19th-c E swimmer]

¹**true** /trooh/ *adj* 1 steadfast, loyal ⟨~ *to one's word*⟩ ⟨*a ~ friend*⟩ 2a in accordance with fact or reality ⟨*a ~ story*⟩ ⟨*a ~ description*⟩ **b** essential ⟨*the ~ nature of socialist economics*⟩

**c** being that which is the case rather than what is claimed or assumed ⟨*the ~ dimensions of the problem*⟩ **d** consistent, conforming ⟨~ *to expectations*⟩ 3a(1) properly so called ⟨*the ~ faith*⟩ ⟨*the ~ stomach*⟩ **a(2)** genuine, real ⟨~ *love*⟩ ⟨~ *gold*⟩ **b(1)** possessing the basic characters of and belonging to the same natural group as ⟨*a whale is a ~ but not a typical mammal*⟩ **b(2)** typical ⟨*the ~ cats*⟩ 4 legitimate, rightful ⟨*our ~ and lawful king*⟩ 5a accurately fitted, adjusted, balanced, or formed **b** conforming to a standard or pattern; accurate ⟨*a ~ voice*⟩ ⟨*a ~ copy*⟩ 6 determined with reference to the earth's axis rather than the MAGNETIC POLES (two points in the N and S hemispheres to which a compass needle points) ⟨~ *north*⟩ 7 logically necessary 8 corrected for error 9 *archaic* truthful ⟨*speak, sad brow and ~ maid* – Shak⟩ [ME *trewe*, fr OE *trēowe* faithful; akin to OHG gi*triuwi* faithful, Skt *dāruṇa* hard, *dāru* wood – more at TREE]

²**true** *n* the quality or state of being accurate (eg in alignment or adjustment) – chiefly in *in/out of true*

³**true** *vt* trueing *also* truing to adjust or restore (eg a mechanical part) to the required shape or degree of accuracy – usu + *up* ⟨~ *up a board*⟩ ⟨~ *up an engine cylinder*⟩ – **truer** *n*

⁴**true** *adv* 1 in accordance with fact or reality ⟨*that story rings ~*⟩ 2a without deviation ⟨*the bullet flew straight and ~*⟩ **b** *genetics* without variation from type ⟨*they breed ~*⟩ – see also RING TRUE [ME *trewe*, fr *trewe*, adj]

**true bill** *n* a document formally accusing someone of a crime that is endorsed by a US GRAND JURY as showing sufficient grounds for him/her to be prosecuted

**,true-'blue** *adj* staunchly loyal; *specif*, *Br* being a staunch supporter of the Conservative party [fr the traditional association of blue with fidelity and its adoption as a party colour by various Br conservative groups since the 17th c] – **true-blue** *n*

**trueborn** /'trooh,bawn/ *adj* genuinely such by birth ⟨*a ~ Englishman* – Shak⟩

**truebred** /'trooh,bred/ *adj* purebred

**true bug** *n* any of a large order (Hemiptera) of insects that have mouthparts adapted to piercing and sucking and usu two pairs of wings, undergo a gradual change from the larval stage into the mature, but structurally similar, adult, and include many important pests

**true-false test** *n* a test consisting of a series of statements to be marked as true or false

**true fly** *n* TWO-WINGED FLY

**truehearted** /,trooh'hahtid/ *adj* faithful, loyal – **trueheartedness** *n*

**truelove** /'trooh,luv/ *n*, *poetic* a sweetheart

**true lover's knot, truelove knot** *n* a complicated ornamental knot not easily untied and symbolic of mutual love

**truepenny** /'trooh,peni/ *n*, *archaic* an honest or trusty person

**true rib** *n* any of the ribs having cartilages connected directly with the breastbone and in human beings constituting the first seven pairs

**truffle** /'trufl/ *n* 1 the usu dark brown edible FRUITING BODY of several European fungi (genus *Tuber*) that grows underground and is eaten as a delicacy; *also* any of these fungi 2 a rich soft creamy sweet made with chocolate ⟨*rum ~s*⟩ [modif of MF *truffe*, fr OProv *trufa*, fr (assumed) VL *tufera*, alter. of L *tuber* – more at TUBER] – **truffled** *adj*

**trug** /trug/ *n*, *Br* a shallow rectangular wooden basket used esp for carrying garden produce (eg fruit, flowers, and vegetables) [perh akin to *trough*]

**truism** /'trooh,iz(ə)m/ *n* an undoubted or self-evident truth; *esp* one too obvious or unimportant to be mentioned – **truistic** *adj*

**trull** /trul/ *n*, *archaic* a prostitute, strumpet [obs Ger *trulle*, fr MHG; akin to ON *troll* giant, demon – more at TROLL]

**truly** /'troohli/ *adv* 1 in agreement with fact or reality; truthfully 2 accurately, exactly 3a indeed – often as an intensive ⟨~, *she is fair*⟩ or interjectionally to express astonishment or doubt ⟨~? *you amaze me!*⟩ **b** genuinely, sincerely ⟨*he was ~ sorry*⟩ 4 properly, duly – compare YOURS TRULY *usage* See ¹FAITHFUL – **well and truly** totally, completely ⟨*well and truly beaten*⟩

¹**trump** /trump/ *n*, *chiefly poetic* a trumpet (call) ⟨*await the last ~ on that holy ground* – Evelyn Waugh⟩ [ME *trompe*, fr OF]

²**trump** *n* 1a a card of a suit any of whose cards will win over a card that is not of this suit ⟨*she played a small ~ as she had no spades, and beat his ace of spades*⟩ **b** *pl* the suit whose cards are trumps for a particular hand ⟨*he led ~s*⟩ 2 *informal* a very

worthy and dependable person – no longer in vogue [alter. of ¹*triumph*] – **come/turn up trumps** *informal* to do what is right, needed, or desirable, esp unexpectedly at the last moment ⟨*she was appalling at rehearsals but* turned up trumps *on the night*⟩

³**trump** *vt* 1 to play a trump on (a card or a set of cards played in one round) when another suit was led 2 to excel, outdo ~ *vi* to play a trump when another suit has been led

**trump up** *vt* to concoct, esp with intent to deceive; fabricate, invent ⟨*he alleged that the charges had been* trumped up *by the authorities*⟩

**trump card** *n* 1 TRUMP 1a 2 a telling argument or decisive factor; a clincher – esp in *play one's trump card*

**trumpery** /'trʌmpəri/ *adj* 1 worthless, useless ⟨*a ~ argument*⟩ 2 cheap, tawdry ⟨*travelling players in their ~ finery*⟩ [ME *tromperie* deceit, fr MF, fr *tromper* to deceive] – **trumpery** *n*

¹**trumpet** /'trʌmpit/ *n* 1a a WIND INSTRUMENT consisting of a conical or cylindrical usu metal tube, a cup-shaped mouthpiece, and a flared free end; *specif* the highest-pitched of the BRASS INSTRUMENTS, that has a cylindrical tube with two turns and finger-operated VALVES to vary the pitch **b** a musical instrument (eg a cornet) resembling a trumpet 2 something that resembles (the flared free end or loud penetrating sound of) a trumpet: eg 2a a funnel-shaped instrument (eg a megaphone) for collecting, directing, or intensifying sound **b** the loud penetrating cry of an elephant [ME *trompette*, fr MF, fr OF *trompe* trump] – **trumpetlike** *adj* – **blow one's own trumpet** *informal* to praise one's own abilities; boast

²**trumpet** *vi* 1 to blow a trumpet 2 to make a sound like that of a trumpet ~ *vt* to sound or proclaim loudly (as if) on a trumpet ⟨*~ ing her praises*⟩

**trumpet creeper** *n* a N American woody climbing plant (*Campsis radicans*) of the jacaranda family with large red trumpetlike flowers

**trumpeter** /'trʌmpitə/ *n* 1 a trumpet player; *specif* one who gives (military) signals with a trumpet 2a any of several large long-legged long-necked birds (genus *Psophia*) related to the cranes that have a dark plumage with lighter patches on the wings and a characteristic hunched posture, live in the jungles of N South America, and feed on berries and insects **b** **trumpeter swan, trumpeter** a rare white N American wild swan (*Cygnus buccinator*) noted for its sonorous voice **c** any of an Asiatic type of domestic pigeon with a rounded crest and heavily feathered feet

**trumpet flower** *n* any of various plants (eg a TRUMPET CREEPER) with trumpet-shaped flowers; *also* a trumpet-shaped flower

**trumpet shell** *n* ¹TRITON 1 (snail-like animal with an elongated conical shell)

¹**truncate** /'trʌŋkeɪt, -'-/ *vt* 1 to shorten (as if) by cutting off a part; lop 2 to cut (the edges or corners off a crystal) [L *truncatus*, pp of *truncare*, fr *truncus* trunk] – **truncation** *n*

²**truncate** *adj* having the end square or even ⟨*the ~ leaves of the tulip tree*⟩

**truncated** /'trʌŋkeɪtid, -'--/ *adj* having the apex replaced by a flat plane, esp one parallel to the base ⟨*~ cone*⟩

¹**truncheon** /'trʌnʧən/ *n* 1 a staff of office or authority; a baton 2 a short club carried esp by policemen [ME *tronchoun* broken spear, cudgel, fr MF *tronchon* broken remnant, fr (assumed) VL *truncion-, truncio*, fr L *truncus* trunk]

²**truncheon** *vt* to beat with a truncheon

¹**trundle** /'trʌndl/ *n* a small wheel or roller [alter. of earlier *trendle*, fr ME, circle, ring, wheel, fr OE *trendel*; akin to OE *trendan* to revolve – more at TREND]

²**trundle** *vi* 1 to roll 2 to move (as if) on wheels ⟨*trams* trundling *up and down the street*⟩ 3 to move heavily or laboriously; lumber ⟨*his horse ~d in last*⟩ ~ *vt* 1 to propel by rotating ⟨*we ~d the boulder down the hill*⟩ 2 to move (as if) on wheels ⟨*he ~d the potatoes home in the shopping basket*⟩

**trundle bed** *n* TRUCKLE BED (low bed)

**trundler** /'trʌndlə/ *n, NZ* 1 a child's pushchair 2 a bag on wheels for carrying golf clubs

**trunk** /trʌŋk/ *n* 1a the main stem of a tree, as distinguished from branches and roots **b(1)** the human or animal body apart from the head, limbs, and other appendages; the torso **b(2)** the region between the head and abdomen of an insect, bearing the wings and legs **c** the main or central part of something (eg a blood vessel or nerve, or a column) 2a a large rigid box used usu for transporting clothing and personal articles **b** the housing for a CENTREBOARD (retractable keel) or rudder 3 PROBOSCIS; *esp* the long flexible muscular proboscis of the elephant 4 *pl*

men's usu close-fitting shorts worn chiefly for swimming or sports 5a a chute, shaft, or similar major supply channel **b** a path over which information is transmitted, esp electrically (eg between telephone exchanges) 6 **trunk line, trunk** 6a a major route of communication: eg 6a(1) a main line of a railway system **a(2)** a telephone line between towns; *esp* a long-distance one **b** a main supply channel 7 *NAm* a car boot [ME *tronke* box, torso, fr MF *tronc*, fr L *truncus* tree-trunk, torso]

**trunk call** *n, chiefly Br* a telephone call made on a TRUNK LINE

**trunked** /'trʌŋkt/ *adj* having a trunk, esp of a specified kind – usu in combination ⟨*a grey-trunked tree*⟩

**trunkfish** /'trʌŋk,fɪʃ/ *n* any of numerous small brightcoloured fishes (family Ostraciidae) of tropical seas with the body and head enclosed in a rigid bony boxlike cover formed from thickened scales – called also BOXFISH

**trunk hose** *n taking pl vb* short full breeches reaching about halfway down the thigh that were worn chiefly in the late 16th and early 17th centuries [prob fr obs *trunk* to truncate]

**trunk road** *n, chiefly Br* a road of primary importance, esp for long distance travel

**trunnel** /'trʌnl/ *n* TREENAIL (wooden peg) [by alter. (prob influenced by ¹*trundle*)]

**trunnion** /'trʌnjən/ *n* a pin or pivot on which something can be rotated or tilted; *esp* either of two opposite projections on which a gun barrel can be tilted vertically [Fr *trognon* core, stump]

¹**truss** /trʌs/ *vt* 1a to secure tightly; bind – often + *up* **b** to bind the wings or legs of (a chicken, turkey, etc) closely in preparation for cooking 2 to support, strengthen, or stiffen with a truss [ME *trussen*, fr OF *trousser*] – **trusser** *n*

²**truss** *n* 1a BRACKET 1, CORBEL (weight-bearing projection) **b** a usu triangular assemblage of members (eg beams) forming a rigid framework (eg in a roof or bridge) 2 a device, usu a pad held in position by a belt, worn to lessen the protrusion of a hernia by pressure 3 a compact flower or fruit cluster (eg of tomatoes)

**truss bridge** *n* a bridge supported mainly by trusses

**trussing** /'trʌsɪŋ/ *n* 1 the members forming a truss 2 the trusses and framework of a structure

¹**trust** /trʌst/ *n* 1 confident belief in or reliance on (the character, ability, strength, honesty, etc of) somebody or something ⟨*take it on ~*⟩ 2 financial credit 3a money or other property held by one person for the benefit of another **b** a combination of companies formed by a legal agreement; *esp, chiefly NAm* one that reduces or threatens to reduce competition 4a a charge or duty imposed in faith or as a condition of some relationship ⟨*a public office is a public ~* – Grover Cleveland⟩ **b** responsible charge or office ⟨*in a position of ~*⟩ **c** care, custody ⟨*the child was committed to his ~*⟩ 5 *archaic* reliability ⟨*there's no ~, no faith, no honesty in men* – Shak⟩ [ME, prob of Scand origin; akin to ON *traust* trust; akin to OE *trēowe* faithful – more at TRUE] – **in trust** in the care or possession of a trustee

²**trust** *vi* to place confidence; depend ⟨*~ in God*⟩ ⟨*~ to luck*⟩ ~ *vt* 1a to place in someone's care or keeping; entrust **b** to permit to do or to be without fear or misgiving ⟨*he won't ~ it out of his sight*⟩ 2a to rely on the truthfulness or accuracy of; believe ⟨*you can't ~ the description in the brochure*⟩ **b** to place confidence in; rely on ⟨*don't ~ that branch to bear your weight*⟩ – also used ironically in the imperative ⟨*~ him to arrive late!*⟩ **c** to expect or hope, esp confidently ⟨*I ~ you are well?*⟩ ⟨*we'll see you soon, I ~*⟩ 3 to extend financial credit to **synonyms** see RELY ON – **trustable** *adj*

**trust company** *n* a company that functions as a trustee for individuals or for companies and institutions and usu also engages in the normal activities of a commercial bank

**trustee** /trʌ'stiː/ *n* 1 a country that supervises a TRUST TERRITORY 2a a person appointed to administer property in trust for a beneficiary (eg a person or a charitable organization) **b** any of a body of people appointed to administer the affairs of a company or institution who occupy a position of trust and perform functions comparable to those of a trustee – **trusteeship** *n*

**truster** /'trʌstə/ *n* one who creates a trust – used in Scots law

**trustful** /'trʌstf(ə)l/ *adj* full of trust; confiding – **trustfully** *adv*, **trustfulness** *n*

**trust fund** *n* property (eg money or shares) held in trust

**trusting** /'trʌstɪŋ/ *adj* having or showing (too great) trust – **trustingly** *adv*

**trust territory** *n* a non-self-governing territory placed under an administrative authority by the United Nations

**trustworthy** /'trust,wuhdhi/ *adj* worthy of confidence; dependable, reliable – **trustworthily** *adv*, **trustworthiness** *n*

¹**trusty** /'trusti/ *adj* reliable ⟨*my ~ sword*⟩ – **trustily** *adv*, **trustiness** *n*

²**trusty** *n* a trusted person; *specif* a convict considered trustworthy and allowed special privileges △ trustee

**truth** /troohth/ *n, pl* **truths** /troohdhz, troohths/ **1** sincerity in action, character, and speech; honesty ⟨*a man of ~*⟩ **2a(1)** the state or quality of being true or factual ⟨*there's ~ in what she says*⟩ **a(2)** reality, actuality ⟨*~ is stranger than fiction*⟩ **a(3)** *often cap* a transcendent (eg spiritual) reality ⟨*let us, in life, in death, Thy steadfast ~ declare* – John Wesley⟩ **b** a judgment, proposition, idea, or body of statements that is (accepted as) true ⟨*scientific ~s*⟩ **c** the body of true statements and propositions, esp in a particular field **3a** the property (eg of a statement) of being in accord with fact or reality **b** conformity to an original or to a standard **4** *archaic* fidelity, constancy ⟨*what should I say since faith is dead and ~ away from you is fled?* – Sir Thomas Wyatt⟩ [ME *trouthe*, fr OE *trēowth* fidelity; akin to OE *trēowe* faithful – more at TRUE]

synonyms **Truth, verity, accuracy, veracity, candour, frankness**, and **verisimilitude** all mean "closeness to fact". **Truth**, the most general word, ranges in meaning from "something accepted as true" ⟨*the* **truths** *of science*⟩ to "conformity with the facts". **Verity** is the quality of being true, but *a* **verity** is often an enduring and valuable truth ⟨*the old* **verities** *upon which human life is based*⟩. **Accuracy** is freedom from factual error, particularly in what is measurable ⟨*doubt the* **accuracy** *of your figures*⟩. **Veracity** is chiefly the human quality of sincerity in describing reality ⟨*question an opponent's* **veracity**⟩. **Candour** and **frankness** are also human qualities, **candour** often implying blunt forthrightness about unwelcome truths, and **frankness** suggesting free directness of expression, often where euphemism might be expected ⟨*told me where it hurt with anatomical* **frankness**⟩. **Verisimilitude** is the quality of being convincing, as in good artistic representation ⟨*add* **verisimilitude** *by really washing her hair on stage*⟩. antonyms falsehood, untruth, error

**truth drug** *n* a substance administered in the belief that it will induce a subject under questioning to tell the truth or talk freely

**truthful** /'troohthf(ə)l/ *adj* telling or disposed to tell the truth – **truthfully** *adv*, **truthfulness** *n*

**truth serum** *n* TRUTH DRUG

**truth table** *n* a table that shows whether a compound statement is true or false in formal logic for each combination of truth-values of its component statements; *also* a similar table (eg for a computer logic circuit) showing the value of the OUTPUT for each value of each INPUT

¹**truth-,value** *n* the truth or falsity of a (logical) statement

¹**try** /trie/ *vt* **1a** to investigate (a case or issue) judicially **b** to conduct the trial of (an accused person) **2a** to make an attempt at ⟨*~ to do it*⟩ ⟨*~ doing it*⟩ ⟨*she* tried *the entrance exam twice, but failed*⟩ **b(1)** to test by experiment or trial – often + *out* ⟨*~ out a new plan*⟩ **b(2)** to investigate the state, capabilities, or potential of, esp for a particular purpose ⟨*~ the shop next door*⟩ ⟨*if you want some money, ~ your uncle*⟩ **c** to subject to something that tests the patience or endurance ⟨*enough to ~ the patience of a saint*⟩ **3** to melt down and obtain in a pure state; render – usu + *out* ⟨*~ out whale oil from blubber*⟩ **4** to fit or finish with accuracy – usu + *up ~ vi* to make an attempt ⟨*tried and* tried *but couldn't do it*⟩ [ME *trien*, fr AF *trier*, fr OF, to pick out, sift, prob fr LL *tritare* to rub to pieces, fr *tritus*, pp of *terere* to rub – more at THROW] – **try and** to try to ⟨*try and do it*⟩ – **try it on** *Br informal* to see how far one can pursue a course of disapproved or forbidden conduct without being stopped or penalized ⟨*some classes always* try it on *with a new teacher*⟩ – see also **try one's** HAND (at), **try on/out for** SIZE

usage The combination **try** and ⟨**try** *and stop him*⟩ has been established in English since the 16th century ⟨*to* **try** *and teach the erring soul* – John Milton⟩. It is perfectly legitimate except in formal writing, where it should be replaced by **try** *to* ⟨**try** *to stop him*⟩. Only **try** *to* can be used in the past tense ⟨*she* **tried** *to stop him*⟩.

**try on** *vt* **1** to put on (a garment) in order to examine the fit or appearance **2** *Br* to attempt to impose on somebody ⟨*don't go* trying *anything on with me, mate*⟩

**try out** *vi, NAm* to compete for a position, esp in an athletic team, or for a part in a play

²**try** *n* **1** an experimental trial; an attempt ⟨*made a good ~ at it*⟩ **2** a score in rugby that is made by touching down the ball

behind the opponent's GOAL LINE and that entitles the scoring side to attempt a kick at the goal for additional points

**trying** /'trie·ing/ *adj* irritating, annoying, or demanding – **tryingly** *adv*

'**try-,on** *n, Br informal* an attempt at imposing (something) on somebody ⟨*take no notice of his threats – it's just a ~*⟩

**tryout** /'trie,owt/ *n* an experimental performance or demonstration: eg **a** a test of the ability (eg of an athlete or actor) to meet requirements **b** a performance of a play before its official opening to determine response and discover weaknesses; a preview ⟨*they cut some of the dialogue after the ~*⟩

**trypanocide** /'tripənoh·sied, tri'panəsied/ *n* an agent that kills trypanosomes – **trypanocidal** *adj*

**trypanosome** /tri'panə,sohm, 'tripənə,sohm, trie-/ *n* any of a genus (*Trypanosoma*) of parasitic PROTOZOANS (single-celled microorganisms) having FLAGELLA (whiplike structures), that infest the blood of various VERTEBRATE animals including human beings, are usu transmitted by the bite of an insect, and include some types that cause SLEEPING SICKNESS and other serious diseases [NL *Trypanosoma*, genus name, fr Gk *trypanon* auger + NL *-soma* -some – more at TREPAN] – **trypanosomal, trypanosomic** *adj*

**trypanosomiasis** /,tripənəsə'mie·əsis, tri,panə-, trie-/ *n, pl* **trypanosomiases** /-seez/ infection with or disease caused by trypanosomes [NL]

**tryparsamide** /tri'pahsəmid/ *n* a synthetic arsenic-containing drug, $AsO(OH)(ONa)C_6H_4NHCH_2CONH_2·H_2O$, used esp in the treatment of trypanosomal African SLEEPING SICKNESS [fr *Tryparsamide*, a trademark]

**trypsin** /'tripsin/ *n* an ENZYME from the digestive juice secreted by the pancreas that breaks down protein in an alkaline medium in the SMALL INTESTINES; *also* any of several similar enzymes [Gk *tryein* to wear down (akin to L *terere* to rub) + ISV *-psin* (as in pepsin) – more at THROW] – **tryptic** *adj*

**trypsinogen** /trip'sinəjin/ *n* the inactive substance released by the pancreas into the first part (DUODENUM) of the SMALL INTESTINE to form the enzyme trypsin [ISV]

**tryptamine** /'triptə,meen/ *n* (any of various hallucinogenic substances derived from) a chemical compound (AMINE), $C_{10}H_{12}N_2$, that is a derivative of tryptophan [*trypt*ophan + *amine*]

**tryptophan** /'triptə,fan/ *n* an AMINO ACID, $C_{11}H_{12}N_2O_2$, that is widely distributed in proteins and is necessary for the synthesis of the vitamin NIACIN, a deficiency of which causes the disease PELLAGRA in human beings [ISV *trypt*ic + *-o-* + *-phane*]

**tryptophane** /'triptə,fayn/ *n* tryptophan

**trysail** /'triesayl/ *naut* 'triesl/ *n* a small FORE-AND-AFT sail used in stormy weather in place of the mainsail to keep a vessel's head to the wind [obs *at try* lying to in a storm, fr ²*try*]

**try square** /trie/ *n* an L-shaped instrument used for marking out right angles and testing whether work (eg brickwork or carpentry) is square

¹**tryst** /trist, triest/ *n, poetic* **1** an agreement, esp by lovers, to meet **2** an appointed meeting or meeting place [ME, fr OF *triste* watch post, prob of Scand origin; akin to ON *traust* trust]

²**tryst** *vi, chiefly Scot or poetic* to make a tryst

**tsar, czar, tzar** /zah/ *n* **1** a male ruler of Russia before 1917 **2** one having great power or authority ⟨*undisputed ~ over taxation*⟩ [Russ *tsar'*, fr Goth *kaisar* emperor, fr Gk or L; Gk, fr L *Caesar* – more at CAESAR]

**tsarevitch, tsarevich** /'zahrəvich/ *n* a son, esp the eldest son, of the Russian tsar [Russ *tsarevich*, fr *tsar'* + *-evich*, patronymic suffix]

**tsarina** /zah'reenə/ *n* the wife of a tsar [prob modif of Ger *zarin*, fr *zar* tsar, fr Russ *tsar'*]

**tsarism** /'zah·riz(ə)m/ *n* **1** the government of Russia under the tsars **2** autocratic rule – **tsarist** *n or adj*

**tsaritsa** /zah'ritsə/ *n* a tsarina [Russ *tsaritsa*, fem of *tsar'*]

**tsetse** /'tetsi, 'tsetsi/, **tsetse fly** *n, pl* **tsetse, tsetses** any of several TWO-WINGED FLIES (genus *Glossina*) that occur in Africa, south of the Sahara desert and transmit diseases, esp SLEEPING SICKNESS, by biting human beings and animals and infecting them with TRYPANOSOMES (parasitic single-celled animals) [Afrik, fr Tswana *tsêtsê*]

**Tshi** /cha'wee, chee/ *n* TWI (W African language)

**Tshiluba** /chi'loohbə/ *n* a major trade language of Zaire, esp in the southern part

'**T-,shirt** /tee/ *n* a collarless upper garment of light stretchy fabric for casual wear [fr its being shaped like the letter T]

**tsotsi** /'tsotsee, 'tsaw-/ *n, SAfr* a young black hooligan [origin unknown]

**T square** *n* a ruler with a crosspiece or head at one end used in making parallel lines

**tsunami** /tsoo'nahmi/ *n* a great sea wave produced by underwater earth movement or volcanic eruption – called also TIDAL WAVE [Jap] – **tsunamic** *adj*

**Tswana** /ch'wahnə, 'swahnə, 'tswahnə/ *n, pl* **Tswanas**, *esp collectively Tswana* a member of any of several BANTU-speaking peoples of S Africa and Botswana; *also* the language spoken by these peoples

**t test** *n* a statistical test using the T DISTRIBUTION

**Tuamotu** /,tooh·ə'mohtooh/ *n* the Polynesian language of the Tuamotu archipelago

**Tuareg** /'twahreg/ *n, pl* **Tuaregs**, *esp collectively* **Tuareg** (the BERBER language of) a member of a nomadic Muslim people of the central and western Sahara and areas along the Middle Niger from Timbuktu to Nigeria [Ar *Tawāriq*]

**tuatara** /,tooh·ə'tahrə/ *n* a large spiny lizardlike reptile (*Sphenodon punctatum*) that has a crest along its neck and back, lives in burrows on islands off the coast of New Zealand, is active at night, and feeds on insects [Maori *tuatára*]

**¹tub** /tub/ *n* **1a** any of various wide low often round vessels typically made of wood, metal, or plastic and used industrially or domestically (e g for washing clothes or holding soil for shrubs) **b** a small round plastic or cardboard container in which cream, ice cream, etc may be bought **2** BATH 4 **3** the amount that a tub will hold **4** *informal* an old or slow boat [ME *tubbe*, fr MD; akin to MLG *tubbe* tub] – **tubful** *n*

**²tub** *vb* **-bb-** *vt* to wash or bath in a tub

**tuba** /'tyoohbə/ *n* the lowest-pitched of the BRASS INSTRUMENTS, that has a long conical convoluted tube, a cup-shaped mouthpiece, and finger-operated VALVES to vary the pitch and is played with the flared free end pointing upwards [It, fr L, trumpet]

**tubal** /'tyoohbl/ *adj* of or involving a tube, esp a FALLOPIAN TUBE connecting an ovary to the womb ⟨*a ~ pregnancy*⟩

**tubby** /'tubi/ *adj* **1** podgy, fat **2** sounding dull and unresonant ⟨*a ~ violin*⟩ [¹*tub* + ¹-*y*] – **tubbiness** *n*

**tube** /tyoohb/ *n* **1a** a hollow elongated cylinder; *esp* one to convey liquids or gases **b(1)** a slender channel within a plant or animal body; a duct **b(2)** the narrow basal part of the COROLLA (the petals collectively) or CALYX (the leaflike sepals collectively) of some flowers in which all the petals or sepals are joined **2** any of various usu cylindrical structures or devices: e g **2a** a small cylindrical container of soft metal or plastic sealed at one end and fitted with a cap at the other from which a paste or other semisolid substance is dispensed by squeezing ⟨*roll up the toothpaste ~ as you use it*⟩ ⟨*a ~ of glue*⟩ **b** TEST TUBE **c** the basically cylindrical section between the mouthpiece and free end of a WIND INSTRUMENT **3** ELECTRON TUBE (device for producing a controlled flow of electrons); *specif, chiefly NAm* THERMIONIC VALVE **4** a CATHODE-RAY TUBE (e g of a television set); *broadly, humorous* the television **5** *Br* (a train running in) an underground railway running through deep bored tunnels **6** *chiefly Austr informal* a can of beer [Fr, fr L *tubus;* akin to L *tuba* trumpet] – **tubed** *adj,* **tubelike** *adj*

**tube foot** *n* any of the small flexible tubular parts of starfish, SEA URCHINS, and other ECHINODERMS that are extensions of the water-circulatory system and are used esp in locomotion and grasping

**tubeless** /'tyoohblis/ *adj* lacking a tube; *specif* being an airfilled tyre that does not depend on an INNER TUBE to be airtight

**tube nucleus** *n* that one of the two nuclei resulting from the first CELL DIVISION in the POLLEN GRAIN of a plant producing seeds that is held to control subsequent growth of the tubular structure (POLLEN TUBE) that grows from the pollen grain into the female reproductive organ to convey the male reproductive cell to the female reproductive cell in the ovary, and that does not divide again – compare GENERATIVE NUCLEUS

**tuber** /'tyoohbə/ *n* **1a** a short fleshy usu underground stem (e g a potato) bearing minute SCALE LEAVES each of which bears a bud that may develop into a new plant ⟨*the bud on a potato ~ is usually called an eye*⟩ – compare BULB, CORM **b** a fleshy root or RHIZOME (underground stem) resembling a tuber **2** an anatomical swelling on an organ or other body part [L, lump, tuber, truffle; akin to L *tumēre* to swell – more at THUMB]

**tubercle** /'tyoohbəkl/ *n* **1** a small knobby prominence, esp on a plant or animal; a nodule: e g **1a** a protuberance near the

head of a rib **b** any of several protuberances in the CENTRAL NERVOUS SYSTEM **c** NODULE **b** (bacteria-containing swelling on the root of esp a clover) **2** a small abnormal lump in the substance of an organ or in the skin; esp one characteristic of tuberculosis [L *tuberculum*, dim. of *tuber*] – **tubercled** *adj*

**tubercle bacillus** *n* the bacterium (*Mycobacterium tuberculosis*) that causes tuberculosis

**tubercul-** /'tyoohbəkl/, **tuberculo-** *comb form* **1** tubercle ⟨tubercul*ar*⟩ **2** tubercle bacillus ⟨tubercul*in*⟩ **3** tuberculosis ⟨tubercul*oid*⟩ [NL, fr L *tuberculum*]

**¹tubercular** /tyoo'buhkyoolə/ *adj* **1** of, like, or being a tubercle **2** characterized by spots, lumps, etc typical of a tuberculous infection ⟨*~ leprosy*⟩ **3** tuberculous ⟨*~ meningitis*⟩ – **tubercularly** *adv*

**²tubercular** *n* someone suffering from tuberculosis

**tuberculate** /tyoo'buhkyoolət/, **tuberculated** /-laytid/ *adj* **1** having a tubercle; characterized by or covered with tubercles **2** TUBERCULAR 1 – **tuberculation** *n*

**tuberculin** /tyoo'buhkyoolin/ *n* a sterile liquid extracted from the TUBERCLE BACILLUS and used in the diagnosis of tuberculosis, esp in humans and cattle [ISV]

**tuberculin test** *n* a test for hypersensitivity to tuberculin as an indication of past or present tubercular infection

**tuberculoid** /tyoo'buhkyooloyd/ *adj* resembling tuberculosis, esp through the presence of tubercles ⟨*~ leprosy*⟩ [ISV]

**tuberculosis** /tyoo,buhkyoo'lohsis, tə-/ *n* a serious infectious disease of human beings and other VERTEBRATE animals caused by the TUBERCLE BACILLUS and characterized by fever and the formation of abnormal lumps in organs and other body parts which in human beings primarily affect the lungs [NL]

**tuberculous** /tyoo'buhkyooləs, tə-/ *adj* **1** of, being, or affected with tuberculosis ⟨*a ~ process*⟩ **2** caused by or resulting from the presence or products of the TUBERCLE BACILLUS ⟨*~ peritonitis*⟩ – **tuberculously** *adv*

**tuberose** /'tyoohbərohs/ *n* a bulbous Mexican plant (*Polianthes tuberosa*) of the daffodil family cultivated for its flower head of fragrant white single or double flowers [NL *tuberosa,* specific epithet, fr L, fem of *tuberosus* tuberous, fr *tuber*]

**tuberosity** /,tyoohbə'rosəti/ *n* a rounded knob; *esp* a large knob on a bone, usu one to which muscles or ligaments are attached

**tuberous** /'tyoohbərəs/ *adj* **1** consisting of, bearing, or resembling a tuber **2** of or being a tuber or tuberous root of a plant

**tuberous root** *n* a thick fleshy storage root like a tuber but lacking buds or SCALE LEAVES – **tuberous-rooted** *adj*

**tubicolous** /tyoo'bikaləs/ *adj, of a segmented worm* (e g a lugworm) living in a self-constructed tube [L *tubus* tube + E -*colous*]

**tubifex** /'tyoohbifeks/ *n, pl* **tubifex, tubifexes** any of a genus (*Tubifex* of the class Oligochaeta) of slender reddish segmented worms related to the earthworm, that live in tubes in fresh or slightly salt water and are widely used as food for aquarium fish [NL *Tubific-, Tubifex,* genus name, fr L *tubus* tube + *facere* to make – more at DO]

**tubificid** /tyoo'bifisid, ,tyoohbi'fisid/ *n or adj* (any) of a family (Tubificidae of the class Oligochaeta) of aquatic segmented worms (e g tubifex) that live at the bottom of deep lakes [NL *Tubificidae,* group name, fr *Tubific-, Tubifex,* type genus]

**tubing** /'tyoohbing/ *n* **1** (a length of) material in the form of a tube **2** a series or system of tubes

**tubocurarine** /,tyoohbohkyoo'rahrin, -reen/ *n* a drug, $C_{38}H_{44}Cl_2N_2O_6.5H_2O$, that is obtained chiefly from the bark and stems of a S American climbing plant (*Chondrodendron tomentosum* of the family Minispermaceae), is the chief active constituent of curare, and is used medically esp as a skeletal muscle relaxant [ISV *tubo-* (fr L *tubus* tube) + *curare* + -*ine;* fr its being shipped in sections of hollow bamboo]

**tub-thumper** /'tub ,thumpə/ *n* an impassioned or ranting public speaker – **tub-thumping** *n or adj*

**tubular** /'tyoohbyoolə/ *adj* **1** *also* **tubulous** /-ləs/ having the form of or consisting of a tube ⟨*a ~ calyx*⟩ **2** made of or fitted with tubes or tube-shaped pieces – **tubularly** *adj,* **tubularity** *n*

**tubule** /'tyoohbyoohl/ *n* a small tube; *esp* a slender tubular structure in a plant or animal ⟨*kidney ~* s⟩ [L *tubulus,* dim. of *tubus*]

**tuchun** /tooh'choohn/ *n* **1** a Chinese military governor (e g of a province) **2** a Chinese warlord [Chin (Pek) *dū zhün* (¹*tu* ¹*chün*)]

**¹tuck** /tuk/ *vt* **1a** to draw or gather up into a fold or folded position **b** to make a tuck or a series of tucks in **2** to place in a snug often concealed or isolated spot ⟨*a cottage* ~ed *away in the hills*⟩ **3** to push in the loose end or ends of so as to make secure or tidy ⟨~ *in your shirt*⟩ **4** to put into a tuck position when diving ~ *vi* **1** to draw together into tucks or folds **2** to fit snugly ⟨*the stool* ~s *neatly under the chair*⟩ [ME *tuken* to pull up sharply, scold, fr OE *tūcian* to ill-treat; akin to OE *togian* to pull – more at TOW]

**tuck away** *vt, informal* to eat up heartily ⟨*he tucks away a good dinner every day*⟩

**tuck in** *vi, informal* to eat heartily ⟨*they all tucked in without delay*⟩

**tuck in/up** *vt* **1** to cover snugly by tucking in bedclothes **2** to settle (a child) in bed for the night ⟨*it's late – I must go upstairs and tuck the children in*⟩

**tuck into** *vt, informal* to eat heartily ⟨*they shouldn't be tuck-ing into chocolate pudding*⟩

²**tuck** *n* **1** a (narrow) fold stitched into cloth to shorten or decorate or to reduce or distribute fullness **2** the part of a vessel where the ends of the lower planks meet under the stern **3** (an act of) tucking **4** a body position (eg in diving) in which the knees are bent, the thighs drawn tightly to the chest, and the hands clasped round the shins **5** *Br* food; *esp* chocolate, cakes, etc as eaten by schoolchildren ⟨*a* ~ *shop*⟩

³**tuck** *n, chiefly Scot* a sound (as if) of a drumbeat [obs *tuk* to beat the drum, fr ME *tukken*, fr ONF *toquer* to touch, strike, fr (assumed) VL *toccare*]

**tuckahoe** /ˈtukəhoh/ *n* **1** either of two American arums (*Peltandra virginica* and *Orantium aquaticum*) with rootstocks used as food by the American Indians **2** the large edible SCLEROTIUM (compact mass of hardened fungal threads containing food reserves) of an underground fungus (*Poria cocos*) [*tocka-whoughe* (in some Algonquian language of Virginia)]

¹**tucker** /ˈtukə/ *n* **1** one who or that which tucks **2** a piece of lace or cloth worn in the neckline of a dress in the 17th to 19th centuries **3** *Austr & NZ informal* food ⟨*a* ~ *bag*⟩

²**tucker** *vt, chiefly NAm* to exhaust – often + *out* [¹*tuck* (in obs sense "to reproach") + -*er* (as in ¹*batter*)]

**tucket** /ˈtukit/ *n, archaic* a fanfare on a trumpet [prob fr obs *tuk* to beat the drum, sound the trumpet]

¹**tuck-₁in** *n, informal* a hearty meal

¹**tuck-₁point** *vt* to finish (the mortar joints between bricks or stones) with a narrow ridge of putty or fine lime mortar

**-tude** /-tyoohd, -choohd/ *suffix* (→ *n*) -ness ⟨*pleni*tude⟩ ⟨*alti*tude⟩ [MF or L; MF, fr L -*tudin-*, -*tudo*]

**Tudor** /ˈtyoohdə/ *adj* **1** of the English royal house that ruled from 1485 to 1603 **2** (characteristic) of the Tudor period [Henry *Tudor* (Henry VII of England) †1509] – **Tudor** *n*

**Tuesday** /ˈtyoohzday, -di/ *n* the 3rd day of the week; the day falling between Monday and Wednesday [ME *tiwesday*, fr OE *tīwesdæg*; akin to OHG *zīostag* Tuesday; both fr a prehistoric WGmc-NGmc compound whose components are represented by OE *Tīw*, god of war & by OE *dæg* day – more at DEITY] – **Tuesdays** *adv*

**tufa** /ˈtyoohfə/ *n* **1** tuff **2** a porous rock formed as a deposit by springs or streams [It *tufo*, fr L *tophus*] – **tufaceous** *adj*

**tuff** /tuf/ *n* a rock composed of the finer kinds of volcanic ash usu fused together by heat [MF *tuf*, fr OIt *tufo* tufa] – **tuffaceous** *adj*

**tuffet** /ˈtufit/ *n* **1** TUFT 1a **2** a low seat (eg a hassock) [alter. of ¹*tuft*]

¹**tuft** /tuft/ *n* **1a** a small cluster of long flexible hairs, feathers, grasses, etc attached or close together at the base **b** a bunch of soft fluffy threads cut off short and used for ornament or as carpet pile **2** a clump, cluster [ME, modif of MF *tufe*, prob of Gmc origin] – **tufty** *adj*

²**tuft** *vt* **1** to provide or adorn with a tuft or tufts ⟨*a pattern of* ~ed *flowers*⟩ ⟨*a bedcover of* ~ed *cotton*⟩ **2a** to make (eg a mattress) firm by stitching at intervals and sewing on tufts **b** to make (a carpet) by fastening tufts of pile into a backing material ⟨*the most common construction nowadays for a carpet is* ~ed – *Which?*⟩ ~ *vi* to form into or grow in tufts – **tufter** *n*

**tufted duck** *n* a European diving duck (*Aythya fuligula*) the male of which has a black tufted head and white flanks

¹**tug** /tug/ *vb* -gg- *vi* to pull hard ~ *vt* **1** to pull or strain hard at **2** to move by pulling hard; haul *synonyms* see ¹PULL [ME *tuggen*; akin to OE *togian* to pull – more at TOW] – **tugger** *n*

²**tug** *n* **1a** a hard pull or jerk **b** a strong pulling force ⟨*she felt the* ~ *of the past*⟩ **2** a struggle between two people or opposite forces **3a** tugboat, tug a strongly built powerful boat used for

towing or pushing large ships (eg into and out of dock) **b** an aircraft that tows a glider

₁**tug-of-ˈlove** *adj, journalistic* of or involving a situation in which an adopted or foster child's real parent tries to reclaim him/her against his/her will from the adoptive or foster parents

₁**tug-of-ˈwar** *n, pl* **tugs-of-war 1** a struggle for supremacy **2** a contest in which teams pulling at opposite ends of a rope attempt to pull each other across a line marked between them

**tugrik, tugric** /ˈtoohgrik/ *n* – see MONEY table [Mongolian *dughurik*, lit., round thing, wheel]

**tui** /ˈtooh·i/ *n* a glossy black New Zealand HONEY EATER (*Prosthemadera novaeseelandiae*) that has a tuft of white feathers at its throat, feeds on nectar, fruit, and insects, has a melodious song and an ability to mimic human speech, and is often kept as a cage bird – called also PARSON BIRD [Maori]

**tuille** /twiəl, tweel/ *n* either or any of the hinged plates protecting the front of the thigh in plate armour [ME *toile*, fr MF *tuille* tile, fr L *tegula* – more at TILE]

**tuition** /tyooh·ish(ə)n/ *n* **1** teaching, instruction ⟨*he pursued his studies under private* ~⟩ **2** *chiefly NAm* the fee for instruction, esp at a college or private school [ME *tuicioun* protection, fr OF *tuicion*, fr L *tuition-*, *tuitio*, fr *tuitus*, pp of *tueri* to look at, look after] – **tuitional** *adj*

**tularaemia** /ˌtoohlə·reemyə, -mi·ə/ *n* an infectious disease of rodents, human beings, and some domestic animals that is caused by a bacterium (*Pasteurella tularensis*), is transmitted esp by insect bites, and in human beings is marked esp by fever [NL, fr *Tulare* County, district of California, where it was first discovered]

**tulip** /ˈtyoohlip/ *n* any of a genus (*Tulipa*) of Eurasian plants of the lily family that grow from bulbs and are widely grown for their showy flowers; *also* the flower of a tulip [NL *tulipa*, fr Turk *tülbend* turban]

**tulip tree** *n* a tall N American tree (*Liriodendron tulipifera*) of the magnolia family with large green-yellow tulip-shaped flowers and soft white wood used esp for cabinetwork and wooden utensils; *broadly* any of various trees with tulip-shaped flowers

**tulipwood** /ˈtyoohlip·wood/ *n* **1** wood of the TULIP TREE; whitewood **2a** any of several showily striped or variegated woods; *esp* the rose-coloured wood of a Brazilian tree (*Physocalymma scabberimum*) of the henna family that is much used by cabinetmakers for inlaying **b** a tree that yields tulipwood

**tulle** /t(y)oohl/ *n* a sheer often stiffened silk, rayon, or nylon net used chiefly for veils, evening dresses, and ballet costumes [Fr, fr *Tulle*, city in France]

**tum** /tum/ *n, humorous* the stomach [short for *tummy*]

¹**tumble** /ˈtumbl/ *vi* **1a** to perform gymnastic feats in tumbling **b** to turn end over end in falling or flight ⟨~d *down the stairs*⟩ **2a** to fall suddenly and helplessly ⟨~s *to the ground*⟩ **b** to suffer a sudden downfall, overthrow, or defeat ⟨*government has* ~d⟩ **c** to decline suddenly and sharply (eg in price); drop ⟨*the stock market* ~d⟩ **d** to fall into ruin; collapse **3** to roll over and over, to and fro, or end over end; toss ⟨*thoughts tumbling about in the brain*⟩ **4** to move hurriedly and confusedly ⟨~d *out of bed*⟩ **5** *informal* to realize suddenly; CATCH ON – often + *to* ~ *vt* **1** to cause to tumble (eg by pushing or toppling) **2a** to throw together in a confused mass; bundle **b** to rumple, disorder **3** to whirl in a TUMBLING BARREL (eg in drying clothes or polishing gemstones) [ME *tumblen*, freq of *tumben* to dance, fr OE *tumbian;* akin to OHG *tūmōn* to reel]

²**tumble** *n* **1a** a confused heap **b** a disorderly state **2** an act or instance of tumbling ⟨*acrobats practising a* ~⟩; *specif;* a fall ⟨*took a nasty* ~⟩

**tumbledown** /ˈtumbl·down/ *adj* dilapidated, ramshackle

₁**tumble-ˈdrier** /ˈdrie·ə/, **tumbler-drier** *n* a machine consisting of a rotating heated drum in which wet laundry is dried – **tumble-dry** *vt*

**tumbler** /ˈtumblə/ *n* **1** one who or that which tumbles: eg **1a** one who performs tumbling feats; an acrobat **b** any of various domestic pigeons that tumble or somersault backwards in flight or on the ground **2** a relatively large drinking vessel of glass or plastic (eg for soft drinks) without a foot, stem, or handle that was originally made with a pointed or convex base but is now flat-bottomed **3a** a movable obstruction (eg a lever, wheel, or pin) in a lock that must be adjusted to a particular position (eg by a key) before the bolt can be moved **b** a spring-operated lever that forces the hammer of a firearm forwards when released by the trigger **c(1)** a projecting piece on a revolving or oscillating shaft for actuating another piece **c(2)** the movable part of a reversing or speed-changing gear **4a** a tumble-drier **b** TUMBLING BARREL – **tumblerful** *n*

**tumbleweed** /'tumbl,weed/ *n* any of various esp N American plants (e g some amaranths) that break away from their roots in the autumn and are driven about by the wind as a light rolling mass

**tumbling** /'tumbling, 'tumbl·ing/ *n* the skill, practice, or sport of executing gymnastic feats, esp somersaults and handsprings, without the use of apparatus

**tumbling barrel** *n* a revolving cask in which objects or materials undergo a process (e g drying, cleaning, or polishing) by being whirled about

**tumbrel, tumbril** /'tumbrəl/ *n* **1** an open-ended farm cart that can be tipped up to empty its contents **2** a vehicle carrying condemned people, esp political prisoners during the French Revolution, to a place of execution [ME *tombrel*, fr OF *tumberel*, fr *tomber* to tumble, of Gmc origin; akin to OHG *tûmôn* to reel – more at TUMBLE]

**tumefacient** /,tyoohmi'faysh(y)ənt/ *also* **tumefactive** /-'faktiv/ *adj* (capable of) producing swelling [L *tumefacient-, tumefaciens*, prp of *tumefacere* to cause to swell]

**tumefaction** /,tyoohmi'faksh(ə)n/ *n* **1** an action or process of swelling or becoming tumorous **2** a swelling [MF, fr L *tumefactus*, pp of *tumefacere* to cause to swell, fr *tumēre* to swell + *facere* to make, do – more at THUMB, DO] – **tumefy** *vb*

**tumescent** /tyooh'mes(ə)nt/ *adj* (becoming or somewhat) swollen or distended; *esp, of the penis or clitoris* filled and swollen with blood, esp in response to sexual stimulation [L *tumescent-, tumescens*, prp of *tumescere* to swell up, incho of *tumēre* to swell] – **tumescence** *n*

**tumid** /'tyoohmid/ *adj* **1** *esp of a body part or tissue* marked by swelling or distension; swollen, enlarged ⟨a badly infected ∼ leg⟩ **2** *formal* bulging, protuberant ⟨sails ∼ in the breeze⟩ **3** *formal* pompous, inflated ⟨a ∼ style of writing⟩ [L *tumidus*, fr *tumēre*] – **tumidly** *adv*, **tumidity** *n*

**tummy** /'tumi/ *n, informal* the stomach [baby talk]

**tummy button** *n, informal* the navel

**tumorigenic** /,tyoohməri'jenik/ *adj* producing or tending to produce tumours, esp cancerous tumours – **tumorigenicity** *n*

**tumour,** *NAm chiefly* **tumor** /'tyoohmə/ *n* an abnormal swelling; *specif* an abnormal mass of tissue that arises without obvious cause from cells of existing tissue, possesses no physiological function, and is characterized by the tendency to grow unrestrainedly and independently of the surrounding tissues [L *tumor*, fr *tumēre* to swell] – **tumorous** *adj*

**tump** /tump/ *n* **1** a clump of vegetation **2** *chiefly W Mid Eng* a mound, hummock [origin unknown]

**tumpline** /'tump,lien/ *n* a strap or band fixed across the forehead or stomach for pulling or carrying a load [*tump* of Algonquian origin; akin to Abnaki *mádûmbi* pack strap]

**tumult** /'tyoohmult/ *n* **1a** noisy and disorderly agitation of a crowd; commotion, uproar **b** a turbulent uprising; a riot **2** a confusion or disordered medley (e g of sounds or colours) **3a** a state of violent mental or emotional agitation **b** a violent outburst [ME *tumulte*, fr MF, fr L *tumultus*; akin to Skt *tumula* noisy, L *tumēre* to swell]

**tumultuary** /tyoo'multyooəri/ *adj, formal* marked by tumult, lawlessness, and confusion; lacking in discipline or organization ⟨a ∼ army⟩ [L *tumultuarius*, fr *tumultus*]

**tumultuous** /tyooh'multyoo-əs, -choo-əs/ *adj* **1** marked by commotion and uproar ⟨∼ applause⟩ **2** causing or disposed to cause a tumult; disorderly **3** marked by violent turbulence or upheaval ⟨∼ passions⟩ [L *tumultuosus*, fr *tumultus*] – **tumultuously** *adv*, **tumultuousness** *n*

**tumulus** /'tyoohmyoolǝs/ *n, pl* **tumuli** /-li/ an artificial mound (e g over a grave); *esp* ¹BARROW [L; akin to L *tumēre* to swell – more at THUMB]

**tun** /tun/ *n* **1** a large cask, esp for wine **2** any of various units of liquid capacity; *esp* a unit equal to about 954 litres (210 gallons) △ ton [ME *tunne*, fr OE, prob of Celt origin – more at TUNNEL]

**¹tuna** /'tyoohnə/ *n* **1** any of various PRICKLY PEARS (genus *Opuntia*) with flattened jointed stems; *esp* one (*Opuntia tuna*) common in tropical America **2** the edible fruit of a tuna [Sp, fr Taino]

**²tuna** *n, pl* tuna, *esp for different types* tunas **1** any of numerous large sea fishes (family Scombridae) related to the mackerels, that have an elongated rounded body tapering to-

wards a forked or crescent-shaped tail and that are widely valued for food; *esp* BLUEFIN TUNA **2** tuna, tuna fish the flesh of a tuna, often canned for use as food □ called also TUNNY [AmerSp, alter. of Sp *atún*, modif of Ar *tūn*, fr L *thunnus*, fr Gk *thynnos*]

**tunable** *also* **tuneable** /'tyoohnəbl/ *adj* **1** capable of being tuned ⟨a ∼ laser⟩ **2** *archaic* sounding in tune – **tunableness** *n*, **tunability** *n*

**tundish** /'tun,dish/ *n* a reservoir in the top part of a mould into which molten metal is poured [ME, funnel for filling a tun]

**tundra** /'tundrə/ *n* a vast level or undulating treeless plain characteristic of arctic and subarctic regions, that consists of a thin layer of black marshy soil overlying a permanently frozen subsoil, and that supports a dense growth of mosses, lichens, and often brightly flowering dwarf shrubs and trees – compare TAIGA [Russ, of Finno-Ugric origin; akin to Lapp *tundar* hill]

**¹tune** /tyoohn/ *n* **1** manner of utterance; intonation; *specif* TONE UNIT (distinctive intonation pattern) **2a** a pleasing succession of musical notes; a melody **b** *the* dominant tune in a musical composition **3** correct musical pitch or harmony **4** accord, harmony ⟨in ∼ with the times⟩ **5** amount, extent – chiefly in *to the tune of* ⟨funded the scheme to the ∼ of a thousand pounds⟩ □ (3&4) chiefly in *in/out of tune* [ME, alter. of *tone*] – **change one's tune** to adopt a different attitude or approach, esp out of self-interest – see also CALL the tune

**²tune** *vi* **1** to bring a musical instrument or instruments into tune, esp to a standard pitch – usu + *up* ⟨the orchestra were tuning up⟩ **2** to become attuned *to* ∼ *vt* **1** to adjust the musical pitch of; *esp* to cause to be in tune ⟨∼d his guitar⟩ **2a** to bring into harmony; attune *to* **b** to adjust for optimum performance – often + *up* ⟨∼d up the engine⟩ **3** to adjust (e g an electronic circuit or a laser) so that RESONANCE (state of maximum vibration) occurs at the desired frequency; *esp* to adjust (a radio or television receiver) to respond to waves of a particular frequency – often + *in*

**tune in** *vi* to adjust a radio, television, etc receiver to respond to waves of a particular frequency; *broadly* to switch on a radio or television and start listening or watching ∼ *vt* to establish radio contact with ⟨tune in *a directional beacon*⟩

**tune into/to** *vt* to adjust a radio, television, etc receiver to respond to waves of (a particular frequency); *broadly* to switch on a radio or television and start listening to or watching (a particular broadcasting channel or programme)

**tune out** *vi* to cease to be attentive ⟨he just tunes out when the politicians start gabbling⟩ ∼ *vt* to adjust a radio, television, etc receiver to avoid the reception of ⟨tuned out *the interference*⟩

**,tuned-'in** *adj* informed about and responsive to current trends, opinions, or ideas ⟨a politician ∼ to popular feeling on the issue⟩

**tuneful** /'tyoohnf(ə)l/ *adj* melodious, musical – **tunefully** *adv*, **tunefulness** *n*

**tuneless** /'tyoohnlis/ *adj* **1** not tuneful **2** not producing music – **tunelessly** *adv*, **tunelessness** *n*

**tuner** /'tyoohnə/ *n* **1** somebody who tunes a usu specified device, esp as an occupation ⟨a piano ∼⟩ ⟨an engine ∼⟩ **2** something used for tuning: e g **2a** a part of a radio or television receiving set used to select a signal of a particular frequency and reject others close to it, and convert the selected signal into audio or visual signals ⟨a UHF ∼ in a television⟩ **b** a radio receiver whose output is an electrical signal that is fed into an amplifier ⟨a hi-fi FM ∼⟩

**tunesmith** /'tyoohn,smith/ *n, informal* a composer, esp of popular songs

**'tune-,up** *n* **1** a general adjustment to ensure operation at peak efficiency **2** a preliminary trial; a warm-up

**tung** /tung/, **tung tree** *n* any of several trees (genus *Aleurites*) of the spurge family whose seeds yield an oil used in paints and varnishes; *esp* a Chinese tree (*Aleurites fordii*) widely grown in warm regions [Chin (Pek) *tóng* (²¹*'ung*)]

**tungst-** /tungst-/ *also* **tungsto-** *comb form* tungsten ⟨tungstate⟩ [ISV, fr *tungsten*]

**tungstate** /'tungstayt/ *n* any of various chemical compounds (SALTS or ESTERS) formed by combination between a TUNGSTIC ACID and a metal atom, an alcohol, or another chemical group

**tungsten** /'tungstən/ *n* a hard heavy grey-white metallic chemical element that has a high melting point, can be drawn into wires, and is used esp for electrical purposes (e g for filaments in electric light bulbs) and in hardening and increasing the strength of alloys (eg steel) [Sw, fr *tung* heavy + *sten* stone]

**tungstic** /'tungstik/ *adj* of or containing tungsten, esp with a VALENCY of six [ISV]

**tungstic acid** *n* any of various oxygen-containing acids (eg $H_2WO_4$) of tungsten

**tungstite** /'tungstiet/ *n* a mineral consisting of an oxide of tungsten, $WO_3$, chemically combined with water molecules and occurring in yellow or yellowish-green crumbly masses

**Tungus** /'toong·goohz, 'tun-/ *n, pl* **Tunguses**, *esp collectively* **Tungus 1** a member of a Mongoloid people widely spread over E Siberia **2** the Tungusic languages of the Tungus peoples [Russ]

**Tungusic** /toong'goohzik, tun-/ *n* a branch of the ALTAIC language family spoken in Manchuria and regions to the north of it – **Tungusic** *adj*

**tunic** /'tyoohnik/ *n* **1** a simple slip-on garment that was usu knee-length or longer and belted or gathered at the waist and was worn as an under or outer garment by men and women in ancient Greece and Rome **2** an enclosing or covering membrane or tissue ⟨*the ~ of a seed*⟩ **3** a long usu plain closely fitting jacket with a high collar, worn esp as part of a uniform **4** a tunicle **5** a usu sleeveless slip-on garment that is hip-length or longer and belted at the waist ⟨*schoolgirl's gym ~*⟩ [L *tunica*, of Sem origin; akin to Heb *kuttōneth* coat]

**tunica** /'tyoohnikə/ *n, pl* **tunicae** /-kie/ an enveloping membrane or layer of body tissue; TUNIC 2 [L, tunic, membrane]

**¹tunicate** /'tyoohnikət, -kayt/ *also* **tunicated** /-kaytid/ *adj* **1a** having or covered with a tunic or tunica **b** *esp of a bulb* having, arranged in, or made up of concentric tissue layers **2** of or belonging to the tunicates [L *tunicatus*, fr *tunica*]

**²tunicate** *n* any of a subphylum (Tunicata syn Urochordata) of marine animals (eg SEA SQUIRTS) that have an unsegmented body protected by a tough outer tunic, have a simple nervous system, are free-floating or live attached to rocks, and feed by filtering particles from the water [NL *Tunicata*, group name, fr neut pl of L *tunicatus* tunicate]

**tunicle** /'tyoohnikl/ *n* a short vestment worn by a SUBDEACON over the ALB (long white vestment) during mass and by a bishop under the ceremonial overgarment (DALMATIC) at certain ceremonies [ME, fr L *tunicula*, dim. of *tunica*]

**tuning fork** /'tyoohning/ *n* a 2-pronged metal implement that gives a fixed tone when struck and is used for tuning musical instruments and ascertaining pitches for singing

**tuning pipe** *n* PITCH PIPE (pipe for ascertaining musical pitch); *specif* any of a set of pitch pipes used esp for tuning stringed instruments

**¹tunnel** /'tunl/ *n* **1** a hollow channel or recess (eg for a PROPELLER SHAFT); a tube **2a** a covered passageway; *specif* a man-made horizontal passageway through or under an obstruction ⟨*the Blackwall ~ under the Thames*⟩ **b** a subterranean passage or corridor (eg in a mine) **c** a burrow [ME *tonel* tube-shaped net, fr MF, *tun*, fr OF, fr *tonne* tun, fr ML *tunna*, of Celt origin; akin to MIr *tonn* skin, hide; akin to L *tondēre* to shear – more at TOME] – **tunnel-like** *adj*

**²tunnel** *vb* **-ll-** (*NAm* **-l-, -ll-**) *vt* **1** to make a passage through or under ⟨*~ling the Alps*⟩ **2** to make (eg one's way) by tunnelling; excavate ⟨*a new metro is being ~led*⟩ ~ *vi* **1** to make or pass through a tunnel ⟨*~ling under the Thames*⟩ **2** *physics* to pass through a POTENTIAL ENERGY barrier by means of the TUNNEL EFFECT ⟨*electrons ~ling through an insulator between semiconductors*⟩ – **tunneller** *n*

**tunnel effect** *n* a phenomenon that can be explained by WAVE MECHANICS, in which something, esp a particle (eg an electron), passes through a POTENTIAL ENERGY barrier that requires the expenditure of more energy to cross than that possessed by the particle

**tunnel vision** *n* **1** a condition in which the edges of the VISUAL FIELD are lost (eg as a result of the growth of a tumour into the OPTIC NERVE), leaving good vision only in the straight-ahead position **2** extreme narrowness of viewpoint; narrow-mindedness

**tunny** /'tuni/ *n, pl* **tunny**, *esp for different types* **tunnies** (the flesh of) a tuna [modif of MF *thon* or OIt *tonno;* both fr OProv *ton*, fr L *thunnus*, fr Gk *thynnos*]

**¹tup** /tup/ *n* **1** a heavy metal body (eg the weight of a pendulum or the head of a steam hammer) **2** *chiefly Br* a male sheep; a ram [ME *tupe* ram]

**²tup** *vt* **-pp-** *chiefly Br, of a ram* to copulate with (a ewe)

**Tupamaro** /ˌtyoohpə'mahrə/ *n, pl* **Tupamaros** any of a group of left-wing Uruguayan URBAN GUERRILLAS [AmerSp, fr *Tupac Amarú* †1781 Peruvian Indian revolutionary]

**tupelo** /'tyoohpəloh/ *n, pl* **tupelos** any of a genus (*Nyssa* of the family Nyssaceae) of mostly N American and E Asian trees with pale soft easily worked wood; *also* the wood of a tupelo [Creek *ito opilwa* swamp tree]

**Tupi** /tooh'pee/ *n, pl* **Tupis**, *esp collectively* **Tupi 1** a member of a group of Tupi-Guaranian peoples of Brazil living esp in the Amazon valley **2** the language of the Tupi people – **Tupian** *adj*

**Tupi-Guarani** /ˌtoohpee ˌgwahrə'nee, toh'pee/ *n* **1** a member of an American Indian people spread over a large area from E Brazil to the Peruvian Andes and from the Guianas to Uruguay **2** TUPI-GUARANIAN

**Tupi-Guaranian** /ˌtoohpee ˌgwahrə'nee-ən, tooh'pee/ *adj or n* (of) a language stock of tropical S America

**-tuple** /-tyoopl/ *suffix* (→ *n*) set of (so many) elements – usu used with reference to mathematical sets with ordered elements ⟨*the ordered 2-*tuple (*a, b*)⟩ [quin*tuple*, sex*tuple*]

**tuppence** /'tup(ə)ns/ *n* (a) twopence

**tuppenny** /'tup(ə)ni/ *adj* twopenny

**Turanian** /tyoo'raynyən, -ni·ən/ *n* **1** a member of any of the peoples of URAL-ALTAIC stock **2** the total body of various language families of Asia which are neither SEMITIC nor INDO-EUROPEAN; *esp* URAL-ALTAIC [Per *Tūrān* Turkestan, region in central Asia] – **Turanian** *adj*

**turban** /'tuhbən/ *n* **1** a headdress worn esp by Muslims and Sikhs and made of a long cloth wound either round a cap or directly round the head **2** a headdress resembling a turban; *esp* a woman's hat [MF *turbant*, fr It *turbante*, fr Turk *tülbend*, fr Per *dulband*] – **turbaned, turbanned** *adj*

**turbellarian** /ˌtuhbi'leəri·ən/ *n* any of a class (Turbellaria) of mostly aquatic and nonparasitic (FREE-LIVING) flatworms; *esp* PLANARIAN [deriv of L *turbellae* (pl) bustle, stir, dim. of *turba* confusion, crowd; fr the tiny eddies created in water by the vibrating hairlike parts covering the animal's body] – **turbellarian** *adj*

**turbid** /'tuhbid/ *adj* **1a** thick or opaque (as if) with disturbed sediment; cloudy ⟨*a ~ stream*⟩ **b** thick with smoke or mist; dense **2** *formal* **2a** not clear or pure; foul, muddy ⟨*~ depths of degradation*⟩ **b** characterized by or producing confusion (eg of mind or emotions) ⟨*an emotionally ~ response*⟩ **synonyms** see TURGID **antonyms** clear, limpid [L *turbidus* confused, turbid, fr *turba* confusion, crowd; akin to OHG *dweran* to stir, L *turbare* to throw into disorder, disturb, Gk *tyrbē* confusion] – **turbidly** *adv*, **turbidness, turbidity** *n*

**turbinal** /'tuhbinl/ *adj or n* (of or being) any of the usu several thin folded or spirally coiled membrane-covered plates of bone or cartilage on the walls of the passages of the nose [L *turbin-*, *turbo* top, whirlwind, whirl]

**¹turbinate** /'tuhbinət, -nayt/ *also* **turbinated** /-naytid/ *adj* **1** shaped like a top or an inverted cone ⟨*a ~ seed capsule*⟩ ⟨*a ~ shell*⟩ **2** turbinal [L *turbinatus*, fr *turbin-*, *turbo*]

**²turbinate** *n* **1** a turbinate structure, esp a shell **2** a turbinal

**turbine** /'tuhbien/ *n* a ROTARY ENGINE whose central driving shaft is fitted with vanes that are rotated by the pressure of water, steam, exhaust gases, etc [Fr, fr L *turbin-*, *turbo* top, whirlwind, whirl; akin to L *turbare* to disturb]

**turbit** /'tuhbit/ *n* a domestic pigeon bred for its short crested head, short beak, frilled breast, and mostly white plumage [origin unknown]

**turbo** /'tuhboh/ *n, pl* **turbos 1** a turbine **2** TURBOSUPERCHARGER (powerful turbine)

**turbo-** /tuhboh-/ *comb form* consisting of, incorporating, or driven by a turbine ⟨*turbojet engine*⟩ ⟨*turbocharger*⟩ [turbine]

**turbocar** /'tuhboh,kah/ *n* a vehicle propelled by a GAS TURBINE engine

**turbocharge** /'tuhboh,chahj/ *vt* to supply an air-fuel charge at a higher-than-normal pressure to (an INTERNAL-COMBUSTION ENGINE) by means of a turbocharger so as to increase the power output; SUPERCHARGE using a turbocharger

**turbocharger** /'tuhboh,chahjə/ *n* a compressor device that is used to SUPERCHARGE (supply an air-fuel charge at a higher-than-normal pressure to) an INTERNAL-COMBUSTION ENGINE and is usu driven by an exhaust-gas turbine

**turboelectric** /ˌtuhboh·i'lektrik/ *adj* involving or depending on electricity produced by turbine-driven generators as a power source ⟨*ships with ~ drive*⟩

**turbofan** /'tuhboh,fan/ *n* **1** a fan that is directly connected to and driven by a turbine and is used to supply air for cooling, ventilation, or combustion; *esp* an extra large fan in front of the main COMPRESSOR of a JET ENGINE **2** a JET ENGINE having a turbofan

**turbojet** /'tuhboh,jet/ *n* **1** an aircraft powered by turbojet engines **2 turbojet engine, turbojet** a JET ENGINE in which a COMPRESSOR driven by power from a turbine supplies compressed air to the combustion chamber and in which thrust is derived from the rearward expulsion of hot gases

**turboprop** /'tuhboh,prop/ *n* **1 turboprop engine, turboprop** a JET ENGINE which has a turbine-driven propeller, like that of an ordinary propeller-driven aircraft, for providing the main thrust and in which additional thrust is provided by the expulsion of hot exhaust gases **2** an aircraft powered by turboprop engines

**turbo-propeller engine** *n* TURBOPROP 1

**turboramjet engine** /,tuhboh'ramjet/ *n* a JET ENGINE consisting essentially of a TURBOJET ENGINE with provision for burning additional fuel in the tail pipe or the portion of the engine to the rear of the turbine

**turboshaft** /'tuhboh,shahft/ *n* a GAS TURBINE engine that is similar in operation to a turboprop but instead of being used to power a propeller is used through a transmission system for powering other devices (e g helicopter rotors and pumps)

**turbosupercharged** /,tuhboh'soohpə,chahjd/ *adj* equipped with a turbosupercharger

**turbosupercharger** /,tuhboh'soohpə,chahjə/ *n* a turbine compressor that is driven by hot exhaust gases and feeds rarefied air at high altitudes into the carburettor of an aircraft engine at sea-level pressure so as to increase power

**turbot** /'tuhbət/ *n, pl* **turbot,** *esp for different types* **turbots** (any of various flatfishes resembling) a large European flatfish (*Scophthalmus maximus*) highly valued for food, that has a brownish upper surface marked with small scattered protrusions and a white undersurface [ME, fr OF *tourbot*]

**turbulence** /'tuhbyooləns/ *n* the quality or state of being turbulent: e g **a** a wild commotion **b** irregular atmospheric motion, esp when characterized by strong currents of rising and falling air **c** departure from a smooth flow in a gas or liquid

**turbulency** /'tuhbyoolənsi/ *n, archaic* turbulence

**turbulent** /'tuhbyoolənt/ *adj* **1** causing unrest, violence, or disturbance **2a** characterized by agitation or tumult; stormy ⟨the ~ years of the revolution⟩ **b** exhibiting physical turbulence [L *turbulentus,* fr *turba* confusion, crowd] – **turbulently** *adv*

**turbulent flow** *n* a gas or liquid flow in which the motion of a particle at a given point varies erratically in amount and direction – compare LAMINAR FLOW

**Turco-, Turko-** /tuhkoh-/ *comb form* **1** Turkic; Turk ⟨Turcophile⟩ **2** Turkish and ⟨Turco-*Greek*⟩ [*Turco-* fr ML *Turcus* Turk; *Turko-* fr *Turk*]

**Turcoman** /'tuhkəmən/ *n, pl* **Turcomans 1** TURKMEN (Near Eastern language) **2** TURKOMAN (people of SE USSR)

**turd** /tuhd/ *n, vulg* **1** a piece of excrement **2** a despicable person [ME *tord, turd,* fr OE *tord;* akin to MD *tort* dung, OE *teran* to tear – more at TEAR]

**turdoid** /'tuhdoyd/ *adj* (characteristic) of or resembling a thrush [L *turdus* thrush]

**tureen** /tyoo'reen, tə-/ *n* a deep usu covered bowl or dish from which a food, esp soup, is served at table [Fr *terrine,* fr MF, fr fem of *terrin* of earth, fr (assumed) VL *terrinus,* fr L *terra* earth – more at TERRACE]

**¹turf** /tuhf/ *n, pl* **turfs, turves** /tuhvz/ **1a(1)** the upper layer of soil bound by grass and plant roots into a thick mat, esp when covered with fine even grass ⟨the ~ of a bowling green⟩ **a(2)** a piece of turf; a sod **b** an artificial substitute for turf (e g on a playing field) – compare ASTROTURF **2a** peat **b** a piece of peat dried for fuel **3a** a racecourse for horse racing; *also* the sport or business of horse racing [ME, fr OE; akin to OHG *zurba* turf, Skt *darbha* tuft of grass] – **turfy** *adj*

**²turf** *vt* to cover with turf

**turf out** *vt, chiefly Br informal* to dismiss or throw out forcibly

**turf accountant** *n, Br* a bookmaker

**turfman** /'tuhfmən/ *n, chiefly NAm* a devotee of horse racing; *esp* one who owns and races horses

**turgescent** /tuh'jes(ə)nt/ *adj* (becoming or somewhat) turgid, distended, or inflated [L *turgescent-, turgescens,* prp of *turgescere* to swell, incho of *turgēre* to be swollen] – **turgescence** *n*

**turgid** /'tuhjid/ *adj* **1a** swollen, distended **b** *of a cell* exhibiting turgor **2** in a pompous but laboured style ⟨~ *prose*⟩ [L *tur-*

*gidus,* fr *turgēre* to be swollen] – **turgidly** *adv,* **turgidness, turgidity** *n*

**synonyms** Turgid literally means "swollen" while turbid means "cloudy". A pompous and confused piece of writing can be both turgid and turbid.

**turgor** /'tuhgə/ *n* the normal state of firmness and tension of a living cell; *esp* the normal rigid condition of a plant cell in which the cell wall is distended by the pressure of the liquid contents [LL, swelling, fr L *turgēre*]

**Turk** /tuhk/ *n* **1** a member of any of numerous Asian peoples speaking Turkic languages who live in the region ranging from the Adriatic to the Okhotsk **2** a native or inhabitant of Turkey **3** a Turkish horse; *specif* any of a Turkish strain of Arab and crossbred horses **4** *archaic* a Muslim; *specif* a Muslim subject of the Turkish sultan **5** *archaic* one who is cruel or tyrannical [ME, fr MF *Turc,* fr ML or Turk; ML *Turcus,* fr Turk *Türk*]

**turkey** /'tuhki/ *n, pl* **turkeys,** *esp collectively* **turkey 1** a large N American bird (*Meleagris gallopavo*) related to the pheasant, domestic fowl, and grouse, that has a heavy rounded body, lustrous bronzy plumage, and a featherless head, and that is farmed for its meat in most parts of the world **2** the flesh of a turkey used as food **3** *NAm slang* a failure, flop **4** *NAm slang* an ineffectual person [*Turkey,* country in W Asia and SE Europe; fr confusion with the guinea fowl, supposed to be imported from Turkish territory] – **talk turkey** *chiefly NAm* to talk, esp about business, openly and frankly

**turkey buzzard** *n* an American vulture (*Cathartes aura*) common in S and Central America and in the southern USA that has blackish-brown plumage and red nearly naked wrinkled skin on the head and foreneck

**'turkey-,cock** *n* **1** a male turkey **2** a strutting pompous person

**Turkey red** *n* **1** a brilliant durable red colour produced in fabrics by means of ALIZARIN (orange to red dye); *also* alizarin **2** red IRON OXIDE used as a pigment [*Turkey*]

**turkey trot** *n* a ragtime dance danced with the feet well apart and with a characteristic rise on the ball of the foot followed by a drop onto the heel [*turkey*]

**Turki** /'tuhki/ *adj* **1** TURKIC 1b **2** of or being any of the central Asian Turkic languages, particularly of the eastern group [Per *turkī,* fr *Turk* Turk] – **Turki** *n*

**Turkic** /'tuhkik/ *adj* **1a** of a branch of the ALTAIC language family including Turkish **b** of the peoples speaking Turkic **2** TURKISH 1 – **Turkic** *n*

**¹Turkish** /'tuhkish/ *adj* **1** of Turkey, the Turks, or Turkish **2** TURKIC 1a

**²Turkish** *n* **1** the Turkic language of the Republic of Turkey **2** Turkish, Turkish tobacco a tobacco grown chiefly in Turkey and Greece that is of small leaf size, typically very aromatic, and used esp for cigarettes

**Turkish bath** *n* a steam bath followed by a rubdown, massage, and cold shower – compare SAUNA

**Turkish coffee** *n* a strong and usu sweetened coffee made from very finely ground beans

**Turkish delight** *n* a jellylike confection usu cut in cubes and dusted with sugar

**Turkish towel** *n* a towel made of cotton cloth with a rough pile of uncut loops

**Turkism** /'tuhkiz(ə)m/ *n* the customs, beliefs, institutions, and principles of the Turks

**Turkmen** /'tuhk,men/ *n* a Turkic language of the area east of the Caspian sea [Per *Turkmen, Turkmān* Turkoman]

**Turkoman, Turcoman** /'tuhkəmən/ *n, pl* **Turkomans, Turcomans** a member of any of a group of peoples of E Turkic stock living chiefly in the Turkmen, Uzbek, and Kazakh republics of the USSR [ML *Turcomannus,* fr Per *Turkmān,* fr *turkmān* resembling a Turk, fr *Turk*]

**Turk's head** *n* an ornamental turban-shaped knot

**turmeric** /'tuhmərik/ *n* **1a** an E Indian plant (*Curcuma longa*) of the ginger family with a large aromatic deep yellow RHIZOME (underground stem) **b** the cleaned, boiled, dried, and usu powdered RHIZOME of the turmeric plant used as a colouring agent or condiment (e g in curries) **c** a yellow to reddish-brown dyestuff obtained from turmeric **2** any of several plants that are closely related to turmeric and yield a similar product [modif of MF *terre merite* saffron, fr ML *terra merita,* lit., deserving or deserved earth]

**turmoil** /'tuhmoyl/ *n* an extremely confused or agitated state or condition [origin unknown]

**¹turn** /tuhn/ *vt* **1a** to cause to move round an axis; make rotate or revolve ⟨~ *a wheel*⟩ ⟨~ *a crank*⟩ **b(1)** to cause to move through an arc of a circle ⟨~ *a key*⟩ ⟨~ *the hands of the clock*⟩ ⟨~ed *his chair to the fire*⟩ **b(2)** to alter the functioning of (eg a mechanical device) (as if) by turning a knob, key, etc ⟨~ed *the oven to a higher temperature*⟩ **c** to perform by rotating or revolving ⟨~ *cartwheels*⟩ **d** to twist out of line or shape; wrench ⟨had ~ed *his ankle*⟩ **2** to cause (eg scales) to move so as to register weight **3a** to reverse the sides or surfaces of so as to expose another side ⟨~ *pancakes*⟩ ⟨~ *the page*⟩: **3a(1)** to dig or plough so as to bring the lower soil to the surface **a(2)** to renew (eg a garment) by reversing the material and resewing ⟨~ *a collar*⟩ **a(3)** to invert (eg a character) feet up and face down in setting type **b** to throw into disorder or confusion as specified ⟨*everything was* ~ed *topsy-turvy*⟩ **c** to disturb the mental balance of; derange, unsettle ⟨*a mind* ~ed *by grief*⟩ **d** to cause to change or reverse direction ⟨~ed *his car in the street*⟩ ⟨~ed *his steps homewards*⟩ **e** to check the course of; keep off ⟨*hat will* ~ *a bullet*⟩ ⟨*used fire hoses to* ~ *the mob*⟩ **4a** to bend or change the course or outcome of ⟨~ *the tide of history*⟩ ⟨*housewives' vote could* ~ *the election*⟩ **b** to go round or about; round ⟨~ed *the corner at full speed*⟩ **c** to reach or go beyond (eg an age or time) ⟨*he's just* ~ed *21*⟩ **5a(1)** to direct or point (eg the face) in a specified direction **a(2)** to present by a change in direction or position ⟨~ing *his back to his guests*⟩ **b** to cause to be applied (eg by aiming or focussing); train ⟨*cannon were* ~ed *on the rioting troops*⟩ **c** to direct (eg the attention or mind) towards or away from something ⟨~ed *his thoughts inwards*⟩ **d** to induce or influence (a person) to change sides or to defect ⟨~ed *the boy against his parents*⟩ **e** to direct the employment of; apply, devote ⟨~ed *his skills to the service of mankind*⟩ **f** to cause to rebound or recoil ⟨~s *their argument against them*⟩ **g(1)** to drive, send ⟨~ *cows out to pasture*⟩ ⟨~ing *hunters off his land*⟩ **g(2)** to direct into or out of a receptacle by inverting ⟨~ *the meat into a pot*⟩ ⟨*police asked her to* ~ *out the contents of her handbag*⟩ **6a(1)** to make acid or sour; curdle, ferment **a(2)** to change the colour of (leaves) **b** to translate, paraphrase **c** to cause to become by change ⟨~ *defeat into victory*⟩ ⟨~ed *him into a fiend*⟩ ⟨*illness* ~ed *her hair white*⟩ **d** to exchange for something specified ⟨~ *pounds into marks*⟩ **7a** to shape, esp in a rounded form, by applying a cutting tool while revolving in a lathe **b** to give a rounded form to ⟨~ *the heel of a sock*⟩ **c** to shape or fashion elegantly or neatly ⟨*well* ~ed *ankles*⟩ ⟨*a knack for* ~ing *a phrase*⟩ **8a** to fold, bend ⟨~ *a lead pipe*⟩ ⟨~ *his collar up*⟩ **b** to cause (the edge of a blade) to bend back or over; blunt, dull **9a** to keep (eg money or goods) moving; *specif* to dispose of (a stock) to make room for another **b** to gain in the course of business – esp in **turn an honest penny** ~ *vi* **1a** to (appear to) move round (as if) on an axis or through an arc of a circle ⟨*the wheel* ~s⟩ ⟨*I tossed and* ~ed *all night*⟩ **b(1)** to become giddy or dizzy; reel ⟨*heights always made his head* ~⟩ **b(2)** *of the stomach* to feel nauseated **c(1)** to hinge ⟨*the argument* ~s *on this point*⟩ **c(2)** to centre on something specific; revolve ⟨*the story* ~s *around a fatal passion*⟩ **c(3)** to arrive by turning pages ⟨~ *to chapter four*⟩ **2a** to direct one's course ⟨*didn't know which way to* ~⟩ **b(1)** to change or reverse direction ⟨*the tide* ~ed⟩ ⟨*his luck* ~ed⟩ ⟨*the main road* ~s *sharply to the right*⟩ **b(2)** to become reversed or inverted **3a** to change position so as to face another way ⟨*they* ~ed *to stare at him*⟩ ⟨*she* ~ed *from the gruesome sight*⟩ **b** to change or reverse one's attitude or position to one of opposition or hostility ⟨*felt the world had* ~ed *against him*⟩ **c** to make a sudden violent physical or verbal assault – usu + *on* or *upon* ⟨*dogs* ~ing *on their masters*⟩ ⟨*she* ~ed *upon him with ferocity*⟩ **4a** to direct one's attention or thoughts to or away from someone or something ⟨~ing *to my main topic . . .*⟩; *also* to be directed in this way ⟨*his thoughts* ~ed *to religion*⟩ **b(1)** to change one's religion **b(2)** to change sides; defect **c** to have recourse; refer, resort ⟨~ed *to a friend for help*⟩ ⟨*didn't know where to* ~ *for help*⟩ ⟨~ed *to his notes for the exact figures*⟩ **d** to direct one's efforts or interests; devote or apply oneself ⟨~ed *to the study of the law*⟩ **5a** to become changed, altered, or transformed: eg **5a(1)** to change colour ⟨*the leaves have* ~ed⟩ **a(2)** to become acid or sour; curdle, ferment ⟨*the milk had* ~ed⟩ **a(3)** to become mentally unbalanced or deranged **b** to become by change ⟨~ed *into a fiend*⟩ ⟨*water had* ~ed *to ice*⟩ ⟨~ *traitor*⟩ ⟨*the weather* ~ed *bad*⟩ ⟨*hair* ~ing *white*⟩ ⟨*they were Lowland farmers* ~ed *distillers – Decanter*⟩ **6** to become folded or bent; *esp* to become blunted by bending ⟨*the edge of the knife had* ~ed⟩ **7** to operate a lathe **8** *of mer-*

*chandise* to be stocked and disposed of; change hands – see also **turn one's** BACK **on, turn the other** CHEEK**, turn a deaf** EAR **(to), turn King's/Queen's/**(*NAm*)**State's** EVIDENCE**, turn a blind** EYE **to, turn on one's** HEEL**, turn one's** NOSE **up (at), turn somebody's** STOMACH**, turn the** TABLES**, turn** TAIL/TURTLE [ME *turnen;* partly fr OE *tyrnan* & *turnian* to turn, fr ML *tornare,* fr L, to turn on a lathe, fr *tornus* lathe, fr Gk *tornos;* partly fr OF *torner, tourner* to turn, fr ML *tornare;* akin to L *terere* to rub – more at THROW] – **turnable** *adj*

**turn away** *vt* **1** to deflect, avert **2a** to send away; reject, dismiss **b** to refuse admittance or acceptance to ~ *vi* to start to go away; depart

**turn back** *vi* **1** to go in the reverse direction; return **2** to refer to an earlier time or place ~ *vt* **1** to drive back or away **2** to stop the advance of **3** to fold back

**turn down** *vi* to be capable of being folded or doubled down ⟨*collar that* turns down⟩ ~ *vt* **1** to fold or double down **2** to turn (a playing card) face downwards **3** to reduce the intensity of by turning a control ⟨turn down *the radio*⟩ **4** to decline to accept; reject ⟨turned down *the offer*⟩

**turn in** *vt* **1** to deliver up; HAND OVER ⟨turn in *unused supplies*⟩; *esp* to deliver up to an authority ⟨*urged the wanted man to* turn *himself* in⟩ **2** to inform on; betray **3** to give, execute ⟨turned in *a good performance*⟩ ~ *vi* **1** to enter by turning from a road or path **2** *informal* to go to bed ⟨turned in *early*⟩

**turn off** *vt* **1** to stop the flow or operation of (as if) by turning a control ⟨turn *the radio* off⟩ ⟨turn *the programme* off⟩ **2** *informal* to cause to lose interest; bore ⟨*a subject that* turned off *a number of students*⟩; *specif* to cause to lose sexual interest **3** *archaic* **3a** to dismiss, discharge **b** to sell; DISPOSE OF ~ *vi* **1** to deviate from a straight course or from a main road ⟨turn off *into a side road*⟩ **2** to lose interest; withdrawn ⟨turned off *when they started talking politics*⟩

**turn on** *vt* **1** to cause to flow or operate (as if) by turning a control ⟨turn *the water on full*⟩ ⟨*she can* turn *on the charm when she has to*⟩ **2** *informal* **2a** to cause to undergo an intense often visionary experience by taking a drug; *broadly* to cause to get high **b** to excite or interest pleasurably ⟨*rock music* turns *her on*⟩; *specif* to excite sexually ~ *vi, informal* to become turned on

**turn out** *vt* **1a** to expel, evict **b** to put (eg a horse) to pasture **2a** to turn inside out ⟨turning out *his pockets*⟩ **b** to empty the contents of, esp for cleaning or rearranging ⟨turn out *the spare room*⟩ **3** to produce, often rapidly or regularly, (as if) by machine; manufacture ⟨turned out *20 cars a day*⟩ **4** to put out by turning a switch ⟨turn out *the lights*⟩ **5** to equip, dress, or finish in a specified way – usu pass ⟨*he was nicely* turned out *in a suit and tie*⟩ **6** to call (eg the guard or a company) out from rest or shelter and into formation **7** to transfer from a receptacle by inverting ⟨turn *the pudding* out *onto a flat dish*⟩ ~ *vi* **1a** to leave one's home for a special purpose ⟨*voters* turned out *in droves*⟩ **b** to get out of bed **2a** to prove to be ultimately ⟨*the play* turned out *to be a flop*⟩ ⟨*nobody thought he'd* turn out *like this*⟩ **b** to end ⟨*stories that* turn out *happily*⟩

**turn over** *vt* **1a** to turn from an upright position; overturn **b** to rotate ⟨turn over *a stiff valve with a wrench*⟩; *also* to cause (an INTERNAL-COMBUSTION ENGINE) to revolve and usu to fire **2** to search through (eg clothes or papers) by shifting one by one **3** to think over; meditate on **4** to deliver, surrender ⟨turned *her* over *to the police*⟩ **5a** to receive and dispose of (a stock of merchandise) **b** to do business to the amount of ⟨turning over *£1000 a week*⟩ **6** *informal* to ransack ⟨*police* turned over *his pad*⟩ ~ *vi* **1** to upset, capsize **2a** to rotate **b** *of an* INTERNAL-COMBUSTION ENGINE to revolve at low speed **3a** *of one's stomach* to heave with nausea **b** *of one's heart* to seem to leap or lurch convulsively with sudden fright **4** *of merchandise* to be stocked and disposed of

**turn round** *vt* to complete the processing of ⟨*can* turn round *a batch of 50 inside two hours*⟩

**turn to** *vi* to apply oneself to work; act vigorously

**turn up** *vt* **1** to find, discover **2** to raise or increase the intensity of (as if) by turning a control ⟨turned up *the radio*⟩ **3** to refer to or consult (a book) **4** to turn (a playing card) face upwards **5** to fold and fix in place (a strip of material) so as to give a double thickness (eg to give the required length to a trouser leg) **6** *informal* to cause to vomit; *broadly* to disgust ~ *vi* **1** to appear to come to light unexpectedly or after being lost **2a** to become evident ⟨*her name is always* turning up *in* *the newspapers*⟩ **b** to appear, arrive; *esp* to arrive at an appointed place or particular time ⟨turned up *half an hour late*⟩ **3** to happen or occur unexpectedly ⟨*something always* turned up *to prevent their meeting*⟩ **4** *of a ship* TACK (change direction) – see also **turn up like a bad** PENNY, **turn up** TRUMPS

²**turn** *n* **1a** the action or an act of turning about a centre or axis; a revolution, rotation **b** any of various rotating or pivoting movements in dancing **2a** the action or an act of giving or taking a different direction; change of course or posture ⟨*illegal left* ~s⟩: eg **2a(1)** a drill manoeuvre in which troops in mass formation change direction without preserving alignment **a(2)** any of various shifts of direction in skiing **a(3)** an interruption of a curve in FIGURE SKATING **b** a deflection, deviation ⟨*the twists and* ~s *of the story*⟩ **c** the action or an act of turning so as to face in the opposite direction; reversal of position or course ⟨*an about* ~⟩ ⟨~ *of the tide*⟩ **d** a change made by reversing or inverting ⟨~ *of the cards*⟩ **e** a place at which a change in direction occurs; a bend, curve **3** a short trip (eg a walk or drive) out and back or round about ⟨*took a* ~ *through the park*⟩ **4** an act or deed of a specified kind affecting another ⟨*one good* ~ *deserves another*⟩ **5a** a period of action or activity; a go, spell; *specif* a bout of wrestling **b** a place, time, or opportunity granted in succession or rotation ⟨*our* ~ *to bat*⟩ ⟨*waiting his* ~ *in the queue*⟩ **c** a period or tour of duty; a shift ⟨*on early* ~⟩ **d** a usu short act or performance (eg in a variety show) ⟨*a comedy* ~⟩; *also* a performer or performers in such an act ⟨*chief* ~ *consisted of four performing elephants* – Osbert Sitwell⟩ **e(1)** an event in any gambling game after which bets are settled **e(2)** the order of the last three cards in the game of FARO – in **call the turn 6a** something that revolves round a centre; *esp* a lathe **b** a musical ornament consisting of four or more notes that wind about the principal note by including the notes next above and below **7** a special purpose or requirement – chiefly in **serve one's turn 8a** an alteration, change ⟨*a nasty* ~ *in the weather*⟩ ⟨*an unusual* ~ *of events*⟩ ⟨*a* ~ *for the better*⟩ **b** a point of change in time ⟨*the* ~ *of the century*⟩ **9a** a style of expression or arrangement of words; *esp* a skilful detail of style – compare TURN OF PHRASE **b** the shape or mould in which something is fashioned; a cast **10a** the state or manner of being coiled or twisted **b** a single coil (eg of rope or wire wound round an object) **11** a natural or special ability or aptitude; a bent, inclination ⟨*a* ~ *for logic*⟩ ⟨*an optimistic* ~ *of mind*⟩ **12** a special twist, construction, or interpretation ⟨*gave the old yarn a new* ~⟩ **13a** a disordering spell or attack (eg of illness, faintness, or dizziness) **b** a nervous start or shock ⟨*gave me quite a* ~⟩ **14a** a complete transaction involving a purchase and sale of securities; *also* a profit from such a transaction **b** TURNOVER 6b **15** something turned or to be turned: eg **15a** a character inverted in setting type **b** a piece of type placed bottom up [ME; partly fr OF *tourn, tour* lathe, circuit, turn (partly fr L *tornus* lathe; partly fr OF *torner, tourner* to turn); partly fr ME *turnen* to turn] – **at every turn** on every occasion; constantly, continually – **by turns** alternately, successively – **in turn** in due order of succession – **on the turn** at the point of turning ⟨*tide is* on the turn⟩ ⟨*milk is* on the turn⟩ – **out of turn 1** not in due order of succession ⟨*play* out of turn⟩ **2** at a wrong time or place; imprudently, unwisely ⟨*talking* out of turn⟩ – **take turns/take it in turns** to act by turns – **to a turn** to perfection ⟨*roasted* to a turn⟩ – **turn and turn about** one after another; BY TURNS

**turnabout** /'tuhnə,bowt/ *n* **1** a change or reversal of direction, trend, policy, or role **2** chiefly NAm a changing from one allegiance to another

**turnaround** /'tuhnə,rownd/ *n, chiefly NAm* TURNROUND ⟨*a five-day* ~ *on medical claims* – The Age (Melbourne)⟩

**turnbuckle** /'tuhn,bukl/ *n* a device that consists of a link with screw threads at both ends or a SCREW THREAD at one end and a swivel at the other, that is turned to bring the ends closer together, and that is used for tightening a wire, rod, etc

**turncoat** /'tuhn,koht/ *n* one who switches to an opposing side or party; *specif* a traitor

**turndown** /'tuhn,down/ *adj* (capable of being) worn turned down ⟨~ *collar*⟩

,**turned-'on** *adj, informal* keenly aware of and responsive to what is new and fashionable

¹**turner** /'tuhnə/ *n* one who or that which turns or is used for turning; *esp* one who works a lathe

²**turner** *n, chiefly NAm* a gymnast [Ger, fr *turnen* to perform gymnastic exercises, fr OHG *turnēn* to turn, fr ML *tornare* – more at TURN]

**Turner's syndrome** /'tuhnəz/ *n* a genetically determined condition in women that is associated with the absence of one X CHROMOSOME (chromosome concerned with the inheritance of sex) and that is characterized by a stocky physique with incomplete and infertile SEX GLANDS [Henry Hubert *Turner b* 1892 US physician]

**turnery** /'tuhnəri/ *n* the work, products, or workshop of a turner

**turning** /'tuhning/ *n* **1** the act or course of one who or that which turns **2** a place of turning, turning off, or turning back ⟨*take the third* ~ *on the right*⟩ **3a** the act or process of forming by use of a lathe; *broadly* the work of a turner **b** *pl* waste produced in turning **4** the amount, esp the width, of cloth that is folded under for a seam or hem

**turning circle** *n* the smallest circle round which a given vehicle can be driven

**turning point** *n* a point at which a significant change occurs

**turnip** /'tuhnip/ *n* **1** either of two plants of the cabbage family with thick fleshy edible roots: **1a** a plant (*Brassica rapa*) with hairy leaves and a white-fleshed root **b** a swede **2** the root of a turnip eaten as a vegetable or fed to stock **3** *informal* a large old-fashioned pocket watch [earlier *turnepe*, prob fr ¹*turn* + *neep*; fr the well-rounded root]

**turnkey** /'tuhn,kee/ *n, archaic* a prison warder

**turnoff** /'tuhn,of/ *n* **1** a turning off **2** a place where one turns off; *esp* a motorway junction **3** *informal* something that turns one off ⟨*finds hairy men a complete* ~⟩

**turn of phrase** *n* a style of expressing oneself ⟨*he had a witty personality and a neat* ~⟩

**turn of speed** *n* ability to go fast; capacity for speed

'**turn-,on** *n, informal* something that turns one on ⟨*finds hairy men a* ~⟩

**turnout** /'tuhn,owt/ *n* **1** an act of turning out **2** a number of people attending a gathering for some purpose ⟨*a good* ~ *at the meeting*⟩ **3** a clearing out and cleaning **4** manner of dress; getup **5** quantity of produce yielded **6** NAm **6a** TURNOFF 2 **b** a widened place on a road enabling vehicles to overtake

¹**turnover** /'tuhn,ohvə/ *n* **1** an act or result of turning over; an upset **2** a turning from one side, place, or direction to its opposite; a shift, reversal **3** something that is turned over **4** a small semicircular filled pastry made by folding half of the crust over the other half ⟨*apple* ~⟩ **5** the amount of business done; *esp* the volume of shares traded on a STOCK EXCHANGE **6a** movement (eg of goods or people) into, through, and out of a place **b** a cycle of purchase, sale, and replacement of a stock of goods; *also* the rate at which this occurs **c** the number of people taken on within a period to replace those leaving a working force; *also* the ratio of this number to the number in the average force maintained **d** the total sales revenue of a business

²**turnover** *adj* capable of being turned over

**turnpike** /'tuhn,piek/ *n* **1** chiefly NAm **1a** a main road; *esp* a motorway **b** a road on which a toll is payable **2** archaic a tollgate [ME *turnepike* revolving frame bearing spikes and serving as a barrier, fr *turnen* to turn + *pike*]

**turnround** /'tuhn,rownd/ *n* **1** (the time taken for) the arrival, unloading, loading, and servicing of a vehicle, aircraft, or ship in preparation for its next journey; *broadly* (the time taken for) the receipt and complete processing of something (eg a claim) **2** a reversal, esp to an opposite situation ⟨*£2¹/₂ billion* ~ *in the nationalized industries' finances* – New Statesman⟩

**turnsole** /'tuhn,sohl/ *n* any of several plants whose flowers or stems are supposed to turn with the direction of the sun; *esp* HELIOTROPE (sunflower) [ME *turnesole*, fr MF *tournesol*, fr OIt *tornasole*, fr *tornare* to turn (fr ML) + *sole* sun, fr L *sol* – more at SOLAR]

**turnspit** /'tuhn,spit/ *n* one who or that which turns a spit; *specif* a small dog formerly used in a treadmill to turn a spit

**turnstile** /'tuhn,stiel/ *n* a post with arms pivoted on the top that is set in a passageway so that people on foot can pass through only one at a time; *also* any similar device for admitting one person at a time

**turnstone** /'tuhn,stohn/ *n* any of a genus (*Arenaria*) of various widely distributed migratory WADING BIRDS resembling the related plovers and sandpipers; *esp* a short-billed bird (*Arenaria interpres*) that has upperparts that are variegated black and chestnut in summer and dark brown in winter, white underparts with a black breast, and short orange legs [fr a habit of turning over stones to find food]

**turntable** /'tuhn,taybl/ *n* a revolvable platform: eg **a** a circular platform for turning wheeled vehicles, esp railway engines **b** a rotating platform that carries a gramophone record – compare RECORD DECK

¹**turn-,up** n, chiefly Br **1** a turned up hem, esp on a pair of trousers; also, pl a pair of trousers with turn-ups **2** informal an unexpected or surprising event – esp in turn-up for the book/ books

²**turn-up** adj **1** turned up ⟨a ~ nose⟩ **2** made or fitted to be turned up ⟨a ~ collar⟩

¹**turpentine** /'tuhpən,tien/ n **1a** a thick sticky yellow to brown OLEORESIN (oily naturally occurring plant product) that exudes from the TEREBINTH (small European tree) **b** any of various OLEORESINS obtained from conifers (eg some pines and firs) as yellowish sticky substances that usu thicken and solidify in air **2a** a colourless or slightly yellow pungent ESSENTIAL OIL (natural plant oil) obtained from turpentine, esp from pines, by distillation and used esp as a solvent and thinner in paints, varnishes, etc **b** a similar oil obtained by distillation of pinewood **3** WHITE SPIRIT [ME terbentyne, turpentyne, fr MF & ML; MF terbentine, tourbentine, fr ML terbentina, fr L terebinthina, fem of terebinthinus of terebinth, fr terebinthus terebinth, fr Gk terebinthos] – **turpentinic, turpentinous** adj

²**turpentine** vt **1** to apply turpentine to **2** to extract turpentine from; esp to tap (pine trees) in order to obtain turpentine

**turpentine tree** n a tree that yields turpentine: eg **a** TEREBINTH **b** any of several Australian trees (eg various eucalyptuses) that yield an oily resinous liquid; esp a eucalyptus (Syncarpia laurifolia) often planted as a shade tree

**turpitude** /'tuhpityoohd/ n, formal (an act of) inherent baseness or depravity ⟨moral ~⟩ [MF, fr L turpitudin-, turpitudo, fr turpis vile, base] – **turpitudinous** adj

**turps** /tuhps/ n taking sing vb turpentine [by shortening & alter.]

**turquoise** /'tuhkwoys, -kwoyz/ n **1** a blue, bluish-green, or greenish-grey mineral, $CuAl_6(PO_4)_4(OH)_8.5H_2O$, consisting of a phosphate of copper and aluminium, that takes a high polish and is valued, esp in its sky blue form, as a gem **2** a light greenish-blue colour [ME turkeis, turcas, fr MF turquoyse, fr fem of turquoys Turkish, fr OF, fr Turc Turk]

**turret** /'turit/ n **1** a little tower; specif an ornamental structure on a corner of a larger structure **2a** a pivoted and rotatable holder (eg for a tool) in a machine **b** a device (eg on a microscope or a television camera) holding several lenses **3a** a tall structure usu moved on wheels and formerly used for carrying soldiers and equipment for breaching or scaling a wall **b** a usu revolving armoured structure on warships, forts, tanks, and aircraft in which guns are mounted [ME touret, fr MF torete, tourete, fr OF, dim. of tor, tur tower – more at TOWER] – **turreted** adj

¹**turtle** /'tuhtl/ n, archaic a turtledove [ME, fr OE turtla, fr L turtur, of imit origin]

²**turtle** n, pl **turtles**, esp collectively **turtle** any of several aquatic, esp marine, reptiles (order Chelonia) that have the body covered by a bony shell and resemble the related tortoises but are adapted for swimming; broadly, NAm any of the land, freshwater, and marine reptiles of this order, including the terrapins and tortoises [prob by folk etymology fr Fr tortue, prob fr (assumed) VL tartaruca, fr LL tartarucha, fem of tartaruchus of Tartarus (the underworld), fr Gk tartarouchos, fr Tartaros Tartarus; fr an ancient notion that the turtle was an infernal creature] – **turn turtle** to capsize, overturn [fr the practice of catching turtles by turning them onto their backs, thereby leaving them helpless]

**turtleback** /'tuhtl,bak/ n a raised convex surface: eg **a** a curved deck on a ship shaped so as to spill the water quickly back into the sea during heavy weather **b** NAm a rounded projection on the rear of a car

**turtledove** /'tuhtl,duv/ n any of several small wild pigeons, esp of a Eurasian and African genus (Streptopelia), noted for their plaintive cooing

**turtleneck** /'tuhtl,nek/ n (a jumper with) a high close-fitting neck; also such a neck on various other garments (eg a knitted dress)

**turtling** /'tuhtling/ n the action or process of catching turtles

**turves** /tuhvz/ pl of TURF

¹**Tuscan** /'tuskən/ n **1** a native or inhabitant of Tuscany **2a** the Italian language of Tuscany **b** the standard literary dialect of Italian [ME, fr L tuscanus, adj, Etruscan, fr L Tusci Etruscans]

²**Tuscan** adj **1** (characteristic) of Tuscany, the Tuscans, or

**Tuscan 2** of a Roman order of architecture that is a modification of the Greek DORIC and is plain in style

**Tuscarora** /,tuskə'rawrə/ n, pl **Tuscaroras**, esp collectively **Tuscarora 1** a member of an American Indian people originally of N Carolina and later of New York State and Ontario **2** the language of the Tuscarora people

**tush** /tush/ interj, archaic – used to express disdain or reproach

**tushery** /'tushəri/ n inferior writing characterized esp by the affected use of archaic words

¹**tusk** /tusk/ n **1** an elongated greatly enlarged tooth of an elephant, boar, walrus, etc, that projects when the mouth is closed and is used for digging for food or as a weapon; broadly a long protruding tooth **2** any of the small projections on a TUSK TENON [ME, alter. of tux, fr OE tūx; akin to OFris tusk tooth] – **tusked** adj, **tusklike** adj

²**tusk** vt to dig up with a tusk; also to gash with a tusk

³**tusk** n, pl **tusks**, esp collectively **tusk** TORSK (marine food fish related to the cod) [Shetland Norse; akin to Norw, Sw, & Dan torsk]

**tusker** /'tuskə/ n an animal with tusks; esp a male elephant with two large tusks

**tusk shell** n TOOTH SHELL (marine animal with a tapering tubular shell)

**tusk tenon** n a TENON (woodwork joint) strengthened by one or more smaller tenons underneath forming a steplike outline

**tussive** /'tusiv/ adj of or caused by coughing – used technically [L tussis cough]

¹**tussle** /'tusl/ vi to struggle roughly; scuffle [ME tussillen, freq of ME -tusen, -tousen to pull roughly – more at TOUSLE]

²**tussle** n **1** a physical contest or struggle; a scuffle **2** a hard struggle, controversy, or argument

**tussock** /'tusək/ n a compact tuft of grass, sedge, etc; also a hummock in marsh, bound together by plant roots [origin unknown] – **tussocky** adj

**tussock grass** n a grass or sedge that typically grows in tussocks

**tussock moth** n any of numerous dull-coloured or white moths (esp family Lymantriidae) that have males with feathery antennae, sometimes wingless females, and larvae with long tufts or brushes of hair

**tussore** /'tusaw/, chiefly NAm **tussah** /'tusə/ n (silk or silk fabric made from a brownish silk filament produced by) any of several oriental silkworms that are larvae of SATURNIID moths (esp Antheraea paphia) [Hindi tasar]

¹**tut** /tut/ or clicked t [ǀ]/, **tut-'tut** interj – used to express disapproval or impatience

²**tut** /tut/, **tut-'tut** vi -**tt**- to express disapproval or impatience by uttering "tut" or "tut-tut"

**tutee** /tyooh'tee/ n one who is being tutored [tutor + -ee]

**tutelage** /'tyoohtilij/ n **1a** the act or action of serving as guardian or protector; guardianship **b** control of one country by another **2** the state or period of being under a guardian or tutor **3** instruction, esp of an individual [L tutela protection, guardian, fr tutus, pp of tueri to look at, guard]

¹**tutelary** /'tyoohtiləri/ also **tutelar** /'tyoohtilə/ adj **1** having the guardianship of a person or thing ⟨a ~ goddess⟩ **2** of a guardian

²**tutelary** also **tutelar** n a tutelary power (eg a deity)

¹**tutor** /'tyoohtə/ n **1** a person charged with the instruction and guidance of another: eg **1a** fem **tutoress** a private teacher **b(1)** a teacher in a British university who gives instruction to students esp individually or in small groups **b(2)** a teacher in a British school or university in charge of the social and moral welfare of a group of pupils or students **c** the guardian of a boy under the age of 14 or of a girl under the age of 12 – used in Scots law **2** Br an instruction book [ME, fr MF & L; MF tuteur, fr L tutor, fr tutus, pp] – **tutorage, tutorship** n

²**tutor** vt **1** to have the guardianship, tutelage, or care of **2** to teach or guide usu individually in a special subject or for a particular purpose; coach ~ vi **1** to do the work of a tutor **2** to receive instruction, esp from a tutor **synonyms** see TEACH

¹**tutorial** /tyooh'tawri·əl/ adj **1** of or involving a tutor **2** involving individual tuition ⟨the ~ system⟩

²**tutorial** n a class conducted by a tutor for one student or a small number of students

¹**tutti** /'toohti/ adj or adv all – used as a direction in ensemble music to indicate a passage for all the players and/or singers [It, masc pl of tutto all]

²**tutti** n, pl **tuttis** a passage or section performed by all the performers

**tutti-frutti** /ˌtoohti 'froohti/ *n, pl* **tutti-fruttis** (a confection, esp an ice cream, containing) a mixture of chopped, dried, or candied fruits [It *tutti frutti*, lit., all fruits]

**tut-tut** /ˌtut 'tut/ *vi or interj* **-tt-** (to) tut

¹**tutu** /'toohtooh/ *n, pl* **tutus** a New Zealand shrub (*Coriaria ruscifolia* of the family Coriariaceae) with poisonous black berries [Maori]

²**tutu** *n, pl* **tutus** a very short projecting skirt worn by a ballerina [Fr, fr (baby talk) *cucu, tutu* backside, alter. of *cul* – more at CULET]

**tu-whit tu-whoo** /tə ˌwit tə 'wooh/ *n* the characteristic cry of a (tawny) owl – often used imitatively [imit]

**tux** /tuks/ *n, NAm* DINNER JACKET [short for *tuxedo*]

**tuxedo** /tuk'seedoh/ *n, pl* **tuxedos, tuxedoes** *NAm* DINNER JACKET [*Tuxedo* Park, resort in New York State, USA]

**tuyere, tuyère** /'tweeyeə/ (*Fr* tyijɛːr)/ *n* a nozzle through which an air blast is delivered to a forge or BLAST FURNACE [Fr *tuyère*, fr MF, fr *tuyau* pipe]

**TV** /ˌtee 'vee/ *n* (a) television [*television*]

**TV dinner** *n* a frozen packaged dinner (e g of meat, potatoes, and a vegetable) that requires only heating before it is served

**twa** /twah/, **twae** /twaw, twee/ *n, adj, or pron, Scot* two

**twaddle** /'twodl/ *vi or n* (to speak or write) rubbish or drivel [prob alter. of E dial. *twattle*] – **twaddler** *n*

¹**twain** /twayn/ *adj or pron, archaic* two [ME, fr OE *twēgen* – more at TWO]

²**twain** *n* 1 two ⟨*split in* ∼⟩ 2 *poetic* a couple, pair

¹**twang** /twang/ *n* 1 a harsh quick ringing sound like that of a plucked bowstring 2 nasal speech or resonance 3a an act of plucking b *NAm & dial Br* a pang, twinge [imit] – **twangy** *adj*

²**twang** *vi* 1 to sound with a twang ⟨*the catch of the gate* ∼ed *and squealed*⟩ 2 to speak with a nasal twang 3 *NAm & dial Br* to throb or twitch with pain or tension ∼ *vt* 1 to cause to sound with a twang 2 to utter or pronounce with a nasal twang 3 to pluck the string of ⟨∼ed *his guitar*⟩

³**twang** *n, NAm & dial Br* a persisting flavour, taste, or smell; a tang; *also* a suggestion, trace [alter. of *tang*]

**twat** /twot/ *n, vulg* 1 the female genitals 2 *Br* a disagreeable or contemptible person [origin unknown]

**twayblade** /'tway,blayd/ *n* any of several orchids (esp genera *Listera* or *Liparis*) having a single pair of leaves arranged on the stem opposite each other; *esp* a European orchid (*Listera ovata*) with yellow-green flowers [E dial. *tway* two]

¹**tweak** /tweek/ *vb* to pinch and pull with a sudden jerk and twist ⟨∼ed *a bud from the stem*⟩ ⟨∼ed *his ear*⟩ [ME *twik-ken*, fr OE *twiccian* to pluck – more at TWITCH]

²**tweak** *n* an act of tweaking; a pinch

**twee** /twee/ *adj* excessively sentimental, pretty, or coy [prob baby-talk alter. of *sweet*] – **tweeness** *n*

**tweed** /tweed/ *n* 1 a rough woollen fabric used esp for suits and coats 2 *pl* tweed clothing; *specif* a tweed suit [alter. (influenced by *Tweed*, river in Scotland) of Sc *tweel* twill, fr ME *twyll*]

**Tweedledum and Tweedledee** /tweedl,dum ən tweedl'dee/ *n pl* two individuals or groups that are practically indistinguishable [*tweedle* (to chirp) + *dum* (imit of a low musical note) & *dee* (imit of a high musical note); orig applied in the 18th c to rival musicians, but popularized by the fat identical characters Tweedledum and Tweedledee in *Through the Looking-Glass* by Lewis Carroll (C L Dodgson) †1898 E writer]

**tweedy** /'tweedi/ *adj* 1 of or resembling tweed 2a given to or associated with wearing tweeds b suggestive of the outdoors in taste or habits; *esp* brisk, healthy, and hearty in manner – **tweediness** *n*

**tween** /tween/ *prep, chiefly poetic* between [ME *twene*, short for *betwene*]

**tweeny** /'tweeni/ *n, Br* a subordinate servant girl in a household – no longer in vogue [by shortening & alter. fr *between-maid* (fr her assisting both the cook and the housemaid)]

**tweet** /tweet/ *vi or n* (to utter) a chirping note [imit]

**tweeter** /'tweetə/ *n* a small loudspeaker that responds only to the higher acoustic frequencies and reproduces sounds of high pitch – compare WOOFER

**tweeze** /tweez/ *vt* to pluck, remove, or handle with tweezers ⟨*eyebrows* ∼d *regularly* – *Fair Lady*⟩ [back-formation fr *tweezers*]

**tweezers** /'tweezəz/ *n pl*, **tweezer** *n* any of various small metal instruments that are usu held between the thumb and forefinger, are used for plucking, holding, or manipulating, and consist of two prongs joined at one end [obs *tweeze* case of

small instruments, short for *etweese*, fr pl of *etwee*, fr Fr *étui* – more at ETUI]

**twelfth** /twel(f)th/ *n* 1 – see NUMBER table 2 *often cap, Br the* twelfth of August on which the grouse-shooting season begins ⟨*the glorious* ∼⟩ [ME *twelfte, twelfthe*, adj & n, fr OE *twelfta*, fr *twelf* twelve + *-ta* -th] – **twelfth** *adj or adv*, **twelfthly** *adv*

**Twelfth Day** *n* EPIPHANY (church festival on January 6) [fr its being the 12th day after Christmas]

**twelfth man** *n* the reserve member of a cricket team

**Twelfth Night** *n* the eve or evening of EPIPHANY (church festival on January 6)

**twelve** /twelv/ *n* 1 – see NUMBER table 2 *cap* **2a**(1) *the* 12 original disciples of Jesus **a**(2) *the* 12 Apostles including Judas's successor Matthias **b** the books of the MINOR PROPHETS in the Jewish Scriptures 3 the 12th in a set or series 4 something having 12 parts or members or a denomination of 12 5 *pl* twelvemo [ME, fr *twelve*, adj, fr OE *twelf*; akin to OHG *zwelif* twelve; both fr a prehistoric Gmc compound whose first element is represented by OE *twā* two, & whose second by OE *-leofan* (in *endleofan* eleven) – more at TWO, ELEVEN] – **twelve** *adj or pron*, **twelvefold** *adj or adv*

**twelvemo** /'twelvmoh/ *n, pl* **twelvemos** DUODECIMO (paper size)

**twelvemonth** /'twelv,munth/ *n, archaic, poetic, or dial Br* a year

**twelve-'note** *adj* twelve-tone

**twelve-,tone** *adj* of or being SERIAL music based on a TONE-ROW (all 12 notes of an octave, including all sharps and flats)

**twenty** /'twenti/ *n* 1 – see NUMBER table 2 *pl the* numbers 20 to 29; *specif* a range of temperature, ages, or dates in a century characterized by those numbers 3 something (e g a bank note) having a denomination of 20 [ME, fr *twenty*, adj, fr OE *twēntig*, n, group of 20, fr *twēn-* (akin to OE *twā* two) + *-tig* group of 10 – more at TWO, -TY] – **twentieth** *adj or n*, **twenty** *adj or pron*, **twentyfold** *adj or adv*

**twenty-'fourmo** /'fawmoh/ *n, pl* **twenty-fourmos** the size of a piece of paper cut 24 from a sheet; *also* a book, a page, or paper of this size

**twenty-'one** *n* 1 – see NUMBER table 2 ²PONTOON (card game) [(2) trans of Fr *vingt-et-un*] – **twenty-one** *adj or pron*

**20/20** *also* ,**twenty-'twenty** *adj, of a person's vision* normal, perfect [fr the assessment of normal vision as the ability to read characters at a distance of 20 ft]

**twenty-'two** *n* 1 – see NUMBER table 2 either of two lines across a rugby pitch 22 metres (about 24 yards) from each goal; *also* the area between such a line and the GOAL LINE 3 *NAm.*22 (small rifle or pistol) – **twenty-two** *adj or pron*

**twerp, twirp** /twuhp/ *n, Br informal* an absurd, stupid, or contemptible person; a fool [origin unknown]

**Twi** /ch'wee, twee, chee/ *n* a dialect of AKAN (W African language); *also* a literary language based on this

**twi-** /twie-/ *prefix* two; double; doubly; twice ⟨twi-*headed*⟩ ⟨twi*bill*⟩ [ME, fr OE; akin to OHG *zwi-* twi-, L *bi-*, Gk *di-*, OE *twā* two]

**twibill** /'twie,bil/ *n* a battle-axe with two blades set at one end of a staff

**twice** /twies/ *adv* 1 on two occasions ⟨∼ *absent*⟩ ⟨∼ *daily*⟩ ⟨∼ *a week*⟩ 2 two times; in doubled quantity or degree ⟨∼ *two is four*⟩ ⟨∼ *as much*⟩ ⟨∼ *the money*⟩ [ME *twiges, twies*, fr OE *twiga*; akin to OE *twi-*]

**twice-,born** *adj* 1 having undergone a definite experience of fundamental moral and spiritual renewal – compare BORN-AGAIN 2 of or forming one of the three upper Hindu caste groups in which boys undergo an initiation symbolizing spiritual birth

**twice-'laid** *adj, of a rope* made from strands of used rope

**twice-'told** *adj* well known from repeated telling – chiefly in *a twice-told tale*

¹**twiddle** /'twidl/ *vi* 1 to play absentmindedly with something; fiddle 2 to turn or twirl lightly ∼ *vt* to rotate lightly or idly ⟨∼d *the knob on the radio*⟩ ⟨∼d *his thumbs*⟩ [prob imit]

²**twiddle** *n* a turn, twist

¹**twig** /twig/ *n* a small woody plant shoot or branch, usu without its leaves [ME *twigge*, fr OE; akin to OHG *zwīg* twig, OE *twā* two] – **twigged** *adj*, **twiggy** *adj*

²**twig** *vb* **-gg-** *informal vt* 1 to notice, observe 2 to grasp, understand to understand; CATCH ON ⟨∼ged *instinctively about things* – H E Bates⟩ [perh fr ScGael *twig* I understand]

**twilight** /'twie,liet/ *n* **1a** the light from the sky halfway between night and day; *esp* the shadowy light between sunset and full night **b** the period between sunset and full night **2a** an intermediate state that is not clearly defined ⟨*lived in the ~ of neutrality – Newsweek*⟩ **b** a period of decline ⟨*elderly ladies in the ~ of their years*⟩ [ME, fr twi- + *light*]

**twilight sleep** *n* a state produced by the injection of morphine and HYOSCINE, in which awareness and memory of pain is dulled or removed

**twilight zone** *n* a decaying urban area

**twilit** /'twie,lit/ *adj* **1** lighted (as if) by twilight **2** in a state of eclipse; shadowy, obscure ⟨*after a period of popularity the work has led a ~ existence*⟩ [*twi*light + *lit*]

**twill** /twil/ *n* **1** a fabric with a twill weave **2** a textile weave in which the crosswise threads (WEFT 1a) are passed over one and under two or more lengthwise threads (WARP 1a(1)) to give an appearance of diagonal lines – compare DOUBLE TWILL [ME *twyll*, fr OE *twilic* having a double thread, modif of L *bilic-, bilix*, fr bi- + *licium* thread] – **twilled** *adj*

**twilling** /'twiling/ *n* (the process of making) twilled fabric

**¹twin** /twin/ *adj* **1** born with one other or as a pair at one birth ⟨*~ brother*⟩ ⟨*~ girls*⟩ **2a** made up of two similar, related, or connected members or parts; double **b** paired in a close or necessary relationship ⟨*the ~ threats of inflation and unemployment*⟩ **c** having or consisting of two identical units ⟨*~ engines*⟩ **d** being one of a pair; *specif* being one of a pair of officially associated towns in two different countries [ME, fr OE *twinn* twofold, two by two; akin to ON *tvinnr* two by two, OE *twā* two]

**²twin** *n* **1** either of two offspring produced at one birth **2** either of two people or things closely related to or resembling each other **3** *twin* **twin crystal** a compound crystal composed of two or more crystals or parts of crystals of the same kind that are grown together in an oriented manner – **twinship** *n*

**³twin** *vb* **-nn-** *vt* **1a** to bring together in close association; couple **b** to associate (a town in one country) officially with a town in another ⟨*Basingstoke is ~ned with Alençon*⟩ **2** to duplicate, match **3** to form into a twin crystal **~** *vi* **1** to become paired or closely associated **2** to give birth to twins **3** to grow as or form a twin crystal

**twin bed** *n* either of a pair of matching SINGLE BEDS

**twinborn** /'twin,bawn/ *adj* born at the same birth as another or each other – not used technically

**¹twine** /twien/ *n* **1** a strong string of two or more strands twisted together **2** a twined or interlaced part or object; a coil, twist **3** an act of twining, interlacing, or embracing [ME *twin*, fr OE *twīn;* akin to MD *twijn* twine, OE *twā* two] – **twiny** *adj*

**²twine** *vt* **1a** to twist together **b** to form by twisting; weave **2a** to interlace ⟨*the girl ~d her hands* – John Buchan⟩ **b** to cause to encircle or enfold ⟨*~d her arms round him*⟩ **c** to cause to be encircled ⟨*~d the pillars with garlands*⟩ **~** *vi* **1** to coil round a support **2** to follow a sinuous or winding course; meander ⟨*the river ~s through the valley*⟩ – **twiner** *n*

**twinflower** /'twin,flowə/ *n* either of two low-growing creeping evergreen shrubs (*Linnaea borealis* of N Europe and Asia and *Linnaea americana* of northern N America) of the honeysuckle family, with fragrant usu pink flowers in pairs

**¹twinge** /twinj/ *vb* **twinging, twingeing** *vt* **1** to affect with a sharp pain or pang **2** *dial* to pluck, tweak **~** *vi* **1** to feel a sudden sharp pain [ME *twengen*, fr OE *twengan*]

**²twinge** *n* **1** a sudden sharp stab of pain **2** a moral or emotional pang ⟨*a ~ of conscience*⟩ △ tinge

**¹twinkle** /'twingkl/ *vi* **1** to shine with a flickering or sparkling light **2** to appear bright with gaiety or amusement ⟨*his eyes ~d*⟩ **3** to move or dart rapidly ⟨*danced with* twinkling *feet*⟩ **~** *vt* **1** to cause to shine with flickering light **2** to move or flicker rapidly **synonyms** see ¹FLASH [ME *twinklen*, fr OE *twinclian;* akin to MHG *zwinken* to blink] – **twinkler** *n*

**²twinkle** *n* **1** a wink of the eyelids **2** the duration of a wink; an instant, twinkling **3** an intermittent radiance; a flicker **4** a rapid flashing movement (e.g of the feet) – **twinkly** *adj*

**twinkling** /'twingkling/ *n* an instant, twinkle ⟨*the kettle will boil in a ~ – Punch*⟩

**Twins** /twinz/ *n pl* Gemini – + *the*

**twin set** *n* a jumper and cardigan designed to be worn together, usu by a woman

**¹twirl** /twuhl/ *vi* to revolve rapidly to cause to rotate rapidly; spin, twist [perh of Scand origin; akin to Norw dial. *tvirla* to twirl; akin to OHG *dweran* to stir – more at TURBID] – **twirler** *n*

**²twirl** *n* **1** an act of twirling **2** a coil, whorl – **twirly** *adj*

**twirp** /twuhp/ *n, informal* a twerp

**¹twist** /twist/ *vt* **1a** to join together by winding ⟨*~ing strands together*⟩ **b** to make by twisting strands together ⟨*~ thread from yarn*⟩ **c** to combine by interlacing; interweave **2** to twine, coil **3a** to wring or wrench so as to dislocate or distort; *esp* to sprain ⟨*~ed my ankle*⟩ **b** to distort the meaning of ⟨*~ed the facts*⟩ **c** to contort ⟨*~ed his face into a grin*⟩ **d** to pull off, turn, or break by twisting **e** to cause to move with a rotating motion **f** to form into a spiral shape **g** to make miserable, debase ⟨*a ~ed and embittered society*⟩ **h** to make (one's way) in a winding or oblique manner to a destination or objective **~** *vi* **1** to follow a winding course; snake **2a** to turn or change shape under bending or wrenching **b** to assume a spiral shape **c** to squirm, writhe **d** to dance the twist **3** to turn round ⟨*~ed round to see him*⟩ **4** to advance while spinning ⟨*autumn leaves ~ing through the air*⟩ **5** to request another card from the dealer in pontoon – compare STICK 4c; see also **twist somebody's ARM, twist somebody round one's little FINGER** [ME *twisten*, fr OE *-twist* rope; akin to MD *twist* quarrel, twine, OE *twā* two]

**²twist** *n* **1** something formed by twisting or winding: e g **1a** a thread, yarn, or cord formed by twisting two or more strands together **b** a strong tightly twisted silk sewing thread ⟨*button-hole ~*⟩ **c** a baked piece of twisted dough **d** tobacco twisted into a thick roll **e** a strip of citrus peel used to flavour a drink ⟨*. . . gin, ice, bitters, and a ~ of lemon*⟩ **2a** twisting or being twisted **b** a dance popular esp in the 1960s and performed with twisting motions of the body – usu + *the* **c** a spiral turn or curve **3a** force causing twisting or turning applied to a body (e g a rod or shaft) **b** the angle through which a thing is twisted **4a** a turning off a straight course; a bend **b** an eccentricity, idiosyncrasy **c** a distortion of meaning or sense **5a** an unexpected turn or development ⟨*a strange ~ of fate*⟩ **b** a clever device; a trick ⟨*questions demanding special ~s of thinking – New Yorker*⟩ **c** a variant approach or method ⟨*a new ~ on an old theme*⟩ **6** a dive in which the diver twists the body sideways for one or more half or full turns before entering the water **7** *Br* a piece of paper twisted so as to contain something (e g powder) ⟨*a ~ of salt*⟩ **8** *chiefly NAm* the spin given to the ball by the hand in any of various games (e g baseball) – **round the twist** *Br informal* crazy, mad – see also **get one's KNICKERS in a twist**

**twist drill** *n* a drill bit having deep spiral grooves extending from the cutting edges

**twister** /'twistə/ *n, informal* **1** *Br* a dishonest person; a swindler **2** *NAm* a tornado, waterspout, etc in which the rotatory ascending movement of a column of air is very apparent **synonyms** see WHIRLWIND

**twisty** /'twisti/ *adj* full of twists; winding ⟨*a ~ road*⟩

**¹twit** /twit/ *vt* **-tt-** to subject to mild ridicule or reproach; taunt ⟨*~ted him with his laziness*⟩ **synonyms** see ²RIDICULE [ME *atwiten* to reproach, fr OE *ætwītan*, fr *æt* at + *wītan* to reproach; akin to OHG *wīzan* to punish, OE *witan* to know]

**²twit** *n* an act of twitting; a taunt

**³twit** *n, Br informal* one who is or appears to be absurd or silly; a fool [prob alter. of *twat*] – **twittish, twitty** *adj*

**¹twitch** /twich/ *vt* to move or pull with a sudden motion; jerk **~** *vi* **1** to pull, pluck ⟨*~ed at my sleeve*⟩ **2** to move jerkily or involuntarily; quiver, jump ⟨*a muscle ~ed in his face*⟩ [ME *twicchen;* akin to OE *twiccian* to pluck, OHG *gizwickan* to pinch] – **twitcher** *n*

**²twitch** *n* **1** an act of twitching; *esp* an act of twitching **2** a physical or mental pang; a twinge **3** a loop of rope or strap that is tightened over a horse's upper lip as a restraining device **4a** (the recurrence of) a short spasmodic contraction of the muscle fibres; a tic **b** a sudden slight jerk of a body part – **twitchy** *adj*, **twitchily** *adv*, **twitchiness** *n*

**³twitch** *n* COUCH GRASS [alter. of *quitch*]

**twite** /twiet/ *n* a finch (*Acanthis flavirostris*) of N Europe that resembles the linnet and has buff coloured plumage streaked with brown and black [imit]

**¹twitter** /'twitə/ *vi* **1** to utter chirps or twitters **2a** to talk in a chattering fashion **b** to giggle, titter **3** to tremble with agitation; flutter **~** *vt* to utter in chirps or twitters ⟨*the robin ~ed his morning song*⟩ [ME *twiteren;* akin to OHG *zwizzirōn* to twitter] – **twitterer** *n*

**²twitter** *n* **1** a nervous agitation; a quiver – esp in *all of a twitter* **2** a small tremulous intermittent sound characteristic of birds – **twittery** *adj*

**twixt** /twikst/ *prep, chiefly poetic* between ⟨*many a slip ~ cup and lip*⟩ [ME *twix*, short for *betwix, betwixt*]

¹**two** /tooh/ *pron taking pl vb* **1** two countable individuals not specified ⟨*only* ~ *were found*⟩ **2** a small approximate number of indicated things ⟨*only a shot or* ~ *were fired*⟩ △ to, too [ME *twa* (adj) two, fr OE *twā* (fem & neut); akin to OE *twēgen* two (masc), OHG *zwēne*, L *duo*, Gk *dyo*] – **put two and two together** to draw the proper inference from given premises – see also **fall between two** STOOLS

²**two** *n, pl* **twos 1** – see NUMBER table **2** the second in a set or series ⟨*the* ~ *of spades*⟩ **3** something having a denomination of two ⟨*this domino is a* ~⟩ **4** *Br* a twopence piece – **two** *adj*, **twofold** *adj or adv*

'**two-**ˌ**bit** *adj, chiefly NAm informal* of little worth or importance; petty, small-time

**two bits** *n taking sing or pl vb, chiefly NAm* the value of a quarter of a dollar

ˌ**two-by-**'**four** *adj, NAm* small or petty of its kind ⟨*this house and its* ~ *garden* – Philip Barry⟩

**two-di**'**mensional** *adj* **1** having two dimensions **2** lacking depth of characterization ⟨~ *fiction*⟩

ˌ**two-**'**edged** *adj* double-edged

ˌ**two-**'**faced** *adj* **1** having two faces **2** double-dealing, hypocritical – **two-facedness** *n*

ˌ**two-**'**fisted** *adj, NAm* marked by vigorous energy

**2,4,5-T** *n* an irritant chemical compound, $Cl_3C_6H_2OCH_2COOH$, used as a defoliant, esp in brush and weed control, that is thought to cause genetic defects [*2,4,5* (fr the substitution of chlorine atoms in positions 2,4,5 in phenoxyatetic acid) *trichlorophenoxyacetic acid*]

ˌ**two-**'**handed** *adj* **1** used with both hands ⟨*a* ~ *sword*⟩ **2** requiring two people ⟨*a* ~ *saw*⟩ **3a** having two hands **b** using both hands equally well; ambidextrous – **twohandedness** *n*

**two-line whip** *n, Br* an instruction from a party to its Members of Parliament that they should attend a debate and vote in the specified way – compare FREE VOTE, THREE-LINE WHIP [fr the double underlining of some words in the written instruction]

ˌ**two-**'**party** *adj* characterized by two major political parties of comparable strength ⟨~ *system*⟩

**twopence** *also* **tuppence** /'tup(ə)ns/ *n* **1** the sum of two pence **2** a coin worth two pence

**twopenny** *also* **tuppenny** /'tup(ə)ni/ *adj* costing or worth twopence

**twopenny-halfpenny** /ˌtup(ə)ni 'haypni/ *adj, chiefly Br informal* of little value or importance

'**two-**ˌ**phase** *adj, physics* having two PHASES; *specif* of, being, or using a supply of electricity consisting of two ALTERNATING CURRENTS having voltages that are 90° out of phase with one another

¹'**two-**ˌ**piece** *adj* forming a clothing outfit with matching top and bottom parts ⟨*a* ~ *suit*⟩

²**two-piece** *n* a garment (eg a swimming costume) that is two-piece

'**two-**ˌ**ply** *adj* **1** consisting of two thicknesses **2a** woven with two sets of lengthwise thread (WARP 1a(1)) and two of crosswise (WEFT 1a) ⟨*a* ~ *carpet*⟩ **b** consisting of two strands ⟨~ *yarn*⟩

ˌ**two-**'**sided** *adj* having two sides; BILATERAL

**twosome** /'toohs(ə)m/ *n taking sing or pl vb* **1** a group of two people or things; a couple **2** a golf match between two people

'**two-**ˌ**star** *adj* of the second rank in a system for grading excellence applied to esp hotels, in which the highest standard is usu represented by the fifth rank ⟨~ *hotel*⟩

'**two-**ˌ**step** *n* **1** a ballroom dance in $\frac{2}{4}$ or $\frac{4}{4}$ time having a basic pattern of step-close-step **2** a piece of music for the two-step – **two-step** *vi*

'**two-**ˌ**stroke** *adj or n* (of, being, or powered by) an INTERNAL-COMBUSTION ENGINE with a cycle of two strokes comprising one up-and-down movement of a piston

**two-tailed test, two-tail test** *n* a statistical test of a hypothesis in which all the possible values of the TEST statistic that would lead to acceptance of the hypothesis fall between two given values, with values greater than one of the given values or less than the other leading to rejection of the hypothesis – compare ONE-TAILED TEST

ˌ**two-**'**time** *vt, informal* **1** to be unfaithful to (a spouse, lover, etc) by having a secret relationship with another **2** to double-cross – **two-timer** *n*

**two-toed sloth** *n* a sloth (*Choloepus didactylus*) that has only two toes on the forefoot and three toes on the hindfoot – called also UNAU; compare THREE-TOED SLOTH

'**two-**ˌ**tone** *adj* **1** *also* **two-toned 1a** coloured in two colours or in two shades of one colour ⟨~ *shoes*⟩ **b** having two sounds or tones ⟨*a* ~ *siren*⟩ **2** of or being popular music played by groups of black, esp W Indian, and white musicians and including elements of reggae and NEW WAVE – **two-tone** *n*

**.22** *also* ˌ**two-**'**two**, *NAm* **twenty-two** *n* a rifle or pistol with a calibre of 0.22 inch (5.6 millimetres)

ˌ**two-**'**up** *n* a game played in Australia and New Zealand in which players bet on the fall of tossed coins

'**two-**ˌ**way** *adj* **1** being a cock or valve that will connect a pipe or channel with either of two others **2** moving or allowing movement in either direction ⟨*a* ~ *bridge*⟩ **3a** involving or allowing an exchange between two individuals or groups ⟨*there must be good* ~ *communication* – Jerrold Orne⟩; *esp* designed for both sending and receiving messages ⟨~ *radio*⟩ **b** involving mutual responsibility or a reciprocal relationship ⟨*political alliance is a* ~ *thing* – T H White⟩ **4** involving two participants ⟨*a* ~ *race*⟩ **5** usable in either of two ways ⟨*a* ~ *lamp*⟩

**two-way mirror** *n* a piece of glass that acts as a mirror when viewed from one side, but that can be seen through as if transparent when viewed from the other side

**two-way switch** *n* either of two electrical switches (eg at the top and bottom of a stairway) controlling a single device, esp a light

**two-winged fly** *n* any of a large order (Diptera) of insects including the housefly, mosquito, and gnat, that have functional front wings, greatly reduced hind wings used to control balance, and segmented often headless, eyeless, and legless larvae

¹**-ty** /-ti/ *suffix* (→ *n*) – used in forming numbers of (so many) times ten ⟨*twenty*⟩ ⟨*fifty*⟩ [ME, fr OE *-tig* group of ten; akin to OE *tīen* ten]

²**-ty** *suffix* (→ *n*) quality or condition of ⟨*puberty*⟩ ⟨*cruelty*⟩ [ME *-te*, fr OF *-té*, fr L *-tat-*, *-tas* – more at -ITY]

    **usage** The suffixes **-ty**, **-ity**, and **-ness** are attached to adjectives, and the abstract nouns so formed mean a quality. One should not form **-ness** words, such as **anxiousness**, where a suitable noun with the same meaning, such as **anxiety**, already exists; but sometimes a pair of such words have developed different meanings. Compare ⟨*casualty*⟩ ⟨*casualness*⟩ ⟨*enormity*⟩ ⟨*enormousness*⟩.

**tycoon** /tie'koohn/ *n* **1** a businessman of exceptional wealth and power; a magnate **2** *archaic* SHOGUN (Japanese military governor) [Jap *taikun*, fr Chin (Pek) *tàijūn* (*t'ai*⁴*chün*¹), fr *tài* (*t'ai*⁴) great + *jūn* (*chün*¹) ruler] – **tycoonery** *n*

**tying** /'tie·ing/ *pres part of* TIE

**tyke, tike** /tiek/ *n* **1** a (mongrel) dog **2** *chiefly Br* a boorish churlish person **3** *chiefly Br informal* a small child **4** *Br informal* a native of Yorkshire **5** *Austr derog* a Roman Catholic [ME *tyke*, fr ON *tík* bitch]

**tymbal** /'timbl/ *n* the membrane in the sound-producing organ of a CICADA, whose vibration produces the characteristic shrill singing noise of the insect [alter. of *timbal*]

**tympan** /'timpən/ *n* **1** a sheet (eg of paper or parchment) placed between the impression surface of a press and the paper to be printed **2** *archaic* a drum [(2) ME, fr OE *timpana*, fr L *tympanum*; (1) ML & L *tympanum*]

**tympani** /'timpəni/ *n pl* timpani

**tympanic bone** /tim'panik/ *n* a bone of the mammalian skull that encloses part of the MIDDLE EAR and supports the TYMPANIC MEMBRANE

**tympanic membrane** *n* a thin membrane that separates the OUTER EAR from the cavity of the MIDDLE EAR and functions in the mechanical reception of sound waves and in their transmission in the form of vibrations to the site of sensory reception – called also EARDRUM

**tympanites** /ˌtimpə'nieteez/ *n* swelling of the abdomen caused by accumulation of gas in the intestines or abdominal cavity [ME, fr LL, fr Gk *tympanitēs*, fr *tympanon*] – **tympanitic** *adj*

**tympanum** /'timpənəm/ *n, pl* **tympana** /-nə/ *also* **tympanums 1a(1)** TYMPANIC MEMBRANE **a(2)** MIDDLE EAR **b** a thin taut membrane covering an organ of hearing of an insect **c** a vibrating membrane in a sound-producing organ **2a** the recessed triangular face of a PEDIMENT (space between the angle of a sloping roof and the horizontal lintel) **b** the space within an arch and above a lintel (eg in a medieval doorway) [ML & L; ML, eardrum, fr L, drum, architectural panel, fr Gk *tympanon* drum, kettledrum; akin to Gk *typtein* to beat] – **tympanic** *adj*

**tympany** /'timpəni/ *n* tympanites [ML *tympanias*, fr Gk, fr *tympanon*]

**tyne** /tien/ *n* TINE (prong or antler)

**Tynwald** /'tinwald, 'tien-/ *also* **Tynwald Court** *n* the Parliament of the Isle of Man [ON *thingvöllr* site of parliamentary meetings, fr *thing* assembly, parliament + *völlr* field]

**typal** /'tiepl/ *adj* of or serving as a type

¹**type** /tiep/ *n* **1a** a person or thing (eg in the Old Testament) regarded as foreshadowing another (eg in the New Testament) **b** one having qualities of a higher category; a model **c** a category in the classification of living organisms, that is selected, usu on the basis of its characteristics, as a reference for a higher category and that is usu the subgroup most perfectly exemplifying the higher category ⟨*a ~ species*⟩; *also* TYPE SPECIMEN **2a(1)** a rectangular block, usu of metal, bearing a raised character from which an inked print can be made **a(2)** a collection of such blocks **a(3)** letters, numbers, etc for printing ⟨*the ~ for this book has been photoset*⟩ **b** **typeface, type b(1)** a design of printing type ⟨*italic ~*⟩ **b(2)** all type of a single design **c** printed letters **d** matter set in type **3a** a set of qualities common to a number of individuals that distinguish them as an identifiable class **b** the form common to all instances of a word or other linguistic form ⟨*the letter* l *is a ~, of which there are two tokens in* sell⟩ – compare TOKEN **2b** **c** a typical specimen exhibiting the distinguishing characteristics of its type ⟨*a dog that is a ~ beagle*⟩ **d(1)** a member of a specified class or variety of people ⟨*sporting ~*s *tend to be hearty*⟩ **d(2)** a person of a specified nature ⟨*he's a peculiar ~*⟩ **e** a particular kind, class, or group: eg **e(1)** a group or smallish category distinguishable on physiological or SEROLOGICAL bases ⟨*a blood ~*⟩ **e(2)** any of a hierarchy of mutually exclusive classes of statement in logic postulated in order to avoid logical paradoxes **e(3)** a particular class of computer data defined in terms of what it represents or its function, organization, numerical value, etc **f** something distinguishable as a variety; a sort ⟨*what ~ of films do you like?*⟩ [LL *typus*, fr L & Gk; L *typus* image, fr Gk *typos* blow, impression, model, fr *typtein* to strike, beat; akin to L *stuprum* defilement]

*synonyms* **Type, kind, sort, species, make, nature, character,** and **description** each refer to a group of people or things that share some common characteristic. **Kind** and **sort** are the most general words of the set ⟨*several* **kinds/sorts** *of spider*⟩ ⟨*he's the* **kind/sort** *of man you can trust*⟩. **Type** is often loosely used with the same generality ⟨*he's the* **type** *of man you can trust*⟩ but strictly implies a more rigid classification by some clear-cut difference from other groups ⟨*this* **type** *of machine has an extra gear*⟩. **Species** is in one sense a category in the classification of living things, but is loosely and often derogatorily used like **kind** or **sort** ⟨*Dante, with his ... various* **species** *of sinners* – Charles Kingsley⟩. A **make** is a named class of manufactured goods ⟨*a* **make** *of car such as the Volvo*⟩. **Nature, character,** and **description** are used in such phrases as ⟨*the unusual* **nature** *of the problem*⟩ ⟨*documents of this* **character**⟩ ⟨*people of her* **description**⟩ which lay emphasis on the qualities shared by the members of the group. *usage* see ¹KIND

²**type** *vt* **1** to represent beforehand as a Biblical type **2** to represent in terms of typical characteristics; typify **3** to write with a typewriter; *also* to keyboard **4a** to identify as belonging to a type **b** to determine the natural type of (eg a blood sample) ~ *vi* to use a typewriter; *also* to use a keyboard similar to that of a typewriter ⟨*typing at a computer terminal*⟩

**-type** *comb form* (*n* → *adj*) of (such) a type; resembling ⟨*Cheddar-type*⟩ ⟨*Goon-type funny voices – Annabel*⟩

**typecase** /'tiep,kays/ *n* ²CASE 4 (tray for holding printing type)

**typecast** /'tiep,kahst/ *vt* **typecast** to cast (an actor) repeatedly in the same type of role; *broadly* to stereotype

**typed** /tiept/ *adj* **1** *of computer data* belonging to a well-defined type **2** *of a computer language* requiring data to be represented as well-defined types ⟨*ADA is a strongly ~ language*⟩

**typefounder** /'tiep,fowndə/ *n* somebody engaged in the design and production of metal printing type for hand composition – **typefounding** *n*, **typefoundry** *n*

**type genus** *n* the genus of a family or subfamily in the biological classification of living organisms from which the name of the family or subfamily is formed

'**type-,high** *adj or adv* having the same height (0.9186 inch or 23.33 millimetres) as printing type

**type metal** *n* an alloy of lead, antimony, and tin, used in making printing type

**type one error** *n* rejection of the NULL HYPOTHESIS in statistical testing when it is true

**typescript** /'tiep,skript/ *n* a typewritten manuscript; *esp* one intended for use as printer's copy [*type* + manu*script*]

**typeset** /'tiep,set/ *vt* **-tt-; typeset** to set in type; COMPOSE

**typesetter** /'tiep,setə/ *n* a person or machine that sets type – **typesetting** *adj or n*

**type specimen** *n* a single specimen or individual that is designated as the reference specimen of a species or lesser group in the biological classification of living organisms, and whose characteristics are used for the description of the characteristics of that group; the single specimen on which the description of a new species is based

**type two error** *n* acceptance of the NULL HYPOTHESIS in statistical testing when it is false

**typewrite** /'tiep,riet/ *vb* **typewrote** /-,roht/; **typewritten** /-,ritn/ to write with or use a typewriter [back-formation fr *typewriter*]

**typewriter** /'tiep,rietə/ *n* **1** a machine with a keyboard for writing in characters similar to those produced by printer's type **2** *NAm* a typist

**typhlosole** /'tiflə,sohl/ *n* a longitudinal fold of the inner surface of the intestinal wall in some INVERTEBRATE animals (eg clams, oysters, earthworms, and starfishes), that forms a ridge that projects into the intestinal cavity [Gk *typhlos* blind + *sōlēn* pipe, channel – more at SYRINGE]

¹**typhoid** /'tiefoyd/ *adj* **1** (suggestive) of typhus **2** of or being typhoid

²**typhoid** *n* **1** **typhoid fever, typhoid** a serious infectious human disease caused by a bacterium (*Salmonella typhosa*) and marked esp by fever, diarrhoea, headache, and intestinal inflammation **2** a disease of domestic animals resembling human typhus or typhoid

**typhoon** /tie'foohn/ *n* a tropical cyclone occurring in the region of the Philippines or the China sea *synonyms* see WHIRLWIND [alter. – influenced by Chin (Cant) *daai fong* (*taaî fung*) typhoon fr *daai* (*taaî*) great + *fong* (*fung*) wind – of earlier *touffon*, fr Ar *ṭūfān* hurricane, fr Gk *typhōn* whirlwind; akin to Gk *typhein* to smoke]

**typhus** /'tiefəs/ *n* a serious human disease caused by a RICKETTSIA (parasitic microorganism) (*Rickettsia prowazekii*) and transmitted esp by BODY LICE, and marked by high fever, stupor alternating with delirium, intense headache, and a dark red rash [NL, fr Gk *typhos* fever; akin to Gk *typhein* to smoke – more at DEAF]

**typical** /'tipikl/ *adj* **1** **typical, typic** constituting or having the nature of a type; symbolic **2a** combining or exhibiting the essential characteristics of a type ⟨*~ suburban houses*⟩ **b** **typical, typic** conforming to a biological type; having (most of) the essential characteristics of a particular biological category ⟨*a specimen ~ of the species*⟩ **c** showing or according with the usual or expected (unfavourable) traits ⟨*just ~ of him to complain*⟩ *synonyms* see ¹CHARACTERISTIC – **typically** *adv*, **typicalness, typicality** *n*

**typify** /'tipifie/ *vt* **1a** to represent in typical fashion (eg by an image, form, or model) ⟨*the anthropologist has tried to ~ the various strata of society – TLS*⟩ **b** to constitute a typical mark or instance of ⟨*realism that* typified *his later work*⟩ **2** to embody the essential or most representative characteristics of; be the type of – **typification** *n*

**typist** /'tiepist/ *n* somebody who uses a typewriter, esp as an occupation

**typo** /'tiepoh/ *n, pl* **typos** *informal* a printing error [short for *typographical (error)*]

**typographer** /tie'pogrəfə/ *n* a person (eg a printer or designer) who is a specialist in typography

**typographic** /,tiepə'grafik/, **typographical** /-kl/ *adj* of, occurring, or used in typography or typeset matter ⟨*a ~ character*⟩ – **typographically** *adv*

**typography** /tie'pogrəfi/ *n* the style, arrangement, appearance, or design of typeset matter or typefaces [ML *typographia*, fr Gk *typos* impression, cast + *-graphia* -graphy – more at TYPE]

**typological** /,tiepə'lojikl/ *adj* of typology or types – **typologically** *adv*

**typology** /tie'poləji/ *n* **1** a doctrine of characters (TYPES 1a) that foreshadow other biblical characters **2** the study or analysis and classification of types – **typologist** *n*

**tyramine** /'tierəmin, 'ti-/ *n* a chemical compound, $C_8H_{11}NO$, derived from the AMINO ACID tyrosine, that occurs in various foods (eg cheese) and has an action on the SYMPATHETIC NERVOUS SYSTEM similar to that of adrenalin [ISV *tyrosine* + *amine*]

**tyrannical** /ti'ranikl/, **tyrannous** /'tirənəs/ *also* **tyrannic** *adj* **1** characteristic of a tyrant or tyranny ⟨*~ rule*⟩ **2** characterized by oppressive, unjust, or arbitrary behaviour or control; despotic ⟨*a ~ father*⟩ [*tyrannical* fr L *tyrannicus*, fr Gk *tyrannikos*, fr *tyrannos* tyrant; *tyrannous* fr L *tyrannus* tyrant] – **tyrannically** *adv*, **tyrannicalness** *n*, **tyrannously** *adv*

**tyrannicide** /ti'ranisied/ *n* **1** the act of killing a tyrant **2** a person who kills a tyrant [Fr, fr L *tyrannicidium* & *tyrannicida*, fr *tyrannus* + -*i*- + -*cidium* & -*cida* – more at -CIDE]

**tyrann·ize, -ise** /'tirəniez/ *vi* to exercise arbitrary oppressive power or severity – usu + *over* to treat tyrannically; oppress – **tyrannizer** *n*

**tyrannosaur** /ti'ranə,saw/ *n* a very large 2-footed flesh-eating dinosaur (*Tyrannosaurus rex*) with small forelegs, of the late CRETACEOUS geological period [NL *Tyrannosaurus*, genus name, deriv of Gk *tyrannos* tyrant + *sauros* lizard]

**tyrannosaurus** /ti,ranə'sawrəs/ *n* a tyrannosaur [NL]

**tyranny** /'tirəni/ *n* **1a** a government in which absolute power is vested in a single ruler; *esp* one characteristic of an ancient Greek city-state **b** the office, authority, and administration of a tyrant **2** oppressive power ⟨*every form of ~ over the mind of man* – Thomas Jefferson⟩; *specif* oppressive power exerted by government ⟨*the ~ of a police state*⟩ **3** something severe, oppressive, or inexorable in effect ⟨*the ~ of the normal*⟩ **4** a tyrannical act [ME *tyrannie*, fr MF, fr ML *tyrannia*, fr L *tyrannus* tyrant]

**tyrant** /'tie(ə)rənt/ *n* **1a** an absolute ruler unrestrained by law or constitution **b** a usurper of sovereignty **2a** a ruler who exercises absolute power oppressively or brutally **b** one resembling such a tyrant in the harsh use of authority or power [ME *tirant*, fr OF *tyran*, *tyrant*, fr L *tyrannus*, fr Gk *tyrannos*]

**tyrant flycatcher** *n* any of various large American FLYCATCHERS (family Tyrannidae) that are usu strictly insecteating, catch their prey while flying, and have a flattened bill often hooked at the tip

**tyre, *NAm chiefly* tire** /tie·ə/ *n* **1** a metal hoop forming the tread of a wheel (e g of a horse-drawn wagon or a railway carriage) **2a** a continuous solid or inflated hollow rubber cushion set round a wheel to absorb shock **b** the external rubber-and-fabric covering of a pneumatic tyre that uses an

INNER TUBE [ME *tire*, prob fr ²*tire* (in the sense "attire, equipment")]

**Tyrian purple** /'tiri·ən/ *n* a crimson or purple dye related to indigo, that was obtained by the ancient Greeks and Romans from certain sea snails and is now made synthetically [*Tyre*, city in ancient Phoenicia]

**tyro, tiro** /'tie·əroh/ *n, pl* **tyros, tiros** a beginner, novice *antonym* expert [ML, fr L *tiro* new soldier, novice]

**tyrocidine** /,tieroh'siedeen, -din/, **tyrocidin** /-din/ *n* a mixture of several antibiotics composed of small closed chains of AMINO ACIDS, that is obtained from a soil bacterium (*Bacillus brevis*) and is applied directly to the skin and lining of the mouth in the treatment of infections [*tyro*- (as in *tyrothricin*) + -*cid*- (as in *gramicidin*) + -*ine*]

**Tyrolean** *also* **Tyrolian** /ti'rohli·ən, ,tirə'lee·ən/ *adj* (characteristic) of the Tyrol [*Tyrol, Tirol*, region of Europe in the Alps]

**tyrosinase** /,tieroh·si'nayz, tiroh-/ *n* an ENZYME widespread in plants and animals, that promotes the conversion of tyrosine to the pigment MELANIN

**tyrosine** /'tierəseen, 'ti-, -sin/ *n* an important AMINO ACID, $OHC_6H_4CH_2CH(NH_2)COOH$, from which adrenalin, THYROXINE (hormone essential for most physiological functions), and the pigment MELANIN are formed [ISV, irreg fr Gk *tyros* cheese – more at BUTTER]

**tyrothricin** /,tieroh'thriesin/ *n* an antibiotic mixture that consists chiefly of tyrocidine and GRAMICIDIN, is usu extracted from a soil bacterium (*Bacillus brevis*), and is used as tyrocidine in the treatment of infections of the skin and mouth by GRAM-POSITIVE bacteria [NL *Tyrothoric-, Tyrothrix*, generic name formerly applied to various bacteria including *Bacillus brevis*]

**tzaddik** /'tsahdik/ *n, pl* **tzaddikim** /-kim/ ZADDIK (highly religious Jew)

**tzar** /zah/ *n* a tsar

**tzigane** /(t)si'gahn/ *n* a gipsy; *esp* a Hungarian gipsy [Fr, fr Hung *cigány*]

**tzitzis** /'tsitsis, tseet'seet/ *n pl* ZIZITH (tassels on ceremonial Jewish garments)

# U

**u, U** /yooh/ *n, pl* **u's, us, U's, Us 1a** the 21st letter of the English alphabet **b** a graphic representation of or device for reproducing the letter *u* **c** a speech counterpart of printed or written *u* **2** one designated *u*, esp as the 21st in order or class **3** something shaped like the letter U

**¹U** *adj, chiefly Br* characteristic of the upper classes [upper class]

**²U** *n or adj* (a film) certified in Britain as suitable for all age groups – compare PG, 15, 18 [*universal*]

**uakari** /wə'kahri/ *n* OUAKARI (S American monkey)

**ubiety** /yooh'bie·əti/ *n, formal* the state of being in a definite place or local relation [L *ubi* where + E *-ety* (as in *society*)]

**ubiquinone** /,yoohbikwi'nohn, ,--'--/ *n* a chemical compound (QUINONE) that functions in the transfer of electrons between compounds in OXIDATIVE PHOSPHORYLATION (series of energy-producing reactions in cells) [blend of L *ubique* everywhere and E *quinone*; fr its widespread occurrence in nature]

**ubiquitous** /yooh'bikwitəs/ *adj* **1** existing or being everywhere at the same time; frequently encountered **2** very widely distributed under varied ecological conditions ⟨~ *species*⟩ [L *ubique* everywhere, fr *ubi* where] – **ubiquitously** *adv*, **ubiquitousness, ubiquity** *n*

**'U-,boat** *n* a German submarine, esp as used in World Wars I and II [trans of Ger *u-boot*, short for *unterseeboot*, fr *unter* under + *see* sea + *boot* boat]

**'U-,bolt** *n* a U-shaped bolt having both arms threaded to receive nuts and used as a fastening device

**udder** /'udə/ *n* **1** a large pouch- or bag-like organ (eg of a cow) consisting of two or more MAMMARY GLANDS in a common enclosing structure, and each having a single nipple **2** a MAMMARY GLAND of an animal (eg a sow) [ME, fr OE *ūder*; akin to OHG *ūtar* udder, L *uber*, Gk *outhar*, Skt *ūdhar*]

**UFO** /'yoohfoh, ,yooh ef 'oh/ *n, pl* **UFO's, UFOs** an unidentified flying object; *esp* FLYING SAUCER [*unidentified flying object*]

**¹Ugaritic** /,oohgə'ritik/ *adj* (characteristic) of the ancient city of Ugarit, its inhabitants, or Ugaritic

**²Ugaritic** *n* the SEMITIC language of ancient Ugarit

**ugh** /ookh, uh/ *interj* – used to indicate the sound of a cough or grunt or to express disgust or horror

**ugli** /'ugli/ *n* (a tree that bears) a large citrus fruit that is a cross between a grapefruit and a tangerine [prob alter. of *ugly*; fr its unattractive wrinkled skin]

**ugly** /'ugli/ *adj* **1** frightful, horrible ⟨*an* ~ *and near-fatal wound*⟩ **2** offensive or displeasing to any of the senses, esp to the sight **3** morally offensive or objectionable; repulsive ⟨~ *behaviour*⟩ **4a** likely to cause inconvenience or discomfort; troublesome ⟨*the* ~ *truth*⟩ **b** dangerous, threatening ⟨*an* ~ *customer*⟩ ⟨~ *weather*⟩ ⟨*the crowd are looking* ~⟩ **c** surly, quarrelsome ⟨*an* ~ *disposition*⟩ **antonym** beautiful [ME, fr ON *uggligr*, fr *uggr* fear; akin to ON *ugga* to fear] – **uglily** *adv*, **ugliness** *n*, **uglify** *vt*

**ugly duckling** *n* one who or that which appears very unpromising but turns out to be highly successful [*The Ugly Duckling*, story by Hans Christian Andersen †1875 Dan writer, in which an ugly "duckling" grows into a beautiful swan]

**Ugrian** /'yoohgri·ən, 'ooh-/ *n* a member of the eastern division of the FINNO-UGRIC peoples [ORuss *Ugre* Hungarians] – **Ugrian** *adj*

**Ugric** /'yoohgrik, 'ooh-/ *adj* of the languages of the Ugrians

**ugsome** /'ugsəm/ *adj, archaic or humorous* frightful, loathsome [ME, fr *uggen* to fear, inspire fear, fr ON *ugga* to fear]

**uh-huh** /u 'hu/ *interj* – used to indicate affirmation, agreement, or gratification

**uhlan** /'oohlahn, 'yoohlən/ *n* any of a body of Prussian light cavalry originally modelled on Tartar lancers [Ger, fr Pol *ulan*, fr Turk *oğlan* boy, servant]

**Uighur, Uigur** /'weegooə/ *n* **1** a member of a TURKIC people powerful in Mongolia and E Turkestan between the 8th and 12th centuries AD who constitute a majority of the population of Chinese Turkestan **2** the TURKIC language of the Uighur – **Uighur, Uigur** *adj*

**Uitlander** /'ayt,landə, owt-/ *n, SAfr* a foreigner; *esp* a British resident in the former republics of the Transvaal and Orange Free State [Afrik, fr D, fr *uit* out + *land* land]

**ukase** /yooh'kayz/ *n* **1** a proclamation by a Russian emperor or government having the force of law **2** an edict [Fr & Russ; Fr, fr Russ *ukaz*, fr *ukazat'* to show, order; akin to OSlav *u-away*, L *au-*, Skt *ava-*, & to OSlav *kazati* to show]

**uke** /yoohk/ *n, informal* a ukelele [by shortening & alter.]

**ukiyo-e** *also* **ukiyo-ye** /,oohkeeyoh'yay/ *n* a movement in Japanese art that flourished from the 17th to the 19th century and produced paintings and prints depicting the everyday life and interests of the common people; *also* these paintings and prints themselves [Jap *ukiyo-e* genre picture, fr *ukiyo* world, life + *e* picture]

**Ukrainian** /yooh'kraynyən, -ni·ən/ *n* **1** a native or inhabitant of the Ukraine **2** the Slavonic language of the Ukrainians [*Ukraine*, region in E Europe, now part of the USSR] – **Ukrainian** *adj*

**ukulele** /,yoohkə'layli/ *n* a small usu 4-stringed guitar of Portuguese origin popularized in light music conveying a Hawaiian or South Seas atmosphere [Hawaiian *'ukulele*, fr *'uku* small person + *lele* jumping]

**ulama, ulema** /,oohlə'mah/ *n* **1** *taking sing or pl vb* the body of theologians and scholars who form the highest religious authority in Islam **2** a member of the ulama – not used technically [Ar, Turk, & Per; Turk & Per *'ulemā*, fr Ar *'ulamā*]

**-ular** /-yoolə/ *suffix* (→ *adj*) of or resembling ⟨*valv*ular⟩ [L *-ularis*, fr *-ulus, -ula, -ulum* -ule + *-aris* -ar]

**ulcer** /'ulsə/ *n* **1** an open sore in skin or MUCOUS MEMBRANE (eg that lining the mouth) that results from disintegration of tissue, often discharges pus, and is slow to heal **2** something that visibly festers and corrupts ⟨*the* ~ *of conflict between Israeli and Arab*⟩ [ME, fr L *ulcer-, ulcus*; akin to Gk *helkos* wound] – **ulcerous** *adj*

**ulcerate** /'ulsə,rayt/ *vb* to (cause to) become affected (as if) with an ulcer

**ulceration** /,ulsə'raysh(ə)n/ *n* **1** the process of becoming ulcerated; *also* the state of being ulcerated **2** an ulcer – **ulcerative** *adj*

**ulcerogenic** /,ulsərə'jenik/ *adj* tending to produce or develop into ulcers or ulceration

**-ule** /-yoohl, -yool/ *suffix* (→ *n*) small kind of ⟨*duct*ule⟩ [Fr & L; Fr, fr L *-ulus* (masc), *-ula* (fem), *-ulum* (neut), dim. suffix]

**-ulent** /-yoolənt/ *suffix* (→ *adj*) abounding in (a specified thing) ⟨*flocc*ulent⟩ [L *-ulentus*] – **-ulence** *suffix* (→ *n*)

**ulexite** /'yoohləksiet/ *n* a BORATE mineral, $NaCaB_5O_9.8H_2O$, that occurs in arid regions, usu in the form of loosely packed white fibres [George *Ulex* †1883 Ger chemist]

**ullage** /'ulij/ *n* the amount by which a container (eg a tank or cask) is less than full through evaporation, leakage, etc; *also* the amount of liquid lost in this way [ME *ulage*, fr MF *eullage* act of filling a cask, fr *eullier* to fill a cask, fr OF *ouil* eye, bunghole, fr L *oculus* eye]

**ulna** /'ulnə/ *n, pl* **ulnae** /'ulnee/, **ulnas** the bone of the human forearm on the little-finger side; *also* a corresponding part of the forelimb of amphibians, reptiles, birds, and mammals [NL, fr L, elbow – more at ELL] – **ulnar** *adj*

**-ulose** /-yoolohz, -ohs/ *suffix* (→ *n*) ketose sugar ⟨*hept*ulose⟩ [*levulose*]

**ulothrix** /'yoohlə,thriks/ *n* any of a genus (*Ulothrix*) of GREEN ALGAE that are found in usu freshwater and consist of a filament of cells that are functionally independent units [NL *Ulothrix*, genus name, fr Gk *oulothrix* curly-haired]

**ulotrichous** /yooh'lotrikəs/ *adj* having woolly or crisp hair [deriv of Gk *oulotrich-*, *oulothrix*, fr *oulos* curly (akin to Gk *eilyein* to roll) + *trich-*, *thrix* hair – more at VOLUBLE, TRICH-] – **ulotrichy** *n*

**-ulous** /-yoolǝs/ *suffix* (→ *adj*) being slightly or minutely (such) ⟨*hirsutulous*⟩ [L *-ulus*, dim. suffix]

**ulster** /'ulstǝ/ *n* a long loose overcoat made of heavy material [*Ulster*, ancient kingdom & province of Ireland (name now used also for its two divisions: **a** Northern Ireland **b** a province of the Irish Republic)]

**Ulsterman** /-mǝn/, *fem* **Ulsterwoman** *n* a native or inhabitant of Ulster

**ult** /ult/ *adj, humorous when spoken* ultimo

**ulterior** /ul'tiǝri-ǝ/ *adj* **1a** further, future **b** more distant; remoter **c** situated beyond **2** underlying what is openly said or shown; *esp* intentionally concealed ⟨~ *motives*⟩ [L, farther, further, compar of (assumed) L *ulter* situated beyond, fr *uls* beyond; akin to L *ollus*, *ille* that one, OIr ind*oll* beyond] – **ulteriorly** *adv*

**ultima** /'ultimǝ/ *n* the last syllable of a word [L, fem of *ultimus* last]

**ultima ratio** /,ooltimǝ 'rahtioh/ *n* the final argument; *also* the last resort (e g force) [NL]

¹**ultimate** /'ultimǝt/ *adj* **1a** most remote in space or time; farthest **b** last in a progression or series; final ⟨*their* ~ *destination was Paris*⟩ **c** eventual ⟨*they hoped for* ~ *success*⟩ **2** finally calculated; total ⟨*the* ~ *cost of the storm will not be known for many weeks*⟩ **3a** fundamental, basic ⟨~ *reality*⟩ **b** incapable of further analysis, division, or separation; elemental **4** greatest, maximum ⟨*the* ~ *sacrifice*⟩ ⟨*the* ~ *stupidity*⟩ [ML *ultimatus* last, final, fr LL, pp of *ultimare* to come to an end, be last, fr L *ultimus* farthest, last, final, superl of (assumed) L *ulter* situated beyond] – **ultimateness** *n*

²**ultimate** *n* something ultimate; *the* highest point ⟨*the* ~ *in stupidity*⟩

**ultimately** /-li/ *adv* in the end; finally

**ultima Thule** /,ooltimǝ 'thoohlay/ *n* a cold, remote, and unknown region [L, farthest Thule – more at THULIUM]

**ultimatum** /,ulti'maytǝm/ *n, pl* **ultimatums**, **ultimata** /-tǝ/ a final proposition, condition, or demand, usu to be met within a stated time; *esp* one whose rejection will end negotiations and cause a resort to direct action (e g force) [NL, fr ML, neut of *ultimatus* final]

**ultimo** /'ultimoh/ *adj* of or occurring in the month preceding the present – compare PROXIMO [L *ultimo mense* in the last month]

**ultimogeniture** /,ultimoh'jenichǝ/ *n* a system of inheritance by which the youngest son succeeds to the estate, property, etc [L *ultimus* last + E *-o-* + *-geniture* (as in *primogeniture*)]

¹**ultra** /'ultrǝ/ *adj* going beyond others or beyond due limit; extreme [*ultra-*]

²**ultra** *n* an extremist [*ultra-*]

**ultra-** /,ultrǝ-/ *prefix* **1** beyond in space; on the other side; trans- ⟨*ultramontane*⟩ ⟨*ultraplanetary*⟩ **2** beyond the range or limits of; transcending; super- ⟨*ultramicroscopic*⟩ ⟨*ultrasound*⟩ **3** excessively; extremely ⟨*ultramodern*⟩ ⟨*ultraconservative*⟩ ⟨*ultrahigh vacuum*⟩ [L, fr *ultra* beyond, adv & prep, fr (assumed) L *ulter* situated beyond – more at ULTERIOR]

**ultrabasic** /,ultrǝ'baysik, -zik/ *adj, of (a) rock* consisting of a low proportion of silica to iron and magnesium minerals – called also ULTRAMAFIC [ISV]

**ultracentrifugal** /,ultrǝsentri'fyoohg(ǝ)l, -sen'trifyoog(ǝ)l/ *adj* of or obtained by means of an ultracentrifuge – **ultracentrifugally** *adv*

¹**ultracentrifuge** /,ultrǝ'sentrifyoohj, -fyoohzh/ *n* a CENTRIFUGE that spins at high speed producing a strong CENTRIFUGAL FORCE which causes COLLOIDAL and other small particles to separate from and settle at the bottom of a liquid and that is used esp in determining sizes of such particles and MOLECULAR WEIGHTS of large molecules

²**ultracentrifuge** *vt* to subject to the action of an ultracentrifuge – **ultracentrifugation** *n*

**ultraconservative** /,ultrǝkǝn'suhvǝtiv/ *adj* extremely conservative; of or belonging to an extreme wing of a conservative party – **ultraconservative** *n*

**ultrafiche** /'ultrǝ,feesh/ *n* a MICROFICHE (sheet of film) containing printed matter reduced 90 or more times

**ultrafiltrate** /'ultrǝ,filtrayt/ *n* material that has been subjected to ultrafiltration

**ultrafiltration** /,ultrafil'traysh(ǝ)n/ *n* filtration through a medium (e g a blood capillary wall) which allows small

molecules (e g of water) to pass but holds back larger ones (e g of protein)

**ultrahigh frequency** /,ultrǝ'hie/ *n* a radio frequency or band of frequencies in the range between 300 megahertz and 3000 megahertz

**ultraism** /'ultrǝ,iz(ǝ)m/ *n* the principles of those who advocate extreme measures; extremism; *also* an instance or example of extremism – **ultraist** *adj or n*, **ultraistic** *adj*

**ultraliberal** /,ultrǝ'lib(ǝ)rǝl/ *adj* extremely liberal ⟨*the doubtful benefits of an* ~ *education*⟩ – **ultraliberal** *n*

**ultramafic** /,ultrǝ'mafik/ *adj, of (a) rock* ULTRABASIC (rich in iron and magnesium minerals)

¹**ultramarine** /,ultrǝmǝ'reen/ *n* **1a** a vivid blue pigment formerly made by powdering LAPIS LAZULI **b** any of several similar or related pigments; *esp* one prepared from kaolin, SODA ASH, sulphur, and charcoal **2** a vivid deep blue colour [ML *ultramarinus* coming from beyond the sea; fr its coming orig from Asia]

²**ultramarine** *adj* situated or coming from beyond the sea [ML *ultramarinus*, fr L *ultra-* + *mare* sea – more at MARINE]

**ultramicroscope** /-'miekrǝ,skohp/ *n* an apparatus using scattered light to make visible particles that are too small to be perceived by the ordinary microscope [back-formation fr *ultramicroscopic*]

**ultramicroscopic** /-,miekrǝ'skopik/ *adj* **1** too small to be seen with an ordinary microscope **2** of an ultramicroscope [ISV] – **ultramicroscopically** *adv*

**ultramicrotome** /,ultrǝ'miekrǝtohm/ *n* a MICROTOME designed to cut extremely thin slices, esp of biological material, for examination with the ELECTRON MICROSCOPE – **ultramicrotomy** *n*

**ultraminiature** /,ultrǝ'minǝchǝ/ *adj, electronics* SUBMINIATURE – **ultraminiaturization** *n*

**ultramodern** /,ultrǝ'modǝn/ *adj* having the very latest ideas, styles, etc – **ultramodernist** *n*

**ultramontane** /-'mon'tayn/ *adj* **1** of countries or peoples beyond the Alps or other mountains **2** favouring greater or absolute supremacy of papal over national or diocesan authority in the Roman Catholic church [ML *ultramontanus*, fr L *ultra-* + *mont-*, *mons* mountain – more at MOUNT] – **ultramontane** *n, often cap*, **ultramontanism** *n*

**ultramundane** /,ultrǝmun'dayn/ *adj, chiefly poetic* situated beyond the earth or the solar system [L *ultramundanus*, fr *ultra* beyond + *mundus* world]

**ultranationalism** /,ultrǝ'nash(ǝ)nl,iz(ǝ)m/ *n* great or excessive devotion to or advocacy of national interests and rights, esp as opposed to international considerations; *broadly* jingoism – **ultranationalist** *n or n*

¹**ultrasonic** /-'sonik/ *adj* **1** *of waves and vibrations* having a frequency above the range of the human ear (e g above about 20000 hertz) **2** using, produced by, or relating to ultrasonic waves or vibrations ⟨*an* ~ *dog whistle*⟩ – **ultrasonically** *adv*

²**ultrasonic** *n* an ultrasonic wave or frequency

**ultrasonics** /,ultrǝ'soniks/ *n pl taking sing vb* the science or technology of ultrasonic waves – called also SUPERSONICS

**ultrasound** /-,sownd/ *n* vibrations of the same physical nature as sound but with frequencies above the upper threshold of human hearing

**ultrastructure** /-,strukchǝ/ *n* the minute structure of biological material as revealed by a microscope, esp an ELECTRON MICROSCOPE – **ultrastructural** *adj*, **ultrastructurally** *adv*

¹**ultraviolet, ultraviolet light** /-'vie-ǝlǝt/ *n* ELECTROMAGNETIC RADIATION having a wavelength between the violet end of the visible spectrum and X rays

²**ultraviolet** *adj* consisting of, relating to, producing, or employing ultraviolet ⟨*an* ~ *lamp*⟩

**ultra vires** /,ooltra 'viǝrayz, 'virayz/ *adv or adj* beyond the legal power or authority of a person or body [NL, lit., beyond power]

**ululate** /'yoohyoo,layt/ *vi* to howl, wail [L *ululatus*, pp of *ululare*, of imit origin] – **ululation** *n*, **ululant** *adj*

**ulva** /'ulvǝ/ *n* SEA LETTUCE [NL, genus name, fr L, sedge]

**U-matic** /,yooh'matik/ *trademark* – used for a method of recording programmes, films, etc on video tape

**umbel** /'umb(ǝ)l/ *n* a flower cluster typical of plants of the carrot family in which the flower stalks arise from a central point to form a flat or rounded surface of small flowers [NL *umbella*, fr L, sunshade] – **umbelled, umbeled** *adj*

**umbellate** /'umbǝlayt, um'belayt/ *adj* **1** bearing, consisting of, or arranged in umbels **2** resembling an umbel in form

**umbellifer** /um'belifǝ/ *n* any of several plants of the carrot

U-Z

family that grow chiefly in north temperate regions and have hollow stems, flower heads made up of simple or compound umbels, and fruits that split into two 1-seeded portions [NL *Umbelliferae*, group name, fem pl of *umbellifer* bearing umbels] – **umbelliferous** *adj*

**¹umber** /'umbə/ *n* **1** an earthy substance rich in OXIDES of the chemical elements iron and manganese, that is green-brown when raw and dark brown when burnt and is used to colour paint, ink, etc – compare BURNT UMBER, RAW UMBER **2** a dark brown or yellowish-brown colour [prob fr obs *umber* shade, colour, fr ME *umbre* shade, shadow, fr MF, fr L *umbra* – more at UMBRAGE]

**²umber** *adj* of the colour umber

**³umber** *vt* to darken (as if) with umber

**umbilical** /um'bilikl, ,umbi'liekl/ *adj* **1** of or near the navel **2a** of or relating to the UMBILICAL CORD **b** of or being a tethering or supply line

**umbilical cord** *n* **1** the ropelike tube connecting the foetus with the placenta and being detached at the navel after birth **2** a cable conveying power to a rocket or spacecraft before takeoff; *also* a tethering or supply line (eg for an astronaut outside a spacecraft or a diver underwater)

**umbilicate** /um'bilikət, -,kayt/, **umbilicated** /-,kaytid/ *adj* **1a** shaped like a navel **b** having a central depression **2** having an umbilicus – **umbilication** *n*

**umbilicus** /um'bilikəs, ,umbi'liekəs/ *n, pl* **umbilici** /-kee, -see/, **umbilicuses** **1a** a small depression on the surface of the abdomen at the point where the UMBILICAL CORD was attached – called also NAVEL **b** any of several depressions comparable to an umbilicus; *esp* HILUM 1a (scar on a seed) **2** a central point; core, heart [L – more at NAVEL]

**umbles** /'umb(ə)lz/ *n pl, archaic* the entrails of an animal, esp a deer, formerly used as food [ME, alter. of *nombles*, fr MF, pl of *nomble* fillet of beef, pork loin, modif of L *lumbulus*, dim. of *lumbus* loin – more at LOIN]

**umbo** /'umboh/ *n, pl* **umbones** /um'bohneez/, **umbos** **1** the BOSS (raised central ornament) of a shield **2a** a rounded anatomical elevation **b** the protuberance on each half of the shell of a mussel, clam, etc that is the oldest part of the shell [L; akin to L *umbilicus* – more at NAVEL] – **umbonal** *adj*, **umbonate** *adj*

**umbra** /'umbrə/ *n, pl* **umbras, umbrae** /'umbrie/ **1** a shaded area **2a** a region of total shadow, esp in an eclipse **b** the central dark region of a sunspot – compare PENUMBRA [L] – **umbral** *adj*

**umbrage** /'umbrij/ *n* **1** a feeling of pique or resentment, often at some fancied slight or insult ⟨*took ~ at the chairman's comment*⟩ **2** *archaic* **2a** shade, shadow **b** shady branches foliage **c** an indistinct indication or semblance of something [ME, fr MF, fr L *umbraticum*, neut of *umbraticus* of shade, fr *umbratus*, pp of *umbrare* to shade, fr *umbra* shade, shadow; akin to Lith *unksna* shadow]

**umbrageous** /um'brayjəs/ *adj, archaic* **1** shadowy, shady **2** inclined to take offence easily – **umbrageously** *adv*, **umbrageousness** *n*

**umbrella** /um'brelə/ *n* **1** a collapsible circular convex shade for protection against rain, consisting of fabric stretched over hinged ribs radiating from a central rod; *esp* one for carrying in the hand – compare SUNSHADE **2** the bell-shaped or saucer-shaped largely gelatinous structure that forms the chief part of the body of most jellyfishes **3a** something that provides protection or cover ⟨*under the ~ of the welfare state*⟩ **b** a protective false roof constructed above another that is being dis-

mantled for reconstruction **4** something that covers or embraces a broad range of elements or factors ⟨*the Electricity Council – ~ of the area electricity boards – The Economist*⟩ ⟨*an ~ organization*⟩ [It *ombrella*, modif of L *umbella*, dim. of *umbra*]

**umbrella bird** *n* any of several tropical American songbirds (genus *Cephalopterus*, esp *Cephalopterus ornatus*) in which the male is black with a radiating crest curving forward over the head

**umbrella stand** *n* an upright rack for holding closed umbrellas and walking sticks

**umbrella tree** *n* **1** an American magnolia (*Magnolia tripetala*) having large leaves clustered at the ends of the branches **2** any of various trees or shrubs resembling an umbrella in overall shape, in the arrangement of leaves, or in the shape of the crown

**Umbrian** /'umbri·ən/ *n* **1a** a member of a people of ancient Italy that occupied Umbria **b** a native or inhabitant of the Italian province of Umbria **2** the ITALIC language of ancient Umbria – **Umbrian** *adj*

**Umbundu** /oom'boondooh/ *n* a Congo language of central Angola

**umfaan** /'umfahn/ *n, SAfr* a boy employed for general duties or looking after small children [Afrik, fr Zulu *umfana* boy, dim. of *umfo* man, person]

**umiak** /'oohmi,ak/ *n* an open Eskimo boat made of a wooden frame covered with hide and usu propelled with broad paddles –compare KAYAK [Eskimo]

**¹umlaut** /'oomlowt, 'um-* (Ger ʊmlaʊt)/*n* **1a** the change of a Germanic vowel (eg from *mann* to *männer*, /man/ → /menə/) caused by the influence of a following vowel or semivowel – compare ABLAUT **b** a vowel resulting from such change **2** a mark ¨ placed esp over a German vowel to indicate umlaut [Ger, fr *um-* around, transformation + *laut* sound]

**²umlaut** *vt* **1** to modify with an umlaut **2** to write or print an umlaut over

**¹umpire** /'umpie·ə/ *n* **1** one having authority to decide finally a controversy or question between parties; an arbiter, judge **2** a referee in any of several sports (eg cricket, tennis, badminton, and hockey) [ME *oumpere*, alter. (by incorrect division of *a noumpere*) of *noumpere*, fr MF *nomper* not equal, not paired, fr *non-* + *per* equal, fr L *par*] – **umpirage** *n*

**²umpire** *vb* to act as umpire in (a match or dispute)

**umpteen** /,ump'teen/ *adj, informal* very many; innumerable [blend of *umpty* (such and such) + *-teen* (as in *thirteen*)] – **umpteen** *n*, **umpteenth** *adj*

**un, 'un** /ən/ *pron, dial* one ⟨*caught a lot of fish but threw the little ~s back*⟩

**¹un-** /un-/ *prefix* **1a** not; in-, non- ⟨*unskilled*⟩ ⟨*undressed*⟩ ⟨*unbelief*⟩ – sometimes in words that have a meaning that merely negates that of the base word and are thereby distinguished from words that prefix *in-* or a variant of it (eg *im-*) to the same base word and have a meaning positively opposite to that of the base word ⟨*unartistic*⟩ ⟨*unmoral*⟩ **b** not yet ⟨*unevolved*⟩ **2** opposite of; contrary to ⟨*ungrateful*⟩ ⟨*unthinking*⟩ ⟨*unrest*⟩ **3** lack of; absence of ⟨*unbias*⟩ ⟨*unsoundness*⟩ **synonyms** see NON- [ME, fr OE; akin to OHG *un-* un-, L *in-*, Gk *a-, an-*, OE *ne* not – more at NO]

**²un-** *prefix* **1** do the opposite of; reverse (a specified action); DE- 1a, DIS- 1a ⟨*unbend*⟩ ⟨*undress*⟩ ⟨*unfold*⟩ **2a** deprive of; remove (something specified) from; remove ⟨*unfrock*⟩ ⟨*unsex*⟩ ⟨*unnerve*⟩ **b** release from; free from ⟨*unhand*⟩ ⟨*untie*⟩ **c(1)** remove from; extract from; take out of ⟨*unearth*⟩ ⟨*unsheathe*⟩ **c(2)** dislodge from ⟨*unhorse*⟩ ⟨*unseat*⟩ **d** cause to cease to be ⟨*un-*

| | | | |
|---|---|---|---|
| **unabbreviated** *adj* | **unacculturated** *adj* | **unadjustable** *adj* | **unafraid** *adj* |
| **unabraded** *adj* | **unachievable** *adj* | **unadjusted** *adj* | **unaged** *adj* |
| **unabsolved** *adj* | **unachieved** *adj* | **unadmirable** *adj* | **unaggresive** *adj* |
| **unabsorbable** *adj* | **unacknowledged** *adj* | **unadmired** *adj* | **unagile** *adj* |
| **unabsorbed** *adj* | **unacquainted** *adj* | **unadmitted** *adj* | **unaided** *adj* |
| **unabsorbent** *adj* | **unacquitted** *adj* | **unadoptable** *adj* | **unaimed** *adj* |
| **unacademic** *adj* | **unactable** *adj* | **unadvantageous** *adj* | **unaired** *adj* |
| **unaccented** *adj* | **unacted** *adj* | **unadventurous** *adj* | **unakin** *adj* |
| **unaccentuated** *adj* | **unactionable** *adj* | **unadvertised** *adj* | **unalarmed** *adj* |
| **unaccepted** *adj* | **unactuated** *adj* | **unadvisable** *adj* | **unalienated** *adj* |
| **unacclimated** *adj* | **unadaptable** *adj* | **unaesthetic** *adj* | **unalike** *adj* |
| **unacclimatized** *adj* | **unadapted** *adj* | **unaffecting** *adj* | **unallayed** *adj* |
| **unaccommodating** *adj* | **unaddressed** *adj* | **unaffiliated** *adj* | **unalleviated** *adj* |
| **unaccomplished** *adj* | **unadjourned** *adj* | **unaffluent** *adj* | **unallied** *adj* |
| **unaccredited** *adj* | **unadjudicated** *adj* | **unaffordable** *adj* | **unallocated** *adj* |

man> **3** completely <un*loose*> <un*thaw*> [ME, fr OE *un-*, *on-*, alter. of *and-* against – more at ANTE-]

**unabashed** /,unə'basht/ *adj* not abashed; unashamed – **unabashedly** *adv*

**unabated** /,una'baytid/ *adj* not abated; being at full strength or force; undiminished – **unabatedly** *adv*

**unable** /un'ayb(ə)l/ *adj* not able; incapable <~ *to understand you*> **synonyms** see INCAPABLE

**unabridged** /,unə'brijd/ *adj* **1** not abridged; complete <*an ~ reprint of a novel*> **2** being the most complete of its class; not based on one larger <*an ~ dictionary*>

**unacceptable** /,unək'septəbl/ *adj* **1** not acceptable; not good enough **2** not tolerable or permissible <*an ~ state of affairs*> – **unacceptably** *adv*, **unacceptability** *n*

**unaccommodated** /,unə'komədaytid/ *adj* not accommodated; unprovided for

**unaccompanied** /,unə'kumpənid/ *adj* not accompanied; *specif* being without instrumental accompaniment

**unaccountable** /,unə'kowntəbl/ *adj* **1** not to be accounted for; inexplicable, strange **2** not to be called to account; not responsible – **unaccountably** *adv*, **unaccountability** *n*

**unaccounted** /,unə'kowntid/ *adj* unexplained; not taken into account – often + *for*

**unaccustomed** /,unə'kustəmd/ *adj* **1** not customary; not usual or common **2** not used *to* <~ *to the good life*> – **unaccustomedly** *adv*

**una corda** /,oohnə 'kawdə/ *adv or adj* with the SOFT PEDAL depressed – used as a direction in piano music [It, lit., one string]

**unadopted** /,unə'doptid/ *adj* **1** not adopted **2** *Br, of a road* not maintained by a local authority

**unadorned** /,unə'dawnd/ *adj* not adorned; lacking embellishment or decoration; plain, simple – **unadornment** *n*

**unadulterated** /,unə'dultəraytid/ *adj* **1** unmixed or undiluted; pure **2** complete, utter <~ *nonsense*> – **unadulteratedly** *adv*

**unadvised** /,unəd'viezd/ *adj* **1** done without due consideration; rash <*a cruel and ~ act*> **2** not prudent; indiscreet <*her ~ love of gossip*> – compare ILL-ADVISED – **unadvisedly** *adv*

**unaffected** /,unə'fektid/ *adj* **1** not influenced or changed by something **2** free from affectation; genuine, natural **synonyms** see ¹NATURAL, SINCERE *antonym* affected – **unaffectedly** *adv*, **unaffectedness** *n*

**unaffectionate** /,unə'fekshənət/ *adj* lacking affection; not affectionate – **unaffectionately** *adv*

**unaging, unageing** /un'ayjing/ *adj* ageless

**unalienable** /un'ayli·ənəbl, -'aylyənəbl/ *adj* inalienable

**unaligned** /,unə'liend/ *adj* nonaligned

**unalloyed** /,unə'loyd, un'aloyd/ *adj* not alloyed; unmixed, unqualified, pure <~ *metals*> <~ *happiness*>

**unalterable** /un'awltərəbl/ *adj* not capable of being altered or changed <*an ~ resolve*> <~ *hatred*> – **unalterably** *adv*, **unalterableness** *n*, **unalterability** *n*

**unambiguous** /,unam'bigyooəs/ *adj* not ambiguous; clear, precise – **unambiguously** *adv*

**unambivalent** /,unam'bivələnt/ *adj* not ambivalent; clear-cut, definite – **unambivalently** *adv*

**un-A'merican** *adj* not American; not characteristic of or consistent with American customs, principles, or traditions; *broadly* radical, subversive

**unanaesthet·ized, -ised** /,unə'neesthətiezd/ *adj* not having been subjected to an anaesthetic

**unaneled** /,unə'niəld, -neeld/ *adj, archaic* not having received EXTREME UNCTION [¹*un-* + *aneled*, pp of arch. *anele* to anoint,

fr ME *anelen*, fr *an* on + *elen* to anoint, fr *ele* oil, fr OE *æle*, fr L *oleum* – more at OIL]

**unanimous** /yoo'naniməs/ *adj* **1** being of one mind; all agreeing **2** characterized by or having the agreement and consent of all <*a ~ decision*> [L *unanimus*, fr *unus* one + *animus* mind – more at ONE, ANIMATE] – **unanimously** *adv*, **unanimity** *n*
**synonyms** A motion is carried **unanimously** if everyone votes for it. If there are some abstainers but nobody votes against it, it is carried **nem con**.

**unanswerable** /un'ahns(ə)rəbl/ *adj* **1** *of a question* having no answer **2** incapable of being argued against; irrefutable – **unanswerably** *adv*, **unanswerability** *n*

**unanticipated** /,unan'tisipaytid/ *adj* not anticipated; unexpected, unforeseen – **unanticipatedly** *adv*

**unapologetic** /,unəpolə'jetik/ *adj* not apologetic; offered or put forward without apology – **unapologetically** *adv*

**unappealable** /,unə'peeləbl, -'piə/ *adj* not appealable; not subject to appeal

**unappealing** /,unə'peeling, -'piə-/ *adj* not appealing; unattractive – **unappealingly** *adv*

**unappeasable** /,unə'peezəbl/ *adj* not to be appeased; implacable – **unappeasably** *adv*

**unappet·izing, -ising** /un'apitiezing/ *adj* not appetizing; insipid, unattractive – **unappetizingly** *adv*

**unappreciative** /,unə'preesh(y)ətiv/ *adj* not appreciative

**unapproachable** /,unə'prohchəbl/ *adj* **1** not approachable; physically inaccessible **2** discouraging friendliness; aloof – **unapproachably** *adv*, **unapproachability** *n*

**unapt** /,un'apt/ *adj* **1** unsuitable, inappropriate *for* <~ *for the job*> **2** not accustomed and not likely *to* <*a man ~ to tolerate carelessness*> **3** dull, backward <~ *scholars*> **synonyms** see INAPT – **unaptly** *adv*, **unaptness** *n*

**unarguable** /un'ahgyooəbl/ *adj* not arguable: e g **a** undoubted **b** untenable – **unarguably** *adv*

**unarm** /,un'ahm/ *vt* to disarm

**unarmed** /,un'ahmd/ *adj* **1** not carrying or using arms or armour <~ *combat*> **2** *of a plant or animal* having no spines, spurs, claws, etc

**unarticulated** /,unah'tikyoolaytid/ *adj* not articulated; *esp* not carefully reasoned or analysed

**unary** /'yoohnəri/ *adj* having, consisting of, or acting on a single element, item, or component [L *unus* one + E *-ary*]

**unashamed** /,unə'shaymd/ *adj* not ashamed; being without guilt, embarrassment, or doubt – **unashamedly** *adv*

**unasked** /,un'ahskt/ *adj* **1** not asked <~ *questions*> **2** not being asked; uninvited **3** not asked for <~ *advice*>

**unassailable** /,unə'sayləbl/ *adj* not assailable; not open to doubt, attack, or question – **unassailably** *adv*, **unassailableness, unassailability,** *n*

**unassertive** /,unə'suhtiv/ *adj* not assertive; modest, shy

**unassisted** /,unə'sistid/ *adj* not assisted; without help

**unassuageable** /,unə'swayjəbl/ *adj* not capable of being assuaged

**unassuming** /,unə'syoohming/ *adj* not arrogant or presumptuous; modest, retiring – **unassumingly** *adv*, **unassumingness** *n*

**unattached** /,unə'tacht/ *adj* **1** not assigned, committed, or connected (e g to a particular task, organization, or person); *esp* not married or engaged **2** not joined or united <~ *polyps*> <~ *buildings*>

**unattended** /,unə'tendid/ *adj* **1** without supervision; not looked after <*do not leave your car ~*> **2** unaccompanied; alone

| | | | |
|---|---|---|---|
| **unallowable** *adj* | **unanimated** *adj* | **unappropriate** *adj* | **unassessed** *adj* |
| **unallowed** *adj* | **unannotated** *adj* | **unappropriated** *adj* | **unassigned** *adj* |
| **unalluring** *adj* | **unannounced** *adj* | **unapproved** *adj* | **unassimilable** *adj* |
| **unaltered** *adj* | **unanswered** *adj* | **unaristocratic** *adj* | **unassimilated** *adj* |
| **unambitious** *adj* | **unapologizing** *adj* | **unarithmetical** *adj* | **unassociated** *adj* |
| **unamenable** *adj* | **unappalled** *adj* | **unarmoured** *adj* | **unassorted** *adj* |
| **unamended** *adj* | **unapparent** *adj* | **unarrested** *adj* | **unassuaged** *adj* |
| **unamiable** *adj* | **unappeased** *adj* | **unarrogant** *adj* | **unassumed** *adj* |
| **unamicable** *adj* | **unapplicable** *adj* | **unartistic** *adj* | **unastronomical** *adj* |
| **unamortized** *adj* | **unapplied** *adj* | **unascertainable** *adj* | **unathletic** *adj* |
| **unamplified** *adj* | **unappointed** *adj* | **unascertained** *adj* | **unatoned** *adj* |
| **unamused** *adj* | **unapportioned** *adj* | **unaspirated** *adj* | **unattainable** *adj* |
| **unamusing** *adj* | **unappreciated** *adj* | **unaspiring** *adj* | **unattained** *adj* |
| **unanalysable** *adj* | **unapprehensive** *adj* | **unassailed** *adj* | **unattempted** *adj* |
| **unanalysed** *adj* | **unapproached** *adj* | **unassembled** *adj* | **unattentive** *adj* |

**unattractive** /ˌunə'traktiv/ *adj* not attractive or pleasing – **unattractively** *adv*, **unattractiveness** *n*

**unau** /'yoohnow/ *n* TWO-TOED SLOTH [Fr, fr Tupi *unáu*]

**unavailable** /ˌunə'vayləbl/ *adj* not available – **unavailability** *n*

**unavailing** /ˌunə'vayling/ *adj* futile, useless – **unavailingly** *adv*, **unavailingness** *n*

**unaverage** /ˌun'av(ə)rij/ *adj* not average; unusual, outstanding

**una voce** /ˌoohnə 'vohkay/ *adv* with one voice; together [L]

**unavoidable** /ˌunə'voydəbl/ *adj* not avoidable; inevitable – **unavoidably** *adv*

**¹unaware** /ˌunə'weə/ *adv*, *chiefly NAm* unawares

**²unaware** *adj* not aware; ignorant – usu + *of* or *that* – **unawarely** *adv*, **unawareness** *n*

**unawares** /ˌunə'weəz/ *adv* 1 without noticing or intending; inadvertently 2 without warning; suddenly, unexpectedly [*un-* + *aware* + *-s*, adv suffix, fr ME, fr *-s*, gen sing. ending of nouns – more at -s]

**unbacked** /ˌun'bakt/ *adj* 1 lacking support or aid 2 *of a horse* 2a never mounted by a rider; not broken in b having no backers in betting 3 having no back ⟨an ~ chair⟩

**¹unbalance** /un'baləns/ *vt* to put out of balance; *esp* to derange mentally

**²unbalance** *n* lack of balance; imbalance, instability

**unbalanced** /un'balənst/ *adj* not balanced: e g a not in equilibrium; unstable b mentally disordered or deranged c not adjusted so as to make credits equal to debts ⟨an ~ account⟩

**unballasted** /un'baləstid/ *adj* not furnished with or steadied by ballast; unsteady

**unbar** /ˌun'bah/ *vt* **-rr-** to remove a bar from; unbolt, open

**unbarred** /un'bahd/ *adj* 1 not secured by a bar; unlocked 2 not marked with bars

**unbated** /un'baytid/ *adj* 1 unabated 2 *archaic, of a sword, foil, etc* not blunted

**unbearable** /un'beərəbl/ *adj* not bearable; unendurable – **unbearably** *adv*

**unbeatable** /un'beetəbl/ *adj* not capable of being defeated or surpassed – **unbeatably** *adv*

**unbeaten** /un'beet(ə)n/ *adj* 1 not pounded or beaten 2 not traversed; untrodden 3 not defeated ⟨an ~ record⟩

**unbeautiful** /un'byoohtif(ə)l/ *adj* not beautiful; unattractive – **unbeautifully** *adv*

**unbecoming** /ˌunbi'kuming/ *adj* not attractive or showing to advantage ⟨an ~ dress⟩; *esp* not suitable; unseemly, improper ⟨~ conduct⟩ – **unbecomingly** *adv*, **unbecomingness** *n*

**unbeknown** /ˌunbi'nohn/ *adv or adj* without the knowledge (of someone); unknown – usu + *to* [¹*un-* + obs *beknown* known]

**unbeknownst** /ˌunbi'nohnst/ *adv or adj* unbeknown

**unbelief** /ˌunbi'leef/ *n* incredulity or scepticism, esp in matters of religious faith

**unbelievable** /ˌunbi'leevəbl/ *adj* 1 too improbable for belief; incredible 2 tremendous, fantastic ⟨the stench was ~⟩ – **unbelievably** *adv*

**unbeliever** /ˌunbi'leevə/ *n* one who does not believe, esp in a particular religion – compare HEATHEN, ATHEIST

**unbelieving** /ˌunbi'leeving/ *adj* marked by unbelief; sceptical – **unbelievingly** *adv*

**unbelted** /un'beltid/ *adj* not furnished with a belt

**unbend** /un'bend/ *vb* **unbent** /-'bent/ *vt* 1 to put into or allow to return to a straight position ⟨~ a bow⟩ 2 to cause (e g the mind) to relax 3a to unfasten (e g a sail) from a spar or stay b to cast loose or untie (e g a rope) ~ *vi* 1 to become more relaxed, informal, or outgoing in manner 2 to cease to be bent;

become straight [²*un-* + *bend*]

**unbendable** /un'bendəbl/ *adj* single-minded, firm

**unbending** /un'bending/ *adj* 1 firm, unyielding, inflexible ⟨an ~ will⟩ 2 aloof or unsocial in manner; reserved [¹*un-* + *bending*]

*usage* Besides meaning "inflexible", **unbending** may be formed from the verb **unbend** and thus may mean "relaxing".

**unbeseeming** /ˌunbi'seeming/ *adj*, *archaic* not befitting; unbecoming

**unbiased, unbiassed** /un'bie·əst/ *adj* 1 free from bias; *esp* free from all prejudice and favouritism; fair 2 *of a statistic* having an observed value equal to the EXPECTED VALUE of the population parameter being estimated *synonyms* see ¹FAIR *antonym* biased – **unbiasedness** *n*

**unbiblical** /un'biblikl/ *adj* contrary to or not sanctioned by the Bible

**unbid** /ˌun'bid/ *adj* unbidden

**unbidden** /un'bidn/ *adj* unasked, uninvited

**unbind** /un'biend/ *vt* **unbound** /-'bownd/ 1 to remove a band from; untie, unfasten 2 to set free; release

**unbitted** /un'bitid/ *adj* unbridled, uncontrolled

**unblenched** /un'blencht/ *adj*, *archaic* not disconcerted; undaunted

**unblessed, unblest** /un'blest/ *adj* 1 not blessed 2 evil, accursed 3 not fortunate or favoured *with*

**unblinded** /un'bliendid/ *adj* not blinded; *esp* free from illusion

**unblinking** /ˌun'blingking/ *adj* 1 not blinking 2 not showing signs of emotion, doubt, or confusion – **unblinkingly** *adv*

**unblock** /un'blok/ *vt* to free from being blocked; remove obstruction from – **unblocker** *n*

**unblushing** /ˌun'blushing/ *adj* not blushing; without shame – **unblushingly** *adv*

**unbodied** /un'bodid/ *adj* 1 having no body; incorporeal; *also* disembodied ⟨~ souls⟩ 2 formless

**unbolt** /un'bohlt/ *vt* to open or unfasten by withdrawing a bolt

**unbolted** /un'bohltid/ *adj* not sifted ⟨~ flour⟩

**unbonneted** /un'bonitid/ *adj*, *archaic* bareheaded; *specif* having removed one's hat as a mark of respect

**unborn** /ˌun'bawn/ *adj* 1 still in the womb; not yet born 2 still to appear; future ⟨~ ages⟩

**unbosom** /un'boozəm/ *vt* 1 to give expression to; disclose, reveal 2 to disclose the thoughts or feelings of (*oneself*) ~ *vi* to unbosom oneself

**unbound** /un'bownd/ *adj* not bound: e g a(1) not fastened a(2) not confined ⟨Prometheus Unbound – P B Shelley⟩ b not having the leaves fastened together ⟨an ~ book⟩ c having no binding or case ⟨~ periodicals⟩ d not held by chemical or physical bonds

**unbounded** /un'bowndid/ *adj* 1 having no mathematical limit 2 having no bounds or constraints – **unboundedness** *n*

**unbowed** /un'bowd/ *adj* not bowed down; *esp* not subdued

**unbox** /un'boks/ *vt* to remove from a box, crate, or packing

**unbrace** /un'brays/ *vt* 1 to free or detach (as if) by untying or removing a brace or bond 2 to remove tension from; relax

**unbraid** /ˌun'brayd/ *vt* to separate the strands of; unravel

**unbranched** /un'brahncht/ *adj* 1 having no branches ⟨a straight ~ trunk⟩ 2 not divided into branches ⟨a leaf with ~ veins⟩

**unbreathable** /un'breedhəbl/ *adj* not fit to breathe

**unbred** /un'bred/ *adj* 1 not taught; untrained 2 *obs* ill-bred

**unbridle** /un'briedl/ *vt* to free or loose from a bridle; *broadly* to set loose; free from restraint

| | | | |
|---|---|---|---|
| **unattenuated** *adj* | **unawed** *adj* | **unbemused** *adj* | **unborrowed** *adj* |
| **unattested** *adj* | **unawesome** *adj* | **unbigoted** *adj* | **unbothered** *adj* |
| **unattributable** *adj* | **unbaked** *adj* | **unbilled** *adj* | **unbought** *adj* |
| **unattributed** *adj* | **unbandage** *vt* | **unbitten** *adj* | **unbowdlerized** *adj* |
| **unattuned** *adj* | **unbanned** *adj* | **unbitter** *adj* | **unbracketed** *adj* |
| **unaudited** *adj* | **unbaptized** *adj* | **unblamable** *adj* | **unbranded** *adj* |
| **unauspicious** *adj* | **unbarbed** *adj* | **unblamed** *adj* | **unbreachable** *adj* |
| **unauthentic** *adj* | **unbarricaded** *adj* | **unbleached** *adj* | **unbreakable** *adj* |
| **unauthenticated** *adj* | **unbeautified** *adj* | **unblemished** *adj* | **unbribable** *adj* |
| **unauthorized** *adj* | **unbefitting** *adj* | **unblenching** *adj* | **unbridgeable** *adj* |
| **unautomated** *adj* | **unbefriended** *adj* | **unblended** *adj* | **unbridged** *adj* |
| **unavenged** *adj* | **unbegotten** *adj* | **unblooded** *adj* | **unbriefed** *adj* |
| **unavowed** *adj* | **unbeholden** *adj* | **unblotted** *adj* | **unbrotherly** *adj* |
| **unawakened** *adj* | **unbelligerent** *adj* | **unboastful** *adj* | **unbruised** *adj* |
| **unawarded** *adj* | **unbeloved** *adj* | **unbookish** *adj* | **unbrushed** *adj* |

**unbridled** /un'briedld/ *adj* **1** not held in check or kept under control by a bridle **2** unrestrained, uncontrolled ⟨*the ~ joy of the lovers at being reunited*⟩

**unbroken** /un'brohkən/ *adj* **1** not violated or infringed ⟨*an ~ rule*⟩ **2** whole, intact **3** not subdued; untamed; *esp* not trained to be ridden or to pull a cart, plough, etc ⟨*~ colts*⟩ **4** uninterrupted ⟨*miles of ~ forest*⟩ **5** *of land* not ploughed; never ploughed **6** not disorganized or in disarray ⟨*advanced in ~ ranks*⟩ **7** *of a record* not beaten or surpassed

**unbuckle** /un'bukl/ *vt* **1** to loose the buckle of; unfasten **2** to relax

**unbudgeable** /un'bujəbl/ *adj* not able to be budged or changed; inflexible – **unbudgeably** *adv*

**unbudging** /un'bujing/ *adj* not budging; resisting movement or change – **unbudgingly** *adv*

**unbuilt** /un'bilt/ *adj* **1** not built; not yet constructed **2** not built on ⟨*an ~ plot*⟩

**unbung** /,un'bung/ *vt* to free (eg a drain) from an obstruction

**unburden** /un'buhd(ə)n/ *vt* **1** to free or relieve (as if) from a burden **2** to relieve (oneself) of cares, fears, worries, etc, esp by relating them *to* someone else ⟨*this doctor was not the kind of man that one could ~ oneself to*⟩

**unbutton** /un'but(ə)n/ *vt* **1** to undo the buttons of **2** to open as if by undoing buttons; *specif* to open the hatches or apertures of (an armoured vehicle) **3** to free from constraint, tension, etc; relax ~ *vi* **1** to undo buttons **2** to become unbuttoned – **unbuttoned** *adj*

**uncage** /un'kayj/ *vt* to release (as if) from a cage; free from restraint

**uncalculated** /un'kalkyoolaytid/ *adj* not planned or thought out beforehand; spontaneous

**uncalculating** /un'kalkyoolayting/ *adj* not based on or marked by calculation

**uncalled-for** /un'kawld/ *adj* **1** not called for or needed; unnecessary **2** unwarranted; unprovoked ⟨*an ~ display of temper*⟩ ⟨*~ insults*⟩

**uncandid** /un'kandid/ *adj* not frank or honest – **uncandidly** *adv*

**uncanny** /un'kani/ *adj* **1a** suggesting the supernatural; eerie, mysterious **b** being beyond what is normal or expected; extraordinary, inexplicable ⟨*an ~ sense of direction*⟩ **2** *chiefly Scot* severe, punishing **3** *chiefly Scot* dangerous *synonyms* see ²WEIRD – **uncannily** *adv*, **uncanniness** *n*

**uncap** /un'kap/ *vt* **-pp-** to remove a cap or covering from; open ⟨*~ ped another bottle of rum and took a hefty swig*⟩

**uncatchable** /un'kachəbl/ *adj* not able to be caught

**uncaused** /un'kawzd/ *adj* having no cause; spontaneous

**unceasing** /un'seesing/ *adj* never ceasing; continuous, incessant – **unceasingly** *adv*

**uncelebrated** /un'selibraytid/ *adj* **1** not formally honoured or commemorated **2** not famous; obscure

**unceremonious** /,unserə'mohnyəs, -ni-əs/ *adj* **1** not ceremonious; informal **2** abrupt, rude ⟨*an ~ dismissal*⟩ – **unceremoniously** *adv*, **unceremoniousness** *n*

**uncertain** /un'suhtn/ *adj* **1** indefinite, indeterminate ⟨*an ~ quantity*⟩ **2** liable to change; not reliable, predictable, or fixed ⟨*~ weather*⟩ **3a** not known beyond doubt; dubious **b** not confident or sure; doubtful ⟨*~ of the truth*⟩ **c** hesitant, tentative ⟨*~ fingers* – Edith Sitwell⟩ – **uncertainly** *adv*, **uncertainness** *n*

**uncertainty** /un'suht(ə)nti/ *n* **1** the quality or state of being uncertain; doubt **2** something uncertain

   *synonyms* Uncertainty, doubt, dubiety, scepticism, sus-

picion, and **mistrust** all mean "lack of sureness". **Uncertainty**, doubt, and the formal **dubiety** imply lack of knowledge, particularly about a possible outcome, and hesitation as to how to act ⟨*complete uncertainty as to our future plans*⟩. **Doubt** and **scepticism** are the usual words in religious contexts ⟨*a doubt about the existence of evil*⟩. **Scepticism** suggests a habitual unwillingness to believe without rational demonstration. **Suspicion** involves the belief that something is not real or right, arising from lack of trust. **Mistrust** is a stronger word than **suspicion**, implying an anticipation of falsehood or bad results. *antonyms* certainty, confidence, assurance

**uncertainty principle** *n* a principle in QUANTUM MECH-ANICS: it is impossible to accurately measure both the momentum and the position of a particle (eg a photon) at the same time

**unchain** /un'chayn/ *vt* to free (as if) by removing a chain; set loose

**unchallengeable** /un'chalinjəbl/ *adj* not able to be challenged or disputed

**unchancy** /un'chahnsi/ *adj, chiefly Scot archaic* ill-fated or dangerous

**unchangeable** /un'chaynjəbl/ *adj* not changing or to be changed; immutable – **unchangeably** *adv*, **unchangeableness**, **unchangeability** *n*

**unchanging** /un'chaynjing/ *adj* constant, invariable – **unchangingly** *adv*, **unchangingness** *n*

**uncharacteristic** /un,karəktə'ristik, ,----'--/ *adj* not characteristic; not typical or distinctive – **uncharacteristically** *adv*

**uncharge** /un'chahj/ *vt, obs* to acquit

**uncharitable** /un'charitəbl/ *adj* lacking in charity; severe in judging others; unkind – **uncharitableness** *n*, **uncharitably** *adv*

**uncharted** /un'chahtid/ *adj* not recorded or plotted on a map, chart, or plan; *broadly* unknown, unexplored △ unchartered

**unchaste** /un'chayst/ *adj* not chaste; impure, promiscuous ⟨*~ thoughts*⟩ – **unchastely** *adv*, **unchasteness**, **unchastity** *n*

**unchivalrous** /un'shivəlrəs/ *adj* not chivalrous; lacking in chivalry – **unchivalrously** *adv*

**unchoke** /un'chohk/ *vt* to clear of obstruction

**unchristian** /un'kristi·ən/ *adj* **1** not of the Christian faith **2a** contrary to the Christian spirit or character; *esp* uncharitable **b** barbarous, uncivilized

**unchurch** /un'chuhch/ *vt, archaic* **1** to expel from a church; excommunicate **2** to deprive of a church or of status as a church

**unchurched** /un'chuhcht/ *adj* not belonging to or connected with a church

**unci** /'unsi, -sie/ *pl of* UNCUS (small hooked structure)

**uncial** /'unsyəl/ *n* (a letter or manuscript written in) a style of handwriting formed of somewhat large rounded separated letters and used esp in Greek and Latin manuscripts of the 4th to the 8th centuries AD [L *uncialis* inch-high, fr *uncia* twelfth part, ounce, inch] – **uncial** *adj*, **uncially** *adv*

**unciform** /'unsi,fawm/ *adj, biology* hook-shaped; uncinate [NL *unciformis*, fr L *uncus* hook + *-formis* -form]

**uncinariasis** /,unsinə'rie·əsis/ *n* ANCYLOSTOMIASIS (infestation with hookworms) [NL, fr *Uncinaria*, genus of hookworms, fr L *uncinus* hook]

**uncinate** /'unsi,nayt/ *adj, of a plant or animal part* bent at the tip like a hook; hooked

**uncinus** /un'sienəs/ *n, pl* **uncini** /-ni, -nie/ a small uncinate structure or projection [NL, fr L, hook, fr *uncus* – more at ANGLE]

---

| | | | |
|---|---|---|---|
| **unbudgeted** *adj* | **uncalibrated** *adj* | **uncatalogued** *adj* | **unchartered** *adj* |
| **unbuffered** *adj* | **uncalloused** *adj* | **uncategorical** *adj* | **unchary** *adj* |
| **unbuild** *vt* | **uncamouflaged** *adj* | **uncategorically** *adv* | **unchastened** *adj* |
| **unbuildable** *adj* | **uncancelled** *adj* | **uncaught** *adj* | **unchauvinistic** *adj* |
| **unbureaucratic** *adj* | **uncanonical** *adj* | **uncensored** *adj* | **uncheckable** *adj* |
| **unburied** *adj* | **uncapitalized** *adj* | **uncensorious** *adj* | **unchecked** *adj* |
| **unburnable** *adj* | **uncaptioned** *adj* | **uncensured** *adj* | **unchewable** *adj* |
| **unburned** *adj* | **uncapturable** *adj* | **uncertified** *adj* | **unchewed** *adj* |
| **unburnished** *adj* | **uncaptured** *adj* | **unchallenged** *adj* | **unchic** *adj* |
| **unburnt** *adj* | **uncareful** *adj* | **unchallenging** *adj* | **unchildlike** *adj* |
| **unbusinesslike** *adj* | **uncaring** *adj* | **unchanged** *adj* | **unchlorinated** *adj* |
| **unbusy** *adj* | **uncarpeted** *adj* | **unchannelled** *adj* | **unchoreographed** *adj* |
| **unbuttered** *adj* | **uncase** *vt* | **unchaperoned** *adj* | **unchristened** *adj* |
| **uncalcified** *adj* | **uncashed** *adj* | **uncharismatic** *adj* | **unchronicled** *adj* |
| **uncalcined** *adj* | **uncastrated** *adj* | **uncharming** *adj* | **unchronological** *adj* |

**uncircumcised** /,un'suhkəm,siezd/ *adj* **1** not circumcised **2a** spiritually impure; heathen **b** gentile; non-Jewish – **uncircumcision** *n*

**uncivil** /un'sivl/ *adj* **1** not civilized; barbarous **2** lacking in courtesy; ill-mannered, impolite – **uncivilly** *adv*

**uncivil·ized, -ised** /un'sivl·iezd/ *adj* **1** not civilized; barbarous **2** remote from settled areas; wild

**unclamp** /un'klamp/ *vt* to loosen the clamp of or on; free from a clamp

**unclarity** /un'klarəti/ *n* lack of clarity; ambiguity, obscurity

**unclasp** /un'klahsp/ *vt* **1** to open the clasp of **2** to open or cause (eg a clenched hand) to be opened ~ *vi* **1** to become unclasped **2** to loosen a hold

**unclassical** /un'klasikl/ *adj* not classical; *esp* unconcerned with the classics

**unclassified** /un'klasified/ *adj* **1** not divided into classes or placed in a class **2** not subject to a security classification

**uncle** /'ungkl/ *n* **1a** the brother of one's father or mother **b** the husband of one's aunt **2** – used as a term of courtesy or affection for a man who is a close friend of a young child or its parents **3** *NAm* – used as a cry of surrender ⟨*was forced to cry* ~⟩ **4** *euph* a man who lives with one's mother ⟨*an unhappy childhood with no father and a succession of* ~s⟩ **5** *slang* a pawnbroker [ME, fr OF, fr L *avunculus* mother's brother; akin to OE *ēam* uncle, OIr *aue* grandson, L *avus* grandfather]

**unclean** /un'kleen/ *adj* **1** morally or spiritually impure **2a** ritually prohibited as food **b** ceremonially unfit or defiled **3a** dirty, filthy **b** not tidy or precise; messy – **uncleanness** *n*

¹**uncleanly** /un'klenli/ *adj* morally or physically unclean – **uncleanliness** *n*

²**uncleanly** /un'kleenli/ *adv* in an unclean manner

**unclench** /un'klench/ *vt* **1** to open from a clenched position **2** to release from a grip ~ *vi* to become unclenched or relaxed

**Uncle Sam** /sam/ *n* ~ the American nation, people, or government [prob jocular expansion of *US*, abbr of *United States*]

**Uncle Tom** /tom/ *n, chiefly derog* a black American eager to win the approval of white people and willing to cooperate with them [*Uncle Tom*, black slave in the novel *Uncle Tom's Cabin* by Harriet Beecher Stowe †1896 US author]

**unclimbable** /un'klieməbl/ *adj* not able to be climbed – **unclimbableness** *n*

**uncloak** /un'klohk/ *vt* **1** to remove a cloak or cover from **2** to reveal, unmask ~ *vi* to take off an outer garment (eg a cloak)

**unclog** /un'klog/ *vt* to free from a difficulty or obstruction

**unclose** /un'klohz/ *vb* to (cause to) open or be revealed

**unclosed** /un'klohzd/ *adj* not closed or settled; not concluded ⟨*after weeks of discussion, the deal still remains* ~⟩

**unclothe** /un'klohdh/ *vt* **1** to strip of clothes **2** to uncover

**unclothed** /un'klohdhd/ *adj* not clothed

**unclouded** /un'klowdid/ *adj* not covered by clouds; not darkened; clear – **uncloudedly** *adv*

¹**unco** /'ungkoh/ *adj, chiefly Scot* **1** strange, unknown, weird **2** extraordinary [ME (Sc) *unkow*, alter. of ME *uncouth*]

²**unco** *adv, chiefly Scot* extremely, remarkably, uncommonly

**uncock** /un'kok/ *vt* to remove the hammer of (a firearm) from a cocked position

**uncoil** /un'koyl/ *vb* to release or be released from a coiled state; unwind

**uncoined** /un'koynd/ *adj* **1** not minted ⟨~ *metal*⟩ **2** not fabricated; natural ⟨~ *constancy* – *Shak*⟩

**uncomfortable** /un'kumftəbl/ *adj* **1** causing discomfort or annoyance ⟨*an* ~ *chair*⟩ ⟨*an* ~ *performance*⟩ **2** feeling discomfort; uneasy ⟨*was* ~ *with the newcomers*⟩ – **uncomfortably** *adv*

**uncommercial** /,unkə'muhsh(ə)l/ *adj* **1** not engaged in or related to commerce **2** not based on commercial principles **3** not commercially viable

**uncommitted** /,unkə'mitid/ *adj* not committed; *specif* not pledged to a particular belief, allegiance, or programme

¹**uncommon** /un'komən/ *adj* **1** not ordinarily encountered; unusual **2** remarkable, exceptional – **uncommonly** *adv*, **uncommonness** *n*

²**uncommon** *adv, archaic or dial* uncommonly, unusually

**uncommunicable** /,unkə'myoohnikəbl/ *adj* incommunicable

**uncommunicative** /,unkə'myoohnikətiv/ *adj* not disposed to talk or impart information; reserved, quiet *synonyms* see SILENT

**uncompassionate** /,unkəm'pash(ə)nət/ *adj* hardhearted, unfeeling

**uncompetitive** /,unkəm'petətiv/ *adj* not competitive; unable to compete – **uncompetitiveness** *n*

**uncomplaining** /,unkəm'playning/ *adj* not complaining; patient – **uncomplainingly** *adv*

**uncomplicated** /un'komplikaytid/ *adj* **1** not complicated by something external; *specif* not involving medical complications ⟨~ *peptic ulcer*⟩ **2** not complex; simple ⟨~ *machinery*⟩

**uncomplimentary** /,unkompli'ment(ə)ri/ *adj* not complimentary; derogatory

**uncomprehending** /,unkompri'hending/ *adj* not comprehending; lacking understanding – **uncomprehendingly** *adv*

**uncompromising** /un'komprəmiezing/ *adj* not making or accepting a compromise; making no concessions; inflexible, unyielding – **uncompromisingly** *adv*

**unconcern** /,unkən'suhn/ *n* **1** lack of care or interest; indifference **2** freedom from excessive concern or anxiety

**unconcerned** /,unkən'suhnd/ *adj* **1** not involved; not having any part or interest **2** not anxious or upset; free of worry *synonyms* see INDIFFERENT – **unconcernedly** *adv*, **unconcernedness** *n*

**unconditional** /,unkən'dish(ə)nl/ *adj* **1** absolute, unqualified, total ⟨~ *surrender*⟩ **2** UNCONDITIONED **2** – **unconditionally** *adv*

**unconditioned** /,unkən'dish(ə)nd/ *adj* **1** UNCONDITIONAL 1 **2a** not dependent on, established by, or subjected to conditioning or learning; natural **b** producing an unconditioned response ⟨~ *stimuli*⟩

**unconformable** /,unkən'fawməbl/ *adj* **1** not conforming *to* **2** exhibiting geological unconformity – **unconformably** *adv*

**unconformity** /,unkən'fawməti/ *n* (the surface of contact between rocks of different ages marking) a break in the sequence of rock strata corresponding to a period of nondeposition or erosion

**uncongenial** /,unkən'jeenyəl, -ni·əl/ *adj* **1** not sympathetic or compatible ⟨~ *roommates*⟩ **2a** not fitted; unsuitable ⟨*a soil* ~ *to most crops*⟩ **b** not to one's taste; disagreeable ⟨*an* ~ *task*⟩ – **uncongeniality** *n*

**unconquerable** /,un'kongk(ə)rəbl/ *adj* **1** incapable of being conquered; indomitable ⟨*an* ~ *will*⟩ **2** incapable of being surmounted ⟨~ *difficulties*⟩ – **unconquerably** *adv*

**unconscionable** /un'konsh(ə)nəbl/ *adj* **1** not guided or con-

| | | | |
|---|---|---|---|
| unciliated *adj* | uncollected *adj* | uncompounded *adj* | unconjugated *adj* |
| uncinematic *adj* | uncollectible *adj* | uncomprehended *adj* | unconnected *adj* |
| unclad *adj* | uncoloured *adj* | uncomprehensible *adj* | unconquered *adj* |
| unclaimed *adj* | uncombative *adj* | uncompromised *adj* | unconscientious *adj* |
| unclarified *adj* | uncombed *adj* | ¹uncomputerized *adj* | unconsecrated *adj* |
| unclassifiable *adj* | uncombined *adj* | uncomradely *adj* | unconsenting *adj* |
| uncleaned *adj* | uncomely *adj* | unconcealed *adj* | unconsolable *adj* |
| uncleared *adj* | uncomforted *adj* | unconceded *adj* | unconsoled *adj* |
| unclichéd *adj* | uncomic *adj* | unconceivable *adj* | unconstrained *adj* |
| unclimbed *adj* | uncommanding *adj* | unconcerted *adj* | unconstricted *adj* |
| uncloying *adj* | uncommendable *adj* | unconcluded *adj* | unconsumed *adj* |
| uncluttered *adj* | uncommercialized *adj* | uncondemned *adj* | unconsummated *adj* |
| uncoated *adj* | uncompanionable *adj* | uncondensed *adj* | uncontainable *adj* |
| uncoded *adj* | uncompelling *adj* | unconducive *adj* | uncontaminated *adj* |
| uncoerced *adj* | uncompensated *adj* | unconfined *adj* | uncontemplated *adj* |
| uncoercive *adj* | uncomplacent *adj* | unconfirmed *adj* | uncontemporary *adj* |
| uncoffined *adj* | uncompleted *adj* | unconfused *adj* | uncontested *adj* |
| | uncompliant *adj* | uncongealed *adj* | uncontracted *adj* |

trolled by conscience; unscrupulous ⟨*an ~ villain*⟩ **2a** excessive, unreasonable ⟨*found an ~ number of defects in the car*⟩ **b** shockingly unfair or unjust ⟨*~ sales practices*⟩ – **unconscionableness** *n*, **unconscionably** *adv*, **unconscionability** *n*

**¹unconscious** /un'konshəs/ *adj* **1** not knowing or perceiving; not aware **2a** not possessing mind or consciousness ⟨*~ matter*⟩ **b(1)** not marked by or resulting from conscious thought, sensation, or feeling ⟨*~ motivation*⟩ **b(2)** of the unconscious **c** having lost consciousness ⟨*was ~ for three days*⟩ **3** not intentional ⟨*~ bias*⟩ □ compare SUBCONSCIOUS – **unconsciously** *adv*, **unconsciousness** *n*

**²unconscious** *n* the part of the mind that does not ordinarily enter a person's awareness but nevertheless, in Freudian psychology, is held to influence behaviour and may be manifested in dreams or slips of the tongue

**unconsidered** /unkən'sidəd/ *adj* **1** not considered or worth consideration **2** not resulting from consideration or study; not thought out ⟨*must avoid ~ opinions*⟩

**unconsolidated** /unkən'solidaytid/ *adj* not forming a solid mass; loosely arranged ⟨*~ soil*⟩

**unconstitutional** /unkonsti'tyoohsh(ə)nl/ *adj* not obeying or consistent with the constitution of a nation, organization, etc – **unconstitutionally** *adv*, **unconstitutionality** *n*

**unconstraint** /unkən'straynt/ *n* freedom from constraint; ease

**uncontrollable** /unkən'trohləbl/ *adj* incapable of being controlled; ungovernable – **uncontrollably** *adv*

**unconventional** /unkən'vensh(ə)nl/ *adj* not bound by or conforming with generally accepted standards or practice; different from the norm – **unconventionally** *adv*, **unconventionality** *n*

**unconvincing** /unkən'vinsing/ *adj* not convincing; implausible – **unconvincingly** *adv*, **unconvincingness** *n*

**uncork** /un'kawk/ *vt* **1** to draw a cork from **2** to release from a sealed or pent-up state

**uncorseted** /un'kawsitid/ *adj* **1** not wearing a corset **2** not controlled or inhibited

**uncounted** /un'kowntid/ *adj* **1** not counted **2** innumerable

**uncouple** /un'kupl/ *vt* **1** to release (dogs) from being fastened together in a couple **2** to detach, disconnect ⟨*~ railway wagons*⟩ – **uncoupler** *n*

**uncouth** /un'koohth/ *adj* **1a** rude or uncultivated in appearance, speech, or manner; boorish **b** strange or clumsy in shape or appearance; outlandish **2a** *archaic* not known or not familiar to one; seldom experienced; rare **b** *obs* mysterious, uncanny [ME, fr OE *uncūth*, fr *un-* + *cūth* familiar, known; akin to OHG *kund* known, OE *can* know – more at CAN] – **uncouthly** *adv*, **uncouthness** *n*

**uncover** /un'kuvə/ *vt* **1** to discover or reveal **2** to take the cover from **3** to remove the hat from (one's head) ~ *vi* to take off the hat as a token of respect

**uncovered** /un'kuvəd/ *adj* **1** having no cover **2** not covered by insurance or social security **3** not covered by COLLATERAL (property pledged as security to a lender) ⟨*an ~ note*⟩

**uncreated** /unkri'aytid/ *adj* **1** existing without having been created; self-existent **2** not yet created

**uncritical** /un'kritikl/ *adj* **1** not critical; showing no discrimination or evaluation **2** showing lack or improper use of critical standards or procedures **synonyms** see SUPERFICIAL – **uncritically** *adv*

**uncross** /un'kros/ *vt* to change from a crossed position

**uncrown** /un'krown/ *vt* to take the crown from; depose, dethrone

**uncrowned** /un'krownd/ *adj* **1** having a specified status in fact but not in name ⟨*the ~ champion*⟩ **2** not having yet been crowned

**uncrumple** /un'krumpl/ *vt* to restore to an original smooth condition

**uncrushable** /un'krushəbl/ *adj* not able to be crushed; *esp* crease-resistant

**uncrystall·ized, -ised** /un'kristəliezd/ *adj* not crystallized; *also* not finally or definitely formed

**unction** /'ungksh(ə)n/ *n* **1** the act of anointing as a rite of consecration or healing – compare EXTREME UNCTION **2** something used for anointing; an ointment, unguent **3a** religious or spiritual fervour or its expression **b** exaggerated, assumed, or superficial earnestness of language or manner; unctuousness [ME *unctioun*, fr L *unction-, unctio*, fr *unctus*, pp of *unguere* to anoint – more at OINTMENT]

**unctuous** /'ungktyoo·əs/ *adj* **1** fatty, oily, or greasy in texture or appearance **2** rich in animal and plant matter and easily workable ⟨*~ soil*⟩ **3** marked by ingratiating smoothness and false sincerity [ME, fr MF or ML; MF *unctueux*, fr ML *unctuosus*, irreg fr L *unctum* ointment, fr neut of *unctus*, pp] – **unctuously** *adv*, **unctuousness** *n*

**uncurl** /un'kuhl/ *vb* to straighten out from a curled or coiled state; unroll

**uncus** /'ungkəs/ *n, pl* **unci** /'unsi -sie/ UNCINUS (small hooked structure) [NL, fr L, hook]

**uncut** /un'kut/ *adj* **1** not cut down or cut into **2** not shaped by cutting ⟨*an ~ diamond*⟩ **3a** *of a book* not having the folds of the leaves trimmed off; *broadly* UNOPENED **2 b** *of cine film* unedited **4** not abridged or curtailed

**uncynical** /un'sinikl/ *adj* not cynical – **uncynically** *adv*

**undauntable** /un'dawntəbl/ *adj* incapable of being daunted; fearless, dauntless

**undaunted** /un'dawntid/ *adj* not discouraged by danger or difficulty – **undauntedly** *adv*

**undebatable** /undi'baytəbl/ *adj* not subject to debate; indisputable – **undebatably** *adv*

**undec-** *comb form* eleven ⟨*undecillion*⟩ [L *undecim*, fr *unus* one + *decem* ten – more at ONE, TEN]

**undeceive** /undi'seev/ *vt* to free from deception, illusion, or error; enlighten

*usage* Besides meaning "freed from error", **undeceived** may be the opposite of **deceived** and thus mean "not deceived".

**undecenoic acid** /undesə'noh·ik/ *n* an acid, $CH_2=CH(CH_2)_8COOH$, found in sweat, obtained commercially from CASTOR OIL, and used to treat fungal infections of the skin [*undec-* + *-ene* + *-oic*]

**undecided** /undi'siedid/ *adj* **1** in doubt **2** without a result ⟨*the match was left ~*⟩ – **undecidedly** *adv*, **undecidedness** *n*

**undecillion** /undi'silyən/ *n* – see NUMBER table [*undec-* + *-illion* (as in *million*)]

**undeclared** /undi'kleəd/ *adj* not declared; not announced or openly acknowledged ⟨*an ~ war*⟩ ⟨*~ profits*⟩

**undecylenic acid** /undesə'lenik/ *n* UNDECENOIC ACID

**undefended** /undi'fendid/ *adj* **1** not defended, protected, or guarded **2** *of a lawsuit* having no defence raised against it

**undemocratic** /undemə'kratik/ *adj* not following democratic practice or ideals, esp in being authoritarian – **undemocratically** *adv*

| | | | |
|---|---|---|---|
| uncontradicted *adj* | uncountable *adj* | uncured *adj* | undecorated *adj* |
| uncontrived *adj* | uncourageous *adj* | uncurious *adj* | undedicated *adj* |
| uncontrolled *adj* | uncourteous *adj* | uncurrent *adj* | undefeated *adj* |
| uncontroversial *adj* | uncourtly *adj* | uncurtained *adj* | undefiled *adj* |
| unconversant *adj* | uncovenanted *adj* | uncustomary *adj* | undefinable *adj* |
| unconverted *adj* | uncracked *adj* | undamaged *adj* | undefined *adj* |
| unconvinced *adj* | uncrate *vt* | undamped *adj* | undeformed *adj* |
| uncooked *adj* | uncreative *adj* | undampened *adj* | undelayed *adj* |
| uncooled *adj* | uncredited *adj* | undanceable *adj* | undelegated *adj* |
| uncooperative *adj* | uncrippled *adj* | undaring *adj* | undeliverable *adj* |
| uncoordinated *adj* | uncriticized *adj* | undated *adj* | undelivered *adj* |
| uncordial *adj* | uncropped *adj* | undazzled *adj* | undeluded *adj* |
| uncorrectable *adj* | uncrossable *adj* | undecadent *adj* | undemanding *adj* |
| uncorrected *adj* | uncrowded *adj* | undecidable *adj* | undemonstrable *adj* |
| uncorrelated *adj* | uncultivable *adj* | undecipherable *adj* | undenied *adj* |
| uncorroborated *adj* | uncultivated *adj* | undeciphered *adj* | undenominational *adj* |
| uncorrupt *adj* | uncultured *adj* | undeclinable *adj* | undependable *adj* |
| uncorrupted *adj* | uncurbed *adj* | undecomposed *adj* | |

**undemonstrative** /ˌundiˈmonstrətiv/ *adj* not easily showing feelings, esp of affection; reserved – **undemonstratively** *adv*, **undemonstrativeness** *n*

**undeniable** /ˌundiˈnie·əbl/ *adj* **1** plainly true; incontestable ⟨ ~ *evidence*⟩ **2** unquestionably excellent or genuine ⟨*an applicant with* ~ *references*⟩ – **undeniably** *adv*, **undeniableness** *n*

¹**under** /ˈundə/ *adv* **1** in or to a position below or beneath something **2a** in or to a lower rank, number, or quantity ⟨ *£10 or* ~⟩ **b** to an inadequate or subnormal degree; deficiently – often in combination ⟨*under-staffed*⟩ **3** in or into a condition of subjection, subordination, or unconsciousness **4** so as to be covered, buried, or sheltered **5** BELOW 5 [ME, *adv* & *prep*, fr OE; akin to OHG *untar* under, L *inferus* situated beneath, lower, *infra* below, Skt *adha*]

²**under** *prep* **1a** below or beneath so as to be overhung, surmounted, covered, protected, or hidden ⟨ ~ *sunny skies*⟩ ⟨ ~ *his coat*⟩ ⟨*swims* ~ *water*⟩ ⟨ ~ *cover of darkness*⟩ ⟨*a soft heart* ~ *a stern exterior*⟩ **b** using as a pseudonym or alias ⟨*wrote* ~ *the name "George Eliot"*⟩ **2a**(1) subject to the authority, control, guidance, or instruction of ⟨*served* ~ *the general*⟩ ⟨*is* ~ *the doctor*⟩ ⟨*studied* ~ *the leading sculptor of that era*⟩ **a**(2) during the rule or control of ⟨*India* ~ *the Raj*⟩ **b** receiving or undergoing the action or effect of ⟨ ~ *pressure*⟩ ⟨*courage* ~ *fire* ⟩ ⟨ ~ *ether*⟩ ⟨ ~ *discussion*⟩ ⟨ ~ *sail*⟩ **c** bearing as a crop ⟨*three fields* ~ *corn*⟩ **3** within the group or designation of ⟨ ~ *this heading*⟩ **4** less than or inferior to (eg in size, amount, or rank) ⟨ ~ *an hour*⟩; *esp* falling short of (a standard or required degree) ⟨ ~ *par*⟩

³**under** *adj* **1a** lying or placed below, beneath, or on the lower side ⟨*under*lip⟩ ⟨*under*growth⟩ **b** facing or pointing downward **2** lower in rank or authority; subordinate ⟨*an* ~ *footman*⟩ **3** lower than is usual, proper, or desired in amount or degree ⟨*an* under*dose of medicine*⟩ □ often in combination

**underachieve** /ˌundərəˈcheev/ *vi* to fail to realize one's full potential – **underachievement** *n*, **underachiever** *n*

**underachiever** /ˌundərəˈcheevə/ *n* a child who fails to achieve his/her scholastic potential

**underact** /-ˈakt/ *vt* **1** to perform (a dramatic part) without adequate force or skill **2** to perform with restraint for greater dramatic impact or personal force ~ *vi* to perform feebly or with restraint □ compare OVERACT

**underactive** /ˌundərˈaktiv/ *adj* being at an abnormally low level of activity – **underactivity** *n*

**underage** /-ˈayj/ *adj* being below the legal or required age: eg **a** not old enough to vote **b** not old enough to buy alcoholic drinks, esp in a pub **c** not old enough to hold a licence to drive a motor vehicle

**underappreciated** /ˌundərəˈpreesiaytid, -shi-/ *adj* not duly appreciated

¹**underarm** /-ˌahm/ *adj* **1** under or along the underside of the arm ⟨ ~ *seams*⟩ **2** of a throw, bowl, or service made with the hand brought forwards and up from below shoulder level

²**underarm** *vt* or *adv* (to throw) with an underarm motion ⟨*bowl!* ~⟩

³**underarm** *n* **1** the armpit **2** the part of a garment that covers the underside of the arm

**underbelly** /-ˌbeli/ *n* the underside of an animal, object, or mass; *also* a vulnerable area ⟨*the soft* ~ *of capitalism*⟩

**underbid** /-ˈbid/ *vb* **-dd-**; **underbid** *vt* **1** to bid less than (a competing bidder) **2** to bid (a hand of cards) at less than the strength of the hand warrants ~ *vi* to bid too low – **underbidder** *n*

**underblanket** /ˈundəˌblangkit/ *n* a blanket placed under the bottom sheet of a bed; *esp* an electrically heated underblanket

**underbody** /-ˌbodi/ *n* the lower or under part of something: eg **a** the underside of an animal's body **b** the under surface of the body of a vehicle

**underbred** /-ˈbred/ *adj* **1** ill-bred, vulgar **2** of inferior or mixed breed ⟨*an* ~ *dog*⟩

**underbrim** /ˈundəˌbrim/ *n* a facing on the underside of a hat brim

**underbrush** /-ˌbrush/ *n*, *chiefly NAm* shrubs, bushes, or small trees growing beneath large trees in a wood or forest; undergrowth

**underbudgeted** /ˌundəˈbujitid/ *adj* provided with an inadequate budget

**undercapital·ize, -ise** /ˌundəˈkapitəliez/ *vt* to provide with too little capital for efficient operation

**undercarriage** /-ˌkarij/ *n* **1** a supporting framework (eg of a motor vehicle) **2** the LANDING GEAR of an aircraft

**undercharge** /-ˈchahj/ *vb* to charge too little – **undercharge** *n*

**underclothes** /-ˌklohdhz/ *n pl* underwear

**underclothing** /-ˌklohdhing/ *n* underwear

**undercoat** /-ˌkoht/ *n* **1** a coat or jacket worn under another **2** a growth of short hair or fur partly concealed by a longer growth ⟨*a dog's* ~⟩ **3** a coat (eg of paint) applied as a base for another coat

**undercoating** /ˈundəˌkohting/ *n*, *NAm* UNDERSEAL (waterproofing on the underside of a car, van, etc)

**undercook** /ˌundəˈkook/ *vt* to cook less than is normal or desirable

**undercover** /-ˌkuvə/ *adj* acting or done in secret; *specif* employed or engaged in spying or secret investigation ⟨*an* ~ *agent*⟩

**undercroft** /-ˌkroft/ *n* a crypt [ME, fr *under* + *crofte* crypt, fr MD, fr ML *crupta*, fr L *crypta*]

**undercup** /ˈundəˌkup/ *n* the lower usu padded half of the cup in a garment (eg a bra)

**undercurrent** /-ˌkurənt/ *n* **1** a current below the upper currents or surface **2** a suppressed or underlying drift in opinion or feeling – **undercurrent** *adj*

¹**undercut** /-ˈkut/ *vb* **-tt-**; **undercut** *vt* **1** to cut away the underpart of ⟨ ~ *a vein of ore*⟩ **2** to cut or erode away material from the underside of so as to leave a portion overhanging ⟨*a cliff* ~ *by wave action*⟩ **3** to set one's prices lower than or work for lower wages than (a competitor) **4** to cut obliquely into (a tree) below the main cut so as to determine the side towards which the tree will fall when felled **5** to strike (a ball) with a downward glancing blow so as to give a backspin or elevation to the shot **6** to undermine or destroy the force or effectiveness of ⟨*a technology that* ~s *democracy*⟩ ~ *vi* to undercut someone or something

²**undercut** /ˈundəˌkut/ *n* **1** the action or result of undercutting **2** a notch cut before felling in the base of a tree to determine the direction of falling and to prevent splitting **3** *Br* the underside of sirloin; a beef tenderloin

**underdeveloped** /-diˈveləpt/ *adj* **1** not normally or adequately developed ⟨ ~ *muscles*⟩ ⟨*an* ~ *film*⟩ **2** without modern industries or the means of financing them and having a very low standard of living – compare THIRD WORLD, DEVELOPING – **underdevelopment** *n*

**underdo** /ˌundəˈdooh/ *vt* **underdoing** /-ˈdooh·ing/; **underdid** /-ˈdid/; **underdone** /-ˈdun/ to do less thoroughly than one can or should; *esp* to undercook

**underdog** /-ˌdog/ *n* **1** a loser or expected loser in a struggle or contest **2** a victim of injustice, persecution, poverty, etc

**underdone** /-ˈdun/ *adj* not thoroughly cooked; rare

**underdress** /-ˈdres/ *vi* to dress less formally than is customary or appropriate – **underdressed** *adj*

**undereducated** /ˌundərˈedyookaytid/ *adj* poorly educated – **undereducation** *n*

**underemphas·ize, -ise** /ˌundərˈemfəsiez/ *vt* to give inadequate emphasis to – **underemphasis** *n*

**underemployed** /ˌundərimˈployd/ *adj* having less than full-time or adequate employment; employed in work that does not make full use of one's talents, capabilities, etc

**underemployment** /-imˈploymənt/ *n* **1** less than full employment of the work force in an economy **2** employment at less than full time; partial or inadequate employment

**underestimate** /-ˈestimayt/ *vt* **1** to estimate as being less than the actual size, quantity, or number **2** to place too low a value on; underrate – **underestimate** *n*, **underestimation** *n*

**underexploited** /ˌundərikˈsploytid/ *adj* not made full or sufficient use of

**underexpose** /-ikˈspohz/ *vt* to expose insufficiently; *esp* to expose (a film) to insufficient light – **underexposure** *n*

**underfeed** /-ˈfeed/ *vt* **underfed** /-ˈfed/ **1** to feed insufficiently **2** to feed with fuel from beneath

**underfelt** /ˈundəˌfelt/ *n* a thick felt underlay for laying under a carpet

**underfinanced** /ˌundəˈfienanst, -fiˈnanst/ *adj* inadequately financed

**underflow** /ˈundəˌfloh/ *n* the generation of a number too small to be stored or displayed in the normal way by a computer or calculator

**underfoot** /-ˈfoot/ *adv* **1** under the feet; on or against the ground ⟨*trampled the flowers* ~⟩ ⟨*warm sand* ~⟩ **2** in the way ⟨*children always getting* ~⟩

**underfur** /ˈundəˌfuh/ *n* the thick soft undercoat of fur lying beneath the longer and coarser hair of a mammal

**undergarment** /'undə,gahmənt/ *n* a garment to be worn under another, esp against the skin

**undergird** /'undə,guhd/ *vt* 1 to support underneath (e g with a rope or chain) 2 to strengthen, support, or bolster ⟨*faith* ~s *morals*⟩ – **undergirding** *n*

**underglaze** /'undə,glayz/ *adj* applied or suitable for applying before the glaze is put on ⟨~ *decorations*⟩ ⟨~ *colours*⟩ – **underglaze** *n*

**undergo** /-'goh/ *vt* **underwent** /-'went/; **undergone** /-'gon/ 1 to be subjected to; endure 2 to go through; experience ⟨underwent *a long period of training*⟩

**undergrad** /-,grad/ *n, informal* an undergraduate

**undergraduate** /-,gradyoo·ət/ *n* a student at a college or university who is studying for a first degree

¹**underground** /-'grownd/ *adv* 1 beneath the surface of the earth 2 in or into hiding or secret operation

²**underground** *adj* 1 occurring, growing, operating, or situated below the surface of the ground 2a conducted in hiding or by secret means b(1) existing outside the establishment ⟨*an* ~ *literary reputation*⟩ b(2) produced, published, or operated outside the establishment, esp by the avant-garde ⟨~ *films*⟩ ⟨~ *newspapers*⟩

³**underground** /'undə,grownd/ *n* 1 the region beneath the ground surface 2a a secret movement or group organized among citizens, esp in an occupied country, for concerted resistance against the occupying forces b a secret conspiratorial organization set up for disruption of civil order c an unofficial usu avant-garde movement or group that is anti-establishment 3 *Br* an underground urban passenger railway system – usu + *the*; called also TUBE

**undergrounder** /'undə,growndə/ *n* 1 a member or supporter of an underground group 2 a person who travels on an underground railway

**Underground Railway** *n* a system of cooperation among active opponents of slavery in the USA before 1863 by which fugitive slaves were secretly helped to reach the North or Canada

**undergrowth** /-,grohth/ *n* vegetation (e g seedlings and saplings, shrubs, and ferns) growing on the floor of a wood or forest

**undergunned** /,undə'gund/ *adj* having less than effective armament

**underhand** /,undə'hand/ *adj* 1 aimed so that the target is seen below the hand holding the bow ⟨~ *shooting at long range*⟩ 2 marked by subterfuge, trickery, and deception; not honest and aboveboard; sly 3 done so as to evade notice; clandestine 4 UNDERARM 2 **synonyms** see ¹SECRET **antonym** aboveboard – **underhand** *adv*

**underhanded** /,undə'handid/ *adj or adv* underhand – **underhandedly** *adv*, **underhandedness** *n*

**underhung** /-'hung/ *adj* 1 *of a lower jaw* projecting beyond the upper jaw – compare PROGNATHOUS 2 having an underhung jaw

**underinsured** /-in'shooəd, -in'shawd/ *adj* insured for less than full value or the amount needed to cover possible loss or damage – **underinsurance** *n*

**underlaid** /-'layd/ *adj* 1 laid or placed underneath 2 having an underlay or underlying layer

**underlap** /,undə'lap/ *vt* to extend under so as to be partly covered

¹**underlay** /-'lay/ *vt* **underlaid** /-'layd/ 1 to cover, line, or traverse the bottom of; give support to on the underside or below 2 to raise by something laid under

> *usage* Underlay (-laid, -laid) and underlie (-lay, -lain) are as easily confused as the verbs lay and lie. Both are transitive, but compare ⟨*we underlaid the carpet with felt* (= put felt under it)⟩ ⟨*the coal underlies* (= lies under) *the sandstone*⟩. See ¹LAY

²**underlay** /'undə,lay/ *n* something that lies or is designed to be laid under something else ⟨*a carpet with foam* ~⟩

**underlet** /,undə'let/ *vt* **-tt-**; **underlet** 1 to let at a price below the real value 2 to sublet

**underlie** /-'lie/ *vb* **underlying**; **underlay** /-'lay/; **underlain** /-'layn/ 1 to lie or be situated under (usu an overlying layer) 2 to be at the basis of; form the foundation of or reason for ⟨*ideas* underlying *the revolution*⟩ 3 *of feelings, motives, etc* to be hidden beneath (a facade or superficial behaviour) ⟨*revenge* ~s *her every action*⟩ 4 to exist as a claim or security superior and prior to (another) *usage* see ¹UNDERLAY

**underline** /-'lien/ *vt* 1 to mark (a word or passage) with a line underneath 2 to emphasize, stress 3 to line (a garment) –

**underline** *n*, **underlining** *n*

**underling** /-'ling/ *n* one who is under the orders of another; a subordinate

**underlip** /-,lip/ *n* the lower lip

**underlying** /,undə'lie·ing/ *adj* 1a lying beneath or below ⟨*the* ~ *rock is shale*⟩ b basic, fundamental ⟨*an investigation of the* ~ *issues*⟩ 2 hidden beneath the surface ⟨~ *hostility*⟩ 3 anterior and prior in claim ⟨~ *mortgage*⟩

**undermanned** /-'mand/ *adj* inadequately staffed

**undermentioned** /-,mensh(ə)nd/ *adj, Br formal* mentioned below on the same page or later in the text

**undermine** /-'mien/ *vt* 1 to excavate the earth beneath 2 to wear away the base or foundations of 3 to subvert, weaken, or ruin insidiously or gradually ⟨*gossip* ~d *the candidate's reputation*⟩ **antonyms** reinforce, repair

**undermost** /'undə,mohst/ *adj* lowest in relative position – **undermost** *adv*

¹**underneath** /,undə'neeth/ *prep* 1a directly below ⟨*write the date* ~ *the address*⟩ b close under, esp so as to be hidden ⟨*treachery lying* ~ *a mask of friendliness*⟩ 2 under subjection to [ME *undernethe*, prep & adv, fr OE *underneothan*, fr *under* + *neothan* below – more at BENEATH]

²**underneath** *adv* 1 under or below an object or a surface; beneath 2 on the lower side

³**underneath** *n* the bottom part or surface ⟨*the* ~ *of the bowl*⟩

**undernoted** /'undə,nohtid/ *adj, formal* noted lower on the same or a following page; noted below

**undernourished** /-'nurisht/ *adj* supplied with less than the minimum amount of the foods essential for health and growth – **undernourishment** *n*

**undernutrition** /,undənyooh'trish(ə)n/ *n* deficient bodily nutrition due to inadequate food intake or faulty absorption by the body

**underpaid** /,undə'payd/ *adj* receiving less than adequate or normal pay ⟨~ *workers*⟩ ⟨*this job is* ~⟩

**underpants** /-,pants/ *n pl* PANTS 1

**underpart** /-,paht/ *n* a part lying on the lower side, esp of a bird or mammal

**underpass** /-,pahs/ *n* a tunnel, subway, or road level passing under another road or a railway at a crossing

**underpin** /-,pin/ *vt* **-nn-** 1 to form part of, strengthen, or replace the foundation of ⟨~ *a structure*⟩ ⟨~ *a sagging building*⟩ 2 to support, substantiate ⟨~ *a thesis with evidence*⟩

**underpinning** /-,pining/ *n* 1 the material and construction (e g a foundation) used for support of a structure 2 something that serves as a foundation; a basis, support – often pl with sing. meaning ⟨*the philosophical* ~s *of psychoanalysis*⟩

**underplay** /-'play/ *vt* 1 to play a card lower than (a high card held in hand) 2 to underact 3 to play down or underemphasize to underact

**underplot** /-,plot/ *n* SUBPLOT (subordinate plot in play)

**underprice** /-'pries/ *vt* to price too low

**underprivileged** /-'priv(i)lijd/ *adj* deprived, usu through social or economic conditions, of some of the rights and opportunities regarded as basic in a civilized society; disadvantaged, poor ⟨~ *children*⟩ ⟨~ *areas of the city*⟩ **synonyms** see POOR **antonym** privileged

**underproduction** /-prə'duksh(ə)n/ *n* the production of less than enough to satisfy demand or of less than is usual or possible

**underproductive** /,undəprə'duktiv/ *adj* not capable of adequate production ⟨*unskilled* ~ *workers*⟩

**underproof** /-'proohf/ *adj* containing less alcohol than PROOF SPIRIT (standard strength water/alcohol mixture)

**underprop** /'undə,prop/ *vt* **-pp-** to prop

**underquote** /-'kwoht/ *vt* 1 to quote a lower price than (another person) 2 to quote a price for (e g goods or services) that is lower than another's offer or the market price

**underrate** /-'rayt/ *vt* to rate too low; undervalue

**underrepresentation** /,undə,reprizen'taysh(ə)n/ *n* the state of being underrepresented; *esp* having representatives in a lower proportion than average

**underrepresented** /,undə,repri'zentid/ *adj* inadequately represented

**underripe** /,undə'riep/ *adj* not fully ripe

¹**underrun** /,undə'run/ *vb* **-nn-**; **underran** /-'ran/ *vi* to finish short of the desired or necessary point in space or time ⟨*don't* ~ *even for two minutes*⟩ ~ *vt* to pass or extend under

²**underrun** /'undə,run/ *n* the amount by which something

produced (e g a quantity of logs) falls below an estimate

**undersaturated** /ˌʌndəˈsachooraytid/ *adj* less than normally or adequately saturated

**¹underscore** /ˌʌndəˈskaw/ *vt* to underline

**²underscore** /ˈʌndəˌskaw/ *n* **1** a line drawn under a word or line, esp for emphasis or to indicate intent to italicize **2** music accompanying the action and dialogue of a film

**¹undersea** /-ˈsee/ *adj* **1** being or carried on under the sea or under the surface of the sea ⟨~ *oil deposits*⟩ ⟨~ *warfare*⟩ **2** designed for use under the surface of the sea ⟨*an* ~ *fleet*⟩

**²undersea, underseas** *adv* beneath the surface of the sea ⟨*photographs taken* ~⟩

**underseal** /ˈʌndəˌseel/, -ˌsiəl/ *n* a protective corrosion-proof substance (e g bitumen) used esp to coat vehicle undersurfaces – **underseal** *vt*

**undersecretary** /-ˈsekrətri, -ˌteri/ *n* a secretary immediately subordinate to a principal secretary ⟨~ *of state*⟩

**undersell** /-ˈsel/ *vb* **undersold** /-ˈsohld/ *vt* **1** to sell articles at a lower price than ⟨~ *a competitor*⟩ **2** to be sold cheaper than ⟨*imported cars that* ~ *domestic ones*⟩ **3** to make little of the merits of ⟨*he undersold himself*⟩; *esp* to promote, advertise, or publicize in a usu deliberately restrained or low-key manner **4** to sell too little of ~ *vi* to fail to attain a specified sales quota

**undersexed** /-ˈsekst/ *adj* deficient in sexual drive or interest

**undershoot** /-ˈshooht/ *vt* **undershot** /-ˈshot/ **1** to shoot short of (a target) **2** *of an aircraft* to land short of (a runway)

**undershot** /-ˈshot/ *adj* **1** having or being a lower jaw that projects beyond the upper jaw; UNDERHUNG **2** moved by water passing beneath ⟨*an* ~ *wheel*⟩

**undershrub** /-ˌshrub/ *n* **1** SUBSHRUB 1 (small woody plant with nonwoody tips) **2** a small low-growing shrub

**underside** /-ˌsied/ *n* **1** the side or surface lying underneath **2** the side usu hidden from sight; *specif* the worse side

**undersigned** /-ˌsiend/ *n, pl* **undersigned** the person who signs his/her name at the end of a document – usu + *the* ⟨*the* ~ *testifies*⟩ ⟨*the* ~ *all agree*⟩

**undersized** /-ˈsiezd/ *also* **undersize** *adj* of a size less than is common, proper, normal, or average ⟨~ *trout*⟩

**underslung** /-ˌslung/ *adj* **1** *of a vehicle frame* suspended below the axles **2** UNDERSHOT 1

**undersow** /ˈʌndəˌsoh/ *vt* **undersown** /-ˌsohn/ to grow (a crop) with or after another crop ⟨*barley undersown with clover*⟩

**underspend** /ˌʌndəˈspend/ *vb* **underspent** /-ˈspent/ to spend less than (an estimated or allotted amount)

**underspin** /-ˌspin/ *n* BACKSPIN

**understaffed** /-ˈstahft/ *adj* undermanned

**understand** /ˌʌndəˈstand/ *vb* **understood** /-ˈstood/ *vt* **1a** to grasp the meaning of ⟨~ *this word*⟩ ⟨~ *a message in code*⟩ **b** to grasp the reasonableness of ⟨*his behaviour is hard to* ~⟩ **c** to have thorough or technical acquaintance with or expertise in ⟨~ *finance*⟩ **d** to be thoroughly familiar with the character and propensities of ⟨*doesn't* ~ *children*⟩ **2** to assume without absolute certainty; suppose ⟨*we* ~ *that he is returning from abroad*⟩ ⟨*was understood to be against the plan*⟩ **3** to interpret in one of a number of possible ways ⟨*as I* ~ *it*⟩ **4** to supply mentally (something implied though not expressed) ⟨*the direct object, though not present, is* understood⟩ ~ *vi* **1** to have a grasp or understanding of something ⟨*the more he learnt the less he* understood⟩ ⟨*felt she* understood *about money*⟩ **2** to believe or infer something to be the case **3** to show a sympathetic or tolerant attitude towards something ⟨*if he loves her he'll* ~⟩ [ME *understanden*, fr OE *understandan*, fr *under* + *standan* to stand] – **understandable** *adj*, **understandably** *adv*, **understandability** *n*

**¹understanding** /-ˈstanding/ *n* **1** a mental grasp; comprehension ⟨*a clear* ~ *of the reasons for his failure*⟩ **2** the power of comprehending; intelligence; *esp* the power to make experience intelligible by applying concepts **3a** a friendly or harmonious relationship **b** an agreement of opinion or feeling; an adjust-

ment of differences **c** an informal mutual agreement, in some degree binding on each side **4** meaning, interpretation ⟨*according to the usual* ~ *of the word*⟩ **5** a sympathetic or tolerant attitude; SYMPATHY 3a *synonyms* see ¹REASON

**²understanding** *adj* tolerant, sympathetic – **understandingly** *adv*

**understate** /-ˈstayt/ *vt* **1** to state or represent as being less than is the case **2** to state or present with restraint; *esp* to avoid emphasis or embellishment of, for greater effect ⟨*the coat . . . is . . . a classic – an* ~d *tweed – New York Times magazine*⟩ – **understatement** *n*

**understeer** /-ˌstiə/ *n* the tendency of a motor vehicle to turn less sharply than the driver intends – **understeer** *vi*

**understock** /ˌʌndəˈstok/ *vt* to stock below requirements or facilities

**understood** /ˌʌndəˈstood/ *adj* **1** fully perceived or grasped **2** agreed upon **3** IMPLICIT 1a

**understorey** /ˈʌndəˌstawri/ *n* (the plants forming) the layer of low vegetation underlying the trees in a forest

**understrapper** /ˈʌndəˌstrapə/ *n* an underling, subordinate [³*under* + *strapper* (one who grooms horses), fr ²*strap* 3]

**understrength** /-ˈstreng(k)th/ *adj* deficient in strength; *esp* lacking the sufficient or prescribed number of staff ⟨*a firm 500* ~⟩

**¹understudy** /ˌʌndəˈstudi, '--,--/ *vi* to study another actor's part in order to take it over in an emergency ~ *vt* to prepare (e g a part) as understudy; *also* to prepare a part as understudy to

**²understudy** /ˈʌndəˌstudi/ *n* one who is prepared to act another's part or take over another's duties

**undersubscribe** /ˌʌndəsəbˈskrieb/ *vt, chiefly Br* **1** to subscribe for less of than is offered for sale **2** to enter for in insufficient numbers ⟨*science courses have been* ~d⟩ – **undersubscription** *n*

**undersupply** /ˌʌndəsəˈplie/ *n* failure to supply enough; *also* an inadequate amount

**¹undersurface** /ˈʌndəˌsuhfis/ *n* the underside

**²undersurface** *adj* existing or moving below the surface

**undertake** /-ˈtayk/ *vb* **undertook** /-ˈtook/; **undertaken** *vt* **1** to take upon oneself as a task ⟨~ *a duty*⟩ **2** to put oneself under obligation to perform; contract, covenant **3** to guarantee, promise **4** to accept as a charge ⟨*the lawyer who* undertook *the case*⟩ ~ *vi, archaic* to give surety or assume responsibility

**undertaker** /-ˌtaykə/ *n* **1** someone who undertakes to do something **2** a person whose business is preparing the dead for burial and arranging and managing funerals

**undertaking** /-ˌtayking/ *n* **1a** the act of someone who undertakes or engages in a project or business **b** the business of an undertaker **2** something undertaken; an enterprise **3** a pledge, guarantee

**undertenant** /-ˌtenənt/ *n* a subtenant

**under-the-'counter** *adj, informal* surreptitious and usu illicit ⟨~ *transactions*⟩ [fr the hiding of illicit goods under the counter of shops where they are sold]

**underthings** /-ˌthingz/ *n pl, informal* underwear

**undertint** /ˈʌndəˌtint/ *n* a subdued tint; *specif* one showing through another

**undertone** /-ˌtohn/ *n* **1** a low or subdued utterance or accompanying sound **2a** a quality (e g of emotion) underlying an utterance or action **b** the underlying tendency of a market **3** a subdued colour; *specif* one seen through and modifying another colour *synonyms* see OVERTONE

**undertow** /-ˌtoh/ *n* **1** an undercurrent that flows in a different direction from the surface current, esp out to sea **2** a hidden tendency often contrary to the one that is publicly apparent

**undertrick** /ˈʌndəˌtrik/ *n* any of the rounds of play (TRICKS) in bridge by which a team falls short of fulfilling its undertaking to win a specified number of tricks – compare OVERTRICK

**underused** /ˌʌndəˈyoohzd/ *adj* not fully used

**underutil·ize, -ise** /ˌʌndəˈyoohtiliez/ *vt* to utilize less than fully

| | | | |
|---|---|---|---|
| **undescribable** *adj* | **undetectable** *adj* | **undifferentiated** *adj* | **undisciplined** *adj* |
| **undeserved** *adj* | **undetected** *adj* | **undigestible** *adj* | **undisclosed** *adj* |
| **undeservedly** *adv* | **undeterminable** *adj* | **undigested** *adj* | **undiscouraged** *adj* |
| **undeserving** *adj* | **undetermined** *adj* | **undignified** *adj* | **undiscoverable** *adj* |
| **undesignated** *adj* | **undeterred** *adj* | **undiluted** *adj* | **undiscovered** *adj* |
| **undesired** *adj* | **undeveloped** *adj* | **undiminished** *adj* | **undiscriminating** *adj* |
| **undestroyed** *adj* | **undiagnosed** *adj* | **undimmed** *adj* | **undiscussed** *adj* |
| **undetachable** *adj* | **undialectical** *adj* | **undiscerning** *adj* | **undismayed** *adj* |
| **undetached** *adj* | **undidactic** *adj* | **undischarged** *adj* | **undisputable** *adj* |

or below the potential use – **underutilization** *n*

**undervalue** /,undə'valyooh/ *vt* to value, rate, or estimate below the real worth ⟨~ *stock*⟩ ⟨*was* ~d *as a poet*⟩ – **undervaluation** *n*

**underwater** /-'wawtə/ *adj* **1** situated, used, or designed to operate below the surface of the water **2** below the waterline of a ship – **underwater** *adv*

**under way** *adv* **1** in motion; moving along **2** into motion from a standstill **3** in progress; afoot ⟨*preparations were* ~⟩ [prob fr D *onderweg*, fr MD *onderwegen*, lit., under or among the ways]

**underwear** /-,weə/ *n* clothing worn next to the skin and under other clothing

**under weigh** *adv* UNDER WAY [by folk etymology (influenced by *weigh* 4)]

**underweight** /,undə'wayt; *noun* '--,-/ *adj or n* (of a) weight below what is normal, average, or requisite

**underwhelm** /,undə'welm/ *vt, humorous* to fail to impress or stimulate ⟨*feeling quite* ~ed *at the thought of yet more so-called "insights"*⟩ [*under* + *-whelm* (as in *overwhelm*)]

**¹underwing** /-,wing/ *n* **1** either of the hind wings of an insect **2** any of various moths (esp genus *Catocala*) that have the hind wings banded with contrasting colours (e g red and black)

**²underwing** *adj* placed or growing underneath the wing ⟨*a bird's* ~ *feathers*⟩

**underwood** /'undə,wood/ *n* undergrowth

**underwool** /'undə,wool/ *n* short woolly underfur

**underworld** /-,wuhld/ *n* **1** the place of departed souls; HADES **2** a social sphere below the level of ordinary life; *esp* the world of organized crime

**underwrite** /-'riet/ *vb* **underwrote** /-'roht/; **underwritten** /-'ritn/ *vt* **1** to write under or at the end of something else **2** to set one's signature to (an insurance policy), thereby assuming liability in case of specified loss or damage; *also* to assume (a sum or risk) by way of insurance **3** to subscribe to; agree to **4a** to agree to purchase (a security issue) usu on a fixed date at a fixed price with a view to public distribution **b** to guarantee financial support of ~ *vi* to carry on the business of an underwriter

**underwriter** /-,rietə/ *n* **1** a person who underwrites something, esp an insurance policy; a guarantor **2** a person who selects risks to be solicited or rates the acceptability of risks solicited **3** a person who underwrites a security issue

**undescended** /,undi'sendid/ *adj, of a testis* retained within the abdomen rather than descending into the scrotum at the normal age

**undesigning** /,undi'ziening/ *adj* having no ulterior or fraudulent purpose; sincere

**¹undesirable** /,undi'zie·ərəbl/ *adj* not desirable; unwanted ⟨~ *elements in society*⟩ – **undesirableness** *n*, **undesirably** *adv*, **undesirability** *n*

**²undesirable** *n* an undesirable person or thing

**undeviating** /un'deeviayting/ *adj* unswerving, constant ⟨~ *kindness*⟩ – **undeviatingly** *adv*

**undies** /'undiz/ *n pl, informal* underwear; *esp* women's underwear [by shortening & alter.]

**undine** /'undien/ *n* any of a group of elemental beings that inhabit water in the theory of Paracelsus; WATER NYMPH [NL *undina*, fr L *unda* wave – more at WATER]

**undiplomatic** /,undiplə'matik/ *adj* not diplomatic; tactless – **undiplomatically** *adv*

**undirected** /,undi'rektid, -die-/ *adj* not planned or guided ⟨~ *efforts*⟩

**undisguised** /,undis'giezd/ *adj* not concealed; frank, open ⟨~ *admiration*⟩ – **undisguisedly** *adv*

**undissociated** /,undi'sohsiaytid, -'sohshi-/ *adj, of a molecule, gas, etc* not dissociated or broken up into simpler components or constituents; *esp, of a dissolved substance* not dissociated

into IONS (electrically charged atoms or groups of atoms)

**undo** /un'dooh/ *vb* **undid** /-'did/; **undone** /-'dun/ *vt* **1** to open or loosen by releasing a fastening **2** to reverse or cancel out the effects of; make null **3a** to ruin the standing, reputation, or hopes of; destroy **b** to disturb the composure of; upset **c** *archaic* SEDUCE **3** ~ *vi* to come open or apart – **undoer** *n*

**undock** /un'dok/ *vi* **1** to move away from a dock (e g at sailing time) **2** to become undocked ~ *vt* to separate (e g two spacecraft) mechanically while in space

**undogmatic** /,undog'matik/ *adj* not committed to dogma – **undogmatically** *adv*

**undoing** /un'dooh·ing/ *n* **1** an act of loosening or opening; an unfastening **2** (a cause of) ruin or downfall ⟨*a redhead was to prove his* ~⟩ **3** an annulment, reversal

**¹undone** /un'dun/ *past part of* UNDO

**²undone** *adj* not performed or finished

**undoubted** /un'dowtid/ *adj* not disputed; genuine **synonyms** see ²DOUBT – **undoubtedly** *adv*

**undramatic** /,undrə'matik/ *adj* lacking dramatic force or quality; unspectacular – **undramatically** *adv*

**undrape** /un'drayp/ *vt* to strip of drapery; unveil

**undreamt** /un'dremt/, **undreamed** /-'dreemd, -'dremt/ *adj* not conceived of; unimagined ⟨*technical advances* ~ *of a few years ago*⟩ – usu + *of*

**¹undress** /un'dres/ *vt* **1** to remove the clothes or covering of **2** to expose, reveal ⟨~ed *his real motive*⟩ ~ *vi* to take off one's clothes

**²undress** *n* **1** informal or ordinary dress – compare FULL DRESS **2** a state of having little or no clothing on

**undressed** /un'drest/ *adj* not dressed: e g **a** partially or completely unclothed **b** improperly or informally clothed **c** not fully processed or finished ⟨~ *hides*⟩ **d** not cared for or tended ⟨*an* ~ *wound*⟩ ⟨~ *fields*⟩

**undrunk** /un'drungk/ *adj* not swallowed ⟨*coffee left* ~⟩

**undue** /un'dyooh/ *adj* **1** not yet payable **2** excessive, immoderate ⟨*with* ~ *haste*⟩

*usage* Expressions such as ⟨*there's no cause for* **undue** *alarm*⟩ seem to mean only that there is no reason for something unreasonable. Some people dislike the use of **undue** to mean simply "great", as in ⟨*it did not require* **undue** *intelligence to foretell the result*⟩.

**undue influence** *n* such influence over another (e g by reason of a close relationship) as is regarded in law as precluding the other's exercise of his/her own will (e g in entering a contract)

**undulant** /'undyoolənt/ *adj* rising and falling in waves; rolling

**undulant fever** /'undyoolənt/ *n* BRUCELLOSIS (long-lasting disease) occurring in human beings and contracted by contact with infected domestic animals or consumption of their products (e g milk)

**¹undulate** /'undyoo,layt/, **undulated** /-,laytid/ *adj* having a wavy surface, edge, or markings ⟨*the* ~ *margin of a leaf*⟩ [L *undulatus*, fr (assumed) L *undula*, dim. of L *unda* wave – more at WATER]

**²undulate** *vi* **1** to rise and fall alternately; fluctuate **2** to have a wavy form or appearance ~ *vt* to cause to move in wavy, sinuous, or flowing manner ⟨~d *her body to the music*⟩ **synonyms** see ¹SWING [LL *undula* small wave, fr (assumed) L]

**undulation** /,undyoo'laysh(ə)n/ *n* **1a** a gentle rising and falling (as if) in waves **b** a wavelike motion; *also* a single wave or gentle rise **2** a wavy appearance, outline, or form

**undulatory** /'undyoolət(ə)ri/ *adj* undulating, wavy ⟨~ *swimming movements*⟩

**unduly** /un'dyoohli/ *adv* excessively

**undutiful** /un'dyoohtif(ə)l/ *adj* not dutiful – **undutifully** *adv*, **undutifulness** *n*

**undying** /un'die·ing/ *adj* eternal, perpetual ⟨~ *love*⟩

**unearned** /un'uhnd, un'uhnt/ *adj* not gained by work, service, or skill; *specif, of income* derived from investments, rents, etc rather than employment

| | | | |
|---|---|---|---|
| undisputed *adj* | undiversified *adj* | undotted *adj* | undyed *adj* |
| undissolved *adj* | undivided *adj* | undoubtable *adj* | undynamic *adj* |
| undistinguishable *adj* | undivulged *adj* | undoubting *adj* | uneager *adj* |
| undistinguished *adj* | undocile *adj* | undrained *adj* | uneasily *adv* |
| undistorted *adj* | undoctored *adj* | undramatized *adj* | uneatable *adj* |
| undistracted *adj* | undoctrinaire *adj* | undrilled *adj* | uneaten *adj* |
| undistressed *adj* | undocumented *adj* | undrinkable *adj* | uneccentric *adj* |
| undistributed *adj* | undomestic *adj* | undulled *adj* | unecological *adj* |
| undisturbed *adj* | undomesticated *adj* | unduplicated *adj* | unedible *adj* |

**unearned increment** *n* an increase in the value of property (eg land) due to increased demand rather than the owner's labour or investment

**unearth** /un'uhth/ *vt* 1 to dig up out of the earth ⟨~ *a hidden treasure*⟩ 2 to make known or public; BRING TO LIGHT ⟨~ *a plot*⟩

**unearthly** /un'uhthli/ *adj* not earthly: eg a not terrestrial ⟨~ *radio sources*⟩ b exceeding what is normal or natural; supernatural ⟨*an* ~ *light*⟩ c weird, eerie ⟨~ *howls*⟩ d not mundane; ideal ⟨~ *love*⟩ e unreasonable, preposterous ⟨*getting up at an* ~ *hour*⟩ – compare UNGODLY 2 *synonyms* see ²WEIRD – **unearthliness** *n*

**unease** /un'eez/ *n* a feeling of mental or emotional discomfort; disquiet, awkwardness

**uneasy** /un'eezi/ *adj* 1 marked by lack of mental or emotional ease; awkward ⟨*gave an* ~ *laugh*⟩ 2 apprehensive, worried 3 restless, disturbed ⟨*an* ~ *sleep*⟩ 4 precarious, unstable ⟨*an* ~ *truce*⟩ – **uneasily** *adv*, **uneasiness** *n*

**uneconomic** /,unekə'nomik, -eekə-/, **uneconomical** /-kl/ *adj* not economically practicable; costly, wasteful

**unedited** /un'editid/ *adj* not edited: eg a left unrevised b still unpublished

**unemotional** /,uni'mohsh(ə)nl/ *adj* not emotional; not showing or involving emotion – **unemotionally** *adv*

**unemphatic** /,unim'fatik/ *adj* lacking emphasis – **unemphatically** *adv*

**unemployable** /,unim'ployəbl/ *adj* not acceptable or fitted for employment ⟨*his handicap makes him virtually* ~⟩ – **unemployable** *n*, **unemployability** *n*

**unemployed** /,unim'ployd/ *adj* not employed: a not being used b not engaged in a job c not invested ⟨~ *wealth*⟩ – **unemployed** *n taking pl vb*

**unemployment** /,unim'ploymənt/ *n* 1 the state of being unemployed; lack of available employment 2 the number or percentage of people out of work in a country, region, etc

**unemployment benefit** *n* a sum of money paid (eg by the state) at regular intervals to an unemployed worker

**unencumbered** /,uning'kumbəd/ *adj* free of any burden, hindrance, or difficulty

**unending** /un'ending/ *adj* never ending; seemingly endless – **unendingly** *adv*

**unendurable** /,unin'dyooərəbl/ *adj* unbearable – **unendurableness** *n*, **unendurably** *adv*

**un-'English** *adj* 1 not characteristically English; foreign 2 not conforming to the standard usage of the English language

**unenthusiastic** /,uninthyoohzi'astik/ *adj* not enthusiastic or excited – **unenthusiastically** *adv*

**¹unequal** /un'eekwəl/ *adj* 1a not of the same measurement, quantity, or number as another b not like in quality, nature, or status c not the same for every member of a group, class, or society ⟨~ *rights*⟩ 2 not uniform; variable, uneven ⟨~ *pulse rate*⟩ ⟨*an* ~ *surface*⟩ 3a badly balanced or matched ⟨*an* ~ *contest*⟩ b contracted between unequals ⟨*an* ~ *treaty*⟩ 4a inadequate, insufficient – + *to* ⟨~ *to the task*⟩ b unsuitable ⟨*bored with work* ~ *to his abilities*⟩ 5 *archaic* not equitable; unjust – **unequally** *adv*

*usage* One is **unequal** *to* a task, or *to* performing it, but not *to* perform it ⟨△ *she was quite* **unequal** *to make the decision*⟩.

**²unequal** *n often pl* one who or that which is not equal to another

**unequalled** /un'eekwəld/ *adj* not equalled; unparalleled ⟨~ *in his field*⟩

**unequivocal** /,uni'kwivəkl/ *adj* leaving no doubt; clear, unambiguous – **unequivocally** *adv*

**unerring** /un'uhring/ *adj* committing no error; faultless, unfailing ⟨~ *judgment*⟩ – **unerringly** *adv*

**unessential** /,uni'sensh(ə)l/ *adj* 1 dispensable, unimportant 2 *archaic* without essence; insubstantial

**uneven** /un'eev(ə)n/ *adj* 1 ODD 3a ⟨~ *numbers*⟩ 2a not level or smooth ⟨*large* ~ *teeth*⟩ ⟨~ *handwriting*⟩ b varying from the straight or parallel c not uniform; irregular ⟨~ *combustion*⟩ d varying in quality ⟨*an* ~ *performance*⟩ 3 UNEQUAL 3a ⟨*an* ~ *confrontation*⟩ *synonyms* see ¹ROUGH *antonym* even – **unevenly** *adv*, **unevenness** *n*

**uneventful** /,uni'ventf(ə)l/ *adj* without any noteworthy or untoward incidents; placid ⟨*an* ~ *journey*⟩ – **uneventfully** *adv*

**unexampled** /,unig'zahmpəld/ *adj* having no example or parallel; unprecedented

**unexceptionable** /,unik'sepsh(ə)nəbl/ *adj* beyond reproach or criticism; unimpeachable [*un-* + obs *exception* to take exception, object]–**unexceptionableness** *n*, **unexceptionably** *adv*

**unexceptional** /,unik'sepsh(ə)nl/ *adj* commonplace, ordinary

**unexceptionally** /,unik'sepsh(ə)nli, -shənəli/ *adv* 1 without exception; in every case 2 in an unexceptional way

**unexpected** /,unik'spektid/ *adj* not expected or foreseen – **unexpectedly** *adv*, **unexpectedness** *n*

**unexploited** /,unik'sploytid/ *adj* not taken advantage of; *esp* undeveloped ⟨~ *lowland tropics*⟩

**unexpressive** /,unik'spresiv/ *adj* 1 failing to convey the feeling or meaning intended 2 *obs* that cannot be put into words; INEFFABLE ⟨~ *anguish*⟩

**unfading** /un'fayding/ *adj* 1 not losing colour or freshness 2 not losing value or effectiveness ⟨~ *pleasures*⟩ – **unfadingly** *adv*

**unfailing** /un'fayling/ *adj* that can be relied on; constant, continuous ⟨*a subject of* ~ *interest*⟩ – **unfailingly** *adv*, **unfailingness** *n*

**unfair** /un'feə/ *adj* 1 unjust, dishonest 2 not equitable, esp in business dealings ⟨~ *competition*⟩ – **unfairly** *adv*, **unfairness** *n*

**unfaith** *n* lack of faith; *esp* religious unbelief

**unfaithful** /un'faythf(ə)l/ *adj* not faithful: a not adhering to vows, allegiance, or duty; disloyal, faithless b not faithful to a marriage partner, lover, etc, esp in having sexual relations with another person c inaccurate, untrustworthy ⟨*an* ~ *account*⟩ – **unfaithfully** *adv*, **unfaithfulness** *n*

**unfaltering** /un'fawltəring/ *adj* not wavering or hesitating; firm – **unfalteringly** *adv*

**unfamiliar** /,unfə'mili·ə, -yə/ *adj* not familiar: a not well-known; strange ⟨*an* ~ *place*⟩ b not well acquainted ⟨~ *with the subject*⟩ – **unfamiliarly** *adv*, **unfamiliarity** *n*

**unfancy** /,un'fansi/ *adj* simple, unpretentious

**unfashionable** /un'fash(ə)nəbl/ *adj* 1 not in keeping with the current fashion ⟨~ *clothes*⟩ 2 not favoured socially ⟨*an* ~ *neighbourhood*⟩ – **unfashionably** *adv*

**unfasten** /un'fahs(ə)n/ *vt* 1 to loosen, undo ⟨~ *a blouse*⟩ ⟨~ *a pin*⟩ 2 to untie, detach ⟨~ *a boat from its moorings*⟩

**unfathered** /un'fahdhəd/ *adj* 1 of unknown paternity; illegitimate 2 having no known origin ⟨~ *slanders*⟩

| | | | |
|---|---|---|---|
| unedifying *adj* | unendowed *adj* | unerotic *adj* | unexercised *adj* |
| uneducable *adj* | unenduring *adj* | unescapable *adj* | unexhausted *adj* |
| uneducated *adj* | unenforceable *adj* | unescorted *adj* | unexotic *adj* |
| unelaborated *adj* | unenforced *adj* | unestablished *adj* | unexpanded *adj* |
| unelectable *adj* | unengaged *adj* | unestimated *adj* | unexpeditious *adj* |
| unelected *adj* | unenjoyable *adj* | unethical *adj* | unexpended *adj* |
| unelectrified *adj* | unenlarged *adj* | unevaluated *adj* | unexperienced *adj* |
| unemancipated *adj* | unenlightened *adj* | unexacting *adj* | unexpiated *adj* |
| unembarrassed *adj* | unenlightening *adj* | unexaggerated *adj* | unexpired *adj* |
| unembellished *adj* | unenriched *adj* | unexamined *adj* | unexplainable *adj* |
| unembittered *adj* | unenrolled *adj* | unexcavated *adj* | unexplained *adj* |
| unemotive *adj* | unentered *adj* | unexceeded *adj* | unexplicit *adj* |
| unempirical *adj* | unenterprising *adj* | unexcelled *adj* | unexploded *adj* |
| unemptied *adj* | unentertaining *adj* | unexchangeable *adj* | unexplored *adj* |
| unenchanted *adj* | unenticing *adj* | unexcitable *adj* | unexposed *adj* |
| unenclosed *adj* | unenviable *adj* | unexcited *adj* | unexpressed *adj* |
| unencouraging *adj* | unenvied *adj* | unexciting *adj* | unexpressible *adj* |
| unendearing *adj* | unenvious *adj* | unexcused *adj* | unexpurgated *adj* |
| unendorsed *adj* | unequipped *adj* | unexecuted *adj* | unextended *adj* |

**unfathomable** /un'fadhəməbl/ *adj* not capable of being fathomed: **a** impossible to comprehend **b** immeasurable ⟨~ *seas*⟩

**unfavourable** /un'fayv(ə)rəbl/ *adj* not favourable: eg **a** expressing disapproval; negative ⟨~ *reviews*⟩ **b** disadvantageous, adverse ⟨*an ~ economic climate*⟩ – **unfavourably** *adv*

**unfavourite** /un'fayvrit/ *adj* not favourite; *esp* least favourite

**unfeathered** /un'fedhəd/ *adj* **1** not having feathers **2** UN-FLEDGED

**unfeeling** /un'feeling/ *adj* **1** devoid of feeling or sensation ⟨*an ~ corpse*⟩ **2** devoid of kindness or sympathy; hardhearted, cruel ⟨*an ~ wretch*⟩ – **unfeelingly** *adv*, **unfeelingness** *n*

**unfeigned** /ˌun'faynd/ *adj* not feigned or hypocritical; genuine, sincere ⟨~ *innocence*⟩ **synonyms** see SINCERE – **unfeignedly** *adv*

**unfetter** /un'fetə/ *vt* **1** to release from fetters ⟨~ *a prisoner*⟩ **2** to free from restraint; emancipate, liberate ⟨~ *the mind from prejudice*⟩

**unfilial** /un'filiəl/ *adj* not observing the obligations of a child to a parent – **unfilially** *adv*

**unfindable** /ˌun'fiendəbl/ *adj* not capable of being found

**unfinished** /un'finisht/ *adj* not finished: **a** not brought to an end or to the desired final state; incomplete **b** subjected to no other processes (eg bleaching or dyeing) after coming from the loom

¹**unfit** /un'fit/ *adj* not fit: **a** not adapted to a purpose; unsuitable, inappropriate **b** not qualified; incapable, incompetent ⟨~ *for duty*⟩ **c** physically or mentally unsound – **unfitly** *adv*, **unfitness** *n*

²**unfit** *vt* **-tt-** to make unfit; disable, disqualify

**unfitted** /un'fitid/ *adj* not adapted; unqualified

**unfitting** /un'fiting/ *adj* unsuitable, inappropriate

**unfix** /ˌun'fiks/ *vt* **1** to loosen from a fastening; detach, disengage **2** to make unstable; unsettle

**unfixed** /un'fikst/ *adj* **1** not fixed ⟨*arrangements remain ~*⟩ **2** having become loosened or unfastened

**unflagging** /un'flaging/ *adj* never flagging; tireless – **unflaggingly** *adv*

**unflappable** /un'flapəbl/ *adj* remaining calm and composed; imperturbable – **unflappability** *n*

**unflattering** /un'flatəring/ *adj* not flattering; *esp* unfavourable ⟨~ *comments*⟩ – **unflatteringly** *adv*

**unfledged** /un'flejd/ *adj* **1** *of a young bird* having not yet developed the feathers necessary for flight; not ready for flight **2** not fully developed; immature, callow ⟨*an ~ writer*⟩

**unflinching** /un'flinching/ *adj* not flinching or shrinking; steadfast – **unflinchingly** *adv*

**unfocussed, unfocused** /un'fohkəst/ *adj* **1** *of a camera, telescope, etc* not having the focus correctly adjusted **2** not concentrated on one point or objective ⟨~ *rage*⟩ ⟨*an ~ attack*⟩

**unfold** /un'fohld/ *vt* **1a** to open the folds of; spread or straighten out ⟨~ed *the map*⟩ **b** to remove (eg a package) from the folds; unwrap **2** to open to the view; reveal; *esp* to make clear by gradual disclosure and often by recital ~ *vi* **1a** to open from a folded state; open out **b** to blossom ⟨*his talent gradually* ~ed⟩ **2** to open out gradually to the view or understanding; become known; develop ⟨*a panorama ~s before their eyes*⟩ ⟨*as the story ~s*⟩ – **unfoldment** *n*

**unforgettable** /ˌunfə'getəbl/ *adj* incapable of being forgotten; memorable ⟨*an ~ occasion*⟩ – **unforgettably** *adv*, **unforgettability** *n*

**unforgiving** /ˌunfə'giving/ *adj* unwilling or unable to forgive – **unforgivingness** *n*

**unformed** /un'fawmd/ *adj* not arranged in regular shape or order; *esp* immature, undeveloped ⟨*an ~ mind*⟩

**unforthcoming** /ˌunfawth'kuming/ *adj, chiefly Br* reticent, closemouthed

¹**unfortunate** /un'fawch(ə)nət/ *adj* **1a** not favoured by fortune; unsuccessful, unlucky ⟨*an ~ young man*⟩ **b** accompanied by or resulting in misfortune ⟨*an ~ decision*⟩ **2a** unsuitable, inappropriate ⟨*an ~ choice of words*⟩ **b** deplorable, regrettable ⟨*an ~ lack of taste*⟩

²**unfortunate** *n* an unfortunate person (eg a social outcast)

**unfortunately** /un'fawch(ə)nətli/ *adv* **1** in an unfortunate manner **2** as is unfortunate ⟨*the matter, ~, is not so simple*⟩

**unfounded** /un'fowndid/ *adj* lacking a sound basis; groundless, unwarranted ⟨~ *accusations*⟩

**unfreeze** /un'freez/ *vb* **unfroze** /-'frohz/; **unfrozen** /-'frohz(ə)n/ **1** to (cause to) thaw **2** to free or escape from restriction ⟨~ *prices*⟩

**unfrequented** /ˌunfri'kwentid, -'freekwəntid/ *adj* not often visited or travelled over

**unfriended** /un'frendid/ *adj* having no friends; friendless

**unfriendly** /un'frendli/ *adj* not friendly: **a** hostile, unsympathetic **b** inhospitable, unfavourable ⟨*an ~ climate*⟩ – **unfriendliness** *n*

**unfrock** /un'frok/ *vt* to deprive (esp a priest) of the right to exercise the functions of office

**unfruitful** /un'froohtf(ə)l/ *adj* not fruitful: eg **a** not producing offspring; barren **b** yielding no valuable result ⟨*an ~ conference*⟩ **synonyms** see STERILE **antonyms** fruitful, prolific – **unfruitfully** *adv*, **unfruitfulness** *n*

**unfunded** /ˌun'fundid/ *adj* **1** not funded; floating ⟨*an ~ debt*⟩ **2** not provided with funds ⟨*the school remains ~ by the state*⟩

**unfurl** /un'fuhl/ *vt* to release from a furled state; unroll ~ *vi* to become unfurled

**unfussy** /ˌun'fusi/ *adj* not fussy

**ungainly** /un'gaynli/ *adj* **1a** lacking in grace or dexterity; clumsy **b** hard to handle; unwieldy **2** having an awkward or inelegant appearance ⟨*a tall, ~ figure*⟩ – **ungainliness** *n*

**ungallant** /ˌun'galənt/ *adj* not gallant – **ungallantly** *adv*

**ungenerous** /un'jen(ə)rəs/ *adj* not generous: **a** petty, uncharitable **b** stingy, illiberal – **ungenerously** *adv*, **ungenerosity** *n*

**ungetatable** /ˌunget'atəbl/ *adj, informal* inaccessible, unapproachable

**ungird** /un'guhd/ *vt* to divest of a restraining band or girdle; unbind ⟨~ *one's sword*⟩

**ungirt** /un'guht/ *adj* having the belt or girdle off or loose

**unglue** /ˌun'glooh/ *vt* to separate (as if) by dissolving an adhesive

**ungodly** /un'godli/ *adj* **1a** denying God or disobedient to him; impious, irreligious **b** contrary to accepted moral standards; sinful, wicked **2** indecent, outrageous ⟨*gets up at an ~ hour*⟩ – compare UNEARTHLY – **ungodliness** *n*

**ungovernable** /un'guv(ə)nəbl/ *adj* not capable of being governed, guided, or restrained ⟨*an ~ temper*⟩ **synonyms** see UNRULY **antonyms** governable, docile

| | | | |
|---|---|---|---|
| unextinguished *adj* | unfenced *adj* | unforeseen *adj* | unfunny *adj* |
| unextraordinary *adj* | unfermentable *adj* | unforested *adj* | unfurnished *adj* |
| unfaded *adj* | unfermented *adj* | unforetold *adj* | unfurrowed *adj* |
| unfading *adj* | unfertile *adj* | unforgivable *adj* | unfused *adj* |
| unfaked *adj* | unfertilized *adj* | unforgiven *adj* | ungarnished *adj* |
| unfamous *adj* | unfilled *adj* | unforgotten *adj* | ungathered *adj* |
| unfanatical *adj* | unfiltered *adj* | unforked *adj* | ungenial *adj* |
| unfashioned *adj* | unfired *adj* | unformatted *adj* | ungenteel *adj* |
| unfastidious *adj* | unflamboyant *adj* | unformulated *adj* | ungentle *adj* |
| unfathomed *adj* | unflashy *adj* | unforsaken *adj* | ungentlemanly *adj* |
| unfatigued *adj* | unflavoured *adj* | unfortified *adj* | ungerminated *adj* |
| unfavoured *adj* | unfleshed *adj* | unfossiliferous *adj* | ungifted *adj* |
| unfazed *adj* | unflexed *adj* | unfought *adj* | ungimmicky *adj* |
| unfeasible *adj* | unflyable *adj* | unframed *adj* | unglamorized *adj* |
| unfeatured *adj* | unfond *adj* | unfrantic *adj* | unglamorous *adj* |
| unfed *adj* | unforbearing *adj* | unfree *vt* | unglazed *adj* |
| unfederated *adj* | unforbidden *adj* | unfrustrated *adj* | ungodlike *adj* |
| unfelt *adj* | unforceable *adj* | unfulfilled *adj* | ungoverned *adj* |
| unfeminine *adj* | unforced *adj* | unfunctional *adj* | ungraded *adj* |

**ungraceful** /un'graysf(ə)l/ *adj* lacking in grace; awkward, inelegant – **ungracefully** *adv,* **ungracefulness** *n*

**ungracious** /un'grayshəs/ *adj* 1 not courteous; rude, impolite 2 not pleasing; disagreeable 3 *archaic* wicked – **ungraciously** *adv,* **ungraciousness** *n*

**ungrammatical** /,ungrə'matikl/ *adj* not following rules of grammar – **ungrammatically** *adv,* **ungrammaticality** *n*

**ungrateful** /un'graytf(ə)l/ *adj* 1 showing no gratitude; making a poor return; thankless 2 disagreeable, unpleasant – **ungratefully** *adv,* **ungratefulness** *n*

**ungrudging** /un'grujing/ *adj* without envy or reluctance; generous, wholehearted – **ungrudgingly** *adv*

**ungual** /'ung·gwəl/ *adj* of, bearing, or resembling a nail, claw, or hoof [L *unguis* nail, claw, hoof – more at NAIL]

**unguarded** /un'gahdid/ *adj* 1 vulnerable to attack; unprotected 2 having or showing poor judgment in conduct, esp in speech; imprudent, incautious ⟨*an ~ tongue*⟩ 3 without a guard or screen ⟨*an ~ fire*⟩ – **unguardedly** *adv,* **unguardedness** *n*

**unguent** /'ung-gwənt/ *n* a soothing or healing salve; an ointment [ME, fr L *unguentum* – more at OINTMENT]

**unguiculate** /ung'gwikyoolət, -layt/ *adj* 1 of an animal having nails or claws 2 of a petal having an unguis [L *unguiculus* fingernail, dim. of *unguis*]

**unguis** /'ung-gwis/ *n, pl* **ungues** /-gweez/ 1 a nail, claw, or hoof, esp on a digit of a VERTEBRATE animal 2 a narrow pointed clawlike or stalklike base of a petal [L]

¹**ungulate** /'ungyoolət, -,layt/ *adj* 1 having hoofs 2 of or belonging to the ungulates [LL *ungulatus,* fr L *ungula* hoof, fr *unguis* nail, hoof]

²**ungulate** *n* any of the group (Ungulata) consisting of the hoofed mammals (eg cattle, pigs, horses, deer, tapirs, and rhinoceroses) of which most are plant-eating and many have horns [NL *Ungulata,* group name, fr neut pl of LL *ungulatus*]

**unguligrade** /'ung·gyooligrayd/ *adj, of an animal* walking on hooves – compare DIGITIGRADE, PLANTIGRADE [L *ungula* hoof + E *-i-* + *-grade*]

**unhallowed** /un'halohd/ *adj* 1 not blessed; unconsecrated, unholy 2a unsanctioned by or showing lack of reverence for religion; impious, profane b contrary to accepted moral standards; ungodly

**unhand** /un'hand/ *vt* to remove the hands from; let go

**unhandsome** /,un'hansəm/ *adj* not handsome: eg a not beautiful; ugly b unbecoming, unseemly c lacking in courtesy or taste; rude – **unhandsomely** *adv*

**unhandy** /,un'handi/ *adj* 1 hard to handle; inconvenient 2 lacking in skill or dexterity; awkward – **unhandily** *adv,* **unhandiness** *n*

**unhappily** /un'hapəli/ *adv* 1 in an unhappy manner 2 as is unfortunate; UNFORTUNATELY 2

**unhappy** /un'hapi/ *adj* 1 not fortunate; unlucky 2 not cheerful or glad; sad, miserable 3a causing or subject to misfortune; inauspicious, unfavourable b unsuitable, inappropriate ⟨*an ~ remark*⟩ – **unhappiness** *n*

**unharness** /un'hahnis/ *vt* to remove the harness from

**unhatched** /,un'hacht/ *adj* not hatched (as if) from the egg ⟨*an ~ chick*⟩ ⟨*an ~ plot*⟩ 2 not fully incubated ⟨*an ~ egg*⟩

**unhealthy** /un'helthi/ *adj* 1 not conducive to good health ⟨*an ~ climate*⟩ 2 not in good health; sickly, diseased 3a bad, harmful ⟨*~ consequences of inflation*⟩ b(1) going beyond the bounds of what is considered decent; unnatural; *esp* morbid ⟨*an ~ interest in death*⟩ b(2) morally contaminated; corrupt, unwholesome c *informal* dangerous, risky – **unhealthily** *adv,*

**unhealthiness** *n*

**unheard** /un'huhd/ *adj* 1 not perceived by the ear 2 not given a hearing; disregarded

**un'heard-of** *adj* previously unknown; unprecedented

**unheeding** /un'heeding/ *adj* not watchful or observing; *esp* not attentive to the needs of other people – **unheedingly** *adv*

**unhelpful** /un'helpf(ə)l/ *adj* not helpful; uncooperative – **unhelpfully** *adv*

**unhesitating** /un'hezitayting/ *adj* not hesitating; not checked or qualified ⟨*~ loyalty*⟩ ⟨*an ~ reply*⟩ – **unhesitatingly** *adv*

**unhinge** /un'hinj/ *vt* 1 to remove (eg a door) from hinges 2 to make unstable; unsettle, disrupt ⟨*~ the balance of world peace*⟩ ⟨*experiences that would ~ a lesser woman*⟩

**unhitch** /un'hich/ *vt* to free (as if) from being hitched

**unholy** /un'hohli/ *adj* 1a showing disregard for what is holy; impious b wicked, reprehensible ⟨*an ~ alliance*⟩ 2 *informal* terrible, awful ⟨*what an ~ racket!*⟩ – **unholiness** *n*

**unhood** /un'hood/ *vt* to remove a hood or covering from ⟨*~ a falcon*⟩

**unhook** /un'hook/ *vt* 1 to remove from a hook 2 to unfasten the hooks of

**unhorse** /un'haws/ *vt* to dislodge (as if) from a horse

**unhouse** /un'howz/ *vt* to deprive of shelter

**unhurried** /un'hurid/ *adj* not hurried; leisurely ⟨*time for an ~ breakfast*⟩ – **unhurriedly** *adv*

**uni-** /yoohni-/ *prefix* one; single ⟨*unicellular*⟩ [ME, fr MF, fr L, fr *unus* – more at ONE]

**Uniat** /'yoohniat/ *n or adj* (a) Uniate

**Uniate** /'yoohniat, -ayt/ *n* a Christian of a church adhering to an Eastern rite and discipline but submitting to papal authority [Russ *uniyat,* fr Pol *uniat,* fr *unja* union, fr LL *unio,* fr L *unus* one] – **Uniate** *adj*

**uniaxial** /,yoohni'aksi·əl/ *adj* of or having only one axis – **uniaxially** *adv*

**unicameral** /-'kamərəl/ *adj* having or consisting of a single legislative chamber [*uni-* + *cameral* (as in *bicameral*)] – **unicamerally** *adv*

**unicellular** /-'selyoolə/ *adj* having or consisting of a single cell; single-celled ⟨*~ algae*⟩ – **unicellularity** *n*

**unicolour** /'yoohni,kulə/ *adj* having only one colour; of uniform colour throughout

**unicorn** /'yoohni,kawn/ *n* a mythical animal generally depicted with the body and head of a white horse, the tail of a lion, and a single horn in the middle of the forehead [ME *unicorne,* fr OF, fr LL *unicornis,* fr L, having one horn, fr *uni-* + *cornu* horn – more at HORN]

**unicostate** /,yoohni'kostayt/ *adj, of a leaf* having a single prominent midrib [*uni-* + *costate*]

**unicycle** /-'siekl/ *n* any of various vehicles that have a single wheel, are propelled usu by pedals, and are used esp by acrobats [*uni-* + *-cycle* (as in *tricycle*)] – **unicyclist** *n*

**unidirectional** /-di'reksh(ə)nl, -die-/ *adj* 1 involving, functioning in, or moving in a single direction 2 not subject to change or reversal of direction ⟨*~ current*⟩ 3 receiving or responding to signals from, or transmitting signals in one main direction ⟨*a ~ aerial*⟩ – **unidirectionally** *adv*

**unifactorial** /,yoohnifak'tawriəl/ *adj* relating to or controlled by a single gene

**unification** /,yoohnifi'kaysh(ə)n/ *n* the act, process, or result of unifying; the state of being unified

**unifilar** /,yoohni'fielə/ *adj* having, involving, or using only one thread, wire, fibre, etc

---

| | | | |
|---|---|---|---|
| ungraspable *adj* | unharrowed *adj* | unhistorical *adj* | unidentified *adj* |
| ungrasping *adj* | unharvested *adj* | unhomogenized *adj* | unideological *adj* |
| ungratifying *adj* | unhealable *adj* | unhonoured *adj* | unidiomatic *adj* |
| ungreedy *adj* | unhealed *adj* | unhopeful *adj* | unidiomatically *adv* |
| ungrounded *adj* | unhealthful *adj* | unhuman *adj* | unignorable *adj* |
| unguided *adj* | unheated *adj* | unhumorous *adj* | unilluminated *adj* |
| unhackneyed *adj* | unhedged *adj* | unhurt *adj* | unilluminating *adj* |
| unhailed *adj* | unheeded *adj* | unhydrated *adj* | unillumined *adj* |
| unhampered *adj* | unheedful *adj* | unhydrolysed *adj* | unillustrated *adj* |
| unhandicapped *adj* | unheralded *adj* | unhygienic *adj* | unillustrative *adj* |
| unhandled *adj* | unheroic *adj* | unhyphenated *adj* | unimaginative *adj* |
| unhanged *adj* | unheroical *adj* | unhypocritical *adj* | unimaginatively *adv* |
| unhardened *adj* | unhesitant *adj* | unhysterical *adj* | unimagined *adj* |
| unharmed *adj* | unhewn *adj* | unideal *adj* | unimbued *adj* |
| unharmonious *adj* | unhindered *adj* | unidealized *adj* | unimpaired *adj* |
| unharmoniously *adv* | unhired *adj* | unidentifiable *adj* | unimpeded *adj* |

**unifoliate** /ˌyoohni'fohliət, -ayt/ *adj* **1** having only one leaf or leaflike part **2** unifoliolate

**unifoliolate** /ˌyoohni'fohliəlayt/ *adj, of a* COMPOUND *leaf* having only a single leaflet

**¹uniform** /'yoohni,fawm/ *adj* **1** having always the same character, form, manner, or degree; not varying or variable ⟨*a* ~ *pace*⟩ **2** of the same form, character, manner, or degree as others; conforming to one rule or mode; consonant **3** presenting an undiversified appearance (e g of surface, pattern, or colour ⟨*row on row of* ~ *houses*⟩ **4** consistent in conduct or opinion ⟨~ *interpretation of laws*⟩ *synonyms* see ¹STEADY *antonym* various [MF *uniforme*, fr L *uniformis*, fr *uni-* + *-formis* -form] – **uniformly** *adv*, **uniformness** *n*

**²uniform** *n* clothing of a distinctive design or fashion worn by members of a particular group and serving as a means of identification – **uniformed** *adj*

**Uniform** *n* – a communications code word for the letter *u*

**uniformitarian** /ˌyoohni,fawmi'teəri·ən/ *n or adj* **1** (an adherent) of uniformitarianism **2** (an advocate) of uniformity – **uniformitarian** *adj*

**uniformitarianism** /ˌyoohni,fawmi'teəri·ə,niz(ə)m/ *n* the theory that all geological changes that have occurred can be accounted for by processes (e g erosion and faulting of rocks) existing and acting as at present

**uniformity** /ˌyoohni'fawməti/ *n* **1** the quality or state of being uniform: e g **1a** lack of variation or diversity; *esp* sameness, monotony **b** consistency in conduct or opinion, esp in religion **2** an instance of uniformity

**unify** /'yoohni,fie/ *vt* to make into a unit or a coherent whole; unite [LL *unificare*, fr L *uni-* + *-ficare* -fy] – **unifiable** *adj*, **unifier** *n*

**unilateral** /-'lat(ə)rəl/ *adj* **1a** done or undertaken by one person or party ⟨~ *disarmament*⟩ **b** of or affecting one side of a subject; one-sided **2a** produced or arranged on, or directed towards one side of an axis ⟨*a stem bearing* ~ *flowers*⟩ **b** affecting or occurring in one side of the body or a body part or organ ⟨~ *paralysis*⟩ **3** having only one side – **unilaterally** *adv*

**unilinear** /ˌyoohni'liniə/ *adj* developing in or involving a series of stages, usu going from the primitive to the more advanced in a single direction ⟨*a* ~ *cultural sequence*⟩

**unilingual** /ˌyoohni'ling·gwəl/ *adj* composed in or using one language only [*uni-* + L *lingua* tongue, language – more at TONGUE] – **unilingualism** *n*

**unillusioned** /ˌuni'loohzh(ə)nd; *also* 'lyooh-/ *adj* free from illusion

**unilocular** /ˌyoohni'lokyoolə/ *adj, esp of a plant part* having or containing a single cavity or chamber ⟨*a* ~ *plant ovary*⟩

**unimaginable** /uni'majinəbl/ *adj* not imaginable or comprehensible – **unimaginably** *adv*

**unimpassioned** /ˌunim'pash(ə)nd/ *adj* not showing intense feeling; *esp* marked by cool or sometimes frigid reasonableness and freedom from purely emotional appeal

**unimpeachable** /ˌunim'peechəbl/ *adj* not to be impeached ⟨*an* ~ *president*⟩: **a** not to be doubted; beyond question **b** not liable to accusation; irreproachable, blameless – **unimpeachably** *adv*

**unimproved** /ˌunim'proohvd/ *adj* not improved: e g **a** not improved for use (e g by being cultivated or built on) ⟨~ *land*⟩ **b** not used or employed advantageously ⟨*regretted all the wasted time and* ~ *opportunities*⟩ **c** not selectively bred for better quality or productiveness **d** not better with regard to health

**uninformative** /ˌunin'fawmətiv/ *adj* not informative – **uninformatively** *adv*

**uninhibited** /ˌunin'hibitid/ *adj* free from inhibition; *also* boisterously informal – **uninhibitedly** *adv*, **uninhibitedness** *n*

**unintelligent** /ˌunin'telij(ə)nt/ *adj* lacking intelligence; unwise, ignorant – **unintelligence** *n*, **unintelligently** *adv*

**unintelligible** /ˌunin'telijəbl/ *adj* not intelligible; obscure △ unintelligent – **unintelligibleness** *n*, **unintelligibly** *adv*, **unintelligibility** *n*

**uninterrupted** /ˌunintə'ruptid/ *adj* not interrupted; continuous – **uninterruptedly** *adv*, **uninterruptedness** *n*

**uninucleate** /ˌyoohni'nyoohkliayt, -ət/ *also* **uninuclear** /-'nyoohkli·ə/ *adj* having a single nucleus ⟨*a* ~ *yeast cell*⟩

**¹union** /'yoohnyən/ *n* **1a** an act or instance of uniting or joining two or more things into one: e g **1a(1)** the formation of a single political unit from two or more separate and independent units ⟨*the act of* Union *of 1707*⟩ **a(2)** a uniting in marriage; *also* SEXUAL INTERCOURSE **a(3)** the growing together of severed parts **b** a unified condition; combination, junction ⟨*a gracious* ~ *of excellence and strength*⟩ **2** something that is made one; something formed by a combining or coalition of parts or members: e g **2a** an association of independent individuals (e g nations or people) for some common purpose **b** a political unit made up from previously independent units (e g England and Scotland in 1707) which have surrendered their principal powers to the government of the whole or to a newly created government (e g the USA in 1789) **c** *cap* STUDENT UNION **d** *maths* the set of all elements belonging to two or more of a given collection of sets – compare INTERSECTION **3** **e** TRADE UNION **3a** an emblem of the union of two or more sovereignties borne on a national flag **b** the upper inner corner of a flag; CANTON 2a **4** any of various devices for connecting parts (e g of a machine); *esp* a coupling for pipes or pipes and fittings *synonyms* see UNITY [ME, fr MF, fr LL *union-*, *unio* oneness, union, fr L *unus* one – more at ONE]

**²union** *adj* of, dealing with, or constituting a union

**union card** *n* **1** a card certifying personal membership of a TRADE UNION **2** something necessary for employment or providing evidence of in-group status

**union cloth** *n* any of various cloths having lengthways (WARP) and crossways (WEFT) threads of different fibres

**Union Flag** *n* UNION JACK

**unionism** /'yoohnyə,niz(ə)m/ *n* the principle or policy of forming or adhering to a union: e g **a** the principles, theory, or system of trade unions; TRADE UNIONISM **b** *cap* adherence to the policy of a firm federal union between the states of the USA, esp during the Civil War period **c** *cap* the principles and policies of the Unionist party

**unionist** /'yoohnyənist/ *n* **1** an advocate or supporter of union or unionism **2** a member of a trade union; TRADE UNIONIST – **unionist** *adj*

**Unionist** /'yoohnyənist/ *adj* of or constituting a political party of N Ireland that supports the union between N Ireland and Britain and draws support generally from the Protestant section of the community – **Unionist** *n*

**union·ization, -isation** /ˌyoohnyənie'zaysh(ə)n/ *n* being unionized; *also* the action of unionizing

**union·ize, -ise** /'yoohnyə,niez/ *vt* to cause to become a member of or subject to the rules of a TRADE UNION; form into a trade union

**Union Jack** /jak/ *n* the national flag of the UK combining

| | | | |
|---|---|---|---|
| unimportance *n* | unindustrialized *adj* | uninspiring *adj* | unintermittent *adj* |
| unimportant *adj* | uninfected *adj* | uninspiringly *adv* | uninterruptible *adj* |
| unimposing *adj* | uninflammable *adj* | uninstructed *adj* | unintimidated *adj* |
| unimpressed *adj* | uninflated *adj* | uninstructive *adj* | uninvaded *adj* |
| unimpressible *adj* | uninflected *adj* | uninsulated *adj* | uninventive *adj* |
| unimpressionable *adj* | uninfluenced *adj* | uninsurable *adj* | uninvested *adj* |
| unimpressive *adj* | uninfluential *adj* | uninsured *adj* | uninvited *adj* |
| unimpressively *adv* | uninformed *adj* | unintegrated *adj* | uninviting *adj* |
| unimprovable *adj* | uninhabitable *adj* | unintellectual *adj* | uninvitingly *adv* |
| uninclined *adj* | uninhabited *adj* | unintended *adj* | uninvoked *adj* |
| unincorporated *adj* | uninitiated *adj* | unintendedly *adv* | uninvolved *adj* |
| unincubated *adj* | uninjured *adj* | unintentional *adj* | unironed *adj* |
| unincumbered *adj* | uninoculated *adj* | unintentionally *adv* | unironically *adv* |
| unindemnified *adj* | uninquisitive *adj* | uninterested *adj* | unirradiated *adj* |
| unindexed *adj* | uninspected *adj* | uninteresting *adj* | unirrigated *adj* |
| unindicted *adj* | uninspired *adj* | unintermitted *adj* | unissued *adj* |

crosses representing its constituent countries England, Scotland, and N Ireland [*jack* 5a]

*usage* A **union jack** is strictly speaking a ship's jack emblematic of any two or more sovereignties, but the term has been used for more than a century for any adaptation of the British **Union Flag**, even when not on a ship.

**union shop** *n* an establishment in which the employer by agreement is free to employ nonmembers as well as members of a union but retains nonmembers on the payroll only on condition of their becoming members of the union within a specified time – compare CLOSED SHOP, OPEN SHOP

**union suit** *n, NAm* COMBINATIONS 3 (undergarment)

**uniovular** /ˌyoohni'ovyoolə/ *adj* of, containing, or derived from a single egg cell or OVULE (immature seed before fertilization); *specif, of twins* IDENTICAL 3b (derived from a single egg)

**uniparous** /yoo'nipərəs/ *adj* 1 producing only one egg or offspring at a time; *also* having produced only one offspring 2 producing only one axis at each branching ⟨*a ~ cyme*⟩

**unipersonal** /ˌyoohni'puhs(ə)nl/ *adj, of a verb* used in only one person and esp in the third person singular

**uniplanar** /ˌyoohni'playnə/ *adj* lying or occurring in one plane; planar

**unipolar** /ˌyoohni'pohlə/ *adj* 1 having, produced by, or acting by a single MAGNETIC POLE (region where magnetic forces are strongest) or electrical POLE (positively or negatively charged point) 2 *of a nerve cell* having only a single projecting structure along which nerve impulses are conducted – **unipolarity** *n*

**unique** /yooh'neek, yoo-/ *adj* 1a being the only one; sole ⟨*his ~ concern was his own comfort*⟩ b producing only one result ⟨*the ~ factorization of a number into prime factors*⟩ 2 without a like or equal; unequalled 3 very rare or unusual ⟨*London is one of the most ~ ecology areas in the world – Punch*⟩ – now in general use though disapproved by many [Fr, fr L *unicus*, fr *unus* one – more at ONE] – **uniquely** *adv*, **uniqueness** *n*

*usage* Since **unique** has traditionally been applied to people or things that are unlike any others of their kind ⟨*the Sphinx is* **unique**⟩ many people feel that the word should not be used in formal writing with *more, rather, most, somewhat,* or *very*; although it has been so used since the early 19th century ⟨*a very* **unique** *child* – Charlotte Brontë⟩ and perhaps *more* **unique** means simply *more nearly* **unique**. **Unique** can correctly be used with *quite, almost, nearly, absolutely, perhaps, surely,* or *really*. **synonyms** see ¹SINGLE, STRANGE

**uniramous** /ˌyoohni'rayməs/ *adj* having only one branch; not dividing ⟨*a ~ antenna of a lobster*⟩ [*uni-* + *ramous* (branched), fr L *ramosus*, fr *ramus* branch]

**unisex** /'yoohniˌseks/ *adj* 1 suitable or meant for either sex ⟨*a ~ hair style*⟩ ⟨*~ clothing*⟩ 2 dealing in unisex products or styles ⟨*a ~ barber's*⟩

**unisexual** /-'seksyooəl, -'seksh(ə)l/ *adj* 1 of or restricted to one sex 2 *of an animal or plant* male or female but not both; having either male or female reproductive organs – **unisexually** *adv*, **unisexuality** *n*

**unison** /'yoohnis(ə)n, -z(ə)n/ *n* 1a identity in musical pitch; the interval between two notes of the same pitch b the state of being tuned or sounded in unison c the writing, playing, or singing of parts in a musical passage at the same pitch or a complete octave apart 2 a harmonious agreement or union; concord [MF, fr ML *unisonus* having the same sound, fr L *uni-* + *sonus* sound – more at SOUND] – **unison** *adj* – **in unison** in perfect agreement; so as to harmonize exactly

**unit** /'yoohnit/ *n* 1a(1) the first and lowest NATURAL NUMBER; the number one (1) a(2) a single quantity regarded as a whole b the number occupying the position immediately to the left of the DECIMAL POINT in the ARABIC notation; *also, pl* this position 2 a determinate quantity (eg of length, time, heat, value, or housing) adopted as a standard of measurement: eg **2a** an amount of work used in education in calculating student credits b an amount of a biologically active substance (eg a vitamin) that produces a standard specific result or biological effect under strictly controlled conditions – compare INTERNATIONAL UNIT **3a** a single thing, person, or group that is a constituent of a whole ⟨*the family is the basic ~ of society*⟩ b a part of a military establishment that has a special function (eg of per-

sonnel and supplies) c a piece or set of apparatus serving to perform one particular function d a part of a school course focussing on a central theme and making use of resources from numerous subject areas and the pupils' own experience e a local congregation of JEHOVAH'S WITNESSES [back-formation fr *unity*] – **unit** *adj*

**unitarian** /ˌyoohni'teəri-ən/ *n* 1a *often cap* a person who rejects the doctrine of the Trinity and believes that God is a single being b *cap* a member of a Christian denomination that stresses individual freedom of belief, the free use of reason in religion, a united world community, and liberal social action 2 an advocate of unity or a unitary system [NL *unitarius*, fr L *unitas* unity] – **unitarian** *adj, often cap*, **unitarianism** *n, often cap*

**unitary** /'yoohnit(ə)ri/ *adj* 1a of a unit b based on or characterized by unity or units 2 undivided, whole – **unitarily** *adv*

**unit cell** *n* the smallest group of atoms, ions, or molecules that contains all the structural characteristics of and by repetition in three dimensions makes up the LATTICE of a crystal

**unit character** *n* a genetically determined characteristic that is inherited as a single whole unit or not at all; *esp* one dependent on the presence or absence of a single gene

**unit circle** *n* a circle whose radius is one unit of length long

**unite** /yoo'niet, yooh-/ *vt* 1a to put together to form a single unit ⟨*need to ~ the workers behind our party*⟩ b to cause to adhere c to link by a legal or moral bond ⟨*~d by marriage*⟩ 2 to possess (eg qualities) in combination ⟨*~d beauty and intelligence*⟩ ~ *vi* 1a to become (as if) one unit b to become combined (as if) by adhesion or mixture 2 to act together for a common purpose **synonyms** see ¹JOIN **antonym** disunite [ME *uniten*, fr LL *unitus*, pp of *unire*, fr L *unus* one – more at ONE] – **uniter** *n*

¹**united** /yoo'nietid, yooh-/ *adj* 1 combined, joined 2 relating to or produced by joint action ⟨*a ~ effort*⟩ 3 formed by or resulting from union 4 in agreement; harmonious ⟨*a ~ family*⟩ – **unitedly** *adv*

²**united** *adv* with the two leading legs on the same side ⟨*a horse should canter ~*⟩

**United Reformed** *adj* of the United Reformed Church formed in 1972 by the union of the Presbyterian Church of England and the Congregational Church of England and Wales

**United States** *n taking sing or pl vb* a federation of states, esp when forming a nation in a usu specified territory ⟨*advocating a ~ of Europe*⟩

**unitive** /'yoohnətiv/ *adj* characterized by or tending to produce union

**unit·ize, -ise** /'yoohnitiez/ *vt* 1 to form or convert into a unit 2 to divide into units ⟨*the added cost of* unitizing *bulk products*⟩ – **unitization** *n*

**unit matrix** *n, maths* a SQUARE MATRIX (arrangement of numbers, letters, etc having an equal number of rows and columns) whose elements are equal to one on the PRINCIPAL DIAGONAL (diagonal running from top left to bottom right) and zero elsewhere – called also IDENTITY MATRIX

**unit membrane** *n* a semipermeable biological membrane structure that consists of a double layer of LIPID (fat) molecules interspersed with protein molecules and that is considered as having three layers made up of two outer layers of lipid parts chemically attracted to water and an inner water-repelling layer [fr its being the basic structural unit of the cell]

**unit rule** *n* a rule under which a delegation to a US Democratic national convention casts its entire vote as a unit as determined by a majority vote within the delegation

**unit trust** *n* any of various British investment companies that minimize the risk to investors by collective purchase of shares in many different enterprises – compare INVESTMENT TRUST

**unit vector** *n* a conventionalized VECTOR having a magnitude of one and specifying some particular direction (eg an axis of a coordinate system)

**unity** /'yoohnəti/ *n* 1a the quality or state of being one or united; oneness, singleness ⟨*strength lies in ~*⟩ b(1) the number one or a definite amount taken as one or that assumes the value of one for the purpose of calculation ⟨*in a table of natural sines the radius of the circle is regarded as ~*⟩ b(2) a

| | | | |
|---|---|---|---|
| **unjaded** *adj* | **unjudged** *adj* | **unjustified** *adj* | **unkingly** *adj* |
| **unjoined** *adj* | **unjustifiable** *adj* | **unkept** *adj* | **unkissed** *adj* |
| **unjointed** *adj* | **unjustifiably** *adv* | **unkindled** *adj* | **unknot** *vt* |

number by which any element of an arithmetical or mathematical system can be multiplied without change in the resultant value **2a** a condition of harmony; concord **b** continuity and agreement (eg in aims or interests) ⟨~ *of purpose*⟩ **3a** the quality or state of being made one; unification **b** singleness of effect or symmetry in a literary or artistic work **4** a whole made up of related parts; something that is a complex or systematic whole **5** any of the three principles of dramatic structure (DRAMATIC UNITIES) regulating the structure of classical plays **6** *cap* a 20th-century American religious movement close to orthodox Christianity and emphasizing health and prosperity [ME *unite*, fr OF *unité*, fr L *unitat-*, *unitas*, fr *unus* one]

**synonyms Unity, solidarity, union, homogeneity,** and **integrity** all mean the quality of a whole that is made up of closely associated parts. **Unity** is the fact of being one, and emphasizes harmony produced by agreement ⟨*attaining* **unity** *of purpose through discussion*⟩. **Solidarity** is a stronger word than **unity** for the sharing of interests and standards that enables a group to act as one. **Union** refers particularly to the act of joining ⟨*the* **union** *of Scotland and England in 1707*⟩ or to the resultant product ⟨*the Steelworkers'* **Union**⟩. **Homogeneity** emphasizes the quality of sameness throughout, resulting from likeness between the components. **Integrity** refers to the quality of being undivided ⟨*the* **integrity** *of the Empire was threatened*⟩. **antonyms** diversity, heterogeneity.

¹**univalent** /ˌyoohni'vaylənt/ *adj* **1** *chemistry* having a VALENCY of one **2** *of a* CHROMOSOME (*strand of gene-carrying material*) remaining unpaired during CELL DIVISION in which chromosomes from each parent associate in pairs [ISV]

²**univalent** *n* a univalent chromosome

¹**univalve** /'yoohni,valv/ *adj* having or being a shell consisting of one piece (VALVE) – compare BIVALVE

²**univalve** *n* (a snail, whelk, or similar INVERTEBRATE animal having) a univalve shell

¹**universal** /ˌyoohni'vuhs(ə)l/ *adj* **1** including or covering all or a whole without limit or exception **2** present or occurring everywhere or under all conditions ⟨~ *cultural patterns*⟩ **3a** including a major part or the greatest portion (eg of mankind) ⟨*a* ~ *state*⟩ ⟨~ *practices*⟩ **b** comprehensively broad and versatile ⟨*a* ~ *genius*⟩ **4a** *philosophy* affirming or denying something of, or denoting, every member of a class ⟨*"no man knows everything" is a* ~ *negative*⟩ ⟨*a* ~ *term*⟩ **5** adapted or adjustable to meet varied requirements (eg of use, shape, or size) ⟨*a* ~ *milling machine*⟩ **antonyms** particular, limited [ME, fr MF, fr L *universalis*, fr *universum* universe] – **universally** *adv*, **universalness** *n*

²**universal** *n* **1a** a universal proposition in logic **b(1)** a general concept or term **b(2)** something in the mind or the external world to which a general term corresponds; ESSENCE **2** a behavioural trait, characteristic, or pattern that exists in all cultures; *also* one that exists among all normal adult members of a particular society

**universal coupling** *n* UNIVERSAL JOINT

**universalism** /ˌyoohni'vuhsəliz(ə)m/ *n* **1** *often cap* a theological doctrine that everyone will eventually be saved **2** the state of being universal; universality; *also* something that is universal in scope – **universalist** *n or adj, often cap*

**universalistic** /ˌyoohni,vuhsə'listik/ *adj* of the whole; universal in range or nature

**universality** /ˌyoohnivuh'saləti/ *n* **1** the quality or state of being universal **2** universal comprehensiveness in range or applicability

**universal-ize, -ise** /ˌyoohni'vuhsəliez/ *vt* to make universal; generalize – **universalization** *n*

**universal joint** *n* a joint uniting two shafts and capable of transmitting rotation from one shaft to another at an angle

**universal language** *n* **1** a mode of expression understood everywhere ⟨*is music a* ~?⟩ **2** an artificial international language (eg Esperanto)

**universal motor** *n* an electric motor that can be used on either an ALTERNATING CURRENT or a DIRECT CURRENT supply

**Universal time** *n* GREENWICH MEAN TIME

**universe** /'yoohni,vuhs/ *n* **1** all things that exist, whether perceived or not; the cosmos **2a** a systematic whole held to arise by and persist through the direct intervention of divine power **b** the whole world; everyone **c** a galaxy **3** *statistics* the complete

set of individuals, objects, etc from which a statistical sample is drawn; POPULATION **4 4a** a set that contains all elements relevant to a particular discussion or problem **5** a great number or quantity [L *universum*, fr neut of *universus* entire, whole, fr *uni-* + *versus* turned towards, fr pp of *vertere* to turn – more at WORTH]

**universe of discourse** *n* an inclusive class of items that is implied or stated as the subject of a discussion or logical proposition

**university** /ˌyoohni'vuhsəti/ *n* **1** an institution of higher education that provides facilities for full-time teaching and research, is authorized to grant academic degrees, and in Britain receives a Treasury grant ⟨*she's at* ~⟩ **2** the premises of a university [ME *universite*, fr OF *université*, fr ML *universitat-*, *universitas*, fr LL, society, corporation, fr L, the whole, fr *universus*]

**usage** The use of **university** without the ⟨*go to* **university**⟩ is British rather than American English.

**university college** *n* **1** a college attached to or affiliated with a university; *also* COLLEGE 3c **2** a college where one may study for an external degree

**university extension** *n* a system by which a university provides public lectures and courses held typically in the evening

**univocal** /yooh'nivəkl, ˌyoohni'vohkəl/ *adj* having one meaning only; unambiguous ⟨~ *terms*⟩ [LL *univocus*, fr L *uni-* + *voc-*, *vox* voice – more at VOICE] – **univocally** *adv*

**univoltine** /ˌyoohni'vohltien/ *adj*, *of an animal, esp an insect* laying eggs or giving birth only once a year; producing only one brood or generation in a year – compare BIVOLTINE, MULTIVOLTINE [Fr, fr *uni-* + *-voltine*]

**unjust** /un'just/ *adj* **1** characterized by injustice; unfair **2** *archaic* dishonest, faithless – **unjustly** *adv*, **unjustness** *n*

**unkempt** /un'kempt/ *adj* **1** not combed; dishevelled ⟨~ *hair*⟩ **2** not neat or tidy ⟨~ *individuals*⟩ ⟨~ *hotel rooms*⟩; *also* rough, unpolished ⟨~ *prose*⟩

**unkenned** /ˌun'kend/ *adj, chiefly dial* unknown, strange

**unkennel** /ˌun'kenl/ *vt* **1a** to drive (eg a fox) from a hiding place or den **b** to free (dogs) from a kennel **2** to bring out into the open; uncover

**unkind** /un'kiend/ *adj* **1** not pleasing or mild; inclement ⟨*an* ~ *climate*⟩ **2** lacking in kindness or sympathy; harsh, cruel – **unkindness** *n*

¹**unkindly** /un'kiendli/ *adj* not kindly ⟨~ *words*⟩ – **unkindliness** *n*

²**unkindly** *adv* in an unkind manner

**unknit** /un'nit/ *vt -tt-; unknit, unknitted* to undo, unravel

**unknowable** /un'noh-əbl/ *adj* not knowable; *esp* lying beyond the limits of human experience or understanding

**unknowing** /un'noh-ing/ *adj* not knowing; unaware – **unknowingly** *adv*

¹**unknown** /un'nohn/ *adj* not known; *also* having an unknown value ⟨*an* ~ *quantity*⟩

²**unknown** *n* **1** one who or that which is not known or not well-known; *esp* a person who is little known (eg to the public) **2** something that requires to be discovered, identified, or clarified: eg **2a** a symbol in a mathematical equation representing an unknown quantity **b** a specimen (eg of bacteria or mixed chemicals) required to be identified as an exercise in appropriate laboratory techniques

**Unknown Soldier** *n* an unidentified soldier whose body is entombed in a national memorial as a representative of all of the same nation who died in a war, esp either of the WORLD WARS

**unlace** /un'lays/ *vt* to undo the lacing of (eg a garment or shoe)

**unlade** /un'layd/ *vb* **unladed; unladed, unladen** /'layd(ə)n/ *vt* to discharge, unload ~ *vi* to discharge cargo

**unlash** /ˌun'lash/ *vt* to untie the rope, cord, etc (LASHING) of

**unlatch** /un'lach/ *vt* to open or loose by lifting a latch ~ *vi* to become unlatched

**unlawful** /un'lawf(ə)l/ *adj* **1** not lawful; illegal **2** not morally right or conventional ⟨~ *pleasures*⟩ – **unlawfully** *adv*, **unlawfulness** *n*

**unlay** /un'lay/ *vt* **unlaid** /-'layd/ to untwist the strands of (eg a rope)

| | | | |
|---|---|---|---|
| **unknowledgeable** *adj* | **unladylike** *adj* | **unleavened** *adj* | **unliberated** *adj* |
| **unlabelled** *adj* | **unlamented** *adj* | **unlethal** *adj* | **unlicensed** *adj* |
| **unlaboured** *adj* | **unlaundered** *adj* | **unliberal** *adj* | **unlighted** *adj* |

**unleaded** /‚un'ledid/ *adj* **1a** stripped of lead **b** not treated or mixed with lead or lead compounds ⟨~ *fuels*⟩ **2** not having metal strips (LEADS) between the lines in printing

**unlearn** /un'luhn/ *vt* **1** to put out of one's knowledge or memory **2** to undo the effect of; discard the habit of; *also* to discover the falsity of (something previously accepted)

**unlearned** /un'luhnd, -'luhnt/ *adj* **1** not educated **2** ignorant **3** not gained by study or training

**unleash** /un'leesh/ *vt* to free (as if) from a leash; loose from restraint or control ⟨~ *a dog*⟩ ⟨~ *latent abilities*⟩

**unless** /ən'les/ *conj* **1** except on the condition that ⟨*won't work ~ you put in some money*⟩ **2** without the accompaniment that; except when ⟨*we swim ~ it's very cold*⟩

**unlettered** /un'letəd/ *adj* **1a** lacking skill in reading and writing and ignorant of the knowledge to be gained from books **b** illiterate **2** not marked with letters ⟨~ *tombstones*⟩

**¹unlike** /‚un'liek/ *prep* not like: eg **a** different from **b** not characteristic of ⟨~ *him to be late*⟩ **c** in a different manner from

**²unlike** *adj* not like: eg **a** marked by dissimilarity; different ⟨*the two books are quite ~*⟩ **b** not faithful ⟨*portrait is utterly ~*⟩ **c** unequal ⟨*contributed ~ amounts*⟩ – **unlikeness** *n*

**unlikely** /un'liekli/ *adj* **1** having a low probability of being or occurring ⟨~ *to succeed*⟩ ⟨*an ~ possibility*⟩ **2** incredible ⟨*an ~ story*⟩ **3** likely to fail; unpromising **4** unforeseen ⟨*the ~ result*⟩ – compare LIKELY – **unlikeliness, unlikelihood** *n*

**unlimber** /un'limbə/ *vt* **1** to detach (a gun) from the LIMBER (part of gun carriage) and so make ready **2a** to prepare for action ⟨~ed *his banjo and began to sing*⟩; *also* to make supple; LIMBER UP ⟨~ *one's muscles*⟩ **b** to release; let fly ⟨*mayor . . .* ~ed *a smooth rendition of "Blue Hawaii" – Saturday Review*⟩ ~ *vi* **1** to perform the task of preparing something for action **2** to relax one's stiffness; unbend [¹*limber*; influenced in meaning (esp in vt 2a and vi 2) by ²*limber*]

**unlimited** /un'limitid/ *adj* **1** lacking any controls or restrictions ⟨~ *power*⟩ **2** boundless, infinite ⟨*an ~ expanse of ocean*⟩ – **unlimitedly** *adv*

**unlink** /un'lingk/ *vt* to unfasten the links of; separate, disconnect ~ *vi* to become unlinked

**unlinked** /un'lingkt/ *adj* being or controlled by genes that do not belong to the same LINKAGE GROUP (set of genes that are inherited together)

**unlisted** /un'listid/ *adj* **1** not appearing on a list **2** being or involving a security not listed formally on a STOCK EXCHANGE; OVER-THE-COUNTER **3** *chiefly NAm* ex-directory

**unload** /un'lohd/ *vt* **1a(1)** to take off or out; remove **a(2)** to take the cargo from **b** to give vent to; pour forth ⟨~ed *her bitter feelings*⟩ **2a** to relieve of something burdensome; take a load from ⟨~ed *the pack animals*⟩ **b** to relieve of something oppressive or difficult ⟨~ed *himself to his friend*⟩ **3** to remove the cartridge or projectile from ⟨~ed *the gun*⟩ **4** to sell, esp in large quantities; DUMP **2** ~ *vi* to perform the act of unloading – **unloader** *n*

**unlock** /un'lok/ *vt* **1** to unfasten the lock of **2** to open, undo **3** to free from restraints or restrictions; release ⟨*the shock* ~ed *a flood of tears*⟩ **4** to provide a key to; disclose, reveal ⟨~ *the secrets of nature*⟩ ~ *vi* to become unlocked

**unlooked-for** /un'lookt faw/ *adj* not foreseen; unexpected

**unloose** /un'loohs/, **unloosen** /-'loohs(ə)n/ *vt* **1** to relax the strain of ⟨~ *a grip*⟩ **2** to release (as if) from restraints; set free **3** to loosen the ties of ⟨~ *traditional social bonds*⟩

**unlovely** /‚un'luvli/ *adj* not likable; disagreeable, unpleasant – **unloveliness** *n*

**unluckily** /un'lukili/ *adv* **1** in an unlucky manner **2** as is unlucky ⟨~, *I can't go*⟩

**unlucky** /un'luki/ *adj* **1** marked by adversity or failure ⟨*an ~ year*⟩ **2** likely to bring misfortune; inauspicious ⟨*an ~ omen*⟩ **3** having or meeting with bad luck ⟨~ *people*⟩ **4** producing dissatisfaction; regrettable ⟨*an ~ remark*⟩ – **unluckiness** *n*

**unmade** /‚un'mayd/ *adj* **1** *of a bed* not put in order for sleeping **2** *Br* unmetalled ⟨~ *roads*⟩

**unmake** /‚un'mayk/ *vt* **unmade** /-'mayd/ **1** to undo, destroy **2** to deprive of rank or office; depose **3** to deprive of essential characteristics; change the nature of

**unmalicious** /‚unmə'lishəs/ *adj* not malicious – **unmaliciously** *adv*

**unman** /‚un'man/ *vt* **-nn-** **1** to deprive of manly vigour, fortitude, or spirit **2** to castrate, emasculate

**unmanly** /un'manli/ *adj* not manly: eg **a** of weak character; cowardly **b** effeminate – **unmanliness** *n*

**unmanned** /‚un'mand/ *adj* **1** not manned ⟨*an ~ spaceflight*⟩ **2** *obs, of a hawk* not trained

**unmannered** /un'manəd/ *adj* **1** lacking good manners; rude **2** characterized by an absence of artificiality; unaffected, sincere – **unmanneredly** *adv*

**¹unmannerly** /un'manəli/ *adv* in an unmannerly fashion

**²unmannerly** *adj* without good manners; discourteous, rude – **unmannerliness** *n*

**unmask** /un'mahsk/ *vt* **1** to remove a mask from **2** to reveal the true nature of; expose ~ *vi* to remove one's mask or disguise

**unmeaning** /un'meening/ *adj* **1** showing a lack of liveliness, expression, or intelligence; dull, uninteresting ⟨*an ~ facial expression*⟩ **2** meaningless, senseless

**unmeant** /un'ment/ *adj* unintentional

**unmeet** /un'meet/ *adj, archaic* not meet; unsuitable, improper

**unmemorable** /un'mem(ə)rəbl/ *adj* not memorable; not worth remembering – **unmemorably** *adv*

**¹unmentionable** /un'mensh(ə)nəbl/ *adj* not fit or proper to be mentioned; unspeakable

**²unmentionable** *n, euph or humorous* something that is unmentionable; *esp, pl* underwear

**unmerciful** /un'muhsif(ə)l/ *adj* **1** not merciful; merciless **2** excessive, extreme ⟨*chatted for an ~ length of time*⟩ – **unmercifully** *adv*

| | | | |
|---|---|---|---|
| **unlikable** *adj* | **unmastered** *adj* | **unmetrical** *adj* | **unnaturalized** *adj* |
| **unlined** *adj* | **unmatchable** *adj* | **unmilitary** *adj* | **unnavigable** *adj* |
| **unlit** *adj* | **unmatched** *adj* | **unmilled** *adj* | **unnavigated** *adj* |
| **unliterary** *adj* | **unmatching** *adj* | **unmingled** *adj* | **unneeded** *adj* |
| **unlivable** *adj* | **unmaterialistic** *adj* | **unmistaken** *adj* | **unneedful** *adj* |
| **unlobed** *adj* | **unmatured** *adj* | **unmitigable** *adj* | **unnegotiable** *adj* |
| **unlocated** *adj* | **unmeasurable** *adj* | **unmixed** *adj* | **unnegotiated** *adj* |
| **unloved** *adj* | **unmeasured** *adj* | **unmodernized** *adj* | **unneighbourly** *adj* |
| **unloving** *adj* | **unmechanical** *adj* | **unmodified** *adj* | **unneurotic** *adj* |
| **unlubricated** *adj* | **unmechanized** *adj* | **unmodish** *adj* | **unnewsworthy** *adj* |
| **unlyrical** *adj* | **unmediated** *adj* | **unmodulated** *adj* | **unnoisy** *adj* |
| **unmagnified** *adj* | **unmedicated** *adj* | **unmolested** *adj* | **unnoteworthy** *adj* |
| **unmailable** *adj* | **unmeditated** *adj* | **unmonitored** *adj* | **unnoticeable** *adj* |
| **unmakable** *adj* | **unmellow** *adj* | **unmortgaged** *adj* | **unnoticeably** *adj* |
| **unmalleable** *adj* | **unmelodious** *adj* | **unmotivated** *adj* | **unnoticed** *adj* |
| **unmanageable** *adj* | **unmelted** *adj* | **unmoulded** *adj* | **unnourished** *adj* |
| **unmanipulated** *adj* | **unmemorized** *adj* | **unmounted** *adj* | **unnurtured** *adj* |
| **unmanufactured** *adj* | **unmended** *adj* | **unmourned** *adj* | **unobjectionable** *adj* |
| **unmapped** *adj* | **unmentioned** *adj* | **unmovable** *adj* | **unobliging** *adj* |
| **unmarked** *adj* | **unmerchantable** *adj* | **unmoved** *adj* | **unobscured** *adj* |
| **unmarketable** *adj* | **unmerited** *adj* | **unmoving** *adj* | **unobservable** *adj* |
| **unmarred** *adj* | **unmerry** *adj* | **unmown** *adj* | **unobservant** *adj* |
| **unmarriageable** *adj* | **unmet** *adj* | **unmusical** *adj* | **unobserved** *adj* |
| **unmarried** *adj* | **unmetabolized** *adj* | **unnameable** *adj* | **unobserving** *adj* |
| **unmasculine** *adj* | **unmethodical** *adj* | **unnamed** *adj* | **unobstructed** *adj* |

**unmetalled** /un'metəld/ *adj* not metalled

**unmindful** /un'miendf(ə)l/ *adj* not taking into account; forgetful *of antonyms* mindful, solicitous

**unmistakable** /ˌunmi'staykəbl/ *adj* not capable of being mistaken or misunderstood; clear, obvious – **unmistakably** *adv*

**unmitigated** /un'mitigaytid/ *adj* 1 not diminished in severity, intensity, etc ⟨*sufferings* ~ *by any hope of early relief*⟩ 2 out-and-out, downright ⟨*the evening was an* ~ *disaster*⟩ ⟨*an* ~ *evil*⟩ – **unmitigatedly** *adv*, **unmitigatedness** *n*

**unmoral** /un'morəl/ *adj* having no moral quality or significance – **unmorality** *n*

**unmuffle** /un'mufl/ *vt* to free from something that muffles

**unmurmuring** /un'muhməring/ *adj* uncomplaining – **unmurmuringly** *adv*

**unmuzzle** /un'muzl/ *vt* to free (as if) from a muzzle

**unmyelinated** /un'mie·oliˌnaytid/ *adj, of a nerve fibre* not covered with a MYELIN SHEATH (fatty insulating sheath)

**unnail** /un'nayl/ *vt* to unfasten by removing nails

**unnatural** /un'nachərəl/ *adj* 1 not in accordance with nature or a normal course of events 2a not in accordance with normal feelings or behaviour; perverse **b** lacking ease and naturalness; contrived ⟨*her manner was forced and* ~ ⟩ **c** inconsistent with what is reasonable or expected ⟨*an* ~ *alliance*⟩ – **unnaturally** *adv*, **unnaturalness** *n*

**unnecessarily** /un'nesəs(ə)rəli, ˌun·nesə'serəli/ *adv* not by necessity; to an unnecessary degree ⟨*an* ~ *harsh punishment*⟩

**unnecessary** /un'nesəs(ə)ri, -ˌseri/ *adj* not necessary

**unnerve** /un'nuhv/ *vt* 1 to deprive of courage, strength, or steadiness 2 to cause to become nervous; upset – **unnervingly** *adv*

**unnilpentium** /ˌunəl'pentyəm, -ti·əm/ *n* HAHNIUM [L *un*us one + *nil* nothing, nought + NL *pent-* + *-ium*]

**unnilquadium** /ˌunəl'kwodyəm, -di·əm/ *n* RUTHERFORDIUM [L *un*us one + *nil* nothing, nought + NL *quadri-* + *-ium*]

**unnumbered** /ˌun'numbəd/ *adj* 1 innumerable 2 not having an identifying number ⟨ ~ *pages*⟩

**unobtrusive** /ˌunəb'troohsiv, -ziv/ *adj* not too easily seen or noticed; inconspicuous – **unobtrusively** *adv*, **unobtrusiveness** *n*

**unoccupied** /un'okyoopied/ *adj* not occupied: eg **a** not busy; unemployed **b** not lived in; empty

**unofficial** /ˌunə'fish(ə)l/ *adj* not official – **unofficially** *adv*

**unopenable** /un'ohp(ə)nəbl/ *adj* incapable of being opened

**unopened** /un'ohpənd/ *adj* 1 not opened 2 *of a book* not having the folds of the leaves slit – compare UNCUT

**unorgan·ized, -ised** /un'awgəniezd/ *adj* 1a not organized into a coherent or well-ordered whole **b** not belonging to a TRADE UNION 2 not having the characteristics of a living organism *usage* see DISORGANIZED

**unorthodox** /un'awthədoks/ *adj* unconventional in behaviour, beliefs, doctrine, etc – **unorthodoxly** *adv*

**unorthodoxy** /un'awthədoksi/ *n* the quality or state of being unorthodox; *also* something (eg an opinion) that is unorthodox

**unpack** /un'pak/ *vt* 1 to remove the contents of ⟨ ~ *a trunk*⟩ 2a to remove or undo from packing or a container ⟨ ~ed *his gear*⟩ **b** to change (computer data stored in a compact form) into an expanded form that requires greater storage space but is more easily understandable ~ *vi* to set about unpacking something – **unpacker** *n*

**unpaged** /un'payjd/ *adj* having pages without identifying numbers

**unpaid** /un'payd/ *adj* 1 not paid 2 not paying a salary or wage ⟨*an* ~ *job*⟩

**unpaired** /ˌun'peəd/ *adj* 1a not paired; *esp* not matched or mated ⟨ ~ *chromosomes*⟩ **b** characterized by the absence of pairing ⟨*electrons in the* ~ *state*⟩ 2 situated in the MEDIAN plane (plane dividing a body into two symmetrical parts) of the body and having no corresponding part ⟨*an* ~ *fin of a fish*⟩

**unpalatable** /un'palətəbl/ *adj* 1 not pleasing to the taste 2 unpleasant, disagreeable – **unpalatability** *n*

**unparalleled** /un'parəleld/ *adj* having no parallel; *esp* having no equal or match; unique *synonyms* see STRANGE

**unparliamentary** /ˌunpahlə'mentəri; *also* -lyə-/ *adj* not in accordance with parliamentary practice

**unpeg** /un'peg/ *vt* **-gg-** to remove a peg from; unfasten

**unperfect** /un'puhfikt/ *adj* imperfect

**unperson** /un'puhs(ə)n/ *n, pl* **unpersons** NONPERSON 1

**unpick** /un'pik/ *vt* to undo (eg sewing) by taking out stitches

**unpin** /un'pin/ *vt* **-nn-** 1 to remove a pin from 2 to loosen, free, or unfasten (as if) by removing a pin

**unplaced** /un'playst/ *adj* not having been placed; *specif, chiefly Br* having failed to finish in a leading place in a competition, esp a horse race

**unpleasant** /un'plez(ə)nt/ *adj* not pleasant or agreeable; displeasing ⟨ ~ *odours*⟩ – **unpleasantly** *adv*

**unpleasantness** /un'plez(ə)ntnis/ *n* 1 the quality or state of being unpleasant 2 an unpleasant situation, experience, or event

**unplug** /un'plug/ *vt* **-gg-** 1a to take a plug out of **b** to remove an obstruction from 2a to remove (eg an electric plug) from a socket or receptacle **b** to disconnect from an electric circuit by removing a plug ⟨ ~ *the refrigerator*⟩

**unplumbed** /un'plumd/ *adj* 1 of unknown depth 2a not thoroughly explored **b** uncomprehended, unsounded

**unpolar·ized, -ised** /un'pohləriezd/ *adj* not polarized; *specif, of light waves or other electromagnetic radiation* having a random pattern of vibrations

**unpolitical** /ˌunpə'litikl/ *adj* not interested or engaged in politics ⟨*an* ~ *person*⟩

**unpopular** /un'popyoolə/ *adj* viewed or received unfavourably by the public – **unpopularity** *n*

**unprecedented** /un'presidentid/ *adj* having no precedent; novel, unexampled – **unprecedentedly** *adv*

    *usage* The pronunciation /un'presidentid/ rather than /un'pree-/ is recommended for BBC broadcasters.

---

| | | | |
|---|---|---|---|
| **unobtainable** *adj* | **unpardoned** *adj* | **unpersuasive** *adj* | **unpoised** *adj* |
| **unobtained** *adj* | **unparenthesized** *adj* | **unperturbable** *adj* | **unpoliced** *adj* |
| **unobtruding** *adj* | **unpartisan** *adj* | **unperturbed** *adj* | **unpolished** *adj* |
| **unobvious** *adj* | **unpartitioned** *adj* | **unphilosophic** *adj* | **unpolled** *adj* |
| **unoffended** *adj* | **unpassable** *adj* | **unphilosophical** *adj* | **unpolluted** *adj* |
| **unoffensive** *adj* | **unpasteurized** *adj* | **unphonetic** *adj* | **unpolymerized** *adj* |
| **unoffered** *adj* | **unpatentable** *adj* | **unphotogenic** *adj* | **unpopulated** *adj* |
| **unofficious** *adj* | **unpatented** *adj* | **unphotographed** *adj* | **unposed** *adj* |
| **unoiled** *adj* | **unpatriotic** *adj* | **unpicturesque** *adj* | **unpossessing** *adj* |
| **unopen** *adj* | **unpatterned** *adj* | **unpitied** *adj* | **unpowered** *adj* |
| **unopposed** *adj* | **unpaved** *adj* | **unpitying** *adj* | **unpracticable** *adj* |
| **unoppressive** *adj* | **unpeaceful** *adj* | **unplanned** *adj* | **unpractical** *adj* |
| **unordained** *adj* | **unpedantic** *adj* | **unplanted** *adj* | **unpractised** *adj* |
| **unordered** *adj* | **unpedigreed** *adj* | **unplausible** *adj* | **unpredicted** *adj* |
| **unorganizable** *adj* | **unpensioned** *adj* | **unplayable** *adj* | **unpremeditated** *adj* |
| **unoriginal** *adj* | **unperceivable** *adj* | **unplayed** *adj* | **unprepossessing** *adj* |
| **unornamental** *adj* | **unperceived** *adj* | **unpleased** *adj* | **unprescribed** *adj* |
| **unornamented** *adj* | **unperceiving** *adj* | **unpleasing** *adj* | **unpresentable** *adj* |
| **unostentatious** *adj* | **unperceptive** *adj* | **unpledged** *adj* | **unpreserved** *adj* |
| **unowned** *adj* | **unperfected** *adj* | **unploughed** *adj* | **unpressed** *adj* |
| **unoxygenated** *adj* | **unperformable** *adj* | **unplucked** *adj* | **unpressured** *adj* |
| **unpacified** *adj* | **unperformed** *adj* | **unplundered** *adj* | **unpresumptuous** *adj* |
| **unpainted** *adj* | **unperplexed** *adj* | **unpoetic** *adj* | **unpretty** *adj* |
| **unparasitized** *adj* | **unpersuadable** *adj* | **unpoetical** *adj* | **unprevailing** *adj* |
| **unpardonable** *adj* | **unpersuaded** *adj* | **unpointed** *adj* | **unpreventable** *adj* |

**unpredictable** /ˌʌnpriˈdiktəbl/ *adj* not predictable ⟨~ *weather*⟩ – **unpredictably** *adv*, **unpredictability** *n*

**unprejudiced** /ʌnˈpredʒoodist, -jə-/ *adj* impartial, fair

**unprepared** /ˌʌnpriˈpeəd/ *adj* not prepared – **unpreparedness** *n*

**unpretending** /ˌʌnpriˈtending/ *adj* unpretentious

**unpretentious** /ˌʌnpriˈtenʃəs/ *adj* not seeking to impress others by means of wealth, standing, etc; modest ⟨~ *homes*⟩ – **unpretentiously** *adv*, **unpretentiousness** *n*

**unpriced** /ˌʌnˈpriest/ *adj* having no price set or indicated

**unprincipled** /ʌnˈprinsip(ə)ld/ *adj* without moral principles; unscrupulous – **unprincipledness** *n*

**unprintable** /ʌnˈprintəbl/ *adj* unfit to be printed

**unprofessed** /ˌʌnprəˈfest/ *adj* not professed ⟨an ~ *aim*⟩

**unprofitable** /ʌnˈprofitəbl/ *adj* not yielding profit; useless, vain – **unprofitableness** *n*, **unprofitably** *adv*

**unpromising** /ʌnˈpromising/ *adj* appearing unlikely to prove worthwhile or have a favourable result – **unpromisingly** *adv*

**unpronounced** /ˌʌnprəˈnownst/ *adj* not pronounced; *esp* mute

**unputdownable** /ˌʌnpootˈdownəbl/ *adj, chiefly Br informal, of a book or story* so interesting or exciting as to demand the reader's continual attention; compulsively readable

**unqualified** /ʌnˈkwolifíed/ *adj* 1 not having the necessary qualifications – compare DISQUALIFY 1 2 not modified or restricted by reservations ⟨~ *approval*⟩ – **unqualifiedly** *adv*

**unquestionable** /ʌnˈkwesch(ə)nəbl/ *adj* not able to be doubted or challenged; indisputable ⟨~ *evidence*⟩ – **unquestionably** *adv*

**unquestioning** /ʌnˈkwesch(ə)ning/ *adj* not expressing doubt or hesitation ⟨~ *obedience*⟩ – **unquestioningly** *adv*

**unquiet** /ʌnˈkwie·ət/ *adj* 1 agitated, turbulent 2 physically, emotionally, or mentally restless; uneasy – **unquietly** *adv*, **unquietness** *n*

**unquote** /ˌʌnˈkwoht/ *n* – used orally to indicate the end of a direct quotation

**unravel** /ʌnˈravl/ *vb* -ll- (*NAm* -l-, -ll-) *vt* 1 to disengage or separate the threads of; disentangle 2 to resolve the intricacy, complexity, or obscurity of; solve ~ *vi* to become unravelled

**unread** /ʌnˈred/ *adj* 1 not read; left unexamined 2 not familiar with or versed in a specified field ⟨~ *in political science*⟩

**unready** /ʌnˈredi/ *adj* unprepared – **unreadiness** *n*

**unreal** /ʌnˈriəl, ˈreel/ *adj* lacking in reality, substance, or genuineness; artificial, illusory

**unrealistic** /ˌʌnriəˈlistik, -ree-/ *adj* inappropriate to reality or fact – **unrealistically** *adv*

**unreality** /ˌʌnriˈaləti/ *n* 1a the quality or state of being unreal; lack of substance or validity b something unreal, insubstantial, or visionary; a figment 2 ineptitude in dealing with reality

**unreason** /ʌnˈreez(ə)n/ *n* the absence of reason or sanity; irrationality, madness

**unreasonable** /ʌnˈreez(ə)nəbl/ *adj* 1a not governed by or acting according to reason ⟨~ *people*⟩ b not complying with reason; absurd ⟨~ *beliefs*⟩ 2 exceeding the bounds of reason or moderation ⟨*working under* ~ *pressure*⟩ – **unreasonableness** *n*, **unreasonably** *adv*

**unreasoning** /ʌnˈreezəning/ *adj* not moderated or controlled by reason ⟨~ *fear*⟩ – **unreasoningly** *adv*

**unrecogn·ized, -ised** /ʌnˈrekəgniezd/ *adj* not recognized

**unreconstructed** /ˌʌnreekənˈstruktid/ *adj, chiefly NAm* not reconciled to some political, economic, or social change; *esp* holding stubbornly to principles, beliefs, or views that are outmoded

**unreel** /ʌnˈriəl, -ˈreel/ *vt* 1 to unwind from a reel 2 to produce as if by unwinding ⟨~ *a story*⟩ ~ *vi* 1 to become unreeled 2 to be presented ⟨*the dress rehearsal* ~ed *flawlessly*⟩

**unreeve** /ʌnˈreev/ *vt* **unrove** /-ˈrohv/ to withdraw (a rope) from an opening (e g a loop or eye)

**unregenerate** /ˌʌnriˈjenərət/ *adj* 1 unrepentant 2a not reformed; unconverted ⟨~ *revolutionaries*⟩ b obstinate, stubborn ⟨*struggling against* ~ *impulses*⟩

**unrelenting** /ˌʌnriˈlenting/ *adj* 1 not weakening in determination; hard, stern ⟨an ~ *leader*⟩ 2 not letting up or weakening in vigour, pace, etc ⟨~ *struggles*⟩ – **unrelentingly** *adv*

**unremarked** /ˌʌnriˈmahkt/ *adj* unnoticed ⟨*his absence went* ~⟩

**unremitting** /ˌʌnriˈmiting/ *adj* constant, incessant **synonyms** see CONTINUAL *antonym* intermittent – **unremittingly** *adv*

**unreserve** /ˌʌnriˈzuhv/ *n* absence of reserve; frankness

**unreserved** /ˌʌnriˈzuhvd/ *adj* 1 entire, unqualified ⟨~ *enthusiasm*⟩ 2 frank and open in manner 3 not set aside for special use – **unreservedly** *adv*, **unreservedness** *n*

**unresponsive** /ˌʌnriˈsponsiv/ *adj* not responsive – **unresponsively** *adv*, **unresponsiveness** *n*

**unrest** /ʌnˈrest/ *n* agitation, turmoil ⟨*political* ~⟩

**unrestrained** /ˌʌnriˈstraynd/ *adj* 1 not held in check; uncontrolled ⟨~ *proliferation of technology*⟩ 2 free of constraint; spontaneous ⟨*felt happy and* ~⟩ – **unrestrainedly** *adv*, **unrestrainedness** *n*

**unrestraint** /ˌʌnriˈstraynt/ *n* freedom from or lack of restraint

**unriddle** /ʌnˈridl/ *vt* to find the explanation of; solve ⟨~ *the murder*⟩

**unrighteous** /ʌnˈriech(y)əs/ *adj* 1 sinful, wicked ⟨an ~ *man*⟩ 2 unjust, unmerited ⟨*intolerable and* ~ *interference*⟩ – **unrighteously** *adv*, **unrighteousness** *n*

**unrip** /ʌnˈrip/ *vt* -pp- 1 to rip or slit up; cut or tear open 2 *archaic* to reveal

**unripe** /ʌnˈriep/ *adj* 1 not ripe; immature 2 unready, unprepared – **unripeness** *n*

**unrivalled**, *NAm chiefly* **unrivaled** /ʌnˈrievld/ *adj* unequalled, unparalleled

**unrobe** /ʌnˈrohb/ *vb* to disrobe, undress

**unroll** /ʌnˈrohl/ *vt* 1 to open out; uncoil 2 to unfold, reveal ⟨*the novel* ~s *itself to the reader*⟩ ~ *vi* to be unrolled

---

| | | | |
|---|---|---|---|
| **unprinted** *adj* | **unprovoked** *adj* | **unrealizable** *adj* | **unrefuted** *adj* |
| **unprivileged** *adj* | **unpruned** *adj* | **unrealized** *adj* | **unregarded** *adj* |
| **unprocessed** *adj* | **unpublicized** *adj* | **unreasoned** *adj* | **unregimented** *adj* |
| **unproclaimed** *adj* | **unpublished** *adj* | **unrebuked** *adj* | **unregistered** *adj* |
| **unprocurable** *adj* | **unpunctual** *adj* | **unreceptive** *adj* | **unregulated** *adj* |
| **unproduced** *adj* | **unpunctuality** *n* | **unreciprocated** *adj* | **unrehearsed** *adj* |
| **unproductive** *adj* | **unpunished** *adj* | **unreckoned** *adj* | **unrelated** *adj* |
| **unprofessional** *adj* | **unpurchasable** *adj* | **unreclaimable** *adj* | **unrelaxed** *adj* |
| **unprogrammable** *adj* | **unpure** *adj* | **unrecognizable** *adj* | **unrelaxing** *adj* |
| **unprogrammed** *adj* | **unpurified** *adj* | **unrecommended** *adj* | **unreliability** *n* |
| **unprogressive** *adj* | **unquantifiable** *adj* | **unrecompensed** *adj* | **unreliable** *adj* |
| **unprohibited** *adj* | **unquelled** *adj* | **unreconcilable** *adj* | **unrelieved** *adj* |
| **unprompted** *adj* | **unquenchable** *adj* | **unreconciled** *adj* | **unrelievedly** *adv* |
| **unpronounceable** *adj* | **unquenched** *adj* | **unrecorded** *adj* | **unreligious** *adj* |
| **unpropertied** *adj* | **unquestioned** *adj* | **unrecoverable** *adj* | **unreluctant** *adj* |
| **unpropitious** *adj* | **unquotable** *adj* | **unrectified** *adj* | **unremarkable** *adj* |
| **unproportionate** *adj* | **unraised** *adj* | **unredeemable** *adj* | **unremedied** *adj* |
| **unproportioned** *adj* | **unranked** *adj* | **unredeemed** *adj* | **unremembered** *adj* |
| **unproposed** *adj* | **unransomed** *adj* | **unredressed** *adj* | **unreminiscent** *adj* |
| **unprosperous** *adj* | **unratified** *adj* | **unrefined** *adj* | **unremitted** *adj* |
| **unprotected** *adj* | **unrationed** *adj* | **unreflecting** *adj* | **unremorseful** *adj* |
| **unprotesting** *adj* | **unravished** *adj* | **unreflective** *adj* | **unremovable** *adj* |
| **unprovable** *adj* | **unreachable** *adj* | **unreformable** *adj* | **unremunerated** *adj* |
| **unproved** *adj* | **unreached** *adj* | **unreformed** *adj* | **unremunerative** *adj* |
| **unproven** *adj* | **unreadable** *adj* | **unrefreshed** *adj* | **unrendered** *adj* |
| **unprovided** *adj* | **unrealism** *n* | **unrefrigerated** *adj* | **unrenewed** *adj* |

**unroof** /un'roohf/ *vt* to strip off the roof or covering of

**unroot** /un'rooht/ *vt* **1** to uproot **2** to get rid of; eradicate

**¹unround** /un'rownd/ *vt* **1** SPREAD 1c (make the lips not rounded) **2** to pronounce (eg the vowel /ee/) with little or no lip rounding

**²unround** *adj* pronounced with the lips not rounded

**unruffled** /un'rufld/ *adj* **1** poised and serene, esp in the face of setbacks or confusion ⟨*a man of ~ calm*⟩ **2** smooth, calm ⟨*~ water*⟩ *antonyms* ruffled, excited

**unruly** /un'roohli/ *adj* difficult to discipline or manage [ME *unreuly*, fr *un-* + *reuly* disciplined, fr *reule* rule] – **unruliness** *n*

   *synonyms* Unruly, ungovernable, intractable, refractory, recalcitrant, wilful, headstrong, wayward, and perverse all mean "not submissive to control". Unruly suggests human lack of or incapacity for discipline ⟨*with judicious officers the most* **unruly** *seamen can at sea be kept in some sort of subjection* – Herman Melville⟩. Ungovernable is a stronger word for things or people that defy all restraint. Intractable implies stubborn resistance to guidance ⟨*display a savage, domineering and* **intractable** *temper* – Robert Graves⟩. Refractory and the stronger recalcitrant suggest protest and rebellion ⟨*became most* **refractory***, breathing nothing but downright mutiny* – Herman Melville⟩ ⟨**recalcitrant** *miner who wanted to quit work ... rushed at me with his pick* – John Steinbeck⟩. Wilful implies the often capricious flouting of authority to achieve one's will ⟨*a* **wilful** *child throwing its plate on the floor*⟩. Headstrong may suggest obstinate impatience of restraint ⟨**headstrong** *enough for it to make it a very difficult task for him to manage her* – Anthony Trollope⟩. Wayward behaviour is primarily irresponsible and erratic. Perverse emphasizes opposition to what is right or reasonable ⟨**perversely** *insists on going today instead of on Tuesday with the rest of us*⟩. *antonyms* tractable, docile

**unsaddle** /un'sadl/ *vt* **1** to take the saddle from **2** to throw (as if) from the saddle ~ *vi* to remove the saddle from a horse

**unsaid** /un'sed/ *adj* not said; *esp* not spoken aloud

**unsaturated** /un'sachooraytid/ *adj* not saturated: e g **a** *of a solution* capable of absorbing or dissolving more of something; containing less dissolved material than a SATURATED solution (solution containing the maximum amount of dissolved material) **b** *of a chemical compound* able to form products by chemical addition; *esp* containing one or more DOUBLE BONDS or TRIPLE BONDS between carbon atoms and capable of reacting to add other atoms or chemical groups to the molecule

**unsaved** /un'sayvd/ *adj* not saved; *esp* not absolved from eternal punishment

**unsavoury** /un'sayvəri/ *adj* **1** unpleasant to taste or smell **2** disagreeable, distasteful ⟨*an ~ assignment*⟩; *esp* morally offensive ⟨*he's an ~ character*⟩ **3** *obs* insipid, tasteless

**unsay** /un'say/ *vt* **unsaid** /-'sed/ to retract or withdraw (e g a statement, opinion, etc)

**unsayable** /un'sayəbl/ *adj* not easily expressed or related

**unscathed** /un'skaydhd/ *adj* entirely unharmed or uninjured

**unschooled** /un'skoohld/ *adj* **1** untaught, untrained **2** not artificial; natural ⟨*~ talent*⟩

**unscientific** /ˌunsie·ən'tifik/ *adj* not scientific: eg **a** not in accordance with the principles and methods of science ⟨*~ management of woodlands*⟩ **b** without scientific knowledge – **unscientifically** *adv*

**unscramble** /ˌun'skrambl/ *vt* **1** to restore to order; disentangle, clarify **2** to restore (scrambled communication) to intelligible form; decode – **unscrambler** *n*

**unscrew** /un'skrooh/ *vt* **1** to remove the screws from **2** to loosen or withdraw by turning ~ *vi* to become unscrewed

**unscripted** /un'skriptid/ *adj*, *of a speech, play, etc* not following a prepared script

**unscrupulous** /un'skroohpyooləs/ *adj* without moral scruples; unprincipled – **unscrupulously** *adv*, **unscrupulousness** *n*

**unseal** /un'seel/ *vt* to break or remove the seal of; open

**unsealed** /un'seeld/ *adj* not sealed

**unseam** /un'seem/ *vt* to open or unfasten the seam or seams of (e g a garment)

**unsearchable** /un'suhchəbl/ *adj* not capable of being searched or explored; inscrutable – **unsearchably** *adv*

**unseasonable** /un'seez(ə)nəbl/ *adj* **1** untimely, inopportune ⟨*an ~ moment to break the news*⟩ **2** not normal for the season of the year ⟨*~ weather*⟩ – **unseasonableness** *n*, **unseasonably** *adv*

**unseat** /ˌun'seet/ *vt* **1** to dislodge from a seat, esp on horseback **2** to remove from a (political) position

**¹unseemly** /un'seemli/ *adj* not conforming to established standards of good behaviour ⟨*~ bickering*⟩ *antonyms* seemly, decorous

**²unseemly** *adv* in an unseemly manner

**¹unseen** /ˌun'seen/ *adj* **1** not seen or perceived; invisible **2** done without previous preparation ⟨*an ~ translation*⟩

**²unseen** *n, chiefly Br* a passage of unprepared translation ⟨*doing Latin ~s*⟩

**unsegregated** /un'segrigaytid/ *adj* not segregated; *esp* free from racial segregation

**unselected** /ˌunsi'lektid, ˌunsə-/ *adj* chosen at random

**unselective** /ˌunsi'lektiv, ˌunsə-/ *adj* random, indiscriminate – **unselectively** *adv*

**unselfish** /un'selfish/ *adj* not selfish; generous – **unselfishly** *adv*, **unselfishness** *n*

**unset** /un'set/ *adj* not set: e g **a** not fixed in a setting; unmounted ⟨*~ diamonds*⟩ **b** not firmed or solidified ⟨*~ concrete*⟩

**unsettle** /un'setl/ *vt* **1** to move from a settled state or condition **2** to perturb, agitate ~ *vi* to become unsettled – **unsettlingly** *adv*

**unsettled** /un'setld/ *adj* not settled: e g **a(1)** not calm or tranquil; disturbed ⟨*~ political conditions*⟩ **a(2)** variable, changeable ⟨*~ weather*⟩ **a(3)** not settled down ⟨*~ dust*⟩ **b** not resolved or worked out; undecided ⟨*an ~ state of mind*⟩ ⟨*an ~ question*⟩ **c** characterized by irregularity ⟨*an ~ life*⟩ **d** not

| | | | |
|---|---|---|---|
| unrenowned *adj* | unresonant *adj* | unridden *adj* | unsatisfying *adj* |
| unrented *adj* | unrespectable *adj* | unrightful *adj* | unscalable *adj* |
| unrepaid *adj* | unrespectful *adj* | unrinsed *adj* | unscaled *adj* |
| unrepaired *adj* | unresponsible *adj* | unripened *adj* | unscanned *adj* |
| unrepealed *adj* | unrested *adj* | unroadworthy *adj* | unscarred *adj* |
| unrepeatable *adj* | unrestful *adj* | unromantic *adj* | unscented *adj* |
| unrepentant *adj* | unrestored *adj* | unromantically *adv* | unscheduled *adj* |
| unreplaceable *adj* | unrestricted *adj* | unromanticized *adj* | unscholarly *adj* |
| unreplaced *adj* | unretentive *adj* | unruled *adj* | unscorched *adj* |
| unreported *adj* | unretracted *adj* | unrushed *adj* | unscratched *adj* |
| unrepresentative *adj* | unreturnable *adj* | unsafe *adj* | unscreened *adj* |
| unrepresentativeness *n* | unreturned *adj* | unsafety *n* | unscriptural *adj* |
| unrepresented *adj* | unrevealed *adj* | unsaintly *adj* | unseasoned *adj* |
| unrepressed *adj* | unrevealing *adj* | unsalable *adj* | unseaworthy *adj* |
| unreprieved *adj* | unrevenged *adj* | unsalaried *adj* | unsecluded *adj* |
| unreprimanded *adj* | unreviewed *adj* | unsalted *adj* | unseconded *adj* |
| unreproduced *adj* | unrevised *adj* | unsalvageable *adj* | unsectarian *adj* |
| unreproved *adj* | unrevoked *adj* | unsanctified *adj* | unsecured *adj* |
| unrequested *adj* | unrevolutionary *adj* | unsanctioned *adj* | unseduced *adj* |
| unrequited *adj* | unrewarded *adj* | unsanitary *adj* | unseeded *adj* |
| unresentful *adj* | unrewarding *adj* | unsaponified *adj* | unseeing *adj* |
| unresistant *adj* | unrhetorical *adj* | unsated *adj* | unsegmented *adj* |
| unresisted *adj* | unrhymed *adj* | unsatiated *adj* | unself-conscious *adj* |
| unresisting *adj* | unrhythmic *adj* | unsatisfactory *adj* | unself-consciously *adv* |
| unresolvable *adj* | unrhythmical *adj* | unsatisfiable *adj* | unsensational *adj* |
| unresolved *adj* | unridable *adj* | unsatisfied *adj* | unsensitive *adj* |

inhabited or populated ⟨~ *land*⟩ **e** mentally unbalanced **f(1)** not disposed of according to law ⟨*an* ~ *estate*⟩ **f(2)** not paid or discharged ⟨~ *debts*⟩ – **unsettledness, unsettlement** *n*

**unsex** /ˌun'seks/ *vt* to deprive of sexual power or the typical qualities of one's sex

**unshackle** /un'shakl/ *vt* to free from shackles or restraints

**unshaped** /un'shaypt/, **unshapen** /un'shayp(ə)n/ *adj* **1** not dressed or finished to final form ⟨*an* ~ *timber*⟩ **2** imperfect in form or formulation ⟨~ *ideas*⟩

**unsheathe** /un'sheedh/ *vt* to draw (as if) from a sheath or scabbard

**unshell** /un'shel/ *vt* to remove or extract (as if) from a shell

**unshelled** /un'sheld/ *adj* having no shell

**unshift** /un'shift/ *vi* to release the SHIFT KEY (lever that adjusts a machine's action) (eg on a typewriter)

**unship** /ˌun'ship/ *vb* **-pp-** *vt* **1** to take out of a ship; discharge, unload **2** to remove (eg an oar or tiller) from position; detach **3** to unseat (*horse* ~ped *its rider*) ~ *vi* to become or be suitable for being detached or removed

**unshockable** /un'shokəbl/ *adj* incapable of being shocked – **unshockability** *n*

**unshod** /un'shod/ *adj* not wearing or provided with shoes

**unsight** /ˌun'siet/ *vt* to prevent from seeing ⟨*the goalkeeper was* ~ed *and missed the ball*⟩

**unsightly** /un'sietli/ *adj* not pleasing to the eye; ugly

**unskilful** /un'skilf(ə)l/ *adj* lacking in skill or proficiency

**unskilled** /ˌun'skild/ *adj* **1** of, being, or requiring workers who are not skilled in any particular branch of work ⟨*an* ~ *labourer*⟩ **2** showing a lack of skill ⟨*produced* ~ *poems*⟩

**unsleeping** /un'sleeping/ *adj* **1** not sleeping or requiring sleep **2** continuing without interruption; ceaseless ⟨*his* ~ *care*⟩

**unsling** /un'sling/ *vt* **unslung** /-slung/ **1** to remove from being slung ⟨unslung *his rifle*⟩ **2** to release from slings ⟨*goods* unslung *from a ship's boat*⟩

**unsnap** /un'snap/ *vt* **-pp-** to loosen or free (as if) by undoing a SNAP (fastener)

**unsnarl** /un'snahl/ *vt* to disentangle

**unsociable** /un'sohsh(i)əbl/ *adj* **1** not liking social activity; reserved, solitary **2** not conducive to sociability ⟨*they live an* ~ *distance from the nearest town*⟩ **synonyms** see UNSOCIAL – **unsociableness** *n*, **unsociably** *adv*, **unsociability** *n*

**unsocial** /un'sohsh(ə)l/ *adj* **1** marked by or showing a dislike for social intercourse ⟨*an* ~ *disposition*⟩ **2** *Br* worked at a time that falls outside the normal working day and prevents participation in social activities ⟨*a pay supplement for working* ~ *hours*⟩ – **unsocially** *adv*

*synonyms* Unsociable is the opposite of sociable and unsocial, asocial, nonsocial, and antisocial are all opposites of social. Unsociable is commoner than unsocial for the meaning "reserved" or "unfriendly", while unsocial may imply a total lack of interest in social life. Asocial often implies "self-centred" or "individualistic" ⟨*dreaming is an asocial act*⟩. Nonsocial means chiefly "not socially oriented" ⟨*nonsocial bees*⟩. Antisocial applies to things thought harmful to society ⟨*it's antisocial to leave litter*⟩. antonyms social, convivial

**unsophisticated** /ˌunsə'fisti̱ˌkaytid/ *adj* **1** pure, unadulterated **2** not socially or culturally sophisticated; natural **3** simple,

straightforward ⟨*an* ~ *approach to a problem*⟩ **synonyms** see ¹NATURAL **antonyms** sophisticated, worldly, complex – **unsophistication** *n*

**unsought** /un'sawt/ *adj* not searched for or sought out ⟨~ *compliments*⟩

**unsound** /ˌun'sownd/ *adj* not sound: eg **a** not healthy or whole **b** mentally abnormal ⟨*of* ~ *mind*⟩ **c** not firmly made, placed, or fixed **d** not valid or true; specious ⟨*an* ~ *argument*⟩ – **unsoundly** *adv*, **unsoundness** *n*

**unsparing** /ˌun'speəring/ *adj* **1** not merciful; hard, ruthless **2** liberal, generous – **unsparingly** *adv*

**unspeakable** /un'speekəbl/ *adj* **1a** incapable of being expressed in words ⟨~ *joy*⟩ **b** inexpressibly bad; horrendous **2** that may not or cannot be spoken ⟨*the bawdy thoughts that come into one's head* – *the* ~ *words* – L P Smith⟩ – **unspeakably** *adv*

**unsphere** /un'sfiə/ *vt* to remove (eg a planet) from a sphere

**unspoken** /un'spohkən/ *adj* not expressed in words

**unspotted** /ˌun'spotid/ *adj* unmarked by spot or stain; *esp* morally blameless ⟨*an* ~ *reputation*⟩

**unsprung** /un'sprung/ *adj* not equipped with springs

**unstable** /un'staybl/ *adj* not stable; not firm or fixed; not constant: eg **a** unsteady, irregular ⟨*an* ~ *pulse*⟩ **b** apt to move, sway, or fall ⟨*an* ~ *tower*⟩ **c(1)** readily changing (eg decomposing) in chemical composition ⟨~ *compounds*⟩ **c(2)** readily losing biological activity ⟨*an* ~ *enzyme*⟩ **c(3)** readily changing in physical state or properties ⟨*an* ~ *emulsion*⟩ **d(1)** of an atom, atomic particle, etc existing only for a short time **d(2)** of an atom or chemical element undergoing spontaneous radioactive decay or decomposition **e** characterized by inability to control the emotions – **unstably** *adv*, **unstableness** *n*

**unstate** /un'stayt/ *vt* to deprive of state, dignity, or rank

**unstated** /un'staytid/ *adj* not stated or put down

¹**unsteady** /un'stedi/ *vt* to make unsteady

²**unsteady** *adj* not steady: eg **a(1)** not firm or stable **a(2)** walking in an erratic or staggering manner **b** changeable, fluctuating ⟨*an* ~ *market*⟩ **c** not uniform or even; irregular ⟨*an* ~ *pulse*⟩ – **unsteadily** *adv*, **unsteadiness** *n*

**unstep** /un'step/ *vt* **-pp-** to remove (a mast) from a STEP (socket or frame for holding a mast)

**unstick** /un'stik/ *vt* **unstuck** /-stuk/ to release (something) from being stuck – **come unstuck** *informal* to go wrong; COME TO GRIEF ⟨*the government* came unstuck *over food prices*⟩

**unstop** /ˌun'stop/ *vt* **-pp-** **1** to free from an obstruction **2** to remove a stopper from

**unstoppable** /un'stopəbl/ *adj* incapable of being stopped; *esp* determined, forceful – **unstoppably** *adv*

**unstrap** /un'strap/ *vt* **-pp-** to remove or loose a strap from

**unstreamed** /ˌun'streemd/ *adj*, *Br* not divided into educational streams

**unstressed** /un'strest/ *adj* **1** not having a stress or accent ⟨~ *syllables*⟩ **2** not subjected to stress ⟨~ *wires*⟩

**unstring** /un'string/ *vt* **unstrung** /-strung/ **1** to loosen or remove the strings of (eg a violin or harp) **2** to remove from a string ⟨~ *beads*⟩ **3** to make mentally disordered or unstable ⟨*was* unstrung *by the news*⟩

**unstructured** /un'strukchəd/ *adj* not structured: eg **a** having

---

| | | | |
|---|---|---|---|
| **unsensitized** *adj* | **unshielded** *adj* | **unsold** *adj* | **unspoken** *adj* |
| **unsensual** *adj* | **unshorn** *adj* | **unsoldierly** *adj* | **unsporting** *adj* |
| **unsentimental** *adj* | **unshowy** *adj* | **unsolicited** *adj* | **unsportsmanlike** *adj* |
| **unseparated** *adj* | **unshrinkable** *adj* | **unsolicitous** *adj* | **unsprayed** *adj* |
| **unserious** *adj* | **unshrinking** *adj* | **unsolid** *adj* | **unspun** *adj* |
| **unserved** *adj* | **unshut** *adj* | **unsolvable** *adj* | **unsquared** *adj* |
| **unserviceable** *adj* | **unsifted** *adj* | **unsolved** *adj* | **unstained** *adj* |
| **unsew** *vt* | **unsigned** *adj* | **unsorted** *adj* | **unstamped** *adj* |
| **unsexual** *adj* | **unsilenced** *adj* | **unsounded** *adj* | **unstandardized** *adj* |
| **unsexy** *adj* | **unsilent** *adj* | **unsoured** *adj* | **unstartling** *adj* |
| **unshaded** *adj* | **unsingable** *adj* | **unsown** *adj* | **unstated** *adj* |
| **unshadowed** *adj* | **unsinkable** *adj* | **unspecialized** *adj* | **unstatesmanlike** *adj* |
| **unshakable** *adj* | **unsized** *adj* | **unspecifiable** *adj* | **unstemmed** *adj* |
| **unshaken** *adj* | **unslacked** *adj* | **unspecific** *adj* | **unsterile** *adj* |
| **unshapely** *adj* | **unslaked** *adj* | **unspecified** *adj* | **unsterilized** *adj* |
| **unshared** *adj* | **unsmart** *adj* | **unspectacular** *adj* | **unstinted** *adj* |
| **unsharp** *adj* | **unsmiling** *adj* | **unspent** *adj* | **unstinting** *adj* |
| **unshaved** *adj* | **unsmokable** *adj* | **unspiritual** *adj* | **unstintingly** *adv* |
| **unshaven** *adj* | **unsmoothed** *adj* | **unsplit** *adj* | **unstitch** *adj* |
| **unshed** *adj* | **unsnuffed** *adj* | **unspoiled** *adj* | **unstrained** *adj* |
| **unsheltered** *adj* | **unsoiled** *adj* | **unspoilt** *adj* | **unstratified** *adj* |

few formal requirements ⟨*an ~ college course*⟩ **b** not having a patterned social organization ⟨*in a neighbourhood gang . . . with a relatively ~ system – Journal of Social Issues*⟩

**unstudied** /ˌunˈstudid/ *adj* not studied: e g **a(1)** not acquired by study **a(2)** unversed *in* **b** not done or planned for effect; spontaneous

**unsubstantial** /ˌunsəbˈstansh(ə)l/ *adj* lacking substance, firmness, or strength – **unsubstantially** *adv,* **unsubstantiality** *n*

**unsuccess** /ˌunsəkˈses/ *n* lack of success; failure

**unsuccessful** /ˌunsəkˈsesf(ə)l/ *adj* not meeting with or producing success – **unsuccessfully** *adv*

**unsuitable** /ˌunˈs(y)oohtəbl/ *adj* not suitable or fitting; inappropriate – **unsuitably** *adv,* **unsuitability** *n*

**unsung** /ˌunˈsung/ *adj* **1** not sung **2a** not celebrated or praised (e g in song or verse) ⟨*an ~ hero*⟩ **b** infrequently referred to; obscure

**unswathe** /ˌunˈswaydh/ *vt* to free from something that covers, wraps, or envelops

**unswear** /ˌunˈsweə/ *vb* **unswore** /ˌunˈswaw/; **unsworn** /-ˈswawn/ *archaic vi* to unsay or retract something sworn ~ *vt* to recant or recall (e g an oath), esp by a second oath

**unswerving** /ˌunˈswuhving/ *adj* **1** not turning aside **2** constant ⟨*~ loyalty*⟩ – **unswervingly** *adv*

**unsymmetrical** /ˌunsiˈmetrik(ə)l/ *adj* not symmetrical; ASYMMETRIC – **unsymmetrically** *adv*

**untack** /ˌunˈtak/ *vt* to remove the saddle and bridle from

**untangle** /ˌunˈtang-gl/ *vt* **1** to loose from tangles or entanglement; unravel **2** to make intelligible; clear up

**untapped** /ˌunˈtapt/ *adj* **1** not yet drawn from ⟨*an ~ keg*⟩ **2** not drawn on or used ⟨*as yet ~ markets*⟩

**untaught** /ˌunˈtawt/ *adj* **1** not trained or educated; ignorant **2** not acquired by teaching; natural, spontaneous ⟨*~ kindness*⟩

**untenable** /ˌunˈtenəbl/ *adj* **1** not able to be defended ⟨*an ~ opinion*⟩ **2** not fit or able to be occupied – **untenability** *n*

**untether** /ˌunˈtedhə/ *vt* to free from a tether

**unthinkable** /ˌunˈthingkəbl/ *adj* **1** not capable of being grasped by the mind; inconceivable **2** contrary to what is acceptable or probable; out of the question – **unthinkably** *adv,* **unthinkability** *n*

  *usage* Some people dislike the use of **unthinkable** for "monstrous", of things which actually exist or are happening ⟨*it's* **unthinkable** *that you're still paying all that tax*⟩.

**unthinking** /ˌunˈthingking/ *adj* **1** not taking thought; heedless, unmindful **2** lacking concern for others; inconsiderate **3** not having the power of thought – **unthinkingly** *adv*

**unthought** /ˌunˈthawt/ *adj* not anticipated; unexpected – often + *of* or *on*

**unthread** /ˌunˈthred/ *vt* **1** to draw or take out a thread from ⟨*~ a string of beads*⟩ **2** to make one's way through ⟨*~ a maze*⟩ **3** to disentangle ⟨*~ one's confused thoughts*⟩

**unthrone** /ˌunˈthrohn/ *vt* to dethrone

¹**untidy** /ˌunˈtiedi/ *adj* not neat; slovenly, disorderly – **untidily** *adv,* **untidiness** *n*

²**untidy** *vt* to make untidy

**untie** /ˌunˈtie/ *vt* **1** to free from something that fastens or restrains **2a** to separate out the knotted parts of **b** to disentangle,

---

resolve ⟨*~ the knotty problem of a traffic jam*⟩ ~ *vi* to become untied

¹**until** /unˈtil, ən-/ *prep* **1** up to as late as ⟨*stayed ~ morning*⟩ ⟨*not available ~ tomorrow*⟩ **2** up to as far as ⟨*stay on the train ~ Birmingham*⟩ [ME, fr *un-* unto, until (akin to OE *oth* to, until, OHG *unt* unto, until, OE *ende* end) + *til, till* till]

  *usage* Until is somewhat more formal than till, but the words are used interchangeably. Some people dislike the combination up until ⟨*up until now I've scarcely worn my wellies*⟩.

²**until** *conj* up to the time that; until such time as ⟨*play continued ~ it got dark*⟩ ⟨*never able to relax ~ he took up fishing*⟩ ⟨*ran ~ he was breathless*⟩ ⟨*~ he comes, let's play darts*⟩

¹**untimely** /unˈtiemli/ *adv, chiefly formal* **1** at an inopportune time; unseasonably **2** before the natural or proper time; prematurely

²**untimely** *adj* **1** occurring before the natural or proper time; premature ⟨*~ death*⟩ **2** inopportune, unseasonable ⟨*an ~ joke*⟩ ⟨*~ frost*⟩ – **untimeliness** *n*

**untitled** /unˈtietld/ *adj* **1** not named ⟨*an ~ novel*⟩ **2** not called by a title ⟨*~ nobility*⟩ **3** *obs* having no title or right to rule

**unto** /ˈuntoo, -tə/ *prep, archaic* TO 1, 2, 3 [ME, fr *un-* unto, until + *to*]

**untold** /unˈtohld/ *adj* **1** incalculable, vast ⟨*~ wealth*⟩ **2** not told or revealed

**untouchability** /ˌunˌtuchəˈbiləti/ *n* being untouchable; *esp* the state of being an untouchable

¹**untouchable** /unˈtuchəbl/ *adj* **1a** that cannot or may not be touched **b** exempt from criticism or control **c** unable to be equalled; unparalleled **2** lying beyond reach ⟨*~ mineral resources buried deep within the earth*⟩ **3** disagreeable or defiling to the touch

²**untouchable** *n* someone or something that is untouchable; *specif, often cap* a member of a large formerly segregated hereditary group in India who in traditional Hindu belief can defile a member of a higher caste by contact or proximity

**untouched** /unˈtucht/ *adj* **1** not touched or handled **2** not described, discussed, or dealt with ⟨*left the history of the town ~*⟩ **3a** *of food or drink* not tasted **b** in the original state or condition; not altered **4** not influenced; unaffected

**untoward** /ˌuntəˈwawd/ *adj* **1** unseemly, improper ⟨*~ behaviour*⟩ **2** marked by trouble or unhappiness; unlucky **3** not favourable; adverse, unfortunate **4** *archaic* difficult to guide, manage, or work with; unruly – **untowardly** *adv,* **untowardness** *n*

  *usage* The pronunciation /ˌuntəˈwawd/ rather than /ˌunˈtawd/ is recommended for BBC broadcasters.

**untrammelled** /unˈtraməld/ *adj* not held in check; given free play

**untread** /unˈtred/ *vt, archaic* to retrace

**untried** /unˈtried/ *adj* **1** not tested or proved by experience **2** not tried in court

**untrod** /unˈtrod/, **untrodden** /-d(ə)n/ *adj* not trod; unexplored

**untroubled** /unˈtrubld/ *adj* **1** not troubled; not made uneasy ⟨*remained ~ by the situation*⟩ **2** calm, tranquil

**untrue** /unˈtrooh/ *adj* **1** not faithful; disloyal **2** not level or exact ⟨*~ doors and windows*⟩ **3** inaccurate, false – **untruly** *adv*

---

| | | | |
|---|---|---|---|
| **unstriped** *adj* | **unsurpassable** *adj* | **unsystematically** *adv* | **unterrified** *adj* |
| **unstuffy** *adj* | **unsurpassed** *adj* | **unsystematized** *adj* | **untestable** *adj* |
| **unstylish** *adj* | **unsurprised** *adj* | **untactful** *adj* | **untested** *adj* |
| **unsubdued** *adj* | **unsurprising** *adj* | **untagged** *adj* | **unthanked** *adj* |
| **unsubmissive** *adj* | **unsurprisingly** *adv* | **untainted** *adj* | **unthankful** *adj* |
| **unsubsidized** *adj* | **unsusceptible** *adj* | **untalented** *adj* | **unthatched** *adj* |
| **unsubstantiated** *adj* | **unsuspected** *adj* | **untamable** *adj* | **unthawed** *adj* |
| **unsubtle** *adj* | **unsuspecting** *adj* | **untamed** *adj* | **untheatrical** *adj* |
| **unsuggestible** *adj* | **unsuspenseful** *adj* | **untanned** *adj* | **unthoughtful** *adj* |
| **unsuggestive** *adj* | **unsuspicious** *adj* | **untarnishable** *adj* | **unthreatened** *adj* |
| **unsuited** *adj* | **unsustainable** *adj* | **untarnished** *adj* | **unthreatening** *adj* |
| **unsullied** *adj* | **unsustained** *adj* | **untasted** *adj* | **unthrifty** *adj* |
| **unsuperstitious** *adj* | **unswayed** *adj* | **untaxed** *adj* | **untillable** *adj* |
| **unsupervised** *adj* | **unsweetened** *adj* | **unteachable** *adj* | **untilled** *adj* |
| **unsupportable** *adj* | **unsworn** *adj* | **untechnical** *adj* | **untired** *adj* |
| **unsupported** *adj* | **unsympathetic** *adj* | **untempered** *adj* | **untiring** *adj* |
| **unsuppressed** *adj* | **unsympathetically** *adv* | **untempted** *adj* | **untraceable** *adj* |
| **unsure** *adj* | **unsympathizing** *adj* | **untenantable** *adj* | **untraced** *adj* |
| **unsurfaced** *adj* | **unsynchronized** *adj* | **untenanted** *adj* | **untracked** *adj* |
| **unsurmountable** *adj* | **unsystematic** *adj* | **untended** *adj* | **untractable** *adj* |
| **unsurmounted** *adj* | **unsystematical** *adj* | **untenured** *adj* | **untraditional** *adj* |

**untruss** /un'trus/ *vb, archaic vt* **1** to untie, unfasten – in *untruss one's points* **2** to undress ~ *vi* to undo or take off one's clothes, esp one's breeches

**untruth** /ˌun'troohth/ *n* **1** lack of truthfulness **2** something untrue; a falsehood **3** *archaic* disloyalty

**untruthful** /un'troohthf(ə)l/ *adj* not telling the truth; false, lying ⟨*an* ~ *report*⟩ – **untruthfully** *adv*, **untruthfulness** *n*

**untuck** /un'tuk/ *vt* to release from being tucked up ~ *vi* to become untucked

**untutored** /un'tyoohtəd/ *adj* **1a** having no formal learning or education **b** naive, unsophisticated **2** not produced by instruction; native ⟨*his* ~ *shrewdness*⟩

**untwine** /un'twien/ *vt* **1** to disentangle **2** to remove, release, etc by unwinding ~ *vi* to become untwined

**untwist** /un'twist/ *vt* to separate the twisted parts of; untwine ~ *vi* to become untwisted

**untwisted** /un'twistid/ *adj* not twisted

**unused** /un'yoohst/ *sense 2* -'yoohzd/ *adj* **1** unaccustomed *to* ⟨~ *to crowds*⟩ **2** not used: eg **2a** fresh, new ⟨*set an* ~ *canvas on the easel*⟩ **b** not put to use ⟨~ *land*⟩ **c** not used up; accrued ⟨~ *leave*⟩

**unusual** /un'yoohzhooəl, -zhəl/ *adj* **1** uncommon, rare **2** different, unique ⟨*an* ~ *painting*⟩ – **unusually** *adv*, **unusualness** *n*

**unutterable** /un'ut(ə)rəbl/ *adj* **1** beyond the powers of description; inexpressible **2** out-and-out, downright ⟨*an* ~ *fool*⟩ – **unutterably** *adv*

**unvalued** /un'valyoohd/ *adj* **1a** not regarded as being of value **b** not appraised or assessed as being worth a certain value or sum **2** *obs* invaluable

**unvarnished** /ˌun'vahnisht/ *adj* **1** not adorned or glossed; plain, straightforward ⟨*told the* ~ *truth*⟩ **2** not varnished

**unveil** /un'vayl/ *vt* **1** to remove a veil or covering from ⟨~ *a statue*⟩ **2** to make public; divulge, reveal ⟨~*ing their plans for the new docks*⟩ ~ *vi* to remove a veil or protective cloak ⟨*modern Muslim women who* ~⟩

**unveiled** /un'vayld/ *adj* open, revealed ⟨~ *contempt*⟩

**unvocal** /un'vohkl/ *adj* **1** not eloquent or outspoken; inarticulate **2** not musical; discordant

**unvoice** /un'voys/ *vt* DEVOICE (pronounce without using the VOCAL CORDS)

**unvoiced** /un'voyst/ *adj* **1** not expressed in words **2** pronounced without vibration of the VOCAL CORDS; not voiced

**unwaged** /un'wayjd/ *adj, euph* out of work

**unwarrantable** /un'worəntəbl/, **unwarranted** /un'worəntid/ *adj* not justifiable; inexcusable – **unwarrantably** *adv*

**unwary** /un'weəri/ *adj* not alert; easily fooled or surprised; heedless – **unwarily** *adv*, **unwariness** *n*

**¹unwashed** /un'wosht/ *adj* not cleaned (as if) with soap and water

**²unwashed** *n* taking *pl vb, derog the* common people; *the* rabble – esp in *the great unwashed*

**unwavering** /un'wayv(ə)ring/ *adj* fixed, steadfast – **unwaveringly** *adv*

**unwearied** /un'wiərid/ *adj* not tired or jaded; fresh – **unweariedly** *adv*

**unweight** /un'wayt/ *vt* to reduce momentarily the force exerted by (eg a ski) on a surface

**unwell** /un'wel/ *adj* **1** in poor health **2** *euph* undergoing menstruation

**unwholesome** /un'hohlsəm/ *adj* **1** detrimental to physical, mental, or moral well-being; unhealthy ⟨~ *food*⟩ ⟨~ *pastimes*⟩ **2** offensive to the senses; loathsome – **unwholesomely** *adv*, **unwholesomeness** *n*

**unwieldy** /un'weeldi/ *adj* difficult to move or handle; cumbersome – **unwieldily** *adv*, **unwieldiness** *n*

**unwilled** /un'wild/ *adj* involuntary

**unwilling** /un'wiling/ *adj* **1** loath, reluctant ⟨*was* ~ *to learn*⟩ **2** done or given reluctantly ⟨*his* ~ *approval*⟩ – **unwillingly** *adv*, **unwillingness** *n*

**unwind** /un'wiend/ *vb* **unwound** /-'wownd/ *vt* to cause to uncoil; unroll ~ *vi* **1** to become unwound **2** to become less tense; relax

**unwisdom** /un'wizdəm/ *n* foolishness, folly

**unwise** /un'wiez/ *adj* foolish, imprudent – **unwisely** *adv*

**unwish** /un'wish/ *vt* **1** to take back (a wish) **2** to wish that (something) would stop or cease to be; wish away

**unwitting** /un'witing/ *adj* **1** not intended; inadvertent ⟨*an* ~ *mistake*⟩ **2** ignorant, unaware ⟨*an* ~ *accomplice*⟩ [ME, fr *un-* + *witting*, prp of *witten* to know – more at WIT] – **unwittingly** *adv*

**unwonted** /un'wohntid, -'won-/ *adj* out of the ordinary; unusual △ unwanted – **unwontedly** *adv*, **unwontedness** *n*

**unworldly** /un'wuhldli/ *adj* **1** not of this world; *specif* spiritual **2** naive, unsophisticated **3** not swayed by material considerations (eg of wealth or personal gain) – **unworldliness** *n*

**unworn** /ˌun'wawn/ *adj* **1** not impaired by use; not worn away **2** never worn; new **3** not jaded; fresh

**unworthy** /un'wuhdhi/ *adj* **1a** lacking in excellence or quality; poor **b** base, dishonourable **2** not deserving of attention **3** not suitable; undeserved ⟨~ *treatment*⟩ **4** not befitting a person's position or condition of life – often + *of* ⟨*behaviour* ~ *of an ambassador*⟩ – **unworthily** *adv*, **unworthiness** *n*

**unwrap** /un'rap/ *vb* **-pp-** *vt* to remove the wrapping from (eg a parcel) ~ *vi* to have the wrapping come off

**unwritten** /un'ritn/ *adj* **1** not (formally) written down; oral, traditional **2** containing no writing; blank

**unwritten constitution** *n* a constitution not written down in a single document but based chiefly on custom and precedent

**unwritten law** *n* a customary rule in a community which is strictly obeyed even though not embodied in a formal enactment

**unyielding** /un'yeelding/ *adj* **1** lacking in softness or flexibility **2** firm, obdurate – **unyieldingly** *adv*

**unyoke** /un'yohk/ *vt* **1** to free from a yoke or harness **2** to set free **3** to disjoin; TAKE APART ~ *vi, archaic* **1** to unharness a draught animal **2** to stop working

**unzip** /un'zip/ *vb* **-pp-** to open or be opened (as if) by means of a zip

**¹up** /up/ *adv* **1a** at or towards a relatively high level; *specif* away from the centre of the earth ⟨*live* ~ *in the mountains*⟩ ⟨~ *onto the roof*⟩ **b** from beneath the ground or water to the surface **c** above the horizon ⟨*sun came* ~⟩ **d** upstream **e** in or to a raised or upright position ⟨*sit* ~⟩ ⟨*hands* ~!⟩ ⟨*keep the windows* ~⟩ ⟨*turn your collar* ~⟩; *specif* out of bed ⟨*soon be* ~ *and about*⟩ **f** off or out of the ground or a surface ⟨*pull* ~ *a daisy*⟩ ⟨*lift the piano* ~⟩ ⟨*flowers coming* ~⟩ ⟨*flying 30 000 feet* ~⟩ **g** UPWARDS 1c **h** from below out through the mouth – compare BRING UP, THROW UP **i** to the top; *esp* so as to be full ⟨*top* ~ *the radiator*⟩ **j** in or into the saddle ⟨*a new jockey* ~⟩ **2a** with greater intensity or activity ⟨*speak* ~⟩ **b** in or into a state of relatively high intensity or activity ⟨*turn the radio* ~⟩ **c** into a faster pace or higher gear ⟨*change* ~ *from second to third*⟩ **3a** in or into a relatively high condition or status ⟨*family went* ~ *in the world*⟩ – sometimes used interjectionally as an expression of approval ⟨~ *BBC 2! – The Listener*⟩ **b** above a normal or former level ⟨*sales are* ~⟩ ⟨*men* ~ *from the ranks*⟩: eg **b(1)** UPWARDS 2 ⟨*from the third form* ~⟩ ⟨*prices going* ~ *and* ~⟩ **b(2)** higher in price ⟨*bacon is* ~⟩ **c** ahead of an opponent ⟨*we're three points* ~⟩ ⟨*two strokes* ~ *after nine holes*⟩ **4a(1)** in or into existence, evidence, prominence, or prevalence ⟨*new houses haven't been* ~ *long*⟩ ⟨*with his sergeant's stripes* ~⟩ – compare PUT UP, SET UP **a(2)** in or into operation or full power ⟨*get* ~ *steam*⟩ **b** under consideration or attention ⟨*bring* ~ *for discussion*⟩ ⟨*licence* ~ *for renewal*⟩; *esp* before a court ⟨~ *for robbery*⟩ **5** so as to be together ⟨*add* ~ *the figures*⟩ ⟨*gather* ~ *the apples*⟩ **6a** entirely, completely ⟨*eat* ~ *your spinach*⟩ ⟨*clean* ~ *the house*⟩

---

| | | | |
|---|---|---|---|
| **untrained** *adj* | **untrimmed** *adj* | **untypically** *adv* | **unveracious** *adj* |
| **untransferable** *adj* | **untroublesome** *adj* | **unusable** *adj* | **unverbalized** *adj* |
| **untransformed** *adj* | **untrusting** *adj* | **unutilized** *adj* | **unverifiable** *adj* |
| **untranslatable** *adj* | **untrustworthy** *adj* | **unuttered** *adj* | **unverified** *adj* |
| **untranslated** *adj* | **untufted** *adj* | **unvaccinated** *adj* | **unversed** *adj* |
| **untravelled** *adj* | **untunable** *adj* | **unvanquished** *adj* | **unvexed** *adj* |
| **untraversed** *adj* | **untuneful** *adj* | **unvaried** *adj* | **unviable** *adj* |
| **untreated** *adj* | **unturned** *adj* | **unvarying** *adj* | **unvisited** *adj* |
| **untrendy** *adj* | **untypical** *adj* | **unventilated** *adj* | **unvulcanized** *adj* |

⟨*sell* ~ *the farm*⟩ **b** so as to be firmly closed, joined, or fastened ⟨*button* ~ *your coat*⟩ ⟨*tie* ~ *the parcel*⟩ ⟨*nail* ~ *the door*⟩ **c** so as to be fully inflated **7** in or into storage ⟨*lay* ~ *supplies*⟩ **8** in a direction conventionally the opposite of down: **8a(1)** to the direction from which the wind is blowing **a(2)** with the rudder in the direction opposite to that from which the wind is blowing – used with reference to a ship's helm **b(1)** in or towards the north **b(2)** to or at the top **c** so as to arrive or approach ⟨*walked* ~ *to her*⟩ – compare TURN UP **d** to or at the rear of a theatrical stage **e** *chiefly Br* to or in the capital of a country or a university city ⟨~ *in London*⟩ **9** in or into parts ⟨*chop* ~⟩ **10** to a stop – usu + *draw, bring, fetch,* or *roll* [partly fr ME *up* upwards, fr OE *ūp;* partly fr ME *uppe* on high, fr OE; both akin to OHG *ūf* up, L *sub* under, Gk *hypo* under, *hyper* over – more at OVER] – **up and down 1** TO AND FRO **2** HERE AND THERE **3** continually getting up and sitting or lying down alternately ⟨*was up and down all night with the child's toothache*⟩ – **up to 1** – used to indicate an upward limit or boundary ⟨*sank up to his knees in mud*⟩ ⟨*up to 50 000 copies a month*⟩ **2** as far as; until ⟨*worked up to the last minute*⟩ ⟨*read up to page 37*⟩ **3a** equal to ⟨*didn't feel up to par*⟩ **b** good enough for ⟨*my German isn't up to reading Schiller*⟩ **4** engaged in ⟨*what's he up to?*⟩ ⟨*up to no good*⟩ **5** being the responsibility of ⟨*it's up to me*⟩ – **up to one's armpits/ears/ eyes/eyebrows/neck** deeply involved; heavily implicated

²**up** *adj* **1a** moving, inclining, or directed upwards ⟨*the* ~ *escalator*⟩ ⟨*on the* ~ *slope*⟩ **b** heading in a direction regarded as up ⟨*the* ~ *train to Oxford*⟩ **2** ready, prepared ⟨*dinner's* ~!⟩ **3** prepared to fight – compare UP IN ARMS **4** GOING ON, TAKING PLACE; *esp* being the matter ⟨*find out what is* ~⟩ **5** at an end ⟨*time's* ~⟩; *esp* hopeless ⟨*it's all* ~ *with him now*⟩ **6a** well informed ⟨*well* ~ *in the subject*⟩ **b** ABREAST 2 ⟨~ *on the news*⟩ ⟨~ *on her homework*⟩ **7** *of a road* being repaired; having a broken surface **8** *of a ball in court games* having bounced only once on the ground or floor after being hit by one's opponent and therefore playable ⟨*not* ~⟩ – **up against** faced with; confronting – **up against it** in great difficulties

³**up** *vb* **-pp-** *informal vi* – used with *and* and another verb to indicate that the action of the following verb is either surprisingly or abruptly initiated ⟨*he* ~*ped and married a showgirl*⟩ ⟨*until one day my husband* ~*ped and left – Spare Rib*⟩ ~ *vt* **1** to increase ⟨*they* ~*ped the price of milk*⟩ **2** to raise ⟨~*ped anchor and sailed away*⟩ **3** RAISE 8c (increase a bet)

⁴**up** *prep* **1a** up along, round, through, towards, in, into, or on ⟨*walk* ~ *the hill*⟩ ⟨*water* ~ *my nose*⟩ **b** at the top of ⟨*the office is* ~ *those stairs*⟩ **2** *Br nonstandard* (up) to ⟨*going* ~ *the West End*⟩

⁵**up** *n* **1** an upward slope **2** *usu pl* a period or state of prosperity or success – compare UPS AND DOWNS **3** the part of a ball's trajectory in which it is still rising after having bounced ⟨*hit the ball on the* ~⟩

‚**up-and-'coming** *adj* likely to advance or succeed

‚**up-and-'down** *adj* **1** marked by alternate upward and downward movement **2** perpendicular or almost so **3** hilly **4** marked by alternate success and failure

‚**up-and-'downer** *n, informal* an argument, quarrel

‚**up-and-'up** *n* – **on the up-and-up** increasingly successful ⟨*his career's* on the up-and-up⟩

**Upanishad** /ooh'panishad, ooh'pahnishahd/ *n* a collection of philosophical treatises forming the main body of Hindu scriptures [Skt *upaniṣad,* lit., act of sitting down near something, fr *upa* near to + *ni* down + *sīdati* he sits] – **Upanishadic** *adj*

**upas** /'yoohpəs/ *n* **1a** a tall Asian and E Indian evergreen tree (*Antiaris toxicaria*) of the fig family with a poisonous milky juice that acts on the heart and is used as an arrow poison **b** a Javanese shrub or tree (*Strychnos tieuté* of the family Loganiaceae) that yields a juice that has effects like strychnine and is used as an arrow poison **2** a poisonous concentrate of the juice of a upas tree [Malay *pohon upas* poison tree, fr *pohon* tree +

*upas* poison]

¹**upbeat** /'up‚beet/ *n* an unaccented (eg the last) beat in a musical bar

²**upbeat** *adj, chiefly NAm informal* optimistic, cheerful

**up-bow** /'up ‚boh/ *n* an upward stroke in playing a bowed instrument (eg a violin) in which the bow is moved across the strings from the tip to the handle (NUT 4b)

**upbraid** /up'brayd/ *vt* to scold or reproach severely *synonyms* see ²SCOLD [ME *upbreyden,* fr OE *ūpbregdan,* prob fr *ūp* up + *bregdan* to move suddenly, snatch – more at BRAID] – **upbraider** *n*

**upbringing** /'up‚bring‚ing/ *n* early training; *esp* a particular way of bringing up a child ⟨*had a strict Calvinist* ~⟩

**upbuild** /up'bild/ *vt* **upbuilt** /up'bilt/ to develop; BUILD UP – **upbuilder** *n*

**upcast** /'up‚kahst/ *n* **1** something cast up (eg by digging) **2** a shaft or passage through which air returns to the surface from a mine – compare DOWNCAST

**upcoast** /'up‚kohst/ *adv or adj* in the direction along the coast regarded as up ⟨*to an* ~ *village*⟩

**upcoming** /'up‚kuming/ *adj, NAm* about to happen; forthcoming

‚**up-'country** *adj* **1** (characteristic) of an inland, upland, or outlying region **2** *chiefly derog* not socially or culturally sophisticated; simple – **up-country** *n or adv*

¹**update** /‚up'dayt/ *vt* to bring up to date

²**update** /'up‚dayt/ *n* an act of updating ⟨*a computer file* ~⟩

**updraught** /'up‚drahft/ *n* an upward movement of air or other gas

**upend** /‚up'end/ *vt* **1** to cause to stand on end ⟨~ *a barrel*⟩ **2** *informal* to affect to the point of being very upset ⟨*a. . . literary shocker, designed to* ~ *the credulous matrons* – Wolcott Gibbs⟩ **3** *informal* to beat, defeat **4** *informal* to knock down ⟨~*ed him with a punch to the jaw*⟩ ~ *vi* to rise up on end

**upfield** /‚up'feeld/ *adv or adj* downfield

**up front** *adj, chiefly NAm* uninhibitedly honest; candid

¹**upgrade** /'up‚grayd/ *n* **1** an increase, rise **2** *NAm* an upward gradient or slope

²**upgrade** /‚up'grayd/ *vt* to raise or improve the grade of: eg **a** to improve (livestock) by breeding with purebred males; GRADE 3 **b** to advance to a job requiring a higher level of skill or greater responsibility **c** to raise the classification and usu the price of (a product) without improving the quality

**upgrowth** /'up‚grohth/ *n* the process of growing upwards; development; *also* a product or result of this

**upgun** /up'gun/ *vt* **-nn-** to replace the gun of (eg a tank) with a larger weapon

**upheaval** /up'heevl/ *n* **1** an upheaving, esp of part of the earth's crust **2** (an instance of) extreme agitation or radical change

**upheave** /‚up'heev/ *vt* to heave up; lift ~ *vi* to move upwards, esp with power – **upheaver** *n*

¹**uphill** /'up‚hil/ *n* rising ground; ascent

²**uphill** /‚up'hil/ *adv* **1** upwards on a hill or incline **2** against difficulties ⟨*seemed to be working* ~⟩

³**uphill** *adj* **1** situated on high ground **2** going up; ascending **3** difficult, laborious ⟨*an* ~ *struggle*⟩

**uphold** /up'hohld/ *vt* **upheld** /-held/ **1a** to give support to; maintain ⟨~ *morale in the besieged city*⟩ **b** to support or defend against an opponent or challenge ⟨~ *the ruling of the lower court*⟩ **2a** to give physical support to; keep erect **b** to lift up; raise *synonyms* see ¹SUPPORT – **upholder** *n*

**upholster** /up'hohlstə, -'hol-/ *vt* to provide with upholstery – compare WELL-UPHOLSTERED [back-formation fr *upholstery*] – **upholsterer** *n*

**upholstery** /-ri/ *n* **1** material (eg fabric, padding, and springs) used to make a soft covering, esp for a seat **2** the work of one who upholsters [ME *upholdester* dealer in small articles, upholsterer, fr *upholden* to uphold, fr *up* + *holden* to hold]

| | | | |
|---|---|---|---|
| unwalled *adj* | unwearying *adj* | unwept *adj* | unworkable *adj* |
| unwanted *adj* | unweathered *adj* | unwifely *adj* | unworked *adj* |
| unwarlike *adj* | unweave *vt* | unwinking *adj* | unworkmanlike *adj* |
| unwarmed *adj* | unwed *adj* | unwinnable *adj* | unworried *adj* |
| unwarned *adj* | unwedded *adj* | unwithered *adj* | unwounded *adj* |
| unwatched *adj* | unweeded *adj* | unwitnessed *adj* | unwoven *adj* |
| unwaxed *adj* | unwelcome *adj* | unwomanly *adj* | unwrinkled *adj* |
| unweaned *adj* | unwelcoming *adj* | unwon *adj* | unwrought *adj* |
| unwearable *adj* | unwelded *adj* | unwooded *adj* | |

**upkeep** /'up,keep/ n (the cost of) maintaining or being maintained in good condition

**upland** /'upland/ n, **uplands** n pl (an area of) high land, esp when inland or some distance from the sea – **upland** adj, **uplander** n

¹**-uple** /-yoopl/ comb form (→ adj) **1** having the specified number of units or members ⟨octuple⟩ **2** being the specified number of times as great or many ⟨octuple⟩ [L -uplus (as in duplus double, quadruplus quadruple)]

²**-uple** comb form (→ vb) to make or become the specified number of times as many (octuple)

¹**uplift** /up'lift/ vt **1a** to raise, elevate **b** to cause (a part of the earth's surface) to be raised above adjacent areas **2** to improve the spiritual, social, or intellectual condition of – **uplifter** n

²**uplift** /'up,lift/ n an act, process, result, or cause of uplifting ⟨bra that gives ~⟩: e g **a(1)** the uplifting of a part of the earth's surface **a(2)** an uplifted mass of land **b** a moral or social improvement **c** an influence intended to uplift

**upmanship** /'upmanship/ n, informal one-upmanship

**up-'market** adj being, producing, dealing in, or using goods designed to appeal (e g in prestige value, quality, or price) to the more prosperous or higher-status section of a market – **up-market** adv

**upmost** /'up,mohst/ adj uppermost

¹**upon** /ə'pon/ prep on – formal except in certain phrases ⟨once ~ a time⟩

²**upon** adv, obs **1** on the surface; on it **2** thereafter, thereon

¹**upper** /'upə/ adj **1a** higher in physical position, rank, or order ⟨the ~ arm⟩ **b** farther inland ⟨the ~ Thames⟩ **2** being the branch of a legislature consisting of two houses that is usu more restricted in membership, is in many cases less powerful, and possesses greater traditional prestige than the lower house ⟨in Britain, the House of Lords is the ~ house⟩ **3a** being a layer of rock relatively near the earth's surface **b** cap of or being a later division of a specified geological or archaeological period, system of rocks, etc ⟨Upper Carboniferous⟩ – see also **get/have the upper** HAND, **(keep a) stiff upper** LIP [ME, fr uppe up + ¹-er]

²**upper** n something that is upper: e g **a** the part of a shoe or boot above the sole **b** an upper tooth or denture – **on one's uppers** at the end of one's resources; esp penniless

³**upper** n, informal a stimulant drug; esp AMPHETAMINE – compare DOWNER 1 [up + ²-er]

**upper atmosphere** n the part of the atmosphere that lies above the TROPOSPHERE (lowest atmospheric layer)

**upper bound** n a number greater than or equal to every element of a given mathematical set

**upper-'case** adj, of a letter capital

**upper case** n **1** a TYPECASE (tray for holding printing type) containing capitals and usu small capitals, fractions, symbols, and accents **2** capital letters [fr its being orig the upper of a pair of typecases]

**upper class** n, **upper classes** n pl the class occupying the highest position in a society; esp the wealthy or the aristocracy – **upper-class** adj

**upper crust** n taking sing or pl vb, informal the highest social class

**uppercut** /'upə,kut/ n a swinging blow (e g in boxing) directed upwards with a bent arm – **uppercut** vb

**upper hand** n the mastery, advantage – + have, get, or gain ⟨was determined not to let his opponent get the ~⟩

**uppermost** /'upə,mohst/ adv in or into the highest or most prominent position – **uppermost** adj

**upperpart** /'upə,paht/ n a part lying on the upper side, esp of an animal

**upper partial** n, music OVERTONE 1a

**upper school** n a school or part of a school for older pupils (e g aged from 14 to 18)

**upper-'second** n a level of honours degree between a first and a LOWER-SECOND

**upper sixth** n, often cap U&S the 2nd (and 3rd) year of a school SIXTH FORM

**uppish** /'upish/ adj **1** hit up and travelling far in the air; also producing when hit an effect in the object hit ⟨an ~ stroke by Boycott⟩ **2** informal UPPITY – **uppishly** adv, **uppishness** n

**uppity** /'upəti/ adj, informal putting on airs of superiority; supercilious, arrogant [prob fr up + -ity (arbitrary suffix)] – **uppityness** n

**upraise** /up'rayz/ vt to raise or lift up; elevate

**uprate** /,up'rayt/ vt **1** to raise in rank, status, size, or power ⟨the weather service officially ~d its caution to "a warning" – The Guardian⟩ **2** to increase, esp in order to keep pace with inflation ⟨~d pensions⟩

**uprear** /up'riə/ vt to lift up; raise ⟨~ed a monument⟩

¹**upright** /'up,riet/ adj **1a(1)** perpendicular, vertical **a(2)** of a photograph PORTRAIT (tall and oblong) **b** erect in carriage or posture **c** having the main part perpendicular ⟨an ~ freezer⟩ **2** characterized by strong moral correctness; honourable synonyms see VERTICAL – **uprightly** adv, **uprightness** n

²**upright** adv in an upright or vertical position

³**upright** n **1** being upright; perpendicular ⟨a pillar out of ~⟩ **2** something that stands upright; esp a vertical support **3** **upright piano, upright** a piano with vertical frame and strings – compare GRAND PIANO **4** the answer to an acrostic, being a word read vertically from the initial or other letters of a list of words discovered from rhyming clues

¹**uprise** /up'riez/ vi **uprose** /up'rohz/; **uprisen** /-'riz(ə)n/ **1a** to rise higher or to a higher position ⟨whisper of gongs and trumpets uprose – James Hilton⟩ **b** to rise from a lying or sitting position; GET UP **2** to come into view, esp from below the horizon – **upriser** n

²**uprise** /'up,riez/ n **1** an act of uprising **2** an upward slope

**uprising** /'up,riezing/ n an act or instance of rising up; esp a usu localized rebellion, esp against an established government synonyms see REBELLION

**upriver** /,up'rivə/ adv or adj towards or at a point nearer the source of a river

**uproar** /'up,raw/ n a state of commotion or violent disturbance [by folk etymology fr D oproer, fr MD, fr op up + roer motion; akin to OE ūp up & to OE hrēran to stir]

**uproarious** /,up'rawri·əs/ adj **1** characterized by noise and disorder **2** very noisy and full ⟨~ laughter⟩ **3** extremely funny ⟨an ~ comedy⟩ – **uproariously** adv, **uproariousness** n

**uproot** /,up'rooht/ vt **1** to remove by pulling up by the roots **2** to remove as if by pulling up; destroy **3** to displace from a country or habitual environment – **uprooter** n

**uprush** /'up,rush/ n **1a** an upward rush (e g of gas or liquid) **b** an upward rush (e g of a feeling or emotion) from the unconscious or subconscious **2** a sudden increase

**upsadaisy** /'upsə,dayzi/ interj upsydaisy

**ups and downs** n pl alternating rises and falls, esp in fortune

¹**upset** /up'set/ vb **-tt-**; **upset** vt **1** to thicken and shorten (e g a heated bar of iron) by hammering on the end **2** to knock over; overturn **3a** to trouble mentally or emotionally ⟨~ting news⟩ **b** to throw into disorder **c** to invalidate, nullify **d** to defeat, esp unexpectedly **4** to make physically unwell or somewhat ill ~ vi to become overturned – **upsetter** n

²**upset** /'up,set/ n **1** an act or result of upsetting; a state of being upset: e g **1a** a minor physical disorder ⟨a stomach ~⟩ **b** an emotional disturbance **c** an unexpected defeat (e g in sports or politics) **2** a part of a metal bar or rod (e g the head on a bolt) that is upset **3** a SWAGE (tool for shaping metal) used in upsetting

**upset price** n the minimum price fixed for property offered at auction or public sale

**upshift** /'upshift/ vi, NAm to put a vehicle into a higher gear – **upshift** n

**upshot** /'up,shot/ n, informal the final result; the outcome [¹up + ¹shot; orig referring to the final shot in an archery contest]

**upside down** /'up,sied/ adv **1** with the upper and the lower parts reversed **2** in or into great disorder or confusion [alter. of ME up so doun, fr up + so + doun down] – **upside-down** adj

¹**upsides** /'upsiedz/ adv, Br informal so as to be even, equal, or revenged – usu + of or with

²**upsides** prep, Br informal level with; beside ⟨jumped the last ... ~ Comedy of Errors – The Guardian⟩

**upsilon** /'upsilon, -'sie-, 'yoohp-/ n the 20th letter of the Greek alphabet [MGk y psilon, lit., simple y; fr the desire to distinguish it from oi, which was pronounced the same in later Greek]

**upspring** /up'spring/ vi **upsprang** /up'sprang/, **upsprung** /up'sprung/ **1** to spring up ⟨~ing curls⟩ **2** to come into being ⟨the ~ing of Romanesque art – Cambridge Medieval History⟩

¹**upstage** /,up'stayj/ adv at the rear of a theatrical stage; also away from the audience or film or television camera

²**upstage** adj **1** of or at the rear of a stage **2** informal haughty, aloof

³**upstage** n the part of a stage that is farthest from the audience or camera

**⁴upstage** *vt* **1** to force (an actor) to face away from the audience by holding a dialogue with him/her from an upstage position **2** to steal attention from; steal the show from **3** *informal* to treat snobbishly

**¹upstairs** /ˌup'steəz/ *adv* **1** up the stairs; to or on a higher floor **2** *informal* to or at a higher position, usu with less responsibility ⟨*quietly moved him* ~ *to the House of Lords*⟩ **3** *informal* in the head ⟨*she's all vacant* ~ – J T Farrell⟩ – **kick upstairs** *informal* to promote to a higher but less desirable position

**²upstairs** *adj* situated above the stairs, esp on an upper floor ⟨*an* ~ *lavatory*⟩

**³upstairs** /'-,-, ,-'-/ *n* **1** the part of a building above the ground floor **2** *taking sing or pl vb* people occupying the upper part of a building; *esp* the householders of a house with servants

**upstanding** /up'standing/ *adj* **1** erect, upright **2** marked by integrity; honest – **upstandingness** *n*

**upstart** /'up,staht/ *n* one who has risen suddenly (e g from a low position to wealth or power); *esp* one who claims more personal importance than he/she warrants [*upstart* (to rise suddenly), fr ME *upsterten*, fr *up* + *sterten* to start] – **upstart** *adj*

**upstate** /'up,stayt/ *adj* in or relating to the (northerly) part of a US state that is away from metropolitan areas – compare DOWNSTATE – **upstate** *adv*, **upstater** *n*

**upstream** /ˌup'streem/ *adv or adj* in the direction opposite to the flow of a stream

**upstroke** /'up,strohk/ *n* an upward stroke ⟨*the* ~ *of a pen*⟩

**upsurge** /'up,suhj/ *n* **1** a rapid or sudden rise **2** a rush, burst ⟨*sudden* ~s *of kindness* – *Punch*⟩

**¹upsweep** /'up,sweep/ *vb* **upswept** /'upswept/ to sweep upwards; curve or slope upwards

**²upsweep** *n* an upward sweep; *esp* a hairstyle in which the hair is brushed up to the top of the head

**upswept** /'up,swept/ *adj* swept, curved, or brushed upwards ⟨*roofs . . . have the familiar* ~ *curves* – *New Yorker*⟩; *specif* brushed up to the top of the head ⟨*an* ~ *hairstyle*⟩

**upswing** /'up,swing/ *n* **1** an upward swing **2** a marked increase or rise (e g in activity)

**upsydaisy** /'upsə,dayzi/ *interj* – used to express comfort and reassurance (e g to a small child after a fall) [irreg fr *up*]

**uptake** /'up,tayk/ *n* **1** a ventilating shaft leading upwards **2** the act or process of physically absorbing and incorporating something; *esp* the uptake of food, nutrients, oxygen, etc by or into a living organism or its cells **3** *informal* understanding, comprehension ⟨*quick on the* ~⟩ [(3) Sc *uptake* to understand]

**up-tempo** /'tempoh/ *adj or n* (played at) a fast-moving tempo (e g in jazz)

**upthrow** /'up,throw/ *n* an upward displacement; an upheaval, upthrust; *esp* an upward displacement or movement of a body of rock on one side of a fault, relative to the rock on the other side

**¹upthrust** /'up,thrust/ *vt* to thrust up; *esp* to raise (a part of the earth's surface) in an upthrust ~ *vi* to rise with an upward thrust

**²upthrust** *n* an upward thrust; *esp* an upheaval or uplift of part of the earth's surface

**uptight** /ˌup'tiet/ *adj, informal* **1** tense, nervous, or uneasy **2** angry, indignant **3** rigidly conventional ⟨*the* ~ *and antiseptic white community* – J M Culkin⟩ – **uptightness** *n*

**uptilt** /up'tilt/ *vt* to tilt upwards

**uptime** /'up,tiem/ *n* the time during which a piece of equipment is functioning or able to function – compare DOWNTIME

**,up-to-'date** *adj* **1** extending up to the present time; including the latest information ⟨~ *maps*⟩ **2** abreast of the times; modern ⟨~ *methods*⟩ **3** fully informed of the latest developments ⟨*keep me* ~ *on your plans*⟩ – **up-to-dateness** *n*

**,up-to-the-'minute** *adj* **1** extending up to the immediate present; including the very latest information **2** completely up-to-date

**'up-to-,weight** *adj* able to carry the necessary weight ⟨*an* ~ *hunter*⟩

**uptown** /up'town/ *adv, adj, or n, chiefly NAm* (to, towards, or in) the upper part or residential district of a town or city

**¹upturn** /ˌup'tuhn/ *vt* **1** to turn up or over **2** to direct upwards ~ *vi* to turn upwards

**²upturn** /'up,tuhn/ *n* an upward turn, esp towards better conditions or higher prices

**upward** /'upwood/ *adj* **1** moving or extending upwards;

ascending ⟨*an* ~ *movement*⟩ **2** rising to a higher pitch – **upwardly** *adv*, **upwardness** *n*

**upwards** /'upwədz/ *adv* **1a** from a lower to a higher place or level; in the opposite direction from down ⟨*the kite rose* ~⟩ **b** upstream **c** so as to expose a particular surface ⟨*held out his hand, palm* ~⟩ **2** from a lower to a higher condition; UP **3a** ⟨*young lawyers moving* ~⟩ **3a** to an indefinitely greater amount, price, figure, or rank ⟨*from £5* ~⟩ **b** towards a higher number, degree, or rate ⟨*attendance figures have risen* ~⟩ **4** towards or into later years ⟨*from his youth* ~⟩ – **upwards of** more than; IN EXCESS OF ⟨*they cost* upwards of £25⟩

**upwell** /up'wel/ *vi* to well up; *specif* to move or flow upwards ⟨*lava* ~ing *from the depths of a fissure*⟩

**upwind** /ˌup'wind/ *adv or adj* in the direction from which the wind is blowing

**up yours** *interj, Br vulg* – used to express contemptuous defiance and dismissal [short for *up your arse*]

**¹ur-, uro-** *comb form* **1** urine ⟨*uric*⟩ **2** urinary tract ⟨*urology*⟩ **3** urinal and ⟨*urogenital*⟩ **4** urea ⟨*uracil*⟩ [NL, fr Gk *our-, ouro-*, fr *ouron* urine – more at URINE]

**²ur-, uro-** *comb form* tail ⟨*urochord*⟩ [NL, fr Gk *our-, ouro-*, fr *oura* tail – more at SQUIRREL]

**Ur-** /ooə, uh/ *prefix* **1** original; primitive ⟨Ur-*form*⟩ **2** original version of ⟨Ur-*Hamlet*⟩ [Ger, fr OHG *ir-, ur-* thoroughly (perfective prefix) – more at ABIDE]

**uracil** /'yooərəsil/ *n* a chemical compound, $C_4H_4N_2O_2$, that is a PYRIMIDINE and one of the four BASES whose order in the chain of repeated units making up RNA constitutes information that codes for the production of proteins – compare ADENINE, CYTOSINE, GUANINE, THYMINE [ISV ¹*ur-* + *ac*etic + *-il* (substance relating to)]

**uraemia** /yoo'reemyə, -mi-ə/ *n* the accumulation in the blood, usu in severe kidney disease, of poisonous substances normally excreted in the urine [NL, fr ¹*-ur* + *-aemia*]

**uraeus** /yoo'rayəs/ *n, pl* **uraei** /-ayie/ a representation of a small cobra (ASP) on the headdress of ancient Egyptian rulers, symbolizing absolute sovereignty [NL, fr LGk *ouraios*, a snake]

**Ural-Altaic** /ˌyooərəl al'tayik/ *n* a hypothetical superfamily of languages comprising the Uralic and Altaic language families – **Ural-Altaic** *adj*

**¹Uralic** /yoo(ə)'ralik, -'ray-/, **Uralian** /yoo(ə)'raliən, -'ray-/ *adj* of or constituting Uralic [*Ural* mountains in NW Asia]

**²Uralic** *n* a language family comprising the Finno-Ugric and Samoyed languages

**uralite** /'yooərəliet/ *n* a usu fibrous and dark green AMPHIBOLE (mineral present in many rocks) resulting from alteration of the mineral PYROXENE [Ger *uralit*, fr *Ural* mountains] – **uralitic** *adj*

**¹uran-, urano-** *comb form* sky; heavens ⟨*urano*metry⟩ [L, fr Gk *ouran-, ourano-*, fr *ouranos*]

**²uran-, urano-** *comb form* uranium ⟨*uran*yl⟩ [Fr, fr NL *uranium*]

**uranic** /yoo(ə)'ranik/ *adj* of or containing uranium, esp with a relatively high VALENCY [ISV]

**uranide** /'yooərənied/ *n* **1** uranium **2** a chemical element having an ATOMIC NUMBER (number of protons in the nucleus of an atom) greater than that of uranium; a TRANSURANIC element

**uraninite** /yooə'raniniet/ *n* a brownish-black radioactive mineral that is the chief source of uranium, consists of an oxide of uranium, $UO_2$, often together with the radioactive chemical element THORIUM, metallic RARE-EARTH ELEMENTS, and lead, and that when heated often gives off a gas consisting chiefly of helium [Ger *uranin* uraninite (fr NL *uranium*) + E *-ite*]

**uranium** /yoo(ə)'raynyəm, -ni·əm/ *n* a silvery heavy radioactive metallic chemical element that is found in several minerals, esp pitchblende and uraninite, and exists naturally as a mixture of three ISOTOPES (forms of an atom containing different numbers of neutrons) of MASS NUMBER (number of protons and neutrons in the nucleus of an atom) 234, 235, and 238 in the proportions of 0.006 per cent, 0.71 per cent, and 99.28 per cent respectively [NL, fr *Uranus*; fr the element being discovered soon after the planet]

**uranium 235** *n* a form of uranium having a MASS NUMBER (number of protons and neutrons in the nucleus of an atom) of 235, that is physically separable from natural uranium, and that when bombarded with slow-moving neutrons undergoes rapid FISSION (splitting) into smaller atoms with the release of neutrons and nuclear energy. It is chiefly used as a fuel in NUCLEAR REACTORS and atomic bombs.

**uranium 238** *n* an ISOTOPE (one of several forms of an atom containing different numbers of neutrons) of uranium of MASS NUMBER (number of protons and neutrons in the nucleus of an atom) 238 that absorbs fast-moving neutrons to form a uranium isotope of mass number 239 which then undergoes radioactive decay through the chemical element NEPTUNIUM to form the element PLUTONIUM of mass number 239. It is used in FAST BREEDER REACTORS as the raw material from which plutonium is produced for use in atomic bombs and NUCLEAR REACTORS.

**uranium hexafluoride** /ˌheksəˈflooəried/ *n* a readily vaporized chemical compound, $UF_6$, of uranium and fluorine that is used in one major process of separating URANIUM 235 from uranium

**uranium trioxide** /trieˈoksied/ *n* a brilliant orange chemical compound, $UO_3$, that is formed in the course of refining uranium and that has been used as a colouring agent for ceramic wares

**uranography** /ˌyooərəˈnogrəfi/ *n* the description and mapping of the heavens and celestial bodies [Gk *ouranographia* description of the heavens, fr *ouran-* uran- + *-graphia* -graphy] – **uranographic, uranographical** *adj*

**uranometry** /ˌyooərəˈnometri/ *n* **1** (the making of) a map or catalogue of celestial bodies, esp stars **2** the measurement of the heavens [NL *uranometria*, fr *uran-* + *-metria* -metry]

**uranous** /ˈyooərənəs/ *adj* of or containing uranium, esp with a relatively low VALENCY

**Uranus** /yoo(ə)ˈraynəs, ˈyooərənəs/ *n* the planet 7th in order from the sun [NL, fr LL *Uranus*, the sky personified as a god in Greco-Roman mythology, fr Gk *Ouranos*, fr *ouranos* sky, heaven]

**uranyl** /ˈyooərənil/ *adj or n* (being or containing) the chemical group $UO_2$, having a VALENCY of two [ISV]

**urate** /ˈyooəˌrayt/ *n* any of various chemical compounds (SALTS) formed by combination between URIC ACID and a metal atom or other chemical group [Fr, fr *urique* uric, fr E *uric*] – **uratic** *adj*

**urban** /ˈuhbən/ *adj* (characteristic) of or constituting a city or town [L *urbanus*, fr *urbs* city]

**urbane** /uhˈbayn/ *adj* notably polite or smooth in manner; suave *synonyms* see SUAVE *antonyms* clownish, bucolic [L *urbanus* urban, elegant, sophisticated] – **urbanely** *adv*

**urban guerrilla** *n* a terrorist who operates typically in towns and cities

**urbanism** /ˈuhbənizm/ *n* **1** the characteristic way of life of urban dwellers **2** *NAm* the study of the character and physical needs of urban societies **3** *NAm* urbanization

**urbanist** /ˈuhbənist/ *n, chiefly NAm* TOWN PLANNER – **urbanistic** *adj,* **urbanistically** *adv*

**urbanite** /ˈuhbəˌniet/ *n, chiefly NAm* a person living in a city

**urbanity** /uhˈbanəti/ *n* **1** being urbane **2** *pl* urbane acts or conduct; civilities

**urban·ize, -ise** /ˈuhbəˌniez/ *vt* **1** to cause to take on urban characteristics ⟨∼d *areas*⟩ **2** to impart an urban way of life to ⟨∼ *migrants from rural areas*⟩ – **urbanization** *n*

**urban renewal** *n* the planned replacement or rehabilitation of substandard urban buildings

**urban sprawl** *n* the uncontrolled and haphazard spread of urban developments (e g houses and shopping centres) on undeveloped land round a city

**urceolate** /ˈuhsi·əˌlət, -ˌlayt/ *adj, biology* shaped like an urn ⟨*the* ∼ *corolla of a bilberry*⟩ [NL *urceolatus*, fr L *urceolus,* dim. of *urceus* jug]

**urchin** /ˈuhchin/ *n* **1** a mischievous and impudent child; *esp* one who is small and scruffy **2** SEA URCHIN **3** *archaic or dial* a hedgehog [ME, hedgehog, fr MF *herichon,* fr L *ericius;* akin to Gk *chēr* hedgehog, L *horrēre* to bristle, tremble – more at HORROR]

**urchin cut** *n* a woman's short spiky haircut

**urd** /uhd/ *n* a bean plant (*Phaseolus mungo*) widely grown in warm regions for its edible blackish seed, for GREEN MANURE, or for animal feed; *also* the seed of this plant [Hindi]

**Urdu** /ˈooədooh, ˈuhdooh/ *n* an INDIC language that is an official language of Pakistan, is written usu in Persian script, and is widely used in India, esp by Muslims *synonyms* see HINDU [Hindi *urdū-zabān,* lit., camp language]

**-ure** /-yooə/ *suffix* (*vb* → *n*) **1** act or process of ⟨*exposure*⟩ ⟨*closure*⟩ **2** body performing (a specified function) ⟨*legislature*⟩ [ME, fr OF, fr L *-ura*]

**urea** /yooˈreeə, ˈyooəriə/ *n* a nitrogen-containing water-soluble chemical compound, $CO(NH_2)_2$, that is formed as the final product of protein breakdown, is present in the urine of mammals and some other animals, and is used, in a synthetic form made from CARBON DIOXIDE and ammonia, in the manufacture of plastics, in fertilizers, and in animal feeds [NL, fr Fr *urée,* fr *urine*]

**urea-formaldehyde resin** /fawˈmaldihied/ *n* a synthetic plastic material made from urea and FORMALDEHYDE and used chiefly in baking enamels, buttons, and electrical fittings

**urease** /ˈyooəriayz/ *n* an ENZYME occurring in many plants and some animal tissues that speeds up the breakdown of urea to CARBON DIOXIDE and ammonia

**uredinium** /ˌyooərəˈdiniəm/ *n, pl* **uredinia** /-iə/ (a spore-bearing structure of a RUST fungus containing) a usu brownish mass of developing urediospores that forms a blisterlike pustule beneath the outer skin (EPIDERMIS) of the plant on which the fungus is a parasite [NL, fr L *uredin-, uredo* burning, blight, fr *urere* to burn – more at EMBER] – **uredinial** *adj*

**urediospore** /yooəˈreedioh͵spaw/ *n* any of the thin-walled orange to reddish spores that are produced, usu in summer, by the uredinia of a RUST fungus and that spread the fungus to other plants [NL *uredium* + E *-o-* + *spore*]

**uredium** /yooəˈreediəm/ *n, pl* **uredia** /-iə/ a uredinium [NL, fr *uredo* uredostage, fr L, burning, blight] – **uredial** *adj*

**uredosorus** /yooə͵reedəˈsawrəs/ *n* a uredinium [NL, fr *uredo* + *sorus*]

**uredospore** /yooəˈreedə͵spaw/ *n* a urediospore

**uredostage** /yooəˈreedə͵stayj/ *n* the stage of a RUST fungus when urediospores are produced

**ureide** /ˈyooəri·ied/ *n* any of various ACYLS (acid-based compounds) derived from urea

**ureotelic** /ˌyooəri·əˈtelik/ *adj* excreting nitrogen mostly in the form of urea ⟨∼ *mammals*⟩ – compare URICOTELIC [*urea* + *-o-* + *tel-* + *-ic;* fr urea being the end product] – **ureotelism** *n*

**ureter** /yoo(ə)ˈreetə/ *n* a duct that carries away urine from a kidney to the bladder or, in birds, reptiles, etc, to the CLOACA [NL, fr Gk *ourētēr,* fr *ourein* to urinate – more at URINE] – **ureteral, ureteric** *adj*

**urethane** /ˈyooərə͵thayn/, **urethan** /ˈyooərəthan/ *n* **1** a chemical compound, $NH_2COOC_2H_5$, that is used esp as a solvent, as an anaesthetic for small animals, and medicinally in the treatment of some tumours **2** POLYURETHANE [Fr *uréthane,* fr $^1$*ur-* + *éth-* eth- + *-ane*]

**urethr-, urethro-** *comb form* urethra ⟨*urethritis*⟩ ⟨*urethroscope*⟩ [NL, fr LL *urethra*]

**urethra** /yoo(ə)ˈreethrə/ *n, pl* **urethras, urethrae** /-thri/ the canal that in most mammals carries urine from the bladder out of the body, and in the male serves also to convey semen [LL, fr Gk *ourēthra,* fr *ourein* to urinate] – **urethral** *adj*

**urethritis** /ˌyooəriˈthrietəs/ *n* inflammation of the urethra [NL]

**urethroscope** /yooəˈreethrə͵skohp/ *n* an instrument for examining the urethra [ISV]

$^1$**urge** /uhj/ *vt* **1** to advocate or demand earnestly or pressingly ⟨∼d *greater cooperation between the government and the unions*⟩ **2** to undertake the accomplishment of with energy or enthusiasm ⟨∼ *the attack*⟩ **3a** to try to persuade or sway ⟨∼ *a guest to stay*⟩ **b** to serve as a motive or reason for **4** to force or impel in a specified direction or to greater speed ⟨*the dog* ∼d *the sheep towards the gate*⟩ **5** to stimulate, provoke ∼ *vi* to urge an argument, claim, etc [L *urgēre* – more at WREAK] – **urger** *n*

$^2$**urge** *n* a force or impulse that urges; *esp* a continuing impulse towards an activity or goal ⟨*felt the* ∼ *to sing*⟩

**urgent** /ˈuhjənt/ *adj* **1a** calling for immediate attention; pressing ⟨∼ *appeals*⟩ **b** conveying a sense of being urgent ⟨∼ *requests*⟩ **2** urging insistently; persistent, demanding [ME, fr MF, fr L *urgent-, urgens,* prp of *urgēre*] – **urgency** *n,* **urgently** *adv*

**-urgy** /-uhji/ *comb form* (→ *n*) technology; art; technique ⟨*metallurgy*⟩ ⟨*dramaturgy*⟩ [NL *-urgia,* fr Gk *-ourgia,* fr *-ourgos* working, fr *-o-* + *ergon* work – more at WORK]

**-uria** /-ˈyooəri·ə/ *comb form* (→ *n*) **1** usu abnormal presence or excess of (a specified substance) in urine ⟨*albumin*uria⟩ ⟨*py*uria⟩ **2** condition of producing (a specified amount of) urine ⟨*poly*uria⟩ [NL, fr Gk *-ouria,* fr *ouron* urine – more at URINE]

**urial, oorial** /ˈooəriəl/ *n* a Himalayan wild sheep (*Ovis vignei*) [Punjabi *hulreāl*]

**uric** /ˈyooərik/ *adj* of or found in urine

**uric acid** *n* a white odourless tasteless nearly insoluble chemical compound, $C_5H_4N_4O_3$, that is present in small quantities in the urine of some mammals and is the chief nitrogen-containing excretory product of birds, most reptiles, and some INVERTEBRATE animals, esp insects

**uricosuric** /ˌyooərikəˈsyooərik, -koh-/ *adj, esp of a drug* of or promoting the excretion of URIC ACID in the urine ⟨*probenecid is a ~ drug*⟩ [irreg fr *uric* + *uric*] – **uricosuric** *n*

**uricotelic** /ˌyooərikohˈtelik/ *adj* excreting nitrogen mostly in the form of URIC ACID ⟨*birds are typical ~ animals*⟩ – compare UREOTELIC [*uric* + *-o-* + *tel-* + *-ic;* fr uric acid being the end product] – **uricotelism** *n*

**uridine** /ˈyooərideen/ *n* a chemical compound (NUCLEOSIDE), $C_9H_{12}N_2O_6$, that forms part of RNA, contains URACIL, and is important in the form of its phosphates in the synthesis and breakdown of carbohydrates in living cells [ISV [1]*ur-* + *-idine*]

**Urim and Thummim** /ˌyooərim ən ˈthumim/ *n pl* sacred objects worn on the breastplate of a Jewish high priest in early times [part trans of Heb *ūrīm wĕthummīm*]

**urin-, urino-** *comb form* [1]UR- ⟨*urinogenital*⟩ ⟨*urinary*⟩ [ME, fr OF, fr L, fr *urina* urine]

**urinal** /yooˈ(ə)ˈrienl/ *n* **1** a container for receiving urine **2** a fixture used for urinating into, esp by men **3** a room, compartment, or building containing a urinal [ME, fr OF, fr LL, fr L *urina*]

**urinalysis** /ˌyooəriˈnaləsis/ *n* chemical analysis of the urine, usu for purposes of medical diagnosis [NL, irreg fr *urin-* + *analysis*]

**urinary** /ˈyooərin(ə)ri/ *adj* **1** of, occurring in, or being the organs concerned with the formation and discharge of urine **2** of or for urine **3** excreted as or in urine ⟨*~ nitrogen*⟩

**urinary bladder** *n* a membranous sac in many VERTEBRATE animals that temporarily stores urine excreted by the kidneys

**urinate** /ˈyooəriˌnayt/ *vi* to discharge urine – **urination** *n*

**urine** /ˈyooərin/ *n* the waste material that is secreted by the kidneys in VERTEBRATE animals, contains the end products of protein breakdown, and that has the form of a clear usu slightly acid pale yellow to amber liquid in mammals and is semisolid in birds and reptiles [ME, fr MF, fr L *urina;* akin to Gk *ouron* urine, *ourein* to urinate, OE *wæter* water] – **urinous** *adj*

**urinogenital** /ˌyooərinohˈjenitl/ *adj* of the genital and urinary organs; GENITOURINARY

**urinometer** /ˌyooəriˈnomitə/ *n* a small HYDROMETER (instrument for determining the density of liquids) used to measure the SPECIFIC GRAVITY (ratio of the density of a substance to that of water) of urine [ISV]

**urn** /uhn/ *n* **1** an ornamental vase on a pedestal used esp for preserving the ashes of the dead after cremation **2** a large closed container, usu with a tap at its base, in which large quantities of tea, coffee, etc may be heated or served [ME *urne*, fr L *urna*]

**uro-** – see [1], [2]UR-

**urocanic acid** /ˌyooərəˈkaynik/ *n* an acid, $C_6H_6N_2O_2$, that is normally present in human skin and probably acts as a screening agent against ultraviolet radiation [[1]*ur-* + *can*ine + *-ic;* fr its being first obtained from the urine of a dog]

**urochord** /ˈyooəroh,kawd/ *n* the NOTOCHORD (firm longitudinal rod analogous to a backbone) of a larva of a TUNICATE (primitive marine animal), which is typically restricted to the tail region [[2]*ur-* + NL *chorda* notochord, fr L, cord] – **urochordal** *adj*

**urochordate** /ˌyooərəˈkawdayt/ *n* TUNICATE (primitive marine animal) [NL *Urochordata*, former group name, fr [2]*ur-* + *chordatus* having a notochord, fr *chorda* notochord] – **urochordate** *adj*

**urochrome** /ˈyooərə,krohm/ *n* a yellow pigment that gives normal urine its colour

**urodele** /ˈyooərə,deel/ *n* any of an order (Urodela) of amphibians, including the newts and salamanders, that have a tail throughout life [Fr *urodèle*, deriv of Gk *oura* tail + *dēlos* evident, showing – more at SQUIRREL] – **urodele** *adj*

**urogenital** /ˌyooərohˈjenitl/ *adj* of the genital and urinary organs; GENITOURINARY [ISV]

**urokinase** /ˌyooərohˈkienayz/ *n* an ENZYME that breaks down protein, that is found in human urine and is used to dissolve blood clots (e g in the heart)

**urolith** /ˈyooərəlith/ *n* a stone in the urinary tract or system [ISV]

**urolithiasis** /ˌyooərohliˈthie•əsis/ *n* a condition characterized by the formation or presence of uroliths [NL, fr ISV *urolith*]

**urological** /ˌyooərəˈlojikl/ **urologic** /-ik/ *adj* of the urinary tract or urology

**urology** /yooˈ(ə)ˈroləji/ *n* a branch of medicine dealing with the urogenital tract – **urologist** *n*

**-uronic** /-yooˈ(ə)ˈronik/ *suffix* (→ *adj*) connected with urine – used in names of certain aldehyde-acids derived from sugars or compounds of such acids ⟨*hyal*uronic⟩ [Gk *ouron* urine]

**uronic acid** /yooəˈronik/ *n* any of a class of acidic chemical compounds of the general formula $HOOC(CHOH)_nCHO$, that contain both CARBOXYL (acid) and ALDEHYDE groups, are derived from sugars, and occur combined in many POLYSACCHARIDES (complex carbohydrates) and in urine

**uropod** /ˈyooərohpod/ *n* either of the pair of flattened structures attached to the segment of the ABDOMEN (rear part of the body) in front of the TELSON (last segment of the body) of a lobster or related animal [ISV [2]*ur-* + Gk *pod-, pous* foot – more at FOOT]

**uropygial gland** /ˌyooəroh'piji•əl/ *n* a large gland at the base of the tail feathers in most birds that secretes an oily fluid used by the bird in preening its feathers

**uropygium** /-'piji•əm/ *n* the prominence at the rear end of a bird's body that supports the tail feathers [NL, fr Gk *ouropygion*, fr *ouro-* [2]*ur-* + *pygē* rump – more at STEATOPYGIA] – **uropygial** *adj*

**urostyle** /ˈyooərə,stiel/ *n* the long bony unsegmented rod that forms the rear part of the backbone of frogs and toads [ISV [2]*ur-* + Gk *stylas* pillar – more at STEER]

**-urous** /-yooərəs/ *comb form* (→ *adj*) -tailed ⟨*macr*urous⟩ [NL *-urus*, fr Gk *-ouros*, fr *oura* taii – more at SQUIRREL]

**Ursa Major** /ˈuhsə/ *n* the most conspicuous of the northern constellations, that contains seven stars pictured as a plough, two of which are in a line indicating the direction of the POLE STAR – called also *the* GREAT BEAR, *the* PLOUGH, *NAm the* BIG DIPPER, CHARLES'S WAIN, *the* WAIN [L, lit., greater bear]

**Ursa Minor** *n* a constellation that includes the NORTH POLE of the heavens and seven stars which resemble URSA MAJOR with the POLE STAR at the tip of the handle [L, lit., lesser bear]

**ursine** /ˈuhsin, -sien/ *adj* of or resembling a bear or the bear family [L *ursinus*, fr *ursus* bear – more at ARCTIC]

**Ursprache** /ˈooə,shprahkhə/ *n* a parent language; *esp* one reconstructed from the evidence of later languages [Ger, fr Ur-Ur- + *sprache* language]

**Ursuline** /ˈuhsyoolien/ *n* a member of any of several Roman Catholic teaching orders of nuns; *esp* a member of a teaching order founded by St Angela Merici in Brescia in 1535 [NL *Ursulina*, fr *Ursula*, legendary Christian martyr]

**urticaria** /uhtiˈkeəri•ə/ *n* an allergic condition marked by raised itchy red or white patches on the skin and caused by a specific factor (e g a food or drug) [NL, fr L *urtica* nettle] – **urticarial** *adj*

**urticate** /ˈuhti,kayt/ *vi* to produce weals or itching; *esp* to induce urticaria [ML *urticatus*, pp of *urticare* to sting, fr L *urtica* nettle] – **urtication** *n*

**urus** /ˈyooərəs/ *n* AUROCHS (extinct wild ox) [L, of Gmc origin; akin to OHG *ūro* urus – more at AUROCHS]

**urushiol** /yooəˈroohshiol/ *n* an oily poisonous irritant liquid present in POISON IVY and some related plants (genus *Rhus*) and as a natural varnish or lacquer in the sap of some Oriental sumach trees [ISV, fr Jap *urushi* lacquer]

**us** /əs; *strong* us/ *pron* **1** *objective case of* WE ⟨*please let ~ go*⟩ – compare LET'S and phrases at [1]ME **2** *chiefly Br nonstandard* me ⟨*give ~ a kiss*⟩ [ME, fr OE *ūs;* akin to OHG *uns* us, L *nos*] *usage* As we, than we are preferable in formal writing to *as us, than us*. See [4]AS, [2]THAN, ME

**usable** *also* **useable** /ˈyoohzəbl/ *adj* **1** capable of being used **2** convenient for use – **usably** *adv*, **usableness, usability** *n*

**usage** /ˈyoohsij, -zij/ *n* **1a** (an instance of) established and generally accepted practice or procedure **b** (an instance of) the way in which words and phrases are actually used in a language **2a** the action, amount, or manner of using ⟨*parts subject to rough ~*⟩ **b** manner of treating ⟨*suffered ill ~ at the hands of his captors*⟩

*synonyms* Usage, rather than use, is the usual word for "treatment" ⟨*received some rough usage*⟩ and for the sense connected with language ⟨*modern English usage*⟩. Use should be preferred for "using" ⟨*excessive use of coal*⟩ and for "usefulness".

**usance** /ˈyoohz(ə)ns/ *n* **1** INTEREST 3 (income from investment) **2** the time allowed by custom for payment of a BILL OF EXCHANGE in foreign commerce **3** *formal* USAGE 1a **4** *formal* use, employment **5** *obs* usury [ME *usaunce* usage, fr ML *usantia*, fr *usant-, usans*, prp of *usare* to use, fr L *usus*, pp of *uti* to use]

**¹use** /yoohs/ *n* **1a** using or being used ⟨*he made good ~ of his time*⟩ ⟨*a dish in daily ~*⟩ **b** a way of using something ⟨*gained practice in the ~ of his calculator*⟩ ⟨*a machine with many different ~s*⟩ **2a** habitual or customary usage **b** a form or observance of public worship; *esp* one with modifications peculiar to a local church or religious order ⟨*~ of Sarum*⟩ **3a** the right or benefit of using something ⟨*gave him the ~ of her car*⟩ **b** the ability or power to use something (eg a limb) ⟨*lost the ~ of his left arm*⟩ **c** the legal enjoyment of property ⟨*she had the ~ of the estate for life*⟩ **4a** a purpose, end ⟨*put learning to practical ~*⟩ ⟨*it's no ~ worrying*⟩ **b** practical worth or application ⟨*saving things that might be of ~*⟩ **c** the occasion or need to use ⟨*took only what he had ~ for*⟩ **5** a favourable attitude; a liking ⟨*had no ~ for modern art*⟩ **synonyms** see USAGE [ME *us*, fr OF, fr L *usus*, pp of *uti* to use]

**²use** /yoohz/ *vb* **used** /*vt and vi sense 2* yoohzd; *vi sense 1* yoohst/ *vt* **1** to put into action or service; employ **2** to consume or take (eg drugs) regularly **3** to carry out something by means of ⟨*~ tact*⟩ **4** to make an involuntary or concealed means to one's own ends ⟨*feels he is being ~d and manipulated*⟩ **5** to expend, consume **6** to treat in a specified manner ⟨*~d the prisoners cruelly*⟩ **7** *archaic* to accustom, habituate ⟨*to ~ himself to speak aloud* – Earl of Chesterfield⟩ ~ *vi* **1** – used in the past with *to* to indicate a former fact or state ⟨*claims winters ~d to be harder*⟩ ⟨*didn't ~d to be so pernickety*⟩ **2** *slang* to take drugs habitually – **user** *n*
  **usage** The correct negative of *he used to* was formerly *he used not to* or *he usedn't to*, but research has shown that the commoner forms in both British and American English are now *he didn't use to* or *he didn't used to*. (One can avoid an awkward choice by preferring *he never used to*.) The commonest question form is now *did he used to*, rather than *did he use to* or the more correct *used he to*; and the commonest negative question is *didn't he use to* or *didn't he used to* rather than the former *he not to* ⟨*didn't he used to dislike fish?*⟩ ⟨*he used to dislike fish, didn't he?*⟩.

**use up** *vt* **1** to consume completely ⟨*used up his supplies*⟩ **2** to deprive wholly of strength or useful properties; exhaust ⟨*land that has been used up*⟩

**used** /*senses 1 and 2* yoohzd; *sense 3* yoohst/ *adj* **1** employed in accomplishing something **2** that has endured use; *specif* secondhand ⟨*a ~ car*⟩ **3** accustomed, habituated – usu + *to* ⟨*I'm not ~ to drinking* – SEU S⟩

**useful** /'yoohsf(ə)l/ *adj* **1** having utility, esp practical worth or applicability; *also* helpful **2** of highly satisfactory quality; commendable ⟨*an animal which has put up several ~ performances on the track* – Roy Genders⟩ – **usefully** *adv*, **usefulness** *n*
  **synonyms** Useful, serviceable, practical, functional, and utilitarian all apply to something that serves an end. Useful, the most general word, implies fitness or sufficiency for a purpose ⟨*no useful rain had fallen for five or six months* – Sydney (Australia) Bulletin⟩. Serviceable emphasizes potential or continued durability ⟨*old shoes are still serviceable*⟩. Practical stresses suitability for a purpose ⟨*change into some more practical shoes*⟩. Functional suggests that an item will fulfil its purpose without needless ornamentation ⟨*functional clothes for children*⟩. Utilitarian carries further the idea that use rather than beauty is the first consideration ⟨*her dark abundant hair was skewered into a utilitarian knob* – Edna Ferber⟩. **antonyms** useless, nonfunctional

**useless** /'yoohslis/ *adj* **1** having or being of no use **2** *informal* inept – **uselessly** *adv*, **uselessness** *n*

**usen't, usedn't** /'yoohsnt/ *chiefly Br* used not ⟨*~ to be so pernickety*⟩

**user** /'yoohzə/ *n* USE 3c (legal enjoyment of property)

**user-friendly** *adj* **1** *of a computer system* designed for easy operation by guiding users along a series of simple steps, providing instructions at each step in courteous jargon-free language **2** easy to operate or understand ⟨*a ~ machine*⟩ ⟨*a textbook that explains everything in ~ terms*⟩ – **user-friendliness** *n*

**¹usher** /'ushə/ *n* **1** an officer or servant who acts as a doorkeeper (eg in a court of law) **2** an officer who walks before a person of rank **3** *fem* **usherette** /,ushə'ret/ a person who shows people to their seats (eg in a theatre) **4** *archaic* an assistant teacher [ME *ussher*, fr MF *ussier*, fr (assumed) VL *ustiarius* doorkeeper, fr L *ostium*, *ustium* door, mouth of a river; akin to L *or-*, *os* mouth – more at ORAL]

**²usher** *vt* **1** to conduct to a place **2** to precede as an usher **3** to inaugurate, introduce – usu + *in* or *into* ⟨*~ in a new era*⟩

**usquebaugh** /'uskwi,baw/ *n*, *Irish & Scot* whisky [IrGael *uisce beathadh*]

**usual** /'yoohzhooəl, -zhəl/ *adj* **1** in accordance with usage, custom, or habit; normal **2** commonly or ordinarily used ⟨*followed his ~ route*⟩ [LL *usualis*, fr L *usus* use] – **usually** *adv*, **usualness** *n* – **as usual** in the accustomed or habitual way ⟨*as usual he was late*⟩
  **synonyms** Usual, customary, habitual, wonted, accustomed, and routine all mean "familiar through constant repetition". Usual applies to what happens often and is not strange ⟨*the usual route to Birmingham is up the M6*⟩. Customary describes the regular practice of an individual or community ⟨*settle down to his customary occupations or amusements* – W M Thackeray⟩. Habitual applies to what by force of habit has become almost instinctive ⟨*I stop ashamed, for I am talking habitual thoughts, and not adapting them to her ear* – W B Yeats⟩. Wonted is a more formal word which may apply to what is purposefully cultivated ⟨*maintained his wonted courtesy*⟩. Accustomed may refer to what has come to be looked for by others as a distinguishing characteristic ⟨*to fling out an arm with some familiar accustomed gesture in a House of Commons* – A T Quiller-Couch⟩. Routine applies to what accords with an established procedure ⟨*a routine medical examination*⟩, and may emphasize boring repetitiousness. **antonyms** unusual, original, occasional

**usufruct** /'yoohz(y)oo,frukt, -s(y)oo-/ *n* **1** the legal right of using and enjoying something belonging to another **2** *formal* the right to use or enjoy something [L *ususfructus*, fr *usus et fructus* use and enjoyment]

**¹usufructuary** /,yoohz(y)oo'fruktyoori/ *n* **1** a person having the usufruct of property **2** *formal* a person having the use or enjoyment of something

**²usufructuary** *adj* (having the character) of a usufruct ⟨*~ title*⟩

**usurer** /'yoohzhərə/ *n* a person who lends money, esp at an exorbitant rate of interest

**usurious** /yooh'zhooəri·əs/ *adj* **1** practising usury **2** involving usury; of the character of usury ⟨*~ rates of interest*⟩ – **usuriously** *adv*, **usuriousness** *n*

**usurp** /yooh'suhp, -'zuhp/ *vt* to seize and possess by force or without right ⟨*~ a throne*⟩ ~ *vi* to seize possession or exercise authority wrongfully – usu + *on* or *upon* [ME *usurpen*, fr MF *usurper*, fr L *usurpare*, lit., to take possession of by use, fr *usu* (abl of *usus* use) + *rapere* to seize – more at RAPID] – **usurper** *n*, **usurpation** *n*

**usury** /'yoohzyəri, -zhəri/ *n* **1** the practice of lending money at interest, esp at an exorbitant or illegal rate of interest **2** an exorbitant rate or amount of interest; *specif* interest in excess of a legal rate charged to a borrower for the use of money **3** *archaic* INTEREST 3 (income from investment) [ME, fr ML *usuria*, alter. of L *usura* use, interest, fr *usus*, pp of *uti* to use]

**ut** /oot, ooht/ *n*, *music* DOH – used in French fixed-doh SOLMIZATION to refer not to the 1st note of any scale, but to the note C in whatever scale or context it may occur [ME, fr ML – more at GAMUT]

**ute** /yooht/ *n*, *NAm & Austr informal* an all-purpose truck [by shortening & alter. fr *utility*]

**Ute** /yooht/ *n*, *pl* **Utes**, *esp collectively* **Ute** a member of an American Indian people originally inhabiting Utah, Colorado, Arizona, and New Mexico

**utensil** /yooh'tens(i)l/ *n* **1** a piece of portable equipment, esp a tool or container, used in the household, esp the kitchen **2** a useful tool or implement ⟨*writing ~s*⟩ **synonyms** see ¹TOOL [ME, vessels for domestic use, fr MF *utensile*, fr L *utensilia*, fr neut pl of *utensilis* useful, fr *uti* to use]

**uter-** /yoohtə-/, **utero-** *comb form* **1** uterus ⟨*uterine*⟩ **2** uterine and ⟨*uteroplacental*⟩ [L *uterus*]

**uterine** /'yoohtərin, -rien/ *adj* **1a** born of the same mother but having a different father ⟨*~ sisters*⟩ **b** related through the female line ⟨*~ kinsmen*⟩; *also* MATRILINEAL **2** of, situated in, or affecting the uterus [ME, fr LL *uterinus*, fr L *uterus*]

**uterus** /'yoohtərəs/ *n*, *pl* **uteri** /-rie/ *also* **uteruses 1** a thick-walled hollow organ of the female mammal that contains and usu nourishes the young during development before birth – called also WOMB **2** a structure in some lower animals analogous to the uterus, in which eggs or young develop [L]

**utile** /'yoohtiel/ *adj*, *chiefly formal* USEFUL **1** [MF, fr L *utilis*]

**¹utilitarian** /yooh,tili'teəri·ən/ *n* an advocate of utilitarianism

**²utilitarian** *adj* **1** marked by utilitarian views or practices **2** of or aiming at utility; *esp* designed for practical use rather than beautiful appearance ⟨*spare ~ furnishings*⟩ **synonyms** see USEFUL

**utilitarianism** /yooh,tili'teəri·ənizm/ *n* **1** a doctrine that the criterion for right conduct should be the usefulness of its consequences; *specif* a theory that the aim of action or social policy should be the greatest happiness of the greatest number 2 utilitarian character, spirit, or quality

¹**utility** /yooh'tiləti/ *n* 1 fitness for some purpose; usefulness 2 something useful or designed for use 3a an organization performing a public service (eg by providing gas, electricity, or transport) and operated privately, by local government, or by the state; PUBLIC UTILITY b a service provided by a PUBLIC UTILITY 4 *Austr* a van with an open-topped or fabric-covered rear compartment; UTE [ME *utilite*, fr MF *utilité*, fr L *utilitat-, utilitas*, fr *utilis* useful, fr *uti* to use]

²**utility** *adj* 1 capable of serving as a substitute in various roles or positions ⟨*bought a ~ player to play midfield or at the back*⟩ 2 *of a domestic animal* kept for work or for the production of a useful product rather than for show or as a pet 3 serving primarily for utility rather than beauty; utilitarian ⟨*~ furniture*⟩ 4 designed or adapted for general use ⟨*a ~ knife*⟩

**utility room** *n* a room in a private house typically having a sink and plenty of storage space, and often containing large items of household equipment (eg a freezer or washing machine)

**util·ize, -ise** /'yoohtiliez/ *vt* to make use of; turn to practical use or account [Fr *utiliser*, fr *utile* useful] – **utilizable** *adj*, **utilization** *n*, **utilizer** *n*

¹**utmost** /'ut,mohst/ *adj* 1 situated at the farthest or most distant point; extreme ⟨*the ~ point of the earth* – John Hunt⟩ 2 of the greatest or highest degree or amount ⟨*a matter of ~ concern*⟩ [ME, alter. of *utmest*, fr OE *ūtmest*, superl adj fr *ūt* out, adv – more at OUT]

²**utmost** *n* 1 the highest point or degree; the extreme limit ⟨*the ~ in reliability*⟩ 2 the best of one's abilities, powers, and resources ⟨*did his ~ to help*⟩

**Uto-Aztecan** /,yoohtoh'aztekən/ *n* an American Indian language group comprising the NAHUATLAN, TARACAHITIAN, PIMAN, and SHOSHONEAN families [*Ute* + *-o-* + *Aztec*] – **Uto-Aztecan** *adj*

**utopia** /yooh'tohpi·ə/ *n* 1 often cap a place or state of ideal perfection, esp with regard to laws, government, and social conditions 2 an impractical scheme for social or political improvement [*Utopia*, imaginary ideal country in *Utopia* by Sir Thomas More †1535 E statesman & writer, fr Gk *ou* not, no + *topos* place]

¹**utopian** /yooh'tohpi·ən/ *adj, often cap* 1 impossibly ideal, esp with regard to social and political organization ⟨*dreams far too ~ to be realized*⟩ 2 advocating impractically ideal social and political schemes ⟨*~ idealists*⟩ – **utopianism** *n, often cap*

²**utopian** *n* 1 someone who believes in human perfectibility and the possibility of creating an unflawed form of society 2 an advocate of utopian schemes

**utricle** /'yoohtrikl/ *n* any of various small pouches or pouched parts of an animal or plant body: eg a the larger of the two connected chambers of the sensory structures of the INNER EAR into which the SEMICIRCULAR CANALS open – compare SACCULE b a small dry single-seeded or few-seeded fruit that usu does not break open (is INDEHISCENT) to release the seeds and has a

thin membranous PERICARP (fruit wall) [L *utriculus*, dim. of *uter* leather bag] – **utricular** *adj*

¹**utter** /'utə/ *adj* absolute, total ⟨*~ desolation*⟩ [ME, remote, extreme, absolute, fr OE *ūtera* outward, outer, compar adj fr *ūt* out, adv – more at OUT] – **utterly** *adv*

²**utter** *vt* 1a to emit as a sound ⟨*~ed a groan*⟩ b to give (verbal) expression to; *esp* to pronounce, speak ⟨*didn't ~ a single word*⟩ ⟨*reluctant to ~ her opinions*⟩ 2 to put (eg currency) into circulation; issue; *esp* to put (forged or counterfeit currency, cheques, etc) into circulation as if legal or genuine – used technically 3 *obs* to offer for sale 4 *obs* to put forth or out; discharge [ME *uttren*, fr *utter* outside, adv, fr OE *ūtor*, compar of *ūt* out] – **utterable** *adj*, **utterer** *n*

¹**utterance** /'ut(ə)rəns/ *n, archaic* the last extremity; BITTER END [ME *uttraunce*, modif of MF *outrance*, fr *outrer* to pass beyond, carry to excess, fr *outre* beyond, in excess, fr L *ultra*]

²**utterance** *n* 1 something uttered; *esp* an oral or written statement 2 vocal expression; speech – esp in *give utterance to* 3 power, style, or manner of speaking

¹**uttermost** /'utəmohst/ *adj* extreme, utmost ⟨*the ~ parts of the earth*⟩ [ME, alter. of *uttermest*, fr ¹*utter* + *-mest* (as in *utmest* utmost)]

²**uttermost** *n* utmost ⟨*to the ~ of our capacity* – H S Truman⟩

**utu** /'ooh,tooh/ *n, NZ* retribution; *esp* that entailing the death of the offender [Maori]

**U-turn** /yooh/ *n* 1 the turning of a vehicle to face the opposite direction without reversing 2 something (eg a reversal of policy) that suggests a U-turn ⟨*a ~ on wage controls* – The Economist⟩

**uvarovite** /(y)ooh'varəviet/ *n* an emerald-green garnet, $Ca_3Cr_2(SiO_4)_3$, containing calcium and chromium [Ger *uwarowit*, fr Count Sergei *Uvarov* †1855 Russ statesman]

**uvea** /yooh'vi·ə/ *n* the rearmost pigment-containing layer of the iris of the eye; *also* the layer of the eye that includes the iris and CILIARY BODY (ringlike muscular body that supports the lens) together with the CHOROID COAT [ML, fr L *uva* grape] – **uveal** *adj*

**uveitis** /,yoohvi'ietəs/ *n* inflammation of the uvea of the eye [NL]

**uvula** /'yoohvyoolə/ *n, pl* **uvulas, uvulae** /-li/ the fleshy lobe hanging in the middle of the back of the SOFT PALATE (rear portion of the roof of the mouth) [ML, dim. of L *uva* grape, uvula; akin to OE *īw* yew]

**uvular** /'yoohvyoolə/ *adj* 1 of the uvula ⟨*~ glands*⟩ 2 *of a consonant* produced with the aid of (vibration of) the uvula ⟨*a French ~* /r/⟩ – **uvularly** *adv*

**uxorial** /uk'sawri·əl/ *adj, formal* (characteristic) of a wife [L *uxorius*]

**uxorious** /uk'sawri·əs, ug'zaw-/ *adj, formal* excessively fond of or submissive to a wife [L *uxorius* uxorious, uxorial, fr *uxor* wife] – **uxoriously** *adv*, **uxoriousness** *n*

**Uzbeg** /'oozbeg, 'uzbeg/ *n* (an) Uzbek

**Uzbek** /'oozbek, 'uzbek/ *n* 1 a member of a Turkic people of Turkestan and esp of the Uzbek Republic of the USSR 2 the Turkic language of the Uzbek people

# V

**v, V** /vee/ *n, pl* **v's, vs, V's, Vs 1a** the 22nd letter of the English alphabet **b** a graphic representation of or device for reproducing the letter *v* **c** a speech counterpart of printed or written *v* **2** five **3** one designated *v*, esp as the 22nd in order or class **4** something shaped like the letter V

**V-1** /ˌvee 'wun/ *n* a jet-engined FLYING BOMB used by the Germans in World War II, esp against targets in S England [Ger *vergeltungswaffe*, fr *vergeltung* retaliation + *waffe* weapon]

**V-2** /ˌvee 'tooh/ *n* a long-range rocket used by the Germans in World War II, esp against targets in S England

**V-8** /ˌvee'ayt/ *n* (a vehicle having) an INTERNAL-COMBUSTION ENGINE with two banks of four cylinders each, the banks being at an angle to each other

**vac** /vak/ *n, Br informal* a college or university vacation

**vacancy** /'vaykənsi/ *n* **1** emptiness of mind; vacuity, inanity **2a** a place (e g a room in a hotel) or property that is not being occupied or used **b** an unfilled position in a factory, office, etc ⟨*we have a ~ in the typing pool*⟩ **3** the time that an office, post, or property is vacant between occupants **4** (an) empty space **5** the state of being vacant; emptiness **6** *archaic* an interval of leisure; unoccupied or leisure time

**vacant** /'vaykənt/ *adj* **1** not occupied by an incumbent, possessor, or officer ⟨*a ~ seat on the board*⟩ **2** without an occupant, esp temporarily ⟨*a ~ seat in a bus*⟩ ⟨*a ~ room*⟩ **3** free from activity or work ⟨*obliged to spend his ~ hours in a comfortless hotel* – Jane Austen⟩ **4a** stupid, foolish **b** showing no thought or emotion; expressionless ⟨*a ~ stare*⟩ **5** marked by a respite from thought or care ⟨*in ~ or in pensive mood* – William Wordsworth⟩ **6a** not lived in or put to use ⟨*~ houses*⟩ **b** having no heir or claimant ⟨*a ~ estate*⟩ [ME, fr OF, fr L *vacant-, vacans*, prp of *vacare* to be empty, be free – more at VACUUM] – **vacantly** *adv*, **vacantness** *n*

*synonyms* While **vacant** may mean simply "empty of thought" ⟨*a vacant smile*⟩ **vacuous** means "fatuously empty" ⟨*a vacuous giggle*⟩.

**vacant possession** *n* ownership of property whose previous owner or tenant has departed, and which is therefore available for immediate occupation

**vacate** /vay'kayt/ *vt* **1** to make legally void; annul **2** to give up the possession or occupancy of **3** to make vacant; leave empty ⟨*with instructions to ~ the cinema*⟩ *~ vi* to vacate an office, post, or tenancy [L *vacatus*, pp of *vacare*]

**¹vacation** /vay'kash(ə)n, və-/ *n* **1** a period during which a university, law court, etc does not hold classes, try cases, or carry out its normal functions; RECESS 3A **2** an act or instance of vacating **3** *chiefly NAm* a holiday ⟨*had a restful ~ at the beach*⟩ *synonyms* see ¹HOLIDAY [ME *vacacioun*, fr MF *vacation*, fr L *vacation-, vacatio* freedom, exemption, fr *vacatus*] – **vacational** *adj*

**²vacation** *vi, chiefly NAm* to take or spend a vacation – **vacationer, vacationist** *n*

**vaccinal** /'vaksinəl/ *adj* of vaccine or vaccination

**vaccinate** /'vaksinayt/ *vt* **1** to inoculate with cowpox virus in order to produce immunity to smallpox **2** to administer a vaccine to, either by injection or orally, in order to produce immunity to a specific disease ⟨*had the children ~d against whooping cough*⟩ *~ vi* to perform or practise vaccination – **vaccinator** *n*

*synonyms* **Vaccinate** is often used in nontechnical parlance with reference to smallpox, and **inoculate** for other diseases.

**vaccination** /ˌvaksi'naysh(ə)n/ *n* **1** the act of administering vaccine **2** the scar left by vaccinating

**¹vaccine** /'vak,seen, -sin/ *adj* of cowpox or vaccination ⟨*a ~ pustule*⟩ [L *vaccinus* of or from cows, fr *vacca* cow; akin to Skt *vaśa* cow]

**²vaccine** *n* **1** a preparation containing the virus of cowpox in a form used for vaccination **2** a preparation of killed microorganisms (e g viruses or bacteria), living inactivated organisms, or living fully infective organisms that is administered usu by injection to produce or artificially increase immunity to a particular disease

**vaccinia** /vak'sini·ə/ *n* cowpox [NL, fr *vaccinus*] – **vaccinial** *adj*

**vacherin** /vashə'ranh (*Fr* vaʃrɛ̃)/ *n* a cake or dessert typically consisting of layers or a shell of meringue sandwiched or filled with whipped cream and often fruit [Fr (orig a type of cheese), fr *vache* cow, fr L *vacca*]

**vacillate** /'vasə,layt/ *vi* **1a** to sway because imperfectly balanced **b** to fluctuate, oscillate **2** to hesitate or waver in choosing between opinions or courses of action [L *vacillatus*, pp of *vacillare* to sway, waver – more at PREVARICATE] – **vacillatingly** *adv*, **vacillator** *n*, **vacillation** *n*

**vacuity** /və'kyooh·əti/ *n* **1** an empty space **2** vacuousness, meaninglessness **3** emptiness of mind **4** something (e g an idea) that is stupid or inane [L *vacuitas*, fr *vacuus* empty]

**vacuolate** /'vakyoo(ə),layt, -lət/, **vacuolated** /-laytid/ *adj* containing one or more vacuoles ⟨*highly ~ cells*⟩

**vacuolation** /ˌvakyooə'laysh(ə)n/ *n* the development or formation of vacuoles

**vacuole** /'vakyoo,ohl/ *n* **1** a small cavity or space in the tissues of an organism containing air or liquid **2** a small gas- or liquid-containing cavity or sac within a cell [Fr, lit., small vacuum, fr L *vacuum*] – **vacuolar** *adj*

**vacuous** /'vakyoo·əs/ *adj* **1** emptied of or lacking content; empty **2** showing lack of ideas or intelligence; stupid, inane ⟨*a ~ mind*⟩ ⟨*a ~ expression*⟩ **3** idle, aimless *synonyms* see VACANT [L *vacuus*] – **vacuously** *adv*, **vacuousness** *n*

**¹vacuum** /'vakyoohm, 'vakyooəm, 'vakyoom/ *n, pl* **vacuums, vacua** /'vakyooh·ə/ **1** a space absolutely devoid of matter **2a** a space from which as much air or other substance as possible has been removed by artificial means (e g an air pump) **b** an air pressure below atmospheric pressure **3a** a vacant space; a void ⟨*his death has left a ~ in our lives*⟩ **b** a state of isolation from outside influences ⟨*people who live in a ~ ... so that the world outside them is of no moment* – Somerset Maugham⟩ **4** VACUUM CLEANER [L, fr neut of *vacuus* empty; akin to L *vacare* to be empty]

**²vacuum** *adj* of, containing, producing, or using a partial vacuum ⟨*separated by means of ~ distillation*⟩

**³vacuum** /'vakyoohm, 'vakyoom/ *vb* to clean using a VACUUM CLEANER

**vacuum aspiration** *n* a method of emptying the womb of its contents (e g for an abortion) whereby a CANNULA (thin tube) is attached to a syringe, inserted into the womb, and the contents then sucked out

**vacuum bottle** *n, chiefly NAm* VACUUM FLASK

**vacuum brake** *n* a brake system worked by vacuum suction and used esp on trains

**vacuum cleaner** *n* an electrical appliance for removing dust and dirt (e g from carpets or upholstery) by suction – **vacuum-clean** *vb*

**vacuum concrete** *n* concrete set by removing excess water by means of a vacuum applied through special shuttering

**vacuum flask** *n, chiefly Br* a cylindrical container that is insulated by means of a double wall of silvered glass in which a vacuum exists, and that is used to keep material (e g liquids or liquefied gases) either hot or cold for considerable periods – compare THERMOS FLASK, DEWAR FLASK

**vacuum gauge** *n* a gauge indicating the degree to which an enclosed space has been evacuated

**'vacuum-,packed** *adj* packed in a wrapping from which most of the air has been removed ⟨*~ bacon*⟩

**vacuum pump** *n* a pump for extracting gas from an enclosed space

**vacuum tube** *n* an ELECTRON TUBE (electronic device that generates and controls a beam of electrons) in which there is a vacuum

**vade mecum** /ˌvaydi 'meekəm, ˌvahday 'maykəm/ *n, pl* **vade mecums** **1** a book for ready reference; a manual **2** something regularly carried about by a person [L, go with me]

**vadose** /'vay‚dohs/ *adj* of or being water or solutions in the earth's crust above the WATER TABLE [L *vadosus* shallow, fr *vadum*, n, shallow, ford; akin to L *vadere* to go – more at WADE]

**vag-** /vayg-/, **vago-** *comb form* vagus nerve ⟨vag*al*⟩ ⟨vago-tomy⟩ [ISV, fr NL *vagus*]

**¹vagabond** /'vagə‚bond/ *adj* **1** moving from place to place without a fixed home; wandering **2a** (characteristic) of a wanderer **b** leading an unsettled, irresponsible, or disreputable life [ME, fr MF, fr L *vagabundus*, fr *vagari* to wander] – **vagabondish** *adj*

**²vagabond** *n* a person who lives an irregular or wandering life; *esp* one thought to be lazy or worthless – **vagabond** *vi*, **vagabondage** *n*, **vagabondism** *n*

**vagal** /'vaygəl/ *adj* of, affected or controlled by, or being the VAGUS (nerve supplying the heart, lungs, and gut) [ISV] – **vagally** *adv*

**vagary** /'vaygəri; *also* və'geəri/ *n* an erratic, unpredictable, or extravagant manifestation, action, or notion; a whim, caprice [prob fr L *vagari* to wander; akin to L *vagus* wandering – more at PREVARICATE] – **vagarious** *adj*

   *usage* The pronunciation /'vaygəri/ is recommended for BBC broadcasters.

**vagile** /'vayjiel/ *adj* free to move about ⟨~ *aquatic animals*⟩ [ISV, fr L *vagus* wandering] – **vagility** *n*

**vagina** /və'jienə/ *n, pl* **vaginae** /-ni/, **vaginas** **1a** a tubular passage in a female mammal that leads from the uterus to the external opening of the reproductive tract **b** a tubular passage that is similar in function or location to the vagina and occurs in various animals other than mammals **2** a sheath; *esp a* leaf base that forms a sheath, usu round the main stem [L, lit., sheath] – **vaginal** *adj*

**vaginismus** /ˌvaji'nizməs/ *n* a painful spasmodic contraction of the muscles of the vagina [NL, fr L *vagina*]

**vaginitis** /ˌvaji'nietəs/ *n* inflammation of the vagina or of a sheathlike covering structure (e g a tendon sheath) [NL]

**vagotomy** /və'gotəmi/ *n* surgical cutting of the vagus nerve (e g to reduce the flow of digestive juices in the treatment of a stomach ulcer) [ISV]

**vagotonia** /ˌvaygə'tohnyə, -niə/ *n* overactivity of the vagus nerve [NL, fr *vag-* + *-tonia*]

**vagotropic** /ˌvaygə'tropik/ *adj* acting selectively on the vagus nerve ⟨~ *drugs*⟩

**¹vagrant** /'vaygrənt/ *n* **1a** a person who has no established residence and wanders from place to place without lawful or visible source of income **b** a person (e g a prostitute or drunkard) whose lack of a fixed address or adequate means of support usu associated with begging or soliciting for money constitutes a public nuisance punishable by law **2** a wanderer [ME *vagraunt*, prob modif of MF *waucrant, wacrant* wandering, fr OF, fr prp of *waucrer, wacrer* to roll, wander, of Gmc origin; akin to OE *wealcan* to roll – more at WALK] – **vagrancy** *n*

**²vagrant** *adj* **1** wandering about from place to place usu with no source of income **2** (characteristic) of a vagrant or vagabond; *esp* idle and disorderly **3** having a fleeting, wayward, or inconstant quality; erratic, random – **vagrantly** *adv*

**vagrom** /'vaygrəm/ *adj, archaic or poetic* vagrant [by alter.]

**vague** /vayg/ *adj* **1a** not clearly expressed; stated in indefinite terms ⟨~ *accusations*⟩ **b** not having a precise meaning ⟨*a ~ term of abuse*⟩ **2a** not clearly defined, known, grasped, or understood; indistinct ⟨*a ~ idea*⟩ **b** not clearly felt or sensed ⟨*a ~ longing*⟩ **3a** not thinking or expressing one's thoughts clearly or precisely **b** not alert; absentminded **4** lacking expression; vacant ⟨*a ~ look*⟩ **5** not sharply outlined; hazy ⟨*a ~ shape*⟩ **synonyms** see ¹OBSCURE **antonyms** definite, specific [MF, fr L *vagus*, lit., wandering] – **vaguely** *adv*, **vagueness** *n*

**vagus** /'vaygəs/, **vagus nerve** *n, pl* **vagi** /-ie/, **vagus nerves** either of the 10th pair of CRANIAL NERVES arising in the brain and supplying chiefly the heart, lungs, liver, and digestive tract [NL *vagus nervus*, lit., wandering nerve]

**vail** /vayl/ *vb, archaic vt* to lower, often as a sign of respect or submission ⟨... *France must ~ her lofty-plumed crest* – Shak⟩ ⟨~ed *her Sunday paper* – Aldous Huxley⟩ ~ *vi* **1** to remove one's hat as a sign of respect **2** to submit, yield ⟨*And*

*Greek itself ~ to our English voice* – George Chapman⟩ [ME *valen*, partly fr MF *valer* (short for *avaler* to let fall) & partly short for ME *avalen* to let fall, fr MF *avaler*, fr OF, fr *aval* downward, fr *a* to (fr L *ad*) + *val* valley]

**vain** /vayn/ *adj* **1** having no real value; idle, worthless **2** unsuccessful, ineffectual ⟨~ *efforts to escape*⟩ **3** having or showing excessive pride in one's appearance, ability, or achievements; conceited **4** *archaic* foolish, silly **synonyms** see ¹PRIDE **antonym** modest △ vane, vein [ME, fr OF, fr L *vanus* empty, vain – more at WANE] – **vainly** *adv*, **vainness** *n* – **in vain** to no end; with no success or result – see also **take God's/the Lord's** NAME **in vain, take somebody's** NAME **in vain**

**vainglorious** /ˌvayn'glawri·əs/ *adj* boastful – **vaingloriously** *adv*, **vaingloriousness** *n*

**vainglory** /ˌvayn'glawri/ *n* **1** excessive pride, esp in one's achievements; vanity **2** ostentation, pomp **synonyms** see ¹PRIDE

**vair** /veə/ *n* **1** the bluish grey and white fur of a squirrel prized for ornamental use in medieval times **2** one of the principal furs in heraldry, represented on a heraldic shield by horizontal rows of alternate blue and silver bells – compare ERMINE 4 [ME *veir*, fr OF *vair*, fr *vair*, adj, variegated, fr L *varius* variegated, various]

**Vaishnava** /ˌviesh'nahvə/ *n* a member of a major Hindu sect devoted to the cult of Vishnu [Skt *vaiṣṇ ava* of Vishnu, fr *Viṣṇu* Vishnu, second of the three chief Hindu gods] – **Vaishnava** *adj*, **Vaishnavism** *n*

**Vaisya** /'viesyə/ *n* a Hindu of an upper caste traditionally assigned to commercial and agricultural occupations [Skt *vaiśya*, fr *viś* settlement; akin to Gk *oikos* house – more at VICINITY]

**valance** /'vayləns, 'va-/ *n* **1** a piece of drapery hung as a border, esp along the edge of a bed, canopy, or shelf **2** a pelmet △ valence [ME *vallance*, perh fr *Valence*, town in SE France] – **valanced** *adj*

**vale** /vayl/ *n, poetic* a valley, dale – often in place-names ⟨*the* Vale *of Evesham*⟩ [ME, fr OF *val*, fr L *valles, vallis*; akin to L *volvere* to roll – more at VOLUBLE]

**valediction** /ˌvalə'diksh(ə)n/ *n, formal* **1** an act of bidding farewell **2** an address or statement of farewell or leave-taking [L *valedictus*, pp of *valedicere* to say farewell, fr *vale* farewell + *dicere* to say – more at DICTION]

**¹valedictory** /ˌvalə'dikt(ə)ri/ *adj, formal* expressing or containing a farewell [L *valedictus*, pp]

**²valedictory** *n, formal* VALEDICTION 2

**valence** /'vayləns/ *n, chiefly NAm* valency

**Valenciennes** /ˌvalən'seenz, -si'en, və‚lensi'en(z) (*Fr* valãsjɛn)/ *n* a fine PILLOW LACE (worked with bobbins) [*Valenciennes*, city in N France]

**valency** /'vaylənsi/ *n* **1** the property of an atom, a chemical group, or a chemical element that determines the number of bonds it can form and therefore the number of other atoms, chemical elements, or groups with which it can combine; the degree of combining power of an atom explained in terms of the number of electrons available to form bonds – compare COVALENCY, ELECTROVALENCY **2** a unit of valency ⟨*the four valencies of carbon*⟩ [LL *valentia* power, capacity, fr L *valent-, valens*, prp of *valēre* to be strong]

**-valent** /-'vaylənt/ *comb form* (→ *adj*) **1** having (such) a valency ⟨*bivalent*⟩ ⟨*multivalent*⟩ **2** having (so many) chromosomal strands or corresponding (HOMOLOGOUS) chromosomes ⟨*univalent*⟩ [ISV, fr L *valent-, valens*]

**valentine** /'valəntien/ *n* **1** a sweetheart chosen or acknowledged with a card or gift on St Valentine's Day **2** a gift or greetings card sent, esp anonymously, to a sweetheart or, as a joke, to a friend on St Valentine's Day

**Valentine Day, Valentine's Day** *n* SAINT VALENTINE'S DAY

**valerate** /'valərayt/ *n* any of various chemical compounds (SALTS or ESTERS) formed by combination between VALERIC ACID and a metal atom, an alcohol, or another chemical group

**valerian** /və'liəri·ən/ *n* any of several plants (genera *Valeriana* and *Centranthus* of the family Valerianaceae, the valerian family) with heads of small red, pink, or white flowers, some of which are grown in gardens and many of which possess medicinal properties [ME, fr MF or ML; MF *valeriane*, fr ML *valeriana*, prob fr fem of *valerianus* of Valeria, fr *Valeria*, Roman province in SE Europe]

**valeric acid** /və'liərik, və'lerik/ *n* any of four FATTY ACIDS, $C_5H_{10}O_2$, or a mixture of these; *esp* a liquid acid of disagreeable smell obtained from valerian or made synthetically and used esp in the synthesis of other chemical compounds

**¹valet** /'valay, 'valit/ n **1** a gentleman's male servant who performs personal services (eg taking care of clothing); *also* an employee (eg of a hotel) who performs similar services for customers or guests **2** a device (eg a rack or stand) for holding clothing or personal effects [MF *vaslet, varlet, valet* young nobleman, page, domestic servant, fr (assumed) ML *vassellittus*, dim. of ML *vassus* servant – more at VASSAL]

**²valet** vb to serve (someone) as a valet

**valeta** /və'leetə/ n VELETA (ballroom dance)

**valet de chambre** /,valay də 'shombr/ n, pl **valets de chambre** /~/ VALET 1 [Fr, lit., chamber valet]

**valetudinarian** /,valityoohdi'neəriən/ n, *formal* a person of a weak or sickly constitution; *esp* a hypochondriac [L *valetudinarius* sickly, invalid, fr *valetudin-, valetudo* state of health, illness, fr *valēre* to be strong, be well] – **valetudinarian** adj, **valetudinarianism** n

**valetudinary** /,vali'tyoohdin(ə)ri/ adj or n, *formal* (of or characteristic of) a valetudinarian [L *valetudinarius*]

**valgus** /'valgəs/ n the position of a bone or part that is turned outwards to an abnormal degree at its joint ⟨*the toe is in* ~⟩ – compare VARUS [NL, fr L, bowlegged – more at WALK]

**Valhalla** /val'halə; *also* vol'holə/ n a place of honour or glorification; a shrine [*Valhalla*, banqueting hall in Norse mythology where the souls of slain heroes were received, fr ON *Valhöll*, fr *valr* the slain + *höll* hall]

**valiance** /'vali·əns/, **valiancy** /-si/ n valour

**valiant** /'vali·ənt/ adj characterized by or showing valour; courageous ⟨~ *soldiers*⟩ ⟨~ *deeds*⟩ **synonyms** see ¹BRAVE [ME *valiaunt*, fr MF *vaillant*, fr OF, fr prp of *valoir* to be of worth, fr L *valēre* to be strong – more at WIELD] – **valiant** n, **valiantly** adv, **valiantness** n

**valid** /'valid/ adj **1a** having legal efficacy or force; *esp* executed according to the proper formalities ⟨*a* ~ *contract*⟩ **b** able to be used lawfully, esp for a stated period or under certain conditions; legally acceptable ⟨*a train ticket* ~ *for three months*⟩ ⟨*a* ~ *passport*⟩ **2a** well-grounded or justifiable; relevant and meaningful ⟨*a* ~ *theory*⟩ **b** (having a conclusion) correctly derived from premises; logically sound ⟨~ *argument*⟩ ⟨~ *inference*⟩ [MF or ML; MF *valide*, fr ML *validus*, fr L, strong, effective, fr *valēre* to be strong] – **validness** n, **validly** adv, **validity** n

*usage* **Valid, sound, cogent, convincing, telling,** and **conclusive,** applied to arguments, principles, and ideas, mean "able to compel attention, and perhaps acceptance". What is **valid** is based on truth or correct reasoning ⟨*a* **valid** *conclusion*⟩. **Sound** stresses solid foundation, the avoidance of fallacy and hasty conclusions, and often shrewd practical wisdom ⟨*has* **sound** *reasons for refusing to join the party*⟩. **Cogent** implies both logical inevitability and forceful presentation ⟨*the most* **cogent** *argument for reform*⟩. **Convincing** emphasizes the power to overcome doubt, perhaps by skilful selection rather than by sound reasoning ⟨*think of a* **convincing** *pretext*⟩. **Telling** stresses an immediate and striking effect, which need not be the result of sound argument ⟨*to edit his woes and select the most* **telling** *ones* – Norman Mailer⟩. A **conclusive** argument cannot be disputed, and so puts an end to all further debate. **antonyms** invalid, fallacious

**validate** /'validayt/ vt **1** to make legally valid **2** to support, corroborate, or authenticate on a sound or authoritative basis ⟨*experiments designed to* ~ *his hypothesis*⟩ **synonyms** see CONFIRM **antonym** invalidate – **validation** n

**valine** /'vay,leen, 'va-/ n an ESSENTIAL AMINO ACID, $(CH_3)_2CHCH(NH_2)COOH$, that is required by the body for normal development and health and forms part of many proteins [ISV, fr *valeric (acid)*]

**valise** /və'leez/ n, *chiefly NAm* TRAVELLING BAG [Fr, fr It *valigia*]

**Valium** /'vali·əm/ *trademark* – used for the tranquillizing drug DIAZEPAM

**Valkyrie** /'valkiri, val'kiəri/ n **1** any of the usu 12 maidens who, in Norse mythology, chose the heroes to be slain in battle and conducted them to an afterlife of feasting and heroic deeds in the hall, Valhalla **2** a usu blonde powerfully built young woman; *broadly* AMAZON 2 [Ger & ON; Ger *walküre*, fr ON *valkyrja*, lit., chooser of the slain, fr a prehistoric WGmc-NGmc compound whose first constituent is represented by ON *valr* the slain & whose second is akin to OE *cēosan* to choose – more at CHOOSE]

**vallate** /'valayt/ adj, *of a body part* having a raised edge sur-

rounding a depression ⟨*a* ~ *taste bud on the tongue*⟩ [L *vallatus*, pp of *vallare* to surround with a wall, fr *vallum* wall, rampart – more at WALL]

**vallecula** /və'lekyoolə/ n, pl **valleculae** /-yooli/ an anatomical groove, channel, or depression; *esp* one between the base of the tongue and the EPIGLOTTIS (small flap at the back of the mouth that closes the windpipe during swallowing) [NL, fr LL, little valley, dim. of L *valles* valley – more at VALE] – **vallecular** adj

**valley** /'vali/ n **1a** an elongated depression of the earth's surface usu between hills or mountains **b** an area drained by a river and its tributaries **2a** a hollow, depression **b** the internal angle formed at the meeting of two roof surfaces – compare ²HIP 2 [ME *valey*, fr OF *valee*, fr *val* valley – more at VALE]

**Valois** /'valwah (Fr valwa)/ adj of or supporting the French royal house that ruled from 1328 to 1589 [Philippe de *Valois* (Philip VI of France) †1350]

**valonia** /və'lohnyə, -ni·ə/ n dried acorn cups, esp from the VALONIA OAK, used in tanning or dressing leather [It *vallonia*, fr MGk *balanidia*, pl of *balanidion*, dim. of Gk *balanos* acorn – more at GLAND]

**valonia oak** n a tall Eurasian evergreen oak (*Quercus aegilops*) whose fruit yields valonia

**valor·ize, -ise** /'valəriez/ vt to (try to) enhance the price, value, or status of by organized usu governmental action ⟨*using subsidies to* ~ *coffee*⟩ [Pg *valorizare*, fr *valor* value, price, fr ML] – **valorization** n

**valorous** /'valərəs/ adj valiant **synonyms** see ¹BRAVE – **valorously** adv

**valour, NAm chiefly valor** /'valə/ n strength of mind or spirit that enables one to encounter danger with firmness; personal bravery [ME, worth, value, courage, fr MF, fr ML *valor*, fr L *valēre* to be strong, be worth]

**Valpolicella** /,valpoli'chelə/ n a light red wine produced in NE Italy in the region of Verona [*Valpolicella*, valley in N Italy]

**valse** /vals/ n a (concert) waltz [Fr, fr Ger *walzer* – more at WALTZ]

**¹valuable** /'valyoo(ə)bl/ adj **1** having high monetary value **2** of great use or worth ⟨~ *advice*⟩ ⟨*a* ~ *friendship*⟩ **synonyms** see INVALUABLE – **valuableness** n, **valuably** adv

**²valuable** n usu pl a usu personal possession (eg a piece of jewellery) of relatively great monetary value

**valuable consideration** n a legally recognized equivalent or compensation having at least token value that is given for something acquired or promised (eg money or marriage) and that may consist either in a benefit accruing to one party or a loss falling upon the other

**valuate** /'valyooayt/ vt to place a value on; appraise [back-formation fr *valuation*]

**valuation** /,valyoo'aysh(ə)n/ n **1** the act or process of valuing something, esp property **2** the estimated or fixed value, esp MARKET VALUE, of a thing **3** judgment or appreciation of worth or character – **valuational** adj, **valuationally** adv

**valuator** /'valyoo,aytə/ n one who judges the value or monetary worth of something

**¹value** /'valyooh/ n **1** a fair return or equivalent in goods, services, or money for something exchanged ⟨*always gets* ~ *for money*⟩ **2** the worth of something in money or commodities; marketable price **3** relative worth, utility, or importance ⟨*had nothing of* ~ *to say*⟩ ⟨*this item has news* ~⟩ **4a** a numerical quantity assigned or computed ⟨*the* ~ *of x is 95*⟩ **b** the amount or extent of a specified measurement of space, time, or quantity **c** precise meaning or significance ⟨~ *of a word*⟩ **5** the relative duration of a musical note **6a** relative lightness or darkness of a colour **b** the relationship between the parts of a picture in terms of light and shade **7** usu pl something (eg a principle or quality) considered important, valuable, or desirable; a priority, standard ⟨*the business world with its regulated system of* ~s – D H Lawrence⟩ **8** the denomination of a note or coin [ME, fr MF, fr (assumed) VL *valuta*, fr fem of *valutus*, pp of L *valēre* to be worth, be strong]

**²value** vt **1a** to estimate the worth of in terms of money ⟨~ *a necklace*⟩ **b** to rate in terms of usefulness, importance, or general worth; evaluate, appraise **2** to consider or rate highly; prize, esteem ⟨~d *his friendship*⟩ **synonyms** see INVALUABLE – **valuer** n

**value-added tax** n an INDIRECT TAX levied on the value added at each stage of the processing of a raw material or the production and distribution of a commodity and passed on to the consumer as a form of PURCHASE TAX – compare PURCHASE TAX

**valued** /'valyoohd/ *adj* having a mathematical value or values, esp of a specified kind or number – usu in combination ⟨*real-valued*⟩

**value judgment** *n* a judgment attributing a value (eg good, evil, or desirable) to a particular action or thing, usu as contrasted with a tolerant, factual, or objective assessment

**valueless** /'valyoohləs, -lis/ *adj* worthless **synonyms** see IN-VALUABLE – **valuelessness** *n*

**valuta** /və'l(y)oohtə/ *n* the agreed or exchange value of a currency [It, value, fr (assumed) VL *valuta*]

**valvate** /'valvayt/ *adj* having valves or parts resembling a valve: **a** meeting at the edges without overlapping in the bud ⟨~ *petals*⟩ **b** opening (as if) by valves

**valve** /valv/ *n* **1** a structure, esp in the heart or a vein, that closes temporarily to obstruct passage of material or that permits movement of a liquid or gas in one direction only **2a** any of numerous mechanical devices by which the flow of liquid, gas, or loose material in bulk may be controlled usu to allow movement in one direction only **b** a device in a brass musical instrument for quickly varying the tube length in order to change the note **c** *chiefly Br* **c(1)** ELECTRON TUBE (electronic device that generates and controls a beam of electrons) **c(2)** THERMIONIC VALVE (electronic device for the regulation of electric current) **3** any of the separate joined pieces that make up the shell of an INVERTEBRATE animal; *specif* either of the two halves of the shell of a mussel, oyster, clam, or other bivalve MOLLUSC **4a** any of the segments or pieces into which a ripe plant capsule or pod separates when dispersing the seeds **b** the part of various ANTHERS (pollen-producing structures in a plant) (eg of the barberry) resembling a lid **c** either of the encasing membranes of a DIATOM (minute single-celled plant with a shell-like cell wall) **5** *archaic* a leaf of a folding or double door [L *valva* leaf of a door; akin to L *volvere* to roll – more at VOLUBLE] – **valved** *adj*, **valveless** *adj*

**valvula** /'valvyoolə/ *n*, *pl* **valvulae** /-li/ a small valve or fold [NL, dim. of *valva* valve]

**valvular** /'valvyoolə/ *adj* **1** resembling or functioning as a valve; *also* opening by valves **2** of a valve, esp of the heart

**valvulitis** /ˌvalvyoo'lietəs/ *n* inflammation of a body valve, esp of the heart [NL]

**vamoose** /va'moohs/ *vi*, *NAm slang* to depart quickly; decamp [Sp *vamos* let us go, suppletive 1st pl imper (fr L *vadere* to go) of *ir* to go, fr L *ire* – more at WADE, ISSUE]

**¹vamp** /vamp/ *n* **1** the part of a shoe upper or boot upper covering esp the front of the foot and sometimes also extending forwards over the toe or backwards to the back seam of the upper **2** a simple improvised musical accompaniment [ME *vampe* sock, fr OF *avantpié*, fr *avant-* fore- + *pié* foot, fr L *ped-*, *pes* – more at VANGUARD, FOOT; (2) ²VAMP]

**²vamp** *vt* to provide (a shoe) with a new vamp ~ *vi* to play a musical vamp – **vamper** *n*

**vamp up** *vt*, *informal* **1** to renovate, improve ⟨*vamped up an old sermon for the occasion*⟩ **2** to invent, fabricate ⟨*always able to* vamp up *an excuse*⟩

**³vamp** *n*, *informal* a woman who uses her charm to seduce and exploit men [short for *vampire*] – **vampish** *adj*

**⁴vamp** *vt* to practise seductive wiles on; entice ~ *vi* to act as a vamp

**vampire** /'vampie-ə/ *n* **1** a dead person believed to come from the grave at night and suck the blood of sleeping people **2** one who lives by preying on and exploiting others **3 vampire bat**, **vampire** any of various S American bats (genera *Desmodus* and *Diphylla* of the family Desmodontidae) that feed on blood and are dangerous to human beings and domestic animals, esp as transmitters of disease (eg rabies); *also* any of several other bats that do not feed on blood but are sometimes reputed to do so **4** a trapdoor on a theatre stage [Fr, fr Ger *vampir*, of Slav origin; akin to Serb *vampir* vampire]

**vampirism** /'vampiriz(ə)m/ *n* **1** belief in vampires **2** the actions of a vampire

**¹van** /van/ *n*, *dial Eng* a winnowing device (eg a fan) [ME, fr MF, fr L *vannus* (cf FAN)]

**²van** *n* a vanguard [by shortening]

**³van** *n* **1** an enclosed motor vehicle used for transport of goods, animals, furniture, etc **2** *chiefly Br* an enclosed railway goods wagon [short for *caravan*]

**vanadate** /'vanədayt/ *n* any of various chemical compounds (SALTS or ESTERS) formed by combination between VANADIC

ACID and a metal atom, an alcohol, or another chemical group

**vanadic** /və'naydik, -'na-/ *adj* of or containing vanadium, esp with a relatively high VALENCY

**vanadic acid** *n* **1** any of various acids that consist of VANADIUM PENTOXIDE chemically combined with water or are known esp in the form of their chemical compounds (SALTS and ESTERS) **2** VANADIUM PENTOXIDE

**vanadinite** /və'naydiˌniet/ *n* a mineral, $Pb_5(VO_4)_3Cl$, consisting of lead vanadate and chloride and occurring in yellowish, brownish, or ruby-red crystals [Ger *vanadinit*, fr *vanadin* vanadium, fr NL *vanadium*]

**vanadium** /və'naydi-əm/ *n* a greyish metallic chemical element that can have several VALENCIES, is easily worked and can be drawn out to form a wire, is found combined in minerals, and is used esp to form alloys (eg vanadium steel) [NL, fr ON *Vanadīs* Freya, Norse goddess of love & beauty]

**vanadium pentoxide** /pen'toksied/ *n* a yellowish-red chemical compound, $V_2O_5$, used esp in making glass and as a catalyst

**vanadous** /'vanədəs/ *adj* of or containing vanadium, esp with a relatively low VALENCY

**Van Allen belt** /van 'alən/ *n* either of two belts of electrically charged particles that surround the earth in the outer atmosphere [James A *Van Allen* b1914 US physicist]

**vandal** /'vandl/ *n* **1** *cap* a member of a Germanic people who overran Gaul, Spain, and N Africa in the 4th and 5th centuries AD, and in 455 sacked Rome **2** a person who wilfully or ignorantly destroys, damages, or defaces property belonging to another or to the public [L *Vandalii* (pl), of Gmc origin] – **vandal** *adj*, *often cap*, **Vandalic** *adj*

**vandalism** /-ˌiz(ə)m/ *n* wilful or malicious destruction or defacement of public or private property – **vandalistic** *adj*

**vandal·ize, -ise** /'vandəliez/ *vt* to destroy or damage, esp ignorantly or maliciously – **vandalization** *n*

**Van de Graaff generator** /ˌvan də 'grahf/ *n* an apparatus for the production of electrical discharges at high voltage, typically consisting of an insulated hollow conducting sphere that accumulates in its interior the charge continuously conveyed from a source of direct current by a belt of flexible nonconducting material [Robert J *Van de Graaff* †1967 US physicist]

**van der Waals forces** /ˌvan də 'wahlz, 'vahlz/ *n pl* the relatively weak attractive forces that are operative between neutral atoms and molecules and that arise because of differences in electric potential [Johannes *van der Waals* †1923 D physicist]

**Vandyke** /ˌvan'diek/ *n* **1a** a wide collar with a deeply indented edge **b** (any of) a series of V-shaped points forming a decorative edging **2** a trim pointed beard [Sir Anthony *Vandyke* (Van Dyck) †1641 Flem painter, in whose paintings such collars and beards often appear] – **vandyked** *adj*

**Vandyke brown** *n* a dark brown pigment; *esp* one obtained from bog earth or peat or lignite deposits [fr its use by the painter Vandyke]

**vane** /vayn/ *n* **1** WEATHER VANE **2** a thin flat or curved object that is rotated about an axis by wind or water ⟨*the* ~s *of a windmill*⟩; *also* a device revolving in a similar manner and moving in water or air ⟨*the* ~s *of a propeller*⟩ **3** the flat expanded part of a feather **4** any of the usu three feathers fastened to the shaft of an arrow near the end that slots into the bowstring **5a** the sliding marker on a surveyor's LEVELLING STAFF **b** any of the sights of a compass or quadrant △ vain, vein [ME (southern), fr OE *fana* banner; akin to OHG *fano* cloth, L *pannus* cloth, rag] – **vaned** *adj*

**vang** /vang/ *n* a rope that runs from the upper end of a GAFF (spar from which a FORE AND AFT sail is suspended) to the deck and is used to control the gaff [alter. of *fang* (in the sense 'instrument for gripping or holding')]

**vanguard** /'vangahd/ *n* **1** *taking sing or pl vb* the troops moving at the head of an army **2** the forefront of an action or movement [ME *vantgard*, fr MF *avant-garde*, fr OF, fr *avant-* fore- (fr *avant* before, fr L *abante*) + *garde* guard – more at AD-VANCE]

**vanilla** /və'nilə/ *n* **1** any of a genus (*Vanilla*) of tropical American climbing orchids whose long capsular fruits yield an important flavouring; *also* VANILLA POD **2** a commercially important extract of the VANILLA POD that is used esp as a flavouring [NL, genus name, fr Sp *vainilla* vanilla (plant and fruit), dim. of *vaina* sheath, fr L *vagina*]

**vanilla bean** *n* VANILLA POD

**vanilla pod** *n* the fruit of a vanilla

**vanillic** /və'nilik/ *adj* of or derived from vanilla or vanillin

**vanillin** /və'nilin/ *n* a chemical compound, $C_8H_8O_3$, that is the chief fragrant component of vanilla and is used esp in flavouring and in perfumery

**vanish** /'vanish/ *vi* **1a** to pass quickly from sight; disappear **b** to (suddenly) cease to exist **2** *maths* to assume the value zero ~ *vt* to cause to disappear ⟨*the magician* ~ed *the rabbit*⟩ [ME *vanisshen*, fr MF *evaniss-*, stem of *evanir*, fr (assumed) VL *exvanire*, alter. of L *evanescere* to dissipate like vapour, vanish, fr *e-* + *vanescere* to vanish, fr *vanus* empty] – **vanisher** *n*

**vanishing cream** /'vanishing/ *n* a light cosmetic cream that is less oily than COLD CREAM and is used as a cleaner, moisturizer, etc

**vanishing point** *n* **1** a point at which receding parallel lines seem to meet when represented in linear perspective **2** a point at which something disappears or ceases to exist

**Vanitory** /'vanit(ə)ri/ *trademark* – used for a unit consisting of a washbasin surrounded by a flat top for use as a dressing table

**vanity** /'vanəti/ *n* **1** something that is vain, empty, or valueless **2** the quality of being vain or futile **3** excessive pride in oneself; conceit **4** an instance or display of being vain **5** *NAm* a powder compact **6** *NAm* DRESSING TABLE *synonyms* see ¹PRIDE *antonym* modesty [ME *vanite*, fr OF *vanité*, fr L *vanitat-*, *vanitas* quality of being empty or vain, fr *vanus* empty, vain – more at WANE]

**vanity case** *n* a woman's small case for carrying toiletries, cosmetics, etc

**vanity fair** *n, often cap V&F* a scene or place of frivolity and ostentation [*Vanity-Fair*, a fair held in the frivolous town of Vanity in *Pilgrim's Progress* by John Bunyan †1688 E preacher & writer]

**vanity press** *n* a publishing house that publishes books at the author's expense

**vanity publisher** *n* VANITY PRESS

**vanquish** /'vangkwish, 'van-/ *vt* **1** to overcome in battle; subdue completely **2** to defeat in a conflict or contest **3** to gain mastery over (an emotion, passion, or temptation) [ME *venquissen*, fr MF *venquis*, preterite of *veintre* to conquer, fr L *vincere* – more at VICTOR] – **vanquishable** *adj*, **vanquisher** *n*

**vantage** /'vahntij/ *n* **1** a position giving a strategic advantage or commanding perspective ⟨*a point of* ~ *on top of the hill*⟩ **2** *Br* ADVANTAGE **4** (first point won in tennis after deuce) **3** *archaic* benefit, gain △ advantage [ME, fr AF, fr MF *avantage* – more at ADVANTAGE]

**vanward** /'vanwod/ *adj* located in the vanguard; forward

**vapid** /'vapid/ *adj* lacking liveliness, interest, or force; flat, insipid [L *vapidus* flat-tasting; akin to L *vappa* flat wine, & prob to L *vapor* steam] – **vapidity** *n*, **vapidly** *adv*, **vapidness** *n*

**vapor·ize, -ise** /'vaypə,riez/ *vt* **1** to convert into vapour (e g by the application of heat or by spraying) **2** to destroy by conversion into vapour ⟨~d *by the nuclear explosion*⟩ ~ *vi* to become vaporized – **vaporizable** *adj*, **vaporization** *n*

**vapor·izer, -iser** /'vaypəriezə/ *n* something that vaporizes: e g **a** an atomizer **b** a device for converting water or a medicated liquid into a vapour for inhalation

**vaporous** /'vayp(ə)rəs/ *adj* **1** resembling, consisting of, or characteristic of vapour **2** producing vapours; volatile **3** containing or obscured by vapours; misty **4** ethereal, unsubstantial ⟨~ *twilight landscapes* – *Time*⟩ – **vaporously** *adv*, **vaporousness** *n*

**¹vapour, *NAm* vapor** /'vaypə/ *n* **1** diffused matter (e g smoke or fog) suspended in the air and making it misty **2** a substance in the gaseous state as distinguished from the liquid or solid state **3** a substance (e g petrol, alcohol, or mercury) vaporized for industrial, therapeutic, or military uses; *also* a mixture (e g the explosive mixture in an internal-combustion engine) of such a vapour with air **4** *archaic* **4a** something unsubstantial or transitory; an illusion **b** a foolish or fanciful idea ⟨*what amazing* ~s *a lonely man may get into his head* – H G Wells⟩ **5** *pl, archaic* **5a** a substance given off by a bodily organ (e g the stomach) held to produce depression, hysteria, or hypochondria **b** a depressed or hysterical condition – usu + *the* [ME *vapour*, fr MF *vapeur*, fr L *vapor* steam, vapour] – **vapoury** *adj*

**²vapour, *NAm chiefly* vapor** *vi* **1** to rise or pass off as vapour ⟨*could see his breath and my own* ~ing *in the freezing air* – H E Bates⟩ **2** to emit vapour **3** *archaic* to indulge in bragging, blustering, or idle talk

**vapour concentration** *n* the mass of water vapour present in a unit volume of air

**vapourer moth** /'vaypərə/ *n* a TUSSOCK MOTH (*Orgyia antiqua*) the female of which has much reduced and nonfunctional wings; *also* any of several related moths

**vapouring** /'vayp(ə)ring/ *n usu pl* an idle, extravagant, or highflown expression or speech

**vapourish** /'vaypərish/ *adj* **1** resembling or suggestive of vapour; vaporous **2** *archaic* given to fits of depression or hysteria

**vapour pressure** *n* the pressure exerted by a vapour that is in equilibrium with its solid or liquid form

**vapour trail** *n* a trail of condensed water vapour created in the air by an aircraft flying at high altitude

**vaquero** /və'keəroh/ *n, pl* **vaqueros** *SW US* a herdsman, cowboy [Sp, fr *vaca* cow, fr L *vacca*]

**vara** /'vahrə/ *n* any of various Spanish, Portuguese, and Latin-American units of length equal to between 0.79 and 0.86 metre (31 and 34 inches) [Sp & Pg, lit., pole, fr L, forked pole, fr fem of *varus* bent, crooked – more at PREVARICATE]

**varactor** /və'raktə/ *n* a SEMICONDUCTOR (made of a substance having limited electrical conducting properties) device that is a component of an electronic circuit (e g a switch) and whose CAPACITANCE (property of a conductor enabling it to store electric charge) depends on the applied voltage – compare VARISTOR [*varying* + *reactor*]

**vari-** /'veəri-/, **vario-** *comb form* varied; diverse ⟨*variform*⟩ ⟨*variocoupler*⟩ [L *varius* – more at VARIOUS]

**¹variable** /'veəri·əbl/ *adj* **1a** able or apt to vary; subject to variation or changes ⟨~ *winds*⟩ **b** fickle, inconstant **2** having the characteristics of a variable ⟨*a* ~ *number*⟩ **3** *of a biological group or character* not true to type; aberrant – **variableness** *n*, **variably** *adv*, **variability** *n*

**²variable** *n* **1** something that is variable **2** (a symbol representing) a quantity that may assume any of a set of values **3** VARIABLE STAR

**variable cost** *n* a cost (e g for labour or materials) that varies directly with the level of production

**variable geometry** *adj, of an aircraft* SWING-WING (having wings whose angle can be varied for best performance at high and low speeds)

**variable star** *n* a star whose brightness changes usu in more or less regular periods

**variance** /'veəri·əns/ *n* **1** the fact, quality, or state of being variable or variant; difference, variation ⟨*yearly* ~ *in crops*⟩ **2** the fact or state of being in disagreement; dissension, dispute **3** *law* an inconsistency, esp between two pieces of evidence that are intended to support one another **5** *statistics* the square of the STANDARD DEVIATION **6** *NAm* permission to depart from the usual rules – **at variance** not in harmony or agreement

*usage* **1** Things are **at variance** *with*, not *from*, one another. **2** It is a common confusion to speak of things as being △ *at* **variants**.

**¹variant** /'veəri·ənt/ *adj* **1** displaying variety, deviation, or disagreement **2** varying usu slightly from the standard form ⟨~ *readings*⟩

**²variant** *n* any of two or more people or things exhibiting usu slight differences: e g a **a** one who or that which exhibits variation from a type or norm **b** any of two or more different spellings, pronunciations, or forms of the same word *usage* see VARIANCE

**variate** /'veəri·ət/ *n* RANDOM VARIABLE (quantity depending on the result of a statistical experiment)

**variation** /,veəri'aysh(ə)n/ *n* **1a** varying or being varied **b** an instance of varying **c** the extent to which or the range in which a thing varies **2** DECLINATION **3** (angle between MAGNETIC NORTH and true north) **3** a change in the average motion or orbit of a celestial body **4** (a measure of) the change in the value of a mathematical variable or function **5** the repetition of a musical theme with modifications in rhythm, tune, harmony, or key **6a** divergence in the characteristics of an organism or its genetic makeup from those typical of its group **b** an individual or group exhibiting variation **7** a solo dance in ballet – **variational** *adj*, **variationally** *adv*

**varicella** /,vari'selə/ *n* CHICKEN POX [NL, irreg dim. of *variola*]

**varicocele** /'varikoh,seel/ *n* a varicose enlargement of the veins of the SPERMATIC CORD in the scrotum [NL, fr L *varic-*, *varix* + *-o-* + *-cele*]

**varicoloured** /'veəri,kuləd/ *adj* having various colours; variegated ⟨~ *nuptial plumage of a bird*⟩

**varicose** /'varikəs, -kohs/ *also* **varicosed** /-,kohst, -kohzd/ *adj* abnormally swollen or dilated ⟨~ *veins*⟩ [L *varicosus* full of dilated veins, fr *varic-*, *varix* dilated vein]

**varicosity** /ˌvariˈkosəti/ *n* **1** the quality or state of being varicose **2** a swollen part; *esp* VARIX (swollen vein, artery, or other vessel)

**varied** /ˈveərid/ *adj* **1** having numerous forms or types; diverse **2** VARIEGATED 2 – **variedly** *adv*

**variegate** /ˈveəri‧ə‧gayt, -riˌgayt/ *vt* **1** to diversify in external appearance, esp with patches of different colours; dapple **2** to give variety to [L *variegatus*, pp of *variegare*, fr *varius* various + *-egare* (akin to L *agere* to drive) – more at AGENT] – **variegator** *n*, **variegation** *n*

**variegated** /ˈveərigaytid/ *adj* **1** VARIED 1 **2** marked with patches of different colours ⟨~ *leaves*⟩

**variegated cutworm** *n* a moth (*Peridroma saucia*) whose destructive larva is a CUTWORM (nocturnal caterpillar) attacking crops in most cultivated areas of the world

**variety** /vəˈrie‧əti/ *n* **1** the state of having different forms or types; diversity **2** a number or collection of different things, esp of a particular class; an assortment **3a** something differing from others of the same general kind; a sort **b** any of various groups of plants or animals ranking below a species; a subspecies **4** theatrical entertainment consisting of separate performances (e g of songs, skits, or acrobatics) [MF or L; MF *variété*, fr L *varietat-*, *varietas*, fr *varius* various]

**variety meat** *n, chiefly NAm* edible offal

**variform** /ˈveəriˌfawm/ *adj* varied in form

**variola** /vəˈrie‧ələ/ *n* smallpox, cowpox, or any of various other virus diseases marked by a rash of pus-filled spots or blisters [NL, fr ML, pustule, pox, fr LL, pustule] – **variolous** *adj*

**varioloid** /ˈveəriˌəloyd/ *n* a modified mild form of smallpox that occurs in people who have had, or have been vaccinated against, smallpox

**variometer** /ˌveəriˈomitə/ *n* **1** an instrument for measuring MAGNETIC DECLINATION (angle between MAGNETIC NORTH and true north) **2** an aeronautical instrument for indicating rate of climb

**variorum** /ˌveəriˈawrəm/ *n* **1** an edition or text with notes by different people **2** an edition of a publication containing variant readings of the text [L *variorum* of various people (gen pl masc of *varius*), in the phrase *cum notis variorum* with the notes of various people] – **variorum** *adj*

**various** /ˈveəri‧əs/ *adj* **1a** of differing kinds; diverse **b** dissimilar in nature or form; unlike ⟨*animals as* ~ *as the jaguar and the sloth*⟩ **2** more than one; several ⟨*stop at* ~ *towns*⟩ **3** individual, separate ⟨*refunds to the* ~ *club members*⟩ **4** *poetic* variegated ⟨*birds of* ~ *plumage* – H W Longfellow⟩ **5** *archaic* having a number of different aspects or characteristics ⟨*one whose conversation was so* ~ *and delightful* – W M Thackeray⟩ **6** *archaic* variable, inconstant **synonyms** see DIFFERENT **antonyms** uniform, homogeneous [L *varius;* prob akin to L *varus* bent, crooked – more at PREVARICATE] – **variousness** *n*

**variously** /ˈveəri‧əsli/ *adv* **1** in various ways; at various times ⟨*was* ~ *occupied in teaching, farming, and writing*⟩ **2** by various designations ⟨*known* ~ *as principal, headmaster, and rector*⟩

**varistor** /vəˈristə/ *n* a SEMICONDUCTOR (made of a substance having limited electrical conducting properties) device that is a component of an electronic circuit and whose electrical RESISTANCE (force opposing flow of electric current) depends on the applied voltage – compare VARACTOR [*vari-* + *resistor*]

**varix** /ˈvariks/ *n, pl* **varices** /ˈvariˌseez/ **1** an abnormally dilated and lengthened vein, artery, or lymph vessel; *esp* a varicose vein **2** any of the prominent ridges across each whorl of the shell of a snail, whelk, limpet, etc [L *varic-*, *varix*]

**varlet** /ˈvahlit/ *n* **1** a knight's page in former times **2** *archaic* a base unprincipled person; a knave, rogue **3** *archaic* an attendant, menial [ME, fr MF *vaslet*, *varlet* young nobleman, page – more at VALET]

**varletry** /ˈvahlətri/ *n taking pl vb, archaic* a group of common people; a rabble

**varmint** /ˈvahmint/ *n, dial or NAm* **1** an animal or bird considered a pest; *specif* an animal classed as vermin and unprotected by game law **2** *informal* an irritating, mischievous, or objectionable person; a rascal [alter. of *vermin*]

[1]**varnish** /ˈvahnish/ *n* **1a** a liquid preparation that when spread and allowed to dry on a surface forms a hard shiny typically transparent coating **b** the covering or glaze given by the application of varnish **2** a superficial and deceptive appearance or show; VENEER 3 ⟨*a* ~ *of respectability*⟩ [ME *vernisch*, fr MF *vernis*, fr OIt or ML; OIt *vernice*, fr ML *veronic-*, *veronix* sandarac (resin)]

[2]**varnish** *vt* **1** to apply varnish to **2** to cover or conceal with something that gives an improving appearance; gloss *over* – **varnisher** *n*

**varnish tree** *n* any of various trees yielding a milky juice from which varnish or lacquer can be prepared; *esp* a Japanese sumach (*Rhus verniciflua*)

**varoom** /vəˈroohm/ *vi, n, or interj* (to) vroom

**varsity** /ˈvahsiti/ *n, Br* a university; *esp* either Oxford or Cambridge – no longer in vogue [by shortening & alter. fr *university*]

**varus** /ˈvayrəs/ *n* the position of a bone or part that is turned inwards at its joint to an abnormal degree – compare VALGUS [NL, fr L, bent, knock-kneed]

**varve** /vahv/ *n* a band of sediment composed of two distinct layers of silt or clay believed to comprise an annual cycle of deposition in a body of still water [Sw *varv* turn, layer; akin to OE *hweorfan* to turn – more at WHARF] – **varved** *adj*

**vary** /ˈveəri/ *vt* **1** to make a partial change in; make different in some attribute or characteristic **2** to ensure variety in; diversify ⟨*the days were not crowded, but they were enviably* varied – Virginia Woolf⟩ ~ *vi* **1** to exhibit or undergo change ⟨*a constantly* ~ing *sky*⟩ **2a** to exhibit variety; differ **b** *maths* to deviate, depart ⟨*values* ~ing *from the mean*⟩ – usu + *from* **3** *maths & statistics* to take on values ⟨*y* varies *inversely with x*⟩ **4** to exhibit biological variation; to differ in structure or physiology from what is typical or usual in the group **synonyms** see [1]CHANGE [ME *varien*, fr MF or L; MF *varier*, fr L *variare*, fr *varius* various] – **varyingly** *adv*

**vas** /vas, vahs/ *n, pl* **vasa** /ˈvaysə, ˈvahsə/ an anatomical vessel; a duct [NL, fr L, vessel] – **vasal** *adj*

**vas-** /vas-, vayz-/, **vaso-** *comb form* **1** vessel (e g blood vessel) ⟨*vasodilator*⟩ **2** vascular and ⟨*vasovagal*⟩ [NL, fr L *vas*]

**vasa efferentia** /ˈvaysə efəˈrenshiə, -siə, -shə, vayzə/ *pl of* VAS EFFERENS

**vascular** /ˈvaskyoolə/ *adj* of or being a channel or system of channels for conducting a body fluid (e g blood or sap) in an animal or plant; *also* supplied with or made up of such channels, esp blood vessels ⟨*a* ~ *tumour*⟩ ⟨*a* ~ *system*⟩ [NL *vascularis*, fr L *vasculum* small vessel, dim. of *vas*] – **vascularity** *n*

**vascular bundle** *n* a single strand of the vascular system of a plant consisting usu of water-conducting tissue (XYLEM), food-conducting tissue (PHLOEM), together with woody fibres and PARENCHYMA (soft thin-walled plant tissue)

**vascular cylinder** *n* STELE (central vascular tissue in the stems and roots of plants)

**vascular-ization, -isation** /ˌvaskyoolərieˈzaysh(ə)n/ *n* the process of becoming vascular; *also* abnormal or excessive formation of blood vessels (e g in the retina or on the cornea of the eye)

**vascular-ize, -ise** /ˈvaskyooləˌriez/ *vb* to make or become vascular

**vascular plant** *n* a plant (e g a fern, conifer, or FLOWERING PLANT) having a specialized liquid-conducting system that includes XYLEM (water-conducting tissue) and PHLOEM (food-conducting tissue)

**vascular ray** *n* any of several wedges of PARENCHYMA (soft thin-walled plant tissue), formed from CAMBIUM, that connect XYLEM (water-conducting tissue) and PHLOEM (food-conducting tissue) in a VASCULAR PLANT

**vascular tissue** *n* plant tissue concerned mainly with conducting liquids; *esp* the specialized tissue of higher plants consisting essentially of XYLEM (water-conducting tissue) and PHLOEM (food-conducting tissue) and forming a continuous conducting system throughout the plant body

**vasculature** /ˈvaskyooləchə/ *n* the arrangement of blood vessels in an organ or part [L *vasculum* vessel + E *-ature* (as in *musculature*)]

**vasculum** /ˈvaskyooləm/ *n, pl* **vascula** /-lə/ a usu metal and commonly cylindrical or flattened covered box used by botanists for storing plants as they are collected [NL, fr L, small vessel]

**vas deferens** /ˌvaz ˈdefərenz, vas/ *n, pl* **vasa deferentia** /ˌvaysə defəˈrenshiə, -siə, -shə, vayzə/ a duct, esp of a higher VERTEBRATE animal, that carries sperm to the copulatory organ (e g the penis) [NL, lit., deferent vessel]

**vase** /vahz/ *n* an ornamental vessel, usu of greater depth than width, that is used esp for holding flowers [Fr, fr L *vas* vessel; akin to Umbrian *vasor* vessels]

**vasectomy** /vəˈsektəmi, va-/ *n* surgical removal of a section of the VAS DEFERENS usu to induce permanent sterility, used as a form of contraception [ISV *vas-* + *-ectomy*] – **vasectomize** *vt*

**vas efferens** /,vaz 'efərenz, vas/ *n, pl* **vasa efferentia** /,vaysə efə'renshiə, -siə, -shə, vayzə/ any of the 12 to 20 tubes that lead from the testes to the VAS DEFERENS and form the compact head of the EPIDIDYMIS [NL, lit., efferent vessel]

**Vaseline** /,vas(ə)l'een/ *trademark* – used for PETROLEUM JELLY

**vasiform** /'vasi,fawm/ *adj* having the form of a hollow tube [NL *vasiformis*, fr L *vas* vessel + *-iformis* -iform]

**vaso-** – see VAS-

**vasoactive** /,vasoh'aktiv, ,vayzoh-/ *adj* affecting the blood vessels, esp by causing them to relax or contract – **vasoactivity** *n*

**vasoconstriction** /,vayzohkən'striksh(ə)n/ *n* narrowing of the diameter of blood vessels, esp as a result of nerve action [ISV] – **vasoconstrictive** *adj*

**vasoconstrictor** /,vayzohkən'striktə/ *n* something (e g a nerve of the SYMPATHETIC NERVOUS SYSTEM or a drug) that induces or initiates vasoconstriction

**vasodilatation** /,vayzohdiela'taysh(ə)n/ *n* vasodilation [ISV]

**vasodilation** /,vayzohdie'laysh(ə)n/ *n* widening of the blood vessels, esp as a result of nerve action

**vasodilator** /,vayzohdie'laytə/ *n* something (e g a nerve of the PARASYMPATHETIC NERVOUS SYSTEM or a drug) that induces or initiates vasodilation

**vasoinhibitor** /'vasoh-in,hibitə, 'vayzoh-/ *n* a drug or other agent that inhibits the action of the vasomotor nerves

**vasomotor** /,vayzə'mohtə/ *adj* of or being nerves or centres controlling the size of blood vessels [ISV]

**vasopressin** /,vayzoh'presin/ *n* a hormone secreted by the back lobe of the PITUITARY GLAND that increases blood pressure and decreases urine flow [fr *Vasopressin*, a trademark]

**vasopressor** /,vayzoh'presə/ *adj* causing a rise in blood pressure by constricting the blood vessels – **vasopressor** *n*

**vasospasm** /'vayzoh,spazm/ *n* sharp and often persistent contraction of a blood vessel reducing its diameter and blood flow [ISV] – **vasospastic** *adj*

**vasotocin** /,vayzə'tohsin/ *n* a hormone of most lower VERTEBRATE animals (e g fish and amphibians) that is secreted by the PITUITARY GLAND and is believed to have properties similar to vasopressin [*vaso-* + *oxytocin*]

**vasovagal** /,vayzoh'vaygl/ *adj* of or involving both the blood circulation and the VAGUS (nerve supplying the heart, lungs, and gut)

**vassal** /'vas(ə)l/ *n* 1 a man, or sometimes a woman, in a feudal society who has vowed homage and loyalty to another as his/her feudal lord in return for protection and often a source of income (FIEF), esp land 2 somebody in a subservient or subordinate position [ME, fr MF, fr ML *vassallus*, fr *vassus* servant, vassal, of Celt origin; akin to W *gwas* boy, servant] – **vassal** *adj*

**vassalage** /'vasl·ij/ *n* 1 the state of being a vassal 2 the homage, fealty, or services due from a vassal 3 a position of subordination or submission (e g to a political power)

**¹vast** /vahst/ *adj* very great in amount, degree, intensity, or esp in extent or range; huge *synonyms* see HUGE *antonyms* restricted, minute [L *vastus*; akin to OIr *fot* length] – **vastly** *adv*, **vastness** *n*

**²vast** *n, poetic* a boundless space; an immensity ⟨*the ~ of heaven* – John Milton⟩

**vastitude** /'vahstityoohd/ *n, archaic* immensity, vastness

**vastity** /'vahstiti/ *n, archaic* vastitude

**vasty** /'vahsti/ *adj, archaic or poetic* vast ⟨*call spirits from the ~ deep* – Shak⟩

**¹vat** /vat/ *n* 1 a tub, barrel, or other large vessel, esp for holding liquids undergoing chemical change or preparations for dyeing or tanning 2 a liquid containing a dye in its soluble form, that, when textile material is steeped in the liquid and exposed to the air, is converted by OXIDATION to the original insoluble dye and deposited in the fibre [ME *fat*, *vat*, fr OE *fæt*; akin to OHG *vaz* vessel, Lith *puodas* pot]

**²vat** *vt* **-tt-** to put into or treat in a vat

**VAT** *also* **vat** /,vee ay 'tee, vat/ *n, Br informal* VALUE-ADDED TAX

**vat dye** *n* a water-insoluble generally fast dye used for dyeing textile materials in a vat – **vat-dyed** *adj*

**vatic** /'vatik/ *adj, formal* prophetic, oracular ⟨*a poem with wild and doom-laden ~ imagery*⟩ [L *vates* seer, prophet; akin to OE *wōth* poetry, OHG *wuot* madness, OIr *fāith* seer, poet]

**Vatican** /'vatikən/ *n* 1 the official residence of the Pope and the administrative centre of Roman Catholicism 2 the papal

government [L *Vaticanus* Vatican Hill (in Rome)] – **Vatican** *adj*

**vaticinal** /və'tisinl/ *adj, formal* prophetic [L *vaticinus*, fr *vaticinari* to prophesy]

**vaticinate** /və'tisi,nayt, va-/ *vb, formal* to prophesy, predict [L *vaticinatus*, pp of *vaticinari*, fr *vates* + *-cinari* (akin to L *canere* to sing) – more at CHANT] – **vaticinator** *n*, **vaticination** *n*

**vatted malt** *n* a MALT WHISKY made from several different malt whiskies blended together

**vaudeville** /'vawdə,vil/ *n* 1 a light often comic theatrical piece frequently combining pantomime, dialogue, dancing, and song 2 *NAm* stage entertainment typical of a music hall; variety – compare BURLESQUE [Fr, fr MF, popular satirical song, alter. of *vaudevire*, fr *vau-de-Vire* valley of Vire, fr *vau*, *val* valley + *de* from, of (fr L) + *Vire*, town in NW France where such songs were composed]

**¹vault** /vawlt, volt/ *n* 1a an arched structure of masonry, usu forming a ceiling or roof b something (e g the sky) resembling a vault c an arched or dome-shaped anatomical structure 2a a space covered by an arched structure; *esp* an underground passage, room, or storage compartment b a room or compartment for the safekeeping of valuables 3a a burial chamber, esp beneath a church or in a cemetery b a prefabricated container, usu of metal or concrete, into which a coffin is placed at burial [ME *voute*, fr MF, fr (assumed) VL *volvita* turn, vault, prob fr *volvitare* to turn, leap]

**²vault** *vt* to form or cover (as if) with a vault

**³vault** *vb* to bound vigorously (over); *esp* to execute a leap (over) using the hands or a pole [MF *volter*, fr OIt *voltare*, fr (assumed) VL *volvitare* to turn, leap, freq of L *volvere* to roll – more at VOLUBLE] – **vaulter** *n*

**⁴vault** *n* an act of vaulting; a leap – compare POLE VAULT

**vaulted** /'vawltid, 'voltid/ *adj* 1 built in the form of a vault; arched 2 covered with a vault

**¹vaulting** /'vawlting, 'volting/ *n* 1 the framework or structure of a vault 2 a vault, vaulted ceiling, or vaults considered collectively

**²vaulting** *adj* 1 reaching or stretching for the heights; esp exaggerated ⟨*~ ambition*⟩ 2 designed for use in vaulting or in gymnastic exercises ⟨*a ~ block*⟩ [(1) fr prp of ³*vault;* (2) fr gerund of ³*vault*]

**vaulting horse** *n* an apparatus like a POMMEL HORSE without pommels that is used for vaulting feats in gymnastics; *also* a gymnastics event in which this is used

**¹vaunt** /vawnt/ *vi, archaic* to boast of one's own worth or attainments; brag ~ *vt* to call attention to proudly and often boastfully ⟨*our ~ed progress has its darker side*⟩ *synonyms* see ²BOAST [ME *vaunten*, fr MF *vanter*, fr LL *vanitare*, fr L *vanitas* vanity] – **vaunter** *n*, **vauntingly** *adv*

**²vaunt** *n* 1 a bragging assertive statement 2 a boastful display

**,vaunt-'courier** *n, archaic* one sent in advance; a forerunner, herald [MF *avant-courrier*, lit., advance courier]

**vavasour, vavasor** /'vavə,sooə/ *n* a feudal tenant ranking directly below a baron [ME *vavasour*, fr OF *vavassor*, prob fr ML *vassus vassorum* vassal of vassals]

**vaward** /'vaw(w)ood/ *n, archaic* the foremost part; the forefront ⟨*the ~ of our youth* – Shak⟩ [ME *vauntwarde*, *vaward*, fr ONF *avantwarde*, fr *avant* before (fr L *abante*) + *warde* guard, fr *warder* to guard – more at ADVANCE, REWARD]

**VD** /,vee 'dee/ *n* VENEREAL DISEASE

**VDT** *also* **vdt** /,vee dee 'tee/ *n* a VDU [*visual display terminal*]

**VDU, vdu** /,vee dee 'yooh/ *n* a device for the visual display of information (e g from a computer) typically in the form of text presented on a CATHODE-RAY TUBE [*visual display unit*]

**'ve** /v/ *vb* have ⟨*we've been there*⟩ [by contr]

**veal** /veel, viəl/ *n* 1 the flesh of a young calf used as food 2 *NAm* a calf; *esp* a vealer [ME *veel*, fr MF, fr L *vitellus* small calf, dim. of *vitulus* calf – more at WETHER] – **vealy** *adj*

**vealer** /'veelə/ *n, NAm* a calf reared for or suitable for veal

**vectograph** /'vektə,grahf/ *n* a picture composed of two superimposed STEREOSCOPIC images that give a three-dimensional effect when viewed through polarizing spectacles [*vector* + *-graph*] – **vectographic** *adj*

**¹vector** /'vektə/ *n* 1a(1) a quantity (e g velocity or force) that has both magnitude and direction and that is usu represented by a straight line with an arrow whose length represents the magnitude and whose orientation in space represents the direction a(2) an element of a VECTOR SPACE b a course or compass direction, esp of an aircraft 2a an organism (e g an insect) that transmits a disease-causing agent b POLLINATOR 1 (agent that pollinates flowers) [NL, fr L, carrier, fr *vectus,* pp of *vehere* to carry – more at WAY] – **vectorial** *adj*

²**vector** *vt* **1** to guide (eg an aircraft, its pilot, or a missile) in flight by means of a radioed vector **2** to change the direction of (the thrust of a jet engine) for steering

**vector product** *n* a vector *c* whose length is the product of the lengths of two vectors *a* and *b* and the sine of their included angle, whose direction is that of a right-handed screw with axis *c* when *a* is rotated into *b*, and that lies in a plane perpendicular to that of *a* and *b*

**vector space** *n, maths* a set whose elements are generalized vectors and which is a COMMUTATIVE group under addition that is also CLOSED under an operation of multiplication by elements of a given FIELD having the properties that $c(A + B) = cA + cB$ and $(c + d)A = cA + dA$, $(cd)A = c(dA)$, and $1A = A$ where *A*, *B* are vectors, *c*, *d* are elements of the field, and 1 is the IDENTITY ELEMENT of the field under multiplication

**vector sum** *n* the sum of vectors that for two vectors is geometrically represented by the diagonal of a parallelogram whose sides represent the two vectors being added

**Veda** /'veedə, 'vay-/ *n* any of four collections of hymns, prayers, and liturgical formulas that comprise the earliest Hindu sacred writings [Skt, lit., knowledge; akin to Gk *eidenai* to know – more at WIT]

**vedalia** /vi'daylyə/ *n* an Australian ladybird (*Rodolia cardinalis*) introduced into many countries to control SCALE INSECTS which are pests on a wide variety of plants [NL]

**Vedanta** /və'dahntə, -'dan-/ *n* an orthodox system of Hindu philosophy developing, esp in a qualified MONISM (belief that the whole of reality is basically a single unit and that diversity is merely an illusion), the speculations of the UPANISHADS (collections of philosophical treatises forming the main body of Hindu scriptures) on ultimate reality and the liberation of the soul [Skt *Vedānta,* lit., end of the Veda, fr *Veda* + *anta* end; akin to OE *ende* end] – **Vedantism** *n,* **Vedantist** *n*

**Vedantic** /və'dantik/ *adj* **1** of the Vedanta philosophy **2** Vedic

**V-E Day** *n* (the anniversary of) the end of hostilities in Europe in World War II on 8 May 1945 [*Victory in Europe*]

**Vedda, Veddah** /'vedə/ *n* a member of an aboriginal people of Sri Lanka [Sinhalese *vedda* hunter]

**vedette** /vi'det/ *n* **1** a mounted sentinel stationed ahead of the outposts positioned in advance of the main body of an army **2** a small naval launch used as a patrol vessel [Fr, fr It *vedetta,* alter. of *veletta,* prob fr Sp *vela* watch, fr *velar* to keep watch, fr L *vigilare* to wake, watch, fr *vigil* awake]

**Vedic** /'veedik, 'vay-/ *adj* of the Vedas, the language in which they are written, or Hindu history and culture between 1500 BC and 500 BC

**vee** /vee/ *n* something shaped like the letter V

**veena** /'veenə/ *n* VINA (Indian stringed instrument)

¹**veer** /viə/ *vt* to let or pay out (eg a rope) [ME *veren,* of LG or D origin; akin to MD *vieren* to slacken, MLG *vīren*]

²**veer** *vi* **1** to change direction, position, or inclination; turn **2** *of the wind* to shift in a clockwise direction – compare BACK 3 to bring a ship onto a different course by turning the front away from the wind ∼ *vt* to direct (a ship) to a different course; *specif* WEAR 6 [MF *virer* – more at ENVIRON] – **veeringly** *adv*

³**veer** *n* a change in direction, position, or inclination

**veg** /vej/ *n, pl* **veg** *Br informal* a vegetable ⟨*meat and two* ∼⟩

**vegan** /'veegən, vaygən/ *n* a strict vegetarian who avoids food or other products derived from animals (eg dairy products or furs) [by contr fr *vegetarian*] – **vegan** *adj,* **veganism** *n*

¹**vegetable** /'vej(i)təbl/ *adj* **1a** of, constituting, or growing like plants **b** consisting of plants **2** made or obtained from plants or plant products [ME, fr ML *vegetabilis* growing, fr *vegetare* to grow, fr L, to animate, fr *vegetus* lively, fr *vegēre* to rouse, excite – more at WAKE] – **vegetably** *adv*

²**vegetable** *n* **1** PLANT 1b **2** a plant (eg the cabbage, bean, or potato) grown for an edible part which is usu eaten with the principal course of a meal; *also* this part of the plant **3a** a person with a dull undemanding existence **b** a person whose physical and esp mental capacities are severely impaired by illness or injury, and who is entirely dependent on the care of others

**vegetable ivory** *n* **1** the hard white opaque nutritive tissue (ENDOSPERM) within the IVORY NUT (seed of a S American palm) that takes a high polish and is used as a substitute for ivory **2** IVORY NUT

**vegetable kingdom** *n* PLANT KINGDOM

**vegetable marrow** *n* any of various large smooth-skinned elongated fruits of a cultivated variety of a climbing plant (*Cucurbita pepo* of the family Cucurbitaceae, the vegetable marrow family), used cooked as a vegetable; *also* a plant that bears vegetable marrows

**vegetable oil** *n* an oil of plant origin; *esp* a fatty oil (eg olive oil) obtained from seeds or fruits

**vegetable oyster** *n* SALSIFY (plant with a white edible root) [fr the oyster-like flavour of its roots]

**vegetable silk** *n* a cottony fibrous material obtained from the coating of tree seeds (eg of a Brazilian tree, *Chorisia speciosa,* of the baobab family) and used esp for stuffing cushions

**vegetable wax** *n* a wax of plant origin secreted commonly in thin flakes by the walls of the cells of the outer layer of plant stems or leaves

**vegetal** /'vejitl/ *adj* **1** vegetable **2** vegetative [ML *vegetare* to grow]

**vegetal pole** *n* the point on the surface of an egg that is diametrically opposite to the ANIMAL POLE and is usu marked by having less active division, more yolk, and dividing into larger BLASTOMERES (cells formed by the first divisions of an egg) than that about the animal pole, and by giving rise to the HYPOBLAST (inner layer of tissue) of the embryo

¹**vegetarian** /ˌveji'teəri·ən/ *n* someone who believes in or practises vegetarianism [²*vegetable* + *-arian*]

²**vegetarian** *adj* **1** of vegetarians or vegetarianism **2** consisting wholly of vegetables ⟨*a* ∼ *diet*⟩

**vegetarianism** /ˌveji'teəri·ənizm/ *n* the often ethically based theory or practice of living on a diet that excludes the flesh of animals and often animal products and that is made up of vegetables, fruits, cereals, and nuts – compare LACTO-VEGE-TARIANISM

**vegetate** /'veji,tayt/ *vi* **1a** to grow in the manner of a plant **b** to produce vegetation **2** *medicine* to produce fleshy or warty outgrowths ⟨*a vegetating tumour*⟩ **3** to lead a passive monotonous existence; stagnate ⟨*feels that she's vegetating in her present job*⟩ [ML *vegetatus,* pp of *vegetare* to grow]

**vegetation** /ˌveji'taysh(ə)n/ *n* **1** the process of vegetating **2** plant life or total plant cover (eg of an area) **3** an abnormal outgrowth on a body part (eg a heart valve) – **vegetational** *adj,* **vegetationally** *adv*

**vegetative** /'vejitətiv/ *adj* **1a(1)** growing or having the power of growing **a(2)** of or engaged in nutritive and growth functions as contrasted with reproductive functions ⟨*a* ∼ *nucleus*⟩ **b** promoting plant growth ⟨*the* ∼ *properties of soil*⟩ **c** of or involving propagation by nonsexual processes or methods **2** relating to, composed of, or suggesting vegetation ⟨∼ *cover*⟩ **3** of the plant kingdom or its members **4** affecting, arising from, or relating to involuntary body functions (eg digestion or circulation) – **vegetatively** *adv,* **vegetativeness** *n*

**vegete** /və'jeet/ *adj, archaic* lively, healthy [L *vegetus* – more at VEGETABLE]

**vegetive** /'vejətiv/ *adj* **1** vegetable **2** vegetative [ML *vegetare* to grow]

**vehement** /'vee·əmənt/ *adj* marked by forceful energy: eg **a** intensely felt; impassioned, fervent **b** forcibly expressed; emphatic [MF, fr L *vehement-, vehemens;* akin to L *vehere* to carry] – **vehemence** *n,* **vehemently** *adv*

**vehicle** /'vee·ək(ə)l/ *n* **1a** an inert medium (eg an oil) in which a medicinally active agent is administered **b** any of various usu liquid media acting esp as solvents, carriers, or binders for chemically active ingredients or pigments **2** a means of transmission; a carrier **3** a medium through which something is expressed or communicated **4a** a means of transporting something; a conveyance **b** MOTOR VEHICLE; *esp* a car **5** a work created to display the talents of a particular performer [Fr *véhicule,* fr L *vehiculum* carriage, conveyance, fr *vehere* to carry – more at WAY]

**vehicular** /vee'ikyoolə/ *adj* of or designed for vehicles, esp motor vehicles

¹**veil** /vayl/ *n* **1a** a length of cloth worn by women as a covering for the head and shoulders and often, esp in eastern countries, the face; *specif* the outer covering of a nun's headdress **b** a length of sheer fabric or netting worn over the head or face or attached for protection or ornament to a hat or headdress **c** any of various cloths used in religious ceremonies; *esp* a cloth used to cover the chalice containing the consecrated wine used at Communion **2** *the* cloistered life of a nun **3** a concealing curtain or cover of cloth **4a** something that hides or obscures like a veil ⟨*a* ∼ *of smoke*⟩ **b** a disguise, pretext ⟨*under the* ∼

*of national defence, preparations for war began*⟩ **5** a covering body part or membrane: eg **5a** VELUM **b** a layer of protective tissue enclosing the developing FRUITING BODY of fungi that in certain types (eg agarics) persists in the mature mushroom as a cuplike bag (VOLVA) enclosing the stem base and a membranous ring joining the edge of the cap to the stem [ME *veile*, fr ONF, fr L *vela*, pl of *velum* sail, awning, curtain, cloth] – **draw a veil over** to avoid mentioning (something unpleasant or undesirable) – **take the veil** to become a nun

²**veil** *vt* to cover, provide, or conceal (as if) with a veil ∼ *vi* to put on or wear a veil

**veiled** /vayld/ *adj* **1a** having or wearing a veil or a concealing cover ⟨*heavily* ∼ *women*⟩ **b** indistinct, muffled **2** disguised ⟨*thinly* ∼ *contempt*⟩

**veiling** /'vayling/ *n* **1** a veil **2** any of various light sheer fabrics

¹**vein** /vayn/ *n* **1a** a narrow water channel in rock or earth, or in ice **b** a deposit of coal, ore, etc, esp in a rock fissure; *also* such a fissure **2a** BLOOD VESSEL – not used technically **b** any of the tubular converging vessels that carry blood from the capillaries towards the heart – compare ARTERY **3a** any of the VASCULAR BUNDLES (strands of food- and water-conducting tissue) forming the framework of a leaf **b** any of the thickened ribs that serve to stiffen the wings of an insect **4** a wavy streak or marking suggesting a vein (eg in marble or cheese) **5a** a distinctive mode of expression; style ⟨*written . . . in the appropriate* ∼ *for commercial correspondence* – G B Shaw⟩ **b** a pervasive element or quality; a strain ⟨*a* ∼ *of irony in his writings*⟩ **c** a frame of mind; a mood, humour **d** a line of thought or action ⚠ vain, vane [ME *veine*, fr OF, fr L *vena*] – **veiny** *adj*

²**vein** *vt* to pattern (as if) with veins

**veined** /vaynd/ *adj* patterned (as if) with veins; having veins ⟨*a* ∼ *leaf*⟩ ⟨∼ *marble*⟩

**veining** /'vayning/ *n* a pattern of veins; venation

**veinlet** /'vaynlət/ *n* a small vein, esp of a leaf

**velamen** /və'laymən/ *n, pl* **velamina** /və'layminə/ the thick corky outer layer of the aerial roots of an EPIPHYTIC (growing but not parasitic on another plant) orchid that absorbs water from the atmosphere [NL, fr L, covering, fr *velare* to cover, fr *velum* veil]

**velamentous** /ˌveləˈmentəs/ *adj* of or resembling a thin membrane [NL *velamentum* membrane, fr L, covering, fr *velare* to cover]

**velar** /'veelə/ *adj* **1** of or forming a VELUM (curtainlike membrane or anatomical partition), esp the SOFT PALATE (rear portion of the roof of the mouth) **2** *of a consonant* formed with the back of the tongue touching or near the SOFT PALATE ⟨*the* ∼ /k/ *of* cool⟩ [NL *velaris*, fr *velum*] – **velar** *n*

**velarium** /vəˈleəri·əm/ *n, pl* **velaria** /-i·ə/ an awning over an ancient Roman theatre or amphitheatre [L, fr *velum* awning]

**velar·ize, -ise** /'veeləriez/ *vt* to modify (a speech sound) by velar articulation – **velarization** *n*

**Velcro** /'velkroh/ *trademark* – used for a fastening device consisting of two pieces, esp strips, of fabric that stick to each other by means of very small hooks that cling to loops

**veld, veldt** /velt, felt/ *n* a usu shrubby or thinly forested grassland, esp of southern Africa – compare PRAIRIE, PAMPAS, SAVANNA [Afrik *veld*, fr MD, fr OE *feld* field]

**veldschoen, veldskoen** /'velt,skoohn, 'felt-/ *n, SAfr* VELSKOEN (type of shoe) [by alter. (influenced by *veld*)]

**veleta, valeta** /və'leetə/ *n* a ballroom dance in waltz time that originated in England in about 1900 and was popular between the two World Wars [Sp *veleta* weathervane, fr *vela* cloth, veil, fr L *vela*, pl of *velum* veil]

**veliger** /'veelijə/ *n* a free-swimming second-stage larva of certain marine MOLLUSCS (eg oysters, whelks, or limpets) that has developed the VELUM (swimming organ) [NL, fr *velum* + -*ger* -gerous]

**velleity** /və'lee·əti/ *n, formal* a slight wish or tendency; an inclination that does not prompt any action [NL *velleitas*, fr L *velle* to wish, will – more at WILL]

**vellicate** /'velikayt/ *vi* to twitch [L *vellicatus*, pp of *vellicare* to nip, pinch, fr *vellere* to pluck, pull]

**vellum** /'veləm/ *n* **1** a fine-grained unsplit lambskin, kidskin, or calfskin prepared esp for writing on or for binding books **2** a strong cream-coloured paper [ME *velim*, fr MF *veelin*, fr *veelin*, adj, of a calf, fr *veel* calf – more at VEAL] – **vellum** *adj*

**veloce** /vay'lohchay/ *adv or adj* in a rapid manner – used as a direction in music [It, fr L *veloc-, velox* swift]

**velocimeter** /ˌveelohˈsimitə, ˌveloh-/ *n* a device for measuring speed (eg of machinery or sound) [*velocity* + -*meter*]

**velocipede** /vəˈlosipeed/ *n* **1** any of several early types of bicycle that were driven forward by the rider pushing with his/her foot on the ground **2** *NAm* a child's tricycle [Fr *vélocipède*, fr L *veloc-, velox* swift + *ped-, pes* foot – more at FOOT]

**velocity** /vəˈlosəti/ *n* **1** quickness of motion of esp inanimate things; speed ⟨*the* ∼ *of sound*⟩ **2** rate of change of distance with time in a given direction; speed in a given direction **3** rate of occurrence or action; rapidity ⟨*the* ∼ *of population growth*⟩ [MF *vélocité*, fr L *velocitat-, velocitas*, fr *veloc-, velox* swift; akin to L *vehere* to carry – more at WAY]

**velodrome** /'velə,drohm/ *n* a stadium or arena for bicycle racing, esp in France [Fr *vélodrome*, fr *vélo* cycle (short for *vélocipède*) + -*drome*]

**velour, velours** /və'looə/ *n, pl* **velours** **1** any of various fabrics with a pile or napped surface resembling velvet used in heavy weights for upholstery and curtains and in lighter weights for clothing (eg coats and jackets) **2** a fur felt finished with a long velvety nap and used esp for hats [Fr *velours* velvet, velour, fr MF *velours, velour*, fr OF *velous*, fr L *villosus* shaggy, fr *villus* shaggy hair]

**velouté** /vəˈloohtay/ *n* a basic white sauce made with a roux and chicken, veal, or fish stock – compare BÉCHAMEL [Fr, lit., velvety, fr MF, fr *velours* velvet]

**velskoen** /'velskoohn, 'fel-/ *n, SAfr* **1** a strong heavy shoe, esp of rawhide **2** DESERT BOOT [Afrik *velskoen*, fr *vel* skin + *skoen* shoe]

**velum** /'veeləm/ *n, pl* **vela** /-lə/ **1** a membrane or membranous part resembling a veil or curtain: eg **1a** SOFT PALATE (rear portion of the roof of the mouth) **b** a ring-shaped membrane projecting inwards from the margin of the UMBRELLA (saucerlike body) in some jellyfishes **2** a swimming organ that is well developed in the later larval stages of certain marine MOLLUSCS (eg oysters, whelks, or limpets) [NL, fr L, curtain, veil]

**velure** /və'l(y)ooə/ *n, obs* (a fabric resembling) velvet [modif of MF *velour*]

**velutinous** /vəˈloohtinəs/ *adj* covered with fine silky hairs; velvety ⟨*a* ∼ *rhizome*⟩ [NL *velutinus*, fr ML *velutum* velvet, prob fr OIt *velluto* shaggy, fr (assumed) VL *villutus*]

¹**velvet** /'velvit/ *n* **1** any of various clothing or upholstery fabrics (eg of silk, rayon, or cotton) with a short soft dense pile produced by cutting WARP (lengthways yarns) **2** something suggesting velvet (eg in softness or smoothness) **3** the soft downy skin containing blood vessels that envelops and nourishes the developing antlers of deer **4** *slang* a profit or gain beyond ordinary expectation ⟨*if one of them is real lucky . . . and finally gets to be well known and makes some money, well, it's so much* ∼ *then* – Louis Armstrong⟩ [ME *veluet, velvet*, fr MF *velu* shaggy, fr (assumed) VL *villutus*, fr L *villus* shaggy hair; akin to L *vellus* fleece – more at WOOL]

²**velvet** *adj* **1** made of or covered with velvet **2** resembling or suggesting velvet, esp in smoothness or softness; velvety

**velvet ant** *n* any of various solitary usu brightly coloured and hairy burrowing insects (family Mutillidae), the females of which are wingless

**velveteen** /ˌvelviˈteen/ *n* a cotton fabric made with a short close pile in imitation of velvet

**velvet glove** *n* outward affability concealing ruthless inflexibility – esp in *the iron hand/fist in the velvet glove*

**velvet scoter** *n* a large SCOTER (type of marine duck) (*Melanitta fusca*) of N Europe and Asia

**velvety** /'velviti/ *adj* **1** soft and smooth like velvet **2** *esp of wines and spirits* smooth to the taste; mild

**ven-** /veen, ven-/, **veni-, veno-** *comb form* vein ⟨*venation*⟩ ⟨*venipuncture*⟩ [L *vena*]

**vena** /'veenə/ *n, pl* **venae** /'veeni/ VEIN 2 – used in anatomical and medical names [ME, fr L]

**vena cava** /ˌveenə 'kayvə/ *n, pl* **venae cavae** /ˌveeni 'kayvi/ any of the large veins by which, in air-breathing VERTEBRATE animals, the blood is returned to the right ATRIUM (upper chamber) of the heart [NL, lit., hollow vein] – **vena caval** *adj*

**venal** /'veenl/ *adj* **1** open to corrupt influence, esp bribery; ready to sell what should not be sold ⟨*a* ∼ *judge*⟩ **2** characterized by corrupt bargaining ⟨*a* ∼ *arrangement with the police*⟩ ⚠ venial [L *venalis*, fr *venum* (acc) sale; akin to Gk *ōneisthai* to buy, Skt *vasna* price] – **venally** *adv*, **venality** *n*

**venatic** /vi'natik/ *adj* **1** of or used in hunting ⟨∼ *equipment*⟩ **2** fond of or living by hunting [L *venaticus*, fr *venatus*, pp of *venari* to hunt – more at VENISON]

**venation** /vee'naysh(ə)n/ *n* an arrangement or system of veins in a leaf, insect wing, etc [L *vena* vein] – **venational** *adj*

**vend** /vend/ *vi* to dispose of something by sale; *also* to engage in selling ~ *vt* 1 to sell (small articles), usu in a public place ⟨*tried to earn a living by* ~ing *matches in the street*⟩ 2 to sell by means of a VENDING MACHINE [L *vendere* to sell, vt, contr of *venum dare* to give for sale] – **vendable, vendible** *adj,* **vendition** *n*

**Venda** /'vendə/ *n* a Bantu language of the N Transvaal

**vendace** /'vendəs/ *n, pl* **vendace** *also* **vendaces** /-seez/ a whitefish (*Coregonus albula*) of various European lakes [NL *vandesius,* fr MF *vandoise,* prob of Celt origin]

**vendee** /ven'dee/ *n, formal* one to whom a thing is sold; a buyer

**vendetta** /ven'detə/ *n* 1 a blood feud between families arising from the murder or injury of a member of one family by a member of the other family and requiring a continuing series of retaliations in kind 2 a prolonged bitter feud [It, lit., revenge, fr L *vindicta* – more at VINDICTIVE]

**vending machine** /'vending/ *n* a coin-operated machine for selling cigarettes, drinks, sweets, etc – compare SLOT MACHINE

**vendor** /'vendə, -daw/, **vender** /-də/ *n* 1 a seller; *specif, Br* the seller of a house 2 VENDING MACHINE

**vendue** /ven'dyooh/ *n, NAm* a public auction [obs Fr, fr MF, fr *vendre* to sell, fr L *vendere*]

**¹veneer** /və'niə/ *n* 1 a thin sheet of a material: eg **1a** a thin layer of wood of superior appearance or hardness used esp to give a decorative finish (eg to joinery); *also* wood prepared in thin layers for this purpose **b** any of the thin layers bonded together to form plywood 2 a protective or ornamental facing (eg of brick or stone) 3 a superficial or deceptively attractive appearance or display; a gloss ⟨*a* ~ *of politeness*⟩ [Ger *furnier,* fr *furnieren* to veneer, fr Fr *fournir* to furnish – more at FURNISH]

**²veneer** *vt* 1 to overlay (eg a cheap or common wood) with veneer; *broadly* to face with a material giving a superior surface 2 to conceal (eg a defect of character) under a superficial and deceptive attractiveness – **veneerer** *n*

**veneering** /və'niəring/ *n* 1 material used as veneer 2 a veneered surface

**venepuncture** *also* **venipuncture** /'veni,pungkchə/ *n* surgical puncture of a vein, esp to withdraw blood or to introduce a drug into the bloodstream

**¹venerable** /'ven(ə)rəbl/ *adj* 1 – used as a title for an Anglican archdeacon or for a deceased Roman Catholic who has been accorded the lowest of three degrees of recognition for sanctity ⟨*the* ~ *Bede*⟩ 2 made sacred, esp by religious or historical association **3a** commanding respect through age, character, and attainments **b** impressive by reason of age ⟨*under* ~ *pines*⟩ 4 ancient ⟨*a* ~ *joke*⟩ **synonyms** see ¹OLD **antonym** youthful [ME, fr L *venerabilis,* fr *venerari* to venerate] – **venerableness** *n,* **venerably** *adv,* **venerability** *n*

**²venerable** *n* an old or venerable person ⟨*such* ~s *as the legendary C B Fry* – *Punch*⟩

**venerate** /'venərayt/ *vt* to regard with reverence or with admiring deference; revere **synonyms** see ¹REVERE [L *veneratus,* pp of *venerari,* fr *vener-, venus* love, charm – more at WIN] – **venerator** *n*

**veneration** /,venə'raysh(ə)n/ *n* 1 the act of venerating; *also* reverential respect, deference, or honour 2 the state of being venerated

**venereal** /və'niəri·əl/ *adj* 1 of sexual desire, sexual enjoyment, or sexual intercourse **2a** resulting from or contracted during sexual intercourse **b** of or affected with VENEREAL DISEASE **c** involving or affecting the genital organs ⟨~ *warts*⟩ [ME *venerealle,* fr L *venereus,* fr *vener-, venus* love, sexual desire]

**venereal disease** *n* a contagious disease (eg gonorrhoea or syphilis) that is typically acquired during sexual intercourse

**venereology** /və,niəri'oləji/ *n* a branch of medicine dealing with venereal diseases [ISV *venere*al + *-o-* + *-logy*] – **venereological** *adj,* **venereologist** *n*

**venerology** /,venə'roləji/ *n* venereology [Ger *venerologie,* fr *venerisch* venereal (fr L *vener-, venus*) + *-o-* + *-logie* -logy]

**¹venery** /'venəri/ *n, archaic* 1 the art, act, or practice of hunting 2 animals that are hunted; game [ME *venerie,* fr MF, fr *vener* to hunt, fr L *venari* – more at VENISON]

**²venery** *n, formal or archaic* 1 the pursuit of sexual pleasure 2 SEXUAL INTERCOURSE [ME *venerie,* fr ML *veneria,* fr L *vener-, venus* sexual desire]

**venesection** *also* **venisection** /'veni,seksh(ə)n/ *n* the operation of opening a vein for letting blood; PHLEBOTOMY [NL *venae section-, venae sectio,* lit., cutting of a vein]

**Veneti** /'venəti/ *also* **Venetes** /-teez/ *n pl* 1 an ancient people in Gaul conquered by Caesar in 56 BC 2 an ancient people in NE Italy allied politically to the Romans [L *Veneti*]

**venetian blind** /və'neesh(ə)n/ *n* a blind (eg for a window) having numerous horizontal slats that may be set at any of several angles so as to vary the amount of light admitted [*Venetian* of Venice, city in NE Italy]

**Venetian glass** *n* coloured and elaborately decorated glassware made at Murano near Venice

**Venetian red** *n* HAEMATITE (type of iron-containing mineral) used as a pigment; *also* a synthetic IRON OXIDE pigment

**Venetic** /və'netik/ *n* the Italic language of the ancient Veneti who inhabited NE Italy [L *veneticus* of the Veneti, fr *Veneti*] – **Venetic** *adj*

**venge** /venj/ *vt, archaic* to avenge [ME *vengen,* fr OF *vengier*]

**vengeance** /'venj(ə)ns/ *n* punishment inflicted in retaliation for injury or offence; retribution, revenge [ME, fr OF, fr *venger, vengier* to avenge, fr L *vindicare* to lay claim to, avenge – more at VINDICATE] – **with a vengeance** 1 with great force or vehemence 2 to an extreme or excessive degree

**vengeful** /'venjf(ə)l/ *adj* revengeful, vindictive: e g **a** seeking to avenge ⟨*Hamlet's* ~ *plans*⟩ **b** serving to gain vengeance ⟨*the prisoner plotted the* ~ *murder of his betrayer*⟩ **synonyms** see VINDICTIVE [obs *venge* (revenge)] – **vengefully** *adv,* **vengefulness** *n*

**¹venial** /'veenyəl, -niəl/ *adj* of a kind that can be remitted; forgivable, pardonable; *also* meriting no particular censure or notice; excusable ⟨~ *faults*⟩ △ venal [ME, fr OF, fr LL *venialis,* fr L *venia* favour, indulgence, pardon; akin to L *venus* love, charm – more at WIN] – **venially** *adv,* **venialness** *n*

**²venial** *n* one who is venial; a minor sinner

**venial sin** *n* a sin that is relatively slight or that is committed without full reflection or consent and so, according to Roman Catholic theology, does not deprive the soul of divine grace – compare MORTAL SIN

**venin** /'venin/ *n* any of various poisonous substances in snake venom [*venom* + *-in*]

**venipuncture** /'veni,pungkchə/ *n* VENEPUNCTURE (surgical puncture of a vein)

**venire facias** /ve,nie·əri 'fayshi,as/ *n* a writ directing a US sheriff to summon people to serve as jurors [ME, fr ML, you should cause to come]

**venisection** /'veni,seksh(ə)n/ *n* VENESECTION (surgical cutting of a vein)

**venison** /'venis(ə)n/ *n* 1 the edible flesh of a wild animal taken by hunting 2 the flesh of a deer [ME, fr OF *veneison* hunting, game, fr L *venation-, venatio,* fr *venari* to hunt, pursue; akin to OE *winnan* to struggle – more at WIN]

**Venite** /vi'nieti/ *n* a chant composed of parts of Psalms 95 and 96 to be sung in a public service [L, O come, fr *venire* to come – more at COME; fr the opening word of Ps 95]

**Venn diagram** /ven/ *n* a diagram that uses circles or other shapes to represent mathematical or logical relations between sets or propositions by the inclusion, exclusion, or intersection of the shapes [John *Venn* †1923 E logician]

**venography** /vi'nogrəfi, vay-/ *n* X-ray photography of a vein after injection of a substance that prevents the passage of X rays [ISV] – **venograph** *n*

**¹venom** /'venəm/ *n* 1 poisonous matter secreted by snakes, scorpions, bees, etc and transmitted to prey or an enemy chiefly by biting or stinging; *broadly* material that is poisonous 2 malevolence; ILL WILL [ME *venim, venom,* fr OF *venim,* fr (assumed) VL *venimen,* alter. of L *venenum* magic charm, drug, poison; akin to L *venus* love, charm]

**²venom** *vt, archaic* to envenom

**venomous** /'venəməs/ *adj* 1 full of venom: e g **1a** poisonous, envenomed **b** noxious, pernicious **c** spiteful, malevolent ⟨~ *criticism*⟩ 2 *of an animal* having a venom-producing gland and able to inflict a poisoned wound ⟨~ *snakes*⟩ – **venomously** *adv,* **venomousness** *n*

**venous** /'veenəs/ *adj* 1 having or consisting of veins ⟨*a* ~ *system*⟩ 2 *of blood* circulating in the veins and containing a higher proportion of CARBON DIOXIDE and less oxygen than the blood in the arteries [L *venosus,* fr *vena* vein] – **venously** *adv,* **venosity** *n*

**¹vent** /vent/ *vt* 1 to provide with a vent **2a** to serve as a vent for ⟨*chimneys* ~ *smoke*⟩ **b** to give often vigorous or emotional expression to 3 to relieve by venting ⟨~ *the pressure in the boiler*⟩ [ME *venten,* prob fr MF *esventer* to expose to the air, fr *es-* ex- (fr L *ex-*) + *vent* wind, fr L *ventus* – more at WIND]

²**vent** *n* **1** a means of escape or release; an outlet – chiefly in *give vent to* ⟨*gave* vent *to his anger by thumping the table*⟩ **2** an opening for the escape of a gas or liquid or for the relief of pressure: e g **2a** the external opening of the digestive tract or CLOACA, esp of a bird or reptile, through which waste matter is excreted; the anus **b** an outlet of a volcano; FUMAROLE **c** an opening at the breech of a gun through which the powder is ignited – **ventless** *adj*

³**vent** *n* a slit in a garment; *specif* an opening in the lower part of a seam (e g of a jacket or skirt) [ME *vente*, alter. of *fente*, fr MF, slit, fissure, fr *fendre* to split, fr L *findere* – more at BITE]

**ventage** /'ventij/ *n* a small hole (e g a finger hole on a flute)

**ventail** /'ventayl/ *n* the lower movable front of a medieval helmet [ME, fr MF *ventaille*, fr *vent* wind]

**venter** /'ventə/ *n* **1** a wife or mother considered as a source of offspring – used in law **2** a rounded or swollen often hollow anatomical structure: e g **2a** the abdomen or belly of a VERTEBRATE animal **b** the enlarged thick or fleshy part of a muscle; BELLY **5 c** a broad smooth shallow inward-curving surface, esp of a bone **d** the swollen base of an ARCHEGONIUM (female sex organ in a moss, fern, etc) in which the egg cell develops [AF, fr L, belly, womb; akin to OHG *wanast* paunch, L *vesica* bladder]

**ventifact** /'ventifakt/ *n* a stone shaped or polished by wind-blown sand [L *ventus* wind + E -*i*- + -*fact* (as in *artefact*)]

**ventilate** /'ventilayt/ *vt* **1** to examine, discuss, or investigate freely and openly; expose publicly ⟨ventilating *family quarrels in public*⟩ **2a** to expose to air, esp to a current of fresh air, for purifying, curing, or refreshing ⟨~ *stored grain*⟩ **b** to increase the oxygen content of (blood); oxygenate, aerate **3a** *of a current of air* to pass or circulate through so as to freshen **b** to cause fresh air to circulate through (e g a room or mine) **4** to provide an opening in (a burning structure) to permit escape of smoke and heat **5** *archaic* to free (grain) from chaff by exposing to a current of air; winnow [LL *ventilatus*, pp of *ventilare*, fr L, to fan, winnow, fr *ventulus*, dim. of *ventus* wind – more at WIND] – **ventilative** *adj*

**ventilation** /ˌventiˈlaysh(ə)n/ *n* **1** ventilating **2a** circulation of air ⟨*a room with good* ~⟩ **b** the exchange of CARBON DIOXIDE and oxygen between the blood circulating in and the air of the lungs, that is the basic process of respiration **3** a system or means of providing fresh air

**ventilator** /'ventiˌlaytə/ *n* one who or that which ventilates; *esp* an apparatus or hole for introducing fresh air or expelling foul or stagnant air

**ventilatory** /'ventiˌlayt(ə)ri/ *adj* of or providing ventilation

**ventr-** /ventr-/, **ventro-** *comb form* ventral and ⟨ventro*lateral*⟩ [L *ventr-*, *venter* belly]

¹**ventral** /'ventral/ *adj* **1a** of, being, or situated near or on the front or lower surface of an animal or body part, opposite the back of or towards the belly or abdomen – compare DORSAL **b** of, being, on, or near a lower surface (e g of an aircraft) opposite the top **2** of, being, or situated on the lower or inner surface of a plant structure on the surface that faces towards the centre or axis [Fr, fr L *ventralis*, fr *ventr-*, *venter*] – **ventrally** *adv*

²**ventral** *n* a ventral part (e g a scale or fin)

**ventral root** *n* the one of the two starting points (ROOTS) of a SPINAL NERVE that passes out from the SPINAL CORD towards the front of the body and consists of fibres carrying nerve impulses that activate muscles

**ventre à terre** /ˌvontrah ˈteə (*Fr* vātr a tɛr)/ *adv* at full speed; FLAT OUT [Fr, lit., belly to the ground]

**ventricle** /'ventrikl/ *n* a cavity of a body part or organ: e g **a** a chamber of the heart that receives blood from a corresponding ATRIUM (chamber that receives blood from the veins) and pumps it into the arteries **b** any of the system of communicating cavities in the brain of a VERTEBRATE animal that contain CEREBROSPINAL FLUID (liquid that nourishes and cushions nerve tissues) and join with the fluid-filled canal that runs up the centre of the SPINAL CORD **c** a ventriculus [ME, fr L *ventriculus*, fr dim. of *ventr-*, *venter* belly]

**ventricose** /'ventrikohs/ *adj*, *biology* markedly swollen, distended, or inflated, esp on one side ⟨~ *pods*⟩ ⟨~ *shells*⟩ [NL *ventricosus*, deriv of L *ventr-*, *venter* belly]

**ventricular** /ven'trikyoolə/ *adj* of, involving, having, or being a ventricle or ventriculus

**ventriculus** /ven'trikyooləs/ *n*, *pl* **ventriculi** /-li/ a digestive cavity: e g **a** the stomach **b** the gizzard of a bird **c** the middle part (MIDGUT) of an insect's digestive tract, where digestion of

food occurs [NL, fr L, dim. of *venter*]

**ventriloquism** /ven'trilə,kwiz(ə)m/ *n* the production of the voice in such a manner that the sound appears to come from a source other than the vocal organs of the speaker and esp from a dummy manipulated by the producer of the sound [LL *ventriloquus* ventriloquist, fr L *ventr-*, *venter* + *loqui* to speak; fr the belief that the voice is produced from the ventriloquist's stomach] – **ventriloquist** *n*, **ventriloquial** *adj*, **ventriloquially** *adv*

**ventriloqu·ize, -ise** /ven'trilə,kwiez/ *vi* to use ventriloquism ~ *vt* to utter in the manner of a ventriloquist

**ventripotent** /ven'tripətənt/ *adj*, *chiefly humorous* gluttonous [Fr, fr L *ventr-*, *venter* belly + *potent-*, *potens* powerful – more at POTENT]

**ventro-** – see VENTR-

**ventrodorsal** /ˌventroh'dawsl/ *adj* extending from the front or lower side or surface to the back or upper side or surface

**ventrolateral** /ˌventroh'lat(ə)rəl/ *adj* of or involving both the front or lower surface and the side; situated towards or at the side of a front or lower region

**ventromedial** /ˌventroh'meediəl/ *adj* of or involving both the front or lower surface and the midline; situated in the middle of a front or lower region

¹**venture** /'venchə/ *vt* **1** to expose to hazard; risk, gamble **2** to undertake the risks and dangers of; brave ⟨~d *the stormy sea*⟩ **3** to offer at the risk of opposition or censure ⟨~ *an opinion*⟩ ~ *vi* to proceed despite danger; dare to go ⟨*don't* ~ *too near the edge*⟩ [ME *venteren*, by shortening & alter. fr *aventuren*, fr *aventure* adventure] – **venturer** *n*

²**venture** *n* **1** an undertaking involving chance, risk, or danger, esp in business **2** something (e g money or property) at risk in a speculative venture **3** *obs* fortune, chance – see also **draw a BOW at a venture** ☐ compare ADVENTURE

**venture capital** *n* RISK CAPITAL (capital invested in new enterprises) provided by individuals or organizations (e g merchant banks) other than those who own the enterprise concerned

**venture scout** *n* a senior member of the British Scout movement aged from 16 to 20

**venturesome** /-s(ə)m/ *adj* **1** ready to take risks; daring ⟨*a* ~ *hunter*⟩ **2** involving risk; hazardous ⟨*a* ~ *journey*⟩ **synonyms** see ¹ADVENTURE – **venturesomely** *adv*, **venturesomeness** *n*

**venturi** /ven'tyooəri/ *n* a short tube that is inserted in a wider pipeline and is used for measuring flow rate of a liquid or gas or for providing suction [G B *Venturi* †1822 It physicist]

**venturous** /'venchərəs/ *adj* venturesome – **venturously** *adv*, **venturousness** *n*

**venue** /'venyooh/ *n* **1** the place in which a legal case is to be tried; *also* the place from which the jury is drawn for such a trial **2** the place where a gathering (e g for a sports event) takes place; *broadly* the scene of any event or activity ⟨*this most unlikely* ~ *for vodka production – The Observer*⟩ [ME *venyw* action of coming, fr MF *venue*, fr *venir* to come, fr L *venire* – more at COME]

**venule** /'venyooh l/ *n* a small vein (e g of a leaf or insect's wing); *esp* any of the very small veins that connect larger veins with the network of CAPILLARIES (tiny blood vessels connecting veins and arteries) [L *venula*, dim. of *vena* vein]

**Venus** /'veenəs/ *n* the planet second in order from the sun that revolves on its axis in RETROGRADE motion (opposite to that of the other planets) [ME, fr L *Vener-*, *Venus*, Roman goddess of love & beauty, fr *vener-*, *venus* sexual desire]

¹**Venusian** /vi'nyoohzh(ə)n, -zyən/ *adj* of or coming from the planet Venus

²**Venusian** *n* a supposed inhabitant of Venus

**Venus's-'flower-ˌbasket, Venus'-flower-basket** *n* a delicate deep-sea sponge (genus *Euplectella*) that has an intricate skeleton of fine glassy SILICA-containing fibres (SPICULES)

**Venus's-'flytrap, Venus'-flytrap** *n* an insect-eating plant (*Dionaea muscipula*) of the sundew family having modified leaves consisting of two hinged spiky-edged lobes that snap together to trap insects

**veracious** /və'rayshəs/ *adj*, *formal* **1** reliable in testimony; truthful **2** true, accurate [L *verac-*, *verax* – more at VERY] – **veraciously** *adv*, **veraciousness** *n*

**veracity** /və'rasəti/ *n*, *formal* **1** the quality of being veracious; truthfulness **2** the power of conveying or perceiving truth or accuracy – used with reference to the senses or to instruments of measurement **3** factual accuracy **4** something true **synonyms** see TRUTH

**veranda, verandah** /və'randə/ *n* a usu roofed open gallery attached to the exterior of a building [Hindi *varaṇḍā*]

**veratridine** /vi'ratrideen/ *n* a poisonous chemical compound, $C_{36}H_{51}NO_{11}$, occurring esp in the seeds of the SABADILLA plant [*veratrine* + *-idine*]

**veratrine** /'verəˌtreen/ *n* a poisonous irritant mixture of chemical compounds obtained from the seeds of the SABADILLA plant and formerly used as a COUNTERIRRITANT to relieve inflammation (eg in muscles and joints) and as an insecticide [NL *veratrina*, fr *Veratrum*, genus of herbs]

**veratrum** /və'raytrəm/ *n* HELLEBORE 2 (poisonous plant of the lily family) [NL, genus name, fr L, hellebore]

**verb** /vuhb/ *n* a word that expresses the doing of an action, the occurrence of an event, or a state of being [ME *verbe*, fr MF, fr L *verbum* word, verb – more at WORD]

¹**verbal** /'vuhbl/ *adj* **1a** of, involving, or expressed in words ⟨~ *instructions*⟩ **b** of or involving words rather than meaning or substance ⟨*an unimportant* ~ *distinction*⟩ **c** consisting of or using words only and not involving action ⟨*a* ~ *protest*⟩ **2** of or formed from a verb ⟨*a* ~ *adjective*⟩ **3** spoken rather than written; oral ⟨*a* ~ *contract*⟩ **4** verbatim, word-for-word ⟨*a* ~ *translation*⟩ **5** of ability in the use and comprehension of words ⟨~ *aptitude*⟩ [MF or LL; MF, fr LL *verbalis*, fr L *verbum* word] – **verbally** *adv*

  *usage* Although **verbal** is widely used to mean "spoken rather than written" ⟨*a* **verbal** *contract*⟩ many writers on usage advise that this idea should be expressed by **oral** ⟨*an* **oral** *message*⟩ and that **verbal** should be confined to the sense "in words", according to which a piece or writing is **verbal** but not **oral**.

²**verbal** *n* **1** a word that combines characteristics of a verb with those of a noun or adjective – compare GERUND, INFINITIVE, PARTICIPLE **2** *Br slang* a spoken statement; *esp* one made to the police admitting or implying guilt and used in evidence

³**verbal** *vt* **-ll-** *Br slang* to implicate in a crime by making false statements or by introducing an admission of guilt

**verbal auxiliary** *n* an AUXILIARY verb (eg *be*, *do*, and *may*)

**verbalism** /'vuhblˌiz(ə)m/ *n* **1a** a verbal expression **b** phrasing, wording **2** an excessive emphasis on words as opposed to the ideas or realities they represent – **verbalist** *n*, **verbalistic** *adj*

**verbal·ize, -ise** /'vuhblˌiez/ *vi* **1** to speak or write wordily **2** to express something in words ~ *vt* **1** to convert into a verb ⟨~ table *into* to table⟩ **2** to name or describe in words – **verbalizer**, **verbalization** *n*

**verbal noun** *n* a noun derived from a verb (eg *singing* from *sing*) and having some of the constructions of a verb; *esp* GERUND

**verbatim** /vuh'baytim/ *adj* in the exact words; word-for-word [ME, fr ML, fr L *verbum* word] – **verbatim** *adv*

**verbena** /vuh'beenə/ *n* any of a genus (*Verbena*) of chiefly N and S American plants and small shrubs of the teak family, that are often cultivated for their heads or spikes of showy white, pink, red, blue, or purplish flowers [NL, genus of herbs or subshrubs, fr L – more at VERVAIN]

**verbiage** /'vuhbi-ij/ *n* wordiness, verbosity [Fr, fr MF *verbier* to chatter, fr *verbe* speech, fr L *verbum* word]

**verbicide** /'vuhbiˌsied/ *n*, *humorous* **1** deliberate distortion of the sense of a word (eg in punning) **2** one who distorts the sense of a word [L *verbum* word + E *-cide*] – **verbicidal** *adj*

**verbid** /'vuhbid/ *n* VERBAL 1

**verbify** /'vuhbiˌfie/ *vt* VERBALIZE 1

**verbigeration** /ˌvuhbijə'raysh(ə)n/ *n* continual and usu pathological repetition of stereotyped phrases (eg in some forms of mental illness) [ISV, fr L *verbigeratus*, pp of *verbigerare* to talk, chat, fr *verbum* word + *gerere* to carry, wield]

**verboojuice** /'vuhbooh·joohs/ *n*, *humorous* verbiage ⟨*sesquipedalian* ~ – H G Wells⟩ [by alter. (prob influenced by *verjuice*)]

**verbose** /vuh'bohs/ *adj* **1** containing more words than necessary ⟨*a* ~ *reply*⟩ **2** given to wordiness ⟨*a* ~ *orator*⟩ – **verbosely** *adv*, **verboseness**, **verbosity** *n*

**verboten** /feə'bohtn, vuh-/ *adj*, *chiefly humorous* forbidden; *esp* prohibited by authority [Ger, fr pp of *verbieten* to forbid]

**verdant** /'vuhd(ə)nt/ *adj*, *chiefly poetic* **1a** green in tint or colour ⟨~ *grass*⟩ **b** green with growing plants ⟨~ *fields*⟩ **2** immature, unsophisticated [modif of MF *verdoyant*, fr prp of *verdoyer* to be green, fr OF *verdoier*, fr *verd*, *vert* green, fr L *viridis*, fr *virēre* to be green] – **verdancy** *n*, **verdantly** *adv*

**verd antique, verde antique** /ˌvuhd an'teek/ *n* **1** a green mottled or veined stone of marble or limestone and SERPENTINE (dullish green mineral) much used for indoor decoration, esp by the ancient Romans **2** any of various greenish often marblelike rocks or stones; *esp* a rock (PORPHYRY) containing crystals of FELDSPAR embedded in a dark green fine-grained base [It *verde antico*, lit., ancient green]

**verderer, verderor** /'vuhdərə/ *n* a former English judicial officer having charge of the royal forests [AF, fr OF *verdier*, fr *verd* green]

**verdict** /'vuhdikt/ *n* **1** the finding or decision of a jury on the matter submitted to them by a court **2** an opinion, judgment [alter. of ME *verdit*, fr AF, fr OF *ver* true (fr L *verus*) + *dit* saying, judgment, fr L *dictum* – more at VERY]

**verdigris** /'vuhdigris; *also* -ˌgree/ *n* **1** a green or greenish-blue poisonous chemical compound (copper ACETATE) formed by the action of ACETIC ACID on copper and used esp as a pigment **2** a green or bluish copper-containing deposit, esp of copper carbonates, formed on copper, brass, or bronze surfaces [ME *vertegrez*, fr OF *vert de Grice*, lit., green of Greece]

**verdure** /'vuhdyə, -jə/ *n*, *chiefly poetic* **1** (the greenness of) growing vegetation **2** a condition of health, freshness, and vigour [ME, fr MF, fr *verd* green] – **verdureless** *adj*, **verdurous** *adj*, **verdurousness** *n*

**verdured** /'vuhdyəd, -jəd/ *adj*, *chiefly poetic* (covered) with verdure

¹**verge** /vuhj/ *n* **1** a rod or staff carried as an emblem of authority or symbol of office **2a** something that borders, limits, or bounds: eg **2a(1)** an outer margin of an object or structural part **a(2)** the edge of a roof projecting over the gable **a(3)** *Br* a surfaced or planted strip of land at the side of a road **b** *the* brink, threshold [ME, penis, rod, fr MF, fr L *virga* rod, stripe – more at WHISK; (2) fr the obs phrase *within the verge* within the area subject to the authority of a verge-bearer]

²**verge** *vt* to edge, border ⟨*a strip of grass* ~s *the road*⟩

  **verge on/upon** *vt* to be close to ⟨*their familiarity* verged on *insolence*⟩

³**verge** *vi*, *of the sun* to incline towards the horizon; sink [L *vergere* to bend, incline – more at WRENCH]

  **verge into** *vt* to gradually change into ⟨*his eccentricity finally* verged into *madness*⟩

  **verge towards** *vt* to move gradually towards ⟨*a track* verging towards *the cliff edge and disappearing*⟩

**verger** /'vuhjə/ *n* **1** a church official who keeps order during services or serves as an usher or SACRISTAN (one who has charge of ceremonial equipment) **2** *chiefly Br* an attendant who carries a verge (eg before a bishop or justice)

**veridical** /vi'ridikl/ *adj*, *formal* **1** truthful, veracious **2** not illusory; genuine [L *veridicus*, fr *verus* true + *dicere* to say – more at VERY, DICTION] – **veridically** *adv*, **veridicality** *n*

**verification** /ˌverifi'kaysh(ə)n/ *n* verifying or being verified

**verifier** /'verifie-ə/ *n* one who or that which verifies; *esp* a device for establishing that punched cards have been correctly punched

**verify** /'verifie/ *vt* **1** to confirm or substantiate in law, esp formally or on oath **2** to ascertain the truth, accuracy, or reality of **3** to fulfil; BEAR OUT ⟨*my fears were* verified⟩ *synonyms* see CONFIRM *antonym* disprove [ME *verifien*, fr MF *verifier*, fr ML *verificare*, fr L *verus* true – more at VERY] – **verifiable** *adj*

**verily** /'verəli/ *adv*, *archaic* **1** indeed, certainly **2** truly, confidently [ME *verraily*, fr *verray* very]

**verisimilar** /ˌveri'similə/ *adj*, *formal* appearing to be true; probable [L *verisimilis*, fr *veri similis* like the truth] – **verisimilarly** *adv*

**verisimilitude** /ˌverisi'milityoohd/ *n*, *formal* **1** the quality or state of appearing to be true **2** a statement that has the appearance of truth *synonyms* see TRUTH [L *verisimilitudo*, fr *verisimilis*] – **verisimilitudinous** *adj*

**verism** /'viəriz(ə)m/ *n* artistic use of contemporary everyday material in preference to the heroic or legendary [It *verismo*, fr *vero* true, fr L *verus*] – **verist** *n or adj*, **veristic** *adj*

**verismo** /ve'rizmoh/ *n* verism, esp in GRAND OPERA [It]

**veritable** /'veritəbl/ *adj* being in fact the thing named and not false, unreal, or imaginary – often used to stress the aptness of a metaphor ⟨*a* ~ *mountain °of references*⟩ *synonyms* see GENUINE – **veritableness** *n*, **veritably** *adv*

**verity** /'veriti/ *n* **1** something (eg a statement) that is true; *esp* a permanently true value or principle ⟨*the eternal* verities⟩ **2** *formal* the quality or state of being true or real **3** *formal* honesty, veracity *synonyms* see TRUTH [ME *verite*, fr MF *verité*, fr L *veritat-*, *veritas*, fr *verus* true]

**verjuice** /'vuhˌjoohs/ *n* **1** the sour juice of CRAB APPLES or of unripe fruit (eg grapes or apples) formerly used in cooking **2** *formal* acidity of disposition or manner [ME *verjus*, fr MF, fr *vert jus*, lit., green juice]

**verkramp** /fiə'krump/ *adj, SAfr* (characteristic) of a ver-krampte [prob modif of Afrik *bekrompe* narrow-minded, fr D *bekrimpen* to shrink, restrict]

**verkrampte** /fiə'krumptə/ *n, SAfr* a person holding ultra-conservative or bigoted views, esp on social, political, or re-ligious matters ⟨*coming mainly from* ~s *in the Nationalist Party – Sunday Times* (*Johannesburg*)⟩ – compare KRAGDADIGE, VERLIGTE [Afrik, fr *verkramp* + *-te*, noun suffix]

**verlig** /fiə'likh/ *adj, SAfr* verligte [Afrik, enlightened, fr D *ver-lichten* to light, enlighten]

¹**verligte** /fiə'likhtə/ *adj, SAfr* liberal ⟨*significant* ~ *moves in the race relations field – The Star* (*Johannesburg*)⟩

²**verligte** *n, SAfr* an advocate of liberal policies – compare KRAGDADIGE, VERKRAMPTE [Afrik, fr *verlig* + *-te*]

**vermeil** /'vuhmayl/ *n* 1 gilded silver, bronze, or copper 2 *poetic* VERMILION (red colour) [MF, fr *vermeil*, adj – more at VER-MILION] – **vermeil** *adj*

**vermi-** /vuhmi-/ *comb form* worm ⟨*vermiform*⟩ [NL, fr LL, fr L *vermis* – more at WORM]

**vermian** /'vuhmyən, -mi·ən/ *adj* of or resembling a worm [ISV]

**vermicelli** /ˌvuhmi'cheli/ *n* 1 pasta in the form of long thin solid threads smaller in diameter than spaghetti 2 small thin sugar strands, usu with the colour and flavour of chocolate, that are used as a decoration (eg on iced cakes) [It, fr pl of *vermicello*, dim. of *verme* worm, fr L *vermis*]

**vermicide** /'vuhmmi'sied/ *n* something (eg a drug) that des-troys worms, esp parasitic worms

**vermicular** /vuh'mikyoolə/ *adj* 1a resembling a worm in ap-pearance or movement b vermiculate 2 of or caused by worms [NL *vermicularis*, fr L *vermiculus*, dim. of *vermis*]

**vermiculate** /vuh'mikyoolət/, **vermiculated** /-ˌlaytid/ *adj* 1a resembling a worm in shape; vermiform b marked with irregu-lar or wavy lines or depressions ⟨*a* ~ *nut*⟩ ⟨~d *stonework*⟩ 2 full of worms; worm-eaten 3 *formal* tortuous, intricate [L *ver-miculatus*, fr *vermiculus*]

**vermiculation** /vuhˌmikyoo'laysh(ə)n/ *n* 1 the state of being worm-eaten 2 (a) wormlike or writhing movement (eg of the intestines) 3 (decorative work consisting of) fine wavy or ir-regular markings

**vermiculite** /vuh'mikyooliet/ *n* any of various minerals derived from MICA (common lustrous mineral), that consist of SILICATES of metals (eg magnesium, iron, and aluminium) chemically combined with water and that expand on heating to form a lightweight highly water-absorbent material used in seed beds and for insulation ⟨*a loft can be insulated with* ... *cork, expanded polystyrene,* ~ *or mineral wool – Reader's Digest Repair Manual*⟩ [L *vermiculus* little worm; fr the worm-like projections produced when it is rapidly heated]

**vermiform** /'vuhmiˌfawm/ *adj* long and slender like a worm [NL *vermiformis*, fr *vermi-* + *-formis* -form]

**vermiform appendix, appendix** *n* a narrow short tube closed at one end, that extends from the CAECUM (pouchlike part of the LARGE INTESTINE) in the lower right-hand part of the ab-domen in some mammals

**vermifuge** /'vuhmiˌfyoohj/ *n or adj* (something, esp a drug) used to destroy or expel parasitic worms; ANTHELMINTIC [deriv of L *vermis* + *fugare* to put to flight – more at -FUGE]

**vermilion, vermillion** /və'milyən/ *n* 1 a bright red pigment consisting of mercuric sulphide 2 a brilliant red colour [ME *vermilioun*, fr OF *vermeillon*, fr *vermeil*, adj, bright red, ver-milion, fr LL *vermiculus* kermes, fr L, little worm] – **vermilion** *adj*

**vermin** /'vuhmin/ *n, pl* **vermin** 1 *pl* 1a lice, rats, or other common small animals that are harmful or objectionable to humans b birds and mammals that prey on game 2 *usu pl* an offensive person [ME, fr MF, fr (assumed) L *vermin-, vermen* worm; akin to L *vermis* worm – more at WORM]

**verminous** /'vuhminəs/ *adj* 1 consisting of, suggestive of, or being vermin 2 forming a breeding place for or infested by vermin ⟨*a* ~ *rubbish tip*⟩ 3 caused by vermin ⟨~ *disease*⟩ – **verminously** *adv*

**vermouth** /'vuhməth/ *n* a dry or sweet alcoholic drink that has a white wine base, is flavoured with aromatic herbs, and is used as an aperitif or in mixed drinks [Fr *vermout*, fr Ger *wermut* wormwood, fr OHG *wermuota* – more at WORMWOOD]

¹**vernacular** /və'nakyoolə/ *adj* 1a expressed or written in a language or dialect native to a region or country rather than in a literary, learned, or foreign language; *also, of a speaker or writer* using such a regional language or dialect b of or being

the normal spoken form of a language 2 of or being the name applied to a plant or animal in the common native speech as distinguished from the Latin name used in scientific classifica-tion 3 (characteristic) of a period, place, or group; *esp* of or being the common building style of a period or place [L *ver-naculus* native, fr *verna* slave born in his master's house, native] – **vernacularly** *adv*

²**vernacular** *n* 1 the local vernacular language 2 the mode of expression of a group or class 3 a vernacular name of a plant or animal *synonyms* see DIALECT

**vernacularism** /vuh'nakyooləˌriz(ə)m/ *n* 1 a vernacular word or idiom 2 the use of the vernacular

**vernal** /'vuhnl/ *adj* 1 of or occurring in the spring ⟨~ *sunshine*⟩ 2 *chiefly poetic* fresh or new like the spring; *also* youthful [L *vernalis,* alter. of *vernus,* fr *ver* spring; akin to Gk *ear* spring] – **vernally** *adv*

**vernal equinox** *n* the time in March when the sun crosses the equator and day and night are everywhere of equal length

**vernal·ize, -ise** /'vuhnlˌiez/ *vt* to cause or hasten the flowering and fruiting of (plants), esp by chilling seeds, bulbs, or seed-lings – **vernalization** *n*

**vernation** /vuh'naysh(ə)n/ *n* the arrangement of leaves within a bud – compare AESTIVATION 2 [NL *vernation-, vernatio,* fr L *vernatus,* pp of *vernare* to behave as in spring, fr *vernus* vernal]

**Verner's law** /'vuhnəz/ *n* a statement in historical linguistics supplementing GRIMM'S LAW: under certain specified con-ditions sounds in the Germanic languages that are now voiced PLOSIVES (eg /b/ and /g/) are derived from earlier FRICATIVES (eg /f/ and /h/) which were in their turn derived from voiceless plosives (eg /p/ and /k/) [Karl *Verner* †1896 Dan philologist]

**vernicle, vernacle** /'vuhnikl/ *n* ²VERONICA [ME *vernicle,* fr MF *veronique, vernicle,* fr ML *veronica*]

¹**vernier** /'vuhnyə, -ni·ə/ *n* 1 a short graduated scale that slides along another main graduated scale allowing fine measure-ments of fractions of the smallest divisions of the main scale to be made 2a a small auxiliary device used with a main device to obtain fine adjustment b **vernier, vernier engine** any of two or more small supplementary rocket engines or gas nozzles on a missile or a rocket vehicle for making fine adjustments in the speed or direction [Pierre *Vernier* †1637 Fr mathematician]

²**vernier** *adj* having or comprising a vernier

**vernier calliper** *n* a device used for measuring the dimensions of small objects, that consists of a main scale with a fixed jaw and a sliding jaw with an attached vernier

**Veronal** /'və'rohnl/ *trademark* – used for the tranquillizing and sedative drug BARBITONE

¹**veronica** /və'ronikə/ *n* SPEEDWELL (small-flowered plant) [NL, genus of herbs]

²**veronica** *n* a copy in metal (eg a small badge) or cloth of the legendary cloth of St Veronica which was said to be imprinted with an image of Christ's face [ML, fr *Veronica* St Veronica]

³**veronica** *n* a movement in bullfighting in which the cape is swung slowly away from the charging bull while the matador keeps his feet in the same position [Sp *verónica,* fr St *Veronica*]

**verruca** /və'roohkə/ *n, pl* **verrucas** *also* **verrucae** /-ki/ 1 a wart or warty growth on the skin 2 a wartlike projection on a plant or animal [L – more at WART]

**verrucose** /'verookohs/ *adj* covered with wartlike projections

¹**versant** /'vuhsənt/ *adj, archaic* 1 mentally engaged or occupied 2 conversant [L *versant-, versans,* prp of *versare, ver-sari* to turn, occupy oneself, meditate]

²**versant** *n* 1 the slope of a mountain or chain of mountains 2 the general slope of land or a region; the inclination [Fr, fr MF, fr prp of *verser* to turn, pour, fr L *versare* to turn; fr its shedding of water]

**versatile** /'vuhsətiel/ *adj* 1 embracing a variety of subjects, fields, or skills; *also* turning with ease from one thing to another 2a(1) capable of turning forwards or backwards ⟨*a* ~ *toe of a bird*⟩ a(2) capable of moving sideways and up and down ⟨*an insect's* ~ *antennae*⟩ b *of an* ANTHER (*pollen-contain-ing flower structure*) having the supporting stalk (FILAMENT) attached at or near the middle and swinging freely in the wind 3 having many uses or applications ⟨~ *building material*⟩ 4 *formal* changing or fluctuating readily; variable ⟨*a* ~ *dis-position*⟩ [Fr or L; Fr, fr L *versatilis* turning easily, fr *versatus,* pp of *versare* to turn, fr *versus,* pp of *vertere*] – **versatilely** *adv,* **versatileness, versatility** *n*

**vers de société** /ˌveə də sohsiə'tay (Fr vɛr də sɔsjete)/ *n* witty and typically ironic light verse [Fr, society verse]

**verse** /vuhs/ *n* 1 a line of metrical writing 2a(1) (an example of) metrical language or writing distinguished from poetry esp by its lower level of intensity **a(2)** POETRY **2 b verses** *pl*, **verse** a poem ⟨~s *on the death of Napoleon*⟩ ⟨*a notebook containing her* ~s *and short stories*⟩ **c** a body of metrical writing (e g of a period or country) ⟨*Elizabethan* ~⟩ **3** a stanza **4** any of the short divisions into which a chapter of the Bible is traditionally divided [ME *vers*, fr OF, fr L *versus*, lit., turning, fr *versus*, pp of *vertere* to turn – more at WORTH]

**versed** /vuhst/ *adj* possessing a thorough knowledge of or skill in something – chiefly in *well versed in* [L *versatus*, pp of *versari* to be active, be occupied (in), passive of *versare* to turn]

**versed sine** *n*, *maths* 1 minus the cosine of an angle [NL *versus* turned, fr L, pp of *vertere*]

**verset** /'vuhsət/ *n* a short verse, esp from a sacred book (e g the Koran) [ME, fr OF, dim. of *vers* verse]

**versicle** /'vuhsikl/ *n* **1** a short verse or sentence (e g from a psalm) said or sung by a leader in public worship and followed by a response from the people **2** a little verse [ME, fr L *versiculus*, dim. of *versus* verse]

**versicolour** /'vuhsi,kulə/, **versicoloured** *adj* **1** having various colours; variegated ⟨~ *flowers*⟩ **2** changeable in colour; iridescent ⟨~ *silk*⟩ [L *versicolor*, fr *versus*, pp + *color* colour]

**versicular** /vuh'sikyoolə/ *adj* of verses or versicles [L *versiculus* little verse]

**versification** /,vuhsifi'kaysh(ə)n/ *n* **1** the making of verses **2** the structure of the metre of verse **3** a version in verse of something originally in prose

**versify** /'vuhsifie/ *vi* to compose verses ~ *vt* to turn into verse – **versifier** *n*

**version** /'vuhsh(ə)n, -zh(ə)n/ *n* **1** a translation from another language; *esp*, *often cap* a translation of (part of) the Bible **2a** an account or description from a particular point of view, esp as contrasted with another account **b** an adaptation of a work of art into another medium ⟨*the film* ~ *of the novel*⟩ **c** an arrangement of a musical composition **3** a form or variant of a type or original ⟨*an experimental* ~ *of the plane*⟩ **4a** a condition in which an organ, esp the womb, is turned from its normal position **b** manual turning of a foetus in the womb to aid delivery [MF, fr ML *version-*, *versio* act of turning, fr L *versus*, pp of *vertere*] – **versional** *adj*

**vers libre** /,veə 'leebrə/ *n*, *pl* **vers libres** /~/ FREE VERSE (verse without fixed metre) [Fr]

**vers-librist** /,veə'leebrist/ *n* a writer of FREE VERSE (verse without fixed metre) [Fr *vers-libriste*]

**verso** /'vuhsoh/ *n*, *pl* **versos** the side of a leaf (e g of a manuscript) that is to be read second **2** a left-hand page – contrasted with *recto* [NL *verso (folio)* the page being turned]

**verst** /veəst, vuhst/ *n* a Russian unit of distance equal to about 1.1 kilometres (0.7 mile) [Fr *verste* & Ger *werst*, fr Russ *versta*; akin to L *vertere* to turn]

**versus** /'vuhsəs/ *prep* **1** against **2** in contrast to or as the alternative of ⟨*free trade* ~ *protection*⟩ [ML, towards, against, fr L, adv, so as to face, fr pp of *vertere* to turn]

**vert** /vuht/ *n* **1** green – used in heraldry **2a** the former right or privilege (e g in England) of cutting living wood or sometimes of pasturing animals in a forest **b** *archaic or poetic* green forest vegetation, esp when forming cover or providing food for deer [ME *verte*, fr MF *vert*, fr *vert* green – more at VERDANT]

**vertebra** /'vuhtibrə/ *n*, *pl* **vertebrae** /-brie/, **vertebras** any of the chain of bone or cartilage segments that make up the backbone (SPINAL COLUMN) and enclose and protect the SPINAL CORD [L, joint, vertebra, fr *vertere* to turn – more at WORTH]

**vertebral** /'vuhtibrəl/ *adj* **1** of or being vertebrae or the VERTEBRAL COLUMN; spinal ⟨~ *canal*⟩ **2** composed of or having vertebrae – **vertebral** *n*, **vertebrally** *adv*

**vertebral column** *n* the backbone; SPINAL COLUMN

¹**vertebrate** /'vuhtibrət, -brayt/ *adj* **1** having a backbone **2** of or being a vertebrate animal [NL *vertebratus*, fr L, jointed, fr *vertebra*]

²**vertebrate** *n* any of a large subphylum (Vertebrata) of CHORDATE animals comprising the fishes, amphibians, reptiles, birds, and mammals, and characterized by the presence of a backbone composed of vertebrae, a bone or cartilage skeleton, and a well-developed head and brain; *broadly* CHORDATE [deriv of NL *vertebratus*]

**vertex** /'vuhteks/ *n*, *pl* **vertices** /'vuhtiseez/ *also* **vertexes 1a(1)** the point opposite to and farthest from the base in a geometrical figure **a(2)** the point from which an angle diverges or at which lines or curves intersect **a(3)** a point where an axis of an ellipse, parabola, or hyperbola intersects the curve **b** ZENITH 1 (point in the sky directly above the observer) **2** the top of the head – used technically **3** the highest point; the summit △ vortex [L *vertic-, vertex*, *vortic-, vortex* whirl, whirlpool, top of the head, summit, fr *vertere* to turn]

**vertical** /'vuhtikl/ *adj* **1a** situated at the highest point; directly overhead **b** being an aerial photograph taken with the camera pointing straight down or nearly so **2a** perpendicular to the plane of the horizon or to an axis considered as horizontal; upright **b** located at right angles to the plane of a supporting surface **3a** combining all stages in the manufacture or sale of a commodity **b(1)** transcending differences of status **b(2)** of or concerning the relationship between people of different rank in a hierarchy – compare HORIZONTAL 2 [MF or LL; MF, fr LL *verticalis*, fr L *vertic-, vertex*] – **vertical** *n*, **vertically** *adv*, **verticalness, verticality** *n*

**synonyms** Vertical, upright, perpendicular, and plumb all mean "forming a right angle with the horizon". Vertical implies a line rising more or less straight up ⟨*valley ... in its lower parts ascended steeply as the roof of a house and farther up seemed almost vertical* – C S Lewis⟩. Upright suggests something solid that stands erect ⟨*upright timbers in a house*⟩. Perpendicular is more likely than vertical to be used of a straight drop ⟨*perpendicular descent of a waterfall*⟩. Plumb is used with precision by builders and architects, and specifies a 90 degree angle that can be measured with a weighted plumb line ⟨*wall was not plumb*⟩. **antonym** horizontal

**vertical circle** *n* a GREAT CIRCLE of the CELESTIAL SPHERE (imaginary sphere encircling the earth) whose plane is perpendicular to that of the horizon

**Vertical Grouping** *n* FAMILY GROUPING (teaching in groups of all ages)

**vertical union** *n*, *chiefly NAm* INDUSTRIAL UNION (union for a whole industry)

**verticil** /'vuhtisil/ *n*, *biology* a circular arrangement of similar parts (e g leaves) about a point on an axis; WHORL 2 [NL *verticillus*, dim. of L *vertex* whirl]

**verticillate** /vuh'tisilət, -layt, ,vuhti'silayt/ *adj*, *biology* (having parts) arranged in verticils; whorled; *esp* (having parts) arranged like the spokes of a wheel ⟨~ *leaves*⟩ ⟨*a* ~ *shell*⟩

**vertiginous** /vuh'tijinəs/ *adj* **1** characterized by or suffering from vertigo; *also*, *formal* dizzy, giddy **2** *formal* inclined to frequent and often pointless change; inconstant **3** *formal* causing or tending to cause dizziness ⟨*the* ~ *heights*⟩ **4** *formal* marked by turning; rotary ⟨*the* ~ *motion of the earth*⟩ [L *vertiginosus*, fr *vertigin-, vertigo*] – **vertiginously** *adv*

**vertigo** /'vuhtigoh/ *n* a disordered state marked by loss of balance and the sensation that one's surroundings are whirling dizzily, that often results from the awareness of being at great height; giddiness [L *vertigin-, vertigo*, fr *vertere* to turn]

**vertu** /vuh'tooh/ *n* VIRTU (artistic worth)

**vervain** /'vuhvayn/ *n* VERBENA; *esp* a European verbena (*Verbena officinalis*) with spikes of small lilac flowers [ME *verveine*, fr MF, fr L *verbena*, sing. of *verbenae* sacred boughs, certain medicinal plants; akin to L *verber* rod, Gk *rhabdos*]

**verve** /vuhv/ *n* **1** the spirit and enthusiasm animating artistic composition or performance; vivacity **2** energy, vitality **3** *archaic* talent [Fr, fantasy, caprice, animation, fr L *verba*, pl of *verbum* word – more at WORD]

**vervet** /'vuhvit/, **vervet monkey** *n* a S and E African grounddwelling GUENON monkey (*Cercopithecus pygerythrus*) with soft dense fur having a greenish tinge, pale yellow to white underparts, and a black face [Fr *vervet*]

¹**very** /'veri/ *adj* **1** properly so called; actual, genuine ⟨*the* ~ *heart of the city*⟩ ⟨*refused for* ~ *shame*⟩ ⟨*the* ~ *man you met*⟩ **2** absolute, unqualified ⟨*this* ~ *minute*⟩ ⟨*the* ~ *thing for the purpose*⟩ ⟨*the veriest fool alive* – John Milton⟩ **3** being no more than; mere ⟨*the* ~ *thought terrified me*⟩ ⟨*its* ~ *walls are full of history*⟩ □ used only before a noun **synonyms** see ¹SAME [ME *verray*, *verry*, fr OF *verai*, fr (assumed) VL *veracus*, alter. of L *verac-, verax* truthful, fr *verus* true; akin to OE *wǣr* true, OHG *wāra* trust, care, Gk *ēra* (acc) favour]

²**very** *adv* **1** to a high degree; exceedingly ⟨*a* ~ *hot day*⟩ ⟨~ *much better*⟩ **2** – used as an intensive to emphasize *same*, *own*, or the superlative degree ⟨*the* ~ *best shop in town*⟩ ⟨*my* ~ *own boat*⟩ ⟨*told the* ~ *same story*⟩ – **very good** – used in respectful acknowledgement of an instruction – **very well 1** – used to express often reluctant consent or agreement ⟨*very well, we'll go tomorrow*⟩ **2** with certainty; unquestionably ⟨*you know* very well *what you should do*⟩

*usage* **Very** is replaced by **much**, or by **very much**, before most past participles ⟨*was* **much** *admired/improved/inconvenienced*⟩ ⟨*the story has been* **very much** *exaggerated by the Press*⟩; but some participles which have come to be treated as ordinary adjectives can take **very** ⟨*was* **very** *tired/pleased/limited*⟩. In marginal cases it is safer to use **much** or **very much** for formal writing ⟨*was* **(very) much** *surprised/amused/interested/disgusted/distressed*⟩.

**very high frequency** *n* a radio frequency or band of frequencies in the range between 30 megahertz and 300 megahertz

**Very light** /'viəri, 'veəri/ *n* a white or coloured ball of fire that is projected from a VERY PISTOL and that is used as a signal flare [Edward W *Very* †1910 US naval officer]

**very low frequency** *n* a radio frequency or band of frequencies in the range between 3 kilohertz and 30 kilohertz

**Very pistol** *n* a pistol for firing VERY LIGHTS

**Very Reverend** *n* – used as a title for various ecclesiastical officials (eg cathedral deans and canons, rectors of Roman Catholic colleges, and superiors of some religious houses)

**vesica** /'vesikə/ *n, pl* **vesicae** /'vesi,kie/ **1** a decorative form (eg in architecture) in the shape of a 2-pointed oval **2** a bladder or bladderlike structure; *esp* URINARY BLADDER [L, bladder, blister – more at VENTER; (2) NL, fr L]

**vesical** /'vesikl/ *adj* of a bladder, esp the URINARY BLADDER [L *vesica* bladder]

**vesicant** /'vesikənt/ *n* a drug, war gas, etc, that induces blistering – **vesicant** *adj*

**vesicate** /'vesikayt/ *vb* to blister [L *vesica* blister]

**vesication** /,vesi'kaysh(ə)n/ *n* **1** blistering **2** a blister

**vesicle** /'vesikl/ *n* **1a** a small bladderlike or globular usu liquid- or gas-filled pouch, cavity, or hollow (eg a cyst or cell) in a plant or animal; *esp* a membrane-surrounded sac or cavity inside a cell **b** a blister **c** a pocket or cavity in the tissue of an embryo, that develops into an organ or major part of an organ (eg the brain) **2** a small cavity in a mineral or rock, usu resulting from the presence of bubbles of steam or gas in the molten material as it cooled and solidified [MF *vesicule*, fr L *vesicula* small bladder, blister, fr dim. of *vesica*]

**vesicular** /ve'sikyoolə/, **vesiculate** /ve'sikyoolət, -layt/ *adj* **1** having the form or structure of a vesicle ⟨*a ~ cavity*⟩ **2** containing, consisting of, or characterized by vesicles ⟨*~ lava*⟩ [NL *vesicula* vesicle, fr L, small bladder] – **vesicularly** *adv*, **vesicularity** *n*

**vesicular stomatitis** /ve,sikyoolə stohmə'tietəs/ *n* a virus disease, esp of horses and mules, that is marked by blisters in and about the mouth and that closely resembles FOOT-AND-MOUTH DISEASE

**¹vesper** /'vespə/ *n* **1** *cap* EVENING STAR (Venus) **2** *archaic* evening, eventide [ME, fr L, evening, evening star – more at WEST]

**²vesper, vesperal** /'vespərəl/ *adj* of vespers or the evening

**vespers** /'vespəz/ *n taking sing or pl vb, often cap* **1** the sixth of the CANONICAL HOURS (seven services at set times of day presented by the Roman Catholic church) that is said or sung in the late afternoon **2** a service of evening worship [Fr *vespres*, fr ML *vesperae*, fr L, pl of *vespera* evening; akin to L *vesper* evening star]

**vespertilian** /,vespə'tilyən/ *adj* of bats [L *vespertilio* bat, fr *vesper*]

**vespertine** /'vespətien/ *also* **vespertinal** /,vespə'tienl/ *adj* **1** active or flourishing in the evening: eg **1a** *of an animal* feeding or flying in early evening **b** *of a flower* opening in the evening **2** *formal* of or occurring in the evening ⟨*~ shadows*⟩ [L *vespertinus*, fr *vesper*]

**vespiary** /'vespi·əri/ *n* a nest of a wasp that lives in organized colonies; *also* the colony inhabiting it [L *vespa* + E *-iary* (as in *apiary*)]

**vespid** /'vespid/ *n* any of a widely distributed family (Vespidae) of insects comprising the wasps that live together in organized colonies like bees [deriv of L *vespa* wasp – more at WASP] – **vespid** *adj*

**vespine** /'vespien/ *adj* of or resembling wasps, esp wasps that live in colonies

**vessel** /'vesl/ *n* **1a** a hollow utensil (eg a jug, bottle, kettle, cup, or bowl) for holding esp liquid **b** somebody into whom some quality (eg grace) is infused **2a** a large hollow structure designed to float on and move through water carrying a crew, passengers, or cargo **b** any of various aircraft **3a** a tube or canal (eg an artery) in which a body liquid (eg blood or LYMPH) is contained and conveyed or circulated **b** a continuous tubular structure in a plant, that is formed by the

joining of a series of cells with the loss or perforation of their cross walls and is used for the longitudinal conduction of material from the roots to the leaves; *specif* any of a series of such structures occurring in XYLEM (water-conducting plant tissue) [ME, fr OF *vaissel*, fr LL *vascellum*, dim. of L *vas* vase, vessel – more at VASE]

**¹vest** /vest/ *vt* **1a** to give (eg property or power) into the possession or discretion of another; *esp* to give to a person a legally fixed immediate right of present or future enjoyment of (eg an estate) – usu + *in* **b** to clothe with a particular authority, right, or property – usu + *with* **2a** to robe in ecclesiastical vestments **b** *poetic* to clothe (as if) with a garment *~ vi* **1** to become legally vested – usu + *in* **2** to robe in ecclesiastical vestments [ME *vesten*, fr MF *vestir* to clothe, invest, fr L *vestire* to clothe, fr *vestis* clothing, garment – more at WEAR]

**²vest** *n* **1** a piece (eg of silk, lace, or embroidered material) used to fill in the front neckline of a woman's outer garment (eg a coat or dress) **2** *chiefly Br* a usu sleeveless undergarment for the upper body **3** *chiefly NAm* a waistcoat **4** *archaic* a loose outer garment; a robe [Fr *veste*, fr It, fr L *vestis* garment] – **vested** *adj*, **vestlike** *adj*

**vesta** /'vestə/ *n* a short match with a wax-coated stick; *also, archaic* a short wooden match [*Vesta*, Roman goddess of the hearth & household, fr L]

**vestal** /'vestl/ *adj* **1** of a VESTAL VIRGIN **2** chaste; *esp* virgin – **vestally** *adv*

**vestal virgin, vestal** *n* **1** a priestess of the Roman goddess Vesta, responsible for tending the sacred fire perpetually kept burning on her altar **2** *chiefly derog* a chaste woman

**vested interest** /'vestid/ *n* **1a** an interest (eg a title to an estate) carrying a legal right of present or future possession and of transfer to another **b** an interest (eg in an existing political, economic, or social arrangement) in which the holder has a strong personal commitment **2** one who or that which has a vested interest in something; *specif* a group enjoying benefits from an existing economic or political privilege

**vestiary** /'vesti·əri, 'vestyəri/ *n* a room where clothing is kept; a vestry [ME *vestiarie*, fr OF – more at VESTRY]

**vestibular** /ve'stibyoolə/ *adj* of or functioning as a vestibule

**vestibule** /'vestibyoohl/ *n* **1a** a lobby or chamber between the outer door and the interior of a building **b** an enclosed entrance at the end of a railway passenger carriage **2** any of various body cavities, esp when serving as or resembling an entrance to some other cavity, passage, or space: eg **2a** the central cavity of the BONY LABYRINTH of the INNER EAR, or the parts of the MEMBRANOUS LABYRINTH (part containing sensory structures concerned with hearing and balance) contained within it **b** the part of the mouth cavity outside the teeth and gums **c** the space or cleft between the LABIA MINORA containing the openings of the URETHRA (canal carrying urine from the bladder) and the vagina [L *vestibulum*] – **vestibuled** *adj*

**vestige** /'vestij/ *n* **1a**(1) a trace or visible sign left by something vanished or lost **a**(2) a minute remaining amount **b** the mark of a foot on the earth; a track **2** a body part or organ that is small and nonfunctional or imperfectly developed in comparison to one more fully developed in an earlier stage of the individual, in a past generation, or in closely related forms **synonyms** see ¹TRACE [Fr, fr L *vestigium* footstep, footprint, track (cf INVESTIGATE)] – **vestigial** *adj*, **vestigially** *adv*

**vestment** /'vestmənt/ *n* **1** an outer garment; *esp* a robe of ceremony or office **2** a covering resembling a garment **3** any of the ceremonial garments and insignia worn by ecclesiastical officiants and assistants as appropriate to their rank and to the rite being celebrated **4** *pl, archaic* clothing [ME *vestement*, fr OF, fr L *vestimentum*, fr *vestire* to clothe] – **vestmental** *adj*

**vest-'pocket** *adj, chiefly NAm* adapted to fit into the waistcoat pocket ⟨*a ~ edition of a book*⟩; *broadly* very small ⟨*a ~ version of his father*⟩

**vestry** /'vestri/ *n* **1a** SACRISTY (room where vestments are kept and clergy dress) **b** a room used for church meetings and classes **2a** the business meeting of an English parish **b** an elected administrative body in an EPISCOPAL parish in the USA [ME *vestrie*, prob modif of MF *vestiarie*, fr ML *vestiarium*, fr L *vestire*; fr its use as a robing room for the clergy]

**vestryman** /'vestrimən/ *n* a member of a vestry

**¹vesture** /'veschə/ *n* **1** *formal* clothing, apparel **2** *poetic* VESTMENT 2 [ME, fr MF, fr *vestir* to clothe – more at VEST]

**²vesture** *vt, formal or poetic* to cover with vesture; clothe

**vesuvianite** /vi's(y)oohviə,niet/, **vesuvian** *n* IDOCRASE (mineral used as a gemstone) [Ger *vesuvian*, fr *Vesuv* Vesuvius, volcano in Italy, in whose larva it is found]

**¹vet** /vet/ *n* one qualified and authorized to treat diseases and injuries of animals [short for *veterinary (surgeon)*]

**²vet** *vt* -tt- **1a** to subject (a person or animal) to a physical examination or checkup ⟨*cats will be* ~ted *before entering the show hall*⟩ **b** *chiefly Br* to provide veterinary care for (an animal) or medical care for (a person) **2** *chiefly Br* to subject to careful and thorough appraisal ⟨*they will first* ~ *your application*⟩ ⟨*jurors ... were* ~ted *and investigated by the Special Branch – Private Eye*⟩ ⟨~ting *the manuscript for possible breach of the Official Secrets Act – The Sun*⟩

**vet in** *vb* to examine (an animal) in an official veterinary inspection immediately before a show, so as to ensure that those admitted are in good health

**³vet** *adj or n, NAm* (a) veteran

**vetch** /vech/ *n* any of a genus (*Vicia*) of nonwoody climbing or twining plants of the pea family with white, pink to red, blue, violet, or yellow flowers, some of which are grown for fodder and for soil-improvement [ME *vecche*, fr ONF *veche*, fr L *vicia*; akin to OE *wicga* insect, L *vincire* to bind, OE *wīr* wire]

**vetchling** /'vechling/ *n* any of various small plants (genus *Lathyrus*) of the pea family that resemble vetches and typically have yellow or red flowers

**¹veteran** /'vet(ə)rən/ *n* **1a** a person who has had long experience of or grown old in an occupation, skill, or (military) service **b** something that has grown old with long use **2 veteran car, veteran** *Br* an old motor car; *specif* one built before 1905 – compare EDWARDIAN CAR, VINTAGE 5 **3** *NAm* a former member of the armed forces [L *veteranus*, fr *veteranus* old, of long experience, fr *veter-, vetus* old – more at WETHER]

**²veteran** *adj* of long service and experience ⟨~ *politicians*⟩

**Veterans Day** *n, chiefly NAm* a day set aside in the USA and Canada in commemoration of the end of hostilities in 1918 and 1945; *esp* November 11 observed as a public holiday in Canada and some states of the USA – compare REMEMBRANCE SUNDAY

**veterinarian** /,vet(ə)ri'neəri·ən/ *n, chiefly NAm* ¹VET

**¹veterinary** /'vet(ə)rinəri/ *adj* of or being the branch of medicine dealing with the (treatment of) diseases and injuries of animals, esp domestic animals [L *veterinarius* of beasts of burden, fr *veterinae* beasts of burden, fr fem pl of *veterinus* of beasts of burden; akin to L *veter-, vetus* old]

**²veterinary,** *Br chiefly* **veterinary surgeon** *n* ¹VET

**¹veto** /'veetoh/ *n, pl* **vetoes 1** an authoritative prohibition **2a** a right formally vested in a person or constitutional body to declare decisions made by others to be inoperative; *esp* a power vested in a chief executive (e g the president of the USA) to prevent permanently or temporarily the enactment of measures passed by a law-making body **b(1)** the exercise of such authority **b(2)** a message communicating the reasons of an executive and the president of the USA for vetoing a proposed law [L, I forbid, fr *vetare* to forbid]

**²veto** *vt* **vetoes; vetoing, vetoed** to subject to a veto – **vetoer** *n*

**vex** /veks/ *vt* **vexed** *also* **vext 1a** to bring distress, discomfort, or agitation to ⟨~ed *by a restless desire for change*⟩ **b** to irritate or annoy by petty provocations; harass ⟨*a father* ~ed *by his children*⟩ **c** to puzzle, baffle ⟨*a problem to* ~ *the keenest wit*⟩ **2** *archaic* to shake or toss (e g the sea) about *synonyms* see ANNOY *antonym* please [ME *vexen*, fr MF *vexer*, fr L *vexare* to agitate, trouble]

**vexation** /vek'saysh(ə)n/ *n* **1** being vexed; irritation ⟨*he tried not to show his* ~ *with the old man*⟩ **2** vexing, harassing ⟨*deliberate* ~ *by the neighbours drove her away*⟩ **3** a cause of trouble; an affliction

**vexatious** /vek'sayshəs/ *adj* **1** causing vexation; distressing **2** intended to harass ⟨*a* ~ *legal action*⟩ – **vexatiously** *adv*, **vexatiousness** *n*

**vexed question** /vekst/ *n* a question that has been discussed in detail and at length, usu without a satisfactory solution being reached

**¹vexillary** /'veksiləri/ *n* **1** a veteran soldier under a special standard in 'an ancient Roman army **2** a standard-bearer [L *vexillarius*, fr *vexillum*]

**²vexillary** *adj* **1** of an ensign or standard **2** of or being a vexillum

**vexillology** /,veksi'loləji/ *n* the study of flags [L *vexillum* flag] – **vexillologist** *n*, **vexillologic, vexillological** *adj*

**vexillum** /vek'siləm/ *n, pl* **vexilla** /-lə/ **1** a square flag of the ancient Roman cavalry **2** STANDARD 8a (large petal in some flowers) **3** the vane of a feather **4** a company of ancient Roman troops serving under one standard [L, prob fr *vehere* to carry]

**via** /'vie·ə/ *prep* **1** passing through or calling at (a place) on the way **2** through the medium of; *also* by means of [L, abl of *via* way; akin to Gk *hiesthai* to hurry – more at VIM]

*usage* Some people dislike the use of *via* for a means or medium ⟨*send a message* via *the milkman*⟩.

**viable** /'vie·əbl/ *adj* **1** capable of living or surviving outside the mother ⟨*a* ~ *foetus*⟩; *esp* born alive with such form and development of organs as to be normally capable of living ⟨~ *offspring*⟩ **2** capable of growing or developing ⟨~ *seeds*⟩ ⟨~ *eggs*⟩ **3a** capable of working; practicable ⟨~ *alternatives*⟩ **b** capable of independent existence and development ⟨*the colony is now a* ~ *state*⟩ [Fr, fr MF, fr *vie* life, fr L *vita* – more at VITAL] – **viably** *adv*, **viability** *n*

**via dolorosa** /,vee·ə ,dolə'rohsə/ *n, often cap V&D* a painfully difficult route or course ⟨*the* Via Dolorosa *of Arab-Israeli relationships – The Times*⟩ [*Via Dolorosa* (fr L, lit., sorrowful road), Christ's route from Pilate's judgment hall to the place of crucifixion]

**viaduct** /'vie·ə,dukt/ *n* **1** a usu long bridge that rests on a series of narrow reinforced concrete or masonry arches and carries a road or railway over a deep valley **2** a steel bridge made up of short spans carried on high steel towers [L *via* way, road + E *-duct* (as in *aqueduct*)]

**vial** /'vie·əl, viel/ *n* **1** a phial **2 vials** *pl*, **vial** *formal* a store of a specified violent feeling ⟨*pour out the* ~s *of his indignation*⟩ △ viol [ME *fiole, viole*, fr MF *fiole*, fr OProv *fiola*, fr L *phiala* – more at PHIAL]

**via media** /,vie·ə 'meedi·ə, ,vee·ə 'maydiə/ *n* a middle way; a compromise [L]

**viand** /'vie·ənd/ *n, formal* **1** an item of food; *esp* a choice or tasty dish **2** *pl* provisions, food [ME, fr MF *viande*, fr ML *vivanda* food, alter. of L *vivenda*, neut pl of *vivendus*, gerundive of *vivere* to live – more at QUICK]

**viaticum** /vie'atikəm/ *n, pl* **viaticums, viatica** /-kə/ **1** an allowance (e g of food or travelling expenses) for a journey **2** Communion given to a person in danger of death [L – more at VOYAGE]

**viator** /vie'aytaw/ *n, formal* a traveller [L, fr *via*]

**vibes** /viebz/ *n pl, informal* **1** *taking sing or pl vb* a vibraphone **2** VIBRATIONS 3b ⟨*get very bad* ~ *from the wheels-and-pollution bit – Punch*⟩ [by shortening & alter.] – **vibist** *n*

**vibrant** /'viebrənt/ *adj* **1a** oscillating or pulsating rapidly **b** pulsating with life, vigour, or activity ⟨*a* ~ *personality*⟩ ⟨*intellectually and emotionally* ~⟩ **2** sounding as a result of vibration; resonant ⟨*a* ~ *voice*⟩ – **vibrantly** *adv*

**vibraphone** /'viebrə,fohn/ *n* a percussion instrument resembling the xylophone but having metal bars and motor-driven resonators for sustaining its sound and producing a vibrato [L *vibrare* + ISV *-phone*] – **vibraphonist** *n*

**vibrate** /vie'brayt/ *vt* **1** to cause to swing or move to and fro; cause to oscillate **2** to emit (e g sound) (as if) with a vibratory motion **3** to mark or measure by oscillation ⟨*a pendulum vibrating seconds*⟩ **4** to set in vibration ~ *vi* **1** to move to and fro; oscillate **2** to have an effect as of vibration; throb ⟨*music vibrating in the memory*⟩ **3** to be in a state of vibration; quiver **4** to respond sympathetically; thrill ⟨~ *to the opportunity*⟩ *synonyms* see ¹SWING [L *vibratus*, pp of *vibrare* to shake, vibrate – more at WIPE]

**vibratile** /'viebrətiel/ *adj* **1** characterized by vibration **2** adapted to or used in vibratory motion ⟨*the* ~ *organs of insects*⟩ – **vibratility** *n*

**vibration** /vie'braysh(ə)n/ *n* **1a** a periodic motion of the particles of an elastic body (e g a stretched string of a musical instrument) or of a physical medium (e g air or water) in alternately opposite directions from the position of equilibrium when that equilibrium has been disturbed (e g when a string is plucked or a wave of sound, water, etc is propagated) **b** the action of vibrating; the state of being vibrated or in vibratory motion: e g **b(1)** an oscillation **b(2)** a quivering or trembling motion; a quiver **2** an instance of vibrating or of vibration; *esp* a single cycle of movement of a particle undergoing vibration **3a** a characteristic aura or spirit felt to emanate from somebody or something and instinctively sensed or experienced **b** **vibrations** *pl*, **vibration** a distinctive usu emotional atmosphere capable of being sensed – **vibrational** *adj*, **vibrationless** *adj*

**vibrato** /vi'brahtoh/ *n, pl* **vibratos** a slightly tremulous effect given to musical tone by slight and rapid variations in pitch, in order to add warmth and expressiveness [It, fr pp of *vibrare* to vibrate, fr L]

**vibrator** /vie'brayto/ *n* **1** one who or that which vibrates or causes vibration: e g **1a** a vibrating electrical apparatus used in massage, esp to provide sexual stimulation **b** a vibrating device (e g in an electric bell or buzzer) **2** a device that converts DIRECT CURRENT of low voltage into pulsating direct current of high voltage or ALTERNATING CURRENT (e g for the operation of a valve-driven car radio)

**vibratory** /'viebrot(ə)ri/, **vibrative** /vie'braytiv/ *adj* **1** consisting in, capable of, or causing vibration or oscillation **2** characterized by vibration; vibrant

**vibrio** /'vibri,oh/ *n, pl* **vibrios** any of a genus (*Vibrio*) of short rigid actively mobile bacteria typically shaped like a comma or an S, including the organism (*Vibrio comma*) that causes cholera [NL *Vibrion-*, *Vibrio*, genus name, fr L *vibrare* to vibrate] –**vibrionic** *adj*

**vibriosis** /,vibri'ohsis/ *n, pl* **vibrioses** /-seez/ infestation with or disease caused by vibrio bacteria [NL, fr *Vibrio*]

**vibrissa** /vie'brisə/ *n, pl* **vibrissae** /-sie/ **1** any of the stiff hairs or whiskers on the face (e g round the nostrils) of many mammals, that often serve as sensitive organs of touch **2** any of the bristly feathers near the mouth or beak of many birds, esp insect-eating ones, that may help to prevent the escape of insects [L; akin to L *vibrare*]

**viburnum** /vie'buhnəm, vi-/ *n* any of a genus (*Viburnum*) of widely distributed often cultivated shrubs (e g the GUELDER ROSE) or trees of the honeysuckle family with white or sometimes pink flowers [NL, genus name, fr L, wayfaring tree]

**vicar** /'vikə/ *n* **1** an administrative deputy **2a** a Church of England clergyman in charge of a parish who in former times did not receive any TITHES from it – compare RECTOR **b** a clergyman or layman having charge of a mission or chapel of the EPISCOPAL church in the USA **c** a clergyman exercising a broad pastoral responsibility as the representative of a bishop or other high-ranking churchman [ME, fr L *vicarius*, fr *vicarius* vicarious] – **vicarship** *n*

**vicarage** /'vikərij/ *n* **1** the BENEFICE (office to which income is attached) of a vicar **2** a vicar's house **3** VICARIATE 1

**vicar apostolic** /,apə'stolik/ *n, pl* **vicars apostolic** a Roman Catholic titular bishop who governs a territory not organized as a diocese

**vicarate** /'vikərət/ *n* a vicariate

**vicar-'general** *n, pl* **vicars-general** an administrative deputy of a Roman Catholic or Anglican bishop or of the head of a religious order

**vicarial** /vie'keəri·əl, vi-/ *adj* **1** VICARIOUS 1 **2** of a vicar [L *vicarius*]

**vicariate** /vie'keəri·ət, vi-/ *n* **1** the office, jurisdiction, or tenure of a vicar **2** the office or district of a governmental administrative deputy [ML *vicariatus*, fr L *vicarius* vicar]

**vicarious** /vie'keəri·əs, vi-/ *adj* **1a** serving instead of someone or something else **b** delegated ⟨~ *authority*⟩ **2** performed or suffered by one person as a substitute for another or to the benefit or advantage of another ⟨*a* ~ *sacrifice*⟩ **3** experienced through imaginative participation in the experience of another ⟨~ *pleasure*⟩ **4** *medicine* occurring in an unexpected or abnormal part of the body instead of the usual one [L *vicarius*, fr *vicis* change, alternation, stead – more at WEEK] – **vicariously** *adv*, **vicariousness** *n*

**Vicar of Christ** *n* the Roman Catholic pope

**¹vice** /vies/ *n* **1a** moral depravity or corruption; wickedness **b** a grave moral fault **c** a habitual and usu trivial fault or shortcoming ⟨*suffered from the* ~ *of curiosity*⟩ **2** often *cap* a character representing one of the vices in a medieval MORALITY PLAY **3** a habitual abnormal behaviour pattern in a domestic animal detrimental to its health or usefulness **4** sexual immorality; *esp* prostitution [ME, fr OF, fr L *vitium* fault, vice]

**²vice**, *NAm chiefly* **vise** /vies/ *n* any of various tools, usu able to be attached to a workbench, that have two jaws that close for holding work by operation of a screw, cam, lever, etc [ME *vis*, *vice* screw, fr MF *vis*, *viz* something winding, fr L *vitis* vine – more at WITHY] – **vicelike** *adj*

**³vice**, *NAm chiefly* **vise** *vt* to hold, secure, or squeeze (as if) with a vice

**⁴vice** *prep, formal* in the place of; succeeding △ vide [L, abl of *vicis* change, alternation, stead – more at WEEK]

**vice-** /vies-/ *prefix* **1** person next in rank below or qualified to act in place of; deputy ⟨vice-*president*⟩ ⟨vice*roy*⟩ **2** office next in rank below ⟨vice-*admiralty*⟩ [ME *vis-*, *vice-*, fr ME, fr LL *vice-*, fr L *vice*, abl of *vicis*]

**vice admiral** *n* – see MILITARY RANKS table [MF *visamiral*, fr *vis-* vice- + *amiral* admiral]

**,vice-'chancellor** *n* an officer ranking next below a chancellor and serving as his/her deputy: e g **a** the administrative head of a British university **b** the head of the CHANCERY DIVISION of the HIGH COURT [ME *vichauncellor*, fr MF *vischancelier*, fr *vis-* + *chancelier* chancellor]

**,vice-'consul** *n* a consular officer subordinate to a CONSUL GENERAL or to a consul

**vicegerent** /,vies'jerənt/ *n* an administrative deputy of a king or magistrate – compare VICE-REGENT [ML *vicegerent-*, *vicegerens*, fr LL *vice-* + L *gerent-*, *gerens*, prp of *gerere* to carry, carry on] – **vicegerency** *n*

**vicennial** /vi'senyəl, -ni·əl/ *adj* occurring once every 20 years [LL *vicennium* period of 20 years, fr L *vicies* 20 times + *annus* year; akin to L *viginti* twenty – more at VIGESIMAL, ANNUAL]

**,vice-'president** *n* an officer next in rank to a president and usu empowered to serve as president in the president's absence, death, or disability – **vice-presidency** *n*, **vice-presidential** *adj*

**viceregal** /,vies'reegl/ *adj* of a viceroy ⟨*the* ~ *lodge*⟩ – **vice-regally** *adv*

**,vice-'regent** *n* a regent's deputy – compare VICEGERENT

**vicereine** /'vies,rayn/ *n* **1** the wife of a viceroy **2** a woman viceroy [Fr, fr *vice-* + *reine* queen, fr L *regina*, fem of *reg-*, *rex* king – more at ROYAL]

**viceroy** /'viesroy/ *n* the governor of a country (e g India under British rule) or province who rules as the representative of his sovereign [MF *vice-roi*, fr *vice-* + *roi* king, fr L *reg-*, *rex*]

**viceroyalty** /vies'royəlti/ *n* the office, jurisdiction, or period of office of a viceroy

**viceroyship** /'viesroyship/ *n* viceroyalty

**vice squad** *n taking sing or pl vb* a police squad responsible for enforcing laws concerning gambling, pornography, and prostitution

**vice versa** /,viesi 'vuhsə, ,viesə, ,vies/ *adv* with the order changed and relations reversed; conversely ⟨*Ann hates Jane and* ~⟩ [L]

**vichyssoise** /,vishi'swahz/ *n* a thick soup made of pureed leeks and potatoes, cream, and chicken stock and usu served cold [Fr, fr fem of *vichyssois* of Vichy, fr *Vichy*, town in France]

**Vichy water** /'veeshi/ *n* a natural sparkling MINERAL WATER from Vichy in France

**vicinage** /'visinij/ *n, formal* vicinity [ME *vesinage*, fr MF, fr *vesin* neighbouring, fr L *vicinus*]

**vicinal** /'visinl/ *adj* **1** of or being subordinate planes or faces on a crystal that sometimes take the place of fundamental faces **2** of, being, or attached to adjacent atoms in a molecule ⟨*a* ~ *disulphide group*⟩; *also* having a vicinal chemical group **3** *formal* of a limited district; local **4** *formal* adjacent, neighbouring [L *vicinalis*, fr *vicinus* neighbour, fr *vicinus* neighbouring]

**vicinity** /vi'sinəti/ *n* **1** a surrounding area or district ⟨*everyone in the* ~ *knew of his success*⟩ **2** neighbourhood ⟨*the total cost will be in the* ~ *of a million pounds*⟩ **3** *formal* being near; proximity ⟨*the* ~ *of Etna accounted for the black rich soil*⟩ [MF *vicinité*, fr L *vicinitat-*, *vicinitas*, fr *vicinus* neighbouring, fr *vicus* row of houses, village; akin to Goth *weihs* village, Gk *oikos*, *oikia* house]

**vicious** /'vishəs/ *adj* **1a** having the nature or quality of vice; depraved ⟨~ *habits*⟩ **b** addicted to vice ⟨*a* ~ *father*⟩ **2a** dangerous, refractory ⟨*a* ~ *horse*⟩ **b** unpleasantly fierce, malignant, or severe ⟨~ *storms*⟩ ⟨*a* ~ *form of flu*⟩ ⟨*a* ~ *blow*⟩ **3** malicious, spiteful ⟨~ *gossip*⟩ **4** worsened by internal causes that reciprocally augment each other ⟨*a* ~ *wage-price spiral*⟩ **5** *formal, esp of language or reasoning* defective, faulty *antonyms* virtuous, innocuous [ME, fr MF *vicieus*, fr L *vitiosus* full of faults, corrupt, fr *vitium* blemish, vice] – **viciously** *adv*, **viciousness** *n*

**vicious circle** *n* **1** a chain of events in which the apparent solution of one difficulty creates a new problem that makes the original difficulty worse **2** the logical fallacy of using one argument or definition to prove or define a second on which the first depends **3** a chain of abnormal medical, psychiatric, etc conditions in which one disorder or disease leads to a second which in turn aggravates the first

**vicissitude** /vi'sisityoohd/ *n* **1** a change or alteration (e g in nature or human affairs) **2** *usu pl* an accident of fortune ⟨*the* ~ *s of daily life*⟩ **3** *formal* being changeable; mutability [MF, fr L *vicissitudin-*, *vicissitudo*, fr *vicissim* in turn, fr *vicis* change, alternation – more at WEEK] -- **vicissitudinous** *adj*

**victim** /'viktim/ *n* **1** a living person or animal offered as a sacrifice in a religious rite **2** one who or that which is adversely affected by a force or agent ⟨*schools that are* ~s *of the social system*⟩: e g **2a(1)** one who is injured, destroyed, or sacrificed under any of various conditions ⟨*a* ~ *of cancer*⟩ ⟨*a* ~ *of the car crash*⟩ **a(2)** one who or that which is subjected to oppression, hardship, or mistreatment ⟨*a frequent* ~ *of severe political attacks*⟩ **b** a dupe, prey ⟨*a con man's* ~⟩ [L *victima;* akin to OHG *wīh* holy, Skt *vinakti* he sets apart]

**victim·ize, -ise** /'viktimiez/ *vt* **1** to make a victim of **2** to subject to deception or fraud; cheat **3** to punish selectively (e g by unfair dismissal) – **victimizer** *n,* **victimization** *n*

**victor** /'viktə/ *n* a person, country, etc that defeats an enemy or opponent; a winner [ME, fr L, fr *victus,* pp of *vincere* to conquer, win; akin to OE *wīgan* to fight, OSlav *věkǔ* strength] – **victor** *adj*

**Victor** – a communications code word for the letter *v*

**victoria** /vik'tawri·ə/ *n* **1** a low four-wheeled pleasure carriage for two with a folding top and a raised seat in front for the driver **2** any of a genus (*Victoria*) of S American water-lilies with large spreading leaves often over 1 metre (about 3 feet) in diameter and immense fragrant rose-pink to white flowers **3** a large red sweet type of plum [*Victoria* †1901 Queen of England]

**Victoria Cross** *n* a bronze MALTESE CROSS that is the highest British military decoration [Queen *Victoria*]

**Victoria Day** *n* the Monday preceding 25 May observed in Canada as a legal holiday

**¹Victorian** /vik'tawri·ən/ *adj* **1** (characteristic) of the reign of Queen Victoria or the art, literature, or taste of her time **2** typical of the moral standards or conduct of the age of Queen Victoria, esp in being prudish or hypocritical **3** of a place called Victoria (e g the state in Australia or the capital of British Columbia)

**²Victorian** *n* **1** a person living during Queen Victoria's reign; *esp* a representative figure of that time ⟨*we were studying Tennyson, Dickens, and other* ~s *in English lessons*⟩ **2** an inhabitant of the state of Victoria

**Victoriana** /vik,tawri'ahnə/ *n* articles, esp ornaments, from the Victorian period [NL, neut pl of *Victorianus* Victorian]

**Victorian·ize, -ise** /vik'tawri,niez/ *vt* to make Victorian (e g in style or taste) – **Victorianization** *n*

**Victoria sandwich** *n* a sponge cake made from a creamed mixture containing equal weights of fat, flour, sugar, and egg and sandwiched with a layer of sweet filling (e g jam or cream)

**victorious** /vik'tawri·əs/ *adj* **1a** having won a victory **b** (characteristic) of victory **2** successful, triumphant – **victoriously** *adv,* **victoriousness** *n*

**victory** /'vikt(ə)ri/ *n* **1** the overcoming of an enemy or antagonist ⟨~ *was ours*⟩ ⟨*Nelson's celebrated* ~ *at Trafalgar*⟩ **2** achievement of mastery or success in a struggle or endeavour [ME, fr MF *victorie,* fr L *victoria,* fr fem of (assumed) L *victorius* of winning or conquest, fr L *victus,* pp of *vincere*]
**synonyms** Victory, conquest, and triumph all mean "success in a contest or struggle". Victory is the most general word, and can replace either of the others. Conquest emphasizes mastery over a human opponent ⟨*the* Roman conquest *of the Greeks*⟩ or difficult undertaking ⟨*the* conquest *of Everest*⟩. Triumph suggests public praise and personal joy for the victor as the result of a notable success. **antonyms** defeat, debacle

**victory sign** *n* V SIGN a

**¹victual** /'vitl/ *n* **1** food usable by human beings **2** *pl* supplies of food, esp as prepared for use; provisions [alter. of ME *vitaille,* fr MF, fr LL *victualia,* pl, provisions, victuals, fr neut pl of *victualis* of nourishment, fr L *victus* nourishment, fr *victus,* pp of *vivere* to live – more at QUICK]

**²victual** *vb* **-ll-** (*NAm* **-l-, -ll-**) *vt* to supply with food ~ *vi* **1** to lay in provisions **2** *archaic* to eat

**victualler,** *NAm also* **victualer** /'vitl·ə/ *n* **1** PUBLICAN 2 **2** one who provisions an army, navy, or ship with food **3** a provisioning ship

**vicuña, vicuna** /vi'kyoohnə/ *n* **1** a wild RUMINANT (cud-chewing) mammal (*Lama vicugna*) of the Andes from Ecuador to Bolivia that is related to the domesticated llama and alpaca and has been hunted almost to extinction for its fine silky wool that is light brown above and paler on the underparts **2a** the wool from the fine lustrous undercoat of the vicuña **b** a fabric made of vicuña wool; *also* a sheep's wool imitation of this [Sp *vicuña,* fr Quechua *wikúña*]

**vide** /'viedi/ *vb imperative* see – used to direct a reader to

another item △ vice, pace [L, fr *vidēre* to see – more at WIT]

**videlicet** /vi'deli,set/ *adv* that is to say; namely – used to introduce one or more examples [ME, fr L, fr *vidēre* to see + *licet* it is permitted, fr *licēre* to be permitted – more at LICENCE]
**usage** Usually abbreviated in writing to **viz,** and replaced in speech by **namely.**

**¹video** /'vidioh/ *adj* **1** of television; *specif* of the reproduction of a television image or used in its transmission or reception ⟨~ *signal*⟩ – compare AUDIO **2** of, using, being, or used in the electronic recording of images for reproduction on a television screen ⟨~ *movies*⟩ [L *vidēre* to see + E *-o* (as in *audio*)]

**²video** *n* **1** (a transmission of) material (e g a film or television programme) recorded on videotape, a videodisc, etc ⟨*we spent the evening watching a* ~⟩ ⟨*he's just taken the last* ~ *back to the hire shop*⟩ ⟨*home* ~s⟩ **2** VIDEOTAPE RECORDER; *also* a machine for playing information recorded on videodisc **3** *chiefly NAm* television

**videocassette** /,vidioh·kə'set/ *n* a cassette containing videotape

**videocassette recorder** *n* a VIDEOTAPE RECORDER using videocassettes

**videodisc** /-disk/ *n* a disc, similar to a gramophone record, on which esp visual information that can be played back (e g through a television screen) is stored in a digital form and that may also be used as a general information storage device (e g a computer memory)

**video frequency** *n* a frequency that is in the range required for the transmission of video information by a television system

**video nasty** *n* a video film of (allegedly) sensational nature, usu including scenes of explicit sex, violence, and horror

**videophone** /'vidioh,fohn/ *n* VIEWPHONE

**videorecorder** /'vidioh·ri,kawdə/ *n* VIDEOTAPE RECORDER

**¹videotape** /'vidioh,tayp/ *n* (a) MAGNETIC TAPE used for recording visual images

**²videotape** *vt* to make a recording of (e g something televised) on videotape

**videotape recorder** *n* a TAPE RECORDER for recording television pictures on videotape and playing back video recordings; *esp* VIDEOCASSETTE RECORDER

**vidicon** /'vidi,kon/ *n, often cap* a television CAMERA TUBE (part of camera where images are converted into electrical impulses) in which light is focussed onto a PHOTOCONDUCTIVE material (material that becomes electrically charged according to the amount of light falling on it) lining the tube, producing a pattern of electrical charge [*video* + *icon*oscope]

**viduity** /vi'dyooh·əti/ *n, formal* widowhood [ME (Sc) *viduite,* fr MF *viduite,* fr L *viduitat-, viduitas,* fr *vidua* widow – more at WIDOW]

**vie** /vie/ *vb* **vying** *vi* to strive for superiority; contend with ⟨~d *with each other for the prize*⟩ ~ *vt, archaic* to hazard at cards; wager *synonyms* see **³**RIVAL [modif of MF *envier* to invite, challenge, wager, fr L *invitare* to invite] – **vier** *n*

**Vietcong** /,vee·et'kong/ *n, pl* **Vietcong** an adherent of the Vietnamese communist movement supported by N Vietnam and engaged esp in guerrilla warfare against the S Vietnamese regime during the Vietnam War [Vietnamese *Viêt Nam côngsan* Vietnam communists]

**Vietminh** /,vee·et'min/ *n, pl* **Vietminh** an adherent of the Vietnamese communist movement [Vietnamese *Viêt Nam Dôc-Lâp Dông-Minh* League for the Independence of Vietnam]

**Vietnamese** /,vee·itnə'meez/ *n, pl* **Vietnamese** a native or inhabitant of Vietnam **2** the official AUSTROASIATIC language of Vietnam [*Vietnam,* country in SE Asia] – **Vietnamese** *adj*

**vieux jeu** /,vyuh 'zhuh/ *adj* out-of-date; OLD HAT [Fr, lit., old game]

**¹view** /vyooh/ *n* **1** the act of seeing or examining; inspection; *also* a survey ⟨*a* ~ *of English literature*⟩ **2** a way of regarding something; an opinion ⟨*in my* ~ *the conference has no chance of success*⟩ **3** a scene, prospect ⟨*the lovely* ~ *from the balcony*⟩; *also* an aspect ⟨*the rear* ~ *of the house*⟩ **4** extent or range of vision; sight ⟨*tried to keep the ship in* ~⟩ **5** an intention, object ⟨*studied hard with a* ~ *to graduating with honour*⟩ **6** the foreseeable future ⟨*no hope in* ~⟩ **7** a pictorial representation ⟨*they bought some lurid coloured* ~s *of Venice by moonlight*⟩ [ME *vewe,* fr MF *veue, vue,* fr OF, fr *veeir, voir* to see, fr L *vidēre* – more at WIT] – **in view of 1** taking the specified feature into consideration ⟨*in view of his age, the police have decided not*

*to prosecute*⟩ **2** able to be seen by or from ⟨in *full* view of *the audience*⟩ – **on view** open to public inspection; on exhibition
**synonyms** A **view** is the appearance of something seen from a particular direction, so that one looks at the rear **view** of a house or sees a **view** of the river from its windows. The **aspect** of a building is the direction in which it faces. Used figuratively, an **aspect** is what one sees from a particular **point of view** ⟨*consider a different* aspect *of the question*⟩ ⟨*look at it from my* **point of view**⟩ while **prospect** and **outlook** mean particularly a mental picture of the future. See OPINION *usage* The phrase **in view of** applies to existing circumstances, and should not be confused with *with the* **view** *of* or *with a* **view** *to*, which refer to future intentions ⟨⚠ *study the subject* **in view of** *finding a solution*⟩.

**²view** *vt* **1a** to see, watch ⟨~ *a television programme*⟩ **b** to look on in a particular light; regard ⟨*he doesn't* ~ *himself as a rebel*⟩ **2** to look at attentively; inspect ⟨~ed *the house but decided not to buy it*⟩ **3** to survey or examine mentally; consider ⟨~ *all sides of a question*⟩ **4** to see (a hunted animal) break cover ~ *vi* to watch television *synonyms* see ¹SEE – **viewable** *adj*

**viewdata** /'vyooh,dahtə, -,daytə/ *n* (a system for providing) information, esp text, that is held in a computer and is accessible to users via a specially modified television set

**viewer** /'vyooh-ə/ *n* one who or that which views: eg **a** an optical device used in viewing **b** somebody who watches or is watching television – **viewership** *n*

**viewfinder** /'vyooh,fiendə/ *n* a device on a camera for showing what will be included in the picture

**view halloo** /ha'looh/ *n, pl* **view halloos** a shout given by a hunter on seeing a fox break cover

**viewless** /-lis/ *adj* **1** affording no view **2** holding no views or opinions – **viewlessly** *adv*

**viewphone** /-,fohn/ *n* a telephonic device that transmits and receives visual images in addition to sound, allowing the user to see the person with whom he/she is in contact on a screen – called also VIDEOPHONE

**viewpoint** /-,poynt/ *n* a standpoint; POINT OF VIEW ⟨*I understand your* ~⟩ ⟨*photographed from an oblique* ~⟩

**viewy** /'vyooh-i/ *adj, informal* **1** opinionated **2** possessing visionary, impractical, or fantastic views **3** arresting in appearance; showy □ (*2&3*) no longer in vogue – **viewiness** *n*

**vigesimal** /vie'jesiməl/ *adj* based on the number 20 [L *vicesimus, vigesimus* twentieth; akin to L *viginti* twenty, Gk *eikosi*]

**vigil** /'vijil/ *n* **1a** a devotional watch formerly kept on the night before a religious festival **b** the day before a religious festival, observed as a day of spiritual preparation ⟨*on the* ~ *of the Epiphany*⟩ **c** vigils *pl*, vigil evening or nighttime devotions or prayers **2** vigils *pl*, vigil the act of keeping awake at times when sleep is customary; *also* a period of wakefulness ⟨*in the long lonely* ~s *of the night*⟩ **3** an act or period of watching or surveillance; a watch ⟨*kept* ~ *by the sick woman's bedside*⟩ [ME *vigile*, fr OF, fr LL & L; LL *vigilia* watch on the eve of a feast, fr L, wakefulness, watch, fr *vigil* awake, watchful; akin to L *vigēre* to be vigorous, *vegēre* to be active, rouse – more at WAKE]

**vigilance committee** /'vijiləns/ *n taking sing or pl vb, NAm* an unauthorized self-appointed committee of vigilantes

**vigilant** /'vijilənt/ *adj* alertly watchful, esp to avoid danger [ME, fr MF, fr L *vigilant-, vigilans*, fr prp of *vigilare* to keep watch, stay awake, fr *vigil* awake] – **vigilance** *n*, **vigilantly** *adv*

**vigilante** /,viji'lanti/ *n* one, esp a member of an organized group, who seeks to suppress and punish crime or immorality without recourse to the established processes of law (eg when these appear inadequate) [Sp, watchman, guard, fr *vigilante* vigilant, fr L *vigilant-, vigilans*]

**vigilantism** /viji'lantiz(ə)m/ *n* **1** (the pursuit of justice through) the summary action resorted to by vigilantes ⟨*what confronts Africa is a choice between a system of collective security and a system of international* ~ – *The Listener*⟩ **2** the attitudes, beliefs, and aims of vigilantes

**vigil light** *n* a candle lighted devotionally (eg in a Roman Catholic church) before a shrine or image

**vigintillion** /,viejin'tilyən/ *n* – see NUMBER table [L *viginti* twenty + E *-illion* (as in *million*)]

**vigneron** /'veenyəronh (*Fr* viɲrɔ̃)/ *n* a winegrower [ME *vigneroun*, fr MF *vigneron*, fr OF *vineron*, fr *vine, vigne* vine, vineyard]

**¹vignette** /vi'nyet/ *n* **1** a decorative design (eg of vine leaves, tendrils, and grapes) on a title page or at the beginning or end of a chapter **2a** a picture (eg an engraving or photograph) that shades off gradually into the surrounding background **b** the

pictorial part of a postage stamp design as distinguished from the frame and lettering **3a** a short descriptive literary sketch **b** a brief incident or scene (eg in a play or film) [Fr, fr MF *vignete*, fr dim. of *vigne* vine – more at VINE] – **vignettist** *n*

**²vignette** *vt* to finish (eg a photograph) in the manner of a vignette ~ *vi, of a camera lens* to allow more light through to the centre of a photographic plate than to the edges or corners – **vignetter** *n*

**vigoroso** /,vigə'rohsoh/ *adj or adv* in an energetic style – used as a direction in music [It, lit., vigorous, fr MF *vigorous*]

**vigorous** /'vigərəs/ *adj* **1** possessing or showing vigour; full of active strength ⟨*a* ~ *youth*⟩ ⟨*a* ~ *plant*⟩ **2** done with vigour; carried out forcefully and energetically ⟨~ *exercises*⟩ *synonyms* see LIVELY ⚠ rigorous [ME, fr MF, fr OF, fr *vigor*] – **vigorously** *adv*, **vigorousness** *n*

**vigour, *NAm* vigor** /'vigə/ *n* **1** active physical or mental strength or force **2** (the capacity for) active healthy well-balanced growth in a plant or animal **3** intensity of action or effect; force [ME, fr MF *vigor*, fr L, fr *vigēre* to be vigorous]

**Viking** /'vieking/ *n* **1** a Norse trader and warrior of the 8th to 10th centuries **2** a Scandinavian [ON *vīkingr*]

**vile** /viel/ *adj* **1a** morally despicable or abhorrent **b** physically repulsive; foul ⟨*a* ~ *slum*⟩ **2** tending to degrade ⟨~ *employments*⟩ **3** disgustingly or utterly bad; contemptible ⟨~ *weather*⟩ ⟨*in a* ~ *temper*⟩ **4** *archaic* of small worth or account; common; *also* mean *synonyms* see ¹MEAN [ME, fr OF *vil*, fr L *vilis*] – **vilely** *adv*, **vileness** *n*

**vilification** /,vilifi'kaysh(ə)n/ *n* **1** vilifying, abuse **2** a defamatory remark

**vilify** /'vilifie/ *vt* **1** to utter slanderous and abusive statements against; defame **2** *archaic* to lower in estimation or importance *synonyms* see ²MALIGN *antonym* eulogize [ME *vilifien* to make less valuable, fr LL *vilificare*, fr L *vilis* + *facere* to make, do] – **vilifier** *n*

**vilipend** /'vilipend/ *vt* **1** *formal* to express a low opinion of; disparage **2** *archaic* to hold or treat as contemptible [ME *vilipenden*, fr MF *vilipender*, fr ML *vilipendere*, fr L *vilis* of small worth + *pendere* to weigh, estimate – more at PENDANT]

**villa** /'vilə/ *n* **1** a country mansion **2** an ancient Roman mansion and the surrounding agricultural estate **3** a holiday home (eg at a resort) **4** *Br* a detached or semidetached urban or suburban house, usu with a garden; *esp* one built before World War I [It, fr L; akin to L *vicus* row of houses – more at VICINITY]

**villafranchian** /,vilə'frangkiən/ *adj* of or being the typical animal life of the earlier part of the PLEISTOCENE epoch [*Villa-franca* d'Asti, town in NW Italy]

**village** /'vilij/ *n* **1** a group of dwellings in the country, larger than a hamlet and smaller than a town **2** *taking sing or pl vb* the residents of a village **3** something (eg a group of burrows or nests) suggesting a village **4** *NAm* a legally constituted minor municipality [ME, fr MF, fr OF, fr *ville* farm, village, fr L *villa* country estate]

**village college** *n* a centre for adult education in a British rural area

**villager** /'vilijə/ *n* **1** an inhabitant of a village **2** a rustic

**villain** /'vilən/ *n* **1** a villein **2** a scoundrel, rascal; *also, chiefly Br slang* a criminal **3** *fem* **villainess** a character in a story or play whose evil actions affect the plot ⟨*the audience hissed the* ~⟩ ⟨*in* Vanity Fair *Becky Sharp is both heroine and* ~⟩ **4** *informal* a person or thing blamed for a particular evil or difficulty ⟨*this plug must be the* ~⟩ **5** *archaic* an uncouth person; a boor [ME *vilain, vilein*, fr MF, peasant, churl, fr ML *villanus*, fr L *villa* country estate]

**villainous** /'vilənəs/ *adj* **1** being, befitting, or characteristic of a villain ⟨*a* ~ *attack*⟩ ⟨*the* ~ *foe*⟩ **2** highly objectionable ⟨~ *weather*⟩ – **villainously** *adv*, **villainousness** *n*

**villainy** /'viləni/ *n* **1** villainous conduct; *also* a villainous act **2** depravity

**villanella** /,vilə'nelə/ *n, pl* **villanelle** /-'neli/ **1** a 16th-century Italian rustic part-song unaccompanied and in free form **2** an instrumental piece in the style of a rustic dance [It, fr *villano* villein, peasant, fr ML *villanus*]

**villanelle** /,vilə'nel/ *n* (a poem in) a chiefly French verse form using two rhymes and consisting of five 3-line stanzas and a final 1-line stanza [Fr, fr It *villanella*]

**villatic** /vi'latik/ *adj, formal* rural [L *villaticus*, fr *villa*]

**-ville** /-,vil/ *suffix* (*adj, n* + *-s-* → *n*), *informal* place or thing of (such) a nature ⟨*an evening with him is sheer dulls*ville⟩ [*-ville*, suffix occurring in names of towns, fr Fr, fr OF, fr *ville* village]

**villeggiatura** /ˌvilijəˈtoohrə/ *n* a country holiday or retirement [It, fr *villeggiare* to live in a country villa, fr *villa*]

**villein** /ˈvilən/ *n* **1** a free common villager or village peasant of any of the feudal classes lower in rank than the THANE **2** an unfree peasant standing as the slave of his feudal lord but free in his legal relations with respect to all others [ME *vilain, vilein* – more at VILLAIN]

**villeinage, villenage** /ˈvilənij/ *n* **1** the tenure by which a villein holds land from his feudal lord **2** the status of a villein [ME *vilenage*, fr MF, fr OF, fr *vilein, vilain*]

**villiform** /ˈviliˌfawm/ *adj* having the form or appearance of a villus or a number of villi; *also* resembling bristles or the pile of velvet ⟨*a fish with* ~ *teeth*⟩ [ISV]

**villosity** /viˈlosəti/ *n* **1** being villous **2** a villous patch, area, or surface

**villous** /ˈviləs/ *adj* **1** of or having villi **2** having or covered with soft long hairs ⟨*leaves* ~ *underneath*⟩ – compare PUBESCENT – **villously** *adv*

**villus** /ˈviləs/ *n, pl* **villi** /ˈvili/ a small slender part or outgrowth: e g **a** any of the many minute finger-shaped projections from the membrane lining the SMALL INTESTINE, that provide a large area for the absorption of digested food **b** any of the branching parts, rich in blood vessels, that project from the surface of the membrane (CHORION) enclosing the developing embryo of most mammals and that form part of the placenta [NL, fr L, tuft of shaggy hair – more at VELVET]

**vim** /vim/ *n, informal* robust energy and enthusiasm [L, acc of *vis* strength; akin to Gk *is* strength, *hiesthai* to hurry, OE *wāth* pursuit]

**vina** /ˈveenə/ *n* an Indian stringed instrument with usu four strings on a long bamboo fingerboard and a gourd resonator at each end [Skt *vīṇā*]

**vinaceous** /vieˈnayshəs/ *adj* of the colour of red wine [L *vinaceus* of wine, fr *vinum* wine – more at WINE]

**vinaigrette** /ˌvinəˈgret/ *n* **1** a small ornamental box or bottle with a perforated top used for holding an aromatic preparation (e g smelling salts) **2** a sharp sauce made of oil and vinegar, salt, pepper, and herbs and used esp on green salads; *also* a dish made with a vinaigrette or containing vinaigrette ingredients ⟨*leeks* ~⟩ [Fr, fr *vinaigre* vinegar]

**vinblastine** /vinˈblasteen/ *n* a chemical compound, $C_{46}H_{58}N_4O_9$, obtained from the shrub MADAGASCAR PERIWINKLE and used as an anticancer drug esp in the treatment of leukaemias and LYMPHOMAS (e g HODGKIN'S DISEASE) [contr of *vincaleukoblastine*, fr *vinca* + *leukoblast* (developing leukocyte), fr *leuk-* + *-blast*]

**vinca** /ˈvingkə/ *n* a periwinkle plant [NL, short for L *pervinca* periwinkle]

**Vincentian** /vinˈsensh(ə)n/ *n* a member of the Roman Catholic Congregation of the Mission founded by St Vincent de Paul in Paris in 1625 and devoted to missions and teaching [St *Vincent de Paul* †1660 Fr priest] – **Vincentian** *adj*

**Vincent's angina** /ˈvinsənts/ *n* an infection of the tonsils and throat, often also affecting adjacent parts, that is marked by ulceration of the lining and covering membranes and is caused by two bacteria (*Leptotrichia buccalis* or *Fusobacterium fusiforme* and *Borrelia vincentii*) [Jean Hyacinthe *Vincent* †1950 Fr bacteriologist]

**Vincent's disease** *n* VINCENT'S INFECTION

**Vincent's infection** *n* infection of the throat, mouth, and gums caused by the same bacteria as those that cause VINCENT'S ANGINA

**vincible** /ˈvinsəbl/ *adj, formal* capable of being overcome or subdued [L *vincibilis*, fr *vincere* to conquer – more at VICTOR] – **vincibleness, vincibility** *n*

**vincristine** /vinˈkristeen/ *n* a chemical compound, $C_{46}H_{56}N_4O_{10}$, obtained from the shrub MADAGASCAR PERIWINKLE and used similarly to vinblastine [*vinca* + L *crista* crest + E *-ine*]

**vinculum** /ˈvingkyooləm/ *n, pl* **vinculums, vincula** /-lə/ **1** a straight horizontal mark placed over two or more members of a compound mathematical expression and equivalent to brackets round them (eg in a $\overline{b-c} = a - [b-c]$) **2** *formal* a unifying bond; a link, tie [L, fr *vincire* to bind – more at VETCH]

**vindaloo** /ˌvindəˈlooh/ *n, pl* **vindaloos** a hot curry; *specif* a curried preparation that includes vinegar as an ingredient [origin unknown]

**vin de pays** /ˌvanh də payˈee/ (*Fr* vẽ də pei)/ *n pl* **vins de pays** /~/ TABLE WINE that is produced in a particular locality and

is usu relatively unsophisticated and inexpensive [Fr, wine of the locality]

**vindicable** /ˈvindikəbl/ *adj, formal* capable of being vindicated – **vindicability** *n*

**vindicate** /ˈvindikayt/ *vt* **1** to exonerate, absolve **2a** to provide justification for; justify **b** to maintain the existence of; uphold ⟨~ *his honour*⟩ **3** *archaic* to avenge [L *vindicatus*, pp of *vindicare* to lay claim to, avenge, fr *vindic-, vindex* claimant, avenger] – **vindicator** *n*

**vindication** /ˌvindiˈkaysh(ə)n/ *n* vindicating or being vindicated; *specif* justification against denial or censure; defence

**vindicatory** /ˈvindiˌkaytəri, -kət(ə)ri/ *adj* **1** providing vindication; justificatory **2** punitive, retributive

**vindictive** /vinˈdiktiv/ *adj* **1a** disposed to seek revenge; vengeful **b** intended as revenge ⟨~ *punishments*⟩ **2** intended to cause anguish; spiteful [L *vindicta* revenge, vindication, fr *vindicare*] – **vindictively** *adv*, **vindictiveness** *n*

  **synonyms** Vindictive, spiteful, revengeful, vengeful, resentful, and rancorous all mean "showing or feeling the desire for vengeance". Vindictive and spiteful both imply the wish to hurt another for a wrong or slight inflicted, but vindictive carries a stronger suggestion of serious vengeance and spiteful of petty malice. Revengeful and vengeful apply to the action or state of mind of one who really takes revenge ⟨vengeful *military force and punishments without remorse* – William Wordsworth⟩ ⟨revengeful *Nature grudged him the crops which she granted to more liberal husbandmen* – W M Thackeray⟩. Resentful, and the stronger word rancorous, emphasize the bitter and lasting ill will which may or may not lead to such action. **antonyms** forgiving, magnanimous

**vine** /vien/ *n* **1** the climbing plant that bears grapes **2a** (any of various plants with) a flexible stem that requires support and that creeps along the ground or climbs up a support by means of tendrils or by twining **b** *chiefly NAm* any of various sprawling nonwoody plants (e g a tomato or potato) that lack specialized adaptations for climbing [ME, fr OF *vigne*, fr L *vinea* vine, vineyard, fr fem of *vineus* of wine, fr *vinum* wine – more at WINE]

**vinedresser** /-ˌdresə/ *n* somebody who cultivates and prunes grapevines, esp as an occupation

**vinegar** /ˈvinigə/ *n* **1** a sour liquid obtained esp by acetic fermentation of wine, cider, beer, etc and used as a condiment or preservative **2** ill humour; sourness [ME *vinegre*, fr OF *vinaigre*, fr *vin* wine (fr L *vinum*) + *aigre* keen, sour – more at EAGER]

**vinegar eel** *n* a minute NEMATODE worm (unsegmented round-bodied worm) (*Turbatrix aceti*) often found in great numbers in vinegar or acidic fermenting vegetable matter

**vinegar fly** *n* DROSOPHILA (small fly much used in research) [fr its breeding in pickles]

**vinegary** /ˈvinig(ə)ri/ *adj* **1** containing or resembling vinegar; sour **2** **vinegary, vinegarish** disagreeable, bitter, or irascible in character or manner

**viner** /ˈvienə/ *n* a machine for separating fresh peas from the pods [*vine* + ²*-er*]

**vinery** /ˈvienəri/ *n* an area or building in which vines are grown

**vine weevil** *n* a dull black wingless weevil (*Otiorhynchus sulcatus*) both the adults and larvae of which are very destructive pests of garden flowers

**vineyard** /ˈvinyahd, -yəd/ *n* a planting of grapevines

**vingt-et-un** /ˌvant ay ˈuhn (*Fr* vẽt e œ̃)/ *n* the game of pontoon [Fr, lit., twenty-one]

**vinic** /ˈvienik, ˈvinik/ *adj* of or derived from wine or alcohol [ISV, fr L *vinum* wine – more at WINE]

**viniculture** /ˈviniˌkulchə/ *n* VITICULTURE (wine growing) [L *vinum* + ISV *-i-* + *culture*]

**viniferous** /viˈnif(ə)rəs/ *adj* yielding or grown for the production of wine [L *vinifer*, fr *vinum* + *-ifer* -iferous]

**vinification** /ˌvinifiˈkaysh(ə)n/ *n* the conversion of a sugar-containing solution (e g a fruit juice) into wine by fermentation [Fr, fr *vin* wine + *-i-* + *-fication*]

**vino** /ˈveenoh/ *n, informal* wine [It & Sp, fr L *vinum*]

**vin ordinaire** /van awdiˈneə/ *n, pl* **vins ordinaires** /~/ TABLE WINE that is undistinguished but sufficiently inexpensive for everyday drinking [Fr, ordinary wine]

**vinosity** /viˈnosəti/ *n* **1** being vinous **2** the characteristic body, flavour, and colour of a wine

**vinous** /ˈvienəs/ *adj* **1** of or made with wine ⟨~ *medications*⟩ **2** (showing the effects of being) addicted to wine **3** VINACEOUS (red) [L *vinosus*, fr *vinum* wine] – **vinously** *adv*

**¹vintage** /'vintij/ *n* **1a(1)** a season's yield of grapes or wine from a vineyard **a(2)** wine; *specif* a wine of a particular type, region, and year and usu of superior quality that is dated and allowed to mature ⟨*a pink champagne ... always sold as a ~ – Decanter*⟩ **b** *taking sing or pl vb* a collection of contemporaneous and similar people or things; a crop **2** the act or time of harvesting grapes or making wine **3** a period of origin or manufacture ⟨*a piano of 1845 ~*⟩ [ME, alter. of *vendage*, fr MF *vendenge*, fr L *vindemia*, fr *vinum* wine, grapes + *demere* to take off, fr *de-* + *emere* to take – more at WINE, REDEEM]

**²vintage** *adj* **1** of a vintage; *esp* being a product of one particular year rather than a blend of wines from different years ⟨*~ port*⟩ **2** of enduring interest or quality; classic **3** old-fashioned, outmoded **4** of the best and most characteristic – with a proper noun ⟨*~ Shaw: a wise and winning comedy – Time*⟩ **5** *Br, of a motor vehicle* built between the years 1919 and 1930 inclusive ⟨*a ~ Rolls*⟩ – compare EDWARDIAN CAR, VETERAN 2

**³vintage** *vt* to harvest (wine grapes)

**vintager** /'vintijə/ *n* somebody concerned with the production of grapes and wine

**vintage year** *n* **1** a year in which a vintage wine is produced **2** a year of outstanding distinction or success

**vintner** /'vintnə/ *n* WINE MERCHANT [ME *vineter*, fr OF *vinetier*, fr ML *vinetarius*, fr L *vinetum* vineyard, fr *vinum* wine]

**vinyl** /'vienl/ *adj or n* **1** (of, being, or containing) the chemical group, $CH_2=CH$, that is derived from ETHYLENE by removal of one hydrogen atom and has a VALENCY of one **2** (made from) a POLYMER (large molecule composed of many identical repeating units) derived from a chemical compound containing the vinyl group; *also* (made from) a plastic, textile fibre, etc consisting of a vinyl polymer ⟨*~ wallpaper*⟩ – compare POLYVINYL CHLORIDE [ISV, fr L *vinum* wine] – **vinylic** *adj*

**vinylidene** /'vie'nilideen/ *adj or n* (of, being, or containing) the chemical group, $CH_2=C$, that is derived from ETHYLENE by removal of two hydrogen atoms from the same carbon atom and has a VALENCY of two [ISV *vinyl* + *-ide* + *-ene*]

**vinylidene resin** /'vie'nilideen/ *n* any of a group of tough plastics made from chemical compounds containing the vinylidene group and capable of being moulded and formed into sheets, films, and filaments

**vinyl resin** *n* any of a group of plastic materials (e g PVC) made from chemical compounds containing the vinyl group

**viol** /'vie·əl/ *n* any of a family of bowed stringed instruments chiefly of the 16th and 17th centuries with usu six strings and a fingerboard with ridges (⁵FRETS) for the fingers, played resting on or between the player's knees △ vial [MF *viole* viol, viola, fr OProv *viola* viol]

**¹viola** /vi'ohlə/ *n* a musical instrument of the violin family that is slightly larger than the violin and is intermediate in range between the violin and cello [It & Sp, viol, viola, fr OProv, viol] – **violist** *n*

**²viola** /'vie·ələ, vie'ohlə/ *n* VIOLET 1; *esp* any of various cultivated hybrid violets with white, yellow, or purple often variegated flowers resembling but smaller than those of pansies [L]

**violable** /'vie·ələbl/ *adj* capable of being violated – **violably** *adv*, **violability** *n*

**violaceous** /,vie·ə'layshəs/ *adj* of the colour violet [L *violaceus*, fr *viola* violet] – **violaceously** *adv*

**viola da braccio** /vi,ohlə də 'brachioh/ *n, pl* **viole da braccio** /vi'ohlay/ a member of the early violin family; *esp* one having roughly the range of the viola [It, arm viol]

**viola da gamba** /'gambə/ *n, pl* **viole da gamba** a bass member of the viol family having a range like that of the cello [It, leg viol]

**viola d'amore** /da'mawri/ *n, pl* **viole d'amore** a bowed stringed instrument which is related to the viol family but has no ridges (⁵FRETS) for the fingers to hold the strings against, is played under the chin, and has seven gut strings played by the bow and seven wire strings that vibrate in response to them [It, viol of love]

**¹violate** /'vie·əlayt/ *vt* **1** to fail to comply with; infringe ⟨*~ the law*⟩ **2** to do harm to the person or esp the chastity of; *specif* to rape **3** to fail to respect; desecrate ⟨*~ a shrine*⟩ **4** to interrupt, disturb ⟨*~ your privacy*⟩ [ME *violaten*, fr L *violatus*, pp of *violare*; akin to L *vis* strength – more at VIM] – **violative** *adj*, **violator** *n*

**²violate** *adj, archaic* subjected to violation

**violation** /,vie·ə'laysh(ə)n/ *n* violating or being violated: e g **a**

an infringement, transgression; *specif* an infringement of the rules in sports that is less serious than a foul and usu involves technicalities of play **b** an act of irreverence or desecration; profanation ⟨*~ of a church*⟩ **c** an interruption, disturbance ⟨*~ of civil order*⟩ **d** *euph* rape

**violence** /'vie·ələns/ *n* **1a** exertion of physical force so as to injure or abuse **b** an instance of violent treatment or procedure **2a** intense or turbulent action or force ⟨*the ~ of the storm*⟩ **b** vehement feeling or expression; fervour; *also* an instance of such expression or feeling **c** the quality of being abrupt or discordant ⟨*the ~ of the contrast*⟩ – **do violence to 1** to outrage, insult ⟨*did violence to her feelings*⟩ **2** to distort or misinterpret the meaning of ⟨*the editor did violence to the text*⟩

**violent** /'vie·ələnt/ *adj* **1** marked by extreme force or sudden intense activity ⟨*a ~ attack*⟩ **2a** powerfully intense or furious ⟨*a ~ denunciation*⟩; *also* excited or mentally disordered to the point of loss of self-control ⟨*the patient became ~ and had to be restrained*⟩ **b** extreme, intense ⟨*~ pain*⟩ **3** caused by force; not natural ⟨*a ~ death*⟩ [ME, fr MF, fr L *violentus*; akin to L *violare* to violate] – **violently** *adv*

**violent storm** *n* STORM 1c(1) **synonyms** see ¹WIND

**violet** /'vie·ələt/ *n* **1** any of a genus (*Viola* of the family Violaceae, the violet family) of plants or shrubs that bear both normal flowers and CLEISTOGAMOUS (remaining closed and self-pollinating) flowers; *esp* one with smallish usu single-coloured typically lilac to bluish-purple and often sweet-scented flowers as distinguished from the often variegated usu larger-flowered violas and pansies **2** a bluish-purplish colour [ME, fr MF *violete*, dim. of *viole* violet, fr L *viola*]

**violin** /,vie·ə'lin/ *n* a musical instrument that has a flat hollow wooden body with curved outlines, a wooden neck, and four strings played with a bow and has the highest range of the standard STRINGED INSTRUMENTS [It *violino*, dim. of *viola*] – **violinist** *n*

**violoncello** /,vie·ələn'cheloh/ *n, pl* **violoncellos** a cello [It, dim. of *violone*, aug of *viola*] – **violoncellist** *n*

**VIP** *n, pl* **VIPs** a person of great influence or prestige; *esp* a high official with special privileges ⟨*gave him the ~ treatment*⟩ **synonyms** see PERSONAGE [*very important person*]

**viper** /'viepə/ *n* **1a** any of various venomous snakes (family Viperidae) of Europe, Asia, and Africa; *esp* a common Eurasian venomous snake (*Vipera berus*) that attains a length of 60 centimetres (about 2 feet), varies in colour from red, brown, or grey with dark markings to black, and is rarely fatal to human beings **b** PIT VIPER (venomous American snake) **2** a malignant or treacherous person [MF *vipere*, fr L *vipera*]

**viperish** /'viepərish/ *adj* spitefully abusive

**viperous** /'viep(ə)rəs/ *adj* **1** viperous, **viperine** /'viepərien/ of or resembling a viper; venomous **2** viperish – **viperously** *adv*

**viper's bugloss** *n* a coarse bristly Eurasian plant (*Echium vulgare*) of the forget-me-not family with showy blue tubular flowers

**viraemia** /vie·ə'reemiə/ *n* the presence of a particular virus in the blood [NL, fr *virus* + *-aemia*]

**virago** /vi'rahgoh/ *n, pl* **viragoes**, **viragos 1** a loud overbearing woman; TERMAGANT **2** *archaic* a woman of great stature, strength, and courage [L *viragin-*, *virago*, fr *vir* man – more at VIRILE] – **viraginous** *adj*

**viral** /'vie·ərəl/ *adj* of or caused by a virus ⟨*~ pneumonia*⟩ – **virally** *adv*

**virelay** /'virilay/ *n* a chiefly French verse form consisting of stanzas of indeterminate length and number with alternating long and short lines and interlaced rhyme (e g *abab bcbc cdcd dada*); *also* a poem in this form [ME, fr MF *virelai*]

**vireo** /'virioh/ *n, pl* **vireos** any of various small insect-eating American songbirds (family Vireonidae) [L, a small bird, fr *virēre* to be green]

**virescence** /vi'res(ə)ns/ *n* the state or condition of becoming green; *esp* such a condition occurring in plant organs (e g petals) that are not normally green due to the development of CHLOROPLASTS (cell structures containing the green pigment chlorophyll) [L *virescent-*, *virescens*, prp of *virescere* to become green, incho of *virēre* to be green] – **virescent** *adj*

**virga** /'vuhgə/ *n taking sing or pl vb* wisps of rain or snow that evaporate before reaching the ground [NL, fr L, branch, rod, streak in the sky suggesting rain – more at WHISK]

**¹virgate** /'vuhgət, -gayt/ *n* any of various old English units of land area; *esp* a unit equal to 30 acres (about 0.12 square kilometre) [ML *virgata*, fr *virga*, a land measure, fr L, rod]

²**virgate** *adj, biology* shaped like a rod or wand ⟨*a ~ one-flowered branch*⟩ [NL *virgatus*, fr L, made of twigs, fr *virga*]

¹**virgin** /'vuhjin/ *n* **1** an unmarried woman devoted to religion **2** an unmarried girl or woman **3a Virgin Mary, Virgin** *the* mother of Jesus **b** *often cap* a statue or picture of the Virgin **4** a person, esp a girl, who has not had sexual intercourse **5** a female animal that has never copulated **6** *cap* Virgo – + the [ME, fr OF *virgine*, fr L *virgin-, virgo* young woman, virgin]

²**virgin** *adj* **1** free of impurity or stain; unsullied **2** being a virgin **3** characteristic of or befitting a virgin; modest **4** untouched, unexploited; *specif* not altered by human activity ⟨*a ~ forest*⟩ **5** initial, maiden **6** occurring naturally; NATIVE **7** ⟨*~ sulphur*⟩ **7** *of metal* produced directly from ore or by smelting

¹**virginal** /'vuhjinl/ *adj* **1** (characteristic) of a virgin or virginity; *esp* pure, chaste **2** untouched, uncorrupted – **virginally** *adv*

²**virginal** *n*, **virginals** *n pl* a small rectangular harpsichord having strings parallel to the length of the keyboard and popular in the 16th and 17th centuries [prob fr L *virginalis* of a virgin, fr *virgin-, virgo*]

**virgin birth** *n* **1** birth from a virgin **2** *often cap V&B* the doctrine that Jesus was born of a virgin mother

**Virginia** /və'jinyə, -ni·ə/ *n* a usu mild-flavoured FLUE-CURED (cured without exposure to smoke) tobacco grown originally in N America and used esp in cigarettes – compare MARYLAND [*Virginia*, state of the USA]

**Virginia creeper** *n* either of two plants (genus *Parthenocissus*) of the grape family that climb by means of tendrils and have leaves that turn red in autumn: **a** a common N American plant (*Parthenocissus quinquefolia*) with leaves composed of five leaflets and bluish-black berries **b** a plant (*Parthenocissus tricuspidata*) with purplish berries, commonly cultivated in Britain

**Virginia ham** *n* a flat lean smoked ham with dark red meat

**Virginia pine** *n* an often shrubby pine (*Pinus virginiana*) of the eastern USA that has short needles

**Virginia reel** *n* an American dance in which two lines of couples face each other and all couples in turn participate in a series of figures

**Virginia stock** *n* a commonly cultivated plant (*Malcolmia maritima*) of the cabbage family with small pink, white, red, or lilac flowers

**virginity** /və'jinəti/ *n* **1** being a virgin **2** unmarried life; celibacy, spinsterhood

**virginium** /və'jinyəm, -niəm/ *n* FRANCIUM (chemical element) – not now used technically [NL, fr *Virginia*]

**Virgin Mary** /'meəri/ *n* VIRGIN 3a

**virgin wool** *n* wool not used before in manufacture

**Virgo** /'vuhgoh/ *n* **1** a constellation of the ZODIAC (imaginary belt in the heavens) lying between Leo and Libra and represented as a woman holding an ear of corn **2a** the 6th sign of the ZODIAC in astrology, held to govern the period August 23 – September 22 approx **b** somebody born under this sign [L (gen *Virginis*), lit., virgin] – **Virgoan** *adj or n*

**virgo intacta** /ˌvuhgoh in'taktə/ *n* a virgin human female with an unbroken hymen [L, untouched virgin]

**virgulate** /'vuhgyoolət, -layt/ *adj, biology* rod-shaped; VIRGATE [L *virgula* little rod]

**virgule** /'vuhgyoohl/ *n* SOLIDUS 2 (punctuation mark) [Fr, fr L *virgula* small stripe, obelus, fr dim. of *virga* rod – more at WHISK]

**viricide, virucide** /'vie·ərəˌsied/ *n* something that destroys or inhibits the growth of viruses [NL *virus* + E -*i-* + -*cide*] – **viricidal** *adj*, **viricidally** *adv*

**virid** /'virid/ *adj* vividly green; VERDANT [L *viridis* green – more at VERDANT]

**viridescent** /ˌviri'des(ə)nt/ *adj* slightly green; tending to green

**viridian** /vi'ridi·ən/ *n* (a pigment that consists of an oxide of chromium, $Cr_2O_3.2H_2O$, and has) a strong bluish-green colour [L *viridis*]

**viridity** /vi'ridəti/ *n* **1** being green **2** *formal* naive innocence [ME *viridite* greenness, fr MF *viridité*, fr L *viriditat-, viriditas*, fr *viridis*]

**virile** /'viriel/ *adj* **1** having the nature, properties, or qualities of a man; *specif* capable of functioning as a male in copulation **2** energetic, vigorous, forceful **3** characteristic of or associated with adult males; masculine *synonyms* see ¹MALE *antonyms* puerile, impotent [MF or L; MF *viril*, fr L *virilis*, fr *vir* man, male; akin to OE & OHG *wer* man, Skt *vīrā*]

**virilism** /'viriˌliz(ə)m/ *n* **1** precocious development of SECONDARY SEX CHARACTERISTICS (eg growth of beard) in the male **2** the abnormal development of male SECONDARY SEX CHARACTERISTICS in the female

**virility** /və'riləti/ *n* being virile: **a** power to procreate **b** manly vigour; masculinity

**virion** /'vie·əriˌon, 'viri-/ *n* a complete virus particle with its outer protein coat intact; the form of a virus that exists outside and can infect a living cell [ISV *viri-* (fr *virus*) + ²-*on*]

**virology** /vie·ə'roləji/ *n* the branch of science that deals with viruses and viral diseases [NL *virus* + ISV -*logy*] – **virologist** *n*, **virological, virologic** *adj*, **virologically** *adv*

**virosis** /vie·ə'rohsis/ *n, pl* **viroses** /-seez/ infection with or disease caused by a virus [NL]

**virtu, vertu** /vuh'tooh/ *n* **1a** a taste for or knowledge of curios or objets d'art **b** excellence (eg artistic worth, rarity, or antiquity) in such objects ⟨*Regency snuffboxes and other objects of ~*⟩ **2** curios, objets d'art, or antiques collectively [It *virtù*, lit., virtue, fr L *virtut-, virtus*]

**virtual** /'vuhchooəl/ *adj* **1** being such in essence or effect though not formally recognized or admitted ⟨*a ~ dictator*⟩ ⟨*a ~ promise*⟩ **2** formed by the apparent rather than the actual convergence of light rays at a point ⟨*a ~ image*⟩ – compare REAL 2d **3** *computers* of, being, or having a storage capacity that appears greater to the user than the physical amount available as a result of the rapid movement of data between different storage areas **4** *physics* of or being a particle that is considered to exist for a very brief time in an interaction between other particles [ME, possessed of certain physical virtues, fr ML *virtualis*, fr L *virtus* strength, virtue]

**virtuality** /ˌvuhchoo'aləti/ *n* the ability to develop into existence; potentiality

**virtually** /'vuhchəli, -chooəli/ *adv* almost entirely; for all practical purposes

**virtue** /'vuhtyooh, -chooh/ *n* **1a** conformity to a standard of right; morality **b** a particular moral excellence ⟨*patience is a ~*⟩ **2** *pl* the fifth of the nine orders of angelic beings in the CELESTIAL HIERARCHY ranking immediately below DOMINATIONS and above POWERS **3** a beneficial or commendable quality ⟨*has the ~ of being small*⟩ **4** *euph* chastity, esp in a woman **5** *archaic* manly strength or courage; valour **6** *archaic* a capacity to act; potency [ME *virtu*, fr OF, fr L *virtut-, virtus* strength, manliness, virtue, fr *vir* man – more at VIRILE] – **virtueless** *adj* – **by/in virtue of** as a result of; because of

**virtuosity** /ˌvuhtyooh'osəti/ *n* **1** a taste for or interest in virtu **2** great technical skill, esp in the playing of a musical instrument

¹**virtuoso** /ˌvuhtyooh'ohsoh, -zoh/ *n, pl* **virtuosos, virtuosi** /-si, -zi/ **1** one skilled in or having a taste for the FINE ARTS **2** somebody who has achieved superb technical skill in some activity; *esp* a highly skilled musical performer (eg on the violin) **3** *obs* an experimenter or investigator, esp in the arts and sciences [It, fr *virtuoso*, adj, virtuous, skilled, fr LL *virtuosus* virtuous, fr L *virtus*] – **virtuosic** *adj*

²**virtuoso** *adj* (characteristic) of a virtuoso; having the manner or style of a virtuoso ⟨*a ~ performance*⟩

**virtuous** /'vuhchoo·əs/ *adj* **1** having or exhibiting virtue; *esp* morally excellent **2** *euph* chaste **3** *archaic* potent, efficacious – **virtuously** *adv*, **virtuousness** *n*

**virucide** /'vie·ərəˌsied/ *n* VIRICIDE (something that destroys viruses) [NL *virus* + E -*cide*] – **virucidal** *adj*, **virucidally** *adv*

**virulence** /'viryooləns, -rə-/, **virulency** /-si/ *n* being virulent: eg **a** extreme bitterness or viciousness of temper; malevolence **b** the ability to cause harm; malignancy, venomousness ⟨*the ~ of a disease*⟩ **c** the relative capacity of a disease-causing agent (eg a virus) to overcome the natural defences of the body and cause disease

**virulent** /'viryoolənt, -rə-/ *adj* **1a** *of a disease, disease condition, or infection* marked by a rapid development and severe or harmful effects **b** *of a disease-causing agent* (easily) able to overcome the natural defence mechanisms of the body and cause disease; spreading easily between and infecting many organisms **2** extremely poisonous or venomous; noxious ⟨*a ~ poison*⟩ **3** full of malice; malignant ⟨*~ racialists*⟩ **4** objectionably harsh or strong ⟨*a ~ purple*⟩ [ME, fr L *virulentus*, fr *virus* poison] – **virulently** *adv*

**viruliferous** /ˌviryoo'lif(ə)rəs, -rə-/ *adj* containing, producing, or conveying a disease-causing agent ⟨*offspring of ~ females*⟩ [*virul*ence + -*iferous*]

**virus** /'vie·ərəs/ *n* **1a** the causative agent of an infectious disease – not now used technically **b** any of a large group of minute parasitic entities that are regarded either as the simplest microorganisms or as extremely complex molecules, typically consist of a protein coat surrounding a core of genetic material (RNA or DNA), are capable of growth and multiplication only in living cells, and that cause various common diseases in animals and plants **c** a disease caused by a virus **2** something that poisons the mind or soul ⟨*the ~ of racialism*⟩ **3** *archaic* venom, poison [L, slimy liquid, poison, stench; akin to OE *wāse* marsh, Gk *ios* poison, Skt *viṣa;* (1) NL, fr L]

**virustatic** /ˌvie·ərə'statik/ *adj* tending to stop or retard the growth of viruses [*virus* + Gk *statikos* causing to stand – more at STATIC]

**¹visa** /'veezə/ *n* an endorsement made on a passport by the proper authorities (eg of a country at entrance or exit) denoting that the bearer may proceed [Fr, fr L, neut pl of *visus,* pp]

**²visa** *vt* **visas; visaing; visaed** to provide (a passport) with a visa

**visage** /'vizij/ *n, archaic or poetic* **1** the face or countenance of a person or sometimes an animal **2** aspect, appearance ⟨*grimy ~ of a mining town*⟩ [ME, fr OF, fr *vis* face, fr L *visus* sight, appearance, fr *visus,* pp of *vidēre* to see – more at WIT] – **visaged** *adj*

**¹vis-à-vis** /ˌveez ah 'vee/ *n, pl* **vis-à-vis 1** a person or thing that is face to face with another **2** a counterpart **3** a private conversation; a tête-à-tête [Fr, lit., face to face]

**²vis-à-vis** *prep* **1** face to face with; opposite **2** in relation to

**³vis-à-vis** *adv* FACE TO FACE

**viscacha** /vis'kachə/ *n* any of several S American burrowing rodents (genera *Lagostomus* and *Lagidium*) closely related to the chinchilla – called also VIZCACHA [Sp *vizcacha,* fr Quechua *Wiskácha*]

**viscera** /'visərə/ *n pl* the heart, liver, intestines, and other internal body organs collectively that are located esp in the great cavity of the trunk [L, pl of *viscus* internal organ]

**visceral** /'visərəl/ *adj* **1** felt (as if) in the viscera ⟨*~ sensation*⟩ **2** instinctive, unreasoning ⟨*a ~ conviction*⟩ **3** dealing with crude emotions; earthy ⟨*a ~ novel*⟩ **4** of, affecting, or located in or among the viscera – **viscerally** *adv*

**viscerogenic** /ˌvisərə'jenik/ *adj* arising within the body as contrasted with the mind ⟨*~ needs*⟩ [L *viscera* + E *-genic*]

**visceromotor** /'visəroh,mohtə/ *adj* causing or concerned with the functional activity of the viscera ⟨*~ nerves*⟩

**viscid** /'visid/ *adj* **1a** adhesive, sticky **b** having a glutinous consistency; viscous **2** covered with a sticky layer ⟨*~ leaves*⟩ [LL *viscidus,* fr L *viscum* birdlime] – **viscidly** *adv,* **viscidity** *n*

**viscometer** /vis'komitə/ *n* an instrument for measuring viscosity [*viscosity* + *-meter*] – **viscometry** *n,* **viscometric** *adj*

**viscose** /'viskohs, -kohz/ *n* **1** a viscous solution made by treating CELLULOSE (constituent of woody or fibrous plant tissue) with strong alkali (eg caustic soda) solution and CARBON DISULPHIDE and used in making rayon and films of regenerated cellulose (eg cellophane) **2** rayon made from viscose *synonyms* see NYLON [obs *viscose* viscous, fr ME, fr LL *viscosus*] – **viscose** *adj*

**viscosimeter** /ˌviskoh'simitə/ *n* a viscometer [ISV *viscosity* + *-meter*] – **viscosimetric** *adj*

**viscosity** /vis'kosəti/ *n* **1** being viscous **2** the property of a liquid, gas, or semifluid substance that enables it to develop and maintain resistance to flow or resistance to the movement of a body through it **3 viscosity, coefficient of viscosity** a measure of the viscosity of a liquid equal to the ratio of the frictional force per unit area to the difference in velocity between layers of the liquid one unit apart

**viscosity index** *n* an arbitrary number assigned as a measure of the constancy of the viscosity of a lubricating oil with change of temperature, with higher numbers indicating viscosities that change little with temperature

**viscount** /'viekownt/ *n* a member of the British peerage ranking below an earl and above a baron [ME *viscounte,* fr MF *viscomte,* fr ML *vicecomit-, vicecomes,* fr LL *vice-* + *comit-, comes* count – more at COUNT] – **viscountcy, viscounty** *n*

**viscountess** /ˌviekown'tes, 'viekowntis/ *n* **1** the wife or widow of a viscount **2** a woman having in her own right the rank of a viscount

**viscous** /'viskəs/ *adj* **1** glutinous, viscid **2** having or characterized by (high) viscosity ⟨*~ flow*⟩ △ vicious [ME *viscouse,* fr LL *viscosus* full of birdlime, sticky, fr L *viscum* mistletoe, birdlime; akin to OHG *wīhsila* cherry, Gk *ixos* mistletoe] – **viscously** *adv,* **viscousness** *n*

**viscus** /'viskəs/ *n, pl* **viscera** /'visərə/ any of the organs that collectively make up the viscera [L]

**vise** /vies/ *vt or n, chiefly NAm* (to hold with) a vice

**¹visé** /'veezay, -'-/ *vt* **visés; viséing; viséd, viséed** *archaic or NAm* to visa [Fr, pp of *viser* to visa, fr *visa*]

**²visé** *n, archaic or NAm* a visa

**visibility** /ˌvizə'biləti/ *n* **1** being visible **2a** the degree to which something is visible (eg because of light or atmospheric clarity); *specif* the greatest distance at which prominent objects can be clearly distinguished with the naked eye ⟨*~ is down to 20 yards*⟩ **b** capability of affording an unobstructed view ⟨*car with good rear ~*⟩ **3** a measure of the ability of light of a particular wavelength to evoke visual sensation

**visible** /'vizəbl/ *adj* **1** capable of being seen; perceptible to vision ⟨*stars ~ to the naked eye*⟩ ⟨*~ light*⟩ **2** exposed to view ⟨*the ~ horizon*⟩ **3** capable of being perceived; noticeable ⟨*her ~ impatience*⟩ ⟨*no ~ means of support*⟩ **4** of or being trade in goods rather than services ⟨*~ exports*⟩ – compare INVISIBLE **5** devised to keep a particular part or item always in full view or readily accessible ⟨*a ~ index*⟩ **6** in the public eye; prominent, well-known ⟨*a very ~ politician*⟩ *usage* see VISUAL [ME, fr MF or L; MF, fr L *visibilis,* fr *visus,* pp] – **visibleness** *n,* **visibly** *adv*

**visible horizon** *n* HORIZON 1a (apparent meeting of sky and land or sea)

**visible speech** *n* a set of phonetic symbols based on the positions made by the mouth when making the sounds they represent

**Visigoth** /'vizi,goth/ *n* a member of the western division of the Goths [LL *Visigothi,* pl] – **Visigothic** *adj*

**¹vision** /'vizh(ə)n/ *n* **1a** something seen in a dream, trance, or ecstasy; *specif* a supernatural appearance that conveys a revelation **b vision, visions** *pl* a mental image of something immaterial ⟨*had ~s of missing the train*⟩ **2a** the power of imagination; *also* the manner of perceiving mental images ⟨*an artist's ~*⟩ **b** discernment, foresight ⟨*a man of ~*⟩ ⟨*he lacks ~*⟩ **c** a supernatural apparition **3a** the act or power of seeing; sight **b** the special sense by which the qualities of an object (eg colour, luminosity, shape, and size) constituting its appearance are perceived and which is mediated by the eye **4a** something seen; *esp* the degree of clarity with which something appears on a television screen ⟨*adjust the ~*⟩ **b** a lovely or charming sight ⟨*she looked a ~ in that dress*⟩ [ME, fr OF, fr L *vision-, visio,* fr *visus,* pp of *vidēre* to see – more at WIT] – **visional** *adj,* **visionally** *adv,* **visionless** *adj*

**²vision** *vt* to envision

**¹visionary** /'vizh(ə)nri, -əri/ *adj* **1a** able or likely to see visions **b** disposed to daydreaming or imagining; dreamy, impractical **2a** of the nature of a vision; illusory **b** impracticable, utopian ⟨*a ~ scheme*⟩ **c** existing only in imagination; unreal **3** of or characterized by visions or the power of vision – **visionariness** *n*

**²visionary** *n* **1** one who sees visions; a seer **2** one whose ideas or projects are impractical; a dreamer

**visioned** /'vizh(ə)nd/ *adj* **1** seen or experienced in a vision ⟨*a ~ face*⟩ **2** endowed with vision; inspired

**¹visit** /'vizit/ *vt* **1a(1)** to afflict ⟨*a city frequently ~ed by the plague*⟩ **a(2)** to inflict, impose ⟨*~ed his wrath upon them*⟩ **b** to inflict punishment for ⟨*~ed the sins of the fathers upon the children*⟩ **c** to strike or overcome momentarily ⟨*was ~ed by a strange notion*⟩ **2a** to pay a call on for reasons of kindness, friendship, ceremony, or business ⟨*~ my aunt*⟩ ⟨*~ ICI*⟩ ⟨*~ing the sick*⟩ **b** to reside with temporarily as a guest **c** to go or come to look at or stay at ⟨*~ Kew gardens*⟩ ⟨*~ Paris*⟩ **d** to go or come officially to inspect or oversee ⟨*a bishop ~ing the parish*⟩ **3** *archaic, of God* to comfort ⟨*~ us with Thy salvation* – Charles Wesley⟩ *~ vi* **1** to make a visit or visits **2** *NAm* to chat, converse ⟨*~ with her on the telephone*⟩ [ME *visiten,* fr OF *visiter,* fr L *visitare,* freq of *visere* to go to see, fr *vidēre* to see]

**²visit** *n* **1a** an act of visiting; a call **b** a temporary residence as a guest **c** an extended but temporary stay ⟨*his annual ~s abroad*⟩ **2** a journey to and stay at a place ⟨*during my ~ to Thailand*⟩ **3** an official or professional call ⟨*a doctor's ~*⟩ **4** the act of a naval officer in boarding a merchant ship in exercise of the right of search

**visitable** /'vizitəbl/ *adj* **1** subject to or allowing visitation or inspection **2** eligible or suitable to be visited

**visitant** /'vizit(ə)nt/ *n* **1a** a visitor **b** a supernatural apparition **2** VISITOR 2 – **visitant** *adj*

**visitation** /ˌvizi'taysh(ə)n/ *n* **1** the act or an instance of visiting; *esp* an official visit (eg for inspection) **2a** a special dispensation of divine favour or wrath **b** a severe trial; an affliction **3** *cap the* visit of the Virgin Mary to Elizabeth recounted in Luke 1:39–56 and celebrated on July 2 by a Christian festival – **visitational** *adj*

**visitatorial** /ˌvizitəˈtawri‑əl/ *adj* of visitation or an official visitor

**visiting card** /ˈviziting/ *n* a small card of introduction bearing the name and sometimes the address and profession of the owner

**visiting professor** *n* a professor invited to join a college or university staff for a limited time

**visiting teacher** *n* an educational officer employed by a state school system to visit the homes of pupils in order to bring about cooperation between school and family, to enforce attendance regulations, or to instruct sick or handicapped pupils unable to attend school

**visitor** /ˈvizitə/ *n* **1a** one who is paying a visit **b** one who makes formal visits of inspection **2** a migratory bird that visits a locality for a short time at regular intervals

**visitors' book** *n* a book in which visitors (eg to a place of interest or hotel) write their names and addresses and sometimes comments

**visor, vizor** /ˈviezə/ *n* **1** the movable part of a helmet that covers the face **2a** a usu movable flat sunshade attached at the top of a vehicle windscreen **b** *chiefly NAm* an eyeshade [ME *viser*, fr AF, fr OF *visiere*, fr *vis* face – more at VISAGE] – **visored** *adj*, **visorless** *adj*

**vista** /ˈvistə/ *n* **1** a distant view through or along an avenue or opening; a prospect **2** an extensive mental view (eg over a stretch of time or a series of events) [It, sight, fr *visto*, pp of *vedere* to see, fr L *vidēre* – more at WIT] – **vistaless** *adj*

**visual** /ˈviz(h)yooəl/ *adj* **1** of or used in vision ⟨∼ *organs*⟩ **2** attained or maintained by sight ⟨∼ *impressions*⟩ **3** optical ⟨*the* ∼ *focus of a lens*⟩ **4** visible ⟨*a* ∼ *display*⟩ **5** producing mental images; vivid **6** done or executed by sight only ⟨∼ *navigation*⟩ **7** of or using VISUAL AIDS **8** of interest to the eye; colourful ⟨*the dancers were very* ∼ *in their bright robes*⟩ [ME, fr LL *visualis*, fr L *visus* sight, fr *visus*, pp of *vidēre* to see] – **visually** *adv*

*usage* Although the two words are sometimes confused, traditionally **visual** means "of seeing" and **visible** means "that can be seen". Compare ⟨*a* **visual** *examination* (= by looking)⟩ ⟨**visible** *symptoms*⟩.

**visual aid** *n* an instructional device (eg a chart, map, model, or film) that appeals chiefly to vision; *esp* an educational film or filmstrip

**visual display terminal** *n* VDU

**visual display unit** *n* VDU

**visual field** *n* the entire expanse of space visible at a given instant without moving the eyes

**visual·ization, -isation** /ˌvizhooəlieˈzaysh(ə)n/ *n* **1** formation of mental visual images **2** the act or process of interpreting in visual terms or of putting into visible form **3a** the process of exposing an organ to view by surgery **b** the process of making an internal organ of the body visible by X-ray photography following the introduction (eg by injection) of a substance that prevents the passage of X-rays

**visual·ize, -ise** /ˈvizhooəˌliez/ *vt* to make visible: eg **a** to see or form a mental image of; envisage **b** to make (an internal part of the body) visible by surgery or by X-ray photography ∼ *vi* to form a mental visual image – **visualizer** *n*

**visual purple** *n* a light-sensitive red or purple pigment in the RODS (cells sensitive to dim light) of the retina of the eye of various VERTEBRATE animals; *specif* RHODOPSIN

**vital** /ˈvietl/ *adj* **1a** existing as a manifestation of life **b** concerned with or necessary to the maintenance of life ⟨∼ *organs*⟩ ⟨*blood and other* ∼ *fluids*⟩ ⟨∼ *functions*⟩ **2** full of life and vigour; animated **3** characteristic of life or living beings **4a** fundamentally concerned with or affecting life or living beings: eg **4a(1)** tending to renew or refresh the living; invigorating **a(2)** destructive to life; mortal **b** of the utmost importance; essential to continued worth or well-being **5** recording data relating to lives **6** of or being the STAINING (colouring with dye) of living tissues, cells, etc for examination under the microscope using a dye that does not kill the specimen *synonyms* see ²NECESSARY [ME, fr MF, fr L *vitalis* of life, fr *vita* life; akin to L *vivere* to live – more at QUICK] – **vitally** *adv*

**vital capacity** *n* the breathing capacity of the lungs expressed as the volume of air that can be forcibly exhaled after the maximum intake of air into the lungs

**vital force** *n* ÉLAN VITAL (hypothetical force causing evolutionary development)

**vitalism** /ˈvietlˌiz(ə)m/ *n* a doctrine that the functions of a living organism are due to a vital principle and are not wholly explicable by the laws of physics and chemistry – compare DYNAMISM, MECHANISM – **vitalist** *n or adj*, **vitalistic** *adj*

**vitality** /vieˈtaləti/ *n* **1a** the quality which distinguishes the living from the dead or inanimate **b** capacity to live and develop; *also* physical or mental liveliness **2** power of enduring ⟨*the* ∼ *of an idiom*⟩

**vital·ize, -ise** /ˈvietlˌiez/ *vt* to endow with vitality; animate – **vitalization** *n*

**vitals** /ˈvietlz/ *n pl* **1** vital organs (eg the heart, liver, lungs, and brain) – not used technically **2** essential parts

**vital signs** *n pl* (the level of) heartbeat, breathing rate, body temperature, and other measurable indicators of body activity and functioning; *broadly* signs that indicate the presence of life or level of activity ⟨*checking the city's* ∼⟩

**vital statistics** *n pl* **1** statistics relating to the population (eg births, deaths, marriages, health, and disease) **2** facts (eg physical dimensions or quantities) considered to be interesting or important; *specif* a woman's bust, waist, and hip measurements

**vitamin** /ˈvitəmin, ˈvie-/ *n* any of various organic chemical substances naturally present in foods, that are essential in minute quantities in the diet of most animals for the maintenance of health and growth and the proper functioning of life-supporting chemical processes, but that do not directly provide energy or serve as building units [L *vita* life + ISV *amine;* fr the former belief that it contained an amino acid]

*usage* The pronunciation /ˈvitəmin/ is recommended for BBC broadcasters.

**vitamin A** *n* any or a mixture of several chemically related fat-soluble vitamins that are obtained from animal products (eg fish liver oils, egg yolk, and milk) and by the chemical conversion in the body of CAROTENES (orange pigments in carrots, spinach, etc), are necessary for the production of the light-sensitive pigments required for vision, and whose prolonged lack results in the failure of vision in dim light and the hardening and toughening of skin and other lining and covering tissues (eg those of the eye); *esp* RETINOL (chief vitamin A)

**vitamin B** *n* any or a mixture of the vitamins of the VITAMIN B COMPLEX

**vitamin B₁** *n* THIAMINE

**vitamin B₂** *n* RIBOFLAVIN

**vitamin B₆** *n* any or a mixture of several chemically related and interconvertible water-soluble compounds that are vitamins of the VITAMIN B COMPLEX concerned with the formation and conversion of AMINO ACIDS: eg **a** PYRIDOXAL **b** PYRIDOXAMINE **c** PYRIDOXINE

**vitamin B₁₂** *n* CYANOCOBALAMIN (vitamin essential for growth and normal blood formation); *also* any or a mixture of several related compounds (COBALAMINS) that have the functions of cyanocobalamin

**vitamin B_c** /ˌbee ˈsee/ *n* FOLIC ACID

**vitamin B complex** *n* a group of water-soluble vitamins found in many foods (eg yeast, seed germs, eggs, liver, milk, cheese, and green vegetables) that act esp in ENZYME-regulated reactions inside the cell (eg in the breakdown of food to release energy), and that include biotin, choline, cyanocobalamin, folic acid, nicotinic acid, pantothenic acid, pyridoxine, riboflavin, and thiamine

**vitamin C** *n* a water-soluble vitamin, $C_6H_8O_6$, that is found in plants, esp in fruits (eg citrus fruits) or leafy vegetables (eg spinach or cabbage), is used as an ANTIOXIDANT for preserving foods, and whose lack results in scurvy – called also ASCORBIC ACID

**vitamin D** *n* any or a mixture of several chemically related fat-soluble vitamins found esp in animal products (eg fish liver oils, egg yolk, and milk), that facilitate the absorption of calcium and phosphate from food and are essential for the development and maintenance of normal bone and tooth structure: eg **a** **vitamin D₂**, **vitamin D** a vitamin, $C_{28}H_{43}OH$, that is prepared synthetically by treating ERGOSTEROL with ultraviolet radiation and is used as a dietary supplement and in the treatment of rickets – called also CALCIFEROL **b** **vitamin D₃**, **vitamin D** the main naturally occurring form of vitamin D, $C_{27}H_{43}OH$, that occurs in most fish liver oils and is formed in the skin of humans on exposure to sunlight – called also CHOLECALCIFEROL

**vitamin E** *n* any or a mixture of several related fat-soluble chemical compounds (TOCOPHEROLS) found esp in green leaves (e g lettuce) and oils made from seeds (e g soya beans), that are essential for the nutrition of many VERTEBRATE animals (e g rats, cattle, and poultry), have ANTIOXIDANT properties, and whose lack in various animals leads to infertility and degeneration of muscle; *esp* one, $C_{29}H_{50}O_2$, obtained esp from seed oils or made synthetically, that has a high degree of vitamin E activity

**vitamin G** *n* RIBOFLAVIN

**vitamin H** *n* BIOTIN

**vitamin·ize, -ise** /'vitəmi,niez, 'vie-/ *vt* to provide or supplement with vitamins – **vitaminization** *n*

**vitamin K** *n* 1 any or a mixture of several chemically related fat-soluble vitamins essential for the clotting of blood that are concerned with the formation of PROTHROMBIN and other clotting factors in the liver and with the maintenance of the normal concentration of prothrombin in the blood: e g **1a vitamin $K_1$**, **vitamin K** a naturally occurring vitamin, $C_{31}H_{46}O_2$, found esp in green plants – called also PHYLLOQUINONE, PHYTOMENADIONE **b vitamin $K_2$**, **vitamin K** a vitamin, $C_{41}H_{56}O_2$, found in putrefying organic matter and synthesized by bacteria in the intestines – called also MENAQUINONE **2a vitamin $K_3$**, **vitamin K** MENADIONE **b** any of several synthetic vitamins closely related chemically to the natural vitamins $K_1$ and $K_2$ and of similar biological activity [Dan *k*oagulation coagulation]

**vitamin P** *n* BIOFLAVONOID – not now used technically [*paprika & permeability*; fr its being obtained from some peppers & its regulating the permeability of the blood capillaries]

**vitamin PP** *n* any of various vitamins (e g NICOTINAMIDE or NICOTINIC ACID) of the VITAMIN B COMPLEX whose lack in the diet results in the disease PELLAGRA – not now used technically [*pellagra-preventive*]

**vitellin** /vi'telin/ *n* a PHOSPHOPROTEIN that is the major protein in egg yolk [*vitellus*]

**vitelline** /vi'telin, -lien/ *adj* 1 resembling the (yellow colour of the) yolk of a domestic fowl's egg 2 of or producing yolk ⟨ ∼ *gland*⟩

**vitelline membrane** *n* a membrane that encloses an egg cell and corresponds to the cell wall of an ordinary cell; *also* FERTILIZATION MEMBRANE (thickened membrane round fertilized egg)

**vitellogenesis** /vie,teloh'jenəsis, vi-/ *n* yolk formation [NL, fr L *vitellus* + NL -*o*- + *genesis*]

**vitellus** /vi'teləs/ *n* the mass of stored food in an egg cell; YOLK 1b [L, lit., small calf – more at VEAL]

**vitiate** /'vishiayt/ *vt* 1 to make ineffective; invalidate ⟨*his argument was* ∼d *by faulty logic*⟩ 2 *formal* to make faulty or defective; corrupt, debase ⟨*a spirit* ∼d *by luxury*⟩ □ often pass [L *vitiatus*, pp of *vitiare*, fr *vitium* fault, vice] – **vitiator** *n*

**viticulture** /'viti,kulchə/ *n* (the branch of science dealing with) the cultivation of grapevines [L *vitis* vine + E *culture* – more at WITHY ] – **viticultural** *adj*, **viticulturist** *n*

**vitiligo** /,viti'liegoh/ *n* a skin disorder marked by smooth white patches on various parts of the body resulting from the loss of pigment from the skin [NL, fr L, tetter]

**vitreous** /'vitri·əs/ *adj* 1 of, derived from, or consisting of glass 2a resembling glass (e g in colour, composition, brittleness, or lustre); glassy ⟨ ∼ *rocks*⟩ **b** characterized by hardness and translucence ⟨ ∼ *china*⟩ 3 of or being the VITREOUS HUMOUR [L *vitreus*, fr *vitrum* glass – more at WOAD] – **vitreously** *adv*, **vitreousness** *n*

**vitreous body** *n* VITREOUS HUMOUR

**vitreous humour** *n* the colourless transparent jellylike substance that fills the eyeball behind the lens – compare AQUEOUS HUMOUR

**vitreous silica** *n* a chemically stable transparent or translucent glass or glassy material made from SILICA – compare QUARTZ GLASS

**vitrify** /'vitrifie/ *vt* to convert into glass or a glassy substance by heat and melting ∼ *vi* to become vitrified [Fr *vitrifier*, fr MF, fr L *vitrum* glass] – **vitrifiable** *adj*, **vitrification** *n*

**vitriol** /'vitri·əl/ *n* **1a** a sulphate of any of various metals (e g copper, iron, or zinc), esp when chemically combined with water **b** concentrated SULPHURIC ACID 2 caustic, venomous, or spiteful speech, writing, etc [ME, fr MF, fr ML *vitriolum*, alter. of LL *vitreolum*, neut of *vitreolus* glassy, fr L *vitreus* vitreous] – **vitriolic** *adj*

**vitta** /'vitə/ *n, pl* **vittae** /'viti/ 1 a tube or receptacle containing oil or oily material occurring in fruits of plants of the carrot family 2 *biology* a stripe, streak, or ridge [NL, fr L, fillet; akin to L *viēre* to plait – more at WIRE]

**vittate** /'vitayt/ *adj* 1 bearing or containing vittae 2 *biology* having longitudinal stripes or ridges

**vittles** /'vitlz/ *n pl, dial or humour* food [alter. of *victuals*]

**vituperate** /vi'tyoohpərayt/ *vb, formal vt* to subject to severe or abusive censure; berate ∼ *vi* to use harsh condemning language [L *vituperatus*, pp of *vituperare*, fr *vitium* fault + *parare* to make – more at PARE] – **vituperator** *n*

**vituperation** /vi'tyoohpə'raysh(ə)n/ *n* 1 sustained, bitter, or abusive censure 2 an act or instance of vituperating *synonyms* see ²ABUSE *antonyms* acclaim, praise

**vituperative** /vi'tyoohp(ə)rətiv/, **vituperatory** /vi'tyoohpərət(ə)ri/ *adj* uttering or given to censure; containing or characterized by verbal abuse – **vituperatively** *adv*

**¹viva** /'veevə/ *interj* – used to express goodwill towards or approval of a usu specified person or thing [It, long live, fr 3 sing. pres subj of *vivere* to live, fr L – more at QUICK]

**²viva** *n, chiefly Br* VIVA VOCE

**vivace** /vi'vahchi/ *adv or adj* in a brisk spirited manner – used as a direction in music [It, vivacious, fr L *vivac-, vivax*]

**vivacious** /vi'vayshəs/ *adj* lively in temper or conduct; animated *antonyms* languid, stolid [L *vivac-, vivax*, lit., long-lived, fr *vivere* to live] – **vivaciously** *adv*, **vivaciousness**, **vivacity** *n*

**vivandière** /vi,von'dyeə (*Fr* vivãdjɛ:r)/ *n* a woman who in former times accompanied European regiments, esp those of France, to sell food and drink [Fr, fem of MF *vivandier*, fr ML *vivanda* food – more at VIAND]

**vivarium** /vie'veəri·əm/ *n, pl* **vivaria** /-riə/, **vivariums** an enclosure for keeping or raising and observing animals or plants indoors; *esp* one for ground-living animals – compare TERRARIUM [L, park, preserve, fr *vivus* alive – more at QUICK]

**¹viva voce** /,veevə 'vohki, 'vohchi/ *adj or adv* by word of mouth [ML, with the living voice]

**²viva voce** *n* an examination for an academic degree conducted by word of mouth rather than in writing

**vivax malaria** /'vievaks/ *n* malaria characterized by attacks that recur at approx 48-hour intervals; TERTIAN malaria [NL *vivax*, specific epithet of *Plasmodium vivax*, parasite causing the disease]

**vive** /veev/ *interj* – used to express acclamation of a specified person or thing [Fr, long live, fr 3 sing. pres subj of *vivre* to live, fr L *vivere*]

**viverrid** /vie'verid/ *n* any of a family (Viverridae) of flesh-eating mammals (e g a civet or mongoose) that are long, slender, and like a weasel in build, are rarely larger than a domestic cat, and have short usu retractable claws and rounded feet [NL *Viverridae*, group name, fr *Viverra*, type genus, fr L *viverra* ferret] – **viverrid** *adj*

**vivid** /'vivid/ *adj* 1 having the appearance of vigorous life or freshness; lively ⟨ ∼ *personality*⟩ 2 *of a light or colour* glaring, intense 3 producing a strong or clear impression on the senses; *specif* producing strong mental images ⟨*a* ∼ *description*⟩ [L *vividus*, fr *vivere* to live – more at QUICK] – **vividly** *adv*, **vividness** *n*

**vivify** /'vivifie/ *vt* 1 to give life or renewed life to; animate 2 to impart vitality or vividness to [MF *vivifier*, fr LL *vivificare*, fr L *vivificus* enlivening, fr *vivus* alive – more at QUICK] – **vivifier** *n*, **vivification** *n*

**viviparous** /vi'vipərəs/ *adj* 1 producing living young rather than eggs from within the body in the manner of nearly all mammals, many reptiles, and a few fishes – compare OVIPAROUS 2a *of a seed* germinating while still attached to the parent plant ⟨*the* ∼ *seed of the mangrove*⟩; *also, of a plant* having viviparous seeds **b** *of a plant* multiplying by means of shoots, buds, BULBILS (small bulbs), etc rather than seeds [L *viviparus*, fr *vivus* + -*parus* -parous] – **viviparously** *adv*, **viviparousness**, **viviparity** *n*

**vivisect** /'vivisekt, --'-/ *vt* to perform vivisection on ∼ *vi* to practise vivisection [back-formation fr *vivisection*] – **vivisector** *n*

**vivisection** /,vivi'seksh(ə)n/ *n* 1 operation or physical experimentation on a living animal, usu for scientific investigation; *broadly* animal experimentation (e g for testing the effects of cigarette smoking), esp if considered to cause distress to the subject 2 unduly ruthless criticism [L *vivus* + E *section*] – **vivisectional** *adj*, **vivisectionally** *adv*, **vivisectionist** *n*

**vixen** /'viks(ə)n/ *n* 1 a female fox 2 a spiteful ill-tempered woman [(assumed) ME (southern) *vixen*, alter. of ME *fixen*, fr OE *fyxe*, fem of *fox*] – **vixenish** *adj*, **vixenishly** *adv*, **vixenishness** *n*

**vizard** /'vizəd/ *n*, *archaic* a mask for disguise or protection [alter. of ME *viser* mask, visor]

**vizcacha** /viz'kachə/ *n* VISCACHA (S American rodent)

**vizier** /vi'ziə/ *n* a high executive officer of various Muslim countries and esp of the former Ottoman Empire [Turk *vezir*, fr Ar *wazīr*] – **vizierate** *n*, **vizierial** *adj*, **viziership** *n*

**vizor** /'viezə/ *n* a visor

**vizsla** /'vizhlə/ *n* (any of) a breed of Hungarian hunting dogs with a rich deep red coat and brown eyes [*Vizsla*, town in Hungary]

**vlei** /flie/ *n*, *pl* **vleis** 1 *SAfr* a marshy depression 2 *NW US* a marsh, swamp [(1) Afrik, meadow valley, fr MD *valeye* valley, field, fr OF *valee* – more at VALLEY; (2) obs D dial., fr MD *valeye*]

**V neck** /vee/ *n* a V-shaped neck of a garment; *also* a garment having such a neck

**vocable** /'vohkəbl/ *n* a term; *specif* a word considered as a combination of sounds or letters without regard to its meaning [MF, word, name, fr L *vocabulum*, fr *vocare* to call – more at VOICE]

**vocabulary** /voh'kabyooləri, və-/ *n* 1 a list of words and sometimes phrases usu arranged alphabetically and defined or translated; a lexicon ⟨a ~ *at the back of the book*⟩ **2a** the words used by a language, group, or individual or in a field of knowledge ⟨*her limited* ~⟩ **b** a list or collection of terms or codes available for use (eg in an indexing or computer data processing system) 3 a supply of expressive techniques or devices (eg of an art form) [MF *vocabulaire*, prob fr ML *vocabularium*, fr neut of *vocabularius* verbal, fr L *vocabulum*]

**¹vocal** /'vohkl/ *adj* **1a** uttered by the voice; oral **b** produced in the larynx; VOICED 2 **2** relating to, composed or arranged for, or sung by the human voice ⟨~ *music*⟩ **3** vocalic **4a** having or exercising the power of producing voice, speech, or sound ⟨~ *organs*⟩ **b** given to strident or insistent expression; outspoken [ME, fr L *vocalis*, fr *voc-*, *vox* voice – more at VOICE] – **vocally** *adv*, **vocality** *n*

**²vocal** *n* 1 a vocal sound 2 *usu pl* (the performance of) a voice part in a piece of popular music ⟨*Paul McCartney on* ~s⟩

**vocal cords** *n pl* either of two pairs of folds of MUCOUS MEMBRANE that project into the cavity of the larynx and one pair of which has free edges that vibrate to produce sound

**¹vocalic** /voh'kalik/, **vocal** *adj* **1** containing or consisting of vowels **2a** being or functioning as a vowel **b** of or associated with a vowel or vowels [L *vocalis* vowel, fr *vocalis* vocal] – **vocalically** *adv*

**²vocalic** *n* a vowel sound or sequence in its function as the most prominent element in a syllable

**vocalise** /'vohkəliez/ *n* 1 an exercise for singers, commonly using vowels or special syllables designed to develop vocal beauty or agility 2 a vocalized melody or passage without words [Fr, fr *vocaliser* to vocalize]

**vocalism** /'vohkl,iz(ə)m/ *n* 1 vocalization 2 vocal art or technique; singing 3 the vowel system of a language

**vocalist** /'vohkl·ist/ *n* a singer

**vocal·ize, -ise** /'vohkl,iez/ *vt* 1 to give voice to; utter; *specif* to sing **2a** to utter while vibrating the VOCAL CORDS; VOICE 3 **b(1)** to convert into a vowel **b(2)** to convert into a separate syllable **3** to provide (eg a Hebrew or Arabic text consisting of consonants) with vowels or VOWEL POINTS ~ *vi* 1 to utter vocal sounds ⟨*a gorilla vocalizing*⟩ 2 to sing; *specif* to sing without words – **vocalization** *n*, **vocalizer** *n*

**vocation** /voh'kaysh(ə)n, və-/ *n* **1a** a summons or strong inclination to a particular state or course of action; *esp* a divine call to the religious life **b** an entry into the priesthood or a religious order **2** the work in which a person is regularly employed; an occupation, career – compare AVOCATION, BUSINESS 3 the special function of an individual or group; a role [ME *vocacioun*, fr L *vocation-*, *vocatio* summons, fr *vocatus*, pp of *vocare* to call – more at VOICE]

**vocational** /voh'kaysh(ə)nl, və-/ *adj* 1 of or concerned with a vocation 2 of or being in training in a skill or trade to be pursued as a career ⟨~ *courses*⟩ – **vocationally** *adv*

**vocationalism** /voh'kayshənə,liz(ə)m, və-/ *n* emphasis on vocational training in education – **vocationalist** *n*

**vocative** /'vokətiv/ *n* a grammatical case expressing the one addressed; *also* a form (eg Latin *Domine*) in this case [ME

*vocatif*, adj, fr MF, fr L *vocativus*, fr *vocatus*] – **vocative** *adj*, **vocatively** *adv*

**vociferate** /voh'sifərayt, və-/ *vb*, *formal vi* to cry out loudly; clamour ~ *vt* to utter loudly; shout [L *vociferatus*, pp of *vociferari*, fr *voc-*, *vox* voice + *ferre* to bear – more at VOICE, BEAR] – **vociferator** *n*, **vociferant** *adj*, **vociferation** *n*

**vociferous** /voh'sif(ə)rəs, və-/ *adj* marked by or given to noisy and insistent outcry ⟨a ~ *complainer*⟩ – **vociferously** *adv*, **vociferousness** *n*

synonyms **Vociferous, clamorous, boisterous, rowdy, obstreperous, strident**, and **blatant** all mean "loud or insistent enough to compel attention". **Vociferous** suggests loud vehement outcry ⟨**vociferous** *protests*⟩. **Clamorous** implies sustained disturbance, not necessarily with any purpose ⟨*street was* **clamorous** *with truck drivers bawling and cursing*⟩. **Boisterous** suggests noisy activity resulting from high spirits and defiance of authority ⟨**boisterous** *revelry*⟩, and **rowdy** is a more censorious word for the same behaviour, implying roughness and coarseness ⟨a **rowdy** *neighbourhood*⟩. **Obstreperous** emphasizes truculent unruliness ⟨*teacher trying to control an* **obstreperous** *class*⟩. A **strident** noise is both insistent and obtrusively harsh ⟨**strident** *electric bell*⟩, and the word is also applied figuratively to anything offensively harsh ⟨**strident** *slogans*⟩. **Blatant** describes whatever is crassly obvious ⟨**blatant** *disregard of the facts*⟩. **antonym** subdued

**vocoder** /'voh,kohdə/ *n* 1 an electronic mechanism that transforms speech signals into low-frequency electrical signals which can be transmitted over a communications system and reconverted into recognizable speech sounds at the receiving end 2 an electronic mechanism that separates speech signals into their component frequencies for transformation by a synthesizer into musical notes that retain the characteristics of speech [*voice coder*]

**vodka** /'vodkə/ *n* a colourless and almost tasteless spirit distilled from a mash (eg of rye or wheat) [Russ, fr *voda* water; akin to OE *wæter* water]

**voe** /voh/ *n* an inlet or narrow bay of the Orkney or Shetland islands [of Scand origin; akin to Norw *vaag* bay inlet, ON *vāgr* creek, bay]

**vogue** /vohg/ *n* 1 the prevailing, esp temporary, fashion ⟨*long skirts were in* ~⟩ 2 popular acceptance or favour; popularity ⟨*book enjoyed a great* ~ *about 1960*⟩ [MF, action of rowing, course, fashion, fr OIt *voga*, fr *vogare* to row; akin to OSp *bogar* to row] – **vogue** *adj*

**Vogul** /'vohgl/ *n* a FINNO-UGRIC language system east of the Ural Mountains

**¹voice** /voys/ *n* **1a** sound produced by VERTEBRATE animals by forcing air from the lungs through the larynx (eg in mammals) or SYRINX (birds' vocal organ); *esp* sound so produced by human beings **b(1)** musical sound produced by the VOCAL CORDS and resonated by the cavities of the head and throat **b(2)** the power or ability to sing or produce musical tones **b(3)** a singer **b(4)** voice, voice part any of the melodic parts in a vocal or instrumental piece of music **b(5)** condition of the vocal organs for singing ⟨*in good* ~⟩ **b(6)** the use of the voice (eg in singing or acting) ⟨*studying* ~⟩ **c** breathing out of air with the VOCAL CORDS drawn close so as to vibrate audibly (eg in uttering consonant sounds such as /v/ or /z/or any vowel) **d** the faculty of utterance; speech **2** a sound suggesting vocal utterance ⟨*the* ~ *of a foghorn*⟩ 3 an instrument or medium of expression ⟨*the party became the* ~ *of the workers*⟩ **4a** the expressed wish or opinion ⟨*claimed to follow the* ~ *of the people*⟩ **b** right of expression; say ⟨*I have no* ~ *in this matter*⟩ **c** expression – esp in *give voice to* 5 distinction of form or a particular system of inflections of a verb to indicate the relation of the subject of the verb to the action which the verb expresses ⟨*the passive* ~⟩ [ME, fr OF *vois*, fr L *voc-*, *vox*; akin to OHG *giwahanen* to mention, L *vocare* to call, Gk *epos* word, speech] – **with one voice** without dissent; unanimously

**²voice** *vt* 1 to express (a feeling or opinion) in words; utter 2 to adjust (eg an organ pipe) in manufacture for producing the proper musical sounds 3 to pronounce with vibration of the VOCAL CORDS

**voice box** *n* the larynx

**voiced** /voyst/ *adj* 1 having a usu specified type of voice ⟨*soft-voiced*⟩ 2 uttered with vibrations of the VOCAL CORDS ⟨/b/ *is a* ~ *consonant*⟩ – **voicedness** *n*

**voice frequency** *n* a radio frequency in the range between 300 and 3000 hertz

**voiceful** /'voysf(ə)l/ *adj* having a (full or loud) voice or vocal quality – **voicefulness** *n*

**voiceless** /-lis/ adj 1 having no voice; mute 2 not voiced ⟨/p/ is a ~ consonant⟩ – **voicelessly** adv, **voicelessness** n

'**voice-,over** n a commentary in a film or television programme or advertisement spoken by an unseen narrator; also the thoughts of a film or television character heard on the soundtrack but not actually spoken by the character

**voiceprint** /-,print/ n a visual representation of a single particular speech utterance (eg a word or short phrase) that is held to be individually distinctive for each person's voice and that is electronically produced by a machine (SPECTROGRAPH) that splits up the sound of the voice into its component frequencies and records them on a graph together with some indication of the strength of the speech sounds [voice + -print (as in fingerprint)]

**voicer** /'voysə/ n one who voices; specif one who voices organ pipes

**voice vote** n, NAm a parliamentary vote taken by calling for ayes and noes and estimating which response is stronger

'**void** /voyd/ adj 1 containing nothing; unoccupied ⟨~ space⟩ 2a devoid ⟨a nature ~ of all malice⟩ b having no members or examples; specif, of a suit having no cards represented in a particular hand ⟨bid a ~ suit as a slam signal⟩ 3a ineffective, useless b having no legal force or effect; null ⟨a ~ contract⟩ 4 formal having no holder or occupant; vacant ⟨a ~ bishopric⟩ – see also NULL and void [ME voide, fr OF, fr (assumed) VL vocitus, deriv of L vacuus – more at VACUUM] – **voidness** n

²**void** n 1a empty space; emptiness, vacuum b an opening, gap 2 a feeling of lack, want, or emptiness 3 absence of cards of a particular suit in a hand

³**void** vt 1 to make empty or vacant; clear 2 discharge, emit ⟨~ excrement⟩ 3 to nullify, annul ⟨~ a contract⟩ 4 archaic to vacate, leave [ME voiden, fr MF vuidier, fr (assumed) VL vocitare, fr vocitus] – **voider** n

**voidable** /'voydəbl/ adj capable of being voided; specif capable of being judged to be legally void – **voidableness** n

**voidance** /'voyd(ə)ns/ n 1 the act of voiding 2 the condition of a BENEFICE (ecclesiastical office) that lacks an incumbent

**voided** /'voydid/ adj, of a heraldic design having the inner part cut away or vacant with a narrow border left at the sides

**voile** /voyl/ n a fine soft sheer fabric used esp for women's summer clothing or curtains [Fr, veil, fr L vela, pl of velum curtain, veil]

**volant** /'vohlənt/ adj 1 of a heraldic bird having the wings extended as if in flight 2 flying or capable of flying 3 poetic quick, nimble [MF, fr L volant-, volans, prp of volare to fly]

**volante** /voh'lantay/ adj moving with light rapidity – used as a direction in music [It, lit., flying, fr L volant-, volans, prp]

**Volapük** /'volapook/ n an artificial international language based largely on English but with some root words from German, French, and Latin [Volapük, lit., world's speech, fr vola of the world (gen of vol world, modif of E world) + pük speech, modif of E speak]

**volar** /'vohlə/ adj relating to the palm of the hand or the sole of the foot; also located on the same side as the palm of the hand ⟨the ~ part of the forearm⟩ [L vola palm of the hand, sole of the foot]

'**volatile** /'volə,tiel/ n 1 a volatile chemical substance 2 archaic a winged creature [ME volatil, fr OF, fr volatilie group of birds, fr ML volatilia, fr L, neut pl of volatilis winged, volatile]

²**volatile** adj 1 capable of being readily vaporized at a relatively low temperature (eg room temperature) 2a lighthearted, lively b dangerously unstable; explosive ⟨a ~ social situation⟩ 3a frivolously changeable; fickle b characterized by rapid change 4 transitory 5 of a computer memory not retaining stored data when the power supply is cut off 6 archaic flying or able to fly [Fr, fr L volatilis, fr volatus, pp of volare to fly] – **volatileness**, **volatility** n

**volatile oil** n an oil that vaporizes readily; esp ESSENTIAL OIL (fragrant natural plant oil)

**volatil·ize, -ise** /və'lati,liez/ vb to (cause to) evaporate as a vapour – **volatilizable** adj, **volatilization** n

**vol-au-vent** /,vol oh 'vonh, '- - ,-/ n a round baked puff-pastry case filled typically with a mixture of meat, poultry, or fish in a thick creamy sauce [Fr, lit., flight in the wind]

**volcanic** /vol'kanik/ adj 1a of or produced by a volcano ⟨~ activity⟩ b characterized by volcanoes ⟨a ~ range⟩ c consisting of or being material, esp lava, erupted from a volcano ⟨~ ash⟩; esp, of a rock EXTRUSIVE 2 explosively violent; volatile ⟨~ emotions⟩ – **volcanically** adv

**volcanic glass** n a glassy rock (eg obsidian) formed from molten lava that has cooled too rapidly to permit crystallization

**volcanism** /'volkə,niz(ə)m/, **volcanicity** /,volkə'nisəti/ n volcanic power or action; specif all the natural processes by which volcanoes or volcanic phenomena (eg lava eruptions and geysers) are produced and by which material is forced onto the earth's surface or into the earth's crust

**volcano** /vol'kaynoh/ n, pl **volcanoes**, **volcanos** 1 an opening or vent in the crust of a planet from which molten or hot rock and steam issue; also a hill or mountain surrounding such a vent and composed wholly or in part of the ejected material 2 a violently forceful creative person; also a state of affairs liable to become violent at any moment [It vulcano, fr L Volcanus, Vulcanus Vulcan, Roman god of fire and metalworking] – **volcanologic, volcanological** adj

**volcanology** /,volkə'noləji/ n a branch of science that deals with volcanoes and volcanic phenomena – **volcanological** also **volcanologic** adj, **volcanologist** n

**vole** n any of various small plant-eating rodents (family Cricetidae, esp genus Microtus) that typically have a stout body, rather blunt nose, and short ears, and that do much damage to crops [earlier vole-mouse, fr vole- (of Scand origin; akin to ON völlr field) + mouse]

**volition** /və'lish(ə)n/ n 1 an act of making a free choice or decision ⟨married of her own ~⟩; also a choice or decision made 2 the power of choosing or determining; will [Fr, fr ML volition-, volitio, fr L vol- (stem of velle to will, wish) + -ition-, -itio (as in L position-, positio position) – more at WILL] – **volitional** adj

**volitive** /'volətiv/ adj 1 linguistics expressing a wish or permission 2 formal of the will

**volkslied** /'folks,leet, 'vohks- (Ger folksli:t)/ n, pl **volkslieder** /-,leedə (Ger -li:dər)/ a folk song [Ger, fr volk people + lied song]

'**volley** /'voli/ n 1a a flight of missiles (eg bullets or arrows) b simultaneous discharge of a number of missile-firing weapons (eg rifles) c a firing of one round per gun in a battery as soon as each gun is ready, without regard to order d(1) a shot, pass, etc made by kicking or hitting a ball (eg in soccer or tennis) or a shuttlecock before it bounces; also the flight of such a ball or shuttlecock before it bounces ⟨hit it on the ~⟩ – compare GROUND STROKE d(2) a rapid succession of volleys in tennis, badminton, etc 2a a burst or emission of many things at once ⟨a ~ of oaths⟩ b a burst of (practically) simultaneous NERVE IMPULSES passing to another nerve or a muscle, gland, etc [MF volee flight, fr voler to fly, fr L volare]

²**volley** vt 1 to discharge (as if) in a volley 2 to propel (an object that has not yet hit the ground), esp with an implement or the hand or foot; esp to hit (a tennis ball) on the volley 3 to play a volley against (an opponent in tennis) ~ vi 1 to become discharged (as if) in a volley 2 to make a volley; specif to volley an object of play (eg in tennis) – **volleyer** n

**volleyball** /-,bawl/ n a game between two teams of usu six players who volley an inflated ball over a high net in the centre of a court using only their hands and arms

**volplane** /'vol,playn/ vi 1 to glide (as if) in an aeroplane 2 GLIDE 3 (glide without power) [Fr vol plané gliding flight]

**Volsci** /'volskee/ n pl a people of ancient Italy who fought against the Romans in the fifth and fourth centuries BC [L]

**Volscian** /'volskiən/ n 1 a member of the Volsci 2 the ITALIC language of the Volsci – **Volscian** adj

**volt** /vohlt, volt/ n the SI unit of electrical POTENTIAL DIFFERENCE (work required to move an electrical charge between two points) and ELECTROMOTIVE FORCE (energy causing an electric current to flow round a circuit) that is equal to the potential difference between two points of a resistive conductor (eg a wire) carrying a constant current of 1 amp when the power given out between these two points is equal to 1 watt [Alessandro Volta †1827 It physicist]

**volta** /'voltə/ n LAVOLTA (lively French dance) [It, lit., turn]

**voltage** /'vohltij, 'voltij/ n the POTENTIAL DIFFERENCE (work required to move an electrical charge between two points) measured in volts

**voltage divider** n POTENTIAL DIVIDER (device for providing various voltages from a single power source)

**voltaic** /vol'tayik/ adj of or involved in the production of a DIRECT CURRENT of electricity by chemical action (eg in a battery); GALVANIC [Alessandro Volta]

**voltaic pile** n ³PILE 4 (early form of battery)

**voltaism** /'voltə,iz(ə)m/ n GALVANISM 1,2

**voltameter** /vohl'tamitə, vol-/ *n* an apparatus for measuring the quantity of electricity passed through a solution by determining the amount of decomposition of or separation of the components of the solution (eg the amount of gas given off or material deposited) [ISV *volt*aic + *-meter*] – **voltametric** *adj*, **voltametry** *n*

,**volt-'ampere** *n* a unit of electrical power in a circuit using ALTERNATING CURRENT, equal to the power required for 1 amp of current to flow in a circuit driven by a POTENTIAL DIFFERENCE of 1 volt – compare WATT

**volte** /volt/ *n* **1** volt, volte a leaping movement in fencing to avoid a thrust **2a** a movement in DRESSAGE in which a horse going sideways traces a complete circle **b** a circle traced by a horse in this movement [Fr, fr It *volta* turn, fr *voltare* to turn, fr (assumed) VL *volvitare*, freq of L *volvere* to roll – more at VOLUBLE]

**volte-face** /,volt 'fahs, fas/ *n* a sudden reversal of attitude or policy; a U-turn [Fr, fr It *voltafaccia*, fr *voltare* to turn + *faccia* face, fr (assumed) VL *facia*]

**-voltine** /-vohlteen/ *comb form* (→ *adj*) having (so many) generations or broods in a season or year; laying eggs or giving birth (so many times) in a season or year 〈*multi*voltine〉〈*uni*-voltine〉 [Fr, fr It *volta* time, occasion, lit., turn]

**voltinism** /'volti,niz(ə)m/ *n* the frequency or number of annual broods, esp of an insect

**voltmeter** /'volt,meetə, 'vohlt-/ *n* an instrument for measuring POTENTIAL DIFFERENCE (work required to move an electrical charge between two points) in volts [ISV]

**voluble** /'volyoobl/ *adj* characterized by ready or rapid speech; talkative *synonyms* see TALKATIVE *antonym* curt [MF or L; MF, variable, rotating, fr L *volubilis*, fr *volvere* to roll; akin to OE *wealwian* to roll, Gk *eilyein* to roll, wrap] – **volubleness** *n*, **volubly** *adv*, **volubility** *n*

**volume** /'volyoohm, 'volyoom/ *n* **1** a scroll **2a** a series of printed sheets bound typically in book form; a book **b** a series of issues of a periodical **3** space occupied as measured in cubic units (eg litres); cubic capacity 〈*the ~ of a sphere*〉 **4a(1)** an amount; *specif* the number of contracts traded in a particular future or share in some specified period of time **a(2)** a bulk, mass **a(3)** **volumes** *pl*, **volume** a considerable quantity; a great deal **b** the amount of a substance occupying a particular volume **c** mass or the representation of mass in art or architecture **5** the degree of loudness or the intensity of a sound; *also* loudness [ME, fr MF, fr L *volumen* roll, scroll, fr *volvere* to roll] – **volumed** *adj*

**volumeter** /vo'lyoohmitə/ *n* any of various instruments for measuring the volume of a gas, liquid, or solid [ISV, blend of *volume* and *-meter*]

**volumetric** /,volyoo'metrik/ *adj* **1** of or involving the measurement of volume **2** of or used in VOLUMETRIC ANALYSIS 〈*a ~ flask*〉〈*a ~ solution*〉 – **volumetrically** *adv*

**volumetric analysis** *n* chemical analysis to determine the quantity of a substance present in a mixture or compound containing the substance: eg **a** the determination of the amount of a substance present in a liquid by measuring the amount of the liquid required to react with a solution of known volume and concentration **b** analysis of gases by volume

**voluminous** /və'lyoohminəs/ *adj* **1** having or containing a large volume; *specif, of a garment* very full 〈*a ~ skirt*〉 **2a** consisting of, filling, or capable of filling a large volume or several volumes 〈*a ~ correspondence*〉 **b** writing much or at great length **3** *archaic* consisting of many folds, coils, or convolutions; winding [LL *voluminosus*, fr L *volumin-*, *volumen*] – **voluminously** *adv*, **voluminousness**, **voluminosity** *n*

**voluntarism** /'voləntə,riz(ə)m/ *n* **1** the principle of relying on voluntary action rather than on compulsion **2** a theory that conceives the will to be the dominant or most basic element in experience or in the world – **voluntarist** *n*, **voluntaristic** *adj*

¹**voluntary** /'volənt(ə)ri/ *adj* **1** arising from free choice or consent **2** acting without compulsion and without payment 〈*~ workers*〉 **3** done by design; intentional rather than accidental 〈*~ manslaughter*〉 **4** of, subject to, or regulated by the will 〈*~ behaviour*〉 **5** having power of free choice 〈*man is a ~ agent*〉 **6** provided or supported by voluntary action 〈*a ~ hospital*〉 **7** acting or done of one's own free will without legal obligation or regard to the financial consequences 〈*a ~ legal transaction*〉 [ME, fr L *voluntarius*, fr *voluntas* will, fr *velle* to will, wish – more at WILL] – **voluntarily** *adv*, **voluntariness** *n*

*synonyms* **Voluntary**, **intentional**, **deliberate**, **wilful**, **willing**, and **spontaneous** all mean "done by free choice". **Voluntary**

emphasizes freedom from compulsion 〈*a voluntary confession*〉 or, in contrast with **involuntary**, control by the will 〈*voluntary muscle movements*〉. **Intentional** contrasts with **accidental** and **inadvertent** in specifying a purpose 〈*an intentional insult*〉. **Deliberate** implies full awareness of what one is doing 〈*an organized and deliberate attack – carefully planned and calculated –* New York Times〉. **Wilful** often suggests an obstinate determination to act 〈*wilful disobedience*〉. **Willing** implies readiness to comply with the wishes of others 〈*willing helpers*〉. **Spontaneous** refers to the natural unprompted expression of one's feelings 〈*spontaneous laughter*〉.

²**voluntary** *n* **1** an often improvised musical piece coming before the main work **2** an organ piece played before or after a religious service

**voluntaryism** /-,iz(ə)m/ *n* voluntarism – **voluntaryist** *n*

**voluntary muscle** *n* muscle (eg that in the arms and legs) under voluntary control that can be caused to move at will

**voluntary school** *n* a school built by an independent usu religious body but partly or wholly maintained by a British LOCAL EDUCATION AUTHORITY: **a** AIDED SCHOOL **b** CONTROLLED SCHOOL

¹**volunteer** /,volən'tiə/ *n* **1** one who undertakes a service of his/her own free will: eg **1a** one who enters into military service voluntarily **b(1)** one who acts without being under any legal obligation to do so **b(2)** one who receives a CONVEYANCE (instrument by which title to property is conveyed) or transfer of property without regard to financial consideration **2** a volunteer plant or crop [obs Fr *voluntaire* (now *volontaire*), fr *voluntaire*, adj, voluntary, fr L *voluntarius*]

²**volunteer** *adj* **1** being, consisting of, or engaged in by volunteers 〈*a ~ army*〉〈*~ activities to help the mentally handicapped*〉 **2** of a plant or crop growing spontaneously without direct human control, cultivation, or supervision, esp from seeds dropped from a previous crop

³**volunteer** *vt* **1** to offer or bestow voluntarily 〈*~ one's services*〉 **2** to communicate voluntarily; say 〈*~ed some information*〉 ~ *vi* to offer oneself as a volunteer

**voluptuary** /və'luptyoo(ə)ri/ *n* one whose chief interest is luxury and sensual pleasure – **voluptuary** *adj*

**voluptuous** /və'luptyoo·əs/ *adj* **1** full of delight or pleasure to the senses; conducive to, occupied with, or arising from sensual gratification; luxurious 〈*a ~ dance*〉〈*~ ornamentation*〉 **2** suggestive of sensual pleasure 〈*a ~ mouth*〉; *broadly* highly attractive sexually [ME, fr L *voluptuosus*, fr *voluptas* pleasure; akin to Gk *elpis* hope, L *velle* to wish – more at WILL] – **voluptuously** *adv*, **voluptuousness** *n*

**volute** /və'lyooht/ *n* **1** a spiral or scroll-shaped form **2** a spiral scroll-shaped ornament characteristic of classical architecture **3a** any of numerous marine INVERTEBRATE animals (family Volutidae of the class Gastropoda, phylum Mollusca) related to the snails, whelks, etc, that have a thick spirally coiled shell **b** the shell of a volute; *also* VOLUTION 2b [L *voluta*, fr fem of *volutus*, pp of *volvere* to roll] – **volute**, **voluted** *adj*

**volutin** /'vol(y)oohtin, və'loohtin/ *n* a substance, probably a NUCLEIC ACID compound, occurring in the form of granules in the CYTOPLASM (jellylike material inside a cell) esp of bacteria and other microorganisms [Ger, fr NL *volutans*, specific epithet of the bacterium *Spirillum volutans* in which it was first found]

**volution** /və'lyoohsh(ə)n, -'looh-/ *n* **1** a rolling or revolving motion **2a** a spiral turn; a twist **b** a single whorl of a spirally coiled shell [L *volutus*, pp]

**volva** /'volvə/ *n* a thin membranous sac or cup round the base of the stalk supporting the cap of some fungi – compare VEIL [NL, fr L *volva*, *vulva* covering, womb – more at VULVA] – **volvate** *adj*

**volvox** /'volvoks/ *n* any of a genus (*Volvox*) of freshwater green single-celled microorganisms that exist combined in spherical colonies and swim by means of FLAGELLA (whiplike structures) [NL, genus name, fr L *volvere* to roll – more at VOLUBLE]

**volvulus** /'volvyooləs/ *n* a twisting of the intestine upon itself, causing obstruction and pain [NL, fr L *volvere*]

**vomer** /'vohmə/ *n* a bone of the skull of most VERTEBRATE animals that in human beings forms part of the wall dividing the nostrils [NL, fr L, ploughshare] – **vomerine** *adj*

¹**vomit** /'vomit/ *n* **1** an act or instance of vomiting; *also* the vomited matter **2** a drug or other substance that induces vomiting; an emetic [ME, fr MF, fr L *vomitus*, fr *vomitus*, pp of *vomere* to vomit; akin to ON *vāma* nausea, Gk *emein* to vomit]

²**vomit** *vi* **1** to bring up the contents of the stomach through

the mouth 2 to spew forth; belch, gush ⟨*the volcano smoked and ~*ed⟩ ~ *vt* 1 to bring up (the contents of the stomach) through the mouth 2 to eject violently or abundantly; spew 3 *archaic* to cause to vomit – **vomiter** *n*

**vomitory** /'vomit(ə)ri/ *n* an entrance in the middle of a bank of seats in an ancient roman amphitheatre, stadium, etc [LL *vomitorium*, fr L *vomitus*, pp; fr its disgorging the spectators]

**vomiturition** /ˌvomityoo'rish(ə)n/ *n* repeated ineffectual attempts at vomiting [*vomit* + *-urition* (as in *micturition*)]

**vomitus** /'vomitəs/ *n* material discharged by vomiting – used technically [L]

**V-'one** /vee/ *n* v-1 (flying bomb)

**¹voodoo** /'voohdooh/ *n, pl* **voodoos** 1 a set of magical beliefs and practices used as a form of religion, chiefly by the people of Haiti, and characterized chiefly by communication with deities while in a trance 2a one who deals in spells and communication with the dead **b(1)** a voodoo spell **b(2)** an object with a spell cast over it; a charm [LaF *voudou*, of African origin; akin to Ewe *vo¹du³* tutelary deity, demon] – **voodoo** *adj*

**²voodoo** *vt* **voodoos; voodooing; voodooed** to bewitch (as if) by means of voodoo

**voodooism** /'voohdooh,iz(ə)m/ *n* 1 VOODOO 1 2 belief in or the practice of voodoo – **voodooist** *n*, **voodooistic** *adj*

**Voortrekker** /'faw,trekə, 'fooə-/ *n* a S African pioneer of Dutch descent who moved north from the Cape of Good Hope in 1838 to evade British rule [Afrik, fr *voor* before, in front + *trekker* emigrant, fr *trek* to pull, emigrate]

**voracious** /və'rayshəs/ *adj* 1 having a huge appetite; ravenous 2 excessively eager; insatiable ⟨*a ~ appetite*⟩ ⟨*a ~ reader*⟩ **synonyms** see RAPACIOUS [L *vorac-, vorax*, fr *vorare* to devour; akin to OHG *querdar* bait, L *gurges* whirlpool] – **voraciously** *adv*, **voraciousness, voracity** *n*

**vorlage** /'faw,lahgə (*Ger* fo:rla:gə)/ *n* the position of a skier leaning forwards from the ankles usu without lifting the heels from the skis, that is used esp during SKI JUMPING [Ger, fr *vor* forward + *lage* position]

**-vorous** /-v(ə)rəs/ *comb form* (→ *adj*) eating; feeding on ⟨*herbi*vorous⟩ [L *-vorus*, fr *vorare* to devour]

**vortex** /'vawteks/ *n, pl* **vortices** /'vawtiseez/ *also* **vortexes** 1a a mass of gas or liquid with a whirling or circular motion that tends to form a cavity or vacuum in the centre of the circle into which material is drawn; *esp* a whirlpool, eddy, or whirlwind **b** a region within a mass of gas or liquid in which the gas or liquid is rotating 2 something that resembles a whirlpool in violent activity or in irresistibly swallowing up those who approach △ vertex [NL *vortic-, vortex*, fr L *vertex, vortex* whirlpool – more at VERTEX] – **vortical** *adj*, **vortically** *adv*, **vorticose** *adj*

**vorticella** /ˌvawti'selə/ *n, pl* **vorticellae** /-li/, **vorticellas** any of a genus (*Vorticella*) of freshwater bell-shaped PROTOZOANS (single-celled organisms) that have a ring of CILIA (small hair-like structures) round the mouth and a long elastic stalk by which they are attached to rocks [NL, genus name, fr L *vortic-, vortex*]

**vorticism** /'vawti,siz(ə)m/ *n* a semiabstract English art movement dating from about 1912 related to CUBISM and FUTURISM [L *vortic-, vortex* whirlpool; fr the characteristic use of forms arranged in arcs or whirls round a central point] – **vorticist** *n or adj*

**vorticity** /vaw'tisəti/ *n* 1 the state of a gas or liquid in swirling or vortical motion; *broadly* vortical motion 2 a measure of swirling or vortical motion; *esp* a VECTOR measure (one having magnitude and direction) of rotation in the flow of a gas or liquid

**votary** /'vohtəri/, **votarist** /'vohtərist/ *n* 1 a staunch admirer, worshipper, or advocate; a devotee 2 *archaic* a sworn adherent [L *votum* vow]

**¹vote** /voht/ *n* 1a a usu formal expression (e g by raising a hand or marking a special card) of opinion or will in response to a proposed decision; *esp* one given as an indication of approval or disapproval of a proposal, motion, or candidate for election **b** the total number of such expressions of opinion made known at a single time (e g at an election) **c** an expression of opinion or preference that resembles a vote **d** BALLOT 1 2 the collective opinion or verdict of a body of people expressed by voting 3 *the* right to cast a vote; *specif the* right of voting in parliamentary elections; SUFFRAGE **4a** the act or process of voting ⟨*brought the question to a ~*⟩ **b** a method of voting ⟨*single transferable ~*⟩ 5 a group of voters with some common

and identifying characteristics ⟨*getting the Labour ~ to the polls*⟩ 6 *chiefly Br* **6a** a proposition to be voted on; *esp* a legislative money item **b** a sum of money voted for a special use ⟨*a ~ of £50 000*⟩ [ME (Sc), fr L *votum* vow, wish – more at VOW] – **voteless** *adj*

**²vote** *vi* 1 to express one's views in response to a poll; *esp* to exercise a political franchise 2 to express an opinion ⟨*~ with one's feet*⟩ ~ *vt* 1 to choose, endorse, decide the disposition of, defeat, or authorize by vote ⟨*~*d *a £100 000 increase to the civil list*⟩ **2a** to adjudge by general agreement; declare ⟨*concert was ~*d *a flop*⟩ **b** *informal* to offer as a suggestion; propose ⟨*I ~ we all go home*⟩

**voter** /'vohtə/ *n* one who votes or has the legal right to vote ⟨*a low poll caused by ~*s *staying at home*⟩

**voting machine** /'vohting/ *n* a mechanical device for recording and counting votes cast in an election

**votive** /'vohtiv/ *adj* 1 offered or performed in fulfilment of a vow and often in gratitude or devotion 2 consisting of or expressing a vow, wish, or desire ⟨*a ~ prayer*⟩ [L *votivus*, fr *votum* vow] – **votively** *adv*, **votiveness** *n*

**votive mass** *n* a mass celebrated for a special intention (e g for a wedding or funeral) in place of the mass of the day

**Votyak** /'vohti,ak/ *n* a FINNO-UGRIC language of the E USSR [Russ]

**vouch** /vowch/ *vt* **1a** to testify the truth of; substantiate **b** to verify (e g a business transaction) by examining documentary evidence 2 *archaic* to cite as authority ~ *vi* 1 to give a guarantee or become surety *for* 2 to supply supporting evidence or personal assurance *for* [ME *vochen, vouchen* to assert, call to witness, fr MF *vocher*, fr L *vocare* to call, summon, fr *voc-, vox* voice – more at VOICE] – **vouchee** *n*

**voucher** /'vowchə/ *n* 1 one who or that which vouches: e g **1a** a piece of supporting evidence; a proof **b** a documentary record providing evidence of a business transaction **c** a written certificate or authorization 2 a ticket or coupon, often of a particular value, that can be exchanged for specific goods or services or that entitles the holder to a particular offer (e g a reduced price or a free gift) – compare LUNCHEON VOUCHER [MF *vocher, voucher* to vouch]

**vouchsafe** /vowch'sayf/ *vt* 1 to grant or provide as a special privilege or in a gracious or condescending manner 2 to condescend or deign *to* do something – **vouchsafement** *n*

**voussoir** /vooh'swah/ *n* any of the wedge-shaped blocks forming an arch or vault [Fr, fr (assumed) VL *volsorium*, fr *volsus*, pp of L *volvere* to roll – more at VOLUBLE]

**¹vow** /vow/ *n* a solemn and often religiously binding promise or assertion; *specif* one by which a person binds him-/herself to an act, service, or condition [ME *vowe*, fr OF *vou*, fr L *votum*, fr neut of *votus*, pp of *vovēre* to vow; akin to Gk *euchesthai* to pray, vow]

**²vow** *vt* 1 to promise solemnly; swear 2 to dedicate or consecrate by a vow 3 to resolve to bring about ⟨*~ revenge*⟩ ~ *vi* to make a vow – **vower** *n*

**³vow** *vt* to avow, declare [ME *vowen*, short for *avowen*]

**vowel** /vowl/ *n* 1 any of a class of speech sounds (e g /ee/, /ie/, /ə/) characterized by lack of closure in the breath channel or lack of audible friction; *broadly* the single most prominent sound in a syllable 2 a letter or other symbol representing a vowel – usu used in English with reference to *a, e, i, o, u*, and sometimes *y* [ME, fr MF *vouel*, fr L *vocalis* – more at VOCALIC]

**vowel gradation** *n* ABLAUT (e g *sing, sang, sung*)

**vowel harmony** *n* a restriction in certain languages (e g Turkish) as to the permissible combinations of vowels in the successive syllables of a word

**vowel-ize, -ise** /'vowliez/ *vt* VOCALIZE 3 (provide a foreign text with vowels)

**vowel mutation** *n* UMLAUT (change of a vowel sound caused by a following vowel sound)

**vowel point** *n* a mark that is placed below or above a consonant in some languages (e g Hebrew) and represents the vowel sound that precedes or follows the consonant

**vox angelica** /ˌvoks an'jelikə/ *n* any of various organ stops having a delicate refined sometimes trembling tone [NL, lit., angelic voice]

**vox humana** /hyooh'mahnə/ *n* an organ stop of REED PIPES that imitates the human voice [NL, lit., human voice]

**vox pop** /ˌvoks 'pop/ *n, informal* VOX POPULI; *also* an interview (e g in the street) to determine public opinion

**vox populi** /ˌvoks 'popyoolie, -li/ *n* the opinion of the general public [L, voice of the people]

**¹voyage** /'voyij/ *n* a considerable course or period of travelling by other than land routes; *broadly* a journey, excursion [ME, fr OF *voiage*, fr LL *viaticum*, fr L, money or provisions for a journey, fr neut of *viaticum* of a journey, fr *via* way – more at VIA]

**²voyage** *vi* to make a voyage; travel ~ *vt* to traverse by a voyage; sail – **voyager** *n*

**voyage policy** *n* a marine insurance policy that covers only a specified voyage – compare TIME POLICY

**voyageur** /,vwah·yah'zhuh, 'voyizhə/ *n* a man employed, esp by a fur company in NW Canada, to transport goods and men to and from remote trading stations [CanF, fr Fr, traveller, fr *voyager* to travel, fr *voyage* voyage, fr OF *voiage*]

**voyeur** /vwah'yuh/ *n* 1 one who obtains sexual gratification from seeing sexual organs and sexual acts; *broadly* one who habitually seeks sexual stimulation by visual means 2 a prying observer who is usu seeking the sordid or the scandalous [Fr, lit., one who sees, fr MF, fr *voir* to see, fr L *vidēre* – more at WIT] – **voyeurism** *n*, **voyeuristic** *adj*, **voyeuristically** *adv*

**¹vroom** /vroom, vroohm/ *vi or n* (to make) the noise of an engine revving up or of a vehicle moving at high speed [imit]

**²vroom** *interj* – used to indicate the sound of an engine revving up or a vehicle moving at high speed

**vrouw, vrow** /froh/ *n*, *SAfr* a Dutch or Afrikaner woman [D *vrouw* & Afrik *vrou*, fr MD *vrouwe* lady, woman; akin to OHG *frouwa* mistress, lady – more at FRAU]

**V sign** /vee/ *n* a gesture made by raising the index finger and the middle finger in a V with the thumb tucked into the palm of the hand: **a** one made with the palm outwards signifying victory, approval, or assent **b** one made with the palm inwards signifying insult or extreme contempt

**,V-'two** /vee/ *n* v-2 (German missile of World War II)

**vug, vugg, vugh** /vug/ *n* a small unfilled or crystal-lined cavity in an ore seam or in rock [Cornish dial. *vooga* underground chamber, fr L *fovea* small pit] – **vuggy** *adj*

**vulcanian** /vul'kayniən/ *adj* 1 volcanic 2 of or being a highly explosive volcanic eruption in which blocks of extremely viscous or already solidified lava are thrown out, together with a usu large cloud of dust, ash, and gas

**vulcanism** /'vulkə,niz(ə)m/, **vulcanicity** /,vulkə'nisəti/ *n* VOLCANISM (volcanic action or processes)

**vulcanite** /'vulkəniet/ *n* a hard vulcanized rubber; EBONITE

**vulcan·izate, -isate** /'vulkənie,zayt/ *n* a vulcanized product [back-formation fr *vulcanization*]

**vulcan·ization, -isation** /,vulkənie'zaysh(ə)n/ *n* the process of chemically treating rubber or a similar material, esp with sulphur or sulphur-containing compounds, to give it useful physical properties (eg elasticity, strength, hardness, and stability)

**vulcan·ize, -ise** /'vulkəniez/ *vb* to subject to or undergo vulcanization [ISV, fr L *Vulcanus* Vulcan, fire] – **vulcanizer** *n*

**vulcanology** /,vulkə'noləji/ *n* VOLCANOLOGY (study of volcanoes) [ISV] – **vulcanological** *also* **vulcanologic** *adj*, **vulcanologist** *n*

**vulgar** /'vulgə/ *adj* 1 of or being the common rather than the Latin name of a plant or animal; VERNACULAR 2 **2a** lacking in cultivation, breeding, or taste; coarse **b** morally crude; gross ⟨~ *ambition*⟩ **c** ostentatious or excessive in expenditure or display; pretentious ⟨*a* ~ *display of wealth*⟩ 3 lewdly or irreverently indecent; offensive, obscene 4 *formal* **4a** generally used, applied, or accepted **b** understood in or having the ordinary sense ⟨*they reject the* ~ *conception of miracle* – W R Inge⟩ 5 *archaic* **5a** of or being the common people; plebeian **b** generally current; public ⟨~ *opinion*⟩ **c** of the usual kind; ordinary *synonyms* see COARSE *antonym* refined [ME, fr L *vulgaris* of the mob, vulgar, fr *volgus, vulgus* mob, common people; akin to Skt *varga* group] – **vulgarly** *adv*

**vulgar fraction** *n* a fraction (eg $\frac{5}{4}$ or $\frac{1}{2}$) in which both the denominator and numerator are WHOLE NUMBERS

**vulgarian** /vul'geəri·ən/ *n* a vulgar and esp rich person

**vulgarism** /'vulgə,riz(ə)m/ *n* 1 a word or expression originated or used chiefly by illiterate people; a coarse or substandard expression 2 vulgarity

**vulgarity** /vul'garəti/ *n* 1 being vulgar 2 something vulgar

**vulgar·ize, -ise** /'vulgəriez/ *vt* 1 to make vulgar; coarsen 2 *archaic* to spread generally; popularize – **vulgarizer** *n*, **vulgarization** *n*

**Vulgar Latin** *n* the popular or informal Latin speech of ancient Rome that was the chief source of the ROMANCE languages

**vulgar Marxism** *n* an oversimplification of Marxism: movements or events on the ideological level (eg in religion, law, or the arts) are determined in a direct and simple manner by events in the material economic sphere

**vulgate** /'vulgayt, -gət/ *n* 1 *cap* a Latin version of the Bible authorized and used by the Roman Catholic church 2 a commonly accepted text or reading [ML *vulgata*, fr LL *vulgata editio* edition in general circulation]

**vulnerable** /'vuln(ə)rəbl, 'vun-/ *adj* 1 capable of being physically wounded 2 open to attack or damage; assailable ⟨*a* ~ *outpost*⟩ ⟨~ *to criticism*⟩ 3 liable to increased penalties but entitled to increased bonuses after winning a game in CONTRACT BRIDGE [LL *vulnerabilis*, fr L *vulnerare* to wound, fr *vulner-, vulnus* wound; akin to Goth *wilwan* to rob, L *vellere* to pluck, Gk *oulē* wound] – **vulnerableness** *n*, **vulnerably** *adv*, **vulnerability** *n*

*usage* The pronunciation /'vuln(ə)rəbl/ rather than /'vun-/ is recommended for BBC broadcasters.

**vulnerary** /'vulnərəri/ *n or adj* (a drug or other remedy) used for or useful in healing wounds – not now used technically [adj L *vulnerarius*, fr *vulner-, vulnus*; n fr adj]

**vulpine** /'vulpien/ *adj* 1 of or resembling a fox 2 *formal* foxy, crafty [L *vulpinus*, fr *vulpes* fox; akin to Gk *alōpēx* fox]

**vulture** /'vulchə/ *n* 1 any of various large birds of prey (families Accipitridae and Cathartidae) related to the hawks, eagles, and falcons, that typically have weak claws, very large wing spans, and a featherless head, and that feed chiefly or entirely on carrion 2 a rapacious or predatory person [ME, fr L *vultur*] – **vulturine, vulturous** *adj*

**vulva** /'vulvə/ *n*, *pl* **vulvas, vulvae** /-vi/ the external parts of the female genital organs; *also* the opening between the projecting external parts [NL, fr L *volva, vulva* covering, womb; akin to Skt *ulva* womb, L *volvere* to roll – more at VOLUBLE] – **vulval, vulvar** *adj*

**vulviform** /'vulvi,fawm/ *adj*, *esp of a plant part* suggesting a cleft with projecting edges [NL *vulva* + E *-iform*]

**vulvitis** /vul'vietəs/ *n* inflammation of the vulva [NL]

**vulvovaginitis** /,vulvoh,vaji'nietəs/ *n* inflammation of both the vulva and vagina [NL]

**vying** /'vie·ing/ *pres part of* VIE

# W

**w, W** /'dubl,yooh/ *n, pl* **w's, ws, W's, Ws 1a** the 23rd letter of the English alphabet **b** a graphic representation of or device for reproducing the letter *w* **c** a speech counterpart of printed or written *w* **2** one designated *w*, esp as the 23rd in order or class **3** something shaped like the letter W

**Waac** /wak/ *n* a member of the Women's Army Auxiliary Corps in World War I [*Women's Army Auxiliary Corps*]

**Waaf** /waf/ *n* a member of the Women's Auxiliary Air Force in and immediately after World War II [*Women's Auxiliary Air Force*]

**wabble** /'wobl/ *vb or n* (to) wobble

**Wac** /wak/ *n* a member of the Women's Army Corps established in the US during World War II [*Women's Army Corps*]

**¹wack** /wak/ *n, Merseyside* – used informally to address someone, esp a man [short for *wacker*, perh fr *whacker* (heavy blow, anything large), fr ¹*whack* + ²*-er*]

**²wack** *n, NAm slang* a wacky person [prob back-formation fr *wacky*]

**wacky** /'waki/ *adj, slang* absurdly or amusingly eccentric or irrational; crazy [perh fr E dial. *whacky* fool] – **wackily** *adv*, **wackiness** *n*

**¹wad** /wod/ *n* **1** a small soft mass, bundle, or tuft: eg **1a** a soft mass esp of a loose fibrous material variously used (eg to stop an aperture, pad a garment, or hold grease round an axle) **b(1)** a soft plug used to retain a powder charge or to fill the gap between the projectile and the bore of a cannon or gun that is loaded at the discharging end **b(2)** a felt, paper, or plastic disc that separates the powder from the shot in a shotgun cartridge **c** *NAm* a small mass of a chewing substance ⟨*a ~ of gum*⟩ **2a** a roll of paper money **b** *NAm informal* a large supply of money ⟨*earned quite a ~*⟩ **3** wads *pl*, wad *chiefly NAm informal* a considerable amount ⟨*getting ~s of publicity*⟩ [origin unknown]

**²wad** *vt* **-dd- 1** to form into a wad or wadding **2a** to insert a wad into ⟨*~ a gun*⟩ **b** to hold in by a wad ⟨*~ a bullet in a gun*⟩ **3** to stuff, pad, or line with some soft substance **4** *chiefly NAm* to roll or crush tightly ⟨*~ded his shirt up into a ball*⟩ – **wadder** *n*

**³wad** *n* a dull brown or black soft earthy mineral substance that consists chiefly of oxides of manganese [origin unknown]

**wadding** /'woding/ *n* **1** (material for making) wads **2** stuffing or padding in the form of a soft mass or sheet of short loose fibres

**¹waddle** /'wodl/ *vi* **1** to walk with short steps, swinging the body from side to side **2** to move clumsily in a manner suggesting a waddle ⟨*car ~d out of the drift* – Len Deighton⟩ [freq of *wade*] – **waddler** *n*

**²waddle** *n* an awkward clumsy swaying gait

**¹waddy** /'wodi/ *n, Austr* a club, stick [native name in Australia]

**²waddy** *vt, Austr* to attack or beat with a waddy

**¹wade** /wayd/ *vi* **1** to walk through a medium (eg water) that offers more resistance than air **2** to proceed *through* with difficulty or effort ⟨*~ through a dull book*⟩ ~ *vt* to cross by wading [ME *waden*, fr OE *wadan*; akin to OHG *watan* to go, wade, L *vadere* to go]

  **wade in** *vi* to begin a determined or vigorous attack ⟨*waded in with his fists flying*⟩

  **wade into** *vt* to attack with determination or vigour ⟨*waded into the task*⟩

**²wade** *n* an act of wading ⟨*a ~ in the brook*⟩

**wader** /'waydə/ *n* **1** one who or that which wades **2** any of many long-legged birds including the shorebirds (eg sandpipers and snipes) and the inland waterbirds (eg cranes and herons) that wade in water in search of food **3** *pl* high waterproof boots used for wading (eg by fishermen)

**wadge** /woj/ *n, Br informal* a thick bundle; a wad [alter. of wedge]

**wadi** /'wodi/ *n, pl* **wadis 1** the bed or valley of a stream in regions of SW Asia and N Africa that is usu dry except during the rainy season and that often forms an oasis; a gully **2** a shallow usu sharply defined depression in a desert region [Ar *wādiy*]

**wading bird** /'wayding/ *n* WADER 2

**wading pool** *n, NAm* PADDLING POOL

**waesucks** /'way,suks/ *interj, Scot* – used to express pity [Sc *wae* woe (fr ME *wa*) + *sucks*, alter. of E *sakes* – more at WOE]

**Waf** /waf/ *n* a member of the women's component of the US Air Force formed after World War II [*Women in the Air Force*]

**¹wafer** /'wayfə/ *n* **1a** a thin crisp biscuit; *also* a biscuit consisting of layers of wafers sometimes sandwiched with a filling **b** a round thin piece of unleavened bread used in Communion **2** an adhesive disc of dried paste used, esp formerly, as a seal **3a** a thin disc or ring resembling a wafer and variously used (eg for a valve or diaphragm) **b** a thin slice of silicon or other material that can be cut into many separate sections for the production of INTEGRATED CIRCUITS, microprocessors, etc [ME, fr ONF *waufre*, of Gmc origin; akin to MD *wafel*, *wafer* waffle]

**²wafer** *vt* **1** to seal, close, or fasten with a wafer **2** to divide (eg a silicon rod) into wafers

**wafer-'thin** *adj* paper-thin

**waff** /wof, waf/ *n, chiefly Scot* **1** a waving motion **2** a puff, gust [E dial. *waff* to wave, fr ME (northern) *waffen*, alter. of ME *waven*]

**¹waffle** /'wofl/ *n* a sweet or savoury cake of batter that is baked in a WAFFLE IRON and has a crisp surface [D *wafel*, fr MD *wafel*, *wafer*; akin to OE *wefan* to weave]

**²waffle** *vi, chiefly Br informal* to talk or write foolishly and noncommittally and usu at length ⟨*can ~... tiresomely off the point* – TLS⟩ [freq of obs *woff* to yelp, of imit origin] – **waffler** *n*

**³waffle** *n, chiefly Br* empty or pretentious words; tripe – **waffly** *adj*

**waffle iron** *n* a cooking utensil having two hinged metal parts that shut on each other and impress surface projections on waffles that are being cooked

**¹waft** /woft/ *vt* to convey lightly (as if) by the impulse of wind or waves ~ *vi* to become wafted (as if) on a buoyant medium (eg air); float [(assumed) ME *waughten* to guard, convoy, fr MD or MLG *wachten* to watch, guard; akin to OE *wæccan* to watch – more at WAKE] – **wafter** *n*

**²waft** *n* **1** something (eg a smell) that is wafted; a whiff **2** a slight breeze **3** a pennant or flag flown on a ship and used to signal or to show wind direction

**¹wag** /wag/ *vb* **-gg-** *vi* **1** to be in motion; proceed, stir – chiefly in *how the world wags* **2** to be moved to and fro, esp with quick jerky motions **3** *of chins, tongues, etc* to move in chatter or gossip **4** to wag the tail ⟨*dogs ~ging and barking*⟩ **5** *Br slang* to play truant **6** *archaic* depart ~ *vt* **1a** to cause to swing to and fro, esp with quick jerky motions ⟨*the dog ~ged its tail*⟩ **b(1)** to shake (a finger) in mock or mild reproof **b(2)** to shake (the head) in disagreement, reproof, etc **2** to move (eg the tongue) animatedly in conversation [ME *waggen*; akin to MHG *wacken* to totter, OE *wegan* to move – more at WAY] – **wagger** *n*

**²wag** *n* **1** an act of wagging; a shake **2** *Br slang* truant ⟨*playing ~*⟩

**³wag** *n* a wit, joker [prob short for obs E *waghalter* gallows bird, fr ¹*wag* + *halter*]

**¹wage** /wayj/ *vt* to engage in or carry on (a war, conflict, etc) [ME *wagen* to pledge, give as security, fr ONF *wagier*, fr *wage*]

**²wage** *n* **1a** wages *pl*, **wage** a payment for work or services, esp of a manual kind, usu according to contract and on an hourly, daily, weekly, or piecework basis – compare SALARY **b** *pl* the share of the NATIONAL PRODUCT attributable to labour as a factor of production **2 wages** *taking sing or pl vb,* **wage** recompense, reward ⟨*the* ∼s *of sin is death* – Rom 6:23 (RSV)⟩ [ME, pledge, wage, fr ONF, of Gmc origin; akin to Goth *wadi* pledge – more at WED] – **wageless** *adj*

**wage earner** *n* one who brings in money (eg to a household) by working

**wage level** *n* the approximate position of wages at any given time in any occupation or trade or esp in industry at large

**wage packet** *n, Br* a pay-packet

¹**wager** /'wayjə/ *n* **1** something (eg a sum of money) risked on an uncertain event; a stake **2** something on which bets are laid; a gamble ⟨*do a stunt as a* ∼⟩ [ME, pledge, bet, fr AF *wageure,* fr ONF *wagier* to pledge]

²**wager** *vt* **1** to risk or venture on an uncertain final outcome; *specif* to lay as a bet ⟨∼ *£5 on a horse*⟩ **2** to state with assurance; bet ⟨*I'll* ∼ *they won't come*⟩ ∼ *vi* to make a bet – **wagerer** *n*

**wage slave** *n, chiefly humorous* a person dependent on wages or a salary for his/her livelihood

**wageworker** /'wayj,wuhkə/ *n, NAm* WAGE EARNER

**waggery** /'wagəri/ *n* **1** mischievous merriment; pleasantry **2** a jest; *esp* PRACTICAL JOKE

**waggish** /'wagish/ *adj* befitting or characteristic of a wag; humorous ⟨*a* ∼ *disposition*⟩ – **waggishly** *adv,* **waggishness** *n*

¹**waggle** /'wagl/ *vi* to reel, sway, or move repeatedly from side to side; wag, wiggle ∼ *vt* to cause to move repeatedly one way and the other; wag [freq of ¹*wag*] – **waggly** *adj*

²**waggle** *n* **1** an instance of waggling **2** a movement of a golf club head back and forth over the ball before the swing

¹**Wagnerian** /vahg'niəriən/ *adj* (suggestive) of the music of Wagner, esp in grandiose scale or dramatic intensity [Richard *Wagner* †1883 Ger composer]

²**Wagnerian** /vahg'niəri·ən/ *n* an admirer of the musical theories and style of Wagner

**Wagner tuba** /'vahgnə (*Ger* vagnər)/ *n* a BRASS INSTRUMENT of mid to low range that somewhat resembles the true tuba but is more closely related to the FRENCH HORN, having its funnel-shaped mouthpiece and smooth tone

**wagon,** *chiefly Br* **waggon** /'wagən/ *n* **1** a usu four-wheeled vehicle for transporting bulky or heavy loads, often having a removable canopy, and drawn originally by animals **2** a trolley; *esp* one used in a dining room or for serving light refreshments (eg afternoon tea) **3** *Br* a railway goods vehicle **4** *chiefly Nam* ESTATE CAR **5** *Br informal* a lorry [D *wagen,* fr MD – more at WAIN] – **off/on the wagon** (no longer) abstaining from alcoholic drink [short for *on the water wagon*]

**wagoner,** *chiefly Br* **waggoner** /'wagənə/ *n* the driver of a wagon

**wagonette** /wagə'net/ *n* a light wagon with two inward-facing seats along the sides behind a forward-facing front seat

**wagon-lit** /,vagonh 'lee/ *n, pl* **wagons-lits, wagon-lits** /-lee(z)/ a sleeping carriage, esp on a continental train [Fr, fr *wagon* railway carriage + *lit* bed]

**wagon train** *n* a column of wagons (eg carrying a group of settlers) travelling overland

**wagtail** /'wag,tayl/ *n* any of numerous chiefly Eurasian birds (family Motacillidae) with trim slender bodies and very long tails that they habitually jerk up and down

**Wahhabi, Wahabi** /wah'habi, wə-/ *n* a member of a puritanical Muslim sect founded in Arabia in the 18th century by Muhammad ibn-Abdul Wahhab and revived by ibn-Saud in the 20th century [Ar *wahhābiy,* fr Muḥammad b 'Abd al-*Wahhāb* (Abdul-Wahhab) †1787 Arab religious reformer] – **Wahhabism** *n,* **Wahhabite** *adj or n*

**wahine** /wah'heeni, -nay/ *n* a Polynesian woman [Maori & Hawaiian]

¹**wahoo** /wah'hooh/ *n, pl* **wahoos** a usu N American shrub or small shrubby tree (*Euonymus atropurpureus*) of the SPINDLE TREE family, that has purple capsules which split open to expose the scarlet-covered seeds [Dakota *wāhu,* lit., arrowwood]

²**wahoo** *interj, chiefly W US* – used to express exuberance or enthusiasm or to attract attention

**wah-wah pedal** /'wah ,wah/ *n* WA-WA PEDAL (device on an amplifier that produces a fluctuating muted effect)

**waif** /wayf/ *n* **1** a piece of property found (eg washed up by the sea) but unclaimed **2a** something found without an owner, *esp* by chance **b** a stray helpless person or animal; esp a home-less child [ME, fr ONF, adj, lost, unclaimed, prob of Scand origin]

¹**wail** /wayl/ *vi* **1** to express sorrow audibly; lament **2** to make a sound suggestive of a mournful cry **3** to express dissatisfaction plaintively; complain ∼ *vt, archaic* to bewail [ME *wailen,* of Scand origin; akin to ON *væla, vāla* to wail; akin to ON *vei* woe – more at WOE] – **wailer** *n*

²**wail** *n* **1** the act or practice of wailing; loud lamentation **2a** a usu loud prolonged high-pitched cry expressing grief or pain **b** a sound suggestive of wailing ⟨*the* ∼ *of an air-raid siren*⟩ **c** a querulous expression of grievance; a complaint

**wailful** /'waylf(ə)l/ *adj, chiefly poetic* sorrowful, mournful – **wailfully** *adv*

**wain** /wayn/ *n* **1** a usu large and heavy wagon for farm use **2** *cap* URSA MAJOR (constellation) – + *the* [ME, wagon, chariot, fr OE *wægn;* akin to MD *wagen* wagon, OE *wegan* to move – more at WAY]

¹**wainscot** /'waynskət/ *n* **1a(1)** a usu panelled wooden lining of an interior wall **a(2)** a lining of an interior wall irrespective of material **b** the lower part of an interior wall when finished differently from the remainder of the wall **2** *Br* a fine grade of oak imported for woodwork [ME, fr MD *wagenschot*]

²**wainscot** *vt* **-t-, -tt-** to line (as if) with boards or panelling

**wainscoting, wainscotting** /'waynskəting, 'waynz,koting/ *n* **1** material used to wainscot a surface **2** WAINSCOT 1

**wainwright** /'wayn,riet/ *n* someone who makes and repairs wagons

¹**waist** /wayst/ *n* **1a** the (narrow) part of the human body between the chest and hips **b** the greatly constricted part of the body of a wasp or similar insect, between the THORAX (middle body segment) and the abdomen **2** the part of something corresponding to or resembling the human waist: eg **2a(1)** the part of a ship's deck between the POOP (superstructure at the stem) and FORECASTLE (deck or superstructure towards the front) **a(2)** the middle part of a sailing ship between foremast and mainmast **b** the middle section of the fuselage of an aircraft **c** the narrowest part of a saddle between the POMMEL and the seat **3** the part of a garment covering the body at the waist or waistline [ME *wast;* akin to OE *weaxan* to grow – more at WAX]

²**waist** *vi* to shrink or become narrow in the middle

**waistband** /'wayst,band/ *n* a band (eg on trousers or a skirt) fitting round the waist

**waistcoat** /'ways,koht/ *n, chiefly Br* a sleeveless upper garment that fastens down the centre front and usu has a V-neck; *esp* such a garment shaped to fit closely and worn under a jacket as part of a man's suit – **waistcoated** *adj*

,**waist-'deep** *adj or adv* waist-high

**waisted** /'waystid/ *adj* **1** having a waist or waistlike part **2** having a waist in a specified position in relation to the average length from the shoulder to the waist – in combination ⟨*long*-waisted⟩ ⟨*high*-waisted⟩

,**waist-'high** *adj or adv* reaching up to the waist

**waistline** /'wayst,lien/ *n* **1** an imaginary line encircling the narrowest part of the waist; *also* the part of a garment corresponding to this line or to the place which fashion dictates this should be ⟨*a high* ∼⟩ **2** body circumference at the waist

¹**wait** /wayt/ *vt* **1** to stay in place in expectation of; await ⟨∼ *your turn*⟩ **2** to delay serving (a meal), esp in expectation of further arrivals **3** *chiefly NAm* to serve as waiter for ⟨∼ *table*⟩ ∼ *vi* **1a** to remain stationary in readiness or expectation ⟨∼ *for a train*⟩ **b** to pause for another to catch up **2a** to look forward expectantly ⟨*just* ∼ing *to see his rival lose*⟩ **b** to hold back expectantly ⟨*have to* ∼ *till Thursday*⟩ **3** to serve at meals – usu in the phrases *wait at table* or NAm *wait on table* **4a** to be ready and available ⟨*slippers* ∼ing *by the bed*⟩ **b** to remain temporarily neglected or unrealized **5** *Br* to park a vehicle for a short period at the edge of a road ⟨*no* ∼ing⟩ – see also **wait on somebody** HAND **and foot** [ME *waiten,* fr ONF *waitier* to watch, of Gmc origin; akin to OHG *wahta* watch, OE *wæccan* to watch – more at WAKE]

*usage* The verbs **wait** and **await** have from time to time been used interchangeably ⟨*tea and coffee* **wait** *your pleasure* – R S Surtees⟩ ⟨*on whom three hundred gold-capped youths* **await** – Alexander Pope⟩; but today **wait** is chiefly intransitive, and **await** is chiefly transitive, meaning **wait** *for.* They should not be confused, as in ⟨⚠ *I'm* **awaiting** *to see*⟩. In educated usage **wait** *for* is preferred rather than **wait on** for the meaning "await". *synonyms* see ³STAY

**wait on⟨upon** *vt* **1** to act as an attendant to; serve **2** to await **3** *archaic* to make a formal call on

**wait out** *vt* to delay in hope of a favourable change in ⟨wait out *a storm*⟩

**wait up** *vi* to delay going to bed, esp in expectation of someone's arrival or return

²**wait** *n* **1** *pl* **1a** a band of public musicians in Britain employed to play for processions or public entertainments; *also* tunes formerly associated with a specified band of waits ⟨*London* ~s⟩ **b** a group who serenade for gratuities, esp at the Christmas season **2a** a hidden or concealed position – chiefly in *lie in wait* **b** a state of watchful expectancy **3** an act or period of waiting ⟨*a long* ~ *for the bus*⟩ [ME *waite* watchman, public musician, act of waiting, fr ONF, watchman, watch, of Gmc origin; akin to OHG *wahta* watch]

**waiter** /'waytə/ *n* **1** someone who waits upon another **2** *fem* **waitress** /'waytrəs, -is/ someone who waits at table (eg in a restaurant), esp as a regular job **3** a tray on which something (eg a tea service) is carried; a salver

**waiting game** /'wayting/ *n* a strategic postponement of action in the hope of a more favourable opportunity later

**waiting list** *n* a list of those waiting (eg for a vacancy or for something to become available), arranged usu in order of application

**waiting room** *n* a room for the use of people who are waiting (eg for a train or to see a doctor)

'**wait-,listed** *adj* included on a waiting list, esp for a seat on an airliner

**waive** /wayv/ *vt* **1a** to relinquish (eg a legal right) voluntarily ⟨~ *a jury trial*⟩ **b** to refrain from pressing or enforcing (eg a rule) **2** to put off from immediate consideration; postpone **3** to dismiss from consideration △ **wave** [ME *weiven* to outlaw, abandon, resign, fr ONF *weyver*, fr *waif* lost, unclaimed]

**waiver** /'wayvə/ *n* the act of intentionally relinquishing or abandoning a right, claim, or privilege; *also* the document giving legal proof of such an act △ **waver** [AF *weyver*, fr. ONF *weyver* to abandon, waive]

**Wakashan** /waw'kashən/ *n* a N American Indian language family of the MOSAN group (PHYLUM)

¹**wake** /wayk/ *vb* **waked, woke** /wohk/, (*vt 1*) **waked; waked, woken** /'wohk(ə)n/, **woke**, (*vt 1*) **waked** *vi* **1** to be or remain awake ⟨*her waking hours*⟩ **2** to awake – often + *up* **3** *archaic* to remain deliberately awake (eg on watch) ~ *vt* **1** to hold a wake over (eg a dead person) **2a** to rouse (as if) from sleep; awake – often + *up* **b** to arouse, evoke ⟨~ *memories*⟩ **c** to arouse conscious interest in; alert – + *to* ⟨~ *him to the fact of her existence*⟩ [partly fr ME *waken* (past *wook*, pp *waken*), fr OE *wacan* to awake (past *wōc*, pp *wacen*) and partly fr ME *wakien, waken* (past & pp *waked*), fr OE *wacian* to be awake (past *wacode*, pp *wacod*); akin to OE *wæccan* to watch, L *vegēre* to rouse, excite] – **waker** *n*

²**wake** *n* **1a(1)** an annual English parish festival formerly held in commemoration of the church's patron saint **a(2)** VIGIL **1a** (watch held the night before a religious festival) **b wakes** *taking sing or pl vb*, **wake** the festivities originally connected with the wake of an English parish church and now marked by an annual holiday, typically in the industrial north of England ⟨*we all go off to Blackpool during* ~s *week*⟩ **2** a watch held over the body of a dead person prior to burial and sometimes accompanied by festivity; *broadly* any festive leavetaking **3** *archaic* the state of being awake

³**wake** *n* the track left by a moving body (eg a ship) in water) or another liquid; *broadly* a track or path left behind after something has passed [of Scand origin; akin to ON *vök* hole in ice; akin to ON *vökr* damp – more at HUMOUR]

**wakeful** /'waykf(ə)l/ *adj* **1** not sleeping or able to sleep **2** spent without sleep ⟨*a* ~ *night*⟩ – **wakefully** *adv*, **wakefulness** *n*

**waken** /'waykən/ *vi* to awake – often + *up* ~ *vt* to rouse out of sleep; wake [ME *waknen*, fr OE *wæcnan*; akin to ON *vakna* to awaken, OE *wæccan* to watch] – **wakener** *n*

**wakerife** /'wayk,rief/ *adj*, *Scot* wakeful, alert [ME (Sc) *walkryfe*, fr *walk* awake (fr *waken, walken* to wake) + *ryfe* rife]

'**wake-,robin** *n*, *Br* any of various ARUM plants; *esp* CUCKOOPINT [prob fr ¹*wake* + *robin*]

**wakey wakey** /,wayki 'wayki/ *interj*, *Br slang* wake up [baby talk]

**wakis** /'vahkis/ *n*, *pl* **wakiste** *SAfr* BOX SEAT [Afrik, fr D *wagen* wagon + *kist* chest]

**Waldenses** /wol'denseez/ *n pl* a Christian sect originating in S France in the 12th century, adopting CALVINIST doctrines in the 16th century, and living chiefly in Piedmont [ME *Walden-*

sis, fr ML *Waldenses, Valdenses*, fr Peter *Waldo* (or *Valdo*), 12th-c Fr heretic] – **Waldensian** *adj or n*.

**Waldorf salad** /'wawldawf/ *n* a salad consisting typically of apples, celery, and walnuts dressed with mayonnaise [*Waldorf-Astoria Hotel* in New York City]

¹**wale** /wayl/ *n* **1a** a streak or raised ridge made on the skin, esp by the stroke of a whip; a weal **b** a narrow raised surface; a ridge **2** *usu pl* any of a number of extra thick and strong planks in the sides of a wooden ship – compare GUNWALE **3a** any of a series of even ribs in a fabric (eg corduroy) **b** the texture, esp of a fabric **4** a horizontal timber used esp to support POLING BOARDS (boards supporting the sides) in a trench [ME, fr OE *walu*; akin to ON *valr* round, L *volvere* to roll – more at VOLUBLE]

²**wale** *vt* to mark with weals

³**wale** *n*, *dial Br* **1** an act of choosing; a choice **2** *the* best part; *the* pick [ME (Sc & northern) *wal*, fr ON *val*; akin to OHG *wala* choice, OE *wyllan* to wish – more at WILL]

⁴**wale** *vb*, *dial Br* to choose

**waler** /'waylə/ *n*, *often cap* a horse from New South Wales; *esp* a rather large rugged riding horse of mixed ancestry formerly exported in quantity from Australia to British India for military use [New South *Wales*, state of Australia]

**waling** /'wayling/ *n* **1** the process of placing wales (eg in shipbuilding) **2** wales

¹**walk** /wawk/ *vi* **1** *of a spirit* to move about in visible form; appear **2a** to move along on foot; advance by steps in such a way that at least one foot is always in contact with the ground **b** to go on foot for exercise or pleasure **c** to go at a walk **3a** to pursue a course of action or way of life; conduct oneself; behave ⟨~ *in darkness* – Jn 8:12 (AV)⟩ **b** to be or act in association; continue in union ⟨*the British and American peoples will* . . . ~ *together side by side in peace* – Sir Winston Churchill⟩ **4a** *of an inanimate object* to move in a manner suggestive of walking **b** to stand with an appearance suggestive of strides ⟨*pylons* ~ing *across the valley*⟩ **5** *of an astronaut* to move about in space outside a spacecraft **6** *obs* to roam, wander ~ *vt* **1a** to pass (as if) on foot through, along, over, or upon ⟨~ *the streets*⟩ ⟨~ *a tightrope*⟩ **b** to perform or accomplish by going on foot ⟨~ *guard*⟩ **2a** to cause (an animal) to go at a walk ⟨~ing *a horse round the paddock*⟩ **b** to take (an animal) for a walk ⟨~ing *a dog*⟩ **c** to cause (an inanimate object) to move in a manner suggestive of walking **3a** to accompany on foot; walk with ⟨~ed *her home*⟩ **b** to compel to walk (eg by a command) **c** to bring to a specified condition by walking ⟨~ed *us off our feet*⟩ **4** to go through, round, or over (something that will be performed at a faster pace) at a walk: eg **4a** to walk round (esp a show jumping course) for the purposes of examining, measuring, etc **b** to rehearse (eg a dance) by walking ⟨~ *a quadrille*⟩ **5** *Br* to take charge of (a hound puppy) at walk – see also **walk the** PLANK, **walk** TALL [partly fr ME *walken* (past *welk*, pp *walken*), fr OE *wealcan* to roll, toss (past *wēolc*, pp *wealcen*), and partly fr ME *walkien* (past *walked*, pp *walked*), fr OE *wealcian* to roll up, muffle up; akin to MD *walken* to knead, press, full, L *valgus* bowlegged]

**walk off with** *vt* **1a** to steal and take away **b** to take away unintentionally **2** to win or gain, esp by outdoing one's competitors without difficulty ⟨walked off with the *the trophy every year*⟩

**walk out** *vi* **1** to go on strike **2** to depart suddenly, often as an expression of protest **3** *chiefly Br* to court ⟨*they are walking out*⟩ – often + *with* ⟨*John is* walking out *with Mary*⟩; no longer in vogue – see also WALKOUT

**walk out on** *vt* to leave in the lurch; abandon, desert

**walk over** *vt* to treat contemptuously ⟨*his wife lets him walk all over her*⟩ ~ *vi*, *of a racehorse* to win a walkover

**walk up** *vi* to approach and enter – usu imper; used esp to attract customers at a fairground, circus, etc ~ *vt* to cause (a game bird or animal) to break cover by approaching on foot – compare DRIVE 5

²**walk** *n* **1a** an act or instance of going on foot, esp for exercise or pleasure ⟨*go for a* ~⟩ **b** SPACE WALK **c** a journey undertaken on foot along a usu agreed route to earn money promised by sponsors for charity ⟨*sponsored* ~⟩ ⟨*charity* ~⟩ ⟨*Christian Aid* Walk⟩ **2** a route for walking ⟨*many delightful* ~s *in the neighbourhood*⟩ **3** a place designed for walking:eg **3a** a path specially arranged or surfaced for walking; a footpath ⟨*gravelled garden* ~s⟩ **b** a railed or colonnaded platform **c** a promenade **d** ROPEWALK (place where ropes are made) **4** a place where animals (eg sheep) are kept with minimal restraint

**5** a forest area under one keeper **6** distance to be walked ⟨*a quarter of a mile's ~ from here*⟩ ⟨*a minute's ~*⟩ **7a** the gait of a 2-legged animal in which the feet are lifted alternately with one foot not clear of the ground before the other touches **b** the gait of a 4-legged animal in which there are always at least two feet on the ground; *specif* a 4-beat gait of a horse in which the feet strike the ground in the sequence left hind, left front, right hind, right front – compare CANTER, GALLOP, RUN, TROT **c** a low rate of speed ⟨*the shortage of raw materials slowed production to a ~*⟩ **8** a route regularly covered by a person (e g a postman or policeman) in the performance of a particular activity **9** manner of walking ⟨*his ~ is just like his father's*⟩ **10** social status; *also* a line of work; a calling – chiefly in *walk of life* **b** range or sphere of action; a field, province **11** *chiefly Br* a place (e g a farm) to which a hound puppy is sent to develop – chiefly in *at walk* **12** *Br* a ceremonial procession

**walkabout** /'wawkə,bowt/ *n* **1** a short period of wandering bush life engaged in by an Australian aborigine for ceremonial reasons as an occasional interruption of normal life **2** the following of a route on foot for a purpose ⟨*palace guards doing their ~*⟩ **3** an informal walk among the crowds by a public figure ⟨*the Queen on her Jubilee ~*⟩ – **go walkabout 1** *Austr* to go on a walkabout **2** *Br* to meet and hold a conversation informally with members of the public during an official engagement or tour ⟨*the Queen going walkabout in Milton Keynes*⟩

**walkaway** /'wawkəway/ *n* an easily won contest

**walker** /'wawkə/ *n* **1** one who or that which walks: e g **1a** a pedlar going on foot **b** a bird that walks rather than hopping **2** something used in walking; *specif* a framework designed to support a baby learning to walk or someone learning to walk again (e g after an injury), or to enable a disabled person to walk

**walkies** /'wawkiz/ *n, pl* **walkies** a walk – used esp to children and dogs; chiefly in *go walkies*

**walkie-talkie** /,wawki 'tawki/ *n* a compact easily transportable battery-operated radio transmitting and receiving set

**'walk-,in** *adj* large enough to be walked into ⟨*a ~ safe*⟩

**'walking** /'wawking/ *n* **1** the action of one who or that which walks ⟨*~ is good exercise*⟩ **2** the condition of a surface for one going on foot ⟨*the ~ is slippery*⟩

**²walking** *adj* **1** that walks: e g **1a** animate; *esp* human ⟨*a ~ encyclopedia*⟩ **b** able to walk ⟨*~ wounded*⟩ **c** not requiring bed rest **2a** used for or in walking ⟨*~ shoes*⟩ **b** characterized by or consisting of walking ⟨*a ~ tour*⟩ **3** that moves or appears to move in a manner suggestive of walking ⟨*a ~ toy*⟩; *esp* that swings or rocks back and forth ⟨*~ beam*⟩ **4** guided or operated by a walker ⟨*a ~ plough*⟩ [(1, 3, 4) fr prp of ¹*walk;* (2) fr gerund of ¹*walk*]

**walking papers** *n pl, NAm* MARCHING ORDERS

**walking stick** *n* a stick used as an aid to walking

**Walkman** /'wawkmən/ *trademark* – used for a small portable tape recorder with earphones

**'walk-,on** *n* (someone who has) a small usu nonspeaking part in a dramatic production

**walkout** /'wawk,owt/ *n* **1** a strike (e g by workers) **2** the action of leaving a meeting or organization as an expression of protest

**walkover** /'wawk,ohvə/ *n* **1** a horse race with only one starter **2** an easily won contest; *also* an advance from one round of a competition to the next without contest, owing to the withdrawal or absence of another contestant

**'walk-,through** *n* a perfunctory performance of a play or acting part (e g in an early stage of rehearsal)

**¹'walk-,up** *adj, NAm* having no lift ⟨*a ~ building*⟩; *also* not accessible by lift ⟨*a ~ office on the 3rd floor*⟩

**²walk-up** *n, NAm* something (e g a building or office) that is walk-up

**walkway** /'wawk,way/ *n* a passage or platform for walking; a walk

**Walkyrie** /vol'kiri,---, wol-, val-, wal- (*Ger* val'ky:rə)/ *n* VALKYRIE (maiden from Norse mythology)

**¹wall** /wawl/ *n* **1** a usu upright and solid structure, esp of masonry or concrete, having considerable height and length in relation to width and serving esp to divide, enclose, retain, or support: e g **1a wall, walls** *pl* a high thick masonry structure forming a long rampart or an enclosure, chiefly for defence ⟨*the city ~s*⟩ **b** a structure bounding a garden, park, or estate **c** any of the upright enclosing structures of a room or house **d** an upright structure serving to hold back pressure (e g of water

or sliding earth); RETAINING WALL **e** the surface of a wall ⟨*the ~ is painted cream*⟩ **2** a material layer enclosing space ⟨*the ~ of a container*⟩ ⟨*heart ~s*⟩ **3** something resembling a wall: e g **3a** an almost vertical rock surface **b** something that acts as a barrier or defence ⟨*tariff ~*⟩ ⟨*~ of silence*⟩ [ME, fr OE *weall;* akin to MHG *wall;* both fr a prehistoric WGmc word borrowed fr L *vallum* rampart, fr *vallus* stake, palisade; akin to ON *völr* round stick, L *volvere* to roll – more at VOLUBLE] – **walled** *adj,* **wall-like** *adj* – **to the wall** into a hopeless position; out of existence ⟨*during the recession several small firms went to the wall*⟩ – **up the wall** *informal* into a state of exasperation ⟨*being at home all day with small children drove her* up the wall⟩ – see also **have one's** BACK **to the wall,** FLY **on the wall, the** WRITING **on the wall**

**²wall** *vt* **1a** to protect or surround (as if) with a wall ⟨*a lake ~ed in by mountains*⟩ **b** to separate or shut out (as if) by a wall ⟨*~ed off half the house*⟩ **2a** to immure **b** to close (an opening) (as if) with a wall □ (2) usu + *up*

**wallaby** /'woləbi/ *n, pl* **wallabies,** *esp collectively* **wallaby** any of various small or medium-sized usu brightly coloured mammals (esp genus *Macropus*) closely related to the kangaroos [*wolabā,* native name in New South Wales, Australia]

**Wallace's line** /'wolisiz/ *n* a hypothetical boundary separating the characteristic Asian flora and fauna from that of Australasia and forming the boundary between the Australian and Oriental BIOGEOGRAPHIC regions [Alfred Russel *Wallace* † 1913 Br naturalist]

**wallah, walla** /'wolə/ *n, Ind informal* a person who does a specified type of work or who performs a specified duty or service ⟨*the book ~ was an itinerant peddler* – George Orwell⟩ – usu in combination ⟨*punkah*-wallah⟩ ⟨*bath*-wallah⟩ [Hindi *-wālā* man, one in charge, fr Skt *pāla* protector; akin to Skt *pāti* he protects – more at FUR]

**wallaroo** /,wolə'rooh/ *n, pl* **wallaroos** EURO (large reddish-grey Australian Kangaroo) [*wolarū,* native name in New South Wales, Australia]

**wallboard** /'wawl,bawd/ *n* a structural boarding of any of various materials (e g wood pulp, gypsum, or plastic) made in large rigid sheets and used esp for lining interior walls and ceilings

**wall creeper** *n* a small S European and Asian bird (*Tichodroma muraria*) related to the NUTHATCHES, that has grey upper parts and blackish wings with crimson patches and that inhabits cliffs and rocky areas, usu in mountainous regions

**wallet** /'wolit/ *n* **1** a bag for carrying miscellaneous articles while travelling **2** a holder for paper money, usu with compartments for other items (e g credit cards and stamps) **3** a flat case or folder ⟨*a ~ of maps*⟩ [ME *walet*]

**walleye** /'wawl,ie/ *n* **1a** an eye with a whitish iris **b** an eye in which the normally transparent cornea is white and opaque; *also* LEUCOMA (patch of dense white tissue in the cornea) **c** an eye that turns outwards, showing more than a normal amount of white **2a** a squint in which the eye turns outwards **b** *pl* eyes affected with outward squint [back-formation fr *walleyed*]

**walleyed** /'wawlied/ *adj* **1** having walleyes or affected with walleye **2** marked by a wild irrational staring of the eyes [by folk etymology fr ME *wawil-eghed,* part trans of ON *vagl-eygr,* fr *vagl* beam, roost + *eygr* eyed]

**wall fern** *n* POLYPODY

**wallflower** /'wawl,flowə/ *n* **1** any of several plants (genera *Cheiranthus* and *Erysimum*) of the cabbage family, many of which are cultivated for their showy flowers; *esp* a hardy European plant (*Cheiranthus cheiri*) widely cultivated for its spikelike clusters of typically golden to brown sweet-scented flowers **2** *informal* a person who from shyness or unpopularity remains on the sidelines of a social activity; *esp* a woman who fails to get partners at a dance [fr the plant's growing wild on old walls]

**wall hanging** *n* a piece of often heavy material (e g drapery or tapestry) hung against a wall for decoration

**walling** /'wawling/ *n* **1** the act or practice of building walls; *also* walls **2** material used for building walls – **waller** *n*

**Walloon** /wo'loohn/ *n* **1** a member of a chiefly Celtic French-speaking people of S and SE Belgium and adjacent parts of France **2** the French dialect of the Walloons [MF *Wallon,* adj & n, of Gmc origin; prob akin to OHG *Walah* Celt, Roman, OE *Wealh* Celt, Welshman – more at WELSH] – **Walloon** *adj*

**¹wallop** /'woləp/ *n* **1** *dial Br* a clumsy body movement; a lurch **2** *informal* **2a** a powerful body blow; a punch – sometimes used interjectionally **b** emotional or psychological force; impact

**c** the ability (eg of a boxer) to hit hard **3** *Br slang* beer [ME, gallop, fr ONF *walop,* fr *waloper* to gallop]

²**wallop** *vi* to move about or progress in a lurching clumsy manner ~ *vt, informal* **1a** to thrash soundly; lambaste **b** to beat by a wide margin; trounce **2** to hit with force; sock [ME *walopen* to gallop, fr ONF *waloper*] – **walloper** *n*

**walloping** /'wolǝpiŋ/ *adj, informal* large, whopping

¹**wallow** /'woloh/ *vi* **1** to roll about, lie around, or pass time lazily or luxuriously ⟨*pigs* ~ing *in mud*⟩ **2** to indulge oneself immoderately; revel ⟨~ing *in self-pity*⟩ **3** to struggle laboriously in or through rough water; *broadly* to lurch, pitch ⟨*ship* ~ed *down the coast*⟩ **4** to become or remain helpless ⟨*allowed them to* ~ *in their ignorance*⟩ [ME *walwen,* fr OE *wealwian* to roll – more at VOLUBLE] – **wallower** *n*

²**wallow** *n* **1** an act or instance of wallowing **2a** a muddy or dusty area used by animals for wallowing **b** a depression formed (as if) by the wallowing of animals

**wall painting** *n* FRESCO

¹**wallpaper** /'wawl,paypǝ/ *n* decorative paper for the walls of a room

²**wallpaper** *vt* to apply wallpaper to; *esp* to wallpaper the walls of (a room) ~ *vi* to put wallpaper on a wall; hang wallpaper

**wall pellitory** /'pelit(ǝ)ri/ *n* ²PELLITORY (plant of the nettle family)

**wall plate** *n* a horizontal structural member (eg a timber) that provides bearing and anchorage, esp for the beams (TRUSSES) of a roof or the rafters

**wall rock** *n* rock through which a fault or vein of ore runs

**wall rocket** *n* (any of several plants of the same genus as) a yellow-flowered European plant (*Diplotaxis muralis*) of the cabbage family, that is a weed of cultivated land

**wall rue** *n* a small delicate SPLEENWORT fern (*Asplenium rutamuraria*) found esp growing from crevices in walls or cliffs

**Wall Street** *n* the influential financial interests of the US economy [*Wall Street* in New York City, site of the New York Stock Exchange]

,**wall-to-'wall** *adj* **1** abutting all the walls that enclose an area; *specif* covering the whole floor ⟨~ *carpeting*⟩ **2** *humorous* continuous, uninterrupted ⟨*film with* ~ *commentary*⟩ ⟨*holiday beaches with* ~ *people*⟩

¹**wally** /'woli/ *adj, Scot* fine, sturdy [prob fr ³*wale*]

²**wally** *adj or n, Br slang* (characteristic of or befitting) an ineffectual, incompetent, or foolish person [prob short for *wallydraigle*]

**wallydraigle** /'woli,draygl/ *n, chiefly Scot* a feeble, imperfectly developed, or slovenly creature [perh fr Sc *waly,* exclamation of sorrow + *draigle* dirty or feeble person, fr *draigle* to soil, straggle, var of E *draggle*]

**walnut** /'wawl,nut/ *n* (the edible nut of) any of a genus (*Juglans* of the family Juglandaceae, the walnut family) of trees with richly grained wood often used for cabinetmaking and veneers; *also* the wood of a walnut [ME *walnot,* fr OE *wealhhnutu,* lit., foreign nut, fr *Wealh* Welshman, foreigner + *hnutu* nut – more at WELSH, NUT; fr its being introduced to Britain from overseas, prob by the Romans]

**Walpurgis Night** /val'pooǝgis/ *n* **1** the eve of MAY DAY on which, according to Germanic legend, witches ride to an appointed rendezvous **2** a nightmarish event or situation [part trans of Ger *walpurgisnacht,* fr *Walpurgis* St Walburga † 777 E saint whose feast day falls on May Day + *nacht* night]

**walrus** /'wawlrǝs/ *n, pl* **walruses,** *esp collectively* **walrus** either of two large sea mammals (*Odobenus rosmarus* and *Odobenus divergens* of the family Odobenidae) of northern seas that are related to the seals and are hunted for their tough heavy hides, their ivory tusks, the oil yielded by their blubber, and locally for their flesh [D, of Scand origin; akin to Dan & Norw *hvalros* walrus, ON *rosmhvalr*]

**walrus moustache** *n* a thick moustache that droops down at each side

**Walter Mitty** /,woltǝ 'miti/ *n* a commonplace unadventurous person who seeks escape from reality through daydreaming [*Walter Mitty,* daydreaming hero of the story "The Secret Life of Walter Mitty" by James Thurber †1961 US writer] – **Walter Mittyish** *adj*

¹**waltz** /wol(t)s, wawl(t)s/ *n* **1** a ballroom dance to music with three beats to the bar with the strong accent on the first beat, and a basic pattern of step-step-close **2** music for a waltz; *also* a concert composition in waltz time [Ger *walzer,* fr *walzen* to roll, dance, fr OHG *walzan* to turn, roll – more at WELTER]

²**waltz** *vi* **1** to dance a waltz **2** to move along in a lively, nimble,

or confident manner **3** to proceed easily, boldly, or successfully; breeze ⟨~ed *through his finals*⟩ ⟨*can't just* ~ *up and introduce ourselves*⟩ ~ *vt* **1** to dance a waltz with **2** to grab and lead (eg a person) unceremoniously; march – **waltzer** *n*

¹**wamble** /'wombl/ *vi, chiefly dial* **1a** to feel nausea **b** *of a stomach* to rumble **2** to move unsteadily or with a weaving or rolling motion [ME *wamlen;* akin to Dan *vamle* to become nauseated, L *vomere* to vomit – more at VOMIT]

²**wamble** *n, chiefly dial* **1** a wambling, esp of the stomach **2** a reeling or staggering gait or movement

**wampum** /'wompǝm/ *n* **1** beads of polished shells strung together and used by N American Indians as money, ceremonial pledges, and ornaments **2** *NAm* money [short for *wampumpeag*]

**wampumpeag** /'wompǝm,peeg/ *n* wampum; *esp* that made of the less valuable white shell beads [Narraganset *wampompeag,* fr *wampan* white + *api* string + -*ag,* pl suffix]

¹**wan** /won/ *adj* -**nn**- **1a** suggestive of poor health; sickly, pallid **b** lacking vitality; feeble **2** dim, faint ⟨*a* ~ *light*⟩ **3** languid ⟨*a* ~ *smile*⟩ **4** *archaic* dark, gloomy ⟨*a* ~ *smile*⟩ [MR, fr OE, dark, livid] – **wanly** *adv,* **wanness** *n*

²**wan** *vi* -**nn**- *chiefly poetic* to become wan; pale ⟨*all his visage,* ~ned - Shak⟩

**wand** /wond/ *n* **1** a slender staff carried as a sign of office **2** a slender rod used by conjurers and magicians **3** a long narrow vertical strip used as a target in archery **4** *poetic* a plant shoot [ME, slender stick, fr ON *vöndr;* akin to OE *windan* to wind, twist – more at WIND]

**wander** /'wondǝ/ *vi* **1** to go idly or aimlessly about; ramble ⟨~ *across the room*⟩ **2** to follow or extend along a winding course; meander **3a** to deviate (as if) from a course; stray ⟨*eyes* ~ed *from the page*⟩ **b** to lose concentration; stray in thought ⟨*the student's mind began to* ~ *as the lecture dragged on*⟩ ~ *vt* to roam over ⟨~ *the hills*⟩ [ME *wandren,* fr OE *wandrian;* akin to MHG *wandern* to wander, OE *windan* to wind, twist] – **wander** *n,* **wanderer** *n*

¹**wandering** /'wondǝriŋ/ *n,* **wanderings** *n pl* **1** a going about from place to place **2** movement away from the proper, normal, or usual course or place

²**wandering** *adj* characterized by aimless, slow, or pointless movement: eg **a** that winds or meanders ⟨*a* ~ *course*⟩ **b** not keeping a rational or sensible course; vagrant **c** nomadic ⟨~ *tribes*⟩ **d** *of a plant* having long runners or tendrils

**wandering albatross** *n* a large albatross (*Diomedea exulans*) of southern oceans that is white with black wing tips

**wandering Jew** *n* any of several plants (genera *Zebrina* and *Tradescantia* of the family Commelinaceae); *esp* either of two trailing or creeping plants (*Zebrina pendula* and *Tradescantia fluminensis*) grown for their decorative often white-striped foliage [the *Wandering Jew,* legendary character condemned to roam the world until doomsday]

**wanderlust** /'wondǝ,lust/ *n* eager longing for or impulse towards travelling in distant lands [Ger, fr *wandern* to wander + *lust* desire, pleasure]

**wanderoo** /,wondǝ'rooh/ *n, pl* **wanderoos** **1** a purple-faced LANGUR (large long-tailed monkey) (*Presbytis cephalopterus*) of Sri Lanka **2** a short-tailed MACAQUE monkey (*Macaca albibarbata*) of the Indian subcontinent [Sinhalese *vanduru,* pl of *vandurā,* fr Skt *vānara* monkey, fr *vanar-, vana* forest]

**wandoo** /won dooh/ *n, pl* **wandoos** a eucalyptus tree (*Eucalyptus redunca*) of W Australia with hard tough durable wood [native name in Australia]

¹**wane** /wayn/ *vi* **1** to decrease in size or extent; dwindle: eg **1a** *of the moon* to diminish in apparent size or amount **b** *of light or colour* to become less brilliant; dim **2** to fall gradually from power, prosperity, or influence; decline [ME *wanen,* fr OE *wanian;* akin to OHG *wanōn* to wane, OE *wan* wanting, deficient, L *vanus* empty, vain]

²**wane** *n* **1** a period or time of waning; *specif* the period from FULL MOON to NEW MOON **2** a defect in prepared timber characterized by bark or lack of wood at a corner or edge – **on the wane** in a state of decline; waning

**waney, wany** /'wayni/ *adj* **1** waning or diminished in some parts **2** *of sawn timber* marked by wane

**wangle** /'wang-gl/ *vb, informal vi* to resort to trickery or devious methods ~ *vt* **1** to adjust or manipulate for personal or fraudulent ends **2** to bring about or get by devious means ⟨~ *an invitation*⟩ [perh alter. of *waggle*] – **wangler** *n*

¹**wank** /wangk/ *vi, Br vulgar* to masturbate [origin unknown]

²**wank** *n, Br vulgar* an act of masturbating

**Wankel engine** /'wangkl/ *n* an INTERNAL-COMBUSTION ENGINE with a triangular rotor that functions as, and in place of, a set of pistons and whose rotation is caused by the explosion of a fuel-air mixture in a chamber formed by the side of the rotor and the hollow in the engine in which the rotor turns [Felix *Wankel b* 1902 Ger engineer]

**wanker** /'wangkə/ *n, Br* **1** *vulgar* someone who masturbates **2** *slang* a foolish, ineffectual, superficial, or incompetent person

**¹want** /wont/ *vt* **1a** to have a desire for ⟨~ed *a chance to rest*⟩ ⟨*he* ~s *to go*⟩ ⟨*she* ~s *this dress shortened*⟩ **b** to have an inclination to; like ⟨*say what you* ~, *he is efficient*⟩ **2a** to have need of; require ⟨*the car* ~s *petrol*⟩ ⟨*the room* ~s *decorating*⟩ **b** to suffer from the lack of; need ⟨*thousands still* ~ *food and shelter*⟩ **3** to wish or demand the presence of ⟨*the boss* ~s *you*⟩ **4** to hunt or seek in order to apprehend ⟨*he is* ~ed *for murder*⟩ **5** ought – + *to* and infinitive ⟨*you* ~ *to see a doctor about that toe*⟩ ⟨*you don't* ~ *to drive too fast*⟩ **6** *formal* to fail to possess, esp in customary or required amount; lack ⟨*his answer* ~s *courtesy*⟩ **7** *formal* to be deficient or short by (a specified amount) ⟨*it* ~s *three minutes to twelve*⟩ ~ *vi* **1** to be needy or destitute **2** to have need; be lacking in the specified respect ⟨*never* ~s *for friends*⟩ **3** *chiefly NAm or Scot* to desire to come or go ⟨~s *out of the syndicate*⟩ [ME *wanten*, fr ON *vanta*; akin to OE *wan* deficient]

*usage* **1** The use of *want* with a present participle ⟨⚠ *we want this changing*⟩ is widely disliked, and should be replaced by ⟨*we want this changed*⟩ unless *want* means "need" ⟨*this wants changing*⟩. **2** The construction *want for* should be used only when it means "lack" ⟨*never* **wanted** *for company*⟩ and not as in ⟨⚠ *I* **want** *for you to go*⟩. synonyms see ¹DESIRE, ¹LACK

**²want** *n* **1a** the quality or state of lacking something required or usual ⟨*he suffers from a* ~ *of good sense*⟩ **b** grave and extreme poverty that deprives one of the necessities of life **2** something wanted; a need, desire ⟨*satisfy your* ~s⟩

**want ad** *n, chiefly NAm* a CLASSIFIED AD stating that something (eg an employee, employment, or a specified item) is wanted

**wanting** /'wonting/ *adj* **1** not present or in evidence; absent **2a** not being up to the required standard or expectation ⟨*a candidate tested and found* ~⟩ **b** lacking in the specified ability or capacity; deficient ⟨~ *in gratitude*⟩ **3** *euph* feebleminded

**¹wanton** /'wont(ə)n/ *adj* **1** mischievous **2** sexually unbridled; promiscuous **3a** having no just foundation or provocation; malicious ⟨~ *indifference to the needs of others*⟩ **b** gratuitously brutal or violent ⟨~ *killing*⟩ **4a** uncontrolled, unbridled ⟨~ *inflation*⟩ **b** *chiefly poetic* luxuriant, lavish **5** *archaic* hard to control; undisciplined, unruly [ME, fr *wan-* deficient, wrong, mis- (fr OE, fr *wan* deficient) + *towen*, pp of *teen* to draw, train, discipline, fr OE *tēon* – more at TOW] – **wantonly** *adv*, **wantonness** *n*

**²wanton** *n, archaic* a wanton person; *esp* a lewd or lascivious woman

**³wanton** *vi, archaic* to be wanton or act wantonly; *esp* to behave licentiously – **wantoner** *n*

**wany** /'wayni/ *adj* WANEY

**wapentake** /'wopəntayk, 'wapən-/ *n* a former subdivision of some English shires, esp in the Midlands and North, corresponding to a HUNDRED [ME, fr OE *wæpentæc*, fr ON *vápnatak* act of grasping weapons, fr *vāpn* weapon + *tak* act of grasping, fr *taka* to take; prob fr the brandishing of weapons as a sign of approval when the chief of the wapentake took office]

**wapiti** /'wopiti/ *n, pl* **wapitis**, *esp collectively* **wapiti** a N American deer (*Cervus canadensis*) that is similar to the European RED DEER but much larger, and that has a reddish-brown body, a pale buff rump patch, and large branched antlers [of Algonquian origin; akin to Cree *wapitew* white, whitish; fr its white rump and tail]

**¹war** /waw/ *n* **1a** a state or period of usu open and declared armed hostile conflict between states or nations **b** the art or science of warfare **2a** a state of hostility, conflict, or antagonism **b** a struggle between opposing forces or for a particular end ⟨*a class* ~⟩ ⟨*a* ~ *against disease*⟩ [ME *werre*, fr ONF, of Gmc origin; akin to OHG *werra* strife; akin to OHG *werran* to confuse, L *verrere* to sweep] – **warless** *adj* – **declare war 1** to make a formal declaration of intention to go to war **2** to make a resolution to counteract, eradicate, or work against ⟨~d *war on untidiness in the office*⟩

**²war** *vi* **-rr-** **1** to engage in warfare **2a** to be in active or vigorous conflict **b** to be opposed or inconsistent ⟨~ring *principles*⟩

**³war** *adv or adj, chiefly Scot* worse [ME *werre*, fr ON *verri*, adj, *verr*, adv – more at WORSE]

**⁴war** *vt* **-rr-** *Scot* to overcome, defeat

**waratah** /'worətah/ *n* any of several Australasian shrubs (genus *Telopea*, esp *Telopea speciosissima* and *Telopea oreades*, of the family Proteaceae) that have clusters of crimson or scarlet flowers [native name in Australia]

**war baby** *n* a child born or conceived during a war

**¹warble** /'wawbl/ *n* **1** a musical trill **2** the action of warbling; *also* a warbled song or tune [ME *werble* tune, fr ONF, of Gmc origin; akin to MHG *wirbel* whirl, tuning peg, OHG *wirbil* whirlwind – more at WHIRL]

**²warble** *vi* **1** to sing or sound in a trilling manner or with many turns and variations **2** to become sounded with trills and rapid modulations in pitch **3** to sing ~ *vt* to render musically, esp in an ornamented or trilling manner

**³warble** *n* **1** a swelling under the hide, esp of the back of cattle, horses, and wild mammals, caused by the maggot of a BOTFLY or WARBLE FLY **2** the maggot of a WARBLE FLY [perh of Scand origin; akin to obs Sw *varbulde* boil, fr *var* pus + *bulde* swelling] – **warbled** *adj*

**warble fly** *n* any of various flies (family Oestridae) whose larvae live under the skin of various mammals and cause swellings

**warbler** /'wawblə/ *n* **1** one who or that which warbles; a singer, songster **2** any of numerous small active insect-eating Eurasian birds (family Sylviidae) that are related to the thrushes and many of which are noted songsters

**war bride** *n* a woman who marries a serviceman, esp of a foreign nation, met during a time of war

**war chest** *n, NAm* a fund accumulated to finance a war; *broadly* a fund earmarked for a specific purpose, action, or campaign

**war clouds** *n pl* a state of affairs that threatens war

**war correspondent** *n* a correspondent employed to report news concerning the conduct of a war, esp events at the scene of a battle

**war crime** *n* a crime (eg GENOCIDE or maltreatment of prisoners) committed during or in connection with war – **war criminal** *n*

**war cry** *n* **1** a cry used during charging or rallying by a body of fighters in war **2** a slogan used esp to rally people to a cause

**¹ward** /wawd/ *n* **1** the action or process of guarding – compare WATCH AND WARD **2** the state of being under guard; *esp* custody **3a** the inner court of a castle or fortress **b** a division (eg a cell or block) of a prison **c** a division in a hospital; *esp* a large room in a hospital where a number of patients usu requiring similar treatment are accommodated **4a** a division of a city or town for representative, electoral, or administrative purposes **b** a former division of some English and Scottish counties corresponding to a HUNDRED **5** a projecting piece of metal in a lock casing or keyhole that prevents either the insertion or the turning of keys that have no corresponding notch; *also* the corresponding notch in the key **6** a person under guard, protection, or surveillance: eg **6a** a person below the age of legal responsibility who is under the care of a guardian **b ward, ward of court** a person who because of incapacity (eg lunacy or being below the age of legal responsibility) is under the protection of a court either directly or through a guardian appointed by the court **7** a means of defence; projection [ME, fr OE *weard*; akin to OHG *warta* act of watching, OE *warian* to beware of, guard – more at WARE]

**²ward** *vt* **1** to assign to or confine in a hospital ward **2** *archaic* to keep watch over; guard [ME *warden* to guard, defend, fr OE *weardian*; akin to OHG *wartēn* to watch, ON *vartha* to guard, OE *weard* ward]

**ward off** *vt* to deflect, avert

**¹-ward** /-wəd/ *also* **-wards** *suffix* (→ *adj*) **1** facing or tending in (such) a direction ⟨*homeward*⟩ ⟨*northward*⟩ **2** occurring or situated in (such) a direction ⟨*leftward*⟩ [*-ward* fr ME, fr OE *-weard*; akin to OHG *-wart*, *-wert* *-ward*, L *vertere* to turn; *-wards* fr *-wards*, adv suffix – more at WORTH]

**²-ward** *suffix* (→ *adv*), *chiefly NAm* **-wards** [ME, fr OE *-weard*, fr *-weard*, adj suffix]

**war dance** *n* a dance performed (eg by N American Indians or other tribal peoples) as preparation for battle or in celebration of victory

**warded** /'wahdid/ *adj* provided with a ward ⟨*a* ~ *lock*⟩

**warden** /'wawd(ə)n/ *n* **1** someone having care or charge of something; a guardian, keeper **2a** the governor of a town, district, or fortress ⟨*Lord* Warden *of the Cinque Ports*⟩ **b** a member of the governing body of a guild **3** an official charged with special supervisory or administrative duties or with the enforcement of specified laws or regulations ⟨*game* ~⟩ ⟨*air raid* ~⟩ ⟨*traffic* ~⟩ **4a** a churchwarden **b** any of various British college officials whose duties range from the administration of academic matters to the supervision of student discipline ⟨*the* Warden *of All Souls, Oxford*⟩ **5** chiefly NAm an official in charge of the operation of a prison [ME *wardein*, fr ONF, fr *warder* to guard, of Gmc origin; akin to OHG *wartēn* to watch] – **wardenship**

**wardening** /'wawd(ə)ning/ *n* close supervision of an area (eg in a nature reserve) to prevent wilful interference with the fauna and flora (eg nesting birds or rare plants) ⟨*careful ~ allowed the ospreys to hatch safely*⟩

**¹warder** /'wawdə/ *n* **1** *fem* **wardress** *Br* a prison guard or jailer **2** *archaic* a watchman, guard [ME, fr AF *wardere*, fr *warde* act of guarding, of Gmc origin; akin to OHG *warta* act of watching] – **wardership** *n*

**²warder** *n* a truncheon formerly used by a king or commander in chief to signal orders [ME, perh fr *warden* to ward]

**ward heeler** /'heelə/ *n, NAm* a worker for a political boss in a local area (eg a ward)

**ward of court** *n* WARD 6b (person under the protection of a court)

**Wardour Street** /'wawdə/ *adj, of English literary style* affectedly archaic [*Wardour Street* in London, formely a centre of the (spurious) antique trade]

**wardrobe** /'waw,drohb/ *n* **1** a place (eg a room or large cupboard) where clothes are kept; *esp* a tall cupboard typically fitted with shelves and a rail or pegs for hanging clothes on **2a** a collection of clothes (eg belonging to one person or used for one activity) ⟨*a summer* ~⟩ **b** a collection of stage costumes and accessories **3** the department of a royal or noble household entrusted with the care of clothes, jewels, and personal articles [ME *warderobe*, fr ONF, fr *warder* to guard + *robe* robe]

**wardroom** /'wawdroohm, -room/ *n* the living quarters of all the officers in a warship except the captain; *specif* the mess assigned to these officers

**-wards** /-woodz/ *suffix, chiefly NAm* **-ward** (→ *adv*) **1** in (such) a spatial or temporal direction ⟨*up*wards⟩ ⟨*after*wards⟩ **2** towards (such) a point, position, or place ⟨*earth*wards⟩ [ME, fr OE *-weardes*, gen sing, neut of *-weard*, adj suffix – more at ¹WARD]

**wardship** /'wawdship/ *n, law* **1** care and protection of a ward **2** the state of being under a guardian

**¹ware** /weə/ *adj* **1** *poetic* aware, conscious **2** *archaic* wary, vigilant [ME *war, ware* careful, aware – more at WARY]

**²ware** *vt* to beware of; avoid – used chiefly as a command to hunting animals [ME *waren*, fr OE *warian;* akin to OHG *biwarōn* to protect, OE *wær* aware]

**³ware** *n* **1a** manufactured articles, products of art or craft, or farm produce; *often* in combination ⟨*tin*ware⟩ **b** *pl* goods for sale **2** articles (eg pottery or dishes) of fired clay; *esp* a specified make of pottery or china ⟨*Parian* ~⟩ **3** *dial Br* potatoes of marketable size [ME, fr OE *waru;* akin to MHG *ware* ware]

**⁴ware** *vt, Scot* to spend, expend [ME *waren*, fr ON *verja* to clothe, invest, spend – more at WEAR]

**¹warehouse** /'weə,hows/ *n* a structure or room for the storage of merchandise or commodities

**²warehouse** *vt* to deposit, store, or stock in a warehouse – **warehouser** *n*

**warehouseman** /'weə,howsmən/ *n* someone who owns, manages, or works in a warehouse

**warfare** /'waw,feə/ *n* **1** military operations between enemies; hostilities, war; *also* an activity undertaken by a political unit (eg a nation) to weaken or destroy another ⟨*economic* ~⟩ **2** struggle between competing entities; conflict [ME, fr *werre*, *warre* war + *fare* journey, passage – more at FARE]

**warfarin** /'wawfərin/ *n* a synthetic chemical compound, $C_{19}H_{16}O_4$, that is used in medicine to prevent the blood clotting (eg in the treatment of thrombosis) and is also used as a rodent poison [*Wisconsin Alumni Research Foundation* (its patentee) + coum*arin*]

**war footing** *n* the condition of being prepared to undertake or maintain war

**'war-,game** *vt* to plan or conduct in the manner of a WAR GAME ⟨~d *an invasion – Newsweek*⟩ ~ *vi* to conduct a WAR GAME – **war-gamer** *n*

**war game** *n* **1** a simulated battle or campaign to test military concepts and strategies, and usu conducted by officers taking the role of commanders of opposing forces **2** a two-sided umpired training manoeuvre with actual elements of the armed forces participating **3** an enactment of a conflict in miniature, using counters or models to represent the combatants

**war-gaming** /'waw,gayming/ *n* the conduct or pastime of WAR GAMES

**war grave** *n* the grave of someone who died in combat, esp one who was killed and buried overseas

**warhead** /'waw,hed/ *n* the section of a missile containing the explosive, chemical, or incendiary charge

**war-horse** /'waw,haws/ *n* **1** a powerful horse used in war; a charger **2** a veteran soldier or public person (eg a politician) **3** a work of art (eg a musical composition) that has become hackneyed from repetition in the standard repertoire

**warlike** /'waw,liek/ *adj* **1** fond of or skilful in war **2** of or useful in war **3** threatening war; hostile

**warload** /'waw,lohd/ *n* the weapons carried by a combat vehicle (eg an aircraft)

**war loan** *n* British government stock issued to finance a war

**warlock** /'wawlok/ *n* a man practising black magic; a sorcerer – compare WITCH [ME *warloghe*, fr OE *wǣrloga* one who breaks faith, the Devil, fr *wǣr* faith, troth (akin to OE *wǣr* true) + *leogan* to lie – more at VERY, LIE]

**warlord** /'waw,lawd/ *n* **1** a supreme military leader **2** a military commander (eg in China in former times) exercising civil power by force – **warlordism** *n*

**¹warm** /wawm/ *adj* **1a** having or giving out heat to a moderate or adequate degree ⟨*a* ~ *bath*⟩; *also* experiencing heat to this degree ⟨*are you* ~ *enough?*⟩ **b** serving to maintain or preserve heat, esp to a satisfactory degree ⟨*a* ~ *sweater*⟩ **c** feeling or causing sensations of heat brought about by strenuous exertion ⟨*a* ~ *climb*⟩ **2a** marked by enthusiasm; ardent, cordial ⟨*a* ~ *welcome*⟩ ⟨~ *friends*⟩ **b** marked by excitement, disagreement, or anger ⟨*a* ~ *debate*⟩ **3** affectionate and outgoing in temperament ⟨*a* ~ *personality*⟩ **4** dangerous, hostile ⟨*got a* ~ *reception from a crowd of angry demonstrators*⟩ **5** newly made; fresh ⟨*a* ~ *scent*⟩ **6** suggestive of warmth in colour or tone; *specif* of a hue in the range yellow through orange to red **7** near to a goal, object, or solution sought – chiefly in children's games **8** *Br* comfortably established; secure ⟨*a* ~ *existence in his old age*⟩ [ME, fr OE *wearm;* akin to OHG *warm* warm, L *formus,* Gk *thermos* warm, hot] – **warmish** *adj,* **warmly** *adv,* **warmness** *n*

**²warm** *vt* **1** to make warm **2** to infuse with a feeling of love, friendship, well-being, or pleasure **3** to reheat (cooked food) for eating – often + *up* or *through* in Br or *over* in NAm **4** to bring to the necessary temperature for comfort or efficient working – often + *up* ⟨~ *the room*⟩ ⟨~ *up the engine*⟩ ~ *vi* **1** to become warm **2** to become ardent, interested, or lively – usu + *up* ⟨*the party began to* ~ *up*⟩ **3** to experience feelings of pleasure; bask **4** to come to the necessary temperature for comfort or efficient working

**warm to** *vt* **1** *also* **warm towards** to become filled with affection or love for; begin to like **2** to begin to treat or expound enthusiastically ⟨*warming to his theme*⟩

**warm up** *vi* **1** to engage in exercise or practice, esp before entering a game or contest; *broadly* to get ready **2a** HOT UP **b** to approach a state of violence, conflict, or danger ~ *vt* to put (an audience) into a receptive mood (eg before a comedy show) – see also WARM-UP

**³warm** *adv* in a warm manner; warmly – usu in combination ⟨*warm-clad*⟩

**⁴warm** *n, chiefly Br* **1** an act of getting or making warm ⟨*come to the fire for a* ~⟩ **2** moderate heat ⟨*sit here in the* ~⟩

**,warm-'blood** *adj, of a horse or breed* having Thoroughbred or Arab blood

**,warm-'blooded** *adj* **1** having warm blood; *specif* having a relatively high and constant body temperature that is internally regulated and therefore more or less independent of the environment – compare COLD-BLOODED **2** fervent or ardent in spirit – **warm-bloodedness** *n*

**,warmed-'over** *adj, NAm* not fresh or new; stale ⟨~ *ideas*⟩

**war memorial** *n* a monument to those (eg members of a regiment) killed in a war

**warmer** /'wawmə/ *n* a device for making or keeping something warm

**warm front** *n* an advancing edge of a warm air mass

**warmhearted** /,wawm'hahtid/ *adj* marked by ready affection, friendliness, generosity, or sympathy – **warmheartedly** adv, **warmheartedness** n

**warming pan** /'wawming/ n a usu long-handled flat covered pan (eg of brass) that in former times was filled with hot coals and used to warm a bed

**warmonger** /'waw,mung·gə/ n one who urges or attempts to stir up war – **warmongering** n

**warm spot** n a sentimental weakness; SOFT SPOT

**warmth** /wawmth/ n **1** the quality or state of being warm **a** in temperature **b** in feeling ⟨a child needing human ~ and family life⟩ **2** a glowing effect that is often produced by the use of warm colours

'**warm-,up** n the act or an instance of warming up; also a procedure (eg a set of exercises) used in warming up

**warm-up lap** n a lap of a motor-racing track by the entire field of competitors before the start of a race to allow the engines and tyres to warm up and often to permit a FLYING START

**warn** /wawn/ vt **1** to give notice to beforehand, esp of danger or evil ⟨~ them of the floods⟩ ⟨~ her against strange dogs⟩ **2** to give admonishing advice to; counsel ⟨~ them not to open the door⟩ **3** to notify, inform ⟨~ them of my intentions⟩ ~ vi to give a warning [ME warnen, fr OE warnian; akin to OHG warnōn to take heed, OE wær careful, aware – more at WARY] – **warner** n

**synonyms** Warn, forewarn, caution, and admonish all mean "tell of danger". Warn is the most general word. Forewarn emphasizes the fact of notifying in advance, and in preparation for some real danger. Caution is used specifically of the warning given to someone under arrest against saying anything that may be used in evidence, but in general implies that one must be careful for fear of unpleasant consequences. Admonish suggests a gentle warning about remissness or error, combined with some positive advice.
*antonym* reassure

**warn off** vt **1** also **warn away** to order to go or stay away **2** to order to go or stay away from ⟨the farmer warned us off his fields⟩

'**warning** /'wawning/ n **1** the act of warning; the state of being warned ⟨he had ~ of his illness⟩ **2** something that warns or serves to warn; also notice of termination of an agreement, employment, etc

²**warning** adj serving as an alarm, signal, summons, or admonition ⟨~ bell⟩ ⟨~ shot⟩ – **warningly** adv

**warning coloration** /ˌkulə'raysh(ə)n/ n the conspicuous coloration of an animal that serves to warn off potential enemies

**war of attrition** n a war of little movement in which the side with the largest reserves (eg of men and supplies) gains the victory

**War Office** n the former British Government department in charge of the army

**war of nerves** n a conflict characterized by the use of psychological tactics (eg bluff and threats) designed primarily to demoralize and confuse the enemy

'**warp** /wawp/ n **1a** a series of yarns extended lengthways in a loom and crossed by the WEFT **b** the cords forming the carcass of a pneumatic tyre **2** a rope for warping a ship or boat; also a rope used to secure a vessel alongside a quay **3** sediment deposited by water (eg in an estuary) **4a** a twist or curve that has developed in something originally flat or straight ⟨a ~ in a door panel⟩ – compare SPACE WARP, TIME WARP **b** a mental twist or aberration **5 warp and woof, warp** chiefly journalistic the fabric, essence ⟨the weaving of the media into the ~ and woof of our daily lives – Punch⟩ [ME, fr OE wearp; akin to OHG warf warp, ON verpa to throw; (4) ²warp] – **warpage** n

**synonyms** The warp is the lengthways threads in weaving, the **woof** or **weft** is the crosswise threads, and the **weft** or **web** is the resultant fabric.

²**warp** vt **1a** to turn or twist (eg planks or gramophone records) out of shape, esp out of flatness or straightness **b** to cause to judge, choose, or act wrongly or crookedly; pervert **c** to falsify, distort ⟨a ~ed sense of humour⟩ **2** to arrange (yarns) so as to form a warp **3** to manoeuvre (eg a ship) by hauling on a line attached to a fixed object ~ vi **1** to become warped **2** ME warpen, fr ¹warp; (vt 3) ¹warp] – **warpage** n, **warper** n

**war paint** n **1** paint put on parts of the body (eg the face) by N American Indians as a sign of going to war **2** informal ceremonial dress; regalia **3** informal facial make-up

**war party** n a group of N American Indians going on a warlike expedition or to war

**warpath** /'waw,pahth/ n **1** the route taken by a WAR PARTY of N American Indians **2** a hostile course of action or frame of mind – usu in on the warpath

**warp beam** n a roll on which the warp is wound for a loom

'**warp-,knitted** adj produced in machine knitting with the yarns running in a lengthways direction

**warplane** /'waw,playn/ n a military aircraft; esp one armed for combat

'**warrant** /'worənt/ n **1a(1)** sanction, authorization; also evidence for or token of authorization **a(2)** a guarantee, security **b** grounds, justification; also confirmation, proof ⟨an assertion totally without ~⟩ **2a** a commission or document giving authority to do something; specif a document that authorizes a person to pay or deliver to another and the other to receive money or other consideration ⟨travel ~⟩ **b** a document issued by a magistrate authorizing an officer to make an arrest, a seizure, a search, etc **c** an official certificate of appointment issued to a NONCOMMISSIONED OFFICER **d(1)** a short-term obligation of a governmental body (eg a municipality) issued in anticipation of revenue **d(2)** a document issued by a corporation giving to the holder the right to buy the capital stock of the corporation at a stated price either prior to a stipulated date or at any future time [ME, protector, warrant, fr. ONF warant, modif of a Gmc noun represented by OHG werēnto guarantor, fr prp of werēn to warrant; akin to OHG wāra trust, care – more at VERY] – **warrantless** adj

²**warrant** vt **1a** to declare or maintain with certainty; state as being true ⟨I'll ~ he'll be here by noon⟩ **b** to assure (a person) of the truth of what is said **2a** to guarantee to a person good title to and undisturbed possession of (eg an estate) **b** to guarantee (eg a fact or statement of fact) to be as represented **c** to guarantee; esp to guarantee (eg goods sold) in respect of the quality or quantity specified ⟨~ed against faulty workmanship⟩ **3** to give warrant or sanction to; authorize ⟨the law ~s this procedure⟩ **4** to prove the authenticity or truth of **5** to serve as or give adequate ground or reason for ⟨nothing could ~ such behaviour⟩ [ME warranten, fr ONF warantir, fr warant]

**warrantable** /'worəntəbl/ adj **1** capable of being warranted; justifiable **2** of a stag old enough to be hunted – **warrantableness** n, **warrantably** adv

**warrantee** /ˌworən'tee/ n the person to whom a warranty is made

**warrant officer** n – see MILITARY RANKS table

**warrant officer first class** n – see MILITARY RANKS table

**warrant officer second class** n – see MILITARY RANKS table

**warrantor** /'worəntə, ˌworən'taw/ also **warranter** /-tə/ n a person who warrants

**warranty** /'worənti/ n **1** a COLLATERAL undertaking (one involving pledged securities) that a fact regarding the subject of a contract is, or will be, as it is declared or promised to be **2** something that authorizes, sanctions, supports, or justifies; a warrant **3** a usu written guarantee of the soundness of a product and of the maker's responsibility for the repair or replacement of defective parts [ME warantie, fr ONF, fr warantir to warrant]

**warren** /'worən/ n **1a(1)** an area (eg of uncultivated ground) where rabbits breed **a(2)** a structure where rabbits are kept or bred **b** taking sing or pl vb the rabbits of a warren **2a** a crowded tenement or district **b** a maze of narrow passageways or cubbyholes; broadly anything intricate, confused, or complex **3** chiefly Br **3a** a place for keeping small game animals (eg hare or pheasant) **b** the privilege of hunting game in a warren [ME warenne, fr ONF]

**warrener** /'worənə/ n **1** a gamekeeper **2** someone who keeps or maintains a rabbit warren

**warrior** /'wori·ə/ n a man engaged or experienced in warfare; esp one experienced in tribal or medieval warfare [ME werriour, fr ONF werreieur, fr werreier to make war, fr werre war]

**warship** /'waw,ship/ n a ship, esp an armed ship, for use in warfare

**warsle, warstle** /'wawsl/ vi, Scot to wrestle, struggle [ME werstelen, warstelen, alter. of wrestlen, wrastlen] – **warsle** n

**wart** /wawt/ n **1** (any of various small lumps or rounded areas on the skin similar to) a horny projection on the skin, usu of the hands or feet, that is caused by a virus **2** a protuberance on a plant resembling a true wart **3** a blemish – often in warts and all **4** chiefly Br school slang an objectionable or obnoxious boy or man – no longer in vogue [ME, fr OE *wearte;* akin to OHG *warza* wart, L *verruca*] – **warted** *adj,* **warty** *adj*

**warthog** /'wawt,hog/ *n* any of a genus (*Phacochoerus*) of African wild pigs with two pairs of rough warty lumps on the face and large protruding tusks

**wartime** /'waw,tiem/ *n* a period during which a war is in progress

**war-weary** /'-,--, ,-'--/ *adj* exhausted and dejected by prolonged war

**war whoop** /woohp/ *n* WAR CRY; *esp* one given by N American Indians

**war widow** *n* a woman whose husband was killed in war

'**war-,work** *n* work done by the civilian population to support a country during a war

**warworn** /'waw,wawn/ *adj* showing the effects of war; *esp* war-weary

**wary** /'weəri/ *adj* marked by caution and watchful prudence in detecting and escaping danger *synonyms* see CAUTIOUS *antonyms* foolhardy, brash [ME *war, ware,* fr OE *wær* careful, aware, wary; akin to OHG *giwar* aware, attentive, L *vereri* to fear, Gk *horan* to see] – **warily** *adv,* **wariness** *n*

**was** /wəz; *strong* woz/ *past 1 & 3 sing of* BE *usage* see WERE [ME, fr OE, 1 & 3 sing. past indic of *wesan* to be; akin to ON *vera* to be, *var* was, Skt *vasati* he lives, dwells]

'**wash** /wosh/ *vt* **1a** to cleanse (as if) by the action of liquid (e g water) **b** to remove (e g dirt) by rubbing or drenching with liquid **2** *of an animal* to clean (a body covering, esp fur) by licking or by rubbing with a paw moistened with saliva **3a** to bathe or moisten (a body part or injury) with a liquid **b(1)** to wet thoroughly; drench **b(2)** to suffuse with light **c** to pass water over or through, esp so as to carry off material from the surface or interior **4** to flow along or dash or overflow against ⟨*waves* ∼ing *the shore*⟩ **5** to move, carry, or deposit (as if) by the force of water in motion ⟨*houses* ∼ed *away by the flood*⟩ **6a** to agitate (e g earth, gravel, or crushed ore) in order to separate valuable material **b** to separate (e g particles of gold) from an ore, gravel, etc by agitation with or in water **c(1)** to pass through a vessel containing a liquid in order to carry off impurities or soluble components **c(2)** to pass (a gas or gaseous mixture) through or over a liquid to achieve purification, esp by removing soluble components **7a** to cover or daub lightly (as if) with an application of a thin liquid (e g whitewash or varnish) **b** to depict or paint by a broad sweep of thin colour with a brush – often + *in* ⟨∼ed *in figures in the background*⟩ **8** to cause to swirl ⟨∼ing *coffee round in his cup*⟩ ∼ *vi* **1a** to wash oneself or a part of one's body **b** to wash articles; do the washing **2** to bear washing without damage ⟨*does this dress* ∼⟩ **3a** to drift along on water **b** to pour, sweep, or flow in a stream or current **4** *informal* to gain acceptance; inspire belief ⟨*his story didn't* ∼ *with me*⟩ ⟨*an interesting story, but it just won't* ∼⟩ – see also **wash one's** HANDS **of, wash one's dirty** LINEN **in public** [ME *washen, wasshen,* fr OE *wascan;* akin to OHG *waskan* to wash, OE *wæter* water]

**wash about** *vi* to float aimlessly (as if) in a liquid

**wash down** *vt* **1** to send downwards by action of a liquid; *esp* to ease the swallowing of (food) with accompanying gulps of liquid **2** to wash the whole surface of ⟨*washed down and scrubbed the front step*⟩

**wash off** *vb* **1** to (cause to) disappear as the result of washing **2** RUB OFF

**wash out** *vt* **1a** to wash free of a usu unwanted substance (e g dirt) ⟨*washed the milkbottles* out *before putting them on the doorstep*⟩ **b** to remove (e g a stain) by washing ⟨*washed the greasemarks* out *of his dungarees*⟩ **2a** to cause to fade by laundering **b** to deplete the strength or vitality of **c** to eliminate as useless or unsatisfactory; reject **3a** to destroy or make useless by the force or action of water ⟨*the storm* washed out *the bridge*⟩ **b** RAIN OFF ∼ *vi* to become depleted of colour or vitality; fade – see also WASHOUT

**wash up** *vi* **1** *Br* to wash the used dishes and utensils, esp after a meal **2** to wash one's face and hands ∼ *vt* **1** to remove (e g from the floor) by washing ⟨*wash up* the split milk⟩ **2** to bring into the shore from the sea or a lake ⟨*a dead whale* washed up *on the beach*⟩ **3** to exhaust, finish **4** *Br* to wash (the dishes and utensils) after a meal – see also WASHING-UP

²**wash** *n* **1a** (an instance of) washing or being washed ⟨*doing the week's* ∼⟩ ⟨*car needs a* ∼⟩ **b washing, wash** articles, esp clothes, that have been or are to be washed **c** an area or structure equipped with facilities for washing a vehicle ⟨*a car* ∼⟩ **2** the surging action of waves **3a** a piece of ground (habitually)

washed by the sea or river **b** a bog, marsh **c** a shallow body of water **4a** worthless esp liquid waste; *also* swill **b** a thin tasteless beverage **c** vapid writing or speech **5a** a thin coat of paint (e g watercolour) **b** **wash drawing, wash** (a) drawing done mainly in washes of ink or watercolour **c** a thin liquid used for coating a surface (e g a wall) **6** an esp antiseptic or soothing lotion **7** loose or eroded surface material of the earth (e g rock debris) transported and deposited by running water **8a** BACKWASH (e g behind a boat) **b** a disturbance in the air produced by the passage of an aircraft – **come out in the wash 1** to become known in the course of time **2** to reach a satisfactory conclusion

**washable** /'woshəbl/ *adj* capable of being washed without damage – **washability** *n*

**wash and wear** *adj* of or being a fabric or garment that needs little or no ironing after washing

**washbasin** /'wosh,bays(ə)n/ *n* a basin or sink, usu connected to a water supply, for washing the hands and face

**washboard** /'wosh,bawd/ *n* **1** a broad plank fastened to and projecting above the side or foredeck of a small craft to keep out spray **2** a board that consists typically of a corrugated rectangular metal surface set into a wooden frame and that is used for scrubbing clothes when washing **3** *chiefly NAm* SKIRTING BOARD

**washbowl** /'wosh,bohl/ *n* a washbasin

**washcloth** /'wosh,kloth/ *n, NAm* a facecloth, flannel

**washday** /'wosh,day/ *n* a day set aside, esp regularly (e g once a week), for washing clothes, linen, etc

,**washed-'out** *adj* **1** faded in colour **2** *informal* depleted in vigour or animation; exhausted

,**washed-'up** *adj, informal* having failed or become no longer useful or effective; finished ⟨*all* ∼ *as a footballer at the age of 28*⟩

**washer** /'woshə/ *n* **1** one who or that which washes; *esp* WASHING MACHINE **2** a thin flat ring or perforated plate used in various mechanical joints and assemblies [(1) ME *wassher,* fr *wasshen* to wash + ²*-er;* (2) ME *whasher,* perh of different origin]

,**washer-'up** *n, chiefly Br informal* a person employed to wash up dishes and utensils

**washerwoman** /'woshə,woomən/ *also* **washwoman** /'wosh,-woomən/, *masc* **washerman** *also* **washman** /-mən/ *n* someone who washes clothes; *esp* one who takes in washing

**Washeteria** /,woshə'tiəri-ə/ *trademark* – used for a launderette

**wash-hand basin** *n, Br* a washbasin

**washhouse** /'wosh,hows/ *n* a building used or equipped for washing clothes

**washing** /'woshing/ *n* **1** the act of one who or that which washes **2** material (e g metal ore) obtained by washing **3** a thin covering or coat ⟨*a* ∼ *of silver*⟩ **4** WASH 1b (articles for washing)

**washing day** *n* washday

**washing machine** *n* a machine for washing; *esp* one for washing clothes and household linen

**washing soda** *n* a transparent crystalline compound of SODIUM CARBONATE chemically combined with water, $Na_2CO_3.10H_2O$, used esp as a household cleaning agent

,**washing-'up** *n, chiefly Br* **1** the act or process of washing dishes and utensils **2** the dishes and utensils to be washed after a meal ⟨*stack the* ∼⟩

**wash-leather** /'wosh,ledhə/ *n* a soft leather similar to CHAMOIS, prepared usu from sheepskin; *also* a piece of this used for washing things (e g windows)

**washman** /'woshmən/ *n* a washerman

**wash'n'wear** /,wosh(ə)n'weə/ *adj* WASH AND WEAR

**washout** /'wosh,owt/ *n* **1a** the washing out or away of something (e g a railway track or road) by a large amount of water **b** a place where something (e g earth) is washed away **2** a failure, fiasco

**washrag** /'wosh,rag/ *n, NAm* a facecloth, flannel

**washroom** /'wosh,roohm, -room/ *n* a room with facilities for washing; *also, chiefly NAm euph* a toilet

**washstand** /'wosh,stand/ *n* **1** a piece of furniture used, esp formerly, to hold articles (e g a basin and jug) needed for washing one's face and hands **2** a washbasin permanently set in place and attached to water and drainpipes

**washtub** /'wosh,tub/ *n* a tub in which clothes are washed or soaked

**washwoman** /'wosh,woomən/ *n* a washerwoman

**washy** /'woshi/ *adj* **1** weak, watery ⟨∼ *tea*⟩ **2** deficient in

colour; pallid **3** lacking in vigour, individuality, or definiteness
– **washiness** *n*

**wasn't** /'woznt/ was not

**wasp** /wosp/ *n* any of numerous largely flesh-eating insects
(order Hymenoptera) that live in colonies or alone, and typically have a slender body with a narrow waist attaching the
abdomen to the THORAX (middle body segment), a black or
dark-coloured body with conspicuous orange, red, or yellow
markings, and often an extremely painful sting; *esp* a very
common wasp (*Vespula vulgaris*) that lives in colonies and has
black and yellow stripes and a painful sting [ME *waspe*, fr OE
*wæps, wæsp;* akin to OHG *wafsa* wasp, L *vespa* wasp, OE *wefan*
to weave – more at WEAVE] – **wasplike** *adj*

**WASP, Wasp** /wosp/ *n* an American of N European, esp British, stock and of Protestant background; *esp* one in N America
considered to be a member of the dominating and the most
privileged class [*white Anglo-Saxon Protestant*] – **Waspish,
Waspy** *adj*

**waspish** /'wospish/ *adj* **1** snappish, petulant **2** resembling a
wasp in form; *esp* slightly built – **waspishly** *adv*, **waspish-
ness** *n*

**wasp waist** *n* a very slender waist – **wasp-waisted** *adj*

¹**wassail** /'wosayl/ *n* **1** an early English toast to someone's
health **2** a drink made of spiced ale or wine and often baked
apples, and served in a large bowl, esp formerly, at Christmas
and other festive occasions **3** *archaic* riotous drinking; revelry
[ME *wæs hæil*, fr ON *ves heill* be well, fr *ves* (imper sing. of
*vera* to be) + *heill* healthy – more at WAS, WHOLE]

²**wassail** *vi* **1** to hold a wassail; carouse **2** *dial Eng* to sing
carols from house to house at Christmas ∼ *vt* to drink to the
health or prosperity of

**wassail bowl** *n* a bowl from which wassail is served

**wassailer** /'wosaylə/ *n* **1** someone who carouses; a reveller **2**
*archaic* someone who goes about singing carols

**Wassermann test, Wassermann** /'vahsəmən, 'wahsəmən/ *n*
a test for the detection of syphilis that uses the COMPLEMENT
FIXATION technique to indicate the presence or absence in
the blood of the specific ANTIBODY produced by the body in
response to infection by the syphilis bacterium

**wast** /wɒst, wəst/ *archaic past 2 sing of* BE

**wastage** /'waystij/ *n* **1a** loss, decrease, or destruction of something (eg by use, decay, erosion, or leakage); *esp* wasteful or
avoidable loss of something valuable **b** waste, refuse **2** reduction or loss in numbers (eg of employees or students), usu
caused by individuals leaving or retiring voluntarily – esp in
*natural wastage*

¹**waste** /wayst/ *n* **1a** a sparsely settled, barren, or devastated
region; a desert **b** uncultivated land **c** a broad and empty expanse (eg of water) **2** wasting or being wasted ⟨*it's a ∼ of
time trying to tell her anything*⟩ **3** gradual loss or decrease by
use, wear, or decay **4a** discarded or unusable material ⟨*there's
no ∼ on this joint*⟩ **b(1)** damaged, defective, or superfluous
material produced by a manufacturing process **b(2)** material
rejected during a textile manufacturing process and used usu
for wiping away dirt and oil ⟨*cotton ∼*⟩ **c** human or animal
refuse; *esp* excrement **d** material derived by mechanical and
chemical weathering of the land and moved down sloping
surfaces or carried by streams to the sea **5** damage to or neglect
of property (eg houses or land) by a temporary or life tenant
to the detriment of the person who will eventually inherit it
[ME *waste, wast;* (1), fr ONF *wast*, fr *wast*, adj, desolate, waste,
fr L *vastus;* akin to OHG *wuosti* desolate, waste, L *vanus*
empty; (2-5), fr ME *wasten* to waste – more at WANE] – **go to
waste** to be squandered or wasted

²**waste** *vt* **1** to lay waste; devastate ⟨*land ∼d by strip-mining*⟩
**2** to cause to be reduced in physical bulk or strength; emaciate,
enfeeble **3a** to wear away gradually; consume **b** to dispose of
as waste **4** to spend or use carelessly or inefficiently; squander
⟨*you're wasting your time trying to tell her anything*⟩ **5** *NAm
slang* to murder ∼ *vi* **1** to lose weight, strength, substance, or
vitality – often + *away* **2** to become consumed gradually and
esp wastefully **3** to spend money or consume property extravagantly or improvidently – see also **waste one's** BREATH [ME
*wasten*, fr ONF *waster*, fr L *vastare*, fr *vastus* desolate, waste]

³**waste** *adj* **1a(1)** wild, uninhabited, desolate **a(2)** arid, empty
**b** not cultivated or used; not productive ⟨∼ *energy*⟩ **2** ruined,
devastated **3** discarded as refuse ⟨∼ *material*⟩ **4** serving to
conduct or hold refuse material [ME *waste, wast*, fr ONF
*wast*]

**wastebasket** /'wayst,bahskit/ *n* WASTEPAPER BASKET

**waste bin** *n, Br* a container for refuse, esp from a kitchen;
*also* WASTEPAPER BASKET

**wasted** /'waystid/ *adj* **1** laid waste; ravaged **2** impaired in
strength or health; emaciated **3** unprofitably used, made, or
expended ⟨∼ *effort*⟩

**wasteful** /'waystf(ə)l/ *adj* given to or marked by waste; lavish,
prodigal – **wastefully** *adv*, **wastefulness** *n*

**waste ground** *n* devastated or barely inhabitable land

**wasteland** /'waystland, -lənd/ *n* **1** a barren or uncultivated
area ⟨*a desert ∼*⟩ **2** an ugly often devastated or barely inhabitable place or area **3** something (eg a way of life) that is
spiritually and emotionally arid and unsatisfying

**wastepaper** /,wayst'paypə/ *n* paper discarded as used,
unwanted, or not fit for use

**wastepaper basket** *n* an open-topped receptacle for small
amounts of dry usu household or office refuse, esp wastepaper

**waste pipe** *n* a pipe for carrying off waste fluid – compare
SOIL PIPE

**waste product** *n* **1** an item of debris resulting from a process
(eg of manufacture) and of no further use to the system producing it **2** material (eg urine) that is formed as a by-product
of the life-supporting processes of a living organism and discharged from or stored in an inert form in the organism

**waster** /'waystə/ *n* **1a(1)** someone who spends or consumes
extravagantly or dissolutely without thought for the future **a(2)**
a good-for-nothing, idler **b** one who or that which causes or
permits the specified form of waste ⟨*a procedure that is a ∼ of
time*⟩ **2** an imperfect or inferior manufactured article or object
**3** one who or that which lays waste; a destroyer ⟨*have created
the ∼ to destroy* – Isa 54:16 (AV)⟩

**wasting** /'waysting/ *adj* **1** undergoing gradual wastage ⟨*a ∼
resource*⟩ **2** undergoing or causing decay or loss of strength
⟨∼ *diseases such as tuberculosis*⟩ – **wastingly** *adv*

**wastrel** /'waystrəl/ *n* **1** a vagabond, waif **2** WASTER 1a [²*waste*
+ *-rel* (as in *scoundrel*)]

¹**watch** /woch/ *vi* **1a** to keep vigil as an act of devotion **b** to
be deliberately awake during the night ⟨∼ *by his bedside*⟩ **2a**
to be attentive or vigilant; wait *for* ⟨∼ed *for a chance to get
her revenge*⟩ **b** to keep guard ⟨∼ *over their flocks*⟩ **3** to be
closely observant of an event or action; look attentively ∼ *vt*
**1** to keep under protective guard **2a** to observe closely, esp in
order to check on action or change ⟨*he's being ∼ed by the
police*⟩ **b** to keep one's eyes fixed on; observe ⟨∼ed *the train
till it moved off*⟩ **c** to look at (an event or moving scene); view
⟨∼ *television*⟩ **3a** to take care of; tend ⟨∼ *the baby*⟩ **b** to be
careful of ⟨∼es *his diet*⟩ **c** to take care that ⟨∼ *you don't spill
it*⟩ **4** to be on the alert for; bide ⟨∼ed *his opportunity*⟩ [ME
*wacchen*, fr OE *wæccan* – more at WAKE] – **watch it** to be
careful; LOOK OUT – usu imper – see also **watch one's** STEP
**watch out** *vi* to be vigilant; LOOK OUT – often + *for*
**watch over** *vt* to have charge of; superintend

²**watch** *n* **1a** the act of keeping awake or alert to guard,
protect, or attend ⟨*kept ∼ by his bed* – Robert Browning⟩ **b** a
wake for a dead person **c** a state of alert and continuous attention; a lookout ⟨*always on the ∼*⟩ ⟨*keep a ∼ for the train*⟩
**d** close observation; surveillance ⟨*kept careful ∼ on the
prisoner*⟩ **2a** any of the definite divisions of the night made
by ancient peoples **b** *usu pl* a wakeful interval during the night
⟨*the silent ∼es of the night*⟩ **3a** someone who watches; a lookout, watchman **b** *taking sing or pl vb* a body of sentinels or
watchmen; *specif* those formerly assigned to patrol the streets
of a town at night, announce the hours, and act as police **4a(1)**
a period of time during which a part of a ship's company is on
duty while another part rests **a(2)** *taking sing or pl vb* the part
of a ship's company on duty during a particular watch **a(3)** a
sailor's period of duty **b** a period of keeping guard **5** a small
portable timepiece powered esp by a spring or a battery and
usu worn on the wrist or carried in the pocket – compare
CLOCK – **on the watch** keeping watch; ON THE ALERT

**watchable** /'wochəbl/ *adj* worth watching

**watch and ward** *n* continuous unbroken vigilance and guard

'**watch-,case** *n* the outside metal case covering the mechanism
of a watch

**watch committee** *n* a British local government committee
that formerly supervised police discipline and public order

**watchdog** /'woch,dog/ *n* **1** a dog kept to guard property **2** a
person or organization (eg a committee) that guards against
loss, waste, theft, or undesirable practices

**watcher** /'wochə/ *n* one who or that which watches; *esp* a
watchman

**watch fire** *n* a fire lit, esp at night, as a signal or for the use of a guard

**watchful** /'wochf(ə)l/ *adj* **1** carefully observant or attentive; on the watch **2** *archaic* wakeful – **watchfully** *adv*, **watchfulness** *n*

**watchglass** /'woch,glahs/ *n* a transparent cover protecting the face of a watch

**watching brief** /'woching/ *n* instructions to a barrister to observe the progress of a case on behalf of one not directly involved in it; *broadly* observation of any proceedings or series of events on behalf of another

**watchmaking** /'woch,mayking/ *n* the making or repairing of watches or clocks – **watchmaker** *n*

**watchman** /'wochmən/ *n* someone who keeps watch; a guard

**watch night** *n* a devotional service lasting until after midnight, esp on New Year's Eve

**watch pocket** *n* a small pocket just below the front waistband of a man's trousers

**watchstrap** /'woch,strap/ *n* the strap or bracelet of a wrist-watch

**watchtower** /'woch,towə/ *n* a tower for a lookout

**watchword** /'woch,wuhd/ *n* **1** a word or phrase used as a sign of recognition among members of the same group – compare PASSWORD **2** a motto that embodies a guiding principle; a slogan

**¹water** /'wawtə/ *n* **1a** the colourless odourless tasteless liquid that falls from the clouds as rain, forms streams, lakes, and seas, and is a major constituent of all living matter. It is an oxide of hydrogen, $H_2O$, that freezes at 0°C and boils at 100°C, is at its densest at 4°C, and is a poor conductor of electricity and a good solvent. **b waters** *pl*, **water** a natural mineral water ⟨*went to Bath to take the* ~s⟩ **2a(1)** *pl* the water occupying or flowing in a particular bed ⟨*the* ~s *of the Nile*⟩ **a(2)** *chiefly Br* a body of water; a lake or river – often used in place-names ⟨*Hawes* Water⟩ ⟨*Derwent* water⟩ **b** a depth of water ⟨*in three feet of* ~⟩ **c(1)** *pl* a stretch of sea abutting on the land of a specified sovereignty and under the control of that sovereignty ⟨*in Soviet* ~s⟩ **c(2) waters** *pl*, **water** the sea of a specified part of the earth ⟨*in tropical* ~s⟩ **d** a water supply ⟨*threatened to turn off the* ~⟩ **3** travel or transport on water ⟨*we went by* ~⟩ **4a** the level of water at a specified state of the tide – compare HIGH WATER, LOW WATER **b** the surface of the water ⟨*swam under* ~⟩ **5** liquid containing or resembling water: eg **5a(1)** a medicinal or cosmetic preparation made with water ⟨*rose* ~⟩ – compare TOILET WATER **a(2)** a solution of a gaseous or readily vaporized substance in water – compare AMMONIA WATER **b(1)** a watery liquid (eg tears, urine, or sap) formed in and secreted from, or circulating in a living body **b(2) waters** *pl*, **water** the watery liquid (AMNIOTIC fluid) surrounding a foetus in the womb ⟨*the* ~s *sometimes break before labour begins*⟩ **6a** the clarity and lustre of a precious stone, esp a diamond **b** degree of excellence ⟨*a scholar of the first* ~⟩ **c** a wavy lustrous pattern (eg of a textile) **7** *archaic* a distilled liquid (eg an essence); *esp* a distilled alcoholic liquor [ME, fr OE *wæteri*; akin to OHG *wazzar* water, Gk *hydōr*, L *unda* wave (cf HYDR-, OTTER, UNDULATE, VODKA, WASH, WET)] – **fish in troubled waters** to try to take advantage of difficult circumstances or of the misfortunes of others – **hold water** to stand up under criticism or analysis – **in deep water** in difficulty or distress; unable to manage – **pass water** *euph* to urinate – **tread water** to keep the body nearly upright in water and the head above water by a treading motion of the feet, usu aided by the hands – **water under the bridge** past events which it is futile to try to alter – see also go **through** FIRE **and water**, FISH **out of water**, **keep one's** HEAD **above water**, **pour** OIL **on troubled waters**

**²water** *vt* **1** to moisten, sprinkle, or soak with water; *esp* to provide (growing plants) with water ⟨~ *the garden*⟩ **2a** to supply with water for drink ⟨~ *the horses*⟩ **b** to supply water to ⟨~ *a ship*⟩ **3** to be a source of water for ⟨*land* ~ed *by the Thames*⟩ **4** to treat (as if) with water; *specif* to impart a lustrous appearance and wavy pattern to (cloth) by CALENDERING (pressing between rollers or plates) ⟨~ed *silk*⟩ **5a** to dilute (as if) by the addition of water ⟨~ *the programme to suit the Radicals – The Times*⟩ – often + *down* ⟨~ *down the punch*⟩ **b** to add to the aggregate PAR VALUE (monetary value assigned to each share of stock) of (securities of a company) by the issue of more stock without a corresponding addition to the assets represented by this stock ~ *vi* **1** to form or secrete water or watery matter (eg tears or saliva) **2** to get or take water: eg **2a** to take on a supply of water **b** *of an animal* to drink water – **waterer** *n*

**water in** *vt* to water (a plant or seed) immediately after planting, esp to settle the surrounding soil

**water bag** *n* BAG OF WATERS (liquid-filled sac enclosing a foetus in the womb)

**water bailiff** *n*, *Br* an official employed to enforce bylaws relating to angling and waters used for angling

**Water Bearer** *n* AQUARIUS 1,2a (constellation and sign of the zodiac)

**water bed** *n* a bed with a water-filled plastic or rubber mattress

**water beetle** *n* any of numerous oval flattened aquatic beetles (esp family Dytiscidae) that swim by means of their fringed hind legs which act together as oars

**waterbird** /'watə,buhd/ *n* a bird that frequents or lives on or near water: eg **a** a swimming bird ⟨*rose* ~⟩ **b** WADING BIRD

**water biscuit** *n* a unsweetened biscuit made with flour and water

**water blister** *n* a blister containing a clear watery liquid but no pus or blood

**water bloom** *n* an accumulation of algae, esp BLUE-GREEN ALGAE, at or near the surface of a body of water; *also* an alga that forms this

**water boatman** *n* **1** any of various WATER BUGS (family Corixidae) with a flattened cylindrical body that live esp on the bottom of ponds and swim using their hair-fringed hind legs as paddles **2** BACK SWIMMER (WATER BUG that swims on its back)

**water bomb** *n* a bag of water thrown at someone, usu as a sign of contempt

**waterborne** /'wawtə,bawn/ *adj* supported or carried by water ⟨~ *commerce*⟩ ⟨~ *infection*⟩

**water bottle** *n* a container (eg of glass, leather, or plastic) for carrying or holding drinking water

**water brush** *n* a brush with soft bristles used esp for dampening a horse's mane and tail and washing its feet and legs

**waterbuck** /'wawtə,buk/ *n*, *pl* **waterbucks**, *esp collectively* **waterbuck** any of various African antelopes that commonly live in herds near streams or wet areas; *esp* either of two large shaggy-haired African antelopes (*Kobus ellipsiprynmus* and *Kobus defassa*)

**water buffalo** *n* an often domesticated Asian buffalo (*Bubalus bubalis*) with large horns

**water bug** *n* any of various small insects (eg the WATER BOATMAN) adapted to living on or under the surface of water

**water bus** *n* a passenger boat operating according to a time-table, esp on a river or lake

**water butt** *n* a cask for catching and storing rainwater

**water caltrop** *n* WATER CHESTNUT 1

**water cannon** *n* a device for shooting out a jet of water with great force (eg to disperse a crowd)

**water carrier** *n* **1** a container for carrying water in **2** *cap W&C* AQUARIUS 1,2a (constellation and sign of the zodiac)

**water cart** *n* a cart or truck equipped with a tank or barrels for hauling or sprinkling water

**water chestnut** *n* **1** any of a genus (*Trapa*, esp *Trapa natans*, of the family Trapaceae, the water-chestnut family) of white-flowered aquatic plants with floating leaves arranged in a rosette and narrow rootlike submerged leaves; *also* the edible nutlike spiny-angled fruit of a water chestnut **2** any of several Asian, esp Chinese, sedges (esp *Eleocharis tuberosa*) that have edible enlarged underground stems (TUBERS) for food storage; *also* the tuber of such a sedge, commonly used in Chinese cookery

**water clock** *n* an instrument designed to measure time by the fall or flow of a quantity of water

**water closet** *also* **closet** *n* **1** a toilet with a bowl that can be flushed with water **2** a room, compartment, or building containing a water closet

**watercolour** /'wawtə,kulə/ *n* **1** a paint made from pigment mixed with water rather than oil **2** the art or method of painting with watercolours **3** a picture or design painted in water-colours

**water-,cool** *vt* to cool by means of water, esp circulating water (eg in a WATER JACKET or radiator)

**watercourse** /'wawtə,kaws/ *n* **1** a natural or man-made channel through which water flows or may flow **2** a stream of water (eg a river, brook, or underground stream)

**watercraft** /'wawtə,krahft/ *n*, *pl* **watercraft** **1** skill in aquatic activities (eg handling boats) **2** a ship, boat, or other vessel for water transport

**watercress** /'wawtə‚kres/ n any of several cresses (esp genus *Rorippa*) that grow in wet places; *esp* either of two cresses (*Rorippa nasturtium-aquaticum* and *Rorippa microphylla X nasturtium aquaticum*) widely grown for their peppery-flavoured dark green leaves used in salads

**water crowfoot** n CROWFOOT 1 (water plant of the buttercup family); *esp* a crowfoot (*Ranunculus aquatilis*) with small white flowers and deeply lobed leaves that float on the surface of the water

**'water-di‚viner** n, *chiefly Br* some who searches for water using a DIVINING ROD (forked rod believed to dip down to indicate presence of water, minerals, etc)

**water dog** n a dog accustomed to the water and usu trained to retrieve waterfowl

**water dropwort** n any of several mostly poisonous European plants (genus *Oenanthe*, esp *Oenanthe fistulosa*) of the carrot family, that resemble COW PARSLEY, have fernlike leaves and umbrella-shaped clusters of small white flowers, and grow in ditches and other wet places – compare DROPWORT

**‚watered-'down** adj modified or reduced in force or effectiveness ⟨a ~ version of the original⟩

**waterer** /'wawtərə/ n one who or that which waters; *esp* a device used for supplying water to livestock and poultry

**waterfall** /'wawtə‚fawl/ n **1a** a perpendicular or very steep descent of the water of a stream **b** an artificial waterfall (e g in a hotel lobby or nightclub) **2** something resembling a waterfall ⟨churned out ~s of ballad singles – Story of Pop⟩

**'water-‚finder** n, *chiefly NAm* a water-diviner

**water flea** n any of various small active dark or brightly coloured aquatic INVERTEBRATE animals (of the group Entomostraca, class Crustacea): e g **a** a daphnia **b** a cyclops

**¹waterflood** /'wawtə‚flud/ vi to pump water into the ground round an oil well in order to loosen and force out oil

**²waterflood** n the process of waterflooding an oil well

**waterfowl** /'wawtə‚fowl/ n, pl **waterfowls**, esp collectively **waterfowl 1** a bird that frequents water; *esp* a duck or similar bird that swims on water **2** pl swimming game birds collectively (e g duck), as distinguished from upland game birds (e g grouse) and shorebirds

**waterfowler** /'wawtə‚fowlə/ n a hunter of waterfowl

**waterfront** /'wawtə‚frunt/ n land, land with buildings, or a section of a town fronting or abutting on a body of water

**water gap** n a pass in a mountain ridge through which a stream runs

**water garden** n a (section of a) garden containing a pond or stream, and often with features such as fountains and artificial waterfalls, that is devoted to water plants, marsh plants, ornamental fish, etc – **water gardening** n

**water gas** n a poisonous inflammable gaseous mixture consisting chiefly of CARBON MONOXIDE and hydrogen, that is usu made by blowing air and then steam over red-hot coke or coal and is used esp as a fuel

**water gate** n **1** a gate giving access to a body of water **2** a floodgate

**water gauge** n an instrument to measure or find the depth or quantity of water, or to indicate the height of its surface, esp in a STEAM BOILER; *also* pressure expressed in terms of the depth of water

**water glass** n **1** an instrument consisting of an open box or tube with a glass bottom, used for examining objects in or under water **2** a sticky syrupy solution of sodium or potassium silicate that is used esp as a cement, as a protective coating and fireproofing agent, and in preserving eggs **3** WATER GAUGE

**water gum** n any of various GUM TREES that grow on wet or swampy land; *esp* one (*Nyssa aquatica*) of the S USA

**water hammer** n (the sound of) a violent shaking or agitation of a moving liquid or gas (e g water or steam) against the sides of a containing pipe or vessel

**water hazard** n an open watercourse (e g a pond or ditch) on a golf course

**water heater** n an apparatus for heating water; *esp* an apparatus (e g in a kitchen or bathroom) that makes available an instant supply of hot water for domestic use by heating cold water as it flows from a storage tank

**water hemlock** n COWBANE (poisonous plant of the carrot family)

**water hen** n any of various aquatic birds (e g a coot or moorhen) related to the RAILS

**water hole** n **1** a natural hole or hollow containing water **2** a hole in a surface of ice

**water hyacinth** n a tropical American floating aquatic plant (*Eichhornia crassipes* of the family Pontederiaceae) with spikes of large showy blue flowers, that grows in dense masses and often clogs waterways

**water ice** n a frozen dessert of water, sugar, and flavouring

**watering** /'wawtəring/ n an application of water to a growing plant

**watering can** /'wawt(ə)ring/ n a vessel with a handle and a long spout often fitted with a perforated head (ROSE 2c), used for watering plants

**watering hole** n **1** a pool or water-filled depression where animals come to drink **2** *humorous* a pub, hotel, or other place used, esp habitually, for convivial drinking

**watering place** n **1** a place where water may be obtained; *esp* one where animals, esp livestock, come to drink **2** a health or recreational resort featuring mineral springs or bathing; *esp* a spa

**watering pot** n, *chiefly NAm* WATERING CAN

**waterish** /'wawtərish/ adj somewhat watery – **waterishness** n

**water jacket** n an outer casing that holds water or through which water circulates to cool the interior; *specif* the enclosed space surrounding the cylinder block of an INTERNAL-COMBUSTION ENGINE and containing the cooling liquid

**water jump** n an obstacle (e g in a steeplechase) consisting of a pool, stream, or ditch of water

**waterless** /'wawtələs/ adj **1** lacking or devoid of water; dry **2** not requiring water (e g for cooling or cooking) – **waterlessly** adv, **waterlessness** n

**water level** n **1** an instrument used to indicate whether something is flat or horizontal by means of the surface of water in a trough or in a U-shaped tube **2** the surface of still water: e g **2a** the level assumed by the surface of a particular body or column of water **b** WATER TABLE

**water lily** n any of a family (Nymphaeaceae, the water-lily family) of aquatic plants with typically large leaves that float on the surface of the water and usu showy flowers

**waterline** /'wawtə‚lien/ n the level on the hull of a vessel to which the surface of the water comes when it is afloat and not leaning to one side; *also* any of several lines marked on the hull to correspond with this level

**waterlogged** /'wawtə‚logd/ adj so filled or soaked with water as to be heavy, useless, or hard to manage ⟨~ boats⟩ ⟨~ soil⟩ [¹water + log (to cause to become like a log)] – **waterlog** vt

**waterloo** /‚wawtə'looh/ n, pl **waterloos** often cap a decisive defeat [*Waterloo*, village in Belgium, scene of Napoleon's defeat by British & Prussian armies in 1815]

**water main** n a pipe or conduit for conveying water

**waterman** /'wawtəmən/ n **1** a man who lives and works mostly in or near water; *esp* a boatman whose boat and services are available for hire **2** a man who engages in water recreations

**watermanship** /'wawtəmənship/ n the business, skill, or art of a waterman or of one who engages in water sports; *esp* ability or expertise in rowing or swimming

**¹watermark** /'wawtə‚mahk/ n **1** a mark indicating the height to which water has risen **2** a marking in paper resulting from differences in thickness, usu produced by a projecting design in the mould or on a processing roll, and visible when the paper is held up to the light; *also* the design or the metal pattern producing the marking

**²watermark** vt **1** to mark (paper) with a watermark **2** to impress (a design) as a watermark

**water meadow** n a meadow of rich lush grass kept moist and fertile by a regular influx of water (e g from the periodic flooding of a bordering river)

**watermelon** /'wawtə‚melən/ n **1** a large oblong or roundish melon with a hard green or white often striped or variegated rind, a sweet watery pink, yellowish, or red pulp, and many seeds **2** a widely cultivated African climbing plant (*Citrullus lanatus*) of the marrow family that bears watermelons

**water milfoil** /'milfoyl/ n any of a genus (*Myriophyllum* of the family Haloragaceae) of aquatic plants with whorls of feathery much divided submerged leaves

**water mill** n a mill whose machinery is moved by water

**water moccasin, moccasin** n a venomous semiaquatic snake (*Agkistrodon piscivorus*) of the PIT VIPER family, that occurs in marshes and swamps in the southern USA

**water nymph** n a nymph (e g a NAIAD or NEREID) associated with a body of water

**water oak** n any of numerous American oaks that thrive in wet soils; *esp* one (*Quercus nigra*) of the southeastern USA

**water of crystallization** *n* WATER OF HYDRATION that is chemically combined in the structure of many crystallized substances and that is usu essential for the maintenance of a particular crystal structure

**water of hydration** *n* water that occurs chemically combined with a substance to form a HYDRATE (compound formed by union of water with another substance) and can be expelled (e g by heating) without essentially altering the composition of the substance

**water ouzel** /'oohzl/ *n* the European DIPPER (diving bird)

**water parting** *n, chiefly NAm* WATERSHED 1 (boundary separating the drainage areas of two rivers)

**water pepper** *n* a plant (*Polygonum hydropiper*) of the dock family that grows in wet places and has greenish or pink flowers, peppery-tasting seeds, and extremely acrid peppery juice

**water pipe** *n* 1 a pipe for conveying water 2 a large chiefly oriental smoking apparatus that functions as a type of pipe and consists of a bowl mounted on a vessel of water through which smoke from burning plant material (e g tobacco) in the bowl is drawn and thus cooled before reaching the mouth

**water pistol** *n* a toy pistol designed to shoot a jet of liquid

**water plantain** *n* any of a genus (*Alisma*, esp *Alisma plantago-aquatica* of the family Alismataceae, the water-plantain family) of marsh or aquatic plants with whitish, pink, or pale lilac flowers and acrid juice

**water polo** *n* a game played in water by teams of seven swimmers using a ball resembling a soccer ball that is thrown or dribbled with the object of putting it into a goal

**waterpower** /'wawtə,powə/ *n* 1 the power derived from movement of a body of water 2 a fall of water suitable for use as power

¹**waterproof** /'wawtə,proohf/ *adj* impervious to water; *esp* covered or treated with a material (e g a solution of rubber) to prevent permeation by water – **waterproofness** *n*

²**waterproof** *n* (a garment made of) waterproof fabric

³**waterproof** *vt* to make waterproof – **waterproofer** *n*

**waterproofing** /'wawtə,proohfing/ *n* **1a** the act or process of making something waterproof **b** the condition of being made waterproof **2** something (e g a coating) capable of imparting waterproofness

**water rail** *n* a Eurasian RAIL (type of marsh bird) (*Rallus aquaticus*) that has olive-brown upperparts, conspicuous black and white bars on the flanks, and a long red bill

**water rat** *n* a rodent that frequents water; *esp* WATER VOLE

**water rate** *n* the charge made to a British householder for the use of the public water supply

'**water-re,pellent** *adj* treated with a finish that is resistant but not impervious to penetration by water

'**water-re,sistent** *adj* WATER-REPELLENT

**water right** *n* a right to the use of water (e g for irrigation); *esp* RIPARIAN RIGHT (right of one owning land by a natural watercourse)

**water sapphire** *n* a deep blue variety of the mineral CORDIERITE sometimes used as a gem

**water scorpion** *n* any of numerous WATER BUGS (family Nepidae) that have the end of the body extended into a long tube through which they breathe air from above the surface of the water

**watershed** /'wawtə,shed/ *n* **1** a boundary line (e g a ridge) dividing and separating the areas of ground whose water is drained by two streams, rivers, etc **2** a crucial dividing point or line ⟨*Culloden was a ~ in Scottish history – Scottish Field*⟩ **3** *chiefly NAm* a region or area bounded by a watershed and draining ultimately to a particular watercourse or body of water

**water shrew** *n* a comparatively large semiaquatic European shrew (*Neomys fodiens*)

¹**waterside** /'wawtə,sied/ *n* the margin of a body of water; a waterfront

²**waterside** *adj* **1** of or located on the waterside ⟨*a ~ café*⟩ **2** employed along the waterside ⟨*~ workers*⟩; *also* of the workers along the waterside ⟨*a ~ strike*⟩

**watersider** /'wawtə,siedə/ *n, Austr & NZ* a docker

**water ski** *n* a board used singly or in pairs for standing on and planing over water while being towed at speed by a usu hand-held line from a powerboat – **water-ski** *vi*, **water-skier** *n*

**water-skiing** /'wawtə,skee·ing/ *n* the art or sport of planing and jumping on water skis

**water sky** *n* a dark appearance of the sky at the horizon when

seen over a body of open water from snow or ice-covered land, due to the fact that water reflects light less than ice or snow

**water snake** *n* any of numerous snakes (esp genus *Natrix*) that frequent or inhabit fresh waters and feed largely on aquatic animals

'**water-,softener** *n* a substance or device for softening hard water by removing the substances, esp calcium or magnesium, that make it hard, from solution

**water spaniel** *n* (any of) a breed of rather large spaniel that has a heavy curly coat and is used esp for retrieving waterfowl

**water spider** *n* a European spider (*Argyroneta aquatica*) that lives under the water in a bell-shaped web filled with air carried down by the spider in the form of small bubbles

**watersplash** /'wawtə,splash/ *n* a stretch of road submerged by water

**waterspout** /'wawtə,spowt/ *n* **1** a pipe, duct, or orifice from which water is spouted or through which it is carried **2** a funnel-shaped or tubular column of rotating cloud-filled wind usu extending from the underside of a CUMULUS or CUMULONIMBUS (large billowy) cloud down to a cloud of spray torn up by the whirling winds from the surface of an ocean or lake *synonyms* see WHIRLWIND

**water sprite** *n* a sprite believed to inhabit or haunt water; WATER NYMPH

**water sprout** *n* a rapidly growing but usu unproductive shoot from a bud on the trunk or a main branch of a tree

**water strider** *n* POND SKATER (long-legged insect that skims over the surface of water)

**water supply** *n* the source, means, or process of supplying water (e g to a town or house), usu including reservoirs, tunnels, and pipelines

**water system** *n* a river with its tributaries

**water table** *n* the level below which the ground is wholly and permanently saturated with water

**watertight** /'wawtə,tiet/ *adj* **1** of such tight construction or fit as to be impermeable to water **2** leaving no possibility of misconstruction or evasion; having no loopholes ⟨*a ~ lease*⟩; *esp, of an argument* impossible to disprove **3** isolated from other ideas, influences, etc; discrete ⟨*experiences can't be divided into ~ compartments*⟩ – **watertightness** *n*

**water tower** *n* **1** a tower supporting a raised water tank to provide the steady pressure necessary for a piped water supply **2** a fire-fighting apparatus that can supply water at various heights and at great pressure

**water vapour** *n* water in the form of vapour, esp when below boiling temperature and diffused (e g in the atmosphere)

**water-vascular system** /,wawtə'vaskyoolə/ *n* a system of vessels in starfishes, SEA URCHINS, and related animals, that contains a circulating watery liquid and provides the mechanism for the movement of tentacles and TUBE FEET (organs of locomotion), and may also function in excretion and respiration

**water vole** *n* a common large vole of W Europe (*Arvicola amphibius*) that lives in holes that it digs in river banks

**water wagon** *n, chiefly NAm* WATER CART (cart or truck equipped for hauling water)

**water wave** *n* a wave set in the hair by dampening it with water prior to forming it into waves – **water-waved** *adj*

**waterway** /'wawtə,way/ *n* **1a** a navigable way or channel for water; a canal **b** a route for water traffic **2** a groove at the edge of a ship's deck for draining the deck **3** a navigable body of water

**waterweed** /'wawtə,weed/ *n* any of various aquatic plants (e g a pondweed) with inconspicuous flowers

**waterwheel** /'wawtə,weel/ *n* **1** a wheel powered by flowing water and usu used to drive machinery: **1a** an OVERSHOT waterwheel **b** an UNDERSHOT waterwheel **2** a wheel for raising water by means of buckets, scoops, etc attached to its rim

**water wings** *n pl* an air-filled float, thin in the middle and ballooning at either end, worn across the chest and projecting under the arms to provide support for someone learning to swim; *also* either of a pair of floats worn round the upper arm to provide support and buoyancy

**water witch** *n, NAm* a dowser, water-diviner – **water witching** *n*

**waterworks** /'wawtə,wuhks/ *n pl* **1** an ornamental fountain or cascade **2a** the system of reservoirs, channels, mains, and pumping and purifying equipment by which a water supply is obtained and distributed (e g to a city) **b** *taking sing vb* a building or establishment for pumping or purifying water **3**

*informal* the shedding of tears; tears ⟨*no need to turn on the ~ just because you can't have your own way*⟩ **4** *chiefly Br euph* the urinary system

**waterworn** /ˈwawtəˌwawn/ *adj* worn, smoothed, or polished by the action of water

**watery** /ˈwawt(ə)ri/ *adj* **1a** consisting of or filled with water **b** containing, sodden with, secreting, or yielding water or a thin liquid ⟨*a ~ solution*⟩ ⟨*~ vesicles*⟩ **2a** resembling or suggesting water or watery matter, esp in thin fluidity, soggy texture, paleness, tearfulness, or lack of flavour ⟨*~ blood*⟩ ⟨*~ sunlight*⟩ ⟨*a ~ soup*⟩ **b** vapid, wishy-washy ⟨*a ~ writing style*⟩ – **waterily** *adv*, **wateriness** *n*

**Watson-Crick** /ˌwots(ə)n ˈkrik/ *adj* of or conforming with the WATSON-CRICK MODEL of DNA ⟨*guanine. . . involved in a ~ base pair – Nature*⟩

**Watson-Crick model** /ˌwots(ə)n ˈkrik/ *n* a model of the structure of a molecule of DNA in which the molecule is visualized as a DOUBLE HELIX consisting of two parallel spirally wound strands linked together by HYDROGEN BONDS (weak chemical bonds between atoms of a molecule) [J D *Watson* b 1928 US biologist and F H C *Crick* b 1916 E biologist]

**watt** /wot/ *n* the SI unit of power equal to the expenditure of 1 joule of energy in 1 second or to the electrical power required for 1 amp of current to flow across a POTENTIAL DIFFERENCE of 1 volt [James *Watt* †1819 Sc engineer]

**wattage** /ˈwotij/ *n* amount of power expressed in watts; *esp* the amount of electrical power required by an appliance

**Watteau** /ˈwotow/ *adj* **1** *of a woman's dress* having back pleats falling loosely from neckline to hem **2** *of a hat* shallow-crowned with a wide brim turned up at the back to hold flower trimmings [Antoine *Watteau* †1721 Fr painter]

**watt-hour** /ˈwotˌowə/ *n* a unit of work or energy equivalent to the power of 1 watt operating for 1 hour

¹**wattle** /ˈwotl/ *n* **1a** a framework of poles interwoven with slender branches or reeds and used formerly in building and for making fences, hurdles, etc **b** material for such construction **c** *pl* poles laid on a roof to support thatch **2a** a loose fleshy protuberance or fold of skin hanging from the head, neck, or throat (eg of a bird or reptile) **b** ²BARBEL (slender sensitive projection on the lip of a fish) **3** *Austr* an acacia tree or shrub [ME *wattel*, fr OE *watel;* akin to OHG *wadal* bandage; (2) perh of different origin] – **wattled** *adj*

²**wattle** *vt* **1** to form or build of or with wattle **2a** to form into wattle; interlace to form wattle **b** to unite or make solid by interweaving light flexible material

**wattle and daub** /ˈdawb/ *n* a framework of woven rods and twigs covered and plastered with clay and used, esp formerly, in building

**wattmeter** /ˈwotˌmeetə/ *n* an instrument for measuring electrical power in watts [ISV]

**Watutsi** /wəˈtootsi/ *n, pl* **Watutsis**, *esp collectively* **Watutsi** a member of a tall Negro people of Rwanda and Burundi in central Africa

**waul** /wawl/ *vi* to howl, wail, or cry like a cat or newborn baby [imit] – **waul** *n*

¹**wave** /wayv/ *vi* **1** to flutter loosely to and fro ⟨*flags waving in the breeze*⟩ **2** to give a signal or salute by moving the hand or something held in it ⟨*~d to them cheerily*⟩ **3** to become flourished or brandished to and fro ⟨*his sword ~d and flashed*⟩ **4** to sway in the wind with a wavelike motion ⟨*field of waving grain*⟩ **5** to follow a curving line or take a wavy form; undulate ~ *vt* **1** to cause to swing to and fro **2a** to direct by waving; flag, signal ⟨*looked at his papers, then ~d him on*⟩ ⟨*~ the car to a halt*⟩ **b** to gesture with (the hand or an object) in greeting, farewell, or homage **c** to convey by waving ⟨*~d farewell*⟩ **3** to brandish, flourish ⟨*~d a pistol menacingly*⟩ **4** to give a curving or undulating shape to ⟨*~d her hair*⟩ [ME *waven,* fr OE *wafian* to wave with the hands; akin to OE *wæfre* restless – more at WEAVER]

²**wave** *n* **1a** a moving ridge or swell on the surface of a liquid (eg the sea) **b waves** *pl*, **wave** *chiefly poetic* open water **2a** a shape or outline having successive curves; *also* one of the crests of such a form or a crest together with its adjacent trough **b** a waviness of the hair **c** an undulating line or streak, or a pattern formed by such lines **3** something that swells and dies away: eg **3a** a surge of sensation or emotion ⟨*a ~ of anger swept over her*⟩ **b** a movement involving large numbers of people in a common activity ⟨*~s of protest*⟩ **c** an esp artistic trend, tendency, or movement ⟨*the new ~ of post war French film directors*⟩ **d** a sudden increase or wide occurrence of a speci-

fied activity ⟨*a ~ of house-buying*⟩ **4** a sweep of hand or arm, or of some object held in the hand, used as a signal or greeting **5** a rolling or undulatory movement, or any one of a series of such movements, passing along a surface or through the air **6** a movement like that of an ocean wave: eg **6a** a surging movement of a group ⟨*a sudden ~ of new arrivals*⟩ **b** any of a succession of influxes of people migrating into a region **c(1)** a moving group of animals of one kind **c(2)** a sudden rapid increase in a population **d** *taking sing or pl vb* a line of attacking or advancing troops, aircraft, etc **7a** a periodic disturbance or variation of a physical quantity (eg electric or magnetic intensity or air pressure) by which energy is transferred progressively from point to point either through space or through a physical medium (eg water or air) by transient local displacement of the particles of the medium but without its permanent movement ⟨*light ~*⟩ ⟨*sound ~*⟩ ⟨*radio ~*⟩ **b** one complete cycle of such a disturbance **c** a graphical representation of a wave; a waveform ⟨*a sine ~*⟩ **8** a marked change in temperature; a period of hot or cold weather **9** an undulating or jagged line constituting a graphical representation of an action (eg the beating of the heart) – **wavelike** *adj*

**wave band** *n* a limited range of wavelengths or frequencies, esp of radio waves

**waved** /wayvd/ *adj* having a wavelike form or outline; *esp* marked by undulations; curving ⟨*the ~ cutting edge of a bread knife*⟩

**wave energy** *n* energy derived from the movement of water waves

**wave equation** *n, physics* a PARTIAL DIFFERENTIAL EQUATION of the second ORDER whose solutions describe the shape of waves

**waveform** /ˈwayvˌfawm/ *n* (the shape of) a graphical representation of a wave obtained by plotting the values of a varying quantity (eg voltage) against some other variable, esp time

**wave front** *n* a surface composed of all the points of the same PHASE that a wave (eg a light wave) is passing through at any one instant in its propagation through a medium or space

**wave function** *n* a function used in QUANTUM MECHANICS whose value is related to the relative probability of finding a given ELEMENTARY PARTICLE (eg an electron) within a specified volume of space

**waveguide** /ˈwayvˌgied/ *n* a tube or analogous structure of such dimensions that it will guide ELECTROMAGNETIC WAVES (eg light waves or microwaves) of a particular frequency along its length

**wavelength** /ˈwayvˌleng(k)th/ *n* **1** the distance in the line of travel of a wave between any one point and the next point of corresponding PHASE (eg from one peak to the next) **2** communicative level ⟨*be on the right ~ with youngsters – Annabel*⟩ – **on somebody's/the same wavelength** sharing (somebody's) views, outlook, etc

**wavelet** /ˈwayvlət/ *n* a little wave; a ripple

**wave mechanics** *n pl taking sing or pl vb* a theory of matter that gives a mathematical interpretation of the structure of matter based on the concept that ELEMENTARY PARTICLES (eg electrons, protons, and neutrons) can behave as waves

**wave number** *n* the number of cycles of a wave per unit distance of a wave of a particular wavelength; the RECIPROCAL of the wavelength

**wave power** *n* WAVE ENERGY

¹**waver** /ˈwayvə/ *vi* **1** to vacillate irresolutely between choices; fluctuate in opinion, allegiance, or direction **2a** to weave or sway unsteadily to and fro; reel, totter **b** to quiver, flicker ⟨*~ing flames*⟩ **c** to hesitate as if about to give way; falter **3** to make a tremulous sound; quaver *synonyms* see ¹SWING [ME *waveren;* akin to OE *wæfre* restless, *wefan* to weave – more at WEAVE] – **waverer** *n*, **waveringly** *adv*

²**waver** *n* an act of wavering

³**waver** *n* someone who waves

**wave theory** *n* the theory that light and other ELECTROMAGNETIC RADIATION consists of and is transmitted as waves

**wave train** *n* a succession of similar waves travelling in the same direction at equally spaced intervals

**wavy** /ˈwayvi/ *adj* **1a** rising or swelling in waves ⟨*a ~ lake*⟩ **b** having waves ⟨*~ hair*⟩ **2** moving with an undulating motion; fluctuating; *also* wavering **3a** marked by undulation; rolling ⟨*~ terrain*⟩ **b** *esp of an edge* (eg of a leaf) having a wavelike form or outline – **wavily** *adv*, **waviness** *n*

**waw** /waw/ *n* the 6th letter of the Hebrew alphabet [Heb *wāw*]

**wa-wa pedal** /ˈwahˌwah/ *n* an electronic device that is connected to an amplifier and operated by a foot pedal and that is used esp with an electric guitar to produce a fluctuating muted effect [imit]

**¹wax** /waks/ *n* **1** beeswax **2** any of various substances resembling beeswax: e g **2a** any of numerous plant or animal substances that form protective waterproof layers on leaves, stems, animal fur, etc and that differ from fats in being less greasy, harder, and more brittle, and in consisting principally of compounds (ESTERS) of FATTY ACIDS and alcohols having relatively large numbers of carbon atoms **b** a solid substance (e g OZOKERITE or paraffin wax) of mineral rather than animal or vegetable origin, consisting usu of HYDROCARBONS (chemical compounds of hydrogen and carbon only) having relatively large numbers of carbon atoms; MINERAL WAX **c** any of various pliable or liquid substances used esp for sealing, taking impressions, or polishing ⟨*floor* ~⟩ **d** a resinous preparation used by shoemakers for rubbing on thread **3** something likened to wax as soft, impressionable, or readily moulded ⟨*he was* ~ *in her hands*⟩ **4** a waxy secretion; *esp* CERUMEN (secretion produced by the ear) **5** *informal* a gramophone record – esp in *put on wax* [ME, fr OE *weax;* akin to OHG *wahs* wax, Lith *vaškas*] – **waxlike** *adj*

**²wax** *vt* **1** to treat or rub with wax, usu for polishing or stiffening **2** to remove hair from (a part of the body) using melted wax **3** *informal* to record on gramophone records

**³wax** *vi* **1** *of the moon, a satellite, etc* to have an increasing area of the illuminated surface visible **2** to assume a specified characteristic, quality, or state ⟨~ *indignant*⟩; *specif* to become, esp in speaking or describing ⟨~ *lyrical about the joys of Greece*⟩ **3** *formal or poetic* to increase in size, numbers, strength, prosperity, intensity, or duration; grow [ME *waxen* to grow, increase, fr OE *weaxan;* akin to OHG *wahsan* to increase, Gk *auxanein,* L *augēre* – more at EKE]

**⁴wax** *n* increase, growth – usu in *on the wax*

**⁵wax** *n, informal* a fit of temper; a rage [perh fr ³*wax*]

**waxberry** /'waksb(ə)ri/ *n* **1** (the wax-coated berry of) the WAX MYRTLE **2** SNOWBERRY

**waxbill** /'waks,bil/ *n* any of numerous African and Asian birds (family Ploceidae, esp genus *Estrilda*) that have white, pink, or reddish bills with a waxy appearance

**waxed paper, wax paper** *n* paper coated or impregnated with wax to make it resistant to water and grease and used esp as a wrapping for food

**waxen** /'waks(ə)n/ *adj* **1** made of or covered with wax **2** resembling wax: e g **2a** easily moulded; pliable **b** seeming to lack vitality or animation; pallid **c** smooth and glossy

**wax insect** *n* a SCALE INSECT (family Coccidae) that secretes a wax from its body; *esp* a Chinese insect (*Ericerus pe-la*) that secretes a hard, crumbly, and commercially important wax

**wax moth** *n* a dull brownish or greyish moth (*Galleria mellonella*) whose larva feeds on the wax of the combs produced by the honeybee

**wax myrtle** *n* any of a genus (*Myrica* of the family Myricaceae) of trees or shrubs with aromatic evergreen leaves; *esp* a N American shrub (*Myrica cerifera*) with small hard berries having a thick coating of white wax

**wax palm** *n* any of several palm trees that yield wax: e g **a** an Andean palm (*Ceroxylon andicolum*) whose stem yields a resinous wax used in candles **b** CARNAUBA (Brazilian palm whose leaves yield a brittle wax)

**waxpod bean** /'waks,pod/, **wax bean** *n* any of several FRENCH BEANS with creamy yellow to bright yellow waxy pods

**waxwing** /'waks,wing/ *n* a Eurasian songbird (*Bombycilla garrulus* of the family Bombycillidae) that has a pinkish-chestnut crest, crimson-tipped wings, and a short yellow-tipped tail [fr the red waxlike tips on some of its feathers]

**waxwork** /'waks,wuhk/ *n* **1** an effigy in wax, usu of a person **2** *pl but taking sing or pl vb* an exhibition of wax effigies (e g of famous historical characters)

**¹waxy** /'waksi/ *adj* **1** made of, full of, or covered with wax; waxen ⟨*a* ~ *surface*⟩ ⟨~ *berries*⟩ **2** resembling wax: e g **2a** readily shaped or moulded **b** lustrously white ⟨*a* ~ *complexion*⟩ – **waxiness** *n*

**²waxy** *adj, informal* highly irritated; angry [⁵*wax*]

**¹way** /way/ *n* **1a** a thoroughfare for travel or transport from place to place ⟨*lives across the* ~⟩ ⟨*the Icknield* Way⟩ **b** an opening for passage ⟨*this door is the only* ~ *out*⟩ **c** space or room, esp for forward movement ⟨*move that chair please, it's in my* ~⟩ ⟨*got out of the* ~⟩ **2** the course to be travelled from one place to another; a route ⟨*ask one's* ~ *to the station*⟩

⟨*lost her* ~⟩ **3a** a course leading in a direction or towards an objective ⟨*took the easy* ~ *out*⟩ ⟨*led the* ~ *to open heart operations*⟩ **b(1)** the course of one's life ⟨*put opportunities in my* ~⟩ **b(2)** what one desires, or wants to do ⟨*always manages to get her own* ~⟩ **c** a possible decision; a possibility ⟨*he was rude – there were no two* ~s *about it*⟩ **4a** the manner in which something is done or happens ⟨*the British* ~ *of life*⟩ ⟨*don't like the* ~ *he's breathing*⟩ – often used adverbially ⟨*do it this* ~⟩ **b** a method of doing or accomplishing; a means ⟨*the best* ~ *to make coffee*⟩ **c** a feature, respect ⟨*useful in more* ~s *than one*⟩ **d** a usu specified degree of participation in an activity or enterprise ⟨*a grocer in a small* ~⟩ **5** characteristic, regular, or habitual manner or mode of being, behaving, or happening ⟨*knows nothing of the* ~s *of women*⟩ ⟨*he's old and set in his* ~s*, he can't face a change*⟩ **6** the length of a course; distance ⟨*a long* ~ *from home*⟩ ⟨*has gone a long* ~ *towards becoming profitable*⟩ **7** an advance accompanied by or achieved through a specific action ⟨*working his* ~ *through college*⟩ ⟨*cough their* ~ *through the concert*⟩ **8a** a direction ⟨*is coming this* ~⟩; *also* a side ⟨*which* ~ *does it face?*⟩ ⟨*stand it the other* ~ *up*⟩ – often in combination ⟨*a three-way junction*⟩ ⟨*a one-way street*⟩ ⟨*a three-way discussion*⟩ **b** *pl* – used adverbially to denote a specified number of participants ⟨*split it four* ~s⟩; compare EACH WAY **c** (the direction of) the area in which one lives ⟨*do drop in if you're ever down my* ~⟩ **9** a state of affairs; condition, state ⟨*that's the* ~ *things are*⟩ **10** *pl* **10a** *sometimes taking sing vb* an inclined structure on which a ship is built or supported in launching **b** the guiding surfaces on the bed of a machine along which a table or carriage moves **11** a category, kind ⟨*not much in the* ~ *of brains*⟩ ⟨*porridge is all right in its* ~⟩ ⟨*need anything in the stationery* ~⟩ **12** motion or speed of a ship or boat through the water **13** *Br informal* a state of agitation [ME, fr OE *weg;* akin to OHG *weg* way, OE *wegan* to move, L *vehere* to carry] – **by the way** incidentally; IN PASSING – **by way of 1** to be considered as; as a sort of ⟨*by way of light relief*⟩ **2** by the route through; via **3** in the form of ⟨*money received* by way of *grants*⟩ – **come one's way** to fall to one's lot – **every which way** *chiefly NAm* in every direction; everywhere ⟨*papers were blown* every which way *in the wind*⟩ – **give way 1a** to retreat, give ground **b** to yield the right of way ⟨give way *to oncoming traffic*⟩ **2** to yield oneself without restraint or control ⟨give way *to tears*⟩ **3a** to yield (as if) to physical stress ⟨*the wind caused the roof to* give way⟩ **b** to yield to entreaty or insistence **4** GIVE PLACE TO – **go all the way 1** to enter into complete agreement **2** to engage in sexual intercourse – **go out of the/one's way** to make a special effort in spite of inconvenience – **go the way of all flesh** to die – **have a way with** to be good at dealing with ⟨*has a way with difficult customers*⟩ – **have a way with one** to be charming, esp persuasively – **have it both ways** to exploit or profit from each of a pair of contradictory positions, circumstances, etc; *also* to maintain two contradictory views simultaneously – **in a way** from one point of view; to some extent – **in the way of** in the form of ⟨*what have we in* the way of *food?*⟩ – **no way** *informal* under no circumstances – **on one's way** ON THE WAY 1 – **on the way 1** (while) moving along a course; in the course of travelling **2** coming approaching; *specif* conceived but not yet born – **on the way out** about to disappear, go out of fashion, be dismissed, etc ⟨*these old customs are* on the way out⟩ ⟨*since he took a bad decision he's* on the way out⟩ – **out of the way 1** unusual, remarkable **2** in or to a secluded or remote place **3** done, completed ⟨*got his homework* out of the way⟩ – **rub up the wrong way**, *chiefly NAm* **rub the wrong way** to arouse the antagonism or displeasure of – **see one's way to** to feel capable of – **under way** in progress, started – see also **out of** HARM'S **way, for** ONCE **in a way**

*usage* Sentences using **way** adverbially ⟨*they don't dress the* way *we do*⟩ should be rephrased, in formal British writing, as ⟨*they don't dress in the* way *we do*⟩.

**²way** *adj, NAm* of, connected with, or constituting an intermediate point on a route ⟨*visited five major countries plus* ~ *points*⟩

**³way** *adv* **1** far ⟨*is* ~ *ahead of the class*⟩ **2** *chiefly NAm* all the way ⟨*pull the switch* ~ *back*⟩ – **way back** long ago ⟨*friends from* way back⟩

**waybill** /'way,bil/ *n* **1** a document showing the number of passengers carried and tickets sold for each journey on a public conveyance (e g a bus) **2** a document prepared by the carrier of a shipment of goods that contains details of the shipment, route, and charges

**wayfarer** /'way,feərə/ *n* a traveller, esp on foot [ME *weyfarere*, fr *wey, way* way + *-farere* traveller, fr *faren* to go – more at FARE]

**wayfaring tree** /'wayfeəring/ *n* a European and W Asian shrub (*Viburnum lantana*) of the honeysuckle family, that has white flowers in dense flat-topped clusters and large oval leaves

**waygoing** /'way,gohing/ *n, chiefly Scot* the act of leaving; a departure

**waylay** /way'lay/ *vt* **waylaid** /-layd/ **1** to attack from ambush **2** to accost

**wayleave** /'way,leev/ *n* a right of way over a person's property (e g as granted to an electricity company for the laying of cables)

**wayless** /'waylas/ *adj* having no road or path

**Way of the Cross** *n* STATIONS OF THE CROSS

**way-'out** *adj, informal* **1** out of the ordinary, esp in being very daring or experimental ⟨*a film far too ~ for normal West-End audiences*⟩ **2** – used, esp in the early 1970s, as a generalized term of approval [*way out* (adverbial phrase), fr ³*way* + *out*]

**ways** /wayz/ *n taking sing vb, NAm* WAY **6** ⟨*a long ~ from home*⟩ [ME *wayes*, fr gen of ¹*way*]

**-ways** /-wayz/ *suffix* (→ *adv*) in (such) a way, direction, or manner ⟨*sideways*⟩ ⟨*lengthways*⟩ [ME, fr *ways, wayes*, gen of *way*]

**ways and means** *n pl* **1** methods and resources for accomplishing something, esp for paying expenses **2** *often cap W&M* methods and resources for raising revenue for the use of government ⟨*discussed in the Committee of* Ways and Means⟩

**wayside** /'way,sied/ *n* the side of or land adjacent to a road or path – **wayside** *adj*

**way station** *n, NAm* an intermediate stopping place between main stations on a railway

**wayward** /'waywəd/ *adj* **1** following one's own capricious or ignoble inclinations; ungovernable **2** following no clear principle or law; unpredictable **3** opposite to what is desired or expected; untoward ⟨*~ fate*⟩ *synonyms* see UNRULY [ME, short for *awayward* turned away, fr *away*, adv + *-ward*] – **waywardly** *adv*, **waywardness** *n*

**wayworn** /'way,wawn/ *adj* wearied by travelling

**W boson** *n* a hypothetical ELEMENTARY PARTICLE (minute particle of matter) that has a relatively large mass and is held to be responsible for the WEAK INTERACTION (basic interaction between elementary particles)

**WC** *n* WATER CLOSET

¹**we** /wi; *strong* wee/ *pron taking pl vb* **1** I and the rest of a group; you and I ⟨*shall ~ dance, Mary?*⟩; you and I and another or others; I and another or others not including you ⟨*may ~ go, Sir*⟩ – compare OUR, OURS, US, I **2** I – used, esp formerly, by sovereigns; used by writers to maintain an impersonal character **3** YOU **1** – used esp to children and the sick ⟨*how are ~ feeling today, Mr Jones?*⟩ **4** *WI* us ⟨*give ~ back we stadium – Trinidad Guardian*⟩ [ME, fr OE *wē*; akin to OHG *wir* we, Skt *vayam*]

²**we** *adj, WI* our ⟨*give we back ~ stadium – Trinidad Guardian*⟩

**weak** /week/ *adj* **1** lacking strength: e g **1a** deficient in physical vigour; feeble, debilitated **b** not able to sustain or exert much weight, pressure, or strain **c** not able to resist external force or withstand attack **2a** lacking a particular mental or intellectual quality (e g decisiveness, judgment, or discernment) **b** not firmly decided; vacillating **c** unable to withstand temptation or persuasion **3** not factually grounded or logically presented ⟨*a ~ argument*⟩ **4a** unable to function properly ⟨*~ eyes*⟩ **b(1)** lacking skill or proficiency ⟨*tutoring for ~er students*⟩ **b(2)** indicative of a lack of skill or aptitude ⟨*maths was his ~est subject*⟩ **c** without vigour of expression or effect ⟨*a ~ retort*⟩ ⟨*a ~ joke*⟩ **5a** deficient in the required quality or ingredient ⟨*~ in trumps*⟩ **b** lacking normal intensity or potency ⟨*~ strain of virus*⟩ **c** deficient in strength or flavour; dilute ⟨*~ coffee*⟩ **6a** not having or exerting authority or political power ⟨*~ government*⟩ **b** ineffective, impotent **7** of or being a verb or verb conjugation that forms the past tense and past participle by adding the suffix *-ed* or *-d* or *-t* – compare STRONG 16 **8a** unstressed ⟨*~ syllables*⟩ **b** having little or no stress and obscured vowel sound ⟨*'d is the ~ form of* would⟩ **9** tending towards a lower price ⟨*a ~ market*⟩ **10** *chemistry* forming IONS (electrically charged atoms or groups of atoms) only slightly in solution ⟨*~ acids and bases*⟩ [ME *weike*, fr ON *veikr*; akin

to OE *wīcan* to yield, L *vicis* change – more at WEEK] – **weaken** *vb*, **weakish** *adj*, **weakly** *adv*

*synonyms* Weak, feeble, frail, flimsy, fragile, infirm, and decrepit all mean "unable to endure stress or effort". Weak is the most general word, and can replace any of the others. It can be used of people ⟨*a sick, weak old man*⟩ or of things ⟨*a weak link in the chain*⟩. Feeble when applied to people implies extreme pitiable weakness ⟨*a feeble invalid*⟩ and when applied to their acts or utterances suggests inadequacy ⟨*a feeble argument*⟩. Frail suggests inherent or acquired delicacy of structure or physique ⟨*chair is too frail to bear his weight*⟩ ⟨*old man is getting very frail now*⟩. Flimsy things are inadequate to their purpose from lack of solidity ⟨*a flimsy building*⟩ ⟨*a flimsy pretext*⟩. Fragile implies something easily destroyed ⟨*a tall fragile vase*⟩. Infirm suggests progressive loss of physical strength, particularly in illness or old age ⟨*getting too infirm to go out in the rain*⟩ or weakness of character ⟨*infirm of purpose! Give me the daggers –* Shak⟩. Decrepit things or people are worn out by age ⟨*a decrepit old bicycle*⟩. *antonyms* strong, robust, powerful

**weaker brethren** *n pl* feebler or less firm associates; *esp* those most liable to yield to temptation

**weaker sex** *n taking sing or pl vb* womankind – + *the;* now usu considered offensively patronizing

**weakhearted** /,week'hahtid/ *adj* lacking courage; fainthearted

**weak interaction** *n* a fundamental interaction between ELEMENTARY PARTICLES (particles of matter) that is responsible for some processes in which particles decay to form others and in which atomic nuclei emit radioactive rays, and for the emission and absorption of NEUTRINOS (uncharged massless elementary particles) by atomic nuclei – compare STRONG INTERACTION

**weak-'kneed** *adj* lacking willpower or resolution; easily intimidated

**weakling** /'weekling/ *n* a person, creature, etc that is weak in body, character, or mind – **weakling** *adj*

**weakly** /'weekli/ *adj* feeble, poorly – **weakliness** *n*

**weak-'minded** *adj* having or indicating a weak mind: **a** lacking in judgment or good sense; foolish **b** lacking willpower or resolution **c** feebleminded – **weak-mindedness** *n*

**weakness** /'weeknis/ *n* **1** the quality or state of being weak; *also* an instance or period of being weak ⟨*agreed in a moment of ~ to go too*⟩ **2** a fault, defect **3** special desire or fondness ⟨*have a ~ for chocolates*⟩; also an object of special desire or fondness

**weak sister** *n, chiefly NAm* a member of a group who needs aid; *also* something that is weak and ineffective as compared with others in the group

**weak spot** *n* SOFT SPOT

¹**weal** /weel, wiəl/ *n* **1** a sound, healthy, or prosperous state; well-being **2** *obs* a commonwealth; BODY POLITIC [ME *wele*, fr OE *wela*; akin to OE *wel* well]

²**weal, wheal** *n* a raised mark on the surface of the body; a welt [alter. of *wale*]

**weal and woe** *n* well-being and adversity

**weald** /weeld, wiəld/ *n* **1** a wild or uncultivated usu upland region **2** *archaic* a heavily wooded area; a forest [the *Weald*, region (formerly wooded) in SE England, fr ME *Weeld*, fr OE *weald* wood, forest (cf WOLD)]

**wealth** /welth/ *n* **1a** the state of being rich **b** abundance of valuable material possessions or resources **2** abundant supply; profusion ⟨*a ~ of detail*⟩ **3a** all property that has a money value or an exchangeable value **b** all material objects that have economic utility; *esp* the stock of useful goods having economic value in existence at any one time ⟨*national ~*⟩ **4** *obs* weal, welfare [ME *welthe*, fr *wele* weal]

**wealth tax** *n* a tax on the value of assets owned by persons and private institutions

**wealthy** /'welthi/ *adj* **1** having wealth; extremely affluent **2** characterized by abundance ⟨*a country ~ in oil*⟩ – **wealthily** *adv*, **wealthiness** *n*

¹**wean** /ween/ *vt* **1** to accustom (a child or other young mammal) to take food other than the mother's milk **2** to detach from a cause of usu unwholesome dependence or preoccupation ⟨*to ~ your minds from hankering after false . . . standards* – A T Quiller-Couch⟩ **3** to cause to grow up under a specified dominating influence – usu passive + *on* ⟨*a generation ~ed on television*⟩ *antonym* addict [ME *wenen*, fr OE *wenian* to accustom, wean; akin to OE *wunian* to be used to – more at WONT]

²**wean** *n, Scot & N Eng* a small child; a bairn [contr of *wee ane* wee one]

**weaner** /'weenə/ *n* a young recently weaned animal (eg a piglet or calf)

**weanling** /'weenling/ *n* a child or young animal newly weaned – **weanling** *adj*

¹**weapon** /'wepən/ *n* 1 an instrument of offensive or defensive combat; something to fight with 2 a means of contending against another [ME *wepen,* fr OE *wǣpen;* akin to ON *vāpn* weapon] – **weaponless** *adj*

²**weapon** *vt* to arm

**weaponry** /'wepənri/ *n* 1 the science of designing and making weapons 2 weapons

**weapon system** *n* an item of military equipment (eg a missile or gun) together with systems (eg radar) for detecting its targets and guidance systems (eg radio control) to ensure that they are effectively engaged

¹**wear** /weə/ *vb* **wore** /waw/; **worn** /wawn/ *vt* **1a** to have or carry on the body as clothing or adornment ⟨wore *a coat*⟩ ⟨wore *the family emeralds*⟩ **b** to dress in (a particular manner, colour, or garment), esp habitually ⟨∼ *green*⟩ ⟨∼s *a tie to work*⟩ **c** to have (hair) in a specified style **2a** to hold the rank or dignity or position signified by (an ornament) ⟨∼ *the royal crown*⟩ **b** to have or show in the appearance ⟨wore *a happy smile*⟩ **c** to show or fly (a flag or colours) on a ship **3** to impair, damage, or diminish by use or attrition; consume or waste gradually ⟨*letters on the stone* worn *away by weathering*⟩ **4** to produce gradually and usu incidentally by friction or attrition ⟨∼ *a hole in the rug*⟩ **5** to exhaust or lessen the strength of; weary, fatigue **6** to bring (a sailing vessel) onto another tack by turning the bows away from the wind until the wind is on her stern and then bringing the bows up towards the wind on the other side – used esp of a SQUARE-RIGGED vessel **7** *chiefly Br informal* to find (a claim or proposal) acceptable; STAND FOR ⟨*a day off? I don't think the boss will* ∼ *it*⟩ – usu neg ∼ *vi* **1a** to endure use; last under use or the passage of time ⟨*material that will* ∼ *for years*⟩; *also* to endure such use to the specified degree ⟨*this material won't* ∼ *well*⟩ **b** to retain quality or vitality to the specified degree ⟨*you've* worn *well*⟩ **2a** to diminish or decay through use ⟨*the heels of his shoes began to* ∼⟩ **b** to go by slowly or tediously ⟨*the day* ∼s *into afternoon – Annabel*⟩ **c** to grow or become by attrition, use, or the passage of time ⟨*hair* ∼ing *thin*⟩ **3** *of a ship* to change to an opposite tack by turning the stern to the wind – used esp of a SQUARE-RIGGED vessel; compare TACK, GYBE – see also **wear THIN, wear the TROUSERS** [ME *weren,* fr OE *werian;* akin to ON *verja* to clothe, invest, spend, L *vestis* clothing, garment, Gk *hennynai* to clothe] – **wearable** *adj,* **wearer** *n*

**wear down** *vt* to weary and overcome by persistent resistance or pressure

**wear off** *vi* to pass away gradually and disappear ⟨*the effect of the drug* wore off⟩

**wear on** *vt* to irritate, fray

**wear out** *vt* 1 to make useless, esp by long or hard usage 2 to tire, exhaust ∼ *vi* to become useless from long or excessive wear or use

²**wear** *n* 1 the act of wearing; the state of being worn; use ⟨*clothes for everyday* ∼⟩ 2 clothing or an article of clothing usu of a specified kind ⟨*men's* ∼⟩; *esp* clothing worn for a specified occasion – often in combination ⟨*baby*wear⟩ ⟨*swim*wear⟩ 3 wearing quality; durability under use ⟨*plenty of* ∼ *left in it*⟩ 4 the result of wearing or use; lessening or impairment due to use ⟨wear-*resistant surface*⟩

**wearable** /'weərəbl/ *adj* capable of being worn; suitable to be worn ⟨*not really* ∼ *for that kind of a party*⟩ – **wearability** *n*

**wear and tear** *n* the deterioration which something suffers in the course of use; *esp* normal depreciation

**weariful** /'wiərif(ə)l/ *adj* 1 wearisome; *esp* tedious 2 full of weariness; wearied – **wearifully** *adv,* **wearifulness** *n*

**weariless** /'wiəriləs/ *adj* tireless – **wearilessly** *adv*

**wearing** /'weəring/ *adj* subjecting to or inflicting wear; *esp* causing fatigue ⟨*a* ∼ *journey*⟩ – **wearingly** *adv*

**wearisome** /'wiəris(ə)m/ *adj* causing weariness; tiresome – **wearisomely** *adv,* **wearisomeness** *n*

¹**weary** /'wiəri/ *adj* 1 exhausted in strength, endurance, vigour, or freshness 2 expressing or characteristic of weariness ⟨*a* ∼ *smile*⟩ 3 having one's patience, tolerance, or pleasure exhausted – + *of* or *with* 4 wearisome [ME *wery,* fr OE *wērig;* akin to OHG *wuorag* intoxicated, Gk *hōrakian* to faint] – **wearily** *adv,* **weariness** *n*

²**weary** *vi* 1 to become weary 2 *chiefly Scot* to feel a desire; long – usu + *on* or *for* ∼ *vt* to make weary

**weasand** /'weezənd/ *n, archaic* the throat, gullet; *also* the windpipe [ME *wesand,* fr (assumed) OE *wǣsend* gullet; akin to OE *wāsend* gullet, OHG *weisunt* windpipe]

¹**weasel** /'weezl/ *n, pl* **weasels,** *esp collectively* **weasel** any of various small slender active flesh-eating mammals (genus *Mustela* of the family Mustelidae, the weasel family) that consume small birds and mammals (eg mice), are mostly reddish-brown with white or yellowish underparts, and, in northern forms, turn white in winter; *esp* a Eurasian weasel (*Mustela nivalis*) [ME *wesele,* fr OE *weosule;* akin to OHG *wisula* weasel, L *virus* slimy liquid, stench – more at VIRUS] – **weaselly** *adj*

²**weasel** *vi* 1 to escape from or evade a situation or obligation – often + *out* 2 *NAm* to use WEASEL WORDS; EQUIVOCATE [*weasel word*]

**weasel word** *n, chiefly NAm* a word used in order to evade or retreat from a direct or forthright statement or position; an equivocation [fr the weasel's reputed habit of sucking the contents out of an egg while leaving the shell superficially intact]

¹**weather** /'wedhə/ *n* 1 state of the atmosphere with respect to heat or cold, wetness or dryness, calm or storm, clearness or cloudiness 2 disagreeable atmospheric conditions: eg 2a rain, storm b cold air with dampness 3 WEATHERING (change in form, composition, etc of objects exposed to the weather) [ME *weder,* fr OE; akin to OHG *wetar* weather, OSlav *vetrŭ* wind] – **make heavy weather of** to carry out in an unnecessarily laborious manner – **under the weather** *informal* mildly ill or depressed; not fully well; *also, euph* drunk

²**weather** *adj* windward

³**weather** *vt* 1 to expose to the open air; subject to the action of the elements 2 to sail or pass to the windward of 3 to bear up against and come safely through ⟨∼ *a storm*⟩ ∼ *vi* to undergo or be resistant to change by weathering ⟨*the stone* ∼ed *to a soft grey*⟩ ⟨*wood* ∼s *better if creosoted*⟩

**weatherability** /ˌwedhərə'bilǝti/ *n* capability of resisting weathering ⟨∼ *of a plastic*⟩

'**weather-ˌbeaten** *adj* 1 worn or damaged by exposure to weather 2 toughened, tanned, or bronzed by the weather ⟨∼ *face*⟩

**weatherboard** /'wedhə,bawd/ *n* 1 a board, usu thicker at one edge than the other, fixed horizontally and usu overlapping the board below to form a protective outdoor wall covering that will throw off water 2 a sloping board fixed to the bottom of a door to keep out rain, snow, etc 3 *Austr* a building, esp a house having walls of weatherboarding

**weatherboarding** /'wedhə,bawding/ *n* a method of constructing the walls of a building using weatherboards

'**weather-ˌbound** *adj* unable to proceed or take place because of bad weather

**weather bureau** *n, NAm* WEATHER CENTRE

**weather centre** *n* an esp regional office that collects weather reports, issues weather forecasts and storm warnings, and compiles weather statistics

**weathercock** /'wedhə,kok/ *n* 1 a vane, often in the figure of a cock, mounted so as to turn freely with the wind and show its direction 2 a person or thing that changes readily or is easily influenced

**weather deck** *n* a deck having no overhead protection from the weather

**weathered** /'wedhəd/ *adj* **1a** seasoned by exposure to the weather b altered in form by weather; *also* altered by artificial means, esp staining, to produce a similar effect ⟨∼ *oak*⟩ 2 made sloping so as to throw off water ⟨∼ *windowsill*⟩

**weather eye** *n* 1 an eye quick to observe coming changes in the weather 2 constant and shrewd vigilance and alertness

**weather forecast** *n* a forecast of the weather based on meteorological observations

**weatherglass** /'wedhə,glahs/ *n* a simple instrument for showing changes in atmospheric pressure by the changing level of liquid in a spout connected to a closed reservoir; *broadly* a barometer

**weather house** *n* a model house containing two figures, one of which emerges in fine weather, the other when it rains

**weathering** /'wedhəring/ *n* 1 the action of wind, rain, frost, etc in altering the colour, texture, composition, or form of exposed objects; *specif* the physical disintegration and chemical decomposition of rock at or near the earth's surface 2 a slope given to a surface so that it will shed water

**weatherly** /'wedhəli/ *adj* able to sail close to the wind with little leeway

**weatherman** /'wedhə,man/ *n* 1 someone who reports and

forecasts the weather, usu on the radio or television; *broadly* a meteorologist **2** *cap* a member of a revolutionary group active in the USA in the 1970s

**weather map** *n* a map or chart showing meteorological conditions at a given time and over an extended region

**weatherproof** /'wedhə‚proohf/ *adj* able to withstand exposure to weather without damage or loss of function – **weatherproof** *vt*, **weatherproofness** *n*

**weather satellite** *n* a satellite for taking, recording, and reporting meteorological observations

**weather ship** *n* a ship for taking, recording, and reporting meteorological observations

**weather shore** *n* a shore lying off a ship's windward side

**weather station** *n* an observatory taking, recording, and reporting meteorological data

**weather strip, weather stripping** *n* a strip of material to cover the joint of a door or window and the sill, casing, or threshold so as to exclude rain, snow, and cold air – **weather-strip** *vt*

**weather vane** *n* a movable device attached to an elevated structure (eg a spire) in order to show the direction of the wind

'**weather-‚wise** *adj* **1** skilful in forecasting the weather **2** skilful in forecasting changes in opinion or feeling ⟨*a* ~ *politician*⟩

**weatherworn** /'wedhə‚wawn/ *adj* weatherbeaten

¹**weave** /weev/ *vb* **wove** /wohv/, **weaved; woven** /'wohv(ə)n/, **weaved** *vt* **1a** to form (cloth) by interlacing strands (eg of yarn); *specif* to make (cloth) on a loom by interlacing WARP and WEFT threads **b** to interlace (eg threads) to form cloth **c** to make (eg a basket) by intertwining **2** *of a spider or an insect* to spin (a web, cocoon, etc) **3** to interlace, esp to form a texture, fabric, or design **4a** to produce by elaborately combining elements into a coherent whole; contrive **b** to introduce as an appropriate element – usu + *in* or *into* **5** to direct (eg the body) in a winding or zigzag course, esp to avoid obstacles ~ *vi* **1** to work at weaving; make cloth by weaving **2** to move in a devious, winding, or zigzag course, esp to avoid obstacles [ME *weven*, fr OE *wefan*; akin to OHG *weban* to weave, Gk *hyphos* web] – **get weaving 1** to start to do something **2** to hurry up

²**weave** *n* **1** something woven; *esp* woven cloth **2** any of the patterns or methods for interlacing the threads of woven fabrics

³**weave** *vb* **weaved** *vi* **1** to move waveringly from side to side; sway **2** to lurch forward or stagger along [ME *weven* to move to and fro, wave; akin to ON *veifa* to wave, Skt *vepate* he trembles]

**weaver** /'weevə/ *n* **1** one who or that which weaves; *specif* someone who weaves as an occupation **2 weaver, weaverbird** /'weevə‚buhd/ any of numerous African and Asian songbirds (family Plocidae) that resemble finches and usu construct elaborate nests of interlaced vegetation

**weaver's knot** *n* SHEET BEND (knot used to attach a rope to a loop in another rope)

¹**web** /web/ *n* **1** a woven fabric; *esp* a length of fabric while still being woven on a loom or in the process of being removed from a loom **2a** SPIDER'S WEB; *also* a similar network spun by an insect or insect larva **b** a snare, entanglement ⟨*caught in a* ~ *of intrigue*⟩ **3** a tissue or membrane of an animal or plant; *esp* that uniting fingers or toes either at their bases (eg in human beings) or along most of their length (eg in ducks and many other water birds) **4a** a thin metal sheet, plate, or strip **b** the plate connecting the upper and lower flanges of a girder or rail **c** the arm of a CRANK (part of an axle or shaft that is bent so that it can be turned) **5** an intricate structure suggestive of something woven; a network **6** the flat part of a bird's feather consisting of the series of BARBS implanted on each side of the central shaft; VANE 3 **7a** a continuous sheet of paper manufactured or undergoing manufacture on a paper machine **b** a roll of such paper for use in a rotary printing press *synonyms* see ¹WARP [ME, fr OE; akin to ON *vefr* web, OE *wefan* to weave] – **weblike** *adj*

²**web** *vb* -**bb**- *vt* **1** to cover with a web or network **2** to entangle, ensnare ~ *vi* to construct or form a web

**webbed** /webd/ *adj* having or being toes or fingers joined by a web

**webbing** /'webing/ *n* a strong narrow closely woven tape designed for bearing weight and used esp for straps, upholstery, or harnesses

**webby** /'webi/ *adj* (consisting) of a web

**weber** /'vaybə, 'webə/ *n* the SI unit of MAGNETIC FLUX (strength of magnetic forces operating in a particular area) equal to that flux which in passing through a circuit consisting of one loop of wire produces in it an ELECTROMOTIVE FORCE of 1 volt as the flux is reduced to zero at a uniform rate in 1 second [Wilhelm *Weber* †1891 Ger physicist]

'**web-‚fed** *adj* of or printed by a WEB PRESS

**webfoot** /'web‚foot/ *n, pl* **webfeet** /-‚feet/ **1** a foot with webbed toes **2** an animal, esp a bird, with webfeet – **web-footed** *adj*

**web offset** *n* OFFSET printing (printing using an inked impression transferred from a plate to a rubber-covered cylinder) by WEB PRESS

**web press** *n* a press that prints onto a continuous roll of paper

**web spinner** *n* an insect that spins a web; *esp* any of an order (Embioptera) of small slender insects with biting mouthparts that spin silken tunnels in which they live

**webster** /'webstə/ *n, archaic* a weaver [ME, fr OE *webbestre* female weaver, fr *webbian* to weave; akin to OE *wefan* to weave]

**wed** /wed/ *vb* -**dd**-; **wedded** *also* **wed** *archaic or journalistic vt* **1** to take for wife or husband by a formal ceremony; marry **2** to join in marriage **3** to unite (as if) by the bond of marriage ~ *vi* to enter into marriage; marry [ME *wedden*, fr OE *weddian*; akin to MHG *wetten* to pledge, OE *wedd* pledge, OHG *wetti*, Goth *wadi*, L *vad-, vas* bail, security] – **wedder** *n*

**we'd** /wid; *strong* weed/ we had; we would; we should

**wedded** /'wedid/ *adj* **1** joined in marriage **2** conjugal, connubial ⟨~ *bliss*⟩ **3** strongly emotionally attached; committed, devoted ⟨~ *to an idea*⟩ ⟨~ *to football*⟩

**wedding** /'weding/ *n* **1** a marriage ceremony, usu with its accompanying festivities; nuptials **2** an act, process, or instance of joining in close association or to form a whole **3** a wedding anniversary or its celebration – usu in combination ⟨*golden* ~⟩ – **wedding** *adj*

> *synonyms* A **wedding** is a ceremony, while a **marriage** is also the process of marrying. One can speak of ⟨*my* **marriage** *to Frederick*⟩ but not of ⟨△ *my* **wedding** *to Frederick*⟩.

**wedding breakfast** *n* a celebratory meal following a marriage ceremony

**wedding march** *n* a slow stately march composed or played to accompany the bridal procession

**wedding ring** *n* a ring usu of plain metal (eg gold) given by one marriage partner to the other during the wedding ceremony and worn thereafter to signify marital status

**wedeln** /'vayd(ə)ln/ *n* a style of downhill skiing in which a skier makes a fluent succession of tight linked turns [Ger, fr *wedeln* to fan, wag the tail, fr *vedel* fan, tail, fr OHG *wadal*; akin to ON *vēl* bird's tail] – **wedeln** *vi*

¹**wedge** /wej/ *n* **1** a piece (eg of wood or iron) that tapers to a thin edge and is used for splitting wood and rocks, raising heavy bodies, or for tightening by being driven into something **2a** something (eg a policy) causing a breach or separation **b** something that initiates an action or development **3** something wedge-shaped ⟨*a* ~ *of pie*⟩: eg **3a** an array of troops or tanks in the form of a wedge **b** a wedge-shaped stroke used in forming CUNEIFORM characters **c** (a shoe having) a wedge-shaped sole that is raised at the heel and tapers towards the toe **d** a metal-headed golf club with a broad face angled for maximum loft [ME *wegge*, fr OE *wecg*; akin to OHG *wecki* wedge, Lith *vagis*]

²**wedge** *vt* **1** to fasten or tighten by driving in a wedge **2a** to force or press into a narrow space; cram **b** to force (one's way) into or through something ⟨~d *his way into the crowd*⟩ **3** to split or force apart (as if) with a wedge ⟨~ *the log open*⟩ ~ *vi* to become wedged

**wedged** /wejd/ *adj* shaped like a wedge

**wedgie** /'weji/ *n* WEDGE 3c

**Wedgwood** /'wejwood/ *trademark* – used for fine ceramic ware made originally by Josiah Wedgwood (1730–1795) and typically decorated with a classical cameo-like design in white relief

**Wedgwood blue** *adj or n, often not cap* (of) a light greyish-blue colour characteristic of much Wedgwood ware

**wedgy** /'weji/ *adj* wedged

**wedlock** /'wedlok/ *n* the state of being married; marriage, matrimony [ME *wedlok*, fr OE *wedlāc* marriage bond, fr *wedd* pledge + *-lāc*, suffix denoting activity] – **out of wedlock** with the natural parents not legally married to each other ⟨*born* out of *wedlock*⟩

**Wednesday** /'wenzday, -di, 'wednz-/ *n* the 4th day of the week; the day falling between Tuesday and Thursday [ME, fr OE *wōdnesdæg;* akin to ON *ōthinsdagr* Wednesday; both fr a prehistoric WGmc-NGmc compound whose components are represented by OE *Wōden* Odin, the chief god in Germanic mythology, & by OE *dæg* day] – **Wednesdays** *adv*

¹**wee** /wee/ *adj* **1** very small; diminutive – often used to or by children or to convey an impression of Scottishness **2** very early ⟨~ *hours of the morning*⟩ **synonyms** see ¹SMALL [ME *we,* fr *we,* n, little bit, fr OE *wæge* weight; akin to OE *wegan* to move, weigh – more at WAY]

²**wee** *n* (an act of passing) urine – used esp by or to children [short for *wee-wee*] – **wee** *vi*

¹**weed** /weed/ *n* **1a(1)** an unwanted (wild) plant growing, usu rapidly and profusely, in an undesired place, and often overgrowing or choking out more desirable plants **a(2)** a growth of weed plants **b** an aquatic plant; *esp* a seaweed **2a** an obnoxious growth or thing **b** something like a weed in detrimental quality; *esp* an animal unfit to breed from **3** *Br informal* a weedy person **4a** *chiefly humorous* tobacco **b** *informal* cannabis; *specif* marijuana □ (**4**) usu + *the* [ME, fr OE *wēod;* akin to OS *wiod* weed] – **weedless** *adj*

²**weed** *vi* to remove weeds or something harmful ~ *vt* **1** to clear of weeds ⟨~ *a garden*⟩ **b** to remove the undesirable parts of ⟨~ *the files*⟩ **2** to get rid of (something undesirable or superfluous) – often + *out*

**weeder** /'weedə/ *n* one who or that which weeds; *specif* any of various devices for freeing an area from weeds

**weedkiller** /'weed,kilə/ *n* any of various substances used for killing weeds

**weeds** /weedz/ *n pl* **1** dress worn as a sign of mourning (eg by a widow) **2** **weed, weeds** *pl* a band of crepe worn on a man's hat as a sign of mourning [ME *wede* garment, fr OE *wǣd, gewǣde;* akin to ON *vāth* cloth, clothing, Lith *austi* to weave]

**weedy** /'weedi/ *adj* **1** covered with or consisting of weeds ⟨~ *pastures*⟩ **2** resembling a weed, esp in rapid and profuse growth **3** *informal* noticeably weakly, scrawny, and ineffectual – **weediness** *n*

**week** /week/ *n* **1a** any of several 7-day cycles used in various calendars **b(1)** a week beginning with a specified day or containing a specified event ⟨*the* ~ *of the 18th*⟩ ⟨*Easter* ~⟩ **b(2)** a week appointed for public recognition of some cause ⟨*Plant a Tree Week*⟩ **2a** a period of seven consecutive days ⟨*it took nearly a* ~⟩ **b** the working days during each 7-day period ⟨*stays in London during the* ~⟩ **c** a weekly period of work ⟨*works a 35-hour* ~⟩ **3** a time seven days before or after a specified day ⟨*next Sunday* ~⟩ [ME *weke,* fr OE *wicu, wucu;* akin to OHG *wehha* week, L *vicis* change, alternation, OE *wīr* wire – more at WIRE] – **week in, week out** for an indefinite or seemingly endless number of weeks

**week after week** *adv* for an indefinite or seemingly endless number of weeks

**weekday** /'week,day/ *n* a day of the week except (Saturday and) Sunday

**weekdays** /'week,dayz/ *adv, chiefly NAm* on weekdays repeatedly; on any weekday ⟨*takes a bus* ~⟩

¹**weekend** /,week'end, '-,-/ *n* the end of the week; *specif* the period between the close of one working week and the beginning of the next

²**weekend** *vi* to spend the weekend (eg at a place) habitually or on a single occasion – **weekender** *n*

**weekends** /,week'endz, '-,-/ *adv, chiefly NAm* on weekends repeatedly; on any weekend ⟨*travels* ~⟩

**weeklong** /'week,long/ *adj* lasting for a week

¹**weekly** /'weekli/ *adv* every week; once a week; by the week

²**weekly** *adj* **1** done, occurring, or published weekly **2** payable or reckoned by the week

³**weekly** *n* a weekly newspaper or periodical

**weeknight** /'week,niet/ *n,* a weekday night

**weeknights** /'week,niets/ *adv, chiefly NAm* on weeknights repeatedly; on any weeknight

**ween** /ween/ *vt, archaic* to imagine [ME *wenen,* fr OE *wēnan;* akin to ON *vana* to hope, L *venus* love, charm – more at WIN]

**weeny** /'weeni/ *also* **weensy** /'weenzi/ *adj, informal* exceptionally small; tiny [*wee* + *tiny*]

**weenybopper** /'weeni,bopə/, **weeny** *also* **weenybop** *n* a pre-adolescent person, esp a girl, who is younger than a TEENY-BOPPER, idolizes pop stars, and follows the latest fashions [*weeny* + *-bopper* (as in *teenybopper*)]

¹**weep** /weep/ *vb* **wept** /wept/ *vt* **1** to express deep sorrow for

usu by shedding tears; bewail **2** to pour forth (tears) from the eyes **3** to exude (a liquid) slowly; ooze **4** to bring to a specified condition by shedding tears ⟨*wept herself to sleep*⟩ ~ *vi* **1** to express passion (eg grief) by shedding tears **2a** to give off or leak liquid slowly; ooze **b** *of a liquid* to flow sluggishly or in drops **3** *of a tree* to droop over; bend [ME *wepen,* fr OE *wēpan;* akin to OHG *wuoffan* to weep, OSlav *vabiti* to call to]

²**weep** *n* a fit of weeping

**weeper** /'weepə/ *n* **1a** one who weeps **b** a professional mourner **2** a small statue of a mourning figure on a funeral monument **3** **weepers** *pl,* **weeper** a sign of mourning (eg a black veil or hatband) worn esp in the 18th and 19th centuries **4** *pl* long flowing side-whiskers

**weep hole** *n* a hole or pipe through a wall that allows the escape of otherwise trapped water

**weepie** /'weepi/ *n, informal* a sad or sentimental film or play; a tearjerker

**weeping** /'weeping/ *adj* **1** tearful **2** rainy **3** *of a plant* having slender drooping branches ⟨~ *silver birch*⟩

**weeping willow** *n* an Asian willow tree (*Salix babylonica*) with long drooping branches that is widely grown for ornament

**weepy** /'weepi/ *adj* inclined to weep; tearful

**weet** /weet/ *vb, archaic* to know [ME *weten,* alter. of *witen* – more at WIT]

**weever** /'weevə/ *n* any of several edible marine fishes (family Trachinidae) with a broad spiny head and venomous spines on the back fin [ONF *wivre* viper – more at WYVERN]

**weevil** /'weevl/ *n* any of numerous mostly small beetles (superfamily Curculionoidea) that have a usu downward-curving head elongated to form a snout bearing jaws at the tip, and many of which cause great damage, esp as larvae, to grain, fruit, and living plants [ME *wevel,* fr OE *wifel;* akin to OHG *wibil* beetle, OE *wefan* to weave] – **weeviled, weevilled** *adj,* **weevily, weevilly** *adj*

**wee-wee** /'wee ,wee/ *vi or n* (to) wee [baby talk]

**weft** /weft/ *n* **1a** the thread or yarn that interlaces the WARP (lengthways yarn) in a fabric; the crosswise yarn in weaving **b** yarn used for the weft **2** something woven; a web, fabric **synonyms** see ¹WARP [ME, fr OE; akin to ON *veptr* weft, OE *wefan* to weave – more at WEAVE]

'**weft-,knitted** *adj* produced in machine knitting with the yarns running crosswise or in a circle

**Wehrmacht** /'veəmakht (Ger 've:rmaχt)/ *n* the German armed forces just before and during World War II [Ger, fr *wehr* defence + *macht* force, might]

**weigela** /wie'jelə, -'jeelə, -'geelə, 'wiegilə/ *n* any of a genus (*Weigela*) of shrubs of the honeysuckle family with showy flowers; *esp* one (*Weigela florida*) of China widely grown for its clusters of pink or red flowers [NL, genus name, fr Christian *Weigel* †1831 Ger physician]

**weigelia** /wie'jeeleə, -'geeleə/ *n* weigela

**weigh** /way/ *vt* **1** to ascertain the heaviness of (as if) by using scales **2a** to outweigh **b** to make heavy; weight – often + *down* **3** to consider carefully, esp by balancing opposing factors, in order to reach a conclusion; evaluate – often + *up* ⟨~ *the pros and cons*⟩ ⟨~ *up the advantages*⟩ **4** to pull up (an anchor) preparatory to sailing **5** to measure or apportion (a definite quantity) (as if) on scales – often + *out* ~ *vi* **1a** to have weight or a specified weight **b** to register a weight (eg on scales) – + *in* or *out;* compare WEIGH IN **2** to be considered important; count ⟨*evidence will* ~ *heavily against him*⟩ **3** to press down (as if) with a heavy weight – often + *on* or *upon* ⟨*her responsibilities* ~ed *upon her*⟩ **4** to weigh anchor [ME *weyen,* fr OE *wegan* to move, carry, weigh – more at WAY] – **weighable** *adj,* **weigher** *n*

**weigh in** *vi* **1a** to have oneself or one's possessions (eg luggage) weighed; *esp* to be weighed in connection with a sports contest **b** to have oneself and one's tack weighed after a horse race **c** to be weighed before a boxing or wresting match – usu + *at* and a specified weight ⟨*the challenger* . . . *weighing in at 64.5 kilos*⟩ **2** to enter as a participant; join in ⟨*a bystander weighed in* to *stop the fight*⟩

**weigh out** *vi* to have oneself and one's tack weighed before a horse race

**weighbridge** /'way,brij/ *n* a platform, usu set level with the surface of the road, onto which vehicles may be driven to be weighed

¹**weight** /wayt/ *n* **1a** the heaviness of a quantity or body; the amount that a quantity or body weighs ⟨*needs to lose* ~⟩

⟨*apples sold by* ~⟩ **b(1)** the standard or established amount that a thing should weigh **b(2)** any of the classes into which contestants in certain sports (eg boxing and wrestling) are divided according to body weight ⟨*what* ~ *does he box at?*⟩ – often in combination **b(3)** the weight of the load required to be carried by a horse in a handicap race; *also* a racehorse carrying a usu specified weight ⟨*the top* ~ *won the race*⟩ **2a** a quantity weighing a certain amount ⟨*equal* ~s *of flour and sugar*⟩ **b** a heavy object (eg a metal ball) thrown or lifted as an athletic exercise or contest; *specif* SHOT **2b**(1) **3a** a system of units of weight or mass ⟨*troy* ~⟩; *also* any of the units of weight used in such a system **b** a piece of material (eg metal) of known weight for use in weighing articles **4a** something heavy; a load **b** a heavy object to hold or press something down or to counterbalance ⟨*the* ~s *of the clock*⟩ **5a** a burden, pressure ⟨*won by sheer* ~ *of numbers*⟩ ⟨*took a* ~ *off my mind*⟩ **b** excessive fatness, corpulence **6a** relative heaviness or ponderousness ⟨~ *is a quality of material substances*⟩ **b** the force with which a body is attracted towards a celestial body (eg the earth) by gravitation and which equals the mass of the body multiplied by the local gravitational pull **7** relative importance, authority, or influence ⟨*his views don't carry much* ~⟩ **8** the quality of a fabric (eg lightness or closeness of weave) that makes it or a garment made from it suitable for a particular use or season – often in combination ⟨*summer*-weight⟩ **9** a number assigned to an item to express its relative importance in a FREQUENCY DISTRIBUTION or in the set of items to which it belongs [ME *wight, weght*, fr OE *wiht;* akin to ON *vætt* weight, OE *wegan* to weigh] – **pull one's weight** to do one's full share of the work ⟨*if you'd only* pull your weight *we could be finished today*⟩ – **throw one's weight around** to exercise influence or authority to an excessive degree or in an objectionable manner

²**weight** *vt* **1a** to load or make heavy (as if) with a weight **b** to increase the heaviness of (eg a fabric) by adding an ingredient (eg size) **2** to oppress with a burden ⟨~ed *down with cares*⟩ **3** to assign a statistical weight to **4** to cause to incline in a particular direction by manipulation ⟨*a wage structure* ~ed *heavily in favour of employees with long service*⟩

'**weight-,carrying** *adj*, *of a horse* able to carry a heavy rider

**weight cloth** *n* a SADDLECLOTH (cloth placed under or over a saddle) that can be fitted with lead weights when a rider's weight is less than the amount his horse must carry in a competitive event

**weighted** /'waytid/ *adj* **1a** having a statistical weight assigned **b** compiled from weighted statistical data ⟨~ *average*⟩ **2** *of a racehorse* carrying or handicapped with a particular weight ⟨*badly* ~ *compared with the favourite*⟩

**weighting** /'wayting/ *n* **1** the act of one who or that which weights **2** *Br* an additional sum paid on top of wages; *esp* one paid to offset the higher cost of living in a particular area ⟨*a London* ~ *of £500*⟩ – compare ALLOWANCE

**weightless** /'waytləs/ *adj* having little weight; lacking apparent gravitational pull ⟨*a* ~ *environment*⟩ – **weightlessly** *adv*, **weightlessness** *n*

'**weight-,lifting** *n* a competitive sport in which contestants attempt to lift a BARBELL (metal bar with weights attached to each end) using a variety of lifting styles (SNATCH, CLEAN and JERK, PRESS), the winner being the competitor lifting the heaviest weight in the least number of attempts **weight-lifter** *n*

**weight training** *n* physical training involving the lifting of usu heavy weights, esp BARBELLS

**weightwatcher** /'wayt,wochə/ *n* someone who is dieting to lose weight, esp in a group or organization with others – **weightwatching** *n*

**weighty** /'wayti/ *adj* **1a** of much importance or consequence; momentous **b** solemn **2** heavy, esp in proportion to bulk ⟨~ *metal*⟩ **3a** burdensome, onerous ⟨*the* ~ *cares of state*⟩ **b** powerful, influential ⟨~ *arguments*⟩ – **weightily** *adv*, **weightiness** *n*

**weimaraner** /,viemə'rahnə/ *n* (any of) a German breed of large grey short-haired gundogs [Ger, fr *Weimar*, city in E Germany]

**weir** /wiə/ *n* **1** a fence or enclosure set in a waterway for trapping fish **2** a dam in a stream to raise the water level or divert its flow [ME *were*, fr OE *wer;* akin to ON *ver* fishing place, OHG *werien, werren* to defend, L a*perire* to open, ope*rire* to close, cover]

'**weird** /wiəd/ *n, chiefly Scot* fate, destiny; *esp* ill fortune – archaic except in *dree one's weird* [ME *wird, werd*, fr OE *wyrd;* akin to ON *urthr* fate, OE *weorthan* to become – more at WORTH]

²**weird** *adj* **1** of or caused by witchcraft or the supernatural; magical **2** *informal* of strange or extraordinary character; odd, fantastic [ME (Sc) *werd* fateful, fr *werd* fate] – **weirdly** *adv*, **weirdness** *n*

synonyms **Weird, eerie, spooky, eldritch, uncanny**, and **unearthly** all refer to the supernatural and mean "mysteriously frightening and fantastic"; but only **eerie**, in British English the informal **spooky**, and the poetic word **eldritch** have continued to be confined to this sense, describing anything that inspires fear and cannot be explained rationally ⟨*let out an* **eldritch** *screech*⟩ ⟨*some* **eerie** *moments among the corpses – TLS*⟩ **Spooky** carries the further suggestion of actual ghosts, and in American English has the extended meaning "nervous" ⟨**spooky** *horses*⟩. In addition to the supernatural sense, **weird** has come to mean "extraordinary and improbable" ⟨*her* **weird** *political opinions*⟩; **uncanny** can mean "puzzling and fascinating" and is used particularly of unusual powers ⟨*machines operating with* **uncanny** *precision*⟩; and **unearthly** has taken on the meaning "preposterous" ⟨*the* **unearthly** *leisureliness of English journalism – New Yorker*⟩. antonyms normal, earthly

**weirdie, weirdy** /'wiədi/ *n, informal* someone who is extraordinarily strange or eccentric

**weirdo** /'wiədoh/ *n, pl* **weirdos** *informal* a weirdie

**welch** /welch/ *vi* to welsh – **welcher** *n*

**Welch** /welsh/ *adj* Welsh – now only in names ⟨*the Royal* ~ *Fusiliers*⟩

'**welcome** /'welkəm/ *interj* – used to express a greeting to a guest or newcomer on his/her arrival [ME, alter. (influenced by *wel* well) of *wilcume*, fr OE *wilcuma* desirable guest, prob fr a prehistoric WGmc compound whose constituents are represented by OE *willa*, *will* desire & by OE *cuma* guest; akin to OE *cuman* to come – more at WILL, COME]

²**welcome** *vt* **1** to greet hospitably and with courtesy or cordiality **2** to greet or receive in the specified, esp unpleasant, way ⟨*they* ~d *the intruder with a hail of bullets*⟩ **3** to accept with pleasure the occurrence of ⟨~s *danger*⟩ – **welcomer** *n*

³**welcome** *adj* **1** received gladly into one's presence or companionship ⟨*was always* ~ *in their home*⟩ **2** giving pleasure; received with gladness or delight, esp in response to a need ⟨*a* ~ *relief*⟩ **3** willingly permitted or given the right ⟨*you're* ~ *to read it*⟩ ⟨*he's* ~ *to my share*⟩ **4** – used in "You're welcome" as a reply to an expression of thanks – **welcomely** *adj*, **welcomeness** *n*

⁴**welcome** *n* **1** a greeting or reception on arrival **2** the hospitable treatment that a guest may expect ⟨*overstayed their* ~⟩

'**weld** /weld/ *vi* to become or be capable of being welded ~ *vt* **1a** to fuse (metallic parts) together, either by heating and allowing the metals to flow together, or by hammering or compressing with or without previous heating – compare BRAZE, SOLDER **b** to unite (plastics) in a similar manner by heating or by using a chemical solvent **c** to repair (eg an article) by this method **d** to produce or create as if by such a process **2** to unite closely or inseparably [alter. of obs *well* to weld, fr ME *wellen* to boil, well, weld] – **weldable** *adj*, **weldability** *n*, **welder** *n*

²**weld** *n* **1** a welded joint **2** union by welding; the state or condition of being welded

'**welfare** /'welfeə/ *n* **1** happiness, comfort, and security; well-being ⟨*concerned for her child's* ~⟩ **2** WELFARE WORK **3** aid in the form of money or necessities for those not well able to provide for themselves (eg through poverty, age, or handicap); *also*, *Br* SUPPLEMENTARY BENEFIT [ME, fr the phrase *wel faren* to fare well]

²**welfare** *adj, NAm* **1** of or concerned with welfare, esp with improvement of the welfare of disadvantaged social groups ⟨~ *legislation*⟩ **2** receiving public welfare benefits ⟨~ *mothers*⟩

**welfare state** *n* **1** a social system based on the assumption by the state of responsibility for the individual and social welfare of its citizens by providing education, medical care, unemployment relief, SUPPLEMENTARY BENEFITS, etc **2** a nation or state in which a welfare state system operates

**welfare work** *n* organized efforts by a community or organization to improve the living conditions of a group (eg the poor or elderly) in society – compare SOCIAL WORK – **welfare worker** *n*

**welkin** /'welkin/ *n, poetic* **1a** the sky, firmament **b** the celestial home of God or the gods; heaven **2** the upper atmosphere [ME, lit., cloud, fr OE *wolcen;* akin to OHG *wolkan* cloud, OSlav *vlaga* moisture]

'**well** /wel/ *n* **1a** (a pool fed by) a spring of water **b** a fountain, wellspring **2** a pit or hole sunk into the earth to reach a supply of water **3a** a vertical shaft in a ship reaching to the lowest part of the hull and designed to contain the pumps and enable the water level in the bilges to be measured **b** a compartment in the hold of a fishing boat in which fish are kept alive **4** a shaft or hole sunk in the earth to reach a natural deposit (eg of oil or gas) **5** an open space extending vertically through floors of a structure ⟨*a stair* ~⟩ **6** a vessel, space, or hole having a construction or shape suggesting a well for water **7a** something resembling a well in being damp, cool, deep, or dark **b** a source from which something springs; a fountainhead **8** a range of values in which a physical variable is at a minimum ⟨*a potential* ~⟩ ⟨*an energy* ~⟩ **9** *Br* the open space in front of the judge in a law court [ME *welle*, fr OE (northern & Midland) *welle;* akin to OHG *wella* wave, OE *weallan* to bubble, boil]

²**well** *vi* **1** to rise to the surface and usu flow forth ⟨*tears* ~ed *from her eyes*⟩ **2** to rise to the surface like a flood of liquid ⟨*longing* ~ed *up in his breast*⟩ ~ *vt* to emit in a copious free flow [ME *wellen*, fr OE (northern & Midland) *wellan* to cause to well; akin to MHG *wellen* to cause to well, OE *weallan* to bubble, boil, L *volvere* to roll – more at VOLUBLE]

³**well** *adv* **better** /'betə/; **best** /best/ **1** in a good or proper manner; rightly **2** in a way appropriate to the circumstances: e g **2a** satisfactorily, advantageously ⟨*did* ~ *in maths*⟩ ⟨*married* ~⟩ **b** with good effect ⟨*carried himself* ~⟩ **c** with skill or aptitude; expertly ⟨*paints* ~⟩ ⟨~ *caught!*⟩ **d** with prudence; sensibly ⟨*would do* ~ *to ask*⟩ ⟨*we may* ~ *wonder*⟩ **3** in a kind or friendly manner; favourably ⟨*spoke* ~ *of your idea*⟩ **4** in a prosperous or affluent manner ⟨*he lives* ~⟩ **5** to an extent approaching completeness; thoroughly ⟨*I know him* ~⟩ ⟨*well-equipped kitchen*⟩ ⟨*after being* ~ *dried with a sponge*⟩ ⟨*listen* ~⟩ ⟨*knew the penalty* ~⟩ ⟨~ *up in the subject*⟩ **6a** easily, fully ⟨~ *deserved the honour*⟩ ⟨*can* ~ *afford a car*⟩ ⟨~ *worth the price*⟩ **b** much, considerably ⟨~ *over a million*⟩ ⟨~ *within the time*⟩ – compare PRETTY WELL **c** in all likelihood; indeed ⟨*may* ~ *be true*⟩ [ME *wel*, fr OE; akin to OHG *wela* well, OE *wyllan* to wish – more at WILL] – **as well 1** in addition; also ⟨*there were other features* as well⟩ ⟨*she's pretty* as well⟩ **2** to the same extent or degree ⟨*open* as well *to the poor as to the rich*⟩ **3** with equivalent or preferable effect ⟨*might just* as well *have stayed home*⟩ ⟨*you may* as well *tell him*⟩ **4** ⁵WELL 2,4 – **as well as** ²BESIDES 2 ⟨*skilful* as well as *strong*⟩ – **well away 1** making good progress **2** *informal* (almost) drunk – **well out of** lucky to be free from

*usage* When **as well as** means "as proficiently as" it is used as a conjunction ⟨*she sings* **as well as** *you do*⟩. When it means "besides" it is used like a preposition and followed by a noun or nounlike construction ⟨*you'll have to pay* **as well as** *Peter*⟩; but it may also be used like **and**, either to join similar parts of a sentence ⟨*you'll have to pay* **as well as** *help with the tea* (= joining *pay* and *help*)⟩ or to form a plural subject ⟨*the cat* **as well as** *the kittens climb trees*⟩. Some writers on usage advise that in sentences like this last one, **as well as** should form a parenthetical phrase between commas, and thus make no difference to whether the following verb is singular or plural ⟨*the cat,* **as well as** *the kittens, climbs trees*⟩.

⁴**well** *interj* **1** – used to express surprise, expostulation, or resignation **2** – used to indicate resumption of a thread of discourse or to introduce a remark

⁵**well** *adj* **better 1** satisfactory, pleasing ⟨*all's* ~ *that ends well*⟩ – compare ALL VERY WELL **2** advisable, desirable ⟨*it might be* ~ *for you to leave*⟩ ⟨*it's as* ~ *to ask*⟩ **3** healthy ⟨*not feeling very* ~⟩; *esp* cured, recovered ⟨*the wound is nearly* ~⟩ – sometimes used before the noun ⟨*not a* ~ *man*⟩ **4** being a cause for thankfulness; fortunate ⟨*it is* ~ *that this has happened*⟩ *usage* see ¹GOOD – **wellness** *n*

**we'll** /wel/ we will; we shall

**well-ad'vised** *adj* **1** acting with wisdom; prudent **2** resulting from or showing wisdom ⟨~ *plans*⟩

**well-ap'pointed** *adj* having good and complete equipment; properly fitted out ⟨*a* ~ *house*⟩

**well-'balanced** *adj* **1** correctly or equally adjusted or balanced **2** sane, sensible; emotionally stable

**well-be'haved** *adj* showing proper manners or conduct

**well-'being** *n* the state of being happy, healthy, or prosperous

**well-be'loved** *adj* **1** sincerely and deeply loved ⟨*my* ~ *wife*⟩ **2** sincerely respected – in various ceremonial forms of address

**wellborn** /ˌwel'bawn/ *adj* born of a respected and esp noble family

**well-'bred** *adj* **1** having or displaying good breeding; refined **2** having a good pedigree ⟨~ *pigs*⟩

**well-'built** *adj* **1** soundly constructed **2** broad and sturdy in physique

**well-'chosen** *adj* chosen with care; apt

**well-con'ditioned** *adj* **1** having or showing proper disposition, morals, or behaviour **2** having a good physical condition; sound ⟨*a* ~ *animal*⟩

**well-con'ducted** *adj* **1** properly managed **2** well-behaved

**well-con'nected** *adj* **1** having important relatives; of good family **2** having useful social contacts

**well-de'fined** *adj* **1** having clearly distinguishable limits, boundaries, or features ⟨*a* ~ *scar*⟩ **2** clearly stated or described ⟨~ *policies*⟩

**well-di'sposed** *adj* having a good, esp favourable or sympathetic, disposition

**well-'done** *adj* **1** rightly or properly performed **2** cooked thoroughly

**Wellerism** /'welərizm/ *n* an expression of comparison comprising a usu well-known quotation followed by a facetious sequel (eg " 'every one to his own taste,' as the actress said to the bishop") [Sam *Weller*, witty servant of Mr Pickwick in the novel *Pickwick Papers* by Charles Dickens †1870 E writer]

**well-'favoured** *adj* good-looking; handsome – no longer in vogue

**well-'fed** *adj* **1** having a good diet **2** plump, fat

**well-'formed** *adj* correctly or properly formed; *specif* satisfying the rules or constraints of a theory or system ⟨*a* ~ *proposition*⟩ – **well-formedness** *n*

**well-'found** *adj* fully furnished; properly equipped ⟨*a* ~ *ship*⟩

**well-'founded** *adj* based on excellent grounds or reasoning ⟨*a* ~ *argument*⟩

**well-'groomed** *adj* **1** well dressed and scrupulously neat **2** made tidy and attractive by careful tending ⟨*a* ~ *lawn*⟩

**well-'grounded** *adj* **1** having a firm foundation ⟨~ *in Latin and Greek*⟩ **2** well-founded

**well-'handled** *adj* managed or administered efficiently

**wellhead** /'wel,hed/ *n* **1** the source of a spring or stream **2** WELL 7b (source or fountainhead) **3** the top of or a structure built over a well

**well-'heeled** *adj, informal* having plenty of money; wealthy

**well-'hung** *adj* **1** *of meat, esp game* hung for a sufficient time to allow the development of flavour and tenderness **2** *vulgar* having a large penis; *also* having large breasts

**wellie, welly** /'weli/ *n, chiefly Br informal* WELLINGTON 2 [by shortening & alter.]

**well-in'formed** *adj* **1** having a good knowledge of a wide variety of subjects **2** having reliable information on a usu specified topic, event, etc

**Wellington, Wellington boot** /'welingt(ə)n/ *n* **1** a leather military boot having a loose top with the front usu coming above the knee **2** *chiefly Br* a usu black rubber boot with no fastenings that reaches to just above the ankle or to the knee; a gumboot [Arthur Wellesley, 1st Duke of *Wellington* †1852 Br general & statesman]

**wellingtonia** /ˌweling'tohnyə, -ni·ə/ *n* BIG TREE (very large Californian coniferous tree) [NL, fr 1st Duke of *Wellington*]

**well-in'tentioned** *adj* well-meaning

**well-'kept** *adj* well looked after or cared for; carefully maintained

**well-'knit** *adj* well constructed; *esp* having a compact usu muscular physique ⟨*a* ~ *athlete*⟩

**well-'known** *adj* fully or widely known; *specif* famous

**well-'lined** *adj* **1** having a proper lining **2** *informal* full of money ⟨~ *coffers*⟩; *also* well-heeled

**well-'mannered** *adj* having good manners; courteous

**well-'meaning** *adj* having or based on good intentions but usu having unfortunate or unintended results ⟨~ *but misguided idealists*⟩

**well-'meant** *adj* based on good intentions, but usu failing to have the desired effect ⟨*his comment was* ~ *but very tactless in the circumstances*⟩

**well-'nigh** *adv* almost, nearly

**well-'off** *adj* **1** being in or suggesting affluent circumstances; well-to-do **2** fortunately situated ⟨*you don't know when you're* ~⟩ **3** well provided ⟨*not very* ~ *for sheets*⟩

**well-'oiled** *adj, chiefly Br informal* drunk

**well-'ordered** *adj* **1** having an orderly procedure or arrangement ⟨*a* ~ *household*⟩ **2** *of a mathematical set* SIMPLY ORDERED with every subset containing a first element

**,well-'ordering** *n* an instance of being well-ordered

**,well-'paid** *adj* earning or entailing good pay

**wellpoint** /'wel,poynt/ *n* a pipe driven into the ground near an excavation through which water can be pumped to lower the ground-water level

**,well-pre'served** *adj* kept in good condition; *esp* retaining an unexpectedly youthful appearance

**well-read** /red/ *adj* well informed through much and varied reading ⟨ ~ *in history*⟩

**,well-'rounded** *adj* fully or broadly developed: eg **a** having or consisting of a background of broad experience or education ⟨*a* ~ *person*⟩ **b** agreeably complete and symmetrical; *esp, humorous* of ample proportions; plump **c** well expressed and constructed ⟨*a* ~ *sentence*⟩ **d** comprehensive and varied ⟨*a* ~ *volume*⟩

**,well-'set** *adj* **1** well or firmly established ⟨ ~ *for the next few overs*⟩ **2** strongly built ⟨*a short but* ~ *young man*⟩

**Wellsian** /'welzi•ən/ *adj* (characteristic) of the writings of H G Wells, esp in describing or foretelling a possible future [H G *Wells* †1946 E writer]

**,well-'spoken** *adj* **1a** having a socially acceptable accent **b** speaking courteously **2** spoken fittingly or with propriety ⟨ ~ *words*⟩

**wellspring** /'wel,spring/ *n* **1** a source of continual supply **2** FOUNTAINHEAD 1 (spring that is the source of a stream)

**,well-'stacked** *adj, vulgar, of a woman* having large breasts

**,well-'taken** *adj* well-grounded, justifiable ⟨*his chief and* ~ *point*⟩

**,well-'thought-of** *adj* being of good repute

**,well-,thought-'out** *adj* soundly devised or reasoned

**,well-'timed** *adj* happening at an opportune moment; timely ⟨*a* ~ *announcement*⟩

**,well-to-'do** *adj* having or showing more than adequate financial resources; prosperous ⟨*a* ~ *family*⟩

**,well-'tried** *adj* thoroughly tested and found reliable

**,well-'turned** *adj* **1** symmetrically shaped or rounded; shapely ⟨*a* ~ *ankle*⟩ **2** concisely and appropriately expressed ⟨*a* ~ *compliment*⟩ **3** expertly rounded or turned ⟨*a* ~ *column*⟩

**,well-up'holstered** *adj, humorous, of a person* plump

**,well-'versed** *adj* having a sound knowledge of a subject; conversant with something – + *in*

**'well-,wisher** *n* one who wishes well to another – **well-wishing** *adj or n*

**,well-'worn** *adj* **1a** having been much used or worn ⟨ ~ *shoes*⟩ **b** made trite by overuse; hackneyed ⟨*a* ~ *quotation*⟩ **2** *archaic* worn well or properly ⟨ ~ *honours*⟩

**welly** /'weli/, **welly-boot** *n, informal* WELLINGTON 2

**wels** /welz/ *n* a large freshwater catfish (*Silurus glanis*) of central and E Europe [Ger, fr MHG]

**Welsbach** /'welz,bak/ *trademark* – used for a burner that produces gaslight by the combustion of a mixture of air and gas or vapour to heat a gas MANTLE (covering for a flame which converts its heat into light) to the point at which it emits light, or for the mantle used with such a burner

**welsh** /welsh/ *vi* **1** to evade an obligation, esp payment of a debt **2** to break one's word □ usu + *on* ⟨ ~ed *on his debts*⟩ ⟨ ~ed *on his promises*⟩ [prob fr *Welsh*, adj] – **welsher** *n*

**Welsh** *n* **1** *taking pl vb* the people of Wales **2** the Celtic language of the Welsh *usage* see BRITISH [ME *Walsche, Welsse*, fr *walisch, welisch*, adj, Welsh, fr OE (northern & Midland) *wælisc, welisc* Celtic, Welsh, foreign, fr OE *Wealh* Celt, Welshman, foreigner, of Celtic origin; akin to the source of L *Volcae*, a Celtic people of SE Gaul] – **Welsh** *adj*

**Welsh cob** *n* (any of) a breed of small sturdy agile horses that originated in Wales

**Welsh corgi, corgi** /'kawgi/ *n* (any of) either of two varieties of short-legged long-backed dogs with foxy heads [W *corgi*, fr *cor* dwarf + *ci* dog; akin to OIr *cū* dog, OE *hund* – more at HOUND]

**Welsh dresser** *n* a kitchen dresser; *specif* one having open shelves above a flat top with drawers and small cupboards below

**Welshman** /'welshmən/, *fem* **Welshwoman** /-woomən/ *n* a native or inhabitant of Wales

**Welsh Mountain pony** *n* (any of) a breed of native Welsh pony under 12 hands in height and suitable for children to ride

**Welsh pony** *n* (any of) a breed of pony under 13.2 hands in height developed originally by crossing the small WELSH MOUNTAIN PONY with the larger WELSH COB; *also, chiefly NAm* WELSH MOUNTAIN PONY

**Welsh poppy** *n* a widely cultivated European poppy (*Meconopsis cambrica*) with large yellow flowers

**Welsh rabbit** *n* WELSH RAREBIT

**Welsh rarebit** /'reəbit/ *n* a savoury or snack consisting of melted cheese sometimes mixed with ale and seasonings, esp mustard, poured over toast – compare BUCK RAREBIT [alter. of *Welsh rabbit*]

**Welsh springer spaniel** *n* (any of) a Welsh breed of red and white or orange and white small-eared SPRINGER SPANIELS

**Welsh terrier** *n* (any of) a breed of wiry-coated terriers resembling but smaller than airedales, developed in Wales for hunting

**¹welt** /welt/ *n* **1** a strip between a shoe sole and upper through which they are fastened together **2** any of several finishes given to an edge or seam of a garment or garment part for reinforcement or decoration, made usu by ribbing (eg for knitted articles), by folding over the fabric on itself, or by binding an edge with an adjoining edge (eg at a seam) or with a separate strip of fabric **3a** a ridge or lump raised on the body usu by a blow **b** a heavy blow [ME *welte*]

**²welt** *vt* **1** to provide (eg a garment) with a welt **2a** to raise a welt on the body of **b** to hit hard

**weltanschauung** /'veltan,showəng (*Ger* 'vɛltanʃaʊʊŋ)/ *n, pl* **weltanschauungs, weltanschauungen** /əng•ən/ *often cap* a particular conception of the nature and purpose of the world; a philosophy of life [Ger, fr *welt* world + *anschauung* view]

**¹welter** /'weltə/ *vi* **1** to writhe, toss; *also* to wallow **2a** to become soaked, sunk, or involved *in* something **b** to be in turmoil [ME *welteren*; akin to MD *welteren* to roll, OHG *walzan*, L *volvere* – more at VOLUBLE]

**²welter** *n* **1** a state of wild disorder; turmoil **2** a chaotic mass or jumble ⟨*a bewildering* ~ *of data*⟩

**welterweight** /'weltə,wayt/ *also* **welter** *n* a boxer who weighs not more than 10 stone 7 pounds (66.7 kilograms) if professional, or between 63.5 and 67 kilograms (between about 10 stone and 10 stone 8 pounds) if amateur [*welter* (a heavy horseman or boxer), prob fr ²*welt*]

**weltschmerz** /'velt,shmeəts (*Ger* 'vɛltʃmɛrts)/ *n, often cap* mental depression caused by contemplation of the state of the world; *esp* sentimental pessimism [Ger, fr *welt* world + *schmerz* pain]

**¹wen** /wen/ *n* **1** a cyst formed by obstruction of a SEBACEOUS gland (skin gland that secretes fatty lubricating material) and filled with fatty material **2** an abnormally large overcrowded city, esp London [ME *wenn*, fr OE; akin to MLG *wene* wen]

**²wen** *n* WYNN (Old English letter *w*)

**¹wench** /wench/ *n* **1** a female servant or rustic working girl **2** *dial or humorous* a young woman; a girl **3** *dial or archaic* a lewd woman; a prostitute [ME *wenche*, short for *wenchel* child, fr OE *wencel*; akin to OHG *winchan* to stagger – more at WINK]

**²wench** *vi, of a man* to consort with lewd women; *esp* to fornicate – **wencher** *n*

**wend** /wend/ *vt* to proceed on (one's way) ~ *vi, archaic* to direct one's course; travel [ME *wenden*, fr OE *wendan*; akin to OHG *wenten* to turn, OE *windan* to twist – more at WIND]

**Wend** /wend/ *n* a member of a SLAVONIC people of eastern Germany [Ger *Wende*, fr OHG *Winida*; akin to OE *Winedas*, pl, Wends] – **Wendish** *adj or n*

**wendy house** /'wendi/ *n, often cap W* **1** *chiefly Br* a small house for children to play in **2** *SAfr* a garden shed or summerhouse [*Wendy*, character in *Peter Pan*, children's book by J M Barrie †1937 Sc writer]

**Wensleydale** /'wenzli,dayl/ *n* **1** a crumbly white to creamy-yellow cheese with a mild flavour **2** (any of) a breed of long-haired sheep [*Wensleydale*, valley in North Yorkshire]

**went** /went/ *past of* GO [ME, past & pp of *wenden*]

**wentletrap** /'wentl,trap/ *n* any of a family (Epitoniidae) of marine snails with spirally coiled tapering usu white shells; *also* the shell of a wentletrap [D *wenteltrap* winding stair, fr MD *wendeltrappe*, fr *wendel* turning + *trappe* stairs]

**were** /wə; *strong* wuh/ *past 2 sing, past pl, substandard past 1 & 3 sing, or past subj of* BE [ME *were* (suppletive sing. past subj & 2 sing. past indic of *been* to be), *weren* (suppletive past pl of *been*), fr OE *wǣre* (sing. past subj & 2 sing. past indic of *wesan* to be), *wǣron* (past pl indic of *wesan*), *wǣren* (past pl subj of *wesan*) – more at WAS]

*usage* The past subjunctive **were** is used instead of **was** in formal modern writing to express a "condition contrary to fact"; although the use of **was** in such situations has been long established in English 〈*as if I* **was** *awake* – John Bunyan〉. Examples are 〈*I wish it* **were** *finished* (but it isn't)〉 〈*suppose it* **were** *true* (but it's false)〉. **Were** follows *if* 〈*if John* **were** *here* (but he isn't) *he would know*〉 〈*if it* **were** *to rain we should get wet*〉 〈*if it* **were** *not for her illness she would have finished it*〉 and as *if* 〈*he spoke as if I* **were** *deaf* (but I'm not)〉 and *as though* 〈*he behaves as though he* **were** *a millionaire*〉. **Were** must be used where such sentences are inverted 〈**were** *this true* (but it's false) *it would be very alarming*〉 and in the set phrases 〈*if I* **were** *you*〉 and 〈*as it* **were**〉. It is not recommended, however, where *if* could be replaced by *whether* 〈*I looked to see if/whether he* **was** *coming*〉 〈*to find out if/whether it* **was** *true*〉 〈*there's some doubt if/whether he* **was** *really her son*〉.

**we're** /wiə/ we are

**weren't** /wuhnt/ were not

**werewolf** /'weə‚woolf, 'wiə-/ *n, pl* **wcrewolves** /-woolvz/ a person transformed into a wolf or capable of assuming a wolf's form; LYCANTHROPE [ME, fr OE *werwulf;* akin to OHG *werwolf* werewolf; both fr a prehistoric WGmc compound whose constituents are represented by OE *wer* man & by OE *wulf* wolf – more at VIRILE, WOLF]

**wergild** /'wuhgild/, **wergeld** /-geld/ *n* money value based on social rank and wealth which was set on an individual's life in Anglo-Saxon and Germanic Law and was exacted as a fine payable by a murderer to the relatives of the deceased [ME *wergeld,* fr OE; akin to OHG *wergelt* wergild; both fr a prehistoric WGmc compound whose constituents are represented by OE *wer* man & by OE *gield, geld* payment, tribute – more at GELD]

**wersh** /wuhsh/ *adj, Scot* **1** of *weather* raw **2** of *food* tasting insipid, bad, or badly cooked [contr of *wearish* (tasteless, sickly), fr ME *werische*]

**wert** /wuht/ *archaic past 2 sing of* BE

**weskit** /'weskit/ *n* a waistcoat [by alter.]

**Wesleyanism** /'wezli‚ə‚niz(ə)m/ *n* METHODISM 1; *specif* the system of Methodism taught by John Wesley [John *Wesley* †1791 E preacher] – **Wesleyan** *adj or n*

**¹west** /west/ *adv* to, towards, or in the west **synonyms** see ¹NORTH [ME, fr OE; akin to OHG *westar* to the west, & prob to L *vesper* evening, Gk *hesperos*] – **go west 1** to die **2** to become damaged, broken, or expended [prob fr the sun's setting in the west]

**²west** *adj* **1** situated towards or at the west 〈*the ~ exit*〉 **2** coming from the west 〈*a ~ wind*〉

**³west** *n* **1a** the direction 90° to the left of north that is the general direction of sunset; *also* the compass point that corresponds to this direction and is directly opposite to east **b** the place on the horizon where the sun sets **2a** *often cap* regions or countries lying to the west of a specified or implied point of orientation; *also, taking sing or pl vb* the inhabitants of these regions **b** *cap* the noncommunist countries of Europe and America **c** *cap* European civilization in contrast with that of the Orient **d** *cap* the part of the USA lying west of the Mississippi **3** the end of a church opposite the CHANCEL (part containing the altar) **4** *often cap* **4a** the one of the four positions at 90-degree intervals that lies to the west or to the left of South **b** a person (e g a bridge player) occupying the West in the course of a specified activity □ (2) usu + *the*

**westbound** /'west‚bownd/ *adj* travelling, he̅ading, or leading west 〈*the ~ carriageway*〉

**west by north** *adj, adv, or n* (from, towards, or in the direction of) the compass point that is one point north of due west; 281° 15′ clockwise from north

**west by south** *adj, adv, or n* (from, towards, or in the direction of) the compass point that is one point south of due west; 258° 45′ clockwise from north

**West Coast** *adj or n* (of) the Pacific seaboard of the USA, esp California

**West Country** *n the* southwest of England, esp Devon, Cornwall, and Somerset – **Westcountry** *adj*

**West End** *n the* fashionable western part of central London where the main shopping centres, theatres, etc are located – **West-End** *adj*

**wester** /'westə/ *vi* to turn or decline westwards 〈*the half moon ~ s low* – A E Housman〉 [ME *westren,* fr ¹*west*]

**¹westerly** /'westəli/ *adj or adv* situated towards, belonging to, or coming from the west; west [obs *wester* western]

**²westerly,** *NAm also* **wester** *n* a wind from the west

**¹western** /'westən/ *adj* **1** *cap* (characteristic) of a region conventionally designated West: e g **1a** steeped in or stemming from European traditions in contrast with those of the Orient 〈*~ thought*〉 **b** of the noncommunist countries of Europe and America **c** of America or the American West **2a** lying or directed towards the west **b** coming from the west 〈*the ~ wind*〉 **3** *cap* of the Roman Catholic or Protestant branches of Christianity as opposed to the Eastern or Eastern Orthodox churches 〈*Western liturgies*〉 **synonyms** see ¹NORTH [ME *westerne,* fr OE; akin to OHG *westrōni* western, OE *west*] – **westernmost** *adj*

**²western** *n, often cap* a novel, story, film, or broadcast dealing with cowboys, frontier life, etc in the W USA, esp during the latter half of the 19th century

**Westerner** /'westənə/ *n* **1** a native or inhabitant of the West; *esp, chiefly NAm* a native or inhabitant of the western part of the USA **2** one advocating the adoption of W European culture, esp in 19th-century Russia

**western hemisphere** *n* the half of the earth comprising N and S America and surrounding waters – compare EASTERN HEMISPHERE

**western‧ize, -ise** /'westəniez/ *vt* to imbue with qualities associated with the West *~ vi* to become westernized – **westernization** *n*

**western saddle** *n, often cap* W STOCK SADDLE (saddle with high pommel used originally by cattlemen)

**West Germanic** *n* a group of the Germanic languages including English, Frisian, Dutch, and German

**West Highland** *n* (any of) a breed of small very hardy beef cattle from the Highlands of Scotland

**West Highland white terrier** *n* (any of) a breed of small white long-coated terriers developed in Scotland

**West Indian** *also* **Westindian** *n* **1** a native or inhabitant of the West Indies **2** a descendant of West Indians [*West Indies* (formerly *West India*), group of islands round the Caribbean Sea] – **West Indian** *adj*

**westing** /'westing/ *n* **1** distance due west in longitude from the preceding point of measurement **2** westerly progress

**Westminster** /'west‚minstə, ‚-'--/ *n* the British Parliament [*Westminster*, district of London in which the Houses of Parliament are situated]

**‚west-north'west** *adj, adv, or n* (from, towards, or in the direction of) the compass point that is midway between west and northwest; 292° 30′ clockwise from north

**Westphalian ham** /west'fayli‧ən, -y(ə)n/ *n* a ham of distinctive flavour produced by smoking over juniper wood [*Westphalia,* region in W Germany]

**West Saxon** *n* **1** a native or inhabitant of the West Saxon kingdom **2** the chief literary dialect of Old English used in England before the Norman conquest

**‚west-south'west** *adj, adv, or n* (from, towards, or in the direction of) the compass point that is midway between west and southwest; 247° 30′ clockwise from north

**¹westward** /'westwood, -wəd/ *adv or adj* moving or extending westwards

**²westward** *n the* westward direction or part

**westwards** /'westwədz/ *adv* towards the west

**¹wet** /wet/ *adj* **-tt-** **1** consisting of, containing, covered with, or soaked with liquid (e g water) **2** rainy **3** still moist enough to smudge or smear 〈*~ paint*〉 **4** permitting the sale or consumption of alcoholic drink 〈*many parts of Wales are now ~ on Sundays*〉 – compare DRY **5** using or done by means of or in the presence of a liquid, esp water 〈*~ extraction of copper*〉 **6** *of an aircraft wing* containing fuel tanks **7** *chiefly Br informal* feebly ineffectual, placid, or dull; *also, of a politician* not having extremely right or left-wing views; moderate **8** *Br vulg, esp of a woman* sexually aroused – see also **wet behind the ears** [ME, partly fr pp of *weten* to wet & partly fr OE *wǣt* wet; akin to ON *vātr* wet, OE *wæter* water] – **wetly** *adv,* **wetness** *n*

**synonyms Wet, sodden, damp, dank, moist,** and **humid** all mean "covered with or soaked in liquid". **Wet** is the most general word, describing not only something covered in liquid 〈**wet** *pavements*〉 or soaked in it 〈**wet** *sponge*〉 but something not yet solidified 〈**wet** *paint*〉. **Sodden** means "absolutely soaked" 〈*fields* **sodden** *after weeks of rain*〉. **Damp** suggests moderate wetness 〈*sheets should be* **damp** *when ironed*〉 which may be unpleasant 〈*a* **damp**, *feverish, unhealthy spot* – R L Stevenson〉. **Dank** has a stronger suggestion of something disagreeable and perhaps smelly 〈*from the jungle a* **dank** *sulphurous breeze exuded* – Norman Mailer〉. **Moist** resembles **damp,** but without the undesirable quality 〈*water the seeds to keep them* **moist**〉. **Humid** refers to debilitating dampness in the air, usually accompanied by warmth 〈*the* **humid** *heat of a New York summer*〉. **antonyms** dry, arid

**²wet** *n* **1** water; *also* moisture, wetness **2** rainy weather; rain **3** *NAm* an advocate of a policy of permitting the sale of intoxicating liquors **4** *chiefly Br informal* a wet person; a drip ⟨*bastards or hopeless* ~s – *TLS*⟩; *also* a moderate (Conservative) politician ⟨*the* ~s *in the Cabinet have been accused of disloyalty . . .*⟩ **5** *chiefly Br slang* an alcoholic drink

**³wet** *vb* **-tt-**; (2) **wet** *vt* **1** to make wet **2** to urinate in or on ~ *vi* to become wet – see also **wet one's** WHISTLE [ME *weten*, fr OE *wǣtan*, fr *wǣt*, adj]
 **usage** It is clearer to use the past participle **wetted** when forming a passive with *be*. Compare ⟨*the bed's been* **wetted** (= Billy has **wet** it)⟩ ⟨*the bed's been* **wet** (= it hasn't been dry)⟩.

**weta** /'waytə/ *n* any of various large wingless long-horned fearsome-looking New Zealand insects (family Stenopelmatidae) that resemble grasshoppers [Maori]

**wet and dry** *n* EMERY PAPER that can be used either moistened or dry

**wet-and-dry-bulb hygrometer** *n* PSYCHROMETER (device for measuring atmospheric humidity)

**wetback** /'wet,bak/ *n, NAm* a Mexican who enters the USA illegally (e g by wading across the Rio Grande)

**wet blanket** *n* someone who quenches or dampens enthusiasm or pleasure

**,wet-'bulb** *adj* of, being, or recorded by the thermometer in a PSYCHROMETER (device for measuring atmospheric humidity) whose bulb is kept moistened and that registers a temperature lower than that of the surrounding air – compare DRY-BULB

**wet cell** *n* a battery cell whose ELECTROLYTE (substance that conducts an electric current) is a liquid – compare DRY CELL

**wet dream** *n* an erotic dream culminating in orgasm

**wet fish** *n, Br* fresh uncooked fish ⟨*a* ~ *merchant*⟩

**wet fly** *n* an artificial angling fly designed to be used under water – compare DRY FLY

**wether** /'wedhə/ *n* a male sheep castrated before sexual maturity [ME, ram, fr OE; akin to OHG *widar* ram, L *vitulus* calf, *vetus* old, Gk *etos* year]

**wetlands** /'wetləndz/ *n pl*, **wetland** *n* land or areas (e g tidal flats or swamps) containing much soil moisture and often important as breeding areas for fish and feeding areas for birds

**'wet-,look** *adj* having a glossy sheen suggesting surface wetness ⟨*a* ~ *coat*⟩ ⟨~ *leather*⟩

**wet-nurse** /'-,-, ,-'-/ *vt* **1** to act as wet nurse to **2** to give constant and often excessive care to ⟨~d *the project through its initial stages*⟩

**wet nurse** *n* a woman who cares for and suckles another's children

**wet rot** *n* **1** a decay of timber caused by any of various fungi that attack wood having a high moisture content **2** a fungus causing wet rot

**wet suit** *n* a close-fitting suit made of material (e g sponge rubber) that admits water but retains body heat so as to insulate its wearer (e g a skin diver or surfer) esp in cold water

**wettable** /'wetəbl/ *adj* capable of being wetted – **wettability** *n*

**wetter** /'wetə/ *n* **1** a worker who wets material in any of several manufacturing processes **2** WETTING AGENT

**wetting agent** /'weting/ *n* a substance that prevents a surface from being repellent to a wetting liquid by lowering the SURFACE TENSION (force between molecules on the surface) of the liquid, and that is used esp in mixing solids with liquids or spreading liquids on surfaces

**we've** /wiv; *strong* weev/ we have

**weymouth** /'waym(ə)th/ *n, often cap* a horse's bit that consists of a straight mouthpiece fixed rigidly to long cheekpieces and that is used as part of a DOUBLE BRIDLE, esp for dressage and showing [perh fr *Weymouth*, town in Dorset in England]

**¹whack** /wak/ *vb, informal vt* **1a** to strike with a smart or resounding blow **b** to cut or produce (as if) with a hard blow ⟨~ *off their heads*⟩ ⟨~ *out a tune on the piano*⟩ **2** *chiefly Br* to get the better of; defeat; *also* surpass ~ *vi* to strike a smart or resounding blow [prob imit] – **whacker** *n*

**²whack** *n, informal* **1** a smart or resounding blow, esp with a stick; *also* the sound (as if) of such a blow **2** a portion, share **3** condition; *esp* proper working order **4** an attempt, go ⟨*have a* ~⟩

**whacked** /wakt/ *adj, chiefly Br informal* completely exhausted; DONE IN

**¹whacking** /'waking/ *adj, informal* extremely big; whopping

**²whacking** *adv, informal* very, extremely ⟨*a* ~ *great oil tanker*⟩

**whacko** /,wak'oh/ *interj, Br informal* – used to express delight [*whack* + ²-*o*]

**whacky** /'waki/ *adj* WACKY (eccentric, crazy)

**¹whale** /wayl/ *n, pl* **whales** (*1*) **whales,** *esp collectively* **whale 1** any of an order (Cetacea) of aquatic mammals that superficially resemble large fish, have tails modified as paddles, and many of which grow to enormous size; *esp* any of the larger whales many of which have been hunted for oil, flesh, or whalebone **2** *informal* something that is impressive, esp in size or qualities – often in *a whale of a* ⟨*a* ~ *of a difference*⟩ ⟨*had a* ~ *of a time*⟩ **3** *Br informal* an expert, enthusiast – + *at* or *for*; no longer in vogue; compare SHARK [ME, fr OE *hwæl*; akin to OHG *hwal* whale]

**²whale** *vi* to engage in whale fishing and processing

**³whale** *vt, NAm informal* to thrash, hit, or defeat soundly [origin unknown]

**whaleback** /'wayl,bak/ *n* something shaped like the back of a whale; *specif* a freight steamer with a convex upper deck

**whaleboat** /'wayl,boht/ *n* a long narrow rowing boat with pointed ends, often steered with an oar, and formerly used for hunting whales; *also* any small whaling boat in modern use

**whalebone** /'wayl,bohn/ *n* **1** a horny material that occurs in two rows of plates up to 4 metres (about 12 feet) long attached along the upper jaw of WHALEBONE WHALES **2** a thin strip of whalebone or some artificially produced substitute used for stiffening corsets, collars, etc

**whalebone whale** *n* any of various usu large whales (suborder Mysticeti) that have whalebone plates instead of teeth, which they use to filter KRILL (small shrimplike animals) from large volumes of sea water – compare TOOTHED WHALE

**whale oil** *n* TRAIN OIL

**whaler** /'waylə/ *n* a person, ship, or boat engaged in whale fishing and processing

**whaling** /'wayling/ *n* the occupation of catching and extracting commercial products from whales

**¹wham** /wam/ *n* **1** the loud sound of a hard impact **2** *informal* a solid blow [imit]

**²wham** *interj, informal* – used to express the noise of a forceful blow or impact

**³wham** *vb* **-mm-** *informal vt* to propel, strike, or beat with a loud impact ~ *vi* to crash or explode with a loud impact

**whammy** /'wami/ *n, NAm* a supernatural power bringing bad luck [prob fr ¹*wham*]

**¹whang** /wang/ *vt, informal* to propel, strike, or work at with force [*whang* (*whang, lash*), alter. of ME *thong, thwang*]

**²whang** *n, informal* a loud sharp vibrant or resonant sound [imit]

**whangee** /wang'ee/ *n* **1** any of several Chinese bamboos (genus *Phyllostachys*) whose stems are used for walking sticks, canes, etc **2** a walking stick, riding crop, etc of whangee [prob fr Chin (Pek) *huáng lí* (*huang² lí²*), fr *huáng* (*huang²*) yellow + *li* (*li²*) bamboo cane]

**whap** /wop/ *vt or n* (to) whop

**whare** /'wori/ *n* **1** a Maori house of traditional design **2** *NZ* a hut, shack [Maori]

**wharf** /wawf/ *n, pl* **wharves** /wawvz/ *also* **wharfs 1** a structure built along or out from the shore of navigable water so that ships may lie alongside for loading and unloading **2** *obs* the bank of a river or the shore of the sea [ME, fr OE *hwearf* embankment, wharf; akin to OE *hweorfan* to turn, OHG *hwerban*, Gk *karpos* wrist]

**wharfage** /'wawfij/ *n* **1a** the use of a wharf **b** the handling or storage of goods on a wharf **2** the charge for the use of a wharf **3** a system of wharves

**wharfie** /'wawfi/ *n, Austr & NZ informal* a docker

**wharfinger** /'wawf,finjə/ *n* the owner or manager of a commercial wharf [irreg fr *wharfage*]

**wharfmaster** /'wawf,mahstə/ *n* the manager of a wharf

**¹what** /wot/ *pron, pl* **what 1a(1)** – used as an interrogative expressing inquiry about the identity, nature, purpose, or value of something ⟨~ *are these?*⟩ ⟨~ *does he earn?*⟩ ⟨~'s *this handle for?*⟩ ⟨*wonder* ~ *he meant*⟩; sometimes used rhetorically with the effect of a negative statement ⟨~ *is wealth without friends?*⟩ **a(2)** – used to ask for repetition of something not properly heard or understood ⟨*he bought* ~?⟩ **b(1)** *archaic* WHO 1 – used as an interrogative **b(2)** – used as an interrogative expressing inquiry about the character, nature, occupation, position, or role of a person ⟨~'s *she like?*⟩ ⟨~ *do*

*you think I am, a fool*⟩ ⟨~ *is she, that all our swains commend her?* –
Shak⟩ **c** – used as an exclamation expressing surprise or excitement and frequently introducing a question ⟨~, *no breakfast?*⟩ **d** – used to direct attention to a statement that the speaker is about to make ⟨*guess* ~⟩ ⟨*you know* ~⟩ **e** *chiefly Br* – used like a question-tag demanding assent ⟨*a clever play,* ~?⟩ – not now in vogue **2** *substandard* [4]THAT **1**, WHICH **3**, WHO **2** ⟨*gilded rat-holes* ~ *pass for public hostelries – Punch*⟩ **3** that which; the one that ⟨*no income but* ~ *he gets from his writing*⟩ – sometimes used in reference to a clause or phrase that is yet to come or is not yet complete ⟨*gave also,* ~ *is more valuable, understanding*⟩ **4a** whatever ⟨*say* ~ *you will*⟩ **b** *obs* whoever **c** how much – used in exclamations ⟨~ *it must cost!*⟩ [ME, fr OE *hwæt,* neut of *hwā* who – more at WHO] – **or what** – used at the end of a question to express inquiry about additional possibilities ⟨*is it raining, snowing,* or what?⟩ – **what about 1** what news or plans have you concerning **2** *also* **what do you say to, what say, what's wrong with** let's; HOW ABOUT – **what d'you call him/her/it, what's his/her/its name** – used to replace a forgotten name ⟨*married* what d'you call her, *the blonde girl*⟩ – **what for 1** for what purpose or reason; why – usu used with the other words of a question between *what* and *for* ⟨what *did you do that* for?⟩ except when used alone **2** punishment, esp by blows or by a sharp reprimand ⟨*gave him* what for *in violent Spanish – New Yorker*⟩ – **what have you, what not** any of various other things that might also be mentioned ⟨*paper clips, pins, and* what have you⟩ – **what if 1** what will or would be the result if **2** what does it matter if – **what it takes** the qualities or resources needed for success or for attainment of a goal – **what next** WHATEVER NEXT – **what of 1** what is the situation with respect to **2** what importance can be assigned to – **what of it** what does it matter – **what's what** the true state of things ⟨*knows* what's what *when it comes to fashion*⟩ – **what with** having as a contributory circumstance or circumstances ⟨*very busy* what with *all these guests to feed*⟩ – **what's yours?** what would you like to drink?

*usage* When **what** means "things that" or "the ones that" the verb that follows it is plural ⟨*eating* **what** *appear to be kippers*⟩. When a **what**-clause is the subject of a sentence with a plural complement, the linking verb may be either singular or plural ⟨**what** *she enjoys is/are power and responsibility*⟩. When **what** is also the subject of such a clause, both verbs may today be either singular ⟨**what** *really matters is the children*⟩ or plural ⟨**what** *really matter are the children*⟩ provided that they match, although the singular construction has traditionally been preferred.

[2]**what** *adv* **1** in what respect; how much ⟨~ *does he care*⟩ **2** *obs* why [ME, fr OE *hwæt,* fr *hwæt,* pron]

[3]**what** *adj* **1a(1)** – used with a following noun as an adjective equivalent in meaning to the interrogative pronoun *what* ⟨~ *minerals do we export?*⟩ ⟨~ *fool told you that?*⟩ **a(2)** *informal* which ⟨~ *size do you take?*⟩ **b** how remarkable or striking – used esp in exclamatory utterances and dependent clauses ⟨~ *mountains!*⟩ ⟨~ *a suggestion*⟩ ⟨~ *a charming girl!*⟩ ⟨*remember* ~ *fun we had*⟩ **2a** whatever, any ⟨*ornament of* ~ *description soever*⟩ **b** the . . . that; as much or as many . . . as ⟨*told him* ~ *little I knew*⟩ ⟨*rescued* ~ *survivors they found*⟩ [[1]*what*]

**whate'er** /wot'eə/ *adj or pron, poetic* whatever

[1]**whatever** /wot'evə/ *pron* **1a** anything or everything that ⟨*take* ~ *you want*⟩ **b** no matter what **2** *informal* what in the world ⟨~ *do you mean?*⟩ *usage* see EVER – **or whatever** *informal* or anything else at all ⟨*buffalo or rhinoceros* or whatever – Alan Moorehead⟩ – **whatever next** – used as an exclamation over something absurd or outrageous

[2]**whatever** *adj* **1a** any . . . that; all . . . that ⟨*buy peace on* ~ *terms could be obtained* – C S Forester⟩ **b** no matter what ⟨*money, in* ~ *hands, will confer power* – Samuel Johnson⟩ **2** of any kind at all – used after the substantive with *any* or with a negative ⟨*of any shape* ~⟩ ⟨*no food* ~⟩

**what ho** /hoh/ *interj* – used in greeting or hailing

**whatnot** /'wot,not/ *n* **1** a nondescript person or thing **2** a lightweight open set of shelves for bric-a-brac **3** other usu related goods, objects, etc ⟨*carrying all his bags and* ~⟩ **4** *pl* underwear, esp of a frivolous kind [*what not?*]

**whatsit** /'wotsit/ *n, informal* **1** a thing of unspecified, nondescript, or mysterious character ⟨*there's a little* ~ *on top that you have to be careful removing*⟩ **2** – used in place of a temporarily forgotten name ⟨*old* Whatsit *rang to ask if you could read some proofs*⟩ [*what's it?*]

**whatsoever** /,wotsoh'evə/ *pron or adj* whatever

**whaup** /wawp/ *n, pl* **whaups,** *esp collectively* **whaup** *Scot* a curlew [imit]

**wheal** /weel/ *n* a weal

**wheat** /weet/ *n* **1** a cereal grain that yields a fine white flour, is the chief constituent of bread in temperate climates, is used in pastas (eg macaroni or spaghetti), and is important in animal feeds **2** any of various grasses (genus *Triticum,* esp *Triticum aestivum*) that are widely cultivated, esp in most temperate areas, for the wheat they yield [ME *whete,* fr OE *hwǣte;* akin to OHG *weizzi* wheat, *hwīz, wīz* white – more at WHITE]

**wheatear** /'weet,i-ə/ *n* any of several small usu white-rumped Eurasian birds (genus *Oenanthe,* esp *Oenanthe oenanthe*) related to the thrushes [back-formation fr earlier *wheatears,* prob by folk etymology or euphemism fr *white* + *arse*]

**wheaten** /'weet(ə)n/ *adj* (made) of wheat, wheat grain, wheat meal, or wheat flour

**wheat germ** *n* the embryo of the wheat kernel separated from the husk in milling and used esp as a source of vitamins

**wheat rust** *n* any of various destructive diseases of wheat caused by RUST fungi and characterized by the formation of orange to reddish-brown lesions on the leaves, stems, etc; *also* a fungus (eg *Puccinia graminis*) causing a wheat rust

**Wheatstone bridge** /'weet,stohn/ *n* an electrical device (BRIDGE) used to measure the RESISTANCE (opposition to the flow of electric current) of an electrical component, that consists of a 4-sided circuit made up of the component together with three others whose resistances are known and alterable by known amounts. A current is applied across two diagonals and the known resistances are adjusted until no current flows between the other two diagonals, at which point all four resistances have a predetermined relationship which allows the unknown resistance to be calculated. [Sir Charles *Wheatstone* †1875 E physicist & inventor]

**whee** /wee/ *interj* – used to express delight or exuberance

**wheedle** /'weedl/ *vb* **wheedling** /'weedling, 'weedl·ing/ *vt* **1** to influence or entice by soft words or flattery **2a** to gain or get by wheedling ⟨~ *his way into favour*⟩ **b** to cause to part with something by wheedling – + *out of* ⟨~ *her out of her last £5*⟩ ~ *vi* to use soft words of flattery [origin unknown]

[1]**wheel** /weel/ *n* **1** a solid or partly solid circular disc of hard material, or a circular frame joined to a usu central hub by spokes, that is attached to and capable of turning on an axle **2** a contrivance or apparatus having a wheel as its principal part: eg **2a** POTTER'S WHEEL **b** SPINNING WHEEL **c** STEERING WHEEL **d** FERRIS WHEEL **e** a wheel that controls the steering gear of a ship **3a** a chiefly medieval instrument of torture usu consisting of a round wooden revolving frame to which the victim was tied while his/her limbs were broken by a metal bar **b** any of many revolving discs or drums that help to produce an arbitrary value on which to gamble ⟨*roulette* ~⟩ **4** an imaginary turning wheel symbolizing the inconstancy of fortune **5** something resembling a wheel in shape or motion; *esp* CATHERINE WHEEL **6a** a curving or circular movement **b** a rotation or turn usu about an axis or centre; *specif* a turning movement of troops or ships in line in which the units preserve alignment and relative positions as they change direction **7a** *pl* the moving or controlling parts of something compared to a machine ⟨*the* ~s *of government*⟩ **b** *chiefly NAm informal* a person of importance, esp in an organization ⟨*a big* ~⟩ **8** *pl, informal* a motor vehicle; *esp* a car **9** *NAm informal* a bicycle [ME, fr OE *hweogol, hwēol;* akin to ON *hvēl* wheel, Gk *kyklos* circle, wheel, Skt *cakra,* L *colere* to cultivate, inhabit, Gk *telos* end] – **wheelless** *adj* – **oil the wheels** to help things run smoothly – see also **put one's** SHOULDER **to the wheel, put a** SPOKE **in somebody's wheel**

[2]**wheel** *vi* **1** to turn (as if) on an axis; revolve **2** to change direction as if revolving on a pivot ⟨~ed *round and walked away*⟩ **3** to alter or reverse one's procedure or opinion – often + *about* or *round* **4** to move or extend in a circle or curve ⟨*birds in* ~ing *flight*⟩ **5** to drive or go (as if) on wheels or in a wheeled vehicle ⟨~ed *down the hill on her bicycle*⟩ ~ *vt* **1** to cause to turn (as if) on an axis; rotate **2** to convey or move (as if) on wheels or in a wheeled vehicle; *esp* to push (a wheeled vehicle or its occupant) ⟨~ *the baby into the shade*⟩ **3** to cause to change direction as if revolving on a pivot **4** to make or perform in a circle or curve – **wheel and deal** to pursue one's own usu commercial interests, esp in a shrewd or unscrupulous manner

**wheel and axle** *n* a simple mechanical device (eg for raising a weight) consisting of a large wheel with an axle round which a cord or chain attached to a load is wound when the wheel is turned

**wheel animal** *also* **wheel animalcule** *n* ROTIFER (minute aquatic animal)

¹**wheelbarrow** /'wheel,baroh/ *n* a load-carrying device that consists of a shallow box supported at one end by usu one wheel and at the other by a stand when at rest, or by handles when being pushed

²**wheelbarrow** *vt* to transport in a wheelbarrow

**wheelbarrow race** *n* a race in which the contestants, usu children, compete in pairs, one walking on his/her hands with the body parallel to the ground, and the other holding his/her legs

**wheelbase** /'weel,bays/ *n* the distance between the front and rear axles of a vehicle

**wheelchair** /'weel,chea/ *n* a chair mounted on wheels, esp for the use of invalids

**wheeled** /weeld/ *adj* equipped with or moving on wheels ⟨~ *vehicles*⟩ – often used in combination ⟨2-wheeled⟩

**wheeler** /'weelə/ *n* **1** a maker of wheels **2** a draught animal (eg a horse) pulling in the position nearest the front wheels of a wagon **3** something (eg a vehicle or ship) that has at least one wheel or PADDLE WHEEL – esp in combination ⟨side-wheeler⟩ **4** *pl* cyclists – esp in names (eg of cycling clubs) ⟨*Herts* Wheelers⟩

,**wheeler-'dealer** *n, chiefly NAm informal* a shrewd operator, esp in business or politics [fr the vb phrase *wheel and deal*] – **wheeler-dealing** *n*

**wheelhorse** /'weel,haws/ *n* **1** a horse acting as wheeler **2** *NAm* a steady and effective worker, esp in a political body

**wheelhouse** /'weel,hows/ *n* a deckhouse for a vessel's helmsman containing the steering wheel, compass, and navigating equipment

**wheelie** /'weeli/ *n* a manoeuvre in which a wheeled vehicle (eg a motorcycle) is momentarily balanced on its rear wheel or wheels

**wheel lock** *n* an obsolete gunlock in which sparks are struck from a flint (or a piece of IRON PYRITES (hard iron-containing mineral)) by a revolving wheel

**wheelman** /'weelmən/ *n* **1** a cyclist **2** *NAm* a helmsman

**wheel ore** *n* BOURNONITE (mineral occurring as wheel-shaped grains)

**wheelsman** /'weelzmən/ *n, NAm* someone who steers with a wheel; *esp* a helmsman

**wheelspin** /'weel,spin, 'wiəl-/ *n* usu rapid turning of a vehicle's wheels but without getting any grip and therefore skidding on the surface upon which they are turning

**wheels within wheels** *n* a series of usu hidden and interrelated circumstances, events, influences, etc often causing complications or having unforeseen effects [fr the reference in Ezek 1:16]

**wheelwork** /'weel,wuhk/ *n* an arrangement of wheels or gears and their connections in a machine or mechanism

**wheelwright** /'weel,riet/ *n* someone who makes or repairs wheels, esp wooden ones for carts

¹**wheen** /ween/ *adj, Scot & NEng* few [ME (Sc) *quheyne*, fr OE *hwǣne, hwēne*, adv, somewhat, fr *hwōn* little, few]

²**wheen** *n, Scot & NEng* a considerable number or amount

¹**wheeze** /weez/ *vi* **1** to breathe with difficulty, usu with a whistling sound **2** to make a sound like that of wheezing ~ *vt* to utter wheezily [ME *whesen*, prob fr Scand origin; akin to ON *hvæsa* to hiss; akin to OE *hwǣst* action of blowing, L *queri* to complain]

²**wheeze** *n* **1** a sound of wheezing **2a** an often repeated and widely known joke used esp by entertainers **b** *informal* a cunning trick or expedient **c** *informal* a trite saying or proverb

**wheezy** /'weezi/ *adj* **1** inclined to wheeze **2** having a wheezing sound **3** *informal* cunning, clever, or ingenious ⟨*a ~ little plan to get them out of their difficulties*⟩ – **wheezily** *adv*, **wheeziness** *n*

¹**whelk** /welk/ *n* any of numerous large marine snails (eg of the genus *Buccinum*); *esp* one (*Buccinum undatum*) much used as food in Europe [ME *welke*, fr OE *weoloc*; akin to L *volvere* to turn – more at VOLUBLE]

²**whelk** *vi* to gather whelks

³**whelk** *n* **1** a small rounded lump or blisterlike elevation on the skin; a pustule, pimple **2** a weal, welt [ME *whelke*, fr OE *hwylca*, fr *hwelian* to suppurate]

**whelm** /welm/ *vt, archaic* **1** to cover or engulf completely and usu disastrously **2** to overcome in thought or feeling; overwhelm [ME *whelmen*]

¹**whelp** /welp/ *n* **1** any of the young of various flesh-eating

mammals, esp a dog **2** a disagreeable or despised child or youth [ME, fr OE *hwelp;* akin to OHG *hwelf* whelp]

²**whelp** *vt* to give birth to (esp a puppy) ~ *vi, esp of a bitch* to give birth to young

¹**when** /wen/ *adv* **1** at what time ⟨~ *will he return?*⟩ ⟨*wonder ~ they open*⟩ **2a** at or during which time ⟨*the day ~ we met*⟩ **b** and then; WHEREUPON **1 3** *chiefly NAm* at a former and usu less prosperous time ⟨*brag fondly of having known him ~* – Vance Packard⟩ [ME, fr OE *hwanne, hwenne;* akin to OHG *hwanne* when, OE *hwā* who – more at WHO]

²**when** *conj* **1a** at or during the time that; while ⟨*went fishing ~ he was a boy*⟩ **b** AS SOON AS ⟨*stop writing ~ the bell rings*⟩ ⟨*will look nice ~ finished*⟩ **c** just at the moment that ⟨*were dancing ~ I came in*⟩ **d** whenever ⟨~ *he listens to music, he falls asleep*⟩ **2** in the event that; if ⟨*a contestant is disqualified ~ he disobeys the rules*⟩ **3a** considering that ⟨*why use water at all ~ you can drown in it* – Stuart Chase⟩ **b** in spite of the fact that; although ⟨*gave up politics ~ he might have made a great career in it*⟩ [ME, fr OE *hwanne, hwenne*, fr *hwanne, hwenne*, adv]

*usage* The use of **when** to define things ⟨*a chantry is* **when** *somebody leaves money for masses to be chanted*⟩ should be avoided in formal writing.

³**when** *pron* what or which time ⟨*in 19:4, since ~ he has been working at landscapes and portraits* – Horizon⟩ – compare SAY WHEN

⁴**when** *n* a date, epoch ⟨*troubled his head very little about the hows and ~s of life* – Laurence Sterne⟩

**whence** /wens/ *adv or conj, chiefly formal* **1a** from where; from what place, source, or cause ⟨~ *spring these doubts?*⟩ – sometimes + *from* **b** from which place, source, or cause – sometimes + *from* ⟨*the village from ~ he came*⟩ **2** to the place from which ⟨*returned ~ they came*⟩ **3** from which preceding fact or premise ⟨*he knows nothing, ~ it follows that he cannot tell us*⟩ [ME *whennes*, fr *whenne* whence (fr OE *hwanon*) + *-s*, adv suffix, fr *-s*, gen sing. ending; akin to OHG *hwanān* whence, OE *hwā* who]

*usage* The construction *from* **whence** has been long established in English, but is today disliked by some people, who prefer to use **whence** alone ⟨*the village* **whence** *he came*⟩.

**whencesoever** /,wens·soh'evə/ *conj, archaic* from whatever place or source

¹**whenever** /wen'evə/ *conj* **1** at any or every time ⟨*roof leaks ~ it rains*⟩ **2** at whatever time ⟨*can go ~ he likes*⟩ ⟨*will give him the message ~ he returns*⟩ **3** in any circumstance ⟨~ *possible, he tries to help*⟩

²**whenever** *adv, informal* when in the world ⟨~ *did you find the time?*⟩ *usage* see EVER – **or whenever** *informal* or at any similar time ⟨*in 1922* or whenever⟩

¹**whensoever** /,wensoh'evə/ *conj, archaic* whenever

²**whensoever** *adv, archaic* at any time whatever

¹**where** /weə/ *adv* **1a** at, in, or to what place ⟨~ *is the house?*⟩ ⟨*knows ~ the house is*⟩ ⟨~ *are we going?*⟩ **b** at, in, or to what situation, direction, circumstances, or respect ⟨~ *does this plan lead?*⟩ ⟨*shows ~ the plan leads*⟩ ⟨~ *is he wrong?*⟩ **2a** at, in, or to which place ⟨*the town ~ she lives*⟩ **b** at, in, or to which ⟨*has reached the size ~ traffic is a problem*⟩ **3** *archaic* here, there ⟨*lo, ~ it comes again* – Shak⟩ [ME, fr OE *hwǣr;* akin to OHG *hwār* where, OE *hwā* who – more at WHO]

*usage* Although one must say ⟨**where** *do you come from?*⟩ one need not add *to* to ⟨*where are you going* [*to*]?⟩ and one should not add *at* to ⟨*where are you* (△ *at*)?⟩.

²**where** *conj* **1a** at, in, or to the place at which ⟨*stay ~ you are*⟩ ⟨*send him away ~ he'll forget*⟩ ⟨~ *I live, there are plenty of sheep*⟩ **b** WHEREVER **2** ⟨*goes ~ he likes*⟩ **c** in a case, situation, or respect in which ⟨*outstanding ~ endurance is called for*⟩ **2** whereas, while ⟨*he wants a house, ~ I would prefer a flat*⟩ – **where it's at** *slang* the real scene of the action – no longer in vogue

³**where** *n* **1** what place or point ⟨~ *are you from?*⟩ **2** a place, point ⟨*bought from any old ~*⟩

**whereabout** /'weərə,bowt/ *adv, conj, or n, chiefly NAm* whereabouts

¹**whereabouts** /,weərə'bowts/ *adv or conj* in what vicinity ⟨~ *is the house?*⟩ ⟨*know ~ he lives*⟩ [ME *wherȝaboutes* (fr *wher aboute* +*-s*, adv suffix) & *wher aboute*, fr *where, wher* where + *about, aboute* about – more at WHENCE]

²**whereabouts** /'weərə,bowts/ *n taking sing or pl vb* the place or general locality where a person or thing is ⟨*his present ~ are a secret*⟩

**¹whereas** /weər'az/ *conj* **1** in view of the fact that; since – used, esp formally, to introduce a preamble **2** while on the contrary; although [ME *where as,* fr *where* + *as*]
**²whereas** *n* **1** a preamble **2** a conditional or qualifying statement
**whereat** /weə'rat/ *conj, formal* **1** at or towards which **2** in consequence of which; whereupon
**¹whereby** /'weəbie/ *conj* **1** in accordance with which ⟨*a law ~ children receive cheap milk*⟩ **2** *formal* by which means
**²whereby** *adv, obs* by what means; how
**where'er** /weə'reə/ *adv or conj, poetic* wherever
**¹wherefore** /'weəfaw, ‚-'-/ *adv, formal* **1** for what reason; why **2** for that reason; therefore [ME *wherfor, wherfore,* fr *where, wher* + *for, fore* for]
**²wherefore** /'weə‚faw/ *n* the reason, cause ⟨*wants to know the whys and ~s*⟩
**wherefrom** /weə'from/ *conj, formal* from which
**¹wherein** /weə'rin/ *adv, formal* in what; how ⟨*~ was he wrong?*⟩ ⟨*showed him ~ he was wrong*⟩
**²wherein** *conj, formal* **1** in which, where ⟨*the city ~ he lived*⟩ **2** during which
**whereinto** /weə'rintooh/ *conj, formal* into which
**whereof** /weə'rov/ *adv or conj, formal* of which, whom, or what
**whereon** /weə'ron/ *adv or conj* **1** whereupon **2** *formal* on which or what ⟨*the base ~ it rests*⟩
**wheresoever** /‚weəsoh'evə/ *conj, archaic* wherever
**wherethrough** /weə'throoh/ *conj, formal* through which
**whereto** /weə'tooh/ *adv or conj, formal* to which or what; whither ⟨*~ tends all this* – Shak⟩
**whereunto** /weə'runtooh/ *adv or conj, informal* whereto
**whereupon** /‚weərə'pon/ *adv or conj* **1** closely following and in consequence of which ⟨*he saw me coming, ~ he offered me his seat*⟩ **2** *formal* on which; whereon
**¹wherever** /weə'revə/ *adv, informal* where in the world ⟨*~ have you been?*⟩ *usage* see EVER – **or wherever** or anywhere else at all ⟨*go to China or wherever*⟩
**²wherever** *conj* **1** at, in, or to every place ⟨*thrives ~ she goes*⟩ **2** at, in, or to whatever place ⟨*can sleep ~ he likes*⟩ **3** WHENEVER **3**
**¹wherewith** /weə'widh, -'with/ *conj, chiefly formal* with or by means of which
**²wherewith** *pron, archaic* that with or by which – + *to* and infin ⟨*had not ~ to feed himself*⟩
**³wherewith** *adv, obs* with what ⟨*~ shall it be salted?* – Mt 5:13 (AV)⟩
**¹wherewithal** /'weəwi‚dhawl/ *conj, formal* wherewith [*where* + *withal*]
**²wherewithal** *pron, archaic* wherewith
**³wherewithal** *n* means, resources; *specif* money ⟨*didn't have the ~ for an expensive dinner*⟩
**wherry** /'weri/ *n* **1** any of various light boats: e g **1a** a long light rowing boat which is pointed at both ends and used to transport passengers on rivers and about harbours **b** *NAm* a racing scull for one person **2** a large light barge, lighter, or fishing boat varying in type in different parts of Britain [ME *whery*]
**¹whet** /wet/ *vt* **-tt-** **1** to sharpen by rubbing on or with something (e g a stone) ⟨*~ a knife*⟩ **2** to make keen or more acute; excite, stimulate ⟨*~ the appetite*⟩ [ME *whetten,* fr OE *hwettan;* akin to OHG *wezzen* to whet, *waz* sharp] – **whetter** *n*
**²whet** *n* **1** something that whets: **1a** a goad, incitement **b** an appetizer **2** *dial* a time, while [(2) orig referring to the time between two whettings of a scythe]
**¹whether** /'wedhə/ *n, archaic* which or whichever one of the two [ME, fr OE *hwæther, hwether;* akin to OHG *hwedar* which of two, L *uter,* Gk *poteros,* OE *hwā* who – more at WHO]
**²whether** *conj* – used usu + *or* or *or whether* to indicate **a** until the early 19th century, a direct question involving alternatives **b** an indirect question involving alternatives ⟨*decide ~ he should agree, protest, or do neither*⟩ or choice between two options ⟨*I wonder ~ he heard*⟩ **c** indifference between alternatives ⟨*seated him next to her, ~ by accident or design*⟩ [ME, fr OE *hwaether, hwether,* fr *hwaether, hwether,* pron] – **whether or no/whether or not** IN ANY CASE ⟨*will go whether or no*⟩
**whetstone** /'wet‚stohn/ *n* **1** SHARPENING STONE **2** something that stimulates or makes keen
**whew** /fyooh/ *n* a sound like a half-formed whistle uttered as an exclamation ⟨*gave a long ~ when he realized the size of the*

*job*⟩ – used interjectionally chiefly to express amazement, discomfort, or relief [imit]
**whey** /way/ *n* the serum or watery part of milk that separates from the clotted part or curd, esp in the process of making cheese, and that is rich in the sugar LACTOSE, minerals, and vitamins [ME, fr OE *hwæg;* akin to MD *wey* whey] – **wheyey** *adj*
**whey-'face** *n* a person having a pale face (e g from fear or ill-health) – **whey-faced** *adj*
**¹which** /wich/ *adj* **1** being what one or ones out of a known or limited group – used as an interrogative ⟨*~ tie should I wear?*⟩ ⟨*kept a record of ~ employees took their holidays in July*⟩ **2** whichever ⟨*it will not fit, turn it ~ way you like*⟩ **3** – used to introduce a NONRESTRICTIVE CLAUSE, by modifying a noun therein which refers either to a preceding word or group or to a whole previous clause ⟨*he may come, in ~ case I'll ask him*⟩ [ME, of what kind, which, fr OE *hwilc;* akin to OHG *wilīh* of what kind, which; both fr a prehistoric Gmc compound whose first constituent is akin to OE *hwā* who & whose second is represented by OE *-līc* -ly – more at WHO, -LY]
**²which** *pron, pl* **which** **1** what one out of a known or specified group – used as an interrogative ⟨*~ of those houses do you live in?*⟩ ⟨*~ of you want tea and ~ want lemonade?*⟩ ⟨*he is swimming or canoeing, I don't know ~*⟩ **2** whichever ⟨*take ~ you like*⟩ **3** – used to introduce a RESTRICTIVE or esp a NONRESTRICTIVE CLAUSE; used in any grammatical relation except that of a possessive; used esp in reference to an animal, thing, or idea ⟨*the office in ~ I work*⟩ ⟨*a large dog, ~ bit me*⟩, or to a human group, esp when a singular verb follows ⟨*this tribe, ~ has aroused much interest among anthropologists*⟩; used freely in reference to people as recently as the 17th century ⟨*our Father ~ art in heaven* – Mt 6:9 (AV)⟩; often used in reference to a whole previous clause or even to a preceding sentence ⟨*can sing, ~ is an advantage*⟩ ⟨*can be overcome by basing these programs on need not race. Which is fine* – Nation Review (Melbourne)⟩; compare THAT, WHO, WHOM
**usage** **1** The use of **which** to refer to a whole sentence ⟨*he can sing,* **which** *is an advantage*⟩ is perfectly correct. It should, however, be avoided where it may lead to ambiguity. In ⟨*she crashed the car,* **which** *was expensive*⟩ does *expensive* apply to the car or the crashing? **2** If one of two linked parts of a sentence entails a **who, which,** or **that,** then the other part must have a **who,** a **which,** or a **that** too, referring to the same thing ⟨*Mr Reagan bends over to inspect two birds* **which/that** *were presented* (not △ *two birds presented*) *to him by the California Turkey Industry Board and* **which** *will grace the table*⟩. See ⁴THAT
**¹whichever** /wi'chevə/ *pron, pl* **whichever** **1** whatever one out of a group ⟨*take two of the four optional papers, ~ you prefer*⟩ **2** no matter which **3** *informal* which in the world ⟨*~ did you choose?*⟩ *usage* see EVER
**²whichever** *adj* being whatever one or ones out of a group; no matter which ⟨*its soothing ... effect will be the same ~ way you take it* – Punch⟩
**whichsoever** /‚wichsoh'evə/ *pron or adj, formal* whichever
**whicker** /'wikə/ *vi* to neigh, whinny [imit] – **whicker** *n*
**whid** /wid/ *vi* **-dd-** *Scot* to move nimbly and silently [Sc *whid* silent rapid motion, perh of Scand origin]
**whidah** /'widə/ *n* WHYDAH (African bird)
**¹whiff** /wif/ *n* **1a** a quick puff or slight gust, esp of air, odour, gas, smoke, or spray **b** an inhalation of odour, gas, or smoke **c** a slight puffing or whistling sound **2** a slight trace ⟨*a ~ of scandal*⟩ [imit]
**²whiff** *vi* **1** to move (as if) with a puff of air **2** to emit whiffs; puff **3** to inhale an odour; sniff **4** to smell unpleasant ~ *vt* **1** to carry or convey (as if) by a whiff; blow **2** to expel or puff out in a whiff; exhale **3** SMOKE **4**
**whiffet** /'wifit/ *n, NAm* a small, young, or unimportant person [orig sense, a small dog; alter. of *whippet*]
**whiffle** /'wifl/ *vi* **1a** *of the wind* to blow unsteadily or in gusts **b** to flicker, flutter **2** to be evasive; vacillate **3** to emit or produce a light whistling or puffing sound ⟨*a whiffling old labrador* – Punch⟩ ~ *vt* to blow, disperse, emit, or expel (as if) with a whiff [prob freq of *whiff*]
**whiffletree** /'wifl‚tree/ *n, chiefly NAm* SWINGLETREE (bar for attaching harness traces) [alter. of *whippletree*]
**Whig** /wig/ *n* **1** a member or supporter of a major British political group of the 18th and early 19th centuries seeking to limit royal authority and increase parliamentary power – compare TORY **2** an American favouring independence from Britain during the American Revolution **3** a member or sup-

porter of an American political party formed about 1834 in opposition to the Jacksonian Democrats, associated chiefly with manufacturing, commercial, and financial interests, and succeeded about 1854 by the Republican party [short for *Whiggamore* (member of a Scottish group that marched to Edinburgh in 1648 to oppose the court party), prob fr Sc *whig* to drive + *more* horse, mare] – **Whig** *adj*, **Whiggish** *adj*, **Whiggism** *n*

**Whiggery** /ˌwigəri/ *n* the principles or practices of Whigs

**¹while** /wiel/ *n* **1** a period of time, esp when short and marked by the occurrence of an action or condition; a time ⟨*stay here for a* ~⟩ – compare BETWEENWHILES **2** the time and effort used (eg in the performance of an action); trouble ⟨*worth your* ~⟩ *usage* see AWHILE [ME, fr OE *hwīl;* akin to OHG *hwīla* time, L *quies* rest, quiet] – **the while** *poetic* meanwhile

**²while** *conj* **1a** during the time that ⟨*take a nap* ~ *I'm out*⟩ ⟨*I read it* ~ *in hospital*⟩ **b** AS LONG AS **1** ⟨~ *there's life, there's hope*⟩ **2a** when on the other hand; whereas ⟨*easy for an expert,* ~ *it is dangerous for a novice*⟩ **b** in spite of the fact that; although ⟨~ *respected, he is not liked*⟩ **3** similarly and at the same time that ⟨~ *the book will be welcomed by scholars, it will make an immediate appeal to the general reader* – *Brit Book News*⟩

  *usage* The use of **while** to mean "whereas" or "although" has been established in English since the 16th century. One should be careful, however, to avoid ambiguity where **while** can mean "during the time that" or "although". A sentence such as ⟨**while** *he is young, he will do the work perfectly well*⟩ has two meanings.

**³while** *prep, archaic or dial* until

**while away, wile away** *vt* to cause (time) to pass, esp without boredom or in a pleasant leisurely manner ⟨*while away the afternoon*⟩

**whiles** /wielz/ *adv, chiefly Scot* sometimes [ME (Sc) *quhilis* sometimes, formerly, fr ME (Sc) *quhile*, ME *while*, fr OE *hwīle* formerly, once, fr *hwīle*, acc of *hwīl* time, while]

**whilst** /wielst/ *conj, chiefly Br* while [ME *whilest*, alter. of *whiles*, fr ²*while* + *-s*, adv suffix (cf AGAINST, AMIDST, AMONGST)]

**whim** /wim/ *n* **1** a sudden, capricious, or eccentric idea or impulse; a fancy **2** a large capstan formerly used in mines for raising ore or water *synonyms* see CAPRICE [short for *whim-wham*]

**whimbrel** /ˈwimbrəl/ *n* a small Eurasian curlew (*Numenius phaeopus*) that has broad stripes on its crown, a whitish rump, is found on mud flats and estuaries, and nests among heather and rough grass [perh imit]

**¹whimper** /ˈwimpə/ *vi* **1** to make low plaintive whining sounds **2** to complain or protest petulantly [imit]

**²whimper** *n* **1** a whimpering cry or sound **2** a petulant complaint or protest

**whimsical** /ˈwimzikl/ *adj* **1** full of whims; capricious **2** resulting from or suggesting whimsy ⟨*a* ~ *hat*⟩; *esp* quizzical, playful ⟨*a* ~ *smile*⟩ [*whimsy* + *-ical*] – **whimsicality** *n*, **whimsically** *adv*, **whimsicalness** *n*

**whimsy, whimsey** /ˈwimzi/ *n* **1** a whim, caprice **2** a fanciful or fantastic device, object, or creation, esp in writing or art **3** the quality of affected quaintness ⟨*to avoid* ~ *when writing for children*⟩ *synonyms* see CAPRICE [irreg fr *whim-wham*] – **whimsied** *adj*

**whim-wham** /ˈwimˌwam/ *n* **1** a whimsical object, esp of ornament or dress; a knick-knack **2** a fancy, whim [origin unknown]

**whin** /win/ *n* FURZE (type of shrub) [ME *whynne*, of Scand origin; akin to Norw *kvein* bent grass]

**whinchat** /ˈwinchat/ *n* a small brown and buff Eurasian songbird (*Saxicola rubetra*) that has a white eye stripe, is found in open countryside where there is bracken, gorse, etc, in marshes, and on commons, and nests in coarse grass [*whin* + ²*chat*]

**¹whine** /wien/ *vi* **1a** to utter a high-pitched plaintive cry **b** to make a sound like such a cry ⟨*the wind* ~d *in the chimney*⟩ **2** to utter a querulous or peevish complaint **3** to move with the sound of a whine ⟨*the bullet* ~d *over our heads*⟩ ~ *vt* to utter or express (as if) with a whine [ME *whinen*, fr OE *hwīnan* to whizz; akin to ON *hvīna* to whizz] – **whiner** *n*, **whiningly** *adv*

**²whine** *n* **1a** a prolonged high-pitched cry, usu expressive of distress or pain **b** a sound like such a cry ⟨*the* ~ *of the engine*⟩ **2** a querulous or peevish complaint – **whiny, whiney** *adj*

**whing-ding** /ˈwingˌding/ *n* WINGDING [by alter.]

**whinge, winge** /winj/ *vi, chiefly Austr & dial Br* to complain,

moan [(assumed) ME *whingen* to whine, fr OE *hwinsian*] – **whinger** *n*

**¹whinny** /ˈwini/ *vi* to utter a whinny ~ *vt* to utter (as if) with a whinny [prob imit]

**²whinny** *n* a low gentle neigh; *also* a similar sound

**whinstone** /ˈwinˌstohn/ *n* any of various dark fine-grained rocks (eg basalt) formed by the cooling and solidification of molten rock material [*whin* (very hard rock), fr ME (northern) *quin*]

**¹whip** /wip/ *vb* **-pp-** *vt* **1** to take, pull, jerk, or move very quickly and forcefully ⟨~*ped out a gun*⟩ **2a(1)** to strike with a slender flexible implement (eg a lash or rod), esp as a punishment **a(2)** to spank **b** to drive or urge on (as if) by using a whip **c** to strike as a lash does ⟨*rain* ~*ping the pavement*⟩ **3a** to bind or wrap (eg a rope or rod) with cord for protection and strength **b** to wind or wrap (eg cord) round something **4** to belabour with stinging words; abuse **5** to oversew (an edge, hem, or seam) with shallow overcasting stitches; *also* to hem or join (eg ribbon or lace) by whipping **6** to fish (water) with rod, line, and artificial bait **7** to beat (eg eggs or cream) into a froth with a utensil (eg a whisk or fork) **8** to gather together or hold together for united action in the manner of a whipper-in or party whip **9** *informal* to overcome decisively; defeat **10** *chiefly Br slang* to snatch suddenly; *esp* to steal ~ *vi* **1** to move, go, or come quickly or violently; whisk ⟨~*ped out of the turning at top speed*⟩ **2** to thrash about flexibly like a whiplash ⟨*flags* ~*ping in the wind*⟩ – see also **whip into** SHAPE [ME *wippen, whippen;* akin to MD *wippen* to move up and down, sway, OE *wīpian* to wipe] – **whipper** *n*

**whip in** *vt* to keep (hounds in a pack) from scattering by use of a whip

**whip up** *vt* **1** to stir up; incite ⟨*whip up the emotions of the crowd*⟩ **2** to produce in a hurry ⟨*whip a meal up in no time at all*⟩

**²whip** *n* **1** an instrument consisting usu of a lash attached to a handle, used for driving and controlling animals and for punishment **2** a stroke or cut (as if) with a whip **3a** a dessert made by whipping some of the ingredients ⟨*prune* ~⟩ **b** WHISK **2a** (utensil) **4** a hoisting apparatus; *esp* one consisting of a single block and a small rope for lifting light articles **5** someone who handles a whip: eg **5a** a driver of horses; a coachman **b** a whipper-in **6a** a member of Parliament or other legislative body appointed by a political party to enforce party discipline and to secure the attendance and votes of party members at important sessions **b** *often cap* an instruction (eg a THREE-LINE WHIP or a TWO-LINE WHIP) to each member of a political party in Parliament to be in attendance for voting **c** membership of the group of MPs that constitutes the official parliamentary representation of a political party, together with the privileges and duties of that membership ⟨*was deprived of the Labour* ~⟩ **7** a whipping or thrashing motion **8** the quality of resembling a whip, esp in being flexible **9** any of various pieces of machinery that operate with a quick vibratory motion (eg a spring in an electrical device for making a circuit) **10** a flexible radio aerial **11** a fairground amusement device of cars which circle with sudden jerks round a central pivot – **whiplike** *adj*

**whipcord** /ˈwipˌkawd/ *n* **1** a thin tough cord made of tightly braided or twisted hemp or catgut **2** a usu cotton or worsted cloth that is made of hard-twisted yarns and that has fine diagonal cords or ribs [fr its use in making whips]

**whip hand** *n* **1** the hand holding the whip in driving **2** the positive control; the advantage ⟨*it's no use arguing; they have the* ~⟩

**whiplash** /ˈwipˌlash/ *n* **1** the lash of a whip **2** WHIPLASH INJURY

**whiplash injury** *n* injury to the neck resulting from a sudden sharp whipping movement of the neck and head (eg of a person in a vehicle that is struck head-on or from the rear by another vehicle)

**whipper-in** /ˈwipə/ *n, pl* **whippers-in** a huntsman's assistant who whips in the hounds

**whippersnapper** /ˈwipəˌsnapə/ *n* a diminutive, insignificant, or presumptuous person [prob alter. of earlier *snippersnapper*, prob fr *snip* + *snap*]

**whippet** /ˈwipit/ *n* (any of) a breed of small swift slender dogs related to greyhounds [prob fr ¹*whip* + *-et*]

**whipping** /ˈwiping/ *n* **1** the act of someone who whips: eg **1a** a severe beating or chastisement **b** the act or result of stitching with whipstitch **2** material used to whip or bind

**whipping boy** *n* **1** a boy formerly educated with a prince and punished in his stead **2** a scapegoat

**whipping post** *n* a post to which offenders were formerly tied to be whipped as a legal penalty

**whippletree** /'wipl,tree/ *n* SWINGLETREE (bar for attaching harness traces) [perh irreg fr *whip* + *tree*]

**whippoorwill** /'wipə,wil/ *n* a N American nightjar (*Caprimulgus vociferus*) that has mottled brown plumage and a vigorous call, lives in woodland that is close to open country, and feeds on insects [imit]

**whippy** /'wipi/ *adj* 1 of or resembling a whip 2 unusually resilient; springy ⟨*a ~ fishing rod*⟩

**'whip-,round** *n, chiefly Br informal* a collection of money made usu for a benevolent purpose ⟨*had a ~ to help the couple pay for a Paris honeymoon – The People*⟩

**'whipsaw** /'wip,saw/ *n* any of various flexible saws (e g a narrow tapering PIT SAW) [²*whip*]

**²whipsaw** *vt, NAm* to worst or victimize in two opposite ways at once

**whip scorpion** *n* any of an order (Pedipalpida of the class Arachnida) of INVERTEBRATE animals somewhat resembling true scorpions but having a long slender tail and no sting

**whip stall** *n* a stall during a vertical climb in which the nose of the aeroplane whips violently forwards and then downwards

**'whipstitch** /'wip,stich/ *vt* WHIP 5

**²whipstitch** *n* 1 a very small overcasting stitch 2 *NAm* a small interval of time

**whipstock** /'wip,stok/ *n* the handle of a whip

**whipworm** /'wip,wuhm/ *n* a parasitic NEMATODE worm (family Trichuridae) with a body that is thickened at the rear, and is very long and slender in front; *esp* one (*Trichuris trichiura*) parasitic in the human intestine

**'whirl** /wuhl/ *vi* 1 to move along a curving or circling course, esp with force or speed ⟨*planets ~ing in their orbits*⟩ 2a to turn usu rapidly round and round on an axis; rotate b to turn abruptly round; wheel ⟨*he ~ed to face me*⟩ 3 to pass quickly or hurriedly ⟨*she ~ed down the hallway*⟩ 4 to become giddy or dizzy; reel ⟨*my head's ~ing*⟩ ~ *vt* 1 to convey rapidly; whisk ⟨*the ambulance ~ed him away*⟩ 2a to cause to turn usu rapidly round and round on an axis; rotate b to cause to turn abruptly round ⟨*he ~ed his head*⟩ [ME *whirlen*, prob of Scand origin; akin to ON *hvirfla* to whirl; akin to OHG *wirbil* whirlwind, OE *hweorfan* to turn – more at WHARF] – **whirler** *n*

**²whirl** *n* 1a a rapid rotating or circling movement b something undergoing such a movement or having a form suggestive of such a movement ⟨*a ~ of foam*⟩ 2a a confused tumult; a bustle ⟨*the social ~*⟩ b a confused or disturbed mental state; turmoil ⟨*my mind is in a ~ all the time* – Arnold Bennett⟩ c *informal* a rapid or hurried trip; a spin ⟨*come for a ~ in the car*⟩ 3 *informal* an experimental or brief attempt; a try ⟨*gave it a ~*⟩

**whirligig** /'wuhli,gig/ *n* 1 a child's toy (e g a top) that whirls 2a something that continuously whirls, moves, or changes b a whirling or circling course (e g of events) [ME *whirlegigg*, fr *whirlen* to whirl + *gigg* top – more at GIG]

**whirligig beetle** *n* any of numerous beetles (family Gyrinidae) that live mainly on the surface of water where they move swiftly about in curves

**whirlpool** /'wuhl,poohl/ *n* 1 water moving rapidly in a circle so as to produce a depression in the centre into which floating objects may be drawn; an eddy, vortex 2a a confused tumult and bustle; a whirl b a magnetic or impelling force by which something may be engulfed ⟨*a seething ~ of competition and intrigue* – David Cecil⟩

**whirlwind** /'wuhl,wind/ *n* 1 a small rotating windstorm of limited extent, marked by an inward and upward spiral motion of the lower air round a core of low pressure 2a a confused rush; a whirl b a destructive force or agency

   *synonyms* Whirlwind, hurricane, typhoon, tornado, cyclone, waterspout, and twister are all words for circulating winds. Hurricane is the top level of wind on the Beaufort scale, but the word is aplied particularly tb a violent tropical cyclone of the West Indies. A similar wind in the Western Pacific or the China Sea is a typhoon. A violent funnel-shaped wind of small diameter passing over land is a tornado, and a similar one over water is a waterspout. Twister is an American word for an obviously revolving tornado or waterspout.

**whirlybird** /'wuhli,buhd/ *n, informal* a helicopter – no longer in vogue

**'whirr, whir** /wuh/ *vb* **-rr-** *vi* to fly, revolve, or dart rapidly with a whirr ~ *vt* to move or carry rapidly with a whirr [ME (Sc) *quirren*, prob of Scand origin; akin to Dan *hvirre* to whirl, whirr; akin to OE *hweorfan* to turn]

**²whirr, whir** *n* a continuous buzzing or vibratory sound made by something in rapid motion

**whirry** /'wuhri/ *vt, Scot* to convey quickly [perh blend of *whirr* and *hurry*]

**'whish** /wish/ *vt* to cause to move with a whish ~ *vi* 1 to make a sibilant sound 2 to move fast; whizz ⟨*trees ~ past the train window*⟩ [imit]

**²whish** *n* a rushing sound; a swish

**whisht** /wist, wisht/ *vi, dial Br* to hush, whist [imit]

**'whisk** /wisk/ *n* 1 a quick light brushing or whipping motion 2a any of various small usu hand-held kitchen utensils consisting typically of coiled wire, a bunch of thick wire loops, or two rotatable beaters attached to a handle and used for whisking food b a bunch of flexible strands of a material (e g twigs, feathers, or straw) attached to a handle for use as a brush – compare FLY WHISK [ME *wisk*, prob of Scand origin; akin to ON *visk* wisp; akin to OE *wiscian* to plait, L *virga* branch, rod]

**²whisk** *vi* to move lightly and swiftly ~ *vt* 1 to convey briskly ⟨*~ed the children off to bed*⟩ 2 to whip or fluff up (as if) by beating with a whisk ⟨*~ egg whites*⟩ 3 to brush or wipe off (e g crumbs) lightly; *also* to clean (a surface) by light brushing or wiping 4 to brandish lightly; flick ⟨*~ed its tail*⟩

**whisk broom** *n* a small brush with a short handle used esp as a clothes brush

**whisker** /'wiskə/ *n* 1a a hair of the beard b *pl* the part of the beard growing on the sides of the face or on the chin – compare SIDE-WHISKERS c a hairsbreadth ⟨*lost the race by a ~*⟩ 2 any of the long projecting hairs or bristles growing near the mouth of an animal (e g a cat or bird) 3a a shred or filament resembling a whisker b a thin hairlike crystal (e g of sapphire or a metal) of exceptional mechanical strength 4 *pl, archaic* a moustache [back-formation fr *whiskers* (moustache), fr ²*whisk* + ²*-er*] – **whiskered** *adj*, **whiskery** *adj*, **whiskeriness** *n*

**whiskey** /'wiski/ *n* whisky produced in Ireland or the USA

**Whiskey** – a communications code word for the letter *w*

**'whisky** /'wiski/ *n* 1 a spirit distilled from fermented mash of grain (e g rye, corn, barley, or wheat) 2 a glass of whisky ⟨*two whiskies, please*⟩ [IrGael *uisce beathadh* & ScGael *uisge beatha*, lit., water of life]

**²whisky, whiskey** *n* a light gig or chaise with a chairlike body suspended on leather braces [²*whisk* + *-y*]

**'whisper** /'wispə/ *vi* 1a to speak softly with little or no vibration of the vocal cords b to talk softly and covertly 2 to make a hissing or rustling sound like whispered speech ~ *vt* 1 to address or order in a whisper 2 to utter in a whisper 3 to report or suggest confidentially ⟨*it is ~ed that he will soon resign*⟩ [ME *whisperen*, fr OE *hwisprian*; akin to OHG *hwispalōn* to whisper, ON *hvīsla* – more at WHISTLE] – **whisperer** *n*

**²whisper** *n* 1a an act or instance of whispering; *esp* speech without vibration of the vocal cords b a hissing or rustling sound like whispered speech 2 something communicated (as if) by whispering: e g 2a a rumour ⟨*~s of scandal*⟩ b a hint, trace – **whispery** *adj*

**'whispering** /'wispəring/ *n* 1a whispered speech b gossip, rumour 2 WHISPER 1b

**²whispering** *adj* 1 making a hissing sound 2 spreading confidential, esp derogatory, reports ⟨*~ tongues can poison truth* – S T Coleridge⟩ – **whisperingly** *adv*

**whispering campaign** *n, chiefly NAm* the systematic dissemination by word of mouth of derogatory rumours or charges, esp against a candidate for public office

**'whist** /wist/ *vi, dial Br* to be silent; hush – often used interjectionally to enjoin silence [imit]

**²whist** *adj, archaic or dial* quiet, silent

**³whist** *n* a card game, usu for four players in two partnerships, that is played with a pack of 52 cards and that scores one point for each trick in excess of six [alter. of earlier *whisk*, prob fr ²*whisk*; fr whisking up the tricks]

**whist drive** *n, Br* a session of whist playing with a periodic change of partners, usu with prizes at the finish

**'whistle** /'wisl/ *n* 1a a small WIND INSTRUMENT in which sound is produced by the passage of breath forced through a slit in a short tube ⟨*police ~*⟩ b a device through which air or steam is forced into a cavity or against a thin edge to produce a loud sound ⟨*a factory ~*⟩ 2 a shrill clear sound produced by whistling or by a whistle 3 a sound that resembles a whistle ⟨*the ~ of the wind*⟩; *esp* a shrill clear note (as if) of a bird [ME, fr OE *hwistle*; akin to ON *hvīsla* to whisper, *hvīna* to whizz – more at WHINE] – **blow the whistle on 1** to bring (something secret) into the open **2** to inform against – **wet one's whistle**

*informal* to take an esp alcoholic drink [*whistle* in the humorous sense "mouth, throat"]

²**whistle** *vi* **1a** to utter a shrill clear sound by blowing or drawing air through the puckered lips **b** to utter a shrill note or call resembling a whistle **c** to make a shrill clear sound, esp by rapid movement; *also* to move rapidly with such a sound ⟨*train* ~d *by*⟩ **d** to blow or sound a whistle **2** to give a signal or issue an order or summons (as if) by whistling ⟨~ *to a dog*⟩ ~ *vt* **1** to send, bring, call, or signal to (as if) by whistling **2** to produce, utter, or express by whistling ⟨~ *a tune*⟩ – see also **whistle in the** DARK – **whistleable** *adj*

**whistle for** *vt* to demand or request in vain ⟨*did a sloppy job so he can* whistle for *his money*⟩

**whistler** /'wislə/ *n* one who or that which whistles: eg **a** any of various birds; *esp* a goldeneye duck **b** a broken-winded horse **c** a signal of ELECTROMAGNETIC WAVES of audio or RADIO FREQUENCY that is generated by a lightning discharge and that travels along the earth's magnetic LINES OF FORCE

¹**whistle-₁stop** *n* **1** *NAm* **1a** a small station at which trains stop only on signal **b** *NAm* a small community **2** *chiefly NAm* a brief personal appearance, esp by a political candidate, during the course of a tour – **whistle-stop** *adj*

²**whistle-stop** *vi*, *chiefly NAm* to make a tour, esp in a political campaign, with many brief personal appearances in small communities

**whistling** /'wisling, 'wisl·ing/ *n* the act or sound of one who or that which whistles; a whistle

**whit** /wit/ *n* the smallest part or particle imaginable; a bit ⟨*not a* ~ *abashed*⟩ [alter. of ME *wiht, wight* creature, thing, bit – more at WIGHT]

**Whit** *adj or n* Whitsun

¹**white** /wiet/ *adj* **1a** free from colour **b** of the colour of new snow or milk; *specif* of the colour white **c** light or pallid in colour ⟨~ *hair*⟩ ⟨*lips* ~ *with fear*⟩ **d** lustrous pale grey; silvery ⟨*a* ~ *alloy*⟩; *also* made of silver **e** *of wine* light yellow or amber in colour ⟨~ *Burgundy*⟩ **f** *Br, of coffee* containing milk or cream **2a** being a member of a group or race characterized by reduced pigmentation and usu specif distinguished from people belonging to groups marked by black, brown, yellow, or red skin coloration; CAUCASIAN **2 b** of, intended for, or consisting of white people ⟨~ *schools*⟩ **3** free from spot or blemish: eg **3a(1)** free from moral impurity; innocent **a(2)** *of a wedding* in which the woman wears white clothes as a symbol of purity **b** not marked by writing or printing **c** not intended to cause harm ⟨*a* ~ *lie*⟩ **d** favourable, fortunate ⟨*one of the* ~ *days of his life* – Sir Walter Scott⟩ **4a** dressed in white **b** snowy ⟨*a* ~ *Christmas*⟩ **5a** heated to the point of whiteness **b** notably ardent; passionate ⟨*in a* ~ *rage*⟩ **6a** ultraconservative or reactionary in political outlook and action – compare RED **6 b** instigated or carried out by reactionary forces as a counterrevolutionary measure ⟨~ *terror*⟩ **7** of or constituting a musical tone quality characterized by a controlled pure sound, a lack of warmth and colour, and a lack of resonance **8** *of electromagnetic radiation, sound, etc* consisting of a wide range of frequencies ⟨~ *noise*⟩ **9** marked by upright fairness ⟨*a* ~ *man if ever there was one*⟩ *usage* see CAUCASIAN [ME, fr OE *hwīt*; akin to OHG *hwīz* white, Skt *śveta*] – **whiteness** *n* – **bleed white** to drain of resources

²**white** *n* **1** the ACHROMATIC object colour of greatest lightness that belongs to objects that reflect diffusely nearly all incident light throughout the visible spectrum **2a** a white or light-coloured part of something: eg **2a(1)** the mass of albumin-containing material surrounding the yolk of an egg **a(2)** the white part of the ball of the eye **a(3)** the light-coloured pieces in a two-handed board game; *also* the player by whom these are played **b(1)** *archaic* a white target **b(2)** the white fifth circle that is usu outermost on an archery target; *also* a shot that hits it **3** something that is or approaches the colour white: eg **3a** whites *pl*, **white** white clothing; *esp* white sports clothing **b** WHITE WINE **c** a white animal (eg a butterfly or pig) **4** *pl* LEUCORRHOEA (white or yellow discharge from the vagina) **5** a person belonging to a light-skinned race **6** a member of an ultraconservative or reactionary political group

³**white** *vt, archaic* to whiten [ME *whiten*, fr *white*, adj]

**white ant** *n* a termite

**whitebait** /'wiet₁bayt/ *n* **1** the young of any of several European herrings (eg the common herring or the sprat) used whole as food **2** any of various small fishes similar to the European whitebait and used as food [¹*white* + ²*bait*]

**whitebeam** /'wiet₁beem/ *n* a European tree (*Sorbus aria*) of

the rose family having leaves covered in fine white hairs on the undersurface, white flowers, and scarlet berries [*white* + *-beam*, deriv of OE *bēam* tree]

**whitebeard** /'wiet₁biəd/ *n* an old man; a greybeard

**white blood cell, white cell** *n* any of the white or colourless BLOOD CELLS that have nuclei, do not contain haemoglobin, and are primarily concerned with body defence mechanisms and repair – compare RED BLOOD CELL, GRANULOCYTE, AGRANULOCYTE

**white blood corpuscle** *n* WHITE BLOOD CELL

**white book** *n, NAm* WHITE PAPER

**white burley** /'buhli/ *n, often cap W&B* BURLEY (kind of tobacco)

**white campion** /'kampi·ən/ *n* a white-flowered Eurasian campion (*Silene alba*) found in hedges, bare places, and often on cultivated ground

**whitecap** /'wiet₁kap/ *n* a wave crest breaking into white foam; *esp* one far from land

**white cedar** *n* any of various esp N American timber trees including true cedars, junipers, and cypress

**white clover** *n* a Eurasian clover (*Trifolium repens*), with round heads of white flowers, that is widely used in lawn and pasture grass-seed mixtures and is an important source of nectar for bees

**₁white-₁collar** *adj* of, associated with, or constituting the class of employees in nonmanual and usu salaried jobs (eg clerical posts) whose duties do not call for the wearing of special work clothes or protective clothing – compare BLUE-COLLAR

**white corpuscle** *n* WHITE BLOOD CELL

**whited** /'wietid/ *adj* made white, esp with whitewash or bleach; whitened

**whited sepulchre** *n* a hypocrite [fr Christ's description of the scribes and Pharisees (Mt 23:27)]

**white Dutch clover** *n* WHITE CLOVER

**white dwarf** *n* a very small whitish star of high surface temperature and low intrinsic brightness, usu with a mass approximately equal to that of the sun but with a density many times larger

**white elephant** *n* **1** an Indian elephant of a pale colour that is sometimes venerated in India, Sri Lanka, Thailand, and Burma **2a** a property requiring much care and expense and yielding little profit **b** an object no longer of value to its owner but perhaps of value to others **c** something of little or no value

**₁white-₁faced** *adj* **1** having a wan pale face **2** having a wholly or partly white face – used esp of an animal otherwise dark in colour

**White Father** *n* a member of the ROMAN CATHOLIC Society of Missionaries of Africa founded in Algiers in 1868 by Charles Lavigerie [fr his white garments]

**white feather** *n* a mark or symbol of cowardice [fr the superstition that a white feather in the plumage of a gamecock is a mark of a poor fighter]

**whitefish** /'wiet₁fish/ *n, pl* **whitefish 1** any of various freshwater fishes (family Salmonidae, esp genus *Coregonus*) related to the salmons and trouts and used for food; *also* any of various similar fishes **2** the flesh of a whitefish, esp as an article of food **3** *Br* any of various market fishes (eg cod) with white flesh that is not oily

**white flag** *n* **1** a flag of plain white used as a flag of truce or as a token of surrender **2** a token of weakness or yielding

**whitefly** /'wiet₁flie/ *n, pl* **whiteflies**, *esp collectively* **whitefly 1** any of numerous small insects (family Aleyrodidae) that are related to the SCALE INSECTS and cause damage to plants by sucking sap **2** an infestation of whitefly

**white friar** *n, often cap W&F* a Carmelite friar [fr his white habit]

**white-fronted goose** *n* a large Eurasian and N American greyish brown goose (*Anser albifrons*)

**white gold** *n* a pale silvery alloy of gold esp with the chemical elements nickel or palladium, that resembles platinum in appearance

**white goods** *n pl* **1** white fabrics, esp of cotton or linen **2** *chiefly NAm* major articles of household equipment (eg cookers and refrigerators) that are typically finished in white enamel **3** *NAm* articles (eg sheets, towels, or curtains) originally or typically made of white cloth

**₁white-₁haired** *adj* **1** having white hair **2** favourite, whiteheaded

**Whitehall** /'wiet₁hawl, ₁-'-/ *n* the British government [*White-*

*hall*, street in London containing the chief offices of British government]

**whitehead** /'wiet,hed/ *n* MILIUM (whitish lump on the skin)

,**white-'headed** *adj* **1** having the hair, fur, or plumage of the head white or very light **2** specially favoured; fortunate – esp in *white-headed boy*

**white heat** *n* **1a** a temperature (e g for copper and iron from 1500° to 1600° Celsius) which is higher than RED HEAT and at which a body emits white light **b** great or glaring heat ⟨*the ~ of the South Australian desert – Sydney National Times*⟩ **2** a state of intense mental or physical strain, emotion, or activity

**white hole** *n* a hypothetical celestial body that emits radiation of all wavelengths and is thought to be the converse of a BLACK HOLE

**white hope** *n* someone from whom much is expected; *esp* a person expected to bring glory to his/her group, country, etc

**White Horde** *n taking sing or pl vb* a Mongolian people powerful in Russia in the 14th century

**white horse** *n* **1** a usu prehistoric figure of a horse made by cutting away the turf from a chalk hillside **2** a wave with a crest breaking into white foam; a whitecap □ not used technically for real horses

,**white-'hot** *adj* **1** at or radiating WHITE HEAT **2** ardently zealous; fervid

**whitehouse** /'wiet,hows/ *vt, Br humorous* to expurgate, bowdlerize [Mary *Whitehouse b* 1910 E writer, broadcaster, & campaigner for higher moral standards]

**White House** *n* **1** *the* executive branch of the US government **2** a residence of the president of the USA [the *White House*, mansion in Washington, DC, official residence of the president of the USA]

**white lead** /led/ *n* any of several white lead-containing pigments; *esp* a heavy poisonous CARBONATE of lead used formerly in exterior paints

**white leather** *n* leather prepared with alum and salt

**white light** *n* light containing all the wavelengths in the visible range at (approximately) equal intensities

**white line** *n* a stripe painted along a road to separate traffic lanes

**white list** *n* a list of approved or favoured items – compare BLACKLIST – **white-listed** *adj*

'**white-,livered** *adj* pusillanimous, lily-livered [fr the former belief that vigour and courage depend on the body's producing large quantities of yellow bile]

**whitely** /'wietli/ *adv* with an effect of whiteness; so as to show or appear white ⟨*water gleamed ~ in the moonlight*⟩

**white magic** *n* magic used for good purposes (e g to cure disease) – compare BLACK MAGIC

**white man's burden** *n* the supposed duty of the white peoples to manage the affairs of less developed peoples until they are sufficiently educated to handle the responsibilities of independence themselves ["The White Man's Burden", poem by Rudyard Kipling †1936 E writer]

**white matter** *n* whitish nerve tissue that consists largely of NERVE FIBRES enclosed in a fatty white sheath and underlies the GREY MATTER of the brain and SPINAL CORD or is gathered into nerves

**white meat** *n* light-coloured meat (e g poultry breast or veal) – compare RED MEAT

**white metal** *n* **1** any of several alloys (e g BABBITT METAL) based on tin or lead and used esp for bearings, fusible plugs, and type metal **2** any of several light-coloured alloys used esp as a base for plated silverware and ornaments

**white mustard** *n* a Eurasian plant (*Sinapis alba*) of the cabbage family that is grown for its seeds which yield mustard and mustard oil

**whiten** /'wiet(ə)n/ *vb* to make or become white or whiter, esp by application of a covering coat ⟨*snow ~ed the hills*⟩ **antonyms** blacken, discolour

**whitener** /'wiet(ə)nə/ *n* a substance that whitens: e g **a** a bleaching agent **b** a milk substitute in powder form (e g for use in tea or coffee)

**white night** *n* a sleepless night [trans of Fr *nuit blanche*]

**whitening** /'wiet(ə)ning/ *n* **1** the act or process of making or becoming white **2** something that is used to make white; *esp* whiting

**white oak** *n* any of various oaks, esp durmast, with acorns that mature in one year and leaf veins that never extend beyond the margin of the leaf; *also* the hard, strong, durable, and moisture-resistant wood of a white oak

**white of egg** *n, pl* **whites of egg, whites of eggs** WHITE 2a(1)

**whiteout** /'wiet,owt/ *n* an atmospheric weather condition of heavy cloud in a polar region in which because of uniform whiteness no object casts a shadow, the horizon cannot be seen, and only dark objects are discernible [*white* + *-out* (as in *blackout*)]

**white paper** *n, often cap W&P* a government report on any subject; *esp* a British publication that is usu less extensive than a BLUE BOOK

**white pepper** *n* a condiment prepared from the husked dried berries of an E Indian plant (*Piper nigrum*) used either whole or ground – compare BLACK PEPPER

**white pine** *n* **1** a tall-growing pine (*Pinus strobus*) of eastern N America; *also* any of several similar conifers **2** the wood of a white pine, which is much used in building construction

**white plague** *n* heroin addiction

**white poplar** *n* a Eurasian poplar (*Populus alba*) that has smooth whitish bark and leaves densely covered with white hairs on the undersurface

**white pudding** *n* a sausage made from minced pork meat and fat – compare BLACK PUDDING

**white rat** *n* a rat of an albino strain of the BROWN RAT that is used extensively in biological experiments

**white rhinoceros** *n* a large slate grey 2-horned rhinoceros (*Diceros simus*) of Central and W Africa with a square upper lip and flattened nose

**White Russian** *n* **1** a Byelorussian **2** a Tsarist Russian; *esp* one living in exile

**white sale** *n* a sale of household linen and cotton goods (e g sheets)

**white sauce** *n* a sauce usu made from a roux combined with milk, cream, or a chicken, veal, or fish stock and seasoning – compare BROWN SAUCE

**white shark** *n* GREAT WHITE SHARK

**white slave** *n* a woman or girl held unwillingly, esp in a foreign country, and forced to be a prostitute

**white slavery** *n* **1** the state of being a WHITE SLAVE; enforced prostitution **2** the white-slave trade – **white-slaver** *n*

**whitesmith** /'wiet,smith/ *n* **1** a tinsmith **2** one who finishes or polishes newly made metal goods

**white space** *n* the areas of a page (e g in a book) not covered by print or pictures

**white spirit** *n* an inflammable liquid distilled from petroleum and used esp as a solvent and thinner for paints and varnishes

**white spruce** *n* **1** any of several spruces; *esp* a widely distributed spruce (*Picea glauca*) of N America that has blue-green neddlelike leaves and slender cones **2** the wood of a white spruce; *esp* the light pale tough straight-grained wood of the common white spruce (*Picea glauca*) used esp for construction and as a source of paper pulp

**white supremacist** /sooh'premsist/ *n* an advocate of or believer in WHITE SUPREMACY

**white supremacy** *n* the doctrine of the inherent superiority of the white race over other races

**whitetail** /'wiet,tayl/ *n* a N American deer (*Odocoileus virginianus*) with forward-arching antlers and a rather long tail that is white on the underside

**white-tailed deer** *n* a whitetail

**white-tailed eagle, white-tailed sea eagle** *n* a bulky long-winged Eurasian and N American SEA EAGLE (*Haliaëtus albicilla*) that is brown with a short white wedge-shaped tail

**whitethroat** /'wiet,throht/ *n* a Eurasian and African warbler (*Sylvia communis*) that has a white throat, reddish-brown wings, and buff underparts tinged with pink, and that is found in scrub

,**white-'tie** *adj* characterized by or requiring the wearing of formal evening dress for men, specif a tail coat and a white bow tie ⟨*a ~ dinner*⟩ – compare BLACK-TIE

**white trash** *n taking pl vb, chiefly NAm derog* POOR WHITES

**white wagtail** *n* a very variable European wagtail (*Motacilla alba alba*) that is a combination of black, white, and grey in colour and has lighter underparts and darker upperparts

**whitewall** /'wiet,wawl/ *n* a car tyre with a white band on the sidewall

**white walnut** *n* **1** a BUTTERNUT tree **2** the light-coloured wood of a white walnut

¹**whitewash** /'wiet,wosh/ *vt* **1** to apply whitewash to **2a** to gloss over or cover up (e g vices or crimes) **b** to exonerate by concealment or through biased presentation of data **3** *informal* to hold (an opponent) scoreless in a contest or game; *also* to defeat overwhelmingly – **whitewasher** *n*

²**whitewash** *n* **1** a liquid composition for whitening a surface; *specif* a liquid mixture (eg of lime and water or whiting, size, and water) for whitening outside walls or similar surfaces **2** an act or instance of glossing over or of exonerating **3** *informal* a defeat in a contest or game in which the loser fails to score; *broadly* an overwhelming defeat

**whitewashing** /'wiet,woshing/ *n* an act or instance of applying whitewash; *also* WHITEWASH 3

**white water** *n* frothy water (eg in breakers, rapids, or waterfalls)

**white way** *n, NAm* a brilliantly lighted street or avenue, esp in a city's business or theatre district [the *Great White Way*, nickname for the theatrical section of Broadway, New York City]

**white whale** *n* BELUGA 2

**white wine** *n* a wine produced from usu light-coloured grapes and ranging in colour from yellow to amber

**whitewood** /'wiet,wood/ *n* **1** any of various trees (eg the lime) with pale or white wood **2** the wood of a whitewood; *esp* the pale soft wood of the TULIP TREE

¹**whitey** /'wieti/ *n, often cap, derog* a white man; *also* white society

²**whitey** *adj* whity

**whither** /'widhə/ *adv or conj, chiefly formal* **1** to or towards what place ⟨~ *shall we fly?*⟩ ⟨*knew* ~ *to go* – Daniel Defoe⟩ – also used in rhetorical questions without a verb ⟨~ *democracy?*⟩ **2** to the place at, in, or to which ⟨*go* ~ *you wish*⟩ **3** to which place ⟨*Crewe,* ~ *I went with father and Julia by car* – SEU W⟩ [ME, fr OE *hwider;* akin to L *quis* who & to OE hi*der* hither – more at WHO, HITHER]

**whithersoever** /,widhəsoh'evə/ *conj, formal* to whatever place ⟨*will go* ~ *you lead*⟩

**whitherward** /'widhəwəd/ *adv, archaic* towards what or which place

**whitherwards** /'widhə,woodz/ *adv, archaic* whitherward

¹**whiting** /'wieting/ *n* any of various marine fishes eaten as food; *esp* a common European fish (*Merlangus merlangus*) related to the cod [ME, fr MD *witinc*, fr *wit* white; akin to OE *hwīt* white]

²**whiting** *n* washed and ground chalk used esp as a pigment and in rubber compounding and paper coating [ME, fr gerund of *whiten* to white]

**whitish** /'wietish/ *adj* having a tinge of white; somewhat white

**whitleather** /'wit,ledhə/ *n* WHITE LEATHER [ME *whitlether*, fr *whit* white + *lether* leather]

**whitlow** /'witloh/ *n* a deep usu pus-producing inflammation of the finger or toe, esp near the end or round the nail [ME *whitflawe, whitflowe, whitlowe,* prob fr *whit* white + *flawe* break, fissure]

**whitmanesque** /,witmə'nesk/ *adj* suggestive of the writings of Walt Whitman, esp in being ruggedly American ⟨*a* ~ *all-American boy* – Donald Davie⟩ [Walt *Whitman* †1892 US poet]

**Whitmonday** /wit'munday, -di/ *n* the day after Whitsunday formerly observed as a public holiday in England, Wales, and N Ireland – compare SPRING HOLIDAY [*Whit*- (as in *Whitsunday*) + *Monday*]

**Whitsun** /'wits(ə)n/ *adj or n* (of, being or observed on or at) Whitsunday or Whitsuntide [ME *Whitson,* fr *Whitsonday*]

**Whitsunday** /wit'sunday, -di/ *n* a Christian feast on the seventh Sunday after Easter commemorating the descent of the HOLY SPIRIT at Pentecost [ME *Whitsonday,* fr OE *hwīta sunnandæg,* lit., white Sunday; prob fr the white robes worn by the newly baptized, who were numerous at this season]

**Whitsuntide** /'wits(ə)n,tied/ *n* Whitsunday and Whitmonday and/or the days of public holiday celebrated together with or in place of these days

¹**whittle** /'witl/ *n, archaic or dial* a large knife [ME *whittel,* alter. of *thwitel,* fr *thwiten* to whittle, fr OE *thwītan;* akin to ON *thveita* to hew]

²**whittle** *vt* **1a** to pare or cut off chips from the surface of (wood) with a knife **b** to shape or form by so paring or cutting **2** to reduce, remove, or destroy gradually as if by cutting off bits with a knife; pare – + *down* or *away* ⟨~ *down expenses*⟩ ~ *vi* to cut or shape something, esp wood, (as if) by paring it with a knife – **whittler** *n*

**whittling** /'witling,'witl-ing/ *n* **1** a piece cut away in whittling **2** the act of someone who whittles

**whity, whitey** /'wieti/ *adj* whitish – usu in combination ⟨~ *grey*⟩

**whiz kid, whizz kid** /'wiz,kid/ *n* a person who is unusually intelligent, clever, or successful, esp at an early age

¹**whizz**, *NAm chiefly* **whiz** /wiz/ *vb* **-zz-** *vi* **1** to buzz, whirr, or hiss like a speeding object (eg an arrow or ball) passing through air **2** *informal* to fly or move swiftly (as if) with a whizz ~ *vt* to cause to whizz; *esp* to rotate very rapidly [imit]

²**whizz**, *NAm chiefly* **whiz** *n* **1** a whizzing sound **2** a swift movement or passage of something, often accompanied by a whizzing sound ⟨*a 72-hour* ~ *round twenty hotels* – Punch⟩

³**whizz**, *NAm chiefly* **whiz** *n, informal* WIZARD 2 ⟨*a* ~ *at maths*⟩ [prob alter. (influenced by ¹*whizz*) of *wiz*]

⁴**whizz**, *NAm chiefly* **whiz** *adj, informal or journalistic* WIZARD 1

¹'**whizz-,bang** *n* **1** a high-explosive shell whose explosion is heard directly after the noise of its flight **2** a firework that is suggestive of a whizz-bang **3** *informal or journalistic* a person or thing that is conspicuous for noise, speed, or startling effect

²**whizz-bang** *adj, informal or journalistic* expert; *esp* slick

**whizzer** /'wizə/ *adj* something that whizzes; *esp* a machine that revolves at high speed for drying grain, sugar, etc

**who** /hoo; *strong* hooh/ *pron, pl* **who 1** what or which person – used as an interrogative ⟨~ *was elected President?*⟩ ⟨*find out* ~ *they are*⟩ **2** – used to introduce a RESTRICTIVE or NON-RESTRICTIVE CLAUSE in reference to a person or animal ⟨*my father,* ~ *was a lawyer*⟩ ⟨*dogs* ~ ... *fawn all over tramps* – Nigel Balchin⟩, or to a human group, esp when a plural verb follows ⟨*an orchestra* ~ *play the wartime hits* – The Observer⟩ **3** *archaic* the person that; whoever ⬚ often used as object of a verb or of a following preposition though still disapproved of by some ⟨*do not know* ~ *the message is from* – G K Chesterton⟩ ⟨*a character* ~ *we are meant to pity* – TLS⟩; compare WHOM, WHICH, THAT [ME, fr OE *hwā;* akin to OHG *hwer,* interrog pron, who, L *quis,* Gk *tis,* L *qui,* rel pron, who] – **who is who/who's who** the identity of and noteworthy facts about each of a number of esp eminent people

*usage* **1** The spelling of **whose** meaning "of whom" as ⚠ **who's** is a common confusion ⟨*the girl* **whose** (not ⚠ **who's**) *flat I'm sharing*⟩. **2 Who** may be correctly used in reference to animals. There is some doubt about whether who should properly refer to countries ⟨*Syria,* **who** *was partly to blame*⟩ or to ships ⟨*Hotspur,* **who** *had lost her rudder*⟩. **3** The use of **who** rather than the more formal **whom** as an object pronoun introducing questions has been established in English since at least the 15th century ⟨**who** *should your grace trust hereafter* – Thomas Cranmer⟩ ⟨**who** *should I see there?* – Joseph Addison⟩. It is particularly justified where a question ends with a preposition ⟨**who** *were you with?*⟩ ⟨**who** *are you writing to?*⟩ ⟨**who** *was it aimed at*⟩ and *with* **whom**, *to* **whom**, *at* **whom** would be pedantic. In formal writing, however, and elsewhere than in direct questions, the object pronoun **whom** should be preferred ⟨*a group* **whom/who** *it is natural to admire*⟩. See ELSE, ⁴THAT, ²WHICH, WHOM

**whoa** /'woh·ə, woh/ *interj* – used as a command (eg to a draught animal) to stand still; compare GEE UP [ME *whoo, who*]

**whodunit** *also* **whodunnit** /,hooh'dunit/ *n* a story dealing with the detection of crime or criminals; *also* a play or film based on such a story [substandard or jocular *who done it*]

**whoever** /hooh'evə/ *pron* **1** whatever person **2** no matter who **3** *informal* who in the world ⟨~ *can it be?*⟩ ⬚ *(1&2)* used in any grammatical relation except that of a possessive ⟨*the parents of* ~ *is giving the party* – Daily Mirror⟩ *usage* see EVER, WHOMEVER

¹**whole** /hohl/ *adj* **1a(1)** free of wound or injury; unhurt **a(2)** restored, recovered **b** free of defect or impairment; intact ⟨*not a cup left* ~⟩ **c** physically sound and healthy; free of disease or deformity **2** having all its proper constituents; unmodified ⟨~ *milk*⟩ **3** each or all of; total, entire ⟨*took three* ~ *weeks*⟩ ⟨*made the* ~ *class stay in*⟩ **4a** constituting an undivided unit; unbroken, uncut ⟨*snake swallowed the rabbit* ~⟩ ⟨~*-hoofed animals*⟩ **b** directed to one end; concentrated ⟨*promised to give it his* ~ *attention*⟩ **5a** seemingly complete or total ⟨*the* ~ *idea is to help, not hinder*⟩ **b** very great – chiefly in *a whole lot* ⟨*feels a* ~ *lot better now*⟩ **6** constituting a person in his/her full intellectual, emotional, physical, and social nature ⟨*educate the* ~ *man*⟩ **7** having the same parents as another ⟨~ *brother*⟩ [ME *hool* healthy, unhurt, entire, fr OE *hāl;* akin to OHG *heil* healthy, unhurt, ON *heill,* OSlav *cělŭ*] – **wholeness** *n*

²**whole** *n* **1** a complete amount or sum; a number, or totality lacking no part, member, or element ⟨*the* ~ *of society*⟩ **2** something constituting a complex unity; a coherent system or

organization of parts – **as a whole** considered all together as a body rather than as individuals – **in whole** to the full or entire extent; wholly – usu in **in whole or in part** – **on the whole 1** in view of all the circumstances or conditions; all things considered **2** in most instances; typically

**wholefood** /'hohl,foohd/ *n* food (eg pulses, grains, and nuts) in a simple and natural form that has undergone minimal processing and refining and thus has a higher nutritional and roughage content than the majority of manufactured foods ⟨*unpolished brown rice, wholemeal flour, and unrefined sugar are* ~s⟩ – compare HEALTH FOOD. JUNK FOOD

**whole gale** *n* wind having a speed of 89 to 102 kilometres per hour (about 55 to 63 miles per hour) *synonyms* see ¹WIND

**wholehearted** /,hohl'hahtid/ *adj* **1** completely and sincerely devoted, determined, or enthusiastic ⟨*a* ~ *student of social problems*⟩ **2** marked by complete earnest commitment; free from all reserve or hesitation ⟨*gave the movement his* ~ *support*⟩ *synonyms* see SINCERE – **wholeheartedly** *adv*

**whole hog** *n, informal* the whole way or farthest limit; all – usu in **go the whole hog** – **whole-hog** *adj*

**whole holiday** *n* a whole day's holiday

**whole-'length** *adj* full-length

**whole-life insurance** *n* life insurance for which premiums are payable as long as the insured person lives

**wholemeal** /'hohl,meel/ *adj* made of ground entire wheat kernels ⟨~ *flour*⟩ ⟨~ *bread*⟩

**whole note** *n, NAm* a semibreve

**whole number** *n* INTEGER

**whole rest** *n, NAm* a musical REST (indicating silence) of the same time value as a semibreve

**¹wholesale** /'hohl,sayl/ *n* the sale of commodities in large quantities usu for resale (eg by a retailer) – compare RETAIL

**²wholesale** *adj* **1** of, concerned with, or engaged in the sale of commodities in large quantities for resale ⟨*a* ~ *grocer*⟩ **2** performed on a large scale, esp without discrimination ⟨~ *slaughter*⟩

**wholesaler** /'hohl,saylə/ *n* a merchant middleman who sells chiefly to retailers, other merchants, or industrial, institutional, and commercial users mainly for resale or business use – **wholesale** *vb*

**wholesome** /'hohls(ə)m/ *adj* **1** promoting health or well-being of mind or spirit ⟨*books that aren't* ~ *for the young*⟩ **2** promoting health of body ⟨*a light* ~ *diet*⟩ **3** having the simple health or soundness of normal domesticity ⟨*rosy* ~*-looking children*⟩ **4** based on well-grounded fear; prudent ⟨*a* ~ *respect for the law*⟩ [ME *holsom, hoolsom,* fr *hol, hool* healthy, whole + *-som* -some] – **wholesomely** *adv,* **wholesomeness** *n*

**whole-'souled** *adj* moved by ardent enthusiasm or single-minded devotion; wholehearted

**whole step** *n, NAm* WHOLE TONE

**whole-'time** *adj* full-time

**whole tone, tone** *n* a musical interval (eg C–D or G–A) comprising two semitones

**whole wheat** *adj* wholemeal

**wholly** /'hohl·li/ *adv* **1** to the full or entire extent; completely ⟨~ *incompetent*⟩ **2** to the exclusion of other things; solely ⟨*a book dealing* ~ *with herbs*⟩ △ holey, holy [ME *hoolly,* fr *hool* whole]

**whom** /hoohm/ *pron, objective case of* WHO – used as an interrogative or relative; used as object of a preceding preposition ⟨*to know for* ~ *the bell tolls* – John Donne⟩; or less frequently as the object of a verb or of a following preposition ⟨*the man* ~ *you wrote to*⟩ though now often considered stilted, esp as an interrogative and esp in oral use; occasionally used in the environment of a verb of which it might mistakenly be considered the subject ⟨*taking no bets on* ~ *The Sex Symbol . . . is supposed to be* – *The Sun*⟩; compare WHO, WHICH, THAT [ME, fr OE *hwām,* dat of *hwā* who]

*usage* **1** Whom should not today be used for **who** as complement of the verb *be,* which requires a subject pronoun, although practice was different in the past. Compare ⟨**whom** *say ye that I am?* – Mt 16:15 (AV)⟩ ⟨*only vaguely aware of* **whom** *Miss Chancellor might be* – Henry James⟩ ⟨*you know* **who** (not △ **whom**) *he is*⟩ ⟨**who** (not △ **whom**) *do you think you are?*⟩ **2** It is common and understandable, but today considered incorrect, to use **whom** for **who** in sentences such as ⟨*Ferdinand,* **whom** *they suppose is drowned* – Shak⟩ ⟨*a creature* **whom** *we pretend is here already* – E M Forster⟩ ⟨*someone* **whom** *they imagined would be a more vigorous President* – Winston Churchill⟩. The choice of **whom** here is usually made because the pronoun is felt to be the object of an inserted parenthesis

such as *they suppose* or *we pretend,* whereas it is more correctly the subject of the main verb ⟨*Ferdinand,* **who** . . . *is drowned*⟩ ⟨*someone* **who** . . . *would be a more vigorous President*⟩. **Whom** is correct, however, in the construction ⟨*Ferdinand,* **whom** *they suppose to be drowned*⟩.

**whomever** /hoohm'evə/ *pron, objective case of* WHOEVER *usage* Although the more formal **whomever** exists, **whoever** has been commonly used as the object of verbs and prepositions since the 16th century ⟨*he can choose* **whoever** *he wants*⟩ ⟨*give it to* **whoever** *you like*⟩.

**whomp** /womp/ *n* a loud slap, crash, or crunch [imit]

**whomso** /'hoohmsoh/ *pron, objective case of* WHOSO

**whomsoever** /,hoohmsoh'evə/ *pron, objective case of* WHOSOEVER

**¹whoop** /woohp/ *vi* **1** to utter a whoop in expression of eagerness, enthusiasm, or enjoyment; shout **2** to utter the loud cry characteristic of certain birds (eg an owl or crane) **3** to make the characteristic whoop of WHOOPING COUGH **4** to go or pass with a loud noise ~ *vt* **1a** to utter or express with a whoop **b** to urge, drive, or cheer on with a whoop **2** to agitate on behalf of **3** boost, raise ⟨~ *up the price*⟩ [ME *whopen,* fr MF *houpper,* of imit origin] – **whooper** *n* – **whoop it up** *informal* to celebrate riotously

**²whoop** *n* **1** a loud yell expressive of eagerness, exuberance, or jubilation **2** the whooping cry characteristic of certain birds (eg an owl or crane) **3** the crowing intake of breath following a paroxysm in WHOOPING COUGH **4** a minimum amount or degree (eg of care or consideration); the least bit ⟨*not worth a* ~⟩

**¹whoopee** /woo'pee/ *interj* – used to express exuberance [irreg fr ²*whoop*]

**²whoopee** /'woopi/ *n, informal* boisterous convivial fun – usu in *make whoopee*

**whoopee cushion** *n* an inflatable trick cushion which produces a vulgar noise when sat on

**whooper swan** /'hoohpə/ *n* a common large white European swan (*Cygnus cygnus*) with a yellow beak that has a loud whooping call

**whooping cough** /'hoohping/ *n* an infectious disease, esp of children, caused by a bacterium (*Bordetella pertussis*) and marked by a convulsive spasmodic cough sometimes followed by a crowing intake of breath – called also PERTUSSIS

**whooping crane** /'hoohping/ *n* a large white nearly extinct N American crane (*Grus americana*) noted for its loud mournful ringing call

**whoops** /woops, woohps/ *interj* oops

**¹whoosh** /woosh, woohsh/ *vi* to rush past or move explosively ⟨*cars* ~*ing along the motorway*⟩ ~ *vt* to transport with an explosive or hissing rush [imit]

**²whoosh** *n* a swift or explosive rush or spurt ⟨*fire suddenly gave a* ~⟩

**¹whop** /wop/ *vt* **-pp-** *informal* **1** to beat, strike **2** to defeat totally [ME *whappen,* alter. of *wappen* to throw violently, strike]

**²whop** *n, informal* a heavy blow; a thump

**whopper** /'wopə/ *n, informal* **1** something unusually large or otherwise extreme of its kind **2** an extravagant or monstrous lie [¹*whop* + ²*-er*]

**¹whopping** /'woping/ *adj, informal* extremely big ⟨*won by a* ~ *majority*⟩ ⟨*told a* ~ *lie*⟩

**²whopping** *adv, informal* very, extremely ⟨*a* ~ *great oil tanker*⟩

**¹whore** /haw/ *n* **1** a female prostitute **2** something showy and falsely enticing ⟨*that old* ~ *London* – Colin MacInnes⟩ [ME *hore,* fr OE *hōre;* akin to ON *hōra* whore, *hōrr* adulterer, L *carus* dear – more at CHARITY]

**²whore** *vi* **1** to have sexual intercourse outside marriage, esp with a female prostitute **2** to pursue a faithless, unworthy, or idolatrous desire ⟨*growth was a false god which had been* ~d *after for too long* – The Guardian⟩

**whoredom** /'hawd(ə)m/ *n* **1** the practice of whoring; prostitution **2** faithless or unworthy practices or pursuits; *also, in the Bible* idolatry [ME *hordom* sexual immorality, idolatrous practices, fr ON *hōrdōmr* adultery, fr *hōrr* adulterer]

**whorehouse** /'haw,hows/ *n* a brothel

**whoremaster** /'haw,mahstə/ *n, archaic* a man who consorts with whores or is given to lechery

**whoremonger** /'haw,mung·gə/ *n, archaic* a whoremaster

**whoreson** /'haws(ə)n/ *n* **1** BASTARD 1 **2** a coarse fellow – used as a generalized term of abuse

**whorl** /wuhl, wawl/ *n* **1** a drum-shaped section on the lower part of a spindle in spinning or weaving machinery serving as a pulley for the tape drive that rotates the spindle **2** an arrangement of similar anatomical parts (eg leaves or petals) in a circle round a point on a stem **3** something spiral in form or movement; a swirl ⟨~s *of smoke*⟩ **4** a single turn of a spiral shell **5** a fingerprint in which the central ridges turn through at least one complete circle [ME *wharle, whorle*, prob alter. of *whirle*, fr *whirlen* to whirl]

**whorled** /wuhld, wawld/ *adj* having or arranged in whorls ⟨~ *leaves*⟩

**whortleberry** /'wuhtlb(ə)ri, -,beri/ *n* a bilberry [alter. of earlier *hurtleberry*, fr ME *hurtilberye*, irreg fr OE *horte* whortleberry + ME *berye* berry]

¹**whose** /hoohz/ *adj* of whom or which, esp as possessor or possessors ⟨~ *hat is this?*⟩, agent or agents ⟨*the courts*, ~ *decisions I uphold*⟩, or object or objects of an action ⟨*the factory in* ~ *construction they were involved*⟩ [ME *whos*, gen of *who, what*]

usage The use of **whose** to mean "of which" as well as "of whom" has been long established in English ⟨*that forbidden tree whose mortal taste Brought death into the world* – John Milton⟩ and only very old-fashioned writers on usage now advise against it. People who still feel awkward about it are obliged to rewrite the third example above as ⟨*the factory in the construction of which they were involved*⟩, which is clumsy. See WHO, ELSE

²**whose** *pron, pl* **whose** that which belongs to whom – used without a following noun as a pronoun equivalent in meaning to the adjective *whose* ⟨*tell me* ~ *it was* – Shak⟩

**whosesoever** /,hoohz·soh'evə/ *adj, archaic or formal* of whomsoever

**whoso** /'hoohsoh/ *pron, archaic or formal* whoever

**whosoever** /,hoohsoh'evə/ *pron, archaic or formal* whoever

**who's who** *n, often cap both Ws* a collection of short biographical sketches of prominent people, usu in a specified field ⟨*a* ~ *of sports figures*⟩

**whump** /wump/ *vi* to bang, thump [imit] – **whump** *n*

¹**why** /wie/ *adv* for what cause, reason, or purpose ⟨~ *did you do it?*⟩ ⟨*know* ~ *they shrink*⟩ [ME, fr OE *hwȳ*, instrumental case of *hwæt* what – more at WHAT] – **why not** – used in making a suggestion ⟨why not *boil them?*⟩

²**why** *conj* **1** the cause, reason, or purpose for which ⟨*that is* ~ *I'm so tired*⟩ **2** on which grounds ⟨*the reason* ~ *I left*⟩

³**why** *n, pl* **whys 1** reason, cause ⟨*wants to know the* ~s *and wherefores*⟩

⁴**why** *interj* – used to express mild surprise, hesitation, approval, disapproval, or impatience ⟨~, *here's what I was looking for*⟩ [¹*why*]

**whydah, whidah** /'widə/ *n* any of various mainly black and white African WEAVERBIRDS (songbirds resembling finches) that are often kept as cage birds and the male of which has long drooping tail feathers during the breeding season [alter. (influenced by *Whydah*, town in Dahomey) of *widow (bird)*; fr its dark plumage suggesting a widow's dress]

¹**wick** /wik/ *n* a cord, strip, or cylinder of loosely woven material through which a liquid (eg paraffin, oil, or melted wax) is drawn by capillary action to the top of a candle, lamp, oil stove, etc for burning [ME *weke, wicke*, fr OE *wēoce*; akin to OHG *wiohha* wick, OIr *figim* I weave]

²**wick** *adj, N Eng* alive [alter. of *quick*]

³**wick** *n* [rhyming slang (*Hampton*) *Wick* prick, penis, fr *Hampton Wick*, district in SW London] – **get on somebody's wick** to annoy somebody intensely

**wicked** /'wikid/ *adj* **1** morally very bad; evil **2** disposed to mischief; roguish ⟨*a* ~ *grin*⟩ **3** *informal* very unpleasant, vicious, or dangerous ⟨~ *weather*⟩ ⟨*a* ~ *waste*⟩ synonyms see ¹BAD [ME, alter. of *wicke* wicked, perh fr OE *wicca* wizard] – **wickedly** *adv*, **wickedness** *n*

**wicker** /'wikə/ *n* **1** a small pliant twig or branch; an osier, withe **2** wickerwork [ME *wiker*, of Scand origin; akin to Sw dial. *vikker* willow, ON *veikr* weak – more at WEAK] – **wicker** *adj*

**wickerwork** /'wikə,wuhk/ *n* work consisting of interlaced osiers, twigs, or rods; basketry

**wicket** /'wikit/ *n* **1** a small gate or door; *esp* one forming part of or placed near a larger gate or door **2** an opening like a window; *esp* a grilled or grated window through which business is transacted (eg at a bank) **3a** either of the two sets of stumps set 22 yards (20.12 metres) apart, at which the ball is bowled and which the batsman defends in cricket **b** the area 12 feet (3.66 metres) wide bounded by these wickets, esp when viewed as suitable for a particular type of bowling or play ⟨*a fast* ~⟩ ⟨*a bland and beautiful batting* ~ – *Sportsworld (London)*⟩ **c** a terminated innings of a batsman ⟨*the fast bowlers took all the* ~s *between them*⟩; *also* a partnership between two batsmen who are in at the same time ⟨*the fourth* ~ *put on 57 runs*⟩ **d** an innings of a batsman that is not completed or never begun ⟨*won by five* ~s⟩ **4** *NAm* SLUICE GATE **5** *NAm* a croquet hoop **6** *informal* a situation or set of circumstances – chiefly in *on a good/bad wicket, on a sticky wicket* ⟨*point out to air hostesses and nurses what a good* ~ *they are on* – *The Sun (Melbourne)*⟩ [ME *wiket*, fr ONF, of Gmc origin; akin to MD *wiket* wicket, OE *wīcan* to yield – more at WEAK]

**wicketkeeper** /'wikit,keepə/ *n* the fieldsman in cricket who is stationed behind the batsman's wicket and whose object is to catch balls missed or hit with the edge of the bat by the batsman and to stump him/her if possible; *also* a cricketer who specializes in wicketkeeping rather than in batting or bowling – **wicketkeeping** *n*

**wicking** /'wiking/ *n* material for wicks

**wickiup** /'wiki,up/ *n* a hut used by the nomadic Indians of the arid regions of the western and southwestern USA with a usu oval base and a rough frame covered with reed mats, grass, or brushwood; *also* a rude temporary shelter or hut [Fox *wikiyap* dwelling]

**widdershins** /'widə,shinz/ *adv* in a left-handed, wrong, or contrary direction; *specif* anticlockwise – compare DEASIL [MLG *weddersinnes*, fr MHG *widersinnen* to go back, fr *wider* back, against, again + *sinnen* to go]

¹**widdle** /'widl/ *vi, euph informal* to urinate ⟨*the puppy* ~d *on the bedroom carpet*⟩ [prob fr *wee-wee* + *piddle*]

²**widdle** *n, euph informal* **1** urine **2** an act of urinating

¹**wide** /wied/ *adj* **1a** having great horizontal extent; vast ⟨*a* ~ *area*⟩ **b** embracing much; COMPREHENSIVE 1 ⟨*reaches a* ~ *public*⟩ ⟨~ *experience*⟩ **2a** having a specified width ⟨*3 metres* ~⟩ **b** having much extent between the sides; broad ⟨*a* ~ *doorway*⟩ **c** having much extent between the units ⟨*a* ~ *gait*⟩ **d** fully opened ⟨wide-*eyed*⟩ **e** *of a speech sound* LAX 4 **3a** extending or fluctuating over a considerable range ⟨*a* ~ *variation*⟩ **b** distant or deviating from something specified ⟨*his remark was* ~ *of the truth*⟩ **4** of, occupying, passing through, or being a fielding position in cricket near a line perpendicular to and equidistant from each wicket ⟨~ *mid-off*⟩ **5** *Br slang* shrewd, astute ⟨~ *boys*⟩ – see also **give a wide** BERTH **to** synonyms see ¹BROAD *antonym* narrow [ME, fr OE *wīd*; akin to OHG *wīt* wide] – **widen** *vb*, **wideness** *n*, **widish** *adj*

²**wide** *adv* **1** over a great horizontal distance or extent; widely ⟨*searched far and* ~⟩ **2a** so as to leave much space or distance between ⟨*legs* ~ *apart*⟩ **b** so as to miss or clear a point by a considerable distance ⟨*the bullet went* ~⟩ **3** to the fullest extent; completely, fully – often as an intensive + *open*

usage **Wide** as an adverb is chiefly used in certain fixed phrases ⟨*far and* **wide**⟩ ⟨**wide** *open/apart/awake*⟩ and for the sense "not hitting the target" ⟨*aim* **wide**⟩. It cannot replace **widely**, whose chief meaning is "over a broad range or area" and which must be used with past participles ⟨**widely** *separated*⟩.

³**wide** *n* a ball bowled in cricket that in the opinion of the umpire is out of reach of the batsman in his/her normal position, and that counts as one run to the batting side if no runs are made otherwise

**-wide** *comb form* (*n* → *adj* or *adv*) over (a specified distance, area, or extent); throughout (a specified area or scope) ⟨*a nation*wide *business*⟩ ⟨*expanded the business country-*wide⟩

'**wide-,angle** *adj* **1** having or covering an angle of view wider than the ordinary – used esp of lenses of shorter than normal FOCAL LENGTH **2** having, involving the use of, or relating to a wide-angle lens ⟨~ *camera*⟩

,**wide-'awake** *adj* **1** fully awake **2** alertly watchful, esp for advantages or opportunities – **wide-awakeness** *n*

,**wide-'eyed** *adj* **1** having the eyes wide open, esp with wonder or astonishment **2** marked by uncritical acceptance or admiration; naive ⟨~ *innocence*⟩

**widely** /'wiedli/ *adv* **1** over a broad range ⟨*fluctuated* ~⟩ **2** to a great extent ⟨*two* ~ *different descriptions*⟩ **3** throughout a large well-dispersed group of people ⟨*a* ~ *known political figure*⟩ **4** over a wide area ⟨*has travelled* ~⟩ *usage* see ²WIDE

**widemouthed** /'wied,mowtht, ,-'-/ *adj* **1** having a wide mouth ⟨~ *jars*⟩ **2** having one's mouth opened wide (eg in awe)

'**wide-,screen** *adj* of or being a projected picture that is substantially wider than it is high

**widespread** /'wied,spred/ *adj* **1** widely extended or spread out **2** widely diffused or prevalent ⟨~ *public interest*⟩

**widespreading** /'wied,spreding/ *adj* widespread

**widgeon** *also* **wigeon** /'wijin/ *n, pl* **widgeons,** *esp collectively* **widgeon** any of several freshwater ducks (genus *Anas*) between the teal and the mallard in size; *esp* a Eurasian duck (*Anas penelope*) that is found on mud flats and marshes, is primarily a grazer, and the male of which has a chestnut head with a lighter crown [origin unknown]

**widget** /'wijit/ *n* **1** a gadget **2** an unnamed article considered for purposes of hypothetical example ⟨*some sort of* ~ *between the handle and door would make it firm*⟩ [alter. of *gadget*]

**widgie** /'wiji/ *n, Austr & NZ informal* an unruly irresponsible female – compare BODGIE [origin unknown]

**¹widow** /'widoh/ *n* **1a** a woman who has lost her husband by death; *esp* one who has not remarried **b** a woman whose husband spends much time away from her pursuing the specified esp sporting activity ⟨*a football* ~⟩ **2** an extra hand, or part of a hand, of cards dealt face down and usu placed at the disposal of the highest bidder **3** a single usu short last line (eg of a paragraph) appearing at the top of a printed page or column [ME *widewe,* fr OE *wuduwe;* akin to OHG *wituwa* widow, L *vidua* widow, *-videre* to separate, Gk *ēitheos* unmarried youth]

**²widow** *vt* **1** to bereave of a spouse; *esp* to cause to become a widow **2** to deprive of something greatly valued or needed **3** *obs* to survive as the widow of ⟨*let me be married to three kings . . . and* ~ *them all* – Shak⟩

**widower** /'widoh·ə/ *n* a man who has lost his wife by death; *esp* one who has not remarried [ME *widewer,* alter. of *wedow* widow, widower, fr OE *wuduwa* widower; akin to OE *wuduwe* widow]

**widowhood** /'widoh,hood/ *n* **1** the quality or state of being a widow **2** the period during which a woman remains a widow

**widow's cruse** *n* an unfailing source of supply [fr the biblical story of a widow whose cruse of oil was made unfailing (I Kings 17:14–16)]

**widow's mite** *n* a small gift, esp of money, ungrudgingly given by one who can least afford it [fr the biblical story of a widow who cast two mites (a farthing) into the temple treasury (Mark 12:42)]

**widow's peak** *n* a peak formed by the downward growth of the hairline in the middle of the forehead [fr its resemblance to the peak of a hood formerly worn by widows]

**width** /wit·th, width/ *n* **1** the measurement taken at right angles to the length; breadth **2** largeness of extent or scope **3** a measured and cut piece of material ⟨*a* ~ *of calico*⟩ [¹*wide* + *-th*]

**widthways** /'wit·th,wayz, 'width-/ *adv* in the direction of the width; crosswise

**widthwise** /'wit·th,wiez, 'width-/ *adv* widthways

**wield** /weeld/ *vt* **1** to handle (eg a tool) effectively ⟨~ *a broom*⟩ **2** to exert, exercise ⟨~ *influence*⟩ **3** *chiefly dial* to deal successfully with; manage [ME *welden* to control, fr OE *wieldan;* akin to OHG *waltan* to rule, L *valēre* to be strong, be worth] – **wielder** *n*

**wieldy** /'wieldi/ *adj* easy to use or wield

**wiener** /'weenə/ *n, NAm* a frankfurter [short for *wienerwurst,* fr Ger, fr *wiener* of Vienna + *wurst* sausage]

**Wiener schnitzel** /'veenə ,shnitsəl/ *n* a thin breadcrumbed fried veal cutlet or escalope served with a garnish [Ger, fr *wiener* of Vienna + *schnitzel* cutlet]

**wife** /wief/ *n, pl* **wives** /wievz/ **1** a woman acting in a specified capacity – in combination ⟨*fishwife*⟩ **2** a married woman, esp in relation to her husband ⟨*John's* ~⟩ **3** *dial* a woman [ME *wif,* fr OE *wīf;* akin to OHG *wīb* wife] – **wifehood** *n,* **wifeless** *adj*

**wifelike** /'wief,liek/ *adj* wifely

**wifely** /'wiefli/ *adj* of or befitting a good wife – **wifeliness** *n*

**'wife-,swapping** *n* the temporary exchange of sexual partners by two or more married couples

**wifey** /'wiefi/ *n, chiefly dial or humorous* WIFE 2

**wig** /wig/ *n* **1** a manufactured covering of natural or synthetic hair for the head **2** TOUPEE 2 [short for *periwig*] – **wigged** *adj,* **wigless** *adj*

**wigan** /'wigən/ *n* a stiff plain-weave cotton fabric [*Wigan,* town in NW England]

**wigeon** /'wijin/ *n* a widgeon

**wigging** /'wiging/ *n, informal* a severe scolding [*wig* (rebuke), perh fr *bigwig*]

**¹wiggle** /'wigl/ *vi* **1** to move to and fro with quick jerky or shaking motions ⟨*his toes* ~d⟩ **2** to proceed (as if) with twisting and turning movements; wriggle ~ *vt* **1** to cause to wiggle **2** to make (one's way) by wiggling [ME *wiglen,* fr or akin to MD or MLG *wiggelen* to totter; akin to OE *wegan* to move – more at WAY] – **wiggler** *n*

**²wiggle** *n* **1a** a wiggling movement **b** a wavy line; squiggle **2** shellfish or fish in cream sauce with peas – **wiggly** *adj*

**¹wight** /wiet/ *n, archaic or humorous* a human being; *esp* an unfortunate one [ME, creature, thing, fr OE *wiht;* akin to OHG *wiht* creature, thing, OSlav *vešti* thing (cf AUGHT, NAUGHT)]

**²wight** *adj, archaic* valiant, stalwart [ME, of Scand origin; akin to ON *vīgr* (neut *vīgt*) skilled in fighting; akin to OE *wīgan* to fight – more at VICTOR]

**wigmaker** /'wig,maykə/ *n* someone who makes or deals in wigs

**¹wigwag** /'wig,wag/ *vb* **-gg-** *vi* to send a signal (as if) by waving a flag or light according to a code **2** to waggle ~ *vt* **1** to signal by wigwagging **2** to cause to wigwag [E dial. *wig* to move + E *wag*]

**²wigwag** *n* **1** the art or practice of wigwagging **2** an act of wigwagging

**wigwam** /'wig,wam/ *n* a hut of the American Indians of the Great Lakes region and eastwards, having typically an arched framework of poles overlaid with bark, rush mats, or hides [Abnaki & Massachuset *wīkwām*]

**wilco** /'wilkoh/ *interj* – used esp in radio and signalling to indicate that a message received will be complied with [*will comply*]

**¹wild** /wield/ *adj* **1a** living in a state of nature and not ordinarily tame or domesticated ⟨*a* ~ *duck*⟩ **b(1)** growing or produced without the aid and care of humans ⟨~ *honey*⟩ **b(2)** related to or resembling a corresponding cultivated or domesticated organism ⟨~ *strawberries*⟩ **b(3)** *of fauna* hard to get near; shy **c** of wild organisms ⟨*the* ~ *state*⟩ **2a** not inhabited or cultivated ⟨~ *land*⟩; *also, of scenery* desolate **b** not amenable to human habitation or cultivation; waste **3a(1)** free from restraint or regulation; uncontrolled, unruly ⟨~ *mobs*⟩ ⟨~ *locks*⟩ ⟨*a* ~ *party*⟩ **a(2)** emotionally overcome ⟨~ *with grief*⟩; *also* passionately eager or enthusiastic ⟨*was* ~ *about punk rock*⟩ **a(3)** very angry; infuriated ⟨*drove me* ~ *with his whining*⟩ **b** marked by turbulent agitation ⟨~ *frenzy*⟩; *also* stormy ⟨*a* ~ *night*⟩ **c** going beyond reasonable or conventional bounds; fantastic ⟨*a* ~ *scheme*⟩ ⟨*beyond my* ~*est dreams*⟩ **d** indicative of strong passion, desire, or emotion ⟨*a* ~ *gleam of delight in his eyes* – *Irish Digest*⟩ **4** uncivilized, barbaric **5** characteristic of, appropriate to, or expressive of wilderness, wildlife, or a simple or uncivilized society ⟨~ *freedom*⟩ **6** deviating from the intended or regular course ⟨~ *grammar*⟩ ⟨*the throw was* ~⟩; *also* haphazard ⟨*a* ~ *guess*⟩ **7** *of a playing card* able to represent any card designated by the holder **8** *informal* fashionably outrageous ⟨*those pants are really* ~⟩ – see *also* SOW ONE'S WILD OATS [ME *wilde,* fr OE; akin to OHG *wildi* wild, W *gwyllt*] – **wildish** *adj,* **wildly** *adv,* **wildness** *n*

**²wild** *n* **1a** a sparsely inhabited or uncultivated region or tract; a wilderness **b** **wilds** *pl,* **wild** the remote country ⟨*out in the* ~s *of Norfolk*⟩ **2** a wild, free, or natural state or existence ⟨*living in the* ~⟩

**³wild** *adv* in a wild manner: eg **a** without regulation or control ⟨*rhododendrons growing* ~⟩ **b** off an intended or expected course

**wild and woolly** /'wooli/ *adj* **1** marked by a boisterous and untamed lack of polish and refinement ⟨*a* ~ *town*⟩ **2** unrestrained by realism or pragmatism; visionary ⟨*a* ~ *idealist*⟩

**wild boar** *n* an African and Eurasian wild pig (*Sus scrofa*) from which most domestic pigs have been derived

**wild carrot** *n* a widely naturalized Eurasian plant (*Daucus carota*) of the carrot family that is probably the original of the cultivated carrot and has an acrid unpleasant-tasting root

**¹wildcat** /'wield,kat/ *n, pl* **wildcats,** (*1b*) **wildcats,** *esp collectively* **wildcat 1a** either of two cats (*Felis sylvestris* of Europe and *Felis ocreata* of Africa) that resemble but are heavier in build than the domestic cat and are usu held to be among the ancestors of the domestic cat **b** any of various small or medium-sized cats (eg the lynx or ocelot) **c** a savage domestic cat **2** a savage quick-tempered person **3a** a wildcat oil or gas well **b** a wildcat strike

**²wildcat** *adj* **1a(1)** financially irresponsible or unreliable ⟨~ *banks*⟩ **a(2)** issued by a financially irresponsible banking establishment ⟨~ *currency*⟩ **b(1)** operating, produced, or carried on outside the bounds of standard or legitimate business practices ⟨*a* ~ *insurance scheme*⟩ **b(2)** operating sporadically and unofficially ⟨*published verse in small* ~ *magazines* – Richard Hughes⟩ **2** of or being an oil or gas well drilled in territory not known to be productive **3** initiated by a group of workers without formal union approval or in violation of a contract ⟨*a* ~ *strike*⟩

³**wildcat** *vi* **-tt-** to prospect and drill an experimental oil or gas well or sink a mine shaft in territory not known to be productive – **wildcatter** *n*

**wildebeest** /'wildə,beest, 'vil-/ *n, pl* **wildebeests**, *esp collectively* **wildebeest** GNU (large African antelope) [Afrik *wildebees* (pl *wildebeeste*), fr *wilde* wild + *bees* ox]

**wilder** /'wieldə/ *vb, archaic vt* **1** to lead astray **2** to bewilder, perplex ~ *vi* to move at random; wander [prob irreg fr *wilderness*]

**wilderness** /'wildənis/ *n* **1a(1)** a usu barren area or region uncultivated and uninhabited by human beings **a(2)** an area that, together with its natural fauna and flora, has been essentially undisturbed by human activity **b** an empty or pathless area or region ⟨*in remote* ~es *of space groups of nebulae are found* – G W Gray †1960⟩ **c** a part of a garden or nature reserve devoted to wild growth **2a** a confusing multitude or mass ⟨*I would not have given it for a* ~ *of monkeys* – Shak⟩ **b** a bewildering situation ⟨*those moral* ~es *of civilized life* – Norman Mailer⟩ **3** the state of being excluded from activity or power (e g political power) **4** *obs* wildness [ME, fr *wildern* wild, fr OE *wilddēoren* of wild beasts]

,**wild-'eyed** *adj* **1** glaring wildly **2** WILD AND WOOLLY 2 ⟨~ *schemes*⟩

**wildfire** /'wield,fie·ə/ *n* **1a** GREEK FIRE **b** something that acts intensely and usu spreads very rapidly – usu in *like wildfire* **2** a phosphorescent glow (e g a will-o'-the-wisp)

**wild flower** *n* a wild or uncultivated plant; *also* the flower of such a plant

**wildfowl** /'wield,fowl/ *n* a game bird; *esp* a game waterfowl (e g a wild duck or goose) – **wildfowler** *n*, **wildfowling** *n*

**wild-goose chase** *n* a hopeless pursuit after something unattainable

**wild horse** *n* a horse (*Equus caballus*) of the Russian Steppes that is grey, has an erect mane and black stripe running along its back, and is the sole surviving wild ancestor of the domestic horse

**wild hyacinth** *n* a common European spring-flowering woodland plant (*Endymion non-scriptus*) of the lily family with flower heads of blue drooping bell-shaped flowers; a bluebell

¹**wilding** /'wielding/ *n* **1a** a plant growing uncultivated in the wild, either as a native or a cultivated plant run wild; *esp* a wild apple or CRAB APPLE **b** the fruit of a wilding **2** a wild animal [¹*wild* + ³-*ing*]

²**wilding** *adj, archaic* WILD 1, 2

**wild land** *n* land that is uncultivated or unfit for cultivation

**wildlife** /'wield,lief/ *n* wild animals; *also* the wild animals and plants collectively of a region

**wildlife park** *n* an open-air zoo in which the animals displayed are often indigenous to the region and are free to move over large areas similar to their natural habitats

**wildling** /'wieldling/ *n* a wilding

**wild man** *n* **1** a savage **2** a radical extremist

**wild oat** *n* **1** any of several wild grasses (genus *Avena*); *esp* a grass (*Avena fatua*) common in meadows and as a weed of arable land and waste places **2** *pl* offences and indiscretions ascribed to youthful exuberance; *esp* premarital promiscuity – usu in *sow one's wild oats*

**wild pansy** *n* a common and long-cultivated European plant (*Viola tricolor*) of the violet family from which most of the garden pansies are derived and that has usu blue or purple mixed with white and yellow flowers

**wild parsley** *n* any of numerous wild plants of the carrot family with finely divided foliage

**wild rice** *n* a tall aquatic N American grass (*Zizania aquatica*) that yields an edible purplish-black grain

**wild service tree, service** *n* a Eurasian tree (*Sorbus torminalis*) of the rose family with bitter-tasting fruits

**wild silk** *n* silk that is produced by wild silkworms and is coarser and stronger than cultivated silk

**wild thyme** *n* a low-growing thyme (*Thymus serpyllum*) of the mint family with clusters of pink flowers

**wild type** *n* the typical form of an organism as ordinarily encountered in nature, in contrast to atypical individuals result-

ing from a change in the CHROMOSOMES or genes in the cells – **wild-type** *adj*

**wild West** *n* the western USA in its frontier period

**wildwood** /'wield,wood/ *n* a wood unaltered or unfrequented by man

¹**wile** /wiel/ *n* **1** a deceitful trick or stratagem; *also* a beguiling or playful trick **2** skill in outwitting; trickery, guile [ME *wil*, fr (assumed) ONF, prob of Gmc origin; akin to OE *wigle* divination – more at WITCH]

²**wile** *vt* to lure (as if) by a magic spell; entice

**wile away** *vt* WHILE AWAY

**wilful,** *NAm chiefly* **willful** /'wilf(ə)l/ *adj* **1** obstinately and often perversely self-willed **2** done deliberately; intentional *synonyms* see ¹VOLUNTARY, UNRULY *antonyms* biddable, accidental – **wilfully** *adv*, **wilfulness** *n*

¹**will** /wil/ *vb, pres sing & pl* **will**; *pres neg* **won't** /wohnt/; *past* **would** /wəd; *strong* wood/ *va* **1** – used to express choice, willingness, or consent or in negative constructions refusal ⟨*can find no one who* ~ *take the job*⟩ ⟨*if we* ~ *all do our best*⟩; used in the question form with the force of a request ⟨~ *you please stop talking*⟩ ⟨*shut the door,* ~ *you?*⟩ or of an offer or suggestion ⟨~ *you have some tea?*⟩ **2** – used to express custom or inevitable tendency ⟨~ *work one day and loaf the next*⟩ ⟨*accidents* ~ *happen*⟩; used with emphatic stress to express exasperation ⟨*he* ~ *call the record-player the "gramophone"* – John Fowles⟩ **3** – used to express futurity ⟨*tomorrow morning I* ~ *wake up in this first-class hotel suite* – Tennessee Williams⟩ **4** can ⟨*back seat* ~ *hold three passengers*⟩ ⟨*door won't shut*⟩ **5** – used to express logical probability ⟨*that* ~ *be the milkman*⟩ **6** – used to express determination ⟨*I have made up my mind to go, and go I* ~⟩ **7** – used to express a command or exhortation ⟨*you* ~ *do as I say, at once*⟩ ~ *vi* **1** to wish, desire ⟨*whether we* ~ *or no*⟩ **2** *archaic* to be about to go ⟨*thither* ~ *I then* – Sir Walter Scott⟩ *usage* see SHALL [ME (1 & 3 sing. pres indic), fr OE *wille* (infin *wyllan*); akin to OHG *wili* (3 sing. pres indic) wills, L *velle* to wish, will]

²**will** *n* **1** a desire, wish: e g **1a** a resolute intention ⟨*where there's a* ~ *there's a way*⟩ ⟨*has no* ~ *to live*⟩ **b** an inclination ⟨*I did it against my* ~⟩ **c** a choice, wish ⟨*the* ~ *of the people*⟩ ⟨*carried her off against her* ~⟩ **2a** what is wished or ordained by the specified agent ⟨*impose his* ~ *on them*⟩ ⟨*God's* ~ *be done*⟩ **b** the part of a summons expressing a royal command **3a** a mental power manifested as wishing, choosing, desiring, or intending ⟨*his lack of all* ~ *or purpose*⟩ ⟨*has a* ~ *of her own*⟩ **b(1)** a disposition to act according to principles or ends ⟨*the* ~ *to believe*⟩ **b(2)** the power to initiate deliberate action ⟨*the freedom of the* ~⟩ **c** a specified disposition towards others ⟨*bear him no ill* ~⟩ **4** willpower, self-control ⟨*a man of iron* ~⟩ **5** a legal declaration of a person's mind as to the manner in which he/she would have his/her property or estate disposed of after his/her death; *esp* a written document legally executed by which one makes disposition of one's estate to take effect after one's death **6** *archaic* a request, command [ME, fr OE *willa* will, desire; akin to OE *wille*; (2b) fr the phrase *our will is* which introduces it] – **will-less** *adj*

³**will** *vt* **1a** to order or direct by a will **b** to dispose of (as if) by a will; bequeath **2a** to determine deliberately; purpose by decree, ordain ⟨*Providence* ~s *it*⟩ **c** to (attempt to) cause by exercise of the will ⟨~ed *her to go away*⟩ ~ *vi* **1** to exercise the will **2** to choose – **willer** *n*

**willable** /'wiləbl/ *adj* capable of being willed, wished, or determined by will

**willed** /wild/ *adj* having a will, esp of a specified kind – usu in combination ⟨*strong*-willed⟩

**willemite** /'wiləmiet/ *n* a mineral consisting of zinc SILICATE, $Zn_2SiO_4$, occurring in hexagonal prisms and in a granular or not clearly crystalline form, and usu white in colour [Ger *willemit*, fr *Willem* (William) I †1843 king of the Netherlands]

**willie** /'wili/ *n, Br euph* a penis [*Willie*, nickname for *William*]

**willies** /'wiliz/ *n pl, informal* a fit of nervousness; the jitters – + *the* [origin unknown]

¹**willing** *adj* **1** inclined or favourably disposed in mind; ready ⟨~ *to work*⟩ **2** prompt to act or respond ⟨*a* ~ *horse*⟩ **3** done, borne, or given without reluctance ⟨~ *help*⟩ **4** of the will or the power of choosing; volitional *synonyms* see ¹VOLUNTARY *antonym* reluctant [(4) fr prp of ³*will*] – **willingly** *adv*, **willingness** *n*

²**willing** *n* cheerful alacrity – in *show willing*

**will-o'-the-wisp** /,wil ə dhə 'wisp/ *n* **1** a light that sometimes appears in the night over marshy ground and is often attributable to the combustion of gas from decomposed organic matter – called also IGNIS FATUUS **2** an enticing but elusive goal **3** an unreliable or elusive person [*Will* (nickname for *William*) + *of* + *the* + *wisp*] – **will-o'-the-wispish** *adj*

**¹willow** /'wiloh/ *n* **1** any of a genus (*Salix* of the family Salicaceae, the willow family) of trees and shrubs bearing catkins of flowers with no petals and including some forms grown for wood or rods used in basketry and some grown for ornament **2** a machine in which cotton or wool is opened and cleaned by a spiked drum revolving in a box studded internally with spikes **3** *informal* an object made of willow wood; *esp* a cricket bat [ME *wilghe, wilowe,* fr OE *welig;* akin to MHG *wilge* willow, Gk *helikē*] – **willowlike** *adj*

**²willow** *vt* to open and clean (textile fibres) with a willow

**willower** /'wilohə/ *n* a textile worker who operates a willow

**willow grouse** *n* a stout thick-beaked N European grouse (*Lagopus lagopus lagopus*) that has red-brown plumage and a black tail and is found on moors and scrub

**willowherb** /'wiloh,huhb/ *n* any of a genus (*Epilobium*) of plants of the fuchsia family; *esp* ROSEBAY WILLOWHERB

**willow pattern** *n* china tableware decorated with a usu blue-and-white story-telling design of oriental style, usu including a willow

**willow warbler** *n* a small greenish Eurasian and African warbler (*Phylloscopus trochilus*) found in open areas and scrub

**willowy** /'wiloh-i/ *adj* **1** full of willows **2a** supple, pliant **b** gracefully tall and slender

**willpower** /'wil,powə/ *n* energetic determination; resoluteness

**will to power** *n* **1** the drive of the superman in the philosophy of Nietzsche **2** a desire to exercise authority over others

**willy-nilly** /,wili 'nili/ *adv* or *adj* **1** by compulsion; without choice **2** (carried out or occurring) in a haphazard or random manner ⟨*distributed the gifts ~ among the crowd*⟩ [alter. of *will I (ye/he) nill I (ye/he),* lit., (whether) I am willing (or) I am unwilling]

**willy-willy** /'wili ,wili/ *n, Austr* a whirlwind [prob fr native name in Australia]

**Wilson's disease** /'wils(ə)nz/ *n* an inherited disease caused by an inability of the body to deal with copper in the diet, leading to accumulation of poisonous concentrations of the metal and resulting in degeneration of the liver, lack of muscular control, and often severe mental disorder [Samuel *Wilson* †1937 E neurologist]

**Wilson's petrel** *n* a PETREL (type of seabird) (*Oceanites oceanicus*) that breeds in Antarctic waters and visits the southern Atlantic in summer [Alexander *Wilson* †1813 US ornithologist]

**¹wilt** /wilt/ *archaic pres 2nd sing of* ¹WILL

**²wilt** *vi* **1** *of a plant* to lose freshness and become limp; droop **2** to grow weak or faint; languish ~ *vt* to cause to wilt [alter. of earlier *welk,* fr ME *welken,* prob fr MD; akin to OHG er-*welkēn* to wilt]

**³wilt** *n* **1** wilting or being wilted **2a** wilt, **wilt disease** a disease (eg one caused by a fungus) of plants in which the soft tissues lose water with subsequent drooping and often shrivelling **b** a virus disease of various caterpillars that causes them to shrivel up

**Wilton** /'wilt(ə)n/ *n* **1** a carpet weave in which pattern is woven into the carpet in loops of cut or uncut pile, rather than being inserted in a backing – compare AXMINSTER **2** a carpet woven by the Wilton method [*Wilton,* town in Wiltshire, England]

**wily** /'wieli/ *adj* crafty, artful *synonyms* see SLY [ME, fr *wil* wile + ¹-*y*] – **wilily** *adv,* **wiliness** *n*

**¹wimble** /'wimbl/ *n* a gimlet, brace and bit, or other tool used for boring holes [ME, fr AF, fr MD *wimmel* auger (cf GIMLET)]

**²wimble** /'wimbl/ *vt* to bore (as if) with a wimble

**¹wimple** /'wimpl/ *n* **1** a cloth covering worn over the head and round the neck and chin, esp by women in the late medieval period and by some nuns **2** *Scot* **2a** a crafty turn; a twist **b** a curve, bend [ME *wimpel,* fr OE; akin to OE *wīpian* to wipe; (2) perh of different origin]

**²wimple** *vt* **1** to cover (as if) with a wimple; veil **2** to cause to ripple ~ *vi* **1** to ripple **2** *chiefly Scot* to follow a winding course; meander **3** *archaic* to fall or lie in folds

**Wimpy** /'wimpi/ *trademark* – used for a fried hamburger, esp when served in a plain bread bun ⟨*a ~ bar*⟩

**¹win** /win/ *vb* **-nn-;** won /wun/ *vi* **1a** to gain the victory in a contest; succeed ⟨*always ~s at chess*⟩ **b** to be right in an argument, dispute, etc; *also* to have one's way ⟨*OK, you ~, we'll go to the theatre*⟩ **2** to succeed in arriving at a place or a

state – esp in *to win free* ~ *vt* **1a** to get possession of by effort or qualities ⟨*~ their approval*⟩; *also* to gain by luck or good fortune ⟨*~ £10 at cards*⟩ **b** to obtain by effort; earn ⟨*striving to ~ a living from the sterile soil*⟩ **2a** to gain (as if) in battle or contest ⟨*~ the victory*⟩ ⟨*~ the Cup*⟩ **b** to be the victor in ⟨*won the war*⟩ **3** to induce (a woman) to accept oneself in marriage – often in *win the hand of* **4a** to obtain (eg ore, coal, or clay) by mining **b** to prepare (eg a vein or bed) for regular mining **c** to recover (eg metal) from ore **5** to reach by expenditure of effort ⟨*~ the summit*⟩ ⟨*~ home*⟩ **6** *chiefly Scot* to dry (eg hay or turf) by heating or exposure to the wind **7** *slang* to steal [ME *winnen,* fr OE *winnan* to struggle; akin to OHG *winnan* to struggle, L *venus* love, charm; (6) perh of different origin]

*synonyms* Win, gain, earn, and acquire can all mean "come into possession of". One wins desirable things, including money, particularly by good fortune or as the result of successful competition ⟨**won** *£1,000 on the pools*⟩. One may also gain desirable things, though not usually money, in competition, but gain emphasizes industry or merit ⟨**gained** *admission to the university*⟩. Earn specifies that what one receives is deserved because of the effort expended, and can be used for what is deserved without actually being received ⟨*he's worked so hard he's* **earned** *a rest*⟩. Acquire makes no suggestion of the means, so is often used where these are mysterious ⟨*she's somehow* **acquired** *a new Jaguar*⟩. antonym lose

**win out** *vi* to be successful; prevail ⟨*her common sense finally won out*⟩

**win over/round** *vt* **1** to convert to one's own point of view; persuade ⟨*she said she wouldn't come but we soon won her over*⟩ **2** to persuade into friendliness ⟨*his smile won her round in a trice*⟩

**win through** *vi* to survive difficulties and reach a desired or satisfactory end ⟨*win through to the final*⟩

**²win** *n* **1** a victory or success, esp in a game or sporting contest **2** first place at the finish, esp of a horse race

**wince** /wins/ *vi* to shrink back involuntarily (eg from pain); flinch ⟨*sarcasm that made him ~*⟩ *synonyms* see ¹RECOIL [ME *wenchen* to be impatient, dart about, fr (assumed) ONF *wenchier,* of Gmc origin; akin to OHG *wankōn* to totter, OE *wincian* to wink] – **wince** *n*

**wincey** /'winsi/ *n* a plain or TWILLED fabric, usu with a cotton or linen WARP (lengthways threads) and wool WEFT (crossways threads) that is used esp for shirts and nightclothes [prob alter. of *linsey* (in *linsey-woolsey*)]

**winceyette** /,winsi'et/ *n* a lightweight usu cotton fabric with a nap on one or both sides [*wincey* + -*ette*]

**¹winch** /winch/ *n* **1** any of various machines or instruments for hoisting or pulling; *esp* a powerful machine with one or more drums on which to coil a rope, cable, or chain for hauling or hoisting; a windlass **2** a crank or handle for giving motion to a machine (eg a grindstone) [ME *winche* roller, reel, fr OE *wince;* akin to OE *wincian* to wink]

**²winch** *vt* to hoist or haul (as if) with a winch – **wincher** *n*

**¹wind** /wind/ *n* **1a** a natural movement of air at any speed; *esp* air in natural motion horizontally **b** a movement of air generated by a fan, bellows, or other artificial means **2** a force or agency that carries along or influences; a tendency, trend ⟨*the ~s of change*⟩ **3a** the power to breathe ⟨*took him five minutes to get his ~ back after running up the stairs*⟩ **b** the air used in breathing or talking ⟨*ran out of ~*⟩ **c** the pit of the stomach; SOLAR PLEXUS **4** gas produced in the stomach or the intestines ⟨*cucumbers always give me ~*⟩ **5** compressed air or gas **6** something that is insubstantial: eg **6a** mere talk; idle words ⟨*his talk was just so much ~*⟩ **b** vain self-satisfaction **7** air carrying a scent (eg of a hunter or game) **8a** musical wind instruments collectively, esp as distinguished from stringed and percussion instruments **b** *taking sing or pl vb* the group of players of such instruments **9a** a direction from which the wind may blow; a point of the compass; *esp* a cardinal point that corresponds to such a direction – often in *the four winds* **b** the direction from which the wind is blowing **10** *archaic* air [ME, fr OE; akin to OHG *wint* wind, L *ventus,* Gk *aēnai* to blow, Skt *vāti* it blows] – **windless** *adj,* **windlessly** *adv,* **windlessness** *n* – **before the wind** in the same direction as the main force of the wind – **break wind** *euph* to expel wind from the anus – **cast/fling/throw to the winds** to abandon, renounce ⟨*cast caution to the winds*⟩ – **close to the wind 1** *nautical* as nearly directly into the wind as possible **2** near to a point of danger or to a limit which it is unwise to cross; *also* risqué – **get/have wind of** to hear a rumour of; become aware of – **in the wind**

about to happen; astir, afoot – **put/get the wind up** to (cause to) become frightened – **take the wind from somebody's sails** to place somebody at a disadvantage, esp by shocking or surprising him/her – **under the wind 1** to leeward **2** in a place protected from the wind; under the lee – see also **three** SHEETS **in the wind, a** STRAW **in the wind**

synonyms Wind is the most general word for moving air. A gentle wind is a **breeze** (zephyr is a more literary word). **Light breeze, gentle breeze, moderate breeze, fresh breeze,** and **strong breeze** are levels on the Beaufort scale. A strong destructive wind is a **gale; moderate gale** or **near gale, fresh gale, strong gale,** and **whole gale** are Beaufort scale levels. A **storm** may entail thunder, rain, etc, but **storm** and **violent storm** are also Beaufort scale wind levels. Some particular winds are the **monsoon**, a seasonal wind of southern Asia; the **simoom, harmattan, khamsin,** and **sirocco**, hot desert winds blowing into the Mediterranean area; and the **mistral**, a cold north wind blowing into southern France. See WHIRLWIND

²**wind** /wind/ vt **1** to detect or follow by scent **2** to expose to the air or wind; dry by exposing to air **3** to make short of breath; esp to make temporarily unable to breathe by a blow in the pit of the stomach **4** to rest (eg a horse) in order to allow the breath to be recovered **5** to help (a baby) to bring up wind; burp ∼ vi to scent game

³**wind** /wiend/ vb **winded, wound** /wownd/ vt **1** to cause (eg a horn) to sound by blowing; blow **2** to sound (eg a call or note) on a horn ⟨wound a rousing call – R L Stevenson⟩ ∼ vi to produce a sound on a horn [¹wind (influenced in pronunciation and conjugation by ⁴wind)]

⁴**wind** /wiend/ vb **wound** /wownd/ also **winded** vi **1** to bend, warp **2** to have a curving course; extend or proceed in curves ⟨path ∼s down the hill⟩ ⟨procession wound through the streets⟩ **3** to coil, twine **4** of a ship to turn when lying at anchor **5** to undergo winding ⟨the car window won't ∼⟩ ∼ vt **1** to introduce sinuously or stealthily; worm, insinuate ⟨∼ himself into my affections⟩ **2a** to surround or wrap with something pliable; bind with loops or layers ⟨∼ the baby in a shawl⟩ **b** to turn completely or repeatedly, esp about an object; coil, twine ⟨∼ the scarf round his neck⟩ ⟨∼ wool into a ball⟩ **c(1)** to hoist or haul by means of a rope or chain and a windlass **c(2)** to move (a ship) by hauling on a capstan **d(1)** to tighten the spring of ⟨∼ a clock⟩ **d(2)** to put into the specified state or position by winding ⟨∼ the speedometer back⟩ **e** to raise to a high level (eg of excitement or tension) – usu + up ⟨wound himself up into a frenzy⟩ **3** to make (one's way or course) (as if) by a curving route – see also **wind somebody round one's little** FINGER [ME winden, fr OE windan to twist, move with speed or force, brandish; akin to OHG wintan to wind, Umbrian ohavendu let him turn aside] – **winder** n

**wind down** vt **1** to bring to an end gradually; cause to cease ⟨are winding their operations in France down for the winter⟩ **2** to relax the tension of ∼ vi to become gradually more relaxed; unwind

**wind off** vt to remove by unwinding

**wind up** vt **1** to bring to a conclusion; end; specif to bring (a business company) to an end by liquidation **2** to put in order; settle **3** to wind completely or tightly ⟨wound up the clock⟩ **4** Br slang to deceive playfully; pull (someone's) leg ∼ vi **1a** to come to a conclusion **b** to arrive in a place, situation, or condition at the end of or because of a course of action ⟨wound up as millionaires⟩ **2** to give a preliminary swing to the arms (eg before bowling) – see also WINDUP

⁵**wind** /wiend/ n **1** a mechanism (eg a winch) for winding **2** winding or being wound **3** a coil, turn **4** a particular method of winding

**windage** /'windij/ n **1a** the space between the projectile of a smoothbore gun and the surface of the bore **b** the difference between the diameter of the bore of a muzzle-loading rifled cannon and that of the projectile cylinder **2a** the amount of compensation that must be made to allow for the effect of any wind when aiming a gun **b(1)** the influence of the wind in deflecting the course of a bullet, shell, etc **b(2)** the amount of deflection due to the wind **3** the disturbance of the air caused by a passing object (eg a shell or bullet) **4** the surface exposed (eg by a ship) to the wind [¹wind + -age]

**wind and weather** n the effects of wind and rain

**windbag** /'wind,bag/ n, informal an excessively talkative person

**windbaggery** /'wind,bagəri/ n, humorous pompous meaningless talk

**windblast** /'wind,blahst/ n the ripping, rubbing, and tearing effects resulting from wind resistance, experienced by a pilot ejecting from a high-speed aircraft

**windblown** /'wind,blohn/ adj **1** blown by the wind; esp shaped or deformed by the prevailing winds ⟨∼ trees⟩ **2** windswept

**windbound** /'wind,bownd/ adj, of a sailing ship unable to sail because of contrary winds

**windbreak** /'wind,brayk/ n a growth of trees or shrubs serving to break the force of wind; broadly a shelter (eg a fence) from the wind

**wind-broken** /wind/ adj, of a horse suffering from BROKEN WIND (lung condition)

**windburn** /'wind,buhn/ n irritation of the skin caused by the wind – **windburned** adj

**windcheater** /'wind,cheetə/ n, chiefly Br a weatherproof or windproof coat or jacket; an anorak

'**wind-,chest** n an airtight box supplying air under pressure to the pipes or reeds of an organ

**windchill** /'wind,chil/, **windchill index** n the still-air temperature that has the same cooling effect on exposed human flesh as a given combination of temperature and wind speed ⟨the ∼ on top of the hill was -40°⟩

**wind-cone** /wind/ n a wind-sock

**winder** /'wiendə/ n that which winds: eg **a** any of various devices or textile machines for winding thread and yarn **b** a key for winding a mechanism (eg a clock) **c** a step that is wider at one end than at the other (eg in a spiral staircase)

¹**windfall** /'wind,fawl/ n **1** something (eg a fruit) blown down by the wind **2** an unexpected gain or advantage; esp a legacy

²**windfall** adj, of profits, dividends, etc unexpectedly large, esp because of some unrepeatable event or circumstances ⟨the earthquake meant ∼ profits for the construction industry⟩

**windflaw** /'wind,flaw/ n a sudden gust of wind; a squall

**windflower** /'wind,flowə/ n ANEMONE 1; esp WOOD ANEMONE

**windgall** /'wind,gawl/ n a soft tumour or swelling on a horse's leg in the region of the FETLOCK joint – **windgalled** adj

**wind gap** n a notch in the crest of a mountain ridge; a pass not occupied by a stream

**wind harp** n AEOLIAN HARP

**windhover** /'wind,hovə/ n, Br chiefly poetic a kestrel [fr its habit of hovering in the wind]

¹**winding** /'wiending/ n **1** material (eg wire) wound or coiled about an object (eg an armature); also a single turn of the wound material **2** the act or manner of winding something **3** a sinuous course, line, or progress ⟨the ∼s of the road down into the valley⟩

²**winding** adj **1** having a pronounced curve; esp spiral ⟨a ∼ stairway⟩ **2** having a course that winds ⟨a ∼ road⟩

**winding-sheet** /'wiending/ n a sheet in which a corpse is wrapped for burial

**wind instrument** /wind/ n a musical instrument (eg a trumpet, clarinet, or organ) that requires air to be passed through it for a sound to be produced; esp a musical instrument that the player blows through

**windjammer** /'wind,jamə/ n **1** a large fast square-rigged sailing vessel **2** Br a windcheater

¹**windlass** /'windləs/ n any of various machines for hoisting or hauling: eg **a** a horizontal drum supported on vertical posts and turned by a crank so that the hoisting rope is wound round the drum **b** a steam or electric winch with a horizontal or vertical shaft and two drums, used to raise a ship's anchor [ME wyndlas, alter. of wyndas, fr ON vindáss, fr vinda to wind (akin to OHG wintan to wind) + áss pole]

²**windlass** vt to hoist or haul with a windlass

**windlestraw** /'windl,straw/ n, Scot & N Eng a dry thin stalk of grass [(assumed) ME, fr OE windelstrēaw, fr windel basket (fr windan to wind) + strēaw straw]

¹**windmill** /'wind,mil/ n **1a** a mill operated by sails that are turned by the wind; esp a wind-driven grain mill **b** a pump or dynamo driven by wind power **2** a toy consisting of lightweight vanes that revolve at the end of a stick – **tilt at windmills** to fight imaginary enemies or evils [fr the action of Don Quixote (see QUIXOTIC) in attacking windmills which he thought to be giants]

²**windmill** vt to cause to move like a windmill ∼ vi to move, esp turn, like a windmill; cartwheel

**window** /'windoh/ n **1** an opening, esp in the wall of a building, for admission of light and air that is usu fitted with casements or sashes containing transparent material (eg glass) and capable of being opened and shut **2** a windowpane ⟨smashed *the* ~> **3a** something (eg a shutter, opening, or valve) suggestive of or functioning like a window **b** something functioning like a window in allowing people to see what is normally hidden from them ⟨*Hong Kong, China's* ~ *on the West*⟩; *also* something functioning like a shop window in displaying new goods or items ⟨*Frankfurt Book Fair, the international* ~ *of the book trade*⟩ **4** the transparent panel of a WINDOW ENVELOPE **5** the framework (eg a shutter or sash with its fittings) that closes a window opening **6** material (eg strips of foil or clusters of fine wires) dropped from an aircraft to reflect radar waves (eg to confuse enemy radar); *also* CHAFF 5 **7** a range of ELECTROMAGNETIC wavelengths that can pass through a planet's atmosphere **8** an interval of time within which a rocket or spacecraft must be launched to accomplish a particular mission; *broadly* an interval during which conditions are appropriate for a task ⟨*the Summer weather* ~⟩ **9** an area at the limits of the earth's atmosphere through which a spacecraft must pass for successful re-entry [ME *windowe*, fr ON *vindauga*, fr *vindr* wind + *auga* eye; akin to OE *wind* & to OE *ēage* eye – more at EYE] – **windowless** *adj*

**window box** *n* **1** either of the hollows in the sides of a window frame for the weights that counterbalance a lifting sash **2** a box designed to hold soil for growing plants on a windowsill

'**window-,dress** *vt* to make appear more attractive or favourable by distortion or adroit presentation [back-formation fr *window dresser*]

**window dressing** *n* **1** the art or an act of arranging a display of merchandise in a shop window **2** the act or an instance of making something appear more attractive or favourable by distortion or adroit presentation – **window dresser** *n*

**window envelope** *n* an envelope with a transparent panel through which the address on the enclosure is visible

'**window-,gardening** *n* the growing of plants either indoors next to a window or outdoors in WINDOW BOXES

'**window-,gaze** *vi* to window-shop

**windowpane** /'windoh,payn/ *n* a panel of transparent material, esp glass, forming (part of) a window

'**window-,shop** *vi* to look at the displays in shop windows for amusement or to assess goods, prices, etc – **window-shopper** *n*

**windowsill** /'windoh,sil/ *n* the shelf or horizontal member at the bottom of a window opening; the sill of a window

**windpipe** /'wind,piep/ *n* TRACHEA – not used technically

'**wind-,pollinated** *adj* pollinated by wind-borne pollen

**wind pump** /wind/ *n* a pump powered by a windmill (eg to raise water or drain land)

**wind rose** /wind/ *n* a diagram showing for a given place the relative frequency or frequency and strength of winds from different directions [Ger *windrose* compass card, fr *wind* wind + *rose* rose]

'**windrow** /'windroh/ *n* **1a** a row of hay raked up to dry before being baled or stored **b** a similar row of cut vegetation (eg grain) for drying **2** a row heaped up (as if) by the wind

²**windrow** *vt* to form (eg hay) into a windrow – **windrower** *n*

**wind scale** /wind/ *n* a scale for indicating the strength of a wind in which wind speeds are assigned numbers or words – compare BEAUFORT SCALE

**windscreen** /'wind,skreen/ *n* **1** a screen that protects against the wind **2** *Br* a transparent screen (eg of glass) at the front of a motor vehicle, motor boat, etc

**windscreen wiper** *n* WIPER 4

**wind shake** /wind/ *n* a flaw or crack along the grain in a piece of timber, attributed to strain from high winds – **wind-shaken** *adj*

**windshield** /'wind,sheeld/ *n, NAm* WINDSCREEN 2

**wind-sleeve** /wind/ *n* a wind-sock

**wind-sock** /wind/ *n* a open tube of cloth, narrowing at one end, mounted in an elevated position to indicate the direction of the wind (eg to pilots of light aircraft)

**Windsor chair** /'winzə, 'windzə/ *n* a wooden chair with a back of turned rods or rails, legs that slant outwards, and usu a slightly concave seat [*Windsor*, town in S England]

**Windsor knot** *n* a wide bulky knot for tying a tie

**Windsor soap** *n* a usu brown perfumed toilet soap

**windstorm** /'wind,stawm/ *n* a storm with high winds, but little or no rain, snow, etc

**wind sucking** /wind/ *n* a vice of horses related to CRIB BITING in which they gnaw (eg at the manger) and swallow quantities of air – **wind sucker** *n*

**wind-surfing** /wind/ *n* the sport of sailing with sailboards

**windswept** /'wind,swept/ *adj* **1** swept by wind ⟨*a* ~ *beach*⟩ **2** dishevelled (as if) from being blown by the wind ⟨*came back from the walk all* ~ *and glowing*⟩ **3** *of hair* cut so that the ends turn outwards and to the front as if blown by a wind from behind

**wind tee** /tee/ *n* a large WEATHER VANE shaped like a horizontal letter T on or near a landing field

**wind tunnel** /wind/ *n* a tunnel-like chamber through which air can be blown at known speeds in order to discover the effects of wind pressure on an object (eg an aircraft part or model or a guided missile) placed inside it

'**windup** /'wiendup/ *n* **1** a conclusion, finish **2** a preliminary swing of the arms (eg before throwing or bowling); *also* a golfer's backswing

²**windup** *adj* having a spring wound up by hand ⟨*is that a quartz watch? No, a* ~ *one*⟩

**wind vane** *n* WEATHER VANE

**windward** /'windwood/ *adj, adv, or n* (in or facing) the side or direction from which the wind is blowing – compare LEEWARD – **to windward of** having the advantage over

**windway** /'wind,way/ *n* a passage for air (eg in an organ pipe)

'**wind-,wing** *n, NAm* QUARTER LIGHT

**windy** /'windi/ *adj* **1a** windswept ⟨*a* ~ *beach*⟩ **b** marked by strong stormy wind **2** causing intestinal wind; flatulent ⟨*cucumbers are a bit* ~ *for me*⟩ **3** verbose, bombastic ⟨*a long, empty, and* ~ *speech*⟩ **4** *chiefly Br informal* frightened, nervous – **windily** *adv*, **windiness** *n*

'**wine** /wien/ *n* **1a** grape juice that has been allowed to ferment to produce a drink containing alcohol and varying amounts of sugar together with other substances that give it bouquet and flavour **b** wine or a substitute used in Christian communion services **2** the usu fermented juice of a plant or fruit used as a drink ⟨*rice* ~⟩ ⟨*cowslip* ~⟩ **3** something that invigorates or intoxicates **4** the colour of red wine [ME *win*, fr OE *wīn*; akin to OHG *wīn* wine; both fr a prehistoric Gmc word borrowed fr L *vinum* wine, of non-IE origin; akin to the source of Gk *oinos* wine]

²**wine** *vb* to entertain with or drink wine – usu in *wine and dine*

**wine bar** *n, Br* an establishment selling wine and often food for consumption on the premises

**winebibber** /'wien,bibə/ *n, formal or humorous* a drunkard, tosspot

**wine cellar** *n* a room for storing wines; *also* a stock of wines

**wine cooler** *n* a vessel or container in which wine is cooled: eg **a** an often lidded metal-lined wooden container on legs used, esp in the 18th and early 19th centuries, for cooling wine **b** a bucket containing ice for cooling wine

**wine gallon** *n* a unit of liquid capacity used in the USA and formerly in Britain, and equal to 8 US pints (about 3.785 litres)

**wineglass** /'wien,glahs/ *n* any of several variously shaped and sized drinking glasses for wine that often have a rounded, concave, or spherical bowl and are usu mounted on a stem and foot

**winegrower** /'wien,grohə/ *n* a person, firm, cooperative, etc that cultivates a vineyard and makes wine – **wine growing** *n*

**wine merchant** *n, Br* **1** a usu wholesale dealer in alcoholic drinks, esp wine **2 wine merchants** *pl*, **wine merchant** a shop selling alcoholic drinks including wine; *broadly* an off-licence

**winepress** /'wien,pres/ *n* a vat in which juice is pressed from grapes either by treading or by mechanical means

**winery** /'wienəri/ *n, chiefly NAm* a wine-making establishment

**wineskin** /'wien,skin/ *n* a bag that is made from the skin of an animal (eg a goat) and is used for holding wine

**wine taster** *n* a person who tests the quality of wine by tasting

**wine tasting** *n* a promotional occasion at which sellers of wine offer potential customers a chance to sample wines before buying them

**winey** /'wieni/ *adj* winy

'**wing** /wing/ *n* **1a(1)** any of the movable feathered or membranous paired limblike structures by means of which a bird, bat, or insect is able to fly; *also* such a structure even though much reduced or nonfunctional possessed by a non-flying bird (eg an ostrich) or insect **a(2)** a wing bone of a chicken, duck, etc together with the skin and meat covering it ⟨*will you have a* ~ *or a drumstick?*⟩ **b** any of various structures providing an animal with means of limited flight: eg **b(1)** a modified fin of a flying fish **b(2)** a broad fold of skin in a flying mammal (eg a flying lemur) **2** a structure or part resembling a wing in shape, appearance, or position: eg **2a** *pl* a device worn round the chest or under the arms to aid a person in swimming or staying afloat; WATER WINGS **b** ALA (winglike projection of an organ or body part) ⟨*the* ~s *of the nose*⟩ **c** *Br* the mudguard of a motor vehicle, esp when forming an integral part of the bodywork ⟨*only grazed the gatepost, but still had to have the whole* ~ *replaced*⟩ **d** a sidepiece at the top of a high-backed armchair **e(1)** a membranous, leaflike, or woody growth in a plant, esp along a stem or on a seedpod ⟨*the* ~ *of a sycamore fruit*⟩ **e(2)** either of two side petals in the flower of a pea, bean, or related plant **f** a sail or vane of a windmill **g** any of the AEROFOILS that develop a major part of the lift which supports a heavier-than-air aircraft **3** *pl* a means of flight or escape ⟨*fear lent me* ~s⟩ **4** the act of flying; flight **5** a part of a building usu projecting from the main or central part ⟨*the main* ~ *of the hospital*⟩ ⟨*the science* ~ *of the school*⟩ **6a** any of the pieces of scenery at the side of a stage **b** *pl* the area at the side of the stage out of sight of the audience **7** a left or right section of (the battle line of) an army or fleet; a flank **8a** the right or left section of a playing field or pitch close to the sidelines or touchlines **b** any of the attacking positions or players on either side of a centre position in certain team sports **9** *taking sing or pl vb* a group or faction holding distinct opinions or policies within an organized body (eg a political party) – compare LEFT WING, RIGHT WING **10** *pl* insignia consisting of an outspread pair of stylized bird's wings which are awarded to a qualified pilot or aircrew member in the British armed forces **11** an operational and administrative unit of an air force; *specif* a unit of the Royal Air Force higher than a squadron and lower than a group [ME *winge*, of Scand origin; akin to Dan & Sw *vinge* wing; akin to Skt *vāti* it blows – more at WIND] – **wing-like** *adj* – **clip the wings of** to restrict the freedom of – **in the wings** in the background; in readiness to act – **on the wing** in flight; flying ⟨*birds* on the wing⟩ – **spread one's wings** to venture out into the world; break away from one's background – **under one's wing** under one's protection; in one's care

²**wing** *vt* **1a** to fit with wings **b** to enable to fly or move swiftly **2a** to wound in the wing; disable the wing of ⟨~ed *the duck*⟩ **b** to wound (eg with a bullet) without killing ⟨~ed *by a sniper*⟩ **3a** to traverse (as if) with wings **b** to make (one's way or course) by flying **4** to let fly; dispatch ⟨*would start to* ~ *punches left and right*⟩ ~ *vi* to go (as if) with wings; fly ⟨*she* ~ed *into international stardom* – *Cosmopolitan*⟩

**wing bar** *n* a line of contrasting colour across the middle of a bird's wing produced by markings on the wing feathers

**wing case** *n* ELYTRON (protective wing cover in some insects)

**wing chair** *n* an upholstered armchair with a high solid back and sidepieces that provide a rest for the head and protection from draughts

**wing collar** *n* a man's stand-up collar having the upper corners turned down and now usu worn only for formal evening dress

**wing commander** *n* – see MILITARY RANKS table

**wingding** /'wing,ding/ *n, NAm informal* **1** a wild, lively, or lavish party **2** a pretended fit or illness [origin unknown]

**winge** /winj/ *vi* to whinge [by alter.]

**winged** /wingd; *sense 2* ¹wingid/ *adj* **1a(1)** having wings ⟨~ *seeds*⟩ **a(2)** having wings of a specified kind – in combination ⟨*strong-*winged⟩ **b** using wings in flight **2a** soaring (as if) with wings; elevated ⟨*then thus, with* ~ *Words, the God began* – John Dryden⟩ **b** swift, rapid ⟨*But at my back I always hear Time's* ~ *chariot hurrying near* – Andrew Marvell⟩ **3** wounded or disabled, esp in the wing [¹wing + *-ed*; (3) pp of ²wing]

**winger** /'wing·ə/ *n, chiefly Br* a player (eg in soccer) in a wing position

¹**wing-,footedd** *adj, poetic* swift ⟨*a* ~ *messenger*⟩

**wing forward** *n* either of the two players in RUGBY UNION positioned on the outside of the second row of the scrum; *also* the position itself

**wingless** /'winglas/ *adj* having no wings or very rudimentary wings – **winglessness** *n*

**winglet** /'winglət/ *n* **1** a very small or rudimentary wing **2** BASTARD WING (part of bird's wing corresponding to a thumb)

**wingman** /'wingmən/ *n* a pilot who flies behind and outside the leader of a flying formation

**wing nut** *n* a nut that has projecting wings or flanges so that it may be turned by finger and thumb – called also BUTTERFLY NUT

**wingover** /'wing,ohvə/ *n* a flight manoeuvre in which an aircraft is put into a climbing turn until nearly stalled, after which the nose is allowed to fall while the turn is continued until normal flight is attained in a direction opposite to that in which the manoeuvre was entered

**wing rib** *n* a large cut of beef from between the sirloin and the front ribs

**wingspan** /'wing,span/ *n* **1** the distance from the tip of one of a pair of wings of a bird, insect, etc to that of the other **2** SPAN 2d (distance between tips of aircraft wings)

**wingspread** /'wing,spred/ *n* wingspan; *specif* the maximum distance between the tips or outer edges of the wings (eg of a bird or insect)

**wing three-quarter** *n* either of the two players in rugby positioned on the outside of the three-quarter-back line; *also* the position itself

**wingy** /'wingi/ *adj* **1a** having wings **b** rapid **2** resembling a wing in shape or position ⟨~ *sleeves*⟩ **3** *formal* soaring (as if) with wings; lofty

¹**wink** /wingk/ *vi* **1** to shut one eye briefly as a signal or in teasing; *also, of an eye* to shut briefly **2** to blink **3** to avoid seeing or noting something; condone something – usu + *at* ⟨~ *at his absence*⟩ **4** to gleam or flash intermittently; twinkle **5** to stop shining usu + *out* **6** to signal a message with a light ~ *vt* **1** to cause (one's eye) to wink **2** to force or drive (as if) by blinking the eyes ⟨~ *back his tears*⟩ **3a** to signal with (a light) by winking; flash **b** to convey (a message) by winking *synonyms* see ¹BLINK [ME *winken*, fr OE *wincian*; akin to OHG *winchan* to stagger, wink, L *vacillare* to sway – more at PREVARICATE]

²**wink** *n* **1** a brief period of sleep; a nap ⟨*didn't get a* ~ *all night*⟩ **2** an act of winking **3** the time of a wink; an instant ⟨*quick as a* ~⟩ **4** *informal* a hint or sign given by winking ⟨*the bloke . . . tipped him the* ~ – Richard Llewellyn⟩

**winker** /'wingkə/ *n* **1** someone who winks **2** *pl* a horse's blinkers **3** *informal* an indicator light on a car, lorry, etc

**winkle** /'wingkl/ *n* a PERIWINKLE (edible sea snail), esp when cooked and eaten [short for *periwinkle*]

**winkle out** *vt, chiefly Br* to displace, extract, or evict from a position; *also* to discover or identify with difficulty ⟨winkling out *the facts about the country's stocks of coal* – The Observer⟩ [¹*winkle*; fr the process of extracting a winkle from its shell]

¹**winkle-,picker** *n, chiefly Br* a (man's) shoe with a very pointed toe

**winkler** /'wingklə/ *n, chiefly Br* who or that which winkles somebody or something out; *specif* a landlord who winkles statutory tenants out of rented property (eg by harassment or neglect of repairs)

**winner** /'winə/ *n* **1** a victor **2** *informal* something successful and admirable ⟨*this product is a real* ~⟩

¹**winning** /'wining/ *n* **1a** the act of one who or that which wins; victory **b** acquisition, gaining **2** *pl* money won by success in a game or competition

²**winning** *adj* **1a** of or used for winning ⟨*the* ~ *post*⟩ **b** successful in competition; that wins or has won ⟨*the* ~ *team*⟩ **2** pleasing or delightful ⟨*a* ~ *smile*⟩ – **winningly** *adv*

**winning hazard** *n* the pocketing of the OBJECT BALL after it has been struck by the CUE BALL in billiards

¹**winnow** /'winoh/ *vt* **1a(1)** to remove (eg chaff) by a current of air **a(2)** to get rid of (something undesirable or unwanted) – often + *out* ⟨~ *out certain inaccuracies* – Stanley Walker⟩ **b** to separate, sift ⟨~ *a mass of evidence*⟩ **2** to treat (eg grain) by exposure to a current of air so that light pieces of undesirable material are blown away **3** to blow on; fan ⟨*the wind* ~ing *his thin white hair* – Time⟩ ~ *vi* **1** to separate chaff from grain by exposure to a current of air **2** to separate desirable and undesirable elements [ME *winewen*, fr OE *windwian* to fan, winnow; akin to OHG *wintōn* to fan, L *vannus* winnowing fan, *ventus* wind – more at WIND] – **winnower** *n*

²**winnow** *n* **1** a device for winnowing **2** the action of winnowing

**wino** /'wienoh/ *n, pl* **winos** *chiefly NAm informal* an esp destitute person who is chronically addicted to drinking wine; *broadly* an alcoholic

**winsome** /'wins(ə)m/ *adj* having a pleasing childlike charm and innocence [ME *winsum*, fr OE *wynsum*, fr *wynn* joy; akin to OHG *wunna* joy, L *venus* love – more at WIN] – **winsomely** *adv*, **winsomeness** *n*

¹**winter** /'wintə/ *n* **1** the season between autumn and spring which in the N hemisphere is usu taken to comprise the months

of December, January, and February; *also* the period from the December SOLSTICE (shortest day of the year) to the March EQUINOX (time when day and night are of equal length) **2** the colder part of the year **3** *usu pl* a year ⟨*a woman of four score* ~s⟩ **4** a period of inactivity or decay or of failing or declining powers [ME, fr OE; akin to OHG *wintar* winter] – **winterless** *adj*, **winterlike** *adj*

²**winter** *adj, of a cereal crop* sown in the autumn and harvested in the following spring or summer ⟨~ *wheat*⟩ ⟨~ *rye*⟩ – compare SPRING

³**winter** *vi* **1** to pass or survive the winter **2** to feed or find food during the winter – + *on* ~ *vt* to keep, feed, or manage (e g livestock) during the winter

**winter aconite** *n* a small African and Eurasian plant (*Eranthis hyemalis*) of the buttercup family grown for its bright yellow flowers which often bloom through snow

**winterer** /'wintərə/ *n* (a bird that is) a winter resident or visitor

**wintergarden** /'wintə,gahd(ə)n/ *n* **1** a garden in which evergreen plants are cultivated **2 wintergarden, winter garden** a large conservatory where flowering plants are grown in winter, often built on to a house or hotel and often used for public concerts or recitals

**wintergreen** /'wintə,green/ *n* **1** any of several evergreen plants (*Pyrola* and related genera of the family Pyrolaceae) related to the heathers; *esp* one (*Pyrola minor*) with small round leaves and pinkish flowers **2a** any of a genus (*Gaultheria*) of the heather family; *esp* a low American evergreen plant (*Gaultheria procumbens*) with white flowers and red berries **b(1)** an ESSENTIAL OIL from this plant **b(2)** the flavour of this oil ⟨~ *lozenges*⟩

**winter·ize, -ise** /'wintəriez/ *vt, chiefly NAm* to make ready for winter or winter use; *esp* to make resistant to or proof against winter weather ⟨~ *a car*⟩ – **winterization** *n*

'**winter-,kill** *vb, NAm vt* to kill (e g a plant) by exposure to winter conditions ~ *vi* to die as a result of exposure to winter conditions – **winterkill** *n*

**winterly** /'wintəli/ *adj* of or occurring in winter; wintry

**winter melon** *n* a MUSKMELON (*Cucumis melo inodorus*) with smooth rind and sweet white or greenish flesh

**winter moth** *n* a moth (*Operophtera brumata*) whose larvae are LOOPERS that damage trees and shrubs

**winter quarters** *n taking sing or pl vb*, *pl* **winter quarters** a winter residence or station (e g of a military unit or a circus)

**winter solstice** *n* the SOLSTICE (time when the sun is furthest from the equator) that occurs in December in the N hemisphere or in June in the S hemisphere

**winter sport** *n* a usu open-air sport on snow or ice (e g skiing or tobogganing)

**wintertide** /'wintə,tied/ *n, poetic* wintertime

**wintertime** /'wintə,tiem/ *n* the season of winter

**wintle** /'wintl/ *vi, Scot* **1** to stagger, reel **2** to wriggle [perh fr Flem *windtelen* to reel]

**wintry, wintery** /'wint(ə)ri/ *adj* **1** characteristic of winter; cold, snowy **2a** weathered (as if) by winter; aged, hoary **b** chilling, cheerless ⟨*a bitter* ~ *smile*⟩ **3** *archaic* of winter – **wintrily** *adv*, **wintriness** *n*

**winy, winey** /'wieni/ *adj* **1** having the taste or qualities of wine; vinous **2** *of the air* crisply fresh; exhilarating

**winze** /winz/ *n, Scot* a curse [Flem or D *wensch* wish]

'**wipe** /wiep/ *vt* **1a** to clean or dry by rubbing, esp with or on something soft ⟨~ *the dishes*⟩ **b** to draw or pass for rubbing or cleaning ⟨~d *a cloth over the table*⟩ **c** to put into the specified state by rubbing ⟨~ *your hands dry*⟩ **2a** to remove (as if) by rubbing ⟨~ *the blood away*⟩ ⟨~ *that smile off your face*⟩ **b** to erase completely; cancel, obliterate ⟨~ *a recording*⟩ ⟨~ *the scene from his memory*⟩ **3a** to spread (as if) by wiping ⟨~ *grease on my skates*⟩ **b** to form (a joint between lead pipes) by applying solder in repeated stages, each individually spread and shaped with greased cloth pads ~ *vi* **1** to make a motion (as if) of wiping something **2** to wipe washing-up dry ⟨*you wash, I'll* ~⟩ – often + *up* – see also **wipe the FLOOR with** [ME *wipen*, fr OE *wīpian*; akin to OHG *wīfan* to wind around, L *vibrare* to vibrate]

**wipe out** *vt* **1** to clean the inside of (something hollow) by wiping **2** to destroy completely; annihilate, **3** to cancel, obliterate **4** to cause (a surfer) to experience a wipeout ~ *vi, of a surfer* to experience a wipeout – see also WIPEOUT

**wipe up** *vt* **1** to remove (e g dropped mess or spilt liquid) (as if) by wiping **2** *Br* to dry (washed plates, cutlery, etc) ⟨*wipe up the supper things*⟩

²**wipe** *n* **1** an act or instance of wiping **2** the power or capacity to wipe ⟨*the amount of* ~ *you need depends upon the wind, rain and mud* – *Annabel*⟩

'**wipe-,clean** *adj* that can be cleaned merely with a wipe

**wiped out** *adj, slang* intoxicated, high

**wipeout** /'wiep,owt/ *n* **1** the act or an instance of wiping out; complete or utter destruction **2** a fall from a surfboard caused usu by loss of control

**wiper** /'wiepə/ *n* **1** something (e g a towel or sponge) used for wiping **2** a mechanical device (CAM) for converting rotational movement into linear movement; *also* a similar device (TAPPET) transmitting motion from the CAMSHAFT in an INTERNAL-COMBUSTION ENGINE **3** a moving contact for making connections with the terminals of an electrical device (e g a RHEOSTAT) **4** windscreen wiper, wiper a mechanically operated rubber strip for cleaning windscreens

'**wire** /wie·ə/ *n* **1a** metal in the form of a usu very flexible thread or slender rod **b** a thread or rod of such material **2a** wirework **b** the mesh of parallel or woven wire on which the wet web of paper forms **3** something (e g a thin plant stem) that resembles wire in appearance **4a** a line of wire for conducting electrical current **b** a telephone or telegraph wire or system **c** a telegram, cablegram **5** fencing or a fence of usu barbed wire **6** a tightrope – chiefly in *high wire* **7** *chiefly NAm* strings [ME, fr OE *wīr;* akin to OHG *wiara* fine gold, L *viēre* to plait, Gk *iris* rainbow] – **wirelike** *adj* – **get one's wires crossed** to become involved in a misunderstanding – see also PULL wires

²**wire** *vt* **1** to provide or connect with wire or wiring **2** to send or send word to by telegraph ~ *vi* to send a telegraphic message – **wirable** *adj*, **wirer** *n*

**wire up** *vt* to connect (an electrically powered device) to a power supply

**wirecoated** *adj, of an animal, esp a dog* having a coat of rough and dense outer hair

**wired** /wie·əd/ *adj* **1** reinforced or bound with wire **2** provided with wires (e g for electrical connections) **3** fenced with wire **4** *chiefly NAm slang* addicted, hooked ⟨~ *on heroin*⟩

**wiredraw** /'wie·ə,draw/ *vt* **wiredrew; wiredrawn 1** to spin out to excessive subtlety or minuteness; attenuate ⟨~n *comparisons*⟩ **2** to draw (metal) into wire – **wiredrawer** *n*

**wire gauge** *n* **1** a gauge for measuring the diameter of wire or the thickness of sheet metal **2** a system of standard sizes used in describing the diameter of wire or the thickness of sheet metal

**wire gauze** *n* a thin fabric of fine wire mesh

**wire glass** *n* a glass with wire netting embedded in it

**wirehaired** /'wie·ə,head,-'-/ *adj, esp of a dog* wirecoated

**wirehaired terrier** *n* a wirehaired FOX TERRIER

'**wireless** /'wie·əlis/ *adj* **1** having no wire or wires **2** *chiefly Br* of or involving the transmission or reception of signals by means of RADIO WAVES

²**wireless** *n* **1** RADIOTELEGRAPHY (communication system using radio transmission) **2** WIRELESS TELEGRAPHY **3** *chiefly Br* (a) radio – used of the receiver and the system

³**wireless** *vt, chiefly Br* to radio

**wireless telegraphy** *n*, **1** *chiefly Br* the transmission and reception of signals, usu voice communications, using ELECTROMAGNETIC WAVES rather than cables or wires; RADIO 1 **2** *chiefly NAm* radiotelegraphy

**wireman** /'wie·əman/ *n* a maker of or worker with wire; *esp* one who wires electric or electronic circuitry

**wire netting** *n* a mesh of coarse woven or twisted wire used esp for fencing

**Wirephoto** /'wie·ə,fohtoh/ *trademark* – used for a photograph transmitted by electrical signals over telephone wires

'**wire-,puller** *n, chiefly NAm* a string-puller – **wire-pulling** *n*

**wire recorder** *n* a recording device that uses thin magnetic metal wire rather than MAGNETIC TAPE

**wire rope** *n* a rope formed either wholly of wires or of wire wound round a hemp core

**wire service** *n* a news agency that sends out syndicated news copy to subscribers telegraphically

**wiretap** /'wie·ə,tap/ *n* an electrical connection for wiretapping

**wiretapping** /'wie·ə,taping/ *n* the act or an instance of tapping a telephone or telegraph wire

**wireway** /'wie·ə,way/ *n* a conduit or channel for wires

**wire wool** *n* an abrasive material consisting of fine wire strands woven into a loose mass and used as a cleaning implement or scourer, esp for kitchen utensils (e g pans)

**wirework** /'wie·ə‚wuhk/ *n* something made of wire or wires; *esp* a mesh, netting, or grill of wire ⟨*plan the ~ for the new circuitry*⟩

**wireworm** /'wie·ə‚wuhm/ *n* any of the slender hard-coated larvae of various CLICK BEETLES that commonly cause damage to plant roots

**wiring** /'wie·əring/ *n* **1** the act of providing or using wire **2** a system of wires; *esp* an arrangement of wires that carries electrical current

**wirra** /'wirə/ *interj, Irish* – used to lament or express grief or concern [*oh wirra,* fr IrGael *a Muire,* lit., O Mary]

**wiry** /'wie·əri/ *adj* **1a** made of wire **b** resembling wire, esp in being thin and flexible ⟨*~ grass*⟩ **c** *of sound* produced (as if) by the vibration of wire **2** lean, supple, and vigorous; sinewy – **wirily** *adv,* **wiriness** *n*

**wis** /wis/ *vb, archaic* to know [by incorrect division of *iwis* (understood as *I wis,* with *wis* taken to be 1 sing. pres indic of ¹*wit*)]

**wisdom** /'wizd(ə)m/ *n* **1a** accumulated philosophic or scientific learning; knowledge **b** the thoughtful application of learning; insight **c** good sense; judgment ⟨*had the ~ to refuse*⟩ **2** a wise attitude or act; *also* a wise principle or precept **3** the teachings of the ancient wise men, esp about abstruse or esoteric matters; *broadly* enlightenment ⟨*Tantric doctrines that confer ~ upon the initiate*⟩ **synonyms** see KNOWLEDGE **antonyms** folly, injudiciousness [ME, fr OE *wīsdōm,* fr *wīs* wise]

**Wisdom, Wisdom of Solomon** *n* – see BIBLE table

**wisdom tooth** *n* any of the four third molar teeth in humans that appear last, and are situated at the back of each side of the upper and lower jaws [fr its appearing usu at an age when one may have acquired some wisdom]

¹**wise** /wiez/ *n, formal* a manner, way – usu in *in any/no wise* ⟨*not in any ~ pleased to learn that the car was a total write-off*⟩ [ME, fr OE *wīse;* akin to OHG *wīsa* manner, Gk *eidos* form, *idein* to see – more at WIT]

²**wise** *adj* **1a** characterized by or showing wisdom; marked by deep understanding, keen discernment, and a capacity for sound judgment **b** judicious, prudent ⟨*not ~ to eat oysters*⟩ **2** well-informed ⟨*I'm none the ~r*⟩ **3** possessing inside knowledge; shrewdly cognizant – often + *to* ⟨*was ~ to what was happening*⟩ **4** *archaic* skilled in magic or divination **antonyms** foolish, imprudent [ME *wis,* fr OE *wīs;* akin to OHG *wīs* wise, OE *witan* to know – more at WIT] – **wisely** *adv,* **wiseness** *n* – **put somebody wise** *informal* to inform or enlighten somebody

³**wise** *vb, chiefly NAm informal vt* to give instruction or enlightenment to; teach ~ *vi* to become informed or enlightened; learn □ usu + *up*

⁴**wise** *vt, chiefly Scot* **1a** to direct, guide **b** to advise, persuade **2** to divert or impel in a given direction; send [ME *wisen,* fr OE *wīsian;* akin to ON *vīsa* to show the way, OE *wīs* wise]

**-wise** /-‚wiez/ *comb form* (*n → adv*) **1a** in the manner of ⟨*entered the room crab*wise⟩ **b** in the position or direction of ⟨*a clock*wise *movement*⟩ ⟨*laid it out length*wise⟩ **2** with regard to; in respect of ⟨*career*wise *it's a good idea*⟩ [ME, fr OE -*wīsan,* fr *wīse* manner]

*usage* Some people dislike the recent overuse of -**wise** to mean "in respect of", and prefer to replace ⟨*career*wise⟩ and ⟨*tax*wise⟩ by ⟨*with regard to my career*⟩ and ⟨*from the point of view of taxation*⟩.

**wiseacre** /'wiezaykə/ *n* someone who pretends to be clever or knowledgeable; SMART ALEC [MD *wijssegger* soothsayer, modif of OHG *wīzzago;* akin to OE *wītega* soothsayer, *witan* to know]

¹**wisecrack** /'wiez‚krak/ *n, informal* a flippant and often uncouth remark or witticism

²**wisecrack** *vi, informal* to make a wisecrack – **wisecracker** *n*

**wise guy** *n, informal* a conceited and self-assertive person; *esp* one who claims to know all about something ⟨*OK ~ , you try and fix it*⟩

**wise man** *n* **1** a man of unusual learning, judgment, or insight; a sage **2** a man with skill in magical or occult arts; *specif* MAGUS 2

**wisenheimer** /'wiez(ə)n‚hiemə/ *n, NAm* WISE GUY [²*wise* + Ger -*enheimer* (as in Ger family names such as *Guggenheimer, Oppenheimer*)]

**wisent** /'vee‚zent/ *n* EUROPEAN BISON [Ger, fr OHG *wisunt* – more at BISON]

**wisewoman, wise woman** /'wiez‚woomən/ *n* a woman with skill in magical or occult arts; *also* a woman with knowledge of traditional folk medicine, the use of medicinal herbs, etc

¹**wish** /wish/ *vt* **1** to have (something, esp something unobtainable) as a desire ⟨*~ed herself dead*⟩ ⟨*~ed he could live his life over again*⟩ **2** to invoke on someone ⟨*I ~ them success*⟩; *esp* to bid ⟨*~ him good night*⟩ **3a** to give form to (a wish) **b** to feel or express a wish for; want ⟨*I ~ to be alone*⟩ **c** to request in the form of a wish; order ⟨*he ~es us to leave*⟩ **4** to confer (something unwanted) on someone; foist ⟨*found the children ~ed on them while the parents were at a conference*⟩ ~ *vi* **1** to have a desire – usu + *for* **2** to make a wish ⟨*~ on a star*⟩ [ME *wisshen,* fr OE *wȳscan;* akin to OHG *wunsken* to wish, L *venus* love, charm – more at WIN] – **wisher** *n*

*usage* Some people dislike the use of **wish** to mean "wish for" or "want" ⟨*does Madam* **wish** *some more gravy?*⟩ as a genteelism. **synonyms** see ¹DESIRE

²**wish** *n* **1a** an act or instance of wishing or desire; *broadly* a hope ⟨*his ~ to become a doctor*⟩ **b** an object of desire; a goal ⟨*you got your ~*⟩ **2a** an expressed will or desire ⟨*obeyed their ~es*⟩ **b** *pl* – used, esp + *good* or *best,* to express conventional regard or salutation ⟨*give him my best ~es for a speedy recovery*⟩ **3** a ritual act of wishing ⟨*stir the pudding and make a ~*⟩

**wisha** /'wishə/ *interj, chiefly Irish* – used as an intensive or to express surprise [IrGael *ō* oh + *muise* indeed]

**wishbone** /'wish‚bohn/ *n* **1** a forked bone in front of the breastbone in a bird consisting chiefly of the two CLAVICLES (collarbones or their equivalent) joined at their middle or lower end **2** something shaped like a wishbone [fr the superstition that when two people pull it apart the one getting the longer piece will have his wish granted]

**wishful** /'wishf(ə)l/ *adj* **1a** expressive of a wish ⟨*~ eyes*⟩ **b** having a wish; desirous ⟨*was ~ to meet you*⟩ **2** according with wishes rather than reality – **wishfully** *adv,* **wishfulness** *n*

**wish fulfilment** /fool'filmənt/ *n* the satisfaction of desires, esp symbolically through dreams and fantasies

**wishful thinking** *n* belief in what one wishes to be true without regard to the true state of affairs

**wishing** /'wishing/ *adj* **1** regarded as having the power to grant wishes ⟨*threw a coin in the ~ well*⟩ **2** *archaic* wishful [(1) fr gerund of ¹*wish;* (2) fr gerund of ²*wish*]

**wisht** /wisht/ *adj, dial Br* dismal, eerie [prob fr pp of ¹*wish* (in the dial. sense "to invoke evil upon, curse")]

**wish-wash** /'wish‚wosh/ *n, informal* **1** a weak drink **2** insipid talk or writing [redupl of ²*wash*]

**wishy-washy** /'wishi ‚woshi/ *adj, informal* **1** without strength or flavour; weak ⟨*a ~ cup of tea*⟩ **2** without character or determination; ineffectual [redupl of *washy*]

¹**wisp** /wisp/ *n* **1** a small handful of hay, straw, etc; *esp, chiefly Br* a twisted or plaited wad of hay or straw (e g for grooming horses **2a** a thin insubstantial strand, streak, or fragment ⟨*a ~ of smoke*⟩ ⟨*a ~ of hair*⟩ **b** something frail, slight, or fleeting ⟨*a ~ of a girl*⟩ ⟨*a ~ of a smile*⟩ **3** a flock of (game) birds (e g snipe) [ME] – **wispish** *adj,* **wisplike** *adj,* **wispy** *adj,* **wispily** *adv*

²**wisp** *vt* **1** to roll into a wisp **2a** to make wisps of ⟨*a cigarette ~ing smoke* – Raymond Chandler⟩ **b** to cover with wisps ⟨*mist ~ing the sky above the fens*⟩ **3** *chiefly Br* to groom with a wisp ~ *vi* to emerge or drift in wisps ⟨*her hair began to ~ into her eyes* – Mary Manning⟩

**wist** /wist/ *past of* WIT

**wisteria, wistaria** /wi'stiəri·ə, -'steə-/ *n* any of a genus (*Wisteria*) of chiefly Asian mostly woody climbing plants of the pea family having hanging clusters of showy blue, white, purple, or rose flowers [NL, genus name, fr Caspar *Wistar* †1818 US physician]

**wistful** /'wistf(ə)l/ *adj* **1** full of unfulfilled desire; yearning **2** musingly sad; pensive [alter. (influenced by *wishful*) of obs *wistly* intently, prob fr ¹*whist* + -*ly*] – **wistfully** *adv,* **wistfulness** *n*

¹**wit** /wit/ *vb, pres 1 & 3 sing* **wot** /wot/; **-tt-;** **wist** /wist/ *archaic* **1** to know **2** to come to know; learn – compare TO WIT [ME *witen* (1 & 3 sing. pres *wot,* past *wiste*), fr OE *witan* (1 & 3 sing. pres *wāt,* past *wisse, wiste*); akin to OHG *wizzan* to know, L *vidēre* to see, Gk *eidenai* to know, *idein* to see] – **to wit** that is to say; namely

²**wit** *n* **1** **wit, wits** *pl* reasoning power; intelligence ⟨*past the ~ of man to understand*⟩ ⟨*a girl with quick ~s and a great sense of fun*⟩ **2** **wit, wits** *pl* **2a** mental soundness; sanity ⟨*frightened her out of her ~s*⟩ **b** mental capability and resourcefulness; ingenuity **3a** the ability to relate seemingly disparate things so as to illuminate or amuse **b(1)** a talent for banter or raillery **b(2)** repartee, satire **4** an imaginatively perceptive and articu-

late individual; *esp* one skilled in banter or raillery **5** *archaic* SENSE 2a ⟨*alone and warming his five* ∼s, *the white owl in the belfry sits* – Alfred Tennyson⟩ **6** *archaic* a person of superior intellect; a thinker [ME, fr OE; akin to OHG *wizzi* knowledge, OE *witan* to know] – **at one's wits' end** at a loss for a means of solving a problem

synonyms **Wit, humour, repartee, sarcasm, irony**, and **satire** are all modes of expression more or less intended to amuse. **Wit** is chiefly verbal, and entails ingenuity and swift perception. It is typically somewhat cutting and pointed, with a certain hard brilliance. **Humour** is kinder and broader, and entails perceiving the absurd and expressing it in some medium. **Repartee** involves quick and clever answering, or the interchange of answers. **Sarcasm** is cruel and taunting, and often makes use of **irony** to cut and wound. **Irony** involves saying the opposite of the intended literal meaning, or the expression or mere awareness of some incongruity between how things are and how they ought to be. **Satire** applies mainly to sustained writing, of a kind that uses wit, irony, and sarcasm to expose vice and folly.

**witan** /'witan/ *n taking pl vb* members of the WITENAGEMOT (Anglo-Saxon assembly) [OE, pl of *wita* sage, adviser; akin to OHG *wizzo* sage, OE *witan* to know]

**¹witch** /wich/ *n* **1** someone who is credited with usu malignant supernatural powers; *esp* a woman practising witchcraft often with the aid of a devil or FAMILIAR SPIRIT – compare WARLOCK **2** an ugly old woman; a hag **3** a fascinating or tempting girl or woman – no longer in vogue [ME *wicche*, fr OE *wicca* (masc) wizard & *wicce* (fem) witch; akin to MHG *wicken* to bewitch, OE *wigle* divination, OHG *wīh* holy – more at VICTIM] – **witchlike** *adj*, **witchy** *adj*

**²witch** *vt* **1** to harm by means of witchcraft **2** *archaic* to fascinate, charm

**witchcraft** /'wich,krahft/ *n* **1** the use of sorcery or magic, esp to cause bad things to happen **2** an irresistible influence or fascination; enchantment

**witch doctor** *n* a professional sorcerer, esp in a tribal society, who often works to cure sickness – compare MEDICINE MAN, SHAMAN

**witch elm** *n* WYCH ELM

**witchery** /'wichəri/ *n* **1** witchcraft, sorcery **2** an irresistible fascination; charm

**witches' brew** *n* a potent or fearsome mixture ⟨*a* ∼ *of untamed sex and brutality* – Harrison Smith⟩

**witches'-'broom** *n* an abnormal growth of tufts of small branches on a tree or shrub caused esp by fungi or viruses

**witchetty, witchetty grub, witchety** /'wichəti/ *n* any of various large white grubs that are larvae, esp of moths (family Cossidae), and are eaten by Australian Aborigines [native name in Australia]

**witch hazel, wych hazel** *n* **1** any of an Asian and N American genus (*Hamamelis* of the family Hamamelidaceae, the witchhazel family) of shrubs with slender-petalled yellow flowers appearing in late autumn or early winter **2** a solution containing chemical ALCOHOLS, obtained from the bark of a witch hazel (*Hamamelis virginiana*), and used externally as a soothing and mildly astringent lotion [*witch, wych* (a tree with pliant branches), fr ME *wyche*, fr OE *wice, wic*]

**'witch-,hunt** *n* **1** a searching out for persecution of people accused of witchcraft **2** a campaign of investigation and deliberate harassment of those (eg political opponents) with views that are unpopular or held, often on the basis of unsubstantiated information, to threaten public safety – **witch-hunter** *n*, **witch-hunting** *n or adj*

**¹witching** /'wiching/ *n* the practice of witchcraft; sorcery

**²witching** *adj* of or suitable for witchcraft; magical ⟨*the very* ∼ *time of night* – Shak⟩

**witching hour** *n* the critical or significant time when something is to happen

**witch of Agnesi** /an'yayzi/ *n, maths* a plane curve that is symmetrical about the y-axis, approaches the x-axis as an ASYMPTOTE, and has the equation $x^2y = 4a^2 (2a - y)$ [Maria Gaetana *Agnesi* †1799 It mathematician; prob fr its resemblance to the outline of a witch's hat]

**¹wite** /wiet/ *n, chiefly Scot* blame, responsibility [ME, fr OE *wīte* punishment; akin to OHG *wīzi* punishment, OE *witan* to know]

**²wite** *vt, chiefly Scot* to blame

**witenagemot, witenagemote** /,witənəgə'moht/ *n taking sing or pl vb* an Anglo-Saxon council made up of a varying number of nobles, representatives of the church, and influential officials

and convened from time to time to advise the king on administrative and judicial matters – compare WITAN [OE *witena gemōt*, fr *witena* (gen pl of *wita* sage, adviser) + *gemōt* assembly, fr *ge-* (perfective prefix) + *mōt* assembly – more at MOOT]

**with** /widh/ *prep* **1a** in opposition to; against ⟨*had a fight* ∼ *his brother*⟩ **b** so as to be separated or detached from ⟨*broke* ∼ *his family*⟩ ⟨*I disagree* ∼ *you*⟩ **2a** in relation to ⟨*no longer has any influence* ∼ *him*⟩ ⟨*the Italian frontier* ∼ *Yugoslavia*⟩ **b** – used to indicate the object of attention, behaviour, or feeling ⟨*get tough* ∼ *him*⟩ ⟨*in love* ∼ *her*⟩ **c** in respect to; so far as concerns ⟨*the trouble* ∼ *this machine*⟩ – sometimes used redundantly ⟨*get it finished* ∼⟩ or interjectionally ⟨*Down* ∼ *Skool*⟩ **d** – used to indicate the object of an adverbial expression of imperative force ⟨*off* ∼ *his head*⟩ **3a** – used to indicate accompaniment or association ⟨*went there* ∼ *her*⟩ ⟨*live* ∼ *the gipsies*⟩ **b** – used to indicate one to whom a usu reciprocal communication is made ⟨*talking* ∼ *a friend*⟩ **c** in the judgment, experience, or practice of ⟨*stood well* ∼ *his classmates*⟩ ⟨*it's winter here* ∼ *us*⟩ **d** – used to express agreement or sympathy ⟨*must conclude,* ∼ *him, that the painting is a forgery*⟩ **e** able to follow the reasoning of ⟨*are you* ∼ *me?*⟩ **4a** on the side of; for ⟨*vote* ∼ *the government*⟩ ⟨*if he's for lower taxes, I'm* ∼ *him*⟩ **b** employed by ⟨*he's a salesman* ∼ *ICI*⟩ **5a** – used to indicate the object of a statement of comparison, equality, or harmony ⟨*level* ∼ *the street*⟩ ⟨*dress doesn't go* ∼ *her shoes*⟩ ⟨*a car identical* ∼ *mine*⟩ **b** as well as ⟨*can ride* ∼ *the best of them*⟩ **c** IN ADDITION TO – used to indicate combination ⟨*heat milk* ∼ *honey*⟩ ⟨*his money,* ∼ *his wife's, comes to a million*⟩ **d** inclusive of ⟨*costs five pounds* ∼ *tax*⟩ **e** by acquisition or addition of ⟨*a cake made* ∼ *eggs*⟩ ⟨*threatened* ∼ *tuberculosis*⟩ **6a** by means of; using ⟨*hit him* ∼ *a stone*⟩ ⟨*bought it* ∼ *your money*⟩ ⟨*he amused the crowd* ∼ *his antics*⟩ **b** through the effect of ⟨*pale* ∼ *anger*⟩ ⟨*wet* ∼ *rain*⟩ **7a** – used to indicate manner of action ⟨*ran* ∼ *effort*⟩ ⟨*acknowledge your contribution* ∼ *thanks*⟩ **b** – used to indicate an attendant or contributory circumstance ⟨*stood there* ∼ *his hat on*⟩ ⟨∼ *John away, there's more room*⟩ **c** in possession of; having, bearing ⟨*came* ∼ *good news*⟩ – compare WITH YOUNG **d** in the possession or care of ⟨*left the money* ∼ *his mother*⟩ ⟨*the decision rests* ∼ *you*⟩ **e** so as to have or receive ⟨*issued him* ∼ *a helmet*⟩ ⟨*got off* ∼ *a light sentence*⟩ **f** characterized by ⟨*a man* ∼ *a sharp nose*⟩ **8a** – used to indicate a close association in time ⟨∼ *the outbreak of war they went home*⟩ ⟨*mellows* ∼ *time*⟩ **b** in proportion to ⟨*the pressure varies* ∼ *the depth*⟩ **9a** notwithstanding; IN SPITE OF ⟨*love her* ∼ *all her faults*⟩ **b** EXCEPT FOR ⟨*very similar,* ∼ *one important difference*⟩ **10** in the direction of ⟨∼ *the wind*⟩ ⟨∼ *the grain*⟩ **11** *archaic* by the direct act of [ME, against, from, with, fr OE; akin to OE *wither* against, OHG *widar* against, back, Skt *vi* apart] – **with that** immediately after that; forthwith

usage Some writers on usage advise that a singular subject to which something else is linked by **with** or by **together** with should correctly take a singular verb ⟨*the Queen* with *her entourage has/have just arrived*⟩.

**¹withal** /wi'dhawl/ *adv* **1** together with this; besides **2** on the other hand; nevertheless **3** *archaic* therewith [ME, fr *with* + *all, al* all]

**²withal** *prep, archaic* with – used after its object, which is usu a pronoun ⟨*I'll tell you who Time ambles* ∼, *who Time trots* ∼, *who Time gallops* ∼, *and who he stands still* ∼ – Shak⟩

**withdraw** /widh'draw/ *vb* **withdrew** /-'drooh/; **withdrawn** /-'drawn/ *vt* **1a** to draw back, away, or aside; remove ⟨∼ *one's hand*⟩ ⟨∼ *her son from the school*⟩ **b** to remove from use or cultivation ⟨*the publishers* withdrew *the book after the case*⟩ **c** to remove (money) from a place of deposit ⟨∼ *one's savings*⟩ **2a** to take back; retract ⟨∼ *my offer*⟩ **b** to recall or remove (a motion) under parliamentary procedure ∼ *vi* **1a** to go back or away; retire from participation **b** to draw back from a battlefield; retreat **2** to become socially or emotionally detached ⟨*had* ∼n *into himself*⟩ **3a** to retract a statement **b** to recall a motion under parliamentary procedure [ME, fr *with* from + *drawen* to draw] – **withdrawable** *adj*

**withdrawal** /widh'drawəl/ *n* **1a** the act or an instance of withdrawing **b** an operation by which a military force disengages from the enemy **c(1)** social or emotional detachment **c(2)** a retreat from or refusal to take an interest in what is going on around one that is characteristic of some forms of mental illness (eg schizophrenia) **2 withdrawal method, withdrawal** the practice of removing the penis from the vagina before ejaculation as a method of birth control; COITUS IN-TERRUPTUS **3** removal from a place of deposit or investment ⟨*the ~ of the family plate from the bank*⟩ **4a** the stopping of the administration or use of a drug **b withdrawal, withdrawal symptoms** *pl* the unpleasant effects resulting from ceasing to use or be given an addictive drug; *broadly* the discomfort associated with breaking a habit

**withdrawing room** /widh'drawing/ *n, archaic* DRAWING ROOM

**withdrawn** /widh'drawn/ *adj* **1** secluded, isolated **2** socially detached and unresponsive; *also* shy, reserved – **withdrawnness** *n*

**withe** /with/ *n* a tough flexible branch or twig; a withy; *esp* one used for binding things together [ME, fr OE *withthe;* akin to OE *wĭthig* withy]

**wither** /'widhə/ *vi* **1** to become dry and sapless; *esp* to shrivel (as if) from loss of bodily moisture **2** to lose vitality, force, or freshness ~ *vt* **1** to cause to wither **2** to make speechless or incapable of action; stun ⟨~ed *him with a look* – Dorothy Sayers⟩ [ME *widren;* prob akin to ME *weder* weather]

**wither away** *vi* to disappear (as if) by withering

**withering** /'widhəring/ *adj* acting or serving to cut down or destroy; devastating ⟨~ *fire from the enemy*⟩ – **witheringly** *adv*

**witherite** /'widhə‚riet/ *n* a mineral consisting of the chemical compound barium carbonate, $BaCO_3$, occurring in the form of white or grey crystals or as columns or masses [Ger *witherit,* irreg fr William *Withering* †1799 E physician]

**withers** /'widhəz/ *n pl* **1** the ridge between the shoulder bones of a horse **2** a part corresponding to the withers in a 4-footed animal other than a horse [prob fr obs *wither-* against, fr ME, fr OE, fr *wither* against; fr the withers being the parts which resist the pull in drawing a load]

**withershins** /'widhə‚shinz/ *adv* WIDDERSHINS (anticlockwise)

**withhold** /widh'hohld/ *vb* **withheld** /-'held/ *vt* **1** to hold back *from* action; check **2** to refrain from granting, giving, or allowing ⟨~ *permission*⟩ ~ *vi* to forbear, refrain ⟨withheld *from giving free rein to his feelings*⟩ **synonyms** see [1]KEEP [ME *withholden,* fr *with* from + *holden* to hold – more at WITH] – **withholder** *n*

[1]**within** /wi'dhin/ *adv* **1** in or into the interior; inside ⟨*enquire ~*⟩ **2** in one's every thoughts, disposition, or character [ME *withinne,* fr OE *withinnan,* fr *with* + *innan* inwardly, within, fr *in*]

[2]**within** *prep* **1** inside – used to indicate enclosure or containment, esp in something large ⟨~ *the castle*⟩ ⟨*felt happier ~ himself*⟩ **2a** – used to indicate situation or circumstance in the limits or compass of: e g **2a(1)** before the end of ⟨*gone ~ a week*⟩ **a(2)** since the beginning of ⟨*been there ~ the last week*⟩ **b(1)** not beyond the quantity, degree, or limitations of ⟨~ *his income*⟩ **b(2)** in or into the scope or sphere of ⟨~ *his rights*⟩ ⟨~ *my powers*⟩ ⟨~ *the jurisdiction of the state*⟩ **b(3)** in or into the range of ⟨~ *reach*⟩ ⟨~ *sight*⟩ **b(4)** – used to indicate a specified difference or margin ⟨~ *a mile of the town*⟩ **3** to the inside of; into

[3]**within** *n* an inner place or area ⟨*revolt from ~*⟩

**withindoors** /wi‚dhin'dawz/ *adv, formal* indoors

**'with-‚it** *adj, informal* socially or culturally up-to-date; fashionable ⟨*no ~ chick wears garments in bed anymore – Isis*⟩ – no longer a completely with-it expression; compare COOL, HIP, GROOVY, LAID-BACK

[1]**without** /wi'dhowt/ *prep* **1** – used to indicate absence or lack of or freedom from ⟨*go ~ sleep*⟩ ⟨*left ~ him*⟩ ⟨*did it ~ difficulty*⟩ ⟨~ *everybody knowing*⟩ **2** *archaic* outside [ME *withoute,* fr OE *withūtan,* fr *with* + *ūtan* outside, fr *ūt* out]

[2]**without** *adv* **1** with something lacking or absent ⟨*has learned to do ~*⟩ **2** on or to the exterior; outside

[3]**without** *conj, chiefly dial* unless ⟨~ *you have a stunt, what is there? – Punch*⟩

[4]**without** *n* an outer place or area ⟨*seen from ~*⟩

**withoutdoors** /wi‚dhowt'dawz/ *adv, formal* out of doors

**withstand** /widh'stand/ *vt* **withstood** /-'stood/ **1a** to resist with determination; *esp* to stand up against successfully **b** to be proof against ⟨*repairs cracks invisibly; even ~s boiling water*⟩ **2** *archaic* to stop or obstruct the course of [ME *withstanden,* fr OE *withstandan,* fr *with* against + *standan* to stand – more at WITH]

**withy** /'widhi/ *n* **1** a willow tree; *esp* OSIER **2** a slender flexible branch or twig (e g of osier); withe [ME, fr OE *wĭthig;* akin to OHG *wĭda* willow, L *vitis* vine, *viēre* to plait – more at WIRE]

**witless** /'witlis/ *adj* **1** lacking wit or understanding; foolish, silly **2** mentally deranged; crazy ⟨*drive one ~ with anxiety* – William Styron⟩

**witling** /'witling/ *n* a would-be wit

[1]**witness** /'witnis/ *n* **1** certifying that a fact is true or an event has happened; testimony **2** a person who gives evidence; *specif* a person who testifies in a legal case or before a judicial tribunal **3** a person asked to be present at a transaction (e g a marriage) so as to be able to testify to its having taken place **4** someone who personally sees or hears an event take place **5a** something serving as evidence; a sign ⟨*the children's health bears ~ to the improvement in their diet*⟩ **b** public affirmation by word or example of usu religious faith or conviction ⟨*a life of Christian ~*⟩ **6** *cap* a member of the JEHOVAH'S WITNESSES [ME *witnesse,* fr OE *witnes* knowledge, testimony, witness, fr [2]*wit*]

[2]**witness** *vt* **1** to testify to; attest **2** to act as legal witness of (e g by signing one's name) ⟨~ed *the will*⟩ **3** to give proof of; betoken ⟨*his appearance ~es what he has suffered*⟩ – often in the subjunctive ⟨*has suffered badly, as ~ his appearance*⟩ **4** to observe personally or directly; see for oneself ⟨~ed *the historic event*⟩ **5** to be the scene or time of ⟨*structures . . . which this striking Dorset hilltop once ~ed – TLS*⟩ ~ *vi* **1** to bear witness; testify **2** to bear witness to one's religious convictions ⟨*opportunity to ~ for Christ* – Billy Graham⟩

**'witness-‚box** *n, chiefly Br* an enclosure in which a witness sits or stands while testifying in court

**witness stand** *n, NAm* a witness-box

**-witted** /-'witid/ *comb form (adj → adj)* having wit or understanding of the specified kind ⟨*dull-*witted⟩ ⟨*quick-*witted⟩ ⟨*half-*witted⟩

**witticism** /'witi‚siz(ə)m/ *n* a cleverly witty and often biting or ironic remark; *also* an uncouth attempt at wit [*witty* + *-cism* (as in *criticism*)]

**wittingly** /'witingli/ *adv* deliberately, intentionally ⟨*wouldn't ~ have shown that she knew his secret*⟩ [*witting* (prp of [1]*wit*) + *-ly*]

**wittol** /'witl/ *n, archaic* an acquiescent cuckold [ME *wetewold,* fr *weten, witen* to know + *-wold* (as in *cokewold* cuckold) – more at WIT]

**witty** /'witi/ *adj* **1** amusingly or ingeniously clever in conception or execution ⟨~ *theatrical costumes*⟩ ⟨*a ~ musical theme*⟩ **2** marked by or full of wit; smartly jocular ⟨*a ~ speaker*⟩ ⟨*a ~ remark*⟩ **3** quick or ready to see or express illuminating or amusing relationships or insights **4** *archaic* having good intellectual capacity; intelligent – **wittily** *adv*, **wittiness** *n*

**wive** /wiev/ *vi* to marry a woman ~ *vt* **1** to provide a wife for **2** to take for a wife [ME *wiven,* fr OE *wĭfian,* fr *wĭf* woman, wife]

**wivern** /'wievən/ *n* WYVERN (mythical creature)

**wives** /wievz/ *pl of* WIFE

**wiz** /wiz/ *n, informal* WIZARD **2** – no longer in vogue

[1]**wizard** /'wizəd/ *n* **1** someone, esp a man, skilled in magic; a magician, sorcerer **2** someone who is very clever or skilful, esp in a specified field **3** *archaic* a wise man; a sage [ME *wysard,* fr *wis, wys* wise]

[2]**wizard** *adj* **1** *chiefly Br informal* worthy of the highest praise; excellent, super **2** *archaic* of wizards or wizardry; enchanted

**wizardly** /'wizədli/ *adj* **1** having characteristics of a wizard **2** marvellous in construction or operation ⟨*uses ~ circuitry to distort images – Time*⟩

**wizardry** /'wizədri/ *n* **1** the art or practices of a wizard; sorcery **2** a seemingly magical power or influence

**wizen** /'wiz(ə)n/ *vi* to become dry, shrunken, and wrinkled, often as a result of aging ~ *vt* to cause to wizen [ME *wisenen,* fr OE *wisnian;* akin to OHG *wesanēn* to wither, L *viēre* to twist together, plait – more at WIRE] – **wizen** *adj*

**wizzo** /'wizoh/ *adj, chiefly Br informal* WIZARD 1 ⟨*all this ~ gadgetry – Melody Maker*⟩ [*wiz* + [1]*-o*]

**wo** /woh/ *interj* whoa

**woad** /wohd/ *n* a European plant (*Isatis tinctoria*) of the cabbage family formerly grown for the blue dyestuff yielded by its leaves; *also* this dyestuff [ME *wod,* fr OE *wād;* akin to OHG *weit* woad, L *vitrum* woad, glass]

**wobbegong** /'wobi‚gong/ *n, Austr* CARPET SHARK [native name in Australia]

[1]**wobble** /'wobl/ *vi* **1a** to proceed with an irregular swerving or staggering motion ⟨~d *down the road on his bicycle*⟩ **b** to rock unsteadily from side to side **c** tremble, quaver **2** to waver,

vacillate ~ *vt* to cause to wobble *synonyms* see ¹SHAKE [prob fr LG *wabbeln;* akin to OE *wǣfre* restless – more at WAVER] – **wobbler** *n,* **wobbliness** *n,* **wobbly** *adj*

²**wobble** *n* **1a** a wobbling or rocking unequal motion (eg of a wheel unevenly hung) **b** an act or instance of vacillating or fluctuating **2** an intermittent variation (eg in volume of sound)

**Wodehousian, Wodehousean** /'wood,howsi·ən, -zi-, ,-'---/ *adj* suggestive of the writings of P G Wodehouse, esp as characterized by upper-class inanity [P G *Wodehouse* †1979 E comic novelist]

**wodge** /woj/ *n, Br informal* a bulky mass or chunk; a lump ⟨*a great ~ of a girl – Daily Mirror*⟩ [prob alter. of *wedge*]

¹**woe** /woh/, **woe is me** *interj* – used to express grief, regret, or distress [ME *wa, wo,* fr OE *wā;* akin to ON *vei,* interj, woe, L *vae*]

²**woe** *n* **1** deep suffering from misfortune, affliction, or grief **2** *usu pl* a calamity, affliction ⟨*economic ~s*⟩ *synonyms* see GRIEF [ME *wo,* fr *wo,* interj]

**woebegone** /'wohbi,gon/ *adj* **1** showing great woe, sorrow, or misery ⟨*a ~ expression*⟩ **2** in a sorry state ⟨*one ~ hollyhock growing out of the nettles*⟩ [ME *wo begon,* fr *wo,* n + *begon,* pp of *begon* to go about, beset, fr OE *begān,* fr *be-* + *gān* to go – more at GO]

**woeful** *also* **woful** /'wohf(ə)l/ *adj* **1** feeling or expressing woe ⟨*~ prophecies*⟩ **2** inspiring woe; grievous ⟨*it was ~ to see him spoiling it* – Henry James⟩ **3** lamentably great ⟨*~ ignorance*⟩ – **woefully** *adv,* **woefulness** *n*

**wog** /wog/ *n, chiefly Br derog* a nonwhite person; *broadly* any dark-skinned foreigner ⟨*~s begin at Dover*⟩ – compare WOP [prob short for *golliwog*]

**woggle** /'wogl/ *n, chiefly Br* a usu leather band used to secure a scout's neckerchief at the throat [prob alter. of *toggle*]

**wok** /wok/ *n* a round-bottomed frying pan used esp in the stir-fry cooking of Chinese food [Chin (Cant) *wôk*]

**woke** /wohk/ *past of* WAKE

**woken** /'wohkən/ *past part of* WAKE

**wold** /wohld/ *n* an upland area of open country [ME *wald, wold,* fr OE *weald, wald* forest; akin to OHG *wald* forest]

**Wolds** *n pl* a hilly or rolling region – used in names of various English geographical areas ⟨*the Yorkshire ~*⟩

¹**wolf** /woolf/ *n, pl* **wolves** /woolvz/, (1) **wolves,** *esp collectively* **wolf 1a** any of various large predatory mammals (genus *Canis,* esp *Canis lupus*) of N America and formerly N Europe and Asia that resemble the related dogs, typically hunt in packs, and may rarely attack man – compare COYOTE, JACKAL **b** the fur of a wolf **2** a fiercely rapacious person **3a** dissonance in some chords produced on instruments (eg organs and pianos) with fixed notes tuned by unequal TEMPERAMENT; *also* an instance of such dissonance **b** a harshness due to faulty vibration in various notes in a bowed instrument **4** *informal* a man who is too insistent in amatory attentions to women [ME, fr OE *wulf;* akin to OHG *wolf,* L *lupus,* Gk *lykos;* (3) Ger, fr the howling sound] – **wolflike** *adj* – **cry wolf** to give false alarms so often that a genuine warning is not heeded [fr the fable of a shepherd boy who hoaxed people by crying "Wolf!", and whose cries were therefore not believed when a wolf really came] – **keep the wolf from the door** to avoid destitution ⟨*kept the wolf from the door after her husband's death by giving piano lessons*⟩ – **wolf in sheep's clothing** somebody who hides hostile intentions behind a friendly or harmless manner

²**wolf** *vt* to eat greedily; devour – often + *down*

**wolf child** *n* a child that has grown up in the wild without contact with other human beings

**wolf cub** *n, Br* CUB SCOUT – no longer used technically

**wolf dog** *n* **1** a wolfhound **2** the offspring of a wolf and a domestic dog

**wolffian body** /'woolfi·ən, 'vol-/ *n, often cap W* MESONEPHROS (middle part of the embryonic kidney) [Kaspar Friedrich *Wolff* †1794 Ger anatomist]

**Wolffian duct** /'woolfi·ən, 'vol-/ *n* the duct of the MESONEPHROS (middle part of the embryonic kidney) persisting in the female as the URETER (duct taking urine from kidney to bladder) and in the male as the duct that carries both urine and semen

**wolffish** /'woolf,fish/ *n* any of several large sea BLENNIES notable for their strong teeth and ferocity; *esp* a N Atlantic blenny (*Anarhichas lupus*) widely used for food – called also CATFISH

**wolfhound** /'woolf,hownd/ *n* any of several (breeds of) large dogs used, esp formerly, for hunting wolves or other large animals

**wolfish** /'woolfish/ *adj* **1** of wolves **2a** suggestive of a wolf (eg in savage appearance) **b** befitting or characteristic of a wolf (eg in fierceness or rapacity) ⟨*a ~ appetite*⟩ – **wolfishly** *adv,* **wolfishness** *n*

**wolf pack** *n taking sing or pl vb* a number of submarines operating as a group (eg in attacking shipping)

**wolfram** /'woolfrəm/ *n* **1** tungsten **2** wolframite [Ger]

**wolframite** /'woolfrə,miet/ *n* a mineral, (Fe,Mn)WO₄, that is a TUNGSTATE of iron and manganese, is usu of a brownish or greyish-black colour with a slightly metallic lustre, occurs as crystals or in masses, and is used as a source of tungsten [Ger *wolframit,* fr *wolfram*]

**wolfsbane** /'woolfs,bayn/ *n* ACONITUM 1 (plant of the buttercup family); *esp* a poisonous plant (*Aconitum vulparia*) that is similar to MONKSHOOD, but bears yellow flowers

**wolf spider** *n* any of various spiders (family Lycosidae) that live on the ground and chase their prey

**wolf whistle** *n* a distinctive whistle sounded by a man to express sexual admiration for a woman – **wolf-whistle** *vi*

**wollastonite** /'wooləstə'niet/ *n* a mineral of a white to grey, red, yellow, or brown colour that consists of calcium silicate, CaSiO₃, and occurs usu in masses that can be split into thin layers or flakes [William *Wollaston* †1828 E chemist]

**Wolof** /'wohlof/ *n* a language of the NIGER-CONGO family, spoken in parts of Senegal and the Gambia

**wolverine** /'woolvəreen/ *n, pl* **wolverines,** *esp collectively* **wolverine** a flesh-eating usu solitary mammal (*Gulo gulo*) of northern forests, that is related to the weasel, has a blackish coat with a light brown band on each side of the body, and is noted esp for its strength and ferocity; *also* its fur [prob irreg fr *wolv-* (as in *wolves*)]

**woman** /'woomən/ *n, pl* **women** /'wimin/ **1a** an adult female human as distinguished from a man or child **b** a woman belonging to a particular category (eg by birth, residence, membership, or occupation) – usu in combination ⟨*councilwoman*⟩ ⟨*chairwoman*⟩ **2** womankind **3** distinctively feminine nature; womanliness ⟨*there's something of the ~ in him*⟩ **4** a charwoman ⟨*the daily ~*⟩ **5** one's personal maid, esp in former times **6a** a female sexual partner; *esp* a mistress ⟨*his new fancy ~*⟩ **b** *chiefly derog* GIRLFRIEND 2 – see also **be one's** OWN **woman** *synonyms* see LADY *antonym* man [ME, fr OE *wīfman,* fr *wīf* woman, wife + *man* human being] – **womanless** *adj*

**womanhood** /'woomən,hood/ *n* **1a** the condition of being an adult female as distinguished from a child or male **b** the distinguishing character or qualities of a woman or of womankind **2** women, womankind

**womanish** /'woomənish/ *adj* **1** characteristic of or suitable to a woman; feminine **2** unsuitable to a man or to a strong character of either sex; effeminate ⟨*~ fears*⟩ *synonyms* see ²FEMALE *antonym* mannish – **womanishly** *adv,* **womanishness** *n*

**woman·ize, -ise** /'wooməniez/ *vt* to make effeminate ~ *vi* to philander with many women – **womanizer** *n*

**womankind** /'woomən,kiend/ *n taking sing or pl vb* female human beings; women as a whole, esp as distinguished from men

¹**womanlike** /'woomən,liek/ *adj* womanly *synonyms* see ²FEMALE *antonym* manlike

²**womanlike** *adv* in the manner of a woman

**womanly** /'woomənli/ *adj* having or showing the good qualities befitting a grown woman – compare MATRONLY *synonyms* see ²FEMALE *antonym* manly – **womanliness** *n*

**woman of the street** *n, euph* a prostitute

**woman of the world** *n* a practical or worldly-wise woman of wide experience

**womb** /woohm/ *n* **1** the uterus **2a** a hollow enveloping cavity or space **b** a place where something is generated ⟨*ideas growing in the ~ of time*⟩ [ME *wamb, womb,* fr OE; akin to OHG *wamba* belly] – **wombed** *adj*

**wombat** /'wombat/ *n* any of several stocky Australian marsupial mammals (family Vombatidae) resembling small bears [native name in New South Wales, Australia]

**womenfolk** /'wimin,fohk/ *also* **womenfolks** *n pl* **1** women in general **2** the women of a family or community

**womenkind** /'wimin,kiend/ *n* womankind

**Women's Institute** *n taking sing or pl vb* a British organization of women, esp in country areas, who meet regularly and engage in various social and cultural activities

**women's lib** /lib/ *n, often cap W&L* feminism; *specif* WOMEN'S LIBERATION

**Women's Liberation** *n* a modern feminist movement that not only works for the elimination of sexual discrimination in the civil and political sphere, but also aims at the development of a view of the status of women and their contribution to art and society; *broadly* WOMEN'S MOVEMENT

**women's movement** *n, often cap W&M the* broad movement working for the improvement of the social and political position of women

**women's rights** *n pl* legal, political, and social rights for women (e g equal pay and maternity leave)

**women's room** *n, chiefly NAm euph* a ladies

**women's studies** *n* studies (e g history, literature, and psychology) relating to the changing role of women in society

¹**won** /wun, wohn/ *vi* -**nn**- *archaic* DWELL 2a, ABIDE 2 [ME *wonen,* fr OE *wunian* – more at WONT]

²**won** /won/ *past of* WIN

³**won** *n, pl* **won** – see MONEY table [Korean *wǎn*]

¹**wonder** /'wundə/ *n* **1a** a cause of astonishment or admiration; a marvel ⟨*it's a ~ he wasn't killed*⟩ **b** a supernatural or extraordinary event; a miracle **2a** rapt attention or astonishment at something awesomely mysterious or new to one's experience ⟨*gazed in ~ at the snow*⟩ **b** a state of wondering; a feeling of uncertainty ⟨*their ~ about what to do next*⟩ [ME, fr OE *wundor;* akin to OHG *wuntar* wonder]

²**wonder** *adj* noted for outstanding success or achievement ⟨*~ drugs*⟩ ⟨*Champion the* Wonder *Horse*⟩

³**wonder** *vi* **1a** to be in a state of wonder; marvel ⟨*~ed at her beauty*⟩ **b** to feel surprise ⟨*I shouldn't ~ if he's late*⟩ ⟨*I ~ you don't leave*⟩ **2** to feel curiosity or doubt; speculate ⟨*~ about his motives*⟩ ~ *vt* **1** to be curious or in doubt about – + a clause ⟨*~ who she is*⟩ **2** – used to express polite tentativeness in making a request ⟨*I ~ if you can help me*⟩ – **wonderer** *n*

**wonderful** /-f(ə)l/ *adj* **1** exciting wonder; marvellous, astonishing ⟨*a sight ~ to behold*⟩ **2** unusually good; admirable – **wonderfully** *adv,* **wonderfulness** *n*

**wonderland** /'wundə,land/ *n* **1** a fairylike imaginary realm **2** a place that excites admiration or wonder

**wonderment** /'wundəmənt/ *n* **1** astonishment, marvelling **2** a cause of or occasion for wonder **3** curiosity about something

**wonderstruck** /'wundə,struk/ *adj* overcome with wonder; astonished

'**wonder-,worker** *n* a performer of wonders – **wonder-working** *adj*

**wondrous** /'wundrəs/ *adj, poetic* wonderful [alter. of ME *wonders,* fr gen of ¹*wonder*] – **wondrous** *adv, archaic,* **wondrously** *adv,* **wondrousness** *n*

**wonky** /'wongki/ *adj, Br informal* **1** unsteady, groggy ⟨*his notoriously ~ knee – Punch*⟩ **2** awry, crooked [alter. of E dial. *wankle,* fr ME *wankel,* fr OE *wancol*]

¹**wont** /wohnt/ *adj, formal* **1** accustomed, used ⟨*places where people are ~ to meet*⟩ **2** inclined, apt ⟨*her letters are ~ to be tedious*⟩ □ + *to* and infin △ won't [ME *woned, wont,* fr pp of *wonen* to dwell, be used to, fr OE *wunian;* akin to OHG *wonēn* to dwell, be used to, L *venus* love, charm – more at WIN]

²**wont** *n, formal* customary practice ⟨*it was his ~ to drink a glass or warm milk each evening before retiring*⟩ **synonyms** see ¹HABIT

³**wont** *vi* wont; **wont, wonted** *archaic* to be accustomed – + *to* and infin

**won't** /wohnt/ will not

**wonted** /'wohntid/ *adj, formal* customary, habitual ⟨*spoke with his ~ slowness*⟩ **synonyms** see USUAL – **wontedly** *adv,* **wontedness** *n*

**wonton, wuntun** /,wun'tun, ,won'ton/ *n* a Chinese food consisting of savoury filled cases of thin dough that are boiled, steamed, or fried and eaten esp in soup [Chin (Cant) *wan tan* (*wan t'an*)]

**woo** /wooh/ *vb* **woos; wooing; wooed** *vt* **1** to try to win the affection of and a commitment to marriage from (a woman); court **2** to solicit or entreat, esp with importunity ⟨*people who were ~ed into buying storage heaters – Evening Gazette (Middlesborough)*⟩ **3** to seek to gain ⟨*~ fame*⟩ ~ *vi* to court a woman [ME *wowen,* fr OE *wōgian*] – **wooer** *n*

¹**wood** /wood/ *adj, archaic* violently mad; berserk [ME, fr OE *wōd* insane; akin to OHG *wuot* madness – more at VATIC]

²**wood** *n* **1a** wood, **woods** *pl* a dense growth of trees, usu greater in extent than a copse and smaller than a forest **b** woodland **2a** a hard fibrous substance that is basically XYLEM (water-conducting tissue) and that makes up the greater part

of the stems and branches of trees or shrubs beneath the bark and is found to a limited extent in other plants **b** wood suitable or prepared for some use (e g burning or building) **3** something made of wood: e g **3a** a golf club with a wooden head **b** ²BOWL 1a **c** a wooden cask ⟨*wine from the ~*⟩ [ME *wode,* fr OE *widu, wudu;* akin to OHG *witu* wood, OIr *fid* tree] – **woodless** *adj* – **not see the wood for the trees** to fail to have overall understanding of a subject, situation, etc as a result of being confused by detail – **out of the wood** *Br* escaped from peril or difficulty – **touch wood 1** with a certain amount of luck ⟨*everything will be all right now,* touch wood⟩ **2** *Br* to touch a wooden surface as a gesture to bring luck – see also NECK **of the woods**

³**wood** *adj* **1** made of or derived from wood; wooden **2** suitable for cutting, storing, or carrying wood ⟨*a ~ saw*⟩ **3** living, growing, or existing in woods

⁴**wood** *vt* to cover or surround with a growth of trees or plant with trees

**wood alcohol** *n* METHANOL

**wood anemone** *n* any of several anemones; *esp* a common Eurasian anemone (*Anemone nemorosa*) that grows esp in woodland and has white or pinkish flowers

**woodbin** /'wood,bin/ *n* a bin for firewood

**woodbine** /'wood,bien/ *n* **1** honeysuckle **2** *NAm* VIRGINIA CREEPER [ME *wodebinde,* fr OE *wudubinde,* fr *wudu* wood + *bindan* to tie, bind; fr its winding round trees]

**woodblock** /'wood,blok/ *n* **1** a woodcut **2** a block for a parquet floor – **wood-block** *adj*

'**wood-,boring** *adj, of an insect* chewing out burrows or galleries in wood in feeding or in constructing a nest

**woodbox** /'wood,boks/ *n* a box for firewood

**woodchat** /'wood,chat/, **woodchat shrike** *n* a European and N African SHRIKE (medium-sized songbird) (*Lanius senator*) of which the male has black-and-white upperparts and a conspicuous chestnut-coloured head [*wood* + ²*chat*]

**woodchopper** /'wood,chopə/ *n* a woodcutter

**woodchuck** /'wood,chuk/ *n* a N American thickset MARMOT (burrowing rodent) (*Marmota monax*) with flecked reddish to brown fur; *also* any of several other marmots of the mountains of western N America [by folk etymology fr Ojibwa *otchig* fisher, marten, or Cree *otcheck*]

**wood coal** *n* LIGNITE (woody-textured coal)

**woodcock** /'wood,kok/ *n, pl* **woodcocks,** (*1*) **woodcocks,** *esp collectively* **woodcock 1** a widespread African and Eurasian wading bird (*Scolopax rusticola*) of wooded regions that is related to the sandpipers, has a long narrow beak, and is often shot for food **2** *archaic* a simpleton [ME *wodecok,* fr OE *wuducocc,* fr *wudu* wood + *cocc* cock; (2) fr the bird's being easily caught in a snare or net]

**woodcraft** /'wood,krahft/ *n* **1** skill and practice in anything relating to woods or forests, esp in surviving, travelling, and hunting in them **2** skill in shaping or making things from wood

**woodcut** /'wood,kut/ *n* **1** a relief-printing surface consisting of a wooden block with a usu pictorial design cut esp with the grain – compare WOOD ENGRAVING **2** a print from a woodcut

**woodcutter** /'wood,kutə/ *n* someone who cuts wood and esp chops down trees – compare LUMBERJACK

**woodcutting** /'wood,kuting/ *n* the action or occupation of cutting wood or timber

**wooded** /'woodid/ *adj* covered with growing trees

**wooden** /'wood(ə)n/ *adj* **1** made or consisting of wood **2** lacking ease or flexibility; awkwardly stiff **3** of or marking a fifth anniversary ⟨*~ wedding*⟩ – **woodenly** *adv,* **woodenness** *n*

**wood engraving** *n* **1** a relief-printing surface consisting of a wooden block with a usu pictorial design cut esp against the grain – compare WOODCUT **2** a print from a wood engraving

**woodenhead** /'wood(ə)n,hed/ *n, informal* a blockhead

**woodenheaded** /,wood(ə)n'hedid/ *adj* dense, stupid

**wooden horse** *n* TROJAN HORSE (someone or something subversive)

**wooden spoon** *n* BOOBY PRIZE [fr the wooden spoon formerly presented to the lowest graduand in the mathematical tripos at Cambridge]

**wood fibre** *n* any of various fibres located in or associated with plant XYLEM (water-conducting tissue)

'**wood-,free** *adj, of paper* of superior quality because containing no pulp that has been ground by machine – compare MECHANICAL 1c

**wood grouse** *n, Br* CAPERCAILLIE (game bird)

**wood hyacinth** *n* a bluebell; WILD HYACINTH

**wood ibis** *n* a large WADING BIRD (*Mycteria americana* of the family Ciconiidae) that lives in wooded swamps of S and Central America and the southern USA

¹**woodland** /'woodlənd/ *n*, **woodlands** *n pl* land covered with woody vegetation; forest – **woodlander** *n*

²**woodland** *adj* 1 of or being woodland ⟨*a* ~ *area*⟩ 2 growing, living, or existing in woodland

**woodlark** /'wood,lahk/ *n* a small European lark (*Lullula arborea*) with a melodious song usu sung in a song flight

**woodlore** /'wood,law/ *n* knowledge of the woods; *also* WOODCRAFT 1

'**wood-,louse** *n, pl* **wood-lice** 1 a ground-living INVERTEBRATE animal (suborder Oniscoidea of the order Isopoda, class Crustacea) with a flattened elongated body often capable of being rolled into a ball in defence 2 any of several small wingless insects (order Psocoptera or Corrodentia) that live under bark, in the crevices of walls, and among old books and papers

**woodman** /'woodmən/ *n* someone who frequents or works in the woods; *specif* a forester or woodcutter

**woodnote** /'wood,noht/ *n* verbal expression that is natural and artless [fr its likeness to the call of a bird in the woods]

**wood nymph** *n* DRYAD (spirit in Greek myth)

**woodpecker** /'wood,pekə/ *n* any of numerous birds (family Picidae) with stiff spiny tail feathers used in climbing or resting on tree trunks, a usu long extendable tongue, a very hard beak used to drill the bark or wood of trees for insect food or to burrow nesting cavities, and generally showy multi-coloured plumage

**woodpigeon** /'wood,pijin/ *n* a large European wild pigeon (*Columba palumbus*)

**woodpile** /'wood,piel/ *n* a pile of wood (e g firewood) – **in the woodpile** doing or responsible for secret mischief ⟨*the No 1 villain* in the woodpile – Howard Whitman⟩ – see also NIGGER **in the woodpile**

**wood pulp** *n* pulp from wood used in the manufacture of cellulose derivatives (e g paper or rayon)

**wood ray** *n* XYLEM RAY

**woodruff** /'wood,ruf/ *n* any of several plants (genera *Asperula* and *Galium*) of the madder family; *esp* a small European sweet-scented plant (*Galium odoratum*) used in perfumery and for flavouring wine [ME *woderove*, fr OE *wudurofe*, fr *wudu* wood + *-rofe* (perh akin to OHG *rāba* turnip) – more at RAPE]

**woods** /woodz/ *adj* living, growing, or existing in woods; WOOD 3

**wood screw** *n* a screw used to secure woodwork; SCREW 2a

**woodshed** /'wood,shed/ *n* a shed for storing wood, esp firewood

**wood shot** *n* 1 a golf shot made with a wooden club (WOOD); *also* a shot that would be best made with a wood 2 a stroke in a racket game in which the ball or shuttle is hit with the wooden part of the racket rather than the strings

**woodsman** /'woodzmən/ *n, chiefly* NAm a woodman

**wood sorrel** *n* any of a genus (*Oxalis* of the family Oxalidaceae, the wood-sorrel family) of plants with acid sap and PALMATE (having lobes radiating from a common point) leaves; *esp* a stemless plant (*Oxalis acetosella*) of shady places with leaves made up of three leaflets that is sometimes held to be the original shamrock

**wood spirit** *n* METHANOL

**wood sugar** *n* 1 XYLOSE 2 a mixture of PENTOSE and HEXOSE sugars (sugars with five and six carbon atoms respectively) obtained by the breakdown of cellulose and related compounds in wood

**woodsy** /'woodzi/ *adj, NAm* characteristic or suggestive of woods

**wood tar** *n* tar obtained by the DESTRUCTIVE DISTILLATION of wood

**woodturning** /'wood,tuhning/ *n* the art of producing wooden articles (e g bowls or chair legs) on a lathe – **woodturner** *n*

**wood turpentine** *n* TURPENTINE 2b (oil obtained from pine-wood)

**wood wasp** *n* any of various wasplike insects (family Siricidae) related to the sawflies but having larvae that burrow in woody plants and a stout hornlike egg-laying organ – called also HORNTAIL

**woodwind** /'wood,wind/ *n* 1 any of a group of wind instruments (e g a clarinet, flute, oboe, or saxophone) that consists of a cylindrical or conical tube of wood or metal usu ending in a slightly flared bell, that produces notes by the vibration of a SINGLE REED or a DOUBLE REED or by the passing of air over a mouth hole, and that usu has finger holes or keys for producing all the notes within the instrument's range 2 **woodwind** *taking sing or pl vb*, **woodwinds** *pl* the woodwind section of a band or orchestra

**woodwool** /'wood,wool/ *n* 1 an insulating material in the form of slabs made of wood shavings bonded together with cement 2 fine wood shavings used esp for packing

**woodwork** /'wood,wuhk/ *n* 1 items made of wood; *esp* wooden interior fittings (e g mouldings or stairways) 2 *chiefly Br* woodworking 3 *informal* the goalposts and crossbar in soccer

¹**woodworking** /'wood,wuhking/ *n* the act, process, or occupation of working with wood – **woodworker** *n*

²**woodworking** *adj* used for woodworking ⟨~ *tools*⟩

**woodworm** /'wood,wuhm/ *n* an insect larva, esp that of the furniture beetle, that bores in dead wood (e g the structural wood of a building); *also* an infestation of woodworm

**woody** /'woodi/ *adj* 1 overgrown with or having many woods ⟨*a* ~ *county*⟩ ⟨*a* ~ *valley*⟩ 2a of or containing wood or wood fibres; LIGNEOUS ⟨~ *tissues*⟩ **b** *of a plant* having woody parts; rich in XYLEM (water-conducting tissue) and associated structures **c** *of a plant stem* tough and fibrous 3 characteristic of or suggestive of wood ⟨*wine with a* ~ *flavour*⟩ – **woodiness** *n*

**woody nightshade** *n* BITTERSWEET 2

¹**woof** /woohf/ *n* 1a the crosswise thread in weaving; WEFT 1a **b** the texture of woven fabric 2 a basic or essential element or material *synonyms* see ¹WARP [alter. (influenced by *weave* & *warp*) of ME *oof*, fr OE *ōwef*, fr *ō-* (fr *on*) + *wefan* to weave – more at WEAVE]

²**woof** /woof/ *n* 1 a low gruff sound characteristic of a dog 2 a low note emitted by sound-reproducing equipment [imit] – **woof** *vi*

**woofer** /'woohfə/ *n* a loudspeaker usu larger than a TWEETER that responds mainly to lower frequencies – compare TWEETER

**wool** /wool/ *n* 1 the soft wavy or curly undercoat of various hairy mammals, esp the sheep, that is made up of fibres of KERATIN (strong fibrous protein) covered with minute scales 2 a product of wool; *esp* a woven woollen fabric or garment ⟨*I always wear* ~ *in the winter*⟩ 3a a matted hairy covering, esp on a plant; TOMENTUM **b** a wiry or fibrous mass (e g of steel or glass) – usu in combination; compare MINERAL WOOL, STEEL WOOL [ME *wolle*, fr OE *wull*; akin to OHG *wolla* wool, L *vellus* fleece, *lana* wool, *lanugo* down] – **woolled** *adj*, **wool-like** *adj* – **keep/lose one's wool** *informal* to keep/lose one's temper [*wool* in the humorous sense "hair"] – **pull the wool over somebody's eyes** to blind somebody to the true situation; hoodwink or deceive somebody

**wool fat** *n* WOOL GREASE, esp after refining; LANOLIN

**woolfell** /'wool,fel/ *n, Br* a sheepskin with the wool still on it

**woolgathering** /'wool,gadh(ə)ring/ *n* indulging in idle daydreaming – **wool-gather** *vi*, **woolgatherer** *n*

**wool grease** *n* a fatty slightly sticky wax coating the surface of the fibres of sheep's wool – compare WOOL FAT

¹**woollen**, *NAm chiefly* **woolen** /'woolən/ *adj* 1 made of wool 2 of or for the manufacture or sale of woollen products ⟨~ *mills*⟩ ⟨*the* ~ *industry*⟩

²**woollen**, *NAm chiefly* **woolen** *n* 1 a fabric made of wool 2 *pl* garments of woollen fabric

¹**woolly**, *NAm also* **wooly** /'wooli/ *adj* 1a of or bearing wool; *also* made of wool **b** resembling wool 2a lacking in clearness or sharpness of outline ⟨*a* ~ *TV picture*⟩ **b** mentally vague or confused ⟨~ *thinking*⟩ 3 boisterously rough – chiefly in *wild and woolly* – **woollily** *adv*, **woolliness** *n*

²**woolly**, **woolie**, *NAm also* **wooly** *n, chiefly Br* a jumper or cardigan made from wool

**woolly aphid** *n* a plant louse (genus *Eriosoma*) covered with a dense coat of white hairy threads

**woolly bear** *n* any of various rather large very hairy moth caterpillars; *esp* one that is the larva of a TIGER MOTH

,**woolly-'headed** *adj* 1 having hair like wool 2 mentally woolly; without a clear grasp of detail

'**wool-,oil** *n* SUINT (sweat of sheep deposited in the wool)

**woolpack** /'wool,pak/ *n* 1 (a wrapper containing) a bale of wool 2 a rounded CUMULUS (billowy) cloud rising from a horizontal base

**woolsack** /-,sak/ *n* 1 the official seat of the Lord Chancellor in the House of Lords 2 *archaic* WOOLPACK 1

**woolshed** /'wool,shed/ *n* a building or range of buildings (e g on an Australian sheep station) in which sheep are sheared and wool is prepared for market

**woolskin** /'wool,skin/ *n, chiefly NAm* WOOLFELL

**woolsorter's disease** /'wool,sawtəz/ *n* anthrax affecting the lungs that results esp from inhalation of bacterial spores (*Bacillus anthracis*) from contaminated wool or hair

**wool stapler** *n* a dealer in wool; *esp* one who grades raw wool before selling it to a manufacturer

**wooly** /'wooli/ *n or adj, NAm* (a) woolly

**woomera** /'woomərə/ *n* a wooden rod that has a hooked end and is used by Australian aborigines for throwing a spear [native name in Australia]

**woops** /woops, woohps/ *interj* oops

**woop woop** /'woop ,woop/ *n, Austr slang* a remote provincial district or settlement [imaginary place-name]

**woosh** /woosh, woohsh/ *vi or n* (to make) a swishing sound [imit]

**woozy** /'woohzi/ *adj, informal* 1 mentally unclear or hazy 2 affected with dizziness, mild nausea, or weakness; sick [perh fr *woolly* + *dizzy*] – **woozily** *adj*, **wooziness** *n*

**wop** /wop/ *n, often cap, derog* an Italian – compare WOG [It dial. *guappo* blusterer, swaggerer, bully, fr Sp *guapo*]

**Worcester** /'woostə/, **Worcester china, Worcester porcelain** *n* a SOFT-PASTE PORCELAIN containing STEATITE produced at Worcester from about 1751 [*Worcester*, city in central England]

**Worcester sauce** /'woostə/ *n* a pungent sauce containing SOY SAUCE, vinegar, and spices [*Worcester*, *Worcestershire*, former county of England (now in *Hereford and Worcester*), where it was orig made]

**Worcestershire sauce** /'woostəshiə, -shə/ *n* WORCESTER SAUCE

¹**word** /wuhd/ *n* **1a** something that is said **b** *pl* **b(1)** talk, discourse ⟨*putting one's feelings into* ∼s⟩ **b(2)** the text of a vocal musical composition; lyrics **c** a short remark, statement, or conversation ⟨*would like to have a* ∼ *with you*⟩ **2a** a meaningful unit of spoken language that can stand alone and is not divisible into similar units (e g *happy* and *happiness* but not *-ness* which is less than a word or *happy man* which is two words); *also* a written or printed symbol that represents a spoken word and is usu set off by spaces on either side ⟨*the number of* ∼s *to a line*⟩ **b(1)** a combination of fundamental signals (e g electrical impulses) that provides a definite piece of information – used in communications work **b(2)** a string of BITS (smallest units of computer information) that is typically longer than a BYTE (group of eight bits) and is processed by a computer as a unit ⟨*a 16-bit* ∼⟩ **3** an order, command ⟨*don't move till I give the* ∼⟩ **4** *often cap* **4a** the divine wisdom manifest in the creation, government, and redemption of the world and identified in Christian thought with the second person of the Trinity, Jesus Christ **b** GOSPEL 1a **c** the expressed or manifested mind and will of God **5a** news, information ⟨*sent* ∼ *that he would be late*⟩ **b** rumour ⟨∼ *has it that they're leaving*⟩ **6** the act of speaking or of making verbal communication ⟨*in* ∼ *and deed*⟩ **7** a promise, declaration ⟨*kept her* ∼⟩ **8** *pl* a quarrelsome utterance or conversation ⟨*been having* ∼s *with my wife*⟩ **9** a verbal signal; a password **10** the most appropriate description ⟨*"hot" wasn't the* ∼ *for it*⟩ ☐ see also MY WORD [ME, fr OE; akin to OHG *wort* word, L *verbum*, Gk *eirein* to say, speak] – **eat one's words** to retract what one has said – **from the word go** from the beginning – **get a word in edgeways** to contribute to a conversation in which others are talking constantly – **in a word** IN SHORT – **in so many words** in plain forthright language ⟨*implied that she was lying but did not say so* in so many words⟩ – **of one's word** who can be relied on to keep a promise ⟨*a woman* of her word⟩ – **put words into somebody's mouth** 1 to tell somebody what to say 2 to represent falsely what somebody has said – **take the words out of somebody's mouth** to utter the exact words about to be used by somebody – **upon my word** – used as a mild exclamation of surprise or irritation; not now in vogue – see also **not** MINCE **one's words**, MUM'S **the word**

²**word** *vt* to express in words; phrase

**wordage** /'wuhdij/ *n* 1 wordiness, verbiage 2 length (e g of an article, story, etc) expressed in words

'**word-,blindness** *n* 1 ALEXIA (loss of the ability to read due to brain damage) 2 dyslexia

**wordbook** /'wuhd,book/ *n* a vocabulary, esp without definitions; *also* a dictionary

**word class** *n* a linguistic FORM CLASS (group of grammatically

similar linguistic items) whose members are words; *esp* PART OF SPEECH

,**word-for-'word** *adj, of a report or translation* in or following the exact words; verbatim – **word for word** *adv*

'**word-,hoard** *n, chiefly poetic* a supply of words; a vocabulary

**wording** /'wuhding/ *n* the act or manner of expressing in words ⟨*the exact* ∼ *of the will*⟩

**wordless** /'wuhdlis/ *adj* 1 not expressed in or accompanied by words 2 silent, inarticulate – **wordlessly** *adv*, **wordlessness** *n*

**wordmonger** /'wuhd,mung·gə/ *n* a writer who uses words for show rather than strictly for conveying ideas – **wordmongering** *n*

**word of honour** *n* a promise pledging one's honour

**word of mouth** *n* spoken communication – **word-of-mouth** *adj*

'**word-,painting** *n* the art or practice of vivid description in words

,**word-'perfect** *adj* having memorized something perfectly

**word picture** *n* a graphic description in words

**wordplay** /-,play/ *n* verbal wit

**word processor** *n* a computer, esp a microcomputer, that stores text which can then be manipulated (e g by adding corrections or inserting new material), and that performs routine or repetitive typing tasks (e g the production of type-written standardized letters) – **word processing** *n*

**word square** *n* a series of words of equal length arranged in a square pattern to read the same across and down ⟨ring, idol, nose, *and* glen *make a* ∼⟩

**word stress** *n* the manner in which emphases (STRESSES 3a) are distributed on the syllables of a word

**wordy** /'wuhdi/ *adj* using or containing (too) many words *antonyms* concise, laconic – **wordily** *adv*, **wordiness** *n*

**wore** /waw/ *past of* WEAR

¹**work** /wuhk/ *n* **1** activity in which one exerts strength or faculties to do or produce something: **1a** sustained physical or mental effort to achieve a result **b** the activities that provide one's accustomed means of livelihood **2a** energy expended by natural phenomena (e g waves, wind, and glaciers) **b** the result of such energy ⟨*sand dunes are the* ∼ *of sea and wind*⟩ **c** *physics* the amount of energy transferred to a body by a force in producing movement of the body, that is measured by multiplying the force by the distance it moves while causing motion of the body; *also* the transference of energy from the force to the body **3a** (the result of) a specified method of working ⟨*the* ∼ *of many hands*⟩ – often in combination ⟨*can't do needle*work⟩ ⟨*clever camera* ∼⟩ **b** something made from a specified material – often in combination ⟨*iron*work⟩ ⟨*porcelain* ∼⟩ **4a** a fortified structure (e g a fort, earth barricade, or trench) **b** *pl* structures in engineering (e g docks, bridges, or embankments) or mining (e g shafts or tunnels) **5** *pl but taking sing or pl vb* a place where industrial activity is carried out; a factory – often in combination ⟨*a water*works⟩ ⟨*a tile*works⟩ **6** *pl* the working or moving parts of a mechanism ⟨∼s *of a clock*⟩ **7** something produced by the exercise of creative talent or effort; an artistic production **8** *pl* the performance of moral or religious acts ⟨*salvation by* ∼s⟩ **9a** effective operation; an effect, result ⟨*wait for time to do its healing* ∼⟩ **b** activity, behaviour, or experience of the specified kind ⟨*dancing reels is thirsty* ∼⟩ **10** a piece of material being worked **11** *pl, slang* **11a** everything possessed, available, or belonging ⟨*the whole* ∼s, *rod, reel, tackle box, went overboard*⟩ **b** subjection to all possible abuse – usu + *get* ⟨*get the* ∼s⟩ *or give* ⟨*gave him the* ∼s⟩ [ME *werk, work*, fr OE *werc, weorc*; akin to OHG *werc*, Gk *ergon*] – **at work** 1 engaged in working, busy; *esp* engaged in one's regular occupation 2 at one's place of work – **have one's work cut out** to be faced with a very difficult or exacting task – **in the works** in the process of preparation, development, or completion – **out of work** unemployed – **set to work** to apply oneself; begin ⟨*he* set to work *to undermine their confidence*⟩

*synonyms* Work, labour, toil, drudgery, and travail all involve sustained activity to achieve a result. Work, but not the others, can be performed by animals and machines as well as by people. Labour, and still more toil, implies that the work is tiring, probably physical rather than mental, and perhaps done under compulsion. Drudgery suggests that the work is boring and perhaps degrading. Travail is a somewhat archaic word for work so strenuous as to involve suffering.

²**work** *adj* 1 suitable for wear while working ⟨∼ *clothes*⟩ 2 used for work ⟨∼ *elephant*⟩

**³work** *vb* **worked,** (*esp vt* 1, 2, 3) **worked, wrought** /rawt/ *vt* **1** to cause to happen; effect ⟨~ *miracles*⟩ **2a** to fashion or create something by expending labour or exertion on; forge, shape ⟨~ *flint into tools*⟩ **b** to make or decorate with needlework; *esp* to embroider ⟨~ *a sampler*⟩ **3** to prepare or form into a desired state for use by manipulation or mechanical processes (eg stirring, hammering, pressing, or kneading) ⟨~ *the icing until smooth and glossy*⟩ ⟨~ *cold steel*⟩ **4** to set or keep in operation ⟨*a pump* ~ed *by hand*⟩ **5a** to cause to labour ⟨~ed *his horses nearly to death*⟩ **b** to make use of; exploit for some end **c** to control the operation of ⟨*switches are* ~ed *from a central tower*⟩ **6** to carry on an operation through, in, or along (a place or area) ⟨*the salesman* ~ed *both sides of the street*⟩ ⟨*fisherman* ~ed *the stream from the bridge down to the pool*⟩ **7** to finance by working ⟨~ed *his way through college*⟩ **8a** to manœuvre (oneself or an object) gradually or with difficulty into or out of a specified condition or position ⟨*the screw* ~ed *itself loose*⟩ **b** to contrive, arrange ⟨*we can* ~ *it so that you can take your holiday early*⟩ **9** to excite, provoke ⟨~ed *himself into a rage*⟩ ~ *vi* **1a** to exert oneself, esp in sustained, purposeful, or necessary effort ⟨~ed *all day over a hot stove*⟩ ⟨~ing *for the cause*⟩ **b** to perform work or fulfil duties regularly for wages or a salary **2** to operate or function, esp according to plan or design ⟨*the lifts don't* ~ *at night*⟩ **3** to exert an influence or tendency ⟨*events have* ~ed *in our favour*⟩ **4** to produce a desired effect; succeed ⟨*hope your plan will* ~⟩ **5a** to make way slowly and with difficulty; move or progress laboriously ⟨*just* ~ing *through her own teen-age rebellion thing – Annabel*⟩ **b** to sail close to the wind **6a** to produce artefacts by shaping or fashioning a specified material ⟨~s *in copper*⟩ **b** to react in a specified way to being worked ⟨*this wood* ~s *easily*⟩ **7a** to be in agitation or restless motion ⟨*her mouth* ~ed *nervously*⟩ **b** to ferment **c** to move slightly in relation to another part **d** to get into a specified condition by slow or imperceptible movements ⟨*the knot* ~ed *loose*⟩ [ME *werken, worken,* fr OE *wyrcan;* akin to OE *weorc*]

**work in** *vt* **1** to cause to penetrate by persistent effort ⟨*work the ointment thoroughly* in⟩ **2** to insinuate unobtrusively ⟨worked in *a few topical jokes*⟩; *also* to find room for **3** RIDE IN (exercise a horse by riding)

**work off** *vt* to dispose of or get rid of by work or activity ⟨work off *a debt*⟩ ⟨work off *one's anger*⟩

**work on** *vt* to strive to influence or persuade

**work out** *vt* **1** to bring about by labour and exertion ⟨work out *your own salvation – Phil* 2:12 (AV)⟩ **2a** to solve or find out by reasoning or calculation ⟨*couldn't* work out *how the prices stayed so low – Cosmopolitan*⟩ **b** to devise by resolving difficulties ⟨work out *an agreement*⟩ **c** to elaborate in detail ⟨work out *a scheme*⟩ **3** to discharge (eg a debt) by labour **4** to exhaust (eg a mine) by working ~ *vi* **1a** to prove effective, practicable, or suitable ⟨*their marriage didn't* work out⟩ **b** to amount to a total or calculated figure – often + *at* or *to* ⟨works out *at £17.50*⟩ ⟨*gas heating might* work out *expensive*⟩ **c** *of a sum* to yield a result ⟨*it won't* work out⟩ **2** to engage in a workout ⟨works out *in the gym every morning*⟩

**work over** *vt* **1** to subject to thorough examination, study, or treatment ⟨*shelf stock would get thoroughly* worked over *by shoppers*⟩ **2** *chiefly NAm* to revise, rework ⟨*saved the play by* working *the first act* over⟩ **3** *informal* to beat up thoroughly; manhandle

**work up** *vt* **1** to stir up; rouse ⟨*can't* work up *much interest*⟩ **2** to produce by mental or physical work ⟨worked up *a comedy act*⟩ ⟨worked up *a sweat in the gymnasium*⟩ **3** to improve, esp by mental work ⟨work up *your French*⟩ ~ *vi* to rise gradually in intensity or emotional tone ⟨work up *to a climax*⟩ – see also WORKED UP

**workable** /'wuhkǝbl/ *adj* **1** capable of being worked ⟨~ *vein of coal*⟩ **2** practicable, feasible – **workableness, workability** *n*

**workaday** /'wuhkǝ‚day/ *adj* **1** of or suited for working days **2** prosaic, ordinary [alter. of earlier *workyday,* fr obs *workyday* working day, fr ME *werkeday,* irreg fr *werk work* + *day*]

**workaholic** /‚wuhkǝ'holik/ *n* somebody with an excessive need to work; a compulsive worker [*work* + connective *-a-* + *-holic*]

**workbag** /'wuhk‚bag/ *n* a bag for implements or materials for work, esp needlework

**workbasket** /-‚bahskit/ *n* a basket for needlework implements and materials

**workbench** /-‚bench/ *n* a bench on which work, esp of mechanics, machinists, or carpenters, is performed

**workbook** /-‚book/ *n* **1** a booklet outlining a course of study **2** a manual of operating instructions **3** a record book of work done **4** a pupil's individual exercise book of problems to be solved directly on the pages

**workbox** /-‚boks/ *n* a box for work instruments and materials, esp for needlework

**workday** /'wuhk‚day/ *n, chiefly NAm* WORKING DAY – **workday** *adj*

**worked** /wuhkt/ *adj* subjected to work; *esp* embroidered

**worked up** *adj* emotionally aroused; excited

**worker** /'wuhkǝ/ *n* **1a** somebody who works, esp at manual or industrial work or with a particular material – often in combination ⟨*steel*worker⟩ **b** a member of the WORKING CLASS **2** any of the sexually underdeveloped and usu sterile female members of a colony of ants, bees, wasps, etc that perform most of the labour and protective duties of the colony

**'worker-‚priest** *n* a Roman Catholic priest who for mission ary purposes spends part of each weekday as a worker in an ordinary job

**workfellow** /'wuhk‚feloh/ *n* a workmate

**workforce** /'wuhk‚faws/ *n taking sing or pl vb* **1** the workers engaged in a specific activity ⟨*the factory's* ~⟩ **2** the number of workers potentially assignable for any purpose ⟨*the nation's* ~⟩

**work function** *n, physics* the minimum amount of energy needed to cause an electron to leave the surface of a particular metal

**'work-‚harden** *vt* to harden and strengthen (a metal) by physical methods (eg hammering or rolling)

**workhorse** /'wuhk‚haws/ *n* **1** a horse used chiefly for labour as distinguished from driving, riding, or racing **2** a markedly useful or durable vehicle, craft, or machine **3** *informal* a willing worker, esp for a voluntary cause

**workhouse** /-‚hows/ *n* **1** *Br* a place formerly maintained at public expense to house needy or dependent people – not now in technical use **2** *NAm* a prison for people guilty of minor crimes

**'work-‚in** *n* a continuous occupation of a place of employment by employees continuing to work normally as a protest, usu against the threat of factory closure and redundancy

**¹working** /'wuhking/ *adj* **1a** adequate to permit effective work to be done ⟨*a* ~ *majority*⟩ **b** able to function or perform labour ⟨*a* ~ *model*⟩ ⟨~ *horses*⟩ **2** serving as a basis for further work ⟨~ *draft*⟩ **3** being time during which one works ⟨~ *hours*⟩; *also* being time during which one discusses business or policy ⟨*a* ~ *lunch*⟩ **4** of a domestic animal trained or bred for useful work ⟨*a* ~ *horse*⟩ [(1a, 2, 3) fr gerund of ³*work;* (1b, 4) fr prp of ³*work*]

**²working** *n,* **workings** *n pl* **1** an excavation or group of excavations made in mining, quarrying, or tunnelling **2** the fact or manner of functioning or operating ⟨*the* ~s *of his mind*⟩

**working asset** *n* an asset that is part of WORKING CAPITAL

**working capital** *n* capital actively turned over in or available for use in the course of business activity: **a** the excess of CURRENT ASSETS (short-term assets) over current liabilities **b** all capital of a business except that invested in CAPITAL ASSETS (long-term assets)

**working class** *n taking sing or pl vb,* **working classes** *n pl* the class of people who do manual labour for wages; *broadly* the class of people in Marxist theory who, regardless of status, are dependent on a wage or salary – compare PROLETARIAT – **working-class** *adj*

**working day,** *chiefly NAm* **workday** /'wuhk‚day/ *n* **1** a day on which work is done, as distinguished from Sunday or a holiday **2** the period of time in a day during which work is performed

**working dog** *n* a dog fitted by size, breeding, or training for useful work (eg herding sheep or guarding buildings), esp as distinguished from one fitted primarily for pet, show, or sporting use

**working drawing** *n* a scale drawing of an object to be made or a structure to be built that is used as a guide by the workman

**working fluid** *n* WORKING SUBSTANCE

**working girl** *n, euph* a prostitute

**working majority** *n* a parliamentary majority of sufficient size to allow the government to get its legislative programme safely through

**workingman** /-‚man/ *n* somebody who works for wages, esp in a manual job

**working party** *n, chiefly Br* a committee appointed (eg by a government) to investigate a particular question or problem and report on its findings

**working substance** *n* a liquid or gas (eg water or steam) that through changes of temperature, volume, and pressure is the means of carrying out processes or cycles involving the conversion between heat and mechanical or other forms of energy (eg in a steam engine or refrigerator)

**working trot** *n* the natural trotting pace of a horse

**working woman** *n* 1 a woman who works for wages or a salary 2 *euph* a prostitute

**workless** /'wuhklis/ *adj* without work; unemployed – **worklessness** *n*

**work load** *n* 1 the amount of work or of working time expected from or assigned to an employee 2 the amount of work (capable of being) performed (eg by a mechanical device) usu within a specific period

**workman** /-mən/ *n* 1 *fem* **workwoman** 1a a workingman b an artisan 2 somebody skilled at his/her trade to a specified degree ⟨*a bad* ~⟩

**workmanlike** /-,liek/ *also* **workmanly** /-,li/ *adj* worthy of a good workman: a skilful b efficient in appearance

**workmanship** /-,ship/ *n* the relative art or skill of a workman; craftsmanship; *also* the finish or execution imparted to a thing in the process of making ⟨*a vase of exquisite* ~⟩

**workmate** /-,mayt/ *n, chiefly Br* a companion at work

**work of art** *n* 1 a product of any of the FINE ARTS; *esp* a painting or sculpture of high artistic quality 2 a human creation that gives high aesthetic satisfaction ⟨*the wedding cake was a* ~⟩

**workout** /-,owt/ *n* a practice or exercise to test or improve physical fitness, ability, or performance

**workpeople** /-,peepl/ *n pl, chiefly Br* workers, employees

**workpiece** /-,pees/ *n* the (piece of) material that is operated on at any stage in the process of manufacture

**workroom** /'wuhk,roohm, -room/ *n* a room used esp for manual work

**works** /wuhks/ *adj* of a place of industrial labour ⟨~ *council*⟩ ⟨~ *doctor*⟩

**work sheet** *n* 1 a document on which work done and in progress is recorded 2 WORKBOOK 4

**workshop** /-,shop/ *n* 1 a room or place (eg in a factory) in which manufacture or repair work is carried out 2 a workroom 3 a brief intensive educational programme for a relatively small group of people in a given field that emphasizes participation

**workshy** /-,shie/ *adj, derog* disliking work; lazy

**work study** *n* the study of working methods and job performance in order to improve the efficiency and organization of labour and operations

**worktable** /-,taybl/ *n* a table often with drawers for holding working materials and implements; *esp* one used for sewing

**worktop** /-,top/ *n* a flat surface (eg of Formica) on a piece of furniture, esp kitchen furniture (eg a cupboard or dresser), that is suitable for working on

**work-to-'rule** *n* an instance of industrial action designed to reduce output by deliberately adhering very rigidly to rules and regulations

**'work-,up** *n* 1 an unintended mark on a printed sheet caused by the rising of spacing material 2 a complete medical examination (eg including urine, blood, and tissue tests)

**¹world** /wuhld/ *n* 1 the earth with its inhabitants and all things on it ⟨*travel round the* ~⟩ 2 the course of human affairs ⟨*knowledge of the* ~⟩ 3 the inhabitants of the earth both dead and living; the human race 4a the earthly state of human existence, as distinguished from heaven and the life to come ⟨*brought three children into the* ~⟩ ⟨*My Kingdom is not of this* ~ – *Jn 18:36 (AV)*⟩ b daily affairs, as distinguished from religious or clerical 5 the system of created things; the universe 6a a division, section, or generation of the inhabitants of the earth distinguished by living together at the same place or at the same time ⟨*the medieval* ~⟩ b a distinctive class of people or their sphere of interest ⟨*the academic* ~⟩ ⟨*woman's* ~⟩ 7a human society as a whole ⟨*all the* ~ *knows*⟩ ⟨*withdraw from the* ~⟩; *also* the public ⟨*announced his discovery to the* ~⟩ b fashionable or respectable people; public opinion ⟨*didn't care what the* ~ *said*⟩ 8 a part or section of the earth that is a separate independent unit – compare THIRD WORLD 9a one's personal environment in the sphere of one's life or work ⟨*the external* ~⟩ ⟨*the* ~ *of Van Gogh*⟩ b a particular aspect of one's life ⟨*the* ~ *of dreams*⟩ 10 an indefinite multitude or a

great quantity or amount ⟨*makes a* ~ *of difference*⟩ ⟨*thinks the* ~ *of you*⟩ 11 KINGDOM 4 ⟨*the animal* ~⟩ 12 a planet; *esp* one that is inhabited ⟨*life on other* ~s⟩ □ *(except 10&12)* + *the* [ME, fr OE *woruld* human existence, this world, age; akin to OHG *werald* age, world; both fr a prehistoric WGmc-NGmc compound whose first constituent is represented by OE *wer* man & whose second is akin to OE *eald* old – more at VIRILE, OLD] – **best of both worlds** the advantages of two alternatives, esp without their disadvantages – **come into the world** to be born – **dead to the world** sleeping soundly – **for all the world** in every way; exactly ⟨*for all the world like the original*⟩ – **for the world** in any circumstances; for anything ⟨*wouldn't hurt her* for the world⟩ – **in the world** among innumerable possibilities; ever ⟨*what* in the world *is it?*⟩ – **out of this world** of extraordinary excellence; superb – see also **set the world on FIRE**, **on TOP of the world**

**²world** *adj* 1 of the whole world ⟨*a* ~ *championship*⟩ 2 extending or found throughout the world; worldwide ⟨*a* ~ *state*⟩ ⟨*brought about* ~ *peace*⟩

**'world-,beater** *n* one who or that which excels all others; a champion

**,world-'class** *adj* of the highest quality in the world, esp in playing a sport or game ⟨*a* ~ *polo player*⟩

**world fair, world's fair** *n* an international exhibition featuring exhibits and participants from all over the world

**,world-'famous** *adj* universally known

**World Federalist** *n* a member of a movement arising after World War II advocating the formation of a federal union of the nations of the world with limited but positive governmental powers – **World Federalism** *n*

**World Island** *n* the landmass consisting of Europe, Asia, and Africa held by experts in political geography to have strategic advantages for mastery of the world

**world language** *n* 1 a language used by a large part of the world's population ⟨*English is a* ~⟩ 2 an artificial language (eg Esperanto) designed to be used for international communication

**worldling** /'wuhldling/ *n* a worldly person; somebody who is not interested in spiritual affairs

**worldly** /'wuhldli/ *adj* 1 of or devoted to this world and its pursuits rather than to religion or spiritual affairs ⟨*my* ~ *goods*⟩ 2 worldly-wise – **worldliness** *n*

**,worldly-'minded** *adj* devoted to or engrossed in worldly interests – **worldly-mindedness** *n*

**,worldly-'wise** *adj* possessing a practical and often shrewd and materialistic understanding of human affairs; sophisticated

**world power** *n* a political unit (eg a nation or state) powerful enough to affect the entire world by its influence or actions

**world premiere** *n* the first official performance (eg of a theatrical production) anywhere in the world

**world series** *n* a series of baseball games played each year between the winners of the major US leagues to decide the professional championship of the USA

**world's fair** *n* WORLD FAIR

**'world-,shaking** *adj, chiefly informal* earthshaking

**world soul** *n* an animating spirit or creative principle held to be related to the world as the soul is to the individual being

**world view** *n* WELTANSCHAUUNG (philosophy of life)

**world war** *n* a war engaged in by all or most of the principal nations of the world; *specif, cap both Ws* either of two such wars of the first half of the 20th century

**'world-,weary** *adj* bored with the life of the world and its material pleasures – **world-weariness** *n*

**worldwide** /-'wied/ *adj* extended throughout or involving the entire world – **worldwide** *adv*

**world without end** *adv* eternally, forever

**¹worm** /wuhm/ *n* 1a any of numerous relatively small elongated INVERTEBRATE animals that typically have a soft cylindrical or flattened body often without any projecting structures, that live on land or in water, and that may exist independently or as parasites: eg 1a(1) ANNELID (worm with a segmented body); *esp* an earthworm a(2) PLATYHELMINTH (tapeworm or related flat-bodied worm) a(3) NEMATODE (parasitic round-bodied or threadlike worm) b any of various invertebrate animals that resemble worms: eg b(1) an insect larva (eg a silkworm); *esp* one that is a destructive grub, caterpillar, or maggot b(2) SHIPWORM (marine clam) b(3) BLINDWORM (limbless lizard) 2a a human being who is an object of contempt, loathing, or pity; a wretch b something that torments or devours from within ⟨*the ~ of conscience*⟩ **3** *pl but taking sing or pl vb* infestation with or disease caused by parasitic worms **4** something (eg a mechanical device) that is spiral in form or appearance: eg **4a** the thread of a screw **b** a short revolving screw whose threads engage with a WORM WHEEL or a rack **c** a spiral tube in which vapour is cooled and turns to liquid during distilling **d** ARCHIMEDES' SCREW; *also* a conveyor working on the principle of such a screw **5** *archaic* a snake, serpent [ME, fr OE *wyrm* serpent, worm; akin to OHG *wurm* serpent, worm, L *vermis* worm] – **wormlike** *adj*

**²worm** *vi* to proceed indirectly or insidiously ~ *vt* **1** to free (eg a dog) from worms – sometimes + *out* **2a** to cause to move or proceed (as if) in the manner of a worm **b** to insinuate or introduce (oneself) by devious or subtle means **c** to proceed or make (one's way) insidiously or deviously ⟨*tried to ~ her way out of the situation*⟩ **3** to wind rope or yarn spirally round and between the strands of (a cable or rope) so as to make the surface smooth **4** to obtain or extract by artful or insidious questioning or by pleading, asking, or persuading – usu + *out of* ⟨*she ~ed the secret out of him*⟩ – **wormer** *n*

**wormcast** /-,kahst/ *n* a small heap of earth excreted by an earthworm on the soil surface

'**worm-,eaten** *adj* **1a** eaten or burrowed into (as if) by worms ⟨*~ timber*⟩ **b** pitted **2** worn-out, antiquated ⟨*~ regulations*⟩

**wormed** /wuhmd/ *adj* WORM-EATEN 1a

**worm gear** *n* **1** WORM WHEEL **2** a gear consisting of a revolving screw (WORM 4b) and a WORM WHEEL working together

**wormhole** /-,hohl/ *n* a hole or passage burrowed by a worm

**wormseed** /'wuhm,seed/ *n* SANTONICA **2** (plant flowerheads used to treat worm infestation)

**worm's-eye view** *n, chiefly humorous* a view from a humble position

**worm snake** *n* any of various small harmless burrowing snakes somewhat resembling earthworms

**worm wheel** *n* a toothed wheel that engages with the thread of a revolving screw (WORM 4b)

**wormwood** /-wood/ *n* **1** ARTEMISIA (strong-smelling plant of the daisy family); *esp* a European artemisia (*Artemisia absinthium*) that yields a bitter slightly aromatic dark green oil used in the drink ABSINTHE **2** something bitter or mortifying; bitterness [ME *wormwode*, alter. (influenced by *worm* & *wode* wood) of *wermode*, fr OE *wermōd*; akin to OHG *wermuota* wormwood]

**wormy** /'wuhmi/ *adj* **1** containing, abounding in, or infested with worms ⟨*~ flour*⟩ ⟨*a ~ dog*⟩; *also* damaged by worms; worm-eaten ⟨*~ timbers*⟩ **2** resembling or suggestive of a worm

**worn** /wawn/ *past part of* WEAR

**,worn-'out** *adj* exhausted or used up (as if) by wear

**worriment** /'wurimənt/ *n, chiefly NAm informal* worrying; *also* trouble, anxiety

**worrisome** /'wuris(ə)m/ *adj* **1** causing distress or worry **2** inclined to worry or fret – **worrisomely** *adv*, **worrisomeness** *n*

**worrit** /'wurit/ *vb, dial Eng* to worry [by alter.]

'**worry** /'wuri/ *vt* **1a** to harass by tearing, biting, or snapping, esp at the throat ⟨*a dog ~ing sheep*⟩ **b** to shake or pull at with the teeth ⟨*a terrier ~ing a rat*⟩ **c** to touch or disturb repeatedly **d** to change the position of or adjust by repeated pushing or hauling **2a** to attack with rough or aggressive treatment; torment **b** to subject to persistent or nagging attention or effort **3** to afflict with mental distress or agitation; make anxious **4** *dial Br* to choke, strangle ~ *vi* **1** to move, progress, or work at something with unceasing or difficult effort; struggle **2** to feel or experience concern or anxiety; fret [ME *worien* to seize by the throat, strangle, fr OE *wyrgan* to strangle; akin to OHG *wurgen* to strangle, Lith *veržti* to constrict] – **worriedly** *adv*, **worrier** *n* – **not to worry** *Br informal* do not worry; do not feel anxious or dispirited

**²worry** *n* **1** (a state of) mental distress or agitation resulting from concern, usu for something impending or anticipated; anxiety **2** a cause of worry; a trouble, difficulty *synonyms see* ¹CARE

**worry beads** *n pl* a string of beads fingered so as to calm oneself and keep one's hands occupied

**worrywart** /'wuri,wawt/ *n, informal* somebody who is inclined to worry unduly

'**worse** /wuhs/ *adj, comparative of* BAD *or* ILL **1** of lower quality **2** in poorer health [ME *werse, worse*, fr OE *wiersa, wyrsa*; akin to OHG *wirsiro* worse] – **worsen** *vb* – **the worse for** harmed by or harming ⟨*none the worse for his fall*⟩ ⟨*it will be the worse for you if you do*⟩ – see also **worse** LUCK

**²worse** *n, pl* **worse** something worse ⟨*a change for the ~*⟩ ⟨*called him a radical or ~*⟩

**³worse** *adv, comparative of* BAD, BADLY, *or* ILL in a worse manner; to a worse extent or degree ⟨*raining ~ than ever*⟩

**,worse-'off** *adj* in poorer economic circumstances

**worser** /'wuhsə/ *adj or adv, archaic or dial* worse ⟨*had chosen the ~ part* – Robert Southey⟩

'**worship** /'wuhship/ *n* **1** (an act of) reverence offered to a divine being or supernatural power **2** a form of religious practice with its set of beliefs and ritual **3** extravagant admiration for or devotion to an object of esteem ⟨*~ of the dollar*⟩ **4** *chiefly Br* a person of importance – used as a title for various officials (eg magistrates and some mayors) ⟨*sent a petition to his* Worship⟩ [ME *worship* worthiness, repute, respect, reverence paid to a divine being, fr OE *weorthscipe* worthiness, repute, respect, fr *weorth* worthy, worth + *-scipe* -ship]

**²worship** *vb* **-pp-** ⟨*NAm* **-p-, -pp-**⟩ *vt* **1** to honour or reverence as a divine being or supernatural power **2** to regard with great, even extravagant respect, honour, or devotion ~ *vi* to perform or take part in (an act of) worship *synonyms see* ¹REVERE – **worshipper** *n*

**worshipful** /-f(ə)l/ *adj* **1** rendering worship or veneration **2** *chiefly Br* – used as a title for various people or groups of rank or distinction ⟨*the* Worshipful *Company of Mercers*⟩ **3** *archaic* notable, distinguished – **worshipfully** *adv*, **worshipfulness** *n*

'**worst** /wuhst/ *adj, superlative of* BAD *or* ILL **1** most productive of evil ⟨*the ~ thing you could have done*⟩ **2** most lacking in quality ⟨*the ~ student*⟩ [ME *werste, worste*, fr OE *wierresta, wyrsta*, superl of the root of OE *wiersa* worse]

**²worst** *n, pl* **worst** **1** the worst state or part ⟨*always at my ~ before breakfast*⟩ ⟨*that's the ~ of keeping rabbits*⟩ **2** one who or that which is worst **3** the utmost harm of which one is capable ⟨*do your ~*⟩; *broadly* one's maximum effort **4** defeat, disadvantage ⟨*got the ~ of the argument*⟩ – **at (the) worst** under the worst circumstances; seen in the worst light – **if the worst comes to the worst** if the very worst thing happens

**³worst** *adv, superlative of* BAD, BADLY, *or* ILL **1** in the worst manner; to the worst extent or degree ⟨*the worst-dressed woman*⟩ ⟨*the old suffered ~*⟩ **2** to the greatest or highest degree ⟨*groups who need the subsidies ~ lose out* – T W Arnold⟩

**⁴worst** *vt* to get the better of; defeat

**worsted** /'woostid/ *n* **1** a smooth compact yarn made from long wool fibres, used esp for firm fabrics with no NAP (downy surface), carpeting, or knitting **2** a fabric made from worsted yarns [ME, fr *Worsted* (now *Worstead*), village in Norfolk, England] – **worsted** *adj*

'**wort** /wuht/ *n* a plant; *esp* a soft or fleshy-stemmed (HERBACEOUS) plant as opposed to a woody plant or shrub – now used only in combination ⟨*stink*wort⟩ [ME, fr OE *wyrt* root, herb, plant – more at ROOT]

**²wort** *n* a dilute solution of sugars obtained from malt by soaking, and fermented to form beer [ME, fr OE *wyrt*; akin to MHG *würze* brewer's wort, OE *wyrt* root, herb]

'**worth** /wuhth/ *vi, archaic* to become [ME *worthen*, fr OE *weorthan*; akin to OHG *werdan* to become, L *vertere* to turn]

**²worth** *prep* **1a** equal in value to **b** having property equal to ⟨*he's ~ £1000000*⟩ **2** deserving of ⟨*well ~ the effort*⟩ ⟨*food's not ~ eating*⟩ *usage see* WORTHWHILE [ME, fr OE *weorth* (adj) worthy, of a (specified) value; akin to OHG *werd* worthy, worth]

**³worth** *n* **1a** monetary value ⟨*farmhouse and lands of little ~*⟩ **b** the equivalent of a specified amount or figure – often in combination ⟨*three quids*worth *of petrol*⟩ **2** value, importance ⟨*a literary heritage of great ~*⟩ **3** moral or personal merit, esp high merit ⟨*proved his ~*⟩ **4** wealth, riches ⟨*his personal ~ is several million*⟩

**worthless** /-lis/ *adj* **1a** lacking worth; valueless ⟨*~ currency*⟩ **b** useless ⟨*~ to continue searching*⟩ **2** contemptible, despicable *synonyms* SEE INVALUABLE – **worthlessly** *adv*, **worthlessness** *n*

**worthwhile** /-'wiel/ *adj* worth the time or effort spent – **worthwhileness** *n*

*usage* **Worthwhile** is an adjective and should not be confused with the preposition **worth**, which needs an object. One can say ⟨*it's* worthwhile *reading/to read this book* (compare *it's easy to read this book*⟩ or ⟨*this book is* worth *reading*⟩, but to say ⟨⚠ *this book is* worthwhile *reading*⟩ is as incorrect as to say ⟨⚠ *this book is* worthwhile *a lot of money*⟩.

'**worthy** /'wuhdhi/ *adj* **1a** having moral worth or value; estimable ⟨*a ~ cause*⟩ **b** honourable, meritorious ⟨*they were* *all honoured and ~ men⟩* **2** having sufficient worth; important enough; deserving ⟨*a deed ~ to be remembered*⟩ ⟨*a ~ opponent*⟩ – **worthily** *adv*, **worthiness** *n*

²**worthy** *n, chiefly archaic or humorous* a worthy or prominent person

**-worthy** */-₁wuhdhi/ comb form (n → adj)* **1** fit or safe for ⟨*a seaworthy vessel*⟩ **2** deserving of ⟨*praiseworthy*⟩ ⟨*noteworthy*⟩

**wossname** /'wos₁naym/ *n, Br slang* WHAT'S HIS NAME, WHAT'S ITS NAME ⟨*look a gift horse in the ~ – Punch*⟩ [by alter.]

¹**wot** /wot/ *pres 1 & 3 sing of* WIT

²**wot** *vb* **-tt-** *chiefly Br formal or humorous* to know – often + *of* ⟨*voted on a motion they ~ted not of – Punch*⟩ [ME *woten*, alter. of *witen* – more at WIT]

**wotcher** /'wochə/ *interj, Br slang* – used as a greeting [alter. of *what cheer*]

**would** /wəd; *strong* wood/ *past of* WILL **1a** to desire, wish ⟨*I ~ I were young again*⟩ ⟨*as ye ~ that men should do to you – Lk 6:31 (AV)*⟩ **b** – used in auxiliary function with *rather* or *soon, sooner* to express preference ⟨*~ sooner die than face them*⟩ **2a** – used in auxiliary function to express wish, desire, or intent ⟨*those who ~ forbid gambling*⟩ or, in negative constructions, reluctance ⟨*~ not hurt a fly*⟩; used in the question form with the force of a polite request ⟨*~ you please help me*⟩ ⟨*shut the door, ~ you?*⟩ or of an offer or suggestion ⟨*~ you like some tea?*⟩ **b** – used in auxiliary function in reported speech to represent *shall* or *will* ⟨*said he ~ come*⟩ ⟨*knew I ~ enjoy the trip*⟩ **3a** used to ⟨*we ~ meet often for lunch*⟩ – used with emphatic stress to express exasperation ⟨*she ~ keep complaining*⟩ **b** – used in auxiliary function with emphatic stress as a comment on the annoyingly typical ⟨*you ~ say that*⟩ **4** – used in auxiliary function to introduce a contingent fact, possibility, or presumption **4a** in the main clause of a conditional sentence ⟨*it ~ break if you dropped it*⟩ ⟨*he ~ have won if he hadn't tripped*⟩ **b** after a verb expressing desire, request, or advice ⟨*wish he ~ go*⟩ **5** could ⟨*barrel ~ hold 20 gallons*⟩ ⟨*door wouldn't open*⟩ **6** – used in auxiliary function to soften direct statement ⟨*I ~ like a bath*⟩ ⟨*the explanation ~ seem satisfactory*⟩ ⟨*~ be glad to know*⟩ ⟨*that ~ be the milkman*⟩ ⟨*I wouldn't know*⟩ **7** *archaic* to wish for; want *usage* see SHOULD, ²BETTER, RATHER [ME *wolde*, fr OE; akin to OHG *wolta* wished, desired]

'**would-be** *adj* desiring or intended to be ⟨*a ~ rapist – Daily Mirror*⟩

**wouldn't** /'woodnt/ would not

**wouldst** /woodst/, **wouldest** /'woodist/ *archaic past 2 sing of* WILL

¹**wound** /woohnd/ *n* **1a** an injury to the body (eg from violence, accident, or surgery) that involves tearing or breaking of a membrane (eg the skin) and usu damage to underlying tissues **b** a cut or break in a plant due to external injury **2** a mental or emotional hurt or blow [ME, fr OE *wund;* akin to OHG *wunta* wound] – **woundless** *adj*

²**wound** *vt* to cause a wound to or in ~ *vi* to inflict a wound *synonyms* see INJURE

³**wound** /wownd/ *past of* WIND

**wounded** /'woohndid/ *adj* injured, hurt by, or suffering from a wound ⟨*a ~ soldier*⟩ ⟨*~ pride*⟩

**woundwort** /'woohnd₁wuht/ *n* any of various plants whose soft downy leaves were formerly used in the dressing of wounds; *esp* any of several plants (genus *Stachys*) of the mint family with yellowish-white, pink, or purplish flowers usu in spikes

¹**wove** /wohv/ *past of* WEAVE

²**wove** *n* paper made in such a way that no fine lines run across the grain – compare LAID

**woven** /'wohv(ə)n/ *past part of* WEAVE

¹**wow** /wow/ *interj, slang* – used to express strong feeling (eg pleasure or surprise)

²**wow** *n, slang* a striking success; a hit [¹*wow*]

³**wow** *vt, slang* to excite to enthusiastic admiration or approval

⁴**wow** *n* a distortion in reproduced sound that is heard as a slow rise and fall in the pitch of the sound and is caused by variations in the speed of the reproducing system – compare FLUTTER [imit]

**wowzer** /'wowzə/ *n, Austr & NZ slang* an oppressively puritanical person; a killjoy [origin unknown]

**W particle** *n, physics* W BOSON (subatomic particle of matter) [*W*, abbr for *weak*]

**WPB** *n, informal* WASTE PAPER BASKET [*wastepaper basket*]

¹**wrack** /rak/ *n* **1** ⁷RACK – chiefly in *wrack and ruin* **2** (a remnant of) something destroyed *usage* see ¹RACK [ME, fr OE *wræc* misery, punishment, something driven by the sea; akin to OE *wrecan* to drive, punish – more at WREAK]

²**wrack** *n* **1a** a wrecked ship **b** a shipwreck **2a** marine vegetation; *esp* any of various usu large brown seaweeds (eg BLADDER WRACK or another FUCUS) **b** dried seaweeds [ME *wrak*, fr MD or MLG; akin to OE *wræc* something driven by the sea]

³**wrack** *n or vt* ³'⁴RACK ⟨*doubt-wracked faces – Punch*⟩ [by alter.]

⁴**wrack** *n or vi, poetic* ¹'²RACK (scudding clouds) [by alter.]

**wraith** /rayth/ *n, pl* **wraiths** /rayths; *also* raydhz/ **1a** an apparition of a living person in his/her exact likeness seen usu just before or after his/her death **b** a ghost, spectre **2** an insubstantial replica or shadow ⟨*looked a mere ~ of her former self*⟩ **3** a barely visible column of gas or vapour △ wreath [Sc, of unknown origin]

¹**wrangle** /'rang·gl/ *vi* **1** to dispute angrily or peevishly; bicker **2** to engage in argument or controversy ~ *vt, NAm* to herd and care for (livestock, esp horses) on the range [ME *wranglen;* akin to OHG *ringan* to struggle – more at WRING]

²**wrangle** *n* an angry, noisy, or prolonged dispute or quarrel *synonyms* see ²QUARREL

**wrangler** /'rang·glə/ *n* **1** a bickering disputant **2** the holder of a first-class Cambridge honours degree in mathematics – compare OPTIME **3** *NAm* a ranch hand who takes care of the riding horses; *broadly* a cowboy – **wranglership** *n*

¹**wrap** /rap/ *vb* **-pp-** *vt* **1a** to muffle, envelop, pack, or enfold in something flexible **b** to coil, fold, draw, or twine about something specified ⟨*~ a blanket round her*⟩ **2a** to obscure or surround with the specified covering ⟨*~ped in mist*⟩ ⟨*the affair was ~ped in scandal*⟩ **b** to involve completely; engross – usu pass + *up in* ⟨*~ped up in his daughter*⟩ ~ *vi* to curl round something; be a wraparound ⟨*skirt that ~s over*⟩ – see also **wrap somebody round one's little** FINGER [ME *wrappen*] **wrap up** *vt, informal* to bring to a usu successful conclusion; end ~ *vi* **1** to protect oneself with outer garments ⟨*wrap up warm*⟩ **2** to be subject to wrapping **3** *Br slang* to stop talking; SHUT UP – usu imper ⟨*wrap up when I'm talking!*⟩

²**wrap** *n* **1** a waterproof wrapping placed round food to be frozen, esp in a domestic freezer; *broadly, chiefly NAm* a wrapping **2** an article of clothing that may be wrapped round a person; *esp* an outer garment (eg a shawl) – **under wraps** concealed from public knowledge; secret

¹**wraparound** /'rapə₁rownd/ *adj* **1a** made to be wrapped round the body ⟨*a ~ skirt*⟩ **b** of or being a flexible printing surface wrapped round a plate cylinder **2** shaped to follow a contour; *esp* made to curve from the front round to the side ⟨*~ windscreen*⟩

²**wraparound** *n* an object or garment that encircles or esp curves and laps over another

**wrapover** /'rap₁ohvə/ *adj* WRAPAROUND 1a

**wrapper** /'rapə/ *n* **1** that in which something is wrapped: eg **1a** a fine quality tobacco leaf used for the outside covering of a cigar **b(1)** DUST JACKET **b(2)** the paper cover of a book not bound in hard covers **c** a paper wrapped round a newspaper or magazine in the post **2** a person or device that wraps **3** an article of clothing (eg a dressing gown) worn wrapped round the body

**wrapping** /'raping/ *n* (a piece of) material used to wrap an object

**wrasse** /ras/ *n* any of numerous long usu brilliantly coloured spiny-finned fishes (family Labridae) of warm seas that include important food fishes [Cornish *gwragh, wragh*]

¹**wrath** /roth/ *n* **1** strong vengeful anger or indignation **2** retributory, esp divine punishment ⟨*the ~ of God*⟩ *synonyms* see ¹ANGER [ME, fr OE *wrǣththo*, fr *wrǣth* angry – more at WROTH]

²**wrath** *adj, archaic* wrathful [alter. of *wroth*]

**wrathful** /'rothf(ə)l/ *adj* **1** filled with wrath; irate **2** arising from or suggesting wrath – **wrathfully** *adv*, **wrathfulness** *n*

**wreak** /reek/ *vt* **1** to inflict (vengeance or punishment) **2** to give free play to (malevolent feeling) ⟨*~ed his wrath on her*⟩ **3** to cause or create (havoc or destruction) **4** *archaic* to avenge [ME *wreken*, fr OE *wrecan* to drive, punish, avenge; akin to OHG *rehhan* to avenge, L *urgēre* to drive on, urge]

*usage* **Wreak** has no connection with the participial adjective **wrought** which means "worked". Pleasant things may be **wrought**, but one can **wreak** only unpleasant ones.

**wreath** /reeth/ *n, pl* **wreaths** /reedhz/ *also* reeths/ **1** something intertwined into a circular shape; *esp* a garland, chaplet ⟨*lay a ~ on the coffin*⟩ **2** a representation of a wreath (e g in heraldry) **3** a drifting and coiling whorl ⟨~s *of smoke*⟩ [ME *wrethe,* fr OE *writha;* akin to OE *wrīthan* to twist – more at WRITHE] – **wreathy** *adj*

**wreathe** /reedh/ *vt* **1a** to shape (e g flowers) into a wreath **b** to coil about something **2** to encircle (as if) with a wreath ⟨*bust* ~d *with laurel*⟩ **3** to cover, suffuse – esp in *wreathed in smiles* ⟨*her face was* ~d *in smiles at the news*⟩ ~ *vi* to twist or move in coils; writhe ⟨*smoke* ~d *from the chimney*⟩ [partly fr *wreath;* partly fr ME *wrethen,* pp of *writhen* to twist, fr OE *wrīthan*]

**¹wreck** /rek/ *n* **1** something cast up on the land by the sea, esp after a shipwreck ⟨*a ~ of the sea is Crown property*⟩ **2a** a shipwreck **b** wrecking or being wrecked; destruction ⟨*after the ~ of our hopes*⟩ **3a** a hulk or the ruins of a wrecked ship **b** the broken remains of something (e g a building or vehicle) wrecked or ruined **c** a person or animal of broken constitution, health, or spirits ⟨*a mere ~ of his former self*⟩ ⟨*felt a ~ the morning after the party*⟩ **d** *informal* something dilapidated or disarranged ⟨*that old ~ he drives around in*⟩ ⟨*my hair's a ~!*⟩ *synonyms* see ¹RUIN [ME *wrek,* fr AF, of Scand origin; akin to ON *rek* wreck; akin to OE *wrecan* to drive]

**²wreck** *vt* **1** to cast ashore **2a** to reduce to a ruinous state by violence ⟨*~ a train*⟩ **b** to cause (a vessel) to be shipwrecked **c** to involve in disaster or ruin ⟨*~ one's marriage*⟩ ~ *vi* **1** to become wrecked **2** to rob, salvage, or repair wreckage or a wreck

**wreckage** /'rekij/ *n* **1** wrecking or being wrecked **2** broken, disrupted, and disordered parts or material from a wrecked structure

**wrecker** /'rekə/ *n* **1** one who or that which wrecks: e g **1a** somebody who wrecks ships (e g by false lights) for plunder **b** somebody whose work is the demolition of buildings **2a** somebody who searches for or works on the wrecks of ships (e g for rescue or for plunder) **b** *NAm* BREAKDOWN LORRY **c** *NAm* somebody who salvages parts and material from scrapped motor vehicles

**wren** /ren/ *n* a very small brown European bird (*Troglodytes troglodytes*) that has a short erect tail and is noted for its loud song [ME *wrenne,* fr OE *wrenna;* akin to OHG *rentilo* wren]

**Wren** *n* a woman serving in the Women's Royal Naval Service [*W*omen's *R*oyal Naval Service]

**¹wrench** /rench/ *vi* **1** to undergo violent twisting **2** to pull or strain at something with violent twisting ⟨*he* ~ed *at the handle*⟩ ~ *vt* **1** to pull or twist violently ⟨*~ the door open*⟩ **2** to injure or disable by a violent twisting or straining ⟨*~ed his shoulder*⟩ **3** to distort, pervert ⟨*~ language*⟩ **4** to snatch forcibly; wrest ⟨*~ the knife from her hand*⟩ **5** to cause to suffer mental anguish; rack [ME *wrenchen,* fr OE *wrencan;* akin to OHG *renken,* L *vergere* to bend, incline] – **wrenchingly** *adv*

**²wrench** *n* **1a** a violent twisting or a sideways pull **b** a sharp twist or sudden jerk straining muscles or ligaments; *also* the resultant injury (e g of a joint) **c** a distorting or perverting alteration **d** acute emotional distress (e g resulting from parting); a sudden distressing mental change **2a** a spanner with adjustable jaws for holding nuts of different sizes **b** *NAm* a spanner

**¹wrest** /rest/ *vt* **1** to obtain or take away by violent wringing or twisting **2** to obtain with difficulty by force or determined labour ⟨*~ a living from the stony soil*⟩ **3** WRENCH 3 ⟨*~ the law*⟩ [ME *wrasten, wresten,* fr OE *wrǣstan;* akin to OE *wrīthan* to twist – more at WRITHE] – **wrester** *n*

**²wrest** *n* the action of wresting; a wrench

**¹wrestle** /'resl/ *vi* **1** to contend with an opponent in wrestling **2** to contend or grapple with a problem or an opposing tendency ⟨*~ with a difficulty*⟩ ⟨wrestling *with his conscience*⟩ **3** to engage in a violent or determined struggle ⟨wrestling *with cumbersome luggage*⟩ ~ *vt* **1a** to engage in (a match, bout, or fall) in wrestling **b** to wrestle with **2** to push, pull, or manhandle by force [ME *wrastlen, wrestlen,* fr OE *wrǣstlian,* freq of *wrǣstan*] – **wrestler** *n*

**²wrestle** *n* the action or an instance of wrestling; a struggle; *esp* a wrestling bout

**wrestling** /'resling/ *n* a sport or contest in which two unarmed individuals struggle hand to hand with each attempting to subdue or unbalance his/her opponent according to agreed rules, and without hitting with the closed fist

**wretch** /rech/ *n* **1** a profoundly unhappy or unfortunate person **2** a base, despicable, or vile person or animal [ME *wrecche,* fr

OE *wrecca* outcast, exile; akin to OE *wrecan* to drive, drive out – more at WREAK]

**wretched** /'rechid/ *adj* **1** deeply afflicted, dejected, or unfortunate **2** deplorably bad ⟨*was in ~ health*⟩ ⟨*~ workmanship*⟩ **3** (appearing) mean, squalid, or contemptible ⟨*dressed in ~ old clothes*⟩ **4** causing annoyance; damned – used as a general expression of annoyance ⟨*lost my ~ socks*⟩ [irreg fr *wretch*] – **wretchedly** *adv,* **wretchedness** *n*

**wrick** /rik/ *vt, chiefly Br* ³RICK ⟨*~ed her neck*⟩

**¹wriggle** /'rigl/ *vi* **1** to move (a part of) the body to and fro with short writhing motions like a worm; squirm **2** to move or advance by twisting and turning **3** to extricate or insinuate oneself by manoeuvring, equivocation, evasion, or ingratiation ⟨*trying to ~ out of her responsibilities*⟩ ~ *vt* **1** to cause to move in short quick contortions ⟨*she* ~d *her hips*⟩ **2** to introduce or insinuate into a state or place by wriggling **3** to make (one's way) by wriggling [ME *wrigglen,* fr or akin to MLG *wriggeln* to wriggle; akin to OE *wrigian* to turn – more at WRY] – **wriggly** *adj*

**²wriggle** *n* **1** a short or quick writhing motion or contortion **2** a formation or marking of sinuous design

**wriggler** /'riglə/ *n* one who or that which wriggles; *esp* the larva or pupa of a mosquito

**wright** /riet/ *n* a craftsman, maker – usu in combination ⟨*ship*wright⟩ ⟨*play*wright⟩ [ME, fr OE *wyrhta, wryhta* worker, maker; akin to OE *weorc* work]

**wring** /ring/ *vb* **wrung** /rung/ *vt* **1** to twist or compress, esp so as to extract liquid ⟨*~ the towel dry*⟩ **2a** to expel or obtain (as if) by twisting and compressing ⟨*~ the water from the towel*⟩ **b** to exact or extort by coercion or with difficulty ⟨*~ a confession from the suspect*⟩ **3a** to twist so as to strain, sprain, or break; contort ⟨*~ a chicken's neck*⟩ **b** to twist together (one's clasped hands) as a sign of anguish **4** to affect painfully as if by wringing; torment ⟨*a tragedy that* ~s *the heart*⟩ **5** to shake (somebody's hand) vigorously in greeting ~ *vi* to squirm or writhe (as if) with pain [ME *wringen,* fr OE *wringan;* akin to OHG *ringan* to struggle, OE *wyrgan* to strangle – more at WORRY] – **wring** *n*

**wringer** /'ring-ə/ *n* one who or that which wrings; *specif* a mangle ⟨*a clothes ~*⟩

**wringing-'wet** *adj* so wet that liquid may be dripping out

**¹wrinkle** /'ringkl/ *n* **1** a small ridge or furrow, esp when formed on a surface by the shrinking or contraction of a smooth substance; a crease; *specif* one in the skin, esp when due to age, worry, or fatigue **2** *informal* a valuable trick or dodge for bringing about a result [ME, back-formation fr *wrinkled* twisted, winding, prob fr OE *gewrinclod,* pp of *gewrinclian* to wind, fr *ge-,* perfective prefix + *-wrinclian* (akin to *wrencan* to wrench)] – **wrinkly** *adj*

**²wrinkle** *vi* to become marked with or contracted into wrinkles ~ *vt* to contract into wrinkles; pucker

**wrist** /rist/ *n* **1** (the region of) the joint between the human hand and the arm; CARPUS; *also* a corresponding part on a VERTEBRATE animal other than a human **2** the part of a garment or glove covering the wrist [ME, fr OE; akin to OE *wrǣstan* to twist, wrest – more at WREST]

**wristband** /-,band/ *n* a band encircling the wrist: e g **a** one on the sleeve of a garment **b** the bracelet or strap of a wristwatch **c** a sweatband worn round the wrist

**wristlet** /'ristlit/ *n* a band encircling the wrist; *esp* a closely fitting knitted band attached to the top of a glove or the end of a sleeve

**wrist pin** *n* a stud or pin that forms a bearing for a CONNECTING ROD (rod transmitting motion from one part of a machine to another)

**wrist shot** *n* a stroke (e g in golf, hockey, or TABLE TENNIS) in which a quick flick of the wrist or wrists provides all or most of the power

**wristwatch** /-,woch/ *n* a small watch that is attached to a bracelet or strap and is worn round the wrist

**wristy** /'risti/ *adj* characterized by or tending to use a lot of wrist movement (e g in hitting a ball with a bat or club) ⟨*a ~ shot to the leg-side boundary*⟩ – **wristily** *adv*

**writ** /rit/ *n* **1a** a formal written document; *specif* a legal instrument in the form of a letter issued under seal in the name of the sovereign **b** an order in writing issued under seal in the name of a court or judicial officer commanding or forbidding an act specified in it ⟨*~ of detinue*⟩ ⟨*~ of entry*⟩ ⟨*~ of execution*⟩ **2** *archaic* something written; writing – chiefly in *holy writ, sacred writ* [ME, fr OE; akin to OE *wrītan* to write]

**write** /riet/ *vb* **wrote** /roht/; **written** /'ritn/ *also* **writ** /rit/ *vt* **1a** to form (legible characters, symbols, or words) on a surface, esp with an instrument ⟨~ *an inscription*⟩ ⟨~ *"I love you"*⟩ **b** to spell in writing ⟨*words* written *alike but pronounced differently*⟩ **c** to cover or fill (in) by writing ⟨wrote *ten pages*⟩ ⟨~ *a cheque*⟩ **2** to set down in writing: e g **2a** to draw up; draft ⟨~ *a will*⟩ **b** to be the author of; compose ⟨~s *poems and essays*⟩ **c** to say by letter ⟨~s *that he is coming*⟩ **d** to use (a specific script or language) in writing ⟨~ *a clear hand*⟩ ⟨~ *shorthand*⟩ ⟨~ *Braille*⟩ ⟨~ *French*⟩ **e** to write contracts or orders for; esp to underwrite ⟨~ *life insurance*⟩ **3** to express, record, or reveal (as if) in writing ⟨*it is* written⟩ ⟨written *on my heart*⟩ **4** to make (a quality or condition) evident ⟨*guilt* written *on his face*⟩ **5** to introduce or remove by writing ⟨~ *a clause into a contract*⟩ ⟨~ *a character out of a serial*⟩ **6** to be the subject of (something worth recording) ⟨*this discovery has* written *a chapter in the history of medicine*⟩ **7** to introduce (information) into a computer memory or transfer (information) from a computer memory to another storage device (e g a disk or tape) – compare READ **8** *chiefly NAm* to communicate with in writing ⟨wrote *them on his arrival*⟩ ~ *vi* **1** to make significant written characters, inscriptions, words, or sentences ⟨*learning to* ~⟩ ⟨~ *in ink*⟩; *also* to permit or be adapted to writing ⟨*pen* ~s *badly*⟩ **2** to compose, communicate by, or send a letter ⟨~ *home*⟩ ⟨~ *for information*⟩ **3** to produce or compose a written work, esp professionally, for publication or performance ⟨~ *for "The Times"*⟩ ⟨~ *for woodwind*⟩ ⟨*his wife* ~s⟩ – see also **nothing to write** HOME **about, writ** LARGE [ME *writen*, fr OE *wrītan* to scratch, draw, inscribe; akin to OHG *rīzan* to tear, Gk *rhinē* file, rasp] – **writable** *adj*

**write down** *vt* **1** to record in written form **2a** to disparage, injure, or minimize by writing **b** to reduce in status, rank, or value; esp to reduce the BOOK VALUE (value in accounting) of (an asset) **c** to play down in writing ~ *vi* to write so as to appeal to a lower level of taste, comprehension, or intelligence – usu + *to* – see also WRITE-DOWN

**write in** *vt* **1** to insert in a document or text **2** *NAm* **2a** to insert (a name not listed on a ballot or voting machine) in an appropriate space **b** to cast (a vote) in this manner – see also WRITE-IN

**write off** *vt* **1** to take off the books; cancel ⟨write off *a bad debt*⟩ **2a** to concede to be irreparably lost, useless, or dead ⟨*this two square miles isn't being* written off *as a ghetto* – Colin MacInnes⟩ **b** *informal* to get (oneself) killed ~ *vi* to write and send a letter ⟨wrote off *for the latest cut-price offer*⟩ – see also WRITE-OFF

**write out** *vt* **1** to put in writing; esp to put into a full and complete written form **2** to exhaust the ideas or resources of (oneself) by writing all one has to say ⟨wrote *himself out on the subject*⟩

**write up** *vt* **1a** to write an account of; describe ⟨write up *the fire*⟩ **b** to put into finished written form ⟨write up *my notes*⟩ **2** to bring up to date the writing of (e g a diary) **3** to praise or maximize in writing **4** *NAm* to increase the BOOK VALUE (value in accounting) of ~ *vi* WRITE OFF – see also WRITE-UP

'write-,down *n* a deliberate reduction in the BOOK VALUE (value in accounting) of an asset (e g to reflect the effect of obsolescence or deflation)

'write-,in *n*, *NAm* **1** a vote cast by writing in the name of a candidate **2** a candidate whose name is written in

'write-,off *n* **1** an elimination of an item from accounts books **2** *informal* something (e g a badly damaged car or aeroplane) regarded as a total loss

**writer** /'rietə/ *n* **1** one who or that which writes; esp one who writes as an occupation; an author **2** *Scot* WRITER TO THE SIGNET

**writer's cramp** *n* a painful spasmodic cramp of muscles of the hand or fingers brought on by prolonged writing

**Writer to the Signet** *n* a Scottish solicitor

'write-,up *n* **1** a written, esp flattering, account **2** *NAm* a deliberate increase in the BOOK VALUE (value in accounting) of an asset (e g to reflect the effect of inflation)

**writhe** /riedh/ *vt* **1** to twist so as to distort; wrench **2** to twist (the body or a body part) in pain ~ *vi* **1** to proceed with twists and turns **2** to twist (as if) from pain or struggling **3** to suffer keenly ⟨~ *under an insult*⟩ [ME *writhen*, fr OE *wrīthan*; akin to ON *rītha* to twist, OE *wrigian* to turn – more at WRY] – **writhe** *n*

**writhen** /'ridhən/ *adj*, *archaic or poetic* twisted, contorted ⟨~ *trees*⟩ ⟨*a* ~ *smile*⟩ [ME, fr OE, fr pp of *wrīthan*]

**writing** /'rieting/ *n* **1a** the act of one who writes ⟨*hurt her hand and found* ~ *difficult*⟩ **b** the act, practice, or occupation of literary composition **2a** written letters or words; esp handwriting ⟨*put it in* ~⟩ ⟨*I can't read your* ~⟩ **b** *usu pl* a written composition ⟨*the* ~s *of Marx*⟩ **c** a written or printed letter, notice, document, or inscription **3** composition in a specified manner or for a specified purpose ⟨*baroque* ~⟩ ⟨*the brass* ~ *in the score*⟩ – **writing on the wall** an omen or sign of future ruin, misery, etc [fr the miraculous writing on a wall which foretold the downfall of King Belshazzar (Daniel 5)]

'writing-,case *n* a portable container for writing materials

**writing desk** *n* a desk that often has a sloping top for writing on; *also* a portable case that contains writing materials and has a surface for writing

**writing paper** *n* a paper treated with SIZE to fill the pores and seal the paper so that it can be written on with ink; esp notepaper

**Writings** /'rietingz/ *n pl* HAGIOGRAPHA (third part of Jewish scriptures) [trans of LHeb *kĕthūbhīm*]

¹**wrong** /rong/ *n* **1a** an injurious, unfair, or unjust act; action or conduct inflicting harm without due provocation or just cause ⟨*suffer* ~ *at their hands*⟩ ⟨*did him a great* ~⟩ **b** *law* a violation or invasion of the legal rights of another; esp TORT **2** what is wrong, immoral, or unethical ⟨*the difference between right and* ~⟩ ⟨*to do no* ~⟩ **3a** the state of being mistaken or incorrect ⟨*my guess was hopelessly in the* ~⟩ **b** the state of being or appearing to be the offender ⟨*put me in the* ~⟩ [ME, fr OE *wrang*, fr (assumed) *wrang*, adj, wrong]

²**wrong** *adj* **1** against moral standards; sinful, immoral ⟨*thought that war was* ~⟩ **2** not right or proper according to a code, standard, or convention; improper ⟨*it was* ~ *not to thank your host*⟩ **3** not according to truth or facts; incorrect ⟨*gave a* ~ *date*⟩; *also* in error; mistaken ⟨*you're quite* ~⟩ **4** not satisfactory (e g in condition, results, health, or temper) ⟨*something* ~ *with my toe*⟩ **5** not in accordance with one's needs, intentions, or expectations ⟨*took the* ~ *bus*⟩ **6a** of or being the side of something that is not meant to be used or exposed ⟨*put it on* ~ *side out*⟩ **b** of or being the less desirable side ⟨*on the* ~ *side of 40*⟩ – see also **get out of** BED **on the wrong side, get the wrong** END **of the stick, rub up the wrong** WAY *antonyms* right, correct [ME, fr (assumed) OE *wrang*, of Scand origin; akin to ON *rangr* awry, wrong; akin to OE *wringan* to wring] – **wrongly** *adv*, **wrongness** *n*

³**wrong** *adv* **1** without accuracy; incorrectly ⟨*guessed* ~⟩ **2** out of proper working order ⟨*washing machine went* ~⟩ **3** in a false light ⟨*don't get me* ~⟩ – see also **put a** FOOT **wrong**

*usage* Wrong is commoner than **wrongly** for the meaning "so as to be wrong" ⟨*spelt it* wrong⟩. **Wrongly** means "in the wrong way" ⟨*acted* wrongly⟩ and is the only one that can be used before a verb or participle ⟨*a* wrongly *addressed letter*⟩ or that can mean "as is wrong" ⟨*he* wrongly *refused* (= he did wrong to refuse)⟩.

⁴**wrong** *vt* **1a** to do wrong to; injure, harm **b** to treat disrespectfully or dishonourably; esp, euph to seduce **2** to mistakenly ascribe an unworthy motive to; misrepresent – **wronger** *n*

**wrongdoer** /,rong'dooh·ə, '-,--/ *n* somebody who does (moral) wrong – **wrongdoing** *n*

'wrong-,foot *vt* **1** to make (an opponent) move in the wrong direction by deception (e g in tennis or football) **2** to put at a disadvantage by a sudden change of approach

**wrongful** /-f(ə)l/ *adj* **1** wrong, unjust **2** having no legal sanction; unlawful ⟨*the* ~ *claimant*⟩ – **wrongfully** *adv*, **wrongfulness** *n*

**wrongheaded** /-'hedid/ *adj* stubborn in adherence to wrong opinion or principles; perverse – **wrongheadedly** *adv*, **wrongheadedness** *n*

**wrong'un** /'rong·ən/ *n*, *informal* **1** GOOGLY (deceptively bowled ball in cricket) **2** a person of bad character; a rogue [alter. of *wrong one*]

**wrote** /roht/ *past of* WRITE

**wroth** /roth/ *adj*, *poetic or humorous* angry [ME, fr OE *wrāth*; akin to OHG *reid* twisted, OE *wrīthan* to writhe]

**wrought** /rawt/ *adj* **1** worked into shape by artistry or effort; fashioned, formed ⟨*carefully* ~ *essays*⟩ **2** elaborately embellished; ornamented **3** processed for use; manufactured ⟨~ *silk*⟩ **4** *of a metal* beaten into shape by tools; hammered – compare WROUGHT IRON **5** deeply stirred; excited – usu + *up* ⟨*gets easily* ~ *up over nothing*⟩ [ME, fr pp of *worken* to work]

**wrought iron** *n* a very pure commercial form of iron that is tough, easily worked, and relatively soft and contains less than 0.3 per cent and usu less than 0.1 per cent carbon – **wrought-iron** *adj*

**wrung** /rung/ *past of* WRING

**wry** /rie/ *adj* **1** bent or twisted, esp with distaste ⟨made a ~ face⟩ **2** ironically or grimly humorous ⟨a ~ smile⟩ ⟨~ wit⟩ [ME *wrien* to twist, writhe, fr OE *wrigian* to turn; akin to MLG *wrīch* twisted, Gk *rhoikos* crooked] – **wryly** *adv*, **wryness** *n*

**wrybill** /'rie,bil/ *n* a New Zealand bird (*Anarhynchus frontalis*) related to the plovers, whose beak is curved sharply to the right

**wryneck** /'rie,nek/ *n* **1** a grey-brown bird (*Jynx torquilla*) that differs from the related woodpeckers in being able to twist the head sideways over the shoulder **2** TORTICOLLIS (twisted condition of the neck)

**Wu** /wooh/ *n* a group of Chinese dialects of the lower Yangtze valley [Chin (Pek) *wú* (*wu²*)]

**wud** /woohd/ *adj, chiefly Scot* insane, mad [alter. of ¹*wood*]

**wulfenite** /'woolfə,niet/ *n* a mineral, PbMoO₄, that is a complex oxide of the chemical elements lead and molybdenum and occurs usu in bright orange-yellow to red, grey, green, or brown flat crystals in veins of other lead ores [Ger *wulfenit*, fr F X von *Wulfen* †1805 Austrian mineralogist]

**wunderkind** /'voondə,kint/ *n, pl* **wunderkinder** /-,kində/ a child prodigy; *also* one who succeeds in a competitive field at an early age [Ger, fr *wunder* wonder + *kind* child]

**wuntun** /,wun'tun, ,won'ton/ *n* WONTON (Chinese food)

**wurley** /'wuhli/ *n, Austr* an aborigine's hut [native name in Australia]

**wurst** /wuhst, wooəst, vooəst/ *n* (a) sausage; *esp* a sausage typical of those made in Germany – usu in combination [Ger; akin to OHG *werran* to confuse – more at WAR]

**wurzel** /'wuhzl/ *n* MANGEL-WURZEL (root vegetable)

**wuther** /'wudhə/ *vi, dial Eng, of wind* to bluster [ME (Sc) *quhediren*, of Scand origin; akin to ON *hvitha* squall of wind]

**wuzzy** /'wuzi/ *adj, informal* woozy [by alter.]

**wyandotte** /'wie-ən,dot/ *n* (any of) an American breed of medium-sized domestic fowls [prob fr *Wyandotte*, a N American Indian people]

**wych elm, witch elm** /wich/ *n* (the wood of) a hardy elm (*Ulmus glabra*) that grows in esp N Europe and Asia [*wych, witch* (a tree with pliant branches) – more at WITCH HAZEL]

**wych hazel** *n* WITCH HAZEL

**Wycliffite** /'wikli,fiet/ *n* LOLLARD (follower of John Wycliffe) [John *Wycliffe* †1384 E religious reformer] – **Wycliffite** *adj*

**wye** /wie/ *n* a Y-shaped part or object

**wynd** /wiend/ *n, chiefly Scot* a very narrow street [ME (Sc) *wynde*, prob fr *wynden* to wind, proceed, go, fr OE *windan* to twist – more at WIND]

**wynn** /win/ *n* a letter Þ used in Old English with the value of Modern English *w* [OE *wen, wyn*]

**wyvern** *also* **wivern** /'wievən/ *n* a mythical and heraldic animal usu represented as a 2-legged winged creature resembling a dragon **synonyms** see GRIFFON [alter. of ME *wyvere* viper, fr ONF *wivre*, modif of L *vipera*]

# X

**¹x, X** /eks/ *n, pl* **x's, xs, X's, Xs 1a** the 24th letter of the English alphabet **b** a graphic representation of or device for reproducing the letter *x* **c** a speech counterpart of printed or written *x* **2** one designated *x*, esp as the 24th in order or class or the 1st in a series that includes x, y, and sometimes z **3** ten **4** somebody or something whose identity is unknown or withheld **5** – used in italic to represent a variable mathematical quantity **6** something shaped like or marked with the letter X

**²x** *vt* **x-ing, x'ing** /'eksing/; **x-ed** *also* **x'd, xed** /ekst/ to mark with an *x*

**X** *n or adj* (a film) certified in Britain as suitable only for people over 18 – not used technically since December 12 1982; compare 18

**Xanadu** /'zanədooh/ *n* a place (e g an estate or village) of idyllic beauty [*Xanadu*, locality in the poem *Kubla Khan* by S T Coleridge †1834 E poet]

**xanth-** /zanth-/, **xantho-** *comb form* yellow ⟨xanth*ene*⟩ ⟨xantho*phyll*⟩ [NL, fr Gk, fr *xanthos*]

**xanthate** /'zanthayt/ *n* any of various chemical compounds (SALTS OR ESTERS) formed by combination between a XANTHIC ACID and a metal atom, an alcohol, or another chemical group

**xanthein** /'zanthi·in/ *n* a water-soluble yellow colouring matter in the cells of some plants and algae

**xanthene** /'zantheen/ *n* (any of various coloured or colourless compounds related to) a chemical compound, $C_{13}H_{10}O$, from which XANTHENE DYES are derived

**xanthene dye** *n* any of various brilliant fluorescent yellow to pink to bluish-red dyes derived from xanthene

**xanthic** /'zanthik/ *adj* **1** of or tending towards a yellow colour **2a** of xanthin or xanthine **b** of or derived from XANTHIC ACID [Fr *xanthique*, fr Gk *xanthos* yellow]

**xanthic acid** *n* any of various unstable sulphur-containing acids; *esp* a colourless oily acid, $C_3H_6OS_2$

**xanthin** /'zanthin/ *n* any of a group of yellow to red pigments chemically similar to the CAROTENES, that occur in many plants (e g sweet corn), animals, and animal products (e g egg yolk and butter) [ISV]

**xanthine** /'zanthien, -theen/ *n* a chemical compound, $C_5H_4N_4O_2$, that occurs widely in living animal and plant tissue, is formed by the breakdown of GUANINE (component of DNA, occurring in most living cells), and is converted into URIC ACID (compound in urine and other excretory matter); *also* any of various derivatives of this (e g caffeine) [ISV]

**Xanthippe** /zan'thipi/ *n* an ill-tempered woman [Gk *Xanthippē*, shrewish wife of the philosopher Socrates]

**xanthochroi** /zan'thokrə,ie/ *n pl* white people with light hair and fair skin [NL, fr *xanth-* + Gk *ōchroi*, nom pl masc of *ōchros* pale] – **xanthochroic** *adj*, **xanthochroid** *adj or n*

**xanthoma** /zan'thohmə/ *n, pl* **xanthomas, xanthomata** /-mətə/ a skin condition characterized by raised yellowish patches (e g on the eyelids, neck, or back) [NL, fr *xanth-* + *-oma*]

**xanthophyll** /'zanthoh,fil, -thə-/ *n* any of several yellow to orange pigments derived from CAROTENES and occurring in plants (e g nettles and the yellow petals of flowers), algae, and animal tissues; *esp* LUTEIN (orange form of xanthophyll) [Fr *xanthophylle*, fr *xanth-* + *-phylle* -phyll] – **xanthophyllic, xanthophyllous** *adj*

**xanthous** /'zanthəs/ *adj* having or being yellow skin or hair

**Xantippe** /zan'tipi/ *n* a Xanthippe

**x-axis** /eks/ *n, maths* **1** the horizontal axis in a CARTESIAN COORDINATE system (system of axes with reference to which points can be placed on a graph) having two axes at right angles **2** the one of the three axes in a CARTESIAN CO-ORDINATE system having three axes at right angles that is not designated as the y-axis or the z-axis

**X chromosome** *n* a SEX CHROMOSOME (strand of gene-carrying material concerned with the inheritance of sex) that usu occurs paired with an identical chromosome in one sex, and with a dissimilar chromosome in the other sex. In many animals, including human beings, the inheritance of two X chromosomes determines that the sex of the animal is female and the inheritance of an X chromosome and a Y CHROMOSOME determines that the sex is male.

**'x-co,ordinate** *n, maths* a COORDINATE that defines the position of a point (e g on a graph) and whose value is determined by measuring along the direction of an x-axis; *esp* ABSCISSA (x-coordinate in a system of two axes)

**xebec** /'zeebek/ *n* a usu 3-masted Mediterranean sailing ship with long overhanging bow and stern and mixed triangular sails and SQUARE SAILS [prob modif of Fr *chebec*, fr Ar *shabbāk*]

**xen-** /zen-/, **xeno-** *comb form* **1** guest; foreigner ⟨xeno*phobia*⟩ **2** strange; foreign ⟨xeno*lith*⟩ [LL, fr Gk, fr *xenos* stranger, guest, host]

**xenia** /'zeeniə, -nyə/ *n, botany* the effect that the genes from a plant male reproductive cell, esp a POLLEN GRAIN, have on the growth, development, etc of the female structures, esp those (e g the fruit) other than the embryo [NL, fr Gk, hospitality, fr *xenos* host]

**xenogamy** /zen'ogəmi/ *n* cross-fertilization [ISV *xen-* + *-gamy*]

**xenogeneic** /,zenohjə'nee·ik/ *adj* derived from or originating in a member of another species; HETEROLOGOUS ⟨*a ~ antibody*⟩ [*xen-* + *-geneic*, alter. of *-genic*]

**xenoglossia** /,zenə'glosyə/ *n* the alleged ability of some psychic mediums, spiritualists, etc to speak a foreign language they have not learned [NL, fr *xen-* + Gk *glōssa* tongue]

**xenograft** /'zenəgrahft, 'zee-/ *n* a tissue,graft carried out between members of different species

**xenolith** /'zenəlith, 'zee-/ *n* a fragment of rock embedded in a rock of a different type – **xenolithic** *adj*

**xenon** /'zeenon, 'zenon/ *n* a heavy, colourless, chemical element that is one of the NOBLE GASES (group of chemically stable unreactive gases including helium and neon) but takes part in some chemical reactions, occurs in air as about one part in 20 million by volume, and is used in some radio valves, flashguns for photography, and stroboscopic lamps [Gk, neut of *xenos* strange]

**xenophile** /'zenə,fiel/ *n* somebody who is attracted to foreign things (e g manners, styles, or people) [ISV *xen-* + *-phile*] – **xenophilous** *adj*

**xenophobe** /'zenəfohb/ *n* somebody who hates or fears what is foreign, esp foreigners [ISV *xen-* + *-phobe*] – **xenophobia** *n*, **xenophobic** *adj*

**xer-, xero-** *comb form* dry ⟨xero*phyte*⟩ ⟨xero*graphy*⟩ [LL, fr Gk *xēr-, xēro-*, fr *xēros* – more at SERENE]

**xerarch** /'ziərahk/ *adj, ecology* developing or originating in a dry place – used with reference to a series of plant communities that succeed one another

**xeric** /'ziərik/ *adj, ecology* of, being, characterized by, or adapted to living in dry conditions ⟨*a ~ habitat*⟩ ⟨*a ~ plant*⟩ – compare HYDRIC, MESIC – **xerically** *adv*

**xeroderma** /,ziəroh'duhmə/ *n, pl* **xerodermas, xerodermata** /-mətə/ a condition characterized by abnormally dry skin resulting from the malfunctioning of sweat glands [NL, fr *xer-* + *-derma*] – **xerodermatous** *adj*

**xerography** /ze'rogrəfi, ziə-/ *n* a photocopying process using the action of light on an electrically charged light-conducting surface. The latent image is developed with a resinous powder and fixed onto a sheet of paper by heating. [ISV *xer-* + *-graphy*] – **xerographic** *adj*, **xerographically** *adv*

**xeromorph** /'zerə,mawf, 'ziə-/ *n* a xerophyte; *esp* one structurally adapted to prevent excessive water loss [ISV *xer-* + *-morph*] – **xeromorphic** *adj*

**xerophilous** /ze'rofiləs, ziə-/, **xerophile** /'zerə,fiel, 'ziə-/ *adj* (characteristic) of or living in a xeric environment – **xerophily** *n*

**xerophthalmia** /,ziərof'thalmiə/ *n* a dry thickened lustreless condition of the eyeball resulting from a severe deficiency of VITAMIN A [LL, fr Gk *xērophthalmia*, fr *xēr-* xer- + *ophthalmia*] – **xerophthalmic** *adj*

**xerophyte** /'ziərə,fiet/ *n* a plant (eg a cactus) adapted for life and growth in dry conditions (eg deserts), esp by means of structural features that limit water loss through the plant surface or that provide for the storage of water – **xerophytic** *adj*, **xerophytically** *adv*, **xerophytism** *n*

**xerothermic** /,ziərə'thuhmik/ *adj*, *ecology* of, being, characterized by, or adapted to living in hot dry conditions

**xerox** /'ziəroks, 'zeroks/ *vt*, *often cap* to copy on a Xerox machine; *broadly* to photocopy

**Xerox** *trademark* – used for a xerographic copier

**x height** *n* the height of a small x used to represent the relative height of small to capital letters in a complete set of type

**Xhosa** /'khawsə/ *n*, *pl* **Xhosas**, *esp collectively* **Xhosa** 1 a member of a people of Cape Province related to the Zulus 2 the BANTU language of the Xhosa people

**xi** /sie, zie/ *n* 1 the 14th letter of the Greek alphabet 2 *physics* an unstable ELEMENTARY PARTICLE (minute particle of matter) existing in electrically uncharged and negatively charged forms with masses respectively 2572 and 2585 times the mass of an electron [Gk *xei*]

**x-'intercept** *n*, *maths* the X-COORDINATE of a point (eg on a graph) where a line, curve, or surface intersects the X-AXIS (fixed reference line)

**xiphisternum** /,ziefə'stuhnəm, zi-/ *n*, *pl* **xiphisterna** /-nə/ the lowest segment of the breastbone [NL, fr Gk *xiphos* sword + NL *sternum*]

**¹xiphoid** /'zifoyd/ *adj* 1 *biology* shaped like a sword ⟨*a ~ leaf*⟩ 2 of or being the xiphisternum [NL *xiphoides*, fr Gk *xiphoeidēs*, fr *xiphos* sword]

**²xiphoid, xiphoid process** *n* the xiphisternum

**xiphosuran** /,ziefə'suhrən, ,zi-/ *n* any of an order (Xiphosura of the phylum Arthropoda) of INVERTEBRATE animals including the HORSESHOE CRABS and extinct related forms [deriv of Gk *xiphos* sword + *oura* tail – more at SQUIRREL] – **xiphosuran** *adj*, **xiphosure** *n*, **xiphosurous** *adj*

**x-ir'radiate** *vt*, *often cap* to subject to X rays – **x-irradiation** *n*

**Xmas** /'eksməs/ *n* Christmas [*X* (symbol for *Christ*, fr the Gk letter chi (X), initial of *Christos* Christ) + *-mas* (in *Christmas*)] *usage* This is a spelling of "Christmas" rather than a synonym for it. It should be confined to commercial or casual writing. Most people prefer to say *Christmas* rather than /'eksməs/ when reading it aloud.

**x-radi'ation** *n*, *often cap* (exposure to) X rays

**Xray** /'eksray/ – a communications code word for the letter x

**x-ray** /'eksray/ *vt*, *often cap* to examine, treat, or photograph with X rays

**X ray** /'eks ray/ *n* 1 an ELECTROMAGNETIC RADIATION of extremely short wavelength in the range $10^{-9}$ to $10^{-12}$ metres that has the properties of IONIZING (causing electrically charged particles to form in) a gas when passing through it, of penetrating various thicknesses of all solids, and of acting like light to expose photographic films and plates 2 X ray, X-ray photograph a photograph (eg of a bone or organ of the body) obtained by use of X rays 3 an examination (eg of a part of the body) by means of X rays

**X-ray astronomy** *n* astronomy dealing with investigations of heavenly bodies by means of the X rays they emit

**x-ray crystallography** *n* the investigation of crystal structure using X-RAY DIFFRACTION methods

**X-ray diffraction** *n* the scattering of a beam of X rays by the atoms of a crystal to produce a characteristic pattern from which the structure of the crystal (eg of a protein) can be determined; *also* the determination of a crystal's structure by this process

**X-ray star** *n* a luminous starlike celestial body that emits a major portion of its radiation in the form of X rays

**X-ray therapy** *n* medical treatment (eg of cancer) by controlled application of X rays

**X-ray tube** *n* a tube in which a vacuum exists and in which a concentrated stream of electrons strikes a metal target and produces X rays

**xtal** /'kristl/ *n or adj* crystal [*x* (taken to stand for *crys-* or *chris-*, by analogy to *Xmas*) + crystal]

**X-word** /'kros ,wuhd/ *n* a crossword

**xyl-** /ziel-/, **xylo-** *comb form* 1 wood ⟨*xylophone*⟩ 2 xylene ⟨*xylic*⟩ [L, fr Gk, fr *xylon*]

**xylan** /'zielan/ *n* a yellow gummy carbohydrate made up of repeating XYLOSE (type of sugar) units that is present in large amounts in plant cell walls and woody tissue [ISV]

**xylary** /'zieləri/ *adj* of or in xylem [*xylem* + *-ary*]

**xylem** /'zieləm, 'zielem/ *n* a complex plant tissue that consists of firm-walled water-conducting tubes (VESSELS or TRACHEIDS), usu together with woody fibres and PARENCHYMA (basic plant tissue in which others are embedded). Xylem functions chiefly in the conduction of water and dissolved mineral salts from the roots to other parts of the plant, gives mechanical strength and support, and forms the woody part of many plant stems (eg tree trunks) and roots. – compare PHLOEM [Ger, fr Gk *xylon* wood]

**xylem ray** *n* (a portion of) a VASCULAR RAY (band or wedge of nonspecialized tissue) located in xylem – compare PHLOEM RAY

**xylene** /'zieleen/ *n* a poisonous inflammable oily chemical compound, $C_6H_4(CH_3)_2$, obtained from WOOD TAR, COAL TAR, or petroleum [ISV]

**xylidine** /'zieli,deen, -,dien, 'zili-/ *n* (any of) a mixture of six poisonous chemical compounds derived from xylene, that have the same formula, $(CH_3)_2C_6H_3NH_2$, but different structural arrangements of atoms, and are used chiefly in the manufacture of dyes [ISV]

**xylography** /zie'logrəfi/ *n* the art of making (prints from) engravings on wood [Fr *xylographie*, fr *xyl-* + *-graphie* -graphy] – **xylographer** *n*, **xylograph** *vb or n*, **xylographic, xylographical** *adj*

**xylol** /'zielol/ *n* xylene – not used technically [ISV]

**xylophagous** /zie'lofəgəs/ *adj* feeding on or in wood ⟨*~ insect larvae*⟩ [Gk *xylophagos*, fr *xyl-* + *-phagos* -phagous]

**xylophilous** /zie'lofiləs/ *adj* growing or living in or on wood

**xylophone** /'zielə,fohn/ *n* a percussion instrument consisting of a series of wooden bars graduated in length to produce the musical scale, mounted horizontally at waist height, supported on belts of straw or felt, and sounded by striking with two small wooden hammers [*xyl-* + *-phone*] – **xylophonist** *n*

**xylose** /'zielohs, -lohz/ *n* a sugar, $C_5H_{10}O_5$, that occurs esp as a constituent of XYLAN in woody plant tissue [ISV]

**xylotomous** /zie'lotəməs/ *adj*, of an insect, insect larva, etc capable of boring or cutting wood

**xyy** *adj*, of a man having twice the normal number of Y CHROMOSOMES (strands of gene-carrying material occurring in men but not women)

# Y

**y, Y** /wie/ *n, pl* **y's, ys, Y's, Ys** **1a** the 25th letter of the English alphabet **b** a graphic representation of or device for reproducing the letter *y* **c** a speech counterpart of printed or written *y* **2** one designated *y*, esp as the 25th in order or class or the 2nd in a series that includes *x, y,* and *z* **3** something shaped like the letter Y **4** *maths* – used in italic to represent a variable mathematical quantity

**¹-y** *also* **-ey** /-i/ *suffix* (*n, vb → adj*) **1a** covered with; full of ⟨*blossomy*⟩ ⟨*dirty*⟩ ⟨*hairy*⟩ **b** having the quality of ⟨*waxy*⟩ ⟨*icy*⟩ ⟨*cheery*⟩ **c** addicted to; enthusiastic about ⟨*horsy*⟩ **d** like; like that of ⟨*wintry*⟩ ⟨*stagy*⟩ **2** tending or inclined to ⟨*sleepy*⟩ ⟨*sticky*⟩ ⟨*curly*⟩ **3** slightly; rather; -ish ⟨*chilly*⟩ [ME, fr OE *-ig;* akin to OHG *-ig, -y,* L *-icus,* Gk *-ikos,* Skt *-ika*]

**²-y** *suffix* (→ *n*) **1** state, condition, or quality of ⟨*beggary*⟩ ⟨*courtesy*⟩ **2** whole body or group sharing (a specified class or state) ⟨*soldiery*⟩ [ME *-ie,* fr OF, fr L *-ia,* fr Gk *-ia, -eia*]

**³-y** *suffix* (*vb → n*) instance of (a specified action) ⟨*entreaty*⟩ ⟨*inquiry*⟩ [ME *-ie,* fr AF, fr L *-ium*]

**⁴-y, -ie** *suffix* (*n → n*) little; dear ⟨*doggy*⟩ ⟨*granny*⟩ – used esp as a pet name by or to children [ME]

**yabber** /'yabə/ *vi or n, Austr* (to) talk, jabber ⟨*all ~ and chatter ceased around the campfires –* Francis Birtles⟩ [prob modif (influenced by *jabber*) of *yabba,* native name in Australia]

**yabby, yabbie** /'yabi/ *n* a small Australian freshwater crayfish, often used as bait [native name in Australia]

**¹yacht** /yot/ *n* any of various relatively small sailing or powered vessels that characteristically have a sharp prow and graceful lines and are used for pleasure cruising or racing [obs D *jaght,* fr MLG *jacht,* short for *jachtschiff,* lit., hunting ship]

**²yacht** *vi* to race or cruise in a yacht – esp in *go yachting*

**yachting** /'yoting/ *n* the action or pastime of racing or cruising in a yacht

**yachtsman** /'yotsmən/ *n* a person who owns or sails a yacht

**yack** /yak/ *n or vi, slang* ²,³YAK

**yackety-yack** /,yakəti 'yak/ *n or vi, slang* ²,³YAK [redupl of *yak*]

**yaff** /yaf/ *vi, Scot* to bark like a dog; *also* to nag [imit]

**yaffle** /'yafl/ *n, Br dial* GREEN WOODPECKER [imit]

**YAG** /yag/ *n* a synthetic garnet of aluminium with the metallic chemical element yttrium, that is extremely hard, has a high REFRACTIVE INDEX (measure of the amount by which light is bent on entering a substance), and is used esp as a gemstone and in laser technology [yttrium *aluminium* garnet]

**Yagi** /'yahgi, 'yagi/, **Yagi aerial** *n* an aerial (eg for a television) that picks up RADIO WAVES from a very small number of directions only, and consists of an array of horizontal closely spaced parallel elements, the line of whose centres is the direction of maximum signal reception [Hidetsugu *Yagi* b 1886 Jap engineer]

**yah** /yah/, **yah-boo** *interj* – used to express disgust, defiance, or derision

**yahoo** /'yah-hooh, 'yay-/ *n, pl* **yahoos 1** *cap* a coarse or brutish person **2** an uncouth, rowdy, or degraded person [*Yahoo,* one of a race of human brutes in *Gulliver's Travels* by Jonathan Swift †1745 Ir satirist]

**Yahveh** /'yahvay/ *n* Yahweh

**Yahweh** /'yahway/ *n* the God of the Hebrews – compare TETRAGRAMMATON [Heb]

**Yahwism** /'yahwiz(ə)m, -viz(ə)m/ *n* the worship of Yahweh among the ancient Hebrews

**Yahwistic** /yah'wistik, -'vis-/ *adj* **1** characterized by the use of *Yahweh* as the name of God **2** of Yahwism

**¹yak** /yak/ *n, pl* **yaks,** *esp collectively* **yak** a large long-haired long-horned wild or domesticated ox (*Bos grunniens*) of Tibet and nearby mountainous parts of central Asia [Tibetan *gyak*]

**²yak** *also* **yack** /yak/ *n, slang* persistent or voluble talk [prob imit]

**³yak** *also* **yack** *vi* **-kk-** *slang* to talk persistently; chatter

**⁴yak** *n, NAm* **1** a laugh **2** a joke, gag [imit]

**yakka, yakker** /'yaka/ *vi or n, Austr informal* (to) work [native name in Australia]

**Yakut** /ya'koot/ *n* a TURKIC language of NE Siberia [Russ]

**yale** /yayl/ *n* a mythical horned and tusked mammal [ME *eale,* fr L, an Ethiopian animal]

**Yale** /yayl/ *trademark* – used for a type of lock used frequently on outside doors that has a revolving cylinder which is prevented from turning by a set of pins until the correct key is inserted

**y'all** /yawl/ *pron, chiefly S US* YOU-ALL

**yam** /yam/ *n* **1a** any of various tropical and subtropical plants (genus *Dioscorea* of the family Dioscoreaceae, the yam family) with inconspicuous greenish flowers, that are cultivated for their edible root **b** the edible starchy swollen root of a yam used as a staple food in tropical areas **2** *NAm* a moist-fleshed usu orange SWEET POTATO [earlier *iname,* fr Pg *inhame* & Sp *ñame,* of W African origin]

**yammer** /'yamə/ *vb, informal* *vi* **1** to wail, whimper **2** to complain, grumble ⟨*~ing at the umpire*⟩ **3** to talk volubly; clamour ⟨*caused the purists to ~ for censorship –* D W Maurer⟩ ~ *vt* to say in voluble complaint [alter. of ME *yomeren* to murmur, be sad, fr OE *gēomrian;* akin to OHG *jāmaron* to be sad] – **yammer** *n*

**yang** /yang/ *n* the masculine active principle in nature that in Chinese philosophy is expressed in positive forces and qualities (eg light, heat, and dryness) and that combines with the feminine principle (YIN) to produce the entire universe [Chin (Pek) *yáng* (*yang²*)]

**¹yank** /yangk/ *n, informal* a strong sudden pull; a jerk [origin unknown]

**²yank** *vb, informal* to pull or extract (something) with a quick vigorous movement ⟨*~ a tooth out*⟩ *synonyms* see ¹PULL

**Yank** *n, chiefly Br slang* a Yankee

**yankee** /'yangki/ *n* **1** *cap* a native or inhabitant of **a** *chiefly Br derog* the USA **b** *chiefly NAm* the N USA **c** *NAm* New England **2** a combination of bets (eg on horse races) covering four selections in different events in their 11 possible permutations of DOUBLES, TREBLES, and a fourfold ACCUMULATOR [perh fr the D names *Jantje* (dim. of *Jan* John) or *Jan Kees* (John Cornelius), allegedly used as nicknames by early Dutch settlers in America] – **Yankee** *adj*

**Yankee** – a communications code word for the letter *y*

**yanqui** /'yahngki/ *n, NAm* a citizen of the USA as distinguished from a Latin American [Sp, fr E *yankee*]

**¹yap** /yap/ *vi* **-pp-** **1** to bark snappishly; yelp **2** *informal* to talk in a shrill insistent querulous way [imit] – **yapper** *n*

**²yap** *n* **1a** a quick sharp bark; a yelp **b** *informal* shrill insistent talk; chatter **2** *slang* a mouth ⟨*shut your ~*⟩

**yapock, yapok** /yə'pok/ *n* a grey and white S American semi-aquatic opossum (*Chironectes minimus*) that has webbed hind feet, dense oily fur, and feeds on small fish, shrimps, etc [*Oyapock, Oyapok,* river in S America]

**yapp binding** /yap/ *n, Br* bookbinding (eg for Bibles) having rounded outer corners and limp overhanging leather covers [*Yapp* fl 1860 E bookseller]

**Yarborough** /'yahb(ə)rə/ *n* a hand in bridge or whist containing no card higher than a nine [2nd Earl of *Yarborough* †1897 E nobleman who allegedly bet 1000 to 1 against the dealing of such a hand]

**¹yard** /yahd/ *n* **1** any of various units of measure: eg **1a** a unit of length equal to 3 feet (about 0.9144 metre) **b** a unit of volume equal to 1 cubic yard (about 0.765 cubic metre) **2** a long spar tapered towards the ends to support and spread the head of a SQUARE SAIL, LATEEN (triangular) sail, or LUGSAIL (4-sided sail) **3 yards** *pl, yard informal* a great length or quantity ⟨*remembered ~s of facts and figures*⟩ [ME *yarde* twig, stick, rod, unit of length, fr OE *geard, gierd*; akin to OHG *gart* stick, L *hasta* spear]

²**yard** *n* **1a** a small usu walled and often paved area open to the sky and adjacent to a building; a courtyard **b** the grounds of a specified building or group of buildings – in combination ⟨*a farm*yard⟩ ⟨*a church*yard⟩ **2a** an enclosure for livestock (e g poultry) **b** an area with its buildings and facilities set aside for a usu specified business or activity – often in combination ⟨*a brick*yard⟩ **c** a system of tracks for the storage and maintenance of railway carriages and wagons and the making up of trains **3** *cap, Br* SCOTLAND YARD – *the* ⟨*Slipper of the* Yard⟩ **4** *NAm* a garden of a house [ME, fr OE *geard* enclosure, yard; akin to OHG *gart* enclosure, L *hortus* garden]

³**yard** *adj* **1** of or used in the yard surrounding a building ⟨*∼ broom*⟩ **2** of or used in a railway yard ⟨*∼ engine*⟩

⁴**yard** *vt* **1** to drive into or confine in a restricted area; herd, pen **2** to deliver to or store in a yard

¹**yardage** /'yahdij/ *n* (the charge made for) the use of a livestock enclosure at a railway station [²*yard*]

²**yardage** *n* **1a** an aggregate number of yards **b** the length, extent, or volume of something as measured in yards **2** PIECE GOODS (fabrics in standard lengths) [¹*yard*]

**yardarm** /'yahd,ahm/ *n* either end of the long spar (¹YARD 2) that supports sails suspended along their top edge

**yard goods** *n pl* PIECE GOODS (fabrics in standard lengths)

**yardman** /'yahdmən, -man/ *n* **1a** somebody who works in the yard of a commercial establishment; *esp* one who supervises the handling of building materials in a timber yard **b** a railwayman employed in yard service **2** *NAm* a man employed to do outdoor work (e g mowing lawns)

**yardmaster** /-,mahstə/ *n* the man in charge of operations in a railway yard

**yard of ale** *n* (the amount contained in) a slender horn-shaped glass 3 feet (about 1 metre) tall that holds 2 or 3 pints (1 or 2 litres)

**yardstick** /-,stik/ *n* **1** a graduated measuring stick 1 yard long **2** a standard basis of calculation or judgment; a criterion

**yare** /yeə/ *adj* **1** *esp of a ship* nimble, lively **2** *archaic* set for action; ready [ME, fr OE *gearu*; akin to OHG *garo* ready] – **yare, yarely** *adv, archaic*

**yarmulke, yarmelke, yarmulka** /'yahməlkə/ *n* a skullcap worn esp by Orthodox and Conservative Jewish males in the synagogue, and by very religious Jews at all times [Yiddish *yarmulke*, fr Ukrainian & Polish *jarmulka* skullcap]

¹**yarn** /yahn/ *n* **1a** a thread; *esp* a spun thread (e g of wool, cotton, or hemp) as prepared and used for weaving, knitting, and rope-making **b** a similar strand of metal, glass, asbestos, paper, or plastic **2** *informal* **2a** a narrative of adventures; *esp* a tall tale **b** a conversation, chat [ME, fr OE *gearn*; akin to OHG *garn* yarn, Gk *chordē* string, L *hernia* rupture] – **spin a yarn** to tell an esp exaggerated or untrue story

²**yarn** *vi, informal* **1** to tell a yarn **2** to chat garrulously

'**yarn-,dye** *vt* to dye before weaving or knitting

**yarrow** /'yaroh/ *n* (any of several plants related to) a widely naturalized strong-scented Eurasian plant (*Achillea millefolium*) of the daisy family with fine feathery leaves and small usu white flowers in dense heads [ME *yarowe*, fr OE *gearwe*; akin to OHG *garwa* yarrow]

**yashmak** /'yashmak/ *also* **yasmak** /∼, 'yas-/ *n* a veil worn by Muslim women round the upper and lower parts of the face so that only the eyes remain exposed [Turk *yaşmak*]

**yataghan** /'yatə,gan, 'yatəgən/ *n* a sword without a guard used formerly by Muslims and typically having a long blade with a single sharpened edge that curves concavely then convexly to the point [Turk *yatağan*]

**yatter** /'yatə/ *vi or n, informal* (to) chatter, prattle [perh blend of *yap* and *chatter*]

**yauld** /yawd, yahd, yahld/ *adj, chiefly Scot* vigorous, energetic [origin unknown]

¹**yaw** /yaw/ *n* **1** the action of yawing; *esp* a side-to-side movement (e g of an aircraft, ship, or missile) **2** the extent of the movement in yawing [origin unknown]

²**yaw** *vi* **1a** *of a ship* to deviate erratically from a course (e g when sailing with a following wind or sea) **b** *of an aircraft, spacecraft, or projectile* to deviate from a straight course by esp side-to-side movement, the nose going to the left while the tail goes to the right and vice versa **2** to become deflected; swerve

¹**yawl** /yawl/ *n* **1** a small boat carried on a ship **2** a FORE-AND-AFT rigged sailing vessel with two masts, the MIZZENMAST

being shorter than the foremast and positioned far aft [LG *jolle*]

²**yawl** *vi or n, dial Br* (to) howl, caterwaul [ME *yaulen*, prob of imit origin]

¹**yawn** /yawn/ *vi* **1** to open wide; gape ⟨*a ∼ing chasm*⟩ **2** to open the mouth wide and inhale usu in reaction to fatigue or boredom ∼ *vt* to utter with a yawn [ME *yenen, yanen*, fr OE *geonian, ginian*; akin to OHG *ginēn* to yawn, L *hiare*, Gk *chainein*] – **yawner** *n*, **yawningly** *adv*

²**yawn** *n* **1** a gap, cavity **2** a deep usu involuntary intake of breath through the wide open mouth **3** *slang* a boring thing or person ⟨*thought the cathedral a big ∼* – Kenneth Tynan⟩

**yawp, yaup** /yawp/ *vi, chiefly NAm informal* **1** to make a raucous noise; squawk **2** to clamour, complain [ME *yolpen*, prob of imit origin] – **yawp** *n*, **yawper** *n*

**yaws** /yawz/ *n taking sing or pl vb* an infectious tropical disease caused by a SPIROCHAETE (spirally twisted bacterium) (*Treponema pertenue*) and marked by skin sores that develop into ulcers [of Cariban origin; akin to Calinago *yáya* yaws]

**y-axis** /wie/ *n, maths* **1** the vertical axis that intersects the horizontal x-axis in a CARTESIAN COORDINATE system (system of axes with reference to which points can be placed on a graph) having two axes at right angles **2** the one of the three axes in a CARTESIAN COORDINATE system having three axes at right angles that is not designated as the x-axis or the z-axis

**Y chromosome** *n* a SEX CHROMOSOME (strand of gene-carrying material concerned with the inheritance of sex) that usu occurs paired with a dissimilar chromosome in one sex and does not occur in the other sex. In many animals, including human beings, the inheritance of a Y chromosome and an X CHROMOSOME determines that the sex of the animal is male.

**yclept, ycleped** /i'klept/ *past part of* CLEPE [ME, fr OE *geclipod*, pp of *clipian* to cry out, name]

,**y-co'ordinate** *n, maths* a COORDINATE that defines the position of a point (e g on a graph) and whose value is determined by measuring along the direction of a y-axis; *esp* ORDINATE (y-coordinate in a system of two axes)

¹**ye** /yee/ *pron, archaic or dial* the ones being addressed; you – used originally only as the subject of a sentence, not the object; compare THOU, YOU [ME, fr OE *gē*; akin to OHG *ir* you – more at YOU]

²**ye** /dhee, yee/ *definite article, archaic* the ⟨Ye Old Gift Shoppe⟩ [alter. of OE *þe* the; fr the use by early printers of the letter *y* to represent *þ* (*th*) of manuscripts]

¹**yea** /yay/ *adv* **1** more than this; NAY 1 ⟨*∼, even unto the second and third generation*⟩ **2** *archaic* yes [ME *ye, ya*, fr OE *gēa*; akin to OHG *jā* yes]

²**yea** *n* **1** affirmation, assent **2** *chiefly NAm* (a person casting) an affirmative vote

**yeah** /yeə/ *adv* yes – used in writing to represent a casual pronunciation [by alter.]

**yean** /yeen/ *vi, of a sheep or goat* to bring forth young [ME *yenen*, fr (assumed) OE *geēanian*, fr OE *ge-*, perfective prefix + *ēanian* to yean; akin to L *agnus* lamb, Gk *amnos*]

**yeanling** /'yeenling/ *n* a lamb, kid

**year** /yiə/ *n* **1** the period of about 365¼ days required for one revolution of the earth round the sun **2a** a cycle in the GREGORIAN CALENDAR (modern Western calendar) of 365 or 366 days divided into 12 months beginning with January and ending with December **b** a period of time equal to one year of the GREGORIAN CALENDAR but beginning at a different time **3** a CALENDAR YEAR, specified usu by a number **4** *pl* a long time ⟨*∼s ago*⟩ **5** *pl* age ⟨*a man in ∼s had a child in understanding*⟩; *also* old age ⟨*beginning to show his ∼s*⟩ **6** a period of time (e g an ACADEMIC YEAR) other than a CALENDAR YEAR **7** *taking sing or pl vb* the body of students who enter school, university, etc in one ACADEMIC YEAR, considered as a group throughout the time that they are taught in that institution [ME *yere*, fr OE *gēar*; akin to OHG *jār* year, Gk *hōros* year, *hōra* season, hour, L *ire* to go – more at ISSUE] – **since the year dot** since a very long time ago – **year in, year out** for an indefinite or seemingly endless number of years

**year after year** *adv* **1** for an indefinite or seemingly endless number of years **2** regularly every year

**yearbook** /-,book/ *n* **1** a book published yearly as a report or summary of statistics or facts **2** a school publication in America that is compiled usu by those in their final year and that serves as a record of the year's activities

¹,**year-'end** *n* the end of the year, esp the financial year

**²year-end** *adj* made at the year-end ⟨a ~ report⟩; occurring or existing at the year-end ⟨a ~ upsurge of prices⟩

**yearling** /'yiəling/ *n* one who or that which is a year old: eg **a** an animal one year old or in its second year **b** a racehorse between January 1st of the year following its birth and the next January 1st – **yearling** *adj*

**yearling bond** *n* a BOND (certificate of debt repayable at a fixed time) with a life of one year, that is usu issued in parcels of £100000 or more, esp by local authorities

**yearlong** /'yiə,long/ *adj* lasting through a year

**¹yearly** /'yiəli/ *adj* **1** payable or reckoned by the year **2** done, occurring, or published once every year; annual

**²yearly** *adv* every year; once a year; by the year

**³yearly** *n* a yearly publication

**Yearly Meeting** *n* an organization uniting several QUARTERLY MEETINGS of the Quakers

**yearn** /yuhn/ *vi* **1** to long persistently, wistfully, or sadly ⟨~ for home⟩ ⟨~ to travel⟩ **2** to feel tenderness or compassion ⟨heart ~ed towards the child⟩ [ME yernen, fr OE giernan; akin to OHG gerōn to desire, L hortari to urge, encourage, Gk chairein to rejoice] – **yearningly** *adv*, **yearner** *n*

**yearning** /'yuhning/ *n* a tender or urgent longing

**year of grace** *n* a year of the Christian era ⟨the ~ 1984⟩

**,year-'round** *adj* effective, employed, or operating for the full year; not seasonal ⟨a ~ resort⟩

**year's mind** *n* an esp Roman Catholic REQUIEM (service for the dead) for a person a year after his/her death

**yea-sayer** /'yay,say·ə/ *n*, *informal* **1** somebody whose attitude is that of confident affirmation **2** a yes-man – **yea-saying** *adj*

**¹yeast** /yeest/ *n* **1a** a yellowish surface froth or sediment that consists largely of cells of a fungus (family Saccharomycetaceae), occurs esp in sweet liquids (eg fruit juices) in which it promotes alcoholic fermentation, and is used esp in the making of alcoholic drinks and as a raising agent in baking **b(1)** a commercial product that is used for fermentation of alcohol or for raising bread and that contains yeast plants in a moist or dry medium **b(2)** a medicinal preparation containing yeast, usu in the form of tablets, used to treat VITAMIN B deficiency **c(1)** a minute fungus (esp Saccharomyces cerevisiae) that is present and functionally active in yeast, usu has little or no MYCELIUM (rootlike network of filaments) and reproduces by budding **c(2)** any of various similar fungi (esp orders Endomycetales and Moniliales) **2** something that causes ferment or activity ⟨the ~ of revolution⟩ [ME yest, fr OE gist; akin to MHG jest foam, Gk zein to boil]

**²yeast** *vi* to ferment, froth

**yeasty** /'yeesti/ *adj* **1** of or resembling yeast **2a** churning with growth and change; turbulent **b** exuberant **c** trivial, frivolous – **yeastily** *adv*, **yeastiness** *n*

**Yeatsian** /'yaytsi·ən/ *adj* relating to or suggestive of the poet W B Yeats or his writing, esp in its visionary or mythic quality [W B Yeats †1939 Ir poet]

**yegg** /yeg, yayg/ *n*, *chiefly NAm slang* a safecracker, burglar [origin unknown]

**¹yell** /yel/ *vi* **1** to utter a sharp loud cry, scream, or shout ⟨~ for help⟩ ⟨~ with laughter⟩ **2** to give an American college yell ~ *vt* to utter or declare (as if) with a scream; shout ⟨~ curses⟩ [ME yellen, fr OE giellan; akin to OHG gellan to yell, OE galan to sing] – **yeller** *n*

**²yell** *n* **1** a scream, shout **2** *NAm* a usu rhythmic shout of set words used to encourage sports teams

**¹yellow** /'yeloh/ *adj* **1a** of the colour yellow **b** of a greyish shade of yellow through age, disease (eg jaundice), or discoloration; sallow **c** having a yellow or light brown complexion or skin **2** featuring sensational or scandalous items or ordinary news sensationally distorted ⟨~ journalism⟩ ⟨the ~ press⟩ **3** *informal* dishonourable, cowardly ⟨too ~ to fight⟩ [ME yelwe, yelow, fr OE geolu; akin to OHG gelo yellow, L helvus light bay, Gk chlōros greenish yellow, Skt hari yellowish] – **yellowish, yellowy** *adj*

**²yellow** *vb* to make or become yellow ⟨~ed by time⟩

**³yellow** *n* **1a** a colour resembling that of ripe lemons and lying between green and orange in the spectrum **b** a pigment or dye that colours yellow **2** something yellow: eg **2a** somebody with yellow or light brown skin **b** the yolk of an egg **c** a yellow ball (eg in snooker) **3** *pl* **3a** jaundice **b** a disease of dogs that is caused by a virus (Leptospira icterohaemorrhagiae), is characterized by jaundice and kidney failure, and can be transmitted to human beings **4** *pl but taking sing vb* any of several plant

diseases caused esp by viruses and marked by yellowing of the leaves and stunting of growth

**yellowback** /'yeloh,bak/ *n* a cheap usu sensational novel popular in the 19th century

**'yellow-,belly** *n*, *informal* a coward

**yellow bile** *n* the one of the four HUMOURS (body fluids believed to determine a person's disposition) in medieval physiology that was believed to be secreted by the liver and to cause bad temper – called also CHOLER

**yellow birch** *n* (the strong hard usu pale wood of) a large birch (Betula alleghaniensis) of NE America with thin shiny yellowish-grey bark

**yellowbird** /'yeloh,buhd/ *n* any of various American goldfinches

**yellow bunting** *n* a yellowhammer

**yellow card** *n* a yellow-coloured card held up by a soccer referee to indicate that a player is having his name taken for committing an offence – not used in English domestic soccer since 1981; compare RED CARD

**yellow fever** *n* an acute often fatal infectious disease of warm regions marked by sudden onset, fever, jaundice, and often bleeding and caused by a virus transmitted by a mosquito

**yellow-fever mosquito** *n* a small dark-coloured mosquito (Aëdes aegypti) that is the usual carrier of YELLOW FEVER

**yellowfin tuna, yellowfin** /'yeloh,fin/ *n* a rather small widely distributed tuna (Thunnus albacares) with yellow-tipped fins and delicate light flesh

**yellow flag** *n* a yellow Eurasian iris (Iris pseudacorus) that grows in damp places

**yellow-green alga** *n* any of a division (Chrysophyta) of algae with the chlorophyll masked by brown or yellow pigment

**yellowhammer** /-,hamə/ *n* a common Eurasian BUNTING (finchlike bird) (Emberiza citrinella) the male of which is largely yellow with a reddish-brown back [alter. of earlier yelambre, fr (assumed) ME yelwambre, fr ME yelwe yellow + (assumed) ME ambre yellowhammer, fr OE amore; akin to OHG amaro yellowhammer, amari emmer]

**yellow jack** *n* **1** YELLOW FEVER **2** a flag raised on ships in quarantine

**yellow jacket** *n* **1** a sedative or hypnotic drug; esp THIOPENTONE **2** *NAm* any of various yellow-marked social wasps (family Vespidae) that commonly nest in the ground

**yellow jasmine** *n* a twining evergreen shrub (Gelsemium sempervirens of the family Loganiaceae) of the southern USA with fragrant yellow flowers

**yellow metal** *n* MUNTZ METAL (brass)

**yellow ochre** *n* **1** an orange-yellow colour **2** a mixture of LIMONITE (iron-containing mineral) usu with clay and silica, used as a pigment – **yellow ochre** *adj*

**Yellow Pages** *n pl* the section of a telephone directory that lists organizations and services alphabetically within sections classified according to the nature of their business

**yellow peril** *n*, *often cap Y&P* a danger to Western civilization held to arise from expansion of the power and influence of Oriental peoples

**yellow pimpernel** *n* a common European pimpernel (Lysimachia nemorum) of the primrose family with creeping stems and small bright yellow flowers

**yellow pine** *n* (the yellowish wood of) any of several N American pines

**yellow poplar** *n* (the pale soft wood of) the American TULIP TREE

**yellow spot** *n* MACULA LUTEA (area of the retina in the eye)

**yellowtail** /'yeloh,tayl/ *n* **1** yellowtail, yellowtail tuna a large fish (Ocyurus chrysurus) hunted in western US coastal waters **2** any of various yellow-tailed fish of various parts of the world

**yellow wagtail** *n* a wagtail (Motacilla flava) with wholly bright yellow underparts and dull olive back and wings

**yellowwood** /'yeloh,wood/ *n* **1** any of various trees having yellowish wood or yielding a yellow extract: eg **1a** a southern US tree (Cladrastis lutea) of the pea family having showy white fragrant flowers and yielding a yellow dye **b** OSAGE ORANGE (ornamental tree of the fig family) **c** SMOKE TREE (small sumach tree) **2** the wood of a yellowwood tree

**yelp** /yelp/ *vi* to utter a sharp quick shrill cry ⟨dogs ~⟩ ~ *vt* to utter with a yelp [ME yelpen to boast, cry out, fr OE gielpan to boast, exult; akin to OHG gelph outcry, Lith gulbinti to praise] – **yelp** *n*, **yelper** *n*

**¹yen** /yen/ *n*, *pl* yen – see MONEY table [Jap en]

**²yen** *n*, *informal* a strong desire or propensity; a longing [obs E slang *yen-yen* craving for opium, fr Chin (Cant) *in-yăn*, fr *in* opium + *yăn* craving]

**³yen** *vi* **-nn-** *informal* to long, yearn

**yeoman** /'yohmən/ *n, pl* **yeomen 1a yeoman of the guard, yeoman warder, yeoman** a member of a military corps attached to the British Royal Household who serve as ceremonial attendants of the sovereign and as warders of the Tower of London – called also BEEFEATER **b** a naval PETTY OFFICER who **(1)** carries out visual signalling in the British navy **(2)** performs clerical duties in the US navy **2** a small farmer who cultivates his own land; *specif* one formerly belonging to a class of English freeholders below the gentry [ME *yoman*, prob contr of *yong man* young man]

**yeomanly** /-li/ *adj* **1** (having the rank) of a yeoman **2** becoming or suitable to a yeoman; sturdy, loyal – **yeomanly** *adv*

**yeomanry** /-ri/ *n taking sing or pl vb* **1** the body of small landed proprietors **2** a British volunteer cavalry force created from yeomen in 1761 as a home defence force and reorganized in 1907 as part of the territorial force

**yeoman's service, yeoman service** *n* great and loyal service, assistance, or support

**yep** /yep/ *adv* yes – used in writing to represent a casual or American pronunciation [by alter.]

**yer** /yə/ *adj* your – used in writing to represent a nonstandard pronunciation [by alter.]

**-yer** /-yə/ – see -ER

**yerba maté** /,yuhbə 'mahtay, ,yeəbə/ *n* MATÉ (drink) [AmerSp *yerba mate*, fr *yerba* herb, plant + *mate* maté]

**yerk** /yuhk/ *n, Scot* a lashing out; a kick [E dial. *yerk* to bind tightly, strike, lash, fr ME *yerken* (cf JERK)]

**¹yes** /yes/ *adv* **1** – used in answers expressing affirmation, agreement, or willingness; contrasted with *no* ⟨*are you ready? Yes, I am*⟩ **2** – used in answers correcting or contradicting a negative assertion or direction ⟨*don't say that! Yes, I will*⟩ **3** YEA 1 ⟨*boys, ∼, and girls too*⟩ **4** – used to indicate uncertainty, polite interest, or attentiveness ⟨Yes? *What do you want?*⟩ [ME, fr OE *gēse*, prob fr *gēa* yea + *sī*, 3 sing. imper of *bēon* to be]

**²yes** *n* an affirmative reply or vote; a yea, aye

**yeshiva, yeshivah** /yə'sheevə/ *n, pl* **yeshivas, yeshivoth** /-,voht, -vohth/ **1** a school for TALMUDIC (Jewish scripture) study **2** an orthodox Jewish college for the training of rabbis **3** a Jewish day school providing religious and nonreligious instruction [LHeb *yĕshībhāh*]

**'yes-,man** *n, informal* somebody who endorses or supports everything that is said to him/her, esp by a superior; a sycophant

**yester** /'yestə/ *adj, archaic* of yesterday

**¹yesterday** /'yestəday, -di/ *adv* **1** on the day before today ⟨*saw him ∼*⟩ **2** at a recent time; only a short time ago ⟨*not born ∼*⟩ [ME *yisterday*, fr OE *giestran dæg*, fr *giestran* yesterday (akin to OHG *gestaron* yesterday, L *heri*, Gk *chthes*) + *dæg* day] – **yesterday** *adj*

**²yesterday** *n* **1** the day before today ⟨*∼'s meeting*⟩ ⟨*∼ morning*⟩ **2** recent time; time not long past ⟨*the fashions of ∼*⟩ **3 yesterdays** *pl,* **yesterday** past time

**yesteryear** /'yestə,yiə/ *n, chiefly poetic* **1** last year **2** the recent past [*yester*day + *year* – **yesteryear** *adv*]

**¹yet** /yet/ *adv* **1a** again, IN ADDITION ⟨*gives ∼ another reason*⟩ **b** EVEN 2b ⟨*a ∼ higher speed*⟩ **2a** up to this or that time; so FAR – not in affirmative statements ⟨*hasn't had breakfast ∼*⟩ ⟨*is it time to go ∼?*⟩ ⟨*John can't crawl ∼, but Ann can already walk*⟩ **b** STILL 1 ⟨*is ∼ unmarried*⟩ ⟨*have ∼ to learn the truth*⟩ **c** at some future time and despite present appearances ⟨*we may win ∼*⟩ **3** nevertheless, however ⟨*strange and ∼ true*⟩ [ME, fr OE *gīet;* akin to OFris *ieta* yet] – **yet again** still one more time
*usage* When yet means "so far", it is not used with the simple past tense except in informal American English ⟨*did you eat yet?*⟩.

**²yet** *conj* but nevertheless; but

**yeti** /'yeti/ *n* ABOMINABLE SNOWMAN [Tibetan]

**yett** /yet/ *n, Scot* a door, gate [ME, fr OE *geat* – more at GATE]

**yew** /yooh/ *n* **1a** any of a genus (*Taxus* of the family Taxaceae, the yew family) of trees and shrubs that have stiff needle-shaped evergreen leaves and that usu have separate male and female plants, the male bearing much smaller cones than those of the true conifers and the female producing usu solitary seeds having a red fleshy cup-shaped outer covering (ARIL) when mature; *esp* a long-lived Eurasian tree (*Taxus baccata*) **b** the wood of a yew **2** *archaic* an archery bow made of yew [ME *ew*, fr OE *īw;* akin to OHG *īwa* yew, OIr *ēo*]

**Y-fronts** /wie/ *n pl* men's closely fitting underpants in which the front seams take the form of an inverted Y

**YHWH** *n* YAHWEH (Hebrew name for God) – compare TETRAGRAMMATON

**yid** /yid/ *n, often cap, chiefly derog* a Jew [Yiddish, fr MHG *Jude, Jüde,* fr OHG *Judo, Judeo,* fr L *Judaeus* – more at JEW]

**Yiddish** /'yidish/ *n* a HIGH GERMAN language with some Hebrew and Slavonic elements that is usu written in Hebrew characters and is spoken by Jews chiefly in or from E Europe [Yiddish *yidish,* short for *yidish daytsh,* lit., Jewish German] – **Yiddish** *adj*

**Yiddisher** /'yidishə/ *adj* **1** in or of Yiddish **2** Jewish [Yiddish *yidisher*]

**¹yield** /yeeld/ *vt* **1** to give or render as fitting, rightfully owed, or required ⟨*∼ed allegiance to his master*⟩ **2** to give up possession of on claim or demand: e g **2a** to give up (e g one's breath) and so die **b** to surrender or relinquish to the physical control of another; hand over possession of **c** to surrender or submit (oneself) to another **d** to give (oneself) up to an inclination, temptation, or habit **e** to relinquish one's possession of (e g a position of advantage or point of superiority) ⟨*∼ precedence*⟩ **3a** to bear or bring forth as a natural product, esp as a result of cultivation ⟨*the tree always ∼s good fruit*⟩ **b** to give as a return or in result of expended effort ⟨*properly handled this soil should ∼ good crops*⟩ **c(1)** to produce as a return from an expenditure or investment; give as profit or interest ⟨*a bond that ∼s 12 per cent*⟩ **c(2)** to produce as revenue; BRING IN ⟨*the tax is expected to ∼ millions*⟩ **4** *archaic* to recompense, reward ∼ *vi* **1** to be fruitful or productive; bear, produce **2** to give up and cease resistance or contention; submit, succumb **3** to give way to pressure or influence; submit to urging, persuasion, or entreaty **4** to give way under physical force (e g bending, stretching, or breaking) **5a** to give place or precedence; acknowledge the superiority of someone else **b** to be inferior ⟨*our beer ∼s to none*⟩ **c** to give way to or be succeeded by somebody or something else **6** to give way to another speaker in a parliament – see also **yield up the** GHOST [ME *yielden,* fr OE *gieldan;* akin to OHG *geltan* to pay] – **yielder** *n*

*synonyms* Yield, submit, capitulate, succumb, relent, defer, and bow all mean that one gives way before a superior force. Yield is the most general word, and implies that one gives way to force or entreaty or in acknowledgment of the rightness of an argument. Submit suggests that one obeys the will of another out of necessity and after previous conflict. Capitulate stresses the fact of coming to terms with an adversary, not necessarily after active opposition and often in the face of an irresistible opposing force. Succumb attributes helplessness to the one that gives way ⟨*the best of constitutions will not prevent ambitious politicians from succumbing ... to the temptations of power* – Aldous Huxley⟩, and often implies a disastrous outcome ⟨*true passion must be crushed before it will succumb* – George Meredith⟩. Relent suggests a yielding through pity, by one who holds the upper hand ⟨*can you hear a good man groan, and not relent?* – Shak⟩. Defer implies a voluntary yielding out of respect or affection ⟨*she deferred in all things to her uncle* – Upton Sinclair⟩. Bow suggests that one is obliged to give way, out of respectful courtesy ⟨*I bow to your superior knowledge*⟩. *antonyms* resist, stand firm

**²yield** *n* **1** something yielded; a product; *esp* the amount or quantity produced ⟨*∼ of wheat per acre*⟩ **2** the capacity of yielding produce ⟨*high ∼ strain of wheat*⟩

**yielding** /'yeelding/ *adj* **1** lacking rigidity or stiffness; flexible **2** disposed to submit or comply

**¹yin** /yin/ *n* the feminine passive principle in nature that in Chinese philosophy is expressed in qualities of darkness, cold, wetness, etc and that combines and interacts with YANG (masculine principle) to produce the entire universe [Chin (Pek) *yīn (yin¹)*]

**²yin** *n, adj, or pron, Scot* one

**Yinglish** /'ying-glish/ *n, informal* English with a considerable number of borrowings from Yiddish [blend of *Yiddish* and *English*]

**y-'intercept** *n, maths* the Y-COORDINATE of a point (e g on a graph) where a line, curve, or surface intersects the Y-AXIS (fixed reference line)

**yip** /yip/ *vi* **-pp-** *chiefly NAm* **1** to bark sharply, quickly, and often continuously **2** to utter a short sharp cry [imit] – **yip** *n*

**yippee** /yi'pee/ *interj* – used to express exuberant delight or triumph

**yippie, yippy** /'yipi/ *n* a politically active hippie, esp in the USA in the 1960s [blend of *Y*outh *I*nternational *P*arty and *hippie*]

**-yl** /-il, iel/ *comb form* (→ *n*) chemical radical ⟨*ethyl*⟩ ⟨*carbonyl*⟩ ⟨*phenyl*⟩ [Gk *hylē* matter, material, lit., wood]

**ylang-ylang, ilang-ilang** /ˌeelang 'eelang/ *n* (a perfume distilled from the fragrant yellow flowers of) a Malayan tree (*Cananga odorata*) of the custard-apple family [Tagalog]

**yob** /yob/ *n, Br slang* a loutish youth; *esp* a hooligan [back slang for *boy*]

**yobbo** /'yoboh/ *n, pl* **yobbos** *Br slang* a yob [*yob* + [1]*-o*]

**yod** /yawd, yood/ *n* the 10th letter of the Hebrew alphabet [Heb *yōdh*]

**[1]yodel** /'yohdl/ *vb* **-ll-** (*NAm* **-l-, -ll-**) to sing (a tune) by suddenly changing from a natural voice to an unnaturally high voice (FALSETTO) and back; *also* to shout or call (a word, phrase, etc) in a similar manner [Ger *jodeln*, of imit origin] – **yodeller** *n*

**[2]yodel** *n* a song or refrain sung by yodelling; *also* a yodelled shout or cry

**yog** /yog/ *n, Cockney* a non-Jew, Gentile [back slang for *goy*]

**yoga** /'yohgə/ *n* **1** *cap* a Hindu philosophy teaching the suppression of all activity of body, mind, and will in order that the self may recognize its distinction from them and attain liberation and union with God **2** a system of exercises for attaining bodily or mental control and well-being [Skt, lit., yoking, fr *yunakti* he yokes; akin to L *jungere* to join – more at YOKE] – **yogic** *adj, often cap*

**yogh** /yohk, yohg, yoh·kh/ *n* a letter ȝ used in Old English for the sound of Modern English *g* and in Middle English chiefly for the sound of Modern English *y* (eg in *year*) and for a sound produced by forcing air past the SOFT PALATE that is not used in Modern English but traces of which survive in the spellings *w* (eg in *own*) and *gh* (eg in *bough*) [ME *yogh*, ȝogh]

**yoghourt, yoghurt, yogurt** /'yogət/ *n* a fermented slightly acid semisolid food made of milk to which cultures of two bacteria (*Lactobacillus bulgaricus* and *Streptococcus thermophilus*) have been added; *also* sweetened yoghourt to which flavouring or colouring have been added that is sold commercially [Turk *yoğurt*]

**yogi** /'yohgi/ *n* **1** somebody who practises yoga **2** *cap* an adherent of Yoga philosophy [Skt *yogin*, fr *yoga*]

**yogin** /'yohgin/ *n* a yogi

**yohimbine** /yoh'himbeen, -bin/ *n* a drug, $C_{21}H_{26}N_2O_3$, obtained from an African tree and used as a tranquillizer and also as an aphrodisiac [ISV, fr *yohimbé, yohimbi* (the tree whose bark yields the drug), of Bantu origin]

**yoicks** /yoyks/ *interj, archaic* – used as a cry of encouragement to foxhounds on the hunting field

**[1]yoke** /yohk/ *n* **1a** a bar or frame by which two draught animals (eg oxen) are joined at the heads or necks for working together **b** an arched device formerly laid on the neck of a defeated person to symbolize his/her defeat, esp in a triumphal procession **c** a frame fitted to somebody's shoulders to carry a load (eg two buckets) in two equal weights **d** a bar by which the end of the pole of a wagon or carriage is suspended from the collars of the harness **e(1)** a crosspiece on the head of a boat's rudder to which steering lines are attached **e(2)** an aircraft lever operating the ELEVATORS (part of the tailfin) and AILERONS (wing flaps) **f** a frame from which a bell is hung **g** a piece (eg a clamp) that embraces two parts to hold or unite them in position **2** *taking sing or pl vb* two animals yoked or worked together **3a** an oppressive force ⟨*under the ~ of tyranny*⟩ **b** a tie, link; *esp* marriage **4** a fitted or shaped piece at the top of a skirt or across the shoulder or chest of a dress, blouse, etc, from which the rest of the garment hangs in gathers or pleats △ yolk [ME *yok*, fr OE *geoc*; akin to OHG *joh* yoke, L *jugum*, Gk *zygon*, L *jungere* to join]

**[2]yoke** *vt* **1a** to couple in or with a yoke **b** to attach a draught animal to; *also* to attach (a draught animal) to something **2** to join (as if) by a yoke ~ *vi* to become linked or joined

**yoke to** *vt, Scot* to tackle (a job) – usu + *it* ⟨*they* yoked to it *with a will*⟩

**yokefellow** /'yohkˌfeloh/ *n, archaic* a close companion; a mate

**yokel** /'yohkl/ *n* a naive or gullible rustic; a country bumpkin [perh fr E dial. *yokel* green woodpecker, of imit origin]

**yolk,** *NAm also* **yoke** /yohk/ *n* **1a** the round yellow mass of stored food that forms the inner portion of the egg of a bird or reptile, is rich in protein and fat, and is surrounded by the white **b** material stored in an OVUM (egg cell) that supplies food to the developing embryo and consists chiefly of proteins and certain fat-containing chemical compounds (LECITHIN and CHOLESTEROL) **2** oily material in unprocessed sheep wool consisting of wool fat, SUINT (dried sweat), and debris [ME *yolke*, fr OE *geoloca*, fr *geolu* yellow – more at YELLOW] – **yolked, yolky** *adj*

**yolk sac** *n* a membranous sac attached to an embryo and containing yolk which passes to the intestine through the YOLK STALK and serves as food for the developing embryo of some animals (eg fishes, amphibians, and reptiles) but is much reduced and nonfunctional in mammals with placentas

**yolk stalk** *n* the narrow tubular stalk connecting the YOLK SAC with the embryo

**Yom Kippur** /ˌyom ki'pooə, 'kipə/ *n* a Jewish holiday observed with fasting and prayer on the 10th day of TISHRI (Jewish month) in accordance with the rites described in Leviticus 16 – called also DAY OF ATONEMENT [Heb *yōm kippūr*, fr *yōm* day + *kippūr* atonement]

**yomp** /yomp/ *vi, Br slang* to march laboriously, esp while carrying heavy baggage [Br military slang, of unknown origin]

**[1]yon** /yon/ *adj, archaic or dial* yonder [ME, fr OE *geon*; akin to OHG *ienēr*, adj, that, Gk *enē* day after tomorrow]

**[2]yon** *pron, pl* **yon** *dial* the one yonder

**yond** /yond/ *adv, archaic or dial* yonder [ME, fr OE *geond*; akin to OE *geon*]

**[1]yonder** /'yondə/ *adv* at, in, or to that more or less distant place usu within sight; over there [ME, fr *yond* + *-er* (as in *hither*)]

**[2]yonder** *adj* **1** more distant; far **2** situated over there

**yoni** /'yohni/ *n* a stylized representation of the female genitals used in Hindu temples to symbolize the feminine principle in Hindu philosophy – compare LINGA [Skt, vulva]

**yonks** /yongks/ *n, Br informal* a long time; ages [origin unknown]

**[1]yoo-,hoo** *interj* – used to attract attention or as a call to people

**[2]yoo-hoo** *vi* to call "yoo-hoo!"

**yore** /yaw/ *n* time (long) past – usu in *of yore* [ME, fr *yore*, adv, long ago, fr OE *geāra*, fr *gēar* year]

**york** /yawk/ *vt* to bowl (a batsman) out with a yorker [back-formation fr *yorker*]

**yorker** /'yawkə/ *n* a ball bowled in cricket that is aimed to bounce on the POPPING CREASE (line on which batsman stands) and so pass under the bat [prob fr *Yorkshire*, where it was allegedly introduced]

**Yorkist** /'yawkist/ *n or adj* (of an adherent of) the English royal house of York that ruled from 1461 to 1485 [Edward, Duke of *York* (Edward IV of England) †1483]

**Yorkshire** /'yawkshiə, -shə/ *n* a white pig of any of several breeds or strains originating in Yorkshire [*Yorkshire*, county in N England]

**Yorkshire fog** *n* a grass (*Holcus lanatus*) with a velvety stem and feathery pinkish-green flowers which is widespread in temperate regions [[1]*fog*]

**Yorkshireman** /'yorkshiəmən, -shə-/, *fem* **Yorkshirewoman** *n* a native of Yorkshire

**Yorkshire pudding** *n* a savoury baked pudding made from a batter and usu served before or with roast beef

**Yorkshire terrier** *n* a very small terrier with long straight silky hair mostly bluish-grey but tan on the head and chest

**Yoruba** /'yoroobə/ *n, pl* **Yorubas,** *esp collectively* **Yoruba 1** a member of a Negro people of the eastern Guinea coast mainly between Dahomey and the lower Niger **2** the KWA language of the Yoruba

**you** /yoo; *strong* yooh/ *pron, pl* **you 1** the one being addressed – used as subject or object ⟨*~ must sit in a row*⟩ ⟨*~ are my friend*⟩ ⟨*can I pour ~ a cup of tea?*⟩; sometimes used in addressing people with exclamations ⟨*~ angel*⟩ ⟨*~ scoundrels*⟩ **2** a person, one ⟨*funny, when ~ come to think of it*⟩ [ME, fr OE *ēow*, dat & accus of *gē* you; akin to OHG *iu*, dat of *ir* you, Skt *yūyam* you] – **you get** there is or are ⟨*within the Chinese language* you get *quite different sounds* – SEU S⟩

*usage* **1** The use of **you** for "one" has been established in English for a long time ⟨**you** *can talk a mob into anything* – John Ruskin⟩, but one may prefer to use **one** in formal writing, as in the present sentence. In any case, either **you** or **one** should be used consistently throughout the same passage. **2** Since **you** may be either subject or object, while **I** is only a subject and **me** only an object ⟨**you** *love* **me** *and* **I** *love* **you**⟩ one must be extra careful, when combining them, to use **you** *and* **I** to mean "we" ⟨**you** *and* **I** *are young*⟩ and **you** *and* **me** to mean "us" ⟨*they've invited* **you** *and* **me**⟩ ⟨*a present for* **you** *and* **me**⟩.

**you-'all** *pron, chiefly S US* you – usu used in addressing two or more people or sometimes one person as representing also another or others

**you'd** /yoohd/ you had; you would

**,you-know-'what** *n, chiefly euph* something understood but unspecified

**,you-know-'where** *n, chiefly euph* a place understood but unspecified

**,you-know-'who** *n, chiefly euph* a person understood but unspecified

**you'll** /yoohl/ you will; you shall

**¹young** /yung/ *adj* **younger** /'yung·gə/; **youngest** /'yung·gist/ **1a** in the first or an early stage of life, growth, or development **b** JUNIOR 1 **c** of an early or tender age for eating or drinking ⟨*fresh* ~ *lamb*⟩ **2** having little experience **3a** recently come into being; new ⟨*a* ~ *industry*⟩ ⟨*the night is* ~⟩ **b** *of a land surface or feature* YOUTHFUL 3 **4** of or having the characteristics (eg vigour or gaiety) of young people ⟨*a* ~ *style of dress*⟩ ⟨*a* ~ *hat*⟩ **5** *cap* representing a new or rejuvenated esp political group or movement **6** tending towards the size of ⟨*the chapel was a* ~ *cathedral*⟩ [ME *yong*, fr OE *geong*; akin to OHG *jung* young, L *juvenis*] – **youngish** *adj*, **youngness** *n*

**synonyms** Young, youthful, juvenile, immature, adolescent, and teenage all refer to people who are not old. Young is the widest in range, extending from birth ⟨*the care of young babies*⟩ to middle age ⟨*she's very young to be a grandma*⟩. Youthful is used particularly of the good qualities typical *of youth* ⟨*preserve his* youthful *vitality after retirement*⟩. Juvenile, immature, and particularly **puerile** imply the less desirable mental and physical qualities of youth ⟨**juvenile**/ **puerile** *humour*⟩ ⟨*still too* immature *for marriage*⟩. Adolescent refers to the period between childhood and adulthood, stressing the difficulties of growing up ⟨*spotty* adolescent *complexion*⟩ while teenage refers to that same period from a more positive point of view, emphasizing particularly the interests and tastes of young people ⟨*teenage fashions*⟩. antonyms old, adult, mature

**²young** *n, pl* young **1a** *pl* young people; youth **b** immature offspring, esp of lower animals **2** a single recently born or hatched animal – **with young** *of a female animal* pregnant

**youngberry** /'yungb(ə)ri/ *n* (the large sweet reddish-black fruit of) a trailing plant that is a cross between a blackberry and a DEWBERRY and is grown in W and S USA [B M *Young* fl 1900 US fruit-grower]

**younger** /'yung·gə/ *adj* inferior in age; junior – used before or after somebody's name to distinguish him/her from his/her father or mother ⟨*William Pitt the* Younger⟩

**youngest** /'yung·gist/ *n, pl* youngest one who or that which is least old; *esp* the youngest child or member of a family

**young lady** *n* somebody's girlfriend; a sweetheart – no longer in vogue

**youngling** /'yungling/ *n* a young person or animal – **youngling** *adj*

**young man** *n* somebody's boyfriend; a sweetheart – no longer in vogue

**young person** *n* somebody between the ages of 14 and 17 – used in English law; compare CHILD

**youngster** /'yungstə/ *n* **1a** a young person **b** a child, baby **2** a young mammal, bird, or plant, esp of a domesticated or cultivated breed or type

**Young Turk** /tuhk/ *n* a member of a political party who agitates for radical change [*Young Turks,* an early 20th-c revolutionary party in Turkey]

**young woman** *n* somebody's girlfriend; a sweetheart – no longer in vogue

**younker** /'yungkə/ *n, archaic* **1** a young man **2** a child, youngster [D *jonker* young nobleman, fr MD *jonchere,* fr *jonc* young + *here* lord, master]

**your** /yə; *strong* yaw/ *adj* **1** of you or yourself or yourselves, esp as possessor or possessors ⟨~ *bodies*⟩, agent or agents ⟨~ *contributions*⟩, or object or objects of an action ⟨~ *discharge*⟩ – used with certain titles when addressing the person ⟨~ *Eminence*⟩ **2** of one or oneself ⟨*when you face north, east is on* ~ *right*⟩ **3** *informal* – used for indicating something well-known and characteristic ⟨~ *typical commuter*⟩ [ME, fr OE *ēower;* akin to OE *ēow* you – more at YOU]

**usage** The spelling of **yours** meaning "the one belonging to **you**" as △ **your's** is a common confusion ⟨*the house became* yours (not △ **your's**)⟩. △ you're

**you're** /yaw, yooə/ you are

**yours** /yawz/ *pron, pl* yours **1** that which or the one who be-

longs to you – used without a following noun as a pronoun equivalent in meaning to the adjective *your;* often used in the complimentary close of a letter ⟨~ *truly*⟩; compare phrases at ²MINE **2** your letter ⟨~ *of the 19th*⟩ **3** – used in sport as an exclamation to indicate to a colleague that he/she should deal with a situation (eg take a catch) *usage* see YOUR [ME, fr *your* + *-s* -'s]

**yourself** /yə'self, yaw'self/ *pron, pl* **yourselves** **1a** that identical person or creature that is you – used reflexively ⟨*enjoy* yourselves, *everyone*⟩, for emphasis ⟨*carry it* ~⟩, or in constructions without a verb; compare ONESELF **b** your normal self ⟨*soon be* ~ *again*⟩ **2** oneself

**youth** /yoohth/ *n, pl* **youths** /yoodhz/ **1a** the time of life when one is young; *esp* adolescence ⟨*lived there in his* ~⟩ **b** the early period of existence, growth, or development **2** *taking sing or pl vb* young people ⟨*modern* ~⟩ **3** the quality or state of being youthful; youthfulness ⟨*preserved her* ~⟩ **4** *sometimes derog* a young male adolescent *synonyms* see GENTLEMAN *antonym* girl [ME *youthe,* fr OE *geoguth;* akin to OE *geong* young – more at YOUNG]

**youthful** /-f(ə)l/ *adj* **1** (characteristic) of youth ⟨~ *complexion*⟩ ⟨~ *optimism*⟩ **2** not yet mature or old; young ⟨~ *dancers*⟩ **3** *of a land surface or feature* having undergone little erosion; characterized by minimum relief – compare MATURE 5, OLD 8b *synonyms* see ¹YOUNG – **youthfully** *adv,* **youthfulness** *n*

**youth hostel** *n* a lodging typically providing inexpensive bed and breakfast accommodation for members of the Youth Hostel Association, esp young travellers or hikers – **youth-hosteller** *n,* **youth-hostelling** *n*

**you've** /yoohv/ you have

**yow** /yow/ *n* a yell of pain – often used interjectionally

**¹yowl** /yowl/ *vi* **1** to utter a loud long cry of grief, pain, or distress; wail **2** to complain or protest (as if) with yowls ~ *vt* to express or utter with yowling [ME *yowlen,* prob of imit origin]

**²yowl** *n* a yowling cry (eg of a cat or dog)

**yo-yo** /'yoh,yoh/ *n, pl* **yo-yos** **1** a toy that consists of two discs separated by a deep groove in which a string is attached and wound and that is made to fall and rise when held and jerked rhythmically by the string **2** *NAm slang* a fool [native name in the Philippines]

**ytterbic** /i'tuhbik/ *adj* of or containing ytterbium, esp when having a VALENCY of three

**ytterbium** /i'tuhbi·əm/ *n* a soft silvery metallic chemical element having a VALENCY of two or three, that is a member of the RARE EARTH group of elements and that resembles yttrium and occurs with it and related elements in several minerals (eg GADOLINITE) [NL, fr *Ytterby,* town in Sweden]

**ytterbous** /i'tuhbəs/ *adj* of or containing ytterbium when having a VALENCY of two

**yttrium** /'itri·əm/ *n* a silvery metallic chemical element having a VALENCY of three, that is usu included among the RARE EARTH metals which it resembles chemically and with which it occurs in minerals (eg in MONAZITE and GADOLINITE), and that is used in various alloys [NL, fr *yttria* (yttrium oxide), irreg fr *Ytterby*]

**yuan** /'yooh·ən, yooh'ahn/ *n, pl* **yuan** – see MONEY table [Chin (Pek) *üan* (*yüan²*)]

**Yucatec** /'yoohkatek/ *n* **1** a member of an American Indian people of the Yucatán peninsula in Mexico **2** a MAYAN language of the Yucatecs [Sp *yucateco,* fr *Yucatán,* peninsula in SE Mexico] – **Yucatecan** *adj or n*

**yucca** /'yukə/ *n* any of a genus (*Yucca*) of sometimes treelike plants of the lily family that are native to southern N America, have long often rigid spiky leaves on a woody base, and bear large clusters of white flowers [NL, genus name, fr Sp *yuca,* prob of Cariban origin]

**yucky** /'yuki/ *adj, slang* disgustingly messy; *also* sickeningly sweet [*yuck* (interj of disgust), prob imit of the noise of retching]

**yuga** /'yoogə/ *n, often cap* any of the four ages of a Hindu world cycle, lasting more than a million years [Skt, yoke, age; akin to L *jugum* yoke – more at YOKE]

**yule** /yoohl/ *n, often cap, archaic* the festival of the birth of Jesus Christ; Christmas [ME *yol,* fr OE *geōl;* akin to ON *jōl* winter feast, Christmas]

**Yule log** *n* a large log formerly put on the hearth on Christmas Eve as the foundation of the fire

**yuletide** /'yoohl,tied/ *n, often cap, archaic* Christmastide

**Yuman** /'yoohmən/ *n* an American Indian language family of the SW USA and N Mexico – **Yuman** *adj*

**yummy** /'yumi/ *adj, informal* highly attractive or pleasing; delectable, delicious [*yum-yum*]

**yum-yum** /,yum'yum/ *interj* – used to express pleasurable satisfaction, esp in the taste of food [imit of the sound of smacking the lips]

**Yurak** /yoo'rak, 'yooərak/ *n* a URALIC language of N Russia and Siberia

**yurt** /yooət/ *n* a circular domed tent of skins or felt stretched over a collapsible lattice framework and used by the Kirghiz and other Mongol nomads of Central Asia [Russ *yurta*, of Turkic origin; akin to Turk *yurt* dwelling]

# Z

**z, Z** /zed; *NAm* zee/ *n, pl* **z's, zs, Z's, Zs 1a** the 26th and last letter of the English alphabet **b** a graphic representation of or device for reproducing the letter *z* **c** a speech counterpart of printed or written *z* **2** one designated *z*, *esp* as the 26th in order or class or 3rd in a series that includes *x*, *y*, and *z* **3** something shaped like the letter Z **4** *maths* – used in italic to represent a variable mathematical quantity

**zabaglione** /ˌzabəˈlyohni/ *n* a mixture of eggs, sugar, and wine, *esp* MARSALA (sweet Italian wine), beaten over hot water until thick and creamy and served warm or cold as a dessert [It]

**Zac, zack** /zak/ *n, Austr slang* a sixpence [perh modif of Ger *sechs* six]

**Zacharias** /ˌzakəˈrie·əs/ *n* – see BIBLE table [LL, Zechariah]

**zaddik, tzaddik** /ˈtsahdik/ *n, pl* **zaddikim, tzaddikim** /tsahˈdikim/ **1** a righteous and saintly person by Jewish religious standards, often credited with supernatural powers **2** the spiritual leader of a modern HASIDIC (mystical sect of Judaism) community [Heb *ṣaddīq* just, righteous]

**zaffre**, *NAm chiefly* **zaffer** /ˈzafə/ *n* an impure cobalt-containing chemical compound used esp as a blue colouring for glass and pottery and in the manufacture of SMALT (deep blue colouring material)

**zag** /zag/ *n* ZIG [*zigzag*]

**zaire** /zahˈiə/ *n, pl* **zaire** – see MONEY table [Fr *zaïre*, fr Zaïre (formerly Congo), country in central Africa]

**zamindar, zemindar** /zəmeenˈdah/ *n* **1** a collector of land taxes of a district during the period of Muslim rule in India **2** a feudal landlord in British India responsible for collecting land taxes [Hindi *zamīndār*, fr Per, fr *zamīn* land + *-dār* holder]

**zamindari, zemindary** /zəmeenˈdahri/ *n, pl* **zamindaris, zemindaries 1** the system of landholding and tax collection by zamindars **2** the land held or administered by a zamindar [Hindi *zamīndārī*, fr Per, fr *zamīndār*]

**zander** /ˈzandə/ *n, pl* **zander, zanders** a freshwater fish (*Stizostedion lucioperca*) of central Europe that is related to the perch [Ger]

**¹zany** /ˈzayni/ *n* **1** a subordinate clown or acrobat in old comedies who mimics ludicrously the tricks of the principal characters **2** somebody who acts the buffoon to amuse others **3** a simpleton △ zombie [It *zanni*, a traditional masked clown, fr It dial. *Zanni*, nickname for Giovanni John]

**²zany** *adj* **1** (having the characteristics) of a zany **2** fantastically or absurdly ludicrous – **zanily** *adv*, **zaniness** *n*

**zanza** /ˈzanzə/ *n* an African musical instrument that consists of a wooden box set with a graduated series of wooden or metal tongues which are plucked with the fingers or thumbs [Ar *ṣanj* castanets, cymbals, fr Per *sanj*]

**¹zap** /zap/ *interj, informal* – used to indicate a sudden or instantaneous occurrence [imit]

**²zap** *n, chiefly NAm slang* ²ZIP 2

**³zap** *vb* **-pp-** *vt* **1** to overwhelm, overcome **2** to propel vigorously **3** *chiefly NAm* to destroy, kill ~ *vi* to move with speed or force

**zapateado** /ˌzahpətayˈahdoh/ *n, pl* **zapateados** a Latin American dance marked by rhythmic stamping or tapping of the feet [Sp, fr *zapatear* to strike or tap with the shoe, fr *zapato* shoe]

**Zapotec** /ˈzahpətek/ *n* a member of an American Indian people of Mexico

**zappy** /ˈzapi/ *adj, informal* **1** energetic, dynamic ⟨the ~ presentation of a TV commercial⟩ **2** fast-moving ⟨a ~ little car⟩

**zaratite** /ˈzarəˌtiet/ *n* an emerald green mineral, $NiCO_3 2Ni(OH)_2.4H_2O$, containing nickel [Sp *zaratita*, fr *Zarate*, 19th-c Spaniard]

**zareba, zariba** /zəˈreebə/ *n* an improvised stockade constructed, esp of thorny bushes, in parts of Africa [Ar *zarībah* enclosure]

**zarzuela** /zahˈzwaylə/ *n* a traditional Spanish comic opera [Sp]

**zax** /zaks/ *n* a tool with a blade and a spike for chopping and making holes in slates [ME *sexe* knife, short sword – more at SEAX]

**z-axis** /zed/ *n, maths* that one of the axes in a three-dimensional system that is not the x- or y-axis

**zayin** /ˈzahyin/ *n* the 7th letter of the Hebrew alphabet [Heb]

**zeal** /zeel/ *n* eagerness and ardent interest in pursuit or support of something (eg a religious or political movement); keenness; *also* fervent application to work **synonyms** see PASSION [ME *zele*, fr LL *zelus*, fr Gk *zēlos*]

**zealot** /ˈzelət/ *n* **1** *cap* a member of a fanatical sect arising in Judea during the first century AD and militantly opposing the Roman domination of Palestine **2** a zealous person; *esp* a fanatical partisan [LL *zelotes*, fr Gk *zēlōtēs*, fr *zēlos* zeal] – **zealot** *adj*, **zealotry** *n*

**zealous** /ˈzeləs/ *adj* filled with or characterized by zeal ⟨~ missionaries⟩ – **zealously** *adv*, **zealousness** *n*

**zeatin** /ˈzee·ətin/ *n* a natural CYTOKININ (plant growth hormone) first isolated from the seeds of maize [NL *Zea*, genus of grasses including maize + *-tin* (as in *kinetin*) – more at ZEIN]

**zebra** /ˈzebrə, ˈzeebrə/ *n, pl* **zebras**, *esp collectively* **zebra** any of several fast-running African mammals (genus *Equus*) related to the horse but distinctively and conspicuously patterned in stripes of black or dark brown and white or buff [It, fr Sp *cebra*, fr OSp *zebra, zebro* wild ass] – **zebrine, zebroid** *adj*

**zebra crossing** *n, Br* a road crossing marked by a series of broad white and black stripes to indicate that pedestrians have the right of way – compare CROSSWALK

**zebra danio** *n* ZEBRA FISH [NL *Danio*, former genus of Cyprinid fishes]

**zebra finch** *n* a small largely grey and white Australian weaverbird (*Poephila castanotis*) that has black bars on the tail feathers and is often kept as a cage bird

**zebra fish** *n* any of various barred fishes; *esp* a very small blue-and-silver-striped Indian fish (*Brachydanio rerio*) often kept in tropical aquariums

**zebrawood** /ˈzebrəˌwood, ˈzee-/ *n* **1** any of several trees or shrubs having mottled or striped wood; *esp* a tropical American, Asian, or African tree (*Connarus guianensis* of the family Connaraceae) with strikingly marked hard wood used in cabinetwork **2** the wood of a zebrawood

**zebu** /ˈzeeb(y)ooh/ *n* a domesticated Asiatic ox (*Bos indicus*) of any of several breeds, used chiefly for drawing wagons and distinguished from European cattle by the presence of a large fleshy hump over the shoulders, a large flap (DEWLAP) of loose skin hanging under the chin, large pendulous ears, and marked resistance to the injurious effects of heat and insect attack [Fr *zébu*]

**zecchino** /zeˈkeenoh/ *n, pl* **zecchini, zecchinos** SEQUIN 1 (coin) [It]

**Zechariah** /ˌzekəˈrie·ə/ *n* – see BIBLE table [Zechariah (Heb *Zĕkharyāh*), 6th-c BC Heb prophet]

**zechin** /ˈzekin, zeˈkeen/ *n* SEQUIN 1 (coin) [It *zecchino*]

**zed** /zed/ *n, chiefly Br* the letter *z* [ME, fr MF *zede*, fr LL *zeta* zeta, fr Gk *zēta*]

**zedoary** /ˈzedoh·əri/ *n* the dried root of an Asian plant (*Curcuma zedoaria*) used in medicine, perfumery, etc [ML *zedoarium*, fr Ar or Per; Ar *zadwār*, fr Per]

**zee** /zee/ *n, NAm* the letter *z*

**zein** /ˈzee·in/ *n* a protein from maize that is used esp in making textile fibres, plastics, printing inks, coatings (eg varnish), and adhesives [NL *Zea*, genus of grasses including maize, fr Gk, wheat; akin to Skt *yava* barley]

**zeitgeist** /ˈtsietˌgiest/ *n* the general intellectual and moral character or cultural climate of an era [Ger, fr *zeit* time + *geist* spirit]

**zemindar** /zə͵meen'dah/ *n* ZAMINDAR (Indian tax collector)

**zemindary** /zəmeen'dahri/ *n* ZAMINDARI

**zemstvo** /'zemstvoh, -və/ *n, pl* **zemstvos** any of the district and provincial assemblies established in Russia in 1864 [Russ; akin to Russ *zemlya* earth, land, L *humus* – more at HUMBLE]

**Zen** /zen/ *n* a Japanese sect of MAHAYANA (widespread liberal sect) Buddhism that aims at enlightenment by direct intuition through meditation (eg on paradoxes) [Jap, religious meditation, fr Chin (Pek) *chán* (*ch'an²*), fr Pali *jhāna*, fr Skt *dhyāna*, fr *dhyayati* he thinks – more at SEMANTIC]

**zenana** /ze'nahnə/ *n* the women's quarters in an eastern, esp Muslim, house [Hindi *zanāna*, fr Per, fr *zan* woman]

**Zend-Avesta** /͵zend ə'vestə/ *n* AVESTA (ancient Persian sacred writings) [Fr, fr MPer *Avastāk va Zand* Avesta and commentary]

**zener diode** /'zeenə/ *n, often cap Z, electronics* a silicon SEMICONDUCTOR device that is used to provide a stable voltage for reference or voltage regulation [Clarence *Zener* b1905 US physicist]

**zenith** /'zenith/ *n* **1** *astronomy* the point of the CELESTIAL SPHERE (imaginary sphere encircling the earth) that is vertically above the observer and directly opposite the NADIR (point vertically below observer) **2** *astronomy* the highest point reached in the heavens by a heavenly body **3** the culminating point; the acme ⟨*at the ~ of his powers* – John Buchan⟩ *synonyms* see SUMMIT *antonym* nadir [ME *senith*, fr MF *cenith*, fr ML, fr OSp *zenit*, modif of Ar *samt* (*ar-ra's*) path (above the head)]

**zenithal** /'zenithəl/ *adj* **1** located at or near the zenith **2** showing correct directions from the centre ⟨*a ~ map*⟩

**zenithal equidistant projection** *n* AZIMUTHAL EQUIDISTANT PROJECTION

**zenithal projection** *n* AZIMUTHAL PROJECTION (map projection onto a tangent plane of a part of the globe)

**zenith distance** *n, astronomy* the distance of a heavenly object from the zenith, expressed in degrees of an angle

**zeolite** /'zee·ə͵liet/ *n* (a synthetic chemical compound resembling) any of various silicon-containing minerals that are similar in composition to the FELDSPARS, occur as secondary minerals in cavities of lavas, and can act as ION-EXCHANGERS (eg in water softening) [Sw *zeolit*, fr Gk *zein* to boil + *-o-* + Sw *-lit* -lite, fr Fr *-lite* – more at YEAST; fr its swelling up when subjected to fierce heat] – **zeolitic** *adj*

**Zephaniah** /͵zefə'nie·ə/ *n* – see BIBLE table [*Zephaniah* (Heb *Sĕphanyāh*), 7th-c BC Heb prophet]

**zephyr** /'zefə/ *n* **1** a gentle breeze, esp from the west **2** any of various lightweight fabrics or articles of clothing *synonyms* see ¹WIND [ME *Zephirus*, west wind (personified), fr L *Zephyrus*, *zephyrus* (god of the) west wind, fr Gk *Zephyros*, *zephyros*]

**zeppelin** /'zep(ə)lin/ *n, often cap* a large rigid cigar-shaped airship of a type built in Germany in the early 20th century, esp for transatlantic flight or military use; *broadly* an airship [Count Ferdinand von *Zeppelin* †1917 Ger general & aeronaut]

**¹zero** /'ziəroh/ *n, pl* **zeros** *also* **zeroes** **1a** the arithmetical symbol O or Ø denoting the absence of all magnitude or quantity **b** an IDENTITY ELEMENT (number that has no effect on a mathematical operation) of a group under addition; *specif* the number between the set of all negative numbers and the set of all positive numbers **c** a value of the INDEPENDENT VARIABLE of a function that makes it equal to zero **2** – see NUMBER table **3a(1)** the point of departure in reckoning; *specif* the point from which the graduation of a scale (eg of a thermometer) begins **a(2)** the temperature represented by the zero mark on a thermometer **b** the setting or adjustment of the sights of a firearm to ensure that its aim is accurate **4a** nothing ⟨*slow down to ~ in the traffic*⟩ **b** the lowest point ⟨*his spirits fell to ~*⟩ [Fr or It; Fr *zéro*, fr It *zero*, fr ML *zephirum*, fr Ar *ṣifr* (cf CIPHER)]

*synonyms* Zero, nought, oh, null, cipher, nil, nothing, nix, and zilch each mean the absence of all quantity. **Zero** is chiefly the quantity represented by O or Ø, rather than the symbol itself. It is used in most mathematical and technical senses, particularly for a point of departure on a graduated scale ⟨*the thermometer read* **zero**⟩. It is used in American English for saying telephone numbers ⟨*five one* **zero** *four*⟩ (see ¹DOUBLE). **Nought** is chiefly the symbol 0 itself ⟨*don't like the way you write your* **noughts**⟩. It is used, except in technical use, for saying numbers before a decimal point ⟨**nought** *point oh four*⟩. **Oh** is used, except in technical use, for saying numbers after a decimal point, for saying dates ⟨*nineteen* **oh** *six*⟩, and in

British English for saying telephone numbers ⟨*five one* **oh** *four*⟩. **Null** is used particularly for the point of departure on a scale. **Cipher** is a somewhat archaic word for the symbol 0. **Nil** is used particularly in sport ⟨*won four* **nil**⟩. **Nothing** is also used in sport ⟨*won four* **nothing**⟩ but is not otherwise much used as a number. **Nix** (*informal*) and **zilch** (*American slang*) have emotional overtones ⟨*paid me practically* **nix/zilch**⟩.

**²zero** *adj* **1a** of or being a zero **b** having no magnitude or quantity ⟨*~ growth*⟩ **c(1)** *linguistics* lacking inflectional realization; not represented by an inflection ⟨*the ~ modification in the past of cut*⟩ **c(2)** having no modified inflectional form ⟨*the ~ plural of* sheep⟩ **2a** *of a cloud ceiling* limiting vision to 15 metres (about 50 feet) or less **b** *of horizontal visibility* limited to 50 metres (about 165 feet) or less

**³zero** *vt* **1** to determine or adjust the zero of (eg a rifle) **2a** to concentrate firepower on the exact range of **b** to bring to bear on the exact range of a target *~ vi* **1** to adjust fire (eg of artillery) on a specific target **2** to move near to or focus attention as if on a target; close ⟨*reporters ~ed in on Miss World*⟩ □ (*except vt 1*) usu + *in on*

**zero grazing** *n* the practice of keeping cattle indoors all year and feeding them on cut grass

**zero growth** *n* a condition of stability in population, productivity, etc

**zero hour** *n* **1** the hour at which a planned military operation is scheduled to start **2** the time at which an event is scheduled to take place [fr its being marked by the count of zero in a countdown]

**'zero-͵sum** *adj* of or being a situation (eg a game or relationship) in which a gain for one side entails a corresponding loss for the other side

**͵zero-'zero** *adj* **1** characterized by or being atmospheric conditions that reduce cloud ceiling and visibility to zero **2** limited to zero by atmospheric conditions

**zest** /zest/ *n* **1** the peel of a citrus fruit used as flavouring **2** piquancy, spice ⟨*danger added ~ to the proceedings*⟩ **3** keen enjoyment; gusto ⟨*her ~ for living*⟩ [obs Fr (now *zeste*)] – **zestful** *adj*, **zestfully** *adv*, **zestfulness** *n*, **zesty** *adj*

**zeta** /'zeetə/ *n* the 6th letter of the Greek alphabet [Gk *zēta*]

**zetetic** /zee'tetik/ *adj, formal* proceeding by inquiry [Gk *zētētikos*, fr *zētētos*, verbal of *zētein* to seek for, inquire]

**zeugma** /'zyoohgmə/ *n* the use of a word to modify or govern two or more words, usu in such a manner that it applies to each in a different sense or makes sense with only one (eg in "opened the door and her heart to the homeless boy") [L, fr Gk, lit., joining, fr *zeugnynai* to join; akin to L *jungere* to join – more at YOKE]

*synonyms* In the terminology of formal rhetoric, **zeugma** is an error that occurs when a word actually fails to make sense with one of those to which it is applied (e g in "kill the boys and the luggage"), while **syllepsis** is no error but merely requires the same word to be understood in different senses; but the two words have long been used interchangeably.

**zho** /zoh/ *n, pl* **zhos**, *esp collectively* **zho** DZO (Tibetan breed of cattle)

**zibeline, zibelline** /'zibəlin, -͵lien, -͵leen/ *n* a soft lustrous wool fabric with mohair, alpaca, or camel hair [MF, sable, fr OIt *zibellino*, of Slav origin; akin to Russ *sobol'* sable]

**zibet** /'zibit/ *n* a common Asian CIVET CAT (*Viverra zibetha*) [It *zibetto* & ML *zibethum*, fr Ar *zabād* civet perfume]

**¹zig** /zig/ *n* any of the sharp turns, angles, or lines in a zigzag – called also ZAG [*zigzag*]

**²zig** *vi* **-gg-** to execute a sharp turn or follow a section of a zigzag course

**ziggurat** /'zigərat/ *n* a temple tower of ancient Mesopotamia consisting of a lofty stepped pyramid with outside staircases and a shrine at the top [Akkadian *ziqqurratu* pinnacle]

**¹zigzag** /'zig͵zag/ *n* a line, course, or pattern consisting of a series of sharp alternate turns or angles ⟨*a blue shirt with red ~s*⟩ [Fr, prob fr Ger *zickzack*, prob of imit origin]

**²zigzag** *adj* forming or going in a zigzag; consisting of zigzags ⟨*a ~ path up the hill*⟩ – **zigzag** *adv*

**³zigzag** *vb* **-gg-** *vt* to form into a zigzag *~ vi* to proceed along or consist of a zigzag course

**zilch** /zilch/ *adj or n, chiefly NAm slang* zero *synonyms* see ¹ZERO [by alter.]

**zillah, zila, zilla** /'zilah/ *n* an Indian administrative district [Hindi *ẓila'*, fr Ar *ḍil'* rib, part]

**zillion** /'zilyən/ *n* an indefinitely large number ⟨*~s of mosquitoes*⟩ [*z* + *-illion* (as in *million*)]

**¹zinc** /zingk/ *n* a bluish white metallic chemical element having a VALENCY of two, that is of low to intermediate hardness, is easily worked when pure but in the commercial form is brittle at ordinary temperatures, occurs abundantly in minerals, is an essential nutrient for both plants and animals, and is used esp as a protective coating for iron and steel [Ger *zink*] – **zincic, zincous** *adj*

**²zinc** *vt* **-c-, -ck-** to treat or coat with zinc; galvanize

**zincate** /'zingkayt/ *n* a chemical compound formed by reaction of ZINC OXIDE or zinc with alkaline solutions

**zinc blende** *n* SPHALERITE (common zinc-containing mineral)

**zinc chloride** *n* a white soluble poisonous chemical compound $ZnCl_2$, used esp as a wood preservative, drying agent, antiseptic, and catalyst to increase the rate of chemical reactions

**zincite** /'zing·kiet/ *n* a brittle reddish-yellow mineral, ZnO, that consists essentially of ZINC OXIDE and occurs in large crystals or in the form of grains [Ger *zinkit*, fr *zink*]

**zincky, zinky, zincy** /'zing·ki/ *adj* containing or having the appearance of zinc

**zinco** /'zing·koh/ *n, pl* **zincos** *Br* a cheap zinc-coated printing block with raised characters [short for *zincograph,* back-formation fr *zincography* (art of engraving on zinc), fr *zinc* + *-o- + -graphy*]

**zinc ointment** *n* a soothing ointment that contains about 20 per cent of ZINC OXIDE and is used in treating skin disorders

**zinc oxide** *n* a white solid, ZnO, used esp as a pigment, in glass making, in compounding rubber, and in medicinal and cosmetic preparations

**zinc spar** *n* SMITHSONITE (zinc-containing mineral)

**zinc sulphate** *n* a colourless soluble powder, $ZnSO_4$, used as a dye fixative, in zinc plating, and in paper manufacture

**zinc sulphide** *n* a fluorescent white to yellowish chemical compound, ZnS, used esp as a white pigment and a PHOSPHOR (luminescent substance)

**zinc white** *n* ZINC OXIDE used as a pigment (eg in paint)

**¹zing** /zing/ *n* **1** a shrill humming noise **2** *informal* energy, vim [imit]

**²zing** *vi, informal* to move briskly or with a humming sound ⟨*a bullet ~ed past her ear*⟩

**Zingaro** /'zing·gəroh/ *n, pl* **Zingari** /-ri/ an Italian Gipsy [It]

**zingy** /'zing·i/ *adj, informal* strikingly exciting or attractive ⟨*a ~ musical*⟩ ⟨*a ~ new outfit*⟩ [¹*zing* + ¹*-y*]

**zinjanthropus** /zin'janthrəpəs/ *n, pl* **zinjanthropi** /-,pie, -pi/, **zinjanthropuses** a fossil prehistoric man (*Australopithecus,* syn *Zinjanthropus, boisei*) based on skeletal remains from the early PLEISTOCENE period of E Africa and characterized by a very low brow and large back teeth [NL, genus name, fr Ar *Zīnj* eastern Africa + Gk *anthrōpos* human being] – **zinjanthropine** *adj or n*

**zinkenite** /'zing·kə,niet/ *n* a steel-grey lead- and antimony-containing mineral, $PbSb_2S_4$, of metallic appearance [Ger *zinkenit,* fr J K L *Zinken* †1862 Ger mineralogist]

**zinky** /'zing·ki/ *adj* zincky

**zinnia** /'zinyə, 'zini·ə/ *n* any of a small genus (*Zinnia*) of tropical American nonwoody plants and low-growing shrubs of the daisy family with showy flower heads and long-lasting flowers of many colours [NL, genus name, fr Johann *Zinn* †1759 Ger botanist]

**Zion** /'zie,on, 'zie·ən/ *n* **1a** the Jewish people; Israel **b** the Jewish homeland that is symbolic of Judaism or of Jewish national aspiration **c** the ideal nation or society envisaged by Judaism **2** heaven [*Zion,* citadel in Palestine which was the nucleus of Jerusalem, fr ME *Sion,* fr OE, fr LL, fr Heb *Sīyōn*]

**Zionism** /'zie·ə,niz(ə)m/ *n* a theory, plan, or movement for setting up a Jewish national or religious homeland in Palestine – **Zionist** *adj or n,* **Zionistic** *adj*

**¹zip** /zip/ *vb* **-pp-** *vi* **1** to move with speed and vigour ⟨*waitresses ~ped by*⟩ **2** to travel with a sharp hissing or humming sound **3** to become open, closed, or attached by means of a zip ~ *vt* **1** to add zest or life to – often + *up* **2** to transport with speed **3a** to close or open (as if) with a zip **b** to enclose by means of a zip ⟨*~ him into his snowsuit*⟩ **4** to cause (a zip) to open or shut [imit of the sound of a speeding object]

**²zip** *n* **1** a light sharp hissing sound **2** energy, liveliness **3** *also* **zipp** *chiefly Br* a fastener that joins two edges of fabric by means of two flexible spirals or rows of teeth brought together by a sliding clip – **zippy** *adj,* **zippily** *adv*

**³zip** *adj* equipped with a zip; zip-up ⟨*a ~ jacket*⟩

**zip code, zip** *n, often cap Z,I,&P* a 5-digit number that is used in the postal address of a place in the USA to assist sorting – compare POSTCODE [*zone improvement plan*]

**zip fastener** /'fahs(ə)nə/ *n, chiefly Br* ²ZIP 3

**zipped** /zipt/ *adj* zip-up

**zipper** /'zipə/ *n, chiefly NAm* ²ZIP 3 [fr *Zipper,* a trademark]

**zippered** /'zipəd/ *adj, chiefly NAm* zip-up

**'zip-,up** *adj* fastened by means of a zip

**ziram** /'zieram/ *n* a zinc-containing chemical compound, $Zn(S_2CN(CH_3)_2)_2$, used in the treatment (VULCANIZATION) of rubber and as an agricultural fungicide [*zinc* + *-ram* (as in *thiram*)]

**zircon** /'zuhkon/ *n* a zirconium-containing mineral, $ZrSiO_4$, occurring in variously coloured square prisms and sometimes in transparent forms which are used as gems [Ger, modif of Fr *jargon* jargoon, zircon, fr It *giargone*]

**zirconia** /zuh'kohnyə, -niə/ *n* ZIRCONIUM OXIDE [NL, fr ISV *zircon*]

**zirconic** /zuh'konik/ *adj* of or containing zirconium

**zirconium** /zuh'kohnyəm, -ni·əm/ *n* a steel-grey strong easily worked chiefly metallic chemical element with a high MELTING POINT, that occurs widely in combined form (e g in zircon), is highly resistant to corrosion, and is used esp in alloys and in heat-resisting ceramic materials [NL, fr ISV *zircon*]

**zirconium oxide** *n* a white insoluble chemical compound, $ZrO_2$, used esp in heat-resisting ceramic materials, in thermal and electrical insulation, in abrasives, and in enamels and glazes

**zither** /'zidhə/ *n* a stringed instrument having usu 30 to 40 strings over a shallow horizontal soundboard and played with PLECTRUM (small wooden or plastic implement) and fingers – compare CITTERN [Ger, fr L *cithara* lyre, fr Gk *kithara*] – **zitherist** *n*

**zizith** /'tsitsis, tsee'tseet/ *n pl* the fringes or tassels worn on traditional or ceremonial garments by Jewish males as reminders of the commandments of Deut 22:12 and Num 15:37–41 [Heb *sīsīth*]

**¹zizz** /ziz/ *n, Br informal* a nap, doze [imit of the sound of a sleeper's breathing]

**²zizz** *vi, Br informal* to take a zizz – often + *off*

**zloty** /'zloti/ *n, pl* **zlotys** /'zloteez/ *also* **zloty** – see MONEY table [Polish *zloty*]

**zo** /zoh/ *n, pl* **zos,** *esp collectively* **zo** DZO (Tibetan breed of cattle)

**zo-** /zoh-/, **zoo-** *comb form* **1** animal; animal kingdom ⟨*zooid*⟩ ⟨*zoology*⟩ **2** exhibiting or capable of movement ⟨*zoospore*⟩ [Gk *zōi-, zōio-,* fr *zōion;* akin to Gk *zōē* life – more at QUICK]

**-zoa** /-'zoh·ə/ *comb form* (→ *n pl*) animals – in TAXA (biological groups) ⟨*Metazoa*⟩ [NL, fr Gk *zōia,* pl of *zōion*]

**zoantharian** /,zoh·ən'theəriən/ *n* any of a subclass (Zoantharia of the class Anthozoa) of marine INVERTEBRATE animals, including most of the recent corals and SEA ANEMONES, that have a six-branched arrangement of tentacles or SEPTA (internal body partitions) or both [deriv of *zo-* + Gk *anthos* flower – more at ANTHOLOGY] – **zoantharian** *adj*

**zodiac** /'zohdiak/ *n* **1a** an imaginary belt in the heavens usu 18 degrees wide that encompasses the apparent paths of all the principal planets except Pluto, has the ECLIPTIC (apparent annual path of the sun) as its central line, and is divided into 12 constellations or signs each taken for astrological purposes to extend 30 degrees of longitude **b** a diagram representing the signs of the zodiac and their symbols **2** a cyclic course ⟨*a ~ of feasts and fasts* – R W Emerson⟩ [ME, fr MF *zodiaque,* fr L *zodiacus,* fr Gk *zōidiakos,* fr *zōidiakos,* adj, of carved figures, fr *zōidion* carved figure, sign of the zodiac, fr dim. of *zōion* living being, animal, figure] – **zodiacal** *adj*

**zodiacal light** /zoh'die·əkl, zə-/ *n* a diffuse glow seen in the west after twilight and in the east before dawn

**zoea** /zoh'eeə/ *n, pl* **zoeae** /zoh'ee·ee/, **zoeas**, **zoaes** an early larval form of many ten-legged INVERTEBRATE animals (of the class Crustacea), esp crabs, that has a relatively large CEPHALOTHORAX (body region combining head and central segment in front of the abdomen), conspicuous eyes, and large fringed antennae and mouthparts used for swimming [NL, fr Gk *zōē* life] – **zoeal** *adj*

**¹-zoic** /-'zoh·ik/ *comb form* (→ *adj*) being an animal that has (such) a mode of existence ⟨*holozoic*⟩ ⟨*saprozoic*⟩ [Gk *zōikos* of animals, fr *zōion* animal]

**²-zoic** *comb form* (→ *adj*) of or being (such) a geological era ⟨*Archaeozoic*⟩ ⟨*Mesozoic*⟩ [Gk *zōē* life]

**zoisite** /'zoy,siet/ *n* a mineral that is a silicate of calcium and aluminium, $Ca_2Al_3Si_3O_{12}OH$, and is related to EPIDOTE (green mineral) [Ger *zoisit*, fr Baron Sigismund *Zois* von Edelstein † 1819 Slovenian nobleman]

**zombie**, *NAm also* **zombi** /'zombi/ *n* **1a** a will-less and speechless human in the W Indies who is capable of automatic movement only and who is held, esp in Haitian voodooism, to have died and been reanimated **b** a supernatural power that according to voodoo belief, esp in Haiti, may enter into and reanimate a dead body **2a** a person who resembles the walking dead; *esp* a shambling automaton **b** a person markedly strange in appearance or behaviour △ zany [of Niger-Congo origin; akin to Kongo *nzambi* god] – **zombielike** *adj*

**zonal** /'zohnl/ *adj* **1** of, affecting, or being a zone ⟨*a ~ boundary*⟩ **2** of or being (a class of) soils marked by well-developed characteristics that are determined primarily by the action of climate and organisms, esp vegetation – compare AZONAL, INTRAZONAL – **zonally** *adv*

**zonate** /'zohnayt/, **zonated** /-aytid/ *adj*, *chiefly ecology* marked with or arranged in zones

**zonation** /zoh'naysh(ə)n/ *n*, *ecology* **1** zonate structure or arrangement **2** the distribution of living organisms in BIOGEOGRAPHIC zones

¹**zone** /zohn/ *n* **1a** any of five great divisions of the earth's surface with respect to latitude and temperature – compare FRIGID ZONE, TEMPERATE ZONE, TORRID ZONE **b** *maths* a portion of the surface of a sphere included between two parallel lines **2a** an encircling anatomical structure **b** *ecology* **b(1)** a subdivision of a biogeographic region that supports a similar collection of animals and plants throughout its extent **b(2)** such a zone dominated by a particular, usu specified, life form ⟨*the barnacle ~ on a rocky shore*⟩ **c** a distinctive belt, layer, or series of layers of earth materials (eg rock) **3** an area distinct from adjoining parts ⟨*an erogenous ~*⟩ **4** any of the sections into which an area is divided for a particular purpose (eg an area on a field of play) ⟨*a smokeless ~*⟩ **5** *archaic* a girdle, belt [L *zona* belt, zone, fr Gk *zōnē*; akin to Lith *juosti* to gird]

²**zone** *vt* **1** to surround with a zone or belt; encircle **2** to arrange in, mark off, or partition into zones **3** to assign to a zone ⟨*neighbourhood has been ~d as residential*⟩ – **zoner** *n*

³**zone** *adj* **1** of or being a zone **2** of or being a system of defence (eg in basketball or AMERICAN FOOTBALL) in which each player guards an assigned area rather than a specified opponent

**zone melting** *n* a technique for the purification of a crystalline material, esp of a metal, in which a molten region travels through the material to be refined and picks up impurities

**zone refine** *vt* to produce or refine by ZONE MELTING – **zone refining** *n*

**zonked** /zongkt/ *adj*, *slang* **1** strongly under the influence of alcohol, hallucinogenic drugs, etc; very high – often + *out* **2** completely exhausted [origin unknown]

**zoo** /zooh/ *n*, *pl* **zoos** a ZOOLOGICAL GARDEN or collection of living animals usu open to the public [short for *zoological garden*]

**zoo-** – see ZO-

**zoogenic** /ˌzoh-ə'jenik/, **zoogenous** /zoh'ojənəs/ *adj* caused by, produced by, or associated with animals or their activities [ISV]

**zoogeography** /ˌzoh-əji'ogrəfi/ *n* a branch of BIOGEOGRAPHY dealing with the geographical distribution of animals, esp the determination of the areas characterized by special groups of animals and the study of the causes and significance of the presence of such groups [ISV] – **zoogeographer** *n*, **zoogeographic** *also* **zoogeographical** *adj*, **zoogeographically** *adv*

**zoogloea**, *chiefly NAm* **zooglea** /ˌzoh-ə'glee-ə/ *n*, *pl* **zoogloeas**, **zoogloeae** /-'glee,ee/, *chiefly NAm* **zoogleas**, **zoogleae** a jelly-like or slimy growth formed by bacteria growing in liquids rich in material derived from plants or animals (eg in a sewage bed) and made up of bacterial bodies embedded in a mass of swollen cell walls [NL, fr *zo-* + MGk *glia*, *gloea* glue – more at CLAY] – **zoogloeal** *adj*

**zooid** /'zoh-oyd/ *n* an entity that resembles but is not wholly the same as a separate individual organism: eg **a** a cell (eg a PHAGOCYTE or a SPERM CELL) capable of independent motion **b** a more or less independent animal produced (eg by splitting or segmented growth) by other than direct sexual methods – **zooidal** *adj*

**zooks** /zooks/ *interj*, *archaic* – used as a mild oath [short for *gadzooks*]

**zoolatry** /zoh'olətri/ *n* animal worship [NL *zoolatria*, fr *zo-* + LL *-latria* -latry]

**zoological** /ˌzooh-ə'lojikl/, ˌzoh-ə-/, *also* **zoologic** *adj* **1** of or concerned with zoology **2** of or affecting animals, often as distinguished from man – **zoologically** *adv*

**zoological garden** *n*, **zoological gardens** *n pl* a garden or park where wild animals are kept for exhibition

**zoology** /zooh'oləji, zoh-/ *n* **1** (a branch of biology that deals with) animals, usu excluding human beings, and animal life in the world **2a** the animal life of a particular region or environment **b** the properties and vital phenomena exhibited by an animal, animal type, or animal group *usage* The pronunciation /zoh'oləji/is recommended for BBC broadcasters. [NL *zoologia*, fr *zo-* + *-logia* -logy] – **zoologist** *n*

¹**zoom** /zoohm/ *vi* **1** to move with a loud low hum or buzz **2** *of an aircraft* to climb for a short time at a steep angle and high speed **3** to focus a camera or microscope using a ZOOM LENS that permits the apparent distance of the object to be varied **4** to increase sharply ⟨*retail sales ~*ed⟩ ~ *vt* **1** to cause to zoom **2** to operate the ZOOM LENS of (eg a camera) [imit]
*usage* Some people dislike the use of **zoom** for a downward movement ⟨*pigeon came zooming down from a lamp post*⟩.

²**zoom** *n* **1** an act or process of zooming; *specif* a sharp upward movement **2** a zooming sound **3 zoom lens, zoom** a camera or projector lens in which the FOCAL LENGTH, and thus the image size, can be varied continuously so that the image remains in focus at all times

**zoomorphic** /ˌzoh-ə'mawfik/ *adj* **1** resembling the form of an animal; *also* having parts or a part of the form of an animal ⟨*a ~ orchid*⟩ **2** of or being a god conceived of in animal form or with the attributes of an animal [ISV]

**-zoon** /-'zoh-ən/ *comb form* (→ *n*), *pl* **-zoa** /-'zoh-ə/ animal; zooid ⟨*haematozoon*⟩ ⟨*spermatozoon*⟩ [NL, fr Gk *zōion*]

**zoonosis** /zoh'onəsis, ˌzoh-ə'nohsis/ *n*, *pl* **zoonoses** /-seez/ a disease (eg rabies or anthrax) communicable from animals to human beings [NL, fr *zo-* + Gk *nosos* disease] – **zoonotic** *adj*

**zooparasite** /ˌzoh-ə'parə,siet/ *n* a parasitic animal – **zoo-parasitic** *adj*

**zoophagous** /zoh'ofəgəs/ *adj* feeding on animals; carnivorous [ISV]

**zoophilia** /ˌzoh-ə'filiə/ *n* sexual attraction to animals; BESTIALITY 2 [NL, fr *zo-* + *-philia*]

**zoophilous** /zoh'ofiləs/, **zoophilic** /ˌzoh-ə'filik/ *adj* having an attraction to or preference for animals: eg **a** adapted to pollination by animals other than insects – compare ENTOMOPHILOUS **b** *of a blood-sucking insect* preferring animals to human beings as a source of food

**zoophyte** /'zoh-ə,fiet/ *n* an INVERTEBRATE animal (eg a coral or sponge) more or less resembling a plant in appearance or mode of growth; *esp* one that forms a branching treelike colony attached to a surface [Gk *zōophyton*, fr *zōi-*, *zō-* zo- + *phyton* plant – more at PHYT-] – **zoophytic** *adj*

**zooplankter** /'zoh-ə,plangktə/ *n* an animal present in plankton [*zo-* + *plankter*]

**zooplankton** /ˌzoh-ə'plangktən, -ton/ *n* animal constituents of plankton – compare PHYTOPLANKTON – **zooplanktonic** *adj*

**zoosperm** /'zoh-ə,spuhm/ *n* a zoospore [ISV]

**zoosporangium** /ˌzoh-əspaw'ranjiəm/ *n* a spore case or SPORANGIUM (plant organ producing spores) that bears zoospores [NL]

**zoospore** /'zoh-ə,spaw/ *n* a spore capable of independent movement: eg **a** an asexual spore, esp of an alga or lower fungus **b** a minute spore produced by some PROTOZOANS (single-celled organisms) by sexual or asexual CELL DIVISION [ISV] – **zoosporal** *adj*

**zoosterol** /zoh'ostə,rol/ *n* a STEROL (fat-containing chemical compound) (eg cholesterol) of animal origin

**zootechnics** /ˌzoh-ə'tekniks/ *n taking sing or pl vb* the care and improving of animals under domestication; the technology of ANIMAL HUSBANDRY – **zootechnical** *adj*

**zootoxin** /ˌzoh-ə'toksin/ *n* any of various poisons (eg snake venom) produced by animals

**zoot suit** /zooht/ *n* a flamboyant suit popularized by black jazz fans in the 1940s and 1950s, typically consisting of a thigh-length draped jacket with wide padded shoulders and wide trousers tapering to narrow turn-ups [*zoot* prob arbitrary rhyme on *suit*] – **zoot-suiter** *n*

**zori** /'zori/ *n*, *pl* **zori** a flat thonged Japanese sandal, usu made of straw, leather, or rubber [Jap *zōri*]

**zoril** /'zoril/ *n* a zorilla

**zorilla** /zo'rilə/ *n* a S African animal (*Ictonyx striatus*) that resembles the weasel and has a long black and white coat [Fr *zorille*, fr Sp *zorrilla*, *zorrillo*, dim. of *zorra*, *zorro* fox]

**Zoroastrianism** /ˌzoroh'astri·əniz(ə)m/ *n* a Persian religion founded in the 6th century BC by the prophet Zoroaster, promulgated in its sacred book, the AVESTA, and characterized by worship of a supreme god AHURA MAZDA who requires people's good deeds for help in his cosmic struggle against the evil spirit AHRIMAN – **Zoroastrian** *adj or n*

**zoster** /'zostə/ *n* SHINGLES (virus disease) [L, fr Gk *zōstēr* girdle; akin to Gk *zōnē* zone]

**Zouave** /zooh'ahv, zwahv/ *n* **1** a member of a former French infantry unit originally composed of Algerians wearing a brilliant uniform and conducting a quick spirited drill **2** a member of a military unit adopting the dress and drill of the Zouaves [Fr, fr Berber *Zwāwa*, an Algerian tribe]

**zounds** /zownz, zoohnz/ *interj, archaic* – used as a mild oath [euphemism for *God's wounds*]

**zucchetto** /tsooh'ketoh, sooh-, zooh-/ *n, pl* **zucchettos** a small round skullcap worn by Roman Catholic ecclesiastics in colours that vary according to the rank of the wearer [It, fr *zucca* gourd, head, fr LL *cucutia* gourd]

**zucchini** /zooh'keeni, tsooh-/ *n, pl* **zucchini, zucchinis** *chiefly NAm* a courgette [It, pl of *zucchino*, dim. of *zucca* gourd]

**¹Zulu** /'zoohlooh/ *n* **1** a member of a BANTU-speaking people of Natal in S Africa **2** a BANTU language of the Zulus – **Zulu** *adj*

**²Zulu** – a communications code word for the letter *z*

**Zuni, Zuñi** /'zoohn(y)ee/ *n, pl* **Zunis, Zuñis,** *esp collectively* **Zuni, Zuñi** (the language of) a member of an American Indian people of W New Mexico – **Zunian, Zuñian** *adj*

**Zunian, Zuñian** /'zoohn(y)ee·ən/ *n* a language family consisting of Zuni only

**zwieback** /'swee,bak, 'zwee-/ *n* a usu sweetened rich bread that is baked and then sliced and toasted until dry and crisp – compare RUSK [Ger, lit., twice baked, fr *zwie-* twice (fr OHG *zwi-*) + *backen* to bake, fr OHG *bahhan* – more at TWI-, BAKE]

**Zwinglian** /'zwing·gli·ən, 'tsving-/ *adj* of Ulrich Zwingli or his teachings, esp his doctrine that Christ's presence in the communion is not actual but symbolic [Ulrich *Zwingli* †1531 Swiss theologian] – **Zwinglian** *n,* **Zwinglianism** *n*

**zwitterion** /'tsvitə,rie·ən/ *n* an ion with both a positive and negative electric charge [Ger, fr *zwitter* hybrid + *ion*] – **zwitterionic** *adj*

**zyg-, zygo-** *comb form* **1** pair ⟨zygo*dactyl*⟩ **2** union; zygosis ⟨zygo*spore*⟩ [NL, fr Gk, fr *zygon* yoke – more at YOKE]

**zygapophysis** /ˌzigə'pofəsis, ˌziegə-/ *n, pl* **zygapophyses** /-seez/ any of the projections of the NEURAL ARCH (part enclosing spinal cord) of a vertebra which articulate with adjoining projections and of which there are usu two at the front and two at the back [NL, fr *zyg-* + *apophysis*]

**zygodactyl** /ˌziegə'daktil/, **zygodactylous** /ˌziegə'daktiləs/ *adj, of a bird* having the toes arranged two in front and two behind [ISV *zyg-* + Gk *daktylos* toe] – **zygodactyl** *n*

**zygoma** /zie'gohmə, zi-/ *n, pl* **zygomata** /-mətə/ *also* **zygomas 1a** ZYGOMATIC ARCH **b** a slender bony projection of the ZYGOMATIC ARCH **2** ZYGOMATIC BONE [NL *zygomat-, zygoma,* fr Gk *zygōma,* fr *zygoun* to join, fr *zygon* yoke]

**zygomatic** /ˌziegə'matik, ˌzi-/ *adj* of, being, or situated in the region of the zygoma, esp the ZYGOMATIC ARCH

**zygomatic arch** *n* the arch of bone that extends along the front or side of the skull beneath the eye socket

**zygomatic bone** *n* a bone of the side of the face below the eye that in mammals forms part of the ZYGOMATIC ARCH and part of the eye socket; a cheekbone

**zygomatic process** *n* any of several bony projections that enter into or strengthen the ZYGOMATIC ARCH

**zygomorphic** /ˌziegoh'mawfik, ˌzi-, -gə-/ *adj* symmetrical about only one longitudinal plane ⟨*the ~ flowers of the toadflax*⟩ – **zygomorphism, zygomorphy** *n*

**zygopteran** /zie'goptərən/ *n* a damselfly [deriv of Gk *zygon* yoke + *pteron* wing]

**zygosity** /zie'gosəti, zi-/ *n* the makeup or characteristics of a particular zygote

**zygospore** /'ziegoh,spaw, 'zi-, -gə-/ *n* a plant spore (eg in some algae) that is formed by union of two similar sexual cells, usu serves as a resting spore, and develops into the phase of the plant that produces asexual spores – compare OOSPORE [ISV] – **zygosporic** *adj*

**zygote** /'ziegoht, 'zigoht/ *n* a cell formed by the union of two GAMETES (reproductive cells); *broadly* the developing individual produced from such a cell [Gk *zygōtos* yoked, fr *zygoun* to join together – more at ZYGOMA] – **zygotic** *adj,* **zygotically** *adv*

**zygotene** /'ziegə,teen/ *n* the stage in MEIOSIS (division of a cell to produce the reproductive cells) in which corresponding CHROMOSOMES (strands of gene-carrying material) form closely associated pairs [ISV *zyg-* + *-tene*]

**-zygous** /-zigəs/ *comb form* (→ *adj*) having (such) a zygotic constitution ⟨*heterozygous*⟩ [Gk *-zygos* yoked, fr *zygon* yoke]

**zym-, zymo-** *comb form* **1** fermentation ⟨zym*urgy*⟩ **2** enzyme ⟨zymo*gen*⟩ [NL, fr Gk, leaven, fr *zymē*]

**zymase** /'ziemayz, -mays/ *n* an ENZYME or enzyme complex that promotes the breakdown of glucose [ISV]

**-zyme** /-ziem/ *comb form* (→ *n*) enzyme ⟨*lysozyme*⟩ [Gk *zymē* leaven]

**zymogen** /'ziem6əjen, -jən/ *n* an inactive protein secreted by living cells and activated by a catalyst (eg a KINASE or an acid) to form an ENZYME [ISV]

**zymogenic** /ˌziemə'jenik/ *adj* **1** producing fermentation **2** of a zymogen

**zymology** /zie'moləji/ *n* a science that deals with fermentation [NL *zymologia,* fr *zym-* + *-logia* -logy]

**zymotic** /zie'motik/ *adj* **1** of, causing, or caused by fermentation **2** relating to, being, or causing an infectious or contagious disease [Gk *zymōtikos,* fr *zymōtos* fermented, fr *zymoun* to ferment, fr *zymē* leaven] – **zymotically** *adv*

**zymurgy** /'ziemuhji/ *n* a branch of applied chemistry that deals with fermentation processes

**zzz** – used as a visual representation of sleep or snoring, esp in cartoons

# Abbreviations

## A

**a 1** acceleration **2** acre **3** answer **4** are – a metric unit of area **5** area **6** atto-
**A 1** ampere **2** Associate
**AA 1** Alcoholics Anonymous **2** antiaircraft **3** Automobile Association
**AAA 1** Amateur Athletic Association **2** American Automobile Association
**AAM** air-to-air missile
**A and M** ancient and modern – used of hymns
**AB 1** able seaman; able-bodied seaman **2** *NAm* bachelor of arts [NL *artium baccalaureus*]
**ABA** Amateur Boxing Association
**ABC 1** American Broadcasting Company **2** Australian Broadcasting Commission
**abl** ablative
**ABM** antiballistic missile
**Abp** archbishop
**abr** abridged; abridgment
**ABRO** Animal Breeding Research Organization
**abs** absolute
**ABS** Association of Broadcasting Staff
**ABTA** /'abtə, ,ay bee tee 'ay/ Association of British Travel Agents
**AC 1** alternating current **2** appellation contrôlée **3** athletic club
**a/c** account
**ACA** Associate of the Institute of Chartered Accountants
**acad** academic; academy
**ACAS** /'aykas, ,ay see ,ay 'es/ Advisory Conciliation and Arbitration Service
**acc 1** according to **2** account **3** accusative
**ACCA** Association of Certified and Corporate Accountants
**acct** account; accountant
**ACCT** Association of Cinematograph and Television Technicians
**accus** accusative
**ACGB** Arts Council of Great Britain
**ACIS** Associate of the Chartered Institute of Secretaries
**ack** acknowledge; acknowledgment
**ACP** African, Caribbean, and Pacific
**acpt** acceptance
**act** active
**ACT** Australian Capital Territory
**actg** acting
**ACTU** Australian Council of Trade Unions
**ACV** air-cushion vehicle
**ACW** aircraftwoman
**AD** anno domini
**ADAS** /'aydas/ Agricultural Development and Advisory Service
**ADC 1** aide-de-camp **2** amateur dramatic club
**addn** addition
**ADH** antidiuretic hormone
**ad inf** ad infinitum
**adj 1** adjective **2** adjustment – used in banking **3** adjutant
**Adm** admiral

**adv 1** adverb; adverbial **2** against [L *adversus*]
**ad val** ad valorem
**advt** advertisement
**AEA** Atomic Energy Authority
**AEB** Associated Examining Board
**AEC** Atomic Energy Commission – a US organization
**AEI** Associated Electrical Industries
**AERE** Atomic Energy Research Establishment
**aet, aetat** of the specified age; aged [L *aetatis*]
**AEU** Amalgamated Engineering Union – now AUEW
**AEW** airborne early warning
**AF 1** Anglo-French **2** audio frequency
**AFA** Amateur Football Association
**AFAM** Ancient Free and Accepted Masons
**AFC 1** Air Force Cross **2** Association Football Club **3** automatic frequency control
**AFL-CIO** American Federation of Labor and Congress of Industrial Organizations
**AFM** Air Force Medal
**Afr** Africa; African
**AFV** armoured fighting vehicle
**AG 1** adjutant general **2** attorney general **3** joint-stock company [Ger *Aktiengesellschaft*]
**AGC** automatic gain control
**agcy** agency
**AGM** *chiefly Br* annual general meeting
**AGR** advanced gas-cooled reactor
**agric** agricultural; agriculture
**agt** agent
**AH** anno hegirae
**AHA** Area Health Authority
**AI 1** artificial insemination **2** artificial intelligence
**AIA** Associate of the Institute of Actuaries
**AIB** Associate of the Institute of Bankers
**AID 1** Agency for International Development – a US agency **2** artificial insemination by donor
**AIDS** /aydz/ Acquired Immune Deficiency Syndrome
**AIH** artificial insemination by husband
**AJC** Australian Jockey Club
**AK** Alaska
**AKA** also known as
**Ala** Alabama
**ALA** Associate of the Library Association
**ald** alderman
**alg** algebra
**ALS** autograph letter signed
**alt 1** alternate **2** altitude **3** alto
**Alta** Alberta
**ALU** arithmetic and logic unit
**am** ante meridiem
**Am 1** America; American **2** Amos – used for the book of the Bible
**AM 1** Albert Medal **2** amplitude modulation **3** associate member **4** *NAm* master of arts [NL *artium magister*]
**AMA 1** American Medical Association **2** Australian Medical Association

**AMDEA** Association of Manufacturers of Domestic Electrical Appliances
**AMDG** to the greater glory of God [L *ad majorem Dei gloriam*]
**amdt** amendment
**Amer** America; American
**AMR** automatic message routing
**amt** amount
**AMU** atomic mass unit
**an** in the year [L *anno*]
**anal 1** analogous, analogy **2** analysis; analytic
**anat** anatomical; anatomy
**Angl** Anglican
**ann 1** annals **2** annual **3** annuity
**anon** anonymous
**ANSI** /'ansi/ American National Standards Institute
**ant** antonym
**Ant** Antrim
**anthrop** anthropological; anthropology
**A/O** account of
**aob** any other business
**AOC** Air Officer Commanding
**AP** Associated Press
**APB** *chiefly NAm* all points bulletin
**APEX** /'aypeks, ,ay pee ee 'eks/ Association of Professional, Executive, Clerical, and Computer Staff
**APO** army post office
**Apoc 1** Apocalypse **2** Apocrypha; apocryphal
**Apocr** Apocrypha
**app 1** apparent; apparently **2** appendix **3** appointed
**appl** applied
**appro** /'aproh/ approval
**approx** /ə'proks/ approximate; approximately
**Apr** April
**apt** apartment
**APT** Advanced Passenger Train
**ar 1** arrival; arrive **2** in the year of the reign [L *anno regni*]
**AR 1** annual return **2** Arkansas **3** autonomous republic
**ARA** Associate of the Royal Academy
**ARAM** Associate of the Royal Academy of Music
**ARC** Agricultural Research Council
**ARCA** Associate of the Royal College of Art
**arch 1** archaic **2** architect; architectural; architecture
**Arch** archbishop
**archaeol** archaeological; archaeology
**ARCM** Associate of the Royal College of Music
**ARCS** Associate of the Royal College of Science
**ARIBA** Associate of the Royal Institute of British Architects
**arith** arithmetic; arithmetical
**Ariz** Arizona
**Ark** Arkansas
**Arm** Armagh
**ARP** air-raid precautions
**arr 1** arranged by – used in music **2** arrival; arrives

**art 1** article **2** artificial **3** artillery
**arty** artillery
**AS 1** airspeed **2** Anglo-Saxon
   **3** antisubmarine
**ASA 1** Advertising Standards Authority
   **2** American Standards Association
   **3** Amateur Swimming Association
**asap** as soon as possible
**ASE** Amalgamated Society of Engineers
**ASEAN** /'asian/ Association of South-East
   Asian Nations
**ASH** /ash/ Action on Smoking and Health
**ASI** airspeed indicator
**ASLEF** /'azlef/ Associated Society of
   Locomotive Engineers and Firemen
**ASSET** /'aset/ Association of Supervisory
   Staffs, Executives and Technicians
**assoc** association
**ASSR** Autonomous Soviet Socialist Republic
**asst** assistant
**asstd** assorted
**ASTMS** /'aztemz, ,ay es ,tee em 'es/
   Association of Scientific, Technical, and
   Managerial Staffs
**astr** astronomer; astronomy
**astrol** astrologer; astrology
**astron** astronomer; astronomy
**at** atomic
**ATC 1** air traffic control **2** Air Training Corps
**atm** atmosphere; atmospheric
**at no** atomic number
**att** attorney
**attn** for the attention of
**attrib** /ə'trib/ attributive; attributively
**atty** attorney
**ATV** Associated Television
**at wt** atomic weight
**AU 1** angstrom unit **2** astronomical unit
**AUEW** Amalgamated Union of Engineering
   Workers
**aug** augmentative – used in grammar
**Aug** August
**AUT** Association of University Teachers
**auth** authorized
**auto** /'awtoh/ automatic
**aux** auxiliary
**av 1** average **2** avoirdupois
**Av** avenue
**AV 1** ad valorem **2** audiovisual **3** Authorized
   Version (of the Bible)
**avdp** avoirdupois
**Ave** avenue
**avge** average
**AVM** Air Vice Marshal
**avn** aviation
**az** azimuth

# B

**b 1** born **2** bowled by – used in cricket
   **3** breadth **4** bye – used in cricket
**B 1** bachelor **2** bel **3** bishop – used in chess
   **4** black – used esp on lead pencils **5** British
**BA 1** Bachelor of Arts **2** British Academy
   **3** British Airways **4** British Association
**BAA** British Airports Authority
**BAC** /,bee ay 'see; *also* bak/ **1** British
   Agricultural Council **2** British Aircraft
   Corporation
**BAFTA** /'baftə/ British Academy of Film and
   Television Arts
**bal** balance – used in bookkeeping
**BALPA** /'balpə/ British Airline Pilots'
   Association
**b and b,** *often cap* B & B, *Br* bed and
   breakfast
**b and w** black and white
**BAOR** British Army of the Rhine
**Bap** Baptist
**bap** baptize; baptized

**BAPS** /,bee ay pee 'es, baps/ British
   Association of Plastic Surgeons
**Bapt** Baptist
**bar** barometer; barometric
**Bar 1** barrister **2** Baruch – used for the book
   of the Apocrypha
**BArch** Bachelor of Architecture
**Bart** baronet
**BB 1** Boys' Brigade **2** double black – used on
   lead pencils
**BBBC** British Boxing Board of Control
**BBC** /bee bee 'see; *humor* beeb/ British
   Broadcasting Corporation
**BBFC** British Board of Film Censors
**BC 1** before Christ **2** British Columbia
   **3** British Council
**BCC** British Council of Churches
**BCD** binary-coded decimal
**BCh** Bachelor of Surgery [ML *baccalaureus*
   *chirurgiae*]
**BCom** Bachelor of Commerce
**BCS** British Computer Society
**bd 1** bond **2** bound
**BD 1** Bachelor of Divinity **2** bank draft
   **3** barrels per day **4** brought down
**BDA** British Dental Association
**bdc** bottom dead centre
**BDS** Bachelor of Dental Surgery
**BE** bill of exchange
**BEA** British European Airways – now BA
**BEd** Bachelor of Education
**Beds** Bedfordshire
**BEF** British Expeditionary Force
**BEM** British Empire Medal
**BEng** Bachelor of Engineering
**Berks** /bahks, buhks/ Berkshire
**bet** between
**BeV** billion electron volts
**bf** bloody fool
**b/f** brought forward
**BFPO** British Forces Post Office
**BG** brigadier general
**BGC** British Gas Council
**BH** Brinell hardness
**B'ham** /often brum/ Birmingham
**bhp** brake horsepower
**BHS** British Home Stores
**Bib** bible; biblical
**bibliog** bibliographical; bibliography
**BIM** British Institute of Management
**biog** biographical; biography
**biol** biological; biology
**BIR** Board of Inland Revenue
**BIS** Bank for International Settlements
**bk** book
**bkg** banking
**BL 1** Bachelor of Law **2** bill of lading
   **3** British Legion **4** British Leyland **5** British
   Library
**bldg** building
**BLitt** Bachelor of Letters [ML *baccalaureus*
   *litterarum*]
**blvd** boulevard
**BM 1** Bachelor of Medicine **2** bench mark
   **3** British Medal **4** British Museum
**BMA** British Medical Association
**BMC** British Medical Council
**BMJ** British Medical Journal
**BMR** basal metabolic rate
**BMTA** British Motor Trade Association
**BMus** Bachelor of Music
**bn** billion
**BNOC** British National Oil Corporation
**BO** body odour – euph
**BOAC** British Overseas Airways Corporation
   – now BA
**BOC** British Oxygen Company
**BOD** biochemical oxygen demand; biological
   oxygen demand
**BOF** beginning of file

**bor** borough
**BOSS** /bos/ Bureau of State Security – a S
   Afr organization
**bot 1** botanical; botany; botanist **2** bottle
**BOT 1** beginning of tape **2** Board of Trade
**BOTB** British Overseas Trade Board
**Bp** bishop
**BP 1** boiling point **2** British Petroleum
   **3** British Pharmacopoeia
**B/P** bill payable
**BPAS** British Pregnancy Advisory Service
**BPC** British Pharmaceutical Codex
**BPD** barrels per day
**BPharm** Bachelor of Pharmacy
**BPhil** /,bee 'fil/ Bachelor of Philosophy
**bpi** bits per inch; bytes per inch
**bps** bits per second
**Bq** becquerel
**br** branch
**Br 1** British **2** brother
**BR** British Rail
**B/R** bill receivable
**BRCS** British Red Cross Society
**Brig** brigade; brigadier
**Brig-Gen** brigadier-general
**Brit** /brit/ Britain; British
**bro** /broh/ brother
**bros, Bros** brothers
**BRS** British Road Services
**BS 1** Bachelor of Surgery **2** balance sheet
   **3** bill of sale **4** British Standard **5** *NAm*
   Bachelor of Science
**BSA** Building Societies Association
**BSc** /,bee es 'see/ Bachelor of Science
**BSC 1** British Steel Corporation **2** British
   Sugar Corporation
**BSI 1** British Standards Institution **2** Building
   Societies Institute
**BSJA** British Show Jumping Association
**BSocSc, BSSc** Bachelor of Social Science
**BST** British Standard Time; British Summer
   Time
**Bt** Baronet
**BTA** British Tourist Authority
**BTh** Bachelor of Theology
**BTO** British Trust for Ornithology
**Btu** British thermal unit
**Bucks** /buks/ Buckinghamshire
**bull** bulletin
**BUPA** /'byoohpə, 'boohpə/ British United
   Provident Association
**bus** business
**BV** Blessed Virgin
**BVA** British Veterinary Association
**BVM** Blessed Virgin Mary
**BVMS, BVM & S** Bachelor of Veterinary
   Medicine and Surgery
**bvt** brevet
**BW** bacteriological warfare; biological
   warfare
**BYOB** bring your own booze; bring your own
   bottle

# C

**c 1** canine – used in dentistry **2** carat **3** caught
   by – used in cricket **4** centi- **5** century
   **6** chapter **7** circa **8** cloudy **9** cold **10** college
   **11** colt **12** copyright **13** cubic
**C 1** calorie **2** castle – used in chess **3** Catholic
   **4** Celsius **5** centigrade **6** *Br* Conservative **7**
   corps **8** coulomb
**ca** circa
**CA 1** California **2** chartered accountant **3**
   chief accountant **4** Consumers' Association
   **5** current account
**CAA** Civil Aviation Authority
**CAB** Citizens' Advice Bureau
**CAD, Cad** /kad/ computer-aided design

**CADCAM, CAD/CAM** /'kadkam/ computer-aided design and manufacture

**CADMAT** /'kadmat/ computer-aided design, manufacture and test; computer-aided design, manufacture, and testing

**CAE, Cae** computer-aided engineering

**CAI** computer-aided instruction; computer-assisted instruction

**cal 1** calibre **2** (small) calorie

**Cal 1** California **2** (large) calorie

**CAL, Cal** /kal/ computer-aided learning; computer-assisted learning

**Calif** California

**CAM, Cam** /kam/ computer-aided manufacture; computer-aided manufacturing

**Cambs** Cambridgeshire

**CAMRA** /'kamrə/ Campaign for Real Ale

**can** canto

**Can** Canada; Canadian

**c and b** caught and bowled by – used in cricket

**C and G** City and Guilds

**C and W** country and western

**Cant** Canticles – used for the book of the Bible

**Cantab** /'kantab/ of Cambridge – used with academic awards <MA ~ > [L *Cantabrigiensis*]

**Cantuar** of Canterbury – used chiefly in the signature of the Archbishop fo Canterbury [L *Cantuariensis*]

**cap 1** capital **2** capitalize; capitalized

**CAP** Common Agricultural Policy

**caps** /(1) *sometimes* kaps/ **1** capital letters **2** capsule

**Capt** captain

**Car** Carlow

**Card** cardinal

**CARD** /kahd, ,see ay ah 'dee/ Campaign Against Racial Discrimination

**CAT 1** College of Advanced Technology **2** computerized axial tomography

**cath 1** cathedral **2** catholic

**cav** cavalry

**CB 1** château-bottled **2** Citizens' Band **3** Companion of the (Order of the) Bath

**CBC** Canadian Broadcasting Corporation

**CBD** Cash before delivery

**CBE** Commander of the (Order of the) British Empire

**CBI** Confederation of British Industry

**CBS** Columbia Broadcasting System

**cc 1** carbon copy **2** chapters **3** cubic centimetre

**CC 1** Chamber of Commerce **2** County Council **3** Cricket Club

**CCF** Combined Cadet Force

**cd** candela

**c/d** carried down

**CD 1** civil defence **2** diplomatic corps [Fr *corps diplomatique*]

**Cdr** Commander

**Cdre** Commodore

**CE 1** Church of England **2** civil engineer **3** Council of Europe

**CEGB** Central Electricity Generating Board

**cemy** cemetery

**CEng** Chartered Engineer

**CENTO** /sentoh/ Central Treaty Organization

**CERN** /suhn/ European Organization for Nuclear Research [Fr *Conseil Européen pour la Recherche Nucléaire*]

**cert** certificate; certified; certify

**CET** Central European Time

**cf** compare [L *confer*, imper of *conferre* to compare – more at CONFER]

**CF** Chaplain to the Forces

**c/f** carried forward

**CFE** College of Further Education

**cfi** cost, freight, and insurance

**CG 1** centre of gravity **2** coast guard **3** consul general

**CGM** Conspicuous Gallantry Medal

**cgs** centimetre-gram-second (system)

**CGS** Chief of General Staff

**CGT** General Confederation of Labour [Fr *Confédération Générale du Travail*]

**ch 1** chain – a unit of length **2** central heating **3** chapter **4** check – used in chess **5** child; children **6** church

**CH 1** clubhouse **2** Companion of Honour

**chap 1** chaplain **2** chapter

**ChB** Bachelor of Surgery [ML *baccalaureus chirurgiae*]

**CHE** Campaign for Homosexual Equality

**chem** chemical; chemist; chemistry

**Ches** Cheshire

**chk** check *n* used in chess

**chm 1** chairman **2** checkmate – used in chess

**ChM** Master of Surgery [ML *chirurgiae magister*]

**chron, chronol** chronological; chronology

**Chron** Chronicles – used for the books of the Bible

**Ci** curie

**CI** Channel Islands

**CIA** Central Intelligence Agency

**cia** company [Sp *compañía*]

**CID** Criminal Investigation Department

**cie** company [Fr *compagnie*]

**CIE 1** Companion of the (Order of the) Indian Empire **2** Transport Organization of Ireland [IrGael *Coras Iompair Eireann*]

**cif** cost, insurance, and freight

**CIGS** Chief of the Imperial General Staff

**CII** Chartered Insurance Institute

**C in C** Commander in Chief

**circ 1** circa **2** *often cap* circus

**CIS** Chartered Institute of Secretaries

**cit** citation; cited

**civ** civil; civilian

**CJ** chief justice

**cl 1** centilitre **2** clerk

**clin** clinical

**CLit** Companion of Literature

**Cllr** *Br* councillor

**Clo** close – used in street names

**cm** centimetre

**cmd** command

**cmdg** commanding

**Cmdr** Commander

**Cmdre** Commodore

**CMG** Companion of (the Order of) St Michael and St George

**cml** commercial

**cmnd** command

**CMS** Church Missionary Society

**CNAA** Council for National Academic Awards

**CND** Campaign for Nuclear Disarmament

**CNS** central nervous system

**co** /(1) *often pronounced* koh *in the phrase* sby and co *eg* Jones and Co/ **1** company **2** county

**CO 1** commanding officer **2** Commonwealth Office **3** conscientious objector

**c/o 1** care of **2** carried over

**COD 1** cash on delivery **2** Concise Oxford Dictionary

**C of A** Certificate of Airworthiness

**C of C** Chamber of Commerce

**C of E 1** Church of England **2** Council of Europe

**C of S** Church of Scotland

**cog** cognate

**COHSE** /'kohzi/ Confederation of Health Service Employees

**COI** Central Office of Information

**col 1** colour; coloured **2** column

**Col 1** Colonel **2** Colorado **3** Colossians – used for the book of the Bible

**coll 1** college **2** colloquial

**colloq** colloquial; colloquially

**Colo** Colorado

**com, comm 1** commerce; commercial **2** commission **3** committee

**Com, Comm 1** Commander **2** Commodore **3** Commonwealth **4** Communist

**comb** combination; combined; combining

**comdg** commanding

**Comdr** Commander

**Comdt** Commandant

**comp 1** comparative; compare **2** compiled; compiler **3** composition **4** comprehensive

**compar** comparative; comparison

**con 1** consolidated **2** consul

**Con, Cons** Conservative

**conc** concentrate; concentrated; concentration

**conf** conference

**conj 1** conjugation **2** conjunction; conjunctive

**Conn** Connecticut

**cons 1** consecrated **2** consigned; consignment **3** consolidated **4** consonant **5** consulting

**const** constant

**constr** construction

**cont 1** containing **2** contents **3** continent; continental **4** continued

**contd** continued

**contr** contralto

**contrib** contribution; contributor

**Copt** Coptic

**Cor 1** Corinthians – used for the books of the Bible **2** coroner

**CORE** /kaw/ Congress of Racial Equality – a US organization

**Corp 1** Corporal **2** corporation

**cos** /koz/ cosine

**COS** chief of staff

**cosec** cosecant

**cosech** hyperbolic cosecant

**cosh** hyperbolic cosine

**cot** cotangent

**coth** hyperbolic cotangent

**Coun** councillor

**coy** company – used esp for a military company

**cp 1** candlepower **2** compare

**CP 1** Communist Party **2** Country Party – an Australian political party

**CPAG** Child Poverty Action Group

**cpd** compound

**Cpl** Corporal

**CPM** Critical Path Method

**CPO 1** Chief Petty Officer **2** *Br* compulsory purchase order

**CPR** Canadian Pacific Railway

**CPRE** Council for the Preservation of Rural England

**cps 1** characters per second **2** cycles per second

**CPSA** Civil and Public Services Association

**CPSU** Communist Party of the Soviet Union

**CPU, cpu** central processing unit

**cr** credit; creditor

**Cr** councillor

**CR** conditioned reflex; conditioned response

**CRAC** Careers Research and Advisory Centre

**CRC** Cancer Research Campaign

**cresc, cres 1** crescendo **2** *often cap* crescent – used esp in street names

**crit** critical; criticism

**CRO 1** cathode ray oscilloscope **2** Criminal Records Office

**CRT** cathode-ray tube

**cs** case; cases

**CS 1** chartered surveyor **2** Civil Service **3** Court of Session – the supreme civil court of Scotland
**CSC 1** Civil Service Commission **2** Conspicuous Service Cross
**CSD** Civil Service Department
**CSE** Certificate of Secondary Education
**CSI** Companion of the (Order of the) Star of India
**CSIRO** Commonwealth Scientific and Industrial Research Organization – an Australian organization
**CSM** Company Sergeant Major
**CSO 1** Central Statistical Office **2** Community Service Order
**ct 1** carat **2** *often cap* court
**CT** Connecticut
**CTC** Cyclists' Touring Club
**ctr** centre
**cu** cubic
**Cumb** Cumbria
**CV** curriculum vitae
**CVO** Commander of the (Royal) Victorian Order
**CW** chemical warfare
**Cwlth** Commonwealth
**CWS** Cooperative Wholesale Society
**cwt** hundredweight

# D

**d 1** date **2** daughter **3** day **4** deca- **5** deci- **6** delete **7** penny; pence – used before introduction of decimal currency [L *denarius, denarii*] **8** density **9** departs **10** diameter **11** died **12** dose **13** drizzle
**D 1** dimensional **2** Duke
**da** deca-
**DA 1** deposit account **2** *NAm* district attorney
**Dak** Dakota
**Dan** Daniel – used for the book of the Bible
**D & C** dilatation and curettage
**dat** dative
**dB** /,dee 'bee/ decibel
**DBE** Dame Commander of the (Order of the) British Empire
**dbl** double
**DBMS, dbms** database management system
**DC 1** from the beginning [It *da capo*] **2** Detective Constable **3** direct current **4** District of Columbia **5** District Commissioner
**DCB** Dame Commander of the (Order of the) Bath
**DCh** Doctor of Surgery [ML *chirurgiae doctor*]
**DCL 1** Distillers Company Limited **2** Doctor of Civil Law
**DCM** Distinguished Conduct Medal
**DCMG** Dame Commander of (the Order of) St Michael and St George
**DCVO** Dame Commander of the (Royal) Victorian Order
**DD 1** direct debit **2** Doctor of Divinity
**DDBS** distributed database
**DDP** distributed data processing
**DDS** Doctor of Dental Surgery
**DE 1** Delaware **2** Department of Employment
**deb** debenture
**dec 1** deceased **2** declared – used esp in cricket **3** declension **4** declination **5** decrease **6** decrescendo
**Dec** December
**def 1** defendant **2** defence **3** deferred – used esp for deferred shares **4** definite **5** definition
**deg** degree

**del** delegate; delegation
**Del** Delaware
**Dem** Democrat; Democratic
**DEng** /,dee 'enj/ Doctor of Engineering
**dent** dental; dentist; dentistry
**dep 1** departs; departure **2** deposed **3** deposit **4** depot **5** deputy
**dept** department
**der, deriv** derivation; derivative; derived
**DES** Department of Education and Science
**det** detached; detachment
**Det** Detective
**Deut** Deuteronomy – used for the book of the Bible
**DF** Defender of the Faith [ML *defensor fidei*]
**DFC** Distinguished Flying Cross
**DFM** Distinguished Flying Medal
**DG 1** by the grace of God [LL *Dei gratia*] **2** director general
**DHSS** Department of Health and Social Security
**DI** Detective Inspector
**diag** diagram
**dial** dialect
**diam** diameter
**dict 1** dictator **2** dictionary
**diff** difference; different
**dim 1** dimension **2** diminuendo **3** diminutive
**DIN** /din/ German Industrial Standards [Ger *Deutsche Industrie-Norm*]
**Dip** Diploma
**DIP** Dual Inline Package
**Dip AD** Diploma in Art and Design
**Dip Ed** /,dip 'ed/ Diploma in Education
**Dip HE** Diploma in Higher Education
**dir** director
**dis** disused
**dist 1** distance **2** distilled **3** district
**div 1** divergence **2** divide; divided **3** dividend **4** division **5** divorced
**DIY** do-it-yourself
**dk** dark
**dl** decilitre
**DLitt** /,dee 'lit/ Doctor of Letters [L *doctor litterarum*]
**DLT** Development Land Tax
**dm** decimetre
**DM** Doctor of Medicine
**DMA** direct memory access
**DMus** Doctor of Music
**DMZ** *NAm* demilitarized zone
**DNB** Dictionary of National Biography
**do** ditto
**DOA** dead on arrival – used chiefly in hospitals
**dob** date of birth
**doc** document
**DOC** Denominazióne d'Origine Contròllata
**DOD** Department of Defense – a US government department
**DOE** Department of the Environment
**dom** domestic
**DOM** to God, the best and greatest [ML *Deo optimo maximo*]
**Don** Donegal
**DOS** /dos/ disk operating system
**DoT** Department of Trade
**doz** *sometimes* duz/ dozen
**DP 1 DP, dp** data processing **2** displaced person
**dpc** damp proof course
**DPH** Diploma in Public Health
**DPhil** /,dee 'fil/ Doctor of Philosophy
**DPM 1 DPM, dpm** data processing manager **2** Diploma in Psychological Medicine
**DPP** Director of Public Prosecutions
**dpt** department
**dr 1** debtor **2** drachma **3** dram **4** drawer
**Dr 1** doctor **2** Drive – used in street names
**DRAW** /draw/ direct read after write – used in computing

**Dri** drive
**DS 1** from the sign [It *dal segno*] **2** Detective Sergeant
**DSc** Doctor of Science
**DSC** Distinguished Service Cross
**DSM** Distinguished Service Medal
**DSO** Distinguished Service Order
**dsp 1** died without issue [L *decessit sine prole*] **2** dessertspoon; dessertspoonful
**DST** daylight saving time
**Dt** Deuteronomy
**DTh, D Theol** Doctor of Theology
**Dunelm** /'dunelm/ of Durham – used with academic awards and in the signature of the Bishop of Durham [L *Dunelmensis*]
**dup** duplicate
**DV** God willing [L *Deo volente*]
**DVLC** Driver and Vehicle Licensing Centre
**dz** dozen

# E

**E 1** Earl **2** earth – used esp on electrical plugs **3** East; Easterly; Eastern **4** energy **5** English **6** exa-
**ea** each
**E and OE** errors and omissions excepted
**EAW** Electrical Association for Women
**EBCDIC** /'ebsədik *also* 'ebkədik/ Extended Binary Coded Decimal Interchange Code
**Ebor** /'eebaw/ of York – used esp in the signature of the Archbishop of York [L *Eboracensis*]
**EBU** European Broadcasting Union
**EC** East Central – a London postal district
**eccl** ecclesiastic; ecclesiastical
**Eccles, Ec** Ecclesiastes – used for the book of the Bible
**Ecclus** Ecclesiasticus – used for the book of the Apocrypha
**ECG** electrocardiogram; electrocardiograph
**ECL** emitter-coupled logic
**ecol** ecological; ecology
**econ** economics; economist; economy
**ECS** European Communication Satellite
**ECSC** European Coal and Steel Community
**ECT** electroconvulsive therapy
**ECU** European Currency Unit
**ed, edit** edited; edition; editor
**Ed 1** editor **2** education
**EDP** electronic data processing
**educ** education; educational
**EE** Early English
**EEC** European Economic Community
**EEG** electroencephalogram; electroencephalograph
**EEROM** /'eerom/ electrically erasable read only memory
**EFTA** /'eftə/ European Free Trade Association
**EFL** English as a foreign language
**e g** for example [L *exempli gratia*]
**EHF** extremely high frequency
**EHT** extremely high tension
**elec, elect** electric; electrical; electricity
**ELF** extremely low frequency
**Eliz** Elizabethan
**ELT** English language teaching
**em** electromagnetic
**EMA** European Monetary Agreement
**embryol** embryology
**emer** emeritus
**emf** electromotive force
**EMI** Electrical and Musical Industries
**Emp** Emperor; Empress
**emu** electromagnetic unit
**enc, encl** enclosed; enclosure
**ency, encyc, encycl** encyclopedia
**ENE** east-northeast

**ENEA** European Nuclear Energy Agency
**eng 1** engine; engineer; engineering
  **2** engraved; engraver; engraving
**Eng** England; English
**ENO** English National Opera
**ENON** English National Opera North
**Ens** ensign
**ENSA** /'ensə/ Entertainments National Service
  Association
**ENT** ear, nose, and throat
**entom** entomological; entomology
**env** envelope
**EO** Executive Officer
**EOC** Equal Opportunities Commission
**EOF** end of file
**EOJ** end of job
**EOT** end of tape
**ep** en passant
**Ep** epistle
**EP** electroplate
**EPA** Environmental Protection Agency
**Eph, Ephes** Ephesians – used for the book of
  the Bible
**Episc** Episcopal; Episcopalian
**EPNS** electroplated nickel silver
**EPROM** /'eeprom/ erasable programmable
  read only memory
**eq** equal
**equiv** equivalent
**ER 1** Eastern Region **2** King Edward [NL
  *Edwardus Rex*] **3** Queen Elizabeth [NL
  *Elizabetha Regina*]
**ESA** European Space Agency
**Esd** Esdras – used for the books of the
  Apocrypha
**ESE** east-southeast
**ESL** English as a second language
**ESN** educationally subnormal
**esp** /esp/ especially
**Esq** *also* **Esqr** esquire
**est 1** established **2** estate **3** estimate; estimated
**EST 1** Eastern Standard Time **2** electro-shock
  treatment
**Esth** Esther – used for the book of the Bible
**esu** electrostatic unit
**ETA** estimated time of arrival
**ETD** estimated time of departure
**ethnol** ethnologist; ethnology
**et seq 1** and the following one [L *et sequens*]
  **2** and the following ones [L *et sequentes*
  (masc & fem pl), or *et sequentia* (neut pl)]
**ETU** Electrical Trades Union
**ety, etym, etymol** etymological; etymologist;
  etymology
**EUA** European Unit of Account
**euph** euphemistic
**eV** electron volt
**EVA** extravehicular activity
**evap** evaporate; evaporated
**ex 1** examined **2** example **3** except **4** exchange
**Ex, Exod** Exodus – used for the book of the
  Bible
**exc** except
**Exc** excellency
**ex div** without dividend
**exec** executive
**ex lib** from the books (of) – used on
  bookplates [L *ex libris*]
**exor** executor
**exp 1** experimental **2** export; exported
  **3** exponential **4** express
**expt** experiment
**exptl** experimental
**exrx** executrix
**ext 1** extension **2** exterior **3** external;
  externally **4** extinct
**Ez, Ezr** Ezra – used for the book of the Bible
**Ezek** Ezekiel – used for the book of the Bible

# F

**f 1** fathom **2** female **3** femto- **4** force **5** forte
  **6** frequency **7** focal length **8** folio **9** following
  (e g page) **10** foot
**F 1** Fahrenheit **2** false **3** farad **4** Fellow **5** filial
  generation **6** fine – used esp on lead pencils
  **7** forward **8** French
**FA** Football Association
**FAA 1** Fleet Air Arm **2** Federal Aviation
  Agency – a US government agency
**fac** facsimile
**Fahr** Fahrenheit
**FAI** International Aeronautical Federation [Fr
  *Fédération aéronautique internationale*]
**F and F** fixtures and fittings
**FANY** /'fani, ,ef ay en 'wie/ First Aid Nursing
  Yeomanry
**FAO** Food and Agriculture Organization (of
  the United Nations)
**fas** free alongside ship
**fath** fathom
**FBA** Fellow of the British Academy
**FBI** Federal Bureau of Investigation
**FBR** fast breeder reactor
**FC 1** Football Club **2** Forestry Commission
**FCA** Fellow of the (Institute of) Chartered
  Accountants
**FCC** Federal Communications Commission – a
  US government organization
**FCII** Fellow of the Chartered Insurance
  Institute
**FCIS** Fellow of the Chartered Institute of
  Secretaries
**FCO** Foreign and Commonwealth Office
**fcp** foolscap
**FCS** Fellow of the Chemical Society
**FD 1** Defender of the Faith [L *Fidei Defensor*]
  **2** full duplex – used in telecommunications
**FDA** Food and Drug Administration – a US
  government organization
**FDM** frequency division multiplexing
**Feb** February
**fec** he/she made it [L *fecit*]
**fed** federal; federation
**fem 1** female **2** feminine – used in grammar
**Ferm** Fermanagh
**FET** field-effect transistor
**ff 1** folios **2** following (e g pages) **3** fortissimo
**FH** fire hydrant
**FIDE** World Chess Federation [Fr *Fédération
  Internationale des Échecs*]
**FIFA** /'feefə/ International Football Federation
  [Fr *Fédération Internationale de Football
  Association*]
**FIFO, fifo** /'fiefoh/ first in first out
**fig 1** figurative; figuratively **2** figure
**FILO, filo** /'fieloh/ first in last out
**fin 1** finance; financial **2** finish
**fl 1** floor **2** flourished – used to indicate a
  period of renown of sby whose dates of birth
  and death are unknown [L *floruit*] **3** fluid
**FL 1** Florida **2** focal length
**Fla** Florida
**fl oz** fluid ounce
**Flt Lt** Flight Lieutenant
**Flt Off** Flight Officer
**Flt Sgt** Flight Sergeant
**fm** fathom
**FM** Field Marshal
**fml** formal
**fo, fol** folio
**FO 1** Field Officer **2** Flying Officer **3** Foreign
  Office
**fob** free on board
**foc** free of charge
**FOC** Father of the Chapel (in a Trade Union)

**FOE** Friends of the Earth
**for 1** free on rail **2** foreign **3** forest; forestry
**fp 1** forte-piano **2** freezing point
**FPA 1** Family Planning Association **2** Foreign
  Press Association
**fpm** feet per minute
**fps 1** feet per second **2** foot-pound-second
**fr** from
**Fr 1** Father **2** French **3** Friar
**FRAeS** Fellow of the Royal Aeronautical
  Society
**FRAM** Fellow of the Royal Academy of Music
**FRAS** Fellow of the Royal Astronomical
  Society
**FRCM** Fellow of the Royal College of Music
**FRCO** Fellow of the Royal College of
  Organists
**FRCOG** Fellow of the Royal College of
  Obstetricians and Gynaecologists
**FRCP** Fellow of the Royal College of
  Physicians
**FRCS** Fellow of the Royal College of Surgeons
**FRCVS** Fellow of the Royal College of
  Veterinary Surgeons
**freq** frequency; frequent; frequentative;
  frequently
**FRGS** Fellow of the Royal Geographical
  Society
**Fri** Friday
**FRIBA** Fellow of the Royal Institute of British
  Architects
**FRIC** Fellow of the Royal Institute of
  Chemistry
**FRICS** Fellow of the Royal Institution of
  Chartered Surveyors
**front** frontispiece
**FRPS** Fellow of the Royal Photographic
  Society
**FRS** Fellow of the Royal Society
**FRSA** Fellow of the Royal Society of Arts
**frt** freight
**FSA** Fellow of the Society of Actuaries
**FSH** follicle-stimulating hormone
**ft 1** feet; foot **2** fort
**FT** Financial Times
**ftd** fitted
**fth, fthm** fathom
**ft lb** foot-pound
**fur** furlong
**fwd 1** foreword **2** forward; forwards
**FWD 1** four-wheel drive **2** front-wheel drive
**FZS** Fellow of the Zoological Society

# G

**g 1** gauge **2** giga **3** good **4** gram
**G 1** gauss **2** German **3** giga-gauss
  **4** acceleration due to gravity **5** gulf
**Ga 1** gate **2** Georgia (USA)
**GA 1** General Assembly **2** Gamblers
  Anonymous
**gal, gall** */sometimes/ gal/ gallon
**Gal** Galatians – used for the book of the Bible
**galv** galvanized
**G and S** Gilbert and Sullivan
**gar** garage
**GATT** /gat/ General Agreement on Tariffs and
  Trade
**gaz** gazette; gazetteer
**GB** Great Britain
**GBE** Knight/Dame Grand Cross of the (Order
  of the) British Empire
**GBH** *Br* grievous bodily harm
**GC** George Cross
**GCB** Knight/Dame Grand Cross of the (Order
  of the) Bath

**GCE** General Certificate of Education
**GCHQ** Government Communications Headquarters
**GCMG** Knight/Dame Grand Cross of (the Order of) St Michael and St George
**GCVO** Knight/Dame Grand Cross of the (Royal) Victorian Order
**gd** good
**Gdns** Gardens – used esp in street names
**GDP** gross domestic product
**GDR** German Democratic Republic
**GEC** General Electric Company
**gen 1** genitive **2** genus
**Gen** Genesis – used for the book of the Bible
**geog** geographic; geographical; geography
**geol** geologic; geological; geology
**geom** geometric; geometrical; geometry
**ger** gerund
**Ger** German
**GHQ** general headquarters
**gi** gill
**GI** gastrointestinal
**Gib** Gibraltar
**Gk** Greek
**Glam** Glamorgan
**GLC 1** Greater London Council **2** gas-liquid chromatography
**Glos** Gloucestershire
**GLS** General Lighting Service
**gm** gram
**GM 1** general manager **2** George Medal **3** guided missile
**GMC 1** General Medical Council **2** general management committee
**GMT** Greenwich Mean Time
**GMWU** General and Municipal Workers Union
**gn** guinea
**GNB** Good News Bible
**GNP** gross national product
**Gnr** gunner
**GOC** General Officer Commanding
**gov 1** government **2** governor
**govt** government
**GP 1** general practitioner **2** Grand Prix
**Gp Capt** Group Captain
**GPDST** Girls' Public Day School Trust
**GPI** general paralysis of the insane
**GPO** general post office
**GQ** general quarters
**gr 1** grade **2** grain **3** gram **4** gravity **5** gross
**Gr** Greek
**GR** King George [L *Georgius Rex*]
**grad** graduate; graduated
**gram** grammar; grammatical
**gro** gross
**Gro** Grove – used in street names
**gr wt** gross weight
**Gs** gauss
**GS** General Staff
**GSO** general staff officer
**gt** great
**GT** grand tourer
**gtd** guaranteed
**GTT** glucose tolerance test
**gyn, gynaecol** gynaecology

# H

**h 1** hect-; hecto **2** height **3** high **4** hot **5** hour **6** husband
**H 1** harbour **2** hard – used esp on lead pencils **3** hardness **4** henry – used in physics **5** hospital
**ha** hectare
**Hab** Habakkuk – used for the book of the Bible
**Hag** Haggai – used for the book of the Bible
**h and c** hot and cold (water)

**Hants** /hants/ Hampshire [OE *Hantescire*, var of *Hamtunscir*]
**HB** hard black – used on lead pencils
**HBM** His/Her Britannic Majesty
**HC 1** Holy Communion **2** House of Commons
**HCF** highest common factor
**HD** half duplex – used in telecommunications
**hdbk** handbook
**HDip** higher diploma
**hdqrs** headquarters
**HE 1** high explosive **2** His Eminence **3** His/Her Excellency
**Heb** Hebrews – used for the book of the Bible
**HEC** Health Education Council
**HEO** Higher Executive Officer
**her** heraldry
**Here, Heref** Herefordshire
**Herts** Hertfordshire
**HEW** Department of Health, Education, and Welfare – a US government department
**hf** half
**HF** high frequency
**hg 1** hectogram **2** haemoglobin
**HG 1** His/Her Grace **2** Home Guard
**HGV** *Br* heavy goods vehicle
**HH 1** double hard – used on lead pencils **2** His/Her Highness **3** His Holiness
**HI** Hawaii
**HIH** His/Her Imperial Highness
**HIM** His/Her Imperial Majesty
**hist** historian; historical; history
**hl** hectolitre
**HL** House of Lords
**hm** hectometre
**HM 1** headmaster **2** headmistress **3** His/Her Majesty
**HMAS** His/Her Majesty's Australian Ship
**HMCS** His/Her Majesty's Canadian Ship
**HMF** His/Her Majesty's Forces
**HMG** His/Her Majesty's Government
**HMI** His/Her Majesty's Inspector (of Schools)
**HMNZS** His/Her Majesty's New Zealand Ship
**HMS** His/Her Majesty's Ship
**HMSO** His/Her Majesty's Stationery Office
**HMV** His Master's Voice
**HNC** Higher National Certificate
**HND** Higher National Diploma
**ho** house
**HO** Home Office
**hon** honour; honourable; honorary
**Hon** (the) Honourable
**Hons** *Br* honours
**Hon Sec** *Br* Honorary Secretary
**hort, hortic** horticultural; horticulture
**Hos** Hosea – used for the book of the Bible
**hos, hosp** hospital
**HP 1** high pressure **2** hire purchase **3** horsepower **4** Houses of Parliament
**HPF** highest possible frequency
**HPLC** high performance liquid chromatography
**HQ** headquarters
**hr** hour
**HR 1** holiday route **2** House of Representatives
**HRH** His/Her Royal Highness
**hrt** hormone replacement therapy
**HRW** heated rear window
**HSH** His/Her Serene Highness
**HSO** Higher Scientific Officer
**HST** high speed train
**ht** height
**HT 1** high-tension **2** under this title [L *hoc titulo*]
**HTR** high-temperature reactor
**HUD** head-up display

**humor** humorous; humorously
**Hung** Hungarian; Hungary
**HV 1** high velocity **2** high-voltage
**HW 1** high water **2** hot water
**HWM** high-water mark
**hwy** highway
**hy** henry – used in physics
**Hz** hertz

# I

**i** intransitive
**I 1** inductance **2** island; isle
**Ia, IA** Iowa
**IA** Institute of Actuaries
**IAA** indoleacetic acid
**IAAF** International Amateur Athletic Federation
**IABA** International Amateur Boxing Association
**IAEA** International Atomic Energy Agency
**IALC** instrument approach and landing chart
**IAM** Institute of Advanced Motorists
**IARU** International Amateur Radio Union
**IAS** indicated airspeed
**IATA** /ie'ahta/ International Air Transport Association
**ib** ibidem
**IB** Institute of Bankers
**IBA** Independent Broadcasting Authority
**ibid** ibidem
**IBM** International Business Machines
**IBRD** International Bank for Reconstruction and Development
**i/c** in charge
**IC** integrated circuit
**ICA** Institute of Contemporary Arts
**ICAO** International Civil Aviation Organization
**ICBM** intercontinental ballistic missile
**ICC** International Cricket Conference
**ICE 1** Institution of Civil Engineers **2** internal-combustion engine
**ICFC** Industrial and Commercial Finance Corporation
**ICFTU** International Confederation of Free Trade Unions
**IChemE** Institute of Chemical Engineers
**ICI** Imperial Chemical Industries
**ICJ** International Court of Justice
**ICL** International Computers Limited
**ICRF** Imperial Cancer Research Fund
**ICS** Indian Civil Service
**id** idem
**ID 1** Idaho **2** (proof of) identification **3** inner diameter **4** intelligence department
**IDA** International Development Association
**IDB** *chiefly S Afr* illicit diamond buying
**i e** that is [L *id est*]
**IE** Indo-European
**IEE** Institution of Electrical Engineers
**IF** intermediate frequency
**IFC** International Finance Corporation
**iff** /if/ if and only if – used in mathematics
**IG** inspector general
**IHS** Jesus [taken as abbr of L *Iesus hominum salvator*; orig, part transliteration of Gk IHΣ, short for IHΣOYΣ *lēsous* Jesus]
**IL** Illinois
**ILEA** /ie el ee 'ay, 'ili·ə/ Inner London Education Authority
**ill, illus, illust** illustrated; illustration
**Ill** Illinois
**ILO 1** International Labour Organization **2** International Labour Office
**ILP** Independent Labour Party
**ILS** instrument landing system
**IM** intramuscular
**IMechE** Institution of Mechanical Engineers

**IMF** International Monetary Fund
**imit** imitative; imitation
**imp 1** Emperor; Empress [L *Imperator, Imperatrix*] **2** imperative **3** imperfect **4** imperial
**imper** imperative
**in** inch
**IN** Indiana
**inc** /(2) *often* ingk/ **1** increase **2** *chiefly NAm* incorporated
**incl** included; including; inclusive
**ind 1** independent **2** indicative **3** industrial; industry
**Ind** Indiana
**indic** indicative
**inf 1** below [L *infra*] **2** infantry **3** infinitive
**infin** infinitive
**infml** informal
**in loc cit** in the place cited [L *in loco citato*]
**INP** International News Photo
**INRI** Jesus of Nazareth, King of the Jews [L *Iesus Nazarenus Rex Iudaeorum*]
**ins** insurance
**INS 1** inertial navigation system **2** International News Service
**insp** inspector
**inst 1** instant **2** institute; institution
**int 1** integral **2** interior **3** intermediate **4** internal **5** international **6** interpreter **7** intransitive
**inter** intermediate
**interj** interjection
**interrog** interrogation; interrogative; interrogatively
**intl** international
**in trans** in transit [L *in transitu*]
**intro** introduction
**I/O** input/output
**IOC** International Olympic Committee
**IOF** Independent Order of Foresters
**IOM** Isle of Man
**IOOF** Independent Order of Odd Fellows
**IOW** Isle of Wight
**IPA** International Phonetic Alphabet
**IPC** International Publishing Corporation
**IPM 1** inches per minute **2** Institute of Personnel Management
**IPPF** International Planned Parenthood Federation
**IPS** inches per second
**IPSE** /'ipsi/ Integrated Programming Support Environment
**IQS** Institute of Quantity Surveyors
**Ir** Irish
**IR 1** information retrieval **2** infrared **3** Inland Revenue
**IRA** Irish Republican Army
**IRBM** intermediate range ballistic missile
**IRN** Independent Radio News
**IRO 1** Inland Revenue Office **2** International Refugee Organization
**is** island; isle
**IS** International Socialist
**Isa, Is** Isiah – used for the book of the Bible
**ISAM** /'iesam/ indexed-sequential access memory; indexed-sequential access method
**ISBN** International Standard Book Number
**ISD** international subscriber dialling
**isl** island
**ISO 1** Imperial Service Order **2** International Standardization Organization
**ISTC** Iron and Steel Trades Confederation
**IStructE** Institution of Structural Engineers
**ISV** International Scientific Vocabulary
**IT 1** Information Technology **2** Intermediate Technology
**ita** initial teaching alphabet
**ITA** Independent Television Authority – now IBA
**ital** italic; italicized

**Ital, It** Italian
**ITB** Industry Training Board
**ITN** Independent Television News
**ITO** International Trade Organization
**ITT** International Telephone and Telegraph (Corporation)
**ITU** International Telecommunications Union
**ITV** Independent Television
**IU** international unit
**IUD** intrauterine device
**IV** intravenous; intravenously
**IVR** International Vehicle Registration
**IW 1** inside width **2** isotopic weight
**IWC** International Whaling Commission
**IWW** Industrial Workers of the World
**IYHF** International Youth Hostels Federation

# J

**J 1** joule **2** Judge **3** Justice
**JA** Judge Advocate
**JA, J/A** joint account
**JAG** judge advocate general
**Jan** January
**Jas** James – used for the book of the Bible
**JC 1** Jesus Christ **2** Julius Caesar
**JCD 1** Doctor of Canon Law [NL *juris canonici doctor*] **2** Doctor of Civil Law [NL *juris civilis doctor*]
**JCL** Job Control Language
**JCR** Junior Common Room
**jct** junction
**Jer** Jeremiah – used for the book of the Bible
**JJ** Justices
**JMB** Joint Matriculation Board
**jnr** junior
**Jo** Joel – used for the book of the Bible
**Jon** Jonah – used for the book of the Bible
**Josh** Joshua – used for the book of the Bible
**journ** journalistic
**JP** Justice of the Peace
**Jr** junior
**jt, jnt** joint
**Jud** Judith – used for the book of the Apocrypha
**JUD** Doctor of both Civil and Canon Law [L *juris utriusque doctor*]
**Judg** Judges – used for the books of the Bible
**Jul** July
**Jun** June

# K

**k 1** carat **2** kilo- **3** kitchen **4** knot **5** kosher
**K 1** kelvin **2** kilobit **3** kilobyte **4** king – used in chess **5** knit
**KANU** /'kahnooh/ Kenya African National Union
**KB 1** King's Bench **2** Knight Bachelor
**KBE** Knight (Commander of the Order of the) British Empire
**kc** kilocycle
**KC 1** Kennel Club **2** King's Counsel
**kcal** /'kay ˌkal/ kilocalorie
**KCB** Knight Commander of the (Order of the) Bath
**KCIE** Knight Commander of the (Order of the) Indian Empire
**KCMG** Knight Commander of (the Order of) St Michael and St George
**KCSI** Knight Commander of the (Order of the) Star of India
**kc/s** kilocycles per second
**KCVO** Knight Commander of the (Royal) Victorian Order

**KD** knocked down
**KE** kinetic energy
**Ker** Kerry
**KeV** kilo-electron volt
**kg 1** keg **2** kilogram
**KG** Knight of the (Order of the) Garter
**KGB** (Soviet) State Security Committee [Russ *Komitet Gosudarstvennoye Bezopastnosti*]
**Kgs** Kings – used for the books of the Bible
**kHz** kilohertz
**Kild** Kildare
**Kilk** Kilkenny
**kit** kitchen
**kJ** kilajoule
**KKK** Ku Klux Klan
**kl** kilolitre
**km** kilometre
**kn** knot
**KP** Knight of (the Order of) St Patrick
**kph** kilometres per hour
**KS** Kansas
**KSAM** /'kaysam/ keyed-sequential access memory; keyed-sequential access method
**KStJ** Knight of (the Order of) St John
**kt** karat
**KT 1** knight – used in chess **2** Knight Templar **3** Knight of the (Order of the) Thistle
**kV** kilovolt
**kW** kilowatt
**KWAC** /kwak/ keyword and context
**kWh, kwh** kilowatt-hour
**KWIC** /kwik/ keyword in context
**KWOC** /kwok/ keyword out of context
**Ky, KY** Kentucky

# L

**l 1** Lady **2** lake **3** large **4** left **5** length **6** Liberal **7** pound [L *libra*] **8** lightning **9** line **10** litre **11** little **12** long **13** last **14** lower **15** lumen
**L 1** Latin **2** live – used esp on electrical plugs **3** *Br* learner (driver)
**La 1** lane – used esp in street names **2** Louisiana
**LA 1** law agent **2** Library Association **3** *Br* local authority **4** Los Angeles **5** Louisiana
**Lab** /(1) lab *in the phrase* Lib/Lab pact/ **1** Labour **2** Labrador
**LAC** Leading Aircraftman
**LACW** Leading Aircraftwoman
**Lam** Lamentations – used for the book of the Bible
**LAN** /lan/ local-area network
**Lancs** /langks/ Lancashire
**lang** language
**lat** latitude
**Lat 1** Latin **2** Latvia
**lb 1** pound [L *libra*] **2** leg bye
**LBC** London Broadcasting Company
**lbf** pound-force
**lbw** leg before wicket
**lc 1** letter of credit **2** in the place cited [L *loco citato*] **3** lowercase
**LC 1** left centre **2** Library of Congress **3** Lord Chamberlain **4** Lord Chancellor
**LCC** London County Council
**lcd 1** liquid crystal display **2** lowest (*or* least) common denominator
**LCJ** Lord Chief Justice
**LCM** lowest (*or* least) common multiple
**LCpl** lance corporal
**ld** load
**Ld** Lord
**LD** lethal dose – often used with a numerical subscript to indicate the percent of a test group of organisms killed by the dose <$LD_{50}$>

**Ldg** Leading – used chiefly in titles
**LDS** Licentiate in Dental Surgery
**LEA** Local Education Authority
**led** light emitting diode
**leg** legato
**Leics** Leicestershire
**Leit** Leitrim
**LEM** lunar excursion module
**Lev, Levit** Leviticus
**lf 1** light face **2** low frequency
**LF** low frequency
**lge** lounge
**lh** left hand
**LH** luteinizing hormone
**LHA** Local Health Authority
**LHD** Doctor of Letters; Doctor of Humanities [L *litterarum humaniorum doctor*]
**LI 1** Light Infantry **2** librarian; library
**Lib** /lib *in the phrase* Lib/Lab pact/ Liberal
**Lieut** Lieutenant
**LIFO** last in, first out
**Lim** Limerick
**Lincs** /lingks/ Lincolnshire
**ling** linguistics
**Linn** Linnaean; Linnaeus
**lit 1** litre **2** literature
**Litt D** doctor of letters; doctor of literature [ML *litterarum doctor*]
**LJ** Lord Justice
**Lk** Luke – used for the book of the Bible
**ll** lines
**LL** Lord Lieutenant
**LLB** Bachelor of Laws [NL *legum baccalaureus*]
**LLD** Doctor of Laws [NL *legum doctor*]
**LLM** Master of Laws [NL *legum magister*]
**lm** lumen
**LMG** light machine gun
**LNG** liquefied natural gas
**LOB** Location of Offices Bureau
**loc cit** in the place cited [L *loco citato*]
**Lond** Londonderry
**long** longitude
**Long** Longford
**loq** he/she speaks [L *loquitur*]
**Lou** Louth
**LP** low pressure
**LPG** liquefied petroleum gas
**LPO** London Philharmonic Orchestra
**LPS** Lord Privy Seal
**LRAM** Licentiate of the Royal Academy of Music
**LS 1** left side **2** Linnaean Society
**LSB** least significant bit; least significant byte
**LSE** London School of Economics
**LSI** large-scale integration
**LSO** London Symphony Orchestra
**lt** light
**LT 1** lieutenant **2** low-tension
**LTA** Lawn Tennis Association
**Lt Cdr** Lieutenant Commander
**Lt Col** Lieutenant Colonel
**Ltd** limited
**Lt Gen** Lieutenant General
**LV 1** low velocity **2** low voltage **3** *Br* luncheon voucher
**LVT 1** landing vehicle, tracked **2** landing vehicle (tank)
**LW 1** long wave **2** low water
**LWB** long wheelbase
**LWM** low-water mark
**LWR** light water reactor
**LWT** London Weekend Television
**lx** lux

# M

**m 1** maiden (over) – used in cricket **2** male **3** married **4** masculine **5** mass **6** metre

**7** middle **8** mile **9** thousand [L *mille*]
**10** milli- **11** million **12** minute – used for the unit of time **13** molar **14** month
**M 1** Mach **2** Master **3** mega- **4** Member **5** Monsieur **6** motorway
**mA** milliampere
**MA 1** Massachusetts **2** Master of Arts [ML *magister artium*] **3** Middle Ages **4** Military Academy
**MAA** Motor Agents' Association
**Mac, Macc** Maccabees – used for the book of the Apocrypha
**mach** machine; machinery; machinist
**MAD** /mad/ mutual assured destruction
**MAFF** Ministry of Agriculture, Fisheries, and Food
**mag 1** magnesium **2** magnetic; magnetism **3** magnitude
**Maj** Major
**Maj Gen** Major General
**Mal** Malachi – used for the book of the Bible
**man** manual
**Man** Manitoba
**M & S** Marks and Spencer
**manuf** manufacture; manufacturing
**mar** maritime
**Mar** March
**MArch** Master of Architecture
**Marq** Marquess; Marquis
**masc** masculine – used in grammar
**MASH** /mash/ *NAm* mobile army surgical hospital
**Mass** Massachusetts
**Matt** Matthew – used for the book of the Bible
**max** /maks/ maximum
**mb** millibar
**MB 1** Bachelor of Medicine [NL *medicinae baccalaureus*] **2** megabyte
**MBA** Master of Business Administration
**MBE** Member of the (Order of the) British Empire
**MBSc** Master of Business Science
**mc 1** megacycle **2** millicurie
**MC 1** Master of Ceremonies **2** Member of Congress **3** Military Cross
**MCA** Monetary Compensatory Amount
**MCC** Marylebone Cricket Club
**mcg** microgram
**MCh, MChir** Master of Surgery [NL *magister chirurgiae*]
**MCom** Master of Commerce
**mcp** male chauvinist pig
**Mc/s** megacycles per second
**Md** Maryland
**MD 1** Managing Director **2** Doctor of Medicine [NL *medicinae doctor*] **3** right hand – used in music [It *mano destra*]
**MDS** Master of Dental Surgery
**Me** Maine
**ME** Middle English
**Mea** Meath
**meas** measure
**mech** mechanic; mechanical; mechanics
**MEcon** Master of Economics
**med** /(1) med/ **1** medical; medicine **2** medieval **3** medium
**MEd** /,em 'ed/ Master of Education
**meg** megohm
**MEng** Master of Engineering
**MEP** Member of the European Parliament
**mer** meridian
**met** /(1) met *in the phrase* met office/ **1** meteorological; meteorology **2** metropolitan
**metal, metall** metallurgical; metallurgy
**meteor, meteorol** meteorological; meteorology
**MeV** mega-electron-volts
**mf 1** medium frequency **2** mezzo forte **3** millifarad

**mfd** manufactured
**mfg** manufacturing
**MFH** Master of Foxhounds
**MFI** Manufacture of Furniture Institute
**mg** milligram
**MG** machine gun
**Mgr 1** Monseigneur **2** Monsignor
**mh** millihenry
**MHD** magnetohydrodynamics
**MHR** Member of the House of Representatives
**MHz** megahertz
**mi** mile; mileage
**MI 1** Michigan **2** military intelligence
**Mic** Micah – used for the book of the Bible
**Mich** Michigan
**MICR** magnetic ink character recognition
**mld** middle
**Middx** Middlesex
**mil, milit** military
**min 1** minimum **2** minor **3** minute – used for the unit of time
**Min** Minister; Ministry
**Minn** Minnesota
**MIO** minimum identifiable odour
**misc** miscellaneous; miscellany
**Miss** Mississippi
**MIT** Massachusetts Institute of Technology
**mixt** mixture
**Mk** Mark
**MKS** metre-kilogram-second
**ml** /(2) *sometimes* mil/ **1** mile **2** millilitre
**mL** millilambert
**MLA** Member of the Legislative Assembly
**MLC 1** Member of the Legislative Council **2** Meat and Livestock Commission
**MLD** minimum lethal dose
**MLitt** /,em 'lit/ Master of Letters [L *magister litterarum*]
**Mlle** mademoiselle [Fr]
**MLR** minimum lending rate
**MLS** microwave landing system
**mm** millimetre
**MM 1** Maelzel's metronome **2** messieurs [Fr] **3** Military Medal
**MMB** Milk Marketing Board
**Mme** madame [Fr]
**Mmes** mesdames [Fr]
**mmf** magnetomotive force
**MN 1** Merchant Navy **2** Minnesota
**mo** *NAm* month
**MO 1** Medical Officer **2** Missouri **3** modus operandi **4** money order
**MoC** Mother of the Chapel (in a Trade Union)
**mod 1** moderate **2** moderato **3** modern **4** modulus
**MoD** /,em oh 'dee, mod/ Ministry of Defence
**MOH** Medical Officer of Health
**mol 1** molecular; molecule **2** mole
**mol wt** molecular weight
**mon** monetary
**Mon 1** Monaghan **2** Monday
**Mont** Montana
**morph** morphological; morphology
**MOS** /mos, ,em oh 'ess/ metal oxide semiconductor
**mp** mezzo piano
**MP 1** Member of Parliament **2** Metropolitan Police **3** Military Police; Military Policeman
**mpg** miles per gallon
**mph** miles per hour
**MPhil** /,em 'fil/ Master of Philosophy
**mpm** metres per minute
**mps** metres per second
**mr** milliroentgen
**Mr** *see entry in main text*
**MR 1** map reference **2** Master of the Rolls
**MRA** Moral Re-Armament
**MRC** Medical Research Council

**MRCA** multi-role combat aircraft
**MRCOG** Member of the Royal College of Obstetricians and Gynaecologists
**MRCP** Member of the Royal College of Physicians
**MRCS** Member of the Royal College of Surgeons
**MRCVS** Member of the Royal College of Veterinary Surgeons
**mRNA** /,em ahr en 'ay/ messenger RNA
**Mrs** *see entry in main text*
**ms** millisecond
**Ms** *see entry in main text*
**MS 1** left hand – used in music [It *mano sinistra*] **2** manuscript **3** Mississippi **4** multiple sclerosis
**MSB** most significant bit; most significant byte
**MSC 1** Manpower Services Commission **2** Metropolitan Special Constabulary
**MSc** /,em es 'see/ Master of Science
**msec** millisecond
**MSG** monosodium glutamate
**Msgr** *chiefly NAm* Monseigneur; Monsignor
**MSI** medium-scale integration
**msl** mean sea level
**MSS** manuscripts
**Mt 1** Matthew **2** Mount
**MT** Montana
**MTB** motor torpedo-boat
**MTBF** mean time between failures
**MTech** /,em 'tek/ Master of Technology
**mth** month
**mun** municipal
**mus 1** museum **2** music; musical; musician
**mv** millivolt
**MV 1** mezza voce **2** motor vessel
**MVO** Member of the (Royal) Victorian Order
**MW 1** Master of Wine **2** medium wave **3** megawatt
**mW** milliwatt
**Mx** maxwell
**MY** motor yacht
**myth, mythol** mythological; mythology

# N

**n 1** name **2** nano- **3** born [L *natus*] **4** net **5** new **6** neuter **7** nominative **8** noon **9** noun **10** numerical aperture
**N 1** knight – used in chess **2** newton **3** North; Northerly; Northern **4** neutral – used esp on electric plugs
**n/a** no account – used in banking
**NA 1** North America **2** not applicable
**NAAFI** /'nafi/ Navy, Army, and Air Force Institutes
**NAD 1** no appreciable disease **2** nothing abnormal detected
**Nah** Nahum – used for the book of the Bible
**NALGO** /'nalgoh/ National and Local Government Officers Association
**NAm** North America; North American
**NASA** /'nasa/ National Aeronautics and Space Administration – a US government organization
**nat** national; nationalist
**natl** national
**NATO** /'naytoh/ North Atlantic Treaty Organization
**NATSOPA** /nat'sohpa/ National Society of Operative Printers, Graphical and Media Personnel
**naut** nautical
**nav** navigable; navigation
**nb** no ball – used in cricket
**NB 1** Nebraska **2** New Brunswick **3** note well [L *nota bene*]

**NBC** National Broadcasting Company – a US company
**nbg** *Br informal* no bloody good
**NBL** National Book League
**NC 1** no charge **2** North Carolina
**NCA** National Cricket Association
**NCB** National Coal Board
**NCC** Nature Conservancy Council
**NCCL** National Council for Civil Liberties
**NCH** National Children's Home
**NCO** non-commissioned officer
**NCP** National Car Parks
**NCR** National Cash Register (Company)
**NCT** National Childbirth Trust
**ncv** no commercial value
**nd** no date
**ND, NDak** North Dakota
**NE 1** modern English [*New English*] **2** New England **3** Northeast; Northeastern
**NEB 1** National Enterprise Board **2** New English Bible
**Nebr, Neb** Nebraska
**NEC** National Executive Committee
**NEDC** National Economic Development Council
**neg** negative
**Neh** Nehemiah – used for the book of the Bible
**NEI** not elsewhere included
**NERC** Natural Environment Research Council
**neut** neuter
**Nev** Nevada
**NF 1** National Front **2** Newfoundland **3** no funds
**Nfld** Newfoundland
**NFS** not for sale
**NFU** National Farmers' Union
**NFWI** National Federation of Women's Institutes
**ng** no good
**NGA** National Graphical Association
**NH** New Hampshire
**NHS** National Health Service
**NI 1** National Insurance **2** Northern Ireland
**NJ** New Jersey
**NL 1** New Latin **2** it is not permitted [L *non licet*]
**NLC** National Liberal Club
**NLF** National Liberation Front
**nm 1** nanometre **2** nautical mile
**NM, N Mex** New Mexico
**NMR** nuclear magnetic resonance
**NNE** north-northeast
**NNW** north-northwest
**no 1** not out – used in cricket **2** number [L *numero*, abl of *numerus*] **3** *NAm* north
**nom** nominative
**NOP** National Opinion Poll
**Nor, Norm** Norman
**Norf** Norfolk
**norm** normal
**Northants** /naw'thants, nawth'hants/ Northamptonshire
**Northumb** Northumberland
**nos** numbers
**Notts** /nots/ Nottinghamshire
**Nov** November
**np** new paragraph
**NP** Notary Public
**NPFA** National Playing Fields Association
**NPL** National Physical Laboratory
**NPN** negative-positive-negative
**nr** near
**NR** Northern Region
**NRA** National Rifle Association
**NS 1** not specified **2** Nova Scotia **3** *NAm* nuclear ship
**NSB** National Savings Bank
**nsec** *also* **ns** nanosecond

**NSF** not sufficient funds
**NSPCC** National Society for the Prevention of Cruelty to Children
**NSU** nonspecific urethritis
**NSW** New South Wales
**NT 1** National Trust **2** New Testament **3** no trumps
**NTP** normal temperature and pressure
**NTS** National Trust for Scotland
**nt wt** net weight
**NUBE** /'nyoohbi/ National Union of Bank Employees
**NUGMW** National Union of General and Municipal Workers
**NUJ** National Union of Journalists
**num** numeral
**Num, Numb** Numbers – used for the book of the Bible
**NUM** National Union of Mineworkers
**NUPE** /'nyoohpi/ National Union of Public Employees
**NUR** National Union of Railwaymen
**NUS 1** National Union of Seamen **2** National Union of Students
**NUT** National Union of Teachers
**NUTGW** National Union of Tailors and Garment Workers
**NV 1** Nevada **2** nonvintage
**NW** Northwest; Northwestern
**NWT** Northwest Territories (of Canada)
**NY** New York
**NYC** New York City
**NYO** National Youth Orchestra
**NZ** New Zealand

# O

**o 1** ohm **2** old
**O** Ohio
**o-** ortho-
**O & M** organization and methods
**OAP** *Br* old-age pensioner
**OAS 1** Organization of American States **2** Organisation de l'Armée Secrète – used for an organization dedicated to retaining French rule in Algeria
**OAU** Organization of African Unity
**ob** he/she died [L *obiit*]
**Ob, Obad** Obadiah – used for the book of the Bible
**OB 1** outside broadcast **2** *Br* old boy
**OBE** Officer of the (Order of the) British Empire
**obj** object; objective – used esp in grammar
**obs 1** obsolete **2** obstetrical; obstetrics
**o/c** overcharge
**OC** *Br* Officer Commanding
**occas** occasionally
**OCR** optical character reader; optical character recognition
**oct** octavo
**Oct** October
**OCTU** Officer Cadets Training Unit
**OD, (2, 5, & 6) O/D 1** officer of the day **2** on demand **3** ordnance datum **4** outer diameter **5** overdraft **6** overdrawn
**OE** Old English
**Oe** oersted
**OECD** Organization for Economic Cooperation and Development
**OED** Oxford English Dictionary
**oem** own equipment manufacturer; original equipment manufacturer
**off** office; officer; official
**OFM** Order of Friars Minor
**OFS** Orange Free State
**OFT** Office of Fair Trading
**OG** *Br* old girl
**OH** Ohio

**ohc** overhead camshaft
**OHMS** On His/Her Majesty's Service
**ohv** overhead value
**OIS** office information system
**OK, Okla** Oklahoma
**OM** Order of Merit
**ONC** Ordinary National Certificate
**OND** Ordinary National Diploma
**ono** or near offer – used with prices of goods for sale
**Ont** Ontario
**op** opus
**OP 1** observation post **2** opposite prompt – used to designate part of the theatrical stage **3** out of print
**op cit** in the work cited [L *opere citato*]
**OPEC** /'ohpek/ Organization of Petroleum Exporting Countries
**opp** opposite
**ops** operations
**opt 1** optative – used in grammar **2** optical; optician; optics **3** optional
**OR 1** operational research **2** Oregon **3** other ranks **4** owner's risk
**orch 1** orchestra; orchestral **2** orchestrated by
**ord 1** order **2** ordinary **3** ordnance
**Oreg, Ore** Oregon
**org 1** organic **2** organization; organized
**orig** original; originally; originator
**Ork** Orkney
**ornith** ornithology
**OS 1** ordinary seaman **2** Ordnance Survey **3** out of stock **4** outsize
**O/S** outstanding
**OSA** Order of St Augustine
**OSB** Order of St Benedict
**OSD** optical scanning device
**OSF** Order of St Francis
**OSI** open system interconnection
**OT 1** occupational therapy; Occupational Therapist **2** Old Testament; **3** overtime
**OTC** Officers' Training Corps
**OU** Open University
**OUDS** Oxford University Dramatic Society
**OXFAM** /'oksfam/ Oxford Committee for Famine Relief
**Oxon** /'okson/ **1** Oxfordshire [L *Oxonia*] **2** of Oxford – used chiefly with academic awards <MA ~> [L *Oxoniensis*]
**oz** ounce; ounces [It *onza*]

# P

**p 1** page **2** participle **3** past **4** pence; penny **5** per **6** piano – used as an instruction in music **7** pico- **8** pint **9** power **10** premolar **11** pressure
**P 1** parental generation **2** parking **3** pawn – used in chess **4** peta-poise **5** poise **6** Prince **7** purl
**pa** per annum
**Pa 1** Pennsylvania **2** pascal
**PA 1** Pennsylvania **2** personal assistant **3** press agent **4** public address (system) **5** purchasing agent
**PABX** *Br* private automatic branch (telephone) exchange
**Pac** Pacific
**PAL** /,pee ay 'el, pal/ phase alternation line – a system of transmitting colour television programmes
**palaeont** palaeontology
**P & L** profit and loss
**P & O** Peninsular and Oriental (Steamship Company)
**p & p** *Br* postage and packing
**par 1** paragraph **2** parallel **3** parish
**part** participial; participle

**PAS 1** para-aminosalicyclic acid **2** Pregnancy Advisory Service
**pass** passive
**pat** patent; patented
**path, pathol** pathological; pathology
**PAX** /paks/ *Br* private automatic (telephone) exchange
**PAYE** pay as you earn
**PBAB** please bring a bottle
**PBX** private branch (telephone) exchange
**pc 1** per cent **2** personal computer **3** postcard
**PC 1** police constable **2** Privy Councillor
**PCB** printed circuit board
**PCC** parochial church council
**pcm** pulse code modulation
**pct** *chiefly NAm* per cent
**pd** paid
**PD 1** per diem **2** potential difference **3** *NAm* police department
**Pde** parade – used in street names
**pdl** poundal
**PDSA** People's Dispensary for Sick Animals
**PDT** Pacific daylight time
**PE** physical education
**ped** pedal
**PEI** Prince Edward Island
**pen** peninsula
**Penn, Penna** Pennsylvania
**PEP** *Br* Political and Economic Planning
**PER** Professional Employment Register
**perf 1** perforated **2** performance
**perh** perhaps
**perm** permanent
**perp** *often cap* perpendicular
**per pro** /,puh 'proh/ by the agency (of) [L *per procurationem*]
**pers** person; personal
**PERT** /puht/ programme evaluation and review technique
**Pet** Peter – used for the book of the Bible
**pF** picofarad
**PF** Procurator Fiscal
**PFA** Professional Footballers' Association
**PFLP** Popular Front for the Liberation of Palestine
**PG 1** paying guest **2** postgraduate
**PGA** Professional Golfers' Association
**PH** public health
**phar, pharm** pharmaceutical; pharmacist; pharmacy
**PhB** /,pee aych 'bee/ Bachelor of Philosophy [L *philosophiae baccalaureus*]
**PhD** /,pee aych 'dee/ Doctor of Philosophy [L *philosophiae doctor*]
**phil** philosophy
**Phil 1** Philippians – used for the book of the Bible **2** Philharmonic
**Philem** Philemon – used for the book of the Bible
**phon** phonetics
**phr** phrase
**phys 1** physical **2** physics
**physiol** physiology
**PI** petrol injection
**pizz** pizzicato
**pk 1** *often cap* park – used esp in street names **2** peck
**pkg** package
**pkt** packet
**pl 1** *often cap* place – used esp in street names **2** platoon **3** plural
**PL** Poet Laureate
**PLA** Port of London Authority
**plc** public limited company
**PLO** Palestine Liberation Organization
**PLP** Parliamentary Labour Party
**PLR** Public Lending Right
**plup** pluperfect
**pm 1** post meridiem **2** premium
**PM 1** postmortem **2** Prime Minister **3** Provost Marshal

**PMB** Potato Marketing Board
**PMG 1** Paymaster General **2** Postmaster General
**PMH** production per man-hour
**PMS** pre-menstrual syndrome
**PMT** pre-menstrual tension
**pn 1** promissory note **2** pronoun
**PNdB** perceived noise decibel
**PNP** positive-negative-positive
**PO 1** Petty Officer **2** Pilot Officer **3** postal order **4** Post Office
**POB** Post Office box
**POD** pay on delivery
**POE 1** port of embarkation **2** port of entry
**pol, polit** political; politics
**pop** population
**POP** *Br* Post Office Preferred
**por 1** pay on receipt **2** pay on return
**pos** positive
**poss 1** possessive – used in grammar **2** possible
**pot 1** potential **2** potentiometer
**POUNC** Post Office Users' National Council
**POW** prisoner of war
**pp 1** pages **2** past participle **3** by proxy [L *per procurationem*] **4** pianissimo
**PP 1** parcel post **2** parish priest
**ppd, PP 1** postpaid **2** prepaid
**PPE** Philosophy, Politics, and Economics
**ppm** parts per million
**PPS 1** Parliamentary Private Secretary **2** further postscript [L *post-postscriptum*]
**ppt** precipitate
**pptn** precipitation
**PQ** Province of Quebec
**pr 1** pair **2** present **3** price **4** pronoun
**Pr 1** Priest **2** Prince
**PR 1** proportional representation **2** public relations **3** Puerto Rico
**PRA** President of the Royal Academy
**PRAM** /pram/ programmable random access memory
**PRB** Pre-Raphaelite Brotherhood
**Preb** Prebendary
**prec** preceding
**pred** predicate
**pref 1** preface **2** preferred **3** prefix
**prelim** preliminary
**prem** premium
**prep 1** preparation; preparatory **2** preposition
**pres** present
**Pres** President
**Presb** Presbyterian
**prev** previous; previously
**Prin** Principal
**PRO 1** Public Records Office **2** public relations officer
**prob** probable; probably
**proc** proceedings
**prod** production
**Prof** Professor
**prom** promontory
**PROM** /prom/ programmable read-only memory
**pron 1** pronoun **2** pronounced; pronunciation
**prop 1** proposition **2** proprietor
**PROP** /prop/ Preservation of the Rights of Prisoners
**pros** prosody
**Prot 1** Protectorate **2** Protestant
**prov 1** province; provincial **2** provisional
**Prov 1** Proverbs – used for the book of the Bible **2** Provost
**prox** proximo
**PRT** petroleum revenue tax
**Ps** Psalms – used for the book of the Bible
**PS 1** Police Sergeant **2** postscript [L *postscriptum*] **3** Private Secretary **4** prompt side – used to designate part of the theatrical stage

**PSA** Property Services Agency
**PSBR** Public Sector Borrowing Requirement
**PSE** Programming Support Environment
**pseud** pseudonym; pseudonymous
**psf** pounds per square foot
**psi** pounds per square inch
**PST** Pacific Standard Time
**PSV** *Br* public service vehicle
**psychol, psych** psychology
**pt** 1 part 2 pint 3 point 4 port
**PT** 1 Pacific time 2 physical training
**PTA** Parent-Teacher Association
**Pte** Private
**PTE** Passenger Transport Executive
**PTFE** polytetrafluoroethylene
**ptg** printing
**PTO** please turn over
**Pty** *chiefly Austr, NZ, & SAfr* Proprietary
**pu** per unit
**pub, pub** 1 public 2 published; publisher; publishing
**PVA** polyvinyl acetate
**PVC** polyvinyl chloride
**Pvt** *chiefly NAm* Private
**pw** per week
**PW** *Br* policewoman
**pwr** power
**PWR** pressurized water reactor
**pwt** pennyweight
**PX** post exchange

## Q

**q** 1 quarto 2 quintal 3 quire
**Q** queen – used in chess
**QB** Queen's Bench
**QC** Queen's Counsel
**QED** which was to be demonstrated [L *quod erat demonstrandum*]
**QEH** Queen Elizabeth Hall (London)
**QF** quick-firing
**QM** quartermaster
**QMG** Quartermaster General
**QMS** Quartermaster Sergeant
**QPM** Queen's Police Medal
**QPR** Queen's Park Rangers
**qq** which (*pl*) see [L *quae vide*]
**qr** 1 quarter 2 quire
**QS** quarter sessions
**QSO** quasi-stellar object
**qt** quart
**qto** quarto
**qty** quantity
**qu, ques** question
**Que** Quebec
**quot** quotation
**qv** which see [L *quod vide*]

## R

**r** 1 radius 2 railway 3 recto 4 resistance 5 right 6 runs – used in cricket
**R** 1 rabbi 2 radical – used in chemistry 3 rain 4 Réaumur 5 rector 6 queen [L *regina*] 7 registered (as a trademark) 8 king [L *rex*] 9 ring road 10 river 11 röntgen 12 rook – used in chess 13 Royal
**RA** 1 Rear Admiral 2 Royal Academician; Royal Academy 3 Royal Artillery
**RAA** Royal Academy of Arts
**RAAF** Royal Australian Air Force
**Rabb** Rabbinic
**RAC** 1 Royal Armoured Corps 2 Royal Automobile Club
**rad** 1 radian 2 radius
**RADA** /ˈrahdə/ Royal Academy of Dramatic Art
**RAE** Royal Aircraft Establishment

**RAEC** Royal Army Educational Corps
**RAF** /ˌahr ay ˈef, raf/ Royal Air Force
**RAFVR** Royal Air Force Volunteer Reserve
**RAH** Royal Albert Hall (London)
**rall** rallentando
**RAM** /(1) ram, ˌahr ay ˈem/ 1 random access memory 2 Royal Academy of Music
**RAMC** Royal Army Medical Corps
**RAN** Royal Australian Navy
**R and A** Royal and Ancient – used as the title of St Andrews Golf Club
**R & B** rhythm and blues
**R and D** research and development
**R and R** *NAm* rest and recreation; rest and recuperation
**RAOC** Royal Army Ordnance Corps
**RAS** Royal Astronomical Society
**RB** Rifle Brigade
**RBA** Royal (Society of) British Artists
**RBC** red blood cells; red blood count
**RBS** Royal (Society of) British Sculptors
**RC** 1 Red Cross 2 reinforced concrete 3 Roman Catholic
**RCA** Royal College of Art
**RCAF** Royal Canadian Air Force
**RCM** Royal College of Music
**RCMP** Royal Canadian Mounted Police
**RCN** 1 Royal Canadian Navy 2 Royal College of Nursing
**RCO** Royal College of Organists
**RCOG** Royal College of Obstetricians and Gynaecologists
**RCP** Royal College of Physicians
**RCS** 1 Royal College of Science 2 Royal College of Surgeons 3 Royal Corps of Signals
**RCT** Royal Corps of Transport
**RCVS** Royal College of Veterinary Surgeons
**rd** *often cap R* road
**RD** having recently had the lees removed [Fr *récemment dégorgé*]
**RDC** Rural District Council
**RE** 1 religious education 2 Royal Engineers
**rec** 1 receipt 2 recommended 3 recreation
**recd** received
**ref** 1 reference 2 referred
**refl** reflex; reflexive
**reg** 1 regiment 2 register; registered 3 registrar; registry 4 regulation 5 regulo
**regd** registered
**Reg Prof** Regius Professor
**regt** regiment
**rel** relating; relation; relative
**REM** /rem/ röntgen equivalent man
**REME** /ˈreemi/ Royal Electrical and Mechanical Engineers
**Rep** 1 republic 2 Republican
**repr** reprint; reprinted
**req** 1 require; required 2 requisition
**reqd** required
**res** 1 reserve 2 residence; resides
**resp** respective; respectively
**ret** 1 retired 2 return; returned
**retd** 1 retired 2 returned
**rev** 1 revenue 2 reverse 3 review; reviewed 4 revised; revision
**Rev** /(2) rev/ 1 Revelation – used for the book of the Bible 2 Reverend
**REV** reentry vehicle
**Revd** Reverend
**REX** /reks/ real-time executive routine
**RF** 1 radio frequency 2 Rugby Football
**RFC** 1 Royal Flying Corps 2 Rugby Football Club
**RFH** Royal Festival Hall (London)
**RFU** Rugby Football Union
**RGS** Royal Geographical Society
**rh** 1 relative humidity 2 right hand
**RH** Royal Highness
**RHA** 1 Road Haulage Association 2 Royal Horse Artillery

**rhet** rhetoric
**RHG** Royal Horse Guards
**rhs** right hand side
**RHS** 1 Royal Historical Society 2 Royal Horticultural Society 3 Royal Humane Society
**RI** 1 refractive index 2 religious instruction 3 Rhode Island
**RIBA** Royal Institute of British Architects
**RIC** Royal Institute of Chemistry
**RICS** Royal Institution of Chartered Surveyors
**RIP** 1 may he rest in peace [L *requiescat in pace*] 2 may they rest in peace [L *requiescant in pace*]
**rit** /rit/ ritardando
**RK** religious knowledge
**RL** Rugby League
**rm** 1 ream 2 room
**RM** 1 Resident Magistrate 2 Royal Mail 3 Royal Marines
**RMA** Royal Military Academy (Sandhurst)
**rms** root-mean-square
**RN** Royal Navy
**RNAS** Royal Naval Air Service
**RNIB** Royal National Institute for the Blind
**RNLI** Royal National Lifeboat Institution
**RNR** Royal Naval Reserve
**RNVR** Royal Naval Volunteer Reserve
**RNZAF** Royal New Zealand Air Force
**RNZN** Royal New Zealand Navy
**ro** run out – used in cricket
**ROC** Royal Observer Corps
**rom** roman (type)
**Rom** Romans – used for the book of the Bible
**ROM** /rom/ read only memory
**Ros, Rosc** Roscommon
**RoSPA** /ˈrospə/ Royal Society for the Prevention of Accidents
**RP** 1 Received Pronunciation 2 Regius Professor
**RPC** Royal Pioneer Corps
**RPI** *Br* retail price index
**rpm** 1 *Br, often cap* retail price maintenance 2 revolutions per minute
**RPO** Royal Philharmonic Orchestra
**rps** revolutions per second
**RPS** Royal Photographic Society
**rpt** 1 repeat 2 report
**RQ** respiratory quotient
**RRB** Race Relations Board
**RS** 1 right side 2 Royal Society
**RSA** 1 Royal Scottish Academician; Royal Scottish Academy 2 Royal Society of Arts
**RSC** Royal Shakespeare Company
**RSE** Royal Society of Edinburgh
**RSFSR** Russian Soviet Federated Socialist Republic [Russ *Rossiĭskaya Sovetskaya Federativnaya Sotsialisticheskaya Respublika*]
**RSG** rate support grant
**RSL** Royal Society of Literature
**RSM** 1 Regimental Sergeant Major 2 Royal Society of Medicine
**RSPB** Royal Society for the Protection of Birds
**RSPCA** Royal Society for the Prevention of Cruelty to Animals
**RSSPCC** Royal Scottish Society for the Prevention of Cruelty to Children
**RSV** Revised Standard Version (of the Bible)
**RSVP** please answer [Fr *répondez s'il vous plaît*]
**rt** right
**RT** 1 radiotelephone; radiotelephony 2 real-time 3 remote terminal 4 room temperature
**RTE** Irish Radio and Television [IrGael *Radio Telefís Éireann*]

**Rt Hon** Right Honourable
**Rt Rev, Rt Revd** Right Reverend
**RU** Rugby Union
**RUC** Royal Ulster Constabulary
**RV** Revised Version (of the Bible)
**RW 1** Right Worshipful **2** Right Worthy
**R/W** read/write – used in computing
**ry, rwy** railway
**RYA** Royal Yachting Association

# S

**s 1** school **2** scruple **3** second **4** shilling **5** singular **6** sire **7** small **8** snow **9** son **10** succeeded
**S 1** saint **2** sea **3** siemens **4** Signor **5** society **6** South; Southerly; Southern **7** sun
**SA 1** Salvation Army **2** sex appeal **3** small arms **4** limited liability company; Ltd [Fr *société anonyme*] **5** Society of Actuaries **6** South Africa **7** South America
**SABC** South African Broadcasting Corporation
**sae** stamped addressed envelope
**SALT** /sawlt/ Strategic Arms Limitation Talks
**Sam, Saml** Samuel – used for the books of the Bible
**SAM** /sam/ **1** sequential access memory; sequential access method; serial access memory **2** surface-to-air missile
**SANROC** /'sanrok/ South African Non-Racial Olympics Committee
**SAS** Special Air Service
**Sask** Saskatchewan
**Sat** Saturday
**SATB** soprano, alto, tenor, bass
**SAYE** save-as-you-earn
**sb** substantive
**SBN** Standard Book Number
**SBS** Special Boat Squadron
**sc 1** scene **2** scilicet **3** small capitals
**s/c** self-contained
**Sc** Scots
**SC 1** South Carolina **2** special constable
**ScD** /,es see 'dee/ Doctor of Science [ML *scientiae doctor*]
**SCE** Scottish Certificate of Education
**SCF** Save the Children Fund
**sch** school
**sci** science; scientific
**SCM 1** State Certified Midwife **2** Student Christian Movement
**Scot** Scotland; Scottish
**SCR 1** senior common room **2** script **3** scripture
**SCS** Society of Civil Servants
**SD 1** sine die **2** Social Democrat **3** South Dakota **4** standard deviation
**SDA 1** Scottish Development Agency **2** Sex Discrimination Act
**S Dak** South Dakota
**SDLP** Social Democratic and Labour Party
**SDP** Social Democratic Party
**SE** southeast; southeastern
**SEATO** /'seetoh/ Southeast Asia Treaty Organization
**sec 1** second; secondary **2** secretary **3** section **4** according to [L *secundum*] **5** secant
**SECAM** /'seekam/ sequence by colour-memory – a system of transmitting colour television programmes [Fr *séquentiel couleur à mémoire*]
**sect** section; sectional
**secy** secretary
**sem** seminary
**Sem** Semitic
**SEM** scanning electron microscope
**sen 1** Senate; Senator **2** Senior

**SEN** State Enrolled Nurse
**Sep, Sept** September
**seq** the following [L *sequens, sequentes, sequentia*]
**seqq** the following [L *sequentes, sequentia*]
**Serg, Sergt** Sergeant
**SET** Selective Employment Tax
**sf** sforzando
**SF** science fiction
**SFA** Scottish Football Association
**SG 1** Solicitor General **2** *often not cap* specific gravity
**sgd** signed
**SGHWR** steam-generating heavy water reactor
**Sgt** Sergeant
**Sgt Maj** Sergeant Major
**Shak** Shakespeare
**SHAPE** /shayp/ Supreme Headquarters Allied Powers Europe
**SHO** senior house officer
**SI** International System of Units [Fr *Système International d'Unités*]
**sig** signature
**Sig** Signor
**sin** sine
**sing** singular
**SIS** Secret Intelligence Service
**sit** situated; situation
**SJ** Society of Jesus
**SLADE** /slayd/ Society of Lithographic Artists, Designers and Etchers
**Slo** Sligo
**SLP** Scottish Labour Party
**SLR** single lens reflex
**sm** small
**SM** Sergeant Major
**SNCF** the French National Railways [Fr *Société nationale des chemins de fer français*]
**SNP** Scottish National Party
**snr** senior
**So** south
**SO 1** Scientific Officer **2** Stationery Office
**soc** /*sometimes* sok/ society
**sociol** sociological; sociologist; sociology
**SOGAT** /'sohgat/ Society of Graphical and Allied Trades
**sol 1** solicitor **2** soluble **3** solution
**Som** Somerset
**sop** soprano
**sp 1** species **2** specific **3** spelling **4** spell out
**SP 1** without issue [L *sine prole*] **2** starting price
**SPCK** Society for Promoting Christian Knowledge
**SPD 1** supplementary petroleum duty **2** the W German Social Democratic Party [Ger *Sozialdemokratische Partei Deutschlands*]
**specif** specific; specifically
**SPG** Special Patrol Group
**sp gr** specific gravity
**SPL** sound pressure level
**spp** species (pl)
**SPQR** the Senate and the people of Rome [L *senatus populusque Romanus*]
**SPR** Society for Psychical Research
**SPRC** Society for the Prevention and Relief of Cancer
**SPUC** Society for the Protection of the Unborn Child
**sq** square
**Sqn Ldr** Squadron Leader
**sr** steradian
**Sr 1** senior **2** Senor **3** Sir **4** Sister
**SR 1** Senior Registrar **2** Southern Region
**SRA** Squash Racquets Association
**SRC** Science Research Council
**SRN** State Registered Nurse
**SRO 1** standing room only **2** Statutory Rules and Orders

**SRV** space rescue vehicle
**SS 1** saints **2** steamship **3** Sunday school
**SSC** Solicitor in the Supreme Court – a Scottish legal officer
**SSE** south-southeast
**SSgt** staff sergeant
**SSM** surface-to-surface missile
**SSR** Soviet Socialist Republic
**SSRC** Social Science Research Council
**SST** supersonic transport
**SSW** south-southwest
**st 1** stanza **2** stitch **3** stone **4** stumped by
**St 1** Saint **2** street
**sta** station; stationary
**Staffs** /stafs/ Staffordshire
**stbd** starboard
**std** standard
**STD 1** doctor of sacred theology [L *sacrae theologiae doctor*] **2** subscriber trunk dialling
**Ste** saint (female) [Fr *sainte*]
**stg** sterling
**sth** south
**STOL** /stol/ short takeoff and landing
**STP** standard temperature and pressure
**str 1** strait **2** stroke – used in rowing
**STUC** Scottish Trades Union Congress
**STV** Scottish Television
**subj 1** subject **2** subjunctive
**suff** suffix
**Sun** Sunday
**sup 1** superior **2** superlative **3** supplement; supplementary **4** supra
**superl** superlative
**supp, suppl** supplement; supplementary
**supt** superintendent
**surg** surgeon; surgery; surgical
**surv** survey; surveying; surveyor
**Sus** Susanna – used for the book of the Apocrypha
**SW 1** shortwave **2** southwest; southwestern
**SWALK** /swalk/ sealed with a loving kiss
**SWAPO** /'swahpoh/ South-West Africa People's Organization
**SWG** standard wire guage
**Sx** Sussex
**SYHA** Scottish Youth Hostels Association
**syl, syll** syllable
**sym** symmetrical
**syn** synonym; synonymous; synonymy
**syst** system

# T

**t 1** time **2** ton; tonne **3** transitive
**T 1** temperature **2** tera- **3** tesla **4** true
**TA** Territorial Army
**TAB** /tab, ,tee ay 'bee/ typhoid-paratyphoid A and B (vaccine)
**TAM** television audience measurement
**T & AVR** Territorial and Army Volunteer Reserve
**tan** /tan/ tangent
**TASS** /tas/ the official news agency of the Soviet Union [Russ *Telegrafnoye agentsvo Sovietskovo Soyuza*]
**TB** tubercle bacillus
**tbs, tbsp** tablespoon; tablespoonful
**TC** technical college
**TCCB** Test and County Cricket Board
**Tce** *Br* terrace – used esp in street names
**TD 1** member of the Dail – used for members of the lower house of parliament of the Republic of Ireland [IrGael *Teachta Dála*] **2** Territorial (Officer's) Decoration
**tech 1** technical; technically; technician **2** technological; technology
**technol** technological; technology
**TEFL** /,tee ee ef 'el, 'tefl/ teaching English as a foreign language

**tel 1** telegram **2** telegraph; telegraphic **3** telephone

**temp 1** temperature **2** temporary **3** in the time of [L *tempore*]

**ten** tenuto

**Tenn** Tennessee

**Terr, Terr 1** terrace – used esp in street names **2** territory

**TES** Times Educational Supplement

**TESL** /,tee ee es 'el, 'tesl/ teaching English as a second language

**Test** Testament

**Tex** Texas

**TG** transformational grammar

**TGIF** thank God it's Friday

**TGWU** Transport and General Workers' Union

**Th** Thursday

**TH** town hall

**ThB** /,tee aych 'bee/ Bachelor of Theology [NL *theologiae baccalaureus*]

**ThD** /,tee aych 'dee/ Doctor of Theology [NL *theologiae doctor*]

**theol** theologian; theological; theology

**THES** /,tee aych ee 'es, thes/ Times Higher Educational Supplement

**Thess** Thessalonians – used for the books of the Bible

**ThM** /,tee aych 'em/ Master of Theology [NL *theologiae magister*]

**Tho, Thos** /*sometimes* thos/ Thomas

**Thur, Thurs** Thursday

**Tim** Timothy – used for the books of the Bible

**tinct** tincture

**Tip** Tipperary

**TIR** International Road Transport [Fr *Transport International Routiers*]

**Tit** Titus – used for the book of the Bible

**TKO** technical knock-out

**TLS** Times Literary Supplement

**TM 1** trademark **2** transcendental meditation

**TN** Tennessee

**TO** telegraph office

**Tob** Tobit – used for the book of the Apocrypha

**topog** topography

**TOPS** /tops/ Training Opportunities Scheme

**tot** total

**tp, TP 1** teleprocessing **2** text processing

**TPI** Town Planning Institute

**Tpr** Trooper

**tr 1** transitive **2** translated; translation; translator **3** transpose **4** trill **5** trustee

**trans 1** transitive **2** translated; translation; translator

**transf** transfer; transferred

**transl** translated; translation

**treas** treasurer; treasury

**trib** tributary

**trop** tropic; tropical

**trs** transpose

**TSB** Trustee Savings Bank

**TSH** thyroid-stimulating hormone

**tsp** teaspoon; teaspoonful

**TT 1** teetotal; teetotaller **2** Tourist Trophy **3** tuberculin tested

**TTL** transistor transistor logic

**TTY** teletype

**TU** trade union

**TUC** Trades Union Congress

**Tue, Tues** Tuesday

**TV** television

**TVP** textured vegetable protein

**TWA** Trans-World Airlines

**TX** Texas

**typ, typog** typographer; typography

**Tyr** Tyrone

# U

**u 1** unit **2** upper

**U 1** uncle **2** Unionist **3** university

**UAE** United Arab Emirates

**UAR** United Arab Republic

**UAU** Universities Athletic Union

**uc** upper case

**UC** University College

**UCATT** Union of Construction, Allied Trades, and Technicians

**UCCA** /'ukə/ Universities Central Council on Admissions

**UCL** University College, London

**UDA** Ulster Defence Association

**UDI** unilateral declaration of independence

**UDR** Ulster Defence Regiment

**UEFA** /'yoohfə, yooh'ayfə/ Union of European Football Associations

**UGC** University Grants Committee

**UHF** ultrahigh frequency

**UHT** ultrahigh temperature

**UJ** universal joint

**UK** United Kingdom

**UKAEA** United Kingdom Atomic Energy Authority

**ult 1** ultimate **2** ultimo

**UMIST** /yoohmist/ University of Manchester Institute of Science and Technology

**UN** United Nations

**UNA** United Nations Association

**unan** unanimous

**UNCTAD** /'ungktad/ United Nations Commission for Trade and Development

**UNESCO** /yooh'neskoh/ United Nations Educational, Scientific, and Cultural Organization

**UNICEF** /'yoohnisef/ United Nations Children's Fund [*United Nations Children's Emergency Fund*, its former name]

**Unit** Unitarian

**univ 1** universal **2** university

**UNO** /'yoohnoh/ United Nations Organization

**UNRWA** /'unrə/ United Nations Relief and Works Agency

**UP** Uttar Pradesh

**UPI** United Press International

**UPOW** Union of Post Office Workers

**UPU** Universal Postal Union

**URC** United Reformed Church

**US** United States

**USA 1** United States Army **2** United States of America

**USAF** United States Air Force

**USDAW** /'uzdaw/ Union of Shop, Distributive, and Allied Workers

**USN** United States Navy

**USS** United States ship

**USSR** Union of Soviet Socialist Republics

**usu** usual; usually

**UT 1** Universal time **2** Utah

**UU** Ulster Unionist

**UV** ultraviolet

**UVF** Ulster Volunteer Force

# V

**v 1** vector **2** verb **3** verse **4** versus **5** very **6** verso **7** vice **8** vide **9** von – used in German personal names

**V 1** velocity **2** volt; voltage **3** volume

**va** verbal auxiliary

**Va** Virginia

**VA 1** Veterans Administration – a US organization **2** Vicar Apostolic **3** Vice-Admiral **4** (Order of) Victoria and Albert **5** Virginia **6** volt-ampere

**vac** vacant

**V & A** Victoria and Albert Museum

**var 1** variable **2** variant **3** variation **4** variety **5** various

**Vat** Vatican

**VAT** /vat, ,vee ay 'tee/ value-added tax

**vb** verb; verbal

**VC 1** Vice Chairman **2** Vice Chancellor **3** Vice Consul **4** Victoria Cross

**VCR** video cassette recorder

**VD** venereal disease

**VDQS** vin délimité de qualité supérieure

**VDU** visual display unit

**VE** Victory in Europe

**VED** Vehicle Excise Duty

**vel** velocity

**Ven** Venerable

**ver** verse

**vert** vertical

**Vet MB** Bachelor of Veterinary Medicine

**VG 1** very good **2** Vicar General

**VHF** very high frequency

**vi 1** verb intransitive **2** see below [L *vide infra*]

**VI** Virgin Islands

**Vic 1** vicar **2** Victoria

**Vis, Visc** Viscount; Viscountess

**viz** videlicet

**VLF** very low frequency

**VLSI** very large-scale integration

**voc** vocative

**vocab** /*sometimes* 'vohkab/ vocabulary

**vol 1** volume **2** volunteer

**VP** Vice-President

**VR 1** Queen Victoria [NL *Victoria Regina*] **2** Volunteer Reserve

**vs** verse

**VS** veterinary surgeon

**VSO** Voluntary Service Overseas

**VSOP** Very Special Old Pale – a type of brandy

**vt** verb transitive

**Vt** Vermont

**VTOL** /'veetol/ vertical takeoff and landing

**VTR** video tape recorder

**vulg** vulgar; vulgarly

**Vulg** Vulgate

**vv 1** verses **2** vice versa **3** volumes

# W

**w 1** week **2** weight **3** white **4** wicket **5** wide **6** width **7** wife **8** with

**W 1** Watt **2** West; Westerly; Western

**WAAC** /wak, ,dubl yooh ,ay ay 'see/ **1** Women's Army Auxiliary Corps – the women's component of the British army from 1914 to 1918 **2** Women's Army Auxiliary Corps – the women's component of the US army from 1942 to 1948

**WAAF** /waf, ,dubl yooh ,ay ay 'ef/ Women's Auxiliary Air Force – the women's component of the RAF from 1939 to 1948

**WAC** /wak, ,dubl yooh ay 'see/ Women's Army Corps – the women's component of the US army

**WAF** /waf, ,dubl yooh ay 'ef/ Women in the Air Force – the women's component of the USAF

**War, Warw** Warwickshire

**WAR** Women Against Rape

**Wash** Washington

**Wat** Waterford

**Wb** weber

**WBA** World Boxing Association

**WBC 1** white blood cells; white blood count **2** World Boxing Council

**WC 1** water closet **2** West Central – a London postal district

**WCC** World Council of Churches

**WCdr** Wing Commander
**WCT** World Championship Tennis
**WD 1** War Department **2** Works Department
**WEA** Workers' Education Association
**Wed, Weds** Wednesday
**wef** with effect from
**Westm** Westmeath
**WEU** Western European Union
**Wex** Wexford
**wf** wrong fount
**WFTU** World Federation of Trade Unions
**Wg Cdr** Wing Commander
**wh** watt-hour
**WHO** World Health Organization
**WI 1** West Indies **2** Wisconsin **3** Women's
Institute
**Wick** Wicklow
**Wilts** /wilts/ Wiltshire
**WIPO** World Intellectual Property
Organization – a branch of the United
Nations
**Wis, Wisc** Wisconsin
**Wisd, Wis** Wisdom – used for the book of the
Apochrypha
**wk 1** week **2** work
**wkly** weekly
**wkt** wicket
**Wlk** walk – used in street names
**Wm** William
**WMO** World Meteorological Organization
**WNP** Welsh National Party
**WNW** west-northwest

**w/o** without
**WO** Warrant Officer
**Worcs** Worcestershire
**WOW** War on Want
**WP** word processing; word processor
**wpb** wastepaper basket
**WPC** Woman Police Constable
**wpm** words per minute
**WPS** Woman Police Sergeant
**WR** Western Region
**WRAC** /rak, ,dubl yooh ,ahr ay 'see/ Women's
Royal Army Corps
**WRAF** Women's Royal Air Force
**WRNS** /renz, 'dubl yooh ,ahr en 'es/ Women's
Royal Naval Service
**WRP** Workers' Revolutionary Party
**WRVS** Women's Royal Voluntary Service
**WS** Writer to the Signet – a Scottish solicitor
**WSW** west-southwest
**wt** weight
**W Va, W V** West Virginia
**WW** World War
**WWF** World Wildlife Fund
**Wyo, Wy** Wyoming

# X

**x 1** ex **2** extra
**X** Christ [Gk *X* (chi), initial letter of *Christos*
Christ]
**XL** extra large

**XT** Christ (Gk *X* (chi), initial letter of *Christos*
Christ]

# Y

**y** year
**yd** yard
**yeo** yeomanry
**YHA** Youth Hostels Association
**YMCA** Young Men's Christian Association
**YMHA** Young Men's Hebrew Association
**Yorks** /yawks/ Yorkshire
**yr 1** year **2** younger **3** your
**YWCA** Young Women's Christian Association
**YWHA** Young Women's Hebrew Association

# Z

**Zach** Zachariah – used for the book of the
Bible
**ZANU** /'zahnooh/ Zimbabwe African National
Union
**ZAPU** /'zahpooh/ Zimbabwe African People's
Union
**Zech** Zechariah – used for the book of the
Bible
**Zeph** Zephaniah – used for the book of the
Bible
**zoo, zool** zoological; zoology
**ZPG** zero population growth

# Handbook of style

## PUNCTUATION

The English writing system uses punctuation marks for the following purposes: to separate groups of words for meaning and emphasis; to convey an idea of the variations of pitch, volume, pauses, and intonations of speech; and to help avoid contextual ambiguity. The following list gives English punctuation marks, together with general rules and bracketed examples of their use.

## Apostrophe (')

| | | |
|---|---|---|
| 1. | indicates the possessive case of nouns and indefinite pronouns (e g anyone, anybody) | \<Alan Brown's camera\> <br> \<the boy's mother\> <br> \<the boys' mothers\> <br> \<It is anyone's guess how much it will cost.\> <br> \<Marks and Spencer's pullovers\> <br> \<Charles's wedding\> <br> \<for goodness' sake\> |
| 2. | marks omissions in contracted words | \<didn't\>  \<o'clock\> |
| 3. | often forms the plural of letters, figures, and words referred to as words <br> (An apostrophe should not be used to form a plural except in the rare instances given here.) | \<You should dot your *i*'s and cross your *t*'s.\> <br> \<His *1*'s and his *7*'s looked alike.\> <br> \<She has trouble pronouncing her *the*'s.\> |

## Colon (:)

| | | |
|---|---|---|
| 1. | introduces a clause or phrase that explains, illustrates, amplifies, or restates what has gone before | \<The bicycle was little use: it lacked both saddle and handlebars.\> |
| 2. | introduces a list or series | \<Three countries were represented: England, France, and Belgium.\> |
| 3. | directs attention to a word or phrase in apposition to another | \<He had only one pleasure: eating.\> |
| 4. | introduces usu lengthy quoted material | \<I quote from the text of Chapter One:\> |
| 5. | introduces the words of a speaker (e g in a play) | \<Macbeth: So foul and fair a day I have not seen.\> |
| 6. | separates data in biblical references and, particularly in American English, in time-telling | \<John 4:10\>  \<8:30 am\> |
| 7. | is used in giving the relationship between one number and another | \<2:1\> |

## Comma (,)

| | | |
|---|---|---|
| 1. | separates main clauses joined by a conjunction (e g *and, but, or, nor,* or *for*) and very short clauses not so joined | \<She knew very little about him, and he disclosed nothing.\> <br> \<I came, I saw, I conquered.\> |
| 2. | sets off an adverbial clause (or a long phrase) that precedes the main clause | \<When he found that his friends had deserted him, he sat down and wept.\> |
| 3. | sets off from the rest of the sentence transitional words and expressions (e g *on the contrary, on the other hand*), conjunctive adverbs (e g *consequently, furthermore, however*), and expressions that introduce an illustration or example (e g *namely, for example*) | \<Your second question, on the other hand, remains open.\> <br> \<The mystery, however, was left unsolved.\> <br> \<She expects to travel through two countries, namely, France and Belgium.\> |

4.  separates a series of three or more words, phrases, or clauses

&lt;He was young, eager, and restless.&gt;
&lt;She decided to sell her house, to rent a small cottage in Wales, and to begin writing her first novel.&gt;

5.  separates parenthetic elements from the rest of the sentence

&lt;Our guide, who wore a tartan skirt, was a seasoned traveller.&gt;
&lt;We visited Bannockburn, the site of a famous battle.&gt;
&lt;The captain, John Fitzpatrick, was an experienced mariner.&gt;

6.  is used with sentences to mark off narrative from a direct quotation that is neither a question nor an exclamation

&lt;John said, 'I am leaving.'&gt;
&lt;'I am leaving,' John said.&gt;
&lt;'I am leaving,' John said with determination, 'even if you want me to stay.'&gt;

7.  sets off words in direct address, absolute phrases, and mild interjections

&lt;You may go, Mary, if you wish.&gt;
&lt;I dread the encounter, his temper being what it is.&gt;
&lt;Ah, that's my idea of a good wine.&gt;

8.  separates a question tag from the rest of the sentence

&lt;It's a fine day, isn't it?&gt;

9.  is used to avoid ambiguity and also to emphasize a particular phrase

&lt;He tried in vain to find her, in his underclothes.&gt;
&lt;The more embroidery on a dress, the higher the price.&gt;

10. is used to group numbers into units of three in separating thousands, millions etc.; however it is not used in pagination, or in years

&lt;Northborough, pop. 100,000&gt;
*but*
&lt;3600 rpm&gt; &lt;the year 1982&gt;
&lt;page 1411&gt;

11. punctuates an inverted name

&lt;Brown, Alan David&gt;

12. separates a proper name from a following academic, honorary, governmental, or military title

&lt;Alan Brown, BSc&gt; &lt;Margaret Anderson, MP&gt;

13. sets off geographical names (e g town from county), items in dates, and addresses from the rest of a text. In American English it is commonly used also to set off the name of a town from the name of a country.

&lt;Gatwick, Sussex, is the site of a large airport.&gt;
&lt;vacationing in Paris, France&gt;
&lt;On Sunday, 23 June, 1940, he was wounded.&gt;
&lt;10 Downing Street, London, is a famous address.&gt;

14. follows the salutation and complimentary close in correspondence

&lt;Dear Alan,&gt;
&lt;Yours faithfully,&gt;

# Dash (–)

1.  marks an abrupt change or break in the continuity of a sentence

&lt;There are many doctors – indeed, some surgeons – who have never witnessed a heart transplant.&gt;

2.  introduces a summary statement that follows a series of words or phrases

&lt;Coal, iron, and steel – these are the backbone of industrialization.&gt;

3.  often precedes the attribution of a question

&lt;My foot is on my native heath . . . – Sir Walter Scott&gt;

4.  indicates halting speech or an unfinished sentence in dialogue (see also ELLIPSIS 3)

&lt;'He–um–er, well I suppose you could say he–er– "borrowed" it.'&gt;
&lt;'Wait until he's shut the door and then —'&gt;

5.  replaces a word or part of a word that is considered taboo (see also ELLIPSIS 2)

&lt;'Where's the —ing key?'&gt;

6.  indicates duration or distance between two points in time or space

&lt;1980–87&gt;
&lt;London–New York&gt;

# Ellipsis (. . .)

1.  indicates the omission of one or more words within a quoted passage

&lt;The head is not more native to the heart . . . than is the throne of Denmark to thy father. –Shak&gt;

2.  replaces a word or part of a word that is considered taboo

&lt;'That's the last . . . time I let you drive my car.'&gt;

3.  indicates halting speech or an unfinished sentence in dialogue

&lt;'I'd like to . . . that is . . . if you don't mind. . . .' He faltered and fell into silence.&gt;

**4.** indicates the omission of one or more sentences within a quoted passage or the omission of words at the end of a sentence by using four spaced dots the last of which represents the full stop

<He adjusted his discourse to their level. . . . He made everything concrete. –William Golding>
<I was so lonely, and more or less housebound, in that mausoleum of a house . . . –Margaret Drabble>

# Exclamation Mark (!)

indicates forceful utterance or strong feeling

<Hurray!> <Get out of here!>

# Full Stop or Period (.)

**1.** terminates sentences that are neither questions nor exclamations

<She came through the door.>
<He asked whether the law had been obeyed.>

**2.** terminates sentence fragments that are neither questions nor exclamations

<Obey the law.>

**3.** follows some abbreviations and contractions

<i.e.> <A.D.> <etc.> <Hon.> <Esq.>

# Hyphen (-)

**1.** marks separation or division at the end of a line terminating with a syllable of a word that is to be carried over to the next line

<mill-
stone>

<pas-
sion>

**2.** separates the prefix of a newly-formed word, or of a word the second part of which begins with a capital letter

<neuro-mechanics>
<pre-Renaissance>

**3.** separates a prefix where juxtaposition would suggest a misleading pronunciation or different sense

<co-opted> <re-ink> <re-cover a sofa>

**4.** is often used between elements of a modifier in attributive position in order to avoid ambiguity

<He is a small-business man.>
<She has grey-green eyes.>
<He looked across to her with a don't-ask-me expression.>

**5.** is used in writing numbers between 21 and 99

<forty-six>
<one hundred and twenty-eight>

**6.** is used between the numerator and the denominator in writing out fractions, especially when they are used as modifiers; however, fractions used as nouns are usually treated as open compounds and therefore are not hyphenated

<a two-thirds majority of the vote>
*but*
<ate two thirds of a box of chocolates>

# Inverted Commas or Quotation Marks (', ")

**1.** indicate the beginning and end of direct quotations

<He said 'I am leaving.'>

**2.** enclose words or phrases borrowed from others or used in a special way

<He called himself 'emperor' but he was really just a director.>

**3.** are sometimes used to disclaim responsibility for an expression

<He was arrested for smuggling 'scag'.>
<Her 'hubby' had bought her a new car.>

**4.** enclose titles of short writings, writings not published separately, chapters of books, short musical compositions, and radio and TV programmes

<The third chapter of *Treasure Island* is entitled 'The Black Spot'.>
<Ravel's 'Bolero'> <BBC's 'Tomorrow's World'>

**5.** are sometimes used in place of italics for the names of vehicles, ships, or aircraft

<Francis Chichester's 'Gypsy Moth IV'>

Inverted commas may be either single or double, although the latter are more used in handwritten material. Whichever form is not used for main quotation is used for quotation within quotation.

<'He said "I am leaving", but stayed until the end.'>

## Question Mark (?)

| | | |
|---|---|---|
| **1.** | terminates a direct question | \<Who threw the brick?\><br>\<'Who threw the brick?' he asked.\><br>\<To ask the question Who threw the brick? is irrelevant.\> |
| **2.** | indicates the writer's uncertainty | \<Omar Khayyám, Persian poet (?–?1123)\> |

## Round Brackets or Parentheses (( ))

| | | |
|---|---|---|
| **1.** | indicate supplementary, parenthetic, or explanatory material when the interruption is more marked than that usually indicated by commas | \<Three old destroyers (all now out of commission) will be scrapped.\><br>\<He is hoping (as we all are) that this time he will succeed.\> |
| **2.** | enclose numbers or letters in a series | \<We must determine (1) our long-term goals, (2) our immediate objectives, and (3) the means at our disposal.\> |

## Semicolon (;)

| | | |
|---|---|---|
| **1.** | links main clauses not joined by conjunctions | \<Some people have the ability to write well; others do not.\> |
| **2.** | links main clauses joined by conjunctive adverbs (e g *consequently, furthermore, however*) | \<Speeding is illegal; furthermore it is very dangerous.\> |
| **3.** | links clauses which themselves contain commas even when such clauses are joined by conjunctions | \<She lived in a small cottage in Wales, miles from the nearest town; the cottage was without gas, water, or electricity.\> |

## Solidus or Virgule (/)

| | | |
|---|---|---|
| **1.** | separates alternatives | \<Engines intended for high-speed and/or high-temperature operation.\><br>\<. . . sit hour after hour . . . and finally year after year in a catatonic/frenzied trance rewriting the Bible – William Saroyan\> |
| **2.** | separates successive divisions (e g months or years) of an extended period of time | \<the tax year 1982/3\> |
| **3.** | serves as a dividing line between continuous lines of poetry | \<In the window full of sunlight/Concentrates her golden shadow – D H Lawrence\> |
| **4.** | indicates abbreviation, especially as a substitute for *per* | \<c/o\> \<20 km/hr\> |

## Square Brackets ([ ])

| | | |
|---|---|---|
| **1.** | indicate extraneous data such as editorial interpolations, especially within quoted material | \<He wrote, 'received [sic] your letter'.\> |
| **2.** | function as brackets within brackets | \<the first witness (Alan Hughes [alias Brown])\> |

# ITALICIZATION

The following are usually italicized in print and underlined in manuscript and typescript:

| | | |
|---|---|---|
| **1.** | titles of books, magazines, newspapers, plays, films, works of art, and music | \<Tolkien's *Lord of the Rings*\> \<*Good Housekeeping*\><br>\<*Daily Express*\> \<Shaffer's *Equus*\><br>\<the film *Gone With the Wind*\> \<Gainsborough's *Blue Boy*\><br>\<Mozart's *Don Giovanni*\> |
| **2.** | names of ships, aircraft, and often spacecraft | \<HMS *Jupiter*\> \<Lindbergh's *Spirit of St Louis*\> \<*Apollo 14*\> |
| **3.** | words, letters, and figures when referred to as such | \<The word *receive* is often misspelt.\><br>\<The *g* in *align* is silent.\><br>\<Some people prefer to cross their *7*'s.\> |
| **4.** | words given special emphasis, esp in speech | \<'He doesn't *dislike* train journeys, but he *would* rather fly.'\> |

5. foreign words and phrases that have not been naturalized in English

&lt;*aere perennius*&gt;
&lt;*che sarà, sarà*&gt;
&lt;*sans peur et sans reproche*&gt;
&lt;*ich dien*&gt;

6. New Latin scientific names of genera, species, subspecies, and varieties (but not groups of higher rank such as phyla, classes, or orders) in botanical and zoological names

&lt;a European carnivorous mammal (*Mustela putorius*)&gt;
&lt;a small bunting (*Emberiza cirlus*)&gt;

# CAPITALIZATION

The following are the most common uses of capital letters:

1. The first word of a sentence or sentence fragment is capitalized.

The play lasted nearly three hours.&gt;
&lt;How are you feeling?&gt;
&lt;Bravo!&gt;

2. The first word of a direct quotation is capitalized.

&lt;And God said, Let there be light. – Gen 1:3 (AV)&gt;
&lt;He replied 'We can only stay for a few minutes.'&gt;

3. The first word of a direct question within a sentence is capitalized.

&lt;That question is this: Is man an ape or an angel? –Benjamin Disraeli&gt;

4. The first word of a line of poetry is capitalized.

&lt;The best lack all conviction, while the worst
Are full of passionate intensity. – W B Yeats&gt;

5. Words in titles are capitalized with the exception of internal conjunctions, prepositions, and articles.

&lt;*The Way of the World*&gt;
&lt;*Of Mice and Men*&gt;
&lt;Deuteronomy&gt;

6. The first word of the salutation of a letter and the first word of the complimentary close are capitalized

&lt;Dear Mary&gt;
&lt;My dear Mr Brown&gt;
&lt;Yours sincerely&gt;

7. Proper nouns are always capitalized.

&lt;Paul Simpson&gt; &lt;Liverpool&gt;
&lt;The Church of England&gt; &lt;Persil&gt;
&lt;The Wars of the Roses&gt; &lt;Apollo 14&gt;
&lt;Italians&gt; &lt;Yiddish&gt;

8. Derivatives of proper nouns are capitalized when used in their primary sense.

&lt;Roman customs&gt;
&lt;the Edwardian era&gt;
*but*
&lt;bowdlerize&gt;
&lt;jeremiad&gt;

9. Words of family relationship preceding the name of a person are capitalized.

&lt;Uncle George&gt; &lt;Aunt Brenda&gt; &lt;Cousin Susan&gt;

10. Titles preceding the name of a person and epithets used instead of a name are capitalized.

&lt;Professor Harris&gt;
&lt;Pope John Paul II&gt;
&lt;Queen Elizabeth&gt;
&lt;The Iron Duke&gt;

11. The pronoun I is capitalized

&lt;I think you and I should discuss this together.&gt;

12. Words designating God (and pronouns referring to Him) are often capitalized.

&lt;We must recognise that He is God, that He is King, we must surrender to Him – Anthony Bloom&gt;

13. The days of the week, the months of the year, public holidays, and holy days are capitalized.

&lt;Tuesday&gt; &lt;June&gt; &lt;Remembrance Sunday&gt; &lt;May Day&gt;
&lt;Easter&gt; &lt;Yom Kippur&gt;

14. Points of the compass are capitalized when used to designate a specific region.

&lt;The North&gt;
&lt;The Middle East&gt;

15. Geological eras, periods, epochs, strata, and names of prehistoric and historic periods are capitalized.

&lt;Silurian period&gt;
&lt;Age of Reptiles&gt;
&lt;Neolithic age&gt;

16. Planets, constellations, asteroids, stars, and groups of stars are capitalized; however, sun, earth, and moon are not capitalized unless they are listed with other capitalized astronomical names.

&lt;Venus&gt;
&lt;The Great Bear&gt;
&lt;Sirius&gt;
&lt;The Pleiades&gt;

17. Genera in binomial scientific names in zoology and botany are capitalized; names of species are not.

&lt;a common buttercup (*Ranunculus acris*)&gt;
&lt;the robin (*Erithacus rubecola*)&gt;
&lt;the haddock (*Melanogrammus aeglefinus*)&gt;

18. New Latin names of classes, families, and all groups above genera in zoology and botany are capitalized; however, their derivative adjectives and nouns are not.

&lt;Gastropoda&gt; but &lt;gastropod&gt;
&lt;Thallophyta&gt; but &lt;thallophyte&gt;

Information about capitalization of specific items is given at vocabulary entries in the main text of this dictionary. See, for example, the entries for **board of trade**, **freemasonry**, and **third world**.

# Ten vexed points in English grammar

There are certain general grammatical questions, not quite within the scope of the conventional dictionary, which cause many people particular concern; which is the 'right' thing to say? Here is some advice on ten important areas of doubt about grammar and usage.

## Agreement of Verbs

Should one say 'The committee **were** furious'?

A verb should be plural after a plural subject <her **wages** *were £17*> and singular after a singular subject <**this pitiful sum** *was her wages*>.

Some nouns such as **cattle** are only plural, and take a plural verb; but a noun that is plural in appearance may refer to a single entity, and be used with a singular verb <**linguistics** (= one subject) *is his hobby*> <*the* **United States** (= one country) *has agreed*> <**The Brothers Karamazov** (= one book) *is Dostoievsky's masterpiece*>.

A noun marked *taking sing or pl vb* in this dictionary often refers to a group of people, such as **government, audience, crowd, committee, nation**, or **clergy**. Such nouns, particularly in British English, are treated as plurals if one thinks of them as naming a number of individuals <*the* **government** (= its members) *do not propose to change the policy*> <**England** (English players) *have just gone in to bat*> <**Vauxhall** (= the car people) *are one of the latest motor manufacturers to announce price increases – Staffordshire Weekly Sentinel*> <*any young* **couple** *want to be assured that their chosen location is going to offer happy and sustaining life – Annabel*>. Group nouns have long been treated as plurals by distinguished writers <*the* **nation** *had lost the bond of union in their sacred edifice –* Edmund Burke> <*the* **club** *all know that he is a disappointed man* – Thomas De Quincey>. Those group nouns that are not names have their own plurals (**army/armies**) which of course behave as plurals in the ordinary way <*ignorant* **armies** *clash by night* – Matthew Arnold>.

A group noun is treated as singular when it is thought of as a single entity <*the* **audience** *was enormous*> and, where there is doubt, the singular construction should be preferred for formal writing. American English treats groups as singular more than British English does, but even the Americans will use a plural where the rest of the sentence requires it <*the* **audience** *are all raising their hands* (not *is raising its hand*)>. It is important that a group should be treated consistently throughout as either singular or plural, and that the grammar should not change, as in < △ *the younger* **generation** *hopes that their demands will be recognized*> < △ *the Colliery Winders'* **Federation** *of Great Britain, to which the Yorkshire Enginemen's* **Association** is affiliated, have decided against a stoppage>.

A group of people in the plural require the pronoun *who* <*they're a* **family** *who quarrel all the time*> while such a group in the singular takes *which or that* <*it's a* **family** *which dates back to the Norman Conquest*>.

Quantities and measurements should correctly take a singular verb if a single unit is implied <*five* **pounds** *is enough*> <10 **miles** *is a long way*> <12 **acres** *of land was sold for housing*>, but a plural verb for a set of individuals <*one* **third** *of the students come by bus*>. Compare <*two* **two's** *are four*> <*twice* **two** *is four*>. See [2]EACH, [3]EITHER, EVERY, [1]KIND, [1]NONE, [1]NUMBER, [2]ONE, [2]THERE, PRINCIPLE OF PROXIMITY.

Compound subjects joined by *and* are correctly plural <*the* **Walrus** *and the* **Carpenter** *were walking close at hand* – Lewis Carroll> unless they are thought of as single entities <*the* **hammer and sickle** (=one flag) *was flying from the flagpole*> <*the* **Bat and Ball** (= one pub) *sells good beer*>.

A subject to which something else is linked by *with, together with, as well as*, or *in addition to* is not a true compound subject, and should correctly take a singular verb <*the* **teacher** *as well as the students was pleased with the book*>. See [3]WELL, WITH.

## Dangling Participle

Should one say '**Climbing** the mountain, the cabin came into view'?

The parts of a verb that end with *-ing* and *-ed* can be used like adjectives with a noun <*a* **frightened** *cat*> <*a* **floating** *log*>. They can introduce a whole phrase that is attached, like an adjective, to the subject of a sentence <**frightened** *by the crash, the cat leapt through the window*> <*the log,* **floating** *down the river, broke our propeller*>; or a similar sort of phrase can be formed with *-ing* and a preposition <*after* **working** *for the firm for 20 years, she decided to leave*>. (Here, **working** is in fact a 'gerund', operating as a noun and not as an adjective, but the phrase is attached to the subject in the same way.) The curious phenomenon known as the 'dangling', 'unattached', 'unrelated', or 'loose' participle occurs when the *-ing* or *-ed* phrase appears to be attached to the wrong noun <**climbing** *the mountain, the cabin came into view*> <*after* **working** *for the firm for 20 years, promotion came as a surprise to her*>: it was not the cabin that *climbed* or the promotion that *worked*. Such a phrase may appear to be attached to no noun at all <**climbing** *the mountain, it seemed we'd never reach the cabin*>.

Many writers of the past used dangling participles freely <**sitting** *within my orchard, a serpent stung me* – Shak> <**awakening** *with a start, the waters heave around me –*

Lord Byron> <**being** *pushed unceremoniously to one side, he usurped my place* – Charlotte Brontë>. These examples are comprehensible enough: nobody really thinks it was the serpent that was *sitting* in the orchard. But the dangling participle is considered an error in modern prose writing, so that it is safer to avoid criticism by rephrasing such sentences <*while I was* **sitting** *in my orchard, a serpent stung me*>.

All of this does not apply to certain -ing and -ed phrases which are by modern convention permitted to 'dangle'. Probably nobody would object to <*strictly* **speaking,** *it shouldn't be allowed*> or to <**considering** *the circumstances, he was quite right*> or to <*five of them, not* **counting** *the baby*> or to <**talking** *of music, what's the programme for Thursday?*> or to <**knowing** *George, it's not surprising*>. Some 'dangling' participles are conventionally used, particularly in commercial or bureaucratic language, to introduce something that is to follow <**referring** *to your recent enquiry . . .*> <**arising** *out of that reply . . .*>. With regard to these and others like them, the safest advice that can be given is that in formal writing one should confine oneself to the well-known forms rather than experimenting with marginal cases, and that when in doubt over something such as <**looking** *to the future, it seems unlikely*> one should use a full clause <*when we* **look** *to the future, it seems unlikely*>.

## Double Negative

Can one say 'I didn't hear **nothing**'?

'Double negatives' are correct in some languages, and were once permissible in English. Today, the English double negative is considered substandard, and is criticized as illogical on the grounds that < △ *I didn't hear* **nothing**> logically means 'I did hear something', although such constructions are perfectly comprehensible and are quite commonly used, to make a negative even stronger. Double negation is accepted in dependent clauses, after *I don't doubt, I wouldn't wonder,* etc <*I shouldn't be surprised if it didn't rain*> <*I shall never agree, not under any circumstances*> and in such expressions as *not uncommon,* where one negative really does cancel out the other.

## Ending with a Preposition

Need one say 'This is the sort of English up **with** which I will not put', as Winston Churchill once ironically did?

A preposition connects a noun or a noun equivalent (e g a pronoun or clause) with the rest of the sentence <*I rested* **after** *lunch*> <*we took the cat* **to** *the vet*> <*the flowers are* **for** *me*> <*I was surprised* **at** *what you said*>.

Normally, prepositions precede the noun, pronoun, etc to which they are attached, but there is no reason why they should. Indeed, as H W Fowler put it, the freedom to put a preposition late in the sentence is 'a valuable idiomatic resource, which has been used freely by all our greatest writers except those whose instinct for English idiom has been overpowered by notions of correctness derived from Latin standards'. This freedom has been available to us for many centuries <*we are such stuff as dreams are made* **on** – Shak> <*houses are built to live* **in** – Francis Bacon>

<*knocking down every beautiful building they could lay their hands* **on** – John Ruskin>. The objection to it, originated apparently by the poet John Dryden in the 17th century, is merely that since a preposition cannot end a Latin sentence it must be wrong for it to end an English one.

There are situations where a sentence would be distorted if one were to avoid putting the preposition in its natural place <*it depends on what they're made* **of**> <*he's not worth talking* **to**> <*murders are interesting to read* **about**>. In particular, some English verbs such as **look after,** or **put up with** in Churchill's jocular example above, have a preposition so closely attached to them that the result constitutes a single unit. If such a verb ends the sentence, its preposition must accompany it <*they're being properly* **looked after**>.

Often, however, there is a choice of where to put a preposition, and one may choose to put it at the end in speech but not in formal writing. Compare <*that's the house we lived* **in**> <*that is the house* **in** *which we lived*> <*who did you speak* **to?**> <**to** *whom did you speak?*> (See WHO.) <*tell me what you object* **to**> <*tell me* **to** *what you object*>.

So strong is our instinct to put a preposition at the end that we sometimes make the mistake of putting it in twice < △ *the weak estate* **in** *which Queen Mary left the realm* **in** – John Milton>. This sort of thing is clearly not permissible, but it illustrates the dilemma.

## False Ellipsis

Can one say 'I never **have** and never shall allow it'?

We often omit part of a sentence to avoid repeating something in it, a process known to grammarians as 'ellipsis'. A sentence such as <*he must and shall go*> is a short way of saying <*he must go and shall go*> by omitting the first **go,** or <*he must go and he shall go*> by omitting **go** and **he**. Such omissions are an essential part of good English style, and the language would be tediously repetitive without them.

The fault known as 'false ellipsis' arises when the part that has been left out does not, in fact, correspond exactly to the part one is trying to avoid repeating. The above sentence < △ *I never have and never shall allow it*> is short for <*I never have* **allowed** *it and (I) never shall* **allow** *it*> but in the shortened form **allowed** has disappeared completely.

One can commit a false ellipsis with things other than verbs. In < △ *he can play as well or better than you can*>it is the second **as** of *as well* **as** that has gone astray. The sentence must be rephrased, either as <*he can play as well or better than you can*> or as <*he can play as well as you can, or better*>. In < △ *an account of what is known and what has been written on the subject*> the missing item is the **of** or **about** of *known* **of** or **about,** since one does not △ *know* **on** a subject. In < △ *Oxford is much larger and quite different from Cambridge*> what is missing is the **than** of *larger* **than.** In < △ *it ought and will improve*> it is the **to** of *ought* **to.**

A slightly less obvious example of false ellipsis is <*unlike Chico, Murray's smile wasn't motivated by a desire to join other men* – Len Deighton>. Here, all would be well with the addition of the necessary '**s** to *Chico*'**s,** since we are comparing the respective smiles of the two men, and not comparing one man with the smile of the other.

Most writers on usage allow one to leave out a part of the verb **be** or **have** which would differ from the part that is actually there. In <*I was in London and you in Glasgow*> the missing item is *were*, since we do not say < △ *you was in Glasgow*>, but the omission seems reasonable here.

## Noun + -ing

Should one say 'He doesn't like **me** standing on my head'?

Should it be **my** *standing on my head*? In <*I insist on* **Miss Sharp** *appearing*>, should it be **Miss Sharp's**? The construction with what corresponds to **me** and **Miss Sharp** has been used by good writers in English since the beginning of the 18th century <*had not entertained any notion of* **my ammunition** *being destroyed* – Daniel Defoe> <*she had calculated on* **her daughters** *remaining at Netherfield* – Jane Austen> <*on account of* **my sister** *being in town* – John Keats>. This was at one time actually considered to be the 'better' form. Today, however, many people prefer to use the possessive forms **my** and **Miss Sharp's**, since it is not **me** whom he doesn't like or **Miss Sharp** whom I insist on; and this is usually the safer choice in formal writing, where it can be managed without clumsiness or ambiguity. Some writers like to use the possessive for pronouns but not for nouns <*I can understand an* **Afghan** *stealing . . . but I can't understand* **his** *crying* – Rudyard Kipling> or for pronouns and names <*I was surprised at* **your**/*at* **John's** *saying that*>.

Sometimes the possessive form is impossible <*I am not surprised at* **young and old** *falling in love with her* – William Thackeray> <*without* **either of us** *knowing* – William Wordsworth> <*there's no chance of* **that** *happening*> and here one must choose between rephrasing the sentence and leaving it alone. In many such examples, everything that follows the main verb constitutes one extended object. In <*I can smell* **fish** *cooking*>, I smell the fish as well as the cooking; in <*I don't want* **them** *crawling all over the place*>, it is them as well as the crawling that I don't want; in <*we watched* **a party of tourists** *being dragged round the cathedral*>, we watched the tourists as well as the dragging. The change to **fish's**, **their**, and **tourists'** would be decidedly wrong here. It might even lead to an unwanted change of meaning, as would the change from <*I can't understand* **John** *writing* ( = the fact that he wrote) > to <*I can't understand* **John's** *writing* ( = his handwriting)>.

## Object Pronoun after Verbs and Prepositions

Should one say 'a girl like **I**'?

Prepositions, and verbs that take an object, should be followed by the objective case of pronouns <*it's bad news for* **us** *farmers* (not △ **we** *farmers*)>. The problem arises only over *me*, *him*, *her*, *us*, *them* and to a lesser extent *whom*, since *you*, *it* and *one* have no separate objective form. (See [4]AS, [2]BUT, [2]THAN, WHO). These objective pronouns are often wrongly replaced by *I, he, she, we*, and *they* in situations where the pronoun is the second of two objects <*take my sister and* **me** (not △ *I*)> <*it's*

*intended for people like you and* **me** (not △ *I*)>. Although great writers have infringed the rule <*you have seen Cassio and* **she** *together* – Shak> it should be obeyed in formal writing today. Those who feel unsure of themselves sometimes avoid the difficulty by using the reflexive pronouns *myself, herself*, etc <*they invited his wife and himself* (neither *him* nor △ *he*)> but this construction is disapproved of by writers on usage. (See [1]BETWEEN, [2]LET, ME.)

## Placement of Negatives

Should one say 'I **don't** think it will rain'?

The negative in English does not work as logically as it does in mathematics or logic. When we say <*all cats* **don't** *scratch the furniture*> we do not mean that cats as a class never do, but that there are cats that do not.

In general, it matters where we put the word that negates all or part of a sentence. Compare <*he* **didn't** *definitely promise*> <*he definitely* **didn't** *promise*>. But there is a certain kind of English sentence in which the negative is attached to the main verb, instead of to the *that*-clause whose truth is actually being denied. It happens with verbs that mean 'believe', such as **think, believe, suppose, fancy, expect, imagine**, and **reckon**. Common negative constructions such as <*I* **don't** *suppose/believe he's paid for it*> or <*he* **doesn't** *expect/reckon that we need worry*> or <*I* **don't** *think/imagine so*> are perfectly normal English, and need not be changed to <*I suppose he* **hasn't** *paid for it*> or <*I think* **not**>.

## Present Tense for Future

Should one say 'We **leave** for France tomorrow'?

The present tense <*we* **leave**> is often used, particularly in spoken English, to announce arrangements or activities in the future <*tomorrow* is *Wednesday*> <*at 9.30 John Jones and Jane Smith* **discuss** *the problem of moles in your lawn*> <*when* is *high tide?*>. Such constructions are perfectly normal English, and need not be changed to **will be** or **will discuss**.

## Split Infinitive

Should one say 'to **critically** review their position'?

Good writers have been putting one or more words between *to* and a following English infinitive verb since the 14th century <*to* **slowly** *trace the forest's shady scene* – Lord Byron> <*in order to* **fully** *appreciate* – T B Macaulay>. The well-known objection to this practice arose only in the 19th century, probably on the view that since it is impossible to split a one-word Latin infinitive such as *amare* it must be wrong to split the corresponding English infinitive *to* **love**. Although infinitive-splitting is fairly common, even in serious writing, it is widely disliked and should be avoided. A whole string of intervening adverbs is particularly liable to adverse comment <*to* **slowly, carefully, and gently** *steam open the letter*>.

Sometimes, however, a change in the word order would lead to distortion, as in <*they expected the student population to* **more than** *double*> where the splitting seems unavoidable without rephrasing. In other cases the avoidance of splitting leads to ambiguity. Compare <*our intention is to* **further** *improve conditions* ( = to make them even better)> <*our intention is* **further** *to improve conditions* ( = 'moreover' to improve them?)> <*she failed to* **entirely** *understand* ( = she partly understood)> <*she failed to understand* **entirely** ( = she understood partly, or not at all?)>.

To insert words between the parts of a compound verb but not directly after *to*, as in <*to be* **usefully** *added*> or <*to have* **just** *arrived*> is not to split an infinitive, and has never been frowned upon.

# Biographical names

This section provides basic information – names, dates of birth and death, nationality, and occupation or status – about thousands of celebrated people, both living and dead, in many fields of human activity.

People are usually entered under the names by which they are best known; in some cases these may be titles or pseudonyms rather than original or 'real' names. With a few exceptions, names including such particles as *de, di, van,* and *von* are not alphabetized under these particles but under the main element of the surname. Names which are not commonly used are shown in parentheses. Any titles, pseudonyms, original names, alternative names, nicknames, and indication of relationship to other people listed, appear in italic type after dates.

At the end of some entries are given the adjectives used to refer to that person's activities, works, etc. Such adjectives (normally ending in *-an, -ic,* or *-esque*) can be formed from any names, but only the most common examples are shown here.

## Abbreviations

| | | | |
|---|---|---|---|
| admin | administrator | | |
| agric | agricultural, agriculturist | Jap | Japanese |
| Am | American, America | | |
| anthropol | anthropologist | Lat | Latin |
| astron | astronomer | | |
| Austral | Australian | manuf | manufacturer |
| | | math | mathematician |
| bacteriol | bacteriologist | Mex | Mexican |
| Belg | Belgian | mil | military |
| biochem | biochemist | min | minister |
| Br | British, Britain | | |
| Braz | Brazilian | Norw | Norwegian |
| bro | brother | nov | novelist |
| | | NZ | New Zealand |
| c | century | | |
| Canad | Canadian | orig | originally, originator |
| chem | chemist | Pers | Persian |
| Chin | Chinese | philos | philosopher |
| criminol | criminologist | physiol | physiologist |
| | | Pol | Polish |
| dau | daughter | polit | politician |
| disc | discovered | Port | Portuguese |
| dram | dramatist | prec | preceding |
| Du | Dutch | pres | president |
| econ | economist | Pruss | Prussian |
| educ | educator | pseud | pseudonym |
| emp | emperor | psychol | psychologist |
| Eng | English, England | | |
| ethnol | ethnologist | relig | religious |
| | | Rom | Roman |
| Flem | Flemish | Russ | Russian |
| Fr | French, France | | |
| | | Scot | Scottish |
| GB | Great Britain | Span | Spanish |
| gen | general | Swed | Swedish |
| Ger | German | | |
| gov | governor | theol | theologian |
| | | Turk | Turkish |
| hist | historian | | |
| Hung | Hungarian | USA | United States of America |
| It | Italian | zool | zoologist |

# A

**Aalto** (Hugo) Alvar (Hendrik) 1898–1976 Finnish architect & furniture designer

**Aaltonen** Wäinö 1894–1966 Finnish artist; pioneer in revival of stone carving

**Aaron** Henry Louis 1934–  *Hank* Am baseball player

**Abbado** Claudio 1933–  Ital conductor

**Abbas I** 1571–1629 *The Great* Shah of Persia

**Abbott** John Joseph Caldwell 1821–1893 Canad polit; prime min (1891–92)

**Abd-el-Kader, Abd-al-Kadir** 1807?–1883 Arab leader in Algeria

**Abd-er-Rahman Khan** 1830?–1901 amir of Afghanistan (1880–1901)

**Abdul-Aziz** 1830–1876 sultan of Turkey (1861–76)

**Abdul Baha** 1844–1921 *Abbas Effendi* Pers Bahai leader

**Abdul-Hamid II** 1842–1918 sultan of Turkey (1876-1909)

**Abdullah-Husein** 1882–1951 ruler of Transjordan; amir (1921–46); king (1946–51)

**Abdul-Medjid, Abdul Mejid** 1823–1861 sultan of Turkey (1839–61)

**Abebe** Bikila 1932–1973 Ethiopian athlete

**Abel** Sir Frederick Augustus 1827–1902 Eng chem

**Abelard** Peter *Fr* Pierre **Abélard, Abailard** 1079–1142 Fr philos & theol

**Abercrombie** Sir (Leslie) Patrick 1879–1957 Eng architect & town planner

**Abercromby** Sir Ralph 1734–1801 Eng gen

**Aberdeen** 4th Earl 1784–1860 *George Hamilton Gordon* Eng polit; prime min (1852–55)

**Abington** Frances *or* Fanny 1737–1815 née *Barton* Eng actress

**Abrahams** Harold Maurice 1899–1978 Eng athlete & amateur athletics admin

**Abruzzi** Duke of the 1873–1933 Prince *Luigi of Savoy-Aosta* Ital naval officer & explorer

**abu-Bakr** *also* **Abu Bekr** 573–634 1st caliph of Mecca

**Abul Kasim** *Lat* **Albucasis** *d* ?1013 Arab surgeon & medical author

**Achebe** Chinua 1930–  Nigerian nov

**Acheson** Dean Gooderham 1893–1971 Am lawyer

**Ackland** Rodney 1908–  Eng dram

**Acton** 1st Baron 1834–1902 *John Emerich Edward Dalberg-Acton* Eng hist

**Adam** Adolphe Charles 1803–1856 Fr composer

**Adam** Robert 1728–1792 & his bro James 1730–1794 Scot architects & furniture designers

**Adams** Francis William Lauderdale 1862–1893 Austral poet & nov

**Adams** Henry Brooks 1838–1918 Am hist

**Adams** John 1735–1826 Am lawyer & 2nd pres of the US (1797–1801)

**Adams** John Couch 1819–1892 Eng astron

**Adams** John Quincy 1767–1848 *son of John* 6th pres of the US (1825–29)

**Adams** William 1564–1620 Eng navigator; shipbuilder in Japan

**Addams** Jane 1860–1935 Am social worker

**Addinsell** Richard Stewart 1904–1977 Eng composer

**Addison** Joseph 1672–1719 Eng essayist & poet – **Addisonian** *adj*

**Addison** Thomas 1793–1860 Eng physician

**Adenauer** Konrad 1876–1967 chancellor of West Germany (1949–63)

**Adler** Alfred 1870–1937 Austrian psychiatrist

**Adler** Larry 1914–  Am harmonica player

**Adrian** Rom emp – see HADRIAN

**Adrian** name of 6 popes: esp **IV** (*Nicholas Breakspear*) 1100?–1159 the only Eng pope (1154–59)

**Adrian** Edgar Douglas 1889–1977 1st Baron *Adrian of Cambridge* Eng physiol

**Æ** – see George William RUSSELL

**Ælfric** *ab* 955–*ab* 1020 Eng abbot & writer

**Aeneas Silvius, Sylvius** – see PIUS II

**Aeschines** 389–314 B C Athenian orator

**Aeschylus** 525–456 B C Greek dram – **Aeschylean** *adj*

**Aesop** *ab* 620–*ab* 560 B C Greek fabulist

**Aga Khan III** 1877–1957 *Aga Sultan Sir Mahomed Shah* head of Ismailian Muslims (1885–1957)

**Aga Khan IV** 1936–  *grandson of prec, Shah Karim* head of Ismailian Muslims (1957–  )

**Agassiz** (Jean) Louis (Rodolphe) 1807–1873 Am (Swiss-born) naturalist

**Agate** James Evershed 1877–1947 Eng drama critic & author

**Agathocles** 361–289 B C tyrant of Syracuse

**Agee** James 1909–1955 Am author

**Agesilaus II** *d ab* 360 B C king of Sparta (*ab* 400–360)

**Agnelli** Giovanni 1866–1945 Ital motor manuf

**Agnes** Saint *d* 304 virgin martyr

**Agnew** Spiro Theodore 1918–  Am polit; vice-pres of the US (1969–73)

**Agnon** Shmuel Yosef 1888–1970 Israeli (Austrian-born) author

**Agostini** Giacomo 1943–  Ital motorcyclist

**Agricola** Gnaeus Julius 37–93 Rom gen

**Agrippa** Marcus Vipsanius 63–12 B C Rom statesman

**Agrippina** the elder 13 B C?–A D 33 *dau of Agrippa, wife of Germanicus, mother of Caligula*

**Agrippina** the younger A D 15?–59 *dau of prec & mother of Emp Nero Caesar*

**Ahmed III** 1673–1736 sultan of Turkey (1703–30)

**Aiken** Conrad Potter 1889–1973 Am author

**Ainley** Henry Hinchliffe 1879–1945 Eng actor

**Ainsworth** (William) Harrison 1805–1882 Eng nov

**Aisha, Ayesha** 611–678 favourite wife of Muhammad

**Aitken** Robert Ingersoll 1878–1949 Am sculptor

**Akbar** 1542–1605 *the Great* emp of Hindustan (1556–1605)

**à Kempis** – see THOMAS À KEMPIS

**Akenside** Mark 1721–1770 Eng poet & physician

**Akhenaten, Akhenaton, Akhnaton** – see IKHNATON

**Alain-Fournier** 1886–1914 pseud of *Henri-Alban Fournier* Fr novelist

**Alanbrooke** Viscount – see Alan Francis BROOKE

**Alarcón, de** Pedro Antonio 1833–1891 Span author & statesman

**Alaric** 370?–410 Visigoth king; conqueror of Rome

**Alaric II** *d* 507 Visigoth king; issued legal code

**Alban** Saint *d*?305 first Br martyr

**Albee** Edward Franklin 1928– Am dram

**Albemarle** Duke of – see George MONCK

**Albéniz** Isaac 1860–1909 Span pianist & composer

**Albers** Josef 1888–1976 Am (Ger-born) artist

**Albert I** 1875–1934 king of Belgium (1909–34)

**Albert of Saxe-Coburg-Gotha** Prince 1819–1861 *consort of Queen Victoria of GB*

**Alberti** Leon Battista 1404–1472 Ital architect

**Albertus Magnus** Saint 1193? (or 1206?)–1280 *Albert Count von Bollstädt* Ger philos & theol

**Alboin** *d* 573 Lombard king (*ab* 565–573)

**Albright** Arthur 1811–1900 Eng industrial chem

**Albucasis** – see ABUL KASIM

**Albuquerque, de** Alfonso 1453–1515 Port viceroy & conqueror in India

**Alcaeus** *fl ab* 600 B C Greek poet

**Alcibiades** *ab* 450–404 B C Athenian gen & polit

**Alcock** Sir John William 1892–1919 Eng pioneer airman

**Alcott** Louisa May 1832–1888 Am author

**Alcuin** 735–804 Eng theol & scholar

**Alda** Frances 1883–1952 née *Francis Davis* NZ-born soprano

**Alder** Kurt 1902-1958 Ger chem

**Aldington** Richard 1892–1962 Eng author

**Aldrin** Edwin Eugene Jr 1930– *Buzz* Am astronaut; 2nd man on the moon

**Aldus Manutius** – see MANUTIUS

**Aleichem** Shalom 1859–1916 pseud of *Solomon Rabinowitz* Am (Russ-born) humorist

**Alekhine** Alexander 1892–1946 né *Aleksandr Aleksandrovich Alyokhin* Fr (Russ-born) chess player

**Alemán** Mateo 1547?–1610 Span nov

**Alembert, d'** Jean Le Rond 1717?–1783 Fr math & philos

**Alencar, de** Jooé Martiniano 1829–1877 Braz nov

**Alexander** name of 3 kings of Scotland: **I** 1080?–1124 (reigned 1107–1124); **II** 1198–1249 (reigned 1214–1249); **III** 1241–1286 (reigned 1249–1286)

**Alexander** *Russ* **Aleksandr** name of 3 emps of Russia: **I** 1777–1825 (reigned 1801–25); **II** 1818–1881 (reigned 1855–81); **III** 1845–1894 (reigned 1881–94)

**Alexander** name of 8 popes: esp **VI** (*Rodrigo Lanzol y Borja*) 1431?–1503 (pope 1492–1503)

**Alexander III of Macedon** 356–323 B C *the Great* king (336–323)

**Alexander I Obrenovich** 1876–1903 king of Serbia (1889–1903)

**Alexander I** 1888–1934 king of Yugoslavia (1921–34)

**Alexander Nevski** 1220?–1263 Russ saint & mil hero

**Alexander of Hillsborough** 1st Earl 1885–1965 *Albert Victor Alexander* Eng polit

**Alexander of Tunis** 1st Earl 1891–1969 *Harold Rupert Leofric George Alexander* Eng field marshal; gov-gen of Canada (1946–52)

**Alexander Severus** 208?–235 Rom emp (222–235)

**Alexandra** 1844–1925 Queen Consort of Edward VII of GB

**Alexeev** Vasili 1942–       Soviet weightlifter

**Alexis I Mikhailovich** 1629–1676 *father of Peter the Great* czar of Russia (1645–76)

**Alexis Petrovich** 1690–1718 *son of Peter the Great* czarevitch of Russia

**Alexius I Comnenus** 1048–1118 Eastern Rom emp (1081–1118)

**Alfieri** Count Vittorio 1749–1803 Ital dram

**Alfonso, Alphonso XIII** 1886–1941 king of Spain (1886–1931)

**Alfonso** *Port* **Alfonso** *older* **Affonso** name of 6 kings of Portugal: esp **I** 1112–1185 (1st king; 1139–85); **V** 1432–1481 (reigned 1438–81)

**Alfred** 849–899 *the Great* king of the West Saxons (871–899)

**Alfven** Hannes 1908–       Swed astrophysicist

**Algardi** Alessandro 1595–1654 Ital sculptor

**Algren** Nelson 1909–1981 Am author

**Ali** *Ar* **Ali ibn-abi-Tālib** 600?–661 *cousin & son-in-law of Muhammad* 4th orthodox caliph (656–661)

**Ali, Ali Pasha** 1741–1822 *the Lion of Janina* Turk pasha

**Ali** Muhammad 1942–       *Muhammad Ali Haj; né Cassius Marcellus Clay* Am boxer

**Allard** Sydney Herbert 1910–1966 Eng racing driver & motor manuf

**Allen** George Oswald Browning 1902–       *Gubby* Eng (Austral-born) cricketer

**Allenby** 1st Viscount 1861–1936 *Edmund Henry Hynman Allenby* Eng field marshal

**Allende Gossens** Salvador 1908–1973 Chilean physician; pres of Chile (1970–73)

**Alleyn** Edward 1566–1626 Eng actor

**Allingham** Margery Louise 1904–1966 Eng nov

**Alliss** Peter 1931–       Eng golfer

**Allston** Washington 1779–1843 Am artist

**Alma-Tadema** Sir Lawrence 1836–1912 Br (Du-born) artist

**Alsen** Herbert 1906–1978 Austrian (Ger-born) bass

**Alva, Alba** Duke of 1508–1582 *Fernando Álvarez de Toledo* Span gen

**Alvarado, de** Pedro 1495?–1541 Span soldier; companion of Cortes in Mexico

**Amati** family of Ital violin makers of Cremona: esp Nicolò or Nicola 1596–1684

**Ambrose** Saint 340?–397 bishop of Milan – **Ambrosian** *adj*

**Amenhotep, Amenophis** name of 4 kings of Egypt: esp **III** (reigned *ab* 1411–1375 B C); **IV** – see IKHNATON

**Amerigo Vespucci** – see VESPUCCI

**Ames** Leslie Ethelbert George 1905–       Eng cricketer

**Amies** (Edwin) Hardy 1909–       Eng couturier

**Amin** Idi 1925?–       pres of Uganda (1971–79)

**Amis** Kingsley 1922–       Eng author

**Ampère** André Marie 1775–1836 Fr physicist

**Amundsen** Roald 1872–1928 Norw polar explorer; disc South Pole (1911)

**Anacreon** 572?–?488 B C Greek philos – **Anaxagorean** *adj*

**Anaximander** 611–547 B C Greek philos & astron – **Anaximandrian** *adj*

**Anders** William Alison 1933–       Am astronaut

**Anders** Wladyslaw 1892–1970 Pol gen

**Andersen** Hans Christian 1805–1875 Danish author of fairy tales

**Anderson** Carl David 1905–       Am physicist

**Anderson** Dame Judith 1898– neé *Frances Margaret Anderson* Austral actress

**Anderson** Marian 1902–       Am contralto

**Anderson** Maxwell 1888–1959 Am dram

**Anderson** Robert Woodruff 1917–       Am dram

**Anderson** Sherwood 1876–1941 Am author

**Andrade** Edward Neville da Costa 1887–1971 Eng physicist

**Andrássy** Count Julius, father 1823–1890 prime min (1867–1871) & son 1860–1929 Hung statesmen

**André** John 1751–1780 Eng major; spy in Am Rev

**Andrea del Sarto** 1486–1531 *Andrea Domenico d'Agnolo di Francesco* Florentine artist

**Andrée** Salomon August 1854–1897 Swed arctic explorer & aeronautical engineer

**Andreev** Andrei Andreevich 1895–1971 Soviet polit

**Andreev, Andreyev** Leonid Nikolaevich 1871–1919 Russ nov, storywriter, & dram

**Andrew** Prince Andrew Albert Christian Edward 1960– *2nd son of Queen Elizabeth II of GB*

**Andrews** Julie Elizabeth 1935– Eng actress & singer

**Andrić** Ivo 1892–1975 Yugoslav author

**Andropov** Yuriy Vladimirovich 1914–1984 Soviet polit; 1st sec of Communist party (1982–84)

**Angela Merici** Saint 1474?–1540 Ital religious; founder of Ursuline order (1535)

**Angelico** Fra – see FIESOLE

**Angell** Sir Norman 1872–1967 *Ralph Norman Angell Lane* Eng author & lecturer

**Angström** Anders Jonas 1814–1874 Swed physicist

**Anna Ivanovna** 1693–1740 empress of Russia (1730–40)

**Anne** 1665–1714 *dau of James II* queen of GB (1702–14)

**Anne** Princess Anne Elizabeth Alice Louise 1950–       *wife of Mark Phillips, daughter of Queen Elizabeth II of GB*

**Anne of Austria** 1601–1666 *consort of Louis XIII of France* regent (1643–61) for her son Louis XIV

**Anne of Cleves** 1515–1557 *4th wife of Henry VIII of Eng*

**Annigoni** Pietro 1910–       Ital artist

**Annunzio, D'** Gabriele – see D'ANNUNZIO

**Anouilh** Jean 1910–       Fr dram

**Anquetil** Jacques 1934–       Fr racing cyclist

**Anselm** Saint 1033–1109 archbishop of Canterbury (1093–1109)

**Anson** George 1697–1762 *1st Baron Anson* Eng admiral

**Anthony** Mark – see Marcus ANTONIUS

**Anthony** Saint *ab* 250–350 Egyptian monk; regarded as founder of Christian monachism

**Anthony of Padua** Saint 1195–1231 Franciscan monk

**Antigonus I** 382–301 B C *Cyclops* gen of Alexander the Great & king of Macedonia (306–301)

**Antiochus** name of 13 Seleucid kings of Syria: esp **III** *the Great* 242–187 B C (reigned 223–187); **IV** (*Epiphanes*) *d* 163 B C (reigned 175–163)

**Antipater** 398?–319 B C Macedonian gen & statesman

**Antisthenes** 444?–after 371 B C Athenian philos; founder of Cynic school

**Antonescu** Ion 1882–1946 Rumanian gen; dictator (1940–44)

**Antoninus** Marcus Aurelius 121–180 *nephew, son-in-law, and adopted son of Antoninus Pius* Rom emp (161–180) & Stoic philos

**Antoninus Pius** 86–161 Rom emp (138–161)

**Antonioni** Michelangelo 1912–       Ital film director

**Antonius** Marcus *Eng* Mark *or* Marc Antony *or* Anthony 83?–30 B C Rom orator, triumvir, & gen

**Apelles** 4th-c B C Greek artist

**Apollinaire** Guillaume 1880–1918 *Guillaume Apollinaire de Kostrowitsky* Fr poet

**Apollonius of Rhodes** 3rd- and 2nd-c B C Greek poet – **Apollonian** *adj*

**Appius Claudius** – see CLAUDIUS

**Appleton** Sir Edward (Victor) 1892–1965 Eng physicist

**Apraksin, Apraxin** Fëdor Matveevich 1671–1728 Russ admiral

**Apuleius** Lucius 2nd-c A D Rom philos & satirist

**Aquinas** Saint Thomas 1225–1274 Ital theol

**Arafat** Yasser 1929–   né *Mohammed Abed Ar'oul Arafat* Palestinian resistance leader

**Aram** Eugene 1704–1759 Eng philologist & murderer

**Arblay, d'** Madame – see Fanny BURNEY

**Arbuckle** Roscoe 1887–1933 *Fatty* Am silent-film actor & director

**Arbuthnot** John 1667–1735 Scot physician & author

**Archer** Frederick James 1857–1886 Eng jockey

**Archer** William 1856–1924 Scot critic & dram

**Archimedes** 287?–212 B C Greek math & inventor – **Archimedean** *adj*

**Archipenko** Alexander 1887–1964 Am (Russ-born) sculptor

**Arden** Elizabeth 1884–1966 Am (Canad-born) beauty expert

**Arden** John 1930–   Eng dram

**Ardizzone** Edward Jeffrey Irving 1900–1979 Eng artist, illustrator, & author

**Aretino** Pietro 1492–1556 Ital satirist

**Ariosto** Lodovico 1474–1533 Ital poet

**Aristarchus** 220?–150 B C Greek grammarian

**Aristarchus of Samos** 3rd-c B C Greek astron

**Aristides, Aristeides** 530?–?468 B C *the Just* Athenian statesman

**Aristippus** 435?–?356 B C Greek philos

**Aristophanes** 448?–?380 B C Athenian dram

**Aristophanes of Byzantium** 257?–?180 B C Greek scholar

**Aristotle** 384–322 B C Greek philos

**Arius** *d* 336 A D Greek theol

**Arkwright** Sir Richard 1732–1792 Eng inventor

**Arlen** Michael 1895–1956 *Dikran Kouyoumdijian* Eng (Bulg-born) nov

**Arminius, Armin** 17 B C?–A D 21 sometimes *Hermann* Ger hero

**Arminius** Jacobus 1560–1609 *Jacob Harmensen* or *Hermansz* Du theol

**Armstrong** (Daniel) Louis 1900–1971 *Satchmo* Am jazz musician

**Armstrong** Neil Alden 1930–   Am astronaut; 1st man on the moon

**Armstrong-Jones** Antony Charles Robert 1930–   Earl of *Snowdon; ex-husband of Princess Margaret* Eng photographer & designer

**Arnaud** Yvonne Germaine 1892–1958 Fr actress in Eng

**Arne** Thomas Augustine 1710–1778 Eng composer

**Arnim, von** Jürgen 1889–   Ger gen

**Arnold** Benedict 1741–1801 Am Revolutionary gen & traitor

**Arnold** Henry Harley 1886–1950 Am gen

**Arnold** Malcolm 1921–   Eng composer

**Arnold** Matthew 1822–1888 *son of Thomas* Eng poet & critic

**Arnold** Thomas 1795–1842 Eng educ

**Arnoldson** Klas Pontus 1844–1916 Swed pacifist

**Arouet** François Marie – see VOLTAIRE

**Arp** Jean (or Hans) 1887–1966 Fr artist & poet

**Arpád** *d* 907 Hung national hero

**Arrau** Claudio 1903–   Chilean pianist

**Arrhenius** Svante August 1859–1927 Swed physicist & chem

**Arsonval, d'** Jacques Arsène 1851–1940 Fr physicist

**Artaxerxes** name of 3 Pers kings: **I** *d* 424 BC (reigned 464-24); **II** *d* 359 BC (reigned 404–359); **III** *d* 338 B C (reigned 359–338)

**Artevelde, van** Jacob 1290?–1345 & his son Philip 1340?–1382 Flem leaders

**Arthur** Chester Alan 1829–1886 21st pres of the US (1881–85)

**Arup** Sir Ove Nyquist 1895–   Eng consultant engineer & architect

**Asbury** Francis 1745–1816 1st Methodist bishop in Am

**Asch** Sholem *or* Shalom *or* Sholom 1880–1957 Am (Pol-born) Yiddish author

**Ascham** Roger 1515–1568 Eng scholar & author

**Asclepiades** 124–?40 BC Greek physician

**Ashburton** Baron – see Alexander BARING

**Ashcroft** Dame Peggy 1907–   neé *Edith Margaret Emily Ashcroft* Eng actress

**Ashkenazy** Vladimir 1937–   Soviet pianist

**Ashton** Eric 1935–   Eng rugby league player

**Ashton** Sir Frederick William Mallandaine 1904–   Eng choreographer

**Ashton** Winifred – see Clemence DANE

**Ashton-Warner** Sylvia 1905–1978 NZ teacher & educ

**Ashurbanipal** *also* **A(s)surbanipal** king of Assyria (669–626 B C)

**Asif** Iqbal 1943–   Pakistan cricketer

**Asimov** Isaac 1920–   Am author & scientist

**Askey** Sir Arthur Bowden 1900–1982 Eng entertainer

**Asoka, Açoka** *d* 232 B C king of Magadha, India (273–232)

**Aspasia** 470?–410 B C *consort of Pericles*

**Asplund** Gunner 1885–1940 Swed architect

**Asquith** Anthony 1902–1968 Eng film director

**Asquith** Herbert Henry 1852–1928 *1st Earl of Oxford and Asquith* Eng statesman

**Assad** Hafiz al- 1928–   pres of Syria (1970–   )

**Asser** Tobias Michael Carel 1838–1913 Du lawyer

**Astaire** Fred 1899–   né *Frederick Austerlitz* Am dancer & actor

**Aston** Francis William 1877–1945 Eng physicist

**Astor** John Jacob 1763–1848 Am (Ger-born) fur trader & capitalist

**Astor** Viscountess 1879–1964 *Nancy Langhorne Astor* 1st woman to take seat in House of Commons

**Asturias** Miguel Angel 1899–1974 Guatemalan author

**Atahualpa** 1500?–1533 last Inca king of Peru

**Athanasius** Saint 293?–373 Greek church father

**Athelstan** 895–940 king of Eng (*ab* 924–940)

**Attar** *ab* 1142–*ab* 1220 Pers poet

**Attila** 406?–453 *the Scourge of God* king of the Huns

**Attlee** 1st Earl 1883–1976 *Clement Richard Attlee* Eng polit; prime min (1945–51)

**Auber** Daniel François Esprit 1782–1871 Fr composer

**Aubrey** John 1626–1697 Eng antiquarian

**Auchincloss** Louis Stanton 1917–   Am author

**Auchinleck** Sir Claude John Eyre 1884–1981 Eng field marshal

**Auden** Wystan Hugh 1907–1973 Eng poet – **Audenesque** *adj*

**Audubon** John James 1785–1851 Am (Haitian-born) artist & naturalist

**Auerbach** Berthold 1812–1882 Ger nov

**Augier** Émile 1820–1889 Fr poet & dram

**Augustine** *also* **Austin** Saint *d* 604 *Apostle of the English* 1st archbishop of Canterbury (601–04)

**Augustine** Saint 354–430 church father; bishop of Hippo (396–430)

**Augustus** 63 B C–A D 14 *Gaius Julius Caesar Octavianus* 1st Rom emp (27 B C–A D 14)

**Aurangzeb, Aurungzeb, Aurungzebe** 1618–1707 emp of Hindustan (1658–1707)

**Aurelian** 212?–275 *Lucius Domitius Aurelianus* Rom emp (270–275)

**Auriol** Vincent 1884–1966 Fr lawyer; 1st pres of 4th Republic (1947–54)

**Austen** Jane 1775–1817 Eng nov

**Austin** Alfred 1835–1913 Eng poet; poet laureate (1896–1913)

**Austin** Henry Wilfred 1906–   *Bunny* Eng tennis player

**Austin** Herbert 1866–1941 1st and only Baron *Austin of Longbridge* Eng motor manuf

**Austral** Florence 1894–1968 pseud of *Florence Wilson* Austral soprano

**Avenzoar** 1091?–1162 Arab physician in Spain

**Avicenna** 980–1037 also *ibn-Sina* Arab (Persian-born) philos & physician

**Avila Camacho** Manuel – see CAMACHO

**Avogadro** Count Amedeo 1776–1856 Ital chem & physicist

**Avon** Earl of – see Anthony EDEN

**Ayckbourn** Alan 1939–   Eng dram

**Ayer** Sir Alfred Jules 1910–   Eng philos

**Aylward** Gladys 1902–1970 Eng missionary in China

**Ayrton** Michael 1921–1975 Eng artist, sculptor & author

**Ayub Khan** Muhammed 1907–1974 pres of Pakistan (1958–69)

**Azaña** Manuel 1880–1940 Span lawyer; pres of Spain (1936–39)

**Azuma** Tokuho 1909–   Jap dancer

# B

**Baal Shem-Tob** 1700?–1760 Jewish (Pol-born) teacher

**Babbage** Charles 1792–1871 Eng math

**Babel** August 1840–1913 Ger Social Democrat leader & author
**Baber, Babur, Babar** 1483–1530 *Zahir ud-Din Muhammad* founder of Mogul dynasty of India; emp (1526–30)
**Babeuf, Baboeuf** François Émile 1760–1797 Fr agitator
**Babington** Anthony 1561–1586 Eng RC conspirator against Queen Elizabeth I
**Bach** Carl Philipp Emanuel 1714–1788 *son of JS* Ger composer
**Bach** Johann Christian 1735–1782 *son of JS* Ger organist & composer
**Bach** Johann Sebastian 1685–1750 Ger organist & composer
**Bach** Wilhelm Friedemann 1710–1784 *son of JS* Ger organist & composer
**Back** Sir George 1796–1878 Eng arctic explorer
**Backhaus** Wilhelm 1884–1969 Ger pianist
**Bacon** Francis 1561–1626 1st Baron *Verulam* & Viscount *St Albans* Eng philos
**Bacon** Francis 1909– Irish artist
**Bacon** John 1740–1799 Eng sculptor
**Bacon** Sir Nicholas 1509–1579 Eng statesman
**Bacon** Roger, Friar 1214?–1294 Eng philos
**Baden-Powell** Robert Stephenson Smyth 1857–1941 1st Baron of *Gilwell* founder of Boy Scout movement
**Bader** Sir Douglas Robert Steuart 1910–1982 Eng airman
**Badoglio** Pietro 1871-1956 Ital gen
**Baedeker** Karl 1801–1859 Ger publisher
**Baer** Karl Ernst von 1792–1876 Ger naturalist
**Baer** Maximilian Adelbert 1909–1959 Am boxer
**Baeyer, von** Adolf 1835–1917 Ger chem
**Baez** Joan 1941– Am folk singer
**Baffin** William 1584–1622 Eng navigator
**Bagehot** Walter 1826–1877 Eng econ & journalist
**Bagnold** Enid 1889–1981 *Lady Jones* Eng author
**Bagration** Prince Pëtr Ivanovich 1765–1812 Russ gen
**Bahadur** Shah II 1775–1862 last Mogul emp of India (1837–58)
**Bahaullah** Mirza Husayn Ali 1817–1892 Pers founder of Bahaism
**Baikie** William Balfour 1825–1864 Scot surgeon, naturalist & explorer
**Bailey** Sir Donald Coleman 1901– Eng engineer; designer of Bailey bridge
**Bailey** Edward Hodges 1788–1867 Eng sculptor; sculpted Nelson's statue, Trafalgar Square, London
**Bailey** Francis 1774–1844 Eng astron
**Bailey** James Anthony 1847–1906 Am circus impresario
**Bailey** Liberty Hyde 1858–1954 Am botanist
**Bailey** Nathan *or* Nathaniel *d* 1742 Eng lexicographer
**Bailey** Pearl Mae 1918– Am singer
**Bailey** Trevor Edward 1923– Eng cricketer
**Baillie** Dame Isobel 1895–1983 Scot soprano
**Baillie** Joanna 1762–1851 Scot dram & poet
**Baillie** Mathew 1761–1823 Eng physician
**Bain** Alexander 1818–1903 Scot psychol
**Bainbridge** Beryl 1934– Eng nov
**Baird** John Logie 1888–1946 *father of television* Scot inventor
**Bairnsfather** Bruce 1888–1959 Eng cartoonist
**Bajer** Fredrik 1837–1922 Dan statesman & author
**Baker** Sir Benjamin 1840–1907 Eng civil engineer
**Baker** Sir Herbert 1862–1946 Eng architect
**Baker** Dame Janet Abbott 1933– Eng mezzo-soprano
**Baker** Josephine 1906–1975 Am dancer & singer
**Baker** Newton Diehl 1871–1937 Am statesman
**Baker** Richard St Barbe 1889– Eng silviculturist; founder of Men of the Trees Soc
**Baker** Sir Samuel White 1821–1893 Eng explorer in Africa
**Baker** Sir Stanley 1928–1976 Welsh film actor
**Bakst** Léon Nikolaevich 1866?–1924 Russ artist
**Bakunin** Mikhail Aleksandrovich 1814–1876 Russ anarchist
**Balaguer** Joaquim 1909– pres of Dominican Republic (1960–1962; 1966)
**Balanchine** George 1904– né *Georgy Melitonovich Balanchivadze* Am (Russ-born) choreographer
**Balas** Colanda 1936– Rumanian high-jumper
**Balbo** Italo 1896–1940 Ital aviator & polit
**Balboa, de** Vasco Núñez 1475–1519 Span explorer; disc Pacific Ocean

**Balcon** Sir Michael 1896–1977 Eng film producer
**Baldwin I** 1058–1118 *bro of Godfrey of Bouillon* king of Jerusalem (1100–18)
**Baldwin** James Arthur 1924– Am black author
**Baldwin** James Mark 1861–1934 Am psychol
**Baldwin** Stanley 1867–1947 1st Earl *Baldwin of Bewdley* Eng polit; prime min (1923–24; 1924–29; 1935–37)
**Balenciaga** Cristóbal 1895– Span couturier
**Balewa** Sir Abubakar Tafawa 1912–1966 prime min of Nigeria (1957–66)
**Balfe** Michael William 1808–1870 Irish composer & singer
**Balfour** 1st Earl of 1848–1930 *Arthur James Balfour* Eng philos & statesman; prime min (1902–05)
**Baliol, de** John 1249–1315 king of Scotland (1292–96)
**Ball** Alan James 1945– Eng footballer
**Ball** John *d* 1381 Eng priest & social agitator
**Ballantyne** James 1772–1833 Scot printer
**Ballantyne** Robert Michael 1825–1894 Scot author of boys' books
**Ballard** James Graham 1930– Eng science-fiction author
**Ballesteros** Severiano 1957– Span golfer
**Baltimore** Lord – see George CALVERT
**Balzac, de** Honoré 1799–1850 Fr nov – **Balzacian** *adj*
**Bancroft** Richard 1544–1610 Eng prelate; archbishop of Canterbury (1604–10)
**Banda** Hastings 1905– orig *Kamuzu Banda* prime min of Malawi (1963–1966); pres (1966– )
**Bandaranaike** Sirimavo 1916– *wife of next* prime min of Sri Lanka (1960–65, 1970–77)
**Bandaranaike** Solomon West Ridgeway Dias 1899–1959 prime min of Ceylon (1956–59)
**Bandello** Matteo 1480?–1562 Ital author
**Bankhead** Tallulah Brockman 1903–1968 Am actress
**Banks** Gordon 1937– Eng footballer
**Banks** Sir Joseph 1743–1820 Eng naturalist
**Bannister** Sir Roger Gilbert 1929– Eng physician & athlete; first man to run mile in under 4 mins
**Banting** Sir Frederick Grant 1891–1941 Canad physician; discovered (with others) insulin treatment of diabetes
**Bantock** Sir Granville 1868–1946 Eng composer
**Baranov** Aleksandr Andreevich 1747–1819 Russ fur trader; 1st gov of Russ America
**Bárány** Robert 1876–1936 Austrian physician
**Barbarossa** – see FREDERICK I
**Barbarossa** name of 2 Algerian corsairs, brothers: **I** 1473?–1518; **II** 1466?–1546
**Barber** Samuel 1910–1981 Am composer
**Barbirolli** Sir John 1899–1970 Eng conductor
**Barbour** John 1316?–1396 Scot poet
**Barbusse** Henri 1873–1935 Fr author
**Barclay** Robert 1648–1690 Scot Quaker author
**Barclay de Tolly** Prince Mikhail 1761–1818 Russ field marshal
**Barcroft** Sir Joseph 1872–1947 Irish physiol
**Bardeen** John 1908– Am physicist
**Bardot** Brigitte 1934– Fr film actress
**Barenboim** Daniel 1942– Israeli (Argentine-born) conductor & pianist
**Barents** Willem *d* 1597 Du navigator
**Baring** Alexander 1774–1848 1st Baron *Ashburton* Eng financier & diplomat
**Baring** Evelyn 1841–1917 1st Earl of *Cromer* Eng diplomat
**Barkla** Charles Glover 1877–1944 Eng physicist
**Barkley** Alben William 1877–1956 Am lawyer & polit; vice-pres of US (1949–53)
**Barlach** Ernst 1870–1938 Ger artist, sculptor, dram, & poet
**Barna** Victor 1911– Eng (Hung-born) table-tennis player
**Barnard** Christiaan Neethling 1922– S African surgeon
**Barnardo** Thomas John 1845–1905 Irish founder of homes for destitute children
**Barnato** Barney 1852–1897 S African (Eng-born) millionaire
**Barnes** Sydney Francis 1873–1967 Eng cricketer
**Barnes** William 1800–1886 Eng poet
**Barnum** Phineas Taylor 1810–1891 Am showman
**Barocchio, Barozzi** Giacomo – see VIGNOLA
**Baroja** Pío 1873–1956 Span author

**Barras** Paul Jean Francis Nicholas 1755–1829 Fr revolutionary

**Barrault** Jean-Louis 1910–    Fr actor & producer

**Barrès** Auguste Maurice 1862–1923 Fr nov & polit

**Barrie** Sir James Matthew 1860–1937 Scot nov & dram

**Barrington** Jonah 1940–    Eng squash player

**Barrington** Kenneth Frank 1930–1981 Eng cricketer

**Barros, de** João 1496–1570 Port hist

**Barrow** Isaac 1630–1677 Eng math & theol

**Barry** Sir Charles 1795–1860 Eng architect

**Barry** Philip 1896–1949 Am dram

**Barrymore** family of Am actors: Maurice 1847–1905 né *Herbert Blythe*; his wife Georgiana Emma 1856–1893; their children Lionel 1878–1954, Ethel 1879–1959, & John Blythe 1882–1942

**Bart, Barth** Jean 1651?–1702 Fr naval hero

**Bart** Lionel 1930–    Eng composer, lyricist, & dram

**Barth** Heinrich 1821–1865 Ger explorer

**Barth** Karl 1886–1968 Swiss theol – **Barthian** *adj*

**Bartholdi** Frédéric Auguste 1834–1904 Fr sculptor

**Bartholomew** John George 1860–1920 Scot cartographer

**Bartlett** Vernon 1894–    Eng author

**Bartolommeo** Fra 1475–1517 *Baccio della Porta* Florentine artist

**Bartók** Béla 1881–1945 Hung composer

**Bartram** William 1739–1823 Am naturalist

**Baruch** Bernard Mannes 1870–1965 Am businessman & statesman

**Basie** William 1904–    *Count Basie* Am bandleader

**Basil, Basilius** Saint 300?–?379 *the Great* church father; bishop of Caesarea

**Baskerville** John 1706–1775 Eng typographer

**Bassey** Hogan 1932–    *Kid* Nigerian boxer

**Bastin** Clifford Sydney 1912–    Eng footballer

**Bate** Stanley 1913–1959 Eng composer & pianist

**Bateman** Henry Mayo 1887–1970 Austral cartoonist in Eng

**Bates** Alan Arthur 1934–    Eng actor

**Bates** Herbert Ernest 1905–1974 Eng author

**Batista y Zaldívar** Fulgencio 1901–1973 Cuban soldier; pres of Cuba (1940–44; 1952–59)

**Battani, al-** *ab* 850–929 *Albategnius* or *Albatenius* Arab astron

**Batten** Jean Gardner 1909–    NZ aviator

**Baudelaire** Charles Pierre 1821–1867 Fr poet

**Baudouin** 1930–    king of Belgium (1951–    )

**Baum** Vicki 1888–1960 Am (Austrian-born) nov

**Baumé** Antoine 1728–1804 Fr chem

**Bax** Sir Arnold Edward Trevor 1883–1953 Eng composer

**Baxter** Richard 1615–1691 Eng Puritan scholar & author

**Bayard, de** Seigneur Pierre Terrail 1473?–1524 Fr mil hero

**Bayle** Pierre 1647–1706 Fr philos & critic

**Baylis** Lilian Mary 1874–1937 Eng theatrical manager

**Bazalgette** Sir Joseph William 1819–1891 Eng civil engineer

**Beaconsfield** Earl of – see Benjamin DISRAELI

**Beadle** George Wells 1903–    Am biologist

**Beale** Dorothea 1831–1906 Eng educ

**Beard** Daniel Carter 1850–1941 Am artist & illustrator; organizer of Boy Scouts in US (1910)

**Beardsley** Aubrey Vincent 1872–1898 Eng illustrator

**Beaton** Sir Cecil Walter Hardy 1904–1980 Eng photographer, costume & style designer, & author

**Beattie** James 1735–1803 Scot poet

**Beaufort** Sir Francis 1774–1857 Eng admiral

**Beaufort** Henry 1377?–1447 Eng cardinal & statesman

**Beauharnais, de** Fr family including: Vicomte Alexandre 1760–1794 gen; his wife Joséphine 1763–1814 later the 1st wife of Napoleon I; their son Eugene 1781–1824 prince of Eichstätt; their daughter Hortense 1783–1837 wife of Louis Bonaparte & mother of Napoleon III

**Beaumarchais, de** Pierre Augustin Caron 1732–1799 Fr dram & man of affairs

**Beaumont** Francis 1584–1616 Eng dram

**Beauregard, de** Pierre Gustave Toutant 1818–1893 Am Confed gen

**Beaurepaire** Sir Frank 1891–1956 Austral swimmer

**Beauvoir, de** Simone 1908–    Fr author

**Beaverbrook** 1st Baron 1879–1964 *William Maxwell Aitken* Eng (Canad-born) newspaper publisher

**Beckenbauer** Franz 1945–    W Ger footballer

**Becket, à** Saint Thomas 1118?–1170 archbishop of Canterbury (1162–70)

**Beckett** Samuel 1906–    Irish author in France

**Beckford** William 1760–1844 Eng author

**Becquerel** family of Fr physicists including: Antoine César 1788–1878; his son Alexandre Edmond 1820–1891; the latter's son Antoine Henri 1852–1908

**Beddoes** Thomas Lovell 1803–1849 Eng author

**Bede, Baeda, Beda** Saint 673–735 *the Venerable Bede* Eng scholar, hist, & theol

**Bedford** Duke of 1389–1435 *John of Lancaster; son of Henry IV of England* regent for Henry V

**Bedser** Alec Victor 1918–    Eng cricketer

**Beecham** Sir Thomas 1879–1961 Eng conductor

**Beecher** Lyman 1775–1863 *father of Harriet Beecher Stowe* Am Presbyterian clergyman

**Beerbohm** Sir Henry Max(imilian) 1872–1956 Eng critic & caricaturist

**Beernaert** Auguste Marie François 1829–1912 Belg statesman

**Beethoven, van** Ludwig 1770–1827 Ger composer – **Beethovian** *also* **Beethovenian** *adj*

**Beeton** Isabella Mary 1836–1865 neé *Mayson* Eng writer on cookery

**Begin** Menachem 1913–    prime min of Israel (1977–83)

**Behan** Brendan Francis 1923–1964 Irish dram

**Behrens** Peter 1868–1940 Ger architect & designer

**Behring, von** Emil 1854–1917 Ger bacteriol

**Beiderbecke** Bix 1903–1931 Am pianist & cornetist

**Belafonte** Harry 1927–    Am singer & actor

**Belasco** David 1853–1931 Am dram & producer

**Belisarius** 505?–565 gen of the Eastern Rom Empire

**Bell** Alexander Graham 1847–1922 Am (Scot-born) inventor of the telephone

**Bell** Gertrude Margaret Lowthian 1868–1926 Eng traveller

**Bellay, du** Joachim 1522–1560 Fr poet

**Bellini** family of Venetian artists including: Iacopo *ab* 1400–*ab* 1470 and his sons Gentile 1429?–1507 and Giovanni 1430?–1516

**Bellini** Vincenzo 1801–1835 Ital composer

**Belloc** (Joseph) Hilaire (Pierre) 1870–1953 Br (Fr-born) author

**Bellow** Saul 1915–    Am (Canad-born) author

**Bellows** George Wesley 1882–1925 Am artist & lithographer

**Beloff** Sir Max 1913–    Eng historian

**Benaud** Richie 1930–    Austral cricketer

**Benavente y Martínez** Jacinto 1866–1954 Span dram

**Benchley** Robert Charles 1889–1945 Am humorist

**Benedict** name of 15 popes: esp **XIV** (*Prospero Lambertini*) 1675–1758 (pope 1740–58); **XV** (*Giacomo della Chiesa*) 1854–1922 (pope 1914–22)

**Benedict of Nursia** Saint 480?–?543 Ital founder of Benedictine order

**Beneš** Eduard 1884–1948 Czech statesman; pres (1935–38; 1939–48)

**Benét** Stephen Vincent 1898–1943 *bro of next* Am author

**Benét** William Rose 1886–1950 Am poet, nov, & editor

**Ben-Gurion** David 1886–1973 Israeli (Pol-born) statesman; prime min of Israel (1949–53; 1955–63)

**Benjamin** Judah Philip 1811–1884 Am Confed statesman & lawyer

**Benn** Anthony Neil Wedgwood 1925–    formerly *Viscount Stansgate* Eng polit

**Bennett** Alan 1934–    Eng actor & dram

**Bennett** (Enoch) Arnold 1867–1931 Eng nov

**Bennett** James Gordon 1795–1872 Am (Scot-born) journalist

**Bennett** Richard Rodney 1936–    Am composer & pianist

**Bennett** Viscount 1870–1947 *Richard Bedford Bennett* Canad prime min (1930–35)

**Benoit de Sainte-Maure** 12th c Fr poet

**Benson** Arthur Christopher 1862–1925 Eng educ & author

**Benson** Edward White 1829–1896 Eng prelate; archbishop of Canterbury (1882–96)

**Benson** Sir Frank Robert 1858–1939 Eng actor-manager

**Bentham** Jeremy 1748–1832 Eng jurist & philos

**Bentinck** Lord William Cavendish 1774–1839 *son of WHC* 1st gov-gen of India (1833)

**Bentinck** William Henry Cavendish 1738–1809 3rd Duke of *Portland* Eng polit; prime min (1783; 1807–09)
**Bentley** Edmund Clerihew 1875–1956 Eng nov and orig of "Clerihew" verse
**Bentley** Nicholas Clerihew 1907–1978 *son of prec* Eng artist, author, & publisher
**Bentley** Phyllis Eleanor 1894–1977 Eng author
**Bentley** Richard 1662–1742 Eng clergyman, scholar, & critic
**Bentley** Walter Owen 1888–1971 Eng car designer & manuf
**Benton** Thomas Hart 1889–1975 Am artist
**Benz** Karl Friedrich 1844–1929 Ger engineer & motor manuf
**Béranger, de** Pierre Jean 1780–1857 Fr poet
**Berdyaev** Nikolai Aleksandrovich 1874–1948 Russ philos
**Berenson** Bernhard 1865–1959 Am art critic
**Berg** Alban 1885–1935 Austrian composer
**Bergerac, de** Cyrano – see CYRANO DE BERGERAC
**Bergius** Friedrich 1884–1949 Ger chem
**Bergman** (Ernst) Ingmar 1918– Swed film director
**Bergman** Ingrid 1915–1982 Swed actress
**Bergson** Henri 1859–1941 Fr philos
**Beria, Beriya** Lavrenti Pavlovich 1899–1953 Soviet polit
**Bering** Vitus 1680–1741 Danish navigator; disc Bering Strait and Bering Sea
**Berkeley** George 1685–1753 Irish bishop & philos
**Berkeley** Sir Lennox Randal 1903– Eng composer
**Berkeley** Sir William 1606–1677 colonial gov of Virginia
**Berlichingen, von** Götz *or* Gottfried 1480–1562 Ger knight
**Berlin** Irving 1888– né *Israel Baline* Am (Russ-born) composer
**Berlin** Sir Isaiah 1909– Eng philosopher
**Berlioz** (Louis) Hector 1803–1869 Fr composer
**Bernadette of Lourdes** Saint 1844–1879 *Bernadette Soubirous* Fr religious
**Bernadotte** Jean Baptiste Jules 1763–1844 Fr gen, king (1818–44) of Sweden as *Charles XIV John* founding present Swed dynasty
**Bernard** Claude 1813–1878 Fr physiol
**Bernard of Clairvaux** Saint 1091–1153 Fr ecclesiastic – **Bernardine** *adj*
**Bernardin de Saint-Pierre** Jacques Henri 1737–1814 Fr author
**Bernhardt** Sarah 1844–1923 née *Henrietta Rosine Bernard* Fr actress
**Bernini** Giovanni Lorenzo 1598–1680 Ital sculptor, architect, & artist
**Bernstein** Leonard 1918– Am conductor & composer
**Bernstorff** Count Johann-Heinrich 1862–1939 Ger diplomat
**Berryman** John 1914–1972 Am poet
**Berthier** Louis Alexandre 1753–1815 Prince *de Neuchâtel*; Duc *de Valangin*; Prince *de Wagram* Fr soldier; marshal of France
**Bertillon** Alphonse 1853–1914 Fr anthropol & criminol
**Berzelius** Baron Jöns Jakob 1779–1848 Swed chem
**Besant** Annie née *Wood* 1847–1933 Eng theosophist
**Bessemer** Sir Henry 1813–1898 Eng engineer
**Best** Charles Herbert 1899–1978 Canad physiol; disc insulin (with others)
**Best** George 1946– N Ireland footballer
**Betancourt** Rómulo 1908–1981 Venezuelan pres (1959–64)
**Bethmann-Hollweg, von** Theobald 1856–1921 Ger statesman; chancellor (1909–17)
**Betjeman** Sir John 1906–1984 Eng author; poet laureate (1972–84)
**Betterton** Thomas 1635?–1710 Eng actor
**Bevan** Aneurin 1897–1960 Br polit
**Beveridge** 1st Baron 1879–1963 *William Henry Beveridge* Br econ
**Bevin** Ernest 1881–1951 Eng polit
**Beyle** Marie Henri – see STENDHAL
**Beza** Theodore 1519–1605 Fr theologian
**Bhumibol Adulyadej , Bumipol Adulet** 1927– *Rama IX* king of Thailand (1946– )
**Bhutto** Zulfikar Ali 1928–1979 Pakistan polit; pres of Pakistan (1971–73); prime min (1973–77)
**Bidault** Georges 1899– Fr statesman
**Biddle** John 1615–1662 founder of Eng Unitarianism
**Bienville, de** Sieur Jean Baptiste Lemoyne 1680–1768 Fr colonial gov of Louisiana

**Bierce** Ambrose (Gwinnett) 1842–?1914 Am author
**Bierstadt** Albert 1830–1902 Am (Ger-born) artist
**Binet** Alfred 1854–1911 Fr psychologist; instigator of Intelligence Test
**Binyon** (Robert) Laurence 1869–1943 Eng poet & art critic
**Bion** 2nd c B C Greek poet
**Birkbeck** George 1776–1841 Eng physician; founder of mechanics' institutes
**Birkenhead** 1st Earl of 1872–1930 *Frederick Edwin Smith* Eng jurist & statesman
**Birkett** William Norman 1883–1962 1st Baron *Birkett* Eng lawyer & polit
**Birmingham** George A – see James Owen HANNAY
**Biró** László 1900– Argentine (Hung-born) inventor
**Biron** Ernst Johann 1691–1772 orig *Bühren*; Duke of *Kurland* Russ statesman
**Birrell** Augustine 1850–1933 Eng author & polit
**Bismarck, von** Prince Otto Eduard Leopold 1815–1898 in full *Bismarck-Schönhausen* 1st chancellor of Ger Empire (1871–90) – **Bismarckian** *adj*
**Bizet** Alexandre César Léopold 1838–1875 *Georges* Fr composer
**Björnson** Björnstjerne 1832–1910 Norw poet, dram, & nov
**Black** Misha 1910–1977 Eng (Russ-born) architect & industrial designer
**Blackett** Patrick Maynard Stuart 1897–1974 Eng physicist
**Blackmore** Richard Doddridge 1825–1900 Eng nov
**Blackstone** Sir William 1723–1780 Eng jurist
**Blackwell** Elizabeth 1821–1910 Am (Eng-born) physician
**Blackwood** Algernon 1869–1951 Eng author
**Blackwood** William 1776–1834 Scot publisher
**Blair** Eric – see George ORWELL
**Blake** Robert 1599–1657 Eng admiral
**Blake** William 1757–1827 Eng artist, poet, & mystic – **Blakean** *adj*
**Blanchflower** Robert Dennis 1926– *Danny* N Ireland footballer
**Blankers-Koen** Francina E 1918– *Fanny* Du athlete
**Blasco-Ibáñez** Vicente 1867–1928 Span nov
**Blavatsky** Elena Petrovna 1831–1891 née (*Helena*) *Hahn* Russ traveller & theosophist
**Blériot** Louis 1872–1936 Fr engineer & pioneer aviator
**Bligh** William 1754–1817 Eng naval officer
**Bliss** Sir Arthur 1891–1975 Eng composer
**Blixen** Karen Christence 1885–1962 Baroness *Blixen-Finecke*; pseud *Isak Dinesen* Danish author
**Bloc** André 1896–1966 Fr sculptor
**Bloch** Ernest 1880–1959 Am (Swiss-born) composer
**Bloch** Felix 1905– Am (Swiss-born) physicist
**Bloom** Claire 1931– Eng actress
**Bloomer** Amelia Jenks 1818–1894 Am reformer
**Bloomer** Stephen 1874–1938 Eng footballer
**Bloomfield** Leonard 1887–1949 Am linguist
**Blücher, von** Gebhard Leberecht 1742–1819 Pruss field marshal
**Blum** Léon 1872–1950 Fr polit; provisional pres (1946)
**Blunden** Edmund Charles 1896–1974 Eng poet & critic
**Bluntschli** Johann Kaspar 1808–1881 Swiss legal scholar
**Blyton** Enid Mary 1897–1968 Eng author of children's books
**Boabdil** *d* 1533 *or* 1534 last Moorish king of Granada
**Boadicea** *d* 62 Queen of the Iceni
**Board** Lilian 1948–1970 Eng athlete
**Boas** Franz 1858–1942 Am (Ger-born) anthropol & ethnol
**Bobadilla, de** Francisco *d* 1502 Span viceroy of Indies
**Boccaccio** Giovanni 1313–1375 Ital author
**Boccherini** Luigi 1743–1805 Ital composer
**Bodley** Sir Thomas 1545–1613 Eng diplomat & founder of Bodleian library
**Bodoni** Giambattista 1740–1813 Ital printer & type designer
**Boerhaave** Hermann 1668–1738 Du physician & botanist
**Boethius** Anicius Manlius Severinus 480?–?524 Rom philos
**Bogarde** Dirk 1920– pseud of *Derek Jules Gaspard Ulric Niven van den Bogaerde* Eng actor & author
**Bogart** Humphrey 1899–1957 Am film actor
**Böhme, Böhm** Jákob 1575–1624 Ger mystic & theosophist

**Bohr** Niels 1885–1962 Danish physicist

**Boiardo** Matteo Maria 1434–1494 Ital poet

**Boileau-Despréaux** Nicolas 1636–1711 Fr critic & poet

**Bojer** Johan 1872–1959 Norw author

**Boleyn** Anne 1507–1536 *2nd wife of Henry VIII of England & mother of Queen Elizabeth I*

**Bolingbroke** 1st Viscount 1678–1751 *Henry St John* Eng statesman

**Bolívar** Simón 1783–1830 S Am liberator

**Böll** Heinrich Theodor 1917–     Ger author

**Bolt** Robert Oxton 1924–     Eng dram

**Bonaparte** *Ital* **Buonaparte** Corsican family including Napoleon I (*qv*) & his bros: Joseph 1768–1844 king of Naples & Spain; Lucien 1775–1840 prince of Canino; Louis 1778–1846 king of Holland & father of Napoleon III; Jérôme 1784–1860 king of Westphalia

**Bonar Law** – see LAW

**Bonaventura, Bonaventure** Saint 1221–1274 *the Seraphic Doctor* Ital philos

**Bondi** Sir Hermann 1919–     Eng (Austrian-born of Am parents) math

**Bone** Sir Muirhead 1876–1953 Scot etcher & artist

**Bonheur** Rosa 1822–1899 *Marie Rosalie* Fr artist

**Bonhoeffer** Dietrich 1906–1945 Ger theologian

**Boniface** name of 9 popes: esp **VIII** (*Benedetto Caetani*) 1235?–1303 (pope 1294–1303)

**Boniface** Saint 680?–755 *Winfrid* or *Wynfrith* Eng missionary in Germany

**Bonington** Chris(tian) John Storey 1934–     Eng mountaineer

**Bonnard** Pierre 1867–1947 Fr artist

**Bonner, Boner** Edmund 1500?–1569 Eng prelate

**Bonnet** Georges 1889–1973 Fr polit & diplomat

**Bonnet** Henri 1888–     Fr hist & diplomat

**Bonney** William H 1859–1881 *Billy the Kid* Am outlaw

**Boole** George 1815–1864 Eng math

**Boone** Daniel 1734–1820 Am pioneer

**Boot** Jesse 1850–1931 1st Baron *Trent* Eng pharmacist & drug manufacturer

**Booth** family of Am actors: Junius Brutus 1796–1852 *b* in England & his sons Edwin Thomas 1833–1893 & John Wilkes 1838–1865 assassin of Lincoln

**Booth** William 1829–1912 Eng founder of Salvation Army & father of: William Bramwell 1856–1929 Salvation Army gen; Evangeline Cory 1865–1950 Salvation Army gen

**Borden** Sir Robert (Laird) 1854–1937 Canad lawyer & statesman; prime min (1911–20)

**Bordet** Jules 1870–1961 Belg bacteriol

**Borg** Björn Rune 1956–     Swed tennis player

**Borges** Jorge Luis 1899–     Argentine author

**Borgia** Cesare 1475 (*or* 1476?)–1507 *son of Rodrigo* Ital cardinal & mil leader

**Borgia** Lucrezia 1480–1519 *dau of Rodrigo* duchess of Ferrara

**Borgia** Rodrigo 1431?–1503 – see Pope ALEXANDER VI

**Borglum** (John) Gutzon (de la Mothe) 1871–1941 Am sculptor

**Borg Olivier** George 1911–1980 prime min of Malta (1950–55; 1965–71)

**Boris III** 1894–1943 czar of Bulgaria (1918–43)

**Borlaug** Norman Ernest 1914–     Am agronomist

**Borman** Frank 1928–     Am astronaut

**Bormann** Martin 1900–?1945 Ger polit; Nazi official

**Borodin** Aleksandr Porfirevich 1834–1887 Russ composer & chem

**Borotra** Jean Robert 1898–     Fr tennis player

**Borromini** Francesco 1599–1667 Ital architect

**Borrow** George 1803–1881 Eng author

**Borzov** Valeriy 1949–     Soviet athlete

**Bosch** Hieronymus *ab* 1450–1516 Du artist

**Bosch** Karl 1874–1940 Ger industrial chem

**Bose** Sir Jagadis Chandra 1858–1937 Indian physicist & plant physiol

**Bose** Satyendranath 1894–1974 Indian physicist

**Bose** Subhas Chandra 1897–1945 Indian polit

**Bossuet** Jacques Bénigne 1627–1704 Fr bishop

**Boston** Ralph 1939–     Am long-jumper

**Boswell** James 1740–1795 *Bozzy* Scot lawyer & author; biographer of Samuel Johnson

**Botha** Louis 1862–1919 Boer gen; 1st prime min of Transvaal (1907) & of Union of S Africa (1910–19)

**Botham** Ian Terrence 1955–     Eng cricketer

**Bothe** Walter 1891–1957 Ger physicist

**Botticelli** Sandro 1444?–1510 *Alessandro di Mariano dei Filipepi* Ital artist

**Boucher** François 1703–1770 Fr artist

**Boucicault, Bourcicault** Dion 1820?–1890 *Dionysius Lardner Boursiquot* Irish actor & dram

**Bougainville, de** Louis Antoine 1729–1811 Fr navigator

**Boulanger** Georges Ernest Jean Marie 1837–1891 Fr gen

**Boulanger** Nadia Juliette 1887– Fr music teacher

**Boulez** Pierre 1925–     Fr composer

**Boult** Sir Adrian Cedric 1889–1983 Eng conductor

**Boulting** John Edward & Roy 1913–     Eng twin film producers & directors

**Boumédienne** Houari 1925–1978 né *Mohammed Boukharouba* pres & prime min of Algeria (1965–1978)

**Bourbon, de** Duc Charles 1490–1527 Fr gen; constable of France

**Bourgeois** Léon Victor Auguste 1851–1925 Fr statesman

**Bourget** (Charles Joseph) Paul 1852–1935 Fr poet, critic, & nov

**Bourguiba** Habib Ben Ali 1903–     Tunisian pres (1957–     )

**Bovet** Daniel 1907–     Ital (Swiss-born) physiol

**Bow** Clara 1905–1965 *It girl* Am film actress

**Bowell** Mackenzie 1823–1917 prime min of Canada (1894–96)

**Bowen** Elizabeth Dorothea Cole 1899–1973 Eng (Irish-born) author

**Bowman** Sir William 1816–1892 Eng histologist & ophthalmic surgeon

**Boycott** Geoffrey 1940–     Eng cricketer

**Boyd Orr** 1st Baron 1880–1971 *John Boyd Orr* Scot agric

**Boyer** Charles 1898–1978 Fr actor

**Boyle** Kay 1903–     Am author

**Boyle** Robert 1627–1691 Br physicist & chem

**Brabazon of Tara** Baron – see MOORE-BRABAZON

**Brabham** Sir John Arthur 1926– *Jack* Austral racing driver & car designer

**Bradbury** Ray Douglas 1920–     Am author

**Braddon** Mary Elizabeth 1837–1915 Eng nov

**Bradford** William 1590–1657 Pilgrim father; 2nd gov of Plymouth colony

**Bradley** Francis Herbert 1846–1924 Eng philos – **Bradleian** *also* **Bradleyan** *adj*

**Bradley** Henry 1845–1923 Eng philologist & lexicographer

**Bradley** Omar Nelson 1893–1981 Am gen

**Bradman** Sir Donald George 1908–     Austral cricketer

**Bragg** Sir William (Henry) 1862–1942 Eng (Austral-born) physicist

**Bragg** Sir (William) Lawrence 1890–1971 *son of prec* Eng physicist

**Bragina** Lyudmila 1943–     Soviet athlete

**Brahe** Tycho 1546–1601 Danish astron

**Brahms** Johannes 1833–1897 Ger composer & pianist – **Brahmsian** *adj*

**Braille** Louis 1809–1852 Fr blind teacher of the blind

**Brain** Aubrey Harold 1893–1955 Eng horn player

**Brain** Dennis 1921–1957 *son of prec* Eng horn player

**Bramah** Ernest 1867–1942 pseud of *Ernest Bramah Smith* Eng author

**Bramante** 1444–1514 *Donato d'Agnolo* or *d'Angelo* Ital architect

**Brancusi** Constantin 1876–1957 Fr (Rumanian-born) sculptor

**Brandes** Georg Morris 1842–1927 Danish lit critic

**Brando** Marlon 1924–     Am actor

**Brandt** Willy 1913–     W Ger polit; chancellor of West Germany (1969–74)

**Brangwyn** Sir Frank 1867–1956 Eng artist

**Branting** Karl Hjalmar 1860–1925 Swed statesman & socialist leader

**Braque** Georges 1882–1963 Fr artist

**Brasher** Chris(topher) 1928–     Eng athlete

**Bratby** John Randall 1928–     Eng artist & author

**Brattain** Walter Houser 1902– Am physicist
**Brauchitsch, von** Heinrich Alfred Hermann Walther 1881–1948 Ger gen
**Braun** Karl Ferdinand 1850–1918 Ger physicist
**Braun, von** Wernher 1912–1977 Am (Ger-born) rocket engineer
**Bream** Julian Alexander 1933– Eng guitarist
**Brearley** (John) Michael 1942– Eng cricketer
**Breasley** Arthur Edward 1914– *Scobie* Austral jockey
**Brecht** Bertolt 1898–1956 Ger dram & poet – **Brechtian** *adj*
**Brendel** Alfred 1931– Austrian pianist
**Breshkovsky** Catherine 1844–1934 Russ revolutionist
**Bresson** Robert 1901– Fr film producer
**Breton** André 1896–1966 Fr surrealist poet
**Brewster** Sir David 1781–1868 Scot physicist
**Brewster** William 1567–1644 Pilgrim father
**Brezhnev** Leonid Ilyich 1906–1982 Soviet polit; pres of USSR (1960–64; 1977–82); 1st sec of Communist party (1964–82)
**Brian** (William) Havergal 1876–1972 Eng composer
**Brian Boru** *Irish* **Brian Boroimhe** 941–1014 king of Ireland (1002–14)
**Briand** Aristide 1862–1932 Fr statesman
**Bridge** Frank 1879–1941 Eng composer
**Bridges** Robert Seymour 1844–1930 Eng poet; poet laureate (1913–30)
**Bridgman** Percy Williams 1882–1961 Am physicist
**Bridie** James 1888–1951 pseud of *Osborne Henry Mavor* Scot physician & dram
**Bright** John 1811–1889 Eng orator & statesman
**Brigid, Brigit, Bridget** Saint 453–523 a patron saint of Ireland
**Brillat-Savarin** Anthelme 1755-1826 Fr gastronome
**Brindley** James 1716–1772 Eng engineer
**Britten** (Edward) Benjamin 1913–1976 Baron *Britten of Aldeburgh* Eng composer
**Brodie** Sir Israel 1895–1979 Eng rabbi
**Brogan** Sir Denis William 1900–1974 Br hist
**Broglie, de** Louis Victor 1892– Fr physicist
**Brontë** a family of Eng authors: Charlotte 1816–1855 & her sisters Emily 1818–1848 & Anne 1820–1849
**Brook** Peter Stephen Paul 1925– Eng theatrical producer & director
**Brooke** Alan Francis 1883–1963 1st Viscount *Alanbrooke of Brookeborough* Eng field marshal
**Brooke** Rupert Chawner 1887–1915 Eng poet
**Broome** David 1940– Eng show jumper
**Brophy** Brigid Antonia 1929– Eng author
**Brosio** Manlio 1897–1980 Ital lawyer & diplomat; sec-gen of NATO (1964–71)
**Brough** Louise 1923– Am tennis player
**Brown** Sir Arthur Whitten 1886–1948 Eng aviator
**Brown** Ford Madox 1821–1893 Eng artist
**Brown** Joe 1930– Eng mountaineer
**Brown** John 1826–1883 Scot personal servant of Queen Victoria
**Brown** John *of Osawatomie* 1800–1859 Am abolitionist
**Brown** Lancelot 1715–1783 *Capability* Eng landscape gardener
**Browne** Charles Farrar 1834–1867 pseud *Artemus Ward* Am humorist
**Browne** Sir Thomas 1605–1682 Eng physician & author
**Browning** Elizabeth Barrett 1806–1861 *wife of next* Eng poet
**Browning** Robert 1812–1889 Eng poet
**Broz, Brozovitch** Josip 1892–1980 *Tito* Yugoslav marshal; prime min (1945–53); pres (1953–80)
**Bruce** Sir David 1855–1931 Eng physician & bacteriol
**Bruce** Robert 1274–1329 liberator & king (1306–29) of Scotland
**Bruce of Melbourne** Viscount 1883–1967 *Stanley Melbourne Bruce* Austral statesman; prime min (1923–29)
**Bruckner** Anton 1824–1896 Austrian composer
**Brueghel, Breughel** family of Flem artists including: Pieter 1520?–1569 & his sons Pieter 1564?–?1638 & Jan 1568–1625
**Brumel** Valeriy 1942– Soviet high-jumper
**Brummell** George Bryan 1778–1840 *Beau Brummell* Eng dandy
**Brundage** Avery 1887–1975 Am sportsman; pres of Am Olympic Committee (1952–1972)
**Brunel** Isambard Kingdom 1806–1859 Eng engineer

**Brunelleschi, Brunellesco** Filippo 1377?–1446 Ital architect
**Brunetière** Vincent de Paul Marie Ferdinand 1849–1906 Fr critic
**Brüning, Bruening** Heinrich 1885–1970 chancellor of Germany (1930–32)
**Bruno** Giordano 1548?–1600 Ital philos
**Brutus** Marcus Junius 85?–42 B C Rom polit; one of Caesar's assassins
**Bryant** Sir Arthur 1899– Eng historian
**Bryce** Viscount 1838–1922 *James Bryce* Br jurist, hist, & diplomat
**Buber** Martin 1878–1965 Israeli (Austrian-born) philos
**Buchan** John 1875–1940 1st Baron *Tweedsmuir* Scot author; gov-gen of Canada (1935–40)
**Buchanan** Jack 1891–1957 Eng actor
**Buchanan** James 1791–1868 Am polit & diplomat; 15th pres of the US (1857–61)
**Buchman** Frank Nathan Daniel 1878–1961 Am evangelist
**Buchner** Eduard 1860–1917 Ger chem
**Buck** Pearl 1892–1973 née *Sydenstricker* Am nov
**Buckingham** 1st & 2nd Dukes of – see George VILLIERS
**Buckner** Simon Bolivar 1823–1914 Am Confed gen & polit
**Buckner** Simon Bolivar 1886–1945 *son of SB* Am gen
**Buddha** – see GAUTAMA BUDDHA
**Budenny** Semën Mikhailovich 1883–1973 Soviet gen
**Budge** (James) Donald 1916– Am tennis player
**Bueno** Maria Esther 1939– Braz tennis player
**Buffalo Bill** – see William Frederick CODY
**Buffon, de** Comte Georges Louis Leclerc 1707–1788 Fr naturalist
**Buisson** Ferdinand 1841–1932 Fr educ
**Bukharin** Nikolai Ivanovich 1888–1938 Soviet leader & editor
**Bulfinch** Charles 1763–1844 Am architect
**Bulganin** Nikolai Aleksandrovich 1895–1975 Soviet polit & marshal
**Bull** Ole Bornemann 1810–1880 Norw violinist
**Bullitt** William Christian 1891–1967 Am diplomat
**Bullock** Alan Louis Charles 1914– *Baron Bullock of Leafield* Eng author & univ administrator
**Bülow, von** Prince Bernhard 1849–1929 Ger diplomat & statesman; chancellor of Germany (1900–09)
**Bulwer** William Henry Lytton Earle 1801–1872 *bro of 1st Baron Lytton* Eng diplomat
**Bulwer-Lytton** – see LYTTON
**Bunche** Ralph Johnson 1904–1971 Am diplomat
**Bunin** Ivan Alekseevich 1870–1953 Russ poet & nov
**Bunsen** Robert Wilhelm 1811–1899 Ger chem
**Buñuel** Luis 1900–1983 Span film director
**Bunyan** John 1628–1688 Eng preacher & author
**Buonaparte** – see BONAPARTE
**Burbage** Richard 1567?–1619 Eng actor
**Burbidge** Eleanor Margaret 1925– Eng (Am-born) astron
**Burchfield** Charles Ephraim 1893–1967 Am artist
**Bürger** Gottfried August 1747–1794 Ger poet
**Burgess** Anthony 1917– pseud of *John Burgess Wilson* Eng author
**Burgess** Guy Francis de Moncy 1910–1963 Eng traitor; defector to USSR
**Burghley, Burleigh** 1st Baron – see William CECIL
**Burgoyne** John 1722–1792 Eng gen in Am & dram
**Burk** Martha Jane 1852?–1903 *Calamity Jane* née *Canary* Am frontier markswoman
**Burke** Edmund 1729–1797 Br statesman & orator – **Burkean, Burkian** *adj*
**Burne-Jones** Sir Edward Coley 1833–1898 orig *Jones* Eng artist & designer
**Burnet** Sir (Frank) Macfarlane 1899– Austral physician
**Burnett** Frances Eliza 1849–1924 née *Hodgson* Am (Eng-born) author
**Burney** Fanny 1752–1840 *Frances; Madame d'Arblay* Eng nov & diarist
**Burnham** (Linden) Forbes (Sampson) 1923– prime min of Guyana (1966–80), pres (1980– )
**Burns** Robert 1759–1796 Scot poet – **Burnsian** *adj*
**Burnside** Ambrose Everett 1824–1881 Am gen

**Burra** Edward John 1905–1976 Eng artist
**Burroughs** Edgar Rice 1875–1950 Am author
**Burroughs** William Seward 1914– Am author
**Burton** Beryl 1937– Eng racing cyclist
**Burton** Richard 1925–1984 né *Jenkins* Welsh actor
**Burton** Sir Richard Francis 1821–1890 Eng explorer & orientalist
**Burton** Robert 1577–1640 Eng clergyman & author
**Busby** Sir Matthew 1909– Eng football manager
**Bush** Alan 1900– Eng composer, conductor & pianist
**Bush** Vannevar 1890–1974 Am electrical engineer
**Busoni** Ferruccio Benvenuto 1866–1924 Ital composer & pianist
**Butenandt** Adolph 1903– Ger chem
**Butler** Joseph 1692–1752 Eng theol
**Butler** Nicholas Murray 1862–1947 Am educ
**Butler** Reginald Cotterell 1913–1981 Eng sculptor & architect
**Butler** Richard Austen 1902–1982 Baron *Butler of Saffron Walden* Eng polit
**Butler** Samuel 1612–1680 Eng satirical poet
**Butler** Samuel 1835–1902 Eng nov & satirist
**Butlin** Sir William Edmund 1899–1980 *Billy* Eng (S African-born) holiday camp promoter
**Butor** Michel Marie François 1926– Fr author
**Butt** Dame Clara 1872–1936 Eng contralto
**Butterworth** George 1885–1916 Eng composer
**Buxtehude** Dietrich 1637?–1707 Danish organist & composer
**Byng** George 1663–1733 Eng admiral
**Byng** Julian Hedworth George 1862–1935 1st Baron *Byng (of Vimy)* Eng gen; gov-gen of Canada (1921–26)
**Byrd** Richard Evelyn 1888–1957 Am admiral & polar explorer
**Byrd** William 1543–1623 Eng composer
**Byron** 6th Baron 1788–1824 *George Gordon Byron* Eng poet

# C

**Caballero** Francisco Largo – see LARGO CABALLERO
**Cabell** James Branch 1879–1958 Am nov & essayist
**Cabeza de Vaca** Álvar Núñez 1490?–?1577 Span explorer.
**Cabot** John 1450–1498 *Giovanni Caboto* Venetian navigator; disc continent of N America for England
**Cabot** Sebastian 1476?–1557 *son of John* Eng navigator
**Cabral** Pedro Álvares 1460?–?1526 Port navigator; claimed Brazil for Portugal
**Cabrillo** Juan Rodríguez *d* 1543 Span (Port-born) explorer in Mex & Calif
**Cabrini** Saint Frances Xavier 1850–1917 *Mother Cabrini* 1st Am citizen canonized (1946)
**Cade** Jack *d* 1450 Eng rebel
**Cadillac** Sieur Antoine de la Mothe 1658–1730 Fr founder of Detroit
**Caedmon** *fl* 670 Anglo-Saxon poet
**Caesar** Gaius Julius 100–44 B C Rom gen, statesman, & writer
**Cage** John Milton 1912– Am composer
**Cagliostro, di** Count Alessandro 1743–1795 real name *Giuseppe Balsamo* Ital impostor
**Caine** Sir (Thomas Henry) Hall 1853–1931 Eng nov
**Calamity Jane** – see Martha Jane BURKE
**Caldecott** Randolph 1846–1886 Eng artist & book illustrator
**Calder** Alexander 1898–1976 Am sculptor
**Calderón de la Barca** Pedro 1600–1681 Span dram & poet
**Caldwell** Erskine 1903–1983 Am nov
**Caldwell** (Janet) Taylor 1900– Am author
**Caligula** 12–41 *Gaius Caesar* Rom emp (37–41)
**Callaghan** (Leonard) James 1912– Eng polit; prime min (1976–79)
**Callaghan** Morley 1903– Canad nov
**Callas** Maria 1923–1977 Am soprano
**Calles** Plutarco Alías 1877–1945 Mex gen; pres of Mexico (1924–28)
**Callimachus** 5th-c B C Greek sculptor
**Callimachus** *b ab* 310 B C Greek scholar & Alexandrian librarian
**Callisthenes** 360?–?328 B C Greek philos & hist

**Callistratus** *d* 355 B C Athenian orator & gen
**Calvert** George 1580?–1632 1st Baron *Baltimore* Eng proprietor in N Am
**Calvin** John 1509–1564 né *Jean Chauvin* or *Caulvin* Fr theol & reformer
•**Camacho** Manuel Avila 1897–1955 Mex gen; pres of Mex (1940–46)
**Cambacérès, de** Duc 1753–1824 *Jean Jacques Régis* Fr jurist; counsellor of Napoleon I
**Cambridge** 1st Baron of – see Edgar Douglas ADRIAN
**Cambyses** *d* 522 B C *son of Cyrus the Great* king of Persia (529–22)
**Camden** William 1551–1623 Eng antiquarian & hist
**Cameron of Lochiel** 1629–1719 Sir *Ewen Cameron* Scot chieftain
**Cammaerts** Émile 1878–1953 Belg poet
**Camões, Vaz de** Eng Camoëns Luiz 1524–1580 Port poet
**Campbell** Colin 1792–1863 né *Macliver*; Baron *Clyde* Eng field marshal
**Campbell** Donald Malcolm 1921–1967 *son of Sir Malcolm* Eng land & water speed record holder
**Campbell** (Ignatius) Roy (Dunnachie) 1901–1957 S African poet & journalist
**Campbell** Sir Malcolm 1885–1949 Eng land & water speed record holder
**Campbell** Mrs Patrick 1865–1940 neé *Beatrice Stella Tanner* Eng actress
**Campbell** Thomas 1777–1844 Scot poet
**Campbell-Bannerman** Sir Henry 1836–1908 Eng polit; prime min (1905–08)
**Campi** Ital family of artists in Cremona including: Galeazzo 1477–1536 & his three sons Giulio *ab* 1502–1572, Antonio *d* 1591?, & Vincenzo 1536–1591
**Campion** Edmund 1540–1581 Eng Jesuit martyr
**Campion** Thomas 1567–1620 Eng poet & musician
**Campoli** Alfredo 1906– Ital violinist in Eng
**Camus** Albert 1913–1960 Fr nov, essayist, & dram
**Canaletto** Antonio 1697–1768 né *Antonio Canale* or *Canal* Ital artist
**Candolle, de** Augustin Pyrame 1778–1841 Swiss botanist
**Canetti** Elias 1905– Austrian author
**Canning** Charles John 1812–1862 Earl *Canning* Eng gov-gen of India (1856–62)
**Canning** George 1770–1827 *father of CJ* Eng statesman; prime min (1827)
**Canning** Stratford 1786–1880 1st Viscount *Stratford de Redcliffe* Eng diplomat
**Canova** Antonio 1757–1822 Ital sculptor
**Canute** 994?–1035 *the Great* king of England (1016–35); of Denmark (1018–35); of Norway (1028–35)
**Capablanca** José Raúl 1888–1942 Cuban chess master; world champion (1921–27)
**Čapek** Karel 1890–1938 Czech nov & dram
**Capes** Geoffrey 1950– Eng shot putter
**Capone** Al(phonse) 1899–1947 Am (Ital-born) gangster
**Capote** Truman 1924–1984 Am author
**Capp** Al 1909–1979 pseud of *Alfred Caplin* Am cartoonist
**Capra** Frank 1897– Am (Ital-born) film director
**Caracalla** 188–217 *Marcus Aurelius Antoninus* orig *Bassianus* Rom emp (211–217)
**Caractacus, Caratacus** Eng **Caradoc** *fl* 43–50 Br chieftain
**Caravaggio, da** Michelangelo 1569?–?1609 *Michelangelo Merisi* Ital artist
**Cárdenas** Lázaro 1895–1970 Mex gen & polit; pres of Mex (1934–40)
**Cardinale** Claudia 1938– Ital film actress
**Carducci** Giosuè 1835–1907 Ital poet
**Cardus** Sir Neville 1889–1975 Eng writer on music & cricket
**Carew** Thomas 1595?–?1645 Eng poet
**Carl XVI Gustaf** 1946– king of Sweden (1973– )
**Carleton** Guy 1724–1808 1st Baron *Dorchester* Eng gen & administrator in Am
**Carlos** Don 1788–1855 infante & pretender to Span throne
**Carlos de Austria** 1545–1568 prince of Asturias & heir to Span throne

**Carlota** *Eng* **Charlotte** 1840–1927 empress of Mexico (1864–67)

**Carlyle** Thomas 1795–1881 Scot essayist & hist – **Carlylian** *adj*

**Carman** (William) Bliss 1861–1929 Canad poet

**Carmichael** Hoagy 1899–1981 Am composer

**Carmona** Antonio Oscar de Fragoso 1869–1951 Port gen; pres of Portugal (1926–51)

**Carné** Marcel 1909–     Fr film director

**Carnegie** Andrew 1835–1919 Am (Scot-born) industrialist & philanthropist

**Carnot** Lazare Nicolas Marguerite 1753–1823 Fr statesman & gen

**Carnot** Marie François Sadi 1837–1894 pres of France (1887–94)

**Caro** Anthony Alfred 1924–     Eng sculptor

**Carol II** 1893–1953 king of Rumania (1930–40)

**Carpaccio** Vittore 1460?–?1525 Ital artist

**Carpentier** Georges 1894–1975 Fr boxer

**Carranza** Venustiano 1859–1920 pres of Mexico (1915–20)

**Carrel** Alexis 1873–1944 Fr surgeon & biologist

**Carroll** Lewis – see Charles Lutwidge DODGSON – **Carrollian** *adj*

**Carson** Christopher 1809–1868 *Kit* Am trapper & frontiersman

**Carson** Rachel Louise 1907–1974 Am scientist & author

**Carte, D'Oyly** Richard 1844–1901 Eng opera impresario

**Carter** Horatio Stratton 1913–     *Raich* Eng footballer

**Carter** Howard 1873–1939 Eng archaeologist

**Carter** James Earl, Jnr 1924–     *Jimmy* Am polit; 39th pres of the US (1977–81)

**Carteret** John 1690–1763 Earl *Granville* Eng statesman

**Cartier** George Étienne 1814–1873 Canad statesman

**Cartier** Jacques 1491–1557 Fr navigator & explorer; disc St Lawrence river

**Cartier-Bresson** Henri 1908–     Fr photographer

**Cartland** Barbara Hamilton 1904–     *Mrs McCorquodale* Eng romantic nov

**Cartwright** Edmund 1743–1823 Eng inventor

**Caruso** Enrico 1873–1921 orig *Errico* Ital tenor

**Carver** George Washington 1864–1943 Am botanist

**Cary** (Arthur) Joyce (Lunel) 1888–1957 Eng author

**Casabianca, de** Louis 1755?–1798 Fr naval officer

**Casals** Pablo 1876–1973 Span-born cellist, conductor, & composer

**Casanova, Casanova de Seingalt** Giacomo Girolamo 1725–1798 also *Giovanni Jacopo* Ital adventurer

**Casaubon** Isaac 1559–1614 Fr theol & scholar

**Casement** Sir Roger David 1864–1916 Irish rebel

**Casey** 1st Baron 1890–1976 *Richard Gardiner Casey* Austral polit; governor-gen (1965–69)

**Casimir-Périer** Jean Paul Pierre 1847–1907 Fr statesman; pres of France (1894–95)

**Caslon** William 1692–1766 Eng typefounder

**Cassin** René 1887–1976 Fr statesman

**Cassiodorus** Flavius Magnus Aurelius *d* A D 575 Rom statesman & author

**Cassius Longinus** Gaius *d* 42 B C Rom gen & conspirator

**Casson** Sir Hugh Maxwell 1910–     Eng architect

**Casson** Sir Lewis 1875–1969 Eng actor-manager & producer

**Castiglione** Conte Baldassare 1478–1529 Ital statesman & author

**Castilho, de** Visconde Antônio Feliciano 1800–1875 Port poet

**Castlereagh** Viscount – see Robert STEWART

**Castro, de** Inés *Eng* Agnes 1320?–1355 Span noblewoman

**Castro (Ruz)** Fidel 1927–     Cuban premier (1959–     )

**Castro** Cipriano 1858?–1924 Venezuelan gen; pres of Venezuela (1902–08)

**Catesby** Robert 1573–1605 Eng conspirator in Gunpowder Plot

**Cather** Willa Sibert 1873–1947 Am nov

**Catherine** name of 1st, 5th, & 6th wives of Henry VIII of England: Catherine of Aragon 1485–1536; Catherine Howard 1520?–1542; Catherine Parr 1512–1548

**Catherine I** 1684?–1727 *wife of Peter the Great* empress of Russia (1725–27)

**Catherine II** 1729–1796 *the Great* empress of Russia (1762–96)

**Catherine de Medicis** *Ital* **Caterina de' Medici** 1519–1589 *queen of Henry II of France*

**Catherine of Braganza** 1638–1705 *queen of Charles II of England*

**Catiline** 108?–62 B C *Lucius Sergius Catilina* Rom polit & conspirator

**Catlin** George 1796–1872 Am artist

**Cato** Marcus Porcius 234–149 B C *the Elder; the Censor* Rom statesman

**Cato** Marcus Porcius 95–46 B C *the Younger; great-grandson of prec* Rom Stoic philos

**Catullus** Gaius Valerius 84?–54 B C Rom poet

**Cavell** Edith Louisa 1865–1915 Eng nurse

**Cavendish** Henry 1731–1810 Eng scientist

**Cavendish** Spencer Compton 1833–1908 8th Duke of *Devonshire* Eng statesman

**Cavendish** Sir William 1505?–1557 Eng statesman

**Cavendish** William 1640–1707 1st Duke of *Devonshire* Eng statesman

**Cavour, di** Conte Camillo Benso 1810–1861 Ital statesman

**Cawley** Evonne Fay 1951–     née *Goolagong* Austral tennis player

**Caxton** William 1422?–1491 first Eng printer

**Cayley** Sir George 1773–1857 Eng aerial navigation pioneer; founder of aerodynamics

**Ceauşescu** Nicolae 1918–     pres of Rumania (1974–     )

**Cecil** (Edgar Algernon) Robert 1864–1958 1st Viscount *Cecil of Chelwood* Eng statesman

**Cecil** Lord (Edward Christian) David 1902–     Eng lit critic & biographer

**Cecil** Robert 1563?–1612 1st Earl of *Salisbury* & 1st Viscount *Cranborne* Eng statesman

**Cecil** Robert Arthur Talbot Gascoyne- 1830–1903 3rd Marquis of *Salisbury* Eng statesman

**Cecil** William 1520–1598 1st Baron *Burghley* or *Burleigh* Eng statesman

**Cellini** Benvenuto 1500–1571 Ital goldsmith & sculptor

**Celsius** Anders 1701–1744 Swed astron

**Celsus** Aulus Cornelius 1st c AD Rom physician

**Cervantes Saavedra, de** Miguel 1547–1616 Span author

**Cézanne** Paul 1839–1906 Fr artist – **Cézannesque** *adj*

**Chabrier** (Alexis) Emmanuel 1814–1894 Fr composer

**Chadwick** Sir James 1891–1974 Eng physicist

**Chagall** Marc 1887–     Russ artist in France

**Chain** Sir Ernst Boris 1906–1979 Br (Ger-born) biochem

**Chaliapin** Feodor Ivanovich 1873–1938 Russ basso

**Chamberlain** Joseph 1836–1914 & his sons Sir (Joseph) Austen 1863–1937 & (Arthur) Neville 1869–1940 Eng statesmen

**Chambers** Ephraim 1680?–1740 Eng encyclopaedist

**Chambers** Robert 1802–1871 Scot publisher & editor

**Chambord, de** Comte 1820–1883 Duc *de Bordeaux* Bourbon claimant to Fr throne

**Champlain, de** Samuel 1567?–1635 Fr explorer in Am; founder of Quebec

**Champollion** Jean François 1790–1832 Fr Egyptologist

**Champollion-Figeac** Jean Jacques 1778–1867 *bro of prec* Fr archaeologist

**Chandler** Raymond Thornton 1888–1959 Am author

**Chandragupta** 4th c B C also *Sandrocottus* or *Sandracottus* Indian ruler of Maurya dynasty

**Chandragupta II** Indian ruler of Gupta dynasty (383?–413)

**Chanel** Gabrielle 1883–1971 *Coco* Fr fashion designer & perfumer

**Chaplin** Sir Charles Spencer 1889–1977 *Charlie* Eng actor & producer

**Chapman** George 1559?–1634 Eng dram & translator

**Chapman** Herbert 1873–1934 Eng footballer & manager

**Chappell** Ian Michael 1943–     & his brother Gregory Stephen 1948–     Austral cricketers

**Charcot** Jean Martin 1825–1893 Fr neurologist

**Charlemagne** 742–814 *Charles the Great* or *Charles I* Frankish king (768–814) & emp of the West (800–814)

**Charles I** *Charles Stuart* king of GB (1625–49)

**Charles II** 1630–1685 *son of Charles I* king of GB (1660–85)

**Charles** 1948–     *Prince Charles Philip Arthur George; son of Elizabeth II* prince of Wales

**Charles I** 1887–1922 *Charles Francis Joseph; nephew of Francis Ferdinand* emp of Austria & (as *Charles IV*) king of Hungary (1916–18)

**Charles I, II** 823–877 *the Bald* king of France as *Charles I* (840–877); emp as *Charles II* (875–877)

**Charles IV** 1294–1328 *the Fair* king of France (1322–28)

**Charles V** 1337–1380 *the Wise* king of France (1364–80)

**Charles V** 1500–1558 Holy Rom emp (1519–56); king of Spain as *Charles I* (1516–56)

**Charles VI** 1368–1422 *the Mad* or *the Beloved* king of France (1380–1422)

**Charles VII** 1403–1461 *the Victorious* king of France (1422–61)

**Charles IX** 1550–1574 king of France (1560–74)

**Charles X** 1757–1836 king of France (1824–30)

**Charles XII** 1682–1718 king of Sweden (1697–1718)

**Charles XIV John** – see BERNADOTTE

**Charles** 1771–1847 archduke of Austria

**Charles** *or* **Karl Ludwig** Prince 1903–     *bro of King Leopold* regent of Belgium (1944–50)

**Charles Edward Stuart** 1720–1788 *the Young Pretender*; (*Bonnie*) *Prince Charlie* Eng prince

**Charles Martel** *ab* 688–741 *grandfather of Charlemagne* Frankish ruler (719–741)

**Charles** Ezzard 1922–1975 Am boxer

**Charles** (William) John 1932–     Welsh footballer

**Charlotte** Empress of Mexico – see CARLOTA

**Charlton** Andrew 1907–1975 *Boy* Austral swimmer

**Charlton** Robert 1937–     *Bobby* Eng footballer

**Charteris** Leslie 1907–     Eng author

**Chataway** Christopher John 1931–     Eng athlete & polit

**Chateaubriand, de** Vicomte François René 1768–1848 Fr author

**Chatham** 1st Earl of – see William PITT

**Chatterji** Bankim Chandra 1838–1894 Indian nov

**Chatterton** Thomas 1752–1770 Eng poet

**Chaucer** Geoffrey 1340?–1400 Eng poet – **Chaucerian** *adj*

**Chautemps** Camille 1885–1963 Fr lawyer & polit; premier (1930; 1933–34; 1937–38)

**Chavannes, de** – see PUVIS DE CHAVANNES

**Chávez** Carlos 1899–1978 Mex conductor & composer

**Chekhov** *also* **Chekov** Anton Pavlovich 1860–1904 Russ dram & writer – **Chekhovian** *adj*

**Chenier, de** André Marie 1762–1794 Fr poet

**Cheops** – see KHUFU

**Chernenko** Konstantin Ustinovich 1911–     Soviet polit; 1st sec of Communist party (1984–     )

**Cheshire** (Geoffrey) Leonard 1917–     Eng bomber pilot & philanthropist

**Chesterfield** 4th Earl of 1694–1773 *Philip Dormer Stanhope* Eng statesman & author

**Chesterton** Gilbert Keith 1874–1936 Eng journalist & author

**Chevalier** Albert 1862–1923 Eng music-hall entertainer

**Chevalier** Gabriel 1895–1969 Fr nov

**Chevalier** Maurice 1888–1972 Fr entertainer

**Chiang Kai-shek** 1887–1975 Chin gen & statesman; pres of China (1948–49; Taiwan, 1950–75)

**Chichester** Sir Francis 1901–1972 Eng airman & yachtsman; made first solo circumnavigation of the world (1966–67)

**Chifley** Joseph Benedict 1885–1951 prime min of Austral (1945–49)

**Chikamatsu Monzaemon** 1653–?1724 *the Shakespeare of Japan* Jap dram

**Childe** Vere Gordon 1892–1957 Eng anthropol & archaeol

**Childers** Erskine Hamilton 1905–1974 Irish (Eng-born) polit; pres of Ireland (1973–74)

**Chippendale** Thomas 1718?–1779 Eng cabinetmaker & designer

**Chirico, de** Giorgio 1888–1978 Ital artist

**Chomsky** (Avram) Noam 1928–     Am linguist

**Chopin** Frédéric François 1810–1849 Pol pianist & composer

**Chou En-lai** 1898–1976 Chin Communist polit

**Chrétien de Troyes** *also* *Chrestien* 12th c Fr trouvère

**Christ** Jesus – see JESUS

**Christian X** 1870–1947 king of Denmark (1912–47)

**Christie** Dame Agatha 1891–1976 née *Mary Clarissa Miller* Eng author

**Christina** 1626–1689 *dau of Gustavus Adolphus* queen of Sweden (1632–54)

**Christophe** Henri 1767–1820 king of Haiti (1811–20)

**Chrysostom** Saint John 345?–407 church father & patriarch of Constantinople

**Chu Teh** 1886–1976 Chin Communist gen

**Church** Richard Thomas 1893–1972 Eng nov & poet

**Churchill** John 1650–1722 1st Duke of *Marlborough* Eng gen

**Churchill** Randolph Henry Spencer 1849–1895 Lord *Randolph Churchill* Eng statesman

**Churchill** Sir Winston Leonard Spencer 1874–1965 *son of Lord Randolph* Eng statesman; prime min (1940–45; 1951–55) – **Churchillian** *adj*

**Churriguera, de** José Benito 1665–1725 Span architect

**Ciano** Conte Galeazzo 1903–1944 *son-in-law of Mussolini* Ital statesman

**Cibber** Colley 1671–1757 Eng dram & actor; poet laureate (1730–57)

**Cicero** Marcus Tullius 106–43 B C Rom statesman, orator, & author – **Ciceronian** *adj*

**Cimabue** Giovanni *ab* 1240–*ab* 1302 né *Cenni de Pepo* Florentine artist

**Cimon** 507?–440 B C Athenian gen & statesman

**Cincinnatus** Lucius Quinctius 5th-c B C Rom gen & statesman

**Civil** Alan 1928–     Eng horn player & composer

**Clair** René 1898–1981 Fr film producer & author

**Clare** John 1793–1864 Eng poet

**Clare** Saint 1194–1253 Ital nun; founder of "Poor Clares" order

**Clarendon** Earl of – see Edward HYDE

**Clark** James 1937–1968 *Jim* Scot racing driver

**Clark** 1st Baron 1903–1983 *Kenneth Mackenzie Clark* Eng art hist

**Clark** Mark Wayne 1896–1984 Am gen

**Clarke** Arthur Charles 1917–     Eng science-fiction author

**Clarke** Charles Cowden 1787–1877 & his wife Mary Victoria Cowden-Clarke 1809–1898 Eng Shakespearean scholars

**Clarke** Don 1933–     NZ rugby union player

**Clarke** Sir Ellis Emmanuel Innocent 1917–     pres of Trinidad & Tobago (1976)

**Clarke** Ron 1937–     Austral athlete

**Claudius** Rom gens including: **Appius Claudius Crassus** consul (471 & 451 B C) & decemvir (451–450 B C); **Appius Claudius Caecus** censor (312–307 B C); **Appius Claudius Caecus** censor (312–307 B C), & dictator who began building of the Appian Way (312 B C)

**Claudius I** 10 B C–A D 54 *Tiberius Claudius Drusus Nero Germanicus* Rom emp (41–54)

**Claudius II** 214–270 *Marcus Aurelius Claudius Gothicus* Rom emp (268–270)

**Clausewitz, von** Karl 1780–1831 Pruss gen & military strategist

**Clayton** Philip Thomas Bayard 1885–1972 *Tubby* Eng clergyman; founder of Toc H

**Cleanthes** 3rd-c B C Greek Stoic philos

**Clemenceau** Georges 1841–1929 *the Tiger* Fr statesman

**Clemens** Samuel Langhorne 1835–1910 pseud *Mark Twain* Am author

**Clement** name of 14 popes: esp **VII** (*Giulio de'Medici*) 1478–1534 (pope 1523–34)

**Clement of Alexandria** 150?–?220 *Titus Flavius Clemens* Greek Christian theologian & church father

**Clementi** Muzio 1752–1832 Ital pianist & composer in Eng

**Clements** Sir John Selby 1910–     Eng actor-manager & producer

**Cleopatra** 69–30 B C queen of Egypt (51–49; 48–30)

**Clerk-Maxwell** James – see James Clerk MAXWELL

**Cleveland** (Stephen) Grover 1837–1908 22nd & 24th pres of the US (1885–89; 1893–97)

**Clinton** Sir Henry 1738?–1795 Eng gen in Am

**Clive** Robert 1725–1774 Baron *Clive of Plassey* Eng gen; founder of the empire of Br India

**Clough** Arthur Hugh 1819–1861 Eng poet

**Clough** Brian 1936–     Eng footballer & manager

**Clouzot** Henri-Georges 1907–1977 Fr film director

**Clovis I** *Ger Chlodwig* 466?–511 Frankish king of Merovingian dynasty (481–511)

**Clyde** Baron – see Colin CAMPBELL

**Cnut** – see CANUTE

**Coates** Joseph Gordon 1878–1943 NZ statesman; prime min (1925–28)

**Cobb** John Rhodes 1899–1952 Eng racing driver

**Cobb** Lee J 1911–1976 Am actor

**Cobbett** William 1763–1835 *Peter Porcupine* Eng polit author

**Cobden** Richard 1804–1865 Eng statesman & econ

**Cobham** Lord – see Sir John OLDCASTLE

**Cochet** Henri 1901– Fr tennis player

**Cochran** Sir Charles Blake 1872–1951 Eng theatrical producer

**Cockcroft** Sir John Douglas 1897–1967 Eng physicist

**Cockerell** Sir Christopher Sydney 1910– Eng radio engineer; hovercraft pioneer

**Cocteau** Jean 1889–1963 Fr author

**Cody** William Frederick 1846–1917 *Buffalo Bill* Am scout, Indian fighter, & showman

**Coe** Sebastian Newbold 1956– Eng athlete

**Coeur de Lion** – see RICHARD I of England

**Coggan** (Frederick) Donald 1909– archbishop of Canterbury (1974–80)

**Cohn** Ferdinand Julius 1828–1898 Ger botanist

**Coke** Sir Edward 1552–1634 *Lord Coke* Eng jurist

**Coke** Thomas William 1752–1842 *Coke of Holkham* 1st Earl *Leicester of Holkham* Eng agric

**Colbert** Jean Baptiste 1619–1683 Fr statesman & financier

**Cole** Nat King 1919–1965 Am singer & pianist

**Cole** Thomas 1801–1848 Am (Eng-born) artist

**Coleridge** Samuel Taylor 1772–1834 Eng poet – **Coleridgean** *also* **Coleridgian** *adj*

**Coleridge-Taylor** Samuel 1875–1921 Eng composer

**Colet** John 1466?–1519 Eng theol & scholar

**Colette** Sidonie Gabrielle Claudine 1873–1954 Fr author

**Coligny, Coligni, de** Gaspard (II) 1519–1572 Fr admiral & Huguenot leader

**Collie** John Norman 1859–1942 Eng chem & mountaineer

**Collins** Michael 1890–1922 Irish revolutionist

**Collins** Michael 1930– Am astronaut

**Collins** Norman Richard 1907– Eng author & administrator

**Collins** William 1721–1759 Eng poet

**Collins** (William) Wilkie 1824–1889 Eng nov

**Colman** George 1732–1794 Eng dram

**Colman** Ronald 1891–1958 Eng film actor

**Colum** Padraic 1881–1972 Am (Irish-born) author

**Columba** *Irish* **Colum, Columcille** Saint 521–597 *apostle of Caledonia* Irish missionary in Scot

**Columbus** Christopher *Ital* Cristoforo Colombo *Span* Cristóbal Colón 1451–1506 Ital navigator; disc Am

**Comenius** *Czech* **Komenský** John Amos 1592–1670 Czech theol & educ

**Comfort** Alexander 1920– Eng medical biologist & author

**Comines, Commines, Commynes, Comynes, de** Philippe 1447?–?1511 Sire *d'Argenton* Fr chronicler

**Commodus** Lucius Aelius Aurelius 161–192 Rom emp (180–192)

**Compton** Arthur Holly 1892–1962 Am physicist

**Compton** Denis Charles Scott 1918– Eng cricketer & footballer

**Compton** Fay 1894–1978 neé *Lillian Emmeline Compton* Eng actress

**Compton-Burnett** Dame Ivy 1892–1969 Eng nov

**Comte** Auguste 1798–1857 *Isidore Auguste Marie François Comte* Fr math & philos

**Conan Doyle** – see DOYLE

**Condé, de** Prince 1621–1687 *Louis II de Bourbon*; Duc *d'Enghien* Fr gen

**Condorcet, de** Marquis 1743–1794 *Marie Jean Antoine Nicholas de Caritat* Fr philos & polit

**Confucius** *Chin* **K'ung Futzu, Kung Futse** *ab* 551–479 B C Chin philos

**Congreve** William 1670–1729 Eng dram

**Coningham** Sir Arthur 1895–1948 Eng air marshal

**Connolly** Maureen 1934–1969 *Little Mo* Am tennis player

**Connors** James Scott 1952– *Jimmy* Am tennis player

**Conrad** Joseph 1857–1924 né *Teodor Józef Konrad Korzeniowski* Br (Ukrainian-born of Pol parents) nov

**Constable** John 1776–1837 Eng artist

**Constant de Rebecque** Benjamin 1767–1830 Fr author & polit

**Constantine I** 280?–337 *the Great* Rom emp (306–337) – **Constantinian** *adj*

**Constantine I** 1868–1923 king of Greece (1913–17; 1920–22)

**Constantine II** 1940– king of Greece (1964–73; deposed)

**Constantine** 1st Baron 1902–1971 *Learie Nicholas Constantine* W Indian cricketer

**Contarini** Venetian family including esp Gasparo 1483–1542 cardinal & diplomat

**Conti, de'** Niccolò 15th-c Venetian traveller

**Cook** Captain James 1728–1779 Eng navigator & explorer

**Cook** Thomas 1808–1892 Eng railway excursion & tourist pioneer

**Cooke** (Alfred) Alistair 1908– Am (Eng-born) essayist & journalist

**Coolidge** (John) Calvin 1872–1933 30th pres of the US (1923–29)

**Coolidge** William Augustus Brevoort 1850–1926 Eng mountaineer & Alpine hist

**Cooper** Anthony Ashley – see SHAFTESBURY

**Cooper** Gary 1901–1961 orig *Frank Cooper* Am film actor

**Cooper** Dame Gladys 1888–1971 Eng actress

**Cooper** Henry 1934– Eng boxer

**Cooper** James Fenimore 1789–1851 Am nov

**Copeland** William Taylor 1797–1868 Eng china manuf

**Copernicus** Nicolaus *Pol* Mikolaj **Kopernik** *or* Niklas **Koppernigk** 1473–1543 Pol astron; founder of modern astronomy

**Copland** Aaron 1900– Am composer

**Copley** John Singleton 1738–1815 Am portrait painter

**Coppard** Alfred Edgar 1878–1957 Eng author

**Coppola** Francis Ford 1939– Am film director

**Coran** Thomas 1668?–1751 Eng philanthropist

**Corbett** James John 1866–1933 *Gentleman Jim* Am boxer

**Corbusier** – see LE CORBUSIER

**Corday** Charlotte 1768–1793 *Marie Anne Charlotte Corday d'Armont* Fr patriot; assassinated Marat

**Corelli** Arcangelo 1653–1713 Ital violinist & composer

**Cori** Carl Ferdinand 1896– & his wife Gerty Theresa 1896–1957 née *Radnitz* Am (Czech-born) biochemists

**Corneille** Pierre 1606–1684 Fr dram

**Cornelia** *d* ?67 B C *wife of Julius Caesar*

**Cornelius, von** Peter 1783–1867 Ger artist

**Cornwallis** 1st Marquis 1738–1805 *Charles Cornwallis* Eng gen & statesman

**Corot** Jean Baptiste Camille 1796–1875 Fr artist

**Correggio** 1494–1534 *Antonio Allegri da Correggio* Ital artist

**Cortes, Cortez** Hernán *or* Hernando 1485–1547 Span conqueror of Mexico

**Cortot** Alfred 1877–1962 Fr pianist & conductor

**Cosgrave** Liam 1920– prime min of Ireland (1973–77)

**Cosgrave** William Thomas 1880–1965 Irish statesman

**Costello** John Aloysius 1891–1976 prime min of Ireland (1948–51; 1954–57)

**Cotman** John Sell 1782–1842 Eng artist

**Cotton** (Thomas) Henry 1907– Eng golfer

**Cottrell** Leonard 1913–1974 Eng author & archaeologist

**Coty** René 1882–1962 Fr lawyer; 2nd pres of 4th Republic (1954–59)

**Coulomb, de** Charles Augustin 1736–1806 Fr physicist

**Couperin** François 1668–1733 Fr composer

**Courbet** Gustave 1819–1877 Fr artist

**Cournand** André Frédéric 1895– Am (Fr-born) physiologist

**Court** Margaret 1942– neé *Smith* Austral tennis player

**Courtenay** Thomas Daniel 1937– *Tom* Eng actor

**Cousins** Frank 1904– Eng trade union leader

**Cousteau** Jacques Yves 1910– Fr marine explorer

**Coutts** Thomas 1735–1822 Eng banker

**Coverdale** Miles 1488–1568 Eng Bible translator

**Coward** Sir Noël Pierce 1899–1973 Eng actor & dram

**Cowdrey** Michael Colin 1932– Eng cricketer

**Cowell** Henry Dixon 1897–1965 Am composer

**Cowley** Abraham 1618–1667 Eng poet

**Cowper** William 1731–1800 Eng poet

**Cox** Mark 1943– Eng tennis player

**Crabbe** George 1754–1832 Eng poet
**Craigavon** 1st Viscount 1871–1940 *James Craig* Br statesman; 1st prime min of Northern Ireland (1921–40)
**Craigie** Sir William Alexander 1867–1957 Scot philologist & lexicographer
**Crampton** Bruce 1935–     Austral golfer
**Cranach** Lucas 1472–1553 Ger artist & engraver
**Cranborne** Viscount – see Robert CECIL
**Crane** Stephen 1871–1900 Am author
**Crane** Walter 1845–1915 Eng artist
**Cranmer** Thomas 1489–1556 Eng reformer; archbishop of Canterbury (1533–56)
**Crassus** Marcus Licinius 115?–53 B C *Dives* Rom polit
**Crawford** Joan 1908–1977 Am film actress
**Crazy Horse** 1849?–1877 *Tashunca-Uitco* Sioux Indian chief
**Creasey** John 1908–1973 Eng author
**Crébillon** 1674–1762 pseud of *Prosper Jolyot* Fr dram
**Cremer** Sir William Randal 1838–1908 Eng pacifist
**Crèvecoeur, de** Michel Guillaume St Jean 1735–1813 Am (Fr-born) essayist
**Crichton** James 1560?–1582 *the Admirable Crichton* Scot prodigy
**Crick** Francis Harry Compton 1916–     Eng biophysicist
**Crippen** Hawley Harvey 1862–1910 Am physician & murderer in Eng
**Cripps** Sir (Richard) Stafford 1889–1952 Eng lawyer & polit
**Crispi** Francesco 1819–1901 Ital statesman; premier (1887–91; 1893–96)
**Crispin** Edmund – see (Robert) Bruce MONTGOMERY
**Croce** Benedetto 1866–1952 Ital philos & statesman
**Crockett** David 1786–1836 *Davy* Am frontiersman & polit
**Croesus** *d* 546 B C king of Lydia (560–546)
**Cromer** 1st earl of – see Evelyn BARING
**Crompton** Richmal 1890–1969 née *Richmal Crompton Lamburn* Eng author
**Crompton** Samuel 1753–1827 Eng inventor of the spinning mule
**Cromwell** Oliver 1599–1658 Eng gen & statesman; lord protector of England (1653–58)
**Cromwell** Richard 1626–1712 *son of Oliver* lord protector (1658–59)
**Cromwell** Thomas 1485?–1540 Earl of *Essex* Eng statesman
**Cronin** Archibald Joseph 1896–1981 Scot physician & nov
**Cronjé** Piet Arnoldus 1840?–1911 Boer leader & gen
**Crookes** Sir William 1832–1919 Eng physicist & chem
**Crosby** Harry Lillis 1904–1977 *Bing* Am singer & film actor
**Cruden** Alexander 1701–1779 Scot compiler of a biblical concordance
**Cruft** Charles 1852–1938 Eng dog breeder & showman
**Cruikshank** George 1792–1878 Eng caricaturist & illustrator
**Cruyff** Johannes 1947–     Du footballer
**Cudworth** Ralph 1617–1688 Eng philos
**Culbertson** Ely 1891–1955 Am bridge player
**Cullis** Stanley 1915–     Eng footballer
**Cummings** Edward Estlin 1894–1962 *e e cummings* Am poet
**Cunha, da** Tristão 1460?–1540 Port navigator & explorer
**Cunningham** Allan 1784–1842 Scot author
**Cunningham** Merce 1922?–     Am choreographer
**Curie** Eve 1904–     *dau of Marie & Pierre* Fr author
**Curie** Marie 1867–1934 née *Marja Sklodowska* Fr (Pol-born) chem
**Curie** Pierre 1859–1906 *husband of prec* Fr chem
**Curie-Joliot** – see JOLIOT-CURIE
**Curry** John 1949–     Eng ice-skater
**Curtin** John 1885–1945 Austral polit; prime min (1941–45)
**Curtis** Cyrus Hermann Kotzschmar 1850–1933 Am publisher
**Curtis** Tony 1925–     né *Bernard Schwarz* Am film actor
**Curtiss** Glenn Hammond 1878–1930 Am aviator & inventor
**Curwen** John 1816–1880 Eng music teacher
**Curzon** Sir Clifford Michael 1907–1982 Br pianist
**Curzon** George Nathaniel 1859–1925 1st Baron & 1st Marquis *Curzon of Kedleston* Eng statesman; viceroy of India (1899–1905)
**Cushing** Harvey 1869–1939 Am surgeon
**Custer** George Armstrong 1839–1876 Am gen

**Cuthbert** Saint 635?–687 Eng monk
**Cuvier** Baron Georges Léopold Chrétien Frédéric Dagobert 1769–1832 Fr naturalist
**Cynewulf, Cynwulf** *fl* 750 Anglo-Saxon poet
**Cyprian** Saint *d* 258 *Thascius Caecilius Cyprianus* Christian martyr; bishop of Carthage (248–258)
**Cyrano de Bergerac, de** Savinien 1619–1655 Fr poet & soldier
**Cyril** Saint 827–869 *Constantine* Slavic apostle
**Cyrus** 600?–529 B C *the Great* or *the Elder* king of Persia (550–529)
**Cyrus** 429?–401 B C *the Younger* Persian prince & satrap
**Czerny** Carl 1791–1857 Austrian pianist & composer

# D

**D', De, Du,** etc – for many names beginning with these elements see the specific family names
**Dacre of Glanton** Baron – see Hugh TREVOR-ROPER
**Daguerre** Louis Jacques Mandé 1789–1851 Fr artist; inventor of the daguerrotype
**Dahl** Roald 1916–     Br author
**Dahrendorf** Ralf 1929–     Ger sociologist
**Daimler** Gottlieb 1834–1900 Ger motor manuf
**Dakin** Henry Drysdale 1880–1952 Eng chem
**Daladier** Édouard 1884–1970 Fr statesman
**Dalcroze** Émile Jaques – see Émile JAQUES-DALCROZE
**Dale** Sir Henry Hallett 1875–1968 Eng physiol
**Dalén** Nils Gustav 1869–1937 Swed engineer
**Daley** Richard Joseph 1902–1976 Am polit & mayor of Chicago
**Dalhousie** Earl & Marquis of – see RAMSEY
**Dali** Salvador 1904–     Span surrealist artist – **Daliesque** *adj*
**Dalrymple** Sir John 1673–1747 2nd Earl of *Stair* Scot gen & diplomat
**Dalton** John 1766–1844 Eng chem & physicist
**Daly** (John) Augustin 1838–1899 Am dram & theatre manager
**Daly** Fred 1911–     Irish golfer
**Dam** (Carl Peter) Henrik 1895–1976 Danish biochem
**Damien de Veuster** Joseph 1840–1889 *Father Damien* Belg RC missionary to lepers on Molokai
**Dampier** William 1652–1715 Eng buccaneer & navigator
**Dane** Clemence 1888–1965 pseud of *Winifred Ashton* Eng nov
**Daniel** Samuel 1562?–1619 Eng poet
**Dankworth** John 1927–     Eng composer & saxophonist
**D'Annunzio** Gabriele 1863–1938 Ital author & soldier
**Dante** 1265–1321 *Dante Alighieri* Ital poet – **Dantean, Dantescan, Dantesque** *adj*
**Danton** Georges Jacques 1759–1794 Fr revolutionist
**Darby** Abraham 1678–1717 Eng ore-smelting expert
**Darby** John Nelson 1800–1882 Eng religious leader
**Darius** name of 3 kings of Persia: esp **I** 558?–486 B C (reigned 521–486) *Darius Hystaspis*; *the Great*
**Darlan** François 1881–1942 Fr admiral & polit; prime min (1941–42)
**Darling** Fred 1884–1953 Eng racehorse trainer
**Darling** Grace Horsley 1815–1842 Eng heroine in sea rescue (1838)
**Darnley** Lord 1545–1567 *Henry Stewart* or *Stuart*; *husband of Mary, Queen of Scots*
**Darrow** Clarence Seward 1857–1938 Am lawyer & author
**Dart** Robert Thurston 1921–1971 Eng conductor, harpsichordist, & pianist
**Darwin** Sir Charles Galton 1887–1962 Eng physicist
**Darwin** Charles Robert 1809–1882 Eng naturalist
**Darwin** Erasmus 1731–1802 *grandfather of CR* Eng physiol & poet
**Darwin** Sir Francis 1848–1925 *son of CR* Eng botanist
**Darwin** Sir George Howard 1845–1912 *son of CR* Eng astron
**Dassault** Marcel 1892–     Fr aircraft manuf
**Daubigny** Charles François 1817–1878 Fr artist
**Daudet** Alphonse 1840–1897 Fr nov
**Daumier** Honoré 1808–1879 Fr caricaturist & artist
**Davenant, D'Avenant** Sir William 1606–1668 Eng poet & dram; poet laureate (1638–68)

**David I** 1084–1153 king of Scotland (1124–53)
**David** Elizabeth 1914–    Eng cookery author
**David** Gerard 1450? or 1460?–1523 Du artist
**David** Jacques Louis 1748–1825 Fr artist
**Davidson** Randall Thomas 1848–1930 archbishop of Canterbury (1903–28)
**Davie** Alan 1920–    Scot artist & jazz musician
**Davie** Donald Alfred 1922–    Eng poet & critic
**Davies** Arthur Bowen 1862–1928 Am artist
**Davies** Sir Henry Walford 1869–1941 Eng composer & organist
**Davies** Lynn 1942–    Welsh long jumper
**Davies** Peter Maxwell 1934–    Eng composer
**Davies** Rhys 1903–1978 Welsh author
**Davies** Sharron 1963–    Eng swimmer
**Davies** William Henry 1871–1940 Welsh poet
**Davis** Angela 1944–    Am Communist activist
**Davis** Bette 1908–    Am film actress
**Davis** Sir Colin Rex 1927–    Eng conductor
**Davis** Jefferson 1808–1889 Am statesman; pres of confed states (1861–65)
**Davis** Joe 1901–1978 Eng billiards & snooker player
**Davis** Sammy Jnr 1925–    Am singer, actor, & dancer
**Davisson** Clinton Joseph 1881–1958 Am physicist
**Davy** Sir Humphry 1778–1829 Eng chem
**Dawes** Charles Gates 1865–1951 Am lawyer & financier; vice-pres of US (1925–29); Nobel Peace Prize (1925)
**Dawes** John 1940–    Welsh rugby union player
**Dawson** Peter 1882–1961 Austral baritone
**Day** Doris 1924–    Am actress & singer
**Day** Sir Robin 1923–    Eng broadcaster & journalist
**Dayan** Moshe 1915–1981 Israeli soldier & statesman
**Day-Lewis** Cecil 1904–1972 pseud *Nicholas Blake* Eng author; poet laureate (1968–72)
**Deakin** Alfred 1856–1919 prime min of Austral (1903–1904; 1905–1908; 1909–1910)
**Dean** Basil 1888–1978 Eng theatrical producer: founder of ENSA
**Dean** James 1931–1955 Am film actor
**Dean** William Ralph 1907–1980 *Dixie* Eng footballer
**Debrett** John 1750?–1822 Eng publisher
**Debussy** Claude Achille 1862–1918 Fr composer
**Debye** Peter Joseph Wilhelm 1884–1966 Du-born physicist in Am
**Decius** 201–251 *Gaius Messius Quintus Trajanus Decius* Rom emp (249–51)
**Deeping** (George) Warwick 1877–1950 Eng nov
**Defoe** Daniel *ab* 1660–1731 Eng journalist & nov
**De Forest** Lee 1873–1961 Am inventor
**Degas** (Hilaire Germain) Edgar 1834–1917 Fr artist
**de Gaulle** Charles André Joseph Marie 1890–1970 Fr gen; interim pres of France (1945–46); pres of Fifth Republic (1959–69)
**De Havilland** Sir Geoffrey 1882–1965 Eng aircraft designer & manuf
**Dekker, Decker** Thomas 1572?–?1632 Eng dram
**de Kooning** Willem 1904–    Am (Du-born) artist
**De La Beche** Sir Henry Thomas 1796–1855 Eng geologist
**Delacroix** (Ferdinand Victor) Eugène 1798–1863 Fr artist
**de la Mare** Walter John 1873–1956 Eng poet & nov
**Delaney** Shelagh 1939–    Eng dram
**De La Rey** Jacobus Hercules 1847–1914 Boer gen & statesman
**De la Roche** Mazo 1885–1961 Canad nov
**De la Rue** Warren 1815–1889 Eng astron
**De La Warr** Baron 1577–1618 *Thomas West; Lord Delaware* Eng colonial administrator in Am
**Deledda** Grazia 1875–1936 Ital author
**Delfont** Sir Bernard 1909–    Br (Russ-born) impresario & film exec
**Delibes** Leo 1836–1891 Fr composer
**Delius** Frederick 1862–1934 Eng composer
**Dell** Ethel Mary 1881–1939 Eng romantic nov
**Deller** Alfred George 1912–1979 Eng counter tenor
**De Mille** Cecil 1881–1959 Am film producer
**Democritus** *b ab* 460 B C *the Laughing Philosopher* Greek philos

**De Morgan** William Frend 1839–1917 Eng artist & nov
**Demosthenes** 385?–322 B C Athenian orator & statesman – **Demosthenic** *adj*
**Dempsey** William Harrison 1895–1983 *Jack* Am boxer
**Denis, Denys** Saint 3rd c 1st bishop of Paris; patron saint of France
**Denning of Whitchurch** Baron 1899–    *Alfred Thompson Denning* Eng lawyer
**De Quincey** Thomas 1785–1859 Eng author
**Derain** André 1880–1954 Fr artist
**Descartes** René 1596–1650 Lat *Renatus Cartesius* Fr math & philos
**de Seversky** Alexander Procofieff 1894–1974 Am (Russ-born) aeronautical engineer
**De Sica** Vittorio 1901–1974 Ital film director & actor
**Desmoulins** Camille 1760–1794 *Lucie Simplice Camille Benoît Desmoulins* Fr revolutionist
**de Soto** Hernando *or* Fernando 1500?–1542 Span explorer in Am
**Des Prez** Josquin 1450?–1521 Du composer
**Dessalines** Jean Jacques 1758–1806 emp as *Jacques I* of Haiti (1804–06)
**Deus Ramos, de** João 1830–1896 Port poet
**De Valera** Eamon 1882–1975 Irish polit; prime min of Ireland (1937–48; 1951–54; 1957–59); pres of Ireland (1959–73)
**de Valois** Dame Ninette 1898–    neé *Edris Stannus* Irish ballet dancer & choreographer
**Devereux** Robert 1566–1601 2nd Earl of *Essex* Eng soldier & courtier
**Devine** George Alexander Cassady 1910–1966 Eng theatre manager, director, & actor
**Devlin** (Josephine) Bernadette 1947–    *Mrs J B McAliskey* N Ireland polit
**Devonshire** dukes of – see CAVENDISH
**De Vries** Hugo 1848–1935 Du botanist
**Dewar** Sir James 1842–1923 Scot chem & physicist
**De Wet** Christiaan Rudolph 1854–1922 Boer soldier & polit
**Dewey** Melvil 1851–1931 Am librarian
**Dexter** Edward Ralph 1935–    Eng (Ital- born) cricketer
**Diaghilev** Sergei Pavlovich 1872–1929 Russ ballet producer & art critic
**Diana** 1961–    formerly *Lady Diana Frances Spencer; wife of Prince Charles* princess of Wales
**Dias, Diaz** Bartholomeu 1450?–1500 Port navigator; disc Cape of Good Hope
**Días de Bivar** – see EL CID
**Dickens** Charles John Huffam 1812–1870 *Boz* Eng nov – **Dickensian** *adj*
**Dickens** Monica 1915–    *granddaughter of prec* Eng author
**Dickinson** Emily Elizabeth 1830–1886 Am poet
**Dick-Read** Grantly 1890–1959 Eng obstetrician
**Diderot** Denis 1713–1784 Fr encyclopedist
**Diefenbaker** John George 1895–1979 prime min of Canada (1957–63)
**Diels** Otto 1876–1954 Ger chem
**Diem Ngo Dinh** 1901–1963 prime min of S Vietnam (1954–63)
**Diesel** Rudolf 1858–1913 Ger mechanical engineer
**Dietrich** Marlene 1904–    neé *Maria Magdalena von Losch* Ger film actress
**Digby** Sir Kenelm 1603–1665 Eng naval commander, diplomat, & author
**Dilland** Harrison 1923–    Am athlete
**Dillon** John 1851–1927 Irish nationalist polit
**DiMaggio** Joseph Paul 1914–    Am baseball player
**Dimbleby** Richard 1913–1965 Eng broadcaster
**Dinesen** Isak – see Karen BLIXEN
**d'Inzeo** Piero 1923–    *bro of next* Ital show jumper
**d'Inzeo** Raimondo 1925–    *bro of prec* Ital show jumper
**Diocletian** 245–313 *Gaius Aurelius Valerius Diocletianus* Rom emp (284–305)
**Diogenes** 412?–323 B C Greek Cynic philos
**Dionysius** 430?–?367 B C the *Elder* Greek tyrant of Syracuse (405–367)
**Dionysius** the *Younger* tyrant of Syracuse (367–356; 347–344 B C)

**Dionysius Exiguus** 6th-c Christian monk; introduced method of reckoning the Christian era

**Dionysius of Alexandria** Saint 3rd-c theol & bishop of Alexandria (247)

**Dionysius of Halicarnassus** *d ab* 7 B C Greek scholar

**Dior** Christian 1905–1957 Fr fashion designer

**Diouf** Abdou 1935– prime min of Senegal (1970–81), pres (1981– )

**Dirac** Paul Adrien Maurice 1902– Eng physicist

**Disney** Walter Elias 1901–1966 Am producer of animated cartoon films

**Disraeli** Benjamin 1804–1881 1st Earl of *Beaconsfield; Dizzy* Eng polit & author; prime min (1868; 1874–80)

**di Stefano** Alfredo 1926– Argentine footballer

**Dobell** Sir William 1899-1970 Austral artist

**Dobson** (Henry) Austin 1840–1921 Eng poet & essayist

**Dod** Charlotte 1871–1960 *Lottie* Eng sportswoman, mainly tennis & golf

**Dodgson** Charles Lutwidge 1832–1898 pseud *Lewis Carroll* Eng math & author

**Doherty** Hugh Lawrence 1874–1910 *Lawrie; bro of next* Eng tennis player

**Doherty** Reginald Frank 1876–1919 *Reggie; bro of prec* Eng tennis player

**Dolci** Danilo 1924– Ital social reformer

**Dolin** Sir Anton 1904–1983 né *Patrick Healey-Kay* Eng ballet dancer & choreographer

**D'Oliveira** Basil Lewis 1931– S African cricketer for England

**Dollfuss** Engelbert 1892–1934 Austrian statesman

**Dolmetsch** Arnold 1858–1940 Br (Fr-born) musicologist

**Domenichino, Il** 1581–1641 *Domenico Zampieri* Ital artist

**Dominic** Saint 1170–1221 *Domingo de Guzmán* Span-born founder of the Dominican order of friars

**Domitian** 51–96 *Titus Flavius Domitianus Augustus* Rom emp (81–96)

**Donat** Robert 1905–1958 Eng actor

**Donatello** 1386?–1466 *Donato di Niccolò di Betto Bardi* Ital sculptor

**Dong Pham Van** 1902– prime min of N Vietnam (1954–76), of Vietnam (1976– )

**Dönitz** Karl 1891–1980 Ger admiral

**Donizetti** Gaetano 1797–1848 Ital composer

**Donne** John *ab* 1572–1631 Eng poet & clergyman – **Donnean, Donnian** *adj*

**Donoghue** Stephen 1884–1945 *Steve* Eng jockey

**Doolittle** James Harold 1896– Am aviator & gen

**Doppler** Christian Johann 1803–1853 Austrian physicist & math

**Dorati** Antal 1906– Am (Hung-born) conductor

**Doré** (Paul) Gustave 1833–1883 Fr illustrator & artist

**d'Oriola** Pierre 1920– Fr show jumper

**Dornberger** Walter 1895– Ger engineer; inventor of V2 rocket

**Dornier** Claude 1884–1969 Ger aeroplane builder

**Dorset** 1st Earl of – see Thomas SACKVILLE

**Dos Passos** John Roderigo 1896–1970 Am author

**Dostoevski, Dostoyevski** Fëdor Mikhailovich 1821–1881 Russ nov – **Dostoevskian** *adj*

**Dotrice** Roy 1925– Eng actor

**Doughty** Charles Montagu 1843–1926 Eng poet & traveller

**Douglas** David 1798–1834 Sc botanist & explorer

**Douglas** (George) Norman 1868–1952 Eng author

**Douglas** John Sholto 1844–1900 8th Marquis & Earl of *Queensberry* Scot boxing patron

**Douglas** John William Henry 1882–1930 Eng footballer, boxer, & cricketer

**Douglas** Kirk 1916– né *Issur Danilovitch Demsky* Am actor & producer

**Douglas** Lloyd Cassel 1887–1951 Am author

**Douglas-Home** – see HOME

**Douglas of Kirtleside** 1st Baron 1893–1969 *William Sholto Douglas* Br air marshal

**Downes** Terry 1936– Eng boxer

**Dowson** Ernest Christopher 1867–1900 Eng lyric poet

**Doyle** Sir Arthur Conan 1859–1930 Br physician, nov, & detective-story author, creator of Sherlock Holmes

**D'Oyly Carte** – see CARTE

**Drabble** Margaret 1939– Eng nov

**Draco** late 7th-c B C Athenian lawgiver

**Drake** Sir Francis 1540?–1596 Eng navigator & admiral

**Draper** John William 1811–1882 Am (Eng-born) scientist & author

**Draper** Ruth 1884–1956 Am actress

**Drayton** Michael 1563–1631 Eng poet

**Dreiser** Theodore Herman Albert 1871–1945 Am editor & nov

**Dreyer** Carl 1889–1968 Danish film director

**Dreyfus** Alfred 1859–1935 Fr army officer

**Drinkwater** John 1882–1937 Eng poet & dram

**Drobny** Jaroslav 1921– Br (Czech-born) tennis player

**Drummond** William 1585–1649 1st Laird of *Hawthornden* Scot poet

**Drummond** William Henry 1854–1907 Canad (Irish-born) poet

**Dryden** John 1631–1700 Eng poet & dram; poet laureate (1670–88) – **Drydenian** *adj*

**Du Barry** Comtesse 1746 (or 1743?)–1793 *Marie Jeanne Bécu; mistress of Louis XV of France*

**Dubček** Alexander 1921– Czech politician

**Dubois** Théodore 1837–1924 Fr composer

**Dubuffet** Jean 1901– Fr artist

**Duchamp** Marcel 1887–1968 Fr artist

**Duckworth** George 1901–1966 Eng cricketer

**Dudevant** Aurore – see George SAND

**Dudley** Sir Edmund 1462?–1510 Eng lawyer

**Dudley** Robert 1532?–1588 1st Earl of *Leicester* Eng courtier

**Dufferin and Ava** 1st Marquis of 1826–1902 *Frederick Temple Hamilton-Temple-Blackwood* Eng diplomat

**Duffy** Sir Charles Gavan 1816–1903 Irish nationalist & Austral polit

**Dufy** Raoul 1877–1953 Fr artist

**Du Gard** Roger Martin – see MARTIN DU GARD

**Duhamel** Georges 1884–1966 pseud of *Denis Thévenin* Fr author

**Dukas** Paul 1865–1935 Fr composer

**Duke** Geoffrey 1922– Eng racing motor cyclist

**Dulac** Edmond 1882–1953 Br (Fr-born) artist & designer

**Dulbecco** Renato 1914– Am (Ital-born) virologist

**Dulles** John Foster 1888–1959 Am lawyer; sec of state (1953–59)

**Dulong** Pierre Louis 1785–1838 Fr physicist & chem

**Dumas** Alexandre 1802–1870 *Dumas père* Fr nov & dram

**Dumas** Alexandre 1824–1895 *Dumas fils* Fr nov & dram

**du Maurier** Dame Daphne 1907– *dau of Gerald* Eng author

**du Maurier** George Louis Palmella Busson 1834–1896 Eng artist & nov

**du Maurier** Sir Gerald 1873–1934 *son of GLPB and father of D* Eng actor-manager

**Dunant** Jean Henri 1828–1910 Swiss philanthropist; founder of the Red Cross

**Dunaway** Faye 1941– Am actress

**Dunbar** William 1460?–?1520 Scot poet

**Duncan** Isadora 1878–1927 Am dancer

**Dundas** Henry 1742–1811 1st Viscount *Melville* & Baron *Dunira* Eng statesman

**Dunham** Katherine 1914– Am dancer & choreographer

**Dunlop** John Boyd 1840–1921 Scot inventor

**Dunmore** 4th Earl of 1732–1809 *John Murray* Scot colonial administrator in Am

**Dunsany** 18th Baron 1878–1957 *Edward John Moreton Drax Plunkett; Lord Dunsany* Irish poet & dram

**Duns Scotus** John 1265?–?1308 Scot scholastic theol

**Dunstan** Saint 925?–988 archbishop of Canterbury (961–988)

**Dunster** Henry 1612?–1659 Eng educ; first pres of Harvard Univ, USA

**Dupleix** Marquis Joseph François 1679–1763 Fr colonial administrator in India

**du Pré** Jacqueline 1945– *Mrs Daniel Barenboim* Eng cellist

**Dürer** Albrecht 1471–1528 Ger artist & engraver – **Düreresque** *adj*

**Durkheim** Émile 1858–1917 Fr sociol

**Durrell** Gerald Malcolm 1925– *bro of next* Eng naturalist & author

**Durrell** Lawrence George 1912–    *bro of prec* Eng author & poet
**Dürrenmatt** Friedrich 1921–    Swiss author
**Duse** Eleonora 1858–1924 Ital actress
**Duvalier** François 1907–1971 *Papa Doc* pres of Haiti (1957–71)
**Duvalier** Jean-Claude 1951–    *son of prec* pres of Haiti (1971–    )
**Duveen of Millbank** 1st Baron 1869–1939 *Joseph Duveen* Eng art dealer
**du Vigneaud** Vincent 1901–    Am biochem
**Dvořák** Anton 1841–1904 Czech composer
**Dworkin** Ronald Myles 1931–    Am jurist & philos
**Dwyfor** Earl of – see LLOYD GEORGE
**Dylan** Bob 1941–    pseud of *Robert Zimmerman* Am singer & composer


# E

**Eads** James Buchanan 1820–1887 Am engineer & inventor
**Eakins** Thomas 1844–1916 Am artist
**Eanes** António dos Santos Ramalho 1935–    Port gen & pres (1976–    )
**Earhart** Amelia 1898–1937 Am aviator
**Earp** Wyatt Berry Stapp 1848–1929 Am law enforcement officer
**Eastman** George 1854–1932 Am inventor & industrialist
**Eastwood** Clint 1930–    Am film actor & director
**Ebert** Friedrich 1871–1925 pres of Germany (1919–25)
**Echegaray y Eizaguirre** José 1832–1916 Span dram
**Echeverría Alvarez** Luis 1922–    pres of Mex (1970–76)
**Eck** Johann 1486–1543 né *Mayer* Ger RC theol
**Eckermann** Johann Peter 1792–1854 Ger author
**Eckhart, Eckart, Eckardt** Johannes 1260?–?1327 Ger Dominican theol; founder of Ger mysticism
**Eddery** Pat 1952–    Irish jockey
**Eddington** Sir Arthur Stanley 1882–1944 Eng astron
**Eddy** Mary Morse 1821–1910 née *Baker* Am founder of the Christian Science Church
**Eddy** Nelson 1901–1967 Am film actor & singer
**Eden** (Robert) Anthony 1897–1977 1st Earl of *Avon* Eng polit; prime min (1955–57)
**Edgeworth** Maria 1767–1849 Eng nov
**Edgeworth** Richard Lovell 1744–1817 Eng inventor & educ
**Edinburgh** Duke of – see PHILIP
**Edison** Thomas Alva 1847–1931 Am inventor
**Edmund, Eadmund II** 980?–1016 *Ironside* king of the English (1016)
**Edward** name of 8 post-Norman Eng (Brit) kings: **I** 1239–1307 (reigned 1272–1307) *Longshanks*
**Edward II** 1284–1327 (reigned 1307–27)
**Edward III** 1312–1377 (reigned 1327–77)
**Edward IV** 1442–1483 (reigned 1461–70; 1471–83)
**Edward V** 1470–1483 (reigned 1483)
**Edward VI** 1537–1553 (reigned 1547–53) *son of Henry VIII & Jane Seymour*
**Edward VII** 1841–1910 (reigned 1901–10) *Albert Edward, son of Victoria*
**Edward VIII** 1894–1972 (reigned 1936; abdicated) Duke of *Windsor, son of George V*
**Edward** 1002?–1066 *the Confessor* king of the English (1042–66)
**Edward** 1330–1376 *the Black Prince; son of Edward III* prince of Wales
**Edwards** Duncan 1936–1958 Eng footballer
**Edwards** Gareth 1947–    Welsh rugby union player
**Edwin** or **Eadwine** 585?–633 king of Northumbria (617–633)
**Egbert** 775?–839 king of the West Saxons (802–839) & 1st king of the English (828–839)
**Egg** Augustus 1816–1863 Eng artist
**Ehrenburg** Ilya Grigorievich 1891–1967 Soviet writer
**Ehrlich** Paul 1854–1915 Ger bacteriologist
**Eichmann** Adolf 1906–1962 Ger Nazi leader
**Eiffel** Alexandre Gustave 1832–1923 Fr engineer
**Eijkman** Christiaan 1858–1930 Du hygienist

**Einstein** Albert 1879–1955 Am (Ger-born) physicist
**Einthoven** Willem 1860–1927 Du physiol
**Eisenhower** Dwight David 1890–1969 Am gen; 34th pres of the US (1953–61)
**Eisenstein** Sergei Mikhailovich 1898–1948 Soviet film director
**Elagabalus** – see HELIOGABALUS
**El Cid** 1040?–1099 *Rodrigo* (or *Ruy*) *Díaz de Bivar* Span soldier & hero
**Elder** James 1934–    Canad show jumper
**Eldon** 1st Earl of 1751–1838 *John Scott* Eng jurist
**Eleanor of Aquitaine** 1122?–1204 *queen of Louis VII of France (divorced 1152) & of Henry II of England*
**Eleanor of Castile** d 1290 *queen of Edward I of England*
**Eleanor of Provence** d 1291 *queen of Henry III of England*
**Elgar** Sir Edward 1857–1934 Eng composer
**Elgin** 7th Earl of 1766–1841 *Thomas Bruce* Br diplomat
**Eliot** George 1819–1880 pseud of *Mary Ann (or Marian) Evans* Eng nov – **Eliotic** *adj*
**Eliot** Thomas Stearns 1888–1965 Br (Am-born) poet & critic
**Elizabeth** name of 2 Eng (Br) queens: **I** 1533–1603 *dau of Henry VIII & Anne Boleyn* (reigned 1558–1603); **II** 1926– *Elizabeth Alexandra Mary; dau of George VI, wife of Prince Philip; mother of Prince Charles* (reigned 1952–    )
**Elizabeth** 1900–    *Elizabeth Angela Marguerite Bowes-Lyon; queen consort of George VI of GB*
**Elizabeth** 1596–1662 *Queen of Hearts; queen of Frederick V of Bohemia*
**Elizabeth** 1843–1916 pseud *Carmen Sylva* queen of Rumania & author
**Elizabeth Petrovna** 1709–1762 empress of Russia (1741–62)
**Ellington** Edward Kennedy 1899–1974 *Duke Ellington* Am band leader & composer
**Elliott** Herb 1938–    Austral athlete
**Ellis (Henry) Havelock** 1859–1939 Eng psychol & author
**Ellis** Jan 1943–    S African rugby union player
**Ellison** Ralph Waldo 1914–    Am author
**Elphinstone** William 1431–1514 Scot bishop & statesman
**El-Sadat** – see SADAT
**Elyot** Sir Thomas 1490?–1546 Eng scholar & diplomat
**Emerson** Ralph Waldo 1803–1882 Am essayist & poet – **Emersonian** *adj*
**Emmet** Robert 1778–1803 Irish nationalist & rebel
**Empedocles** 5th-c B C Greek philos & statesman
**Empson** Sir William 1906–1984 Eng poet
**Ender** Kornelia 1958–    E Ger swimmer
**Enders** John Franklin 1897–    Am bacteriol
**Endo** Yukio 1937–    Jap gymnast
**Enesco** Georges 1881–1955 Rumanian composer
**Engels** Friedrich 1820–1895 Ger socialist; collaborator with Karl Marx
**Enver Pasha** 1881–1922 *Enver Bey* Turk soldier & polit
**Epictetus** 1st–2nd c A D Greek Stoic philos in Rome – **Epictetian** *adj*
**Epicurus** 342?–270 B C Greek philos
**Epstein** Sir Jacob 1880–1959 Br (Am-born) sculptor
**Erasmus** Desiderius 1466?–1536 *Gerhard Gerhards* or *Geert Geerts* Du scholar – **Erasmian** *adj*
**Eratosthenes** 3rd c B C Greek astron
**Erhard** Ludwig 1897–1977 chancellor of West Germany (1963–66)
**Eric** 10th c *the Red* Norw navigator; explored Greenland coast
**Ericson** Leif *Old Norse* Leifr **Eiriksson** *fl* 1000 *son of Eric the Red* Norw mariner; disc "Vinland"
**Ericsson** John 1803–1889 Am (Swed-born) engineer & inventor
**Erigena** Johannes Scotus 815?–?877 Scot–Irish (?) philos & theol
**Erlanger** Joseph 1874–1965 Am physiol
**Ernst** Max 1891–1976 Ger artist
**Ervine** St John Greer 1883–1971 Irish dram & nov
**Esenin** – see YESENIN
**Eshkol** Levi 1895–1969 premier of Israel (1963–69)
**Essex** Earl of – see Thomas CROMWELL
**Essex** 2nd Earl of – see DEVEREUX
**Estaing, d'** Comte Jean Baptiste Charles Henri Hector 1729–1794 Fr admiral

**Este** Ital princely family beginning with *Alberto Azzo II* 996–1097 & ending with *Ercole III Rinaldo* 1727–1803

**Esterhazy** Marie Charles Ferdinand Walsin 1847–1923 Fr army officer

**Estienne, Étienne** Fr family of printers & booksellers including esp Henri I *d* 1520; his son Robert 1503–1559; & Robert's son Henri II 1528?–1598

**Estournelles de Constant, d'** Baron Constant de Rebecque 1852–1924 *Paul Henri Benjamin Balluat* Fr diplomat & polit

**Ethelbert** 552?–616 king of Kent

**Ethelred II** 968?–1016 *the Unready* king of England (978–1016)

**Etherege** Sir George 1635?–1691 Eng dram

**Etty** William 1787–1849 Eng artist

**Eucken** Rudolf Christoph 1846–1926 Ger philos

**Euclid** *fl ab* 300 B C Greek math

**Eugene, Eugène** 1663–1736 *François Eugène de Savoie-Carignan* prince of Savoy & Austrian gen

**Eugénie** 1826–1920 *Eugénie Marie de Montijo de Guzman; wife of Napoleon III* empress of the French (1853–71)

**Euler** Leonhard 1707–1783 Swiss math & physicist

**Euler-Chelpin, von** Hans August Simon 1873–1964 Swed (Ger-born) chem

**Euripides** 480?–?406 B C Greek dram – **Euripidean** *adj*

**Eusebio da Silva** Ferreira 1942– Port (Mozambique-born) footballer

**Eusebius of Caesarea** 260?–?340 theol & church hist

**Eustachio** Bartolommeo 1520–1574 Ital anatomist

**Evans** Sir Arthur John 1851–1941 Eng archaeologist

**Evans** Dame Edith 1888–1976 Eng actress

**Evans** Sir Geraint Llewellyn 1922– Welsh baritone

**Evans** (Thomas) Godfrey 1920– Eng cricketer

**Evatt** Herbert Vere 1894–1965 Austral lawyer & statesman

**Evelyn** John 1620–1706 Eng diarist

**Everest** Sir George 1790–1866 Eng surveyor & geographer; Mt Everest named after him

**Evershed** John 1864–1956 Eng astron

**Evert-Lloyd** Christine Marie 1954– Am tennis player

**Ewald, Evald** Johannes 1743–1781 Danish poet & dram

**Ewbank** Thomas 1792–1870 Am (Eng-born) inventor of carpet sweeper

**Ewins** Arthur James 1882–1957 Eng chem

**Eyck, van** Hubert *or* Huybrecht 1366?–1426 & his bro **Jan** 1370?–1440 Flem artists

**Eyre** Edward John 1815–1901 Eng explorer & colonial administrator

**Eysenck** Hans Jurgen 1916– Br psychol

**Ezra** Derek 1919– *Baron Ezra* Eng chairman of Nat Coal Board (1971–82)

# F

**Fabergé** Peter Carl 1846–1920 Russ jeweller

**Fabiola** 1928– *wife of King Baudouin I of Belgium*

**Fabius** *d* 203 B C *Quintus Fabius Maximus Verrucosus Cunctator* Rom gen against Hannibal

**Fabre** Jean Henri 1823–1915 Fr entomologist

**Fadden** Sir Arthur William 1895–1973 Austral statesman

**Fahrenheit** Gabriel Daniel 1686–1736 Ger physicist

**Fairbairn** Douglas 1862–1938 Austral oarsman; founded London's Head of the River race on Thames

**Fairbairn** Sir William 1789–1874 Eng engineer

**Fairbanks** Douglas Elton 1883–1939 né *Ulman* Am actor

**Fairbanks** Douglas Jnr 1909– *son of prec* Am actor

**Fairburn** Arthur Rex Dugard 1904–1957 NZ poet

**Fairey** Sir Charles Richard 1887–1956 Eng aircraft manuf

**Fairfax** Baron Thomas 1612–1671 Eng gen

**Fairfax** Baron Thomas 1692–1782 proprietor in Virginia

**Faisal, Feisal, Feisul I** 1885–33 king of Syria (1920), of Iraq (1921–33)

**Faisal, Feisal, Feisul II** 1935–1958 king of Iraq (1939–58)

**Faisal** 1906?–1975 king of Saudi Arabia (1964–75)

**Falkner** William – see FAULKNER

**Falla, de** Manuel 1876–1946 Span composer

**Fangio** Juan Manuel 1911– Argentine racing driver

**Fantin-Latour** Ignace Henri Jean Théodore 1836–1904 Fr artist

**Faraday** Michael 1791–1867 Eng chem & physicist

**Farina** Giuseppe 1906–1966 *Nino* Ital racing driver

**Farman** Henri 1874–1958 & his brother Maurice 1877-1964 Fr pioneer aviators & aeroplane manufacturers

**Farmer** Ken 1910– Austral rules footballer

**Farnese** Alessandro 1545–1592 Duke of *Parma* Ital gen in Span service

**Farquhar** George 1678–1707 Eng dram

**Farrar** Frederic William 1831–1903 Eng clergyman & author

**Farrell** James Gordon 1935–1979 Eng nov

**Farrell** James Thomas 1904–1979 Am nov

**Farrelly** Bernard 1944– *Midget* Austral surfer

**Faruk, Farouk** 1920–1965 king of Egypt (1936–52; abdicated); citizen of Monaco (1959–65)

**Fastolf** Sir John 1378?–1459 Eng soldier & administrator; Shakespeare's "Falstaff"

**Fatima** 606–632 *dau of Muhammad*

**Faulkner** Max 1916– Eng golfer

**Faulkner** William Cuthbert 1897–1962 né *Falkner* Am nov

**Faulkner of Downpatrick** Baron 1921–1977 *Arthur Brian Deane Faulkner* N Ireland prime min (1971–72)

**Faure** François Félix 1841–1899 Fr statesman; pres of France (1895–99)

**Fauré** Gabriel Urbain 1845–1924 Fr composer

**Fawcett** Dame Millicent Garrett 1847–1929 Eng suffragette

**Fawcett** Percy Harrison 1867–?1925 Eng explorer; disappeared on Brazil expedition

**Fawkes** Guy 1570–1606 Eng RC conspirator

**Feather** Baron 1908–1976 *Victor Grayson Hardie Feather* Eng trade-union leader

**Fechner** Gustav Theodor 1801–1887 Ger physicist & psychol

**Feininger** Lyonel Charles Adrian 1871–1956 Am artist

**Fellini** Federico 1920– Ital film director

**Fenby** Eric William 1906– Eng composer & arranger

**Fenton** Roger 1819–1869 Eng pioneer photographer

**Fénelon** François de Salignac de La Mothe 1651–1715 Fr prelate & author

**Ferber** Edna 1887–1968 Am author

**Ferdinand I** 1861–1948 *Maximilian Karl Leopold Maria* king of Bulgaria (1908–18)

**Ferdinand I** *d* 1065 *the Great* king of Castile (1033-65); of Navarre and Leon (1037–65); emp of Spain (1056–65)

**Ferdinand I** 1503–1564 Holy Rom emp (1556–64)

**Ferdinand II** 1578-1637 king of Bohemia (1617–19; 1620–37) & of Hungary (1621–37); Holy Rom emp (1619–37)

**Ferdinand III** 1608–1657 king of нungary (1625–57); Holy Rom emp (1637–57)

**Ferdinand V** of Castile *or* **II** of Aragon 1452–1516 *the Catholic* king of Castile (1474–1504), of Aragon (1479-1516); of Naples (1504–16); founder of the Span monarchy

**Ferdinand VII** 1784–1833 king of Spain (1808; 1814–33)

**Ferguson** Harry 1884–1960 Eng engineer; designer of agric machinery

**Ferguson** James 1710–1776 Scot astron

**Fermat, de** Pierre 1601–1665 Fr math

**Fermi** Enrico 1901–1954 Am (Ital-born) physicist

**Fernandel** 1903–1971 pseud of *Fernand Joseph Désiré Constandin* Fr comedian & actor

**Fernández** Juan 1536–?1602 Span navigator

**Ferrari** Enzo 1898– Ital motor manuf & racing driver

**Ferrer** José Vicente 1909– Am actor, producer & director

**Ferrier** Kathleen 1912–1953 Eng contralto

**Feuchtwanger** Lion 1884–1958 Ger nov & dram

**Feydeau** Georges 1862–1921 Fr dram

**Fibiger** Johannes 1867–1928 Danish pathologist

**Fichte** Johann Gottlieb 1762–1814 Ger philos – **Fichtean** *adj*

**Fiedler** Arthur 1894–1979 Am conductor

**Field** Marshall 1834–1906 Am merchant

**Fielding** Henry 1707–1754 Eng nov

**Fields** Dame Gracie 1898–1979 neé *Stansfield* Eng singer & comedienne

**Fields** W C 1880–1946 pseud of *William Claude Dukenfield* Am comedian

**Fiennes** Celia 1662–1741 Eng diarist

**Fiesole, da** Giovanni 1387–1455 *Fra Angelico* orig *Guido di Pietro* Ital artist

**Figueiredo** João Baptista de Oliveira 1918– pres of Brazil (1979– )

**Fillmore** Millard 1800–1874 13th pres of the US (1850–53)

**Finch** Peter 1916–1977 Eng actor

**Finlay** Carlos Juan 1833–1915 Cuban physician & biologist

**Finney** Albert 1936– Eng actor

**Finney** Thomas 1922– Eng footballer

**Finsen** Niels Ryberg 1860–1904 Danish physician

**Finzi** Gerald 1901–1956 Eng composer

**Firbank** (Arthur Annesley) Ronald 1886–1926 Eng nov

**Firdausi, Firdusi** 940?–?1020 *Abul Qasim Mansur* or *Hasan* Pers epic poet

**Fischer** Emil 1852–1919 Ger chem

**Fischer** Ernst Otto 1918– Ger chem

**Fischer** Hans 1881–1945 Ger chem

**Fischer** Robert James 1943– *Bobby* Am chess player

**Fischer-Dieskau** Dietrich 1925– Ger baritone

**Fisher** Andrew 1862–1928 Austral (Scot-born) prime min (1908–1909; 1910–1913)

**Fisher** Geoffrey Francis 1887–1972 archbishop of Canterbury (1945–61)

**Fisher** Herbert Albert Laurens 1865–1940 Eng hist & educ

**Fisher** John Arbuthnot 1841–1920 1st Baron *Fisher of Kilverstone* Br admiral

**Fitch** John 1743–1798 Am inventor

**Fittipaldi** Emerson 1947– Braz racing driver

**FitzGerald** Edward 1809–1883 Eng poet & translator

**Fitzgerald** Ella 1918– Am singer

**Fitzgerald** Francis Scott Key 1896–1940 Am author

**FitzGerald** Garret 1926– prime min of Irish Republic (1982– )

**Fitzherbert** Maria Anne 1756–1837 née *Smythe; wife of George IV of England*

**Fitzsimmons** Robert 1862–1917 *Bob* Eng boxer

**Flagstad** Kirsten 1895–1962 Norw soprano

**Flaherty** Robert Joseph 1884–1951 Am pioneer director of documentary films

**Flammarion** Camille 1842–1925 Fr astron & author

**Flamsteed** John 1646–1719 Eng astron

**Flaubert** Gustave 1821–1880 Fr nov – **Flaubertian** adj

**Flaxman** John 1755–1826 Eng sculptor

**Flecker** (Herman) James Elroy 1884–1915 Eng poet & dram

**Fleming** Sir Alexander 1881–1955 Scot bacteriol

**Fleming** Ian Lancaster 1908–1964 Eng writer

**Fleming** Sir John Ambrose 1849–1945 Eng electrical engineer

**Fletcher** Graham 1951– Eng show jumper

**Fletcher** John 1579–1625 Eng dram

**Fleury** Claude 1640–1723 Fr ecclesiastical hist

**Flinders** Mathew 1774–1814 Eng navigator

**Flint** Sir (William) Russell 1880–1969 Scot artist

**Flores** Juan José 1800–1864 Ecuadorian soldier; pres of Ecuador (1830–35; 1839–45)

**Florey** Sir Howard Walter 1898–1968 Br pathologist

**Florio** John 1553?–1625 Eng lexicographer & translator

**Flory** Paul John 1910– Am chem

**Flynn** John 1880–1951 Austral missionary; pioneer of Flying Doctor service

**Foch** Ferdinand 1851–1929 Fr gen; marshal of France

**Fokine** Michel 1880–1942 Am (Russ-born) choreographer

**Fokker** Anthony Herman Gerard 1890–1939 Am (Du-born) aircraft designer & builder

**Foley** John Henry 1818–1874 Irish sculptor

**Fonda** Henry 1905–1982 Am actor

**Fonda** Jane 1937– dau of prec Am film actress

**Fontane** Theodor 1819–1898 Ger author

**Fontanne** Lynn 1887?–1983 *wife of Alfred Lunt* Am (Eng-born) actress

**Fonteyn** Dame Margot 1919– née *Margot Hookham* Eng dancer

**Foot** Michael 1913– Br polit

**Forbes** George William 1869–1947 prime min of NZ (1930–35)

**Forbes-Robertson** Sir Johnston 1853–1937 Eng actor

**Ford** Ford Madox 1873–1939 né *Hueffer* Eng author

**Ford** Gerald Rudolph 1913– Am polit; 38th pres of the US (1974–77)

**Ford** Henry 1863–1947 Am motor manuf

**Ford** John 1586?–1639 Eng dram

**Ford** John 1895–1973 Am film director

**Foreman** George 1949– Am boxer

**Forester** Cecil Scott 1899–1966 Eng author

**Forman** Milos 1932– Czech film director

**Formby** George 1904–1961 Eng music-hall comedian & singer

**Forssmann** Werner Theodor Otto 1904–1979 Ger surgeon

**Forster** Edward Morgan 1879–1970 Eng nov – **Forsterian** adj

**Forsyth** Alexander John 1769–1843 Scot clergyman & inventor

**Fosbury** Richard 1947– *Dick* Am high jumper; orig of "Fosbury Flop"

**Foster** Brendan 1948- Eng athlete

**Foucault** Jean Bernard Léon 1819–1868 Fr physicist

**Fougasse** 1887–1965 pseud of *Kenneth Bird* Eng cartoonist

**Fournier** Pierre 1926– Fr cellist

**Fowler** Henry Watson 1858–1933 Eng lexicographer

**Fowles** John 1926– Eng author

**Fox** Charles James 1749–1806 Eng statesman & orator

**Fox** George 1624–1691 Eng preacher; founder of Society of Friends (Quakers)

**Fox** Henry 1705–1774 1st Baron *Holland* Eng statesman

**Fox** Sir Uffa 1898–1972 Eng boat designer & builder

**Foxe** John 1517–1587 Eng martyrologist

**Fragonard** Jean Honoré 1732–1806 Fr artist & engraver

**France** Anatole 1844–1924 pseud of *Jacques Anatole François Thibault* Fr nov & satirist

**Francesca da Rimini** d 1284? née *Francesca da Polenta* Ital adulteress

**Francesca, della** Piero 1420?–1492 *Piero dei Franceschi* Ital artist

**Francis I** 1494–1547 king of France (1515–47)

**Francis II** 1768–1835 last Holy Rom emp (1792–1806); emp of Austria (as *Francis I*) 1804–35

**Francis Ferdinand** 1863–1914 archduke of Austria; assassinated

**Francis Joseph** 1830–1916 emp of Austria (1848–1916)

**Francis of Assisi** Saint 1182–1226 *Giovanni Francesco Bernardone* Ital friar; founder of Franciscan order

**Francis of Sales** Saint 1567–1622 Fr RC bishop of Geneva

**Francis** Clare 1947– Eng yachtswoman

**Franck** César Auguste 1822–1890 Belg-Fr organist & composer

**Franck** James 1882–1964 Am (Ger-born) physicist

**Franco** Francisco 1892–1975 *Francisco Paulino Hermenegildo Teódulo Franco-Bahamonde* Span gen & head of Span state (1936–75)

**Frankel** Benjamin 1906–1973 Eng composer

**Franklin** Benjamin 1706–1790 Am statesman & philos

**Franklin** Sir John 1786–1847 Eng arctic explorer

**Fraser** Lady Antonia 1932– Eng author

**Fraser** Dawn 1937– Austral swimmer

**Fraser** (John) Malcolm 1930– prime min of Austral (1975–83)

**Fraser** Neale Andrew 1933– Austral tennis player

**Fraser** Peter 1884–1950 NZ statesman; prime min (1940–49)

**Fraser** Simon 1667?–1747 12th Baron *Lovat* Scot Jacobite

**Fraunhofer, von** Joseph 1787–1826 Bavarian optician & physicist

**Frazer** Sir James George 1854–1941 Scot anthropol

**Frazier** Joe 1944– Am boxer

**Frederick I** 1123?–1190 *Frederick Barbarossa* Holy Rom emp (1152–90)

**Frederick I** 1657–1713 king of Prussia (1701–13)

**Frederick II** 1194–1250 Holy Rom emp (1215–50); king of Sicily (1198–1250)

**Frederick II** 1712–1786 *Frederick the Great* king of Prussia (1740–86)

**Frederick IX** 1899–1972 king of Denmark (1947–72)

**Frederick William** *the great Elector* elector of Brandenburg (1640–88)

**Frederick William** name of 4 kings of Prussia: **I** 1688–1740 (reigned 1713–40); **II** 1744–1797 (reigned 1786–97); **III** 1770–1840 (reigned 1797–1840); **IV** 1795–1861 (reigned 1840–61)

**Freneau** Philip Morin 1752–1832 Am poet
**Fréchette** Louis Honoré 1839–1908 Canad journalist & poet
**Frémont** John Charles 1813–1890 Am gen & explorer
**Frescobaldi** Girolamo 1583–1643 Ital composer
**Fresnel** Augustin Jean 1788–1827 Fr physicist
**Freud** Anna 1895–1982 *daughter of S* Austrian psychiatrist
**Freud** Lucian 1922– Eng artist
**Freud** Sigmund 1856–1939 Austrian neurologist; founder of psychoanalysis
**Freyberg** 1st Baron 1889–1963 *Bernard Cyril Freyberg* NZ gen
**Fried** Alfred Hermann 1864–1921 Austrian pacifist
**Friedman** Milton 1912– Am econ
**Friese-Greene** William 1855-1921 Eng cinematography pioneer
**Friml** Charles Rudolf 1879-1972 Am composer
**Frink** Elisabeth 1930– Eng artist
**Frisch** Karl von 1886– Austrian zoologist
**Frobisher** Sir Martin 1535?–1594 Eng navigator
**Froebel, Fröbel** Friedrich 1782–1852 Ger educ
**Froissart** Jean 1333?–?1400 Fr chronicler
**Frondizi** Arturo 1908– Argentine pres (1958–62)
**Frontenac, de** Comte *de Palluau et* 1620–1698 *Louis de Buade* Fr gen & colonial administrator
**Frost** David Paradine 1939– Eng producer & TV interviewer
**Frost** Robert Lee 1874–1963 Am poet – **Frostian** *adj*
**Froude** James Anthony 1818–1894 Eng hist
**Fry** Charles Burgess 1872–1956 Eng cricketer & athlete
**Fry** Christopher 1907– pseud of *Christopher Harris* Eng dram
**Fry** Elizabeth 1780–1845 Eng social worker & prison reformer
**Fry** Maxwell 1899– Eng architect
**Fry** Roger Eliot 1866–1934 Eng artist & art critic
**Fuad I** 1868–1936 orig *Ahmed Fuad Pasha* sultan (1917–22) & king (1922–36) of Egypt
**Fuchs** Sir Vivian Ernest 1908– Eng explorer & geologist
**Fuentes** Carlos 1928– Mex author
**Fulbright** (James) William 1905– Am polit
**Fuller** (Richard) Buckminster 1895–1983 Am engineer & inventor
**Fuller** Roy Broadbent 1912– Eng poet & nov
**Fulton** Robert 1765–1815 Am engineer & inventor
**Fundin** Ove 1933– Swed speedway rider
**Furse** Roger Kemble 1903–1972 Eng film & stage designer & artist
**Furtseva** Ekaterina Alekseyevna 1910–1974 Soviet polit
**Furtwängler** Wilhelm 1886–1954 Ger conductor
**Fyffe** Will 1885–1947 Scot comedian


# G

**Gabin** Jean 1904–1976 pseud of *Jean Alexis Moncorgé* Fr film actor
**Gable** (William) Clark 1901–1960 Am film actor
**Gabo** Naum 1890–1977 né *Naum Pevsner* Am (Russ-born) sculptor
**Gabor** Dennis 1900–1979 Br (Hung-born) physicist
**Gabriel** Jacques Ange 1698–1782 Fr architect
**Gabrieli** Giovanni 1557–1612 Ital composer
**Gaddafi** – see QADDAFI
**Gagarin** Yuri Alekseyevich 1934–1968 Soviet astronaut; first man in space (1961)
**Gainsborough** Thomas 1727–1788 Eng artist
**Gainsford** John 1938– S African rugby union player
**Gaitskell** Hugh Todd Naylor 1906–1963 Eng polit
**Gaius, Caius** 2nd c A D Rom jurist
**Galbraith** John Kenneth 1908– Am (Canad-born) econ
**Galen** *ab* 130– *ab* 200 Greek physician & writer
**Galerius** *d* 311 *Gaius Galerius Valerius Maximianus* Rom emp (305–311)
**Galilei** Galileo 1564–1642 *Galileo* Ital astron & physicist
**Gallacher** Hugh Kilpatrick 1903–1957 *Hughie* Scot footballer
**Gallico** Paul William 1897–1976 Am author
**Galli-Curci** Amelita 1889–1963 née *Galli* Am (Ital-born) soprano

**Gallup** George Horace 1901– Am statistician
**Galois** Evariste 1811–1832 Fr math
**Galsworthy** John 1867–1933 Eng nov & dram
**Galt** John 1779–1839 Scot nov
**Galton** Sir Francis 1822–1911 Eng scientist – **Galtonian** *adj*
**Galvani** Luigi *or* Aloisio 1737–1798 Ital physician & physicist
**Gama, da** Vasco 1469?–1524 Port navigator
**Gambetta** Léon 1838–1882 Fr lawyer & statesman
**Gandhi** Indira Priyadarshini Nehru 1917–1984 *dau of Jawaharlal Nehru* prime min of India (1966–77; 1980–1984)
**Gandhi** Mohandas Karamchand 1869–1948 *Mahatma Gandhi* Hindu nationalist leader
**Garamond** Claude *d* 1561 Fr type-founder
**Garbo** Greta 1905– neé *Greta Lovisa Gustafsson* Swed film actress
**García Gutiérrez** Antonio 1813–1884 Span dram
**García Lorca** Federico 1899–1936 Span poet & dram
**García Márquez** Gabriel 1928– Colombian nov
**Garcilaso de la Vega** 1539?–1616 *El Inca* Peruvian hist
**Garden** Mary 1874–1967 Am (Scot-born) soprano
**Gardner** Erle Stanley 1889–1970 Am author
**Gardner** Jack 1920-1978 Eng boxer
**Garfield** James Abram 1831–1881 20th pres of the US (1881)
**Garfunkel** Arthur 1942– Am singer; "Simon & Garfunkel"
**Garibaldi** Giuseppe 1807–1882 Ital patriot – **Garibaldian** *adj*
**Garland** Judy 1922–1969 née *Frances Gumm* Am film actress & singer
**Garner** Alan 1934– Eng author
**Garnett** Constance 1862–1946 née *Black* Eng translator
**Garnett** David 1892–1981 Eng author
**Garrick** David 1717–1779 Eng actor
**Garvey** Marcus Moziah 1887–1940 Jamaican Negro leader
**Gascoigne** George 1535?–1577 Eng poet
**Gaskell** Elizabeth Cleghorn 1810–1865 née *Stevenson* Eng nov & biographer
**Gassendi** Pierre 1592–1655 Fr philos & math
**Gasser** Herbert Spencer 1888–1963 Am physiol
**Gasset** – see José ORTEGA Y GASSET
**Gates** Horatio 1728?–1806 Am gen in Revolution
**Gaudí** Antonio 1852–1926 Span architect
**Gauguin** (Eugène Henri) Paul 1848–1903 Fr artist – **Gauguinesque** *adj*
**Gauss** Karl Friedrich 1777–1855 Ger math & astron
**Gautama Buddha** 563?–?483 B C orig Prince *Siddhartha* Indian philos; founder of Buddhism
**Gautier** Théophile 1811–1872 Fr author
**Gavaskar** Sunil Manohar 1949– Indian cricketer
**Gaveston** Piers *d* 1312 Eng favourite of Edward II
**Gay** John 1685–1732 Eng poet & dram
**Gay-Lussac** Joseph Louis 1778–1850 Fr chem & physicist
**Geber, Gebir** *ab* 721–*ab* 815 *Abū Mūsā Jābir ibn Hayyān* Arab alchemist & mystic
**Geiger** Hans Wilhelm 1881–1945 Ger physicist
**Geikie** Sir Archibald 1835–1924 Scot geologist
**Geisel** Theodor Seuss 1904– pseud *Dr Seuss* Am author & illustrator
**Gellée** Claude – see Claude LORRAIN
**Genée** Dame Adelle 1878–1970 née *Anita Jensen* Br (Danish-born) ballet dancer
**Genet** Jean 1910– Fr dram & nov
**Genghis Khan** 1162–1227 Mongol conqueror
**Genseric, Gaiseric** *d* 477 king of the Vandals (482–477)
**Gentile da Fabriano** 1370?–?1427 *Gentile Massi* Ital artist
**Geoffrey of Monmouth** 1100?–1154 Eng ecclesiastic & chronicler
**George** Saint *d ab* 303 Christian martyr & patron saint of Eng
**George** name of 6 kings of GB: **I** 1660–1727 (reigned 1714–27); **II** 1683–1760 (reigned 1727–60); **III** 1738–1820 (reigned 1760–1820); **IV** 1762–1830 (reigned 1820–30); **V** 1865–1936 (reigned 1910–36); **VI** 1895–1952 (reigned 1936–52)
**George I** 1845–1913 king of Greece (1863–1913)
**George II** 1890–1947 king of Greece (1922–23; 1935–47)
**George** David Lloyd – see David LLOYD GEORGE
**Gérard** Comte Étienne Maurice 1773–1852 Fr Napoleonic gen; marshal of France

**Géricault** (Jean Louis André) Théodore 1791–1824 Fr artist
**Germanicus Caesar** 15 B C–A D 19 Rom gen
**Geronimo** 1829–1909 Apache chieftain
**Gersed** Ernesto 1908–     Brazil soldier; pres of Brazil (1974)
**Gershwin** George 1898–1937 Am composer
**Gesner, von** Konrad 1516–1565 Swiss naturalist
**Getty** Jean Paul 1892–1976 Am business executive & art collector
**Ghiberti** Lorenzo 1378–1455 Florentine goldsmith, artist, & sculptor
**Ghirlandaho** Domenico 1449–1494 Florentine artist & mosaicist
**Ghose** Sri Aurobindo 1872–1950 Indian philos & nationalist statesman
**Giacometti** Alberto 1901–1966 Swiss artist
**Gibberd** Sir Frederick 1908–1984 Eng architect
**Gibbon** Edward 1737–1794 Eng hist
**Gibbons** Grinling 1648–1721 Eng wood carver
**Gibbons** Orlando 1538–1625 Eng organist & composer
**Gibbons** Stella Dorothea 1902–     Eng author
**Gibbs** James 1682–1754 Scot architect
**Gibbs** Josiah Willard 1839–1903 Am math & physicist
**Gibbs** Lancelot Richard 1934–     W Indian cricketer
**Gibbs** Sir Philip 1877–1962 Eng journalist & nov
**Gibson** Sir Alexander Drummond 1926– Eng conductor
**Gibson** Althea 1927–     Am tennis player
**Gibson** Charles Dana 1867–1944 Am illustrator
**Gibson** Mike 1942–     Irish rugby union player
**Gide** André 1869–1951 Fr nov, critic, & essayist
**Gielgud** Sir (Arthur) John 1904–     Eng actor
**Gieseking** Walter Wilhelm 1895–1956 Ger (Fr-born) pianist
**Gifford** Henri 1823–1882 Fr engineer
**Gigli** Beniamino 1890–1957 Ital tenor
**Gilbert** Cass 1859–1934 Am architect
**Gilbert** Sir Humphrey 1539?–1583 Eng navigator
**Gilbert** William 1540–1603 Eng physician & physicist
**Gilbert** Sir William Schwenck 1836–1911 Eng librettist & poet; collaborator with Sir Arthur Sullivan
**Gill** (Arthur) Eric (Rowton) 1881–1940 Eng engraver & sculptor
**Gillen** Francis James 1856–1912 Austral anthropol
**Gillespie** John Birks 1917–     *Dizzy* Am bandleader & jazz pianist
**Gillette** King Camp 1855–1932 Am inventor & manuf
**Gillray** James 1757–1815 Eng caricaturist
**Gilroy** Norman Thomas 1896–1977 Austral cardinal
**Gilwell** 1st Baron of – see BADEN-POWELL
**Gingold** Hermione Ferdinanda 1897–     Eng actress
**Ginsberg** Allen 1926–     Am poet
**Giorgione** *ab* 1478–1511 *Giorgione da Castelfranco,* orig *Giorgio Barbarelli* Venetian artist
**Giotto** 1266?–1337 *Giotto di Bondone* Florentine artist, architect, & sculptor
**Giraudoux** Jean 1882–1944 Fr author
**Girtin** Thomas Joseph 1775–1802 Eng founder of art of modern watercolour painting
**Giscard d'Estaing** Valéry 1926–     pres of France (1974–81)
**Gish** Dorothy 1898–1968 Am film actress
**Gish** Lillian Diana 1896–     Am actress
**Gissing** George Robert 1857–1903 Eng nov
**Gjellerup** Karl 1857–1919 Dan author
**Gladstone** William Ewart 1809–1898 Eng statesman; prime min (1868–74; 1880–85;1886;1892–94)
**Glaser** Donald Arthur 1926–     Am physicist
**Glasgow** Ellen Anderson Gholson 1874–1945 Am nov
**Glaspell** Susan 1882–1948 Am nov & dram
**Glazunov** Aleksandr 1865–1936 Russ composer
**Glendower** Owen 1359?–?1416 Welsh chieftain & rebel against Henry IV of Eng
**Glenn** John Herschel 1921–     Am astronaut & polit; first Am to orbit the earth (1962)
**Glinka** Mikhail Ivanovich 1803–1857 Russ composer
**Glossop** Peter 1928– Eng baritone
**Gloucester** Duke of – see HUMPHREY
**Glover** Sarah Ann 1785–1867 Eng music teacher; invented tonic sol-fa system of notation
**Gluck** Christoph Willibald 1714–1787 Ger composer

**Glyn** Elinor 1864–1943 née *Sutherland* Eng nov
**Gobat** Charles Albert 1843–1914 Swiss statesman
**Gobbi** Tito 1915–1984 Ital baritone
**Godard** Jean-Luc 1930– Fr film director
**Goddard** Robert Hutchings 1882–1945 Am physicist
**Godfrey of Bouillon** *Fr* **Godefroy de Bouillon** 1061?–1100 Fr crusader
**Godiva** Lady *d* ?1080 Eng benefactress; wife of Leofric, Earl of Mercia
**Godolphin** Sidney 1645–1712 1st Earl of *Godolphin* Eng statesman
**Godunov** Boris Fëdorovich 1551?–1605 czar of Russia (1598–1605)
**Godwin** *d* 1053 earl of the West Saxons
**Godwin** William 1756–1836 Eng philos & nov – **Godwinian** *adj*
**Godwin-Austen** Henry Haversham 1834–1923 Eng explorer & geologist
**Goebbels** Joseph Paul 1897–1945 Ger Nazi propagandist
**Goering** – see GÖRING
**Goes** Hugo van der 1440?–1482 Du artist
**Goethe, von** Johann Wolfgang 1749–1832 Ger poet & dram – **Goethean** *adj*
**Gogh, van** Vincent 1853–1890 Du artist
**Gogol** Nikolai Vasilievich 1809–1852 Russ author – **Gogolian** *adj*
**Going** Sid 1943–     NZ rugby union player
**Golding** William Gerald 1911–     Eng author
**Goldoni** Carlo 1707–1793 Ital dram
**Goldsmith** Oliver 1728–1774 Eng author
**Goldwyn** Samuel 1882–1974 né *Samuel Goldfish* Am (Pol-born) film producer
**Golgi** Camillo 1844–1926 Ital physician
**Gollancz** Sir Victor 1893–1967 Eng publisher
**Gómez** Juan Vicente 1857?–1935 Venezuelan gen & polit; dictator (1908–35)
**Gomulka** Wladyslaw 1905–1982 Pol polit
**Gonçalves** Vasco dos Santos 1921–     Port polit; prime min (1974–75)
**Gonçalves Dias** Antônio 1823–1864 Braz poet
**Goncharov** Ivan Alexandrovich 1812–1891 Russ novelist
**Goncourt, de** Edmond Louis Antoine 1822–1896 & his bro Jules Alfred Huot 1830–1870 Fr nov
**Gonzaga** Saint Aloysius 1568–1591 Ital Jesuit cleric
**Gonzales** Richard A 1928–     *Pancho* Am tennis player
**Goodman** Benny 1909–     Am musician
**Goodyear** Charles 1800–1860 Am inventor
**Goolagong** Evonne Fay – see Evonne Fay CAWLEY
**Gordon** Charles George 1833–1885 *Chinese Gordon, Gordon Pasha* Eng soldier
**Gordon** Lord George 1751–1793 Eng polit agitator
**Gordon** Richard 1921–     pseud of *Gordon Ostlere* Eng author
**Gordon-Watson** Mary 1951– Eng show jumper
**Goremykin** Ivan Longinovich 1839–1917 Russ statesman; prime min (1906; 1914–16)
**Göring** Hermann Wilhelm 1893–1946 Ger Nazi polit
**Gorki** Maksim *also* Maxim **Gorky** 1868–1936 pseud of *Aleksei Maksimovich Peshkov* Russ author
**Gorky** Arshile 1904–1948 Am (Turk-born) artist
**Gort** 6th Viscount 1886–1946 *John Standish Surtees Prendergast Vereker* Eng field marshal
**Gorton** John Grey 1911–     Austral polit; prime minister (1968–71)
**Gosse** Sir Edmund William 1849–1928 Eng poet & critic
**Gotama Buddah** – see GAUTAMA BUDDHA
**Goudy** Frederic William 1865–1947 Am type designer
**Gould** Glenn 1932–1982 Canad pianist & composer
**Gould** Shane Elizabeth 1956–     Austral swimmer
**Gounod** Charles François 1818–1893 Fr composer
**Gower** David Ivon 1957–     Eng cricketer
**Gower** John 1325?–1408 Eng poet
**Goya y Lucientes, de** Francisco José 1746–1828 Span painter – **Goyaesque, Goyesque** *adj*
**Graaff, van de** Robert Jemison 1901–1967 Am physicist
**Gracchus** Gaius Sempronius 153–121 B C & his bro Tiberius Sempronius 163–133 B C *the Gracchi* Rom statesmen

**Grace** W(illiam) G(ilbert) 1848–1915 Eng cricketer

**Graham** Martha 1894?– Am dancer

**Graham** Thomas 1805–1869 Scot chem

**Graham** William Franklin 1918– *Billy* Am evangelist

**Grahame** Kenneth 1859–1932 Scot author

**Grahame-White** Claude 1879–1959 Eng pioneer airman

**Grainger** Percy Aldridge 1882–1961 Austral composer & pianist

**Gramme** Zénobe Théophile 1826–1901 Belg electrician

**Gramont, de** Comte Philibert 1621?–1707 Fr soldier & courtier

**Gramsci** Antonio 1891–1937 Ital polit theorist; founder of Ital Communist party

**Granados** Enrique 1867–1916 Span composer

**Grandi** Count (di Mordano) Dino 1895– Ital Fascist polit

**Grant** Cary 1904– né *Alexander Archibald Leach* Am (Eng-born) film actor

**Grant** Duncan James Corrowr 1885–1978 Br artist

**Grant** Ulysses Simpson 1822–1885 *Ulysses Hiram* (baptized *Hiram Ulysses*) *Grant* Am gen; 18th pres of the US (1869–77)

**Granville-Barker** Harley Granville 1877–1946 Eng actor-manager & dram

**Grass** Günter Wilhelm 1927– Ger author

**Grasse, de** Comte François Joseph Paul 1722–1788 Marquis *de Grasse-Tilly* Fr naval officer

**Gratian** *Lat* **Flavius Gratianus** 359–383 Rom emp (375–383)

**Grattan** Henry 1746–1820 Irish orator & statesman

**Grau San Martín** Ramón 1887–1969 Cuban physician & polit; pres of Cuba (1944–48)

**Graveney** Thomas William 1927– Eng cricketer

**Graves** Robert Ranke 1895– Eng author

**Gray** Thomas 1716–1771 Eng poet

**Graziani** Rodolfo 1882–1955 Marchese *di Neghelli* Ital marshal & colonial administrator

**Greaves** James Peter 1940– *Jimmy* Eng footballer

**Greco, El** 1548?–?1614 or ?1625 *Domenico Teotocopulo* Span (Cretan-born) artist

**Greeley** Horace 1811–1872 Am journalist & polit

**Greely** Adolphus Washington 1844–1935 Am gen & arctic explorer

**Green** Henry 1905–1973 pseud of *Henry Vincent Yorke* Eng nov

**Green** John Richard 1837–1883 Eng hist

**Green** Julian 1900– Am (Fr-born) nov

**Greenaway** Catherine 1846–1901 *Kate* Eng artist & illustrator

**Greene** Graham 1904– Eng nov

**Greene** Nathanael 1742–1786 Am Revolutionary gen

**Greene** Robert 1558–1592 Eng poet & dram

**Greenough** Horatio 1805–1852 Am sculptor

**Gregory** name of 16 popes: esp **I** Saint 540?–604 *the Great* (pope 590–604); **VII** Saint (*Hildebrand*) 1020?–1085 (pope 1073–85); **XIII** (*Ugo Buoncompagni*) 1502–1585 (pope 1572–85)

**Gregory of Nyssa** Saint 331?–?396 Eastern church father

**Gregory of Tours** Saint 538?–593 Frankish ecclesiastic & hist

**Gregory** Lady Isabella Augusta 1859?–1932 née *Persse* Irish dram

**Greig** Anthony William 1946– *Tony* S African cricketer; played for England

**Grenfell** Joyce Irene 1910–1979 Eng entertainer & author

**Grenfell** Julian 1888–1915 Eng poet

**Grenfell** Sir Wilfred Thomason 1865–1940 Eng medical missionary to Labrador

**Grenville, Greynville** George 1712–1770 Eng statesman

**Grenville** Sir Richard 1541?–1591 Eng admiral

**Gresham** Sir Thomas 1519?–1579 Eng financier

**Gretzky** Wayne 1961– Canad ice hockey player

**Greuze** Jean Baptiste 1725–1805 Fr artist

**Grévy** François Paul Jules 1807–1891 Fr lawyer; 3rd pres of the republic (1879–87)

**Grey** Beryl 1927– Eng ballet dancer

**Grey** 2nd Earl 1764–1845 *Charles Grey* Eng statesman; prime min (1830–34)

**Grey** Edward 1862–1933 Viscount *Grey of Fallodon* Eng statesman

**Grey** Lady Jane 1537–1554 Eng noblewoman beheaded as a possible rival for the throne

**Grey** (Pearl) Zane 1875–1939 Am nov

**Grieg** Edvard Hagerup 1843–1907 Norw composer

**Grierson** John 1898–1972 Eng critic & film maker; pioneer of documentary films

**Grieve** Christopher Murray – see Hugh MACDIARMID

**Griffith** Arthur 1872–1922 Irish polit; founder of Irish Free State

**Griffith** Charles Christopher 1938– W Indian cricketer

**Griffith** David Lewelyn Wark 1875–1948 Am film producer

**Grignard** Victor 1871–1934 Fr chem

**Grillparzer** Franz 1791–1872 Austrian dram & poet

**Grimaldi** Joseph 1779–1837 *Joey the Clown* Eng clown

**Grimm** Jacob 1785–1863 & his bro Wilhelm 1786–1859 Ger philologists & fairy tale writers

**Grinham** Judith Brenda 1939– *Judy* Eng swimmer

**Gris** Juan 1887–1927 Span artist in France

**Grivas** George 1898–1974 Greek Cypriot general

**Grock** 1880–1959 pseud of *Charles Adrien Wettach* Swiss clown

**Grolier de Servières** Jean 1479–1565 Fr bibliophile

**Gromyko** Andrei Andreevich 1909– Soviet econ & diplomat

**Gronchi** Giovanni 1887–1978 Ital polit; pres (1955–62)

**Gropius** Walter 1883–1969 Ger-born architect in Am

**Grosvenor** Gilbert Hovey 1875–1966 Am geographer

**Grosz** George 1893–1959 Ger artist

**Grote** George 1794–1871 Eng hist

**Grotius** Hugo 1583–1645 *Huig de Groot* Du jurist & statesman

**Grouchy, de** Marquis Emmanuel 1766–1847 Fr gen

**Grove** Sir George 1820–1900 Eng writer on music

**Groves** Sir Charles Barnard 1915– Eng conductor

**Grünewald** Matthias *fl* 1500–1530 Ger artist

**Gryphius** Andreas 1616–1664 *Ger* **Greif** Ger poet & dram

**Guarneri** *Lat* **Guarnerius** family of Italian violin makers: esp Giuseppe Antonio 1687–1745

**Guedalla** Philip 1889–1944 Eng author

**Guesde** Jules 1845–1922 *Mathieu Basile* Fr socialist

**Guevara** Ernesto 1928–1967 *Ché* Latin-Am revolutionary leader

**Guido d' Arezzo, Guido Aretino** 995?–?1050 Benedictine monk & music reformer

**Guillaume** Charles Édouard 1861–1938 Fr physicist

**Guinness** Sir Alec 1914– Eng actor

**Guiscard** Robert 1015?–1085 Norman conqueror in Italy

**Guise, de** 2nd duc 1519–1563 *François de Lorraine; le Balafré* Fr soldier & polit

**Guise, de** 3rd duc 1550–1588 *Henri I de Lorraine; also le Balafré* Fr soldier & polit

**Guitry** Sacha 1885–1957 Fr actor & dram

**Guizot** François Pierre Guillaume 1787–1874 Fr hist & statesman

**Gulbenkian** Calouste Sarkis 1869–1955 Turk-Persian financier

**Gullstrand** Allvar 1862–1930 Swed ophthalmologist

**Gunnarsson** Gunnar 1889–1975 Icelandic author

**Gunter** Edmund 1581–1626 Eng math

**Gustavus** name of 6 kings of Sweden: **I** (*Gustavus Vasa*) 1496–1560 (reigned 1523–60); **II** (*Gustavus Adolphus*) 1594–1632 (reigned 1611–32); **III** 1746–1792 (reigned 1771–92); **IV** (*Gustavus Adolphus*) 1778–1837 (reigned 1792–1809); **V** (*Gustaf*) 1858–1950 (reigned 1907–50); **VI** (*Gustavus Adolphus*) 1882–1973 (reigned 1950–73)

**Gutenberg** Johann 1400?–?1468 *Johann Gensfleisch* Ger inventor of printing from movable type

**Guthrie** Sir (William) Tyrone 1900–1971 Eng stage director & dram

**Guthrie** Woodrow Wilson 1912–1967 *Woody* Am folk singer

**Gutzkow** Karl 1811–1878 Ger journalist, nov, & dram

**Guzmán Blanco** Antonio 1829–1899 Venezuelan soldier & statesman; pres of Venezuela (alternate terms of two years 1870–89)

**Gwyn, Gwynne** Eleanor 1650–1687 *Nell* Eng actress; *mistress of Charles II*

# H

**Haakon VII** 1872–1957 king of Norway (1905–57)

**Haber** Fritz 1868–1934 Ger chem

**Habyarimana** Juvénal 1937–    Rwanda soldier & polit; pres (1973–    )

**Hackman** Gene 1931–    Am film actor

**Hadfield** Sir Robert Abbott 1858–1940 Eng metallurgist

**Hadley** John 1682–1744 Eng inventor

**Hadow** Sir (William) Henry 1859–1937 Eng educ & writer on music

**Hadrian** 76–138 Rom emp (117–138)

**Hadrian** – see ADRIAN

**Haeckel** Ernst Heinrich 1834–1919 Ger biologist & philos

**Hafiz** 14th c *Shams ud-din Mohammed* Pers poet

**Hagen** Walter Charles 1892–1969 Am golfer

**Hägg** Gunder 1918–    Swed athlete

**Haggard** Sir (Henry) Rider 1856–1925 Eng nov

**Hahn** Kurt 1886–1968 Ger educ; founder of Gordonstoun school

**Hahn** Otto 1879–1968 Ger physical chem

**Hahnemann** (Christian Friedrich) Samuel 1755–1843 Ger physician; founder of homoeopathy

**Haig** 1st Earl 1861–1928 *Douglas Haig* Eng field marshal

**Haile Selassie** 1892–1975 Ras *Taffari* or *Tafari* emp of Ethiopia (1930–36; 1941–74)

**Hailey** Arthur 1920–    Canad (Eng-born) nov

**Hailsham of St Marylebone** Baron 1907–    *Quintin McGarel Hogg* Eng lawyer & polit

**Hailwood** Stanley Michael Bailey 1940–1981 *Mike* Eng motorcyclist & racing driver

**Hakluyt** Richard 1552?–1616 Eng geographer & hist

**Haldane** John Burdon Sanderson 1892–1964 Eng scientist

**Haldane** Richard Burdon 1856–1928 Viscount *Haldane of Cloan* Eng lawyer, philos, & statesman

**Hale** George Ellery 1868–1938 Am astron

**Hale** Nathan 1755–1776 Am Revolutionary officer; executed as a spy by the British

**Halévy** 1799–1862 pseud of *Jacques Fromental Élie Lévy* Fr composer

**Halévy** Ludovic 1834–1908 *nephew of prec* Fr dram & nov

**Haley** Bill 1925–1981 Am rock' n' roll singer

**Halifax** Earl of 1881–1959 *Edward Frederick Lindley Wood* Eng statesman & diplomat

**Hall** Charles Francis 1821–1871 Am arctic explorer

**Hall** Sir Peter Reginald Frederick 1930–    Eng theatrical director

**Hall** Wesley Winfield 1938–    W Indian cricketer

**Hallam** Henry 1777–1859 Eng hist

**Hallé** Sir Charles 1819–1895 Eng conductor

**Halley** Edmund 1656–1742 Eng astron

**Hallgrímsson** Geir 1925–    prime min of Iceland (1974–78)

**Hals** Frans 1580?–1666 Du artist

**Halsey** William Frederick 1882–1959 Am admiral

**Halsted** William Stewart 1852–1922 Am surgeon

**Hamilcar Barca** 270?–228 B C *father of Hannibal* Carthaginian gen

**Hamilton** Lady Emma 1761?–1815 née *Lyon, mistress of Lord Nelson*

**Hamilton** Sir William Rowan 1805–1865 Eng math

**Hammarskjöld** Dag Hjalmar Agné Carl 1905–1961 Swed UN official; sec gen (1953–61)

**Hammerstein** Oscar 1847?–1919 Ger-born theatre manager in Am

**Hammerstein** Oscar 1895–1960 *grandson of prec* Am dram

**Hammett** Dashiell 1894–1961 Am nov

**Hammond** Dame Joan Hood 1912–    Austral (NZ-born) soprano

**Hammond** Walter Reginald 1903–1965 Eng cricketer

**Hammurabi** king of Babylon (*ab* 1955-1913 B C or earlier)

**Hampden** John 1594–1643 Eng statesman

**Hampton** Wade 1818–1902 Am polit & Confed gen

**Hamsun** Knut 1859–1952 pseud of *Knut Pedersen* Norw author

**Hancock** Anthony John 1924–1968 *Tony* Eng comedian & actor

**Handel** George Frederick 1685–1759 Br (Ger-born) composer – **Handelian** *adj*

**Handy** William Christopher 1873–1958 *WC* Am blues musician

**Hanif** Mohammed 1934–    Pakistan cricketer

**Hannay** James Owen 1865–1950 Irish clergyman & nov; pseud *George A Birmingham*

**Hannibal** 247–183 B C *son of Hamilcar Barca* Carthaginian gen

**Hansard** Luke 1752–1828 Eng printer

**Hapgood** Edris Albert 1907–1973 *Eddie* Eng footballer

**Hardecanute** 1019?–1042 king of Denmark (1035–42) and of Eng (1040–42)

**Harden** Sir Arthur 1865–1940 Eng chem

**Hardie** James Keir 1856–1915 Eng polit; founder of Labour party

**Harding** Warren Gamaliel 1865–1923 29th pres of the US (1921–23)

**Hardwick** Elizabeth 1518–1608 *Bess of Hardwick* Eng gentlewoman; Chatsworth House & Hardwick Hall built on her land

**Hardwicke** Sir Cedric Webster 1893–1964 Eng actor

**Hardy** Oliver 1892–1957 Am film comedian; "Laurel and Hardy"

**Hardy** Thomas 1840–1928 Eng nov & poet

**Hare** David 1947–    Eng dram, producer, & director

**Hargreaves** James *d* 1778 Eng inventor of the spinning jenny

**Harley** Robert 1661–1724 1st Earl of *Oxford* Eng statesman

**Harlow** Jean 1911–1937 Am film actress

**Harmsworth** Alfred Charles William 1865–1922 Viscount *Northcliffe* Eng publisher & polit

**Harmsworth** Harold Sidney 1868–1940 1st Viscount *Rothermere; bro of ACW* Eng publisher & polit

**Harold** name of 3 kings of Norway; esp **III** *Haardraade* 1015–1066 (reigned 1047–66)

**Harold I** *d* 1040 *Harold Harefoot* king of Eng (1035–40)

**Harold II** 1022?–1066 king of Eng (1066)

**Harriman** William Averell 1891– Am businessman, diplomat, & polit

**Harrington, Harington** Sir John 1561–1612 Eng author & translator

**Harris** Frank 1856–1931 Am (Irish-born) author

**Harris** Joel Chandler 1848–1908 Am author

**Harris** Reginald Hargreaves 1920–    Eng racing cyclist

**Harris** Roy 1898–1979 Am composer

**Harrison** Benjamin 1833–1901 *grandson of WH Harrison* 23rd pres of the US (1889–93)

**Harrison** George 1943–    Eng musician; member of Beatles

**Harrison** James 1816–1893 Austral journalist & inventor

**Harrison** John 1693–1776 Eng horologist; inventor of chronometer

**Harrison** Sir Rex Carey 1908–    Eng actor

**Harrison** William Henry 1773–1841 9th pres of the US (1841)

**Hart** Basil Henry Liddell – see LIDDELL HART

**Hart** Doris 1925–    Am tennis player

**Hart** Moss 1904–1961 Am librettist & dram

**Harte** Francis Brett 1836–1902 *Bret* Am author

**Hartley** Leslie Poles 1895–1972 Eng nov

**Hartono Kurniawan** Rudy 1948–    Indonesian badminton player

**Harty** Sir (Herbert) Hamilton 1879–1941 Irish conductor & composer

**Harun al-Rashid** 764?–809 caliph of Bagdad (786–809)

**Harvard** John 1607–1638 Eng clergyman in Am

**Harvey** Sir John Martin 1863–1944 Eng actor & producer

**Harvey** Len 1907–1976 Eng boxer

**Harvey** Robert Neil 1928–    Austral cricketer

**Harvey** William 1578–1657 Eng physician & anatomist

**Hasdrubal** *d* 207 B C *bro of Hannibal* Carthaginian gen

**Hašek** Jaroslav 1883–1923 Czech nov & journalist

**Hastings** 1st Marquis of 1754–1826 *Francis Rawdon Hastings* Eng gen & colonial administrator

**Hastings** Warren 1732–1818 Eng statesman & administrator in India

**Haston** Dougal 1940–1977 Scot mountaineer

**Hatfield** John Gatenby 1893–1965 *Jack* Eng swimmer

**Hatry** Clarence 1888–1965 Eng financier; served prison sentence for fraud

**Hauptmann** Gerhart 1862–1946 Ger author

**Haussmann** Baron Georges Eugène 1809–1891 Fr administrator; improver of Paris

**Hawke** 1st Baron 1705–1781 *Edward Hawke* Eng admiral

**Hawke** Robert James Lee 1929–     Austral polit; prime min (1983–     )
**Hawkins** Sir Anthony Hope 1863–1933 pseud *Anthony Hope* Eng nov & dram
**Hawkins, Hawkyns** Sir John 1532–1595 Eng admiral
**Hawks** Howard 1896–1977 Am film director
**Haworth** Sir (Walter) Norman 1883–1950 Eng chem
**Hawthorn** John Michael 1929–1958 *Mike* Eng racing driver
**Hawthorne** Nathaniel 1804–1864 Am author
**Haydn** (Franz) Joseph 1732–1809 Austrian composer
**Hayek, von** Friedrich August 1899–     Austrian econ
**Hayes** Helen 1900– *Helen Hayes Brown, wife of Charles MacArthur* Am actress
**Hayes** Rutherford Birchard 1822–1893 19th pres of the US (1877–81)
**Haynes** John Norman 1934–     Eng footballer
**Hazlitt** William 1778–1830 Eng essayist
**Headley** George Alphonso 1909–1983 W Indian cricketer
**Healy** Timothy Michael 1855–1931 Irish statesman
**Heaney** Seamus Justin 1939–     Irish poet
**Hearst** William Randolph 1863–1951 Am newspaper publisher
**Heath** Edward Richard George 1916– Eng polit; prime min (1970–74)
**Hebbel** Friedrich 1813–1863 Ger dram
**Hedin** Sven Anders 1865–1952 Swed explorer
**Heenan** John Carmell 1905–1975 Eng cardinal; archbishop of Westminster (1963–75)
**Hegel** Georg Wilhelm Friedrich 1770–1831 Ger philos
**Heidegger** Martin 1889–1976 Ger philos
**Heidenstam, von** Verner 1859–1940 Swed author
**Heifetz** Jascha 1901–     Am (Russ-born) violinist
**Heilbron** Dame Rose 1914–     Eng judge
**Heine** Heinrich 1797–1856 Ger poet & critic
**Heisenberg** Werner Karl 1901–1976 Ger physicist
**Heliogabalus** 204–222 *Varius Avitus Bassianus* Rom emp (218–222)
**Heller** Joseph 1923–     Am nov
**Hellman** Lillian 1905–1984 Am dram
**Helmholtz, von** Hermann Ludwig Ferdinand 1821–1894 Ger physicist, anatomist, & physiol
**Heloïse** 1101?–1164 *wife of Abelard* Fr abbess
**Helpmann** Sir Robert Murray 1909–     Austral ballet dancer & actor
**Helvetius** Claude Adrien 1715–1771 Fr philos
**Hemery** David 1944–     Eng athlete
**Hemingway** Ernest Miller 1899–1961 Am author
**Henderson** Arthur 1863–1935 Br polit
**Henderson** Sir Nevile Meyrick 1882–1942 Eng diplomat
**Hendren** Elias Henry 1889–1962 *Patsy* Eng cricketer
**Hengist** *and* **Horsa** d 488 and 455 A D respec*tively bros* Jute invaders of Britain (*ab* 449)
**Henie** Sonja 1913–1969 Norw ice figure skater & film actress
**Hennepin** Louis 1640?–1701 Belg friar & explorer in Am
**Henry** name of 8 kings of Eng: **I** 1068–1135 (reigned 1100–35); **II** 1133–1189 (reigned 1154–89); **III** 1207–1272 (reigned 1216–72); **IV** 1367–1413 (reigned 1399–1413); **V** 1387–1422 (reigned 1413–22); **VI** 1421–1471 (reigned 1422–61 & 1470–71); **VII** 1457–1509 (reigned 1485–1509); **VIII** 1491–1547 (reigned 1509–47)
**Henry** name of 4 kings of France: **I** 1008–1060 (reigned 1031–60); **II** 1519–1559 (reigned 1547–59); **III** 1551–1589 (reigned 1574–89); **IV of Navarre** 1553–1610 (reigned 1589–1610)
**Henry** 1394–1460 *the Navigator* Port prince
**Henry** Joseph 1797–1878 Am physicist
**Henry** O – see William Sydney PORTER
**Henry** Patrick 1736–1799 Am statesman & orator
**Henze** Hans Werner 1926–     Ger composer
**Hepburn** Audrey 1929–     neé *Golda Hepburn van Heemstra* Belg actress
**Hepburn** Katharine 1909–     Am actress
**Hepplewhite** George *d* 1786 Eng cabinetmaker
**Hepworth** Dame Barbara 1903–1975 Eng sculptor
**Heraclitus** 6th–5th c B c Greek philos – **Heraclitean** *adj*
**Heraclius** 575?–641 Byzantine emp (610–641)
**Herbart** Johann Friedrich 1776–1841 Ger philos & educ

**Herbert** Sir Alan Patrick 1890–1971 Eng author & polit
**Herbert** George 1593–1633 Eng divine & poet
**Herder, von** Johann Gottfried 1744–1803 Ger philos & author
**Hereward the Wake** 11th c Anglo-Saxon leader
**Heriot** George 1563–1624 Scot goldsmith & philanthropist
**Hero, Heron** 1st c A D Greek scientist
**Herod** 73?–4 B C *the Great* Rom king of Judea (37–4)
**Herod Antipas** 21 B C–A D 39 *son of prec* Roman tetrarch of Galilee (4 B C–A D 39)
**Herodotus** 5th c B C Greek hist – **Herodotean** *adj*
**Herrick** Robert 1591–1674 Eng poet
**Herriot** James 1916–     pseud of *James Alfred Wight* Eng vet & author
**Herschel** Sir John Frederick William 1792–1871 & his father Sir William 1738–1822 Eng astronomers
**Hertz** Gustav Ludwig 1887–1975 Ger physicist
**Hertz** Heinrich Rudolf 1857–1894 Ger physicist
**Hertzog** James Barry Munnik 1866–1942 S African gen
**Heseltine** Philip – see Peter WARLOCK
**Hesiod** 8th c B C Greek poet
**Hess** Dame Myra 1890–1965 Eng pianist
**Hess** Victor Franz 1883–1964 Austrian physicist
**Hess** (Walter Richard) Rudolf 1894–     Ger Nazi polit
**Hess** Walter Rudolf 1881–1973 Swiss physiol
**Hesse** Hermann 1877–1962 Ger author
**Hevesy, de** George Charles 1885–1966 Hung chem
**Heydrich** Reinhard 1904–1942 *the Hangman* Ger Nazi administrator
**Heyer** Georgette 1904–1974 Eng nov
**Heyerdahl** Thor 1914–     Norw explorer & author
**Heymans** Corneille 1892–1968 Belg physiol
**Heyrovsky** Jaroslav 1890–1967 Czech chem
**Heyse, von** Paul Johann Ludwig 1830–1914 Ger nov, dram, & poet
**Heywood** John 1497?–?1580 Eng author
**Heywood** Thomas 1574?–1641 Eng dram
**Hickok** James Butler 1837–1876 *Wild Bill* Am scout & US marshal
**Hieronymus** Saint Eusebius – see JEROME
**Highsmith** Patricia 1921–     Am author
**Hildebrand** – see Pope GREGORY VII
**Hill** Archibald Vivian 1886–1977 Eng physiol
**Hill** Geoffrey 1932–     Eng poet
**Hill** Graham 1929–1975 Eng racing driver
**Hill** Octavia 1838–1912 Eng housing reformer; founder of National Trust
**Hill** Sir Rowland 1795–1879 Eng postal reformer
**Hillary** Sir Edmund Percival 1919–     NZ mountaineer & explorer
**Hiller** Dame Wendy 1912–     Eng actress
**Hilliard** Nicholas 1547?–1619 Eng miniaturist & goldsmith
**Hilton** Conrad Nicholson 1887–1979 Am hotel chain owner
**Hilton** James 1900–1954 Eng nov
**Himmler** Heinrich 1900–1945 Ger Nazi polit
**Hindemith** Paul 1895–1963 Am (Ger-born) violist & composer
**Hindenburg, von** Paul 1847–1934 *Paul Ludwig Hans Anton von Beneckendorff und von Hindenburg* Ger field marshal; pres of Germany (1925–34)
**Hinshelwood** Sir Cyril Norman 1897–1967 Eng chem
**Hipparchus** 6th c B C tyrant of Athens
**Hipparchus** *fl* 130 B C Greek astron
**Hippias** 6th c B C *bro of Hipparchus* ruled Athens with his brother
**Hippocrates** 460?–?377 B C *father of medicine* Greek physician
**Hirohito** 1901–     emp of Japan (1926–     )
**Hiroshige** Ando 1797–1858 Jap artist
**Hitchcock** Sir Alfred Joseph 1899–1980 Eng film director
**Hitchcock** Ethan Allen 1835–1909 Am diplomat & administrator
**Hitler** Adolf 1889–1945 Ger chancellor & führer
**Hoad** Lewis 1934–     Austral tennis player
**Hoare** Sir Samuel John Gurney 1880–1959 Viscount *Templewood* Eng statesman
**Hobbema** Meindert 1638–1709 Du artist
**Hobbes** Thomas 1588–1679 Eng philos

**Hobbs** Carleton Percy 1898–1978 Eng actor, mainly in radio drama

**Hobbs** Sir John Berry 1882–1963 *Jack* Eng cricketer

**Hoccleve** Thomas 1368–*ab* 1450 Eng poet

**Ho Chi Minh** 1890–1969 pres of North Vietnam (1954–69)

**Hockney** David 1937– Eng artist

**Hodgkin** Sir Alan Lloyd 1914– Eng physiol

**Hodgkin** Dorothy Mary Crowfoot 1910– Eng chem

**Hoffmann** August Heinrich 1798–1874 Ger poet, philologist, & hist

**Hoffmann** Ernst Theodor Wilhelm 1776–1822 *Ernst Theodor Amadeus* Ger composer, author, & illustrator

**Hofmann** Hans 1880–1966 Am (Ger-born) artist

**Hofmann** Josef Casimir 1876–1957 Pol pianist

**Hofmann, von** August Wilhelm 1818–1892 Ger chem

**Hofmannsthal, von** Hugo 1874–1929 Austrian poet & dram

**Hogan** Ben 1912– Am golfer

**Hogarth** William 1697–1764 Eng artist & engraver

**Hogben** Lancelot Thomas 1895–1975 Eng scientist & author

**Hogg** James 1770–1835 Scot poet

**Hohenzollern** Michael – see MICHAEL

**Hokusai** Katsushika 1760–1849 Jap artist

**Holbein** Hans father 1465?–1524 & son 1497?–1543 Ger artists

**Holford** Sir William Graham 1907–1975 Eng architect

**Holinshed, Hollingshead** Raphael *d ab* 1580 Eng chronicler

**Holland** John Philip 1840–1914 Irish-born inventor in Am

**Holland** Sir Sidney George 1893–1961 prime min of NZ (1945–57)

**Hollerith** Herman 1860–1929 Am inventor

**Holm** Ian 1931– né *Ian Holm Cuthbert* Eng actor

**Holman-Hunt** William – see Holman HUNT

**Holmes** Oliver Wendell 1809–1894 Am physician & author

**Holst** Gustav Theodore 1874–1934 Eng composer

**Holt** Harold Edward 1908–1967 Austral polit; prime min (1966–67)

**Holyoake** Sir Keith Jacka 1904–1983 prime min of NZ (1960–72)

**Home** Alexander Frederick Douglas- 1903– Baron *Home of the Hirsel* Br polit; prime min (1963–64)

**Home** William Douglas- 1912– Br dram

**Homer** *fl* 850? B C; traditional Greek epic poet

**Homer** Winslow 1836–1910 Am artist

**Honecker** Erich 1912– E Ger polit; head of state (1976– )

**Honegger** Arthur 1892–1955 Fr composer

**Honorius** Flavius 384–423 Rom emp of the West (395–423)

**Hood** Samuel 1st Viscount 1724–1816 Eng admiral

**Hood** Thomas 1799–1845 Eng poet

**Hooke** Robert 1635–1703 Eng experimental philos

**Hooker** Sir Joseph Dalton 1817–1911 Eng botanist

**Hooker** Richard 1554–1600 Eng theol

**Hooker** Thomas 1586?–1647 Eng Puritan clergyman; a founder of Connecticut

**Hoover** Herbert Clark 1874–1964 31st pres of the US (1929–33)

**Hoover** John Edgar 1895–1972 Am criminologist; FBI director (1924–72)

**Hope** Anthony – see Sir Anthony Hope HAWKINS

**Hope** Bob 1903– né *Leslie Townes Hope* Am (Eng-born) comedian & actor

**Hope** Victor Alexander John 1887–1951 *son of prec* 8th Earl of *Hopetoun* & 2nd Marquis of *Linlithgow* Eng soldier; viceroy of India (1936–43)

**Hopkins** Sir Frederick Gowland 1861–1947 Eng biochem

**Hopkins** Gerard Manley 1844–1889 Eng poet

**Horace** 65–8 B C *Quintus Horatius Flaccus* Rom poet & satirist

**Hordern** Sir Michael Murray 1911– Eng actor

**Hore-Belisha** Leslie 1893–1957 Eng polit

**Horowitz** Vladimir 1904– Am (Russ-born) pianist

**Horrocks** Sir Brian Gwynne 1895– Eng general & author

**Horsa** – see HENGIST

**Horsley** Colin 1920– NZ pianist

**Hortense de Beauharnais** – see BEAUHARNAIS

**Horthy** Miklós von Nagybánya 1868–1957 Hung admiral; regent of Hungary (1920–44)

**Houdini** Harry 1874–1926 né *Ehrich Weiss* Am magician & escapologist

**Houdon** Jean Antoine 1741–1828 Fr sculptor

**Housman** Alfred Edward 1859–1936 Eng classical scholar & poet

**Housman** Laurence 1865–1959 *bro of prec* Eng author & illustrator

**Houssay** Bernardo Alberto 1887–1971 Argentine physiol

**Howard** Catherine – see CATHERINE

**Howard** Sir Ebenezer 1850–1928 Eng town planner

**Howard** Elizabeth Jane 1923– Eng nov

**Howard** Henry 1517?–1547 Earl of *Surrey* Eng soldier & poet

**Howe** Elias 1819–1867 Am inventor

**Howe** Julia 1819–1910 née *Ward* Am suffragist & reformer

**Howe** Earl 1726–1799 *Richard Howe* Eng admiral

**Howe** 5th Viscount 1729–1814 *William Howe* Eng gen in Am

**Howells** Herbert 1892– Eng composer

**Howells** William Dean 1837–1920 Am author

**Hoxha** Enver 1908– First Sec of the Central Committee of the Albanian Communist Party (1954– )

**Hoyle** Sir Fred 1915– Eng astron & author

**Hsüan-t'ung** 1906–1967 *Henry P'u-yi* Chin emp (1908–12); last of Manchu dynasty; puppet emp of Manchukuo (1934–45)

**Hua Kuo-feng** 1920– Chin prime min (1976–80)

**Huáscar** 1495?–1533 Inca prince

**Hubble** Edwin Powell 1889–1953 Am astron

**Huddlestone** (Ernest Urban) Trevor 1913– Eng clergyman; bishop of Mauritius (1977– )

**Hudson** Henry *d* 1611 erroneously *Hendrick* Eng navigator & explorer

**Hudson** William Henry 1841–1922 Eng naturalist & author

**Huggins** Sir William 1824–1910 Eng astron

**Hughes** Howard Robard 1905–1976 Am businessman, aviator, & film producer

**Hughes** Richard Arthur Warren 1900–1976 Eng nov

**Hughes** Ted 1930– Eng poet

**Hughes** Thomas 1822–1896 Eng jurist, reformer, & writer

**Hughes** William Morris 1864–1952 Austral statesman

**Hugo** Victor Marie 1802–1885 Fr poet, nov, & dram – **Hugoesque** *adj*

**Huizinga** Johan 1872–1945 Du hist

**Hulagu** 1217–1265 *grandson of Genghis Khan* Mongol ruler

**Hull** Cordell 1871–1955 Am statesman; US sec of state (1933–44)

**Humbert I** *Ital* **Umberto** 1844–1900 king of Italy (1878–1900)

**Humbert II** 1904– Prince of *Piedmont*; Count of *Sarre*; king of Italy (1946)

**Humboldt, von** Baron (Friedrich Heinrich) Alexander 1769–1859 Ger naturalist, traveller, & statesman

**Humboldt, von** Baron Wilhelm 1767–1835 *bro of prec* Ger philologist & diplomat

**Hume** David 1711–1776 Scot philos & hist – **Humean, Humian** *adj*

**Humperdinck** Engelbert 1854–1921 Ger composer

**Humphrey** 1391–1447 *son of Henry IV*; Duke of *Gloucester* (*the Good Duke*) & Earl of *Pembroke* Eng statesman & book collector

**Humphrey** Hubert Horatio 1911–1978 Am polit; vice-pres of the US (1965–69)

**Hung-wu** 1328–1398 *Chu Yüan-chang* Chin emp (1368–98); founder of Ming dynasty

**Hunt** Sir (Henry Cecil) John 1910– Eng mountaineer & explorer

**Hunt** (James Henry) Leigh 1784–1859 Eng author

**Hunt** (William) Holman 1827–1910 Eng artist

**Hunter** Evan 1926– né *Salvatore Lombino*; pseud *Ed McBain* Am author

**Hunter** John 1728–1793 Eng anatomist & surgeon

**Hunyadi , Hunyady** János 1387?–1456 Hung soldier & hero

**Hurry** Leslie 1909–1978 Eng artist & theatrical designer

**Hurst** Fannie 1889–1968 Am author

**Hurst** Geoffrey Charles 1941– Eng footballer

**Husák** Gustáv 1913– Czech polit; pres (1975– )

**Husein ibn-Ali** 1856–1931 first king of the Hejaz (1916–24)

**Huss, Hus** John *or* Jan *ab* 1374–1415 *Johannes Hus von Husinetz* Bohemian religious reformer

**Hussein I** 1935– king of Jordan (1953– )

**Husserl** Edmund 1859–1938 Ger philos

**Huston** John 1906–          Am film director

**Hutten, von** Ulrich 1488–1523 Ger humanist & supporter of Luther

**Hutton** John Campbell 1906–1978 NZ artist

**Hutton** Sir Leonard 1916–          Eng cricketer

**Huxley** Aldous Leonard 1894–1963 *bro of JS* Eng nov & critic – **Huxleian** *or* **Huxleyan** *adj*

**Huxley** Sir Andrew Fielding 1917–          Eng physiol & educ

**Huxley** Elspeth Josceline 1907–          Eng author

**Huxley** Sir Julian Sorell 1887–1975 *grandson of TH* Eng biologist

**Huxley** Thomas Henry 1825–1895 Eng biologist

**Huygens, Huyghens** Christian 1629–1695 Du math, physicist, & astron

**Huysmans** Joris Karl 1848–1907 né *Charles Marie Georges* Fr nov

**Hyde** Douglas 1860–1949 Irish author; pres of Republic of Ireland (1938–45)

**Hyde** Edward 1609–1674 1st Earl of *Clarendon* Eng statesman & hist

**Hyder Ali** – see HAIDAR ALI

# I

**Ibáñez** Vicente Blasco– – see BLASCO-IBÁÑEZ

**Ibbotson** Derek 1932–          Eng athlete

**Iberville, d'** Sieur 1661–1706 *Pierre Lemoyne* Fr-Canad explorer; founder of Louisiana

**ibn-Saud** Abdul-Aziz 1880–1953 king of Saudi Arabia (1932–53)

**Ibrahim Pasha** 1789–1848 Egyptian gen & viceroy

**Ibsen** Henrik 1828–1906 Norw poet & dram – **Ibsenian** *adj*

**Ickx** Jacky 1945–          Belg racing driver

**Ictinus** 5th c B C Greek architect

**Ignatius** Saint 1st–2nd c *Theophorus* bishop of Antioch & church father

**Ignatius of Loyola** Saint – see LOYOLA – **Ignatian** *adj*

**Ikhnaton** *Amenhotep IV* king of Egypt (*ab* 1375–1358 B C); religious reformer

**Illingworth** Raymond 1932–          Eng cricketer

**Imran Khan** Niazi 1952–          Pakistan cricketer

**Imtiaz** Ahmed 1928–          Pakistan cricketer

**Indy, d'** Vincent 1851–1931 Fr composer

**Inés de Castro** – see CASTRO

**Inge** William 1913–1973 Am dram

**Inge** William Ralph 1860–1954 Eng prelate & author

**Ingram** Arthur Foley Winnington 1858–1946 Eng prelate; bishop of London (1901–39)

**Ingres** Jean Auguste Dominique 1780–1867 Fr artist

**Innes** Michael 1906–          pseud of *John Innes Mackintosh Stewart* Br author

**Innocent** name of 13 popes; esp **II** *d* 1143 (pope 1130–43); **III** 1161–1216 (pope 1198–1216); **IV** *d* 1254 (pope 1243–54); **XI** 1611–1689 (pope 1676–89)

**Innocenti** Ferdinando 1891–1966 Ital motor manuf

**Inönü** Ismet 1884–1973 Turk statesman; pres of Turkey (1938–50); premier (1961–65)

**Intikhab** Alam Khan 1941–          Pakistan cricketer

**Ionesco** Eugene 1912–          Fr (Rumanian-born) dram

**Ireton** Henry 1611–1651 Eng Parliamentary commander & regicide

**Ironside** William Edmund 1880–1959 1st Baron of *Archangel and Ironside* Br field marshal

**Irving** Sir Henry 1838–1905 né *John Henry Brodribb* Eng actor

**Irving** Washington 1783–1859 Am essayist, nov, & hist

**Isaacs** Sir Isaac Alfred 1855–1948 Austral jurist & statesman; gov-gen of Australia (1931–36)

**Isaacs** Rufus Daniel – see Marquis of READING

**Isabella** 1292–1358 *wife of Edward II of England*

**Isabella I** 1451–1504 *wife of Ferdinand II of Aragon* queen of Castile (1474–1504); aided Columbus

**Isherwood** Christopher William Bradshaw 1904–          Am (Eng-born) author

**Isidore of Seville** Saint *ab* 570–636 *Isidorus Hispalensis* Span prelate & scholar

**Ismail Pasha** 1830–1895 *Ismail I* khedive of Egypt (1863–79)

**Isocrates** 436–338 B C Athenian orator

**Issigonis** Sir Alec Arnold Constantine 1906–          Br (Turk-born) engineer & car designer

**Iturbi** José 1895–1980 Span-born pianist & conductor

**Ivan III Vasilievich** 1440–1505 *Ivan the Great* grand duke of Russia (1462–1505)

**Ivan IV Vasilievich** 1530–1584 *Ivan the Terrible* ruler of Russia (1533–84)

**Ives** Charles Edward 1874–1954 Am composer – **Ivesian** *adj*

# J

**Jabir** – see GEBER

**Jack** David Bone Nightingale 1899–1958 Eng footballer

**Jacklin** Anthony 1944–          *Tony* Eng golfer

**Jackson** Andrew 1767–1845 Am gen; 7th pres of the US (1829–37)

**Jackson** Sir Barry Vincent 1879–1961 Eng theatre manager & director

**Jackson** Donald 1940–          Canad figure ice-skater

**Jackson** Glenda 1936–          Eng actress

**Jackson** Marjorie 1931–          *Blue Streak* Austral athlete

**Jackson** Thomas 1925–          Eng trade-union leader

**Jackson** Thomas Jonathan 1824–1863 *Stonewall Jackson* Am Confed gen

**Jacob** François 1920–          Fr biologist

**Jacobs** Helen Hull 1908–          Am tennis player

**Jacobsen** Arne 1902–1971 Danish architect & industrial designer

**Jacquard** Joseph Marie 1752–1834 Fr inventor

**Jacques I** – see Jean Jacques DESSALINES

**Jagan** Cheddi 1918–          Br Guiana prime min (1961–64)

**Jagatai** *d* 1242 2nd *son of Genghis Khan* Mongol ruler

**Jahangir** 1569–1627 emp of Hindustan (1605–27)

**Jakobson** Roman 1896–1982 Am (Russian-born) linguist

**James** name of 6 kings of Scot & 2 kings of GB: esp **VI** 1566–1625 of Scot (reigned 1567–1603) *or* **I** of GB (reigned 1603–25); **II** 1633–1701 (reigned 1685–88)

**James** Alex 1902–1953 Scot footballer

**James** Henry 1843–1916 Br (Am-born) writer

**James** Jesse Woodson 1847–1882 Am outlaw

**James** William 1842–1910 *bro of Henry* Am psychol & philos

**James Edward Stuart** 1688–1766 *the Old Pretender* Eng prince

**Jameson** Sir Leander Starr 1853–1917 *Doctor Jameson* Scot physician & administrator in S Africa

**Jami** 1414–1492 Pers poet & mystic

**Janáček** Leoš 1854–1928 Czech composer

**Janes** Christine 1941–          neé *Truman* Eng tennis player

**Jaques-Dalcroze** Émile 1865–1950 Swiss composer & creator of eurythmics

**Jardine** Douglas Robert 1900–1958 Eng cricketer

**Jarry** Alfred 1873–1907 Fr author

**Jaruzelski** Wojciech Witold 1923–          Pol gen & polit; 1st sec of the Communist Party in Poland (1981–    )

**Jarvis** John Arthur 1872–1933 Eng swimmer

**Jarvis** Sir John Layton 1887–1968 Eng jockey & racehorse trainer

**Jaspers** Karl 1883–1969 Ger philos

**Jauregg** Julius Wagner von – see WAGNER VON JAUREGG

**Jaurès** Jean Léon 1858–1914 Fr socialist

**Jeanne d'Arc** – see JOAN OF ARC

**Jeans** Sir James Hopwood 1877–1946 Eng physicist, astron, & author

**Jefferies** Richard 1848–1887 Eng nov & naturalist

**Jefferson** Thomas 1743–1826 3rd pres of the US (1801–09)

**Jeffreys** George *d* 1685 Eng composer

**Jeffreys** George 1648–1689 1st Baron *Jeffreys of Wem* Eng judge

**Jeffreys** Sir Harold 1891–          Eng astron & geophysicist

**Jekyll** Gertrude 1843–1932 Eng artist, gardener, & author

**Jellicoe** 1st Earl 1859–1935 *John Rushworth Jellicoe* Eng admiral

**Jenghiz Khan** – see GENGHIS KHAN

**Jenkins** (David) Clive 1926– Welsh trade-union leader

**Jenkins** Roy Harris 1920– Eng polit

**Jenner** Edward 1749–1823 Eng physician – **Jennerian** *adj*

**Jensen** Johannes Vilhelm 1873–1950 Danish poet & nov

**Jerome** Saint 340?–420 *Eusebius Hieronymus* Latin church father

**Jerome** Jerome Klapka 1859–1927 Eng author

**Jervis** John 1735–1823 Earl *St Vincent* Eng admiral

**Jesus , Jesus Christ, Christ Jesus** 4–8? B C–A D ?29 *Jesus of Nazareth; the Son of Mary* source of the Christian religion & Saviour in the Christian faith

**Jevons** William Stanley 1835–1882 Eng econ

**Jex-Blake** Sophia Louisa 1840–1912 Eng physician

**Jiménez** Juan Ramón 1881–1958 Span poet

**Jiménez de Cisneros** Francisco 1436–1517 Span prelate & statesman

**Jinnah** Mohammed Ali 1876–1948 Muslim lawyer; 1st gov-gen of dominion of Pakistan (1947–48)

**Jipcho** Ben 1943– Kenyan athlete

**Joachim** Joseph 1831–1907 Hung violinist

**Joan of Arc** *Fr* **Jeanne d'Arc** Saint 1412–1431 *the Maid of Orleans* Fr national heroine

**Jodl** Alfred 1892?–1946 Ger gen

**Joffre** Joseph Jacques Césaire 1852–1931 Fr field marshal; marshal of France

**John** name of 21 popes: esp **XXIII** (*Angelo Giuseppe Roncalli*) 1881–1963 (pope 1958–63)

**John** 1167?–1216 *John Lackland* king of England (1199–1216)

**John I** 1357–1433 *the Great* king of Portugal (1385–1433)

**John** Augustus Edwin 1878–1961 Eng artist & etcher

**John** Barry 1945– Welsh rugby union player

**John** Elton 1947– né *Reginald Dwight* Eng rock singer

**John of Austria** 1547–1578 Don *John* Span gen

**John of Gaunt** 1340–1399 Duke of *Lancaster; son of Edward III of Eng*

**John of Lancaster** – see Duke of BEDFORD

**John of Salisbury** *d* 1180 Eng ecclesiastic

**John III Sobieski** 1624–1696 king of Poland (1674–96)

**John Paul I** Pope 1912–1978 (*Albino Luciani*) pope (1978)

**John Paul II** Pope 1920– (*Karol Wojtyla*) pope (1978– )

**Johnson** Amy 1903–1941 Eng aviator

**Johnson** Andrew 1808–1875 17th pres of the US (1865–69) – **Johnsonian** *adj*

**Johnson** Dame Celia 1908–1982 Eng actress

**Johnson** Hewlett 1874–1966 *Red Dean* Eng clergyman; dean of Canterbury (1931–63)

**Johnson** Lyndon Baines 1908–1973 Am polit; 36th pres of the US (1963–69) – **Johnsonian** *adj*

**Johnson** Pamela Hansford 1912–1981 *Lady Snow* Eng author

**Johnson** Samuel 1709–1784 *Dr Johnson* Eng lexicographer & author – **Johnsonian** *adj*

**Joinville, de** Jean 1224?–1317 Fr chronicler

**Jókai** Maurus *or* Móricz 1825–1904 Hung nov & dram

**Joliet, Jolliet** Louis 1645–1700 Fr-Canad explorer

**Joliot-Curie** Frédéric 1900–1958 orig *Joliot* Fr physicist

**Joliot-Curie** Irène 1897–1956 formerly *Irène Curie-Joliot, dau of Marie & Pierre Curie & wife of prec* Fr physicist

**Jolyot** Prosper – see CRÉBILLON

**Jones** Adrianne Shirley 1938– *Ann* neé *Haydon* Eng tennis & table-tennis player

**Jones** Gwyneth 1936– Welsh soprano

**Jones** Inigo 1573–1652 Eng architect

**Jones** James Larkin 1913– *Jack* Eng trade-union leader

**Jones** John Paul 1747–1792 orig in full *John Paul* Am (Scot-born) naval officer

**Jones** Lewis 1931– Welsh rugby union and rugby league player

**Jones** Robert Tyre 1902–1971 *Bobby* Am golfer

**Jonson** Ben 1573?–1637 orig *Benjamin* Eng dram – **Jonsonian** *adj*

**Joplin** Scott 1868–1917 Am pianist & composer

**Josephine** Empress – see BEAUHARNAIS

**Josephson** Brian David 1940– Eng physicist

**Josephus** Flavius 37–?100 Jewish hist

**Joubert** Joseph 1754–1824 Fr essayist & moralist

**Joubert** Petrus Jacobus 1834–1900 *Piet* Boer gen & statesman

**Jouhaux** Léon 1879–1954 Fr trade-union leader

**Joule** James Prescott 1818–1889 Eng physicist

**Jourdan** Comte Jean Baptiste 1762–1833 Fr soldier; marshal of France

**Jowett** Benjamin 1817–1893 Eng classical scholar

**Joyce** Eileen 1912– Austral pianist

**Joyce** James Augustine 1882–1941 Irish author – **Joycean** *adj*

**Joyce** William 1906–1946 *Lord Haw-haw* Eng (Am-born) anti-Br propagandist

**Juan Carlos** 1938– king of Spain (1975– )

**Juan Manuel** Don 1282–1349 Span author

**Juantorena** Alberto 1951– *White Lightning* Cuban athlete

**Juárez** Benito Pablo 1806–1872 Mex lawyer; pres of Mexico (1861–65; 1867–72)

**Judas Maccabaeus** *d* 160 B C Jewish patriot; with 4 bros (the Maccabees) revolted against Antiochus Epiphanes

**Julian** 331–363 *Flavius Claudius Julianus, the Apostate* Rom emp (361–363)

**Juliana** 1909– *dau of Wilhelmina* queen of the Netherlands (1948–80)

**Jung** Carl Gustav 1875–1961 Swiss psychol

**Junkers** Hugo 1859–1935 Ger aeroplane designer & builder

**Justin** Saint 100?–?165 *Justin (the) Martyr* church father

**Justinian I** 483–565 *the Great* Byzantine emp (527–565)

**Juvenal** 60?–?140 *Decimus Junius Juvenalis* Rom poet & satirist – **Juvenalian** *adj*

# K

**Kádár** János 1912– prime min of Hung (1956–58; 1961–65)

**Kafka** Franz 1883–1924 Austrian author – **Kafkaesque** *adj*

**Kalidasa** 5th c Hindu dram & poet

**Kalinin** Mikhail Ivanovich 1875–1946 Soviet polit; pres of USSR (1923–46)

**Kallio** Kyösti 1873–1940 pres of Finland (1937–40)

**Kamehameha** 1758?–1819 *the Great* king of Hawaii (1795–1819)

**Kamenev** Lev Borisovich 1883–1936 Soviet Communist leader

**Kamerlingh Onnes** Heike 1853–1926 Du physicist

**Kandinski** Vasili 1866–1944 Soviet artist

**Kane** Elisha Kent 1820–1857 Am arctic explorer

**Kanhai** Rohan Babulal 1935– W Indian cricketer

**Kant** Immanuel 1724–1804 Ger philos

**Karajan** Herbert von 1908– Austrian conductor

**Karamanlis** Konstantinos 1907– prime min (1955–63; 1974–80) & pres (1980– ) of Greece

**Karlfeldt** Erik Axel 1864–1931 Swed poet

**Karloff** Boris 1887–1969 né *William Henry Pratt* Eng film actor

**Károlyi** Count Mihály 1875–1955 Hung polit

**Karrer** Paul 1889–1971 Swiss chemist

**Karsavina** Tamara 1885–1978 Russ dancer

**Karsh** Yousef 1908– Canad (Turk-born) photographer

**Kästner** Erich 1899–1974 Ger author

**Katchen** Julius 1926–1969 Am pianist

**Kato** Komei Takaaki 1860–1926 prime min of Jap (1924–26)

**Katsura** Taro 1847–1913 prime min of Jap (1901–06; 1908–11; 1912–13)

**Katz** Sir Bernard 1911– Br (Ger-born) biophysicist

**Katzir** Ephraim 1916– Israeli biophysicist; pres of Israel (1973–78)

**Kaufman** George Simon 1889–1961 Am dram

**Kaunda** (David) Kenneth 1924– Zambian polit; pres (1964– )

**Kaunitz, von** Count Wenzel Anton 1711–1794 Prince *von Kaunitz-Rietberg* Austrian statesman

**Kawabata** Yasunari 1899–1972 Jap author

**Kaye** Danny 1913– pseud of *David Daniel Kominski* Am actor & singer

**Kazantzakis** Nikos 1885–1957 Greek poet, nov, & translator

**Kean** Edmund 1787–1833 Eng actor
**Keaton** Joseph Francis 1895–1966 *Buster* Am film comedian
**Keats** John 1795–1821 Eng poet – **Keatsian** *adj*
**Keble** John 1792–1866 Eng clergyman & poet
**Keegan** (Joseph) Kevin 1951– Eng footballer
**Keino** Kipchoge 1940– Kenyan athlete
**Keitel** Wilhelm 1882–1946 Ger field marshal
**Kekkonen** Urho Kaleva 1900– pres of Finland (1956–82)
**Keller** Helen Adams 1880–1968 Am deaf & blind lecturer
**Kellogg** Frank Billings 1856–1937 Am statesman
**Kelly** Gene 1912– Am film actor, dancer, choreographer, & director
**Kelly** Sir Gerald Festus 1879–1972 Eng artist
**Kelvin** 1st Baron 1824–1907 *William Thomson* Scot math & physicist
**Kemal Atatürk** 1881–1938 *Mustafa* or *Mustapha Kemal* Turk gen; pres of Turkey (1923–38)
**Kemble** Frances Anne 1809–1893 *Fanny* Eng actress
**Kemble** John Philip 1757–1823 Eng actor
**Kempe** Rudolph 1910–1976 Ger conductor
**Kempis** Thomas à – see THOMAS À KEMPIS
**Ken, Kenn** Thomas 1637–1711 Eng prelate & hymn writer
**Kendall** Edward Calvin 1886–1972 Am biochem
**Kendall** Henry Clarence 1839–1882 Austral poet
**Kendrew** Sir John Cowdery 1917– Eng biochem
**Keneally** Thomas Michael 1935– Austral nov
**Kennan** George Frost 1904– Am hist & diplomat
**Kennedy** John Fitzgerald 1917–1963 Am polit; 35th pres of the US (1961–63)
**Kennedy** Joseph Patrick 1888–1969 *father of JF & RF* Am businessman & diplomat
**Kennedy** Robert Francis 1925–1968 Am polit & lawyer; atty gen of the US (1961–64)
**Kennelly** Arthur Edwin 1861–1939 Am engineer
**Kennington** Eric Henri 1888–1960 Eng artist & sculptor
**Kenny** Elizabeth 1886–1952 Austral nurse & physiotherapist
**Kent** Rockwell 1882–1971 Am painter
**Kent** William 1684–1748 Eng architect
**Kenton** Stanley Newcomb 1912– Am bandleader & composer
**Kenyatta** Jomo 1893?–1978 Kenyan polit; pres (1964–78)
**Kenyon** Dame Kathleen 1906–1978 Eng archaeologist
**Kepler** Johannes 1571–1630 Ger astron
**Keppel** 1st Viscount 1725–1786 *Augustus Keppel* Eng admiral
**Kerenski** Aleksandr Feodorovich 1881–1970 Russ revolutionist
**Kern** Jerome David 1885–1945 Am composer
**Kerouac** Jack 1922–1969 Am author
**Kerr** Deborah Jane 1921– Eng actress
**Kesselring** Albert 1887–1960 Ger field marshal
**Ketch** John *d* 1686 *Jack* Eng public hangman
**Kett** Robert *d* 1549 Eng peasant leader
**Key** Francis Scott 1779–1843 Am lawyer; author of "The Star-Spangled Banner"
**Keynes** Sir Geoffrey Langdon 1887–1982 *bro of next* Eng surgeon & author
**Keynes** John Maynard 1883–1946 1st Baron *Keynes of Tilton* Eng econ
**Keyserling** Count Hermann Alexander 1880–1946 Ger philos & author
**Khachaturian** Aram Ilych 1903–1978 Russ-Armenian composer
**Khalid** 1913–1982 king of Saudi Arabia (1975–82)
**Khama** Sir Seretse 1921–1980 pres of Botswana (1966–80)
**Khan** Majid Jahangir 1946– Pakistan cricketer
**Khayyám** Omar – see OMAR KHAYYÁM
**Kheraskov** Mikhail Matveevich 1733–1807 Russ poet
**Khomeini** Ruhollah 1900– *Ayatollah Khomeini* Islamic leader of Iran (1979– )
**Khrushchev** Nikita Sergeevich 1894–1971 Soviet polit; premier of Soviet Union (1958–64) – **Khrushchevian, Khrushchevite** *adj*
**Khufu** *Greek* **Cheops** king of Egypt (*ab* 2900–2877 B C) & pyramid builder
**Kidd** William 1645?–1701 *Captain Kidd* Scot pirate
**Kiepura** Jan 1902–1966 Pol tenor

**Kierkegaard** Sören Aabye 1813–1855 Danish philos & theol – **Kierkegaardian** *adj*
**Kiesinger** Kurt Georg 1904– chancellor of West Germany (1966–69)
**Killanin** 3rd Baron 1914– *Michael Morris Killanin* Irish author & film producer; pres of International Olympic Committee (1972–80)
**Killy** Jean-Claude 1944– Fr ski racer
**Kim Il Sung** 1912– N Korean leader (1948– ) & pres (1972– )
**King** Billie-Jean 1943– née *Moffitt* Am tennis player
**King** Ernest Joseph 1878–1956 Am admiral
**King** Hetty 1883–1972 Eng music-hall entertainer
**King** Martin Luther 1929–1968 Am clergyman & civil-rights leader
**King** Sir Truby 1858–1938 NZ physician
**King** William Lyon Mackenzie 1874–1950 Canad statesman; prime min (1921–26; 1926–30; 1935–48)
**Kinglake** Alexander William 1809–1891 Eng hist
**Kingsford-Smith** Sir Charles Edward 1897–1935 Austral airman
**Kingsley** Charles 1819–1875 Eng clergyman & nov
**Kinnock** Neil Gordon 1942– Br polit
**Kinsey** Alfred Charles 1894–1956 Am zoologist
**Kipling** (Joseph) Rudyard 1865–1936 Eng author – **Kiplingesque** *adj*
**Kirchhoff** Gustav Robert 1824–1887 Ger physicist
**Kirchner** Ernst Ludwig 1880–1938 Ger artist
**Kirk** Norman Eric 1923–1974 prime min of NZ (1972–74)
**Kirov** Sergei Mironovich 1886–1934 Russ revolutionist
**Kissinger** Henry Alfred 1923– Am (Ger-born) scholar & govt official; US sec of state (1973–77)
**Kitchener** Horatio Herbert 1850–1916 1st Earl *Kitchener of Khartoum and of Broome* Br field marshal
**Kittredge** George Lyman 1860–1941 Am educ
**Klee** Paul 1879–1940 Swiss artist
**Kleist, von** Heinrich 1777–1811 Ger dram
**Klemperer** Otto 1885–1973 Ger conductor
**Klopstock** Friedrich Gottlieb 1724–1803 Ger poet
**Kneller** Sir Godfrey 1646–1723 né *Gottfried Kniller* Ger-born portrait painter in Eng
**Knight** Dame Laura 1877–1970 Eng artist
**Knott** Alan Philip Eric 1946– Eng cricketer
**Knox** John 1514?–1572 Scot reformer & statesman
**Knox** Ronald Arbuthnott Hilary 1888–1957 Eng priest & author
**Knox-Johnston** Robin 1939– Eng yachtsman
**Knudsen** William Signius 1879–1948 Am (Danish-born) industrialist & administrator
**Knut** – see CANUTE
**Koch** Ludwig 1881–1974 Ger naturalist
**Koch** Robert 1843–1910 Ger bacteriologist
**Kocher** Emil Theodor 1841–1917 Swiss surgeon
**Kodály** Zoltán 1882–1967 Hung composer
**Koestler** Arthur 1905–1983 Br (Hung-born) author
**Kohl** Helmut 1930– chancellor of W Germany (1982– )
**Koiso** Kuniaki 1880–1950 Jap gen
**Kok** Ada 1947– Du swimmer
**Kokoschka** Oskar 1886–1980 Br (Austrian-born) artist
**Kolchak** Aleksandr Vasilievich 1874–1920 Russ admiral & counterrevolutionist
**Kollwitz** Käthe 1867–1945 née *Schmidt* Ger artist
**Konoye** Prince Fumimaro 1891–1945 Jap statesman
**Koo** Vi Kyuin Wellington 1887– né *Ku Weichün* Chin statesman & diplomat
**Kopa** Raymond 1931– né *Kopaszewski* Fr footballer
**Kopernik, Koppernigk** – see COPERNICUS
**Kops** Bernard 1926– Eng dram
**Korbut** Olga 1955– Soviet gymnast
**Korda** Sir Alexander 1893–1956 Br (Hung-born) film director
**Kornberg** Arthur 1918– Am biochem
**Kornilov** Lavr Georgievich 1870–1918 Russ gen & counterrevolutionist
**Korzybski** Alfred Habdank Skarbek 1879–1950 Am (Pol-born) scientist & author
**Kosciuszko** Thaddeus 1746–1817 Pol patriot
**Kossel** Albrecht 1853–1927 Ger biochem

**Kossuth** Lajos 1802–1894 Hung patriot & statesman
**Kostelanetz** André 1901–1980 Am (Russ-born) conductor
**Kosygin** Aleksei Nikolaevich 1904–1980 Soviet polit; premier of Soviet Union (1964–80)
**Kotzebue, von** August Friedrich Ferdinand 1761–1819 Ger dram
**Koussevitzky** Serge 1874–1951 *Sergei Alexandrovitch* Russ-born conductor
**Krafft-Ebing, von** Baron Richard 1840–1902 Ger neurologist
**Krag** Jens Otto 1915–1978 prime min of Denmark (1962–68)
**Kramer** John Albert 1921– *Jack* Am tennis player, promoter, & commentator
**Kramer** Stanley 1913– Am film producer
**Kraus** Lili 1908– Br (Hung-born) pianist
**Krebs** Sir Hans (Adolf) 1900–1981 Br (Ger-born) biochem
**Kreisler** Fritz 1875–1962 Am (Austrian-born) violinist
**Krips** Josef 1902–1974 Austrian conductor
**Krogh** August 1874–1949 Danish physiol
**Kropotkin** Prince Pëtr Alekseevich 1842–1921 Russ geographer & revolutionist
**Kruger** Stephanus Johannes Paulus 1825–1904 *Oom Paul* S African statesman
**Krupp** family of Ger munition makers including: Friedrich 1787–1826; his son Alfred 1812–1887; Alfred's son Friedrich Alfred 1854–1902; Friedrich Alfred's daughter Bertha 1886–1957; & Bertha's son Alfred-Felix 1907–1967
**Kubitschek** Juscelino 1901–1976 pres of Brazil (1956–61)
**Kublai Khan** 1216–1294 founder of Mongol dynasty in China
**Kubrick** Stanley 1928– Am film director
**Kuhn** Richard 1900–1967 Austrian chem
**Kuibyshev** Valerian Vladimirovich 1888–1935 Russ Bolshevik
**Kun** Béla 1885–1937 Hung Communist
**Küng** Hans 1928– Swiss Catholic theologian
**Kurosawa** Akira 1910– Jap film director
**Kurusu** Saburo 1888–1954 Jap diplomat
**Kusch** Polykarp 1911– Am (Ger-born) physicist
**Kuts** Vladimir 1927–1975 Soviet athlete
**Kutuzov** Mikhail Ilarionovich 1745–1813 Prince of *Smolensk* Russ field marshal
**Kyd , Kid** Thomas 1558–1594 Eng dram
**Kynewulf** – see CYNEWULF

# L

**Labouchère** Henry du Pré 1831–1912 Eng polit & publicist
**La Bruyère, de** Jean 1645–1696 Fr moralist
**Ladd** Alan 1913–1964 Am film actor
**La Farge** Oliver Hazard Perry 1901–1963 Am author & anthropol
**Lafayette, de** Marquis 1757–1834 *Marie Joseph Paul Yves Roch Gilbert du Motier* Fr gen & statesman
**Laffite, Lafitte** Jean *ab* 1780–*ab* 1826 Fr pirate
**La Follette** Robert Marion 1855–1925 Am polit
**Lafontaine** Henri 1854–1943 Belg lawyer & statesman
**La Fontaine, de** Jean 1621–1695 Fr fabulist
**Laforgue** Jules 1800–1887 Fr poet & lit critic
**Lagerkvist** Pär Fabian 1891–1974 Swed dram, poet, & nov
**Lagerlöf** Selma Ottiliana Lovisa 1858–1940 Swed nov & poet
**Lagrange** Comte Joseph Louis 1736–1813 Fr geometer & astron
**La Guardia** Fiorello Henry 1882–1947 Am lawyer & polit
**Laine** Clementina Dinah 1927– *Cleo; Mrs John Dankworth* Eng jazz singer
**Laing** Ronald David 1927– Br psychiatrist
**Lake** Veronica 1919–1973 pseud of *Constance Kean* Am film actress
**Laker** Sir Frederick Alfred 1922– Eng airlines director
**Laker** James Charles 1922– Eng cricketer
**Lalique** René 1860–1945 Fr jeweller
**Lamarck, de** Chevalier 1744–1829 *Jean Baptiste Pierre Antoine de Monet* Fr naturalist
**Lamartine, de** Alphonse Marie Louis de Prat 1790–1869 Fr poet & statesman
**Lamb** Charles 1775–1834 Eng essayist & critic

**Lamb** Henry 1883–1960 Eng artist
**Lamb** William 1779–1848 2nd Viscount *Melbourne* Eng statesman
**Lamb** Willis Eugene 1913– Am physicist
**Lambert** Constant 1905–1951 Eng conductor & composer
**Lambert** John 1619–1683 Eng parliamentary gen
**Lamming** George 1927– W Indian nov
**Lampedusa, di** Giuseppe Tomasi 1896–1957 Ital nov
**Lancaster** Sir Osbert 1908– Eng cartoonist, author, & stage designer
**Landau** Lev Davidovich 1908–1968 Soviet physicist
**Landor** Walter Savage 1775–1864 Eng author
**Landowska** Wanda Louise 1879–1959 Pol pianist
**Landseer** Sir Edwin Henry 1802–1873 Eng artist
**Landsteiner** Karl 1868–1943 Austrian-born pathologist in Am
**Land** Edwin Herbert 1909– Am inventor & industrialist
**Lane** Sir Allen 1902–1970 Eng publisher
**Lane** Edward William 1801–1876 Eng orientalist
**Lane** Dame Elizabeth Kathleen 1905– Eng lawyer; first woman High Court judge (1965)
**Lanfranc** 1005?–1089 Ital-born prelate in Eng
**Lang** Andrew 1844–1912 Scot scholar & author
**Lang** Cosmo Gordon 1864–1945 Eng prelate; archbishop of Canterbury (1928–42)
**Lang** Fritz 1890–1976 Am (Ger-born) film director
**Lange** Christian Louis 1869–1938 Norw pacifist & hist
**Langer** Susanne Knauth 1895– Am philos
**Langevin** Paul 1872–1946 Fr physicist
**Langland** *also* **Langley** William 1332?–?1400 Eng poet
**Langley** Samuel Pierpont 1834–1906 Am astron & aeroplane pioneer
**Langmuir** Irving 1881–1957 Am chem
**Langton** Stephen *d* 1228 Eng theol, hist, & poet
**Langtry** Lillie 1853–1929 née (*Emilie Charlotte*) *Le Breton;* the *Jersey Lily* Br actress
**Lanier** Sidney 1842–1881 Am poet
**Lankester** Sir Edwin Ray 1847–1929 Eng zool
**Lansbury** Angela Brigid 1925–Am (Eng-born) actress
**La Pérouse, de** Comte 1741–1788 *Jean François de Galoup* Fr navigator & explorer
**Laplace, de** Marquis Pierre Simon 1749–1827 Fr astron & math
**La Rochefoucauld, de** Duc François 1613–1680 Fr author & moralist
**Lardner** Ring 1885–1933 *Ringgold Wilmer Lardner* Am author
**Largo Caballero** Francisco 1869–1946 Span labour leader; prime min (1936–37)
**Larkin** Philip Arthur 1922– Eng poet & nov
**Larousse** Pierre Athanase 1817–1875 Fr grammarian & lexicographer
**Larsson** Gunnar 1951– Swed swimmer
**Larwood** Harold 1904– Eng cricketer
**La Salle, de** Sieur 1643–1687 *René Robert Cavelier* Fr explorer in Am
**Las Casas, de** Bartolomé 1474–1566 Span Dominican missionary & hist
**Lasdun** Sir Denys Louis 1914– Eng architect
**Lasker** Emanuel 1868–1941 Ger chess player & math
**Laski** Harold Joseph 1893–1950 Eng polit scientist
**Laski** Marghanita 1915– Eng nov & critic
**Lastman** Pieter Pieterszoon 1583–1633 Du artist
**Latimer** Hugh 1485?–1555 Eng Protestant martyr
**Latrobe** Benjamin Henry 1764–1820 Am (Eng-born) architect & engineer
**Laud** William 1573–1645 Eng prelate; archbishop of Canterbury (1633–45)
**Lauda** Niki 1949– Austrian racing driver
**Lauder** Sir Harry 1870–1950 né *MacLennan* Scot singer
**Laue, von** Max 1879–1960 Ger physicist
**Laughton** Charles 1899–1962 Am (Eng-born) actor
**Laurel** Stan 1890–1965 né *Arthur Stanley Jefferson* Am (Eng-born) film comedian; "Laurel and Hardy"
**Laurencin** Marie 1885–1956 Fr artist
**Laurier** Sir Wilfrid 1841–1919 Canad statesman
**Lautrec** – see TOULOUSE-LAUTREC
**Laval** Pierre 1883–1945 Fr lawyer & polit

**Laver** Rodney George 1938– Austral tennis player
**Laveran** Charles Louis Alphonse 1845–1922 Fr physiol & bacteriol
**Lavery** Sir John 1856–1941 Eng artist
**Lavoisier** Antoine Laurent 1743–1794 Fr chem
**Law** (Andrew) Bonar 1858–1923 Br (Canad-born) statesman
**Law** Denis 1940– Scot footballer
**Law** John 1671–1729 Scot financier & speculator
**Law** William 1686–1761 Eng devotional writer
**Lawes** Henry 1596–1662 Eng composer
**Lawes** Sir John Bennett 1814–1900 Eng agric
**Lawrence** David Herbert 1885–1930 Eng nov
**Lawrence** Ernest Orlando 1901–1958 Am physicist
**Lawrence** Gertrude 1901–1952 née *Gertrud Alexandra Dagmar Lawrence Klasen* Eng actress
**Lawrence** Sir Thomas 1769–1830 Eng artist
**Lawrence** Thomas Edward 1888–1935 *Lawrence of Arabia* later surname *Shaw* Eng archaeologist, soldier, & author
**Lawrie** Lee 1877–1963 Am sculptor
**Lawton** Thomas 1919– Eng footballer
**Laxness** Halldór Kiljan 1902– Icelandic author
**Layamon** *fl* 1200 Eng poet
**Layard** Sir Austen Henry 1817–1894 Eng archaeologist & diplomat
**Laye** Evelyn 1900– Eng actress & singer
**Leach** Bernard Howell 1887–1979 Eng potter
**Leach** David 1911– *son of prec* Eng potter
**Leach** Johnny 1922– Eng table-tennis player
**Leacock** Stephen Butler 1869–1944 Canad econ & humorist
**Leadbelly** – see Huddie LEDBETTER
**Leakey** Louis Seymour 1903–1972 and wife Mary 1913– Eng palaeontologists
**Lean** David 1908– Eng film producer, director & scriptwriter
**Lear** Edward 1812–1888 Eng artist & nonsense poet
**Leavis** Frank Raymond 1895–1978 Eng literary critic
**Lebrun** Albert 1871–1950 Fr statesman; pres of France (1932–40)
**Lebrun** Mme Vigée – see VIGÉE-LEBRUN
**Le Brun, Lebrun** Charles 1619–1690 Fr artist
**Le Carré** John 1931– pseud of *David John Moore Cornwell* Eng author
**Leconte de Lisle** Charles Marie 1818–1894 orig *Leconte* Fr poet
**Le Corbusier** 1887–1965 pseud of *Charles Édouard Jeanneret* Fr (Swiss-born) architect, artist, & author
**Ledbetter** Huddie 1888–1949 *Leadbelly* Am folk singer
**Lederberg** Joshua 1925– Am geneticist
**Lee** Ann 1736–1784 Eng mystic; founder of Shaker society in US
**Lee** Gypsy Rose 1914–1970 pseud of *Rose Louise Hovick* Am entertainer; alleged orig of "striptease"
**Lee** Laurie 1914– Eng author
**Lee** Robert Edward 1807–1870 Am Confed gen
**Lee** Tsung-Dao 1926– Chin physicist
**Leech** John 1817–1864 Eng caricaturist & illustrator
**Lee Kuan Yew** 1923– prime min of Singapore (1959– )
**Leeuwenhoek, Leuwenhoek, van** Anton 1632–1723 Du naturalist
**Le Fanu** Joseph Sheridan 1814–1873 Irish author
**Lefebvre** François Joseph 1755–1820 Duc *de Dantzig* Fr gen; marshal of France
**Legendre** Adrien Marie 1752–?1833 Fr math
**Léger** Alexis Saint-Léger 1887–1975 pseud *St John Perse* Fr diplomat & poet
**Léger** Fernand 1881–1955 Fr artist
**Lehár** Franz 1870–1948 Hung composer
**Lehmann** Beatrix 1903–1979 Eng actress
**Lehmann** Lotte 1888–1976 Ger soprano
**Leibniz, Leibnitz, von** Baron Gottfried Wilhelm 1646–1716 Ger philos & math
**Leicester** 1st Earl of – see Robert DUDLEY; see also de MONTFORT
**Leif Ericson** – see ERICSON
**Leigh** Vivien 1913–1967 neé *Hartley* Eng actress
**Leigh-Mallory** Sir Trafford Leigh 1892–1944 Eng air marshal
**Leighton** Clare 1899– Eng illustrator, print-maker, & author

**Leighton** Frederick 1830–1896 Baron *Leighton of Stretton* Eng artist
**Leighton** Margaret 1922–1976 Eng actress
**Leinsdorf** Erich 1912– Am (Austrian-born) conductor
**Leland, Leyland** John 1506?–1552 Eng antiquarian
**Lely** Sir Peter 1618–1680 né *Pieter Van der Faes* Du artist in Eng
**Lemaître** Abbé Georges Henri 1894–1966 Belg astrophysicist
**Lemass** Seán Francis 1899–1971 prime min of Ireland (1959–66)
**Lemmon** Jack 1925– Am film actor
**Lemoyne** Pierre – see IBERVILLE
**Lenard** Philipp 1862–1947 Ger physicist
**Lenárt** Jozef 1915– prime min of Czech (1963–68)
**Lenclos** Anne 1620–1705 *Ninon de Lenclos* Fr wit & lady of fashion
**Lenglen** Suzanne 1899–1938 Fr tennis player
**Lenin** V I 1870–1924 *Vladimir Ilyich Ulyanov* Soviet Communist leader
**Lennon** John Ono 1940–1980 Eng pop musician; member of the Beatles
**Leo** name of 13 popes; esp **I** Saint 390?–461 (pope 440–61); **III** Saint 750?–816 (pope 795–816); **XIII** 1810–1903 (pope 1878–1903)
**Leonardo da Vinci** – see Leonardo da VINCI
**Leoncavallo** Ruggiero 1858–1919 Ital composer & librettist
**Leonidas** 5th c B C Greek hero; king of Sparta (490?–480)
**Leopardi** Conte Giacomo 1798–1837 Ital poet
**Leopold I** 1790–1865 king of Belgium (1831–65)
**Leopold I** 1640–1705 king of Hungary (1655–1705) & Holy Rom emp (1658–1705)
**Leopold II** 1835–1909 king of Belgium (1865–1909)
**Leopold II** 1747–1792 Holy Rom emp (1790–92)
**Leopold III** 1901–1983 king of Belgium (1934–51)
**Lepidus** Marcus Aemilius *d* 13 B C Rom triumvir
**Lermontov** Mikhail Yurievich 1814–1841 Russ poet & nov
**Lerner** Alan Jay 1918– Am dram
**Lesage** Alain René 1668–1747 Fr nov & dram
**Leschetizky** Theodor 1830–1915 Pol pianist & composer
**Lesseps, de** Vicomte Ferdinand Marie 1805–1894 Fr diplomat; promoter of Suez Canal
**Lessing** Doris May 1919– Rhodesian nov & dram
**Lessing** Gotthold Ephraim 1729–1781 Ger critic & dram
**Lester** Richard 1932– Am film director
**L'Estrange** Sir Roger 1616–1704 Eng journalist & translator
**Lever** Charles James 1806–1872 Irish nov
**Lévi-Strauss** Claude 1908– Fr (Belg-born) social anthropol
**Lewes** George Henry 1817–1878 Eng philos & critic
**Lewis** Alun 1915–1944 Welsh poet & short story author
**Lewis** Cecil Day – see DAY-LEWIS
**Lewis** Clive Staples 1898–1963 Eng nov & essayist
**Lewis** (Harry) Sinclair 1885–1951 Am nov
**Lewis** Jerry 1926– Am film director & comedian
**Lewis** John Aaron 1920– Am jazz composer & pianist
**Lewis** Matthew Gregory 1775–1818 *Monk Lewis* Eng author
**Lewis** Meriwether 1774–1809 Am explorer
**Lewis** (Percy) Wyndham 1884–1957 Eng artist & author
**Ley** Robert 1890–1945 Ger Nazi leader
**Leyden** John 1775–1811 Scot poet & orientalist
**Libby** Willard Frank 1908–1980 Am chem
**Lichine** David 1910–1972 Soviet ballet dancer & choreographer
**Lichtenstein** Roy 1923– Am artist
**Licinius** 270?–325 *Valerius Licinianus Licinius* Rom emp (308–324)
**Liddell Hart** Sir Basil Henry 1895–1970 Eng military scientist
**Lidman** Sara 1923– Swed nov & dram
**Lie** Jonas 1833–1909 Norw nov & dram
**Lie** Jonas 1880–1940 *nephew of prec* Norw-born artist in Am
**Lie** Trygve Halvdan 1896–1968 Norw lawyer; sec-gen of UN (1946–52)
**Liebig, von** Baron Justus 1801–1873 Ger chem
**Liebknecht** Karl 1871–1919 Ger socialist leader
**Lifar** Serge 1905– Russ dancer
**Lilienthal** Otto 1848–1896 Ger aeronautical engineer
**Lillee** Denis 1949– Austral cricketer
**Lillie** Beatrice 1898– Br (Canad-born) actress & comedienne

**Linacre** Thomas 1460?–1524 Eng humanist & physician
**Lincoln** Abraham 1809–1865 16th pres of the US (1861–65)
**Lind** Jenny 1820–1887 *Johanna Maria; the Swedish Nightingale* Swed soprano
**Lindbergh** Anne Spencer 1906– née *Morrow; wife of next* Am author
**Lindbergh** Charles Augustus 1902–1974 Am aviator
**Lindley** John 1799–1865 Eng botanist – **Lindleyan** *adj*
**Lindrum** Walter 1899–1960 Austral billiards player
**Lindsay** Howard 1889–1968 Am dram & actor
**Lindsay** (Nicholas) Vachel 1879–1931 Am poet
**Lindsay** Norman Alfred William 1879–1969 Austral artist
**Lindwall** Raymond Russell 1921– Austral cricketer
**Linklater** Eric 1899–1974 Br author
**Linlithgow** Marquis of – see HOPE
**Linnaeus** Carolus 1707–1778 *Carl von Linné* Swed botanist – **Linnaean, Linnean** *adj*
**Lin Yutang** 1895–1976 Chin author & philologist
**Lipchitz** Jacques 1891–1973 Am (Latvian-born) sculptor
**Lipmann** Fritz Albert 1899– Am (Ger-born) biochem
**Li Po** *d* 762 A D Chin poet
**Lippi** Fra Filippo *or* Lippo 1406?–1469 Florentine artist
**Lippi** Filippo *or* Filippino 1457?–1504 *son of prec* Florentine artist
**Lippman** Walter 1889–1974 Am journalist & author
**Lippmann** Gabriel 1845–1921 Fr physicist
**Lipton** Sir Thomas Johnstone 1850–1931 Eng merchant & yachtsman
**Lisle, de** – see LECONTE DE LISLE, ROUGET DE LISLE
**Lister** Joseph 1827–1912 1st Baron *Lister of Lyme Regis* Eng surgeon
**Liston** Charles 1932–1971 *Sonny* Am boxer
**Liszt** Franz 1811–1886 Hung pianist & composer – **Lisztian** *adj*
**Littlewood** Joan Maud 1914– Eng theatre director & actress
**Littré** Maximilien Paul Émile 1801–1881 Fr lexicographer
**Liu Shao-ch'i** 1898–1974 Chin Communist
**Livingston** Robert R 1746–1813 Am statesman
**Livingstone** David 1813–1873 Scot explorer in Africa
**Livy** 59 B C–A D 17 *Titus Livius* Rom hist
**Llewellyn** Sir Harry 1911– Welsh show jumper
**Llewellyn** Richard 1907–1983 pseud of *Richard Llewellyn Lloyd* Welsh author
**Lloyd** Clive Hubert 1944– W Indian cricketer
**Lloyd** Harold Clayton 1893–1971 Am film comedian
**Lloyd** Marie 1870–1922 neé *Matilda Wood* Eng music-hall entertainer
**Lloyd George** David 1863–1945 1st Earl of *Dwyfor* Br statesman; prime min (1916–22)
**Lloyd Webber** Andrew 1948– Eng composer
**Loach** Kenneth 1936– Eng film & television director
**Lobachevski** Nikolai Ivanovich 1793–1856 Russ math
**Lobengula** 1833–1894 Zulu king of the Matabele
**Lock** Graham Anthony Richard 1929– *Tony* Eng cricketer
**Locke** Arthur D'Arcy 1917– *Bobby* S African golfer
**Locke** John 1632–1704 Eng philos
**Locke** Matthew 1630?–1677 Eng composer
**Lockhart** John Gibson 1794–1854 Scot nov & biographer
**Lockwood** Margaret Mary 1916– Eng actress
**Lockyer** Sir Joseph Norman 1836–1920 Eng astron
**Lodge** Sir Oliver Joseph 1851–1940 Eng physicist
**Lodge** Thomas 1558–1625 Eng poet & dram
**Loeb** Jacques 1859–1924 Ger-born physiol in Am
**Loewe** Frederick 1901– Am (Austrian-born) composer
**Loewi** Otto 1873–1961 Am (Ger-born) pharmacologist
**Löffler** Friedrich August Johannes 1852–1915 Ger bacteriol
**Lofting** Hugh 1886–1947 Am (Eng-born) author
**Lomax** Alan 1915– *son of next* Am folksinger
**Lomax** John Avery 1872–1948 Am folklorist
**Lombard** Peter 1100?–1160 or 1164 *Petrus Lombardus* Ital theol
**Lombroso** Cesare 1836–1909 Ital physician & psychiatrist
**London** Brian 1931– Eng boxer
**London** John Griffith 1876–1916 *Jack* Am author
**Longfellow** Henry Wadsworth 1807–1882 Am poet
**Longinus** Dionysius Cassius *d* A D 273 Greek philos

**Longley** Charles Thomas 1794–1868 archbishop of Canterbury (1862–68)
**Lönnrot** Elias 1802–1884 Finnish scholar
**Lonsborough** Anita 1941– Eng swimmer
**Lonsdale** Frederick 1881–1954 Eng dram
**López de Segura** Ruy *fl* 1560 Span writer on chess
**Lorca** Federico García – see Federico GARCÍA LORCA
**Loren** Sophia 1934– Ital film actress
**Lorentz** Hendrik Antoon 1853–1928 Du physicist
**Lorenz** Konrad 1903– Austrian ethnologist & author
**Lorrain** Claude 1600–1682 pseud of *Claude Gellée* Fr artist
**Lorre** Peter 1904–1964 né *Laszlo Löwenstein* Hung film actor
**Losey** Joseph 1909–1984 Am film director
**Lothair I** 795?–855 king of Germany (840–43) & Holy Rom emp (840–55)
**Lothair II** (*or* **III**) 1070?–1137 *the Saxon* king of Germany & Holy Rom emp (1125–37)
**Loti** Pierre 1850–1923 pseud of *Louis Marie Julien Viaud* Fr naval officer & nov
**Louis** name of 18 kings of France: esp **I** (*le Débonnaire*) 778–840 (reigned 814–840); **V** (*le Fainéant*) 966?–987 (reigned – last Carolingian – 986–987); **IX** (*Saint*) 1214–1270 (reigned 1226–70); **XI** 1423–1483 (reigned 1461–83); **XII** 1462–1515 (reigned 1498–1515); **XIII** 1601–1643 (reigned 1610-43); **XIV** 1638–1715 (reigned 1643–1715); **XV** 1710–1774 (reigned 1715–74); **XVI** 1754–1793 (reigned 1774–92; guillotined); **XVII** 1785–1795 (nominally reigned 1793–95); **XVIII** 1755–1824 (reigned 1814–15; 1815–24)
**Louis II de Bourbon** – see CONDÉ
**Louis IV** 1287?–1347 *Duke of Bavaria* king of Germany & Holy Rom emp (1314–47)
**Louis** Joe 1914–1981 né *Joseph Louis Barrow* Am boxer
**Louis Napoleon** – see NAPOLEON III
**Louis Philippe** 1773–1850 *the Citizen King* king of the French (1830–48)
**L'Ouverture** – see Pierre Dominique TOUSSAINT L'OUVERTURE
**Lovat** 12th Baron – see Simon FRASER
**Lovelace** Richard 1618–1658 Eng Cavalier poet
**Loveless** George 1797–1874 Eng leader of Tolpuddle martyrs
**Lovell** Sir (Alfred Charles) Bernard 1913– Eng radio astron
**Lovell** James Arthur jr 1928– Am astronaut
**Lover** Samuel 1797–1868 Irish nov
**Low** Sir David Alexander Cecil 1891–1963 NZ cartoonist in Eng
**Lowell** Amy 1874–1925 Am poet & critic
**Lowell** James Russell 1819–1891 Am poet, essayist, & dram
**Lowell** Percival 1855–1916 *bro of Amy* Am astron
**Lowell** Robert Traill Spence 1917–1977 Am poet
**Lowry** (Clarence) Malcolm 1909–1957 Eng nov
**Lowry** Lawrence Stanley 1887–1976 Eng artist
**Loyola** Saint Ignatius of 1491–1556 *Iñigo de Oñez y Loyola* Span soldier & ecclesiastic; founder of the Society of Jesus
**Lu Hsun** 1881–1936 Chin author
**Lubitsch** Ernst 1892–1947 Am film director
**Lübke** Heinrich 1894–1972 W Ger pres (1959–69)
**Lucan** 39–65 *Marcus Annaeus Lucanus* Rom poet
**Luce** Clare 1903– née *Boothe; wife of HR* Am dram, polit, & diplomat
**Luce** Henry Robinson 1898–1967 Am editor & publisher
**Lucretius** 96?–55 B C *Titus Lucretius Carus* Rom poet & philos – **Lucretian** *adj*
**Lucullus** Lucius Licinius *fl* 79?–?57 B C Rom gen & epicure
**Ludendorff** Erich Friedrich Wilhelm 1865–1937 Ger gen
**Lully** Jean Baptiste 1632–1687 Fr (Ital-born) composer
**Lumet** Sidney 1924– Am film director
**Lunt** Alfred 1893–1977 Am actor
**Luther** Martin 1483–1546 Ger Reformation leader
**Luthuli** Albert John 1898–1967 S African reformer
**Lutyens** (Agnes) Elisabeth 1906– Eng composer
**Lutyens** Sir Edwin Landseer 1869–1944 Eng architect
**Luxemburg** Rosa 1870–1919 Ger (Pol-born) socialist leader
**Lycurgus** 9th C B C Spartan lawgiver
**Lydgate** John 1370?–?1451 Eng poet
**Lyell** Sir Charles 1797–1875 Eng geologist
**Lyly** John 1554?–1606 Eng author
**Lympany** Moura 1916– Eng pianist

**Lynch** Benny 1913–1946 Scot boxer
**Lynch** John Mary 1917–          *Jack* prime min of Ireland (1966–73, 1977–79)
**Lyndsay** Sir David 1486?–1555 Scot poet
**Lynn** Dame Vera 1917–          Eng singer
**Lyons** Joseph Aloysius 1879–1939 Austral statesman; prime min (1932–39)
**Lysander** *d* 395 B C Spartan commander
**Lysenko** Trofim Denisovich 1898–1976 Soviet scientist
**Lysias** 450?–?380 B C Athenian orator
**Lysippus** 4th c B C Greek sculptor
**Lytton** 1st Baron 1803–1873 *Edward George Earle Lytton Bulwer-Lytton; bro of Sir Henry Bulwer* Eng author
**Lytton** 1st Earl of 1831–1891 *Edward Robert Bulwer-Lytton*; pseud *Owen Meredith; son of prec* Eng statesman & poet
**Lytton** 2nd Earl of 1876–1947 *Victor Alexander George Robert Lytton; son of 1st Earl* Eng administrator & author

# M

**Mac-** – see also MC-
**MacArthur** Douglas 1880–1964 Am gen
**MacArthur** John 1767–1834 Austral (Eng-born) pioneer of wool industry
**Macaulay** Dame Rose 1881–1958 Eng nov
**Macaulay** 1st Baron 1800–1859 *Thomas Babington Macaulay* Eng hist, author, & statesman
**Macbeth** *d* 1057 king of Scotland (1040–57)
**MacBeth** George Mann 1932–          Scot poet
**MacDiarmid** Hugh 1892–1978 pseud of *Christopher Murray Grieve* Scot poet
**Macdonald** Flora 1722–1790 Scot heroine
**Macdonald** George 1824–1905 Scot nov & poet
**Macdonald** (James) Ramsay 1866–1937 Br statesman; prime min (1924; 1929–35)
**Macdonald** Sir John Alexander 1815–1891 Canad statesman; 1st prime min of Dominion of Canada (1867–73) and again (1878–91)
**Macdonald** Ross 1915–1983 pseud of *Kenneth Millar* Am author
**MacDowell** Edward Alexander 1861–1908 Am composer
**Mach** Ernst 1838–1916 Austrian physicist & philos
**Machen** Arthur Llewellyn 1863–1947 Welsh author
**Machiavelli** Niccolò 1469–1527 Ital statesman & polit philos
**Mackay** David 1935–          Scot footballer
**Mackenzie** Alexander 1822–1892 Canad (Scot-born) statesman; prime min (1873–78)
**Mackenzie** Sir Alexander Campbell 1847–1935 Eng composer & conductor
**Mackenzie** Sir (Edward Montague) Compton 1883–1972 Eng author
**Mackerras** Sir Alan Charles 1925–          Austral conductor
**Mackintosh** Charles 1766–1843 Scot chem & inventor
**Mackintosh** Charles Rennie 1868–1928 Scot architect, artist, & designer
**Mackmurdo** Arthur 1851–1942 Eng architect & pioneer of arts & crafts movement
**MacLennan** Hugh 1907–          Canad nov
**Macleod** John James Rickard 1876–1935 Scot physiol
**MacMahon, Macmahon, de** Comte Marie Patrice Maurice 1808–1893 marshal (1859) & pres (1873–79) of France
**MacMillan** Donald Baxter 1874–1970 Am arctic explorer
**MacMillan** Kenneth 1929–          Eng dancer & choreographer
**MacMillan** (Maurice) Harold 1894–          Earl of *Stockton* Eng statesman; prime min (1957–63)
**MacNeice** Louis 1907–1963 Br (Irish-born) poet
**Maconchy** Elizabeth 1907–          Eng composer
**Macpherson** James 1736–1796 Scot author
**Macready** William Charles 1793–1873 Eng actor
**Madison** James 1751–1836 4th pres of the US (1809–17) – **Madisonian** *adj*
**Maes, Maas** Nicolaes 1632–1693 Du artist

**Maeterlinck** Count Maurice 1862–1949 Belg poet, dram, & essayist – **Maeterlinckian** *adj*
**Magellan** Ferdinand 1480?–1521 *Fernão de Magalhães* Port navigator
**Maginot** André 1877–1932 Fr polit
**Magritte** René 1898–1967 Belg artist
**Mahler** Gustav 1860–1911 Austrian composer
**Mahomet, Mahomed** – see MUHAMMAD
**Mailer** Norman 1923–          Am author
**Mailey** Arthur 1888–1967 Austral cricketer
**Maillol** Aristide 1861–1944 Fr sculptor
**Maimonides** 1135–1204 Rabbi *Moses ben Maimon* Span-born philos
**Maintenon, de** Marquise 1635–1719 *Françoise d'Aubigné; consort of Louis XIV*
**Makarios III** Archbishop 1913–1977 pres of Cyprus (1960–77)
**Mäkinen** Timo 1938–          Finnish rally driver & speedboat racer
**Malamud** Bernard 1914–          Am author
**Malan** Daniel François 1874–1959 S African editor; prime min (1948–54)
**Malcolm X** 1925–1965 *Malcolm Little* Am civil-rights leader
**Malenkov** Georgi Maximilianovich 1902–          Soviet polit; premier (1953–55)
**Malherbe, de** François 1555–1628 Fr poet
**Malinovsky** Rodion Yakovlevich 1898–1967 Soviet gen
**Malinowski** Bronislaw Kasper 1884–1942 Pol-born anthropologist
**Mallarmé** Stéphane 1842–1898 Fr poet
**Mallory** George Herbert Leigh 1886–1924 Eng mountaineer
**Mallowan** Sir Max Edgar Lucien 1904–1978 Eng archaeologist
**Malory** Sir Thomas *fl* 1470 Eng author
**Malpighi** Marcello 1628–1694 Ital anatomist
**Malraux** André 1901–1976 Fr author & polit
**Malthus** Thomas Robert 1766–1834 Eng econ
**Mandel** Georges 1885–1943 né *Jéroboam Rothschild* Fr polit
**Mandeville** Sir John *d* 1372 pseud of an unidentified author of travel books
**Manet** Édouard 1832–1883 Fr artist
**Mankowitz** Wolf 1924–          Eng author & dram
**Manley** Michael Norman 1924–          *son of next* prime min of Jamaica (1972–80)
**Manley** Norman Washington 1893–1969 prime min of Jamaica (1959–62)
**Mann** Thomas 1875–1955 Ger author
**Mannerheim, von** Baron Carl Gustaf Emil 1867–1951 Finn gen & statesman
**Manning** Edward 1808–1892 Eng cardinal
**Mansfield** Katherine 1888–1923 pseud of *Kathleen Murry* née *Beauchamp* Br (NZ-born) writer
**Manson** Sir Patrick 1844–1922 Br parasitologist
**Mantegna** Andrea 1431–1506 Ital artist & engraver
**Manuel** Don Juan – see JUAN MANUEL
**Manutius** Aldus 1450–1515 *Teobaldo Mannucci* or *Manuzio* Ital printer & classical scholar
**Manzoni** Alessandro Francesco Tommaso Antonio 1785–1873 Ital nov & poet
**Mao Tse-tung, Mao Zedong** 1893–1976 Chin Communist; leader of People's Republic of China (1949–76)
**Marat** Jean Paul 1743–1793 Fr (Swiss-born) revolutionist
**Marble** Alice 1913–          Am tennis player
**Marceau** Marcel 1923–          Fr mime
**Marcellus** Marcus Claudius 268?–208 B C Rom gen
**March** 1st Earl of – see Roger de MORTIMER
**Marciano** Rocky 1923–1969 né *Rocco Francis Marchegiano* Am boxer
**Marconi** Marchese Guglielmo 1874–1937 Ital electrical engineer & inventor
**Marco Polo** – see POLO
**Marcos** Ferdinand Edralin 1917– pres of the Philippine Republic (1965–          )
**Marcus Aurelius** – see Marcus Aurelius ANTONINUS
**Marcuse** Herbert 1898–1979 Am (Ger-born) philos
**Margaret of Anjou** 1430–1482 *queen of Henry VI of England*
**Margaret of Navarre** 1492–1549 queen of Navarre (1544–49) & writer

**Margaret Rose** 1930– *ex-wife of Earl of Snowdon* princess of GB
**Margrethe II** 1940– queen of Denmark (1972– )
**Maria Theresa** 1717–1780 *wife of Emp Francis I* queen of Hungary & Bohemia
**Marie** 1875–1938 queen of Rumania (1914–27); dowager queen (1927–38)
**Marie Antoinette** 1755–1793 *dau of Maria Theresa & wife of Louis XVI of France*
**Marie de Medicis** 1573–1642 *2nd wife of Henry IV of France*
**Marie Louise** 1791–1847 *dau of Francis I of Austria & 2nd wife of Napoleon I*
**Marin** John Cheri 1872–1953 Am artist
**Marinetti** Emilio Filippo Tommaso 1876–1944 Ital poet
**Marius** Gaius 155?–86 B C Rom gen
**Mark Antony** or **Anthony** – see Marcus ANTONIUS
**Markova** Dame Alicia 1910– *Lilian Alicia Marks* Eng dancer
**Marlborough** 1st Duke of – see John CHURCHILL
**Marlowe** Christopher 1564–1593 Eng dram – **Marlovian** *adj*
**Marmont, de** Auguste Frédéric Louis Viesse 1774–1852 Duc *de Raguse* Fr gen; marshal of France
**Marot** Clément 1495?–1544 Fr poet
**Marquand** John Phillips 1893–1960 Am author
**Marquette** Jacques 1637–1675 *Père Marquette* Fr Jesuit missionary & explorer in Am
**Marquis** Donald Robert Perry 1878–1937 *Don* Am humorist
**Marquis** Frederick James – see WOOLTON
**Marryat** Frederick 1792–1848 Eng naval commander & nov
**Marsh** Dame (Edith) Ngaio 1899–1982 NZ author
**Marshall** George Catlett 1880–1959 Am gen & diplomat
**Marshall** John 1755–1835 Am judge; chief justice US Supreme Court (1801–35)
**Marshall** John Ross 1912– prime min of NZ (1972)
**Martel** Charles – see CHARLES MARTEL
**Martial** *ab* 40–*ab* 102 *Marcus Valerius Martialis* Rom epigrammatist
**Martin** Saint 315?–?399 *Martin of Tours* patron saint of France
**Martin** Archer John Porter 1910– Eng chem
**Martin** Louis George 1937– Eng (Jamaica-born) weight lifter
**Martin du Gard** Roger 1881–1958 Fr nov
**Martineau** Harriet 1802–1876 Eng nov & econ
**Martinet** Jean *d* 1672 Fr soldier
**Martini** Simone 1283?–1344 Ital artist
**Marvell** Andrew 1621–1678 Eng poet & satirist
**Marx** Karl Heinrich 1818–1883 Ger polit philos & socialist
**Marx Brothers** Am actors; Leonard 1891–1961 *Chico*; Arthur 1893–1964 *Harpo*; Julius 1895–1977 *Groucho*; Milton 1894–1977 *Gummo*; Herbert 1901–1979 *Zeppo*
**Mary** 1867–1953 Princess *Victoria Mary of Teck; queen consort of George V of Br*
**Mary I** 1516–1558 *Mary Tudor; Bloody Mary* queen of Eng (1553–58)
**Mary II** 1661–1694 joint Br sovereign with William III
**Mary Stuart** 1542–1587 *Mary, Queen of Scots* queen of Scot (1542–67)
**Masaccio** 1401–1428 né *Tommaso Guidi* Ital artist
**Masaryk** Jan Garrigue 1886–1948 *son of T G* Czech diplomat & polit
**Masaryk** Tomáš Garrigue 1850–1937 Czech philos; 1st pres of Czechoslovakia (1918–35)
**Mascagni** Pietro 1863–1945 Ital composer
**Masefield** John 1878–1967 Eng author; poet laureate (1930–67)
**Mason** Charles 1730–1787 Eng astron & surveyor
**Mason** James 1909– Eng film actor
**Massenet** Jules Émile Frédéric 1842–1912 Fr composer
**Massey** Raymond 1896–1983 Am (Canad-born) actor
**Massey** William Ferguson 1856–1925 NZ statesman; prime min (1912–1925)
**Massine** Léonide 1896–1979 Am (Russ–born) dancer & choreographer
**Massinger** Philip 1583–1640 Eng dram
**Masters** Edgar Lee 1869–1950 Am author
**Masters** John 1914–1983 Eng author

**Mata Hari** 1876–1917 pseud of *Margaretha Geertruida Zelle* Du courtesan & double agent
**Mathias** Robert Bruce 1930– Am athlete & polit
**Mathieson** Muir 1911–1975 Scot conductor & composer
**Matisse** Henri 1869–1954 Fr artist
**Matthes** Roland 1950– E Ger swimmer
**Matthews** Denis 1919– Eng pianist
**Matthews** Sir Stanley 1915– Eng footballer
**Maufe** Sir Edward 1883–1974 Eng architect
**Mauger** Ivan 1940– NZ speedway rider
**Maugham** (William) Somerset 1874–1965 Eng nov & dram
**Maupassant, de** (Henri René Albert) Guy 1850–1893 Fr short-story author
**Mauriac** François 1885–1970 Fr author
**Maurice of Nassau** 1567–1625 Prince of *Orange* Du gen & statesman
**Maurois** André 1885–1967 pseud of *Émile Salomon Wilhelm Herzog* Fr author
**Maury** Matthew Fontaine 1806–1873 Am naval official & oceanographer
**Mauser** Peter Paul 1838–1914 & his bro Wilhelm 1834–1882 Ger inventors
**Mawson** Sir Douglas 1882–1958 Eng antarctic explorer & geologist
**Maxim** Sir Hiram Stevens 1840–1916 Br (Am–born) inventor
**Maxim** Hudson 1853–1927 *bro of Hiram* Am inventor & explosives expert
**Maximilian** 1832–1867 *bro of Francis Joseph I of Austria* emp of Mexico (1864–67)
**Maximilian I** 1459–1519 Holy Rom emp (1493–1519)
**Maximilian II** 1527–1576 Holy Rom emp (1564–76)
**Maxwell** James Clerk 1831–1879 Scot physicist
**May** Peter Barker Howard 1929– Eng cricketer
**May** Sir Thomas Erskine 1815–1886 1st Baron *Farnborough* Eng constitutional jurist
**Mayakovski** Vladimir Vladimirovich 1893–1930 Russ poet
**Mayo** Robert Hobart 1890–1957 Eng aircraft designer
**Mazarin** Jules 1602–1661 Fr cardinal & statesman
**Mazzini** Giuseppe 1805–1872 Ital patriot
**Mboya** Thomas Joseph 1930–1969 Kenyan polit
**Mc-** – see also MAC-
**McAdam** John Loudon 1756–1836 Scot engineer; invented macadam road surface
**McBain** Ed – see Evan HUNTER
**McBride** Séan 1904– Irish polit
**McBride** William John 1940– *Willie John* Irish rugby union player
**McCabe** Stanley Joseph 1910–1968 Austral cricketer
**McCarthy** Joseph Raymond 1908–1957 Am polit
**McCarthy** Mary Therese 1912– Am author
**McCartney** Paul 1942– Eng pop musician; member of the Beatles
**McClure** Sir Robert John le Mesurier 1807–1873 Eng arctic explorer
**McCormack** John 1884–1945 Am (Irish-born) tenor
**McCracken** William 1883–1979 Irish footballer
**McCrae** Hugh Raymond 1876–1958 Austral author
**McCullers** Carson 1917–1967 née *Smith* Am author
**McEnroe** John Patrick 1959– Am tennis player
**McGonagall** William 1830–1902 Scot doggerel author
**McGregor** Robert Bilsland 1944– *Bobby* Scot swimmer
**McGrory** James Edward 1904– *Jimmy* Scot footballer
**McIndoe** Sir Archibald Hector 1900–1960 NZ plastic surgeon
**McKay** Heather Pamela 1941– Austral squash rackets player
**McKenna** Siobhán 1923– Irish actress
**McKenzie** Sir Alexander 1755–1850 Canad (Scot-born) fur trader & explorer
**McKenzie** Stuart 1937– Austral oarsman
**McKie** Sir William Neil 1901– Austral organist
**McKinley** Charles 1941– *Chuck* Am tennis player
**McKinley** William 1843–1901 25th pres of the US (1897–1901)
**McLaren** Bruce 1937–1970 NZ racing driver
**McLauchlan** Ian 1942– *Mighty Mouse* Scot rugby union player
**McLuhan** (Herbert) Marshall 1911–1980 Canad educ

**McMahon** William 1908–   prime min of Austral (1971–72)
**McPherson** Aimee Semple 1890–1944 Am evangelist
**Mead** Margaret 1901–1978 Am anthropol
**Meade** Richard John Hannay 1938–   Eng horse trials rider
**Meads** Colin Earl 1935–   NZ rugby union player
**Medawar** Sir Peter Brian 1915–   Eng anatomist
**Medici, de** Catherine – see CATHERINE DE MEDICIS
**Medici, dé'** Cosimo *or* Cosmo 1389–1464 Florentine financier & polit
**Medici, dé'** Cosimo I 1519–1574 *Cosimo the Great*; Duke of *Florence*; Grand Duke of *Tuscany*
**Medici, dé'** Giulio – see CLEMENT VII
**Medici, dé'** Lorenzo 1449–1492 *Lorenzo the Magnificent* Florentine statesman, ruler, & patron
**Medina-Sidonia** 7th Duke of 1550–1615 *Alonso Pérez de Guzmán* Span admiral
**Meegeren, van** Hans 1889–1947 Du artist & forger
**Meer van Delft, van der** – see Jan VERMEER
**Mehemet Ali, Mohammed Ali** 1769–1849 viceroy of Egypt (1805–48)
**Meighen** Arthur 1874–1960 Canad statesman; prime min (1920–21; 1926)
**Meir** Golda 1898–1978 *Goldie Mabovitz* or *Mabovich* Russ-born prime min of Israel (1969–1974)
**Meissonier** (Jean Louis) Ernest 1815–1891 Fr artist
**Meitner** Lise 1878–1968 Ger physicist
**Melanchthon** 1497–1560 *Philipp Schwarzert* Ger scholar & religious reformer
**Melba** Dame Nellie 1861–1931 née *Helen Porter Mitchell* Austral soprano
**Melchior** Lauritz Lebrecht Hommel 1890–1973 Am (Danish-born) tenor
**Melville** Herman 1819–1891 Am nov
**Memling, Memlinc** Hans 1430?–1495 Flem artist
**Menander** 343?–?291 B C Greek dram
**Mencius** 372?–?289 B C *Mêng-tzŭ* or *Meng-tse* Chin philos
**Mendel** Gregor Johann 1822–1884 Austrian botanist
**Mendeleev, Mendeleyev** Dmitri Ivanovich 1834–1907 Russ chem
**Mendelssohn** Moses 1729–1786 Ger philos
**Mendelssohn-Bartholdy** (Jakob Ludwig) Felix 1809–1847 *grandson of Moses Mendelssohn* Ger composer, pianist, & conductor
**Mendès-France** Pierre 1907–1982 Fr statesman
**Mendoza, de** Antonio 1485?–1552 Span colonial administrator
**Menelik II** 1844–1913 emp of Ethiopia (1889–1913)
**Menes** *fl* 3400 (3500?) B C Egyptian king; uniter of north & south kingdoms
**Menotti** Gian-Carlo 1911–   Am (Ital-born) composer
**Menuhin** Yehudi 1916–   Am violinist
**Menzies** Sir Robert Gordon 1894–1978 Austral statesman; prime min (1939–41; 1949–66)
**Mercador** Ramon 1914–1978 Span assassinator of Leo Trotsky
**Mercator** Gerhardus 1512–1594 *Gerhard Kremer* Flem geographer
**Mercer** David 1928–   Eng dram
**Mercer** Joe 1915–   Eng footballer
**Mercer** Johnny 1909–1976 Am singer & songwriter
**Merckx** Eddy 1945–   Belg racing cyclist
**Meredith** George 1828–1909 Eng nov & poet
**Meredith** Owen – see E R Bulwer LYTTON
**Meredith** William 1874–1958 Welsh footballer
**Mergenthaler** Ottmar 1854–1899 Am (Ger-born) inventor
**Mérimée** Prosper 1803–1870 Fr author
**Merman** Ethel 1909–   Am singer & actress
**Merton** Thomas 1915–1968 Am clergyman & author
**Mesmer** Franz *or* Friedrich Anton 1734–1815 Austrian physician
**Messalina** Valeria *d* A D 48 *3rd wife of Emp Claudius*
**Messel** Oliver Hilary Sambourne 1904–1978 Eng stage designer
**Messenger** Herbert Henky 1883–1964 *Dally; The Master* Austral rugby league player
**Messerschmitt** Willy 1898–1978 Ger aircraft designer & manuf
**Messier** Charles 1730–1817 Fr astron
**Meštrović** Ivan 1883–1962 Am (Yugoslavian-born) sculptor

**Metalious** Grace 1924–1964 Am nov
**Metaxas** Ioannis 1871–1941 Greek gen & dictator
**Metchnikoff** Elie 1845–1916 Russ zool & bacteriol
**Metternich** Prince Klemens Wenzel Nepomuk Lothar 1773–1859 Austrian statesman
**Meyer** Deborah 1952–   Am swimmer
**Meyerbeer** Giacomo 1791–1864 né *Jakob Liebmann Beer* Ger composer
**Meyerhof** Otto 1884–1951 Ger physiol
**Michael** *Rumanian* Mihai 1921–   *Michael Hohenzollern* king of Rumania (1927–30; 1940–47); abdicated
**Michelangelo Buonarroti** 1475–1564 Ital sculptor, artist, architect, & poet – **Michelangelesque** *adj*
**Michelson** Albert Abraham 1852–1931 Am (Ger-born) physicist
**Mickiewicz** Adam 1798–1855 Pol poet
**Middleton** Thomas 1570–1627 Eng dram
**Mies van der Rohe** Ludwig 1886–1969 Am (Ger-born) architect
**Mihajlović, Mikhailovitch** Draža *or* Draja 1893?–1946 Yugoslav gen
**Mikoyan** Anastas Ivanovich 1895–1978 Soviet polit; pres of USSR (1964–65)
**Miles** Sir Bernard 1907–   Eng actor-manager & director
**Milhaud** Darius 1892–1974 Fr composer
**Mill** James 1773–1836 Scot philos, hist, & econ
**Mill** John Stuart 1806–1873 *son of James* Eng philos & econ
**Millais** Sir John Everett 1829–1896 Eng artist
**Millay** Edna St Vincent 1892–1950 Am poet
**Miller** Arthur 1915–   Am dram & nov
**Miller** Henry 1891–1980 Am author
**Miller** Hugh 1802–1856 Scot geologist & author
**Miller** Johnny Lawrence 1947–   Am golfer
**Miller** Keith Ross 1919–   Austral cricketer
**Millet** Jean François 1814–1875 Fr artist
**Milligan** Terence Alan 1918–   *Spike* Eng comedian & author
**Millikan** Robert Andrews 1868–1953 Am physicist
**Millin** Sarah Gertrude 1889–1968 S African nov
**Mills** Frederick 1919–1965 Eng boxer
**Mills** Sir John 1908–   Eng actor
**Milne** Alan Alexander 1882–1956 Eng poet & dram
**Miltiades** 540?–?489 B C Athenian gen
**Milton** John 1608–1674 Eng poet – **Miltonian, Miltonic** *adj*
**Mindszenty** Jozsef 1892–1975 Hung cardinal
**Minnelli** Liza 1946–   *daughter of next* Am singer & actress
**Minnelli** Vincente 1913–   Am film director & producer
**Mintoff** Dominic 1916–   prime min of Malta (1971–   )
**Minton** Thomas 1765–1836 Eng pottery manuf
**Mirabeau, de** Comte 1749–1791 *Honoré Gabriel Victor Riqueti* Fr orator & revolutionist
**Miró** Joan 1893–1983 Span artist
**Mishima** Yukio 1925–1970 Jap author
**Mistral** Frédéric 1830–1914 Provençal poet
**Mistral** Gabriela 1889-1957 *Lucila Godoy de Alcayaga* Chilean poet & educ
**Mitchell** Margaret 1900–1949 Am nov
**Mitchell** Maria 1818–1889 Am astron
**Mitchell** Reginald Joseph 1895–1937 Eng aircraft designer
**Mitchell** Sir Thomas Livingstone 1792–1855 Austral (Scot-born) explorer
**Mitchum** Robert 1917–   Am film actor
**Mitford** Jessica 1917–   *sister of Nancy* Eng author
**Mitford** Mary Russell 1787–1855 Eng nov & dram
**Mitford** Nancy 1904–1973 *sister of Jessica* Eng author
**Mithridates VI** *ab* 132–63 B C *the Great* king of Pontus (120–63)
**Mitterrand** François Maurice 1916–   pres of France (1981–)
**Mix** Tom 1880–1940 Am actor-director of silent films
**Mobutu** Sese Seko 1930–   né *Joseph-Désiré Mobutu* pres of Zaire (1976–   )
**Moctezuma** – see MONTEZUMA
**Modigliani** Amedeo 1884–1920 Ital artist in France
**Mohammad Reza Pahlavi, Pahlevi** 1919–1980 shah of Iran (1941–79)
**Mohammed** – see MUHAMMAD

**Moissan** (Ferdinand Fréderic) Henri 1852–1907 Fr chem
**Molière** 1622–1673 pseud of *Jean Baptiste Poquelin* Fr actor & dram
**Molina, de** Tirso – see TIRSO DE MOLINA
**Molnár** Ferenc 1878–1952 Hung author
**Molotov** Vyacheslav Mikhailovich 1890– orig *Skryabin* Soviet statesman
**Moltke, von** Count Helmuth 1800–1891 Pruss field marshal
**Mommsen** Theodor 1817–1903 Ger classical scholar & hist
**Monck , Monk** George 1608–1670 1st Duke of *Albemarle* Eng gen
**Mondale** Walter Frederick 1928– Am polit; vice-pres of the US (1977–81)
**Mondrian** Piet 1872–1944 *Pieter Cornelis Mondriaan* Du artist
**Monet** Claude 1840–1926 Fr artist
**Monet** Jean 1888–1979 Fr polit
**Moneta** Ernesto Teodoro 1833–1918 Ital journalist & pacifist
**Moniz** António Caetano de Abreu Freire Egas 1874–1955 Port medical scientist
**Monmouth** Duke of 1649–1685 *James Scott, son of Charles II of Eng* Eng rebel & claimant to the throne
**Monroe** James 1758–1831 5th pres of US (1817–25)
**Monroe** Marilyn 1926–1962 neé *Norma Jean Baker* Am film actress
**Monsarrat** Nicholas John Turney 1910–1979 Eng author
**Montagna** Bartolommeo 1450?–1523 Ital artist
**Montagu** Lady Mary Wortley 1689–1762 Eng letter writer
**Montaigne, de** Michel Eyquem 1533–1592 Fr essayist
**Montale** Eugenio 1896–1981 Ital poet
**Montand** Yves 1921– Fr (Ital-born) film actor
**Montcalm de Saint-Véran, de** Marquis Louis Joseph 1712–1759 Fr field marshal in Canada
**Montespan, de** Marquise 1641–1707 née (*Françoise Athénaïs*) *Rochechouart* mistress of Louis XIV
**Montesquieu, de** Baron *de La Brède et* 1689–1755 *Charles de Secondat* Fr lawyer & polit philos
**Montessori** Maria 1870–1952 Ital physician & educ
**Monteux** Pierre 1875–1964 Am (Fr-born) conductor
**Monteverdi** Claudio Giovanni Antonio 1567–1643 Ital composer
**Montezuma II, Moctezuma** 1480?–1520 last Aztec emp of Mexico (1502–20)
**Montfort, de** Simon 1208?–1265 Earl of *Leicester* Eng soldier & statesman
**Montgolfier** Joseph Michel 1740–1810 & his bro Jacques Étienne 1745–1799 Fr inventors & aviators
**Montgomery** Bernard Law 1887–1976 1st Viscount *Montgomery of Alamein* Br field marshal
**Montgomery** (Robert) Bruce 1921–1978 Eng composer & (as *Edmund Crispin*) detective-story author
**Montmorency, de** Duc Anne 1493–1567 Fr soldier; constable (1537)
**Montrose** 1st Marquis of 1612–1650 *James Graham* Scot Royalist
**Moody** Helen Wills 1905– Am tennis player
**Moon** Sun Myung 1920– Korean industrialist & religious leader
**Moore** Ann 1950– Eng show jumper
**Moore** Archie 1913– Am boxer
**Moore** Brian 1921– Canad (Irish-born) nov
**Moore** George 1852–1933 Irish author
**Moore** George Edward 1873–1958 Eng philos
**Moore** Gerald 1899– Eng pianist
**Moore** Henry 1898– Eng sculptor
**Moore** Marianne Craig 1887–1972 Am poet
**Moore** Patrick 1923– Eng astron, author, & broadcaster
**Moore** Robert Frederick 1941– *Bobby* Eng footballer
**Moore** Ronnie 1933– NZ speedway rider
**Moore** Stanford 1913–1982 Am biochem
**Moore** Thomas 1779–1852 Irish poet
**Moore-Brabazon** John Theodore Cuthbert 1884–1964 1st Baron *Brabazon of Tara* Eng aviator & administrator
**Moorehead** Alan McCrae 1910–1983 Eng author
**Moravia** Alberto 1907– pseud of *Alberto Pincherle* Ital author

**More** Hannah 1745–1833 Eng author of religious works
**More** Sir Thomas 1478–1535 *Saint* Eng statesman & author
**Moreau** Jean Victor 1763–1813 Fr gen
**Morgan** Clifford Isaac 1930– Welsh rugby union player
**Morgan** Sir Henry 1635?–1688 Eng buccaneer
**Morgan** Thomas Hunt 1866–1945 Am zool
**Morison** Elsie 1924– Austral soprano
**Morison** Stanley 1889–1968 Eng type designer
**Morisot** Berthe 1841–1895 Fr artist
**Morley** John 1838–1923 Viscount *Morley of Blackburn* Eng statesman & author
**Morley** Robert 1908– Eng actor & dram
**Morphy** Paul Charles 1837–1884 Am chess player
**Morris** William 1834–1896 Eng poet, artist, & socialist
**Morrison** Herbert Stanley 1888–1965 Baron *Morrison of Lambeth* Eng polit
**Morse** Samuel Finley Breese 1791–1872 Am artist & inventor
**Mortimer** John Clifford 1923– Eng dram, nov, & lawyer
**Mortimer, de** Roger (IV) 1287–1330 1st Earl of *March* Welsh rebel & paramour of Isabella, Queen of Edward II of Eng
**Morton** Jelly Roll 1885–1941 né *Ferdinand Joseph La Menthe Morton* Am jazz pianist, bandleader & composer
**Moscicki** Ignacy 1867–1946 Pol chem; pres of Poland (1926–39)
**Moses** Anna Mary née *Robertson* 1860–1961 *Grandma Moses* Am artist
**Mosley** Sir Oswald Ernald 1896–1980 Eng polit
**Moss** Stirling 1929– Eng racing driver
**Motherwell** Robert 1915– Am artist
**Mott** Sir Nevill Francis 1905– Eng scientist
**Mould** Marion 1947– neé *Coates* Eng show jumper
**Moulton** Forest Ray 1872–1952 Am astron
**Mountbatten** Louis, Earl 1900–1979 Prince *Louis of Battenberg* Eng admiral; 1st gov-gen of India (1947–48); chief of defence staff (1959–65)
**Mountbatten** Philip, Duke of Edinburgh – see PHILIP
**Mozart** Wolfgang Amadeus 1756–1791 Austrian composer – **Mozartean** *also* **Mozartian** *adj*
**Mubarak** Muhammad Hosni 1929– pres of Egypt (1981– )
**Mugabe** Robert Gabriel 1924– prime min of Zimbabwe (1980– )
**Muhammad** 570–632 Arab prophet & founder of Islam
**Muhammad** Elijah 1897–1975 né *E Poole* Am religious leader
**Muir** John 1838–1914 Am (Scot-born) naturalist
**Muir** Karen Yvette 1952– S African swimmer
**Muldoon** Robert David 1921– prime min of NZ (1975– )
**Muller** Gerhardt 1945– W Ger footballer
**Muller** Hermann Joseph 1890–1967 Am geneticist
**Müller** (Friedrich) Max 1823–1900 Br (Ger-born) philologist
**Müller** Johann 1436–1476 *Regiomontanus* Ger astron
**Müller** Paul Hermann 1899–1965 Swiss chem
**Mumford** Lewis 1895– Am author
**Munch** Charles 1891–1968 Fr-born conductor
**Munch** Edvard 1863–1944 Norw artist
**Münchhausen, von** Baron Karl Friedrich Hieronymus 1720–1797 Baron *Munchausen* Ger hunter, soldier, & supposed teller of absurdly exaggerated stories
**Munnings** Sir Alfred James 1878–1959 Eng artist
**Munro** H H – see SAKI
**Munthe** Axel Martin Fredrik 1857–1949 Swed author & psychiatrist
**Murasaki** Baroness 11th c *Murasaki Shikibu* Jap nov
**Murat** Joachim 1767?–1815 Fr gen; marshal of France; king of Naples (1808–15)
**Murchison** Sir Roderick Ampey 1792–1871 Scot geologist
**Murdoch** (Jean) Iris 1919– Br (Irish-born) author
**Murdoch** (Keith) Rupert 1931– Austral newspaper publisher
**Murillo** Bartolomé Esteban 1617–1682 Span artist
**Murless** Sir (Charles Francis) Noel 1910– Eng race-horse trainer
**Murphy** Alexander John 1939– Eng rugby league player
**Murray** (George) Gilbert (Aimé) 1866–1957 Br classical scholar
**Murray** Sir James Augustus Henry 1837–1915 Scot lexicographer

**Murray** Lionel 1922– *Len* Eng trade-union leader; sec of Trades Union Congress (1973–1984)
**Murrow** Edward Roscoe 1908–1965 Am news commentator
**Mushtaq** Mohammed 1943– Pakistan cricketer
**Musil** Robert 1880–1942 Austrian nov
**Musset, de** (Louis Charles) Alfred 1810–1857 Fr poet
**Mussolini** Benito 1883–1945 *Il Duce* Ital Fascist premier (1922–45)
**Mussorgsky, Moussorgsky** Modest Petrovich 1835–1881 Russ composer
**Mustafa** (*or* **Mustapha**) **Kemal Pasha** – see KEMAL ATATÜRK
**Myers** Leopold Hamilton 1881–1944 Eng nov
**Myron** 5th c B C Greek sculptor

# N

**Naber** John 1956– Am swimmer
**Nabokov** Vladimir Vladimirovich 1899–1977 Am (Russ-born) nov
**Nader** Ralph 1934– Am lawyer & author
**Nagy** Imre 1896–1958 Hung statesman; prime min (1953–55; 1956)
**Naidu** Sarojini 1879–1949 Hindu poet & reformer
**Naipaul** Vidiadhar Surajprasad 1932– W Indian author
**Naismith** James 1861–1939 Am sportsman; orig of basketball
**Namby-Pamby** – see Ambrose PHILIPS
**Namier** Sir Lewis Bernstein 1888–1960 Br hist
**Nanak** 1469–1538 founder of the Sikh faith in India
**Nansen** Fridtjof 1861–1930 Norw arctic explorer, zool, & statesman
**Napier** Sir Charles James 1782–1853 Eng gen
**Napier** John 1550–1617 Laird of *Merchiston* Scot math
**Napier** Robert Cornelis 1810–1880 1st Baron *Napier of Magdala* Br field marshal
**Napoleon, Napoleon Bonaparte** 1769–1821 emp of the French (1804–15)
**Napoleon II** 1811–1832 *L'Aiglon;* Duc *de Reichstadt; son of Napoleon I & Marie Louise*
**Napoleon III** 1808–1873 *Louis Napoleon; son of Louis Bonaparte & Hortense de Beauharnais* emp of the French (1852–70)
**Narayan** Rasipuram Krishnaswamy 1906– Indian author
**Narváez, de** Pánfilo 1480?–1528 Span soldier in Am
**Nash** John 1752–1835 Eng architect & town planner
**Nash** John Northcote 1893–1977 *bro of P* Eng artist & wood engraver
**Nash** Ogden 1902–1971 Am poet
**Nash** Paul 1889–1946 *bro of JN* Eng artist
**Nash** Richard 1674–1762 *Beau* Eng dandy
**Nash** Walter 1882–1968 prime min of NZ (1957–60)
**Nashe , Nash** Thomas 1567–1601 Eng satirist & dram
**Nasmyth** Alexander 1758–1840 Scot artist
**Nasmyth** James 1808–1890 Scot engineer & inventor
**Nasser** Gamal Abdel 1918–1970 Egyptian polit; pres of Egypt (1956–70)
**Nathan** George Jean 1882–1958 Am editor & dram critic
**Navratilova** Martina 1956– Am (Czech-born) tennis player
**Neagle** Dame Anna 1904– pseud of *Dame Marjorie Wilcox* née *Robertson* Eng actress
**Neave** Airey Middleton Sheffield 1916–1979 Eng polit; assassinated
**Nebuchadnezzar, Nebuchadrezzar** *d* 562 B C Chaldean king of Babylon (605–562)
**Necker** Jacques 1732–1804 *father of Mme de Staël* Fr (Swiss-born) financier & statesman
**Neel** Louis Boyd 1905–1981 Eng conductor
**Nehru** Jawaharlal 1889–1964 *son of Motilal* Indian nationalist; prime min (1947–64)
**Nehru** Pundit Motilal 1861–1931 Indian nationalist
**Neill** Alexander Sutherland 1883–1973 Eng educ
**Neilson** James Beaumont 1792–1865 Scot inventor
**Nelson** Viscount 1758–1805 *Horatio Nelson* Eng admiral
**Neri, de'** San Filippo 1515–1595 Saint *Philip Neri* Ital founder (1564) of "Fathers of the Oratory"

**Nernst** Walther Hermann 1864–1941 Ger physicist & chem
**Nero** 37–68 *Nero Claudius Caesar Drusus Germanicus* orig *Lucius Domitius Ahenobarbus* Rom emp 54–68 – **Neronian, Neronic** *adj*
**Neruda** Pablo 1904–1973 *Neftalí Ricardo Reyes (Basoalto)* Chilean poet & diplomat
**Nerva** Marcus Cocceius 35?–98 Rom emp (96–98)
**Nervi** Pier Luigi 1891–1979 Ital structural engineer
**Nesbit** Edith 1858–1924 Eng author of children's books
**Nestorius** *d ab* 451 patriarch of Constantinople (428–431)
**Nestroy** Johann 1801–1862 Austrian dram
**Nevelson** Louise 1900– Am (Russ-born) sculptor
**Neville** Richard – see Earl of WARWICK
**Newbery** John 1713–1767 Eng publisher
**Newbolt** Sir Henry John 1862–1938 Eng author
**Newby** Percy Howard 1918– Eng author
**Newcombe** John 1944– Austral tennis player
**Newcomen** Thomas 1663–1729 Eng engineer & inventor
**Newman** John Henry 1801–1890 Eng cardinal & author
**Newman** Paul 1925– Am film actor, producer, & director
**Newton** Sir Isaac 1642–1727 Eng math & natural philos
**Ney** Michel 1769–1815 Duc *d'Elchingen;* Prince *de la Moskova* Fr soldier; marshal of France
**Nicholas** Saint 4th c Christian prelate; patron saint of children
**Nicholas I** 1796–1855 czar of Russia (1825–55)
**Nicholas II** 1868–1918 czar of Russia (1894–1917)
**Nicholas** Grand Duke 1856–1929 Russ gen & monarchist
**Nicholas of Cusa** 1401–1464 Ger prelate, math, & philos
**Nichols** Peter Richard 1927– Eng dram
**Nicholson** Ben 1894–1982 Eng artist
**Nicholson** Jack 1937– Am film actor
**Nicklaus** Jack William 1940– Am golfer
**Nicol** William 1768–1851 Scot physicist
**Nicolet** Jean 1598–1642 Fr explorer in North America
**Nicolle** Charles Jean Henri 1866–1936 Fr physician & bacteriol
**Nicolson** Sir Harold George 1886–1968 Eng biographer & diplomat
**Nielsen** Carl August 1865–1931 Danish composer
**Niemeyer** Oscar 1907– Braz architect
**Niemöller** (Friedrich Gustav Emil) Martin 1892– Ger anti-Nazi Protestant theol
**Nietzsche** Friedrich Wilhelm 1844–1900 Ger philos – **Nietzschean** *adj*
**Nightingale** Florence 1820–1910 Eng nurse & philanthropist
**Nijinska** Bronislava 1891–1972 *sister of following* Russ dancer & choreographer
**Nijinsky** Waslaw 1890–1950 Russ dancer
**Nilsson** Birgit 1918– Swed soprano
**Nilsson** Gunnar 1948–1978 Swed racing driver
**Nimitz** Chester William 1885–1966 Am admiral
**Niven** (James) David (Graham) 1910–1983 Eng actor & author
**Nixon** Richard Milhous 1913– Am lawyer; 37th pres of the US (1969–74)
**Nkomo** Joshua 1917– Zimbabwean polit
**Nkrumah** Kwame 1909–1972 Ghanaian prime min (1957–60); 1st pres (1960–66)
**Nobel** Alfred Bernhard 1833–1896 Swed manuf, inventor, & philanthropist
**Nobile** Umberto 1885–1978 Ital arctic explorer & aeronautical engineer
**Noel-Baker** Baron 1889–1982 *Philip John Noel-Baker* Eng polit; Nobel Peace Prize (1959)
**Noguchi** Hideyo 1876–1928 Am (Jap-born) bacteriol
**Noguchi** Isamu 1904– Am sculptor
**Nolan** Sidney Robert 1917– Austral artist
**Nomura** Kichisaburo 1877–1964 Jap admiral & diplomat
**Nordenskjöld** Baron (Nils) Adolf Erik 1832–1901 Swed arctic explorer
**Norodom Sihanouk** 1922– King of Cambodia (1941–55); prime min (1955–60); head of state (1960–70; 1975–76)
**Norrish** Ronald George Wreyford 1897–1978 Eng chem
**North** Frederick 1732–1792 *Lord North* Eng statesman; prime min (1770–82)
**Northcliffe** Viscount – see HARMSWORTH
**Northrop** John Howard 1891– Am scientist

**Nostradamus** 1503–1566 né *Michel de Notredame* Fr physician & astrologer

**Novello** Ivor 1893–1951 pseud of *Ivor Novello Davies* Welsh actor, composer, songwriter, & dram

**Novotný** Antonin 1904–1975 pres of Czech (1957–68)

**Noyes** Alfred 1880-1958 Eng poet

**Nureyev** Rudolf Hametovich 1938–     Br (Russ-born) ballet dancer & choreographer

**Nurmi** Paavo Johannes 1897–1973 Finnish athlete

**Nuvolari** Tazio Giorgio 1892–1953 Ital racing driver

**Nyerere** Julius Kambarage 1922–     pres of Tanzania (1964– )

# O

**Oakley** Annie 1860–1926 pseud of *Phoebe Anne Oakley Mozee* née *Moses* Am entertainer; expert shot

**Oates** Joyce Carol 1938–     Am author

**Oates** Captain Lawrence Edward Grace 1880–1912 Eng explorer

**Oates** Titus 1649–1705 Eng fabricator of the Popish Plot

**Oberth** Hermann Julius 1894–     Ger physicist

**Obote** (Apollo) Milton 1924–     prime min & pres of Uganda (1966–71; 1979–     )

**Obrenović** Alexander I – see ALEXANDER

**O'Brien** Edna 1936–     Irish nov

**O'Brien** Flann 1911–1966 pseud of *Brian O'Nolan* Irish author

**O'Brien** William Smith 1803–1864 Irish polit & nationalist

**O'Casey** Sean 1880–1964 Irish dram

**Occam , Ockham** William of 1300?–?1349 Eng philos – **Occamistic, Ockhamistic** *adj*

**Occleve** – see Thomas HOCCLEVE

**Ochoa** Severo 1905–     Am (Span-born) biochem

**Ochs** Adolph Simon 1858–1935 Am newspaper publisher

**O'Connell** Daniel 1775–1847 Irish polit

**O'Connor** Thomas Power 1848–1929 *Tay Pay* Irish journalist

**Octavian, Octavianus** – see AUGUSTUS

**Odets** Clifford 1906–1963 Am dram

**Odinga** (Ajuma) Oginga 1911–     Kenyan polit

**Odoacer** 434?–493 1st barbarian ruler of Italy (476–493)

**Oehlenschläger** Adam Gottlob 1779–1850 Danish poet & dram

**Oerter** Alfred 1936–     Am discus thrower

**O'Faoláin** Seán 1900–     Irish author

**Offenbach** Jacques 1819–1880 Fr composer

**O'Flaherty** Liam 1896–     Irish nov

**Ogdon** John Andrew Howard 1937–     Eng pianist & composer

**Oglethorpe** James Edward 1696–1785 Eng philanthropist & gen; founder of Georgia

**O'Hara** John Henry 1905–1970 Am author

**O'Higgins** Bernardo 1778–1842 *Liberator of Chile* Chilean soldier & statesman

**Ohm** Georg Simon 1787–1854 Ger physicist

**Oistrakh** David Fyodorovich 1908–1974 Russ violinist

**O'Kelly** Seán Thomas 1883–1966 Irish journalist; pres of Republic of Ireland (1945–59)

**Olaf I** 969–1000 *Olaf Tryggvason* king of Norway (995–1000)

**Olaf II** 995?–1030 *Saint Olaf* king of Norway (1016–28)

**Olaf V** 1903–     king of Norway (1957–     )

**Olbers** Heinrich Wilhelm Matthias 1758–1840 Ger astron & physician

**Oldcastle** Sir John 1377?–1417 Baron *Cobham* Eng Lollard leader

**Oldfield** William Albert Stanley 1897–1976 *Bertie* Austral cricketer

**Oliphant** Sir Marcus Laurence Elwin 1901–     Austral nuclear physicist

**Olivier** Laurence Kerr 1907–     Baron *Olivier of Brighton* Eng actor

**Olmsted** Frederick Law 1822–1903 Am landscape architect

**Omar Khayyám** *d ab* 1123 Pers poet & astron

**Onassis** Aristotle Socrates 1906–1975 Greek shipping owner

**O'Neill** Eugene Gladstone 1888–1953 Am dram

**O'Neill** Terence Marne 1914–     Baron *O'Neill of the Maine* N Ireland prime min (1963–69)

**O'Nolan** Brian – see Flann O'BRIEN

**Oppenheimer** Sir Ernest 1880–1957 S African industrialist

**Oppenheimer** (Julius) Robert 1904–1967 Am physicist

**Orcagna** Andrea 1308?–?1368 *Andrea di Cione* Florentine artist, sculptor, & architect

**Orczy** Baroness Emmuska 1865–1947 Br (Hung-born) nov & dram

**O'Reilly** Anthony John Francis 1936–     Irish rugby union player

**Orff** Carl 1895–1982 Ger composer

**Origen** 185?–?254 Greek author, teacher, & church father

**Orlando** Vittorio Emanuele 1860–1952 Ital statesman

**Ormandy** Eugene 1899–     Am (Hung-born) conductor

**Orozco** José Clemente 1883–1949 Mex artist

**Ortega y Gasset** José 1883–1955 Span philos, author, & statesman

**Ortiz** Manuel 1917–1970 Mex-Am boxer

**Orton** John Kingsley 1933–1967 *Joe* Eng dram

**Orwell** George 1903–1950 pseud of *Eric Blair* Eng author – **Orwellian** *adj*

**Osborn** Sir Frederick James 1885–1978 Eng town & country planner

**Osborne** John James 1929–     Eng dram & actor

**Oscar II** 1829–1907 king of Sweden (1872–1907) & of Norway (1872–1905)

**Osler** Sir William 1849–1919 Canad physician

**Osman, Othman** 1259–1326 founder of the Ottoman Empire

**Ossietzky, von** Carl 1889–1938 Ger author & pacifist

**Ostwald** Wilhelm 1853–1932 Ger physical chem & philos

**Oswald** Saint 605?–641 King of Northumbria (633–641)

**Otis** Elisha Graves 1811–1861 Am inventor of lifts & escalators

**O'Toole** Peter 1932–     Irish actor

**Otto I** 912–973 *the Great* Holy Rom emp (936–973)

**Otway** Thomas 1652–1685 Eng dram

**Ouida** – see Marie Louise de la RAMÉE

**Ovett** Steve 1956–     Eng athlete

**Ovid** 43 B C–?A D 17 *Publius Ovidius Naso* Rom poet – **Ovidian** *adj*

**Owen** Alun Davies 1925–     Welsh dram

**Owen** David Anthony Llewellyn 1938–     Eng politician

**Owen** Robert 1771–1858 Welsh social reformer

**Owen** Wilfred 1893–1918 Eng poet

**Owens** James Cleveland 1913–1980 *Jesse* Am athlete

**Oxenstierna, Oxenstjerna, Oxenstiern** Count Axel Gustafsson 1583–1654 Swed statesman

**Oxford** Earl of – see Robert HARLEY

**Oxley** John Joseph William Molesworth 1781–1828 Eng explorer of Australia

# P

**Paasikivi** Juho Kusti 1870–1956 Finnish businessman; pres of Finland (1946–56)

**Packard** Vance Oakley 1914–     Am author & social critic

**Packer** Kerry Francis Bullmore 1937–     Austral businessman & organizer of World Series cricket tournament in Austral

**Packer** Michael 1435–1498 Austrian sculptor & artist

**Paderewski** Ignace Jan 1860–1941 Pol pianist & statesman

**Paganini** Niccolò 1782–1840 Ital violinist

**Page** Sir Earle Christmas Grafton 1880–1961 Austral polit; founder of Country Party

**Page** Sir Frederick Handley 1885–1962 Am aeronautical engineer & aircraft manuf

**Paget** Sir James 1814–1899 Eng surgeon & pathologist

**Paine** Thomas 1737–1809 Am (Eng-born) polit philos & author

**Paisley** Ian Richard Kyle 1926–     N Ireland polit & relig leader

**Palestrina, da** Giovanni Pierluigi 1526?–1594 Ital composer

**Palgrave** Francis Turner 1824–1897 Eng poet & anthologist

**Palladio** Andrea 1508–1580 Ital architect

**Palmer** Arnold Daniel 1929–     Am golfer

**Palmer** Samuel 1805–1881 Eng artist

**Palmerston** 3rd Viscount 1784–1865 *Henry John Temple* Eng statesman; prime min (1859–65) – **Palmerstonian** *adj*
**Pandit** Vijaya Lakshmi 1900– Indian diplomat
**Pankhurst** Dame Christabel 1880–1958 *daughter of next* Eng suffragette
**Pankhurst** Emmeline 1858–1928 *Emily* née *Goulden* Eng suffragette
**Panufnik** Andrzej 1914– Pol conductor & composer
**Papandreou** Georgios 1888–1968 prime min of Greece (1964–65)
**Papen, von** Franz 1879–1969 Ger diplomat
**Papp** László 1926– Hung boxer
**Paracelsus** Theophrastus 1493–1541 *Philippus Aureolus Theophrastus Bombastus von Hohenheim* Swiss-born alchemist & physician
**Paré** Ambroise 1510–1590 Fr surgeon
**Pares** Sir Bernard 1867–1949 Eng hist
**Pareto** Vilfredo 1848–1923 Ital econ & sociol
**Paris** Matthew 1200?–1259 Eng monk & hist
**Park** Chung Hee 1917–1979 pres of S Korea (1963–79); assassinated
**Park** Mungo 1771–1806 Scot explorer in Africa
**Parker** Dorothy 1893–1967 née *Rothschild* Am author
**Parker** Matthew 1504–1575 Eng theol; Archbishop of Canterbury (1559–75)
**Parkes** Sir Henry 1815–1896 Austral statesman
**Parkinson** Cyril Northcote 1909– Eng satirist & hist; orig of "Parkinson's Law"
**Parmenides** 5th c B c Greek philos
**Parmigianino, Parmigiano** Il 1503–1540 *Girolamo Francesco Maria Mazzuoli* or *Mazzola* Ital painter
**Parnell** Charles Stewart 1846–1891 Irish nationalist
**Parnell** Thomas 1679–1718 Irish poet
**Parr** Catherine – see CATHERINE
**Parr** Thomas 1483?–1635 *Old Parr* Englishman alleged to have lived for 152 years
**Parry** Sir Charles Hubert Hastings 1848–1918 Eng composer
**Parry** John 1710–1782 *Blind Parry* Welsh music collector & harpist
**Parry** Sir William Edward 1790–1855 Eng arctic explorer
**Parsons** William 1800–1867 3rd Earl of *Rosse* Irish astron
**Partridge** Eric Honeywood 1894–1979 NZ philologist & author
**Pascal** Blaise 1623–1662 Fr math & philos
**Pasmore** (Edwin John) Victor 1908– Eng artist
**Pasolini** Pier Paolo 1922–1975 Ital nov, poet, & film director
**Passfield** 1st Baron – see Sidney James WEBB
**Passy** Frédéric 1822–1912 Fr econ & statesman
**Pasternak** Boris Leonidovich 1890–1960 Soviet poet, nov, & translator
**Pasteur** Louis 1822–1895 Fr chem – **Pasteurian** *adj*
**Pater** Walter Horatio 1839–1894 Eng essayist & critic
**Paterson** Andrew Barton 1864–1941 *Banjo* Austral nov & poet; author of "Waltzing Matilda"
**Paterson** William 1658–1719 Scot financier; founder of Bank of England
**Pathé** Charles 1863–1957 Fr pioneer film producer
**Patmore** Coventry Kersey Dighton 1823–1896 Eng poet
**Paton** Alan Stewart 1903– S African writer
**Paton** Sir Joseph Noel 1821–1901 Scot artist
**Patrick** Saint 389?–?461 apostle & patron saint of Ireland
**Patterson** Floyd 1935– Am boxer
**Patti** Adelina 1843–1919 Ital (Span-born) operatic soprano
**Patton** George Smith 1885–1945 Am gen
**Paul** name of 6 popes: esp **III** 1468–1549 (pope 1534–49); **V** 1552–1621 (pope 1605–1621); **VI** (*Giovanni Battista Montini*) 1897–1978 (pope 1963–1978)
**Paul I** 1754–1801 emp of Russia (1796–1801)
**Paul I** 1901–1964 king of Greece (1947–64)
**Paul** Jean – see RICHTER
**Pauli** Wolfgang 1900–1958 Am (Austrian-born) physicist
**Pauling** Linus Carl 1901– Am chem
**Paulus** Julius 2nd–3rd c A D Rom jurist
**Pavese** Cesare 1908–1950 Ital poet
**Pavlov** Ivan Petrovich 1849–1936 Soviet physiol
**Pavlova** Anna 1885–1931 Russ ballerina

**Paxton** Sir Joseph 1803–1865 Eng architect & landscape gardener
**Paz** Octavio 1914– Mex author
**Peabody** George 1795–1869 Am merchant & philanthropist
**Peacock** Thomas Love 1785–1866 Eng nov & poet
**Peale** Charles Wilson 1741–1827 & his bro James 1749–1831 & Charles's son Rembrandt 1778–1860 Am artists
**Pears** Sir Peter 1910– Eng tenor
**Pearson** Sir Cyril Arthur 1866–1921 Eng publisher & newspaper owner
**Pearson** Lester Bowles 1897–1972 prime min of Canada (1963–68)
**Peary** Robert Edwin 1856–1920 Am arctic explorer
**Peck** (Eldred) Gregory 1916– Am film actor
**Pedro I** 1798–1834 *Dom* emp of Brazil (1822–31); king of Portugal (1826)
**Pedro II** 1825–1891 *son of prec* emp of Brazil (1831–89)
**Peel** Sir Robert 1788–1850 Eng statesman
**Peele** George 1556–1596 Eng dram & poet
**Peirce** Charles Sanders 1839–1914 Am physicist, math, & logician
**Peisistratus** – see PISISTRATUS
**Pelagius** 360?–?420 Br monk & theol
**Pelé** 1940– né *Edson Arantes do Nascimento* Braz footballer
**Pelham** Henry 1696–1754 Eng polit; prime min (1743–54)
**Pelletier** Pierre Joseph 1788–1842 Fr chem
**Penderecki** Krzysztof 1933– Pol composer
**Penn** Sir William 1621–1670 Eng admiral
**Penn** William 1644–1718 *son of prec* Eng Quaker; founder of Pennsylvania
**Penney** William George 1909– Baron *Penney of East Hendred* Eng scientist
**Pepin the Short** 714?–768 king of the Franks (751–768)
**Pepusch** Johann Christoph 1667–1752 Br (Ger-born) composer
**Pepys** Samuel 1633–1703 Eng diarist & Admiralty official – **Pepysian** *adj*
**Percival** Spencer 1762–1812 Eng polit; prime min (1809–1812); assassinated
**Percy** Sir Henry 1364–1403 *Hotspur* Eng soldier
**Perelman** Sidney Joseph 1904–1979 Am author
**Pérez Galdós** Benito 1843–1920 Span nov & dram
**Perez Rodriguez** Carlos Andrés 1922– pres of Venezuela (1974–79)
**Pergolesi** Giovanni Battista 1710–1736 Ital composer
**Pericles** *d* 429 B c Athenian statesman – **Periclean** *adj*
**Perkin** Sir William Henry 1838–1907 Eng chem
**Perón** Eva Duarte de 1919–1952 *Evita; 2nd wife of JD* Argentine polit leader
**Perón** Juan Domingo 1895–1974 Argentine polit; pres of Argentina (1946–55; 1973–74)
**Perón** María Estela 1931– *3rd wife of JD* pres of Argentine (1974–76)
**Perrault** Charles 1628–1703 Fr author of fairy tales
**Perret** Auguste 1874–1954 Fr architect
**Perrin** Jean Baptiste 1870–1942 Fr physicist
**Perry** Fred(erick) John 1909– Eng tennis & table-tennis player
**Perse** St John – see Alexis Saint-Léger LÉGER
**Pershing** John Joseph 1860–1948 Am gen
**Persius** 34–62 *Aulus Persius Flaccus* Rom satirist
**Perugino, Il** 1446–1523 *Pietro Vannucci* Ital artist
**Perutz** Max Ferdinand 1914– Eng biochem
**Pestalozzi** Johann Heinrich 1746–1827 Swiss educ
**Pétain** Henri Philippe 1856–1951 Fr gen; marshal of France; premier of Vichy France (1940–44)
**Peter** Saint *d* A D ?67 disciple of Jesus; regarded, esp by Roman Catholics, as vicar of Christ on earth [Mt 16:16–19]
**Peter I** 1672–1725 *the Great* czar of Russia (1682–1725)
**Peter I Karageorgevich** 1844–1921 king of Serbia (1903–21)
**Peter II** 1923–1970 king of Yugoslavia (1934–45)
**Peter the Hermit** 1050?–?1115 Fr preacher of the 1st Crusade
**Peters** Mary Elizabeth 1939– N Ireland athlete
**Peterson** Oscar (Emmanuel) 1925– Am jazz pianist
**Peterson** Ronnie 1944–1978 Swed racing driver

**Petrarch, Petrarca** Francesco 1304–1374 Ital poet – **Petrarchan** *adj*

**Petrie** Sir (William Matthew) Flinders 1853–1942 Eng Egyptologist

**Petronius** Gaius 1st c A D *Arbiter Elegantiae* Rom satirist – **Petronian** *adj*

**Petty** Sir William 1623–1687 Eng polit econ

**Pevsner** Antoine 1886–1962 *bro of Naum Gabo* Fr (Russ-born) sculptor & artist

**Pevsner** Sir Nikolaus 1902–1983 Br (Ger-born) art hist

**Phaedrus** 5th c B c Greek philos

**Phaedrus** 1st c A D Rom fabulist

**Phelps** Brian Eric 1944–     Eng diver

**Phelps** Samuel 1804–1878 Eng actor-manager

**Phidias** 5th c B c Greek sculptor

**Philidor** François André 1726–1796 né *Danican* Fr composer & chess player

**Philip** name of 6 kings of France: esp **II, Philip Augustus** 1165–1223 (reigned 1180–1223); **IV** (*the Fair*) 1268–1314 (reigned 1285–1314); **VI** 1293–1350 (reigned 1328–50)

**Philip** name of 5 kings of Spain: esp **II** 1527–1598 (reigned 1556–98); **V** 1683–1746 (reigned 1700–46)

**Philip II** 382–336 B c king of Macedon (359–336)

**Philip** Prince 1921–     *consort of Queen Elizabeth II of GB* 3rd Duke of Edinburgh

**Philip the Good** 1396–1467 Duke of Burgundy (1419–67)

**Philipe** Gérard 1922–1959 Fr actor

**Philips** Ambrose 1675?–1749 *Namby-Pamby* Eng poet & dram

**Phillips** Mark Anthony Peter 1948–     *husband of Princess Anne* Eng horse-trials rider

**Phillpotts** Eden 1862–1960 Eng nov & dram

**Philo Judaeus** 1st c B c-1st c A D Hellenistic Jewish philos of Alexandria

**Piaf** Edith 1915–1963 neé *Edith Giovanna Gassion* Fr cabaret singer

**Piaget** Jean 1896–1980 Swiss psychol

**Piatigorsky** Gregor 1903–1976 Am (Russ-born) cellist

**Picard** Jean 1620–1682 Fr astron

**Picasso** Pablo 1881–1973 Span artist & sculptor in Fr

**Piccard** Auguste 1884–1962 Swiss physicist & aviator

**Piccard** Jacques Ernst *son of Auguste* 1922–     Swiss (Belg-born) oceanographer; developer of bathyscaphe

**Pickering** Edward Charles 1846–1919 & his bro William Henry 1858–1938 Am astronomers

**Pickford** Mary 1893–1979 neé *Gladys Mary Smith* Am film actress

**Pico della Mirandola** Count Giovanni 1463–1494 Ital humanist

**Pieck** Wilhelm 1876–1960 Ger Communist

**Pierce** Franklin 1804–1869 14th pres of the US (1853–57)

**Piero della Francesca** – see FRANCESCA

**Piggott** Lester Keith 1935–     Eng jockey

**Pigou** Arthur Cecil 1877–1959 Eng econ

**Pilate** Pontius 1st c A D Rom procurator of Judea; tried & condemned Jesus Christ

**Pilsudski** Józef Klemens 1867–1935 Pol gen & statesman

**Pindar** 522?–443 B c Greek poet

**Pinero** Sir Arthur Wing 1855–1934 Eng dram

**Pinkerton** Allan 1819–1884 Scot-born detective in Am

**Pinochet Ugarte** Augusto 1915–     pres of Chile (1973–     )

**Pinter** Harold 1930–     Eng dram

**Pinturicchio** 1454–1513 *Bernardino di Betto di Biago* Ital artist

**Pinza** Ezio 1892–1957 Ital bass

**Pinzón** Martín Alonso 1440?–1493 & his bro Vicente Yáñez 1460?–?1524 Span navigators with Columbus

**Piozzi** Hester Lynch 1741–1821 *Mrs Thrale* Eng author

**Piper** John Egerton Christmas 1903–     Eng artist & author

**Pirandello** Luigi 1867–1936 Ital author – **Pirandellian** *adj*

**Piranesi** Giovanni Battista 1720–1778 Ital architect & engraver

**Pire** Dominique-Georges 1910–1969 Belg priest; founder of charitable organization

**Pirie** (Douglas Alastair) Gordon 1931–     Eng athlete

**Pisano** Giovanni 1245–1314 & his father Nicola 1220–1284 Ital sculptors

**Pisistratus , Peisistratus** *d* 527 B c tyrant of Athens

**Pissarro** Camille 1830–1903 Fr artist

**Pitman** Sir Isaac 1813–1897 Eng shorthand inventor

**Pitt** William 1708–1778 Earl of *Chatham; the Elder Pitt* Eng statesman; prime min (1756–61, 1766–68)

**Pitt** William 1759–1806 *the Younger Pitt; son of prec* Eng statesman; prime min (1783–1801, 1804–06)

**Pitt-Rivers** Augustus Henry 1827–1900 Eng archaeologist

**Pius** name of 12 popes: esp **II** (*Enea Silvio Piccolomini* or *Aeneas Silvius* or *Sylvius*) 1405–1464 (pope 1458–64); **VII** 1742–1823 (pope 1800–23); **IX** 1792–1878 (pope 1846–78); **X** 1835–1914 (pope 1903–14); **XI** (*Achille Ratti*) 1857–1939 (pope 1922–39); **XII** (*Eugenio Pacelli*) 1876–1958 (pope 1939–58)

**Pizarro** Francisco 1470?–1541 Span conqueror of Peru

**Planck** Max Karl Ernst Ludwig 1858–1947 Ger physicist

**Plath** Sylvia 1932–1963 Am poet

**Plato** 427?–347 B c Greek philos

**Plautus** Titus Maccius 254?–184 B c Rom dram – **Plautine** *adj*

**Player** Gary 1936–     S African golfer

**Pleasence** Donald 1919– Eng actor

**Plekhanov** Georgi Valentinovich 1857–1918 Russ Marxist philos

**Plimsoll** Samuel 1824–1898 *the Sailor's Friend* Eng shipping reformer

**Pliny** 23–79 *Gaius Plinius Secundus; the Elder* Rom scholar

**Pliny** 72–113 *Gaius Plinius Caecilius Secundus; the Younger; nephew of prec* Rom author

**Plisetskaya** Maiya Mikhailovna 1925–     Soviet ballet dancer

**Plomer** William Charles Franklyn 1903–1973 Br (S African-born) author

**Plotinus** 205?–270 Rom (Egyptian-born) philos – **Plotinian** *adj*

**Plowright** Joan Ann 1929–     *Lady Olivier* Eng actress

**Plutarch** 46?–120 Greek biographer & moralist – **Plutarchan, Plutarchian** *adj*

**Pocahontas** 1595?–1617 *dau of Powhatan* Am Indian

**Podgorny** Nikolai Viktorovich 1903–1983 Soviet polit; pres of USSR (1965–77)

**Poe** Edgar Allan 1809–1849 Am poet & storywriter

**Pohl** Frederick 1919–     Am science-fiction author

**Poincaré** Jules Henri 1854–1912 Fr math

**Poincaré** Raymond Nicholas Landry 1860–1934 *cousin of J H* Fr statesman; pres of France (1913–20)

**Poisson** Siméon Denis 1781–1840 Fr math

**Poitier** Sidney 1924–     Am actor

**Polanski** Roman 1933–     Pol actor & director

**Pole** Reginald 1500–1558 Eng cardinal; archbishop of Canterbury (1556–58)

**Polk** James Knox 1795–1849 11th pres of the US (1845–49)

**Pollard** Albert Frederick 1869–1948 Eng hist

**Pollock** Jackson 1912–1956 Am artist

**Pollock** (Robert) Graeme 1944–     S African cricketer

**Polo** Marco 1254?–?1324 Ital traveller

**Polycarp** Saint 69?–?155 Christian martyr & Apostolic Father; bishop of Smyrna

**Polyclitus, Polycleitus** 5th c B c Greek sculptor & architect

**Polygnotus** 5th c B c Greek artist

**Pompadour, de** Marquise 1721–1764 *Jeanne Antoinette Poisson* mistress of Louis XV

**Pompey** 106–48 B c *Gnaeus Pompeius Magnus; the Great* Rom gen & statesman

**Pompidou** Georges Jean Raymond 1911–1974 Fr polit; premier of France (1962–68); pres of France (1969–74)

**Ponce de León** Juan 1460?–1521 Span explorer; disc Florida

**Ponchielli** Amilcare 1834–1886 Ital composer

**Pons** Lily 1904–1976 Am (Fr-born) soprano

**Ponti** Giovanni 1891–1979 Ital architect & stage designer

**Pontoppidan** Henrik 1857–1943 Danish nov

**Pontormo, da** Jacopo 1494–1557 né *Jacobo Carrucci* Ital artist

**Pope** Alexander 1688–1744 Eng poet – **Popian** *also* **Popean** *adj*

**Popper** Sir Karl Raimund 1902–     Br (Austrian-born) philos

**Porritt** Sir Arthur Espie 1900–     Baron *Porritt of Wanganui and of Hampstead* Br (NZ-born) surgeon

**Portal** Charles Frederick Algernon 1893–1971 1st Viscount *Portal of Hungerford* Eng air marshal

**Porter** Cole Albert 1891–1964 Am composer & songwriter

**Porter** Edwin 1870–1941 Am inventor

**Porter** Eric Richard 1928–     Eng actor

**Porter** Gene 1868–1924 née *Stratton* Am nov
**Porter** Hugh 1940– Eng track cyclist
**Porter** William Sydney 1862–1910 pseud *O Henry* Am short-story author
**Portland** Duke of – see BENTINCK
**Post** Emily 1873?–1960 née *Price* Am columnist & author
**Postgate** Raymond William 1896–1971 Eng hist & nov
**Potĕmkin** Grigori Aleksandrovich 1739–1791 Russ field marshal & statesman
**Potter** (Helen) Beatrix 1866–1943 Eng author & illustrator
**Potter** Paul 1625–1654 Du artist
**Poulenc** Francis 1899–1963 Fr composer
**Pound** Ezra Loomis 1885–1972 Am poet
**Poussin** Nicolas 1594–1665 Fr artist
**Powell** Anthony Dymoke 1905– Eng author
**Powell** Cecil Frank 1903–1969 Eng physicist
**Powell** Maud 1868–1920 Am violinist
**Powhatan** 1550?–1618 *father of Pocahontas* Am Indian chief
**Powys** John Cowper 1872–1963 & his bros Theodore Francis 1875–1953 & Llewelyn 1884–1939 Eng authors
**Prajadhipok** 1893–1941 king of Siam (1925–35)
**Pratt** Edwin John 1883–1964 Canad poet
**Praxiteles** 4th c B C Athenian sculptor – **Praxitelean** *adj*
**Pregl** Fritz 1869–1930 Austrian chem
**Preminger** Otto Ludwig 1906– Am film director
**Prescott** Alan 1927– Eng rugby league player
**Prescott** William Hickling 1796–1859 Am hist
**Presley** Elvis Aron 1935–1977 Am pop singer
**Pretorius** Andries Wilhelmus Jacobus 1799–1853 & his son Marthinus Wessels 1819–1901 S African Du colonizers & soldiers
**Previn** André George 1929– Am (Ger-born) conductor, composer & pianist
**Prévost d'Exiles** Antoine François 1697–1763 Fr abbé & writer
**Price** Vincent 1911– Am actor
**Pride** Thomas *d* 1658 Eng Parliamentary commander
**Priestley** John Boynton 1894–1984 Eng author
**Priestley** Joseph 1733–1804 Eng clergyman & chem
**Primo de Rivera y Orbaneja** Miguel 1870–1930 Marqués *de Estella* Span gen & polit; dictator of Spain (1923–30)
**Primrose** Archibald Philip – see ROSEBERY
**Prior** Matthew 1664–1721 Eng poet
**Pritchard** Sir John Michael 1921– Eng conductor
**Proclus** 410?–485 Greek philos
**Prokofiev** Sergei Sergeevich 1891–1953 Russ composer – **Prokofievian** *adj*
**Propertius** Sextus 50?–?15 B C Rom poet
**Protagoras** 5th c B C Greek philos – **Protagorean** *adj*
**Protopopov** Oleg 1932– and wife Ludmila 1935– neé *Belousova* Soviet ice figure skaters
**Proudhon** Pierre Joseph 1809–1865 Fr journalist
**Proust** Marcel 1871–1922 Fr nov – **Proustian** *adj*
**Prynne** William 1600–1669 Eng Puritan pamphleteer
**Przhevalski** Nikolai Mikhailovich 1839–1888 Russ explorer
**Ptolemy** name of 15 kings of Egypt (323–30 B C)
**Ptolemy** 2nd c A D *Claudius Ptolemaeus* Alexandrian astron
**Puccini** Giacomo 1858–1924 Ital composer
**Pudney** John Sleigh 1909–1977 Eng author
**Pugin** Augustus Welby Northmore 1812–1852 Eng architect
**Pulitzer** Joseph 1847–1911 Am (Hung-born) journalist
**Pullman** George Mortimer 1831–1897 Am inventor
**Pupin** Michael Idvorsky 1858–1935 Am (Yugoslavian-born) physicist & inventor
**Purcell** Henry 1658?–1695 Eng composer
**Purdy** Alfred Wellington 1918– Canad poet
**Purkinje** Johannes Evangelista 1787–1869 Czech physiol
**Pusey** Edward Bouverie 1800–1882 Eng theol
**Pushkin** Aleksander Sergeevich 1799–1837 Russ poet – **Pushkinian** *adj*
**Puskas** Ferenc 1926– Hung footballer
**Puvis de Chavannes** Pierre 1824–1898 Fr artist, esp of murals
**P'u-yi** Henry – see HSÜAN-T'UNG
**Pym** John 1584–1643 Eng Parliamentary statesman
**Pyrrhus** 318?–272 B C king of Epirus (306–272 B C)
**Pythagoras** *d ab* 497 B C Greek philos & math

# Q

**Qaddafi , Qadhafi, Kadhafi, Gaddafi** Muammar Muhammad al-1942– Libyan polit & army officer
**Quant** Mary 1934– Eng fashion designer
**Quarles** Francis 1592–1644 Eng poet
**Quasimodo** Salvatore 1901–1968 Ital poet & critic
**Queensberry** Marquis of – see DOUGLAS
**Quennell** Peter 1905– Eng author
**Quezon y Molina** Manuel Luis 1878–1944 *Manuel Quezon* pres of the Philippine Commonwealth (1935–44)
**Quiller-Couch** Sir Arthur Thomas 1863–1944 pseud *Q* Eng author
**Quilter** Roger 1877–1953 Eng composer
**Quintero, Alvarez** Serafín 1871–1938 & his bro Joaquín 1873–1944 Span dramatists
**Quintilian** 1st c A D *Marcus Fabius Quintilianus* Rom rhetorician
**Quoirez** Françoise – see Françoise SAGAN

# R

**Rabelais** François 1494?–1553 Fr humorist & satirist
**Rabi** Isidor Isaac 1898– Am (Austrian-born) physicist
**Rabin** Itzhak 1922– prime min of Israel (1974–77)
**Rabinowitz** Solomon – see Shalom ALEICHEM
**Rachel** Élisa 1820–1858 pseud of *Élisa Félix* Fr actress
**Rachmaninoff** Sergei Wassilievitch 1873–1943 Russ composer, pianist, & conductor
**Racine** Jean 1639–1699 Fr dram
**Rackham** Arthur 1867–1939 Eng illustrator
**Radcliffe** Ann 1764–1823 née *Ward* Eng nov
**Radcliffe-Brown** Alfred Reginald 1881–1955 Eng anthropol
**Radek** Karl 1885–?1939 Russ revolutionary
**Radetzky** Joseph Wenzel 1766–1858 count *Radetzky von Radetz* Austrian field marshal
**Radmilovic** Paulo 1886–1968 Br swimmer
**Raeburn** Sir Henry 1756–1823 Scot artist
**Raffles** Sir Thomas Stamford 1781–1826 Eng colonial administrator; estab port of Singapore
**Raglan** 1st Baron 1788–1855 *Fitzroy James Henry Somerset* Eng field marshal
**Rahman Putra** Tunku Abdul 1903– prime min of Malaysia (1963–70)
**Rahner** Karl 1904–1984 Ger Catholic theologian
**Raimondi** Marcantonio 1475?–?1534 Ital engraver
**Rainaldi** Carlo 1611–1691 Ital architect
**Raine** Kathleen Jessie 1908– Eng poet
**Rainey** Gertrude 1886–1939 *Mother of the Blues* Am blues singer
**Rainier III** 1923– *Rainier Louis Henri Maxence Bertrand de Grimaldi* Prince of Monaco
**Rainwater** Leo James 1917– Am physicist
**Rais, de** Gilles 1404–1440 *Bluebeard* Fr soldier & murderer
**Raleigh, Ralegh** Sir Walter 1552?–1618 Eng courtier, navigator, & hist
**Ramakrishna** 1836–1886 Hindu saint
**Raman** Sir Chandrasekhara Venkata 1888–1970 Indian physicist
**Rambert** Dame Marie 1888–1982 neé *Cynthia Rabbam* Br (Pol-born) ballet dancer, teacher, & choreographer
**Rameau** Jean Philippe 1683–1764 Fr composer
**Ramée, de la** Marie Louise 1839–1908 pseud *Ouida* Eng nov
**Ramón y Cajal** Santiago 1852–1934 Span histologist
**Ramsay** Allan 1686–1758 Scot poet
**Ramsay** Sir William 1852–1916 Scot chem
**Ramses, Rameses** name of 12 kings of Egypt: esp **II** (reigned 1292–1225 B C); **III** (reigned 1198–1167 B C)
**Ramsey** Sir Alfred Ernest 1920– Eng footballer & manager
**Ramsey** (Arthur) Michael 1904– Baron *Ramsey of Canterbury* archbishop of Canterbury (1961–74)
**Rand** Mary Denise 1940– neé *Bignal;* now *Mrs P Toomey* Eng athlete

**Ranjit Singh** Maharaja 1780–1839 founder of Sikh kingdom
**Ranjitsinhji** Kumar Shri 1872–1933 *Maharajah Jam Sahib of Nawanagar; Ranji* Indian cricketer, played for Eng
**Rank** Joseph Arthur 1888–1972 Eng industrialist & film magnate
**Rankine** William John Macquorn 1820–1872 Scot engineer & physicist
**Ransome** Arthur Mitchell 1884–1967 Eng author
**Raper** Johnny 1939–    Austral rugby league player
**Raphael** 1483–1520 *Raffaello Santi* or *Sanzio* Ital artist – **Raphaelesque** *adj*
**Rasmussen** Knud Johan 1879–1933 Danish arctic explorer & ethnologist
**Rasputin** Grigori Efimovich 1871?–1916 Russ monk
**Ratsiraka** Didier 1936–    Malagasy pres (1976–    )
**Rattigan** Sir Terence Mervyn 1911–1977 Eng dram
**Ravel** Maurice Joseph 1875–1937 Fr composer
**Raven** Simon Arthur Noël 1927–    Eng author
**Ravenscroft** George 1618–1681 Eng glassmaker
**Rawlinson** Sir Henry Creswicke 1810–1895 Eng Assyriologist
**Rawsthorne** Alan 1905–1971 Eng composer
**Ray** John 1627?–1705 Eng naturalist
**Ray** Satyajit 1921–    Indian film director
**Rayleigh** 3rd Baron 1842–1919 *John William Strutt* Eng math & physicist
**Read** Sir Herbert 1893–1968 Eng author
**Read** Philip William 1939–    Eng motorcyclist
**Reade** Charles 1814–1884 Eng nov & dram
**Reading** 1st Marquis of 1860–1935 *Rufus Daniel Isaacs* Eng statesman; viceroy of India (1921–26)
**Reagan** Ronald Wilson 1911–    Am actor & polit; 40th pres of the US (1981–    )
**Réaumur, de** René Antoine Ferchault 1683–1757 Fr naturalist & physicist
**Récamier** Jeanne François Julie Adélaïde 1777–1849 Fr society wit
**Redford** Robert 1937–    Am film actor
**Redgrave** Lynn 1943–    *dau of next* Eng actress
**Redgrave** Sir Michael Scudamore 1908–    Eng actor
**Redgrave** Vanessa 1937–    *dau of prec* Eng actress
**Redon** Odilon 1840–1916 Fr artist
**Redouté** Pierre Joseph 1759–1840 Belg artist & engraver
**Reed** Sir Carol 1906–1976 Eng film director
**Reed** Oliver 1938–    Eng film actor
**Reeves** Jim 1924–1964 Am singer
**Reichstein** Tadeus 1897–    Swiss (Pol-born) chem
**Reid** Thomas 1710–1796 Scot philos
**Reinhardt** Max 1873–1943 orig *Goldmann* Austrian theatre director
**Reisner** George Andrew 1867–1942 Am Egyptologist
**Remarque** Erich Maria 1898–1970 né *Erich Remark* Am (Ger-born) nov
**Rembrandt van Rijn , Ryn** 1606–1669 Du artist – **Rembrandtesque** *adj*
**Remington** Philo 1816–1889 Am inventor
**Remsen** Ira 1846–1927 Am chem
**Renan** Joseph Ernest 1823–1892 Fr philologist & hist
**Renault** Louis 1843–1918 Fr jurist & pacifist
**Renault** Mary 1905–1983 pseud of *Mary Challans* Eng author
**Reni** Guido 1575–1642 Ital artist
**Rennell** James 1742–1830 Eng cartographer & oceanographer
**Renner** Karl 1870–1950 Austrian statesman; pres of Austria (1945–50)
**Renoir** Jean 1894–1979 *son of next* Fr film director & author
**Renoir** Pierre Auguste 1841–1919 Fr artist
**Repton** Humphrey 1752–1818 Eng landscape gardener
**Respighi** Ottorino 1879–1936 Ital composer
**Reuchlin** Johann 1455–1522 *Capnio* Ger humanist
**Reuter, von** Baron Paul Julius 1816–1899 né *Israel Beer Josaphat* Br (Ger-born) founder of news agency
**Revere** Paul 1735–1818 Am patriot & silversmith
**Reymont** Wladyslaw Stanislaw 1867–1925 Pol nov
**Reynaud** Paul 1878–1966 premier of France (1940)
**Reynolds** Sir Joshua 1723–1792 Eng artist
**Rhee** Syngman 1875–1965 S Korean polit; pres of S Korea (1948–60)

**Rhodes** Cecil John 1853–1902 Eng administrator & financier in S Africa
**Rhodes** Wilfred 1877–1973 Eng cricketer
**Ribbentrop, von** Joachim 1893–1946 Ger diplomat
**Ribera, de** Jusepe 1588–1652 *Lo Spagnoletto* Span artist & etcher
**Ricardo** David 1772–1823 Eng econ
**Rice** Elmer Leopold 1892–1967 orig *Elmer Reizenstein* Am dram
**Richard** name of 3 kings of England: **I** (*Coeur de Lion*) 1157–1199 (reigned 1189–99); **II** 1367–1400 (reigned 1377–99); **III** 1452–1485 (reigned 1483–85)
**Richard** Cliff 1940–    pseud of *Harold Webb* Eng pop singer
**Richards** Barry Anderson 1945–    S African cricketer
**Richards** Dickinson Woodruff 1895–1973 Am physician
**Richards** Frank 1875–1961 pseud of *Charles Hamilton* Eng author of boys' stories
**Richards** Sir Gordon 1904–    Eng jockey
**Richards** Isaac Vivian Alexander 1952–    W Indian cricketer
**Richards** Ivor Armstrong 1893–1979 Eng lit critic
**Richards** Theodore William 1868–1928 Am chem
**Richardson** Dorothy 1873–1957 Eng nov
**Richardson** Henry Handel 1870–1946 pseud of *Ethel Florence Lindesay Richardson* Austral nov
**Richardson** Sir Owen Willans 1879–1959 Eng physicist
**Richardson** Sir Ralph David 1902–1983 Eng actor
**Richardson** Samuel 1689–1761 Eng nov
**Richardson** Tony 1928–    Eng film & stage director
**Richelieu, de** Duc 1585–1642 *Armand Jean du Plessis* Fr cardinal & statesman
**Richler** Mordecai 1931–    Canad nov
**Richter** Hans 1843–1916 Austrian (Hung-born) conductor
**Richter** Jean Paul Friedrich 1763–1825 pseud *Jean Paul* Ger author
**Richter** Sviatoslav 1915–    Soviet pianist
**Richthofen, von** Manfred 1892–1918 *Red Baron* Ger airman
**Rickenbacker** Edward Vernon 1890–1973 Am aviator
**Ridley** Arnold 1896–    Eng dram, actor, & producer
**Ridley** Nicholas 1500?–1555 Eng reformer & martyr
**Riefenstahl** Leni 1902–    Ger film director
**Riemann** Georg Friedrich Bernhard 1826–1866 Ger math – **Riemannian** *adj*
**Rienzi, Rienzo, di** Cola 1313–1354 *Niccolò Gabrini; Last of the Romans* Ital patriot; tribune of Rome
**Riley** Bridget Louise 1931–    Eng artist
**Riley** James Whitcomb 1849–1916 Am poet
**Rilke** Rainer Maria 1875–1926 Ger poet
**Rimbaud** (Jean Nicholas) Arthur 1854–1891 Fr poet
**Rimini** Francesca da – see FRANCESCA DA RIMINI
**Rimski-Korsakov** Nikolai Andreevich 1844–1908 Russ composer
**Rindt** Karl-Jochen 1942–1970 Austrian (Ger-born) racing driver
**Risman** Augustus Beverley Walter 1937–    *Bev; son of next* Eng rugby league player
**Risman** Augustus John Ferdinand 1911–    *Gus* Eng rugby league player
**Rivera** Diego 1886–1957 Mex artist
**Rivers** Larry 1923–    Am artist
**Riza Shah Pahlavi, Pahlevi** 1877–1944 shah of Iran (1925–41)
**Rizzio, Riccio** David 1533?–1566 Ital musician & favourite of Mary, Queen of Scots
**Robbe-Grillet** Alain 1922–    Fr author
**Robbia, della** Luca 1400?–1482 Florentine sculptor
**Robbins** Frederick Chapman 1916–    Am physician
**Robbins** Harold 1916–    Am nov
**Robbins** Jerome 1918–    Am dancer & choreographer
**Robert** – see Robert BRUCE
**Robert I** *d* 1035 *Robert the Devil* Duke of Normandy (1028–35); father of William the Conqueror
**Roberton** Sir Hugh Stevenson 1874–1952 Eng choral conductor
**Roberts** Sir Charles George Douglas 1860–1943 Canad poet & short story author
**Roberts** Frederick Sleigh 1832–1914 1st Earl *Roberts of Kandahar, Pretoria, and Waterford* Br field marshal
**Roberts** Thomas William 1856–1931 Austral artist

**Roberts** William 1895–1980 Eng artist
**Robeson** Paul Bustill 1898–1976 Am actor & singer
**Robeson** Peter 1929–       Eng show jumper
**Robespierre, de** Maximilien François Marie Isidore 1758–1794 Fr revolutionist
**Robey** Sir George Edward 1869–1954 *Prime Minister of Mirth* né *George Edward Wade* Eng comedian & actor
**Robinson** Edward G 1893–1973 né *Emanuel Goldenberg* Am film actor
**Robinson** Henry Crabb 1775–1867 Eng diarist
**Robinson** Henry Peach 1830–1901 Eng photographer
**Robinson** Sir Robert 1886–1975 Eng chem
**Robinson** Stanford 1904–       Eng conductor & composer
**Robinson** Sugar Ray 1920–       né *Walker Smith* Am boxer
**Robinson** W Heath 1872–1944 Eng cartoonist
**Robinson** William 1838–1935 Br gardener & author
**Robsart** Amy 1525–1560 Eng wife of Robert Dudley, favourite of Queen Elizabeth I
**Robson** Dame Flora 1902–1984 Eng actress
**Rockefeller** John Davison father 1839–1937 & son 1874–1960 Am oil magnates & philanthropists
**Rockefeller** Nelson Aldrich 1908–1979 *grandson & son of prec* Am polit; vice-pres of the US (1974–77)
**Rockingham** 2nd Marquis of 1730–1782 *Charles Watson-Wentworth* Eng statesman
**Rockwell** Norman 1894–1978 Am illustrator
**Rodgers** Richard 1902–1979 Am composer
**Rodin** (François) Auguste (René) 1840–1917 Fr sculptor
**Rodney** George Brydges 1719–1792 1st Baron *Rodney* Eng admiral
**Rodnina** Irena 1949–       Soviet ice figure skater
**Rodriguez** Pedro 1940–1971 Mex racing driver
**Roeg** Nicholas 1928–       Eng film director
**Roentgen, Röntgen** Wilhelm Conrad 1845–1923 Ger physicist
**Rogers** Bruce 1870–1957 Am printer & book designer
**Rogers** Derek 1939–       *Budge* Eng rugby union player
**Rogers** Ginger 1911–       née *Virginia McMath* Am actress & dancer
**Rogers** William Penn Adair 1879–1935 *Will* Am actor & humorist
**Roget** Peter Mark 1779–1869 Eng physician & scholar
**Rolfe** Frederick William 1860–1913 pseud *Baron Corvo* Eng author
**Rolfe** John 1585–1622 *husband of Pocahontas* Eng colonist
**Rolland** Romain 1866–1944 Fr author
**Rollo, Hrol** 860?–?931 Norse chieftain
**Rolls** Charles Stewart 1877–1910 Eng motor manuf, motor trials driver, & aviator
**Romains** Jules 1885–1972 pseud of *Louis Farigoule* Fr author
**Romanov, Romanoff** Mikhail Feodorovich 1596–1645 1st czar (1613–45) of Russ Romanov dynasty (1613–1917)
**Romberg** Sigmund 1887–1951 Hung-born composer in Am
**Rommel** Erwin 1891–1944 Ger field marshal
**Romney** George 1734–1802 Eng artist
**Ronsard, de** Pierre 1524–1585 Fr poet
**Roosevelt** (Anna) Eleanor 1884–1962 née *Roosevelt, wife of FD* Am lecturer & author
**Roosevelt** Franklin Delano 1882–1945 32nd pres of the US (1933–45)
**Roosevelt** Theodore 1858–1919 26th pres of the US (1901–09)
**Rosa** Salvator 1615–1673 Ital artist & poet
**Rose** Sir Alec 1908–       Eng yachtsman; round the world single-handed
**Rose** Murray 1939–       Austral (Eng-born) swimmer
**Rosebery** 5th Earl of 1847–1929 *Archibald Philip Primrose* Eng statesman; prime min (1894–95)
**Rosenberg** Alfred 1893–1946 Ger Nazi & author
**Rosenfeld** Albert Aaron 1885–1970 Austral rugby league player
**Rosewall** Kenneth Ronald 1934–       Austral tennis player
**Ross** Sir James Clark 1800–1862 Scot polar explorer
**Ross** Sir John 1777–1856 *uncle of prec* Scot arctic explorer
**Ross** Sir Ronald 1857–1932 Br physician
**Rosse** Earl of – see William PARSONS
**Rossellini** Roberto 1906–1977 Ital film director & producer

**Rossetti** Christina Georgina 1830–1894 *sister of next* Eng poet
**Rossetti** Dante Gabriel 1828–1882 Eng artist & poet
**Rossini** Gioacchino Antonio 1792–1868 Ital composer
**Rostand** Edmond 1868–1918 Fr poet & dram
**Rostropovich** Mstislav Leopoldovich 1927–       Soviet cellist
**Roth** Philip 1933–       Am author
**Rothko** Mark 1903–1970 Am (Russ-born) artist
**Rothschild** Mayer Amschel 1743–1812 Ger financier
**Rothschild** Nathan Mayer 1777–1836 *son of prec* financier in London
**Rouault** Georges 1871–1958 Fr artist
**Rouget de Lisle** Claude Joseph 1760–1836 Fr army officer & composer of the "Marseillaise"
**Rous** Sir Stanley Ford 1895–       Eng football admin
**Rousseau** Henri 1844–1910 *le Douanier* Fr artist
**Rousseau** Jean Jacques 1712–1778 Fr (Swiss-born) philos & author
**Rousseau** Théodore 1812–1867 Fr artist
**Rowe** Nicholas 1674–1718 Eng poet & dram; poet laureate (1715–18)
**Rowlandson** Thomas 1756–1827 Eng caricaturist
**Rowley** William 1585?–?1642 Eng actor & dram
**Rowling** Wallace Edward 1927–       prime min of NZ (1974–75)
**Rowntree** (Benjamin) Seebohm 1871–1954 *son of next* Eng businessman & sociologist
**Rowntree** Joseph 1836–1925 Eng social reformer & manuf
**Rowse** Alfred Leslie 1903–       Eng hist
**Royce** Sir (Frederick) Henry 1863–1933 Eng engineer; co-founder of Rolls-Royce Ltd
**Rubbra** Edmund 1901–       Eng composer
**Rubens** Peter Paul 1577–1640 Flem artist – **Rubenesque, Rubensian** *adj*
**Rubinstein** Anton 1829–1894 Russ pianist & composer
**Rubinstein** Arthur 1888–       Pol-born pianist in Am
**Rubinstein** Helena 1871?–1965 Pol cosmetician
**Ruck** Berta 1878–1978 Eng romantic nov
**Rudolf, Rudolph of Hapsburg** 1858–1889 archduke & crown prince of Austria
**Rudolf I of Hapsburg** 1218–1291 Holy Rom emp (1273–91); 1st of the Hapsburgs
**Ruisdael, Ruysdael, van** Jacob 1628?–1682 & his uncle Salomon 1600?–1670 Du artists
**Rumford** – see Benjamin THOMPSON
**Runcie** Robert Alexander Kennedy 1921–       archbishop of Canterbury (1980–       )
**Rundstedt, von** Karl Rudolf Gerd 1875–1953 Ger field marshal
**Runeberg** Johan Ludvig 1804–1877 Finnish poet
**Runjit Singh** – see RANJIT SINGH
**Runyon** (Alfred) Damon 1884–1946 Am author
**Rupert** Prince 1619–1682 *nephew of Charles I of Eng* Ger-Eng gen & admiral
**Rupert, Rupprecht** 1869–1955 crown prince of Bavaria & Ger field marshal
**Ruskin** John 1819–1900 Eng essayist, critic, & reformer – **Ruskinian** *adj*
**Russell** Bertrand Arthur William 1872–1970 3rd Earl *Russell* Eng math & philos
**Russell** George William 1867–1935 pseud *AE* Irish author
**Russell** Lord John 1792–1878 1st Earl *Russell of Kingston Russell* Eng statesman; prime min (1846–52, 1865–66)
**Russell** Ken 1927–       Eng film director
**Russell** Sir William Howard 1820–1907 Eng (Irish-born) journalist
**Ruth** George Herman 1895–1948 *Babe* Am baseball player
**Rutherford** Ernest 1871–1937 1st Baron *Rutherford of Nelson* Br (NZ-born) physicist
**Rutherford** Dame Margaret 1892–1972 Eng actress
**Růžička** Leopold Stephen 1887–1976 Yugoslav chem
**Ryder** Albert Pinkham 1847–1917 Am artist
**Ryle** Gilbert 1900–1976 Eng philos
**Ryle** Sir Martin 1918–       Eng astron
**Ryun** James Ronald 1947–       *Jim* Am athlete

# S

**Sabatini** Rafael 1875–1950 Br (Ital-born) author
**Sabin** Albert Bruce 1906–    Am virologist
**Sabine** Sir Edward 1788–1883 Br astron
**Sacco** Nicola 1891–1927 & **Vanzetti** Bartolomeo 1888–1927 Am (Ital-born) anarchists
**Sachs** Hans 1494–1576 Ger cobbler & Meistersinger
**Sachs** Nelly 1891–1970 Swed dram & poet
**Sackville** Thomas 1536–1608 1st Earl of *Dorset* Eng poet & diplomat
**Sackville-West** Victoria Mary 1892–1962 *Vita* Eng author
**Sadat, el-** Anwar Mohamed 1918–1981 pres of Egypt (1970–81); assassinated
**Sade, de** Comte Donatien Alphonse François 1740–1814 Marquis *de Sade* Fr soldier, author, & sadist
**Sagan** Françoise 1935–    pseud of *Françoise Quoirez* Fr author
**Sailer** Toni 1935–    Austrian alpine ski racer
**Saint-Cyr** Marquis Laurent de Gouvion 1764–1830 Fr gen under Napoleon; marshal of France
**Sainte-Beuve** Charles Augustin 1804–1869 Fr critic & author
**St John** Henry – see BOLINGBROKE
**Saint-Just, de** Louis Antoine Léon 1767–1794 Fr revolutionist
**St Laurent** Louis Stephen 1882–1973 Canad lawyer; prime min (1948–57)
**St Laurent** Yves-Mathieu 1936–    Fr fashion designer
**Saint-Leon** Arthur 1821–1870 Fr ballet dancer & choreographer
**Saint-Martin** Yves 1941–    Fr jockey
**Saint-Pierre** – SEE BERNARDIN DE SAINT-PIERRE
**Saint-Saëns** (Charles) Camille 1835–1921 Fr composer
**Saint-Simon, de** Duc 1675–1755 *Louis de Rouvroy* Fr soldier, statesman, & author
**Saint-Simon, de** Comte 1760–1825 *Claude Henri de Rouvroy* Fr philos & social scientist
**Saintsbury** George Edward Bateman 1845–1933 Eng critic
**Saki** 1870–1916 pseud of *Hector Hugh Munro* Br author
**Saladin** 1138–1193 sultan of Egypt & Syria
**Salazar** Antonio de Oliveira 1889–1970 Port chief of state (1933–68)
**Salinger** Jerome David 1919–    Am nov
**Salisbury** 1st Earl of & 3rd Marquis of – see CECIL
**Salk** Jonas Edward 1914–    Am physician
**Sallust** 86–34 B C *Gaius Sallustius Crispus* Rom hist & polit – **Sallustian** *adj*
**Salote** 1900–1965 queen of Tonga (1918–65)
**Salt** Sir Titus 1803–1876 Eng textile manuf & inventor
**Salvini** Tommaso 1829–1916 Ital actor
**Sand** George 1804–1876 pseud of *Amandine Aurore Lucie* née *Dupin*; Baronne *Dudevant* Fr author
**Sandburg** Carl 1878–1967 né *Charles August Sandburg* Am author
**Sandracottus, Sandrocottus** – see CHANDRAGUPTA
**Sangallo, da** Giuliano 1445–1516 Florentine architect & sculptor
**Sanger** Frederick 1918–    Eng chem
**San Martín, de** José 1778–1850 S Am soldier & statesman
**Sanmicheli** Michele 1484?–1559 Ital architect & engineer
**Sansom** William 1912–1976 Eng author
**Sansovino** Jacopo 1486–1570 Ital architect & sculptor
**Santa Anna, Santa Ana, de** Antonio López 1795?–1876 Mex gen & pres
**Santander** Francisco de Paula 1792–1840 gen & polit of New Granada
**Santayana** George 1863–1952 Am (Span-born) poet & philos
**Santos-Dumont** Albert 1873–1932 Braz aviator in France
**Sapper** 1888–1937 pseud of *Herman Cyril McNeile* Eng nov
**Sappho** *fl ab* 600 B C Greek poet
**Saragat** Giuseppe 1898–    pres of Italy (1964–71)
**Sarazen** Gene 1902–    Am golfer
**Sardou** Victorien 1831–1908 Fr dram
**Sargent** Sir (Harold) Malcolm (Watts) 1895–1967 Eng conductor

**Sargent** John Singer 1856–1925 Am artist
**Sarkis** Elias 1924–    Lebanese banker & polit; pres of Lebanon (1976–   )
**Saroyan** William 1908–1981 Am author
**Sarraute** Nathalie 1902–    née *Tcherniak* Fr (Russ-born) author
**Sartre** Jean-Paul 1905–1980 Fr philos, dram, & nov – **Sartrian** *adj*
**Sassoon** Siegfried Lorraine 1886–1967 Eng author
**Satie** Erik Alfred Leslie 1866–1925 Fr composer
**Sato** Eisaku 1901–1975 Jap prime min (1964–1972); Nobel Peace Prize (1974)
**Saud Ibn Abdul** 1902–1969 king of Saudi Arabia (1953–64)
**Saussure, de** Ferdinand 1857–1913 Swiss linguist
**Savage** Michael Joseph 1872–1940 prime min of NZ (1935–40)
**Savery** Thomas 1650–1715 Eng engineer & inventor
**Savonarola** Girolamo 1452–1498 Ital reformer
**Sawchuk** Terrance Gordon 1929–1970 Canad ice-hockey player
**Sax** (Antoine Joseph) Adolphe 1814–1894 Belg musician; inventor of saxophone
**Saxo Grammaticus** 1150?–?1220 Danish hist
**Sayem** Abu Sadat Mohammad 1916–    pres of Bangladesh (1975–77)
**Sayers** Dorothy Leigh 1893–1957 Eng author
**Scaliger** Joseph Justus 1540–1609 Ital-born physician & scholar
**Scaliger** Julius Caesar 1484–1558 *father of prec* Ital physician
**Scanlon** Baron 1913–    *Hugh Parr Scanlon* Eng trade-union leader
**Scarfe** Gerald 1936–    Eng cartoonist
**Scarlatti** Alessandro 1659–1725 & his son Domenico 1685–1757 Ital composers
**Scarron** Paul 1610–1660 Fr author
**Schacht** (Horace Greeley) Hjalmar 1877–1970 Ger financier
**Scharnhorst, von** Gerhard Johann David 1755–1813 Pruss gen
**Scheel** Walter 1919–    W Ger pres (1974–   )
**Schelling, von** Friedrich Wilhelm Joseph 1775–1854 Ger philos – **Schellingian** *adj*
**Schiaparelli** Giovanni Virginio 1835–1910 Ital astron
**Schick** Béla 1877–1967 Am (Hung-born) paediatrician
**Schiller, von** (Johann Christoph) Friedrich 1759–1805 Ger poet & dram
**Schirach, von** Baldur 1907–1974 Ger Nazi polit
**Schlegel, von** August Wilhelm 1767–1845 Ger author
**Schlegel, von** Friedrich 1772–1829 *bro of prec* Ger philos & author
**Schleiermacher** Friedrich Ernst Daniel 1768–1834 Ger theol & philos
**Schlesinger** John Richard 1926–    Eng film director
**Schliemann** Heinrich 1822–1890 Ger archaeologist
**Schmidt** Helmut 1918–    chancellor of W Germany (1974–82)
**Schmitz** Ettore – see Italo SVEVO
**Schnabel** Artur 1882–1951 Am (Austrian-born) pianist & composer
**Schnitzler** Arthur 1862–1931 Austrian physician, dram, & nov
**Schockemohle** Alwin 1937–    W Ger show jumper
**Schönberg** Arnold 1874–1951 Am (Austrian-born) composer
**Schopenhauer** Arthur 1788–1860 Ger philos
**Schreiner** Olive Emilie Albertina 1855–1920 S African nov
**Schrödinger** Erwin 1887–1961 Austrian physicist
**Schubert** Franz Peter 1797–1828 Austrian composer
**Schuman** Robert 1886–1963 Fr statesman
**Schuman** William Howard 1910–    Am composer
**Schumann** Clara Josephine 1819–1896 née *Wiéck; wife of Robert* Ger pianist
**Schumann** Elizabeth 1895–1952 Am (Ger-born) soprano
**Schumann** Robert Alexander 1810–1856 Ger composer
**Schuschnigg, von** Kurt 1897–1977 Austrian statesman
**Schwarz** Rudolf 1905–    Eng (Austrian-born) conductor
**Schwarzkopf** Elisabeth 1915–    Ger soprano
**Schweitzer** Albert 1875–1965 Fr Protestant clergyman, philos, physician, & music scholar
**Scipio Aemilianus Africanus Numantinus** Publius Cornelius 185–129 B C *Scipio the Younger* Rom gen

**Scipio Africanus** Publius Cornelius 237–183 B C *Scipio the Elder* Rom gen
**Scofield** (David) Paul 1922–     Eng actor
**Scoresby** William 1789–1857 Eng scientist & arctic explorer
**Scott** George Campbell 1927–     Am actor
**Scott** Sir George Gilbert 1811–1878 Eng architect
**Scott** Sir Giles Gilbert 1880–1960 *grandson of prec* Eng architect
**Scott** Paul Mark 1920–1978 Eng nov
**Scott** Sir Peter Markham 1909–     *son of next* Eng ornithologist & artist
**Scott** Robert Falcon 1868–1912 Eng antarctic explorer
**Scott** Robert William Henry 1921–     NZ rugby union player
**Scott** Sheila Christine 1927–     Eng aviator
**Scott** Sir Walter 1771–1832 Scot poet & nov
**Scotto** Renata 1934–     Ital soprano
**Scotus** Duns – see DUNS SCOTUS
**Scotus** Johannes – see ERIGENA
**Scriabin, Scriabine** Alexander 1872–1915 Russ composer
**Scribe** Augustin Eugène 1791–1861 Fr dram
**Scrope** Richard 1350?–1405 Eng prelate
**Seaborg** Glen Theodore 1912–     Am chem
**Seaman** Richard John Beattie 1913–1939 Eng racing driver
**Searle** Humphrey 1915–1982 Eng composer
**Searle** Ronald William Fordham 1920–     Eng artist & cartoonist
**Secombe** Sir Harry Donald 1921–     Welsh singer & comedian
**Seddon** Richard John 1845–1906 *King Dick* prime min of NZ (1893–1906)
**Sedgman** Francis Arthur 1927–     *Frank* Austral tennis player
**Seeger** Peter 1919–     *Pete* Am folk singer
**Seferiades** Giorgos Stylianou 1900–1971 pseud *George Seferis* Greek diplomat & poet
**Segovia** Andrés 1893–     Span guitarist & composer
**Segrave** Sir Henry O'Neal de Hane 1896–1930 Eng racing driver & water speed racer
**Seidler** Harry 1923–     Austral (Austrian-born) architect
**Selden** John 1584–1654 Eng jurist & antiquarian
**Seleucus** 358?–280 B C ruler (306–280) of a Greek dynasty in Syria
**Selfridge** Henry Gordon 1864?–1947 Br (Am-born) businessman; founder of department store
**Selkirk** Alexander 1676–1721 Scot sailor marooned on one of Juan Fernández islets; original of Defoe's Robinson Crusoe
**Sellers** Peter Richard Henry 1925–1980 Eng actor
**Selwyn** George Augustus 1809–1878 Eng missionary; first bishop of NZ (1841)
**Seménov** Nikolai Nikolaevitch 1896–     Soviet chem
**Seneca** Lucius Annaeus 4 B C?–A D 65 Rom statesman, philos, & dram – **Senecan** *adj*
**Senghor** Léopold Sédar 1906–     pres of Senegal (1960–80)
**Sennacherib** *d* 681 B C king of Assyria (705–681)
**Sennett** Mack 1884–1960 Am film actor, producer, & director
**Sequoya** 1770?–1843 Cherokee Indian scholar
**Serkin** Rudolf 1903–     Am (Bohemian-born) pianist
**Serlio** Sebastiano 1475–1554 Ital architect
**Serra** Junípero 1713–1784 orig *Miguel José* Span missionary in Mexico & California
**Servetus** Michael 1511–1553 Span theol & martyr
**Service** Robert William 1874–1958 Canad author
**Sessions** Roger 1896–     Am composer
**Seton** Ernest Thompson 1860–1946 orig surname *Thompson* Eng-born author & illustrator in Am
**Seurat** Georges 1859–1891 Fr artist
**Seuss** – see Theodor Seuss GEISEL
**Severus** Lucius Septimius 146–211 Rom emp (193–211)
**Sévigné, de** Marquise 1626–1696 née *Marie de Rabutin-Chantal* Fr author & lady of fashion
**Sewell** Anna 1820–1878 Eng author
**Seymour** Jane 1509?–1537 *3rd wife of Henry VIII of Eng & mother of Edward VI*
**Seyss-Inquart, von** Artur 1892–1946 Ger Nazi polit
**Shackleton** Sir Ernest Henry 1874–1922 Br antarctic explorer

**Shadwell** Thomas 1642?–1692 Eng dram; poet laureate (1688–92)
**Shaffer** Peter Levin 1926–     Eng dram
**Shaftesbury** 1st Earl of 1621–1683 *Anthony Ashley Cooper* Eng statesman
**Shah Jahan** 1592–1666 Mogul emp of Hindustan (1628–58)
**Shahn** Ben 1898–1969 Am (Lithuanian-born) artist
**Shakespeare, Shakspere** William 1564–1616 Eng dram & poet
**Shakhlin** Boris 1932–     Soviet gymnast
**Shankar** Ravi 1920–     Indian musician
**Shapiro** Karl Jay 1913–     Am poet & critic
**Shapley** Harlow 1885–1972 Am astron
**Sharp** Cecil James 1859–1924 Eng folk musician
**Shastri** Shri Lal Bahadur 1904–1966 Indian polit; prime min of India (1964–66)
**Shaw** George Bernard 1856–1950 Irish dram, essayist, critic, & pamphleteer
**Shaw** Irwin 1913–     Am author
**Shaw** Richard Norman 1831–1912 Eng architect
**Shaw** Robert 1927–1978 Eng actor & author
**Shaw** Thomas Edward – see T E LAWRENCE
**Shearer** Norma 1902–1983 Canad film actress
**Sheene** Barry 1950–     Eng motor cycle racer
**Shelley** Mary Wollstonecraft 1797–1851 née *Godwin: wife of P B* Eng nov
**Shelley** Percy Bysshe 1792–1822 Eng poet – **Shelleyan, Shelleyesque** *adj*
**Shepard** Alan Bartlett 1923–     Am astronaut; 1st Am in space (1961)
**Shepard** Ernest Howard 1879–1976 Eng artist
**Sheppard** David Stuart 1929–     Eng clergyman & cricketer
**Sheppard** Hugh Richard Lawrie 1880–1937 *Dick* Eng clergyman & pacifist
**Sheppard** Jack 1702–1724 Eng robber; hanged at Tyburn
**Sheraton** Thomas 1751–1806 Eng furniture maker
**Sheridan** Richard Brinsley 1751–1816 Irish dram & orator
**Sherriff** Robert Cedric 1896–1975 Eng author
**Sherrington** Sir Charles Scott 1861–1952 Eng physiol
**Sherwood** Robert Emmet 1896–1955 Am dram
**Shih Huang-ti** 259–210 B C Chin emp
**Shinwell** Emanuel 1884–     Baron *Shinwell of Easington* Eng polit
**Shipton** Eric Earle 1907–1977 Eng explorer & mountaineer
**Shirley** James 1596–1666 Eng dram
**Sholokhov** Mikhail Aleksandrovich 1905–1984 Soviet nov
**Shostakovich** Dimitri Dimitrievich 1906–1975 Soviet composer
**Shovel** Sir Cloudesley 1650–1707 Eng sailor
**Shute** Nevil 1899–1960 pseud of *Nevil Shute Norway* Eng aeronautical engineer & author
**Sibelius** Jean 1865–1957 Finnish composer
**Sickert** Walter Richard 1860–1942 Eng artist
**Siddons** Sarah 1755–1831 née *Kemble* Eng actress
**Sidney** Sir Philip 1554–1586 Eng poet, statesman, & soldier
**Siegbahn** Karl Manne Georg 1886–1978 Swed physicist
**Siemens** Sir William 1823–1883 Br (Ger-born) inventor
**Sienkiewicz** Henryk 1846–1916 Pol nov
**Sigismund** 1368–1437 Holy Rom emp (1411–37)
**Signoret** Simone 1921–     pseud of *Simone Henriette Charlotte Montand* née *Kaminker* Fr actress
**Sigurdsson** Jón 1811–1879 Icelandic statesman & author
**Sihanouk** Norodom – see NORODOM SIHANOUK
**Sikorski** Wladyslaw 1881–1943 Pol gen & statesman
**Sikorsky** Igor Ivan 1889–1972 Am (Soviet-born) aeronautical engineer
**Sillanpää** Frans Eemil 1888–1964 Finnish nov
**Sillitoe** Alan 1928–     Eng author
**Siloe, de** Diego 1495?–1563 Span architect & sculptor
**Silone** Ignazio 1900–1978 pseud of *Secondo Tranquilli* Ital author
**Silvester** Victor Marlborough 1900–1978 Eng dance band leader
**Simenon** Georges Joseph Christian 1903–     Fr (Belg-born) author
**Simeon Stylites** Saint 390?–459 Syrian ascetic & stylite

**Simnel** Lambert 1475?–1535 Eng impostor
**Simon** Paul 1942–   Am singer & songwriter; "Simon and Garfunkel"
**Simonides of Ceos** 6th–5th c B C Greek poet
**Simpson** Sir James Young 1811–1870 Scot physician & obstetrician
**Simpson** Norman Frederick 1919–   Eng dram
**Simpson** Thomas 1937–1967 Eng road racing cyclist
**Sims** William Sowden 1858–1936 Am admiral
**Sinatra** Francis Albert 1915–   *Frank* Am singer & film actor
**Sinclair** Sir Clive Marles 1940–   Eng inventor
**Sinclair** Upton Beall 1878–1968 Am author & polit
**Singer** Isaac Bashevis 1904–   Am (Pol-born) author
**Singer** Isaac Merritt 1811–1875 Am inventor
**Siqueiros** David Alfaro 1898–1974 Mex mural painter
**Sisley** Alfred 1839–1899 Eng-born artist in France
**Sitter, de** Willem 1872–1934 Du astron
**Sitting Bull** 1834–1890 Sioux leader & medicine man
**Sitwell** Sir George Reresby 1860–1943 & his 3 children: Dame Edith 1887–1964; Sir Osbert 1892–1969; & Sir Sacheverell 1897–   Eng authors
**Skalkottas** Nikos 1904–1949 Greek composer
**Skeat** Walter William 1835–1912 Eng philologist
**Skelton** John 1460?–1529 Eng poet – **Skeltonic** *adj*
**Skinner** Burrhus Frederic 1904–   Am psychol
**Skoblikova** Lydia 1939–   Soviet ice skater
**Slessor** Sir John Cotesworth 1897–   Eng air-marshal
**Sloane** Sir Hans 1660–1753 Eng naturalist & physician
**Smart** Christopher 1722–1771 Eng poet
**Smeaton** John 1724–1794 Eng engineer
**Smellie** William 1740?–1795 Scot printer & natural hist
**Smetana** Bedřich 1824–1884 Czech pianist, composer, & conductor
**Smiles** Samuel 1812–1904 Scot author
**Smith** Adam 1723–1790 Scot econ
**Smith** Bessie 1894–1937 Am blues singer
**Smith** Cyril 1909–1974 Eng pianist
**Smith** Dodie 1896–   Eng dram & nov
**Smith** Florence Margaret 1902–1971 *Stevie* Eng poet
**Smith** Harvey 1938–   Eng show jumper
**Smith** Ian Douglas 1919–   Rhodesian prime min (1964–79)
**Smith** John 1580–1631 Eng colonist in Am
**Smith** Joseph 1805–1844 Am founder of Mormon Church
**Smith** Madeleine Hamilton 1835–1928 Scot defendant in murder trial (1857)
**Smith** Maggie 1934–   *Margaret Natalie Cross* née *Smith* Eng actress
**Smith** Sydney 1771–1845 Eng essayist, clergyman, & wit
**Smith** William 1769–1839 Eng geologist
**Smith** William Henry 1825–1891 Eng newsagent, bookseller, & poet
**Smith** Sir William Sidney 1764–1840 Eng admiral
**Smithson** James 1765–1829 Eng chem & mineralogist & founder of Smithsonian Institute
**Smollett** Tobias George 1721–1771 Br author
**Smuts** Jan Christiaan 1870–1950 S African field marshal; prime min (1919–24; 1939–48)
**Smyth** Dame Ethel 1858–1944 Eng composer
**Smythe** Francis Sydney 1900–1949 Eng mountaineer & author
**Smythe** Patricia Rosemary 1928–   Eng show jumper
**Snead** Samuel Jackson 1912–   Am golfer
**Snell** Peter George 1938–   NZ athlete
**Snorri Sturluson** 1178–1241 Icelandic statesman & hist
**Snow** 1st Baron 1905–1980 *Charles Percy Snow* Eng nov & physicist
**Snow** John Augustine 1941–   Eng cricketer
**Snowdon** Earl of – see ARMSTRONG-JONES
**Soane** Sir John 1753–1837 Eng architect
**Sobers** Sir Garfield St Aubrun 1936–   *Gary* W Indian cricketer
**Sobieski** John – see JOHN III SOBIESKI
**Socrates** 470?–399 B C Greek philos
**Soddy** Frederick 1877–1956 Eng chem
**Söderblom** Nathan 1866–1931 Swed theol
**Sodoma, Il** 1477?–1549 *Giovanni Antonio de' Bazzi* Ital artist

**Sokolova** Lydia 1896–1974 neé *Hilda Munnings* Eng ballet dancer
**Solon** 638?–?559 B C Athenian lawgiver
**Solti** Sir George 1912–   Br (Hung-born) conductor
**Solyman** – see SULEIMAN
**Solzhenitsyn** Aleksandr Isayevich 1918–   Soviet nov
**Somare** Michael Thomas 1936–   Papua New Guinea prime min (1975–   )
**Somes** Michael George 1917–   Eng dancer & ballet director
**Sophocles** 496?–406 B C Greek dram – **Sophoclean** *adj*
**Soult** Nicolas Jean de Dieu 1769–1851 *Duc de Dalmatie* Fr soldier; marshal of France
**Souphanouvong** Prince 1912–   pres of Lao People's Democratic Republic (1975–   )
**Sousa** John Philip 1854–1932 *the March King* Am bandmaster & composer
**Southey** Robert 1774–1843 Eng author; poet laureate (1813–43)
**Soutine** Chaim 1894–1943 Lith-born artist in France
**Spaak** Paul-Henri Charles 1899–1972 Belg lawyer & polit; premier (1938–39; 1947–49); sec- gen of NATO (1957–61)
**Spark** Muriel Sarah 1918–   née *Camberg* Br author
**Spartacus** *d* 71 B C Rom slave & insurrectionist
**Spassky** Boris Vasilyevich 1937–   Soviet chess player
**Speaight** Robert William 1904–1976 Eng actor & author
**Spear** Ruskin 1911–   Eng artist
**Spearman** Charles Edward 1863–1945 Eng psychologist
**Speer** Albert 1905–   Ger architect & Nazi official
**Speke** John Hanning 1827–1864 Eng soldier & explorer
**Spemann** Hans 1869–1941 Ger zool
**Spence** Sir Basil Urwin 1907–1976 Eng architect
**Spencer** Herbert 1820–1903 Eng philos
**Spencer** Sir Stanley 1891–1956 Eng artist
**Spender** Sir Stephen Harold 1909–   Eng poet & critic
**Spengler** Oswald 1880–1936 Ger philos
**Spenser** Edmund 1552–1599 Eng poet – **Spenserian** *adj*
**Sperry** Elmer Ambrose 1860–1930 Am inventor
**Spillane** Frank Morrison 1918–   *Mickey* Am author
**Spilsbury** Sir Bernard Henry 1877–1947 Eng pathologist
**Spinoza** Baruch *or* Benedict 1632–1677 Du philos – **Spinozistic** *adj*
**Spitteler** Carl 1845–1924 pseud *Felix Tandem* Swiss author
**Spitz** Mark Andrew 1950–   Am swimmer
**Spock** Benjamin McLane 1903–   Am physician
**Spode** Josiah 1754–1827 Eng potter
**Spofforth** Frederick Robert 1853–1926 *The Demon* Austral cricketer
**Spooner** William Archibald 1844–1930 Eng clergyman & educ; orig of "spoonerisms"
**Spring** Howard 1889–1965 Eng nov
**Staël, de** Mme Anne Louise Germaine 1766–1817 *Baronne de Staël Holstein*; née *Necker* Fr author
**Stahl** Georg Ernst 1660–1734 Ger chemist
**Stair** Earl of – see DALRYMPLE
**Stalin** Joseph 1879–1953 *Iosif Vissarionovich Dzhugashvili* Soviet leader
**Stanhope** Philip Dormer – see CHESTERFIELD
**Stanislas I Leszczyński** 1677–1766 king of Poland (1704–09; 1733–35)
**Stanislavski** Konstantin 1863–1938 Russ actor, director, & teacher
**Stanley** Edward George Geoffrey Smith 1799–1869 *Earl of Derby* Eng statesman
**Stanley** Sir Henry Morton 1841–1904 né *John Rowlands* Eng explorer in Africa
**Stanley** Wendell Meredith 1904–1971 Am biochem
**Stanton** Elizabeth 1815–1902 née *Cady* Am suffragette
**Stark** Dame Freya Madeline 1893–   Eng explorer
**Stark** Johannes 1874–1957 Ger physicist
**Starr** Ringo 1940–   pseud of *Richard Starkey* Eng drummer; member of Beatles
**Statham** (John) Brian 1930–   Eng cricketer
**Staudinger** Hermann 1881–1965 Ger chem
**Staunton** Howard 1810–1874 Eng chess player & scholar
**Stead** Christina Ellen 1902–   Austral nov

**Stecher** Renate 1950–   née *Meissner* E Ger athlete
**Steel** David Martin Scott 1938–   Scot polit
**Steele** Sir Richard 1672–1729 Br essayist & dram
**Steen** Jan 1626–1679 Du artist
**Steenken** Harting 1941–   W Ger show jumper
**Steer** Philip Wilson 1860–1942 Eng artist
**Stein** Gertrude 1874–1946 Am author
**Stein** John 1923–   *Jock* Scot footballer & manager
**Steinbeck** John Ernst 1902–1968 Am nov
**Steiner** Rudolf 1861–1925 Austrian philos & educ
**Steinitz** Wilhelm 1836–1900 Czech chess player
**Steinkraus** William 1925–   Am show jumper
**Stendhal** 1783–1842 pseud of *Marie Henri Beyle* Fr author – **Stendhalian** *adj*
**Stepanova** Galina 1948–   Soviet swimmer
**Stephen** 1097?–1154 king of England (1135–54)
**Stephen** Sir Leslie 1832–1904 Eng philos, critic, & biographer
**Stephens** James 1882–1950 Irish poet & nov
**Stephenson** George 1781–1848 Eng inventor & founder of railways
**Stephenson** Robert 1803–1859 *son of prec* Eng engineer
**Stern** Isaac 1920–   Russ-born violinist in Am
**Stern** Otto 1888–1969 Am (Ger-born) physicist
**Sterne** Laurence 1713–1768 Eng nov
**Stevens** Wallace 1879–1955 Am poet
**Stevenson** Adlai Ewing 1900–1965 Am lawyer & diplomat
**Stevenson** Robert Louis Balfour 1850–1894 Scot author
**Stevenson** Teophilo 1951–   Cuban boxer
**Stewart** Dugald 1753–1828 Scot philos
**Stewart** James Maitland 1902–   Am film actor
**Stewart** John Innes Mackintosh – see Michael INNES
**Stewart** John Young 1939–   *Jackie* Scot racing driver
**Stewart** Robert 1769–1822 Viscount *Castlereagh* Eng statesman
**Steyn** Martinus Theunis 1857–1916 S African lawyer & statesman
**Stilicho** Flavius 359?–408 Rom gen & statesman
**Still** Andrew Taylor 1828–1917 Am physician; founder of osteopathy
**Stockhausen** Karlheinz 1928–   Ger composer
**Stockmar, von** Baron Christian Friedrich 1787–1863 Anglo-Belg statesman
**Stoker** Bram 1847–1912 Br author
**Stokes** Sir George Gabriel 1819–1903 Br math & physicist
**Stokowski** Leopold Antoni Stanislaw 1882–1977 Eng-born conductor in Am
**Stones** Dwight 1953–   Am high jumper
**Stopes** Marie Charlotte Carmichael 1880–1958 Eng birth-control pioneer
**Stoppard** Tom 1937–   Eng (Czech-born) dram
**Storey** David Malcolm 1933–   Eng dram & nov
**Stout** Sir Robert 1844–1930 NZ (Scot-born) prime min (1884–87)
**Stow** John 1525?–1605 Eng hist & antiquarian
**Stowe** Harriet Elizabeth 1811–1896 née *Beecher* Am author
**Strabo** 63 B C?–?A D 24 Greek geographer
**Strachey** (Evelyn) John St Loe 1901–1963 Eng socialist & author
**Strachey** (Giles) Lytton 1880–1932 Eng biographer
**Strachey** John St Loe 1860–1927 *father of Evelyn* Eng journalist
**Stradivari** Antonio 1644–1737 *Antonius Stradivarius* Ital violin maker
**Strafford** 1st Earl of 1593–1641 *Thomas Wentworth* Eng statesman
**Stratford de Redcliffe** Viscount – see CANNING
**Strathcona and Mount Royal** 1st Baron 1820–1914 *Donald Alexander Smith* Canad (Scot-born) railroad builder & administrator
**Straus** Oskar 1870–1954 Fr (Austrian-born) composer
**Strauss** Johann father 1804–1849 & his sons Johann 1825–1899 & Josef 1827–1870 Austrian composers
**Strauss** Richard 1864–1949 Ger composer
**Stravinsky** Igor Fëdorovich 1882–1971 Am (Russ-born) composer – **Stravinskyan, Stravinskian** *adj*
**Streeton** Arthur 1867–1943 Austral artist

**Streicher** Julius 1885–1946 Ger Nazi administrator
**Streisand** Barbra 1942–   Am actress & singer
**Strijdom** Johannes Garhardus 1893–1958 prime min of S Africa (1954–58)
**Strindberg** August 1849–1912 Swed dram & nov – **Strindbergian** *adj*
**Stroheim, von** Erich 1885–1957 Am (Austrian-born) actor & film director
**Strudwick** Herbert 1880–1970 Eng cricketer
**Struther** Jan 1901–1953 pseud of *Joyce Maxtone Graham* née *Anstruther* Eng author
**Strutt** Jedediah 1726–1797 Eng knitting-machine inventor
**Strutt** John William – see RAYLEIGH
**Stuart** Charles *the Young Pretender* – see CHARLES EDWARD STUART
**Stuart** Gilbert Charles 1755–1828 Am artist
**Stuart** James Francis Edward *the Old Pretender* – see JAMES
**Stubbs** George 1724–1806 Eng artist
**Stubbs** William 1825–1901 Eng hist & prelate
**Sturgeon** William 1783–1850 Eng electrical engineer
**Sturluson** – see SNORRI STURLUSON
**Sturt** Charles 1795–1869 Eng explorer of Australia
**Stuyvesant** Peter 1592–1672 Du administrator in Am
**Suckling** Sir John 1609–1642 Eng Cavalier poet
**Sucre, de** Antonio José 1795–1830 S Am liberator
**Suetonius** 2nd c A D *Gaius Suetonius Tranquillus* Rom biographer & hist
**Suggia** Guilhermina 1888–1950 Port cellist
**Suharto** General 1921–   Indonesian pres & prime min (1968–   )
**Sukarno** Achmed 1901–1970 pres of Indonesian Republic (1945–67)
**Suleiman I** 1496?–1566 *the Magnificent* Ottoman sultan (1520–66)
**Sulla** 138–78 B C *Lucius Cornelius Sulla Felix* Rom gen & polit
**Sullivan** Sir Arthur Seymour 1842–1900 Eng composer; collaborator with Sir William Schwenck Gilbert
**Sullivan** James 1903–   Eng rugby league player
**Sullivan** John Lawrence 1858–1918 Am boxer
**Sullivan** Louis Henri 1856–1924 Am architect
**Sully, de** Duc 1560–1641 *Maximilien de Béthune* Baron de *Rosny* Fr statesman
**Sully Prudhomme** René François Armand 1839–1907 Fr poet & critic
**Sumner** James Batcheller 1887–1955 Am biochem
**Sumner** John Bird 1780–1862 archbishop of Canterbury (1848–62)
**Sumner** William Graham 1840–1910 Am sociologist & educ
**Sun** Yatsen 1866–1925 Chin statesman
**Surrey** Earl of – see Henry HOWARD
**Surtees** John 1934–   Eng motor cyclist & motor racing driver
**Surtees** Robert Smith 1803–1864 Eng nov & editor
**Susskind** (Jan) Walter 1913–1980 Br (Czech-born) conductor
**Sutcliffe** Herbert 1894–1978 Eng cricketer
**Sutherland** Graham Vivian 1903–1980 Eng artist
**Sutherland** Dame Joan 1926–   Austral operatic soprano
**Suttner, von** Bertha 1843–1914 née *Kinsky* Austrian author & pacifist
**Sverdrup** Otto Neumann 1855–1930 Norw arctic explorer
**Sverre, Sverrir** 1152?–1202 *Sverre Sigurdsson* king of Norway (1184–1202)
**Svevo** Italo 1861–1928 pseud of *Ettore Schmitz* Ital nov
**Swan** Sir Joseph Wilson 1828–1914 Eng scientist; designed first electric light bulb
**Swanson** Gloria May Josephine 1899–   Am film actress
**Swedenborg** Emanuel 1688–1772 né *Svedberg* Swed philos & religious writer
**Sweet** Henry 1845–1912 Eng phonetician & philologist
**Swift** Frank Victor 1914–1958 Eng footballer
**Swift** Jonathan 1667–1745 Br (Irish-born) satirist – **Swiftian** *adj*
**Swinburne** Algernon Charles 1837–1909 Eng poet – **Swinburnian** *adj*
**Swinnerton** Frank Arthur 1884–1982 Eng nov & critic
**Swinton** 1st Earl of 1884–1972 *Philip Cunliffe-Lister* Eng statesman

**Sydenham** Thomas 1624–1689 Eng physician
**Sylva** Carmen – see ELIZABETH Queen of Rumania
**Symonds** John Addington 1840–1893 Eng scholar
**Symons** Julian Gustave 1912–　　Eng author
**Synge** John Millington 1871–1909 Irish poet & dram
**Synge** Richard Laurence Millington 1914–　　Eng biochem
**Szell** George 1897–1970 Am (Hung-born) conductor
**Szent-Györgyi von Nagyrapolt** Albert 1893–　　Hung chem
**Szewinska** Irena 1946–　　neé *Kirszenstein* Pol athlete

# T

**Tacitus** Cornelius 55?–after 117 Rom hist – **Tacitean** *adj*
**Taft** William Howard 1857–1930 27th pres of the US (1909–13); chief justice US Supreme Court (1921–30)
**Taglioni** Filippo 1777–1871 Ital ballet dancer & choreographer
**Taglioni** Maria 1804–1884 *dau of prec* Ital ballet dancer
**Tagore** Rabindranath 1861–1941 Indian poet & philosopher
**Tailleferre** Germaine 1892–1983 Fr composer
**Tait** Archibald Campbell 1811–1882 archbishop of Canterbury (1869–82)
**Talleyrand-Périgord, de** Charles Maurice 1754–1838 Prince *de Bénévent* Fr statesman
**Tallis** Thomas 1505–1585 Eng composer
**Talon** Jean-Baptiste 1625?–1694 Fr colonial administrator in Can
**Tamerlane , Tamburlaine** 1336?–1405 *Timur Lenk* also *Timour* Eastern conqueror
**Tamm** Igor Yevgenievich 1895–1971 Soviet physicist
**Tanaka** Kakuei 1918–　　Jap premier (1972–74)
**Tancred** 1078?–1112 Norman leader in 1st crusade
**Tandy** James Napper 1740–1803 Irish revolutionary
**Tange** Kenzo 1913–　　Jap architect
**Tapies** Antoni 1923–　　Span artist
**Tarkington** (Newton) Booth 1869–1946 Am nov
**Tarleton** Sir Banastre 1754–1833 Eng soldier
**Tarleton** Richard *d*1588 Eng actor & jester
**Tasman** Abel Janszoon 1603–1659 Du mariner
**Tasso** Torquato 1544–1595 Ital poet
**Tate** Nahum 1652–1715 Eng dram; poet laureate (1692–1715)
**Tate** Phyllis 1911–　　Eng composer
**Tati** Jacques 1908–1982 pseud of *Jacques Tatischeff* Fr music-hall artist & film actor
**Tatum** Arthur 1910–1956 *Art* Am jazz pianist
**Tauber** Richard 1892–1948 Br (Austrian-born) tenor
**Tawney** Richard Henry 1880–1962 Eng economic hist
**Taylor** Alan John Percivale 1906–　　Eng historian
**Taylor** Cecil 1933–　　Am jazz pianist
**Taylor** Elizabeth 1932–　　Am (Eng-born) film actress
**Taylor** Sir Geoffrey Ingram 1886–1975 Eng physicist & meteorologist
**Taylor** Jeremy 1613–1667 Eng prelate & author
**Taylor** Sir Robert 1714–1788 Eng architect
**Taylor** Zachary 1784–1850 12th pres of the US (1849–50)
**Tchaikovsky** Pëtr Ilich 1840–1893 Russ composer – **Tchaikovskyan, Tchaikovskian** *adj*
**Tchekhov** – see CHEKHOV
**Tedder** 1st Baron 1890–1967 *Arthur William Tedder* Br air marshal
**Teilhard de Chardin** Pierre 1881–1955 Fr priest & author
**Telemann** Georg Philipp 1681–1767 Ger composer
**Telford** Thomas 1757–1834 Scot civil engineer
**Teller** Edward 1908–　　Am (Hung-born) physicist
**Téllez** Gabriel – see TIRSO DE MOLINA
**Temple** Frederick 1821–1902 archbishop of Canterbury (1896–1902)
**Temple** Shirley 1928–　　*Mrs Shirley Temple Black* Am child film actress & polit
**Temple** Sir William 1628–1699 Eng statesman
**Temple** William 1881–1944 *son of Frederick* archbishop of Canterbury (1942–44)
**Templer** Sir Gerald Walter Robert 1898–1979 Eng field marshal
**Templewood** Viscount – see HOARE

**Teng Hsiao-p'ing** 1904–　　Chin Communist leader (1977–)
**Teniers** David father 1582–1649 & son 1610–1690 Flemish artists
**Tenniel** Sir John 1820–1914 Eng cartoonist & illustrator
**Tennyson** 1st Baron 1809–1892 *Alfred Tennyson* Eng poet; poet laureate (1850–92) – **Tennysonian** *adj*
**Tenzing** Norgay 1914?–　　Tibetan mountaineer
**Terborch, Ter Borch** Gerard 1617–1681 Du artist
**Terence** 190?–159 B C *Publius Terentius Afer* Rom dram
**Tereshkova** Valentina Vladimirovna 1937–　　Soviet astronaut; first woman in space (1963)
**Terry** Dame Ellen Alicia *or* Alice 1847–1928 Eng actress
**Tertis** Lionel 1876–1975 Eng viola player
**Tertullian** 160?–?230 *Quintus Septimius Florens Tertullianus* Carthaginian church father
**Tesla** Nikola 1856–1943 Am (Austrian-born) electrician & inventor
**Te Wiata** Inia 1915–1971 Maori bass
**Teyte** Dame Maggie 1888–1976 *Dame Margaret Cottingham* Eng soprano
**Thackeray** William Makepeace 1811–1863 Eng author – **Thackerayan** *adj*
**Thalben-Ball** George Thomas 1896–　　Austral organist & composer
**Thales** 640?–546 B C Greek philos – **Thalesian** *adj*
**Thant** U 1909–1974 Burmese UN official; sec-gen (1961–71)
**Thatcher** Margaret Hilda 1925–　　née *Roberts* Eng polit; prime min (1979– )
**Theiler** Max 1899–1972 S African-born specialist in tropical medicine in US
**Themistocles** 524?–?460 B C Athenian gen & statesman
**Thenard** Louis Jacques 1777–1857 Fr chem
**Theocritus** 3rd c B C Greek poet
**Theodorakis** Mikis 1925–　　Greek composer
**Theodoric** 454?–526 *the Great* king of the Ostrogoths (474–526)
**Theodosius I** 346?–395 *the Great* Rom gen & emp (379–395)
**Theophrastus** *ab* 371–287 B C Greek philos & naturalist
**Theorell** Axel Hugo Theodor 1903–1982 Swed biochem
**Theresa , Teresa** Saint 1515–1582 Span Carmelite nun
**Thesiger** Wilfred Patrick 1910–　　Eng explorer & author
**Thespis** 6th c B C Greek poet
**Thiers** Louis Adolphe 1797–1877 Fr statesman & hist
**Thomas** Dylan Marlais 1914–1953 Br poet
**Thomas** (Philip) Edward 1878–1917 Eng poet
**Thomas** Sidney Gilchrist 1850–1885 Eng metallurgist
**Thomas à Becket** – see BECKET
**Thomas à Kempis** 1380–1471 Ger ecclesiastic & author
**Thompson** Benjamin 1753–1814 Count *Rumford* Eng (Am-born) physicist & statesman
**Thompson** Daley 1958–　　Eng pentathlete
**Thompson** Donald James 1933–　　Eng track & road walker
**Thompson** Sir Edward Maunde 1840–1929 Eng palaeographer
**Thompson** Francis 1859–1907 Eng poet
**Thompson** Sir John Sparrow David 1844–1894 Canad statesman; prime min (1892–94)
**Thomson** Sir Charles Wyville 1830–1882 Scot naturalist
**Thomson** Sir George Paget 1892–1975 *son of Sir Joseph John* Eng physicist
**Thomson** James 1700–1748 Scot poet
**Thomson** James Merriman Archer 1863–1912 Welsh mountaineer
**Thomson** Jeffrey 1950–　　Austral cricketer
**Thomson** Joseph 1858–1895 Scot explorer
**Thomson** Sir Joseph John 1856–1940 Eng physicist
**Thomson** Peter W 1929–　　Austral golfer
**Thomson** Virgil Garnett 1896–　　Am composer & critic
**Thomson** William – see Baron KELVIN
**Thomson of Fleet** 1st Baron 1894–1976 *Roy Herbert Thomson* Canad newspaper proprietor
**Thomson of Fleet** 2nd Baron 1923–　　*Kenneth Roy Thomson; son of prec* Canad newspaper proprietor
**Thorburn** Archibald 1860–1935 Eng naturalist, author, & artist
**Thoreau** Henry David 1817–1862 né *David Henry Thoreau* Am author – **Thoreauvian** *adj*

**Thorndike** Dame Sybil 1882–1976 *wife of Sir Lewis Casson* Eng actress

**Thornett** John 1930– Austral rugby union player

**Thornhill** Sir James 1675–1734 Eng artist

**Thorpe** James Francis 1888–1953 Am athlete

**Thorpe** (John) Jeremy 1929– Eng polit

**Thorvaldsen, Thorwaldsen** Bertel 1768–1844 Danish sculptor

**Thucydides** 471?–?400 B C Greek hist – **Thucydidean** *adj*

**Thurber** James Grover 1894–1961 Am author

**Thutmose, Thothmes** name of 4 kings of Egypt: esp **III** *d*1450 B C (reigned 1504–1450 B C)

**Thyssen** Fritz 1873–1951 Ger industrialist

**Tibbett** Lawrence Mervil 1896–1960 Am baritone

**Tiberius** 42 B C–A D 37 *Tiberius Claudius Nero Caesar* Rom emp (14–37)

**Tibullus** Albius 54?–?18 B C Rom poet

**Tieck** Ludwig 1773–1853 Ger author

**Tiepolo** Giovanni Battista 1696–1770 Ital artist

**Tiglath-pileser III** *d* 727 B C king of Assyria (745–727)

**Tilden** William Tatem 1893–1953 *Big Bill* Am tennis player

**Tildy** Zoltán 1889–1961 Hung polit

**Tillett** Benjamin 1860–1943 Eng trade-union leader

**Tilley** Vesta 1864–1952 pseud of *Lady de Frece*, née *Matilda Alice Powles* Eng music-hall entertainer

**Tillich** Paul Johannes 1886–1965 Am (Ger-born) theol

**Timoshenko** Semën Konstantinovich 1895–1970 Soviet marshal

**Timour, Timur, Timur Lenk** – see TAMERLANE

**Tinbergen** Jan 1903– Du econ

**Tinbergen** Nikolaas 1907– *bro of Jan* Du ethologist

**Tindemans** Leo 1922– prime min of Belg (1974–78)

**Tintoretto, Il** 1518–1594 *Jacopo Robusti* Ital artist

**Tippett** Sir Michael Kemp 1905– Eng composer

**Tipu Sahib, Tippoo Sahib** 1751–1799 sultan of Mysore (1782–99)

**Tirpitz, von** Alfred 1849–1930 Ger admiral

**Tirso de Molina** 1571?–1648 pseud of *Gabriel Téllez* Span dram

**Tiselius** Arne Wilhelm Kaurin 1902–1971 Swed biochem

**Titchener** Edward Bradford 1867–1927 Eng psychol

**Titian** 1477–1576 *Tiziano Vecellio* Ital artist – **Titianesque** *adj*

**Tito** – see BROZ

**Titus** 40?–81 *Titus Flavius Sabinus Vespasianus* Rom emp (79–81)

**Tocqueville, de** Alexis Charles Henri Maurice Clérel 1805–1859 Fr statesman & author

**Todd** Sir Alexander Robertus 1907– Baron *Todd of Trumpington* Scot chem

**Todd** Mike 1907–1958 Am stage & film producer

**Todd** (Reginald Stephen) Garfield 1908– Rhodesian (NZ-born) prime min (1953–58)

**Todt** Fritz 1891–1942 Ger military engineer

**Tojo** Hideki 1885–1948 Jap gen & polit; prime min (1941–44).

**Tolbert** William Richard 1913–1980 pres of Liberia (1971–80)

**Tolkien** John Ronald Reuel 1892–1973 Eng author

**Toller** Ernst 1893–1939 Ger dram & polit

**Tolstoy, Tolstoi** Count Lev Nikolaevich 1828–1910 Russ nov, philos, & mystic – **Tolstoyan, Tolstoian** *adj*

**Tombaugh** Clyde William 1906– Am astron; disc Pluto

**Tommasini** Vincenzo 1878–1950 Ital composer

**Tone** (Theobald) Wolfe 1763–1798 Irish revolutionist

**Tooke** (John) Horne 1736–1812 Eng polit radical & philologist

**Topolski** Feliks 1907– Br (Pol-born) artist

**Torquemada, de** Tomás 1420?–1498 Span grand inquisitor

**Torrens** William Torrens McCullagh 1813–1894 Eng social reformer

**Torricelli** Evangelista 1608–1647 Ital math & physicist

**Toscanini** Arturo 1867–1957 Ital conductor

**Toulouse-Lautrec, de** Henri 1864–1901 Fr artist

**Toussaint L'Ouverture** Pierre Dominique 1743–1803 Haitian gen & liberator

**Toynbee** Arnold Joseph 1889–1975 Eng hist

**Trabert** Marian Anthony 1930– Am tennis player

**Tracy** Spencer 1900–1967 Am film actor

**Traherne** Thomas 1637–1674 Eng author

**Trajan** 52 *or* 53–117 *Marcus Ulpius Trajanus* Rom emp (98–117)

**Travers** Ben 1886–1980 Eng dram

**Travers** Pamela Lyndon 1906– Br (Austral-born) author

**Tree** Sir Herbert Draper Beerbohm 1853–1917 Eng actor-manager

**Trench** Richard Chenevix 1807–1886 Irish poet & prelate

**Trenchard** Hugh Montague 1873–1956 1st Viscount *Trenchard* Eng airman & administrator

**Trésagnet** Pierre Marie Jérome 1716–1796 Fr civil engineer

**Tressel** Robert 1871–1911 pseud of *Robert Noonan* Irish author

**Trevelyan** George Macaulay 1876–1962 Eng hist

**Trevelyan** Sir George Otto 1838–1928 *father of prec* Eng polit, biographer, & hist

**Treves** Sir Frederick 1853–1923 Eng surgeon; founder of Br Red Cross Soc

**Trevino** Lee Buck 1939– Am golfer

**Treviranus** Gottfried Reinhold 1776–1837 Ger naturalist

**Trevithick** Richard 1771–1833 Eng engineer & inventor

**Trevor-Roper** Hugh Redwald 1914– Baron *Dacre of Glanton* Eng hist & author

**Trollope** Anthony 1815–1882 Eng nov – **Trollopian** *adj*

**Trotsky , Trotski** Leon 1879–1940 *Leib* or *Lev Davydovich Bronstein* Soviet Communist

**Trudeau** Pierre–Elliott 1919– Canad polit; prime min (1968–79; 1980– )

**Trueman** Frederick Sewards 1931– *Freddie* Eng cricketer

**Truffaut** François 1932–1984 Fr film director

**Truman** Harry S 1884–1972 33rd pres of the US (1945–53)

**Trumper** Victor Thomas 1877–1915 Austral cricketer

**Tsatsos** Konstantinos 1899– Greek philos, lawyer, & polit

**Tschaikovsky** – see TCHAIKOVSKY

**Tshombe** Moise Kapenda 1919–1969 Congolese mil leader & polit

**Tubman** William Vacanarat Shadrach 1895–1971 Liberian lawyer; pres of Liberia (1944–71)

**Tudor** Antony 1908– Eng ballet dancer & choreographer

**Tu fu** 712–770 Chin poet

**Tull** Jethro 1674–1741 Eng agric

**Tulsi Das** 1532–1623 Hindu poet

**Tunnicliffe** Charles Frederick 1901–1979 Eng artist & illustrator

**Tupou IV** 1918– King Taufa'ahau of Tonga (1965– )

**Turenne, de** Vicomte 1611–1675 *Henri de la Tour d'Auvergne* Fr marshal

**Turgenev** Ivan Sergeevich 1818–1883 Russ nov

**Turgot** Anne Robert Jacques 1727–1781 Baron *de l'Aulne* Fr statesman & econ

**Turitscheva** Ludmilla 1952– Soviet gymnast

**Turner** Glenn Maitland 1947– NZ cricketer

**Turner** Joseph Mallord William 1775–1851 Eng artist

**Turpin** Dick 1706–1739 Eng highwayman

**Turrall** Jenny 1960– Austral swimmer

**Tussaud** Marie 1760–1850 née *Grosholtz* Swiss waxwork modeller

**Tutankhamen, Tutenkhamon** *fl ab* 1358 B C king of Egypt

**Tutin** Dorothy 1931– Eng actress

**Twain** Mark – see CLEMENS

**Tweedsmuir** – see BUCHAN

**Tyler** John 1790–1862 10th pres of the US (1841–45)

**Tyler** Wat *or* Walter *d* 1381 Eng leader of Peasants' revolt (1381)

**Tylor** Sir Edward Burnet 1832–1917 Eng anthrop

**Tynan** Kenneth Peacock 1927–1980 Eng theatre critic

**Tyndale** William 1492?–1536 Eng reformer & martyr

**Tyndall** John 1820–1893 Ir physicist

# U

**Uccello** Paolo 1397–1475 *Paolo di Dono* Florentine artist

**Udall, Uvedale** Nicholas 1505–1556 Eng schoolmaster & dram

**Uhland** Johann Ludwig 1787–1862 Ger poet & hist

**Ulbricht** Walter 1893–1973 East German statesman

**Unamuno y Jugo, de** Miguel 1864–1936 Span philos & author

**Undset** Sigrid 1882–1949 Norw nov

**Updike** John Hoyer 1932– Am author

**Upham** Charles Hazlitt 1908– NZ soldier & farmer

**Urban** name of 8 popes: esp **II** (*Odo* or *Udo*) 1042?–1099 (pope 1088–99)
**Urey** Harold Clayton 1893–1981 Am chem
**Urquhart** Sir Thomas 1611–1660 Scot author & translator
**Ussher** James 1581–1656 Irish archbishop
**Ustinov** Peter Alexander 1921–    Eng dram, author, actor, & raconteur
**Utamaro** Kitagawa 1753–1806 Jap artist
**Utrillo** Maurice 1883–1955 Fr artist
**Utzon** Jøern 1918–    Danish architect; designer of Sydney Opera House

# V

**Vadim** Roger 1927–    Fr film director & author
**Vaillant** Jean Baptiste Philibert 1790–1872 Fr army officer; marshal of France
**Valdemar** – see WALDEMAR
**Valdivia, de** Pedro 1500?–1553 Span conqueror of Chile
**Valentinian** *Lat* **Valentinianus** name of 3 Rom emperors: **I** 321–375 (reigned 364–375); **II** 372–392 (reigned 375–392); **III** 419–455 (reigned 425–455)
**Valentino** Rudolph 1895–1926 Am (Ital-born) film actor
**Valera** Eamon de – see DE VALERA
**Valera y Alcalá Galiano** Juan 1824–1905 Span author & statesman
**Valerian** d 269? *Publius Licinius Valerianus* Rom emp (253–260)
**Valéry** Paul Ambroise 1871–1945 Fr poet & philos
**Van Allen** James Alfred 1914–    Am physicist
**Vanbrugh** Sir John 1664–1726 Eng dram & architect
**Van Buren** Martin 1782–1862 8th pres of the US (1837–41)
**Vancouver** George 1757–1798 Eng navigator & explorer
**Van de Graaff** – see GRAAFF
**Vanderbilt** Cornelius 1794–1877 Am capitalist
**Van der Post** Laurens Jan 1906–    S African author, farmer, & explorer
**Van Dine** – see Willard Huntington WRIGHT
**van Dongen** Cornelius 1877–1968 *Kees van Dongen* Fr (Dutch-born) artist
**Vandyke , Van Dyck** Sir Anthony 1599–1641 Flem-born artist in Eng
**Vane** Sir Henry *or* Harry 1613–1662 Eng statesman
**Van Gogh** Vincent –see GOGH
**Vansittart** Robert Gilbert 1881–1957 1st Baron *Vansittart of Denham* Eng diplomat
**van't Hoff** Jacobus Hendricus 1852–1911 Du physical chem
**Vanzetti** Bartolomeo – see Nicola SACCO
**Varah** (Edward) Chad 1911–    Eng clergyman; founder of the Samaritans
**Vardon** Harry 1870–1937 Eng golfer
**Varèse** Edgard 1883–1965 Am (Fr-born) composer
**Vargas** Getulio Dornelles 1883–1954 Braz lawyer; pres of Brazil (1930–45; 1951–54)
**Varro** Marcus Terentius 116–27 B C Rom author
**Vasari** Giorgio 1511–1574 Ital artist & author
**Vasco da Gama** – see Vasco da GAMA
**Vauban, de** Marquis 1633–1707 *Sébastien Le Prestre* Fr mil engineer; marshal of France
**Vaughan** Henry 1622–1695 *the Silurist* Br poet
**Vaughan Williams** Ralph 1872–1958 Eng composer
**Vega, de** Lope 1562–1635 *Lope Félix de Vega Carpio* Span dram
**Veidt** Conrad 1893–1943 Ger film actor
**Velázquez, Velásquez** Diego Rodríguez de Silva y 1599–1660 Span artist
**Vendôme, de** Duc Louis Joseph 1654–1712 Fr soldier; marshal of France
**Venizelos** Eleutherios 1864–1936 Greek statesman
**Ventris** Michael 1922–1956 Eng architect & archaeologist
**Verdi** Giuseppe 1813–1901 Ital composer – **Verdian** *adj*
**Vereker** – see GORT
**Vereshchagin** Vasili Vasilievich 1842–1904 Russ artist

**Vergil, Virgil** 70–19 B C *Publius Vergilius Maro* Rom poet – **Vergilian, Virgilian** *adj*
**Verity** Hedley 1905–1943 Eng cricketer
**Verlaine** Paul 1841–1896 Fr poet
**Vermeer** Jan 1632–1675 *Jan van der Meer van Delft* Du artist
**Verne** Jules 1828–1905 Fr author
**Vernier** Pierre 1580–1637 Fr math
**Vernon** Edward 1684–1757 Eng admiral
**Veronese** Paolo 1528–1588 né *Paolo Cagliari* Ital artist
**Verrazano, Verrazzano, da** Giovanni 1485?–?1528 Florentine navigator
**Verrocchio, del** Andrea 1435–1488 né *Andrea di Michele Cione* Florentine sculptor & artist
**Verulam** – see Francis BACON
**Verwoerd** Hendrik Frensch 1901–1966 S African polit; prime min (1958–66)
**Vesalius** Andreas 1514–1564 Belgian anatomist & artist
**Vespasian** 9–79 *Titus Flavius Sabinus Vespasianus* Rom emp (69–79)
**Vespucci** Amerigo 1454–1512 *Americus Vespucius* Ital navigator; alleged discoverer of American mainland
**Vian** Sir Philip Louis 1894–1968 Eng admiral
**Vickers** Jon 1926–    Canad tenor
**Victor Emmanuel I** 1759–1824 king of Sardinia (1802–21)
**Victor Emmanuel II** 1820–1878 king of Sardinia (1849–61) & 1st king of Italy (1861–78)
**Victor Emmanuel III** 1869–1947 king of Italy (1900–46)
**Victoria** Alexandrina 1819–1901 queen of GB (1837–1901)
**Victoria** Tomás Luis de 1540?–1611 Span composer
**Vida** Marco Girolamo 1480?–1566 Ital poet
**Vidal** Gore 1925–    Am author
**Vigée-Lebrun** Marie Louise Élisabeth 1755–1842 Fr artist
**Vignola, da** Giacomo 1507–1573 *Giacomo Barocchio* or *Barozzi* Ital architect
**Vigny, de** Comte Alfred Victor 1797–1863 Fr author
**Villa** Francisco *or* Pancho 1877–1923 né *Doroteo Arango* Mex bandit & revolutionist
**Villa-Lobos** Heitor 1887–1959 Braz composer
**Villard** Paul 1860–1934 Fr physicist
**Villars, de** Duc Claude Louis Hector 1653–1734 Fr soldier; marshal of France
**Villiers** George 1592–1628 1st Duke of *Buckingham* Eng statesman & admiral
**Villiers** George 1628–1687 2nd Duke of *Buckingham, son of prec* Eng courtier & dram
**Villon** François 1431–after 1462 né *François de Montcorbier* Fr poet
**Villon** Jacques 1875–1963 né *Gaston Duchamp* Fr artist
**Vincent de Paul** Saint 1581?–1660 Fr priest
**Vinci, da** Leonardo 1452–1519 Florentine artist, sculptor, architect, & engineer
**Viollet-le-Duc** Eugène Emmanuel 1814–1879 Fr architect
**Virchow** Rudolf 1821–1902 Ger pathologist
**Viren** Lasse Artturi 1949–    Finnish athlete
**Virgil** – see VERGIL
**Virtanen** Artturi Ilmari 1895–1973 Finnish biochem
**Visconti** Luchino 1906–1976 Ital stage & film director
**Vivaldi** Antonio 1675?–1741 Ital composer
**Vladimir** 956?–1015 *the Great* ruler of Russia (980–1015)
**Vlaminck, de** Maurice 1876–1958 Fr artist
**Vlasov** Yuri 1935–    Soviet weight lifter
**Vogel** Sir Julius 1835–1899 NZ (Eng-born) prime min (1873–75)
**Vogel** Renate 1955–    E Ger swimmer
**Vogt, van** Alfred Elton 1912–    Canad science-fiction author
**Volta** Count Alessandro 1745–1827 Ital physicist
**Voltaire** 1694–1778 né *François Marie Arouet* Fr author – **Voltairean, Voltairian** *adj*
**Von Braun** Wernher – see BRAUN
**Voroshilov** Kliment Efremovich 1881–1969 Soviet marshal; pres of USSR (1953–60)
**Vorster** Balthazar Johannes 1915–1983 prime min of Republic of South Africa (1966–78)
**Vuillard** (Jean) Édouard 1868–1940 Fr artist
**Vyshinsky** Andrei Yanuarievich 1883–1954 Soviet lawyer & statesman

# W

**Waals, van der** Johannes Diderik 1837–1923 Du physicist
**Wace** 12th c Anglo-Norman poet
**Waddell** Helen Jane 1889–1965 Eng author; specialist in medieval studies
**Wade** (Sarah) Virginia 1945– Eng tennis player
**Wagner** (Wilhelm) Richard 1813–1883 Ger composer
**Wagner von Jauregg** Julius 1857–1940 Austrian neurologist & psychiatrist
**Wagstaff** Harold 1891–1939 Eng rugby league player
**Wain** John Barrington 1925– Eng author
**Wakefield** Edward Gibbon 1796–1862 Eng colonial reformer
**Waksman** Selman Abraham 1888–1973 Am (Ukrainian-born) microbiologist
**Walcott** Joe 1914– *Jersey Joe;* né *Arnold Raymond Cream* Am boxer
**Waldemar, Valdemar** name of 4 kings of Denmark: esp **I** (*the Great*) 1131–1182 (reigned 1157–82)
**Waldheim** Kurt 1918– Austrian UN official; sec-gen (1972–82)
**Waldo, Valdo** Peter *fl* 1173–1179 Fr heretic
**Walesa** Lech 1943– Pol trade-union leader
**Waley** Arthur Schloss 1889–1966 Eng oriental scholar & poet
**Walker** John 1952– NZ athlete
**Wallace** Alfred Russel 1823–1913 Eng naturalist
**Wallace** Edgar 1875–1932 Eng nov & dram
**Wallace** Sir William 1272?–1305 Scot patriot
**Wallach** Otto 1847–1931 Ger chem
**Wallenstein, von** Albrecht Eusebius Wenzel 1583–1634 Duke of *Friedland and Mecklenburg;* Prince of *Sagan* Austrian gen
**Waller** Edmund 1606–1687 Eng poet
**Wallis** Alfred 1855–1942 Eng primitive artist
**Wallis** Sir Barnes Neville 1887–1979 Eng aeronautical engineer & inventor
**Walpole** Horace *or* Horatio 1717–1797 4th Earl of *Orford* Eng author
**Walpole** Sir Hugh Seymour 1884–1941 Eng nov
**Walpole** Sir Robert 1676–1745 1st Earl of *Orford; father of Horace* Eng statesman – **Walpolian** *adj*
**Walsingham** Sir Francis 1532?–1590 Eng statesman
**Walter** Bruno 1876–1962 né *Bruno Schlesinger* Am (Ger-born) conductor
**Walter** Hubert *d* 1202 Eng statesman, prelate, & judge; archbishop of Canterbury (1193)
**Walter** John 1739–1812 Eng journalist
**Walton** Ernest Thomas Sinton 1903– Irish physicist
**Walton** Izaak 1593–1683 Eng author
**Walton** Sir William Turner 1902–1983 Eng composer
**Wanamaker** Sam 1919– Am actor & director
**Wangchuk** Jigme Sinhe 1955– King of Bhutan (1972– )
**Wanova** Galina Sergeyevna 1910– Soviet ballet dancer
**Warbeck** Perkin 1474–1499 Walloon impostor; pretender to the Eng throne
**Warburg** Otto Heinrich 1883–1970 Ger physiol
**Ward** Artemus – see Charles Farrar BROWNE
**Ward** Barbara Mary 1914–1981 Baroness *Jackson of Lodsworth* Eng econ
**Ward** Mrs Humphrey 1851–1920 neé *Mary Augusta Arnold* Eng (Austral-born) nov & philanthropist
**Ward** Sir Joseph George 1856–1930 NZ statesman; prime min (1906–12; 1926–30)
**Warhol** Andy 1931– Am artist & filmmaker
**Warlock** Peter 1894–1930 pseud of *Philip Heseltine* Eng composer
**Warner** Sir Pelham Francis 1873–1963 *Plum* Eng cricketer
**Warner** Rex 1905– Eng nov & poet
**Warren** Robert Penn 1905– Am author & educ
**Warton** Thomas 1728–1790 Eng literary hist & critic; poet laureate (1785–90)
**Warwick** Earl of 1428–1471 *Richard Neville; the Kingmaker* Eng soldier & statesman
**Washington** George 1732–1799 Am gen; 1st pres of the US (1789–97) – **Washingtonian** *adj*

**Wassermann, von** August 1866–1925 Ger bacteriol
**Watkins** David 1942– Welsh rugby union player
**Watson** Tom 1949– Am golfer
**Watson-Watt** Sir Robert Alexander 1892–1973 Scot physicist
**Watt** James 1736–1819 Scot inventor
**Watteau** Jean Antoine 1684–1721 Fr artist
**Watts** George Frederic 1817–1904 Eng artist & sculptor
**Watts** Isaac 1674–1748 Eng theol & hymn writer
**Watts-Dunton** Walter Theodore 1832–1914 Eng critic & poet
**Waugh** Evelyn Arthur St John 1903–1966 Eng author
**Wavell** 1st Earl 1883–1950 *Archibald Percival Wavell* Eng field marshal; viceroy of India (1943–47)
**Wayne** John 1907–1980 né *Marion Michael Morrison* Am film actor
**Webb** Sir Aston 1849–1930 Eng architect
**Webb** Beatrice 1858-1943 née *Potter; wife of SJ* Eng socialist
**Webb** Mary Gladys 1881–1927 née *Meredith* Eng author
**Webb** Matthew 1848–1883 Eng swimmer; first to swim English Channel
**Webb** Philip 1831–1915 Eng architect
**Webb** Sidney James 1859–1947 1st Baron *Passfield* Eng socialist
**Weber, von** Karl Maria Friedrich Ernst 1786–1826 Ger composer & conductor
**Weber** Max 1864–1930 Ger sociologist & econ – **Weberian** *adj*
**Webern** Anton von 1883–1945 Austrian composer
**Webster** Daniel 1782–1852 Am statesman & orator
**Webster** John 1580?–?1625 Eng dram
**Webster** Noah 1758–1843 Am lexicographer & author
**Weddell** James 1787–1834 Eng antarctic explorer
**Wedekind** Frank 1864–1918 Ger dram
**Wedgwood** Dame Cicely Veronica 1910– Eng historian
**Wedgwood** Josiah 1730–1795 Eng potter
**Wedgwood Benn** – see BENN
**Weekes** Everton de Courcy 1925– W Indian cricketer
**Weighell** Sidney 1922– Eng trade-union leader
**Weill** Kurt 1900–1950 Ger-born composer in the US
**Weismann** August 1834–1914 Ger biologist
**Weissmuller** Johnny 1904– Am swimmer & film actor
**Weizmann** Chaim 1874–1952 Israeli (Russ-born) chem; 1st pres of Israel (1948–52)
**Welensky** Sir Roy (Roland) 1907– prime min of Rhodesia (1956–63)
**Welles** (George) Orson 1915– Am actor & producer
**Wellesley** 1st Marquis 1760–1842 *Richard Colley Wellesley* Brit statesman; gov-gen of India (1797–1805)
**Wellington** 1st Duke of 1769–1852 *Arthur Wellesley; the Iron Duke* Eng gen & statesman
**Wells** Herbert George 1866–1946 Eng nov & hist – **Wellsian** *adj*
**Wells** William 1888–1967 *Bombardier Billy Wells* Eng boxer
**Wenceslaus** *Ger Wenzel* 1361–1419 king of Germany & Holy Rom Emp (1378–1400) & (as Wenceslaus IV) king of Bohemia (1378–1419)
**Wenden** Michael 1949– Austral swimmer
**Wentworth** William Charles 1793–1872 Austral statesman
**Werner** Alfred 1866–1919 Swiss chem
**Wesker** Arnold 1932– Eng dram & director
**Wesley** Charles 1707–1788 *bro of John* Eng Methodist preacher & hymn writer
**Wesley** John 1703–1791 Eng theol, evangelist, & founder of Methodism
**West** Benjamin 1738–1820 Am artist in Eng
**West** Nathanael 1903–1940 né *Nathan Wallenstein Weinstein* Am nov
**West** Dame Rebecca 1892–1983 pseud of *Cicily Isabel Andrews* née *Fairfield* Eng critic & nov
**West** Thomas – see DE LA WARR
**Westinghouse** George 1846–1914 Am inventor
**Weyden, van der** Rogier 1399?–1464 Flem artist
**Weygand** Maxime 1867–1965 Fr gen
**Wharton** Edith Newbold 1862–1937 née *Jones* Am nov
**Wheatcroft** Harry 1899–1977 Eng rose grower
**Wheatley** Dennis Yates 1897–1977 Eng author
**Wheatley** Francis 1747–1801 Eng artist
**Wheatstone** Sir Charles 1802–1875 Eng physicist & inventor
**Wheeler** Sir Charles Thomas 1892–1974 Eng sculptor

**Wheeler** Sir (Robert Eric) Mortimer 1890–1976 Eng archaeologist

**Whillans** Donald Desbrow 1933–　　Eng mountaineer

**Whinfield** John Rex 1901–1966 Eng chem

**Whinneray** Wilson James 1935–　　NZ rugby union player

**Whistler** James Abbott McNeill 1834–1903 Am artist & etcher – **Whistlerian** *adj*

**Whistler** Laurence 1912–　　*bro of next* Eng glass engraver & author

**Whistler** Reginald John 1905–1944 *Rex; bro of prec* Eng artist & stage designer

**White** Edward Higgins II 1930–1967 Am astronaut; first to walk in space

**White** Gilbert 1720–1793 Eng clergyman & naturalist

**White** Patrick Victor Martindale 1912–　　Austral author

**White** Terence Hanbury 1906–1964 Eng author

**Whitefield** George 1714–1770 Eng Methodist revivalist

**Whitehead** Alfred North 1861–1947 Eng math & philos

**Whitehouse** Mary 1910– Eng journalist; leader of "Clean up TV" campaign

**Whiteman** Paul 1890–1967 Am bandleader

**Whitlam** Edward Gough 1916–　　prime min of Austral (1972–75)

**Whitman** Walt 1819–1892 orig *Walter* Am poet – **Whitmanes-que, Whitmanian** *adj*

**Whitney** Eli 1765–1825 Am inventor

**Whittier** John Greenleaf 1807–1892 *the Quaker Poet* Am poet

**Whymper** Edward 1840–1911 Eng mountaineer

**Wiclif, Wickliffe** – see WYCLIFFE

**Widor** Charles Marie 1845–1937 Fr organist & composer

**Wieland** Christoph Martin 1733–1813 Ger author

**Wieland** Heinrich 1877–1957 Ger chem

**Wien** Wilhelm 1864–1928 Ger physicist

**Wiener** Norbert 1894–1964 Am math

**Wiggin** Kate Douglas 1856–1923 née *Smith* Am author & educ

**Wigner** Eugene Paul 1902–　　Am (Hung-born) physicist

**Wilberforce** William 1759–1833 Eng philanthropist & abolitionist

**Wilbur** Richard Purdy 1921–　　Am author

**Wild** Jonathan 1682?–1725 Eng criminal; hanged at Tyburn

**Wilde** Jimmy 1892–1969 Eng boxer

**Wilde** Oscar Fingal O'Flahertie Wills 1854–1900 Eng (Irish-born) author

**Wilder** Billy 1906–　　Am (Austrian-born) film director

**Wilder** Thornton Niven 1897–1975 Am author

**Wilhelmina** 1880–1962 queen of the Netherlands (1890–1948)

**Wilkes** Charles 1798–1877 Am naval officer & explorer

**Wilkes** John 1727–1797 Eng polit reformer

**Wilkie** Sir David 1785–1841 Scot artist

**Wilkie** David 1954–　　Scot swimmer

**Wilkins** Sir George Hubert 1888–1958 Austral polar explorer

**Wilkinson** Diana 1944–　　Eng swimmer

**Wilkinson** Ellen Cicely 1891–1947 Eng feminist & polit

**William** name of 4 kings of Eng: **I** (*the Conqueror*) 1027–1087 (reigned 1066–87); **II** (*Rufus*) 1056?–1100 (reigned 1087–1100); **III** 1650–1702 (reigned 1689–1702 – see MARY); **IV** 1765–1837 (reigned 1830–37)

**William** 1982–　　*Prince William Arthur Philip Louis; Prince William of Wales; son of Prince Charles*

**William** 1882–1951 *Friedrich Wilhelm Victor August Ernst* crown prince of Germany (1888–1918)

**William I** 1533–1584 *the Silent* prince of Orange & founder of the Dutch Republic

**William I** 1797–1888 king of Prussia (1861–88) & Ger emp (1871–88)

**William II** 1859–1941 Ger emp & king of Prussia (1888–1918)

**William of Malmesbury** between 1090 and 1096–?1143 Eng hist

**Williams** Elizabeth Mary 1943–　　N Ireland peace movement organizer; Nobel Peace Prize (1976)

**Williams** Emlyn 1905–　　Welsh actor & dram

**Williams** Sir (Evan) Owen 1890–1969 Eng architect

**Williams** John Peter Rhys 1949–　　Welsh rugby union player

**Williams** Ralph Vaughan – see Ralph VAUGHAN WILLIAMS

**Williams** Roger 1603?–1683 Eng-born clergyman; founder of Rhode Island colony

**Williams** Ted 1912–　　Eng show jumper & racing greyhound trainer

**Williams** Tennessee 1911–1982 *Thomas Lanier Williams* Am dram

**Williams** William Carlos 1883–1963 Am author

**Williams-Ellis** Sir (Bertram) Clough 1883–1978 Eng architect

**Williamson** Henry 1895–1977 Eng nov

**Williamson** Malcolm 1931–　　Austral composer, organist, & pianist

**Willis** Thomas 1621–1673 Eng physician

**Willstätter** Richard 1872–1942 Ger chem

**Wilson** Angus 1913–　　pseud of *Angus Frank Johnstone-Wilson* Eng nov

**Wilson** Charles Thomson Rees 1869–1959 Scot physicist

**Wilson** Colin Henry 1931–　　Eng author

**Wilson** Edmund 1895–1972 Am author

**Wilson** (James) Harold 1916–　　Baron *Wilson of Rievaulx* Eng polit; prime min (1964–70; 1974–76) – **Wilsonian** *adj*

**Wilson** Sandy 1924–　　Eng composer & lyricist

**Wilson** (Thomas) Woodrow 1856–1924 28th pres of the US (1913–21) – **Wilsonian** *adj*

**Winchester** Oliver Fisher 1810–1880 Am gun manuf

**Winckelmann** Johann Joachim 1717–1768 Ger archaeol & art hist

**Windaus** Adolf 1876–1959 Ger chem

**Windisch-Graetz, zu** Prince Alfred Candidus Ferdinand 1787–1862 Austrian field marshal

**Windsor** Duke of – see EDWARD VIII

**Wingate** Orde Charles 1903–1944 Eng gen

**Winkler** Hans Günter 1926–　　W Ger show jumper

**Winn** Godfrey Herbert 1908–1971 Eng journalist & author

**Winner** Michael Robert 1935–　　Eng film director

**Winter** Frederick Thomas 1926–　　Eng jockey & racehorse trainer

**Winterhalter** Franz Xavier 1806–1873 Ger artist & engraver

**Wirtanen** Artturi – see Artturi VIRTANEN

**Wirth** Karl Joseph 1879–1956 Ger statesman; chancellor of Weimar Republic (1921–22)

**Wisden** John 1826–1884 Eng cricketer; compiler of cricketers' almanac

**Wise** Stephen Samuel 1874–1949 Am (Hung-born) rabbi

**Wise** Thomas James 1859–1937 Eng bibliophile & forger

**Wiseman** Nicholas Patrick Stephen 1802–1865 Eng cardinal & author

**Wishart** George 1513?–1546 Scot religious reformer; burnt at stake

**Wither, Withers** George 1588–1667 Eng poet & pamphleteer

**Witte** Count Sergei Yulievich 1849–1915 Russ statesman

**Wittekind, Widukind** *d ab* 807 Saxon warrior

**Wittgenstein** Ludwig 1889–1951 Br (Austrian-born) philos – **Wittgensteinian** *adj*

**Wodehouse** Sir Pelham Grenville 1881–1975 Am (Eng-born) author

**Woffington** Margaret 1714?–1760 *Peg* Irish actress

**Wolf** Friedrich August 1759–1824 Ger philologist

**Wolf** Hugo 1860–1903 Austrian composer

**Wolf** Max 1863–1932 Ger astron

**Wolfe** James 1727–1759 Br gen

**Wolfe** Thomas Clayton 1900–1938 Am nov

**Wolfenden** John Frederick 1906–　　Baron *Wolfenden of Westcott* Eng administrator & philos

**Wolfit** Sir Donald 1902–1968 Eng actor

**Wolfram von Eschenbach** 1170?–?1220 Ger poet

**Wolgemut** Michael 1434–1519 Ger artist

**Wollaston** William Hyde 1766–1828 Eng chem & physicist

**Wollstonecraft** Mary 1759–1797 *Mrs Mary Wollstonecraft Godwin* Eng author

**Wolseley** 1st Viscount 1833–1913 *Garnet Joseph Wolseley* Br field marshal

**Wolsey** Thomas 1475?–1530 Eng cardinal & statesman

**Wood** Haydn 1881–1959 Eng composer

**Wood** Mrs Henry 1814–1887 neé *Eileen Price* Eng nov

**Wood** Sir Henry Joseph 1869–1944 Eng conductor

**Woodcock** George 1904–1979 Eng trade-union leader

**Wooderson** Sydney Charles 1914–　　Eng athlete

**Woodforde** James 1740–1803 Eng clergyman & diarist
**Woodfull** William Maldon 1897–1965 Austral cricketer
**Woodham-Smith** Cecil Blanche 1897–1977 Eng author
**Woodward** Sir Arthur Smith 1864–1944 Eng geologist
**Woolf** Leonard Sidney 1880–1969 *husband of next* Eng author & publisher
**Woolf** Virginia 1882–1941 née *Stephen* Eng author
**Woollcott** Alexander 1887–1943 Am author
**Woolley** Sir Charles Leonard 1880–1960 Eng archaeol
**Woolley** Frank Edward 1887–1978 Eng cricketer
**Woolton** 1st Baron 1883–1964 *Frederick James Marquis* Eng businessman & administrator
**Woolworth** Frank Winfield 1852–1919 Am merchant
**Wootton** Barbara Frances 1897– Baroness *Wootton of Abinger* Eng economist
**Wordsworth** William 1770–1850 Eng poet; poet laureate (1843–50) – **Wordsworthian** *adj*
**Worrell** Sir Frank Mortimer Maglinne 1924–1967 W Indian cricketer
**Wotton** Sir Henry 1568–1639 Eng diplomat & poet
**Wouk** Herman 1915– Am nov
**Wrangel** Baron Pëtr Nikolaevich 1878–1928 Russ gen & counterrevolutionist
**Wren** Sir Christopher 1632–1723 Eng architect
**Wren** Percival Christopher 1885–1941 Eng nov
**Wright** Frank Lloyd 1869–1959 Am architect
**Wright** Judith 1915– Austral poet
**Wright** Orville 1871–1948 & his bro Wilbur 1867–1912 Am pioneers in aviation
**Wright** Willard Huntington 1888–1939 pseud *S S Van Dine* Am author
**Wright** William Ambrose 1924– *Billy* Eng footballer
**Wulstan** Saint 1012?–1095 Eng ecclesiastic
**Wundt** Wilhelm 1832–1920 Ger physiol & psychol
**Wyatt, Wyat** James 1746–1813 Eng architect
**Wyatt** Sir Thomas 1503–1543 Eng poet & diplomat
**Wycherley** William 1640?–1716 Eng dram
**Wycliffe** John 1320?–1384 Eng religious reformer & Bible translator – **Wycliffian** *adj*
**Wyler** William 1902– Am film director
**Wyndham** Sir Charles 1837–1919 né *Charles Culverwell* Eng actor-manager
**Wyndham** John 1903–1969 pseud of *John Wyndham Beynon Harris* Eng science-fiction author
**Wynne** David 1926– Eng artist & sculptor

# X

**Xanthippe, Xantippe** 5th c B C *wife of Socrates*
**Xavier** Saint Francis 1506–1552 *Francisco Javier; Apostle of the Indies* Span Jesuit missionary
**Xenocrates** 396–314 B C Greek philos
**Xenophanes** 6th c B C Greek philos
**Xenophon** 434?–?355 B C Greek hist, essayist, & soldier
**Xerxes I** 519?–465 B C *the Great* king of Persia (486–465)

# Y

**Yale** Linus 1821–1868 Am locksmith
**Yalow** Rosalyn Sussman 1921– Am biochem
**Yamagata** Prince Aritomo 1838–1922 Jap gen & statesman
**Yang Chen Ning** 1922– Chin physicist
**Yashin** Lev 1929– Soviet footballer
**Yates** Dornford 1885–1960 pseud of *Cecil William Mercer* Eng nov
**Yeats** Jack Butler 1871–1957 *bro of next* Irish artist & author
**Yeats** William Butler 1865–1939 Irish poet & dram – **Yeatsian** *adj*
**Yeremenko** Andrei Ivanovich 1892–1970 Soviet gen
**Yersin** Alexandre-Émile-John 1863–1943 Swiss bacteriol

**Yesenin** Sergey Aleksandrovich 1895–1925 Russ poet
**Yevtushenko** Yevgeny 1933– Soviet author
**Yonge** Charlotte Mary 1823–1901 Eng nov
**Yoshihito** 1879–1926 emp of Japan (1912–26)
**Young** Brigham 1801–1877 Am Mormon leader
**Young** Charles Mayne 1777–1856 Eng actor
**Young** Edward 1683–1765 Eng poet
**Young** Francis Brett 1884–1954 Eng nov
**Young** Geoffrey Winthrop 1876–1958 Eng mountaineer
**Younghusband** Sir Francis Edward 1863–1942 Eng soldier & explorer
**Yüan Shihk'ai** 1859–1916 Chin statesman; pres of China (1913–16)
**Yukawa** Hideki 1907–1981 Jap physicist

# Z

**Zadkine** Ossip 1890–1967 Russ sculptor
**Zaharias** Mildred 1914–1956 née *Didrikson* Am athlete, golfer, & basketball player
**Zaharoff** Sir Basil 1850–1936 né *Basileios Zacharias* Fr (Russ-born) banker & armament contractor
**Zamenhof** Ludwik Lejzer 1859–1917 Pol oculist; inventor of Esperanto
**Zamora** Ricardo 1901– Span footballer
**Zamora y Torres** Niceto Alcalá 1877–1949 Span polit; pres of Spain (1931–36)
**Zápotocký** Antonín 1884–1957 prime min of Czech (1948–53), pres (1953–57)
**Zátopek** Emil 1922– Czech athlete
**Zeami** Motokiyo 1363–1443 Jap dram & actor
**Zeeman** Pieter 1865–1943 Du physicist
**Zeffirelli** Franco Corse 1923– Ital film, opera, & stage director
**Zeiss** Carl 1816–1888 Ger manuf of optical instruments
**Zeno** 4th–3rd c B C Greek philos; founder of Stoic school
**Zeno of Elea** 5th c B C Greek philos
**Zenobia** *d* after 272 queen of Palmyra (267–272)
**Zeppelin, von** Count Ferdinand 1838–1917 Ger gen & airship constructor
**Zetterling** Mai Elizabeth 1925– Swed actress & film director
**Zhukov** Georgi Konstantinovich 1896–1974 Soviet marshal
**Ziegfeld** Florenz 1869–1932 Am theatrical producer
**Ziegler** Karl 1898–1973 Ger chem
**Zimbalist** Efrem 1889– Am (Russ-born) violinist
**Zimmermann** Arthur 1864–1940 Ger statesman
**Zinnemann** Fred 1907– Am (Austrian-born) film director
**Zinzendorf, von** Count Nikolaus Ludwig 1700–1760 Ger leader of the Bohemian Brethren
**Zog I, Zogu I** 1895–1961 *Scanderbeg III*; né *Ahmed Bey Zogu* king of the Albanians (1928–46)
**Zola** Émile 1840–1902 Fr nov – **Zolaesque** *adj*
**Zoroaster, Zarathustra** 6th c B C founder of ancient Pers religion
**Zorrilla y Moral** José 1817–1893 Span poet & dram
**Zuckerman** Sir Solly 1904– Baron *Zuckerman of Burnham Thorpe* Br (S African-born) scientist
**Zurbarán** Francisco 1598–?1664 Span artist
**Zweig** Arnold 1887–1968 Ger author
**Zweig** Stefan 1881–1942 Austrian author
**Zwingli** Huldreich *or* Ulrich 1484–1531 Swiss Reformation leader

# Geographical names

This section provides basic information about the countries of the world and their most important regions, cities, and physical features. Statistical data are included for most entries.

Many derivative forms are included, e g:

**Aberdeen** ... – **Aberdonian** *adj or n*
**Alaska** ... – **Alaskan** *adj or n*
**Andes** ... – **Andean** *n*

Abbreviations used in this appendix are listed below. The letters N, E, S, and W indicate direction and are not part of a place-name; thus N Vietnam indicates northern Vietnam and not North Vietnam. The symbol ✳ denotes a capital. Areas, altitudes, and lengths are given first in metric units, followed by conventional equivalents in parentheses.

## Abbreviations

| | | | |
|---|---|---|---|
| *ab* | about | | |
| AD | anno Domini | L | Latin |
| *anc* | ancient | Lith | Lithuanian |
| Ar | Arabic | LL | Late Latin |
| Assoc | Association | *m* | metres |
| BC | before Christ | max | maximum |
| bet | between | Mex Sp | Mexican Spanish |
| *bib* | biblical | ML | Medieval Latin |
| Brit | British | Mt | Mount |
| Bulg | Bulgarian | N | North |
| | | N | northern |
| *cen* | central | NGk | New Greek |
| Co | County | Norw | Norwegian |
| Czech | Czechoslovakian | | |
| D | Dutch | orig | originally |
| Dan | Danish | Pol | Polish |
| E | East | *pop* | population |
| E | eastern | Port | Portuguese |
| esp | especially | *prov* | provisional |
| *est* | estimated | Rum | Rumanian |
| F | French | Russ | Russian |
| Finn | Finnish | S | South |
| Flem | Flemish | s | southern |
| *ft* | feet | Sp | Spanish |
| G | German | *sq km* | square kilometres |
| Gael | Gaelic | *sq miles* | square miles |
| Gen | General | St | Saint |
| Gk | Greek | Swed | Swedish |
| Heb | Hebrew | Turk | Turkish |
| HQ | Headquarters | Univ | University |
| Hung | Hungarian | US | United States |
| I | Island | USA | United States of America |
| It | Italian | USSR | Union of Soviet Socialist Republics |
| Jap | Japanese | usu | usually |
| *km* | kilometres | W | West |
| | | w | western |

# A

**Aachen,** F **Aix-la-Chapelle** city w Germany near Belgian & Dutch borders *pop* 243,900 (1980)

**Abadan** city & port in w Iran in Shatt-al-Arab delta *pop* 296,081 (1976)

**Abbeville** town N France on the Somme NW of Amiens *pop* 25,000 (1973)

**Aberdeen** city and seaport Grampian region, NE Scotland *pop* 181,785 (1971) – **Aberdonian** *adj or n*

**Abidjan** city & port ✳ of Ivory Coast *pop* 1,700,000 (1979 *est*)

**Abu Dhabi 1** sheikhdom United Arab Emirates on s coast of Persian Gulf *area* 63,333 *sq km* (26,000 *sq miles*), *pop* 450,000 (1980 *est*) **2** city & port, its ✳ & ✳ of United Arab Emirates *pop* 350,000 (1980 *est*)

**Abu Simbel, Impsambul** locality s Egypt on left bank of the Nile sw of Aswân; site of two rock temples which were moved 1964–66 to higher ground when area was flooded after completion of Aswân High Dam

**Abyssinia** – see ETHIOPIA

**Accra, Akkra** city & port ✳ of Ghana on Gulf of Guinea *pop* 851,614 (1970 *prov*)

**Aconcagua** mountain 6,960m (22,834 *ft*) w Argentina WNW Mendoza near Chilean border; highest in Andes & western hemisphere

**Açores** – see AZORES

**Acre,** Heb **Akko, Accho,** *anc* **Ptolemais** city & port NW Israel at N end of Bay of Acre N of Mt Carmel *pop* 33,900 (1974)

**Addis Ababa** city ✳ of Ethiopia *pop* 912,000 (1977 *est*)

**Adelaide** city Australia ✳ of S Australia *pop* (with suburbs) 952,700 (1981)

**Aden** city & port, a ✳ of People's Democratic Republic of Yemen (Southern Yemen) & former ✳ of Aden colony & protectorate *pop* 270,000 (1977 *est*)

**Admiralty** islands w Pacific N of New Guinea in Bismarck archipelago *area* 2,072 *sq km* (800 *sq miles*), *pop* 23,000 (1971)

**Adriatic** sea arm of the Mediterranean between Italy & Balkan peninsula

**Aegean 1** sea arm of the Mediterranean between Asia Minor & Greece **2** islands Aegean sea including the Cyclades & the Northern & Southern Sporades

**Aetna** – see ETNA

**Afars and the Issas, French Territory of the** – see DJIBOUTI

**Afghanistan** country w Asia E of Iran; a republic ✳ Kabul *area* 647,497 *sq km* (250,000 *sq miles*), *pop* 15,500,000 (1979 *est*) – **Afghanistani** *n*

**Afognak** island s Alaska N of Kodiak I

**Africa** continent of the eastern hemisphere s of the Mediterranean & adjoining Asia on NE *area ab* 30,244,050 *sq km* (11,677,240 *sq miles*), *pop* 401,000,000 (1975 *est*)

**Agadir** city & port sw Morocco *pop* 61,192 (1971)

**Agana** town ✳ of Guam on w coast *pop* 2,119 (1971)

**Agincourt** – see AZINCOURT

**Agri Dagi** – see ARARAT

**Ahmadabad, Ahmedabad** city w India N of Bombay in Gujarat state *pop* 1,741,522 (1971)

**Ailsa Craig** small rocky island Scotland s of Arran at mouth of Firth of Clyde *area* 2.58 *sq km* (1 *sq mile*)

**Aintree** town in Merseyside NW of Liverpool; scene of annual Grand National steeplechase *pop* 8,271 (1971)

**Aire** river 112 *km* (70 *miles*) N England in w Yorkshire flowing to the Ouse; its valley is **Airedale**

**Aix, Aix-en-Provence** city SE France N of Marseilles *pop* 102,000 (1975)

**Aix-la-Chapelle** – see AACHEN

**Ajaccio** city & port France in Corsica *pop* 51,770 (1980 *est*)

**Ajman** sheikhdom United Arab Emirates *area* 267 *sq km* (100 *sq miles*), *pop* 36,000 (1980 *est*)

**Akkra** – see ACCRA

**Akosombo Dam** on river Volta, Ghana 113 *m* (370 *ft*) high

**Alabama** state SE USA ✳ Montgomery *area* 134,183 *sq km* (51,609 *sq miles*), *pop* 3,890,061 (1980) – **Alabaman** *adj or n*

**Alaska** state (territory 1912–59) of the USA NW North America ✳ Juneau *area* 1,524,671 *sq km* (586,412 *sq miles*), *pop* 400,481 (1980) – **Alaskan** *adj or n*

**Albania** country s Europe in Balkan peninsula on the Adriatic; a republic ✳ Tirane *area* 28,748 *sq km* (11,101 *sq miles*), *pop* 2,670,600 (1980)

**Albany** city ✳ of New York on Hudson river *pop* 101,727 (1980)

**Alberta** province w Canada ✳ Edmonton *area* 646,880 *sq km* (248,800 *sq miles*), *pop* 2,237,724 (1981) –**Albertan** *adj or n*

**Albert Canal** waterway in NE Belgium linking Liège with Antwerp; 130 *km* (80 *miles*) long

**Alcatraz** island California in San Francisco Bay

**Aldeburgh** coastal town in E Suffolk; venue for annual music festival *pop* 2,800 (1971)

**Aldermaston** village in Berkshire; site of atomic weapons establishment

**Alderney** island in English channel, northernmost of the Channel islands ✳ St Anne *area* 8 *sq km* (3 *sq miles*), *pop* 2,000 (1981)

**Aldershot** town in NE Hampshire; site of military camp and barracks *pop* 33,400 (1971)

**Aleppo, Alep,** Ar **Haleb, Halab,** *anc* **Beroea, Bereo** city N Syria *pop* 1,862,713 (1979) – **Aleppine** *adj or n*

**Aletsch** glacier, largest in Bernese Alps, Switzerland; 16 *km* (10 *miles*) long *area* 171 *sq km* (66 *sq miles*)

**Aleutian** islands sw Alaska extending in an arc 1,800 *km* (1,100 *miles*) sw & w from Alaska peninsula

**Alexandria** city & port N Egypt between Lake Mareotis & the Mediterranean *pop* 2,521,000 (1980 *est*) – **Alexandrian** *adj or n*

**Algeciras** city & port sw Spain w of Gibraltar on Bay of Algeciras *pop* 81,662 (1970)

**Algeria** country NW Africa bordering on the Mediterranean ✳ Algiers *area* 2,381,741 *sq km* (919,397 *sq miles*), *pop* 18,250,000 (1981 *est*) – **Algerian** *adj or n*

**Algiers 1** former Barbary state N Africa now Algeria **2 Algiers,** F **Alger,** Ar **Aljezair** city & port ✳ of Algeria on Bay of Algiers *pop* 3,250,000 (1981 *est*) – **Algerine** *adj or n*

**Al Hijaz** – see HEJAZ

**Alma-Ata,** *formerly* **Vernyi** city USSR in Soviet Central Asia ✳ of Kazakhstan *pop* 910,000 (1979)

**Alps** mountain system s cen Europe extending *ab* 1,200 *km* (745 *miles*) from Mediterranean coast at border between France & Italy into NW & w Yugoslavia – see MONT BLANC

**Amazon** river *ab* 6,500 *km* (4,000 *miles*) long N South America flowing from Peruvian Andes into the Atlantic in N Brazil

**America 1** either continent (North America or South America) of the western hemisphere **2 America, the Americas** the lands of the western hemisphere including North, Central, & South America & the West Indies *pop* 561,000,000 (1975 *est*) **3** – see UNITED STATES OF AMERICA

**Amiens** city N France on the Somme *pop* 131,013 (1975 *prov*)

**Amman** *anc* **Philadelphia,** *bib* **Rabbah, Rabbath** city ✳ of Jordan *pop* 750,000 (1980)

**Amsterdam** city & port, official ✳ of Netherlands *pop* 965,246 (1978)

**Amur, Heilungkiang** river 2,824 *km* (1,755 *miles*) long E Asia formed by junction of Shilka & Argun rivers, flowing into the Pacific at N end of Tatar strait, & forming part of boundary between China & Soviet Russia, Asia

**Anapurna** – see ANNAPURNA

**Anatolia** the part of Turkey comprising the peninsula of Asia Minor

**Andes** mountain system of South America extending *ab* 8,900 *km* (5,500 *miles*) along w coast from Panama to Tierra del Fuego – **Andean** *adj,* **Andine** *adj*

**Andorra** country sw Europe in E Pyrenees between France & Spain; a republic ✳ Andorra la Vella *area* 453 *sq km* (175 *sq miles*), *pop* 31,000 (1981 *est*) – **Andorran** *adj or n*

**Andorra la Vella** town ✳ of Andorra *pop* 11,750 (1981 *est*)

**Andros** island, largest of the Bahamas *pop* 8,845 (1970)

**Angel Falls** waterfall 979 *m* (3,212 *ft*) SE Venezuela on Auyántepuí Mountain in a headstream of the Caroní river

**Anglesey** island in Gwynedd Wales off NW coast separated from mainland by Menai strait; *area* 718 *sq km* (276 *sq miles*), *pop* 63,200 (1971)

**Angola,** *formerly* **Portuguese West Africa** country sw Africa s of mouth of the Congo river; until 1975 a dependency of Portugal ✳ Luanda *area* 1,246,700 *sq km* (481,351 *sq miles*), *pop* 5,798,000 (1972 *est*) – **Angolan** *adj or n*

**Anguilla** island Brit West Indies nw of St Kitts *area* 91 *sq km* (35 *sq miles*), *pop* 7,000 (1981 *est*)

**Aniakchak Crater** active volcano 1,347 *m* (4,420 *ft*) sw Alaska on Alaska peninsula; crater 10 *km* (6 *miles*) in diameter

**Ankara,** *formerly* **Angora** , *anc* **Ancyra** city ✳ of Turkey in n *cen* Anatolia *pop* 3,196,460 (1980)

**Annaba,** *formerly* **Bône** town & port ne Algeria *pop* 313,174 (1974 *est*)

**Annapolis** city & port ✳ of Maryland *pop* 31,740 (1980)

**Annapurna, Anapurna** massif n Nepal in the Himalayas; highest peak Annapurna I 8,078 *m* (26,503 *ft*)

**Antarctic 1** ocean surrounding Antarctica including the southern regions of South Atlantic, South Pacific, & Indian oceans esp s of *ab* 60° s **2** the Antarctic regions **3 Antarctic,** *formerly* **Palmer peninsula, Graham Land** peninsula 1,931 *km* (1,200 *miles*) long w Antarctica s of s end of South America **4 Antarctic, Palmer archipelago** islands w of n end of Antarctic peninsula in Falkland Islands Dependencies

**Antarctica, Antarctic continent** body of land around the S Pole; a plateau 1,828 to 3,048 *m* (6,000 to 10,000 *ft*) covered by a great ice cap & having mountain peaks 3,048 to 4,572 *m* (10,000 to 15,000 *ft*) high; *area ab* 14,244,945 *sq km* (5,500,000 *sq miles*); divided into **West Antarctica** (including Antarctic peninsula) & **East Antarctica** by Transantarctic mountains

**Antigua** island Brit West Indies in the Leewards *area* 281 *sq km* (108 *sq miles*); with Barbuda an independent nation (**Antigua and Barbuda**) since 1981 *pop* 74,500 (1981) – **Antiguan** *adj or n*

**Antrim** county e Northern Ireland ✳ Belfast *area* 3,100 *sq km* (1,200 *sq miles*), *pop* 338,302 (1971) town, Co Antrim *pop* 45,303 (1981)

**Antwerp,** F **Anvers,** Flem **Antwerpen 1** province n Belgium *area* 2,861 *sq km* (1,104 *sq miles*), *pop* 1,535,680 (1971) **2** city & port, its ✳, on the Scheldt river *pop* 918,144 (1981)

**Aorangi** – see **cook** (Mount)

**Apennines** mountain chain Italy extending the length of the peninsula – **Apennine** *adj*

**Apia** town & port Samoa ✳ of Western Samoa on Upolu I *pop* 33,100 (1981)

**Apo, Mount** volcano 2,953 *m* (9,689 *ft*) s Philippines; highest peak in the Philippines

**Arab Emirates** – see **united arab emirates**

**Araguaia, Araguaya** river 2,627 *km* (1,632 *miles*) long *cen* Brazil flowing n into the Tocantins

**Aral sea, Lake Aral** brackish lake USSR in sw Soviet Central Asia between Kazakhstan & Uzbekistan *area* 68,681 *sq km* (26,518 *sq miles*)

**Aran** islands w Ireland off coast of Galway; largest island Inishmore *area* 47 *sq km* (18 *sq miles*), *pop ab* 2,600

**Ararat, Agri Dagi** mountain 5,185 *m* (17,011 *ft*) e Turkey near border of Iran

**Archangel** – see **archangelsk**

**Archangel, Gulf of** – see **dvina gulf**

**Arctic 1** ocean n of the Arctic circle **2** the Arctic regions **3** archipelago n Canada in Arctic ocean constituting larger part of Franklin District, Northwest Territories

**Arden, Forest of** wooded region of n Warwickshire 27 *km* (17 *miles*) long 19 *km* (12 *miles*) wide

**Ardennes** wooded plateau region in ne France, w Luxembourg, & se Belgium e of the Meuse

**Arecibo** city & port n Puerto Rico *pop* 83,300 (1980)

**Arena, Point** promontory n California in the Pacific *ab* midway between Cape Mendocino & San Francisco Bay

**Arequipa** city s Peru *pop* 561,338 (1976)

**Argentina, Argentine Republic, the Argentine** country s South America between the Andes & the Atlantic s of Pilcomayo river; a federal republic ✳ Buenos Aires *area* 2,776,889 *sq km* (1,072,156 *sq miles*), *pop* 27,862,771 (1980) – **Argentine** *adj or n,* **Argentinean, Argentinian** *adj or n*

**Arizona** state sw USA ✳ Phoenix *area* 296,163 *sq km* (113,909 *sq miles*), *pop* 2,717,866 (1980) – **Arizonan, Arizonian** *adj or n*

**Arkansas 1** river 2,330 *km* (1,450 *miles*) long sw *cen* USA rising in *cen* Colorado & flowing e & se through s Kansas, ne Oklahoma, & Arkansas into the Mississippi **2** state s *cen* USA ✳ Little Rock *area* 138,070 *sq km* (53,104 *sq miles*), *pop* 2,285,513 (1980) – **Arkansan** *adj or n*

**Arkhangelsk, Archangel** city & port USSR in n Soviet Russia, Europe, on the Northern Dvina *pop* 391,000 (1977)

**Armagh 1** county s Northern Ireland *area* 1,266 *sq km* (489 *sq miles*), *pop* 133,969 (1971) **2** urban district, its ✳ *pop* 48,169 (1981)

**Arnhem** town e Netherlands ✳ of Gelderland province *pop* 284,244 (1978)

**Arnhem Land** region n Australia on n coast of Northern Territory *area ab* 155,399 *sq km* (60,000 *sq miles*)

**Arran** island sw Scotland in Firth of Clyde *area* 428 *sq km* (165 *sq miles*), *pop* 3,576 (1971)

**Arras** city n France ssw of Lille *pop* 48,494 (1981)

**Ascension** island in s Atlantic at 7°55′s, 14°25′w belonging to Brit colony of St Helena *area* 88 *sq km* (34 *sq miles*), *pop* 1,051 (1982)

**Ascot** town in Berkshire 10 *km* (6 *miles*) sw of Windsor; site of racecourse *pop* 15,630 (1971)

**Ashby-de-la-Zouche** town in Leicestershire; site of 15th century castle *pop* 8,300 (1971)

**Ashdod** city & port in Israel w of Jerusalem *pop* 37,600 (1974)

**Ashford** town in Kent 22 *km* (14 *miles*) sw of Canterbury *pop* 36,130 (1972 *est*)

**Ashington** town in Northumberland 22 *km* (14 *miles*) n of Newcastle-upon-Tyne *pop* 25,950 (1971)

**Ashkelon, Ascalon** ancient city & port sw Palestine, site in Israel wsw of Jerusalem

**Ashkhabad,** *formerly* **Poltoratsk** city USSR in Soviet Central Asia ✳ of Turkmen Republic *pop* 312,000 (1979)

**Ashton-in-Makerfield** town in Greater Manchester 3 *km* (5 *miles*) s of Wigan *pop* 21,120 (1971)

**Ashton-under-Lyne** town in Greater Manchester *pop* 48,760 (1972 *est*)

**Asia** continent of the eastern hemisphere n of equator forming a single landmass with Europe (the conventional dividing line between Asia & Europe being the Ural mountains & main range of the Caucasus mountains); has numerous large offshore islands including Cyprus, Sri Lanka, Malay archipelago, Taiwan, the Japanese chain, & Sakhalin; *area* 44,391,206 *sq km* (17,139,445 *sq miles*), *pop* 2,256,000,000 (1975 *est*)

**Asia Minor** peninsula forming w extremity of Asia between Black sea on n, Mediterranean sea on s, & Aegean sea on w – see **anatolia**

**Asir** province s Saudi Arabia on Red sea se of Hejaz ✳ As Sabya *area* 36,028 *sq km* (13,857 *sq miles*), *pop* 1,850,000 (1976 *est*)

**Asmara** city n Ethiopia ✳ of Eritrea *pop* 250,000 (1977 *est*)

**Asunción** city ✳ of Paraguay on Paraguay river at confluence with the Pilcomayo *pop* 437,000 (1970)

**Aswân, Assouan, Assuan,** *anc* **Syene** city s Egypt on right bank of the Nile near site of dam built 1898–1902 & of **Aswân High Dam** (completed 1970) to form **Lake Nasser** *pop* 521,000 (1966)

**Atacama** desert n Chile between Copiapó & Peru border

**Antananarivo,** *formerly* **Tananarive** city ✳ of Madagascar *pop* 400,000 (1981 *est*)

**Athens,** NGk **Athínai,** *anc* **Athenae** city ✳ of Greece *pop* (with Piraeus and suburbs) 2,540,241 (1971)

**Atherstone** market town in Warwickshire 6 *km* (4 *miles*) nw of Nuneaton *pop* 10,170 (1971)

**Atlanta** city nw *cen* Georgia, its ✳ *pop* 425,022 (1980) – **Atlantan** *adj or n*

**Atlantic** ocean separating North & South America from Europe & Africa *area* 106,400,000 *sq km* (41,100,000 *sq miles*) ˙

**Atlas** mountains nw Africa extending from sw Morocco to ne Tunisia; extent *ab* 2,000 *km* (1,200 *miles*) its highest peaks are in the **Grand,** or **High, Atlas** in sw *cen* Morocco

**Auckland** city & port n New Zealand on North I *pop* 649,700 (1971)

**Augusta** city ✳ of Maine on the Kennebec river *pop* 21,819 (1980)

**Austin** city ✳ of Texas on the Colorado river *pop* 345,496 (1980)

**Australasia 1** Australia, Tasmania, New Zealand, & Melanesia **2** the Brit Commonwealth nations of the sw Pacific: Australia, New Zealand, Fiji, & Western Samoa – **Australasian** *adj or n*

**Australia 1** continent of the eastern hemisphere SE of Asia & s of the equator *area* 7,636,238 *sq km* (2,948,366 *sq miles*) **2 Australia, Commonwealth of Australia** dominion of the British Commonwealth of Nations including the continent of Australia & island of Tasmania ✳ Canberra *area* 7,686,848 *sq km* (2,967,909 *sq miles*), *pop* 14,926,800 (1981)

**Australian Capital Territory,** *formerly* **Federal Capital Territory** district SE Australia including two areas, one around Canberra & the other on Jervis Bay, surrounded by New South Wales ✳ Canberra *area* 2,441 *sq km* (939 *sq miles*), *pop* 227,300 (1981)

**Austria, Österreich** country *cen* Europe in & N of E Alps with the Danube crossing it in N; a republic *area* 83,848 *sq km* (32,367 *sq miles*), *pop* 7,553,380 (1981) – **Austrian** *adj or n*

**Avon**[1] name of four British rivers: **1** Warwickshire or Upper Avon rises in Northamptonshire, flows sw through Stratford-on-Avon to join river Severn at Tewkesbury 155 *km* (96 *miles*) long **2** Bristol or Lower Avon rises in Cotswold Hills in Gloucestershire flows s and then w through Bristol to enter Severn estuary at Avonmouth 121 *km* (75 *miles*) long **3** Wiltshire or East Avon rises near Devizes and flows s into English Channel 77 *km* (48 *miles*) long **4** Scottish Avon flows s into Firth of Forth 29 *km* (18 *miles*) long

**Avon**[2] county in sw England on Bristol Channel formed in 1974 from county boroughs of Bath and Bristol and parts of former counties of Gloucestershire and Somerset *urea* 1,346 *sq km* (520 *sq miles*), *pop* 923,600 (1981)

**Aycliffe** town in Durham on river Skerne; developed as "new town" 1947; *pop* 25,000 (1981)

**Azincourt,** *earlier* **Agincourt** village N France wnw of Arras *pop* 276 (1968)

**Azores,** Port **Açores** islands N Atlantic belonging to Portugal & lying *ab* 1,190 *km* (740 *miles*) off coast of Portugal; chief town Ponta Delgada *area* 2,344 *sq km* (905 *sq miles*), *pop* 292,200 (1978) – **Azorean, Azorian** *adj or n*

# B

**Baalbek** town E Lebanon N of Damascus on site of ancient city of **Heliopolis** *pop* 17,670 (1970)

**Babylon** ancient city ✳ of Babylonia; its site *ab* 80 *km* (50 *miles*) s of Baghdad near the Euphrates

**Baffin** island NE Canada N of Hudson strait; largest in Arctic archipelago *area* 476,070 *sq km* (183,810 *sq miles*)

**Baghdad, Bagdad** city ✳ of Iraq on the middle Tigris *pop* 3,205,645 (1977) – **Baghdadi** *n*

**Bahama** islands in the Atlantic SE of Florida; an independent member of Brit Commonwealth since 1973 (officially **Commonwealth of the Bahamas**) ✳ Nassau *area* 13,935 *sq km* (5,380 *sq miles*), *pop* 237,070 (1980) – **Bahamian, Bahaman** *adj or n*

**Bahrain, Bahrein** islands in Persian gulf off coast of Arabia; an independent sultanate ✳ Manama (on Bahrain I) *area* 663 *sq km* (256 *sq miles*), *pop* 358,857 (1981) – **Bahraini, Bahreini** *adj or n*

**Baikal, Baykal** lake USSR in s Soviet Russia, Asia, in mountains N of Mongolia; *area* 31,500 *sq km* (12,200 *sq miles*); 636 *km* (395 *miles*) long; max depth 1,620 *m* (5,315 *ft*)

**Baku** city USSR ✳ of Azerbaijan (republic) on w shore of Caspian sea *pop* 1,550,000 (1979)

**Bala Lake** in Gwynedd, N Wales; *ab* 6 *km* (4 *miles*) long and 1.6 *km* (1 *mile*) wide; largest natural lake in Wales

**Baleares 1** the Balearic islands **2** province E Spain comprising the Balearic islands ✳ Palma *area* 5,034 *sq km* (1,936 *sq miles*)

**Balearic** islands E Spain in the w Mediterranean – see BALEARES, IBIZA, MAJORCA, MINORCA

**Bali** island Indonesia off E end of Java; chief town Singaradja *area* 5,623 *sq km* (2,171 *sq miles*), *pop* 2,174,105 (1981) – **Balinese** *adj or n*

**Balkan** peninsula SE Europe bet Adriatic & Ionian seas on w & Aegean & Black seas on E – **Balkan, Balkanic** *adj*

**Balkan States, Balkans** the countries occupying the Balkan peninsula: Yugoslavia, Rumania, Bulgaria, Albania, Greece, & Turkey in Europe

**Ballarat** city SE Australia in *cen* Victoria wnw of Melbourne *pop* 60,737 (1976)

**Balmoral Castle** royal residence in Grampian region, NE Scotland 10 *km* (6 *miles*) NE of Braemar

**Baltic** sea arm of the Atlantic N Europe enclosed by Denmark & the Scandinavian peninsula *area ab* 420,400 *sq km* (160,000 *sq miles*)

**Bamako** city ✳ of Mali on the Niger *pop* 404,000 (1978)

**Bandar Seri Begawan,** *formerly* **Brunei** town, ✳ of Brunei *pop* 58,000 (1979 *est*)

**Bandung,** D **Bandoeng** city Indonesia in w Java SE of Jakarta *pop* 1,202,000 (1976)

**Bangalore** city s India w of Madras ✳ of Karnataka state *pop* 1,633,779 (1971)

**Bangka, Banka** island, Indonesia off SE Sumatra; chief town Pangkalpinang *area* 11,330 *sq km* (4,375 *sq miles*), *pop* 303,804 (1971)

**Bangkok** city & port ✳ of Thailand on the Chao Phraya river *ab* 32 *km* (20 *miles*) above its mouth *pop* 5,153,902 (1980)

**Bangladesh** country s Asia E of India on Bay of Bengal; a republic in Brit Commonwealth since 1971 ✳ Dacca *area* 142,776 *sq km* (55,126 *sq miles*), *pop* 89,940,000 (1981) – **Bangladeshi** *n*

**Bangor 1** coastal town in Co Down, Northern Ireland *pop* 35,105 (1971) **2** city & port in Gwynedd, NW Wales on Menai strait; home of Univ College of N Wales *pop* 14,500 (1971)

**Bangui** city ✳ of Central African Republic *pop* 350,000 (1975 *est*)

**Banjul,** *formerly* **Bathurst** city & port ✳ of Gambia on Island of St Mary in Gambia river *pop* 50,000 (1981 *est*)

**Bannockburn** town and moor in Central region, Scotland; site of battle 1314 *pop* 5,889 (1971)

**Baracoa** city & port E Cuba on N coast near E tip of island *pop* (municipality) 105,070 (1970)

**Barbados** island Brit West Indies in Lesser Antilles E of the Windward group; a dominion of the Brit Commonwealth since 1966 ✳ Bridgetown *area* 430 *sq km* (166 *sq miles*), *pop* 248,983 (1980) – **Barbadian** *adj or n*

**Barbary** former name of region N Africa on **Barbary Coast** extending from Egyptian border to the Atlantic & including the former **Barbary States** (Morocco, Algiers, Tunis, & Tripoli)

**Barbuda** island Brit West Indies in the Leewards *area* 161 *sq km* (62 *sq miles*) – see ANTIGUA

**Barcelona 1** province NE Spain in Catalonia on the Mediterranean *area* 7,733 *sq km* (2,986 *sq miles*), *pop* 3,929,194 (1970) **2** city & port, its ✳ *pop* 1,750,000 (1970) **3** city NE Venezuela near coast *pop* 76,410 (1971) – **Barcelonese** *adj or n*

**Barents** sea comprising the part of the Arctic ocean between Spitsbergen & Novaya Zemlya

**Bari,** *anc* **Barium** town & port SE Italy ✳ of Apulia region on the Adriatic *pop* 370,781 (1981 *est*)

**Barnsley** town in S Yorkshire *pop* 75,330 (1971)

**Barra** island of Outer Hebrides, Western Isles, Scotland *area* 91 *sq km* (35 *sq miles*), *pop* 1,087 (1971)

**Barranquilla** city & port N Colombia on the Magdalena river *pop* 721,900 (1972)

**Barrow, Point** most northerly point of Alaska & of the USA, at *ab* 71°25′N, 156°30′w

**Basel,** F **Bâle,** *older* **Basle 1** former canton NW Switzerland, now divided into two cantons (formerly half cantons): **Basel-Land** (✳ Liestal *pop* 439,834 (1970)) & **Basel-Stadt** (✳ Basel *pop* 182,143 (1980)) **2** city NW Switzerland ✳ of Basel-Stadt

**Basildon** town in Essex 40 *km* (25 *miles*) ENE of London "new town" 1949; *pop* 100,100 (1981)

**Basra, Busra** city & port s Iraq on Shatt-al-Arab *pop* 333,684 (1970 *est*)

**Bass** strait separating Tasmania & continent of Australia

**Basseterre** town & port Brit West Indies ✳ of St Kitts I & of St Kitts-Nevis state *pop* 15,000 (1981)

**Basse-Terre 1** island French West Indies constituting the w part of Guadeloupe *area* 946 *sq km* (364 *sq miles*) **2** town & port ✳ of Guadeloupe *pop* 15,778 (1974)

**Bass Rock** islet in Firth of Forth, Scotland *ab* 107 *m* (350 *ft*) high

**Bastia** city & port France on NE coast of Corsica *pop* 52,000 (1980 *est*)

**Basutoland** – see LESOTHO

**Bata** city * Mbini *pop* 30,474 (1981)

**Batavia** – see JAKARTA

**Bath** city and health resort in Avon, on right bank of river Avon 19 *km* (12 *miles*) SE of Bristol, *pop* 84,670 (1971) – **Bathonian** *adj or n*

**Bathurst** – see BANJUL

**Baton Rouge** city * of Louisiana on Mississippi river *pop* 219,419 (1980)

**Battle** town in E Sussex; named after Battle of Hastings

**Bayreuth** city w Germany in Bavaria state NE of Nuremberg *pop* 60,600 (1971)

**Beachy Head** headland SE England on coast of E Sussex

**Beaconsfield** town in Buckinghamshire 37 *km* (23 *miles*) WNW of London, *pop* 12,000 (1971)

**Béarn** region & former province sw France in Pyrenees sw of Gascony

**Bedford** town in Bedfordshire on river Ouse *pop* 73,064 (1971)

**Bedfordshire** county in *cen* s England *area* 1,235 *sq km* (477 *sq miles*), *pop* 508,300 (1981)

**Beersheba** city s Israel in N Negev, in Bible times marking extreme s limit of Palestine *pop* (with district) 275,800 (1980 *est*)

**Beirut, Bayrut , Beyrouth,** *anc* **Berytus** city & port * of Lebanon *pop* 702,000 (1981 *est*)

**Belém, Pará** city N Brazil * of Pará state on Pará river *pop* 934,330 (1980)

**Belfast** city & county borough & port * of Northern Ireland & of Co Antrim at head of **Belfast Lough** (inlet) *pop* 345,800 (1980)

**Belgian Congo** – see ZAIRE

**Belgium, F Belgique, Flem België** country w Europe bordering on North sea; a constitutional monarchy * Brussels *area* 30,513 *sq km* (11,781 *sq miles*), *pop* 9,848,647 (1981)

**Belgrade, Beograd** city * of Yugoslavia & of Serbia *pop* 1,455,000 (1981)

**Belgravia** district of w *cen* London, in Kensington and Chelsea borough s of Hyde Park

**Belize** 1 city & port, former * of Brit Honduras *pop* 49,661 (1970) 2 **Belize,** *formerly* **British Honduras** country Central America on the Caribbean; until 1981 a Brit colony, * Belmopan *area* 22,963 *sq km* (8,866 *sq miles*), *pop* 144,857 (1980 *prov*) – **Belizean** *adj or n*

**Belmopan** city * of Belize *pop* 4,000 (1975 *est*)

**Bengal, Bay of** arm of the Indian ocean between India & Sri Lanka on the w & Burma & Malay peninsula on the E

**Benghazi, Bengasi, Bengasi,** *anc* **Berenice** city & port NE Libya, a * of Libya *pop* 371,515 (1976)

**Benin** 1 former kingdom w Africa on the lower Niger; incorporated in Nigeria after 1897 2 **Benin,** *formerly* **Dahomey** county w Africa on Gulf of Guinea; a republic, formerly a territory of French West Africa * **Porto-Novo** *area* 112,600 *sq km* (43,480 *sq miles*), *pop* 3,200,000 (1976 *est*) 3 **Benin, Benin City** city sw Nigeria in w delta of the Niger *pop* 119,692 (1970) – **Beninese** *adj or n*

**Ben Nevis** – see NEVIS (Ben)

**Berchtesgaden** village in SE Bavaria, Germany; Hitler's country home; *pop* 6,000 (1970)

**Bergen** city & port sw Norway *pop* 207,419 (1981)

**Bering** 1 sea arm of the N Pacific between Alaska & NE Siberia & between the Aleutians & Bering strait *area* 2,292,000 *sq km* (885,000 *sq miles*) 2 strait *ab* 88 *km* (56 *miles*) wide at narrowest point separating Asia (USSR) from North America (Alaska)

**Berkshire** county in s *cen* England *area* 1,255 *sq km* (485 *sq miles*), *pop* 707,000 (1981)

**Berlin** city E *cen* Germany on Spree river, before 1945 * of Germany & of Prussia, divided under postwar occupation between East & West Germany, East Berlin being made * of East Germany (1949) & West Berlin a state (not formally incorporated) of West Germany, (West) Federal Republic of Germany *area* 480 *sq km* (185 *sq miles*), *pop* 1,896,200 (1980) (East) German Democratic Republic *area* 403 *sq km* (156 *sq miles*), *pop* 1,152,529 (1980) – **Berliner** *n*

**Bermuda** islands w Atlantic ESE of Cape Hatteras; a Brit self-governing colony * Hamilton *area* 53 *sq km* (21 *sq miles*), *pop* 54,670 (1980) – **Bermudian, Bermudan** *adj or n*

**Bern** 1 canton NW & w *cen* Switzerland *area* 6,911 *sq km* (2,658 *sq miles*), *pop* 983,296 (1981) 2 city, its * & * of Switzerland on the Aare river *pop* 145,254 (1980) – **Bernese** *adj or n*

**Bethlehem** city Palestine in Judea sw of Jerusalem; now in w Jordan *pop* 16,300 (1972)

**Beyrouth** – see BEIRUT

**Bhakra Dam** hydroelectric & irrigation dam 207*m* (680 *ft*) high N India in Punjab state NW of Bilaspur in gorge of the Sutlej river

**Bhutan** country Asia in Himalayas on NE border of India; a protectorate of India * Thimbu *area* 47,000 *sq km* (18,000 *sq miles*), *pop* 1,247,000 (1978) – **Bhutani** *adj or n*

**Bikini** island (atoll) w Pacific in Marshall islands at NW end of Ratak chain

**Bilbao** city N Spain * of Vizcaya province *pop* 410,490 (1970)

**Birkenhead** seaport and town in Merseyside, on Mersey estuary opposite Liverpool *pop* 137,738 (1971)

**Birmingham** city in West Midlands 160 *km* (100 *miles*) NW of London; second largest city in England; *pop* 1,014,670 (1971)

**Biscay, Bay of** inlet of the Atlantic between w coast of France & N coast of Spain

**Biskra** city NE Algeria at an oasis on s edge of Atlas mountains *pop* 53,177 (1971)

**Bisley** village in Surrey wNw of Woking: National Rifle Assoc ranges

**Bismarck** 1 sea comprising the part of the w Pacific enclosed by the islands of the Bismarck archipelago 2 archipelago w Pacific N or E end of New Guinea *area* 49,658 *sq km* (19,173 *sq miles*) 3 city * of North Dakota on Missouri river *pop* 44,485 (1980)

**Bissau, Bissāo** city & port * of Guinea-Bissau *pop* 65,000 (1971 *est*)

**Bitter Lakes** two lakes (Great Bitter Lake & Little Bitter Lake) in NE Egypt N of Suez; connected & traversed by the Suez canal

**Bizerte, Bizerta** city & port N Tunisia on **Lake Bizerte** (a deep lagoon) *pop* 62,000 (1976 *est*)

**Blackburn** town in Lancashire 32 *km* (20 *miles*) NW of Manchester *pop* 101,816 (1971)

**Black Forest, G Schwarzwald** forested mountain region sw Germany along the upper Rhine between the Neckar river & Swiss border

**Blackpool** town and seaside resort in Lancashire with 11 *km* (7 *miles*) of promenades and 152 *m* (500 *ft*) tower *pop* 151,860 (1971)

**Black sea, Euxine sea,** *anc* **Pontus Euxinus, Pontus** sea between Europe & Asia connected with Aegean sea through the Bosporus, Sea of Marmara, & Dardanelles *area* 423,000 *sq km* (163,000 *sq miles*)

**Blanc, Cape** cape N Tunisia; northernmost point of Africa, at 37°15′N

**Blanc, Mont** – see MONT BLANC

**Blantyre-Limbe** city s Malawi *pop* 169,000 (1971 *est*)

**Blarney** town in Co Cork Rep of Ireland; in wall of 15th century castle is Blarney Stone; *pop* 1,130 (1971)

**Blide** city N Algeria sw of Algiers *pop* 158,947 (1974 *est*)

**Bloemfontein** city Republic of South Africa * of Orange Free State & judicial * of the Republic *pop* 182,329 (1970)

**Blue Nile** river 1,368 *km* (850 *miles*) long Ethiopia & Sudan flowing from Lake Tana NNW into the Nile at Khartoum

**Bognor Regis** town and seaside resort in W Sussex *pop* 34,000 (1972 *est*)

**Bogotá** city * of Colombia on plateau in the Andes *pop* 5,000,000 (1978 *est*)

**Bois de Boulogne** park France w of Paris *area* 873 *hectares* (2,155 *acres*)

**Bolan** mountain pass 1,798 *m* (5,900 *ft*) Pakistan in N Baluchistan province

**Bolívar, Cero, La Parida** iron mountain 803 *m* (2,631 *ft*) E Venezuela

**Bolívar, Pico, La Columna** mountain 5,002 *m* (16,411 *ft*) w Venezuela highest in Venezuela

**Bolivia** country w *cen* South America; a republic; administrative ✳ La Paz, constitutional ✳ Sucre *area* 1,098,581 *sq km* (424,165 *sq miles*), *pop* 4,700,000 (1976 *est*) – **Bolivian** *adj or n*

**Bologna,** *anc* **Bononia** town N Italy ✳ of Emilia-Romagna region at foot of the Apennines *pop* 455,853 (1981 *est*) – **Bolognan, Bolognese** *adj or n*

**Bolton** town in Greater Manchester 18 *km* (11 *miles*) NW of Manchester *pop* 153,977 (1971)

**Boma** city & port w Congo on Congo river *pop* 79,230 (1967 *est*)

**Bombay** city & port w India ✳ of Maharashtra state & of former Bombay state *pop* 5,970,575 (1971)

**Bône** – see ANNABA

**Bonn** city w Germany on Rhine SSE of Cologne ✳ of Federal Republic of Germany (often called **Bonn Republic**) *pop* 288,100 (1980)

**Bonneville, Lake** prehistoric lake *area ab* 49,210 *sq km* (19,000 *sq miles*) in Utah, E Nevada, & s Idaho; its remnant is Great Salt Lake

**Bonneville Salt Flats, Bonneville Flats** broad level area of Great Salt Lake desert, Utah *area* 260 *sq km* (100 *sq miles*)

**Boothia** peninsula N Canada w of Baffin I; its N tip (at *ab* 72°N, 94°w) is the northernmost point on North American mainland

**Borås** city sw Sweden E of Göteborg *pop* 102,129 (1980)

**Bordeaux** city & port sw France on the Garonne river *pop* 226,281 (1980 *est*)

**Borders** region in SE Scotland formed in 1975 from former counties of Berwickshire, Peebles, Roxburgh and Selkirk and small part of Midlothian *area* 4,671 *sq km* (1,803 *sq miles*), *pop* 100,470 (1981)

**Borneo** island Malay archipelago sw of Philippines *area ab* 743,330 *sq km* (287,000 *sq miles*), *pop* 6,968,000 (1971 *est*) – **Bornean** *adj or n*

**Bosporus , Bosphorus** strait *ab* 29 *km* (18 *miles*) long between Turkey in Europe & Turkey in Asia connecting Sea of Marmara & Black sea – **Bosporan** *adj*

**Boston 1** city & port ✳ of Massachusetts on Massachusetts Bay *pop* 562,994 (1980) **2** seaport town in Lincolnshire on river Witham 6 *km* (4 *miles*) from its mouth; St Botolph England's largest parish church, its tower "Boston stump" a landmark for seamen; *pop* 25,995 (1971) – **Bostonese** *adj,* **Bostonian** *adj or n*

**Botafogo Bay** inlet of Guanabara Bay in Rio de Janeiro, Brazil

**Botany Bay** inlet of the s Pacific SE Australia in New South Wales on s border of city of Sydney

**Botswana** country s Africa N of Molopo river; an independent republic since 1966, formerly Brit protectorate of **Bechuanaland** ✳ Gaborone *area ab* 569,797 *sq km* (222,000 *sq miles*), *pop* 937,000 (1981 *est*)

**Bougainville** island s Pacific, largest of the Solomons; chief town Kieta *area* 10,049 *sq km* (3,880 *sq miles*), *pop* 96,363 (1971)

**Boulder Dam** – see HOOVER DAM

**Boulogne, Boulogne-sur-Mer** city & port N France on English channel *pop* 50,138 (1973)

**Bournemouth** town s England in Dorset on English channel sw of Southampton *pop* 153,869 (1971)

**Boyne** river 110 *km* (70 *miles*) long E Ireland in Leinster flowing to Irish sea s of Drogheda

**Bracknell** town in Berkshire; developed as "new town" 1949; *pop* 50,000 (1981)

**Bradford** city N England in W Yorkshire *pop* 294,177 (1971)

**Brahmaputra** river *ab* 2,900 *km* (1,800 *miles*) long s Asia flowing from the Himalayas in Tibet to the Ganges delta in E India (subcontinent)

**Braila** city E Rumania on the Danube *pop* 151,650 (1970)

**Brasília** city ✳ of Brazil in Federal District in E Goiás state *pop* 1,176,748 (1980)

**Bratislava,** G **Pressburg,** Hung **Pozsony** city Czechoslavakia, chief city of Slovakia, on the Danube *pop* 374,860 (1979)

**Brazil,** Port **Brasil** country E South America; a federal republic ✳ Brasília *area* 8,511,965 *sq km* (3,286,486 *sq miles*), *pop* 119,098,922 (1980) – **Brazilian** *adj or n*

**Brazzaville** city & port ✳ of Congo Republic on w bank of Congo river *pop* 156,000 (1981 *est*)

**Brecon Beacons, Brecknock Beacons** two mountain peaks SE Wales in s Powys; highest Pen y Fan 886 *m* (2,907 *ft*)

**Breda** town s Netherlands *pop* 151,102 (1978)

**Bremen 1** former duchy N Germany between the lower Weser & the lower Elbe rivers **2** state NW Germany *area* 404 *sq km* (156 *sq miles*), *pop* 721,000 (1979) **3** city & port, its ✳ *pop* 555,100 (1980)

**Bremerhaven** city & port NW Germany in Bremen state at mouth of the Weser; includes former city of Wesermünde *pop* 138,700 (1980)

**Brenner** mountain pass 1,137 *m* (4,498 *ft*) in the Alps between Austria & Italy

**Brest 1** town & port NW France in Brittany *pop* 172,176 (1980 *est*) **2 Brest, Brest Litovsk** city USSR in sw Belorussia on the Bug river *pop* 122,000 (1972)

**Bridgetown** city & port Brit West Indies ✳ of Barbados *pop* 17,552 (1980 *est*)

**Brighton** borough s England in E Sussex on English channel *pop* 161,351 (1971)

**Brindisi,** *anc* **Brundisium** city & port SE Italy in Apulia region *pop* 82,700 (1971)

**Brisbane** city & port E Australia ✳ of Queensland on Brisbane river near its mouth *pop* (with suburbs) 1,086,470 (1981)

**Bristol** university city & port in Avon 13 *km* (8 *miles*) from mouth of river Avon and 11 *km* (7 *miles*) from Bristol Channel *pop* 426,657 (1971)

**Bristol Channel** seaward extension of Severn estuary 137 *km* (85 *miles*) long and 8 *km* (5 *miles*) to 69 *km* (43 *miles*) wide

**British Columbia** province w Canada on Pacific coast ✳ Victoria *area* 934,125 *sq km* (359,279 *sq miles*), *pop* 2,744,467 (1981)

**British Commonwealth of Nations, British Commonwealth** Great Britain & Northern Ireland, the Brit dominions & republics, & the Brit dependencies

**British Isles** island group w Europe comprising Great Britain, Ireland, & adjacent islands

**British Malaya, Malaya** former dependencies of Great Britain on Malay peninsula & in Malay archipelago including Malaya (federation), Singapore, N Borneo, Sarawak, & Brunei

**British Solomon Islands** Brit protectorate comprising the Solomons (except Bougainville, Buka, & adjacent small islands) & the Santa Cruz islands ✳ Honiara *area* 29,785 *sq km* (11,500 *sq miles*), *pop* 196,823 (1976)

**British Virgin Islands** the E islands of the Virgin islands group; a Brit possession ✳ Road Town (on Tortola I) *area* 155 *sq km* (60 *sq miles*), *pop* 12,034 (1980)

**British West Indies** islands of the West Indies including Jamaica, the Bahamas, Caymans, Brit Virgin islands, Brit Leeward & Windward islands, Trinidad, & Tobago

**Brno,** G **Brünn** city *cen* Czechoslovakia, chief city of Moravia *pop* 372,793 (1979)

**Broads, Norfolk Broads** region of shallow lakes and marshland mainly in Norfolk, England with small part in Suffolk, England centred on river Bure and tributaries Ant and Thame

**Broadstairs** town and seaside resort in NE Kent *pop* 21,050 (1972 *est*)

**Broken Hill** – see KABWE

**Bronx, The Bronx** borough of New York City on the mainland NE of Manhattan I *pop* 1,471,701 (1970)

**Brooklyn** borough of New York City at sw end of Long I *pop* 2,602,012 (1970) – **Brooklynite** *n*

**Bruges,** Flem **Brugge** town NW Belgium ✳ of West Flanders province *pop* 252,430 (1981)

**Brunei 1** sultanate & Brit protectorate NW Borneo ✳ Bandar Seri Begawan *area* 5,765 *sq km* (2,226 *sq miles*), *pop* 212,840 (1979 *est*) **2** – see BANDAR SERI BEGAWAN – **Bruneian** *adj or n*

**Brussels,** F **Bruxelles,** Flem **Brussel** city ✳ Belgium & of Brabant province *pop* (with suburbs) 997,293 (1981)

**Bucharest,** Rum **Bucuresti** city ✳ of Rumania *pop* 1,960,097 (1979)

**Buckinghamshire, Buckingham, Bucks** county SE *cen* England ✳ Aylesbury *area* 1,878 *sq km* (727 *sq miles*), *pop* 577,400 (1981)

**Budapest** city ✳ of Hungary on the Danube *pop* 2,093,000 (1979)

**Buenos Aires** city & port ✳ of Argentina on Río de la Plata *pop* 2,908,000 (1980) (with suburbs) 9,677,200

**Bujumbura,** *formerly* **Usumbura** city ✳ of Burundi on Lake Tanganyika *pop* 150,000 (1977 *est*)

**Buka** island w Pacific in the Solomons N of Bougainville

**Bulawayo, Buluwayo** city sw Rhodesia, chief town of Matabeleland province *pop* 340,000 (1976 *est*)

**Bulgaria** country SE Europe on Black sea; a republic ✳ Sofia *area* 110,912 *sq km* (42,823 *sq miles*), *pop* 8,730,000 (1975) – **Bulgar** *n*

**Burma** country SE Asia on Bay of Bengal; a federal republic ✳ Rangoon *area* 678,000 *sq km* (261,789 *sq miles*), *pop* 33,310,000 (1979 *est*) – **Burman** *adj or n*

**Burundi,** *formerly* **Urundi** country E cen Africa; a republic ✳ Bujumbura *area* 27,834 *sq km* (10,747 *sq miles*), *pop* 3,900,000 (1977 *est*) – **Burundian** *adj or n*

**Bute** island sw Scotland w of Firth of Clyde

# C

**Cádiz,** *anc* **Gadir, Gades** city & port, on Bay of Cádiz NW of Gibraltar *pop* 135,743 (1970)

**Caernarvon, Caernarfon** town NW Wales ✳ of Gwynedd *pop* 8,840 (1973 *est* )

**Cagliari** commune & port Italy ✳ of Sardinia *pop* 255,812 (1976 *est*)

**Cairngorm 1** mountain range of the Grampians NE cen Scotland; highest point Ben Macdhui 1,309 *m* (4,296 *ft*) **2** mountain 1,245 *m* (4,084 *ft*) high in Cairngorm mountains on boundary between Highland and Grampian regions

**Cairo** city N Egypt ✳ of Egypt *pop* 11,000,000 (1981*est*) – **Cairene** *adj or n*

**Calais** city & port N France on Strait of Dover *pop* 78,820 (1975 *prov*)

**Calcutta** city & port E India on Hooghly river ✳ of West Bengal state *pop* 7,031,382 (1971) – **Calcuttan** *n*

**Caledonian Canal** ship canal N Scotland connecting Loch Linnhe & Moray Firth & uniting lochs Ness, Oich, Lochy, & Eil 96 *km* (60 *miles*) long

**California** state sw USA ✳: Sacramento *area* 412,602 *sq km* (158,693 *sq miles*), *pop* 23,668,562 (1980)

**Cam** river 64 *km* (40 *miles*) long E cen England in Cambridgeshire flowing into the Ouse

**Cambodia,** *officially* **Democratic Kampuchea,** *1970–75* **Khmer Republic** country SE Asia bordering on Gulf of Siam ✳ Phnom Penh *area* 181,652 *sq km* (69,866 *sq miles*), *pop* 6,000,000 (1981)

**Cambridge** university city in Cambridgeshire on river Cam 82 *km* (51 *miles*) N of London *pop* 98,840 (1972 *est*)

**Cambridgeshire** county in E England formed in 1974 by amalgamation of former county of Cambridgeshire and Isle of Ely with Huntingdonshire and Peterborough; *area* 3,409 *sq km* (1,316 *sq miles*), *pop* 595,600 (1981)

**Cameroon 1 Cameroon, Fako** massif 407 *m* (13,353 *ft*) Republic of Cameroon NW of Buea near coast **2 Cameroon, Cameroun** country w equatorial Africa in Cameroons region; a republic, formerly a trust territory under France ✳ Yaoundé *area* 465,054 *sq km* (179,557 *sq miles*), *pop* 8,320,000 (1980 *est*) – **Cameroonian** *adj or n*

**Canada** country N North America including Newfoundland & Arctic islands N of mainland; a dominion of the British Commonwealth ✳ Ottawa (including fresh water) *area* 9,220,974 *sq km* (3,851,809 *sq miles*), *land area* 9,976,139 *sq km* (3,560,238 *sq miles*), *pop* 24,343,181 (1981)

**Canal Zone, Panama Canal Zone** strip of territory Panama under perpetual lease to the USA for Panama canal; administrative centre Balboa Heights; *area* 1,432 *sq km* (553 *sq miles*), *pop* 44,198 (1975 *est*)

**Canary** islands in the Atlantic off NW coast of Africa s of Madeira belonging to Spain *area* 7,273 *sq km* (2,807 *sq miles*), *pop* 1,170,224 (1970) – **Canarian** *adj or n*

**Canberra** city ✳ of Australia in Australian Capital Territory sw of Sydney *pop* 220,423 (1981)

**Canea,** NGk **Khania,** *anc* **Cydonia** city & port Greece ✳ of Crete *pop* 40,564 (1971)

**Cannes** town & port SE France sw of Nice *pop* 66,590 (1976 *est*)

**Canterbury 1** city SE Australia in E New South Wales, sw suburb of Sydney *pop* 130,334 (1971) **2** city in Kent on river Stour *pop* 36,300 (1972 *est*)

**Canterbury Plains** area of grassland on E coast of South Island, New Zealand *ab* 10,000 *sq km* (4,000 *sq miles*)

**Cape of Good Hope 1** – see GOOD HOPE (Cape of) **2 Cape of Good Hope, Cape Province,** Afrikaans **Kaapland,** *formerly* **Cape Colony** province s Republic of South Africa ✳ Cape Town *area* 721,000 *sq km* (278,400 *sq miles*), *pop* 6,731,820 (1970)

**Cape Town, Capetown,** Afrikaans **Kaapstad** city & port, legislative ✳ of Republic of South Africa & ✳ of Cape of Good Hope, on Table Bay *pop* 1,107,764 (1970) – **Capetonian** *n*

**Cape Verde** islands in the Atlantic off w Africa; a republic; until 1975 belonged to Portugal ✳ Praia (on São Tiago) *area* 4,048 *sq km* (1,557 *sq miles*), *pop* 306,046 (1978 *est*) – **Cape Verdean** *adj or n*

**Capri,** *anc* **Capreae** island Italy s Bay of Naples *area* 10 *sq km* (4 *sq miles*), *pop* 8,025 (1971 *prov*)

**Caracas** city ✳ of Venezuela near Caribbean coast *pop* 3,507,800 (1979)

**Cardiff,** Welsh **Caerdydd** city & port in s Glamorgan, Wales ✳ of Wales, on river Severn estuary at mouth of rivers Taff, Rhymney and Ely *pop* 278,900 (1981)

**Caribbean** sea arm of Atlantic ocean bounded on N & E by West Indies, on s by South America, & on w by Central America

**Caroline** islands w Pacific E of s Philippines; part of Trust Territory of the Pacific Islands *area* 1,130 *sq km* (450 *sq miles*)

**Carrantuohill** mountain 1,041 *m* (3,414 *ft*) sw Ireland in Co Kerry; highest in Macgillicuddy's Reeks & in Ireland

**Carson City** city ✳ of Nevada E of Lake Tahoe *pop* 32,022 (1980)

**Carstensz** – see DJAJA (Mount)

**Casablanca,** Ar **Dar el Beida** city & port w Morocco on the Atlantic *pop* 2,537,200 (1979)

**Caspian** sea (salt lake) between Europe & Asia; below sea level *area* 393,896 *sq km* (152,083 *sq miles*)

**Castries, Port Castries** city & port Brit West Indies in the Windward islands ✳ of St Lucia *pop* 48,782 (1980 *est*)

**Caucasus 1** mountain system USSR **2 Caucasus, Caucasia** region USSR bet the Black & Caspian seas: divided by Caucasus mountains into **Ciscaucasia** (to the N) & **Transcaucasia** (to the s)

**Cayenne** city & port ✳ of French Guiana an island in Cayenne river near the coast *pop* 20,000 (1974)

**Cayman** islands West Indies NW of Jamaica; a Brit colony ✳ Georgetown (on **Grand Cayman,** chief island) *area* 200 *sq km* (125 *sq miles*), *pop* 17,955 (1981) – **Cayman Islander** *n*

**Celebes 1 Celebes, Sulawesi** island Indonesia E of Borneo ✳ Makassar *area,* including adjacent islands, 224,654 *sq km* (87,897 *sq miles*), *pop* 8,535,000 (1971) **2** sea arm of sw Pacific enclosed on N by Mindanao & Sulu archipelago, on s by Celebes, & on w by Borneo – **Celebesian** *adj*

**Central** region of Scotland created in 1975 to include most of Stirlingshire, county of Clackmannan and Bo'ness area of W Lothian *area* 2,590 *sq km* (1,000 *sq miles*), *pop* 273,012 (1981)

**Central African Republic** country N cen Africa, formerly Uban-gi-Shari; a republic ✳ Bangui *area* 624,977 *sq km* (241,305 *sq miles*), *pop* 3,200,000 (1975 *est*)

**Central America 1** the narrow s portion of North America connecting that continent with South America & extending from the Isthmus of Tehuantepec to the Isthmus of Panama **2** the republics of Guatemala, El Salvador, Honduras, Nicaragua, & Costa Rica & often also Panama & Belize

**Ceuta** city & port N Morocco opposite Gibraltar; a Spanish presidio *pop* 67,187 (1970)

**Cévennes** mountain range s France w of the Rhone at E edge of Massif Central

**Ceylon, Lanka 1** Ceylon, Ar **Serendib,** L & Gk **Taprobane** island *area* 64,643 *sq km* (24,959 *sq miles*) in Indian ocean off s India **2** – see SRI LANKA – **Sinhalese** *adj or n*

**Chad,** F **Tchad** country N cen Africa ✳ Ndjamena; a republic; until 1959 a territory of French Equatorial Africa *area* 1,284,000 *sq km* (495,752 *sq miles*), *pop* 4,000,000 (1981 *est*) – **Chadian** *adj or n*

**Chalfont St Peter** town in Buckinghamshire 13 km (8 miles) ESE of High Wycombe pop 18,760 (1971)

**Champlain, Lake** lake 1,127 km (435 miles) long between New York & Vermont extending N into Quebec area 172 km (107 miles)

**Channel Islands** islands in English channel; a possession of Brit Crown area 194 sq km (75 sq miles), pop 133,034 (1981) – see ALDERNEY, GUERNSEY, JERSEY, SARK

**Chargres** river Panama flowing through Gatun Lake to the Caribbean

**Charleston** city ✳ of W Virginia on the Kanawha river pop 63,968 (1980)

**Charlestown** town & port ✳ of Nevis pop 1,200 (1981)

**Charlotte Amalie,** formerly **Saint Thomas** city & port ✳ of Virgin Islands of the United States, on St Thomas I

**Chatham** islands s Pacific belonging to New Zealand & comprising two islands (Chatham & Pitt) area 967 sq km (372 sq miles), pop 751 (1981)

**Chemnitz, Karl-Marx-Stadt** city E Germany SE of Leipzig pop 1,930,087 (1980)

**Chemulpo** – see INCHON

**Chequers** official country residence of British Prime Ministers in Buckinghamshire near Wendover

**Cherbourg** city & port NW France on Cotentin peninsula on English channel pop 37,933 (1970)

**Cherwell** river 48 km (30 miles) long cen England in Northamptonshire & Oxfordshire flowing s into the Thames at Oxford

**Chesapeake Bay** inlet of the Atlantic 311 km (193 miles) long in Virginia & Maryland

**Cheshire** county in NW England ✳ Chester area 2,629 sq km (1,013 sq miles), pop 935,100 (1981)

**Chesil Bank** shingle bank on coast of Dorset 19 km (11 miles) long

**Cheviot** hills extending NE to sw along English-Scottish border

**Cheyenne** city ✳ of Wyoming pop 47,283 (1980)

**Chicago** city & port NE Illinois on Lake Michigan pop 3,366,957 (1970)

**Chile** country s South America between the Andes & Pacific ocean; a republic ✳ Santiago area 756,945 sq km (292,256 sq miles), pop 11,000,000 (1979 est) – **Chilean** adj or n

**Chiltern** hills s cen England in Oxfordshire, Buckinghamshire, Hertfordshire, & Bedfordshire

**China** country E Asia; a republic, until 1912 an empire ✳ Peking; area ab 9,597,000 sq km (3,704,400 sq miles), pop 982,550,000 (1980 est) – see FORMOSA

**China sea** the E & S China seas

**Chindwin** river 840 km (520 miles) long NW Burma flowing s into the Irrawaddy

**Chittagong** city & port SE Bangladesh on Bay of Bengal pop 416,733 (1974)

**Cho Oyu** mountain 8,153 m (26,750 ft) Nepal Tibet in the Himalayas; 6th highest in the world

**Christchurch** city New Zealand on E coast of South I pop 321,720 (1981)

**Christiania** – see OSLO

**Christmas 1** island E Indian ocean s of w end of Java; administered by Australia area 135 sq km (52 sq miles), pop 3,308 (1980) **2** island (atoll) in the Line islands belonging to Great Britain; largest atoll in the Pacific area (including lagoon) 359 sq km (139 sq miles), pop 674 (1973)

**Chungking, Pahsien** city ✳ of China 1937–46 in SE Szechwan province on the Yangtze pop 6,200,000 (1979)

**Cinque Ports** group of seaport towns SE England on coast of Kent & Sussex, orig five (Dover, Sandwich, Romney, Hastings, & Hythe) to which were later added Winchelsea, Rye, & other minor places, granted special privileges (abolished in 19th century) in return for services in coast defence

**Ciudad Juárez, Juárez** city Mexico in Chihuahua State on Rio Grande opposite El Paso, Texas pop 520,539 (1975 est)

**Cleveland** county in NE England formed in 1974 from parts of former counties of Durham and Yorkshire and county boroughs of Hartlepool and Teeside area 583 sq km (225 sq miles), pop 566,400 (1981) – **Clevelander** n

**Clwyd** county in N Wales formed in 1974 from former counties of Flintshire, part of Denbigh and Merioneth area 2,426 sq km (937 sq miles), pop 392,000 (1981)

**Clyde** river 170 km (106 miles) long sw Scotland flowing NW into **Firth of Clyde** (estuary)

**Coblenz** – see KOBLENZ

**Cochinos Bay** – see PIGS (Bay of)

**Cocos, Keeling** islands E Indian ocean belonging to Australia area 2.6 sq km (1 sq mile), pop 487 (1980)

**Cologne,** G **Köln** city w Germany in N Rhine-Westphalia state on the Rhine pop 976,700 (1980)

**Colombey-les-Deux-Églises** village in Haute-Marne, France; home and burial places of Gen de Gaulle pop 390 (1973)

**Colombia** country NW South America bordering on Caribbean sea & Pacific ocean ✳ Bogotá area ab 1,138,914 sq km (456,737 sq miles), pop 27,729,847 (1980 est) – **Colombian** adj or n

**Colombo** city & port ✳ of Sri Lanka pop 585,776 (1981)

**Colón Archipelago** – see GALAPAGOS ISLANDS

**Colorado 1** river 2,320 km (1,440 miles) long sw USA & NW Mexico rising in N Colorado & flowing sw into Gulf of California **2** river 965 km (600 miles) long s Texas flowing SE into Gulf of Mexico **3** river 850 km (530 miles) long, cen Argentina flowing SE to the Atlantic **4** State w USA ✳ Denver area 271,042 sq km (104,247 sq miles), pop 2,888,834 (1980) – **Coloradan** adj or n, **Coloradoan** adj or n

**Columbia 1** river 1,953 km (1,214 miles) long sw Canada & NW USA rising in SE British Columbia & flowing s & w into the Pacific **2** city ✳ of South Carolina pop 99,296 (1980) – **Columbian** adj or n

**Columbus** city cen Ohio, its ✳ pop 564,871 (1980)

**Columna, La** – see BOLIVAR (Pico)

**Communism Peak** – see GARMO PEAK

**Como** town N Italy in Lombardy region at sw end of **Lake Como** (59 km or 37 miles long), pop 97,395 (1971)

**Comoro** islands off SE Africa between Mozambique & Madagascar; formerly a French possession, a republic (except for Mayotte I, which remains French) since 1975 ✳ Moroni area 1,797 sq km (694 sq miles), pop 385,000 (1979 est) – **Comoranian** adj or n, **Comoro** adj or n

**Conakry, Konakry** city & port ✳ of Guinea on the Atlantic pop 120,000 (1978 est)

**Concepción** city s cen Chile pop 170,000 (1979 est)

**Concord** city ✳ of New Hampshire on the Merrimack river pop 30,400 (1980)

**Coney Island** resort section of New York City in s Brooklyn; formerly an island 3 km (2 miles) long

**Congo 1** Congo, **Congo Republic,** formerly **Middle Congo** country w cen Africa w of the town Congo ✳ Brazzaville area 343,320 sq km (132,046 sq miles), pop 2,100,000 (1981 est) – see FRENCH EQUATORIAL AFRICA **2** – see ZAIRE – **Congolese** adj or n

**Connacht,** formerly **Connaught** province w Republic of Ireland comprising counties Galway, Leitrim, Mayo, Roscommon, & Sligo area 17,189 sq km (6,611 sq miles), pop 389,763 (1981)

**Connecticut** state NE USA ✳ Hartford area 13,023 sq km (5,009 sq miles), pop 3,107,576 (1980)

**Constance, Lake,** G **Bodensee** lake area 543 sq km (210 sq miles) w Europe on border between Germany, Austria, & Switzerland

**Constantine** city NE Algeria pop 350,183 (1974)

**Constantinople** – see ISTANBUL

**Constantsa** city & port SE Rumania on Black sea pop 279,308 (1979)

**Cook 1** islands s Pacific sw of Society islands; belong to New Zealand ✳ Avarua (on Rarotonga I) area 240 sq km (93 sq miles), pop 18,000 (1980) **2** strait New Zealand between North I & South I **3** inlet of the Pacific s Alaska w of Kenai peninsula

**Cook, Mount, Aorangi** mountain 3,764 m (12,349 ft) high New Zealand in w cen South I; highest peak in Southern Alps & New Zealand

**Copenhagen,** Dan **København** city & port ✳ of Denmark on E Sjaelland I & N Amager I pop 579,145 (1981) Greater Copenhagen 1,202,790 (1981) – **Copenhagener** n

**Copiapó 1** volcano 6,080 m (19,947 ft) N cen Chile **2** city w of the volcano pop 36,767 (1981)

**Coquilhatville** – see MBANDAKA

**Coral** sea arm of the sw Pacific bounded on w by Queensland, Australia, on N by the Solomons, & on E by New Hebrides & New Caledonia

**Corby** town in Northamptonshire; created "new town" 1950; *pop* 47,000 (1981)

**Córdoba 1** province s Spain *area* 13,718 *sq km* (5,297 *sq miles*), *pop* 161,423 (1970) **2 Córdoba, Cordova** city, its ✻, on the Guadalquivir river *pop* 229,407 (1970) **3** city N *cen* Argentina *pop* 781,565 (1970) – **Cordoban** *adj or n*

**Corfe Castle** village on Isle of Purbeck, Dorset *pop* 1,400 (1974 *est*)

**Corfu**, NGk **Kérkyra, Kérkira,** *anc* **Corcyra 1** island NW Greece, one of the Ionian islands *area* 592 *sq km* (227 *sq miles*) **2** city & port on E Corfu *pop* 28,630 (1971) – **Corfiote** *n*

**Corinth**, NGk **Kórinthos 1 Corinth, Corinthia** region of ancient Greece occupying most of Isthmus of Corinth & part of NE Peloponnesus **2** city & port Greece on Isthmus of Corinth at head of Gulf of Corinth NE of site ancient city of Corinth *pop* 20,733 (1971)

**Corinth, Gulf of, Gulf of Lepanto** inlet of Ionian sea *cen* Greece w of **Isthmus of Corinth** (neck of land 32 *km or* 20 *miles* long connecting Peloponnesus region with rest of Greece)

**Cork 1** county sw Ireland in Munster *area* 7,462 *sq km* (2,881 *sq miles*), *pop* 351,735 (1971) **2** city & county borough & port, its ✻, at head of Cork Harbour *pop* 136,269 (1981 *prov*)

**Cornwall** county in sw England and including Isles of Scilly *area* 3,512 *sq km* (1,356 *sq miles*), *pop* 429,300 (1981)

**Corsica**, F **Corse** island France in the Mediterranean N of Sardinia *area* 8,681 *sq km* (3,352 *sq miles*), *pop* 230,100 (1981) – **Corsican** *adj or n*

**Costa Brava** coast region NE Spain in Catalonia on the Mediterranean extending NE from Barcelona

**Costa del Sol** coast region s Spain on the Mediterranean extending E from Gibraltar

**Costa Rica** country Central America between Nicaragua & Panama; a republic ✻ San José *area* 50,900 *sq km* (19,653 *sq miles*), *pop* 2,183,625 (1979) – **Costa Rican** *adj or n*

**Côte d'Azur** coast region SE France on the Mediterranean; part of the Riviera

**Côte d'Ivoire** – see IVORY COAST

**Côte d'Or** range of hills E France sw of Dijon

**Cotentin** peninsula NW France projecting into English channel w of mouth of the Seine

**Cotonou** city & port s Benin *pop* 178,000 (1976)

**Cotopaxi** volcano 5,896 *m* (19,344 *ft*) N *cen* Ecuador

**Cotswolds** range of hills in Avon-Gloucestershire *ab* 80 *km* (50 *miles*) long; average height *ab* 200 *m* (600 *ft*); highest point Cleave Cloud 314 *m* (1,031 *ft*)

**Coventry** city & borough *cen* England in W Midlands *pop* 335,238 (1971)

**Cracow** – see KRAKOW

**Craiova** city s Rumania *pop* 197,820 (1975)

**Crawley** town in W Sussex; created "new town" 1956; 11 *km* (7 *miles*) NE of Horsham *pop* 72,500 (1981)

**Crécy, Cressy, Crécy-en-Ponthieu** town N France NW of Amiens *pop* 1,400 (1973)

**Cremona** town N Italy in Lombardy region on the Po ESE of Milan *pop* 80,798 (1968 *est*)

**Crete**, NGk **Kríti** island Greece in the E Mediterranean ✻ Canea *area* 8,259 *sq km* (3,189 *sq miles*), *pop* 456,208 (1971) – **Cretan** *adj or n*

**Creuse** river *cen* France 255 *km* (158 *miles*) long flowing from Plateau des Millevaches to Vienne river

**Crimea**, Russ **Krim** peninsula USSR in s Soviet Russia, Europe, extending into Black sea sw of Sea of Azov – **Crimean** *adj*

**Croatia 1** region sE Europe in NW Yugoslavia incl of Slovenia **2** constituent republic of Yugoslavia comprising Croatia, Slavonia, & most of Istria & the Dalmatian coast ✻ Zagreb *area* 56,538 *sq km* (21,829 *sq miles*), *pop* 4,426,000 (1971)

**Crocodile** – see LIMPOPO

**Cuba** island in the West Indies N of Caribbean sea *area* 110,822 *sq km* (42,827 *miles*), *pop* 9,700,000 (1978 *est*) – **Cuban** *adj or n*

**Cúcuta** city N Colombia *pop* 259,400 (1973)

**Cuernavaca** city s *cen* Mexico s of Mexico City ✻ of Morelos *pop* 273,986 (1975 *est*)

**Culloden Moor** moorland N Scotland in N Highland region E of Inverness; scene of battle 1746

**Cumbernauld** town in Strathclyde region Scotland; established "new town" 1956; *pop* 50,850 (1981)

**Cumbria** county in NW England formed in 1974 from former counties of Cumberland, Westmorland and parts of Yorkshire and Lancashire; *area* 6,808 *sq km* (2,629 *sq miles*), *pop* 468,500 (1981) – **Cumbrian** *adj or n*

**Cumbrian** mountains NW England chiefly in Cumbria & Lancashire – see SCAFELL PIKE

**Curaçao** island Netherlands Antilles in the s Caribbean; chief town Willemstad *area* 471 *sq km* (182 *sq miles*), *pop* 154,928 (1974)

**Cwmbran** town in Gwent, Wales; established as "new town" 1949; *pop* 45,700 (1981)

**Cymru** – see WALES

**Cyprus 1** island E Mediterranean s of Turkey **2** country coextensive with the island; a republic of the Brit Commonwealth ✻ Nicosia *area* 9,251 *sq km* (3,572 *sq miles*), *pop* 618,300 (1978 *est*) – **Cypriot, Cypriote** *adj or n*, **Cyprian** *adj or n*

**Czechoslovakia** country *cen* Europe; a republic ✻ Prague *area* 127,877 *sq km* (49,365 *sq miles*), *pop* 15,237,788 (1979) – **Czechoslovak** *adj or n*, **Czechoslovakian** *adj or n*

# D

**Dacca** city ✻ of Bangladesh *pop* 3,458,602 (1974)

**Dahomey** – see BENIN – **Dahoman** *adj or n*, **Dahomean** *adj or n*, **Dahomeyan** *adj or n*

**Dakar** city & port ✻ of Senegal *pop* 581,000 (1978)

**Damascus**, Ar **Esh Sham** city ✻ of Syria *pop* 2,250,000 (1979 *est*)

**Danube**, G **Donau**, *anc* **Danubius, Ister** river 2,859 *km* (1,770 *miles*) long, *cen* & SE Europe flowing SE from s Germany into Black sea – **Danubian** *adj*

**Danzig 1** – see GDANSK **2** territory surrounding & including Danzig that (1920–39) constituted a free city under the League of Nations *area* 1,952 *sq km* (754 *sq miles*)

**Dapsang** – see GODWIN AUSTEN

**Dardanelles, Hellespont,** *anc* **Hellespontus** strait NW Turkey connecting Sea of Marmara with the Aegean

**Dar es Salaam** city & port ✻ of Tanzania & of Tanganyika on Indian ocean *pop* 757,346 (1978)

**Darling 1** river 2,740 *km* (1,702 *miles*) SE Australia in Queensland & New South Wales flowing sw into the Murray **2** mountain range sw Western Australia extending *ab* 800 *km* (500 *miles*) N–s along coast; highest point Mt Cooke 583 *m* (1,910 *ft*)

**Dartmoor** moorland sw England in s Devonshire *area* 945 *sq km* (365 *sq miles*)

**Dead sea,** *bib* **Salt sea,** L **Lacus Asphaltites** salt lake on boundary between Israel & Jordan *area* 1,049 *sq km* (405 *sq miles*), surface 395 *m* (1,296 *ft*) below sea level

**Deal** town in Kent, England; one of Cinque Ports; *pop* 25,432 (1971)

**Dean, Forest of** forested district sw England in w Gloucestershire between Severn & Wye rivers; an ancient royal forest

**Death Valley** arid valley E California & s Nevada containing lowest point in the USA 85 *m* (280 *ft*) below sea level; most of area included in **Death Valley National Monument** *area* 7,488 *sq km* (2,891 *sq miles*)

**Dee 1** river 140 *km* (87 *miles*) long NE Scotland flowing E into North sea **2** river 110 *km* (70 *miles*) long Wales & w England flowing E & N into Irish sea

**Delaware** state E USA ✻ Dover *area* 5,348 *sq km* (2,057 *sq miles*), *pop* 595,225 (1980)

**Delhi 1** territory N India w of Uttar Pradesh state ✻ Delhi *area* 1,486 *sq km* (578 *sq miles*), *pop* 4,044,338 (1971) **2** city, its ✻ *pop* 4,065,698 (1971) – see NEW DELHI

**Denali** – see MCKINLEY (Mount)

**Denmark**, Dan **Danmark 1** country N Europe occupying most of Jutland peninsula & adjacent islands in Baltic & North seas; a kingdom ✻ Copenhagen *area* 43,074 *sq km* (16,631 *sq miles*), *pop* 5,119,155 (1981 *est*) **2** strait 209 *km* (130 *miles*) wide 483 *km* (300 *miles*) long between SE Greenland & Iceland connecting Arctic ocean with the Atlantic

**Dent Blanche** mountain 4,359 *m* (14,304 *ft*) S Switzerland in Pennine Alps

**Denver** city NE *cen* Colorado, its ✳ *pop* 492,365 (1980) – **Denverite** *n*

**Derby** borough N *cen* England in Derbyshire *pop* 219,348 (1971)

**Derbyshire** county in N *cen* England *area* 2,631 *sq km* (1,016 *sq miles*), *pop* 910,000 (1981)

**Derry** – see LONDONDERRY

**Derwent 1** river 190 *km* (120 *miles*) long Australia in Tasmania flowing SE into Tasman sea **2** river in North Yorkshire, England 92 *km* (57 *miles*) long; rises on North Yorkshire moors and flows SSW to join river Ouse

**Derwent Water** lake NW England in Lake District in Cumbria *ab* 5 *km* (3 *miles*) long; 2 *km* (1.25 *miles*) wide

**Des Moines** city ✳ of Iowa on Des Moines river *pop* 191,003 (1980)

**Detroit** city SE Michigan *pop* 1,492,507 (1970) – **Detroiter** *n*

**Devon** county in SW England, bordered by English Channel and Bristol Channel, *area* 6,711 *sq km* (2,591 *sq miles*), *pop* 962,700 (1981)

**Dhaulagiri** mountain 8,172 *m* (27,810 *ft*) W *cen* Nepal in the Himalayas

**Didcot** town in Oxfordshire 16 *km* (10 *miles*) S of Oxford *pop* 12,990 (1971)

**Dieppe** city & port N France N of Rouen *pop* 29,970 (1975 *prov*)

**Dijon** city E France *pop* 156,787 (1980 *est*)

**Dinnington** town in S Yorkshire 11 *km* (7 *miles*) SE of Rotherham *pop* 15,380 (1971)

**District of Columbia** federal district E USA coextensive with city of Washington *area* 174 *sq km* (67 *sq miles*), *pop* 637,651 (1980)

**Djaja, Mount,** *formerly* **Mount Carstensz** mountain 5,030*m* (16,503 *ft*) Indonesia in W Irian province in Sudirman range; highest in New Guinea

**Djakarta** – see JAKARTA

**Djambi, Jambi** city & port Indonesia in SE *cen* Sumatra on Hari river *pop* 939,000 (1971)

**Djibouti 1** Djibouti, *formerly* **French Territory of the Afars and the Issas, earlier French Somaliland** country E Africa on Gulf of Aden; a republic *area* 23,088 *sq km* (8,800 *sq miles*), *pop* 300,000 (1981 *est*) **2** Djibouti, Jibuti city, its ✳ – **Djibutian, Jibutian** *adj or n*

**Dnieper** river 2,250 *km* (1,400 *miles*) long USSR rising in S Valdai hills & flowing S through Ukraine into Black sea

**Dodecanese** islands Greece in the SE Aegean comprising the Southern Sporades S of Icaria & Samos; belonged to Italy 1923–47 *area* 2,663 *sq km* (1,028 *sq miles*), *pop* 121,017 (1971) – see RHODES – **Dodecanesian** *adj or n*

**Dogger Bank** submerged sandbank *ab* 115 *km* (70 *miles*) off Yorkshire coast; average depth 18 to 36 *m* (60 to 120 *ft*)

**Doha** city & port ✳ of Qatar on Persian Gulf *pop* 200,000 (1982 *est*)

**Dominica** island Brit West Indies in the Leeward islands ✳ Roseau *area* 728 *sq km* (289 *sq miles*), *pop* 74,069 (1981) – **Dominican** *adj or n*

**Dominican Republic,** *formerly* **Santo Domingo, San Domingo** country West Indies on E Hispaniola; a republic ✳ Santo Domingo *area* 48,442 *sq km* (18,604 *sq miles*), *pop* 5,647,977 (1981) – **Dominican** *adj or n*

**Don** river 1,900 *km* (1,200 *miles*) long USSR in SW Soviet Russia, Europe, flowing SE & then SW into Sea of Azov

**Doncaster** town N England in S Yorkshire *pop* 82,668 (1971)

**Dordogne** river 490 *km* (300 *miles*) long SW France flowing SW & W to unite with the Garonne forming the Gironde estuary

**Dorking** town in Surrey on river Mole *pop* 22,530 (1971)

**Dorset** county in SW England on English Channel *area* 2,520 *sq km* (973 *sq miles*), *pop* 604,500 (1981)

**Dortmund** city W Germany in the Ruhr district *pop* 608,300 (1980)

**Douglas** borough ✳ of Isle of Man *pop* 19,944 (1981)

**Dover 1** market town and seaport on SE coast of Kent, England; one of Cinque Ports *pop* 34,395 (1971) **2** city *cen* Delaware, its ✳ *pop* 23,512 (1980)

**Dover, Strait of,** F **Pas de Calais** channel between SE England & N France, easternmost section of English channel; *ab* 35 *km* (22 *miles*) long and 34 *km* (21 *miles*) wide

**Down** county SE Northern Ireland ✳ Downpatrick *area* 2,466 *sq km* (952 *sq miles*), *pop* 311,266 (1971)

**Downpatrick** urban district SE Northern Ireland ✳ of Co Down

**Drammen** city & port SE Norway *pop* 50,098 (1981)

**Dresden** city E Germany in Saxony *pop* 1,806,401 (1980)

**Drina** river 257 *km* (160 *miles*) long *cen* Yugoslavia flowing N along the border between Bosnia & Serbia into the Sava river

**Dubai 1** sheikhdom E United Arab Emirates *area* 157,579 *sq km* (59,029 *sq miles*), *pop* 350,000 (1980 *est*) **2** city & port, its ✳ *pop* 59,092 (1968)

**Dubawnt 1** lake N Canada in SE Northwest Territories E of Great Slave Lake *area* 4,100 *sq km* (1,654 *sq miles*) **2** river 935 *km* (580 *miles*) long N Canada flowing NE through Dubawnt Lake to **Baker Lake** (W expansion of Chesterfield inlet)

**Dublin,** Gael **Baile Atha Cliath 1** county E Ireland in Leinster *area* 922 *sq km* (356 *sq miles*), *pop* 849,542 (1971) **2** city & county borough & port ✳ of Republic of Ireland & Co Dublin at mouth of the Liffey on **Dublin Bay** (inlet of Irish sea) *pop* 525,360 (1981) – **Dubliner** *n*

**Dubrovnik,** It **Ragusa** city & port SW Yugoslavia in Croatia *pop* 20,000 (1971)

**Dudley** town in W Midlands 13 *km* (8 *miles*) NW of Birmingham *pop* 185,581 (1971)

**Duisburg,** *formerly* **Duisburg-Hamborn** city W W Germany at junction of Rhine & Ruhr rivers *pop* 558,100 (1980)

**Dumbarton** town in Strathclyde region W *cen* Scotland on Clyde estuary *pop* 25,240 (1971)

**Dumfries** burgh S Scotland ✳ of Dumfries and Galloway *pop* 29,384 (1971)

**Dumfries and Galloway** region in S Scotland formed in 1975 from former counties of Dumfrieshire, Kirkcudbrightshire and Wigtownshire *area* 6,475 *sq km* (2,500 *sq miles*), *pop* 144,218 (1981)

**Dundee** city & port E Scotland ✳ of Tayside on Firth of Tay *pop* 181,243 (1974)

**Dunedin** city New Zealand on SE coast of South I at head of Otago Harbour *pop* 82,216 (1971)

**Dunfermline** town in Fife region E Scotland near Firth of Forth and including naval base of Rosyth *pop* 49,882 (1971)

**Dungeness** headland of shingle and sand on S coast of Kent projecting into Strait of Dover

**Dunkerque, Dunkirk** city & port N France on Strait of Dover *pop* 83,091 (1975 *prov*)

**Dun Laoghaire, Dunleary,** *formerly* **Kingstown** borough & port E Ireland in Leinster on Dublin Bay *pop* 54,405 (1981 *prov*)

**Dunnet Head** headland N Scotland on N coast W of John o' Groats; northernmost point of mainland, at 58°50′N

**Duque de Caxias** city SE Brazil in Rio de Janeiro state N of city of Rio de Janeiro *pop* 431,397 (1970)

**Durban** city & port E Republic of South Africa in E Natal on Natal Bay *pop* 350,935 (1970)

**Durham** county in NE England facing North sea formed in 1974 *area* 2,436 *sq km* (941 *sq miles*), *pop* 606,600 (1981)

**Dushanbe,** *formerly* **Stalinabad** city USSR in Soviet Central Asia ✳ of Tadzhik Republic *pop* 494,000 (1979)

**Düsseldorf** city W Germany on the Rhine N of Cologne ✳ of N Rhine-Westphalia state *pop* 590,500 (1980)

**Dutch Guiana** – see SURINAM

**Dvina Gulf, Dvina Bay,** *formerly* **Gulf of Archangel** arm of White sea USSR in N Soviet Russia, Europe

**Dyfed** county in SW Wales formed in 1974 from former counties of Cardigan, Carmarthen and Pembroke *area* 5,765 *sq km* (2,226 *sq miles*), *pop* 327,600 (1981)

# E

**E¹** – see LHOTSE

**East Anglia** region E England including Norfolk & Suffolk; one of kingdoms in Anglo-Saxon heptarchy – **East Anglian** *adj or n*

**Easter, Rapa Nui,** Sp **Isla de Pascua** island SE Pacific w of Chilean coast belonging to Chile *area* 119 *sq km* (46 *sq miles*), *pop* 1,100

**Eastern Ghats** chain of mountains SE India extending SW & S from near delta of Mahanadi river in Orissa to w Madras & s Kerala; 1,400 *km* (875 *miles*) long; average height 600 *m* (1,970 *ft*) – see WESTERN GHATS

**East Germany** the German Democratic Republic – see GERMANY

**East Kilbride** town in Strathclyde region Scotland; developed as "new town" 1947; *pop* 76,100 (1981)

**Eastleigh** town in Hampshire 8 *km* (5 *miles*) NNE of Southampton *pop* 45,361 (1971)

**East Sussex** county in SE England *area* 3,674 *sq km* (1,419 *sq miles*), *pop* 663,200 (1981)

**Ecuador** country w South America bordering on the Pacific; a republic ✻ Quito *area* 283,561 *sq km* (109,483 *sq miles*), *pop* 8,000,000 (1981) – **Ecuadoran** *adj or n*, **Ecuadorian** *adj or n*

**Edinburgh** city and capital of Scotland in Lothian region near s shore of Firth of Forth *pop* 475,042 (1974 *est*)

**Edo** – see TOKYO

**Egypt,** Ar **Misr** country NE Africa & Sinai peninsula bordering on Mediterranean & Red seas ✻ Cairo *area* 1,002,000 *sq km* (386,900 *sq miles*), *pop* 44,000,000 (1981 *est*)

**Eiger** mountain 3,975 *m* (13,040 *ft*) w *cen* Switzerland NE of the Jungfrau

**Eindhoven** commune s Netherlands in N Brabant province *pop* 362,982 (1978)

**Eire** – see IRELAND

**Elba** island Italy in the Mediterranean between Corsica & mainland; chief town Portoferraio *area* 223 *sq km* (86 *sq miles*), *pop* 29,000 (1971)

**El Faiyûm, El Fayum** – see FAIYÛM

**El Giza, El Gizeh** – see GIZA

**Elisabethville** – see LUBUMBASHI

**Ellesmere Port** town in Cheshire, England on s bank of Manchester Ship Canal 14 *km* (9 *miles*) SSE of Liverpool *pop* 61,637 (1971)

**Ellice** – see TUVALU

**El Mansûra** – see MANSURA

**El Salvador** country Central America bordering on the Pacific; a republic ✻ San Salvador *area* 21,393 *sq km* (8,259 *sq miles*), *pop* 4,539,000 (1977)

**Elsinore** – see HELSINGOR

**Ely** city in Cambridgeshire, England on river Ouse 24 *km* (15 *miles*) NE of Cambridge *pop* 9,020 (1971)

**England 1** England, LL Anglia country s Great Britain; a division of the United Kingdom of Great Britain & Northern Ireland ✻ London *area* 130,360 *sq km* (50,331 *sq miles*), *pop* 46,221,000 (1981) **2** England & Wales **3** UNITED KINGDOM

**English channel,** F **La Manche** channel between s England & N France connecting North sea & Atlantic ocean

**Enniskillen, Inniskilling** municipal borough SW Northern Ireland ✻ of Co Fermanagh

**Enschede** town E Netherlands in Overijssel province near German frontier *pop* 241,184 (1978)

**Entebbe** town s Uganda on N shore of Lake Victoria; former ✻ of Uganda *pop* 10,900 (1969)

**Ephraim** – see ISRAEL

**Epping Forest** forested region SE England in Essex NE of London & s of town of **Epping**

**Equatorial Guinea,** *formerly* Spanish Guinea country w Africa on Bight of Biafra including Mbini, Fernando Po & other islands ; an independent republic since 1968 ✻ Malabo *area* 28,051 *sq km* (10,831 *sq miles*), *pop* 150,000 (1980 *est*) – **Equatorial Guinean** *adj or n*

**Erebus, Mount** volcano 3,795 *m* (12,450 *ft*) E Antarctica on Ross I in SW Ross sea

**Erevan** city USSR ✻ of Armenia *pop* 1,019,000 (1979)

**Erfurt** city E Germany wsw of Leipzig *pop* 1,238,576 (1980)

**Erie, Lake** lake E *cen* North America on boundary between the USA & Canada; one of the Great Lakes *area* 25,667 *sq km* (9,910 *sq miles*)

**Eritrea** former country NE Africa bordering on Red sea ✻ Asmara; incorporated (1962) into Ethiopia *area* 119,600 *sq km* (46,000 *sq miles*) – **Eritrean** *adj or n*

**Esbjerg** city & port SW Denmark in SW Jutland peninsula on North sea *pop* 79,992 (1981)

**Esfahan** – see ISFAHAN

**España** – see SPAIN

**Essen** city w Germany in the Ruhr district *pop* 647,600 (1980)

**Essex** county in SE England *area* 3,674 *sq km* (1,419 *sq miles*), *pop* 1,482,600 (1981)

**Estonia, Esthonia** country N Europe bordering on Baltic sea; one of the Baltic Provinces of Russia 1721–1917, an independent republic 1918–40, since 1940 a constituent republic (**Estonian Republic**) of the USSR ✻ Tallin *area* 45,100 *sq km* (17,410 *sq miles*), *pop* 1,447,000 (1977)

**Ethiopia 1** ancient country NE Africa s of Egypt bordering on Red sea **2 Ethiopia, Abyssinia** country E Africa; formerly an empire, since 1975 a republic ✻ Addis Ababa *area* 1,221,900 *sq km* (471,800 *sq miles*), *pop* 29,416,000 (1977 *est*)

**Etna, Aetna** volcano 3,340 *m* (10,958 *ft*), Italy in NE Sicily

**Ettrick Forest** region, formerly a forest & hunting ground, in SE Scotland in Borders region

**Euphrates** river 3,598 *km* (2,235 *miles*) long SW Asia flowing from E Turkey SW & SE to unite with the Tigris forming the Shatt-al-Arab

**Europe 1** continent of the eastern hemisphere between Asia & the Atlantic *area ab* 10,360,000 *sq km* (4,000,000 *sq miles*), *pop* 473,000,000 (1975 *est*) **2** the European continent as distinguished from the British Isles

**Euxine sea** – see BLACK SEA

**Everest, Mount,** Tibetan **Chomolungma** mountain 8,848 *m* (29,028 *ft*), s Asia on border between Nepal & Tibet in the Himalayas; highest in the world

**Evesham** town in Hereford and Worcester, on river Avon *pop* 14,150 (1972)

**Exeter** city in Devon, on river Exe *pop* 95,729 (1971)

**Exmoor** moorland SW England in Somerset & Devonshire *area* 686 *sq km* (265 *sq miles*)

**Eyre, Lake** intermittent lake *cen* Australia in NE South Australia *area ab* 9,324 *sq km* (3,600 *sq miles*), max depth 1.2 *m* (4 *ft*)

# F

**Faeroe, Faroe** islands Denmark in the NE Atlantic NW of the Shetlands ✻ Thorshavn *area* 1,399 *sq km* (540 *sq miles*), *pop* 41,211 (1976)

**Faiyûm, Fayum, El Faiyûm, El Fayum** city N Egypt ssw of Cairo *pop* 167,000 (1974 *est*)

**Faka** – see CAMEROON

**Falkland,** Sp **Islas Malvinas** islands SW Atlantic E of s end of Argentina; a Brit crown colony ✻ Stanley *area* 11,961 *sq km* (4,618 *sq miles*), *pop* 2,045 (1975 *est*)

**Falkland Islands Dependencies** islands & territories in the s Atlantic & in Antarctica administered by the British from Falkland islands, including S Orkney, S Sandwich, & S Shetland islands, S Georgia I, Antarctic peninsula, & Antarctic archipelago; chief town Stanley on E Falkland *pop* 1,813 (1980)

**Famagusta** city & port E Cyprus on **Famagusta Bay** (inlet of the Mediterranean) *pop* 39,400 (1975 *est*)

**Far East** the countries of Asia & the Malay archipelago – usu considered as comprising the Asian countries bordering on the Pacific but sometimes as including also India, Sri Lanka, Bangladesh, Tibet, & Burma – **Far Eastern** *adj*

**Farnborough** town in Hants, N of Aldershot; site of Royal Airforce Establishment *pop* 41,680 (1972 *est*)

**Federal Capital Territory** – see AUSTRALIAN CAPITAL TERRITORY

**Fengtien** – see MUKDEN

**Fermanagh** county SW Northern Ireland ✻ Enniskillen *area* 1,852 *sq km* (715 *sq miles*), *pop* 50,255 (1971)

**Fernando Po, Fernando Poo** island Equatorial Guinea in Bight of Biafra *area* 2,017 *sq km* (778 *sq miles*), *pop* 61,197 (1970 *est*) – see MALABO

**Ferrara** town N Italy in Emilia-Romagna region NE of Bologna near the Po *pop* 155,172 (1976)

**Fez, Fès** city N *cen* Morocco *pop* 744,900 (1979)

**Fife** region in E *cen* Scotland, changed from county to region in 1975 *area* 1,305 *sq km* (504 *sq miles*), *pop* 340,182 (1981)

**Fiji** islands SW Pacific E of New Hebrides constituting (with Rotuma I) an independent dominion of Brit Commonwealth ✳ Suva (on Viti Levu) *area* 18,272 *sq km* (7,055 *sq miles*), *pop* 634,151 (1980)

**Fingal's Cave** sea cave W Scotland on Staffa I

**Finger Lakes** group of long narrow lakes W *cen* New York comprised of Cayuga, Seneca, Keuka, Canandaigua, Skaneateles, Owasco, & several smaller lakes

**Finland, Finn Suomi** country N Europe bordering on Gulf of Bothnia & Gulf of Finland; a republic ✳ Helsinki *area* 337,009 *sq km* (130,092 *sq miles*), *pop* 4,811,391 (1981) – **Finlander** *n*

**Finland, Gulf of** arm of Baltic sea between Finland & Estonia

**Fleetwood** port in Lancashire *pop* 29,530 (1972 *est*)

**Flinders 1** river 840 *km* (520 *miles*) long Australia in *cen* Queensland flowing NW into Gulf of Carpentaria **2** mountain ranges Australia in E South Australia E of Lake Torrens

**Flodden** hill N England in N Northumberland near Scottish border; site of battle of Flodden Field (1513) which surrounds it

**Florence, It Firenze** town *cen* Italy on the Arno river ✳ of Tuscany *pop* 453,293 (1981 *est*) – **Florentine** *adj or n*

**Flores 1** island NW Azores *area* 142 *sq km* (55 *sq miles*), *pop* 5,302 (1970) **2** island Indonesia in Lesser Sunda islands *area* 14,250 *sq km* (5,500 *sq miles*), *pop* 6,556 (1970)

**Florida** state SE USA ✳ Tallahassee *area* 152,256 *sq km* (58,560 *sq miles*), *pop* 9,739,992 – **Floridian, Floridan** *adj or n*

**Flushing** – see VLISSINGEN

**Foggia** town SE Italy in Apulia region *pop* 153,334 (1976)

**Formosa** – see TAIWAN – **Formosan** *adj or n*

**Fort-de-France** city French West Indies ✳ of Martinique on W coast *pop* 100,576 (1974)

**Forth** river 80 *km* (50 *miles*) long S *cen* Scotland flowing E into **Firth of Forth** (estuary 97 *km* (48 *miles*) long, inlet of North sea)

**Fort Knox** military reservation N *cen* Kentucky SSW of Louisville; location of USA Gold Bullion Depository

**Fort-Lamy** – see N'DJAMENA

**Four Forest Cantons, Lake of the** – see LUCERN (Lake of)

**France** country W Europe between English channel & the Mediterranean; a republic ✳ Paris *area* 551,000 *sq km* (212,742 *sq miles*), *pop* 53,962,000 (1981)

**Frankfort** city ✳ of Kentucky *pop* 25,973 (1980)

**Frankfurt, Frankfort 1 Frankfurt, Frankfurt am Main, Frankfort on the Main** city W Germany on Main river *pop* 629,400 (1980) **2 Frankfurt , Frankfurt an der Oder, Frankfort on the Oder** city E Germany on Oder river *pop* 62,011 (1971)

**Frederiksberg** city Denmark on Sjaelland I, W suburb of Copenhagen *pop* 260,825 (1971 *est*)

**Freetown** city & port ✳ Sierra Leone on the Atlantic *pop* 274,000 (1981)

**Fréjus, Massif du** mountain on border between France & Italy at SW end of Graian Alps

**Fremantle** city Australia in SW Western Australia at mouth of Swan river; port for Perth *pop* 25,284 (1976)

**French Equatorial Africa, French Congo** former country W *cen* Africa N of Congo river comprising a federation of Chad, Gabon, Middle Congo, & Ubangi-Shari territories ✳ Brazzaville

**French Guiana** country N South America; an overseas department of France ✳ Cayenne *area* 90,000 *sq km* (34,750 *sq miles*), *pop* 50,000 (1971)

**French Guinea** – see GUINEA

**French Polynesia,** *formerly* **French Oceania** islands in S Pacific belonging to France & including Society, Marquesas, Tuamotu, Gambier, & Tubai groups ✳ Papeete (on Tahiti) *pop* 119,200 (1971 *est*)

**French Somaliland** – see DJIBOUTI

**French Sudan** – see MALI

**French Territory of the Afars and the Issas** – see DJIBOUTI

**French West Indies** islands of the West Indies belonging to France and including Guadeloupe, Martinique, Désirade, Les Saintes, Marie Galante, St Barthélemy, & part of St Martin

**Friendly Islands** – see TONGA

**Frisian** islands NW Europe in North sea including **West Frisian** islands (off N coast of Netherlands), **East Frisian** islands (off NW coast of Germany), & **North Frisian** islands (off coast of Germany & Denmark, including Helgoland & Sylt)

**Frunze,** *formerly* **Pishpek** city USSR on Chu river ✳ of Kirghiz Republic *pop* 533,000 (1979)

**Fujeirah 1** Sheikhdom United Arab Emirates *area* 1,200 *sq km* (450 *sq miles*), *pop* 40,000 (1980 *est*) **2** town, its ✳ on coast of Gulf of Oman

**Fuji, Fujiyama, Fuji-san** mountain 3,775 *m* (12,388 *ft*) Japan in S *cen* Honshu; highest in Japan

**Fukuoka** city & port Japan on N Kyushu on inlet of Tsushima strait *pop* 1,109,344 (1982)

**Funafuti** island (atoll) S Pacific in *cen* Tuvalu islands; contains ✳ of group *pop* 2,120 (1979 *est*)

**Funchal** city & port Portugal ✳ of Madeira I *pop* 54,068 (1978)

**Futuna 1 Futuna, Hooru** islands SW Pacific NE of Fiji; formerly a French protectorate, since 1959 part of Wallis and Futuna islands territory *pop* 8,550 (1971 *est*) **2** island SW Pacific in Futuna group

# G

**Gabon** country W Africa on the Atlantic; formerly a territory of French Equatorial Africa, since 1958 a republic ✳ Libreville *area* 267,677 *sq km* (103,346 *sq miles*), *pop* 950,000 (1974 *est*) – **Gabonese** *adj or n*

**Gaborone,** *formerly* **Gaberones** town ✳ of Botswana *pop* 60,000 (1981 *est*)

**Galápagos islands, Colón archipelago** island group Ecuador in the Pacific ✳ San Cristóbal *area tab* 8,000 *sq km* (3,000 *sq miles*), *pop* 4,000 (1973)

**Galilee, Sea of,** *bib* **Lake of Gennesaret, Sea of Tiberias, Sea of Chinnereth,** Heb **Yam Kinneret** lake *area* 166 *sq km* (64 *sq miles*) N Israel on Syrian border traversed by the Jordan; 209 *m* (686 *ft*) below sea level

**Gallipoli, Gelibolu** peninsula Turkey in Europe between the Dardanelles & Saros gulf

**Galloway** district SW Scotland comprising area formerly in counties of Wigtown & Kirkcudbright – see DUMFRIES AND GALLOWAY – **Galwegian** *adj or n*

**Gambia 1** river *ab* 1,000 *km* (620 *miles*) long W Africa flowing from Fouta Djallon in W Guinea W through Senegal into the Atlantic in Gambia **2 Gambia, The Gambia** country W Africa; a republic in the Brit Commonwealth ✳ Banjul *area ab* 11,000 *sq km* (4,000 *sq miles*), *pop* 620,000 (1981 *est*) – **Gambian** *adj or n*

**Gana** – see GHANA

**Ganges** river 2,506 *km* (1,557 *miles*) long N India flowing from the Himalayas SE & E to unite with the Brahmaputra & empty into Bay of Bengal through the vast **Ganges delta** – **Gangetic** *adj*

**Garmo Peak, Stalin Peak,** *since 1961* **Communism Peak** mountain 7,495 *m* (24,590 *ft*) Soviet Central Asia in SE Tadzhik Republic in the Pamir mountains; highest in the USSR

**Garonne** river 571 *km* (355 *miles*) long SW France flowing NW to unite with the Dordogne forming the Gironde estuary

**Gateshead** borough N England in Tyne and Wear county on the Tyne opposite Newcastle *pop* 94,469 (1971)

**Gaya** city NE India in *cen* Bihar state *pop* 179,826 (1971)

**Gaza,** Ar **Ghazze** city S Palestine near the Mediterranean; with surrounding coastal district (**Gaza Strip,** adjoining Sinai peninsula *area* 260 *sq km* (100 *sq miles*), *pop* 365,000 (1971)), administered 1949-67 by Egypt, since 1967 by Israel city *pop* 118,300 (1971 *est*)

**Gdansk,** G **Danzig** city & port N Poland on Gulf of Gdansk *pop* 434,000 (1977)

**Gdansk, Gulf of** in Gulf of Danzig inlet of S Baltic sea in N Poland & W USSR

**Gdynia** city & port N Poland on Gulf of Gdansk NNW of Gdansk *pop* 225,000 (1977)

**Gelibolu** – see GALLIPOLI

**Geneva,** F **Genève,** G **Genf 1** canton sw Switzerland, *pop* 321,100 (1970) **2** city, its ✳, at sw tip of Lake Geneva on the Rhone *pop* 156,505 (1980) – **Genevese** *adj or n*

**Genoa,** It **Genova,** *anc* **Genua** town & port NW Italy ✳ of Liguria province at foot of the Apennines & at head of **Gulf of Genoa** (arm of Ligurian sea) *pop* 760,300 (1981 *est*) – **Genoese** *adj or n,* **Genovese** *adj or n*

**George Town 1 George Town, Penang, Pinang** city & port Federation of Malaysia ✳ of Penang on Penang I *pop* 269,247 (1970) **2** town ✳ of Cayman I on Grand Cayman *pop* 8,200 (1981)

**Georgetown** city & port ✳ of Guyana on the Atlantic *pop* 185,000 (1980 *est*)

**Georgia** state SE USA ✳ Atlanta *area* 153,078 *sq km* (58,876 *sq miles*), *pop* 5,464,265 (1980)

**German Southwest Africa** – see NAMIBIA

**Germany,** G **Deutschland** country *cen* Europe bordering on North & Baltic seas, since 1949 constituting two republics: the Federal Republic of Germany (✳ Bonn, *area* 248,577 *sq km* (95,976 *sq miles*), *pop* 61,657,900 (1980)) & the East German Democratic Republic (✳ East Berlin, *area* 108,178 *sq km* (41,610 *sq miles*), *pop* 16,740,000 (1980))

**Ghana 1 Ghana, Gana** ancient empire w Africa in what is now w Mali; flourished 4th–13th centuries **2 Ghana,** *formerly* **Gold Coast** country w Africa bordering on Gulf of Guinea; a republic within Brit Commonwealth; formerly (as Gold Coast) a Brit territory comprising Gold Coast colony, Ashanti, Northern Territories, & Togoland trust territory ✳ Accra *area* 238,305 *sq km* (92,100 *sq miles*), *pop* 8,545,561 (1970) – **Ghanaian** *adj or n,* **Ghanian** *adj or n,* **Ghanese** *adj*

**Ghats** – see EASTERN GHATS, WESTERN GHATS

**Giant's Causeway** formation of prismatic basaltic columns Northern Ireland on N coast of Antrim

**Gibraltar** town & port on Rock of Gibraltar; a Brit colony *area* 6.5 *sq km* (2.5 *sq miles*), *pop* 29,648 (1981 *prov*) – **Gibraltarian** *adj or n*

**Gibraltar, Rock of,** *anc* **Calpe** headland on s coast of Spain at E end of Strait of Gibraltar; highest point 425 *m* (1,396 *ft*) – see PILLARS OF HERCULES

**Gibraltar, Strait of** passage between Spain & Africa connecting the Atlantic & Mediterranean 58 *km* (36 *miles*) long; 13 *km* (8 *miles*) wide at narrowest point

**Gilbert** – see KIRIBATI – **Gilbertese** *n or adj*

**Gilbert and Ellice** island group w Pacific SSE of the Marshalls; until 1976 comprising a Brit colony; now divided into the independent countries of Kiribati and Tuvalo

**Giza, Gizeh, El Giza, El Gizeh** city N Egypt on w bank of the Nile near Cairo *pop* 854,000 (1974 *est*)

**Glamorgan** – see MID GLAMORGAN, SOUTH GLAMORGAN, WEST GLAMORGAN

**Glasgow** city & port s *cen* Scotland on the Clyde ✳ of Strathclyde *pop* 897,483 (1971)

**Glenrothes** town in Fife region Scotland 10 *km* (6 *miles*) N of Kirkaldy; developed as "new town" 1948; *pop* 38,000 (1981)

**Gloucester** city & port in Gloucestershire, on river Severn *pop* 90,232 (1971)

**Gloucestershire** county in sw England *area* 2,642 *sq km* (1,020 *sq miles*), *pop* 503,500 (1981)

**Gobi** desert E *cen* Asia in Mongolia *ab* 1,600 *km* (1,000 *miles*) long & 800 *km* (500 *miles*) wide *area ab* 1,295,000 *sq km* (500,000 *sq miles*)

**Godthaab** town ✳ of Greenland on sw coast

**Godwin Austen, K2, Dapsang** mountain 8,611 *m* (28,250 *ft*) N Kashmir in Karakoram range; 2nd highest mountain in the world

**Golan Heights** hilly region between NE Israel & sw Syria NE of Sea of Galilee

**Gold Coast 1** region w Africa on N shore of Gulf of Guinea between the Ivory Coast (on w) & the Slave Coast (on E) **2** – see GHANA **3** former Brit colony in s Gold Coast region ✳ Accra; now part of Ghana

**Golden Gate** strait 8 *km* (5 *miles*) long; 1.5 *km* (1 *mile*) to 3 *km* (2 *miles*) wide w California connecting San Francisco Bay with Pacific ocean

**Golden Horn** inlet of the Bosporus, Turkey in Europe; harbour of Istanbul

**Gondar** city NW Ethiopia N of Lake Tana ✳ of Amhara & former ✳ of Ethiopia *pop* 43,040 (1974)

**Good Hope, Cape of** cape s Republic of South Africa in sw Cape Province w of False Bay, at 34°21′s – see CAPE OF GOOD HOPE

**Goodwin Sands** shoals SE England in Strait of Dover off E coast of Kent

**Goodwood** racecourse in Sussex, England NE of Chichester

**Gorki, Gorky, Gorkiy,** *formerly* **Nizhni Novgorod** city USSR in *cen* Soviet Russia, Europe, at confluence of Oka & Volga rivers *pop* 1,367,000 (1979)

**Göteborg, Gothenburg** city & port sw Sweden *pop* 431,273 (1980)

**Gotland, Gottland** island Sweden in the Baltic off SE coast; chief town Visby *area* 3,172 *sq km* (1,225 *sq mile*), *pop* 54,621 (1976)

**Göttingen** city w Germany ssw of Brunswick *pop* 129,700 (1980)

**Graham Land 1** – see ANTARCTIC **2** the N section of the Antarctic peninsula

**Grampian 1** hills *cen* Scotland between the Lowlands & the Great Glen – see NEVIS (Ben) **2** region in NE Scotland formed in 1975 from former counties of Aberdeen, Kincardine, Banffshire and most of Moray area *ab* 8,550 *sq km* (3,300 *sq miles*), *pop* 483,000 (1981)

**Granada 1** province s Spain in Andalusia bordering on the Mediterranean *area* 12,530 *sq km* (4,838 *sq miles*), *pop* 733,375 (1970) **2** city, its ✳, in the Sierra Nevada *pop* 190,429 (1970)

**Grand Canal** main waterway in Venice, Italy **3** *km* (2 *miles*) long

**Grand Canary, Gran Canaria** island Spain in the Canaries; chief city Las Palmas *area* 1,533 *sq km* (592 *sq miles*)

**Grand Canyon** gorge of the Colorado NW Arizona extending from mouth of the Little Colorado w to the Grand Wash Cliffs; over 1.5 *km* (1 *mile*) deep; area largely comprised in **Grand Canyon National Park & Grand Canyon National Monument**

**Grande-Terre** island French West Indies constituting the E portion of Guadeloupe *area* 572 *sq km* (220 *sq miles*)

**Grand Turk** – see TURKS AND CAICOS

**Grasmere** lake 1.5 *km* (1 *mile*) long NW England in Cumbria in Lake District

**Great Barrier Reef** coral reef 2,000 *km* (1,242 *miles*) long Australia off NE coast of Queensland

**Great Basin** region w USA between Sierra Nevada & Wasatch mountains including most of Nevada & parts of California, Idaho, Utah, Wyoming & Oregon & having no drainage to ocean; contains many isolated mountain ranges (the **Basin ranges**)

**Great Bear** lake Canada in N Mackenzie District, Northwest Territories *area* 31,792 *sq km* (12,275 *sq miles*)

**Great Dividing Range** mountain system E Australia extending from Cape York peninsula to s Victoria & interrupted by Bass Strait, into Tasmania

**Greater Antilles** group of islands in the West Indies including Cuba, Hispaniola, Jamaica, & Puerto Rico

**Greater London** administrative area in SE England formed in 1974 from former county boroughs of London and City of London, most of former county of Middlesex and parts of former counties of Surrey, Kent, Essex and Hertfordshire *area* 1,580 *sq km* (610 *sq miles*), *pop* 6,795,300 (1981)

**Greater London Boroughs** *pop* 1982 (*est*): **1** Barking 152,600 **2** Barnet 296,600 **3** Bexley 217,000 **4** Brent 253,275 **5** Bromley 295,400 **6** Camden 186,000 **7** Croydon 319,100 **8** Ealing 277,000 **9** Enfield 257,200 **10** Greenwich 213,500 **11** Hackney 177,800 **12** Hammersmith 141,750 **13** Haringey 212,000 **14** Harrow 198,000 **15** Havering 239,800 **16** Hillingdon 288,710 **17** Hounslow 201,000 **18** Islington 169,700 **19** Kensington and Chelsea 125,892 **20** Kingston upon Thames 132,300 **21** Lambeth 243,400 **22** Lewisham 235,200 **23** Merton 164,600 **24** Newham 209,300 **25** Redbridge 226,300 **26** Richmond-on-Thames 159,800 **27** Southwark 210,000 **28** Sutton 167,000 **29** Tower Hamlets 143,000 **30** Waltham Forest 215,000 **31** Wandsworth 253,000 **32** Westminster 210,400

**Greater Manchester** metropolitan county in NW England formed in 1974 from parts of former counties of Cheshire,

**Lancashire** and including former county borough of Manchester *area* 1,284 *sq km* (496 *sq miles*), *pop* 2,590,000 (1981)

**Great Lakes 1** chain of five lakes (Superior, Michigan, Huron, Erie, & Ontario) *cen* North America in the USA & Canada **2** group of lakes E *cen* Africa including Lakes Rudolf, Albert, Victoria, Tanganyika, & Malawi

**Great Rift Valley** depression sw Asia & E Africa extending with several breaks from valley of the Jordan s to *cen* Mozambique

**Great Saint Bernard** mountain pass 2,469 *m* (8,111 *ft*) through Pennine Alps between Switzerland & Italy

**Great Salt** lake N Utah having strongly saline waters & no outlet *area* varies greatly, average depth usually less than 5 *m* (15 *ft*)

**Great Yarmouth** – see YARMOUTH

**Greece** , Gk **Hellas**, NGk **Ellás** country s Europe at s end of Balkan peninsula; a republic ✻ Athens *area* 131,986 *sq km* (50,960 *sq miles*), *pop* 8,768,641 (1971)

**Greenland 1** island in N Atlantic off NE North America belonging to Denmark ✻ Godthaab *area ab* 2,175,000 *sq km* (840,000 *sq miles*), *pop* 49,666 (1976) **2** sea arm of Arctic ocean between Greenland and Spitsbergen – **Greenlander** *n*

**Greenwich Village** section of New York City in Manhattan on lower w side

**Grenada** island Brit West Indies in s Windward islands; with s Grenadines, independent member of Brit Commonwealth since 1974 ✻ St George's *area* 344 *sq km* (133 *sq miles*), *pop* 109,200 (1980) – **Grenadian** *adj or n*

**Grenadines** islands Brit West Indies in *cen* Windwards between Grenada & St Vincent; divided administratively between Grenada & St Vincent

**Grenoble** city SE France *pop* 169,740 (1980 *est*)

**Grimsby** borough E England in Humberside near mouth of the Humber *pop* 95,540 (1971)

**Groningen 1** province NE Netherlands *area* 2,419 *sq km* (934 *sq miles*), *pop* 544,264 (1976 *est*) **2** city, its ✻ *pop* 199,827 (1978)

**Grossglockner** mountain 3,797 *m* (12,457 *ft*) sw Austria, highest in the Hohe Tauern & in Austria

**Guadalajara** city w *cen* Mexico ✻ of Jalisco *pop* 1,725,107 (1977 *est*)

**Guadalcanal** island w Pacific in the SE Solomons *area* 6,475 *sq km* (2,500 *sq miles*), *pop* 31,677 (1976)

**Guadeloupe** two islands, Basse-Terre (or Guadeloupe proper) & Grande-Terre, in French West Indies in *cen* Leeward islands; an overseas department of France & Barre-Terre (on Basse-Terre I) *area* 1,516 *sq km* (583 *sq miles*), *pop* 324,530 (1974)

**Guam** island w Pacific in s Marianas belonging to USA ✻ Agana *area* 551 *sq km* (212 *sq miles*), *pop* 105,816 (1980)

**Guatemala 1** country Central America s of Mexico bordering on the Pacific & the Caribbean; a republic *area* 108,889 *sq km* (42,042 *sq miles*), *pop* 6,835,900 (1981) **2 Guatemala, Guatemala City** city, its ✻ *pop* 1,500,000 (1981) – **Guatemalan** *adj or n*

**Guernsey** island in the English channel, one of the Channel islands ✻ St Peter Port *area* 78 *sq km* (30 *sq miles*), *pop* 54,380 (1981)

**Guiana** region N South America bordering on the Atlantic & bounded on w & s by the Orinoco, the Negro, & the Amazon rivers; includes Guyana, French Guiana, Surinam, & adjoining parts of Brazil & Venezuela – **Guianan** *adj or n*, **Guianese** *adj or n*

**Guinea**, F **Guinée 1** region w Africa bordering on Africa from Gambia (on N) to Angola (on s) **2 Guinea**, *formerly* **French Guinea** republic w Africa bordering on the Atlantic; formerly a territory of French West Africa ✻ Conakry *area* 281,983 *sq km* (108,455 *sq miles*), *pop* 5,133,000 (1978 *est*) – **Guinean** *adj or n*

**Guinea, Gulf of** arm of the Atlantic w *cen* Africa; includes bights of Benin & Biafra

**Guinea-Bissau,** *formerly* **Portuguese Guinea** republic of w Africa s of Senegal; until 1974 a Portuguese colony ✻ Bissau *area* 36,265 *sq km* (13,948 *sq miles*), *pop* 800,000 (1978 *est*) – **Guinean** *adj or n*

**Gulf Stream** warm ocean current in N Atlantic flowing from Gulf of Mexico NE along coast of USA to Nantucket I & thence to Brit Isles

**Gustavo A Madero** city *cen* Mexico in Federal District N of Mexico City *pop* 1,182,895

**Guyana,** *formerly* **British Guiana** country N South America on Atlantic coast; a republic within Brit Commonwealth since 1970 ✻ Georgetown *area* 214,970 *sq km* (83,000 *sq miles*), *pop* 795,000 (1980 *est*) – **Guyanese** *adj or n*

**Gwent** county in SE Wales formed in 1974 from most of former county of Monmouthshire and part of Brecknockshire *area* 1,376 *sq km* (531 *sq miles*), *pop* 436,300 (1981)

**Gwynedd** county in NW Wales formed in 1974 from former counties of Anglesey, Caernarvon, most of Merioneth and part of Denbighshire *area* 3,866 *sq km* (1,493 *sq miles*), *pop* 226,900 (1981)

# H

**Haarlem, Harlem** city w Netherlands ✻ of N Holland province *pop* 228,536 (1978)

**Habana** – see HAVANA

**Hague, The,** D s **Gravenhage** city sw Netherlands in S Holland province near w coast of North sea; de facto ✻ of the Netherlands *pop* 673,391 (1978)

**Haifa** city & port NW Israel *pop* (with district) 566,400 (1980 *est*)

**Haiti,** *formerly* **Hayti** country West Indies on w Hispaniola; a republic ✻ Port-au-Prince *area* 27,750 *sq km* (10,714 *sq miles*), *pop* 6,000,000 (1981)

**Haleakala Crater** crater of dormant volcano 3,055 *m* (10,023 *ft*) Hawaii in E Maui I; 829 *m* (2,720 *ft*) deep, 32 *km* (20 *miles*) in circumference

**Halifax 1** city & port Canada ✻ of Nova Scotia *pop* 122,035 (1974) **2** borough N England in W Yorkshire *pop* 91,171 (1971)

**Halle** city sw E Germany on the Saale river NW of Leipzig *pop* 1,833,135 (1980)

**Hälsingborg** city & port sw Sweden on Oresund strait opposite Helsingör, Denmark *pop* 102,137 (1974)

**Hama,** *bib* **Hamath** city w Syria on the Orontes river *pop* 747,578 (1979 *est*)

**Hamburg** city & port w Germany on the Elbe river; since 1948 a state of the Bonn Republic *area* 753 *sq km* (291 *sq miles*), *pop* 1,645,100 (1980) – **Hamburger** *n*

**Hamilton** town & port ✻ of Bermuda *pop* 1,617 (1980)

**Hammerfest** town & port N Norway on island in Arctic ocean; northernmost town in Europe, at 70°38′ N

**Hampshire** county in s England bordering English Channel *area* 3,782 *sq km* (1,460 *sq miles*), *pop* 1,481,000 (1981)

**Hangchow** city E China ✻ of Chekiang at head of **Hangchow Bay** (inlet of East China sea) *pop* 1,000,000 (1970 *est*)

**Hannover, Hanover** city w Germany WNW of Brunswick *pop* 534,600 (1980)

**Hanoi** city ✻ of Vietnam in Tonkin on Red river; formerly ✻ of French Indochina & of N Vietnam *pop* 2,543,800 (1981)

**Harare** – see SALISBURY

**Harlem 1** section of New York city in NE Manhattan bordering on Harlem & East rivers **2** HAARLEM – **Harlemite** *n*

**Harlow** town in Essex, developed as "new town" 1947; *pop* 79,000 (1981)

**Harris** – see LEWIS WITH HARRIS

**Harrisburg** city ✻ of Pennsylvania *pop* 53,264 (1980)

**Harrogate** town & spa in N Yorkshire *pop* 62,427 (1971)

**Hartford** city N *cen* Connecticut, its ✻ *pop* 136,392 (1980)

**Hartlepool** town and seaport in Cleveland *pop* 97,094 (1971)

**Harwell** research establishment of United Kingdom Atomic Energy Authority near village of Harwell, Berkshire

**Harwich** town & seaport in Essex on peninsula at the end of Stour and Orwell estuary *pop* 14,926 (1971)

**Hastings** town in E Sussex; one of Cinque Ports *pop* 72,410 (1971)

**Hatfield** town in Hertfordshire, developed as "new town" 1948; *pop* 29,000 (1981)

**Havana, Habana,** Sp **La Habana** city & port ✻ of Cuba on Gulf of Mexico *pop* 1,924,886 (1981 *est*) – **Havanan** *adj or n*

**Havant and Waterloo** market town in Hampshire, England 10 *km* (6 *miles*) NE of Portsmouth *pop* 108,999 (1971)

**Hawaii 1** Hawaii, Hawaiian islands, *formerly* Sandwich islands group of islands *cen* Pacific belonging to USA **2** island SE Hawaii, largest of the group; chief city Hilo **3** state of the USA comprising Hawaiian islands except Midway islands; annexed 1898, a territory 1900–59 ✳ Honolulu *area* 16,770 *sq km* (6,450 *sq miles*), *pop* 965,000 (1980)

**Hayling Island** island off SE coast of Hampshire, England 6 *km* (4 *miles*) long and 2 *km* (1.5 *miles*) wide *pop* 10,560 (1971)

**Hayti** – see HAITI

**Hebrides, Western** islands w Scotland in the Atlantic divided by Little Minch into **Inner Hebrides** (near the mainland) *area* 4,400 *sq km* (1,700 *sq miles*) & **Outer Hebrides** (to NW) *area* 2,900 *sq km* (1,120 *sq miles*), *pop* 60,000 (1971) – see LEWIS WITH HARRIS, WESTERN ISLES – **Hebridean** *adj or n*

**Heidelberg** city w Germany on the Neckar river SE of Mannheim *pop* 133,200 (1980)

**Heilungkiang** – see AMUR

**Hejaz, Hedjaz, Al Hijaz** region w Saudi Arabia on Red sea; a viceroyalty ✳ Mecca *area* 388,500 *sq km* (150,000 *sq miles*), *pop* 2,300,000 (1976 *est*)

**Helena** city ✳ of Montana *pop* 23,938 (1980)

**Helgoland, Heligoland** island NW Germany in North sea, in N Frisian islands

**Hellespont** – see DARDANELLES

**Helsingör, Elsinore** city & port Denmark on N Sjaelland I *pop* 56,318 (1981)

**Helsinki,** Swed **Helsingfors** city & port ✳ of Finland on Gulf of Finland *pop* 482,800 (1981)

**Helvellyn** mountain 950 *m* (3,118 *ft*) NW England in Cumbria sw of Ullswater

**Hemel Hempstead** market town in Hertfordshire; developed as "new town" 1946; *pop* 77,579 (1981)

**Herculaneum** ancient city s Italy on Tyrrhenian sea SE of Naples; destroyed A D 79 by eruption of Mt Vesuvius

**Hereford and Worcester** county in w *cen* England formed in 1974 from former counties of Herefordshire & Worcestershire *area* 3,926 *sq km* (1,516 *sq miles*), *pop* 636,400 (1981)

**Herisau** town NE Switzerland ✳ of Appenzell Outer Rhodes canton

**Hermon, Mount** mountain 2,814 *m* (9,232 *ft*) on border between Syria & Lebanon; highest in Anti-Lebanon mountains

**Herstmonceux, Hurstmonceux** village s England in E Sussex NE of Eastbourne; site of Royal Observatory

**Hertfordshire** county in SE England, N of greater London *area* 1,634 *sq km* (632 *sq miles*), *pop* 960,500 (1981)

**Highland** region in N Scotland formed in 1975 from former counties of Caithness, Ross and Cromarty, Sutherland, Inverness (excluding Western Isles) Nairn and parts of Argyll & Moray *area* 25,130 *sq km* (9,735 *sq miles*), *pop* 191,966 (1981)

**Highlands** the chiefly mountainous N part of Scotland N of a line connecting Firth of Clyde & Firth of Tay

**Hijaz, Al** – see HEJAZ

**Hilversum** city *cen* Netherlands in N Holland province SE of Amsterdam *pop* 111,645 (1978)

**Himalaya** mountains s Asia on border between India & Tibet & in Kashmir, Nepal, & Bhutan – see EVEREST – **Himalayan** *adj*

**Hiroshima** city & port Japan in sw Honshu on Inland sea *pop* 853,000 (1975)

**Hispaniola, San Domingo** island West Indies in the Greater Antilles; divided between Haiti (on w) & Dominican Republic (on E) *area* 76,192 *sq km* (29,418 *sq miles*), *pop* 9,281,000 (1975 *est*)

**Hobart** city & port Australia ✳ of Tasmania *pop* (with suburbs) 128,603 (1981)

**Ho Chi Minh** – see SAIGON

**Hodeida** city & port w Yemen Arab Republic *pop* 100,000 (1975)

**Hofuf** city NE Saudi Arabia in E Nejd; chief town of Hasa region *pop* 85,000 (1974 *est*)

**Hokkaido, Yezo** island N Japan N of Honshu *area* 78,508 *sq km* (30,265 *sq miles*), *pop* 5,171,000 (1970)

**Holland** – see NETHERLANDS

**Hollywood 1** section of Los Angeles, California NW of the downtown district **2** city SE Florida N of Miami *pop* 106,873 (1970)

**Holy Island 1** Holy Island, **Lindisfarne** island N England off NE coast of Northumberland **2** Holy Island, **Holyhead** island NW Wales in St George's channel off w coast of Anglesey

**Homs,** *anc* **Emesa** city w Syria on the Orontes river *pop* 821,703 (1979)

**Honduras** country Central America bordering on the Caribbean & the Pacific; a republic ✳ Tegucigalpa *area* 112,088 *sq km* (43,277 *sq miles*), *pop* 3,500,000 (1979 *est*) – **Honduran** *adj or n*

**Hong Kong, Hongkong** Brit crown colony on SE coast of China E of mouth of Pearl river including Hong Kong I, Kowloon & adjacent area (New Territories) on mainland, & nearby islands ✳ Victoria *area* 1,036 *sq km* (400 *sq miles*), *pop* 5,108,000 (1981 *est*)

**Honiara** town w Pacific ✳ of Solomon Islands on Guadalcanal I *pop* 14,942 (1976)

**Honolulu** city & port ✳ of Hawaii on Oahu I *pop* 365,048 (1980) – **Honolulan** *n*

**Honshu, Hondo** island Japan, chief island of the group *area* 228,800 *sq km* (88,000 *sq miles*)

**Hook of Holland** headland sw Netherlands in S Holland province on coast

**Hooru** – see FUTUNA

**Hoover Dam, Boulder Dam** dam 221 *m* ( 726 *ft*) high; 378 *m* (1,244 *ft*) long in Colorado river between Nevada & Arizona

**Horeb, Sinai** mountain where according to the Bible the Law was given to Moses; thought to be in the Gebel Musa on Sinai peninsula

**Horn, Cape** headland s Chile on Horn I in Tierra del Fuego; southernmost point of South America, at 55°59′s

**Horn of Africa** the easternmost projection of Africa s of Gulf of Aden including Somalia & SE Ethiopia; its E tip is Cape Guardafui

**Houston** city & port SE Texas NW of Galveston; connected with Galveston Bay by ship canal *pop* 1,232,802 (1970) – **Houstonian, Houstonite** *n*

**Huang** – see YELLOW

**Huddersfield** town in W Yorkshire on river Colne *pop* 131,190 (1971)

**Hudson 1** river 492 *km* (306 *miles*) long E New York flowing from Adirondack mountains s into New York Bay **2** bay inlet of the Atlantic in N Canada; an island sea *ab* 1,368 *km* (850 *miles*) long **3** strait 724 *km* (450 *miles*) long NE Canada between s Baffin I & N Quebec connecting Hudson Bay with the Atlantic – **Hudsonian** *adj*

**Hull 1** city Canada in sw Quebec on Ottawa river opposite Ottawa, Ontario *pop* 63,580 (1971) **2 Hull, Kingston upon Hull** city and port in Humberside, England on bank of Humber estuary *pop* 272,400 (1971)

**Humber** estuary 59 *km* (37 *miles*) NE England formed by the Ouse & Trent & flowing E & SE into North sea

**Humberside** county in NE England created in 1974 from parts of former counties of Yorkshire, East Riding and N Lincolnshire *area* 3,512 *sq km* (1,356 *sq miles*), *pop* 852,600 (1981)

**Hungary,** Hung **Magyarorszag** country *cen* Europe; formerly a kingdom, since 1946 a republic ✳ Budapest *area* 93,033 *sq km* (35,912 *sq miles*), *pop* 10,710,000 (1980)

**Huron, Lake** lake E *cen* North America between the USA & Canada; one of the Great Lakes *area* 59,296 *sq km* (23,010 *sq miles*), max depth 229 *m* (750 *ft*)

**Hwang Ho** – see YELLOW

**Hythe** town and seaside resort on s coast of Kent; one of Cinque Ports 8 *km* (5 *miles*) w of Folkestone *pop* 11,959 (1971)

# I

**Ibadan** city sw Nigeria *pop* 847,000 (1975 *est*)

**Iberian** peninsula sw Europe between the Mediterranean & the Atlantic occupied by Spain & Portugal

**Ibiza, Iviza** island Spain in the Balearics sw of Majorca *area* 527 *sq km* (221 *sq miles*), *pop* 45,075 (1970)

**Iceland,** Dan **Island,** Icelandic **Island** island between the Arctic & the Atlantic SE of Greenland; a republic formerly (1380–

1918) belonging to Denmark, later (1918–1944) an independent kingdom in personal union with Denmark ✳ Reykjavik *area* 103,000 *sq km* (39,769 *sq miles*), *pop* 231,608 (1980) – **Icelander** *n*

**Idaho** state NW USA ✳ Boise *area* 217,248 *sq km* (83,557 *sq miles*), *pop* 943,935 (1980) – **Idahoan** *adj or n*

**Illinois** state *cen* USA ✳ Springfield *area* 146,640 *sq km* (56,400 *sq miles*), *pop* 11,418,461 (1980) – **Illinoisan** *adj or n*

**Impsambul** – see ABU SIMBEL

**Inchon, Chemulpo** city & port NW South Korea w of Seoul *pop* 1,084,000 (1980)

**India 1** peninsula region (often called a subcontinent) s Asia s of the Himalayas between Bay of Bengal & Arabian sea occupied by India, Pakistan & Bangladesh & formerly often considered as also including Burma (but not Ceylon) **2** those parts of India until 1947 under Brit rule or protection together with Baluchistan & the Andaman & Nicobar Islands &, prior to 1937, Burma **3 India, Indian Union, Bharat** country comprising major portion of peninsula; a republic within the Brit Commonwealth; until 1947 a part of the Brit Empire ✳ New Delhi *area* 3,268,090 *sq km* (1,261,810 *sq miles*), *pop* 683,880,051 (1981)

**Indian** ocean E of Africa, s of Asia, w of Australia & Tasmania, & N of Antarctica *area* 73,600,000 *sq km* (28,400,000 *sq miles*)

**Indiana** state E *cen* USA ✳ Indianapolis *area* 94,357 *sq km* (36,291 *sq miles*), *pop* 5,490,179 (1980) – **Indianan, Indianian** *adj or n*

**Indianapolis** city ✳ of Indiana *pop* 744,624 (1970)

**Indonesia 1** country SE Asia in Malay archipelago comprising Sumatra, Java, s & E Borneo, Celebes, Timor, w New Guinea, the Moluccas, & many adjacent smaller islands; a republic since 1949; formerly (as *Netherlands East Indies*) an overseas territory of the Netherlands ✳ Jakarta *area* 2,027,087 *sq km* (782,663 *sq miles*), *pop* 147,000,000 (1981 *est*) **2** the Malay archipelago

**Indus** river *ab* 2,900 *km* (1,800 *miles*) long s Asia flowing from Tibet NW & ssw through Pakistan into Arabian sea

**Inniskilling** – see ENNISKILLEN

**Innsbruck** city w Austria *pop* 115,197 (1971)

**Interlaken** commune w *cen* Switzerland in Bern canton on the Aare river between Lake of Thun & Lake of Brienz

**Inverness** town NW Scotland ✳ of Highland region *pop* 34,870 (1971)

**Iona** island Scotland in s Inner Hebrides off sw tip of Mull I 5 *km* (3 *miles*) long; 2 *km* (1.5 *miles*) wide *pop* 150 (1971)

**Iowa** state *cen* USA ✳ Des Moines *area* 146,354 *sq km* (56,290 *sq miles*), *pop* 2,913,387 (1980) – **Iowan** *adj or n*

**Ipswich** town SE England ✳ of Suffolk *pop* 122,814 (1971)

**Iran**, *esp formerly* **Persia** country sw Asia bordering in N on Caspian sea & in s on Persian gulf & Gulf of Oman; ✳ Tehran *area* 1,648,000 *sq km* (636,296 *sq miles*), *pop* 39,190,000 (1982 *est*) – **Irani** *adj or n*, **Iranian** *adj or n*

**Iraq, Irak** country sw Asia in Mesopotamia; a republic since 1958, formerly a kingdom ✳ Baghdad *area* 437,522 *sq km* (168,927 *sq miles*), *pop* 12,171,480 (1977) – **Iraqi** *adj or n*, **Iraqian** *adj or n*

**Ireland 1 Ireland,** L **Hibernia** island w Europe in the Atlantic, one of the Brit Isles *area* 83,851 *sq km* (32,375 *sq miles*) divided between Republic of Ireland & Northern Ireland **2 Ireland, Republic of Ireland, Irish Republic, Eire** country occupying major portion of island; a republic since 1949; a division of the United Kingdom of Great Britain & Ireland 1801–1921 & (as **Irish Free State**) a dominion of the Brit Commonwealth 1922–37 ✳ Dublin *area* 68,894 *sq km* (26,602 *sq miles*), *pop* 3,440,427 (1981) **3** – see NORTHERN IRELAND

**Irish** sea arm of the Atlantic between Great Britain & Ireland

**Irrawaddy** river 2,100 *km* (1,300 *miles*) long Burma flowing s into Bay of Bengal through several mouths

**Irtysh, Irtish** river 4,444 *km* (2,760 *miles*) long *cen* Asia flowing from Altai mountains in Sinkiang, China, NW & N into the Orb river in USSR

**Irvine** town in Strathclyde region, Scotland; developed as "new town" 1966; *pop* 58,000 (1981)

**Isfahan, Esfahan, Ispahan** city w *cen* Iran; former ✳ of Persia *pop* 671,825 (1976)

**Isis** the Thames river, England, at & above Oxford

**Iskenderun, Iskenderon,** *formerly* **Alexandretta** city & port s Turkey on **Gulf of Iskenderun** (inlet of the Mediterranean) *pop* 79,291 (1970)

**Islamabad** city ✳ of Pakistan in NE Pakistan in Murree hills NE of Rawalpindi *pop* 201,000 (1981)

**Islay** island Scotland in s Inner Hebrides *area* 609 *sq km* (234 *sq miles*), *pop* 3,825 (1971)

**Isle of Man** – see MAN (Isle of)

**Isle of Pines,** Sp **Isla de Pinos** island w Cuba in the Caribbean *area* 3,056 *sq km* (1,180 *sq miles*)

**Isle of Wight** – see WIGHT (Isle of)

**Ismailia** city NE Egypt on the Suez canal *pop* 400,000 (1981 *est*)

**Israel 1** ancient kingdom Palestine comprising the lands occupied by the Hebrew people; established *ab* 1025 B C; divided *ab* 933 B C into a s kingdom (Judah) & a N kingdom (Israel) **2 Israel, Northern Kingdom, Ephraim** the N portion of the Hebrew kingdom after the division ✳ Samaria **3** country Palestine bordering on the Mediterranean; a republic established 1948 ✳ Jerusalem *area* 20,700 *sq km* (7,903 *sq miles*), *pop* 3,921,700 1980 *est*) – see PALESTINE

**Issyk Kul** lake USSR in Soviet Central Asia in NE Kirgiz Republic *area* 6,332 *sq km* (2,445 *sq miles*)

**Istanbul,** *formerly* **Constantinople,** *anc* **Byzantium** city NW Turkey on the Bosporus & Sea of Marmara; former ✳ of Turkey & of Ottoman Empire *pop* 4,870,747 (1980)

**Italy,** It **Italia,** L **Italia 1** peninsula 1,223 *km* (760 *miles*) long s Europe projecting into the Mediterranean between Adriatic & Tyrrhenian seas **2** country comprising the peninsula of Italy, Sicily, Sardinia, & numerous other islands; a republic since 1946, formerly a kingdom ✳ Rome *area* 301,245 *sq km* (116,311 *sq miles*), *pop* 56,500,000 (1981)

**Iviza** – see IBIZA

**Ivory Coast, Côte d'Ivoire 1** region w Africa bordering on the Atlantic w of the Gold Coast **2** country w Africa including the Ivory Coast & its hinterland; a republic; formerly a territory of French West Africa ✳ Abidjan *area* 319,822 *sq km* (123,483 *sq miles*), *pop* 7,000,000 (1979 *est*) – **Ivory Coaster** *n*, **Ivorian** *adj or n*

**Izmir, Smyrna** city & port w Turkey in Asia on an inlet of the Aegean *pop* 1,968,614 (1980)

**Iztaccihuatl, Ixtacihuatl** extinct volcano 5,286 *m* (17,342 *ft*) s Mexico N of Popocatepetl

# J

**Jackson** city ✳ of Mississippi on Pearl river *pop* 202,895 (1980)

**Jakarta, Djakarta,** *formerly* **Batavia** city & port ✳ of Indonesia in NW Java *pop* 6,503,449 (1981 *est*)

**Jamaica** island West Indies in the Greater Antilles; a dominion of Brit Commonwealth since 1962; formerly a Brit colony ✳ Kingston *area* 10,991 *sq km* (4,244 *sq miles*), *pop* 2,223,400 (1981) – **Jamaican** *adj or n*

**Jambi** – see DJAMBI

**Jamestown** town ✳ of St Helena *pop* 1,516 (1978)

**Japan,** Jap **Nippon, Nihon** country E Asia comprising Honshu, Hokkaido, Kyushu, Shikoku, & other islands in the w Pacific; an empire ✳ Tokyo *area* 377,535 *sq km* (145,766 *sq miles*), *pop* 118,390,000 (1982)

**Java,** Indonesian **Djawa 1** island Indonesia SE of Sumatra; chief city Jakarta *area* 126,501 *sq km* (48,842 *sq miles*), *pop* 78,201,001 (1971) **2** sea arm of the Pacific bounded on s by Java, on w by Sumatra, on N by Borneo, & on E by Celebes

**Jefferson City** city ✳ of Missouri on Missouri river *pop* 33,619 (1980)

**Jersey** island in the English channel, one of the Channel islands ✳ St Helier *area* 117 *sq km* (45 *sq miles*), *pop* 76,050 (1981) – **Jerseyan** *n*, **Jerseyite** *n*

**Jerusalem,** *anc* **Hierosolyma** city *cen* Palestine NW of Dead sea; divided since 1948 between Jordan (old city) & Israel (new city) ✳ of Israel since 1950 & formerly ✳ of ancient kingdoms of Israel & Judah *pop* 448,200 (1980 *est*)

**Jibuti** – see DJIBOUTI

**Jidda, Jedda** city w Saudi Arabia in Hejaz on Red sea; port for Mecca *pop* 300,000 (1974 *est*)

**Johannesburg** city NE Republic of South Africa in s Transvaal in *cen* Witwatersrand *pop* 1,441,335 (1970)

**John o'Groat's, John o'Groat's House** locality N Scotland; popularly considered the northernmost point of mainland of Scotland & Great Britain – see DUNNET HEAD

**Jönköping** city s Sweden at s end of Vättern Lake *pop* 107,561 (1980)

**Jordan 1** river 360 *km* (223 *miles*) long NE Palestine flowing from Anti-Lebanon mountains s through Sea of Galilee into Dead sea **2 Jordan,** *formerly* **Transjordan,** *officially* **Hashemite Kingdom of Jordan** country sw Asia in NW Arabia ✳ Amman *area* 97,740 *sq km* (37,737 *sq miles*), *pop* 2,150,000 (1979) – **Jordanian** *adj or n*

**Juárez** – see CIUDAD JUÁREZ

**Jubuti** – see DJIBOUTI

**Jugoslavia** – see YUGOSLAVIA – **Jugoslav Jugoslavian** *adj or n*

**Juneau** city & port ✳ of Alaska in SE coastal strip *pop* 19,528 (1980)

**Jungfrau** mountain 4,158 *m* (13,642 *ft*) sw *cen* Switzerland in Bernese Alps between Bern & Valais cantons

**Jurua** river 3,283 *km* (2,040 *m*) long NW *cen* South America flowing from E *cen* Peru NE into the Solimoes river in NW Brazil

**Jutland,** Dan **Jylland 1** peninsula N Europe projecting into North sea & comprising mainland of Denmark & N portion of Schleswig-Holstein state, Germany **2** the mainland of Denmark

# K

**K2** – see GODWIN AUSTEN

**Kabul** city ✳ of Afghanistan on Kabul river *pop* 970,000 (1979 *est*) – **Kabuli** *adj or n*

**Kabwe,** *formerly* **Broken Hill** city *cen* Zambia *pop* 98,000 (1976)

**Kaffeklubben** island in Arctic ocean off N coast of Greenland; northernmost point of land in the world, at 83°40′N

**Kaiserslautern** city w Germany w of Ludwigshafen *pop* 100,383 (1976)

**Kalahari** desert region South Africa N of Orange river & s of Lake Ngami in Botswana & NW Republic of South Africa

**Kama** river 1,805 *km* (1,222 *miles*) long USSR in E Soviet Russia, Europe, flowing sw into the Volga s of Kazan

**Kamet** mountain 7,756 *m* (25,447 *ft*) N India in Uttar Pradesh state in the NW Himalayas

**Kampala** city ✳ of Uganda N of Lake Victoria *pop* 331,000 (1980 *est*)

**Kampuchea, Democratic** – see CAMBODIA – **Kampuchean** *adj or n*

**Kananga,** *formerly* **Luluabourg** city s *cen* Zaire *pop* 595,954 (1974)

**Kanchenjunga, Kangchenjunga, Kinchinjunga** mountain 8,598 *m* (20,208 *ft*) Nepal & Sikkim in the Himalayas; 3rd highest in world

**Kandahar** city SE Afghanistan *pop* 115,000 (1976 *est*)

**Kandy** city w *cen* Sri Lanka ENE of Colombo *pop* 93,602 (1971)

**Kano** city N *cen* Nigeria *pop* 399,000 (1975 *est*)

**Kanpur** city N India in s Uttar Pradesh state on the Ganges *pop* 1,275,242 (1971)

**Kansas** state *cen* USA ✳ Topeka *area* 213,886 *sq km* (82,264 *sq miles*), *pop* 2,363,208 (1980) – **Kansan** *adj or n*

**Kansas City 1** city NE Kansas adjacent to Kansas City, Missouri *pop* 168,213 (1970) **2** city w Missouri *pop* 507,087 (1970)

**Kaolan** – see LANCHOW

**Kara** sea arm of Arctic ocean off coast of N USSR E of Novaya Zemla

**Karachi** city & port s Pakistan *pop* 5,103,000 (1981)

**Kara Kum** desert USSR in Turkmen Republic s of Lake Aral between the Caspian sea & the Amu Darya river *area* 300,000 *sq km* (115,830 *sq miles*)

**Kariba** lake 280 *km* (175 *miles*) long 32 *km* (20 *miles*) wide SE Zambia & N Rhodesia formed in the Zambezi by **Kariba Dam**

**Karl-Marx-Stadt** – see CHEMNITZ

**Karlsruhe** city w Germany in Baden-Württemberg state on the Rhine *pop* 271,900 (1980)

**Karnak** town s Egypt on the Nile N of Luxor on N part of site of ancient Thebes

**Kástron** town Greece on Lemnos

**Katar** – see QATAR

**Katmandu, Kathmandu, Khatmandu** city ✳ of Nepal *pop ab* 235,000 (1981)

**Katowice** city s Poland in Silesia *pop* 349,000 (1977)

**Kawasaki** city Japan in E Honshu on Tokyo Bay, s suburb of Tokyo *pop* 1,047,284 (1982)

**Keeling** – see COCOS

**Kent** county in SE England *area* 3,732 *sq km* (1,441 *sq miles*), *pop* 1,469,700 (1981)

**Kentucky** state E *cen* USA ✳ Frankfort *area* 105,027 *sq km* (40,395 *sq miles*), *pop* 3,661,433 (1980) – **Kentuckian** *adj or n*

**Kenya 1** extinct volcano highest peak Batian 5,199 *m* (17,058 *ft*), *cen* Kenya near equator **2** republic E Africa s of Ethiopia bordering on Indian ocean; member of Brit Commonwealth, formerly Brit crown colony & protectorate ✳ Nairobi *area* 582,646 *sq km* (224,960 *sq miles*), *pop* 15,332,000 (1981 *est*) – **Kenyan** *adj or n*

**Kerintji** volcano 3,805 *m* (12,484 *ft*) Indonesia in w *cen* Sumatra; highest on the island

**Kermadec** islands sw Pacific NE of New Zealand; belong to New Zealand *area* 34 *sq km* (13 *sq miles*), *pop* 5 (1981)

**Khan Tengri** – see TENGRI KHAN

**Khartoum, Khartum** city ✳ of Sudan at junction of the White Nile & Blue Nile *pop* 194,000 (1981 *est*)

**Khmer Republic** – see CAMBODIA

**Khyber** mountain pass 53 *km* (33 *miles*) long on border between Afghanistan & Pakistan in Safed Koh range WNW of Peshawar

**Kibo** mountain peak 5,895 *m* (19,340 *ft*) Tanzania in NE Tanganyika; highest peak of Kilimanjaro & highest point in Africa

**Kiel 1** city & port N Germany ✳ of Schleswig-Holstein state on SE coast of Jutland peninsula *pop* 250,100 (1980) **2** ship canal 98 *km* (61 *miles*) N Germany across base of Jutland peninsula connecting Baltic sea & North sea

**Kiev, Kiyev** city USSR ✳ of Ukrainian Republic on the Dneiper river *pop* 2,144,000 (1979) – **Kievan** *adj*

**Kigali** city *cen* Rwanda, its ✳ *pop* 7,000 (1981 *est*)

**Kilimanjaro** mountain Tanzania in NE Tanganyika near Kenya border – see KIBO

**King's Lynn** town & port in Norfolk, at mouth of Great Ouse *pop* 30,200 (1972 *est*)

**Kingston** city & port ✳ of Jamaica on **Kingston Harbour** (inlet of the Caribbean) *pop* (with St Andrew) 662,501 (1979)

**Kingston upon Hull** – see HULL

**Kingstown 1** town & port ✳ of St Vincent and the Grenadines on St Vincent I at head of Kingstown Bay *pop* 34,000 (1979) **2** – see DUN LAOGHAIRE

**Kinshasa,** *formerly* **Léopoldville** city ✳ of Zaire on Congo river *pop* 2,500,000 (1980 *est*)

**Kiribati,** *formerly* **Gilbert** islands w Pacific SSE of the Marshalls; a Brit territory 1976 – 79; became an independent member of the Commonwealth 1979 ✳ Tarawa *area* 265 *sq km* (102 *sq miles*), *pop* 56,452 (1978) – **Kiribatian** *adj or n*

**Kirkwall** burgh & port N Scotland ✳ of Orkney, on Mainland I *pop* 4,618 (1971)

**Kishinev,** Rum **Chisinau** city USSR ✳ of Moldavia *pop* 503,000 (1979)

**Kitakyushu** city & port Japan in N Kyushu formed 1963 by amalgamation of former cities of Kokura, Moji, Tobata, Wakamatsu, & Yahata *pop* 1,065,512 (1982)

**Kivu, Lake** lake 90 *km* (55 *miles*) long E Zaire in Great Rift valley N of Lake Tanganyika *area* 2,700 *sq km* (1,042 *sq miles*)

**Klagenfurt** city s Austria ✳ of Carinthia state wsw of Graz *pop* 82,512 (1981)

**Kobé** city & port Japan in s Honshu on Osaka Bay *pop* 1,376,759 (1982)

**Koblenz, Coblenz** city w Germany SSE of Cologne at confluence of the Rhine & the Moselle *pop* 113,700 (1980)

**Kodiak** island s Alaska in Gulf of Alaska E of Alaska peninsula *area* 9,009 *sq km* (3,465 *sq miles*)

**Kola** peninsula *area ab* 100,000 *sq km* (40,000 *sq miles*), USSR in NW Soviet Russia, Europe, between Barents & White seas

**Kolyma, Kolima 1** river 2,129 *km* (1,323 *miles*) long USSR in NE Soviet Russia, Asia, flowing from Kolyma range NE into East Siberian sea **2** mountain range Soviet Russia, Asia, in NE Khabarovsk Territory parallel to coast of Penzhinskaya Bay

**Konakry** – see CONAKRY

**Konkan** region W India in W Maharashtra state bordering on Arabian sea & extending from Bombay S to Goa

**Korea 1** peninsula 966 *km* (600 *miles*) long & 217 *km* (135 *miles*) wide E Asia between Yellow sea & Sea of Japan **2** strait 193 *km* (120 *miles*) wide between S Korea & SW Japan connecting Sea of Japan & Yellow sea **3 Korea,** Jap **Chosen** country coextensive with Korea peninsula; once a kingdom & (1910–1945) a Japanese dependency ✳ Seoul; divided 1948 at 38th parallel into republics of **North Korea** (✳ Pyongyang) *area* 121,200 *sq km* (46,800 *sq miles*), *pop* 18,000,000 (1982 *est*) & **South Korea** (✳ Seoul) *area* 98,477 *sq km* (38,022 *sq miles*), *pop* 37,600,000 (1982 *est*)

**Kosciusko, Mount** mountain 2,230 *m* (7,316 *ft*) SE Australia in SE New South Wales; highest in Great Dividing range & in Australia

**Kosice** city E Czechoslovakia *pop* 200,943 (1979)

**Kowloon 1** peninsula SE China in Hong Kong colony opposite Hong Kong I **2** city on Kowloon peninsula *pop* 715,440 (1971)

**Krakow, Cracow** city S Poland on the Vistula *pop* 701,000 (1977)

**Krefeld,** *formerly* **Krefeld-Uerdingen** city W Germany on the Rhine WSW of Essen *pop* 224,000 (1980)

**Kristiania** – see OSLO

**Kristiansand** city & port SW Norway on the Skagerrak SW of Oslo *pop* 61,476 (1981)

**Kruger National Park** game reserve NE Republic of South Africa in E Transvaal on Mozambique border *area* 21,000 *sq km* (8,000 *sq miles*)

**Kuala Lumpur** city ✳ of Malaysia in Peninsular Malaysia *pop* 937,875 (1980)

**Kunming,** *formerly* **Yunnan, Yunnanfu** city S China ✳ of Yunnan province *pop* 1,700,000 (1970 *est*)

**Kutch, Rann of** salt marsh in S Pakistan & W India stretching in an arc from the mouth of the Indus to the head of Gulf of Kutch

**Kuwait, Kuweit, Kowait, Al Kuwait 1** country SW Asia in Arabia at head of Persian gulf; a sheikhdom, before 1961 under Brit protection *area* 17,000 *sq km* (6,560 *sq miles*), *pop* 1,562,000 (1982) **2** city & port, its ✳ *pop* 400,000 (1982) – **Kuwaiti** *adj or n*

**Kwei** river 322 *km* (200 *miles*) long SE China in E Kwangsi region flowing S into West river

**Kyongsong** – see SEOUL

**Kyoto** city Japan in W *cen* Honshu NNE of Osaka; formerly (794–1869) ✳ of Japan *pop* 1,469,891 (1982)

**Kyushu** island S Japan S of W end of Honshu *area* 42,224 *sq km* (16,240 *sq miles*)

# L

**Labrador 1** peninsula E Canada between Hudson Bay & the Atlantic; divided bet Quebec & Newfoundland **2** the section of the peninsula belonging to Newfoundland *area* 383,300 *sq km* (156,185 *sq miles*), *pop* 557,725 (1976) **3** sea arm of the Atlantic between Labrador & Greenland – **Labradorean, Labradorian** *adj or n*

**Ladrone** – see MARIANA

**Lagos** city & port ✳ of Nigeria on an offshore island in Bight of Benin & on mainland opposite *pop* 3,000,000 (1981 *est*)

**Lahore** city Pakistan in E Punjab state province near the Ravi river *pop* 2,920,000 (1981)

**Lahti** city S Finland NNE of Helsinki *pop* 94,700 (1981)

**Lake District** area NW England in S Cumbria & NW Lancashire containing many lakes & peaks

**Lambaréné** city W Gabon, Africa *pop* 10,385 (1970)

**Lancashire** county of England, between N and W Yorkshire to the East and the Irish Sea to the West, reconstituted in 1974; *area* 5,885 *sq km* (2,272 *sq miles*), *pop* 1,374,100 (1981)

**Lanchow, Kaolan** city N *cen* China ✳ of Kansu province *pop* 1,500,000 (1970 *est*)

**Lands End, Land's End** cape SW England at SW tip of Cornwall; extreme W point of England, at 5°41'W

**Langdale Pikes** two mountain peaks NW England in Cumbria in Lake District

**Lansing** city S Michigan, its ✳ *pop* 130,414 (1980)

**Laos** country SE Asia; a republic, until 1975 a kingdom; formerly a state of French Indochina; ✳ Vientiane *area* 236,800 *sq km* (91,482 *sq miles*), *pop ab* 3,000,000 (1976 *est*)

**La Palma** island Spain in Canary islands; chief town Santa Cruz de la Palma *area* 728 *sq km* (280 *sq miles*), *pop* 65,291 (1970)

**La Paz** city, administrative ✳ of Bolivia E of Lake Titicaca at altitude of 3,630 *m* (11,910 *ft*), *pop* 654,700 (1976)

**Lapland** region N Europe above the arctic circle in N Norway, N Sweden, N Finland, & Kola peninsula of the USSR – **Laplander** *n*

**La Plata** city E Argentina SE of Buenos Aires *pop* 391,000 (1970)

**Las Palmas 1** province Spain comprising the E Canary islands *area* 3,325 *sq km* (1,279 *sq miles*) **2** city & port, its ✳, in NE Grand Canary I *pop* 287,038 (1970)

**Lassa** – see LHASA

**Lassen Peak, Mount Lassen** volcano 3,187 *m* (10,457 *ft*) N California at S end of Cascade range; central feature of **Lassen Volcanic National Park**

**Las Vegas** city SE Nevada *pop* 125,787 (1970)

**Latakia 1** region NW Syria bordering on the Mediterranean **2 Latakia,** *anc* **Laodicea** city & port, its chief town on the Mediterranean *pop* 563,173 (1979)

**Latvia** country N *cen* Europe bordering on the Baltic; an independent republic 1918–40, since 1940 a constituent republic (**Latvian Republic**) of the USSR ✳ Riga *area* 63,700 *sq km* (25,590 *sq miles*), *pop* 2,500,000 (1977)

**Launceston** city & port Australia in N Tasmania *pop* (with suburbs) 64,555 (1981)

**Lausanne** town W Switzerland ✳ of Vaud canton on Lake Geneva *pop* 127,349 (1980)

**Lebanon** country SW Asia bordering on the Mediterranean; a republic since 1944, formerly (1920–44) a French mandate ✳ Beirut *area* 10,230 *sq km* (3,950 *sq miles*), *pop* 2,550,000 (1975 *est*) – **Lebanese** *adj or n*

**Leeds** city in W Yorkshire, on river Aire *pop* 494,971 (1971)

**Leeward 1** island chain *cen* Pacific extending 2,011 *km* (1,250 *miles*) WNW from main islands of the Hawaiian group; includes Nihoa, Necker, Laysan, Midway, & Kure islands **2 Leeward,** F **Iles sous le Vent** islands S Pacific, W group of the Society islands **3** islands West Indies in the N Lesser Antilles extending from Virgin islands (on N) to Dominica (on S) **4** former colony Brit West Indies in the Leewards including territories of Antigua, St Kitts-Nevis, & Montserrat

**Le Havre,** *formerly* **Le Havre-de-Grâce** city & port N France on English channel on N side of Seine estuary *pop* 219,853 (1980 *est*)

**Leicester** city in Leicestershire, on river Soar *pop* 287,350 (1973 *est*)

**Leicestershire** midland county of England, reformed in 1974 to include county of Rutland *area* 2,553 *sq km* (986 *sq miles*), *pop* 845,600 (1981)

**Leiden, Leyden** city W Netherlands in S Holland province on a branch of the lower Rhine *pop* 170,804 (1978)

**Leinster** province E Republic of Ireland comprising counties Carlow, Dublin, Kildare, Kilkenny, Laoighis, Longford, Louth, Meath, Offaly, Westmeath, Wexford, & Wicklow *area* 19,708 *sq km* (7,580 *sq miles*), *pop* 1,494,544 (1981)

**Leipzig, Leipsic** city E Germany in Saxony SSW of Berlin *pop* 1,412,037 (1980)

**Le Mans** city NW France *pop* 155,245 (1980 *est*)

**Lemnos,** NGk **Límnos** island Greece in the Aegean ESE of Chalcidice peninsula; chief town Kástron *area* 476 *sq km* (184 *sq miles*), *pop* 17,367 (1971)

**Leningrad,** *formerly* (1703–1914) **Saint Petersburg,** (1914–24) **Petrograd** city USSR in NW Soviet Russia, Europe, at E end of Gulf of Finland ✳ of Russian empire 1712–1917 *pop* 4,676,000 (1981) – **Leningrader** *n*

**Lenin Peak** mountain 7,128 *m* (23,386 *ft*) on border between Kirgiz & Tadzhik republics; highest in Trans Alai range

**Léopoldville** – see KINSHASA

**Lerwick** burgh & port N Scotland ✳ of Shetland on Mainland I *pop* 6,107 (1971)

**Lesbos, Mytilene,** NGk **Lésvos, Mitilíni** island Greece in the Aegean off NW coast of Turkey *area* 1,630 *sq km* (629 *sq miles*), *pop* 97,008 (1971)

**Lesotho,** *formerly* **Basutoland** country s Africa surrounded by Republic of South Africa; a constitutional monarchy, in Brit Commonwealth ✳ Maseru *area* 30,355 *sq km* (11,716 *sq miles*), *pop* 1,204,000 (1981 *est*)

**Lesser Antilles** islands in the West Indies including Virgin, Leeward, & Windward islands, Trinidad, Barbados, Tobago, & islands in the s Caribbean N of Venezuela

**Letchworth** town in Hertfordshire, founded in 1903 as first Brit garden city *pop* 27,150 (1971)

**Letzeburg** – see LUXEMBOURG

**Lewis with Harris** island NW Scotland in the Outer Hebrides divided administratively into **Lewis** (in the N; chief town & port Stornoway) & **Harris** (in the s); largest of the Hebrides, in Western Isles regional division *area* 1,769 *sq miles* (683 *sq miles*)

**Leyden** – see LEIDEN

**Lhasa, Lassa** city sw China in Tibet *pop* 175,000 (1970)

**Lhotse, E**[1] mountain 8,511 *m* (27,923 *ft*) in Mt Everest massif s of Mt Everest; 4th highest in the world

**Liberia** country w Africa; a republic ✳ Monrovia *area* 111,800 *sq km* (43,000 *sq miles*), *pop* 1,481,524 (1974) – **Liberian** *adj or n*

**Libreville** city & port ✳ of Gabon at mouth of Gabon river *pop* 169,200 (1975 *est*)

**Libya 1** the part of Africa N of the Sahara between Egypt & Syrtis Major (Gulf of Sidra) – an ancient name **2** northern Africa w of Egypt – an ancient name **3 Libya, Libyan Arab Republic** country N Africa bordering on the Mediterranean; a colony of Italy 1912–43, an independent kingdom 1951–69, a republic since 1969 ✳ ✳ Tripoli & Benghazi *area* 1,748,700 *sq km* (675,200 *sq miles*), *pop* 2,900,000 (1977 *est*)

**Liechtenstein** country w Europe between Switzerland & Austria bordering on the Rhine; a principality ✳ Vaduz *area* 160 *sq km* (62 *sq miles*), *pop* 26,125 (1981) – **Liechtensteiner** *n*

**Liège,** Flem **Luik 1** province E Belgium *area* 3,949 *sq km* (1,525 *sq miles*) **2** city, its ✳ *pop* 605,123 (1981)

**Liffey** river 80 *km* (50 *miles*) long E Ireland flowing into Dublin Bay

**Likasi,** *formerly* **Jadotville** city SE Zaire in SE Shaba province *pop* 146,394 (1974)

**Lille,** *formerly* **Lisle** city N France; medieval ✳ of Flanders *pop* 177,218 (1980 *est*)

**Lilongwe** city ✳ of Malawi *pop* 102,924 (1977)

**Lima** city ✳ of Peru on the Rúmac river *pop* 3,595,000 (1976)

**Limoges** city sw cen France *pop* 143,689 (1975 *prov*)

**Limpopo, Crocodile** river 1,600 *km* (1,000 *miles*) long s Africa flowing from Transvaal, Republic of South Africa, into Indian ocean in Mozambique

**Lincoln 1** city in Lincolnshire, on river Witham *pop* 73,260 (1974 *est*) **2** city SE Nebraska, its ✳ *pop* 171,932 (1980)

**Lincolnshire** county in E England reconstituted in 1974 *area* 5,885 *sq km* (2,272 *sq miles*), *pop* 550,900 (1981)

**Lindisfarne** – see HOLY ISLAND

**Line** islands Kiribati in cen Pacific s of Hawaii formerly divided bet the USA (Kingman Reef & Palmyra) & Great Britain (Washington, Fanning, & Christmas)

**Linköping** city SE Sweden *pop* 112,600 (1980)

**Lisbon,** Port **Lisboa** city & port ✳ of Portugal on estuary of the Tagus river *pop* 1,707,500 (1974 *est*) – **Lisboan** *n*

**Lisle** – see LILLE

**Lithuania,** Lith **Lietuva** country N cen Europe bordering on the Baltic; remnant of a medieval principality extending from Baltic sea to Black sea; a republic 1918–40, since 1940 a constituent republic (**Lithuanian Republic**) of the USSR ✳ Vilnius *area* 65,200 *sq km* (25,200 *sq miles*), *pop* 3,317,000 (1977)

**Little Rock** city ✳ of Arkansas on Arkansas river *pop* 158,461 (1980)

**Liverpool** city & seaport in Merseyside, on right bank of river Mersey 5 *km* (3 *miles*) from Irish sea *pop* 606,834 (1971) – **Liverpudlian** *adj or n*

**Livingston** town in W Lothian region, Scotland; developed as "new town" 1962; *pop* 38,677 (1981)

**Ljubljana** city NW Yugoslavia ✳ of Slovenia on the Sava river *pop* 253,000 (1981)

**Llanfairpwllgwyngyllgogerchwyrndrobwllysiliogogo-goch, Llanfairpwll, Llanfair PG** village in Anglesey; longest place name in Britain

**Loanda** – see LUANDA

**Lódz** city cen Poland wsw of Warsaw *pop* 810,000 (1976)

**Lofoten** island group Norway off NW coast sw of Vesterålen *area* 1,425 *sq km* (550 *sq miles*), *pop* 62,917 (1971 *est*)

**Logan, Mount** mountain 6,050 *m* (19,850 *ft*) Canada in sw Yukon Territory; highest in St Elias & Coast ranges & in Canada & 2nd highest in North America

**Loire** river 1,020 *km* (634 *miles*) long cen France flowing from the Massif Central NW & w into Bay of Biscay

**Lombok** island Indonesia in the Lesser Sundas E of Bali; chief town Mataram *area* 5,435 *sq km* (2,098 *sq miles*), *pop* 1,300,234 (*est*)

**Lomé** city & port ✳ of Toga *pop* 247,000 (1979)

**Lomond, Ben** mountain 973 *m* (3,192 *ft*) s cen Scotland on E side of Loch Lomond

**Lomond, Loch** freshwater lake partly in Strathclyde region and partly in Central region, Scotland *area* 70 *sq km* (25 *sq miles*), 39 *km* (24 *miles*) long

**London 1** city & port SE England formerly constituting an administrative county ✳ of United Kingdom; comprises City of London & 12 inner boroughs of Greater London *area* 303 *sq km* (117 *sq miles*), *pop* 2,723,483 (1971) **2 London, City of London,** anc **Londinium** city within Greater London, on the Thames *area* 273 *hectares* (675 *acres*), *pop* 5,500 (1971) **3** GREATER LONDON – **Londoner** *n*

**Londonderry, Derry 1** county NW Northern Ireland *area* 2,082 *sq km* (804 *sq miles*), *pop* 130,556 (1971) **2** borough & port, its ✳, on the Foyle river *pop* 51,617 (1971)

**Long Island** island SE New York s of Connecticut *area* 4,463 *sq km* (1,723 *sq miles*), *pop* 7,141,515 (1970)

**Lord Howe** island Australia in Tasman sea ENE of Sydney belonging to New South Wales *area* 13 *sq km* (5 *sq miles*), *pop* 287 (1981)

**Los Angeles** city & port sw California on the Pacific *pop* 2,816,061 (1970)

**Lothian** region s Scotland bordering on Firth of Forth, established 1975 ✳ Edinburgh *area* 1812 *sq km* (678 *sq miles*), *pop* 735,892 (1981); formerly divided into three counties (the **Lothians**): E Lothian, Midlothian, & West Lothian

**Louisiana** state s USA ✳ Baton Rouge *area* 126,160 *sq km* (48,523 *sq miles*), *pop* 4,203,972 (1980) – **Louisianan, Louisianian** *adj or n*

**Louisiana Purchase** region w cen USA between the Mississippi & the Rockies purchased (1803) from France *area* 2,292,141 *sq km* (885,000 *sq miles*)

**Lourdes** town sw France on the Gave de Pau river ssw of Tarbes *pop* 18,130 (1973)

**Lourenço-Marques** – see MAPUTO

**Low Countries** region w Europe bordering on North sea & comprising modern Belgium, Luxembourg, & the Netherlands

**Lowlands** the cen & E part of Scotland lying between the Highlands & the Southern Uplands

**Loyalty** islands sw Pacific E of New Caledonia; a dependency of New Caledonia *area ab* 1,970 *sq km* (760 *sq miles*), *pop* 12,248 (1971)

**Luanda , Loanda** city & port ✳ of Angola *pop* 480,613 (1972 *est*)

**Lübeck** city & port N Germany NE of Hamburg *pop* 220,600 (1980)

**Lublin** city E Poland SE of Warsaw *pop* 281,900 (1976)

**Lubumbashi,** *formerly* **Elisabethville** city SE Zaire in SE Shaba province *pop* 403,623 (1980)

**Lucerne,** G **Luzern 1** canton cen Switzerland *area* 1,496 *sq km* (579 *sq miles*), *pop* 289,641 (1970) **2** town, its ✳, on Lake of Lucerne *pop* 63,278 (1980)

**Lucerne, Lake of,** Lake of the Four Forest Cantons lake 39 *km* (24 *miles*) long *cen* Switzerland *area* 114 *sq km* (44 *sq miles*)

**Lucknow** city N India ESE of Delhi ✳ of Uttar Pradesh state *pop* 826,246 (1971)

**Ludwigshafen** city W Germany on the Rhine opposite Mannheim *pop* 159,400 (1980)

**Lugano, Lake** lake on border between Switzerland & Italy E of Lake Maggiore *area* 50 *sq km* (19 *sq miles*)

**Luluabourg** – see KANANGA

**Lundy** island SW England at mouth of Bristol channel off coast of Devon *area* 5 *sq km* (2 *sq miles*), *pop* 20 (1981)

**Lusaka** city ✳ of Zambia *pop* 641,000 (1980 *est*)

**Luton** town in Bedfordshire *pop* 161,405 (1971)

**Luxembourg, Luxemburg, Letzeburg 1** province SE Belgium ✳ Arlon *area* 4,418 *sq km* (1,706 *sq miles*), *pop* 219,186 (1971) **2** country W Europe between Belgium, France, & Germany; a grand duchy *area* 2,586 *sq km* (999 *sq miles*), *pop* 365,100 (1980) **3** city, its ✳ *pop* 79,600 (1979) – **Luxembourger, Luxemburger** *n*, **Luxembourgian, Luxemburgian** *adj*

**Luxor ,** Ar **El Uqsor** city S Egypt on the Nile on S part of site of ancient Thebes *pop* 84,600 (1970 *est*)

**Luzon** island N Philippines, chief island of the group *area* 104,688 *sq km* (40,420 *sq miles*), *pop ab* 18,000,000 (1970)

**Lyons, Lyon,** *anc* **Lugdunum** city SE *cen* France *pop* 462,841 (1980 *est*)

# M

**Maastricht, Maestricht** town SE Netherlands on the Meuse ✳ of Limburg province *pop* 145,209 (1978)

**Macao, Macau 1** island SE China in Kwangtung province W of Hong Kong **2** Portuguese colony comprising peninsula on SE Macao I & adjacent islands *area* 16 *sq km* (6 *sq miles*), *pop* 248,316 (1981) **3** city & port, its ✳ *pop* 157,175 (1981) – **Macoan** *adj or n*, **Macanese** *n*

**Maceió** city NE Brazil ✳ of Alagoas *pop* 249,000 (1970)

**Macgillicuddy's Reeks** mountain range SW Ireland in County Kerry – see CARRANTUOHILL

**Machu Picchu** site SE Peru of ancient Inca city on a mountain NW of Cuzco

**Mackenzie 1** river 1,705 *km* (1,060 *miles*) long NW Canada flowing from Great Slave Lake NW into Beaufort sea; sometimes considered to include the Finlay, Peace, & Slave rivers (total length 4,240 *km* (2,635 *miles*)) **2** mountain range NW Canada in the Rockies in Yukon Territory & Mackenzie District **3** district Canada in W Northwest Territories in basin of Mackenzie river *area* 1,366,190 *sq km* (527,490 *sq miles*), *pop* 23,655 (1971)

**Mâcon** city E *cen* France *pop* 33,445 (1970 *est*)

**Macquarie** river 950 *km* (590 *miles*) SE Australia in E *cen* New South Wales flowing NNW to Darling river

**Madagascar** island W Indian ocean off SE coast of Africa; formerly a French territory; became (1958), as the **Malagasy Republic** *or* F **République Malgache**, a republic of the French Community ✳ Antananarivo *area* 586,486 *sq km* (226,444 *sq miles*), *pop* 8,000,000 (1981 *est*) – **Madagascan** *adj or n*

**Madeira 1** islands in N Atlantic N of the Canaries belonging to Portugal ✳ Funchal *area* 798 *sq km* (308 *sq miles*), *pop* 265,600 (1978) **2** island chief of group – **Madeiran** *adj or n*

**Madison** city S Wisconsin, its ✳ *pop* 170,616 (1980)

**Madras 1** – see TAMIL NADU **2** city & port ✳ of Tamil Nadu *pop* 3,169,930 (1971)

**Madrid 1** province *cen* Spain in NW New Castile *area* 7,993 *sq km* (3,084 *sq miles*), *pop* 3,792,561 (1970) **2** city, its ✳ & ✳ of Spain *pop* 3,146,071 (1970) – **Madrilenian** *adj or n*

**Madura, D Madoera** island Indonesia off coast of NE Java *area* (with adjacent islands) 5,290 *sq km* (2,042 *sq miles*), *pop* 1,858,183 (1974 *est*) – **Madurese** *adj or n*

**Maestricht** – see MAASTRICHT

**Mafeking** town S Republic of South Africa in N Cape Province near W Transvaal border *pop* 6,493 (1971)

**Magdeburg** city W East Germany on the Elbe WSW of Berlin *pop* 1,268,360 (1980)

**Magellan, Strait of** strait 560 *km* (350 *miles*) long at S end of South America between mainland & Tierra del Fuego archipelago

**Maggiore, Lake** lake *area* 212 *sq km* (82 *sq miles*) N Italy & S Switzerland traversed by the Ticino river

**Mahón, Port Mahon** city & port Spain on Minorca I *pop* 16,547 (1970)

**Maiden Castle** prehistoric fort and later earthworks at Fordington Hall, near Dorchester, Dorset

**Maine** state NE USA ✳ Augusta *area* 86,359 *sq km* (33,215 *sq miles*), *pop* 1,124,660 (1980) – **Mainer** *n*

**Mainz,** F **Mayence** city W Germany on the Rhine ✳ of Rhineland-Palatinate state *pop* 187,400 (1980)

**Majorca, Mallorca** island Spain, largest of the Balearic islands; chief city Palma *area* 3,639 *sq km* (1,405 *sq miles*), *pop* 460,030 (1970) – **Majorcan** *adj or n*

**Makalu** mountain 8,481 *m* (27,824 *ft*) in the Himalayas in NE Nepal SE of Mt Everest; 5th highest in world

**Makka** – see MECCA

**Malabo,** *formerly* **Santa Isabel** city ✳ of Equatorial Guinea on Fernando Po I *pop* 25,000 (1980 *est*)

**Malacca, Strait of** channel 804 *km* (500 *miles*) long between S Malay peninsula & island of Sumatra

**Malagasy Republic** – see MADAGASCAR

**Malawi,** *formerly* **Nyasaland** country SE Africa bordering on Lake Malawi; formerly a Brit protectorate; independent member of Brit Commonwealth since 1964; a republic since 1966 ✳ Lilongwe *area* 118,484 *sq km* (45,747 *sq miles*), *pop* 5,547,460 (1977) – **Malawian** *adj or n*

**Malay 1** archipelago SE Asia including Sumatra, Java, Borneo, Celebes, Moluccas, & Timor; usu considered as including also the Philippines & sometimes New Guinea **2** peninsula 1,126 *km* (700 *miles*) long SE Asia divided bet Thailand & Malaysia **3** sea SE Asia surrounding the Malay archipelago

**Malaya 1** BRITISH MALAYA **2 Malaya, Federation of Malaya** former country SE Asia; a Brit dominion 1957–63, since 1963 a territory (now called **Peninsular Malaysia**) of Malaysia ✳ Kuala Lumpur *area* 131,587 *sq km* (50,806 *sq miles*), *pop* 8,980,000 (1970)

**Malaysia 1** the Malay archipelago **2 Malaysia, Federation of Malaysia** country SE Asia, a union of Malaya, Sabah (N Borneo), Sarawak, & (until 1965) Singapore; a limited constitutional monarchy in Brit Commonwealth ✳ Kuala Lumpur *area* 329,740 *sq km* (127,313 *sq miles*), *pop* 13,435,588 (1980) – **Malaysian** *adj or n*

**Maldive** islands in Indian ocean S of the Laccadives; a sultanate under Brit protection until 1965; now **Republic of Maldives** ✳ Male *area* 298 *sq km* (115 *sq miles*), *pop* 143,469 (1978) – **Maldivian** *adj or n*

**Male** island (atoll) chief of the Maldives

**Mali 1** federation 1959–60 of Senegal & Sudanese Republic **2 Mali,** *formerly* **Sudanese Republic** country W Africa in W Sahara & Sudan regions; a republic; before 1958 constituted **French Sudan** (a territory of France) ✳ Bamako *area* 1,240,142 *sq km* (478,822 *sq miles*), *pop* 6,297,000 (1978) – **Malian** *adj or n*

**Mallorca** – see MAJORCA

**Malmö** city & port SW Sweden on Öresund strait opposite Copenhagen, Denmark *pop* 233,803 (1980)

**Malta,** *anc* **Melita 1 Malta, Maltese islands** group of islands in Mediterranean S of Sicily; a dominion of Brit Commonwealth since 1964 ✳ Valletta *area* 316 *sq km* (122 *sq miles*), *pop* 316,850 (1980 *est*) **2** island, chief of the group *area* 246 *sq km* (95 *sq miles*)

**Malvern 1** hills W England in Hereford and Worcester; highest point 425 *m* (1,395 *ft*) **2** town and spa in Hereford and Worcester, on side of Malvern hills *pop* 31,000 (1972 *est*)

**Manado, Menado** city & port Indonesia in NE Celebes I on Celebes sea *pop* 217,159 (1981*est*)

**Managua** city ✳ of Nicaragua on Lake Managua *pop* 615,000 (1980)

**Manama** city ✳ Bahrain *pop* 120,000 (1979)

**Manaus, Manaos** city W Brazil ✳ of Amazonas state on the Negro river 11 *km* (7 *miles*) from its junction with the Amazon *pop* 284,118 (1970)

**Manchester** city in Greater Manchester, on river Irwell *pop* 533,560 (1974 *est*) – **Mancunian** *adj or n*

**Mandalay** city *cen* Burma *pop* 781,819 (1973)

**Manhattan 1** island 21 *km* (13 *miles*) long SE New York on New York Bay **2** borough of New York City comprising Manhattan I, several small adjacent islands, & a small area (**Marble Hill**) on mainland *pop* 1,539,233 (1970) – **Manhattanite** *n*

**Manila** city & port Philippines on w coast of Luzon on **Manila Bay** (inlet of s China sea) ✳ of the Philippines until 1948 & present seat of government *pop* 1,438,253 (1975) (with suburbs) 3,356,404 (1975) – see QUEZON CITY

**Man, Isle of,** *anc* **Monapla, Mona** island Brit Isles in Irish sea; a possession of the Brit Crown; has own legislature & laws ✳ Douglas *area* 572 *sq km* (221 *sq miles*), *pop* 64,679 (1981) – **Manxman** *n*

**Manitoba** province s *cen* Canada ✳ Winnipeg *area* 652,600 *sq km* (251,000 *sq miles*), *pop* 1,026,241 (1981)

**Manitoba, Lake** lake 193 *km* (120 *miles*) long Canada in s Manitoba *area* 4,706 *sq km* (1,817 *sq miles*)

**Manitoulin** island 160 *km* (100 *miles*) long in Ontario in Lake Huron; largest freshwater island in the world *area* 2,766 *sq km* (1,068 *sq miles*)

**Mannheim** city w Germany at confluence of the Rhine & the Neckar rivers *pop* 304,300 (1980)

**Mansûra, El Mansûra** city N Egypt in Nile delta *pop* 120,000 (1981 *est*)

**Maputo,** *formerly* **Lourenço Marques** city & port ✳ of Mozambique on Delagoa Bay *pop* 600,000 (1982 *est*)

**Maracaibo** city NW Venezuela on channel between **Lake Maracaibo** (*area* 16,380 *sq km* or 6,300 *sq miles*) & Gulf of Venezuela *pop* 650,000 (1979)

**Mar del Plata** city & port E Argentina SSE of Buenos Aires *pop* 298,979 (1970)

**Mariana,** *formerly* **Ladrone** islands w Pacific s of Bonin islands; comprise commonwealth of **Northern Mariana** islands & Guam

**Maribor** city NW Yugoslavia *pop* 97,167 (1971)

**Marmara, Sea of, Sea of Marmora,** *anc* **Propontis** sea NW Turkey connected with Black sea by the Bosporus & with Aegean sea by the Dardanelles *area* 11,472 *sq km* (4,429 *sq miles*)\

**Marrakech, Marrakesh,** *formerly* **Morocco** city *cen* Morocco in foothills of the Grand Atlas *pop* 1,224,100 (1979)

**Marseilles, Marseille,** *anc* **Massilia** city & port SE France on Gulf of Lions *pop* 914,356 (1980 *est*)

**Marshall** islands w Pacific E of the Carolines comprising the **Ratak** (in the E) & **Ralik** (in the w) chains; a Japanese mandate 1920–45; now part of Trust Territory of the Pacific Islands administered by the USA *area* 149 *sq km* (70 *sq miles*), *pop* 20,200 (1970 *est*) – **Marshallese** *adj or n*

**Martinique** island West Indies in the Windwards; department of France ✳ Fort-de-France *area* 1,166 *sq km* (431 *sq miles*), *pop* 324,832 (1974)

**Maryland** state E USA ✳ Annapolis *area* 27,500 *sq km* (10,577 *sq miles*), *pop* 4,216,446 (1980) – **Marylander** *n*

**Mascarene** islands w Indian ocean E of Madagascar including Mauritius, Réunion, & Rodrigues

**Maseru** city ✳ of Lesotho *pop* 240,081 (1981)

**Maskat, Masqat** – see MUSCAT

**Massachusetts** state NE USA ✳ Boston *area* 21,468 *sq km* (8,257 *sq miles*), *pop* 5,737,037 (1980)

**Massif Central** plateau *cen* France rising sharply just w of the Rhône- Saône valley & sloping N to the Paris basin & w to the basin of Aquitaine

**Matadi** town & port w Zaire *pop* 142,808 (1974)

**Matterhorn, F Mont Cervin** mountain 4,477 *m* (14,690 *ft*) in Pennine Alps on border between Switzerland & Italy

**Mauna Loa** volcano 4,169 *m* (13,680 *ft*) Hawaii in s *cen* Hawaii I in **Hawaii Volcanoes National Park**

**Mauritania, F Mauritanie** country NW Africa bordering on the Atlantic N of Senegal river; a republic (**Islamic Republic of Mauritania**) within the French Community, formerly a territory ✳ Nouakchott *area* 1,030,700 *sq km* (398,000 *sq miles*), *pop* 1,545,000 (1978 *est*) – **Mauritanian** *adj or n*

**Mauritius** island in Indian ocean in *cen* Mascarenes; constitutes with Rodrigues & other dependencies a dominion of the Brit Commonwealth ✳ Port Louis *area* 2,046 *sq km* (790 *sq miles*), *pop* 924,243 (1979 *est*) – **Mauritian** *adj or n*

**Mayfair** district of w London, England, in Westminster borough

**Mbabane** town ✳ of Swaziland *pop* 25,000 (1981 *est*)

**Mbandaka,** *formerly* **Coquilhatville** city w Zaire on Congo river *pop* 136,877 (1974)

**Mbini,** *formerly* **Rio Muni** mainland portion of Equatorial Guinea bordering on Gulf of Guinea ✳ Bata *area* 26,104 *sq km* (10,040 *sq miles*)

**McKinley, Mount, Denali** mountain 6,194 *m* (20,320 *ft*) *cen* Alaska in Alaska range; highest in USA & North America

**McMurdo Sound** inlet of w Ross sea Antarctica between Ross I & coast of Victoria Land

**Mecca, Makka** city w Saudi Arabia ✳ of Hejaz province *pop* 366,801 (1974) – **Meccan** *adj or n*

**Medan** city Indonesia in NE Sumatra *pop* 635,562 (1971)

**Medellín** city NW Colombia NW of Bogotá *pop* 1,269,900 (1973)

**Medina** city w Saudi Arabia *pop* 198,186 (1974)

**Mediterranean** sea area 2,509,972 *sq km* (969,100 *sq miles*) between Europe & Africa connecting with the Atlantic through Strait of Gibraltar & with Red sea through Suez canal

**Médoc** district sw France N of Bordeaux

**Medway** river 110 *km* (70 *miles*) long SE England in Kent flowing NE into the Thames

**Meknes** city N Morocco wsw of Fez; former ✳ of Morocco *pop* 774,100 (1979)

**Mekong** river *ab* 4,000 *km* (2,500 *miles*) long SE Asia flowing from s Tsinghai, China, s & SE into S China sea in s Vietnam

**Melanesia** the islands in the Pacific NE of Australia & s of Micronesia including Bismarck archipelago, the Solomons, New Hebrides, New Caledonia, & the Fijis

**Melbourne** city & port SE Australia ✳ of Victoria on Port Philip Bay *pop* (with suburbs) 2,578,527 (1981) – **Melburnian** *n*

**Melilla** city & port NE Morocco on coast NE of Fez; a Spanish presidio *pop* 64,942 (1970)

**Menado** – see MANADO

**Menai** strait 24 *km* (15 *miles*) long N Wales between Anglesey I & mainland

**Mendip** hills sw England in NE Somerset; highest Blackdown 326 *m* (1,068 *ft*)

**Mersey** river 110 *km* (70 *miles*) long NW England flowing NW & w into Irish sea through a large estuary

**Merseyside** metropolitan county NW England ✳ Liverpool *area* 646 *sq km* (250 *sq miles*), *pop* 1,508,940 (1981)

**Mesopotamia 1** region sw Asia between Tigris & Euphrates rivers extending from the mountains of E Asia Minor to the Persian gulf **2** the entire Tigris-Euphrates valley – **Mesopotamian** *adj or n*

**Messina,** *anc* **Messana, Zancle** city & port Italy in NE Sicily *pop* 265,318 (1976)

**Messina, Strait of** channel between s Italy & NE Sicily

**Meuse, D Maas** river 950 *km* (590 *miles*) long w Europe flowing from NE France through s Belgium into North sea in the Netherlands

**Mexico, Sp Méjico, MexSp México 1** Mexico, **Estados Unidos Mexicanos** country s North America s of the USA; a republic ✳ Mexico *area* 1,967,183 *sq km* (761,530 *sq miles*), *pop* 62,500,000 (1981 *est*) **2** state s *cen* Mexico ✳ Toluca *area* 1,967,183 *sq km* (759,530 *sq miles*), *pop* 48,382,000 (1970) **3** **Mexico, Mexico City** city ✳ of Republic of Mexico in Federal District (area surrounded on three sides by state of Mexico) *pop* 8,941,912 (1977 *est*)(metropolitan area) 12,578,420 (1977 *est*)

**Michigan** state N USA in Great Lakes region including an upper (NW) & a lower (SE) peninsula ✳ Lansing *area* 151,362 *sq km* (58,216 *sq miles*), *pop* 9,258,344 (1980) – **Michigander** *n,* **Michiganite** *n*

**Michigan, Lake** lake N *cen* USA, one of the Great Lakes 517 *km* (321 *miles*) long

**Micronesia** the islands of the w Pacific E of the Philippines & N of Melanesia including the Caroline, Gilbert, Mariana & Marshall groups

**Middleton** town in Greater Manchester, England on river Irk 8 *km* (5 *miles*) NNE of Manchester *pop* 53,512 (1971)

**Mid Glamorgan** county SE Wales ✳ Cardiff *area* 1,019 *sq km* (393 *sq miles*), *pop* 539,400 (1981)

**Midlands** the central counties of England usu considered as comprising Bedfordshire, Buckinghamshire, Cambridgeshire, Derbyshire, Leicestershire, Lincolnshire, Northamptonshire, Nottinghamshire, Oxfordshire, Staffordshire, Warwickshire, W Midlands, & part of Hereford and Worcester

**Midway** islands (atoll) *cen* Pacific 2,100 *km* (1,300 *miles*) WNW of Honolulu belonging to the USA, in Hawaiian group but not incorporated in state of Hawaii *area* 5 *sq km* (2 *sq miles*), *pop* 2,220 (1970)

**Milan**, It Milano, *anc* Mediolanum town N Italy ✳ of Lombardy region *pop* 1,634,638 (1981 *est*) – **Milanese** *adj or n*

**Milton Keynes** town in Buckinghamshire, planned "new town" 1969; HQ of Open Univ *pop* 107,000 (1981)

**Mindanao** 1 island S Philippines *area* (including adjacent islands) 94,996 *sq km* (36,537 *sq miles*) 2 sea S Philippines N of Mindanao

**Minnesota** state N USA ✳ Saint Paul *area* 218,577 *sq km* (84,068 *sq miles*), *pop* 4,077,148 (1980) – **Minnesotan** *adj or n*

**Minorca**, Sp Menorca island Spain in the Balearic islands ENE of Majorca; chief city Mahón *area* 702 *sq km* (271 *sq miles*), *pop* 50,217 (1970) – **Minorcan** *adj or n*

**Minsk** city USSR ✳ of Belorussia *pop* 1,276,000 (1979)

**Miquelon** island off S coast of Newfoundland, Canada, belonging to France – see SAINT PIERRE

**Mississippi** 1 river 3,779 *km* (2,348 *miles*) long, *cen* USA flowing from N *cen* Minnesota to Gulf of Mexico 2 state S USA ✳ Jackson *area* 124,062 *sq km* (47,716 *sq miles*), *pop* 2,250,638 (1980)

**Missouri** 1 river *ab* 4,318 *km* (2,683 *miles*) long W USA flowing from SW Montana into the Mississippi in E Missouri 2 state *cen* USA ✳ Jefferson City *area* 181,184 *sq km* (69,686 *sq miles*), *pop* 4,917,444 (1980)

**Mogadishu**, Mogadiscio city & port ✳ of Somalia on Indian ocean *pop* 450,000 (1981 *est*)

**Mojave**, Mohave desert S California SE of S end of the Sierra Nevada

**Moluccas**, Spice, Indonesian Maluku islands Indonesia in Malay archipelago between Celebes & New Guinea *area* 74,505 *sq km* (28,767 *sq miles*), *pop ab* 1,000,000 (1971) – **Molucca**, **Moluccan** *adj*

**Monaco** 1 country S Europe on the Mediterranean coast of France; a principality *area* 1.5 *sq km* (0.6 *sq miles*) *pop* 25,029 (1976) 2 town, its ✳ *pop* 1,443 (1975) – **Monacan** *adj or n*, **Monegasque** *adj or n*

**Mönchen-Gladbach**, G München-Gladbach city W Germany W of Düsseldorf *pop* 258,400 (1980)

**Mongolia** 1 region E Asia W of Khingan mountains & E of Altai mountains; includes Gobi desert 2 Mongolia, Mongolian Republic, Outer Mongolia country E Asia comprising major portion of Mongolia region; a republic ✳ Ulan Bator *area* 1,565,000 *sq km* (610,350 *sq miles*), *pop* 1,641,000 (1981) 3 Mongolia, Inner Mongolia region N China in SE Mongolia & W Manchuria ✳ Huhehot *area* 1,182,046 *sq km* (454,633 *sq miles*), *pop* 13,000,000 (1971)

**Monrovia** city & port ✳ of Liberia on the Atlantic *pop* 220,000 (1981 *est*)

**Montana** state NW USA ✳ Helena *area* 382,559 *sq km* (147,138 *sq miles*), *pop* 786,690 (1980) – **Montanan** *adj or n*

**Mont Blanc** 1 mountain 4,807 *m* (15,771 *ft*) SE France on Italian border in Savoy Alps; highest of the Alps 2 tunnel 11 *km* (7 *miles*) long France & Italy under Mont Blanc

**Monte Carlo** town Monaco

**Montevideo** city & port ✳ of Uruguay on N shore of Rio de la Plata *pop* 1,289,546 (1979 *est*)

**Montgomery** city ✳ of Alabama on Alabama river *pop* 177,857 (1980)

**Montpelier** city ✳ of Vermont *pop* 8,241 (1980)

**Montpellier** city S France WNW Marseilles *pop* 195,603 (1980 *est*)

**Montreal**, Montréal city & port Canada in S Quebec on Montreal Island *pop* 1,080,546 (1976) – **Montrealer** *n*

**Montserrat** island Brit West Indies in the Leewards SW of Antigua ✳ Plymouth *area* 104 *sq km* (40 *sq miles*), *pop* 12,073 (1980) *n* **Montserratian** *adj or n*

**Monza** town N Italy in Lombardy region SE of Milan *pop* 116,257 (1971)

**Morocco** country NW Africa bordering on the Atlantic & the Mediterranean; a kingdom ✳ Rabat, summer ✳ Tangier *area ab* 458,730 *sq km* (177,117 *sq miles*), *pop* 19,470,000 (1979) – **Moroccan** *adj or n*

**Moroni** city ✳ of Comoro *pop* 15,900 (1973)

**Moscow**, Russ Moskva 1 river 507 *km* (315 *miles*) long USSR in W *cen* Soviet Russia, Europe, flowing E into the Oka 2 city ✳ of USSR & of the Russian Republic on Moscow river *pop* 8,203,000 (1981)

**Mostaganem** city & port NW Algeria ENE of Oran *pop* 101,780 (1974 *est*)

**Mozambique**, Port Moçambique 1 Mozambique, *formerly* Portuguese East Africa country SE Africa bordering on Mozambique channel; a republic, until 1975 a dependency of Portugal ✳ Maputo *area* 773,900 *sq km* (297,654 *sq miles*), *pop* 850,000 (1982 *est*) 2 channel 1,592 *km* (950 *miles*) long SE Africa bet Madagascar & Mozambique – **Mozambican** *adj or n*

**Mukden**, Shenyang, *formerly* Fengtien city NE China ✳ of Liaoning province on Hun river; chief city of Manchuria region *pop* 4,400,000 (1977)

**Mülheim**, G Mülheim an der Ruhr city W Germany on Ruhr river *pop* 187,677 (1976)

**Mull** island W Scotland in the Inner Hebrides *area* 909 *sq km* (351 *sq miles*), *pop* (incl Iona) 1,560 (1971)

**Munich**, G München city S Germany ✳ of Bavaria state on the Isar river *pop* 1,298,900 (1980)

**Munster** province S Republic of Ireland comprising counties Clare, Cork, Kerry, Limerick, Tipperary, & Waterford *area* 24,224 *sq km* (9,317 *sq miles*), *pop* 880,000 (1981)

**Münster** city W Germany; formerly ✳ of Westphalia state *pop* 266,083 (1976)

**Murmansk** city & port USSR in NW Soviet Russia, Europe, on Kola peninsula on an inlet of Barents sea *pop* 374,000 (1977)

**Murray** river 2,589 *km* (1,609 *miles*) long SE Australia flowing from near Mt Kosciusko in E Victoria W into Indian ocean in SE South Australia

**Murrumbidgee** river 1,690 *km* (1,050 *miles*) long SE Australia in New South Wales flowing W into the Murray

**Muscat**, Masqat, Maskat town & port ✳ of Oman on Gulf of Oman *pop* 7,000 (1982 *est*)

**Muscat and Oman** – see OMAN

**Mweru** lake *area* 4,920 *sq km* (1,900 *sq miles*) on border between Zaire & Zambia SW of Lake Tanganyika

**Mytilene** – see LESBOS

# N

**Nagasaki** city & port Japan in W Kyushu on E China sea *pop* 450,000 (1975)

**Nagoya** city Japan in S *cen* Honshu *pop* 2,081,465 (1982)

**Nairobi** city ✳ of Kenya *pop* 1,000,000 (1981 *est*)

**Najd** – see NEJD

**Namibia, South-West Africa**, *formerly* German Southwest Africa territory SW Africa on the Atlantic; belonged to Germany before 1919, assigned as mandate by League of Nations to Union of South Africa 1919 ✳ Windhoek *area* 827,057 *sq km* (318,099 *sq miles*), *pop* 1,039,400 (1982) – **Namibian** *adj or n*

**Nanda Devi** mountain 7,821 *m* (25,645 *ft*) N India in the Himalayas in Uttar Pradesh state

**Nanga Parbat** mountain 8,126 *m* (26,660 *ft*) NW Kashmir in the W Himalayas

**Nanking** city E China on the Yangtze ✳ of Kiangsu & (1928–37 & 1946–49) ✳ of China *pop* 2,400,000 (1974 *est*)

**Nantes** city NW France on the Loire *pop* 263,689 (1980 *est*)

**Napier** borough & port New Zealand in E North I on Hawke Bay *pop* 40,186 (1971)

**Naples**, It Napoli, *anc* Neapolis city & port S Italy on Bay of Naples (inlet of Tyrrhenian sea) ✳ of Campania *pop* 1,210,503 (1981 *est*)

**Nashville** city N *cen* Tennessee, its ✳ *pop* 446,027 (1980)

**Nassau** city & port ✳ of the Bahamas on New Providence I *pop* 135,437 (1980)

**Natal 1** city & port NE Brazil ✳ of Rio Grande do Norte state *pop* 250,787 (1970) **2** province E Republic of South Africa between Drakensberg mountains & Indian ocean ✳ Pietermaritzburg *area* 86,967 *sq km* (33,578 *sq miles*), *pop* 4,236,770 (1970)

**Nauru,** *formerly* **Pleasant** island (atoll) w Pacific; formerly a joint Brit, New Zealand, & Australian trust territory; since 1968 an independent republic *area* 21 *sq km* (8 *sq miles*), *pop* 7,245 (1977) – **Nauruan** *adj or n*

**Navigators** – see SAMOA

**Návpaktos,** It **Lepanto,** *anc* **Naupactus** town & port Greece on N shore of strait connecting gulfs of Corinth & Patras

**Nazareth** city N Israel in Galilee SE of Haifa *pop* 34,000 (1970 *est*)

**N'Djamena,** *formerly* **Fort-Lamy** city on the Chari river ✳ of Chad *pop* 150,000 (1981 *est*)

**Neagh, Lough** lake *cen* Northern Ireland *area* 388 *sq km* (150 *sq miles*) largest in British Isles

**Nebraska** state *cen* USA ✳ Lincoln *area* 200,790 *sq km* (77,227 *sq miles*), *pop* 1,570,006 (1980) – **Nebraskan** *adj or n*

**Negev, Negeb** region S Israel, a triangular wedge of desert touching Gulf of Aqaba in S

**Negro 1** river 1,044 *km* (700 *miles*) long S *cen* Argentina flowing E into the Atlantic **2** river *ab* 2,000 *km* (1,250 *miles*) long E Colombia & N Brazil flowing into the Amazon **3** river *ab* 800 *km* (500 *miles*) long *cen* Uruguay flowing SW into Uruguay river

**Nejd, Najd** region *cen* & E Saudi Arabia; a viceroyalty ✳ Riyadh *area* 1,162,200 *sq km* (447,000 *sq miles*), *pop* 2,000,000 (1976 *est*) – **Nejdi** *adj or n*

**Nelson** city & port New Zealand on N coast of South I *pop* 28,300 (1972 *est*)

**Nepal** country Asia on NE border of India in the Himalayas; a kingdom ✳ Katmandu *area* 140,797 *sq km* (54,362 *sq miles*), *pop* 15,000,000 (1981 *est*) – **Nepalese** *adj or n*

**Ness, Loch** lake 38 *km* (24 *miles*) long NW Scotland in Highland region

**Netherlands 1** LOW COUNTRIES – an historical usage **2 Netherlands, Holland, Nederland** country NW Europe on North sea; a kingdom, official ✳ Amsterdam, de facto ✳ The Hague *area* 41,160 *sq km* (15,892 *sq miles*), *pop* 14,208,586 (1980 *est*) – **Netherland** *adj,* **Netherlander** *n,* **Netherlandish** *adj*

**Netherlands Antilles** the islands of the West Indies belonging to the Netherlands: Aruba, Bonaire, Curaçao, Saba, St Eustachius, & S part of St Martin; an overseas territory ✳ Willemstad (on Curaçao) *area* 1,048 *sq km* (403 *sq miles*), *pop* 250,000 (1978)

**Netherlands East Indies** – see INDONESIA

**Netherlands Guiana** – see SURINAM

**Netherlands Timor** – see TIMOR

**Nevada** state w USA ✳ Carson City *area* 287,404 *sq km* (110,540 *sq miles*), *pop* 799,184 (1980) – **Nevadan, Nevadian** *adj or n*

**Nevis** island Brit West Indies, part of St Kitts-Nevis Associated State, in the Leewards; chief town Charlestown *area* 129 *sq km* (50 *sq miles*), *pop* 9,300 (1981)

**Nevis, Ben** mountain 1,340 *m* (4,406 *ft*) w Scotland in Grampian mountains; highest in Great Britain

**New Amsterdam** town founded 1625 on Manhattan I by the Dutch: renamed New York 1664 by the British

**New Brunswick** province SE Canada bordering on Gulf of St Lawrence & Bay of Fundy ✳ Fredericton *area* 72,761 *sq km* (27,985 *sq miles*), *pop* 677,250

**New Caledonia** island SW Pacific SW of Vanuatu; with nearby islands, constitutes an overseas department of France ✳ Nouméa *area* 22,225 *sq km* (8,548 *sq miles*), *pop* 100,600 (1971 *est*)

**Newcastle upon Tyne** city & port N England ✳ of Tyne and Wear *pop* 222,209 (1971)

**New Delhi** city ✳ of India in Delhi Territory S of city of (Old) Delhi *pop* 292,857 (1971)

**New England** the NE section of the USA comprising the states of Maine, New Hampshire, Vermont, Rhode Island, & Connecticut

**New Forest** forested area S England in Hampshire between the Avon & Southampton Water; once a royal hunting ground

**Newfoundland 1** island Canada in the Atlantic E of Gulf of St Lawrence *area* 112,300 *sq km* (43,359 *sq miles*) **2** province E Canada comprising Newfoundland I & Labrador ✳ St John's *area* 404,517 *sq km* (156,185 *sq miles*), *pop* 567,681 (1981) – **Newfoundlander** *n*

**New Guinea 1 New Guinea, Papua,** Indonesian **Irian** island in Malay archipelago N of E Australia divided between West Irian on w & Papua New Guinea on E *area ab* 777,000 *sq km* (300,000 *sq miles*), *pop* 3,600,000 (1973 *est*) **2** the NE portion of the island of New Guinea with the Bismarck archipelago, Bougainville, Buka, & adjacent small islands; part of Papua New Guinea – **New Guinean** *n or adj*

**New Hampshire** state NE USA ✳ Concord *area* 24,190 *sq km* (9,304 *sq miles*), *pop* 920,610 (1980) – **New Hampshireman** *n,* **New Hampshirite** *n*

**New Hebrides** – see VANUATU

**New Jersey** state E USA ✳ Trenton *area* 20,374 *sq km* (7,836 *sq miles*), *pop* 7,364,158 (1980) – **New Jerseyite** *n*

**Newmarket** town in Suffolk, England; HQ of the Jockey Club; *pop* 11,350 (1971)

**New Mexico** state SW USA ✳ Santa Fe *area* 316,332 *sq km* (121,666 *sq miles*), *pop* 1,299,968 (1980) – **New Mexican** *adj or n*

**New Orleans** city & port SE Louisiana between Lake Pontchartrain & the Mississippi *pop* 593,471 (1970) – **New Orleanian** *n*

**New South Wales** state SE Australia bordering on the Pacific ✳ Sydney *area* 801,396 *sq km* (309,432 *sq miles*), *pop* 5,237,100 (1981)

**Newtown** town in Powys, Wales on river Severn; developed as "new town" 1967; *pop* 8,660 (1981 *prov*)

**New York 1** state NE USA ✳ Albany *area* 121,898 *sq km* (49,576 *sq miles*), *pop* 17,557,288 (1980) **2 New York, New York City** city & port SE New York at mouth of the Hudson; includes boroughs of Bronx, Brooklyn, Manhattan, Queens, & Staten Island *pop* 11,572,000 (1973) **3** the borough of Manhattan in New York City – **New Yorker** *n*

**New Zealand** country SW Pacific ESE of Australia comprising chiefly North I & South I; a dominion of the Brit Commonwealth ✳ Wellington *area* 268,676 *sq km* (103,736 *sq miles*), *pop* 3,175,737 (1981) – **New Zealander** *n*

**Niagara Falls 1** waterfalls on border between New York & Ontario in the **Niagara** river; divided by Goat I into Horseshoe, or Canadian Falls 48 *m* (158 *ft*) high and 792 *m* (2,600 *ft*) wide & American Falls 51 *m* (167 *ft*) high and 305 *m* (1,000 *ft*) wide **2** city w New York at the falls *pop* 85,615 (1971) **3** city Canada in SE Ontario *pop* 67,163 (1970)

**Niamey** city ✳ of Niger *pop* 130,299 (1975)

**Nicaragua** country Central America bordering on the Pacific & the Caribbean; a republic ✳ Managua *area* 148,000 *sq km* (57,150 *sq miles*), *pop* 2,700,000 (1980) – **Nicaraguan** *adj or n*

**Nice,** *anc* **Nicaea** city & port SE France on the Mediterranean *pop* 346,620 (1980 *est*)

**Nicobar** islands India in Indian ocean S of Andaman islands *area* 1,645 *sq km* (635 *sq miles*), *pop* 115,000 (1971)

**Nicosia** city ✳ of Cyprus *pop* 233,500 (1974 *est*)

**Niger 1** river 4,185 *km* (2,600 *miles*) long w Africa flowing from Fouta Djallon NE, SE, & S into Gulf of Guinea **2** country w Africa; a republic, until 1958 a territory of French West Africa ✳ Niamey *area* 1,187,000 *sq km* (458,874 *sq miles*), *pop* 4,030,000 (1972) – **Nigerien** *adj or n*

**Nigeria** country w Africa bordering on Gulf of Guinea; a republic within the Brit Commonwealth, formerly a colony & protectorate ✳ Lagos *area* 923,769 *sq km* (356,669 *sq miles*), *pop* 90,000,000 (1981 *est*) – **Nigerian** *adj or n*

**Nijmegen, Nimwegen, Nimeguen** town E Netherlands in Gelderland province on the Waal river S of Arnhem *pop* 216,088 (1978)

**Nile** river 6,648 *km* (4,132 *miles*) long E Africa from Lake Victoria in Uganda N into Mediterranean in Egypt, in various sections called specifically; **Victoria,** *or* **Somerset, Nile,** between Lake Victoria & Lake Albert; **Albert Nile,** between Lake Albert & Lake No; & **White Nile,** from Lake No to Khartoum –see BLUE NILE

**Nineveh, L Ninus** ancient city ✳ of Assyria; ruins in Iraq on the Tigris opposite Monsul

**Niue** island s *cen* Pacific w of Cook Islands; a dependency of New Zealand *area* 260 *sq km* (100 *sq miles*), *pop* 3,226 (1980)

**Norfolk 1** county on E coast of England, *area* 5,515 *sq km* (2,129 *sq miles*), *pop* 699,200 (1981) **2** island s Pacific between New Caledonia & New Zealand; administered by Australia *area* 34 *sq km* (13 *sq miles*), *pop* 2,175 (1981)

**Norfolk Broads** – see BROADS

**Norrköping** city & port SE Sweden sw of Stockholm at head of an inlet of the Baltic *pop* 119,238 (1980)

**North** island N New Zealand *area* 114,729 *sq km* (44,297 *sq miles*), *pop* 2,322,989 (1981)

**North America** continent of the western hemisphere NW of South America bounded by Atlantic, Arctic, & Pacific oceans *area ab* 24,400,000 *sq km* (9,420,000 *sq miles*) – **North American** *adj or n*

**Northampton** town in Northamptonshire, on river Nene *pop* 160,000 (1981)

**Northamptonshire** county in central England *area* 2,367 *sq km* (914 *sq miles*), *pop* 543,700 (1981)

**North Carolina** state E USA ✳ Raleigh *area* 136,724 *sq km* (52,586 *sq miles*), *pop* 5,874,429 (1980) – **North Carolinian** *adj or n*

**North Dakota** state NW *cen* USA ✳ Bismarck *area* 183,729 *sq km* (70,665 *sq miles*), *pop* 652,695 (1980) – **North Dakotan** *adj or n*

**North Downs** hills s England chiefly in Kent & Surrey

**Northern Dvina,** Russ **Severnaya Dvina** river 1,770 *km* (1,100 *miles*) and USSR in N Soviet Russia, Europe, flowing NW into White sea

**Northern Ireland** country NE Ireland; a division of the United Kingdom of Great Britain and Northern Ireland ✳ Belfast *area* 14,147 *sq km* (5,461 *sq miles*), *pop* 1,547,300 (1980)

**Northern Kingdom** – see ISRAEL

**North sea** arm of the Atlantic 966 *km* (600 *miles*) long & 563 *km* (350 *miles*) wide E of Great Britain

**Northern Territory** territory *cen* & N Australia bordering on Arafura sea ✳ Darwin *area* 1,361,412 *sq km* (523,620 *sq miles*), *pop* 122,800 (1981)

**North Riding** – see NORTH YORKSHIRE

**Northumbria** county in N of England reconstituted in 1974 *area* 5,034 *sq km* (1,944 *sq miles*), *pop* 296,000 (1981)

**Northwest Territories** territory N Canada comprising the Arctic islands, the mainland N of 60° between Yukon Territory & Hudson Bay, & the islands in Hudson Bay; divided into Mackenzie, Keewatin, & Franklin districts ✳ Yellowknife *area* 3,379,689 *sq km* (1,304,903 *sq miles*), *pop* 45,741 (1981)

**North Yorkshire** county in N England, formed in 1974 from parts of N, E and w Ridings of Yorkshire *area* 8,309 *sq km* (3,208 *sq miles*), *pop* 668,800 (1981)

**Norway,** Norw **Norge** country N Europe in Scandinavia bordering on Atlantic & Arctic oceans; a kingdom ✳ Oslo *area* 323,883 *sq km* (125,051 *sq miles*), *pop* 4,107,063 (1981 *est*)

**Norwich** city in Norfolk, on river Wensun *pop* 122,083 (1971)

**Nottaway** river 644 *km* (400 *miles*) long Canada in sw Quebec flowing NW into James Bay

**Nottingham** city in Nottinghamshire, at confluence of rivers Lear and Trent *pop* 300,630 (1971)

**Nottinghamshire** county in midland area of England, slightly reconstructed in 1974, *area* 2,108 *sq km* (814 *sq miles*), *pop* 977,000 (1981)

**Nouakchott** city ✳ of Mauritania *pop* 135,000 (1978 *est*)

**Nouméa** city & port ✳ of New Caledonia *pop* 12,000 (1971 *est*)

**Novara** town NW Italy in Piedmont region *pop* 102,132 (1976)

**Nova Scotia** province SE Canada comprising a peninsula (600 *km or* 375 *miles* long) & Cape Breton Is ✳ Halifax *area* 54,868 *sq km* (21,103 *sq miles*), *pop* 847,442 (1981) – **Nova Scotian** *adj or n*

**Novaya Zemla** two islands USSR in NE Soviet Russia, Europe, in Arctic ocean bet Barents sea & Kara sea *area* 93,600 *sq km* (36,000 *sq miles*)

**Novi Sad** city NE Yugoslavia on the Danube; chief city of Vojvodina *pop* 169,000 (1981)

**Nukualofa** town ✳ of Tonga on Tongatapu I *pop* 18,396 (1981 *est*)

**Nuremberg,** G **Nurnberg** city w Germany in N *cen* Bavaria state on Pegnitz river *pop* 484,400 (1980)

**Nyasaland** – see MALAWI

**Oberammergau** town sw Germany in Bavaria state ssw of Munich; famous for its Passion play

**Oceania, Oceanica** the lands of the *cen* & s Pacific including Micronesia, Melanesia, Polynesia (including New Zealand), often Australia, & sometimes the Malay archipelago *pop* 21,000,000 (1975 *est*) – **Oceanian** *n*

**Odense** city Denmark in N Fyn I *pop* 169,943 (1981)

**Odessa** city & port USSR in s Ukraine on Black sea *pop* 1,039,000 (1977)

**Ohio** state E *cen* USA ✳ Columbus *area* 107,177 *sq km* (41,222 *sq miles*), *pop* 10,797,419 (1980) – **Ohioan** *n*

**Okinawa 1** island group Japan in *cen* Ryukyu islands ✳ Naha; occupied by the USA 1945-1972 **2** island in the group; largest in the Ryukyus *area* 1,256 *sq km* (485 *sq miles*), *pop* 934,000 (1970)

**Oklahoma** state s *cen* USA ✳ Oklahoma City *area* 181,789 *sq km* (69,919 *sq miles*), *pop* 3,025,266 (1980) – **Oklahoman** *adj or n*

**Oklahoma City** city ✳ of Oklahoma on the N Canadian river *pop* 403,213 (1980)

**Oland** island Sweden in Baltic sea off SE coast; chief town Borgholm *area* 1,344 *sq km* (519 *sq miles*), *pop* 20,249 (1971)

**Oldham** town in Greater Manchester, England 11 *km* (7 *miles*) NE of Manchester *pop* 105,913 (1971)

**Olives, Mount of, Olivet** mountain ridge 808 *m* (2,652 *ft*) w Jordan running N & s on E side of Jerusalem

**Olympia** city ✳ of Washington on Puget Sound *pop* 27,447 (1980)

**Omagh** town w Northern Ireland ✳ of Tyrone

**Oman,** *formerly* **Muscat and Oman** country sw Asia in SE Arabia bordering on Arabian sea; a sultanate ✳ Muscat *area* 212,000 *sq km* (82,000 *sq miles*), *pop* 850,000 (1982 *est*) – **Omani** *adj or n*

**Omsk** city USSR in sw Soviet Russia, Asia, at confluence of Irtysh & Om rivers *pop* 1,026,000 (1977)

**Ontario** province E Canada bet Great Lakes & Hudson bay ✳ Toronto *area* 944,533 *sq km* (363,282 *sq miles*), *pop* 8,625,107 (1981)

**Ontario, Lake** lake USA & Canada in New York & Ontario; easternmost of the Great Lakes *area* 19,550 *sq km* (7,550 *sq miles*)

**Oporto** , **Pôrto** city & port NW Portugal on the Douro river *pop* 1,389,800 (1974 *est*)

**Oran** city & port NW Algeria *pop* 327,493 (1970)

**Orange** river 2,100 *km* (1,300 *miles*) long s Africa flowing from the Drakensberg mountains in Lesotho w into the Atlantic

**Örebro** city s *cen* Sweden *pop* 116,969 (1980)

**Oregon** state NW USA ✳ Salem *area* 252,151 *sq km* (96,981 *sq miles*), *pop* 2,632,663 (1980) – **Oregonian** *adj or n*

**Orinoco** river 2,150 *km* (1,336 *miles*) long Venezuela flowing from Brazilian border to Colombia border & thence into the Atlantic through wide delta

**Orkney** islands off N coast of Scotland, created island area in 1975; *area* 984 *sq km* (380 *sq miles*), *pop* 18,862 (1981)

**Orléans** town N *cen* France *pop* 100,200 (1973)

**Osaka** city & port Japan in s Honshu *pop* 2,629,395 (1982)

**Oslo,** *formerly* **Christiania, Kristiania** city ✳ of Norway at N end of **Oslo Fjord** (inlet of the Skagerrak) *pop* 450,386 (1981)

**Osnabrück** city NW Germany *pop* 157,400 (1980)

**Ostend,** Flem **Oostende,** F **Ostende** city & port NW Belgium *pop* 270,800 (1981)

**Österreich** – see AUSTRIA

**Ottawa 1** river 1,120 *km* (696 *miles*) long E Canada in SE Ontario & s Quebec flowing E into the St Lawrence **2** city ✳ of Canada in SE Ontario *pop* 300,678 (1981) – **Ottawan** *n*

**Ottoman Empire** former Turkish sultanate (✳ Constantinople) in SE Europe, w Asia, & N Africa including at greatest extent Turkey, Syria, Mesopotamia, Palestine, Arabia, Egypt, Barbary States, Balkan States, & parts of Russia & Hungary

**Ouagadougou** city *cen* Upper Volta, its ✳ *pop* 200,000 (1979 *est*)

**Oujda** city NE Morocco *pop* 769,100 (1979)

**Ouse 1 Ouse, Great Ouse** river *ab* 250 *km* (160 *miles*) long *cen* & E England flowing into the Wash **2** river 92 *km* (57 *miles*) long NE England flowing SE to unite with the Trent forming the Humber

**Oxford** university city in Oxfordshire, on river Thames (or Isis) at confluence into river Cherwell *pop* 108,805 (1971)

**Oxfordshire** county in S *cen* England, reformed in 1974 to include large area of NW Berkshire *area* 2,612 *sq km* (1,008 *sq miles*), *pop* 554,700 (1981)

# P

**Pacific** ocean extending from the Arctic circle to the Antarctic regions & from W North America & W South America to E Asia & Australia *area ab* 166,000,000 *sq km* (64,000,000 *sq miles*)

**Pacific Islands, Trust Territory of the** islands in W Pacific under US administration: the Marianas (except Guam), the Carolines (including the Palaus), & the Marshalls ✳ Tanapag, on Saipan I; a Japanese mandate 1919–45, *land area* 1,860 *sq km* (717 *sq miles*), *pop* 116,662 (1980)

**Padua,** It **Padova** town NE Italy W of Venice *pop* 242,186 (1976) – **Paduan** *adj or n*

**Pahsien** – see CHUNGKING

**Pakistan** country S Asia orig comprising an eastern division & a western division; a dominion 1947–56 & a republic 1956–72 of the Brit Commonwealth, formed from parts of former Brit India; ✳ Islamabad *area* 796,095 *sq km* (307,374 *sq miles*), *pop* 83,780,000 (1981) – **Pakistani** *adj or n*

**Palawan** island W Philippines W of the Visayan islands *area* 11,785 *sq km* (4,550 *sq miles*), *pop* (with adjacent islands) 236,635 (1970)

**Palermo,** *anc* **Panormus, Panhormus** city & port Italy ✳ of Sicily *pop* 699,691 (1981 *est*) – **Palermitan** *adj or n*

**Palestine,** L **Palaestina 1** ancient region SW Asia bordering on E coast of the Mediterranean & extending E of the Jordan **2** former country bordering on the Mediterranean on W & Dead sea on E; a part of the Ottoman Empire 1516–1917, a Brit mandate 1923–48; now divided between Israel & Jordan, with Gaza Strip administered by Egypt – **Palestinian** *adj or n*

**Palma, Palma de Mallorca** town & port Spain ✳ of Baleares province on Majorca *pop* 234,098 (1970)

**Palmer archipelago, Palmer peninsula** – see ANTARCTIC

**Palmer Land** the S section of the Antarctic peninsula

**Panama,** Sp **Panamá 1** country S Central America; a republic; before 1903 part of Colombia *area* (including Canal Zone) 75,650 *sq km* (29,208 *sq miles*), *pop* 1,718,000 (1976 *est*) **2 Panama, Panama City** city & port, its ✳, on Gulf of Panama *pop* 460,000 (1976 *est*) **3** ship canal 82 *km* (51 *miles*) long *cen* Panama in the Canal Zone connecting the Atlantic (Caribbean sea) & the Pacific (Gulf of Panama) – **Panamanian** *adj or n*

**Panama Canal Zone** – see CANAL ZONE

**Pão de Açúcar, Sugarloaf Mountain** peak 404 *m* (1,325 *ft*) SE Brazil in city of Rio de Janeiro on W side of entrance to Guanabara Bay

**Papeete** commune & port Society islands on Tahiti ✳ of French Polynesia *pop* 15,220 (1971 *est*)

**Papua** – see NEW GUINEA

**Papua New Guinea** country comprising territories of Papua & New Guinea; independent from 1975, formerly a UN trust territory administered by Australia ✳ Port Moresby *area* 461,260 *sq km* (178,260 *sq miles*), *pop* 3,006,799 (1981 *est*)

**Paraguay 1** river 2,550 *km* (1,585 *miles*) long, *cen* South America flowing from Mato Grosso plateau in Brazil S into the Paraná river in Paraguay **2** country *cen* South America traversed by Paraguay river; a republic ✳ Asunción *area* 406,750 *sq km* (157,006 *sq miles*), *pop* 3,167,900 (1980 *est*) – **Paraguayan** *adj or n*

**Paramaribo** city & port ✳ of Surinam on Surinam river *pop* 110,000 (1971)

**Parida, La** – see BOLIVAR (Cero)

**Paris ,** *anc* **Lutetia** city ✳ of France on the Seine *pop* (town) 2,050,500 (1980 *est*)(with suburbs) 10,033,700 (1980 *est*) – **Parisian** *adj or n*

**Parnassus,** NGk **Parnassós** mountain 2,457 *m* (8,060 *ft*), *cen* Greece N of Gulf of Corinth

**Pearl Harbour** inlet Hawaii on S coast of Oahu I W of Honolulu

**Peking,** *formerly* **Peiping** municipality ✳ of China *pop* 8,706,000 (1980)

**Penang, Pinang** – see GEORGE TOWN

**Pennine Chain** mountains N England extending S from Scottish border to Derbyshire & Staffordshire; highest Cross Fell 893 *m* (2,930 *ft*)

**Pennsylvania** state NE USA ✳ Harrisburg *area* 117,866 *sq km* (45,333 *sq miles*), *pop* 11,866,728 (1980)

**Pentland 1** firth channel between Orkneys & mainland of Scotland **2** hills S Scotland in Borders, Lothian, & Strathclyde regions; highest peak Scald Law 579 *m* (1,898 *ft*)

**People's Democratic Republic of Yemen** – see YEMEN

**Pernambuco** – see RECIFE

**Persia** – see IRAN

**Persian Gulf** arm of Arabian sea between SW Iran & Arabia

**Perth 1** city ✳ of Western Australia on Swan river *pop* (with suburbs & Fremantle) 918,000 (1981) – see FREMANTLE **2** town *cen* Scotland *pop* 44,066 (1974 *est*)

**Peru** country W South America; a republic ✳ Lima *area* 1,285,215 *sq km* (496,224 *sq miles*), *pop* 15,839,000 (1975 *est*) – **Peruvian** *n or adj*

**Peterborough** borough E *cen* England *pop* 122,440 (1981)

**Peterlee** town in Durham; created as "new town" 1946; *pop* 23,000 (1981)

**Petra** ancient city of NW Arabia on slope of Mt Hor, site now in SW Jordan

**Petrograd** – see LENINGRAD

**Philippines, Republic of the Philippines,** Sp **Republica de Filipinas,** Pilipino **Republika ng Pilipinas** country E Asia comprising the Philippine islands; a republic, once a Spanish possession & (1898-1945) a US possession ✳ Manila, official ✳ Quezon City *land area* 298,558 *sq km* (114,830 *sq miles*), *pop* 42,759,000 (1975) – **Philippine** *adj*

**Phnom Penh** city ✳ of Cambodia, on the Mekong *pop* 393,995 (1981)

**Phoenix** city ✳ of Arizona on Salt river *pop* 789,704 (1980)

**Pierre** city ✳ of South Dakota on Missouri river *pop* 11,973 (1980)

**Pietermaritzburg** city E Republic of S Africa ✳ of Natal *pop* 160,847 (1970)

**Pigs, Bay of, Cochinos Bay** bay W Cuba on S coast

**Pilcomayo** river 1,609 *km* (1,000 *miles*) S *cen* South America rising in Bolivia & flowing SE on Argentina- Paraguay boundary into Paraguay river

**Pillars of Hercules** the two promontories at E end of Strait of Gibraltar: Rock of Gibraltar (in Europe) & Jebel Musa (in Africa)

**Piraeus** city E Greece; port for Athens *pop* 187,458 (1971)

**Pisa** town W *cen* Italy in Tuscany region on the Arno river *pop* 103,479 (1976) – **Pisan** *adj or n*

**Pishpek** – see FRUNZE

**Pitcairn** island S Pacific SE of Tuamotu archipelago; a Brit colony, with several smaller islands

**Pittsburgh** city SW Pennsylvania *pop* 520,117 (1970)

**Plata, Río de la, River Plate** estuary of Paraná & Uruguay rivers South America between Uruguay & Argentina; *area* 35,000 *sq km* (13,500 *sq miles*)

**Pleasant** – see NAURU

**Pleven, Plevna** city NW Bulgaria *pop* 127,716 (1980)

**Ploesti** city SE *cen* Rumania *pop* 178,256 (1975)

**Plymouth 1** city and seaport in Devon, *pop* 239,452 (1971) **2** town ✳ of Montserrat *pop* 1,623 (1980)

**Po,** *anc* **Padus** river *ab* 668 *km* (415 *miles*) long N Italy flowing from slopes of Mt Viso E into the Adriatic through several mouths

**Poland,** Pol **Polska** country E *cen* Europe bordering on Baltic sea; in medieval period a kingdom, at one time extending to the lower Dnieper; partitioned 1772, 1793, 1795 among Russia, Prussia, & Austria; again a kingdom 1815–30; lost autonomy 1830–1918; since 1918 a republic ✳ Warsaw *area* 312,677 *sq km* (120,725 *sq miles*), *pop* 35,032,000 (1978)

**Poltoratsk** – see ASHKHABAD

**Polynesia** the islands of the *cen* & s Pacific including Hawaii, the Line, Ellice, Phoenix, Tonga, Cook, & Samoa islands, Easter I, French Polynesia, & often New Zealand

**Pompeii** ancient city s Italy SE of Naples destroyed A D 79 by eruption of Mt Vesuvius – **Pompeian, Pompeiian** *adj or n*

**Ponta Delgada** city & port Azores on São Miguel I *pop* 21,347 (1978)

**Poole** town in Dorset, on **Poole harbour** 8 *km* (5 *miles*) w of Bournemouth *pop* 106,161 (1971)

**Poona** city w India in Maharashtra state ESE of Bombay *pop* 853,225 (1971)

**Popocatepetl** volcano 5,452 *m* (17,887 *ft*) SE *cen* Mexico in Puebla

**Port-au-Prince** city & port ✳ of Republic of Haiti *pop* 506,525 (1971)

**Port Castries** – see CASTRIES

**Port Elizabeth** city & port s Republic of South Africa in SE Cape Province on Algoa Bay *pop* 475,869 (1970)

**Port Louis** city & port ✳ of Mauritius *pop* (with suburbs) 145,817 (1980)

**Port Mahon** – see MAHON

**Port Moresby** city & port SE New Guinea in Papua ✳ of Papua New Guinea *pop* 131,000 (1981 *est*)

**Pôrto** – see OPORTO

**Port of Spain** city & port ✳ of Trinidad and Tobago, on NW Trinidad I *pop* 120,000 (1978 *est*)

**Porton Down** Wiltshire, England; site of Microbiological Research and Chemical Defence Experimental Establishment of Ministry of Defence

**Porto-Novo** city & port ✳ of Benin *pop* 104,000 (1976 *est*)

**Port Said** city & port NE Egypt on the Mediterranean at N end of Suez canal *pop* 285,000 (1981 *est*)

**Portsmouth** city s England in Hampshire on **Portsea** (island in English channel) *pop* 197,431 (1971)

**Port Stanley** – see STANLEY

**Portugal,** *anc* **Lusitania** country sw Europe in w Iberian peninsula bordering on the Atlantic; a republic, before 1910 a kingdom ✳ Lisbon *area* (not including Azores & Madeira) 91,641 *sq km* (35,383 *sq miles*), *pop* 9,862,700 (1979)

**Portuguese East Africa** – see MOZAMBIQUE

**Portuguese Guinea** – see GUINEA-BISSAU

**Portuguese Timor** – see TIMOR

**Portuguese West Africa** – see ANGOLA

**Potomac** river 462 *km* (287 *miles*) long E USA flowing from W Virginia into Chesapeake Bay & forming s boundary of Maryland

**Potsdam** city E Germany sw of Berlin *pop* 1,117,523 (1980)

**Potteries, The** district in upper Trent basin of N Staffordshire, England; centre of china and earthenware industry

**Powys** county in E *cen* Wales *area* 5,077 *sq km* (1,960 *sq miles*), *pop* 110,100 (1981)

**Poznan,** G **Posen** city w *cen* Poland on the Warta river *pop* 527,000 (1977)

**Prague,** Czech **Praha** city ✳ of Czechoslovakia in Bohemia on Vltava river *pop* 1,191,125 (1979)

**Praia** town ✳ of Cape Verde on São Tiago I *pop* 6,000 (1970)

**Pretoria** city, administrative ✳ of Republic of South Africa & ✳ of Transvaal *pop* 563,384 (1970)

**Prince Edward Island** island SE Canada in Gulf of St Lawrence off E New Brunswick & N Nova Scotia; a province ✳ Charlottetown *area* 5,657 *sq km* (2,184 *sq miles*), *pop* 122,506 (1981)

**Principé** island w Africa in Gulf of Guinea N of Sao Tomé *area* 151 *sq km* (58 *sq miles*), – see SAO TOME

**Providence** city & port N Rhode Island, its ✳ *pop* 156,804 (1980)

**Puerto Rico,** *formerly* **Porto Rico** island West Indies E of Hispaniola; a self-governing commonwealth in union with the USA ✳ San Juan *area* 8,891 *sq km* (3,435 *sq miles*), *pop* 3,187,570 (1980) – **Puerto Rican** *adj or n*

**Purbeck, Isle of** peninsula region s England in Dorset extending E into English channel

**Pusan** city & port SE S Korea on Korea strait *pop* 3,160,000 (1980)

**Pyongyang** city ✳ of N Korea on the Taedong *pop* 1,500,000 (1982 *est*)

# Q

**Qatar, Katar** country E Arabia on peninsula projecting into Persian gulf; an independent emirate ✳ Doha *area* 11,400 *sq km* (4,400 *sq miles*), *pop* 250,000 (1982 *est*) – **Qatari** *adj or n*

**Quebec, Québec 1** province E Canada extending from Hudson Bay to Gaspé peninsula *area* 1,540,680 *sq km* (594,860 *sq miles*), *pop* 6,438,403 (1981) **2** city & port, its ✳, on the St Lawrence *pop* 166,474 (1981) – **Quebecer, Quebecker** *n*

**Queensland** state NE Australia ✳ Brisbane *area* 1,728,000 *sq km* (667,000 *sq miles*), *pop* 2,345,300 (1980) – **Queenslander** *n*

**Quezaltenango** city sw Guatemala *pop* 65,733 (1981)

**Quezon City** city Philippines in Luzon NE Manila; official ✳ of the Philippines *pop* 960,341 (1975)

**Quito** city ✳ of Ecuador *pop* 800,000 (1981 *est*)

# R

**Rabat** city ✳ of Morocco on Atlantic coast *pop* 865,100 (1979)

**Raleigh** city E *cen* North Carolina, its ✳ *pop* 150,255 (1980)

**Rangoon** city & port ✳ of Burma on Rangoon river 34 *km* (21 *miles*) from its mouth *pop* 3,186,886 (1973)

**Rapa Nui** – see EASTER

**Rarotonga** island s Pacific in sw part of Cook islands; site of Avarua, ✳ of the group

**Ras al Khaimah 1** sheikhdom United Arab Emirates *area* 1,733 *sq km* (650 *sq miles*), *pop* 80,000 (1980 *est*) **2** town, its ✳

**Reading** town in Berkshire, on river Thames at junction with river Kennet *pop* 132,939 (1971)

**Recife,** *formerly* **Pernambuco** city & port NE Brazil ✳ of Pernambuco state *pop* 1,204,794 (1980)

**Red** sea *area ab* 438,000 *sq km* (169,000 *sq miles*); *ab* 2,000 *km* (1,200 *miles*) long; 160 to 320 *km* (100 to 200 *miles*) wide between Arabia & NE Africa

**Redditch** town in Hereford and Worcester, England, developed as "new town" 1965; *pop* 64,700 (1981)

**Reggio 1 Reggio, Reggio di Calabria, Reggio Calabria,** *anc* **Rhegium** town & port s Italy on Strait of Messina *pop* 177,883 (1976) **2 Reggio, Reggio nell'Emilia, Reggio Emilia** town N Italy in Emilia-Romagna region NW of Bologna *pop* 129,674 (1976)

**Reims, Rheims** city NE France ENE of Paris *pop* 183,610 (1980 *est*)

**Rennes** city NW France N of Nantes *pop* 205,733 (1980 *est*)

**Réunion** island w Indian ocean in the w Mascarenes ✳ St-Denis; an overseas department of France *area* 2,500 *sq km* (970 *sq miles*), *pop* 476,675 (1974)

**Reval, Revel** – see TALLINN

**Reykjavík** city & port ✳ of Iceland *pop* 84,469 (1981)

**Rhine, G Rhein, F Rhin, D Rijn** river 1,320 *km* (820 *miles*) long w Europe flowing from SE Switzerland to North sea in the Netherlands – **Rhenish** *adj*

**Rhode Island,** *officially* **Rhode Island and Providence Plantation** state NE USA ✳ Providence *area* 3,156 *sq km* (1,214 *sq miles*), *pop* 947,154 (1980) – **Rhode Islander** *n*

**Rhodes,** NGk **Ródhos 1** island off Greece in the SE Aegean, chief island of the Dodecanese *area* 1,400 *sq km* (545 *sq miles*) **2** city, its ✳ *pop* 32,092 (1971) – **Rhodian** *adj or n*

**Rhodesia 1** region *cen* s Africa s of Zaire comprising Zambia & Zimbabwe; contains rich archaeological findings **2** – see ZIMBABWE – **Rhodesian** *adj or n*

**Rhondda** coal mining town in Mid Glamorgan, Wales *pop* 88,994 (1971)

**Rhone, F Rhône** river 800 *km* (500 *miles*) long Switzerland & France flowing through Lake Geneva into the Mediterranean

**Richmond** city ✳ of Virginia on the James river *pop* 219,214 (1980)

**Riga** city & port USSR ✳ of Latvia *pop* 835,000 (1979)

**Rijeka, Rieka,** It **Fiume** city & port NW Yugoslavia in Croatia *pop* 133,000 (1981)

**Rimini,** *anc* **Ariminum** town & port N Italy on the Adriatic ESE of Ravenna *pop* 125,816 (1976)

**Rio de Janeiro 1** city & port SE Brazil ✳ of Guanabara state on Guanabara Bay; former ✳ of Brazil *pop* 5,094,396 (1980) **2** state SE Brazil ✳ Niterói *area* 44,268 *sq km* (17,092 *sq miles*), *pop* 9,110,324 (1970)

**Rio Muni** – see MBINI

**Ripon** city in N Yorkshire, on river Ure *pop* 10,989 (1971)

**Riyadh** city ✳ of the Nejd & Saudi Arabia *pop* 1,000,000 (1976 *est*)

**Road Town** town ✳ of Brit Virgin Islands on SE Tortola I *pop* 2,479 (1980)

**Rochdale** town in Greater Manchester 16 *km* (10 *miles*) NE of Manchester *pop* 91,454 (1971)

**Rochester** city in Kent, on river Medway *pop* 55,519 (1971)

**Rockall** islet N Atlantic NW of Ireland, at 57°36′N, 13°41′W

**Rocky** mountains W North America extending from N Alaska SE to *cen* New Mexico

**Romania, Rumania, Roumania** country SE Europe bordering on Black sea ✳ Bucharest *area* 237,500 *sq km* (91,699 *sq miles*), *pop* 22,048,305 (1979)

**Rome,** It **Roma,** *anc* **Roma** city ✳ of Italy on the Tiber *pop* 2,830,569 (1980)

**Romney Marsh** area of drained marshland on Kent coast, between Hythe and Rye *area* 176 *sq km* (68 *sq miles*)

**Roseau** seaport ✳ of Dominica *pop* 8,346 (1981)

**Ross Dependency** section of Antarctica lying bet 160°E and 150°W long; claimed by New Zealand

**Rostock** city & port E Germany on Warnow river near the Baltic coast *pop* 887,820 (1980)

**Rosyth** naval base and dockyard in Fife region Scotland

**Rotterdam** city & port SW Netherlands on the Nieuwe Maas river *pop* 1,017,136 (1978)

**Rouen** city & port N France on the Seine *pop* 114,415 (1975 *prov*)

**Ruapehu** volcano 2,797 *m* (9,175 *ft*) New Zealand, highest peak in North I, in Tongariro National Park

**Rum, Isle of, Rhum** island of Outer Hebrides, Highland region Scotland *area* 109 *sq km* (42 *sq miles*)

**Runcorn** town in Cheshire, designated "new town" 1964; *pop* 64,700 (1981)

**Runnymede** meadow S England in Surrey at Egham on S bank of the Thames

**Rushmore, Mount** mountain 1,745 *m* (5,725 *ft*) above sea level; over 150 *m* (500 *ft*) above the valley W S Dakota, in Black hills on which are carved gigantic faces of Washington, Jefferson, Lincoln, Theodore Roosevelt; a national memorial

**Rwanda,** *formerly* **Ruanda** country E *cen* Africa; a republic ✳ Kigali *area* 26,330 *sq km* (10,116 *sq miles*), *pop* 4,500,000 (1981 *est*) – **Rwandan** *n or adj*

# S

**Saarbrücken** city W Germany ✳ of Saarland state *pop* 193,600 (1980)

**Sacramento** city ✳ of California on Sacramento river *pop* 275,741 (1980)

**Saghalien** – see SAKHALIN

**Sahara** desert region *area* 8,600,000 *sq km* (3,520,000 *sq miles*) N Africa N of the Sudan region extending from the Atlantic coast to Red sea or, as sometimes considered, to the Nile – **Saharan** *adj*

**Saigon, Ho Chi Minh** city & port S Vietnam; formerly ✳ of S Vietnam *pop* 3,500,000 (1974) – **Saigonese** *adj or n*

**Saint Christopher** – see SAINT KITTS

**Saint Davids** city in Dyfed, Wales, Cathedral is largest church in Wales *pop* 1,700 (1972 *est*)

**Saint-Denis** commune ✳ of Réunion I *pop* 104,603 (1974)

**Saint-Etienne** city SE *cen* France *pop* 221,775 (1980 *est*)

**Saint Gall 1** canton NE Switzerland *area* 2,080 *sq km* (800 *sq miles*), *pop* 384,475 (1981) **2** commune, its ✳ *pop* 75,847 (1980)

**Saint George's** town ✳ of Grenada *pop* 7,500 (1980)

**Saint George's channel** strait British Isles between SW Wales & Ireland extending for 160 *km* (100 *miles*)

**Saint Gotthard, Saint Gothard,** G **Sankt Gotthard 1** mountains Switzerland in Lepontine Alps between Uri & Ticino cantons **2** mountain pass 2,109 *m* (6,916 *ft*) in St Gotthard range

**Saint Helena** island S Atlantic; a Brit colony ✳ Jamestown *area* 122 *sq miles* (47 *sq miles*), *pop* 5,146 (1976)

**Saint Helens** borough NW England in Merseyside ENE of Liverpool *pop* 104,341 (1971)

**Saint Johns** town Brit West Indies ✳ Antigua on Antigua I *pop* 22,000 (1981)

**Saint Kilda** island group Western Isles, Scotland 80 *km* (50 *miles*) W of Harris

**Saint Kitts, Saint Christopher** island Brit West Indies in the Leewards; chief town Basseterre *area* 176 *sq km* (68 *sq miles*), *pop* 35,000 (1981 *est*); with Nevis, forms **Saint Kitts-Nevis** Associated State ✳ Basseterre *area* 352 *sq km* (136 *sq miles*), *pop* 52,020

**Saint Lawrence 1** river *ab* 1,046 *km* (650 *miles*) long E Canada in Ontario & Quebec bordering on the USA in New York, flowing from Lake Ontario NE into the Atlantic, & forming at its mouth a wide bay (the **Gulf of Saint Lawrence**) **2** seaway Canada & USA in & along the St Lawrence between Lake Ontario & Montreal 217 *km* (135 *miles*) long

**Saint Lucia** island Brit West Indies in the Windwards S of Martinique; an Associated State ✳ Castries *area* 603 *sq km* (233 *sq miles*), *pop* 120,300 (1980 *est*)

**Saint Paul** city E Minnesota, its ✳ *pop* 270,230 (1980) – **Saint Paulite** *n*

**Saint Petersburg** – see LENINGRAD

**Saint Pierre** island in the Atlantic off S Newfoundland; with nearby island of Miquelon and others, constitutes French territory of **Saint Pierre and Miquelon** ✳ St Pierre *area* 242 *sq km* (93 *sq miles*), *pop* 5,200 (1968)

**Saint Thomas** – see CHARLOTTE AMALIE

**Saint Vincent** island Brit West Indies in *cen* Windwards; with N Grenadines, constitutes an Associated State ✳ Kingstown *area* 389 *sq km* (150 *sq miles*), *pop* 119,942 (1979 *est*)

**Sakhalin,** *formerly* **Saghalien,** Jap **Karafuto** island USSR in Sea of Okhotsk N of Hokkaido; formerly (1905–45) divided bet Russia & Japan *area* 63,856 *sq km* (24,560 *sq miles*)

**Salé, Salli,** *formerly* **Sallee** city & port NW Morocco, N suburb of Rabat *pop* 75,799 (1971)

**Salem** city ✳ of Oregon on Williamette river *pop* 89,223 (1980)

**Salisbury, Harare** city ✳ of Zimbabwe *pop* 601,000 (1977)

**Salisbury Plain** plateau S England in Wiltshire NW of Salisbury *area ab* 775 *sq km* (300 *sq miles*)

**Salonika, Salonica, Thessalonica,** NGk **Thessaloniki, Saloniki** city & port N Greece in Macedonia region *pop* 557,360 (1971)

**Salop** county in W England; changed name from Shropshire 1974; *area* 3,490 *sq km* (1,347 *sq miles*), *pop* 381,000 (1981) **Salopian** *adj or n*

**Salt Lake City** city N Utah, its ✳ *pop* 163,033 (1980)

**Salzburg** city W Austria *pop* 128,845 (1971)

**Samoa,** *formerly* **Navigators** islands SW *cen* Pacific N of Tonga islands; divided at long 171°W into American, or Eastern, Samoa & Western Samoa *area* 2,842 *sq km* (1,097 *sq miles*), *pop* 146,650 (1971)

**San'a** city S Arabia ✳ of Yemen Arab Republic *pop* 277,817 (1981)

**San Domingo** – see HISPANIOLA

**Sandringham** village in Norfolk; Sandringham House is royal residence

**Sandwich** market town in Kent; one of Cinque Ports, on river Stour *pop* 4,467 (1971)

**San Francisco** city & port W California on **San Francisco Bay** & the Pacific *pop* 715,674 (1970) – **San Franciscan** *adj or n*

**San José** city *cen* Costa Rica, its ✳ *pop* 808,919 (1979)

**San Juan** city & port NE Puerto Rico, its ✳ *pop* 518,700 (1980)

**San Marino 1** country S Europe on Italian peninsula SSW of Rimini; a republic *area* 61 *sq km* (24 *sq miles*), *pop* 21,359 (1980) **2** town its ✳ – **San Marinese** *adj or n*

**San Salvador** city w *cen* El Salvador, its ✳ *pop* 425,119 (1980 *est*)

**Santa Cruz de Tenerife 1** province Spain comprising w Canary islands *area* 3,973 *sq km* (1,528 *sq miles*) **2** city & port, its ✳, on NE Tenerife I *pop* 151,361 (1970)

**Santa Fe** city ✳ of New Mexico *pop* 48,953 (1980) – **Santa Fean** *n*

**Santa Isabel** –see MALABO

**Santiago** city ✳ of Chile *pop* 4,000,000 (1979 *est*)

**Santo Domingo** city & port ✳ of Dominican Republic on Caribbean sea *pop* 1,550,739 (1981) – **Santo Domingan** *adj or n*

**Saône** river 480 *km* (300 *miles*), long E France flowing ssw into the Rhone

**São Tomé** island w Africa in Gulf of Guinea; with Principé I, forms the Republic (until 1975 a Portuguese territory) of **São Tomé and Principé** (✳São Tomé *area* 980 *sq km or* 377 *sq miles*, *pop* 82,000 (1981)) – **Sao Tomean** *adj or n*

**Sarajevo, Serajevo** city *cen* Yugoslavia ✳ of Bosnia and Herzegovina republic *pop* 447,000 (1981)

**Sarawak** country N Borneo bordering on S China sea; formerly a Brit colony, since 1963 a territory of Malaysia ✳ Kuching *area* 122,000 *sq km* (47,000 *sq miles*), *pop* 1,150,279 (1976 *est*)

**Sardinia, It Sardegna** island Italy s of Corsica; with surrounding smaller islands, constitutes a region of Italy ✳ Cagliari *area* 14,964 *sq km* (9,298 *sq miles*), *pop* 1,470,000 (1971)

**Sark** island in the English channel, one of the Channel islands; a dependency of Guernsey *area* 5 *sq km* (2 *sq miles*), *pop* 604 (1981)

**Saskatchewan 1** river 547 *km* (340 *miles*) long s *cen* Canada formed by confluence in *cen* Saskatchewan of two branches rising in the Rockies in Alta, the **North Saskatchewan** 1,223 *km* (760 *miles*) long & the **South Saskatchewan** 885 *km* (550 *miles*) long, & flowing E into Lake Winnipeg **2** province sw Canada ✳ Regina *area* 651,900 *sq km* (251,700 *sq miles*), *pop* 968,313 (1981) – **Saskatchewanian** *adj or n,* **Saskatchewaner** *n*

**Saudi Arabia** country sw Asia occupying most of Arabian peninsula; a kingdom, comprising former kingdoms of Nejd & Hejaz & principality of Asir ✳ Riyadh *area* 2,149,690 *sq km* (829,995 *sq miles*), *pop* 9,160,000 (1976 *est*) – **Saudi** *adj or n,* **Saudi Arabian** *adj or n*

**Scafell** mountain 964 *m* (3,162 *ft*) NW England in Cumbrians sw of Keswick; second highest peak in England

**Scafell Pike** mountain 978 *m* (3,210 *ft*) NW England in Cumbria NE of Scafell; highest in the Cumbrians & in England

**Scandinavia 1** peninsula N Europe occupied by Norway & Sweden **2** Denmark, Norway, Sweden, & sometimes also Iceland, the Faeroe islands, & Finland

**Scapa Flow** sea basin N Scotland in the Orkneys

**Scilly** island group sw England off Lands End comprising 140 islands ✳ Hugh Town (on St Mary's, largest island) *area* 16 *sq km* (6.3 *sq miles*), *pop* 2,428 (1971) – see CORNWALL – **Scillonian** *adj or n*

**Scotland** , L **Caledonia, ML Scotia** country N Great Britain; a division of United Kingdom of Great Britain & Northern Ireland ✳ Edinburgh *area* 78,764 *sq km* (30,411 *sq miles*), *pop* 5,117,000 (1981)

**Seattle** city & port w Washington, between Puget Sound & Lake Washington *pop* 530,831 (1970) – **Seattleite** *n*

**Sedgemoor** tract of moorland sw England in *cen* Somerset; scene of battle (1685)

**Seine** river 780 *km* (480 *miles*) long N France flowing NW into **Bay of the Seine** (inlet of English Channel)

**Selborne** village in Hampshire 8 *km* (5 *miles*) SSE of Aston; made famous by *The Natural History of Selborne* by Gilbert White (1789)

**Senegal 1** river *ab* 1,633 *km* (1,015 *miles*) long w Africa flowing from Fouta Djallon district NW & w into the Atlantic **2** country w Africa on the Atlantic; a republic of the French Community, formerly a territory of French West Africa ✳ Dakar *area* 197,000 *sq km* (76,000 *sq miles*), *pop* 5,377,000 (1978) – **Senegalese** *adj or n*

**Seoul, Kyongsong** city s Korea on Han river; formerly ✳ of Korea, since 1948 ✳ of s Korea *pop* 8,367,000 (1980)

**Severn 1** river 980 *km* (610 *miles*) long Canada in NW Ontario flowing NE into Hudson Bay **2** river 338 *km* (210 *miles*) long

Great Britain flowing from E *cen* Wales into Bristol Channel in England

**Seville, Sp Sevilla 1** province sw Spain *area* 14,001 *sq km* (5,406 *sq miles*), *pop* 1,327,190 (1970) **2** city, its ✳ *pop* 546,000 (1970)

**Seychelles** island group w Indian ocean NE of Madagascar; formerly a Brit colony, a republic in Brit commonwealth since 1976 ✳ Victoria (on Mahe I) *area* 278 *sq km* (107 *sq miles*), *pop* 64,303 (1980 *est*) – **Seychellois** *adj or n*

**Shanghai** municipality & port E China in SE Kiangsu province on the Hwang Pu river near the Yangtze estuary *pop* 11,320,000 (1980)

**Shannon** river 370 *km* (230 *miles*) long w Ireland flowing s & w into the Atlantic

**Sharjah 1** sheikhdom United Arab Emirates *area* 2,667 *sq km* (1,000 *sq miles*), *pop* 120,000 (1980 *est*) **2** city, its ✳

**Shatt-al-Arab** river 193 *km* (120 *miles*) SE Iraq formed by the Tigris & the Euphrates & flowing SE into Persian Gulf

**Sheffield** city N England in S Yorkshire *pop* 520,327 (1971)

**Shenyang** –see MUKDEN

**Sherwood Forest** ancient royal forest *cen* England chiefly in Nottinghamshire

**Shetland 1** islands N Scotland NE of the Orkneys **2 Shetland, Zetland** country comprising the Shetlands ✳ Lerwick (on Mainland I) *area* 1,424 *sq km* (550 *sq miles*), *pop* 25,812 (1981) – **Shetlander** *n*

**Shikoku** island s Japan E of Kyushu *area* 18,840 *sq km* (7,246 *sq miles*)

**Shropshire** – see SALOP

**Siam** – see THAILAND

**Sicily, It Sicilia,** *anc* **Sicilia, Trinacria** island s Italy in the Mediterranean; a region ✳ Palermo *area* 25,709 *sq km* (9,926 *sq miles*), *pop* 4,667,315 (1971) – **Sicilian** *adj or n*

**Sidi-bel-Abbès** town NW Algeria s of Oran *pop* 105,000 (1970)

**Sierra Leone** country w Africa on the Atlantic; a dominion of Brit Commonwealth ✳ Freetown *area* 72,325 *sq km* (27,925 *sq miles*), *pop* 14,600,000 (1981) – **Sierra Leonean** *adj or n*

**Sierra Nevada 1** mountain range E California – see WHITNEY (Mount) **2** mountain range s Spain; highest peak Mulhacén 3,478 *m* (11,411 *ft*)

**Simla** city N India N of Delhi ✳ of Himachal Pradesh state & former summer ✳ of India *pop* 45,000 (1971)

**Simplon 1** mountain pass 2,005 *m* (6,578 *ft*) in Lepontine Alps between Switzerland & Italy in Valais canton & Piedmont region **2** tunnel *ab* 19 *km* (12 *miles*) long through Monte Leone near the pass

**Sinai 1** peninsula extension of continent of Asia NE Egypt between Red sea & the Mediterranean **2** – see HOREB – **Sinaitic** *adj*

**Singapore 1** island Malay archipelago in S China sea off s end of Malay peninsula; formerly a Brit crown colony, from 1963 to 1965 a state of Federation of Malaysia, an independent republic in Brit Commonwealth since 1965, *area* 585 *sq km* (225 *sq miles*), *pop* 2,362,700 (1980) **2** city & port, its ✳, on Singapore Strait *pop* 2,074,507 (1977 *est*) – **Singaporean** *adj or n*

**Skagerrak** arm of the North sea bet Norway & Denmark

**Skelmersdale** town in Lancashire; developed as "new town" 1962; *pop* 41,300 (1981)

**Skiddaw** mountain 930 *m* (3,054 *ft*) NW England in NW *cen* Cumbria

**Skoplje, Skopje, Turk Uskub** city s Yugoslavia ✳ of Macedonia region on Vardar river *pop* 503,000 (1981)

**Skye** island Scotland, one of the Inner Hebrides *area* 1,665 *sq km* (643 *sq miles*), *pop* 7,372 (1971)

**Slough** town in Berkshire *pop* 101,580 (1974 *est*)

**Smyrna** –see IZMIR

**Snowdon** mountain 1,085 *m* (3,560 *ft*) NW Wales in Gwynedd; highest point in Wales

**Snowdonia** mountain region NW Wales around Snowdon

**Snowy 1** mountains SE Australia in SE New South Wales **2** river *ab* 435 *km* (270 *miles*) long SE Australia flowing from Snowy mountains to the Pacific in SE Victoria

**Society Islands, F Îles de la Société** islands s Pacific belonging to France ✳ Papeete (on Tahiti) *area* 1,690 *sq km* (650 *sq miles*), *pop* 81,424 (1981)

**Sofia, Bulg Sofiya,** *anc* **Serdica, Sardica** city ✳ of Bulgaria *pop* 1,056,945 (1980)

**Soho** district of *cen* London in Westminster

**Solent, The** channel s England between Isle of Wight & the mainland *ab* 24 *km* (15 *miles*) long

**Solihull** borough *cen* England in West Midlands SE of Birmingham *pop* 107,095 (1971)

**Solingen** city w Germany in the Ruhr valley ESE of Düsseldorf *pop* 166,100 (1980)

**Solomon 1** islands w Pacific E of New Guinea divided between Papua New Guinea & the Brit Solomon islands *area* 10,600 *sq km* (4,100 *sq miles*), *pop* 196,823 (1976) **2** sea arm of Coral sea w of Solomon islands

**Somalia, Somali Republic** E Africa bordering on Gulf of Aden & Indian ocean; formed 1960 by union of Brit Somaliland & Italian Somaliland ✳ Mogadishu *area* 638,000 *sq km* (246,300 *sq miles*), *pop* 4,000,000 (1981 *est*) – **Somalian** *adj or n*

**Somerset** county in sw England *area* 3,450 *sq km* (1,332 *sq miles*), *pop* 427,200 (1981)

**Somme** river 236 *km* (147 *miles*) N France flowing NW into the English channel

**South** island s New Zealand *area* 151,039 *sq km* (58,092 *sq miles*), *pop* 852,748 (1981)

**South Africa, Republic of** country s Africa s of the Limpopo, Molopo, & Orange rivers bordering on Atlantic & Indian oceans; a republic, until 1961 (as **Union of South Africa**) a Brit dominion; administrative ✳ Pretoria, legislative ✳ Cape Town, judicial ✳ Bloemfontein *area* 1,221,037 *sq km* (471,445 *sq miles*), *pop* 23,894,000 (1978 *est*)

**South America** continent of the western hemisphere lying between the Atlantic & Pacific oceans SE of North America & chiefly s of the equator *area* 17,805,200 *sq km* (6,874,600 *sq miles*) – **South American** *adj or n*

**Southampton** city & port s England in Hampshire on **Southampton Water** (estuary of Test river) *pop* 215,118 (1971)

**South Arabia, Federation of** – see YEMEN

**South Australia** state s Australia ✳ Adelaide *area* 984,375 *sq km* (380,070 *sq miles*), *pop* 1,319,300 (1981)

**South Carolina** state SE USA ✳ Columbia *area* 80,743 *sq km* (31,055 *sq miles*), *pop* 3,119,208 (1980) – **South Carolinian** *adj or n*

**South Dakota** state NW *cen* USA ✳ Pierre *area* 200,322 *sq km* (77,047 *sq miles*), *pop* 690,178 (1980) – **South Dakotan** *adj or n*

**South Glamorgan** county in s Wales on Bristol Channel formed in 1974 from parts of former counties of Glamorganshire and Monmouthshire *area* 416 *sq km* (161 *sq miles*), *pop* 391,600 (1981)

**South-West Africa** –see NAMIBIA

**South Yorkshire** county in N England formed in 1974 from part of the W Riding of Yorkshire *area* 1,562 *sq km* (603 *sq miles*), *pop* 1,300,900 (1981)

**Soviet Union** – see UNION OF SOVIET SOCIALIST REPUBLICS

**Spain, Sp España** country sw Europe in the Iberian peninsula; a kingdom ✳ Madrid *area* 503,556 *sq km* (194,424 *sq miles*), *pop* 37,682,355 (1981)

**Spanish Guinea** –see EQUATORIAL GUINEA

**Spice** –see MOLUCCAS

**Spitsbergen** group of islands in Arctic ocean N of Norway; belongs to Norway *area* 62,050 *sq km* (29,958 *sq miles*) –see SVALBARD

**Split, Spljet,** It **Spalato** city & port w Yugoslavia in Croatia on Dalmatian coast *pop* 152,000 (1981)

**Springfield** city ✳ of Illinois on the Sangamon river *pop* 99,637 (1980)

**Sri Lanka,** *formerly* **Ceylon** country coextensive with island of Ceylon; an independent republic in Brit Commonwealth ✳ Colombo *area* 65,600 *sq km* (25,332 *sq miles*), *pop* 14,800,001 (1981) – **Sri Lankan** *adj or n*

**Staffa** islet w Scotland in the Inner Hebrides w of Mull – see FINGAL'S CAVE

**Staffordshire** county in w *cen* England *area* 2,716 *sq km* (1,049 *sq miles*), *pop* 1,019,700 (1981)

**St Albans** town in Hertfordshire *pop* 52,174 (1971)

**Stalinabad** –see DUSHANBE

**Stalin Peak** –see GARMO PEAK

**Stanley, Port Stanley** town ✳ of the Falklands *pop* 1,050 (1980)

**St Austell** market town in Cornwall *pop* 30,000 (1972 *est*)

**Stavanger** city sw Norway *pop* 91,021 (1981)

**Stevenage** town in Hertfordshire; developed as "new town" 1946; *pop* 73,000 (1981)

**Stewart** island New Zealand s of South I *area* 1,742 *sq km* (670 *sq miles*), *pop* 600 (1981)

**Stirling** burgh *cen* Scotland ✳ of Central region *pop* 29,769 (1971)

**Stockholm** city & port ✳ of Sweden on Lake Malar *pop* 647,214 (1980) Greater Stockholm 1,386,980 (1980) – **Stockholmer** *n*

**Stockport** town in Greater Manchester on river Mersey *pop* 139,633 (1971)

**Stockton-on-Tees** town in Cleveland 8 *km* (5 *miles*) above mouth of river Tees *pop* 162,580 (1974 *est*)

**Stoke Newington** former metropolitan borough N London, now part of Hackney

**Stoke-on-Trent** city in Staffordshire *pop* 265,256 (1971)

**Stonehenge** assemblage of megaliths s England in Wiltshire on Salisbury Plain erected by a prehistoric people

**Stormont** E suburb of Belfast, Northern Ireland; site of Parliament House of Northern Ireland

**Stornoway** town and fishing port of Outer Hebrides on E coast of Lewis, region of Western Isles, Scotland *pop* 5,266 (1971)

**Stour 1** English river 76 *km* (47 *miles*) long flowing E along Essex and Suffolk border into North sea at Harwich **2** English river 88 *km* (55 *miles*) long in Dorset and Hampshire flowing SE to join river Avon near Christchurch **3 Stour, Great Stour** English river 64 *km* (40 *miles*) long in Kent flowing NE into the North sea **4** English river 32 *km* (20 *miles*) long in Oxfordshire and Warwickshire flowing into river Avon **5** English river 32 *km* (20 *miles*) long in Staffordshire and Hereford and Worcester flowing s to join river Severn at Stourport-on-Severn

**Strasbourg, G Strassburg** city NE France on Ill river *pop* 257,303 (1980 *est*)

**Stratford-upon-Avon** market town in Warwickshire; birthplace of William Shakespeare *pop* 19,449 (1971)

**Strathclyde 1** Celtic kingdom of 6th to 11th centuries s Scotland & NW England ✳ Dumbarton; its s part called **Cumbria 2** region of Scotland created in 1975 from counties of Ayrshire, Bute, Dumbartonshire, Lanarkshire and Renfrewshire and parts of Argyll and Stirlingshire *area* 13,727 *sq km* (5,300 *sq miles*), *pop* 2,400,000 (1981)

**Stromboli,** *anc* **Strongyle 1** island Italy in Lipari islands **2** volcano 926 *km* (3,038 *ft*) on the island

**Stuttgart** city w Germany ✳ of Baden-Württemberg state on the Neckar river *pop* 580,600 (1980)

**Sucre** city, constitutional ✳ of Bolivia, SE of La Paz *pop* 63,000 (1976)

**Sudan, F Soudan 1** region N Africa between the Atlantic & the upper Nile s of the Sahara including basins of Lake Chad & the Niger & upper Nile **2** country NE Africa s of Egypt; a republic, until 1956 a territory (**Anglo-Egyptian Sudan**) under joint Brit & Egyptian rule ✳ Khartoum *area* 2,505,805 *sq km* (967,500 *sq miles*), *pop* 19,500,000 (1981 *est*) – **Sudanese** *adj or n*

**Sudanese Republic** –see MALI

**Suez 1** city & port NE Egypt at s end of Suez canal on **Gulf of Suez** (arm of Red sea) *pop* 368,000 (1974) **2** canal 148 *km* (92 *miles*) long NE Egypt traversing Isthmus of Suez & connecting Mediterranean and Red seas

**Suffolk** county in E England *area* 3,807 *sq km* (1,470 *sq miles*), *pop* 608,400 (1981)

**Sugarloaf Mountain** – see PAO DE ACUCAR

**Sulawesi** –see CELEBES

**Sulu 1** archipelago sw Philippines sw of Mindanao **2** sea w Philippines N of Celebes sea

**Sumatra** island w Indonesia s of Malay peninsula *area* 427,350 *sq km* (165,000 *sq miles*), *pop* 20,812,700 (1971) – **Sumatran** *adj or n*

**Sunderland** borough N England in Tyne and Wear on North sea at mouth of the Wear *pop* 217,079 (1971)

**Superior, Lake** lake USA & Canada; largest, northernmost, & westernmost of the Great Lakes *area* 82,475 *sq km* (31,820 *sq miles*)

**Surabaja, D Soerabaja** city & port Indonesia in NE Java on **Surabaja strait** (between Java & w end of Madura) *pop* 1,600,000 (1971)

**Surinam,** *formerly* **Dutch Guiana, Netherlands Guiana** country N South America bet Guyana & French Guiana; a republic, until 1975 territory of the Netherlands ✳ Paramaribo *area* 143,369 *sq km* (55,142 *sq miles*), *pop* 375,000 (1981) – **Surinamese** *adj or n*

**Surrey** county in SE England *area* 1,679 *sq km* (648 *sq miles*), *pop* 1,008,500 (1981)

**Sutherland Falls** waterfall 580 *m* (1,904 *ft*) New Zealand in sw South I

**Suva** city & port ✳ of Fiji, on Viti Levu I *pop* 66,018 (1980)

**Svalbard** islands in the Arctic ocean including Spitsbergen, Bear I, & other small islands *area* 65,000 *sq km* (25,000 *sq miles*) under Norwegian administration

**Swansea** city and port in W Glamorgan, Wales *pop* 186,589 (1981)

**Swaziland** country SE Africa N of Natal between Transvaal & Mozambique; a former Brit protectorate, an independent kingdom since 1968 ✳ Mbabane *area* 17,366 *sq km* (6,705 *sq miles*), *pop* 600,000 (1981 *est*) – **Swazi** *adj or n*

**Sweden,** Swed **Sverige** country N Europe on Scandinavian peninsula w of Baltic sea; a kingdom ✳ Stockholm *area* 449,700 *sq km* (173,629 *sq miles*), *pop* 8,318,000 (1980)

**Switzerland,** F **Suisse,** G **Schweiz,** It **Svizzera,** L **Helvetia** country w Europe in the Alps; a federal republic ✳ Bern *area* 41,288 *sq km* (15,940 *sq miles*), *pop* 6,365,900 (1979 *est*)

**Sydney** city & port SE Australia on Port Jackson ✳ of New South Wales *pop* (with suburbs) 3,204,211 (1982) – **Sydneyite** *n*

**Syria 1** ancient region sw Asia bordering on the Mediterranean & covering modern Syria, Lebanon, Israel, & Jordan **2** former French mandate (1920–44) comprising the **Levant States** (Syria, Lebanon, Latakia, & Jebel ed Druz), administrative ✳ Beirut, legislative ✳ Damascus *area* 196,916 *sq km* (76,030 *sq miles*) **3 Syria, Syrian Arab Republic** country sw Asia bordering on the Mediterranean; a republic 1944–58 & since 1961; a province of United Arab Republic 1958–61 ✳ Damascus *area* 186,000 *sq km* (72,000 *sq miles*), *pop* 9,622,632 (1979) – **Syrian** *adj or n*

**Syrian** desert w Asia between Mediterranean coast & the Euphrates covering N Saudi Arabia, NE Jordan, SE Syria, & w Iraq

**Szczecin** city & port NW Poland on the Oder near its mouth *pop* 376,400 (1976)


# T

**Table Mountain** mountain highest point 1,086 *m* (3,567 *ft*) Republic of South Africa s of Cape Town

**Taegu** city SE South Korea NNW of Pusan *pop* 1,607,000 (1980)

**Tahiti** island s Pacific in Windward group of the Society Islands; chief town Papeete *area* 1,040 *sq km* (402 *sq miles*), *pop* 79,494 (1971)

**Taipei** city ✳ of (Nationalist) China on Taiwan *pop* 2,196,237 (1979)

**Taiwan** island China off SE coast E of Fukien; belonged to Japan 1895–1945; since 1949 seat of (Nationalist) Republic of China (✳ Taipei) *area* 35,981 *sq km* (13,892 *sq miles*), *pop* 18,203,000 (1982) – **Taiwanese** *adj or n*

**Tallahassee** city ✳ of Florida *pop* 81,548 (1980)

**Tallinn,** *formerly* **Reval, Revel** city & port USSR ✳ of Estonia *pop* 430,000 (1979)

**Tamil Nadu,** *formerly* **Madras** state SE India bordering on Bay of Bengal ✳ Madras *area* 129,785 *sq km* (50,110 *sq miles*)

**Tananarive** –see ANTANANARIVO

**Tanganyika, Lake** lake E Africa in Great Rift valley between Zaire & Tanzania *area* 32,892 *sq km* (12,700 *sq miles*)

**Tangier, Tangiers,** Sp **Tánger** city & port N Morocco on Strait of Gibraltar; summer ✳ of Morocco *pop* 377,600 (1979) – **Tangerine** *adj or n*

**Tanzania** republic E Africa formed 1964 by union of Tanganyika & Zanzibar ✳ Dar es Salaam *area* 945,087 *sq km* (364,898 *sq miles*), *pop* 17,551,925 (1978) – **Tanzanian** *adj or n*

**Tarawa** island *cen* Pacific ✳ of Kiribati *area* 21 *sq km* (8 *sq miles*), *pop* 20,000 (1978 *est*)

**Tashkent** city USSR in Soviet Central Asia E of the Syr Darya ✳ of Uzbek Republic *pop* 1,780,000 (1979)

**Tasman** sea comprising the part of the s Pacific between SE Australia & w New Zealand

**Tasmania,** *formerly* **Van Diemen's Land** island SE Australia s of Victoria; a state ✳ Hobart *area* 68,332 *sq km* (26,383 *sq miles*), *pop* 427,300 (1981) – **Tasmanian** *adj or n*

**Tay** river 193 *km* (120 *miles*) long E *cen* Scotland flowing into North sea through **Firth of Tay** (estuary 40 *km* (25 *miles*) long)

**Tayside** region in N *cen* and E Scotland created in 1975 from former counties of Angus, Kinross and most of Perth ✳ Dundee *area* 7,665 *sq km* (2,959 *sq miles*), *pop* 391,529 (1981)

**Tbilisi, Tiflis** city USSR ✳ of Georgia on the Kura *pop* 1,066,000 (1979)

**Tees** river 110 *km* (70 *miles*) long N England flowing E into North sea near Middlesbrough

**Tegucigalpa** city ✳ of Honduras *pop* 472,700 (1980 *est*)

**Tehran, Teheran** city ✳ of Iran at foot of s slope of Elburz mountains *pop* 6,200,000 (1982 *est*)

**Tel Aviv** city w Israel *pop* (with district) 1,005,000 (1980 *est*)

**Telford** town in Salop; developed as "new town" 1963; *pop* 105,000 (1981)

**Tenerife,** *formerly* **Teneriffe** island Spain, largest of the Canary islands; chief town Santa Cruz de Tenerife *area* 2,059 *sq km* (795 *sq miles*)

**Tengri Khan, Khan Tengri** mountain 6,995 *m* (22,949 *ft*) on border between Kirgiz Republic (USSR) & Sinkiang (China) in Tien Shan

**Tennessee** state SE *cen* USA ✳ Nashville *area* 109,834 *sq km* (42,244 *sq miles*), *pop* 4,590,750 (1980) – **Tennessean, Tennesseean** *adj or n*

**Texas** state s USA ✳ Austin *area* 695,081 *sq km* (267,339 *sq miles*), *pop* 14,228,383 (1980) – **Texan** *adj or n*

**Thailand,** *formerly* **Siam** country SE Asia of Gulf of Siam; a kingdom ✳ Bangkok *area* 514,000 *sq km* (198,250 *sq miles*), *pop* 47,600,000 (1980 *est*) – **Thailander** *n*

**Thames** river 339 *km* (209 *miles*) long s England flowing from the Cotswolds in Gloucestershire E into the North sea – see ISIS

**Thanet, Isle of** tract of land SE England in NE Kent cut off from mainland by arms of Stour river *area* 103 *sq km* (40 *sq miles*)

**The Hague** – see HAGUE (The)

**Thessalonica** –see SALONIKA

**Thimbu, Thimphu** city w *cen* Bhutan, its ✳

**Thorshavn, Tórshavn** town & port ✳ of the Faeroe islands, on Strömö I

**Thun, Lake of,** G **Thunersee** lake 16 *km* (10 *miles*) long *cen* Switzerland; an expansion of the Aare river

**Tiber,** It **Tevere** river 405 *km* (252 *miles*) long *cen* Italy flowing through Rome into Tyrrhenian sea

**Tierra del Fuego 1** archipelago off s South America s of Strait of Magellan; in Argentina & Chile *area* 71,760 *sq km* (27,600 *sq miles*) **2** chief island of the archipelago; divided bet Chile and Argentina *area* 48,178 *sq km* (18,530 *sq miles*)

**Tiflis** –see TBILISI

**Tigris** river 1,900 *km* (1,180 *miles*) long Iraq & SE Turkey flowing sse & uniting with the Euphrates to form the Shatt-al-Arab

**Tilburg** commune s Netherlands SE Rotterdam *pop* 213,502 (1978)

**Timor 1** island E Indonesia in Lesser Sunda islands *area* 33,857 *sq km* (13,074 *sq miles*), *pop* 3,000,000 (1970 *est*); w part (formerly **Netherlands Timor**) belonged to the Dutch until 1946, E part (formerly **Portuguese Timor**) to Portugal until 1975 **2** sea between Timor I & Australia – **Timorese** *n*

**Tirane, Tirana** city ✳ of Albania *pop* 200,000 (1980)

**Tirol, Tyrol,** It **Tirolo** region Europe in E Alps chiefly in Austria; the section s of Brenner pass has belonged since 1919 to Italy – **Tirolean** *adj or n,* **Tirolese** *adj or n*

**Tobago** island SE West Indies, a territory of Trinidad and Tobago; chief town Scarborough *area* 300 *sq km* (116 *sq miles*), *pop* 40,950 (1978 *est*) – **Tobagan** *adj or n*

**Tobruk** city & port NE Libya *pop* 28,000 (1970 *est*)

**Tocantins** river 2,736 *km* (1,700 *miles*) long E *cen* & NE Brazil rising in s *cen* Goiás & flowing N into Pará river

**Togo, Togoland 1** region w Africa on Gulf of Guinea between Benin & Ghana; until 1919 a German protectorate, then divided into two trust territories: **British Togoland** (in w, since 1957 part of Ghana) & **French Togo** (in E, since 1958 the Republic of Togo) **2** republic w Africa ✳ Lomé *area* 56,000 *sq km* (21,850 *sq miles*), *pop* 2,348,000 (1977) – **Togolese** *adj or n*, **Togolander** *n*

**Tokelau** islands *cen* Pacific N of Samoa belonging to New Zealand – **Tokelauan** *n*

**Tokyo,** *formerly* **Edo, Yedo** city ✳ of Japan in SE Honshu on **Tokyo Bay** (inlet of the Pacific) *pop* 11,648,378 (1982) – **Tokyoite** *n*

**Tonga, Friendly** islands sw Pacific E of Fiji islands; a kingdom in Brit Commonwealth ✳ Nukualofa *area* 700 *sq km* (270 *sq miles*), *pop* 98,000 (1981 *est*)

**Tongariro** volcano 1,968 *m* (6,458 *ft*) New Zealand in *cen* North I in **Tongariro National Park**

**Torbay** district in s Devon, created 1968 by union of Paignton, Torquay and Brixham *pop* 108,700 (1974 *est*)

**Toronto** city & port Canada ✳ of Ontario on Lake Ontario *pop* 2,131,159 (1981) – **Torontonian** *adj or n*

**Torrens, Lake** salt lake Australia in E South Australia N of Spencer Gulf; *area* 5,776 *sq km* (2,230 *sq miles*)

**Tórshavn** –see THORSHAVN

**Toulon** commune & port SE France on the Garonne *pop* 185,050 (1980 *est*)

**Toulouse** city sw France on the Garonne *pop* 383,176 (1980 *est*)

**Transjordan** –see JORDAN

**Trent 1** river 270 *km* (170 *miles*) long *cen* England flowing NNE & uniting with the Ouse to form the Humber **2 Trent, Trento,** G **Trient,** *anc* **Tridentum** town N Italy ✳ of Trentino-Alto Adige region on Adige river *pop* 88,544 (1970)

**Trenton** city ✳ of New Jersey on Delaware river *pop* 92,124 (1980)

**Trieste,** G **Triest,** Serbo-Croatian **Trist** city & port NE Italy on **Gulf of Trieste** (inlet at head of the Adriatic NW of the Istrian peninsula) *pop* 267,857 (1976); once belonged to Austria; part of Italy 1919–47; in 1947 made with surrounding territory the **Free Territory of Trieste** under administration of the United Nations; city with N part of Free Territory returned to Italy 1953, s part of territory having previously been absorbed into Yugoslavia – **Triestine** *adj*

**Trinidad** island SE West Indies off coast of NE Venezuela; with Tobago, a dominion (**Trinidad and Tobago**) of Brit Commonwealth since 1962; formerly a Brit colony ✳ Port of Spain *area* 4,828 *sq km* (1,864 *sq miles*), *pop* 1,136,900 (1978 *est*) – **Trinidadian** *adj or n*

**Tripoli,** Ar **Tarabulus 1 Tripoli,** *anc* **Oea** city & port NW Libya a ✳ of Libya *pop* 837,169 (1976) **2 Tripoli,** *anc* **Tripolis** city & port NW Lebanon *pop* 175,000 (1981) – **Tripolitan** *adj or n*

**Tristan da Cunha** island s Atlantic, chief of the Tristan da Cunha islands attached to Brit colony of St Helena *area* 98 *sq km* (38 *sq miles*); volcanic eruptions 1961

**Trondheim** city & port *cen* Norway on **Trondheim Fjord** (129 *km or* 80 *miles* long), *pop* 134,690 (1980)

**Trucial States, Trucial Oman** –see UNITED ARAB EMIRATES

**Tunis 1** city ✳ of Tunisia near site of ancient Carthage *pop* 1,133,000 (1981 *est*) **2** –see TUNISIA – used esp of the former Barbary state

**Tunisia** country N Africa bordering on the Mediterranean; formerly one of the Barbary states; a French protectorate 1881–1956, a monarchy 1956–57, & a republic since 1957 ✳ Tunis *area* 164,150 *sq km* (63,376 *sq miles*), *pop* 6,520,000 (1981 *est*) – **Tunisian** *adj or n*

**Turin ,** It **Torino** town NW Italy on the Po ✳ of Piedmont region *pop* 1,103,520 (1980 *est*) – **Turinese** *adj or n*

**Turkey** country w Asia (**Turkey in Asia**) & SE Europe (**Turkey in Europe**) between Mediterranean & Black seas; formerly centre of an empire ( ✳ Constantinople), since 1923 a republic ✳ Ankara *area* 779,452 *sq km* (300,947 *sq miles*), *pop* 45,217,556 (1980) – see OTTOMAN EMPIRE

**Turks and Caicos** two groups of islands (Turks islands and Caicos islands) Brit West Indies at SE end the Bahamas; a Brit colony; seat of government Grand Turk on **Grand Turk** island

(11 *km or* 7 *miles* long) *area* 432 *sq km* (166 *sq miles*), *pop* 7,436 (1981)

**Tuvalu,** *formerly* **Ellice** islands w Pacific N of Fiji; a Brit territory 1976–78; became an independent member of the Commonwealth 1978 ✳ Funafuti *area* 23 *sq km* (9 *sq miles*), *pop* 7,349 (1979) – **Tuvalese** *adj or n*

**Tweed** river 155 *km* (96 *miles*) long SE Scotland & NE England flowing E into North sea

**Tyne** river 48 *km* (30 *miles*) long N England flowing E into North sea

**Tyne and Wear** county in NE England formed in 1974 from parts of former counties of Northumberland and Durham and including former county borough of Newcastle- upon-Tyne *area* 540 *sq km* (208 *sq miles*), *pop* 1,130,432 (1981)

**Tyrol** –see TIROL

**Tyrone** county w *cen* Northern Ireland ✳ Omagh *area* 3,155 *sq km* (1,218 *sq miles*), *pop* 139,075 (1971)

# U

**Uganda** republic E Africa N of Lake Victoria; member of Brit Commonwealth ✳ Kampala *area* 236,000 *sq km* (93,981 *sq miles*), *pop* 12,600,000 (1980 *est*) – **Ugandan** *adj or n*

**Ulan Bator,** *formerly* **Urga** city N *cen* Mongolia (republic), its ✳ *pop* 420,000 (1981)

**Ullswater** lake 12 *km* (7 *miles*) long NW England in Cumbria

**Ulster 1** region N Ireland comprising Northern Ireland & N Republic of Ireland; ancient kingdom, later a province comprising nine counties three of which in 1921 joined Irish Free State (now Republic of Ireland) while the rest remained with United Kingdom **2** province N Republic of Ireland comprising counties Cavan, Donegal, & Monaghan *area* 8,010 *sq km* (3,093 *sq miles*), *pop* 208,283 (1971) **3** Northern Ireland comprising counties Antrim, Armagh, Down, Fermanagh, Londonderry, & Tyrone ✳ Belfast

**Umm al Qaiwain** sheikhdom United Arab Emirates *area* 800 *sq km* (300 *sq miles*), *pop* 25,000 (1980 *est*)

**Union of South Africa** – see SOUTH AFRICA (Republic of)

**Union of Soviet Socialist Republics, Soviet Union** country E Europe & N Asia bordering on the Arctic & Pacific oceans & Baltic & Black seas; a union of 15 constituent republics ✳ Moscow *area* 22,400,000 *sq km* (8,650,000 *sq miles*), *pop* 268,800,000 (1982)

**United Arab Emirates,** *formerly* **Trucial States** *or* **Trucial Oman** country NE Arabia on Persian Gulf between Qatar & Oman; a republic composed of seven sheikhdoms (Abu Dhabi, Ajman, Dubai, Fujaira, Ras al Khaima, Sharja, & Umm al Qaiwan) formerly under Brit protection ✳ Abu Dhabi *area* 92,100 *sq km* (32,300 *sq miles*), *pop* 1,000,000 (1980 *est*)

**United Kingdom 1 United Kingdom, United Kingdom of Great Britain and Northern Ireland** country w Europe in British Isles comprising Great Britain & Northern Ireland ✳ London *area* 230,609 *sq km* (89,038 *sq miles*), *pop* 55,576,000 (1981) **2 United Kingdom, United Kingdom of Great Britain and Ireland** country 1801–1921 comprising Great Britain & all of Ireland

**United States of America, United States 1** country North America bordering on Atlantic, Pacific, & Arctic oceans; a federal republic ✳ Washington *area* 9,363,123 *sq km* (3,614,343 *sq miles*), *pop* 226,074,825 (1980) **2** the United States of America with dependencies & possessions

**Upolu** island South Pacific in Western Samoa

**Upper Volta,** F **Haute-Volta** country w Africa N of Ivory Coast, Ghana & Togo; a republic; until 1958 a French territory ✳ Ouagadougou *area* 274,200 *sq km* (105,869 *sq miles*), *pop* 6,600,000 (1979 *est*) – **Upper Voltan** *adj or n*

**Uppsala, Upsala** city E Sweden NW of Stockholm *pop* 146,192 (1980)

**Ural 1** river 2,428 *km* (1,509 *miles*) long USSR rising at s end of Ural mountains & flowing s into the Caspian **2** mountain system USSR extending from Kara sea to steppes N of Lake Aral; usu considered the dividing line between Asia & Europe; highest point Narodnaya 2,799 *m* (6,182 *ft*)

**Urga** –see ULAN BATOR

**Uruguay 1** river *ab* 1,600 *km* (1,000 *miles*) long SE South America rising in Brazil & flowing into the Río de la Plata **2 Uruguay, República Oriental del Uruguay** country SE South America between the lower Uruguay & the Atlantic; a republic ✳ Montevideo *area* 186,926 *sq km* (72,172 *sq miles*), *pop* 2,886,187 (1979 *est*) – **Uruguayan** *adj or n*

**Urundi** –see BURUNDI

**Usk** river *ab* 113 *km* (70 *miles*) long s Wales & w England flowing E & s into Severn estuary

**Usumbura** –see BUJUMBURA

**Utah** state w USA ✳ Salt Lake City *area* 220,782 *sq km* (84,916 *sq miles*), *pop* 1,461,037 (1980) – **Utahn** *n*

**Utrecht** city *cen* Netherlands ✳ *pop* 471,897 (1978)

# V

**Vaduz** commune ✳ of Liechtenstein on the upper Rhine *pop* 4,980 (1981)

**Valletta, Valetta** city & port ✳ of Malta *pop* 14,042 (1979 *est*)

**Valparaiso,** Sp **Valparaíso** city & port *cen* Chile WNW of Santiago *pop* 500,000 (1979 *est*)

**Vancouver 1** island w Canada in British Columbia off sw coast; chief city Victoria *area* 32,136 *sq km* (12,408 *sq miles*) **2** city & port Canada in sw British Columbia on Burrard Inlet *pop* 410,188 (1976)

**Van Diemen's Land** – see TASMANIA

**Vanuatu,** *formerly* **New Hebrides** islands sw Pacific NE of New Caledonia & w of Fiji; formerly under joint Brit & French administration, a republic since 1980 ✳ Vila (on Efate) *area* 14,820 *sq km* (5,700 *sq miles*), *pop* 112,596 (1979) – **Vanuatuan** *adj or n*

**Västerås** city E Sweden on Lake Malar NW of Stockholm *pop* 117,487 (1980)

**Vatican City, Vatican City State,** It **Cittàdel Vaticano** independent papal state within town of Rome, Italy; created Feb 11, 1929 *area* 0.4 *sq km* (109 *acres*), *pop* 731 (1978)

**Venezuela** country N South America; a republic ✳ Caracas *area* 912,049 *sq km* (352,141 *sq miles*), *pop* 16,000,000 (1981 *est*) – **Venezuelan** *adj or n*

**Venice,** It **Venezia,** L **Venetia** city & port NE Italy ✳ of Veneto region, on islands in **Lagoon of Venice** (inlet of Gulf of Venice) *pop* 362,494 (1976) – **Venetian** *adj or n*

**Vermont** state NE USA ✳ Montpelier *area* 24,983 *sq km* (9,609 *sq miles*), *pop* 511,456 (1980) – **Vermonter** *n*

**Véroia ,** *anc* **Berea, Beroea** town NE Greece in Macedonia region w of Salonika

**Verona** town NE Italy on the Adige river *pop* 271,381 (1976) – **Veronese** *adj or n*

**Versailles** city N France, wsw suburb of Paris *pop* 94,915 (1973)

**Vesuvius,** It **Vesuvio** volcano 1,280 *m* (4,198 *ft*) Italy on Bay of Naples – **Vesuvian** *adj*

**Victoria 1** city Canada ✳ of British Columbia on SE Vancouver I *pop* 61,761 (1976) **2** island N Canada SE of Banks I *area* 212,198 *sq km* (81,930 *sq miles*) **3** river 563 *km* (350 *miles*) long Australia in NW Northern Territory flowing N & NW to Timor sea **4** state SE Australia ✳ Melbourne *area* 227,618 *sq km* (87,884 *sq miles*), *pop* 3,948,600 (1981) **5** lake E Africa in Tanganyika, Kenya, & Uganda *area* 69,484 *sq km* (26,828 *sq miles*) **6 Victoria, Hong Kong** city & port ✳ of Hong Kong colony on NW Hong Kong I *pop* 633,138 (1975 *est*) **7** town ✳ of Seychelles on NE of Mahé I *pop* 25,000 (1981) – **Victorian** *adj or n*

**Victoria Falls** waterfall 120 *m* (400 *ft*) high & 1,700 *m* (5,580 *ft*) wide s Africa on the Zambezi on border between Zambia & Rhodesia

**Vienna,** G **Wien** city ✳ of Austria on the Danube *pop* 1,580,600 (1981) – **Viennese** *adj or n*

**Vientiane** city ✳ of Laos, near Thailand border *pop* 90,000 (1978 *est*)

**Vietnam, Viet-Nam, Viet Nam** country SE Asia in Indochina; state, including Tonkin & N Annam, set up 1945–46; with s Annam & Cochin China, an associated state of French Union 1950–54; after civil war, divided 1954–1975 at 17th parallel into republics of **North Vietnam** (✳ Hanoi) & **South Vietnam** (✳ Saigon) reunited 1975 (✳ Hanoi) & renamed 1976 as **Socialist Republic of Vietnam** *area* 338,392 *sq km* (130,653 *sq miles*), *pop* 55,000,000 (1981 *est*)

**Vila** town & port ✳ of Vanuatu in sw Efate I *pop* 14,801 (1979)

**Vilnius** city USSR ✳ of Lithuania *pop* 481,000 (1979)

**Vinson Massif** mountain 5,140 *m* (16,860 *ft*) w Antarctica s of Ellsworth Land in Sentinel range of Ellsworth mountains; highest in Antarctica

**Virginia** state E USA ✳ Richmond *area* 106,124 *sq km* (40,817 *sq miles*), *pop* 5,346,279 (1980) – **Virginian** *adj or n*

**Virgin Islands of the United States** the w islands of the Virgin islands group including St Criox, St John, & St Thomas; a territory ✳ Charlotte Amalie (on St Thomas I) *area* 343 *sq km* (132 *sq miles*), *pop* 95,591 (1981)

**Vistula,** Pol **Wisla,** Russ **Visla,** G **Weichsel** river 1,068 *km* (664 *miles*) long Poland flowing N from the Carpathian mountains into Gulf of Gdansk

**Vladivostok** city & port USSR in SE Soviet Russia, Asia ✳ of Maritime Territory *pop* 565,000 (1981)

**Vlissingen, Flushing** city & port sw Netherlands on Walcheren I *pop* 43,415 (1977)

**Volga** river 3,692 *km* (2,293 *miles*) long USSR in Soviet Russia, Europe, rising in Valdai hills & flowing into the Caspian sea

**Volta** river *ab* 161 *km* (100 *miles*) long w Africa flowing from **Lake Volta** (reservoir *area* 8,482 *sq km* (3,275 *sq miles*)) receiving the **Black Volta** (869 *km* (540 *miles*)) & **White Volta** (724 *km* (450 *miles*)) in N *cen* Ghana & flowing s into Bight of Benin

# W

**Wales,** Welsh **Cymru,** ML **Cambria** principality sw Great Britain; a division of the United Kingdom ✳ Cardiff *area ab* 21,000 *sq km* (8,000 *sq miles*), *pop* 2,790,000 (1981)

**Wallis** islands sw Pacific NE of Fiji islands; with Futuna islands, constitute a French overseas territory (**Wallis and Futuna Islands**) *pop* 8,550 (1971 *est*)

**Walsall** town in W Midlands 13 *km* (8 *miles*) NW of Birmingham *pop* 184,734 (1971)

**Warrington** town in Cheshire on river Mersey; developed as "new town" 1969; *pop* 140,200 (1981)

**Warsaw,** Pol **Warszawa** city ✳ of Poland on the Vistula *pop* 1,316,000 (1977)

**Warwickshire** county in *cen* England partly reformed in 1974 *area* 1,981 *sq km* (765 *sq miles*), *pop* 480,100 (1981)

**Washington 1** state NW USA ✳ Olympia *area* 177,299 *sq km* (68,192 *sq miles*), *pop* 4,130,163 (1980) **2** city ✳ of the USA, coextensive with District of Columbia *pop* 637,651 (1980) **3** town in Tyne and Wear, on river Wear; developed as "new town" 1964; *pop* 52,415 (1981) – **Washingtonian** *adj or n*

**Wash, The** inlet of North sea E England between Norfolk & Lincoln 29 *km* (18 *miles*) long and up to 24 *km* (15 *miles*) wide

**Weimar Republic** the German republic 1919–33

**Wellington 1** market town in Salop, 16 *km* (10 *miles*) E of Shrewsbury *pop* 67,600 (1971) **2** city & port ✳ of New Zealand in sw North I on Port Nicholson (Wellington Harbour) on Cook strait *pop* 343,982 (1981)

**Welwyn Garden City** town in Hertfordshire; developed as "new town" 1946; *pop* 47,000 (1981)

**Weser** river 443 *km* (280 *miles*) long w Germany formed by confluence of the Fulda & Werra rivers & flowing into North sea

**West Bromwich** town in W Midlands 8 *km* (5 *miles*) NW of Birmingham *pop* 166,593 (1971)

**Western Australia** state w Australia on Indian ocean ✳ Perth *area* 2,527,632 *sq km* (975,920 *sq miles*), *pop* 1,273,624 (1981)

**Western Ghats** chain of mountains sw India extending SSE parallel to coast from mouth of Tapti river to Cape Comorin; average height 1,000 *m* (3,000 *ft*) – see EASTERN GHATS

**Western Isles** the Outer Hebrides, constituting since 1975 a regional division of w Scotland ✳ Stornoway *area* 2,901 *sq km* (1,120 *sq miles*), *pop* 30,691 (1981)

**Western Samoa** group of islands of Samoa w of 171°w; an independent state; until 1962 a territory administered by New

**Zealand** \* Apia (on Upolu I) *area* 2,842 *sq km* (1,097 *sq miles*), *pop* 158,130 (1981)

**West Germany** the Federal Republic of Germany – see GERMANY

**West Glamorgan** county in s Wales formed in 1974 from part of former county of Glamorgan and county borough of Swansea *area* 816 *sq km* (315 *sq miles*), *pop* 364,350 (1981)

**West Indies 1** the islands lying between SE North America & N South America bordering the Caribbean & comprising the Greater Antilles, Lesser Antilles, & Bahamas **2 West Indies, West Indies Federation** former country including all of the Brit West Indies except the Bahamas & the Brit Virgin islands; established 1958, dissolved 1961

**West Midlands** county in *cen* England formed in 1974 from parts of counties of Staffordshire, Worcestershire and Warwickshire *area* 899 *sq km* (347 *sq miles*), *pop* 2,686,700 (1981)

**West Riding** – see WEST YORKSHIRE

**West Sussex** county in SE England formed in 1974 from administrative district of w Sussex in former county of Sussex and parts of administrative districts of E Sussex and Surrey *area* 2,016 *sq km* (778 *sq miles*), *pop* 663,900 (1981)

**West Virginia** state E USA \* Charleston *area* 62,871 *sq km* (24,181 *sq miles*), *pop* 1,949,644 (1980) – **West Virginian** *adj or n*

**West Yorkshire** county in N England formed in 1974 from parts of former West Riding of Yorkshire *area* 2,039 *sq km* (789 *sq miles*), *pop* 2,018,000 (1981)

**White,** Russ **Beloye More** sea, inlet of Barents sea USSR on N coast of Soviet Russia, Europe, enclosed on the N by Kola peninsula

**Wight, Isle of** island s England in English channel constituting **Isle of Wight** county (\* Newport *area* 381 *sq km* (147 *sq miles*), *pop* 115,400 (1981))

**Wiltshire** county in sw England *area* 3,481 *sq km* (1,344 *sq miles*), *pop* 527,700 (1981)

**Winchester** city in Hampshire on river Itchen *pop* 31,107 (1971)

**Windermere** lake 17 *km* (10 *miles*) long NW England in Cumbria; largest in England

**Windhoek** city \* of South-West Africa *pop* 61,260 (1970)

**Windsor** town in Berkshire on river Thames; **Windsor Castle** royal residence *pop* 30,065 (1971)

**Windward** islands West Indies in the s Lesser Antilles extending s from Martinique but not including Barbados, Tobago, or Trinidad

**Winnipeg, Lake** lake 425 *km* (264 *miles*) long Canada in s *cen* Manitoba drained by Nelson river *area* 24,510 *sq km* (9,460 *sq miles*)

**Wisconsin** state N *cen* USA \* Madison *area* 146,026 *sq km* (56,164 *sq miles*), *pop* 4,705,335 (1980) – **Wisconsinite** *n*

**Wolds, The** chalk hills NE England in n Yorkshire, Humberside, & N Lincolnshire

**Wolverhampton** town in W Midlands 21 *km* (13 *miles*) NW of Birmingham *pop* 268,200 (1971)

**Worcester** city in Hereford and Worcester on river Severn *pop* 73,445 (1971)

**Wrangell, Mount** active volcano 4,269 *m* (14,006 *ft*) s Alaska in Wrangell mountains NW of Mt Blackburn

**Wroclaw,** G **Breslau** city sw Poland, chief city of Silesia *pop* 585,000 (1977)

**Wuhan** city E *cen* China \* of Hupei province at junction of Han & Yangtze rivers; formed from the former separate cities of Hankow, Hanyang, & Wuchang *pop* 3,500,000 (1976)

**Wye** river 210 *km* (130 *miles*) long E Wales & w England flowing into the Severn

**Wyoming** state NW USA \* Cheyenne *area* 254,576 *sq km* (97,914 *sq miles*), *pop* 470,816 (1980) – **Wyomingite** *n*

# Y

**Yakutsk** city USSR in E *cen* Soviet Russia, Asia \* of Yakutsk Republic *pop* 108,000 (1970)

**Yalta** city & port USSR in s Soviet Russia, Europe, on s coast of Crimea *pop* 34,500 (1972)

**Yangtze, Yangtse, Yangtze Kiang** river 5,980 *km* (3,716 *miles*) long *cen* China flowing from Kunlun Shan in sw Tsinghai province E into East China sea

**Yaoundé, Yaunde** city s *cen* Cameroon, its \* *pop* 337,000 (1980 *est*)

**Yarmouth, Great Yarmouth** borough & port E Norfolk on North sea *pop* 50,152 (1971)

**Yedo** –see TOKYO

**Yellow 1 Yellow, Hwang Ho, Huang** river 4,410 *km* (2,740 *miles*) long N China flowing from Kunlun mountains in Tsinghai province E into **Po Hai** (arm of Yellow sea) **2** sea inlet of East China sea between N China & Korea

**Yemen 1 Yemen, Yemen Arab Republic** country sw Arabia bordering on Red sea; republic since 1962 \* San°a *area* 195,000 *sq km* (75,290 *sq miles*), *pop* 8,556,974 (1981) **2 Yemen, People's Democratic Republic of Yemen , Southern Yemen** country s Arabian peninsula on Gulf of Aden formed 1967 from former **Federation of South Arabia** (Brit protectorate comprising crown colony of Aden & numerous semi-independent Arab sultanates & emirates ) \* \* Aden & Medina as-Shaab *area* 287,680 *sq km* (111,074 *sq miles*), *pop* 1,800,000 (1977 *est*) – **Yemeni** *adj or n*

**Yezo** –see HOKKAIDO

**Yokohama** city & port Japan in SE Honshu on Tokyo Bay s of Tokyo *pop* 2,817,479 (1982)

**York 1 York,** *anc* **Eboracum** city in North Yorkshire, on river Ouse *pop* 104,513 (1971) **2 York, Yorkshire** – see HUMBERSIDE, NORTH YORKSHIRE, SOUTH YORKSHIRE, WEST YORKSHIRE

**Yugoslavia, Jugoslavia** country s Europe bordering on the Adriatic; established 1918 as a kingdom (**Kingdom of the Serbs, Croats, and Slovenes**), became a federal republic 1945 \* Belgrade *area* 255,874 *sq km* (98,740 *sq miles*), *pop* 22,420,000 (1981) – **Yugoslav, Yugoslavian** *adj or n*

**Yukon Territory** territory NW Canada bet Alaska & British Columbia bordering on Arctic ocean \* Whitehorse *area* 533,900 *sq km* (205,346 *sq miles*), *pop* 23,153 (1981)

**Yunnan, Yunnanfu** –see KUNMING

# Z

**Zabrze,** G **Hindenburg** city sw Poland in Silesia *pop* 204,200 (1976)

**Zagazig, Zaqaziq** city N Egypt NNE of Cairo *pop* 195,000 (1974 *est*)

**Zagreb** city NW Yugoslavia \* of Croatia *pop* 763,000 (1981)

**Zaïre 1 Zaire, Congo** river 4,828 *km* (3,000 *miles*) long *cen* Africa flowing N, w, & sw into the Atlantic **2 Zaire,** *formerly* **Congo, Republic of the Congo,** *earlier* **Belgian Congo** country *cen* Africa comprising most of Congo river basin E of lower Congo river; a republic \* Kinshasa *area* 2,344,885 *sq km* (905,365 *sq miles*), *pop* 21,637,000 (1970) – **Zairian** *adj or n*

**Zambezi, Zambesi** river 3,540 *km* (2,200 *miles*) long SE Africa flowing from NW Zambia into Mozambique channel

**Zambia,** *formerly* **Northern Rhodesia** country s Africa; formerly a Brit protectorate; independent republic within the Brit Commonwealth since 1964 \* Lusaka *area* 752,614 *sq km* (290,586 *sq miles*), *pop* 5,834,000 (1980 *est*) – **Zambian** *adj or n*

**Zanzibar 1** island E Africa off NE Tanganyika *area* 1,651 *sq km* (637 *sq miles*), *pop* 122,004 (1973 *est*); formerly a sultanate, with Pemba & adjacent islands forming a Brit protectorate; became independent 1963; united 1964 with Tanganyika in United Republic of Tanzania **2** city & port \* of the island & protectorate *pop* 68,490 (1973 *est*) – **Zanzibari** *n*

**Zetland** –see SHETLAND

**Zimbabwe** country s Africa s of Zambezi river; formerly **Southern Rhodesia** self-governing Brit colony; unilaterally declared itself a republic 1970; became independent republic 1980 \* Salisbury *area* 390,622 *sq km* (150,820 *sq miles*), *pop* 7,260,000 (1979 *est*) – **Zimbabwean** *adj or n*

**Zurich,** G **Zürich 1** canton N Switzerland *area* 1,729 *sq km* (668 *sq miles*), *pop* 1,107,788 (1970) **2** city, its \*, at NW end of Lake of Zurich *pop* 369,522 (1980)

**Zwickau,** city s E Germany s of Leipzig, *pop* 88,436 (1980)

| Name | Symbol | Subdivision | Country |
|---|---|---|---|
| afghani | Af | 100 puls | Afghanistan |
| baht or tical | B | 100 satang | Thailand |
| balboa | B or B/ | 100 centesimos | Panama |
| birr | E$ or EB | 100 cents | Ethiopia |
| bolivar | B | 100 centimos | Venezuela |
| cedi | ¢ | 100 pesewas | Ghana |
| colon | ¢ | 100 centimos | Costa Rica |
| colon | ¢ | 100 centavos | El Salvador |
| cordoba | C$ | 100 centavos | Nicaragua |
| cruzeiro | $ or Cr$ | 100 centavos | Brazil |
| dalasi | D | 100 bututs | Gambia |
| deutschemark | DM | 100 pfennigs | West Germany |
| dinar | DA | 100 centimes | Algeria |
| dinar | BD | 1000 fils | Bahrain |
| dinar | ID | 1000 fils | Iraq |
| dinar | JD | 1000 fils | Jordan |
| dinar | KD | 1000 fils | Kuwait |
| dinar | LD | 1000 dirhams | Libya |
| dinar | £SY | 1000 fils | Southern Yemen |
| dinar | D | 1000 millimes | Tunisia |
| dinar | Din | 100 paras | Yugoslavia |
| dirham | DH | 100 centimes | Morocco |
| dirham | UD | 10 dinar/1000 fils | United Arab Emirates |
| dobra | | 100 centavos | Sao Tome and Principe |
| dollar | $ | 100 cents | Anguilla |
| dollar | $ | 100 cents | Antigua |
| dollar | $A | 100 cents | Australia |
| dollar | B$ | 100 cents | Bahamas |
| dollar | Bds$ | 100 cents | Barbados |
| dollar | $ | 100 cents | Belize (British Honduras) |
| dollar | $ | 100 cents | Bermuda |
| dollar | B$ | 100 sen | Brunei |
| dollar | $ | 100 cents | Canada |
| dollar | $ | 100 cents | Cayman Islands |
| dollar or yuan | NT$ | 100 cents or chiao | China (Taiwan) |
| dollar | $ | 100 cents | Dominica |
| dollar | $F | 100 cents | Fiji |
| dollar | $ | 100 cents | Grenada |
| dollar | G$ | 100 cents | Guyana |
| dollar | HK$ | 100 cents | Hong Kong |
| dollar | $ or J$ | 100 cents | Jamaica |
| dollar | $A | 100 cents | Kiribati |
| dollar | $ | 100 cents | Liberia |
| dollar | $A | 100 cents | Montserrat |
| dollar | $A | 100 cents | Nauru |
| dollar | NZ$ | 100 cents | Pitcairn Islands |
| dollar | NZ$ | 100 cents | New Zealand |
| dollar | $ | 100 cents | St Kitts – Nevis |
| dollar | $ | 100 cents | St Lucia |
| dollar | $ | 100 cents | St Vincent and the Grenadines |
| dollar | S$ | 100 cents | Singapore |
| dollar | | 100 cents | Solomon Islands |
| dollar | TT$ | 100 cents | Trinidad and Tobago |
| dollar | $ | 100 cents | United States |
| dollar | Z$ | 100 cents | Zimbabwe |
| dong | D | 100 hào | Vietnam |
| drachma | Dr | 100 lepta | Greece |
| ekuele | E | 100 centimos | Equatorial Guinea |
| escudo | Esc | 100 centavos | Cape Verde |
| escudo | $ or Esc | 100 centavos | Portugal |
| escudo—see PESO, below | | | |
| florin or gulden or guilder | F or Fl or G | 100 cents | Netherlands |
| florin or gulden or guilder | F or Fl or G | 100 cents | Netherlands Antilles |
| florin or gulden or guilder | F or Fl or G | 100 cents | Surinam |
| forint | F or Ft | 100 fillers | Hungary |
| franc | Fr or F | 100 centimes | Andorra |
| franc | BF | 100 centimes | Belgium |
| franc | Fr or F | 100 centimes | Benin |
| franc | FBu | 100 centimes | Burundi |
| franc | Fr or F | 100 centimes | Cameroon |
| franc | Fr or F | 100 centimes | Central African Republic |
| franc | Fr or F | 100 centimes | Chad |
| franc | Fr or F | 100 centimes | Comoros |
| franc | Fr or F | 100 centimes | Congo |
| franc | DjFr | 100 centimes | Djibouti |
| franc | Fr or F | 100 centimes | France |
| franc | Fr or F | 100 centimes | Gabon |
| franc | SFr | 100 centimes | Ivory Coast |
| franc | Fr or F | 100 centimes | Liechtenstein |
| franc | Fr or F | 100 centimes | Luxembourg |
| franc | FMG | 100 centimes | Madagascar |
| franc | MF | 100 centimes | Mali |
| franc | Fr or F | 100 centimes | Monaco |
| franc | Fr or F | 100 centimes | Niger |
| franc | Fr or F | 100 centimes | Rwanda |
| franc | Fr or F | 100 centimes | Senegal |
| franc | SFr | 100 centimes or rappen | Switzerland |
| franc | Fr or F | 100 centimes | Togo |
| franc | Fr or F | 100 centimes | Tuvalu (formerly Ellice Islands) |
| franc | Fr or F | 100 centimes | Upper Volta |
| franc | Fr or F | 100 centimes | Vanuatu (formerly New Hebrides) |
| gourde | G or Gde | 100 centimes | Haiti |
| guarani | G or G̃ | 100 centimes | Paraguay |
| gulden—see FLORIN | | | |
| kina | K | 100 toea | Papua New Guinea |
| kip | K | 100 at | Laos |
| koruna | Kčs | 100 halers | Czechoslovakia |
| krona | IKr or Kr | 100 aurar | Iceland |
| krona | Skr or Kr | 100 öre | Sweden |
| krone | Kr or DKr | 100 öre | Denmark |
| krone | Kr or NKr | 100 öre | Norway |
| kwacha | K | 100 tambala | Malawi |
| kwacha | K | 100 ngwee | Zambia |
| kwanza | | 100 lweis | Angola |
| kyat | K | 100 pyas | Burma |
| lek | L | 100 qindarka | Albania |
| lempira | L | 100 centavos | Honduras |
| leone | Le | 100 cents | Sierra Leone |
| leu | L | 100 bani | Romania |
| lev | Lv | 100 stotinki | Bulgaria |
| lilangeni (pl emalangeni) | | 100 cents | Swaziland |
| lira | L or Lit | 100 centesimi | Italy |
| lira | L or Lit | 100 centesimi | San Marino |
| lira or pound | £T or Lt | 100 kurus or piastres | Turkey |
| loti (pl maloti) | | 100 lisente | Lesotho |
| mark or ostmark | M or OM | 100 pfennigs | East Germany |
| mark—see DEUTSCHMARK, above | | | |
| markka | Mk or Fmk | 100 pennia | Finland |
| metical | | 100 centavos | Mozambique |
| naira | N | 100 kobo | Nigeria |
| ngultrum | N | 100 chetrums | Bhutan |
| ostmark—see MARK, above | | | |
| ouguiya | | 100 khoums | Mauritania |
| pa'anga | TS | 100 seniti | Tonga |
| pataca | P or $ | 100 avos | Macao |
| peseta | Pta or P (pl Pts) | 100 centimos | Andorra |
| peseta | Pta or P (pl Pts) | 100 centimos | Spain |
| peso | $ | 100 centavos | Argentina |
| peso | $B | 100 centavos | Bolivia |
| peso | $ | 100 centavos 1000 escudos | Chile |
| peso | $ or P | 100 centavos | Colombia |
| peso | $ | 100 centavos | Cuba |
| peso | RD$ | 100 centavos | Dominican Republic |
| peso or escudo | Esc | 100 centavos | Guinea-Bissau |
| peso | $ | 100 centavos | Mexico |
| peso | P | 100 sentimos or centavos | Philippines |
| peso | $ | 100 centesimos | Uruguay |
| pound | £ | 1000 mils | Cyprus |
| pound | £E | 100 piastres 1000 milliemes | Egypt |
| pound | FI£ | 100 pence | Falkland Islands |
| pound | Gib£ | 100 pence | Gibraltar |
| punt | £ | 100 pence | Ireland |
| pound | L£ or LL | 100 piastres | Lebanon |
| pound | £ | 100 pence 1000 mils | Malta |
| pound | £ | 100 pence | St Helena |
| pound | £S or LSd | 100 piastres 1000 milliemes | Sudan |
| pound | £S or LS | 100 piastres | Syria |
| pound | £ | 100 pence | United Kingdom |
| pound—see LIRA, above | | | |
| pula | P | 100 thebe | Botswana |
| quetzal | Q | 100 centavos | Guatemala |
| rand | R | 100 cents | Namibia |
| rand | R | 100 cents | South Africa |
| rial | R or RI | 100 dinars | Iran |
| rial | RO | 1000 baizas | Oman |
| rial or riyal | | 40 buqshas 100 fils | Yemen Arab Republic |
| riel | ៛ or CR | 100 sen | Kampuchea (Cambodia) |
| ringgit | $ | 100 sen | Malaysia |
| riyal | QDR | 100 dirhams | Qatar |
| riyal | R or SR | 20 qursh 100 halala | Saudi Arabia |
| riyal—see RIAL | | | |
| rouble | R or Rub | 100 kopecks | USSR |
| rupee | Re (pl Rs) | 100 paise | India |
| rupee | Re (pl Rs) | 100 laris | Maldive Islands |
| rupee | Re (pl Rs) | 100 cents | Mauritius |
| rupee | Re (pl Rs) | 100 paise | Nepal |
| rupee | Re (pl Rs) or PRe (pl PRs) | 100 paise | Pakistan |
| rupee | Re (pl Rs) | 100 cents | Seychelles |
| rupee | Re (pl Rs) | 100 cents | Sri Lanka |
| rupiah | Rp | 100 sen | Indonesia |
| schilling | S or Sch | 100 groschen | Austria |
| shekel | I£ | 100 agorot | Israel |
| shilingi—see SHILLING, below | | | |
| shilling | Sh | 100 cents | Kenya |
| shilling | Sh or SoSh | 100 cents | Somalia |
| shilling or shilingi | Sh or TSh | 100 senti or cents | Tanzania |
| shilling | Sh | 100 cents | Uganda |
| sol | S/ or $ | 100 centavos | Peru |
| sucre | S/ | 100 centavos | Ecuador |
| syli | GS | 100 cauris | Guinea |
| taka | Tk | 100 paise | Bangladesh |
| tala | WS$ | 100 sene | Western Samoa |
| tical—see BAHT, above | | | |
| tugrik | Tug | 100 mongo | Mongolia |
| won | W | 100 jun | North Korea |
| won | W | 100 jeon | South Korea |
| yen | ¥ or Y | 100 sen | Japan |
| yuan | Y | 100 fen | China (mainland) |
| yuan—see DOLLAR, above | | | |
| zaire | Z | 100 makuta (sing likuta), 10,000 sengi | Zaire |
| zloty | Zl | 100 groszy | Poland |

# Number

## Cardinal numbers

| | Arabic[1] | Roman[2] |
|---|---|---|
| zero or nought | 0 | |
| one | 1 | I |
| two | 2 | II |
| three | 3 | III |
| four | 4 | IV |
| five | 5 | V |
| six | 6 | VI |
| seven | 7 | VII |
| eight | 8 | VIII |
| nine | 9 | IX |
| ten | 10 | X |
| eleven | 11 | XI |
| twelve | 12 | XII |
| thrirteen | 13 | XIII |
| fourteen | 14 | XIV |
| fifteen | 15 | XV |
| sixteen | 16 | XVI |
| seventeen | 17 | XVII |
| eighteen | 18 | XVIII |
| nineteen | 19 | XIX |
| twenty | 20 | XX |
| twenty-one | 21 | XXI |
| twenty-two | 22 | XXII |
| twenty-three | 23 | XXIII |
| twenty-four | 24 | XXIV |
| twenty-five | 25 | XXV |
| twenty-six | 26 | XXVI |
| twenty-seven | 27 | XXVII |
| twenty-eight | 28 | XXVIII |
| twenty-nine | 29 | XXIX |
| thirty | 30 | XXX |
| thirty-one | 31 | XXXI |
| thirty-two, etc | 32 | XXXII |
| forty | 40 | XL |
| forty-one, etc | 41 | XLI |
| fifty | 50 | L |
| sixty | 60 | LX |
| seventy | 70 | LXX |
| eighty | 80 | LXXX |
| ninety | 90 | XC |
| one hundred | 100 | C |
| one hundred (and) one | 101 | CI |
| one hundred and two, etc | 102 | CII |
| two hundred | 200 | CC |
| three hundred | 300 | CCC |
| four hundred | 400 | CD |
| five hundred | 500 | D |
| six hundred | 600 | DC |
| seven hundred | 700 | DCC |
| eight hundred | 800 | DCCC |
| nine hundred | 900 | CM |
| one thousand *or* ten hundred, etc | 1,000 *or* 1000 | M |
| two thousand, etc | 2,000 *or* 2000 | MM |
| five thousand | 5,000 *or* 5000 | V̄ |
| ten thousand | 10,000 *or* 10000 | X̄ |
| one hundred thousand | 100,000 *or* 100000 | |
| one million | 1,000,000 *or* 1000000 | C̄ M̄ |

## Ordinal numbers

| | Arabic[3] |
|---|---|
| first | 1st |
| second | 2nd *or* 2d |
| third | 3rd *or* 3d |
| fourth | 4th |
| fifth | 5th |
| sixth | 6th |
| seventh | 7th |
| eighth | 8th |
| ninth | 9th |
| tenth | 10th |
| eleventh | 11th |
| twelfth | 12th |
| thirteenth | 13th |
| fourteenth | 14th |
| fifteenth | 15th |
| sixteenth | 16th |
| seventeenth | 17th |
| eighteenth | 18th |
| nineteenth | 19th |
| twentieth | 20th |
| twenty-first | 21st |
| twenty-second | 22nd *or* 22d |
| twenty-third | 23rd *or* 23d |
| twenty-fourth | 24th |
| twenty-fifth | 25th |
| twenty-sixth | 26th |
| twenty-seventh | 27th |
| twenty-eighth | 28th |
| twenty-ninth | 29th |
| thirtieth | 30th |
| thirty-first | 31st |
| thirty-second, etc | 32nd *or* 32d |
| fortieth | 40th |
| forty-first | 41st |
| forty-second, etc | 42nd *or* 42d |
| fiftieth | 50th |
| sixtieth | 60th |
| seventieth | 70th |
| eightieth | 80th |
| ninetieth | 90th |
| hundredth or one hundredth | 100th |
| hundred and first or one hundred and first | 101st |
| hundred and second, etc | 102nd *or* 102d |
| two hundredth | 200th |
| three hundredth | 300th |
| four hundredth | 400th |
| five hundredth | 500th |
| six hundredth | 600th |
| seven hundredth | 700th |
| eight hundredth | 800th |
| nine hundredth | 900th |
| thousandth *or* one thousandth | 1,000th *or* 1000th |
| two thousandth, etc | 2,000th *or* 2000th |
| ten thousandth | 10,000th *or* 10000th |
| hundred thousandth *or* one hundred thousandth | 100,000th *or* 100000th |
| millionth *or* one millionth | 1,000,000th *or* 1000000th |

1 Arabic numerals from 1,000 to 9,999 are often written without commas or spaces (1000, 9999). Year numbers are always written without commas (1783).

2 The Roman numerals are written either in capitals or in lower-case letters (VIII or viii).

3 The Arabic symbols for the cardinal numbers may be read as ordinals in certain contexts (January 1 = January first; 2 Samuel = Second Samuel). The Roman numerals are sometimes read as ordinals (Henry IV = Henry the Fourth); sometimes they are written with the ordinal suffixes (XIXth dynasty).

## Denominations above one million

| | British system | | | | American system | | |
|---|---|---|---|---|---|---|---|
| Name | Value in powers of ten | Number of zeros | Powers of 1,000,000 | Name | Value in powers of ten | Number of zeros | Number of groups of three 0s after 1,000 |
| gillion | $10^9$ | 9 | — | billion | $10^9$ | 9 | 2 |
| †billion | $10^{12}$ | 12 | 2 | trillion | $10^{12}$ | 12 | 3 |
| trillion | $10^{18}$ | 18 | 3 | quadrillion | $10^{15}$ | 15 | 4 |
| quadrillion | $10^{24}$ | 24 | 4 | quintillion | $10^{18}$ | 18 | 5 |
| quintillion | $10^{30}$ | 30 | 5 | sextillion | $10^{21}$ | 21 | 6 |
| sextillion | $10^{36}$ | 36 | 6 | septillion | $10^{24}$ | 24 | 7 |
| septillion | $10^{42}$ | 42 | 7 | octillion | $10^{27}$ | 27 | 8 |
| octillion | $10^{48}$ | 48 | 8 | nonillion | $10^{30}$ | 30 | 9 |
| nonillion | $10^{54}$ | 54 | 9 | decillion | $10^{33}$ | 33 | 10 |
| decillion | $10^{60}$ | 60 | 10 | undecillion | $10^{36}$ | 36 | 11 |
| undecillion | $10^{66}$ | 66 | 11 | duodecillion | $10^{39}$ | 39 | 12 |
| duodecillion | $10^{72}$ | 72 | 12 | tredecillion | $10^{42}$ | 42 | 13 |
| tredecillion | $10^{78}$ | 78 | 13 | quattuordecillion | $10^{45}$ | 45 | 14 |
| quattuordecillion | $10^{84}$ | 84 | 14 | quindecillion | $10^{48}$ | 48 | 15 |
| quindecillion | $10^{90}$ | 90 | 15 | sexdecillion | $10^{51}$ | 51 | 16 |
| sexdecillion | $10^{96}$ | 96 | 16 | septendecillion | $10^{54}$ | 54 | 17 |
| septendecillion | $10^{102}$ | 102 | 17 | octodecillion | $10^{57}$ | 57 | 18 |
| octodecillion | $10^{108}$ | 108 | 18 | novemdecillion | $10^{60}$ | 60 | 19 |
| novemdecillion | $10^{114}$ | 114 | 19 | vigintillion | $10^{63}$ | 63 | 20 |
| vigintillion | $10^{120}$ | 120 | 20 | centillion | $10^{303}$ | 303 | 100 |
| centillion | $10^{600}$ | 600 | 100 | | | | |

† The American system is now replacing the British in this case.

# Weights and measures

## Length

| | | | | | | |
|---|---|---|---|---|---|---|
| | 1 inch | = | 25.4 mm | | | |
| 12 inches | = | 1 foot | = | 0.305 mm | | |
| 3 feet | = | 1 yard | = | 0.914 m | | |
| 1760 yards | = | 1 mile | = | 1.61 km | | |

| | | | | |
|---|---|---|---|---|
| | 1 millimetre | = | 0.039 in | |
| 10 mm | = | 1 centimetre | = | 0.394 in |
| 10 cm | = | 1 decimetre | = | 3.937 in |
| 10 dm | = | 1 metre | = | 39.37 in |
| 1000 m | = | 1 kilometre | = | 0.6214 mile |

1 light year = $9.46070 \times 10^{15}$ metres = $5.87848 \times 10^{12}$ miles
1 Astronomical Unit = $1.496 \times 10^{11}$ metres
1 parsec = $3.0857 \times 10^{16}$ metres = 3.2616 light years

| | 1 digit | = | 1.9 cm | = | ¾ in |
|---|---|---|---|---|---|
| | 1 hand | = | 10 cm | = | 4 in |
| | 1 palm (length) | = | 20 cm approx | = | 8 in |
| | (breadth) | = | 10 cm approx | = | 4 in |
| | 1 span | = | 23 cm approx | = | 9 in |
| | 1 cubit | = | 46 cm approx | = | 18 in |
| | 1 pace | = | 75 cm approx | = | 30 in |
| | 1 link | = | 20.1 cm | = | 7¹¹⁄₁₂ in |
| | 1 ell | = | 1.14 m | = | 45 in |
| | 1 fathom | = | 1.83 m | = | 6 ft |
| | 1 rod, pole, or perch | = | 5.03 m | = | 5½ yd |
| | 1 chain | = | 20.1 m | = | 22 yd |
| | 1 furlong | = | 201 m | = | 220 yd |
| | 1 league (variable) | = | 5 km | = | 3 mi |

| | m | cm | in | ft | yd | km | mi | n.mi |
|---|---|---|---|---|---|---|---|---|
| 1 metre | 1 | 100 | 39.3701 | 3.28084 | 1.09361 | | | |
| 1 centimetre | 0.01 | 1 | 0.393701 | 0.0328084 | 0.0109361 | | | |
| 1 inch | 0.0254 | 2.54 | 1 | 0.0833333 | 0.0277778 | | | |
| 1 foot | 0.3048 | 30.48 | 12 | 1 | 0.3333333 | | | |
| 1 yard | 0.9144 | 91.44 | 36 | 3 | 1 | | | |
| 1 kilometre | | | | | | 1 | 0.621371 | 0.539957 |
| 1 mile | | | | | | 1.60934 | 1 | 0.868976 |
| 1 nautical mile | | | | | | 1.85300 | 1.15078 | 1 |

## Area

| | | | |
|---|---|---|---|
| | 1 square inch | = | 6.452 cm² |
| 144 sq in | = 1 square foot | = | 9.29 dm² |
| 9 sq ft | = 1 square yard | = | 0.836 m² |
| 4840 sq yd | = 1 acre | = | 4046.86 m² |
| | | = | 0.4047 ha |
| 640 acres | = 1 square mile | = | 258.99 ha |
| | | = | 2.59 km² |

| | | | |
|---|---|---|---|
| | 1 sq centimetre | = | 0.155 in² |
| 100 cm² | = 1 sq metre | = | 1.196 yd² |
| 100 m² | = 1 are | = | 119.6 yd² |
| 100 ares | = 1 hectare | = | 2.471 acres |
| 100 ha | = 1 sq kilometre | = | 0.387 mi² |

## Cubic measure

| | | | |
|---|---|---|---|
| | 1 cubic inch | = | 16.4 cm³ |
| 1728 cu in | = 1 cubic foot | = | 0.0283 m³ |
| 27 cu ft | = 1 cubic yard | = | 0.765 m³ |

| | | | |
|---|---|---|---|
| | 1 cu centimetre | = | 0.061 in³ |
| 1000 cu cm | = 1 cu decimetre | = | 0.035 ft³ |
| 1000 cu dm | = 1 cu metre | = | 1.308 yd³ |

## Capacity measure

| | | | |
|---|---|---|---|
| | 1 fluid ounce | = | 28.4 ml |
| 5 fl oz | = 1 gill | = | 0.142 l |
| 4 gill | = 1 pint | = | 0.568 l |
| 2 pt | = 1 quart | = | 1.136 l |
| 4 qt | = 1 gallon | = | 4.546 l |

| | | | |
|---|---|---|---|
| | 1 millilitre | = | 0.002 pt |
| 10 ml | = 1 centilitre | = | 0.018 pt |
| 10 cl | = 1 decilitre | = | 0.176 pt |
| 10 dl | = 1 litre | = | 1.76 pt |
| 1000 l | = 1 kilolitre | = | 220 gall |

## Apothecaries weight

| | | | |
|---|---|---|---|
| | 1 grain | = | 0.0648 g |
| 20 grains | = 1 scruple | = | 1.296 g |
| 3 scruples (60 grains) | = 1 drachm | = | 3.888 g |
| 8 drachms (480 grains) | = 1 ounce | = | 31.1035 g |

## Apothecaries capacity measure

| | | | |
|---|---|---|---|
| | 1 minim | = | 0.059 ml |
| 60 minims | = 1 fluid drachm | = | 3.55 ml |
| 8 fl drachm | = 1 fluid ounce | = | 28.4 ml |
| 20 fl oz | = 1 pint | = | 0.568 l |
| 8 pt | = 1 gallon | = | 4.546 l |

## Weight

| | | | | | |
|---|---|---|---|---|---|
| | | 1 grain | = | 64.8 mg | |
| | | 1 dram | = | 1.772 g | |
| 16 drams | = | 1 ounce | = | 28.35 g | |
| 16 oz | = | 1 pound | = | 0.4536 kg | |
| 14 pounds | = | 1 stone | = | 6.35 kg | |
| 2 stones | = | 1 quarter | = | 12.7 kg | |
| 4 quarters | = | 1 hundredweight | = | 50.8 kg | |
| 20 cwt | = | 1 (long) ton | = | 1.016 tonnes | |

| | | | | |
|---|---|---|---|---|
| | | 1 milligram | = | 0.015 grain |
| 10 mg | = | 1 centigram | = | 0.154 grain |
| 10 cg | = | 1 decigram | = | 1.543 grains |
| 10 dg | = | 1 gram | = | 15.43 grains |
| | | | = | 0.035 oz |
| 1000 g | = | 1 kilogram | = | 2.205 lb |
| 1000 kg | = | 1 tonne | | |
| | | (metric ton) | = | 0.984 (long) ton |
| 1 slug | = | 14.5939 kg | = | 32.174 lb |

## Troy weight

| | | | |
|---|---|---|---|
| | 1 grain | = | 0.0648 g |
| 24 grains | = 1 pennyweight (dwt) | = | 1.555 g |
| 20 dwt (480 grains) | = 1 ounce | = | 31.1035 g |
| 12 oz (5760 grains) | = 1 pound | = | 373.27 g |

## US measures

### Capacity measure

| | | | |
|---|---|---|---|
| | 1 minim | = | 0.062 ml |
| 60 minims | = 1 fluid dram | = | 3.6966 ml |
| 8 fl drams | = 1 fluid ounce | = | 0.296 dl |
| 16 fl oz | = 1 pint | = | 0.473 l |
| 2 pt | = 1 quart | = | 0.946 l |
| 4 qt | = 1 gallon | = | 3.785 l |

### Dry measure

| | | | |
|---|---|---|---|
| | 1 pint | = | 0.551 l |
| 2 pt | = 1 quart | = | 1.101 l |
| 8 qt | = 1 peck | = | 8.809 l |
| 4 pecks | = 1 bushel | = | 35.238 l |

### Weight

| | | | | | |
|---|---|---|---|---|---|
| 25 lb | = | 1 US quarter | = | 12.7 kg |
| 4 quarters (100 lb) | = | 1 US hundredweight (cwt) | = | 45.36 kg |
| 20 cwt (2000 lb) | = | 1 US (short) ton | = | 907.19 kg |

# Weights and measures

## Velocity

|                     | m/sec    | km/hr    | mi/hr    | ft/sec   |
|---------------------|----------|----------|----------|----------|
| 1 metre per second  | 1        | 3.6      | 2.23694  | 3.28084  |
| 1 kilometre per hour| 0.277778 | 1        | 0.621371 | 0.911346 |
| 1 mile per hour     | 0.44704  | 1.609344 | 1        | 1.46667  |
| 1 foot per second   | 0.3048   | 1.09728  | 0.681817 | 1        |

1 knot = 1 nautical mile per hour = 0.514444 metre per second

## Pressure

|                                     | N/m²(Pa)              | kg/cm²                 | lb/in²                  | atmos                   |
|-------------------------------------|-----------------------|------------------------|-------------------------|-------------------------|
| 1 newton per square metre (pascal)  | 1                     | $1.01972 \times 10^{-5}$ | $1.45038 \times 10^{-4}$ | $9.86923 \times 10^{-6}$ |
| 1 kilogram per square centimetre    | $980.665 \times 10^2$   | 1                      | 14.2234                 | 0.967841                |
| 1 pound per square inch             | $6.89476 \times 10^3$   | 0.0703068              | 1                       | 0.068046                |
| 1 atmosphere                        | $1.01325 \times 10^5$   | 1.03323                | 14.6959                 | 1                       |

1 pascal = 1 newton per square metre = 10 dynes per square centimetre
1 bar = $10^5$ newtons per square metre = 0.986923 atmosphere
1 torr = 133.322 newtons per square metre = 1/760 atmosphere
1 atmosphere = 760 mm Hg = 29.92 in Hg = 33.90 ft water (all at 0°C.)

## Work and energy

|                        | J                   | cal                    | kWhr                    | btu                     |
|------------------------|---------------------|------------------------|-------------------------|-------------------------|
| 1 joule                | 1                   | 0.238846               | $2.77778 \times 10^{-7}$ | $9.47813 \times 10^{-4}$ |
| 1 calorie              | 4.1868              | 1                      | $1.16300 \times 10^{-6}$ | $3.96831 \times 10^{-3}$ |
| 1 kilowatt hour        | $3.6 \times 10^6$     | $8.59845 \times 10^5$    | 1                       | 3412.14                 |
| 1 British Thermal Unit | 1055.06             | 251.997                | $2.93071 \times 10^{-4}$ | 1                       |

1 joule = 1 newton metre = 1 watt second = $10^7$ ergs = 0.737561 ft lb
1 electron volt = $1.602\ 19 \times 10^{-19}$ joule

## Force

|                   | N         | kg                     | dyne                   | poundal                 | lb                      |
|-------------------|-----------|------------------------|------------------------|-------------------------|-------------------------|
| 1 newton          | 1         | 0.101972               | $10^5$                   | 7.23300                 | 0.224809                |
| 1 kilogram force  | 9.80665   | 1                      | $9.80665 \times 10^5$    | 70.9316                 | 2.20462                 |
| 1 dyne            | $10^{-5}$   | $1.01972 \times 10^{-6}$ | 1                      | $7.23300 \times 10^{-5}$  | $2.24809 \times 10^{-6}$  |
| 1 poundal         | 0.138255  | $1.40981 \times 10^{-2}$ | $1.38255 \times 10^4$    | 1                       | 0.031081                |
| 1 pound force     | 4.44822   | 0.453592               | $4.44823 \times 10^5$    | 32.174                  | 1                       |

## Temperature

° Fahrenheit = $(\tfrac{9}{5} \times \chi°C) + 32$

° Centigrade = $\tfrac{5}{9} \times (\chi°F - 32)$

where $\chi$ is the temperature needing converting

## Metric prefixes

|         | symbol | value       |
|---------|--------|-------------|
| tera-   | T      | $10^{12}$     |
| giga-   | G      | $10^9$        |
| mega-   | M      | $10^6$        |
| kilo-   | k      | $10^3$        |
| hecto-  | h      | $10^2$        |
| deca-   | da     | 10          |
| deci-   | d      | $10^{-1}$     |
| centi-  | c      | $10^{-2}$     |
| milli-  | m      | $10^{-3}$     |
| micro-  | $\mu$  | $10^{-6}$     |
| nano-   | n      | $10^{-9}$     |
| pico-   | p      | $10^{-12}$    |
| femto-  | f      | $10^{-15}$    |
| atto-   | a      | $10^{-18}$    |

## UK cookery measures

| 1 teaspoonful    | = | 6 ml   |
|------------------|---|--------|
| 1 dessertspoonful| = | 12 ml  |
| 1 tablespoonful  | = | 18 ml  |
| 1 cupful         | = | 284 ml |

## US cookery measures

| 1 teaspoonful   | = | 5 ml   |
|-----------------|---|--------|
| 1 tablespoonful | = | 15 ml  |
| 1 cupful        | = | 237 ml |

## Periodic table of chemical elements

**Key**

| 4 |
|---|
| **Be** |
| Beryllium |
| 9.012 |

atomic number
symbol
element
atomic weight

| | IA | IIA | IIIA | IVA | VA | VIA | VIIA | VIII | | | IB | IIB | IIIB | IVB | VB | VIB | VIIB | 0 |
|---|---|---|---|---|---|---|---|---|---|---|---|---|---|---|---|---|---|---|
| **1** | 1 **H** Hydrogen 1.008 | | | | | | | | | | | | | | | | | 2 **He** Helium 4.003 |
| **2** | 3 **Li** Lithium 6.94 | 4 **Be** Beryllium 9.012 | | | | | | | | | | | 5 **B** Boron 10.81 | 6 **C** Carbon 12.011 | 7 **N** Nitrogen 14.007 | 8 **O** Oxygen 15.999 | 9 **F** Fluorine 18.998 | 10 **Ne** Neon 20.17 |
| **3** | 11 **Na** Sodium 22.990 | 12 **Mg** Magnesium 24.305 | | | | | | | | | | | 13 **Al** Aluminium 26.982 | 14 **Si** Silicon 28.08 | 15 **P** Phosphorus 30.974 | 16 **S** Sulphur 32.06 | 17 **Cl** Chlorine 35.453 | 18 **Ar** Argon 39.94 |
| **4** | 19 **K** Potassium 39.09 | 20 **Ca** Calcium 40.08 | 21 **Sc** Scandium 44.956 | 22 **Ti** Titanium 47.9 | 23 **V** Vanadium 50.941 | 24 **Cr** Chromium 51.996 | 25 **Mn** Manganese 54.938 | 26 **Fe** Iron 55.84 | 27 **Co** Cobalt 58.933 | 28 **Ni** Nickel 58.7 | 29 **Cu** Copper 63.54 | 30 **Zn** Zinc 65.38 | 31 **Ga** Gallium 69.72 | 32 **Ge** Germanium 72.5 | 33 **As** Arsenic 74.922 | 34 **Se** Selenium 78.9 | 35 **Br** Bromine 79.904 | 36 **Kr** Krypton 83.80 |
| **5** | 37 **Rb** Rubidium 85.467 | 38 **Sr** Strontium 87.62 | 39 **Y** Yttrium 88.906 | 40 **Zr** Zirconium 91.22 | 41 **Nb** Niobium 92.906 | 42 **Mo** Molybdenum 95.9 | 43 **Tc** Technetium 97 | 44 **Ru** Ruthenium 101.0 | 45 **Rh** Rhodium 102.906 | 46 **Pd** Palladium 106.4 | 47 **Ag** Silver 107.868 | 48 **Cd** Cadmium 112.40 | 49 **In** Indium 114.82 | 50 **Sn** Tin 118.6 | 51 **Sb** Antimony 121.7 | 52 **Te** Tellurium 127.6 | 53 **I** Iodine 126.905 | 54 **Xe** Xenon 131.30 |
| **6** | 55 **Cs** Caesium 132.905 | 56 **Ba** Barium 137.34 | 57 **La** Lanthanum 138.905 * | 72 **Hf** Hafnium 178.4 | 73 **Ta** Tantalum 180.947 | 74 **W** Tungsten 183.8 | 75 **Re** Rhenium 186.2 | 76 **Os** Osmium 190.2 | 77 **Ir** Iridium 192.2 | 78 **Pt** Platinum 195.0 | 79 **Au** Gold 196.967 | 80 **Hg** Mercury 200.5 | 81 **Tl** Thallium 204.3 | 82 **Pb** Lead 207.2 | 83 **Bi** Bismuth 208.980 | 84 **Po** Polonium 209 | 85 **At** Astatine 210 | 86 **Rn** Radon 222 |
| **7** | 87 **Fr** Francium 223 | 88 **Ra** Radium 226.025 | 89 **Ac** Actinium 227 † | 104 **Rf** Rutherfordium 261 | 105 **Hn** Hahnium 260 | 106 263 | | | | | | | | | | | | |

*Lanthanide Series

| 58 **Ce** Cerium 140.12 | 59 **Pr** Praseodymium 140.908 | 60 **Nd** Neodymium 144.2 | 61 **Pm** Promethium 147 | 62 **Sm** Samarium 150.4 | 63 **Eu** Europium 151.96 | 64 **Gd** Gadolinium 157.2 | 65 **Tb** Terbium 158.925 | 66 **Dy** Dysprosium 162.5 | 67 **Ho** Holmium 164.930 | 68 **Er** Erbium 167.2 | 69 **Tm** Thulium 168.934 | 70 **Yb** Ytterbium 173.0 | 71 **Lu** Lutetium 174.97 |
|---|---|---|---|---|---|---|---|---|---|---|---|---|---|

†Actinide Series

| 90 **Th** Thorium 232.038 | 91 **Pa** Protactinium 231.036 | 92 **U** Uranium 238.029 | 93 **Np** Neptunium 237.048 | 94 **Pu** Plutonium 244 | 95 **Am** Americium 243 | 96 **Cm** Curium 247 | 97 **Bk** Berkelium 247 | 98 **Cf** Californium 251 | 99 **Es** Einsteinium 254 | 100 **Fm** Fermium 257 | 101 **Md** Mendelevium 257 | 102 **No** Nobelium 255 | 103 **Lr** Lawrencium 256 |
|---|---|---|---|---|---|---|---|---|---|---|---|---|---|

## Books of the Old Testament

| Protestant canon | Roman Catholic canon | Jewish scripture | Protestant apocrypha |
|---|---|---|---|
| Genesis | Genesis | *Law* | 1 & 2 Esdras |
| Exodus | Exodus | Genesis | Tobit |
| Leviticus | Leviticus | Exodus | Judith |
| Numbers | Numbers | Leviticus | Additions to Esther |
| Deuteronomy | Deuteronomy | Numbers | Wisdom of Solomon |
| Joshua | Josue | Deuteronomy | Ecclesiasticus or the Wisdom of |
| Judges | Judges | | Jesus Son of Sirach |
| Ruth | Ruth | | Baruch |
| 1 & 2 Samuel | 1 & 2 Kings | *Prophets* | Prayer of Azariah and the Song of |
| 1 & 2 Kings | 3 & 4 Kings | Joshua | the Three Holy Children |
| 1 & 2 Chronicles | 1 & 2 Paralipomenon | Judges | Susanna |
| Ezra | 1 Esdras | 1 & 2 Samuel | Bel and the Dragon |
| Nehemiah | 2 Esdras | 1 & 2 Kings | The Prayer of Manasses |
| | Tobias | Isaiah | 1 & 2 Maccabees |
| | Judith | Jeremiah | |
| Esther | Esther | Ezekiel | |
| Job | Job | Hosea | |
| Psalms | Psalms | Joel | |
| Proverbs | Proverbs | Amos | |
| Ecclesiastes | Ecclesiastes | Obadiah | **Books of the New Testament** |
| Song of Solomon | Canticle of Canticles | Jonah | |
| | Wisdom | Micah | Matthew |
| | Ecclesiasticus | Nahum | Mark |
| Isaiah | Isaias | Habakkuk | Luke |
| Jeremiah | Jeremias | Zephaniah | John |
| Lamentations | Lamentations | Haggai | Acts of the Apostles |
| | Baruch | Zechariah | Romans |
| Ezekiel | Ezechiel | Malachi | 1 & 2 Corinthians |
| Daniel | Daniel | | Galatians |
| Hosea | Osee | | Ephesians |
| Joel | Joel | *Hagiographa* | Philippians |
| Amos | Amos | Psalms | Colossians |
| Obadiah | Abdias | Proverbs | 1 & 2 Thessalonians |
| Jonah | Jonas | Job | 1 & 2 Timothy |
| Micah | Micheas | Song of Songs | Titus |
| Nahum | Nahum | Ruth | Philemon |
| Habakkuk | Habacuc | Lamentations | Hebrews |
| Zephaniah | Sophonias | Ecclesiastes | James |
| Haggai | Haggeus | Esther | 1 & 2 Peter |
| Zechariah | Zacharias | Daniel | 1, 2, 3 John |
| Malachi | Malachias | Ezra | Jude |
| | 1 & 2 Machabees | Nehemiah | Revelation (Roman Catholic |
| | | 1 & 2 Chronicles | canon: Apocalypse) |

## Principal calendars

| Gregorian[1] | | Jewish | | Islamic | | Hindu[5] |
|---|---|---|---|---|---|---|
| name | days | name | days | name | days | name |
| January | 31 | Tishri | 30 | Muharram[4] | 30 | Chait[6] (March-April) |
| begins 10 days after the | | the seventh month in the | | in A.H. 1404 began 8 | | Baisakh (April-May) |
| winter solstice | | Hebrew calendar | | October 1983 | | |
| February | 28 | Heshvan | 29/30 | Safar | 29 | Jeth (May-June) |
| in leap years | 29 | Kislev | 29/30 | Rabi I | 30 | Asarh (June-July) |
| March | 31 | Tebet | 29 | Rabi II | 29 | Sawan (July-August) |
| April | 30 | Shebat | 30 | Jumada I | 30 | Bhadon (August-September) |
| May | 31 | Adar[2] | 29/30 | Jumada II | 29 | Asin (September-October) |
| June | 30 | Nisan[3] | 30 | Rajab | 30 | Kartik (October-November) |
| July | 31 | Iyar | 29 | Sha'ban | 29 | Aghan (November-December) |
| August | 31 | Sivan | 30 | Ramadan | 30 | Pus (December-January) |
| September | 30 | Tammuz | 29 | Shawwal | 29 | Magh (January-February) |
| October | 31 | Ab | 30 | Dhu'l-Qa'dah | 30 | Phagun (February-March) |
| November | 30 | Elul | 29 | Dhu'l-Hijja | 29 | |
| December | 31 | | | in leap years | 30 | |

[1] The equinoxes occur about 21 March and 23 September, the solstices about 22 June and 22 December.

[2] In leap years Adar is followed by Vendar or Adar Sheni, an intercalary month of 29 days.

[3] Anciently called Abib; the first month of the postexilic calendar; sometimes called the first month of the ecclesiastical year.

[4] Retrogresses through the seasons; the Islamic year is lunar and each month begins at the approximate new moon; the year 1 A.H. began on Friday, 16 July, A.D. 622.

[5] An extra month is inserted after every month in which two new moons occur (once in three years). The intercalary month has the name of the one that precedes it.

[6] Baisakh is sometimes considered the first month of the Hindu year.

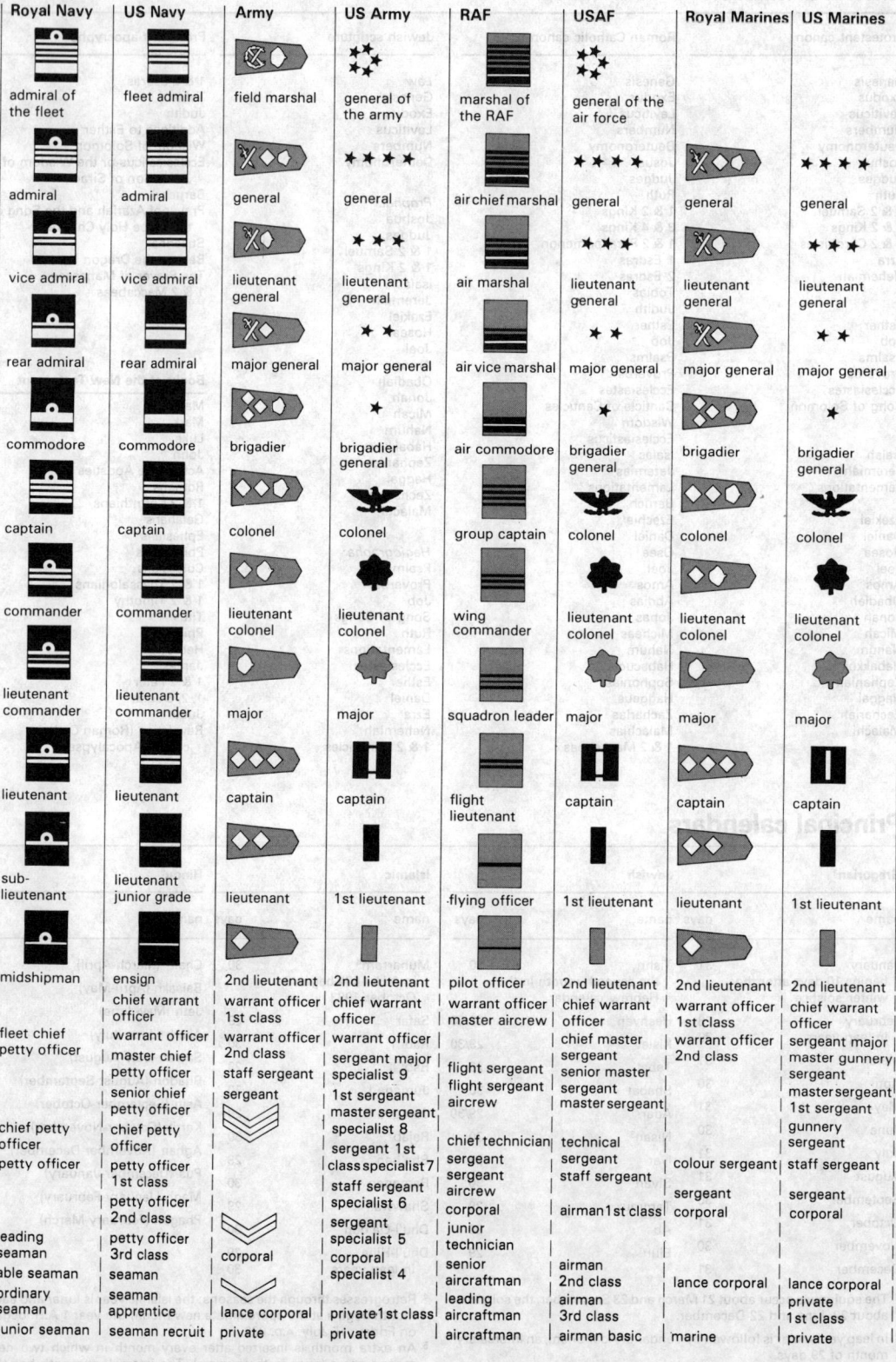

| Royal Navy | US Navy | Army | US Army | RAF | USAF | Royal Marines | US Marines |
|---|---|---|---|---|---|---|---|
| admiral of the fleet | fleet admiral | field marshal | general of the army | marshal of the RAF | general of the air force | | |
| admiral | admiral | general | general | air chief marshal | general | general | general |
| vice admiral | vice admiral | lieutenant general | lieutenant general | air marshal | lieutenant general | lieutenant general | lieutenant general |
| rear admiral | rear admiral | major general | major general | air vice marshal | major general | major general | major general |
| commodore | commodore | brigadier | brigadier general | air commodore | brigadier general | brigadier | brigadier general |
| captain | captain | colonel | colonel | group captain | colonel | colonel | colonel |
| commander | commander | lieutenant colonel | lieutenant colonel | wing commander | lieutenant colonel | lieutenant colonel | lieutenant colonel |
| lieutenant commander | lieutenant commander | major | major | squadron leader | major | major | major |
| lieutenant | lieutenant | captain | captain | flight lieutenant | captain | captain | captain |
| sub-lieutenant | lieutenant junior grade | lieutenant | 1st lieutenant | flying officer | 1st lieutenant | lieutenant | 1st lieutenant |
| midshipman | ensign | 2nd lieutenant | 2nd lieutenant | pilot officer | 2nd lieutenant | 2nd lieutenant | 2nd lieutenant |

**Warrant / enlisted ranks**

| Royal Navy | US Navy | Army | US Army | RAF | USAF | Royal Marines | US Marines |
|---|---|---|---|---|---|---|---|
| | chief warrant officer | warrant officer 1st class | chief warrant officer | master aircrew | chief warrant officer | warrant officer 1st class | chief warrant officer |
| fleet chief petty officer | warrant officer | warrant officer 2nd class | warrant officer | | chief master sergeant | warrant officer 2nd class | sergeant major |
| | master chief petty officer | staff sergeant | sergeant major specialist 9 | flight sergeant | senior master sergeant | | master gunnery sergeant |
| | senior chief petty officer | sergeant | 1st class master sergeant specialist 8 | flight sergeant aircrew | master sergeant | | master sergeant 1st sergeant |
| chief petty officer | chief petty officer | | sergeant 1st class specialist 7 | chief technician | technical sergeant | | gunnery sergeant |
| petty officer | petty officer 1st class | | staff sergeant specialist 6 | sergeant aircrew | staff sergeant | colour sergeant | staff sergeant |
| | petty officer 2nd class | | sergeant specialist 5 | corporal | airman 1st class | sergeant | sergeant |
| leading seaman | petty officer 3rd class | corporal | junior technician | airman 2nd class | corporal | corporal |
| able seaman | seaman | | corporal specialist 4 | senior aircraftman | airman 2nd class | lance corporal | lance corporal |
| ordinary seaman | seaman apprentice | lance corporal | private 1st class | leading aircraftman | airman 3rd class | | private 1st class |
| junior seaman | seaman recruit | private | private | aircraftman | airman basic | marine | private |